DRUG INFORMATION HANDBOOK

A Comprehensive Resource for all Clinicians and Healthcare Professionals

Charles F. Lacy, RPh, PharmD, FCSHP
Lora L. Armstrong, RPh, PharmD, BCPS
Morton P. Goldman, RPh, PharmD, BCPS
Leonard L. Lance, RPh, BSPharm

Lexi-Comp is the official drug reference for the American Pharmacists Association

APhA

15th Edition

LEXI-COMP

DRUG INFORMATION HANDBOOK

A Comprehensive Resource for all Clinicians and Healthcare Professionals

Charles F. Lacy, PharmD, FCSHP
Vice President, Information Technologies
Professor, Pharmacy Practice
Professor, Business Leadership
University of Southern Nevada
Las Vegas, Nevada

Lora L. Armstrong, PharmD, BCPS
Vice President, Clinical Affairs
Pharmacy & Therapeutics Formulary Process
Clinical Program Oversight
CaremarkRx
Northbrook, Illinois

Morton P. Goldman, PharmD, BCPS, FCCP
Director of Pharmacotherapy Services
Department of Pharmacy
Cleveland Clinic Foundation
Cleveland, Ohio

Leonard L. Lance, RPh, BSPharm
Pharmacist
Lexi-Comp, Inc.
Hudson, Ohio

 LEXI-COMP

 APhA

NOTICE

This handbook is intended to serve the user as a handy quick reference and not as a complete drug information resource. It does not include information on every therapeutic agent available. The publication covers commonly used drugs and is specifically designed to present certain important aspects of drug data in a more concise format than is generally found in medical literature or product material supplied by manufacturers.

The nature of drug information is that it is constantly evolving because of ongoing research and clinical experience and is often subject to interpretation. While great care has been taken to ensure the accuracy of the information presented, the reader is advised that the authors, editors, reviewers, contributors, and publishers cannot be responsible for the continued currency of the information or for any errors, omissions, or the application of this information, or for any consequences arising therefrom. Therefore, the author(s) and/or the publisher shall have no liability to any person or entity with regard to claims, loss, or damage caused, or alleged to be caused, directly or indirectly, by the use of information contained herein. Because of the dynamic nature of drug information, readers are advised that decisions regarding drug therapy must be based on the independent judgment of the clinician, changing information about a drug (eg, as reflected in the literature and manufacturer's most current product information), and changing medical practices. The editors are not responsible for any inaccuracy of quotation or for any false or misleading implication that may arise due to the text or formulas as used or due to the quotation of revisions no longer official. Further, the reader/user, herewith, is advised that information shown under the heading **Dosage** is provided only as an indication of the amount of the drug typically given or taken during therapy. Actual dosing amount for any specific drug should be based on an in-depth evaluation of the individual patient's therapy requirement and strong consideration given to such issues as contraindications, warnings, precautions, adverse reactions, along with the interaction of other drugs. The manufacturers most current product information or other standard recognized references should always be consulted for such detailed information prior to drug use.

The editors, authors, and contributors have written this book in their private capacities. No official support or endorsement by any federal agency or pharmaceutical company is intended or inferred.

The publishers have made every effort to trace the copyright holders for borrowed material. If they have inadvertently overlooked any, they will be pleased to make the necessary arrangements at the first opportunity.

If you have any suggestions or questions regarding any information presented in this handbook, please contact our drug information pharmacists at (330) 650-6506.

This manual was produced using Lexi-Comp's Information Management System™ (LIMS) — a complete publishing service of Lexi-Comp Inc.

LEXI-COMP
1100 Terex Road
Hudson, Ohio 44236
(330) 650-6506

ISBN 978-1-59195-203-9 (North American Edition)

TABLE OF CONTENTS

About the Authors.. 2

Editorial Advisory Panel 4

Acknowledgments... 10

Description of Sections and Fields Used in This Handbook 11

FDA Pregnancy Categories 13

Safe Writing 14

FDA Name Differentiation Project - Tall-Man Letters..................... 15

ALPHABETICAL LISTING OF DRUGS 17

APPENDIX
(see Appendix Table of Contents for expanded listing) 1829

    Abbreviations and Measurements 1832

    Assessment of Liver Function 1853

    Assessment of Renal Function 1854

    Comparative Drug Charts 1858

    Cytochrome P450 and Drug Interactions 1899

    Desensitization and Skin Testing Guidelines 1913

    Immunizations and Vaccinations 1929

    Infectious Disease - Prophylaxis 1941

    Infectious Disease - Treatment 1976

    Parenteral Nutrition... 2021

    Therapy Recommendations 2023

    Toxicology 2075

    Miscellaneous 2095

PHARMACOLOGIC CATEGORY INDEX........................... 2119

ABOUT THE AUTHORS

Charles F. Lacy, PharmD, FCSHP

Dr Lacy is the Vice President for Information Technologies, Professor of Pharmacy Practice, and Professor of Business Leadership at the University of Southern Nevada. In his capacity at the university, Dr. Lacy oversees the directors of the Library and Learning Resources Center and the University Information Systems. Additionally, Dr Lacy is also a co-founder of the University. Currently, Dr Lacy is also the Director of International Programs for the university, which includes the College of Pharmacy, the College of Business Administration, and the College of Nursing. Previously, Dr Lacy was the Facilitative Officer for Clinical Programs for the College of Pharmacy where he managed the clinical curriculum, clinical faculty activities, student experiential programs, pharmacy residency programs, and the college's continuing education programs.

Prior to co-founding the Nevada College of Pharmacy, Dr Lacy was the Clinical Coordinator for the Department of Pharmacy at Cedars-Sinai Medical Center. With 20 years of clinical experience, he has developed a reputation as an acknowledged expert in drug information, pharmacy practice, and critical care drug therapy.

Dr Lacy received his doctorate from the University of Southern California School of Pharmacy. Presently, Dr Lacy holds teaching affiliations with the University of Southern Nevada, the University of Southern California, the University of the Pacific School of Pharmacy, Western University of Health Sciences School of Pharmacy, Hokkaido College of Pharmacy in Otaru, Japan, and the University of Alberta at Edmonton, School of Pharmacy and Health Sciences.

Dr Lacy is an active member of numerous professional associations including the American Society of Health-System Pharmacists (ASHP), the American College of Clinical Pharmacy (ACCP), the American Society of Consultant Pharmacists (ASCP), the American Association of Colleges of Pharmacy (AACP), American Pharmacists Association (APhA), and the California Society of Hospital Pharmacists (CSHP), through which he has chaired many committees and subcommittees.

Lora Armstrong, PharmD, BCPS

Dr Armstrong received her bachelor's degree in pharmacy from Ferris State University and her Doctor of Pharmacy degree from Midwestern University. Dr Armstrong is a Board-Certified Pharmacotherapy Specialist (BCPS).

In her current position, Dr Armstrong serves as Vice President of Clinical Affairs with responsibility for the National Pharmacy & Therapeutics Committee process, Clinical Program Oversight process, and Pharmaceutical Pipeline Services at Caremark. Caremark is a prescription benefit management company (PBM). Dr Armstrong is also responsible for monitoring drug surveillance and communicating Pharmacy & Therapeutics Committee Formulary information to Caremark's internal and external customers.

Prior to joining Caremark, Inc, Dr Armstrong served as the Director of Drug Information Services at the University of Chicago Hospitals. She obtained 17 years of experience in a variety of clinical settings including critical care, hematology, oncology, infectious diseases, and clinical pharmacokinetics. Dr Armstrong played an active role in the education and training of medical, pharmacy, and nursing staff. She coordinated the Drug Information Center, the medical center's Adverse Drug Reaction Monitoring Program, and the continuing Education Program for pharmacists. She also maintained the hospital's strict formulary program and was the editor of the University of Chicago Hospitals' *Formulary of Accepted Drugs* and the drug information center's monthly newsletter *Topics in Drug Therapy*.

Dr Armstrong is an active member of the Academy of Managed Care Pharmacy (AMCP), the American Society of Health-Systems Pharmacists (ASHP), the American Pharmaceutical Association (APhA), the American College of Clinical Pharmacy (ACCP), and the Pharmacy & Therapeutics Society (P & T Society). Dr Armstrong wrote the chapter entitled "Drugs and Hormones Used in Endocrinology" in the 4th edition of the textbook *Endocrinology*. She is an Adjunct Clinical Instructor of Pharmacy Practice at Midwestern University. Dr Armstrong currently serves on the Drug Information Advisory Board for pharmacist.com and on the American Pharmaceutical Association Scientific Review Panel for Evaluations of Drug Interactions (EDI).

Morton P. Goldman, PharmD, BCPS, FCCP

Dr Goldman received his bachelor's degree in pharmacy from the University of Pittsburgh, College of Pharmacy and his Doctor of Pharmacy degree from the University of Cincinnati, Division of Graduate Studies and Research. He completed his concurrent 2-year hospital pharmacy residency at the VA Medical Center in Cincinnati. Dr Goldman is presently the Director of Pharmacotherapy Services for the Department of Pharmacy at the Cleveland Clinic Foundation (CCF) after having spent over 4 years at CCF as an Infectious Disease pharmacist and 10 years as Clinical Manager/Assistant Director. He holds faculty appointments from The University of Toledo, College of Pharmacy and Case Western Reserve University, College of Medicine and is the Pharmacology Curriculum Director Coordinator for the new Cleveland Clinic Lerner College of Medicine. Dr Goldman is a Board-Certified Pharmacotherapy Specialist (BCPS) with added qualifications in infectious diseases.

In his capacity as Director of Pharmacotherapy Services at CCF, Dr Goldman remains actively involved in patient care and clinical research with the Department of Infectious Disease, as well as the continuing education of the medical and pharmacy staff. He is an editor of CCF's *Guidelines for Antibiotic Use* and participates in their annual Antimicrobial Review retreat. He is a member of the Pharmacy and Therapeutics Committee and many of its subcommittees. Dr Goldman has authored numerous journal articles and lectures locally and nationally on infectious diseases topics and current drug therapies. He is currently a reviewer for the *Clinical Infectious Diseases* and the *Journal of the American Medical Association*, an editorial board member of the *Journal of Infectious Disease Pharmacotherapy*, and coauthor of the *Infectious Diseases Handbook* and the *Drug Information Handbook for the Allied Health Professional* produced by Lexi-Comp, Inc. He also provides technical support to Lexi-Comp's Clinical Reference Library™ publications.

Dr Goldman is an active member of the Ohio College of Clinical Pharmacy, the Society of Infectious Disease Pharmacists, the American College of Clinical Pharmacy (and is a Fellow of the College), and the American Society of Health-Systems Pharmacists.

Leonard L. Lance, RPh, BSPharm

Leonard L. (Bud) Lance has been directly involved in the pharmaceutical industry since receiving his bachelor's degree in pharmacy from Ohio Northern University in 1970. Upon graduation from ONU, Mr Lance spent four years as a navy pharmacist in various military assignments and was instrumental in the development and operation of the first whole hospital I.V. admixture program in a military (Portsmouth Naval Hospital) facility. His last 15 months in the Navy were spent on the USS Independence CV-62.

After completing his military service, he entered the retail pharmacy field and has managed both an independent and a home I.V. franchise pharmacy operation. Since the late 1970s, Mr Lance has focused much of his interest on using computers to improve pharmacy service. The independent pharmacy he worked for was one of the first retail pharmacies in the State of Ohio to computerize (1977).

His love for computers and pharmacy lead him to Lexi-Comp, Inc. in 1988. He was the first pharmacist at Lexi-Comp and helped develop Lexi-Comp's first drug database in 1989 and was involved in the editing and publishing of Lexi-Comp's first *Drug Information Handbook* in 1990.

As a result of his strong publishing interest, he presently serves in the capacity of pharmacy editor and technical advisor as well as pharmacy (information) database coordinator for Lexi-Comp. Along with authoring the *Drug Information Handbook for the Allied Health Professional* and *Lippincott Williams & Wilkins Quick Look Drug Book*, he provides technical support to Lexi-Comp's reference publications. Mr Lance also assists over 300 major hospitals in producing their own formulary (pharmacy) publications through Lexi-Comp's custom publishing service. Mr Lance is also Manager of the Dosage Forms database in the Medical Sciences Division at Lexi-Comp.

Mr Lance is past president (1984) of the Summit Pharmaceutical Association (SPA). He is a member of the Ohio Pharmacists Association (OPA), the American Pharmaceutical Association (APhA), and the American Society of Health-System Pharmacists (ASHP).

EDITORIAL ADVISORY PANEL

5

EDITORIAL ADVISORY PANEL *(Continued)*

Kay Kyllonen, PharmD
Clinical Specialist
The Cleveland Clinic Children's Hospital
Cleveland, Ohio

Charles Lacy, RPh, PharmD, FCSHP
Vice President, Information Technologies
Professor, Pharmacy Practice
Professor, Business Leadership
University of Southern Nevada
Las Vegas, Nevada

Brenda R. Lance, RN, MSN
Program Development Director
Northcoast HealthCare Management Company
Northcoast Infusion Therapies
Oakwood Village, Ohio

Leonard L. Lance, RPh, BSPharm
Clinical Pharmacist
Lexi-Comp Inc
Hudson, Ohio

Jerrold B. Leikin, MD, FACP, FACEP, FACMT, FAACT
Director, Medical Toxicology
Evanston Northwestern Healthcare-OMEGA
Glenbrook Hospital
Glenview, Illinois
Associate Director
Toxikon Consortium at Cook County Hospital
Chicago, Illinois
Professor of Medicine
Pharmacology and Health Systems Management
Rush Medical College
Chicago, Ilinois
Professor of Medicine
Feinberg School of Medicine
Northwestern University
Chicago, Ilinois

Jeffrey D. Lewis, PharmD
Pharmacotherapy Specialist
Lexi-Comp, Inc
Hudson, Ohio

Jennifer K. Long, PharmD, BCPS
Infectious Diseases Clinical Specialist
The Cleveland Clinic Foundation
Cleveland, Ohio

Laurie S. Mauro, BS, PharmD
Associate Professor of Clinical Pharmacy
Department of Pharmacy Practice
College of Pharmacy
The University of Toledo
Toledo, Ohio

Vincent F. Mauro, BS, PharmD, FCCP
Professor of Clinical Pharmacy
College of Pharmacy
The University of Toledo
Adjunct Professor of Medicine
College of Medicine
Medical University of Ohio at Toledo
Toledo, Ohio

Barrie McCombs, MD, FCFP
Medical Information Service Coordinator
The Alberta Rural Physician Action Plan
Calgary, Alberta, Canada

Timothy F. Meiller, DDS, PhD
Professor
Diagnostic Sciences and Pathology
Baltimore College of Dental Surgery
Professor of Oncology
Greenebaum Cancer Center
University of Maryland Baltimore
Baltimore, Maryland

EDITORIAL ADVISORY PANEL *(Continued)*

Dominic A. Solimando, Jr, MA, FAPhA, FASHP, BCOP
Oncology Pharmacist
President, Oncology Pharmacy Services, Inc
Arlington, VA

Joni Lombardi Stahura, BS, PharmD, RPh
Pharmacotherapy Specialist
Lexi-Comp, Inc
Hudson, Ohio

Carol K. Taketomo, PharmD
Pharmacy Manager
Children's Hospital Los Angeles
Los Angeles, California

Mary Temple, PharmD
Pediatric Clinical Research Specialist
Hillcrest Hospital
Mayfield Heights, Ohio

Elizabeth A. Tomsik, PharmD, BCPS
Pharmacotherapy Specialist
Lexi-Comp, Inc
Hudson, Ohio

Jennifer Trofe, PharmD
Clinical Transplant Pharmacist
Hospital of The University of Pennsylvania
Philadelphia, Pennsylvania

Beatrice B. Turkoski, RN, PhD
Associate Professor, Graduate Faculty
Advanced Pharmacology
College of Nursing
Kent State University
Kent, Ohio

Amy VanOrman, PharmD
Pharmacotherapy Specialist
Lexi-Comp, Inc
Hudson, Ohio

David M. Weinstein, PhD, RPh
Pharmacotherapy Specialist
Lexi-Comp, Inc.
Hudson, Ohio

Anne Marie Whelan, PharmD
College of Pharmacy
Dalhouise University
Halifax, Nova Scotia

Richard L. Wynn, PhD
Professor of Pharmacology
Baltimore College of Dental Surgery
Dental School
University of Maryland Baltimore
Baltimore, Maryland

ACKNOWLEDGMENTS

The *Drug Information Handbook* exists in its present form as the result of the concerted efforts of the following individuals: Robert D. Kerscher, publisher and chief executive officer of Lexi-Comp, Inc; Steven Kerscher, president and chief operating officer; Mark F. Bonfiglio, BS, PharmD, RPh, chief content officer; Stacy S. Robinson, editorial manager; David C. Marcus, chief information officer; Leslie Jo Hoppes, pharmacology database manager; Ginger Stein, project manager; Alexandra Hart, composition specialist; Tracey J. Henterly, senior graphic designer; and Julian I. Graubart, American Pharmacists Association (APhA), Senior Director, Books and Electronic Products.

Special acknowledgment goes to all Lexi-Comp staff for their contributions to this handbook.

Much of the material contained in this book was a result of pharmacy contributors throughout the United States and Canada. Lexi-Comp has assisted many medical institutions to develop hospital-specific formulary manuals that contain clinical drug information as well as dosing. Working with these clinical pharmacists, hospital pharmacy and therapeutics committees, and hospital drug information centers, Lexi-Comp has developed an evolutionary drug database that reflects the practice of pharmacy in these major institutions.

In addition, the authors wish to thank their families, friends, and colleagues who supported them in their efforts to complete this handbook.

DESCRIPTION OF SECTIONS AND FIELDS USED IN THIS HANDBOOK

The *Drug Information Handbook, 15th Edition* is divided into four sections.

The first section is a compilation of introductory text pertinent to the use of this book.

The drug information section of the handbook, in which all drugs are listed alphabetically, details information pertinent to each drug. Extensive cross-referencing is provided by U.S. brand names, Canadian brand names, and index terms. Many combination monographs have been added to this edition; however, they have been condensed with only brand names and forms available. For more information on these products, see the individual components.

The third section is an invaluable appendix which offers a compilation of tables, guidelines, nomograms, algorithms, and conversion information which can be helpful when considering patient care.

The last section of this handbook contains a Pharmacologic Category Index which lists all drugs in this handbook in their unique pharmacologic class.

The **Alphabetical Listing of Drugs** is presented in a consistent format and provides the following fields of information:

Generic Name	U.S. adopted name
Pronunciation	Phonetic pronunciation guide
U.S. Brand Names	Trade names (manufacturer-specific) found in the United States. The symbol [DSC] appears after trade names that have been recently discontinued.
Canadian Brand Names	Trade names found in Canada
Index Terms	Includes names or accepted abbreviations of the generic drug; may include common brand names no longer available; this field is used to create cross-references to monographs
Pharmacologic Category	Unique systematic classification of medications
Additional Appendix Information	Cross-reference to other pertinent drug information found in the appendix section of this handbook
Use	Information pertaining to appropriate FDA-approved indications of the drug.
Unlabeled/ Investigational Use	Information pertaining to non-FDA approved and investigational indications of the drug.
Restrictions	The controlled substance classification from the Drug Enforcement Agency (DEA). U.S. schedules are I-V. Schedules vary by country and sometimes state (ie, Massachusetts uses I-VI)
Pregnancy Risk Factor	Five categories established by the FDA to indicate the potential of a systemically absorbed drug for causing birth defects.
Pregnancy Implications	Information pertinent to or associated with the use of the drug as it relates to clinical effects on the fetus and clinical effects on the infant
Lactation	Information describing characteristics of using the drug listed in the monograph while breast-feeding (where recommendation of American Academy of Pediatrics differs, notation is made).
Medication Safety Issues	In an effort to promote the safe use of medications, this field is intended to highlight possible sources of medication errors such as look-alike/sound-alike drugs or highly concentrated formulations which require vigilance on the part of healthcare professionals. In addition, medications which have been associated with severe consequences in the event of a medication error are also identified in this field.
Contraindications	Information pertaining to inappropriate use of the drug
Warnings/Precautions	Precautionary considerations, hazardous conditions related to use of the drug, and disease states or patient populations in which the drug should be cautiously used

DESCRIPTION OF SECTIONS AND FIELDS USED IN THIS HANDBOOK *(Continued)*

Adverse Reactions	Side effects are grouped by percentage of incidence (if known) and/or body system; in the interest of saving space, <1% effects are grouped only by percentage
Overdosage/ Toxicology	Comments and/or considerations are offered when appropriate and include signs/symptoms of excess drug and suggested management of the patient
Drug Interactions	
Cytochrome P450 Effect	Describes which cytochrome P450 enzymes are responsible for metabolizing the drug and/or which enzymes might be induced or inhibited by the drug.
Increased Effect/ Toxicity	Drug combinations that result in an increased or toxic therapeutic effect between the drug listed in the monograph and other drugs or drug classes.
Decreased Effect	Drug combinations that result in a decreased therapeutic effect between the drug listed in the monograph and other drugs or drug classes.
Ethanol/Nutrition/Herb Interactions	Information regarding potential interactions with food, nutritionals, herbal products, vitamins, or ethanol.
Stability	Information regarding storage of product or steps for reconstitution. Provides the time and conditions for which a solution or mixture will maintain full potency. For example, some solutions may require refrigeration after reconstitution while stored at room temperature prior to preparation. Also includes compatibility information. **Note:** Professional judgment of the individual pharmacist in application of this information is imperative. While drug products may exhibit stability over longer durations of time, it may not be appropriate to utilize the drug product due to concerns in sterility.
Mechanism of Action	How the drug works in the body to elicit a response
Pharmacodynamics/ Kinetics	The magnitude of a drug's effect depends on the drug concentration at the site of action. The pharmacodynamics are expressed in terms of onset of action and duration of action. Pharmacokinetics are expressed in terms of absorption, distribution (including appearance in breast milk and crossing of the placenta), protein binding, metabolism, bioavailability, half-life, time to peak serum concentration, and elimination.
Dosage	The amount of the drug to be typically given or taken during therapy for children and adults; also includes any dosing adjustment/comments for renal impairment or hepatic impairment and other suggested dosing adjustments (eg, hematological toxicity)
Dietary Considerations	Includes information on how the medication should be taken relative to meals or food.
Administration	Information regarding the recommended final concentrations, rates of administration for parenteral drugs, or other guidelines when giving the medication
Monitoring Parameters	Laboratory tests and patient physical parameters that should be monitored for safety and efficacy of drug therapy
Reference Range	Therapeutic and toxic serum concentrations listed including peak and trough levels
Test Interactions	Listing of assay interferences when relevant; (B) = Blood; (S) = Serum; (U) = Urine
Additional Information	Information about sodium content and/or pertinent information about specific brands
Dosage Forms	Information with regard to form, strength, and availability of the drug
Extemporaneous Preparations	Directions for preparing liquid formulations from solid drug products. May include stability information and references.

FDA PREGNANCY CATEGORIES

Throughout this book there is a field labeled Pregnancy Risk Factor (PRF) and the letter A, B, C, D or X immediately following which signifies a category. The FDA has established these five categories to indicate the potential of a systemically absorbed drug for causing birth defects. The key differentiation among the categories rests upon the reliability of documentation and the risk:benefit ratio. Pregnancy Category X is particularly notable in that if any data exists that may implicate a drug as a teratogen and the risk:benefit ratio is clearly negative, the drug is contraindicated during pregnancy.

These categories are summarized as follows:

A   Controlled studies in pregnant women fail to demonstrate a risk to the fetus in the first trimester with no evidence of risk in later trimesters. The possibility of fetal harm appears remote.

B   Either animal-reproduction studies have not demonstrated a fetal risk but there are no controlled studies in pregnant women, or animal-reproduction studies have shown an adverse effect (other than a decrease in fertility) that was not confirmed in controlled studies in women in the first trimester and there is no evidence of a risk in later trimesters.

C   Either studies in animals have revealed adverse effects on the fetus (teratogenic or embryocidal effects or other) and there are no controlled studies in women, or studies in women and animals are not available. Drugs should be given only if the potential benefits justify the potential risk to the fetus.

D   There is positive evidence of human fetal risk, but the benefits from use in pregnant women may be acceptable despite the risk (eg, if the drug is needed in a life-threatening situation or for a serious disease for which safer drugs cannot be used or are ineffective).

X   Studies in animals or human beings have demonstrated fetal abnormalities or there is evidence of fetal risk based on human experience, or both, and the risk of the use of the drug in pregnant women clearly outweighs any possible benefit. The drug is contraindicated in women who are or may become pregnant.

SAFE WRITING

Health professionals and their support personnel frequently produce handwritten copies of information they see in print; therefore, such information is subjected to even greater possibilities for error or misinterpretation on the part of others. Thus, particular care must be given to how drug names and strengths are expressed when creating written healthcare documents.

The following are a few examples of safe writing rules suggested by the Institute for Safe Medication Practices, Inc.*

1. There should be a space between a number and its units as it is easier to read. There should be no periods after the abbreviations mg or mL.

Correct	Incorrect
10 mg	10mg
100 mg	100mg

2. Never place a decimal and a zero after a whole number (2 mg is correct and 2.0 mg is **incorrect**). If the decimal point is not seen because it falls on a line or because individuals are working from copies where the decimal point is not seen, this causes a tenfold overdose.

3. Just the opposite is true for numbers less than one. Always place a zero before a naked decimal (0.5 mL is correct, .5 mL is **incorrect**).

4. Never abbreviate the word unit. The handwritten U or u, looks like a 0 (zero), and may cause a tenfold overdose error to be made.

5. IU is not a safe abbreviation for international units. The handwritten IU looks like IV. Write out international units or use int. units.

6. Q.D. is not a safe abbreviation for once daily, as when the Q is followed by a sloppy dot, it looks like QID which means four times daily.

7. O.D. is not a safe abbreviation for once daily, as it is properly interpreted as meaning "right eye" and has caused liquid medications such as saturated solution of potassium iodide and Lugol's solution to be administered incorrectly. There is no safe abbreviation for once daily. It must be written out in full.

8. Do not use chemical names such as 6-mercaptopurine or 6-thioguanine, as sixfold overdoses have been given when these were not recognized as chemical names. The proper names of these drugs are mercaptopurine or thioguanine.

9. Do not abbreviate drug names (5FC, 6MP, 5-ASA, MTX, HCTZ, CPZ, PBZ, etc) as they are misinterpreted and cause error.

10. Do not use the apothecary system or symbols.

11. Do not abbreviate microgram as μg; instead use mcg as there is less likelihood of misinterpretation.

12. When writing an outpatient prescription, write a complete prescription. A complete prescription can prevent the prescriber, the pharmacist, and/or the patient from making a mistake and can eliminate the need for further clarification. The legible prescriptions should contain:

    a. patient's full name

    b. for pediatric or geriatric patients: their age (or weight where applicable)

    c. drug name, dosage form and strength; if a drug is new or rarely prescribed, print this information

    d. number or amount to be dispensed

    e. complete instructions for the patient, including the purpose of the medication

    f. when there are recognized contraindications for a prescribed drug, indicate to the pharmacist that you are aware of this fact (ie, when prescribing a potassium salt for a patient receiving an ACE inhibitor, write "K serum level being monitored")

---

*From "Safe Writing" by Davis NM, PharmD and Cohen MR, MS, Lecturers and Consultants for Safe Medication Practices, 1143 Wright Drive, Huntington Valley, PA 19006. Phone: (215) 947-7566.

FDA NAME DIFFERENTIATION PROJECT
THE USE OF TALL-MAN LETTERS

Confusion between similar drug names is an important cause of medication errors. For years, The Institute For Safe Medication Practices (ISMP), has urged generic manufacturers to use a combination of large and small letters as well as bolding (ie, chlorpro**MAZINE** and chlorpro**PAMIDE**) to help distinguish drugs with look-alike names, especially when they share similar strengths. Recently the FDA's Division of Generic Drugs began to issue recommendation letters to manufacturers suggesting this novel way to label their products to help reduce this drug name confusion. Although this project has had marginal success, the method has successfully eliminated problems with products such as diphenhydr**AMINE** and dimenhy**DRINATE**. Hospitals should also follow suit by making similar changes in their own labels, preprinted order forms, computer screens and printouts, and drug storage location labels.

Lexi-Comp Medical Publishing will use "Tall-Man" letters for the drugs suggested by the FDA.

The following is a list of product names and recommended FDA revisions.

Drug Product	Recommended Revision
acetazolamide	aceta**ZOLAMIDE**
acetohexamide	aceto**HEXAMIDE**
bupropion	bu**PROP**ion
buspirone	bus**PIR**one
chlorpromazine	chlorpro**MAZINE**
chlorpropamide	chlorpro**PAMIDE**
clomiphene	clomi**PHENE**
clomipramine	clomi**PRAMINE**
cycloserine	cyclo**SERINE**
cyclosporine	cyclo**SPORINE**
daunorubicin	**DAUNO**rubicin
dimenhydrinate	dimenhy**DRINATE**
diphenhydramine	diphenhydr**AMINE**
dobutamine	**DOBUT**amine
dopamine	**DOP**amine
doxorubicin	**DOXO**rubicin
glipizide	glipi**ZIDE**
glyburide	gly**BURIDE**
hydralazine	hydr**ALAZINE**
hydroxyzine	hydr**OXY**zine
medroxyprogesterone	medroxy**PROGESTER**one
methylprednisolone	methyl**PREDNIS**olone
methyltestosterone	methyl**TESTOSTER**one
nicardipine	ni**CAR**dipine
nifedipine	**NIFE**dipine
prednisolone	predniso**LONE**
prednisone	predni**SONE**
sulfadiazine	sulfa**DIAZINE**
sulfisoxazole	sulfi**SOXAZOLE**
tolazamide	**TOLAZ**amide
tolbutamide	**TOLBUT**amide
vinblastine	vin**BLAS**tine
vincristine	vin**CRIS**tine

Institute for Safe Medication Practices. "New Tall-Man Lettering Will Reduce Mix-Ups Due to Generic Drug Name Confusion," *ISMP Medication Safety Alert*, September 19, 2001. Available at: http://www.ismp.org.

Institute for Safe Medication Practices. "Prescription Mapping, Can Improve Efficiency While Minimizing Errors With Look-Alike Products," *ISMP Medication Safety Alert*, October 6, 1999. Available at: http://www.ismp.org.

U.S. Pharmacopeia, "USP Quality Review: Use Caution-Avoid Confusion," March 2001, No. 76. Available at: http://www.usp.org.

ALPHABETICAL LISTING OF DRUGS

♦ **1370-999-397** *see* Anagrelide *on page 128*

♦ **A200® Lice [OTC]** *see* Permethrin *on page 1348*

♦ **A-200® Maximum Strength [OTC]** *see* Pyrethrins and Piperonyl Butoxide *on page 1461*

♦ **A and D® Original [OTC]** *see* Vitamin A and Vitamin D *on page 1794*

Abacavir (a BAK a veer)

U.S. Brand Names Ziagen®

Canadian Brand Names Ziagen®

Index Terms Abacavir Sulfate; ABC

Pharmacologic Category Antiretroviral Agent, Reverse Transcriptase Inhibitor (Nucleoside)

Additional Appendix Information

Antiretroviral Therapy for HIV Infection: Adults and Adolescents *on page 1988*

Management of Healthcare Worker Exposures to HBV, HCV, and HIV *on page 1941*

Use Treatment of HIV infections in combination with other antiretroviral agents

Restrictions An FDA-approved medication guide and warning card (summarizing symptoms of hypersensitivity) must be distributed when dispensing an outpatient prescription (new or refill) where this medication is to be used without direct supervision of a healthcare provider. Medication guides are available at http://www.fda.gov/cder/Offices/ODS/medication_guides.htm.

Pregnancy Risk Factor C

Pregnancy Implications It is not known if abacavir crosses the human placenta. No increased risk of overall birth defects has been observed following 1st trimester exposure according to data collected by the antiretroviral pregnancy registry. Cases of lactic acidosis/hepatic steatosis syndrome have been reported in pregnant women receiving nucleoside analogues. It is not known if pregnancy itself potentiates this known side effect; however, pregnant women may be at increased risk of lactic acidosis and liver damage. Hepatic enzymes and electrolytes should be monitored frequently during the 3rd trimester of pregnancy in women receiving nucleoside analogues. Dose adjustment is not needed for pregnancy. The Perinatal HIV Guidelines Working Group considers abacavir to be an alternative NRTI in dual nucleoside combination regimens. Health professionals are encouraged to contact the antiretroviral pregnancy registry to monitor outcomes of pregnant women exposed to antiretroviral medications (1-800-258-4263 or www.APRegistry.com).

Lactation Excretion in breast milk unknown/contraindicated

Contraindications Hypersensitivity to abacavir or any component of the formulation (do not rechallenge patients who have experienced hypersensitivity to abacavir); moderate-to-severe hepatic impairment

Warnings/Precautions Abacavir should always be used as a component of a multidrug regimen. **[U.S. Boxed Warning]: Serious and sometimes fatal hypersensitivity reactions have occurred.** Patients exhibiting symptoms from two or more of the following: Fever, skin rash, constitutional symptoms (malaise, fatigue, aches), respiratory symptoms (eg, pharyngitis, dyspnea, cough), and GI symptoms (eg, abdominal pain, diarrhea, nausea, vomiting) should discontinue therapy immediately and call for medical attention. Abacavir should be permanently discontinued if hypersensitivity cannot be ruled out, even when other diagnoses are possible. Abacavir SHOULD NOT be restarted because more severe symptoms may occur within hours, including LIFE-THREATENING HYPOTENSION AND DEATH. Fatal hypersensitivity reactions have occurred following the reintroduction of abacavir in patients whose therapy was interrupted (ie, interruption in drug supply, temporary discontinuation while treating other conditions). Reactions occurred within hours. In some cases, signs of hypersensitivity may have been previously present, but attributed to other medical conditions (eg, acute onset respiratory diseases, gastroenteritis, reactions to other medications). If abacavir is restarted following an interruption in therapy, evaluate the patient for previously unsuspected symptoms of hypersensitivity. Do not restart if hypersensitivity is suspected or if hypersensitivity cannot be ruled out. To report these events on abacavir hypersensitivity, a registry has been established (1-800-270-0425). Use with caution in patients with mild hepatic dysfunction (contraindicated in moderate-to-severe dysfunction). **[U.S. Boxed Warning]: Lactic acidosis and severe hepatomegaly with steatosis (sometimes fatal) have occurred with antiretroviral nucleoside analogues.** Female gender, prior liver disease, obesity, and prolonged treatment may increase the risk of hepatotoxicity. May be associated with fat redistribution. Immune reconstitution syndrome may develop; further evaluation and treatment may be required. Safety and efficacy in children <3 months of age have not been established.

Adverse Reactions Hypersensitivity reactions (which may be fatal) occur in ~5% of patients (see Warnings/Precautions). Symptoms may include anaphylaxis, fever, rash (including erythema multiforme), fatigue, diarrhea, abdominal pain; respiratory symptoms (eg, pharyngitis, dyspnea, cough, adult respiratory distress syndrome, or respiratory failure); headache, malaise, lethargy, myalgia, myolysis, arthralgia, edema, paresthesia, nausea and vomiting, mouth ulcerations, conjunctivitis, lymphadenopathy, hepatic failure, and renal failure.

Note: Rates of adverse reactions were defined during combination therapy with other antiretrovirals (lamivudine and efavirenz **or** lamivudine and zidovudine). Only reactions which occurred at a higher frequency in adults (except where noted) than in the comparator group are noted. Adverse reaction rates attributable to abacavir alone are not available.

>10%:

Central nervous system: Headache (7% to 13%)

Gastrointestinal: Nausea (7% to 19%, children 9%)

1% to 10%:

Central nervous system: Depression (6%), fever/chills (6%, children 9%), anxiety (5%)

Dermatologic: Rash (5% to 6%, children 7%)

Endocrine & metabolic: Triglycerides increased (2% to 6%)

Gastrointestinal: Diarrhea (7%), vomiting (children 9%), amylase increased (2%)

Hematologic: Thrombocytopenia (1%)

Hepatic: AST increased (6%)

Neuromuscular and skeletal: Musculoskeletal pain (5% to 6%)

Miscellaneous: Hypersensitivity reactions (2% to 9%; may include reactions to other components of antiretroviral regimen), infection (EENT 5%)

<1% (Limited to important or life-threatening): Erythema multiforme, fat redistribution, GGT increased, hepatic steatosis, hepatomegaly, hepatotoxicity, lactic acidosis, pancreatitis, Stevens-Johnson syndrome, toxic epidermal necrolysis

Overdosage/Toxicology Treatment should be symptom-directed and supportive. Benefit of dialysis is unknown.

Drug Interactions

Increased Effect/Toxicity: Ganciclovir/valganciclovir may increase the adverse/toxic effects of nucleoside reverse transcriptase inhibitors. Concomitant use of ribavirin with or without interferon alfa and nucleoside analogues may increase the risk of developing hepatic decompensation or other signs of mitochondrial toxicity, including pancreatitis or lactic acidosis.

Ethanol/Nutrition/Herb Interactions Ethanol: Ethanol may increase the risk of toxicity.

Stability Store oral solution and tablets at controlled room temperature of 20°C to 25°C (68°F to 77°F). Oral solution may be refrigerated; do not freeze.

Mechanism of Action Nucleoside reverse transcriptase inhibitor. Abacavir is a guanosine analogue which is phosphorylated to carbovir triphosphate which interferes with HIV viral RNA-dependent DNA polymerase resulting in inhibition of viral replication.

Pharmacodynamics/Kinetics

Absorption: Rapid and extensive absorption

Distribution: V_d: 0.86 L/kg

Protein binding: 50%

Metabolism: Hepatic via alcohol dehydrogenase and glucuronyl transferase to inactive carboxylate and glucuronide metabolites

Bioavailability: 83%

Half-life elimination: 1.5 hours

Time to peak: 0.7-1.7 hours

Excretion: Primarily urine (as metabolites, 1.2% as unchanged drug); feces (16% total dose)

Dosage Oral:

Children: 3 months to 16 years: 8 mg/kg body weight twice daily (maximum: 300 mg twice daily) in combination with other antiretroviral agents

Adults: 300 mg twice daily or 600 mg once daily in combination with other antiretroviral agents

Dosage adjustment in hepatic impairment:

Mild dysfunction (Child-Pugh score 5-6): 200 mg twice daily (oral solution is recommended)

Moderate-to-severe dysfunction: Use is contraindicated by the manufacturer

Dietary Considerations May be taken with or without food.

Administration May be administered with or without food.

Additional Information A high rate of early virologic nonresponse was observed when abacavir, lamivudine, and tenofovir were used as the initial regimen in treatment-naive patients. Use of this combination is not recommended; patients currently on this regimen should be closely monitored for modification of therapy.

Dosage Forms

Solution, oral:

Ziagen®: 20 mg/mL (240 mL) [strawberry-banana flavor]

Tablet:

300 mg

Abacavir and Lamivudine (a BAK a veer & la MI vyoo deen)

U.S. Brand Names Epzicom™

Canadian Brand Names Kivexa™

Index Terms Abacavir Sulfate and Lamivudine; Lamivudine and Abacavir

Pharmacologic Category Antiretroviral Agent, Reverse Transcriptase Inhibitor (Nucleoside)

Additional Appendix Information

Antiretroviral Therapy for HIV Infection: Adults and Adolescents on page 1988

Management of Healthcare Worker Exposures to HBV, HCV, and HIV on page 1941

Use Treatment of HIV infections in combination with other antiretroviral agents

Restrictions An FDA-approved medication guide and warning card (summarizing symptoms of hypersensitivity) must be distributed when dispensing an outpatient prescription (new or refill) where this medication is to be used without direct supervision of a healthcare provider. Medication guides are available at http://www.fda.gov/cder/Offices/ODS/medication_guides.htm.

Pregnancy Risk Factor C

Dosage Oral: Adults: HIV: One tablet (abacavir 600 mg and lamivudine 300 mg) once daily

Dosage adjustment in renal impairment: Cl_{cr} <50 mL/minute: Use not recommended

Dosage adjustment in hepatic impairment: Use contraindicated.

Additional Information Complete prescribing information for this medication should be consulted for additional detail.

Dosage Forms

Tablet:

Epzicom™: Abacavir 600 mg and lamivudine 300 mg

Abacavir, Lamivudine, and Zidovudine

(a BAK a veer, la MI vyoo deen, & zye DOE vyoo deen)

U.S. Brand Names Trizivir®

Index Terms Azidothymidine, Abacavir, and Lamivudine; AZT, Abacavir, and Lamivudine; Compound S, Abacavir, and Lamivudine; Lamivudine, Abacavir, and Zidovudine; 3TC, (Continued)

Abacavir, Lamivudine, and Zidovudine *(Continued)*

Abacavir, and Zidovudine; ZDV, Abacavir, and Lamivudine; Zidovudine, Abacavir, and Lamivudine

Pharmacologic Category Antiretroviral Agent, Reverse Transcriptase Inhibitor (Nucleoside)

Additional Appendix Information

Antiretroviral Therapy for HIV Infection: Adults and Adolescents *on page 1988*

Management of Healthcare Worker Exposures to HBV, HCV, and HIV *on page 1941*

Use Treatment of HIV infection (either alone or in combination with other antiretroviral agents) in patients whose regimen would otherwise contain the components of Trizivir®

Restrictions An FDA-approved medication guide and warning card (summarizing symptoms of hypersensitivity) must be distributed when dispensing an outpatient prescription (new or refill) where this medication is to be used without direct supervision of a healthcare provider. Medication guides are available at http://www.fda.gov/cder/Offices/ODS/medication_guides.htm.

Pregnancy Risk Factor C

Dosage Oral:

Adolescents ≥40 kg and Adults: 1 tablet twice daily

Elderly: Use with caution

Dosage adjustment in renal impairment: Because lamivudine and zidovudine require dosage adjustment in renal impairment, Trizivir® should not be used in patients with Cl_{cr} ≤50 mL/minute

Dosage adjustment in hepatic impairment: Use contraindicated.

Additional Information Complete prescribing information for this medication should be consulted for additional detail.

Dosage Forms

Tablet:

Trizivir®: Abacavir 300 mg, lamivudine 150 mg, and zidovudine 300 mg

♦ **Abacavir Sulfate** *see* Abacavir *on page 18*

♦ **Abacavir Sulfate and Lamivudine** *see* Abacavir and Lamivudine *on page 19*

Abarelix *(a ba REL iks)*

U.S. Brand Names Plenaxis™ [DSC]

Index Terms PPI-149; R-3827

Pharmacologic Category Gonadotropin Releasing Hormone Antagonist

Use Palliative treatment of advanced prostate cancer; treatment is limited to men who are not candidates for LHRH therapy, refuse surgical castration, and have one or more of the following complications due to metastases or local encroachment: 1) risk of neurological compromise, 2) ureteral or bladder outlet obstruction, or 3) severe bone pain (persisting despite narcotic analgesia)

Restrictions Abarelix is not distributed through retail pharmacies. Prescribing and distribution of abarelix is limited to physicians and hospital pharmacies participating in the Plenaxis™ PLUS program. See Additional Information, or contact Praecis Pharmaceuticals at www.plenaxisplus.com or by calling 1-877-772-3247.

Pregnancy Risk Factor X

Pregnancy Implications Not indicated for use in women; may cause fetal harm if administered to a pregnant woman.

Lactation Excretion in breast milk unknown/not indicated in women

Contraindications Hypersensitivity to abarelix or any component of the formulation

Warnings/Precautions Hazardous agent - use appropriate precautions for handling and disposal. **[U.S. Boxed Warning]: Has been associated with immediate-onset allergic reactions; may occur with initial dose and risk increases with duration of treatment. Observe for signs/symptoms of allergic reactions (which may include hypotension and/or syncope) for at least 30 minutes following each injection.** Abarelix may cause prolongation of the QT interval; consider risk:benefit in patients with baseline QT_c values >450 msec or patients receiving concurrent medications which prolong the QT_c interval (class Ia and class III antiarrhythmics). **[U.S. Boxed Warning]: Efficacy may diminish during prolonged treatment,** particularly in patients weighing >225 pounds; monitor serum testosterone levels to identify treatment failures. Monitor transaminase levels and hepatic function during therapy. Extended treatment may result in a decrease in bone mineral density. **[U.S. Boxed Warning]: May only be prescribed by physicians enrolled in the Plenaxis™ Plus Program.**

Adverse Reactions

>10%:

Cardiovascular: Hot flushes (79%), peripheral edema (15%)

Central nervous system: Sleep disturbance (44%), pain (31%), dizziness (12%), headache (12%)

Endocrine & metabolic: Breast enlargement (30%), nipple discharge/tenderness (20%)

Gastrointestinal: Constipation (15%), diarrhea (11%)

Neuromuscular & skeletal: Back pain (17%)

Respiratory: Upper respiratory infection (12%)

1% to 10%:

Central nervous system: Fatigue (10%)

Endocrine & metabolic: Serum triglycerides increased (10%)

Gastrointestinal: Nausea (10%)

Genitourinary: Dysuria (10%), micturition frequency (10%), urinary retention (10%), urinary tract infection (10%)

Hepatic: Transaminases increased (2% to 8%)

Miscellaneous: Allergic reactions (urticaria, pruritus, syncope, hypotension); risk increases with prolonged treatment

Overdosage/Toxicology No experience in overdose. Treatment is symptomatic and supportive.

Drug Interactions
Increased Effect/Toxicity: When used with other QT$_c$-prolonging agents, additive QT$_c$ prolongation may occur. Life-threatening ventricular arrhythmias may result; example drugs include class Ia and class III antiarrhythmics, cisapride, selected quinolones, erythromycin, pimozide, mesoridazine, and thioridazine.

Stability Store at room temperature: 25°C (77°F); excursions permitted to 15°C to 30°C (58°F to 86°F). Reconstitute vial with 2.2 mL of NS; reconstituted solutions contain abarelix 50 mg/mL. Reconstituted solution is stable for at least 8 hours at 30°C.

Mechanism of Action Competes with naturally-occurring GnRH for binding on receptors of the pituitary. Suppresses LH and FSH, resulting in decreased testosterone.

Pharmacodynamics/Kinetics
Distribution: V$_d$: 4040 L (± 1607)
Metabolism: Hepatic, via peptide hydrolysis
Half-life elimination: 13 days
Time to peak, serum: 3 days (following I.M. administration)
Excretion: Urine (13% as unchanged drug)

Dosage I.M.: Male prostate cancer: 100 mg administered on days 1, 15, 29 (week 4), then every 4 weeks

Administration Administer intramuscularly (to the buttock).

Monitoring Parameters Signs/symptoms of allergic reaction (for at least 30 minutes after each injection). Obtain transaminase levels at baseline and periodically during treatment. Serum testosterone (to identify treatment failure) just prior to abarelix administration, beginning on day 29 and every 8 weeks thereafter. PSA and bone mineral density may be monitored as needed.

Reference Range Efficacy may be monitored by suppression of serum testosterone <50 ng/dL

Additional Information Prior to distribution, Praecis Pharmaceuticals must enroll prescribing physicians and/or hospital pharmacies in the Plenaxis™ user safety program (Plenaxis™ PLUS). A Physician Attestation form must be used to document the physician's qualifications and acceptance of responsibilities concerning patient education and adverse effect reporting. Physicians must obtain the patient's signature and personally cosign the two-part Plenaxis™ Patient Information leaflet. The original signed copy should be retained in the patient's medical record while the other copy should be given to the patient. Hospital pharmacies must submit a hospital pharmacy agreement form to allow dispensing, which will be limited to physicians enrolled in the prescriber's registry. Confirmation of physician enrollment may be obtained by calling 1-866-753-6294. All doses must be dispensed with a Patient Information leaflet. Distributors must restrict shipment to physicians or hospital pharmacies enrolled in the Plenaxis™ prescribing program. Additional details and/or forms may be obtained through Praecis Pharmaceuticals at www.plenaxisplus.com or by calling 1-877-772-3247.

Dosage Forms [DSC] = Discontinued product
Injection, powder for reconstitution [preservative free]: 113 mg [provides 100 mg/2 mL depot suspension when reconstituted; packaged with diluent and syringe] [DSC]

Abatacept (ab a TA sept)

U.S. Brand Names Orencia®
Index Terms CTLA-4Ig
Pharmacologic Category Antirheumatic, Disease Modifying
Use Treatment of rheumatoid arthritis not responsive to other disease-modifying antirheumatic drugs (DMARD); may be used as monotherapy or in combination with other DMARDs (**not** in combination with TNF-blocking agents)

Pregnancy Risk Factor C
Pregnancy Implications Teratogenic effects were not observed in animal studies. There are no adequate and well-controlled studies in pregnant women. Due to the potential risk for development of autoimmune disease in the fetus, use during pregnancy only if clearly needed.

Lactation Excretion in breast milk unknown/not recommended

Contraindications Hypersensitivity to abatacept or any component of the formulation; concurrent use with tumor necrosis factor (TNF) blocking agents (eg, adalimumab, etanercept, infliximab)

Warnings/Precautions Caution should be exercised when considering the use of abatacept in patients with a history of recurrent infections, with conditions that predispose them to infections, or with chronic, latent, or localized infections. Patients who develop a new infection while undergoing treatment should be monitored closely. If a patient develops a serious infection, abatacept should be discontinued. Screen patients for latent tuberculosis infection prior to initiating abatacept; safety in tuberculosis-positive patients has not been established. Patients receiving abatacept in combination with TNF-blocking agents had higher rates of infections (including serious infections) than patients on TNF-blocking agents alone. The manufacturer does not recommend concurrent use with anakinra. Due to the affect of T-cell inhibition on host defenses, abatacept may affect immune responses against infections and malignancies; impact on the development and course of malignancies is not fully defined.

Use caution with chronic obstructive pulmonary disease (COPD), higher incidences of adverse effects (COPD exacerbation, cough, rhonchi, dyspnea) have been observed; monitor closely. May cause hypersensitivity, anaphylaxis, or anaphylactoid reactions; medications for the treatment of hypersensitivity reactions should be available for immediate use. Patients should be brought up to date with all immunizations before initiating therapy. Live vaccines should not be given concurrently; there is no data available concerning secondary transmission of live vaccines in patients receiving therapy. Safety and efficacy in children have not been established.

Adverse Reactions Note: Percentages not always reported; COPD patients experienced a higher frequency of COPD-related adverse reactions (COPD exacerbation, cough, dyspnea, pneumonia, rhonchi)
(Continued)

Abatacept (Continued)

>10%:
Central nervous system: Headache (18%)
Gastrointestinal: Nausea
Respiratory: Nasopharyngitis (12%), upper respiratory tract infection
Miscellaneous: Infection
1% to 10%:
Cardiovascular: Hypertension (7%)
Central nervous system: Dizziness (9%)
Dermatologic: Rash (4%)
Gastrointestinal: Dyspepsia (6%)
Genitourinary: Urinary tract infection (6%)
Neuromuscular & skeletal: Back pain (7%), limb pain (3%)
Respiratory: Cough (8%), bronchitis, pneumonia, rhinitis, sinusitis
Miscellaneous: Infusion-related reactions (9%), herpes simplex, influenza
<1% (Limited to important or life-threatening): Anaphylaxis, anaphylactoid reactions, cellulitis, diverticulitis, dyspnea, flushing, hypersensitivity, hypotension, lung cancer, lymphoma, pruritus, pyelonephritis, urticaria, wheezing

Overdosage/Toxicology Doses up to 50 mg/kg have been tolerated. In the event of an overdose, monitor for signs and symptoms of adverse reactions; treatment should be symptom-directed and supportive.

Drug Interactions

Increased Effect/Toxicity: Abatacept may increase the risk of infections associated with vaccines (live organism). TNF-blocking agents used in combination with abatacept is contraindicated (may increase risk of infections).

Decreased Effect: Abatacept may decrease the efficacy of immune response to live vaccines.

Stability Prior to reconstitution, store at 2°C to 8°C (36°F to 46°F); protect from light. Reconstitute each vial with 10 mL SWFI using a silicone-free disposable syringe (discard solutions accidentally reconstituted with siliconized syringe as they may develop translucent particles). Inject SWFI down the side of the vial to avoid foaming. Gently rotate or swirl vial to dissolve; do not shake. Upon dissolution, vent vial to dissipate foaming. After reconstitution, each mL will contain 25 mg abatacept. Further dilute (using a silicone-free syringe) to a final concentration of 5-10 mg/mL in 100 mL NS; gently mix.

After dilution, may be stored for up to 24 hours at room temperature or refrigerated at 2°C to 8°C (36°F to 46°F). Must be used within 24 hours of reconstitution.

Mechanism of Action Selective costimulation modulator; inhibits T-cell (T-lymphocyte) activation by binding to CD80 and CD86 on antigen presenting cells (APC), thus blocking the required CD28 interaction between APCs and T cells. Activated T lymphocytes are found in the synovium of rheumatoid arthritis patients.

Pharmacodynamics/Kinetics
Distribution: V_{ss}: 0.02-0.13 L/kg
Half-life elimination: 8-25 days

Dosage I.V.:
Adults: Dosing is according to body weight: Repeat dose at 2 weeks and 4 weeks after initial dose, and every 4 weeks thereafter:
<60 kg: 500 mg
60-100 kg: 750 mg
>100 kg: 1000 mg
Elderly: Refer to adult dosing; due to potential for higher rates of infections and malignancies, use caution.
Dosage adjustment for toxicity: Withhold therapy for patients with serious infections.

Administration Infuse over 30 minutes. Administer through a 0.2-1.2 micron low protein-binding. filter

Monitoring Parameters Signs and symptoms of infection

Dosage Forms Injection, powder for reconstitution [preservative free]: 250 mg

♦ **Abbokinase® [DSC]** see Urokinase on page 1761
♦ **Abbott-43818** see Leuprolide on page 991
♦ **ABC** see Abacavir on page 18
♦ **ABCD** see Amphotericin B Cholesteryl Sulfate Complex on page 115

Abciximab (ab SIK si mab)

U.S. Brand Names ReoPro®
Canadian Brand Names Reopro®
Index Terms C7E3; 7E3
Pharmacologic Category Antiplatelet Agent, Glycoprotein IIb/IIIa Inhibitor
Additional Appendix Information
Glycoprotein Antagonists on page 1884

Use Prevention of acute cardiac ischemic complications in patients at high risk for abrupt closure of the treated coronary vessel and patients at risk of restenosis; an adjunct with heparin to prevent cardiac ischemic complications in patients with unstable angina not responding to conventional therapy when a percutaneous coronary intervention (PCI) is scheduled within 24 hours

Unlabeled/Investigational Use Acute MI — combination regimen of abciximab (full dose), tenecteplase (half dose), and heparin (unlabeled dose)

Pregnancy Risk Factor C

Pregnancy Implications Animal reproduction studies have not been conducted. In vitro studies have shown only small amounts of abciximab to cross the placenta. It is not known whether abciximab can cause fetal harm when administered to a pregnant woman or can affect reproduction capacity.

Lactation Excretion in breast milk unknown/use caution

Contraindications Hypersensitivity to abciximab, to murine proteins, or any component of the formulation; active internal hemorrhage or recent (within 6 weeks) clinically-significant GI or GU bleeding; history of cerebrovascular accident within 2 years or cerebrovascular accident with significant neurological deficit; clotting abnormalities or administration of oral anticoagulants within 7 days unless prothrombin time (PT) is ≤1.2 times control PT value; thrombocytopenia (<100,000 cells/µL); recent (within 6 weeks) major surgery or trauma; intracranial tumor, arteriovenous malformation, or aneurysm; severe uncontrolled hypertension; history of vasculitis; use of dextran before PTCA or intent to use dextran during PTCA; concomitant use of another parenteral GP IIb/IIIa inhibitor

Warnings/Precautions Administration of abciximab is associated with increased frequency of major bleeding complications, including retroperitoneal bleeding, pulmonary bleeding, spontaneous GI or GU bleeding, and bleeding at the arterial access. Risk may be increased with patients weighing <75 kg, elderly patients (>65 years of age), history of previous GI disease, and recent thrombolytic therapy. Avoid the creation of venous access at noncompressible sites.

The risk of major bleeds may increase with concurrent use of thrombolytics. Anticoagulation, such as with heparin, may contribute to the risk of bleeding. In serious, uncontrolled bleeding, abciximab and heparin should be stopped. Increased risk of hemorrhage during or following angioplasty is associated with unsuccessful PTCA, PTCA procedure >70 minutes duration, or PTCA performed within 12 hours of symptom onset for acute myocardial infarction. Prior to pulling the sheath, heparin should be discontinued for 3-4 hours and ACT ≤175 seconds or aPTT ≤50 seconds. Use standard compression techniques after sheath removal. Watch the site closely afterwards for further bleeding.

Administration of abciximab may result in human antichimeric antibody formation that can cause hypersensitivity reactions (including anaphylaxis), thrombocytopenia, or diminished efficacy. Readmingation of abciximab within 30 days or in patients with human antichimeric antibodies (HACA) increases the incidence and severity of thrombocytopenia. Safety and efficacy have not been established in children.

Adverse Reactions As with all drugs which may affect hemostasis, bleeding is associated with abciximab. Hemorrhage may occur at virtually any site. Risk is dependent on multiple variables, including the concurrent use of multiple agents which alter hemostasis and patient susceptibility.

>10%:
  Cardiovascular: Hypotension (14.4%), chest pain (11.4%)
  Gastrointestinal: Nausea (13.6%)
  Hematologic: Minor bleeding (4.0% to 16.8%)
  Neuromuscular & skeletal: Back pain (17.6%)
1% to 10%:
  Cardiovascular: Bradycardia (4.5%), peripheral edema (1.6%)
  Central nervous system: Headache (6.45)
  Gastrointestinal: Vomiting (7.3%), abdominal pain (3.1%)
  Hematologic: Major bleeding (1.1% to 14%), thrombocytopenia: <100,000 cells/mm^3 (2.5% to 5.6%); <50,000 cells/mm^3 (0.4% to 1.7%)
  Local: Injection site pain (3.6%)
<1% (Limited to important or life-threatening): Abnormal thinking, allergic reactions/anaphylaxis (possible), AV block, bronchospasm, bullous eruption, coma, confusion, diabetes mellitus, embolism, hyperkalemia, ileus, inflammation, intracranial hemorrhage, myalgia, nodal arrhythmia, pleural effusion, pulmonary embolism, prostatitis, pruritus, stroke, urinary retention, ventricular tachycardia, xerostomia

Overdosage/Toxicology The antiplatelet effects can be quickly reversed with the administration of platelets.

Drug Interactions
  Increased Effect/Toxicity: The risk of bleeding is increased when abciximab is given with heparin, other anticoagulants, thrombolytics, or antiplatelet drugs. However, aspirin and heparin were used concurrently in the majority of patients in the major clinical studies of abciximab. Allergic reactions may be increased in patients who have received diagnostic or therapeutic monoclonal antibodies due to the presence of HACA antibodies. Concomitant use of other glycoprotein IIb/IIIa antagonists is contraindicated.

Stability Vials should be stored at 2°C to 8°C; do not freeze or shake. After admixture, the prepared solution is stable for 12 hours.

Mechanism of Action Fab antibody fragment of the chimeric human-murine monoclonal antibody 7E3; this agent binds to platelet IIb/IIIa receptors, resulting in steric hindrance, thus inhibiting platelet aggregation

Pharmacodynamics/Kinetics Half-life elimination: ~30 minutes

Dosage
  Acute coronary syndromes: PCI: I.V.: 0.25 mg/kg bolus administered 10-60 minutes before the start of intervention followed by an infusion of 0.125 mcg/kg/minute (maximum: 10 mcg/minute) for 12 hours
  Patients with unstable angina not responding to conventional medical therapy and who are planning to undergo percutaneous coronary intervention within 24 hours may be treated with abciximab 0.25 mg/kg intravenous bolus followed by an 18- to 24-hour intravenous infusion of 10 mcg/minute, concluding 1 hour after the percutaneous coronary intervention.
  Acute MI combination regimen (unlabeled): Half-dose tenecteplase (15-25 mg based on weight), abciximab 0.25 mg/kg bolus then 0.125 mcg/kg/minute (maximum: 10 mcg/minute) for 12 hours and heparin dosing as follows: Concurrent bolus of 40 units/kg (maximum: 3000 units), then 7 units/kg/hour (maximum: 800 units/hour) as continuous infusion. Adjust to aPTT target of 50-70 seconds.

Administration Abciximab is intended for coadministration with aspirin postangioplasty and heparin infused and weight adjusted to maintain a therapeutic bleeding time (eg, ACT 300-500 seconds). Solution must be filtered prior to administration. Do not shake the vial.
(Continued)

Abciximab *(Continued)*

Bolus dose: Aseptically withdraw the necessary amount of abciximab for the bolus dose into a syringe using a 0.2 or 5 micron low protein-binding syringe filter (or equivalent); the bolus should be administered 10-60 minutes before the procedure.

Continuous infusion: Aseptically withdraw 4.5 mL (9 mg) of abciximab for the infusion through a 0.2 or 5 micron low protein-binding syringe filter into a syringe; inject this into 250 mL of NS or D_5W to make a solution with a final concentration of 35 mcg/mL. Infuse at a rate of 17 mL/hour (10 mcg/minute) for 12 hours via pump. If a syringe filter was not used when preparing the infusion, administer using an in-line 0.02 or 0.22 low protein-binding filter.

Monitoring Parameters Prothrombin time, activated partial thromboplastin time (aPTT), hemoglobin, hematocrit, platelet count, fibrinogen, fibrin split products, transfusion requirements, signs of hypersensitivity reactions, guaiac stools, Hemastix® urine. Platelet count should be monitored at baseline, 2-4 hours following bolus infusion, and at 24 hours (or prior to discharge, if before 24 hours). To minimize risk of bleeding:

Abciximab initiated 18-24 hours prior to PCI: Maintain aPTT between 60-85 seconds during the heparin/abciximab infusion period

During PCI: Maintain ACT between 200-300 seconds

Following PCI (if anticoagulation is maintained): Maintain aPTT between 50-75 seconds

Sheath removal should not occur until aPTT is ≤50 seconds or ACT ≤175 seconds.

Maintain bleeding precautions, avoid unnecessary arterial and venous punctures, use saline or heparin lock for blood drawing, assess sheath insertion site and distal pulses of affected leg every 15 minutes for the first hour and then every 1 hour for the next 6 hours. Arterial access site care is important to prevent bleeding. Care should be taken when attempting vascular access that only the anterior wall of the femoral artery is punctured, avoiding a Seldinger (through and through) technique for obtaining sheath access. Femoral vein sheath placement should be avoided unless needed. While the vascular sheath is in place, patients should be maintained on complete bedrest with the head of the bed at a 30° angle and the affected limb restrained in a straight position.

Observe patient for mental status changes, hemorrhage; assess nose and mouth mucous membranes, puncture sites for oozing, ecchymosis, and hematoma formation; and examine urine, stool, and emesis for presence of occult or frank blood; gentle care should be provided when removing dressings.

Dosage Forms Injection, solution: 2 mg/mL (5 mL)

- ♦ **Abelcet®** *see* Amphotericin B (Lipid Complex) *on page 118*
- ♦ **Abenol® (Can)** *see* Acetaminophen *on page 28*
- ♦ **Abilify®** *see* Aripiprazole *on page 151*
- ♦ **Abilify® Discmelt™** *see* Aripiprazole *on page 151*
- ♦ **ABLC** *see* Amphotericin B (Lipid Complex) *on page 118*
- ♦ **A/B Otic** *see* Antipyrine and Benzocaine *on page 137*
- ♦ **Abraxane™** *see* Paclitaxel (Protein Bound) *on page 1297*
- ♦ **Abreva® [OTC]** *see* Docosanol *on page 533*
- ♦ **ABX-EGF** *see* Panitumumab *on page 1305*
- ♦ **AC 2993** *see* Exenatide *on page 676*

Acamprosate *(a kam PROE sate)*

U.S. Brand Names Campral®

Index Terms Acamprosate Calcium; Calcium Acetylhomotaurinate

Pharmacologic Category GABA Agonist/Glutamate Antagonist

Use Maintenance of alcohol abstinence

Pregnancy Risk Factor C

Pregnancy Implications Teratogenic in animal studies. No adequate or well-controlled studies in pregnant women; use only if potential benefit outweighs possible risk to the fetus.

Lactation Excretion in breast milk unknown/use caution

Contraindications Hypersensitivity to acamprosate or any component of the formulation; severe renal impairment (Cl_{cr} <30 mL/minute).

Warnings/Precautions Should be used as part of a comprehensive program to treat alcohol dependence. Treatment should be initiated as soon as possible following the period of alcohol withdrawal, when the patient has achieved abstinence. Acamprosate does not eliminate or diminish the symptoms of alcohol withdrawal. Use caution in moderate renal impairment (Cl_{cr} 30-50 mL/minute). Suicidal ideation, attempted and completed suicides have occurred in acamprosate-treated patients; monitor for depression and/or suicidal thinking. Traces of sulfites may be present in the formulation. Safety and efficacy have not been established in pediatric patients.

Adverse Reactions

Note: Many adverse effects associated with treatment may be related to alcohol abstinence; reported frequency range may overlap with placebo.

>10%: Gastrointestinal: Diarrhea (10% to 17%)

1% to 10%:

Cardiovascular: Syncope, palpitation, edema (peripheral)

Central nervous system: Insomnia (6% to 9%), anxiety (5% to 8%), depression (4% to 8%), dizziness (3% to 4%), pain (2% to 4%), paresthesia (2% to 3%), headache, somnolence, amnesia, tremor, chills

Dermatologic: Pruritus (3% to 4%), rash

Endocrine and metabolic: Weight gain, libido decreased

Gastrointestinal: Anorexia (2% to 5%), flatulence (1% to 3%), nausea (3% to 4%), abdominal pain, dry mouth (1% to 3%), vomiting, dyspepsia, constipation, appetite increased, taste perversion

Genitourinary: Impotence

Neuromuscular & skeletal: Weakness (5% to 7%), back pain, myalgia, arthralgia

Ocular: Abnormal vision
Respiratory: Rhinitis, dyspnea, pharyngitis, bronchitis
Miscellaneous: Diaphoresis (2% to 3%), suicide attempt
<1%, postmarketing, and/or case reports (limited to important or life-threatening): Angina, asthma, exfoliative dermatitis, gastrointestinal hemorrhage, hallucinations, hypothyroidism, MI, ophthalmitis, pancreatitis, photosensitivity, psychosis, pulmonary embolus, renal calculus, renal failure, seizure, suicidal ideation, suicide attempts, suicide completion

Overdosage/Toxicology Symptoms may include diarrhea and (in chronic overdose) hypercalcemia. Treatment is symptom-directed and supportive.

Drug Interactions
Decreased Effect: No clinically-significant drug-to-drug interactions have been identified.

Ethanol/Nutrition/Herb Interactions
Ethanol: Abstinence is required during treatment. Ethanol does not affect the pharmacokinetics of acamprosate; however, the continued use of ethanol will decrease desired efficacy of acamprosate.
Food: Food decreases absorption of acamprosate (not clinically significant).

Stability Store at 25°C (77°F); excursions permitted to 15°C to 30°C (59°F to 86°F).

Mechanism of Action Mechanism not fully defined. Structurally similar to gamma-amino butyric acid (GABA), acamprosate appears to increase the activity of the GABA-ergic system, and decreases activity of glutamate within the CNS, including a decrease in activity at N-methyl D-aspartate (NMDA) receptors; may also affect CNS calcium channels. Restores balance to GABA and glutamate activities which appear to be disrupted in alcohol dependence. During therapeutic use, reduces alcohol intake, but does not cause a disulfiram-like reaction following alcohol ingestion.

Pharmacodynamics/Kinetics
Distribution: V_d: 1 L/kg
Protein binding: Negligible
Metabolism: Not metabolized
Bioavailability: 11%
Half-life elimination: 20-33 hours
Excretion: Urine (as unchanged drug)

Dosage Oral: Adults: Alcohol abstinence: 666 mg 3 times/day (a lower dose may be effective in some patients)
Adjustment in patients with low body weight (unlabeled): A lower dose (4 tablets/day) may be considered in patients with low body weight (eg, <60 kg).
Note: Treatment should be initiated as soon as possible (following the period of alcohol withdrawal) when the patient has achieved abstinence.
Dosage adjustment in renal impairment:
Cl_{cr} 30-50 mL/minute: Initial dose should be reduced to 333 mg 3 times/day.
Cl_{cr} <30 mL/minute: Contraindicated in severe renal impairment.

Dietary Considerations May be taken without regard to meals. Each 333 mg tablet contains 33 mg of elemental calcium.

Administration May be administered without regard to meals. Tablet should be swallowed whole; do not crush or chew.

Dosage Forms Tablet, enteric coated, delayed release, as calcium: 333 mg [contains calcium 33 mg and sulfites]

♦ **Acamprosate Calcium** see Acamprosate on page 24

Acarbose (AY car bose)

U.S. Brand Names Precose®
Canadian Brand Names Prandase®
Pharmacologic Category Antidiabetic Agent, Alpha-Glucosidase Inhibitor
Additional Appendix Information
Diabetes Mellitus Management, Adults on page 2040
Hyperglycemia- or Hypoglycemia-Causing Drugs on page 2057
Use
Monotherapy, as indicated as an adjunct to diet to lower blood glucose in patients with type 2 diabetes mellitus (noninsulin dependent, NIDDM) whose hyperglycemia cannot be managed on diet alone
Combination with a sulfonylurea, metformin, or insulin in patients with type 2 diabetes mellitus (noninsulin dependent, NIDDM) when diet plus acarbose do not result in adequate glycemic control. The effect of acarbose to enhance glycemic control is additive to that of other hypoglycemic agents when used in combination.
Pregnancy Risk Factor B
Pregnancy Implications Abnormal blood glucose levels are associated with a higher incidence of congenital abnormalities. Insulin is the drug of choice for the control of diabetes mellitus during pregnancy.
Lactation Excretion in breast milk unknown/use caution
Medication Safety Issues
Sound-alike/look-alike issues:
Precose® may be confused with PreCare®

International issues:
Precose® may be confused with Precosa® which is a brand name for saccharomyces boulardii in Denmark, Finland, Norway, and Sweden
Contraindications Hypersensitivity to acarbose or any component of the formulation; patients with diabetic ketoacidosis or cirrhosis; patients with inflammatory bowel disease, colonic ulceration, partial intestinal obstruction, or in patients predisposed to intestinal obstruction; patients who have chronic intestinal diseases associated with marked disorders of digestion or absorption, and in patients who have conditions that may deteriorate as a result of increased gas formation in the intestine
(Continued)

Acarbose *(Continued)*

Warnings/Precautions Acarbose given In combination with a sulfonylurea will cause a further lowering of blood glucose and may increase the hypoglycemic potential of the sulfonylurea. Treatment-emergent elevations of serum transaminases (AST and/or ALT) occurred in 15% of acarbose-treated patients in long-term studies. These serum transaminase elevations appear to be dose related. At doses >100 mg 3 times/day, the incidence of serum transaminase elevations greater than 3 times the upper limit of normal was 2-3 times higher in the acarbose group than in the placebo group. These elevations were asymptomatic, reversible, more common in females, and, in general, were not associated with other evidence of liver dysfunction. It may be necessary to discontinue acarbose and administer insulin if the patient is exposed to stress (ie, fever, trauma, infection, surgery). Safety and efficacy have not been established in children.

Adverse Reactions
>10%:
  Gastrointestinal: Abdominal pain (21%) and diarrhea (33%) tend to return to pretreatment levels over time, and the frequency and intensity of flatulence (77%) tend to abate with time
  Hepatic: Transaminases increased
<1% (Limited to important or life-threatening): Severe gastrointestinal distress

Overdosage/Toxicology An overdose of acarbose will not result in hypoglycemia. An overdose may result in transient increases in flatulence, diarrhea, and abdominal discomfort which shortly subside. However, acarbose may complicate the treatment of hypoglycemia from other causes, since it will inhibit the absorption of oral disaccharides (sucrose). Oral glucose (dextrose) should be used in mild-to-moderate hypoglycemia; severe hypoglycemia should be treated with I.V. glucose. In cases of overdosage, the patient should not be given fluids or food containing carbohydrates (polysaccharides, oligosaccharides, or disaccharides) for 4-6 hours following overdose.

Drug Interactions
  Increased Effect/Toxicity: Acarbose may increase the risk of hypoglycemia when used with oral hypoglycemics. See Warnings/Precautions.
  Decreased Effect: The effect of acarbose is antagonized/decreased by thiazide and related diuretics, corticosteroids, phenothiazines, thyroid products, estrogens, oral contraceptives, phenytoin, nicotinic acid, sympathomimetics, calcium channel-blocking drugs, isoniazid, intestinal adsorbents (eg, charcoal), and digestive enzyme preparations (eg, amylase, pancreatin). Acarbose decreases the absorption/serum concentration of digoxin.

Ethanol/Nutrition/Herb Interactions Ethanol: Limit ethanol.

Stability Store at <25°C (77°F); protect from moisture.

Mechanism of Action Competitive inhibitor of pancreatic α-amylase and intestinal brush border α-glucosidases, resulting in delayed hydrolysis of ingested complex carbohydrates and disaccharides and absorption of glucose; dose-dependent reduction in postprandial serum insulin and glucose peaks; inhibits the metabolism of sucrose to glucose and fructose

Pharmacodynamics/Kinetics
Absorption: <2% as active drug
Metabolism: Exclusively via GI tract, principally by intestinal bacteria and digestive enzymes; 13 metabolites identified
Bioavailability: Low systemic bioavailability of parent compound; acts locally in GI tract
Excretion: Urine (~34%)

Dosage Oral:
  Adults: Dosage must be individualized on the basis of effectiveness and tolerance while not exceeding the maximum recommended dose
    Initial dose: 25 mg 3 times/day with the first bite of each main meal
    Maintenance dose: Should be adjusted at 4- to 8-week intervals based on 1-hour postprandial glucose levels and tolerance. Dosage may be increased from 25 mg 3 times/day to 50 mg 3 times/day. Some patients may benefit from increasing the dose to 100 mg 3 times/day.
    Maintenance dose ranges: 50-100 mg 3 times/day.
    Maximum dose:
      ≤60 kg: 50 mg 3 times/day
      >60 kg: 100 mg 3 times/day
  Patients receiving sulfonylureas: Acarbose given in combination with a sulfonylurea will cause a further lowering of blood glucose and may increase the hypoglycemic potential of the sulfonylurea. If hypoglycemia occurs, appropriate adjustments in the dosage of these agents should be made.
  Dosing adjustment in renal impairment: Cl_{cr} <25 mL/minute: Peak plasma concentrations were 5 times higher and AUCs were 6 times larger than in volunteers with normal renal function; however, long-term clinical trials in diabetic patients with significant renal dysfunction have not been conducted and treatment of these patients with acarbose is not recommended.

Administration Should be administered with the first bite of each main meal.

Monitoring Parameters Postprandial glucose, glycosylated hemoglobin levels, serum transaminase levels should be checked every 3 months during the first year of treatment and periodically thereafter.

Dosage Forms Tablet: 25 mg, 50 mg, 100 mg

- **A-Caro-25** *see Beta-Carotene on page 211*
- **Accolate®** *see Zafirlukast on page 1805*
- **AccuNeb®** *see Albuterol on page 57*
- **Accupril®** *see Quinapril on page 1469*
- **Accuretic®** *see Quinapril and Hydrochlorothiazide on page 1471*
- **Accutane®** *see Isotretinoin on page 948*
- **Accuzyme®** *see Papain and Urea on page 1309*
- **ACE** *see Captopril on page 281*

Acebutolol (a se BYOO toe lole)

U.S. Brand Names Sectral® [DSC]
Canadian Brand Names Apo-Acebutolol®; Gen-Acebutolol; Monitan®; Novo-Acebutolol; Nu-Acebutolol; Rhotral; Rhoxal-acebutolol; Sandoz-Acebutolol; Sectral®
Index Terms Acebutolol Hydrochloride
Pharmacologic Category Antiarrhythmic Agent, Class II; Beta Blocker With Intrinsic Sympathomimetic Activity
Additional Appendix Information
Beta-Blockers *on page 1875*
Use Treatment of hypertension, ventricular arrhythmias, angina
Pregnancy Risk Factor B (manufacturer); D (2nd and 3rd trimesters - expert analysis)
Pregnancy Implications Acebutolol crosses the placenta. Beta-blockers have been associated with persistent bradycardia, hypotension, and IUGR; IUGR is probably related to maternal hypertension. Available evidence suggests beta-blockers are generally safe during pregnancy (JNC 7). Cases of neonatal hypoglycemia have been reported following maternal use of beta-blockers at parturition or during breast-feeding. Monitor breast-fed infant for symptoms of beta-blockade.
Lactation Enters breast milk/use caution
Medication Safety Issues
Sound-alike/look-alike issues:
Sectral® may be confused with Factrel®, Seconal®, Septra®
Contraindications Hypersensitivity to beta-blocking agents; uncompensated congestive heart failure; cardiogenic shock; bradycardia or second- and third-degree heart block (except in patients with a functioning artificial pacemaker); sinus node dysfunction; pregnancy (2nd and 3rd trimesters)
Warnings/Precautions Consider pre-existing conditions such as sick sinus syndrome before initiating. Beta-blocker therapy should not be withdrawn abruptly (particularly in patients with CAD), but gradually tapered to avoid acute tachycardia, hypertension, and/or ischemia. Use with caution in diabetic patients. Beta-blockers may impair glucose tolerance, potentiate hypoglycemia, and/or mask symptoms of hypoglycemia in a diabetic patient. Use with caution in bronchospastic lung disease, hepatic impairment, myasthenia gravis, psychiatric disease (may cause CNS depression), peripheral vascular disease or renal dysfunction (especially the elderly). Beta-blockers with intrinsic sympathomimetic activity do not appear to be of benefit in CHF and should be avoided. Adequate alpha-blockade is required prior to use of any beta-blocker for patients with untreated pheochromocytoma. Safety and efficacy have not been established in children.
Adverse Reactions
>10%: Central nervous system: Fatigue (11%)
1% to 10%:
Cardiovascular: Chest pain (2%), edema (2%), bradycardia, hypotension, CHF
Central nervous system: Headache (6%), dizziness (6%), insomnia (3%), depression (2%), abnormal dreams (2%), anxiety, hyperesthesia, hypoesthesia, impotence
Dermatologic: Rash (2%), pruritus
Gastrointestinal: Constipation (4%), diarrhea (4%), dyspepsia (4%), nausea (4%), flatulence (3%), vomiting, abdominal pain
Genitourinary: Micturition frequency (3%), dysuria, nocturia, impotence (2%)
Neuromuscular & skeletal: Arthralgia (2%), myalgia (2%), back pain, joint pain
Ocular: Abnormal vision (2%), conjunctivitis, dry eyes, eye pain
Respiratory: Dyspnea (4%), rhinitis (2%), cough (1%), pharyngitis, wheezing
<1% (Limited to important or life-threatening): AV block, exacerbation of pre-existing renal insufficiency, hepatotoxic reaction, impotence, lichen planus, pleurisy, pneumonitis, pulmonary granulomas, systemic lupus erythematosus, urinary retention, ventricular arrhythmia

Potential adverse effects (based on experience with other beta-blocking agents) include reversible mental depression, disorientation, catatonia, short-term memory loss, emotional lability, slightly clouded sensorium, laryngospasm, respiratory distress, allergic reactions, erythematous rash, agranulocytosis, purpura, thrombocytopenia, mesenteric artery thrombosis, ischemic colitis, alopecia, Peyronie's disease, claudication
Overdosage/Toxicology Symptoms include cardiac disturbances, CNS toxicity, bronchospasm, hypoglycemia, and hyperkalemia. The most common cardiac symptoms include hypotension and bradycardia. Atrioventricular block, intraventricular conduction disturbances, cardiogenic shock, and asystole may occur with severe overdose, especially with membrane-depressant drugs (eg, propranolol). CNS effects include convulsions, coma, and respiratory arrest is commonly seen with propranolol and other membrane-depressant and lipid-soluble drugs. Treatment is symptomatic for seizures, hypotension, hyperkalemia, and hypoglycemia. Bradycardia and hypotension resistant to atropine, isoproterenol or pacing, may respond to glucagon. Wide QRS defects caused by membrane-depressant poisoning may respond to hypertonic sodium bicarbonate. Repeat-dose charcoal, hemoperfusion, or hemodialysis may be helpful.
Drug Interactions
Cytochrome P450 Effect: Inhibits CYP2D6 (weak)
Increased Effect/Toxicity: Acebutolol may increase the effects of other drugs which slow AV conduction (digoxin, verapamil, diltiazem), alpha-blockers (prazosin, terazosin), and alpha-adrenergic stimulants (epinephrine, phenylephrine). Acebutolol may mask the tachycardia from hypoglycemia caused by insulin and oral hypoglycemics. In patients receiving concurrent therapy, the risk of hypertensive crisis is increased when either clonidine or the beta-blocker is withdrawn. Reserpine has been shown to enhance the effect of acebutolol. Beta-blockers may increase the action or levels of ethanol, disopyramide, nondepolarizing muscle relaxants, and theophylline although the effects are difficult to predict.
Decreased Effect: Decreased effect of acebutolol with aluminum salts, barbiturates, calcium salts, cholestyramine, colestipol, NSAIDs, penicillins (ampicillin), rifampin, and
(Continued)

Acebutolol (Continued)

salicylates due to decreased bioavailability and plasma levels. The effect of sulfonylureas may be decreased by beta-blockers; however, the decreased effect has not been shown with tolbutamide.

Ethanol/Nutrition/Herb Interactions
Food: Peak serum acebutolol levels may be slightly decreased if taken with food.
Herb/Nutraceutical: Avoid dong quai if using for hypertension (has estrogenic activity). Avoid yohimbe, ginseng (may worsen hypertension).

Stability Store at room temperature of ~25°C (77°F). Protect from light and dispense in a light-resistant, tight container.

Mechanism of Action Competitively blocks beta$_1$-adrenergic receptors with little or no effect on beta$_2$-receptors except at high doses; exhibits membrane stabilizing and intrinsic sympathomimetic activity

Pharmacodynamics/Kinetics
Onset of action: 1-2 hours
Duration: 12-24 hours
Absorption: Oral: 40%
Protein binding: 5% to 15%
Metabolism: Extensive first-pass effect
Half-life elimination: 6-7 hours
Time to peak: 2-4 hours
Excretion: Feces (~55%); urine (35%)

Dosage Oral:
Adults:
Hypertension: 400-800 mg/day (larger doses may be divided); maximum: 1200 mg/day; usual dose range (JNC 7): 200-800 mg/day in 2 divided doses
Ventricular arrhythmias: Initial: 400 mg/day in divided doses; maintenance: 600-1200 mg/day in divided doses
Elderly: Initial: 200-400 mg/day; dose reduction due to age-related decrease in Cl_{cr} will be necessary; do not exceed 800 mg/day
Dosing adjustment in renal impairment:
Cl_{cr} 25-49 mL/minute/1.73 m^2: Reduce dose by 50%.
Cl_{cr} <25 mL/minute/1.73 m^2: Reduce dose by 75%.
Dosing adjustment in hepatic impairment: Use with caution.

Dietary Considerations May be taken without regard to meals.

Administration To discontinue therapy, taper dose gradually. May be administered without regard to meals.

Monitoring Parameters Blood pressure, orthostatic hypotension, heart rate, CNS effects, ECG

Test Interactions Increased triglycerides, potassium, uric acid, cholesterol (S), glucose, thyroxine (S); decreased HDL

Dosage Forms [DSC] = Discontinued product
Capsule, as hydrochloride: 200 mg, 400 mg
Sectral®: 200 mg, 400 mg [DSC]

♦ **Acebutolol Hydrochloride** *see Acebutolol on page 27*
♦ **Aceon®** *see Perindopril Erbumine on page 1346*
♦ **Acephen™ [OTC]** *see Acetaminophen on page 28*
♦ **Acetadote®** *see Acetylcysteine on page 39*
♦ **Aceta-Gesic [OTC]** *see Acetaminophen and Phenyltoloxamine on page 32*

Acetaminophen (a seet a MIN oh fen)

U.S. Brand Names Acephen™ [OTC]; Apra Children's [OTC]; Aspirin Free Anacin® Maximum Strength [OTC]; Cetafen® [OTC]; Cetafen Extra® [OTC]; Comtrex® Sore Throat Maximum Strength [OTC]; FeverALL® [OTC]; Genapap™ [OTC]; Genapap™ Children [OTC]; Genapap™ Extra Strength [OTC]; Genapap™ Infant [OTC]; Genebs [OTC]; Genebs Extra Strength [OTC]; Infantaire [OTC]; Mapap [OTC]; Mapap Children's [OTC]; Mapap Extra Strength [OTC]; Mapap Infants [OTC]; Nortemp Children's [OTC]; Pain Eze [OTC]; Silapap® Children's [OTC]; Silapap® Infants [OTC]; Tycolene [OTC]; Tycolene Maximum Strength [OTC]; Tylenol® [OTC]; Tylenol® 8 Hour [OTC]; Tylenol® Arthritis Pain [OTC]; Tylenol® Children's [OTC]; Tylenol® Children's with Flavor Creator [OTC]; Tylenol® Extra Strength [OTC]; Tylenol® Infants [OTC]; Tylenol® Junior [OTC]; Valorin [OTC]; Valorin Extra [OTC]
Canadian Brand Names Abenol®; Apo-Acetaminophen®; Atasol®; Novo-Gesic; Pediatrix; Tempra®; Tylenol®
Index Terms APAP; N-Acetyl-P-Aminophenol; Paracetamol
Pharmacologic Category Analgesic, Miscellaneous
Additional Appendix Information
Toxicology Information *on page 2081*
Use Treatment of mild-to-moderate pain and fever (antipyretic/analgesic); does not have antirheumatic or anti-inflammatory effects
Pregnancy Risk Factor B
Lactation Enters breast milk/compatible
Medication Safety Issues
Sound-alike/look-alike issues:
Acephen® may be confused with AcipHex®
FeverALL® may be confused with Fiberall®
Tylenol® may be confused with atenolol, timolol, Tuinal®, Tylox®

International issues:
Paralen® [Czech Republic] may be confused with Aralen® which is a brand name for chloroquine in the U.S.
Duorol® may be confused with Diuril® which is a brand name for chlorothiazide in the U.S.

Contraindications Hypersensitivity to acetaminophen or any component of the formulation

Warnings/Precautions Limit dose to <4 g/day. May cause severe hepatic toxicity on acute overdose; in addition, chronic daily dosing in adults has resulted in liver damage in some patients. Use with caution in patients with alcoholic liver disease; consuming ≥3 alcoholic drinks/day may increase the risk of liver damage. Use caution in patients with known G6PD deficiency.

OTC labeling: When used for self-medication, patients should be instructed to contact health-care provider if used for fever lasting >3 days or for pain lasting >10 days in adults or >5 days in children.

Adverse Reactions Frequency not defined.

Dermatologic: Rash

Endocrine & metabolic: May increase chloride, uric acid, glucose; may decrease sodium, bicarbonate, calcium

Hematologic: Anemia, blood dyscrasias (neutropenia, pancytopenia, leukopenia)

Hepatic: Bilirubin increased, alkaline phosphatase increased

Renal: Ammonia increased, nephrotoxicity with chronic overdose, analgesic nephropathy

Miscellaneous: Hypersensitivity reactions (rare)

Overdosage/Toxicology Symptoms include hepatic necrosis, transient azotemia, renal tubular necrosis with acute toxicity, anemia, and GI disturbances with chronic toxicity. Acetyl-cysteine 140 mg/kg orally (loading) followed by 70 mg/kg every 4 hours for 17 doses. Therapy should be initiated based upon laboratory analysis suggesting high probability of hepatotoxic potential. Activated charcoal is very effective at binding acetaminophen.

Drug Interactions

Cytochrome P450 Effect: Substrate (minor) of CYP1A2, 2A6, 2C9, 2D6, 2E1, 3A4; **Inhibits** CYP3A4 (weak)

Increased Effect/Toxicity: Barbiturates, carbamazepine, hydantoins, isoniazid, rifampin, sulfinpyrazone may increase the hepatotoxic potential of acetaminophen. Chronic ethanol abuse increases risk for acetaminophen toxicity; effect of warfarin may be enhanced.

Decreased Effect: Barbiturates, carbamazepine, hydantoins, rifampin, and sulfinpyrazone may decrease the analgesic effect of acetaminophen. Cholestyramine may decrease acet-aminophen absorption (separate dosing by at least 1 hour).

Ethanol/Nutrition/Herb Interactions

Ethanol: Excessive intake of ethanol may increase the risk of acetaminophen-induced hepa-totoxicity. Avoid ethanol or limit to <3 drinks/day.

Food: Rate of absorption may be decreased when given with food.

Herb/Nutraceutical: St John's wort may decrease acetaminophen levels.

Stability Do not freeze suppositories.

Mechanism of Action Inhibits the synthesis of prostaglandins in the central nervous system and peripherally blocks pain impulse generation; produces antipyresis from inhibition of hypothalamic heat-regulating center

Pharmacodynamics/Kinetics

Onset of action: <1 hour

Duration: 4-6 hours

Absorption: Incomplete; varies by dosage form

Protein binding: 8% to 43% at toxic doses

Metabolism: At normal therapeutic dosages, hepatic to sulfate and glucuronide metabolites, while a small amount is metabolized by CYP to a highly reactive intermediate (acetylimido-quinone) which is conjugated with glutathione and inactivated; at toxic doses (as little as 4 g daily) glutathione conjugation becomes insufficient to meet the metabolic demand causing an increase in acetylimidoquinone concentration, which may cause hepatic cell necrosis

Half-life elimination: Prolonged following toxic doses

Neonates: 2-5 hours

Adults: 1-3 hours (may be increased in elderly; however, this should not affect dosing)

Time to peak, serum: Oral: 10-60 minutes; may be delayed in acute overdoses

Excretion: Urine (2% to 5% unchanged; 55% as glucuronide metabolites; 30% as sulphate metabolites)

Dosage Oral, rectal:

Children <12 years: 10-15 mg/kg/dose every 4-6 hours as needed; do **not** exceed 5 doses (2.6 g) in 24 hours; alternatively, the following age-based doses may be used; see table.

Acetaminophen Dosing

Age	Dosage (mg)	Age	Dosage (mg)
0-3 mo	40	4-5 y	240
4-11 mo	80	6-8 y	320
1-2 y	120	9-10 y	400
2-3 y	160	11 y	480

Note: Higher rectal doses have been studied for use in preoperative pain control in children. However, specific guidelines are not available and dosing may be product dependent. The safety and efficacy of alternating acetaminophen and ibuprofen dosing has not been established.

Adults: 325-650 mg every 4-6 hours or 1000 mg 3-4 times/day; do **not** exceed 4 g/day

Dosing interval in renal impairment:

Cl_{cr} 10-50 mL/minute: Administer every 6 hours

Cl_{cr} <10 mL/minute: Administer every 8 hours (metabolites accumulate)

Hemodialysis: Moderately dialyzable (20% to 50%)

Dosing adjustment/comments in hepatic impairment: Use with caution. Limited, low-dose therapy is usually well tolerated in hepatic disease/cirrhosis. However, cases of hepatotox-icity at daily acetaminophen dosages <4 g/day have been reported. Avoid chronic use in hepatic impairment.

(Continued)

Acetaminophen *(Continued)*

Dietary Considerations Chewable tablets may contain phenylalanine (amount varies, ranges between 3-12 mg/tablet); consult individual product labeling.

Administration

Suppositories: Do not freeze.

Suspension, oral: Shake well before pouring a dose.

Monitoring Parameters Relief of pain or fever

Reference Range

Therapeutic concentration (analgesic/antipyretic): 10-30 mcg/mL

Toxic concentration (acute ingestion) with probable hepatotoxicity: >200 mcg/mL at 4 hours or 50 mcg/mL at 12 hours after ingestion

Test Interactions Increased chloride, bilirubin, uric acid, glucose, ammonia (B), chloride (S), uric acid (S), alkaline phosphatase (S), chloride (S); decreased sodium, bicarbonate, calcium (S)

Dosage Forms [DSC] = Discontinued product

Caplet: 500 mg

Cetafen Extra® Strength, Genapap™ Extra Strength, Genebs Extra Strength, Mapap Extra Strength, Tycolene Maximum Strength, Tylenol® Extra Strength: 500 mg

Caplet, extended release:

Tylenol® 8 Hour, Tylenol® Arthritis Pain: 650 mg

Capsule: 500 mg

Elixir: 160 mg/5 mL (120 mL, 480 mL, 3780 mL)

Apra Children's: 160 mg/5 mL (120 mL, 480 mL, 3780 mL) [alcohol free; contains benzoic acid; cherry and grape flavors]

Mapap Children's: 160 mg/5 mL (120 mL) [alcohol free; contains benzoic acid and sodium benzoate; cherry flavor]

Gelcap:

Mapap Extra Strength, Tylenol® Extra Strength: 500 mg

Geltab:

Tylenol® Extra Strength: 500 mg

Geltab, extended release:

Tylenol® 8 Hour: 650 mg [DSC]

Liquid, oral: 500 mg/15 mL (240 mL)

Comtrex® Sore Throat Maximum Strength: 500 mg/15 mL (240 mL) [contains sodium benzoate; honey lemon flavor]

Genapap™ Children: 160 mg/5 mL (120 mL) [contains sodium benzoate; cherry and grape flavors]

Silapap®: 160 mg/5 mL (120 mL, 240 mL, 480 mL) [sugar free; contains sodium benzoate; cherry flavor]

Tylenol® Extra Strength: 500 mg/15 mL (240 mL) [contains sodium benzoate; cherry flavor]

Solution, oral: 160 mg/5 mL (120 mL, 480 mL)

Solution, oral [drops]: 80 mg/0.8 mL (15 mL) [droppers are marked at 0.4 mL (40 mg) and at 0.8 mL (80 mg)]

Genapap™ Infant: 80 mg/0.8 mL (15 mL) [fruit flavor]

Infantaire: 80 mg/0.8mL (15 mL, 30 mL)

Silapap® Infant's: 80 mg/0.8 mL (15 mL, 30 mL) [contains sodium benzoate; cherry flavor]

Suppository, rectal: 120 mg, 325 mg, 650 mg

Acephen™: 120 mg, 325 mg, 650 mg

FeverALL®: 80 mg, 120 mg, 325 mg, 650 mg

Mapap: 125 mg, 650 mg

Suspension, oral:

Mapap Children's: 160 mg/5 mL (120 mL) [contains sodium benzoate; cherry flavor]

Nortemp Children's: 160 mg/5 mL (120 mL) [alcohol free; contains sodium benzoate; cotton candy flavor]

Tylenol® Children's: 160 mg/5 mL (120 mL, 240 mL) [contains sodium benzoate; bubble gum yum, cherry blast, dye free cherry, grape splash, and very berry strawberry flavors]

Tylenol® Children's with Flavor Creator: 160 mg/5 mL (120 mL) [contains sodium 2 mg/5 mL and sodium benzoate; cherry blast flavor; packaged with apple (4), bubblegum (8), chocolate (4), & strawberry (4) sugar free flavor packets]

Suspension, oral [drops]:

Mapap Infants: 80 mg/0.8 mL (15 mL, 30 mL) [contains sodium benzoate; cherry flavor]

Tylenol® Infants: 80 mg/0.8 mL (15 mL, 30 mL) [contains sodium benzoate; cherry, dye free cherry, and grape flavors]

Tablet: 325 mg, 500 mg

Aspirin Free Anacin® Extra Strength, Genapap™ Extra Strength, Genebs Extra Strength, Mapap Extra Strength, Pain Eze, Tylenol® Extra Strength, Valorin Extra: 500 mg

Cetafen®, Genapap™, Genebs, Mapap, Tycolene, Tylenol®, Valorin: 325 mg

Tablet, chewable: 80 mg

Genapap™ Children: 80 mg [contains phenylalanine 6 mg/tablet; fruit and grape flavors]

Mapap Children's: 80 mg [contains phenylalanine 3 mg/tablet; bubble gum, fruit, and grape flavors]

Mapap Junior Strength: 160 mg [contains phenylalanine 12 mg/tablet; grape flavor]

Tablet, orally disintegrating: 80 mg, 160 mg

Tylenol® Children's Meltaways: 80 mg [bubble gum, grape, and watermelon flavors]

Tylenol® Junior Meltaways: 160 mg [bubble gum and grape flavors]

♦ **Acetaminophen and Chlorpheniramine** *see* Chlorpheniramine and Acetaminophen *on page 349*

Acetaminophen and Codeine (a seet a MIN oh fen & KOE deen)

U.S. Brand Names Capital® and Codeine; Tylenol® With Codeine
Canadian Brand Names ratio-Emtec; ratio-Lenoltec; Triatec-8; Triatec-8 Strong; Triatec-30; Tylenol Elixir with Codeine; Tylenol No. 1; Tylenol No. 1 Forte; Tylenol No. 2 with Codeine; Tylenol No. 3 with Codeine; Tylenol No. 4 with Codeine
Index Terms Codeine and Acetaminophen
Pharmacologic Category Analgesic, Opioid
Use Relief of mild-to-moderate pain
Restrictions C-III; C-V
   Note: In countries outside of the U.S., some formulations of Tylenol® with Codeine (eg, Tylenol® No. 3) include caffeine.
Pregnancy Risk Factor C
Medication Safety Issues
   Sound-alike/look-alike issues:
      Capital® may be confused with Capitrol®
      Tylenol® may be confused with atenolol, timolol, Tuinal®, Tylox®

      T3 is an error-prone abbreviation (mistaken as liothyronine)
Dosage Doses should be adjusted according to severity of pain and response of the patient. Adult doses ≥60 mg codeine fail to give commensurate relief of pain but merely prolong analgesia and are associated with an appreciably increased incidence of side effects. Oral:

   Children: Analgesic:
      Codeine: 0.5-1 mg codeine/kg/dose every 4-6 hours
      Acetaminophen: 10-15 mg/kg/dose every 4 hours up to a maximum of 2.6 g/24 hours for children <12 years; **alternatively, the following can be used:**
         3-6 years: 5 mL 3-4 times/day as needed of elixir
         7-12 years: 10 mL 3-4 times/day as needed of elixir
         >12 years: 15 mL every 4 hours as needed of elixir
   Adults:
      Antitussive: Based on codeine (15-30 mg/dose) every 4-6 hours (maximum: 360 mg/24 hours based on codeine component)
      Analgesic: Based on codeine (30-60 mg/dose) every 4-6 hours (maximum: 4000 mg/24 hours based on acetaminophen component)
   Dosing adjustment in renal impairment: See individual agents.
   Dosing adjustment in hepatic impairment: Use with caution. Limited, low-dose therapy is usually well tolerated in hepatic disease/cirrhosis; however, cases of hepatotoxicity at daily acetaminophen dosages <4 g/day have been reported. Avoid chronic use in hepatic impairment.
Additional Information Complete prescribing information for this medication should be consulted for additional detail.
Dosage Forms [DSC] = Discontinued product; [CAN] = Canadian brand name

   Caplet:
      ratio-Lenoltec No. 1 [CAN], Tylenol No. 1 [CAN]: Acetaminophen 300 mg, codeine phosphate 8 mg, and caffeine 15 mg [not available in the U.S.]
      Tylenol No. 1 Forte [CAN]: Acetaminophen 500 mg, codeine phosphate 8 mg, and caffeine 15 mg [not available in the U.S.]
   Elixir, oral [C-V]: Acetaminophen 120 mg and codeine phosphate 12 mg per 5 mL (5 mL, 10 mL, 12.5 mL, 15 mL, 120 mL, 480 mL) [contains alcohol 7%]
      Tylenol® with Codeine [DSC]: Acetaminophen 120 mg and codeine phosphate 12 mg per 5 mL (480 mL) [contains alcohol 7%; cherry flavor]
      Tylenol Elixir with Codeine [CAN]: Acetaminophen 160 mg and codeine phosphate 8 mg per 5 mL (500 mL) [contains alcohol 7%, sucrose 31%; cherry flavor; not available in the U.S.]
   Suspension, oral [C-V] (Capital® and Codeine): Acetaminophen 120 mg and codeine phosphate 12 mg per 5 mL (480 mL) [alcohol free; fruit punch flavor]
   Tablet [C-III]: Acetaminophen 300 mg and codeine phosphate 15 mg; acetaminophen 300 mg and codeine phosphate 30 mg; acetaminophen 300 mg and codeine phosphate 60 mg
      ratio-Emtec [CAN], Triatec-30 [CAN]: Acetaminophen 300 mg and codeine phosphate 30 mg [not available in the U.S.]
      ratio-Lenoltec No. 1 [CAN]: Acetaminophen 300 mg, codeine phosphate 8 mg, and caffeine 15 mg [not available in the U.S.]
      ratio-Lenoltec No. 2 [CAN], Tylenol No. 2 with Codeine [CAN]: Acetaminophen 300 mg, codeine phosphate 15 mg, and caffeine 15 mg [not available in the U.S.]
      ratio-Lenoltec No. 3 [CAN], Tylenol No. 3 with Codeine [CAN]: Acetaminophen 300 mg, codeine phosphate 30 mg, and caffeine 15 mg [not available in the U.S.]
      ratio-Lenoltec No. 4 [CAN], Tylenol No. 4 with Codeine [CAN]: Acetaminophen 300 mg and codeine phosphate 60 mg [not available in the U.S.]
      Triatec-8 [CAN]: Acetaminophen 325 mg, codeine phosphate 8 mg, and caffeine 30 mg [not available in the U.S.]
      Triatec-8 Strong [CAN]: Acetaminophen 500 mg, codeine phosphate 8 mg, and caffeine 30 mg [not available in the U.S.]
      Tylenol® with Codeine No. 3: Acetaminophen 300 mg and codeine phosphate 30 mg [contains sodium metabisulfite]
      Tylenol® with Codeine No. 4: Acetaminophen 300 mg and codeine phosphate 60 mg [contains sodium metabisulfite]

Acetaminophen and Diphenhydramine
(a seet a MIN oh fen & dye fen HYE dra meen)

U.S. Brand Names Excedrin® P.M. [OTC]; Goody's PM® [OTC]; Legatrin PM® [OTC]; Percogesic® Extra Strength [OTC]; Tylenol® PM [OTC]; Tylenol® Severe Allergy [OTC]
(Continued)

Acetaminophen and Diphenhydramine *(Continued)*

Index Terms Diphenhydramine and Acetaminophen
Pharmacologic Category Analgesic, Miscellaneous
Use Aid in the relief of insomnia accompanied by minor pain
Medication Safety Issues
Sound-alike/look-alike issues:
Excedrin® may be confused with Dexatrim®, Dexedrine®
Percogesic® may be confused with paregoric, Percodan®
Tylenol® may be confused with atenolol, timolol, Tuinal®, Tylox®
Dosage Oral: Adults: 50 mg of diphenhydramine HCl (76 mg diphenhydramine citrate) at bedtime or as directed by physician; do not exceed recommended dosage; not for use in children <12 years of age
Dosing adjustment in hepatic impairment: Use with caution. Limited, low-dose therapy is usually well tolerated in hepatic disease/cirrhosis; however, cases of hepatotoxicity at daily acetaminophen dosages <4 g/day have been reported. Avoid chronic use in hepatic impairment.
Additional Information Complete prescribing information for this medication should be consulted for additional detail.
Dosage Forms
Caplet: Acetaminophen 500 mg and diphenhydramine hydrochloride 25 mg
Excedrin® P.M.: Acetaminophen 500 mg and diphenhydramine citrate 38 mg
Legatrin PM®: Acetaminophen 500 mg and diphenhydramine hydrochloride 50 mg
Percogesic® Extra Strength: Acetaminophen 500 mg and diphenhydramine hydrochloride 25 mg
Tylenol® PM: Acetaminophen 500 mg and diphenhydramine hydrochloride 25 mg [also available in vanilla caplets]
Tylenol® Severe Allergy: Acetaminophen 500 mg and diphenhydramine hydrochloride 12.5 mg
Gelcap:
Tylenol® PM: Acetaminophen 500 mg and diphenhydramine hydrochloride 25 mg
Geltab: Acetaminophen 500 mg and diphenhydramine hydrochloride 25 mg
Excedrin® P.M.: Acetaminophen 500 mg and diphenhydramine citrate 38 mg
Tylenol® PM: Acetaminophen 500 mg and diphenhydramine hydrochloride 25 mg
Liquid:
Tylenol® PM: Acetaminophen 500 mg and diphenhydramine hydrochloride 25 mg per 15 mL (240 mL) [contains sodium benzoate; vanilla flavor]
Powder for oral solution:
Goody's PM®: Acetaminophen 500 mg and diphenhydramine citrate 38 mg [contains potassium 41.9 mg and sodium 3.15 mg per powder]
Tablet: Acetaminophen 500 mg and diphenhydramine hydrochloride 25 mg
Excedrin® P.M.: Acetaminophen 500 mg and diphenhydramine citrate 38 mg

♦ **Acetaminophen and Hydrocodone** *see* Hydrocodone and Acetaminophen *on page 848*
♦ **Acetaminophen and Oxycodone** *see* Oxycodone and Acetaminophen *on page 1289*

Acetaminophen and Phenyltoloxamine
(a seet a MIN oh fen & fen il to LOKS a meen)

U.S. Brand Names Aceta-Gesic [OTC]; Dologesic®; Flextra 650; Flextra-DS; Genasec™ [OTC]; Hyflex-DS®; Percogesic® [OTC]; Phenagesic [OTC]; Phenylgesic [OTC]; RhinoFlex™; RhinoFlex 650; Staflex
Index Terms Phenyltoloxamine Citrate and Acetaminophen
Pharmacologic Category Analgesic, Miscellaneous
Use Relief of mild pain
Pregnancy Risk Factor C
Medication Safety Issues
Sound-alike/look-alike issues:
Percogesic® may be confused with paregoric, Percodan®
Dosage Oral:
Analgesic: Based on acetaminophen component:
Children: 10-15 mg/kg/dose every 4-6 hours as needed (maximum: 5 doses/24 hours
Adults: 325-650 mg every 4-6 hours as needed (maximum: 4 g/day)

Product-specific labeling:
Flextra-650:
Children 6 to <12 years: $^1/_2$ tablet every 6 hours (maximum: 2 tablets/day)
Children ≥12 years and Adults: $^1/_2$-1 tablet every 6 hours (maximum: 4 tablets/day)
Flextra-DS, Hyflex-DS®, RhinoFlex™, RhinoFlex™-650:
Children 6 to <12 years: $^1/_2$ tablet every 4 hours (maximum: 2.5 tablets/day)
Children ≥12 years and Adults: $^1/_2$-1 tablet every 4 hours (maximum: 5 tablets/day)
Percogesic®:
Children 6-12 years: 1 tablet every 4 hours (maximum: 4 tablets/24 hours)
Adults: 1-2 tablets every 4 hours (maximum: 8 tablets/24 hours)

Dosing adjustment in renal impairment: Specific dosing adjustment not available; monitor renal function with severe impairment

Dosing adjustment in hepatic impairment: Use with caution. Limited, low-dose therapy is usually well tolerated in hepatic disease/cirrhosis; however, cases of hepatotoxicity at daily acetaminophen dosages <4 g/day have been reported. Avoid chronic use in hepatic impairment.
Additional Information Complete prescribing information for this medication should be consulted for additional detail.

Dosage Forms
Caplet:
    Dologesic®: Acetaminophen 500 mg and phenyltoloxamine citrate 30 mg
    Staflex: Acetaminophen 500 mg and phenyltoloxamine citrate 55 mg
Capsule:
    Dologesic®: Acetaminophen 500 mg and phenyltoloxamine citrate 30 mg
Liquid:
    Dologesic®: Acetaminophen 500 mg and phenyltoloxamine citrate 30 mg per 15 mL (180 mL)
Tablet: Acetaminophen 325 mg and phenyltoloxamine citrate 30 mg
    Aceta-Gesic, Genasec™, Percogesic®, Phenagesic, Phenylgesic: Acetaminophen 325 mg and phenyltoloxamine citrate 30 mg
    Flextra-650: Acetaminophen 650 mg and phenyltoloxamine citrate 60 mg
    Flextra-DS, Hyflex-DS®, RhinoFlex™: Acetaminophen 500 mg and phenyltoloxamine citrate 50 mg
    RhinoFlex™-650: Acetaminophen 650 mg and phenyltoloxamine citrate 50 mg

♦ **Acetaminophen and Propoxyphene** see Propoxyphene and Acetaminophen on page 1445

Acetaminophen and Pseudoephedrine
(a seet a MIN oh fen & soo doe e FED rin)

U.S. Brand Names Allerest® Allergy and Sinus Relief [OTC]; Genapap™ Sinus Maximum Strength [OTC]; Mapap Sinus Maximum Strength [OTC]; Medi-Synal [OTC]; Oranyl Plus [OTC]; Ornex® [OTC]; Ornex® Maximum Strength [OTC]; Sinus-Relief [OTC] [DSC]; Sudafed® Multi-Symptom Sinus and Cold [OTC]; Tylenol® Cold Daytimo, Children's [OTO]; Tylenol® Cold, Infants [OTC]; Tylenol® Sinus Daytime [OTC]
Canadian Brand Names Contac® Cold and Sore Throat, Non Drowsy, Extra Strength; Dristan® N.D.; Dristan® N.D., Extra Strength; Sinutab® Non Drowsy; Sudafed® Head Cold and Sinus Extra Strength; Tylenol® Decongestant; Tylenol® Sinus
Index Terms Pseudoephedrine and Acetaminophen
Pharmacologic Category Alpha/Beta Agonist; Analgesic, Miscellaneous
Use Relief of mild-to-moderate pain; relief of congestion
Medication Safety Issues
Sound-alike/look-alike issues:
    Ornex® may be confused with Orexin®, Orinase®
    Sudafed® may be confused with Sufenta®
    Tylenol® may be confused with atenolol, timolol, Tuinal®, Tylox®
Dosage Oral:
Analgesic: Based on acetaminophen component:
    Children: 10-15 mg/kg/dose every 4-6 hours as needed; do **not** exceed 5 doses in 24 hours
    Adults: 325-650 mg every 4-6 hours as needed; do **not** exceed 4 g/day
Decongestant: Based on pseudoephedrine component:
    Children:
        2-6 years: 15 mg every 4 hours; do **not** exceed 90 mg/day
        6-12 years: 30 mg every 4 hours; do **not** exceed 180 mg/day
    Children >12 years and Adults: 60 mg every 4 hours; do **not** exceed 360 mg/day

Product labeling:
Children's Tylenol® Cold Daytime: Children:
    2-5 years (24-47 lb): 1 teaspoonful every 4-6 hours (maximum: 4 doses/24 hours)
    6-11 years (48-95 lb): 2 teaspoonfuls every 4-6 hours (maximum: 4 doses/24 hours)
Infants' Tylenol® Cold: Children 2-3 years (24-35 lb): 1.6 mL every 4-6 hours (maximum: 4 doses/24 hours)
Sudafed® Multi-Symptom Sinus and Cold: Children ≥12 years and Adults: 2 capsules every 4-6 hours (maximum: 8 capsules/24 hours)
Tylenol® Sinus Daytime: Children ≥12 years and Adults: 2 caplets or gelcaps every 4-6 hours (maximum: 8 caplets or gelcaps/24 hours)

Dosing adjustment in hepatic impairment: Use with caution. Limited, low-dose therapy is usually well tolerated in hepatic disease/cirrhosis; however, cases of hepatotoxicity at daily acetaminophen dosages <4 g/day have been reported. Avoid chronic use in hepatic impairment.
Additional Information Complete prescribing information for this medication should be consulted for additional detail.
Dosage Forms [DSC] = Discontinued product
Caplet:
    Allerest® Allergy and Sinus Relief, Ornex®: Acetaminophen 325 mg and pseudoephedrine hydrochloride 30 mg
    Genapap™ Sinus Maximum Strength, Mapap Sinus Maximum Strength, Ornex® Maximum Strength, Tylenol® Sinus Daytime: Acetaminophen 500 mg and pseudoephedrine hydrochloride 30 mg
Capsule, liquid:
    Sudafed® Multi-Symptom Sinus and Cold: Acetaminophen 325 mg and pseudoephedrine hydrochloride 30 mg [contains sodium 16 mg]
Gelcap:
    Tylenol® Sinus Daytime: Acetaminophen 500 mg and pseudoephedrine hydrochloride 30 mg
Liquid:
    Childrens Tylenol® Cold Daytime: Acetaminophen 160 mg and pseudoephedrine hydrochloride 15 mg per 5 mL (120 mL) [contains sodium benzoate; fruit flavor[
Liquid, oral [drops]:
    Infants Tylenol® Cold: Acetaminophen 80 mg and pseudoephedrine 7.5 mg per 0.8 mL [contains sodium benzoate; bubble gum flavor]
(Continued)

Acetaminophen and Pseudoephedrine *(Continued)*

Tablet:
Medi-Synal, Sinus-Relief [DSC]: Acetaminophen 325 mg and pseudoephedrine hydrochloride 30 mg
Oranyl Plus: Acetaminophen 500 mg and pseudoephedrine hydrochloride 30 mg

Acetaminophen and Tramadol (a seet a MIN oh fen & TRA ma dole)

U.S. Brand Names Ultracet™
Canadian Brand Names Tramacet
Index Terms APAP and Tramadol; Tramadol Hydrochloride and Acetaminophen
Pharmacologic Category Analgesic, Miscellaneous; Analgesic, Nonopioid
Use Short-term (≤5 days) management of acute pain
Pregnancy Risk Factor C
Dosage Oral: Adults: Acute pain: Two tablets every 4-6 hours as needed for pain relief (maximum: 8 tablets/day); treatment should not exceed 5 days
Dosage adjustment in renal impairment: Cl_{cr} <30 mL/minute: Maximum of 2 tablets every 12 hours; treatment should not exceed 5 days
Dosage adjustment in hepatic impairment: Use is not recommended.
Additional Information Complete prescribing information for this medication should be consulted for additional detail.
Dosage Forms Tablet: Acetaminophen 325 mg and tramadol hydrochloride 37.5 mg

Acetaminophen, Aspirin, and Caffeine (a seet a MIN oh fen, AS pir in, & KAF een)

U.S. Brand Names Excedrin® Extra Strength [OTC]; Excedrin® Migraine [OTC]; Fem-Prin® [OTC]; Genaced™ [OTC]; Goody's® Extra Strength Headache Powder [OTC]; Goody's® Extra Strength Pain Relief [OTC]; Pain-Off [OTC]; Vanquish® Extra Strength Pain Reliever [OTC]
Index Terms Aspirin, Acetaminophen, and Caffeine; Aspirin, Caffeine and Acetaminophen; Caffeine, Acetaminophen, and Aspirin; Caffeine, Aspirin, and Acetaminophen
Pharmacologic Category Analgesic, Miscellaneous
Use Relief of mild-to-moderate pain; mild-to-moderate pain associated with migraine headache
Pregnancy Risk Factor D
Medication Safety Issues
Sound-alike/look-alike issues:
Excedrin® may be confused with Dexatrim®, Dexedrine®
Dosage Oral: Adults:
Analgesic:
Based on **acetaminophen** component:
Mild-to-moderate pain: 325-650 mg every 4-6 hours as needed; do **not** exceed 4 g/day
Mild-to-moderate pain associated with migraine headache: 500 mg/dose (in combination with 500 mg aspirin and 130 mg caffeine) every 6 hours while symptoms persist; do not use for longer than 48 hours
Based on **aspirin** component:
Mild-to-moderate pain: 325-650 mg every 4-6 hours as needed; do **not** exceed 4 g/day
Mild-to-moderate pain associated with migraine headache: 500 mg/dose (in combination with 500 mg acetaminophen and 130 mg caffeine) every 6 hours; do not use for longer than 48 hours

Product labeling:
Excedrin® Extra Strength, Excedrin® Migraine: Children >12 years and Adults: 2 doses every 6 hours (maximum: 8 doses/24 hours)
Note: When used for migraine, do not use for longer than 48 hours
Goody's® Extra Strength Headache Powder: Children >12 years and Adults: 1 powder, placed on tongue or dissolved in water, every 4-6 hours (maximum: 4 powders/24 hours)
Goody's® Extra Strength Pain Relief Tablets: Children >12 years and Adults: 2 tablets every 4-6 hours (maximum: 8 tablets/24 hours)
Vanquish® Extra Strength Pain Reliever: Children >12 years and Adults: 2 tablets every 4 hours (maximum: 12 tablets/24 hours)

Dosing adjustment in hepatic impairment: Use with caution. Limited, low-dose therapy is usually well tolerated in hepatic disease/cirrhosis; however, cases of hepatotoxicity at daily acetaminophen dosages <4 g/day have been reported. Avoid chronic use in hepatic impairment.
Additional Information Complete prescribing information for this medication should be consulted for additional detail.
Dosage Forms
Caplet:
Excedrin® Extra Strength, Excedrin® Migraine: Acetaminophen 250 mg, aspirin 250 mg, and caffeine 65 mg
Vanquish® Extra Strength Pain Reliever: Acetaminophen 194 mg, aspirin 227 mg, and caffeine 33 mg
Geltab (Excedrin® Extra Strength, Excedrin® Migraine): Acetaminophen 250 mg, aspirin 250 mg, and caffeine 65 mg
Powder (Goody's® Extra Strength Headache Powder): Acetaminophen 260 mg, aspirin 520 mg, and caffeine 32.5 mg [contains lactose]
Tablet:
Excedrin® Extra Strength, Excedrin® Migraine, Genaced™, Pain-Off: Acetaminophen 250 mg, aspirin 250 mg, and caffeine 65 mg
Fem-Prin®: Acetaminophen 194.4 mg, aspirin 226.8 mg, and caffeine 32.4 mg
Goody's® Extra Strength Pain Relief: Acetaminophen 130 mg, aspirin 260 mg, and caffeine 16.25 mg

♦ **Acetaminophen, Butalbital, and Caffeine** see Butalbital, Acetaminophen, and Caffeine on page 259

♦ **Acetaminophen, Caffeine, Hydrocodone, Chlorpheniramine, and Phenylephrine** see Hydrocodone, Chlorpheniramine, Phenylephrine, Acetaminophen, and Caffeine on page 852

Acetaminophen, Chlorpheniramine, and Pseudoephedrine
(a sect a MIN oh fen, klor fen IR a meen, & soo doe e FED rin)

U.S. Brand Names Actifed® Cold and Sinus [OTC]; Alka-Seltzer® Plus Cold Liqui-Gels® [OTC]; Comtrex® Flu Therapy Day/Night [OTC]; Comtrex® Flu Therapy Nighttime [OTC]; Drinex [OTC]; Kolephrin® [OTC]; Sinutab® Sinus Allergy Maximum Strength [OTC]; Tylenol® Allergy Complete [OTC] [DSC]; Tylenol® Children's Plus Cold Nighttime [OTC]

Canadian Brand Names Sinutab® Sinus & Allergy; Tylenol® Allergy Sinus

Index Terms Acetaminophen, Pseudoephedrine, and Chlorpheniramine; Chlorpheniramine, Acetaminophen, and Pseudoephedrine; Chlorpheniramine, Pseudoephedrine, and Acetaminophen; Pseudoephedrine, Acetaminophen, and Chlorpheniramine; Pseudoephedrine, Chlorpheniramine, and Acetaminophen

Pharmacologic Category Analgesic, Miscellaneous; Antihistamine

Use Temporary relief of sinus symptoms

Pregnancy Risk Factor B

Medication Safety Issues
Sound-alike/look-alike issues:
Thera-Flu® may be confused with Tamiflu®, Thera-Flur-N®
Tylenol® may be confused with atenolol, timolol, Tuinal®, Tylox®

Dosage Oral:
Analgesic: Based on **acetaminophen** component:
Children: 10-15 mg/kg/dose every 4-6 hours as needed; do **not** exceed 5 doses in 24 hours
Adults: 325-650 mg every 4-6 hours as needed; do **not** exceed 4 g/day
Antihistamine: Based on **chlorpheniramine maleate** component:
Children:
2-6 years: 1 mg every 4-6 hours (maximum: 6 mg/24 hours)
6-12 years: 2 mg every 4-6 hours (maximum: 12 mg/24 hours)
Children >12 years and Adults: 4 mg every 4-6 hours (maximum: 24 mg/24 hours)
Decongestant: Based on **pseudoephedrine** component:
Children:
2-6 years: 15 mg every 4 hours (maximum: 90 mg/24 hours)
6-12 years: 30 mg every 4 hours (maximum: 180 mg/24 hours)
Children >12 years and Adults: 60 mg every 4 hours (maximum: 360 mg/24 hours)

Product labeling:
Alka-Seltzer Plus® Cold Medicine Liqui-Gels®:
Children 6-12 years: 1 softgel every 4 hours with water (maximum: 4 doses/24 hours)
Children >12 years and Adults: 2 softgels every 4 hours with water (maximum: 4 doses/24 hours)
Sinutab® Sinus Allergy Maximum Strength: Children >12 years and Adults: 2 tablets/caplets every 6 hours (maximum: 8 doses/24 hours)

Dosing adjustment in hepatic impairment: Use with caution. Limited, low-dose therapy is usually well tolerated in hepatic disease/cirrhosis; however, cases of hepatotoxicity at daily acetaminophen dosages <4 g/day have been reported. Avoid chronic use in hepatic impairment.

Additional Information Complete prescribing information for this medication should be consulted for additional detail.

Dosage Forms [DSC] = Discontinued product
Caplet: Acetaminophen 325 mg, chlorpheniramine maleate 2 mg, and pseudoephedrine hydrochloride 30 mg
Actifed® Cold and Sinus, Sinutab® Sinus Allergy Maximum Strength, Tylenol® Allergy Complete [DSC]: Acetaminophen 500 mg, chlorpheniramine maleate 2 mg, and pseudoephedrine hydrochloride 30 mg
Kolephrin®: Acetaminophen 325 mg, chlorpheniramine maleate 2 mg, and pseudoephedrine hydrochloride 30 mg
Capsule, softgel:
Alka-Seltzer® Plus Cold Liqui-Gels®: Acetaminophen 325 mg, chlorpheniramine maleate 2 mg, and pseudoephedrine hydrochloride 30 mg [contains potassium 25 mg]
Combination package: (Comtrex® Flu Therapy Day/Night):
Caplet [Daytime]: Acetaminophen 500 mg and pseudoephedrine hydrochloride 30 mg
Caplet [Nighttime]: Acetaminophen 500 mg, chlorpheniramine maleate 2 mg, and pseudoephedrine hydrochloride 30 mg
Liquid:
Comtrex® Flu Therapy Nighttime: Acetaminophen 100 mg, chlorpheniramine maleate 4 mg, and pseudoephedrine hydrochloride 60 mg per 30 mL (240 mL) [contains alcohol; cherry flavor]
Tylenol® Children's Plus Cold Nighttime: Acetaminophen 160 mg, chlorpheniramine maleate 1 mg, and pseudoephedrine hydrochloride 15 mg per 5 mL (120 mL) [contains sodium benzoate; grape flavor]
Tablet:
Drinex: Acetaminophen 650 mg, chlorpheniramine maleate 4 mg, and pseudoephedrine hydrochloride 60 mg

Acetaminophen, Dextromethorphan, and Pseudoephedrine
(a seet a MIN oh fen, deks troe meth OR fan, & soo doe e FED rin)

U.S. Brand Names Comtrex® Non-Drowsy Cold and Cough Relief [OTC] [DSC]; Infants' Tylenol® Cold Plus Cough Concentrated Drops [OTC] [DSC]; Sudafed® Severe Cold [OTC]; (Continued)

Acetaminophen, Dextromethorphan, and Pseudoephedrine
(Continued)

Triaminic® Cough and Sore Throat Formula [OTC] [DSC]; Tylenol® Cold Day Non-Drowsy [OTC]; Tylenol® Flu Non-Drowsy Maximum Strength [OTC]; Vicks® DayQuil® Multi-Symptom Cold and Flu [OTC] [DSC]

Canadian Brand Names Contac® Complete; Contac® Cough, Cold and Flu Day & Night™; Sudafed® Cold & Cough Extra Strength; Tylenol® Cold Daytime

Index Terms Dextromethorphan, Acetaminophen, and Pseudoephedrine; Pseudoephedrine, Acetaminophen, and Dextromethorphan; Pseudoephedrine, Dextromethorphan, and Acetaminophen

Pharmacologic Category Antihistamine; Antitussive

Use Treatment of mild-to-moderate pain and fever; symptomatic relief of cough and congestion

Medication Safety Issues
Sound-alike/look-alike issues:
Sudafed® may be confused with Sufenta®
Thera-Flu® may be confused with Tamiflu®, Thera-Flur-N®
Tylenol® may be confused with atenolol, timolol, Tuinal®, Tylox®

Dosage Oral:
Analgesic: Based on acetaminophen component:
Children: 10-15 mg/kg/dose every 4-6 hours as needed; do **not** exceed 5 doses/24 hours
Adults: 325-650 mg every 4-6 hours as needed; do **not** exceed 4 g/day
Cough suppressant: Based on dextromethorphan component:
Children 6-12 years: 15 mg every 6-8 hours; do **not** exceed 60 mg/24 hours
Children >12 years and Adults: 10-20 mg every 4-8 hours **or** 30 mg every 8 hours; do **not** exceed 120 mg/24 hours
Decongestant: Based on pseudoephedrine component:
Children:
2-6 years: 15 mg every 4 hours (maximum: 90 mg/24 hours)
6-12 years: 30 mg every 4 hours (maximum: 180 mg/24 hours)
Children >12 years and Adults: 60 mg every 4 hours (maximum: 360 mg/24 hours)

Product labeling:
Infants' Tylenol® Cold Plus Cough Concentrated Drops: Children 2-3 years (24-55 lb): 2 dropperfuls every 4-6 hours (maximum: 4 doses/24 hours)
Sudafed® Severe Cold, Tylenol® Flu Non-Drowsy Maximum Strength: Children >12 years and Adults: 2 doses every 6 hours (maximum: 8 doses/24 hours)
Tylenol® Cold Non-Drowsy:
Children 6-11 years: 1 dose every 6 hours (maximum: 4 doses/24 hours)
Children ≥12 years and Adults: 2 doses every 6 hours (maximum: 8 doses/24 hours)

Dosing adjustment in hepatic impairment: Use with caution. Limited, low-dose therapy is usually well tolerated in hepatic disease/cirrhosis; however, cases of hepatotoxicity at daily acetaminophen dosages <4 g/day have been reported. Avoid chronic use in hepatic impairment.

Additional Information Complete prescribing information for this medication should be consulted for additional detail.

Dosage Forms [DSC] = Discontinued product
Caplet:
Comtrex® Non-Drowsy Cold and Cough Relief: Acetaminophen 500 mg, dextromethorphan hydrobromide 15 mg, and pseudoephedrine hydrochloride 30 mg [contains benzoic acid] [DSC]
Tylenol® Cold Day Non-Drowsy: Acetaminophen 325 mg dextromethorphan hydrobromide 15 mg, and pseudoephedrine hydrochloride 30 mg
Capsule, liquid:
Vicks® DayQuil® Multi-Symptom Cold and Flu: Acetaminophen 250 mg, dextromethorphan hydrobromide 10 mg, and pseudoephedrine hydrochloride 30 mg [DSC]
Gelcap:
Tylenol® Cold Day Non-Drowsy: Acetaminophen 325 mg, dextromethorphan hydrobromide 15 mg, and pseudoephedrine hydrochloride 30 mg [contains benzyl alcohol] [DSC]
Tylenol® Flu Non-Drowsy Maximum Strength: Acetaminophen 500 mg, dextromethorphan hydrobromide 15 mg, and pseudoephedrine hydrochloride 30 mg
Liquid:
Triaminic® Cough and Sore Throat Formula: Acetaminophen 160 mg, dextromethorphan hydrobromide 7.5 mg, and pseudoephedrine hydrochloride 15 mg per 5 mL (120 mL, 240 mL) [contains benzoic acid; grape flavor] [DSC]
Vicks® DayQuil® Multi-Symptom Cold and Flu: Acetaminophen 325 mg, dextromethorphan hydrobromide 10 mg, and pseudoephedrine hydrochloride 30 mg per 15 mL (175 mL) [DSC]
Suspension, oral [drops]:
Infants' Tylenol® Cold Plus Cough Concentrated Drops: Acetaminophen 160 mg, dextromethorphan hydrobromide 5 mg, and pseudoephedrine hydrochloride 15 mg per 1.6 mL (15 mL) [1.6 mL = 2 dropperfuls] [cherry flavor] [DSC]

♦ **Acetaminophen, Dichloralphenazone, and Isometheptene** see Acetaminophen, Isometheptene, and Dichloralphenazone on page 36

Acetaminophen, Isometheptene, and Dichloralphenazone
(a seet a MIN oh fen, eye soe me THEP teen, & dye KLOR al FEN a zone)

U.S. Brand Names Amidrine [DSC]; Duradrin®; Midrin®; Migquin; Migratine; Migrazone®; Migrin-A
Index Terms Acetaminophen, Dichloralphenazone, and Isometheptene; Dichloralphenazone, Acetaminophen, and Isometheptene; Dichloralphenazone, Isometheptene, and Acetaminophen; Isometheptene, Acetaminophen, and Dichloralphenazone; Isometheptene, Dichloralphenazone, and Acetaminophen

Pharmacologic Category Analgesic, Miscellaneous
Use Relief of migraine and tension headache
Restrictions C-IV
Medication Safety Issues
Sound-alike/look-alike issues:
Midrin® may be confused with Mydfrin®
Dosage Oral: Adults:
Migraine headache: 2 capsules to start, followed by 1 capsule every hour until relief is obtained (maximum: 5 capsules/12 hours)
Tension headache: 1-2 capsules every 4 hours (maximum: 8 capsules/24 hours)

Dosing adjustment in hepatic impairment: Use with caution. Limited, low-dose therapy is usually well tolerated in hepatic disease/cirrhosis; however, cases of hepatotoxicity at daily acetaminophen dosages <4 g/day have been reported. Avoid chronic use in hepatic impairment.

Additional Information Complete prescribing information for this medication should be consulted for additional detail.
Dosage Forms [DSC] = Discontinued product
Capsule: Acetaminophen 325 mg, isometheptene mucate 65 mg, dichloralphenazone 100 mg
Amidrine [DSC], Duradrin®, Midrin®, Migquin, Migrazone®, Migratine, Migrin-A: Acetaminophen 325 mg, isometheptene mucate 65 mg, and dichloralphenazone 100 mg

♦ **Acetaminophen, Pseudoephedrine, and Chlorpheniramine** see Acetaminophen, Chlorpheniramine, and Pseudoephedrine on page 35

♦ **Acetasol® HC** see Acetic Acid, Propylene Glycol Diacetate, and Hydrocortisone on page 38

AcetaZOLAMIDE (a set a ZOLE a mide)

U.S. Brand Names Diamox® Sequels®
Canadian Brand Names Apo-Acetazolamide®; Diamox®
Pharmacologic Category Anticonvulsant, Miscellaneous; Carbonic Anhydrase Inhibitor; Diuretic, Carbonic Anhydrase Inhibitor; Ophthalmic Agent, Antiglaucoma
Additional Appendix Information
Epilepsy on page 2048
Glaucoma Drug Therapy on page 2050
Sulfonamide Derivatives on page 1897
Use Treatment of glaucoma (chronic simple open-angle, secondary glaucoma, preoperatively in acute angle-closure); drug-induced edema or edema due to congestive heart failure (adjunctive therapy); centrencephalic epilepsies (immediate release dosage form); prevention or amelioration of symptoms associated with acute mountain sickness
Unlabeled/Investigational Use Urine alkalinization; respiratory stimulant in COPD; metabolic alkalosis
Pregnancy Risk Factor C
Medication Safety Issues
Sound-alike/look-alike issues:
AcetaZOLAMIDE may be confused with acetoHEXAMIDE
Diamox® Sequels® may be confused with Dobutrex®, Trimox®
Dosage Note: I.M. administration is not recommended because of pain secondary to the alkaline pH

Children:
Glaucoma:
Oral: 8-30 mg/kg/day or 300-900 mg/m²/day divided every 8 hours
I.V.: 20-40 mg/kg/24 hours divided every 6 hours, not to exceed 1 g/day
Edema: Oral, I.V.: 5 mg/kg or 150 mg/m² once every day
Epilepsy: Oral: 8-30 mg/kg/day in 1-4 divided doses, not to exceed 1 g/day; extended release capsule is not recommended for treatment of epilepsy
Adults:
Glaucoma:
Chronic simple (open-angle): Oral: 250 mg 1-4 times/day or 500 mg extended release capsule twice daily
Secondary, acute (closed-angle): I.V.: 250-500 mg, may repeat in 2-4 hours to a maximum of 1 g/day
Edema: Oral, I.V.: 250-375 mg once daily
Epilepsy: Oral: 8-30 mg/kg/day in 1-4 divided doses; **extended release capsule is not recommended for treatment of epilepsy**
Metabolic alkalosis (unlabeled use): I.V.: 250 mg every 6 hours for 4 doses or 500 mg single dose; reassess need based upon acid-base status
Mountain sickness: Oral: 250 mg every 8-12 hours (or 500 mg extended release capsules every 12-24 hours)
Therapy should begin 24-48 hours before and continue during ascent and for at least 48 hours after arrival at the high altitude
Note: In situations of rapid ascent (such as rescue or military operations), 1000 mg/day is recommended.
Urine alkalinization (unlabeled use): Oral: 5 mg/kg/dose repeated 2-3 times over 24 hours
Respiratory stimulant in COPD (unlabeled use): Oral, I.V.: 250 mg twice daily
Elderly: Oral: Initial: 250 mg twice daily; use lowest effective dose
Dosing adjustment in renal impairment:
Cl_{cr} 10-50 mL/minute: Administer every 12 hours
Cl_{cr} <10 mL/minute: Avoid use (ineffective)
Hemodialysis: Moderately dialyzable (20% to 50%)
Peritoneal dialysis: Supplemental dose is not necessary
Additional Information Complete prescribing information for this medication should be consulted for additional detail.
(Continued)

AcetaZOLAMIDE *(Continued)*

Dosage Forms
Capsule, extended release:
Diamox® Sequels®: 500 mg
Injection, powder for reconstitution: 500 mg
Tablet: 125 mg, 250 mg

Acetic Acid *(a SEE tik AS id)*

U.S. Brand Names VoSol® [DSC]
Index Terms Ethanoic Acid
Pharmacologic Category Otic Agent, Anti-infective; Topical Skin Product
Use Irrigation of the bladder; treatment of superficial bacterial infections of the external auditory canal
Pregnancy Risk Factor C
Medication Safety Issues
Sound-alike/look-alike issues:
VoSol® may be confused with Vexol®
Dosage
Irrigation (**Note:** Dosage of an irrigating solution depends on the capacity or surface area of the structure being irrigated):
For continuous irrigation of the urinary bladder with 0.25% acetic acid irrigation, the rate of administration will approximate the rate of urine flow; usually 500-1500 mL/24 hours
For periodic irrigation of an indwelling urinary catheter to maintain patency, about 50 mL of 0.25% acetic acid irrigation is required
Otic: Insert saturated wick; keep moist 24 hours; remove wick and instill 5 drops 3-4 times/day
Additional Information Complete prescribing information for this medication should be consulted for additional detail.
Dosage Forms [DSC] = Discontinued product
Solution for irrigation: 0.25% (250 mL, 500 mL, 1000 mL)
Solution, otic (VōSol® [DSC]): 2% (15 mL)

♦ **Acetic Acid, Hydrocortisone, and Propylene Glycol Diacetate** *see* Acetic Acid, Propylene Glycol Diacetate, and Hydrocortisone *on page 38*

Acetic Acid, Propylene Glycol Diacetate, and Hydrocortisone
(a SEE tik AS id, PRO pa leen GLY kole dye AS e tate, & hye droe KOR ti sone)

U.S. Brand Names Acetasol® HC; VoSol® HC
Index Terms Acetic Acid, Hydrocortisone, and Propylene Glycol Diacetate; Hydrocortisone, Acetic Acid, and Propylene Glycol Diacetate; Propylene Glycol Diacetate, Acetic Acid, and Hydrocortisone
Pharmacologic Category Otic Agent, Anti-infective
Use Treatment of superficial infections of the external auditory canal caused by organisms susceptible to the action of the antimicrobial, complicated by swelling
Dosage Children ≥3 years and Adults: Otic: Instill 3-5 drops in ear(s) every 4-6 hours
Additional Information Complete prescribing information for this medication should be consulted for additional detail.
Dosage Forms Solution, otic drops: Acetic acid 2%, propylene glycol diacetate 3%, and hydrocortisone 1% (10 mL)

♦ **Acetoxymethylprogesterone** *see* MedroxyPROGESTERone *on page 1065*

Acetylcholine *(a se teel KOE leen)*

U.S. Brand Names Miochol®-E
Canadian Brand Names Miochol®-E
Index Terms Acetylcholine Chloride
Pharmacologic Category Cholinergic Agonist; Ophthalmic Agent, Miotic
Use Produces complete miosis in cataract surgery, keratoplasty, iridectomy, and other anterior segment surgery where rapid miosis is required
Pregnancy Risk Factor C
Pregnancy Implications Acetylcholine is used primarily in the eye and there are no reports of its use in pregnancy. Because it is ionized at physiologic pH, transplacental passage would not be expected.
Medication Safety Issues
Sound-alike/look-alike issues:
Acetylcholine may be confused with acetylcysteine
Contraindications Hypersensitivity to acetylcholine chloride or any component of the formulation; acute iritis and acute inflammatory disease of the anterior chamber
Warnings/Precautions During cataract surgery, use only after lens is in place. Systemic effects rarely occur but can cause problems for patients with acute cardiac failure, bronchial asthma, peptic ulcer, hyperthyroidism, GI spasm, urinary tract obstruction, and Parkinson's disease; open under aseptic conditions only.
Adverse Reactions Frequency not defined.
Cardiovascular: Bradycardia, flushing, hypotension
Central nervous system: Headache
Ocular: Clouding, corneal edema, decompensation
Respiratory: Dyspnea
Miscellaneous: Diaphoresis

Overdosage/Toxicology Treatment includes flushing eyes with water or normal saline and supportive measures. If accidentally ingested, induce emesis or perform gastric lavage.

Drug Interactions
 Increased Effect/Toxicity: Effect may be prolonged or enhanced in patients receiving tacrine.
 Decreased Effect: May be decreased with flurbiprofen and suprofen, ophthalmic.

Stability Store unopened vial at 4°C to 25°C (39°F to 77°F); prevent from freezing. Prepare solution immediately before use and discard unused portion. Acetylcholine solutions are unstable; reconstitute immediately before use.

Mechanism of Action Causes contraction of the sphincter muscles of the iris, resulting in miosis and contraction of the ciliary muscle, leading to accommodation spasm

Pharmacodynamics/Kinetics
 Onset of action: Rapid
 Duration: ~10 minutes

Dosage Adults: Intraocular: 0.5-2 mL of 1% injection (5-20 mg) instilled into anterior chamber before or after securing one or more sutures

Administration Open under aseptic conditions only. Attach filter before irrigating eye.

Dosage Forms
 Powder for solution, intraocular, as chloride:
  Miochol®-E: 1:100 [20 mg; packaged with diluent (2 mL)]

♦ **Acetylcholine Chloride** see Acetylcholine on page 38

Acetylcysteine (a se teel SIS teen)

U.S. Brand Names Acetadote®
Canadian Brand Names Acetylcysteine Solution; Mucomyst®; Parvolex®
Index Terms Acetylcysteine Sodium; Mercapturic Acid; Mucomyst; NAC; *N*-Acetylcysteine; *N*-Acetyl-L-cysteine
Pharmacologic Category Antidote; Mucolytic Agent
Additional Appendix Information
 Management of Overdosages on page 2075
Use Adjunctive mucolytic therapy in patients with abnormal or viscid mucous secretions in acute and chronic bronchopulmonary diseases; pulmonary complications of surgery and cystic fibrosis; diagnostic bronchial studies; antidote for acute acetaminophen toxicity
Unlabeled/Investigational Use Prevention of radiocontrast-induced renal dysfunction (oral, I.V.); distal intestinal obstruction syndrome (DIOS, previously referred to as meconium ileus equivalent)
Pregnancy Risk Factor B
Pregnancy Implications Based on limited reports using acetylcysteine to treat acetaminophen overdose in pregnant women, acetylcysteine has been shown to cross the placenta and may provide protective levels in the fetus.
Lactation Excretion in breast milk unknown/use caution
Medication Safety Issues
 Sound-alike/look-alike issues:
  Acetylcysteine may be confused with acetylcholine
  Mucomyst® may be confused with Mucinex®
Contraindications Hypersensitivity to acetylcysteine or any component of the formulation
Warnings/Precautions
 Inhalation: Since increased bronchial secretions may develop after inhalation, percussion, postural drainage, and suctioning should follow. If bronchospasm occurs, administer a bronchodilator; discontinue acetylcysteine if bronchospasm progresses.
 Intravenous: Acute flushing and erythema have been reported; usually occurs within 30-60 minutes and may resolve spontaneously. Serious anaphylactoid reactions have also been reported. Acetylcysteine infusion may be interrupted until treatment of allergic symptoms is initiated; the infusion can then be carefully restarted. Treatment for anaphylactic reactions should be immediately available. Use caution with asthma or history of bronchospasm.
 Acetaminophen overdose: The modified Rumack-Matthew nomogram allows for stratification of patients into risk categories based on the relationship between the serum acetaminophen level and time after ingestion. There are several situations where the nomogram is of limited use. Serum acetaminophen levels obtained prior to 4-hour postingestion are not interpretable; patients presenting late may have undetectable serum concentrations, but have received a lethal dose. The nomogram is less predictive in a chronic ingestion or in an overdose with an extended release product. Acetylcysteine should be administered for any signs of hepatotoxicity even if acetaminophen serum level is low or undetectable. The nomogram also does not take into account patients at higher risk of acetaminophen toxicity (eg, alcoholics, malnourished patients).
Adverse Reactions
 Inhalation: Frequency not defined.
  Central nervous system: Drowsiness, chills, fever
  Gastrointestinal: Vomiting, nausea, stomatitis
  Local: Irritation, stickiness on face following nebulization
  Respiratory: Bronchospasm, rhinorrhea, hemoptysis
  Miscellaneous: Acquired sensitization (rare), clamminess, unpleasant odor during administration
 Intravenous:
  >10%: Miscellaneous: Anaphylactoid reaction (~17%; reported as severe in 1% or moderate in 10% of patients within 15 minutes of first infusion; severe in 1% or mild to moderate in 6% to 7% of patients after 60-minute infusion)
  1% to 10%:
   Cardiovascular: Angioedema (2% to 8%), vasodilation (1% to 6%), hypotension (1% to 4%), tachycardia (1% to 4%), syncope (1% to 3%), chest tightness (1%), flushing (1%)
   Central nervous system: Dysphoria (<1% to 2%)
 (Continued)

Acetylcysteine *(Continued)*

Dermatologic: Urticaria (2% to 7%), rash (1% to 5%), facial erythema (≤1%), palmar erythema (≤1%), pruritus (≤1% to 3%), pruritus with rash and vasodilation (2% to 9%)

Gastrointestinal: Vomiting (<1% to 10%), nausea (1% to 10%), dyspepsia (≤1%)

Neuromuscular & skeletal: Gait disturbance (<1% to 2%)

Ocular: Eye pain (<1% to 3%)

Otic: Ear pain (1%)

Respiratory: Bronchospasm (1% to 6%), cough (1% to 4%), dyspnea (<1% to 3%), pharyngitis (1%), rhinorrhea (1%), rhonchi (1%), throat tightness (1%)

Miscellaneous: Diaphoresis (≤1%)

Overdosage/Toxicology The treatment of acetylcysteine toxicity is usually aimed at reversing anaphylactoid symptoms or controlling nausea and vomiting. The use of epinephrine, antihistamines, and steroids may be beneficial.

Drug Interactions

Decreased Effect: Adsorbed by activated charcoal; clinical significance is minimal, though, once a pure acetaminophen ingestion requiring N-acetylcysteine is established; further charcoal dosing is unnecessary once the appropriate initial charcoal dose is achieved (5-10 g:g acetaminophen)

Stability

Solution for injection (Acetadote®): Store vials at room temperature, 20°C to 25°C (68°F to 77°F). Following reconstitution with D_5W, solution is stable for 24 hours at room temperature. A color change may occur in opened vials (light purple) and does not affect the safety or efficacy.

Loading dose: Dilute 150 mg/kg in D_5W 200 mL.

Initial maintenance dose: Dilute 50 mg/kg in D_5W 500 mL.

Second maintenance dose: Dilute 100 mg/kg in D_5W 1000 mL.

Note: To avoid fluid overload in patients <40 kg and those requiring fluid restriction, decrease volume of D_5W proportionally. Discard unused portion.

Solution for inhalation (Mucomyst®): Store unopened vials at room temperature; once opened, store under refrigeration and use within 96 hours. The 20% solution may be diluted with sodium chloride or sterile water; the 10% solution may be used undiluted. A color change may occur in opened vials (light purple) and does not affect the safety or efficacy.

Intravenous administration of solution for inhalation (unlabeled route): Using D_5W, dilute acetylcysteine 20% oral solution to a 3% solution.

Mechanism of Action Exerts mucolytic action through its free sulfhydryl group which opens up the disulfide bonds in the mucoproteins thus lowering mucous viscosity. The exact mechanism of action in acetaminophen toxicity is unknown; thought to act by providing substrate for conjugation with the toxic metabolite.

Pharmacodynamics/Kinetics

Onset of action: Inhalation: 5-10 minutes

Duration: Inhalation: >1 hour

Distribution: 0.47 L/kg

Protein binding, plasma: 83%

Half-life elimination:

Reduced acetylcysteine: 2 hours

Total acetylcysteine: Adults: 5.5 hours; Newborns: 11 hours

Time to peak, plasma: Oral: 1-2 hours

Excretion: Urine

Dosage

Acetaminophen poisoning: Children and Adults:

Oral: 140 mg/kg; followed by 17 doses of 70 mg/kg every 4 hours; repeat dose if emesis occurs within 1 hour of administration; therapy should continue until acetaminophen levels are undetectable and there is no evidence of hepatotoxicity.

I.V. (Acetadote®): Loading dose: 150 mg/kg over 60 minutes; **Note:** Extended infusion time recommended by manufacturer as of February, 2006. Loading dose is followed by 2 additional infusions: Initial maintenance dose of 50 mg/kg infused over 4 hours, followed by a second maintenance dose of 100 mg/kg infused over 16 hours. Total dosage: 300 mg/kg administered over 21 hours.

Patients <40 kg: Reduce fluid volume according to the following table.

Acetadote® Dosing/Fluid Volume Guidelines for Patients <40 kg

Body Weight (kg)	Loading Dose 150 mg/kg over 1 h		Second Dose 50 mg/kg over 4 h		Third Dose 100 mg/kg over 16 h	
	Acetadote® (mL)	D_5W (mL)	Acetadote® (mL)	D_5W (mL)	Acetadote® (mL)	D_5W (mL)
30	22.5	100	7.5	250	15	500
25	18.75	100	6.25	250	12.5	500
20	15	60	5	140	10	280
15	11.25	45	3.75	105	7.5	210
10	7.5	30	2.5	70	5	140

Note: If commercial I.V. form is unavailable, the following dose has been reported using solution for oral inhalation (unlabeled): Loading dose: 140 mg/kg, followed by 70 mg/kg every 4 hours, for a total of 13 doses (loading dose and 48 hours of treatment); infuse each dose over 1 hour through a 0.2 micron Millipore filter (in-line).

Experts suggest that the duration of acetylcysteine administration may vary depending upon serial acetaminophen levels and liver function tests obtained during treatment. In general, patients without measurable acetaminophen levels and without significant LFT elevations (>3 times the ULN) can safely stop acetylcysteine after ≤24 hours of treatment. The patients who still have detectable levels of acetaminophen, and/or LFT elevations (>1000 units/L) continue to benefit from additional acetylcysteine administration.

Adjuvant therapy in respiratory conditions: **Note:** Patients should receive an aerosolized bronchodilator 10-15 minutes prior to acetylcysteine.

Inhalation, nebulization (face mask, mouth piece, tracheostomy): Acetylcysteine 10% and 20% solution (dilute 20% solution with sodium chloride or sterile water for inhalation); 10% solution may be used undiluted

Infants: 1-2 mL of 20% solution or 2-4 mL of 10% solution until nebulized given 3-4 times/day

Children and Adults: 3-5 mL of 20% solution or 6-10 mL of 10% solution until nebulized given 3-4 times/day; dosing range: 1-10 mL of 20% solution or 2-20 mL of 10% solution every 2-6 hours

Inhalation, nebulization (tent, croupette): Children and Adults: Dose must be individualized; may require up to 300 mL solution/treatment

Direct instillation: Adults:

Into tracheostomy: 1-2 mL of 10% to 20% solution every 1-4 hours

Through percutaneous intratracheal catheter: 1-2 mL of 20% or 2-4 mL of 10% solution every 1-4 hours via syringe attached to catheter

Diagnostic bronchogram: Nebulization or intratracheal: Adults: 1-2 mL of 20% solution or 2-4 mL of 10% solution administered 2-3 times prior to procedure

Prevention of radiocontrast-induced renal dysfunction (unlabeled use): Adults: Oral: 600 mg twice daily for 2 days (beginning the day before the procedure); may be given as powder in capsules, some centers use solution (diluted in cola beverage or juice). Hydrate patient with saline concurrently.

Administration

Inhalation: Acetylcysteine is incompatible with tetracyclines, erythromycin, amphotericin B, iodized oil, chymotrypsin, trypsin, and hydrogen peroxide. Administer separately. Intermittent aerosol treatments are commonly given when patient arises, before meals, and just before retiring at bedtime.

Oral: For treatment of acetaminophen overdosage, administer orally as a 5% solution. Dilute the 20% solution 1:3 with a cola, orange juice, or other soft drink. Use within 1 hour of preparation. Unpleasant odor becomes less noticeable as treatment progresses. If patient vomits within 1 hour of dose, readminister.

I.V. : Intravenous formulation (Acetadote®): Administer loading dose of 150 mg/kg over 60 minutes (see **"Note"**), followed by 2 separate maintenance infusions: 50 mg/kg over 4 hours followed by 100 mg/kg over 16 hours. If not using commercially available I.V. formulation, use a 0.2-μ millipore filter (in-line).

Note: Extended infusion time recommended by manufacturer as of February, 2006.

Monitoring Parameters Acetaminophen overdose: AST, ALT, bilirubin, PT, serum creatinine, BUN, serum glucose, and electrolytes. Acetaminophen levels at ~4 hours postingestion (every 4-6 hours if extended release acetaminophen; plot on the nomogram) and every 4-6 hours to assess serum levels, and LFTs for possible hepatotoxicity. Assess patient for nausea, vomiting, and skin rash following oral administration for treatment of acetaminophen poisoning. If administered I.V., monitor for anaphylaxis/anaphylactoid reactions.

Reference Range Determine acetaminophen level as soon as possible, but no sooner than 4 hours after ingestion (to ensure peak levels have been obtained); administer for acetaminophen level >150 mcg/mL at 4 hours following ingestion; toxic concentration with probable hepatotoxicity: >200 mcg/mL at 4 hours or 50 mcg at 12 hours

Dosage Forms

Injection, solution:

Acetadote®: 20% [200 mg/mL] (30 mL) [contains disodium edetate]

Solution, inhalation/oral: 10% [100 mg/mL] (4 mL, 10 mL, 30 mL); 20% [200 mg/mL] (4 mL, 10 mL, 30 mL)

♦ **Acetylcysteine Sodium** see Acetylcysteine on page 39
♦ **Acetylcysteine Solution (Can)** see Acetylcysteine on page 39
♦ **Acetylsalicylic Acid** see Aspirin on page 160
♦ **Achromycin** see Tetracycline on page 1659
♦ **Aciclovir** see Acyclovir on page 44
♦ **Acidulated Phosphate Fluoride** see Fluoride on page 722
♦ **Acilac (Can)** see Lactulose on page 971
♦ **AcipHex®** see Rabeprazole on page 1477
♦ **Acitfed® Cold and Allergy [OTC] [reformulation]** see Chlorpheniramine and Phenylephrine on page 349

Acitretin (a si TRE tin)

U.S. Brand Names Soriatane®

Canadian Brand Names Soriatane®

Pharmacologic Category Retinoid-Like Compound

Use Treatment of severe psoriasis

Restrictions An FDA-approved medication guide must be distributed when dispensing an outpatient prescription (new or refill) where this medication is to be used without direct supervision of a healthcare provider. Medication guides are available at http://www.fda.gov/cder/Offices/ODS/medication_guides.htm.

Pregnancy Risk Factor X

Pregnancy Implications Acitretin is teratogenic in humans. Severe birth defects have been reported when conception occurred during treatment or after therapy was complete. Not for use by women who want to become pregnant; patient should not get pregnant for at least 3 years after discontinuation. In addition, because ethanol forms a teratogenic metabolite and would increase the duration of teratogenic potential, ethanol should not be consumed during

(Continued)

Acitretin *(Continued)*

treatment or for 2 months after discontinuation. Limited amounts of acitretin are found in seminal fluid; although it appears this poses little risk to a fetus, the actual risk of teratogenicity is not known. Any pregnancy which occurs during treatment, or within 3 years after treatment is discontinued, should be reported to the manufacturer at 1-888-500-3376 or to the FDA at 1-800-FDA-1088.

Lactation Enters breast milk/not recommended

Medication Safety Issues

Sound-alike/look-alike issues:

Soriatane® may be confused with Loxitane®

Contraindications Hypersensitivity to acitretin, other retinoids, or any component of the formulation; patients who are pregnant or intend on becoming pregnant; ethanol ingestion; severe hepatic or renal dysfunction; chronically-elevated blood lipid levels; concomitant use with methotrexate or tetracycline

Acitretin is contraindicated in females of childbearing potential unless all of the following conditions apply.

1) Patient has severe psoriasis unresponsive to other therapy or if clinical condition contraindicates other treatments.
2) Patient must have two negative urine or serum pregnancy tests prior to therapy.
3) Patient must commit to using two effective forms of birth control starting 1 month prior to acitretin treatment and for 3 years after discontinuation.
4) Patient is reliable in understanding and carrying out instructions.
5) Patient has received, and acknowledged, understanding of a careful oral and printed explanation of the hazards of fetal exposure to acitretin and the risk of possible contraception failure; this explanation may include showing a line drawing to the patient of an infant with the characteristic external deformities resulting from retinoid exposure during pregnancy. Patient must sign an agreement/informed consent document stating that she understands these risks and that she should not consume ethanol during therapy or for 2 months after discontinuation.
6) All patients (male and female) should not donate blood during and for 3 years following treatment with acitretin.

Warnings/Precautions [U.S. Boxed Warning]: Not for use by women who want to become pregnant; patient should not get pregnant for at least 3 years after discontinuation. **[U.S. Boxed Warning]: All patients (male and female) should abstain from ethanol or ethanol-containing products during therapy and for 2 months after discontinuation. [U.S. Boxed Warning]: All patients should be advised not to donate blood during therapy or for 3 years following completion of therapy.** Monitor for hepatotoxicity; discontinue if elevations of liver enzymes occur. Use with caution in patients at risk of hypertriglyceridemias. Rarely associated with pseudotumor cerebri. Discontinue if visual changes occur. May cause a decrease in night vision or decreased tolerance to contact lenses. **[U.S. Boxed Warning]: All patients must be provided with a medication guide each time acitretin is dispensed. Female patients must also sign an informed consent prior to therapy.** Safety and efficacy for pediatric patients have not been established; growth potential may be affected.

Adverse Reactions

>10%:

Central nervous system: Hyperesthesia (10% to 25%)

Dermatologic: Cheilitis (>75%), alopecia (50% to 75%), skin peeling (50% to 75%), dry skin (25% to 50%), nail disorder (25% to 50%), pruritus (25% to 50%), erythematous rash (10% to 25%), skin atrophy (10% to 25%), sticky skin (10% to 25%), paronychia (10% to 25%)

Endocrine & metabolic: Hypercholesterolemia (25% to 50%), hypertriglyceridemia (50% to 75%), HDL decreased (25% to 50%), phosphorus increased (10% to 25%), potassium increased (10% to 25%), sodium increased (10% to 25%), magnesium increased/decreased (10% to 25%), fasting blood sugar increased (25% to 50%), fasting blood sugar decreased (10% to 25%)

Gastrointestinal: Xerostomia (10% to 25%)

Hematologic: Reticulocytes increased (25% to 50%), hematocrit decreased (10% to 25%), hemoglobin decreased (10% to 25%), WBC increased/decreased (10% to 25%), haptoglobin increased (10% to 25%), neutrophils increased (10% to 25%)

Hepatic: Liver function tests increased (25% to 50%), alkaline phosphatase increased (10% to 25%), direct bilirubin increased (10% to 25%), GGTP increased (10% to 25%)

Neuromuscular & skeletal: Paresthesia (10% to 25%), arthralgia (10% to 25%), rigors (10% to 25%), CPK increased (25% to 50%), spinal hyperostosis progression (10% to 25%)

Ocular: Xerophthalmia (10% to 25%),

Renal: Uric acid increased (10% to 25%), acetonuria (10% to 25%), hematuria (10% to 25%), RBC in urine (10% to 25%)

Respiratory: Rhinitis (25% to 50%), epistaxis (10% to 25%)

1% to 10%:

Cardiovascular: Flushing, edema

Central nervous system: Headache, pain, depression, insomnia, somnolence, fatigue

Dermatologic: Skin odor, hair texture change, bullous eruption, dermatitis, diaphoresis increased, psoriasiform rash, purpura, pyogenic granuloma, rash, seborrhea, ulcers, fissures, sunburn

Endocrine & metabolic: Hot flashes, potassium decreased, phosphorus decreased, sodium decreased, calcium increased or decreased, chloride increased or decreased

Gastrointestinal: Gingival bleeding, gingivitis, saliva increased, stomatitis, thirst, ulcerative stomatitis, abdominal pain, diarrhea, nausea, taste disturbance, anorexia, appetite increased, tongue disorder

Hepatic: Total bilirubin increased

Neuromuscular & skeletal: Arthritis, back pain, hypertonia, myalgia, osteodynia, peripheral joint hyperostosis, Bell's palsy

Ocular: Blurred vision, blepharitis, conjunctivitis, night blindness, photophobia, corneal epithelial abnormality, eye pain, eyebrow or eyelash loss, diplopia, cataract

Otic: Earache, tinnitus

Renal: BUN increased, creatinine increased, glycosuria, proteinuria

Respiratory: Sinusitis

<1% (Limited to important or life-threatening): Anxiety, bleeding time increased, chest pain, cirrhosis, conjunctival hemorrhage, constipation, corneal ulceration, cyanosis, deafness, diplopia, dizziness, dyspepsia, dysphonia, dysuria, eczema, esophagitis, fever, furunculosis, gastritis, glossitis, gum hyperplasia, hair discoloration, healing impaired, hemorrhage, hepatic dysfunction, hepatitis, hyperkeratosis, hypertrichosis, hypoesthesia, intermittent claudication, itchy eyes, jaundice, leukorrhea, malaise, melena, MI, moniliasis, myopathy, nervousness, neuritis, pancreatitis, papilledema, peripheral ischemia, photosensitivity, pseudotumor cerebri, scleroderma, skin fragility or thinning, spinal hyperostosis (new lesion), stroke, taste loss, tendonitis, thromboembolism

Overdosage/Toxicology Symptoms of acute hypervitaminosis A (headache, vertigo) would be expected; vomiting has also been reported. Pregnancy test for women of childbearing age; counseling regarding potential for birth defects and appropriate contraceptive use.

Drug Interactions

Increased Effect/Toxicity: Additive toxic effects with vitamin A or other systemic retinoids, methotrexate, or tetracycline. Ethanol may lead to formation of teratogenic metabolite. Glucose-lowering effect of sulfonylureas may be potentiated.

Decreased Effect: Acitretin causes decreased efficacy of progestin "mini-pill" preparations.

Ethanol/Nutrition/Herb Interactions Ethanol: Use leads to formation of etretinate, a teratogenic metabolite with a prolonged half-life; concomitant use of ethanol or ethanol-containing products is contraindicated.

Stability Store between 15°C to 25°C (59°F to 77°F); avoid high temperatures and humidity. Protect from light.

Pharmacodynamics/Kinetics Etretinate has been detected in serum for up to 3 years following therapy, possibly due to storage in adipose tissue.

Onset: May take 2-3 months for full effect; improvement may be seen within 8 weeks.

Absorption: Oral: ~72% absorbed when given with food

Protein binding: >99% bound, primarily to albumin

Metabolism: Metabolized to *cis*-acitretin; both compounds are further metabolized. Concomitant ethanol use leads to the formation of etretinate (active).

Half-life elimination: Acitretin: 49 hours (range: 33-96); *cis*-acitretin: 63 hours (range: 28-157); etretinate: 120 days (range: 84-168 days)

Excretion: Feces (34% to 54%); urine (16% to 53%)

Dosage Oral: Adults: Individualization of dosage is required to achieve maximum therapeutic response while minimizing side effects

Initial therapy: Therapy should be initiated at 25-50 mg/day, given as a single dose with the main meal

Maintenance doses of 25-50 mg/day may be given after initial response to treatment; the maintenance dose should be based on clinical efficacy and tolerability

Dietary Considerations Administer with food. Avoid ingestion of additional sources of exogenous vitamin A (in excess of RDA); use of ethanol and ethanol-containing products is contraindicated.

Monitoring Parameters Lipid profile (baseline and at 1- to 2-week intervals for 4-8 weeks); liver function tests (baseline, and at 1- to 2-week intervals until stable, then as clinically indicated); blood glucose in patients with diabetes; bone abnormalities (with long-term use)

Additional Information Female patients are required to use two forms of birth control, at least one of which is a primary form, unless they have undergone a hysterectomy or are postmenopausal. Both forms of birth control must be used simultaneously for at least 1 month prior to therapy and for at least 3 years after discontinuation. Primary forms of birth control include tubal ligation, partner's vasectomy, IUD, or hormonal birth control products. Microdosed progestin products, referred to as "mini-pills," have been shown to be less effective when used with acitretin, and are not recommended. Secondary forms of contraception include diaphragms, latex condoms and cervical caps, all if used with a spermicide.

Dosage Forms Capsule: 10 mg, 25 mg

♦ **Aclasta®** **(Can)** *see* Zoledronic Acid *on page 1820*
♦ **Aclovate®** *see* Alclometasone *on page 59*

Acrivastine and Pseudoephedrine (AK ri vas teen & soo doe e FED rin)

U.S. Brand Names Semprex®-D

Index Terms Pseudoephedrine Hydrochloride and Acrivastine

Pharmacologic Category Antihistamine

Use Temporary relief of nasal congestion, decongest sinus openings, running nose, itching of nose or throat, and itchy, watery eyes due to hay fever or other upper respiratory allergies

Pregnancy Risk Factor B

Dosage Oral: Adults: 1 capsule 3-4 times/day

Dosing comments in renal impairment: Do not use

Additional Information Complete prescribing information for this medication should be consulted for additional detail.

Dosage Forms Capsule: Acrivastine 8 mg and pseudoephedrine hydrochloride 60 mg

♦ **ACT** *see* Dactinomycin *on page 444*
♦ **ACT®** **[OTC]** *see* Fluoride *on page 722*
♦ **Act-D** *see* Dactinomycin *on page 444*
♦ **ActHIB®** *see* Haemophilus b Conjugate Vaccine *on page 824*
♦ **Acthrel®** *see* Corticorelin *on page 419*
♦ **Acticin®** *see* Permethrin *on page 1348*
♦ **Actidose-Aqua®** **[OTC]** *see* Charcoal *on page 330*

♦ **Actidose® with Sorbitol [OTC]** *see Charcoal on page 338*
♦ **Actifed® (Can)** *see Triprolidine and Pseudoephedrine on page 1749*
♦ **Actifed® Cold and Allergy [OTC] [DSC]** *see Triprolidine and Pseudoephedrine on page 1749*
♦ **Actifed® Cold and Sinus [OTC]** *see Acetaminophen, Chlorpheniramine, and Pseudoephedrine on page 35*
♦ **Actigall®** *see Ursodiol on page 1762*
♦ **Actimmune®** *see Interferon Gamma-1b on page 929*
♦ **Actinomycin** *see Dactinomycin on page 444*
♦ **Actinomycin D** *see Dactinomycin on page 444*
♦ **Actinomycin Cl** *see Dactinomycin on page 444*
♦ **Actiq®** *see Fentanyl on page 693*
♦ **Activase®** *see Alteplase on page 79*
♦ **Activase® rt-PA (Can)** *see Alteplase on page 79*
♦ **Activated Carbon** *see Charcoal on page 338*
♦ **Activated Charcoal** *see Charcoal on page 338*
♦ **Activated Ergosterol** *see Ergocalciferol on page 603*
♦ **Activated Protein C, Human, Recombinant** *see Drotrecogin Alfa on page 561*
♦ **Activella®** *see Estradiol and Norethindrone on page 624*
♦ **Actonel®** *see Risedronate on page 1515*
♦ **Actonel® and Calcium** *see Risedronate and Calcium on page 1517*
♦ **Actoplus Met™** *see Pioglitazone and Metformin on page 1374*
♦ **Actos®** *see Pioglitazone on page 1372*
♦ **ACT® Plus [OTC]** *see Fluoride on page 722*
♦ **ACT® x2™ [OTC]** *see Fluoride on page 722*
♦ **Acular®** *see Ketorolac on page 963*
♦ **Acular LS™** *see Ketorolac on page 963*
♦ **Acular® PF** *see Ketorolac on page 963*
♦ **ACV** *see Acyclovir on page 44*
♦ **Acycloguanosine** *see Acyclovir on page 44*

Acyclovir (ay SYE kloe veer)

U.S. Brand Names Zovirax®
Canadian Brand Names Apo-Acyclovir®; Gen-Acyclovir; Nu-Acyclovir; ratio-Acyclovir; Zovirax®
Index Terms Aciclovir; ACV; Acycloguanosine
Pharmacologic Category Antiviral Agent
Additional Appendix Information
   Treatment of Sexually Transmitted Infections *on page 2007*
   USPHS / IDSA Guidelines for the Prevention of Opportunistic Infections in Persons Infected With HIV *on page 1966*
Use Treatment of genital herpes simplex virus (HSV), herpes labialis (cold sores), herpes zoster (shingles), HSV encephalitis, neonatal HSV, mucocutaneous HSV in immunocompromised patients, varicella-zoster (chickenpox)
Unlabeled/Investigational Use Prevention of HSV reactivation in HIV-positive patients; prevention of HSV reactivation in hematopoietic stem-cell transplant (HSCT); prevention of HSV reactivation during periods of neutropenia in patients with acute leukemia
Pregnancy Risk Factor B
Pregnancy Implications Teratogenic effects were not observed in animal studies. Acyclovir has been shown to cross the human placenta. There are no adequate and well-controlled studies in pregnant women. Results from a pregnancy registry, established in 1984 and closed in 1999, did not find an increase in the number of birth defects with exposure to acyclovir when compared to those expected in the general population. However, due to the small size of the registry and lack of long-term data, the manufacturer recommends using during pregnancy with caution and only when clearly needed. Data from the pregnancy registry may be obtained from GlaxoSmithKline.
Lactation Enters breast milk/use with caution (AAP rates "compatible")
Medication Safety Issues
   Sound-alike/look-alike issues:
      Zovirax® may be confused with Zostrix®, Zyvox™

   International issues:
      Opthavir® [Mexico] may be confused with Optivar® which is a brand name for azelastine in the U.S.
Contraindications Hypersensitivity to acyclovir, valacyclovir, or any component of the formulation
Warnings/Precautions Use with caution in immunocompromised patients; thrombocytopenic purpura/hemolytic uremic syndrome (TTP/HUS) has been reported. Use caution in the elderly, pre-existing renal disease, or in those receiving other nephrotoxic drugs. Maintain adequate hydration during oral or intravenous therapy. Use I.V. preparation with caution in patients with underlying neurologic abnormalities, serious hepatic or electrolyte abnormalities, or substantial hypoxia.

Safety and efficacy of oral formulations have not been established in pediatric patients <2 years of age.

Chickenpox: Treatment should begin within 24 hours of appearance of rash; oral route not recommended for routine use in otherwise healthy children with varicella, but may be effective in patients at increased risk of moderate to severe infection (>12 years of age, chronic cutaneous or pulmonary disorders, long-term salicylate therapy, corticosteroid therapy).

Genital herpes: Physical contact should be avoided when lesions are present; transmission may also occur in the absence of symptoms. Treatment should begin with the first signs or symptoms.

Herpes labialis: For external use only to the lips and face; do not apply to eye or inside the mouth or nose. Treatment should begin with the first signs or symptoms.

Herpes zoster: Acyclovir should be started within 72 hours of appearance of rash to be effective.

Adverse Reactions

Systemic: Oral:

>10%: Central nervous system: Malaise (12%)

1% to 10%:

Central nervous system: Headache (2%)

Gastrointestinal: Nausea (2% to 5%), vomiting (3%), diarrhea (2% to 3%)

Systemic: Parenteral:

1% to 10%:

Dermatologic: Hives (2%), itching (2%), rash (2%)

Gastrointestinal: Nausea/vomiting (7%)

Hepatic: Liver function tests increased (1% to 2%)

Local: Inflammation at injection site or phlebitis (9%)

Renal: BUN increased (5% to 10%), creatinine increased (5% to 10%), acute renal failure

Topical:

>10%: Dermatologic: Mild pain, burning, or stinging (ointment 30%)

1% to 10%: Dermatologic: Pruritus (ointment 4%), itching

All forms: <1% (Limited to important or life-threatening): Abdominal pain, aggression, agitation, alopecia, anaphylaxis, anemia, angioedema, anorexia, ataxia, coma, confusion, consciousness decreased, delirium, desquamation, diarrhea, disseminated intravascular coagulopathy (DIC), dizziness, dry lips, dysarthria, encephalopathy, erythema multiforme, fatigue, fever, gastrointestinal distress, hallucinations, hematuria, hemolysis, hepatitis, hyperbilirubinemia, hypotension, insomnia, jaundice, leukocytoclastic vasculitis, leukocytosis, leukopenia, local tissue necrosis (following extravasation), lymphadenopathy, mental depression, myalgia, neutrophilia, paresthesia, peripheral edema, photosensitization, pruritus, psychosis, renal failure, seizure, somnolence, sore throat, Stevens-Johnson syndrome, thrombocytopenia, thrombocytopenic purpura/hemolytic uremic syndrome (TTP/HUS), thrombocytosis, toxic epidermal necrolysis, tremor, urticaria, visual disturbances

Overdosage/Toxicology Overdoses of up to 20 g have been reported. Symptoms of overdose include agitation, seizures, somnolence, confusion, elevated serum creatinine, and renal failure. In the event of overdose, sufficient urine flow must be maintained to avoid drug precipitation within renal tubules. Hemodialysis has resulted in up to 60% reduction in serum acyclovir levels.

Ethanol/Nutrition/Herb Interactions Food: Does not affect absorption of oral acyclovir.

Stability

Capsule, tablet: Store at controlled room temperature of 15°C to 25°C (59°F to 77°F); protect from moisture.

Cream, suspension: Store at controlled room temperature of 15°C to 25°C (59°F to 77°F) in a dry place.

Ointment: Store at controlled room temperature of 15°C to 25°C (59°F to 77°F) in a dry place.

Injection: Store powder at controlled room temperature of 15°C to 25°C (59°F to 77°F). Reconstitute acyclovir 500 mg with SWFI 10 mL; do not use bacteriostatic water containing benzyl alcohol or parabens. For intravenous infusion, dilute to a final concentration ≤7 mg/mL. Concentrations >10 mg/mL increase the risk of phlebitis. Reconstituted solutions remain stable for 12 hours at room temperature. Do not refrigerate reconstituted solutions as they may precipitate. Once diluted for infusion, use within 24 hours.

Mechanism of Action Acyclovir is converted to acyclovir monophosphate by virus-specific thymidine kinase then further converted to acyclovir triphosphate by other cellular enzymes. Acyclovir triphosphate inhibits DNA synthesis and viral replication by competing with deoxyguanosine triphosphate for viral DNA polymerase and being incorporated into viral DNA.

Pharmacodynamics/Kinetics

Absorption: Oral: 15% to 30%

Distribution: V_d: 0.8 L/kg (63.6 L): Widely (eg, brain, kidney, lungs, liver, spleen, muscle, uterus, vagina, CSF)

Protein binding: 9% to 33%

Metabolism: Converted by viral enzymes to acyclovir monophosphate, and further converted to diphosphate then triphosphate (active form) by cellular enzymes

Bioavailability: Oral: 10% to 20% with normal renal function (bioavailability decreases with increased dose)

Half-life elimination: Terminal: Neonates: 4 hours; Children 1-12 years: 2-3 hours; Adults: 3 hours

Time to peak, serum: Oral: Within 1.5-2 hours

Excretion: Urine (62% to 90% as unchanged drug and metabolite)

Dosage Note: Obese patients should be dosed using ideal body weight

Genital HSV:

I.V.: Children ≥12 years and Adults (immunocompetent): Initial episode, severe: 5 mg/kg every 8 hours for 5-7 days

Oral:

Children:

Initial episode (unlabeled use): 40-80 mg/kg/day divided into 3-4 doses for 5-10 days (maximum: 1 g/day)

Chronic suppression (unlabeled use; limited data): 80 mg/kg/day in 3 divided doses (maximum: 1 g/day), re-evaluate after 12 months of treatment

Adults:

Initial episode: 200 mg every 4 hours while awake (5 times/day) for 10 days (per manufacturer's labeling), 400 mg 3 times/day for 5-10 days has also been reported

(Continued)

Acyclovir *(Continued)*

Recurrence: 200 mg every 4 hours while awake (5 times/day) for 5 days (per manufacturer's labeling; begin at earliest signs of disease); 400 mg 3 times/day for 5 days has also been reported

Chronic suppression: 400 mg twice daily or 200 mg 3-5 times/day, for up to 12 months followed by re-evaluation (per manufacturer's labeling); 400-1200 mg/day in 2-3 divided doses has also been reported

Topical: Adults (immunocompromised): Ointment: Initial episode: ½" ribbon of ointment for a 4" square surface area every 3 hours (6 times/day) for 7 days

Herpes labialis (cold sores): Topical: Children ≥12 years and Adults: Cream: Apply 5 times/day for 4 days

Herpes zoster (shingles):

Oral: Adults (immunocompetent): 800 mg every 4 hours (5 times/day) for 7-10 days

I.V.:

Children <12 years (immunocompromised): 20 mg/kg/dose every 8 hours for 7 days

Children ≥12 years and Adults (immunocompromised): 10 mg/kg/dose or 500 mg/m²/dose every 8 hours for 7 days

HSV encephalitis: I.V.:

Children 3 months to 12 years: 20 mg/kg/dose every 8 hours for 10 days (per manufacturer's labeling); dosing for 14-21 days also reported

Children ≥12 years and Adults: 10 mg/kg/dose every 8 hours for 10 days (per manufacturer's labeling); 10-15 mg/kg/dose every 8 hours for 14-21 days also reported

Mucocutaneous HSV:

I.V.:

Children <12 years (immunocompromised): 10 mg/kg/dose every 8 hours for 7 days

Children ≥12 years and Adults (immunocompromised): 5 mg/kg/dose every 8 hours for 7 days (per manufacturer's labeling); dosing for up to 14 days also reported

Oral: Adults (immunocompromised, unlabeled use): 400 mg 5 times a day for 7-14 days

Topical: Ointment: Adults (nonlife-threatening, immunocompromised): ½" ribbon of ointment for a 4" square surface area every 3 hours (6 times/day) for 7 days

Neonatal HSV: I.V.: Neonate: Birth to 3 months: 10 mg/kg/dose every 8 hours for 10 days (manufacturer's labeling); 15 mg/kg/dose or 20 mg/kg/dose every 8 hours for 14-21 days has also been reported

Varicella-zoster (chickenpox): Begin treatment within the first 24 hours of rash onset:

Oral:

Children ≥2 years and ≤40 kg (immunocompetent): 20 mg/kg/dose (up to 800 mg/dose) 4 times/day for 5 days

Children >40 kg and Adults (immunocompetent): 800 mg/dose 4 times a day for 5 days

I.V.:

Children <1 year (immunocompromised, unlabeled use): 10 mg/kg/dose every 8 hours for 7-10 days

Children ≥1 year and Adults (immunocompromised, unlabeled use): 1500 mg/m²/day divided every 8 hours or 10 mg/kg/dose every 8 hours for 7-10 days

Prevention of HSV reactivation in HIV-positive patients, for use only when recurrences are frequent or severe (unlabeled use): Oral:

Children: 80 mg/kg/day in 3-4 divided doses

Adults: 200 mg 3 times/day or 400 mg 2 times/day

Prevention of HSV reactivation in HSCT (unlabeled use): Note: Start at the beginning of conditioning therapy and continue until engraftment or until mucositis resolves (~30 days)

Oral: Adults: 200 mg 3 times/day

I.V.:

Children: 250 mg/m²/dose every 8 hours or 125 mg/m²/dose every 6 hours

Adults: 250 mg/m²/dose every 12 hours

Bone marrow transplant recipients (unlabeled use): I.V.: Children and Adults: Allogeneic patients who are HSV and CMV seropositive: 500 mg/m²/dose (10 mg/kg) every 8 hours; for clinically-symptomatic CMV infection, consider replacing acyclovir with ganciclovir

Dosing adjustment in renal impairment:

Oral:

Cl_{cr} 10-25 mL/minute/1.73 m²: Normal dosing regimen 800 mg every 4 hours: Administer 800 mg every 8 hours

Cl_{cr} <10 mL/minute/1.73 m²:

Normal dosing regimen 200 mg every 4 hours, 200 mg every 8 hours, or 400 mg every 12 hours: Administer 200 mg every 12 hours

Normal dosing regimen 800 mg every 4 hours: Administer 800 mg every 12 hours

I.V.:

Cl_{cr} 25-50 mL/minute/1.73 m²: Administer recommended dose every 12 hours

Cl_{cr} 10-25 mL/minute/1.73 m²: Administer recommended dose every 24 hours

Cl_{cr} <10 mL/minute/1.73 m²: Administer 50% of recommended dose every 24 hours

Hemodialysis: Administer dose after dialysis

Peritoneal dialysis: No supplemental dose needed

CAVH: 3.5 mg/kg/day

CVVHD/CVVH: Adjust dose based upon Cl_{cr} 30 mL/minute

Dietary Considerations May be taken with or without food. Acyclovir 500 mg injection contains sodium ~50 mg (~2 mEq).

Administration

Oral: May be administered with or without food.

I.V.: Avoid rapid infusion; infuse over 1 hour to prevent renal damage; maintain adequate hydration of patient; check for phlebitis and rotate infusion sites

Topical: Not for use in the eye. Apply using a finger cot or rubber glove to avoid transmission to other parts of the body or to other persons.

Monitoring Parameters Urinalysis, BUN, serum creatinine, liver enzymes, CBC
Dosage Forms [DSC] = Discontinued product
Capsule: 200 mg
Zovirax®: 200 mg
Cream, topical:
Zovirax®: 5% (2 g, 5 g)
Injection, powder for reconstitution, as sodium: 500 mg, 1000 mg
Zovirax®: 500 mg [DSC]
Injection, solution, as sodium [preservative free]: 25 mg/mL (20 mL, 40 mL); 50 mg/mL (10 mL, 20 mL)
Ointment, topical:
Zovirax®: 5% (15 g)
Suspension, oral: 200 mg/5 mL (480 mL)
Zovirax®: 200 mg/5 mL (480 mL) [banana flavor]
Tablet: 400 mg, 800 mg
Zovirax®: 400 mg, 800 mg

- **Aczone**™ see Dapsone *on page 450*
- **AD3L** see Valrubicin *on page 1770*
- **Adacel**™ see Diphtheria, Tetanus Toxoids, and Acellular Pertussis Vaccine *on page 521*
- **Adagen**® see Pegademase Bovine *on page 1319*
- **Adalat® XL® (Can)** see NIFEdipine *on page 1226*
- **Adalat® CC** see NIFEdipine *on page 1226*

Adalimumab (a da LIM yoo mah)

U.S. Brand Names Humira®
Canadian Brand Names Humira®
Index Terms Antitumor Necrosis Factor Apha (Human); D2E7; Human Antitumor Necrosis Factor Alpha
Pharmacologic Category Antirheumatic, Disease Modifying; Monoclonal Antibody; Tumor Necrosis Factor (TNF) Blocking Agent
Use Treatment of active rheumatoid arthritis, active psoriatic arthritis (moderate to severe), or ankylosing spondylitis
  Note: May be used alone or in combination with disease-modifying antirheumatic drugs (DMARDs).
Pregnancy Risk Factor B
Pregnancy Implications Teratogenic effects were not observed in animal studies, however, there are no adequate and well-controlled studies in pregnant women. Use during pregnancy only if clearly needed. A pregnancy registry has been established to monitor outcomes of women exposed to adalimumab during pregnancy (877-311-8972).
Lactation Excretion in breast milk unknown/not recommended
Medication Safety Issues
Sound-alike/look-alike issues:
Humira® may be confused with Humulin®
Contraindications Hypersensitivity to adalimumab or any component of the formulation
Warnings/Precautions [U.S. Boxed Warnings]: Patients should be evaluated for latent tuberculosis infection with a tuberculin skin test prior to therapy. Treatment of latent tuberculosis should be initiated before adalimumab is used. Tuberculosis (disseminated or extrapulmonary) has been reactivated while on adalimumab. Most cases have been reported within the first 8 months of treatment. **Patients with initial negative tuberculin skin tests should receive continued monitoring for tuberculosis throughout treatment; active tuberculosis has developed in this population during treatment.** Rare reactivation of hepatitis B has occurred in chronic virus carriers; evaluate prior to initiation and during treatment. Adalimumab may affect defenses against infections and malignancies.

[U.S. Boxed Warning]: Serious and potential fatal infections (including invasive fungal and other opportunistic infections) have been reported in patients receiving TNF-blocking agents, including adalimumab. Use caution with chronic infection, history of recurrent infection, or predisposition to infection. Do not give to patients with an active chronic or localized infection. Many of the serious infections have occurred in patients on concomitant immunosuppressive therapy. Other opportunistic infections included*Histoplasma, Aspergillus,* and *Nocardia.* Use caution in patients who have resided in regions where histoplasmosis is endemic. Patients who develop a new infection while undergoing treatment with adalimumab should be monitored closely. If a patient develops a serious infection or sepsis, adalimumab should be discontinued. Rare cases of lymphoma have also been reported in association with adalimumab. Impact on the development and course of malignancies is not fully defined.

May exacerbate pre-existing or recent-onset demyelinating CNS disorders. Worsening and new-onset CHF has been reported; use caution in patients with decreased left ventricular function. Use caution in patients with CHF. Patients should be brought up to date with all immunizations before initiating therapy. No data are available concerning the effects of adalimumab on vaccination. Live vaccines should not be given concurrently. No data are available concerning secondary transmission of live vaccines in patients receiving adalimumab. Rare cases of pancytopenia (including aplastic anemia) have been reported with TNF-blocking agents; with significant hematologic abnormalities, consider discontinuing therapy. Positive antinuclear antibody titers have been detected in patients (with negative baselines) treated with adalimumab. Rare cases of autoimmune disorder, including lupus-like syndrome, have been reported; monitor and discontinue adalimumab if symptoms develop. May cause hypersensitivity reactions, including anaphylaxis; monitor. Safety and efficacy have not been established in pediatric patients.

Adverse Reactions Frequency > placebo in rheumatoid arthritis studies:
>10%:
Central nervous system: Headache (12%)
(Continued)

Adalimumab *(Continued)*

Dermatologic: Rash (12%)

Local: Injection site reaction (8% to 20%; includes erythema, itching, hemorrhage, pain, swelling)

Respiratory: Upper respiratory tract infection (17%), sinusitis (11%)

5% to 10%:

Cardiovascular: Hypertension (5%)

Endocrine & metabolic: Hyperlipidemia (7%), hypercholesterolemia (6%)

Gastrointestinal: Nausea (9%), abdominal pain (7%)

Genitourinary: Urinary tract infection (8%)

Hepatic: Alkaline phosphatase increased (5%)

Local: Injection site reaction (8%; other than erythema, itching, hemorrhage, pain, swelling)

Neuromuscular & skeletal: Back pain (6%)

Renal: Hematuria (5%)

Miscellaneous: Accidental injury (10%), flu-like syndrome (7%)

<5%:

Cardiovascular: Arrhythmia, atrial fibrillation, chest pain, CHF, coronary artery disorder, heart arrest, MI, palpitation, pericardial effusion, pericarditis, peripheral edema, syncope, tachycardia, thrombosis (leg), vascular disorder

Central nervous system: Confusion, fever, hypertensive encephalopathy, multiple sclerosis, subdural hematoma

Dermatologic: Cellulitis, erysipelas

Endocrine & metabolic: Dehydration, menstrual disorder, parathyroid disorder

Gastrointestinal: Diverticulitis, esophagitis, gastroenteritis, gastrointestinal hemorrhage, vomiting

Genitourinary: Cystitis, pelvic pain

Hematologic: Agranulocytosis, granulocytopenia, leukopenia, pancytopenia, paraproteinemia, polycythemia

Hepatic: Cholecystitis, cholelithiasis, hepatic necrosis

Neuromuscular & skeletal: Arthritis, bone fracture, bone necrosis, joint disorder, muscle cramps, myasthenia, pain in extremity, paresthesia, pyogenic arthritis, synovitis, tendon disorder, tremor

Ocular: Cataract

Renal: Kidney calculus, pyelonephritis

Respiratory: Asthma, bronchospasm, dyspnea, lung function decreased, pleural effusion, pneumonia

Miscellaneous: Adenoma, allergic reactions (1%), carcinoma (including breast, gastrointestinal, skin, urogenital), healing abnormality, herpes zoster, ketosis, lupus erythematosus syndrome, lymphoma, melanoma, postsurgical infection, sepsis, tuberculosis (reactivation of latent infection; miliary, lymphatic, peritoneal and pulmonary)

Postmarketing and/or case reports: Anaphylactoid reaction, anaphylaxis, angioneurotic edema, aplastic anemia, cutaneous vasculitis, cytopenia, fixed drug eruption, infections (viral, fungal and protozoal), interstitial lung disease (eg, pulmonary fibrosis), septic arthritis, thrombocytopenia, transaminases increased, urticaria

Overdosage/Toxicology Doses of up to 10 mg/kg have been tolerated in clinical trials. In case of overdose, treatment should be symptom-directed and supportive.

Drug Interactions

Increased Effect/Toxicity: Concomitant use with abatacept or anakinra may increase risk of infections; not recommended. Allergic reactions to abciximab may be increased in patients who received therapeutic or diagnostic monoclonal antibodies.

Decreased Effect: Concomitant use with vaccines (live) has not been studied; due to potential for vaccinal infection, concurrent use is not recommended. The response to vaccines (dead organism) may be diminished in patients receiving adalimumab; monitor closely.

Ethanol/Nutrition/Herb Interactions Herb/nutraceutical: Echinacea may decrease the therapeutic effects of adalimumab; avoid concurrent use.

Stability Store under refrigeration at 2°C to 8°C (36°F to 46°F); do not freeze. Protect from light.

Mechanism of Action Adalimumab is a recombinant monoclonal antibody that binds to human tumor necrosis factor alpha (TNF-alpha), thereby interfering with binding to TNFα receptor sites and subsequent cytokine-driven inflammatory processes. Elevated TNF levels in the synovial fluid are involved in the pathologic pain and joint destruction in immune-mediated arthritis. Adalimumab decreases signs and symptoms of psoriatic arthritis, rheumatoid arthritis, and ankylosing spondylitis. It inhibits progression of structural damage of rheumatoid and psoriatic arthritis.

Pharmacodynamics/Kinetics

Distribution: V_d: 4.7-6 L; Synovial fluid concentrations: 31% to 96% of serum

Bioavailability: Absolute: 64%

Half-life elimination: Terminal: ~2 weeks (range 10-20 days)

Time to peak, serum: SubQ: 131 ± 56 hours

Excretion: Clearance increased in the presence of antiadalimumab antibodies; decreased in patients 40 years and older

Dosage SubQ: Adults:

Rheumatoid arthritis: 40 mg every other week; may be administered with other DMARDs; patients not taking methotrexate may increase dose to 40 mg every week

Ankylosing spondylitis, psoriatic arthritis: 40 mg every other week

Administration For SubQ injection; rotate injection sites. Do not use if solution is discolored. Do not administer to skin which is red, tender, bruised, or hard.

Monitoring Parameters Place and read PPD before initiation. Monitor improvement of symptoms and physical function assessments; CBC; signs of infection, bleeding or bruising.

Dosage Forms
Injection, solution [preservative free]:
Humira®: 40 mg/0.8 mL (1 mL) [prefilled glass syringe or Humira® pen; packaged with alcohol preps; needle cover contains latex]

♦ **Adamantanamine Hydrochloride** see Amantadine on page 86

Adapalene (a DAP a leen)

U.S. Brand Names Differin®
Canadian Brand Names Differin®; Differin® XP
Pharmacologic Category Acne Products; Topical Skin Product, Acne
Use Treatment of acne vulgaris
Pregnancy Risk Factor C
Pregnancy Implications There are no adequate and well-controlled studies in pregnant women. Use only if benefit outweighs the potential risk to fetus.
Lactation Excretion in breast milk unknown/use caution
Contraindications Hypersensitivity to adapalene or any component in the vehicle gel
Warnings/Precautions Use with caution in patients with eczema. Avoid excessive exposure to sunlight and sunlamps. Avoid contact with abraded skin, mucous membranes, eyes, mouth, angles of the nose.

Certain cutaneous signs and symptoms such as erythema, dryness, scaling, burning, or pruritus may occur during treatment; these are most likely to occur during the first 2-4 weeks and will usually lessen with continued use.
Adverse Reactions
>10%: Dermatologic: Erythema, scaling, dryness, pruritus, burning, pruritus or burning immediately after application
<1% (Limited to important or life-threatening): Acne flares, conjunctivitis, contact dermatitis, dermatitis, eczema, eyelid edema, skin discoloration, skin irritation, stinging sunburn, rash (topical cream)
Overdosage/Toxicology Toxic signs of an overdose commonly respond to drug discontinuation, and generally return to normal spontaneously within a few days to weeks. When confronted with signs of increased intracranial pressure, treatment with mannitol (0.25 g/kg I.V. up to 1 g/kg/dose repeated every 5 minutes as needed), dexamethasone (1.5 mg/kg I.V. load followed with 0.375 mg/kg every 6 hours for 5 days), and/or hyperventilation should be employed.
Mechanism of Action Retinoid-like compound which is a modulator of cellular differentiation, keratinization, and inflammatory processes, all of which represent important features in the pathology of acne vulgaris
Pharmacodynamics/Kinetics
Absorption: Topical: Minimal
Excretion: Bile
Dosage Topical: Children >12 years and Adults: Apply once daily at bedtime; therapeutic results should be noticed after 8-12 weeks of treatment
Dosage Forms [DSC] = Discontinued product
Cream, topical: 0.1% (15 g, 45 g)
Gel, topical: 0.1% (15 g, 45 g) [alcohol free]
Pledget, topical: 0.1% (60s) [DSC]
Solution, topical: 0.1% (30 mL) [DSC]

♦ **Adderall®** see Dextroamphetamine and Amphetamine on page 487
♦ **Adderall XR®** see Dextroamphetamine and Amphetamine on page 487

Adefovir (a DEF o veer)

U.S. Brand Names Hepsera™
Index Terms Adefovir Dipivoxil
Pharmacologic Category Antiretroviral Agent, Reverse Transcriptase Inhibitor (Nucleoside)
Use Treatment of chronic hepatitis B with evidence of active viral replication (based on persistent elevation of ALT/AST or histologic evidence), including patients with lamivudine-resistant hepatitis B
Pregnancy Risk Factor C
Pregnancy Implications There are no adequate and well-controlled studies in pregnant women. Use in pregnancy only when clearly needed. Pregnant women exposed to adefovir should be registered with the pregnancy registry (800-258-4263).
Lactation Excretion in breast milk unknown/not recommended
Contraindications Hypersensitivity to adefovir or any component of the formulation
Warnings/Precautions [U.S. Boxed Warning]: **Use with caution in patients with renal dysfunction or in patients at risk of renal toxicity (including concurrent nephrotoxic agents or NSAIDs).** Chronic administration may result in nephrotoxicity. Dosage adjustment is required in patients with renal dysfunction or in patients who develop renal dysfunction during therapy. **[U.S. Boxed Warnings]: May cause the development of resistance in patients with unrecognized or untreated HIV infection. Lactic acidosis and severe hepatomegaly with steatosis (sometimes fatal) have occurred with antiretroviral nucleoside analogues.** Female gender, obesity, and prolonged treatment may increase the risk of hepatotoxicity. Treatment should be discontinued in patients with lactic acidosis or signs/symptoms of hepatotoxicity (which may occur without marked transaminase elevations). **[U.S. Boxed Warning]: Acute exacerbations of hepatitis may occur (in up to 25% of patients) when antihepatitis therapy is discontinued.** Exacerbations typically occur within 12 weeks and may be self-limited or resolve upon resuming treatment; monitor patients following discontinuation of therapy. Safety and efficacy in pediatric patients have not been established.
(Continued)

Adefovir (Continued)

Adverse Reactions For a majority of adverse reactions, the incidence in adefovir-receiving patients was similar to or less than that observed with placebo treatment.

>10%:
Hepatic: ALT increased (20% grade ≥3)
Renal: Hematuria (11% grade ≥3)

1% to 10%:
Central nervous system: Headache (9%)
Dermatologic: Rash, pruritus
Endocrine & metabolic: Hypophosphatemia (1% to 2%)
Gastrointestinal: Abdominal pain (9%), nausea (5%), amylase increased (4% grade ≥3), flatulence (4%), dyspepsia (3%), vomiting, diarrhea
Hepatic: AST increased (8% grade ≥3), abnormal liver function, hepatic failure
Neuromuscular & skeletal: Weakness (13%)
Renal: Serum creatinine increased (2% to 10%; 7% grade ≥3), glycosuria (1% grade ≥3), renal failure, renal insufficiency

> **Note:** In liver transplant patients with baseline renal dysfunction, frequency of increased serum creatinine has been observed to be as high as 32% to 53%; considering the concomitant use of other potentially nephrotoxic medications, baseline renal insufficiency, and predisposing comorbidities, the role of adefovir in these changes could not be established.

Respiratory: Cough increased, sinusitis, pharyngitis
Postmarketing and/or case reports: Hepatitis, hepatomegaly with steatosis, lactic acidosis, nephrotoxicity

Overdosage/Toxicology Limited experience in acute overdose. Chronic overdose may be associated with renal toxicity and gastrointestinal adverse effects. Hemodialysis may be effective in the removal of adefovir (35% of a 10 mg dose removed in 4 hours).

Drug Interactions
Increased Effect/Toxicity: Ibuprofen increases the bioavailability of adefovir. Concurrent use of nephrotoxic agents (including aminoglycosides, cyclosporine, NSAIDs, tacrolimus, vancomycin) may increase the risk of nephrotoxicity. Use of Ganciclovir (valganciclovir) may increase the incidence of adverse effects/toxicity of adefovir. Concomitant use of ribavirin with or without interferon alfa and nucleoside analogues may increase the risk of developing hepatic decompensation or other signs of mitochondrial toxicity, including pancreatitis or lactic acidosis.

Ethanol/Nutrition/Herb Interactions
Ethanol: Should be avoided in hepatitis B infection due to potential hepatic toxicity.
Food: Does not have a significant effect on adefovir absorption.

Stability Store at 25°C (77 °F); excursions permitted to 15°C to 30°C (59°F to 86°F).

Mechanism of Action Acyclic nucleotide reverse transcriptase inhibitor (adenosine analog) which interferes with HBV viral RNA-dependent DNA polymerase resulting in inhibition of viral replication.

Pharmacodynamics/Kinetics
Distribution: 0.35-0.39 L/kg
Protein binding: ≤4%
Metabolism: Prodrug; rapidly converted to adefovir (active metabolite) in intestine
Bioavailability: 59%
Half-life elimination: 7.5 hours; prolonged in renal impairment
Time to peak: 1.75 hours
Excretion: Urine (45% as active metabolite within 24 hours)

Dosage Oral: Adults: 10 mg once daily
Dosage adjustment in renal impairment:
Cl_{cr} 20-49 mL/minute: 10 mg every 48 hours
Cl_{cr} 10-19 mL/minute: 10 mg every 72 hours
Hemodialysis: 10 mg every 7 days (following dialysis)
Dosage adjustment in hepatic impairment: No adjustment necessary

Dietary Considerations May be taken without regard to food.

Administration May be administered without regard to food.

Monitoring Parameters HIV status (prior to initiation of therapy); serum creatinine (prior to initiation and during therapy); viral load; LFTs for several months following discontinuation of adefovir

Additional Information Adefovir dipivoxil is a prodrug, rapidly converted to the active component (adefovir). It was previously investigated as a treatment for HIV infections (at dosages substantially higher than the approved dose for hepatitis B). The NDA was withdrawn, and no further studies in the treatment of HIV are anticipated (per manufacturer).

Dosage Forms Tablet, as dipivoxil: 10 mg

♦ **Adefovir Dipivoxil** see Adefovir on page 49
♦ **Adenocard**® see Adenosine on page 50
♦ **Adenoscan**® see Adenosine on page 50

Adenosine (a DEN oh seen)

U.S. Brand Names Adenocard®; Adenoscan®
Canadian Brand Names Adenocard®; Adenoscan®; Adenosine Injection, USP
Index Terms 9-Beta-D-Ribofuranosyladenine
Pharmacologic Category Antiarrhythmic Agent, Class IV; Diagnostic Agent
Use
Adenocard®: Treatment of paroxysmal supraventricular tachycardia (PSVT) including that associated with accessory bypass tracts (Wolff-Parkinson-White syndrome); when clinically advisable, appropriate vagal maneuvers should be attempted prior to adenosine

administration; **not effective in atrial flutter, atrial fibrillation, or ventricular tachycardia**

Adenoscan®: Pharmacologic stress agent used in myocardial perfusion thallium-201 scintigraphy

Unlabeled/Investigational Use Adenoscan®: Acute vasodilator testing in pulmonary artery hypertension

Pregnancy Risk Factor C

Pregnancy Implications Reports of administration during pregnancy have indicated no adverse effects on fetus or newborn attributable to adenosine.

Lactation Excretion in breast milk unknown

Contraindications Hypersensitivity to adenosine or any component of the formulation; second- or third-degree AV block or sick sinus syndrome (except in patients with a functioning artificial pacemaker), atrial flutter, atrial fibrillation, and ventricular tachycardia (this drug is not effective in converting these arrhythmias to sinus rhythm). The manufacturer states that Adenoscan® should be avoided in patients with known or suspected bronchoconstrictive or bronchospastic lung disease.

Warnings/Precautions Adenosine may produce first-, second-, or third-degree heart block. Use caution in patients with first-degree AV block or bundle branch block; avoid use of adenosine for pharmacologic stress testing in patients with high-grade AV block or sinus node dysfunction (unless a functional pacemaker is in place). Rare, prolonged episodes of asystole have been reported. Use caution in patients receiving other drugs which slow AV conduction. Drugs which affect adenosine (theophylline, caffeine) should be withheld for five half-lives prior to adenosine use. Avoid dietary caffeine for 12-24 hours prior to pharmacologic stress testing.

Adenosine may also produce profound vasodilation with subsequent hypotension. When used as a bolus dose (PSVT), effects are generally self-limiting. When used as a continuous infusion (pharmacologic stress testing), effects may be more pronounced and persistent. Adenosine infusions should be used with caution in patients with autonomic dysfunction, stenotic valvular heart disease, pericarditis, pleural effusion, carotid stenosis (with cerebrovascular insufficiency), or uncorrected hypovolemia. Use caution in elderly patients. May cause bronchoconstriction in patients with asthma; use caution in patients with obstructive lung disease not associated with bronchoconstriction (eg, emphysema, bronchitis).

Adenocard®: Transient AV block is expected. Administer as a rapid bolus, either directly into a vein or (if administered into an I.V. line), as close to the patient as possible (followed by saline flush).

Adverse Reactions Note: Frequency varies based on use; higher frequency of infusion-related effects, such as flushing and lightheadedness, were reported with continuous infusion (Adenoscan®).

>10%:
Cardiovascular: Facial flushing (18% to 44%)
Central nervous system: Headache (2% to 18%), lightheadedness (2% to 12%)
Neuromuscular & skeletal: Discomfort of neck, throat, jaw (<1% to 15%)
Respiratory: Dyspnea (12% to 28%), chest pressure/discomfort (7% to 40%)
1% to 10%:
Cardiovascular: Hypotension (<1% to 2%), AV block (infusion 6%; third degree <1%), ST segment depression (3%), palpitation, chest pain
Central nervous system: Dizziness, nervousness (2%), apprehension
Gastrointestinal: Nausea (3%)
Neuromuscular & skeletal: Upper extremity discomfort (up to 4%), numbness (up to 2%), paresthesia (up to 2%)
Respiratory: Hyperventilation
Miscellaneous: Diaphoresis
<1% (Limited to important or life-threatening): Asystole (prolonged), atrial fibrillation, back discomfort, bradycardia, bronchospasm, blurred vision, burning sensation, hypertension (transient), injection site reaction, intracranial pressure increased, metallic taste, pressure in groin, respiratory arrest, seizure, torsade de pointes, ventricular fibrillation, ventricular tachycardia

Overdosage/Toxicology Since the half-life of adenosine is <10 seconds, any adverse effects are rapidly self-limiting. Intoxication is usually short-lived since the half-life of the drug is very short. Treatment of prolonged effects requires individualization. Theophylline and other methylxanthines are competitive inhibitors of adenosine and may have a role in reversing its toxic effects. To reverse the effects of Adenoscan®, administer theophylline 50-125 mg slow I.V. push.

Drug Interactions
Increased Effect/Toxicity: Dipyridamole potentiates effects of adenosine. Use with carbamazepine may increase heart block.
Decreased Effect: Methylxanthines (eg, caffeine, theophylline) antagonize the effect of adenosine.

Ethanol/Nutrition/Herb Interactions Food: Avoid food or drugs with caffeine. Adenosine's therapeutic effect may be decreased if used concurrently with caffeine. Avoid dietary caffeine for 12-24 hours prior to pharmacologic stress testing.

Stability Store at controlled room temperature of 15°C to 30°C (59°F to 86°F). Do **not** refrigerate; precipitation may occur (may dissolve by warming to room temperature).

Mechanism of Action Slows conduction time through the AV node, interrupting the re-entry pathways through the AV node, restoring normal sinus rhythm

Pharmacodynamics/Kinetics
Onset of action: Rapid
Duration: Very brief
Metabolism: Blood and tissue to inosine then to adenosine monophosphate (AMP) and hypoxanthine
Half-life elimination: <10 seconds
(Continued)

Adenosine *(Continued)*

Dosage

Adenocard®: **Rapid I.V. push (over 1-2 seconds) via peripheral line:**
Infants and Children:
Manufacturer's recommendation:
<50 kg: 0.05-0.1 mg/kg. If conversion of PSVT does not occur within 1-2 minutes, may increase dose by 0.05-0.1 mg/kg. May repeat until sinus rhythm is established or to a maximum single dose of 0.3 mg/kg or 12 mg. Follow each dose with normal saline flush.
≥50 kg: Refer to Adult dosing
Pediatric advanced life support (PALS): Treatment of SVT: I.V., I.O.: 0.1 mg/kg; if not effective, administer 0.2 mg/kg of PSVT; medium dose required: 0.15 mg/kg; maximum single dose: 12 mg. Follow each dose with normal saline flush.
Adults: 6 mg; if not effective within 1-2 minutes, 12 mg may be given; may repeat 12 mg bolus if needed
Maximum single dose: 12 mg
Follow each I.V. bolus of adenosine with normal saline flush

Note: Preliminary results in adults suggest adenosine may be administered via a central line at lower doses (ie, initial adult dose: 3 mg).

Adenoscan®:
Stress testing: Continuous I.V. infusion via peripheral line: 140 mcg/kg/minute for 6 minutes using syringe or columetric infusion pump; total dose: 0.84 mg/kg. Thallium-201 is injected at midpoint (3 minutes) of infusion.
Acute vasodilator testing (unlabeled use): I.V.: Initial: 50 mcg/kg/minute increased by 50 mcg/kg/minute every 2 minutes to a maximum dose of 500 mcg/kg/minute; acutely assess vasodilator response

Hemodialysis: Significant drug removal is unlikely based on physiochemical characteristics.
Peritoneal dialysis: Significant drug removal is unlikely based on physiochemical characteristics.
Note: Higher doses may be needed for administration via peripheral versus central vein.

Dietary Considerations Avoid dietary caffeine for 12-24 hours prior to pharmacologic stress testing.

Administration For rapid bolus I.V. use only; administer I.V. push over 1-2 seconds at a peripheral I.V. site as proximal as possible to trunk (not in lower arm, hand, lower leg, or foot); follow each bolus with normal saline flush. **Note:** Preliminary results in adults suggest adenosine may be administered via central line at lower doses (eg, adults initial dose: 3 mg)

Monitoring Parameters ECG monitoring, heart rate, blood pressure

Dosage Forms

Injection, solution [preservative free]: 3 mg/mL (2 mL, 4 mL)
Adenocard®: 3 mg/mL (2 mL, 4 mL)
Adenoscan®: 3 mg/mL (20 mL, 30 mL)

♦ **Adenosine Injection, USP (Can)** *see* Adenosine *on page 50*
♦ **Adept®** *see* Icodextrin *on page 877*
♦ **ADH** *see* Vasopressin *on page 1779*
♦ **Adipex-P®** *see* Phentermine *on page 1356*
♦ **Adoxa®** *see* Doxycycline *on page 555*
♦ **Adrenalin®** *see* Epinephrine *on page 589*
♦ **Adrenaline** *see* Epinephrine *on page 589*
♦ **ADR (error-prone abbreviation)** *see* DOXOrubicin *on page 549*
♦ **Adria** *see* DOXOrubicin *on page 549*
♦ **Adriamycin® (Can)** *see* DOXOrubicin *on page 549*
♦ **Adriamycin PFS®** *see* DOXOrubicin *on page 549*
♦ **Adriamycin RDF®** *see* DOXOrubicin *on page 549*
♦ **Adrucil®** *see* Fluorouracil *on page 725*
♦ **Adsorbent Charcoal** *see* Charcoal *on page 338*
♦ **Advair Diskus®** *see* Fluticasone and Salmeterol *on page 742*
♦ **Advair® HFA** *see* Fluticasone and Salmeterol *on page 742*
♦ **Advantage-S™ [OTC]** *see* Nonoxynol 9 *on page 1239*
♦ **Advate** *see* Antihemophilic Factor (Recombinant) *on page 135*
♦ **Advicor®** *see* Niacin and Lovastatin *on page 1221*
♦ **Advil® [OTC]** *see* Ibuprofen *on page 873*
♦ **Advil® (Can)** *see* Ibuprofen *on page 873*
♦ **Advil® Children's [OTC]** *see* Ibuprofen *on page 873*
♦ **Advil® Cold, Children's [OTC]** *see* Pseudoephedrine and Ibuprofen *on page 1456*
♦ **Advil® Cold & Sinus [OTC]** *see* Pseudoephedrine and Ibuprofen *on page 1456*
♦ **Advil® Cold & Sinus (Can)** *see* Pseudoephedrine and Ibuprofen *on page 1456*
♦ **Advil® Infants' [OTC]** *see* Ibuprofen *on page 873*
♦ **Advil® Junior [OTC]** *see* Ibuprofen *on page 873*
♦ **Advil® Migraine [OTC]** *see* Ibuprofen *on page 873*
♦ **Aerius® (Can)** *see* Desloratadine *on page 475*
♦ **AeroBid®** *see* Flunisolide *on page 720*
♦ **AeroBid®-M** *see* Flunisolide *on page 720*
♦ **aeroKid™** *see* Chlorpheniramine, Phenylephrine, and Methscopolamine *on page 353*
♦ **Aerospan™** *see* Flunisolide *on page 720*
♦ **Afeditab™ CR** *see* NIFEdipine *on page 1226*
♦ **AG** *see* Aminoglutethimide *on page 95*

Agalsidase Beta (aye GAL si days BAY ta)

U.S. Brand Names Fabrazyme®
Canadian Brand Names Fabrazyme®
Index Terms Alpha-Galactosidase-A (Human, Recombinant); r-h α-GAL
Pharmacologic Category Enzyme
Use Replacement therapy for Fabry disease
Pregnancy Risk Factor B
Pregnancy Implications There are no adequate and well-controlled studies in pregnant women. Women of childbearing potential are encouraged to enroll in Fabry registry.
Lactation Excretion in breast milk unknown/use caution
Medication Safety Issues
Sound-alike/look-alike issues:
   Agalsidase beta may be confused with alglucerase, alglucosidase alfa
Contraindications No known contraindications
Warnings/Precautions Infusion reactions are common, and may be severe; pretreatment with antipyretics is advised. Use caution in cardiovascular disease (risk related to infusion reactions may be increased). A registry has been created to monitor therapeutic responses and adverse effects during long-term treatment; patients should be encouraged to register (www.fabryregistry.com or 1-800-745-4447). Safety and efficacy in pediatric patients have not been established (studies limited to patients ≥16 years of age).
Adverse Reactions Note: The most common and serious adverse reactions are infusion reactions (symptoms may include fever, tachycardia, hypertension, throat tightness, dyspnea, chills, abdominal pain, pruritus, urticaria, vomiting).

>10%:
   Cardiovascular: Edema (21%), chest pain (17%), hypotension (14%)
   Central nervous system: Fever (48%), headache (45%), anxiety (28%), pain (21%), dizziness (14%), paresthesia (14%)
   Dermatologic: Pallor (14%)
   Gastrointestinal: Nausea (28%)
   Neuromuscular & skeletal: Rigors (52%), skeletal pain (21%)
   Respiratory: Rhinitis (38%), pharyngitis (28%)
   Miscellaneous: Infusion reactions (alteration of temperature sensation 17%)
1% to 10%:
   Cardiovascular: Cardiomegaly (10%), hypertension (10%)
   Central nervous system: Depression (10%)
   Gastrointestinal: Dyspepsia (10%)
   Genitourinary: Testicular pain (7%)
   Neuromuscular & skeletal: Arthrosis (10%)
   Respiratory: Bronchitis (10%), bronchospasm (7%), laryngitis (7%), sinusitis (7%)
   Other reported severe reactions (frequency not established): Arrhythmia, ataxia, bradycardia, cardiac arrest, cardiac output decreased, nephritic syndrome, stroke, vertigo
Stability Store vials between 2°C and 8 °C (36°F and 46°F). Final infusion should be used immediately if possible, but may be stored for up to 24 hours between 2°C and 8 °C (36°F and 46°F). Each vial should be reconstituted with 7.2 mL SWFI; inject down internal side wall of vial; roll and tilt gently. Resulting solution contains 5 mg/mL. To make final infusion, add the desired amount of reconstituted solution (based on patient weight) to make a final volume of 500 mL in NS (do not use filter needle to prepare). Avoid vigorous shaking or agitation.
Mechanism of Action Agalsidase beta is a recombinant form of the enzyme alpha-galactosidase-A, which is required for the hydrolysis of GL-3 and other glycosphingolipids. The compounds may accumulate (over many years) within the tissues of patients with Fabry disease, leading to renal and cardiovascular complications. In clinical trials of limited duration, agalsidase been noted to reduce tissue inclusions of a key sphingolipid (GL-3). It is believed that long-term enzyme replacement may reduce clinical manifestations of renal failure, cardiomyopathy, and stroke. However, the relationship to a reduction in clinical manifestations has not been established.
Pharmacodynamics/Kinetics Half-life elimination: 42-102 minutes (nonlinear)
Dosage I.V.: Adults: 1 mg/kg every 2 weeks
   Dosage adjustment in renal impairment: No dosage adjustment required
Administration Antipyretics should be administered prior to infusion. Initial infusion rate should not exceed 0.25 mg/minute (15 mg/hour). Decrease rate in the event of an infusion reaction. After patient tolerance to the infusion is established, rate may be increased in increments of 0.05-0.08 mg/minute (3-5 mg/hour) with each subsequent infusion. A 0.2 micron low protein-binding filter may be used.
Monitoring Parameters Development of IgG or IgE antibodies in patients with suspected allergic reactions (test available from manufacturer).
Dosage Forms Injection, powder for reconstitution: 5 mg [contains mannitol 33 mg; derived from Chinese hamster cells]; 35 mg [contains mannitol 222 mg/vial; derived from Chinese hamster cells]

♦ Agenerase® see Amprenavir on page 125
♦ Aggrastat® see Tirofiban on page 1693
♦ Aggrenox® see Aspirin and Dipyridamole on page 163
♦ AGN 1135 see Rasagiline on page 1488
♦ AgNO₃ see Silver Nitrate on page 1566
♦ Agrylin® see Anagrelide on page 128
♦ AGT see Aminoglutethimide on page 95
♦ AH-Chew® see Chlorpheniramine, Phenylephrine, and Methscopolamine on page 353
♦ AH-Chew II see Chlorpheniramine, Phenylephrine, and Methscopolamine on page 353
♦ AH-chew® D [OTC] [DSC] see Phenylephrine on page 1358
♦ AHF (Human) see Antihemophilic Factor (Human) on page 133

♦ **AHF (Human)** *see* Antihemophilic Factor/von Willebrand Factor Complex (Human) *on page 136*

♦ **AHF (Recombinant)** *see* Antihemophilic Factor (Recombinant) *on page 135*

♦ **A-hydroCort** *see* Hydrocortisone *on page 852*

♦ **AICC** *see* Anti-inhibitor Coagulant Complex *on page 137*

♦ **Airomir (Can)** *see* Albuterol *on page 57*

♦ **AK-Con™** *see* Naphazoline *on page 1198*

♦ **AK-Dilate®** *see* Phenylephrine *on page 1358*

♦ **AK-Fluor** *see* Fluorescein Sodium *on page 722*

♦ **Akne-Mycin®** *see* Erythromycin *on page 609*

♦ **AK-Pentolate® [DSC]** *see* Cyclopentolate *on page 428*

♦ **AK-Poly-Bac™** *see* Bacitracin and Polymyxin B *on page 192*

♦ **AKTob®** *see* Tobramycin *on page 1696*

♦ **AK-Tracin® [DSC]** *see* Bacitracin *on page 191*

♦ **AK-Trol® [DSC]** *see* Neomycin, Polymyxin B, and Dexamethasone *on page 1211*

♦ **Alamag [OTC]** *see* Aluminum Hydroxide and Magnesium Hydroxide *on page 85*

♦ **Alamag Plus [OTC]** *see* Aluminum Hydroxide, Magnesium Hydroxide, and Simethicone *on page 85*

♦ **Alamast®** *see* Pemirolast *on page 1329*

♦ **Alavert® [OTC]** *see* Loratadine *on page 1033*

♦ **Alavert™ Allergy and Sinus [OTC]** *see* Loratadine and Pseudoephedrine *on page 1034*

♦ **Albalon®** *see* Naphazoline *on page 1198*

Albendazole (al BEN da zole)

U.S. Brand Names Albenza®

Pharmacologic Category Anthelmintic

Use Treatment of parenchymal neurocysticercosis caused by *Taenia solium* and cystic hydatid disease of the liver, lung, and peritoneum caused by *Echinococcus granulosus*

Unlabeled/Investigational Use Albendazole has activity against *Ascaris lumbricoides* (roundworm); *Ancylostoma caninum; Ancylostoma duodenale* and *Necator americanus* (hookworms); cutaneous larva migrans; *Enterobius vermicularis* (pinworm); *Gnathostoma spinigerum; Gongylonema* sp; *Hymenolepis nana* sp (tapeworms); *Mansonella perstans* (filariasis); *Opisthorchis sinensis* and *Opisthorchis viverrini* (liver flukes); *Strongyloides stercoralis* and *Trichuris trichiura* (whipworm); visceral larva migrans (toxocariasis); activity has also been shown against the liver fluke *Clonorchis sinensis, Giardia lamblia, Cysticercus cellulosae,* and *Echinococcus multilocularis.* Albendazole has also been used for the treatment of intestinal microsporidiosis (*Encephalitozoon intestinalis*), disseminated microsporidiosis (*E. hellem, E. cuniculi, E. intestinalis, Pleistophora* sp, *Trachipleistophora* sp, *Brachiola vesicularum*), and ocular microsporidiosis (*E. hellem, E. cuniculi, Vittaforma corneae*).

Pregnancy Risk Factor C

Pregnancy Implications Albendazole has been shown to be teratogenic in laboratory animals and should not be used during pregnancy, if at all possible. Women should be advised to avoid pregnancy for at least 1 month following therapy. Discontinue if pregnancy occurs during treatment.

Lactation Excretion in breast milk unknown/not recommended

Medication Safety Issues

International issues:

Albenza® may be confused with Avanza® which is a brand name for mirtazapine in Australia

Contraindications Hypersensitivity to albendazole or any component of the formulation

Warnings/Precautions Discontinue therapy if LFT elevations are significant; may restart treatment when decreased to pretreatment values. Becoming pregnant within 1 month following therapy is not advised.

Neurocysticercosis: Corticosteroids should be administered 1-2 days before albendazole therapy to minimize inflammatory reactions. Steroid and anticonvulsant therapy should be used concurrently during the first week of therapy to prevent cerebral hypertension. If retinal lesions exist, weigh risk of further retinal damage due to albendazole-induced changes to the retinal lesion vs benefit of disease treatment.

Adverse Reactions

N = Neurocysticercosis; H = Hydatid disease

>10%:

Central nervous system: Headache (11% - N; 1% - H)

Hepatic: LFTs increased (~15% - H; <1% - N)

1% to 10%:

Central nervous system: Dizziness, vertigo, fever (≤1%), intracranial pressure increased (1% - N), meningeal signs (1% - N)

Dermatologic: Alopecia (2% - H; <1% - N)

Gastrointestinal: Abdominal pain (6% - H; 0% - N), nausea/vomiting (3% to 6%)

Hematologic: Leukopenia (reversible) (<1%)

Miscellaneous: Allergic reactions (<1%)

<1% (Limited to important or life-threatening): Acute renal failure, agranulocytopenia, allergic reaction, granulocytopenia, pancytopenia, rash, thrombocytopenia, urticaria

Drug Interactions

Cytochrome P450 Effect: Substrate (minor) of CYP1A2, 3A4; **Inhibits** CYP1A2 (weak)

Ethanol/Nutrition/Herb Interactions Food: Albendazole serum levels may be increased if taken with a fatty meal (increases the oral bioavailability by 4-5 times).

Mechanism of Action Active metabolite, albendazole, causes selective degeneration of cytoplasmic microtubules in intestinal and tegmental cells of intestinal helminths and larvae; glycogen is depleted, glucose uptake and cholinesterase secretion are impaired, and desecratory substances accumulate intracellulary. ATP production decreases causing energy depletion, immobilization, and worm death.

Pharmacodynamics/Kinetics

Absorption: <5%; may increase up to 4-5 times when administered with a fatty meal

Distribution: Well inside hydatid cysts and CSF

Protein binding: 70%

Metabolism: Hepatic; extensive first-pass effect; pathways include rapid sulfoxidation (major), hydrolysis, and oxidation

Half-life elimination: 8-12 hours

Time to peak, serum: 2-2.4 hours

Excretion: Urine (<1% as active metabolite); feces

Dosage Oral:

Children:

Cysticercus cellulosae (unlabeled use): 15 mg/kg/day (maximum: 800 mg/day) in 2 divided doses for 8-30 days; may be repeated as necessary

Echinococcus granulosus (tapeworm) (unlabeled use): 15 mg/kg/day (maximum: 800 mg) divided twice daily for 1-6 months

Children and Adults:

Neurocysticercosis:

<60 kg: 15 mg/kg/day in 2 divided doses (maximum: 800 mg/day) for 8-30 days

≥60 kg: 400 mg twice daily for 8-30 days

Note: Give concurrent anticonvulsant and steroid therapy during first week.

Hydatid:

<60 kg: 15 mg/kg/day in 2 divided doses (maximum: 800 mg/day)

≥60 kg: 400 mg twice daily

Note: Administer dose for three 28-day cycles with a 14-day drug-free interval in between.

Ancylostoma caninum, Ascaris lumbricoides (roundworm), *Ancylostoma duodenale*, and *Necator americanus* (hookworms) (unlabeled use): 400 mg as a single dose

Clonorchis sinensis (Chinese liver fluke) (unlabeled use): 10 mg/kg for 7 days

Cutaneous larva migrans (unlabeled use): 400 mg once daily for 3 days

Enterobius vermicularis (pinworm) (unlabeled use): 400 mg as a single dose; may repeat in 2 weeks

Gnathostoma spinigerum (unlabeled use): 400 mg twice daily for 21 days

Gongylonemiasis (unlabeled use): 10 mg/kg/day for 3 days

Mansonella perstans (unlabeled use): 400 mg twice daily for 10 days

Visceral larva migrans (toxocariasis) (unlabeled use): 400 mg twice daily for 5 days

Adults:

Cysticercus cellulosae (unlabeled use): 400 mg twice daily for 8-30 days; may be repeated as necessary

Disseminated microsporidiosis (unlabeled use): 400 mg twice daily

Echinococcus granulosus (tapeworm) (unlabeled use): 400 mg twice daily for 1-6 months

Intestinal microsporidiosis (unlabeled use): 400 mg twice daily for 21 days

Ocular microsporidiosis (unlabeled use): 400 mg twice daily, in combination with fumagillin

Dietary Considerations Should be taken with a high-fat meal.

Administration Administer with meals. Administer anticonvulsant and steroid therapy during first week of neurocysticercosis therapy.

Monitoring Parameters Monitor fecal specimens for ova and parasites for 3 weeks after treatment; if positive, retreat; monitor LFTs and clinical signs of hepatotoxicity; CBC at start of each 28-day cycle and every 2 weeks during therapy

Dosage Forms Tablet: 200 mg

♦ **Albenza®** *see* Albendazole *on page 54*
♦ **Albert® Glyburide (Can)** *see* GlyBURIDE *on page 803*
♦ **Albert® Pentoxifylline (Can)** *see* Pentoxifylline *on page 1343*
♦ **Albumarc®** *see* Albumin *on page 55*

Albumin (al BYOO min)

U.S. Brand Names Albumarc®; Albuminar®; AlbuRx™; Albutein®; Buminate®; Flexbumin; Plasbumin®

Canadian Brand Names Plasbumin®-5; Plasbumin®-25

Index Terms Albumin (Human); Normal Human Serum Albumin; Normal Serum Albumin (Human); Salt Poor Albumin; SPA

Pharmacologic Category Blood Product Derivative; Plasma Volume Expander, Colloid

Use Plasma volume expansion and maintenance of cardiac output in the treatment of certain types of shock or impending shock; may be useful for burn patients, ARDS, and cardiopulmonary bypass; other uses considered by some investigators (but not proven) are retroperitoneal surgery, peritonitis, and ascites; unless the condition responsible for hypoproteinemia can be corrected, albumin can provide only symptomatic relief or supportive treatment

Unlabeled/Investigational Use In cirrhotics, administered with diuretics to help facilitate diuresis; large volume paracentesis; volume expansion in dehydrated, mildly-hypotensive cirrhotics

Pregnancy Risk Factor C

Lactation Excretion in breast milk unknown/compatible

Medication Safety Issues

Sound-alike/look-alike issues:

Albutein® may be confused with albuterol

Buminate® may be confused with bumetanide

Contraindications Hypersensitivity to albumin or any component of the formulation; patients with severe anemia or cardiac failure

Warnings/Precautions Use with caution in patients with hepatic or renal failure because of added protein load; rapid infusion of albumin solutions may cause vascular overload. All patients should be observed for signs of hypervolemia such as pulmonary edema. Use with (Continued)

Albumin *(Continued)*

caution in those patients for whom sodium restriction is necessary. Avoid 25% concentration in preterm infants due to risk of intraventricular hemorrhage. Nutritional supplementation is not an appropriate indication for albumin.

Adverse Reactions Frequency not defined.
Cardiovascular: CHF precipitation, edema, hyper-/hypotension, hypervolemia, tachycardia
Central nervous system: Chills, fever, headache
Dermatologic: Pruritus, rash, urticaria
Gastrointestinal: Nausea, vomiting
Respiratory: Bronchospasm, pulmonary edema
Miscellaneous: Anaphylaxis

Overdosage/Toxicology Symptoms include hypervolemia, congestive heart failure, and pulmonary edema.

Drug Interactions
Increased Effect/Toxicity: ACE inhibitors: May have increased risk of atypical reactions; withhold ACEIs for at least 24 hours prior to plasma exchanges using large volumes of albumin

Stability Store at a temperature ≤30°C (86°F); do not freeze. Do not use solution if it is turbid or contains a deposit; use within 4 hours after opening vial; discard unused portion.

If 5% human albumin is unavailable, it may be prepared by diluting 25% human albumin with 0.9% sodium chloride or 5% dextrose in water. Do not use sterile water to dilute albumin solutions, as this has been associated with hypotonic-associated hemolysis.

Mechanism of Action Provides increase in intravascular oncotic pressure and causes mobilization of fluids from interstitial into intravascular space

Dosage I.V.:
5% should be used in hypovolemic patients or intravascularly-depleted patients
25% should be used in patients in whom fluid and sodium intake must be minimized
Dose depends on condition of patient:
Children: Hypovolemia: 0.5-1 g/kg/dose (10-20 mL/kg/dose of albumin 5%); maximum dose: 6 g/kg/day
Adults: Usual dose: 25 g; initial dose may be repeated in 15-30 minutes if response is inadequate; no more than 250 g should be administered within 48 hours
Hypoproteinemia: 0.5-1 g/kg/dose; repeat every 1-2 days as calculated to replace ongoing losses
Hypovolemia: 5% albumin: 0.5-1 g/kg/dose; repeat as needed. **Note:** May be considered after inadequate response to crystalloid therapy and when nonprotein colloids are contraindicated. The volume administered and the speed of infusion should be adapted to individual response.

Dietary Considerations
Albumarc®, Albuminar®, Albutein®, Buminate®, Flexbumin: 5% [50 mg/mL] and 25% [250 mg/mL] contain sodium 130-160 mEq/L
Plasbumin®: 5% [50 mg/mL] and 25% [250 mg/mL] contain sodium ~145 mEq/L

Administration For I.V. administration only. Use within 4 hours after opening vial; discard unused portion. In emergencies, may administer as rapidly as necessary to improve clinical condition. After initial volume replacement:
5%: Do not exceed 2-4 mL/minute in patients with normal plasma volume; 5-10 mL/minute in patients with hypoproteinemia
25%: Do not exceed 1 mL/minute in patients with normal plasma volume; 2-3 mL/minute in patients with hypoproteinemia

Do not dilute 5% solution. Rapid infusion may cause vascular overload. Albumin 25% may be given undiluted or diluted in normal saline. May give in combination or through the same administration set as saline or carbohydrates. Do not use with ethanol or protein hydrolysates, precipitation may form.

Monitoring Parameters Blood pressure, pulmonary edema, hematocrit

Additional Information Albumin 5% and 25% solutions contain 130-160 mEq/L sodium and are considered isotonic with plasma. Dilution of albumin 25% solution with sterile water produces a hypotonic solution; administration of such can cause hemolysis and/or renal failure. An albumin 5% solution is osmotically equivalent to an equal volume of plasma, whereas a 25% solution is osmotically equivalent to 5 times its volume of plasma. Albumin solutions are heated to 60°C for 10 hours, decreasing any possible risk of viral hepatitis transmission. To date, there have been no reports of viral transmission using these products.

Dosage Forms
Injection, solution [preservative free; human]:
Albuminar®: 5% [50 mg/mL] (50 mL, 250 mL, 500 mL) [contains sodium 130-160 mEq/L and potassium ≤1 mEq/L; packaging contains dry natural rubber]; 25% [250 mg/mL] (20 mL, 50 mL, 100 mL) [contains sodium 130-160 mEq/L and potassium ≤1 mEq/L; packaging contains dry natural rubber]
AlbuRx™: 5% [50 mg/mL] (250 mL, 500 mL) [contains sodium 130-160 mEq/L and potassium ≤2 mEq/L]; 25% [250 mg/mL] (50 mL, 100 mL) [contains sodium 130-160 mEq/L and potassium ≤2 mEq/L]
Albutein®: 5% [50 mg/mL] (250 mL, 500 mL) [contains sodium 130-160 mEq/L and potassium ≤2 mEq/L]; 25% [250 mg/mL] (50 mL, 100 mL) [contains sodium 130-160 mEq/L and potassium ≤2 mEq/L]
Buminate®: 5% [50 mg/mL] (250 mL, 500 mL) [contains sodium 130-160 mEq/L and potassium ≤2 mEq/L]; 25% [250 mg/mL] (20 mL, 50 mL, 100 mL) [contains sodium 130-160 mEq/L and potassium ≤2 mEq/L]
Flexbumin: 25% [250 mg/mL] (50 mL, 100 mL) [contains sodium 130-160 and potassium ≤2 mEq/L]
Human Albumin Grifols®: 25% [250 mg/mL] (50 mL, 100 mL) [contains sodium 130-160 mEq/L and potassium ≤2 mEq/L]
Plasbumin®: 5% [50 mg/mL] (50 mL, 250 mL) [contains sodium ~145 mEq/L and potassium ≤2 mEq/L]; 25% [250 mg/mL] (20 mL, 50 mL, 100 mL) [contains sodium ~145 mEq/L and potassium ≤2 mEq/L]

♦ **Albuminar**® see Albumin on page 55
♦ **Albumin (Human)** see Albumin on page 55
♦ **AlbuRx**™ see Albumin on page 55
♦ **Albutein**® see Albumin on page 55

Albuterol (al BYOO ter ole)

U.S. Brand Names AccuNeb®; ProAir™ HFA; Proventil®; Proventil® HFA; Ventolin® HFA; VoSpire ER®

Canadian Brand Names Airomir; Alti-Salbutamol; Apo-Salvent®; Apo-Salvent® CFC Free; Apo-Salvent® Respirator Solution; Apo-Salvent® Sterules; Gen-Salbutamol; PMS-Salbutamol; ratio-Inspra-Sal; ratio-Salbutamol; Rhoxal-salbutamol; Salbu-2; Salbu-4; Ventolin®; Ventolin® Diskus; Ventolin® HFA; Ventrodisk

Index Terms Albuterol Sulfate; Salbutamol

Pharmacologic Category Beta$_2$-Adrenergic Agonist

Additional Appendix Information
Bronchodilators on page 1077

Use Bronchodilator in reversible airway obstruction due to asthma or COPD; prevention of exercise-induced bronchospasm

Pregnancy Risk Factor C

Pregnancy Implications Albuterol crosses the placenta; tocolytic effects, fetal tachycardia, fetal hypoglycemia secondary to maternal hyperglycemia with oral or intravenous routes reported. Available evidence suggests safe use during pregnancy.

Lactation Excretion in breast milk unknown/use caution

Medication Safety Issues
Sound-alike/look-alike issues:
Albuterol may be confused with Albutein®, atenolol
Proventil® may be confused with Bentyl®, Prilosec® Prinivil®
Salbutamol may be confused with salmeterol
Ventolin® may be confused with phentolamine, Benylin®, Vantin®
Volmax® may be confused with Flomax®

Contraindications Hypersensitivity to albuterol, adrenergic amines, or any component of the formulation

Warnings/Precautions Optimize anti-inflammatory treatment before initiating maintenance treatment with albuterol. Do not use as a component of chronic therapy without an anti-inflammatory agent. Only the mildest forms of asthma (Step 1 and/or exercise-induced) would not require concurrent use based upon asthma guidelines. Patient must be instructed to seek medical attention in cases where acute symptoms are not relieved or a previous level of response is diminished. The need to increase frequency of use may indicate deterioration of asthma, and treatment must not be delayed.

Use caution in patients with cardiovascular disease (arrhythmia or hypertension or CHF), convulsive disorders, diabetes, glaucoma, hyperthyroidism, or hypokalemia. Beta agonists may cause elevation in blood pressure, heart rate, and result in CNS stimulation/excitation. Beta$_2$ agonists may increase risk of arrhythmia, increase serum glucose, or decrease serum potassium.

Immediate hypersensitivity reactions (urticaria, angioedema, rash, bronchospasm) have been reported. Do not exceed recommended dose; serious adverse events, including fatalities, have been associated with excessive use of inhaled sympathomimetics. Rarely, paradoxical bronchospasm may occur with use of inhaled bronchodilating agents; this should be distinguished from inadequate response. All patients should utilize a spacer device when using a metered-dose inhaler; in addition, face masks should be used in children <4 years of age.

Because of its minimal effect on beta$_1$-receptors and its relatively long duration of action, albuterol is a rational choice in the elderly when an inhaled beta agonist is indicated. Oral use should be avoided in the elderly due to adverse effects. Patient response may vary between inhalers that contain chlorofluorocarbons and those which are chlorofluorocarbon-free.

Adverse Reactions Incidence of adverse effects is dependent upon age of patient, dose, and route of administration.

Cardiovascular: Angina, atrial fibrillation, chest discomfort, extrasystoles, flushing, hypertension, palpitation, tachycardia

Central nervous system: CNS stimulation, dizziness, drowsiness, headache, insomnia, irritability, lightheadedness, migraine, nervousness, nightmares, restlessness, sleeplessness, tremor

Dermatologic: Angioedema, erythema multiforme, rash, Stevens-Johnson syndrome, urticaria

Endocrine & metabolic: Hypokalemia, serum glucose increased, serum potassium decreased

Gastrointestinal: Diarrhea, dry mouth, gastroenteritis, nausea, unusual taste, vomiting, tooth discoloration

Genitourinary: Micturition difficulty

Neuromuscular & skeletal: Muscle cramps, weakness

Otic: Otitis media, vertigo

Respiratory: Asthma exacerbation, bronchospasm, cough, epistaxis, laryngitis, oropharyngeal drying/irritation, oropharyngeal edema

Miscellaneous: Allergic reaction, lymphadenopathy

Overdosage/Toxicology Symptoms include tachycardia, tremor, hypertension, angina, and seizures. Hypokalemia also may occur. Cardiac arrest and death may be associated with abuse of beta-agonist bronchodilators. Treatment includes immediate discontinuation and symptomatic and supportive therapies. Cautious use of beta-adrenergic blocking agents may be considered in severe cases.

(Continued)

Albuterol *(Continued)*

Drug Interactions

Cytochrome P450 Effect: Substrate of CYP3A4 (major)

Increased Effect/Toxicity: When used with inhaled ipratropium, an increased duration of bronchodilation may occur. Cardiovascular effects are potentiated in patients also receiving MAO inhibitors, tricyclic antidepressants, and sympathomimetic agents (eg, amphetamine, dopamine, dobutamine). Albuterol may increase the risk of malignant arrhythmias with inhaled anesthetics (eg, enflurane, halothane).

Decreased Effect: When used with nonselective beta-adrenergic blockers (eg, propranolol) the effect of albuterol is decreased. Levels/effects of albuterol may be decreased by aminoglutethimide, carbamazepine, nafcillin, nevirapine, phenobarbital, phenytoin, rifamycins, and other CYP3A4 inducers.

Ethanol/Nutrition/Herb Interactions

Food: Avoid or limit caffeine (may cause CNS stimulation).

Herb/Nutraceutical: Avoid ephedra, yohimbe (may cause CNS stimulation).

Stability

HFA aerosols: Store at 15°C to 25°C (59°F to 77°F).

Ventolin® HFA: Discard after using 200 actuations or 3 months after removal from protective pouch, whichever comes first. Store with mouthpiece down.

Inhalation solution: AccuNeb®: Store at 2°C to 25°C (36°F to 77°F). Do not use if solution changes color or becomes cloudy. Use within 1 week of opening foil pouch.

Nebulization 0.5% solution: Store at 2°C to 30°C (36°F to 86°F). To prepare a 2.5 mg dose, dilute 0.5 mL of solution to a total of 3 mL with normal saline; also compatible with cromolyn or ipratropium nebulizer solutions.

Syrup: Store at 2°C to 30°C (36°F to 86°F).

Mechanism of Action

Relaxes bronchial smooth muscle by action on beta$_2$-receptors with little effect on heart rate

Pharmacodynamics/Kinetics

Onset of action: Peak effect:

Nebulization/oral inhalation: 0.5-2 hours

  CFC-propelled albuterol: 10 minutes

  Ventolin® HFA: 25 minutes

Oral: 2-3 hours

Duration: Nebulization/oral inhalation: 3-4 hours; Oral: 4-6 hours

Metabolism: Hepatic to an inactive sulfate

Half-life elimination: Inhalation: 3.8 hours; Oral: 3.7-5 hours

Excretion: Urine (30% as unchanged drug)

Dosage

Oral:

Children: Bronchospasm (treatment):

2-6 years: 0.1-0.2 mg/kg/dose 3 times/day; maximum dose not to exceed 12 mg/day (divided doses)

6-12 years: 2 mg/dose 3-4 times/day; maximum dose not to exceed 24 mg/day (divided doses)

Extended release: 4 mg every 12 hours; maximum dose not to exceed 24 mg/day (divided doses)

Children >12 years and Adults: Bronchospasm (treatment): 2-4 mg/dose 3-4 times/day; maximum dose not to exceed 32 mg/day (divided doses)

Extended release: 8 mg every 12 hours; maximum dose not to exceed 32 mg/day (divided doses). A 4 mg dose every 12 hours may be sufficient in some patients, such as adults of low body weight.

Elderly: Bronchospasm (treatment): 2 mg 3-4 times/day; maximum: 8 mg 4 times/day

Inhalation: MDI 90 mcg/puff:

Children ≤12 years:

Bronchospasm (acute): 4-8 puffs every 20 minutes for 3 doses, then every 1-4 hours; spacer/holding-chamber device should be used

Exercise-induced bronchospasm (prophylaxis): 1-2 puffs 5 minutes prior to exercise

Children >12 years and Adults:

Bronchospasm (acute): 4-8 puffs every 20 minutes for up to 4 hours, then every 1-4 hours as needed

Exercise-induced bronchospasm (prophylaxis): 2 puffs 5-30 minutes prior to exercise

Children ≥4 years and Adults: Bronchospasm (chronic treatment): 1-2 inhalations every 4-6 hours; maximum: 12 inhalations/day

NIH guidelines: 2 puffs 3-4 times a day as needed; may double dose for mild exacerbations

Nebulization:

Children ≤12 years:

Bronchospasm (treatment): 0.05 mg/kg every 4-6 hours; minimum dose: 1.25 mg, maximum dose: 2.5 mg

2-12 years: AccuNeb®: 0.63 mg or 1.25 mg 3-4 times/day, as needed, delivered over 5-15 minutes

Children >40 kg, patients with more severe asthma, or children 11-12 years: May respond better with a 1.25 mg dose

Bronchospasm (acute): Solution 0.5%: 0.15 mg/kg (minimum dose: 2.5 mg) every 20 minutes for 3 doses, then 0.15-0.3 mg/kg (up to 10 mg) every 1-4 hours as needed; may also use 0.5 mg/kg/hour by continuous infusion. Continuous nebulized albuterol at 0.3 mg/kg/hour has been used safely in the treatment of severe status asthmaticus in children; continuous nebulized doses of 3 mg/kg/hour ± 2.2 mg/kg/hour in children whose mean age was 20.7 months resulted in no cardiac toxicity; the optimal dosage for continuous nebulization remains to be determined.

Note: Use of the 0.5% solution should be used for bronchospasm (acute or treatment) in children <15 kg. AccuNeb® has not been studied for the treatment of acute bronchospasm; use of the 0.5% concentrated solution may be more appropriate.

Children >12 years and Adults:
  Bronchospasm (treatment): 2.5 mg, diluted to a total of 3 mL, 3-4 times/day over 5-15 minutes
    NIH guidelines: 1.25-5 mg every 4-8 hours
  Bronchospasm (acute) in intensive care patients: 2.5-5 mg every 20 minutes for 3 doses, then 2.5-10 mg every 1-4 hours as needed, **or** 10-15 mg/hour continuously
Hemodialysis: Not removed
Peritoneal dialysis: Significant drug removal is unlikely based on physiochemical characteristics

Dietary Considerations Oral forms should be administered with water 1 hour before or 2 hours after meals.

Administration
Inhalation: MDI: Shake well before use; prime prior to first use, and whenever inhaler has not been used for >2 weeks or when it has been dropped, by releasing 4 test sprays into the air (away from face)
Oral: Do not crush or chew extended release tablets.

Monitoring Parameters FEV$_1$, peak flow, and/or other pulmonary function tests; blood pressure, heart rate; CNS stimulation; serum glucose, serum potassium; asthma symptoms; arterial or capillary blood gases (If patients condition warrants)

Test Interactions Increased renin (S), increased aldosterone (S)

Dosage Forms
Aerosol, for oral inhalation: 90 mcg/metered inhalation (17 g) [200 metered inhalations; contains chlorofluorocarbons]
  Proventil®: 90 mcg/metered inhalation (17 g) [200 metered inhalations; contains chlorofluorocarbons]
Aerosol, for oral inhalation:
  ProAir™ HFA: 90 mcg/metered inhalation (8.5 g) [200 metered inhalations; chlorofluorocarbon free]
  Proventil® HFA: 90 mcg/metered inhalation (6.7 g) [200 metered inhalations; chlorofluorocarbon free]
  Ventolin® HFA: 90 mcg/metered inhalation (18 g) [200 metered inhalations; chlorofluorocarbon free]
Solution for nebulization: 0.042% (3 mL); 0.083% (3 mL); 0.5% (0.5 mL, 20 mL)
  AccuNeb® [preservative free]: 0.63 mg/3 mL (3 mL) [0.021%]; 1.25 mg/3 mL (3 mL) [0.042%]
  Proventil®: 0.083% (3 mL) [preservative free]; 0.5% (20 mL) [contains benzalkonium chloride]
Syrup, as sulfate: 2 mg/5 mL (480 mL)
Tablet: 2 mg, 4 mg
Tablet, extended release:
  VoSpire ER®: 4 mg, 8 mg

- **Albuterol and Ipratropium** *see Ipratropium and Albuterol on page 934*
- **Albuterol Sulfate** *see Albuterol on page 57*
- **Alcaine®** *see Proparacaine on page 1440*
- **Alcalak [OTC]** *see Calcium Carbonate on page 269*

Alclometasone (al kloe MET a sone)

U.S. Brand Names Aclovate®
Index Terms Alclometasone Dipropionate
Pharmacologic Category Corticosteroid, Topical
Additional Appendix Information
  Corticosteroids *on page 1879*
Use Treatment of inflammation of corticosteroid-responsive dermatosis (low potency topical corticosteroid)
Pregnancy Risk Factor C
Medication Safety Issues
  Sound-alike/look-alike issues:
    Aclovate® may be confused with Accolate®
Dosage Topical: Apply a thin film to the affected area 2-3 times/day. Therapy should be discontinued when control is achieved; if no improvement is seen, reassessment of diagnosis may be necessary.
Dosage Forms
  Cream, as dipropionate: 0.05% (15 g, 45 g, 60 g)
  Ointment, as dipropionate: 0.05% (15 g, 45 g, 60 g)

- **Alclometasone Dipropionate** *see Alclometasone on page 59*
- **Alcomicin® (Can)** *see Gentamicin on page 793*
- **Aldactazide®** *see Hydrochlorothiazide and Spironolactone on page 847*
- **Aldactazide 25® (Can)** *see Hydrochlorothiazide and Spironolactone on page 847*
- **Aldactazide 50® (Can)** *see Hydrochlorothiazide and Spironolactone on page 847*
- **Aldactone®** *see Spironolactone on page 1596*
- **Aldara™** *see Imiquimod on page 890*

Aldesleukin (al des LOO kin)

U.S. Brand Names Proleukin®
Canadian Brand Names Proleukin®
Index Terms Epidermal Thymocyte Activating Factor; ETAF; IL-2; Interleukin-2; Lymphocyte Mitogenic Factor; NSC-373364; T-Cell Growth Factor; TCGF; Thymocyte Stimulating Factor
Pharmacologic Category Biological Response Modulator
Use Treatment of metastatic renal cell cancer, melanoma
(Continued)

Aldesleukin *(Continued)*

Unlabeled/Investigational Use Investigational: Multiple myeloma, HIV infection, and AIDS; may be used in conjunction with lymphokine-activated killer (LAK) cells, tumor-infiltrating lymphocyte (TIL) cells, interleukin-1, and interferons; colorectal cancer; non-Hodgkin's lymphoma

Pregnancy Risk Factor C

Pregnancy Implications There are no adequate and well-controlled studies in pregnant women; use during pregnancy only if benefits to the mother outweigh potential risk to the fetus. Contraception is recommended for fertile males or females using this medication.

Lactation Enters breast milk/contraindicated

Medication Safety Issues

Sound-alike/look-alike issues:

Aldesleukin may be confused with oprelvekin

Proleukin® may be confused with oprelvekin

High alert medication: The Institute for Safe Medication Practices (ISMP) includes this medication among its list of drugs which have a heightened risk of causing significant patient harm when used in error.

Contraindications Hypersensitivity to aldesleukin or any component of the formulation; patients with abnormal thallium stress or pulmonary function tests; patients who have had an organ allograft; retreatment in patients who have experienced sustained ventricular tachycardia (≥5 beats), refractory cardiac rhythm disturbances, recurrent chest pain with ECG changes consistent with angina or myocardial infarction, intubation ≥72 hours, pericardial tamponade, renal dialysis for ≥72 hours, coma or toxic psychosis lasting ≥48 hours, repetitive or refractory seizures, bowel ischemia/perforation, GI bleeding requiring surgery

Warnings/Precautions Hazardous agent - use appropriate precautions for handling and disposal. **[U.S. Boxed Warning]: High-dose aldesleukin therapy has been associated with capillary leak syndrome (CLS) resulting in hypotension and reduced organ perfusion which may be severe and can result in death. Therapy should be restricted to patients with normal cardiac and pulmonary functions as defined by thallium stress and formal pulmonary function testing.** Extreme caution should be used in patients with a history of prior cardiac or pulmonary disease. Patients must have a serum creatinine ≤1.5 mg/dL prior to treatment.

[U.S. Boxed Warning]: Should be administered under the supervision of an experienced cancer chemotherapy physician in a facility with cardiopulmonary or intensive specialists and intensive care facilities available. Adverse effects are frequent and sometimes fatal. May exacerbate pre-existing or initial presentation of autoimmune diseases and inflammatory disorders. Patients should be evaluated and treated for CNS metastases and have a negative scan prior to treatment. Mental status changes (irritability, confusion, depression) can occur and may indicate bacteremia, hypoperfusion, CNS malignancy, or CNS toxicity.

[U.S. Boxed Warning]: Impaired neutrophil function is associated with treatment; patients are at risk for sepsis, bacterial endocarditis, and central line-related gram-positive infections. Antibiotic prophylaxis which has been associated with a reduced incidence of staphylococcal infections in aldesleukin studies includes the use of oxacillin, nafcillin, ciprofloxacin, or vancomycin.

[U.S. Boxed Warning]: Withhold treatment for patients developing moderate-to-severe lethargy or somnolence; continued treatment may result in coma. Standard prophylactic supportive care during high-dose aldesleukin treatment includes acetaminophen to relieve constitutional symptoms and an H_2 antagonist to reduce the risk of GI ulceration and/or bleeding.

Adverse Reactions

>10%:

Cardiovascular: Sensory dysfunction, sinus tachycardia, arrhythmia, pulmonary congestion; hypotension (dose-limiting toxicity) which may require vasopressor support and hemodynamic changes resembling those seen in septic shock can be seen within 2 hours of administration; chest pain, acute MI, SVT with hypotension has been reported, edema

Central nervous system: Dizziness, pain, fever, chills, cognitive changes, fatigue, malaise, disorientation, somnolence, paranoid delusion, and other behavioral changes; reversible and dose related; however, may continue to worsen for several days even after the infusion is stopped

Dermatologic: Pruritus, erythema, rash, dry skin, exfoliative dermatitis, macular erythema

Gastrointestinal: Nausea, vomiting, weight gain, diarrhea, stomatitis, anorexia, GI bleeding

Hematologic: Anemia, thrombocytopenia, leukopenia, eosinophilia, coagulation disorders

Hepatic: Transaminases increased, alkaline phosphatase increased, jaundice

Neuromuscular & skeletal: Weakness, rigors which can be decreased or ameliorated with acetaminophen or a nonsteroidal agent and meperidine

Renal: Oliguria, anuria, proteinuria; renal failure (dose-limiting toxicity) manifested by oliguria noted within 24-48 hours of initiation of therapy; marked fluid retention, azotemia, and increased serum creatinine seen, which may return to baseline within 7 days of discontinuation of therapy; hypophosphatemia

Respiratory: Dyspnea, pulmonary edema

1% to 10%: Cardiovascular: Increase in vascular permeability: Capillary-leak syndrome manifested by severe peripheral edema, ascites, pulmonary infiltration, and pleural effusion; occurs in 2% to 4% of patients and is resolved after therapy ends

<1% (Limited to important or life-threatening): Alopecia, coma, CHF, pancreatitis, polyuria, seizure

Overdosage/Toxicology Side effects following the use of aldesleukin are dose related. Administration of more than the recommended dose has been associated with a more rapid onset of expected dose-limiting toxicities. Adverse reactions generally will reverse when the drug is stopped, particularly because of its short serum half-life. Provide supportive treatment of any continuing symptoms. Life-threatening toxicities have been ameliorated by the I.V. administration of dexamethasone, which may decrease the therapeutic effect of aldesleukin.

Drug Interactions

Increased Effect/Toxicity: Aldesleukin may affect central nervous function; therefore, interactions could occur following concomitant administration of psychotropic drugs (eg, narcotics, analgesics, antiemetics, sedatives, tranquilizers).

Concomitant administration of drugs possessing nephrotoxic (eg, aminoglycosides, indomethacin), myelotoxic (eg, cytotoxic chemotherapy), cardiotoxic (eg, doxorubicin), or hepatotoxic effects with aldesleukin may increase toxicity in these organ systems.

Beta-blockers and other antihypertensives may potentiate the hypotension seen with aldesleukin.

Decreased Effect: Corticosteroids have been shown to decrease toxicity of aldesleukin, but may reduce the efficacy of the lymphokine.

Ethanol/Nutrition/Herb Interactions Ethanol: May increase CNS adverse effects.

Stability Store vials of lyophilized injection in a refrigerator at 2°C to 8°C (36°F to 46°F). Reconstitute vials with 1.2 mL SWFI. Gently swirl; do not shake. Further dilute with 50 mL of D_5W. Smaller volumes of D_5W should be used for doses <1.5 mg; avoid concentrations <30 mcg/mL and >70 mcg/mL (an increased variability in drug delivery has been seen). Reconstituted vials and solutions diluted for infusion are stable for 48 hours at room temperature or refrigerated, per the manufacturer. Solution diluted with D_5W to a concentration of 220 mg/mL and repackaged into tuberculin syringes was reported to be stable for 14 days refrigerated.
Note: Filtration will result in significant loss of bioactivity

Recommendations for aldesleukin dilution: See table.

Final Dilution Concentration (mcg/mL)	Final Dilution Concentration (10^6 int. units/mL)	Stability
<30	<0.49	Albumin must be added to bag **prior to addition** of aldesleukin at a final concentration of 0.1% (1 mg/mL) albumin; stable at room temperature or at ≥32°C (89°F) for 6 days[1,2]
≥30 to ≤70	≥0.49 to ≤1.1	Stable at room temperature at 6 days without albumin added or at ≥32°C (89°F) for 6 days only if albumin is added (0.1%)[1,2]
70-100	1.2-1.6	Unstable; avoid use
>100 500	1.7 8.2	Stable at room temperature and at ≥32°C (89°F) for 6 days[1,2]

[1]These solutions do not contain a preservative; use for more than 24 hours may not be advisable.

[2]Continuous infusion via ambulatory infusion device raises aldesleukin to this temperature.

Mechanism of Action Aldesleukin promotes proliferation, differentiation, and recruitment of T and B cells, natural killer (NK) cells, and thymocytes; causes cytolytic activity in a subset of lymphocytes and subsequent interactions between the immune system and malignant cells; can stimulate lymphokine-activated killer (LAK) cells and tumor-infiltrating lymphocytes (TIL) cells.

Pharmacodynamics/Kinetics

Distribution: V_d: 4-7 L; primarily in plasma and then in the lymphocytes

Bioavailability: I.M.: 37%

Half-life elimination: Initial: 6-13 minutes; Terminal: 80-120 minutes

Dosage Refer to individual protocols.

I.V.:

Renal cell carcinoma: 600,000 int. units/kg every 8 hours for a maximum of 14 doses; repeat after 9 days for a total of 28 doses per course. Retreat if needed 7 weeks after previous course.

Melanoma:

Single-agent use: 600,000 int. units/kg every 8 hours for a maximum of 14 doses; repeat after 9 days for a total of 28 doses per course. Retreat if needed 7 weeks after previous course.

In combination with cytotoxic agents: 24 million int. units/m^2 days 12-16 and 19-23

SubQ:

Single-agent doses: 3-18 million int. units/day for 5 days each week, up to 6 weeks

In combination with interferon:

5 million int. units/m^2 3 times/week

1.8 million int. units/m^2 twice daily 5 days/week for 6 weeks

Investigational regimen: SubQ: 11 million int. units (flat dose) daily for 4 days per week for 4 consecutive weeks; repeat every 6 weeks

Dosage adjustment in renal impairment: No specific recommendations by manufacturer. Use with caution.

Administration Administer as I.V. infusion over 15 minutes; may be administered by SubQ injection

Management of symptoms related to vascular leak syndrome:

If actual body weight increases >10% above baseline, or rales or rhonchi are audible:

Administer furosemide at dosage determined by patient response

Administer dopamine hydrochloride 2-4 mcg/kg/minute to maintain renal blood flow and urine output

If patient has dyspnea at rest: Administer supplemental oxygen by face mask

If patient has severe respiratory distress: Intubate patient and provide mechanical ventilation; administer ranitidine (as the hydrochloride salt) 50 mg I.V. every 8-12 hours as prophylaxis against stress ulcers

Monitoring Parameters

The following clinical evaluations are recommended for all patients prior to beginning treatment and then frequently during drug administration:

Standard hematologic tests including CBC, differential, and platelet counts; blood chemistries including electrolytes, renal and hepatic function tests

Chest x-rays

(Continued)

Aldesleukin *(Continued)*

Monitoring during therapy should include vital signs (temperature, pulse, blood pressure, and respiration rate) and weight; in a patient with a decreased blood pressure, especially <90 mm Hg, cardiac monitoring for rhythm should be conducted. If an abnormal complex or rhythm is seen, an ECG should be performed; vital signs in these hypotension patients should be taken hourly and central venous pressure (CVP) checked.

During treatment, pulmonary function should be monitored on a regular basis.

Additional Information
1 Cetus unit = 6 int. units
1.1 mg = 18 x 10^6 int. units (or 3 x 10^6 Cetus units)
1 Roche unit (Teceleukin) = 3 int. units

Dosage Forms Injection, powder for reconstitution: 22 x 10^6 int. units [18 million int. units/mL = 1.1 mg/mL when reconstituted]

♦ **Aldex**™ *see* Guaifenesin and Phenylephrine *on page 818*

♦ **Aldomet** *see* Methyldopa *on page 1117*

♦ **Aldoril**® *see* Methyldopa and Hydrochlorothiazide *on page 1117*

♦ **Aldroxicon I [OTC]** *see* Aluminum Hydroxide, Magnesium Hydroxide, and Simethicone *on page 85*

♦ **Aldroxicon II [OTC]** *see* Aluminum Hydroxide, Magnesium Hydroxide, and Simethicone *on page 85*

♦ **Aldurazyme**® *see* Laronidase *on page 980*

Alefacept *(a LE fa sept)*

U.S. Brand Names Amevive®
Canadian Brand Names Amevive®
Index Terms B 9273; BG 9273; Human LFA-3/IgG(1) Fusion Protein; LFA-3/IgG(1) Fusion Protein, Human
Pharmacologic Category Monoclonal Antibody
Use Treatment of moderate to severe chronic plaque psoriasis in adults who are candidates for systemic therapy or phototherapy
Restrictions Alefacept will be distributed directly to physician offices or to a specialty pharmacy; injections are intended to be administered in the physician's office
Pregnancy Risk Factor B
Pregnancy Implications Effects in pregnancy are not known. Teratogenic effects have not been observed in animal studies. Patients who become pregnant during therapy or within 8 weeks of treatment are advised to enroll in pregnancy registry (866-263-8483).
Lactation Excretion in breast milk unknown/not recommended
Contraindications Hypersensitivity to alefacept or any component of the formulation; history of severe malignancy; patients with HIV infection or other clinically-important infections
Warnings/Precautions Alefacept induces a decline in circulating T-lymphocytes (CD4+ and CD8+); CD4+ lymphocyte counts should be monitored every 2 weeks throughout therapy. Do not initiate in pre-existing depression of CD4+ lymphocytes and withhold treatment in any patient who develops a depressed CD4+ lymphocyte count (<250 cells/μL) during treatment; permanently discontinue if CD4+ lymphocyte counts remain <250 cells/μL for 1 month.

Alefacept may increase the risk of malignancies; use caution in patients at high risk for malignancy. Discontinue if malignancy develops during therapy. Alefacept may increase the risk of infection and may reactivate latent infection; monitor for new infections. Avoid use in patients receiving other immunosuppressant drugs or phototherapy. May cause serious liver damage; discontinue if signs and symptoms of hepatic injury occur. Safety and efficacy of live or attenuated vaccines have not been evaluated. Safety and efficacy have not been established in pediatric patients.

Adverse Reactions
≥10%:
Hematologic: Lymphopenia (up to 10% of patients required temporary discontinuation, up to 17% during a second course of therapy)
Local: Injection site reactions (up to 16% of patients; includes pain, inflammation, bleeding, edema, or other reaction)
1% to 10%:
Central nervous system: Chills (6%; primarily during intravenous administration), dizziness (≥2%)
Dermatologic: Pruritus (≥2%)
Gastrointestinal: Nausea (≥2%)
Neuromuscular & skeletal: Myalgia (≥2%)
Respiratory: Pharyngitis (≥2%), cough increased (≥2%)
Miscellaneous: Malignancies (1% vs 0.5% in placebo), antibodies to alefacept (3%; significance unknown), infection (1% requiring hospitalization)
<1% (Limited to important or life-threatening): Anaphylaxis, allergic reaction, angioedema, headache, MI, transaminases increased (≥3 times ULN), urticaria

Overdosage/Toxicology No specific experience in overdose. Symptoms observed at 0.75 mg/kg I.V. included chills, headache, arthralgia, and sinusitis. Reductions in lymphocyte populations should be closely monitored. Treatment is supportive.

Drug Interactions
Increased Effect/Toxicity: No formal drug interaction studies have been completed.
Decreased Effect: No formal drug interaction studies have been completed.
Ethanol/Nutrition/Herb Interactions Ethanol: Avoid ethanol (may increase risk of liver toxicity).
Stability Store under refrigeration at 2°C to 8°C (36°F to 46°F); protect from light. Reconstitute 15 mg vial for I.M. solution with 0.6 mL of SWFI (supplied); 0.5 mL of reconstituted solution

contains 15 mg of alefacept. Gently swirl to avoid foaming. Do not filter reconstituted solutions. Following reconstitution, may be stored for up to 4 hours at 2°C to 8°C (36°F to 46°F). Discard any unused solution after 4 hours.

Mechanism of Action Binds to CD2, a receptor on the surface of lymphocytes, inhibiting their interaction with leukocyte functional antigen 3 (LFA-3). Interaction between CD2 and LFA-3 is important for the activation of T lymphocytes in psoriasis. Activated T lymphocytes secrete a number of inflammatory mediators, including Interferon gamma, which are involved in psoriasis. Since CD2 is primarily expressed on T lymphocytes, treatment results in a reduction in $CD4^+$ and $CD8^+$ T lymphocytes, with lesser effects on other cell populations (NK and B lymphocytes).

Pharmacodynamics/Kinetics

Distribution: V_d: 0.094 L/kg

Bioavailability: 63% (following I.M. administration)

Half-life: 270 hours (following I.V. administration)

Excretion: Clearance: 0.25 mL/hour/kg

Dosage Adults:

I.M.: 15 mg once weekly; usual duration of treatment: 12 weeks

A second course of treatment may be initiated at least 12 weeks after completion of the initial course of treatment, provided $CD4^+$ T-lymphocyte counts are within the normal range.

Note: $CD4^+$ T-lymphocyte counts should be monitored before initiation of treatment and every 2 weeks during therapy. Dosing should be withheld if $CD4^+$ counts are <250 cells/μL, and dosing should be permanently discontinued if $CD4^+$ lymphocyte counts remain at <250 cell/μL for longer than 1 month.

Elderly: Refer to adult dosing

Dosage adjustment in renal impairment: No dosage adjustment required

Administration I.M. injections should be administered at least 1 inch from previous administration sites.

Monitoring Parameters Baseline $CD4^+$ T-lymphocyte counts prior to initiation and every 2 weeks during treatment course; severity of psoriatic lesions; signs and symptoms of infection

Dosage Forms

Injection, powder for reconstitution:

Amevive®: 15 mg [for I.M. administration; contains sucrose 12.5 mg; supplied with SWFI]

Alemtuzumab (ay lem TU zoo mab)

U.S. Brand Names Campath®

Index Terms C1H; Campath-1H; DNA-Derived Humanized Monoclonal Antibody; Humanized IgG1 Anti-CD52 Monoclonal Antibody

Pharmacologic Category Antineoplastic Agent, Monoclonal Antibody

Use Treatment of B-cell chronic lymphocytic leukemia (B-CLL)

Unlabeled/Investigational Use Treatment of refractory T-cell prolymphocytic leukemia (T-PLL); rheumatoid arthritis; graft-versus-host disease; multiple myeloma; preconditioning regimen for stem-cell transplantation and renal and liver transplantation; post-transplant rejection (renal)

Pregnancy Risk Factor C

Pregnancy Implications Human IgG is known to cross the placental barrier; therefore, alemtuzumab may also cross the barrier and cause fetal B- and T-lymphocyte depletion. Well-controlled human trials have not been done. Use during pregnancy only if the benefit to the mother outweighs the potential risk to the fetus.

Lactation Excretion in breast milk unknown/contraindicated

Medication Safety Issues

High alert medication: The Institute for Safe Medication Practices (ISMP) includes this medication among its list of drugs which have a heightened risk of causing significant patient harm when used in error.

Contraindications Known type 1 hypersensitivity or anaphylactic reaction to alemtuzumab or any component of the formulation; hypersensitivity to another monoclonal antibody; active systemic infections; underlying immunodeficiency (eg, seropositive for HIV)

Warnings/Precautions Hazardous agent - use appropriate precautions for handling and disposal. **[U.S. Boxed Warnings]: Serious infections (bacterial, viral, fungal, and protozoan) have been reported. Prophylactic therapy against PCP pneumonia and herpes viral infections is recommended. Serious and potentially fatal infusion-related reactions (acute respiratory distress syndrome, bronchospasm, cardiac arrest, cardiac arrhythmias, chills, fever, hypotension, myocardial infarction, pulmonary infiltrates, rash, rigors, shortness of breath, syncope) may occur;** gradual escalation to the recommended maintenance dose is required at initiation and after interruption of therapy for ≥7 days to minimize infusion-related reactions. **[U.S. Boxed Warning]: Severe, prolonged myelosuppression, autoimmune anemia, and autoimmune thrombocytopenia have occurred.** Single doses >30 mg and cumulative weekly doses >90 mg are associated with an increased incidence of pancytopenia and should not be administered. Permanently discontinue if autoimmune anemia or autoimmune thrombocytopenia occurs. Patients receiving blood products should only receive irradiated blood products due to the potential for GVHD during lymphopenia. Patients should not be immunized with live, viral vaccines during or recently after treatment. Women of childbearing potential and men of reproductive potential should use effective contraceptive methods during treatment and for a minimum of 6 months following therapy. **[U.S. Boxed Warning]: Should be administered under the supervision of an experienced cancer chemotherapy physician.** Safety and efficacy have not been established in pediatric patients.

Adverse Reactions

>10%:

Cardiovascular: Hypotension (32%), peripheral edema (13%), hypertension (11%), tachycardia/SVT (11%)

Central nervous system: Fever (85%), fatigue (34%), headache (24%), dysthesias (15%), dizziness (12%)

(Continued)

Alemtuzumab *(Continued)*

Dermatologic: Rash (40%), urticaria (30%), pruritus (24%)

Gastrointestinal: Nausea (54%), vomiting (41%), anorexia (20%), diarrhea (22%), stomatitis/mucositis (14%), abdominal pain (11%)

Hematologic: Neutropenia (85%; grade 3/4: 64%; median duration: 28 days), anemia (80%; grade 3/4: 38%), thrombocytopenia (72%; grade 3/4: 50%; median duration: 21 days)

Neuromuscular & skeletal: Rigors (86%), skeletal muscle pain (24%), weakness (13%), myalgia (11%)

Respiratory: Dyspnea (26%), cough (25%), bronchitis/pneumonitis (21%), pneumonia (16%), pharyngitis (12%)

Miscellaneous: Infection (43% to 66%; incidence is lower if prophylaxis anti-infectives are utilized), diaphoresis (19%), sepsis (15%), herpes simplex (11%)

1% to 10%:

Cardiovascular: Chest pain (10%)

Central nervous system: Insomnia (10%), neutropenic fever (10%), malaise (9%), depression (7%), temperature change sensation (5%), somnolence (5%)

Dermatologic: Purpura (8%)

Gastrointestinal: Dyspepsia (10%), constipation (9%)

Hematologic: Pancytopenia/marrow hypoplasia (5% to 6%; grade 3/4: 3%), positive Coombs' test without hemolysis (2%), autoimmune thrombocytopenia (2%), autoimmune hemolytic anemia (1%)

Neuromuscular & skeletal: Back pain (10%), tremor (7%)

Respiratory: Bronchospasm (9%), epistaxis (7%), rhinitis (7%)

Miscellaneous: Moniliasis (8%)

<1% (Limited to important or life-threatening): Acidosis, acute renal failure, agranulocytosis, alkaline phosphatase increased, allergic reactions, anaphylactoid reactions, angina pectoris, angioedema, anuria, aphasia, ascites, asthma, atrial fibrillation, biliary pain, bone marrow aplasia, bronchitis, capillary fragility, cardiac arrest, cardiac failure, cellulitis, cerebral hemorrhage, cerebrovascular disorder, coagulation abnormality, coma, COPD, coronary artery disorder, cyanosis, deep vein thrombosis, disseminated intravascular coagulation (DIC), duodenal ulcer, fluid overload, gastrointestinal hemorrhage, hallucinations, haptoglobin decreased, hematemesis, hematoma, hematuria, hemolysis, hemolytic anemia, hemoptysis, hepatic failure, hepatocellular damage, hyperbilirubinemia, hyper-/hypoglycemia, hyper-/hypokalemia, hyperthyroidism, hypoalbuminemia, hyponatremia, hypovolemia, hypoxia, idiopathic thrombocytopenic purpura (ITP), interstitial pneumonitis, intestinal obstruction, intestinal perforation, intracranial hemorrhage, lymphadenopathy, lymphopenia, marrow depression, melena, meningitis, MI, optic neuropathy, osteomyelitis, otitis media, pancreatitis, paralysis, paralytic ileus, paroxysmal nocturnal hemoglobinuria-like monocytes, pericarditis, peritonitis, plasma cell dyscrasia, phlebitis, pleural effusion, pleurisy, pneumothorax, progressive multifocal leukoencephalopathy, pseudomembranous colitis, pulmonary edema, pulmonary embolism, pulmonary fibrosis, pulmonary infiltration, purpuric rash, renal dysfunction, respiratory alkalosis, respiratory depression, respiratory insufficiency, seizure (grand mal), splenic infarction, splenomegaly, subarachnoid hemorrhage, syncope, toxic nephropathy, thrombocythemia, thrombophlebitis, throat tightness, tumor lysis syndrome, ureteral obstruction, ventricular arrhythmia, ventricular tachycardia

Overdosage/Toxicology Symptoms are likely to be extensions of adverse events (may include hematologic toxicity, respiratory distress, bronchospasm, anuria, tumor lysis syndrome). Cumulative doses >90 mg/week have been associated with pancytopenia and severe (and occasionally fatal) ITP. Treatment is symptom-directed and supportive.

Drug Interactions

Increased Effect/Toxicity: Monoclonal antibodies may increase the risk for allergic reactions to alemtuzumab due to the presence of HACA antibodies; avoid administration of live vaccines in immunosuppressive therapy.

Stability Prior to dilution, store at 2°C to 8°C (36°F to 46°F); do not freeze. Following dilution, use within 8 hours. Store at room temperature or refrigerate; protect from light. Gently invert the bag to mix the solution. Do not shake prior to use. Dilute with 100 mL NS or D_5W.

Mechanism of Action Binds to CD52, a nonmodulating antigen present on the surface of B and T lymphocytes, a majority of monocytes, macrophages, NK cells, and a subpopulation of granulocytes. After binding to CD52$^+$ cells, an antibody-dependent lysis occurs.

Pharmacodynamics/Kinetics

Distribution: V_d: 0.18 L/kg

Metabolism: Clearance decreases with repeated dosing (due to loss of CD52 receptors in periphery), resulting in a sevenfold increase in AUC.

Half-life elimination: Initial: 11 hours; 6 days following repeated dosing

Dosage Note: **Dose escalation is required;** usually accomplished in 3-7 days. Do not exceed single doses >30 mg or cumulative doses >90 mg/week.

I.V. infusion, SubQ (unlabeled route): Adults: B-CLL:

Initial: 3 mg/day; increase to 10 mg/day, then to 30 mg/day as tolerated

Maintenance: 30 mg/day 3 times/week on alternate days for up to 12 weeks

Dosage adjustment for hematologic toxicity (severe neutropenia or thrombocytopenia, not autoimmune):

First occurrence: ANC <250/μL and/or platelet count ≤25,000/μL: Hold therapy; resume at same dose when ANC ≥500/μL and platelet count ≥50,000/μL. If delay between dosing is ≥7 days, restart at 3 mg/day and escalate as tolerated.

Second occurrence: ANC <250/μL and/or platelet count ≤25,000/μL: Hold therapy; resume at 10 mg/day when ANC ≥500/μL and platelet count ≥50,000/μL. If delay between dosing is ≥7 days, restart at 3 mg/day and escalate to a maximum of 10 mg/day as tolerated.

Third occurrence: ANC <250/μL and/or platelet count ≤25,000/μL: Permanently discontinue therapy

Patients with a baseline ANC ≤500/μL and/or a baseline platelet count ≤25,000/μL at initiation of therapy: If ANC and/or platelet counts decrease to ≤50% of the baseline value, hold therapy. When ANC and/or platelet count return to baseline, resume therapy. If delay between dosing is ≥7 days, restart at 3 mg/day and escalate as tolerated.

Administration Administer by I.V. infusion over 2 hours. Consider premedicating with diphenhydramine 50 mg and acetaminophen 650 mg 30 minutes before initiation of infusion. Hydrocortisone 200 mg has been effective in decreasing severe infusion-related events. Start anti-infective prophylaxis. Other drugs should not be added to or simultaneously infused through the same I.V. line. Do not give I.V. bolus or push.

Monitoring Parameters Vital signs; carefully monitor BP especially in patient with ischemic heart disease or on antihypertensive medications; CBC and platelets (weekly); signs and symptoms of infection; CD4+ lymphocyte counts (after treatment until recovery). Monitor closely for infusion reactions (including hypotension, rigors, fever, shortness of breath, bronchospasm, chills, and/or rash).

Test Interactions May interfere with diagnostic serum tests that utilize antibodies.

Dosage Forms [DSC] = Discontinued product
Injection, solution [ampul]: 10 mg/mL (3 mL) [DSC]
Injection, solution [vial]: 30 mg/mL (1 mL)

Alendronate (a LEN droe nate)

U.S. Brand Names Fosamax®

Canadian Brand Names Apo-Alendronate®; CO Alendronate; Fosamax®; Gen-Alendronate; Novo-Alendronate; PMS-Alendronate; ratio-Alendronate; Riva-Alendronate

Index Terms Alendronate Sodium

Pharmacologic Category Bisphosphonate Derivative

Use Treatment and prevention of osteoporosis in postmenopausal females; treatment of osteoporosis in males; Paget's disease of the bone in patients who are symptomatic, at risk for future complications, or with alkaline phosphatase ≥2 times the upper limit of normal; treatment of glucocorticoid-induced osteoporosis in males and females with low bone mineral density who are receiving a daily dosage ≥7.5 mg of prednisone (or equivalent)

Pregnancy Risk Factor C

Pregnancy Implications Safety and efficacy have not been established in pregnant women. Animal studies have shown delays in delivery and fetal/neonatal death (secondary to hypocalcemia). Bisphosphonates are incorporated into the bone matrix and gradually released over time. Theoretically, there may be a risk of fetal harm when pregnancy follows the completion of therapy. Based on limited case reports with pamidronate, serum calcium levels in the newborn may be altered if administered during pregnancy.

Lactation Excretion in breast milk unknown/use caution

Medication Safety Issues
Sound-alike/look-alike issues:
Fosamax® may be confused with Flomax®

International issues:
Fosamax® may be confused with Fisamox® which is a brand name for amoxicillin in Australia

Contraindications Hypersensitivity to alendronate, other bisphosphonates, or any component of the formulation; hypocalcemia; abnormalities of the esophagus which delay esophageal emptying such as stricture or achalasia; inability to stand or sit upright for at least 30 minutes; oral solution should not be used in patients at risk of aspiration

Warnings/Precautions Use caution in patients with renal impairment (not recommended for use in patients with Cl$_{cr}$ <35 mL/minute); hypocalcemia must be corrected before therapy initiation; ensure adequate calcium and vitamin D intake. May cause irritation to upper gastrointestinal mucosa. Esophagitis, esophageal ulcers, esophageal erosions, and esophageal stricture (rare) have been reported; risk increases in patients unable to comply with dosing instructions. Use with caution in patients with dysphagia, esophageal disease, gastritis, duodenitis, or ulcers (may worsen underlying condition).

Bisphosphonate therapy has been associated with osteonecrosis, primarily of the jaw; this has been observed mostly in cancer patients, but also in patients with postmenopausal osteoporosis and other diagnoses. Dental exams and preventative dentistry should be performed prior to placing patients with risk factors on chronic bisphosphonate therapy. Invasive dental procedures should be avoided during treatment.

Infrequently, severe (and occasionally debilitating) bone, joint, and/or muscle pain have been reported during bisphosphonate treatment. The onset of pain ranged from a single day to several months. Symptoms usually resolve upon discontinuation. Some patients experienced recurrence when rechallenged with same drug or another bisphosphonate; avoid use in patients with a history of these symptoms in association with bisphosphonate therapy.

Safety and efficacy in children have not been established.

Adverse Reactions Note: Incidence of adverse effects (mostly GI) increases significantly in patients treated for Paget's disease at 40 mg/day.

>10%: Endocrine & metabolic: Hypocalcemia (transient, mild, 18%); hypophosphatemia (transient, mild, 10%)

1% to 10%:
Central nervous system: Headache (up to 3%)
Gastrointestinal: Abdominal pain (1% to 7%), acid reflux (1% to 4%), dyspepsia (1% to 4%), nausea (1% to 4%), flatulence (up to 4%), diarrhea (1% to 3%), gastroesophageal reflux disease (1% to 3%), constipation (up to 3%), esophageal ulcer (up to 2%), abdominal distension (up to 1%), gastritis (up to 1%), vomiting (up to 1%), dysphagia (up to 1%), gastric ulcer (1%), melena (1%)
Neuromuscular & skeletal: Musculoskeletal pain (up to 6%), muscle cramps (up to 1%)

<1% (Limited to important or life-threatening): Anastomotic ulcer, angioedema; bone, muscle, or joint pain (occasionally severe, considered incapacitating in rare cases); duodenal ulcer, episcleritis, erythema, esophageal erosions, esophageal perforation, esophageal stricture, (Continued)

Alendronate *(Continued)*

esophagitis, fever, flu-like syndrome, hypersensitivity reactions, hypocalcemia (symptomatic), lymphocytopenia, malaise, myalgia, oropharyngeal ulceration, osteonecrosis (jaw), photosensitivity (rare), pruritus, rash, scleritis (rare), Stevens-Johnson syndrome, taste perversion, toxic epidermal necrolysis, urticaria, uveitis (rare)

Overdosage/Toxicology Symptoms include hypocalcemia, hypophosphatemia, and upper GI adverse events (upset stomach, heartburn, esophagitis, gastritis or ulcer). Treat with milk or antacids to bind alendronate. Dialysis would not be beneficial. Do not induce vomiting (due to the risk of esophageal irritation); keep fully upright.

Drug Interactions

Increased Effect/Toxicity: Aminoglycosides may lower serum calcium levels with prolonged administration; concomitant use may have an additive hypocalcemic effect. NSAIDs may enhance the gastrointestinal adverse/toxic effects (increased incidence of GI ulcers) of bisphosphonate derivatives. Bisphosphonate derivatives may enhance the hypocalcemic effect of phosphate supplements.

Decreased Effect: The following agents may decrease the absorption of oral bisphosphonate derivatives: Antacids (aluminum, calcium, magnesium), oral calcium salts, oral iron salts, and oral magnesium salts.

Ethanol/Nutrition/Herb Interactions

Ethanol: Avoid ethanol (may increase risk of osteoporosis and gastric irritation).

Food: All food and beverages interfere with absorption. Coadministration with caffeine may reduce alendronate efficacy. Coadministration with dairy products may decrease alendronate absorption. Beverages (especially orange juice and coffee) and food may reduce the absorption of alendronate as much as 60%.

Stability Store tablets and oral solution at room temperature of 15°C to 30°C (59°F to 86°F). Keep in well-closed container.

Mechanism of Action A bisphosphonate which inhibits bone resorption via actions on osteoclasts or on osteoclast precursors; decreases the rate of bone resorption, leading to an indirect increase in bone mineral density. In Paget's disease, characterized by disordered resorption and formation of bone, inhibition of resorption leads to an indirect decrease in bone formation; but the newly-formed bone has a more normal architecture.

Pharmacodynamics/Kinetics

Distribution: 28 L (exclusive of bone)

Protein binding: ~78%

Metabolism: None

Bioavailability: Fasting: 0.6%; reduced 60% with food or drink

Half-life elimination: Exceeds 10 years

Excretion: Urine; feces (as unabsorbed drug)

Dosage Oral: Adults: **Note:** Patients treated with glucocorticoids and those with Paget's disease should receive adequate amounts of calcium and vitamin D.

Osteoporosis in postmenopausal females:

Prophylaxis: 5 mg once daily **or** 35 mg once weekly

Treatment: 10 mg once daily **or** 70 mg once weekly

Osteoporosis in males: 10 mg once daily **or** 70 mg once weekly

Osteoporosis secondary to glucocorticoids in males and females: Treatment: 5 mg once daily; a dose of 10 mg once daily should be used in postmenopausal females who are not receiving estrogen.

Paget's disease of bone in males and females: 40 mg once daily for 6 months

Retreatment: Relapses during the 12 months following therapy occurred in 9% of patients who responded to treatment. Specific retreatment data are not available. Following a 6-month post-treatment evaluation period, retreatment with alendronate may be considered in patients who have relapsed based on increases in serum alkaline phosphatase, which should be measured periodically. Retreatment may also be considered in those who failed to normalize their serum alkaline phosphatase.

Elderly: No dosage adjustment is necessary

Dosage adjustment in renal impairment:

Cl_{cr} 35-60 mL/minute: None necessary

Cl_{cr} <35 mL/minute: Alendronate is not recommended due to lack of experience

Dosage adjustment in hepatic impairment: None necessary

Dietary Considerations Ensure adequate calcium and vitamin D intake; however, wait at least 30 minutes after taking alendronate before taking any supplement. Alendronate must be taken with plain water first thing in the morning and at least 30 minutes before the first food or beverage of the day.

Administration Alendronate must be taken with plain water (tablets 6-8 oz; oral solution follow with 2 oz) first thing in the morning and ≥30 minutes before the first food, beverage, or other medication of the day. Do not take with mineral water or with other beverages. Patients should be instructed to stay upright (not to lie down) for at least 30 minutes **and** until after first food of the day (to reduce esophageal irritation). Patients should receive supplemental calcium and vitamin D if dietary intake is inadequate.

Monitoring Parameters Alkaline phosphatase should be periodically measured; serum calcium and phosphorus; monitor pain and fracture rate; hormonal status (male and female) prior to therapy; bone mineral density (should be done prior to initiation of therapy and after 6-12 months of combined glucocorticoid and alendronate treatment)

Reference Range Calcium (total): Adults: 9.0-11.0 mg/dL (2.05-2.54 mmol/L), may slightly decrease with aging; phosphorus: 2.5-4.5 mg/dL (0.81-1.45 mmol/L)

Test Interactions Bisphosphonates may interfere with diagnostic imaging agents such as technetium-99m-diphosphonate in bone scans.

Dosage Forms Note: Strength expressed as free acid

Solution, oral, as monosodium trihydrate:

Fosamax™: 70 mg/75 mL [contains parabens; raspberry flavor]

Tablet, as sodium:

Fosamax™: 5 mg, 10 mg, 35 mg, 40 mg, 70 mg

Alendronate and Cholecalciferol (a LEN droe nate & kole e kal SI fer ole)

U.S. Brand Names Fosamax Plus D™
Canadian Brand Names Fosavance
Index Terms Alendronate Sodium and Cholecalciferol; Cholecalciferol and Alendronate; Vitamin D₃
Pharmacologic Category Bisphosphonate Derivative; Vitamin D Analog
Use Treatment of osteoporosis in postmenopausal females; increase bone mass in males with osteoporosis
Pregnancy Risk Factor C
Dosage Oral: Adults: One tablet once weekly
  Dosage adjustment in renal impairment: Cl_{or} <35 mL/minute: Not recommended
Additional Information Complete prescribing information for this medication should be consulted for additional detail.
Dosage Forms
  Tablet:
    Fosamax Plus D™: 70/2800: Alendronate 70 mg and cholecalciferol 2800 int. units

- ◆ **Alendronate Sodium** see Alendronate on page 65
- ◆ **Alendronate Sodium and Cholecalciferol** see Alendronate and Cholecalciferol on page 67
- ◆ **Alenic Alka Tablet [OTC]** see Aluminum Hydroxide and Magnesium Trisilicate on page 85
- ◆ **Aler-Cap [OTC]** see DiphenhydrAMINE on page 515
- ◆ **Aler-Dryl [OTC]** see DiphenhydrAMINE on page 515
- ◆ **Aler-Tab [OTC]** see DiphenhydrAMINE on page 515
- ◆ **Alertec® (Can)** see Modafinil on page 1161
- ◆ **Alesse®** see Ethinyl Estradiol and Levonorgestrel on page 653
- ◆ **Aleve® [OTC]** see Naproxen on page 1199
- ◆ **Aleve® Cold & Sinus [OTC]** see Naproxen and Pseudoephedrine on page 1201
- ◆ **Aleve® Sinus & Headache [OTC]** see Naproxen and Pseudoephedrine on page 1201
- ◆ **Alfenta®** see Alfentanil on page 67

Alfentanil (al FEN ta nil)

U.S. Brand Names Alfenta®
Canadian Brand Names Alfenta®; Alfentanil Injection, USP
Index Terms Alfentanil Hydrochloride
Pharmacologic Category Analgesic, Opioid
Additional Appendix Information
  Narcotic Agonists on page 1888
Use Analgesic adjunct given by continuous infusion or in incremental doses in maintenance of anesthesia with barbiturate or N₂O or a primary anesthetic agent for the induction of anesthesia in patients undergoing general surgery in which endotracheal intubation and mechanical ventilation are required
Restrictions C-II
Pregnancy Risk Factor C
Medication Safety Issues
  Sound-alike/look-alike issues:
    Alfentanil may be confused with Anafranil®, fentanyl, remifentanil, sufentanil
    Alfenta® may be confused with Sufenta®
Contraindications Hypersensitivity to alfentanil hydrochloride, to narcotics, or any component of the formulation; increased intracranial pressure, severe respiratory depression
Warnings/Precautions Use with caution in patients with drug dependence, head injury, morbid obesity, acute asthma and respiratory conditions; hypotension has occurred in neonates with respiratory distress syndrome; use caution when administering to patients with bradyarrhythmias; rapid I.V. infusion may result in skeletal muscle and chest wall rigidity, impaired ventilation, or respiratory distress/arrest; inject slowly over 3-5 minutes; nondepolarizing skeletal muscle relaxant may be required. Alfentanil may produce more hypotension compared to fentanyl, therefore, be sure to administer slowly and ensure patient has adequate hydration. Shares the toxic potentials of opiate agonists, and precautions of opiate agonist therapy should be observed. Should be administered by trained individuals. Safety and efficacy have not been established in children <12 years old.
Adverse Reactions
  >10%:
    Cardiovascular: Bradycardia, peripheral vasodilation
    Central nervous system: Drowsiness, sedation, intracranial pressure increased
    Endocrine & metabolic: Antidiuretic hormone release
    Gastrointestinal: Nausea, vomiting, constipation
    Ocular: Miosis
  1% to 10%:
    Cardiovascular: Cardiac arrhythmia, orthostatic hypotension
    Central nervous system: Confusion, CNS depression
    Ocular: Blurred vision
  <1% (Limited to important or life-threatening): Convulsions, mental depression, paradoxical CNS excitation or delirium, dizziness, dysesthesia, rash, urticaria, itching, biliary tract spasm, urinary tract spasm, respiratory depression, bronchospasm, laryngospasm, physical and psychological dependence with prolonged use; cold, clammy skin
Overdosage/Toxicology Symptoms include miosis, respiratory depression, seizures, and CNS depression. Treatment includes naloxone 2 mg I.V. (0.01 mg/kg for children), with repeat administration as necessary, up to a total of 10 mg. May precipitate withdrawal.
(Continued)

Alfentanil *(Continued)*

Drug Interactions

Cytochrome P450 Effect: Substrate of CYP3A4 (major)

Increased Effect/Toxicity: Dextroamphetamine may enhance the analgesic effect of morphine and other opiate agonists. CNS depressants (eg, benzodiazepines, barbiturates, tricyclic antidepressants), erythromycin, reserpine, beta-blockers may increase the toxic effects of alfentanil. Alfentanil levels/effects may be increased by azole antifungals, clarithromycin, diclofenac, doxycycline, erythromycin, imatinib, isoniazid, nefazodone, nicardipine, propofol, protease inhibitors, quinidine, verapamil, telithromycin, and other inhibitors of CYP3A4.

Stability Store unopened ampuls at 20°C to 25°C (68°F to 77°F). Protect from light. For infusion, dilute in D_5W, NS, LR, or D_5NS to a concentration of 25-80 mcg/mL.

Mechanism of Action Binds with stereospecific receptors at many sites within the CNS, increases pain threshold, alters pain perception, inhibits ascending pain pathways; is an ultra short-acting narcotic

Pharmacodynamics/Kinetics

Onset of action: Rapid

Duration (dose dependent): 30-60 minutes

Distribution: V_d: Newborns, premature: 1 L/kg; Children: 0.163-0.48 L/kg; Adults: 0.46 L/kg

Half-life elimination: Newborns, premature: 5.33-8.75 hours; Children: 40-60 minutes; Adults: 83-97 minutes

Dosage Doses should be titrated to appropriate effects; wide range of doses is dependent upon desired degree of analgesia/anesthesia

Children <12 years: Dose not established

Adults: Dose should be based on ideal body weight as follows (see table):

Alfentanil

Indication	Approx Duration of Anesthesia (min)	Induction Period (Initial Dose) (mcg/kg)	Maintenance Period (Increments/ Infusion)	Total Dose (mcg/kg)	Effects
Incremental injection	≤30	8-20	3-5 mcg/kg or 0.5-1 mcg/kg/min	8-40	Spontaneously breathing or assisted ventilation when required.
	30-60	20-50	5-15 mcg/kg	Up to 75	Assisted or controlled ventilation required. Attenuation of response to laryngoscopy and intubation.
Continuous infusion	>45	50-75	0.5-3 mcg/kg/min average infusion rate 1-1.5 mcg/kg/min	Dependent on duration of procedure	Assisted or controlled ventilation required. Some attenuation of response to intubation and incision, with intraoperative stability.
Anesthetic induction	>45	130-245	0.5-1.5 mcg/kg/ min or general anesthetic	Dependent on duration of procedure	Assisted or controlled ventilation required. Administer slowly (over 3 minutes). Concentration of inhalation agents reduced by 30% to 50% for initial hour.

Administration Administer I.V. slowly over 3-5 minutes or by I.V. continuous infusion.

Monitoring Parameters Respiratory rate, blood pressure, heart rate

Reference Range 100-340 ng/mL (depending upon procedure)

Additional Information Alfentanil may produce more muscle rigidity compared to fentanyl, therefore, be sure to administer slowly.

Dosage Forms

Injection, solution [preservative free]: 500 mcg/mL (2 mL, 5 mL, 10 mL)

Alfenta®: 500 mcg/mL (2 mL, 5 mL, 10 mL, 20 mL)

♦ **Alfentanil Hydrochloride** *see* Alfentanil *on page 67*

♦ **Alfentanil Injection, USP (Can)** *see* Alfentanil *on page 67*

♦ **Alferon® N** *see* Interferon Alfa-n3 *on page 926*

Alfuzosin *(al FYOO zoe sin)*

U.S. Brand Names Uroxatral®

Canadian Brand Names Xatral

Index Terms Alfuzosin Hydrochloride

Pharmacologic Category Alpha₁ Blocker

Use Treatment of the functional symptoms of benign prostatic hyperplasia (BPH)

Pregnancy Risk Factor B

Pregnancy Implications Teratogenic effects were not observed in animal studies; however, alfuzosin is not indicated for use in women.

Lactation Not indicated for use in women

Contraindications Hypersensitivity to alfuzosin or any component of the formulation; moderate or severe hepatic insufficiency (Child-Pugh class B and C); potent CYP3A4 inhibitors (eg, itraconazole, ketoconazole, ritonavir)

Warnings/Precautions Not intended for use as an antihypertensive drug. May cause significant orthostatic hypotension and syncope, especially with first dose; anticipate a similar effect if therapy is interrupted for a few days, if dosage is rapidly increased, or if another antihypertensive drug (particularly vasodilators) or a PDE5 inhibitor is introduced. Discontinue if symptoms of angina occur or worsen. Patients should be cautioned about performing hazardous tasks when starting new therapy or adjusting dosage upward. Discontinue if symptoms of angina occur or worsen. Rule out prostatic carcinoma before beginning therapy. Use caution with renal or mild hepatic impairment; not recommended in moderate to severe hepatic impairment. Intraoperative floppy iris syndrome has been observed in cataract surgery patients who were on or were previously treated with alpha₁ blockers. Causality has not been established and there appears to be no benefit in discontinuing alpha blocker therapy prior to surgery. Safety and efficacy in children have not been established.

Adverse Reactions
1% to 10%:
Central nervous system: Dizziness (6%), fatigue (3%), headache (3%), pain (1% to 2%)
Gastrointestinal: Abdominal pain (1% to 2%), constipation (1% to 2%), dyspepsia (1% to 2%), nausea (1% to 2%)
Genitourinary: Impotence (1% to 2%)
Respiratory: Upper respiratory tract infection (3%), bronchitis (1% to 2%), pharyngitis (1% to 2%), sinusitis (1% to 2%)
<1% (Limited to important or life-threatening): Chest pain, hypotension, intraoperative floppy iris syndrome (with cataract surgery), postural hypotension, priapism, rash, syncope, tachycardia

Overdosage/Toxicology Hypotension would be expected in case of overdose. Treatment is symptom-directed and supportive. Dialysis not likely to benefit.

Drug Interactions
Cytochrome P450 Effect: Substrate of CYP3A4 (major)
Increased Effect/Toxicity: Alfuzosin levels/effects may be increased by azole antifungals, clarithromycin, diclofenac, doxycycline, erythromycin, imatinib, isoniazid, nefazodone, nicardipine, propofol, protease inhibitors, quinidine, verapamil, telithromycin, and other CYP3A4 inhibitors. Concurrent use of itraconazole, ketoconazole, or ritonavir is contraindicated.
Decreased Effect: Levels/effects of alfuzosin may be decreased by aminoglutethimide, carbamazepine, nafcillin, nevirapine, phenobarbital, phenytoin, rifamycins, and other CYP3A4 inducers.

Ethanol/Nutrition/Herb Interactions Food: Food increases the extent of absorption.
Stability Store at controlled room temperature of 15°C to 30°C (59°F to 86°F). Protect from light and moisture.
Mechanism of Action An antagonist of alpha₁ adrenoreceptors in the lower urinary tract. Smooth muscle tone is mediated by the sympathetic nervous stimulation of alpha₁ adrenoreceptors, which are abundant in the prostate, prostatic capsule, prostatic urethra, and bladder neck. Blockade of these adrenoreceptors can cause smooth muscles in the bladder neck and prostate to relax, resulting in an improvement in urine flow rate and a reduction in symptoms of BPH.
Pharmacodynamics/Kinetics
Absorption: Decreased 50% under fasting conditions
Distribution: V_d: 3.2 L/kg
Protein binding: 82% to 90%
Metabolism: Hepatic, primarily via CYP3A4; metabolism includes oxidation, O-demethylation, and N-dealkylation; forms metabolites (inactive)
Bioavailability: 49% following a meal
Half-life elimination: 10 hours
Time to peak, plasma: 8 hours following a meal
Excretion: Feces (69%); urine (24%)
Dosage Oral: Adults: 10 mg once daily
Dosage adjustment in renal impairment: Bioavailability and maximum serum concentrations are increased by ~50% with mild, moderate, or severe renal impairment
Note: Safety has not been evaluated in patients with creatinine clearances <30 mL/minute.
Dosage adjustment in hepatic impairment:
Mild hepatic impairment: Use has not been studied
Moderate or severe hepatic impairment (Child-Pugh class B and C): Clearance is decreased ⅓ to ¼ and serum concentration is increased three- to fourfold; use is contraindicated
Dietary Considerations Take following a meal at the same time each day.
Administration Tablet should be swallowed whole; do not crush or chew. Administer once daily (with a meal); should be taken at the same time each day.
Monitoring Parameters Urine flow; blood pressure
Dosage Forms Tablet, extended release, as hydrochloride: 10 mg

♦ **Alfuzosin Hydrochloride** see Alfuzosin on page 68

Alglucerase (al GLOO ser ase)

U.S. Brand Names Ceredase®
Index Terms Glucocerebrosidase
Pharmacologic Category Enzyme
Use Replacement therapy for Gaucher's disease (type 1)
Pregnancy Risk Factor C
Pregnancy Implications Animal studies have not been conducted.
Lactation Excretion in breast milk unknown/use caution
Medication Safety Issues
Sound-alike/look-alike issues:
Alglucerase may be confused with agalsidase beta, alglucosidase alfa
Ceredase® may be confused with Cerezyme®
Contraindications Hypersensitivity to any component of the formulation
Warnings/Precautions Prepared from pooled human placental tissue that may contain the causative agents of some viral diseases. Patients who develop IgG antibodies may be at a higher risk for developing hypersensitivity. Use caution with androgen-sensitive malignancies
(Continued)

Alglucerase *(Continued)*

or prior allergies to hCG. May cause early virilization in males <10 years of age. Safety and efficacy have not been established in children <2 years of age.

Adverse Reactions Frequency not defined.

Cardiovascular: Peripheral edema

Central nervous system: Chills, fatigue, fever, headache, lightheadedness

Endocrine & metabolic: Hot flashes, menstrual abnormalities

Gastrointestinal: Abdominal discomfort, diarrhea, nausea, oral ulcerations, vomiting

Local: Injection site: Abscess, burning, discomfort, pruritus, swelling

Neuromuscular & skeletal: Backache, weakness

Miscellaneous: Dysosmia; hypersensitivity reactions (abdominal cramping, angioedema, chest discomfort, flushing, hypotension, nausea, pruritus, respiratory symptoms, urticaria); IgG antibody formation (~13%)

Overdosage/Toxicology No obvious toxicity was detected after single doses of up to 234 units/kg.

Stability Refrigerate (4°C); do not freeze. Contains no preservatives. Do not store opened vials for future use. Dilute with NS to a final volume ≤200 mL. Do not shake. Once diluted, 100 mL and 200 mL solutions for infusion are stable for 18 hours when stored at 2°C to 8°C.

Mechanism of Action Alglucerase is a modified form of glucocerebrosidase; it is prepared from human placental tissue. Glucocerebrosidase is an enzyme deficient in Gaucher's disease. It is needed to catalyze the hydrolysis of glucocerebroside to glucose and ceramide.

Pharmacodynamics/Kinetics Half-life elimination: ~3-11 minutes

Dosage I.V.: Children and Adults: Initial: 30-60 units/kg every 2 weeks; dosing is individualized based on disease severity; average dose: 60 units/kg every 2 weeks. Range: 2.5 units/kg 3 times/week to 60 units/kg 1-4 times/week. Once patient response is well established, dose may be reduced every 3-6 months to determine maintenance therapy.

Administration I.V.: Infuse I.V. over 1-2 hours. Use of an in-line filter is recommended. Do not shake solution as it denatures the enzyme.

Monitoring Parameters CBC, platelets, liver function tests, IgG antibody formation, acid phosphatase (AP); MRI or CT of liver and spleen, skeletal x-rays, physical exam every 6-12 months

Test Interactions False-positive pregnancy tests

Dosage Forms [DSC] = Discontinued product

Injection, solution [preservative free]: 10 units/mL (5 mL) [DSC]; 80 units/mL (5 mL) [contains human albumin 1%]

♦ **Alglucosidase** *see* Alglucosidase Alfa *on page 70*

Alglucosidase Alfa (al gloo KOSE i dase AL fa)

U.S. Brand Names Myozyme®

Index Terms Alglucosidase; GAA; rhGAA

Pharmacologic Category Enzyme

Use Replacement therapy for Pompe disease (infantile onset)

Pregnancy Risk Factor B

Medication Safety Issues

Sound-alike/look-alike issues:

Alglucosidase alfa may be confused with agalsidase beta, alglucerase

Dosage I.V.: Children 1 month to 3.5 years (at first infusion): 20 mg/kg over ~4 hours every 2 weeks

Additional Information Complete prescribing information for this medication should be consulted for additional detail.

Dosage Forms

Injection, powder for reconstitution [preservative free]:

Myozyme®: 50 mg [contains mannitol 210 mg; polysorbate 80; derived from Chinese hamster ovary cells]

♦ **Alimta®** *see* Pemetrexed *on page 1328*

♦ **Alinia®** *see* Nitazoxanide *on page 1232*

Alitretinoin (a li TRET i noyn)

U.S. Brand Names Panretin®

Canadian Brand Names Panretin®

Pharmacologic Category Antineoplastic Agent, Miscellaneous

Use Orphan drug: Topical treatment of cutaneous lesions in AIDS-related Kaposi's sarcoma

Unlabeled/Investigational Use Cutaneous T-cell lymphomas

Pregnancy Risk Factor D

Pregnancy Implications Potentially teratogenic and/or embryotoxic; limb, craniofacial, or skeletal defects have been observed in animal models. If used during pregnancy or if the patient becomes pregnant while using alitretinoin, the woman should be advised of potential harm to the fetus. Women of childbearing potential should avoid becoming pregnant.

Lactation Excretion in breast milk unknown/not recommended

Medication Safety Issues

Sound-alike/look-alike issues:

Panretin® may be confused with pancreatin

High alert medication: The Institute for Safe Medication Practices (ISMP) includes this medication among its list of drugs which have a heightened risk of causing significant patient harm when used in error.

Contraindications Hypersensitivity to alitretinoin, other retinoids, or any component of the formulation; pregnancy

Warnings/Precautions Hazardous agent - use appropriate precautions for handling and disposal. May cause fetal harm if absorbed by a woman who is pregnant. May be photosensitizing (based on experience with other retinoids); minimize sun or other UV exposure of treated areas. Do not use concurrently with topical products containing DEET. Safety in pediatric patients or geriatric patients has not been established.

Adverse Reactions

>10%.

Central nervous system: Pain (0% to 34%)
Dermatologic: Rash (25% to 77%), pruritus (8% to 11%)
Neuromuscular & skeletal: Paresthesia (3% to 22%)

5% to 10%:

Cardiovascular: Edema (3% to 8%)
Dermatologic: Exfoliative dermatitis (3% to 9%), skin disorder (0% to 8%)

Overdosage/Toxicology There has been no experience with human overdosage of alitretinoin, and overdose is unlikely following topical application. Treatment is symptomatic and supportive.

Drug Interactions

Increased Effect/Toxicity: Increased toxicity of DEET may occur if products containing this compound are used concurrently with alitretinoin. Due to limited absorption after topical application, interaction with systemic medications is unlikely.

Stability Store at room temperature.

Mechanism of Action Binds to retinoid receptors to inhibit growth of Kaposi's sarcoma

Pharmacodynamics/Kinetics Absorption: Not extensive

Dosage Topical: Apply gel twice daily to cutaneous lesions

Administration Do not use occlusive dressings.

Dosage Forms Gel: 0.1% (60 g tube)

- ◆ **Alka-Mints® [OTC]** see Calcium Carbonate on page 269
- ◆ **Alka-Seltzer® Plus Cold Liqui-Gels® [OTC]** see Acetaminophen, Chlorpheniramine, and Pseudoephedrine on page 35
- ◆ **Alkeran®** see Melphalan on page 1074
- ◆ **Allanfil 405** see Chlorophyllin, Papain, and Urea on page 345
- ◆ **Allanfil Spray** see Chlorophyllin, Papain, and Urea on page 345
- ◆ **AllanFol RX** see Folic Acid, Cyanocobalamin, and Pyridoxine on page 750
- ◆ **AllanTan Pediatric** see Chlorpheniramine and Phenylephrine on page 349
- ◆ **Allanzyme** see Papain and Urea on page 1309
- ◆ **Allanzyme 650** see Papain and Urea on page 1309
- ◆ **Allegra®** see Fexofenadine on page 705
- ◆ **Allegra-D® (Can)** see Fexofenadine and Pseudoephedrine on page 706
- ◆ **Allegra-D® 12 Hour** see Fexofenadine and Pseudoephedrine on page 706
- ◆ **Allegra-D® 24 Hour** see Fexofenadine and Pseudoephedrine on page 706
- ◆ **Allerdryl® (Can)** see DiphenhydrAMINE on page 515
- ◆ **Allerest® Allergy and Sinus Relief [OTC]** see Acetaminophen and Pseudoephedrine on page 33
- ◆ **Allerest® Maximum Strength Allergy and Hay Fever [OTC]** see Chlorpheniramine and Pseudoephedrine on page 350
- ◆ **Allerfrim® [OTC]** see Triprolidine and Pseudoephedrine on page 1749
- ◆ **Allergen®** see Antipyrine and Benzocaine on page 137
- ◆ **AllerMax® [OTC]** see DiphenhydrAMINE on page 515
- ◆ **Allernix (Can)** see DiphenhydrAMINE on page 515
- ◆ **Allersol®** see Naphazoline on page 1198
- ◆ **Allerx™-D** see Pseudoephedrine and Methscopolamine on page 1457
- ◆ **AlleRx™ Suspension** see Chlorpheniramine and Phenylephrine on page 349
- ◆ **Allfen-DM** see Guaifenesin and Dextromethorphan on page 816
- ◆ **Allfen Jr** see Guaifenesin on page 814
- ◆ **Alloprin® (Can)** see Allopurinol on page 71

Allopurinol (al oh PURE i nole)

U.S. Brand Names Aloprim™; Zyloprim®
Canadian Brand Names Alloprin®; Apo-Allopurinol®; Novo-Purol; Zyloprim®
Index Terms Allopurinol Sodium
Pharmacologic Category Xanthine Oxidase Inhibitor
Additional Appendix Information
Desensitization Protocols on page 1913
Use
Oral: Prevention of attack of gouty arthritis and nephropathy; treatment of secondary hyperuricemia which may occur during treatment of tumors or leukemia; prevention of recurrent calcium oxalate calculi
I.V.: Treatment of elevated serum and urinary uric acid levels when oral therapy is not tolerated in patients with leukemia, lymphoma, and solid tumor malignancies who are receiving cancer chemotherapy
Pregnancy Risk Factor C
Pregnancy Implications There are few reports describing the use of allopurinol during pregnancy; no adverse fetal outcomes attributable to allopurinol have been reported in humans; use only if potential benefit outweighs the potential risk to the fetus.
Lactation Enters breast milk/use caution (AAP rates "compatible")
Medication Safety Issues
Sound-alike/look-alike issues:
Allopurinol may be confused with Apresoline
(Continued)

71

Allopurinol *(Continued)*

Zyloprim® may be confused with Xylo-Pfan®, ZORprin®

Contraindications Hypersensitivity to allopurinol or any component of the formulation

Warnings/Precautions Do not use to treat asymptomatic hyperuricemia. Discontinue at first signs of rash. Caution in renal impairment, dosage adjustments needed. Use with caution in patients taking diuretics concurrently. Risk of skin rash may be increased in patients receiving amoxicillin or ampicillin. The risk of hypersensitivity may be increased in patients receiving thiazides, and possibly ACE inhibitors. Use caution with mercaptopurine or azathioprine.

Adverse Reactions

>1%:

Dermatologic: Rash (increased with ampicillin or amoxicillin use, 1.5% per manufacturer, >10% in some reports)

Gastrointestinal: Nausea (1.3%), vomiting (1.2%)

Renal: Renal failure/impairment (1.2%)

<1% (Limited to important or life-threatening): Acute tubular necrosis, agranulocytosis, angioedema, aplastic anemia, bronchospasm, cataracts, exfoliative dermatitis, granuloma annulare, granulomatous hepatitis, hypersensitivity syndrome, interstitial nephritis, macular retinitis, nephrolithiasis, neuritis, pancreatitis, paresthesia, peripheral neuropathy, Stevens-Johnson syndrome, toxic epidermal necrolysis, toxic pustuloderma, vasculitis

Overdosage/Toxicology At high dosages, it is a theoretical possibility that oxypurinol stones could be formed but no record of such occurrence in overdose exists. Alkalinization of the urine and forced diuresis can help prevent potential xanthine stone formation.

Drug Interactions

Increased Effect/Toxicity: Allopurinol may increase the effects of azathioprine, chlorpropamide, mercaptopurine, theophylline, and oral anticoagulants. An increased risk of bone marrow suppression may occur when given with myelosuppressive agents (cyclophosphamide, possibly other alkylating agents). Amoxicillin/ampicillin, ACE inhibitors, and thiazide diuretics have been associated with hypersensitivity reactions when combined with allopurinol (rare), and the incidence of rash may be increased with penicillins (ampicillin, amoxicillin). Urinary acidification with large amounts of vitamin C may increase kidney stone formation.

Decreased Effect: Ethanol decreases effectiveness.

Ethanol/Nutrition/Herb Interactions

Ethanol: May decrease effectiveness.

Iron supplements: Hepatic iron uptake may be increased.

Vitamin C: Large amounts of vitamin C may acidify urine and increase kidney stone formation.

Stability

Powder for injection: Store at controlled room temperature of 15°C to 30°C (59°F to 86°F). Further dilution with NS or D_5W (50-100 mL) to ≤6 mg/mL is recommended. Following reconstitution, intravenous solutions should be stored at 20°C to 25°C (68°F to 77°F). Do not refrigerate reconstituted and/or diluted product. Must be administered within 10 hours of solution preparation.

Tablet: Store at controlled room temperature of 15°C to 25°C (59°F to 77°F).

Mechanism of Action Allopurinol inhibits xanthine oxidase, the enzyme responsible for the conversion of hypoxanthine to xanthine to uric acid. Allopurinol is metabolized to oxypurinol which is also an inhibitor of xanthine oxidase; allopurinol acts on purine catabolism, reducing the production of uric acid without disrupting the biosynthesis of vital purines.

Pharmacodynamics/Kinetics

Onset of action: Peak effect: 1-2 weeks

Absorption: Oral: ~80%; Rectal: Poor and erratic

Distribution: V_d: ~1.6 L/kg; V_{ss}: 0.84-0.87 L/kg; enters breast milk

Protein binding: <1%

Metabolism: ~75% to active metabolites, chiefly oxypurinol

Bioavailability: 49% to 53%

Half-life elimination:

Normal renal function: Parent drug: 1-3 hours; Oxypurinol: 18-30 hours

End-stage renal disease: Prolonged

Time to peak, plasma: Oral: 30-120 minutes

Excretion: Urine (76% as oxypurinol, 12% as unchanged drug)

Allopurinol and oxypurinol are dialyzable

Dosage

Oral: Doses >300 mg should be given in divided doses.

Children ≤10 years: Secondary hyperuricemia associated with chemotherapy: 10 mg/kg/day in 2-3 divided doses **or** 200-300 mg/m²/day in 2-4 divided doses, maximum: 800 mg/24 hours

Alternative (manufacturer labeling): <6 years: 150 mg/day in 3 divided doses; 6-10 years: 300 mg/day in 2-3 divided doses

Children >10 years and Adults:

Secondary hyperuricemia associated with chemotherapy: 600-800 mg/day in 2-3 divided doses for prevention of acute uric acid nephropathy for 2-3 days starting 1-2 days before chemotherapy

Gout: Mild: 200-300 mg/day; Severe: 400-600 mg/day; to reduce the possibility of acute gouty attacks, initiate dose at 100 mg/day and increase weekly to recommended dosage.

Recurrent calcium oxalate stones: 200-300 mg/day in single or divided doses

Elderly: Initial: 100 mg/day, increase until desired uric acid level is obtained

I.V.: Hyperuricemia secondary to chemotherapy: Intravenous daily dose can be given as a single infusion or in equally divided doses at 6-, 8-, or 12-hour intervals. A fluid intake sufficient to yield a daily urinary output of at least 2 L in adults and the maintenance of a neutral or, preferably, slightly alkaline urine are desirable.

Children ≤10 years: Starting dose: 200 mg/m²/day

Children >10 years and Adults: 200-400 mg/m²/day (maximum: 600 mg/day)

Dosing adjustment in renal impairment: Must be adjusted due to accumulation of allopurinol and metabolites:

Oral: Removed by hemodialysis; adult maintenance doses of allopurinol (mg) based on creatinine clearance (mL/minute): See table.

Adult Maintenance Doses of Allopurinol[1]

Creatinine Clearance (mL/min)	Maintenance Dose of Allopurinol (mg)
140	400 daily
120	350 daily
100	300 daily
80	250 daily
60	200 daily
40	150 daily
20	100 daily
10	100 every 2 days
0	100 every 3 days

[1]This table is based on a standard maintenance dose of 300 mg of allopurinol per day for a patient with a creatinine clearance of 100 mL/min.

Hemodialysis: Administer dose posthemodialysis or administer 50% supplemental dose

I.V.:
Cl_{cr} 10-20 mL/minute: 200 mg/day
Cl_{cr} 3-10 mL/minute: 100 mg/day
Cl_{cr} <3 mL/minute: 100 mg/day at extended intervals

Dietary Considerations Should administer oral forms after meals with plenty of fluid. Fluid intake should be administered to yield neutral or slightly alkaline urine and an output of ~2 L (in adults).

Administration

Oral: Should administer oral forms after meals with plenty of fluid.

I.V.: Infuse over 15-60 minutes. The rate of infusion depends on the volume of the infusion. Whenever possible, therapy should be initiated at 24-48 hours before the start of chemotherapy known to cause tumor lysis (including adrenocorticosteroids). I.V. daily dose can be administered as a single infusion or in equally divided doses at 6-, 8-, or 12-hour interval.

Monitoring Parameters CBC, serum uric acid levels, I & O, hepatic and renal function, especially at start of therapy

Reference Range Uric acid, serum: An increase occurs during childhood

Adults:

Male: 3.4-7 mg/dL or slightly more

Female: 2.4-6 mg/dL or slightly more

Values >7 mg/dL are sometimes arbitrarily regarded as hyperuricemia, but there is no sharp line between normals on the one hand, and the serum uric acid of those with clinical gout. Normal ranges cannot be adjusted for purine ingestion, but high purine diet increases uric acid. Uric acid may be increased with body size, exercise, and stress.

Dosage Forms

Injection, powder for reconstitution, as sodium (Aloprim™): 500 mg

Tablet (Zyloprim®): 100 mg, 300 mg

Extemporaneous Preparations Crush tablets to make a 5 mg/mL suspension in simple syrup; stable 14 days under refrigeration

Nahata MC and Hipple TF, *Pediatric Drug Formulations*, 1st ed, Harvey Whitney Books Co, 1990.

♦ **Allopurinol Sodium** *see* Allopurinol *on page 71*

♦ **All-*trans*-Retinoic Acid** *see* Tretinoin (Oral) *on page 1730*

♦ **Almacone® [OTC]** *see* Aluminum Hydroxide, Magnesium Hydroxide, and Simethicone *on page 85*

♦ **Almacone Double Strength® [OTC]** *see* Aluminum Hydroxide, Magnesium Hydroxide, and Simethicone *on page 85*

♦ **Almora® [OTC]** *see* Magnesium Gluconate *on page 1047*

Almotriptan (al moh TRIP tan)

U.S. Brand Names Axert™

Canadian Brand Names Axert™

Index Terms Almotriptan Malate

Pharmacologic Category Antimigraine Agent; Serotonin 5-HT$_{1B, 1D}$ Receptor Agonist

Additional Appendix Information

Antimigraine Drugs: 5-HT$_1$ Receptor Agonists *on page 1871*

Use Acute treatment of migraine with or without aura

Pregnancy Risk Factor C

Pregnancy Implications There are no adequate and well-controlled studies in pregnant women. Use in pregnancy should be limited to situations where benefit outweighs risk to fetus. In some (but not all) animal studies, administration was associated with embryolethality, fetal malformations, and decreased pup weight.

Lactation Excretion in breast milk unknown/use caution

Medication Safety Issues

Sound-alike/look-alike issues:

Axert™ may be confused with Antivert®

(Continued)

Almotriptan *(Continued)*

Contraindications Hypersensitivity to almotriptan or any component of the formulation; use as prophylactic therapy for migraine; hemiplegic or basilar migraine; cluster headache; known or suspected ischemic heart disease (angina pectoris, MI, documented silent ischemia, coronary artery vasospasm, Prinzmetal's variant angina); peripheral vascular syndromes (including ischemic bowel disease); uncontrolled hypertension; use within 24 hours of another 5-HT$_1$ agonist; use within 24 hours of ergotamine derivative; concurrent administration or within 2 weeks of discontinuing an MAO inhibitor (specifically MAO type A inhibitors)

Warnings/Precautions Almotriptan is indicated only in patients ≥18 years of age with a clear diagnosis of migraine headache. If a patient does not respond to the first dose, the diagnosis of migraine should be reconsidered. Do not give to patients with risk factors for CAD until a cardiovascular evaluation has been performed; if evaluation is satisfactory, the healthcare provider should administer the first dose and cardiovascular status should be periodically re-evaluated. Cardiac events (coronary artery vasospasm, transient ischemia, myocardial infarction, ventricular tachycardia/fibrillation, cardiac arrest, and death), cerebral/subarachnoid hemorrhage, stroke, peripheral vascular ischemia, and colonic ischemia have been reported with 5-HT$_1$ agonist administration. Significant elevation in blood pressure, including hypertensive crisis, has also been reported on rare occasions in patients with and without a history of hypertension. Use with caution in liver or renal dysfunction. Symptoms of agitation, confusion, hallucinations, hyperreflexia, myoclonus, shivering, and tachycardia (serotonin syndrome) may occur with concomitant proserotonergic drugs (ie, SSRIs/SNRIs or triptans) or agents which reduce almotriptan's metabolism. Safety and efficacy in pediatric patients have not been established.

Adverse Reactions
1% to 10%:
  Central nervous system: Headache (>1%), dizziness (>1%), somnolence (>1%)
  Gastrointestinal: Nausea (1% to 2%), xerostomia (1%)
  Neuromuscular & skeletal: Paresthesia (1%)
<1% (Limited to important or life-threatening): Colitis, coronary artery vasospasm, hypertension, myocardial ischemia, MI, neuropathy, rash, syncope, tachycardia, ventricular fibrillation, ventricular tachycardia, vertigo

Overdosage/Toxicology Hypertension or more serious cardiovascular symptoms may occur. Clinical and electrocardiographic monitoring is needed for at least 20 hours even if patient is asymptomatic. Treatment is symptom-directed and supportive.

Drug Interactions
  Cytochrome P450 Effect: Substrate (minor) of CYP2D6, 3A4
  Increased Effect/Toxicity: Ergot-containing drugs prolong vasospastic reactions; ketoconazole increases almotriptan serum concentration; SSRIs/SNRIs or other serotonin agonists may increase symptoms of hyper-reflexia, weakness, and incoordination; MAO inhibitors may increase toxicity

Stability Store at 15°C to 30°C (59°F to 86°F).

Mechanism of Action Selective agonist for serotonin (5-HT$_{1B}$, 5-HT$_{1D}$, 5-HT$_{1F}$ receptors) in cranial arteries; causes vasoconstriction and reduce sterile inflammation associated with antidromic neuronal transmission correlating with relief of migraine

Pharmacodynamics/Kinetics
  Absorption: Well absorbed
  Distribution: V$_d$: 180-200 L
  Protein binding: ~35%
  Metabolism: MAO type A oxidative deamination (~27% of dose); via CYP3A4 and 2D6 (~12% of dose) to inactive metabolites
  Bioavailability: 70%
  Half-life elimination: 3-4 hours
  Time to peak: 1-3 hours
  Excretion: Urine (40% as unchanged drug); feces (13% unchanged and metabolized)

Dosage Oral: Adults: Migraine: Initial: 6.25-12.5 mg in a single dose; if the headache returns, repeat the dose after 2 hours; no more than 2 doses in 24-hour period
  Note: If the first dose is ineffective, diagnosis needs to be re-evaluated. Safety of treating more than 4 migraines/month has not been established.
  Dosage adjustment in renal impairment: Initial: 6.25 mg in a single dose; maximum daily dose: ≤12.5 mg
  Dosage adjustment in hepatic impairment: Initial: 6.25 mg in a single dose; maximum daily dose: ≤12.5 mg

Dietary Considerations May be taken without regard to meals

Dosage Forms Tablet, as malate: 6.25 mg, 12.5 mg

♦ **Almotriptan Malate** *see* Almotriptan *on page 73*
♦ **Alocril®** *see* Nedocromil *on page 1205*
♦ **Aloe Vesta® 2-n-1 Antifungal [OTC]** *see* Miconazole *on page 1137*
♦ **Alomide®** *see* Lodoxamide *on page 1026*
♦ **Alophen® [OTC]** *see* Bisacodyl *on page 223*
♦ **Aloprim™** *see* Allopurinol *on page 71*
♦ **Alora®** *see* Estradiol *on page 620*
♦ **Aloxi®** *see* Palonosetron *on page 1299*

Alpha-Galactosidase (AL fa ga lak TOE si days)

U.S. Brand Names beano® [OTC]
Index Terms Aspergillus niger
Pharmacologic Category Enzyme
Use Prevention of flatulence and bloating attributed to a variety of grains, cereals, nuts, and vegetables containing the sugars raffinose, stachyose, and/or verbascose

Dosage Oral: Children ≥12 years and Adults:

Drops: Take 5 drops per serving of problem food; adjust according to number of problem foods per meal; usual dose/meal: 10-15 drops

Tablet: One tablet per serving of problem food; adjust according to number of problem foods per meal; usual dose/meal: 2-3 tablets

Additional Information Complete prescribing information for this medication should be consulted for additional detail.

Dosage Forms

Drops: 150 GalU/5 drops

beano® Drops: 150 GalU/5 drops [contains sodium 5 mg/5 drops]

Tablet: 150 GalU

beano®: 150 GalU/5 tablets

- ◆ **Alpha-Galactosidase-A (Human, Recombinant)** see Agalsidase Beta on page 53
- ◆ **Alphagan® (Can)** see Brimonidine on page 239
- ◆ **Alphagan® P** see Brimonidine on page 239
- ◆ **Alphanate®** see Antihemophilic Factor (Human) on page 133
- ◆ **AlphaNine® SD** see Factor IX on page 679
- ◆ **Alphaquin HP®** see Hydroquinone on page 859
- ◆ **Alph-E [OTC]** see Vitamin E on page 1794
- ◆ **Alph-E-Mixed [OTC]** see Vitamin E on page 1794

Alprazolam (al PRAY zoe lam)

U.S. Brand Names Alprazolam Intensol®; Niravam™; Xanax®; Xanax XR®

Canadian Brand Names Alti-Alprazolam; Apo-Alpraz®; Apo-Alpraz® TS; Gen-Alprazolam; Novo-Alprazol; Nu-Alprax; Xanax®; Xanax TS™

Pharmacologic Category Benzodiazepine

Additional Appendix Information

Benzodiazepines on page 1874

Use Treatment of anxiety disorder (GAD); panic disorder, with or without agoraphobia; anxiety associated with depression

Unlabeled/Investigational Use Anxiety in children

Restrictions C-IV

Pregnancy Risk Factor D

Pregnancy Implications Benzodiazepines have the potential to cause harm to the fetus, particularly when administered during the first trimester. In addition, withdrawal symptoms may occur in the neonate following *in utero* exposure. Use during pregnancy should be avoided.

Lactation Enters breast milk/not recommended (AAP rates "of concern")

Medication Safety Issues

Sound-alike/look-alike issues:

Alprazolam may be confused with alprostadil, lorazepam, triazolam

Xanax® may be confused with Lanoxin®, Tenex®, Tylox®, Xopenex®, Zantac®, Zyrtec®

Contraindications Hypersensitivity to alprazolam or any component of the formulation (cross-sensitivity with other benzodiazepines may exist); narrow-angle glaucoma; concurrent use with ketoconazole or itraconazole; pregnancy

Warnings/Precautions Rebound or withdrawal symptoms, including seizures, may occur 18 hours to 3 days following abrupt discontinuation or large decreases in dose (more common in patients receiving >4 mg/day or prolonged treatment). Breakthrough anxiety may occur at the end of dosing interval. Use with caution in patients receiving concurrent CYP3A4 inhibitors. Use with caution in renal impairment or predisposition to urate nephropathy. Use with caution in elderly or debilitated patients, patients with hepatic disease (including alcoholics), renal impairment, or obese patients.

Causes CNS depression (dose related) which may impair physical and mental capabilities. Patients must be cautioned about performing tasks that require mental alertness (eg, operating machinery or driving). Effects with other sedative drugs or ethanol may be potentiated. Benzodiazepines have been associated with falls and traumatic injury and should be used with extreme caution in patients who are at risk of these events (especially the elderly). Use with caution in patients with respiratory disease or impaired gag reflex.

Use caution in patients with depression, particularly if suicidal risk may be present. Episodes of mania or hypomania have occurred in depressed patients treated with alprazolam. May cause physical or psychological dependence. Acute withdrawal may be precipitated in patients after administration of flumazenil.

Benzodiazepines have been associated with anterograde amnesia. Paradoxical reactions have been reported with benzodiazepines, particularly in adolescent/pediatric or psychiatric patients. Does not have analgesic, antidepressant, or antipsychotic properties.

Adverse Reactions

>10%:

Central nervous system: Abnormal coordination, cognitive disorder, depression, drowsiness, fatigue, irritability, lightheadedness, memory impairment, sedation, somnolence

Gastrointestinal: Appetite increased/decreased, constipation, salivation decreased, weight gain/loss, xerostomia

Genitourinary: Micturition difficulty

Neuromuscular & skeletal: Dysarthria

1% to 10%:

Cardiovascular: Hypotension

Central nervous system: Agitation, attention disturbance, confusion, depersonalization, derealization, disorientation, disinhibition, dizziness, dream abnormalities, fear, hallucinations, hypersomnia, nightmares, seizure, talkativeness

Dermatologic: Dermatitis, pruritus, rash

Endocrine & metabolic: Libido decreased/increased, menstrual disorders

Gastrointestinal: Salivation increased

(Continued)

Alprazolam *(Continued)*

Genitourinary: Incontinence
Hepatic: Bilirubin increased, jaundice, liver enzymes increased
Neuromuscular & skeletal: Arthralgia, ataxia, myalgia, paresthesia
Ocular: Diplopia
Respiratory: Allergic rhinitis, dyspnea
<1% (Limited to important or life-threatening): Amnesia, falls, galactorrhea, gynecomastia, hepatic failure, hepatitis, hyperprolactinemia, Stevens-Johnson syndrome

Overdosage/Toxicology Symptoms include somnolence, confusion, coma, and diminished reflexes. Treatment for benzodiazepine overdose is supportive. Mechanical ventilation is rarely required. Flumazenil has been shown to selectively block the binding of benzodiazepines to CNS receptors, resulting in a reversal of benzodiazepine-induced sedation; however, its use may not alter the course of overdose.

Drug Interactions

Cytochrome P450 Effect: Substrate of CYP3A4 (major)

Increased Effect/Toxicity: Alprazolam serum levels/effects may be increased by azole antifungals, clarithromycin, diclofenac, doxycycline, erythromycin, fluoxetine, imatinib, isoniazid, nefazodone, nicardipine, oral contraceptives, propofol, protease inhibitors, quinidine, telithromycin, verapamil, and other inhibitors of CYP3A4. Contraindicated with itraconazole or ketoconazole. Alprazolam potentiates the CNS depressant effects of opioid analgesics, barbiturates, phenothiazines, ethanol, antihistamines, MAO inhibitors, sedative-hypnotics, and cyclic antidepressants. Alprazolam increases plasma concentrations of imipramine and desipramine.

Decreased Effect: Aminoglutethimide, carbamazepine, nafcillin, nevirapine, phenobarbital, phenytoin, rifamycins, and other CYP3A4 inducers may decrease the levels/effects of alprazolam.

Ethanol/Nutrition/Herb Interactions

Cigarette smoking: May decrease alprazolam concentrations up to 50%.
Ethanol: Avoid ethanol (may increase CNS depression).
Food: Alprazolam serum concentration is unlikely to be increased by grapefruit juice because of alprazolam's high oral bioavailability. The C_{max} of the extended release formulation is increased by 25% when a high-fat meal is given 2 hours before dosing. T_{max} is decreased 30% when food is given immediately prior to dose. T_{max} is increased by 30% when food is given ≥1 hour after dose.
Herb/Nutraceutical: St John's wort may decrease alprazolam levels. Avoid valerian, St John's wort, kava kava, gotu kola (may increase CNS depression).

Stability Orally-disintegrating tablet: Store at room temperature of 20°C to 25°C (68°F to 77°F). Protect from moisture. Seal bottle tightly and discard any cotton packaged inside bottle.

Mechanism of Action Binds to stereospecific benzodiazepine receptors on the postsynaptic GABA neuron at several sites within the central nervous system, including the limbic system, reticular formation. Enhancement of the inhibitory effect of GABA on neuronal excitability results by increased neuronal membrane permeability to chloride ions. This shift in chloride ions results in hyperpolarization (a less excitable state) and stabilization.

Pharmacodynamics/Kinetics

Distribution: V_d: 0.9-1.2 L/kg; enters breast milk
Protein binding: 80%
Metabolism: Hepatic via CYP3A4; forms two active metabolites (4-hydroxyalprazolam and α-hydroxyalprazolam)
Bioavailability: 90%
Half-life elimination:
Adults: 11.2 hours (range: 6.3-26.9)
Elderly: 16.3 hours (range: 9-26.9 hours)
Alcoholic liver disease: 19.7 hours (range: 5.8-65.3 hours)
Obesity: 21.8 hours (range: 9.9-40.4 hours)
Time to peak, serum: 1-2 hours
Excretion: Urine (as unchanged drug and metabolites)

Dosage Oral: **Note:** Treatment >4 months should be re-evaluated to determine the patient's continued need for the drug

Children: Anxiety (unlabeled use): Immediate release: Initial: 0.005 mg/kg/dose or 0.125 mg/dose 3 times/day; increase in increments of 0.125-0.25 mg, up to a maximum of 0.02 mg/kg/dose or 0.06 mg/kg/day (0.375-3 mg/day)

Adults:
Anxiety: Immediate release: Effective doses are 0.5-4 mg/day in divided doses; the manufacturer recommends starting at 0.25-0.5 mg 3 times/day; titrate dose upward; usual maximum: 4 mg/day. Patients requiring doses >4 mg/day should be increased cautiously. Periodic reassessment and consideration of dosage reduction is recommended.

Anxiety associated with depression: Immediate release: Average dose required: 2.5-3 mg/day in divided doses

Ethanol withdrawal (unlabeled use): Immediate release: Usual dose: 2-2.5 mg/day in divided doses

Panic disorder:
Immediate release: Initial: 0.5 mg 3 times/day; dose may be increased every 3-4 days in increments ≤1 mg/day. Mean effective dosage: 5-6 mg/day; many patients obtain relief at 2 mg/day, as much as 10 mg/day may be required

Extended release: 0.5-1 mg once daily; may increase dose every 3-4 days in increments ≤1 mg/day (range: 3-6 mg/day)

Switching from immediate release to extended release: Patients may be switched to extended release tablets by taking the total daily dose of the immediate release tablets and giving it once daily using the extended release preparation.

Preoperative sedation: 0.5 mg in evening at bedtime and 0.5 mg 1 hour before procedure

Dose reduction: Abrupt discontinuation should be avoided. Daily dose may be decreased by 0.5 mg every 3 days, however, some patients may require a slower reduction. If withdrawal symptoms occur, resume previous dose and discontinue on a less rapid schedule.

Elderly: Initial: 0.125-0.25 mg twice daily; increase by 0.125 mg/day as needed. The smallest effective dose should be used. **Note:** Elderly patients may be more sensitive to the effects of alprazolam including ataxia and oversedation. The elderly may also have impaired renal function leading to decreased clearance. Titrate gradually, if needed.
Immediate release: Initial: 0.25 mg 2-3 times/day
Extended release: Initial: 0.5 mg once daily

Dosing adjustment in renal impairment: No guidelines for adjustment; use caution

Dosing adjustment in hepatic impairment: Reduce dose by 50% to 60% or avoid in cirrhosis

Administration

Immediate release preparations: Can be administered sublingually with comparable onset and completeness of absorption.

Extended release tablet: Should be taken once daily in the morning; do not crush, break, or chew.

Orally-disintegrating tablets: Using dry hands, place tablet on top of tongue. If using one-half of tablet, immediately discard remaining half (may not remain stable). Administration with water is not necessary.

Monitoring Parameters Respiratory and cardiovascular status

Additional Information Not intended for management of anxieties and minor distresses associated with everyday life. Treatment longer than 4 months should be re-evaluated to determine the patient's need for the drug. Patients who become physically dependent on alprazolam tend to have a difficult time discontinuing it; withdrawal symptoms may be severe. To minimize withdrawal symptoms, taper dosage slowly; do not discontinue abruptly. Abrupt discontinuation after sustained use (generally >10 days) may cause withdrawal symptoms.

Dosage Forms

Solution, oral [concentrate]:
Alprazolam Intensol®: 1 mg/mL (30 mL)
Tablet: 0.25 mg, 0.5 mg, 1 mg, 2 mg
Xanax®: 0.25 mg, 0.5 mg, 1 mg, 2 mg
Tablet, extended release: 0.5 mg, 1 mg, 2 mg, 3 mg
Xanax® XR: 0.5 mg, 1 mg, 2 mg, 3 mg
Tablet, orally disintegrating [scored]:
Niravam™: 0.25 mg, 0.5 mg, 1 mg, 2 mg [orange flavor]

♦ **Alprazolam Intensol®** see Alprazolam on page 75

Alprostadil (al PROS ta dill)

U.S. Brand Names Caverject®; Caverject Impulse®; Edex®; Muse®; Prostin VR Pediatric®
Canadian Brand Names Caverject®; Muse® Pellet; Prostin® VR
Index Terms PGE₁; Prostaglandin E₁
Pharmacologic Category Prostaglandin

Use

Prostin VR Pediatric®: Temporary maintenance of patency of ductus arteriosus in neonates with ductal-dependent congenital heart disease until surgery can be performed. These defects include cyanotic (eg, pulmonary atresia, pulmonary stenosis, tricuspid atresia, Fallot's tetralogy, transposition of the great vessels) and acyanotic (eg, interruption of aortic arch, coarctation of aorta, hypoplastic left ventricle) heart disease.

Caverject®: Treatment of erectile dysfunction of vasculogenic, psychogenic, or neurogenic etiology; adjunct in the diagnosis of erectile dysfunction

Edex®, Muse®: Treatment of erectile dysfunction of vasculogenic, psychogenic, or neurogenic etiology

Unlabeled/Investigational Use Investigational: Treatment of pulmonary hypertension in infants and children with congenital heart defects with left-to-right shunts

Pregnancy Risk Factor X/C (Muse®)

Pregnancy Implications Alprostadil is embryotoxic in animal studies. It is not indicated for use in women. The manufacturer of Muse® recommends a condom barrier when being used during sexual intercourse with a pregnant women.

Lactation Not indicated for use in women

Medication Safety Issues

Sound-alike/look-alike issues:
Alprostadil may be confused with alprazolam

Contraindications Hypersensitivity to alprostadil or any component of the formulation; hyaline membrane disease or persistent fetal circulation and when a dominant left-to-right shunt is present; respiratory distress syndrome; conditions predisposing patients to priapism (sickle cell anemia, multiple myeloma, leukemia); patients with anatomical deformation of the penis, penile implants; use in men for whom sexual activity is inadvisable or contraindicated; pregnancy

Warnings/Precautions Use cautiously in neonates with bleeding tendencies. **[U.S. Boxed Warning]: Apnea may occur in 10% to 12% of neonates with congenital heart defects, especially in those weighing <2 kg at birth.** Apnea usually appears during the first hour of drug infusion.

When used in erectile dysfunction, priapism may occur; treat immediately to avoid penile tissue damage and permanent loss of potency; discontinue therapy if signs of penile fibrosis develop (penile angulation, cavernosal fibrosis, or Peyronie's disease). When used in erectile dysfunction (Muse®), syncope occurring within 1 hour of administration has been reported. The potential for drug-drug interactions may occur when Muse® is prescribed concomitantly with antihypertensives.

Adverse Reactions

Intraurethral:
>10%: Genitourinary: Penile pain, urethral burning
(Continued)

Alprostadil *(Continued)*

2% to 10%:
Central nervous system: Headache, dizziness, pain
Genitourinary: Vaginal itching (female partner), testicular pain, urethral bleeding (minor)
<2% (Limited to important or life-threatening): Tachycardia, perineal pain, leg pain

Intracavernosal injection:
>10%: Genitourinary: Penile pain
1% to 10%:
Cardiovascular: Hypertension
Central nervous system: Headache, dizziness
Genitourinary: Prolonged erection (>4 hours, 4%), penile fibrosis, penis disorder, penile rash, penile edema
Local: Injection site hematoma and/or bruising
<1% (Limited to important or life-threatening): Balanitis, injection site hemorrhage, priapism (0.4%)

Intravenous:
>10%:
Cardiovascular: Flushing
Central nervous system: Fever
Respiratory: Apnea
1% to 10%:
Cardiovascular: Bradycardia, hyper-/hypotension, tachycardia, cardiac arrest, edema
Central nervous system: Seizures, headache, dizziness
Endocrine & metabolic: Hypokalemia
Gastrointestinal: Diarrhea
Hematologic: Disseminated intravascular coagulation
Neuromuscular & skeletal: Back pain
Respiratory: Upper respiratory infection, flu syndrome, sinusitis, nasal congestion, cough
Miscellaneous: Sepsis, localized pain in structures other than the injection site
<1% (Limited to important or life-threatening): Anemia, anuria, bleeding, bradypnea, bronchial wheezing, cerebral bleeding, CHF, gastric regurgitation, hematuria, hyperbilirubinemia, hyperemia, hyperextension of neck, hyperirritability, hyperkalemia, hypoglycemia, hypothermia, jitteriness, lethargy, peritonitis, second degree heart block, shock, stiffness, supraventricular tachycardia, thrombocytopenia, ventricular fibrillation

Overdosage/Toxicology Symptoms when treating patent ductus arteriosus include apnea, bradycardia, hypotension, and flushing. If hypotension or pyrexia occurs, the infusion rate should be reduced until the symptoms subside, while apnea or bradycardia requires drug discontinuation. If intracavernous overdose occurs, supervise until any systemic effects have resolved or until penile detumescence has occurred.

Drug Interactions
Increased Effect/Toxicity: Risk of hypotension and syncope may be increased with antihypertensives.

Ethanol/Nutrition/Herb Interactions Ethanol: Avoid concurrent use (vasodilating effect).

Stability
Caverject® Impulse™: Store at controlled room temperature of 15°C to 30°C (59°F to 86°F). Provided as a dual-chamber syringe with diluent in one chamber. To mix, hold syringe with needle pointing upward and turn plunger clockwise; turn upside down several times to mix. Device can be set to deliver specified dose, each device can be set at various increments. Following reconstitution, use within 24 hours and discard any unused solution.
Caverject® powder: The 5 mcg, 10 mcg, and 20 mcg vials should be stored at or below 25°C (77°F). The 40 mcg vial should be stored at 2°C to 8°C until dispensed. After dispensing, stable for up to 3 months at or below 25°C. Use only the supplied diluent for reconstitution (ie, bacteriostatic/sterile water with benzyl alcohol 0.945%). Following reconstitution, all strengths should be stored at or below 25°C (77°F); do not refrigerate or freeze; use within 24 hours.
Caverject® solution: Prior to dispensing, store frozen at -20°C to -10°C (-4°F to -14°F); once dispensed, may be stored frozen for up to 3 months, or under refrigeration at 2°C to 8°C (36°F to 46°F) for up to 7 days. Do not refreeze. Once removed from foil wrap, solution may be allowed to warm to room temperature prior to use. If not used immediately, solution should be discarded. Shake well prior to use.
Edex®: Store at controlled room temperature of 15°C to 30°C (59°F to 86°F); following reconstitution with NS, use immediately and discard any unused solution.
Muse®: Refrigerate at 2°C to 8°C (36°F to 46°F); may be stored at room temperature for up to 14 days.
Prostin VR Pediatric®: Refrigerate at 2°C to 8°C (36°F to 46°F); prior to infusion, dilute with D5W or NS; use within 24 hours.

Mechanism of Action Causes vasodilation by means of direct effect on vascular and ductus arteriosus smooth muscle; relaxes trabecular smooth muscle by dilation of cavernosal arteries when injected along the penile shaft, allowing blood flow to and entrapment in the lacunar spaces of the penis (ie, corporeal veno-occlusive mechanism)

Pharmacodynamics/Kinetics
Onset of action: Rapid
Duration: <1 hour
Distribution: Insignificant following penile injection
Protein binding, plasma: 81% to albumin
Metabolism: ~75% by oxidation in one pass via lungs
Half-life elimination: 5-10 minutes
Excretion: Urine (90% as metabolites) within 24 hours

Dosage
Patent ductus arteriosus (Prostin VR Pediatric®):
I.V. continuous infusion into a large vein, or alternatively through an umbilical artery catheter placed at the ductal opening: 0.05-0.1 mcg/kg/minute with therapeutic response, rate is reduced to lowest effective dosage; with unsatisfactory response, rate is increased gradually; maintenance: 0.01-0.4 mcg/kg/minute

PGE₁ is usually given at an infusion rate of 0.1 mcg/kg/minute, but it is often possible to reduce the dosage to ½ or even ¹/₁₀ without losing the therapeutic effect. The mixing schedule is as follows. Infusion rates deliver 0.1 mcg/kg/minute: See table.

Alprostadil

Add 1 Ampul (500 mcg) to:	Concentration (mcg/mL)	Infusion Rate	
		mL/min/kg Needed to Infuse 0.1 mcg/kg/min	mL/kg/24 h
250 mL	2	0.05	72
100 mL	5	0.02	28.8
50 mL	10	0.01	14.4
25 mL	20	0.005	7.2

Therapeutic response is indicated by increased pH in those with acidosis or by an increase in oxygenation (PO₂) usually evident within 30 minutes

Erectile dysfunction:

Caverject®, Edex®: Intracavernous: Individualize dose by careful titration; doses >40 mcg (Edex®) or >60 mcg (Caverject®) are not recommended: Initial dose must be titrated in physician's office. Patient must stay in the physician's office until complete detumescence occurs; if there is no response, then the next higher dose may be given within 1 hour; if there is still no response, a 1-day interval before giving the next dose is recommended; increasing the dose or concentration in the treatment of impotence results in increasing pain and discomfort

Vasculogenic, psychogenic, or mixed etiology: Initiate dosage titration at 2.5 mcg, increasing by 2.5 mcg to a dose of 5 mcg and then in increments of 5-10 mcg depending on the erectile response until the dose produces an erection suitable for intercourse, not lasting >1 hour; if there is absolutely no response to initial 2.5 mcg dose, the second dose may be increased to 7.5 mcg, followed by increments of 5-10 mcg

Neurogenic etiology (eg, spinal cord injury): Initiate dosage titration at 1.25 mcg, increasing to a dose of 2.5 mcg and then 5 mcg; increase further in increments 5 mcg until the dose is reached that produces an erection suitable for intercourse, not lasting >1 hour

Maintenance: Once appropriate dose has been determined, patient may self-administer injections at a frequency of no more than 3 times/week with at least 24 hours between doses

Muse® Pellet: Intraurethral:

Initial: 125-250 mcg

Maintenance: Administer as needed to achieve an erection; duration of action is about 30-60 minutes; use only two systems per 24-hour period

Elderly: Elderly patients may have a greater frequency of renal dysfunction; lowest effective dose should be used. In clinical studies with Edex®, higher minimally effective doses and a higher rate of lack of effect were noted.

Administration Erectile dysfunction: Use a ½ inch, 27- to 30-gauge needle. Inject into the dorsolateral aspect of the proximal third of the penis, avoiding visible veins; alternate side of the penis for injections.

Monitoring Parameters Arterial pressure, respiratory rate, heart rate, temperature, degree of penile pain, length of erection, signs of infection

Dosage Forms

Injection, powder for reconstitution:

Caverject®: 20 mcg, 40 mcg [contains lactose; diluent contains benzyl alcohol]

Caverject Impulse®: 10 mcg, 20 mcg [prefilled injection system; contains lactose; diluent contains benzyl alcohol]

Edex®: 10 mcg, 20 mcg, 40 mcg [contains lactose; packaged in kits containing diluent, syringe, and alcohol swab]

Injection, solution: 500 mcg/mL (1 mL)

Prostin VR Pediatric®: 500 mcg/mL (1 mL) [contains dehydrated alcohol]

Pellet, urethral (Muse®): 125 mcg (6s), 250 mcg (6s), 500 mcg (6s), 1000 mcg (6s)

♦ **Alrex**® see Loteprednol on page 1039
♦ **Altace**® see Ramipril on page 1482
♦ **Altachlore [OTC]** see Sodium Chloride on page 1576
♦ **Altafrin** see Phenylephrine on page 1358
♦ **Altamist [OTC]** see Sodium Chloride on page 1576
♦ **Altarussin DM [OTC]** see Guaifenesin and Dextromethorphan on page 816
♦ **Altaryl [OTC]** see DiphenhydrAMINE on page 515

Alteplase (AL te plase)

U.S. Brand Names Activase®; Cathflo® Activase®

Canadian Brand Names Activase® rt-PA; Cathflo® Activase®

Index Terms Alteplase, Recombinant; Alteplase, Tissue Plasminogen Activator, Recombinant; tPA

Pharmacologic Category Thrombolytic Agent

Use Management of acute myocardial infarction for the lysis of thrombi in coronary arteries; management of acute ischemic stroke

Acute myocardial infarction (AMI): Chest pain ≥20 minutes, ≤12-24 hours; S-T elevation >0.1 mV in at least two ECG leads

(Continued)

Alteplase *(Continued)*

Acute pulmonary embolism (APE): Age ≤75 years: Documented massive pulmonary embolism by pulmonary angiography or echocardiography or high probability lung scan with clinical shock

Cathflo® Activase®: Restoration of central venous catheter function

Unlabeled/Investigational Use Acute peripheral arterial occlusive disease

Pregnancy Risk Factor C

Lactation Excretion in breast milk unknown/use caution

Medication Safety Issues

Sound-alike/look-alike issues:

Alteplase may be confused with Altace®

"tPA" abbreviation should not be used when writing orders for this medication; has been misread as TNKase (tenecteplase)

High alert medication: The Institute for Safe Medication Practices (ISMP) includes this medication (I.V.) among its list of drugs which have a heightened risk of causing significant patient harm when used in error.

Contraindications Hypersensitivity to alteplase or any component of the formulation

Treatment of acute MI or PE: Active internal bleeding; history of CVA; recent intracranial or intraspinal surgery or trauma; intracranial neoplasm; arteriovenous malformation or aneurysm; known bleeding diathesis; severe uncontrolled hypertension

Treatment of acute ischemic stroke: Evidence of intracranial hemorrhage or suspicion of subarachnoid hemorrhage on pretreatment evaluation; recent (within 3 months) intracranial or intraspinal surgery; prolonged external cardiac massage; suspected aortic dissection; serious head trauma or previous stroke; history of intracranial hemorrhage; uncontrolled hypertension at time of treatment (eg, >185 mm Hg systolic or >110 mm Hg diastolic); seizure at the onset of stroke; active internal bleeding; intracranial neoplasm; arteriovenous malformation or aneurysm; known bleeding diathesis including but not limited to: current use of anticoagulants or an INR >1.7, administration of heparin within 48 hours preceding the onset of stroke and an elevated aPTT at presentation, platelet count <100,000/mm^3.

Other exclusion criteria (NINDS recombinant tPA study): Stroke or serious head injury within 3 months, major surgery or serious trauma within 2 weeks, GI or urinary tract hemorrhage within 3 weeks, aggressive treatment required to lower blood pressure, glucose level <50 mg/dL or >400 mg/dL, arterial puncture at a noncompressible site or lumbar puncture within 1 week, clinical presentation suggesting post-MI pericarditis, pregnancy, breast-feeding.

Warnings/Precautions Concurrent heparin anticoagulation may contribute to bleeding. Monitor all potential bleeding sites. Doses >150 mg are associated with increased risk of intracranial hemorrhage. Intramuscular injections and nonessential handling of the patient should be avoided. Venipunctures should be performed carefully and only when necessary. If arterial puncture is necessary, use an upper extremity vessel that can be manually compressed. If serious bleeding occurs, the infusion of alteplase and heparin should be stopped.

For the following conditions, the risk of bleeding is higher with use of thrombolytics and should be weighed against the benefits of therapy: Recent major surgery (eg, CABG, obstetrical delivery, organ biopsy, previous puncture of noncompressible vessels), cerebrovascular disease, recent gastrointestinal or genitourinary bleeding, recent trauma, hypertension (systolic BP >175 mm Hg and/or diastolic BP >110 mm Hg), high likelihood of left heart thrombus (eg, mitral stenosis with atrial fibrillation), acute pericarditis, subacute bacterial endocarditis, hemostatic defects including ones caused by severe renal or hepatic dysfunction, significant hepatic dysfunction, pregnancy, diabetic hemorrhagic retinopathy or other hemorrhagic ophthalmic conditions, septic thrombophlebitis or occluded AV cannula at seriously infected site, advanced age (eg, >75 years), patients receiving oral anticoagulants, any other condition in which bleeding constitutes a significant hazard or would be particularly difficult to manage because of location.

Coronary thrombolysis may result in reperfusion arrhythmias. Treatment of patients with acute ischemic stroke more than 3 hours after symptom onset is not recommended. Treatment of patients with minor neurological deficit or with rapidly improving symptoms is not recommended.

Cathflo® Activase®: When used to restore catheter function, use Cathflo® cautiously in those patients with known or suspected catheter infections. Evaluate catheter for other causes of dysfunction before use. Avoid excessive pressure when instilling into catheter.

Adverse Reactions As with all drugs which may affect hemostasis, bleeding is the major adverse effect associated with alteplase. Hemorrhage may occur at virtually any site. Risk is dependent on multiple variables, including the dosage administered, concurrent use of multiple agents which alter hemostasis, and patient predisposition. Rapid lysis of coronary artery thrombi by thrombolytic agents may be associated with reperfusion-related atrial and/or ventricular arrhythmia. **Note:** Lowest rate of bleeding complications expected with dose used to restore catheter function.

1% to 10%:

Cardiovascular: Hypotension

Central nervous system: Fever

Dermatologic: Bruising (1%)

Gastrointestinal: GI hemorrhage (5%), nausea, vomiting

Genitourinary: GU hemorrhage (4%)

Hematologic: Bleeding (0.5% major, 7% minor: GUSTO trial)

Local: Bleeding at catheter puncture site (15.3%, accelerated administration)

<1% (Limited to important or life-threatening): Allergic reactions: Anaphylaxis, anaphylactoid reactions, laryngeal edema, rash, and urticaria (<0.02%); epistaxis; gingival hemorrhage; intracranial hemorrhage (0.4% to 0.87% when dose is ≤100 mg); pericardial hemorrhage; retroperitoneal hemorrhage

Additional cardiovascular events associated **with use in MI:** AV block, cardiogenic shock, heart failure, cardiac arrest, recurrent ischemia/infarction, myocardial rupture, electromechanical dissociation, pericardial effusion, pericarditis, mitral regurgitation, cardiac tamponade, thromboembolism, pulmonary edema, asystole, ventricular tachycardia, bradycardia, ruptured intracranial AV malformation, seizure, hemorrhagic bursitis, cholesterol crystal embolization

Additional events associated **with use in pulmonary embolism:** Pulmonary re-embolization, pulmonary edema, pleural effusion, thromboembolism

Additional events associated **with use in stroke:** Cerebral edema, cerebral herniation, seizure, new ischemic stroke

Overdosage/Toxicology Symptoms include increased incidence of intracranial bleeding.

Drug Interactions

Increased Effect/Toxicity: The potential for hemorrhage with alteplase is increased by oral anticoagulants (warfarin), heparin, low molecular weight heparins, and drugs which affect platelet function (eg, NSAIDs, dipyridamole, ticlopidine, clopidogrel, IIb/IIIa antagonists). Concurrent use with aspirin and heparin may increase the risk of bleeding. However, aspirin and heparin were used concomitantly with alteplase in the majority of patients in clinical studies.

Decreased Effect: Aminocaproic acid (an antifibrinolytic agent) may decrease the effectiveness of thrombolytic therapy. Nitroglycerin may increase the hepatic clearance of alteplase, potentially reducing lytic activity (limited clinical information).

Ethanol/Nutrition/Herb Interactions Herb/Nutraceutical: Avoid cat's claw, dong quai, evening primrose, feverfew, red clover, horse chestnut, garlic, green tea, ginseng, ginkgo (all have additional antiplatelet activity).

Stability

Activase®: The lyophilized product may be stored at room temperature (not to exceed 30°C/86°F), or under refrigeration. Once reconstituted it should be used within 8 hours. Reconstitution:

50 mg vial: Use accompanying diluent (50 mL sterile water for injection); do not shake. Final concentration: 1 mg/mL.

100 mg vial: Use transfer set with accompanying diluent (100 mL vial of sterile water for injection); no vacuum is present in 100 mg vial; final concentration: 1 mg/mL.

Cathflo® Activase®: Store lyophilized product under refrigeration. Reconstitution: Add 2.2 mL SWFI to vial; do not shake. Final concentration: 1 mg/mL. Once reconstituted, store at 2°C to 30°C (36°F to 86°F) and use within 8 hours. Do not mix other medications into infusion solution.

Mechanism of Action Initiates local fibrinolysis by binding to fibrin in a thrombus (clot) and converts entrapped plasminogen to plasmin

Pharmacodynamics/Kinetics

Duration: >50% present in plasma cleared ~5 minutes after infusion terminated, ~80% cleared within 10 minutes

Excretion: Clearance: Rapidly from circulating plasma (550-650 mL/minute), primarily hepatic; >50% present in plasma is cleared within 5 minutes after the infusion is terminated, ~80% cleared within 10 minutes

Dosage

I.V.:

Coronary artery thrombi: Front loading dose (weight-based):

Patients >67 kg: Total dose: 100 mg over 1.5 hours; infuse 15 mg over 1-2 minutes. Infuse 50 mg over 30 minutes. Infuse remaining 35 mg of alteplase over the next hour. See "Note."

Patients ≤67 kg: Infuse 15 mg I.V. bolus over 1-2 minutes, then infuse 0.75 mg/kg (not to exceed 50 mg) over next 30 minutes, followed by 0.5 mg/kg over next 60 minutes (not to exceed 35 mg). See "Note."

Note: Concurrently, begin heparin 60 units/kg bolus (maximum: 4000 units) followed by continuous infusion of 12 units/kg/hour (maximum: 1000 units/hour) and adjust to aPTT target of 1.5-2 times the upper limit of control.

Acute pulmonary embolism: 100 mg over 2 hours.

Acute ischemic stroke: Doses should be given within the first 3 hours of the onset of symptoms; recommended total dose: 0.9 mg/kg (maximum dose should not exceed 90 mg) infused over 60 minutes.

Load with 0.09 mg/kg (10% of the 0.9 mg/kg dose) as an I.V. bolus over 1 minute, followed by 0.81 mg/kg (90% of the 0.9 mg/kg dose) as a continuous infusion over 60 minutes. Heparin should not be started for 24 hours or more after starting alteplase for stroke.

Intracatheter: Central venous catheter clearance: Cathflo® Activase® 1 mg/mL:

Patients <30 kg: 110% of the internal lumen volume of the catheter, not to exceed 2 mg/2 mL; retain in catheter for 0.5-2 hours; may instill a second dose if catheter remains occluded

Patients ≥30 kg: 2 mg (2 mL); retain in catheter for 0.5-2 hours; may instill a second dose if catheter remains occluded

Intra-arterial: Acute peripheral arterial occlusive disease (unlabeled use): 0.02-0.1 mg/kg/hour for up to 36 hours

Advisory Panel to the Society for Cardiovascular and Interventional Radiology on Thrombolytic Therapy recommendation: ≤2 mg/hour and subtherapeutic heparin (aPTT <1.5 times baseline)

Administration

Activase®: Acute MI: Accelerated infusion:

Bolus dose may be prepared by one of three methods:

1) removal of 15 mL reconstituted (1 mg/mL) solution from vial

2) removal of 15 mL from a port on the infusion line after priming

3) programming an infusion pump to deliver a 15 mL bolus at the initiation of infusion

Remaining dose may be administered as follows:

50 mg vial: Either PVC bag or glass vial and infusion set

(Continued)

Alteplase *(Continued)*

100 mg vial: Insert spike end of the infusion set through the same puncture site created by transfer device and infuse from vial

If further dilution is desired, may be diluted in equal volume of 0.9% sodium chloride or D₅W to yield a final concentration of 0.5 mg/mL AD

Cathflo® Activase®: Intracatheter: Instill dose into occluded catheter. Do not force solution into catheter. After a 30-minute dwell time, assess catheter function by attempting to aspirate blood. If catheter is functional, aspirate 4-5 mL of blood in patients ≥10 kg or 3 mL in patients <10 kg to remove Cathflo® Activase® and residual clots. Gently irrigate the catheter with NS. If catheter remains nonfunctional, let Cathflo® Activase® dwell for another 90 minutes (total dwell time: 120 minutes) and reassess function. If catheter function is not restored, a second dose may be instilled.

Monitoring Parameters

When using for central venous catheter clearance: Assess catheter function by attempting to aspirate blood.

When using for management of acute myocardial infarction: Assess for evidence of cardiac reperfusion through resolution of chest pain, resolution of baseline ECG changes, preserved left ventricular function, cardiac enzyme washout phenomenon, and/or the appearance of reperfusion arrhythmias; assess for bleeding potential through clinical evidence of GI bleeding, hematuria, gingival bleeding, fibrinogen levels, fibrinogen degradation products, prothrombin times, and partial thromboplastin times.

Reference Range

Not routinely measured; literature supports therapeutic levels of 0.52-1.8 mcg/mL

Fibrinogen: 200-400 mg/dL

Activated partial thromboplastin time (aPTT): 22.5-38.7 seconds

Prothrombin time (PT): 10.9-12.2 seconds

Test Interactions Altered results of coagulation and fibrinolytic agents

Dosage Forms

Injection, powder for reconstitution, recombinant:

Activase®: 50 mg [29 million int. units; contains polysorbate 80; packaged with diluent]; 100 mg [58 million int. units; contains polysorbate 80; packaged with diluent and transfer device]

Cathflo® Activase®: 2 mg [contains polysorbate 80]

♦ **Alteplase, Recombinant** *see Alteplase on page 79*

♦ **Alteplase, Tissue Plasminogen Activator, Recombinant** *see Alteplase on page 79*

♦ **ALternaGel® [OTC]** *see Aluminum Hydroxide on page 83*

♦ **Alti-Alprazolam (Can)** *see Alprazolam on page 75*

♦ **Alti-Amiodarone (Can)** *see Amiodarone on page 97*

♦ **Alti-Amoxi-Clav (Can)** *see Amoxicillin and Clavulanate Potassium on page 112*

♦ **Alti-Azathioprine (Can)** *see Azathioprine on page 183*

♦ **Alti-Captopril (Can)** *see Captopril on page 281*

♦ **Alti-Clindamycin (Can)** *see Clindamycin on page 389*

♦ **Alti-Clonazepam (Can)** *see Clonazepam on page 397*

♦ **Alti-Desipramine (Can)** *see Desipramine on page 473*

♦ **Alti-Diltiazem CD (Can)** *see Diltiazem on page 509*

♦ **Alti-Divalproex (Can)** *see Valproic Acid and Derivatives on page 1767*

♦ **Alti-Doxazosin (Can)** *see Doxazosin on page 544*

♦ **Alti-Flunisolide (Can)** *see Flunisolide on page 720*

♦ **Alti-Fluoxetine (Can)** *see Fluoxetine on page 727*

♦ **Alti-Flurbiprofen (Can)** *see Flurbiprofen on page 735*

♦ **Alti-Fluvoxamine (Can)** *see Fluvoxamine on page 747*

♦ **Alti-Ipratropium (Can)** *see Ipratropium on page 932*

♦ **Alti-Metformin (Can)** *see Metformin on page 1098*

♦ **Alti-Minocycline (Can)** *see Minocycline on page 1149*

♦ **Alti-MPA (Can)** *see MedroxyPROGESTERone on page 1065*

♦ **Alti-Nadolol (Can)** *see Nadolol on page 1187*

♦ **Alti-Nortriptyline (Can)** *see Nortriptyline on page 1243*

♦ **Alti-Ranitidine (Can)** *see Ranitidine on page 1485*

♦ **Alti-Salbutamol (Can)** *see Albuterol on page 57*

♦ **Alti-Sotalol (Can)** *see Sotalol on page 1592*

♦ **Alti-Sulfasalazine (Can)** *see Sulfasalazine on page 1615*

♦ **Alti-Terazosin (Can)** *see Terazosin on page 1647*

♦ **Alti-Ticlopidine (Can)** *see Ticlopidine on page 1683*

♦ **Alti-Timolol (Can)** *see Timolol on page 1687*

♦ **Alti-Trazodone (Can)** *see Trazodone on page 1727*

♦ **Alti-Verapamil (Can)** *see Verapamil on page 1784*

♦ **Altoprev®** *see Lovastatin on page 1040*

Altretamine *(al TRET a meen)*

U.S. Brand Names Hexalen®

Canadian Brand Names Hexalen®

Index Terms Hexamethylmelamine; HEXM; HMM; HXM; NSC-13875

Pharmacologic Category Antineoplastic Agent, Miscellaneous

Use Palliative treatment of persistent or recurrent ovarian cancer

Pregnancy Risk Factor D

Pregnancy Implications Teratogenic effects were noted in animal studies. There are no adequate and well-controlled studies in pregnant women. Women of childbearing potential should avoid becoming pregnant while on therapy.

Lactation Excretion in breast milk unknown/not recommended

Medication Safety Issues

High alert medication: The Institute for Safe Medication Practices (ISMP) includes this medication among its list of drugs which have a heightened risk of causing significant patient harm when used in error.

International issues:

Hexalen®: Brand name for hexetidine in Greece

Contraindications Hypersensitivity to altretamine or any component of the formulation; pre-existing severe bone marrow suppression or severe neurologic toxicity; pregnancy

Warnings/Precautions Hazardous agent - use appropriate precautions for handling and disposal. **[U.S. Boxed Warning]: Peripheral blood counts and neurologic examinations should be done routinely before and after drug therapy.** Myelosuppression and neurotoxicity are common; use with caution in patients previously treated with other myelosuppressive drugs or with pre-existing neurotoxicity. Use with caution in patients with renal or hepatic dysfunction. **[U.S. Boxed Warning]: Should be administered under the supervision of an experienced cancer chemotherapy physician.** Safety and efficacy in children have not been established.

Adverse Reactions

>10%:

Central nervous system: Peripheral sensory neuropathy (31%; moderate-to-severe 9%), neurotoxicity (21%; may be progressive and dose-limiting)

Gastrointestinal: Nausea/vomiting (33% to 70%; severe 1%), diarrhea (48%)

Hematologic: Anemia (33%), leukopenia (5% to 15%; grade 4: 1%), neutropenia

1% to 10%:

Central nervous system: Fatigue (1%), seizure (1%)

Gastrointestinal: Stomach cramps, anorexia (1%)

Hematologic: Thrombocytopenia (9%)

Hepatic: Alkaline phosphatase increased (9%)

<1% (Limited to important or life-threatening): Alopecia, ataxia, depression, dizziness, hepatotoxicity, mood disorders, pruritus, rash, tremor, vertigo

Overdosage/Toxicology Symptoms include nausea, vomiting, peripheral neuropathy, and severe bone marrow suppression. Treatment is symptom-directed and supportive.

Drug Interactions

Increased Effect/Toxicity: Altretamine may enhance the hypotensive effects of MAO inhibitors and tricyclic antidepressants.

Decreased Effect: Pyridoxine may diminish the effect of altretamine.

Stability Store at 15°C to 30°C (59°F to 86°F).

Mechanism of Action Although altretamine's clinical antitumor spectrum resembles that of alkylating agents, the drug has demonstrated activity in alkylator-resistant patients. The drug selectively inhibits the incorporation of radioactive thymidine and uridine into DNA and RNA, inhibiting DNA and RNA synthesis; reactive intermediates covalently bind to microsomal proteins and DNA; can spontaneously degrade to demethylated melamines and formaldehyde which are also cytotoxic.

Pharmacodynamics/Kinetics

Absorption: Well absorbed (75% to 89%)

Distribution: Highly concentrated hepatically and renally; low in other organs

Protein binding: 50% to 94%

Metabolism: Hepatic; rapid and extensive demethylation to active metabolites (pentamethylmelamine and tetramethylmelamine)

Half-life elimination: 13 hours

Time to peak, plasma: 0.5-3 hours

Excretion: Urine (90%, <1% as unchanged drug)

Dosage Refer to individual protocols. Oral: Adults:

Ovarian cancer: 260 mg/m²/day in 4 divided doses for 14 or 21 days of a 28-day cycle

Alternatively (unlabeled use): 4-12 mg/kg/day in 3-4 divided doses for 21-90 days

Alternatively (unlabeled use): 240-320 mg/m²/day in 3-4 divided doses for 21 days, repeated every 6 weeks

Alternatively (unlabeled use): 150 mg/m²/day in 3-4 divided doses for 14 days of a 28-day cycle

Dosage adjustment for toxicity: Temporarily withhold for 14 days or longer, and resume dose at 200 mg/m²/day for any of the following:

Platelet count <75,000/mm³

White blood cell count <2000/mm³ or granulocyte count <1000/mm³

Progressive neurotoxicity

Gastrointestinal intolerance not responsive to antiemetic regimens

Dietary Considerations Should be taken after meals at bedtime.

Administration Administer total daily dose as 3-4 divided doses after meals and at bedtime.

Monitoring Parameters CBC with differential; liver function tests; neurologic examination

Dosage Forms

Gelcap:

Hexalen®: 50 mg

Aluminum Hydroxide (a LOO mi num hye DROKS ide)

U.S. Brand Names ALternaGel® [OTC]; Dermagran® [OTC]

Canadian Brand Names Amphojel®; Basaljel®

Pharmacologic Category Antacid; Antidote; Protectant; Topical

Use Treatment of hyperacidity; hyperphosphatemia; temporary protection of minor cuts, scrapes, and burns

(Continued)

Aluminum Hydroxide *(Continued)*

Pregnancy Risk Factor C

Pregnancy Implications No data available on clinical effects on the fetus; available evidence suggests safe use during pregnancy and breast-feeding.

Lactation Excretion in breast milk unknown

Contraindications Hypersensitivity to aluminum salts or any component of the formulation

Warnings/Precautions Oral: Hypophosphatemia may occur with prolonged administration or large doses; aluminum intoxication and osteomalacia may occur in patients with uremia. Use with caution in patients with CHF, renal failure, edema, cirrhosis, and low sodium diets, and patients who have recently suffered gastrointestinal hemorrhage; uremic patients not receiving dialysis may develop osteomalacia and osteoporosis due to phosphate depletion.

Elderly may be predisposed to constipation and fecal impaction. Careful evaluation of possible drug interactions must be done. When used as an antacid in ulcer treatment, consider buffer capacity (mEq/mL) to calculate dose.

Topical: Not for application over deep wounds, puncture wounds, infected areas, or lacerations. When used for self medication (OTC use), consult with healthcare provider if needed for >7 days or for use in children <6 months of age.

Adverse Reactions Frequency not defined.

Gastrointestinal: Constipation, stomach cramps, fecal impaction, nausea, vomiting, discoloration of feces (white speckles)

Endocrine & metabolic: Hypophosphatemia, hypomagnesemia

Overdosage/Toxicology Aluminum antacids may cause constipation, phosphate depletion, and bezoar or fecalith formation. In patients with renal failure, aluminum may accumulate to toxic levels. Deferoxamine, traditionally used as an iron chelator, has been shown to increase urinary aluminum output. Deferoxamine chelation of aluminum has resulted in improvements of clinical symptoms and bone histology; however, remains an experimental treatment for aluminum poisoning and has a significant potential for adverse effects.

Drug Interactions

Decreased Effect: Aluminum hydroxide may decrease the absorption of allopurinol, antibiotics (tetracyclines, quinolones, some cephalosporins), bisphosphonate derivatives, corticosteroids, cyclosporine, delavirdine, iron salts, imidazole antifungals, isoniazid, mycophenolate, penicillamine, phosphate supplements, phenytoin, phenothiazines, trientine. Absorption of aluminum hydroxide may be decreased by citric acid derivatives.

Mechanism of Action Neutralizes hydrochloride in stomach to form Al (Cl)$_3$ salt + H$_2$O

Dosage

Oral:

Hyperphosphatemia:

Children: 50-150 mg/kg/24 hours in divided doses every 4-6 hours, titrate dosage to maintain serum phosphorus within normal range

Adults: Initial: 300-600 mg 3 times/day with meals

Antacid: Adults: 600-1200 mg between meals and at bedtime

Topical: Apply to affected area as needed; reapply at least every 12 hours

Dietary Considerations Should be taken 1-3 hours after meals when used as an antacid. When used to decrease phosphorus, should be taken within 20 minutes of a meal.

Administration

Oral: Dose should be followed with water.

Topical: Apply as needed to affected area; reapply at least every 12 hours.

Monitoring Parameters Monitor phosphorus levels periodically when patient is on chronic therapy.

Test Interactions Decreased phosphorus, inorganic (S)

Dosage Forms

Ointment:

Dermagran®: 0.275% (120 g)

Suspension, oral: 320 mg/5 mL (473 mL)

ALternaGel®: 600 mg/5 mL (360 mL)

Aluminum Hydroxide and Magnesium Carbonate

(a LOO mi num hye DROKS ide & mag NEE zhum KAR bun nate)

U.S. Brand Names Gaviscon® Extra Strength [OTC]; Gaviscon® Liquid [OTC]

Index Terms Magnesium Carbonate and Aluminum Hydroxide

Pharmacologic Category Antacid

Use Temporary relief of symptoms associated with gastric acidity

Dosage Oral: Adults:

Liquid:

Gaviscon® Regular Strength: 15-30 mL 4 times/day after meals and at bedtime

Gaviscon® Extra Strength Relief: 15-30 mL 4 times/day after meals

Tablet (Gaviscon® Extra Strength Relief): Chew 2-4 tablets 4 times/day

Additional Information Complete prescribing information for this medication should be consulted for additional detail.

Dosage Forms

Liquid:

Gaviscon®: Aluminum hydroxide 31.7 mg and magnesium carbonate 119.3 mg per 5 mL (355 mL) [contains sodium 0.57 mEq/5 mL]

Gaviscon® Extra Strength: Aluminum hydroxide 84.6 mg and magnesium carbonate 79.1 mg per 5 mL (355 mL) [contains sodium 0.9 mEq/5 mL]

Tablet, chewable (Gaviscon® Extra Strength): Aluminum hydroxide 160 mg and magnesium carbonate 105 mg [contains sodium 1.3 mEq/tablet]

Aluminum Hydroxide and Magnesium Hydroxide
(a LOO mi num hye DROKS ide & mag NEE zhum hye DROK side)

U.S. Brand Names Alamag [OTC]; Rulox [OTC]; Rulox No. 1 [DSC]
Canadian Brand Names Diovol®; Diovol® Ex; Gelusil® Extra Strength; Mylanta™
Index Terms Magnesium Hydroxide and Aluminum Hydroxide
Pharmacologic Category Antacid
Use Antacid, hyperphosphatemia in renal failure
Pregnancy Risk Factor C
Medication Safety Issues
Sound-alike/look-alike issues:
Maalox® may be confused with Maox®, Monodox®
Dosage Oral: 5-10 mL 4-6 times/day, between meals and at bedtime; may be used every hour for severe symptoms
Additional Information Complete prescribing information for this medication should be consulted for additional detail.
Dosage Forms [DSC] – Discontinued product
Suspension: Aluminum hydroxide 225 mg and magnesium hydroxide 200 mg per 5 mL (360 mL)
Alamag, Rulox: Aluminum hydroxide 225 mg and magnesium hydroxide 200 mg per 5 mL (360 mL)
Tablet, chewable:
Alamag: Aluminum hydroxide 300 mg and magnesium hydroxide 150 mg
Rulox No. 1: Aluminum hydroxide 200 mg and magnesium hydroxide 200 mg [DSC]

Aluminum Hydroxide and Magnesium Trisilicate
(a LOO mi num hye DROKS ide & mag NEE zhum trye SIL i kate)

U.S. Brand Names Alenic Alka Tablet [OTC]; Gaviscon® Tablet [OTC]; Genaton Tablet [OTC]
Index Terms Magnesium Trisilicate and Aluminum Hydroxide
Pharmacologic Category Antacid
Use Temporary relief of hyperacidity
Pregnancy Risk Factor C
Dosage Oral: Adults: Chew 2-4 tablets 4 times/day or as directed by healthcare provider
Additional Information Complete prescribing information for this medication should be consulted for additional detail.
Dosage Forms
Tablet, chewable: Aluminum hydroxide 80 mg and magnesium trisilicate 20 mg
Alenic Alka: Aluminum hydroxide 80 mg and magnesium trisilicate 20 mg [butterscotch flavor]
Gaviscon®: Aluminum hydroxide 80 mg and magnesium trisilicate 20 mg [contains sodium 0.8 mEq/tablet; butterscotch flavor]
Genaton: Aluminum hydroxide 80 mg and magnesium trisilicate 20 mg

Aluminum Hydroxide, Magnesium Hydroxide, and Simethicone
(a LOO mi num hye DROKS ide, mag NEE zhum hye DROKS ide, & sye METH i kone)

U.S. Brand Names Alamag Plus [OTC]; Aldroxicon I [OTC]; Aldroxicon II [OTC]; Almacone® [OTC]; Almacone Double Strength® [OTC]; Gelusil® [OTC]; Maalox® [OTC]; Maalox® Max [OTC]; Mi-Acid [OTC]; Mi-Acid Maximum Strength [OTC]; Mintox Extra Strength [OTC]; Mintox Plus [OTC]; Mylanta® Liquid [OTC]; Mylanta® Maximum Strength Liquid [OTC]
Canadian Brand Names Diovol Plus®; Gelusil®; Mylanta® Double Strength; Mylanta® Extra Strength; Mylanta® Regular Strength
Index Terms Magnesium Hydroxide, Aluminum Hydroxide, and Simethicone; Simethicone, Aluminum Hydroxide, and Magnesium Hydroxide
Pharmacologic Category Antacid; Antiflatulent
Use Temporary relief of hyperacidity associated with gas; may also be used for indications associated with other antacids
Pregnancy Risk Factor C
Medication Safety Issues
Sound-alike/look-alike issues:
Maalox® may be confused with Maox®, Monodox®
Mylanta® may be confused with Mynatal®

Maalox® is a different formulation than Maalox® Total Stomach Relief®
Dosage Oral: Adults: 10-20 mL or 2-4 tablets 4-6 times/day between meals and at bedtime; may be used every hour for severe symptoms
Additional Information Complete prescribing information for this medication should be consulted for additional detail.
Dosage Forms
Liquid: Aluminum hydroxide 200 mg, magnesium hydroxide 200 mg, and simethicone 20 mg per 5 mL (360 mL); aluminum hydroxide 400 mg, magnesium hydroxide 400 mg, and simethicone 40 mg per 5 mL (360 mL)
Aldroxicon I: Aluminum hydroxide 200 mg, magnesium hydroxide 200 mg, and simethicone 20 mg per 5 mL (30 mL)
Aldroxicon II: Aluminum hydroxide 400 mg, magnesium hydroxide 400 mg, and simethicone 40 mg per 5 mL (30 mL)
Almacone®: Aluminum hydroxide 200 mg, magnesium hydroxide 200 mg, and simethicone 20 mg per 5 mL (360 mL)
Almacone Double Strength®: Aluminum hydroxide 400 mg, magnesium hydroxide 400 mg, and simethicone 40 mg per 5 mL (360 mL)
(Continued)

Aluminum Hydroxide, Magnesium Hydroxide, and Simethicone (Continued)

Maalox®: Aluminum hydroxide 200 mg, magnesium hydroxide 200 mg, and simethicone 20 mg per 5 mL (360 mL, 770 mL) [lemon and mint flavors]

Maalox® Max: Aluminum hydroxide 400 mg, magnesium hydroxide 400 mg, and simethicone 40 mg per 5 mL (360 mL, 770 mL) [cherry, vanilla creme, and wild berry flavors]

Mi-Acid: Aluminum hydroxide 200 mg, magnesium hydroxide 200 mg, and simethicone 20 mg per 5 mL (360 mL)

Mi-Acid Maximum Strength: Aluminum hydroxide 400 mg, magnesium hydroxide 400 mg, and simethicone 40 mg per 5 mL (360 mL)

Mintox Extra Strength: Aluminum hydroxide 500 mg, magnesium hydroxide 450 mg, and simethicone 40 mg per 5 mL (360 mL) [lemon creme flavor]

Mylanta®: Aluminum hydroxide 200 mg, magnesium hydroxide 200 mg, and simethicone 20 mg per 5 mL (180 mL, 360 mL, 720 mL) [original, cherry, and mint flavors]

Mylanta® Maximum Strength: Aluminum hydroxide 400 mg, magnesium hydroxide 400 mg, and simethicone 40 mg per 5 mL (180 mL, 360 mL, 720 mL) [original, cherry, orange creme, and mint flavors]

Suspension (Alamag Plus): Aluminum hydroxide 225 mg, magnesium hydroxide 200 mg, and simethicone 25 mg per 5 mL (360 mL)

Tablet, chewable: Aluminum hydroxide 200 mg, magnesium hydroxide 200 mg, and simethicone 25 mg

Alamag Plus: Aluminum hydroxide 200 mg, magnesium hydroxide 200 mg, and simethicone 25 mg [cherry flavor]

Almacone®: Aluminum hydroxide 200 mg, magnesium hydroxide 200 mg, and simethicone 20 mg [peppermint flavor]

Gelusil®: Aluminum hydroxide 200 mg, magnesium hydroxide 200 mg, and simethicone 25 mg [peppermint flavor]

Mintox Plus: Aluminum hydroxide 200 mg, magnesium hydroxide 200 mg, and simethicone 25 mg

♦ **Aluminum Sucrose Sulfate, Basic** see Sucralfate on page 1606

Aluminum Sulfate and Calcium Acetate

(a LOO mi num SUL fate & KAL see um AS e tate)

U.S. Brand Names Domeboro® [OTC]; Gordon Boro-Packs [OTC]; Pedi-Boro® [OTC]

Index Terms Calcium Acetate and Aluminum Sulfate

Pharmacologic Category Topical Skin Product

Use Astringent wet dressing for relief of inflammatory conditions of the skin; reduce weeping that may occur in dermatitis

Dosage Topical: Soak affected area in the solution 2-4 times/day for 15-30 minutes or apply wet dressing soaked in the solution for more extended periods; rewet dressing with solution 2-4 times/day every 15-30 minutes

Additional Information Complete prescribing information for this medication should be consulted for additional detail.

Dosage Forms

Powder, for topical solution:

Domeboro®: Aluminum sulfate 1191 mg and calcium acetate 938 mg per packet (12s, 100s)

Gordon Boro-Packs: Aluminum sulfate 49% and calcium acetate 51% per packet (100s)

Pedi-Boro®: Aluminum sulfate 49% and calcium acetate 51% per packet (12s, 100s)

♦ **Alupent®** see Metaproterenol on page 1096

Amantadine (a MAN ta deen)

U.S. Brand Names Symmetrel®

Canadian Brand Names Endantadine®; PMS-Amantadine; Symmetrel®

Index Terms Adamantanamine Hydrochloride; Amantadine Hydrochloride

Pharmacologic Category Anti-Parkinson's Agent, Dopamine Agonist; Antiviral Agent, Adamantane

Additional Appendix Information

Community-Acquired Pneumonia in Adults on page 1999

Parkinson's Agents on page 1895

USPHS / IDSA Guidelines for the Prevention of Opportunistic Infections in Persons Infected With HIV on page 1966

Use Prophylaxis and treatment of influenza A viral infection (per manufacturer labeling; also refer to current CDC guidelines for recommendations during current flu season); treatment of parkinsonism; treatment of drug-induced extrapyramidal symptoms

Pregnancy Risk Factor C

Pregnancy Implications Teratogenic effects were observed in animal studies; limited data in humans. Impaired fertility has also been reported during animal studies and during human in vitro fertilization.

Lactation Enters breast milk/not recommended

Medication Safety Issues

Sound-alike/look-alike issues:

Amantadine may be confused with ranitidine, rimantadine

Symmetrel® may be confused with Synthroid®

International issues:

Symmetrel® may be confused with Somatrel® which is a brand name for somatorelin in Denmark

Contraindications Hypersensitivity to amantadine, rimantadine, or any component of the formulation

Warnings/Precautions Use with caution in patients with liver disease, a history of recurrent and eczematoid dermatitis, uncontrolled psychosis or severe psychoneurosis, seizures and in those receiving CNS stimulant drugs; reduce dose in renal disease; when treating Parkinson's disease, do not discontinue abruptly. In many patients, the therapeutic benefits of amantadine are limited to a few months. Elderly patients may be more susceptible to the CNS effects (using 2 divided daily doses may minimize this effect). Use with caution in patients with CHF, peripheral edema, or orthostatic hypotension. Avoid in angle closure glaucoma. Due to increased resistance, in June 2006, the CDC recommended that amantadine no longer be used for the treatment or prophylaxis of influenza A in the United States until susceptibility has been re-established.

Adverse Reactions
1% to 10%:
    Cardiovascular: Orthostatic hypotension, peripheral edema
    Central nervous system: Insomnia, depression, anxiety, irritability, dizziness, hallucinations, ataxia, headache, somnolence, nervousness, dream abnormality, agitation, fatigue, confusion
    Dermatologic: Livedo reticularis
    Gastrointestinal: Nausea, anorexia, constipation, diarrhea, xerostomia
    Respiratory: Dry nose
<1% (Limited to important or life-threatening): Amnesia, CHF, convulsions, dyspnea, eczematoid dermatitis, euphoria, hyperkinesis, hypertension, leukopenia, libido decreased, neutropenia, oculogyric episodes, photosensitivity, psychosis, rash, slurred speech, urinary retention, visual disturbances, vomiting, weakness; withdrawal reactions may include delirium, hallucinations, and psychosis

Overdosage/Toxicology Symptoms include nausea, vomiting, slurred speech, blurred vision, lethargy, hallucinations, seizures, and myoclonic jerking. Acute toxicity may be primarily due to anticholinergic effects. The minimum lethal dose may be as low as 1 g. Following GI decontamination, treatment should be directed at reducing CNS stimulation and at maintaining cardiovascular function. Seizures can be treated with diazepam, while lidocaine infusion may be required for cardiac dysrhythmias.

Drug Interactions
    Increased Effect/Toxicity: Anticholinergics (benztropine and trihexyphenidyl) may potentiate CNS side effects of amantadine. Hydrochlorothiazide, triamterene, and/or trimethoprim may increase toxicity of amantadine; monitor for altered response.

Ethanol/Nutrition/Herb Interactions Ethanol: Avoid ethanol (may increase CNS adverse effects).

Stability Store at 15°C to 30°C (59°F to 86°F); protect from freezing.

Mechanism of Action As an antiviral, blocks the uncoating of influenza A virus preventing penetration of virus into host; antiparkinsonian activity may be due to its blocking the reuptake of dopamine into presynaptic neurons or by increasing dopamine release from presynaptic fibers

Pharmacodynamics/Kinetics
Onset of action: Antidyskinetic: Within 48 hours
Absorption: Well absorbed
Distribution: V_d: Normal: 1.5-6.1 L/kg; Renal failure: 5.1 ± 0.2 L/kg; in saliva, tear film, and nasal secretions; in animals, tissue (especially lung) concentrations higher than serum concentrations; crosses blood-brain barrier
Protein binding: Normal renal function: ~67%; Hemodialysis: ~59%
Metabolism: Not appreciable; small amounts of an acetyl metabolite identified
Bioavailability: 86% to 90%
Half-life elimination: Normal renal function: 16 ± 6 hours (9-31 hours); End-stage renal disease: 7-10 days
Excretion: Urine (80% to 90% unchanged) by glomerular filtration and tubular secretion
    Total clearance: 2.5-10.5 L/hour

Dosage Oral:
Children:
    Influenza A treatment:
        1-9 years: 5 mg/kg/day in 2 divided doses (manufacturers range: 4.4-8.8 mg/kg/day); maximum dose: 150 mg/day
        ≥10 years and <40 kg: 5 mg/kg/day; maximum dose: 150 mg/day
        ≥10 years and ≥40 kg: 100 mg twice daily
        Note: Initiate within 24-48 hours after onset of symptoms; discontinue as soon as possible based on clinical response (generally within 3-5 days or within 24-48 hours after symptoms disappear)
    Influenza A prophylaxis: Refer to "Influenza A treatment" dosing
        Note: Continue treatment throughout the peak influenza activity in the community or throughout the entire influenza season in patients who cannot be vaccinated. Development of immunity following vaccination takes ~2 weeks; amantadine therapy should be considered for high-risk patients from the time of vaccination until immunity has developed. For children <9 years receiving influenza vaccine for the first time, amantadine prophylaxis should continue for 6 weeks (4 weeks after the first dose and 2 weeks after the second dose).
Adults:
    Drug-induced extrapyramidal symptoms: 100 mg twice daily; may increase to 300-400 mg/day, if needed
    Parkinson's disease or Creutzfeldt-Jakob disease (unlabeled use): 100 mg twice daily as sole therapy; may increase to 400 mg/day if needed with close monitoring; initial dose: 100 mg/day if with other serious illness or with high doses of other anti-Parkinson drugs
    Influenza A viral infection: 100 mg twice daily; initiate within 24-48 hours after onset of symptoms; discontinue as soon as possible based on clinical response (generally within 3-5 days or within 24-48 hours after symptoms disappear)
    Influenza A prophylaxis: 100 mg twice daily
(Continued)

Amantadine (Continued)

Note: Continue treatment throughout the peak influenza activity in the community or throughout the entire influenza season in patients who cannot be vaccinated. Development of immunity following vaccination takes ~2 weeks; amantadine therapy should be considered for high-risk patients from the time of vaccination until immunity has developed.

Elderly: Adjust dose based on renal function; some patients tolerate the drug better when it is given in 2 divided daily doses (to avoid adverse neurologic reactions).

Influenza A prophylaxis or treatment: ≤100 mg/day in patients ≥65 years

Dosing interval in renal impairment:
Cl_{cr} 30-50 mL/minute: Administer 200 mg on day 1, then 100 mg/day
Cl_{cr} 15-29 mL/minute: Administer 200 mg on day 1, then 100 mg on alternate days
Cl_{cr} <15 mL/minute: Administer 200 mg every 7 days
Hemodialysis: Administer 200 mg every 7 days
Peritoneal dialysis: No supplemental dose is needed
Continuous arteriovenous or venous-venous hemofiltration: No supplemental dose is needed

Monitoring Parameters Renal function, Parkinson's symptoms, mental status, influenza symptoms, blood pressure

Additional Information Patients with intolerable CNS side effects often do better with rimantadine.

Dosage Forms
Capsule, as hydrochloride: 100 mg
Syrup, as hydrochloride: 50 mg/5 mL (480 mL)
Tablet, as hydrochloride: 100 mg
Symmetrel®: 100 mg

♦ **Amantadine Hydrochloride** see Amantadine on page 86

♦ **Amaryl®** see Glimepiride on page 797

♦ **Amatine® (Can)** see Midodrine on page 1142

♦ **Ambien®** see Zolpidem on page 1824

♦ **Ambien CR™** see Zolpidem on page 1824

♦ **Ambifed-G** see Guaifenesin and Pseudoephedrine on page 819

♦ **Ambifed-G DM** see Guaifenesin, Pseudoephedrine, and Dextromethorphan on page 821

♦ **AmBisome®** see Amphotericin B (Liposomal) on page 119

Amcinonide (am SIN oh nide)

U.S. Brand Names Cyclocort® [DSC]

Canadian Brand Names Amcort®; Cyclocort®; ratio-Amcinonide; Taro-Amcinonide

Pharmacologic Category Corticosteroid, Topical

Additional Appendix Information
Corticosteroids on page 1879

Use Relief of the inflammatory and pruritic manifestations of corticosteroid-responsive dermatoses (high potency corticosteroid)

Pregnancy Risk Factor C

Contraindications Hypersensitivity to amcinonide or any component of the formulation; use on the face, groin, or axilla

Warnings/Precautions Adverse systemic effects may occur when used on large areas of the body, denuded areas, for prolonged periods of time, with an occlusive dressing, and/or in infants or small children. Occlusive dressings should not be used in presence of infection or weeping lesions.

Adverse Reactions Frequency not defined.
Dermatologic: Acne, hypopigmentation, allergic dermatitis, maceration of the skin, skin atrophy, striae, miliaria, telangiectasia
Endocrine & metabolic: Cushing's syndrome, growth retardation (long-term use), HPA suppression, hyperglycemia; these reactions occur more frequently with occlusive dressings
Local: Burning, itching, irritation, dryness, folliculitis, hypertrichosis
Miscellaneous: Secondary infection

Overdosage/Toxicology Symptoms with long-term use only include cushingoid appearance (systemic), muscle weakness (systemic), and osteoporosis (systemic). When consumed in excessive quantities for prolonged periods, systemic hypercorticism and adrenal suppression may occur. In those cases, discontinuation and withdrawal of the corticosteroid should be done judiciously.

Mechanism of Action Stimulates the synthesis of enzymes needed to decrease inflammation, suppress mitotic activity, and cause vasoconstriction

Pharmacodynamics/Kinetics
Absorption: Adequate through intact skin; increases with skin inflammation or occlusion
Metabolism: Hepatic
Excretion: Urine and feces

Dosage Topical: Adults: Apply in a thin film 2-3 times/day. Therapy should be discontinued when control is achieved; if no improvement is seen, reassessment of diagnosis may be necessary.

Dosage Forms [DSC] = Discontinued product
Cream: 0.1% (15 g, 30 g, 60 g) [contains benzyl alcohol]
Lotion: 0.1% (60 mL)
Cyclocort®: 0.1% (20 mL, 60 mL) [contains benzyl alcohol] [DSC]
Ointment: 0.1% (30 g, 60 g) [contains benzyl alcohol]
Cyclocort®: 0.1% (15 g, 30 g, 60 g) [contains benzyl alcohol] [DSC]

♦ **Amcort® (Can)** see Amcinonide on page 88

♦ **Amdry-D** see Pseudoephedrine and Methscopolamine on page 1457

♦ **Amerge®** see Naratriptan on page 1202
♦ **Americaine® [OTC]** see Benzocaine on page 204
♦ **Americaine® Hemorrhoidal [OTC]** see Benzocaine on page 204
♦ **A-Methapred** see MethylPREDNISolone on page 1122
♦ **Amethocaine Hydrochloride** see Tetracaine on page 1659
♦ **Amethopterin** see Methotrexate on page 1111
♦ **Ametop™ (Can)** see Tetracaine on page 1659
♦ **Amevive®** see Alefacept on page 62
♦ **Amfepramone** see Diethylpropion on page 499
♦ **AMG 073** see Cinacalcet on page 371
♦ **Amibid DM** see Guaifenesin and Dextromethorphan on page 816
♦ **Amicar®** see Aminocaproic Acid on page 93
♦ **Amidal** see Guaifenesin and Phenylephrine on page 818
♦ **Amidate®** see Etomidate on page 668
♦ **Amidrine [DSC]** see Acetaminophen, Isometheptene, and Dichloralphenazone on page 36

Amifostine (am i FOS teen)

U.S. Brand Names Ethyol®
Canadian Brand Names Ethyol®
Index Terms Ethiofos; Gammaphos; WR-2721; YM-08310
Pharmacologic Category Adjuvant, Chemoprotective Agent (Cytoprotective); Antidote
Use Reduce the incidence of moderate to severe xerostomia in patients undergoing postoperative radiation treatment for head and neck cancer, where the radiation port includes a substantial portion of the parotid glands; reduce the cumulative renal toxicity associated with repeated administration of cisplatin
Pregnancy Risk Factor C
Pregnancy Implications Animal studies have demonstrated embryotoxicity. There are no adequate and well-controlled studies in pregnant women.
Lactation Excretion in breast milk unknown/not recommended
Medication Safety Issues
Sound-alike/look-alike issues:
Ethyol® may be confused with ethanol
Contraindications Hypersensitivity to amifostine, aminothiol compounds, or any component of the formulation
Warnings/Precautions Patients who are hypotensive or dehydrated should not receive amifostine. Interrupt antihypertensive therapy for 24 hours before amifostine. Patients who cannot safely stop their antihypertensives 24 hours before amifostine should not receive it. Patients should be adequately hydrated prior to amifostine infusion and kept in a supine position during the infusion. Blood pressure should be monitored every 5 minutes during the infusion. If hypotension requiring interruption of therapy occurs, patients should be placed in the Trendelenburg position and given an infusion of normal saline using a separate I.V. line; subsequent infusions may require a dose reduction. Use caution in patients with cardiovascular and cerebrovascular disease and any other patients in whom the adverse effects of hypotension and nausea/vomiting may have serious adverse events.

It is recommended that antiemetic medication, including dexamethasone 20 mg I.V. and a serotonin 5-HT$_3$ receptor antagonist be administered prior to and in conjunction with amifostine. Rare hypersensitivity reactions, including anaphylaxis and severe cutaneous reaction, have been reported with a higher frequency in patients receiving amifostine as a radioprotectant. Discontinue if allergic reaction occurs; do not rechallenge.

Reports of clinically-relevant hypocalcemia are rare, but serum calcium levels should be monitored in patients at risk of hypocalcemia, such as those with nephrotic syndrome. Safety and efficacy in children have not been established.
Adverse Reactions
>10%:
Cardiovascular: Hypotension (15% to 62%; grades 3/4: 3% to 8%; dose dependent)
Gastrointestinal: Nausea/vomiting (53% to 96%; grades 3/4: 8% to 30%; dose dependent)
<1% (Limited to important or life-threatening): Apnea, anaphylactoid reactions, anaphylaxis, arrhythmia, atrial fibrillation, atrial flutter, back pain, bradycardia, cardiac arrest, chest pain, chest tightness, chills, cutaneous eruptions, dizziness, erythema multiforme, exfoliative dermatitis, extrasystoles, dyspnea, fever, flushing, hiccups, hypersensitivity reactions (fever, rash, hypoxia, dyspnea, laryngeal edema), hypertension (transient), hypocalcemia, hypoxia, myocardial ischemia, pruritus, rash (mild), renal failure, respiratory arrest, rigors, seizure, sneezing, somnolence, Stevens-Johnson syndrome, supraventricular tachycardia, syncope, tachycardia, toxic epidermal necrolysis, toxoderma, urticaria
Overdosage/Toxicology Symptoms include hypotension, nausea, vomiting, anxiety and reversible urinary retention. Treatment includes infusion of normal saline for hypotension and supportive measures as clinically indicated.
Drug Interactions
Increased Effect/Toxicity: Antihypertensives may potentiate the hypotensive effects of amifostine.
Stability Store intact vials of lyophilized powder at room temperature of 20°C to 25°C (68°F to 77°F). For I.V. infusion, reconstitute intact vials with 9.7 mL 0.9% sodium chloride injection and dilute in 0.9% sodium chloride to a final concentration of 5-40 mg/mL. For SubQ administration, reconstitute with 2.5 mL NS or SWFI. Reconstituted solutions (500 mg/10 mL) and solutions for infusion are chemically stable for up to 5 hours at room temperature (25°C) or up to 24 hours under refrigeration (2°C to 8°C).
Mechanism of Action Prodrug that is dephosphorylated by alkaline phosphatase in tissues to a pharmacologically-active free thiol metabolite. The free thiol is available to bind to, and
(Continued)

Amifostine *(Continued)*

detoxify, reactive metabolites of cisplatin; and can also act as a scavenger of free radicals that may be generated in tissues.

Pharmacodynamics/Kinetics

Distribution: V_d: 3.5 L

Metabolism: Hepatic dephosphorylation to two metabolites (active-free thiol and disulfide)

Half-life elimination: 8-9 minutes

Excretion: Urine

Clearance, plasma: 2.17 L/minute

Dosage Note: Antiemetic medication, including dexamethasone 20 mg I.V. and a serotonin 5-HT$_3$ receptor antagonist, is recommended prior to and in conjunction with amifostine.

Adults:

Cisplatin-induced renal toxicity, reduction: I.V.: 740-910 mg/m^2 over 15 minutes once daily 30 minutes prior to cytotoxic therapy

Note: Doses >740 mg/m^2 are associated with a higher incidence of hypotension and may require interruption of therapy or dose modification for subsequent cycles. For 910 mg/m^2 doses, the manufacturer suggests the following blood pressure-based adjustment schedule:

The infusion of amifostine should be interrupted if the systolic blood pressure decreases significantly from baseline, as defined below:

Decrease of 20 mm Hg if baseline systolic blood pressure <100

Decrease of 25 mm Hg if baseline systolic blood pressure 100-119

Decrease of 30 mm Hg if baseline systolic blood pressure 120-139

Decrease of 40 mm Hg if baseline systolic blood pressure 140-179

Decrease of 50 mm Hg if baseline systolic blood pressure ≥180

If blood pressure returns to normal within 5 minutes (assisted by fluid administration and postural management) and the patient is asymptomatic, the infusion may be restarted so that the full dose of amifostine may be administered. If the full dose of amifostine cannot be administered, the dose of amifostine for subsequent cycles should be 740 mg/m^2.

Xerostomia from head and neck cancer, reduction:

I.V.: 200 mg/m^2/day over 3 minutes 15-30 minutes prior to radiation therapy **or**

SubQ (unlabeled route): 500 mg/day prior to radiation therapy

Administration I.V.: Administer over 3-15 minutes; administration as a longer infusion is associated with a higher incidence of side effects. Patients should be kept in supine position during infusion. **Note:** SubQ administration has been used.

Monitoring Parameters Blood pressure should be monitored every 5 minutes during the infusion and after administration if clinically indicated; serum calcium levels (in patients at risk for hypocalcemia)

Additional Information Mean onset of hypotension is 14 minutes into the 15-minute infusion and the mean duration 6 minutes.

Dosage Forms

Injection, powder for reconstitution:

Ethyol®: 500 mg

♦ **Amigesic®** *see Salsalate on page 1544*

Amikacin *(am i KAY sin)*

U.S. Brand Names Amikin®

Canadian Brand Names Amikacin Sulfate Injection, USP; Amikin®

Index Terms Amikacin Sulfate

Pharmacologic Category Antibiotic, Aminoglycoside

Additional Appendix Information

Aminoglycoside Dosing and Monitoring *on page 1858*

Antimicrobial Drugs of Choice *on page 1981*

Tuberculosis *on page 2010*

Use Treatment of serious infections due to organisms resistant to gentamicin and tobramycin, including *Pseudomonas, Proteus, Serratia,* and other gram-negative bacilli (bone infections, respiratory tract infections, endocarditis, and septicemia); documented infection of mycobacterial organisms susceptible to amikacin

Pregnancy Risk Factor D

Lactation Enters breast milk/compatible

Medication Safety Issues

Sound-alike/look-alike issues:

Amikacin may be confused with Amicar®, anakinra

Amikin® may be confused with Amicar®

Contraindications Hypersensitivity to amikacin sulfate or any component of the formulation; cross-sensitivity may exist with other aminoglycosides

Warnings/Precautions [U.S. Boxed Warning]: Amikacin may cause neurotoxicity, nephrotoxicity, and/or neuromuscular blockade and respiratory paralysis; usual risk factors include pre-existing renal impairment, concomitant neuro-/nephrotoxic medications, advanced age and dehydration. Dose and/or frequency of administration must be monitored and modified in patients with renal impairment. Drug should be discontinued if signs of ototoxicity, nephrotoxicity, or hypersensitivity occur. Ototoxicity is proportional to the amount of drug given and the duration of treatment. Tinnitus or vertigo may be indications of vestibular injury and impending bilateral irreversible damage. Renal damage is usually reversible. Use with caution in patients with neuromuscular disorders, hearing loss and hypocalcemia. Prolonged use may result in superinfection, including pseudomembranous colitis. Solution contains sodium metabisulfate; use caution in patients with sulfite allergy.

Adverse Reactions

1% to 10%:

Central nervous system: Neurotoxicity

Otic: Ototoxicity (auditory), ototoxicity (vestibular)

Renal: Nephrotoxicity

<1% (Limited to important or life-threatening): Allergic reaction, dyspnea, eosinophilia

Overdosage/Toxicology Symptoms include ototoxicity, nephrotoxicity, and neuromuscular toxicity. Treatment of choice, following a single acute overdose, appears to be the maintenance of good urine output of at least 3 mL/kg/hour. Dialysis is of questionable value in the enhancement of aminoglycoside elimination. If required, hemodialysis is preferred over peritoneal dialysis in patients with normal renal function.

Drug Interactions

Increased Effect/Toxicity: Amikacin may increase or prolong the effect of neuromuscular blocking agents. Concurrent use of amphotericin (or other nephrotoxic drugs) may increase the risk of amikacin-induced nephrotoxicity. The risk of ototoxicity from amikacin may be increased with other ototoxic drugs.

Stability Store at controlled room temperature. Following admixture at concentrations of 0.25-5 mg/mL, amikacin is stable for 24 hours at room temperature and 2 days at refrigeration when mixed in D_5W, NS, and LR.

Mechanism of Action Inhibits protein synthesis in susceptible bacteria by binding to 30S ribosomal subunits

Pharmacodynamics/Kinetics

Absorption:

I.M.: Rapid

Oral: Poorly absorbed

Distribution: Primarily into extracellular fluid (highly hydrophilic); penetrates blood-brain barrier when meninges inflamed; crosses placenta

Relative diffusion of antimicrobial agents from blood into CSF: Good only with inflammation (exceeds usual MICs)

CSF:blood level ratio: Normal meninges: 10% to 20%; Inflamed meninges: 15% to 24%

Protein-binding: 0% to 11%

Half-life elimination (renal function and age dependent):

Infants: Low birth weight (1-3 days): 7-9 hours; Full-term >7 days: 4-5 hours

Children: 1.6-2.5 hours

Adults: Normal renal function: 1.4-2.3 hours; Anuria/end-stage renal disease: 28-86 hours

Time to peak, serum: I.M.: 45-120 minutes

Excretion: Urine (94% to 98%)

Dosage Note: Individualization is critical because of the low therapeutic index

Use of ideal body weight (IBW) for determining the mg/kg/dose appears to be more accurate than dosing on the basis of total body weight (TBW)

In morbid obesity, dosage requirement may best be estimated using a dosing weight of IBW + 0.4 (TBW - IBW)

Initial and periodic peak and trough plasma drug levels should be determined, particularly in critically-ill patients with serious infections or in disease states known to significantly alter aminoglycoside pharmacokinetics (eg, cystic fibrosis, burns, or major surgery)

Usual dosage range:

Infants and Children: I.M., I.V.: 5-7.5 mg/kg/dose every 8 hours

Adults: I.M., I.V.: 5-7.5 mg/kg/dose every 8 hours

Note: Some clinicians suggest a daily dose of 15-20 mg/kg for all patients with normal renal function. This dose is at least as efficacious with similar, if not less, toxicity than conventional dosing.

Indication-specific dosing:

Adults: I.V.:

Hospital-acquired pneumonia (HAP): 20 mg/kg/day with antipseudomonal beta-lactam or carbapenem (American Thoracic Society/ATS guidelines)

Meningitis (*Pseudomonas aeruginosa*): 5 mg/kg every 8 hours (administered with another bacteriocidal drug)

Mycobacterium fortuitum, M. chelonae, or M. abscessus: 10-15 mg/kg daily for at least 2 weeks with high dose cefoxitin

Dosing interval in renal impairment: Some patients may require larger or more frequent doses if serum levels document the need (ie, cystic fibrosis or febrile granulocytopenic patients)

Cl_{cr} ≥60 mL/minute: Administer every 8 hours

Cl_{cr} 40-60 mL/minute: Administer every 12 hours

Cl_{cr} 20-40 mL/minute: Administer every 24 hours

Cl_{cr} <20 mL/minute: Loading dose, then monitor levels

Hemodialysis: Dialyzable (50% to 100%); administer dose postdialysis or administer $2/3$ normal dose as a supplemental dose postdialysis and follow levels

Peritoneal dialysis: Dose as Cl_{cr} <20 mL/minute: Follow levels

Continuous arteriovenous or venovenous hemodiafiltration effects: Dose as for Cl_{cr} 10-40 mL/minute and follow levels

Dietary Considerations Sodium content of 1 g: 29.9 mg (1.3 mEq)

Administration Administer around-the-clock to promote less variation in peak and trough serum levels. Do not mix with other drugs, administer separately.

I.M.: Administer I.M. injection in large muscle mass.

I.V.: Infuse over 30-60 minutes.

Some penicillins (eg, carbenicillin, ticarcillin, and piperacillin) have been shown to inactivate *in vitro*. This has been observed to a greater extent with tobramycin and gentamicin, while amikacin has shown greater stability against inactivation. Concurrent use of these agents may pose a risk of reduced antibacterial efficacy *in vivo*, particularly in the setting of profound renal impairment. However, definitive clinical evidence is lacking. If combination penicillin/aminoglycoside therapy is desired in a patient with renal dysfunction, separation of doses (if feasible), and routine monitoring of aminoglycoside levels, CBC, and clinical response should be considered.

Monitoring Parameters Urinalysis, BUN, serum creatinine, appropriately timed peak and trough concentrations, vital signs, temperature, weight, I & O, hearing parameters

(Continued)

Amikacin *(Continued)*

Some penicillin derivatives may accelerate the degradation of aminoglycosides *in vitro*. This may be clinically-significant for certain penicillin (ticarcillin, piperacillin, carbenicillin) and aminoglycoside (gentamicin, tobramycin) combination therapy in patients with significant renal impairment. Close monitoring of aminoglycoside levels is warranted.

Reference Range

Sample size: 0.5-2 mL blood (red top tube) or 0.1-1 mL serum (separated)

Therapeutic levels:

Peak:

Life-threatening infections: 25-30 mcg/mL

Serious infections: 20-25 mcg/mL

Urinary tract infections: 15-20 mcg/mL

Trough:

Serious infections: 1-4 mcg/mL

Life-threatening infections: 4-8 mcg/mL

The American Thoracic Society (ATS) recommends trough levels of <4-5 mcg/mL for patients with hospital-acquired pneumonia.

Toxic concentration: Peak: >35 mcg/mL; Trough: >10 mcg/mL

Timing of serum samples: Draw peak 30 minutes after completion of 30-minute infusion or at 1 hour following initiation of infusion or I.M. injection; draw trough within 30 minutes prior to next dose

Test Interactions Some penicillin derivatives may accelerate the degradation of aminoglycosides *in vitro*, leading to a potential underestimation of aminoglycoside serum concentration.

Additional Information Aminoglycoside levels measured from blood taken from Silastic® central catheters can sometimes give falsely high readings (draw levels from alternate lumen or peripheral stick, if possible).

Dosage Forms [DSC] = Discontinued product

Injection, solution, as sulfate: 50 mg/mL (2 mL, 4 mL); 62.5 mg/mL (8 mL) [DSC]; 250 mg/mL (2 mL, 4 mL)

Amikin®: 50 mg/mL (2 mL); 250 mg/mL (2 mL, 4 mL) [contains metabisulfite]

♦ **Amikacin Sulfate** *see* Amikacin *on page 90*

♦ **Amikacin Sulfate Injection, USP (Can)** *see* Amikacin *on page 90*

♦ **Amikin®** *see* Amikacin *on page 90*

Amiloride *(a MIL oh ride)*

U.S. Brand Names Midamor® [DSC]

Canadian Brand Names Apo-Amiloride®

Index Terms Amiloride Hydrochloride

Pharmacologic Category Diuretic, Potassium-Sparing

Additional Appendix Information

Heart Failure (Systolic) *on page 2051*

Use Counteracts potassium loss induced by other diuretics in the treatment of hypertension or edematous conditions including CHF, hepatic cirrhosis, and hypoaldosteronism; usually used in conjunction with more potent diuretics such as thiazides or loop diuretics

Unlabeled/Investigational Use Investigational: Cystic fibrosis; reduction of lithium-induced polyuria

Pregnancy Risk Factor B

Lactation Excretion in breast milk unknown/contraindicated

Medication Safety Issues

Sound-alike/look-alike issues:

Amiloride may be confused with amiodarone, amlodipine, amrinone

Contraindications Hypersensitivity to amiloride or any component of the formulation; presence of elevated serum potassium levels (>5.5 mEq/L); if patient is receiving other potassium-conserving agents (eg, spironolactone, triamterene) or potassium supplementation (medicine, potassium-containing salt substitutes, potassium-rich diet); anuria; acute or chronic renal insufficiency; evidence of diabetic nephropathy. Patients with evidence of renal impairment or diabetes mellitus should not receive this medicine without close, frequent monitoring of serum electrolytes and renal function.

Warnings/Precautions [U.S. Boxed Warning]: Hyperkalemia can occur; patients at risk include those with renal impairment, diabetes, the elderly, and the severely ill. Serum potassium levels must be monitored at frequent intervals especially when dosages are changed or with any illness that may cause renal dysfunction. Excess amounts can lead to profound diuresis with fluid and electrolyte loss; close medical supervision and dose evaluation are required. Watch for and correct electrolyte disturbances; adjust dose to avoid dehydration. In cirrhosis, avoid electrolyte and acid/base imbalances that might lead to hepatic encephalopathy. Use with extreme caution in patients with diabetes mellitus; monitor closely. Discontinue amiloride 3 days prior to glucose tolerance testing. Use with caution in patients who are at risk for metabolic or respiratory acidosis (eg, cardiopulmonary disease, uncontrolled diabetes).

Adverse Reactions

1% to 10%:

Central nervous system: Headache, fatigue, dizziness

Endocrine & metabolic: Hyperkalemia (up to 10%; risk reduced in patients receiving kaliuretic diuretics), hyperchloremic metabolic acidosis, dehydration, hyponatremia, gynecomastia

Gastrointestinal: Nausea, diarrhea, vomiting, abdominal pain, gas pain, appetite changes, constipation

Genitourinary: Impotence

Neuromuscular & skeletal: Muscle cramps, weakness

Respiratory: Cough, dyspnea

<1% (Limited to important or life-threatening): Alopecia, arrhythmia, bladder spasms, chest pain, dyspnea, dysuria, GI bleeding, intraocular pressure increased, jaundice, orthostatic hypotension, palpitation, polyuria

Overdosage/Toxicology Clinical signs are consistent with dehydration and electrolyte disturbance. Large amounts may result in life-threatening hyperkalemia (>6.5 mEq/L). This can be treated with I.V. glucose (dextrose 25% in water), with rapid-acting insulin, with concurrent I.V. sodium bicarbonate and, if needed, Kayexalate® oral or rectal solutions in sorbitol. Persistent hyperkalemia may require dialysis.

Drug Interactions

Increased Effect/Toxicity: Increased risk of amiloride-associated hyperkalemia with triamterene, spironolactone, ACE inhibitors or angiotensin receptor antagonists, potassium preparations, cyclosporine, tacrolimus, and indomethacin. Amiloride may increase the toxicity of amantadine and lithium by reduction of renal excretion. Quinidine and amiloride together may increase risk of malignant arrhythmias.

Decreased Effect: Decreased effect of amiloride with use of NSAIDs. Amoxicillin's absorption may be reduced with concurrent use.

Ethanol/Nutrition/Herb Interactions Food: Hyperkalemia may result if amiloride is taken with potassium-containing foods.

Mechanism of Action Interferes with potassium/sodium exchange (active transport) in the distal tubule, cortical collecting tubule, and collecting duct by inhibiting sodium, potassium-ATPase; decreases calcium excretion; increases magnesium loss

Pharmacodynamics/Kinetics
Onset of action: 2 hours
Duration: 24 hours
Absorption: ~15% to 25%
Distribution: V_d: 350-380 L
Protein binding: 23%
Metabolism: No active metabolites
Half-life elimination: Normal renal function: 6-9 hours; End-stage renal disease: 8-144 hours
Time to peak, serum: 6-10 hours
Excretion: Urine and feces (equal amounts as unchanged drug)

Dosage Oral:
Children: Although safety and efficacy in children have not been established by the FDA, a dosage of 0.625 mg/kg/day has been used in children weighing 6-20 kg.
Adults: 5-10 mg/day (up to 20 mg)
Hypertension (JNC 7): 5-10 mg/day in 1-2 divided doses
Elderly: Initial: 5 mg once daily or every other day
Dosing adjustment in renal impairment:
Cl_{cr} 10-50 mL/minute: Administer at 50% of normal dose.
Cl_{cr} <10 mL/minute: Avoid use.

Dietary Considerations Take with food or meals to avoid GI upset. Do not use salt substitutes or low salt milk without checking with your healthcare provider; too much potassium can be as harmful as too little.

Administration Administer with food or meals to avoid GI upset.

Monitoring Parameters I & O, daily weights, blood pressure, serum electrolytes, renal function

Test Interactions Increased potassium (S)

Additional Information Medication should be discontinued if potassium level exceeds 6.5 mEq/L. Combined with hydrochlorothiazide as Moduretic®. Amiloride is considered an alternative to triamterene or spironolactone.

Dosage Forms Tablet, as hydrochloride: 5 mg

Amiloride and Hydrochlorothiazide
(a MIL oh ride & hye droe klor oh THYE a zide)

Canadian Brand Names Apo-Amilzide®; Gen-Amilazide; Moduret; Novamilor; Nu-Amilzide
Index Terms Hydrochlorothiazide and Amiloride
Pharmacologic Category Diuretic, Combination
Use Potassium-sparing diuretic; antihypertensive
Pregnancy Risk Factor B
Dosage Adults: Oral: Start with 1 tablet/day; may be increased to 2 tablets/day if needed; usually given in a single dose
Elderly: Initial: 1/2 to 1 tablet/day
Dosage adjustment in renal impairment: See individual agents.
Additional Information Complete prescribing information for this medication should be consulted for additional detail.
Dosage Forms Tablet: 5/50: Amiloride hydrochloride 5 mg and hydrochlorothiazide 50 mg

◆ **Amiloride Hydrochloride** see Amiloride on page 92
◆ **2-Amino-6-Mercaptopurine** see Thioguanine on page 1669
◆ **2-Amino-6-Methoxypurine Arabinoside** see Nelarabine on page 1207
◆ **2-Amino-6-Trifluoromethoxy-benzothiazole** see Riluzole on page 1512
◆ **Aminobenzylpenicillin** see Ampicillin on page 122

Aminocaproic Acid (a mee noe ka PROE ik AS id)

U.S. Brand Names Amicar®
Index Terms Epsilon Aminocaproic Acid
Pharmacologic Category Hemostatic Agent
Use Treatment of excessive bleeding from fibrinolysis
Unlabeled/Investigational Use Treatment of traumatic hyphema; control bleeding in thrombocytopenia; control oral bleeding in congenital and acquired coagulation disorders
(Continued)

Aminocaproic Acid *(Continued)*

Pregnancy Risk Factor C

Pregnancy Implications Reproductive studies have not been conducted.

Lactation Excretion in breast milk unknown/use caution

Medication Safety Issues
Sound-alike/look-alike issues:
Amicar® may be confused with amikacin, Amikin®, Omacor®

Contraindications Hypersensitivity to aminocaproic acid or any component of the formulation; disseminated intravascular coagulation (without heparin); evidence of an intravascular clotting process

Warnings/Precautions Avoid rapid I.V. administration. Aminocaproic acid may accumulate in patients with decreased renal function. Intrarenal obstruction may occur. Do not use in hematuria of upper urinary tract origin unless possible benefits outweigh risks. Use with caution in patients with cardiac, renal, or hepatic disease. Do not administer without a definite diagnosis of laboratory findings indicative of hyperfibrinolysis. Inhibition of fibrinolysis may promote clotting or thrombosis; more likely due to the presence of DIC. Subsequently, use with great caution in patients with, or at risk for, veno-occlusive disease of the liver. Benzyl alcohol is used as a preservative. Do not administer with factor IX complex concentrates or anti-inhibitor coagulant complexes.

Adverse Reactions Frequency not defined.
Cardiovascular: Arrhythmia, bradycardia, hypotension, peripheral ischemia, syncope, thrombosis
Central nervous system: Confusion, delirium, dizziness, fatigue, hallucinations, headache, intracranial hypertension, malaise, seizure, stroke
Dermatologic: Rash, pruritus
Gastrointestinal: Abdominal pain, anorexia, cramps, diarrhea, GI irritation, nausea
Genitourinary: Dry ejaculation
Hematologic: Agranulocytosis, bleeding time increased, leukopenia, thrombocytopenia
Neuromuscular & skeletal: CPK increased, myalgia, myositis, myopathy, rhabdomyolysis (rare), weakness
Ophthalmic: Watery eyes, vision decreased
Otic: Tinnitus
Renal: Failure (rare), myoglobinuria (rare)
Respiratory: Dyspnea, nasal congestion, pulmonary embolism

Overdosage/Toxicology Symptoms include acute renal failure, delirium, diarrhea, hepatic necrosis, nausea, seizures, transient hypotension, and thromboembolism. Aminocaproic acid may be removed by hemodialysis.

Drug Interactions
Increased Effect/Toxicity: Increased risk of hypercoagulability with oral contraceptives, estrogens. Should not be administered with factor IX complex concentrate or anti-inhibitor complex concentrates due to an increased risk of thrombosis.

Stability Store at 15°C to 30°C (59°F to 86°F). Dilute I.V. solution (1 g/50 mL of diluent) with D_5W, 0.9% sodium chloride, or lactated Ringer's.

Mechanism of Action Competitively inhibits activation of plasminogen to plasmin, also, a lesser antiplasmin effect

Pharmacodynamics/Kinetics
Onset of action: ~1-72 hours
Distribution: Widely through intravascular and extravascular compartments
V_d: Oral: 23 L, I.V.: 30 L
Metabolism: Minimally hepatic
Half-life elimination: 2 hours
Time to peak: Oral: Within 2 hours
Excretion: Urine (65% as unchanged drug, 11% as metabolite)

Dosage
Acute bleeding syndrome:
Children (unlabeled use): Oral, I.V.: 100-200 mg/kg during the first hour, followed by continuous infusion at 33.3 mg/kg/hour or 100 mg/kg (oral or I.V.) every 6 hours
Adults: Oral, I.V.: 4-5 g during the first hour, followed by 1 g/hour for 8 hours or until bleeding controlled (maximum daily dose: 30 g)
Control bleeding in thrombocytopenia (unlabeled use): Adults:
Initial: I.V.: 0.1 g/kg over 30-60 minutes
Maintenance: Oral: 1-3 g every 6 hours
Control oral bleeding in congenital and acquired coagulation disorder (unlabeled use): Adults:
Oral: 50-60 mg/kg every 4 hours
Traumatic hyphema (unlabeled use): Children and Adults: Oral: 100 mg/kg/dose every 4 hours (maximum daily dose: 30 g)
Dosing adjustment in renal impairment: May accumulate in patients with decreased renal function.

Administration I.V.: May be administered over 30-60 minutes or by continuous infusion; rapid I.V. injection (IVP) should be avoided due to possible hypotension, bradycardia, and arrhythmia.

Monitoring Parameters Fibrinogen, fibrin split products, creatine phosphokinase (with long-term therapy)

Reference Range Therapeutic concentration: >130 mcg/mL (concentration necessary for inhibition of fibrinolysis)

Test Interactions Increased potassium, creatine phosphokinase [CPK] (S)

Dosage Forms
Injection, solution: 250 mg/mL (20 mL)
Amicar®: 250 mg/mL (20 mL) [contains benzyl alcohol]
Solution, oral: 1.25 g/5 mL (240 mL, 480 mL)
Syrup:
Amicar®: 1.25 g/5 mL (480 mL) [raspberry flavor]
Tablet [scored]: 500 mg, 1000 mg
Amicar®: 500 mg, 1000 mg

♦ **Amino-Cerv™** *see Urea on page 1758*

Aminoglutethimide (a mee noe gloo TETH i mide)

U.S. Brand Names Cytadren®
Index Terms AG; AGT; BA-16038; Elipten
Pharmacologic Category Antineoplastic Agent, Aromatase Inhibitor; Enzyme Inhibitor; Hormone Antagonist, Anti-Adrenal; Nonsteroidal Aromatase Inhibitor
Use Suppression of adrenal function in selected patients with Cushing's syndrome
Unlabeled/Investigational Use Treatment of breast and prostate cancer (androgen synthesis inhibitor)
Pregnancy Risk Factor D
Medication Safety Issues
Sound-alike/look-alike issues:
Cytadren® may be confused with cytarabine
Dosage Oral: Adults:
Adrenal suppression: 250 mg every 6 hours may be increased at 1- to 2-week intervals to a total of 2 g/day
Breast cancer, prostate cancer (unlabeled use): 250 mg 4 times/day
Dosing adjustment in renal impairment: Dose reduction may be necessary
Additional Information Complete prescribing information for this medication should be consulted for additional detail.
Dosage Forms Tablet [scored]: 250 mg

Aminolevulinic Acid (a MEE noh lev yoo lin ik AS id)

U.S. Brand Names Levulan® Kerastick®
Canadian Brand Names Levulan®
Index Terms Aminolevulinic Acid Hydrochloride
Pharmacologic Category Photosensitizing Agent, Topical; Topical Skin Product
Use Treatment of minimally to moderately thick actinic keratoses (grade 1 or 2) of the face or scalp; to be used in conjunction with blue light illumination
Pregnancy Risk Factor C
Pregnancy Implications Animal reproduction studies have not been conducted, and there are no adequate and well-controlled studies in pregnant women. Use during pregnancy only if clearly needed.
Lactation Excretion in breast milk unknown/use caution
Contraindications Hypersensitivity to aminolevulinic acid or any component of the formulation; individuals with cutaneous photosensitivity at wavelengths of 400-450 nm; porphyria; allergy to porphyrins
Warnings/Precautions For external use only. Do not apply to eyes or mucous membranes. Treatment site will become photosensitive following application. Patients should be instructed to avoid exposure to sunlight, bright indoor lights, or tanning beds during the period prior to blue light treatment. Should be applied by a qualified health professional to avoid application to perilesional skin. Has not been tested in individuals with coagulation defects (acquired or inherited).
Adverse Reactions Transient stinging, burning, itching, erythema, and edema result from the photosensitizing properties of this agent. Symptoms subside between 1 minute and 24 hours after turning off the blue light illuminator. Severe stinging or burning was reported in at least 50% of patients from at least 1 lesional site treatment.

>10%: Dermatologic: Severe stinging or burning (50%), scaling of the skin/crusted skin (64% to 71%), hyper-/hypopigmentation (22% to 36%), itching (14% to 25%), erosion (2% to 14%)
1% to 10%:
Central nervous system: Dysesthesia (up to 2%)
Dermatologic: Skin ulceration (2% to 4%), vesiculation (4% to 5%), pustular drug eruption (up to 4%), skin disorder (5% to 12%)
Hematologic: Bleeding/hemorrhage (2% to 4%)
Local: Wheal/flare (2% to 7%), local pain (1%), tenderness (1% to 2%), edema (1%), scabbing (up to 2%), ulceration (2% to 4%), excoriation (1%)
Overdosage/Toxicology Monitoring and supportive care are recommended. Patients should be advised to avoid incidental exposure to intense light sources for at least 40 hours. Consequences of exceeding the recommended topical dosage are not known.
Drug Interactions
Increased Effect/Toxicity: Photosensitizing agents such as griseofulvin, thiazide diuretics, sulfonamides, sulfonylureas, phenothiazines, and tetracyclines theoretically may increase the photosensitizing potential of aminolevulinic acid.
Stability Store at 25°C (77°F). Prepare solution by holding applicator tube with cap pointing up. Apply finger pressure to "Position A" on cardboard sleeve to crush ampul containing solution vehicle. Apply finger pressure to "Position B" to crush ampul containing aminolevulinic acid powder. Shake gently for at least 3 minutes to dissolve; point applicator cap away from face while shaking tube. Remove cap; dab dry applicator tip on gauze pad until wet with solution. Once prepared, the topical solution should be used immediately and application must be completed within 2 hours.
Mechanism of Action Aminolevulinic acid is a metabolic precursor of protoporphyrin IX (PpIX), which is a photosensitizer. Photosensitization following application of aminolevulinic acid topical solution occurs through the metabolic conversion to PpIX. When exposed to light of appropriate wavelength and energy, accumulated PpIX produces a photodynamic reaction.
(Continued)

Aminolevulinic Acid (Continued)

Pharmacodynamics/Kinetics
PpIX:
Peak fluorescence intensity: 11 hours ± 1 hour
Half-life, mean clearance for lesions: 30 ± 10 hours

Dosage Adults: Topical: Apply to actinic keratoses (**not** perilesional skin) followed 14-18 hours later by blue light illumination. Application/treatment may be repeated at a treatment site after 8 weeks.

Administration Dab lesion gently with wet applicator tip. Do not apply to periorbital area, ocular tissue, or mucosal surfaces. Allow to dry, then reapply to same lesion. Apply to either scalp or facial lesions, but not to both simultaneously. Follow application with blue light exposure in 14-18 hours.

Additional Information Use in conjunction with the BLU-U™ Blue Light Photodynamic Therapy Illuminator.

Dosage Forms
Powder for topical solution:
Levulan® Kerastick®: 20% (6s) [2-component system containing aminolevulinic acid hydrochloride 354 mg (powder) and diluent containing ethanol 48% (1.5 mL) packaged together in an applicator tube]

♦ **Aminolevulinic Acid Hydrochloride** see Aminolevulinic Acid on page 95
♦ **Aminophylline** see Theophylline Salts on page 1664
♦ **Aminosalicylate Sodium** see Aminosalicylic Acid on page 96

Aminosalicylic Acid (a mee noe sal i SIL ik AS id)

U.S. Brand Names Paser®
Index Terms Aminosalicylate Sodium; 4-Aminosalicylic Acid; Para-Aminosalicylate Sodium; PAS; Sodium PAS
Pharmacologic Category Salicylate
Use Adjunctive treatment of tuberculosis used in combination with other antitubercular agents
Unlabeled/Investigational Use Crohn's disease
Pregnancy Risk Factor C
Pregnancy Implications Teratogenic effects have been reported in animals, however, adequate studies have not been done in humans. Use during pregnancy only if clearly needed.
Lactation Enters breast milk/not recommended
Contraindications Hypersensitivity to aminosalicylic acid or any component of the formulation
Warnings/Precautions Use with caution in patients with hepatic or renal dysfunction and patients with gastric ulcer.
Adverse Reactions Frequency not defined.
Cardiovascular: Pericarditis, vasculitis
Central nervous system: Encephalopathy, fever
Dermatologic: Skin eruptions
Endocrine & metabolic: Goiter (with or without myxedema), hypoglycemia
Gastrointestinal: Abdominal pain, diarrhea, nausea, vomiting
Hematologic: Agranulocytosis, anemia (hemolytic), leukopenia, thrombocytopenia
Hepatic: Hepatitis, jaundice
Ocular: Optic neuritis
Respiratory: Eosinophilic pneumonia
Overdosage/Toxicology Acute overdose results in crystalluria and renal failure, nausea, and vomiting. Alkalinization of urine with sodium bicarbonate and forced diuresis can prevent crystalluria and nephrotoxicity.
Drug Interactions
Decreased Effect: Aminosalicylic acid may decrease serum levels of digoxin and vitamin B_{12}.
Stability Prior to dispensing, store granules below 15°C (59°F). Once dispensed, packets may be stored at room temperature for short periods of time. Do not use if packet is swollen or if granules are dark brown or purple.
Mechanism of Action Aminosalicylic acid (PAS) is a highly-specific bacteriostatic agent active against *M. tuberculosis*. Structurally related to para-aminobenzoic acid (PABA) and its mechanism of action is thought to be similar to the sulfonamides, a competitive antagonism with PABA; disrupts plate biosynthesis in sensitive organisms.
Pharmacodynamics/Kinetics
Absorption: Readily, >90%
Protein binding: 50% to 60%
Metabolism: Hepatic (>50%) via acetylation
Half-life elimination: Reduced with renal impairment
Time to peak, serum: 6 hours
Excretion: Urine (>80% as unchanged drug and metabolites)
Dosage Oral:
Children: Tuberculosis: 200-300 mg/kg/day in 3-4 equally divided doses
Adults:
Tuberculosis: 150 mg/kg/day in 2-3 equally divided doses
Crohn's disease (unlabeled use): 1.5 g/day
Dosing adjustment in renal impairment:
Cl_{cr} 10-50 mL/minute: Administer 50% to 75% of dose
Cl_{cr} <10 mL/minute: Administer 50% of dose
Administer after hemodialysis: Administer 50% of dose
Continuous arteriovenous hemofiltration: Dose for Cl_{cr} <10 mL/minute
Dosing adjustment in hepatic impairment: Use with caution.
Dietary Considerations May be taken with food.

Administration Do not use granules if packet is swollen or if granules are discolored (ie, brown or purple). Granules may be sprinkled on applesauce or yogurt (do not chew) or suspended in tomato or orange juice.

Dosage Forms
Granules, delayed release:
Paser®: 4 g/packet (30s)

♦ **4-Aminosalicylic Acid** *see* Aminosalicylic Acid *on page 96*

♦ **5-Aminosalicylic Acid** *see* Mesalamine *on page 1089*

♦ **Aminoxin® [OTC]** *see* Pyridoxine *on page 1463*

Amiodarone (a MEE oh da rone)

U.S. Brand Names Cordarone®; Pacerone®

Canadian Brand Names Alti-Amiodarone; Amiodarone Hydrochloride for Injection®; Apo-Amiodarone®; Cordarone®; Gen-Amiodarone; Novo-Amiodarone; Rhoxal-amiodarone; Sandoz-Amiodarone

Index Terms Amiodarone Hydrochloride

Pharmacologic Category Antiarrhythmic Agent, Class III

Use Management of life-threatening recurrent ventricular fibrillation (VF) or hemodynamically-unstable ventricular tachycardia (VT) refractory to other antiarrhythmic agents or in patients intolerant of other agents used for these conditions

Unlabeled/Investigational Use
Conversion of atrial fibrillation to normal sinus rhythm; maintenance of normal sinus rhythm
Prevention of postoperative atrial fibrillation during cardiothoracic surgery
Paroxysmal supraventricular tachycardia (SVT)
Control of rapid ventricular rate due to accessory pathway conduction in pre-excited atrial arrhythmias [ACLS guidelines]
Cardiac arrest with persistent ventricular tachycardia (VT) or ventricular fibrillation (VF) if defibrillation, CPR, and vasopressor administration have failed [ACLS/PALS guidelines]
Control of hemodynamically-stable VT, polymorphic VT with a normal QT interval, or wide-complex tachycardia of uncertain origin [ACLS/PALS guidelines]

Restrictions An FDA-approved medication guide must be distributed when dispensing an outpatient prescription (new or refill) where this medication is to be used without direct supervision of a healthcare provider. Medication guides are available at http://www.fda.gov/cder/Offices/ODS/medication_guides.htm.

Pregnancy Risk Factor D

Pregnancy Implications May cause fetal harm when administered to a pregnant woman, leading to congenital goiter and hypo- or hyperthyroidism.

Lactation Enters breast milk/not recommended (AAP rates "of concern")

Medication Safety Issues
Sound-alike/look-alike issues:
Amiodarone may be confused with amiloride, amrinone
Cordarone® may be confused with Cardura®, Cordran®

High alert medication: The Institute for Safe Medication Practices (ISMP) includes this medication among its list of drugs which have a heightened risk of causing significant patient harm when used in error.

Contraindications Hypersensitivity to amiodarone, iodine, or any component of the formulation; severe sinus-node dysfunction; second- and third-degree heart block (except in patients with a functioning artificial pacemaker); bradycardia causing syncope (except in patients with a functioning artificial pacemaker); cardiogenic shock; pregnancy

Warnings/Precautions [U.S. Boxed Warning]: Only indicated for patients with life-threatening arrhythmias because of risk of toxicity. Monitor for pulmonary toxicity. Lung damage (abnormal diffusion capacity) may occur without symptoms. Pre-existing pulmonary disease does not increase risk of developing pulmonary toxicity, but if pulmonary toxicity develops then the prognosis is worse. Liver toxicity is common, but usually mild with evidence of increased liver enzymes. Severe liver toxicity can occur and has been fatal in a few cases.

Amiodarone can exacerbate the arrhythmia (including torsade de pointes), making it more difficult to tolerate or reverse. Other types of arrhythmias have occurred (eg, significant heart block, sinus bradycardia). Proarrhythmic effects may be prolonged. Use very cautiously and with close monitoring in patients with thyroid or liver disease. May cause hyper- or hypothyroidism. Hyperthyroidism may result in thyrotoxicosis and may aggravate or cause break-through arrhythmias. If any new signs of arrhythmia appear, hyperthyroidism should be considered. Thyroid function should be monitored prior to treatment and periodically thereafter. May cause optic neuropathy and/or optic neuritis, usually resulting in visual impairment. Corneal microdeposits occur in a majority of patients, and may cause visual disturbances in some patients (blurred vision, halos); these are not generally considered a reason to discontinue treatment. Corneal refractive laser surgery is generally contraindicated in amiodarone users.

[U.S. Boxed Warning]: Alternative therapies should be tried first before using amiodarone. Patients should be hospitalized when amiodarone is initiated. Due to complex pharmacokinetics, it is difficult to predict when an arrhythmia or interaction with a subsequent treatment will occur following discontinuation of amiodarone.

Amiodarone is a potent inhibitor of CYP enzymes and transport proteins (including p-glycoprotein), which may lead to increased serum concentrations/toxicity of a number of medications. Particular caution must be used when a drug with QT_c-prolonging potential relies on metabolism via these enzymes, since the effect of elevated concentrations may be additive with the effect of amiodarone. Carefully assess risk:benefit of coadministration of other drugs which may prolong QT_c interval. Correct electrolyte disturbances, especially hypokalemia or hypomagnesemia, prior to use and throughout therapy.
(Continued)

Amiodarone *(Continued)*

May cause hypotension and bradycardia (infusion-rate related). Caution in surgical patients; may enhance hemodynamic effect of anesthetics; associated with increased risk of adult respiratory distress syndrome (ARDS) postoperatively. Injection contains benzyl alcohol, which has been associated with "gasping syndrome" in neonates. Safety and efficacy of amiodarone in children has not been fully established.

Adverse Reactions In a recent meta-analysis, patients taking lower doses of amiodarone (152-330 mg daily for at least 12 months) were more likely to develop thyroid, neurologic, skin, ocular, and bradycardic abnormalities than those taking placebo (Vorperian, 1997). Pulmonary toxicity was similar in both the low dose amiodarone group and in the placebo group but there was a trend towards increased toxicity in the amiodarone group. Gastrointestinal and hepatic events were seen to a similar extent in both the low dose amiodarone group and placebo group. As the frequency of adverse events varies considerably across studies as a function of route and dose, a consolidation of adverse event rates is provided by Goldschlager, 2000.

Cardiovascular: Hypotension (I.V. 16%, refractory in rare cases)

Central nervous system (3% to 40%): Abnormal gait/ataxia, dizziness, fatigue, headache, malaise, impaired memory, involuntary movement, insomnia, poor coordination, peripheral neuropathy, sleep disturbances, tremor

Dermatologic: Photosensitivity (10% to 75%)

Endocrine & Metabolic: Hypothyroidism (1% to 22%)

Gastrointestinal: Nausea, vomiting, anorexia, and constipation (10% to 33%)

Hepatic: AST or ALT level >2x normal (15% to 50%)

Ocular: Corneal microdeposits (>90%; causes visual disturbance in <10%)

1% to 10%:

Cardiovascular: CHF (3%), bradycardia (3% to 5%), AV block (5%), conduction abnormalities, SA node dysfunction (1% to 3%), cardiac arrhythmia, flushing, edema. Additional effects associated with I.V. administration include asystole, cardiac arrest, electromechanical dissociation, ventricular tachycardia, and cardiogenic shock.

Dermatologic: Slate blue skin discoloration (<10%)

Endocrine & metabolic: Hyperthyroidism (3% to 10%; more common in iodine-deficient regions of the world), libido decreased

Gastrointestinal: Abdominal pain, abnormal salivation, abnormal taste (oral)

Hematologic: Coagulation abnormalities

Hepatic: Hepatitis and cirrhosis (<3%)

Local: Phlebitis (I.V., with concentrations >3 mg/mL)

Ocular: Visual disturbances (2% to 9%), halo vision (<5% occurring especially at night), optic neuritis (1%)

Respiratory: Pulmonary toxicity has been estimated to occur at a frequency between 2% and 7% of patients (some reports indicate a frequency as high as 17%). Toxicity may present as hypersensitivity pneumonitis; pulmonary fibrosis (cough, fever, malaise); pulmonary inflammation; interstitial pneumonitis; or alveolar pneumonitis. ARDS has been reported in up to 2% of patients receiving amiodarone, and postoperatively in patients receiving oral amiodarone.

Miscellaneous: Abnormal smell (oral)

<1% (Limited to important or life-threatening): Acute intracranial hypertension (I.V.), acute renal failure, agranulocytosis, alopecia, anaphylactic shock, angioedema, aplastic anemia, bone marrow granuloma, bronchiolitis obliterans organizing pneumonia (BOOP), bronchospasm, confusion, disorientation, dyspnea, encephalopathy, epididymitis (noninfectious), erectile dysfunction, erythema multiforme, exfoliative dermatitis, hallucination, hemolytic anemia, hemoptysis, hyperglycemia, hypertriglyceridemia, hypotension (oral), hypoxia, impotence, injection site reactions, leukocytoclastic vasculitis, muscle weakness, myopathy, neutropenia, optic neuropathy, pancreatitis, pancytopenia, parkinsonian symptoms, photophobia, pleuritis, proarrhythmia, pruritus, pseudotumor cerebri, pulmonary edema, pulmonary mass, QT interval increased, rash, renal impairment, renal insufficiency, respiratory failure, rhabdomyolysis, SIADH, sinus arrest, spontaneous ecchymosis, Stevens-Johnson syndrome, thrombocytopenia, thyroid nodules, thyroid cancer, thyrotoxicosis, toxic epidermal necrolysis, vasculitis, ventricular fibrillation, wheezing

Overdosage/Toxicology Symptoms include extensions of pharmacologic effect, sinus bradycardia and/or heart block, hypotension and QT prolongation. Patients should be monitored for several days following ingestion. Intoxication with amiodarone necessitates ECG monitoring. Bradycardia may be atropine resistant. Injectable isoproterenol or a temporary pacemaker may be required. Dialysis is not beneficial.

Drug Interactions

Cytochrome P450 Effect: Substrate of CYP1A2 (minor), 2C8 (major at low concentration), 2C19 (minor), 2D6 (minor), 3A4 (major); **Inhibits** CYP1A2 (weak), 2A6 (moderate), 2B6 (weak), 2C9 (moderate), 2C19 (weak), 2D6 (moderate), 3A4 (moderate)

Increased Effect/Toxicity: The effect of drugs which prolong the QT interval, including amitriptyline, azole antifungals, bepridil, cisapride, clarithromycin, disopyramide, erythromycin, gatifloxacin, haloperidol, imipramine, moxifloxacin, quinidine, pimozide, procainamide, sotalol, sparfloxacin, theophylline, and thioridazine may be increased. Cisapride and sparfloxacin are contraindicated. Use of amiodarone with diltiazem, verapamil, digoxin, beta-blockers, and other drugs which delay AV conduction may cause excessive AV block (amiodarone may also decrease the metabolism of some of these agents - see below).

Amiodarone may increase the levels of digoxin (reduce dose by 50% on initiation), flecainide (decrease dose up to 33%), phenothiazines, procainamide (reduce dose), and quinidine. Amiodarone may increase the levels/effects of aminophylline, amphetamines, selected benzodiazepines, selected beta-blockers, calcium channel blockers, cyclosporine, dexmedetomidine, dextromethorphan, fluoxetine, fluvoxamine, glimepiride, glipizide, ifosfamide, imatinib, isoniazid, lidocaine, mexiletine, mirtazapine, nateglinide, nefazodone, paroxetine, phenytoin, pioglitazone, risperidone, ritonavir, ropinirole, rosiglitazone, sildenafil (and other PDE-5 inhibitors), sertraline, tacrolimus, telithromycin, theophylline, thioridazine, trazodone, tricyclic antidepressants, trifluoperazine, venlafaxine, warfarin, and other CYP2A6, 2C9, CYP2D6, and/or CYP3A4 substrates. Selected benzodiazepines (midazolam, triazolam), cisapride, ergot alkaloids, selected HMG-CoA reductase inhibitors (lovastatin and simvastatin), mesoridazine, pimozide, and thioridazine are generally contraindicated with strong CYP3A4 inhibitors; example CYP3A4 inhibitors include azole antifungals, clarithromycin, diclofenac, doxycycline, erythromycin, imatinib, isoniazid, nefazodone, nicardipine, propofol, protease inhibitors, quinidine, telithromycin, and verapamil. When used with strong CYP3A4 inhibitors, dosage adjustment/limits are recommended for sildenafil and other PDE-5 inhibitors; consult individual monographs.

The levels/effects of amiodarone may be increased by atazanavir, gemfibrozil, ritonavir, and other CYP2C8 inhibitors.

Concurrent use of fentanyl may lead to bradycardia, sinus arrest, and hypotension. Amiodarone may alter thyroid function and response to thyroid supplements. Amiodarone enhances the myocardial depressant and conduction effects of inhalation anesthetics (monitor).

Decreased Effect: Levels/effects of amiodarone may be decreased by aminoglutethimide, carbamazepine, nafcillin, nevirapine, phenobarbital, phenytoin, rifampin, rifapentine, secobarbital, and other CYP2C8 inducers and CYP3A4 inducers. Amiodarone may decrease the levels/effects of codeine, hydrocodone, oxycodone, tramadol, and other prodrug substrates of CYP2D6. Amiodarone may alter thyroid function and response to thyroid supplements; monitor closely.

Ethanol/Nutrition/Herb Interactions
Food: Increases the rate and extent of absorption of amiodarone. Grapefruit juice increases bioavailability of oral amiodarone by 50% and decreases the conversion of amiodarone to N-DEA (active metabolite); altered effects are possible; use should be avoided during therapy.

Herb/Nutraceutical: St John's wort may decrease amiodarone levels or enhance photosensitization. Avoid ephedra (may worsen arrhythmia). Avoid dong quai.

Stability Store at room temperature; protect from light. When admixed in D_5W to a final concentration of 1-6 mg/mL, the solution is stable at room temperature for 24 hours in polyolefin or glass, or for 2 hours in PVC. Infusions >2 hours must be administered in glass or polyolefin bottles.

Mechanism of Action Class III antiarrhythmic agent which inhibits adrenergic stimulation (alpha- and beta-blocking properties), affects sodium, potassium, and calcium channels, prolongs the action potential and refractory period in myocardial tissue; decreases AV conduction and sinus node function

Pharmacodynamics/Kinetics
Onset of action: Oral: 2 days to 3 weeks; I.V.: May be more rapid
Peak effect: 1 week to 5 months
Duration after discontinuing therapy: 7-50 days
Note: Mean onset of effect and duration after discontinuation may be shorter in children than adults
Distribution: V_d: 66 L/kg (range: 18-148 L/kg); crosses placenta; enters breast milk in concentrations higher than maternal plasma concentrations
Protein binding: 96%
Metabolism: Hepatic via CYP2C8 and 3A4 to active N-desethylamiodarone metabolite; possible enterohepatic recirculation
Bioavailability: Oral: ~50%
Half-life elimination: Terminal: 40-55 days (range: 26-107 days); shorter in children than adults
Excretion: Feces; urine (<1% as unchanged drug)

Dosage Note: Lower loading and maintenance doses are preferable in women and all patients with low body weight.

Oral:
  Children: Arrhythmias (unlabeled use):
    Loading dose: 10-20 mg/kg/day in 1-2 doses for 4-14 days or until adequate control of arrhythmia or prominent adverse effects occur; alternative loading dose in children <1 year: 600-800 mg/1.73 m²/day in 1-2 divided doses/day
    Maintenance dose: Dose may be reduced to 5 mg/kg/day for several weeks (or 200-400 mg/1.73 m²/day given once daily); if no recurrence of arrhythmia, dose may be further reduced to 2.5 mg/kg/day; maintenance doses may be given 5-7 days/week

  Adults:
    Ventricular arrhythmias: 800-1600 mg/day in 1-2 doses for 1-3 weeks, then when adequate arrhythmia control is achieved, decrease to 600-800 mg/day in 1-2 doses for 1 month; maintenance: 400 mg/day. Lower doses are recommended for supraventricular arrhythmias.
    Prophylaxis of atrial fibrillation following open heart surgery (unlabeled use): 400 mg twice daily (starting in postop recovery) for up to 7 days. An alternative regimen of amiodarone 600 mg/day for 7 days prior to surgery, followed by 200 mg/day until hospital discharge, has also been shown to decrease the risk of postoperative atrial fibrillation. **Note:** A variety of regimens have been used in clinical trials.
    Recurrent atrial fibrillation (unlabeled use): No standard regimen defined; examples of regimens include: Initial: 10 mg/kg/day for 14 days; followed by 300 mg/day for 4 weeks, followed by maintenance dosage of 100-200 mg/day (Roy D, 2000). Other regimens have been described and are used clinically (ie, 400 mg 3 times/day for 5-7 days, then 400 mg/day for 1 month, then 200 mg/day).

  I.V.:
    Children:
      Arrhythmias (unlabeled use, dosing based on limited data): Loading dose: 5 mg/kg over 30 minutes; may repeat up to 3 times if no response. Maintenance dose: 2-20 mg/kg/day (5-15 mcg/kg/minute) by continuous infusion
      Note: I.V. administration at low flow rates (potentially associated with use in pediatrics) may result in leaching of plasticizers (DEHP) from intravenous tubing. DEHP may

(Continued)

Amiodarone (Continued)

adversely affect male reproductive tract development. Alternative means of dosing and administration (1 mg/kg aliquots) may need to be considered.

Pulseless VF or VT (PALS dosing): 5 mg/kg rapid I.V. bolus or I.O.; repeat up to a maximum dose of 15 mg/kg (300 mg)

Perfusing tachycardias (PALS dosing): Loading dose: 5 mg/kg I.V. over 20-60 minutes or I.O.; may repeat up to maximum dose of 15 mg/kg/day

Adults:

Breakthrough VF or VT: 150 mg supplemental doses in 100 mL D_5W over 10 minutes

Pulseless VF or VT: I.V. push: Initial: 300 mg in 20-30 mL NS or D_5W; if VF or VT recurs, supplemental dose of 150 mg followed by infusion of 1 mg/minute for 6 hours, then 0.5 mg/minute (maximum daily dose: 2.1 g)

Prophylaxis of atrial fibrillation following open heart surgery (unlabeled use): 1000 mg infused over 24 hours (starting at postop recovery) for 2 days has been shown to reduce the risk of postoperative atrial fibrillation. **Note:** A variety of regimens have been used in clinical trials.

Stable VT or SVT (unlabeled use): First 24 hours: 1050 mg according to following regimen

Step 1: 150 mg (100 mL) over first 10 minutes (mix 3 mL in 100 mL D_5W)

Step 2: 360 mg (200 mL) over next 6 hours (mix 18 mL in 500 mL D_5W): 1 mg/minute

Step 3: 540 mg (300 mL) over next 18 hours: 0.5 mg/minute

Note: After the first 24 hours: 0.5 mg/minute utilizing concentration of 1-6 mg/mL

Note: When switching from I.V. to oral therapy, use the following as a guide:

<1-week I.V. infusion: 800-1600 mg/day

1- to 3-week I.V. infusion: 600-800 mg/day

>3-week I.V. infusion: 400 mg/day

Recommendations for conversion to intravenous amiodarone after oral administration: During long-term amiodarone therapy (ie, ≥4 months), the mean plasma-elimination half-life of the active metabolite of amiodarone is 61 days. Replacement therapy may not be necessary in such patients if oral therapy is discontinued for a period <2 weeks, since any changes in serum amiodarone concentrations during this period may **not** be clinically significant.

Elderly: No specific guidelines available. Dose selection should be cautious, at low end of dosage range, and titration should be slower to evaluate response.

Hemodialysis: Not dialyzable (0% to 5%); supplemental dose is not necessary.

Peritoneal dialysis effects: Not dialyzable (0% to 5%); supplemental dose is not necessary.

Dosing adjustment in hepatic impairment: Dosage adjustment is probably necessary in substantial hepatic impairment. No specific guidelines available. If hepatic enzymes exceed 3 times normal or double in a patient with an elevated baseline, consider decreasing the dose or discontinuing amiodarone.

Dietary Considerations Administer consistently with regard to meals. Amiodarone is a potential source of large amounts of inorganic iodine; ~3 mg of inorganic iodine per 100 mg of amiodarone is released into the systemic circulation. Recommended daily allowance for iodine in adults is 150 mcg.

Grapefruit juice is not recommended.

Administration

Oral: Administer consistently with regard to meals. Take in divided doses with meals if high daily dose or if GI upset occurs. If GI intolerance occurs with single-dose therapy, use twice daily dosing.

I.V.: Adjust administration rate to urgency (give more slowly when perfusing arrhythmia present). Give I.V. therapy using an infusion pump at a concentration <2 mg/mL. Slow the infusion rate if hypotension or bradycardia develops. Infusions >2 hours must be administered in glass or polyolefin bottles. **Note:** I.V. administration at lower flow rates (potentially associated with use in pediatrics) and higher concentrations than recommended may result in leaching of plasticizers (DEHP) from intravenous tubing. DEHP may adversely affect male reproductive tract development. Alternative means of dosing and administration (1 mg/kg aliquots) may need to be considered. Use only volumetric infusion pump; use of drop counting may lead to under-dosing. Administer through I.V. line with in-line filter.

Monitoring Parameters Blood pressure, heart rate (ECG) and rhythm throughout therapy; assess patient for signs of lethargy, edema of the hands or feet, weight loss, and pulmonary toxicity (baseline pulmonary function tests); liver function tests; monitor serum electrolytes, especially potassium and magnesium. Assess thyroid function tests before initiation of treatment and then periodically thereafter (some experts suggest every 3-6 months). If signs or symptoms of thyroid disease or arrhythmia breakthrough/exacerbation occur then immediate re-evaluation is necessary. Amiodarone partially inhibits the peripheral conversion of thyroxine (T_4) to triiodothyronine (T_3); serum T_4 and reverse triiodothyronine (rT_3) concentrations may be increased and serum T_3 may be decreased; most patients remain clinically euthyroid, however, clinical hypothyroidism or hyperthyroidism may occur.

Perform regular ophthalmic exams.

Reference Range Therapeutic: 0.5-2.5 mg/L (SI: 1-4 μmol/L) (parent); desethyl metabolite is active and is present in equal concentration to parent drug

Dosage Forms [DSC] = Discontinued product

Injection, solution, as hydrochloride: 50 mg/mL (3 mL, 9 mL, 18 mL) [contains benzyl alcohol and polysorbate (Tween®) 80] [DSC]

Cordarone®: 50 mg/mL (3 mL) [contains benzyl alcohol and polysorbate (Tween®) 80]

Tablet, as hydrochloride [scored]: 200 mg, 400 mg

Cordarone®: 200 mg

Pacerone®: 100 mg [not scored], 200 mg, 300 mg [DSC], 400 mg

Extemporaneous Preparations A 5 mg/mL oral suspension has been made from tablets and has an expected stability of 91 days under refrigeration; three 200 mg tablets are crushed in a mortar, 90 mL of methylcellulose 1%, and 10 mL of syrup (syrup NF [85% sucrose in water) or flavored syrup] are added in small amounts and triturated until uniform; purified water USP is used to make a quantity sufficient to 120 mL

Nahata MC and Hipple TF, *Pediatric Drug Formulations*, 2nd ed, Cincinnati, OH: Harvey Whitney Books Co, 1992.

♦ **Amiodarone Hydrochloride** *see* Amiodarone *on page 97*
♦ **Amiodarone Hydrochloride for Injection**® **(Can)** *see* Amiodarone *on page 97*
♦ **Ami-Tex LA** *see* Guaifenesin and Phenylephrine *on page 818*
♦ **Amitiza**™ *see* Lubiprostone *on page 1044*

Amitriptyline (a mee TRIP ti leen)

Canadian Brand Names Apo-Amitriptyline®; Levate®; Novo-Triptyn; PMS-Amitriptyline
Index Terms Amitriptyline Hydrochloride; Elavil
Pharmacologic Category Antidepressant, Tricyclic (Tertiary Amine)
Additional Appendix Information
Antidepressant Agents *on page 1866*
Use Relief of symptoms of depression
Unlabeled/Investigational Use Analgesic for certain chronic and neuropathic pain; prophylaxis against migraine headaches; treatment of depressive disorders in children
Restrictions An FDA-approved medication guide concerning the use of antidepressants in children and teenagers must be distributed when dispensing an outpatient prescription (new or refill) where this medication is to be used without direct supervision of a healthcare provider. Medication guides are available at http://www.fda.gov/cder/Offices/ODS/medication_guides.htm. Dispense to parents or guardians of children and teenagers receiving this medication.
Pregnancy Risk Factor C
Pregnancy Implications Teratogenic effects have been observed in animal studies. Amitriptyline crosses the human placenta; CNS effects, limb deformities and developmental delay have been noted in case reports.
Lactation Enters breast milk/not recommended (AAP rates "of concern")
Medication Safety Issues
Sound-alike/look-alike issues:
Amitriptyline may be confused with aminophylline, imipramine, nortriptyline
Elavil® may be confused with Aldoril®, Eldepryl®, enalapril, Equanil®, Mellaril®, Oruvail®, Plavix®
Contraindications Hypersensitivity to amitriptyline or any component of the formulation (cross-sensitivity with other tricyclics may occur); use of MAO inhibitors within past 14 days; acute recovery phase following myocardial infarction; concurrent use of cisapride
Warnings/Precautions [U.S. Boxed Warning]: Antidepressants increase the risk of suicidal thinking and behavior in children and adolescents with major depressive disorder (MDD) and other depressive disorders; consider risk prior to prescribing. All patients must be closely monitored for clinical worsening, suicidality, or unusual changes in behavior, especially during the initiation of therapy or following an increase or decrease in dosage. When used in children, the child's family or caregiver should be instructed to closely observe the patient and communicate condition with healthcare provider. A medication guide should be dispensed with each prescription. **Amitriptyline is not FDA approved for use in children <12 years of age.**

The possibility of a suicide attempt is inherent in major depression and may persist until remission occurs. Use caution in high-risk patients. Worsening depression and severe abrupt suicidality that are not part of the presenting symptoms may require discontinuation or modification of drug therapy. The patient's family or caregiver should be alerted to monitor patients for the emergence of suicidality and associated behaviors (such as agitation, irritability, hostility, impulsivity, and hypomania) and notify healthcare provider.

May worsen psychosis in some patients or precipitate a shift to mania or hypomania in patients with bipolar disorder. Patients presenting with depressive symptoms should be screened for bipolar disorder. Monotherapy in patients with bipolar disorder should be avoided. **Amitriptyline is not FDA approved for bipolar depression.**

The degree of sedation, anticholinergic effects, orthostasis, and conduction abnormalities are high relative to other antidepressants. Amitriptyline often causes drowsiness/sedation, resulting in impaired performance of tasks requiring alertness (eg, operating machinery or driving). Sedative effects may be additive with other CNS depressants and/or ethanol. Use with caution in patients with a history of cardiovascular disease (including previous MI, stroke, tachycardia, or conduction abnormalities). Use with caution in patients with urinary retention, benign prostatic hyperplasia, narrow-angle glaucoma, xerostomia, visual problems, constipation, or a history of bowel obstruction.

May alter glucose control - use with caution in patients with diabetes. May cause hyponatremia/SIADH. Consider discontinuing, when possible, prior to elective surgery. Therapy should not be abruptly discontinued in patients receiving high doses for prolonged periods. May lower seizure threshold - use caution in patients with a previous seizure disorder or condition predisposing to seizures such as brain damage, alcoholism, or concurrent therapy with other drugs which lower the seizure threshold. May increase the risks associated with electroconvulsive therapy. Use with caution in hyperthyroid patients or those receiving thyroid supplementation. Use with caution in patients with hepatic or renal dysfunction and in elderly patients.

Adverse Reactions Anticholinergic effects may be pronounced; moderate to marked sedation can occur (tolerance to these effects usually occurs).

Frequency not defined.
Cardiovascular: Orthostatic hypotension, tachycardia, ECG changes (nonspecific), AV conduction changes, cardiomyopathy (rare), MI, stroke, heart block, arrhythmia, syncope, hypertension, palpitation
Central nervous system: Restlessness, dizziness, insomnia, sedation, fatigue, anxiety, cognitive function impaired, seizure, extrapyramidal symptoms, coma, hallucinations, confusion, disorientation, coordination impaired, ataxia, headache, nightmares, hyperpyrexia
(Continued)

Amitriptyline *(Continued)*

Dermatologic: Allergic rash, urticaria, photosensitivity, alopecia

Endocrine & metabolic: Syndrome of inappropriate ADH secretion

Gastrointestinal: Weight gain, xerostomia, constipation, paralytic ileus, nausea, vomiting, anorexia, stomatitis, peculiar taste, diarrhea, black tongue

Genitourinary: Urinary retention

Hematologic: Bone marrow depression, purpura, eosinophilia

Neuromuscular & skeletal: Numbness, paresthesia, peripheral neuropathy, tremor, weakness

Ocular: Blurred vision, mydriasis, ocular pressure increased

Otic: Tinnitus

Miscellaneous: Diaphoresis, withdrawal reactions (nausea, headache, malaise)

Postmarketing and/or case reports: Neuroleptic malignant syndrome (rare), serotonin syndrome (rare)

Overdosage/Toxicology Symptoms include agitation, confusion, hallucinations, urinary retention, hypothermia, hypotension, ventricular tachycardia, and seizures. Following initiation of essential overdose management, toxic symptoms should be treated. Sodium bicarbonate is indicated when the QRS interval is >0.10 seconds or the QT_c is >0.42 seconds. Ventricular arrhythmias often respond to phenytoin 15-20 mg/kg (adults) with concurrent systemic alkalinization (sodium bicarbonate 0.5-2 mEq/kg I.V.). Arrhythmias unresponsive to this therapy may respond to lidocaine 1 mg/kg I.V. followed by a titrated infusion. Physostigmine (1-2 mg slow I.V. for adults or 0.5 mg slow I.V. for children) may be indicated in reversing cardiac arrhythmias that are due to vagal blockade, or for anticholinergic effects, but should only be used as a last measure in life-threatening situations. Seizures usually respond to diazepam I.V. boluses (5-10 mg for adults up to 30 mg or 0.25-0.4 mg/kg/dose for children up to 10 mg/dose). If seizures are unresponsive or recur, phenytoin or phenobarbital may be required.

Drug Interactions

Cytochrome P450 Effect: Substrate of CYP1A2 (minor), 2B6 (minor), 2C9 (minor), 2C19 (minor), 2D6 (major), 3A4 (minor); **Inhibits** CYP1A2 (weak), 2C9 (weak), 2C19 (weak), 2D6 (weak), 2E1 (weak)

Increased Effect/Toxicity: Amitriptyline increases the effects of amphetamines, anticholinergics, other CNS depressants (sedatives, hypnotics, or ethanol), carbamazepine, tolazamide, chlorpropamide, and warfarin. When used with MAO inhibitors, hyperpyrexia, hypertension, tachycardia, confusion, seizures, and **deaths have been reported** (serotonin syndrome). Serotonin syndrome has also been reported with ritonavir (rare). Levels/effects of amitriptyline may be increased by chlorpromazine, delavirdine, fluoxetine, miconazole, paroxetine, pergolide, quinidine, quinine, ritonavir, ropinirole, and other CYP2D6 inhibitors. Cimetidine, fenfluramine, grapefruit juice, indinavir, methylphenidate, diltiazem, valproate, and verapamil may increase the serum concentrations of tricyclic antidepressants (TCAs). Use of lithium with a TCA may increase the risk for neurotoxicity. Phenothiazines may increase concentration of some TCAs and TCAs may increase the concentration of phenothiazines. Pressor response to I.V. epinephrine, norepinephrine, and phenylephrine may be enhanced in patients receiving TCAs. (**Note:** Effect is unlikely with epinephrine or levonordefrin dosages typically administered as infiltration in combination with local anesthetics.) Combined use of beta-agonists or drugs which prolong QT_c (including quinidine, procainamide, disopyramide, cisapride, sparfloxacin, gatifloxacin, moxifloxacin) with TCAs may predispose patients to cardiac arrhythmias.

Decreased Effect: Amitriptyline inhibits the antihypertensive response to bethanidine, clonidine, debrisoquin, guanadrel, guanethidine, guanabenz, or guanfacine. Cholestyramine and colestipol may bind TCAs and reduce their absorption.

Ethanol/Nutrition/Herb Interactions

Ethanol: Avoid ethanol (may increase CNS depression).

Food: Grapefruit juice may inhibit the metabolism of some TCAs and clinical toxicity may result.

Herb/Nutraceutical: St John's wort may decrease amitriptyline levels. Avoid valerian, St John's wort, kava kava, gotu kola (may increase CNS depression).

Stability Protect injection and Elavil® 10 mg tablets from light.

Mechanism of Action Increases the synaptic concentration of serotonin and/or norepinephrine in the central nervous system by inhibition of their reuptake by the presynaptic neuronal membrane

Pharmacodynamics/Kinetics

Onset of action: Migraine prophylaxis: 6 weeks, higher dosage may be required in heavy smokers because of increased metabolism; Depression: 4-6 weeks, reduce dosage to lowest effective level

Distribution: Crosses placenta; enters breast milk

Metabolism: Hepatic to nortriptyline (active), hydroxy and conjugated derivatives; may be impaired in the elderly

Half-life elimination: Adults: 9-27 hours (average: 15 hours)

Time to peak, serum: ~4 hours

Excretion: Urine (18% as unchanged drug); feces (small amounts)

Dosage

Children:

Chronic pain management (unlabeled use): Oral: Initial: 0.1 mg/kg at bedtime, may advance as tolerated over 2-3 weeks to 0.5-2 mg/kg at bedtime

Depressive disorders (unlabeled use): Oral: Initial doses of 1 mg/kg/day given in 3 divided doses with increases to 1.5 mg/kg/day have been reported in a small number of children (n=9) 9-12 years of age; clinically, doses up to 3 mg/kg/day (5 mg/kg/day if monitored closely) have been proposed

Migraine prophylaxis (unlabeled use): Oral: Initial: 0.25 mg/kg/day, given at bedtime; increase dose by 0.25 mg/kg/day to maximum 1 mg/kg/day. Reported dosing ranges: 0.1-2 mg/kg/day; maximum suggested dose: 10 mg.

Adolescents: Depressive disorders: Oral: Initial: 25-50 mg/day; may administer in divided doses; increase gradually to 100 mg/day in divided doses

Adults:
Depression:
Oral: 50-150 mg/day single dose at bedtime or in divided doses; dose may be gradually increased up to 300 mg/day
Migraine prophylaxis (unlabeled use): Oral: Initial: 10-25 mg at bedtime; usual dose: 150 mg; reported dosing ranges: 10-400 mg/day
Pain management (unlabeled use): Oral: Initial: 25 mg at bedtime; may increase as tolerated to 100 mg/day
Elderly: Depression: Oral: Initial: 10-25 mg at bedtime; dose should be increased in 10-25 mg increments every week if tolerated; dose range: 25-150 mg/day
Dosing interval in hepatic impairment: Use with caution and monitor plasma levels and patient response
Hemodialysis: Nondialyzable
Monitoring Parameters Monitor blood pressure and pulse rate prior to and during initial therapy; evaluate mental status; monitor weight; ECG in older adults and patients with cardiac disease
Reference Range Therapeutic: Amitriptyline and nortriptyline 100-250 ng/mL (SI: 360-900 nmol/L); nortriptyline 50-150 ng/mL (SI: 190-570 nmol/L); Toxic: >0.5 mcg/mL; plasma levels do not always correlate with clinical effectiveness
Test Interactions May cause false-positive reaction to EMIT immunoassay for imipramine
Dosage Forms
Tablet, as hydrochloride: 10 mg, 25 mg, 50 mg, 75 mg, 100 mg, 150 mg

Amitriptyline and Chlordiazepoxide
(a mee TRIP ti leen & klor dye az e POKS ide)

U.S. Brand Names Limbitrol®; Limbitrol® DS
Canadian Brand Names Limbitrol®
Index Terms Chlordiazepoxide and Amitriptyline Hydrochloride
Pharmacologic Category Antidepressant, Tricyclic (Tertiary Amine); Benzodiazepine
Use Treatment of moderate to severe anxiety and/or agitation and depression
Restrictions C-IV
An FDA-approved medication guide concerning the use of antidepressants in children and teenagers must be distributed when dispensing an outpatient prescription (new or refill) where this medication is to be used without direct supervision of a healthcare provider. Medication guides are available at http://www.fda.gov/cder/Offices/ODS/medication_guides.htm. Dispense to parents or guardians of children and teenagers receiving this medication.
Pregnancy Risk Factor D
Dosage Initial: 3-4 tablets in divided doses; this may be increased to 6 tablets/day as required; some patients respond to smaller doses and can be maintained on 2 tablets
Additional Information Complete prescribing information for this medication should be consulted for additional detail.
Dosage Forms
Tablet: 12.5/5: Amitriptyline hydrochloride 12.5 mg and chlordiazepoxide 5 mg; 25/10: Amitriptyline hydrochloride 25 mg and chlordiazepoxide 10 mg
Limbitrol®: 12.5/5: Amitriptyline hydrochloride 12.5 mg and chlordiazepoxide 5 mg
Limbitrol® DS: 25/10: Amitriptyline hydrochloride 25 mg and chlordiazepoxide 10 mg

Amitriptyline and Perphenazine (a mee TRIP ti leen & per FEN a zeen)

Canadian Brand Names Etrafon®
Index Terms Perphenazine and Amitriptyline Hydrochloride
Pharmacologic Category Antidepressant, Tricyclic (Tertiary Amine); Antipsychotic Agent, Typical, Phenothiazine
Use Treatment of patients with moderate to severe anxiety and depression
Unlabeled/Investigational Use Depression with psychotic features
Restrictions An FDA-approved medication guide concerning the use of antidepressants in children and teenagers must be distributed when dispensing an outpatient prescription (new or refill) where this medication is to be used without direct supervision of a healthcare provider. Medication guides are available at http://www.fda.gov/cder/Offices/ODS/medication_guides.htm. Dispense to parents or guardians of children and teenagers receiving this medication.
Pregnancy Risk Factor D
Dosage Oral: 1 tablet 2-4 times/day
Additional Information Complete prescribing information for this medication should be consulted for additional detail.
Dosage Forms Tablet:
2-10: Amitriptyline hydrochloride 10 mg and perphenazine 2 mg
2-25: Amitriptyline hydrochloride 25 mg and perphenazine 2 mg
4-10: Amitriptyline hydrochloride 10 mg and perphenazine 4 mg
4-25: Amitriptyline hydrochloride 25 mg and perphenazine 4 mg
4-50: Amitriptyline hydrochloride 50 mg and perphenazine 4 mg

♦ **Amitriptyline Hydrochloride** see Amitriptyline on page 101

♦ **AMJ 9701** see Palifermin on page 1298

Amlexanox (am LEKS an oks)

U.S. Brand Names Aphthasol®
Pharmacologic Category Anti-inflammatory, Locally Applied
Use Treatment of aphthous ulcers (ie, canker sores)
(Continued)

Amlexanox *(Continued)*

Unlabeled/Investigational Use Allergic disorders

Pregnancy Risk Factor B

Dosage Topical: Administer (0.5 cm - ¼") directly on ulcers 4 times/day following oral hygiene, after meals, and at bedtime

Additional Information Complete prescribing information for this medication should be consulted for additional detail.

Dosage Forms Paste: 5% (5 g) [contains benzyl alcohol]

Amlodipine *(am LOE di peen)*

U.S. Brand Names Norvasc®

Canadian Brand Names Norvasc®

Index Terms Amlodipine Besylate

Pharmacologic Category Calcium Channel Blocker

Additional Appendix Information
Calcium Channel Blockers *on page 1878*

Use Treatment of hypertension; treatment of symptomatic chronic stable angina, vasospastic (Prinzmetal's) angina (confirmed or suspected); prevention of hospitalization due to angina with documented CAD (limited to patients without heart failure or ejection fraction <40%)

Pregnancy Risk Factor C

Pregnancy Implications Embryotoxic effects have been demonstrated in small animals. No well-controlled studies have been conducted in pregnant women. Use in pregnancy only when clearly needed and when the benefits outweigh the potential hazard to the fetus.

Lactation Excretion in breast milk unknown/not recommended

Medication Safety Issues
Sound-alike/look-alike issues:
Amlodipine may be confused with amiloride
Norvasc® may be confused with Navane®, Norvir®, Vascor®

Contraindications Hypersensitivity to amlodipine or any component of the formulation

Warnings/Precautions Increased angina and/or MI has occurred with initiation or dosage titration of calcium channel blockers. Symptomatic hypotension with or without syncope can rarely occur; blood pressure must be lowered at a rate appropriate for the patient's clinical condition. Use caution in severe aortic stenosis and/or hypertrophic cardiomyopathy. Use caution in patients with hepatic impairment. The most common side effect is peripheral edema; occurs within 2-3 weeks of starting therapy. Reflex tachycardia may occur with use. Dosage titration should occur after 7-14 days on a given dose. Initiate at a lower dose in the elderly. Safety and efficacy have not been established in children <6 years of age.

Adverse Reactions
>10%: Cardiovascular: Peripheral edema (2% to 15% dose related)
1% to 10%:
Cardiovascular: Flushing (1% to 3%), palpitation (1% to 4%)
Central nervous system: Headache (7%; similar to placebo 8%), dizziness (1% to 3%), fatigue (4%), somnolence (1% to 2%)
Dermatologic: Rash (1% to 2%), pruritus (1% to 2%)
Endocrine & metabolic: Male sexual dysfunction (1% to 2%)
Gastrointestinal: Nausea (3%), abdominal pain (1% to 2%), dyspepsia (1% to 2%), gingival hyperplasia
Neuromuscular & skeletal: Muscle cramps (1% to 2%), weakness (1% to 2%)
Respiratory: Dyspnea (1% to 2%), pulmonary edema (15% from PRAISE trial, CHF population)
<1% (Limited to important or life-threatening): Abnormal dreams, agitation alopecia, amnesia, anxiety, apathy, arrhythmia, ataxia, bradycardia, cardiac failure, cholestasis, depersonalization, depression, erythema multiforme, exfoliative dermatitis, extrapyramidal symptoms, gastritis, gynecomastia, hepatitis, hypotension, jaundice, leukocytoclastic vasculitis, migraine, nonthrombocytopenic purpura, paresthesia, peripheral ischemia, photosensitivity, postural hypotension, purpura, rash, skin discoloration, Stevens-Johnson syndrome, syncope, thrombocytopenia, tinnitus, transaminases increased, urticaria, weight loss, vertigo, xerophthalmia

Overdosage/Toxicology Primary cardiac symptoms of calcium blocker overdose include hypotension and bradycardia. Hypotension is caused by peripheral vasodilation, myocardial depression, and bradycardia. Bradycardia results from sinus bradycardia, second- or third-degree atrioventricular block, or sinus arrest with junctional rhythm. Intraventricular conduction is usually not affected, so QRS duration is normal (verapamil prolongs the PR interval and bepridil prolongs the QT interval and may cause ventricular arrhythmias, including torsade de pointes).

Noncardiac symptoms include confusion, stupor, nausea, vomiting, metabolic acidosis, and hyperglycemia. Following initial gastric decontamination, if possible, repeated calcium administration may promptly reverse depressed cardiac contractility (but not sinus node depression or peripheral vasodilation). Glucagon, epinephrine, and inamrinone (amrinone) may treat refractory hypotension. Glucagon and epinephrine also increase the heart rate (outside the U.S., 4-aminopyridine may be available as an antidote). Dialysis and hemoperfusion are not effective in enhancing elimination, although repeat-dose activated charcoal may serve as an adjunct with sustained-release preparations.

In a few reported cases, overdose with calcium channel blockers has been associated with hypotension and bradycardia, initially refractory to atropine, but becoming more responsive to this agent when larger doses (approaching 1 g/hour for more than 24 hours) of calcium chloride were administered.

Drug Interactions
Cytochrome P450 Effect: Substrate of CYP3A4 (major); **Inhibits** CYP1A2 (moderate), 2A6 (weak), 2B6 (weak), 2C8 (weak), 2C9 (weak), 2D6 (weak), 3A4 (weak)

Increased Effect/Toxicity: Amlodipine may increase the levels/effects of aminophylline, fluvoxamine, mexiletine, mirtazapine, ropinirole, theophylline, trifluoperazine and other CYP1A2 substrates. Levels/effects of amlodipine may be increased by azole antifungals, clarithromycin, diclofenac, doxycycline, erythromycin, imatinib, isoniazid, nefazodone, nicardipine, propofol, protease inhibitors, quinidine, telithromycin, verapamil, and other CYP3A4 inhibitors. Cyclosporine levels may be increased by amlodipine. Blood pressure-lowering effects of sildenafil, tadalafil, and vardenafil are additive with amlodipine (use caution).

Decreased Effect: Calcium may reduce the calcium channel blocker's hypotensive effects. Levels/effects of amlodipine may be decreased by aminoglutethimide, carbamazepine, nafcillin, nevirapine, phenobarbital, phenytoin, rifamycins, and other CYP3A4 inducers.

Ethanol/Nutrition/Herb Interactions
Food: Grapefruit juice may modestly increase amlodipine levels.
Herb/Nutraceutical: St John's wort may decrease amlodipine levels. Avoid dong quai if using for hypertension (has estrogenic activity). Avoid ephedra, yohimbe, ginseng (may worsen hypertension). Avoid garlic (may have increased antihypertensive effects).

Stability Store at room temperature of 15°C to 30°C (59°F to 86°F).

Mechanism of Action Inhibits calcium ion from entering the "slow channels" or select voltage-sensitive areas of vascular smooth muscle and myocardium during depolarization, producing a relaxation of coronary vascular smooth muscle and coronary vasodilation; increases myocardial oxygen delivery in patients with vasospastic angina

Pharmacodynamics/Kinetics
Onset of action: Antihypertensive: 30-50 minutes
Duration of antihypertensive effect: 24 hours
Absorption: Oral: Well absorbed
Distribution: V_d: 21 L/kg
Protein binding: 93% to 98%
Metabolism: Hepatic (>90%) to inactive metabolite
Bioavailability: 64% to 90%
Half-life elimination: 30-50 hours; increased with hepatic dysfunction
Time to peak, plasma: 6-12 hours
Excretion: Urine (10% as parent, 60% as metabolite)

Dosage Oral:
Children 6-17 years: Hypertension: 2.5-5 mg once daily
Adults:
Hypertension: Initial dose: 5 mg once daily; maximum dose: 10 mg once daily. In general, titrate in 2.5 mg increments over 7-14 days. Usual dosage range (JNC 7): 2.5-10 mg once daily.
Angina: Usual dose: 5-10 mg; lower dose suggested in elderly or hepatic impairment; most patients require 10 mg for adequate effect
Elderly: Dosing should start at the lower end of dosing range due to possible increased incidence of hepatic, renal, or cardiac impairment. Elderly patients also show decreased clearance of amlodipine.
Hypertension: 2.5 mg once daily
Angina: 5 mg once daily
Dialysis: Hemodialysis and peritoneal dialysis does not enhance elimination. Supplemental dose is not necessary.
Dosage adjustment in hepatic impairment:
Angina: Administer 5 mg once daily.
Hypertension: Administer 2.5 mg once daily.

Dietary Considerations May be taken without regard to meals.

Administration May be administered without regard to meals.

Dosage Forms
Tablet:
Norvasc®: 2.5 mg, 5 mg, 10 mg

Extemporaneous Preparations A 1 mg/mL suspension was stable for 91 days when refrigerated or 56 days when kept at room temperature when compounded as follows: Triturate fifty 5 mg tablets in a mortar, reduce to a fine powder. In a graduate, mix Ora-Sweet® 125 mL and Ora-Plus® 125 mL together. Add small amount of this mixture to the powder to make a paste. Add the remainder in small quantities while mixing. Shake well before using.
Nahata MC, Morosco RS, and Hipple TF, 4th ed, *Pediatric Drug Formulations*, Cincinnati, OH: Harvey Whitney Books Co, 2000.

Amlodipine and Atorvastatin (am LOW di peen & a TORE va sta tin)

U.S. Brand Names Caduet®
Canadian Brand Names Caduet®
Index Terms Atorvastatin Calcium and Amlodipine Besylate
Pharmacologic Category Antilipemic Agent, HMG-CoA Reductase Inhibitor; Calcium Channel Blocker
Use For use when treatment with both amlodipine and atorvastatin is appropriate:
Amlodipine: Treatment of hypertension; treatment of symptomatic chronic stable angina, vasospastic (Prinzmetal's) angina (confirmed or suspected); prevention of hospitalization due to angina with documented CAD (limited to patients without heart failure or ejection fraction <40%)
Atorvastatin: Treatment of dyslipidemias or primary prevention of cardiovascular disease (atherosclerotic) as detailed here:
Primary prevention of cardiovascular disease (high-risk for CVD): To reduce the risk of MI or stroke in patients without evidence of heart disease who have multiple CVD risk factors or type 2 diabetes. Treatment reduces the risk for angina or revascularization procedures in patients with multiple risk factors.
Treatment of dyslipidemias: To reduce elevations in total cholesterol, LDL-C, apolipoprotein B, and triglycerides in patients with elevations of one or more components, and/or to increase HDL-C as present in heterozygous hypercholesterolemia (Fredrickson type IIa
(Continued)

Amlodipine and Atorvastatin *(Continued)*

hyperlipidemias); treatment of primary dysbetalipoproteinemia (Fredrickson type III), elevated serum TG levels (Fredrickson type IV), and homozygous familial hypercholesterolemia

Treatment of heterozygous familial hypercholesterolemia (HeFH) in adolescent patients (10-17 years of age, females >1 year postmenarche) having LDL-C ≥190 mg/dL or LDL-C ≥160 mg/dL with positive family history of premature cardiovascular disease (CVD) or with two or more CVD risk factors.

Pregnancy Risk Factor X

Dosage Oral:

Amlodipine:

Children >10 years: Hypertension: 2.5-5 mg once daily. **Note:** Use in ages >10 years because of atorvastatin content.

Adults:

Hypertension: Initial dose: 5 mg once daily; maximum dose: 10 mg once daily; in general, titrate in 2.5 mg increments over 7-14 days. Usual dosage range (JNC 7): 2.5-10 mg once daily

Angina: Usual dose: 5-10 mg; lower dose suggested in elderly or hepatic impairment; most patients require 10 mg for adequate effect

Elderly: Dosing should start at the lower end of dosing range due to possible increased incidence of hepatic, renal, or cardiac impairment. Elderly patients also show decreased clearance of amlodipine.

Hypertension: 2.5 mg once daily

Angina: 5 mg once daily

Atorvastatin:

Children 10-17 years (females >1 year postmenarche): HeFH: 10 mg once daily (maximum: 20 mg/day)

Adults:

Hyperlipidemias: Initial: 10-20 mg once daily; patients requiring >45% reduction in LDL-C may be started at 40 mg once daily; range: 10-80 mg once daily

Primary prevention of CVD: 10 mg once daily

Dosage adjustment in renal impairment: No dosage adjustment is necessary.

Dosage adjustment in hepatic impairment: Do not use in active liver disease.

Additional Information Complete prescribing information for this medication should be consulted for additional detail.

Dosage Forms Tablet:

2.5/10: Amlodipine 2.5 mg and atorvastatin 10 mg

2.5/20: Amlodipine 2.5 mg and atorvastatin 20 mg

2.5/40: Amlodipine 2.5 mg and atorvastatin 40 mg

5/10: Amlodipine 5 mg and atorvastatin 10 mg

5/20: Amlodipine 5 mg and atorvastatin 20 mg

5/40: Amlodipine 5 mg and atorvastatin 40 mg

5/80: Amlodipine 5 mg and atorvastatin 80 mg

10/10: Amlodipine 10 mg and atorvastatin 10 mg

10/20: Amlodipine 10 mg and atorvastatin 20 mg

10/40: Amlodipine 10 mg and atorvastatin 40 mg

10/80: Amlodipine 10 mg and atorvastatin 80 mg

Amlodipine and Benazepril *(am LOE di peen & ben AY ze pril)*

U.S. Brand Names Lotrel®

Index Terms Benazepril Hydrochloride and Amlodipine Besylate

Pharmacologic Category Antihypertensive Agent, Combination

Use Treatment of hypertension

Pregnancy Risk Factor C/D (2nd and 3rd trimesters)

Dosage Oral:

Adults: 2.5-10 mg (amlodipine) and 10-40 mg (benazepril) once daily; maximum: Amlodipine: 10 mg/day; benazepril: 40 mg/day

Elderly: Initial dose: 2.5 mg based on amlodipine component

Dosage adjustment in renal impairment: Cl$_{cr}$ ≤30 mL/minute: Use of combination product is not recommended.

Dosage adjustment in hepatic impairment: Initial dose: 2.5 mg based on amlodipine component

Additional Information Complete prescribing information for this medication should be consulted for additional detail.

Dosage Forms Capsule:

Lotrel® 2.5/10: Amlodipine 2.5 mg and benazepril hydrochloride 10 mg

Lotrel® 5/10: Amlodipine 5 mg and benazepril hydrochloride 10 mg

Lotrel® 5/20: Amlodipine 5 mg and benazepril hydrochloride 20 mg

Lotrel® 5/40: Amlodipine 5 mg and benazepril hydrochloride 40 mg

Lotrel® 10/20: Amlodipine 10 mg and benazepril hydrochloride 20 mg

Lotrel® 10/40: Amlodipine 10 mg and benazepril hydrochloride 40 mg

♦ **Amlodipine Besylate** *see* Amlodipine *on page 104*

♦ **Ammens® Medicated Deodorant [OTC]** *see* Zinc Oxide *on page 1817*

♦ **Ammonapse** *see* Sodium Phenylbutyrate *on page 1582*

Ammonium Chloride *(a MOE nee um KLOR ide)*

Pharmacologic Category Electrolyte Supplement, Parenteral

Use Treatment of hypochloremic states or metabolic alkalosis

Pregnancy Risk Factor C

Pregnancy Implications Reproduction studies have not been conducted.

Contraindications Severe hepatic or renal dysfunction

Warnings/Precautions Use caution in patients with primary respiratory acidosis or pulmonary insufficiency. Safety and efficacy have not been established in children.

Adverse Reactions Frequency not defined.

Central nervous system: Headache, coma, drowsiness, EEG abnormalities, mental confusion, seizure

Dermatologic: Rash

Endocrine & metabolic: Calcium-deficient tetany, hyperchloremia, hypokalemia, metabolic acidosis, potassium and sodium may be decreased

Gastrointestinal: Abdominal pain, gastric irritation, nausea, vomiting

Hepatic: Ammonia may be increased

Local: Pain at site of injection

Neuromuscular & skeletal: Twitching

Respiratory: Hyperventilation

Overdosage/Toxicology Symptoms of overdose include abdominal pain, apnea, bradycardia, confusion, coma, diuresis, headache, hyperchloremic hypokalemic metabolic acidosis, hyperventilation, hypomagnesemia, hypovolemia, nausea, pulmonary edema, seizures, vomiting. Administer electrolytes as indicated.

Stability Prior to use, vials should be stored at controlled room temperature of 15°C to 30°C (59°F to 86°F). Solution may crystallize if exposed to low temperatures. If crystals are observed, warm vial to room temperature in a water bath prior to use. Dilute prior to use; final concentration should not exceed 1% to 2% ammonium chloride. Suggested dilution: Mix contents of 1-2 vials (100-200 mEq) in 500-1000 mL NS.

Mechanism of Action Increases acidity by increasing free hydrogen ion concentration

Pharmacodynamics/Kinetics

Metabolism: Hepatic; forms urea and hydrochloric acid

Excretion: Urine

Dosage Metabolic alkalosis: The following equations represent different methods of correction utilizing either the serum HCO_3^-, the serum chloride, or the base excess

Dosing of mEq NH_4Cl via the chloride-deficit method (hypochloremia):

Dose of mEq NH_4Cl = [0.2 L/kg x body weight (kg)] x [103 - observed serum chloride]; administer 50% of dose over 12 hours, then re-evaluate

Note: 0.2 L/kg is the estimated chloride volume of distribution and 103 is the average normal serum chloride concentration (mEq/L)

Dosing of mEq NH_4Cl via the bicarbonate-excess method (refractory hypochloremic metabolic alkalosis):

Dose of NH_4Cl = [0.5 L/kg x body weight (kg)] x (observed serum HCO_3^- - 24); administer 50% of dose over 12 hours, then re-evaluate

Note: 0.5 L/kg is the estimated bicarbonate volume of distribution and 24 is the average normal serum bicarbonate concentration (mEq/L)

These equations will yield different requirements of ammonium chloride

Administration Administer by slow intravenous infusion to avoid local irritation and adverse effects. Rate of infusion should not exceed 5 mL/minute in an adult.

Monitoring Parameters Serum bicarbonate; signs and symptoms of ammonia toxicity

Dosage Forms Injection, solution: Ammonium 5 mEq/mL and chloride 5 mEq/mL (20 mL) [equivalent to ammonium chloride 267.5 mg/mL]

♦ **Ammonul®** see Sodium Phenylacetate and Sodium Benzoate *on page 1582*

♦ **Amnesteem™** see Isotretinoin *on page 948*

Amobarbital (am oh BAR bi tal)

U.S. Brand Names Amytal®

Canadian Brand Names Amytal®

Index Terms Amobarbital Sodium; Amylobarbitone

Pharmacologic Category Barbiturate

Use Hypnotic in short-term treatment of insomnia; reduce anxiety and provide sedation preoperatively

Unlabeled/Investigational Use Therapeutic or diagnostic "Amytal® Interviewing"; Wada test

Restrictions C-II

Pregnancy Risk Factor D

Dosage

Children:

Sedative: I.M., I.V. : 6-12 years: Manufacturer's dosing range: 65- 500 mg

Hypnotic: I.M.: 2-3 mg/kg (maximum: 500 mg)

Adults:

Hypnotic: I.M., I.V.: 65-200 mg at bedtime (maximum I.M. dose: 500 mg)

Sedative: I.M., I.V.: 30-50 mg 2-3 times/day

"Amytal® interview" (unlabeled use): I.V.: 50-100 mg/minute for total dose of 200-1000 mg or until patient experiences drowsiness, impaired attention, slurred speech, or nystagmus

Wada test (unlabeled use): Intra-arterial: 100 mg over 4-5 seconds via percutaneous transfemoral catheter

Dosing adjustment in renal/hepatic impairment: Dosing should be reduced; specific recommendations not available.

Additional Information Complete prescribing information for this medication should be consulted for additional detail.

Dosage Forms Injection, powder for reconstitution, as sodium: 500 mg

Amobarbital and Secobarbital (am oh BAR bi tal & see koe BAR bi tal)

U.S. Brand Names Tuinal® [DSC]
Index Terms Amobarbital Sodium and Secobarbital Sodium; Secobarbital and Amobarbital
Pharmacologic Category Barbiturate
Use Short-term treatment of insomnia
Restrictions C-II
Pregnancy Risk Factor D
Medication Safety Issues
Sound-alike/look-alike issues:
Tuinal® may be confused with Luminal®, Tylenol®
Dosage Adults: Oral: 1-2 capsules at bedtime
Additional Information Complete prescribing information for this medication should be consulted for additional detail.
Dosage Forms Capsule: Amobarbital 50 mg and secobarbital 50 mg

♦ **Amobarbital Sodium** see Amobarbital on page 107
♦ **Amobarbital Sodium and Secobarbital Sodium** see Amobarbital and Secobarbital on page 108
♦ **Amoclan** see Amoxicillin and Clavulanate Potassium on page 112

Amoxapine (a MOKS a peen)

Index Terms Asendin [DSC]
Pharmacologic Category Antidepressant, Tricyclic (Secondary Amine)
Additional Appendix Information
Antidepressant Agents on page 1866
Use Treatment of depression, psychotic depression, depression accompanied by anxiety or agitation
Restrictions An FDA-approved medication guide concerning the use of antidepressants in children and teenagers must be distributed when dispensing an outpatient prescription (new or refill) where this medication is to be used without direct supervision of a healthcare provider. Medication guides are available at http://www.fda.gov/cder/Offices/ODS/medication_guides.htm. Dispense to parents or guardians of children and teenagers receiving this medication.
Pregnancy Risk Factor C
Lactation Enters breast milk/contraindicated (AAP rates "of concern")
Medication Safety Issues
Sound-alike/look-alike issues:
Amoxapine may be confused with amoxicillin, Amoxil®
Asendin may be confused with aspirin
Contraindications Hypersensitivity to amoxapine or any component of the formulation; use of MAO inhibitors within past 14 days; acute recovery phase following myocardial infarction
Warnings/Precautions [U.S. Boxed Warning]: Antidepressants increase the risk of suicidal thinking and behavior in children and adolescents with major depressive disorder (MDD) and other depressive disorders; consider risk prior to prescribing. All patients must be closely monitored for clinical worsening, suicidality, or unusual changes in behavior, especially during the initiation of therapy or following an increase or decrease in dosage. When used in children, the child's family or caregiver should be instructed to closely observe the patient and communicate condition with healthcare provider. A medication guide should be dispensed with each prescription. **Amoxapine is not FDA approved for use in patients <16 years of age.**

The possibility of a suicide attempt is inherent in major depression and may persist until remission occurs. Use caution in high-risk patients. Worsening depression and severe abrupt suicidality that are not part of the presenting symptoms may require discontinuation or modification of drug therapy. The patient's family or caregiver should be alerted to monitor patients for the emergence of suicidality and associated behaviors (such as agitation, irritability, hostility, impulsivity, and hypomania) and notify the healthcare provider.

May worsen psychosis in some patients or precipitate a shift to mania or hypomania in patients with bipolar disorder. Patients presenting with depressive symptoms should be screened for bipolar disorder. Monotherapy in patients with bipolar disorder should be avoided. **Amoxapine is not FDA approved for bipolar depression.** May cause extrapyramidal symptoms, including pseudoparkinsonism, acute dystonic reactions, akathisia, and tardive dyskinesia (risk of these reactions is low). May be associated with neuroleptic malignant syndrome.

The degree of sedation, anticholinergic effects, orthostasis, and conduction abnormalities are moderate relative to other antidepressants. May cause drowsiness/sedation, resulting in impaired performance of tasks requiring alertness (eg, operating machinery or driving). Sedative effects may be additive with other CNS depressants and/or ethanol. Use with caution in patients with a history of cardiovascular disease (including previous MI, stroke, tachycardia, or conduction abnormalities). Use with caution in patients with urinary retention, benign prostatic hyperplasia, narrow-angle glaucoma, xerostomia, visual problems, constipation, or a history of bowel obstruction.

Consider discontinuing, when possible, prior to elective surgery. Therapy should not be abruptly discontinued in patients receiving high doses for prolonged periods. May lower seizure threshold - use caution in patients with a previous seizure disorder or condition predisposing to seizures such as brain damage, alcoholism, or concurrent therapy with other drugs which lower the seizure threshold. May increase the risks associated with electroconvulsive therapy. Use with caution in hyperthyroid patients or those receiving thyroid supplementation. Use with caution in patients with hepatic or renal dysfunction and in elderly patients.

Adverse Reactions
>10%:
    Central nervous system: Drowsiness
    Gastrointestinal: Xerostomia, constipation
1% to 10%:
    Central nervous system: Dizziness, headache, confusion, nervousness, restlessness, insomnia, ataxia, excitement, anxiety
    Dermatologic: Edema, skin rash
    Endocrine: Prolactin levels increased
    Gastrointestinal: Nausea
    Neuromuscular & skeletal: Tremor, weakness
    Ocular: Blurred vision
    Miscellaneous: Diaphoresis
<1% (Limited to important or life-threatening): Agranulocytosis, allergic reactions, diarrhea, extrapyramidal symptoms, galactorrhea, hypertension, impotence, incoordination, intraocular pressure increased, leukopenia, menstrual irregularity, mydriasis, neuroleptic malignant syndrome, numbness, painful ejaculation, paresthesia, photosensitivity, seizure, SIADH, syncope, tardive dyskinesia, testicular edema, tinnitus, urinary retention, vomiting

Overdosage/Toxicology Symptoms include grand mal convulsions, acidosis, coma, and renal failure. Following initiation of essential overdose management, toxic symptoms should be treated. Sodium bicarbonate is indicated when the QRS interval is >0.10 seconds or the QT_c is >0.42 seconds. Ventricular arrhythmias often respond to phenytoin 15-20 mg/kg (adults) with concurrent systemic alkalinization (sodium bicarbonate 0.5-2 mEq/kg I.V.). Arrhythmias unresponsive to this therapy may respond to lidocaine 1 mg/kg I.V. followed by a titrated infusion. Physostigmine (1-2 mg slow I.V. for adults or 0.5 mg slow I.V. for children) may be indicated in reversing cardiac arrhythmias that are due to vagal blockade, or for anticholinergic effects, but should only be used as a last measure in life-threatening situations. Seizures usually respond to diazepam I.V. boluses (5-10 mg for adults up to 30 mg or 0.25-0.4 mg/kg/dose for children up to 10 mg/dose). If seizures are unresponsive or recur, phenytoin or phenobarbital may be required.

Drug Interactions
    Cytochrome P450 Effect: Substrate of CYP2D6 (major)
    Increased Effect/Toxicity: Amoxapine increases the effects of amphetamines, anticholinergics, other CNS depressants (sedatives, hypnotics, or ethanol), chlorpropamide, tolazamide, and warfarin. When used with MAO inhibitors, hyperpyrexia, hypertension, tachycardia, confusion, seizures, and **deaths have been reported** (serotonin syndrome). Serotonin syndrome has also been reported with ritonavir (rare). CYP2D6 inhibitors may increase the levels/effects of amoxapine; example inhibitors include chlorpromazine, delavirdine, fluoxetine, miconazole, paroxetine, pergolide, quinidine, quinine, ritonavir, and ropinirole. Use of lithium with a TCA may increase the risk for neurotoxicity. Phenothiazines may increase concentration of some TCAs and TCAs may increase the concentration of phenothiazines. Pressor response to I.V. epinephrine, norepinephrine, and phenylephrine may be enhanced in patients receiving TCAs (**Note:** Effect is unlikely with epinephrine or levonordefrin dosages typically administered as infiltration in combination with local anesthetics). Combined use of beta-agonists or drugs which prolong QT_c (including quinidine, procainamide, disopyramide, cisapride, sparfloxacin, gatifloxacin, moxifloxacin) with TCAs may predispose patients to cardiac arrhythmias.

    Decreased Effect: Amoxapine inhibits the antihypertensive effects of bethanidine, clonidine, debrisoquin, guanadrel, guanethidine, guanabenz, or guanfacine. Cholestyramine and colestipol may bind TCAs and reduce their absorption.

Ethanol/Nutrition/Herb Interactions
    Ethanol: Avoid ethanol (may increase CNS depression).
    Food: Grapefruit juice may inhibit the metabolism of some TCAs and clinical toxicity may result.
    Herb/Nutraceutical: Avoid valerian, St John's wort, SAMe, kava kava.

Mechanism of Action Reduces the reuptake of serotonin and norepinephrine. The metabolite, 7-OH-amoxapine has significant dopamine receptor blocking activity similar to haloperidol.

Pharmacodynamics/Kinetics
    Onset of antidepressant effect: Usually occurs after 1-2 weeks, but may require 4-6 weeks
    Absorption: Rapid and well absorbed
    Distribution: V_d: 0.9-1.2 L/kg; enters breast milk
    Protein binding: 80%
    Metabolism: Primarily hepatic
    Half-life elimination: Parent drug: 11-16 hours; Active metabolite (8-hydroxy): Adults: 30 hours
    Time to peak, serum: 1-2 hours
    Excretion: Urine (as unchanged drug and metabolites)

Dosage Oral:
    Children: Not established in children <16 years of age.
    Adolescents: Initial: 25-50 mg/day; increase gradually to 100 mg/day; may administer as divided doses or as a single dose at bedtime
    Adults: Initial: 25 mg 2-3 times/day, if tolerated, dosage may be increased to 100 mg 2-3 times/day; may be given in a single bedtime dose when dosage <300 mg/day
    Elderly: Initial: 25 mg at bedtime increased by 25 mg weekly for outpatients and every 3 days for inpatients if tolerated; usual dose: 50-150 mg/day, but doses up to 300 mg may be necessary
    Maximum daily dose:
        Inpatient: 600 mg
        Outpatient: 400 mg

Administration May be administered with food to decrease GI distress.

Monitoring Parameters Monitor blood pressure and pulse rate prior to and during initial therapy evaluate mental status; monitor weight; ECG in older adults.

(Continued)

Amoxapine *(Continued)*

Reference Range Therapeutic: Amoxapine: 20-100 ng/mL (SI: 64-319 nmol/L); 8-OH amoxa-pine: 150-400 ng/mL (SI: 478-1275 nmol/L); both: 200-500 ng/mL (SI: 637-1594 nmol/L)

Test Interactions Increased glucose, liver function tests; decreased WBC

Additional Information Extrapyramidal reactions and tardive dyskinesia may occur.

Dosage Forms Tablet: 25 mg, 50 mg, 100 mg, 150 mg

Amoxicillin *(a moks i SIL in)*

U.S. Brand Names Amoxil®

Canadian Brand Names Apo-Amoxi®; Gen-Amoxicillin; Lin-Amox; Novamoxin®; Nu-Amoxi; PHL-Amoxicillin; PMS-Amoxicillin

Index Terms Amoxicillin Trihydrate; Amoxycillin; *p*-Hydroxyampicillin

Pharmacologic Category Antibiotic, Penicillin

Additional Appendix Information
  Animal and Human Bites *on page 1976*
  Antimicrobial Drugs of Choice *on page 1981*
  Community-Acquired Pneumonia in Adults *on page 1999*
  Helicobacter pylori Treatment *on page 2056*
  Prevention of Bacterial Endocarditis *on page 1960*
  Treatment of Sexually Transmitted Infections *on page 2007*

Use Treatment of otitis media, sinusitis, and infections caused by susceptible organisms involving the respiratory tract, skin, and urinary tract; prophylaxis of bacterial endocarditis in patients undergoing surgical or dental procedures; as part of a multidrug regimen for *H. pylori* eradication

Unlabeled/Investigational Use Postexposure prophylaxis for anthrax exposure with documented susceptible organisms

Pregnancy Risk Factor B

Lactation Enters breast milk/compatible

Medication Safety Issues
  Sound-alike/look-alike issues:
    Amoxicillin may be confused with amoxapine, Amoxil®, Atarax®
    Amoxil® may be confused with amoxapine, amoxicillin
  International issues:
    Fisamox® [Australia] may be confused with Fosamax® which is a brand name for alen-dronate in the U.S.
    Fisamox® [Australia] may be confused with Vigamox™ which is a brand name for moxiflox-acin in the U.S.

Contraindications Hypersensitivity to amoxicillin, penicillin, or any component of the formulation

Warnings/Precautions In patients with renal impairment, doses and/or frequency of administration should be modified in response to the degree of renal impairment. A high percentage of patients with infectious mononucleosis have developed rash during therapy with amoxicillin. A low incidence of cross-allergy with other beta-lactams and cephalosporins exists.

Adverse Reactions Frequency not defined.
  Central nervous system: Hyperactivity, agitation, anxiety, insomnia, confusion, convulsions, behavioral changes, dizziness
  Dermatologic: Acute exanthematous pustulosis, erythematous maculopapular rash, erythema multiforme, Stevens-Johnson syndrome, exfoliative dermatitis, toxic epidermal necrolysis, hypersensitivity vasculitis, urticaria
  Gastrointestinal: Nausea, vomiting, diarrhea, hemorrhagic colitis, pseudomembranous colitis, tooth discoloration (brown, yellow, or gray; rare)
  Hematologic: Anemia, hemolytic anemia, thrombocytopenia, thrombocytopenia purpura, eosinophilia, leukopenia, agranulocytosis
  Hepatic: AST (SGOT) and ALT (SGPT) increased, cholestatic jaundice, hepatic cholestasis, acute cytolytic hepatitis
  Renal: Crystalluria

Overdosage/Toxicology Symptoms of penicillin overdose include neuromuscular hypersensitivity (eg, agitation, hallucinations, asterixis, encephalopathy, confusion, and seizures). Interstitial nephritis and/or crystalluria, possibly resulting in renal failure, may occur; hydration and diuresis may be beneficial. Electrolyte imbalance may occur if the preparation contains potassium or sodium salts, especially in renal failure. A study of 51 pediatric overdose victims suggests that ingestion of doses ≤250 mg/kg does not manifest significant clinical symptoms, and thus does not require gastric lavage. Hemodialysis may be helpful to aid in removal of the drug from blood; otherwise, treatment is symptom-directed and supportive.

Drug Interactions
  Increased Effect/Toxicity: Disulfiram and probenecid may increase amoxicillin levels. Amoxicillin may increase the effects of oral anticoagulants (warfarin). Theoretically, allopurinol taken with amoxicillin has an additive potential for amoxicillin rash. Penicillins may increase the exposure to methotrexate during concurrent therapy; monitor.
  Decreased Effect: Decreased effectiveness with tetracyclines and chloramphenicol. Although anecdotal reports suggest that oral contraceptive efficacy could be reduced by penicillins, this has been refuted by more rigorous scientific and clinical data.

Stability Amoxil®: Oral suspension remains stable for 14 days at room temperature or if refrigerated (refrigeration preferred). Unit-dose antibiotic oral syringes are stable for 48 hours.

Mechanism of Action Inhibits bacterial cell wall synthesis by binding to one or more of the penicillin-binding proteins (PBPs) which in turn inhibits the final transpeptidation step of peptidoglycan synthesis in bacterial cell walls, thus inhibiting cell wall biosynthesis. Bacteria eventually lyse due to ongoing activity of cell wall autolytic enzymes (autolysins and murein hydrolases) while cell wall assembly is arrested.

Pharmacodynamics/Kinetics
  Absorption: Oral: Rapid and nearly complete; food does not interfere

Distribution: Widely to most body fluids and bone; poor penetration into cells, eyes, and across normal meninges

Pleural fluids, lungs, and peritoneal fluid; high urine concentrations are attained; also into synovial fluid, liver, prostate, muscle, and gallbladder; penetrates into middle ear effusions, maxillary sinus secretions, tonsils, sputum, and bronchial secretions; crosses placenta; low concentrations enter breast milk

CSF:blood level ratio: Normal meninges: <1%; Inflamed meninges: 8% to 90%

Protein binding: 17% to 20%

Metabolism: Partially hepatic

Half-life elimination:

Neonates, full-term: 3.7 hours

Infants and Children: 1-2 hours

Adults: Normal renal function: 0.7-1.4 hours

Cl_{cr} <10 mL/minute: 7-21 hours

Time to peak: Capsule: 2 hours; Suspension: 1 hour

Excretion: Urine (80% as unchanged drug); lower in neonates

Dosage

Usual dosage range:

Children ≤3 months: Oral: 20-30 mg/kg/day divided every 12 hours

Children >3 months and <40 kg: Oral: 20-50 mg/kg/day in divided doses every 8-12 hours

Adults: Oral: 250-500 mg every 8 hours or 500-875 mg twice daily

Indication-specific dosing:

Children >3 months and <40 kg: Oral:

Acute otitis media: 80-90 mg/kg/day divided every 12 hours

Anthrax exposure (CDC guidelines): Note: Postexposure prophylaxis only with documented susceptible organisms: 80 mg/kg/day in divided doses every 8 hours (maximum: 500 mg/dose)

Community-acquired pneumonia:

4 months to <5 years: 80-100 mg/kg/day divided every 8 hours

5-15 years: 100 mg/kg/day divided every 8 hours; **Note:** Treatment with a macrolide or doxycycline (if age >8 years) is preferred due to higher prevalence of atypical pathogens in this age group

Ear, nose, throat, genitourinary tract, or skin/skin structure infections:

Mild to moderate: 25 mg/kg/day in divided doses every 12 hours **or** 20 mg/kg/day in divided doses every 8 hours

Severe: 45 mg/kg/day in divided doses every 12 hours **or** 40 mg/kg/day in divided doses every 8 hours

Endocarditis (subacute bacterial) prophylaxis: 50 mg/kg 1 hour before procedure

Lower respiratory tract infections: 45 mg/kg/day in divided doses every 12 hours **or** 40 mg/kg/day in divided doses every 8 hours

Lyme disease: 25-50 mg/kg/day divided every 8 hours (maximum: 500 mg)

Adults: Oral:

Anthrax exposure (CDC guidelines): Note: Postexposure prophylaxis in pregnant or nursing women only with documented susceptible organisms: 500 mg every 8 hours

Ear, nose, throat, genitourinary tract, or skin/skin structure infections:

Mild to moderate: 500 mg every 12 hours **or** 250 mg every 8 hours

Severe: 875 mg every 12 hours **or** 500 mg every 8 hours

Endocarditis prophylaxis: 2 g 1 hour before procedure

Helicobacter pylori **eradication:** 1000 mg twice daily; requires combination therapy with at least one other antibiotic and an acid-suppressing agent (proton pump inhibitor or H_2 blocker)

Lower respiratory tract infections: 875 mg every 12 hours **or** 500 mg every 8 hours

Lyme disease: 500 mg every 6-8 hours (depending on size of patient) for 21-30 days

Dosing interval in renal impairment: The 875 mg tablet should not be used in patients with Cl_{cr} <30 mL/minute.

Cl_{cr} 10-30 mL/minute: 250-500 mg every 12 hours

Cl_{cr} <10 mL/minute: 250-500 mg every 24 hours

Dialysis: Moderately dialyzable (20% to 50%) by hemo- or peritoneal dialysis; approximately 50 mg of amoxicillin per liter of filtrate is removed by continuous arteriovenous or venovenous hemofiltration; dose as per Cl_{cr} <10 mL/minute guidelines

Dietary Considerations May be taken with food. Amoxil® chewable contains phenylalanine 1.82 mg per 200 mg tablet, phenylalanine 3.64 mg per 400 mg tablet.

Administration Administer around-the-clock to promote less variation in peak and trough serum levels. The appropriate amount of suspension may be mixed with formula, milk, fruit juice, water, ginger ale, or cold drinks; administer dose immediately after mixing.

Some penicillins (eg, carbenicillin, ticarcillin, and piperacillin) have been shown to inactivate aminoglycosides *in vitro*. This has been observed to a greater extent with tobramycin and gentamicin, while amikacin has shown greater stability against inactivation. Concurrent use of these agents may pose a risk of reduced antibacterial efficacy *in vivo*, particularly in the setting of profound renal impairment. However, definitive clinical evidence is lacking. If combination penicillin/aminoglycoside therapy is desired in a patient with renal dysfunction, separation of doses (if feasible), and routine monitoring of aminoglycoside levels, CBC, and clinical response should be considered.

Monitoring Parameters With prolonged therapy, monitor renal, hepatic, and hematologic function periodically; assess patient at beginning and throughout therapy for infection; monitor for signs of anaphylaxis during first dose

Test Interactions May interfere with urinary glucose tests using cupric sulfate (Benedict's solution, Clinitest®)

Some penicillin derivatives may accelerate the degradation of aminoglycosides *in vitro*, leading to a potential underestimation of aminoglycoside serum concentration.

Dosage Forms

Capsule: 250 mg, 500 mg

Amoxil®: 500 mg

(Continued)

Amoxicillin *(Continued)*

Powder for oral suspension: 125 mg/5 mL (80 mL, 100 mL, 150 mL); 200 mg/5 mL (50 mL, 75 mL, 100 mL); 250 mg/5 mL (80 mL, 100 mL, 150 mL); 400 mg/5 mL (50 mL, 75 mL, 100 mL)

Amoxil®: 200 mg/5 mL (50 mL, 75 mL, 100 mL) [contains sodium benzoate; bubble gum flavor]; 250 mg/5 mL (100 mL, 150 mL) [contains sodium benzoate; bubble gum flavor]; 400 mg/5 mL (5 mL, 50 mL, 75 mL, 100 mL) [contains sodium benzoate; bubble gum flavor]

Powder for oral suspension [drops]:

Amoxil®: 50 mg/mL (30 mL) [contains sodium benzoate; bubble gum flavor]

Tablet: 500 mg, 875 mg

Amoxil®: 500 mg, 875 mg

Tablet, chewable: 125 mg, 200 mg, 250 mg, 400 mg

Amoxil®: 200 mg [contains phenylalanine 1.82 mg/tablet; cherry banana peppermint flavor]; 400 mg [contains phenylalanine 3.64 mg/tablet; cherry banana peppermint flavor]

Amoxicillin and Clavulanate Potassium
(a moks i SIL in & klav yoo LAN ate poe TASS ee um)

U.S. Brand Names Amoclan; Augmentin®; Augmentin ES-600®; Augmentin XR®

Canadian Brand Names Alti-Amoxi-Clav; Apo-Amoxi-Clav®; Augmentin®; Clavulin®; Novo-Clavamoxin; ratio-Aclavulanate

Index Terms Amoxicillin and Clavulanic Acid; Clavulanic Acid and Amoxicillin

Pharmacologic Category Antibiotic, Penicillin

Additional Appendix Information

Animal and Human Bites *on page 1976*

Antimicrobial Drugs of Choice *on page 1981*

Community-Acquired Pneumonia in Adults *on page 1999*

Use Treatment of otitis media, sinusitis, and infections caused by susceptible organisms involving the lower respiratory tract, skin and skin structure, and urinary tract; spectrum same as amoxicillin with additional coverage of beta-lactamase producing *B. catarrhalis, H. influenzae, N. gonorrhoeae,* and *S. aureus* (not MRSA). The expanded coverage of this combination makes it a useful alternative when amoxicillin resistance is present and patients cannot tolerate alternative treatments.

Pregnancy Risk Factor B

Pregnancy Implications Both amoxicillin and clavulanate potassium cross the human placenta. Teratogenic effects have not been reported. Use in women with premature rupture of fetal membranes may increase risk of necrotizing enterocolitis in neonates.

Lactation Enters breast milk/use caution (AAP rates "compatible")

Medication Safety Issues

Sound-alike/look-alike issues:

Augmentin® may be confused with Azulfidine®

Contraindications Hypersensitivity to amoxicillin, clavulanic acid, penicillin, or any component of the formulation; history of cholestatic jaundice or hepatic dysfunction with amoxicillin/clavulanate potassium therapy; Augmentin XR™: severe renal impairment (Cl_{cr} <30 mL/minute) and hemodialysis patients

Warnings/Precautions Hypersensitivity reactions, including anaphylaxis (some fatal), have been reported. Prolonged use may result in superinfection, including *Pseudomembranous colitis*. In patients with renal impairment, doses and/or frequency of administration should be modified in response to the degree of renal impairment. High percentage of patients with infectious mononucleosis have developed rash during therapy. Incidence of diarrhea is higher than with amoxicillin alone. Due to differing content of clavulanic acid, not all formulations are interchangeable. Low incidence of cross-allergy with cephalosporins exists. Some products contain phenylalanine.

Adverse Reactions

>10%: Gastrointestinal: Diarrhea (3% to 34%; incidence varies upon dose and regimen used)

1% to 10%:

Dermatologic: Diaper rash, skin rash, urticaria

Gastrointestinal: Abdominal discomfort, loose stools, nausea, vomiting

Genitourinary: Vaginitis, vaginal mycosis

Miscellaneous: Moniliasis

<1% (Limited to important or life-threatening): Cholestatic jaundice, flatulence, headache, hepatic dysfunction, prothrombin time increased, thrombocytosis

Additional adverse reactions seen with **ampicillin-class antibiotics:** Agitation, agranulocytosis, alkaline phosphatase increased, anaphylaxis, anemia, angioedema, anxiety, behavioral changes, bilirubin increased, black "hairy" tongue, confusion, convulsions, crystalluria, dizziness, enterocolitis, eosinophilia, erythema multiforme, exanthematous pustulosis, exfoliative dermatitis, gastritis, glossitis, hematuria, hemolytic anemia, hemorrhagic colitis, indigestion, insomnia, hyperactivity, interstitial nephritis, leukopenia, mucocutaneous candidiasis, pruritus, pseudomembranous colitis, serum sickness-like reaction, Stevens-Johnson syndrome, stomatitis, transaminases increased, thrombocytopenia, thrombocytopenic purpura, tooth discoloration, toxic epidermal necrolysis

Overdosage/Toxicology Symptoms of overdose may include abdominal pain, diarrhea, drowsiness, rash, hyperactivity, stomach pain, and vomiting. Interstitial nephritis and/or crystalluria, possibly resulting in renal failure, may occur; hydration and diuresis may be beneficial. Electrolyte imbalance may occur, especially in renal failure. A study of 51 pediatric overdose victims suggests that ingestion of amoxicillin at doses ≤250 mg/kg do not manifest significant clinical symptoms, and thus do not require gastric lavage. Hemodialysis may be helpful to aid in removal of the drug from blood; otherwise, treatment is supportive or symptom-directed.

Drug Interactions

Increased Effect/Toxicity: Probenecid may increase amoxicillin levels (concomitant use is not recommended). Increased effect of anticoagulants with amoxicillin. Allopurinol taken with Augmentin® has an additive potential for rash. Penicillins may increase the exposure to methotrexate during concurrent therapy; monitor.

Decreased Effect: Although anecdotal reports suggest oral contraceptive efficacy could be reduced by penicillins, this has been refuted by more rigorous scientific and clinical data.

Stability

Powder for oral suspension: Store dry powder at room temperature of 25°C (77°F). Reconstitute powder for oral suspension with appropriate amount of water as specified on the bottle. Shake vigorously until suspended. Reconstituted oral suspension should be kept in refrigerator. Discard unused suspension after 10 days. Unit-dose antibiotic oral syringes are stable for 48 hours.

Tablet: Store at room temperature of 25°C (77°F).

Mechanism of Action Clavulanic acid binds and inhibits beta-lactamases that inactivate amoxicillin resulting in amoxicillin having an expanded spectrum of activity. Amoxicillin inhibits bacterial cell wall synthesis by binding to one or more of the penicillin-binding proteins (PBPs) which in turn inhibits the final transpeptidation step of peptidoglycan synthesis in bacterial cell walls, thus inhibiting cell wall biosynthesis. Bacteria eventually lyse due to ongoing activity of cell wall autolytic enzymes (autolysins and murein hydrolases) while cell wall assembly is arrested.

Pharmacodynamics/Kinetics Amoxicillin pharmacokinetics are not affected by clavulanic acid.

Amoxicillin: See Amoxicillin.

Clavulanic acid:

Metabolism: Hepatic

Excretion: Urine (30% to 40% as unchanged drug)

Dosage Note: Dose is based on the amoxicillin component; see "Augmentin® Product-Specific Considerations" table.

Augmentin® Product-Specific Considerations

Strength	Form	Consideration
125 mg	CT, S	q8h dosing
	S	For adults having difficulty swallowing tablets, 125 mg/5 mL suspension may be substituted for 500 mg tablet.
200 mg	CT, S	q12h dosing
	CT	Contains phenylalanine
	S	For adults having difficulty swallowing tablets, 200 mg/5 mL suspension may be substituted for 875 mg tablet.
250 mg	CT, S, T	q8h dosing
	CT	Contains phenylalanine
	T	Not for use in patients <40 kg
	CT, T	Tablet and chewable tablet are not interchangeable due to differences in clavulanic acid.
	S	For adults having difficulty swallowing tablets, 250 mg/5 mL suspension may be substituted for 500 mg tablet.
400 mg	CT, S	q12h dosing
	CT	Contains phenylalanine
	S	For adults having difficulty swallowing tablets, 400 mg/5 mL suspension may be substituted for 875 mg tablet.
500 mg	T	q8h or q12h dosing
600 mg	S	q12h dosing
		Contains phenylalanine
		Not for use in adults or children ≥40 kg
		600 mg/5 mL suspension is not equivalent to or interchangeable with 200 mg/5 mL or 400 mg/5 mL due to differences in clavulanic acid.
875 mg	T	q12h dosing; not for use in Cl$_{cr}$ <30 mL/minute
1000 mg	XR	q12h dosing
		Not for use in children <16 years of age
		Not interchangeable with two 500 mg tablets
		Not for use if Cl$_{cr}$ <30 mL/minute or hemodialysis

Legend: CT = chewable tablet, S = suspension, T = tablet, XR = extended release.

Usual dosage range:

Infants <3 months: Oral: 30 mg/kg/day divided every 12 hours using the 125 mg/5 mL suspension

Children ≥3 months and <40 kg: Oral: 20-90 mg/kg/day divided every 8-12 hours

Children >40 kg and Adults: Oral: 250-500 mg every 8 hours or 875 mg every 12 hours

Indication-specific dosing:

Children ≥3 months and <40 kg: Oral:

Lower respiratory tract infections, severe infections, sinusitis: 45 mg/kg/day divided every 12 hours **or** 40 mg/kg/day divided every 8 hours

Mild-to-moderate infections: 25 mg/kg/day divided every 12 hours or 20 mg/kg/day divided every 8 hours

Otitis media (Augmentin® ES-600): 90 mg/kg/day divided every 12 hours for 10 days in children with severe illness and when coverage for β-lactamase-positive *H. influenzae* and *M. catarrhalis* is needed.

Children ≥16 years and Adults: Oral:

Acute bacterial sinusitis: Extended release tablet: Two 1000 mg tablets every 12 hours for 10 days

Bite wounds (animal/human): 875 mg every 12 hours **or** 500 mg every 8 hours

Chronic obstructive pulmonary disease: 875 mg every 12 hours **or** 500 mg every 8 hours

Diabetic foot: Extended release tablet: Two 1000 mg tablets every 12 hours for 7-14 days

(Continued)

Amoxicillin and Clavulanate Potassium *(Continued)*

Diverticulitis, perirectal abscess: Extended release tablet: Two 1000 mg tablets every 12 hours for 7-10 days

Erysipelas: 875 mg every 12 hours **or** 500 mg every 8 hours

Febrile neutropenia: 875 mg every 12 hours

Pneumonia:

Aspiration: 875 mg every 12 hours

Community-acquired: Extended release tablet: Two 1000 mg tablets every 12 hours for 7-10 days

Pyelonephritis (acute, uncomplicated): 875 mg every 12 hours **or** 500 mg every 8 hours

Skin abscess: 875 mg every 12 hours

Dosing interval in renal impairment:

Cl_{cr} <30 mL/minute: Do not use 875 mg tablet or extended release tablets

Cl_{cr} 10-30 mL/minute: 250-500 mg every 12 hours

Cl_{cr} <10 mL/minute: 250-500 every 24 hours

Hemodialysis: Moderately dialyzable (20% to 50%)

250-500 mg every 24 hours; administer dose during and after dialysis. Do not use extended release tablets.

Peritoneal dialysis: Moderately dialyzable (20% to 50%)

Amoxicillin: Administer 250 mg every 12 hours

Clavulanic acid: Dose for Cl_{cr} <10 mL/minute

Continuous arteriovenous or venovenous hemofiltration effects:

Amoxicillin: ~50 mg of amoxicillin/L of filtrate is removed

Clavulanic acid: Dose for Cl_{cr} <10 mL/minute

Dietary Considerations May be taken with meals or on an empty stomach; take with meals to increase absorption and decrease GI intolerance; may mix with milk, formula, or juice. Extended release tablets should be taken with food. Some products contain phenylalanine. If you have phenylketonuria or PKU, avoid use. All dosage forms contain potassium.

Administration Administer around-the-clock to promote less variation in peak and trough serum levels. Administer with food to decrease stomach upset; shake suspension well before use. Extended release tablets should be administered with food.

Some penicillins (eg, carbenicillin, ticarcillin, and piperacillin) have been shown to inactivate aminoglycosides *in vitro*. This has been observed to a greater extent with tobramycin and gentamicin, while amikacin has shown greater stability against inactivation. Concurrent use of these agents may pose a risk of reduced antibacterial efficacy *in vivo*, particularly in the setting of profound renal impairment. However, definitive clinical evidence is lacking. If combination penicillin/aminoglycoside therapy is desired in a patient with renal dysfunction, separation of doses (if feasible), and routine monitoring of aminoglycoside levels, CBC, and clinical response should be considered.

Monitoring Parameters Assess patient at beginning and throughout therapy for infection; with prolonged therapy, monitor renal, hepatic, and hematologic function periodically; monitor for signs of anaphylaxis during first dose

Test Interactions May interfere with urinary glucose tests using cupric sulfate (Benedict's solution, Clinitest®, Fehling's solution); may inactivate aminoglycosides *in vitro*.

Some penicillin derivatives may accelerate the degradation of aminoglycosides *in vitro*, leading to a potential underestimation of aminoglycoside serum concentration.

Additional Information Two 250 mg tablets are not equivalent to a 500 mg tablet (both tablet sizes contain equivalent clavulanate). Two 500 mg tablets are not equivalent to a single 1000 mg extended release tablet.

Dosage Forms

Powder for oral suspension: 200: Amoxicillin 200 mg and clavulanate potassium 28.5 mg per 5 mL (50 mL, 75 mL, 100 mL) [contains phenylalanine]; 400: Amoxicillin 400 mg and clavulanate potassium 57 mg per 5 mL (50 mL, 75 mL, 100 mL) [contains phenylalanine]; 600: Amoxicillin 600 mg and clavulanic potassium 42.9 mg per 5 mL (75 mL, 125 mL, 200 mL) [contains phenylalanine]

Amoclan:

200: Amoxicillin 200 mg and clavulanate potassium 28.5 mg per 5 mL (50 mL, 75 mL, 100 mL) [contains phenylalanine 7 mg/5 mL and potassium 0.14 mEq/5 mL; fruit flavor]

400: Amoxicillin 400 mg and clavulanate potassium 57 mg per 5 mL (50 mL, 75 mL, 100 mL) [contains phenylalanine 7 mg/5 mL and potassium 0.29 mEq/5 mL; fruit flavor]

Augmentin®:

125: Amoxicillin 125 mg and clavulanate potassium 31.25 mg per 5 mL (75 mL, 100 mL, 150 mL) [contains potassium 0.16 mEq/5 mL; banana flavor]

200: Amoxicillin 200 mg and clavulanate potassium 28.5 mg per 5 mL (50 mL, 75 mL, 100 mL) [contains phenylalanine 7 mg/5 mL and potassium 0.14 mEq/5 mL; orange flavor]

250: Amoxicillin 250 mg and clavulanate potassium 62.5 mg per 5 mL (75 mL, 100 mL, 150 mL) [contains potassium 0.32 mEq/5 mL; orange flavor]

400: Amoxicillin 400 mg and clavulanate potassium 57 mg per 5 mL (50 mL, 75 mL, 100 mL) [contains phenylalanine 7 mg/5 mL and potassium 0.29 mEq/5 mL; orange flavor]

Augmentin ES-600®: Amoxicillin 600 mg and clavulanic potassium 42.9 mg per 5 mL (75 mL, 125 mL, 200 mL) [contains phenylalanine 7 mg/5 mL and potassium 0.23 mEq/5 mL; strawberry cream flavor]

Tablet: 250: Amoxicillin 250 mg and clavulanate potassium 125 mg; 500: Amoxicillin 500 mg and clavulanate potassium 125 mg; 875: Amoxicillin 875 mg and clavulanate potassium 125 mg

Augmentin®:

250: Amoxicillin 250 mg and clavulanate potassium 125 mg [contains potassium 0.63 mEq/tablet]

500: Amoxicillin 500 mg and clavulanate potassium 125 mg [contains potassium 0.63 mEq/tablet]

875: Amoxicillin 875 mg and clavulanate potassium 125 mg [contains potassium 0.63 mEq/tablet]

Tablet, chewable: 200: Amoxicillin 200 mg and clavulanate potassium 28.5 mg [contains phenylalanine]; 400: Amoxicillin 400 mg and clavulanate potassium 57 mg [contains phenylalanine]

Augmentin®:
125: Amoxicillin 125 mg and clavulanate potassium 31.25 mg [contains potassium 0.16 mEq/tablet; lemon-lime flavor]
200: Amoxicillin 200 mg and clavulanate potassium 28.5 mg [contains phenylalanine 2.1 mg/tablet and potassium 0.14 mEq/tablet; cherry-banana flavor]
250: Amoxicillin 250 mg and clavulanate potassium 62.5 mg [contains potassium 0.32 mEq/tablet; lemon-lime flavor]
400: Amoxicillin 400 mg and clavulanate potassium 57 mg [contains phenylalanine 4.2 mg/tablet and potassium 0.29 mEq/tablet; cherry-banana flavor]

Tablet, extended release:
Augmentin XR®: Amoxicillin 1000 mg and clavulanic acid 62.5 mg [contains potassium 29.3 mg (1.27 mEq) and sodium 12.6 mg (0.32 mEq) per tablet; packaged in either a 7-day or 10-day package]

- ♦ **Amoxicillin and Clavulanic Acid** see Amoxicillin and Clavulanate Potassium on page 112
- ♦ **Amoxicillin, Lansoprazole, and Clarithromycin** see Lansoprazole, Amoxicillin, and Clarithromycin on page 979
- ♦ **Amoxicillin Trihydrate** see Amoxicillin on page 110
- ♦ **Amoxil®** see Amoxicillin on page 110
- ♦ **Amoxycillin** see Amoxicillin on page 110
- ♦ **Amphetamine and Dextroamphetamine** see Dextroamphetamine and Amphetamine on page 487
- ♦ **Amphocin®** see Amphotericin B (Conventional) on page 116
- ♦ **Amphojel® (Can)** see Aluminum Hydroxide on page 83
- ♦ **Amphotec®** see Amphotericin B Cholesteryl Sulfate Complex on page 115
- ♦ **Amphotec® (Can)** see Amphotericin B (Lipid Complex) on page 118

Amphotericin B Cholesteryl Sulfate Complex
(am foe TER i sin bee kole LES te ril SUL fate KOM plecks)

U.S. Brand Names Amphotec®
Canadian Brand Names Amphotec®
Index Terms ABCD; Amphotericin B Colloidal Dispersion
Pharmacologic Category Antifungal Agent, Parenteral
Use Treatment of invasive aspergillosis in patients who have failed amphotericin B deoxycholate treatment, or who have renal impairment or experience unacceptable toxicity which precludes treatment with amphotericin B deoxycholate in effective doses.
Unlabeled/Investigational Use Effective in patients with serious *Candida* species infections
Pregnancy Risk Factor B
Lactation Excretion in breast milk unknown/contraindicated
Medication Safety Issues
Safety issues:
Lipid-based amphotericin formulations (Amphotec®) may be confused with conventional formulations (Amphocin®, Fungizone®)
Large overdoses have occurred when conventional formulations were dispensed inadvertently for lipid-based products. Single daily doses of conventional amphotericin formulation never exceed 1.5 mg/kg.

Contraindications Hypersensitivity to amphotericin B or any component of the formulation
Warnings/Precautions Anaphylaxis has been reported with amphotericin B-containing drugs. If severe respiratory distress occurs, the infusion should be immediately discontinued. During the initial dosing, the drug should be administered under close clinical observation. Infusion reactions, sometimes severe, usually subside with continued therapy - manage with decreased rate of infusion and pretreatment with antihistamines/corticosteroids.

Adverse Reactions
>10%: Central nervous system: Chills, fever
1% to 10%:
Cardiovascular: Hypotension, tachycardia
Central nervous system: Headache
Dermatologic: Rash
Endocrine & metabolic: Hypokalemia, hypomagnesemia
Gastrointestinal: Nausea, diarrhea, abdominal pain
Hematologic: Thrombocytopenia
Hepatic: LFT change
Neuromuscular & skeletal: Rigors
Renal: Creatinine increased
Respiratory: Dyspnea
Note: Amphotericin B colloidal dispersion has an improved therapeutic index compared to conventional amphotericin B, and has been used safely in patients with amphotericin B-related nephrotoxicity; however, continued decline of renal function has occurred in some patients.

Overdosage/Toxicology Symptoms include renal dysfunction, anemia, thrombocytopenia, granulocytopenia, fever, nausea, and vomiting. Treatment is supportive.

Drug Interactions
Increased Effect/Toxicity: Toxic effect with other nephrotoxic drugs (eg, cyclosporine and aminoglycosides) may be additive. Corticosteroids may increase potassium depletion caused by amphotericin. Amphotericin B may predispose patients receiving digitalis glycosides or neuromuscular blocking agents to toxicity secondary to hypokalemia.

(Continued)

Amphotericin B Cholesteryl Sulfate Complex *(Continued)*

Decreased Effect: Pharmacologic antagonism may occur with azole antifungals (eg, keto-conazole, miconazole).

Stability

Store intact vials under refrigeration.

Reconstitute 50 mg and 100 mg vials with 10 mL and 20 mL of SWI, respectively. The reconstituted vials contain 5 mg/mL of amphotericin B. Shake the vial gently by hand until all solid particles have dissolved. After reconstitution, the solution should be refrigerated at 2°C to 8°C (36°F to 46°F) and used within 24 hours.

Further dilute amphotericin B colloidal dispersion with dextrose 5% in water. Concentrations of 0.1-2 mg/mL in dextrose 5% in water are stable for 14 days at 4°C and 23°C if protected from light, however, due to the occasional formation of subvisual particles, solutions should be used within 48 hours.

Mechanism of Action Binds to ergosterol altering cell membrane permeability in susceptible fungi and causing leakage of cell components with subsequent cell death. Proposed mechanism suggests that amphotericin causes an oxidation-dependent stimulation of macrophages (Lyman, 1992).

Pharmacodynamics/Kinetics

Distribution: V_d: Total volume increases with higher doses, reflects increasing uptake by tissues (with 4 mg/kg/day = 4 L/kg); predominantly distributed in the liver; concentrations in kidneys and other tissues are lower than observed with conventional amphotericin B

Half-life elimination: 28-29 hours; prolonged with higher doses

Dosage Children and Adults: I.V.:

Premedication: For patients who experience chills, fever, hypotension, nausea, or other nonanaphylactic infusion-related immediate reactions, premedicate with the following drugs 30-60 minutes prior to drug administration: A nonsteroidal (eg, ibuprofen, choline magnesium trisalicylate) with or without diphenhydramine **or** acetaminophen with diphenhydramine **or** hydrocortisone 50-100 mg. If the patient experiences rigors during the infusion, meperidine may be administered.

Range: 3-4 mg/kg/day (infusion of 1 mg/kg/hour); maximum: 7.5 mg/kg/day

Administration Avoid injection faster than 1 mg/kg/hour. For a patient who experiences chills, fever, hypotension, nausea, or other nonanaphylactic infusion-related reactions, premedicate with the following drugs 30-60 minutes prior to drug administration: A nonsteroidal (eg, ibuprofen, choline magnesium trisalicylate) with or without diphenhydramine **or** acetaminophen with diphenhydramine **or** hydrocortisone 50-100 mg. If the patient experiences rigors during the infusion, meperidine may be administered. If severe respiratory distress occurs, the infusion should be immediately discontinued.

Monitoring Parameters Liver function tests, electrolytes, BUN, Cr, temperature, CBC, I/O, signs of hypokalemia (muscle weakness, cramping, drowsiness, ECG changes)

Additional Information Controlled trials which compare the original formulation of amphotericin B to the newer liposomal formulations (ie, Amphotec®) are lacking. Thus, comparative data discussing differences among the formulations should be interpreted cautiously. Although the risk of nephrotoxicity and infusion-related adverse effects may be less with Amphotec®, the efficacy profiles of Amphotec® and the original amphotericin formulation are comparable. Consequently, Amphotec® should be restricted to those patients who cannot tolerate or fail a standard amphotericin B formulation.

Dosage Forms Injection, powder for reconstitution: 50 mg, 100 mg

♦ **Amphotericin B Colloidal Dispersion** *see* Amphotericin B Cholesteryl Sulfate Complex *on page 115*

Amphotericin B (Conventional) (am foe TER i sin bee con VEN sha nal)

U.S. Brand Names Amphocin®

Canadian Brand Names Fungizone®

Index Terms Amphotericin B Desoxycholate

Pharmacologic Category Antifungal Agent, Parenteral

Additional Appendix Information

Antifungal Agents *on page 1869*

Desensitization Protocols *on page 1913*

USPHS / IDSA Guidelines for the Prevention of Opportunistic Infections in Persons Infected With HIV *on page 1966*

Use Treatment of severe systemic and central nervous system infections caused by susceptible fungi such as *Candida* species, *Histoplasma capsulatum*, *Cryptococcus neoformans*, *Aspergillus* species, *Blastomyces dermatitidis*, *Torulopsis glabrata*, and *Coccidioides immitis*; fungal peritonitis; irrigant for bladder fungal infections; used in fungal infection in patients with bone marrow transplantation, amebic meningoencephalitis, ocular aspergillosis (intraocular injection), candidal cystitis (bladder irrigation), chemoprophylaxis (low-dose I.V.), immuno-compromised patients at risk of aspergillosis (intranasal/nebulized), refractory meningitis (intrathecal), coccidioidal arthritis (intra-articular/I.M.)

Low-dose amphotericin B has been administered after bone marrow transplantation to reduce the risk of invasive fungal disease.

Pregnancy Risk Factor B

Lactation Excretion in breast milk unknown/contraindicated

Medication Safety Issues

Safety issues:

Conventional amphotericin formulations (Amphocin®, Fungizone®) may be confused with lipid-based formulations (AmBisome®, Abelcet®, Amphotec®).

Large overdoses have occurred when conventional formulations were dispensed inadvertently for lipid-based products. Single daily doses of conventional amphotericin formulation never exceed 1.5 mg/kg.

Contraindications Hypersensitivity to amphotericin or any component of the formulation

Warnings/Precautions Anaphylaxis has been reported with amphotericin B-containing drugs. During the initial dosing, the drug should be administered under close clinical observation. Avoid use with other nephrotoxic drugs; drug-induced renal toxicity usually improves with interrupting therapy, decreasing dosage, or increasing dosing interval. Infusion reactions are most common 1-3 hours after starting the infusion and diminish with continued therapy. Use amphotericin B with caution in patients with decreased renal function.

Adverse Reactions

Systemic:

>10%:

Cardiovascular: Hypotension, tachypnea

Central nervous system: Fever, chills, headache (less frequent with I.T.), malaise

Endocrine & metabolic: Hypokalemia, hypomagnesemia

Gastrointestinal: Anorexia, nausea (less frequent with I.T.), vomiting (less frequent with I.T.), diarrhea, heartburn, cramping epigastric pain

Hematologic: Normochromic-normocytic anemia

Local: Pain at injection site with or without phlebitis or thrombophlebitis (incidence may increase with peripheral infusion of admixtures)

Neuromuscular & skeletal: Generalized pain, including muscle and joint pains (less frequent with I.T.)

Renal: Decreased renal function and renal function abnormalities including azotemia, renal tubular acidosis, nephrocalcinosis (>0.1 mg/mL)

1% to 10%:

Cardiovascular: Hypertension, flushing

Central nervous system: Delirium, arachnoiditis, pain along lumbar nerves (especially I.T. therapy)

Genitourinary: Urinary retention

Hematologic: Leukocytosis

Neuromuscular & skeletal: Paresthesia (especially with I.T. therapy)

<1% (Limited to important or life-threatening): Acute liver failure, agranulocytosis, anuria, bone marrow suppression, cardiac arrest, coagulation defects, convulsions, dyspnea, hearing loss, leukopenia, maculopapular rash, renal failure, renal tubular acidosis, thrombocytopenia, vision changes

Overdosage/Toxicology Symptoms include cardiac arrest, renal dysfunction, anemia, thrombocytopenia, granulocytopenia, fever, nausea, and vomiting. Treatment is supportive.

Drug Interactions

Increased Effect/Toxicity: Use of amphotericin with other nephrotoxic drugs (eg, cyclosporine and aminoglycosides) may result in additive toxicity. Amphotericin may increase the toxicity of flucytosine. Antineoplastic agents may increase the risk of amphotericin-induced nephrotoxicity, bronchospasms, and hypotension. Corticosteroids may increase potassium depletion caused by amphotericin. Amphotericin B may predispose patients receiving digitalis glycosides or neuromuscular-blocking agents to toxicity secondary to hypokalemia.

Decreased Effect: Pharmacologic antagonism may occur with azole antifungal agents (ketoconazole, miconazole).

Stability Store intact vials under refrigeration; protect from light. Add 10 mL of SWFI (without a bacteriostatic agent) to each vial of amphotericin B. Further dilute with 250-500 mL D$_5$W; final concentration should not exceed 0.1 mg/mL (peripheral infusion) or 0.25 mg/mL (central infusion).

Reconstituted vials are stable, protected from light, for 24 hours at room temperature and 1 week when refrigerated. Parenteral admixtures are stable, protected from light, for 24 hours at room temperature and 2 days under refrigeration. Short-term exposure (<24 hours) to light during I.V. infusion does **not** appreciably affect potency.

Mechanism of Action Binds to ergosterol altering cell membrane permeability in susceptible fungi and causing leakage of cell components with subsequent cell death. Proposed mechanism suggests that amphotericin causes an oxidation-dependent stimulation of macrophages (Lyman, 1992).

Pharmacodynamics/Kinetics

Distribution: Minimal amounts enter the aqueous humor, bile, CSF (inflamed or noninflamed meninges), amniotic fluid, pericardial fluid, pleural fluid, and synovial fluid

Protein binding, plasma: 90%

Half-life elimination: Biphasic: Initial: 15-48 hours; Terminal: 15 days

Time to peak: Within 1 hour following a 4- to 6-hour dose

Excretion: Urine (2% to 5% as biologically active form); ~40% eliminated over a 7-day period and may be detected in urine for at least 7 weeks after discontinued use

Dosage

Premedication: For patients who experience infusion-related immediate reactions, premedicate with the following drugs 30-60 minutes prior to drug administration: NSAID (with or without diphenhydramine) **or** acetaminophen with diphenhydramine **or** hydrocortisone 50-100 mg. If the patient experiences rigors during the infusion, meperidine may be administered.

Infants and Children: I.V.:

Test dose: 0.1 mg/kg/dose to a maximum of 1 mg; infuse over 30-60 minutes. Many clinicians believe a test dose is unnecessary.

Maintenance dose: 0.25-1 mg/kg/day given once daily; infuse over 2-6 hours. Once therapy has been established, amphotericin B can be administered on an every-other-day basis at 1-1.5 mg/kg/dose; cumulative dose: 1.5-2 g over 6-10 weeks.

Adults: I.V.:

Test dose: 1 mg infused over 20-30 minutes. Many clinicians believe a test dose is unnecessary.

Maintenance dose: Usual: 0.25-1.5 mg/kg/day; 1-1.5 mg/kg over 4-6 hours every other day may be given once therapy is established; aspergillosis, mucormycosis, rhinocerebral phycomycosis often require 1-1.5 mg/kg/day; do not exceed 1.5 mg/kg/day

Duration of therapy varies with nature of infection: Usual duration is 4-12 weeks or cumulative dose of 1-4 g

(Continued)

Amphotericin B (Conventional) *(Continued)*

Meningitis, coccidioidal or cryptococcal: I.T.:
Children.: 25-100 mcg every 48-72 hours; increase to 500 mcg as tolerated
Adults: Initial: 25-300 mcg every 48-72 hours; increase to 500 mcg to 1 mg as tolerated; maximum total dose: 15 mg has been suggested

Bone marrow transplantation (prophylaxis): Adults: I.V.: Low-dose amphotericin B 0.1-0.25 mg/kg/day has been administered after bone marrow transplantation to reduce the risk of invasive fungal disease.

Bladder irrigation: Candidal cystitis: Irrigate with 50 mcg/mL solution instilled periodically or continuously for 5-10 days or until cultures are clear

Note: Alternative routes of administration and extemporaneous preparations have been used when standard antifungal therapy is not available (eg, inhalation, intraocular injection, subconjunctival application, intracavitary administration into various joints and the pleural space).

Dosing adjustment in renal impairment: If renal dysfunction is due to the drug, the daily total can be decreased by 50% or the dose can be given every other day; I.V. therapy may take several months

Dialysis: Poorly dialyzed; no supplemental dosage necessary when using hemo- or peritoneal dialysis or continuous arteriovenous or venovenous hemodiafiltration effects

Administration in dialysate: Children and Adults: 1-2 mg/L of peritoneal dialysis fluid either with or without low-dose I.V. amphotericin B (a total dose of 2-10 mg/kg given over 7-14 days). Precipitate may form in ionic dialysate solutions.

Administration May be infused over 4-6 hours. For a patient who experiences chills, fever, hypotension, nausea, or other nonanaphylactic infusion-related reactions, premedicate with the following drugs 30-60 minutes prior to drug administration: A nonsteroidal (eg, ibuprofen, choline magnesium trisalicylate) with or without diphenhydramine **or** acetaminophen with diphenhydramine **or** hydrocortisone 50-100 mg. If the patient experiences rigors during the infusion, meperidine may be administered. Bolus infusion of normal saline immediately preceding, or immediately preceding and following amphotericin B may reduce drug-induced nephrotoxicity. Risk of nephrotoxicity increases with amphotericin B doses >1 mg/kg/day. Infusion of admixtures more concentrated than 0.25 mg/mL should be limited to patients absolutely requiring volume contraction.

Monitoring Parameters Renal function (monitor frequently during therapy), electrolytes (especially potassium and magnesium), liver function tests, temperature, PT/PTT, CBC; monitor input and output; monitor for signs of hypokalemia (muscle weakness, cramping, drowsiness, ECG changes, etc)

Reference Range Therapeutic: 1-2 mcg/mL (SI: 1-2.2 µmol/L)

Test Interactions Increased BUN (S), serum creatinine, alkaline phosphate, bilirubin; decreased magnesium, potassium (S)

Additional Information Premedication with diphenhydramine and acetaminophen may reduce the severity of acute infusion-related reactions. Meperidine reduces the duration of amphotericin B-induced rigors and chilling. Hydrocortisone may be used in patients with severe or refractory infusion-related reactions. Bolus infusion of normal saline immediately preceding, or immediately preceding and following amphotericin B may reduce drug-induced nephrotoxicity. Risk of nephrotoxicity increases with amphotericin B doses >1 mg/kg/day. Infusion of admixtures more concentrated than 0.25 mg/mL should be limited to patients absolutely requiring volume restriction. Amphotericin B does not have a bacteriostatic constituent, subsequently admixture expiration is determined by sterility more than chemical stability.

Dosage Forms Injection, powder for reconstitution, as desoxycholate: 50 mg

♦ **Amphotericin B Desoxycholate** *see* Amphotericin B (Conventional) *on page 116*

Amphotericin B (Lipid Complex) (am foe TER i sin bee LIP id KOM pleks)

U.S. Brand Names Abelcet®
Canadian Brand Names Abelcet®; Amphotec®
Index Terms ABLC
Pharmacologic Category Antifungal Agent, Parenteral
Use Treatment of aspergillosis or any type of progressive fungal infection in patients who are refractory to or intolerant of conventional amphotericin B therapy
Unlabeled/Investigational Use Effective in patients with serious *Candida* species infections
Pregnancy Risk Factor B
Lactation Enters breast milk/contraindicated
Medication Safety Issues
Safety issues:
Lipid-based amphotericin formulations (Abelcet®) may be confused with conventional formulations (Amphocin®, Fungizone®)
Large overdoses have occurred when conventional formulations were dispensed inadvertently for lipid-based products. Single daily doses of conventional amphotericin formulation never exceed 1.5 mg/kg.

Contraindications Hypersensitivity to amphotericin or any component of the formulation
Warnings/Precautions Anaphylaxis has been reported with amphotericin B-containing drugs. If severe respiratory distress occurs, the infusion should be immediately discontinued. During the initial dosing, the drug should be administered under close clinical observation. Acute reactions (including fever and chills) may occur 1-2 hours after starting an intravenous infusion. These reactions are usually more common with the first few doses and generally diminish with subsequent doses.

Adverse Reactions Nephrotoxicity and infusion-related hyperpyrexia, rigor, and chilling are reduced relative to amphotericin deoxycholate.

>10%:
Central nervous system: Chills, fever
Renal: Serum creatinine increased

Miscellaneous: Multiple organ failure

1% to 10%:

Cardiovascular: Hypotension, cardiac arrest

Central nervous system: Headache, pain

Dermatologic: Rash

Endocrine & metabolic: Bilirubinemia, hypokalemia, acidosis

Gastrointestinal: Nausea, vomiting, diarrhea, gastrointestinal hemorrhage, abdominal pain

Renal: Renal failure

Respiratory: Respiratory failure, dyspnea, pneumonia

Drug Interactions

Increased Effect/Toxicity: See Drug Interactions - Increased Effect/Toxicity in Amphotericin B (Conventional).

Decreased Effect: See Drug Interactions - Decreased Effect in Amphotericin B (Conventional).

Stability Intact vials should be stored at 2°C to 8°C (35°F to 46°F) and protected from exposure to light; do not freeze intact vials. Solutions for infusion are stable for 48 hours under refrigeration and for 6 hours at room temperature. Shake the vial gently until there is no evidence of any yellow sediment at the bottom. Dilute with D_6W to 1-2 mg/mL. Protect from light.

Do not dilute with saline solutions or mix with other drugs or electrolytes - compatibility has not been established

Do not use an in-line filter during administration.

Mechanism of Action Binds to ergosterol altering cell membrane permeability in susceptible fungi and causing leakage of cell components with subsequent cell death. Proposed mechanism suggests that amphotericin causes an oxidation-dependent stimulation of macrophages.

Pharmacodynamics/Kinetics

Distribution: V_d: Increases with higher doses; reflects increased uptake by tissues (131 L/kg with 5 mg/kg/day)

Half-life elimination: ~24 hours

Excretion: Clearance: Increases with higher doses (5 mg/kg/day): 400 mL/hour/kg

Dosage Children and Adults: I.V.:

Premedication: For patients who experience infusion-related immediate reactions, premedicate with the following drugs 30-60 minutes prior to drug administration: A nonsteroidal anti-inflammatory agent ± diphenhydramine **or** acetaminophen with diphenhydramine **or** hydrocortisone 50-100 mg. If the patient experiences rigors during the infusion, meperidine may be administered.

Range: 2.5-5 mg/kg/day as a single infusion

Dosing adjustment in renal impairment: None necessary; effects of renal impairment are not currently known

Hemodialysis: No supplemental dosage necessary

Peritoneal dialysis: No supplemental dosage necessary

Continuous arteriovenous or venovenous hemofiltration: No supplemental dosage necessary

Administration For patients who experience nonanaphylactic infusion-related reactions, premedicate 30-60 minutes prior to drug administration with a nonsteroidal anti-inflammatory agent ± diphenhydramine **or** acetaminophen with diphenhydramine **or** hydrocortisone 50-100 mg. If the patient experiences rigors during the infusion, meperidine may be administered.

Invert infusion container several times prior to administration and every 2 hours during infusion.

Monitoring Parameters Renal function (monitor frequently during therapy), electrolytes (especially potassium and magnesium), liver function tests, temperature, PT/PTT, CBC; monitor input and output; monitor for signs of hypokalemia (muscle weakness, cramping, drowsiness, ECG changes, etc)

Test Interactions Increased BUN (S), serum creatinine, alkaline phosphate, bilirubin; decreased magnesium, potassium (S)

Additional Information As a modification of dimyristoyl phosphatidylcholine:dimyristoyl phosphatidylglycerol 7:3 (DMPC:DMPG) liposome, amphotericin B lipid-complex has a higher drug to lipid ratio and the concentration of amphotericin B is 33 M. ABLC is a ribbon-like structure, not a liposome.

Controlled trials which compare the original formulation of amphotericin B to the newer liposomal formulations (ie, Abelcet®) are lacking. Thus, comparative data discussing differences among the formulations should be interpreted cautiously. Although the risk of nephrotoxicity and infusion-related adverse effects may be less with Abelcet®, the efficacy profiles of Abelcet® and the original amphotericin formulation are comparable. Consequently, Abelcet® should be restricted to those patients who cannot tolerate or fail a standard amphotericin B formulation.

Dosage Forms Injection, suspension [preservative free]: 5 mg/mL (20 mL)

Amphotericin B (Liposomal) (am foe TER i sin bee lye po SO mal)

U.S. Brand Names AmBisome®

Canadian Brand Names AmBisome®

Index Terms L-AmB

Pharmacologic Category Antifungal Agent, Parenteral

Use Empirical therapy for presumed fungal infection in febrile, neutropenic patients; treatment of patients with *Aspergillus* species, *Candida* species, and/or *Cryptococcus* species infections refractory to amphotericin B desoxycholate, or in patients where renal impairment or unacceptable toxicity precludes the use of amphotericin B desoxycholate; treatment of cryptococcal meningitis in HIV-infected patients; treatment of visceral leishmaniasis

Unlabeled/Investigational Use Effective in patients with serious *Candida* species infections

Pregnancy Risk Factor B

Lactation Excretion in breast milk unknown/contraindicated

(Continued)

Amphotericin B (Liposomal) *(Continued)*

Medication Safety Issues

Safety issues:

Lipid-based amphotericin formulations (AmBisome®) may be confused with conventional formulations (Amphocin®, Fungizone®)

Large overdoses have occurred when conventional formulations were dispensed inadvertently for lipid-based products. Single daily doses of conventional amphotericin formulation never exceed 1.5 mg/kg.

Contraindications Hypersensitivity to amphotericin B or any component of the formulation

Warnings/Precautions Although amphotericin B (liposomal) has been shown to be significantly less toxic than amphotericin B desoxycholate, adverse events may still occur. Patients should be under close clinical observation during initial dosing. As with other amphotericin B-containing products, anaphylaxis has been reported. Facilities for cardiopulmonary resuscitation should be available during administration. Acute reactions (including fever and chills) may occur 1-2 hours after starting infusions; reactions are more common with the first few doses and generally diminish with subsequent doses. Immediately discontinue infusion if severe respiratory distress occurs; the patient should not receive further infusions. Safety and efficacy have not been established in patients <1 year of age.

Adverse Reactions Percentage of adverse reactions is dependent upon population studied and may vary with respect to premedications and underlying illness. Incidence of decreased renal function and infusion-related events are lower than rates observed with amphotericin B deoxycholate.

>10%:

Cardiovascular: Peripheral edema (15%), edema (12% to 14%), tachycardia (9% to 18%), hypotension (7% to 14%), hypertension (8% to 20%), chest pain (8% to 12%), hypervolemia (8% to 12%)

Central nervous system: Chills (29% to 48%), insomnia (17% to 22%), headache (9% to 20%), anxiety (7% to 14%), pain (14%), confusion (9% to 13%)

Dermatologic: Rash (5% to 25%), pruritus (11%)

Endocrine & metabolic: Hypokalemia (31% to 51%), hypomagnesemia (15% to 50%), hyperglycemia (8% to 23%), hypocalcemia (5% to 18%), hyponatremia (8% to 12%)

Gastrointestinal: Nausea (16% to 40%), vomiting (10% to 32%), diarrhea (11% to 30%), abdominal pain (7% to 20%), constipation (15%), anorexia (10% to 14%)

Hematologic: Anemia (27% to 48%), blood transfusion reaction (9% to 18%), leukopenia (15% to 17%), thrombocytopenia (6% to 13%)

Hepatic: Alkaline phosphatase increased (7% to 22%), BUN increased (7% to 21%), bilirubinemia (9% to 18%), ALT increased (15%), AST increased (13%), liver function tests abnormal (not specified) (4% to 13%)

Local: Phlebitis (9% to 11%)

Neuromuscular & skeletal: Weakness (6% to 13%), back pain (12%)

Renal: Creatinine increased (18% to 40%), hematuria (14%)

Respiratory: Dyspnea (18% to 23%), lung disorder (14% to 18%), cough increased (2% to 18%), epistaxis (8% to 15%), pleural effusion (12%), rhinitis (11%)

Miscellaneous: Sepsis (7% to 14%), infection (11% to 12%)

2% to 10% (Limited to important or life-threatening):

Cardiovascular: Arrhythmia, atrial fibrillation, bradycardia, cardiac arrest, cardiomegaly, postural hypotension

Central nervous system: Agitation, coma, convulsion, depression, dizziness (7% to 8%), hallucinations, malaise, somnolence

Dermatologic: Alopecia, rash, petechia, purpura, skin discoloration, urticaria

Endocrine & metabolic: Acidosis, hypernatremia (4%), hyperchloremia, hyperkalemia, hypermagnesemia, hyperphosphatemia, hypophosphatemia

Gastrointestinal: Gastrointestinal hemorrhage (10%), hematemesis, gum/oral hemorrhage, ileus, ulcerative stomatitis

Genitourinary: Vaginal hemorrhage

Hematologic: Coagulation disorder, hemorrhage, prothrombin decreased, thrombocytopenia

Hepatic: Hepatocellular damage, veno-occlusive liver disease

Local: Injection site inflammation

Neuromuscular & skeletal: Arthralgia, bone pain, dystonia, paresthesia, rigors, tremor

Ocular: Conjunctivitis, eye hemorrhage

Renal: Acute kidney failure, toxic nephropathy

Respiratory: Asthma, atelectasis, hemoptysis, pulmonary edema, respiratory alkalosis, respiratory failure, hypoxia (6% to 8%)

Miscellaneous: Allergic reaction, cell-mediated immunological reaction, flu-like syndrome, procedural complication (8% to 10%), diaphoresis (7%)

<1% (Limited to important or life-threatening): Agranulocytosis, angioedema, cyanosis/hypoventilation, erythema, hemorrhagic cystitis, pulmonary edema, urticaria

Overdosage/Toxicology Toxicity due to overdose has not been defined. Repeated daily doses up to 7.5 mg/kg have been administered in clinical trials with no reported dose-related toxicity. If overdosage should occur, cease administration immediately. Symptomatic supportive measures should be instituted. Particular attention should be given to monitoring renal function.

Drug Interactions

Increased Effect/Toxicity: Drug interactions have not been studied in a controlled manner; however, drugs that interact with conventional amphotericin B may also interact with amphotericin B liposome for injection. See Drug Interactions - Increased Effect/Toxicity in Amphotericin B (Conventional) monograph.

Stability Unopened vials should be refrigerated at 2°C to 8°C (36°F to 46°F). Vials reconstituted with SWFI are stable for 24 hours under refrigeration. Infusion should begin within 6 hours of dilution with D_5W.

Reconstitution: Add 12 mL SWFI to vial. The use of any solution other than those recommended, or the presence of a bacteriostatic agent in the solution, may cause precipitation. **Shake the vial vigorously** for 30 seconds.

Filtration and dilution: The 5-micron filter should be on the syringe used to remove the reconstituted AmBisome®. Dilute to a final concentration of 1-2 mg/mL (0.2-0.5 mg/mL for infants and small children).

Mechanism of Action Binds to ergosterol altering cell membrane permeability in susceptible fungi and causing leakage of cell components with subsequent cell death. Proposed mechanism suggests that amphotericin causes an oxidation-dependent stimulation of macrophages (Lyman, 1992).

Pharmacodynamics/Kinetics

Distribution: V_d: 131 L/kg

Half-life elimination: Terminal: 174 hours

Dosage

Usual dosage range:

Children: I.V.: 3-5 mg/kg/day

Adults: I.V.: 2-6 mg/kg/day; **Note:** Higher doses (15 mg/kg/day) have been used clinically.

Note: Premedication: For patients who experience nonanaphylactic infusion-related immediate reactions, premedicate with the following drugs 30-60 minutes prior to drug administration: A nonsteroidal anti-inflammatory agent ± diphenhydramine; **or** acetaminophen with diphenhydramine; **or** hydrocortisone 50-100 mg. If the patient experiences rigors during the infusion, meperidine may be administered.

Indication-specific dosing:

Children: I.V.:

Candidal infection:

Endocarditis: 3-6 mg/kg/day with flucytosine 25-37.5 mg/kg 4 times daily

Meningitis: 5 mg/kg/day with flucytosine 100 mg/kg/day

Cryptococcal meningitis (HIV-positive): 6 mg/kg/day

Note: IDSA guidelines (April, 2000) report doses of 3-6 mg/kg/day, noting that 4 mg/kg/day was effective in a small, open-label trial. The manufacturer's labeled dose of 6 mg/kg/day was approved in June, 2000.

Empiric therapy: 3 mg/kg/day

Systemic fungal infections *(Aspergillus, Candida, Cryptococcus)*: 3-5 mg/kg/day

Visceral leishmaniasis:

Immunocompetent: 3 mg/kg/day on days 1-5, and 3 mg/kg/day on days 14 and 21; a repeat course may be given in patients who do not achieve parasitic clearance

Note: Alternate regimen of 10 mg/kg/day for 2 days has been reportedly effective.

Immunocompromised: 4 mg/kg/day on days 1-5, and 4 mg/kg/day on days 10, 17, 24, 31, and 38

Adults: I.V.:

Candidal infection:

Endocarditis: 3-6 mg/kg/day with flucytosine 25-37.5 mg/kg 4 times daily

Meningitis: 5 mg/kg/day with flucytosine 100 mg/kg/day

Cryptococcal meningitis (HIV-positive): 6 mg/kg/day

Note: IDSA guidelines (April, 2000) report doses of 3-6 mg/kg/day, noting that 4 mg/kg/day was effective in a small, open-label trial. The manufacturer's labeled dose of 6 mg/kg/day was approved in June, 2000.

Empiric therapy: 3 mg/kg/day

Fungal sinusitis: 5-7.5 mg/kg/day

Note: Use azole antifungal if causative organism is *Pseudallescheria boydii* (*Scedosporium* sp).

Systemic fungal infections *(Aspergillus, Candida, Cryptococcus)*: 3-5 mg/kg/day

Visceral leishmaniasis:

Immunocompetent: 3 mg/kg/day on days 1-5, and 3 mg/kg/day on days 14 and 21; a repeat course may be given in patients who do not achieve parasitic clearance

Note: Alternate regimen of 2 mg/kg/day for 5 days has been reportedly effective.

Immunocompromised: 4 mg/kg/day on days 1-5, and 4 mg/kg/day on days 10, 17, 24, 31, and 38

Dosing adjustment in renal impairment: None necessary; effects of renal impairment are not currently known

Hemodialysis: No supplemental dosage necessary

Peritoneal dialysis effects: No supplemental dosage necessary

Continuous arteriovenous or venovenous hemofiltration: No supplemental dosage necessary

Administration Administer via intravenous infusion, over a period of approximately 2 hours. Infusion time may be reduced to approximately 1 hour in patients in whom the treatment is well-tolerated. If the patient experiences discomfort during infusion, the duration of infusion may be increased. Administer at a rate of 2.5 mg/kg/hour. Existing intravenous line should be flushed with D_5W prior to infusion (if not feasible, administer through a separate line). An in-line membrane filter (not less than 1 micron) may be used.

Monitoring Parameters Renal function (monitor frequently during therapy), electrolytes (especially potassium and magnesium), liver function tests, temperature, PT/PTT, CBC; monitor input and output; monitor for signs of hypokalemia (muscle weakness, cramping, drowsiness, ECG changes, etc)

Additional Information Amphotericin B (liposomal) is a true single bilayer liposomal drug delivery system. Liposomes are closed, spherical vesicles created by mixing specific proportions of amphophilic substances such as phospholipids and cholesterol so that they arrange themselves into multiple concentric bilayer membranes when hydrated in aqueous solutions. Single bilayer liposomes are then formed by microemulsification of multilamellar vesicles using a homogenizer. Amphotericin B (liposomal) consists of these unilamellar bilayer liposomes with amphotericin B intercalated within the membrane. Due to the nature and quantity of amphophilic substances used, and the lipophilic moiety in the amphotericin B molecule, the drug is an integral part of the overall structure of the amphotericin B liposomal liposomes. Amphotericin B (liposomal) contains true liposomes that are <100 nm in diameter. (Continued)

Amphotericin B (Liposomal) *(Continued)*

Dosage Forms
Injection, powder for reconstitution:
AmBisome®: 50 mg [contains soy and sucrose]

Ampicillin *(am pi SIL in)*

Canadian Brand Names Apo-Ampi®; Novo-Ampicillin; Nu-Ampi

Index Terms Aminobenzylpenicillin; Ampicillin Sodium; Ampicillin Trihydrate

Pharmacologic Category Antibiotic, Penicillin

Additional Appendix Information
Animal and Human Bites *on page 1976*
Antibiotic Treatment of Adults With Infective Endocarditis *on page 1977*
Antimicrobial Drugs of Choice *on page 1981*
Community-Acquired Pneumonia in Adults *on page 1999*
Desensitization Protocols *on page 1913*
Prevention of Bacterial Endocarditis *on page 1960*

Use Treatment of susceptible bacterial infections (nonbeta-lactamase-producing organisms); susceptible bacterial infections caused by streptococci, pneumococci, nonpenicillinase-producing staphylococci, *Listeria*, meningococci; some strains of *H. influenzae*, *Salmonella*, *Shigella*, *E. coli*, *Enterobacter*, and *Klebsiella*

Pregnancy Risk Factor B

Pregnancy Implications Teratogenic effects were not observed in animal studies. Ampicillin crosses the human placenta.

Lactation Enters breast milk/use caution

Medication Safety Issues
Sound-alike/look-alike issues:
Ampicillin may be confused with aminophylline

Contraindications Hypersensitivity to ampicillin, any component of the formulation, or other penicillins

Warnings/Precautions Dosage adjustment may be necessary in patients with renal impairment. A low incidence of cross-allergy with other beta-lactams exists. High percentage of patients with infectious mononucleosis have developed rash during therapy with ampicillin. Appearance of a rash should be carefully evaluated to differentiate a nonallergic ampicillin rash from a hypersensitivity reaction. Ampicillin rash occurs in 5% to 10% of children receiving ampicillin and is a generalized dull red, maculopapular rash, generally appearing 3-14 days after the start of therapy. It normally begins on the trunk and spreads over most of the body. It may be most intense at pressure areas, elbows, and knees.

Adverse Reactions Frequency not defined.
Central nervous system: Fever, penicillin encephalopathy, seizure
Dermatologic: Erythema multiforme, exfoliative dermatitis, rash, urticaria
Note: Appearance of a rash should be carefully evaluated to differentiate (if possible) nonallergic ampicillin rash from hypersensitivity reaction. Incidence is higher in patients with viral infection, *Salmonella* infection, lymphocytic leukemia, or patients that have hyperuricemia.
Gastrointestinal: Black hairy tongue, diarrhea, enterocolitis, glossitis, nausea, pseudomembranous colitis, sore mouth or tongue, stomatitis, vomiting
Hematologic: Agranulocytosis, anemia, hemolytic anemia, eosinophilia, leukopenia, thrombocytopenia purpura
Hepatic: AST increased
Renal: Interstitial nephritis (rare)
Respiratory: Laryngeal stridor
Miscellaneous: Anaphylaxis, serum sickness-like reaction

Overdosage/Toxicology Symptoms of penicillin overdose include neuromuscular hypersensitivity (agitation, hallucinations, asterixis, encephalopathy, confusion, and seizures) and electrolyte imbalance (with potassium or sodium salts), especially in renal failure. Hemodialysis may be helpful to aid in the removal of the drug from the blood, otherwise most treatment is supportive or symptom-directed.

Drug Interactions
Increased Effect/Toxicity: Ampicillin increases the effect of disulfiram and anticoagulants. Probenecid may increase penicillin levels. Theoretically, allopurinol taken with ampicillin has an additive potential for rash. Penicillins may increase the exposure to methotrexate during concurrent therapy; monitor.

Decreased Effect: Although anecdotal reports suggest oral contraceptive efficacy could be reduced by penicillins, this has been refuted by more rigorous scientific and clinical data.

Ethanol/Nutrition/Herb Interactions Food: Food decreases ampicillin absorption rate; may decrease ampicillin serum concentration.

Stability
Oral: Oral suspension is stable for 7 days at room temperature or for 14 days under refrigeration.
I.V.:
I.V. minimum volume: Concentration should not exceed 30 mg/mL due to concentration-dependent stability restrictions. Solutions for I.M. or direct I.V. should be used within 1 hour. Solutions for I.V. infusion will be inactivated by dextrose at room temperature. If dextrose-containing solutions are to be used, the resultant solution will only be stable for 2 hours versus 8 hours in the 0.9% sodium chloride injection. D_5W has limited stability.
Stability of parenteral admixture in NS at room temperature (25°C) is 8 hours.
Stability of parenteral admixture in NS at refrigeration temperature (4°C) is 2 days.
Standard diluent: 500 mg/50 mL NS; 1 g/50 mL NS; 2 g/100 mL NS

Mechanism of Action Inhibits bacterial cell wall synthesis by binding to one or more of the penicillin-binding proteins (PBPs) which in turn inhibits the final transpeptidation step of peptidoglycan synthesis in bacterial cell walls, thus inhibiting cell wall biosynthesis. Bacteria eventually lyse due to ongoing activity of cell wall autolytic enzymes (autolysins and murein hydrolases) while cell wall assembly is arrested.

Pharmacodynamics/Kinetics

Absorption: Oral: 50%

Distribution: Bile, blister, and tissue fluids; penetration into CSF occurs with inflamed meninges only, good only with inflammation (exceeds usual MICs)

Normal meninges: Nil; Inflamed meninges: 5% to 10%

Protein binding: 15% to 25%

Half-life elimination:

Children and Adults: 1-1.8 hours

Anuria/end-stage renal disease: 7-20 hours

Time to peak: Oral: Within 1-2 hours

Excretion: Urine (~90% as unchanged drug) within 24 hours

Dosage

Usual dosage range:

Infants and Children:

Oral: 50-100 mg/kg/day in doses divided every 6 hours (maximum: 2-4 g/day)

I.M., I.V.: 100-400 mg/kg/day in divided doses every 6 hours (maximum: 12 g/day)

Adults: Oral, I.M., I.V.: 250-500 mg every 6 hours

Indication-specific dosing:

Infants and Children:

Endocarditis prophylaxis:

Dental, oral, respiratory tract, or esophageal procedures: I.M., I.V.: 50 mg/kg within 30 minutes prior to procedure in patients unable to take oral amoxicillin

Genitourinary and gastrointestinal tract (except esophageal) procedures: I.M., I.V.:

High-risk patients: 50 mg/kg (maximum: 2 g) within 30 minutes prior to procedure, followed by ampicillin 25 mg/kg (or amoxicillin 25 mg/kg orally) 6 hours later; must be used in combination with gentamicin.

Moderate-risk patients: 50 mg/kg within 30 minutes prior to procedure

Mild-to-moderate infections:

Oral: 50-100 mg/kg/day in doses divided every 6 hours (maximum: 2-4 g/day)

I.M., I.V.: 100-150 mg/kg/day in divided doses every 6 hours (maximum: 2-4 g/day)

Severe infections, meningitis: I.M., I.V.: 200-400 mg/kg/day in divided doses every 6 hours (maximum: 6-12 g/day)

Adults:

Actinomycosis: I.V.: 50 mg/kg/day for 4-6 weeks then oral amoxicillin

Cholangitis (acute): I.V.: 2 g every 4 hours with gentamicin

Diverticulitis: I.M., I.V.: 2 g every 6 hours with metronidazole

Endocarditis:

Infective: I.V.: 12 g/day via continuous infusion or divided every 4 hours

Prophylaxis: Dental, oral, respiratory tract, or esophageal procedures: I.M., I.V.: 2 g within 30 minutes prior to procedure in patients unable to take oral amoxicillin

Genitourinary and gastrointestinal tract (except esophageal) procedures:

High-risk patients: I.M., I.V.: 2 g within 30 minutes prior to procedure, followed by ampicillin 1 g (or amoxicillin 1g orally) 6 hours later; must be used in combination with gentamicin.

Moderate-risk patients: I.M., I.V.: 2 g within 30 minutes prior to procedure

Group B strep prophylaxis (intrapartum): I.V.: 2 g initial dose, then 1 g every 4 hours until delivery

Listeria infections: I.V.: 200 mg/kg/day divided every 6 hours

Sepsis/meningitis: I.M., I.V.: 150-250 mg/kg/day divided every 3-4 hours (range: 6-12 g/day)

Urinary tract infections (enterococcus suspected): I.V.: 1-2 g every 6 hours with gentamicin

Dosing interval in renal impairment:

Cl_{cr} >50 mL/minute: Administer every 6 hours

Cl_{cr} 10-50 mL/minute: Administer every 6-12 hours

Cl_{cr} <10 mL/minute: Administer every 12-24 hours

Hemodialysis: Moderately dialyzable (20% to 50%); administer dose after dialysis

Peritoneal dialysis: Moderately dialyzable (20% to 50%)

Administer 250 mg every 12 hours

Continuous arteriovenous or venovenous hemofiltration effects: Dose as for Cl_{cr} 10-50 mL/minute; ~50 mg of ampicillin per liter of filtrate is removed

Dietary Considerations Take on an empty stomach 1 hour before or 2 hours after meals.

Sodium content of 5 mL suspension (250 mg/5 mL): 10 mg (0.4 mEq)

Sodium content of 1 g: 66.7 mg (3 mEq)

Administration Administer around-the-clock to promote less variation in peak and trough serum levels.

Oral: Administer on an empty stomach (ie, 1 hour prior to, or 2 hours after meals) to increase total absorption.

I.V.: Administer over 3-5 minutes (125-500 mg) or over 10-15 minutes (1-2 g). More rapid infusion may cause seizures. Ampicillin and gentamicin should not be mixed in the same I.V. tubing.

Some penicillins (eg, carbenicillin, ticarcillin, and piperacillin) have been shown to inactivate aminoglycosides *in vitro*. This has been observed to a greater extent with tobramycin and gentamicin, while amikacin has shown greater stability against inactivation. Concurrent use of these agents may pose a risk of reduced antibacterial efficacy *in vivo*, particularly in the setting of profound renal impairment. However, definitive clinical evidence is lacking. If combination penicillin/aminoglycoside therapy is desired in a patient with renal dysfunction, separation of doses (if feasible), and routine monitoring of aminoglycoside levels, CBC, and clinical response should be considered.

Monitoring Parameters With prolonged therapy, monitor renal, hepatic, and hematologic function periodically; observe signs and symptoms of anaphylaxis during first dose

(Continued)

123

Ampicillin *(Continued)*

Test Interactions May interfere with urinary glucose tests using cupric sulfate (Benedict's solution, Clinitest®)

Some penicillin derivatives may accelerate the degradation of aminoglycosides *in vitro*, leading to a potential underestimation of aminoglycoside serum concentration.

Dosage Forms

Capsule: 250 mg, 500 mg

Injection, powder for reconstitution, as sodium: 125 mg, 250 mg, 500 mg, 1 g, 2 g, 10 g

Powder for oral suspension: 125 mg/5 mL (100 mL, 200 mL); 250 mg/5 mL (100 mL, 200 mL)

Ampicillin and Sulbactam *(am pi SIL in & SUL bak tam)*

U.S. Brand Names Unasyn®

Canadian Brand Names Unasyn®

Index Terms Sulbactam and Ampicillin

Pharmacologic Category Antibiotic, Penicillin

Additional Appendix Information

Antimicrobial Drugs of Choice *on page 1981*

Community-Acquired Pneumonia in Adults *on page 1999*

Treatment of Sexually Transmitted Infections *on page 2007*

Use Treatment of susceptible bacterial infections involved with skin and skin structure, intra-abdominal infections, gynecological infections; spectrum is that of ampicillin plus organisms producing beta-lactamases such as *S. aureus, H. influenzae, E. coli, Klebsiella, Acinetobacter, Enterobacter*, and anaerobes

Pregnancy Risk Factor B

Lactation Enters breast milk/use caution

Contraindications Hypersensitivity to ampicillin, sulbactam, penicillins, or any component of the formulations

Warnings/Precautions Dosage adjustment may be necessary in patients with renal impairment. A low incidence of cross-allergy with other beta-lactams exists. High percentage of patients with infectious mononucleosis have developed rash during therapy with ampicillin. Appearance of a rash should be carefully evaluated to differentiate a nonallergic ampicillin rash from a hypersensitivity reaction.

Adverse Reactions Also see Ampicillin.

>10%: Local: Pain at injection site (I.M.)

1% to 10%:

Dermatologic: Rash

Gastrointestinal: Diarrhea

Local: Pain at injection site (I.V.), thrombophlebitis

Miscellaneous: Allergic reaction (may include serum sickness, urticaria, bronchospasm, hypotension, etc)

<1% (Limited to important or life-threatening): Abdominal distension, candidiasis, chest pain, chills, dysuria, edema, epistaxis, erythema, facial swelling, fatigue, flatulence, glossitis, hairy tongue, headache, interstitial nephritis, itching, liver enzymes increased, malaise, mucosal bleeding, nausea, pseudomembranous colitis, seizure, substernal pain, throat tightness, thrombocytopenia, urine retention, vomiting

Overdosage/Toxicology Symptoms of penicillin overdose include neuromuscular hypersensitivity (agitation, hallucinations, asterixis, encephalopathy, confusion, and seizures) and electrolyte imbalance (with potassium or sodium salts), especially in renal failure. Hemodialysis may be helpful to aid in the removal of the drug from the blood; otherwise, most treatment is supportive or symptom-directed.

Drug Interactions

Increased Effect/Toxicity: Disulfiram or probenecid can increase ampicillin levels. Theoretically, allopurinol taken with ampicillin has an additive potential for rash. Penicillins may increase the exposure to methotrexate during concurrent therapy; monitor.

Decreased Effect: Although anecdotal reports suggest oral contraceptive efficacy could be reduced by penicillins, this has been refuted by more rigorous scientific and clinical data.

Stability Prior to reconstitution, store at ≤30°C (86°F).

I.M. and direct I.V. administration: Use within 1 hour after preparation. Reconstitute with sterile water for injection or 0.5% or 2% lidocaine hydrochloride injection (I.M.). Sodium chloride 0.9% (NS) is the diluent of choice for I.V. piggyback use. Solutions made in NS are stable up to 72 hours when refrigerated whereas dextrose solutions (same concentration) are stable for only 4 hours.

Mechanism of Action The addition of sulbactam, a beta-lactamase inhibitor, to ampicillin extends the spectrum of ampicillin to include some beta-lactamase-producing organisms; inhibits bacterial cell wall synthesis by binding to one or more of the penicillin-binding proteins (PBPs) which in turn inhibits the final transpeptidation step of peptidoglycan synthesis in bacterial cell walls, thus inhibiting cell wall biosynthesis. Bacteria eventually lyse due to ongoing activity of cell wall autolytic enzymes (autolysins and murein hydrolases) while cell wall assembly is arrested.

Pharmacodynamics/Kinetics

Ampicillin: See Ampicillin.

Sulbactam:

Distribution: Bile, blister, and tissue fluids

Protein binding: 38%

Half-life elimination: Normal renal function: 1-1.3 hours

Excretion: Urine (~75% to 85% as unchanged drug) within 8 hours

Dosage Note: Unasyn® (ampicillin/sulbactam) is a combination product. Dosage recommendations for Unasyn® are based on the ampicillin component.

Usual dosage range:
Children ≥1 year: I.V.: 100-400 mg ampicillin/kg/day divided every 6 hours (maximum: 8 g ampicillin/day, 12 g Unasyn®). **Note:** The American Academy of Pediatrics recommends a dose of up to 300 mg/kg/day for severe infection in infants >1 month of age.

Adults: I.M., I.V.: 1-2 g ampicillin (1.5-3 g Unasyn®) every 6 hours (maximum: 8 g ampicillin/day, 12 g Unasyn®)

Indication-specific dosing:
Children:
Epiglottitis: I.V.: 100-200 mg ampicillin/kg/day divided in 4 doses
Mild-to-moderate infections: I.M., I.V.: 100-200 mg ampicillin/kg/day (150-300 mg Unasyn®) divided every 6 hours (maximum: 8 g ampicillin/day, 12 g Unasyn®)
Peritonsillar and retropharyngeal abscess: I.V.: 50 mg ampicillin/kg/dose every 6 hours
Severe infections: I.M., I.V.: 200-400 mg ampicillin/kg/day divided every 6 hours (maximum: 8 g ampicillin/day, 12 g Unasyn®)
Adults: Doses expressed as ampicillin/sulbactam combination:
Amnionitis, cholangitis, diverticulitis, endometritis, endophthalmitis, epididymitis/ orchitis, liver abscess, osteomyelitis (diabetic foot), peritonitis: I.V.: 3 g every 6 hours
Endocarditis: I.V.: 3 g every 6 hours with gentamicin or vancomycin for 4-6 weeks
Orbital cellulitis: I.V.: 1.5 g every 6 hours
Parapharyngeal space infections: I.V.: 3 g every 6 hours
***Pasteurella multocida* (human, canine/feline bites):** I.V.: 1.5-3 g every 6 hours
Pelvic inflammatory disease: I.V.: 3 g every 6 hours with doxycycline
Peritonitis (CAPD): Intraperitoneal:
Anuric, intermittent: 3 g every 12 hours
Anuric, continuous: Loading dose: 1.5 g; maintenance dose: 150 mg
Pneumonia:
Aspiration, community-acquired: I.V.: 1.5-3 g every 6 hours
Hospital-acquired: I.V.: 3 g every 6 hours
Urinary tract infections, pyelonephritis: I.V.: 3 g every 6 hours for 14 days
Dosing interval in renal impairment:
Cl$_{cr}$ 15-29 mL/minute: Administer every 12 hours
Cl$_{cr}$ 5-14 mL/minute: Administer every 24 hours

Dietary Considerations Sodium content of 1.5 g injection: 115 mg (5 mEq)

Administration Administer around-the-clock to promote less variation in peak and trough serum levels. Administer by slow injection over 10-15 minutes or I.V. over 15-30 minutes. Ampicillin and gentamicin should not be mixed in the same I.V. tubing.

Some penicillins (eg, carbenicillin, ticarcillin, and piperacillin) have been shown to inactivate aminoglycosides *in vitro*. This has been observed to a greater extent with tobramycin and gentamicin, while amikacin has shown greater stability against inactivation. Concurrent use of these agents may pose a risk of reduced antibacterial efficacy *in vivo*, particularly in the setting of profound renal impairment. However, definitive clinical evidence is lacking. If combination penicillin/aminoglycoside therapy is desired in a patient with renal dysfunction, separation of doses (if feasible), and routine monitoring of aminoglycoside levels, CBC, and clinical response should be considered.

Monitoring Parameters With prolonged therapy, monitor hematologic, renal, and hepatic function; monitor for signs of anaphylaxis during first dose

Test Interactions May interfere with urinary glucose tests using cupric sulfate (Benedict's solution, Clinitest®).

Some penicillin derivatives may accelerate the degradation of aminoglycosides. *in vitro*, leading to a potential underestimation of aminoglycoside serum concentration.

Dosage Forms
Injection, powder for reconstitution: Injection, powder for reconstitution: 1.5 g: Ampicillin 1 g and sulbactam 0.5 g [contains sodium 115 mg (5 mEq)/1.5 g)]; 3 g: Ampicillin 2 g and sulbactam 1 g [contains sodium 115 mg (5 mEq)/1.5 g)]; 15 g: Ampicillin 10 g and sulbactam 5 g [bulk package; contains sodium 115 mg (5 mEq)/1.5 g)]
Unasyn®:
1.5 g: Ampicillin 1 g and sulbactam 0.5 g [contains sodium 115 mg (5 mEq)/1.5 g)]
3 g: Ampicillin 2 g and sulbactam 1 g [contains sodium 115 mg (5 mEq)/1.5 g)]
15 g: Ampicillin 10 g and sulbactam 5 g [bulk package; contains sodium 115 mg (5 mEq)/ 1.5 g)]

♦ **Ampicillin Sodium** *see* Ampicillin *on page 122*
♦ **Ampicillin Trihydrate** *see* Ampicillin *on page 122*

Amprenavir *(am PREN a veer)*

U.S. Brand Names Agenerase®
Canadian Brand Names Agenerase®
Pharmacologic Category Antiretroviral Agent, Protease Inhibitor
Additional Appendix Information
Antiretroviral Therapy for HIV Infection: Adults and Adolescents *on page 1988*
Management of Healthcare Worker Exposures to HBV, HCV, and HIV *on page 1941*
Use Treatment of HIV infections in combination with at least two other antiretroviral agents; oral solution should only be used when capsules or other protease inhibitors are not therapeutic options
Pregnancy Risk Factor C
Pregnancy Implications It is not known if amprenavir crosses the human placenta and there are no clinical studies currently underway to evaluate its use in pregnant women. Use of oral solution is contraindicated during pregnancy. Pregnancy and protease inhibitors are both associated with an increased risk of hyperglycemia. Glucose levels should be closely monitored. Health professionals are encouraged to contact the antiretroviral pregnancy registry to (Continued)

Amprenavir (Continued)

monitor outcomes of pregnant women exposed to antiretroviral medications (1-800-258-4263 or www.APRegistry.com).

Lactation Excretion in breast milk unknown/contraindicated

Contraindications Hypersensitivity to amprenavir or any component of the formulation; concurrent therapy with cisapride, ergot derivatives, midazolam, pimozide, and triazolam; severe previous allergic reaction to sulfonamides; oral solution is contraindicated in infants or children <4 years of age, pregnant women, patients with renal or hepatic failure, and patients receiving concurrent metronidazole or disulfiram

Warnings/Precautions Use with caution in patients taking strong CYP3A4 inhibitors, moderate or strong CYP3A4 inducers and major CYP3A4 substrates (see drug interactions); consider alternative agents that avoid or lessen the potential for CYP-mediated interactions. New onset or worsening diabetes mellitus and hyperglycemia have been reported, including cases of diabetic ketoacidosis; use with caution in patients with impaired glucose control. Use with caution in patients with sulfonamide allergy, hepatic impairment, or hemophilia. Redistribution of fat may occur (eg, buffalo hump, peripheral wasting, cushingoid appearance). Immune reconstitution syndrome may develop resulting in the occurrence of an inflammatory response to an indolent or residual opportunistic infection; further evaluation and treatment may be required.

Amprenavir formulations contain vitamin E; additional vitamin E supplements should be avoided. **[U.S. Boxed Warning]: Certain ethnic populations (Asians, Eskimos, Native Americans) may be at increased risk of propylene glycol-associated adverse effects; therefore, use of the oral solution of amprenavir should be avoided.** Use oral solution only when capsules or other protease inhibitors are not options. Safety and efficacy in children <4 years of age have not been established.

Adverse Reactions

>10%:
Central nervous system: Depression/mood disorder (9% to 16%), paresthesia (peripheral 10% to 14%)

Dermatologic: Rash (20% to 27%)

Endocrine & metabolic: Hyperglycemia (>160 mg/dL: 37% to 41%), hypertriglyceridemia (>399 mg/dL: 36% to 47%; >750 mg/dL: 8% to 13%)

Gastrointestinal: Nausea (43% to 74%), vomiting (24% to 34%), diarrhea (39% to 60%), abdominal symptoms

Miscellaneous: Perioral tingling/numbness (26% to 31%)

1% to 10%:
Central nervous system: Headache, fatigue

Dermatologic: Stevens-Johnson syndrome (1% of total, 4% of patients who develop a rash)

Endocrine & metabolic: Hypercholesterolemia (>260 mg/dL: 4% to 9%), hyperglycemia (>251 mg/dL: 2% to 3%), fat redistribution

Gastrointestinal: Taste disorders (2% to 10%), amylase increased (3% to 4%)

Hepatic: AST increased (3% to 5%), ALT increased (4%)

<1% (Limited to important or life-threatening): New-onset diabetes

Overdosage/Toxicology Monitor for signs and symptoms of propylene glycol toxicity (seizures, stupor, tachycardia, hyperosmolality, lactic acidosis, renal toxicity, hemolysis) if the oral solution is administered.

Drug Interactions

Cytochrome P450 Effect: Substrate of CYP2C9 (minor), 3A4 (major); **Inhibits** CYP2C19 (weak), 3A4 (strong)

Increased Effect/Toxicity: Concurrent use of cisapride, midazolam, pimozide, quinidine, or triazolam is contraindicated. Concurrent use of ergot alkaloids (dihydroergotamine, ergotamine, ergonovine, methylergonovine) with amprenavir is also contraindicated (may cause vasospasm and peripheral ischemia). Concurrent use of oral solution with disulfiram or metronidazole is contraindicated, due to the risk of propylene glycol toxicity.

Serum concentrations of amiodarone, bepridil, lidocaine, quinidine, and other antiarrhythmics may be increased, potentially leading to toxicity; when amprenavir is coadministered with ritonavir, flecainide and propafenone are contraindicated. HMG-CoA reductase inhibitors serum concentrations may be increased by amprenavir, increasing the risk of myopathy/rhabdomyolysis; lovastatin and simvastatin are not recommended; fluvastatin and pravastatin may be safer alternatives.

Amprenavir may increase the levels/effects of selected benzodiazepines (midazolam and triazolam are contraindicated), calcium channel blockers, cyclosporine, mirtazapine, nateglinide, nefazodone, quinidine, sildenafil (and other PDE-5 inhibitors), tacrolimus, venlafaxine, and other CYP3A4 substrates. Amprenavir may increase the levels/effects of trazodone (monitor for signs of hypotension/syncope); reduce dose of trazodone. When used with strong CYP3A4 inhibitors, dosage adjustment/limits are recommended for sildenafil and other PDE-5 inhibitors; refer to individual monographs. Amprenavir may increase the levels/effects of inhaled corticosteroids; monitor for adrenal suppression, Cushing's syndrome; concomitant use of fluticasone with amprenavir/ritonavir is not recommended.

Concurrent therapy with ritonavir may result in increased serum concentrations: dosage adjustment is recommended; avoid concurrent use of amprenavir and ritonavir oral solutions due to metabolic competition between formulation components. Clarithromycin, indinavir, nelfinavir may increase serum concentrations of amprenavir.

Decreased Effect: Serum concentrations of estrogen (oral contraceptives) may be decreased, use alternative (nonhormonal) forms of contraception. Serum concentrations of delavirdine may be decreased; may lead to loss of virologic response and possible resistance to delavirdine; concomitant use is not recommended. Efavirenz and nevirapine may decrease serum concentrations of amprenavir (dosing for combinations not established). Avoid St John's wort (may lead to subtherapeutic concentrations of amprenavir). Effect of amprenavir may be diminished when administered with methadone (consider alternative antiretroviral); in addition, effect of methadone may be reduced (dosage increase may be required). The levels/effects of amprenavir may be decreased by include aminoglutethimide, carbamazepine, nafcillin, nevirapine, phenobarbital, phenytoin, rifamycins, and other CYP3A4 inducers. The administration of antacids and didanosine (buffered formulation) should be separated from amprenavir by 1 hour to limit interaction between formulations.

Ethanol/Nutrition/Herb Interactions
Ethanol: Avoid ethanol with amprenavir oral solution.
Food: Levels increased sixfold with high-fat meals.
Herb/Nutraceutical: Amprenavir serum concentration may be decreased by St John's wort; avoid concurrent use. Formulations contain vitamin E; avoid additional supplements.

Mechanism of Action Binds to the protease activity site and inhibits the activity of the enzyme. HIV protease is required for the cleavage of viral polyprotein precursors into individual functional proteins found in infectious HIV. Inhibition prevents cleavage of these polyproteins, resulting in the formation of immature, noninfectious viral particles.

Pharmacodynamics/Kinetics
Absorption: 63%
Distribution: 430 L
Protein binding: 90%
Metabolism: Hepatic via CYP (primarily CYP3A4)
Bioavailability: Not established; increased sixfold with high-fat meal; oral solution: 86% relative to capsule formulation (14% less bioavailable than capsule)
Half-life elimination: 7.1-10.6 hours
Time to peak: 1-2 hours
Excretion: Feces (75%, ~68% as metabolites); urine (14% as metabolites)

Dosage Oral: Note: Capsule and oral solution are **not** interchangeable on a mg-per-mg basis.
Capsule:
Children 4-12 years **or** 13-16 years (<50 kg): 20 mg/kg twice daily or 15 mg/kg 3 times daily; maximum: 2400 mg/day
Children >13 years (≥50 kg) and Adults: 1200 mg twice daily
Note: Dosage adjustments for amprenavir when administered in combination therapy:
Efavirenz: Adjustments necessary for both agents:
Amprenavir 1200 mg 3 times/day (single protease inhibitor) **or**
Amprenavir 1200 mg twice daily plus ritonavir 200 mg twice daily
Ritonavir: Adjustments necessary for both agents:
Amprenavir 1200 mg plus ritonavir 200 mg once daily **or**
Amprenavir 600 mg plus ritonavir 100 mg twice daily
Note: Oral solution of ritonavir and amprenavir should not be coadministered.
Solution:
Children 4-12 years **or** 13-16 years (<50 kg): 22.5 mg/kg twice daily or 17 mg/kg 3 times daily; maximum: 2800 mg/day
Children >13 years (≥50 kg) and Adults: 1400 mg twice daily
Dosage adjustment in renal impairment: Oral solution is contraindicated in renal failure.
Dosage adjustment in hepatic impairment:
Child-Pugh score between 5-8:
Capsule: 450 mg twice daily
Solution: 513 mg twice daily; contraindicated in hepatic failure
Child-Pugh score between 9-12:
Capsule: 300 mg twice daily
Solution: 342 mg twice daily; contraindicated in hepatic failure

Dietary Considerations May be taken with or without food; do not take with high-fat meal. The 50 mg capsules contain 36.3 int. units of vitamin E per capsule; oral solution contains 46 int. units of vitamin E per mL; avoid additional vitamin E-containing supplements.

Additional Information Propylene glycol is included in the oral solution; a dose of 22.5 mg/kg twice daily corresponds to an intake of 1650 mg/kg of propylene glycol. Capsule and oral solution are not interchangeable on a mg-per-mg basis.

Dosage Forms
Capsule:
Agenerase®: 50 mg [contains vitamin E 36.3 int. units (as TPGS)]
Solution, oral:
Agenerase®: 15 mg/mL (240 mL) [contains propylene glycol 550 mg/mL and vitamin E 46 int. units/mL; grape-bubble gum-peppermint flavor]

♦ **AMPT** see Metyrosine on page 1134
♦ **Amrinone Lactate** see Inamrinone on page 897

Amyl Nitrite (AM il NYE trite)

Index Terms Isoamyl Nitrite
Pharmacologic Category Antidote; Vasodilator
Use Coronary vasodilator in angina pectoris; adjunct in treatment of cyanide poisoning; produce changes in the intensity of heart murmurs
Pregnancy Risk Factor X
Dosage Nasal inhalation:
Cyanide poisoning: Children and Adults: Inhale the vapor from a 0.3 mL crushed ampul every minute for 15-30 seconds until I.V. sodium nitrite infusion is available
Angina: Adults: 1-6 inhalations from 1 crushed ampul; may repeat in 3-5 minutes
Additional Information Complete prescribing information for this medication should be consulted for additional detail.
Dosage Forms Vapor for inhalation [crushable covered glass capsules]: Amyl nitrite USP (0.3 mL)

♦ **Amylobarbitone** see Amobarbital on page 107
♦ **Amytal®** see Amobarbital on page 107
♦ **AN100226** see Natalizumab on page 1203

♦ **Anadrol**® *see* Oxymetholone *on page 1290*
♦ **Anafranil**® *see* ClomiPRAMINE *on page 395*

Anagrelide (an AG gre lide)

U.S. Brand Names Agrylin®
Canadian Brand Names Agrylin®; Gen-Anagrelide; PMS-Anagrelide; Rhoxal-anagrelide; Sandoz-Anagrelide
Index Terms 1370-999-397; Anagrelide Hydrochloride; BL4162A; 6,7-Dichloro-1,5-Dihydroimidazo [2,1b] quinazolin-2(3H)-one Monohydrochloride
Pharmacologic Category Phospholipase A_2 Inhibitor
Use Treatment of essential thrombocythemia (ET) and thrombocythemia associated with chronic myelogenous leukemia (CML), polycythemia vera, and other myeloproliferative disorders
Pregnancy Risk Factor C
Dosage Note: Maintain for ≥1 week, then adjust to the lowest effective dose to reduce and maintain platelet count <600,000/μL ideally to the normal range; the dose must not be increased by >0.5 mg/day in any 1 week; maximum dose: 10 mg/day or 2.5 mg/dose

Oral:
  Children: Initial: 0.5 mg/day (range: 0.5 mg 1-4 times/day)
  Adults: 0.5 mg 4 times/day or 1 mg twice daily
  Elderly: There are no special requirements for dosing in the elderly
  Dosage adjustment in hepatic impairment:
    Moderate impairment: Initial: 0.5 mg once daily; maintain for 1 week with careful monitoring of cardiovascular status
    Severe impairment: Contraindicated
Additional Information Complete prescribing information for this medication should be consulted for additional detail.
Dosage Forms Capsule: 0.5 mg, 1 mg

♦ **Anagrelide Hydrochloride** *see* Anagrelide *on page 128*

Anakinra (an a KIN ra)

U.S. Brand Names Kineret®
Canadian Brand Names Kineret®
Index Terms IL-1Ra; Interleukin-1 Receptor Antagonist
Pharmacologic Category Antirheumatic, Disease Modifying; Interleukin-1 Receptor Antagonist
Use Reduction of signs and symptoms of moderately- to severely-active rheumatoid arthritis in adult patients who have failed one or more disease-modifying antirheumatic drugs (DMARDs); may be used alone or in combination with DMARDs (other than tumor necrosis factor-blocking agents)
Pregnancy Risk Factor B
Pregnancy Implications No evidence of impaired fertility or harm to fetus in animal models; however, there are no controlled trials in pregnant women. Women exposed to anakinra during pregnancy may contact the Organization of Teratology Information Services (OTIS), Rheumatoid Arthritis and Pregnancy Study at 1-877-311-8972.
Lactation Excretion in breast milk unknown/use caution
Medication Safety Issues
Sound-alike/look-alike issues:
  Anakinra may be confused with amikacin
Contraindications Hypersensitivity to *E. coli*-derived proteins, anakinra, or any component of the formulation; patients with active infections (including chronic or local infection)
Warnings/Precautions Anakinra may affect defenses against infections and malignancies. Safety and efficacy in patients with immunosuppression or chronic infections have not been evaluated. Discontinue administration if patient develops a serious infection. Do not start drug administration in patients with an active infection. Patients with asthma may be at an increased risk of serious infections. Should not be used in combination with tumor necrosis factor antagonists, unless no satisfactory alternatives exist, and then only with extreme caution. Impact on the development and course of malignancies is not fully defined. As compared to the general population, an increased risk of lymphoma has been noted in clinical trials; however, rheumatoid arthritis has been previously associated with an increased rate of lymphoma.

Use caution in patients with a history of significant hematologic abnormalities; has been associated with uncommon, but significant decreases in hematologic parameters (particularly neutrophil counts). Patients must be advised to seek medical attention if they develop signs and symptoms suggestive of blood dyscrasias. Discontinue if significant hematologic abnormalities are confirmed.

Patients should be brought up to date with all immunizations before initiating therapy. Live vaccines should not be given concurrently. Patients with a significant exposure to varicella virus should temporarily discontinue anakinra. Hypersensitivity reactions may occur. Impact on the development and course of malignancies is not fully defined. Safety and efficacy have not been established in children.
Adverse Reactions
>10%:
  Central nervous system: Headache (12%)
  Local: Injection site reaction (majority mild, typically lasting 14-28 days, characterized by erythema, ecchymosis, inflammation, and pain; up to 71%)
  Miscellaneous: Infection (39% versus 37% in placebo; serious infection in 3% to 2%)
1% to 10%:
  Gastrointestinal: Nausea (8%), diarrhea (7%), abdominal pain (5%)

Hematologic: WBCs decreased (8%)
Respiratory: Sinusitis (7%)
Miscellaneous: Flu-like syndrome (6%)
<1% (Limited to important or life-threatening): Neutropenia (0.3%)

Overdosage/Toxicology No serious toxicities have been reported following administration of high doses of anakinra (up to 35 times the typical dosage for rheumatoid arthritis).

Drug Interactions

Increased Effect/Toxicity: Concurrent use of anakinra and etanercept has been associated with an increased risk of serious infection while American College of Rheumatology (ACR) response rates were not improved, as compared to etanercept alone. Use caution with other drugs known to block or decrease the activity of tumor necrosis factor (TNF); includes infliximab and thalidomide.

Stability Store in refrigerator at 2°C to 8°C (36°F to 46°F); do not freeze. Protect from light.

Mechanism of Action Binds to the interleukin-1 (IL-1) receptor. IL-1 is induced by inflammatory stimuli and mediates a variety of immunological responses, including degradation of cartilage (loss of proteoglycans) and stimulation of bone resorption.

Pharmacodynamics/Kinetics
Bioavailability: SubQ: 95%
Half-life elimination: Terminal: 4-6 hours
Time to peak: SubQ: 3-7 hours

Dosage Adults: SubQ: Rheumatoid arthritis: 100 mg once daily (administer at approximately the same time each day)

Dosage adjustment in renal impairment: No specific guidelines for adjustment (clearance decreased by 70% to 75% in patients with Cl_{cr} <30 mL/minute)

Administration Rotate injection sites (thigh, abdomen, upper arm); injection should be given at least 1 inch away from previous injection site. Do not shake. Provided in single-use, preservative free syringes with 27-gauge needles; discard any unused portion.

Monitoring Parameters Neutrophil counts should be assessed prior to initiation of treatment and repeated every month for the first 3 months of treatment, then quarterly up to 1 year.

Additional Information Anakinra is produced by recombinant DNA/*E. coli* technology.

Dosage Forms Injection, solution [preservative free]: 100 mg/0.67 mL (1 mL) [prefilled syringe]

♦ **Analpram-HC**® *see* Pramoxine and Hydrocortisone *on page 1409*
♦ **Anandron**® **(Can)** *see* Nilutamide *on page 1228*
♦ **Anaprox**® *see* Naproxen *on page 1199*
♦ **Anaprox**® **DS** *see* Naproxen *on page 1199*
♦ **Anaspaz**® *see* Hyoscyamine *on page 866*

Anastrozole (an AS troe zole)

U.S. Brand Names Arimidex®
Canadian Brand Names Arimidex®
Index Terms ICI-D1033; NSC-719344; ZD1033
Pharmacologic Category Antineoplastic Agent, Aromatase Inhibitor
Use Treatment of locally-advanced or metastatic breast cancer (ER-positive or hormone receptor unknown) in postmenopausal women; treatment of advanced breast cancer in postmenopausal women with disease progression following tamoxifen therapy; adjuvant treatment of early ER-positive breast cancer in postmenopausal women

Pregnancy Risk Factor D

Pregnancy Implications Fetotoxicity was observed in animal studies. Safety and efficacy have not been established in premenopausal women; exclude pregnancy prior to treatment.

Lactation Excretion in breast milk unknown/use caution

Contraindications Hypersensitivity to anastrozole or any component of the formulation; pregnancy

Warnings/Precautions Hazardous agent - use appropriate precautions for handling and disposal. Use with caution in patients with hyperlipidemias; total cholesterol and LDL-cholesterol increase in patients receiving anastrozol; exclude pregnancy before initiating therapy. Anastrozole may be associated with a reduction in bone mineral density. Safety and efficacy in premenopausal women or pediatric patients have not been established.

Adverse Reactions

>10%:
Cardiovascular: Vasodilatation (25% to 36%), hypertension (2% to 13%)
Central nervous system: Mood disturbance (19%), fatigue (19%), pain (11% to 17%), headache (9% to 13%), depression (5% to 13%)
Dermatologic: Rash (6% to 11%)
Endocrine & metabolic: Hot flashes (12% to 36%)
Gastrointestinal: Nausea (11% to 19%), vomiting (8% to 13%)
Neuromuscular & skeletal: Weakness (16% to 19%), arthritis (17%), arthralgia (2% to 15%), back pain (10% to 12%), bone pain (6% to 11%), osteoporosis (11%)
Respiratory: Pharyngitis (6% to 14%), cough increased (8% to 11%)

1% to 10%:
Cardiovascular: Peripheral edema (5% to 10%), chest pain (5% to 7%), ischemic cardiovascular disease (4%), venous thromboembolic events (3% to 4%), ischemic cerebrovascular events (2%), angina (2%)
Central nervous system: Insomnia (2% to 10%), dizziness (6% to 8%), anxiety (2% to 6%), fever (2% to 5%), malaise (2% to 5%), confusion (2% to 5%), nervousness (2% to 5%), somnolence (2% to 5%), lethargy (1%)
Dermatologic: Alopecia (2% to 5%), pruritus (2% to 5%)
Endocrine & metabolic: Hypercholesterolemia (9%), breast pain (2% to 8%)
Gastrointestinal: Constipation (7% to 9%), abdominal pain (7% to 9%), diarrhea (8% to 9%), anorexia (5% to 7%), xerostomia (6%), dyspepsia (7%), weight gain (2% to 9%), weight loss (2% to 5%)

(Continued)

Anastrozole *(Continued)*

Genitourinary: Urinary tract infection (2% to 8%), vulvovaginitis (6%), pelvic pain (5%), vaginal bleeding (1% to 5%), vaginitis (4%), vaginal discharge (4%), vaginal hemorrhage (2% to 4%), leukorrhea (2% to 3%), vaginal dryness (2%)

Hematologic: Anemia (2% to 5%), leukopenia (2% to 5%)

Hepatic: Liver function tests increased (2% to 5%), alkaline phosphatase increased (2% to 5%), gamma GT increased (2% to 5%)

Local: Thrombophlebitis (2% to 5%)

Neuromuscular & skeletal: Fracture (2% to 10%), arthrosis (7%), paresthesia (5% to 7%), joint disorder (6%), myalgia (2% to 6%), neck pain (2% to 5%), hypertonia (3%)

Ocular: Cataracts (6%)

Respiratory: Dyspnea (8% to 10%), sinusitis (2% to 6%), bronchitis (2% to 5%), rhinitis (2% to 5%)

Miscellaneous: Lymph edema (10%), infection (2% to 9%), flu-like syndrome (2% to 7%), diaphoresis (2% to 5%), cyst (5%), tumor flare (3%)

<1% (Limited to important or life-threatening): Anaphylaxis, angioedema, CVA, cerebral ischemia, cerebral infarct, endometrial cancer, erythema multiforme, joint pain, joint stiffness, MI, myocardial ischemia, pulmonary embolus, retinal vein thrombosis, Stevens-Johnson syndrome, urticaria

Overdosage/Toxicology Symptoms include severe irritation to the stomach (necrosis, gastritis, ulceration and hemorrhage). Treatment is symptom-directed and supportive. Vomiting may be induced if the patient is alert. Dialysis may be helpful because anastrozole is not highly protein bound. Treatment consists of general supportive care, including frequent monitoring of all vital signs and close observation.

Drug Interactions

Cytochrome P450 Effect: Inhibits CYP1A2 (weak), 2C8 (weak), 2C9 (weak), 3A4 (weak)

Decreased Effect: Estrogen derivatives and tamoxifen may decrease the levels/effects of anastrozole.

Ethanol/Nutrition/Herb Interactions Herb/Nutraceutical: Avoid black cohosh, hops, licorice, red clover, thyme, and dong quai.

Stability Store at 20°C to 25°C (68°F to 77°F).

Mechanism of Action Potent and selective nonsteroidal aromatase inhibitor. By inhibiting aromatase, the conversion of androstenedione to estrone, and testosterone to estradiol, is prevented. Anastrozole causes an 85% decrease in estrone sulfate levels.

Pharmacodynamics/Kinetics

Onset of estradiol reduction: 70% reduction after 24 hours; 80% after 2 weeks therapy

Duration of estradiol reduction: 6 days

Absorption: Well absorbed; not affected by food

Protein binding, plasma: 40%

Metabolism: Extensively hepatic (~85%) via N-dealkylation, hydroxylation, and glucuronidation; primary metabolite inactive

Half-life elimination: ~50 hours

Excretion: Urine (10% as unchanged drug; 60% as metabolites)

Dosage Breast cancer: Adults: Oral (refer to individual protocols): 1 mg once daily

Dosage adjustment in renal impairment: Dosage adjustment not necessary

Dosage adjustment in hepatic impairment: Mild-to-moderate impairment: Plasma concentrations in subjects with stable hepatic cirrhosis were within the range concentrations in normal subjects across all clinical trials; therefore, no dosage adjustment required; however, patients should be monitored for side effects. Safety and efficacy in severe hepatic impairment have not been established.

Monitoring Parameters Bone mineral density; total cholesterol and LDL

Test Interactions Lab test abnormalities: GGT, AST, ALT, alkaline phosphatase, total cholesterol, and LDL increased; threefold elevations of mean serum GGT levels have been observed among patients with liver metastases. These changes were likely related to the progression of liver metastases in these patients, although other contributing factors could not be ruled out. Mean serum total cholesterol levels increased by 0.5 mmol/L among patients.

Dosage Forms

Tablet:

Arimidex®: 1 mg

♦ **Anbesol® [OTC]** *see* Benzocaine *on page 204*

♦ **Anbesol® Baby [OTC]** *see* Benzocaine *on page 204*

♦ **Anbesol® Baby (Can)** *see* Benzocaine *on page 204*

♦ **Anbesol® Cold Sore Therapy [OTC]** *see* Benzocaine *on page 204*

♦ **Anbesol® Jr. [OTC]** *see* Benzocaine *on page 204*

♦ **Anbesol® Maximum Strength [OTC]** *see* Benzocaine *on page 204*

♦ **Ancef®** *see* Cefazolin *on page 306*

♦ **Ancobon®** *see* Flucytosine *on page 714*

♦ **Andehist DM NR Drops [DSC]** *see* Carbinoxamine, Pseudoephedrine, and Dextromethorphan *on page 291*

♦ **Andehist NR Drops [DSC]** *see* Carbinoxamine and Pseudoephedrine *on page 290*

♦ **Andehist NR Syrup** *see* Brompheniramine and Pseudoephedrine *on page 243*

♦ **Andriol® (Can)** *see* Testosterone *on page 1653*

♦ **Androderm®** *see* Testosterone *on page 1653*

♦ **AndroGel®** *see* Testosterone *on page 1653*

♦ **Android®** *see* MethylTESTOSTERone *on page 1125*

♦ **Andropository (Can)** *see* Testosterone *on page 1653*

♦ **Anestacon®** *see* Lidocaine *on page 1010*

♦ **Aneurine Hydrochloride** *see* Thiamine *on page 1668*

♦ **Anexate® (Can)** *see* Flumazenil *on page 718*

- **Anexsia®** *see* Hydrocodone and Acetaminophen *on page 848*
- **Angiomax®** *see* Bivalirudin *on page 227*
- **Angiscein®** *see* Fluorescein Sodium *on page 722*

Anidulafungin (ay nid yoo la FUN jin)

U.S. Brand Names Eraxis™
Index Terms LY303366
Pharmacologic Category Antifungal Agent, Parenteral; Echinocandin
Additional Appendix Information
Antifungal Agents *on page 1869*
Use Treatment of candidemia and other forms of *Candida* infections (including those of intra-abdominal, peritoneal, and esophageal locus)
Pregnancy Risk Factor C
Pregnancy Implications Skeletal teratogenic effects were noted in animal studies. There are no adequate and well-controlled studies in pregnant women. Use only if benefit outweighs risk.
Lactation Excretion in breast milk unknown/use caution
Contraindications Hypersensitivity to anidulafungin, other echinocandins, or any component of the formulation
Warnings/Precautions Histamine-mediated reactions (eg, urticaria, flushing, hypotension) have been observed; these may be related to infusion rate. Elevated liver function tests, hepatitis, and worsening hepatic failure have been reported. Monitor for progressive hepatic impairment if increased transaminase enzymes noted. Safety and efficacy in pediatric patients, neutropenic patients, or other *Candida* infections (eg, endocarditis, osteomyelitis, meningitis) have not been established.
Adverse Reactions
2% to 10%:
Endocrine & metabolic: Hypokalemia (3%)
Gastrointestinal: Diarrhea (3%)
Hepatic: Transaminase increased (<1% to 2%)
<2% (Limited to important or life-threatening): Abdominal pain, alkaline phosphatase increased, amylase increased, angioneurotic edema, atrial fibrillation, back pain, bilirubin increased, bundle branch block (right), candidiasis, cholestasis, clostridial infection, coagulopathy, constipation, cough, CPK increased, creatinine increased, diaphoresis, diarrhea, dizziness, DVT, dyspepsia, ECG abnormality (including QT prolongation), erythema, eye pain, fecal incontinence, flushing, fungemia, GGT increased, headache, hepatic necrosis, hepatitis, hepatic dysfunction, hot flushes, hypercalcemia, hyperglycemia, hyperkalemia, hypernatremia, hyper-/hypotension, hypomagnesemia, infusion-related reaction, leukopenia (0.7%), lipase increased, nausea, neutropenia (1%), peripheral edema, phlebitis, platelet count increased, prothrombin time prolonged, pruritus, pyrexia, rash, rigors, seizure, sinus arrhythmia, thrombocytopenia, thrombophlebitis, urea increased, urticaria, ventricular extrasystoles, vision blurred, visual disturbance, vomiting
Overdosage/Toxicology Treatment should be symptom-directed and supportive. Not removed by dialysis.
Stability Store at 15°C to 30°C (59°F to 86°F). Aseptically add 15 mL of companion diluent (20% w/w dehydrated alcohol in water for injection) to each 50 mg vial; swirl to dissolve; do not shake. Further dilute 50 mg, 100 mg, or 200 mg in 100 mL, 250 mL, or 500 mL, respectively, of D$_5$W or NS. Reconstituted and diluted solutions are stable for 24 hours at room temperature. Do not freeze.
Mechanism of Action Noncompetitive inhibitor of 1,3-beta-D-glucan synthase resulting in reduced formation of 1,3-beta-D-glucan, an essential polysaccharide comprising 30% to 60% of *Candida* cell walls (absent in mammalian cells); decreased glucan content leads to osmotic instability and cellular lysis
Pharmacodynamics/Kinetics
Distribution: 30-50 L
Protein binding: 84%
Metabolism: No hepatic metabolism observed; undergoes slow chemical hydrolysis to open-ring peptide-lacking antifungal activity
Half-life elimination: 27 hours
Excretion: Feces (30%, 10% as unchanged drug); urine (<1%)
Dosage I.V.: Adults:
Candidemia, intra-abdominal or peritoneal candidiasis: 200 mg loading dose on day 1, followed by 100 mg daily for at least 14 days after last positive culture
Esophageal candidiasis: 100 mg loading dose on day 1, followed by 50 mg daily for at least 14 days and for at least 7 days after symptom resolution

Dosage adjustment in renal impairment: No adjustment necessary, including dialysis patients
Dosage adjustment in hepatic impairment: No adjustment necessary
Administration For intravenous use only; infusion rate should not exceed 1.1 mg/minute
Monitoring Parameters Liver function tests
Dosage Forms
Injection, powder for reconstitution [preservative free]:
Eraxis™: 50 mg [contains polysorbate 80; packaged with 20% (w/w) dehydrated alcohol (15 mL) as diluent]

- **Anolor 300** *see* Butalbital, Acetaminophen, and Caffeine *on page 259*
- **Ansaid® [DSC]** *see* Flurbiprofen *on page 735*
- **Ansaid® (Can)** *see* Flurbiprofen *on page 735*
- **Ansamycin** *see* Rifabutin *on page 1507*
- **Antabuse®** *see* Disulfiram *on page 528*
- **Antara™** *see* Fenofibrate *on page 689*

♦ **Anthraforte® (Can)** *see Anthralin on page 132*

Anthralin (AN thra lin)

U.S. Brand Names Dritho-Scalp®; Psoriatec™
Canadian Brand Names Anthraforte®; Anthranol®; Anthrascalp®; Micanol®
Index Terms Dithranol
Pharmacologic Category Antipsoriatic Agent; Keratolytic Agent
Use Treatment of psoriasis (quiescent or chronic psoriasis)
Pregnancy Risk Factor C
Dosage Children (unlabeled) and Adults: Topical: Generally, apply once a day or as directed. The irritant potential of anthralin is directly related to the strength being used and each patient's individual tolerance. Always commence treatment using a short, daily contact time (5-10 minutes) for at least 1 week using the lowest strength possible. Contact time may be gradually increased (to 20-30 minutes) as tolerated.

Skin application: Apply sparingly only to psoriatic lesions and rub gently and carefully into the skin until absorbed. Avoid applying an excessive quantity which may cause unnecessary soiling and staining of the clothing or bed linen.

Scalp application: Comb hair to remove scalar debris, wet hair and, after suitably parting, rub cream well into the lesions, taking care to prevent the cream from spreading onto the forehead,

Remove by washing or showering; optimal period of contact will vary according to the strength used and the patient's response to treatment. Continue treatment until the skin is entirely clear (ie, when there is nothing to feel with the fingers and the texture is normal).
Additional Information Complete prescribing information for this medication should be consulted for additional detail.
Dosage Forms
Cream:
Dritho-Scalp®: 0.5% (50 g)
Psoriatec™: 1% (50 g)

♦ **Anthranol® (Can)** *see Anthralin on page 132*
♦ **Anthrascalp® (Can)** *see Anthralin on page 132*

Anthrax Vaccine Adsorbed (AN thraks vak SEEN ad SORBED)

U.S. Brand Names BioThrax™
Index Terms AVA
Pharmacologic Category Vaccine
Use Immunization against *Bacillus anthracis*. Recommended for individuals who may come in contact with animal products which come from anthrax endemic areas and may be contaminated with *Bacillus anthracis* spores; recommended for high-risk persons such as veterinarians and other handling potentially infected animals. Routine immunization for the general population is not recommended.

The Department of Defense is implementing an anthrax vaccination program against the biological warfare agent anthrax, which will be administered to all active duty and reserve personnel.
Unlabeled/Investigational Use Postexposure prophylaxis in combination with antibiotics
Restrictions Not commercially available in the U.S.; presently, all anthrax vaccine lots are owned by the U.S. Department of Defense. The Centers for Disease Control (CDC) does not currently recommend routine vaccination of the general public.
Pregnancy Risk Factor D
Pregnancy Implications Reproduction studies have not been conducted. Use during pregnancy only if clearly needed. Unpublished data from the Department of Defense suggest the vaccine may be linked with an increased number of birth defects when given during pregnancy.
Lactation Excretion in breast milk unknown/use caution
Contraindications Hypersensitivity to anthrax vaccine or any component of the formulation; severe anaphylactic reaction to a previous dose of anthrax vaccine; history of anthrax; history of Guillain-Barré syndrome; pregnancy
Warnings/Precautions Immediate treatment for anaphylactic/anaphylactoid reaction should be available during vaccine use. Patients with a history of Guillain-Barré syndrome should not be given the vaccine unless there is a clear benefit that outweighs the potential risk of recurrence. Defer dosing during acute respiratory disease or other active infection; defer dosing during short-term corticosteroid therapy, chemotherapy, or radiation; additional dose required in patients on long-term corticosteroid therapy; discontinue immunization in patients with chills or fever associated with administration; use caution with latex allergy; immune response may be decreased with immunodeficiency; safety and efficacy in children <18 years of age or adults >65 years of age have not been established
Adverse Reactions (Includes pre- and postlicensure data; systemic reactions reported more often in women than in men)

>10%:
Central nervous system: Malaise (4% to 11%)
Local: Tenderness (58% to 71%), erythema (12% to 43%), subcutaneous nodule (4% to 39%), induration (8% to 21%), warmth (11% to 19%), local pruritus (7% to 19%)
Neuromuscular & skeletal: Arm motion limitation (7% to 12%)
1% to 10%:
Central nervous system: Headache (4% to 7%), fever (<1% to 7%)
Gastrointestinal: Anorexia (4%), vomiting (4%), nausea (<1% to 4%)
Local: Mild local reactions (edema/induration <30 mm) (9%), edema (8%)
Neuromuscular & skeletal: Myalgia (4% to 7%)
Respiratory: Respiratory difficulty (4%)

<1% (Limited to important or life-threatening): Anaphylaxis, arthralgia, cardiomyopathy, cellulitis, chills, body aches, delayed hypersensitivity reaction (started approximately day 17), dizziness, encephalitis, facial palsy, fatigue, Guillain-Barré syndrome, idiopathic thrombocytopenia purpura, inflammatory arthritis, injection site pain/tenderness, moderate local reactions (edema/induration >30 mm and <120 mm), peripheral swelling, seizure, severe local reactions (edema/induration >120 mm in diameter or accompanied by marked limitation of arm motion or marked axillary node tenderness), sudden cardiac arrest, systemic lupus erythematosus

Drug Interactions
Decreased Effect: Effect of vaccine may be decreased with chemotherapy, corticosteroids (high doses, ≥14 days), immunosuppressant agents, and radiation therapy; consider waiting at least 3 months between discontinuing therapy and administering vaccine.

Stability Store under refrigeration at 2°C to 8°C (36°F to 46°F); do not freeze.

Mechanism of Action Active immunization against *Bacillus anthracis*. The vaccine is prepared from a cell-free filtrate of *B. anthracis*, but no dead or live bacteria.

Pharmacodynamics/Kinetics Duration: Unknown; may be 1-2 years following two inoculations based on animal data

Dosage SubQ:
Children <18 years: Safety and efficacy have not been established
Children ≥18 years and Adults:
Primary immunization: Three injections of 0.5 mL each given 2 weeks apart, followed by three additional injections given at 6-, 12-, and 18 months; it is not necessary to restart the series if a dose is not given on time; resume as soon as practical
Subsequent booster injections: 0.5 mL at 1-year intervals are recommended for immunity to be maintained
Elderly: Safety and efficacy have not been established for patients >65 years of age

Administration Administer SubQ; shake well before use. Do not use if discolored or contains particulate matter. Do not use the same site for more than one injection. Do not mix with other injections. After administration, massage injection site to disperse the vaccine. Federal law requires that the date of administration, the vaccine manufacturer, lot number of vaccine, and the administering person's name, title, and address be entered into the patient's permanent medical record.

Monitoring Parameters Monitor for local reactions, chills, fever, anaphylaxis

Additional Information Not commercially available in the U.S.
Local reactions increase in severity by the fifth dose. Moderate local reactions (>5 cm) may be pruritic and may occur if given to a patient with a previous history of anthrax infection. Federal law requires that the date of administration, the vaccine manufacturer, lot number of vaccine, and the administering person's name, title, and address be entered into the patient's permanent medical record.

Dosage Forms Injection, suspension: 5 mL [vial stopper contains dry natural rubber]

♦ **Anti-4 Alpha Integrin** *see* Natalizumab *on page 1203*
♦ **131 I Anti-B1 Antibody** *see* Tositumomab and Iodine I 131 Tositumomab *on page 1713*
♦ **131 I-Anti-B1 Monoclonal Antibody** *see* Tositumomab and Iodine I 131 Tositumomab *on page 1713*
♦ **Anti-CD11a** *see* Efalizumab *on page 570*
♦ **Anti-CD20 Monoclonal Antibody** *see* Rituximab *on page 1523*
♦ **Anti-CD20-Murine Monoclonal Antibody I-131** *see* Tositumomab and Iodine I 131 Tositumomab *on page 1713*
♦ **Antidigoxin Fab Fragments, Ovine** *see* Digoxin Immune Fab *on page 504*
♦ **Antidiuretic Hormone** *see* Vasopressin *on page 1779*

Antihemophilic Factor (Human) (an tee hee moe FIL ik FAK tor HYU man)

U.S. Brand Names Alphanate®; Hemofil M; Koāte®-DVI; Monarc-M™; Monoclate-P®
Canadian Brand Names Hemofil M
Index Terms AHF (Human); Factor VIII (Human)
Pharmacologic Category Antihemophilic Agent; Blood Product Derivative
Use Prevention and treatment of hemorrhagic episodes in patients with hemophilia A (classic hemophilia); perioperative management of hemophilia A; can be of significant therapeutic value in patients with acquired factor VIII inhibitors not exceeding 10 Bethesda units/mL
Orphan status: Alphanate®: Management of von Willebrand disease

Pregnancy Risk Factor C

Pregnancy Implications Reproduction studies have not been conducted. Safety and efficacy in pregnant women have not been established. Use during pregnancy only if clearly needed. Parvovirus B19 or hepatitis A, which may be present in plasma-derived products, may affect a pregnant woman more seriously than nonpregnant women.

Lactation Excretion in breast milk unknown/use caution

Contraindications Hypersensitivity to any component of the formulation

Warnings/Precautions [U.S. Boxed Warning]: Risk of viral transmission is not totally eradicated. Because antihemophilic factor is prepared from pooled plasma, it may contain the causative agent of viral hepatitis and other viral diseases. Hepatitis B vaccination is recommended for all patients. Hepatitis A vaccination is also recommended for seronegative patients. Antihemophilic factor contains trace amounts of blood groups A and B isohemagglutinins and when large or frequently repeated doses are given to individuals with blood groups A, B, and AB, the patient should be monitored for signs of progressive anemia and the possibility of intravascular hemolysis should be considered. The dosage requirement will vary in patients with factor VIII inhibitors; optimal treatment should be determined by clinical response. Natural rubber latex is a component of Hemofil M and Monarc-M™ packaging. Hemofil M, Monoclate-P®, and Monarc-M™ contain trace amounts of mouse protein. Products vary by preparation method; final formulations contain human albumin. Products contain naturally-occurring von Willebrand factor for stabilization, however efficacy has not been established for the treatment of von Willebrand disease. Natural rubber latex is a
(Continued)

Antihemophilic Factor (Human) *(Continued)*

component of Hemofil M packaging. Products vary by preparation method; final formulations contain human albumin.

Adverse Reactions <1% (Limited to important or life-threatening): Acute hemolytic anemia, AHF inhibitor development, allergic reactions (rare), anaphylaxis (rare), bleeding tendency increased, blurred vision, chest tightness, chills, fever, headache, hyperfibrinogenemia, jittery feeling, lethargy, nausea, somnolence, stinging at the infusion site, stomach discomfort, tingling, urticaria, vasomotor reactions with rapid infusion, vomiting

Overdosage/Toxicology Massive doses have been reported to cause acute hemolytic anemia, increased bleeding tendency, or hyperfibrinogenemia. Occurrence is rare.

Stability Store under refrigeration, 2°C to 8°C (36°F to 46°F); avoid freezing. If refrigerated, the dried concentrate and diluent should be warmed to room temperature before reconstitution. Gently swirl or rotate vial after adding diluent; do not shake vigorously. Use within 3 hours of reconstitution. Do not refrigerate after reconstitution, precipitation may occur.

Alphanate®: May also be stored at room temperature not to exceed 30°C (86°F) for ≤2 months.

Hemofil M, Monarc-M™: May also be stored at room temperature not to exceed 30°C (86°F).

Koāte®-DVI; Monoclate-P®: May also be stored at room temperature of 25°C (77°F) for ≤6 months.

Mechanism of Action Protein (factor VIII) in normal plasma which is necessary for clot formation and maintenance of hemostasis; activates factor X in conjunction with activated factor IX; activated factor X converts prothrombin to thrombin, which converts fibrinogen to fibrin, and with factor XIII forms a stable clot

Pharmacodynamics/Kinetics Half-life elimination: Mean: 8-27 hours

Dosage Children and Adults: I.V.: Individualize dosage based on coagulation studies performed prior to treatment and at regular intervals during treatment. In general, administration of factor VIII 1 int. unit/kg will increase circulating factor VIII levels by ~2 int. units/dL. (General guidelines presented; consult individual product labeling for specific dosing recommendations.)

Dosage based on desired factor VIII increase (%):

To calculate dosage needed based on desired factor VIII increase (%):

Body weight (kg) x 0.5 int. units/kg x desired factor VIII increase (%) = int. units factor VIII required

For example:

50 kg x 0.5 int. units/kg x 30 (% increase) = 750 int. units factor VIII

Dosage based on expected factor VIII increase (%):

It is also possible to calculate the **expected** % factor VIII increase:

(# int. units administered x 2%/int. units/kg) divided by body weight (kg) = expected % factor VIII increase

For example:

(1400 int. units x 2%/int. units/kg) divided by 70 kg = 40%

General guidelines:

Minor hemorrhage: 10-20 int. units/kg as a single dose to achieve FVIII plasma level ~20% to 40% of normal. Mild superficial or early hemorrhages may respond to a single dose; may repeat dose every 12-24 hours for 1-3 days until bleeding is resolved or healing achieved.

Moderate hemorrhage/minor surgery: 15-25 int. units/kg to achieve FVIII plasma level 30% to 50% of normal. If needed, may continue with a maintenance dose of 10-15 int. units/kg every 8-12 hours.

Major to life-threatening hemorrhage: Initial dose 40-50 int. units/kg, followed by a maintenance dose of 20-25 int. units/kg every 8-12 hours until threat is resolved, to achieve FVIII plasma level 80% to 100% of normal.

Major surgery: 50 int. units/kg given preoperatively to raise factor VIII level to 100% before surgery begins. May repeat as necessary after 6-12 hours initially and for a total of 10-14 days until healing is complete. Intensity of therapy may depend on type of surgery and postoperative regimen.

Bleeding prophylaxis: May be administered on a regular basis for bleeding prophylaxis. Doses of 24-40 int. units/kg 3 times/week have been reported in patients with severe hemophilia to prevent joint bleeding.

If bleeding is not controlled with adequate dose, test for presence of inhibitor. It may not be possible or practical to control bleeding if inhibitor titers are >10 Bethesda units/mL.

Elderly: Response in the elderly is not expected to differ from that of younger patients; dosage should be individualized

Dietary Considerations Alphanate® contains sodium ≤10 mEq/vial

Administration Administer I.V. over 5-10 minutes (maximum: 10 mL/minute). Infuse Monoclate-P® at 2 mL/minute.

Monitoring Parameters Heart rate and blood pressure (before and during I.V. administration); AHF levels prior to and during treatment; in patients with circulating inhibitors, the inhibitor level should be monitored; hematocrit; monitor for signs and symptoms of intravascular hemolysis; bleeding

Reference Range Classification of hemophilia; normal is defined as 1 int. unit/mL of factor VIII

Severe: Factor level <1% of normal

Moderate: Factor level 1% to 5% of normal

Mild: Factor level >5% to <40% of normal

Dosage Forms

Injection, powder for reconstitution:

Alphanate®: Vial labeled with international units [contains sodium ≤10 mEq/vial and albumin]

Hemofil M: Vial labeled with international units [contains albumin; derived from mouse proteins; packaging may contain natural rubber latex]

Koate®-DVI: ~250 int. units, ~500 int. units, ~1000 int. units [contains albumin]

Monarc-M™: Vial labeled with international units [contains albumin; derived from mouse proteins; packaging may contain natural rubber latex]

Monoclate-P®: ~250 int. units, ~500 int. units, ~1000 int. units, ~1500 int. units [contains albumin; derived from mouse proteins]

Antihemophilic Factor (Recombinant)
(an tee hee moe FIL ik FAK tor ree KOM be nant)

U.S. Brand Names Advate; Helixate® FS; Kogenate® FS; Recombinate; ReFacto®

Canadian Brand Names Helixate® FS; Kogenate®; Kogenate® FS; Recombinate; ReFacto®

Index Terms AHF (Recombinant); Factor VIII (Recombinant); rAHF

Pharmacologic Category Antihemophilic Agent

Use Prevention and treatment of hemorrhagic episodes in patients with hemophilia A (classic hemophilia); perioperative management of hemophilia A; can be of significant therapeutic value in patients with acquired factor VIII inhibitors ≤10 Bethesda units/mL

Pregnancy Risk Factor C

Pregnancy Implications Animal reproduction studies have not been conducted. Safety and efficacy in pregnant women has not been established. Use during pregnancy only if clearly needed.

Lactation Excretion in breast milk unknown/use caution

Contraindications Hypersensitivity to any component of the formulation

Warnings/Precautions Monitor for signs of formation of antibodies to factor VIII; may occur at anytime but more common in young children with severe hemophilia. The dosage requirement will vary in patients with factor VIII inhibitors; optimal treatment should be determined by clinical response. Monitor for allergic hypersensitivity reactions. Products vary by preparation method. Recombinate is stabilized using human albumin. Helixate® FS and Kogenate® FS are stabilized with sucrose. Advate, Helixate® FS, Kogenate® FS and ReFacto® may contain trace amounts of mouse or hamster protein. Recombinate may contain mouse, hamster or bovine protein. Products may contain vonWillebrand factor for stabilization; however, efficacy has not been established for the treatment of von Willebrand's disease.

Adverse Reactions Actual frequency may vary by product.

>1%:

Central nervous system: Chills, dizziness, fever, headache, pain

Dermatologic: Pruritus

Gastrointestinal: Nausea, taste perversion

Hematologic: Hemorrhage

Local: Injection site pain

Neuromuscular & skeletal: Arthralgia, weakness

Respiratory: Dyspnea, nasopharyngitis, pharyngolaryngeal pain

Miscellaneous: Catheter thrombosis, factor VIII inhibitor formation

≤1% (Limited to important or life-threatening): Abdominal pain, adenopathy, allergic reactions, anaphylaxis, anemia, anorexia, arthralgia, chest discomfort, constipation, depersonalization, diaphoresis, diarrhea, edema, epistaxis, facial flushing, factor VIII decreased, fatigue, fever, GI hemorrhage, hot flashes, hyper-/hypotension (slight), infection, Injection site reactions, joint swelling, lethargy, otitis media, pallor, rash, rhinitis, rigors, SGOT increased, somnolence, urinary tract infection, urticaria, vasodilation, venous catheter access complications, vomiting

Overdosage/Toxicology Massive doses of antihemophilic factor (human) have been reported to cause acute hemolytic anemia, increased bleeding tendency, or hyperfibrinogenemia. Occurrence is rare.

Stability Store under refrigeration, 2°C to 8°C (36°F to 46°F); avoid freezing. Use within 3 hours of reconstitution. Gently agitate or rotate vial after adding diluent, do not shake vigorously. Do not refrigerate after reconstitution, a precipitation may occur.

Advate: May also be stored at room temperature for up to 6 months.

Helixate® FS, Kogenate® FS, ReFacto®: May also be stored at room temperature for up to 3 months; avoid prolonged exposure to light during storage.

Recombinate: May also be stored at room temperature, not to exceed 30°C (86°F).

If refrigerated, the dried concentrate and diluent should be warmed to room temperature before reconstitution. Gently swirl or rotate vial after adding diluent, do not shake vigorously.

Mechanism of Action Factor VIII replacement, necessary for clot formation and maintenance of hemostasis. It activates factor X in conjunction with activated factor IX; activated factor X converts prothrombin to thrombin, which converts fibrinogen to fibrin, and with factor XIII forms a stable clot.

Pharmacodynamics/Kinetics Half-life elimination: Mean: 9-19 hours

Dosage Children and Adults: I.V.: Individualize dosage based on coagulation studies performed prior to treatment and at regular intervals during treatment. In general, administration of factor VIII 1 int. unit/kg will increase circulating factor VIII levels by ~2 int. units/dL. (General guidelines presented; consult individual product labeling for specific dosing recommendations.)

Dosage based on desired factor VIII increase (%):

To calculate dosage needed based on desired factor VIII increase (%):

[Body weight (kg) x desired factor VIII increase (%)] divided by 2%/int. units/kg = int. units factor VIII required

For example:

50 kg x 30 (% increase) divided by 2%/int. units/kg = 750 int. units factor VIII

Dosage based on expected factor VIII increase (%):

It is also possible to calculate the **expected** % factor VIII increase:

(# int. units administered x 2%/int. units/kg) divided by body weight (kg) = expected % factor VIII increase

For example:

(1400 int. units x 2%/int. units/kg) divided by 70 kg = 40%

(Continued)

Antihemophilic Factor (Recombinant) *(Continued)*

General guidelines:

Minor hemorrhage: 10-20 int. units/kg as a single dose to achieve FVIII plasma level ~20% to 40% of normal. Mild superficial or early hemorrhages may respond to a single dose; may repeat dose every 12-24 hours for 1-3 days until bleeding is resolved or healing achieved.

Moderate hemorrhage/minor surgery: 15-30 int. units/kg to achieve FVIII plasma level 30% to 60% of normal. May repeat 1 dose at 12-24 hours if needed. Some products suggest continuing for ≥3 days until pain and disability are resolved

Major to life-threatening hemorrhage: Initial dose 40-50 int. units/kg followed by a maintenance dose of 20-25 int. units/kg every 8-12 hours until threat is resolved, to achieve FVIII plasma level 80% to 100% of normal.

Major surgery: 50 int. units/kg given preoperatively to raise factor VIII level to 100% before surgery begins. May repeat as necessary after 6-12 hours initially and for a total of 10-14 days until healing is complete. Intensity of therapy may depend on type of surgery and postoperative regimen.

Bleeding prophylaxis: May be administered on a regular basis for bleeding prophylaxis. Doses of 24-40 int. units/kg 3 times/week have been reported in patients with severe hemophilia to prevent joint bleeding.

If bleeding is not controlled with adequate dose, test for presence of inhibitor. It may not be possible or practical to control bleeding if inhibitor titers >10 Bethesda units/mL.

Elderly: Response in the elderly is not expected to differ from that of younger patients; dosage should be individualized

Dietary Considerations Advate contains sodium 108 mEq/L; Helixate® FS and Kogenate® FS contain sodium 27-36 mEq/L; Recombinate contains sodium 180 mEq/L

Administration I.V. infusion over 5-10 minutes (maximum: 10 mL/minute).

Advate: Infuse over ≤5 minutes (maximum: 10 mL/minute).

Monitoring Parameters Heart rate and blood pressure (before and during I.V. administration); AHF levels prior to and during treatment; development of factor VIII inhibitors; bleeding

Reference Range Classification of hemophilia; normal is defined as 1 int. unit/mL of factor VIII

Severe: Factor level <1% of normal

Moderate: Factor level 1% to 5% of normal

Mild: Factor level >5% to <40% of normal

Dosage Forms

Injection, powder for reconstitution, recombinant [preservative free]:

Advate: 250 int. units, 500 int. units, 1000 int. units, 1500 int. units, 2000 int. units [plasma/albumin free; contains sodium 108 mEq/L, mannitol; derived from hamster or mouse proteins]

Helixate® FS, Kogenate® FS: 250 int. units, 500 int. units, 1000 int. units [albumin free; contains sucrose 28 mg/vial, sodium 27-36 mEq/L; derived from hamster or mouse protein]

Recombinate: 250 int. units, 500 units, 1000 int. units [contains human albumin, sodium 180 mEq/L; derived from bovine, hamster or mouse proteins; packaging contains natural rubber latex]

ReFacto®: 250 int. units, 500 units, 1000 int. units, 2000 int. units [contains sucrose; derived from hamster or mouse proteins]

Antihemophilic Factor/von Willebrand Factor Complex (Human)

(an tee hee moe FIL ik FAK tor von WILL le brand FAK tor KOM plex HYU man)

U.S. Brand Names Humate-P®

Index Terms AHF (Human); Factor VIII (Human); FVIII/vWF

Pharmacologic Category Antihemophilic Agent; Blood Product Derivative

Use Prevention and treatment of hemorrhagic episodes in patients with hemophilia A (classical hemophilia); treatment of spontaneous bleeding in patients with severe von Willebrand disease (vWD) and in mild or moderate vWD where use of desmopressin is known or suspected to be inadequate

Pregnancy Risk Factor C

Dosage Children and Adults: I.V.:

Hemophilia A: Individualize dosage based on coagulation studies performed prior to treatment and at regular intervals during treatment; in general, administration of factor VIII 1 int. unit/kg will increase circulating factor VIII levels by ~2 int. units/dL.

Minor hemorrhage: Loading dose: FVIII:C 15 int. units/kg to achieve FVIII:C plasma level ~30% of normal. If second infusion is needed, half the loading dose may be given once or twice daily for 1-2 days.

Moderate hemorrhage: Loading dose: FVIII:C 25 int. units/kg to achieve FVIII:C plasma level ~50% of normal; Maintenance: FVIII:C 15 int. units/kg every 8-12 hours for 1-2 days in order to maintain FVIII:C plasma levels at 30% of normal. Repeat the same dose once or twice daily for up to 7 days or until adequate wound healing.

Life-threatening hemorrhage: Loading dose: FVIII:C 40-50 int. units/kg; Maintenance: FVIII:C 20-25 int. units/kg every 8 hours to maintain FVIII:C plasma levels at 80% to 100% of normal for 7 days. Continue same dose once or twice daily for another 7 days in order to maintain FVIII:C levels at 30% to 50% of normal.

von Willebrand disease (vWD): Individualize dosage based on coagulation studies performed prior to treatment and at regular intervals during treatment; in general, administration of factor VIII 1 int. unit/kg would be expected to raise circulating vWF:RCo approximately 3.5-4 int. units/dL.

Type 1, mild (if desmopressin is not appropriate): Major hemorrhage:

Loading dose: vWF:RCo 40-60 int. units/kg

Maintenance dose: vWF:RCo 40-50 int. units/kg every 8-12 hours for 3 days, keeping vWF:RCo nadir >50%; follow with 40-50 int. units/kg daily for up to 7 days

Type 1, moderate or severe:

Minor hemorrhage: vWF:RCo 40-50 int. units/kg for 1-2 doses

Major hemorrhage:
  Loading dose: vWF:RCo 50-75 int. units/kg
  Maintenance dose: vWF:RCo 40-60 int. units/kg every 8-12 hours for 3 days to keep the VWF:RCo nadir >50%, then 40-60 int. units/kg daily for a total of up to 7 days
Types 2 and 3:
  Minor hemorrhage: vWF:RCo 40-50 int. units/kg for 1-2 doses
  Major hemorrhage:
  Loading dose: vWF:RCo 60-80 int. units/kg
  Maintenance dose: vWF:RCo 40-60 int. units/kg every 8-12 hours for 3 days, keeping the VWF:RCo nadir >50%; follow with 40-60 int. units/kg daily for a total of up to 7 days

Elderly: Response in the elderly is not expected to differ from that of younger patients; dosage should be individualized

Additional Information Complete prescribing information for this medication should be consulted for additional detail.

Dosage Forms

Injection, powder for reconstitution:
  Humate-P®: FVIII 250 int. units and vWF:RCo 600 int. units [human derived; contains albumin; packaged with diluent]; FVIII 500 int. units and vWF:RCo 1200 int. units [human derived; contains albumin; packed with diluent]; FVIII 1000 int. units and vWF:RCo 2400 int. units [human derived; contains albumin; packaged with diluent]

Anti-inhibitor Coagulant Complex
(an tee-in HI bi tor coe AG yoo lant KOM pleks)

U.S. Brand Names Autoplex® T [DSC]; Feiba VH
Canadian Brand Names Feiba VH Immuno
Index Terms AICC; Coagulant Complex Inhibitor
Pharmacologic Category Activated Prothrombin Complex Concentrate (aPCC); Antihemophilic Agent; Blood Product Derivative
Use Hemophilia A & B patients with factor VIII inhibitors who are to undergo surgery or those who are bleeding
Pregnancy Risk Factor C
Dosage I.V.: Children and Adults:
  Autoplex® T: Dosage range: 25-100 factor VIII correctional units per kg depending on the severity of hemorrhage; may repeat in ~ 6 hours if needed. Adjust dose based on patient response.
  Feiba VH: General dosing guidelines: 50-100 units/kg (maximum 200 units/kg)
    Joint hemorrhage: 50 units/kg every 12 hours; may increase to 100 units/kg; continue until signs of clinical improvement occur
    Mucous membrane bleeding: 50 units/kg every 6 hours; may increase to 100 units/kg (maximum: 2 administrations/day or 200 units/kg/day)
    Soft tissue hemorrhage: 100 units/kg every 12 hours (maximum: 200 units/kg/day)
    Other severe hemorrhage: 100 units/kg every 12 hours; may be used every 6 hours if needed; continue until clinical improvement
Additional Information Complete prescribing information for this medication should be consulted for additional detail.
Dosage Forms Injection, powder for reconstitution:
  Autoplex® T: Each bottle is labeled with correctional units of factor VIII [contains heparin 2 units/mL and sodium 162-192 mEg/L; packaging contains natural rubber latex] [DSC]
  Feiba VH: Each bottle is labeled with Immuno units of factor VIII [heparin free; contains sodium 8 mg/mL; packaging contains natural rubber latex]

Antipyrine and Benzocaine (an tee PYE reen & BEN zoe kane)

U.S. Brand Names A/B Otic; Allergen®; Aurodex
Canadian Brand Names Auralgan®
Index Terms Benzocaine and Antipyrine
Pharmacologic Category Otic Agent, Analgesic; Otic Agent, Cerumenolytic
Use Temporary relief of pain and reduction of swelling associated with acute congestive and serous otitis media, swimmer's ear, otitis externa; facilitates ear wax removal
Pregnancy Risk Factor C
Medication Safety Issues
Sound-alike/look-alike issues:
  Auralgan® may be confused with Ophthalgan®
Dosage Children and Adults: Otic: Fill ear canal; moisten cotton pledget, place in external ear, repeat every 1-2 hours until pain and congestion are relieved; for ear wax removal instill drops 3-4 times/day for 2-3 days
Additional Information Complete prescribing information for this medication should be consulted for additional detail.
Dosage Forms
Solution, otic [drops]: Antipyrine 5.4% and benzocaine 1.4% (10 mL)
  A/B Otic, Allergen®, Aurodex: Antipyrine 5.4% and benzocaine 1.4% (15 mL)

Antithrombin III (an tee THROM bin three)

U.S. Brand Names Thrombate III®
Canadian Brand Names Thrombate III®
Index Terms AT III; Heparin Cofactor I
Pharmacologic Category Anticoagulant; Blood Product Derivative
Use Treatment of hereditary antithrombin III deficiency in connection with surgical procedures, obstetrical procedures, or thromboembolism
(Continued)

Antithrombin III *(Continued)*

Unlabeled/Investigational Use Acquired antithrombin III deficiencies related to disseminated intravascular coagulation (DIC)

Pregnancy Risk Factor B

Pregnancy Implications Teratogenic effects were not observed in animal studies. Although FDA indicated for obstetrical procedures, there are no adequate and well-controlled studies in pregnant women.

Lactation Excretion in breast milk unknown/use caution

Contraindications Hypersensitivity to any component of the formulation

Warnings/Precautions Product of human plasma; may potentially contain infectious agents which could transmit disease; screening of donors, as well as testing and/or inactivation or removal of certain viruses, reduces this risk. Infections thought to be transmitted by this product should be reported to Talecris Biotherapeutics at 1-800-520-2807. Safety and efficacy in children have not been established.

Adverse Reactions

1% to 10%: Central nervous system: Dizziness (2%)

<1% (Limited to important or life-threatening): Bowel fullness, chest pain, chest tightness, chills, cramps, dyspnea, fever, film over eye, foul taste, hematoma, hives, lightheadedness, nausea

Drug Interactions

Increased Effect/Toxicity: Heparin's anticoagulant effects are potentiated by antithrombin III (half-life of antithrombin III is decreased by heparin). Risk of hemorrhage with antithrombin III may be increased by drotrecogin alfa, thrombolytic agents, oral anticoagulants (warfarin), treprostinil, and drugs which affect platelet function (eg, aspirin, NSAIDs, dipyridamole, ticlopidine, clopidogrel, and IIb/IIIa antagonists).

Ethanol/Nutrition/Herb Interactions Herb/Nutraceutical: Recent use/intake of herbs with anticoagulant or antiplatelet activity (including cat's claw, dong quai, evening primrose, garlic, ginkgo and ginseng) may increase the risk of bleeding.

Stability Store vials under refrigeration at 2°C to 8°C (36°F to 46°F); avoid freezing. Bring drug and diluent to room temperature prior to reconstitution. Reconstitute with sterile water for injection. Do not shake; swirl to mix to avoid foaming. Filter through sterile filter needle provided prior to administration. Administer within 3 hours of mixing.

Mechanism of Action Antithrombin III is the primary physiologic inhibitor of *in vivo* coagulation. It is an alpha$_2$-globulin. Its principal actions are the inactivation of thrombin, plasmin, and other active serine proteases of coagulation, including factors IXa, Xa, XIa, and XIIa. The inactivation of proteases is a major step in the normal clotting process. The strong activation of clotting enzymes at the site of every bleeding injury facilitates fibrin formation and maintains normal hemostasis. Thrombosis in the circulation would be caused by active serine proteases if they were not inhibited by antithrombin III after the localized clotting process.

Pharmacodynamics/Kinetics Half-life elimination: Biologic: 2.5 days (immunologic assay); 3.8 days (functional AT-III assay). Half-life may be decreased following surgery, with hemorrhage, acute thrombosis, and/or during heparin administration.

Dosage Adults:

Initial dose: Dosing is individualized based on pretherapy AT-III levels. The initial dose should raise antithrombin III levels (AT-III) to 120% and may be calculated based on the following formula:

[desired AT-III level % - baseline AT-III level %] x body weight (kg)
divided by 1.4%/int. units/kg

For example, if a 70 kg adult patient had a baseline AT-III level of 57%, the initial dose would be

[(120% - 57%) x 70] divided by 1.4 = 3150 int. units

Maintenance dose: Subsequent dosing should be targeted to keep levels between 80% to 120% which may be achieved by administering 60% of the initial dose every 24 hours. Adjustments may be made by adjusting dose or interval. Maintain level within normal range for 2-8 days depending on type of procedure.

Dietary Considerations Contains sodium 110-210 mEq/L

Administration I.V.: Infuse over 10-20 minutes.

Monitoring Parameters Monitor antithrombin III peak and trough levels (preinfusion and 20 minutes postinfusion) for each dose and monitor levels 12 hours after initial loading dose; liver function tests; monitor antithrombin III levels in neonates of parents with hereditary antithrombin III deficiency immediately after birth

Reference Range Maintain antithrombin III level in plasma >80%; plasma AT-III levels are ~60% lower near term infants than levels observed in adults; premature infants may have levels lower than other neonates.

Additional Information Thromboembolism has been reported in children of women with hereditary antithrombin III (AT-III) deficiency; AT-III levels in neonates of parents with hereditary AT-III deficiency should be measured immediately after birth. Plasma AT-III levels are typically lower in neonates and infants than in adults. Low plasma AT-III levels in neonates may not be indicative of deficiency; consultation with a coagulation expert is recommended.

Dosage Forms Injection, powder for reconstitution [preservative free]: 500 int. units, 1000 int. units [contains heparin, sodium chloride 110-210 mEq/L; packaged with diluent]

Antithymocyte Globulin (Equine) *(an te THY moe site GLOB yu lin, E kwine)*

U.S. Brand Names Atgam®

Canadian Brand Names Atgam®

Index Terms Antithymocyte Immunoglobulin; ATG; Horse Antihuman Thymocyte Gamma Globulin; Lymphocyte Immune Globulin

Pharmacologic Category Immunosuppressant Agent

Use Prevention and treatment of acute renal allograft rejection; treatment of moderate to severe aplastic anemia in patients not considered suitable candidates for bone marrow transplantation

Unlabeled/Investigational Use Prevention and treatment of other solid organ allograft rejection; prevention of graft-versus-host disease following bone marrow transplantation

Pregnancy Risk Factor C

Pregnancy Implications Reproduction studies have not been conducted; use during pregnancy is not recommended. Women exposed to Atgam® during pregnancy may be enrolled in the National Transplantation Pregnancy Registry (877-955-6877).

Lactation Excretion in breast milk unknown/use caution

Medication Safety Issues
Sound-alike/look-alike issues:
Atgam® may be confused with Ativan®

Contraindications Hypersensitivity to lymphocytic immune globulin, any component of the formulation, or other equine gamma globulins

Warnings/Precautions Must be administered via central line due to chemical phlebitis. **[U.S. Boxed Warning]: Should only be used by physicians experienced in immunosuppressive therapy or management of solid organ or bone marrow transplant patients. Adequate laboratory and supportive medical resources must be readily available in the facility for patient management.** Rash, dyspnea, hypotension, or anaphylaxis precludes further administration of the drug. Discontinue if severe and unremitting thrombocytopenia and/or leukopenia occur. Dose must be administered over at least 4 hours; patient may need to be pretreated with an antipyretic, antihistamine, and/or corticosteroid. Intradermal skin testing is recommended prior to first-dose administration.

Adverse Reactions
>10%:
Central nervous system: Fever, chills
Dermatologic: Pruritus, rash, urticaria
Hematologic: Leukopenia, thrombocytopenia
1% to 10%:
Cardiovascular: Bradycardia, chest pain, CHF, edema, encephalitis, hyper-/hypotension, myocarditis, tachycardia
Central nervous system: Agitation, headache, lethargy, lightheadedness, listlessness, seizure
Gastrointestinal: Diarrhea, nausea, stomatitis, vomiting
Hepatic: Hepatosplenomegaly, liver function tests abnormal
Local: Pain at injection site, phlebitis, thrombophlebitis, burning soles/palms
Neuromuscular & skeletal: Myalgia, back pain, arthralgia
Ocular: Periorbital edema
Renal: Abnormal renal function tests
Respiratory: Dyspnea, respiratory distress
Miscellaneous: Anaphylaxis, serum sickness, viral infection, night sweats, diaphoresis, lymphadenopathy
<1% (Limited to important or life-threatening): Acute renal failure, anemia, aplasia, confusion, cough, deep vein thrombosis, disorientation, dizziness, epigastric pain, faintness, GI bleeding, granulocytopenia, hemolysis, herpes simplex reactivation, hiccups, hyperglycemia, iliac vein obstruction, infection, kidney enlarged, laryngospasm, malaise, neutropenia, nosebleed, pancytopenia, paresthesia, pulmonary edema, renal artery thrombosis, serum sickness, toxic epidermal necrosis, vasculitis, weakness, wound dehiscence

Stability Ampuls must be refrigerated; do not freeze. Dilute into inverted bottle of sterile vehicle to ensure that undiluted lymphocyte immune globulin does not contact air. Gently rotate or swirl to mix. Final concentration should be 4 mg/mL. May be diluted in NS, $D_5$1/4NS, $D_5$1/2NS. Diluted solution is stable for 24 hours (including infusion time) at refrigeration.

Mechanism of Action May involve elimination of antigen-reactive T lymphocytes (killer cells) in peripheral blood or alteration of T-cell function

Pharmacodynamics/Kinetics
Distribution: Poorly into lymphoid tissues; binds to circulating lymphocytes, granulocytes, platelets, bone marrow cells
Half-life elimination, plasma: 1.5-12 days
Excretion: Urine (~1%)

Dosage An intradermal skin test is recommended prior to administration of the initial dose of ATG; use 0.1 mL of a 1:1000 dilution of ATG in normal saline. A positive skin reaction consists of a wheal ≥10 mm in diameter. If a positive skin test occurs, the first infusion should be administered in a controlled environment with intensive life support immediately available. A systemic reaction precludes further administration of the drug. The absence of a reaction does **not** preclude the possibility of an immediate sensitivity reaction.

Premedication with diphenhydramine, hydrocortisone, and acetaminophen is recommended prior to first dose.

Children: I.V.:
Aplastic anemia protocol: 10-20 mg/kg/day for 8-14 days; then administer every other day for 7 more doses; addition doses may be given every other day for 21 total doses in 28 days
Renal allograft: 5-25 mg/kg/day
Adults: I.V.:
Aplastic anemia protocol: 10-20 mg/kg/day for 8-14 days, then administer every other day for 7 more doses, for a total of 21 doses in 28 days
Renal allograft:
Rejection prophylaxis: 15 mg/kg/day for 14 days followed by 14 days of alternative day therapy at the same dose; the first dose should be administered within 24 hours before or after transplantation
Rejection treatment: 10-15 mg/kg/day for 14 days, then administer every other day for 10-14 days up to 21 doses in 28 days
(Continued)

Antithymocyte Globulin (Equine) *(Continued)*

Administration Infuse dose over at least 4 hours. Any severe systemic reaction to the skin test, such as generalized rash, tachycardia, dyspnea, hypotension, or anaphylaxis, should preclude further therapy. Epinephrine and resuscitative equipment should be nearby. Patient may need to be pretreated with an antipyretic, antihistamine, and/or corticosteroid. Mild itching and erythema can be treated with antihistamines. Infuse into a vascular shunt, arterial venous fistula, or high-flow central vein through a 0.2-1 micron in-line filter.

First dose: Premedicate with diphenhydramine orally 30 minutes prior to and hydrocortisone I.V. 15 minutes prior to infusion and acetaminophen 2 hours after start of infusion.

Monitoring Parameters Lymphocyte profile, CBC with differential and platelet count, vital signs during administration

Dosage Forms Injection, solution: 50 mg/mL (5 mL)

Antithymocyte Globulin (Rabbit) (an te THY moe site GLOB yu lin (RAB bit)

U.S. Brand Names Thymoglobulin®
Index Terms Antithymocyte Immunoglobulin; ATG
Pharmacologic Category Immune Globulin
Use Treatment of renal transplant acute rejection in conjunction with concomitant immunosuppression
Pregnancy Risk Factor C
Pregnancy Implications Reproduction studies have not been conducted.
Lactation Excretion in breast milk unknown/use caution
Contraindications History of allergy or anaphylaxis to rabbit proteins; acute viral illness
Warnings/Precautions Infusion may produce fever and chills. To minimize, the first dose should be infused over a minimum of 6 hours into a high-flow vein. Also, premedication with corticosteroids, acetaminophen, and/or an antihistamine and/or slowing the infusion rate may reduce reaction incidence and intensity.

Prolonged use or overdosage of Thymoglobulin® in association with other immunosuppressive agents may cause overimmunosuppression resulting in severe infections and may increase the incidence of lymphoma or post-transplant lymphoproliferative disease (PTLD) or other malignancies. Appropriate antiviral, antibacterial, antiprotozoal, and/or antifungal prophylaxis is recommended.

[U.S. Boxed Warning]: Thymoglobulin® should only be used by physicians experienced in immunosuppressive therapy for the treatment of renal transplant patients. Medical surveillance is required during the infusion. In rare circumstances, anaphylaxis has been reported with use. In such cases, the infusion should be terminated immediately. Medical personnel should be available to treat patients who experience anaphylaxis. Emergency treatment such as 0.3-0.5 mL aqueous epinephrine (1:1000 dilution) subcutaneously and other resuscitative measures including oxygen, intravenous fluids, antihistamines, corticosteroids, pressor amines, and airway management, as clinically indicated, should be provided. Thymoglobulin® or other rabbit immunoglobulins should not be administered again for such patients. Thrombocytopenia or neutropenia may result from cross-reactive antibodies and is reversible following dose adjustments.

Adverse Reactions
>10%:
    Cardiovascular: Hypertension, peripheral edema, tachycardia
    Central nervous system: Chills, fever, headache, pain, malaise
    Dermatologic: Rash
    Endocrine & metabolic: Hyperkalemia
    Gastrointestinal: Abdominal pain, diarrhea, nausea
    Hematologic: Leukopenia, thrombocytopenia
    Neuromuscular & skeletal: Weakness
    Respiratory: Dyspnea
    Miscellaneous: Systemic infection
1% to 10%: Central nervous system: Dizziness
Postmarketing and/or case reports: Anaphylaxis

Stability Store powder under refrigeration at 2°C to 8°C (36°F to 46°F); do not freeze. Protect from light. Allow vials to reach room temperature, then reconstitute using provided diluent. Rotate vial gently until dissolved. Prior to administration, further dilute one vial in 50 mL saline or dextrose (total volume is usually 50-500 mL depending on total number of vials needed per dose). Mix by gently inverting infusion bag once or twice. Reconstituted vials should be used within 4 hours. Use immediately following dilution for infusion.

Mechanism of Action May involve elimination of antigen-reactive T lymphocytes (killer cells) in peripheral blood or alteration of T-cell function

Pharmacodynamics/Kinetics Half-life elimination, plasma: 2-3 days

Dosage I.V.: 1.5 mg/kg/day for 7-14 days
    Dosage adjustment for toxicity:
        WBC count 2000-3000 cells/mm^3 or platelet count 50,000-75,000 cells/mm^3: Reduce dose by 50%
        WBC count <2000 cells/mm^3 or platelet count <50,000 cells/mm^3: Consider discontinuing treatment

Administration The first dose should be infused over at least 6 hours through a high-flow vein. Subsequent doses should be administered over at least 4 hours. Administer through an in-line 0.22 micron filter. Premedication with corticosteroids, acetaminophen, and/or an antihistamine may reduce infusion-related reactions.

Monitoring Parameters Lymphocyte profile, CBC with differential and platelet count, vital signs during administration; any severe systemic reaction to the skin test (eg, generalized rash, tachycardia, dyspnea, hypotension, or anaphylaxis) should preclude further therapy; T-lymphocyte count prior to retreatment (verify T-cell depletion).

Dosage Forms Injection, powder for reconstitution: 25 mg [packaged with diluent]

- **Antithymocyte Immunoglobulin** *see* Antithymocyte Globulin (Equine) *on page 138*
- **Antithymocyte Immunoglobulin** *see* Antithymocyte Globulin (Rabbit) *on page 140*
- **Antitumor Necrosis Factor Apha (Human)** *see* Adalimumab *on page 47*
- **Anti-VEGF Monoclonal Antibody** *see* Bevacizumab *on page 217*
- **Antivert®** *see* Meclizine *on page 1063*
- **Antizol®** *see* Fomepizole *on page 755*
- **Anucort-HC®** *see* Hydrocortisone *on page 852*
- **Anu-Med [OTC]** *see* Phenylephrine *on page 1358*
- **Anusol-HC®** *see* Hydrocortisone *on page 852*
- **Anusol® HC-1 [OTC]** *see* Hydrocortisone *on page 852*
- **Anuzinc (Can)** *see* Zinc Sulfate *on page 1817*
- **Anzemet®** *see* Dolasetron *on page 536*
- **APAP** *see* Acetaminophen *on page 28*
- **APAP and Tramadol** *see* Acetaminophen and Tramadol *on page 34*
- **ApexiCon™** *see* Diflorasone *on page 499*
- **ApexiCon™ E** *see* Diflorasone *on page 499*
- **Aphthasol®** *see* Amlexanox *on page 103*
- **Apidra®** *see* Insulin Glulisine *on page 911*
- **Aplisol®** *see* Tuberculin Tests *on page 1754*
- **Aplonidine** *see* Apraclonidine *on page 144*
- **Apo-Acebutolol® (Can)** *see* Acebutolol *on page 27*
- **Apo-Acetaminophen® (Can)** *see* Acetaminophen *on page 28*
- **Apo-Acetazolamide® (Can)** *see* AcetaZOLAMIDE *on page 37*
- **Apo-Acyclovir® (Can)** *see* Acyclovir *on page 44*
- **Apo-Alendronate® (Can)** *see* Alendronate *on page 65*
- **Apo-Allopurinol® (Can)** *see* Allopurinol *on page 71*
- **Apo-Alpraz® (Can)** *see* Alprazolam *on page 75*
- **Apo-Alpraz® TS (Can)** *see* Alprazolam *on page 75*
- **Apo-Amiloride® (Can)** *see* Amiloride *on page 92*
- **Apo-Amilzide® (Can)** *see* Amiloride and Hydrochlorothiazide *on page 93*
- **Apo-Amiodarone® (Can)** *see* Amiodarone *on page 97*
- **Apo-Amitriptyline® (Can)** *see* Amitriptyline *on page 101*
- **Apo-Amoxi® (Can)** *see* Amoxicillin *on page 110*
- **Apo-Amoxi-Clav® (Can)** *see* Amoxicillin and Clavulanate Potassium *on page 112*
- **Apo-Ampi® (Can)** *see* Ampicillin *on page 122*
- **Apo-Atenidone® (Can)** *see* Atenolol and Chlorthalidone *on page 169*
- **Apo-Atenol® (Can)** *see* Atenolol *on page 167*
- **Apo-Azathioprine® (Can)** *see* Azathioprine *on page 183*
- **Apo-Azithromycin® (Can)** *see* Azithromycin *on page 186*
- **Apo-Baclofen® (Can)** *see* Baclofen *on page 193*
- **Apo-Beclomethasone® (Can)** *see* Beclomethasone *on page 198*
- **Apo-Benazepril® (Can)** *see* Benazepril *on page 202*
- **Apo-Benztropine® (Can)** *see* Benztropine *on page 208*
- **Apo-Bisacodyl® (Can)** *see* Bisacodyl *on page 223*
- **Apo-Bisoprolol® (Can)** *see* Bisoprolol *on page 226*
- **Apo-Brimonidine® (Can)** *see* Brimonidine *on page 239*
- **Apo-Bromocriptine® (Can)** *see* Bromocriptine *on page 240*
- **Apo-Buspirone® (Can)** *see* BusPIRone *on page 256*
- **Apo-Butorphanol® (Can)** *see* Butorphanol *on page 261*
- **Apo-Cal® (Can)** *see* Calcium Carbonate *on page 269*
- **Apo-Calcitonin® (Can)** *see* Calcitonin *on page 264*
- **Apo-Capto® (Can)** *see* Captopril *on page 281*
- **Apo-Carbamazepine® (Can)** *see* Carbamazepine *on page 284*
- **Apo-Carvedilol® (Can)** *see* Carvedilol *on page 299*
- **Apo-Cefaclor® (Can)** *see* Cefaclor *on page 303*
- **Apo-Cefadroxil® (Can)** *see* Cefadroxil *on page 305*
- **Apo-Cefuroxime® (Can)** *see* Cefuroxime *on page 326*
- **Apo-Cephalex® (Can)** *see* Cephalexin *on page 331*
- **Apo-Cetirizine® (Can)** *see* Cetirizine *on page 334*
- **Apo-Chlorax® (Can)** *see* Clidinium and Chlordiazepoxide *on page 388*
- **Apo-Chlordiazepoxide® (Can)** *see* Chlordiazepoxide *on page 342*
- **Apo-Chlorpropamide® (Can)** *see* ChlorproPAMIDE *on page 358*
- **Apo-Chlorthalidone® (Can)** *see* Chlorthalidone *on page 359*
- **Apo-Cimetidine® (Can)** *see* Cimetidine *on page 369*
- **Apo-Ciproflox® (Can)** *see* Ciprofloxacin *on page 372*
- **Apo-Citalopram® (Can)** *see* Citalopram *on page 381*
- **Apo-Clindamycin® (Can)** *see* Clindamycin *on page 389*
- **Apo-Clomipramine® (Can)** *see* ClomiPRAMINE *on page 395*
- **Apo-Clonazepam® (Can)** *see* Clonazepam *on page 397*
- **Apo-Clonidine® (Can)** *see* Clonidine *on page 399*
- **Apo-Clorazepate® (Can)** *see* Clorazepate *on page 403*
- **Apo-Clozapine® (Can)** *see* Clozapine *on page 406*
- **Apo-Cromolyn® (Can)** *see* Cromolyn *on page 423*
- **Apo-Cyclobenzaprine® (Can)** *see* Cyclobenzaprine *on page 427*

- **Apo-Desipramine® (Can)** *see* Desipramine *on page 473*
- **Apo-Desmopressin® (Can)** *see* Desmopressin *on page 476*
- **Apo-Dexamethasone® (Can)** *see* Dexamethasone *on page 479*
- **Apo-Diazepam® (Can)** *see* Diazepam *on page 488*
- **Apo-Diclo® (Can)** *see* Diclofenac *on page 492*
- **Apo-Diclo Rapide® (Can)** *see* Diclofenac *on page 492*
- **Apo-Diclo SR® (Can)** *see* Diclofenac *on page 492*
- **Apo-Diflunisal® (Can)** *see* Diflunisal *on page 500*
- **Apo-Diltiaz® (Can)** *see* Diltiazem *on page 509*
- **Apo-Diltiaz CD® (Can)** *see* Diltiazem *on page 509*
- **Apo-Diltiaz® Injectable (Can)** *see* Diltiazem *on page 509*
- **Apo-Diltiaz SR® (Can)** *see* Diltiazem *on page 509*
- **Apo-Dimenhydrinate® (Can)** *see* DimenhyDRINATE *on page 511*
- **Apo-Dipyridamole FC® (Can)** *see* Dipyridamole *on page 525*
- **Apo-Divalproex® (Can)** *see* Valproic Acid and Derivatives *on page 1767*
- **Apo-Docusate-Sodium® (Can)** *see* Docusate *on page 533*
- **Apo-Doxazosin® (Can)** *see* Doxazosin *on page 544*
- **Apo-Doxepin® (Can)** *see* Doxepin *on page 545*
- **Apo-Doxy® (Can)** *see* Doxycycline *on page 555*
- **Apo-Doxy Tabs® (Can)** *see* Doxycycline *on page 555*
- **Apo-Erythro Base® (Can)** *see* Erythromycin *on page 609*
- **Apo-Erythro E-C® (Can)** *see* Erythromycin *on page 609*
- **Apo-Erythro-ES® (Can)** *see* Erythromycin *on page 609*
- **Apo-Erythro-S® (Can)** *see* Erythromycin *on page 609*
- **Apo-Etodolac® (Can)** *see* Etodolac *on page 666*
- **Apo-Famotidine® (Can)** *see* Famotidine *on page 683*
- **Apo-Famotidine® Injectable (Can)** *see* Famotidine *on page 683*
- **Apo-Fenofibrate® (Can)** *see* Fenofibrate *on page 689*
- **Apo-Feno-Micro® (Can)** *see* Fenofibrate *on page 689*
- **Apo-Ferrous Gluconate® (Can)** *see* Ferrous Gluconate *on page 703*
- **Apo-Ferrous Sulfate® (Can)** *see* Ferrous Sulfate *on page 704*
- **Apo-Flavoxate® (Can)** *see* Flavoxate *on page 710*
- **Apo-Flecainide® (Can)** *see* Flecainide *on page 710*
- **Apo-Fluconazole® (Can)** *see* Fluconazole *on page 712*
- **Apo-Flunisolide® (Can)** *see* Flunisolide *on page 720*
- **Apo-Fluoxetine® (Can)** *see* Fluoxetine *on page 727*
- **Apo-Fluphenazine® (Can)** *see* Fluphenazine *on page 731*
- **Apo-Fluphenazine Decanoate® (Can)** *see* Fluphenazine *on page 731*
- **Apo-Flurazepam® (Can)** *see* Flurazepam *on page 733*
- **Apo-Flurbiprofen® (Can)** *see* Flurbiprofen *on page 735*
- **Apo-Flutamide® (Can)** *see* Flutamide *on page 737*
- **Apo-Fluvoxamine® (Can)** *see* Fluvoxamine *on page 747*
- **Apo-Folic® (Can)** *see* Folic Acid *on page 749*
- **Apo-Fosinopril® (Can)** *see* Fosinopril *on page 766*
- **Apo-Furosemide® (Can)** *see* Furosemide *on page 773*
- **Apo-Gabapentin® (Can)** *see* Gabapentin *on page 775*
- **Apo-Gain® (Can)** *see* Minoxidil *on page 1151*
- **Apo-Gemfibrozil® (Can)** *see* Gemfibrozil *on page 787*
- **Apo-Glyburide® (Can)** *see* GlyBURIDE *on page 803*
- **Apo-Haloperidol® (Can)** *see* Haloperidol *on page 826*
- **Apo-Haloperidol LA® (Can)** *see* Haloperidol *on page 826*
- **Apo-Hydralazine® (Can)** *see* HydrALAZINE *on page 843*
- **Apo-Hydro® (Can)** *see* Hydrochlorothiazide *on page 845*
- **Apo-Hydroxyquine® (Can)** *see* Hydroxychloroquine *on page 862*
- **Apo-Hydroxyurea® (Can)** *see* Hydroxyurea *on page 863*
- **Apo-Hydroxyzine® (Can)** *see* HydrOXYzine *on page 865*
- **Apo-Ibuprofen® (Can)** *see* Ibuprofen *on page 873*
- **Apo-Imipramine® (Can)** *see* Imipramine *on page 888*
- **Apo-Indapamide® (Can)** *see* Indapamide *on page 898*
- **Apo-Indomethacin® (Can)** *see* Indomethacin *on page 901*
- **Apo-Ipravent® (Can)** *see* Ipratropium *on page 932*
- **Apo-ISDN® (Can)** *see* Isosorbide Dinitrate *on page 945*
- **Apo-ISMN (Can)** *see* Isosorbide Mononitrate *on page 947*
- **Apo-K® (Can)** *see* Potassium Chloride *on page 1396*
- **Apo-Keto® (Can)** *see* Ketoprofen *on page 961*
- **Apo-Ketoconazole® (Can)** *see* Ketoconazole *on page 959*
- **Apo-Keto-E® (Can)** *see* Ketoprofen *on page 961*
- **Apo-Ketorolac® (Can)** *see* Ketorolac *on page 963*
- **Apo-Ketorolac Injectable® (Can)** *see* Ketorolac *on page 963*
- **Apo-Keto SR® (Can)** *see* Ketoprofen *on page 961*
- **Apo-Ketotifen® (Can)** *see* Ketotifen *on page 965*
- **Apo-Labetalol® (Can)** *see* Labetalol *on page 967*
- **Apo-Lactulose® (Can)** *see* Lactulose *on page 971*
- **Apo-Lamotrigine® (Can)** *see* Lamotrigine *on page 974*

- **Apo-Leflunomide®** **(Can)** *see* Leflunomide *on page 982*
- **Apo-Levobunolol®** **(Can)** *see* Levobunolol *on page 996*
- **Apo-Levocarb®** **(Can)** *see* Levodopa and Carbidopa *on page 999*
- **Apo-Levocarb® CR (Can)** *see* Levodopa and Carbidopa *on page 999*
- **Apo-Lisinopril®** **(Can)** *see* Lisinopril *on page 1021*
- **Apo-Lithium® Carbonate (Can)** *see* Lithium *on page 1023*
- **Apo-Lithium® Carbonate SR (Can)** *see* Lithium *on page 1023*
- **Apo-Loperamide®** **(Can)** *see* Loperamide *on page 1027*
- **Apo-Loratadine®** **(Can)** *see* Loratadine *on page 1033*
- **Apo-Lorazepam®** **(Can)** *see* Lorazepam *on page 1035*
- **Apo-Lovastatin®** **(Can)** *see* Lovastatin *on page 1040*
- **Apo-Loxapine®** **(Can)** *see* Loxapine *on page 1042*
- **Apo-Medroxy®** **(Can)** *see* MedroxyPROGESTERone *on page 1065*
- **Apo-Mefenamic®** **(Can)** *see* Mefenamic Acid *on page 1068*
- **Apo-Mefloquine®** **(Can)** *see* Mefloquine *on page 1069*
- **Apo-Megestrol®** **(Can)** *see* Megestrol *on page 1071*
- **Apo-Meloxicam®** **(Can)** *see* Meloxicam *on page 1072*
- **Apo-Metformin®** **(Can)** *see* Metformin *on page 1098*
- **Apo-Methazide®** **(Can)** *see* Methyldopa and Hydrochlorothiazide *on page 1117*
- **Apo-Methazolamide®** **(Can)** *see* Methazolamide *on page 1105*
- **Apo-Methotrexate®** **(Can)** *see* Methotrexate *on page 1111*
- **Apo-Methyldopa®** **(Can)** *see* Methyldopa *on page 1117*
- **Apo-Methylphenidate®** **(Can)** *see* Methylphenidate *on page 1119*
- **Apo-Methylphenidate® SR (Can)** *see* Methylphenidate *on page 1119*
- **Apo-Metoclop®** **(Can)** *see* Metoclopramide *on page 1126*
- **Apo-Metoprolol®** **(Can)** *see* Metoprolol *on page 1129*
- **Apo-Metronidazole®** **(Can)** *see* Metronidazole *on page 1132*
- **Apo-Midazolam®** **(Can)** *see* Midazolam *on page 1139*
- **Apo-Midodrine®** **(Can)** *see* Midodrine *on page 1142*
- **Apo-Minocycline®** **(Can)** *see* Minocycline *on page 1149*
- **Apo-Misoprostol®** **(Can)** *see* Misoprostol *on page 1154*
- **Apo-Nabumetone®** **(Can)** *see* Nabumetone *on page 1185*
- **Apo-Nadol®** **(Can)** *see* Nadolol *on page 1187*
- **Apo-Napro-Na®** **(Can)** *see* Naproxen *on page 1199*
- **Apo-Napro-Na DS®** **(Can)** *see* Naproxen *on page 1199*
- **Apo-Naproxen®** **(Can)** *see* Naproxen *on page 1199*
- **Apo-Naproxen EC®** **(Can)** *see* Naproxen *on page 1199*
- **Apo-Naproxen SR®** **(Can)** *see* Naproxen *on page 1199*
- **Apo-Nifed®** **(Can)** *see* NIFEdipine *on page 1226*
- **Apo-Nifed PA®** **(Can)** *see* NIFEdipine *on page 1226*
- **Apo-Nitrofurantoin®** **(Can)** *see* Nitrofurantoin *on page 1233*
- **Apo-Nizatidine®** **(Can)** *see* Nizatidine *on page 1238*
- **Apo-Norflox®** **(Can)** *see* Norfloxacin *on page 1241*
- **Apo-Nortriptyline®** **(Can)** *see* Nortriptyline *on page 1243*
- **Apo-Oflox®** **(Can)** *see* Ofloxacin *on page 1254*
- **Apo-Ofloxacin®** **(Can)** *see* Ofloxacin *on page 1254*
- **Apo-Omeprazole®** **(Can)** *see* Omeprazole *on page 1264*
- **Apo-Orciprenaline®** **(Can)** *see* Metaproterenol *on page 1096*
- **Apo-Oxaprozin®** **(Can)** *see* Oxaprozin *on page 1279*
- **Apo-Oxazepam®** **(Can)** *see* Oxazepam *on page 1281*
- **Apo-Oxybutynin®** **(Can)** *see* Oxybutynin *on page 1285*
- **Apo-Paclitaxel®** **(Can)** *see* Paclitaxel *on page 1295*
- **Apo-Paroxetine®** **(Can)** *see* Paroxetine *on page 1314*
- **Apo-Pentoxifylline SR®** **(Can)** *see* Pentoxifylline *on page 1343*
- **Apo-Pen VK®** **(Can)** *see* Penicillin V Potassium *on page 1336*
- **Apo-Perphenazine®** **(Can)** *see* Perphenazine *on page 1349*
- **Apo-Pimozide®** **(Can)** *see* Pimozide *on page 1370*
- **Apo-Pindol®** **(Can)** *see* Pindolol *on page 1371*
- **Apo-Piroxicam®** **(Can)** *see* Piroxicam *on page 1378*
- **Apo-Pravastatin®** **(Can)** *see* Pravastatin *on page 1409*
- **Apo-Prazo®** **(Can)** *see* Prazosin *on page 1411*
- **Apo-Prednisone®** **(Can)** *see* PredniSONE *on page 1416*
- **Apo-Primidone®** **(Can)** *see* Primidone *on page 1422*
- **Apo-Procainamide®** **(Can)** *see* Procainamide *on page 1424*
- **Apo-Prochlorperazine®** **(Can)** *see* Prochlorperazine *on page 1429*
- **Apo-Propafenone®** **(Can)** *see* Propafenone *on page 1439*
- **Apo-Propranolol®** **(Can)** *see* Propranolol *on page 1446*
- **Apo-Quinidine®** **(Can)** *see* Quinidine *on page 1471*
- **Apo-Quinine®** **(Can)** *see* Quinine *on page 1474*
- **Apo-Ranitidine®** **(Can)** *see* Ranitidine *on page 1485*
- **Apo-Risperidone®** **(Can)** *see* Risperidone *on page 1517*
- **Apo-Salvent®** **(Can)** *see* Albuterol *on page 57*
- **Apo-Salvent® CFC Free (Can)** *see* Albuterol *on page 57*
- **Apo-Salvent® Respirator Solution (Can)** *see* Albuterol *on page 57*

- **Apo-Salvent® Sterules (Can)** *see* Albuterol *on page 57*
- **Apo-Selegiline® (Can)** *see* Selegiline *on page 1552*
- **Apo-Sertraline® (Can)** *see* Sertraline *on page 1557*
- **Apo-Simvastatin® (Can)** *see* Simvastatin *on page 1567*
- **Apo-Sotalol® (Can)** *see* Sotalol *on page 1592*
- **Apo-Sulfatrim® (Can)** *see* Sulfamethoxazole and Trimethoprim *on page 1613*
- **Apo-Sulfatrim® DS (Can)** *see* Sulfamethoxazole and Trimethoprim *on page 1613*
- **Apo-Sulfatrim® Pediatric (Can)** *see* Sulfamethoxazole and Trimethoprim *on page 1613*
- **Apo-Sulin® (Can)** *see* Sulindac *on page 1618*
- **Apo-Sumatriptan® (Can)** *see* Sumatriptan *on page 1620*
- **Apo-Tamox® (Can)** *see* Tamoxifen *on page 1631*
- **Apo-Temazepam® (Can)** *see* Temazepam *on page 1640*
- **Apo-Terazosin® (Can)** *see* Terazosin *on page 1647*
- **Apo-Terbinafine® (Can)** *see* Terbinafine *on page 1648*
- **Apo-Tetra® (Can)** *see* Tetracycline *on page 1659*
- **Apo-Ticlopidine® (Can)** *see* Ticlopidine *on page 1683*
- **Apo-Timol® (Can)** *see* Timolol *on page 1687*
- **Apo-Timop® (Can)** *see* Timolol *on page 1687*
- **Apo-Tizanidine® (Can)** *see* Tizanidine *on page 1695*
- **Apo-Tolbutamide® (Can)** *see* TOLBUTamide *on page 1701*
- **Apo-Trazodone® (Can)** *see* Trazodone *on page 1727*
- **Apo-Trazodone D® (Can)** *see* Trazodone *on page 1727*
- **Apo-Triazide® (Can)** *see* Hydrochlorothiazide and Triamterene *on page 847*
- **Apo-Triazo® (Can)** *see* Triazolam *on page 1738*
- **Apo-Trifluoperazine® (Can)** *see* Trifluoperazine *on page 1740*
- **Apo-Trihex® (Can)** *see* Trihexyphenidyl *on page 1742*
- **Apo-Trimethoprim® (Can)** *see* Trimethoprim *on page 1744*
- **Apo-Trimip® (Can)** *see* Trimipramine *on page 1747*
- **Apo-Valproic® (Can)** *see* Valproic Acid and Derivatives *on page 1767*
- **Apo-Verap® (Can)** *see* Verapamil *on page 1784*
- **Apo-Verap® SR (Can)** *see* Verapamil *on page 1784*
- **Apo-Warfarin® (Can)** *see* Warfarin *on page 1800*
- **Apo-Zidovudine® (Can)** *see* Zidovudine *on page 1812*
- **APPG** *see* Penicillin G Procaine *on page 1335*
- **Apra Children's [OTC]** *see* Acetaminophen *on page 28*

Apraclonidine (a pra KLOE ni deen)

U.S. Brand Names Iopidine®
Canadian Brand Names Iopidine®
Index Terms Aplonidine; Apraclonidine Hydrochloride; p-Aminoclonidine
Pharmacologic Category Alpha₂ Agonist, Ophthalmic
Additional Appendix Information
   Glaucoma Drug Therapy *on page 2050*
Use Prevention and treatment of postsurgical intraocular pressure (IOP) elevation; short-term, adjunctive therapy in patients who require additional reduction of IOP
Pregnancy Risk Factor C
Medication Safety Issues
   Sound-alike/look-alike issues:
      Iopidine® may be confused with indapamide, iodine, Lodine®
Dosage Adults: Ophthalmic:
   0.5%: Instill 1-2 drops in the affected eye(s) 3 times/day
   1%: Instill 1 drop in operative eye 1 hour prior to anterior segment laser surgery, second drop in eye immediately upon completion of procedure
   Dosing adjustment in renal impairment: Although the topical use of apraclonidine has not been studied in renal failure patients, structurally-related clonidine undergoes a significant increase in half-life in patients with severe renal impairment; close monitoring of cardiovascular parameters in patients with impaired renal function is advised.
   Dosing adjustment in hepatic impairment: Close monitoring of cardiovascular parameters in patients with impaired liver function is advised because the systemic dosage form of clonidine is partially metabolized in the liver.
Additional Information Complete prescribing information for this medication should be consulted for additional detail.
Dosage Forms
   Solution, ophthalmic:
      Iopidine®: 0.5% (5 mL, 10 mL); 1% (0.1 mL) [contains benzalkonium chloride]

- **Apraclonidine Hydrochloride** *see* Apraclonidine *on page 144*

Aprepitant (ap RE pi tant)

U.S. Brand Names Emend®
Index Terms L 754030; MK 869
Pharmacologic Category Antiemetic; Substance P/Neurokinin 1 Receptor Antagonist
Use Prevention of acute and delayed nausea and vomiting associated with moderately- and highly-emetogenic chemotherapy in combination with a corticosteroid and 5-HT₃ receptor antagonist; prevention of postoperative nausea and vomiting (PONV)
Pregnancy Risk Factor B

Pregnancy Implications Teratogenic effects were not observed in animal studies. There are no adequate and well-controlled studies in pregnant women; use only if clearly needed.

Lactation Excretion in breast milk unknown/not recommended

Contraindications Hypersensitivity to aprepitant or any component of the formulation; use with cisapride or pimozide

Warnings/Precautions Use caution with agents primarily metabolized via CYP3A4; aprepitant is a 3A4 inhibitor. Effect on orally administered 3A4 substrates is greater than those administered intravenously. Use caution with hepatic impairment. Not intended for treatment of existing nausea and vomiting or for chronic continuous therapy. Safety and efficacy in pediatric patients have not been established.

Adverse Reactions Note: Adverse reactions reported as part of a combination chemotherapy regimen or with general anesthesia.

>10%:
    Central nervous system: Fatigue (18% to 22%)
    Gastrointestinal: Nausea (7% to 13%), constipation (9% to 12%)
    Neuromuscular & skeletal: Weakness (3% to 18%)
    Miscellaneous: Hiccups (11%)
1% to 10%:
    Cardiovascular: Hypotension (6%), bradycardia (4%)
    Central nervous system: Dizziness (>0.5% to 7%)
    Endocrine & metabolic: Dehydration (6%), hot flushing (3%)
    Gastrointestinal: Diarrhea (6% to 10%), dyspepsia (8%), abdominal pain (5%), stomatitis (5%), epigastric discomfort (4%), gastritis (4%), mucous membrane disorder (3%), throat pain (3%), vomiting (3%)
    Hematologic: Neutropenia (3% to 0%), leukopenia (0%), hemoglobin decreased (2% to 5%)
    Hepatic: ALT increased (1% to 6%), AST increased (3%)
    Renal: BUN increased (5%), proteinuria (7%), serum creatinine increased (4%)
>0.5% (Limited to important or life-threatening): Acid reflux, acne, albumin decreased, alkaline phosphatase increased, anemia, anxiety, appetite decreased, back pain, bilirubin increased, candidiasis, confusion, conjunctivitis, cough, deglutition disorder, depression, diabetes mellitus, diaphoresis, dry mouth, DVT, dysgeusia, dysphagia, dyspnea, dysuria, edema, eructation, erythrocyturia, flatulence, flushing, hyperglycemia, hyper-/hypotension, hypokalemia, hyponatremia, hypovolemia, hypoxia, glucosuria, leukocytes increased, leukocyturia, malaise, MI, muscular weakness, musculoskeletal pain, myalgia, nasal secretion, obstipation, pelvic pain, peripheral neuropathy, pharyngitis, pneumonitis, pulmonary embolism, rash, renal insufficiency, respiratory infection, respiratory insufficiency, rigors, salivation, sensory neuropathy, septic shock, syncope, tachycardia, taste disturbance, thrombocytopenia, tremor, urinary tract infection, vocal disturbance, weight loss

Overdosage/Toxicology Single doses up to 600 mg and daily doses of 375 mg for up to 42 days were well-tolerated in healthy subjects; drowsiness and headache were noted at a dose of 1440 mg. In cancer patients, a single dose of 375 mg followed by 250 mg on days 2 to 5 was well tolerated. In case of overdose, treatment should be symptom-directed and supportive. Not removed by hemodialysis.

Drug Interactions
Cytochrome P450 Effect: Substrate of CYP1A2 (minor), 2C19 (minor), 3A4 (major); **Inhibits** CYP2C9 (weak), 2C19 (weak), 3A4 (moderate); **Induces** CYP2C9 (weak), 3A4 (weak)

Increased Effect/Toxicity: Use with cisapride or pimozide is contraindicated. CYP3A4 inhibitors may increase the levels/effects of aprepitant; example inhibitors include azole antifungals, clarithromycin, diclofenac, diltiazem, doxycycline, erythromycin, imatinib, isoniazid, nefazodone, nicardipine, propofol, protease inhibitors, quinidine, telithromycin, and verapamil. Aprepitant may increase the bioavailability of corticosteroids; dose adjustment of dexamethasone and methylprednisolone is needed. Aprepitant may increase the levels/effects of CYP3A4 substrates; example substrates include benzodiazepines, calcium channel blockers, ergot derivatives, mirtazapine, nateglinide, nefazodone, tacrolimus, and venlafaxine. Aprepitant may increase the levels/effects of pimecrolimus.

Decreased Effect: CYP3A4 inducers may decrease the levels/effects of aprepitant; example inducers include aminoglutethimide, carbamazepine, nafcillin, nevirapine, phenobarbital, phenytoin, and rifamycins. Metabolism of warfarin may be induced; monitor INR following the start of each cycle. Efficacy of hormone-containing contraceptives (estrogens) may be decreased (plasma levels of ethinyl estradiol and norethindrone decreased with concomitant use).

Ethanol/Nutrition/Herb Interactions
Food: Aprepitant serum concentration may be increased when taken with grapefruit juice; avoid concurrent use.
Herb/Nutraceutical: St John's wort may decrease aprepitant levels.

Stability Store at controlled room temperature of 20°C to 25°C (68°F to 77°F).

Mechanism of Action Prevents acute and delayed vomiting at the substance P/neurokinin 1 (NK$_1$) receptor; augments the antiemetic activity of the 5-HT$_3$ receptor antagonist and corticosteroid and inhibits both acute and delayed phases of cisplatin-induced emesis.

Pharmacodynamics/Kinetics
Distribution: V_d: 70 L; crosses the blood brain barrier
Protein binding: >95%
Metabolism: Extensively hepatic via CYP3A4 (major); CYP1A2 and CYP2C19 (minor); forms seven metabolites (weakly active)
Bioavailability: 60% to 65%
Half-life elimination: Terminal: 9-13 hours
Time to peak, plasma: 4 hours

Dosage Oral: Adults:
Prevention of chemotherapy induced nausea/vomiting: 125 mg on day 1, followed by 80 mg on days 2 and 3 in combination with a corticosteroid and 5-HT$_3$ receptor antagonist
Prevention of PONV: 40 mg within 3 hours prior to induction
(Continued)

Aprepitant *(Continued)*

Dosage adjustment in renal impairment: No dose adjustment necessary in patients with renal disease or end-stage renal disease maintained on hemodialysis.

Dosage adjustment in hepatic impairment:
Mild-to-moderate impairment (Child-Pugh score 5-9): No adjustment necessary
Severe impairment (Child-Pugh score >9): No data available

Dietary Considerations May be taken with or without food.

Administration Administer with or without food.
Chemotherapy induced nausea/vomiting: First dose should be given 1 hour prior to antineoplastic therapy; subsequent doses should be given in the morning.
PONV: Administer within 3 hours of induction

Dosage Forms
Capsule:
Emend®: 40 mg, 80 mg, 125 mg
Combination package: Capsule 80 mg (2s), capsule 125 mg (1s)

♦ **Apresazide [DSC]** *see* Hydralazine and Hydrochlorothiazide *on page 845*

♦ **Apresoline [DSC]** *see* HydrALAZINE *on page 843*

♦ **Apresoline® (Can)** *see* HydrALAZINE *on page 843*

♦ **Apri®** *see* Ethinyl Estradiol and Desogestrel *on page 645*

♦ **Aprodine® [OTC]** *see* Triprolidine and Pseudoephedrine *on page 1749*

Aprotinin *(a proe TYE nin)*

U.S. Brand Names Trasylol®

Canadian Brand Names Trasylol®

Pharmacologic Category Blood Product Derivative; Hemostatic Agent

Use Prevention of perioperative blood loss in patients who are at increased risk for blood loss and blood transfusions in association with cardiopulmonary bypass in coronary artery bypass graft surgery

Pregnancy Risk Factor B

Pregnancy Implications Teratogenic effects were not observed in animal studies. There are no adequate and well-controlled studies in pregnant women.

Lactation Excretion in breast milk unknown/use caution

Contraindications Hypersensitivity to aprotinin or any component of the formulation; known or suspected exposure (including through fibrin sealant products that contain aprotinin) within the past 12 months

Warnings/Precautions [U.S. Boxed Warning]: Anaphylactic reactions are possible. Hypersensitivity reactions are more common with repeated use; the risk of fatal reactions appears to be greater upon re-exposure within 12 months of previous use. Patients with a history of allergic reactions may also be more likely to develop a reaction. All patients should receive a test dose at least 10 minutes before the loading dose, although the test dose does not fully predict a patient's risk. Fatal hypersensitivity reactions have occurred in patients who tolerated the test dose. Epinephrine, steroids, and facilities for cardiopulmonary resuscitation should be available in case such a reaction occurs. In order to administer in a more controlled setting, patients should be in the OR, intubated and ready for rapid cannulation and initiation of cardiopulmonary bypass before the test dose is administered. Delay adding aprotinin to the pump prime solution until after the loading dose has been safely administered. Hypotension is the most frequently reported sign of the hypersensitivity reaction.

Aprotinin has been linked to an increased risk of death, serious kidney damage, and heart failure in observational studies. Renal dysfunction (elevations of >0.5 mg/dL over baseline serum creatinine) may occur with use and may increase the need for dialysis in the perioperative period. Patients at greatest risk are those with pre-existing renal dysfunction (Cl_{cr} <60 mL/minute) or those receiving potential nephrotoxins (eg, aminoglycosides). Monitor renal function closely following administration. Safety and efficacy in children have not been established.

Adverse Reactions
>10%:
Central nervous system: Fever (15%)
Gastrointestinal: Nausea (11%)
1% to 10%:
Cardiovascular: Atrial flutter (6%), ventricular extrasystoles (6%), ventricular tachycardia (1% to 5%), heart failure (1% to 5%), arrhythmia (4%), supraventricular tachycardia (4%), bradycardia (1% to 2%), thrombosis (1% to 2%), bundle branch block (1% to 2%), cardiac arrest (1% to 2%), heart block (1% to 2%), hemorrhage (1% to 2%), myocardial ischemia (1% to 2%), pericardial effusion (1% to 2%), , ventricular fibrillation (1% to 2%), shock (<1% to 2%)
Central nervous system: Agitation (1% to 2%), anxiety (1% to 2%), dizziness (1% to 2%), seizure (1% to 2%)
Endocrine & metabolic: Creatinine phosphokinase increase (2%), acidosis (1% to 2%), hyperglycemia (1% to 2%), hypervolemia (1% to 2%), hypokalemia
Gastrointestinal: Diarrhea (3%), dyspepsia (1% to 2%), gastrointestinal hemorrhage (1% to 2%)
Hematologic: Disseminated intravascular coagulation (DIC), leukocytosis (1% to 2%), prothrombin decreased (1% to 2%), thrombocytopenia (1% to 2%)
Hepatic: Jaundice (1% to 2%), hepatic failure (1% to 2%)
Neuromuscular & skeletal: Arthralgia (1% to 2%)
Renal: Serum creatinine increase of >0.5 mg/dL above baseline (high dose: 9%), oliguria (1% to 2%), tubular necrosis (1% to 2%), kidney failure (1%)
Respiratory: Hypoxia (2%), pulmonary hypertension (1% to 2%), pneumonia (1% to 2%), apnea (1% to 2%), cough increased (1% to 2%)
Miscellaneous: Sepsis (1% to 2%), multisystem organ failure (1% to 2%)

<1% (Limited to important or life-threatening): Anaphylactic reaction/hypersensitivity (no prior exposure: <0.1%; re-exposure within 6 months 5%; re-exposure >6 months <1%), hemoperitoneum, skin discoloration

Overdosage/Toxicology The maximum amount of aprotinin that can safely be given has not yet been determined. Doses as high as 17.5 million KIU/24 hours have been tolerated. However, one case report of aprotinin overdose (>15 million KIU/24 hours) was associated with the development of hepatic and renal failure and eventually death. Autopsy demonstrated severe hepatic necrosis and extensive renal tubular and glomerular necrosis. The patient had pre-existing hepatic dysfunction.

Drug Interactions

Decreased Effect: Aprotinin decreases the effects of thrombolytics. The antihypertensive effects of captopril (and other ACE inhibitors) may be blocked.

Stability Store at 2°C to 25°C (36°F to 77°F); protect from freezing.

Mechanism of Action Bleeding from CABG surgery is thought to result from a systemic inflammatory response induced by the procedure. Contact of blood cells with the cardiopulmonary bypass (CPB) equipment leads to deregulated activation of the coagulation and fibrinolysis systems, with concurrent upregulation of proinflammatory cytokines. Aprotinin is a broad spectrum serine protease inhibitor that attenuates the coagulation, fibrinolytic and inflammatory pathways by interfering with the chemical mediators (thrombin, plasmin, kallikrein). Additionally, it protects platelet-expressed glycoproteins from mechanical shear forces. This preserves normal hemostatic activity through protease receptor-independent mechanisms (eg, via ADP, IIb/IIIa), while blocking CPB-induced thrombin-mediated aggregation.

Pharmacodynamics/Kinetics

Distribution: Extracellular space; renal phagolysosomes

Metabolism: Aprotinin is slowly degraded by lysosomal enzymes.

Half-life elimination: 2.5 hours (plasma); terminal: 10 hours

Excretion: Urine (25% to 40%; <10% as unchanged drug)

Dosage Adults: Test dose: **All** patients should receive a 1 mL (1.4 mg) I.V. test dose at least 10 minutes prior to the loading dose to assess the potential for allergic reactions.

Notes:

The loading dose should be given after induction of anesthesia but prior to sternotomy. In patients with previous exposure to aprotinin, administer loading dose just prior to cannulation. A constant infusion is continued until surgery is complete.

To avoid physical incompatibility with heparin when adding to pump-prime solution, each agent should be added during recirculation to assure adequate dilution.

Regimen A (standard dose):

2 million KIU (280 mg; 200 mL) loading dose I.V. over 20-30 minutes

2 million KIU (280 mg; 200 mL) into pump prime volume

500,000 KIU/hour (70 mg/hour; 50 mL/hour) I.V. during operation

Regimen B (low dose):

1 million KIU (140 mg; 100 mL) loading dose I.V. over 20-30 minutes

1 million KIU (140 mg; 100 mL) into pump prime volume

250,000 KIU/hour (35 mg/hour; 25 mL/hour) I.V. during operation

Dosage adjustment in renal impairment: No adjustment required, but increased risk of worsening renal dysfunction with use; monitor closely

Dosage adjustment in hepatic impairment: No information available

Administration Administer through a central line. Infuse loading dose over 20-30 minutes, then continuous infusion at 50 mL/hour (regimen A) or 25 mL/hour (regimen B). Rapid infusion (<20 minutes) can cause transient blood pressure decrease; to avoid incompatibility with heparin, add while recirculating the prime fluid of the cardiac bypass circuit.

Monitoring Parameters Bleeding times, prothrombin time, activated clotting time, platelet count, red blood cell counts, hematocrit, hemoglobin and fibrinogen degradation products; for toxicity also include renal function tests and blood pressure

Because aPTT and ACT are difficult to interpret with aprotinin use, the manufacturer recommends two different ways to administer heparin:

1). Fixed heparin dosing where a standard loading dose of heparin plus the quantity of heparin added to the prime volume of the CPB circuit should total at least 350 units/kg. Additional heparin should be administered based on patient's weight and duration of CPB.

2). Heparin dosing based upon a protamine titration method. A heparin dose response, assessed by protamine titration, should be performed prior to administration of aprotinin to determine the heparin loading dose.

Reference Range Antiplasmin effects occur when plasma aprotinin concentrations are 125 KIU/mL and antikallikrein effects occur when plasma levels are 250-500 KIU/mL; it remains unknown if these plasma concentrations are required for clinical benefits to occur during cardiopulmonary bypass; **Note:** KIU = Kallikrein inhibitor unit

While institutional protocols may vary, a minimal celite ACT of 750 seconds or kaolin-ACT of 480 seconds is recommended in the presence of aprotinin. Consult the manufacturer's information on specific ACT test interpretation in the presence of aprotinin.

Test Interactions Aprotinin significantly increases aPTT and celite Activated Clotting Time (ACT) which may not reflect the actual degree of anticoagulation by heparin. Kaolin-based ACTs are not affected by aprotinin to the same degree as celite ACTs.

Dosage Forms

Injection, solution:

Trasylol®: 1.4 mg/mL [10,000 KIU/mL] (100 mL, 200 mL) [bovine derived]

♦ **Aptivus®** see Tipranavir on page 1692

♦ **Aquacare® [OTC]** see Urea on page 1758

♦ **Aquachloral® Supprettes®** see Chloral Hydrate on page 339

♦ **Aquacort® (Can)** see Hydrocortisone on page 852

♦ **AquaMEPHYTON® (Can)** see Phytonadione on page 1366

♦ **Aquanil™ HC [OTC]** see Hydrocortisone on page 852

- ◆ **Aquaphilic® With Carbamide [OTC]** *see* Urea *on page 1758*
- ◆ **Aquasol A®** *see* Vitamin A *on page 1793*
- ◆ **Aquasol E® [OTC]** *see* Vitamin E *on page 1794*
- ◆ **Aquatensen® (Can)** *see* Methyclothiazide *on page 1116*
- ◆ **Aquavit-E [OTC]** *see* Vitamin E *on page 1794*
- ◆ **Aqueous Procaine Penicillin G** *see* Penicillin G Procaine *on page 1335*
- ◆ **Ara-C** *see* Cytarabine *on page 437*
- ◆ **Arabinosylcytosine** *see* Cytarabine *on page 437*
- ◆ **Aralen®** *see* Chloroquine *on page 347*
- ◆ **Aranelle™** *see* Ethinyl Estradiol and Norethindrone *on page 655*
- ◆ **Aranesp®** *see* Darbepoetin Alfa *on page 453*
- ◆ **Arava®** *see* Leflunomide *on page 982*
- ◆ **Aredia®** *see* Pamidronate *on page 1300*

Arformoterol (ar for MOE ter ol)

U.S. Brand Names Brovana™
Index Terms Arformoterol Tartrate; (R,R)-Formoterol L-Tartrate
Pharmacologic Category Beta$_2$-Adrenergic Agonist
Additional Appendix Information
Bronchodilators *on page 1877*
Use Long-term maintenance treatment of bronchoconstriction in chronic obstructive pulmonary disease (COPD), including chronic bronchitis and emphysema
Restrictions An FDA-approved medication guide must be distributed when dispensing an outpatient prescription (new or refill) where this medication is to be used without direct supervision of a healthcare provider. Medication guides are available at http://www.fda.gov/cder/Offices/ODS/medication_guides.htm.
Pregnancy Risk Factor C
Pregnancy Implications Teratogenic effects, decreased fetal weight and increased fetal loss were observed in animal studies. There are no adequate and well-controlled studies in pregnant women. Beta agonists may interfere with uterine contractility if administered during labor. Use in pregnancy and/or during labor should be limited to situations where benefit outweighs risk to fetus.
Lactation Excretion in breast milk unknown/use caution
Contraindications Hypersensitivity to arformoterol, racemic formoterol, or any component of the formulation
Warnings/Precautions [U.S. Boxed Warning]: Long-acting beta$_2$-agonists may increase the risk of asthma-related deaths. In a large, randomized clinical trial (SMART, 2006), salmeterol was associated with a small, but statistically significant increase in asthma-related deaths (when added to usual asthma therapy); risk may be greater in African-American patients versus Caucasians. Data is not available to determine whether rate of death is increased with long-acting beta$_2$-agonists in COPD setting. Rarely, paradoxical bronchospasm may occur with use of inhaled bronchodilating agents; this should be distinguished from inadequate response. Immediate hypersensitivity reactions (urticaria, angioedema, rash, bronchospasm) have been reported. Do not exceed recommended dose; serious adverse events, including fatalities, have been associated with excessive use of inhaled sympathomimetics.

Use with caution in patients with cardiovascular disease (eg, arrhythmia, hypertension, CHF); beta agonists may cause elevation in blood pressure, heart rate and result in CNS stimulation/excitation. Beta$_2$-agonists may also increase risk of arrhythmias and prolong QT$_c$ interval. Arformoterol should only be used for long-term maintenance treatment and should not be used as rescue therapy in treatment of acute episodes. It should not be initiated in patients with acutely deteriorating COPD or combined with other long-acting beta$_2$-agonists. Use with caution in patients with diabetes mellitus; beta$_2$-agonists may increase serum glucose. Use caution in hepatic impairment; systemic clearance prolonged in hepatic dysfunction. Use with caution in hyperthyroidism; may stimulate thyroid activity. Use with caution in patients with hypokalemia; beta$_2$-agonists may decrease serum potassium. Use with caution in patients with seizure disorders; beta$_2$-agonists may result in CNS stimulation/excitation.

Tolerance/tachyphylaxis to the bronchodilator effect, measured by FEV$_1$, has been observed in studies. Patients using inhaled, short-acting beta$_2$-agonists should be instructed to discontinue routine use of these medications prior to beginning treatment; short-acting agents should be reserved for symptomatic relief of acute symptoms. Patients must be instructed to seek medical attention in cases where acute symptoms are not relieved or a previous level of response is diminished. The need to increase frequency of use may indicate deterioration of COPD, and treatment must not be delayed. Safety and efficacy have not been established in children.

Adverse Reactions
2% to 10%:
  Cardiovascular: Chest pain (7%), peripheral edema (3%)
  Central nervous system: Pain (8%)
  Dermatologic: Rash (4%)
  Gastrointestinal: Diarrhea (6%)
  Neuromuscular & skeletal: Back pain (6%), leg cramps (4%)
  Respiratory: Dyspnea (4%), sinusitis (5%), congestive conditions (2%)
  Miscellaneous: Flu-like syndrome (3%)
<2% (Limited to important or life-threatening): Abscess, agitation, allergic reaction, arteriosclerosis, arthralgia, arthritis, atrial flutter, AV block, bone disorder, calcium crystalluria, cystitis, cerebral infarct, CHF, circumoral paresthesia, constipation, dehydration, dry skin, ECG changes, edema, fever, gastritis, glaucoma, glucose tolerance decreased, glycosuria, gout, heart block, hematuria, hyper-/hypoglycemia, hyperlipemia, hypokalemia, hypokinesia, inverted T-wave, kidney calculus, lung carcinoma, melena, MI, neck rigidity,

neoplasm, nocturia, oral moniliasis, paradoxical bronchospasm, paralysis, pelvic pain, periodontal abscess, PSA increased, pyuria, QT interval increased, rectal hemorrhage, retroperitoneal hemorrhage, rheumatoid arthritis, skin discoloration, skin hypertrophy, somnolence, supraventricular tachycardia, tendinous contracture, tremor, urinary tract disorder, urine abnormality, viral infection, vision abnormalities, voice alteration

Overdosage/Toxicology Symptoms of excessive beta-adrenergic stimulation include hyperglycemia, metabolic acidosis, arrhythmias, tachycardia, tremor, hypertension, angina, and seizures. Hypokalemia also may occur. Cardiac arrest and death may be associated with abuse of beta-agonist bronchodilators. Treatment should be symptom-directed and supportive. Cautious use of cardioselective beta-adrenergic blocking agents may be considered in severe cases.

Drug Interactions

Cytochrome P450 Effect: Substrate of CY2D6 (minor) and CYP2C19 (minor)

Increased Effect/Toxicity: Atomoxetine may enhance the tachycardia effect of beta$_2$ agonists. Sympathomimetics may enhance the toxic/adverse effects of arformoterol.

Decreased Effect: Beta$_2$ agonists may diminish the bradycardia effect of beta-blockers (beta$_1$ selective). Alpha-/beta-blockers, beta-blockers (nonselective), and betahistine may diminish the therapeutic effect of beta$_2$ agonists.

Stability Prior to dispensing, store in protective foil pouch under refrigeration at 2°C to 8°C (36°F to 46°F). Protect from light and excessive heat. After dispensing, unopened foil pouches may be stored at room temperature at 20°C to 25°C (68°F to 77°F) for up to 6 weeks. Only remove vial from foil pouch immediately before use.

Mechanism of Action Arformoterol, the (R,R)-enantiomer of the racemic formoterol, is a long-acting beta$_2$ agonist that relaxes bronchial smooth muscle by selective action on beta$_2$ receptors with little effect on cardiovascular system.

Pharmacodynamics/Kinetics

Onset of action: 7-20 minutes

Peak effect: 1-3 hours

Absorption: A portion of inhaled dose is absorbed into systemic circulation

Protein binding: 52% to 65%

Metabolism: Hepatic via direct glucuronidation and secondarily via O-demethylation; CYP2D6 and CYP2C19 (to a lesser extent) involved in O-demethylation

Half-life elimination: 26 hours

Time to peak: 0.5-3 hours

Dosage Nebulization: Adults: COPD: 15 mcg twice daily; maximum: 30 mcg/day

Dosage adjustment in renal impairment: No adjustment required

Dosage adjustment in hepatic impairment: No dosage adjustment required, but use caution; systemic drug exposure prolonged (1.3- to 2.4-fold)

Administration Nebulization: Remove each vial from individually sealed foil pouch immediately before use. Use with standard jet nebulizer connected to an air compressor, administer with mouthpiece or face mask. Administer vial undiluted and do not mix with other medications in nebulizer.

Monitoring Parameters FEV$_1$, peak flow, and/or other pulmonary function tests; blood pressure, heart rate; CNS stimulation; serum glucose, serum potassium. Monitor for increased use of short-acting beta$_2$-agonist inhalers; may be marker of a deteriorating COPD condition.

Dosage Forms

Solution for nebulization:

Brovana™: 15 mcg/2 mL (30s, 60s)

♦ **Arformoterol Tartrate** see Arformoterol on page 148

Argatroban (ar GA troh ban)

Pharmacologic Category Anticoagulant, Thrombin Inhibitor

Use Prophylaxis or treatment of thrombosis in adults with heparin-induced thrombocytopenia; adjunct to percutaneous coronary intervention (PCI) in patients who have or are at risk of thrombosis associated with heparin-induced thrombocytopenia

Pregnancy Risk Factor B

Pregnancy Implications No adequate and well-controlled studies have been done in pregnant women. Argatroban should be used in pregnant women only if clearly needed.

Lactation Excretion in breast milk unknown/not recommended

Medication Safety Issues

Sound-alike/look-alike issues:

Argatroban may be confused with Aggrastat®

Contraindications Hypersensitivity to argatroban or any component of the formulation; overt major bleeding

Warnings/Precautions Hemorrhage can occur at any site in the body. Extreme caution should be used when there is an increased danger of hemorrhage, such as severe hypertension, immediately following lumbar puncture, spinal anesthesia, major surgery (including brain, spinal cord, or eye surgery), congenital or acquired bleeding disorders, and gastrointestinal ulcers. Use caution in critically-ill patients; reduced clearance may require dosage reduction. Use caution with hepatic dysfunction. Concomitant use with warfarin will cause increased prolongation of the PT and INR greater than that of warfarin alone; alternative guidelines for monitoring therapy should be followed. Safety and efficacy for use with other thrombolytic agents has not been established. Discontinue all parenteral anticoagulants prior to starting therapy. Allow reversal of heparin's effects before initiation. Patients with hepatic dysfunction may require >4 hours to achieve full reversal of argatroban's anticoagulant effect following treatment. Avoid use during PCI in patients with elevations of ALT/AST (>3 times ULN); the use of argatroban in these patients has not been evaluated. For adult use; safety and efficacy in children <18 years of age have not been established.

Adverse Reactions As with all anticoagulants, bleeding is the major adverse effect of argatroban. Hemorrhage may occur at virtually any site. Risk is dependent on multiple variables, including the intensity of anticoagulation and patient susceptibility.

(Continued)

Argatroban *(Continued)*

>10%:
    Cardiovascular: Chest pain (<1% to 15%), hypotension (7% to 11%)
    Gastrointestinal: Gastrointestinal bleed (minor, 3% to 14%)
    Genitourinary: Genitourinary bleed and hematuria (minor, 2% to 12%)

1% to 10%:
    Cardiovascular: Cardiac arrest (6%), ventricular tachycardia (5%), bradycardia (5%), myocardial infarction (PCI: 4%), atrial fibrillation (3%), angina (2%), CABG-related bleeding (minor, 2%), myocardial ischemia (2%), cerebrovascular disorder (<1% to 2%), thrombosis (<1% to 2%)
    Central nervous system: Fever (<1% to 7%), headache (5%), pain (5%), intracranial bleeding (1% to 4%)
    Gastrointestinal: Nausea (5% to 7%), diarrhea (6%), vomiting (4% to 6%), abdominal pain (3% to 4%), bleeding (major, <1% to 2%)
    Genitourinary: Urinary tract infection (5%)
    Hematologic: Hemoglobin (<2 g/dL) and hematocrit (minor, 2% to 10%) decreased
    Local: Bleeding at injection or access site (minor, 2% to 5%)
    Neuromuscular & skeletal: Back pain (8%)
    Renal: Abnormal renal function (3%)
    Respiratory: Dyspnea (8% to 10%), cough (3% to 10%), hemoptysis (minor, <1% to 3%), pneumonia (3%)
    Miscellaneous: Sepsis (6%), infection (4%)

<1% (Limited to important or life-threatening): Aortic stenosis, genitourinary bleeding and hematuria (major), GERD, hemoglobin/hematocrit decreased (major), limb and below-the-knee stump bleed, pulmonary edema, multisystem hemorrhage and DIC, retroperitoneal bleeding, vascular disorder

Overdosage/Toxicology No specific antidote is available. Treatment should be symptomatic and supportive. Discontinue or decrease infusion to control excessive anticoagulation with or without bleeding. Reversal of anticoagulant effects may be longer than 4 hours in patients with hepatic impairment. Hemodialysis may remove up to 20% of the drug; however, this is considered clinically insignificant.

Drug Interactions
    Cytochrome P450 Effect: Substrate of CYP3A4 (minor)
    Increased Effect/Toxicity:
        Drugs which affect platelet function (eg, aspirin, NSAIDs, dipyridamole, ticlopidine, clopidogrel), anticoagulants, or thrombolytics may potentiate the risk of hemorrhage. Sufficient time must pass after heparin therapy is discontinued; allow heparin's effect on the aPTT to decrease.
        Concomitant use of argatroban with warfarin increases PT and INR greater than that of warfarin alone. Argatroban is commonly continued during the initiation of warfarin therapy to assure anticoagulation and to protect against possible transient hypercoagulability.

Stability Prior to use, store at 15°C to 30°C (59°F to 86°F). Protect from light. The prepared solution is stable for 24 hours at 15°C to 30°C (59°F to 86°F) in ambient indoor light. Do not expose to direct sunlight. May be mixed with 0.9% sodium chloride injection, 5% dextrose injection, or lactated Ringer's injection. Do not mix with other medications.

To prepare solution for I.V. administration, dilute each 250 mg vial with 250 mL of diluent. Mix by repeated inversion for 1 minute. Once mixed, final concentration should be 1 mg/mL. A slight but brief haziness may occur prior to mixing. Prepared solutions that are protected from light and kept at controlled room temperature of 20°C to 25°C (68°F to 77°F) or under refrigeration at 2°C to 8°C (36°F to 46°F) are stable for up to 96 hours.

Mechanism of Action A direct, highly-selective thrombin inhibitor. Reversibly binds to the active thrombin site of free and clot-associated thrombin. Inhibits fibrin formation; activation of coagulation factors V, VIII, and XIII; protein C; and platelet aggregation.

Pharmacodynamics/Kinetics
    Onset of action: Immediate
    Distribution: 174 mL/kg
    Protein binding: Albumin: 20%; α_1-acid glycoprotein: 35%
    Metabolism: Hepatic via hydroxylation and aromatization. Metabolism via CYP3A4/5 to four known metabolites plays a minor role. Unchanged argatroban is the major plasma component. Plasma concentration of metabolite M1 is 0% to 20% of the parent drug and is three- to fivefold weaker.
    Half-life elimination: 39-51 minutes; Hepatic impairment: ≤181 minutes
    Time to peak: Steady-state: 1-3 hours
    Excretion: Feces (65%); urine (22%); low quantities of metabolites M2-4 in urine

Dosage I.V.: Adults:
    Heparin-induced thrombocytopenia:
        Initial dose: 2 mcg/kg/minute
        Maintenance dose: Measure aPTT after 2 hours, adjust dose until the steady-state aPTT is 1.5-3.0 times the initial baseline value, not exceeding 100 seconds; dosage should not exceed 10 mcg/kg/minute
        Conversion to oral anticoagulant: Because there may be a combined effect on the INR when argatroban is combined with warfarin, loading doses of warfarin should not be used. Warfarin therapy should be started at the expected daily dose.
        Patients receiving ≤2 mcg/kg/minute of argatroban: Argatroban therapy can be stopped when the combined INR on warfarin and argatroban is >4; repeat INR measurement in 4-6 hours; if INR is below therapeutic level, argatroban therapy may be restarted. Repeat procedure daily until desired INR on warfarin alone is obtained.
        Patients receiving >2 mcg/kg/minute of argatroban: Reduce dose of argatroban to 2 mcg/kg/minute; measure INR for argatroban and warfarin 4-6 hours after dose reduction; argatroban therapy can be stopped when the combined INR on warfarin and argatroban is >4. Repeat INR measurement in 4-6 hours; if INR is below therapeutic

level, argatroban therapy may be restarted. Repeat procedure daily until desired INR on warfarin alone is obtained.

Note: Critically-ill patients with normal hepatic function became excessively anticoagulated with FDA-approved or lower starting doses of argatroban (Reichert MG, 2003). Doses between 0.15-1.3 mcg/kg/minute were required to maintain aPTTs in the target range. Another report of a cardiac patient with anasarca secondary to acute renal failure had a reduction in argatroban clearance similar to patients with hepatic dysfunction (de Denus S, 2003). Reduced clearance may have been attributed to reduced perfusion to the liver. Consider reducing starting dose to 0.5-1 mcg/kg/minute in critically-ill patients who may have impaired hepatic perfusion (eg, patients requiring vasopressors, having decreased cardiac output, having fluid overload). In a retrospective review of critical care patients (Baghdasarian SB, 2004), patients with three organ system failure required 0.5 mcg/kg/FDA. The mean argatroban dose of ICU patients was 0.9 mcg/kg/minute.

Percutaneous coronary intervention (PCI):
Initial: Begin infusion of 25 mcg/kg/minute and administer bolus dose of 350 mcg/kg (over 3-5 minutes). ACT should be checked 5-10 minutes after bolus infusion; proceed with procedure if ACT >300 seconds. Following initial bolus:
ACT <300 seconds: Give an additional 150 mcg/kg bolus, and increase infusion rate to 30 mcg/kg/minute (recheck ACT in 5-10 minutes)
ACT >450 seconds: Decrease infusion rate to 15 mcg/kg/minute (recheck ACT in 5-10 minutes)
Once a therapeutic ACT (300-450 seconds) is achieved, infusion should be continued at this dose for the duration of the procedure.
If dissection, impending abrupt closure, thrombus formation during PCI, or inability to achieve ACT >300 seconds: An additional bolus of 150 mcg/kg, followed by an increase in infusion rate to 40 mcg/kg/minute may be administered.
Note: Post-PCI anticoagulation, if required, may be achieved by continuing infusion at a reduced dose of 2-10 mcg/kg/minute, with close monitoring of aPTT.

Dosage adjustment in renal impairment: Removal during hemodialysis and continuous venovenous hemofiltration is clinically insignificant. No dosage adjustment required.

Dosage adjustment in hepatic impairment: Decreased clearance and increased elimination half-life are seen with hepatic impairment; dose should be reduced. Initial dose for moderate hepatic impairment is 0.5 mcg/kg/minute. **Note:** During PCI, avoid use in patients with elevations of ALT/AST (>3 times ULN); the use of argatroban in these patients has not been evaluated.

Elderly: No adjustment is necessary for patients with normal liver function

Administration Solution **must be diluted to 1 mg/mL** prior to administration.

Monitoring Parameters Obtain baseline aPTT prior to start of therapy. Check aPTT 2 hours after start of therapy to adjust dose, keeping the steady-state aPTT 1.5-3 times the initial baseline value (not exceeding 100 seconds). Monitor hemoglobin, hematocrit, signs and symptoms of bleeding.

PCI: Monitor ACT before dosing, 5-10 minutes after bolus dosing, and after any change in infusion rate and at the end of the procedure. Additional ACT assessments should be made every 20-30 minutes during extended PCI procedures.

Additional Information Platelet counts recovered by day 3 in 53% of patients with heparin-induced thrombocytopenia and in 58% of patients with heparin-induced thrombocytopenia with thrombosis syndrome.

Dosage Forms Injection, solution: 100 mg/mL (2.5 mL) [contains dehydrated alcohol 1000 mg/mL]

Arginine (AR ji neen)

U.S. Brand Names R-Gene®
Index Terms Arginine Hydrochloride
Pharmacologic Category Diagnostic Agent
Use Pituitary function test (growth hormone)
Unlabeled/Investigational Use Management of severe, uncompensated, metabolic alkalosis (pH ≥7.55) **after** optimizing therapy with sodium and potassium supplements
Pregnancy Risk Factor B
Dosage I.V.: Pituitary function test:
Children: 500 mg/kg/dose administered over 30 minutes
Adults: 30 g (300 mL) administered over 30 minutes
Additional Information Complete prescribing information for this medication should be consulted for additional detail.
Dosage Forms Injection, solution, as hydrochloride: 10% [100 mg/mL = 950 mOsm/L] (300 mL) [contains chloride 0.475 mEq/mL]

- ◆ Arginine Hydrochloride see Arginine on page 151
- ◆ 8-Arginine Vasopressin see Vasopressin on page 1779
- ◆ Aricept® see Donepezil on page 538
- ◆ Aricept® ODT see Donepezil on page 538
- ◆ Aricept® RDT (Can) see Donepezil on page 538
- ◆ Arimidex® see Anastrozole on page 129

Aripiprazole (ay ri PIP ray zole)

U.S. Brand Names Abilify®; Abilify® Discmelt™
Index Terms BMS 337039; OPC-14597
Pharmacologic Category Antipsychotic Agent, Atypical
Additional Appendix Information
Antipsychotic Agents on page 1872
(Continued)

Aripiprazole *(Continued)*

Use Treatment of schizophrenia; stabilization and maintenance therapy of bipolar disorder (with acute manic or mixed episodes); agitation associated with schizophrenia or bipolar mania

Unlabeled/Investigational Use Depression with psychotic features; aggression (children); bipolar disorder (children); conduct disorder (children); Tourette syndrome (children)

Pregnancy Risk Factor C

Pregnancy Implications Aripiprazole demonstrated developmental toxicity and teratogenic effects in animal models. There are no adequate and well-controlled trials in pregnant women. Should be used in pregnancy only when potential benefit to mother outweighs possible risk to the fetus.

Lactation Excretion in breast milk unknown/not recommended

Medication Safety Issues
Sound-alike/look-alike issues:
Aripiprazole may be confused with proton pump inhibitors (eg, rabeprazole)

Contraindications Hypersensitivity to aripiprazole or any component of the formulation

Warnings/Precautions [U.S. Boxed Warning]: Patients with dementia-related behavioral disorders treated with atypical antipsychotics are at an increased risk of death compared to placebo. An increased incidence of cerebrovascular adverse events (including fatalities) has been reported in elderly patients with dementia-related psychosis. Risk may be increased by dehydration; use caution with concurrent diuretics. Aripiprazole is not approved for this indication.

May cause extrapyramidal symptoms, including pseudoparkinsonism, acute dystonic reactions, akathisia, and tardive dyskinesia (risk of these reactions is very low relative to typical/conventional antipsychotics, frequencies reported are similar to placebo). May be associated with neuroleptic malignant syndrome (NMS).

May be sedating, use with caution in disorders where CNS depression is a feature. May cause orthostatic hypotension (although reported rates are similar to placebo); use caution in patients at risk of this effect or those who would not tolerate transient hypotensive episodes (cerebrovascular disease, cardiovascular disease, or other medications which may predispose).

Use caution in patients with Parkinson's disease; predisposition to seizures; and severe cardiac disease. May alter cardiac conduction; life-threatening arrhythmias have occurred with therapeutic doses of antipsychotics. Esophageal dysmotility and aspiration have been associated with antipsychotic use; use caution in patients at risk of pneumonia (ie, Alzheimer's disease). May alter temperature regulation. Significant weight gain has been observed with antipsychotic therapy; incidence varies with product.

Atypical antipsychotics have been associated with development of hyperglycemia; in some cases, may be extreme and associated with ketoacidosis, hyperosmolar coma, or death. Reports of hyperglycemia with aripiprazole therapy have been few and specific risk associated with this agent is not known. Use caution in patients with diabetes or other disorders of glucose regulation; monitor for worsening of glucose control.

The possibility of a suicide attempt is inherent in psychotic illness or bipolar disorder; use caution in high-risk patients during initiation of therapy. Prescriptions should be written for the smallest quantity consistent with good patient care. Abilify® Discmelt™: Use caution in phenylketonuria; contains phenylalanine. Safety and efficacy in pediatric patients have not been established.

Adverse Reactions Unless otherwise noted, frequency of adverse reactions is shown as reported for oral administration.
>10%:
Central nervous system: Headache (31%; injection 12%), agitation (25%), anxiety (20%), insomnia (20%), extrapyramidal symptoms (6% to 17%), somnolence (12% to 15%, dose related; injection 7%), akathisia (12% to 15%; injection 2%), lightheadedness (11%)
Gastrointestinal: Nausea (16%; injection 9%), dyspepsia (15%; injection 1%), constipation (11% to 13%), vomiting (11%; injection 3%), weight gain (8% to 30%, highest frequency in patients with BMI <23)
1% to 10%:
Cardiovascular: Edema (peripheral 2%), hypertension (2%), tachycardia, hypotension, bradycardia, chest pain
Central nervous system: Abnormal dreams, confusion, delusion, depression, fever, hallucination, hostility, mania, nervousness, paranoid reaction, schizophrenic reaction, suicidal thought
Dermatologic: Bruising, dry skin, skin ulcer
Endocrine & metabolic: Dehydration
Gastrointestinal: Salivation increased (3%), xerostomia (injection 1%), weight loss
Genitourinary: Urinary incontinence, pelvic pain
Hematologic: Anemia
Neuromuscular & skeletal: Tremor (4% to 9%), weakness (8%), myalgia (4%), neck pain, neck rigidity, muscle cramp, CPK increased, abnormal gait
Ocular: Blurred vision (3%), conjunctivitis
Respiratory: Rhinitis (4%), pharyngitis (4%), cough (3%), asthma, dyspnea, pneumonia, sinusitis
Miscellaneous: Accidental injury (5% to 6%), flu-like syndrome, diaphoresis
<1% (Limited to important or life-threatening): Albuminuria, alkaline phosphatase increased, ALT increased, anaphylactic reaction, angina, angioedema, apnea, arthralgia, arthrosis, aspiration pneumonia, AST increased, ataxia, atrial fibrillation, atrial flutter, AV block, bacteriuria, bilirubinemia, body temperature increased, bone pain, bradykinesia, BUN increased, bundle branch block, cardiomegaly, cardiopulmonary failure, cataract, cerebral ischemia, cerebrovascular accident, chest tightness, CHF, cholecystitis, cholelithiasis, colitis, cyanosis, cystitis, deafness, deep vein thrombosis, delirium, dementia, diabetes

mellitus, duodenal ulcer, eosinophilia, erectile dysfunction, extrasystoles, fecal impaction, hematemesis, hematuria, hemoptysis, hemorrhage, hepatitis, hepatomegaly, hyper-/hypoglycemia, hyper-/hypokalemia, hyper-/hyponatremia, hyper-/hypothyroidism, hyperacusis, hypercholesterolemia, hyperuricemia, hypoesthesia, hypokinesia, hypotonia, hypoxia, intestinal obstruction, intestinal perforation, laryngospasm, LDH increased, leukocytosis, leukopenia, maculopapular rash, melena, Mendelson's syndrome, MI, migraine, moniliasis, myoclonus, myopathy, neuroleptic malignant syndrome, neuropathy, nightmare, oculogyric crisis, palpitation, pancreatitis, panic attack, peptic ulcer, phlebitis, pruritus, pulmonary edema, pulmonary embolism, QT prolongation, renal calculus, renal failure, respiratory failure, rhabdomyolysis, seborrhea, serum creatinine increased, stroke, suicide attempt, tardive dyskinesia, throat tightness, thrombocythemia, thrombocytopenia, tongue edema, T-wave abnormality, urosepsis, urticaria, UTI, vesiculobullous rash

Overdosage/Toxicology Ingestion of 1080 mg has been reported, with full recovery. Common symptoms of overdose include somnolence, tremor, and vomiting. Treatment is supportive and symptom-directed. An ECG should be obtained and cardiac monitoring initiated if QT_c prolongation is present. Administration of 50 g activated charcoal 1 hour after a 15 mg dose reportedly decreased AUC and C_{max} values by 50%. Due to the high degree of protein binding, hemodialysis is unlikely to be effective in removing aripiprazole.

Drug Interactions
Cytochrome P450 Effect: Substrate (major) of CYP2D6, 3A4

Increased Effect/Toxicity: CYP2D6 inhibitors may increase the levels/effects of aripiprazole; example inhibitors include chlorpromazine, delavirdine, fluoxetine, miconazole, paroxetine, pergolide, quinidine, quinine, ritonavir, and ropinirole. CYP3A4 inhibitors may increase the levels/effects of aripiprazole; example inhibitors include azole antifungals, clarithromycin, diclofenac, doxycycline, erythromycin, imatinib, isoniazid, nefazodone, nicardipine, propofol, protease inhibitors, quinidine, telithromycin, and verapamil. Manufacturer recommends a 50% reduction in dose during concurrent ketoconazole therapy. Similar reductions in dose may be required with other potent inhibitors. CNS depressants may increase adverse effects/toxicity of aripiprazole. Acetylcholinesterase inhibitors (central) may increase the risk of antipsychotic-related extrapyramidal symptoms. Lithium may increase neurotoxicity of antipsychotics.

Decreased Effect: CYP3A4 inducers may decrease the levels/effects of aripiprazole; example inducers include aminoglutethimide, carbamazepine, nafcillin, nevirapine, phenobarbital, phenytoin, and rifamycins. Manufacturer recommends a doubling of the aripiprazole dose when carbamazepine is added. Similar increases may be required with other inducers.

Ethanol/Nutrition/Herb Interactions
Ethanol: Avoid ethanol (may increase CNS depression).
Food: Ingestion with a high-fat meal delays time to peak plasma level.
Herb/Nutraceutical: St John's wort may decrease aripiprazole levels. Avoid kava kava, gotu kola, valerian, St John's wort (may increase CNS depression).

Stability
Injection solution: Store at 15°C to 30°C (59°F to 86°F). Protect from light.
Oral solution: Store at 15°C to 30°C (59°F to 86°F). Use within 6 months after opening.
Tablet: Store at 15°C to 30°C (59°F to 86°F).

Mechanism of Action Aripiprazole is a quinolinone antipsychotic which exhibits high affinity for D_2, D_3, $5-HT_{1A}$, and $5-HT_{2A}$ receptors; moderate affinity for D_4, $5-HT_{2C}$, $5-HT_7$, alpha$_1$ adrenergic, and H_1 receptors. It also possesses moderate affinity for the serotonin reuptake transporter; has no affinity for muscarinic (cholinergic) receptors. Aripiprazole functions as a partial agonist at the D_2 and $5-HT_{1A}$ receptors, and as an antagonist at the $5-HT_{2A}$ receptor.

Pharmacodynamics/Kinetics
Onset: Initial: 1-3 weeks
Absorption: Well absorbed
Distribution: V_d: 4.9 L/kg
Protein binding: ≥99%, primarily to albumin
Metabolism: Hepatic, via CYP2D6, CYP3A4 (dehydro-aripiprazole metabolite has affinity for D_2 receptors similar to the parent drug and represents 40% of the parent drug exposure in plasma)
Bioavailability: I.M.: 100%; Tablet: 87%
Half-life elimination: Aripiprazole: 75 hours; dehydro-aripiprazole: 94 hours
CYP2D6 poor metabolizers: Aripiprazole: 146 hours
Time to peak, plasma: I.M.: 1-3 hours; Tablet: 3-5 hours
With high-fat meal: Aripiprazole: Delayed by 3 hours; dehydro-aripiprazole: Delayed by 12 hours
Excretion: Feces (55%, ~18% unchanged drug); urine (25%, <1% unchanged drug)

Dosage Note: Oral solution may be substituted for the oral tablet on a mg-per-mg basis, up to 25 mg. Patients receiving 30 mg tablets should be given 25 mg oral solution. Orally disintegrating tablets (Abilify® Discmelt™) are bioequivalent to the immediate release tablets (Abilify®).

Children: Oral: Aggression, bipolar disorder, conduct disorder, Tourette syndrome (unlabeled uses): 5-20 mg/day
Adults:
Acute agitation (schizophrenia/bipolar mania): I.M.: 9.75 mg as a single dose (range: 5.25-15 mg); repeated doses may be given at ≥2-hour intervals to a maximum of 30 mg/day. **Note:** If ongoing therapy with aripiprazole is necessary, transition to oral therapy as soon as possible.
Schizophrenia: Oral: 10-15 mg once daily; may be increased to a maximum of 30 mg once daily (efficacy at dosages above 10-15 mg has not been shown to be increased). Dosage titration should not be more frequent than every 2 weeks.
Depression (unlabeled use): Oral: 5-30 mg/day
Bipolar disorder (acute manic or mixed episodes): Oral:
Stabilization: 30 mg once daily; may require a decrease to 15 mg based on tolerability (15% of patients had dose decreased); safety of doses >30 mg/day has not been evaluated
(Continued)

Aripiprazole *(Continued)*

Maintenance: Continue stabilization dose for up to 6 weeks; efficacy of continued treatment >6 weeks has not been established

Dosage adjustment with concurrent CYP450 inducer or inhibitor therapy: Oral:

CYP3A4 inducers (eg, carbamazepine): Aripiprazole dose should be doubled (20-30 mg/day); dose should be subsequently reduced (10-15 mg/day) if concurrent inducer agent discontinued.

CYP3A4 inhibitors (eg, ketoconazole): Aripiprazole dose should be reduced to $\frac{1}{2}$ of the usual dose, and proportionally increased upon discontinuation of the inhibitor agent.

CYP2D6 inhibitors (eg, fluoxetine, paroxetine): Aripiprazole dose should be reduced to $\frac{1}{2}$ of the usual dose, and proportionally increased upon discontinuation of the inhibitor agent.

Dosage adjustment in renal impairment: No dosage adjustment required

Dosage adjustment in hepatic impairment: No dosage adjustment required

Dietary Considerations May be taken with or without food. Oral solution contains sucrose 400 mg/mL and fructose 200 mg/mL. Orally disintegrating tablet contains phenylalanine; avoid use in phenylketonuria.

Administration

Injection: For I.M. use only; do not administer SubQ or I.V.; inject slowly into deep muscle mass

Oral: May be administered with or without food. Tablet and oral solution may be interchanged on a mg-per-mg basis, up to 25 mg. Doses using 30 mg tablets should be exchanged for 25 mg oral solution. Orally disintegrating tablets (Abilify® Discmelt™) are bioequivalent to the immediate release tablets (Abilify®).

Orally-disintegrating tablet: Remove from foil blister by peeling back (do not push tablet through the foil). Place tablet in mouth immediately upon removal. Tablet dissolves rapidly in saliva and may be swallowed without liquid. If needed, can be taken with liquid. Do not split tablet.

Monitoring Parameters Vital signs; fasting lipid profile and fasting blood glucose/Hb A_{1c} (prior to treatment, at 3 months, then annually); BMI, personal/family history of diabetes, waist circumference, blood pressure, mental status, abnormal involuntary movement scale (AIMS), extrapyramidal symptoms (EPS). Weight should be assessed prior to treatment, at 4 weeks, 8 weeks, 12 weeks, and then at quarterly intervals. Consider titrating to a different antipsychotic agent for a weight gain ≥5% of the initial weight.

Dosage Forms

Injection, solution:
Abilify®: 7.5 mg/mL (1.3 mL)

Solution, oral:
Abilify®: 1 mg/mL (150 mL) [contains sucrose 400 mg/mL and fructose 200 mg/mL; orange cream flavor]

Tablet:
Abilify®: 2 mg, 5 mg, 10 mg, 15 mg, 20 mg, 30 mg

Tablet, orally disintegrating:
Abilify® Discmelt™: 10 mg [contains phenylalanine 1.12 mg; creme de vanilla flavor]; 15 mg [contains phenylalanine 1.68 mg; creme de vanilla flavor]

♦ **Aristocort® [DSC]** *see* Triamcinolone *on page 1734*
♦ **Aristocort® A [DSC]** *see* Triamcinolone *on page 1734*
♦ **Aristospan®** *see* Triamcinolone *on page 1734*
♦ **Arixtra®** *see* Fondaparinux *on page 757*
♦ **A.R.M® [OTC]** *see* Chlorpheniramine and Pseudoephedrine *on page 350*
♦ **Armour® Thyroid** *see* Thyroid *on page 1676*
♦ **Aromasin®** *see* Exemestane *on page 674*
♦ **Arranon®** *see* Nelarabine *on page 1207*

Arsenic Trioxide *(AR se nik tri OKS id)*

U.S. Brand Names Trisenox®

Index Terms As_2O_3; NSC-706363

Pharmacologic Category Antineoplastic Agent, Miscellaneous

Use Induction of remission and consolidation in patients with relapsed or refractory acute promyelocytic leukemia (APL) which is specifically characterized by t(15;17) translocation or PML/RAR-alpha gene expression.

Orphan drug: Treatment of myelodysplastic syndrome; multiple myeloma; chronic myeloid leukemia (CML); acute myelocytic leukemia (AML)

Pregnancy Risk Factor D

Pregnancy Implications Animal studies have demonstrated teratogenicity and fetal loss. There are no adequate and well-controlled studies in pregnant women. May cause harm to the fetus. Pregnancy should be avoided.

Lactation Excretion in breast milk unknown/contraindicated

Medication Safety Issues

High alert medication: The Institute for Safe Medication Practices (ISMP) includes this medication among its list of drugs which have a heightened risk of causing significant patient harm when used in error.

Contraindications Hypersensitivity to arsenic or any component of the formulation; pregnancy

Warnings/Precautions Hazardous agent - use appropriate precautions for handling and disposal. **[U.S. Boxed Warnings]: May prolong the QT interval. May lead to torsade de pointes or complete AV block.** Risk factors for torsade de pointes include CHF, a history of torsade de pointes, pre-existing QT interval prolongation, patients taking potassium-wasting diuretics, and conditions which cause hypokalemia or hypomagnesemia. If possible, discontinue all medications known to prolong the QT interval. **[U.S. Boxed Warning]: A baseline**

12-lead ECG, serum electrolytes (potassium, calcium, magnesium), and creatinine should be obtained. Correct electrolyte abnormalities prior to treatment and monitor potassium and magnesium levels during therapy (potassium should stay >4 mEq/dL and magnesium >1.8 mg/dL). Correct QT_c >500 msec prior to treatment. Discontinue therapy and hospitalize patient if QT_c >500 msec, syncope, or irregular heartbeats develop during therapy; do not reinitiate until QT_c<460 msec. **[U.S. Boxed Warning]: May cause retinoic-acid-acute promyelocytic leukemia (RA-APL) syndrome or APL differentiation syndrome;** high-dose steroids (eg, dexamethasone 10 mg I.V. twice daily for at least 3 days) have been used for treatment. May lead to the development of hyperleukocytosis. Use with caution in renal impairment. **[U.S. Boxed Warning]: Should be administered under the supervision of an experienced cancer chemotherapy physician.** Safety and efficacy in children <5 years of age have not been established (limited experience with children 5-16 years of age).

Adverse Reactions

>10%:

Cardiovascular: Tachycardia (55%), edema (40%), QT interval >500 msec (40%), chest pain (25%), hypotension (25%)

Central nervous system: Fatigue (63%), fever (63%), headache (60%), insomnia (43%), anxiety (30%), dizziness (23%), depression (20%), pain (15%)

Dermatologic: Dermatitis (43%), pruritus (33%), bruising (20%), dry skin (13%)

Endocrine & metabolic: Hypokalemia (50%), hyperglycemia (45%), hypomagnesemia (45%), hyperkalemia (18%)

Gastrointestinal: Nausea (75%), abdominal pain (58%), vomiting (58%), diarrhea (53%), sore throat (35% to 40%), constipation (28%), anorexia (23%), appetite decreased (15%), weight gain (13%)

Genitourinary: Vaginal hemorrhage (13%)

Hematologic: Leukocytosis (50%), APL differentiation syndrome (23%), anemia (20%), thrombocytopenia (18%), febrile neutropenia (13%)

Hepatic: ALT increased (20%), AST increased (13%)

Local: Injection site: Pain (20%), erythema (13%)

Neuromuscular & skeletal: Neuropathy (43%), rigors (38%), arthralgia (33%), paresthesia (33%), myalgia (25%), bone pain (23%), back pain (18%), limb pain (13%), neck pain (13%), tremor (13%)

Respiratory: Cough (65%), dyspnea (38% to 53%), epistaxis (25%), hypoxia (23%), pleural effusion (20%), sinusitis (20%), postnasal drip (13%), upper respiratory tract infection (13%), wheezing (13%)

Miscellaneous: Herpes simplex (13%)

1% to 10%:

Cardiovascular: Hypertension (10%), flushing (10%), pallor (10%), palpitation (10%), facial edema (8%), abnormal ECG (not QT prolongation) (7%)

Central nervous system: Convulsion (8%), somnolence (8%), agitation (5%), coma (5%), confusion (5%)

Dermatologic: Erythema (10%), hyperpigmentation (8%), petechia (8%), skin lesions (8%), urticaria (8%), local exfoliation (5%)

Endocrine & metabolic: Hypocalcemia (10%), hypoglycemia (8%), acidosis (5%)

Gastrointestinal: Dyspepsia (10%), loose stools (10%), abdominal distension (8%), abdominal tenderness (8%), xerostomia (8%), fecal incontinence (8%), gastrointestinal hemorrhage (8%), hemorrhagic diarrhea (8%), oral blistering (8%), weight loss (8%), oral candidiasis (5%)

Genitourinary: Intermenstrual bleeding (8%), incontinence (5%)

Hematologic: Neutropenia (10%), DIC (8%), hemorrhage (8%), lymphadenopathy (8%)

Local: Injection site edema (10%)

Neuromuscular & skeletal: Weakness (10%)

Ocular: Blurred vision (10%), eye irritation (10%), dry eye (8%), eyelid edema (5%), painful eye (5%)

Otic: Earache (8%), tinnitus (5%)

Renal: Renal failure (8%), renal impairment (8%), oliguria (5%)

Respiratory: Crepitations (10%), breath sounds decreased (10%), rales (10%), hemoptysis (8%), rhonchi (8%), tachypnea (8%), nasopharyngitis (8%)

Miscellaneous: Diaphoresis increased (10%), bacterial infection (8%), herpes zoster (8%), night sweats (8%), hypersensitivity (5%), sepsis (5%)

Postmarketing and/or case reports: Atrial dysrhythmia, AV block, torsade de pointes

Overdosage/Toxicology Symptoms of arsenic toxicity include convulsions, muscle weakness, and confusion. Discontinue treatment and consider chelation therapy. One suggested adult protocol is dimercaprol 3 mg/kg I.M. every 4 hours. Continue until life-threatening toxicity has subsided. Follow with penicillamine 250 mg orally up to 4 times/day (total daily dose ≤1 g).

Drug Interactions

Increased Effect/Toxicity: Use caution with medications causing hypokalemia or hypomagnesemia (ampho B, aminoglycosides, diuretics, cyclosporin). Use caution with medications that prolong the QT interval, avoid concurrent use if possible; includes type Ia and type III antiarrhythmic agents, selected quinolones (sparfloxacin, gatifloxacin, moxifloxacin, grepafloxacin), cisapride, dolasetron, palonosetron, thioridazine, and other agents.

Ethanol/Nutrition/Herb Interactions Herb/Nutraceutical: Avoid homeopathic products (arsenic is present in some homeopathic medications). Avoid hypoglycemic herbs, including alfalfa, bilberry, bitter melon, burdock, celery, damiana, fenugreek, garcinia, garlic, ginger, ginseng, gymnema, marshmallow, and stinging nettle (may enhance the hypoglycemic effect of arsenic trioxide).

Stability Store at room temperature, 25°C (77°F); do not freeze. Following dilution, stable for 24 hours at room temperature or 48 hours when refrigerated. Dilute in 100-250 mL D_5W or 0.9% NaCl. Discard unused portion.

Mechanism of Action Not fully understood; causes *in vitro* morphological changes and DNA fragmentation to NB4 human promyelocytic leukemia cells; also damages or degrades the fusion protein PML-RAR alpha

(Continued)

Arsenic Trioxide *(Continued)*

Pharmacodynamics/Kinetics
Metabolism: Hepatic; pentavalent arsenic is reduced to trivalent arsenic (active) by arsenate reductase; trivalent arsenic is methylated to monomethylarsinic acid, which is then converted to dimethylarsinic acid via methyltransferases

Excretion: Urine (as methylated metabolite); disposition not yet studied

Dosage I.V.: Children >5 years and Adults:
Induction: 0.15 mg/kg/day; administer daily until bone marrow remission; maximum induction: 60 doses

Consolidation: 0.15 mg/kg/day starting 3-6 weeks after completion of induction therapy; maximum consolidation: 25 doses over 5 weeks

Dosage adjustment in renal impairment: Safety and efficacy have not been established; use with caution due to renal elimination

Dosage adjustment in hepatic impairment: Safety and efficacy have not been established

Elderly: Safety and efficacy have not been established; clinical trials included patients ≤72 years of age; use with caution due to the increased risk of renal impairment in the elderly

Administration Administer as I.V. infusion over 1-2 hours. If acute vasomotor reactions occur, infuse over a maximum of 4 hours. Does not require administration via a central venous catheter.

Monitoring Parameters Baseline then weekly 12-lead ECG, baseline then twice weekly serum electrolytes, hematologic and coagulation profiles at least twice weekly; more frequent monitoring may be necessary in unstable patients

Additional Information Arsenic is stored in liver, kidney, heart, lung, hair, and nails. Arsenic trioxide is a human carcinogen.

Dosage Forms
Injection, solution [preservative free]:
Trisenox®: 1 mg/mL (10 mL)

♦ **Artane** *see* Trihexyphenidyl *on page 1742*

♦ **Arthrotec®** *see* Diclofenac and Misoprostol *on page 494*

♦ **As₂O₃** *see* Arsenic Trioxide *on page 154*

♦ **ASA** *see* Aspirin *on page 160*

♦ **5-ASA** *see* Mesalamine *on page 1089*

♦ **Asacol®** *see* Mesalamine *on page 1089*

♦ **Asacol® 800 (Can)** *see* Mesalamine *on page 1089*

♦ **Asaphen (Can)** *see* Aspirin *on page 160*

♦ **Asaphen E.C. (Can)** *see* Aspirin *on page 160*

Ascorbic Acid *(a SKOR bik AS id)*

U.S. Brand Names C-500-GR™ [OTC]; Cecon® [OTC]; Cevi-Bid® [OTC]; C-Gram [OTC]; Dull-C® [OTC]; Vita-C® [OTC]

Canadian Brand Names Proflavanol C™; Revitalose C-1000®

Index Terms Vitamin C

Pharmacologic Category Vitamin, Water Soluble

Use Prevention and treatment of scurvy; acidify the urine

Unlabeled/Investigational Use Investigational: In large doses, to decrease the severity of "colds"; dietary supplementation; a 20-year study was recently completed involving 730 individuals which indicates a possible decreased risk of death by stroke when ascorbic acid at doses ≥45 mg/day was administered

Pregnancy Risk Factor A/C (dose exceeding RDA recommendation)

Lactation Enters breast milk/compatible

Medication Safety Issues
International issues:
Rubex® [Ireland] may be confused with Revex® which is a brand name for nalmefene in the U.S.

Rubex® [Ireland]: Brand name for doxurbicin in the U.S.

Warnings/Precautions Patients with diabetes and patients prone to recurrent renal calculi (eg, dialysis patients) should not take excessive doses for extended periods of time (some studies point to as little as 100 mg/day).

Adverse Reactions
1% to 10%: Renal: Hyperoxaluria (incidence dose related)

<1% (Limited to important or life-threatening): Dizziness, faintness, fatigue, flank pain, headache

Overdosage/Toxicology Symptoms include renal calculi, nausea, gastritis, and diarrhea. Diuresis with forced fluids may be useful following massive ingestion.

Drug Interactions
Increased Effect/Toxicity: Ascorbic acid enhances iron absorption from the GI tract. Concomitant ascorbic acid taken with oral contraceptives may increase contraceptive effect.

Decreased Effect: Ascorbic acid and fluphenazine may decrease fluphenazine levels. Ascorbic acid and warfarin may decrease anticoagulant effect. Changes in dose of ascorbic acid when taken with oral contraceptives may reduce the contraceptive effect.

Stability Injectable form should be stored under refrigeration (2°C to 8°C). Protect oral dosage forms from light. Rapidly oxidized when in solution in air and alkaline media.

Mechanism of Action Not fully understood; necessary for collagen formation and tissue repair; involved in some oxidation-reduction reactions as well as other metabolic pathways, such as synthesis of carnitine, steroids, and catecholamines and conversion of folic acid to folinic acid

Pharmacodynamics/Kinetics
Absorption: Oral: Readily absorbed; an active process thought to be dose dependent

Distribution: Large

Metabolism: Hepatic via oxidation and sulfation

Excretion: Urine (with high blood levels)

Dosage Oral, I.M., I.V., SubQ:

Recommended daily allowance (RDA):

<6 months: 30 mg

6 months to 1 year: 35 mg

1-3 years: 15 mg; upper limit of intake should not exceed 400 mg/day

4-8 years: 25 mg; upper limit of intake should not exceed 650 mg/day

9-13 years: 45 mg; upper limit of intake should not exceed 1200 mg/day

14-18 years: Upper limit of intake should not exceed 1800 mg/day

Male: 75 mg

Female: 65 mg

Adults: Upper limit of intake should not exceed 2000 mg/day

Male: 90 mg

Female: 75 mg

Pregnant female:

≤18 years: 80 mg; upper limit of intake should not exceed 1800 mg/day

19-50 years: 85 mg; upper limit of intake should not exceed 2000 mg/day

Lactating female:

≤18 years: 15 mg; upper limit of intake should not exceed 1800 mg/day

19-50 years: 20 mg; upper limit of intake should not exceed 2000 mg/day

Adult smoker: Add an additional 35 mg/day

Children:

Scurvy: 100-300 mg/day in divided doses for at least 2 weeks

Urinary acidification: 500 mg every 6-8 hours

Dietary supplement: 35-100 mg/day

Adults:

Scurvy: 100-250 mg 1-2 times/day for at least 2 weeks

Urinary acidification: 4-12 g/day in 3-4 divided doses

Prevention and treatment of colds: 1-3 g/day

Dietary supplement: 50-200 mg/day

Dietary Considerations Sodium content of 1 g: ~5 mEq

Administration Avoid rapid I.V. injection.

Monitoring Parameters Monitor pH of urine when using as an acidifying agent

Test Interactions False-positive urinary glucose with cupric sulfate reagent, false-negative urinary glucose with glucose oxidase method; false-negative stool occult blood 48-72 hours after ascorbic acid ingestion

Dosage Forms

Capsule: 500 mg, 1000 mg

C-500-GR™: 500 mg

Capsule, timed release: 500 mg

Crystal (Vita-C®): 4 g/teaspoonful (100 g)

Injection, solution: 250 mg/mL (2 mL, 30 mL); 500 mg/mL (50 mL)

Cenolate®: 500 mg/mL (1 mL, 2 mL) [contains sodium hydrosulfite]

Powder, solution (Dull-C®): 4 g/teaspoonful (100 g, 500 g)

Solution, oral (Cecon®): 90 mg/mL (50 mL)

Tablet: 100 mg, 250 mg, 500 mg, 1000 mg

C-Gram: 1000 mg

Tablet, chewable: 100 mg, 250 mg, 500 mg [some products may contain aspartame]

Tablet, timed release: 500 mg, 1000 mg, 1500 mg

Cevi-Bid®: 500 mg

♦ **Ascorbic Acid and Ferrous Sulfate** see Ferrous Sulfate and Ascorbic Acid on page 705

♦ **Ascriptin® [OTC]** see Aspirin on page 160

♦ **Ascriptin® Extra Strength [OTC]** see Aspirin on page 160

♦ **Asendin [DSC]** see Amoxapine on page 108

♦ **Asmanex® Twisthaler®** see Mometasone Furoate on page 1165

Asparaginase (a SPEAR a ji nase)

U.S. Brand Names Elspar®

Canadian Brand Names Elspar®; Erwinase®; Kidrolase®

Index Terms E. coli Asparaginase; Erwinia Asparaginase; L-asparaginase; NSC-106977 (Erwinia); NSC-109229 (E. coli)

Pharmacologic Category Antineoplastic Agent, Miscellaneous

Use Treatment of acute lymphocytic leukemia

Unlabeled/Investigational Use Treatment of lymphoma

Pregnancy Risk Factor C

Pregnancy Implications Decreased weight gain, resorptions, gross abnormalities, and skeletal abnormalities were observed in animal studies. There are no adequate and well-controlled studies in pregnant women. Use during pregnancy only if clearly needed.

Lactation Excretion in breast milk unknown/not recommended

Medication Safety Issues

Sound-alike/look-alike issues:

Asparaginase may be confused with pegaspargase

Elspar® may be confused with Elaprase™

High alert medication: The Institute for Safe Medication Practices (ISMP) includes this medication among its list of drugs which have a heightened risk of causing significant patient harm when used in error.

Contraindications Hypersensitivity to asparaginase or any component of the formulation; history of anaphylaxis to asparaginase; pancreatitis (active or any history of); if a reaction occurs with use of E. coli-derived asparaginase (Elspar®), pegaspargase may be used cautiously

(Continued)

Asparaginase *(Continued)*

Warnings/Precautions [U.S. Boxed Warnings]: Hazardous agent - use appropriate precautions for handling and disposal. Should be administered under the supervision of an experienced cancer chemotherapy physician and in a hospital setting. Monitor for severe allergic reactions; immediate treatment for hypersensitivity reactions should be available during administration. May alter hepatic function; use caution with pre-existing liver impairment. Use cautiously in patients with an underlying coagulopathy. Monitor blood glucose; may cause hyperglycemia. May cause pancreatitis; discontinue permanently if pancreatitis develops. Appropriate measures must be taken to prevent hyperuricemia and uric acid nephropathy; monitor, consider allopurinol, hydration and urinary alkalization.

Risk factors for allergic reactions:

Route of administration: I.V. administration is more likely to cause a reaction than I.M. or SubQ.

Prolonged therapy dose: Doses >6000-12,000 units/m^2 increase the risk of a reaction.

Previous therapy: Patients who have received previous cycles of asparaginase have an increased risk.

Intermittent therapy: Intervals of even a few days between doses increase the risk.

Up to 33% of patients who have an allergic reaction to *E. coli* asparaginase will also react to the *Erwinia* form or pegaspargase.

A test dose may be administered prior to the first dose of asparaginase, or prior to restarting therapy after a hiatus of several days. **False-negative rates of up to 80% to test doses of 2-50 units are reported.** Desensitization may be performed in patients found to be hypersensitive by the intradermal test dose or who have received previous courses of therapy with the drug.

Adverse Reactions Note: Immediate effects: Fever, chills, nausea, and vomiting occur in 50% to 60% of patients.

>10%:

Central nervous system: Fatigue, fever, chills, depression, agitation, seizure (10% to 60%), somnolence, stupor, confusion, coma (25%)

Endocrine & metabolic: Hyperglycemia (10%)

Gastrointestinal: Nausea, vomiting (50% to 60%), anorexia, abdominal cramps (70%), acute pancreatitis (15%, may be severe in some patients)

Hematologic: Hypofibrinogenemia and depression of clotting factors V and VIII, variable decrease in factors VII and IX, severe protein C deficiency and decrease in antithrombin III (may be dose limiting or fatal)

Hepatic: Transaminases, bilirubin, and alkaline phosphatase increased (transient)

Hypersensitivity: Acute allergic reactions (fever, rash, urticaria, arthralgia, hypotension, angioedema, bronchospasm, anaphylaxis (15% to 35%); may be dose limiting in some patients, may be fatal)

Renal: Azotemia (66%)

1% to 10%:

Endocrine & metabolic: Hyperuricemia

Gastrointestinal: Stomatitis

<1% (Limited to important or life-threatening) and/or frequency not defined: Acute renal failure, albumin decreased, cerebrovascular thrombosis, cough, disorientation, drowsiness, fatty liver, fibrinogen decreased, glucosuria, hallucinations, headache, hemorrhagic pancreatitis, hyper-/hypolipidemia, hyperthermia, hypocholesterolemia, hypotension, insulin-dependent diabetes, intracranial hemorrhage, irritability, ketoacidosis, laryngospasm, malabsorption syndrome, pancreatic pseudocyst, Parkinsonism symptoms (including tremor and increased muscle tone), peripheral edema, polyuria, proteinuria, pruritus, rash, renal insufficiency, serum ammonia increased, serum cholesterol decreased, sinus thrombosis, urticaria, venous thrombosis, weight loss; mild-to-moderate myelosuppression, leukopenia, anemia, thrombocytopenia (onset: 7 days, nadir: 14 days, recovery: 21 days)

Overdosage/Toxicology Symptoms include nausea and diarrhea. Treatment is symptom-directed and supportive.

Drug Interactions

Increased Effect/Toxicity: Asparaginase (I.V.) may increase the toxicity of vincristine and prednisone.

Decreased Effect: Asparaginase may diminish the effects of methotrexate.

Stability Intact vials of powder should be refrigerated (<8°C). Lyophilized powder should be reconstituted with 1-5 mL sterile water for injection or NS for I.V. administration; NS for I.M. use. Shake well, but not too vigorously. A 5 micron filter may be used to remove fiber-like particles in the solution (do not use a 0.2 micron filter; has been associated with loss of potency). Reconstituted solutions are stable 1 week refrigerated (8°C).

Standard I.M. dilution: 2000, 5000, or 10,000 int. units/mL

Standard I.V. dilution: Dilute in 50-250 mL NS or D$_5$W; solutions for I.V. infusion are stable for 8 hours at room temperature or under refrigeration

Test dose preparation: Reconstitute a 10,000 unit vial with 5 mL NS or SWFI (concentration = 2000 units/mL); withdraw 0.1 mL and add to 9.9 mL NS (concentration = 20 units/mL); test dose is 0.1 mL (2 units)

Mechanism of Action Asparaginase inhibits protein synthesis by hydrolyzing asparagine to aspartic acid and ammonia. Leukemia cells, especially lymphoblasts, require exogenous asparagine; normal cells can synthesize asparagine. Asparaginase is cycle-specific for the G$_1$ phase.

Pharmacodynamics/Kinetics

Absorption: I.M.: Produces peak blood levels 50% lower than those from I.V. administration

Distribution: V$_d$: 4-5 L/kg; 70% to 80% of plasma volume; <1% CSF penetration

Metabolism: Systemically degraded

Half-life elimination: I.M.: 39-49 hours; I.V.: 8-30 hours

Time to peak, plasma: I.M.: 14-24 hours

Dosage Refer to individual protocols.
Children:
I.V.:
Infusion for induction: 1000 units/kg/day for 10 days
Consolidation: 6000-10,000 units/m²/day for 14 days
I.M.: 6000 units/m² on days 4, 7, 10, 13, 16, 19, 22, 25, 28
Adults:
I.V. infusion single agent for induction:
200 units/kg/day for 28 days **or**
5000-10,000 units/m²/day for 7 days every 3 weeks **or**
10,000-40,000 units every 2-3 weeks
I.M. as single agent: 6000-12,000 units/m²; reconstitution to 10,000 units/mL may be
necessary

Test dose: A test dose is often recommended prior to the first dose of asparaginase, or prior
to restarting therapy after a hiatus of several days. Most commonly, 0.1 mL of a 20 units/mL
(2 units) asparaginase dilution is injected intradermally, and the patient observed for at least
1 hour. False-negative rates of up to 80% to test doses of 2-50 units are reported.

Some practitioners recommend an asparaginase desensitization regimen for patients who
react to a test dose, or are being retreated following a break in therapy. Doses are doubled
and given every 10 minutes until the total daily dose for that day has been administered. One
schedule begins with a total of 1 unit given I.V. and doubles the dose every 10 minutes until
the total amount given is the planned dose for that day. For example, if a patient was to
receive a total dose of 4000 units, he/she would receive injections 1 through 12 during the
desensitization. See table.

Asparaginase Desensitization

Injection No.	Elspar Dose (int. units)	Accumulated Total Dose
1	1	1
2	2	3
3	4	7
4	8	15
5	16	31
6	32	63
7	64	127
8	128	255
9	256	511
10	512	1023
11	1024	2047
12	2048	4095
13	4096	8191
14	8192	16,383
15	16,384	32,767
16	32,768	65,535
17	65,536	131,071
18	131,072	262,143

Administration May be administered I.M., I.V., or intradermal (skin test only)
I.M.: Doses should be given as a deep intramuscular injection into a large muscle
**Note: I.V. administration greatly increases the risk of allergic reactions and should be
avoided if possible.**
I.V.: I.V. infusion in 50-250 mL of D₅W or NS over at least 30-60 minutes. The manufacturer
recommends a test dose (0.1 mL of a dilute 20 unit/mL solution) prior to initial administration and when given after an interval of 7 days or more. Institutional policies vary. The skin
test site should be observed for at least 1 hour for a wheal or erythema. Note that a
negative skin test does not preclude the possibility of an allergic reaction. Desensitization
may be performed in patients who have been found to be hypersensitive by the intradermal
skin test or who have received previous courses of therapy with the drug. Have epinephrine, diphenhydramine, and hydrocortisone at the bedside. Have a running I.V. in place. A
physician should be readily accessible.

Gelatinous fiber-like particles may develop on standing. Filtration through a 5-micron filter
during administration will remove the particles with no loss of potency.
Monitoring Parameters Vital signs during administration, CBC, urinalysis, amylase, liver
enzymes, prothrombin time, renal function tests, urine dipstick for glucose, blood glucose,
uric acid. Be prepared to treat anaphylaxis at each administration; monitor for onset of
abdominal pain and mental status changes.
Test Interactions Decreased thyroxine and thyroxine-binding globulin
Additional Information Some institutions recommended the following precautions for asparaginase administration: Parenteral epinephrine, diphenhydramine, and hydrocortisone available at bedside; freely running I.V. in place; physician readily accessible; monitor the patient
closely for 30-60 minutes; avoid administering at night.
The *E. coli* and the *Erwinia* strains of asparaginase differ slightly in their gene sequencing,
and have slight differences in their enzyme characteristics. Both are highly specific for
asparagine and have <10% activity for the D-isomer. The *E. coli* form is more commonly
used. The *Erwinia* variety is no longer commercially available in the U.S., although may be
obtained through clinical trials or on a compassionate use basis.
Dosage Forms
Injection, powder for reconstitution:
Elspar®: 10,000 units

- ◆ **Aspart Insulin** *see* Insulin Aspart *on page 909*
- ◆ **Aspercin [OTC]** *see* Aspirin *on page 160*
- ◆ **Aspercin Extra [OTC]** *see* Aspirin *on page 160*
- ◆ *Aspergillus niger* *see* Alpha-Galactosidase *on page 74*
- ◆ **Aspergum® [OTC]** *see* Aspirin *on page 160*

Aspirin (AS pir in)

U.S. Brand Names Ascriptin® [OTC]; Ascriptin® Extra Strength [OTC]; Aspercin [OTC]; Aspercin Extra [OTC]; Aspergum® [OTC]; Bayer® Aspirin [OTC]; Bayer® Aspirin Extra Strength [OTC]; Bayer® Aspirin Regimen Adult Low Strength [OTC]; Bayer® Aspirin Regimen Children's [OTC]; Bayer® Aspirin Regimen Regular Strength [OTC]; Bayer® Extra Strength Arthritis Pain Regimen [OTC]; Bayer® Plus Extra Strength [OTC]; Bayer® Women's Aspirin Plus Calcium [OTC]; Bufferin® [OTC]; Bufferin® Extra Strength [OTC]; Buffinol [OTC]; Buffinol Extra [OTC]; Easprin®; Ecotrin® [OTC]; Ecotrin® Low Strength [OTC]; Ecotrin® Maximum Strength [OTC]; Halfprin® [OTC]; St. Joseph® Adult Aspirin [OTC]; Sureprin 81™ [OTC]; ZORprin®

Canadian Brand Names Asaphen; Asaphen E.C.; Entrophen®; Novasen

Index Terms Acetylsalicylic Acid; ASA

Pharmacologic Category Salicylate

Additional Appendix Information
Salicylates *on page 2080*

Use Treatment of mild-to-moderate pain, inflammation, and fever; may be used as prophylaxis of myocardial infarction; prophylaxis of stroke and/or transient ischemic episodes; management of rheumatoid arthritis, rheumatic fever, osteoarthritis, and gout (high dose); adjunctive therapy in revascularization procedures (coronary artery bypass graft [CABG], percutaneous transluminal coronary angioplasty [PTCA], carotid endarterectomy), stent implantation

Unlabeled/Investigational Use Low doses have been used in the prevention of pre-eclampsia, complications associated with autoimmune disorders such as lupus or anti-phospholipid syndrome

Pregnancy Risk Factor C/D (full-dose aspirin in 3rd trimester - expert analysis)

Pregnancy Implications Salicylates have been noted to cross the placenta and enter fetal circulation. Adverse effects reported in the fetus include mortality, intrauterine growth retardation, salicylate intoxication, bleeding abnormalities, and neonatal acidosis. Use of aspirin close to delivery may cause premature closure of the ductus arteriosus. Adverse effects reported in the mother include anemia, hemorrhage, prolonged gestation, and prolonged labor. Aspirin has been used for the prevention of pre-eclampsia; however, the ACOG currently recommends that it not be used in low-risk women. Low-dose aspirin is used to treat complications resulting from antiphospholipid syndrome in pregnancy (either primary or secondary to SLE). In general, low doses during pregnancy needed for the treatment of certain medical conditions have not been shown to cause fetal harm, however, discontinuing therapy prior to delivery is recommended. Use of safer agents for routine management of pain or headache should be considered.

Lactation Enters breast milk/use caution

Medication Safety Issues
Sound-alike/look-alike issues:
Aspirin may be confused with Afrin®, Asendin®
Ascriptin® may be confused with Aricept®
Ecotrin® may be confused with Akineton®, Edecrin®, Epogen®
Halfprin® may be confused with Halfan®, Haltran®
ZORprin® may be confused with Zyloprim®

International issues:
Cartia® [multiple international markets] may be confused with Cartia XT™ which is a brand name for diltiazem in the U.S.

Contraindications Hypersensitivity to salicylates, other NSAIDs, or any component of the formulation; asthma; rhinitis; nasal polyps; inherited or acquired bleeding disorders (including factor VII and factor IX deficiency); do not use in children (<16 years of age) for viral infections (chickenpox or flu symptoms), with or without fever, due to a potential association with Reye's syndrome; pregnancy (3rd trimester especially)

Warnings/Precautions Use with caution in patients with platelet and bleeding disorders, renal dysfunction, dehydration, erosive gastritis, or peptic ulcer disease. Heavy ethanol use (>3 drinks/day) can increase bleeding risks. Avoid use in severe renal failure or in severe hepatic failure. Discontinue use if tinnitus or impaired hearing occurs. Caution in mild-to-moderate renal failure (only at high dosages). Patients with sensitivity to tartrazine dyes, nasal polyps, and asthma may have an increased risk of salicylate sensitivity. Surgical patients should avoid ASA if possible, for 1-2 weeks prior to surgery, to reduce the risk of excessive bleeding (except in patients with cardiac stents that have not completed their full course of dual antiplatelet therapy [aspirin, clopidogrel]; patient-specific situations need to be discussed with cardiologist; AHA/ACC/SCAI/ACS/ADA Science Advisory provides recommendations).

When used for self-medication (OTC labeling): Children and teenagers who have or are recovering from chickenpox or flu-like symptoms should not use this product. Changes in behavior (along with nausea and vomiting) may be an early sign of Reye's syndrome; patients should be instructed to contact their healthcare provider if these occur.

Adverse Reactions As with all drugs which may affect hemostasis, bleeding is associated with aspirin. Hemorrhage may occur at virtually any site. Risk is dependent on multiple variables including dosage, concurrent use of multiple agents which alter hemostasis, and patient susceptibility. Many adverse effects of aspirin are dose related, and are extremely rare at low dosages. Other serious reactions are idiosyncratic, related to allergy or individual sensitivity. Accurate estimation of frequencies is not possible.

Cardiovascular: Hypotension, tachycardia, dysrhythmias, edema

Central nervous system: Fatigue, insomnia, nervousness, agitation, confusion, dizziness, headache, lethargy, cerebral edema, hyperthermia, coma

Dermatologic: Rash, angioedema, urticaria

Endocrine & metabolic: Acidosis, hyperkalemia, dehydration, hypoglycemia (children), hyperglycemia, hypernatremia (buffered forms)

Gastrointestinal: Nausea, vomiting, dyspepsia, epigastric discomfort, heartburn, stomach pain, gastrointestinal ulceration (6% to 31%), gastric erosions, gastric erythema, duodenal ulcers

Hematologic: Anemia, disseminated intravascular coagulation (DIC), prothrombin times prolonged, coagulopathy, thrombocytopenia, hemolytic anemia, bleeding, iron-deficiency anemia

Hepatic: Hepatotoxicity, transaminases increased, hepatitis (reversible)

Neuromuscular & skeletal: Rhabdomyolysis, weakness, acetabular bone destruction (OA)

Otic: Hearing loss, tinnitus

Renal: Interstitial nephritis, papillary necrosis, proteinuria, renal failure (including cases caused by rhabdomyolysis), BUN increased, serum creatinine increased

Respiratory: Asthma, bronchospasm, dyspnea, laryngeal edema, hyperpnea, tachypnea, respiratory alkalosis, noncardiogenic pulmonary edema

Miscellaneous: Anaphylaxis, prolonged pregnancy and labor, stillbirths, low birth weight, peripartum bleeding, Reye's syndrome

Postmarketing and/or case reports: Colonic ulceration, esophageal stricture, esophagitis with esophageal ulcer, esophageal hematoma, oral mucosal ulcers (aspirin-containing chewing gum), coronary artery spasm, conduction defect and atrial fibrillation (toxicity), delirium, ischemic brain infarction, colitis, rectal stenosis (suppository), cholestatic jaundice, periorbital edema, rhinosinusitis

Overdosage/Toxicology Symptoms include tinnitus, headache, dizziness, confusion, metabolic acidosis, hyperpyrexia, hypoglycemia, and coma. Treatment should also be based upon symptomatology.

Drug Interactions

Cytochrome P450 Effect: Substrate of CYP2C9 (minor)

Increased Effect/Toxicity: Aspirin may increase methotrexate serum levels/toxicity and may displace valproic acid from binding sites which can result in toxicity. NSAIDs and aspirin increase GI adverse effects (ulceration). Aspirin with oral anticoagulants (warfarin), thrombolytic agents, heparin, low molecular weight heparins, and antiplatelet agents (ticlopidine, clopidogrel, dipyridamole, NSAIDs, and IIb/IIIa antagonists) may increase risk of bleeding. Bleeding times may be additionally prolonged with verapamil. The effects of older sulfonylurea agents (tolazamide, tolbutamide) may be potentiated due to displacement from plasma proteins. This effect does not appear to be clinically significant for newer sulfonylurea agents (glyburide, glipizide, glimepiride).

Decreased Effect: The effects of ACE inhibitors may be blunted by aspirin administration (may be significant only at higher aspirin dosages). Aspirin may decrease the effects of beta-blockers, loop diuretics (furosemide), thiazide diuretics, and probenecid. Aspirin may cause a decrease in NSAIDs serum concentration and decrease the effects of probenecid. Increased serum salicylate levels when taken with with urine acidifiers (ammonium chloride, methionine). Ibuprofen, and possibly other COX-1 inhibitors, may reduce the cardioprotective effects of aspirin.

Ethanol/Nutrition/Herb Interactions

Ethanol: Avoid ethanol (may enhance gastric mucosal damage).

Food: Food may decrease the rate but not the extent of oral absorption.

Folic acid: Hyperexcretion of folate; folic acid deficiency may result, leading to macrocytic anemia.

Iron: With chronic aspirin use and at doses of 3-4 g/day, iron-deficiency anemia may result.

Sodium: Hypernatremia resulting from buffered aspirin solutions or sodium salicylate containing high sodium content. Avoid or use with caution in CHF or any condition where hypernatremia would be detrimental.

Benedictine liqueur, prunes, raisins, tea, and gherkins: Potential salicylate accumulation.

Fresh fruits containing vitamin C: Displace drug from binding sites, resulting in increased urinary excretion of aspirin.

Herb/Nutraceutical: Avoid cat's claw, dong quai, evening primrose, feverfew, garlic, ginger, ginkgo, red clover, horse chestnut, green tea, ginseng (all have additional antiplatelet activity). Limit curry powder, paprika, licorice; may cause salicylate accumulation. These foods contain 6 mg salicylate/100 g. An ordinarily American diet contains 10-200 mg/day of salicylate.

Stability Keep suppositories in refrigerator; do not freeze. Hydrolysis of aspirin occurs upon exposure to water or moist air, resulting in salicylate and acetate, which possess a vinegar-like odor. Do not use if a strong odor is present.

Mechanism of Action Inhibits prostaglandin synthesis, acts on the hypothalamus heat-regulating center to reduce fever, blocks prostaglandin synthetase action which prevents formation of the platelet-aggregating substance thromboxane A_2

Pharmacodynamics/Kinetics

Duration: 4-6 hours

Absorption: Rapid

Distribution: V_d: 10 L; readily into most body fluids and tissues

Metabolism: Hydrolyzed to salicylate (active) by esterases in GI mucosa, red blood cells, synovial fluid, and blood; metabolism of salicylate occurs primarily by hepatic conjugation; metabolic pathways are saturable

Bioavailability: 50% to 75% reaches systemic circulation

Half-life elimination: Parent drug: 15-20 minutes; Salicylates (dose dependent): 3 hours at lower doses (300-600 mg), 5-6 hours (after 1 g), 10 hours with higher doses

Time to peak, serum: ~1-2 hours

Excretion: Urine (75% as salicyluric acid, 10% as salicylic acid)

(Continued)

Aspirin (Continued)

Dosage

Children:

Analgesic and antipyretic: Oral, rectal: 10-15 mg/kg/dose every 4-6 hours, up to a total of 4 g/day

Anti-inflammatory: Oral: Initial: 60-90 mg/kg/day in divided doses; usual maintenance: 80-100 mg/kg/day divided every 6-8 hours; monitor serum concentrations

Antiplatelet effects: Adequate pediatric studies have not been performed; pediatric dosage is derived from adult studies and clinical experience and is not well established; suggested doses have ranged from 3-5 mg/kg/day to 5-10 mg/kg/day given as a single daily dose. Doses are rounded to a convenient amount (eg, $1/2$ of 80 mg tablet).

Mechanical prosthetic heart valves: 6-20 mg/kg/day given as a single daily dose (used in combination with an oral anticoagulant in children who have systemic embolism despite adequate oral anticoagulation therapy (INR 2.5-3.5) and used in combination with low-dose anticoagulation (INR 2-3) and dipyridamole when full-dose oral anticoagulation is contraindicated)

Blalock-Taussig shunts: 3-5 mg/kg/day given as a single daily dose

Kawasaki disease: Oral: 80-100 mg/kg/day divided every 6 hours; monitor serum concentrations; after fever resolves: 3-5 mg/kg/day once daily; in patients without coronary artery abnormalities, give lower dose for at least 6-8 weeks or until ESR and platelet count are normal; in patients with coronary artery abnormalities, low-dose aspirin should be continued indefinitely

Antirheumatic: Oral: 60-100 mg/kg/day in divided doses every 4 hours

Adults:

Analgesic and antipyretic: Oral, rectal: 325-650 mg every 4-6 hours up to 4 g/day

Anti-inflammatory: Oral: Initial: 2.4-3.6 g/day in divided doses; usual maintenance: 3.6-5.4 g/day; monitor serum concentrations

Myocardial infarction prophylaxis: 75-325 mg/day; use of a lower aspirin dosage has been recommended in patients receiving ACE inhibitors

Acute myocardial infarction: 160-325 mg/day (have patient chew tablet if not taking aspirin before presentation)

CABG: 75-325 mg/day starting 6 hours following procedure; if bleeding prevents administration at 6 hours after CABG, initiate as soon as possible

PTCA: Initial: 80-325 mg/day starting 2 hours before procedure; longer pretreatment durations (up to 24 hours) should be considered if lower dosages (80-100 mg) are used

Stent implantation: Oral: 325 mg 2 hours prior to implantation and 160-325 mg daily thereafter

Carotid endarterectomy: 81-325 mg/day preoperatively and daily thereafter

Acute stroke: 160-325 mg/day, initiated within 48 hours (in patients who are not candidates for thrombolytics and are not receiving systemic anticoagulation)

Stroke prevention/TIA: 30-325 mg/day (dosages up to 1300 mg/day in 2-4 divided doses have been used in clinical trials)

Pre-eclampsia prevention (unlabeled use): 60-80 mg/day during gestational weeks 13-26 (patient selection criteria not established)

Dosing adjustment in renal impairment: Cl_{cr} <10 mL/minute: Avoid use.

Hemodialysis: Dialyzable (50% to 100%)

Dosing adjustment in hepatic disease: Avoid use in severe liver disease.

Dietary Considerations Take with food or large volume of water or milk to minimize GI upset.

Administration Do not crush sustained release or enteric coated tablet. Administer with food or a full glass of water to minimize GI distress. For acute myocardial infarction, have patient chew tablet.

Reference Range Timing of serum samples: Peak levels usually occur 2 hours after ingestion. Salicylate serum concentrations correlate with the pharmacological actions and adverse effects observed. The serum salicylate concentration (mcg/mL) and the corresponding clinical correlations are as follows: See table.

Serum Salicylate: Clinical Correlations

Serum Salicylate Concentration (mcg/mL)	Desired Effects	Adverse Effects / Intoxication
~100	Antiplatelet Antipyresis Analgesia	GI intolerance and bleeding, hypersensitivity, hemostatic defects
150-300	Anti-inflammatory	Mild salicylism
250-400	Treatment of rheumatic fever	Nausea/vomiting, hyperventilation, salicylism, flushing, sweating, thirst, headache, diarrhea, and tachycardia
>400-500		Respiratory alkalosis, hemorrhage, excitement, confusion, asterixis, pulmonary edema, convulsions, tetany, metabolic acidosis, fever, coma, cardiovascular collapse, renal and respiratory failure

Test Interactions False-negative results for glucose oxidase urinary glucose tests (Clinistix®); false-positives using the cupric sulfate method (Clinitest®); also, interferes with Gerhardt test, VMA determination; 5-HIAA, xylose tolerance test and T_3 and T_4

Dosage Forms

Caplet:

Bayer® Aspirin: 325 mg

Bayer® Aspirin Extra Strength: 500 mg

Bayer® Extra Strength Arthritis Pain Regimen: 500 mg [enteric coated]

Bayer® Women's Aspirin Plus Calcium: 81 mg [contains elemental calcium 300 mg]

Caplet, buffered (Ascriptin® Extra Strength): 500 mg [contains aluminum hydroxide, calcium carbonate, and magnesium hydroxide]

Gelcap (Bayer® Aspirin Extra Strength): 500 mg
Gum (Aspergum®): 227 mg [cherry or orange flavor]
Suppository, rectal: 300 mg, 600 mg
Tablet: 325 mg
    Aspercin: 325 mg
    Aspercin Extra: 500 mg
    Bayer® Aspirin: 325 mg [film coated]
Tablet, buffered: 325 mg
    Ascriptin®: 325 mg [contains aluminum hydroxide, calcium carbonate, and magnesium hydroxide]
    Bayer® Plus Extra Strength: 500 mg [contains calcium carbonate]
    Bufferin®: 325 mg [contains citric acid]
    Bufferin® Extra Strength: 500 mg [contains citric acid]
    Buffinol: 325 mg [contains magnesium oxide]
    Buffinol Extra: 500 mg [contains magnesium oxide]
Tablet, chewable: 81 mg
    Bayer® Aspirin Regimen Children's Chewable: 81 mg [cherry, mint or orange flavor]
    St. Joseph® Adult Aspirin: 81 mg [orange flavor]
Tablet, controlled release (ZORprin®): 800 mg
Tablet, enteric coated: 81 mg, 325 mg, 500 mg, 650 mg
    Bayer® Aspirin Regimen Adult Low Strength, Ecotrin® Low Strength, St. Joseph Adult Aspirin: 81 mg
    Bayer® Aspirin Regimen Regular Strength, Ecotrin®: 325 mg
    Easprin®: 975 mg
    Ecotrin® Maximum Strength: 500 mg
    Halfprin®: 81 mg, 162 mg
    Sureprin 81™: 81 mg

♦ **Aspirin, Acetaminophen, and Caffeine** see Acetaminophen, Aspirin, and Caffeine on page 34

♦ **Aspirin and Carisoprodol** see Carisoprodol and Aspirin on page 295

Aspirin and Dipyridamole (AS pir in & dye peer ID a mole)

U.S. Brand Names Aggrenox®

Canadian Brand Names Aggrenox®

Index Terms Aspirin and Extended-Release Dipyridamole; Dipyridamole and Aspirin

Pharmacologic Category Antiplatelet Agent

Use Reduction in the risk of stroke in patients who have had transient ischemia of the brain or completed ischemic stroke due to thrombosis

Pregnancy Risk Factor D

Pregnancy Implications Animal reproduction studies have shown an increase in aspirin-related fetal toxicity with this combination. Use during pregnancy is not recommended; should not be used in the 3rd trimester of pregnancy. Maternal aspirin use during later pregnancy may result in low infant birth weight, stillbirth, neonatal death, and an increased incidence of intracranial hemorrhage in premature infants.

Lactation Enters breast milk/use caution

Medication Safety Issues
Sound-alike/look-alike issues:
    Aggrenox® may be confused with Aggrastat®

Contraindications Hypersensitivity to dipyridamole, aspirin, or any component of the formulation; allergy to NSAIDs; patients with asthma, rhinitis, and nasal polyps; bleeding disorders (factor VII or IX deficiencies); children <16 years of age with viral infections; pregnancy (aspirin)

Warnings/Precautions Patients who consume ≥3 alcoholic drinks per day are at risk of bleeding. Cautious use in patients with inherited or acquired bleeding disorders including those of liver disease or vitamin K deficiency. Watch for signs and symptoms of GI ulcers and bleeding. Avoid use in patients with active peptic ulcer disease. Discontinue use if dizziness, tinnitus, or impaired hearing occurs. Discontinue 1-2 weeks before elective surgical procedures to avoid bleeding. Use caution in the elderly who are at high risk for adverse events. Cautious use in patients with hypotension, patients with unstable angina, recent MI, and hepatic dysfunction. Avoid in patients with severe renal failure. Dose of aspirin in this combination is inadequate to prevent MI. Safety and efficacy in children have not been established.

Adverse Reactions
>10%:
    Central nervous system: Headache (38%)
    Gastrointestinal: Dyspepsia, abdominal pain (18%), nausea (16%), diarrhea (13%)
1% to 10%:
    Cardiovascular: Cardiac failure (2%), syncope (1%)
    Central nervous system: Pain (6%), seizure (2%), fatigue (6%), malaise (2%), amnesia (2%), confusion (1%), somnolence (1%)
    Dermatologic: Purpura (1%)
    Gastrointestinal: Vomiting (8%), bleeding (4%), rectal bleeding (2%), hemorrhoids (1%), hemorrhage (1%), anorexia (1%)
    Hematologic: Anemia (2%)
    Neuromuscular & skeletal: Back pain (5%), weakness (2%), arthralgia (6%), arthritis (2%), arthrosis (1%), myalgia (1%)
    Respiratory: Cough (2%), upper respiratory tract infection (1%), epistaxis (2%)
(Continued)

Aspirin and Dipyridamole *(Continued)*

<1% (Limited to important or life-threatening): Allergic reaction, allergic vasculitis, alopecia, anaphylaxis, anemia (aplastic), angina pectoris, angioedema, antepartum and postpartum bleeding, arrhythmia, bronchospasm, cerebral edema, cerebral hemorrhage, cholelithiasis, coma, deafness, disseminated intravascular coagulation (DIC), dyspnea, hematemesis, hemoptysis, hepatic failure, hepatitis, interstitial nephritis, intracranial hemorrhage (0.6%), jaundice, lower weight infants, pancreatitis, pancytopenia, papillary necrosis, paresthesia, PT time prolonged, pruritus, pulmonary edema, rash, renal failure, Reye's syndrome, rhabdomyolysis, Stevens-Johnson syndrome, stillbirths, subarachnoid hemorrhage, tachypnea, thrombocytopenia, ulceration, urticaria, uterine hemorrhage

Overdosage/Toxicology Symptoms of dipyridamole overdose might predominate because of the ratio of dipyridamole to aspirin. Symptoms may include hypotension and peripheral vasodilation. Treatment is symptom-directed and supportive. Treatment would include I.V. fluids and possibly vasopressors. Careful medical management is necessary.

Drug Interactions

Cytochrome P450 Effect: Aspirin: **Substrate** of CYP2C9 (minor)

Increased Effect/Toxicity: See individual agents.

Decreased Effect: See individual agents.

Ethanol/Nutrition/Herb Interactions Ethanol: Avoid ethanol (due to GI irritation).

Stability Store at 25°C (77°F); excursions permitted to 15°C to 30°C (59°F to 86°F). Protect from excessive moisture.

Mechanism of Action The antithrombotic action results from additive antiplatelet effects. Dipyridamole inhibits the uptake of adenosine into platelets, endothelial cells, and erythrocytes. Aspirin inhibits platelet aggregation by irreversible inhibition of platelet cyclooxygenase and thus inhibits the generation of thromboxane A_2.

Pharmacodynamics/Kinetics See individual agents.

Dosage Adults: Oral: 1 capsule (dipyridamole 200 mg, aspirin 25 mg) twice daily

Dosage adjustment in renal impairment: Avoid use in patients with severe renal dysfunction (Cl_{cr} <10 mL/minute). Studies have not been done in patients with renal impairment.

Dosage adjustment in hepatic impairment: Avoid use in patients with severe hepatic impairment. Studies have not been done in patients with varying degrees of hepatic impairment.

Elderly: Plasma concentrations were 40% higher, but specific dosage adjustments have not been recommended.

Dietary Considerations May be taken with or without food.

Administration Capsule should be swallowed whole; do not crush or chew. May be given with or without food.

Monitoring Parameters Hemoglobin, hematocrit, signs or symptoms of bleeding, signs or symptoms of stroke or transient ischemic attack

Dosage Forms

Capsule, variable release:

Aggrenox®: Aspirin 25 mg (immediate release) and dipyridamole 200 mg (extended release)

♦ **Aspirin and Extended-Release Dipyridamole** *see Aspirin and Dipyridamole on page 163*

♦ **Aspirin and Hydrocodone** *see Hydrocodone and Aspirin on page 849*

Aspirin and Meprobamate *(AS pir in & me proe BA mate)*

U.S. Brand Names Equagesic®

Canadian Brand Names 292 MEP®

Index Terms Meprobamate and Aspirin

Pharmacologic Category Antianxiety Agent, Miscellaneous

Use Adjunct to treatment of skeletal muscular disease in patients exhibiting tension and/or anxiety

Restrictions C-IV

Pregnancy Risk Factor D

Dosage Oral: 1 tablet 3-4 times/day

Additional Information Complete prescribing information for this medication should be consulted for additional detail.

Dosage Forms Tablet: Aspirin 325 mg and meprobamate 200 mg

♦ **Aspirin and Oxycodone** *see Oxycodone and Aspirin on page 1289*

Aspirin and Pravastatin *(AS pir in & PRA va stat in)*

U.S. Brand Names Pravigard™ PAC [DSC]

Canadian Brand Names PravASA

Index Terms Buffered Aspirin and Pravastatin Sodium; Pravastatin and Aspirin

Pharmacologic Category Antilipemic Agent, HMG-CoA Reductase Inhibitor; Salicylate

Use Combination therapy in patients who need treatment with aspirin and pravastatin to reduce the incidence of cardiovascular events, including myocardial infarction, stroke, and death

Pregnancy Risk Factor X

Dosage Oral: Adults:

Initial: Pravastatin 40 mg with aspirin (either 81 mg or 325 mg); both medications taken once daily. If pravastatin 40 mg does not achieve the desired cholesterol result, dosage may be increased to 80 mg once daily with aspirin (either 81 mg or 325 mg) once daily. Some patients may achieve/maintain goal cholesterol levels at a pravastatin dosage of 20 mg.

See Pravastatin for dosing in renal or hepatic impairment, as well as, dosing with concurrent immunosuppressant therapy.

Additional Information Complete prescribing information for this medication should be consulted for additional detail.

Dosage Forms [DSC] = Discontinued product
Combination package (Pravigard™ PAC) [each administration card contains] [DSC]:
81/20:
    Tablet: Aspirin, buffered 81 mg (5/card) [contains calcium carbonate, and magnesium oxide, and magnesium carbonate]
    Tablet (Pravachol®): Pravastatin sodium 20 mg (5/card) [contains lactose]
81/40:
    Tablet: Aspirin, buffered 81 mg (5/card) [contains calcium carbonate, and magnesium oxide, and magnesium carbonate]
    Tablet (Pravachol®): Pravastatin sodium 40 mg (5/card) [contains lactose]
81/80:
    Tablet: Aspirin, buffered 81 mg (5/card) [contains calcium carbonate, and magnesium oxide, and magnesium carbonate]
    Tablet (Pravachol®): Pravastatin sodium 80 mg (5/card) [contains lactose]
325/20:
    Tablet: Aspirin, buffered 325 mg (5/card) [contains calcium carbonate, and magnesium oxide, and magnesium carbonate]
    Tablet (Pravachol®): Pravastatin sodium 20 mg (5/card) [contains lactose]
325/40:
    Tablet: Aspirin, buffered 325 mg (5/card) [contains calcium carbonate, and magnesium oxide, and magnesium carbonate]
    Tablet (Pravachol®): Pravastatin sodium 40 mg (5/card) [contains lactose]
325/80:
    Tablet: Aspirin, buffered 325 mg (5/card) [contains calcium carbonate, and magnesium oxide, and magnesium carbonate]
    Tablet (Pravachol®): Pravastatin sodium 80 mg (5/card) [contains lactose]

♦ **Aspirin, Caffeine and Acetaminophen** *see* Acetaminophen, Aspirin, and Caffeine *on page 34*
♦ **Aspirin, Caffeine, and Butalbital** *see* Butalbital, Aspirin, and Caffeine *on page 260*
♦ **Aspirin, Caffeine, and Propoxyphene** *see* Propoxyphene, Aspirin, and Caffeine *on page 1446*
♦ **Aspirin, Carisoprodol, and Codeine** *see* Carisoprodol, Aspirin, and Codeine *on page 295*
♦ **Aspirin Free Anacin® Maximum Strength [OTC]** *see* Acetaminophen *on page 28*
♦ **Aspirin, Orphenadrine, and Caffeine** *see* Orphenadrine, Aspirin, and Caffeine *on page 1273*
♦ **Astelin®** *see* Azelastine *on page 185*
♦ **Astramorph/PF™** *see* Morphine Sulfate *on page 1171*
♦ **AT-III** *see* Antithrombin III *on page 137*
♦ **Atacand®** *see* Candesartan *on page 270*
♦ **Atacand HCT™** *see* Candesartan and Hydrochlorothiazide *on page 278*
♦ **Atacand® Plus (Can)** *see* Candesartan and Hydrochlorothiazide *on page 278*
♦ **Atarax® (Can)** *see* HydrOXYzine *on page 865*
♦ **Atasol® (Can)** *see* Acetaminophen *on page 28*

Atazanavir (at a za NA veer)

U.S. Brand Names Reyataz®
Canadian Brand Names Reyataz®
Index Terms Atazanavir Sulfate; BMS-232632
Pharmacologic Category Antiretroviral Agent, Protease Inhibitor
Additional Appendix Information
    Antiretroviral Therapy for HIV Infection: Adults and Adolescents *on page 1988*
    Management of Healthcare Worker Exposures to HBV, HCV, and HIV *on page 1941*
Use Treatment of HIV-1 infections in combination with at least two other antiretroviral agents
    Note: In patients with prior virologic failure, coadministration with ritonavir is recommended.
Pregnancy Risk Factor B
Pregnancy Implications Teratogenic effects not observed in animal studies. It is not known if atazanavir crosses the human placenta. Pregnancy and protease inhibitors are both associated with an increased risk of hyperglycemia. Glucose levels should be closely monitored. It is not known if atazanavir will exacerbate hyperbilirubinemia in neonates. There are no adequate and well-controlled studies in pregnant women. Health professionals are encouraged to contact the antiretroviral pregnancy registry to monitor outcomes of pregnant women exposed to antiretroviral medications (1-800-258-4263 or www.APRegistry.com).
Lactation Excretion in breast milk unknown/contraindicated
Contraindications Hypersensitivity to atazanavir or any component of the formulation; concurrent therapy with cisapride, ergot derivatives (dihydroergotamine, ergonovine, ergotamine, methylergonovine), indinavir, irinotecan, lovastatin, midazolam, pimozide, proton pump inhibitors (esomeprazole, lansoprazole, omeprazole), rifampin, simvastatin, St John's wort, or triazolam
Warnings/Precautions Use with caution in patients taking strong CYP3A4 inhibitors, moderate or strong CYP3A4 inducers and major CYP3A4 substrates (see drug interactions); consider alternative agents that avoid or lessen the potential for CYP-mediated interactions.

Atazanavir may prolong PR interval, use with caution in patients with pre-existing conduction abnormalities or with medications which prolong AV conduction (dosage adjustment required with some agents); rare cases of AV block have been reported. May exacerbate pre-existing hepatic dysfunction; use caution in patients with hepatitis B or C or in patients with elevated transaminases. Asymptomatic elevations in bilirubin (unconjugated) occur commonly during therapy with atazanavir; consider alternative therapy if bilirubin is >5 times ULN. Evaluate alternative etiologies if transaminase elevations also occur.
(Continued)

Atazanavir *(Continued)*

Use with caution in patients with hemophilia A or B; increased bleeding during protease inhibitor therapy has been reported. Changes in glucose tolerance, hyperglycemia, exacerbation of diabetes, DKA, and new-onset diabetes mellitus have been reported in patients receiving protease inhibitors. May be associated with fat redistribution (buffalo hump, increased abdominal girth, breast engorgement, facial atrophy). Atazanavir has been associated with development of rash (median onset 8 weeks); if mild to moderate, treatment may be continued (rash may resolve); discontinue therapy in cases of severe rash. Immune reconstitution syndrome may develop resulting in the occurrence of an inflammatory response to an indolent or residual opportunistic infection; further evaluation and treatment may be required. Optimal dosing in pediatric patients has not been established; do not use in children <3 months of age due to potential for kernicterus.

Adverse Reactions Includes data from both treatment-naive and treatment-experienced patients.

>10%:
    Dermatologic: Rash (21%; median onset 8 weeks)
    Endocrine & metabolic: Cholesterol increased (≥240 mg/dL: 6% to 25%)
    Gastrointestinal: Nausea (6% to 14%), amylase increased (up to 14%)
    Hepatic: Bilirubin increased (≥2.6 times ULN: 35% to 49%)
    Neuromuscular & skeletal: CPK increased (6% to 11%)
2% to 10%:
    Cardiovascular: AV block (1st degree: 6%)
    Central nervous system: Headache (1% to 6%), peripheral neuropathy (<1% to 4%), insomnia (<1% to 3%), depression (2%), fever (2%), dizziness (<1% to 2%)
    Endocrine & metabolic: Triglycerides increased (<1% to 8%), hyperglycemia (≥251 mg/dL: up to 5%)
    Gastrointestinal: Lipase increased (1% to 5%), abdominal pain (4%), vomiting (3% to 4%), diarrhea (1% to 3%)
    Hematologic: Neutropenia (3% to 7%), hemoglobin decreased (<1% to 5%), thrombocytopenia (up to 2%)
    Hepatic: ALT increased (>5 times ULN: 4% to 9%; 15% to 25% in patients seropositive for hepatitis B and/or C), AST increased (>5 times ULN: 2% to 7%; 9% to 10% in patients seropositive for hepatitis B and/or C), jaundice (7% to 9%)
    Neuromuscular & skeletal: Myalgia (4%)
<2%, postmarketing and/or case reports: Alopecia, arthralgia, AV block (second degree, rare), diabetes mellitus, edema, erythema multiforme, immune reconstitution syndrome, macropapular rash, pancreatitis, pruritus, Stevens-Johnson syndrome

Overdosage/Toxicology Limited experience in overdose. A single case report of ingestion of 29 g resulted in asymptomatic bifascicular block and PR interval prolongation. High doses may be expected to produce jaundice and PR interval changes. Treatment is symptom-directed and supportive. Dialysis is not likely to remove significant amounts of drug.

Drug Interactions

Cytochrome P450 Effect: Substrate of CYP3A4 (major); **Inhibits** CYP1A2 (weak), 2C8 (strong), 2C9 (weak), 3A4 (strong)

Increased Effect/Toxicity: Serum concentrations of medications significantly metabolized by CYP2C8, CYP3A4, or UGT1A1 may be elevated by atazanavir. Concurrent therapy with cisapride, ergot derivatives (dihydroergotamine, ergonovine, ergotamine, methylergonovine), indinavir, irinotecan, lovastatin, midazolam, pimozide, simvastatin, or triazolam is contraindicated (or not recommended, per manufacturer).

Atazanavir may increase the levels/effects of selected benzodiazepines, calcium channel blockers, cyclosporine, delavirdine, fentanyl, mirtazapine, nateglinide, nefazodone, quinidine, sildenafil (and other PDE-5 inhibitors), tacrolimus, telithromycin, tenofovir, venlafaxine, and other CYP3A4 substrates. When used with strong CYP3A4 inhibitors, dosage adjustment/limits are recommended for sildenafil and other PDE-5 inhibitors; consult individual monographs. Serum concentrations of antiarrhythmics (amiodarone, lidocaine, and quinidine) may be increased; monitor serum concentrations of these agents. Serum concentrations/effects of trazodone may be increased; use caution and reduce trazodone dose.

The levels/effects of atazanavir may be increased by azole antifungals, clarithromycin, delavirdine, diclofenac, doxycycline, erythromycin, imatinib, isoniazid, nefazodone, nicardipine, propofol, protease inhibitors, quinidine, telithromycin, verapamil, and other CYP3A4 inhibitors. Serum concentrations of atazanavir are increased by ritonavir; specific dosing adjustment of atazanavir in combination with ritonavir and efavirenz has been established. Serum concentrations of saquinavir may be increased by atazanavir; dosing recommendations for the combination have not been established. Tenofovir concentrations are increased by atazanavir. Concurrent use of indinavir may increase the risk of hyperbilirubinemia; concomitant administration is not recommended. Serum concentrations of orally inhaled corticosteroids (fluticasone, budesonide) may be increased by atazanavir (with or without ritonavir) resulting in decreased serum cortisol, HPA axis suppression; concurrent use with atazanavir plus ritonavir not recommended.

Atazanavir may increase serum concentrations of clarithromycin, potentially increasing the risk of QT$_c$ prolongation. A 50% reduction in clarithromycin dose or an alternative agent (except in *M. avium* complex infections) should be considered. An increase in rifabutin plasma AUC (>200%) has been observed when coadministered with atazanavir (decrease rifabutin's dose by up to 75%).

Decreased Effect: Concurrent use of proton pump inhibitors may reduce atazanavir absorption; avoid concurrent use. Antacids and buffered formulations (eg, didanosine pediatric oral solution) may reduce the serum concentrations of atazanavir. Administer atazanavir 2 hours before or 1 hour after these medications. H$_2$ antagonists may reduce the absorption of atazanavir; avoid concurrent use or administer H$_2$ antagonist at least 10 hours before or 2 hours after atazanavir. Serum levels/effects of enteric-coated didanosine may be decreased by atazanavir

The levels/effects of atazanavir may be decreased by aminoglutethimide, carbamazepine, nafcillin, nevirapine, phenobarbital, phenytoin, rifamycins, and other CYP3A4 inducers. Rifampin decreases bioavailability of protease inhibitors by ~90%; loss of virologic response and resistance may occur; the two drugs should not be administered together. St John's wort (*Hypericum perforatum*) decreases serum concentrations of protease inhibitors and may lead to treatment failures; concurrent use is contraindicated. Tenofovir may decrease serum concentrations of atazanavir, resulting in a loss of virologic response (specific atazanavir dosing recommendations provided by manufacturer).

Ethanol/Nutrition/Herb Interactions
Food: Atazanavir taken with food increases bioavailability.
Herb/Nutraceutical: St John's wort (*Hypericum perforatum*) decreases serum concentrations of protease inhibitors and may lead to treatment failures; concurrent use is contraindicated.

Stability Store at 25°C (77°F); excursions permitted to 15°C to 30°C (59°F to 86°F).

Mechanism of Action Inhibits the HIV-1 protease; inhibition of the viral protease prevents cleavage of the gag-pol polyprotein resulting in the production of immature, noninfectious virus

Pharmacodynamics/Kinetics
Absorption: Rapid; enhanced with food
Protein binding: 86%
Metabolism: Hepatic, via multiple pathways including CYP3A4; forms two metabolites (inactive)
Half-life elimination: Unboosted therapy: 7-8 hours; Boosted therapy (with ritonavir): 9-18 hours
Time to peak, plasma: 2-3 hours
Excretion: Feces (79%, 20% as unchanged drug); urine (13%, 7% as unchanged drug)

Dosage Oral: Adolescents ≥16 years and Adults:
Antiretroviral-naive patients: 400 mg once daily
Antiretroviral-experienced patients: 300 mg once daily **plus** ritonavir 100 mg once daily
Coadministration with efavirenz:
Antiretroviral-naive patients: Atazanavir 300 mg plus ritonavir 100 mg given with efavirenz 600 mg (all as a single daily dose)
Antiretroviral-experienced patients: Recommendations have not been established.
Coadministration with didanosine buffered or enteric-coated formulations: Administer atazanavir 2 hours before or 1 hour after didanosine buffered formulations
Coadministration with H2 antagonists: Administer atazanavir (with or without ritonavir) at least 2 hours before, or 10 hours after, the H2 receptor antagonist
Coadministration with tenofovir: Atazanavir 300 mg plus ritonavir 100 mg be given with tenofovir 300 mg (all as a single daily dose)
Dosage adjustment in renal impairment: No recommendation
Dosage adjustment in hepatic impairment:
Moderate hepatic insufficiency (Child-Pugh Class B): Reduce dose to 300 mg once daily if no prior virologic failure
Severe hepatic insufficiency (Child-Pugh Class C): Avoid use
Note: Data unavailable for patients with underlying hepatitis B or C, or with combination therapy (with ritonavir) in patients with hepatic impairment.

Dietary Considerations Should be taken with food to enhance absorption.

Administration Administer with food.

Monitoring Parameters Viral load, CD4, serum glucose; liver function tests, bilirubin, drug levels (with certain concomitant medications), ECG monitoring in patients with prolonged PR interval or with concurrent AV nodal blocking drugs

Additional Information A listing of medications that should not be used is available with each bottle and patients should be provided with this information.

Dosage Forms
Capsule, as sulfate:
Reyataz®: 100 mg, 150 mg, 200 mg, 300 mg

♦ **Atazanavir Sulfate** *see Atazanavir on page 165*

Atenolol (a TEN oh lole)

U.S. Brand Names Tenormin®
Canadian Brand Names Apo-Atenol®; Gen-Atenolol; Novo-Atenol; Nu-Atenol; PMS-Atenolol; RAN™-Atenolol; Rhoxal-atenolol; Riva-Atenolol; Sandoz-Atenolol; Tenolin; Tenormin®
Pharmacologic Category Beta Blocker, Beta1 Selective
Additional Appendix Information
Beta-Blockers *on page 1875*
Hypertension *on page 2063*
Use Treatment of hypertension, alone or in combination with other agents; management of angina pectoris, postmyocardial infarction patients
Unlabeled/Investigational Use Acute ethanol withdrawal, supraventricular and ventricular arrhythmias, and migraine headache prophylaxis
Pregnancy Risk Factor D
Pregnancy Implications Atenolol crosses the placenta; beta-blockers have been associated with persistent bradycardia, hypotension, and IUGR; IUGR is probably related to maternal hypertension. Available evidence suggests beta-blockers are generally safe during pregnancy (JNC 7). Cases of neonatal hypoglycemia have been reported following maternal use of beta-blockers at parturition or during breast-feeding. Monitor breast-fed infant for symptoms of beta-blockade.
Lactation Enters breast milk/use caution
Medication Safety Issues
Sound-alike/look-alike issues:
Atenolol may be confused with albuterol, Altenol®, timolol, Tylenol®
Tenormin® may be confused with Imuran®, Norpramin®, thiamine, Trovan®
(Continued)

Atenolol *(Continued)*

International issues:

Betanol® [Bangladesh] may be confused with Patanol® which is a brand name for olopatadine in the U.S.

Contraindications Hypersensitivity to atenolol or any component of the formulation; sinus bradycardia; sinus node dysfunction; heart block greater than first-degree (except in patients with a functioning artificial pacemaker); cardiogenic shock; uncompensated cardiac failure; pulmonary edema; pregnancy

Warnings/Precautions Consider pre-existing conditions such as sick sinus syndrome before initiating. Administer cautiously in compensated heart failure and monitor for a worsening of the condition (efficacy of atenolol in heart failure has not been established). Beta-blocker therapy should not be withdrawn abruptly (particularly in patients with CAD), but gradually tapered to avoid acute tachycardia, hypertension, and/or ischemia. Use caution with concurrent use of beta-blockers and either verapamil or diltiazem; bradycardia or heart block can occur. Avoid concurrent I.V. use of both agents. Beta-blockers should be avoided in patients with bronchospastic disease (asthma). Atenolol, with B_1 selectivity, has been used cautiously in bronchospastic disease with close monitoring. Use cautiously in peripheral arterial disease, especially if severe disease is present. Use cautiously in patients with diabetes - may mask hypoglycemic symptoms. Use cautiously in the renally impaired (dosage adjustment required). Use care with anesthetic agents which decrease myocardial function. Caution in myasthenia gravis or psychiatric disease (may cause CNS depression). Adequate alpha-blockade is required prior to use of any beta-blocker for patients with untreated pheochromocytoma. Safety and efficacy have not been established in children.

Adverse Reactions

1% to 10%:

Cardiovascular: Persistent bradycardia, hypotension, chest pain, edema, heart failure, second- or third-degree AV block, Raynaud's phenomenon

Central nervous system: Dizziness, fatigue, insomnia, lethargy, confusion, mental impairment, depression, headache, nightmares

Gastrointestinal: Constipation, diarrhea, nausea

Genitourinary: Impotence

Miscellaneous: Cold extremities

<1% (Limited to important or life-threatening): Alopecia, dyspnea (especially with large doses), hallucinations, impotence, liver enzymes increased, lupus syndrome, Peyronie's disease, positive ANA, psoriaform rash, psychosis, thrombocytopenia, wheezing

Overdosage/Toxicology Symptoms include cardiac disturbances, CNS toxicity, bronchospasm, hypoglycemia, and hyperkalemia. The most common cardiac symptoms include hypotension and bradycardia. Atrioventricular block, intraventricular conduction disturbances, cardiogenic shock, and asystole may occur with severe overdose, especially with membrane-depressant drugs (eg, propranolol). CNS effects include convulsions, coma, and respiratory arrest (commonly seen with propranolol and other membrane-depressant and lipid-soluble drugs). Treatment is symptomatic for seizures, hypotension, hyperkalemia, and hypoglycemia. Bradycardia and hypotension resistant to atropine, isoproterenol, or pacing may respond to glucagon. Wide QRS defects caused the membrane-depressant poisoning may respond to hypertonic sodium bicarbonate. Repeat-dose charcoal, hemoperfusion, or hemodialysis may be helpful in removal of only those beta-blockers with a small V_d, long half-life, or low intrinsic clearance (acebutolol, atenolol, nadolol, sotalol).

Drug Interactions

Increased Effect/Toxicity: Atenolol may increase the effects of other drugs which slow AV conduction (digoxin, verapamil, diltiazem), alpha-blockers (prazosin, terazosin), and alpha-adrenergic stimulants (epinephrine, phenylephrine). Atenolol may mask the tachycardia from hypoglycemia caused by insulin and oral hypoglycemics. In patients receiving concurrent therapy, the risk of hypertensive crisis is increased when either clonidine or the beta-blocker is withdrawn. Reserpine has been shown to enhance the effect of atenolol. Beta-blockers may increase the action or levels of ethanol, disopyramide, nondepolarizing muscle relaxants, and theophylline although the effects are difficult to predict.

Decreased Effect: Decreased effect of atenolol with aluminum salts, barbiturates, calcium salts, cholestyramine, colestipol, NSAIDs, penicillins (ampicillin), rifampin, salicylates, and sulfinpyrazone due to decreased bioavailability and plasma levels. Beta-blockers may decrease the effect of sulfonylureas.

Ethanol/Nutrition/Herb Interactions

Food: Atenolol serum concentrations may be decreased if taken with food.

Herb/Nutraceutical: Avoid dong quai if using for hypertension (has estrogenic activity). Avoid ephedra, yohimbe, ginseng (may worsen hypertension). Avoid garlic (may have increased antihypertensive effect).

Stability Protect from light.

Mechanism of Action Competitively blocks response to beta-adrenergic stimulation, selectively blocks beta₁-receptors with little or no effect on beta₂-receptors except at high doses

Pharmacodynamics/Kinetics

Onset of action: Peak effect: Oral: 2-4 hours

Duration: Normal renal function: 12-24 hours

Absorption: Incomplete

Distribution: Low lipophilicity; does not cross blood-brain barrier

Protein binding: 3% to 15%

Metabolism: Limited hepatic

Half-life elimination: Beta:

Neonates: ≤35 hours; Mean: 16 hours

Children: 4.6 hours; children >10 years may have longer half-life (>5 hours) compared to children 5-10 years (<5 hours)

Adults: Normal renal function: 6-9 hours, prolonged with renal impairment; End-stage renal disease: 15-35 hours

Excretion: Feces (50%); urine (40% as unchanged drug)

Dosage

Oral:

Children: 0.8-1 mg/kg/dose given daily; range of 0.8-1.5 mg/kg/day; maximum dose: 2 mg/kg/day

Adults:

Hypertension: 25-50 mg once daily, may increase to 100 mg/day. Doses >100 mg are unlikely to produce any further benefit.

Angina pectoris: 50 mg once daily, may increase to 100 mg/day. Some patients may require 200 mg/day.

Postmyocardial infarction: Follow I.V. dose with 100 mg/day or 50 mg twice daily for 6-9 days postmyocardial infarction.

I.V.:

Hypertension: Dosages of 1.25-5 mg every 6-12 hours have been used in short-term management of patients unable to take oral enteral beta-blockers

Postmyocardial infarction: Early treatment: 5 mg slow I.V. over 5 minutes; may repeat in 10 minutes. If both doses are tolerated, may start oral atenolol 50 mg every 12 hours or 100 mg/day for 6-9 days postmyocardial infarction.

Dosing interval for oral atenolol in renal impairment:

Cl_{cr} 15-35 mL/minute: Administer 50 mg/day maximum.

Cl_{cr} <15 mL/minute: Administer 50 mg every other day maximum.

Hemodialysis: Moderately dialyzable (20% to 50%) via hemodialysis; administer dose postdialysis or administer 25-50 mg supplemental dose.

Peritoneal dialysis: Elimination is not enhanced; supplemental dose is not necessary.

Dietary Considerations May be taken without regard to meals.

Administration When administered acutely for cardiac treatment, monitor ECG and blood pressure. The injection can be administered undiluted or diluted with a compatible I.V. solution. May administer by rapid infusion (I.V. push) at a rate of 1 mg/minute or by slow infusion over ~30 minutes. Necessary monitoring for surgical patients who are unable to take oral beta-blockers (prolonged ileus) has not been defined. Some institutions require monitoring of baseline and postinfusion heart rate and blood pressure when a patient's response to beta-blockade has not been characterized (ie, the patient's initial dose or following a change in dose). Consult individual institutional policies and procedures.

Monitoring Parameters Acute cardiac treatment: Monitor ECG and blood pressure with I.V. administration; heart rate and blood pressure with oral administration

Test Interactions Increased glucose; decreased HDL

Dosage Forms

Injection, solution: 0.5 mg/mL (10 mL)

Tablet: 25 mg, 50 mg, 100 mg

Extemporaneous Preparations A 2 mg/mL atenolol oral liquid compounded from tablets and a commercially available oral diluent was found to be stable for up to 40 days when stored at 5°C or 25°C.

Garner SS, Wiest DB, and Reynolds ER, "Stability of Atenolol in an Extemporaneously Compounded Oral Liquid," *Am J Hosp Pharm*, 1994, 51(4):508-11.

Atenolol and Chlorthalidone (a TEN oh lole & klor THAL i done)

U.S. Brand Names Tenoretic®

Canadian Brand Names Apo-Atenidone®; Tenoretic®

Index Terms Chlorthalidone and Atenolol

Pharmacologic Category Antihypertensive Agent, Combination

Use Treatment of hypertension with a cardioselective beta-blocker and a diuretic

Pregnancy Risk Factor D

Dosage Adults: Oral: Initial (based on atenolol component): 50 mg once daily, then individualize dose until optimal dose is achieved

Dosage adjustment in renal impairment:

Cl_{cr} 15-35 mL/minute: Administer 50 mg/day.

Cl_{cr} <15 mL/minute: Administer 50 mg every other day.

Additional Information Complete prescribing information for this medication should be consulted for additional detail.

Dosage Forms Tablet:

50: Atenolol 50 mg and chlorthalidone 25 mg

100: Atenolol 100 mg and chlorthalidone 25 mg

♦ **ATG** see Antithymocyte Globulin (Equine) on page 138

♦ **ATG** see Antithymocyte Globulin (Rabbit) on page 140

♦ **Atgam®** see Antithymocyte Globulin (Equine) on page 138

♦ **Ativan®** see Lorazepam on page 1035

Atomoxetine (AT oh mox e teen)

U.S. Brand Names Strattera®

Canadian Brand Names Strattera®

Index Terms Atomoxetine Hydrochloride; LY139603; Methylphenoxy-Benzene Propanamine; Tomoxetine

Pharmacologic Category Norepinephrine Reuptake Inhibitor, Selective

Use Treatment of attention deficit/hyperactivity disorder (ADHD)

Restrictions An FDA-approved medication guide must be distributed when dispensing an outpatient prescription (new or refill) for this medication. Medication guides are available at http://www.fda.gov/cder/Offices/ODS/medication_guides.htm. Dispense to all patients or parents or guardians of children and teenagers receiving this medication.

Pregnancy Risk Factor C

(Continued)

Atomoxetine *(Continued)*

Pregnancy Implications Decreased pup weight and survival were observed in animal studies. There are no adequate and well-controlled studies in pregnant women. Use only if potential benefit to the mother outweighs possible risk to fetus.

Lactation Excretion in breast milk unknown/use caution

Contraindications Hypersensitivity to atomoxetine or any component of the formulation; use with or within 14 days of MAO inhibitors; narrow-angle glaucoma

Warnings/Precautions [U.S. Boxed Warning]: Use caution in pediatric patients; may be an increased risk of suicidal ideation. Closely monitor for clinical worsening, suicidality, or unusual changes in behavior; the child's family or caregiver should be instructed to closely observe the patient and communicate condition with healthcare provider. Patients should be observed for, especially during the initial few months of a course of drug therapy, or at times of dose changes, either increases or decreases. Atomoxetine is not approved for major depressive disorder. Patients presenting with depressive symptoms should be screened for bipolar disorder. A medication guide should be dispensed with each prescription.

Use caution with hepatic (dosage adjustments necessary in hepatic impairment). Use may be associated with rare but severe hepatotoxicity; discontinue and do not restart if signs or symptoms of hepatotoxic reaction (eg, jaundice, pruritus, flu-like symptoms) are noted. Use caution in patients who are poor metabolizers of CYP2D6 metabolized drugs ("poor metabolizers"), bioavailability increases.

May cause increased heart rate or blood pressure; use caution with hypertension or other cardiovascular disease. Use caution with renal impairment. May cause urinary retention/hesitancy; use caution in patients with history of urinary retention or bladder outlet obstruction. Allergic reactions (including angioneurotic edema, urticaria, and rash) may occur.

Growth should be monitored during treatment. Height and weight gain may be reduced during the first 9-12 months of treatment, but should recover by 3 years of therapy. Safety and efficacy have not been evaluated in pediatric patients <6 years of age.

Adverse Reactions Percentages as reported in children and adults; some adverse reactions may be increased in "poor metabolizers" (CYP2D6).

>10%:
  Central nervous system: Headache (17% to 27%), insomnia (16%)
  Gastrointestinal: Xerostomia (4% to 21%), abdominal pain (20%), vomiting (11% to 15%), appetite decreased (10% to 14%), nausea (12%)
  Respiratory: Cough (11%)

1% to 10%:
  Cardiovascular: Palpitations (4%), diastolic pressure increased (<1% to 5%), systolic blood pressure increased (2% to 9%), orthostatic hypotension (2%), tachycardia (2% to 3%)
  Central nervous system: Fatigue/lethargy (7% to 9%), irritability (≤8%), somnolence (7%), dizziness (6%), mood swings (2% to 5%), abnormal dreams (4%), sleep disturbance (4%), pyrexia (3%), rigors (3%), crying (2%), flushing (<2%), tearfulness (<2%)
  Dermatologic: Dermatitis (2% to 4%)
  Endocrine & metabolic: Dysmenorrhea (7%), libido decreased (6%), menstruation disturbance (2% to 3%), hot flashes (3%), orgasm abnormal (2%)
  Gastrointestinal: Dyspepsia (4% to 6%), diarrhea (4%), flatulence (2%), constipation (3% to 10%), weight loss (2%), anorexia (<2%)
  Genitourinary: Urinary hesitation/retention (8%), erectile disturbance (7%), ejaculatory disturbance (5%), prostatitis (3%), impotence (3%)
  Neuromuscular & skeletal: Paresthesia (4%), myalgia (3%)
  Ocular: Mydriasis (<2%)
  Otic: Ear infection (3%)
  Respiratory: Sinusitis (6%), rhinorrhea (4%), sinus headache (3%)
  Miscellaneous: Diaphoresis increased (4%), influenza (≤3%)

<1% (Limited to important or life-threatening): Abdominal pain (right upper quadrant), aggressiveness, agitation, akathisia, allergy, angioedema, anxiety, flu-like syndrome, hepatotoxicity, hostility, hypomania, insomnia, irritability, jaundice, mania, panic attacks, peripheral vascular instability, pruritus, QT prolongation, Raynaud's phenomenon, suicidal ideation, syncope

Overdosage/Toxicology Somnolence, agitation, hyperactivity, abnormal behavior, mydriasis, tachycardia, dry mouth and GI symptoms have been reported with acute and chronic overdose. Gastric emptying and use of activated charcoal may prevent drug absorption; monitor patient and provide supportive care. Dialysis is not likely to provide benefit.

Drug Interactions

Cytochrome P450 Effect: Substrate of CYP2C19 (minor), 2D6 (major)

Increased Effect/Toxicity: MAO inhibitors may increase risk of CNS toxicity (combined use is contraindicated). CNS depressants may enhance the adverse/toxic effect of atomoxetine. CYP2D6 inhibitors may increase the levels/effects of atomoxetine (dose adjustment may be needed in patients who are extensive metabolizers of CYP2D6); example inhibitors include chlorpromazine, delavirdine, fluoxetine, miconazole, paroxetine, pergolide, quinidine, quinine, ritonavir, and ropinirole. Albuterol may increase risk of cardiovascular toxicity.

Ethanol/Nutrition/Herb Interactions Ethanol: Avoid ethanol (may increase CNS depression).

Stability Store at room temperature of 25°C (77°F).

Mechanism of Action Selectively inhibits the reuptake of norepinephrine (Ki 4.5nM) with little to no activity at the other neuronal reuptake pumps or receptor sites.

Pharmacodynamics/Kinetics

Absorption: Rapid

Distribution: V_d: I.V.: 0.85 L/kg

Protein binding: 98%, primarily albumin

Metabolism: Hepatic, via CYP2D6 and CYP2C19; forms metabolites (4-hydroxyatomoxetine, active, equipotent to atomoxetine; N-desmethylatomoxetine in poor metabolizers, limited activity)

Bioavailability: 63% in extensive metabolizers; 94% in poor metabolizers

Half-life elimination: Atomoxetine: 5 hours (up to 24 hours in poor metabolizers); Active metabolites: 4-hydroxyatomoxetine: 6-8 hours; N-desmethylatomoxetine: 6-8 hours (34-40 hours in poor metabolizers)

Time to peak, plasma: 1-2 hours

Excretion: Urine (80%, as conjugated 4-hydroxy metabolite); feces (17%)

Dosage Oral: **Note:** Atomoxetine may be discontinued without the need for tapering dose.

Children and Adolescents ≤70 kg: ADHD: Initial: 0.5 mg/kg/day, increase after minimum of 3 days to ~1.2 mg/kg/day; may administer as either a single daily dose or 2 evenly divided doses in morning and late afternoon/early evening. Maximum daily dose: 1.4 mg/kg or 100 mg, whichever is less.

Dosage adjustment in patients receiving strong CYP2D6 inhibitors (eg, paroxetine, fluoxetine, quinidine): Do not exceed 1.2 mg/kg/day; dose adjustments should occur only after 4 weeks.

Children and Adolescents >70 kg and Adults: ADHD: Initial: 40 mg/day, increased after minimum of 3 days to ~80 mg/day; may administer as either a single daily dose or two evenly divided doses in morning and late afternoon/early evening. May increase to 100 mg in 2-4 additional weeks to achieve optimal response.

Dosage adjustment in patients receiving strong CYP2D6 inhibitors (eg, paroxetine, fluoxetine, quinidine): Do not exceed 80 mg/day; dose adjustments should occur only after 4 weeks.

Elderly: Use has not been evaluated in the elderly

Dosage adjustment in renal impairment: No adjustment needed

Dosage adjustment in hepatic impairment:

Moderate hepatic insufficiency (Child-Pugh class B): All doses should be reduced to 50% of normal

Severe hepatic insufficiency (Child-Pugh class C): All doses should be reduced to 25% of normal

Dietary Considerations May be taken with or without food.

Administration May be administered with or without food. Swallow capsules whole; do not open.

Monitoring Parameters Patient growth (weight/height gain in children); attention, hyperactivity, anxiety, worsening of aggressive behavior or hostility; blood pressure, pulse

Family members and caregivers need to monitor patient daily for emergence of irritability, agitation, unusual changes in behavior, and suicidal ideation. Pediatric patients should be monitored closely for suicidality, clinical worsening, or unusual changes in behavior, especially during the initial for months of therapy or at times of dose changes. Appearance of symptoms needs to be immediately reported to healthcare provider. Weekly office visits from patient or caregiver are necessary for the first 4 weeks, then every other week for the next 4 weeks, then at 12 weeks, and as clinically indicated beyond 12 weeks. Additional contact may be required between office visits.

Dosage Forms

Capsule:

Strattera®: 10 mg, 18 mg, 25 mg, 40 mg, 60 mg, 80 mg, 100 mg

♦ **Atomoxetine Hydrochloride** see Atomoxetine on page 169

Atorvastatin (a TORE va sta tin)

U.S. Brand Names Lipitor®

Canadian Brand Names Lipitor®

Pharmacologic Category Antilipemic Agent, HMG-CoA Reductase Inhibitor

Additional Appendix Information

Hyperlipidemia Management on page 2058

Lipid-Lowering Agents on page 1887

Use Treatment of dyslipidemias or primary prevention of cardiovascular disease (atherosclerotic) as detailed below:

Primary prevention of cardiovascular disease (high-risk for CVD): To reduce the risk of MI or stroke in patients without evidence of heart disease who have multiple CVD risk factors or type 2 diabetes. Treatment reduces the risk for angina or revascularization procedures in patients with multiple risk factors.

Treatment of dyslipidemias: To reduce elevations in total cholesterol, LDL-C, apolipoprotein B, and triglycerides in patients with elevations of one or more components, and/or to increase HDL-C as present in Fredrickson type IIa, IIb, III, and IV hyperlipidemias; treatment of primary dysbetalipoproteinemia, homozygous familial hypercholesterolemia

Treatment of heterozygous familial hypercholesterolemia (HeFH) in adolescent patients (10-17 years of age, females >1 year postmenarche) having LDL-C ≥190 mg/dL or LDL-C ≥160 mg/dL with positive family history of premature cardiovascular disease (CVD) or with two or more CVD risk factors.

Pregnancy Risk Factor X

Pregnancy Implications Cholesterol biosynthesis may be important in fetal development. Contraindicated in pregnancy. Administer to women of childbearing potential only when conception is highly unlikely and patients have been informed of potential hazards.

Lactation Enters breast milk/contraindicated

Medication Safety Issues

Sound-alike/look-alike issues:

Lipitor® may be confused with Levatol®

Contraindications Hypersensitivity to atorvastatin or any component of the formulation; active liver disease; unexplained persistent elevations of serum transaminases; pregnancy

Warnings/Precautions Secondary causes of hyperlipidemia should be ruled out prior to therapy. Liver function must be monitored by periodic laboratory assessment. May cause hepatic dysfunction. Use with caution in patients who consume large amounts of ethanol or have a history of liver disease. Monitoring is recommended. Rhabdomyolysis with acute renal failure has occurred. Risk is dose related and is increased with concurrent use of (Continued)

Atorvastatin *(Continued)*

lipid-lowering agents which may cause rhabdomyolysis (gemfibrozil, fibric acid derivatives, or niacin at doses ≥1 g/day) or during concurrent use with potent CYP3A4 inhibitors (including amiodarone, clarithromycin, cyclosporine, erythromycin, itraconazole, ketoconazole, nefazodone, nelfinavir, or ritonavir). Weigh the risk versus benefit when combining any of these drugs with atorvastatin. Discontinue in any patient experiencing an acute or serious condition predisposing to renal failure secondary to rhabdomyolysis. Use with caution in patients with advanced age, these patients are predisposed to myopathy. Safety and efficacy have not been established in patients <10 years of age or in premenarcheal girls.

Adverse Reactions

>10%: Central nervous system: Headache (3% to 17%)

2% to 10%:

Cardiovascular: Chest pain, peripheral edema

Central nervous system: Insomnia, dizziness

Dermatologic: Rash (1% to 4%)

Gastrointestinal: Abdominal pain (up to 4%), constipation (up to 3%), diarrhea (up to 4%), dyspepsia (1% to 3%), flatulence (1% to 3%), nausea

Genitourinary: Urinary tract infection

Hepatic: Transaminases increased (2% to 3% with 80 mg/day dosing)

Neuromuscular & skeletal: Arthralgia (up to 5%), arthritis, back pain (up to 4%), myalgia (up to 6%), weakness (up to 4%)

Respiratory: Sinusitis (up to 6%), pharyngitis (up to 3%), bronchitis, rhinitis

Miscellaneous: Infection (3% to 10%), flu-like syndrome (up to 3%), allergic reaction (up to 3%)

<2% (Limited to important or life-threatening): Alopecia, anaphylaxis, angina, angioneurotic edema, arrhythmia, bullous rash, cholestatic jaundice, deafness, dyspnea, erythema multiforme, esophagitis, facial paralysis, fatigue, glaucoma, gout, hepatitis, hyperkinesias, impotence, migraine, myasthenia, myopathy, myositis, nephritis, pancreatitis, paresthesia, peripheral neuropathy, petechiae, photosensitivity, postural hypotension, pruritus, rectal hemorrhage, rhabdomyolysis, somnolence, Stevens-Johnson syndrome, syncope, tendinous contracture, thrombocytopenia, tinnitus, torticollis, toxic epidermal necrolysis, urticaria, vaginal hemorrhage, vomiting

Overdosage/Toxicology Treatment is supportive.

Drug Interactions

Cytochrome P450 Effect: Substrate of CYP3A4 (major); **Inhibits** CYP3A4 (weak)

Increased Effect/Toxicity: CYP3A4 inhibitors may increase the levels/effects of atorvastatin; example inhibitors include azole antifungals, clarithromycin, diclofenac, doxycycline, erythromycin, imatinib, isoniazid, nefazodone, nicardipine, propofol, protease inhibitors, quinidine, telithromycin, and verapamil. The risk of myopathy and rhabdomyolysis due to concurrent use of a CYP3A4 inhibitor with atorvastatin is probably less than lovastatin or simvastatin. Cyclosporine, clofibrate, diltiazem, fenofibrate, gemfibrozil, and niacin may also increase the risk of myopathy and rhabdomyolysis. The effect/toxicity of levothyroxine may be increased by atorvastatin. Levels of digoxin and ethinyl estradiol may be increased by atorvastatin.

Decreased Effect: Colestipol, antacids decreased plasma concentrations but effect on LDL-cholesterol was not altered. Cholestyramine may decrease absorption of atorvastatin when administered concurrently.

Ethanol/Nutrition/Herb Interactions

Ethanol: Avoid excessive ethanol consumption (due to potential hepatic effects).

Food: Atorvastatin serum concentrations may be increased by grapefruit juice; avoid concurrent intake of large quantities (>1 quart/day). Red yeast rice contains an estimated 2.4 mg lovastatin per 600 mg rice.

Herb/Nutraceutical: St John's wort may decrease atorvastatin levels.

Mechanism of Action Inhibitor of 3-hydroxy-3-methylglutaryl coenzyme A (HMG-CoA) reductase, the rate-limiting enzyme in cholesterol synthesis (reduces the production of mevalonic acid from HMG-CoA); this then results in a compensatory increase in the expression of LDL receptors on hepatocyte membranes and a stimulation of LDL catabolism

Pharmacodynamics/Kinetics

Onset of action: Initial changes: 3-5 days; Maximal reduction in plasma cholesterol and triglycerides: 2 weeks

Absorption: Rapid

Distribution: V_d: 318 L

Protein binding: ≥98%

Metabolism: Hepatic; forms active ortho- and parahydroxylated derivates and an inactive beta-oxidation product

Half-life elimination: Parent drug: 14 hours

Time to peak, serum: 1-2 hours

Excretion: Bile; urine (2% as unchanged drug)

Dosage Oral: **Note:** Doses should be individualized according to the baseline LDL-cholesterol levels, the recommended goal of therapy, and patient response; adjustments should be made at intervals of 2-4 weeks

Children 10-17 years (females >1 year postmenarche): HeFH: 10 mg once daily (maximum: 20 mg/day)

Adults:

Hyperlipidemias: Initial: 10-20 mg once daily; patients requiring >45% reduction in LDL-C may be started at 40 mg once daily; range: 10-80 mg once daily

Primary prevention of CVD: 10 mg once daily

Dosing adjustment in renal impairment: No dosage adjustment is necessary.

Dosing adjustment in hepatic impairment: Do not use in active liver disease.

Dietary Considerations May take with food if desired; may take without regard to time of day. Before initiation of therapy, patients should be placed on a standard cholesterol-lowering diet for 3-6 months and the diet should be continued during drug therapy. Red yeast rice contains an estimated 2.4 mg lovastatin per 600 mg rice.

Administration May be administered with food if desired; may take without regard to time of day.

Monitoring Parameters Lipid levels after 2-4 weeks; LFTs, CPK

It Is recommended that liver function tests (LFTs) be performed prior to and at 12 weeks following both the initiation of therapy and any elevation in dose, and periodically (eg, semiannually) thereafter

Dosage Forms Tablet: 10 mg, 20 mg, 40 mg, 80 mg

♦ **Atorvastatin Calcium and Amlodipine Besylate** see Amlodipine and Atorvastatin on page 105

Atovaquone (a TOE va kwone)

U.S. Brand Names Mepron®
Canadian Brand Names Mepron®
Pharmacologic Category Antiprotozoal
Additional Appendix Information
Malaria Treatment on page 2003
USPHS / IDSA Guidelines for the Prevention of Opportunistic Infections in Persons Infected With HIV on page 1966
Use Acute oral treatment of mild-to-moderate Pneumocystis carinii pneumonia (PCP) in patients who are intolerant to co-trimoxazole; prophylaxis of PCP in patients intolerant to co-trimoxazole; treatment/suppression of Toxoplasma gondii encephalitis; primary prophylaxis of HIV-infected persons at high risk for developing Toxoplasma gondii encephalitis
Pregnancy Risk Factor C
Lactation Excretion in breast milk unknown/use caution
Contraindications Life-threatening allergic reaction to the drug or formulation
Warnings/Precautions Has only been indicated in mild-to-moderate PCP. Use with caution in elderly patients due to potentially impaired renal, hepatic, and cardiac function.
Adverse Reactions Note: Adverse reaction statistics have been compiled from studies including patients with advanced HIV disease. Consequently, it is difficult to distinguish reactions attributed to atovaquone from those caused by the underlying disease or a combination thereof.

>10%:
    Central nervous system: Headache, fever, insomnia, anxiety
    Dermatologic: Rash
    Gastrointestinal: Nausea, diarrhea, vomiting
    Respiratory: Cough
1% to 10%:
    Central nervous system: Dizziness
    Dermatologic: Pruritus
    Endocrine & metabolic: Hypoglycemia, hyponatremia
    Gastrointestinal: Abdominal pain, amylase increased, constipation, anorexia, heartburn
    Hematologic: Anemia, neutropenia, leukopenia
    Hepatic: Liver enzymes increased
    Neuromuscular & skeletal: Weakness
    Renal: BUN/creatinine increased
    Miscellaneous: Oral Monilia

Drug Interactions
    Increased Effect/Toxicity: Possible increased toxicity with other highly protein-bound drugs.
    Decreased Effect: Rifamycins (rifampin) used concurrently decrease the steady-state plasma concentrations of atovaquone.
Ethanol/Nutrition/Herb Interactions Food: Ingestion with a fatty meal increases absorption.
Stability Do not freeze.
Mechanism of Action Has not been fully elucidated; may inhibit electron transport in mitochondria inhibiting metabolic enzymes
Pharmacodynamics/Kinetics
    Absorption: Significantly increased with a high-fat meal
    Distribution: 3.5 L/kg
    Protein binding: >99%
    Metabolism: Undergoes enterohepatic recirculation
    Bioavailability: Tablet: 23%; Suspension: 47%
    Half-life elimination: 2-3 days
    Excretion: Feces (94% as unchanged drug)
Dosage Oral: Adolescents 13-16 years and Adults:
    Prevention of PCP: 1500 mg once daily with food
    Treatment of mild-to-moderate PCP: 750 mg twice daily with food for 21 days
Dosage Forms Suspension, oral: 750 mg/5 mL (5 mL, 210 mL) [contains benzyl alcohol; citrus flavor]

Atovaquone and Proguanil (a TOE va kwone & pro GWA nil)

U.S. Brand Names Malarone®
Canadian Brand Names Malarone®; Malarone® Pediatric
Index Terms Proguanil and Atovaquone
Pharmacologic Category Antimalarial Agent
Additional Appendix Information
Malaria Treatment on page 2003
Use Prevention or treatment of acute, uncomplicated P. falciparum malaria
(Continued)

Atovaquone and Proguanil *(Continued)*

Pregnancy Risk Factor C

Pregnancy Implications Use in pregnant women only if the potential benefit outweighs the possible risk to the fetus. Because falciparum malaria can cause maternal death and fetal loss, pregnant women traveling to malaria-endemic areas must use personal protection against mosquito bites.

Lactation

Atovaquone: Excretion in breast milk unknown/use caution

Proguanil: Enters breast milk (small amounts)/use caution

Contraindications Hypersensitivity to atovaquone, proguanil, or any component of the formulation; prophylactic use in severe renal impairment

Warnings/Precautions Not indicated for severe or complicated malaria. Absorption of atovaquone may be decreased in patients who have diarrhea or vomiting; monitor closely and consider use of an antiemetic. If severe, consider use of an alternative antimalarial. Administer with caution to patients with pre-existing renal disease. Not for use in patients <5 kg (treatment) or <11 kg (prophylaxis). Delayed cases of *P. falciparum* malaria may occur after stopping prophylaxis. Recrudescent infections or infections following prophylaxis with this agent should be treated with an alternative agent(s).

Adverse Reactions The following adverse reactions were reported in patients being treated for malaria. When used for prophylaxis, reactions are similar to those seen with placebo.

>10%: Gastrointestinal: Abdominal pain (17%), nausea (12%), vomiting (children 10% to 13%, adults 12%)

1% to 10%:

Central nervous system: Headache (10%), dizziness (5%)

Dermatologic: Pruritus (children 6%)

Gastrointestinal: Diarrhea (children 6%, adults 8%), anorexia (5%)

Neuromuscular & skeletal: Weakness (8%)

Postmarketing and/or case reports: Anaphylaxis, angioedema, erythema multiforme, hallucinations, photosensitivity, psychotic episodes, rash, seizure, Stevens-Johnson syndrome, urticaria

Overdosage/Toxicology

Atovaquone: Overdoses of up to 31,500 mg have been reported. Rash has been reported as well as methemoglobinemia in one patient also taking dapsone. There is no known antidote and it is unknown if it is dialyzable.

Proguanil: Single doses of 1500 mg and 700 mg twice daily for 2 weeks have been reported without toxicity. Reversible hair loss, scaling of skin, reversible aphthous ulceration, and hematologic side effects have occurred. Epigastric discomfort and vomiting would also be expected.

There have been no reported overdoses with the atovaquone/proguanil combination.

Drug Interactions

Cytochrome P450 Effect: Proguanil: **Substrate** (minor) of 1A2, 2C19, 3A4

Decreased Effect: Metoclopramide decreases bioavailability of atovaquone. Rifabutin decreases atovaquone levels by 34%. Rifampin decreases atovaquone levels by 50%. Tetracycline decreases plasma concentrations of atovaquone by 40%.

Ethanol/Nutrition/Herb Interactions Food: Atovaquone taken with dietary fat increases the rate and extent of absorption.

Stability Store tablets at 25°C (77°F).

Mechanism of Action

Atovaquone: Selectively inhibits parasite mitochondrial electron transport.

Proguanil: The metabolite cycloguanil inhibits dihydrofolate reductase, disrupting deoxythymidylate synthesis. Together, atovaquone/cycloguanil affect the erythrocytic and exoerythrocytic stages of development.

Pharmacodynamics/Kinetics

Atovaquone: See Atovaquone.

Proguanil:

Absorption: Extensive

Distribution: 42 L/kg

Protein binding: 75%

Metabolism: Hepatic to active metabolites, cycloguanil (via CYP2C19) and 4-chlorophenylbiguanide

Half-life elimination: 12-21 hours

Excretion: Urine (40% to 60%)

Dosage Oral:

Children (dosage based on body weight):

Prevention of malaria: Start 1-2 days prior to entering a malaria-endemic area, continue throughout the stay and for 7 days after returning. Take as a single dose, once daily.

11-20 kg: Atovaquone/proguanil 62.5 mg/25 mg

21-30 kg: Atovaquone/proguanil 125 mg/50 mg

31-40 kg: Atovaquone/proguanil 187.5 mg/75 mg

>40 kg: Atovaquone/proguanil 250 mg/100 mg

Treatment of acute malaria: Take as a single dose, once daily for 3 consecutive days.

5-8 kg: Atovaquone/proguanil 125 mg/50 mg

9-10 kg: Atovaquone/proguanil 187.5 mg/75 mg

11-20 kg: Atovaquone/proguanil 250 mg/100 mg

21-30 kg: Atovaquone/proguanil 500 mg/200 mg

31-40 kg: Atovaquone/proguanil 750 mg/300 mg

>40 kg: Atovaquone/proguanil 1 g/400 mg

Adults:

Prevention of malaria: Atovaquone/proguanil 250 mg/100 mg once daily; start 1-2 days prior to entering a malaria-endemic area, continue throughout the stay and for 7 days after returning

Treatment of acute malaria: Atovaquone/proguanil 1 g/400 mg as a single dose, once daily for 3 consecutive days

Elderly: Use with caution due to possible decrease in renal and hepatic function, as well as possible decreases in cardiac function, concomitant diseases, or other drug therapy.

Dosage adjustment in renal impairment: Should not be used as prophylaxis in severe renal impairment (Cl$_{cr}$ <30 mL/minute). Alternative treatment regimens should be used in patients with Cl$_{cr}$ <30 mL/minute. No dosage adjustment required in mild-to-moderate renal impairment.

Dosage adjustment in hepatic impairment: No dosage adjustment required in mild-to-moderate hepatic impairment. No data available for use in severe hepatic impairment.

Dietary Considerations Must be taken with food or a milky drink.

Administration Administer with food or milk at the same time each day. If vomiting occurs within 1 hour of administration, repeat the dose. For children who have difficulty swallowing tablets, tablets may be crushed and mixed with condensed milk just prior to administration.

Dosage Forms
Tablet: Atovaquone 250 mg and proguanil hydrochloride 100 mg
Tablet, pediatric: Atovaquone 62.5 mg and proguanil hydrochloride 25 mg

♦ **ATRA** see Tretinoin (Oral) on page 1730

Atracurium (a tra KYOO ree um)

Canadian Brand Names Atracurium Besylate Injection
Index Terms Atracurium Besylate
Pharmacologic Category Neuromuscular Blocker Agent, Nondepolarizing
Additional Appendix Information
Neuromuscular Blocking Agents on page 1890
Use Adjunct to general anesthesia to facilitate endotracheal intubation and to relax skeletal muscles during surgery; to facilitate mechanical ventilation in ICU patients; does not relieve pain or produce sedation
Pregnancy Risk Factor C
Lactation Excretion in breast milk unknown/use caution
Medication Safety Issues
High alert medication: The Institute for Safe Medication Practices (ISMP) includes this medication among its list of drugs which have a heightened risk of causing significant patient harm when used in error.
Contraindications Hypersensitivity to atracurium besylate or any component of the formulation
Warnings/Precautions Reduce initial dosage and inject slowly (over 1-2 minutes) in patients in whom substantial histamine release would be potentially hazardous (eg, patients with clinically-important cardiovascular disease). Maintenance of an adequate airway and respiratory support is critical. Certain clinical conditions may result in potentiation or antagonism of neuromuscular blockade:
    Potentiation: Electrolyte abnormalities, severe hyponatremia, severe hypocalcemia, severe hypokalemia, hypermagnesemia, neuromuscular diseases, acidosis, acute intermittent porphyria, renal failure, hepatic failure
    Antagonism: Alkalosis, hypercalcemia, demyelinating lesions, peripheral neuropathies, diabetes mellitus

Increased sensitivity in patients with myasthenia gravis, Eaton-Lambert syndrome; resistance in burn patients (>30% of body) for period of 5-70 days postinjury; resistance in patients with muscle trauma, denervation, immobilization, infection, chronic treatment with atracurium. Cross-sensitivity with other neuromuscular-blocking agents may occur; use extreme caution in patients with previous anaphylactic reactions. Bradycardia may be more common with atracurium than with other neuromuscular-blocking agents since it has no clinically-significant effects on heart rate to counteract the bradycardia produced by anesthetics.

Adverse Reactions Mild, rare, and generally suggestive of histamine release

1% to 10%: Cardiovascular: Flushing
<1%: Bronchial secretions, erythema, hives, itching, wheezing
Postmarketing and/or case reports: Allergic reaction, bradycardia, bronchospasm, dyspnea, hypotension, injection site reaction, seizure, acute quadriplegic myopathy syndrome (prolonged use), laryngospasm, myositis ossificans (prolonged use), tachycardia, urticaria
Causes of prolonged neuromuscular blockade: Excessive drug administration; cumulative drug effect, metabolism/excretion decreased (hepatic and/or renal impairment); accumulation of active metabolites; electrolyte imbalance (hypokalemia, hypocalcemia, hypermagnesemia, hypernatremia); hypothermia

Overdosage/Toxicology Symptoms include respiratory depression and cardiovascular collapse. Neostigmine 1-3 mg slow I.V. push in adults (0.5 mg in children) antagonizes the neuromuscular blockade and should be administered with or immediately after atropine 1-1.5 mg I.V. push (adults). This may be especially useful in the presence of bradycardia.

Drug Interactions
Increased Effect/Toxicity: Increased effects are possible with aminoglycosides, beta-blockers, clindamycin, calcium channel blockers, halogenated anesthetics, imipenem, ketamine, lidocaine, loop diuretics (furosemide), macrolides (case reports), magnesium sulfate, procainamide, quinidine, quinolones, tetracyclines, and vancomycin. May increase risk of myopathy when used with high-dose corticosteroids for extended periods.
Decreased Effect: Effect of nondepolarizing neuromuscular blockers may be reduced by carbamazepine (chronic use), corticosteroids (also associated with myopathy - see increased effect), phenytoin (chronic use), sympathomimetics, and theophylline.

Stability Refrigerate intact vials at 2°C to 8°C (36°F to 46°F). Protect from freezing. Use vials within 14 days upon removal from the refrigerator to room temperature of 25°C (77°F). Dilutions of 0.2 mg/mL or 0.5 mg/mL in 0.9% sodium chloride, dextrose 5% in water, or 5% dextrose in sodium chloride 0.9% are stable for up to 24 hours at room temperature or under refrigeration. Atracurium should not be mixed with alkaline solutions.
(Continued)

Atracurium *(Continued)*

Mechanism of Action Blocks neural transmission at the myoneural junction by binding with cholinergic receptor sites

Pharmacodynamics/Kinetics

Onset of action (dose dependent): 2-3 minutes

Duration: Recovery begins in 20-35 minutes following initial dose of 0.4-0.5 mg/kg under balanced anesthesia; recovery to 95% of control takes 60-70 minutes

Metabolism: Undergoes ester hydrolysis and Hofmann elimination (nonbiologic process independent of renal, hepatic, or enzymatic function); metabolites have no neuromuscular blocking properties; laudanosine, a product of Hofmann elimination, is a CNS stimulant and can accumulate with prolonged use. Laudanosine is hepatically metabolized.

Half-life elimination: Biphasic: Adults: Initial (distribution): 2 minutes; Terminal: 20 minutes

Excretion: Urine (<5%)

Dosage I.V. (not to be used I.M.): Dose to effect; doses must be individualized due to interpatient variability; use ideal body weight for obese patients

Children 1 month to 2 years: Initial: 0.3-0.4 mg/kg followed by maintenance doses as needed to maintain neuromuscular blockade

Children >2 years to Adults: 0.4-0.5 mg/kg, then 0.08-0.1 mg/kg 20-45 minutes after initial dose to maintain neuromuscular block, followed by repeat doses of 0.08-0.1 mg/kg at 15- to 25-minute intervals

Initial dose after succinylcholine for intubation (balanced anesthesia): Adults: 0.2-0.4 mg/kg

Pretreatment/priming: 10% of intubating dose given 3-5 minutes before initial dose

Continuous infusion:

Surgery: Initial: 9-10 mcg/kg/minute at initial signs of recovery from bolus dose; block usually maintained by a rate of 5-9 mcg/kg/minute under balanced anesthesia

ICU: Block usually maintained by rate of 11-13 mcg/kg/minute (rates for pediatric patients may be higher)

See table.

Atracurium Besylate Infusion Chart

Drug Delivery Rate (mcg/kg/min)	Infusion Rate (mL/kg/min) 0.2 mg/mL (20 mg/100 mL)	Infusion Rate (mL/kg/min) 0.5 mg/mL (50 mg/100 mL)
5	0.025	0.01
6	0.03	0.012
7	0.035	0.014
8	0.04	0.016
9	0.045	0.018
10	0.05	0.02

Dosage adjustment for hepatic or renal impairment is not necessary

Administration May be given undiluted as a bolus injection; not for I.M. injection due to tissue irritation; administration via infusion requires the use of an infusion pump; use infusion solutions within 24 hours of preparation

Monitoring Parameters Vital signs (heart rate, blood pressure, respiratory rate); degree of muscle relaxation (via peripheral nerve stimulator and presence of spontaneous movement); renal function (serum creatinine, BUN) and liver function when in ICU

In the ICU setting, prolonged paralysis and generalized myopathy, following discontinuation of agent, may be minimized by appropriately monitoring degree of blockade.

Additional Information Atracurium is classified as an intermediate-duration neuromuscular-blocking agent. It does not appear to have a cumulative effect on the duration of blockade. It does not relieve pain or produce sedation.

Dosage Forms

Injection, as besylate: 10 mg/mL (10 mL) [contains benzyl alcohol]

Injection, as besylate [preservative free]: 10 mg/mL (5 mL)

♦ **Atracurium Besylate** *see Atracurium on page 175*

♦ **Atracurium Besylate Injection (Can)** *see Atracurium on page 175*

♦ **Atripla™** *see Efavirenz, Emtricitabine, and Tenofovir on page 573*

♦ **AtroPen®** *see Atropine on page 176*

Atropine *(A troe peen)*

U.S. Brand Names AtroPen®; Atropine-Care®; Isopto® Atropine; Sal-Tropine™

Canadian Brand Names Dioptic's Atropine Solution; Isopto® Atropine

Index Terms Atropine Sulfate

Pharmacologic Category Anticholinergic Agent; Anticholinergic Agent, Ophthalmic; Antidote; Antispasmodic Agent, Gastrointestinal; Ophthalmic Agent, Mydriatic

Additional Appendix Information

Cycloplegic Mydriatics *on page 1882*

Management of Overdosages *on page 2075*

Use

Injection: Preoperative medication to inhibit salivation and secretions; treatment of symptomatic sinus bradycardia; AV block (nodal level); ventricular asystole; antidote for organophosphate pesticide poisoning

Ophthalmic: Produce mydriasis and cycloplegia for examination of the retina and optic disc and accurate measurement of refractive errors; uveitis

Oral: Inhibit salivation and secretions

Unlabeled/Investigational Use Pulseless electric activity, asystole, neuromuscular blockade reversal; treatment of nerve agent toxicity (chemical warfare) in combination with pralidoxime

Restrictions The AtroPen® formulation is available for use primarily by the Department of Defense.

Pregnancy Risk Factor C

Pregnancy Implications Animal reproduction studies have not been conducted. Atropine has been found to cross the human placenta.

Lactation Enters breast milk (trace amounts)/use caution (AAP rates "compatible")

Medication Safety Issues
International issues:
Genatropine® [France] may be confused with Genotropin®

Contraindications Hypersensitivity to atropine or any component of the formulation; narrow-angle glaucoma; adhesions between the iris and lens; tachycardia; obstructive GI disease; paralytic ileus; intestinal atony of the elderly or debilitated patient; severe ulcerative colitis; toxic megacolon complicating ulcerative colitis; hepatic disease; obstructive uropathy; renal disease; myasthenia gravis (unless used to treat side effects of acetylcholinesterase inhibitor); asthma; thyrotoxicosis; Mobitz type II block

Warnings/Precautions Use with caution in children with spastic paralysis; use with caution in elderly patients. Low doses cause a paradoxical decrease in heart rates. Some commercial products contain sodium metabisulfite, which can cause allergic-type reactions. May accumulate with multiple inhalational administration, particularly in the elderly. Heat prostration may occur in hot weather. Use with caution in patients with autonomic neuropathy, prostatic hyperplasia, hyperthyroidism, CHF, cardiac arrhythmias, chronic lung disease, biliary tract disease; anticholinergic agents are generally not well tolerated in the elderly and their use should be avoided when possible. Atropine is rarely used except as a preoperative agent or in the acute treatment of bradyarrhythmias.

AtroPen®: There are no absolute contraindications for the use of atropine in organophosphate poisonings, however, use caution in those patients where the use of atropine would be otherwise contraindicated. Formulation for use by trained personnel only.

Adverse Reactions Severity and frequency of adverse reactions are dose related and vary greatly; listed reactions are limited to significant and/or life-threatening.

Cardiovascular: Arrhythmia, flushing, hypotension, palpitation, tachycardia
Central nervous system: Ataxia, coma, delirium, disorientation, dizziness, drowsiness, excitement, fever, hallucinations, headache, insomnia, nervousness
Dermatologic: Anhidrosis, urticaria, rash, scarlatiniform rash
Gastrointestinal: Bloating, constipation, delayed gastric emptying, loss of taste, nausea, paralytic ileus, vomiting, xerostomia
Genitourinary: Urinary hesitancy, urinary retention
Neuromuscular & skeletal: Weakness
Ocular: Angle-closure glaucoma, blurred vision, cycloplegia, dry eyes, mydriasis, ocular tension increased
Respiratory: Dyspnea, laryngospasm, pulmonary edema
Miscellaneous: Anaphylaxis

Overdosage/Toxicology Symptoms include dilated, unreactive pupils; blurred vision; hot, dry flushed skin; dryness of mucous membranes; difficulty in swallowing, foul breath, diminished or absent bowel sounds, urinary retention, tachycardia, hyperthermia, and hypertension, increased respiratory rate. Anticholinergic toxicity is caused by strong binding of the drug to cholinergic receptors. Anticholinesterase inhibitors reduce acetylcholinesterase, the enzyme that breaks down acetylcholine, and thereby allow acetylcholine to accumulate and compete for receptor binding with the offending anticholinergic. For anticholinergic overdose with severe life-threatening symptoms, physostigmine 1-2 mg (0.5 mg or 0.02 mg/kg for children) SubQ or slow I.V. may be given to reverse these effects.

Drug Interactions
Increased Effect/Toxicity: Antihistamines, phenothiazines, TCAs, and other drugs with anticholinergic activity may increase anticholinergic effects of atropine when used concurrently. Sympathomimetic amines may cause tachyarrhythmias; avoid concurrent use.
Decreased Effect: Effect of some phenothiazines may be antagonized. Levodopa effects may be decreased (limited clinical validation). Drugs with cholinergic mechanisms (metoclopramide, cisapride, bethanechol) decrease anticholinergic effects of atropine.

Stability Store injection at controlled room temperature of 15°C to 30°C (59°F to 86°F); avoid freezing. In addition, AtroPen® should be protected from light.

Mechanism of Action Blocks the action of acetylcholine at parasympathetic sites in smooth muscle, secretory glands, and the CNS; increases cardiac output, dries secretions, antagonizes histamine and serotonin

Pharmacodynamics/Kinetics
Onset of action: I.V.: Rapid
Absorption: Complete
Distribution: Widely throughout the body; crosses placenta; trace amounts enter breast milk; crosses blood-brain barrier
Metabolism: Hepatic
Half-life elimination: 2-3 hours
Excretion: Urine (30% to 50% as unchanged drug and metabolites)

Dosage
Neonates, Infants, and Children: Doses <0.1 mg have been associated with paradoxical bradycardia.
Inhibit salivation and secretions (preanesthesia): Oral, I.M., I.V., SubQ:
<5 kg: 0.02 mg/kg/dose 30-60 minutes preop then every 4-6 hours as needed. Use of a minimum dosage of 0.1 mg in neonates <5 kg will result in dosages >0.02 mg/kg. There is no documented minimum dosage in this age group.
>5 kg: 0.01-0.02 mg/kg/dose to a maximum 0.4 mg/dose 30-60 minutes preop; minimum dose: 0.1 mg
Alternate dosing:
3-7 kg (7-16 lb): 0.1 mg
8-11 kg (17-24 lb): 0.15 mg
11-18 kg (24-40 lb): 0.2 mg
(Continued)

Atropine *(Continued)*

18-29 kg (40-65 lb): 0.3 mg

>30 kg (>65 lb): 0.4 mg

Bradycardia: I.V., intratracheal: 0.02 mg/kg, minimum dose 0.1 mg, maximum single dose: 0.5 mg in children and 1 mg in adolescents; may repeat in 5-minute intervals to a maximum total dose of 1 mg in children or 2 mg in adolescents. (**Note:** For intratracheal administration, the dosage must be diluted with normal saline to a total volume of 1-5 mL). When treating bradycardia in neonates, reserve use for those patients unresponsive to improved oxygenation and epinephrine.

Infants and Children: Nerve agent toxicity management (unlabeled use): See **Note** under adult dosing.

Prehospital ("in the field"): I.M.:

Birth to <2 years: Mild-to-moderate symptoms: 0.05 mg/kg; severe symptoms: 0.1 mg/kg

2-10 years: Mild-to-moderate symptoms: 1 mg; severe symptoms: 2 mg

>10 years: Mild-to-moderate symptoms: 2 mg; severe symptoms: 4 mg

Hospital/emergency department: I.M.:

Birth to <2 years: Mild-to-moderate symptoms: 0.05 mg/kg I.M. **or** 0.02 mg/kg I.V.; severe symptoms: 0.1 mg/kg I.M. **or** 0.02 mg/kg I.V.

2-10 years: Mild-to-moderate symptoms: 1 mg; severe symptoms: 2 mg

>10 years: Mild-to-moderate symptoms: 2 mg; severe symptoms: 4 mg

Note: Pralidoxime is a component of the management of nerve agent toxicity; consult Pralidoxime for specific route and dose. For prehospital ("in the field") management, repeat atropine I.M. (children: 0.05-0.1 mg/kg) at 5-10 minute intervals until secretions have diminished and breathing is comfortable or airway resistance has returned to near normal. For hospital management, repeat atropine I.M. (infants 1 mg; all others: 2 mg) at 5-10 minute intervals until secretions have diminished and breathing is comfortable or airway resistance has returned to near normal.

Children: Organophosphate or carbamate poisoning:

I.V.: 0.03-0.05 mg/kg every 10-20 minutes until atropine effect, then every 1-4 hours for at least 24 hours

I.M. (AtroPen®): Mild symptoms: Administer dose listed below as soon as exposure is known or suspected. If severe symptoms develop after first dose, 2 additional doses should be repeated in 10 minutes; do not administer more than 3 doses. Severe symptoms: Immediately administer 3 doses as follows:

<6.8 kg (15 lb): Use of **AtroPen® formulation not recommended;** administer atropine 0.05 mg/kg

6.8-18 kg (15-40 lb): 0.5 mg/dose

18-41 kg (40-90 lb): 1 mg/dose

>41 kg (>90 lb): 2 mg/dose

Adults (doses <0.5 mg have been associated with paradoxical bradycardia):

Asystole or pulseless electrical activity:

I.V.: 1 mg; repeat in 3-5 minutes if asystole persists; total dose of 0.04 mg/kg.

Intratracheal: Administer 2-2.5 times the recommended I.V. dose; dilute in 10 mL NS or distilled water. **Note:** Absorption is greater with distilled water, but causes more adverse effects on PaO_2.

Inhibit salivation and secretions (preanesthesia):

I.M., I.V., SubQ: 0.4-0.6 mg 30-60 minutes preop and repeat every 4-6 hours as needed

Oral: 0.4 mg; may repeat in 4 hours if necessary; 0.4 mg initial dose may be exceeded in certain cases and may repeat in 4 hours if necessary

Bradycardia: I.V.: 0.5-1 mg every 5 minutes, not to exceed a total of 3 mg or 0.04 mg/kg; may give intratracheally in 10 mL NS (intratracheal dose should be 2-2.5 times the I.V. dose)

Neuromuscular blockade reversal: I.V.: 25-30 mcg/kg 30-60 seconds before neostigmine or 7-10 mcg/kg 30-60 seconds before edrophonium

Organophosphate or carbamate poisoning:

I.V.: 2 mg, followed by 2 mg every 5-60 minutes until adequate atropinization has occurred; initial doses of up to 6 mg may be used in life-threatening cases

I.M. (AtroPen®): Mild symptoms: Administer 2 mg as soon as exposure is known or suspected. If severe symptoms develop after first dose, 2 additional doses should be repeated in 10 minutes; do not administer more than 3 doses. Severe symptoms: Immediately administer three 2 mg doses.

Nerve agent toxicity management (unlabeled use): I.M.: See **Note.** Prehospital ("in the field") or hospital/emergency department: Mild-to-moderate symptoms: 2-4 mg; severe symptoms: 6 mg

Note: Pralidoxime is a component of the management of nerve agent toxicity; consult Pralidoxime for specific route and dose. For prehospital ("in the field") management, repeat atropine I.M. (2 mg) at 5-10 minute intervals until secretions have diminished and breathing is comfortable or airway resistance has returned to near normal. For hospital management, repeat atropine I.M. (2 mg) at 5-10 minute intervals until secretions have diminished and breathing is comfortable or airway resistance has returned to near normal.

Mydriasis, cycloplegia (preprocedure): Ophthalmic (1% solution): Instill 1-2 drops 1 hour before procedure.

Uveitis: Ophthalmic:

1% solution: Instill 1-2 drops 4 times/day

Ointment: Apply a small amount in the conjunctival sac up to 3 times/day; compress the lacrimal sac by digital pressure for 1-3 minutes after instillation

Elderly, frail patients: Nerve agent toxicity management (unlabeled use): I.M.: See **Note** under adult dosing.

Prehospital ("in the field"): Mild-to-moderate symptoms: 1 mg; severe symptoms: 2-4 mg

Hospital/emergency department: Mild-to-moderate symptoms: 1 mg; severe symptoms: 2 mg

Administration

I.M.: AtroPen®: Administer to outer thigh. May be given through clothing as long as pockets at the injection site are empty. Hold autoinjector in place for 10 seconds following injection; massage the injection site.

I.V.: Administer undiluted by rapid I.V. injection; slow injection may result in paradoxical bradycardia.

Intratracheal: Dilute in NS or distilled water. Absorption is greater with distilled water, but causes more adverse effects on PaO_2. Pass catheter beyond tip of tracheal tube, stop compressions, spray drug quickly down tube. Follow immediately with several quick insufflations and continue chest compressions.

Monitoring Parameters Heart rate, blood pressure, pulse, mental status; intravenous administration requires a cardiac monitor

Dosage Forms

Injection, solution, as sulfate: 0.05 mg/mL (5 mL); 0.1 mg/mL (5 mL, 10 mL); 0.4 mg/0.5 mL (0.5 mL); 0.4 mg/mL (0.5 mL, 1 mL, 20 mL); 1 mg/mL (1 mL)

AtroPen® [prefilled autoinjector]: 0.5 mg/0.7 mL (0.7 mL); 1 mg/0.7 mL (0.7 mL); 2 mg/0.7 mL (0.7 mL)

Ointment, ophthalmic, as sulfate: 1% (3.5 g)

Solution, ophthalmic, as sulfate: 1% (2 mL, 5 mL, 15 mL)

Atropine-Care®: 1% (2 mL) [contains benzalkonium chloride]

Isopto® Atropine: 1% (5 mL, 15 mL) [contains benzalkonium chloride]

Tablet, as sulfate (Sal-Tropine™): 0.4 mg

- ♦ **Atropine and Difenoxin** see Difenoxin and Atropine on page 499
- ♦ **Atropine and Diphenoxylate** see Diphenoxylate and Atropine on page 518
- ♦ **Atropine-Care®** see Atropine on page 176
- ♦ **Atropine, Hyoscyamine, Scopolamine, and Phenobarbital** see Hyoscyamine, Atropine, Scopolamine, and Phenobarbital on page 868
- ♦ **Atropine Sulfate** see Atropine on page 176
- ♦ **Atropine Sulfate and Edrophonium Chloride** see Edrophonium and Atropine on page 570
- ♦ **Atrovent®** see Ipratropium on page 932
- ♦ **Atrovent® HFA** see Ipratropium on page 932
- ♦ **A/T/S®** see Erythromycin on page 609
- ♦ **Attenuvax®** see Measles Virus Vaccine (Live) on page 1058
- ♦ **Atuss® HX** see Hydrocodone and Guaifenesin on page 849
- ♦ **Augmentin®** see Amoxicillin and Clavulanate Potassium on page 112
- ♦ **Augmentin ES-600®** see Amoxicillin and Clavulanate Potassium on page 112
- ♦ **Augmentin XR®** see Amoxicillin and Clavulanate Potassium on page 112
- ♦ **Auralgan® (Can)** see Antipyrine and Benzocaine on page 137

Auranofin (au RANE oh fin)

U.S. Brand Names Ridaura®

Canadian Brand Names Ridaura®

Pharmacologic Category Gold Compound

Use Management of active stage of classic or definite rheumatoid arthritis in patients who do not respond to or tolerate other agents; psoriatic arthritis; adjunctive or alternative therapy for pemphigus

Pregnancy Risk Factor C

Lactation Enters breast milk/contraindicated

Medication Safety Issues

Sound-alike/look-alike issues:

Ridaura® may be confused with Cardura®

Contraindications Hypersensitivity to auranofin or any component of the formulation; renal disease, history of blood dyscrasias, congestive heart failure, exfoliative dermatitis, necrotizing enterocolitis, history of anaphylactic reactions

Warnings/Precautions [U.S. Boxed Warning]: The possibility of adverse effects should be explained, as well as their manifestations; patients should be instructed to contact the prescriber with symptoms which may suggest toxicity. Hematologic toxicity, renal toxicity (hematuria, proteinuria), mucosal (stomatitis or persistent diarrhea), and dermatologic toxicities (pruritus, rash) may occur. Laboratory monitoring should be completed prior to each new prescription. Therapy should be discontinued if platelet count falls to <100,000/mm³. WBC <4000, granulocytes <1500/mm³. NSAIDs and corticosteroids may be discontinued after starting gold therapy. Use with caution in patients with renal or hepatic impairment.

Adverse Reactions

>10%:

Dermatologic: Itching, rash

Gastrointestinal: Stomatitis

Ocular: Conjunctivitis

Renal: Proteinuria

1% to 10%:

Dermatologic: Urticaria, alopecia

Gastrointestinal: Glossitis

Hematologic: Eosinophilia, leukopenia, thrombocytopenia

Renal: Hematuria

<1% (Limited to important or life-threatening): Agranulocytosis, anemia, angioedema, aplastic anemia, dysphagia, GI hemorrhage, gingivitis, hepatotoxicity, interstitial pneumonitis, metallic taste, peripheral neuropathy, ulcerative enterocolitis

Overdosage/Toxicology Symptoms include hematuria, proteinuria, fever, nausea, vomiting, and diarrhea. Signs of gold toxicity include decrease in hemoglobin, leukopenia, granulocytes and platelets, proteinuria, hematuria, pruritus, stomatitis or persistent diarrhea. Advise

(Continued)

Auranofin *(Continued)*

patients to report any symptoms of toxicity. Metallic taste may indicate stomatitis. For mild gold poisoning, dimercaprol 2.5 mg/kg 4 times/day for 2 days, or for more severe forms of gold intoxication, dimercaprol 3 mg/kg every 4 hours for 2 days, should be initiated. After 2 days the initial dose should be repeated twice daily on the third day and once daily thereafter for 10 days. Other chelating agents have been used with some success.

Drug Interactions

Increased Effect/Toxicity: Toxicity of penicillamine, antimalarials, hydroxychloroquine, cytotoxic agents, and immunosuppressants may be increased.

Stability Store in tight, light-resistant containers at 15°C to 30°C.

Mechanism of Action The exact mechanism of action of gold is unknown; gold is taken up by macrophages which results in inhibition of phagocytosis and lysosomal membrane stabilization; other actions observed are decreased serum rheumatoid factor and alterations in immunoglobulins. Additionally, complement activation is decreased, prostaglandin synthesis is inhibited, and lysosomal enzyme activity is decreased.

Pharmacodynamics/Kinetics

Onset of action: Delayed; therapeutic response may require as long as 3-4 months

Duration: Prolonged

Absorption: Oral: ~20% gold in dose is absorbed

Protein binding: 60%

Half-life elimination (single or multiple dose dependent): 21-31 days

Time to peak, serum: ~2 hours

Excretion: Urine (60% of absorbed gold); remainder in feces

Dosage Oral:

Children: Initial: 0.1 mg/kg/day divided daily; usual maintenance: 0.15 mg/kg/day in 1-2 divided doses; maximum: 0.2 mg/kg/day in 1-2 divided doses

Adults: 6 mg/day in 1-2 divided doses; after 3 months may be increased to 9 mg/day in 3 divided doses; if still no response after 3 months at 9 mg/day, discontinue drug

Dosing adjustment in renal impairment:

Cl_{cr} 50-80 mL/minute: Reduce dose to 50%

Cl_{cr} <50 mL/minute: Avoid use

Monitoring Parameters Monitor urine for protein; CBC and platelets; monitor for mouth ulcers and skin reactions; may monitor auranofin serum levels

Reference Range Gold: Normal: 0-0.1 mcg/mL (SI: 0-0.0064 µmol/L); Therapeutic: 1-3 mcg/mL (SI: 0.06-0.18 µmol/L); Urine: <0.1 mcg/24 hours

Test Interactions May enhance the response to a tuberculin skin test

Dosage Forms Capsule: 3 mg [29% gold]

- ◆ **Aurodex** *see* Antipyrine and Benzocaine *on page 137*
- ◆ **Aurolate®** *see* Gold Sodium Thiomalate *on page 808*
- ◆ **Autoplex® T [DSC]** *see* Anti-inhibitor Coagulant Complex *on page 137*
- ◆ **AVA** *see* Anthrax Vaccine Adsorbed *on page 132*
- ◆ **Avagard™ [OTC]** *see* Chlorhexidine Gluconate *on page 344*
- ◆ **Avage™** *see* Tazarotene *on page 1635*
- ◆ **Avalide®** *see* Irbesartan and Hydrochlorothiazide *on page 935*
- ◆ **Avandamet®** *see* Rosiglitazone and Metformin *on page 1537*
- ◆ **Avandaryl™** *see* Rosiglitazone and Glimepiride *on page 1536*
- ◆ **Avandia®** *see* Rosiglitazone *on page 1535*
- ◆ **Avapro®** *see* Irbesartan *on page 934*
- ◆ **Avapro® HCT** *see* Irbesartan and Hydrochlorothiazide *on page 935*
- ◆ **AVAR™** *see* Sulfur and Sulfacetamide *on page 1618*
- ◆ **AVAR™-e** *see* Sulfur and Sulfacetamide *on page 1618*
- ◆ **AVAR™-e Green** *see* Sulfur and Sulfacetamide *on page 1618*
- ◆ **AVAR™ Green** *see* Sulfur and Sulfacetamide *on page 1618*
- ◆ **Avastin®** *see* Bevacizumab *on page 217*
- ◆ **Avaxim® (Can)** *see* Hepatitis A Vaccine *on page 833*
- ◆ **Avaxim®-Pediatric (Can)** *see* Hepatitis A Vaccine *on page 833*
- ◆ **Avelox®** *see* Moxifloxacin *on page 1175*
- ◆ **Avelox® I.V.** *see* Moxifloxacin *on page 1175*
- ◆ **Aventyl® (Can)** *see* Nortriptyline *on page 1243*
- ◆ **Aviane™** *see* Ethinyl Estradiol and Levonorgestrel *on page 653*
- ◆ **Avinza®** *see* Morphine Sulfate *on page 1171*
- ◆ **Avita®** *see* Tretinoin (Topical) *on page 1732*
- ◆ **Avitene®** *see* Collagen Hemostat *on page 416*
- ◆ **Avitene® Flour** *see* Collagen Hemostat *on page 416*
- ◆ **Avitene® Ultrafoam** *see* Collagen Hemostat *on page 416*
- ◆ **Avitene® UltraWrap™** *see* Collagen Hemostat *on page 416*
- ◆ **Avodart™** *see* Dutasteride *on page 565*
- ◆ **Avonex®** *see* Interferon Beta-1a *on page 926*
- ◆ **Axert™** *see* Almotriptan *on page 73*
- ◆ **Axid®** *see* Nizatidine *on page 1238*
- ◆ **Axid® AR [OTC]** *see* Nizatidine *on page 1238*
- ◆ **AY-25650** *see* Triptorelin *on page 1750*
- ◆ **Ayr® Baby Saline [OTC]** *see* Sodium Chloride *on page 1576*
- ◆ **Ayr® Saline [OTC]** *see* Sodium Chloride *on page 1576*
- ◆ **Ayr® Saline No-Drip [OTC]** *see* Sodium Chloride *on page 1576*
- ◆ **5-Aza-2'-deoxycytidine** *see* Decitabine *on page 463*
- ◆ **5-AzaC** *see* Decitabine *on page 463*

Azacitidine (ay za SYE ti deen)

U.S. Brand Names Vidaza™
Index Terms AZA-CR; 5-Azacytidine; 5-AZC; Ladakamycin; NSC-102816
Pharmacologic Category Antineoplastic Agent, Antimetabolite (Pyrimidine)
Use Treatment of myelodysplastic syndrome (MDS)
Unlabeled/Investigational Use Investigational: Refractory acute lymphocytic and myelogenous leukemia
Pregnancy Risk Factor D
Pregnancy Implications Embryotoxicity, fetal death, and fetal abnormalities were observed in animal studies. Women of childbearing potential should be advised to avoid pregnancy during treatment. In addition, males should be advised to avoid fathering a child while on azacitidine therapy.
Lactation Excretion in breast milk unknown/not recommended
Medication Safety Issues
  High alert medication: The Institute for Safe Medication Practices (ISMP) includes this medication among its list of drugs which have a heightened risk of causing significant patient harm when used in error.
Contraindications Hypersensitivity to azacitidine, mannitol, or any component of the formulation; advanced malignant hepatic tumors; pregnancy
Warnings/Precautions Hazardous agent - use appropriate precautions for handling and disposal. Azacitidine may be hepatotoxic, use caution with hepatic impairment. Progressive hepatic coma leading to death has been reported (rare) in patients with extensive tumor burden, especially those with a baseline albumin <30 g/L. Use caution with renal impairment; dose adjustment may be required.
Adverse Reactions Note: Percentages reported are following SubQ administration unless otherwise noted.

  >10%:
    Cardiovascular: Hypotension (7%; I.V. 6% to 66% - incidence may be related to dose and rate of infusion), chest pain (16%), pallor (15%), peripheral edema (19%), pitting edema (14%)
    Central nervous system: Pyrexia (52%), fatigue (13% to 36%), headache (22%), dizziness (19%), anxiety (13%), depression (12%), insomnia (11%), malaise (11%), pain (11%)
    Dermatologic: Alopecia (I.V. 20%), bruising (30%), petechiae (24%), erythema (17%), skin lesion (14%), rash (14%)
    Gastrointestinal: Nausea (58% to 85%; more common/more severe with I.V. administration), vomiting (54%; more common/more severe with I.V. administration), mucositis (I.V. 23% to 45%), diarrhea (36%), constipation (34%), anorexia (21%), weight loss (16%), abdominal pain (15%), appetite decreased (13%), abdominal tenderness (12%)
    Hematologic: Anemia (70%), thrombocytopenia (66%), leukopenia (48%), neutropenia (32%), febrile neutropenia (16%)
    Nadir: Day 10-17
    Recovery: Day 28-31
    Hepatic: Hepatic enzymes increased (I.V. 37%)
    Local: Injection site:
      I.V.: Redness, irritation, and induration (80%)
      SubQ: Erythema (35%), pain (23%), bruising (14%)
    Neuromuscular & skeletal: Weakness (30%), rigors (26%), arthralgia (22%), limb pain (20%), back pain (19%), myalgia (16%)
    Respiratory: Cough (30%), dyspnea (5% to 30%), pharyngitis (20%), epistaxis (16%), nasopharyngitis (14%), upper respiratory tract infection (13%), productive cough (11%), pneumonia (11%)
    Miscellaneous: Contusion (19%)
  5% to 10%:
    Cardiovascular: Cardiac murmur (10%), tachycardia (9%), peripheral swelling (7%), syncope (6%), chest wall pain (5%), hypoesthesia (5%), postprocedural pain (5%)
    Central nervous system: Lethargy (8%)
    Dermatologic: Cellulitis (8%), urticaria (6%), dry skin (5%), skin nodule (5%)
    Gastrointestinal: Upper abdominal pain (10%), gingival bleeding (9%), oral mucosal petechiae (8%), stomatitis (8%), dyspepsia (7%), hemorrhoids (7%), abdominal distension (6%), loose stools (6%), dysphagia (5%), tongue ulceration (5%)
    Genitourinary: Dysuria (8%), urinary tract infection (8%)
    Hematologic: Hematoma (9%), postprocedural hemorrhage (6%)
    Local: Injection site: Pruritus (7%), granuloma (5%), pigmentation change (5%), swelling (5%)
    Neuromuscular & skeletal: Muscle cramps (6%)
    Respiratory: Crackles (10%), rhinorrhea (10%), wheezing (9%), breath sounds decreased (8%), pleural effusion (6%), postnasal drip (6%), rhonchi (6%), nasal congestion (5%), atelectasis (5%), sinusitis (5%)
    Miscellaneous: Diaphoresis (10%), lymphadenopathy (9%), herpes simplex (9%), night sweats (9%), transfusion reaction (7%), mouth hemorrhage (5%)
  <5% (Limited to important or life-threatening): Agranulocytosis, anaphylactic shock, bone marrow depression, CHF, convulsions, dehydration, diverticulitis, hypersensitivity reaction, pyoderma gangrenosum, splenomegaly; myalgia, weakness, and lethargy progressing to somnolence, stupor, or coma (<1%)
Overdosage/Toxicology Diarrhea, nausea, and vomiting were reported following a single I.V. dose of 290 mg/m². Treatment should be supportive.
Stability
  SubQ: Prior to reconstitution, store powder at room temperature of 15°C to 30°C (59°F to 86°F). To reconstitute, slowly add 4 mL SWFI to each vial. Invert vial 2-3 times and gently rotate until a suspension is formed. Following reconstitution, suspension may be stored at room temperature for up to 1 hour, or immediately refrigerated at 2°C to 8°C (36°F to 46°F) and stored for up to 8 hours.
  (Continued)

Azacitidine *(Continued)*

I.V.: **Solutions for injection have very limited stability and must be prepared fresh immediately prior to each dose.** Reconstitute vial with 19.9 mL of lactated Ringer's injection, 0.9% sodium chloride, or 5% dextrose to form a 5 mg/mL solution. Mix in 50-250 mL (final concentration ≥2 mg/mL) lactated Ringer's injection for infusion. Solutions (≥2 mg/mL) in lactated Ringer's injection are stable for 3 hours; solutions in 5% dextrose in water or 0.9% sodium chloride injection are only stable for ~1 hour.

Mechanism of Action Antineoplastic effects may be a result of azacitidine's ability to promote hypomethylation of DNA leading to direct toxicity of abnormal hematopoietic cells in the bone marrow.

Pharmacodynamics/Kinetics

Absorption: SubQ: Rapid and complete

Bioavailability: SubQ: 89%

Distribution: V_d: 76 ± 26 L; does not cross blood-brain barrier

Metabolism: Hepatic; hydrolysis to several metabolites

Half-life elimination: ~4 hours

Time to peak concentration: 30 minutes

Excretion: Urine (50% to 85%); feces (minor)

Dosage

I.V. (unlabeled use, doses reported in combination regimens):

Children:

Pediatric AML and ANLL: 250 mg/m² days 4 and 5 every 4 weeks

Pediatric AML induction: 300 mg/m² days 5 and 6

Adults:

Acute leukemia:

50-150 mg/m² days 1 through 5 of induction

200 mg/m² CIVI days 7 through 9 of induction

CML (accelerated phase and blast crisis): 50-150 mg/m² days 1 through 5 of induction

AML induction: 150 mg/m² days 3 through 5 and 8 through 10, **then**

150 mg/m² days 1 through 5 and 8 through 10 (cycle 2 consolidation)

AML consolidation: 150 mg/m² CIVI days 1 through 7 for 3 cycles

AML maintenance: 150 mg/m² days 1 through 3 every 6 weeks

MDS: 75-150 mg/m² CIVI days 1 through 7 every 4 weeks

SubQ: Adults: MDS: 75 mg/m²/day for 7 days repeated every 4 weeks. Dose may be increased to 100 mg/m²/day if no benefit is observed after 2 cycles and no toxicity other than nausea and vomiting have occurred. Treatment is recommended for at least 4 cycles.

Dosage adjustment based on hematology: Adults: SubQ:

For baseline WBC ≥3.0 x 10⁹/L, ANC ≥1.5 x 10⁹/L, and platelets ≥75 x 10⁹/L:

Nadir count: ANC <0.5 x 10⁹/L and platelets <25 x 10⁹/L: Administer 50% of dose during next treatment course

Nadir count: ANC 0.5-1.5 x 10⁹/L and platelets 25-50 x 10⁹/L: Administer 67% of dose during next treatment course

Nadir count: ANC >1.5 x 10⁹/L and platelets >50 x 10⁹/L: Administer 100% of dose during next treatment course

For baseline WBC <3 x 10⁹/L, ANC 1.5 x 10⁹/L, or platelets <75 x 10⁹/L: Adjust dose as follows based on nadir counts and bone marrow biopsy cellularity at the time of nadir, unless clear improvement in differentiation at the time of the next cycle:

WBC or platelet nadir decreased 50% to 75% from baseline and bone marrow biopsy cellularity at time of nadir 30% to 60%: Administer 100% of dose during next treatment course

WBC or platelet nadir decreased 50% to 75% from baseline and bone marrow biopsy cellularity at time of nadir 15% to 30%: Administer 50% of dose during next treatment course

WBC or platelet nadir decreased 50% to 75% from baseline and bone marrow biopsy cellularity at time of nadir <15%: Administer 33% of dose during next treatment course

WBC or platelet nadir decreased >75% from baseline and bone marrow biopsy cellularity at time of nadir 30% to 60%: Administer 75% of dose during next treatment course

WBC or platelet nadir decreased >75% from baseline and bone marrow biopsy cellularity at time of nadir 15% to 30%: Administer 50% of dose during next treatment course

WBC or platelet nadir decreased >75% from baseline and bone marrow biopsy cellularity at time of nadir <15%: Administer 33% of dose during next treatment course

Note: If a nadir defined above occurs, administer the next treatment course 28 days after the start of the preceding course as long as WBC and platelet counts are >25% above the nadir and rising. If a >25% increase above the nadir is not seen by day 28, reassess counts every 7 days. If a 25% increase is not seen by day 42, administer 50% of the scheduled dose.

Dosage adjustment base on serum electrolytes: The manufacturer recommends that if serum bicarbonate falls to <20 mEq/L (unexplained decrease): Reduce dose by 50% for next treatment course

Dosage adjustment in renal impairment: If increases in BUN or serum creatinine occur, delay next cycle until values reach baseline or normal, then reduce dose by 50% for next treatment course.

Administration

SubQ: Premedication for nausea and vomiting is recommended. Volumes >2 mL may be divided into two syringes and injected into two separate sites. Allow refrigerated suspensions to come to room temperature (up to 30 minutes) prior to administration. Resuspend by gently rolling the syringe between the palms for 30 seconds. If azacitidine suspension comes in contact with the skin, immediately wash with soap and water.

Premedication for nausea and vomiting is recommended. Administer as short (15 minutes to 2 hours) bolus or continuous (24 hours) infusion. Due to azacitidine's limited stability, for continuous infusions the daily dose should be divided by 12, and a freshly prepared bag, using a freshly reconstituted vial, started every 2 hours.

Monitoring Parameters Liver function tests, electrolytes, CBC, renal function tests (BUN and serum creatinine) should be obtained prior to initiation of therapy. Electrolytes, renal function (BUN and creatinine), CBC should be monitored periodically to monitor response and toxicity. At a minimum, CBC should be repeated prior to each cycle.

Dosage Forms

Injection, powder for suspension [preservative free]:
Vidaza™: 100 mg [contains mannitol 100 mg]

♦ AZA-CR *see* Azacitidine *on page 181*

♦ Azactam® *see* Aztreonam *on page 189*

♦ 5-Azacytidine *see* Azacitidine *on page 181*

♦ Azasan® *see* Azathioprine *on page 183*

Azathioprine (ay za THYE oh preen)

U.S. Brand Names Azasan®; Imuran®

Canadian Brand Names Alti-Azathioprine; Apo-Azathioprine®; Gen-Azathioprine; Imuran®; Novo-Azathioprine

Index Terms Azathioprine Sodium

Pharmacologic Category Immunosuppressant Agent

Use Adjunctive therapy in prevention of rejection of kidney transplants; active rheumatoid arthritis

Unlabeled/Investigational Use Adjunct in prevention of rejection of solid organ (nonrenal) transplants; steroid-sparing agent for corticosteroid-dependent Crohn's disease (CD) and ulcerative colitis (UC); maintenance of remission in CD; fistulizing Crohn's disease

Pregnancy Risk Factor D

Pregnancy Implications Azathioprine was found to be teratogenic in animal studies; temporary depression in spermatogenesis and reduction in sperm viability and sperm count were also reported in mice. Azathioprine crosses the placenta in humans; congenital anomalies, immunosuppression, and intrauterine growth retardation have been reported. There are no adequate and well-controlled studies in pregnant women. Azathioprine should not be used to treat arthritis during pregnancy. The potential benefit to the mother versus possible risk to the fetus should be considered when treating other disease states.

Lactation Enters breast milk/not recommended

Medication Safety Issues

Sound-alike/look-alike issues:

Azathioprine may be confused with azatadine, azidothymidine, Azulfidine®

Imuran® may be confused with Elmiron®, Enduron®, Imdur®, Inderal®, Tenormin®

Azathioprine is metabolized to mercaptopurine; concurrent use of these commercially-available products has resulted in profound myelosuppression.

Contraindications Hypersensitivity to azathioprine or any component of the formulation; pregnancy

Warnings/Precautions [U.S. Boxed Warning]: Chronic immunosuppression increases the risk of neoplasia and serious infections. Azathioprine has mutagenic potential to both men and women and with possible hematologic toxicities; hematologic toxicities are dose related and may be more severe with renal transplants undergoing rejection. Gastrointestinal toxicity may occur within the first several weeks of therapy and is reversible. Symptoms may include severe nausea, vomiting, diarrhea, rash, fever, malaise, myalgia, hypotension, and liver enzyme abnormalities. Use with caution in patients with liver disease, renal impairment; monitor hematologic function closely. Patients with genetic deficiency of thiopurine methyltransferase (TPMT) or concurrent therapy with drugs which may inhibit TPMT may be sensitive to myelosuppressive effects. Azathioprine is metabolized to mercaptopurine; concomitant use may result in profound myelosuppression and should be avoided.

Adverse Reactions Frequency not defined; dependent upon dose, duration, and concomitant therapy.

Central nervous system: Chills, fever, malaise

Dermatologic: Alopecia, rash (erythematous or maculopapular)

Gastrointestinal: Diarrhea, nausea, pancreatitis, vomiting

Hematologic: Bleeding, leukopenia, macrocytic anemia, pancytopenia, thrombocytopenia

Hepatic: Hepatotoxicity, hepatic veno-occlusive disease, steatorrhea

Neuromuscular & skeletal: Arthralgia, myalgia

Respiratory: Interstitial pneumonitis

Miscellaneous: Hypersensitivity reactions (rare), infection secondary to immunosuppression, neoplasia

Overdosage/Toxicology Symptoms include nausea, vomiting, diarrhea, and hematologic toxicity. Following initiation of essential overdose management, symptomatic and supportive treatment should be instituted. Dialysis has been reported to remove significant amounts of the drug and its metabolites, and should be considered as a treatment option in those patients who deteriorate despite established forms of therapy.

Drug Interactions

Increased Effect/Toxicity: Allopurinol may increase serum levels of azathioprine's active metabolite (mercaptopurine). Decrease azathioprine dose to $\frac{1}{3}$ to $\frac{1}{4}$ of normal dose. Azathioprine and ACE inhibitors may induce anemia and severe leukopenia. Aminosalicylates (olsalazine, mesalamine, sulfasalazine) may inhibit TPMT, increasing toxicity/myelosuppression of azathioprine. Azathioprine is metabolized to mercaptopurine; concomitant use may result in profound myelosuppression and should be avoided.

Decreased Effect: Azathioprine may result in decreased action of warfarin.

Ethanol/Nutrition/Herb Interactions Herb/Nutraceutical: Avoid cat's claw, echinacea (have immunostimulant properties).

Stability

Tablet: Store at room temperature of 15°C to 25°C (59°F to 77°F); protect from light. (Continued)

Azathioprine (Continued)

Powder for injection: Store at room temperature of 15°C to 25°C (59°F to 77°F) and protect from light. Parenteral admixture is stable at room temperature (25°C) for 24 hours, and stable under refrigeration (4°C) for 16 days.

Mechanism of Action Azathioprine is an imidazolyl derivative of mercaptopurine; antagonizes purine metabolism and may inhibit synthesis of DNA, RNA, and proteins; may also interfere with cellular metabolism and inhibit mitosis. The 6-thioguanine nucleotides appear to mediate the majority of azathioprine's immunosuppressive and toxic effects.

Pharmacodynamics/Kinetics

Distribution: Crosses placenta

Protein binding: ~30%

Metabolism: Hepatic, to 6-mercaptopurine (6-MP), possibly by glutathione S-transferase (GST). Further metabolism of 6-MP (in the liver and GI tract), via three major pathways: Hypoxanthine guanine phosphoribosyltransferase (to 6-thioguanine-nucleotides, or 6-TGN), xanthine oxidase (to 6-thiouric acid), and thiopurine methyltransferase (TPMT), which forms 6-methylmercaptopurine (6-MMP).

Half-life elimination: Parent drug: 12 minutes; mercaptopurine: 0.7-3 hours; End-stage renal disease: Slightly prolonged

Time to peak, plasma: 1-2 hours (including metabolites)

Excretion: Urine (primarily as metabolites)

Dosage I.V. dose is equivalent to oral dose (dosing should be based on ideal body weight):

Children (unlabeled) and Adults:

Renal transplantation: Oral, I.V.: Initial: 3-5 mg/kg/day usually given as a single daily dose, then 1-3 mg/kg/day maintenance

Rheumatoid arthritis: Oral:

Initial: 1 mg/kg/day given once daily or divided twice daily for 6-8 weeks; increase by 0.5 mg/kg every 4 weeks until response or up to 2.5 mg/kg/day; an adequate trial should be a minimum of 12 weeks

Maintenance dose: Reduce dose by 0.5 mg/kg every 4 weeks until lowest effective dose is reached; optimum duration of therapy not specified; may be discontinued abruptly

Adults: Oral:

Adjunctive management of severe recurrent aphthous stomatitis (unlabeled use): 50 mg once daily in conjunction with prednisone

Reduction of steroid use in CD or UC, maintenance of remission in CD or fistulizing disease (unlabeled uses): Initial: 50 mg daily; may increase by 25 mg/day every 1-2 weeks as tolerated to target dose of 2-3 mg/kg/day

Dosing adjustment in renal impairment:

Cl_{cr} 10-50 mL/minute: Administer 75% of normal dose daily

Cl_{cr} <10 mL/minute: Administer 50% of normal dose daily

Hemodialysis: Dialyzable (~45% removed in 8 hours)

Administer dose posthemodialysis: CAPD effects: Unknown; CAVH effects: Unknown

Dietary Considerations May be taken with food.

Administration

I.V.: Azathioprine can be administered IVP over 5 minutes at a concentration not to exceed 10 mg/mL **or** azathioprine can be further diluted with normal saline or D_5W and administered by intermittent infusion usually over 30-60 minutes; may be extended up to 8 hours.

Oral: Administering tablets after meals or in divided doses may decrease adverse GI events.

Monitoring Parameters CBC, platelet counts, total bilirubin, liver function tests, TPMT genotyping or phenotyping

For use as immunomodulatory therapy in CD or UC, monitor CBC with differential weekly for 1 month, then biweekly for 1 month, followed by monitoring every 1-2 months throughout the course of therapy. LFT's should be assessed every 3 months.

Dosage Forms

Injection, powder for reconstitution: 100 mg

Tablet [scored]: 50 mg

Azasan®: 75 mg, 100 mg

Imuran®: 50 mg

Extemporaneous Preparations A 50 mg/mL oral suspension can be prepared by crushing one hundred twenty (120) 50 mg tablets in a mortar (reducing to a fine powder), and then mixing in a small amount of vehicle (a 1:1 combination of Ora-Sweet® or Ora-Sweet® SF and Ora-Plus®) to create a uniform paste. Continue to add vehicle in geometric amounts (while mixing) until near-final volume is achieved. Transfer to a graduate and add sufficient quantity to make 120 mL. Label "shake well" and "refrigerate." Refrigerated stability is 60 days.

Allen LV Jr and Erickson MA III, "Stability of Acetazolamide, Allopurinol, Azathioprine, Clonazepam, and Flucytosine in Extemporaneously Compounded Oral Liquids," Am J Health Syst Pharm, 1996, 53(16):1944-9.

Nahata MC, Morosco RS, and Hipple TF, 4th ed, Pediatric Drug Formulations, Cincinnati, OH: Harvey Whitney Books Co, 2000.

♦ **Azathioprine Sodium** see Azathioprine on page 183

♦ **5-AZC** see Azacitidine on page 181

Azelaic Acid (a zeh LAY ik AS id)

U.S. Brand Names Azelex®; Finacea®

Pharmacologic Category Topical Skin Product, Acne

Use Topical treatment of inflammatory papules and pustules of mild-to-moderate rosacea; mild-to-moderate inflammatory acne vulgaris

Finacea®: Not FDA-approved for the treatment of acne

Pregnancy Risk Factor B

Dosage Topical:

Adolescents ≥12 years and Adults: Acne vulgaris: Cream 20%: After skin is thoroughly washed and patted dry, gently but thoroughly massage a thin film of azelaic acid cream into the affected areas twice daily, in the morning and evening. The duration of use can vary and depends on the severity of the acne. In the majority of patients with inflammatory lesions, improvement of the condition occurs within 4 weeks.

Adults: Rosacea: Gel 15%: Massage gently into affected areas of the face twice daily; use beyond 12 weeks has not been studied

Additional Information Complete prescribing information for this medication should be consulted for additional detail.

Dosage Forms
Cream:
Azelex®: 20% (30 g, 50 g) [contains benzoic acid and propylene glycol]
Gel:
Finacea®: 15% (30 g) [contains benzoic acid and propylene glycol]

Azelastine (a ZEL as teen)

U.S. Brand Names Astelin®; Optivar®
Canadian Brand Names Astelin®
Index Terms Azelastine Hydrochloride
Pharmacologic Category Antihistamine
Use
Nasal spray: Treatment of the symptoms of seasonal allergic rhinitis such as rhinorrhea, sneezing, and nasal pruritus in children ≥5 years of age and adults; treatment of the symptoms of vasomotor rhinitis in children ≥12 years of age and adults
Ophthalmic: Treatment of itching of the eye associated with seasonal allergic conjunctivitis in children >3 years of age and adults

Pregnancy Risk Factor C
Pregnancy Implications There are no adequate and well-controlled studies in pregnant women. Animal reproduction studies have shown toxic effects to the fetus at maternally toxic doses. Use during pregnancy only if the potential benefit to the mother outweighs the possible risk to the fetus.

Lactation Excretion in breast milk unknown/use caution
Medication Safety Issues
Sound-alike/look-alike issues:
Optivar® may be confused with Optiray®

International issues:
Optivar® may be confused with Opthavir® which is a brand name for acyclovir in Mexico
Contraindications Hypersensitivity to azelastine or any component of the formulation
Warnings/Precautions
Nasal spray: May cause drowsiness in some patients; instruct patient to use caution when driving or operating machinery. Effects may be additive with CNS depressants and/or ethanol. Safety and efficacy in children <5 years of age have not been established.
Ophthalmic: Solution contains benzalkonium chloride; wait at least 10 minutes after instilling solution before inserting soft contact lenses. Do not use contact lenses if eyes are red.
Adverse Reactions
Nasal spray:
>10%:
Central nervous system: Headache (8% to 15%), somnolence (<1% to 12%)
Gastrointestinal: Bitter taste (8% to 20%)
Respiratory: Cold symptoms/rhinitis (2% to 17%), cough (11%)
2% to 10%:
Central nervous system: Dysesthesia (8%), dizziness (2%), fatigue (2%)
Gastrointestinal: Nausea (3%), weight gain (2%), dry mouth (3%)
Ocular: Conjunctivitis (<2% to 5%)
Respiratory: Asthma (5%), nasal burning (4%), pharyngitis (4%), paroxysmal sneezing (3%), sinusitis (3%), epistaxis (2% to 3%)
<2%:
Cardiovascular: Flushing, hypertension, tachycardia
Central nervous system: Abnormal thinking, anxiety, depersonalization, depression, drowsiness, fever, hypoesthesia, malaise, nervousness, sleep disorder, vertigo
Dermatologic: Contact dermatitis, eczema, furunculosis, hair and follicle infection
Endocrine & metabolic: Amenorrhea, breast pain
Gastrointestinal: Abdominal pain, ALT increased, aphthous stomatitis, appetite increased, constipation, diarrhea, gastroenteritis, glossitis, ulcerative stomatitis, toothache, vomiting
Genitourinary: Albuminuria, hematuria, polyuria
Hepatic: Liver enzymes increased
Neuromuscular & skeletal: Back pain, extremity pain, hyperkinesia, myalgia, rheumatoid arthritis, temporomandibular dislocation
Ocular: Eye pain, watery eyes
Respiratory: Bronchitis, bronchospasm, laryngitis, nasal congestion, nocturnal dyspnea, postnasal drip, sinus hypersecretion, throat burning
Miscellaneous: Allergic reactions, viral infection
<1%, postmarketing, and/or case reports: Anaphylactoid reaction, chest pain, nasal congestion, confusion, diarrhea, dyspnea, facial edema, involuntary muscle contractions, paresthesia, parosmia, pruritus, rash, skin irritation, tolerance, urinary retention, visual abnormalities, xerophthalmia
Ophthalmic:
>10%:
Central nervous system: Headache (15%)
Ocular: Transient burning/stinging (30%)
1% to 10%:
Central nervous system: Fatigue
Gastrointestinal: Bitter taste (10%)
Ocular: Conjunctivitis, eye pain, blurred vision (temporary)
(Continued)

Azelastine (Continued)

Respiratory: Asthma, dyspnea, pharyngitis
Miscellaneous: Flu-like syndrome

Overdosage/Toxicology There have been no reported overdoses with azelastine. Increased somnolence is likely to occur. Supportive measures should be employed.

Drug Interactions

Cytochrome P450 Effect: Substrate (minor) of CYP1A2, 2C19, 2D6, 3A4; **Inhibits** CYP2B6 (weak), 2C9 (weak), 2C19 (weak), 2D6 (weak), 3A4 (weak)

Increased Effect/Toxicity: Azelastine may increase the CNS effects of ethanol and the arrhythmogenic effects of antipsychotics agents (phenothiazines). Other anticholinergics, cimetidine, CNS depressants and pramlintide may enhance the effects of azelastine.

Decreased Effect: Acetylcholinesterase inhibitors (central) may decreased the effects of azelastine; azelastine may diminish the effects of acetylcholinesterase inhibitors.

Ethanol/Nutrition/Herb Interactions Ethanol: Avoid ethanol (may cause increased somnolence or fatigue).

Stability

Nasal spray: Store upright at controlled room temperature of 20°C to 25°C (68°F to 77°F). Protect from freezing.

Ophthalmic solution: Store upright between 2°C to 25°C (36°F to 77°F).

Mechanism of Action Competes with histamine for H_1-receptor sites on effector cells and inhibits the release of histamine and other mediators involved in the allergic response; when used intranasally, reduces hyper-reactivity of the airways; increases the motility of bronchial epithelial cilia, improving mucociliary transport

Pharmacodynamics/Kinetics

Onset of action: Peak effect: Nasal spray: 3 hours; Ophthalmic solution: 3 minutes
Duration: Nasal spray: 12 hours; Ophthalmic solution: 8 hours
Protein binding: 88%
Metabolism: Hepatic via CYP; active metabolite, desmethylazelastine
Bioavailability: Intranasal: 40%
Half-life elimination: 22 hours
Time to peak, serum: 2-3 hours

Dosage

Children 5-11 years: Seasonal allergic rhinitis: Intranasal: 1 spray each nostril twice daily
Children ≥3 years and Adults: Itching eyes due to seasonal allergic conjunctivitis: Ophthalmic: Instill 1 drop into affected eye(s) twice daily
Children ≥12 years and Adults:
  Seasonal allergic rhinitis: Intranasal: 1-2 sprays (137 mcg/spray) each nostril twice daily
  Vasomotor rhinitis: Intranasal: 2 sprays each nostril twice daily.

Administration Intranasal: Before initial use of the nasal spray, the delivery system should be primed with 4 sprays or until a fine mist appears. If 3 or more days have elapsed since last use, the delivery system should be reprimed with 2 sprays or until a fine mist appears.

Dosage Forms

Solution, intranasal, as hydrochloride [spray]:
  Astelin®: 1 mg/mL(30 mL) [contains benzalkonium chloride; 137 mcg/spray; 200 metered sprays]
Solution, ophthalmic, as hydrochloride:
  Optivar®: 0.05% (6 mL) [contains benzalkonium chloride]

♦ **Azelastine Hydrochloride** see Azelastine on page 185
♦ **Azelex®** see Azelaic Acid on page 184
♦ **Azidothymidine** see Zidovudine on page 1812
♦ **Azidothymidine, Abacavir, and Lamivudine** see Abacavir, Lamivudine, and Zidovudine on page 19
♦ **Azilect®** see Rasagiline on page 1488

Azithromycin (az ith roe MYE sin)

U.S. Brand Names Zithromax®; Zmax™
Canadian Brand Names Apo-Azithromycin®; CO Azithromycin; GMD-Azithromycin; Novo-Azithromycin; PMS-Azithromycin; ratio-Azithromycin; Sandoz-Azithromycin; Zithromax®
Index Terms Azithromycin Dihydrate; Zithromax® TRI-PAK™; Zithromax® Z-PAK®
Pharmacologic Category Antibiotic, Macrolide

Additional Appendix Information

Antimicrobial Drugs of Choice on page 1981
Community-Acquired Pneumonia in Adults on page 1999
Prevention of Bacterial Endocarditis on page 1960
Treatment of Sexually Transmitted Infections on page 2007
USPHS / IDSA Guidelines for the Prevention of Opportunistic Infections in Persons Infected With HIV on page 1966

Use Treatment of acute otitis media due to H. influenzae, M. catarrhalis, or S. pneumoniae; pharyngitis/tonsillitis due to S. pyogenes; treatment of mild-to-moderate upper and lower respiratory tract infections, infections of the skin and skin structure, community-acquired pneumonia, pelvic inflammatory disease (PID), sexually-transmitted diseases (urethritis/cervicitis), pharyngitis/tonsillitis (alternative to first-line therapy), and genital ulcer disease (chancroid) due to susceptible strains of C. trachomatis, M. catarrhalis, H. influenzae, S. aureus, S. pneumoniae, Mycoplasma pneumoniae, and C. psittaci; acute bacterial exacerbations of chronic obstructive pulmonary disease (COPD) due to H. influenzae, M. catarrhalis, or S. pneumoniae; acute bacterial sinusitis

Unlabeled/Investigational Use Prevention of (or to delay onset of) or treatment of MAC in patients with advanced HIV infection; prophylaxis of bacterial endocarditis in patients who are allergic to penicillin and undergoing surgical or dental procedures; pertussis

Pregnancy Risk Factor B

Pregnancy Implications Azithromycin has been shown to cross the placenta. It has been used as an alternative treatment of *Chlamydia* in late-term pregnancy. There are no adequate and well-controlled studies in pregnant women; use during pregnancy only if clearly needed.

Lactation Enters breast milk/use caution

Medication Safety Issues
Sound-alike/look-alike issues:
Azithromycin may be confused with erythromycin
Zithromax® may be confused with Zinacef®

Contraindications Hypersensitivity to azithromycin, other macrolide antibiotics, or any component of the formulation

Warnings/Precautions Use with caution in patients with hepatic dysfunction; hepatic impairment with or without jaundice has occurred chiefly in older children and adults. It may be accompanied by malaise, nausea, vomiting, abdominal colic, and fever; discontinue use if these occur. May mask or delay symptoms of incubating gonorrhea or syphilis, so appropriate culture and susceptibility tests should be performed prior to initiating azithromycin. Pseudomembranous colitis has been reported with use of macrolide antibiotics; use caution with renal dysfunction. Prolongation of the QT$_c$ interval has been reported with macrolide antibiotics; use caution in patients at risk of prolonged cardiac repolarization. Safety and efficacy have not been established in children <6 months of age with acute otitis media, acute bacterial sinusitis, or community-acquired pneumonia, or in children <2 years of age with pharyngitis/tonsillitis. Suspensions (immediate release and extended release) are not interchangeable.

Adverse Reactions
>10%: Gastrointestinal: Diarrhea (4% to 11%)
1% to 10%:
Central nervous system: Headache
Gastrointestinal: Nausea, abdominal pain, cramping, vomiting (especially with high single-dose regimens)
<1% (Limited to important or life-threatening): Acute renal failure, allergic reaction, aggressive behavior, anaphylaxis, angioedema, arrhythmia (including ventricular tachycardia), cholestatic jaundice, constipation, convulsion, deafness, dehydration, enteritis, erythema multiforme (rare), hearing loss, hepatic necrosis (rare), hepatitis, hypertrophic pyloric stenosis, hypotension, interstitial nephritis, leukopenia, LFTs increased, neutropenia, oral candidiasis, oral moniliasis, palpitations, pancreatitis, paresthesia, pruritus, pseudomembranous colitis, QT$_c$ prolongation (rare), seizure, somnolence, Stevens-Johnson syndrome (rare), syncope, taste perversion, thrombocytopenia, tinnitus, tongue discoloration (rare), torsade de pointes (rare), urticaria, vertigo

Overdosage/Toxicology Symptoms include nausea, vomiting, diarrhea, and prostration. Treatment is supportive and symptomatic.

Drug Interactions
Cytochrome P450 Effect: Substrate of CYP3A4 (minor); **Inhibits** CYP3A4 (weak)
Increased Effect/Toxicity: Concurrent use of pimozide is contraindicated due to potential cardiotoxicity. The manufacturer warns that azithromycin potentially may increase levels of tacrolimus, phenytoin, ergot alkaloids, alfentanil, bromocriptine, carbamazepine, cyclosporine, digoxin, disopyramide, and triazolam. However, azithromycin did not affect the response/levels of carbamazepine, theophylline, or warfarin in specific interaction studies; caution is advised when administered together. Nelfinavir may increase azithromycin serum levels (monitor for adverse effects).
Decreased Effect: Decreased azithromycin peak serum concentrations with aluminum- and magnesium-containing antacids (by 24%), however, total absorption is unaffected.

Ethanol/Nutrition/Herb Interactions Food: Rate and extent of GI absorption may be altered depending upon the formulation. Azithromycin suspension, not tablet form, has significantly increased absorption (46%) with food.

Stability
Injection (Zithromax®): Store intact vials of injection at room temperature. Reconstitute the 500 mg vial with 4.8 mL of sterile water for injection and shake until all of the drug is dissolved. Each mL contains 100 mg azithromycin. Reconstituted solution is stable for 24 hours when stored below 30°C (86°F). Use of a standard syringe is recommended due to the vacuum in the vial (which may draw additional solution through an automated syringe). The initial solution should be further diluted to a concentration of 1 mg/mL (500 mL) to 2 mg/mL (250 mL) in 0.9% sodium chloride, 5% dextrose in water, or lactated Ringer's. The diluted solution is stable for 24 hours at or below room temperature (30°C or 86°F) and for 7 days if stored under refrigeration (5°C or 41°F).
Suspension, immediate release (Zithromax®): Store dry powder below 30°C (86°F). Following reconstitution, store at 5°C to 30°C (41°F to 86°F).
Suspension, extended release (Zmax™): Store dry powder below 30°C (86°F). Following reconstitution, store at 15°C to 30°C (59°F to 86°F); do not freeze. Should be consumed within 12 hours following reconstitution.
Tablet (Zithromax®): Store between 15°C to 30°C (59°F to 86°F).

Mechanism of Action Inhibits RNA-dependent protein synthesis at the chain elongation step; binds to the 50S ribosomal subunit resulting in blockage of transpeptidation

Pharmacodynamics/Kinetics
Absorption: Rapid
Distribution: Extensive tissue; distributes well into skin, lungs, sputum, tonsils, and cervix; penetration into CSF is poor; I.V.: 33.3 L/kg; Oral: 31.1 L/kg
Protein binding (concentration dependent): 7% to 51%
Metabolism: Hepatic
Bioavailability: 38%, decreased by 17% with extended release suspension; variable effect with food (increased with immediate or delayed release oral suspension, unchanged with tablet)
Half-life elimination: Terminal: Immediate release: 68-72 hours; Extended release: 59 hours
Time to peak, serum: Immediate release: 2-3 hours; Extended release: 5 hours
Excretion: Biliary (major route); urine (6%)
(Continued)

Azithromycin *(Continued)*

Dosage Note: Extended release suspension (Zmax™) is not interchangeable with immediate release formulations. Use should be limited to approved indications. All doses are expressed as immediate release azithromycin unless otherwise specified.

Usual dosage range:

Children ≥6 months: Oral: 5-12 mg/kg given once daily (maximum: 500 mg/day) **or** 30 mg/kg as a single dose (maximum: 1500 mg)

Adolescents ≥16 years and Adults:

Oral: 250-600 mg once daily **or** 1-2 g as a single dose

I.V.: 250-500 mg once daily

Indication-specific dosing:

Children: Oral:

Bacterial sinusitis: 10 mg/kg once daily for 3 days (maximum: 500 mg/day)

Cat scratch disease (unlabeled use): <45.5 kg: 10 mg/kg as a single dose, then 5 mg/kg once daily for 4 days

Community-acquired pneumonia: 10 mg/kg on day 1 (maximum: 500 mg/day) followed by 5 mg/kg/day once daily on days 2-5 (maximum: 250 mg/day)

Disseminated *M. avium* (unlabeled use):

HIV-infected patients: 5 mg/kg/day once daily (maximum: 250 mg/day) or 20 mg/kg (maximum: 1200 mg) once weekly given alone or in combination with rifabutin

Treatment and secondary prevention in HIV-negative patients: 5 mg/kg/day once daily (maximum: 250 mg/day) in combination with ethambutol, with or without rifabutin

Endocarditis, prophylaxis (unlabeled use): 15 mg/kg 1 hour before procedure (maximum: 500 mg)

Otitis media:

1-day regimen: 30 mg/kg as a single dose (maximum: 1500 mg)

3-day regimen: 10 mg/kg once daily for 3 days (maximum: 500 mg/day)

5-day regimen: 10 mg/kg on day 1 (maximum: 500 mg/day) followed by 5 mg/kg/day once daily on days 2-5 (maximum: 250 mg/day)

Pharyngitis, tonsillitis: Children ≥2 years: 12 mg/kg/day once daily for 5 days (maximum: 500 mg/day)

Pertussis (CDC guidelines):

Children <6 months: 10 mg/kg/day for 5 days

Children ≥6 months: 10 mg/kg on day 1 (maximum: 500 mg/day) followed by 5 mg/kg/day once daily on days 2-5 (maximum: 250 mg/day)

Uncomplicated chlamydial urethritis or cervicitis (unlabeled use): Children ≥45 kg: 1 g as a single dose

Adolescents ≥16 years and Adults:

Bacterial sinusitis: Oral: 500 mg/day for a total of 3 days

Extended release suspension (Zmax™): 2 g as a single dose

Cat scratch disease (unlabeled use): Oral: >45.5 kg: 500 mg as a single dose, then 250 mg once daily for 4 days

Chancroid due to *H. ducreyi*: Oral: 1 g as a single dose

Community-acquired pneumonia:

Oral (Zmax™): 2 g as a single dose

I.V.: 500 mg as a single dose for at least 2 days, follow I.V. therapy by the oral route with a single daily dose of 500 mg to complete a 7- to 10-day course of therapy.

Disseminated *M. avium* complex disease in patients with advanced HIV infection (unlabeled use): Oral:

Prophylaxis: 1200 mg once weekly (may be combined with rifabutin)

Treatment: 600 mg daily (in combination with ethambutol 15 mg/kg)

Endocarditis, prophylaxis (unlabeled use): Oral: 500 mg 1 hour prior to the procedure

Mild-to-moderate respiratory tract, skin, and soft tissue infections: Oral: 500 mg in a single loading dose on day 1 followed by 250 mg/day as a single dose on days 2-5

Alternative regimen: Bacterial exacerbation of COPD: 500 mg/day for a total of 3 days

Pelvic inflammatory disease (PID): I.V.: 500 mg as a single dose for 1-2 days, follow I.V. therapy by the oral route with a single daily dose of 250 mg to complete a 7-day course of therapy

Pertussis (CDC guidelines): Oral: 500 mg on day 1 followed by 250 mg/day on days 2-5 (maximum: 500 mg/day)

Urethritis/cervicitis: Oral:

Due to C. trachomatis: 1 g as a single dose

Due to N. gonorrhoeae: 2 g as a single dose

Dosage adjustment in renal impairment: Use caution in patients with Cl_cr <10 mL/minute

Dosage adjustment in hepatic impairment: Use with caution due to potential for hepatotoxicity (rare). Specific guidelines for dosing in hepatic impairment have not been established.

Dietary Considerations

Oral suspension, immediate release, may be administered with or without food.

Oral suspension, extended release, should be taken on an empty stomach (at least 1 hour before or 2 hours following a meal).

Tablet may be administered with food to decrease GI effects.

Sodium content:

Injection: 114 mg (4.96 mEq) per vial

Oral suspension, immediate release: 3.7 mg per 100 mg/5 mL of constituted suspension; 7.4 mg per 200 mg/5 mL of constituted suspension; 37 mg per 1 g single-dose packet

Oral suspension, extended release: 148 mg per 2 g constituted suspension

Tablet: 0.9 mg/250 mg tablet; 1.8 mg/500 mg tablet; 2.1 mg/600 mg tablet

Administration

I.V.: Infusate concentration and rate of infusion for azithromycin for injection should be either 1 mg/mL over 3 hours or 2 mg/mL over 1 hour. Other medications should not be infused simultaneously through the same I.V. line.

Oral: Immediate release suspension and tablet may be taken without regard to food; extended release suspension should be taken on an empty stomach (at least 1 hour before or 2 hours following a meal), within 12 hours of reconstitution.

Monitoring Parameters Liver function tests, CBC with differential

Additional Information Zithromax® tablets and immediate release suspension may be interchanged (eg, two Zithromax® 250 mg tablets may be substituted for one Zithromax® 500 mg tablet or the tablets may be substituted with the immediate release suspension); however, the extended release suspension (Zmax™) is not bioequivalent with Zithromax® and therefore should not be interchanged.

Dosage Forms Note: Strength expressed as base

Injection, powder for reconstitution, as dihydrate: 500 mg
  Zithromax®: 500 mg [contains sodium 114 mg (4.96 mEq) per vial]

Injection, powder for reconstitution, as monohydrate: 500 mg

Microspheres for oral suspension, extended release, as dihydrate:
  Zmax™: 2 g [single-dose bottle; contains sodium 148 mg per bottle; cherry and banana flavor]

Injection, powder for reconstitution, as monohydrate: 500 mg

Powder for oral suspension, as monohydrate: 100 mg/5 mL (15 mL); 200 mg/5 mL (15 mL, 22.5 mL, 30 mL)

Powder for oral suspension, immediate release, as dihydrate:
  Zithromax®: 100 mg/5 mL (15 mL) [contains sodium 3.7 mg/ 5 mL; cherry creme de vanilla and banana flavor]; 200 mg/5 mL (15 mL, 22.5 mL, 30 mL) [contains sodium 7.4 mg/5 mL; cherry creme de vanilla and banana flavor]; 1 g [single-dose packet; contains sodium 37 mg per packet; cherry creme de vanilla and banana flavor]

Tablet, as dihydrate:
  Zithromax®: 250 mg [contains sodium 0.9 mg per tablet]; 500 mg [contains sodium 1.8 mg per tablet]; 600 mg [contains sodium 2.1 mg per tablet]
  Zithromax® TRI-PAK™ [unit-dose pack]: 500 mg (3s) [contains sodium 1.8 mg per tablet]
  Zithromax® Z-PAK® [unit-dose pack]: 250 mg (6s) [contains sodium 0.9 mg per tablet]

Tablet, as monohydrate: 250 mg, 500 mg, 600 mg

♦ **Azithromycin Dihydrate** see Azithromycin on page 186
♦ **Azmacort®** see Triamcinolone on page 1734
♦ **AZO-Gesic® [OTC]** see Phenazopyridine on page 1351
♦ **Azopt®** see Brinzolamide on page 240
♦ **AZO-Standard® [OTC]** see Phenazopyridine on page 1351
♦ **AZT™ (Can)** see Zidovudine on page 1812
♦ **AZT + 3TC (error-prone abbreviation)** see Zidovudine and Lamivudine on page 1815
♦ **AZT, Abacavir, and Lamivudine** see Abacavir, Lamivudine, and Zidovudine on page 19
♦ **AZT (error-prone abbreviation)** see Zidovudine on page 1812
♦ **Azthreonam** see Aztreonam on page 189

Aztreonam (AZ tree oh nam)

U.S. Brand Names Azactam®
Canadian Brand Names Azactam®
Index Terms Azthreonam
Pharmacologic Category Antibiotic, Miscellaneous
Additional Appendix Information
  Antimicrobial Drugs of Choice on page 1981
  Community-Acquired Pneumonia in Adults on page 1999

Use Treatment of patients with urinary tract infections, lower respiratory tract infections, septicemia, skin/skin structure infections, intra-abdominal infections, and gynecological infections caused by susceptible gram-negative bacilli

Pregnancy Risk Factor B

Pregnancy Implications Teratogenic effects were not observed in animal studies. Aztreonam crosses the human placenta and enters fetal circulation.

Lactation Enters breast milk/not recommended (AAP rates "compatible")

Medication Safety Issues
  Sound-alike/look-alike issues:
    Aztreonam may be confused with azidothymidine

Contraindications Hypersensitivity to aztreonam or any component of the formulation

Warnings/Precautions Rare cross-allergenicity to penicillins and cephalosporins has been reported. Use caution in renal impairment; dosing adjustment required.

Adverse Reactions As reported in adults:
  1% to 10%:
    Dermatologic: Rash
    Gastrointestinal: Diarrhea, nausea, vomiting
    Local: Thrombophlebitis, pain at injection site
  <1% (Limited to important or life-threatening): Abdominal cramps, abnormal taste, anaphylaxis, anemia, angioedema, aphthous ulcer, breast tenderness, bronchospasm, *C. difficile*-associated diarrhea, chest pain, confusion, diaphoresis, diplopia, dizziness, dyspnea, eosinophilia, erythema multiforme, exfoliative dermatitis, fever, flushing, halitosis, headache, hepatitis, hypotension, insomnia, jaundice, leukopenia, liver enzymes increased, muscular aches myalgia, neutropenia, numb tongue, pancytopenia, paresthesia, petechiae, pruritus, pseudomembranous colitis, purpura, seizure, sneezing, thrombocytopenia, tinnitus, toxic epidermal necrolysis, urticaria, vaginitis, vertigo, weakness, wheezing

Overdosage/Toxicology Symptoms include seizures. If necessary, dialysis can reduce the drug concentration in the blood.

Drug Interactions
  Decreased Effect: Avoid antibiotics that induce beta-lactamase production (cefoxitin, imipenem),
  (Continued)

Aztreonam *(Continued)*

Stability Prior to reconstitution, store at room temperature; avoid excessive heat. Reconstituted solutions are colorless to light yellow straw and may turn pink upon standing without affecting potency. Use reconstituted solutions and I.V. solutions (in NS and D_5W) within 48 hours if kept at room temperature (25°C) or 7 days under refrigeration (4°C).

I.M.: Reconstitute with at least 3 mL SWFI, sterile bacteriostatic water for injection, NS, or bacteriostatic sodium chloride.

I.V.:

Bolus injection: Reconstitute with 6-10 mL SWFI.

Infusion: Reconstitute to a final concentration ≤2%; the final concentration should not exceed 20 mg/mL. Solution for infusion may be frozen at less than -2°C (less than -4°F) for up to 3 months. Thawed solution should be used within 24 hours if thawed at room temperature or within 72 hours if thawed under refrigeration. **Do not refreeze.**

Mechanism of Action Inhibits bacterial cell wall synthesis by binding to one or more of the penicillin binding proteins (PBPs) which in turn inhibits the final transpeptidation step of peptidoglycan synthesis in bacterial cell walls, thus inhibiting cell wall biosynthesis. Bacteria eventually lyse due to ongoing activity of cell wall autolytic enzymes (autolysins and murein hydrolases) while cell wall assembly is arrested. Monobactam structure makes cross-allergenicity with beta-lactams unlikely.

Pharmacodynamics/Kinetics

Absorption: I.M.: Well absorbed; I.M. and I.V. doses produce comparable serum concentrations

Distribution: Widely to most body fluids and tissues; crosses placenta; enters breast milk

V_d: Children: 0.2-0.29 L/kg; Adults: 0.2 L/kg

Relative diffusion of antimicrobial agents from blood into CSF: Good only with inflammation (exceeds usual MICs)

CSF:blood level ratio: Meninges: Inflamed: 8% to 40%; Normal: ~1%

Protein binding: 56%

Metabolism: Hepatic (minor %)

Half-life elimination:

Children 2 months to 12 years: 1.7 hours

Adults: Normal renal function: 1.7-2.9 hours

End-stage renal disease: 6-8 hours

Time to peak: I.M., I.V. push: Within 60 minutes; I.V. infusion: 1.5 hours

Excretion: Urine (60% to 70% as unchanged drug); feces (~13% to 15%)

Dosage

Children >1 month: I.M., I.V.:

Mild-to-moderate infections: I.M., I.V.: 30 mg/kg every 8 hours

Moderate-to-severe infections: I.M., I.V.: 30 mg/kg every 6-8 hours; maximum: 120 mg/kg/day (8 g/day)

Cystic fibrosis: I.V.: 50 mg/kg/dose every 6-8 hours (ie, up to 200 mg/kg/day); maximum: 8 g/day

Adults:

Urinary tract infection: I.M., I.V.: 500 mg to 1 g every 8-12 hours

Moderately-severe systemic infections: 1 g I.V. or I.M. or 2 g I.V. every 8-12 hours

Severe systemic or life-threatening infections (especially caused by *Pseudomonas aeruginosa*): I.V.: 2 g every 6-8 hours; maximum: 8 g/day

Meningitis (gram-negative): I.V.: 2 g every 6-8 hours

Dosing adjustment in renal impairment: Adults: Following initial dose, maintenance doses should be given as follows:

Cl_{cr} 10-30 mL/minute: 50% of usual dose at the usual interval

Cl_{cr} <10 mL/minute: 25% of usual dosage at the usual interval

Hemodialysis: Moderately dialyzable (20% to 50%); ⅛ of initial dose after each hemodialysis session (given in addition to the maintenance doses)

Peritoneal dialysis: Administer as for Cl_{cr} <10 mL/minute

Continuous arteriovenous or venovenous hemofiltration: Dose as for Cl_{cr} 10-30 mL/minute

Administration Doses >1 g should be administered I.V.

I.M.: Administer by deep injection into large muscle mass, such as upper outer quadrant of gluteus maximus or the lateral part of the thigh

I.V.: Administer by slow I.V. push over 3-5 minutes or by intermittent infusion over 20-60 minutes.

Monitoring Parameters Periodic liver function test; monitor for signs of anaphylaxis during first dose

Test Interactions May interfere with urine glucose tests containing cupric sulfate (Benedict's solution, Clinitest®); positive Coombs' test

Additional Information Although marketed as an agent similar to aminoglycosides, aztreonam is a monobactam antimicrobial with almost pure gram-negative aerobic activity. It cannot be used for gram-positive infections. Aminoglycosides are often used for synergy in gram-positive infections.

Dosage Forms

Infusion [premixed]: 1 g (50 mL); 2 g (50 mL)

Injection, powder for reconstitution: 500 mg, 1 g, 2 g

♦ **Azulfidine®** *see* Sulfasalazine *on page 1615*

♦ **Azulfidine® EN-tabs®** *see* Sulfasalazine *on page 1615*

♦ **B1** *see* Tositumomab and Iodine I 131 Tositumomab *on page 1713*

♦ **B1 Antibody** *see* Tositumomab and Iodine I 131 Tositumomab *on page 1713*

♦ **B2036-PEG** *see* Pegvisomant *on page 1327*

♦ **B 9273** *see* Alefacept *on page 62*

♦ **BA-16038** *see* Aminoglutethimide *on page 95*

♦ **BabyBIG®** *see* Botulism Immune Globulin (Intravenous-Human) *on page 238*

♦ **Bacid® [OTC]** *see* Lactobacillus *on page 969*

♦ **Bacid® (Can)** *see* Lactobacillus *on page 969*

♦ **Baciguent®** [OTC] *see* Bacitracin *on page 191*
♦ **Baciguent®** (Can) *see* Bacitracin *on page 191*
♦ **BaciIM®** *see* Bacitracin *on page 191*
♦ **Baciject®** (Can) *see* Bacitracin *on page 191*
♦ **Bacillus Calmette-Guérin (BCG) Live** *see* BCG Vaccine *on page 197*

Bacitracin (bas i TRAY sin)

U.S. Brand Names AK-Tracin® [DSC]; Baciguent® [OTC]; BaciIM®
Canadian Brand Names Baciguent®; Baciject®
Pharmacologic Category Antibiotic, Miscellaneous; Antibiotic, Ophthalmic; Antibiotic, Topical
Use Treatment of susceptible bacterial infections mainly; has activity against gram-positive bacilli; due to toxicity risks, systemic and irrigant uses of bacitracin should be limited to situations where less toxic alternatives would not be effective
Unlabeled/Investigational Use Oral administration: Successful in antibiotic-associated colitis; has been used for enteric eradication of vancomycin-resistant enterococci (VRE)
Pregnancy Risk Factor C
Lactation Excretion in breast milk unknown/use caution
Medication Safety Issues
Sound-alike/look-alike issues:
Bacitracin may be confused with Bactrim®, Bactroban®
Contraindications Hypersensitivity to bacitracin or any component of the formulation; I.M. use is contraindicated in patients with renal impairment
Warnings/Precautions [U.S. Boxed Warning]: I.M. use may cause renal failure due to tubular and glomerular necrosis; monitor renal function daily. Prolonged use may result in overgrowth of nonsusceptible organisms. Do not administer intravenously because severe thrombophlebitis occurs.
Adverse Reactions 1% to 10%:
Cardiovascular: Hypotension, edema of the face/lips, chest tightness
Central nervous system: Pain
Dermatologic: Rash, itching
Gastrointestinal: Anorexia, nausea, vomiting, diarrhea, rectal itching
Hematologic: Blood dyscrasias
Miscellaneous: Diaphoresis
<1%: Rare cases of anaphylaxis have been reported in association with topical and intraoperative exposures.
Overdosage/Toxicology Symptoms include nephrotoxicity (parenteral), nausea, and vomiting (oral).
Drug Interactions
Increased Effect/Toxicity: Nephrotoxic drugs, neuromuscular blocking agents, and anesthetics (increased neuromuscular blockade).
Stability For I.M. use. Bacitracin sterile powder should be dissolved in 0.9% sodium chloride injection containing 2% procaine hydrochloride. Once reconstituted, bacitracin is stable for 1 week under refrigeration (2°C to 8°C). Sterile powder should be stored in the refrigerator. Do not use diluents containing parabens.
Mechanism of Action Inhibits bacterial cell wall synthesis by preventing transfer of mucopeptides into the growing cell wall
Pharmacodynamics/Kinetics
Duration: 6-8 hours
Absorption: Poor from mucous membranes and intact or denuded skin; rapidly following I.M. administration; not absorbed by bladder irrigation, but absorption can occur from peritoneal or mediastinal lavage
Distribution: CSF: Nil even with inflammation
Protein binding, plasma: Minimal
Time to peak, serum: I.M.: 1-2 hours
Excretion: Urine (10% to 40%) within 24 hours
Dosage Do not administer I.V.:
Infants: I.M.:
≤2.5 kg: 900 units/kg/day in 2-3 divided doses
>2.5 kg: 1000 units/kg/day in 2-3 divided doses
Children: I.M.: 800-1200 units/kg/day divided every 8 hours
Adults: Oral:
Antibiotic-associated colitis: 25,000 units 4 times/day for 7-10 days
VRE eradication (unlabeled use): 25,000 units 4 times/day for 7-10 days
Children and Adults:
Topical: Apply 1-5 times/day
Ophthalmic, ointment: Instill ¼" to ½" ribbon every 3-4 hours into conjunctival sac for acute infections, or 2-3 times/day for mild-to-moderate infections for 7-10 days
Irrigation, solution: 50-100 units/mL in normal saline, lactated Ringer's, or sterile water for irrigation; soak sponges in solution for topical compresses 1-5 times/day or as needed during surgical procedures
Administration For I.M. administration only, **do not administer I.V.** Confirm any orders for parenteral use. pH of urine should be kept >6 by using sodium bicarbonate. Bacitracin sterile powder should be dissolved in 0.9% sodium chloride injection containing 2% procaine hydrochloride. Do not use diluents containing parabens.
Monitoring Parameters I.M.: Urinalysis, renal function tests
Additional Information 1 unit is equivalent to 0.026 mg
Dosage Forms [DSC] = Discontinued product
Injection, powder for reconstitution (BaciIM®): 50,000 units
Ointment, ophthalmic (AK-Tracin® [DSC]): 500 units/g (3.5 g)
Ointment, topical: 500 units/g (0.9 g, 15 g, 30 g, 120 g, 454 g)
Baciguent®: 500 units/g (15 g, 30 g)
(Continued)

Bacitracin (Continued)

Extemporaneous Preparations In some institutions, oral formulations have been prepared either by preparation of capsules from powder or oral administration of I.V. solution.

Bacitracin and Polymyxin B (bas i TRAY sin & pol i MIKS in bee)

U.S. Brand Names AK-Poly-Bac™; Betadine® First Aid Antibiotics + Moisturizer [OTC] [DSC]; Polysporin® [OTC]

Canadian Brand Names LID-Pack®; Optimyxin®

Index Terms Polymyxin B and Bacitracin

Pharmacologic Category Antibiotic, Ophthalmic; Antibiotic, Topical

Use Treatment of superficial infections caused by susceptible organisms

Pregnancy Risk Factor C

Medication Safety Issues

Sound-alike/look-alike issues:

Betadine® may be confused with Betagan®, betaine

Dosage Children and Adults:

Ophthalmic ointment: Instill 1/2" ribbon in the affected eye(s) every 3-4 hours for acute infections or 2-3 times/day for mild-to-moderate infections for 7-10 days

Topical ointment/powder: Apply to affected area 1-4 times/day; may cover with sterile bandage if needed

Additional Information Complete prescribing information for this medication should be consulted for additional detail.

Dosage Forms [DSC] = Discontinued product

Ointment, ophthalmic: Bacitracin 500 units and polymyxin B 10,000 units per g (3.5 g)

AK-Poly-Bac™: Bacitracin 500 units and polymyxin 10,000 units per g (3.5 g)

Ointment, topical: Bacitracin 500 units and polymyxin B 10,000 units per g in white petrolatum (15 g, 30 g)

Betadine® First Aid Antibiotics + Moisturizer: Bacitracin 500 units and polymyxin B 10,000 units per g (14 g) [DSC]

Polysporin®: Bacitracin 500 units and polymyxin B 10,000 units per g (0.9 g, 15 g, 30 g)

Powder, topical:

Polysporin®: Bacitracin 500 units and polymyxin B 10,000 units per g (10 g)

Bacitracin, Neomycin, and Polymyxin B

(bas i TRAY sin, nee oh MYE sin, & pol i MIKS in bee)

U.S. Brand Names Neosporin® Neo To Go® [OTC]; Neosporin® Ophthalmic Ointment [DSC]; Neosporin® Topical [OTC]

Canadian Brand Names Neosporin® Ophthalmic Ointment

Index Terms Neomycin, Bacitracin, and Polymyxin B; Polymyxin B, Bacitracin, and Neomycin; Triple Antibiotic

Pharmacologic Category Antibiotic, Ophthalmic; Antibiotic, Topical

Use Helps prevent infection in minor cuts, scrapes, and burns; short-term treatment of superficial external ocular infections caused by susceptible organisms

Pregnancy Risk Factor C

Dosage Children and Adults:

Ophthalmic: Ointment: Instill 1/2" into the conjunctival sac every 3-4 hours for 7-10 days for acute infections

Topical: Apply 1-3 times/day to infected area; may cover with sterile bandage as needed

Additional Information Complete prescribing information for this medication should be consulted for additional detail.

Dosage Forms [DSC] = Discontinued product

Ointment, ophthalmic (Neosporin® [DSC]): Bacitracin 400 units, neomycin 3.5 mg, and polymyxin B 10,000 units per g (3.5 g)

Ointment, topical: Bacitracin 400 units, neomycin 3.5 mg, and polymyxin B 5000 units per g (0.9 g, 15 g, 30 g, 454 g)

Neosporin®: Bacitracin 400 units, neomycin 3.5 mg, and polymyxin B 5000 units per g (15 g, 30 g)

Neosporin® Neo To Go®: Bacitracin 400 units, neomycin 3.5 mg, and polymyxin B 5000 units per g (0.9 g)

Bacitracin, Neomycin, Polymyxin B, and Hydrocortisone

(bas i TRAY sin, nee oh MYE sin, pol i MIKS in bee, & hye droe KOR ti sone)

U.S. Brand Names Cortisporin® Ointment

Canadian Brand Names Cortisporin® Topical Ointment

Index Terms Hydrocortisone, Bacitracin, Neomycin, and Polymyxin B; Neomycin, Bacitracin, Polymyxin B, and Hydrocortisone; Polymyxin B, Bacitracin, Neomycin, and Hydrocortisone

Pharmacologic Category Antibiotic, Ophthalmic; Antibiotic, Otic; Antibiotic, Topical; Corticosteroid, Ophthalmic; Corticosteroid, Otic; Corticosteroid, Topical

Use Prevention and treatment of susceptible inflammatory conditions where bacterial infection (or risk of infection) is present

Pregnancy Risk Factor C

Dosage Children and Adults:

Ophthalmic: Ointment: Instill 1/2" ribbon to inside of lower lid every 3-4 hours until improvement occurs

Topical: Apply sparingly 2-4 times/day. Therapy should be discontinued when control is achieved; if no improvement is seen, reassessment of diagnosis may be necessary.

Additional Information Complete prescribing information for this medication should be consulted for additional detail.

Dosage Forms

Ointment, ophthalmic: Bacitracin 400 units, neomycin 3.5 mg, polymyxin B 10,000 units, and hydrocortisone 10 mg per g (3.5 g)

Ointment, topical:

Cortisporin®: Bacitracin 400 units, neomycin 3.5 mg, polymyxin B 5000 units, and hydrocortisone 10 mg per g (15 g)

Baclofen (BAK loe fen)

U.S. Brand Names Lioresal®

Canadian Brand Names Apo-Baclofen®; Gen-Baclofen; Lioresal®; Liotec; Nu-Baclo; PMS-Baclofen

Pharmacologic Category Skeletal Muscle Relaxant

Use Treatment of reversible spasticity associated with multiple sclerosis or spinal cord lesions

Orphan drug: Intrathecal: Treatment of intractable spasticity caused by spinal cord injury, multiple sclerosis, and other spinal disease (spinal ischemia or tumor, transverse myelitis, cervical spondylosis, degenerative myelopathy)

Unlabeled/Investigational Use Intractable hiccups, intractable pain relief, bladder spasticity, trigeminal neuralgia, cerebral palsy, Huntington's chorea

Pregnancy Risk Factor C

Lactation Enters breast milk (small amounts)/compatible

Medication Safety Issues

Sound-alike/look-alike issues:

Baclofen may be confused with Bactroban®

Lioresal® may be confused with lisinopril, Lotensin®

Contraindications Hypersensitivity to baclofen or any component of the formulation

Warnings/Precautions Use with caution in patients with seizure disorder or impaired renal function. **[U.S. Boxed Warning]: Avoid abrupt withdrawal of the drug; abrupt withdrawal of intrathecal baclofen has resulted in severe sequelae (hyperpyrexia, obtundation, rebound/exaggerated spasticity, muscle rigidity, and rhabdomyolysis), leading to organ failure and some fatalities.** Risk may be higher in patients with injuries at T-6 or above, history of baclofen withdrawal, or limited ability to communicate. Elderly are more sensitive to the effects of baclofen and are more likely to experience adverse CNS effects at higher doses.

Adverse Reactions

>10%:

Central nervous system: Drowsiness, vertigo, dizziness, psychiatric disturbances, insomnia, slurred speech, ataxia, hypotonia

Neuromuscular & skeletal: Weakness

1% to 10%:

Cardiovascular: Hypotension

Central nervous system: Fatigue, confusion, headache

Dermatologic: Rash

Gastrointestinal: Nausea, constipation

Genitourinary: Polyuria

<1% (Limited to important or life-threatening): Chest pain, dyspnea, dysuria, enuresis, hematuria, impotence, inability to ejaculate, nocturia, palpitation, syncope, urinary retention; withdrawal reactions have occurred with abrupt discontinuation (particularly severe with intrathecal use).

Overdosage/Toxicology Symptoms include vomiting, muscle hypotonia, salivation, drowsiness, coma, seizures, and respiratory depression. Atropine has been used to improve ventilation, heart rate, blood pressure, and core body temperature. Following initiation of essential overdose management, symptomatic and supportive treatment should be instituted.

For toxicity following intrathecal administration: For adults, administer physostigmine 2 mg I.M. or I.V. (not to exceed 1 mg/minute). For pediatric patients, administer physostigmine 0.02 mg/kg I.M. or I.V. (not to exceed 0.5 mg/minute). Consider withdrawal of 30-40 mL of CSF to reduce baclofen concentration. Abrupt withdrawal of intrathecal baclofen has resulted in severe sequelae (hyperpyrexia, obtundation, muscle rigidity, and rhabdomyolysis).

Drug Interactions

Increased Effect/Toxicity: Effects may be additive with CNS depressants.

Ethanol/Nutrition/Herb Interactions

Ethanol: Avoid ethanol (may increase CNS depression).

Herb/Nutraceutical: Avoid valerian, St John's wort, kava kava, gotu kola.

Mechanism of Action Inhibits the transmission of both monosynaptic and polysynaptic reflexes at the spinal cord level, possibly by hyperpolarization of primary afferent fiber terminals, with resultant relief of muscle spasticity

Pharmacodynamics/Kinetics

Onset of action: 3-4 days

Peak effect: 5-10 days

Absorption (dose dependent): Oral: Rapid

Protein binding: 30%

Metabolism: Hepatic (15% of dose)

Half-life elimination: 3.5 hours

Time to peak, serum: Oral: Within 2-3 hours

Excretion: Urine and feces (85% as unchanged drug)

Dosage

Oral (avoid abrupt withdrawal of drug):

Children:

2-7 years: Initial: 10-15 mg/24 hours divided every 8 hours; titrate dose every 3 days in increments of 5-15 mg/day to a maximum of 40 mg/day

≥8 years: Maximum: 60 mg/day in 3 divided doses

(Continued)

Baclofen *(Continued)*

Adults: 5 mg 3 times/day, may increase 5 mg/dose every 3 days to a maximum of 80 mg/day

Hiccups: Adults: Usual effective dose: 10-20 mg 2-3 times/day

Intrathecal: Children and Adults:

Test dose: 50-100 mcg, doses >50 mcg should be given in 25 mcg increments, separated by 24 hours. A screening dose of 25 mcg may be considered in very small patients. Patients not responding to screening dose of 100 mcg should not be considered for chronic infusion/implanted pump.

Maintenance: After positive response to test dose, a maintenance intrathecal infusion can be administered via an implanted intrathecal pump. Initial dose via pump: Infusion at a 24-hour rate dosed at twice the test dose. Avoid abrupt discontinuation.

Elderly: Oral (the lowest effective dose is recommended): Initial: 5 mg 2-3 times/day, increasing gradually as needed; if benefits are not seen, withdraw the drug slowly.

Dosing adjustment in renal impairment: May be necessary to reduce dosage in renal impairment, but there are no specific guidelines available

Hemodialysis: Poor water solubility allows for accumulation during chronic hemodialysis. Low-dose therapy is recommended. There have been several case reports of accumulation of baclofen resulting in toxicity symptoms (organic brain syndrome, myoclonia, deceleration and steep potentials in EEG) in patients with renal failure who have received normal doses of baclofen.

Administration Intrathecal: For screening dosages, dilute with preservative-free sodium chloride to a final concentration of 50 mcg/mL for bolus injection into the subarachnoid space. For maintenance infusions, concentrations of 500-2000 mcg/mL may be used.

Test Interactions Increased alkaline phosphatase, AST, glucose, ammonia (B); decreased bilirubin (S)

Dosage Forms

Injection, solution, intrathecal [preservative free]:

Lioresal®: 50 mcg/mL (1 mL); 500 mcg/mL (20 mL); 2000 mcg/mL (5 mL, 20 mL)

Tablet: 10 mg, 20 mg

Extemporaneous Preparations Make a 5 mg/mL suspension by crushing fifteen 20 mg tablets; wet with glycerin, gradually add 45 mL simple syrup in 3 x 5 mL aliquots to make a total volume of 60 mL; refrigerate; stable 35 days

Johnson CE and Hart SM, "Stability of an Extemporaneously Compounded Baclofen Oral Liquid," *Am J Hosp Pharm,* 1993, 50:2353-5.

- ◆ **BactoShield® CHG [OTC]** *see* Chlorhexidine Gluconate *on page 344*
- ◆ **Bactrim™** *see* Sulfamethoxazole and Trimethoprim *on page 1613*
- ◆ **Bactrim™ DS** *see* Sulfamethoxazole and Trimethoprim *on page 1613*
- ◆ **Bactroban®** *see* Mupirocin *on page 1179*
- ◆ **Bactroban® Nasal** *see* Mupirocin *on page 1179*
- ◆ **Baking Soda** *see* Sodium Bicarbonate *on page 1575*
- ◆ **BAL** *see* Dimercaprol *on page 512*
- ◆ **Balacet 325™** *see* Propoxyphene and Acetaminophen *on page 1445*
- ◆ **BAL in Oil®** *see* Dimercaprol *on page 512*
- ◆ **Balmex® [OTC]** *see* Zinc Oxide *on page 1817*
- ◆ **Balminil Decongestant (Can)** *see* Pseudoephedrine *on page 1454*
- ◆ **Balminil DM D (Can)** *see* Pseudoephedrine and Dextromethorphan *on page 1455*
- ◆ **Balminil DM + Decongestant + Expectorant (Can)** *see* Guaifenesin, Pseudoephedrine, and Dextromethorphan *on page 821*
- ◆ **Balminil DM E (Can)** *see* Guaifenesin and Dextromethorphan *on page 816*
- ◆ **Balminil Expectorant (Can)** *see* Guaifenesin *on page 814*

Balsalazide (bal SAL a zide)

U.S. Brand Names Colazal®

Index Terms Balsalazide Disodium

Pharmacologic Category 5-Aminosalicylic Acid Derivative; Anti-inflammatory Agent

Use Treatment of mild-to-moderate active ulcerative colitis

Pregnancy Risk Factor B

Pregnancy Implications Teratogenic effects were not observed in animal studies. There are no adequate and well-controlled studies have been done in pregnant women. Balsalazide should be used in pregnant women only if clearly needed.

Lactation Excretion in breast milk unknown/use caution

Medication Safety Issues

Sound-alike/look-alike issues:

Colazal® may be confused with Clozaril®

Contraindications Hypersensitivity to balsalazide, metabolites to balsalazide, salicylates, or any component of the formulation

Warnings/Precautions Pyloric stenosis may prolong gastric retention of balsalazide capsules. Renal toxicity has been observed with other mesalamine (5-aminosalicylic acid) products; use with caution in patients with known renal disease. May exacerbate symptoms of ulcerative colitis. Safety and efficacy of use beyond 12 weeks in adults or 8 weeks in children has not been established. Safety and efficacy have not been established in children <5 years of age.

Adverse Reactions

>10%:

Central nervous system: Headache (children 15%; adults 8%)

Gastrointestinal: Abdominal pain (children 12% to 13%; adults 6%)

1% to 10%:
Central nervous system: Insomnia (adults 2%), fatigue (children 4%; adults2%), fever (children 6%; adults 2%)
Endocrine & metabolic: Dysmenorrhea (children 3%)
Gastrointestinal: Diarrhea (children 9%; adults 5%), ulcerative colitis exacerbation (children 6%; adults 1%), nausea (children 4%; adults 5%), vomiting (children 10%; adults 4%), hematochezia (children 4%), stomatitis (children 3%), anorexia (adults 2%), dyspepsia (adults 2%), flatulence (adults 2%), cramps (adults 1%), constipation (adults 1%), dry mouth (adults 1%)
Genitourinary: Urinary tract infection (adults 1%)
Neuromuscular & skeletal: Arthralgia (adults 4%), back pain (adults 2%), myalgia (adults 1%)
Respiratory: Respiratory infection (adults 4%), cough (children 3%; adults 2%), pharyngitis (children 6%; adults 2%), pharyngolaryngeal pain (children 3%), rhinitis (adults 2%)
Miscellaneous: Flu-like syndrome (children 4%; adults 1%)
<1% (Limited to important or life-threatening): Alopecia, anemia, bradycardia, bronchospasm, chest pain, cholestatic jaundice, cirrhosis, dysphonia, edema, epigastric pain, erythema nodosum, fecal incontinence, glossitis, hematuria, hemorrhage, hepatocellular damage, hepatotoxicity, hypertension, interstitial nephritis, jaundice, Kawasaki-like syndrome, liver failure, liver necrosis, liver function tests increased, menstrual disorder, palpitation, pancreatitis, pericarditis, pruritus, tinnitus, tongue discoloration, tremor
Overdosage/Toxicology Treatment is symptom-directed and supportive, and should include correction of electrolyte abnormalities.
Drug Interactions
Increased Effect/Toxicity: 5-ASA derivatives may decrease the metabolism of azathioprine, mercaptopurine, thioguanine
Decreased Effect: 5-ASA derivatives may decrease the absorption of digoxin.
Stability Store at room temperature of 15°C to 30°C (59°F to 86°F).
Mechanism of Action Balsalazide is a prodrug, converted by bacterial azoreduction to 5-aminosalicylic acid (mesalamine, active), 4-aminobenzoyl-β-alanine (inert), and their metabolites. 5-aminosalicylic acid may decrease inflammation by blocking the production of arachidonic acid metabolites topically in the colon mucosa.
Pharmacodynamics/Kinetics
Onset of action: Delayed; may require several days to weeks
Absorption: Very low and variable
Protein binding: Balsalazide: ≥99%
Metabolism: Azoreduced in the colon to 5-aminosalicylic acid (active), 4-aminobenzoyl-β-alanine (inert), and N-acetylated metabolites
Half-life elimination: Primary effect is topical (colonic mucosa); systemic half-life not determined
Time to peak: Balsalazide: 1-2 hours
Excretion: Feces (65% as 5-aminosalicylic acid, 4-aminobenzoyl-β-alanine, and N-acetylated metabolites); urine (25% as N-acetylated metabolites); Parent drug: Urine or feces (<1%)
Dosage Oral:
Children 5-17 years: 750 mg 3 times/day for up to 8 weeks **or** 2.25 g (three 750 mg capsules) 3 times/day for 8 weeks
Adults: 2.25 g (three 750 mg capsules) 3 times/day for 8-12 weeks
Elderly: No specific dosage adjustment available
Dosage adjustment in renal impairment: No information available with balsalazide; renal toxicity has been observed with other 5-aminosalicylic acid products, use with caution
Dosage adjustment in hepatic impairment: No specific dosage adjustment available
Dietary Considerations Colazal® 750 mg capsule contains sodium 86 mg.
Administration Capsules should be swallowed whole or may be opened and sprinkled on applesauce. Applesauce mixture may be chewed; swallow immediately, do not store mixture for later use. When sprinkled on food, may cause staining of teeth or tongue.
Monitoring Parameters Worsening of symptoms
Additional Information Balsalazide 750 mg is equivalent to mesalamine 267 mg
Dosage Forms
Capsule, as disodium:
Colazal®: 750 mg [contains sodium 86 mg]

♦ **Balsalazide Disodium** see Balsalazide on page 194
♦ **Balsam Peru, Trypsin, and Castor Oil** see Trypsin, Balsam Peru, and Castor Oil on page 1754
♦ **Baltussin** see Dihydrocodeine, Chlorpheniramine, and Phenylephrine on page 506
♦ **Band-Aid® Hurt-Free™ Antiseptic Wash [OTC]** see Lidocaine on page 1010
♦ **Banophen® [OTC]** see DiphenhydrAMINE on page 515
♦ **Banophen® Anti-Itch [OTC]** see DiphenhydrAMINE on page 515
♦ **Baraclude™** see Entecavir on page 586
♦ **Baridium® [OTC]** see Phenazopyridine on page 1351
♦ **Basaljel® (Can)** see Aluminum Hydroxide on page 83
♦ **Base Ointment** see Zinc Oxide on page 1817

Basiliximab (ba si LIK si mab)

U.S. Brand Names Simulect®
Canadian Brand Names Simulect®
Pharmacologic Category Monoclonal Antibody
Use Prophylaxis of acute organ rejection in renal transplantation
Pregnancy Risk Factor B (manufacturer)
Pregnancy Implications Teratogenic effects were not observed in animal studies. IL-2 receptors play an important role in the development of the immune system. Use in pregnant women only when benefit exceeds potential risk to the fetus. Women of childbearing potential
(Continued)

Basiliximab *(Continued)*

should use effective contraceptive measures before beginning treatment and for 4 months after completion of therapy with this agent.

Lactation Excretion in breast milk unknown/not recommended

Contraindications Hypersensitivity to basiliximab, murine proteins, or any component of the formulation

Warnings/Precautions To be used as a component of immunosuppressive regimen which includes cyclosporine and corticosteroids. The incidence of lymphoproliferative disorders and/or opportunistic infections may be increased by immunosuppressive therapy. Severe hypersensitivity reactions, occurring within 24 hours, have been reported. Reactions, including anaphylaxis, have occurred both with the initial exposure and/or following re-exposure after several months. Use caution during re-exposure to a subsequent course of therapy in a patient who has previously received basiliximab. Discontinue the drug permanently if a reaction occurs. Medications for the treatment of hypersensitivity reactions should be available for immediate use. Treatment may result in the development of human antimurine antibodies (HAMA); however, limited evidence suggesting the use of muromonab-CD3 or other murine products is not precluded. **[U.S. Boxed Warning]: Should be administered under the supervision of a physician experienced in immunosuppression therapy.**

Adverse Reactions Administration of basiliximab did not appear to increase the incidence or severity of adverse effects in clinical trials. Adverse events were reported in 96% of both the placebo and basiliximab groups.

>10%:
  Cardiovascular: Hypertension, peripheral edema
  Central nervous system: Fever, headache, insomnia, pain
  Dermatologic: Acne, wound complications
  Endocrine & metabolic: Hypercholesterolemia, hyperglycemia, hyper-/hypokalemia, hyper-uricemia, hypophosphatemia
  Gastrointestinal: Abdominal pain, constipation, diarrhea, dyspepsia, nausea, vomiting
  Genitourinary: Urinary tract infection
  Hematologic: Anemia
  Neuromuscular & skeletal: Tremor
  Respiratory: Dyspnea, infection (upper respiratory)
  Miscellaneous: Viral infection

3% to 10%:
  Cardiovascular: Abnormal heart sounds, angina pectoris, arrhythmia, atrial fibrillation, cardiac failure, chest pain, generalized edema, hypotension, tachycardia
  Central nervous system: Agitation, anxiety, depression, dizziness, fatigue, hypoesthesia, malaise, neuropathy, rigors
  Dermatologic: Cyst, hypertrichosis, pruritus, rash, skin disorder, skin ulceration
  Endocrine & metabolic: Acidosis, dehydration, diabetes mellitus, fluid overload, hyper-/hypocalcemia, hyperlipidemia, hypertriglyceridemia, hypoglycemia, hypomagnesemia, hyponatremia
  Gastrointestinal: Abdomen enlarged, esophagitis, flatulence, gastroenteritis, GI hemorrhage, gingival hyperplasia, melena, moniliasis, stomatitis (including ulcerative), weight gain
  Genitourinary: Albuminuria, bladder disorder, dysuria, genital edema, hematuria, impotence, oliguria, renal function abnormal, renal tubular necrosis, ureteral disorder, urinary frequency, urinary retention
  Hematologic: Hematoma, hemorrhage, leukopenia, polycythemia, purpura, thrombocytopenia, thrombosis
  Neuromuscular & skeletal: Arthralgia, arthropathy, back pain, cramps, fracture, hernia, leg pain, myalgia, paresthesia, weakness
  Ocular: Abnormal vision, cataract, conjunctivitis
  Respiratory: Bronchitis, bronchospasm, cough, pharyngitis, pneumonia, pulmonary edema, sinusitis, rhinitis
  Miscellaneous: Accidental trauma, facial edema, glucocorticoids increased, herpes infection, sepsis
Postmarketing and/or case reports: Capillary leak syndrome, cytokine release syndrome; severe hypersensitivity reactions, including anaphylaxis, have been reported (symptoms may include hypotension, tachycardia, cardiac failure, dyspnea, bronchospasm, pulmonary edema, urticaria, rash, pruritus, sneezing, and respiratory failure)

Overdosage/Toxicology The maximum tolerated dose has not been determined. Single doses up to 60 mg and divided doses up to 120 mg were administered without adverse event in clinical trials; a pediatric patient received a single 20 mg dose without adverse event. Treatment is symptom-directed and supportive.

Drug Interactions
  Increased Effect/Toxicity: Allergic reactions may be increased in patients who have received diagnostic or therapeutic monoclonal antibodies due to the presence of human antichimeric antibody (HACA). Basiliximab may increase the risk of vaccinial infection with live organism vaccine administration.
  Decreased Effect: Basiliximab may decrease the effect of vaccines (dead organisms).

Ethanol/Nutrition/Herb Interactions Herb/Nutraceutical: Echinacea may diminish the therapeutic effect of basiliximab. Avoid hypoglycemic herbs, including alfalfa, bilberry, bitter melon, burdock, celery, damiana, fenugreek, garcinia, garlic, ginger, ginseng, gymnema, marshmallow, and stinging nettle (may enhance the hypoglycemic effect of basiliximab).

Stability Store intact vials under refrigeration 2°C to 8°C (36°F to 46°F). Reconstitute vials with sterile water for injection, USP. Shake the vial gently to dissolve. It is recommended that after reconstitution, the solution should be used immediately. If not used immediately, it can be stored at 2°C to 8°C for up to 24 hours or at room temperature for up to 4 hours. Discard the reconstituted solution within 24 hours. Further dilute reconstituted solution with 25-50 mL 0.9% sodium chloride or dextrose 5% in water. When mixing the solution, gently invert the bag to avoid foaming. Do not shake.

Mechanism of Action Chimeric (murine/human) monoclonal antibody which blocks the alpha-chain of the interleukin-2 (IL-2) receptor complex; this receptor is expressed on activated T lymphocytes and is a critical pathway for activating cell-mediated allograft rejection

Pharmacodynamics/Kinetics

Duration: Mean: 36 days (determined by IL-2R alpha saturation)

Distribution: Mean: V_d: Children 1-11 years: 4.8 ± 2.1 L; Adolescents 12-16 years: 7.8 ± 5.1 L; Adults: 8.6 ± 4.1 L

Half-life elimination: Children 1-11 years: 9.5 days; Adolescents 12-16 years: 9.1 days; Adults: Mean: 7.2 days

Excretion: Clearance: Children 1-11 years: 17 mL/hour; Adolescents 12-16 years: 31 mL/hour; Adults: Mean: 41 mL/hour

Dosage Note: Patients previously administered basiliximab should only be re-exposed to a subsequent course of therapy with extreme caution.

I.V.:

Children <35 kg: Renal transplantation: 10 mg within 2 hours prior to transplant surgery, followed by a second 10 mg dose 4 days after transplantation; the second dose should be withheld if complications occur (including severe hypersensitivity reactions or graft loss)

Children ≥35 kg and Adults: Renal transplantation: 20 mg within 2 hours prior to transplant surgery, followed by a second 20 mg dose 4 days after transplantation; the second dose should be withheld if complications occur (including severe hypersensitivity reactions or graft loss)

Dosing adjustment/comments in renal or hepatic impairment: No specific dosing adjustment recommended

Administration For intravenous administration only. Infuse as a bolus or I.V. infusion over 20-30 minutes. (Bolus dosing is associated with nausea, vomiting, and local pain at the injection site.)

Monitoring Parameters Signs and symptoms of acute rejection

Dosage Forms

Injection, powder for reconstitution [preservative free]:
Simulect®: 10 mg, 20 mg

 ♦ **BAY 43-9006** *see Sorafenib on page 1590*
 ♦ **Bayer® Aspirin [OTC]** *see Aspirin on page 160*
 ♦ **Bayer® Aspirin Extra Strength [OTC]** *see Aspirin on page 160*
 ♦ **Bayer® Aspirin Regimen Adult Low Strength [OTC]** *see Aspirin on page 160*
 ♦ **Bayer® Aspirin Regimen Children's [OTC]** *see Aspirin on page 160*
 ♦ **Bayer® Aspirin Regimen Regular Strength [OTC]** *see Aspirin on page 160*
 ♦ **Bayer® Extra Strength Arthritis Pain Regimen [OTC]** *see Aspirin on page 160*
 ♦ **Bayer® Plus Extra Strength [OTC]** *see Aspirin on page 160*
 ♦ **Bayer® Women's Aspirin Plus Calcium [OTC]** *see Aspirin on page 160*
 ♦ **BayGam® [DSC]** *see Immune Globulin (Intramuscular) on page 891*
 ♦ **BayGam® (Can)** *see Immune Globulin (Intramuscular) on page 891*
 ♦ **BayHep B® [DSC]** *see Hepatitis B Immune Globulin on page 834*
 ♦ **BayHep B® (Can)** *see Hepatitis B Immune Globulin on page 834*
 ♦ **BayRab® [DSC]** *see Rabies Immune Globulin (Human) on page 1478*
 ♦ **BayRab™ (Can)** *see Rabies Immune Globulin (Human) on page 1478*
 ♦ **BayRho-D® Full-Dose [DSC]** *see Rh₀(D) Immune Globulin on page 1499*
 ♦ **BayRho-D® Full-Dose (Can)** *see Rh₀(D) Immune Globulin on page 1499*
 ♦ **BayRho-D® Mini-Dose [DSC]** *see Rh₀(D) Immune Globulin on page 1499*
 ♦ **BayTet™ [DSC]** *see Tetanus Immune Globulin (Human) on page 1656*
 ♦ **BayTet™ (Can)** *see Tetanus Immune Globulin (Human) on page 1656*
 ♦ **Baza® Antifungal [OTC]** *see Miconazole on page 1137*
 ♦ **Baza® Clear [OTC]** *see Vitamin A and Vitamin D on page 1794*
 ♦ **B-Caro-T™** *see Beta-Carotene on page 211*
 ♦ **BCG, Live** *see BCG Vaccine on page 197*

BCG Vaccine (bee see jee vak SEEN)

U.S. Brand Names TheraCys®; TICE® BCG

Canadian Brand Names ImmuCyst®; Oncotice™; Pacis™

Index Terms Bacillus Calmette-Guérin (BCG) Live; BCG, Live; BCG Vaccine U.S.P. *(percutaneous use product)*

Pharmacologic Category Biological Response Modulator; Vaccine

Use Immunization against tuberculosis and immunotherapy for cancer; treatment and prophylaxis of carcinoma *in situ* of the bladder; prophylaxis of primary or recurrent superficial papillary tumors following transurethral resection

Pregnancy Risk Factor C

Medication Safety Issues

High alert medication: The Institute for Safe Medication Practices (ISMP) includes this medication among its list of drugs which have a heightened risk of causing significant patient harm when used in error.

Dosage

Immunization against tuberculosis: Percutaneous: **Note:** Initial lesion usually appears after 10-14 days consisting of small, red papule at injection site and reaches maximum diameter of 3 mm in 4-6 weeks.

Children <1 month: 0.2-0.3 mL (half-strength dilution). Administer tuberculin test (5 TU) after 2-3 months; repeat vaccination after 1 year of age for negative tuberculin test if indications persist.

Children >1 month and Adults: 0.2-0.3 mL (full strength dilution); conduct postvaccinal tuberculin test (5 TU of PPD) in 2-3 months; If test is negative, repeat vaccination

(Continued)

BCG Vaccine (Continued)

Immunotherapy for bladder cancer: Intravesicular: Adults:
> TheraCys®: One dose instilled into bladder (for 2 hours) once weekly for 6 weeks followed by one treatment at 3, 6, 12, 18, and 24 months after initial treatment
>
> TICE® BCG: One dose instilled into the bladder (for 2 hours) once weekly for 6 weeks followed by once monthly for 6-12 months

Additional Information Complete prescribing information for this medication should be consulted for additional detail.

Dosage Forms

Injection, powder for reconstitution, intravesical [preservative free]:
> TheraCys®: 81 mg [with diluent]
> TICE® BCG: 50 mg

Injection, powder for reconstitution, percutaneous [preservative free]:
> BCG Vaccine U.S.P.: 50 mg

- ♦ **BCG Vaccine U.S.P. (percutaneous use product)** see BCG Vaccine on page 197
- ♦ **BCI-Fluoxetine (Can)** see Fluoxetine on page 727
- ♦ **BCI-Gabapentin (Can)** see Gabapentin on page 775
- ♦ **BCI-Metformin (Can)** see Metformin on page 1098
- ♦ **BCI-Ranitidine (Can)** see Ranitidine on page 1485
- ♦ **BCI-Simvastatin (Can)** see Simvastatin on page 1567
- ♦ **BCNU** see Carmustine on page 296
- ♦ **beano® [OTC]** see Alpha-Galactosidase on page 74
- ♦ **Bebulin® VH** see Factor IX Complex (Human) on page 681

Becaplermin (be KAP ler min)

U.S. Brand Names Regranex®
Canadian Brand Names Regranex®
Index Terms Recombinant Human Platelet-Derived Growth Factor B; rPDGF-BB
Pharmacologic Category Growth Factor, Platelet-Derived; Topical Skin Product
Use Debridement adjunct for the treatment of diabetic ulcers that occur on the lower limbs and feet
Pregnancy Risk Factor C
Medication Safety Issues
Sound-alike/look-alike issues:
> Regranex® may be confused with Granulex®, Repronex®

Contraindications Hypersensitivity to becaplermin or any component of the formulation; known neoplasm(s) at the site(s) of application; active infection at ulcer site
Warnings/Precautions Concurrent use of corticosteroids, cancer chemotherapy, or other immunosuppressive agents; ulcer wounds related to arterial or venous insufficiency. Thermal, electrical, or radiation burns at wound site. Malignancy (potential for tumor proliferation, although unproven; topical absorption is minimal). Should not be used in wounds that close by primary intention. For external use only.
Adverse Reactions <1%: Erythema with purulent discharge, exuberant granulation tissue, local pain, skin ulceration, tunneling of ulcer, ulcer infection
Stability Refrigerate at 2°C to 8°C (36°F to 46°F); do not freeze.
Mechanism of Action Recombinant B-isoform homodimer of human platelet-derived growth factor (rPDGF-BB) which enhances formation of new granulation tissue, induces fibroblast proliferation and differentiation to promote wound healing
Pharmacodynamics/Kinetics
Onset of action: Complete healing: 15% of patients within 8 weeks, 25% at 10 weeks
Absorption: Minimal
Distribution: Binds to PDGF-beta receptors in normal skin and granulation tissue
Dosage Topical: Adults:
Diabetic ulcers: Apply appropriate amount of gel once daily with a cotton swab or similar tool, as a coating over the ulcer
The amount of becaplermin to be applied will vary depending on the size of the ulcer area. To calculate the length of gel applied to the ulcer, measure the greatest length of the ulcer by the greatest width of the ulcer in inches. Tube size will determine the formula used in the calculation. For a 15 or 7.5 g tube, multiply length x width x 0.6. For a 2 g tube, multiply length x width x 1.3.
> **Note:** If the ulcer does not decrease in size by ~30% after 10 weeks of treatment or complete healing has not occurred in 20 weeks, continued treatment with becaplermin gel should be reassessed.

Monitoring Parameters Ulcer volume (pressure ulcers); wound area; evidence of closure; drainage (diabetic ulcers); signs/symptoms of toxicity (erythema, local infections)
Dosage Forms
Gel, topical:
> Regranex®: 0.01% (2 g, 15 g)

Beclomethasone (be kloe METH a sone)

U.S. Brand Names Beconase® AQ; QVAR®
Canadian Brand Names Apo-Beclomethasone®; Gen-Beclo; Nu-Beclomethasone; Propaderm®; QVAR®; Rivanase AQ; Vanceril® AEM
Index Terms Beclomethasone Dipropionate
Pharmacologic Category Corticosteroid, Inhalant (Oral); Corticosteroid, Nasal
Additional Appendix Information
Asthma on page 2029

Use

Oral inhalation: Maintenance and prophylactic treatment of asthma; includes those who require corticosteroids and those who may benefit from a dose reduction/elimination of systemically-administered corticosteroids. Not for relief of acute bronchospasm.

Nasal aerosol: Symptomatic treatment of seasonal or perennial rhinitis; prevent recurrence of nasal polyps following surgery.

Pregnancy Risk Factor C

Pregnancy Implications Teratogenic effects were observed in animal studies. No human data on beclomethasone crossing the placenta or effects on the fetus. A decrease in fetal growth has not been observed with inhaled corticosteroid use during pregnancy. Inhaled corticosteroids are recommended for the treatment of asthma (most information available using budesonide) and allergic rhinitis during pregnancy.

Lactation Excretion in breast milk unknown/use caution

Medication Safety Issues

Sound-alike/look-alike issues:

Vanceril® may be confused with Vancenase®

Contraindications Hypersensitivity to beclomethasone or any component of the formulation; status asthmaticus

Warnings/Precautions May cause hypercorticism or suppression of hypothalamic-pituitary-adrenal (HPA) axis, particularly in younger children or in patients receiving high doses for prolonged periods. HPA axis suppression may lead to adrenal crisis. Withdrawal and discontinuation of a corticosteroid should be done slowly and carefully. Particular care is required when patients are transferred from systemic corticosteroids to inhaled products due to possible adrenal insufficiency or withdrawal from steroids, including an increase in allergic symptoms. Patients receiving >20 mg per day of prednisone (or equivalent) may be most susceptible. Fatalities have occurred due to adrenal insufficiency in asthmatic patients during and after transfer from systemic corticosteroids to aerosol steroids; aerosol steroids do not provide the systemic steroid needed to treat patients having trauma, surgery, or infections.

Bronchospasm may occur with wheezing after inhalation; if this occurs stop steroid and treat with a fast-acting bronchodilator. Supplemental steroids (oral or parenteral) may be needed during stress or severe asthma attacks. Not to be used in status asthmaticus or for the relief of acute bronchospasm. Corticosteroid use may cause psychiatric disturbances, including depression, euphoria, insomnia, mood swings, and personality changes. Pre-existing psychiatric conditions may be exacerbated by corticosteroid use. Prolonged use of corticosteroids may also increase the incidence of secondary infection, mask acute infection (including fungal infections), prolong or exacerbate viral infections, or limit response to vaccines. Exposure to chickenpox should be avoided; corticosteroids should not be used to treat ocular herpes simplex. Corticosteroids should not be used for cerebral malaria. Close observation is required in patients with latent tuberculosis and/or TB reactivity; restrict use in active TB (only in conjunction with antituberculosis treatment). Prolonged treatment with corticosteroids has been associated with the development of Kaposi's sarcoma (case reports); if noted, discontinuation of therapy should be considered.

Use with caution in patients with thyroid disease, hepatic impairment, renal impairment, cardiovascular disease, diabetes, glaucoma, cataracts, myasthenia gravis, patients at risk for osteoporosis, patients at risk for seizures, or GI diseases (diverticulitis, peptic ulcer, ulcerative colitis) due to perforation risk. Use caution following acute MI (corticosteroids have been associated with myocardial rupture). Because of the risk of adverse effects, systemic corticosteroids should be used cautiously in the elderly in the smallest possible effective dose for the shortest duration. Avoid nasal corticosteroid use in patients with recent nasal septal ulcers, nasal surgery or nasal trauma until healing has occurred.

Orally-inhaled and intranasal corticosteroids may cause a reduction in growth velocity in pediatric patients (~1 centimeter per year [range 0.3-1.8 cm per year] and related to dose and duration of exposure). To minimize the systemic effects of orally-inhaled and intranasal corticosteroids, each patient should be titrated to the lowest effective dose. Growth should be routinely monitored in pediatric patients. Safety and efficacy have not been established in children <5 years of age. There have been reports of systemic corticosteroid withdrawal symptoms (eg, joint/muscle pain, lassitude, depression) when withdrawing oral inhalation therapy.

Adverse Reactions Frequency not defined.

Central nervous system: Agitation, depression, dizziness, dysphonia, headache, lightheadedness, mental disturbances

Dermatologic: Acneiform lesions, angioedema, atrophy, bruising, pruritus, purpura, striae, rash, urticaria

Endocrine & metabolic: Cushingoid features, growth velocity reduction in children and adolescents, HPA function suppression

Gastrointestinal: Dry/irritated nose, throat and mouth, hoarseness, localized *Candida* or *Aspergillus* infection, loss of smell, loss of taste, nausea, unpleasant smell, unpleasant taste, vomiting, weight gain

Local: Nasal spray: Burning, epistaxis, localized *Candida* infection, nasal septum perforation (rare), nasal stuffiness, nosebleeds, rhinorrhea, sneezing, transient irritation, ulceration of nasal mucosa (rare)

Ocular: Cataracts, glaucoma, intraocular pressure increased

Respiratory: Cough, paradoxical bronchospasm, pharyngitis, sinusitis, wheezing

Miscellaneous: Anaphylactic/anaphylactoid reactions, death (due to adrenal insufficiency, reported during and after transfer from systemic corticosteroids to aerosol in asthmatic patients); immediate and delayed hypersensitivity reactions

Overdosage/Toxicology Symptoms include irritation and burning of the nasal mucosa, sneezing, intranasal and pharyngeal *Candida* infections, nasal ulceration, epistaxis, rhinorrhea, nasal stuffiness, and headache. When consumed in excessive quantities, systemic hypercorticism and adrenal suppression may occur; in those cases, discontinuation and withdrawal of the corticosteroid should be done judiciously.

(Continued)

Beclomethasone *(Continued)*

Drug Interactions
Increased Effect/Toxicity: The addition of salmeterol has been demonstrated to improve response to inhaled corticosteroids (as compared to increasing steroid dosage).

Stability Do not store near heat or open flame. Do not puncture canisters. Store at room temperature. Rest QVAR® on concave end of canister with actuator on top.

Mechanism of Action Controls the rate of protein synthesis; depresses the migration of polymorphonuclear leukocytes, fibroblasts; reverses capillary permeability and lysosomal stabilization at the cellular level to prevent or control inflammation

Pharmacodynamics/Kinetics
Onset of action: Therapeutic effect: 1-4 weeks

Absorption: Readily; quickly hydrolyzed by pulmonary esterases prior to absorption

Distribution: Beclomethasone: 20 L; active metabolite: 424 L

Protein binding: 87%

Metabolism: Hepatic via CYP3A4 to active metabolites

Bioavailability: Of active metabolite, 44% following nasal inhalation (43% from swallowed portion)

Half-life elimination: Initial: 3 hours

Excretion: Feces (60%); urine (12%)

Dosage Nasal inhalation and oral inhalation dosage forms are not to be used interchangeably

Inhalation, nasal: Rhinitis, nasal polyps (Beconase® AQ): Children ≥6 years and Adults: 1-2 inhalations each nostril twice daily; total dose 168-336 mcg/day

Inhalation, oral: Asthma (doses should be titrated to the lowest effective dose once asthma is controlled) (QVAR®):

Children 5-11 years: Initial: 40 mcg twice daily; maximum dose: 80 mcg twice daily

Children ≥12 years and Adults:

Patients previously on bronchodilators only: Initial dose 40-80 mcg twice daily; maximum dose: 320 mcg twice day

Patients previously on inhaled corticosteroids: Initial dose 40-160 mcg twice daily; maximum dose: 320 mcg twice daily

NIH Asthma Guidelines (NAEPP, 2002; NIH, 1997): HFA formulation (eg, QVAR®): Administer in divided doses:

Children ≤12 years:

"Low" dose: 80-160 mcg/day

"Medium" dose: 160-320 mcg/day

"High" dose: >320 mcg/day

Children >12 years and Adults:

"Low" dose: 80-240 mcg/day

"Medium" dose: 240-480 mcg/day

"High" dose: >480 mcg/day

Administration
Beconase AQ®: Shake well before use. Nasal applicator and dust cap may be washed in warm water and dry thoroughly.

QVAR®: Rinse mouth and throat after use to prevent *Candida* infection. Do not wash or put inhaler in water; mouth piece may be cleaned with a dry tissue or cloth. Prime canister before using.

Additional Information Effects of inhaled/intranasal steroids on growth have been observed in the absence of laboratory evidence of HPA axis suppression, suggesting that growth velocity is a more sensitive indicator of systemic corticosteroid exposure in pediatric patients than some commonly used tests of HPA axis function. The long-term effects of this reduction in growth velocity associated with orally-inhaled and intranasal corticosteroids, including the impact on final adult height, are unknown. The potential for "catch up" growth following discontinuation of treatment with inhaled corticosteroids has not been adequately studied.

Dosage Forms
Aerosol for oral inhalation, as dipropionate:

QVAR®: 40 mcg/inhalation [100 metered actuations] (7.3 g); 80 mcg/inhalation [100 metered actuations] (7.3 g)

Suspension, intranasal, as dipropionate [aqueous spray]:

Beconase® AQ: 42 mcg/inhalation [180 metered sprays (25 g)

- ◆ **Beclomethasone Dipropionate** *see* Beclomethasone *on page 198*
- ◆ **Beconase® AQ** *see* Beclomethasone *on page 198*
- ◆ **Behenyl Alcohol** *see* Docosanol *on page 533*
- ◆ **Belladonna Alkaloids With Phenobarbital** *see* Hyoscyamine, Atropine, Scopolamine, and Phenobarbital *on page 868*

Belladonna and Opium (bel a DON a & OH pee um)

U.S. Brand Names B&O Supprettes®

Index Terms Opium and Belladonna

Pharmacologic Category Analgesic Combination (Opioid); Antispasmodic Agent, Urinary

Use Relief of moderate-to-severe pain associated with ureteral spasms not responsive to nonopioid analgesics and to space intervals between injections of opiates

Restrictions C-II

Pregnancy Risk Factor C

Pregnancy Implications Reproduction studies have not been conducted with this product. Refer to Atropine and Morphine Sulfate monographs for additional information.

Lactation Excretion in breast milk unknown/use caution

Contraindications Hypersensitivity to belladonna, opium, or any component of the formulation; glaucoma; severe renal or hepatic disease; bronchial asthma; respiratory depression; convulsive disorders; acute alcoholism; premature labor

Warnings/Precautions Usual precautions of opiate agonist therapy should be observed. Use caution with known idiosyncrasy to atropine or atropine-like compounds; hypersensitivity reactions to other phenanthrene derivative opioid agonists (codeine, hydrocodone, hydromorphone, levorphanol, oxycodone, oxymorphone); persons dependent upon morphine; cardiac disease; prostatic hyperplasia; increased intracranial pressure; toxic psychosis; myxedema; the elderly. Not recommended for use in children ≤12 years of age.

Adverse Reactions Frequency not defined.
Cardiovascular: Palpitation
Central nervous system: Dizziness, drowsiness
Dermatologic: Pruritus, urticaria
Gastrointestinal: Constipation, nausea, vomiting, xerostomia
Genitourinary: Urinary retention
Ocular: Blurred vision, photophobia

Overdosage/Toxicology Primary attention should be directed to ensuring adequate respiratory exchange. Opiate agonist-induced respiratory depression may be reversed with parenteral naloxone hydrochloride. Anticholinergic toxicity may be caused by strong binding of a belladonna alkaloid to cholinergic receptors. Anticholinesterase inhibitors reduce acetylcholinesterase, the enzyme that breaks down acetylcholine and thereby allows acetylcholine to accumulate and compete for receptor binding with the offending anticholinergic. For an overdose with severe life-threatening symptoms, physostigmine 1-2 mg (0.5 mg or 0.02 mg/kg for children) SubQ or slow I.V., may be given to reverse these effects.

Drug Interactions
Increased Effect/Toxicity: Additive effects with CNS depressants. Coadministration with other anticholinergic agents (phenothiazines, tricyclic antidepressants, amantadine, and antihistamines) may increase effects such as dry mouth, constipation, and urinary retention. Hypotensive and anticholinergic effects may be enhanced with concomitant use of phenothiazines. Opioid analgesics may enhance the serotonergic effect of SSRIs.
Decreased Effect: May decrease effects of drugs with cholinergic mechanisms.

Ethanol/Nutrition/Herb Interactions Ethanol: Avoid ethanol (may increase sedation).

Stability Store at 15°C to 30°C. Do not refrigerate.

Mechanism of Action The pharmacologically active agents present in the belladonna component are atropine and scopolamine. Atropine blocks the action of acetylcholine at parasympathetic sites in smooth muscle, secretory glands, and the CNS causing a relaxation of smooth muscle and drying of secretions. The principle agent in opium is morphine. Morphine binds to opiate receptors in the CNS, causing inhibition of ascending pain pathways, altering the perception of and response to pain.

Pharmacodynamics/Kinetics Absorption: Rectal absorption is dependent upon body hydration, not temperature

Dosage Rectal: Children >12 years and Adults: 1 suppository 1-2 times/day, up to 4 doses/day

Administration Prior to rectal insertion, the finger and suppository should be moistened. Assist with ambulation.

Dosage Forms
Suppository: Belladonna extract 16.2 mg and opium 30 mg; belladonna extract 16.2 mg and opium 60 mg
B&O Supprettes® #15 A: Belladonna extract 16.2 mg and opium 30 mg
B&O Supprettes® #16 A: Belladonna extract 16.2 mg and opium 60 mg

---

Belladonna, Phenobarbital, and Ergotamine
(bel a DON a, fee noe BAR bi tal, & er GOT a meen)

U.S. Brand Names Bellamine S; Bel-Tabs [DSC]; Eperbel-S; Spastrin®
Canadian Brand Names Bellergal® Spacetabs®
Index Terms Ergotamine Tartrate, Belladonna, and Phenobarbital; Phenobarbital, Belladonna, and Ergotamine Tartrate
Pharmacologic Category Ergot Derivative
Use Management and treatment of menopausal disorders, GI disorders, and recurrent throbbing headache
Pregnancy Risk Factor X
Dosage Oral: 1 tablet each morning and evening
Additional Information Complete prescribing information for this medication should be consulted for additional detail.
Dosage Forms [DSC] = Discontinued product
Tablet:
Bel-Tabs [DSC], Bellamie S, Eperbel-S, Spastrin®: Belladonna alkaloids 0.2 mg, phenobarbital 40 mg, and ergotamine 0.6 mg

♦ **Bellamine S** see Belladonna, Phenobarbital, and Ergotamine on page 201
♦ **Bellergal® Spacetabs® (Can)** see Belladonna, Phenobarbital, and Ergotamine on page 201
♦ **Bel-Tabs [DSC]** see Belladonna, Phenobarbital, and Ergotamine on page 201
♦ **Benadryl® (Can)** see DiphenhydrAMINE on page 515
♦ **Benadryl-D™ Allergy and Sinus Fastmelt™ [OTC]** see Diphenhydramine and Pseudoephedrine on page 517
♦ **Benadryl-D™ Children's Allergy and Sinus [OTC]** see Diphenhydramine and Pseudoephedrine on page 517
♦ **Benadryl® Allergy [OTC]** see DiphenhydrAMINE on page 515
♦ **Benadryl® Children's Allergy [OTC]** see DiphenhydrAMINE on page 515
♦ **Benadryl® Children's Allergy and Cold Fastmelt™ [OTC]** see Diphenhydramine and Pseudoephedrine on page 517
♦ **Benadryl® Children's Allergy Fastmelt® [OTC]** see DiphenhydrAMINE on page 515
♦ **Benadryl® Dye-Free Allergy [OTC]** see DiphenhydrAMINE on page 515
♦ **Benadryl® Injection** see DiphenhydrAMINE on page 515
♦ **Benadryl® Itch Stopping [OTC]** see DiphenhydrAMINE on page 515
♦ **Benadryl® Itch Stopping Extra Strength [OTC]** see DiphenhydrAMINE on page 515

Benazepril (ben AY ze pril)

U.S. Brand Names Lotensin®
Canadian Brand Names Apo-Benazepril®; Lotensin®
Index Terms Benazepril Hydrochloride
Pharmacologic Category Angiotensin-Converting Enzyme (ACE) Inhibitor
Additional Appendix Information
Angiotensin Agents *on page 1860*
Use Treatment of hypertension, either alone or in combination with other antihypertensive agents
Pregnancy Risk Factor C (1st trimester)/D (2nd and 3rd trimesters)
Pregnancy Implications Decreased placental blood flow, low birth weight, fetal hypotension, preterm delivery, and fetal death have been noted with the use of some ACE inhibitors (ACEIs) in animal studies. Neonatal hypotension, skull hypoplasia, anuria, renal failure, oligohydramnios (associated with fetal limb contractures, craniofacial deformities, hypoplastic lung development), prematurity, intrauterine growth retardation, and patent ductus arteriosus have been reported with the use of ACEIs, primarily in the 2nd and 3rd trimesters. The risk of neonatal toxicity has been considered less when ACEIs have been used in the 1st trimester; however, major congenital malformations have been reported. The cardiovascular and/or central nervous systems are most commonly affected. Unless alternative agents are not appropriate, ACEIs should be discontinued as soon as possible once pregnancy is detected.
Lactation Enters breast milk/compatible
Medication Safety Issues
Sound-alike/look-alike issues:
Benazepril may be confused with Benadryl®
Lotensin® may be confused with Lioresal®, lovastatin

International issues:
Lotensin® may be confused with Latensin® which is a brand name for bacillus cereus in Germany
Contraindications Hypersensitivity to benazepril or any component of the formulation; angioedema or serious hypersensitivity related to previous treatment with an ACE inhibitor; bilateral renal artery stenosis; patients with idiopathic or hereditary angioedema; pregnancy (2nd and 3rd trimesters)
Warnings/Precautions Anaphylactic reactions can occur. Angioedema can occur at any time during treatment (especially following first dose). Angioedema can occur at any time during treatment (especially following first dose). It may involve head and neck (potentially affecting the airway) or the intestine (presenting with abdominal pain). Prolonged monitoring may be required especially if tongue, glottis, or larynx are involved as they are associated with airway obstruction. Those with a history of airway surgery in this situation have a higher risk. Careful blood pressure monitoring with first dose (hypotension can occur especially in volume-depleted patients). **[U.S. Boxed Warning]: Based on human data, ACEIs can cause injury and death to the developing fetus when used in the second and third trimesters. ACEIs should be discontinued as soon as possible once pregnancy is detected.** Dosage adjustment needed in renal impairment. Use with caution in hypovolemia; collagen vascular diseases; valvular stenosis (particularly aortic stenosis); hyperkalemia; or before, during, or immediately after anesthesia. Hyperkalemia may occur. Avoid rapid dosage escalation which may lead to renal insufficiency. Rare toxicities associated with ACE inhibitors include cholestatic jaundice (which may progress to hepatic necrosis) and neutropenia/agranulocytosis with myeloid hyperplasia. Hypersensitivity reactions may be seen during hemodialysis with high-flux dialysis membranes (eg, AN69). May be associated with deterioration of renal function and/or increases in serum creatinine, particularly in patients dependent on renin-angiotensin-aldosterone system. Use with caution in unilateral renal artery stenosis and pre-existing renal insufficiency; if patient has renal impairment then a baseline WBC with differential and serum creatinine should be evaluated and monitored closely during the first 3 months of therapy. Safety and efficacy have not been established in children <6 years of age.
Adverse Reactions
1% to 10%:
Cardiovascular: Postural dizziness (1.5%)
Central nervous system: Headache (6.2%), dizziness (3.6%), fatigue (2.4%), somnolence (1.6%)
Endocrine & metabolic: Hyperkalemia (1%), uric acid increased
Gastrointestinal: Nausea (1.3%)
Renal: Serum creatinine increased (2%), worsening of renal function may occur in patients with bilateral renal artery stenosis or hypovolemia
Respiratory: Cough (1.2% to 10%)
<1% (Limited to important or life-threatening): Alopecia, angina, angioedema, asthma, dermatitis, dyspnea, hemolytic anemia, hypersensitivity, hypotension, impotence, insomnia, pancreatitis, paresthesia, photosensitivity, postural hypotension (0.3%), rash, shock, Stevens-Johnson syndrome, syncope, thrombocytopenia, vomiting
Eosinophilic pneumonitis, neutropenia, anaphylaxis, renal insufficiency, and renal failure have been reported with other ACE inhibitors. In addition, a syndrome including fever, myalgia, arthralgia, interstitial nephritis, vasculitis, rash, eosinophilia, and elevated ESR has been reported to be associated with ACE inhibitors.
Overdosage/Toxicology Mild hypotension has been the only toxic effect seen with acute overdose; bradycardia may also occur. Hyperkalemia occurs even with therapeutic doses, especially in patients with renal insufficiency and those taking NSAIDs. Following initiation of essential overdose management, toxic symptom treatment and supportive treatment should be initiated. Hypotension usually responds to I.V. fluids or Trendelenburg positioning.
Drug Interactions
Increased Effect/Toxicity: Potassium supplements, co-trimoxazole (high dose), angiotensin II receptor antagonists (eg, candesartan, losartan, irbesartan), or potassium-sparing diuretics (amiloride, spironolactone, triamterene) may result in elevated serum potassium

levels when combined with benazepril. ACE inhibitor effects may be increased by phenothiazines or probenecid (increases levels of captopril). ACE inhibitors may increase serum concentrations/effects of lithium. Diuretics have additive hypotensive effects with ACE inhibitors, and hypovolemia increases the potential for adverse renal effects of ACE inhibitors. In patients with compromised renal function, coadministration with NSAIDs may result in further deterioration of renal function. Allopurinol and ACE inhibitors may cause a higher risk of hypersensitivity reaction when taken concurrently. ACE inhibitors may enhance the adverse/toxic effects (nitritoid reaction) of gold sodium thiomalate.

Decreased Effect: Aspirin (high dose) may reduce the therapeutic effects of ACE inhibitors; at low dosages this does not appear to be significant. Rifampin may decrease the effect of ACE inhibitors. Antacids may decrease the bioavailability of ACE inhibitors (may be more likely to occur with captopril); separate administration times by 1-2 hours. NSAIDs, specifically indomethacin, may reduce the hypotensive effects of ACE inhibitors.

Ethanol/Nutrition/Herb Interactions Herb/Nutraceutical: Avoid dong quai if using for hypertension (has estrogenic activity). Avoid ephedra, yohimbe, ginseng (may worsen hypertension). Avoid garlic (may have increased antihypertensive effect).

Mechanism of Action Competitive inhibition of angiotensin I being converted to angiotensin II, a potent vasoconstrictor, through the angiotensin I-converting enzyme (ACE) activity, with resultant lower levels of angiotensin II which causes an increase in plasma renin activity and a reduction in aldosterone secretion

Pharmacodynamics/Kinetics

Reduction in plasma angiotensin-converting enzyme (ACE) activity:
Onset of action: Peak effect: 1-2 hours after 2-20 mg dose
Duration: >90% inhibition for 24 hours after 5-20 mg dose

Reduction in blood pressure:
Peak effect: Single dose: 2-4 hours; Continuous therapy: 2 weeks

Absorption: Rapid (37%); food does not alter significantly; metabolite (benazeprilat) itself unsuitable for oral administration due to poor absorption

Distribution: V_d: ~8.7 L

Metabolism: Rapidly and extensively hepatic to its active metabolite, benazeprilat, via enzymatic hydrolysis; extensive first-pass effect

Half-life elimination: Benazeprilat: Effective: 10-11 hours; Terminal: Children: 5 hours, Adults: 22 hours

Time to peak: Parent drug: 0.5-1 hour

Excretion: Clearance: Nonrenal clearance (ie, biliary, metabolic) appears to contribute to the elimination of benazeprilat (11% to 12%), particularly patients with severe renal impairment; hepatic clearance is the main elimination route of unchanged benazepril

Dialysis: ~6% of metabolite removed within 4 hours of dialysis following 10 mg of benazepril administered 2 hours prior to procedure; parent compound not found in dialysate

Dosage Oral: Hypertension:
Children ≥6 years: Initial: 0.2 mg/kg/day as monotherapy; dosing range: 0.1-0.6 mg/kg/day (maximum dose: 40 mg/day)

Adults: Initial: 10 mg/day in patients not receiving a diuretic; 20-40 mg/day as a single dose or 2 divided doses; the need for twice-daily dosing should be assessed by monitoring peak (2-6 hours after dosing) and trough responses.

Note: Patients taking diuretics should have them discontinued 2-3 days prior to starting benazepril. If they cannot be discontinued, then initial dose should be 5 mg; restart after blood pressure is stabilized if needed.

Elderly: Oral: Initial: 5-10 mg/day in single or divided doses; usual range: 20-40 mg/day; adjust for renal function; also see **Note** in adult dosing.

Dosing interval in renal impairment: Cl_{cr} <30 mL/minute:
Children: Use is not recommended.
Adults: Administer 5 mg/day initially; maximum daily dose: 40 mg.
Hemodialysis: Moderately dialyzable (20% to 50%); administer dose postdialysis or administer 25% to 35% supplemental dose.
Peritoneal dialysis: Supplemental dose is not necessary.

Monitoring Parameters CBC, renal function tests, electrolytes

Dosage Forms
Tablet, as hydrochloride: 5 mg, 10 mg, 20 mg, 40 mg
Lotensin®: 5 mg, 10 mg, 20 mg, 40 mg

Extemporaneous Preparations To prepare a 2 mg/mL suspension, mix 15 benazepril 20 mg tablets in a bottle with Ora-Plus® 75 mL. Shake for 2 minutes, allow suspension to stand for ≥1 hour, then shake again for at least 1 additional minute. Add Ora-Sweet® 75 mL to suspension and shake to disperse. Will make 150 mL of a 2 mg/mL suspension. Store under refrigeration at 2°C to 8°C (36°F to 46°F) for up to 30 days. Shake prior to each use.

Benazepril and Hydrochlorothiazide
(ben AY ze pril & hye droe klor oh THYE a zide)

U.S. Brand Names Lotensin® HCT
Index Terms Hydrochlorothiazide and Benazepril
Pharmacologic Category Antihypertensive Agent, Combination
Use Treatment of hypertension
Pregnancy Risk Factor C/D (2nd and 3rd trimesters)
Dosage Oral: Dose is individualized (range: benazepril: 5-20 mg; hydrochlorothiazide: 6.25-25 mg/day)
Cl_{cr} <30 mL/minute: Not recommended; loop diuretics are preferred.
Additional Information Complete prescribing information for this medication should be consulted for additional detail.
Dosage Forms
Tablet: 5/6.25: Benazepril hydrochloride 5 mg and hydrochlorothiazide 6.25 mg; 10/12.5: Benazepril hydrochloride 10 mg and hydrochlorothiazide 12.5 mg; 20/12.5: Benazepril (Continued)

Benazepril and Hydrochlorothiazide *(Continued)*

hydrochloride 20 mg and hydrochlorothiazide 12.5 mg; 20/25: Benazepril hydrochloride 20 mg and hydrochlorothiazide 25 mg

Lotensin® HCT 5/6.25: Benazepril hydrochloride 5 mg and hydrochlorothiazide 6.25 mg
Lotensin® HCT 10/12.5: Benazepril hydrochloride 10 mg and hydrochlorothiazide 12.5 mg
Lotensin® HCT 20/12.5: Benazepril hydrochloride 20 mg and hydrochlorothiazide 12.5 mg
Lotensin® HCT 20/25: Benazepril hydrochloride 20 mg and hydrochlorothiazide 25 mg

♦ **Benazepril Hydrochloride** *see Benazepril on page 202*
♦ **Benazepril Hydrochloride and Amlodipine Besylate** *see Amlodipine and Benazepril on page 106*
♦ **BeneFix®** *see Factor IX on page 679*
♦ **Beneflur® (Can)** *see Fludarabine on page 716*
♦ **Benemid [DSC]** *see Probenecid on page 1423*
♦ **Benicar®** *see Olmesartan on page 1260*
♦ **Benicar HCT®** *see Olmesartan and Hydrochlorothiazide on page 1261*

Bentoquatam (BEN toe kwa tam)

U.S. Brand Names IvyBlock® [OTC]
Index Terms Quaternium-18 Bentonite
Pharmacologic Category Topical Skin Product
Use Skin protectant for the prevention of allergic contact dermatitis to poison oak, ivy, and sumac
Contraindications Hypersensitivity to bentoquatam or any component of the formulation
Warnings/Precautions Use with caution in patients with history of allergic-type responses to medications (especially topical formulations); open wounds, psoriatic lesions, or other cutaneous conditions. Use with caution in patients who are postexposure to poison oak, ivy, or sumac (lack of efficacy).
Adverse Reactions <1% (Limited to important or life-threatening): Erythema
Mechanism of Action An organoclay substance which is capable of absorbing or binding to urushiol, the active principle in poison oak, ivy, and sumac. Bentoquatam serves as a barrier, blocking urushiol skin contact/absorption.
Pharmacodynamics/Kinetics Absorption: Has not been studied
Dosage Children >6 years and Adults: Topical: Apply to skin 15 minutes prior to potential exposure to poison ivy, poison oak, or poison sumac, and reapply every 4 hours
Monitoring Parameters Signs and symptoms of exposure to poison oak, ivy, or sumac (rash, swelling, blisters)
Dosage Forms
Lotion:
IvyBlock®: 5% (120 mL) [contains alcohol 25% and benzyl alcohol]

♦ **Bentyl®** *see Dicyclomine on page 496*
♦ **Bentylol® (Can)** *see Dicyclomine on page 496*
♦ **Benuryl™ (Can)** *see Probenecid on page 1423*
♦ **Benylin® 3.3 mg-D-E (Can)** *see Guaifenesin, Pseudoephedrine, and Codeine on page 820*
♦ **Benylin® D for Infants (Can)** *see Pseudoephedrine on page 1454*
♦ **Benylin® DM-D (Can)** *see Pseudoephedrine and Dextromethorphan on page 1455*
♦ **Benylin® DM-D-E (Can)** *see Guaifenesin, Pseudoephedrine, and Dextromethorphan on page 821*
♦ **Benylin® DM-E (Can)** *see Guaifenesin and Dextromethorphan on page 816*
♦ **Benylin® E Extra Strength (Can)** *see Guaifenesin on page 814*
♦ **Benylin® Expectorant [OTC] [DSC]** *see Guaifenesin and Dextromethorphan on page 816*
♦ **Benzalkonium Chloride, Benzocaine, Butyl Aminobenzoate, and Tetracaine Hydrochloride** *see Benzocaine, Butyl Aminobenzoate, Tetracaine, and Benzalkonium Chloride on page 207*
♦ **Benzamycin®** *see Erythromycin and Benzoyl Peroxide on page 613*
♦ **Benzamycin® Pak** *see Erythromycin and Benzoyl Peroxide on page 613*
♦ **Benzathine Benzylpenicillin** *see Penicillin G Benzathine on page 1332*
♦ **Benzathine Penicillin G** *see Penicillin G Benzathine on page 1332*
♦ **Benzazoline Hydrochloride** *see Tolazoline on page 1701*
♦ **Benzene Hexachloride** *see Lindane on page 1016*
♦ **Benzhexol Hydrochloride** *see Trihexyphenidyl on page 1742*
♦ **Benzmethyzin** *see Procarbazine on page 1428*

Benzocaine (BEN zoe kane)

U.S. Brand Names Americaine® [OTC]; Americaine® Hemorrhoidal [OTC]; Anbesol® [OTC]; Anbesol® Baby [OTC]; Anbesol® Cold Sore Therapy [OTC]; Anbesol® Jr. [OTC]; Anbesol® Maximum Strength [OTC]; Benzodent® [OTC]; Cepacol® Sore Throat [OTC]; Chiggerex® [OTC]; Chiggertox® [OTC]; Cylex® [OTC]; Dentapaine [OTC]; Dent's Extra Strength Toothache [OTC]; Dent's Maxi-Strength Toothache [OTC]; Dermoplast® Antibacterial [OTC]; Dermoplast® Pain Relieving [OTC]; Detane® [OTC]; Foille® [OTC]; HDA® Toothache [OTC]; Hurricaine® [OTC]; Ivy-Rid® [OTC]; Kanka® Soft Brush™ [OTC]; Lanacane® [OTC]; Lanacane® Maximum Strength [OTC]; Mycinettes® [OTC]; Orabase® with Benzocaine [OTC]; Orajel® Baby Daytime and Nighttime [OTC]; Orajel® Baby Teething [OTC]; Orajel® Baby Teething Nighttime [OTC]; Orajel® Denture Plus [OTC]; Orajel® Maximum Strength [OTC]; Orajel® Medicated Toothache [OTC]; Orajel® Mouth Sore [OTC]; Orajel® Multi-Action Cold Sore [OTC]; Orajel PM® [OTC]; Orajel® Ultra Mouth Sore [OTC]; Oticaine; Otocaine™; Outgro® [OTC]; Red Cross™ Canker Sore [OTC]; Rid-A-Pain Dental Drops [OTC]; Skeeter

Stik [OTC]; Sting-Kill [OTC]; Tanac® [OTC]; Thorets [OTC]; Trocaine® [OTC]; Zilactin®-B [OTC]; Zilactin Toothache and Gum Pain® [OTC]

Canadian Brand Names Anbesol® Baby; Zilactin-B®; Zilactin Baby®

Index Terms Ethyl Aminobenzoate

Pharmacologic Category Local Anesthetic

Use Temporary relief of pain associated with pruritic dermatosis, pruritus, minor burns, acute congestive and serous otitis media, swimmer's ear, otitis externa, bee stings, insect bites; mouth and gum irritations (toothache, minor sore throat pain, canker sores, dentures, orthodontia, teething, mucositis, stomatitis); sunburn; hemorrhoids; anesthetic lubricant for passage of catheters and endoscopic tubes

Pregnancy Risk Factor C

Pregnancy Implications Reproduction studies have not been conducted.

Lactation Excretion in breast milk unknown/use caution

Medication Safety Issues

Sound-alike/look-alike issues:

Orabase®-B may be confused with Orinase®

Contraindications Hypersensitivity to benzocaine, other ester-type local anesthetics, or any component of the formulation; secondary bacterial infection of area; ophthalmic use; otic preparations are also contraindicated in the presence of perforated tympanic membrane

Warnings/Precautions Methemoglobinemia has been reported following topical use (rare), particularly with higher concentration (14% to 20%) spray formulations applied to the mouth or mucous membranes. When applied as a spray to the mouth or throat, multiple sprays (or sprays of longer than indicated duration) are not recommended. Use caution with breathing problems (asthma, bronchitis, emphysema, in smokers), inflamed/damaged mucosa, heart disease, children <6 months of age, and homoglobin or enzyme abnormalities (glucose-6-phosphodiesterase deficiency, hemoglobin-M disease, NADH-methemoglobin reductase deficiency, pyruvate-kinase deficiency). Alternatives to benzocaine sprays, such as topical lidocaine preparations, should be considered for patients at higher risk of this reaction.

The classical clinical finding of methemoglobinemia is chocolate brown-colored arterial blood. However, suspected cases should be confirmed by co-oximetry, which yields a direct and accurate measure of methemoglobin levels. Standard pulse oximetry readings or arterial blood gas values are not reliable. Clinically significant methemoglobinemia requires immediate treatment.

When used for self-medication (OTC), notify healthcare provider if condition worsens or does not improve within 7 days, or if swelling, rash, or fever develops. Do not use on open wounds. Avoid contact with the eyes.

Adverse Reactions Frequency not defined.

Hematologic: Methemoglobinemia

Local: Burning, contact dermatitis, edema, erythema, pruritus, rash, stinging, tenderness, urticaria

Miscellaneous: Hypersensitivity

Overdosage/Toxicology Methemoglobinemia has been reported with benzocaine in oral overdose. Treatment is primarily symptomatic and supportive. Termination of anesthesia by pneumatic tourniquet inflation should be attempted when the agent is administered by infiltration or regional injection. The classical clinical finding of methemoglobinemia is chocolate brown-colored arterial blood. However, suspected cases should be confirmed by co-oximetry, which yields a direct and accurate measure of methemoglobin levels. Standard pulse oximetry readings or arterial blood gas values are not reliable. Clinically significant methemoglobinemia requires immediate treatment. Methemoglobinemia may be treated with methylene blue, 1-2 mg/kg I.V. infused over several minutes. Seizures commonly respond to diazepam, while hypotension responds to I.V. fluids and Trendelenburg positioning. Bradyarrhythmias (when the heart rate is <60) can be treated with I.V., I.M., or SubQ atropine 15 mcg/kg. With the development of metabolic acidosis, I.V. sodium bicarbonate 0.5-2 mEq/kg and ventilatory assistance should be instituted.

Drug Interactions

Decreased Effect: May antagonize actions of sulfonamides.

Mechanism of Action Ester local anesthetic blocks both the initiation and conduction of nerve impulses by decreasing the neuronal membrane's permeability to sodium ions, which results in inhibition of depolarization with resultant blockade of conduction

Pharmacodynamics/Kinetics

Absorption: Topical: Poor to intact skin; well absorbed from mucous membranes and traumatized skin

Metabolism: Hepatic (to a lesser extent) and plasma via hydrolysis by cholinesterase

Excretion: Urine (as metabolites)

Dosage Note: These are general dosing guidelines; refer to specific product labeling for dosing instructions.

Children ≥4 months: Topical (oral): Teething pain: 7.5% to 10%: Apply to affected gum area up to 4 times daily

Children ≥2 years and Adults:

Topical:

Bee stings, insect bites, minor burns, sunburn: 5% to 20%: Apply to affected area 3-4 times a day as needed. In cases of bee stings, remove stinger before treatment.

Lubricant for passage of catheters and instruments: 20%: Apply evenly to exterior of instrument prior to use.

Topical (oral): Mouth and gum irritation: 10% to 20%: Apply thin layer to affected area up to 4 times daily

Children ≥5 years and Adults: Oral: Sore throat: Allow one lozenge (10-15 mg) to dissolve slowly in mouth; may repeat every 2 hours as needed

Children ≥12 years and Adults: Rectal: Hemorrhoids: 5% to 20%: Apply externally to affected area up to 6 times daily

Adults: Otic: 20%: Instill 4-5 drops into external auditory canal; may repeat in 1-2 hours if needed

(Continued)

Benzocaine *(Continued)*

Monitoring Parameters

Monitor patients for signs and symptoms of methemoglobinemia such as pallor, cyanosis, nausea, muscle weakness, dizziness, confusion, agitation, dyspnea and tachycardia. The classical clinical finding of methemoglobinemia is chocolate brown-colored arterial blood. However, suspected cases should be confirmed by co-oximetry, which yields a direct and accurate measure of methemoglobin levels. Standard pulse oximetry readings or arterial blood gas values are not reliable. Clinically significant methemoglobinemia requires immediate treatment.

Dosage Forms

Aerosol, oral spray (Hurricaine®): 20% (60 mL) [dye free; cherry flavor]

Aerosol, topical spray:

Americaine®: 20% (60 mL)

Dermoplast® Antibacterial: 20% (83 mL) [contains aloe vera, benzethonium chloride, menthol]

Dermoplast® Pain Relieving: 20% (60 mL, 83 mL) [contains menthol]

Foille®: 5% (92 g) [contains chloroxylenol 0.63% and corn oil]

Ivy-Rid®: 2% (83 mL)

Lanacane® Maximum Strength: 20% (120 mL) [contains alcohol]

Solarcaine®: 20% (120 mL) [contains triclosan 0.13%, alcohol 35%]

Combination package (Orajel® Baby Daytime and Nighttime):

Gel, oral [Daytime Regular Formula]: 7.5% (5.3 g)

Gel, oral [Nighttime Formula]: 10% (5.3 g)

Cream, oral:

Benzodent®: 20% (7.5 g, 30 g)

Orajel PM®: 20% (5.3 g, 7 g)

Cream, topical:

Lanacane®: 6% (30 g, 60 g)

Lanacane® Maximum Strength: 20% (30 g)

Gel, oral:

Anbesol®: 10% (7.5 g) [contains benzyl alcohol; cool mint flavor]

Anbesol® Baby: 7.5% (7.5 g) [contains benzoic acid; grape flavor]

Anbesol® Jr.: 10% (7 g) [contains benzyl alcohol; bubble gum flavor]

Anbesol® Maximum Strength: 20% (7.5 g, 10 g) [contains benzyl alcohol]

Dentapaine: 20% (11 g) [contains clove oil]

HDA® Toothache: 6.5% (15 mL) [contains benzyl alcohol]

Hurricaine®: 20% (5 g) [dye free; wild cherry flavor]; (30 g) [dye free; mint, pina colada, watermelon, and wild cherry flavors]

Kanka® Soft Brush™: 20% (2 mL) [packaged in applicator with brush tip]

Orabase® with Benzocaine®: 20% (7 g) [contains ethyl alcohol 48%; mild mint flavor]

Orajel®: 10% (5.3 g, 7 g, 9.4 g)

Orajel® Baby Teething: 7.5% (9.4 g, 11.9 g) [cherry flavor]

Orajel® Baby Teething Nighttime: 10% (5.3 g)

Orajel® Denture Plus: 15% (9 g) [contains menthol 2%, ethyl alcohol 66.7%]

Orajel® Maximum Strength: 20% (5.3 g, 7 g, 9.4 g, 11.9 g)

Orajel® Mouth Sore: 20% (5.3 g, 9.4 g, 11.9 g) [contains benzalkonium chloride 0.02%, zinc chloride 0.1%]

Orajel® Multi-Action Cold Sore: 20% (9.4 g) [contains allantoin 0.5%, camphor 3%, dimethicone 2%]

Orajel® Ultra Mouth Sore: 15% (9.4 g) [contains ethyl alcohol 66.7%, menthol 2%]

Zilactin®-B: 10% (7.5 g)

Gel, topical (Detane®): 7.5% (15 g)

Liquid, oral:

Anbesol®: 10% (9 mL) [cool mint flavor]

Anbesol® Maximum Strength: 20% (9 mL) [contains benzyl alcohol]

Hurricaine®: 20% (30 mL) [pina colada and wild cherry flavors]

Orajel® Baby Teething: 7.5% (13 mL) [very berry flavor]

Orajel® Maximum Strength: 20% (13 mL) [contains ethyl alcohol 44%, tartrazine]

Liquid, oral drop:

Dent's Maxi-Strength Toothache: 20% (3.7 mL) [contains alcohol 74%]

Rid-A-Pain Dental Drops: 6.3% (30 mL) [contains alcohol 70%]

Liquid, topical:

Chiggertox®: 2% (30 mL)

Outgro®: 20% (9 mL)

Skeeter Stik: 5% (14 mL) [contains menthol]

Tanac®: 10% (13 mL) [contains benzalkonium chloride]

Lozenge: 6 mg (18s) [contains menthol]; 15 mg (10s)

Cepacol® Sore Throat: 10 mg (18s) [contains cetylpyridinium, menthol; cherry, citrus, honey lemon, and menthol flavors]

Cepacol® Sore Throat: 10 mg (16s) [sugar free; contains cetylpyridinium, menthol; cherry and menthol flavors]

Cylex®: 15 mg [sugar free; contains cetylpyridinium chloride 5 mg; cherry flavor]

Mycinettes®: 15 mg (12s) [sugar free; contains sodium 9 mg; cherry or regular flavor]

Thorets: 18 mg (500s) [sugar free]

Trocaine®: 10 mg (40s, 400s)

Ointment, oral:

Anbesol® Cold Sore Therapy: 20% (7.1 g) [contains benzyl alcohol, allantoin, aloe, camphor, menthol, vitamin E]

Red Cross™ Canker Sore: 20% (7.5 g) [contains coconut oil]

Ointment, rectal (Americaine® Hemorrhoidal): 20% (30 g)

Ointment, topical:

Chiggerex®: 2% (50 g) [contains aloe vera]

Foille®: 5% (3.5 g, 14 g, 28 g) [contains chloroxylenol 0.1%, benzyl alcohol; corn oil base]

Pads, topical (Sting-Kill): 20% (8s) [contains menthol and tartrazine]
Paste, oral (Orabase® with Benzocaine): 20% (6 g)
Solution, otic drops (Oticaine, Otocaine™): 20% (15 mL)
Swabs, oral:
Hurricaine®: 20% (6s, 100s) [dye free; wild cherry flavor]
Orajel® Baby Teething: 7.5% (12s) [berry flavor]
Orajel® Medicated Mouth Sore, Orajel® Medicated Toothache: 20% (8s, 12s) [contains tartrazine]
Zilactin® Toothache and Gum Pain: 20% (8s) [grape flavor]
Swabs, topical (Sting-Kill): 20% (5s) [contains menthol and tartrazine]
Wax, oral (Dent's Extra Strength Toothache Gum): 20% (1 g)

♦ **Benzocaine and Antipyrine** see Antipyrine and Benzocaine on page 137

Benzocaine, Butamben, and Tetracaine
(BEN zoe kane, byoo TAM ben, & TET ra kane)

U.S. Brand Names Exactacain™
Index Terms Benzocaine, Butamben, and Tetracaine Hydrochloride; Butamben, Tetracaine, and Benzocaine; Tetracaine, Benzocaine, and Butamben
Pharmacologic Category Local Anesthetic
Use Topical anesthetic to control pain in surgical or endoscopic procedures; anesthetic for accessible mucous membranes except for the eyes
Dosage Topical anesthetic:
Children: Dose has not been established; dose reduction is suggested
Adults: 3 metered sprays (maximum dose: 6 metered sprays); decrease dose in the acutely ill patient
Elderly: Dose reduction is suggested
Additional Information Complete prescribing information for this medication should be consulted for additional detail.
Dosage Forms
Aerosol, topical:
Exactacain™: Benzocaine 14%, butamben 2%, and tetracaine hydrochloride 2% (60 g) [contains benzalkonium chloride; cherry flavor; packaged with 100 disposable applicators]

♦ **Benzocaine, Butamben, and Tetracaine Hydrochloride** see Benzocaine, Butamben, and Tetracaine on page 207

Benzocaine, Butyl Aminobenzoate, Tetracaine, and Benzalkonium Chloride
(BEN zoe kane, BYOO til a meen oh BENZ oh ate, TET ra kane, & benz al KOE nee um KLOR ide)

U.S. Brand Names Cetacaine®
Index Terms Benzalkonium Chloride, Benzocaine, Butyl Aminobenzoate, and Tetracaine Hydrochloride; Butyl Aminobenzoate, Tetracaine Hydrochloride, Benzocaine, and Benzalkonium Chloride; Tetracaine Hydrochloride, Benzocaine, Butyl Aminobenzoate, and Benzalkonium Chloride
Pharmacologic Category Local Anesthetic
Use Topical anesthetic to control pain or gagging, pain in surgical or endoscopic procedures; anesthetic for accessible mucous membranes except for the eyes.
Dosage Apply to affected area for approximately 1 second
Additional Information Complete prescribing information for this medication should be consulted for additional detail.
Dosage Forms
Aerosol, topical: Benzocaine 14%, butyl aminobenzoate 2%, tetracaine hydrochloride 2%, and benzalkonium chloride 0.5% (56 g) [also packaged in a kit with various sized cannulas]
Gel, topical: Benzocaine 14%, butyl aminobenzoate 2%, tetracaine hydrochloride 2%, and benzalkonium chloride 0.5% (29 g)
Liquid, topical: Benzocaine 14%, butyl aminobenzoate 2%, tetracaine hydrochloride 2%, and benzalkonium chloride 0.5% (56 mL)

♦ **Benzodent® [OTC]** see Benzocaine on page 204

Benzonatate (ben ZOE na tate)

U.S. Brand Names Tessalon®
Canadian Brand Names Tessalon®
Pharmacologic Category Antitussive
Use Symptomatic relief of nonproductive cough
Pregnancy Risk Factor C
Lactation Excretion in breast milk unknown/use caution
Contraindications Hypersensitivity to benzonatate, related compounds (such as tetracaine), or any component of the formulation
Adverse Reactions 1% to 10%:
Central nervous system: Sedation, headache
Dermatologic: Rash
Gastrointestinal: Constipation, nausea, vomiting, GI upset
Neuromuscular & skeletal: Chest numbness
Ocular: Burning sensation in eyes
Respiratory: Nasal congestion
(Continued)

Benzonatate *(Continued)*

Overdosage/Toxicology Symptoms include restlessness, tremor, and CNS stimulation. The drug's local anesthetic activity can reduce the patient's gag reflex and, therefore, may contraindicate the use of ipecac following ingestion. This is especially true when the capsules are chewed. Gastric lavage may be indicated if initiated early on following an acute ingestion or in comatose patients. The remaining treatment is supportive and symptomatic.

Mechanism of Action Tetracaine congener with antitussive properties; suppresses cough by topical anesthetic action on the respiratory stretch receptors

Pharmacodynamics/Kinetics
Onset of action: Therapeutic: 15-20 minutes
Duration: 3-8 hours

Dosage Children >10 years and Adults: Oral: 100 mg 3 times/day or every 4 hours up to 600 mg/day

Administration Swallow capsule whole (do not break or chew).

Monitoring Parameters Monitor patient's chest sounds and respiratory pattern

Dosage Forms
Capsule, softgel: 100 mg, 200 mg
Tessalon®: 100 mg, 200 mg

♦ **Benzoyl Peroxide and Erythromycin** *see* Erythromycin and Benzoyl Peroxide *on page 613*

Benzoyl Peroxide and Hydrocortisone
(BEN zoe il peer OKS ide & hye droe KOR ti sone)

U.S. Brand Names Vanoxide-HC®
Canadian Brand Names Vanoxide-HC®
Index Terms Hydrocortisone and Benzoyl Peroxide
Pharmacologic Category Acne Products; Topical Skin Product; Topical Skin Product, Acne
Use Treatment of acne vulgaris and oily skin
Pregnancy Risk Factor C
Dosage Adolescents and Adults: Topical: Shake well; apply thin film 1-3 times/day; gently massage into skin
Additional Information Complete prescribing information for this medication should be consulted for additional detail.
Dosage Forms Lotion: Benzoyl peroxide 5% and hydrocortisone acetate 0.5% (25 mL)

Benztropine (BENZ troe peen)

U.S. Brand Names Cogentin®
Canadian Brand Names Apo-Benztropine®
Index Terms Benztropine Mesylate
Pharmacologic Category Anti-Parkinson's Agent, Anticholinergic; Anticholinergic Agent
Additional Appendix Information
Parkinson's Agents *on page 1895*
Use Adjunctive treatment of Parkinson's disease; treatment of drug-induced extrapyramidal symptoms (except tardive dyskinesia)
Pregnancy Risk Factor C
Lactation Excretion in breast milk unknown/use caution
Medication Safety Issues
Sound-alike/look-alike issues:
Benztropine may be confused with bromocriptine
Contraindications Hypersensitivity to benztropine or any component of the formulation; pyloric or duodenal obstruction, stenosing peptic ulcers; bladder neck obstructions; achalasia; myasthenia gravis; children <3 years of age
Warnings/Precautions Use with caution in older children (dose has not been established). Use with caution in hot weather or during exercise. May cause anhidrosis and hyperthermia, which may be severe. The risk is increased in hot environments, particularly in the elderly, alcoholics, patients with CNS disease, and those with prolonged outdoor exposure.

Elderly patients frequently develop increased sensitivity and require strict dosage regulation - side effects may be more severe in elderly patients with atherosclerotic changes. Use with caution in patients with tachycardia, cardiac arrhythmias, hypertension, hypotension, prostatic hyperplasia (especially in the elderly), any tendency toward urinary retention, liver or kidney disorders, and obstructive disease of the GI or GU tract. When given in large doses or to susceptible patients, may cause weakness and inability to move particular muscle groups.

May be associated with confusion or hallucinations (generally at higher dosages). Intensification of symptoms or toxic psychosis may occur in patients with mental disorders.

Adverse Reactions Frequency not defined.
Cardiovascular: Tachycardia
Central nervous system: Confusion, disorientation, memory impairment, toxic psychosis, visual hallucinations
Dermatologic: Rash
Endocrine & metabolic: Heat stroke, hyperthermia
Gastrointestinal: Xerostomia, nausea, vomiting, constipation, ileus
Genitourinary: Urinary retention, dysuria
Ocular: Blurred vision, mydriasis
Miscellaneous: Fever

Overdosage/Toxicology Symptoms include CNS depression, confusion, nervousness, hallucinations, dizziness, blurred vision, nausea, vomiting, and hyperthermia. For anticholinergic overdose with severe life-threatening symptoms, physostigmine 1-2 mg (0.5 mg or 0.02 mg/kg for children) SubQ or slow I.V., may be given to reverse these effects. Anticholinergic toxicity is caused by strong binding of the drug to cholinergic receptors. Anticholinesterase inhibitors reduce acetylcholinesterase, the enzyme that breaks down acetylcholine and thereby allows acetylcholine to accumulate and compete for receptor binding with the offending anticholinergic.

Drug Interactions
Cytochrome P450 Effect: Substrate of CYP2D6 (minor)
Increased Effect/Toxicity: Central and/or peripheral anticholinergic syndrome can occur when benztropine is administered with amantadine, rimantadine, narcotic analgesics, phenothiazines and other antipsychotics (especially with high anticholinergic activity), tricyclic antidepressants, quinidine and some other antiarrhythmics, and antihistamines. Benztropine may increase the absorption of digoxin.
Decreased Effect: May increase gastric degradation of levodopa and decrease the amount of levodopa absorbed by delaying gastric emptying. Therapeutic effects of cholinergic agents (tacrine, donepezil) and neuroleptics may be antagonized.

Ethanol/Nutrition/Herb Interactions Ethanol: Avoid ethanol (may increase CNS depression).

Mechanism of Action Possesses both anticholinergic and antihistaminic effects. *In vitro* anticholinergic activity approximates that of atropine; *in vivo* it is only about half as active as atropine. Animal data suggest its antihistaminic activity and duration of action approach that of pyrilamine maleate. May also inhibit the reuptake and storage of dopamine and thereby, prolong the action of dopamine.

Pharmacodynamics/Kinetics
Onset of action: Oral: Within 1 hour; Parenteral: Within 15 minutes
Duration: 6-48 hours
Metabolism: Hepatic (N-oxidation, N-dealkylation, and ring hydroxylation)
Bioavailability: 29%

Dosage Use in children ≤3 years of age should be reserved for life-threatening emergencies
Drug-induced extrapyramidal symptom: Oral, I.M., I.V.:
Children >3 years: 0.02-0.05 mg/kg/dose 1-2 times/day
Adults: 1-4 mg/dose 1-2 times/day
Acute dystonia: Adults: I.M., I.V.: 1-2 mg
Parkinsonism: Oral:
Adults: 0.5-6 mg/day in 1-2 divided doses; if one dose is greater, administer at bedtime; titrate dose in 0.5 mg increments at 5- to 6-day intervals
Elderly: Initial: 0.5 mg once or twice daily; increase by 0.5 mg as needed at 5-6 days; maximum: 4 mg/day

Monitoring Parameters Symptoms of EPS or Parkinson's, pulse, anticholinergic effects
Additional Information No significant difference in onset of I.M. or I.V. injection, therefore, there is usually no need to use the I.V. route. Improvement is sometimes noticeable a few minutes after injection.

Dosage Forms
Injection, solution, as mesylate (Cogentin®): 1 mg/mL (2 mL)
Tablet, as mesylate: 0.5 mg, 1 mg, 2 mg

- ♦ **Benztropine Mesylate** *see* Benztropine *on page 208*
- ♦ **Benzylpenicillin Benzathine** *see* Penicillin G Benzathine *on page 1332*
- ♦ **Benzylpenicillin Potassium** *see* Penicillin G (Parenteral/Aqueous) *on page 1333*
- ♦ **Benzylpenicillin Sodium** *see* Penicillin G (Parenteral/Aqueous) *on page 1333*

Benzylpenicilloyl-polylysine (BEN zil pen i SIL oyl pol i LIE seen)

U.S. Brand Names Pre-Pen® [DSC]
Index Terms Penicilloyl-polylysine; PPL
Pharmacologic Category Diagnostic Agent
Use Adjunct in assessing the risk of administering penicillin (penicillin or benzylpenicillin) in adults with a history of clinical penicillin hypersensitivity
Pregnancy Risk Factor C
Pregnancy Implications Safety for use during pregnancy has not been established.
Contraindications Known hypersensitivity to penicillin or any component of the formulation
Warnings/Precautions PPL test alone does not identify those patients who react to a minor antigenic determinant and does not appear to predict reliably the occurrence of late reactions. A negative skin test is associated with an incidence of allergic reactions <5% after penicillin administration and a positive skin test is associated with a >20% incidence of allergic reaction after penicillin administration; have epinephrine 1:1000 available.
Adverse Reactions Frequency not defined.
Cardiovascular: Hypotension
Dermatologic: Angioneurotic edema, pruritus, erythema, urticaria
Local: Intense local inflammatory response at skin test site, wheal (locally)
Respiratory: Dyspnea
Miscellaneous: Systemic allergic reactions occur rarely
Drug Interactions
Decreased Effect: Corticosteroids and other immunosuppressive agents may inhibit the immune response to the skin test.
Stability Refrigerate; discard if left at room temperature for longer than 1 day.
Mechanism of Action Elicits IgE antibodies which produce type I accelerate urticarial reactions to penicillins
Dosage PPL is administered by a scratch technique or by intradermal injection. For initial testing, PPL should always be applied via the scratch technique. **Do not administer intradermally to patients who have positive reactions to a scratch test.** PPL test alone does not identify those patients who react to a minor antigenic determinant and does not appear to predict reliably the occurrence of late reactions.
(Continued)

Benzylpenicilloyl-polylysine *(Continued)*

Scratch test: Use scratch technique with a 20-gauge needle to make 3-5 mm nonbleeding scratch on epidermis, apply a small drop of solution to scratch, rub in gently with applicator or toothpick. A positive reaction consists of a pale wheal surrounding the scratch site which develops within 10 minutes and ranges from 5-15 mm or more in diameter.

Intradermal test: Use intradermal test with a tuberculin syringe with a 26- to 30-gauge short bevel needle; a dose of 0.01-0.02 mL is injected intradermally. A control of 0.9% sodium chloride should be injected at least 1.5" from the PPL test site. Most skin responses to the intradermal test will develop within 5-15 minutes.

Interpretation:

(-) Negative: No reaction

(±) Ambiguous: Wheal only slightly larger than original bleb with or without erythematous flare and larger than control site

(+) Positive: Itching and marked increase in size of original bleb

Control site should be reactionless

Administration PPL is administered by a scratch technique or by intradermal injection. For initial testing, PPL should always be applied via the scratch technique. Do not give intradermally to patients who have positive reactions to a scratch test. Have epinephrine 1:1000 immediately available.

Dosage Forms [DSC] = Discontinued product

Injection, solution: 6×10^{-5} M (0.25 mL) [DSC]

Beractant *(ber AKT ant)*

U.S. Brand Names Survanta®

Canadian Brand Names Survanta®

Index Terms Bovine Lung Surfactant; Natural Lung Surfactant

Pharmacologic Category Lung Surfactant

Use Prevention and treatment of respiratory distress syndrome (RDS) in premature infants

Prophylactic therapy: Body weight <1250 g in infants at risk for developing, or with evidence of, surfactant deficiency (administer within 15 minutes of birth)

Rescue therapy: Treatment of infants with RDS confirmed by x-ray and requiring mechanical ventilation (administer as soon as possible - within 8 hours of age)

Medication Safety Issues

Sound-alike/look-alike issues:

Survanta® may be confused with Sufenta®

Warnings/Precautions Rapidly affects oxygenation and lung compliance and should be restricted to a highly-supervised use in a clinical setting with immediate availability of clinicians experienced with intubation and ventilatory management of premature infants. If transient episodes of bradycardia and decreased oxygen saturation occur, discontinue the dosing procedure and initiate measures to alleviate the condition. Produces rapid improvements in lung oxygenation and compliance that may require immediate reductions in ventilator settings and FiO_2.

Adverse Reactions During the dosing procedure:

>10%: Cardiovascular: Transient bradycardia

1% to 10%: Respiratory: Oxygen desaturation

<1% (Limited to important or life-threatening): Apnea, endotracheal tube blockage, hypercarbia, hyper-/hypotension, post-treatment nosocomial sepsis probability increased, pulmonary air leaks, pulmonary interstitial emphysema, vasoconstriction

Drug Interactions

Increased Effect/Toxicity: No data reported

Decreased Effect: No data reported

Stability Refrigerate; protect from light. Prior to administration, warm by standing at room temperature for 20 minutes or held in hand for 8 minutes. **Artificial warming methods should not be used.** Unused, unopened vials warmed to room temperature may be returned to the refrigerator within 8 hours of warming only once.

Mechanism of Action Replaces deficient or ineffective endogenous lung surfactant in neonates with respiratory distress syndrome (RDS) or in neonates at risk of developing RDS. Surfactant prevents the alveoli from collapsing during expiration by lowering surface tension between air and alveolar surfaces.

Pharmacodynamics/Kinetics Excretion: Clearance: Alveolar clearance is rapid

Dosage

Prophylactic treatment: Administer 100 mg phospholipids (4 mL/kg) intratracheal as soon as possible; as many as 4 doses may be administered during the first 48 hours of life, no more frequently than 6 hours apart. The need for additional doses is determined by evidence of continuing respiratory distress; if the infant is still intubated and requiring at least 30% inspired oxygen to maintain a PaO_2 ≤80 torr.

Rescue treatment: Administer 100 mg phospholipids (4 mL/kg) as soon as the diagnosis of RDS is made; may repeat if needed, no more frequently than every 6 hours to a maximum of 4 doses

Administration

For intratracheal administration only

Suction infant prior to administration. Inspect solution to verify complete mixing of the suspension.

Administer intratracheally by instillation through a 5-French end-hole catheter inserted into the infant's endotracheal tube.

Administer the dose in four 1 mL/kg aliquots. Each quarter-dose is instilled over 2-3 seconds; each quarter-dose is administered with the infant in a different position. Slightly downward inclination with head turned to the right, then repeat with head turned to the left; then slightly upward inclination with head turned to the right, then repeat with head turned to the left.

Monitoring Parameters Continuous ECG and transcutaneous O_2 saturation should be monitored during administration; frequent arterial blood gases are necessary to prevent postdosing hyperoxia and hypocarbia

Additional Information Each mL contains 25 mg phospholipids suspended in 0.9% sodium chloride solution. Contents of 1 mL: 0.5-1.75 mg triglycerides, 1.4-3.5 mg free fatty acids, and <1 mg protein.

Dosage Forms
Suspension, intratracheal [preservative free; bovine derived]:
Survanta®: 25 mg/mL (4 mL, 8 mL)

◆ **9-Beta-D-Ribofuranosyladenine** *see Adenosine on page 50*
◆ **Betacaine® (Can)** *see Lidocaine on page 1010*

Beta-Carotene (BAY ta KARE oh teen)

U.S. Brand Names A-Caro-25; B-Caro-T™; Lumitene™
Pharmacologic Category Vitamin, Fat Soluble
Unlabeled/Investigational Use Prophylaxis and treatment of polymorphous light eruption; prophylaxis against photosensitivity reactions in erythropoietic protoporphyria
Pregnancy Risk Factor C
Dosage Oral:
Children <14 years: 30-150 mg/day
Adults: 30-300 mg/day
Additional Information Complete prescribing information for this medication should be consulted for additional detail.
Dosage Forms
Capsule, softgel: 10,000 int. units (6 mg); 25,000 int. units (15 mg)
A-Caro-25: 25,000 int. units (15 mg) [contains soy]
B-Caro-T™: 25,000 int. units (15 mg) [contains soybean lecithin and soybean oil]
Capsule:
Lumitene™: 50,000 int. units (30 mg)
Tablet: 10,000 int. units

◆ **Betaderm (Can)** *see Betamethasone on page 211*
◆ **Betadine® [OTC]** *see Povidone-Iodine on page 1404*
◆ **Betadine® (Can)** *see Povidone-Iodine on page 1404*
◆ **Betadine® First Aid Antibiotics + Moisturizer [OTC] [DSC]** *see Bacitracin and Polymyxin B on page 192*
◆ **Betadine® Ophthalmic** *see Povidone-Iodine on page 1404*
◆ **Betagan®** *see Levobunolol on page 996*
◆ **Beta-HC®** *see Hydrocortisone on page 852*

Betaine (BAY ta een)

U.S. Brand Names Cystadane®
Canadian Brand Names Cystadane®
Index Terms Betaine Anhydrous
Pharmacologic Category Homocystinuria, Treatment Agent
Use Treatment of homocystinuria (eg, deficiencies or defects in cystathionine beta-synthase [CBS], 5,10-methylene tetrahydrofolate reductase [MTHFR], and cobalamin cofactor metabolism [CBL])
Pregnancy Risk Factor C
Medication Safety Issues
Sound-alike/look-alike issues:
Betaine may be confused with Betadine®
Cystadane® may be confused with cysteamine, cysteine
Dosage Oral:
Children <3 years: Initial dose: 100 mg/kg/day given once daily or in 2 divided doses; increase weekly by 50 mg/kg increments, as needed
Children ≥3 years and Adults: Usual dose: 6 g/day administered in divided doses of 3 g twice daily; dosages of up to 20 g/day have been necessary to control homocysteine levels in some patients
Note: Dosage in all patients can be gradually increased until plasma total homocysteine is undetectable or present only in small amounts. One study in six patients with CBS deficiency, ranging from 6-17 years of age, showed minimal benefit from exceeding a twice daily dosing schedule and a 150 mg/kg/day dosage.
Additional Information Complete prescribing information for this medication should be consulted for additional detail.
Dosage Forms
Powder for oral solution:
Cystadane®: 1 g/scoop (180 g) [1 scoop = 1.7 mL]

◆ **Betaine Anhydrous** *see Betaine on page 211*
◆ **Betaject™ (Can)** *see Betamethasone on page 211*
◆ **Betaloc® (Can)** *see Metoprolol on page 1129*
◆ **Betaloc® Durules® (Can)** *see Metoprolol on page 1129*

Betamethasone (bay ta METH a sone)

U.S. Brand Names Beta-Val®; Celestone®; Celestone® Soluspan®; Diprolene®; Diprolene® AF; Luxiq®; Maxivate®
(Continued)

Betamethasone *(Continued)*

Canadian Brand Names Betaderm; Betaject™; Betnesol®; Betnovate®; Celestone® Soluspan®; Diprolene® Glycol; Diprosone®; Ectosone; Prevex® B; Taro-Sone®; Topilene®; Topisone®; Valisone® Scalp Lotion

Index Terms Betamethasone Dipropionate; Betamethasone Dipropionate, Augmented; Betamethasone Sodium Phosphate; Betamethasone Valerate; Flubenisolone

Pharmacologic Category Corticosteroid, Systemic; Corticosteroid, Topical

Use Inflammatory dermatoses such as seborrheic or atopic dermatitis, neurodermatitis, anogenital pruritus, psoriasis, inflammatory phase of xerosis

Pregnancy Risk Factor C

Pregnancy Implications Teratogenic effects were noted in animal studies. There are no reports linking the use of betamethasone with congenital defects in the literature. Betamethasone is often used in patients with premature labor [26-34 weeks gestation] to stimulate fetal lung maturation.

Lactation Excretion in breast milk unknown/use caution

Medication Safety Issues

Sound-alike/look-alike issues:

Luxiq® may be confused with Lasix®

International issues:

Beta-Val® may be confused with Betanol® which is a brand name for metipranolol in Monaco

Contraindications Hypersensitivity to betamethasone, other corticosteroids, or any component of the formulation; systemic fungal infections

Warnings/Precautions

Very high potency topical products are not for treatment of rosacea, perioral dermatitis; not for use on face, groin, or axillae; not for use in a diapered area. Avoid concurrent use of other corticosteroids.

May cause hypercorticism or suppression of hypothalamic-pituitary-adrenal (HPA) axis, particularly in younger children or in patients receiving high doses for prolonged periods. HPA axis suppression may lead to adrenal crisis. Withdrawal and discontinuation of a corticosteroid should be done slowly and carefully. Particular care is required when patients are transferred from systemic corticosteroids to inhaled products due to possible adrenal insufficiency or withdrawal from steroids, including an increase in allergic symptoms. Patients receiving >20 mg per day of prednisone (or equivalent) may be most susceptible. Fatalities have occurred due to adrenal insufficiency in asthmatic patients during and after transfer from systemic corticosteroids to aerosol steroids; aerosol steroids do not provide the systemic steroid needed to treat patients having trauma, surgery, or infections. In stressful situations, HPA axis-suppressed patients should receive adequate supplementation with natural glucocorticoids (hydrocortisone or cortisone) rather than betamethasone (due to lack of mineralocorticoid activity).

Acute myopathy has been reported with high dose corticosteroids, usually in patients with neuromuscular transmission disorders; may involve ocular and/or respiratory muscles; monitor creatine kinase; recovery may be delayed. Corticosteroid use may cause psychiatric disturbances, including depression, euphoria, insomnia, mood swings, and personality changes. Pre-existing psychiatric conditions may be exacerbated by corticosteroid use. Prolonged use of corticosteroids may also increase the incidence of secondary infection, mask acute infection (including fungal infections), prolong or exacerbate viral infections, or limit response to vaccines. Exposure to chickenpox should be avoided; corticosteroids should not be used to treat ocular herpes simplex. Corticosteroids should not be used for cerebral malaria. Close observation is required in patients with latent tuberculosis and/or TB reactivity; restrict use in active TB (only in conjunction with antituberculosis treatment). Prolonged treatment with corticosteroids has been associated with the development of Kaposi's sarcoma (case reports); if noted, discontinuation of therapy should be considered.

Use with caution in patients with thyroid disease, hepatic impairment, renal impairment, cardiovascular disease, diabetes, glaucoma, cataracts, myasthenia gravis, patients at risk for osteoporosis, patients at risk for seizures, or GI diseases (diverticulitis, peptic ulcer, ulcerative colitis) due to perforation risk. Use caution following acute MI (corticosteroids have been associated with myocardial rupture). Because of the risk of adverse effects, systemic corticosteroids should be used cautiously in the elderly in the smallest possible effective dose for the shortest duration. Do not use occlusive dressings on weeping or exudative lesions and general caution with occlusive dressings should be observed; adverse effects may be increased. Discontinue if skin irritation or contact dermatitis should occur; do not use in patients with decreased skin circulation. Withdraw therapy with gradual tapering of dose. May affect growth velocity; growth should be routinely monitored in pediatric patients. Topical use in patients ≤12 years of age is not recommended.

Adverse Reactions

Systemic:

Cardiovascular: Congestive heart failure, edema, hyper-/hypotension

Central nervous system: Dizziness, headache, insomnia, intracranial pressure increased, lightheadedness, nervousness, pseudotumor cerebri, seizure, vertigo

Dermatologic: Ecchymoses, facial erythema, fragile skin, hirsutism, hyper-/hypopigmentation, perioral dermatitis (oral), petechiae, striae, wound healing impaired

Endocrine & metabolic: Amenorrhea, Cushing's syndrome, diabetes mellitus, growth suppression, hyperglycemia, hypokalemia, menstrual irregularities, pituitary-adrenal axis suppression, protein catabolism, sodium retention, water retention

Gastrointestinal: Abdominal distention, appetite increased, hiccups, indigestion, peptic ulcer, pancreatitis, ulcerative esophagitis

Local: Injection site reactions (intra-articular use), sterile abscess

Neuromuscular & skeletal: Arthralgia, muscle atrophy, fractures, muscle weakness, myopathy, osteoporosis, necrosis (femoral and humeral heads)

Ocular: Cataracts, glaucoma, intraocular pressure increased

Miscellaneous: Anaphylactoid reaction, diaphoresis, hypersensitivity, secondary infection
Topical:
Dermatologic: Acneiform eruptions, allergic dermatitis, burning, dry skin, erythema, folliculitis, hypertrichosis, irritation, miliaria, pruritus, skin atrophy, striae, vesiculation
Endocrine and metabolic effects have occasionally been reported with topical use.

Overdosage/Toxicology When consumed in excessive quantities for prolonged periods, systemic hypercorticism and adrenal suppression may occur; in those cases, discontinuation and withdrawal of the corticosteroid should be done judiciously.

Drug Interactions
Cytochrome P450 Effect: Inhibits CYP3A4 (weak)
Increased Effect/Toxicity: Inhibitors of CYP3A4 (including erythromycin, diltiazem, itraconazole, ketoconazole, quinidine, and verapamil) may decrease metabolism of betamethasone.
Decreased Effect: May induce cytochrome P450 enzymes, which may lead to decreased effect of any drug metabolized by P450 (ie, barbiturates, phenytoin, rifampin). Decreased effectiveness of salicylates when taken with betamethasone.

Ethanol/Nutrition/Herb Interactions
Ethanol: Avoid ethanol (may enhance gastric mucosal irritation).
Food: Betamethasone interferes with calcium absorption.
Herb/Nutraceutical: Avoid cat's claw, echinacea (have immunostimulant properties).

Mechanism of Action Controls the rate of protein synthesis; depresses the migration of polymorphonuclear leukocytes, fibroblasts; reverses capillary permeability and lysosomal stabilization at the cellular level to prevent or control inflammation

Pharmacodynamics/Kinetics
Protein binding: 64%
Metabolism: Hepatic
Half-life elimination: 6.5 hours
Time to peak, serum: I.V.: 10-36 minutes
Excretion: Urine (<5% as unchanged drug)

Dosage Base dosage on severity of disease and patient response
Children: Use lowest dose listed as initial dose for adrenocortical insufficiency (physiologic replacement)
I.M.: 0.0175-0.125 mg base/kg/day divided every 6-12 hours **or** 0.5-7.5 mg base/m²/day divided every 6-12 hours
Oral: 0.0175-0.25 mg/kg/day divided every 6-8 hours **or** 0.5-7.5 mg/m²/day divided every 6-8 hours
Topical:
≤12 years: Use is not recommended.
≥13 years: Use minimal amount for shortest period of time to avoid HPA axis suppression
Gel, augmented formulation: Apply once or twice daily; rub in gently. **Note:** Do not exceed 2 weeks of treatment or 50 g/week.
Lotion: Apply a few drops twice daily
Augmented formulation: Apply a few drops once or twice daily; rub in gently. **Note:** Do not exceed 2 weeks of treatment or 50 mL/week.
Cream/ointment: Apply once or twice daily.
Augmented formulation: Apply once or twice daily. **Note:** Do not exceed 2 weeks of treatment or 45 g/week.
Adolescents and Adults:
Oral: 2.4-4.8 mg/day in 2-4 doses; range: 0.6-7.2 mg/day
I.M.: Betamethasone sodium phosphate and betamethasone acetate: 0.6-9 mg/day (generally, ¹/₃ to ¹/₂ of oral dose) divided every 12-24 hours
Adults:
Intrabursal, intra-articular, intradermal: 0.25-2 mL
Intralesional: Rheumatoid arthritis/osteoarthritis:
Very large joints: 1-2 mL
Large joints: 1 mL
Medium joints: 0.5-1 mL
Small joints: 0.25-0.5 mL
Topical:
Foam: Apply to the scalp twice daily, once in the morning and once at night
Gel, augmented formulation: Apply once or twice daily; rub in gently. **Note:** Do not exceed 2 weeks of treatment or 50 g/week.
Lotion: Apply a few drops twice daily
Augmented formulation: Apply a few drops once or twice daily; rub in gently. **Note:** Do not exceed 2 weeks of treatment or 50 mL/week.
Cream/ointment: Apply once or twice daily
Augmented formulation: Apply once or twice daily. **Note:** Do not exceed 2 weeks of treatment or 45 g/week.
Dosing adjustment in hepatic impairment: Adjustments may be necessary in patients with liver failure because betamethasone is extensively metabolized in the liver

Dietary Considerations May be taken with food to decrease GI distress.

Administration
Oral: Not for alternate day therapy; once daily doses should be given in the morning.
I.M.: Do **not** give injectable sodium phosphate/acetate suspension I.V.
Topical: Apply topical sparingly to areas. Not for use on broken skin or in areas of infection. Do not apply to wet skin unless directed; do not cover with occlusive dressing. Do not apply very high potency agents to face, groin, axillae, or diaper area.
Foam: Invert can and dispense a small amount onto a saucer or other cool surface. Do not dispense directly into hands. Pick up small amounts of foam and gently massage into affected areas until foam disappears. Repeat until entire affected scalp area is treated.

Additional Information
Very high potency. Augmented betamethasone dipropionate ointment, lotion
(Continued)

Betamethasone *(Continued)*

High potency: Augmented betamethasone dipropionate cream, betamethasone dipropionate cream and ointment

Intermediate potency: Betamethasone dipropionate lotion, betamethasone valerate cream

Dosage Forms

Note: Potency expressed as betamethasone base.

Cream, topical, as dipropionate: 0.05% (15 g, 45 g)

Maxivate®: 0.05% (45 g)

Cream, topical, as dipropionate augmented (Diprolene® AF): 0.05% (15 g, 50 g)

Cream, topical, as valerate (Beta-Val®): 0.1% (15 g, 45 g)

Foam, topical, as valerate (Luxiq®): 0.12% (50 g, 100 g, 150 g) [contains alcohol 60.4%]

Gel, topical, as dipropionate augmented: 0.05% (15 g, 50 g)

Injection, suspension (Celestone® Soluspan®): Betamethasone sodium phosphate 3 mg/mL and betamethasone acetate 3 mg/mL [6 mg/mL] (5 mL)

Lotion, topical, as dipropionate (Maxivate®): 0.05% (60 mL)

Lotion, topical, as dipropionate augmented (Diprolene®): 0.05% (30 mL, 60 mL)

Lotion, topical, as valerate (Beta-Val®): 0.1% (60 mL)

Ointment, topical, as dipropionate: 0.05% (15 g, 45 g)

Maxivate®: 0.05% (45 g)

Ointment, topical, as dipropionate augmented (Diprolene®): 0.05% (15 g, 50 g)

Ointment, topical, as valerate: 0.1% (15 g, 45 g)

Syrup, as base (Celestone®): 0.6 mg/5 mL (118 mL)

Betamethasone and Clotrimazole (bay ta METH a sone & kloe TRIM a zole)

U.S. Brand Names Lotrisone®

Canadian Brand Names Lotriderm®

Index Terms Clotrimazole and Betamethasone

Pharmacologic Category Antifungal Agent, Topical; Corticosteroid, Topical

Use Topical treatment of various dermal fungal infections (including tinea pedis, cruris, and corpora in patients ≥17 years of age)

Pregnancy Risk Factor C

Medication Safety Issues

Sound-alike/look-alike issues:

Lotrisone® may be confused with Lotrimin®

Dosage

Children <17 years: Do not use

Children ≥17 years and Adults:

Allergic or inflammatory diseases: Topical: Apply to affected area twice daily, morning and evening

Tinea corporis, tinea cruris: Topical: Massage into affected area twice daily, morning and evening; do not use for longer than 2 weeks; re-evaluate after 1 week if no clinical improvement; do not exceed 45 g cream/week or 45 mL lotion/week

Tinea pedis: Topical: Massage into affected area twice daily, morning and evening; do not use for longer than 4 weeks; re-evaluate after 2 weeks if no clinical improvement; do not exceed 45 g cream/week or 45 mL lotion/week

Elderly: Use with caution; skin atrophy and skin ulceration (rare) have been reported in patients with thinning skin; do not use for diaper dermatitis or under occlusive dressings

Additional Information Complete prescribing information for this medication should be consulted for additional detail.

Dosage Forms

Cream: Betamethasone dipropionate 0.05% (base) and clotrimazole 1% (15 g, 45 g) [contains benzyl alcohol]

Lotrisone®: Betamethasone dipropionate 0.05% (base) and clotrimazole 1% (15 g, 45 g) [contains benzyl alcohol]

Lotion: Betamethasone dipropionate 0.05% (base) and clotrimazole 1% (30 mL) [contains benzyl alcohol]

Lotrisone®: Betamethasone dipropionate 0.05% (base) and clotrimazole 1% (30 mL) [contains benzyl alcohol]

♦ **Betamethasone Dipropionate** *see* Betamethasone *on page 211*

♦ **Betamethasone Dipropionate and Calcipotriene Hydrate** *see* Calcipotriene and Betamethasone *on page 264*

♦ **Betamethasone Dipropionate, Augmented** *see* Betamethasone *on page 211*

♦ **Betamethasone Sodium Phosphate** *see* Betamethasone *on page 211*

♦ **Betamethasone Valerate** *see* Betamethasone *on page 211*

♦ **Betapace®** *see* Sotalol *on page 1592*

♦ **Betapace AF®** *see* Sotalol *on page 1592*

♦ **Betasept® [OTC]** *see* Chlorhexidine Gluconate *on page 344*

♦ **Betaseron®** *see* Interferon Beta-1b *on page 928*

♦ **Beta-Val®** *see* Betamethasone *on page 211*

♦ **Betaxin® (Can)** *see* Thiamine *on page 1668*

Betaxolol (be TAKS oh lol)

U.S. Brand Names Betoptic® S; Kerlone®

Canadian Brand Names Betoptic® S; Sandoz-Betaxolol

Index Terms Betaxolol Hydrochloride

Pharmacologic Category Beta Blocker, Beta₁ Selective

Use Treatment of chronic open-angle glaucoma and ocular hypertension; management of hypertension

Pregnancy Risk Factor C (manufacturer); D (2nd and 3rd trimesters - expert analysis)

Pregnancy Implications Teratogenic effects were not observed in animal studies; however, there was drug-related postimplantation loss in rats and rabbits.

Lactation Oral: Enters breast milk/use caution

Medication Safety Issues
Sound-alike/look-alike issues:
Betaxolol may be confused with bethanechol, labetalol

Contraindications Hypersensitivity to betaxolol or any component of the formulation; sinus bradycardia; heart block greater than first-degree (except in patients with a functioning artificial pacemaker); cardiogenic shock; uncompensated cardiac failure; pulmonary edema; pregnancy (2nd and 3rd trimester)

Warnings/Precautions Consider pre-existing conditions such as sick sinus syndrome before initiating. Administer cautiously in compensated heart failure and monitor for a worsening of the condition. Beta-blocker therapy should not be withdrawn abruptly (particularly in patients with CAD), but gradually tapered to avoid acute tachycardia, hypertension, and/or ischemia. Use caution with concurrent use of beta-blockers and either verapamil or diltiazem; bradycardia or heart block can occur. Use caution in patients with PVD (can aggravate arterial insufficiency). In general, beta-blockers should be avoided in patients with bronchospastic disease. Betaxolol, with beta$_1$ selectivity, should be used cautiously in bronchospastic disease with close monitoring. Use cautiously in diabetics because it can mask prominent hypoglycemic symptoms. Dosage adjustment required in severe renal impairment and in patients on dialysis. Use care with anesthetic agents which decrease myocardial function. Use with caution in patients with myasthenia gravis or psychiatric disease (may cause CNS depression). Adequate alpha-blockade is required prior to use of any beta-blocker for patients with untreated pheochromocytoma. Safety and efficacy in pediatric patients have not been established.

Adverse Reactions
Ophthalmic:
>10%: Ocular: Short-term discomfort (25%)
<1% (Limited to important or life-threatening): Alopecia, asthma, bradycardia, bronchospasm, depression, dizziness, dyspnea, glossitis, heart block, heart failure, headache, hives, insomnia, myasthenia gravis exacerbation, respiratory failure, toxic epidermal necrolysis, vertigo
Frequency not defined: Ocular: Anisocoria, blurred vision, corneal sensitivity decreased, corneal staining, crusty lashes, discharge, dry eyes, edema, erythema, foreign body sensation, inflammation, itching sensation, keratitis, photophobia, tearing, visual acuity decreased
Systemic:
>10%:
Central nervous system: Drowsiness, insomnia
Endocrine & metabolic: Sexual ability decreased
1% to 10%:
Cardiovascular: Bradycardia, palpitation, edema, CHF, peripheral circulation reduced
Central nervous system: Mental depression
Gastrointestinal: Diarrhea or constipation, nausea, vomiting, stomach discomfort
Respiratory: Bronchospasm
Miscellaneous: Cold extremities
<1% (Limited to important or life-threatening): Chest pain, thrombocytopenia

Overdosage/Toxicology Symptoms of intoxication include cardiac disturbances, CNS toxicity, bronchospasm, hypoglycemia, and hyperkalemia. The most common cardiac symptoms include hypotension and bradycardia. Atrioventricular block, intraventricular conduction disturbances, cardiogenic shock, and asystole may occur with severe overdose, especially with membrane-depressant drugs (eg, propranolol). CNS effects include convulsions, coma, and respiratory arrest (commonly seen with propranolol and other membrane-depressant and lipid-soluble drugs). Treatment is symptomatic for seizures, hypotension, hyperkalemia, and hypoglycemia. Bradycardia and hypotension resistant to atropine, isoproterenol, or pacing may respond to glucagon. Wide QRS defects caused by membrane-depressant poisoning may respond to hypertonic sodium bicarbonate. Repeat-dose charcoal, hemoperfusion, or hemodialysis may be helpful in removal of only those beta-blockers with a small V_d, long half-life, or low intrinsic clearance (acebutolol, atenolol, nadolol, sotalol).

Drug Interactions
Cytochrome P450 Effect: Substrate (major) of CYP1A2, 2D6; **Inhibits** CYP2D6 (weak)
Increased Effect/Toxicity: Acetylcholinesterase inhibitors, amiodarone, cardiac glycosides, dipyridamole, disopyramide, and SSRIs may enhance the bradycardic effects of beta-blockers. Beta-blockers may enhance the vasopressor effects of alpha-/beta-agonists, the orthostatic effects of alpha$_1$-agonists, and the rebound hypertensive effect of alpha$_2$-agonists after abrupt withdrawal. Aminoquinolones (antimalarial), antipsychotic agents, calcium channel blockers, CYP1A2 inhibitors, CYP2D6 inhibitors, and propoxyphene may increase the effects of beta-blockers. Beta-blockers may enhance the effects of insulin(hypoglycemia), lidocaine, and sulfonylureas (hypoglycemia).
Decreased Effect: Barbiturates, CYP1A2 inducers, NSAIDs, penicillins, and rifamycin derivatives may decrease the effects of beta-blockers. Beta$_2$-agonists may decrease the bradycardic effect of beta-blockers. Beta-blockers may decrease the bronchodilatory effect of theophylline.

Ethanol/Nutrition/Herb Interactions Herb/Nutraceutical: Avoid bayberry; blue cohosh, cayenne, ephedra, ginger, ginseng (American), gotu kola, and licorice (may worsen hypertension). Avoid black cohosh, California poppy, coleus, golden seal, hawthorn, mistletoe, periwinkle, quinine, shepherd's purse (may have increased antihypertensive effects).

Stability Avoid freezing. Store ophthalmic drops at room temperature.

Mechanism of Action Competitively blocks beta$_1$-receptors, with little or no effect on beta$_2$-receptors; ophthalmic reduces intraocular pressure by reducing the production of aqueous humor

Pharmacodynamics/Kinetics
Onset of action: Ophthalmic: 30 minutes; Oral: 1-1.5 hours
Duration: Ophthalmic: ≥12 hours
Absorption: Ophthalmic: Some systemic; Oral: ~100%
(Continued)

Betaxolol *(Continued)*

Metabolism: Hepatic to multiple metabolites
Protein binding: Oral: 50%
Bioavailability: Oral: 89%
Half-life elimination: Oral: 12-22 hours
Time to peak: Ophthalmic: ~2 hours; Oral: 1.5-6 hours
Excretion: Urine

Dosage Adults:
Ophthalmic: Instill 1-2 drops twice daily.
Oral: 5-10 mg/day; may increase dose to 20 mg/day after 7-14 days if desired response is not achieved. Initial dose in elderly: 5 mg/day.
Dosage adjustment in renal impairment: Administer 5 mg/day. Can increase every 2 weeks up to a maximum of 20 mg/day.
Cl_{cr} <10 mL/minute: Administer 50% of usual dose.

Administration Ophthalmic: Shake suspension well before using. Tilt head back and instill in eye. Keep eye open and do not blink for 30 seconds. Apply gentle pressure to lacrimal sac for 1 minute. Wipe away excess from skin. Do not touch applicator to eye and do not contaminate tip of applicator.

Monitoring Parameters Ophthalmic: Intraocular pressure. Systemic: Blood pressure, pulse.

Dosage Forms
Solution, ophthalmic: 0.5% (5 mL, 10 mL, 15 mL) [contains benzalkonium chloride]
Suspension, ophthalmic:
Betoptic® S: 0.25% (2.5 mL, 5 mL, 10 mL, 15 mL) [contains benzalkonium chloride]
Tablet, as hydrochloride: 10 mg, 20 mg
Kerlone®: 10 mg, 20 mg

♦ **Betaxolol Hydrochloride** *see* Betaxolol *on page 214*

Bethanechol (be THAN e kole)

U.S. Brand Names Urecholine®
Canadian Brand Names Duvoid®; Myotonachol®; PMS-Bethanechol
Index Terms Bethanechol Chloride
Pharmacologic Category Cholinergic Agonist
Use Nonobstructive urinary retention and retention due to neurogenic bladder
Unlabeled/Investigational Use Treatment and prevention of bladder dysfunction caused by phenothiazines; diagnosis of flaccid or atonic neurogenic bladder; gastroesophageal reflux
Pregnancy Risk Factor C
Lactation Excretion in breast milk unknown/contraindicated
Medication Safety Issues
Sound-alike/look-alike issues:
Bethanechol may be confused with betaxolol
Contraindications Hypersensitivity to bethanechol or any component of the formulation; mechanical obstruction of the GI or GU tract or when the strength or integrity of the GI or bladder wall is in question; hyperthyroidism, peptic ulcer disease, epilepsy, obstructive pulmonary disease, bradycardia, vasomotor instability, atrioventricular conduction defects, hypotension, or parkinsonism
Warnings/Precautions Potential for reflux infection if the sphincter fails to relax as bethanechol contracts the bladder. Safety and efficacy in children have not been established.
Adverse Reactions Frequency not defined.
Cardiovascular: Hypotension, tachycardia, flushed skin
Central nervous system: Headache, malaise
Gastrointestinal: Abdominal cramps, diarrhea, nausea, vomiting, salivation, eructation
Genitourinary: Urinary urgency
Ocular: Lacrimation, miosis
Respiratory: Asthmatic attacks, bronchial constriction
Miscellaneous: Diaphoresis
Overdosage/Toxicology Symptoms include nausea, vomiting, abdominal cramps, diarrhea, involuntary defecation, flushed skin, hypotension, and bronchospasm. Atropine is the treatment of choice for intoxications manifesting with significant muscarinic symptoms. Atropine I.V. 0.6 mg every 30-60 minutes (or 0.01 mg/kg I.V. every 2 hours if needed for children) should be repeated to control symptoms and then continued as needed for 1-2 days following the acute ingestion. Epinephrine 0.1-1 mg SubQ may be useful in reversing severe cardiovascular or pulmonary sequelae.
Drug Interactions
Increased Effect/Toxicity: Bethanechol and ganglionic blockers may cause a critical fall in blood pressure. Cholinergic drugs or anticholinesterase agents may have additive effects with bethanechol.
Decreased Effect: Procainamide, quinidine may decrease the effects of bethanechol. Anticholinergic agents (atropine, antihistamines, TCAs, phenothiazines) may decrease effects.
Stability Store at room temperature of 15°C to 30°C (59°F to 86°F).
Mechanism of Action Stimulates cholinergic receptors in the smooth muscle of the urinary bladder and gastrointestinal tract resulting in increased peristalsis, increased GI and pancreatic secretions, bladder muscle contraction, and increased ureteral peristaltic waves
Pharmacodynamics/Kinetics
Onset of action: 30-90 minutes
Duration: Up to 6 hours
Absorption: Variable
Dosage Oral:
Children:
Urinary retention (unlabeled use): 0.6 mg/kg/day divided 3-4 times/day

Gastroesophageal reflux (unlabeled use): 0.1-0.2 mg/kg/dose given 30 minutes to 1 hour before each meal to a maximum of 4 times/day

Adults:
Urinary retention, neurogenic bladder, and/or bladder atony:
Oral: Initial: 10-50 mg 2-4 times/day (some patients may require dosages of 50-100 mg 4 times/day). To determine effective dose, may initiate at a dose of 5-10 mg, with additional doses of 5-10 mg hourly until an effective cumulative dose is reached. Cholinergic effects at higher oral dosages may be cumulative.

SubQ: Initial: 2.575 mg, may repeat in 15-30 minutes (maximum cumulative initial dose: 10.3 mg); subsequent doses may be given 3-4 times daily as needed (some patients may require more frequent dosing at 2.5- to 3-hour intervals). Chronic neurogenic atony may require doses of 7.5-10 mg every 4 hours.

Gastroesophageal reflux (unlabeled): Oral: 25 mg 4 times/day

Elderly: Use the lowest effective dose

Dietary Considerations Should be taken 1 hour before meals or 2 hours after meals.

Monitoring Parameters Observe closely for side effects.

Test Interactions Increased lipase, AST, amylase (S), bilirubin, aminotransferase [ALT (SGPT)/AST (SGOT)] (S)

Dosage Forms Tablet, as chloride: 5 mg, 10 mg, 25 mg, 50 mg

♦ **Bethanechol Chloride** see Bethanechol on page 216
♦ **Betimol®** see Timolol on page 1687
♦ **Betnesol® (Can)** see Betamethasone on page 211
♦ **Betnovate® (Can)** see Betamethasone on page 211
♦ **Betoptic® S** see Betaxolol on page 214

Bevacizumab (be vuh SIZ uh mab)

U.S. Brand Names Avastin®
Canadian Brand Names Avastin®
Index Terms Anti-VEGF Monoclonal Antibody; NSC-704865; rhuMAb-VEGF
Pharmacologic Category Antineoplastic Agent, Monoclonal Antibody; Vascular Endothelial Growth Factor (VEGF) Inhibitor
Use Treatment of metastatic colorectal cancer; treatment of nonsquamous, nonsmall cell lung cancer
Unlabeled/Investigational Use Breast cancer, malignant mesothelioma, prostate cancer, ovarian cancer (early stage), renal cell cancer
Pregnancy Risk Factor C
Pregnancy Implications There are no adequate or well-controlled studies in pregnant women, however, bevacizumab is teratogenic in animal models. Angiogenesis is of critical importance to fetal development, and bevacizumab is likely to have adverse consequences in terms of fetal development. Adequate contraception during therapy is recommended. The risk and benefit of treatment should be evaluated in pregnant women. Patients should also be counseled regarding prolonged exposure following discontinuation of therapy due to the long half-life of bevacizumab.

Based on animal studies, bevacizumab may disrupt normal menstrual cycles and impair fertility by several effects, including reduced endometrial proliferation and follicular developmental arrest. Some parameters do not recover completely, or recover very slowly following discontinuation.

Lactation Excretion in breast milk unknown/not recommended
Medication Safety Issues
Sound-alike/look-alike issues:
Bevacizumab may be confused with cetuximab

High alert medication: The Institute for Safe Medication Practices (ISMP) includes this medication among its list of drugs which have a heightened risk of causing significant patient harm when used in error.

Contraindications Hypersensitivity to bevacizumab, murine proteins, or any component of the formulation
Warnings/Precautions [U.S. Boxed Warning]: Gastrointestinal perforation, intra-abdominal abscess, and wound dehiscence have been reported in patients receiving bevacizumab (not related to treatment duration); monitor patients for signs/symptoms of abdominal pain, constipation, or vomiting. Permanently discontinue in patients who develop these complications. The appropriate intervals between administration of bevacizumab and surgical procedures to avoid impairment in wound healing has not been established. Do not initiate therapy within 28 days of major surgery and only following complete healing of the incision. Bevacizumab should be discontinued prior to elective surgery and the estimated half-life (20 days) should be considered.

Use with caution in patients with cardiovascular disease; patients with significant recent cardiovascular disease were excluded from clinical trials. An increased risk for arterial thromboembolic events (eg, stroke, MI, TIA, angina) is associated with bevacizumab use in combination with chemotherapy. History of arterial thromboembolism or ≥65 years of age may present an even greater risk; permanently discontinue if serious arterial thromboembolic events occur.

May cause CHF and/or potentiate cardiotoxic effects of anthracyclines. CHF is more common with prior anthracycline exposure and/or left chest wall irradiation. Bevacizumab may cause and/or worsen hypertension significantly; use caution in patients with pre-existing hypertension and monitor BP closely in all patients. Permanent discontinuation is recommended in patients who experience a hypertensive crisis or encephalopathy. Temporarily discontinue in patients who develop uncontrolled hypertension. Cases of reversible posterior leukoencephalopathy syndrome (RPLS) have been reported. Symptoms (which include headache, seizure, confusion, lethargy, blindness and/or other vision, or neurologic disturbances), may occur (Continued)

Bevacizumab *(Continued)*

from 16 hours to 1 year after treatment initiation. RPLS may be associated with hypertension; discontinue bevacizumab and begin management of hypertension, if present.

[U.S. Boxed Warning]: Avoid use in patients with recent hemoptysis (>2.5 mL blood); significant pulmonary bleeding has been reported in patients receiving bevacizumab (primarily in patients with nonsmall cell lung cancer with squamous cell histology). Avoid use in patients with CNS metastases; patients with CNS metastases were excluded from clinical trials due to concerns for bleeding. Other serious bleeding events may occur, but with a lower frequency; discontinuation of treatment is recommended in all patients with serious hemorrhage.

Interrupt therapy in patients experiencing severe infusion reactions; there are no data to address reinstitution of therapy in patients who experience CHF and/or severe infusion reactions. Proteinuria and/or nephrotic syndrome has been associated with bevacizumab; discontinue in patients with nephrotic syndrome. When used in combination with myelosuppressive chemotherapy, increased rates of severe or febrile neutropenia and neutropenic infection were reported. Safety and efficacy in children have not been established.

Adverse Reactions Percentages reported as part of combination chemotherapy regimens.
>10%:
  Cardiovascular: Hypertension (8% to 67%; grades 3/4: 8% to 18%), thromboembolism (18%); hypotension (7% to 15%)
  Central nervous system: Pain (61% to 62%), headache (2% to 26%), dizziness (19% to 26%), fatigue (5% to 19%), sensory neuropathy (1% to 17%)
  Dermatologic: Alopecia (6% to 32%), dry skin (7% to 20%), exfoliative dermatitis (3% to 19%), skin discoloration (2% to 16%)
  Endocrine & metabolic: Weight loss (15% to 16%), hypokalemia (12% to 16%)
  Gastrointestinal: Abdominal pain (8% to 61%), diarrhea (2% to 18%; grades 3/4: 34%), vomiting (6% to 52%), anorexia (35% to 43%), constipation (29% to 40%), stomatitis (30% to 32%), gastrointestinal hemorrhage (19% to 24%), dyspepsia (17% to 24%), taste disorder (14% to 21%), flatulence (11% to 19%), nausea (6% to 12%)
  Hematologic: Leukopenia (grades 3/4: 37%), neutropenia (grades 3/4: 21% to 27%)
  Neuromuscular & skeletal: Weakness (73% to 74%), myalgia (8% to 15%)
  Ocular: Tearing increased (6% to 18%)
  Renal: Proteinuria (36%)
  Respiratory: Upper respiratory infection (40% to 47%), epistaxis (32% to 35%), dyspnea (25% to 26%)
  Miscellaneous: Infection (serious: 14%; pneumonia, catheter, or wound infections)
1% to 10%:
  Cardiovascular: DVT (6% to 9%; grades 3/4: 9%); arterial thrombosis (3% to 4%), syncope (grades 3/4: 3%), intra-abdominal venous thrombosis (grades 3/4: 3%), cardio-/cerebro-vascular arterial thrombotic event (2% to 4%), CHF (2%)
  Central nervous system: Confusion (1% to 6%), abnormal gait (1% to 5%)
  Dermatologic: Nail disorder (2% to 8%), skin ulcer (6%), wound dehiscence (1%)
  Endocrine & metabolic: Dehydration (6% to 10%)
  Gastrointestinal: Xerostomia (4% to 7%), colitis (1% to 6%), ileus (4% to 5%), gingival bleeding (2%), fistula (1%), gastrointestinal perforation (<1% to 4%), intra-abdominal abscess (1%)
  Genitourinary: Polyuria/urgency (3% to 6%), vaginal hemorrhage (4%)
  Hematologic: Neutropenic fever (5%), thrombocytopenia (5%), hemorrhage (4% to 5%)
  Hepatic: Bilirubinemia (1% to 6%)
  Respiratory: Voice alteration (6% to 9%), hemoptysis (nonsquamous histology 2%)
  Miscellaneous: Infusion reactions (<3%)
<1% (Limited to important or life-threatening): Anastomotic ulceration, angina, cerebral infarction, hemorrhagic stroke, hypertensive crises, hypertensive encephalopathy, hyponatremia, intestinal necrosis, intestinal obstruction, mesenteric venous occlusion, MI, nasal septum perforation, nephrotic syndrome, pancytopenia, polyserositis, pulmonary embolism, pulmonary hemorrhage, reversible posterior leukoencephalopathy syndrome (RPLS), subarachnoid hemorrhage, transient ischemic attack, ureteral stricture, wound healing complications

Overdosage/Toxicology No information available on overdoses. Doses up to 20 mg/kg have been used in clinical trials. Treatment is symptom-directed and supportive.

Drug Interactions
  Increased Effect/Toxicity: Bevacizumab may potentiate the cardiotoxic effects of anthracyclines. Serum concentrations of irinotecan's active metabolite may be increased by bevacizumab; an approximate 33% increase has been observed.

Stability Store vials at 2°C to 8°C (36°F to 46°F). Protect from light; do not freeze or shake. Prior to infusion, dilute prescribed dose of bevacizumab in 100 mL NS. Do not mix with dextrose-containing solutions. Diluted solutions are stable for up to 8 hours under refrigeration.

Mechanism of Action Bevacizumab is a recombinant, humanized monoclonal antibody which binds to, and neutralizes, vascular endothelial growth factor (VEGF), preventing its association with endothelial receptors. VEGF binding initiates angiogenesis (endothelial proliferation and the formation of new blood vessels). The inhibition of microvascular growth is believed to retard the growth of all tissues (including metastatic tissue).

Pharmacodynamics/Kinetics
  Distribution: V_d: 46 mL/kg
  Half-life elimination: 20 days (range: 11-50 days)
  Excretion: Clearance: 2.75-5 mL/kg/day

Dosage I.V.: Adults:
  Colorectal cancer: 5 or 10 mg/kg every 2 weeks (5 mg/kg in combination with fluorouracil based or irinotecan/fluorouracil/ leucovorin treatment; 10 mg/kg when given in combination with FOLFOX4 regimen)
  Lung cancer, nonsquamous cell nonsmall cell: 15 mg/kg every 3 weeks
  Breast cancer (unlabeled use): 3 mg/kg or 10 mg/kg or 20 mg/kg every 2 weeks

Head and neck cancer (unlabeled use): 5 mg/kg or 10 mg/kg, or 15 mg/kg every 3 weeks

Prostate cancer (unlabeled use): 10 mg/kg every 2 weeks

Renal cell cancer (unlabeled use): 3 mg/kg or 10 mg/kg every 2 weeks

Dosage adjustment for toxicity: Temporary suspension is recommended in moderate-to-severe proteinuria or in patients with severe hypertension which is not controlled with medical management. Permanent discontinuation is recommended (by the manufacturer) in patients who develop wound dehiscence requiring intervention, gastrointestinal perforation, hypertensive crisis, serious bleeding, severe arterial thrombotic event, nephrotic syndrome, or reversible posterior leukoencephalopathy syndrome.

Administration I.V. infusion, usually after the other antineoplastic agents. Infuse the initial dose over 90 minutes. Infusion may be shortened to 60 minutes if the initial infusion is well tolerated. The third and subsequent infusions may be shortened to 30 minutes if the 60-minute infusion is well tolerated. Monitor closely during the infusion for signs/symptoms of an infusion reaction.

Monitoring Parameters Monitor closely during the infusion for signs/symptoms of an infusion reaction. Monitor CBC with differential; signs/symptoms of gastrointestinal perforation or abscess (including abdominal pain, constipation, and vomiting); signs/symptoms of bleeding, including hemoptysis, gastrointestinal, and/or CNS bleeding, and/or epistaxis. Monitor blood pressure every 2-3 weeks; more frequently if hypertension develops during therapy. Continue to monitor blood pressure after discontinuing due to bevacizumab-induced hypertension. Monitor for proteinuria/nephrotic syndrome.

Dosage Forms

Injection, solution [preservative free]:

Avastin®: 25 mg/mL (4 mL, 16 mL)

Bexarotene (beks AIR oh teen)

U.S. Brand Names Targretin®

Canadian Brand Names Targretin®

Pharmacologic Category Antineoplastic Agent, Miscellaneous

Use

Oral: Treatment of cutaneous manifestations of cutaneous T-cell lymphoma in patients who are refractory to at least one prior systemic therapy

Topical: Treatment of cutaneous lesions in patients with refractory cutaneous T-cell lymphoma (stage 1A and 1B) or who have not tolerated other therapies

Pregnancy Risk Factor X

Pregnancy Implications Bexarotene caused birth defects when administered orally to pregnant rats. It must not be given to a pregnant woman or a woman who intends to become pregnant. If a woman becomes pregnant while taking the drug, it must be stopped immediately and appropriate counseling be given. Women of childbearing potential should use two forms of reliable contraception, one should be nonhormonal.

Lactation Excretion in breast milk unknown/contraindicated

Medication Safety Issues

High alert medication: The Institute for Safe Medication Practices (ISMP) includes this medication among its list of drugs which have a heightened risk of causing significant patient harm when used in error.

Contraindications Hypersensitivity to bexarotene or any component of the formulation; pregnancy

Warnings/Precautions Hazardous agent - use appropriate precautions for handling and disposal. **[U.S. Boxed Warning]: Bexarotene is a retinoid, a drug class associated with birth defects in humans; do not administer during pregnancy.** Pregnancy test needed 1 week before initiation and every month thereafter. Effective contraception must be in place 1 month before initiation, during therapy, and for at least 1 month after discontinuation. Male patients with sexual partners who are pregnant, possibly pregnant, or who could become pregnant, must use condoms during sexual intercourse during treatment and for 1 month after last dose. Induces significant lipid abnormalities in a majority of patients (triglyceride, total cholesterol, and HDL); reversible on discontinuation. Use extreme caution in patients with underlying hypertriglyceridemia. Pancreatitis secondary to hypertriglyceridemia has been reported. Monitor for liver function test abnormalities and discontinue drug if tests are three times the upper limit of normal values for AST (SGOT), ALT (SGPT), or bilirubin. Hypothyroidism occurs in about a third of patients. Monitor for signs and symptoms of infection about 4-8 weeks after initiation (leukopenia may occur). Any new visual abnormalities experienced by the patient should be evaluated by an ophthalmologist (cataracts can form, or worsen, especially in the geriatric population). May cause photosensitization. Safety and efficacy are not established in the pediatric population. Avoid use in hepatically-impaired patients. Limit additional vitamin A intake to <15,000 int. units/day. Use caution with diabetic patients.

Adverse Reactions First percentage is at a dose of 300 mg/m²/day; the second percentage is at a dose >300 mg/m²/day.

>10%:

Cardiovascular: Peripheral edema (13% to 11%)

Central nervous system: Headache (30% to 42%), chills (10% to 13%)

Dermatologic: Rash (17% to 23%), exfoliative dermatitis (10% to 28%)

Endocrine & metabolic: Hyperlipidemia (about 79% in both dosing ranges), hypercholesteremia (32% to 62%), hypothyroidism (29% to 53%)

Hematologic: Leukopenia (17% to 47%)

Neuromuscular & skeletal: Weakness (20% to 45%)

Miscellaneous: Infection (13% to 23%)

<10% (Limited to important or life-threatening):

Cardiovascular: Hemorrhage, hypertension, angina pectoris, right heart failure, tachycardia, cerebrovascular accident, syncope

Central nervous system: Fever (5% to 17%), insomnia (5% to 11%), subdural hematoma, depression, agitation, ataxia

(Continued)

Bexarotene *(Continued)*

Dermatologic: Dry skin (about 10% for both dosing ranges), alopecia (4% to 11%), skin ulceration, maculopapular rash, vesicular bullous rash, cheilitis

Endocrine & metabolic: Hypoproteinemia, hyperglycemia

Gastrointestinal: Abdominal pain (11% to 4%), nausea (16% to 8%), diarrhea (7% to 42%), vomiting (4% to 13%), anorexia (2% to 23%), colitis, gastroenteritis, gingivitis, melena, pancreatitis

Genitourinary: Albuminuria, hematuria, dysuria

Hematologic: Hypochromic anemia (4% to 13%), anemia (6% to 25%), eosinophilia, thrombocythemia, coagulation time increased, lymphocytosis, thrombocytopenia

Hepatic: LDH increased (7% to 13%), hepatic failure

Neuromuscular & skeletal: Back pain (2% to 11%), arthralgia, myalgia, myasthenia, neuropathy

Ocular: Conjunctivitis, blepharitis, corneal lesion, visual field defects, keratitis

Otic: Ear pain, otitis externa

Renal: Renal dysfunction

Respiratory: Pharyngitis, rhinitis, dyspnea, pleural effusion, bronchitis, cough increased, lung edema, hemoptysis, hypoxia

Miscellaneous: Flu-like syndrome (4% to 13%), infection (1% to 13%)

Topical:

Cardiovascular: Edema (10%)

Central nervous system: Headache (14%), weakness (6%), pain (30%)

Dermatologic: Rash (14% to 72%), pruritus (6% to 40%), contact dermatitis (14%), exfoliative dermatitis (6%)

Hematologic: Leukopenia (6%), lymphadenopathy (6%)

Neuromuscular & skeletal: Paresthesia (6%)

Respiratory: Cough (6%), pharyngitis (6%)

Miscellaneous: Diaphoresis (6%), infection (18%)

Overdosage/Toxicology Doses up to 1000 mg/m^2/day have been used in humans without acute toxic effects. Any overdose should be treated with supportive care focused on the symptoms exhibited.

Drug Interactions

Cytochrome P450 Effect: Substrate of CYP3A4 (minor); **Induces** CYP3A4 (weak)

Increased Effect/Toxicity: Bexarotene plasma concentrations may be increased by gemfibrozil. Bexarotene may increase the toxicity of DEET.

Decreased Effect: Bexarotene may decrease the plasma levels of hormonal contraceptives and tamoxifen.

Ethanol/Nutrition/Herb Interactions

Food: Take with a fat-containing meal. Bexarotene serum levels may be increased by grapefruit juice; avoid concurrent use.

Herb/Nutraceutical: Avoid dong quai, St John's wort (may also cause photosensitization). St John's wort may decrease bexarotene levels. Additional vitamin A supplements may lead to vitamin A toxicity (dry skin, irritation, arthralgias, myalgias, abdominal pain, hepatic changes).

Stability Store at 2°C to 25°C (36°F to 77°F); protect from light.

Mechanism of Action The exact mechanism is unknown. Binds and activates retinoid X receptor subtypes. Once activated, these receptors function as transcription factors that regulate the expression of genes which control cellular differentiation and proliferation. Bexarotene inhibits the growth *in vitro* of some tumor cell lines of hematopoietic and squamous cell origin.

Pharmacodynamics/Kinetics

Absorption: Significantly improved by a fat-containing meal

Protein binding: >99%

Metabolism: Hepatic via CYP3A4 isoenzyme; four metabolites identified; further metabolized by glucuronidation

Half-life elimination: 7 hours

Time to peak: 2 hours

Excretion: Primarily feces; urine (<1% as unchanged drug and metabolites)

Dosage Adults:

Oral: 300-400 mg/m^2/day taken as a single daily dose.

Topical: Apply once every other day for first week, then increase on a weekly basis to once daily, 2 times/day, 3 times/day, and finally 4 times/day, according to tolerance

Dosing adjustment in renal impairment: No studies have been conducted; however, renal insufficiency may result in significant protein binding changes and alter pharmacokinetics of bexarotene

Dosing adjustment in hepatic impairment: No studies have been conducted; however, hepatic impairment would be expected to result in decreased clearance of bexarotene due to the extensive hepatic contribution to elimination

Dietary Considerations It is preferable to take the oral capsule following a fat-containing meal.

Administration

Oral: Administer capsule following a fat-containing meal.

Topical: Allow gel to dry before covering with clothing. Avoid application to normal skin. Use of occlusive dressings is not recommended.

Monitoring Parameters If female, pregnancy test 1 week before initiation then monthly while on bexarotene; lipid panel before initiation, then weekly until lipid response established and then at 8-week intervals thereafter; baseline LFTs, repeat at 1, 2, and 4 weeks after initiation then at 8-week intervals thereafter if stable; baseline and periodic thyroid function tests; baseline CBC with periodic monitoring

Dosage Forms

Capsule:

Targretin®: 75 mg

Gel: 1% (60 g)

Targretin®: 1% (60 g) [contains dehydrated alcohol]

◆ **Bexxar**® *see* Tositumomab and Iodine I 131 Tositumomab *on page 1713*

◆ **BG 9273** *see* Alefacept *on page 62*

◆ **BI-007** *see* Paclitaxel (Protein Bound) *on page 1297*

◆ **Biaxin**® *see* Clarithromycin *on page 385*

◆ **Biaxin**® **XL** *see* Clarithromycin *on page 385*

Bicalutamide (bye ka LOO ta mide)

U.S. Brand Names Casodex®
Canadian Brand Names Casodex®; CO Bicalutamide; Novo-Bicalutamide; PMS-Bicalutamide; ratio-Bicalutamide; Sandoz-Bicalutamide
Index Terms CDX; ICI-176334; NC-722665
Pharmacologic Category Antineoplastic Agent, Antiandrogen
Use In combination therapy with LHRH agonist analogues in treatment of metastatic prostate cancer
Unlabeled/Investigational Use Monotherapy for locally-advanced prostate cancer
Pregnancy Risk Factor X
Pregnancy Implications Animal studies have demonstrated teratogenicity. Bicalutamide is not indicated for women.
Lactation Excretion in breast milk unknown/contraindicated
Contraindications Hypersensitivity to bicalutamide or any component of the formulation; female patients; pregnancy
Warnings/Precautions Hazardous agent - use appropriate precautions for handling and disposal. Rare cases of death or hospitalization due to hepatitis have been reported postmarketing. Use with caution in moderate-to-severe hepatic dysfunction. Hepatotoxicity generally occurs within the first 3-4 months of use; patients should be monitored for signs and symptoms of liver dysfunction. Bicalutamide should be discontinued if patients have jaundice or ALT is >2 times the upper limit of normal. May cause gynecomastia, breast pain, or lead to spermatogenesis inhibition.
Adverse Reactions Adverse reaction percentages reported as part of combination regimen with an LHRH analogue.

>10%:
  Cardiovascular: Peripheral edema (13%)
  Central nervous system: Pain (35%)
  Endocrine & metabolic: Hot flashes (53%)
  Gastrointestinal: Constipation (22%), nausea (15%), diarrhea (12%), abdominal pain (11%)
  Genitourinary: Pelvic pain (21%), nocturia (12%), hematuria (12%)
  Hematologic: Anemia (11%)
  Neuromuscular & skeletal: Back pain (25%), weakness (22%)
  Respiratory: Dyspnea (13%)
  Miscellaneous: Infection (18%)
≥2% to 10%:
  Cardiovascular: Chest pain (8%), hypertension (8%), angina pectoris (2% to <5%), CHF (2% to <5%), edema (2% to <5%), MI (2% to <5%), coronary artery disorder (2% to <5%), syncope (2% to <5%)
  Central nervous system: Dizziness (10%), headache (7%), insomnia (7%), anxiety (5%), depression (4%), chills (2% to <5%), confusion (2% to <5%), fever (2% to <5%), nervousness (2% to <5%), somnolence (2% to <5%)
  Dermatologic: Rash (9%), alopecia (2% to <5%), dry skin (2% to <5%), pruritus (2% to <5%), skin carcinoma (2% to <5%)
  Endocrine & metabolic: Gynecomastia (9%), breast pain (6%; up to 39% as monotherapy), hyperglycemia (6%), dehydration (2% to <5%), gout (2% to <5%), hypercholesterolemia (2% to <5%), libido decreased (2% to <5%)
  Gastrointestinal: Dyspepsia (7%), weight loss (7%), anorexia (6%), flatulence (6%), vomiting (6%), weight gain (5%), dysphagia (2% to <5%), gastrointestinal carcinoma (2% to <5%), melena (2% to <5%), periodontal abscess (2% to <5%), rectal hemorrhage (2% to <5%), xerostomia (2% to <5%)
  Genitourinary: Urinary tract infection (9%), impotence (7%), polyuria (6%), urinary retention (5%), urinary impairment (5%), urinary incontinence (4%), dysuria (2% to <5%), urinary urgency (2% to <5%)
  Hepatic: LFTs increased (7%), alkaline phosphatase increased (5%)
  Neuromuscular & skeletal: Bone pain (9%), paresthesia (8%), myasthenia (7%), arthritis (5%), pathological fracture (4%), hypertonia (2% to <5%), leg cramps (2% to <5%), myalgia (2% to <5%), neck pain (2% to <5%), neuropathy (2% to <5%)
  Ocular: Cataract (2% to <5%)
  Renal: BUN increased, creatinine increased, hydronephrosis
  Respiratory: Cough (8%), pharyngitis (8%), bronchitis (6%), pneumonia (4%), rhinitis (4%), asthma (2% to <5%), epistaxis (2% to <5%), sinusitis (2% to <5%)
  Miscellaneous: Flu syndrome (7%), diaphoresis (6%), cyst (2% to <5%), hernia (2% to <5%), herpes zoster (2% to <5%), sepsis (2% to <5%)
  Postmarketing and/or case reports: Bilirubin increased, hemoglobin decreased, hepatitis, hypersensitivity reactions (including angioneurotic edema and urticaria), interstitial pneumonitis, pulmonary fibrosis, WBC decreased
Overdosage/Toxicology Doses up to 200 mg daily have been well tolerated in long term clinical trials. Symptoms of overdose may include hypoactivity, ataxia, anorexia, vomiting, slow respiration, and lacrimation. Vomiting may be induced if the patient is alert. Vital signs should be monitored frequently. Treatment is symptom-directed and supportive. Dialysis is of no benefit.
Stability Store at room temperature of 20°C to 25°C (68°F to 77°F).
(Continued)

Bicalutamide *(Continued)*

Mechanism of Action Pure nonsteroidal antiandrogen that binds to androgen receptors; specifically a competitive inhibitor for the binding of dihydrotestosterone and testosterone; prevents testosterone stimulation of cell growth in prostate cancer

Pharmacodynamics/Kinetics

Absorption: Rapid and complete

Protein binding: 96%

Metabolism: Extensively hepatic; glucuronidation and oxidation of the R (active) enantiomer to inactive metabolites

Half-life elimination: Active enantiomer ~6 days, ~10 days in severe liver disease

Time to peak, plasma: 31 hours

Excretion: Urine (36%, as inactive metabolites); feces (42%, as unchanged drug and inactive metabolites)

Dosage Adults: Oral:

Metastatic prostate cancer: 50 mg once daily (in combination with an LHRH analogue)

Locally-advanced prostate cancer (unlabeled use): Oral: 150 mg once daily (as monotherapy)

Dosage adjustment in renal impairment: No adjustment required

Dosage adjustment in hepatic impairment: No adjustment required for mild, moderate, or severe hepatic impairment; use caution with moderate-to-severe impairment. Discontinue if ALT >2 times ULN or patient develops jaundice.

Dietary Considerations May be taken with or without food.

Administration Dose should be taken at the same time each day with or without food. Treatment should be started concomitantly with an LHRH analogue.

Monitoring Parameters Periodically monitor CBC, ECG, echocardiograms, serum testosterone, luteinizing hormone, and prostate specific antigen. Liver function tests should be obtained at baseline and repeated regularly during the first 4 months of treatment, and periodically thereafter; monitor for signs and symptoms of liver dysfunction (discontinue if jaundice is noted or ALT is >2 times the upper limit of normal).

Dosage Forms Tablet: 50 mg

◆ **Bicillin® L-A** *see* Penicillin G Benzathine *on page 1332*

◆ **Bicillin® C-R** *see* Penicillin G Benzathine and Penicillin G Procaine *on page 1333*

◆ **Bicillin® C-R 900/300** *see* Penicillin G Benzathine and Penicillin G Procaine *on page 1333*

◆ **Bicitra®** *see* Sodium Citrate and Citric Acid *on page 1579*

◆ **BiCNu®** *see* Carmustine *on page 296*

◆ **Bidhist** *see* Brompheniramine *on page 242*

◆ **BiDil®** *see* Isosorbide Dinitrate and Hydralazine *on page 947*

◆ **BIG-IV** *see* Botulism Immune Globulin (Intravenous-Human) *on page 238*

◆ **Biltricide®** *see* Praziquantel *on page 1411*

Bimatoprost *(bi MAT oh prost)*

U.S. Brand Names Lumigan®

Canadian Brand Names Lumigan®

Pharmacologic Category Ophthalmic Agent, Antiglaucoma; Prostaglandin, Ophthalmic

Use Reduction of intraocular pressure (IOP) in patients with open-angle glaucoma or ocular hypertension

Pregnancy Risk Factor C

Pregnancy Implications Decreased gestation, decreased body weight, increased late resorptions, and increased mortality were observed in animal studies with oral doses achieving serum levels >33 times human exposure. There are no adequate and well-controlled studies in pregnant women.

Lactation Excretion in breast milk unknown/use caution

Contraindications Hypersensitivity to bimatoprost or any component of the formulation

Warnings/Precautions May cause permanent changes in eye color (increases the amount of brown pigment in the iris), the eyelid skin, and eyelashes. In addition, may increase the length and/or number of eyelashes (may vary between eyes). Use caution in patients with intraocular inflammation, aphakic patients, pseudophakic patients with a torn posterior lens capsule, or patients with risk factors for macular edema. Contains benzalkonium chloride (may be adsorbed by contact lenses). Safety and efficacy have not been determined for use in patients with renal impairment or angle-closure, inflammatory, or neovascular glaucoma. Safety and efficacy in pediatric patients not established.

Adverse Reactions

>10%: Ocular (15% to 45%): Conjunctival hyperemia, growth of eyelashes, ocular pruritus

1% to 10%:

Central nervous system: Headache (1% to 5%)

Dermatologic: Hirsutism (1% to 5%)

Hepatic: Liver function tests abnormal (1% to 5%)

Neuromuscular & skeletal: Weakness (1% to 5%)

Ocular:

3% to 10%: Blepharitis, burning, cataract, dryness, eyelid redness, eyelash darkening, foreign body sensation, irritation, pain, pigmentation of periocular skin, superficial punctate keratitis, visual disturbance

1% to 3%: Allergic conjunctivitis, asthenopia, conjunctival edema, discharge, iris pigmentation increased, photophobia, tearing

Respiratory: Upper respiratory tract infection (10%)

<1% (Limited to important or life-threatening): Bacterial keratitis (caused by inadvertent contamination of multiple-dose ophthalmic solutions), iritis, macular edema

Overdosage/Toxicology No information available. Treatment is symptom-directed and supportive.

Drug Interactions
Increased Effect/Toxicity:
Combination therapy with latanoprost may result in increased IOP than either agent alone.
Stability Store between 2°C to 25°C (36°F to 77°F).
Mechanism of Action As a synthetic analog of prostaglandin with ocular hypotensive activity, bimatoprost decreases intraocular pressure by increasing the outflow of aqueous humor.
Pharmacodynamics/Kinetics
Onset of action: Reduction of IOP: ~4 hours
Peak effect: Maximum reduction of IOP: ~8-12 hours
Distribution: 0.67 L/kg
Protein binding: ~88%
Metabolism: Undergoes oxidation, N-demethylation, and glucuronidation after reaching systemic circulation; forms metabolites
Half-life elimination: I.V.: 45 minutes
Time to peak: 10 minutes
Excretion: Urine (67%); feces (25%)
Dosage Ophthalmic: Adults: Open-angle glaucoma or ocular hypertension: Instill 1 drop into affected eye(s) once daily in the evening; do not exceed once-daily dosing (may decrease IOP-lowering effect). If used with other topical ophthalmic agents, separate administration by at least 5 minutes.
Administration May be used with other eye drops to lower intraocular pressure. If using more than one ophthalmic product, wait at least 5 minutes in between application of each medication. Remove contact lenses prior to administration and wait 15 minutes before reinserting.
Additional Information The IOP-lowering effect was shown to be 7-8 mm Hg in clinical studies.
Dosage Forms
Solution, ophthalmic:
Lumigan®: 0.03% (2.5 mL, 5 mL, 7.5 mL) [contains benzalkonium chloride]

◆ Biocef® *see* Cephalexin *on page 331*
◆ Biolon™ [DSC] *see* Hyaluronate and Derivatives *on page 841*
◆ BioQuin® Durules™ (Can) *see* Quinidine *on page 1471*
◆ Bio-Statin® *see* Nystatin *on page 1250*
◆ BioThrax™ *see* Anthrax Vaccine Adsorbed *on page 132*
◆ Biphentin® (Can) *see* Methylphenidate *on page 1119*
◆ Bisac-Evac™ [OTC] *see* Bisacodyl *on page 223*

Bisacodyl (bis a KOE dil)

U.S. Brand Names Alophen® [OTC]; Bisac Evac™ [OTC]; Bisacodyl Uniserts® [OTC]; Correctol® Tablets [OTC]; Doxidan® [OTC]; Dulcolax® [OTC]; Femilax™ [OTC]; Fleet® Bisacodyl Enema [OTC]; Fleet® Stimulant Laxative [OTC]; Modane Tablets® [OTC]; Veracolate [OTC]
Canadian Brand Names Apo-Bisacodyl®; Carter's Little Pills®; Dulcolax®; Gentlax®
Pharmacologic Category Laxative, Stimulant
Additional Appendix Information
Laxatives, Classification and Properties *on page 1886*
Use Treatment of constipation; colonic evacuation prior to procedures or examination
Pregnancy Risk Factor C
Medication Safety Issues
Sound-alike/look-alike issues:
Doxidan® may be confused with doxepin
Modane® may be confused with Matulane®, Moban®
Contraindications Hypersensitivity to bisacodyl or any component of the formulation; abdominal pain or obstruction, nausea, or vomiting
Adverse Reactions <1% (Limited to important or life-threatening): Electrolyte and fluid imbalance (metabolic acidosis or alkalosis, hypocalcemia); mild abdominal cramps, nausea, rectal burning, vertigo, vomiting
Drug Interactions
Decreased Effect: Milk or antacids may decrease the effect of bisacodyl. Bisacodyl may decrease the effect of warfarin.
Ethanol/Nutrition/Herb Interactions Food: Milk or dairy products may disrupt enteric coating, increasing stomach irritation.
Mechanism of Action Stimulates peristalsis by directly irritating the smooth muscle of the intestine, possibly the colonic intramural plexus; alters water and electrolyte secretion producing net intestinal fluid accumulation and laxation
Pharmacodynamics/Kinetics
Onset of action: Oral: 6-10 hours; Rectal: 0.25-1 hour
Absorption: Oral, rectal: Systemic: <5%
Dosage
Children:
Oral: >6 years: 5-10 mg (0.3 mg/kg) at bedtime or before breakfast
Rectal suppository:
<2 years: 5 mg as a single dose
>2 years: 10 mg
Adults:
Oral: 5-15 mg as single dose (up to 30 mg when complete evacuation of bowel is required)
Rectal suppository: 10 mg as single dose
Dietary Considerations Should not be administered within 1 hour of milk, any dairy products, or taking an antacid, to protect the coating. Should be administered with a glass of water on an empty stomach for rapid effect.
(Continued)

Bisacodyl (Continued)

Administration Administer with a glass of water on an empty stomach for rapid effect. Do not administer within 1 hour of milk, any dairy products, or taking an antacid, to protect the coating.

Dosage Forms

Enema:
Fleet® Bisacodyl Enema: 10 mg/30 mL (37 mL)

Suppository, rectal: 10 mg
Bisac-Evac™, Bisacodyl Uniserts®, Dulcolax®: 10 mg

Tablet, enteric coated: 5 mg
Alophen®, Bisac-Evac™, Correctol®, Dulcolax®, Femilax™, Fleet® Stimulant Laxative, Modane®, Veracolate: 5 mg

Tablet, delayed release:
Doxidan®: 5 mg

♦ **Bisacodyl Uniserts® [OTC]** see Bisacodyl on page 223

♦ **bis-chloronitrosourea** see Carmustine on page 296

♦ **Bismatrol** see Bismuth on page 224

♦ **Bismatrol [OTC]** see Bismuth on page 224

♦ **Bismatrol Maximum Strength [OTC]** see Bismuth on page 224

Bismuth (BIZ muth)

U.S. Brand Names Bismatrol [OTC]; Bismatrol Maximum Strength [OTC]; Diotame® [OTC]; Kaopectate® [OTC]; Kaopectate® Extra Strength [OTC]; Kao-Tin [OTC]; Kapectolin [OTC]; Maalox® Total Stomach Relief® [OTC]; Pepto-Bismol® [OTC]; Pepto-Bismol® Maximum Strength [OTC]

Index Terms Bismatrol; Bismuth Subgallate; Bismuth Subsalicylate; Pink Bismuth

Pharmacologic Category Antidiarrheal

Use

Subsalicylate formulation: Symptomatic treatment of mild, nonspecific diarrhea; control of traveler's diarrhea (enterotoxigenic *Escherichia coli*); as part of a multidrug regimen for *H. pylori* eradication to reduce the risk of duodenal ulcer recurrence

Subgallate formulation: An aid to reduce fecal odors from a colostomy or ileostomy

Pregnancy Risk Factor C/D (3rd trimester)

Lactation Excretion in breast milk unknown (salicylates enter breast milk)/use caution

Medication Safety Issues

Sound-alike/look-alike issues:

Kaopectate® may be confused with Kayexalate®

Maalox® Total Stomach Relief® is a different formulation than Maalox®

Contraindications Hypersensitivity to bismuth or any component of the formulation

Subsalicylate formulation: Do not use subsalicylate in patients with influenza or chickenpox because of risk of Reye's syndrome; hypersensitivity to salicylates or any component of the formulation; history of severe GI bleeding; history of coagulopathy; pregnancy (3rd trimester)

Warnings/Precautions Subsalicylate should be used with caution if patient is taking aspirin; use with caution in children, especially those <3 years of age and those with viral illness; may be neurotoxic with very large doses.

When used for self-medication (OTC labeling): Children and teenagers who have or are recovering from chickenpox or flu-like symptoms should not use subsalicylate. Changes in behavior (along with nausea and vomiting) may be an early sign of Reye's syndrome; patients should be instructed to contact their healthcare provider if these occur. Patients should be instructed to contact healthcare provider for diarrhea lasting >2 days, hearing loss, or ringing in the ears. Not labeled for OTC use in children <12 years of age.

Adverse Reactions Frequency not defined; subsalicylate formulation:

Central nervous system: Anxiety, confusion, headache, mental depression, slurred speech

Gastrointestinal: Discoloration of the tongue (darkening), grayish black stools, impaction may occur in infants and debilitated patients

Neuromuscular & skeletal: Muscle spasms, weakness

Ocular: Hearing loss, tinnitus

Overdosage/Toxicology

Symptoms of toxicity: **Subsalicylate**: Hyperpnea, nausea, vomiting, tinnitus, hyperpyrexia, metabolic acidoses/respiratory alkalosis, tachycardia, and confusion; seizures in severe overdose, pulmonary or cerebral edema, respiratory failure, cardiovascular collapse, coma, and death. Note: Each 262.4 mg tablet of bismuth subsalicylate contains an equivalent of 130 mg aspirin; 150 mg/kg of aspirin is considered to be toxic. Serious life-threatening toxicity occurs with >300 mg/kg.

Treatment: Gastrointestinal decontamination (activated charcoal for immediate release formulations (10x dose of ASA in g), whole bowel irrigation for enteric coated tablets, or when serially increasing ASA plasma levels indicate the presence of an intestinal bezoar); supportive and symptomatic treatment with emphasis on correcting fluid, electrolyte, blood glucose, and acid-base disturbances. Elimination is enhanced with urinary alkalinization (sodium bicarbonate infusion with potassium), multiple-dose activated charcoal, and hemodialysis.

Symptoms of toxicity: **Bismuth**: Rare with short-term administrations of bismuth salts; encephalopathy, methemoglobinemia, seizures

Treatment: Gastrointestinal decontamination; chelation with dimercaprol in doses of 3 mg/kg or penicillamine 100 mg/kg/day for 5 days can hasten recovery from bismuth-induced encephalopathy; methylene blue 1-2 mg/kg in a 1% sterile aqueous solution I.V. push over 4-6 minutes for methemoglobinemia. This may be repeated within 60 minutes if necessary, up to a total dose of 7 mg/kg. Seizures usually respond to I.V. diazepam.

Drug Interactions
Increased Effect/Toxicity: Toxicity of aspirin, warfarin, and/or hypoglycemics may be increased.

Decreased Effect: The effects of tetracyclines and uricosurics may be decreased.

Mechanism of Action Bismuth subsalicylate exhibits both antisecretory and antimicrobial action. This agent may provide some anti-inflammatory action as well. The salicylate moiety provides antisecretory effect and the bismuth exhibits antimicrobial directly against bacterial and viral gastrointestinal pathogens.

Pharmacodynamics/Kinetics
Absorption: Bismuth: <1%; Subsalicylate: >90%
Metabolism: Bismuth subsalicylate is converted to salicylic acid and insoluble bismuth salts in the GI tract.
Half-life elimination: Terminal: Bismuth: Highly variable
Excretion: Bismuth: Urine and feces; Salicylate: Urine

Dosage Oral:
Treatment of nonspecific diarrhea, control/relieve traveler's diarrhea: Subsalicylate (doses based on 262 mg/15 mL liquid or 262 mg tablets):
Children: Up to 8 doses/24 hours:
3-6 years: $^1/_3$ tablet or 5 mL every 30 minutes to 1 hour as needed
6-9 years: $^2/_3$ tablet or 10 mL every 30 minutes to 1 hour as needed
9-12 years: 1 tablet or 15 mL every 30 minutes to 1 hour as needed
Children >12 years and Adults: 2 tablets or 30 mL every 30 minutes to 1 hour as needed up to 8 doses/24 hours
Helicobacter pylori eradication: Adults: 524 mg 4 times/day with meals and at bedtime; requires combination therapy
Control of fecal odor in ileostomy or colostomy: Children ≥12 years and Adults: Subgallate: 200-400 mg up to 4 times/day

Dosing adjustment in renal impairment: Should probably be avoided in patients with renal failure

Dietary Considerations Drink plenty of fluids to help prevent dehydration caused by diarrhea. Different dosage forms contain variable amounts of sodium; consult individual product labeling.

Administration Subsalicylate tablets should be taken at least 3 hours apart from other medications.

Test Interactions Increased uric acid, increased AST; bismuth absorbs x-rays and may interfere with diagnostic procedures of GI tract

Dosage Forms
Caplet, as subsalicylate: 262 mg
Pepto-Bismol®: 262 mg [sugar free; contains sodium 2 mg]
Liquid, as subsalicylate: 262 mg/15 mL (240 mL, 360 mL, 480 mL); 525 mg/15 mL (240 mL, 360 mL)
Bismatrol: 262 mg/15 mL (240 mL)
Bismatrol Maximum Strength: 525 mg/15 mL (240 mL)
Diotame®: 262 mg/15 mL (30 mL)
Kaopectate®: 262 mg/15 mL (180 mL, 240 mL, 360 mL) [contains sodium 10 mg/15 mL; regular and peppermint flavor]
Kaopectate® Extra Strength: 525 mg/15 mL (240 mL) [contains sodium 11 mg/15 mL; peppermint flavor]
Kaotin: 262 mg/15 mL (240 mL, 480 mL)
Maalox® Total Stomach Relief®: 525 mg/15 mL (360 mL) [contains sodium 3.3 mg/15mL; strawberry and peppermint flavor]
Pepto-Bismol®: 262 mg/15 mL (120 mL, 240 mL, 360 mL, 480 mL) [sugar free; contains sodium 6 mg/15 mL and benzoic acid; wintergreen flavor]
Pepto-Bismol® Maximum Strength: 525 mg/15 mL (120 mL, 240 mL, 360 mL) [sugar free; contains sodium 6 mg/15 mL and benzoic acid; wintergreen flavor]
Suspension:
Kapectolin: 262 mg/15 mL (480 mL) [mint flavor]
Tablet, chewable, as subsalicylate: 262 mg
Bismatrol: 262 mg
Diotame®: 262 mg
Pepto-Bismol®: 262 mg [sugar free; contains sodium <1 mg; cherry flavor]

◆ **Bismuth Subgallate** *see* Bismuth *on page 224*
◆ **Bismuth Subsalicylate** *see* Bismuth *on page 224*

Bismuth Subsalicylate, Metronidazole, and Tetracycline
(BIZ muth sub sa LIS i late, me troe NI da zole, & tet ra SYE kleen)

U.S. Brand Names Helidac®
Index Terms Bismuth Subsalicylate, Tetracycline, and Metronidazole; Metronidazole, Bismuth Subsalicylate, and Tetracycline; Tetracycline, Metronidazole, and Bismuth Subsalicylate
Pharmacologic Category Antibiotic, Tetracycline Derivative; Antidiarrheal
Use In combination with an H_2 antagonist, as part of a multidrug regimen for *H. pylori* eradication to reduce the risk of duodenal ulcer recurrence
Pregnancy Risk Factor D (tetracycline); B (metronidazole)
Dosage Adults: Chew 2 bismuth subsalicylate 262.4 mg tablets, swallow 1 metronidazole 250 mg tablet, and swallow 1 tetracycline 500 mg capsule 4 times/day at meals and bedtime, plus an H_2 antagonist (at the appropriate dose) for 14 days; follow with 8 oz of water; the H_2 antagonist should be continued for a total of 28 days
Additional Information Complete prescribing information for this medication should be consulted for additional detail.
Dosage Forms Combination package [each package contains 14 blister cards (2-week supply); each card contains the following]:
Capsule: Tetracycline hydrochloride: 500 mg (4)
(Continued)

Bismuth Subsalicylate, Metronidazole, and Tetracycline
(Continued)

Tablet: Bismuth subsalicylate [chewable]: 262.4 mg (8)
Tablet: Metronidazole: 250 mg (4)

♦ **Bismuth Subsalicylate, Tetracycline, and Metronidazole** *see* Bismuth Subsalicylate, Metronidazole, and Tetracycline *on page 225*

Bisoprolol (bis OH proe lol)

U.S. Brand Names Zebeta®
Canadian Brand Names Apo-Bisoprolol®; Monocor®; Novo-Bisoprolol; Sandoz-Bisoprolol; Zebeta®
Index Terms Bisoprolol Fumarate
Pharmacologic Category Beta Blocker, Beta₁ Selective
Use Treatment of hypertension, alone or in combination with other agents
Unlabeled/Investigational Use Angina pectoris, supraventricular arrhythmias, PVCs, CHF
Pregnancy Risk Factor C (manufacturer); D (2nd and 3rd trimesters - expert analysis)
Pregnancy Implications No data available on whether bisoprolol crosses the placenta. Beta-blockers have been associated with persistent bradycardia, hypotension, and IUGR; IUGR is probably related to maternal hypertension. Available evidence suggests beta-blockers are generally safe during pregnancy (JNC 7). Cases of neonatal hypoglycemia have been reported following maternal use of beta-blockers at parturition or during breast-feeding. Monitor breast-fed infant for symptoms of beta-blockade.
Lactation Enters breast milk/use caution
Medication Safety Issues
Sound-alike/look-alike issues:
Zebeta® may be confused with DiaBeta®
Contraindications Hypersensitivity to bisoprolol or any component of the formulation; sinus bradycardia; heart block greater than first-degree (except in patients with a functioning artificial pacemaker); cardiogenic shock; uncompensated cardiac failure; pulmonary edema; pregnancy (2nd and 3rd trimesters)
Warnings/Precautions Consider pre-existing conditions such as sick sinus syndrome before initiating. Use with caution in patients with inadequate myocardial function, myasthenia gravis, psychiatric disease (may cause CNS depression), bronchospastic disease, undergoing anesthesia; and in those with impaired hepatic function. Beta-blocker therapy should not be withdrawn abruptly (particularly in patients with CAD), but gradually tapered to avoid acute tachycardia, hypertension, and/or ischemia. Use caution in patients with PVD (can aggravate arterial insufficiency). Use caution with concurrent use with verapamil or diltiazem; bradycardia or heart block can occur. Bisoprolol, with B₁selectivity, has been used cautiously in bronchospastic disease with close monitoring. Use cautiously in diabetics because it can mask prominent hypoglycemic symptoms. Use care with anesthetic agents which decrease myocardial function. Adequate alpha-blockade is required prior to use of any beta-blocker for patients with untreated pheochromocytoma. Safety and efficacy have not been established in children.
Adverse Reactions
>10%:
Central nervous system: Drowsiness, insomnia
Endocrine & metabolic: Sexual ability decreased
1% to 10%:
Cardiovascular: Bradycardia, palpitation, edema, CHF, peripheral circulation reduced
Central nervous system: Mental depression
Gastrointestinal: Diarrhea, constipation, nausea, vomiting, stomach discomfort
Ocular: Mild ocular stinging and discomfort, tearing, photophobia, corneal sensitivity decreased, keratitis
Respiratory: Bronchospasm
Miscellaneous: Cold extremities
<1% (Limited to important or life-threatening): Angioedema, arrhythmia, bronchospasm, confusion (especially in the elderly), depression, dyspnea, exfoliative dermatitis, hallucinations, leukopenia, orthostatic hypotension, Peyronie's disease, psoriasiform eruption, syncope, thrombocytopenia, vasculitis
Overdosage/Toxicology Symptoms include cardiac disturbances, CNS toxicity, bronchospasm, hypoglycemia, and hyperkalemia. The most common cardiac symptoms include hypotension and bradycardia. Atrioventricular block, intraventricular conduction disturbances, cardiogenic shock, and asystole may occur with severe overdose, especially with membrane-depressant drugs (eg, propranolol). CNS effects include convulsions, coma, and respiratory arrest (commonly seen with propranolol and other membrane-depressant and lipid-soluble drugs). Treatment is symptomatic for seizures, hypotension, hyperkalemia, and hypoglycemia. Bradycardia and hypotension resistant to atropine, isoproterenol, or pacing may respond to glucagon. Wide QRS defects caused by membrane-depressant poisoning may respond to hypertonic sodium bicarbonate. Repeat-dose charcoal, hemoperfusion, or hemodialysis may be helpful in removal of only those beta-blockers with a small V_d, long half-life, or low intrinsic clearance (acebutolol, atenolol, nadolol, sotalol).
Drug Interactions
Cytochrome P450 Effect: Substrate of CYP2D6 (minor), 3A4 (major)
Increased Effect/Toxicity: Bisoprolol may increase the effects of other drugs which slow AV conduction (digoxin, verapamil, diltiazem), alpha-blockers (prazosin, terazosin), and alpha-adrenergic stimulants (epinephrine, phenylephrine). Bisoprolol may mask the tachycardia from hypoglycemia caused by insulin and oral hypoglycemics. In patients receiving concurrent therapy, the risk of hypertensive crisis is increased when either clonidine or the beta-blocker is withdrawn. Reserpine has been shown to enhance the effect of beta-blockers. Beta-blockers may increase the action or levels of ethanol, disopyramide, nondepolarizing muscle relaxants, and theophylline although the effects are difficult to

predict. CYP3A4 inhibitors may increase the levels/effects of bisoprolol; example inhibitors include azole antifungals, clarithromycin, diclofenac, doxycycline, erythromycin, imatinib, isoniazid, nefazodone, nicardipine, propofol, protease inhibitors, quinidine, telithromycin, and verapamil.

Decreased Effect: Decreased effect of bisoprolol with aluminum salts, calcium salts, cholestyramine, colestipol, NSAIDs, penicillins (ampicillin), and salicylates due to decreased bioavailability and plasma levels. The effect of sulfonylureas may be decreased by beta-blockers. CYP3A4 inducers may decrease the levels/effects of bisoprolol; example inducers include aminoglutethimide, carbamazepine, nafcillin, nevirapine, phenobarbital, phenytoin, and rifamycins.

Ethanol/Nutrition/Herb Interactions Herb/Nutraceutical: Avoid dong quai if using for hypertension (has estrogenic activity). Avoid ephedra, yohimbe, ginseng (may worsen hypertension). Avoid garlic (may have increased antihypertensive effect).

Mechanism of Action Selective inhibitor of beta$_1$-adrenergic receptors; competitively blocks beta$_1$-receptors, with little or no effect on beta$_2$-receptors at doses <10 mg

Pharmacodynamics/Kinetics
Onset of action: 1-2 hours
Absorption: Rapid and almost complete
Distribution: Widely; highest concentrations in heart, liver, lungs, and saliva; crosses blood-brain barrier; enters breast milk
Protein binding: 26% to 33%
Metabolism: Extensively hepatic; significant first-pass effect
Half-life elimination: 9-12 hours
Time to peak: 1.7-3 hours
Excretion: Urine (3% to 10% as unchanged drug); feces (<2%)

Dosage Oral:
Adults: 2.5-5 mg once daily; may be increased to 10 mg and then up to 20 mg once daily, if necessary
Hypertension (JNC 7): 2.5-10 mg once daily
CHF (unlabeled use): Initial: 1.25 mg once daily; maximum recommended dose: 10 mg once daily
Elderly: Initial dose: 2.5 mg/day; may be increased by 2.5-5 mg/day; maximum recommended dose: 20 mg/day
Dosing adjustment in renal/hepatic impairment: Cl$_{cr}$ <40 mL/minute: Initial: 2.5 mg/day; increase cautiously.
Hemodialysis: Not dialyzable

Dietary Considerations May be taken without regard to meals.

Monitoring Parameters Blood pressure, ECG, neurologic status

Test Interactions Increased thyroxine (S), cholesterol (S), glucose, triglycerides, uric acid; decreased HDL

Dosage Forms Tablet, as fumarate: 5 mg, 10 mg

Bisoprolol and Hydrochlorothiazide
(bis OH proe lol & hye droe klor oh THYE a zide)

U.S. Brand Names Ziac®
Canadian Brand Names Ziac®
Index Terms Hydrochlorothiazide and Bisoprolol
Pharmacologic Category Antihypertensive Agent, Combination
Use Treatment of hypertension
Pregnancy Risk Factor C/D (2nd and 3rd trimesters)
Medication Safety Issues
Sound-alike/look-alike issues:
Ziac® may be confused with Tiazac®, Zerit®
Dosage Oral: Adults: Dose is individualized, given once daily
Dosage adjustment in hepatic impairment: Caution should be used in dosing/titrating patients.
Additional Information Complete prescribing information for this medication should be consulted for additional detail.
Dosage Forms Tablet:
2.5/6.25: Bisoprolol fumarate 2.5 mg and hydrochlorothiazide 6.25 mg
5/6.25: Bisoprolol fumarate 5 mg and hydrochlorothiazide 6.25 mg
10/6.25: Bisoprolol fumarate 10 mg and hydrochlorothiazide 6.25 mg

♦ **Bisoprolol Fumarate** see Bisoprolol on page 226
♦ **Bistropamide** see Tropicamide on page 1752

Bivalirudin (bye VAL i roo din)

U.S. Brand Names Angiomax®
Canadian Brand Names Angiomax®
Index Terms Hirulog
Pharmacologic Category Anticoagulant, Thrombin Inhibitor
Use Anticoagulant used in conjunction with aspirin for patients with unstable angina undergoing percutaneous transluminal coronary angioplasty (PTCA) or percutaneous coronary intervention (PCI) with provisional glycoprotein IIb/IIIa inhibitor; anticoagulant used in patients undergoing PCI with (or at risk of) heparin-induced thrombocytopenia (HIT) / thrombosis syndrome (HITTS)
Pregnancy Risk Factor B
Pregnancy Implications Although animal studies have not shown harm to the fetus, safety and efficacy for use in pregnant women have not been established. Bivalirudin is used in conjunction with aspirin, which may lead to maternal or fetal adverse effects, especially during the third trimester. Use during pregnancy only if clearly needed.
(Continued)

Bivalirudin (Continued)

Lactation Excretion in breast milk unknown/use caution

Contraindications Hypersensitivity to bivalirudin or any component of the formulation; active major bleeding

Warnings/Precautions Not for intramuscular use. Safety and efficacy have not been established in patients with unstable angina or acute coronary syndromes who are not undergoing PTCA or PCI. Increased risk of thrombus formation (some fatal) has been reported with bivalirudin use in gamma brachytherapy. As with all anticoagulants, bleeding may occur at any site and should be considered following an unexplained fall in blood pressure or hematocrit, or any unexplained symptom. Use with caution in patients with disease states associated with increased risk of bleeding. Use with caution in patients with renal impairment; dosage reduction required. Safety and efficacy in pediatric patients have not been established.

Adverse Reactions As with all anticoagulants, bleeding is the major adverse effect of bivalirudin. Hemorrhage may occur at virtually any site. Risk is dependent on multiple variables, including the intensity of anticoagulation and patient susceptibility. Additional adverse effects are often related to idiosyncratic reactions, and the frequency is difficult to estimate. Adverse reactions reported were generally less than those seen with heparin.

>10%:
Cardiovascular: Hypotension (3% to 12%)
Central nervous system: Pain (15%), headache (3% to 12%)
Gastrointestinal: Nausea (3% to 15%)
Neuromuscular & skeletal: Back pain (9% to 42%)
1% to 10%:
Cardiovascular: Hypertension (6%), bradycardia (5%), angina (up to 5%)
Central nervous system: Insomnia (7%), anxiety (6%), fever (5%), nervousness (5%)
Gastrointestinal: Vomiting (6%), dyspepsia (5%), abdominal pain (5%)
Genitourinary: Urinary retention (4%)
Hematologic: Major hemorrhage (2% to 4%, compared to 4% to 9% with heparin); transfusion required (1% to 2%, compared to 2% to 6% with heparin), thrombocytopenia (<1% to 4%)
Local: Injection site pain (3% to 8%)
Neuromuscular & skeletal: Pelvic pain (6%)
<1% (Limited to important or life-threatening): Allergic reaction (including anaphylaxis), cerebral ischemia, confusion, facial paralysis, fatal bleeding, intracranial bleeding, kidney failure, pulmonary edema, retroperitoneal bleeding, syncope, thrombus formation (during PCI, including intracoronary brachytherapy), ventricular fibrillation

Overdosage/Toxicology Single bolus doses of up to 7.5 mg/kg have been reported without bleeding complications or other adverse events. Discontinue bivalirudin and monitor patients for signs of bleeding. Bivalirudin is hemodialyzable (~25% removed).

Drug Interactions
Increased Effect/Toxicity: Aspirin may increase anticoagulant effect of bivalirudin (**Note:** All clinical trials included coadministration of aspirin). Other anticoagulants may increase the risk of bleeding complications (monitor).Treprostinil may increase risk of bleeding.

Stability Store unopened vials at 15°C to 30°C. Reconstitute each 250 mg with 5 mL SWFI. Gently swirl to dissolve. Further dilution in D_5W or NS (50 mL to make 5 mg/mL solution **or** 500 mL to make 0.5 mg/mL solution) is required prior to infusion. Do not administer in same line with other medications. Following reconstitution, vials should be stored at 2°C to 8°C. Do not freeze. Final dilutions of 0.5 mg/mL or 5 mg/mL are stable at room temperature for up to 24 hours.

Mechanism of Action Bivalirudin acts as a specific and reversible direct thrombin inhibitor; it binds to the catalytic and anionic exosite of both circulating and clot-bound thrombin. Catalytic binding site occupation functionally inhibits coagulant effects by preventing thrombin-mediated cleavage of fibrinogen to fibrin monomers, and activation of factors V, VIII, and XIII. Shows linear dose- and concentration-dependent prolongation of ACT, aPTT, PT, and TT.

Pharmacodynamics/Kinetics
Onset of action: Immediate
Duration: Coagulation times return to baseline ~1 hour following discontinuation of infusion
Distribution: 0.2 L/kg
Protein binding, plasma: Does not bind other than thrombin
Half-life elimination: Normal renal function: 25 minutes; Cl_{cr} 10-29 mL/minute: 57 minutes
Excretion: Urine, proteolytic cleavage

Dosage I.V.: Adults: Anticoagulant in patients undergoing PTCA/PCI or PCI with HITS/HITTS (treatment should be started just prior to procedure): Initial: Bolus: 0.75 mg/kg, followed by continuous infusion: 1.75 mg/kg/hour for the duration of procedure and up to 4 hours postprocedure if needed; determine ACT 5 minutes after bolus dose; may administer additional bolus of 0.3 mg/kg if necessary.
A glycoprotein IIb/IIIa inhibitor may be administered concomitantly during the procedure. If needed, infusion may be continued beyond initial 4 hours at 0.2 mg/kg/hour for up to 20 hours.

Dosage adjustment in renal impairment: Infusion dose should be reduced based on degree of renal impairment; initial bolus dose remains unchanged; monitor activated coagulation time (ACT)
Cl_{cr} ≥30 mL/minute: No adjustment required
Cl_{cr} 10-29 mL/minute: Decrease infusion rate to 1 mg/kg/hour
Dialysis-dependent patients (off dialysis): Decrease infusion rate to 0.25 mg/kg/hour
Clearance of bivalirudin remains 1.8-fold greater than the glomerular filtration rate, regardless of the degree in renal impairment.

Dosage adjustment in hepatic impairment: No dosage adjustment is needed
Elderly: No dosage adjustment is needed in elderly patients with normal renal function. Puncture site hemorrhage and catheterization site hemorrhage were seen in more patients ≥65 years of age than in patients <65 years of age

Administration For I.V. administration only.

Monitoring Parameters ACT; depending upon indication for use of bivalirudin: aPTT, PT
Dosage Forms Injection, powder for reconstitution: 250 mg

- **BL4162A** see Anagrelide on page 128
- **Blenoxane®** see Bleomycin on page 229
- **Bleo** see Bleomycin on page 229

Bleomycin (blee oh MYE sin)

U.S. Brand Names Blenoxane®
Canadian Brand Names Blenoxane®; Bleomycin Injection, USP
Index Terms Bleo; Bleomycin Sulfate; BLM; NSC-125066
Pharmacologic Category Antineoplastic Agent, Antibiotic
Use Treatment of squamous cell carcinomas, melanomas, sarcomas, testicular carcinoma, Hodgkin's lymphoma, and non-Hodgkin's lymphoma; sclerosing agent for malignant pleural effusion
Pregnancy Risk Factor D
Pregnancy Implications Animal studies have demonstrated teratogenic and abortifacient effects. There are no adequate and well-controlled studies in pregnant women. Women of childbearing potential should avoid becoming pregnant during treatment.
Lactation Excretion in breast milk unknown/not recommended
Medication Safety Issues
Sound-alike/look-alike issues:
Bleomycin may be confused with Cleocin®

High alert medication: The Institute for Safe Medication Practices (ISMP) includes this medication among its list of drugs which have a heightened risk of causing significant patient harm when used in error.
Contraindications Hypersensitivity to bleomycin or any component of the formulation; severe pulmonary disease; pregnancy
Warnings/Precautions Hazardous agent - use appropriate precautions for handling and disposal. **[U.S. Boxed Warnings]: Occurrence of pulmonary fibrosis (commonly presenting as pneumonitis) is higher in elderly patients, patients receiving >400 units total lifetime dose or single doses >30 units, smokers, and patients with prior radiation therapy or receiving concurrent oxygen. A severe idiosyncratic reaction consisting of hypotension, mental confusion, fever, chills, and wheezing (similar to anaphylaxis) has been reported in 1% of lymphoma patients treated with bleomycin.** Since these reactions usually occur after the first or second dose, careful monitoring is essential after these doses. Use caution when administering O_2 during surgery to patients who have received bleomycin. Use caution with renal impairment, may require dose adjustment. May cause renal or hepatic toxicity. **[U.S. Boxed Warning]: Should be administered under the supervision of an experienced cancer chemotherapy physician.**
Adverse Reactions
>10%:
Dermatologic: Pain at the tumor site, phlebitis. About 50% of patients develop erythema, rash, striae, induration, hyperkeratosis, vesiculation, and peeling of the skin, particularly on the palmar and plantar surfaces of the hands and feet. Hyperpigmentation (50%), alopecia, nailbed changes may also occur. These effects appear dose related and reversible with discontinuation.
Gastrointestinal: Stomatitis and mucositis (30%), anorexia, weight loss
Respiratory: Tachypnea, rales, acute or chronic interstitial pneumonitis, and pulmonary fibrosis (5% to 10%); hypoxia and death (1%). Symptoms include cough, dyspnea, and bilateral pulmonary infiltrates. The pathogenesis is not certain, but may be due to damage of pulmonary, vascular, or connective tissue. Response to steroid therapy is variable and somewhat controversial.
Miscellaneous: Acute febrile reactions (25% to 50%)
1% to 10%:
Dermatologic: Skin thickening, diffuse scleroderma, onycholysis, pruritus
Miscellaneous: Anaphylactoid-like reactions (characterized by hypotension, confusion, fever, chills, and wheezing); onset may be immediate or delayed for several hours); idiosyncratic reactions (1% in lymphoma patients)
<1% (Limited to important or life-threatening): Angioedema, cerebrovascular accident, cerebral arteritis, hepatotoxicity, malaise, MI, nausea, Raynaud's phenomenon, renal toxicity, scleroderma-like skin changes, thrombotic microangiopathy, vomiting; Myelosuppression (rare); Onset: 7 days, Nadir: 14 days, Recovery: 21 days
Overdosage/Toxicology Symptoms include chills, fever, pulmonary fibrosis, and hyperpigmentation. Treatment is symptom-directed and supportive.
Drug Interactions
Increased Effect/Toxicity: Cisplatin may decrease bleomycin elimination.
Decreased Effect: Bleomycin may decrease plasma levels of digoxin. Concomitant therapy with phenytoin results in decreased phenytoin levels.
Stability
Refrigerate intact vials of powder. Intact vials are stable for up to 1 month at 45°C. Solutions for infusion are stable for 96 hours at room temperature and 14 days under refrigeration. Reconstitute powder with 1-5 mL BWFI or BNS which is stable at room temperature or under refrigeration for 28 days.
Standard I.V. dilution: Dose/50-1000 mL NS.
Mechanism of Action Inhibits synthesis of DNA; binds to DNA leading to single- and double-strand breaks
Pharmacodynamics/Kinetics
Absorption: I.M. and intrapleural administration: 30% to 50% of I.V. serum concentrations; intraperitoneal and SubQ routes produce serum concentrations equal to those of I.V.
Distribution: V_d: 22 L/m^2; highest concentrations in skin, kidney, lung, heart tissues; lowest in testes and GI tract; does not cross blood-brain barrier
(Continued)

Bleomycin *(Continued)*

Protein binding: 1%
Metabolism: Via several tissues including hepatic, GI tract, skin, pulmonary, renal, and serum
Half-life elimination: Biphasic (renal function dependent):
  Normal renal function: Initial: 1.3 hours; Terminal: 9 hours
  End-stage renal disease: Initial: 2 hours; Terminal: 30 hours
Time to peak, serum: I.M.: Within 30 minutes
Excretion: Urine (50% to 70% as active drug)

Dosage Maximum cumulative lifetime dose: 400 units; refer to individual protocols; 1 unit = 1 mg

May be administered I.M., I.V., SubQ, or intracavitary

Children and Adults:
Test dose for lymphoma patients: I.M., I.V., SubQ: Because of the possibility of an anaphylactoid reaction, administer 1-2 units of bleomycin before the first 1-2 doses; monitor vital signs every 15 minutes; wait a minimum of 1 hour before administering remainder of dose; if no acute reaction occurs, then the regular dosage schedule may be followed.
  Note: Test doses may produce false-negative results.

Single-agent therapy:
  I.M./I.V./SubQ: Squamous cell carcinoma, lymphoma, testicular carcinoma: 0.25-0.5 units/kg (10-20 units/m^2) 1-2 times/week
  CIV: 15 units/m^2 over 24 hours daily for 4 days

Pleural sclerosing: Intrapleural: 60 units as a single instillation (some recommend limiting the dose in the elderly to 40 units/m^2; usual maximum: 60 units). Dose may be repeated at intervals of several days if fluid continues to accumulate (mix in 50-100 mL of NS); may add lidocaine 100-200 mg to reduce local discomfort.

Dosing adjustment in renal impairment:
  Cl_{cr} 10-50 mL/minute: Administer 75% of normal dose
  Cl_{cr} <10 mL/minute: Administer 50% of normal dose

Administration
I.V. doses should be administered slowly (over 10-60 minutes).
I.M. or SubQ: May cause pain at injection site
Intrapleural: 60 units in 50-100 mL NS; use of topical anesthetics or narcotic analgesia is usually not necessary

Monitoring Parameters Pulmonary function tests (total lung volume, forced vital capacity, carbon monoxide diffusion), renal function, liver function, chest x-ray, temperature initially; check body weight at regular intervals

Dosage Forms Injection, powder for reconstitution, as sulfate: 15 units, 30 units

- ◆ **Bleomycin Injection, USP (Can)** *see* Bleomycin *on page 229*
- ◆ **Bleomycin Sulfate** *see* Bleomycin *on page 229*
- ◆ **Bleph®-10** *see* Sulfacetamide *on page 1609*
- ◆ **Blephamide®** *see* Sulfacetamide and Prednisolone *on page 1610*
- ◆ **Blis-To-Sol® [OTC]** *see* Tolnaftate *on page 1704*
- ◆ **BLM** *see* Bleomycin *on page 229*
- ◆ **Blocadren®** *see* Timolol *on page 1687*
- ◆ **BMS-232632** *see* Atazanavir *on page 165*
- ◆ **BMS 337039** *see* Aripiprazole *on page 151*
- ◆ **BMS-354825** *see* Dasatinib *on page 458*
- ◆ **Bonamine™ (Can)** *see* Meclizine *on page 1063*
- ◆ **Bondronat® (Can)** *see* Ibandronate *on page 869*
- ◆ **Bonine® [OTC]** *see* Meclizine *on page 1063*
- ◆ **Bonine® (Can)** *see* Meclizine *on page 1063*
- ◆ **Boniva®** *see* Ibandronate *on page 869*
- ◆ **Boostrix®** *see* Diphtheria, Tetanus Toxoids, and Acellular Pertussis Vaccine *on page 521*

Bortezomib *(bore TEZ oh mib)*

U.S. Brand Names Velcade®
Canadian Brand Names Velcade®
Index Terms LDP-341; MLN341; NSC-681239; PS-341
Pharmacologic Category Antineoplastic Agent; Proteasome Inhibitor
Use Treatment of relapsed or refractory multiple myeloma; relapsed or refractory mantle cell lymphoma
Unlabeled/Investigational Use Treatment of non-Hodgkin's lymphomas (other than mantle cell lymphoma)
Pregnancy Risk Factor D
Pregnancy Implications Adverse effects (fetal loss and decreased fetal weight) were observed in animal studies. There are no adequate and well-controlled studies in pregnant women. Effective contraception is recommended for women of childbearing potential.
Lactation Excretion in breast milk unknown/not recommended
Medication Safety Issues
  High alert medication: The Institute for Safe Medication Practices (ISMP) includes this medication among its list of drugs which have a heightened risk of causing significant patient harm when used in error.
Contraindications Hypersensitivity to bortezomib, boron, mannitol, or any component of the formulation; pregnancy
Warnings/Precautions Hazardous agent - use appropriate precautions for handling and disposal. May cause peripheral neuropathy (usually sensory but may be mixed sensorimotor); risk may be increased with previous use of neurotoxic agents or pre-existing peripheral neuropathy; adjustment of dose and schedule may be required. May cause hypotension;

use caution with dehydration, history of syncope, or medications associated with hypotension. Has been associated with the development or exacerbation of congestive heart failure; use caution in patients with risk factors or existing heart disease. Has also been associated with QT_c prolongation.

Pulmonary disorders including pneumonitis, interstitial pneumonia, lung infiltrates, and acute respiratory distress syndrome (ARDS) have been reported. May cause tumor lysis syndrome; risk is increased in patients with large tumor burden prior to treatment. Reversible posterior leukoencephalopathy syndrome (RPLS) has been reported (rarely). Symptoms of RPLS include confusion, headache, hypertension, lethargy, seizure, blindness and/or other vision, or neurologic disturbances; discontinue if RPLS occurs. Hematologic toxicity with severe thrombocytopenia may occur; risk is increased in patients with pretreatment platelet counts <75,000/μL; frequent monitoring is required throughout treatment; withhold treatment for platelets <25,000/μL. Acute liver failure has been reported (rarely) in patients receiving multiple concomitant medications; hepatitis, transaminase increases, and hyperbilirubinemia have also been reported. Use caution in patients with hepatic dysfunction; toxicities may be increased. Use caution with renal impairment. Safety and efficacy have not been established in pediatric patients.

Adverse Reactions

>10%:

Cardiovascular: Edema (11% to 28%), hypotension (12% to 15%; grades 3/4: 3%)

Central nervous system: Fever (19% to 37%), psychiatric disturbance (35%), headache (17% to 26%), dysesthesia (9% to 27%), insomnia (18% to 21%), dizziness (14% to 23%; excludes vertigo), anxiety (5% to 11%)

Dermatologic: Rash (17% to 28%), pruritus (11%)

Endocrine & metabolic: Dehydration (7% to 11%)

Gastrointestinal: Diarrhea (47% to 57%), nausea (44% to 57%), constipation (40% to 50%), anorexia (34% to 39%), vomiting (27% to 35%), abdominal pain (14% to 16%), abnormal taste (13%), dyspepsia (13%)

Hematologic: Thrombocytopenia (21% to 38%; grade 4: 4%; nadir: Day 11; recovery: days 12-21), anemia (17% to 30%; grade 4: <1%), neutropenia (6% to 19%; grade 4: 2%)

Neuromuscular & skeletal: Weakness (61% to 72%; grades 3/4: 12% to 19%), peripheral neuropathy (36% to 55%; grades 3/4: 7% to 13%), paresthesia (9% to 27%), arthralgia (13% to 18%), limb pain (5% to 17%), bone pain (2% to 16%), back pain (<1 % to 15%), myalgia (10% to 12%), muscle cramps (5% to 12%), rigors (11%)

Ocular: Blurred vision (11%)

Respiratory: Dyspnea (20% to 23%), cough (19% to 21%), lower respiratory infection (15%), upper respiratory tract infection (11% to 15%), nasopharyngitis (8% to 14%), pneumonia (9% to 12%)

Miscellaneous: Herpes virus infections (7% to 13%)

1% to 10%:

Cardiovascular: Syncope (2%)

Endocrine & metabolic: Hypercalcemia (grade 4: 2%)

Frequency not defined (limited to important or life-threatening): Acute diffuse infiltrative pulmonary disease, acute respiratory distress syndrome, allergic reaction, anaphylaxis, angina, angioedema, ascites, aspergillosis, atelectasis, atrial fibrillation, atrial flutter, AV block, bacteremia, bradycardia, cardiac amyloidosis, cardiac arrest, cardiac tamponade, cardiogenic shock, cerebral hemorrhage, cerebrovascular accident, CHF, cholestasis, coma, confusion, cranial palsy, deafness, deep venous thrombosis, diplopia, disseminated intravascular coagulation (DIC), duodenitis (hemorrhagic), dysautonomia, dysphagia, edema (facial), encephalopathy, embolism, epistaxis, fecal impaction, fracture, gastritis (hemorrhagic), gastroenteritis, glomerular nephritis, hematemesis, hematuria, hemoptysis, hemorrhagic cystitis, hepatic failure, hepatic hemorrhage, hepatitis, herpes meningoencephalitis, hyperbilirubinemia, hyper-/hypoglycemia, hyper-/hypokalemia, hyper-/hyponatremia, hypersensitivity, hyperuricemia, hypocalcemia, hypoxia, immune complex hypersensitivity, injection site reaction, intestinal obstruction, intestinal perforation, ischemic colitis, laryngeal edema, leukocytoclastic vasculitis, leukopenia, listeriosis, lymphopenia, melena, MI, myocardial ischemia, neuralgia, neutropenic fever, oral candidiasis, pancreatitis, paralytic ileus, paraplegia, pericardial effusion, pericarditis, peritonitis, pleural effusion, pneumonia, pneumonitis, portal vein thrombosis, proliferative glomerular nephritis, pulmonary edema, pulmonary embolism, pulmonary hypertension, psychosis, QT_c prolongation, renal calculus, renal failure, respiratory insufficiency, reversible posterior leukoencephalopathy syndrome (RPLS), seizure, septic shock, sepsis, sinus arrest, spinal cord compression, stomatitis, stroke (hemorrhagic), stroke, subdural hematoma, suicidal ideation, torsade de pointes, toxic epidermal necrolysis, toxoplasmosis, transient ischemic attack, tumor lysis syndrome, urinary incontinence, urinary retention, urinary tract infection, urticaria, ventricular tachycardia

Overdosage/Toxicology Doses of 2.6 mg/m^2 have been associated with fatal hypotension and thrombocytopenia. In case of overdose, monitor vital signs, maintain blood pressure and body temperature; treatment is otherwise symptom-directed and supportive.

Drug Interactions

Cytochrome P450 Effect: Substrate of CYP1A2 (minor), 2C9 (minor), 2C19 (major), 2D6 (minor), 3A4 (major); Inhibits CYP1A2 (weak), 2C9 (weak), 2C19 (moderate), 2D6 (weak), 3A4 (weak)

Increased Effect/Toxicity: Bortezomib may increase the levels/effects citalopram, diazepam, methsuximide, phenytoin, propranolol, sertraline, and other CYP2C19 substrates. Levels/effects of bortezomib may be increased by azole antifungals, clarithromycin, delavirdine, diclofenac, doxycycline, erythromycin, fluconazole, fluvoxamine, gemfibrozil, imatinib, isoniazid, nefazodone, nicardipine, omeprazole, propofol, protease inhibitors, quinidine, telithromycin, ticlopidine, verapamil, and other CYP2C19 and CYP3A4 inhibitors.

Decreased Effect: Levels/effects of bortezomib may be decreased by aminoglutethimide, carbamazepine, nafcillin, nevirapine, phenobarbital, phenytoin, rifamycins, rifapentane, and other CYP2C19 and CYP3A4 inducers.

Ethanol/Nutrition/Herb Interactions Herb/Nutraceutical: St John's wort may decrease bortezomib levels.

(Continued)

Bortezomib (Continued)

Stability Prior to reconstitution, store at room temperature, 15°C to 30°C (59°F to 86°F); protect from light. Dilute each 3.5 mg vial with 3.5 mL NS. Once reconstituted, may be stored at room temperature for up to 3 days, or under refrigeration for up to 5 days, in vial or syringe; protect from light.

Mechanism of Action Bortezomib inhibits proteasomes, enzyme complexes which regulate protein homeostasis within the cell. Specifically, it reversibly inhibits chymotrypsin-like activity at the 26S proteasome, leading to activation of signaling cascades, cell-cycle arrest, and apoptosis.

Pharmacodynamics/Kinetics

Distribution: 498-1884 L/m^2

Protein binding: ~83%

Metabolism: Hepatic primarily via CYP2C19 and 3A4 and to a lesser extent CYP1A2; forms metabolites (inactive) via deboronation followed by hydroxylation

Half-life elimination: Single dose: 9-15 hours; multiple dosing: 1 mg/m^2: 40-193 hours; 1.3 mg/m^2: 76-108 hours

Dosage I.V.: Adults:

Multiple myeloma, mantle cell lymphoma: 1.3 mg/m^2 twice weekly for 2 weeks on days 1, 4, 8, 11 of a 21-day treatment cycle. Consecutive doses should be separated by at least 72 hours. Therapy extending beyond 8 cycles may be given once weekly for 4 weeks (days 1, 8, 15, and 22), followed by a 13-day rest (days 23 through 35).

Non-hodgkin's lymphoma, other than mantle cell (unlabeled use): 1.5 mg/m^2 twice weekly for 2 weeks on days 1, 4, 8, 11 of a 21-day treatment cycle.

Dosage adjustment in renal impairment: Specific guidelines are not available; studies did not include patients with Cl_{cr} <13 mL/minute and patients on hemodialysis. Monitor closely for toxicity.

Dosage adjustment in hepatic impairment: Specific guidelines are not available; clearance may be decreased; monitor closely for toxicity

Dosage adjustment for toxicity:

Grade 3 nonhematological (excluding neuropathy) or Grade 4 hematological toxicity: Withhold until toxicity resolved; may reinitiate with a 25% dose reduction

Neuropathic pain and/or peripheral sensory neuropathy:

Grade 1 without pain or loss of function: No action needed

Grade 1 with pain or Grade 2 interfering with function but not activities of daily living: Reduce dose to 1 mg/m^2

Grade 2 with pain or Grade 3 interfering with activities of daily living: Withhold until toxicity resolved, may reinitiate at 0.7 mg/m^2 once weekly

Grade 4: Discontinue therapy

Administration Administer via rapid I.V. push (3-5 seconds)

Monitoring Parameters Signs/symptoms of peripheral neuropathy, dehydration, or hypotension; CBC; platelets should be monitored frequently throughout therapy, renal function, pulmonary function (with new or worsening pulmonary symptoms), liver function tests (in patients with existing hepatic impairment)

Dosage Forms

Injection, powder for reconstitution [preservative free]:

Velcade®: 3.5 mg [contains mannitol 35 mg]

Bosentan (boe SEN tan)

U.S. Brand Names Tracleer®

Canadian Brand Names Tracleer®

Pharmacologic Category Endothelin Antagonist

Use Treatment of pulmonary artery hypertension (PAH) (WHO Group I) in patients with World Health Organization (WHO) Class III or IV symptoms to improve exercise capacity and decrease the rate of clinical deterioration

Unlabeled/Investigational Use Investigational: Congestive heart failure

Restrictions Bosentan (Tracleer®) is available only through a limited distribution program directly from the manufacturer (Actelion Pharmaceuticals 1-866-228-3546). It will not be available through wholesalers or individual pharmacies. An FDA-approved medication guide must be distributed when dispensing an outpatient prescription (new or refill) where this medication is to be used without direct supervision of a healthcare provider. Medication guides are available at http://www.fda.gov/cder/Offices/ODS/medication_guides.htm.

Pregnancy Risk Factor X

Pregnancy Implications Based on animal studies, bosentan is likely to produce major birth defects if used by pregnant women. Pregnancy must be excluded prior to initiation of therapy and follow-up pregnancy tests should be obtained monthly. Effective contraception must be maintained throughout treatment. Hormonal contraception is not recommended as the sole contraceptive therapy due to a potential lack of efficacy in patients receiving bosentan. Women of childbearing potential should avoid exposure to dust generated from broken or split tablets, especially if repeated exposure is expected (tablet splitting is currently outside of product labeling). Irreversible testicular atrophy and decreased fertility in males was observed in animal studies with long-term exposure.

Lactation Excretion in breast milk unknown/not recommended

Contraindications Hypersensitivity to bosentan or any component of the formulation; concurrent use of cyclosporine or glyburide; pregnancy

Warnings/Precautions [U.S. Boxed Warning]: Avoid use in moderate-to-severe hepatic impairment. Has been associated with a high incidence (11%) of significant transaminase elevations, and rare cases of unexplained hepatic cirrhosis have occurred, including after long-term therapy. Transaminase elevations are dose dependent, generally asymptomatic, occur both early and late in therapy, progress slowly, and are usually reversible. Avoid use in patients with elevated serum transaminases (>3 times upper limit of normal) at baseline. Monitor hepatic function closely (at least monthly) for the duration of treatment. Treatment should be stopped in patients who develop elevated transaminases (ALT or AST) in combination with symptoms of hepatic injury (unusual fatigue, jaundice, nausea, vomiting, abdominal pain, and/or fever) or elevated serum bilirubin ≥2 times upper limit of normal.

[U.S. Boxed Warning]: Use in pregnancy is contraindicated; exclude pregnancy prior to initiation of therapy. Pregnancy must be excluded prior to shipment of each monthly refill. Efficacy of hormonal contraceptive may be decreased, and should not be the sole contraceptive method in patients receiving bosentan. Women of childbearing potential should avoid excessive handling broken tablets. Use caution in patients with low hemoglobin levels or ischemic cardiovascular disease. May cause dose-related decreases in hemoglobin and hematocrit (monitoring of hemoglobin is recommended). May cause fluid retention evidenced by signs and symptoms of CHF, weight gain, and leg edema. Bosentan should be discontinued in any patient with signs of pulmonary edema due to the possibility of pulmonary veno-occlusive disease (PVOD). Safety and efficacy in pediatric patients ≤12 years of age have not been established.

Adverse Reactions
>10%:
Central nervous system: Headache (16% to 22%)
Hematologic: Hemoglobin decreased (≥1 g/dL in up to 57%; typically in first 6 weeks of therapy)
Hepatic: Transaminases increased (>3 times upper limit of normal; up to 11%)
Respiratory: Nasopharyngitis (11%)
1% to 10%:
Cardiovascular: Flushing (7% to 9%), edema (lower limb, 8%; generalized 4%), hypotension (7%), palpitation (5%)
Central nervous system: Fatigue (4%)
Dermatologic: Pruritus (4%)
Gastrointestinal: Dyspepsia (4%)
Hematologic: Anemia (3%)
Hepatic: Abnormal hepatic function (6% to 8%)
<1% (Limited to important or life-threatening): Angioneurotic edema, CHF (exacerbation), cirrhosis (prolonged therapy), hypersensitivity, leukocytoclastic vasculitis, liver failure (rare), peripheral edema, rash, weight gain

Overdosage/Toxicology No specific experience in overdose. Single doses of 2400 mg or 2000 mg/day for 2 months have been tolerated. Symptoms may include headache, nausea, vomiting, and hypotension. Treatment is symptom-directed and supportive.

Drug Interactions
Cytochrome P450 Effect: Substrate (major) of CYP2C9, 3A4; **Induces** CYP2C9 (strong), 3A4 (strong)

Increased Effect/Toxicity: An increased risk of serum transaminase elevations was observed during concurrent therapy with glyburide; concurrent use is contraindicated. Cyclosporine increases serum concentrations of bosentan (approximately 3-4 times baseline). Concurrent use of cyclosporine is contraindicated.

CYP2C9 inhibitors may increase the levels/effects of bosentan; example inhibitors include delavirdine, fluconazole, gemfibrozil, ketoconazole, nicardipine, NSAIDs, pioglitazone, and sulfonamides. CYP3A4 inhibitors may increase the levels/effects of bosentan; example inhibitors include azole antifungals, clarithromycin, diclofenac, doxycycline, erythromycin, imatinib, isoniazid, nefazodone, nicardipine, propofol, protease inhibitors, quinidine, telithromycin, and verapamil. Sildenafil may increase the serum concentration of bosentan.

Decreased Effect: Bosentan may enhance the metabolism of cyclosporine, decreasing its serum concentrations by ~50%; effect on sirolimus and/or tacrolimus has not been specifically evaluated, but may be similar. Concurrent use of cyclosporine is contraindicated. CYP2C9 inducers may decrease the levels/effects of bosentan; example inducers include carbamazepine, phenobarbital, phenytoin, rifampin, rifapentine, and secobarbital. Bosentan may decrease the levels/effects of CYP2C9 substrates; example substrates include celecoxib, dapsone, fluoxetine, glimepiride, glipizide, losartan, montelukast, nateglinide, paclitaxel, phenytoin, sulfonamides, trimethoprim, warfarin, and zafirlukast. Bosentan may increase the metabolism, via CYP isoenzymes, of sildenafil.

CYP3A4 inducers may decrease the levels/effects of bosentan; example inducers include aminoglutethimide, carbamazepine, nafcillin, nevirapine, phenobarbital, phenytoin, and rifamycins. Bosentan may enhance the metabolism of methadone resulting in methadone withdrawal. Bosentan may decrease the levels/effects of CYP3A4 substrates; example substrates include benzodiazepines, calcium channel blockers, ergot derivatives, mirtazapine, nateglinide, nefazodone, tacrolimus, and venlafaxine. Bosentan may decrease levels of hormonal contraceptives; additional methods of contraception are recommended.

Ethanol/Nutrition/Herb Interactions
Food: Bioavailability of bosentan is not affected by food.
Herb/Nutraceutical: Avoid St John's wort (may decrease serum concentrations of bosentan).

Stability Store at 20°C to 25°C (68°F to 77°F).

Mechanism of Action Blocks endothelin receptors on vascular endothelium and smooth muscle. Stimulation of these receptors is associated with vasoconstriction. Although bosentan blocks both ET_A and ET_B receptors, the affinity is higher for the A subtype. Improvement in symptoms of pulmonary artery hypertension and a decrease in the rate of clinical deterioration have been demonstrated in clinical trials.

Pharmacodynamics/Kinetics
Distribution: V_d: 18 L
Protein binding, plasma: >98% primarily to albumin
Metabolism: Hepatic via CYP2C9 and 3A4 to three primary metabolites (one contributing ~10% to 20% pharmacologic activity)
Bioavailability: 50%
Half-life elimination: 5 hours; prolonged with heart failure, possibly in PAH
Time to peak, plasma: 3-5 hours
(Continued)

Bosentan (Continued)

Excretion: Feces (as metabolites); urine (<3% as unchanged drug)

Dosage Oral:

Children ≤12 years (unlabeled use):

10-20 kg: Initial: 31.25 mg once daily for 4 weeks; increase to maintenance dose of 31.25 mg twice daily

>20-40 kg: Initial: 31.25 mg twice daily for 4 weeks; increase to maintenance dose of 62.5 mg twice daily

>40 kg: Initial: 62.5 mg twice daily for 4 weeks; increase to maintenance dose of 125 mg twice daily

Adolescents >12 years and ≥40 kg and Adults: Initial: 62.5 mg twice daily for 4 weeks; increase to maintenance dose of 125 mg twice daily; patients <40 kg should be maintained at 62.5 mg twice daily. Doses >125 mg twice daily do not appear to confer additional clinical benefit but may increase risk of liver toxicity.

Note: When discontinuing treatment, consider a reduction in dosage to 62.5 mg twice daily for 3-7 days (to avoid clinical deterioration).

Dosage adjustment in renal impairment: No dosage adjustment required.

Dosage adjustment in hepatic impairment: Avoid use in patients with **pretreatment** moderate to severe hepatic insufficiency.

Modification based on transaminase elevation:

If any elevation, regardless of degree, is accompanied by clinical symptoms of hepatic injury (unusual fatigue, nausea, vomiting, abdominal pain, fever, or jaundice) or a serum bilirubin ≥2 times the upper limit of normal, treatment should be stopped.

AST/ALT >3 times but ≤5 times upper limit of normal: Confirm with additional test; if confirmed, reduce dose or interrupt treatment. Monitor transaminase levels at least every 2 weeks. May continue or reintroduce treatment, as appropriate, following return to pretreatment values. Begin with initial dose (above) and recheck transaminases within 3 days

AST/ALT >5 times but ≤8 times upper limit of normal: Confirm with additional test; if confirmed, stop treatment. Monitor transaminase levels at least every 2 weeks. May reintroduce treatment, as appropriate, at starting dose, following return to pretreatment values. Recheck within 3 days and thereafter following reinitiation.

AST/ALT >8 times upper limit of normal: Stop treatment. No experience with reintroduction.

Dietary Considerations May be taken with or without food.

Administration May be administered with or without food, once in the morning and once in the evening. Women of childbearing potential should avoid excessive handling broken tablets.

Monitoring Parameters Serum transaminase (AST and ALT) and bilirubin should be determined prior to the initiation of therapy and at monthly intervals thereafter. A woman of childbearing potential must have a negative pregnancy test prior to the initiation of therapy and monthly thereafter (prior to shipment of monthly refill). Hemoglobin and hematocrit should be measured at baseline, at 1 month and 3 months of treatment, and every 3 months thereafter. Monitor for clinical signs and symptoms of liver injury.

Dosage Forms

Tablet:

Tracleer®: 62.5 mg, 125 mg

Extemporaneous Preparations Use a commercial pill cutter to prepare a 31.25 mg dose from the 62.5 mg tablet. Half-cut 62.5 mg tablets are stable for up to 4 weeks, when stored at room temperature in the high-density polyethylene plastic bottle provided by the manufacturer of the drug.

To prepare a suspension, dissolve the 62.5 mg tablet in 5-25 mL water. Tablets will disintegrate rapidly without crushing (within ~5 minutes); stirring will accelerate disintegration. An appropriate aliquot of the suspension can be used to deliver the prescribed dose. The suspension is stable for up to 24 hours when stored at room temperature in a 10 mL syringe. A new syringe should be used each day. Bosentan should not be mixed or dissolved in liquids with an acidic pH (eg, fruit juices) due to poor solubility; the drug is most soluble in solutions with a pH >8.5.

Women of childbearing potential should avoid exposure to dust generated from broken or split tablets, especially if repeated exposure is expected.

♦ **B&O Supprettes®** see Belladonna and Opium on page 200

♦ **Botox®** see Botulinum Toxin Type A on page 235

♦ **Botox® Cosmetic** see Botulinum Toxin Type A on page 235

Botulinum Pentavalent (ABCDE) Toxoid

(BOT yoo lin num pen ta VAY lent [aye, bee, cee, dee, ee] TOKS oyd)

Index Terms Botulinum Toxoid, Pentavalent Vaccine (Against Types A / B / C / D / E Strains of C. botulinum)

Pharmacologic Category Toxoid

Unlabeled/Investigational Use Investigational: Prophylaxis for C. botulinum exposure (high-risk research laboratory personnel actively working with, or expect to work with, known cultures and purified botulinum toxin)

Dosage Do not inject intracutaneously or into superficial structures.

Initial vaccination series: 0.5 mL deep SubQ at 0-, 2-, and 12 weeks

First booster: 0.5 mL deep SubQ 12 months after first injection of the initial series

Subsequent boosters: 0.5 mL deep SubQ at 2-year intervals based on antitoxin titers as checked by CDC

Additional Information Complete prescribing information for this medication should be consulted for additional detail.

Botulinum Toxin Type A (BŌT yoo lin num TOKS in type aye)

U.S. Brand Names Botox®; Botox® Cosmetic
Canadian Brand Names Botox®; Botox® Cosmetic
Index Terms BTX-A
Pharmacologic Category Neuromuscular Blocker Agent, Toxin; Ophthalmic Agent, Toxin
Use Treatment of strabismus and blepharospasm associated with dystonia (including benign essential blepharospasm or VII nerve disorders in patients ≥12 years of age); cervical dystonia (spasmodic torticollis) in patients ≥16 years of age; temporary improvement in the appearance of lines/wrinkles of the face (moderate to severe glabellar lines associated with corrugator and/or procerus muscle activity) in adult patients ≤65 years of age; treatment of severe primary axillary hyperhidrosis in adults not adequately controlled with topical treatments

Orphan drug: Treatment of dynamic muscle contracture in pediatric cerebral palsy patients
Unlabeled/Investigational Use Treatment of oromandibular dystonia, spasmodic dysphonia (laryngeal dystonia) and other dystonias (ie, writer's cramp, focal task-specific dystonias); migraine treatment and prophylaxis
Pregnancy Risk Factor C (manufacturer)
Pregnancy Implications Decreased fetal body weight, delayed ossification, maternal toxicity, abortions, and fetal malformations were observed in animal studies. Human reproduction studies have not been conducted. Avoid use in pregnancy.
Lactation Excretion in breast milk unknown/not recommended
Contraindications Hypersensitivity to albumin, botulinum toxin, or any component of the formulation; infection at the proposed injection site(s); pregnancy. Relative contraindications include diseases of neuromuscular transmission; coagulopathy including therapeutic anticoagulation; uncooperative patient.
Warnings/Precautions Higher doses or more frequent administration may result in neutralizing antibody formation and loss of efficacy. Product contains albumin and may carry a remote risk of virus transmission. Use caution if there is inflammation, excessive weakness, or atrophy at the proposed injection site(s). Have appropriate support in case of anaphylactic reaction. Use with caution in patients with neuromuscular diseases (such as myasthenia gravis), neuropathic disorders (such as amyotrophic lateral sclerosis), or patients taking aminoglycosides or other drugs that interfere with neuromuscular transmission. Ensure adequate contraception in women of childbearing years. Long-term effects of chronic therapy unknown.

Cervical dystonia: Dysphagia is common. It may be severe requiring alternative feeding methods. Risk factors include smaller neck muscle mass, bilateral injections into the sternocleidomastoid muscle, or injections into the levator scapulae. Dysphasia may be associated with increased risk of upper respiratory infection.

Blepharospasm: Reduced blinking from injection of the orbicularis muscle can lead to corneal exposure and ulceration.

Strabismus: Retrobulbar hemorrhages may occur from needle penetration into orbit. Spatial disorientation, double vision, or past pointing may occur if one or more extraocular muscles are paralyzed. Covering the affected eye may help. Careful testing of corneal sensation, avoidance of lower lid injections, and treatment of epithelial defects are necessary.

Primary axillary hyperhidrosis: Evaluate for secondary causes prior to treatment (eg, hyperthyroidism). Safety and efficacy for treatment of hyperhidrosis in other areas of the body have not been established.

Temporary reduction in glabellar lines: Do not use more frequently than every 3 months. Patients with marked facial asymmetry, ptosis, excessive dermatochalasis, deep dermal scarring, thick sebaceous skin, or the inability to substantially lessen glabellar lines by physically spreading them apart were excluded from clinical trials. Reduced blinking from injection of the orbicularis muscle can lead to corneal exposure and ulceration. Spatial disorientation, double vision, or past pointing may occur if one or more extraocular muscles are paralyzed.

Adverse Reactions Adverse effects usually occur in 1 week and may last up to several months

>10%:
  Central nervous system: Headache (cervical dystonia up to 11%, reduction of glabellar lines up to 13%; can occur with other uses)
  Gastrointestinal: Dysphagia (cervical dystonia 19%)
  Neuromuscular & skeletal: Neck pain (cervical dystonia 11%)
  Ocular: Ptosis (blepharospasm 10% to 40%, strabismus 1% to 38%, reduction of glabellar lines 1% to 5%), vertical deviation (strabismus 17%)
  Respiratory: Upper respiratory infection (cervical dystonia 12%)
2% to 10%:
  Central nervous system: Anxiety (primary axillary hyperhidrosis), dizziness (cervical dystonia, reduction of glabellar lines), drowsiness (cervical dystonia), fever (cervical dystonia, primary axillary hyperhidrosis), speech disorder (cervical dystonia)
  Dermatologic: Nonaxillary sweating (primary axillary hyperhidrosis), pruritus (primary axillary hyperhidrosis)
  Gastrointestinal: Xerostomia (cervical dystonia), nausea (cervical dystonia, reduction of glabellar lines)
  Local: Injection site reaction
  Neuromuscular & skeletal: Back pain (cervical dystonia), facial pain (reduction of glabellar lines), hypertonia (cervical dystonia), weakness (cervical dystonia, reduction of glabellar lines)
  Ocular: Dry eyes (blepharospasm 6%), superficial punctate keratitis (blepharospasm 6%)
  Respiratory: Cough (cervical dystonia), infection (reduction of glabellar lines, primary axillary hyperhidrosis), pharyngitis (primary axillary hyperhidrosis), rhinitis (cervical dystonia)
(Continued)

Botulinum Toxin Type A *(Continued)*

Miscellaneous: Flu syndrome (cervical dystonia, reduction of glabellar lines, primary axillary hyperhidrosis)

<2%: Stiffness, diplopia (cervical dystonia, blepharospasm), ptosis (cervical dystonia), dyspnea (cervical dystonia), numbness (cervical dystonia), ectropion (blepharospasm), lagophthalmos (blepharospasm), facial weakness (blepharospasm), ecchymoses (blepharospasm), eyelid edema (blepharospasm), tearing (blepharospasm), photophobia (blepharospasm), entropion (blepharospasm)

Postmarketing and/or case reports: Allergic reactions, arrhythmia, erythema multiforme, MI, pruritus, psoriasiform eruption, skin rash, urticaria

Reported following treatment of cervical dystonia: Brachial plexopathy, dysphonia, aspiration

Reported following treatment of blepharospasm: Reduced blinking leading to corneal ulceration, corneal perforation, acute angle-closure glaucoma, focal facial paralysis, exacerbation of myasthenia gravis, syncope, vitreous hemorrhage

Reported following treatment of strabismus: Retrobulbar hemorrhage, ciliary ganglion damage, anterior segment eye ischemia

Reported following reduction of glabellar lines: Exacerbation of myasthenia gravis, retinal vein occlusion, abnormal hearing/hearing loss, glaucoma, vertigo with nystagmus

Overdosage/Toxicology Systemic weakness or muscle paralysis could occur for up to several weeks after overdose. Signs and symptoms of overdose are not apparent immediately. An antitoxin is available if there is immediate knowledge of an overdose or misinjection. Contact Allergan for additional information at (800) 433-8871 or (714) 246-5954. The antitoxin will not reverse toxin-induced muscle weakness already present.

Drug Interactions

Increased Effect/Toxicity: Aminoglycosides, neuromuscular-blocking agents, and other agents which may block neuromuscular transmission.

Stability Store undiluted vials under refrigeration at 2°C to 8°C for up to 24 months. Administer within 4 hours after the vial is reconstituted. Reconstitute with sterile normal saline without a preservative. Mix gently. After reconstitution, store in refrigerator (2°C to 8°C) and use within 4 hours (does not contain preservative). Do not freeze.

Botox®: Reconstitute vials with 1 mL of diluent to get 10 units per 0.1 mL; 2 mL of diluent to get 5 units per 0.1 mL; 4 mL of diluent to get 2.5 units per 0.1 mL; 8 mL of diluent to get 1.25 units per 0.1 mL.

Botox® Cosmetic: Reconstitute vials with 2.5 mL of diluent to get 0.4 units per 0.1 mL (20 units per 0.5 mL).

Mechanism of Action Botulinum A toxin is a neurotoxin produced by *Clostridium botulinum*, spore-forming anaerobic bacillus, which appears to affect only the presynaptic membrane of the neuromuscular junction in humans, where it prevents calcium-dependent release of acetylcholine and produces a state of denervation. Muscle inactivation persists until new fibrils grow from the nerve and form junction plates on new areas of the muscle-cell walls.

Pharmacodynamics/Kinetics

Onset of action (improvement):

Blepharospasm: ~3 days

Cervical dystonia: ~2 weeks

Strabismus: ~1-2 days

Reduction of glabellar lines (Botox® Cosmetic): 1-2 days, increasing in intensity during first week

Duration:

Blepharospasm: ~3 months

Cervical dystonia: <3 months

Strabismus: ~2-6 weeks

Primary axillary hyperhidrosis: 201 days (mean)

Reduction of glabellar lines (Botox® Cosmetic): Up to 3 months

Absorption: Not expected to be present in peripheral blood at recommended doses

Time to peak:

Blepharospasm: 1-2 weeks

Cervical dystonia: ~6 weeks

Strabismus: Within first week

Dosage

Cervical dystonia: Children ≥16 years and Adults: I.M.: For dosing guidance, the mean dose is 236 units (25th to 75th percentile range 198-300 units) divided among the affected muscles in patients previously treated with botulinum toxin. Initial dose in previously untreated patients should be lower. Sequential dosing should be based on the patient's head and neck position, localization of pain, muscle hypertrophy, patient response, and previous adverse reactions. The total dose injected into the sternocleidomastoid muscles should be ≤100 units to decrease the occurrence of dysphagia.

Blepharospasm: Children ≥12 years and Adults: I.M.: Initial dose: 1.25-2.5 units injected into the medial and lateral pretarsal orbicularis oculi of the upper and lower lid; dose may be increased up to twice the previous dose if the response from the initial dose lasted ≤2 months; maximum dose per site: 5 units; cumulative dose in a 30-day period: ≤200 units. Tolerance may occur if treatments are given more often than every 3 months, but the effect is not usually permanent.

Strabismus: Children ≥12 years and Adults: I.M.:

Initial dose:

Vertical muscles and for horizontal strabismus <20 prism diopters: 1.25-2.5 units in any one muscle

Horizontal strabismus of 20-50 prism diopters: 2.5-5 units in any one muscle

Persistent VI nerve palsy >1 month: 1.5-2.5 units in the medial rectus muscle

Re-examine patients 7-14 days after each injection to assess the effect of that dose. Subsequent doses for patients experiencing incomplete paralysis of the target may be increased up to twice the previous administered dose. The maximum recommended dose as a single injection for any one muscle is 25 units. Do not administer subsequent injections until the effects of the previous dose are gone.

Primary axillary hyperhidrosis: Adults ≥18 years: Intradermal: 50 units/axilla. Injection area should be defined by standard staining techniques. Injections should be evenly distributed into multiple sites (10-15), administered in 0.1-0.2 mL aliquots, ~1-2 cm apart.

Reduction of glabellar lines: Adults ≤65 years: I.M.: An effective dose is determined by gross observation of the patient's ability to activate the superficial muscles injected. The location, size and use of muscles may vary markedly among individuals. Inject 0.1 mL dose into each of five sites, two in each corrugator muscle and one in the procerus muscle (total dose 0.5 mL).

Elderly: No specific adjustment recommended

Dosage adjustment in renal impairment: No specific adjustment recommended

Dosage adjustment in hepatic impairment: No specific adjustment recommended

Administration

Cervical dystonia: Use 25-, 27-, or 30-gauge needle for superficial muscles and a longer 22-gauge needle for deeper musculature; electromyography may help localize the involved muscles.

Blepharospasm: Use a 27- or 30-gauge needle without electromyography guidance. Avoid injecting near the levator palpebrae superioris (may decrease ptosis); avoid medial lower lid injections (may decrease diplopia). Apply pressure at the injection site to prevent ecchymosis in the soft eyelid tissues.

Strabismus injections: Must use surgical exposure or electromyographic guidance; use the electrical activity recorded from the tip of the injections needle as a guide to placement within the target muscle. Local anesthetic and ocular decongestant should be given before injection. The volume of injection should be 0.05-0.15 mL per muscle. Many patients will require additional doses because of inadequate response to initial dose.

Primary axillary hyperhidrosis: Inject each dose intradermally to a depth of ~2 mm and at a 45° angle. Do not inject directly into areas marked in ink (to avoid permanent tattoo effect). Prior to administration, injection area should be defined by standard staining techniques such as Minor's Iodine-Starch Test.

Instructions for Minor's Iodine-Starch Test: Patient should shave underarms and refrain from using deodorants or antiperspirants for 24 hours prior to test. At 30 minutes prior to test, patient should be at rest, no exercise, and not consume hot beverages. Underarm area should be dried and immediately painted with iodine solution. After area dries, lightly sprinkle with starch powder. Gently blow off excess powder. A deep blue-black color will develop over the hyperhidrotic area in ~10 minutes.

Reduction of glabellar lines (Botox® Cosmetic): Use a 30-gauge needle. Ensure injected volume/dose is accurate and where feasible keep to a minimum. Avoid injection near the levator palpebrae superioris. Medial corrugator injections should be at least 1 cm above the bony supraorbital ridge. Do not inject toxin closer than 1 cm above the central eyebrow.

Additional Information Units of biological activity of Botox® cannot be compared with units of any other botulinum toxin.

Dosage Forms Injection, powder for reconstitution [preservative free]: Clostridium botulinum toxin type A 100 units [contains human albumin]

Botulinum Toxin Type B (BOT yoo lin num TOKS in type bee)

U.S. Brand Names Myobloc®

Pharmacologic Category Neuromuscular Blocker Agent, Toxin

Use Treatment of cervical dystonia (spasmodic torticollis)

Unlabeled/Investigational Use Treatment of cervical dystonia in patients who have developed resistance to botulinum toxin type A

Pregnancy Risk Factor C (manufacturer)

Pregnancy Implications Neither animal or human reproduction studies have been conducted. Avoid use in pregnancy.

Lactation Excretion in breast milk unknown/not recommended

Contraindications Hypersensitivity to albumin, botulinum toxin, or any component of the formulation; infection at the injection site(s); pregnancy; coadministration of agents known to potentiate neuromuscular blockade. Relative contraindications include diseases of neuromuscular transmission; coagulopathy, including therapeutic anticoagulation; inability of patient to cooperate.

Warnings/Precautions Higher doses or more frequent administration may result in neutralizing antibody formation and loss of efficacy. Product contains albumin and may carry a remote risk of virus transmission. Use caution if there is inflammation, excessive weakness, or atrophy at the proposed injection site(s). Concurrent use of botulinum toxin type A or within <4 months of type B is not recommended. Have appropriate support in case of anaphylactic reaction. Use with caution in patients taking aminoglycosides or other drugs that interfere with neuromuscular transmission. Ensure adequate contraception in women of childbearing years. Long-term effects of chronic therapy unknown. Increased risk of dysphagia and respiratory complications. Safety and efficacy in children have not been established.

Adverse Reactions

>10%:
  Central nervous system: Headache (10% to 16%), pain (6% to 13%; placebo 10%)
  Gastrointestinal: Dysphagia (10% to 25%), xerostomia (3% to 34%)
  Local: Injection site pain (12% to 16%)
  Neuromuscular & skeletal: Neck pain (up to 17%; placebo: 16%)
  Miscellaneous: Infection (13% to 19%; placebo: 15%)

1% to 10%:
  Cardiovascular: Chest pain, vasodilation, peripheral edema
  Central nervous system: Dizziness (3% to 6%), fever, malaise, migraine, anxiety, tremor, hyperesthesia, somnolence, confusion, vertigo
  Dermatologic: Pruritus, bruising
  Gastrointestinal: Nausea (3% to 10%; placebo: 5%), dyspepsia (up to 10%; placebo: 5%), vomiting, stomatitis, taste perversion

(Continued)

Botulinum Toxin Type B *(Continued)*

Genitourinary: Urinary tract infection, cystitis, vaginal moniliasis

Hematologic: Serum neutralizing activity

Neuromuscular & skeletal: Torticollis (up to 8%; placebo: 7%), arthralgia (up to 7%; placebo: 5%), back pain (3% to 7%; placebo: 3%), myasthenia (3% to 6%; placebo: 3%), weakness (up to 6%; placebo: 4%), arthritis

Ocular: Amblyopia, abnormal vision

Otic: Otitis media, tinnitus

Respiratory: Cough (3% to 7%; placebo: 3%), rhinitis (1% to 5%; placebo: 6%), dyspnea, pneumonia

Miscellaneous: Flu-syndrome (6% to 9%), allergic reaction, viral infection, abscess, cyst

Overdosage/Toxicology Systemic weakness or muscle paralysis could occur for up to several weeks after overdose. Signs and symptoms of overdose are not apparent immediately. An antitoxin is available if there is immediate knowledge of an overdose or misinjection. Contact Elan Pharmaceuticals for additional information at (888) 638-7605 and your State Health Department to process a request for antitoxin through the CDC. The antitoxin will not reverse toxin-induced muscle weakness already present.

Drug Interactions

Increased Effect/Toxicity: Aminoglycosides, neuromuscular-blocking agents, botulinum toxin type A, and other agents which may block neuromuscular transmission

Stability Store vials under refrigeration at 2°C to 8°C (36°F to 46°F) for up to 21 months. May be diluted with normal saline; once diluted, use within 4 hours. Does not contain preservative. Single-use vial. Do not shake; do not freeze.

Mechanism of Action Botulinum B toxin is a neurotoxin produced by *Clostridium botulinum*, spore-forming anaerobic bacillus. It cleaves synaptic Vesicle Association Membrane Protein (VAMP; synaptobrevin) which is a component of the protein complex responsible for docking and fusion of the synaptic vesicle to the presynaptic membrane. By blocking neurotransmitter release, botulinum B toxin paralyzes the muscle.

Pharmacodynamics/Kinetics

Duration: 12-16 weeks

Absorption: Not expected to be present in peripheral blood at recommended doses

Dosage

Children: Not established in pediatric patients

Adults: Cervical dystonia: I.M.: Initial: 2500-5000 units divided among the affected muscles in patients **previously treated** with botulinum toxin; initial dose in **previously untreated** patients should be lower. Subsequent dosing should be optimized according to patient's response.

Elderly: No dosage adjustments required, but limited experience in patients ≥75 years old

Dosage adjustment in renal impairment: No specific adjustment recommended

Dosage adjustment in hepatic impairment: No specific adjustment recommended

Additional Information Units of biological activity of Myobloc® cannot be compared with units of any other botulinum toxin.

Dosage Forms

Injection, solution [preservative free]:

Myobloc®: 5000 units/mL (0.5 mL, 1 mL, 2 mL) [contains albumin 0.05%]

♦ **Botulinum Toxoid, Pentavalent Vaccine (Against Types A / B / C / D / E Strains of *C. botulinum*)** see Botulinum Pentavalent (ABCDE) Toxoid *on page 234*

Botulism Immune Globulin (Intravenous-Human)

(BOT yoo lism i MYUN GLOB you lin, in tra VEE nus, YU man)

U.S. Brand Names BabyBIG®

Index Terms BIG-IV

Pharmacologic Category Immune Globulin

Use Treatment of infant botulism caused by toxin type A or B

Restrictions Available from the California Department of Health

Pregnancy Implications Reproduction studies have not been conducted.

Contraindications Hypersensitivity to human immune globulin preparations or any component of the formulation; selective immunoglobulin A deficiency

Warnings/Precautions Use caution with renal dysfunction or those at increased risk for renal disease, including concomitant nephrotoxic drugs, diabetes mellitus, paraproteinemia, sepsis, or volume depletion. Patients should not be volume depleted prior to therapy. For I.V. infusion only; do not exceed recommended rate of administration. Not indicated for use in adults or children; safety and efficacy established for infants <1 year of age.

Adverse Reactions Percentages reported in open-label study except where otherwise noted; may reflect pathophysiology of infant botulism.

>10%:

Cardiovascular: Blood pressure increased (transient, 75%), pallor (28%), edema (18%); blood pressure decreased (transient, 16%), cardiac murmur (15%)

Central nervous system: Irritability (41%), pyrexia (17%), body temperature decreased (16%)

Dermatologic: Contact dermatitis (24%), erythematous rash (22%, reported as 14% vs 8% in placebo-controlled study)

Gastrointestinal: Dysphagia (65%), loose stools (25%), vomiting (20%), abdominal distension (11%)

Otic: Otitis media (11%, reported in placebo-controlled study)

Respiratory: Atelectasis (39%), rhonchi (34%), nasal congestion (18%), oxygen saturation decreased (17%), cough (13%), rales (13%)

1% to 10%:

Cardiovascular: Tachycardia (7%), peripheral coldness (7%)

Central nervous system: Agitation (10%)

Endocrine & metabolic: Dehydration (10%), hyponatremia (6%), metabolic acidosis (5%)

Hematologic: Hemoglobin decreased (9%), anemia (5%)

Local: Injection site reaction (7%), injection site erythema (5%)

Renal: Neurogenic bladder

· Respiratory: Breath sounds decreased (10%), stridor (9%), lower respiratory tract infection (8%), dyspnea (6%), tachypnea (5%)

Miscellaneous: Oral candidiasis (8%), intubation (5%), infusion rate reactions (<5%, includes chills, back pain, fever, muscle cramps, nausea, vomiting, wheezing)

Overdosage/Toxicology Limited data; adverse reactions related to volume overload may be expected

Drug Interactions

Decreased Effect: Immune globulins may interfere with live virus vaccines; defer vaccination for ~5 months following therapy; revaccinations may be needed if given shortly before or after BIG-IV administration.

Stability Prior to reconstitution, store between 2°C to 8°C (35.6°F to 46.4°F). Infusion should begin within 2 hours of reconstitution and be completed within 4 hours of reconstitution. Reconstitute with SWFI 2 mL. Swirl gently to wet powder; do not shake. Powder should dissolve in ~30 minutes.

Mechanism of Action BIG-IV is purified immunoglobulin derived from the plasma of adults immunized with botulinum toxoid types A and B. BIG-IV provides antibodies to neutralize circulating toxins.

Pharmacodynamics/Kinetics

Duration: Protective neutralizing antibody levels: 6 months

Half-life elimination: 28 days

Dosage I.V.: Children <1 year: Infant botulism: 1 mL/kg (50 mg/kg) as a single dose; infuse at 0.5 mL/kg/hour (25 mg/kg/hour) for the first 15 minutes; if well tolerated, may increase to 1 mL/kg/hour (50 mg/kg/hour)

Administration For I.V. infusion only. Do not administer if solution is turbid. Epinephrine should be available for the treatment of acute allergic reaction. Administer using low volume tubing and infusion pump with an in-line or syringe tip 18 μm filter. Infuse at 0.5 mL/kg/hour (25 mg/kg/hour) for the first 15 minutes; if well tolerated, may increase to 1 mL/kg/hour (50 mg/kg/hour). Infusion should take ~67.5 minutes. Infusion should be slowed or temporarily interrupted for minor side effects; discontinue in case of hypotension or anaphylaxis.

Monitoring Parameters Renal function (BUN, serum creatinine, urinary output); vital signs (continuously during infusion); aseptic meningitis syndrome (may occur hours to days following IGIV therapy), signs of relapse (may occur up to 1 month following recovery)

Dosage Forms Injection, powder for reconstitution [preservative free]: ~100 mg [contains albumin 1% and sucrose 5%; packaged with SWFI]

♦ **Boudreaux's® Butt Paste [OTC]** see Zinc Oxide on page 1817

♦ **Bovine Lung Surfactant** see Beractant on page 210

♦ **Bravelle®** see Urofollitropin on page 1759

♦ **Breathe Right® Saline [OTC]** see Sodium Chloride on page 1576

♦ **Brethaire [DSC]** see Terbutaline on page 1650

♦ **Brevibloc®** see Esmolol on page 616

♦ **Brevicon®** see Ethinyl Estradiol and Norethindrone on page 655

♦ **Brevicon® 0.5/35 (Can)** see Ethinyl Estradiol and Norethindrone on page 655

♦ **Brevicon® 1/35 (Can)** see Ethinyl Estradiol and Norethindrone on page 655

♦ **Brevital® (Can)** see Methohexital on page 1110

♦ **Brevital® Sodium** see Methohexital on page 1110

♦ **Bricanyl [DSC]** see Terbutaline on page 1650

♦ **Bricanyl® (Can)** see Terbutaline on page 1650

Brimonidine (bri MOE ni deen)

U.S. Brand Names Alphagan® P

Canadian Brand Names Alphagan®; Apo-Brimonidine®; PMS-Brimonidine Tartrate; ratio-Brimonidine

Index Terms Brimonidine Tartrate

Pharmacologic Category Alpha$_2$ Agonist, Ophthalmic; Ophthalmic Agent, Antiglaucoma

Additional Appendix Information

Glaucoma Drug Therapy on page 2050

Use Lowering of intraocular pressure (IOP) in patients with open-angle glaucoma or ocular hypertension

Pregnancy Risk Factor B

Medication Safety Issues

Sound-alike/look-alike issues:

Brimonidine may be confused with bromocriptine

Dosage Ophthalmic: Children ≥2 years of age and Adults: Glaucoma: Instill 1 drop in affected eye(s) 3 times/day (approximately every 8 hours)

Additional Information Complete prescribing information for this medication should be consulted for additional detail.

Dosage Forms

Solution, ophthalmic, as tartrate: 0.2% (5 mL, 10 mL, 15 mL) [may contain benzalkonium chloride]

(Continued)

Brimonidine *(Continued)*

Alphagan® P: 0.1% (5 mL, 10 mL, 15 mL) [contains Purite® as preservative]; 0.15% (5 mL, 10 mL, 15 mL) [contains Purite® as preservative]

♦ **Brimonidine Tartrate** *see* Brimonidine *on page 239*

Brinzolamide *(brin ZOH la mide)*

U.S. Brand Names Azopt®
Canadian Brand Names Azopt®
Pharmacologic Category Carbonic Anhydrase Inhibitor; Ophthalmic Agent, Antiglaucoma
Additional Appendix Information
Glaucoma Drug Therapy *on page 2050*
Use Lowers intraocular pressure in patients with ocular hypertension or open-angle glaucoma
Pregnancy Risk Factor C
Dosage Ophthalmic: Adults: Instill 1 drop in affected eye(s) 3 times/day
Additional Information Complete prescribing information for this medication should be consulted for additional detail.
Dosage Forms Suspension, ophthalmic: 1% (5 mL, 10 mL, 15 mL) [contains benzalkonium chloride]

♦ **Brioschi® [OTC]** *see* Sodium Bicarbonate *on page 1575*
♦ **British Anti-Lewisite** *see* Dimercaprol *on page 512*
♦ **BRL 43694** *see* Granisetron *on page 811*
♦ **Brofed®** *see* Brompheniramine and Pseudoephedrine *on page 243*
♦ **Bromaline® [OTC]** *see* Brompheniramine and Pseudoephedrine *on page 243*
♦ **Bromaxefed RF** *see* Brompheniramine and Pseudoephedrine *on page 243*

Bromfenac *(BROME fen ak)*

U.S. Brand Names Xibrom™
Index Terms Bromfenac Sodium
Pharmacologic Category Nonsteroidal Anti-inflammatory Drug (NSAID), Ophthalmic
Use Treatment of postoperative inflammation and reduction in ocular pain following cataract removal
Pregnancy Risk Factor C/D (3rd trimester)
Dosage Ophthalmic: Adults: Instill 1 drop into affected eye(s) twice daily beginning 24 hours after surgery and continuing for 2 weeks postoperative
   Dosage adjustment in renal impairment: No adjustment required
Additional Information Complete prescribing information for this medication should be consulted for additional detail.
Dosage Forms
Solution, ophthalmic:
   Xibrom™: 0.09% (5 mL) [contains benzalkonium chloride and sodium sulfite]

♦ **Bromfenac Sodium** *see* Bromfenac *on page 240*
♦ **Bromfenex®** *see* Brompheniramine and Pseudoephedrine *on page 243*
♦ **Bromfenex® PD** *see* Brompheniramine and Pseudoephedrine *on page 243*
♦ **Bromhist-NR** *see* Brompheniramine and Pseudoephedrine *on page 243*
♦ **Bromhist Pediatric** *see* Brompheniramine and Pseudoephedrine *on page 243*

Bromocriptine *(broe moe KRIP teen)*

U.S. Brand Names Parlodel®; Parlodel® SnapTabs®
Canadian Brand Names Apo-Bromocriptine®; Parlodel®; PMS-Bromocriptine
Index Terms Bromocriptine Mesylate
Pharmacologic Category Anti-Parkinson's Agent, Dopamine Agonist; Ergot Derivative
Additional Appendix Information
Parkinson's Agents *on page 1895*
Use Treatment of hyperprolactinemia associated with amenorrhea with or without galactorrhea, infertility, or hypogonadism; treatment of prolactin-secreting adenomas; treatment of acromegaly; treatment of Parkinson's disease
Unlabeled/Investigational Use Neuroleptic malignant syndrome
Pregnancy Risk Factor B
Pregnancy Implications No evidence of teratogenicity or fetal toxicity in animal studies. Bromocriptine is used for ovulation induction in women with hyperprolactinemia. In general, therapy should be discontinued if pregnancy is confirmed unless needed for treatment of macroprolactinoma. Data collected from women taking bromocriptine during pregnancy suggest the incidence of birth defects is not increased with use. However, the majority of women discontinued use within 8 weeks of pregnancy. Women not seeking pregnancy should be advised to use appropriate contraception.
Lactation Enters breast milk/contraindicated
Medication Safety Issues
Sound-alike/look-alike issues:
   Bromocriptine may be confused with benztropine, brimonidine
   Parlodel® may be confused with pindolol, Provera®
Contraindications Hypersensitivity to bromocriptine, ergot alkaloids, or any component of the formulation; ergot alkaloids are contraindicated with potent inhibitors of CYP3A4 (includes protease inhibitors, azole antifungals, and some macrolide antibiotics); uncontrolled hypertension; severe ischemic heart disease or peripheral vascular disorders; pregnancy (risk to benefit evaluation must be performed in women who become pregnant during treatment for

acromegaly, prolactinoma, or Parkinson's disease - hypertension during treatment should generally result in efforts to withdraw)

Warnings/Precautions Complete evaluation of pituitary function should be completed prior to initiation of treatment. Use caution in patients with impaired renal or hepatic function, a history of peptic ulcer disease, dementia, psychosis, or cardiovascular disease (myocardial infarction, arrhythmia). Symptomatic hypotension may occur in a significant number of patients. In addition, hypertension, seizures, MI, and stroke have been rarely associated with bromocriptine therapy. Severe headache or visual changes may precede events. The onset of reactions may be immediate or delayed (often may occur in the second week of therapy).

Concurrent antihypertensives or drugs which may alter blood pressure should be used with caution. Concurrent use with levodopa has been associated with an increased risk of hallucinations. Consider dosage reduction and/or discontinuation in patients with hallucinations. Hallucinations may require weeks to months before resolution.

In the treatment of acromegaly, discontinuation is recommended if tumor expansion occurs during therapy. Digital vasospasm (cold sensitive) may occur in some patients with acromegaly; may require dosage reduction. Patients who receive bromocriptine during and immediately following pregnancy as a continuation of previous therapy (eg, acromegaly) should be closely monitored for cardiovascular effects. Should not be used post-partum in women with coronary artery disease or other cardiovascular disease. Use of bromocriptine to control or prevent lactation or in patients with uncontrolled hypertension is not recommended.

Monitoring and careful evaluation of visual changes during the treatment of hyperprolactinemia is recommended to differentiate between tumor shrinkage and traction on the optic chiasm; rapidly progressing visual field loss requires neurosurgical consultation. Discontinuation of bromocriptine in patients with macroadenomas has been associated with rapid regrowth of tumor and increased prolactin serum levels. Pleural and retroperitoneal fibrosis have been reported with prolonged daily use. Cardiac valvular fibrosis has also been associated with ergot alkaloids. Safety and effectiveness in patients <15 years of age (for pituitary adenoma) have not been established.

Adverse Reactions Note: Frequency of adverse effects may vary by dose and/or indication.

>10%:
    Cardiovascular: Hypotension (up to 30%)
    Central nervous system: Headache, dizziness
    Gastrointestinal: Nausea, constipation
1% to 10%:
    Cardiovascular: Orthostasis, vasospasm (cold-sensitive), Raynaud's syndrome, syncope
    Central nervous system: Fatigue, lightheadedness, drowsiness
    Gastrointestinal: Anorexia, vomiting, abdominal cramps, diarrhea, dyspepsia, GI bleeding, xerostomia
    Respiratory: Nasal congestion
<1% (Limited to important or life-threatening): Arrhythmias, erythromelalgia, ethanol potentiation, hallucinations (visual), hypertension, MI, paranoia, paresthesia, psychosis, pulmonary infiltrates, pleural effusion, peritoneal fibrosis, rash, retroperitoneal fibrosis, skin mottling, status epilepticus, vasovagal reaction, vertigo, visual changes
Withdrawal reactions: Abrupt discontinuation has resulted in rare cases of a withdrawal reaction with symptoms similar to neuroleptic malignant syndrome.

Overdosage/Toxicology Symptoms include nausea, vomiting, and hypotension. Hypotension, when unresponsive to I.V. fluids or Trendelenburg positioning, often responds to norepinephrine infusions started at 0.1-0.2 mcg/kg/minute followed by a titrated infusion.

Drug Interactions
    Cytochrome P450 Effect: Substrate of CYP3A4 (major); **Inhibits** CYP1A2 (weak), 3A4 (weak)
        Increased Effect/Toxicity: Effect/toxiicty of bromocriptine may be increased by alpha agonists/sympathomimetics, antifungals (azole derivatives), macrolide antibiotics, protease inhibitors, and MAO inhibitors. Bromocriptine may increase the effects of sibutramine and other serotonin agonists (serotonin syndrome). CYP3A4 inhibitors may increase the levels/effects of bromocriptine; example inhibitors include azole antifungals, clarithromycin, diclofenac, doxycycline, erythromycin, imatinib, isoniazid, nefazodone, nicardipine, propofol, protease inhibitors, quinidine, telithromycin, and verapamil. Concurrent use of bromocriptine with antihypertensive agents may increase the risk of hypotension. Concurrent use of levodopa may increase the risk of hallucinations (dose-dependant).
        Decreased Effect: Effects of bromocriptine may be diminished by antipsychotics, metoclopramide.

Ethanol/Nutrition/Herb Interactions
    Ethanol: Avoid ethanol (may increase GI side effects or ethanol intolerance).
    Herb/Nutraceutical: St John's wort may decrease bromocriptine levels.

Mechanism of Action Semisynthetic ergot alkaloid derivative and a dopamine receptor agonist which activates postsynaptic dopamine receptors in the tuberoinfundibular (inhibiting pituitary prolactin secretion) and nigrostriatal pathways (enhancing coordinated motor control).

Pharmacodynamics/Kinetics
    Bioavailability: 28%
    Protein binding: 90% to 96%
    Metabolism: Primarily hepatic
    Half-life elimination: Biphasic: Initial: 6-8 hours; Terminal: 50 hours
    Time to peak, serum: 1-2 hours
    Excretion: Feces; urine (2% to 6% as unchanged drug)

Dosage Oral:
    Children: Hyperprolactinemia:
        11-15 years (based on limited information): Initial: 1.25-2.5 mg daily; dosage may be increased as tolerated to achieve a therapeutic response (range: 2.5-10 mg daily).
        ≥16 years: Refer to adult dosing
    (Continued)

Bromocriptine *(Continued)*

Adults:

Parkinsonism: 1.25 mg twice daily, increased by 2.5 mg/day in 2- to 4-week intervals (usual dose range is 30-90 mg/day in 3 divided doses), though elderly patients can usually be managed on lower doses

Neuroleptic malignant syndrome (unlabeled use): 2.5-5 mg 3 times/day

Acromegaly: Initial: 1.25-2.5 mg daily increasing by 1.25-2.5 mg daily as necessary every 3-7 days; usual dose: 20-30 mg/day (maximum: 100 mg/day)

Hyperprolactinemia: Initial: 1.25-2.5 mg/day; may be increased by 2.5 mg/day as tolerated every 2-7 days until optimal response (range: 2.5-15 mg/day)

Dosing adjustment in hepatic impairment: No guidelines are available, however, may be necessary

Dietary Considerations May be taken with food to decrease GI distress.

Monitoring Parameters Monitor blood pressure closely as well as hepatic, hematopoietic, and cardiovascular function; visual field monitoring is recommended (prolactinoma); pregnancy test during amenorrheic peroid; growth hormone and prolactin levels.

Additional Information Usually used with levodopa or levodopa/carbidopa to treat Parkinson's disease. When adding bromocriptine, the dose of levodopa/carbidopa can usually be decreased.

Dosage Forms

Capsule, as mesylate: 5 mg
   Parlodel®: 5 mg
Tablet, as mesylate: 2.5 mg
   Parlodel® SnapTabs®: 2.5 mg

♦ **Bromocriptine Mesylate** *see* Bromocriptine *on page 240*

Brompheniramine *(brome fen IR a meen)*

U.S. Brand Names Bidhist; BroveX™; BroveX™ CT; B-Vex; Lodrane® 12 Hour; Lodrane® 24; Lodrane® XR; LoHist-12; TanaCof-XR

Index Terms Brompheniramine Maleate; Brompheniramine Tannate

Pharmacologic Category Antihistamine

Use Symptomatic relief of perennial and seasonal allergic rhinitis, vasomotor rhinitis, and other respiratory allergies

Pregnancy Risk Factor C

Dosage Allergic rhinitis, allergic symptoms, vasomotor rhinitis: Oral:

Children:

1-2 years (B-Vex, BroveX™): 1.25 mL every 12 hours (maximum: 2.5 mL/day)

2-6 years:

B-Vex, BroveX™: 2.5 mL every 12 hours (maximum: 5 mL/day)
BroveX™ CT: ½ tablet every 12 hours (maximum: 1 tablet/day)
Lodrane® XR, TanaCof-XR: 1.25 mL every 12 hours (maximum: 2.5 mL/day)

6-12 years:

B-Vex, BroveX™: 5 mL every 12 hours (maximum: 10 mL/day)
BroveX™ CT: ½ to 1 tablet every 12 hours (maximum: 2 tablets/day)
Lodrane® 12 Hour, LoHist-12: One tablet every 12 hours (maximum: 2 tablets/day)
Lodrane® 24: One capsule once daily
Lodrane® XR, TanaCof-XR: 2.5 mL every 12 hours (maximum: 5 mL/day)

>12 years (B-Vex, BroveX™, BroveX™ CT, Lodrane® 12 Hour, Lodrane® 24, Lodrane® XR, LoHist-12, TanaCof-XR): Refer to adult dosing

Adults:

B-Vex, BroveX™: 5-10 mL every 12 hours (maximum: 20 mL/day)
BroveX™ CT: 1-2 tablets every 12 hours (maximum: 4 tablets/day)
Lodrane® 12 Hour, LoHist: 1-2 tablets every 12 hours (maximum: 4 tablets/day)
Lodrane® 24: 1-2 capsules once daily
Lodrane® XR, TanaCof-XR: 5 mL every 12 hours (maximum: 10 mL/day)

Elderly (also refer to adult dosing): Initial:

B-Vex, BroveX™: 5 mL every 12 hours
BroveX™ CT, Lodrane® 12 Hour, LoHist: 1 tablet every 12 hours
Lodrane® 24: 1 capsule/24 hours
Lodrane® XR, TanaCof-XR: 2.5 mL every 12 hours

Additional Information Complete prescribing information for this medication should be consulted for additional detail.

Dosage Forms

Suspension, as tannate:

B-Vex, BroveX™: 12 mg/5 mL (120 mL) [contains sodium benzoate and tartrazine; banana flavor]
Lodrane® XR: 8 mg/5 mL (480 mL) [alcohol free, sugar free; strawberry flavor]
TanaCof-XR: 8 mg/5 mL (480 mL) [alcohol free, sugar free; contains phenylalanine; strawberry creme flavor]

Tablet, chewable, as tannate:

BroveX™ CT: 12 mg [banana flavor]

Tablet, extended release, as maleate [scored]:

Bidhist: 6 mg
Lodrane® 12 Hour, LoHist-12: 6 mg [dye free]
Lodrane® 24: 12 mg [dye free]

Tablet, timed release, as maleate: 6 mg

Brompheniramine and Pseudoephedrine
(brome fen IR a meen & soo doe e FED rin)

U.S. Brand Names Andehist NR Syrup; Brofed®; Bromaline® [OTC]; Bromaxefed RF; Bromfenex®; Bromfenex® PD; Bromhist-NR; Bromhist Pediatric; Children's Dimetapp® Elixir Cold & Allergy [OTC]; Histex™ SR; Lodrano®; Lodrane® 12D; Lodrane® LD; Touro™ Allergy

Index Terms Brompheniramine Maleate and Pseudoephedrine Hydrochloride; Brompheniramine Maleate and Pseudoephedrine Sulfate; Pseudoephedrine and Brompheniramine

Pharmacologic Category Antihistamine/Decongestant Combination

Use Temporary relief of symptoms of seasonal and perennial allergic rhinitis, and vasomotor rhinitis, including nasal obstruction

Pregnancy Risk Factor C

Medication Safety Issues
Sound-alike/look-alike issues:
Bromfed® may be confused with Bromphen®

Dosage Oral:
Capsule, long acting:
Based on 60 mg pseudoephedrine:
Children 6-12 years: 1 capsule every 12 hours
Children ≥12 years and Adults: 1-2 capsules every 12 hours
Based on 120 mg pseudoephedrine: Children ≥12 years and Adults: 1 capsule every 12 hours
Liquid:
Based on brompheniramine 1 mg/pseudoephedrine 15 mg per 1 mL: Children:
1-3 months: 0.25 mL 4 times/day
3-6 months: 0.5 mL 4 times/day
6-12 months: 0.75 mL 4 times/day
12-24 months: 1 mL 4 times/day
Based on brompheniramine 1 mg/pseudoephedrine 15 mg per 5 mL: Children:
6-11 months (6-8 kg): 2.5 mL every 6-8 hours (maximum: 4 doses/24 hours)
12-23 months (8-10 kg): 3.75 mL every 6-8 hours (maximum: 4 doses/24 hours)
2-6 years: 5 mL every 6-8 hours (maximum: 4 doses/24 hours)
6-12 years: 10 mL every 6-8 hours (maximum: 4 doses/24 hours)
>12 years and Adults: 20 mg every 4 hours (maximum: 4 doses/24 hours)
Based on brompheniramine 4 mg/pseudoephedrine 30 mg:
Children 2-6 years: 2.5 mL 3 times/day
Children >6 years and Adults: 5 mL 3 times/day
Brompheniramine 4 mg/pseudoephedrine 45 mg per 5 mL:
Children 2-6 years: 2.5 mL 4 times/day
Children >6 years and Adults: 5 mL 4 times/day
Tablet, extended release: Based on pseudoephedrine 45 mg:
Children 6-12 years: 1 tablet every 12 hours
Children ≥12 years and Adults: 1-2 tablets every 12 hours

Additional Information Complete prescribing information for this medication should be consulted for additional detail.

Dosage Forms
Capsule, extended release: Brompheniramine maleate 6 mg and pseudoephedrine hydrochloride 60 mg; brompheniramine maleate 12 mg and pseudoephedrine hydrochloride 120 mg
Bromfenex®: Brompheniramine maleate 12 mg and pseudoephedrine hydrochloride 120 mg
Bromfenex® PD, Lodrane® LD: Brompheniramine maleate 6 mg and pseudoephedrine hydrochloride 60 mg
Histex™ SR: Brompheniramine maleate 10 mg and pseudoephedrine hydrochloride 120 mg
Capsule, sustained release:
Touro™ Allergy: Brompheniramine maleate 5.75 mg and pseudoephedrine hydrochloride 60 mg
Elixir: Brompheniramine maleate 1 mg and pseudoephedrine hydrochloride 15 mg per 5 mL (120 mL, 480 mL)
Children's Dimetapp® Elixir Cold & Allergy: Brompheniramine maleate 1 mg and pseudoephedrine hydrochloride 15 mg per 5 mL (240 mL) [alcohol free; contains sodium benzoate; grape flavor]
Liquid:
Lodrane®: Brompheniramine maleate 4 mg and pseudoephedrine hydrochloride 60 mg per 5 mL (480 mL) [alcohol free, dye free, sugar free; cherry flavor]
Liquid, oral [drops]:
Bromhist NR: Brompheniramine maleate 1 mg and pseudoephedrine hydrochloride 12.5 mg per 1 mL (30 mL) [cherry flavor]
Bromhist Pediatric: Brompheniramine maleate 1 mg and pseudoephedrine hydrochloride 15 mg per 1 mL (30 mL) [cherry flavor]
Solution (Bromaline®): Brompheniramine maleate 1 mg and pseudoephedrine hydrochloride 15 mg per 5 mL (120 mL, 480 mL) [alcohol free; contains sodium benzoate; grape flavor]
Syrup: Brompheniramine maleate 4 mg and pseudoephedrine sulfate 45 mg per 5 mL (120 mL, 480 mL)
Andehist NR: Brompheniramine maleate 4 mg and pseudoephedrine sulfate 45 mg per 5 mL (473 mL) [raspberry flavor]
Brofed®: Brompheniramine maleate 4 mg and pseudoephedrine hydrochloride 30 mg per 5 mL (480 mL) [mint flavor]
Bromaxefed RF: Brompheniramine maleate 4 mg and pseudoephedrine hydrochloride 45 mg per 5 mL (120 mL, 480 mL) [alcohol free; cherry flavor]
Tablet, extended release:
Lodrane® 12D: Brompheniramine maleate 6 mg and pseudoephedrine hydrochloride 45 mg

- **Brompheniramine Maleate** *see* Brompheniramine *on page 242*
- **Brompheniramine Maleate and Pseudoephedrine Hydrochloride** *see* Brompheniramine and Pseudoephedrine *on page 243*
- **Brompheniramine Maleate and Pseudoephedrine Sulfate** *see* Brompheniramine and Pseudoephedrine *on page 243*
- **Brompheniramine Tannate** *see* Brompheniramine *on page 242*
- **Broncho Saline® [OTC]** *see* Sodium Chloride *on page 1576*
- **Brontex®** *see* Guaifenesin and Codeine *on page 815*
- **Brovana™** *see* Arformoterol *on page 148*
- **BroveX™** *see* Brompheniramine *on page 242*
- **BroveX™ CT** *see* Brompheniramine *on page 242*
- **BTX-A** *see* Botulinum Toxin Type A *on page 235*
- **B-type Natriuretic Peptide (Human)** *see* Nesiritide *on page 1215*
- **Budeprion™ SR** *see* BuPROPion *on page 252*

Budesonide (byoo DES oh nide)

U.S. Brand Names Entocort® EC; Pulmicort Respules®; Pulmicort Turbuhaler®; Rhinocort® Aqua®

Canadian Brand Names Entocort®; Gen-Budesonide AQ; Pulmicort®; Rhinocort® Turbuhaler®

Pharmacologic Category Corticosteroid, Inhalant (Oral); Corticosteroid, Nasal; Corticosteroid, Systemic

Additional Appendix Information
Asthma *on page 2029*

Use
Intranasal: Children ≥6 years of age and Adults: Management of symptoms of seasonal or perennial rhinitis

Nebulization: Children 12 months to 8 years: Maintenance and prophylactic treatment of asthma

Oral capsule: Treatment of active Crohn's disease (mild to moderate) involving the ileum and/or ascending colon; maintenance of remission (for up to 3 months) of Crohn's disease (mild to moderate) involving the ileum and/or ascending colon

Oral inhalation: Maintenance and prophylactic treatment of asthma; includes patients who require corticosteroids and those who may benefit from systemic dose reduction/elimination

Pregnancy Risk Factor C/B (Pulmicort Respules® and Turbuhaler®, Rhinocort® Aqua®)

Pregnancy Implications Use only if potential benefit to the mother outweighs the possible risk to the fetus. Studies of pregnant women using inhaled budesonide have not demonstrated an increased risk of abnormalities. Hypoadrenalism has been reported in infants.

Lactation Enters breast milk/use caution

Contraindications Hypersensitivity to budesonide or any component of the formulation
Inhalation: Contraindicated in primary treatment of status asthmaticus, acute episodes of asthma; not for relief of acute bronchospasm

Warnings/Precautions May cause hypercorticism or suppression of hypothalamic-pituitary-adrenal (HPA) axis, particularly in younger children or in patients receiving high doses for prolonged periods. HPA axis suppression may lead to adrenal crisis. Withdrawal and discontinuation of a corticosteroid should be done slowly and carefully. Particular care is required when patients are transferred from systemic corticosteroids to inhaled products due to possible adrenal insufficiency or withdrawal from steroids, including an increase in allergic symptoms. Patients receiving >20 mg per day of prednisone (or equivalent) may be most susceptible. Fatalities have occurred due to adrenal insufficiency in asthmatic patients during and after transfer from systemic corticosteroids to aerosol steroids; aerosol steroids do not provide the systemic steroid needed to treat patients having trauma, surgery, or infections. Do not use this product to transfer patients from oral corticosteroid therapy.

Bronchospasm may occur with wheezing after inhalation; if this occurs stop steroid and treat with a fast-acting bronchodilator. Supplemental steroids (oral or parenteral) may be needed during stress or severe asthma attacks. Not to be used in status asthmaticus or for the relief of acute bronchospasm. Acute myopathy has been reported with high dose corticosteroids, usually in patients with neuromuscular transmission disorders; may involve ocular and/or respiratory muscles; monitor creatine kinase; recovery may be delayed. Corticosteroid use may cause psychiatric disturbances, including depression, euphoria, insomnia, mood swings, and personality changes. Pre-existing psychiatric conditions may be exacerbated by corticosteroid use. Prolonged use of corticosteroids may also increase the incidence of secondary infection, mask acute infection (including fungal infections), prolong or exacerbate viral infections, or limit response to vaccines. Exposure to chickenpox should be avoided; corticosteroids should not be used to treat ocular herpes simplex. Corticosteroids should not be used for cerebral malaria. Close observation is required in patients with latent tuberculosis and/or TB reactivity; restrict use in active TB (only in conjunction with antituberculosis treatment). Prolonged treatment with corticosteroids has been associated with the development of Kaposi's sarcoma (case reports); if noted, discontinuation of therapy should be considered.

Use with caution in patients with thyroid disease, hepatic impairment, renal impairment, cardiovascular disease, diabetes, glaucoma, cataracts, myasthenia gravis, patients at risk for osteoporosis, patients at risk for seizures, or GI diseases (diverticulitis, peptic ulcer, ulcerative colitis) due to perforation risk. Use caution following acute MI (corticosteroids have been associated with myocardial rupture). Because of the risk of adverse effects, systemic corticosteroids should be used cautiously in the elderly in the smallest possible effective dose for the shortest duration. Avoid nasal corticosteroid use in patients with recent nasal septal ulcers, nasal surgery or nasal trauma until healing has occurred.

Orally-inhaled and intranasal corticosteroids may cause a reduction in growth velocity in pediatric patients (~1 centimeter per year [range 0.3-1.8 cm per year] and related to dose and duration of exposure). To minimize the systemic effects of orally-inhaled and intranasal corticosteroids, each patient should be titrated to the lowest effective dose. Growth should be routinely monitored in pediatric patients. Withdraw systemic therapy with gradual tapering of dose. There have been reports of systemic corticosteroid withdrawal symptoms (eg, joint/muscle pain, lassitude, depression) when withdrawing oral inhalation therapy. Enteric-coated capsules should not be crushed or chewed.

Adverse Reactions Reaction severity varies by dose and duration; not all adverse reactions have been reported with each dosage form.

>10%:
Central nervous system: Headache (up to 21%)
Gastrointestinal: Nausea (up to 11%)
Respiratory: Respiratory infection, rhinitis
Miscellaneous: Symptoms of HPA axis suppression and/or hypercorticism may occur in >10% of patients following administration of dosage forms which result in higher systemic exposure (ie, oral capsule), but may be less frequent than rates observed with comparator drugs (prednisolone). These symptoms may be rare (<1%) following administration via methods which result in lower exposures (topical).

1% to 10%:
Cardiovascular: Chest pain, edema, flushing, hypertension, palpitation, syncope, tachycardia
Central nervous system: Dizziness, dysphonia, emotional lability, fatigue, fever, insomnia, migraine, nervousness, pain, vertigo
Dermatologic: Acne, alopecia, bruising, contact dermatitis, eczema, hirsutism, pruritus, pustular rash, rash, striae
Endocrine & metabolic: Adrenal insufficiency, hypokalemia, menstrual disorder
Gastrointestinal: Abdominal pain, anorexia, diarrhea, dry mouth, dyspepsia, flatulence, gastroenteritis, oral candidiasis, taste perversion, vomiting, weight gain
Genitourinary: Dysuria, hematuria, nocturia, pyuria
Hematologic: Cervical lymphadenopathy, leukocytosis, purpura
Hepatic: Alkaline phosphatase increased
Neuromuscular & skeletal: Arthralgia, back pain, fracture, hyperkinesis, hypertonia, myalgia, neck pain, weakness, paresthesia
Ocular: Conjunctivitis, eye infection
Otic: Earache, ear infection, external ear infection
Respiratory: Bronchitis, bronchospasm, cough, epistaxis, nasal irritation, pharyngitis, sinusitis, stridor
Miscellaneous: Abscess, allergic reaction, C-reactive protein increased, erythrocyte sedimentation rate increased, fat distribution (moon face, buffalo hump), flu-like syndrome, herpes simplex, infection, moniliasis, viral infection, voice alteration

<1% (Limited to important or life-threatening): Aggressive reactions, alopecia, angioedema, avascular necrosis of the femoral head, benign intracranial hypertension, depression, dyspnea, growth suppression, hoarseness, hypersensitivity reactions (immediate and delayed; includes rash, contact dermatitis, angioedema, bronchospasm), intermenstrual bleeding, irritability, nasal septum perforation, osteoporosis, psychosis, somnolence

Overdosage/Toxicology Symptoms with inhaled formulations include irritation and burning of the nasal mucosa, sneezing, intranasal and pharyngeal *Candida* infections, nasal ulceration, epistaxis, rhinorrhea, nasal stuffiness, and headache. When consumed in excessive quantities, systemic hypercorticism and adrenal suppression may occur. In those cases, discontinuation and withdrawal of the corticosteroid should be done judiciously. Treatment should be symptomatic and supportive.

Drug Interactions
Cytochrome P450 Effect: Substrate of CYP3A4 (major)
Increased Effect/Toxicity: Cimetidine may decrease the clearance and increase the bioavailability of budesonide, increasing its serum concentrations. In addition, CYP3A4 inhibitors may increase the serum level and/or toxicity of budesonide this effect was shown with ketoconazole, but not erythromycin. Other potential inhibitors include amiodarone, cimetidine, clarithromycin, delavirdine, diltiazem, dirithromycin, disulfiram, fluoxetine, fluvoxamine, grapefruit juice, indinavir, itraconazole, ketoconazole, nefazodone, nevirapine, propoxyphene, quinupristin-dalfopristin, ritonavir, saquinavir, telithromycin, verapamil, zafirlukast, and zileuton. The addition of salmeterol has been demonstrated to improve response to inhaled corticosteroids (as compared to increasing steroid dosage).
Decreased Effect: Theoretically, proton pump inhibitors (omeprazole, pantoprazole) alter gastric pH and may affect the rate of dissolution of enteric-coated capsules. Administration with omeprazole did not alter kinetics of budesonide capsules.

Ethanol/Nutrition/Herb Interactions
Food: Grapefruit juice may double systemic exposure of orally-administered budesonide. Administration of capsules with a high-fat meal delays peak concentration, but does not alter the extent of absorption.
Herb/Nutraceutical: St John's wort may decrease budesonide levels.

Stability
Nebulizer: Store upright at 20°C to 25°C (68°F to 77°F) and protect from light. Do not refrigerate or freeze. Once aluminum package is opened, solution should be used within 2 weeks. Continue to protect from light.
Nasal inhaler: Store with valve up at 15°C to 30°C (59°F to 86°F). Use within 6 months after opening aluminum pouch. Protect from high humidity.
Nasal spray: Store with valve up at 20°C to 25°C (68°F to 77°F) and protect from light. Do not freeze.

Mechanism of Action Controls the rate of protein synthesis; depresses the migration of polymorphonuclear leukocytes, fibroblasts; reverses capillary permeability and lysosomal stabilization at the cellular level to prevent or control inflammation

Pharmacodynamics/Kinetics
Onset of action: Respules®: 2-8 days; Rhinocort® Aqua®: ~10 hours; Turbuhaler®: 24 hours
(Continued)

Budesonide *(Continued)*

Peak effect: Respules®: 4-6 weeks; Rhinocort® Aqua®: ~2 weeks; Turbuhaler®: 1-2 weeks
Distribution: 2.2-3.9 L/kg
Protein binding: 85% to 90%
Metabolism: Hepatic via CYP3A4 to two metabolites: 16 alpha-hydroxyprednisolone and 6 beta-hydroxybudesonide; minor activity
Bioavailability: Limited by high first-pass effect; Capsule: 9% to 21%; Respules®: 6%; Turbuhaler®: 6% to 13%; Nasal: 34%
Half-life elimination: 2-3.6 hours
Time to peak: Capsule: 0.5-10 hours (variable in Crohn's disease); Respules®: 10-30 minutes; Turbuhaler®: 1-2 hours; Nasal: 1 hour
Excretion: Urine (60%) and feces as metabolites

Dosage

Nasal inhalation: (Rhinocort® Aqua®): Children ≥6 years and Adults: 64 mcg/day as a single 32 mcg spray in each nostril. Some patients who do not achieve adequate control may benefit from increased dosage. A reduced dosage may be effective after initial control is achieved.
Maximum dose: Children <12 years: 128 mcg/day; Adults: 256 mcg/day

Nebulization: Children 12 months to 8 years: Pulmicort Respules®: Titrate to lowest effective dose once patient is stable; start at 0.25 mg/day or use as follows:
Previous therapy of bronchodilators alone: 0.5 mg/day administered as a single dose or divided twice daily (maximum daily dose: 0.5 mg)
Previous therapy of inhaled corticosteroids: 0.5 mg/day administered as a single dose or divided twice daily (maximum daily dose: 1 mg)
Previous therapy of oral corticosteroids: 1 mg/day administered as a single dose or divided twice daily (maximum daily dose: 1 mg)

Oral inhalation:
Children ≥6 years:
Previous therapy of bronchodilators alone: 200 mcg twice initially which may be increased up to 400 mcg twice daily
Previous therapy of inhaled corticosteroids: 200 mcg twice initially which may be increased up to 400 mcg twice daily
Previous therapy of oral corticosteroids: The highest recommended dose in children is 400 mcg twice daily
Adults:
Previous therapy of bronchodilators alone: 200-400 mcg twice initially which may be increased up to 400 mcg twice daily
Previous therapy of inhaled corticosteroids: 200-400 mcg twice initially which may be increased up to 800 mcg twice daily
Previous therapy of oral corticosteroids: 400-800 mcg twice daily which may be increased up to 800 mcg twice daily
NIH Guidelines (NIH, 1997) (give in divided doses twice daily):
Children:
"Low" dose: 100-200 mcg/day
"Medium" dose: 200-400 mcg/day (1-2 inhalations/day)
"High" dose: >400 mcg/day (>2 inhalation/day)
Adults:
"Low" dose: 200-400 mcg/day (1-2 inhalations/day)
"Medium" dose: 400-600 mcg/day (2-3 inhalations/day)
"High" dose: >600 mcg/day (>3 inhalation/day)

Oral: Adults: Crohn's disease (active): 9 mg once daily in the morning for up to 8 weeks; recurring episodes may be treated with a repeat 8-week course of treatment
Note: Patients receiving CYP3A4 inhibitors should be monitored closely for signs and symptoms of hypercorticism; dosage reduction may be required. If switching from oral prednisolone, prednisolone dosage should be tapered while budesonide (Entocort™ EC) treatment is initiated.
Maintenance of remission: Following treatment of active disease (control of symptoms with CDAI <150), treatment may be continued at a dosage of 6 mg once daily for up to 3 months. If symptom control is maintained for 3 months, tapering of the dosage to complete cessation is recommended. Continued dosing beyond 3 months has not been demonstrated to result in substantial benefit.

Dosage adjustment in hepatic impairment: Monitor closely for signs and symptoms of hypercorticism; dosage reduction may be required.
Dietary Considerations Avoid grapefruit juice when using oral capsules.
Administration
Inhalation: Inhaler should be shaken well immediately prior to use. While activating inhaler, deep breathe for 3-5 seconds, hold breath for ~10 seconds, and allow ≥1 minute between inhalations. Rinse mouth with water after use to reduce aftertaste and incidence of candidiasis.
Nebulization: Shake well before using. Use Pulmicort Respules® with jet nebulizer connected to an air compressor; administer with mouthpiece or facemask. Do not use ultrasonic nebulizer. Do not mix with other medications in nebulizer. Rinse mouth following treatments to decrease risk of oral candidiasis (wash face if using face mask).
Oral capsule: Capsule should be swallowed whole; do not crush or chew.
Monitoring Parameters Monitor growth in pediatric patients.
Additional Information Effects of inhaled/intranasal steroids on growth have been observed in the absence of laboratory evidence of HPA axis suppression, suggesting that growth velocity is a more sensitive indicator of systemic corticosteroid exposure in pediatric patients than some commonly used tests of HPA axis function. The long-term effects of this reduction in growth velocity associated with orally-inhaled and intranasal corticosteroids, including the impact on final adult height, are unknown. The potential for "catch up" growth following discontinuation of treatment with inhaled corticosteroids has not been adequately studied.

Dosage Forms [CAN] = Canadian brand name
 Capsule, enteric coated (Entocort® EC): 3 mg
 Powder for oral inhalation:
  Pulmicort Turbuhaler®: 200 mcg/inhalation (104 g) [delivers ~160 mcg/inhalation; 200 metered actuations]
  Pulmicort Turbuhaler® [CAN]: 100 mcg/inhalation [delivers 200 metered actuations]; 200 mcg/inhalation [delivers 200 metered actuations]; 400 mcg/Inhalation [delivers 200 metered actuations] [not available in the U.S.]
 Suspension, intranasal [spray]:
  Rhinocort® Aqua®: 32 mcg/inhalation (8.6 g) [120 metered actuations]
 Suspension for nebulization:
  Pulmicort Respules®: 0.25 mg/2 mL (30s), 0.5 mg/2 mL (30s)

♦ **Budesonide and Eformoterol** *see* Budesonide and Formoterol *on page 247*

Budesonide and Formoterol (byoo DES oh nide & for MOH te rol)

U.S. Brand Names Symbicort®
Canadian Brand Names Symbicort®
Index Terms Budesonide and Eformoterol; Eformoterol and Budesonide; Formoterol Fumarate Dehydrate and Budesonide
Pharmacologic Category Beta$_2$-Adrenergic Agonist; Corticosteroid, Inhalant (Oral)
Use Treatment of asthma in patients ≥12 years of age where combination therapy is indicated
Restrictions An FDA-approved medication guide must be distributed when dispensing an outpatient prescription (new or refill) where this medication is to be used without direct supervision of a healthcare provider. Medication guides are available at http://www.fda.gov/cder/Offices/ODS/medication_guides.htm.
Pregnancy Risk Factor C
Dosage Oral inhalation: Children ≥12 years and Adults:
 Symbicort® 80/4.5, Symbicort® 160/4.5: 2 inhalations twice daily. Patients currently receiving a low-to-medium dose inhaled corticosteroid may be started on the lower strength combination; those receiving a medium-to-high dose inhaled corticosteroid may be started on the higher strength combination. Consider the higher dose combination for patients not adequately controlled on the lower combination following 1-2 weeks of therapy. Do not use more than 2 inhalations twice daily of either strength.
 Symbicort® Turbuhaler®: 1-2 inhalations once or twice daily
  Maximum long-term maintenance dose: 4 inhalations/day; in periods of worsening asthma, this may be temporarily increased to 4 inhalations twice daily
  Manufacturer's recommendation: Initial: Symbicort® 200 once or twice daily to establish symptom control. Following the establishment of response/symptom control: Titrate to the lowest dosage possible to maintain control (may substitute Symbicort® 100).
Additional Information Complete prescribing information for this medication should be consulted for additional detail.
Dosage Forms [CAN] = Canadian brand name
 Powder for oral inhalation:
  Symbicort® 80/4.5: Budesonide 80 mcg and formoterol fumarate dehydrate 4. 5mcg per actuation (10.2 g) [120 metered inhalations]
  Symbicort® 160/4.5: Budesonide 160 mcg and formoterol fumarate dehydrate 4. 5mcg per actuation (10.2 g) [120 metered inhalations]
  Symbicort® 100 Turbuhaler® [CAN]: Budesonide 100 mcg and formoterol dehydrate 6 mcg per inhalation (available in 60 or 120 metered doses) [delivers ~80 mcg budesonide and 4.5 mcg formoterol per inhalation; contains lactose] [not available in the U.S]
  Symbicort® 200 Turbuhaler® [CAN]: Budesonide 200 mcg and formoterol dehydrate 6 mcg per inhalation (available in 60 or 120 metered doses) [delivers ~160 mcg budesonide and 4.5 mcg formoterol per inhalation; contains lactose] [not available in the U.S]

♦ **Buffered Aspirin and Pravastatin Sodium** *see* Aspirin and Pravastatin *on page 164*
♦ **Bufferin® [OTC]** *see* Aspirin *on page 160*
♦ **Bufferin® Extra Strength [OTC]** *see* Aspirin *on page 160*
♦ **Buffinol [OTC]** *see* Aspirin *on page 160*
♦ **Buffinol Extra [OTC]** *see* Aspirin *on page 160*

Bumetanide (byoo MET a nide)

U.S. Brand Names Bumex®
Canadian Brand Names Bumex®; Burinex®
Pharmacologic Category Diuretic, Loop
Additional Appendix Information
 Heart Failure (Systolic) *on page 2051*
 Sulfonamide Derivatives *on page 1897*
Use Management of edema secondary to congestive heart failure or hepatic or renal disease including nephrotic syndrome; may be used alone or in combination with antihypertensives in the treatment of hypertension; can be used in furosemide-allergic patients
Pregnancy Risk Factor C (manufacturer); D (expert analysis)
Lactation Excretion in breast milk unknown/use caution
Medication Safety Issues
 Sound-alike/look-alike issues:
  Bumetanide may be confused with Buminate®
  Bumex® may be confused with Brevibloc®, Buprenex®, Permax®
Contraindications Hypersensitivity to bumetanide, any component of the formulation, or sulfonylureas; anuria; patients with hepatic coma or in states of severe electrolyte depletion until the condition improves or is corrected; pregnancy (based on expert analysis)
(Continued)

Bumetanide *(Continued)*

Warnings/Precautions [U.S. Boxed Warning]: Excessive amounts can lead to profound diuresis with fluid and electrolyte loss; close medical supervision and dose evaluation are required. In cirrhosis, avoid electrolyte and acid/base imbalances that might lead to hepatic encephalopathy. *In vitro* studies using pooled sera from critically-ill neonates have shown bumetanide to be a potent displacer of bilirubin; avoid use in neonates at risk for kernicterus. Coadministration of antihypertensives may increase the risk of hypotension.

Monitor fluid status and renal function in an attempt to prevent oliguria, azotemia, and reversible increases in BUN and creatinine; close medical supervision of aggressive diuresis required. Rapid I.V. administration, renal impairment, excessive doses, and concurrent use of other ototoxins is associated with ototoxicity. Asymptomatic hyperuricemia has been reported with use.

Chemical similarities are present among sulfonamides, sulfonylureas, carbonic anhydrase inhibitors, thiazides, and loop diuretics (except ethacrynic acid). Use in patients with sulfonyl-urea allergy is specifically contraindicated in product labeling, however, a risk of cross-reaction exists in patients with allergy to any of these compounds; avoid use when previous reaction has been severe. Discontinue if signs of hypersensitivity are noted.

Adverse Reactions
>10%:
Endocrine & metabolic: Hyperuricemia (18%), hypochloremia (15%), hypokalemia (15%)
Renal: Azotemia (11%)
1% to 10%:
Central nervous system: Dizziness (1%)
Endocrine & metabolic: Hyponatremia (9%); hyperglycemia (7%); variations in phosphorus (5%), CO_2 content (4%), bicarbonate (3%), and calcium (2%)
Neuromuscular & skeletal: Muscle cramps (1%)
Otic: Ototoxicity (1%)
Renal: Serum creatinine increased (7%)
<1% (Limited to important or life-threatening): Asterixis, dehydration, encephalopathy, hearing impaired, hypernatremia, hypotension, orthostatic hypotension, pruritus, rash, renal failure, vertigo, vomiting

Overdosage/Toxicology Symptoms include electrolyte and volume depletion. Treatment is primarily symptomatic and supportive.

Drug Interactions
Increased Effect/Toxicity: Bumetanide-induced hypokalemia may predispose to digoxin toxicity and may increase the risk of arrhythmia with drugs which may prolong QT interval, including type Ia and type III antiarrhythmic agents, cisapride, and some quinolones (spar-floxacin, gatifloxacin, and moxifloxacin). The risk of toxicity from lithium and salicylates (high dose) may be increased by loop diuretics. Hypotensive effects and/or adverse renal effects of ACE inhibitors and NSAIDs are potentiated by bumetanide-induced hypovolemia. The effects of peripheral adrenergic-blocking drugs or ganglionic blockers may be increased by bumetanide.

Bumetanide may increase the risk of ototoxicity with other ototoxic agents (aminoglyco-sides, cis-platinum), especially in patients with renal dysfunction. Synergistic diuretic effects occur with thiazide-type diuretics. Diuretics tend to be synergistic with other antihy-pertensive agents, and hypotension may occur.
Decreased Effect: Glucose tolerance may be decreased by loop diuretics, requiring adjust-ment of hypoglycemic agents. Cholestyramine or colestipol may reduce bioavailability of bumetanide. Indomethacin (and other NSAIDs) may reduce natriuretic and hypotensive effects of diuretics. Hypokalemia may reduce the efficacy of some antiarrhythmics.

Ethanol/Nutrition/Herb Interactions Herb/Nutraceutical: Avoid ephedra, yohimbe, ginseng (may worsen hypertension). Avoid dong quai if using for hypertension (has estrogenic activity). Avoid garlic (may have increased antihypertensive effect).

Stability
I.V.: Store vials at 15°C to 30°C (59°F to 86°F). Infusion solutions should be used within 24 hours after preparation. Light sensitive; discoloration may occur when exposed to light.
Tablet: Store at 15°C to 30°C (59°F to 86°F).

Mechanism of Action Inhibits reabsorption of sodium and chloride in the ascending loop of Henle and proximal renal tubule, interfering with the chloride-binding cotransport system, thus causing increased excretion of water, sodium, chloride, magnesium, phosphate, and calcium; it does not appear to act on the distal tubule

Pharmacodynamics/Kinetics
Onset of action: Oral, I.M.: 0.5-1 hour; I.V.: 2-3 minutes
Duration: 4-6 hours
Distribution: V_d: 13-25 L/kg
Protein binding: 95%
Metabolism: Partially hepatic
Half-life elimination: Neonates: ~6 hours; Infants (1 month): ~2.4 hours; Adults: 1-1.5 hours
Excretion: Primarily urine (as unchanged drug and metabolites)

Dosage
Oral, I.M., I.V.:
Neonates (see Warnings/Precautions): 0.01-0.05 mg/kg/dose every 24-48 hours
Infants and Children: 0.015-0.1 mg/kg/dose every 6-24 hours (maximum dose: 10 mg/day)
Adults:
Edema:
Oral: 0.5-2 mg/dose (maximum dose: 10 mg/day) 1-2 times/day
I.M., I.V.: 0.5-1 mg/dose; may repeat in 2-3 hours for up to 2 doses if needed (maximum dose: 10 mg/day)
Continuous I.V. infusion: Initial: 1 mg I.V. load then 0.5-2 mg/hour (ACC/AHA 2005 practice guidelines for chronic heart failure)
Hypertension: Oral: 0.5 mg daily (maximum dose: 5 mg/day); usual dosage range (JNC 7): 0.5-2 mg/day in 2 divided doses

Dietary Considerations May require increased intake of potassium-rich foods.

Administration Administer I.V. slowly, over 1-2 minutes. An alternate-day schedule or a 3-4 daily dosing regimen with rest periods of 1-2 days in between may be the most tolerable and effective regimen for the continued control of edema. Reserve I.V. administration for those unable to take oral medications.

Monitoring Parameters Blood pressure, serum electrolytes, renal function

Dosage Forms

Injection, solution: 0.25 mg/mL (2 mL, 4 mL, 10 mL) [contains benzyl alcohol]

Tablet (Bumex®): 0.5 mg, 1 mg, 2 mg

♦ **Bumex®** *see* Bumetanide *on page 247*

♦ **Buminate®** *see* Albumin *on page 55*

♦ **Bupap** *see* Butalbital and Acetaminophen *on page 259*

♦ **Buphenyl®** *see* Sodium Phenylbutyrate *on page 1582*

Bupivacaine (byoo PIV a kane)

U.S. Brand Names Marcaine®; Marcaine® Spinal; Sensorcaine®; Sensorcaine®-MPF; Sensorcaine®-MPF Spinal

Canadian Brand Names Marcaine®; Sensorcaine®

Index Terms Bupivacaine Hydrochloride

Pharmacologic Category Local Anesthetic

Use Local anesthetic (injectable) for peripheral nerve block, infiltration, sympathetic block, caudal or epidural block, retrobulbar block

Pregnancy Risk Factor C

Pregnancy Implications Decreased pup survival and embryocidal effects were observed in animal studies. Bupivacaine is approved for use at term in obstetrical anesthesia or analgesia. Bupivacaine 0.75% solutions have been associated with cardiac arrest following epidural anesthesia in obstetrical patients and use of this concentration is not recommended for this purpose. Use in obstetrical paracervical block anesthesia is contraindicated.

Lactation Enters breast milk/not recommended

Medication Safety Issues

Sound-alike/look-alike issues:

Bupivacaine may be confused with mepivacaine, ropivacaine

Marcaine® may be confused with Narcan®

Contraindications Hypersensitivity to bupivacaine hydrochloride, amide-type local anesthetics, or any component of the formulation; obstetrical paracervical block anesthesia

Warnings/Precautions Use with caution in patients with hepatic impairment. Not recommended for use in children <12 years of age. The solution for spinal anesthesia should not be used in children <18 years of age. **Do not use solutions containing preservatives for caudal or epidural block.** Local anesthetics have been associated with rare occurrences of sudden respiratory arrest; convulsions due to systemic toxicity leading to cardiac arrest have also been reported, presumably following unintentional intravascular injection. **[U.S. Boxed Warning]: The 0.75% is not recommended for obstetrical anesthesia.** A test dose is recommended prior to epidural administration (prior to initial dose) and all reinforcing doses with continuous catheter technique. Use caution with cardiovascular dysfunction. Use caution in debilitated, elderly, or acutely ill patients; dose reduction may be required.

Adverse Reactions Note: Incidence of adverse reactions is difficult to define. Most effects are dose related, and are often due to accelerated absorption from the injection site, unintentional intravascular injection, or slow metabolic degradation. The development of any central nervous system symptoms may be an early indication of more significant toxicity (seizure).

Cardiovascular: Hypotension, bradycardia, palpitation, heart block, ventricular arrhythmia, cardiac arrest

Central nervous system: Restlessness, anxiety, dizziness, seizure (0.1%); rare symptoms (usually associated with unintentional subarachnoid injection during high spinal anesthesia) include persistent anesthesia, paresthesia, paralysis, headache, septic meningitis, and cranial nerve palsies

Gastrointestinal: Nausea, vomiting; rare symptoms (usually associated with unintentional subarachnoid injection during high spinal anesthesia) include fecal incontinence and loss of sphincter control

Genitourinary: Rare symptoms (usually associated with unintentional subarachnoid injection during high spinal anesthesia) include urinary incontinence, loss of perineal sensation, and loss of sexual function

Neuromuscular & skeletal: Weakness

Ocular: Blurred vision, pupillary constriction

Otic: Tinnitus

Respiratory: Apnea, hypoventilation (usually associated with unintentional subarachnoid injection during high spinal anesthesia)

Miscellaneous: Allergic reactions (urticaria, pruritus, angioedema), anaphylactoid reactions

Overdosage/Toxicology Treatment is primarily symptomatic and supportive. Termination of anesthesia by pneumatic tourniquet inflation should be attempted when the agent is administered by infiltration or regional injection. Seizures commonly respond to diazepam, while hypotension responds to I.V. fluids and Trendelenburg positioning. Bradyarrhythmias (when the heart rate is <60) can be treated with I.V. or SubQ atropine 15 mcg/kg. With the development of metabolic acidosis, I.V. sodium bicarbonate 0.5-2 mEq/kg and ventilatory assistance should be instituted. Methemoglobinemia should be treated with methylene blue 1-2 mg/kg in a 1% sterile aqueous solution I.V. push over 4-6 minutes, repeated up to a total dose of 7 mg/kg.

Drug Interactions

Cytochrome P450 Effect: Substrate (minor) of CYP1A2, 2C19, 2D6, 3A4

Stability Store at controlled room temperature of 15°C to 30°C (59°F to 86°F).

(Continued)

Bupivacaine (Continued)

Mechanism of Action Blocks both the initiation and conduction of nerve impulses by decreasing the neuronal membrane's permeability to sodium ions, which results in inhibition of depolarization with resultant blockade of conduction

Pharmacodynamics/Kinetics

Onset of action: Anesthesia (route and dose dependent): 1-17 minutes

Duration (route and dose dependent): 2-9 hours

Protein binding: ~95%

Metabolism: Hepatic; forms metabolite (PPX)

Half-life elimination (age dependent): Neonates: 8.1 hours; Adults: 1.5-5.5 hours

Excretion: Urine (~6% unchanged)

Dosage Dose varies with procedure, depth of anesthesia, vascularity of tissues, duration of anesthesia, and condition of patient. Do not use solutions containing preservatives for caudal or epidural block.

Children >12 years and Adults:

Local anesthesia: Infiltration: 0.25% infiltrated locally; maximum: 175 mg

Caudal block (preservative free): 15-30 mL of 0.25% or 0.5%

Epidural block (other than caudal block; preservative free): Administer in 3-5 mL increments, allowing sufficient time to detect toxic manifestations of inadvertent I.V. or I.T. administration: 10-20 mL of 0.25% or 0.5%

Surgical procedures requiring a high degree of muscle relaxation and prolonged effects **only**: 10-20 mL of 0.75% (**Note:** Not to be used in obstetrical cases)

Peripheral nerve block: 5 mL of 0.25 or 0.5%; maximum: 400 mg/day

Sympathetic nerve block: 20-50 mL of 0.25%

Retrobulbar anesthesia: 2-4 mL of 0.75%

Adults: Spinal anesthesia: Preservative free solution of 0.75% bupivacaine in 8.25% dextrose:

Lower extremity and perineal procedures: 1 mL

Lower abdominal procedures: 1.6 mL

Normal vaginal delivery: 0.8 mL (higher doses may be required in some patients)

Cesarean section: 1-1.4 mL

Administration Solutions containing preservatives should not be used for epidural or caudal blocks.

Monitoring Parameters Vital signs, state of consciousness; signs of CNS toxicity; fetal heart rate during paracervical anesthesia

Dosage Forms

Injection, solution, as hydrochloride [preservative free]: 0.25% [2.5 mg/mL] (10 mL, 20 mL, 30 mL, 50 mL); 0.5% [5 mg/mL] (10 mL, 20 mL, 30 mL); 0.75% [7.5 mg/mL] (10 mL, 20 mL, 30 mL)

Marcaine®: 0.25% [2.5 mg/mL] (10 mL, 30 mL); 0.5% [5 mg/mL] (10 mL, 30 mL); 0.75% [7.5 mg/mL] (10 mL, 30 mL)

Marcaine® Spinal: 0.75% [7.5 mg/mL] (2 mL) [in dextrose 8.25%]

Sensorcaine®-MPF: 0.25% [2.5 mg/mL] (10 mL, 30 mL); 0.5% [5 mg/mL] (10 mL, 30 mL); 0.75% [7.5 mg/mL] (10 mL, 30 mL)

Sensorcaine®-MPF Spinal: 0.75% [7.5 mg/mL] (2 mL) [in dextrose 8.25%]

Injection, solution, as hydrochloride:

Marcaine®, Sensorcaine®: 0.25% [2.5 mg/mL] (50 mL); 0.5% [5 mg/mL] (50 mL) [contains methylparaben]

♦ **Bupivacaine and Lidocaine** see Lidocaine and Bupivacaine on page 1014

♦ **Bupivacaine Hydrochloride** see Bupivacaine on page 249

♦ **Buprenex®** see Buprenorphine on page 250

Buprenorphine (byoo pre NOR feen)

U.S. Brand Names Buprenex®; Subutex®

Canadian Brand Names Buprenex®; Subutex®

Index Terms Buprenorphine Hydrochloride

Pharmacologic Category Analgesic, Opioid

Additional Appendix Information

Narcotic Agonists on page 1888

Use

Injection: Management of moderate to severe pain

Tablet: Treatment of opioid dependence

Unlabeled/Investigational Use Injection: Heroin and opioid withdrawal

Restrictions Injection: C-V; Tablet: C-III

Prescribing of tablets for opioid dependence is limited to physicians who have met the qualification criteria and have received a DEA number specific to prescribing this product. Tablets will be available through pharmacies and wholesalers which normally provide controlled substances.

Pregnancy Risk Factor C

Pregnancy Implications Withdrawal has been reported in infants of women receiving buprenorphine during pregnancy. Onset of symptoms ranged from day 1 to day 8 of life, most occurring on day 1.

Lactation Enters breast milk/not recommended

Medication Safety Issues

Sound-alike/look-alike issues:

Buprenex® may be confused with Brevibloc®, Bumex®

Contraindications Hypersensitivity to buprenorphine or any component of the formulation

Warnings/Precautions An opioid-containing analgesic regimen should be tailored to each patient's needs and based upon the type of pain being treated (acute versus chronic), the route of administration, degree of tolerance for opioids (naive versus chronic user), age, weight, and medical condition. The optimal analgesic dose varies widely among patients. Doses should be titrated to pain relief/prevention.

May cause CNS depression, which may impair physical or mental abilities. Effects with other sedative drugs or ethanol may be potentiated. Elderly may be more sensitive to CNS depressant and constipating effects. May cause respiratory depression - use caution in patients with respiratory disease or pre-existing respiratory depression. Potential for drug dependency exists, abrupt cessation may precipitate withdrawal. Use caution in elderly, debilitated, pediatric patients, depression or suicidal tendencies. Tolerance, psychological and physical dependence may occur with prolonged use. Partial antagonist activity may precipitate acute narcotic withdrawal in opioid-dependent individuals.

Use with caution in patients with hepatic, pulmonary, or renal function impairment. Also use caution in patients with head injury or increased ICP, biliary tract dysfunction, patients with history of hyperthyroidism, morbid obesity, adrenal insufficiency, prostatic hyperplasia, urinary stricture, CNS depression, toxic psychosis, pancreatitis, alcoholism, delirium tremens, or kyphoscoliosis. May cause hypotension; use with caution in patients with hypovolemia, cardiovascular disease (including acute MI), or drugs which may exaggerate hypotensive effects (including phenothiazines or general anesthetics). May obscure diagnosis or clinical course of patients with acute abdominal conditions.

Tablets, which are used for induction treatment of opioid dependence, should not be started until effects of withdrawal are evident.

Adverse Reactions

Injection:

>10%: Central nervous system: Sedation

1% to 10%:
Cardiovascular: Hypotension
Central nervous system: Respiratory depression, dizziness, headache
Gastrointestinal: Vomiting, nausea
Ocular: Miosis
Otic: Vertigo
Miscellaneous: Diaphoresis

<1% (Limited to important or life-threatening): Agitation, allergic reaction, apnea, appetite decreased, blurred vision, bradycardia, confusion, constipation, convulsion, coma, cyanosis, depersonalization, depression, diplopia, dyspnea, dysphoria, euphoria, fatigue, flatulence, flushing, hallucinations, hypertension, injection site reaction, malaise, nervousness, pallor, paresthesia, pruritus, psychosis, rash, slurred speech, tachycardia, tinnitus, tremor, urinary retention, urticaria, weakness, Wenckebach block, xerostomia

Tablet:

>10%:
Central nervous system: Headache (30%), pain (24%), insomnia (21% to 25%), anxiety (12%), depression (11%)
Gastrointestinal: Nausea (10% to 14%), abdominal pain (12%), constipation (8% to 11%)
Neuromuscular & skeletal: Back pain (14%), weakness (14%)
Respiratory: Rhinitis (11%)
Miscellaneous: Withdrawal syndrome (19%; placebo 37%), infection (12% to 20%), diaphoresis (12% to 13%)

1% to 10%:
Central nervous system: Chills (6%), nervousness (6%), somnolence (5%), dizziness (4%), fever (3%)
Gastrointestinal: Vomiting (5% to 8%), diarrhea (5%), dyspepsia (3%)
Ocular: Lacrimation (5%)
Respiratory: Cough (4%), pharyngitis (4%)
Miscellaneous: Flu-like syndrome (6%)

Overdosage/Toxicology Symptoms include CNS depression, pinpoint pupils, hypotension, and bradycardia. Treatment is supportive. Naloxone may have limited effects in reversing respiratory depression; doxapram has also been used to stimulate respirations.

Drug Interactions

Cytochrome P450 Effect: Substrate of CYP3A4 (major); **Inhibits** CYP1A2 (weak), 2A6 (weak), 2C19 (weak), 2D6 (weak)

Increased Effect/Toxicity: Barbiturate anesthetics and other CNS depressants may produce additive respiratory and CNS depression. Respiratory and CV collapse was reported in a patient who received diazepam and buprenorphine. Effects may be additive with other CNS depressants. CYP3A4 inhibitors may increase the levels/effects of buprenorphine; example inhibitors include azole antifungals, clarithromycin, diclofenac, doxycycline, erythromycin, imatinib, isoniazid, nefazodone, nicardipine, propofol, protease inhibitors, quinidine, and verapamil.

Decreased Effect: CYP3A4 inducers may decrease the levels/effects of buprenorphine; example inducers include aminoglutethimide, carbamazepine, nafcillin, nevirapine, phenobarbital, phenytoin, and rifamycins. Naltrexone may antagonize the effect of opioid analgesics; concurrent use or use within 7-10 days of injection for pain relief is contraindicated.

Ethanol/Nutrition/Herb Interactions

Ethanol: Avoid ethanol (may increase CNS depression).
Herb/Nutraceutical: Avoid valerian, St John's wort, kava kava, gotu kola (may increase CNS depression).

Stability

Injection: Protect from excessive heat >40°C (>104°F) and light.
Tablet: Store at room temperature of 25°C (77°F).

Mechanism of Action Buprenorphine exerts its analgesic effect via high affinity binding to μ opiate receptors in the CNS; displays both agonist and antagonist activity

Pharmacodynamics/Kinetics

Onset of action: Analgesic: 10-30 minutes
Duration: 6-8 hours
Absorption: I.M., SubQ: 30% to 40%
Distribution: V_d: 97-187 L/kg
(Continued)

Buprenorphine *(Continued)*

Protein binding: High

Metabolism: Primarily hepatic; extensive first-pass effect

Half-life elimination: 2.2-3 hours

Excretion: Feces (70%); urine (20% as unchanged drug)

Dosage Long-term use is not recommended

Note: These are guidelines and do not represent the maximum doses that may be required in all patients. Doses should be titrated to pain relief/prevention. In high-risk patients (eg, elderly, debilitated, presence of respiratory disease) and/or concurrent CNS depressant use, reduce dose by one-half. Buprenorphine has an analgesic ceiling.

Acute pain (moderate to severe):

Children 2-12 years: I.M., slow I.V.: 2-6 mcg/kg every 4-6 hours

Children ≥13 years and Adults:

I.M.: Initial: Opiate-naive: 0.3 mg every 6-8 hours as needed; initial dose (up to 0.3 mg) may be repeated once in 30-60 minutes after the initial dose if needed; usual dosage range: 0.15-0.6 mg every 4-8 hours as needed

Slow I.V.: Initial: Opiate-naive: 0.3 mg every 6-8 hours as needed; initial dose (up to 0.3 mg) may be repeated once in 30-60 minutes after the initial dose if needed

Elderly: I.M., slow I.V.: 0.15 mg every 6 hours; elderly patients are more likely to suffer from confusion and drowsiness compared to younger patients

Heroin or opiate withdrawal (unlabeled use): Children ≥13 years and Adults: I.M., slow I.V.: Variable; 0.1-0.4 mg every 6 hours

Sublingual: Children ≥16 years and Adults: Opioid dependence:

Induction: Range: 12-16 mg/day (doses during an induction study used 8 mg on day 1, followed by 16 mg on day 2; induction continued over 3-4 days). Treatment should begin at least 4 hours after last use of heroin or short-acting opioid, preferably when first signs of withdrawal appear. Titrating dose to clinical effectiveness should be done as rapidly as possible to prevent undue withdrawal symptoms and patient drop-out during the induction period.

Maintenance: Target dose: 16 mg/day; range: 4-24 mg/day; patients should be switched to the buprenorphine/naloxone combination product for maintenance and unsupervised therapy

Administration

I.V.: Administer slowly, over at least 2 minutes.

Sublingual: Tablet should be placed under the tongue until dissolved; should not be swallowed. If two or more tablets are needed per dose, all may be placed under the tongue at once, or two at a time. To ensure consistent bioavailability, subsequent doses should always be taken the same way.

Monitoring Parameters Pain relief, respiratory and mental status, CNS depression, blood pressure; LFTs

Additional Information

Buprenorphine injection: 0.3 mg = 10 mg morphine or 75 mg meperidine, has longer duration of action than either agent

Subutex® (buprenorphine) should be limited to supervised use whenever possible; patients should be switched to Suboxone® (buprenorphine/naloxone) for maintenance and unsupervised therapy

Dosage Forms

Injection, solution (Buprenex®): 0.3 mg/mL (1 mL)

Tablet, sublingual (Subutex®): 2 mg, 8 mg

Additional dosage strength available in Canada: 0.4 mg

Buprenorphine and Naloxone *(byoo pre NOR feen & nal OKS one)*

U.S. Brand Names Suboxone®

Index Terms Buprenorphine Hydrochloride and Naloxone Hydrochloride Dihydrate; Naloxone and Buprenorphine; Naloxone Hydrochloride Dihydrate and Buprenorphine Hydrochloride

Pharmacologic Category Analgesic, Opioid

Use Treatment of opioid dependence

Restrictions C-III; Prescribing of tablets for opioid dependence is limited to physicians who have met the qualification criteria and have received a DEA number specific to prescribing this product. Tablets will be available through pharmacies and wholesalers which normally provide controlled substances.

Pregnancy Risk Factor C

Dosage Sublingual: Children ≥16 years and Adults: Opioid dependence: **Note:** This combination product is not recommended for use during the induction period; initial treatment should begin using buprenorphine oral tablets. Patients should be switched to the combination product for maintenance and unsupervised therapy.

Maintenance: Target dose (based on buprenorphine content): 16 mg/day; range: 4-24 mg/day

Additional Information Complete prescribing information for this medication should be consulted for additional detail.

Dosage Forms Tablet, sublingual: Buprenorphine 2 mg and naloxone 0.5 mg; buprenorphine 8 mg and naloxone 2 mg [lemon-lime flavor]

♦ **Buprenorphine Hydrochloride** *see* Buprenorphine *on page 250*

♦ **Buprenorphine Hydrochloride and Naloxone Hydrochloride Dihydrate** *see* Buprenorphine and Naloxone *on page 252*

♦ **Buproban™** *see* BuPROPion *on page 252*

BuPROPion *(byoo PROE pee on)*

U.S. Brand Names Budeprion™ SR; Buproban™; Wellbutrin®; Wellbutrin SR®; Wellbutrin XL™; Zyban®

Canadian Brand Names Novo-Bupropion SR; Wellbutrin®; Wellbutrin XL™; Zyban®

Pharmacologic Category Antidepressant, Dopamine-Reuptake Inhibitor; Smoking Cessation Aid

Additional Appendix Information
Antidepressant Agents *on page 1866*

Use Treatment of major depressive disorder, including seasonal affective disorder (SAD); adjunct in smoking cessation

Unlabeled/Investigational Use Attention-deficit/hyperactivity disorder (ADHD); depression associated with bipolar disorder

Restrictions An FDA-approved medication guide concerning the use of antidepressants in children and teenagers must be distributed when dispensing an outpatient prescription (new or refill) where this medication is to be used without direct supervision of a healthcare provider. Medication guides are available at http://www.fda.gov/cder/Offices/ODS/medication_guides.htm. Dispense to parents or guardians of children and teenagers receiving this medication.

Pregnancy Risk Factor C

Pregnancy Implications A slight increase in malformations was observed in some animal studies. The manufacturer provides results from a retrospective database study conducted in women taking bupropion during pregnancy. The study showed no greater risk of congenital malformations following bupropion exposure in comparison to other antidepressant agents. There are no adequate and well-controlled studies in pregnant women. Bupropion should be used during pregnancy only if the potential benefit outweighs the possible risks. A registry has been established for women exposed to bupropion during pregnancy (800-336-2176).

Lactation Enters breast milk/not recommended (AAP rates "of concern")

Medication Safety Issues
Sound-alike/look-alike issues:
BuPROPion may be confused with busPIRone
Wellbutrin SR® may be confused with Wellbutrin XL™
Wellbutrin XL™ may be confused with Wellbutrin SR®
Zyban® may be confused with Zagam®

Contraindications Hypersensitivity to bupropion or any component of the formulation; seizure disorder; anorexia/bulimia; use of MAO inhibitors within 14 days; patients undergoing abrupt discontinuation of ethanol or sedatives (including benzodiazepines); patients receiving other dosage forms of bupropion

Warnings/Precautions [U.S. Boxed Warning]: Antidepressants increase the risk of suicidal thinking and behavior in children and adolescents with major depressive disorder (MDD) and other depressive disorders; consider risk prior to prescribing. All patients must be closely monitored for clinical worsening, suicidality, or unusual changes in behavior, especially during the initiation of therapy or following an increase or decrease in dosage. When used in children, the child's family or caregiver should be instructed to closely observe the patient and communicate condition with healthcare provider. A medication guide should be dispensed with each prescription. **Bupropion is not FDA approved for use in children.**

The possibility of a suicide attempt is inherent in major depression and may persist until remission occurs. Use caution in high-risk patients. Worsening depression and severe abrupt suicidality that are not part of the presenting symptoms may require discontinuation or modification of drug therapy. The patient's family or caregiver should be alerted to monitor patients for the emergence of suicidality and associated behaviors (such as agitation, irritability, hostility, impulsivity, and hypomania) and notify the healthcare provider.

May worsen psychosis in some patients or precipitate a shift to mania or hypomania in patients with bipolar disorder. Patients presenting with depressive symptoms should be screened for bipolar disorder. Monotherapy in patients with bipolar disorder should be avoided. **Bupropion is not FDA approved for bipolar depression.**

The risk of seizures is dose-dependent and increased in patients with a history of seizures, anorexia/bulimia, head trauma, CNS tumor, severe hepatic cirrhosis, abrupt discontinuation of sedative-hypnotics or ethanol, medications which lower seizure threshold (antipsychotics, antidepressants, theophyllines, systemic steroids), stimulants, or hypoglycemic agents. Discontinue and do not restart in patients experiencing a seizure. May cause CNS stimulation (restlessness, anxiety, insomnia) or anorexia. May increase the risks associated with electroconvulsive therapy. Consider discontinuing, when possible, prior to elective surgery. May cause weight loss; use caution in patients where weight loss is not desirable. The incidence of sexual dysfunction with bupropion is generally lower than with SSRIs.

Use caution in patients with cardiovascular disease, history of hypertension, or coronary artery disease; treatment-emergent hypertension (including some severe cases) has been reported, both with bupropion alone and in combination with nicotine transdermal systems. Use with caution in patients with hepatic or renal dysfunction and in elderly patients; reduced dose recommended. Elderly patients may be at greater risk of accumulation during chronic dosing. May cause motor or cognitive impairment in some patients; use with caution if tasks requiring alertness such as operating machinery or driving are undertaken. Arthralgia, myalgia, and fever with rash and other symptoms suggestive of delayed hypersensitivity resembling serum sickness have been reportedreported.

Extended release tablet: Insoluble tablet shell may remain intact and be visible in the stool.

Adverse Reactions Frequencies, when reported, reflect highest incidence reported with sustained release product.

>10%:
Cardiovascular: Tachycardia (11%)
Central nervous system: Headache (25% to 34%), insomnia (11% to 20%), dizziness (6% to 11%)
Gastrointestinal: Xerostomia (17% to 26%), weight loss (14% to 23%), nausea (1% to 18%)
Respiratory: Pharyngitis (3% to 13%)
(Continued)

BuPROPion (Continued)

1% to 10%:

Cardiovascular: Palpitation (2% to 6%), arrhythmias (5%), chest pain (3% to 4%), hypertension (2% to 4%, may be severe), flushing (1% to 4%), hypotension (3%)

Central nervous system: Agitation (2% to 9%), confusion (8%), anxiety (5% to 7%), hostility (6%), nervousness (3% to 5%), sleep disturbance (4%), sensory disturbance (4%), migraine (1% to 4%), abnormal dreams (3%), irritability (2% to 3%), somnolence (2% to 3%), pain (2% to 3%), memory decreased (up to 3%), fever (1% to 2%), CNS stimulation (1% to 2%), depression

Dermatologic: Rash (1% to 5%), pruritus (2% to 4%), urticaria (1% to 2%)

Endocrine & metabolic: Menstrual complaints (2% to 5%), hot flashes (1% to 3%), libido decreased (3%)

Gastrointestinal: Constipation (5% to 10%), abdominal pain (2% to 9%), diarrhea (5% to 7%), flatulence (6%), anorexia (3% to 5%), appetite increased (4%), taste perversion (2% to 4%), vomiting (2% to 4%), dyspepsia (3%), dysphagia (up to 2%)

Genitourinary: Urinary frequency (2% to 5%), urinary urgency (up to 2%), vaginal hemorrhage (up to 2%), UTI (up to 1%)

Neuromuscular & skeletal: Tremor (3% to 6%), myalgia (2% to 6%), weakness (2% to 4%), arthralgia (1% to 4%), arthritis (2%), akathisia (2%), paresthesia (1% to 2%), twitching (1% to 2%), neck pain

Ocular: Amblyopia (2%), blurred vision (2% to 3%)

Otic: Tinnitus (3% to 6%), auditory disturbance (5%)

Respiratory: Upper respiratory infection (9%), cough increased (1% to 4%), sinusitis (1% to 5%)

Miscellaneous: Infection (8% to 9%), diaphoresis increased (5% to 6%), allergic reaction (including anaphylaxis, pruritus, urticaria)

Postmarketing and/or case reports: Accommodation abnormality, aggression, akinesia, alopecia, amnesia, anemia, angioedema, aphasia, ataxia, atrioventricular block, bronchospasm, bruxism, chills, colitis, coma, coordination abnormal, cystitis, deafness, delirium, delusions, depersonalization, derealization, diplopia, dry eye, dysarthria, dyskinesia, dyspareunia, dysphoria, dystonia, ecchymosis, EEG abnormality, ejaculation abnormality, emotional lability, esophagitis, euphoria, exfoliative dermatitis, extrapyramidal syndrome, extrasystoles, facial edema, fever with rash (and other symptoms suggestive of delayed hypersensitivity resembling serum sickness), gastric reflux, gastrointestinal hemorrhage, gingivitis, glossitis, glycosuria, gum hemorrhage, gynecomastia, hallucinations, hepatic damage, hepatitis, hirsutism, hostility, hyper-/hypokinesia, hypertonia, hypoesthesia, hyper-/hypoglycemia, hypomania, impotence, intestinal perforation, intraocular pressure increased, jaundice, leg cramps, leukocytosis, leukopenia, libido increased, liver function abnormal, lymphadenopathy, maculopapular rash, malaise, manic reaction, menopause, MI, mouth ulcers, muscle rigidity, muscle weakness, musculoskeletal chest pain, mydriasis, myoclonus, neuralgia, neuropathy, painful erection, pancreatitis, pancytopenia, paranoia, paranoid reaction, phlebitis, pneumonia, photosensitivity, postural hypotension, prostate disorder, pulmonary embolism, restlessness, rhabdomyolysis, salivation increased, salpingitis, sciatica, seizure, SIADH, stomach ulcer, stomatitis, stroke, suicidal ideation, syncope, tardive dyskinesia, thirst, thrombocytopenia, tongue edema, urinary incontinence, urinary retention, vaginitis, vasodilation, vertigo

Overdosage/Toxicology Ingestion of up to 30 g has been reported. Symptoms include labored breathing, salivation, ataxia, convulsions (~33% of all cases), sedation, coma, and respiratory depression, especially with coingestion of ethanol. Bupropion may cause sinus tachycardia and seizures. Treatment should include cardiac and EEG monitoring for the first 48 hours, but is otherwise supportive following initial decontamination with activated charcoal (lavage with massive and recent doses). Treat seizures with I.V. benzodiazepines and supportive therapies. Dialysis may be of limited value after drug absorption because of slow tissue-to-plasma diffusion.

Drug Interactions

Cytochrome P450 Effect: Substrate of CYP1A2 (minor), 2A6 (minor), 2B6 (major), 2C9 (minor), 2D6 (minor), 2E1 (minor), 3A4 (minor); **Inhibits** CYP2D6 (weak)

Increased Effect/Toxicity: Treatment-emergent hypertension may occur in patients treated with bupropion and nicotine patch. Toxicity of bupropion is enhanced by levodopa and phenelzine (MAO inhibitors). Risk of seizures may be increased with agents that may lower seizure threshold (antipsychotics, antidepressants, theophylline, abrupt discontinuation of benzodiazepines, systemic steroids). Effect of warfarin may be altered by bupropion. Concomitant therapy with metoprolol may result in bradycardia. Concurrent use with amantadine or CNS depressants appears to result in a higher incidence of adverse effects; use caution. CYP2B6 inhibitors may increase the levels/effects of bupropion; example inhibitors include desipramine, paroxetine, and sertraline. Combined use of CYP2B6 inhibitors (orphenadrine, thiotepa, cyclophosphamide) with bupropion may increase serum concentrations and may result in seizures.

Decreased Effect: CYP2B6 inducers may decrease the levels/effects of bupropion; example inducers include carbamazepine, nevirapine, phenobarbital, phenytoin, and rifampin.

Ethanol/Nutrition/Herb Interactions

Ethanol: Avoid ethanol (may increase CNS depression).

Herb/Nutraceutical: Avoid valerian, St John's wort, SAMe, gotu kola, kava kava (may increase CNS depression).

Stability

Store at controlled room temperature of 20°C to 25°C (68°F to 77°F).

Wellbutrin XL™: Store at 15°C to 30°C (59°F to 86°F).

Mechanism of Action Aminoketone antidepressant structurally different from all other marketed antidepressants; like other antidepressants the mechanism of bupropion's activity is not fully understood. Bupropion is a relatively weak inhibitor of the neuronal uptake of serotonin, norepinephrine, and dopamine, and does not inhibit monoamine oxidase. Metabolite inhibits the reuptake of norepinephrine. The primary mechanism of action is thought to be dopaminergic and/or noradrenergic.

Pharmacodynamics/Kinetics

Absorption: Rapid

Distribution: V_d: 19-21 L/kg

Protein binding: 82% to 88%

Metabolism: Extensively hepatic via CYP2B6 to hydroxybupropion; non-CYP-mediated metabolism to erythrohydrobupropion and threohydrobupropion. Metabolite activity ranges from 20% to 50% potency of bupropion.

Bioavailability: 5% to 20% in animals

Half-life:

Distribution: 3-4 hours

Elimination: 21 ± 9 hours; Metabolites: Hydroxybupropion: 20 ± 5 hours; Erythrohydrobupropion: 33 ± 10 hours; Threohydrobupropion: 37 ± 13 hours

Time to peak, serum: Bupropion: ~3 hours; bupropion extended release: ~5 hours

Metabolites: Hydroxybupropion, erythrohydrobupropion, threohydrobupropion: 6 hours

Excretion: Urine (87%); feces (10%)

Dosage Oral:

Children and Adolescents: ADHD (unlabeled use): 1.4-6 mg/kg/day

Adults:

Depression:

Immediate release: 100 mg 3 times/day; begin at 100 mg twice daily; may increase to a maximum dose of 450 mg/day

Sustained release: Initial: 150 mg/day in the morning; may increase to 150 mg twice daily by day 4 if tolerated; target dose: 300 mg/day given as 150 mg twice daily; maximum dose: 400 mg/day given as 200 mg twice daily

Extended release: Initial: 150 mg/day in the morning; may increase as early as day 4 of dosing to 300 mg/day, maximum dose: 450 mg/day

SAD (Wellbutrin XL™): Initial: 150 mg/day in the morning; if tolerated, may increase after 1 week to 300 mg/day

Note: Prophylactic treatment should be reserved for those patients with frequent depressive episodes and/or significant impairment. Initiate treatment in the Autumn prior to symptom onset, and discontinue in early Spring with dose tapering to 150 mg/day for 2 weeks

Smoking cessation (Zyban®): Initiate with 150 mg once daily for 3 days; increase to 150 mg twice daily; treatment should continue for 7-12 weeks

Elderly: Depression: 50-100 mg/day, increase by 50-100 mg every 3-4 days as tolerated; there is evidence that the elderly respond at 150 mg/day in divided doses, but some may require a higher dose

Dosing conversion between immediate, sustained, and extended release products: Convert using same total daily dose (up to the maximum recommended dose for a given dosage form), but adjust frequency as indicated for sustained (twice daily) or extended (once daily) release products.

Dosing adjustment/comments in renal Impairment: Effect of renal disease on bupropion's pharmacokinetics has not been studied; elimination of the major metabolites of bupropion may be affected by reduced renal function. Patients with renal failure should receive a reduced dosage initially and be closely monitored.

Dosing adjustment in hepatic impairment:

Note: The mean AUC increased by ~1.5-fold for hydroxybupropion and ~2.5-fold for erythro/threohydrobupropion; median T_{max} was observed 19 hours later for hydroxybupropion, 31 hours later for erythro/threohydrobupropion; mean half-life for hydroxybupropion increased fivefold, and increased twofold for erythro/threohydrobupropion in patients with severe hepatic cirrhosis compared to healthy volunteers.

Mild-to-moderate hepatic impairment: Use with caution and/or reduced dose/frequency

Severe hepatic cirrhosis: Use with extreme caution; maximum dose:

Wellbutrin®: 75 mg/day

Wellbutrin SR®: 100 mg/day or 150 mg every other day

Wellbutrin XL™: 150 mg every other day

Zyban®: 150 mg every other day

Administration May be taken without regard to meals. Zyban® and extended release tablets should be swallowed whole; do not crush, chew, or divide. The insoluble shell of the extended-release tablet may remain intact during GI transit and is eliminated in the feces. Data from the manufacturer states that dividing Wellbutrin® SR tablets resulted in an increased rate of release at 15 minutes: "However, the divided tablet retained its sustained-release characteristics with similar increases of released bupropion at each sampling point beyond 15 minutes when compared to the intact Wellbutrin® SR tablet..." Bupropion is hydroscopic and therefore should be stored in a dry place. Splitting of large quantities in advance of administration is not advised since loss of potency may result. If necessary, splitting should be done cleanly without crushing.

Monitoring Parameters Body weight; mental status for depression, suicidal ideation (especially at the beginning of therapy or when doses are increased or decreased), anxiety, social functioning, mania, panic attacks

Reference Range Therapeutic levels (trough, 12 hours after last dose): 50-100 ng/mL

Additional Information Risk of seizures: When using immediate release tablets, seizure risk is increased at total daily dosage >450 mg, individual dosages >150 mg, or by sudden, large increments in dose. Data for the immediate-release formulation of bupropion revealed a seizure incidence of 0.4% in patients treated at doses in the 300-450 mg/day range. The estimated seizure incidence increases almost 10-fold between 450 mg and 600 mg per day. Data for the sustained release dosage form revealed a seizure incidence of 0.1% in patients treated at a dosage range of 100-300 mg/day, and increases to ~0.4% at the maximum recommended dose of 400 mg/day.

Dosage Forms

Tablet, as hydrochloride (Wellbutrin®): 75 mg, 100 mg

Tablet, extended release, as hydrochloride:

Budeprion™ SR: 100 mg [contains tartrazine; equivalent to Wellbutrin® SR], 150 mg [equivalent to Wellbutrin® SR]

(Continued)

BuPROPion (Continued)

Buproban™: 150 mg [equivalent to Zyban®]
Wellbutrin XL™: 150 mg, 300 mg
Tablet, sustained release, as hydrochloride: 100 mg, 150 mg [equivalent to Wellbutrin® SR], 150 mg [equivalent to Zyban®]
Wellbutrin® SR: 100 mg, 150 mg, 200 mg
Zyban®: 150 mg

♦ **Burinex®** (Can) *see* Bumetanide *on page 247*
♦ **Burnamycin [OTC]** *see* Lidocaine *on page 1010*
♦ **Burn Jel [OTC]** *see* Lidocaine *on page 1010*
♦ **Burn-O-Jel [OTC]** *see* Lidocaine *on page 1010*
♦ **Buscopan®** (Can) *see* Scopolamine Derivatives *on page 1550*
♦ **BuSpar®** *see* BusPIRone *on page 256*
♦ **Buspirex (Can)** *see* BusPIRone *on page 256*

BusPIRone (byoo SPYE rone)

U.S. Brand Names BuSpar®
Canadian Brand Names Apo-Buspirone®; BuSpar®; Buspirex; Bustab®; Gen-Buspirone; Lin-Buspirone; Novo-Buspirone; Nu-Buspirone; PMS-Buspirone
Index Terms Buspirone Hydrochloride
Pharmacologic Category Antianxiety Agent, Miscellaneous
Use Management of generalized anxiety disorder (GAD)
Unlabeled/Investigational Use Management of aggression in mental retardation and secondary mental disorders; major depression; potential augmenting agent for antidepressants; premenstrual syndrome
Pregnancy Risk Factor B
Lactation Excretion in breast milk unknown/not recommended
Medication Safety Issues
Sound-alike/look-alike issues:
BusPIRone may be confused with buPROPion
Contraindications Hypersensitivity to buspirone or any component of the formulation
Warnings/Precautions Use in hepatic or renal impairment is not recommended; does not prevent or treat withdrawal from benzodiazepines. Low potential for cognitive or motor impairment. Use with MAO inhibitors may result in hypertensive reactions.
Adverse Reactions
>10%: Central nervous system: Dizziness
1% to 10%:
Central nervous system: Drowsiness, EPS, serotonin syndrome, confusion, nervousness, lightheadedness, excitement, anger, hostility, headache
Dermatologic: Rash
Gastrointestinal: Diarrhea, nausea
Neuromuscular & skeletal: Muscle weakness, numbness, paresthesia, incoordination, tremor
Ocular: Blurred vision, tunnel vision
Miscellaneous: Diaphoresis, allergic reactions
Overdosage/Toxicology Symptoms include dizziness, drowsiness, pinpoint pupils, nausea, and vomiting. There is no known antidote for buspirone. Treatment is supportive.
Drug Interactions
Cytochrome P450 Effect: Substrate of CYP2D6 (minor), 3A4 (major)
Increased Effect/Toxicity: Concurrent use of buspirone with SSRIs or trazodone may cause serotonin syndrome. Buspirone should not be used concurrently with an MAO inhibitor due to reports of increased blood pressure; theoretically, a selective MAO type B inhibitors (selegiline) has a lower risk of this reaction. Concurrent use of buspirone with nefazodone may increase risk of CNS adverse events; limit buspirone initial dose (eg, 2.5 mg/day). CYP3A4 inhibitors may increase the levels/effects of buspirone; example inhibitors include azole antifungals, clarithromycin, diclofenac, doxycycline, erythromycin, imatinib, isoniazid, nefazodone, nicardipine, propofol, protease inhibitors, quinidine, telithromycin, and verapamil.
Decreased Effect: CYP3A4 inducers may decrease the levels/effects of buspirone; example inducers include aminoglutethimide, carbamazepine, nafcillin, nevirapine, phenobarbital, phenytoin, and rifamycins.
Ethanol/Nutrition/Herb Interactions
Ethanol: Ethanol (may increase CNS depression).
Food: Food may decrease the absorption of buspirone, but it may also decrease the first-pass metabolism, thereby increasing the bioavailability of buspirone. Grapefruit juice may cause increased buspirone concentrations; avoid concurrent use.
Herb/Nutraceutical: St John's wort may decrease buspirone levels or increase CNS depression. Avoid valerian, gotu kola, kava kava (may increase CNS depression).
Mechanism of Action The mechanism of action of buspirone is unknown. Buspirone has a high affinity for serotonin 5-HT$_{1A}$ and 5-HT$_2$ receptors, without affecting benzodiazepine-GABA receptors. Buspirone has moderate affinity for dopamine D$_2$ receptors.
Pharmacodynamics/Kinetics
Absorption: Oral: ~100%
Distribution: V$_d$: 5.3 L/kg
Protein binding: 95%
Metabolism: Hepatic via oxidation; extensive first-pass effect
Bioavailability: ~4%
Half-life elimination: Mean: 2.4 hours (range: 2-11 hours)
Time to peak, serum: Within 0.7-1.5 hours
Excretion: Urine: 65%; feces: 35%; ~1% dose excreted unchanged

Dosage Oral:
Generalized anxiety disorder:
Children and Adolescents: Initial: 5 mg daily; increase in increments of 5 mg/day at weekly intervals as needed, to a maximum dose of 60 mg/day divided into 2-3 doses
Adults: 15 mg/day (7.5 mg twice daily); may increase in increments of 5 mg/day every 2-4 days to a maximum of 60 mg/day; target dose for most people is 30 mg/day (15 mg twice daily)
Elderly: Initial: 5 mg twice daily, increase by 5 mg/day every 2-3 days as needed up to 20-30 mg/day; maximum daily dose: 60 mg/day.
Dosing adjustment in renal or hepatic impairment: Buspirone is metabolized by the liver and excreted by the kidneys. Patients with impaired hepatic or renal function demonstrated increased plasma levels and a prolonged half-life of buspirone. Therefore, use in patients with severe hepatic or renal impairment cannot be recommended.
Monitoring Parameters Mental status, symptoms of anxiety
Test Interactions Increased AST, ALT, growth hormone(s), prolactin (S)
Additional Information Has shown little potential for abuse; needs continuous use. Because of slow onset, not appropriate for "as needed" (prn) use or for brief, situational anxiety. Ineffective for treatment of benzodiazepine or ethanol withdrawal.
Dosage Forms
Tablet, as hydrochloride: 5 mg, 7.5 mg, 10 mg, 15 mg, 30 mg
BuSpar®: 5 mg, 10 mg, 15 mg, 30 mg

♦ **Buspirone Hydrochloride** see BusPIRone on page 256
♦ **Bustab® (Can)** see BusPIRone on page 256

Busulfan (byoo SUL fan)

U.S. Brand Names Busulfex®; Myleran®
Canadian Brand Names Busulfex®; Myleran®
Index Terms NSC-750
Pharmacologic Category Antineoplastic Agent, Alkylating Agent
Use
Oral: Chronic myelogenous leukemia; conditioning regimens for bone marrow transplantation
I.V.: Combination therapy with cyclophosphamide as a conditioning regimen prior to allogeneic hematopoietic progenitor cell transplantation for chronic myelogenous leukemia
Unlabeled/Investigational Use Oral: Bone marrow disorders, such as polycythemia vera and myeloid metaplasia; thrombocytosis
Pregnancy Risk Factor D
Pregnancy Implications Animal studies have demonstrated teratogenic effects. May cause fetal harm if administered during pregnancy. There are no adequate and well-controlled studies in pregnant women. Women of childbearing potential should avoid pregnancy while receiving treatment.
Lactation Excretion in breast milk unknown/contraindicated
Medication Safety Issues
Sound-alike/look-alike issues:
Busulfan may be confused with Butalan®
Myleran® may be confused with melphalan, Mylicon®

High alert medication: The Institute for Safe Medication Practices (ISMP) includes this medication among its list of drugs which have a heightened risk of causing significant patient harm when used in error.
Contraindications Hypersensitivity to busulfan or any component of the formulation; failure to respond to previous courses; pregnancy
Warnings/Precautions Hazardous agent - use appropriate precautions for handling and disposal. **[U.S. Boxed Warning]: May induce severe bone marrow suppression.** Seizures have been reported with use; use caution in patients predisposed to seizures; initiate prophylactic anticonvulsant therapy (eg, phenytoin) prior to treatment; use caution with history of seizures or head trauma. May cause delayed pulmonary toxicity (known as "busulfan lung" — bronchopulmonary dysplasia with pulmonary fibrosis); the average onset is 4 years. Busulfan has been causally related to the development of secondary malignancies (tumors and acute leukemias). Busulfan has been associated with ovarian failure (including failure to achieve puberty). High busulfan area under the concentration versus time curve (AUC) values (>1500 μM/minute) are associated with increased risk of hepatic veno-occlusive disease during conditioning for allogenic BMT. **[U.S. Boxed Warning]: Should be administered under the supervision of an experienced cancer chemotherapy physician.**
Adverse Reactions Frequency not always defined.
Cardiovascular: Arrhythmia, atrial fibrillation, chest pain, edema, hyper-/hypotension, hypervolemia, tachycardia, tamponade (children with thalassemia: 2%), third degree heart block, thrombosis, vasodilation, ventricular extrasystoles
Central nervous system: Anxiety, chills, depression, dizziness, fever, headache, insomnia, pain, seizure (2%)
Dermatologic: Alopecia, erythema, hyperpigmentation of skin (busulfan tan 5% to 10%), pruritus, rash, urticaria
Endocrine & metabolic: Amenorrhea, hyperglycemia, hypocalcemia, hypokalemia, hypomagnesemia
Gastrointestinal: Abdominal fullness, abdominal pain, anorexia, constipation, diarrhea, dyspepsia, hematemesis, ileus, mucositis/stomatitis, nausea, pancreatitis, vomiting, weight gain, xerostomia
Hematologic: Anemia (I.V.: 69%), bone marrow suppression, leukopenia, lymphopenia, neutropenia (I.V.: ≤100%; onset: 4 days; recovery: 9-22 days), severe pancytopenia, thrombocytopenia (I.V.: ≤98%; onset 5-6 days)
Hepatic: ALT increased, hyperbilirubinemia, veno-occlusive disease (stem cell transplantation: 8% to 12%)
Local: Injection site pain and inflammation
(Continued)

Busulfan (Continued)

Neuromuscular & skeletal: Back pain, weakness

Renal: Creatinine increased

Respiratory: Cough, dyspnea, epistaxis, lung disorder, pneumonia, rhinitis

Miscellaneous: Allergic reaction, infection

Infrequent, postmarketing, and/or case reports: Adrenal suppression, alopecia (permanent), aplastic anemia, blurred vision, cataracts, cheilosis, cholestatic jaundice, corneal thinning, dry skin, endocardial fibrosis, erythema multiforme, erythema nodosum, esophageal varices, gynecomastia, hemorrhagic cystitis, hepatic dysfunction, hyperuricemia, hyperuricosuria, interstitial pulmonary fibrosis (busulfan lung; manifested by a diffuse interstitial pulmonary fibrosis and persistent cough, fever, rales, and dyspnea; may be relieved by corticosteroids); malignant tumors, myasthenia gravis, ocular (lens) changes, ovarian supression, porphyria cutanea tarda, prothrombin time increased, radiation myelopathy, sepsis, sterility, testicular atrophy

Overdosage/Toxicology Symptoms include leukopenia and thrombocytopenia. Induction of vomiting or gastric lavage with charcoal is indicated for recent ingestions. The effects of dialysis are unknown. Treatment is symptom-directed and supportive.

Drug Interactions

Cytochrome P450 Effect: Substrate of CYP3A4 (major)

Increased Effect/Toxicity: CYP3A4 inhibitors may increase the levels/effects of busulfan; example inhibitors include azole antifungals, clarithromycin, diclofenac, doxycycline, erythromycin, imatinib, isoniazid, nefazodone, nicardipine, propofol, protease inhibitors, quinidine, telithromycin, and verapamil. Metronidazole may increase busulfan plasma levels. Pulmonary toxicity of other cytotoxic agents may be additive.

Decreased Effect: CYP3A4 inducers may decrease the levels/effects of busulfan; example inducers include aminoglutethimide, carbamazepine, nafcillin, nevirapine, phenobarbital, phenytoin, and rifamycins.

Ethanol/Nutrition/Herb Interactions

Ethanol: Avoid ethanol due to GI irritation.

Food: No clear or firm data on the effect of food on busulfan bioavailability.

Herb/Nutraceutical: St John's wort may decrease busulfan levels.

Stability

Injection: Store unopened ampuls under refrigeration at 2°C to 8°C (36°F to 46°F). Dilute (using manufacturer provided 5-micron filters) in 0.9% sodium chloride injection or dextrose 5% in water. The dilution volume should be ten times the volume of busulfan injection, ensuring that the final concentration of busulfan is 0.5 mg/mL. This solution is stable for up to 8 hours at room temperature (25°C); the infusion must also be completed within that 8-hour timeframe. Dilution of busulfan injection in 0.9% sodium chloride is stable for up to 12 hours at refrigeration (2°C to 8°C); the infusion must be completed within that 12-hour timeframe.

Tablet: Store at room temperature at 15°C to 30°C (59°F to 86°F).

Mechanism of Action Reacts with N-7 position of guanosine and interferes with DNA replication and transcription of RNA. Busulfan has a more marked effect on myeloid cells than on lymphoid cells. The drug is also very toxic to hematopoietic stem cells. Busulfan exhibits little immunosuppressive activity. Interferes with the normal function of DNA by alkylation and cross-linking the strands of DNA.

Pharmacodynamics/Kinetics

Duration: 28 days

Absorption: Rapid and complete

Distribution: V_d: ~1 L/kg; into CSF and saliva with levels similar to plasma

Protein binding: ~14% to 32%

Metabolism: Extensively hepatic (may increase with multiple doses); glutathione conjugation followed by oxidation

Half-life elimination: After first dose: 3.4 hours; After last dose: 2.3 hours

Time to peak, serum: Oral: Within 4 hours; I.V.: Within 5 minutes

Excretion: Urine (10% to 50% as metabolites) within 24 hours (<2% as unchanged drug)

Dosage

Children:

For remission induction of CML: Oral: 0.06-0.12 mg/kg/day **or** 1.8-4.6 mg/m²/day; titrate dosage to maintain leukocyte count above 40,000/mm³; reduce dosage by 50% if the leukocyte count reaches 30,000-40,000/mm³; discontinue drug if counts fall to ≤20,000/mm³

BMT marrow-ablative conditioning regimen:

Oral: 1 mg/kg/dose (ideal body weight) every 6 hours for 16 doses

I.V.:

≤12 kg: 1.1 mg/kg/dose (ideal body weight) every 6 hours for 16 doses

>12 kg: 0.8 mg/kg/dose (ideal body weight) every 6 hours for 16 doses

Adjust dose to desired AUC [1125 μmol(min)] using the following formula:

Adjusted dose (mg) = Actual dose (mg) x [target AUC μmol(min) / actual AUC μmol(min)]

Adults:

For remission induction of CML: Oral: 4-8 mg/day (may be as high as 12 mg/day); Maintenance doses: 1-4 mg/day to 2 mg/week to maintain WBC 10,000-20,000 cells/mm³

BMT marrow-ablative conditioning regimen:

Oral: 1 mg/kg/dose (ideal body weight) every 6 hours for 16 doses

I.V.: 0.8 mg/kg (ideal body weight or actual body weight, whichever is lower) every 6 hours for 4 days (a total of 16 doses)

Polycythemia vera (unlabeled use): Oral: 2-6 mg/day

Thrombocytosis (unlabeled use): Oral: 4-6 mg/day

Administration Intravenous busulfan should be administered as a 2-hour infusion.

BMT only: To facilitate ingestion of high oral doses, insert multiple tablets into gelatin capsules.

Monitoring Parameters CBC with differential and platelet count, hemoglobin, liver function tests (evaluate transaminases, alkaline phosphatase, and bilirubin for at least 28 days post transplant)

Additional Information The solvent in I.V. busulfan, DMA, may impair fertility and is associated with teratogenic effects. DMA may also be associated with hepatotoxicity, hallucinations, somnolence, lethargy, and confusion.

Dosage Forms
Injection, solution:
Busulfex®: 6 mg/mL (10 mL)
Tablet:
Myleran®: 2 mg

♦ **Busulfex**® *see* Busulfan *on page 257*

Butabarbital (byoo ta BAR bi tal)

U.S. Brand Names Butisol Sodium®
Pharmacologic Category Barbiturate
Use Sedative; hypnotic
Restrictions C-III
Pregnancy Risk Factor D
Medication Safety Issues
Sound-alike/look-alike issues:
Butabarbital may be confused with butalbital
Dosage Oral:
Children: Preoperative sedation: 2-6 mg/kg/dose (maximum: 100 mg)
Adults:
Sedative: 15-30 mg 3-4 times/day
Hypnotic: 50-100 mg
Preop: 50-100 mg 1-1½ hours before surgery
Elderly: Not recommeded for use in the elderly
Additional Information Complete prescribing information for this medication should be consulted for additional detail.
Dosage Forms
Elixir, as sodium: 30 mg/5 mL (480 mL) [contains alcohol 7% and tartrazine]
Tablet, as sodium: 30 mg, 50 mg [contains tartrazine]

Butalbital, Acetaminophen, and Caffeine
(byoo TAL bi tal, a seet a MIN oh fen, & KAF een)

U.S. Brand Names Anolor 300; Dolgic® LQ; Dolgic® Plus; Esgic®; Esgic-Plus™; Fioricet®; Medigesic®; Repan®; Zebutal™
Index Terms Acetaminophen, Butalbital, and Caffeine
Pharmacologic Category Barbiturate
Use Relief of the symptomatic complex of tension or muscle contraction headache
Pregnancy Risk Factor C
Medication Safety Issues
Sound-alike/look-alike issues:
Fioricet® may be confused with Fiorinal®, Lorcet®
Repan® may be confused with Riopan®
Dosage
Adults: Oral: 1-2 tablets or capsules (or 15-30 mL elixir) every 4 hours; not to exceed 6 tablets or capsules (or 180 mL elixir) daily
Elderly: Not recommended for use in the elderly
Dosing interval in renal or hepatic impairment: Should be reduced
Additional Information Complete prescribing information for this medication should be consulted for additional detail.
Dosage Forms
Capsule:
Anolor 300, Esgic®, Medigesic®: Butalbital 50 mg, acetaminophen 325 mg, and caffeine 40 mg
Dolgic® Plus: Butalbital 50 mg, acetaminophen 750 mg, and caffeine 40 mg
Esgic-Plus™, Zebutal™: Butalbital 50 mg, acetaminophen 500 mg, and caffeine 40 mg
Elixir:
Dolgic® LQ: Butalbital 50 mg, acetaminophen 325 mg, and caffeine 40 mg per 15 mL (480 mL) [contains alcohol 7%; fruit flavor]
Tablet: Butalbital 50 mg, acetaminophen 325 mg, and caffeine 40 mg; butalbital 50 mg, acetaminophen 500 mg, and caffeine 40 mg
Esgic®, Fioricet®, Repan®: Butalbital 50 mg, acetaminophen 325 mg, and caffeine 40 mg

---

Butalbital and Acetaminophen (byoo TAL bi tal & a seet a MIN oh fen)

U.S. Brand Names Bupap; Cephadyn; Phrenilin®; Phrenilin® Forte; Promacet; Sedapap®
Index Terms Butalbital and Acetaminophen
Pharmacologic Category Analgesic, Miscellaneous; Barbiturate
Use Relief of the symptomatic complex of tension or muscle contraction headache
Pregnancy Risk Factor C
Dosage Oral: Adults: One tablet/capsule every 4 hours as needed (maximum dose: 6 tablets/day)
Phrenilin®: 1-2 tablets every 4 hours as needed (maximum 6 tablets in 24 hours)
Elderly: Use with caution, see adult dosing
(Continued)

Butalbital and Acetaminophen *(Continued)*

Dosage adjustment in renal impairment: Mild-to-moderate: Should decrease dose; in severe impairment, use with caution

Dosage adjustment in hepatic impairment: Mild-to-moderate: Should decrease dose; in severe impairment, use with caution

Additional Information Complete prescribing information for this medication should be consulted for additional detail.

Dosage Forms
Tablet:
Phrenilin®: Butalbital 50 mg and acetaminophen 325 mg
Bupap, Cephadyn, Promacet, Sedapap®: Butalbital 50 mg and acetaminophen 650 mg
Capsule:
Phrenilin® Forte: Butalbital 50 mg and acetaminophen 650 mg

♦ **Butalbital and Acetaminophen** *see* Butalbital and Acetaminophen *on page 259*

Butalbital, Aspirin, and Caffeine (byoo TAL bi tal, AS pir in, & KAF een)

U.S. Brand Names Fiorinal®
Canadian Brand Names Fiorinal®
Index Terms Aspirin, Caffeine, and Butalbital; Butalbital Compound
Pharmacologic Category Barbiturate
Use Relief of the symptomatic complex of tension or muscle contraction headache
Restrictions C-III
Pregnancy Risk Factor C/D (prolonged use or high doses at term)
Medication Safety Issues
Sound-alike/look-alike issues:
Fiorinal® may be confused with Fioricet®, Florical®, Florinef®
Dosage
Oral: Adults: 1-2 tablets or capsules every 4 hours; not to exceed 6/day
Elderly: Not recommended for use in the elderly
Dosing interval in renal or hepatic impairment: Should be reduced
Additional Information Complete prescribing information for this medication should be consulted for additional detail.
Dosage Forms Capsule: Butalbital 50 mg, caffeine 40 mg, and aspirin 325 mg

♦ **Butalbital Compound** *see* Butalbital, Aspirin, and Caffeine *on page 260*
♦ **Butamben, Tetracaine, and Benzocaine** *see* Benzocaine, Butamben, and Tetracaine *on page 207*

Butenafine (byoo TEN a feen)

U.S. Brand Names Lotrimin® Ultra™ [OTC]; Mentax®
Index Terms Butenafine Hydrochloride
Pharmacologic Category Antifungal Agent, Topical
Use Topical treatment of tinea pedis (athlete's foot), tinea cruris (jock itch), tinea corporis (ringworm), and tinea versicolor
Pregnancy Risk Factor B
Medication Safety Issues
Sound-alike/look-alike issues:
Lotrimin may be confused with Lotrisone®, Otrivin®
Dosage Children >12 years and Adults: Topical:
Tinea corporis, tinea cruris, or tinea versicolor: Apply once daily for 2 weeks to affected area and surrounding skin
Tinea pedis: Apply once daily for 4 weeks or twice daily for 7 days to affected area and surrounding skin (7-day regimen may have lower efficacy)
Dosage Forms Cream, as hydrochloride:
Lotrimin® Ultra™: 1% (12 g, 24 g) [contains benzyl alcohol and sodium benzoate]
Mentax®: 1% (15 g, 30 g) [contains benzyl alcohol and sodium benzoate]

♦ **Butenafine Hydrochloride** *see* Butenafine *on page 260*
♦ **Butisol Sodium®** *see* Butabarbital *on page 259*

Butoconazole (byoo toe KOE na zole)

U.S. Brand Names Gynazole-1®; Mycelex®-3 [OTC]
Canadian Brand Names Femstat® One; Gynazole-1®
Index Terms Butoconazole Nitrate
Pharmacologic Category Antifungal Agent, Vaginal
Additional Appendix Information
Treatment of Sexually Transmitted Infections *on page 2007*
Use Local treatment of vulvovaginal candidiasis
Pregnancy Risk Factor C (use only in 2nd or 3rd trimester)
Pregnancy Implications No adequate and well-controlled studies have been conducted in pregnant women. However, butoconazole has been used during pregnancy. Use should be limited to the 2nd or 3rd trimesters only.
Lactation Excretion in breast milk unknown/use caution
Medication Safety Issues
Sound-alike/look-alike issues:
Mycelex® may be confused with Myoflex®
Contraindications Hypersensitivity to butoconazole or any component of the formulation

Warnings/Precautions If irritation or sensitization occurs, discontinue use. Contains mineral oil which may weaken latex or rubber products (condoms, vaginal contraceptive diaphragms); do not use these products within 72 hours of treatment. HIV infection should be considered in sexually-active women with difficult to eradicate recurrent vaginal yeast infections. OTC product is not for use in women with a first-time vaginal yeast infection. Safety and efficacy in females <12 years have not been established.

Adverse Reactions Frequency not defined.
Gastrointestinal: Abdominal pain or cramping
Genitourinary: Pelvic pain; vulvar/vaginal burning, itching, soreness, and swelling

Stability Store at 15°C to 30°C (59°F to 86°F).

Mechanism of Action Increases cell membrane permeability in susceptible fungi (*Candida*)

Pharmacodynamics/Kinetics
Absorption: 2%
Metabolism: Not reported
Time to peak: 12-24 hours

Dosage Adults: Female:
Femstat®-3 [OTC]: Insert 1 applicatorful (~5 g) intravaginally at bedtime for 3 consecutive days
Gynazole-1®: Insert 1 applicatorful (~5 g) intravaginally as a single dose; treatment may need to be extended for up to 6 days in pregnant women (use in pregnancy during 2nd or 3rd trimester only)

Additional Information Gynazole-1®: This product is delivered in a base allowing the active ingredient to remain vaginally for 4 days. It is associated with less leakage and can therefore be applied at any time during the day or night (per product information, Gynazole-1®).

Dosage Forms Cream, vaginal, as nitrate:
Mycelex®-3: 2% (5 g) [prefilled applicator], (20 g) [with disposable applicator]
Gynazole-1®: 2% (5 g) [prefilled applicator]

◆ **Butoconazole Nitrate** see Butoconazole on page 260

Butorphanol (byoo TOR fa nole)

U.S. Brand Names Stadol®
Canadian Brand Names Apo-Butorphanol®; PMS-Butorphanol
Index Terms Butorphanol Tartrate
Pharmacologic Category Analgesic, Opioid
Additional Appendix Information
Narcotic Agonists on page 1888
Use
Parenteral: Management of moderate-to-severe pain; preoperative medication; supplement to balanced anesthesia; management of pain during labor
Nasal spray: Management of moderate-to-severe pain, including migraine headache pain
Restrictions C-IV
Pregnancy Risk Factor C/D (prolonged use or high doses at term)
Lactation Enters breast milk/use caution (AAP rates "compatible")
Medication Safety Issues
Sound-alike/look-alike issues:
Stadol® may be confused with Haldol®, sotalol
Contraindications Hypersensitivity to butorphanol or any component of the formulation; avoid use in opiate-dependent patients who have not been detoxified, may precipitate opiate withdrawal; pregnancy (prolonged use or high doses at term)
Warnings/Precautions An opioid-containing analgesic regimen should be tailored to each patient's needs and based upon the type of pain being treated (acute versus chronic), the route of administration, degree of tolerance for opioids (naive versus chronic user), age, weight, and medical condition. The optimal analgesic dose varies widely among patients. Doses should be titrated to pain relief/prevention. May cause CNS depression; use with caution in patients with head trauma, morbid obesity, thyroid dysfunction, hepatic/renal dysfunction, adrenal insufficiency, prostatic hyperplasia and/or urinary stricture, may elevate CSF pressure, may increase cardiac workload; tolerance of drug dependence may result from extended use. Use with caution in patients with biliary tract dysfunction; acute pancreatitis may cause constriction of sphincter of Oddi.

Partial antagonist activity may precipitate acute narcotic withdrawal in opioid-dependent individuals. Use with caution in patients with pre-existing respiratory compromise (hypoxia and/or hypercapnia), COPD or other obstructive pulmonary disease; critical respiratory depression may occur, even at therapeutic dosages. May cause hypotension; use with caution in patients with hypovolemia, cardiovascular disease (including acute MI), or drugs which may exaggerate hypotensive effects (including phenothiazines or general anesthetics). May obscure diagnosis or clinical course of patients with acute abdominal conditions.

Concurrent use of sumatriptan nasal spray and butorphanol nasal spray may increase risk of transient high blood pressure. Healthcare provider should be alert to problems of abuse, misuse, and diversion. Use with caution in the elderly and debilitated patients; may be more sensitive to adverse effects. Safety and efficacy have not been established in children.

Adverse Reactions
>10%:
Central nervous system: Drowsiness (43%), dizziness (19%), insomnia (Stadol® NS)
Gastrointestinal: Nausea/vomiting (13%)
Respiratory: Nasal congestion (Stadol® NS)
1% to 10%:
Cardiovascular: Vasodilation, palpitation
Central nervous system: Lightheadedness, headache, lethargy, anxiety, confusion, euphoria, somnolence
Dermatologic: Pruritus
Gastrointestinal: Anorexia, constipation, xerostomia, stomach pain, unpleasant aftertaste
(Continued)

Butorphanol *(Continued)*

Neuromuscular & skeletal: Tremor, paresthesia, weakness

Ocular: Blurred vision

Otic: Ear pain, tinnitus

Respiratory: Bronchitis, cough, dyspnea, epistaxis, nasal irritation, pharyngitis, rhinitis, sinus congestion, sinusitis, upper respiratory infection

Miscellaneous: Diaphoresis increased

<1% (Limited to important or life-threatening): Dependence (with prolonged use), depression, difficulty speaking (transient), dyspnea, hallucinations, hypertension, nightmares, paradoxical CNS stimulation, rash, respiratory depression, syncope, tinnitus, vertigo, withdrawal symptoms

Stadol® NS: Apnea, chest pain, convulsions, delusions, depressions, edema, hypertension, shallow breathing, tachycardia

Overdosage/Toxicology Symptoms include respiratory depression, cardiac and CNS depression. Treatment includes airway support, establishment of an I.V. line and administration of naloxone 2 mg I.V. (0.01 mg/kg for children), with repeat administration as necessary, up to a total of 10 mg.

Drug Interactions

Increased Effect/Toxicity: Increased toxicity with CNS depressants, phenothiazines, barbiturates, skeletal muscle relaxants, alfentanil, guanabenz, and MAO inhibitors.

Ethanol/Nutrition/Herb Interactions

Ethanol: Avoid or limit ethanol (may increase CNS depression). Watch for sedation.

Herb/Nutraceutical: Avoid valerian, St John's wort, kava kava, gotu kola (may increase CNS depression).

Stability Store at room temperature. Protect from freezing.

Mechanism of Action Mixed narcotic agonist-antagonist with central analgesic actions; binds to opiate receptors in the CNS, causing inhibition of ascending pain pathways, altering the perception of and response to pain; produces generalized CNS depression

Pharmacodynamics/Kinetics

Onset of action: I.M.: 5-10 minutes; I.V.: <10 minutes; Nasal: Within 15 minutes

Peak effect: I.M.: 0.5-1 hour; I.V.: 4-5 minutes

Duration: I.M., I.V.: 3-4 hours; Nasal: 4-5 hours

Absorption: Rapid and well absorbed

Protein binding: 80%

Metabolism: Hepatic

Bioavailability: Nasal: 60% to 70%

Half-life elimination: 2.5-4 hours

Excretion: Primarily urine

Dosage Note: These are guidelines and do not represent the maximum doses that may be required in all patients. Doses should be titrated to pain relief/prevention. Butorphanol has an analgesic ceiling.

Adults:

Parenteral:

Acute pain (moderate to severe):

I.M.: Initial: 2 mg, may repeat every 3-4 hours as needed; usual range: 1-4 mg every 3-4 hours as needed

I.V.: Initial: 1 mg, may repeat every 3-4 hours as needed; usual range: 0.5-2 mg every 3-4 hours as needed

Preoperative medication: I.M.: 2 mg 60-90 minutes before surgery

Supplement to balanced anesthesia: I.V.: 2 mg shortly before induction and/or an incremental dose of 0.5-1 mg (up to 0.06 mg/kg), depending on previously administered sedative, analgesic, and hypnotic medications

Pain during labor (fetus >37 weeks gestation and no signs of fetal distress):

I.M., I.V.: 1-2 mg; may repeat in 4 hours

Note: Alternative analgesia should be used for pain associated with delivery or if delivery is anticipated within 4 hours

Nasal spray:

Moderate to severe pain (including migraine headache pain): Initial: 1 spray (~1 mg per spray) in 1 nostril; if adequate pain relief is not achieved within 60-90 minutes, an additional 1 spray in 1 nostril may be given; may repeat initial dose sequence in 3-4 hours after the last dose as needed

Alternatively, an initial dose of 2 mg (1 spray in each nostril) may be used in patients who will be able to remain recumbent (in the event drowsiness or dizziness occurs); additional 2 mg doses should not be given for 3-4 hours

Note: In some clinical trials, an initial dose of 2 mg (as 2 doses 1 hour apart or 2 mg initially - 1 spray in each nostril) has been used, followed by 1 mg in 1 hour; side effects were greater at these dosages

Elderly:

I.M., I.V.: Initial dosage should generally be ½ of the recommended dose; repeated dosing must be based on initial response rather than fixed intervals, but generally should be at least 6 hours apart

Nasal spray: Initial dose should not exceed 1 mg; a second dose may be given after 90-120 minutes

Dosage adjustment in renal impairment:

I.M., I.V.: Initial dosage should generally be ½ of the recommended dose; repeated dosing must be based on initial response rather than fixed intervals, but generally should be at least 6 hours apart

Nasal spray: Initial dose should not exceed 1 mg; a second dose may be given after 90-120 minutes

Dosage adjustment in hepatic impairment:
I.M., I.V.: Initial dosage should generally be ½ of the recommended dose; repeated dosing must be based on initial response rather than fixed intervals, but generally should be at least 6 hours apart

Nasal spray: Initial dose should not exceed 1 mg; a second dose may be given after 90-120 minutes

Administration Intranasal: Consider avoiding simultaneous intranasal migraine sprays; may want to separate by at least 30 minutes

Monitoring Parameters Pain relief, respiratory and mental status, blood pressure

Reference Range 0.7-1.5 ng/mL

Dosage Forms

Injection, solution, as tartrate [preservative free] (Stadol®): 1 mg/mL (1 mL); 2 mg/mL (1 mL, 2 mL)

Injection, solution, as tartrate [with preservative] (Stadol®): 2 mg/mL (10 mL)

Solution, intranasal, as tartrate [spray]: 10 mg/mL (2.5 mL) [14-15 doses]

- ◆ **Butorphanol Tartrate** see Butorphanol on page 261
- ◆ **Butyl Aminobenzoate, Tetracaine Hydrochloride, Benzocaine, and Benzalkonium Chloride** see Benzocaine, Butyl Aminobenzoate, Tetracaine, and Benzalkonium Chloride on page 207
- ◆ **B-Vex** see Brompheniramine on page 242
- ◆ **BW-430C** see Lamotrigine on page 974
- ◆ **BW524W91** see Emtricitabine on page 576
- ◆ **Byetta™** see Exenatide on page 676
- ◆ **C1H** see Alemtuzumab on page 63
- ◆ **C2B8** see Rituximab on page 1523
- ◆ **C2B8 Monoclonal Antibody** see Rituximab on page 1523
- ◆ **C7E3** see Abciximab on page 22
- ◆ **311C90** see Zolmitriptan on page 1822
- ◆ **C225** see Cetuximab on page 336
- ◆ **C-500-GR™ [OTC]** see Ascorbic Acid on page 156

Cabergoline (ca BER goe leen)

U.S. Brand Names Dostinex®

Canadian Brand Names Dostinex®

Pharmacologic Category Ergot Derivative

Use Treatment of hyperprolactinemic disorders, either idiopathic or due to pituitary adenomas

Unlabeled/Investigational Use Adjunct for the treatment of Parkinson's disease

Pregnancy Risk Factor B

Dosage Initial dose: Oral: 0.25 mg twice weekly; the dose may be increased by 0.25 mg twice weekly up to a maximum of 1 mg twice weekly according to the patient's serum prolactin level. Dosage increases should not occur more rapidly than every 4 weeks. Once a normal serum prolactin level is maintained for 6 months, the dose may be discontinued and prolactin levels monitored to determine if cabergoline is still required. The durability of efficacy beyond 24 months of therapy has not been established.

Elderly: No dosage recommendations suggested, but start at the low end of the dosage range

Additional Information Complete prescribing information for this medication should be consulted for additional detail.

Dosage Forms
Tablet: 0.5 mg
Dostinex®: 0.5 mg

- ◆ **Caduet®** see Amlodipine and Atorvastatin on page 105
- ◆ **CaEDTA** see Edetate Calcium Disodium on page 566
- ◆ **Caelyx® (Can)** see DOXOrubicin (Liposomal) on page 552
- ◆ **Caffeine, Acetaminophen, and Aspirin** see Acetaminophen, Aspirin, and Caffeine on page 34
- ◆ **Caffeine, Aspirin, and Acetaminophen** see Acetaminophen, Aspirin, and Caffeine on page 34
- ◆ **Caffeine, Hydrocodone, Chlorpheniramine, Phenylephrine, and Acetaminophen** see Hydrocodone, Chlorpheniramine, Phenylephrine, Acetaminophen, and Caffeine on page 852
- ◆ **Caffeine, Orphenadrine, and Aspirin** see Orphenadrine, Aspirin, and Caffeine on page 1273
- ◆ **Caffeine, Propoxyphene, and Aspirin** see Propoxyphene, Aspirin, and Caffeine on page 1446
- ◆ **Calan®** see Verapamil on page 1784
- ◆ **Calan® SR** see Verapamil on page 1784
- ◆ **Calcarb 600 [OTC]** see Calcium Carbonate on page 269
- ◆ **Calci-Chew® [OTC]** see Calcium Carbonate on page 269
- ◆ **Calciferol™** see Ergocalciferol on page 603
- ◆ **Calcijex®** see Calcitriol on page 266
- ◆ **Calcimar® (Can)** see Calcitonin on page 264
- ◆ **Calci-Mix® [OTC]** see Calcium Carbonate on page 269
- ◆ **Calcionate [OTC]** see Calcium Glubionate on page 273

Calcipotriene (kal si POE try een)

U.S. Brand Names Dovonex®
Pharmacologic Category Topical Skin Product; Vitamin D Analog
Use Treatment of plaque psoriasis
Pregnancy Risk Factor C
Dosage Topical: Adults: Apply in a thin film to the affected skin twice daily and rub in gently and completely
Additional Information Complete prescribing information for this medication should be consulted for additional detail.
Dosage Forms
Cream: 0.005% (60 g, 120 g)
Ointment: 0.005% (60 g, 120 g)
Solution, topical: 0.005% (60 mL)

Calcipotriene and Betamethasone
(kal si POE try een & bay ta METH a sone)

U.S. Brand Names Taclonex®
Canadian Brand Names Dovobet®
Index Terms Betamethasone Dipropionate and Calcipotriene Hydrate; Calcipotriol and Betamethasone Dipropionate
Pharmacologic Category Corticosteroid, Topical; Vitamin D Analog
Use Treatment of psoriasis vulgaris
Unlabeled/Investigational Use Treatment of corticosteroid-responsive dermatoses
Pregnancy Risk Factor C
Dosage Topical: Adults: Psoriasis vulgaris: Apply to affected area once daily for up to 4 weeks (maximum recommended dose: 100 g/week). Application to >30% of body surface area is not recommended.
  Dosing adjustment in renal impairment: Safety and efficacy have not been established with severe renal impairment.
  Dosing adjustment in hepatic impairment: Safety and efficacy have not been established with severe hepatic impairment.
Additional Information Complete prescribing information for this medication should be consulted for additional detail.
Dosage Forms [CAN] = Canadian brand name
Cream, topical:
  Dovobet® [CAN]: Calcipotriol 50 mcg and betamethasone 0.5 mg per gram (3 g, 30 g, 60 g, 100 g, 120 g) [not available in the U. S.]
Ointment, topical:
  Taclonex®: Calcipotriene 0.005% and betamethasone 0.064% (60 g)

♦ **Calcipotriol and Betamethasone Dipropionate** *see* Calcipotriene and Betamethasone *on page 264*
♦ **Calcite-500 (Can)** *see* Calcium Carbonate *on page 269*

Calcitonin (kal si TOE nin)

U.S. Brand Names Fortical®; Miacalcin®
Canadian Brand Names Apo-Calcitonin®; Calcimar®; Caltine®; Miacalcin® NS
Index Terms Calcitonin (Salmon)
Pharmacologic Category Antidote; Hormone
Use Calcitonin (salmon): Treatment of Paget's disease of bone (osteitis deformans); adjunctive therapy for hypercalcemia; postmenopausal osteoporosis
Pregnancy Risk Factor C
Pregnancy Implications Decreased birth weight was observed in animal studies. Calcitonin does not cross the placental barrier. There are no adequate and well-controlled studies in pregnant women.
Lactation Excretion in breast milk unknown/not recommended
Medication Safety Issues
Sound-alike/look-alike issues:
  Calcitonin may be confused with calcitriol
  Miacalcin® may be confused with Micatin®
Contraindications Hypersensitivity to calcitonin salmon or any component of the formulation
Warnings/Precautions A skin test should be performed prior to initiating therapy of calcitonin salmon in patients with suspected sensitivity; have epinephrine immediately available for a possible hypersensitivity reaction. A detailed skin testing protocol is available from the manufacturers. Temporarily withdraw use of nasal spray if ulceration of nasal mucosa occurs. Safety and efficacy have not been established in pediatric patients.
Adverse Reactions Unless otherwise noted, frequencies reported are with nasal spray.

>10%: Respiratory: Rhinitis (12%)
1% to 10%:
  Cardiovascular: Flushing (nasal spray: <1%; injection: 2% to 5%), angina (1% to 3%), hypertension (1% to 3%)
  Central nervous system: Depression (1% to 3%), dizziness (1% to 3%), fatigue (1% to 3%)
  Dermatologic: Erythematous rash (1% to 3%)
  Gastrointestinal: Abdominal pain (1% to 3%), constipation (1% to 3%), diarrhea (1% to 3%), dyspepsia (1% to 3%), nausea (injection: 10%; nasal spray: 1% to 3%)
  Genitourinary: Cystitis (1% to 3%)
  Hematologic: Lymphadenopathy (1% to 3%)
  Local: Injection site reactions (injection: 10%)

Neuromuscular & skeletal: Back pain (5%), arthrosis (1% to 3%), myalgia (1% to 3%), paresthesia (1% to 3%)

Ocular: Conjunctivitis (1% to 3%), lacrimation abnormality (1% to 3%)

Respiratory: Bronchospasm (1% to 3%), sinusitis (1% to 3%), upper respiratory tract infection (1% to 3%)

Miscellaneous: Flu-like syndrome (1% to 3%), infection (1% to 3%)

<1% (Limited to important or life-threatening): Agitation, allergic reactions, alopecia, anaphylaxis, anemia, anorexia, anxiety, appetite increased, arthritis, blurred vision, bronchitis, bundle branch block, cerebrovascular accident, cholelithiasis, cough, diaphoresis, dry mouth, dyspnea, earache, eczema, fever, flatulence, gastritis, goiter, hearing loss, hematuria, hepatitis, hyperthyroidism, insomnia, migraine, myocardial infarction, neuralgia, nocturia, palpitation, parosmia, periorbital edema, pharyngitis, pneumonia, polymyalgia rheumatica, pruritus, pyelonephritis, rash, renal calculus, skin ulceration, stiffness, tachycardia, taste perversion, thirst, thrombophlebitis, tinnitus, vertigo, vitreous floater, vomiting, weight gain

Overdosage/Toxicology Symptoms include nausea, vomiting, hypocalcemia, and tetany. Treatment should be symptom-directed and supportive.

Ethanol/Nutrition/Herb Interactions Ethanol: Avoid ethanol (may increase risk of osteoporosis).

Stability

Injection: Store under refrigeration at 2°C to 8°C (36°F to 46°F); protect from freezing. NS has been recommended for the dilution to prepare a skin test in patients with suspected sensitivity.

Nasal: Store unopened bottle under refrigeration at 2°C to 8°C (36°F to 46°F)

Fortical®: After opening, store for up to 30 days at 20°C to 25°C (68°F to 77°F); excursions permitted to 15°C to 30°C (59°F to 86°F). Store in upright position.

Miacalcin®: After opening, store for up to 35 days at room temperature of 15°C to 30°C (59°F to 86°F). Store in upright position.

Mechanism of Action Peptide sequence similar to human calcitonin; functionally antagonizes the effects of parathyroid hormone. Directly inhibits osteoclastic bone resorption; promotes the renal excretion of calcium, phosphate, sodium, magnesium, and potassium by decreasing tubular reabsorption; increases the jejunal secretion of water, sodium, potassium, and chloride

Pharmacodynamics/Kinetics

Hypercalcemia: I.M. or SubQ:

Onset of action: ~2 hours

Duration: 6-8 hours

Absorption: Nasal: ~3% of I.M. level (range: 0.3% to 31%)

Distribution: Does not cross placenta

Half-life elimination: SubQ: 1.2 hours; Nasal: 43 minutes

Time to peak: Nasal: ~30-40 minutes

Excretion: Urine (as inactive metabolites)

Dosage

Children: Dosage not established

Adults:

Paget's disease (Miacalcin®): I.M., SubQ: Initial: 100 units/day; maintenance: 50 units/day or 50-100 units every 1-3 days

Hypercalcemia (Miacalcin®): Initial: I.M., SubQ: 4 units/kg every 12 hours; may increase up to 8 units/kg every 12 hours to a maximum of every 6 hours

Postmenopausal osteoporosis:

I.M., SubQ: Miacalcin®: 100 units/every other day

Intranasal: Fortical®, Miacalcin®: 200 units (1 spray)/day

Dietary Considerations Adequate vitamin D and calcium intake is essential for preventing/treating osteoporosis. Patients with Paget's disease and hypercalcemia should follow a low calcium diet as prescribed.

Administration

Injection solution: Administer I.M. or SubQ; intramuscular route is recommended over the subcutaneous route when the volume of calcitonin to be injected exceeds 2 mL.

Nasal spray: Before first use, allow bottle to reach room temperature, then prime pump by releasing at least 5 sprays until full spray is produced. To administer, place nozzle into nostril with head in upright position. Alternate nostrils daily. Do not prime pump before each daily use. Discard after 30 doses.

Monitoring Parameters Serum electrolytes and calcium; alkaline phosphatase and 24-hour urine collection for hydroxyproline excretion (Paget's disease), bone mineral density

Nasal formulation: Visualization of nasal mucosa, turbinate, septum, and mucosal blood vessels)

Reference Range Therapeutic: <19 pg/mL (SI: 19 ng/L) basal, depending on the assay

Dosage Forms

Injection, solution, calcitonin-salmon: (Miacalcin®): 200 int. units/mL (2 mL)

Solution, nasal spray, calcitonin-salmon:

Fortical®: 200 int. units/0.09 mL (3.7 mL) [rDNA origin; contains benzyl alcohol; delivers 30 doses, 200 units/actuation]

Miacalcin®: 200 int. units/0.09 mL (3.7 mL) [contains benzalkonium chloride; delivers 30 doses, 200 units/actuation]

◆ **Calcitonin (Salmon)** see Calcitonin on page 264

◆ **Cal Citrate® 250 [OTC]** see Calcium Citrate on page 272

Calcitriol (kal si TRYE ole)

U.S. Brand Names Calcijex®; Rocaltrol®

Canadian Brand Names Calcijex®; Rocaltrol®

Index Terms 1,25 Dihydroxycholecalciferol

Pharmacologic Category Vitamin D Analog

Use Management of hypocalcemia in patients on chronic renal dialysis; management of secondary hyperparathyroidism in moderate-to-severe chronic renal failure; management of hypocalcemia in hypoparathyroidism and pseudohypoparathyroidism

Unlabeled/Investigational Use Decrease severity of psoriatic lesions in psoriatic vulgaris; vitamin D-resistant rickets

Pregnancy Risk Factor C (manufacturer); A/D (dose exceeding RDA recommendation) (expert analysis)

Lactation Enters breast milk/not recommended

Medication Safety Issues
Sound-alike/look-alike issues:
Calcitriol may be confused with calcifediol, Calciferol®, calcitonin
Dosage is expressed in mcg (micrograms), **not** mg (milligrams); rare cases of acute overdose have been reported

Contraindications Hypercalcemia; vitamin D toxicity; abnormal sensitivity to the effects of vitamin D; pregnancy (dose exceeding RDA)

Warnings/Precautions Adequate dietary (supplemental) calcium is necessary for clinical response to vitamin D. Monitor serum calcium and phosphate concentrations. Avoid hypercalcemia; calcium-phosphate product (serum calcium times phosphorus) must not exceed 70. Immobilization or excessive dosage may increase risk of hypercalcemia and/or hypercalciuria. Maintain adequate hydration. Use caution in patients with malabsorption syndromes (efficacy may be limited and/or response may be unpredictable).

Adverse Reactions
>10%: Endocrine & metabolic: Hypercalcemia (33%)
Frequency not defined:
Cardiovascular: Cardiac arrhythmia, hyper-/hypotension
Central nervous system: Headache, irritability, seizure (rare), somnolence, psychosis
Dermatologic: Pruritus, erythema multiforme
Endocrine & metabolic: Hypermagnesemia, hyperphosphatemia, polydipsia
Gastrointestinal: Anorexia, constipation, metallic taste, nausea, pancreatitis, vomiting, xerostomia
Hepatic: LFTs increased
Neuromuscular & skeletal: Bone pain, myalgia, dystrophy, soft tissue calcification
Ocular: Conjunctivitis, photophobia
Renal: Polyuria

Overdosage/Toxicology Symptoms of overdose include hypercalcemia, hyperphosphatemia, and hypercalciuria. Following withdrawal of the drug, treatment consists of bedrest, liberal intake of fluids, reduced calcium intake, and cathartic administration. Severe hypercalcemia requires I.V. hydration and forced diuresis. Urine output should be monitored and maintained at >3 mL/kg/hour during the acute treatment phase. I.V. saline can quickly and significantly increase excretion of calcium into urine. Calcitonin, cholestyramine, prednisone, sodium EDTA, bisphosphonates, and mithramycin have all been used successfully to treat the more resistant cases of vitamin D-induced. Correction of hyperphosphatemia may be necessary.

Drug Interactions
Cytochrome P450 Effect: Induces CYP3A4 (weak)
Increased Effect/Toxicity: Risk of hypercalcemia with thiazide diuretics. Risk of hypermagnesemia with magnesium-containing antacids. Risk of digoxin toxicity may be increased (if hypercalcemia occurs).
Decreased Effect: Cholestyramine and colestipol decrease absorption/effect of calcitriol. Thiazide diuretics and corticosteroids may reduce the effect of calcitriol.

Stability Store in tight, light-resistant container; calcitriol degrades upon prolonged exposure to light.

Mechanism of Action Promotes absorption of calcium in the intestines and retention at the kidneys thereby increasing calcium levels in the serum; decreases excessive serum phosphatase levels, parathyroid hormone levels, and decreases bone resorption; increases renal tubule phosphate resorption

Pharmacodynamics/Kinetics
Onset of action: ~2-6 hours
Duration: 3-5 days
Absorption: Oral: Rapid
Protein binding: 99.9%
Metabolism: Primarily to 1,24,25-trihydroxycholecalciferol and 1,24,25-trihydroxy ergocalciferol
Half-life elimination: 3-8 hours
Excretion: Primarily feces; urine (4% to 6%)

Dosage Individualize dosage to maintain calcium levels of 9-10 mg/dL
Renal failure:
Children:
Oral: 0.25-2 mcg/day have been used (with hemodialysis); 0.014-0.041 mcg/kg/day (not receiving hemodialysis); increases should be made at 4- to 8-week intervals
I.V.: 0.01-0.05 mcg/kg 3 times/week if undergoing hemodialysis
Adults:
Oral: 0.25 mcg/day or every other day (may require 0.5-1 mcg/day); increases should be made at 4- to 8-week intervals
I.V.: 0.5 mcg/day 3 times/week (may require from 0.5-3 mcg/day given 3 times/week) if undergoing hemodialysis

Hypoparathyroidism/pseudohypoparathyroidism: Oral (evaluate dosage at 2- to 4-week intervals):

Children:

    <1 year: 0.04-0.08 mcg/kg once daily

    1-5 years: 0.25-0.75 mcg once daily

    Children ≥6 years and Adults: 0.5-2 mcg once daily

Vitamin D-dependent rickets: Children and Adults: Oral: 1 mcg once daily

Vitamin D-resistant rickets (familial hypophosphatemia): Children and Adults: Oral: Initial: 0.015-0.02 mcg/kg once daily; maintenance: 0.03-0.06 mcg/kg once daily; maximum dose: 2 mcg once daily

Hypocalcemia in premature infants: Oral: 1 mcg once daily for 5 days

Hypocalcemic tetany in premature infants: I.V.: 0.05 mcg/kg once daily for 5-12 days

Elderly: No dosage recommendations, but start at the lower end of the dosage range

Dosage adjustment for toxicity: Hypercalcemia: Adults:

Dialysis or hypoparathyroidism: Discontinue calcitriol and calcium supplements; initiate low-calcium diet. In dialysis patients with persistent hypercalcemia, may dialyze against calcium-free dialysate.

Predialysis:

Discontinue or reduce calcium supplements.

If taking calcitriol 0.5 mcg once daily, reduce to 0.25 mcg once daily.

If taking calcitriol 0.25 mcg once daily, discontinue until serum calcium normalizes. Restart at 0.25 mcg every other day.

Dietary Considerations May be taken without regard to food. Give with meals to reduce GI problems.

Administration May be administered without regard to food. Give with meals to reduce GI problems. May be administered as a bolus dose I.V. through the catheter at the end of hemodialysis.

Monitoring Parameters Monitor symptoms of hypercalcemia (weakness, fatigue, somnolence, headache, anorexia, dry mouth, metallic taste, nausea, vomiting, cramps, diarrhea, muscle pain, bone pain, and irritability). If patient becomes hypercalcemic on therapy, check serum calcium daily until normalized, then twice weekly on new dose. If hypercalcemia persists in predialysis patient, monitor PTH.

Reference Range Calcium (serum): 9-10 mg/dL (4.5-5 mEq/L) but do not include the I.V. dosages; phosphate: 2.5-5 mg/dL

Test Interactions Increased calcium, cholesterol, magnesium, BUN, AST, ALT, calcium (S), cholesterol (S); decreased alkaline phosphatase

Dosage Forms

Capsule (Rocaltrol®): 0.25 mcg, 0.5 mcg [each strength contains coconut oil]

Injection, solution: 1 mcg/mL (1 mL); 2 mcg/mL (2 mL)

Calcijex®: 1 mcg/mL (1 mL)

Solution, oral (Rocaltrol®): 1 mcg/mL (15 mL) [contains palm seed oil]

Calcium Acetate (KAL see um AS e tate)

U.S. Brand Names PhosLo®

Pharmacologic Category Antidote; Calcium Salt; Phosphate Binder

Use

Oral: Control of hyperphosphatemia in end-stage renal failure; does not promote aluminum absorption

I.V.: Calcium supplementation in parenteral nutrition therapy

Pregnancy Risk Factor C

Medication Safety Issues

Sound-alike/look-alike issues:

PhosLo® may be confused with Phos-Flur®, ProSom™

Contraindications Hypersensitivity to any component of the formulation; hypercalcemia, renal calculi

Warnings/Precautions Calcium absorption is impaired in achlorhydria (common in elderly - try alternate salt, administer with food); administration is followed by increased gastric acid secretion within 2 hours of administration. While hypercalcemia and hypercalciuria may result when therapeutic replacement amounts are given for prolonged periods, they are most likely to occur in hypoparathyroid patients receiving high doses of vitamin D.

Adverse Reactions

Mild hypercalcemia (calcium: >10.5 mg/dL to ≤12 mg/dL) may be asymptomatic or manifest itself as constipation, anorexia, nausea, and vomiting

More severe hypercalcemia (calcium: >12 mg/dL) is associated with confusion, delirium, stupor, and coma

Postmarketing and/or case reports: Pruritus, allergic reaction

Overdosage/Toxicology Acute single ingestions of calcium salts may produce mild gastrointestinal distress, but hypercalcemia or other toxic manifestations are extremely unlikely. Treatment is supportive.

Drug Interactions

Increased Effect/Toxicity: High doses of calcium with thiazide diuretics may result in milk-alkali syndrome and hypercalcemia; monitor response. Calcium salts may decrease T_4 absorption; separate dose from levothyroxine by at least 4 hours. Calcium acetate may potentiate digoxin toxicity.

Decreased Effect: Absorption of tetracycline, atenolol (and potentially other beta-blockers), iron, quinolone antibiotics, alendronate, sodium fluoride, and zinc absorption may be significantly decreased; space administration times. Effects of calcium channel blockers (eg, verapamil) effects may be diminished. Polystyrene sulfonate's potassium-binding ability may be reduced; avoid concurrent administration.

Mechanism of Action Combines with dietary phosphate to form insoluble calcium phosphate which is excreted in feces

(Continued)

Calcium Acetate *(Continued)*

Pharmacodynamics/Kinetics

Absorption: Requires vitamin D; minimal unless chronic, high doses are given; calcium is absorbed in soluble, ionized form; solubility of calcium is increased in an acid environment

Distribution: Crosses placenta; enters breast milk

Excretion: Primarily feces (as unabsorbed calcium); urine (20%)

Dosage

Dietary Reference Intake:

0-6 months: 210 mg/day

7-12 months: 270 mg/day

1-3 years: 500 mg/day

4-8 years: 800 mg/day

Adults, Male/Female:

9-18 years: 1300 mg/day

19-50 years: 1000 mg/day

≥51 years: 1200 mg/day

Female: Pregnancy/Lactating: Same as for Adults, Male/Female

Oral: Adults, on dialysis: Initial: 1334 mg with each meal, can be increased gradually to bring the serum phosphate value to <6 mg/dL as long as hypercalcemia does not develop (usual dose: 2001-2868 mg calcium acetate with each meal); do not give additional calcium supplements

I.V.: Dose is dependent on the requirements of the individual patient; in central venous total parental nutrition (TPN), calcium is administered at a concentration of 5 mEq (10 mL)/L of TPN solution; the additive maintenance dose in neonatal TPN is 0.5 mEq calcium/kg/day (1mL/kg/day)

Neonates: 70-200 mg/kg/day

Infants and Children: 70-150 mg/kg/day

Adolescents: 18-35 mg/kg/day

Dietary Considerations Oral dosage forms must be administered with meals to be effective.

Administration Administer with meals.

Monitoring Parameters Serum calcium, serum phosphate; for control of hypophosphatemia, serum calcium times phosphate should not exceed 66

Reference Range

Serum calcium: 8.4-10.2 mg/dL

Due to a poor correlation between the serum ionized calcium (free) and total serum calcium, particularly in states of low albumin or acid/base imbalances, direct measurement of ionized calcium is recommended.

In low albumin states, the corrected **total** serum calcium may be estimated by the following equation (assuming a normal albumin of 4 g/dL).

Corrected total calcium = total serum calcium + 0.8 (4.0 - measured serum albumin)

or

Corrected calcium = measured calcium - measured albumin + 4.0

Additional Information Calcium acetate binds to phosphorus in the GI tract better than other calcium salts due to its lower solubility and subsequent reduced absorption and increased formation of calcium phosphate.

12.7 mEq calcium/g; 250 mg/g elemental calcium (25% elemental calcium)

Dosage Forms [DSC] = Discontinued product. **Note:** Elemental calcium listed in brackets:

Gelcap (PhosLo®): 667 mg [169 mg]

Injection, solution: 0.5 mEq/mL (10 mL, 50 mL, 100 mL)

Tablet (PhosLo®): 667 mg [169 mg] [DSC]

♦ **Calcium Acetate and Aluminum Sulfate** *see* Aluminum Sulfate and Calcium Acetate *on page 86*

♦ **Calcium Acetylhomotaurinate** *see* Acamprosate *on page 24*

♦ **Calcium and Risedronate** *see* Risedronate and Calcium *on page 1517*

Calcium and Vitamin D *(KAL see um & VYE ta min dee)*

U.S. Brand Names Cal-CYUM [OTC]; Caltrate® 600+D [OTC]; Caltrate® 600+ Soy™ [OTC]; Caltrate® ColonHealth™ [OTC]; Chew-Cal [OTC]; Liqua-Cal [OTC]; Os-Cal® 500+D [OTC]; Oysco 500+D [OTC]; Oysco D [OTC]; Oyst-Cal-D [OTC]; Oyst-Cal-D 500 [OTC]

Index Terms Vitamin D and Calcium Carbonate

Pharmacologic Category Calcium Salt; Electrolyte Supplement, Oral; Vitamin, Fat Soluble

Use Dietary supplement, antacid

Dosage Oral: Adults: Refer to individual monographs for dietary reference intake.

Dosage adjustment in renal impairment: Use caution in severe renal impairment

Additional Information Complete prescribing information for this medication should be consulted for additional detail.

Dosage Forms

Capsule, softgel: Calcium 500 mg and vitamin D 500 int. units; calcium 600 mg and vitamin D 100 int. units; calcium 600 mg and vitamin D 200 int. units

Liqua-Cal: Calcium 600 mg and vitamin D 200 int. units [contains beeswax, lecithin, and soybean oil]

Tablet: Calcium 250 mg and vitamin D 125 int. units; calcium 500 mg and vitamin D 125 int. units; calcium 500 mg and vitamin D 200 int. units; calcium 600 mg and vitamin D 125 int. units; calcium 600 mg and vitamin D 200 int. units

Caltrate® 600+D: Calcium 600 mg and vitamin D 200 int. units [contains soybean oil]

Caltrate® 600+ Soy™: Calcium 600 mg and vitamin D 200 int. units [contains soy isoflavones 25 mg]

Caltrate® ColonHealth™: Calcium 600 mg and vitamin D 200 int. units [contains soybean oil]

Oysco D: Calcium 250 mg and vitamin D 125 int. units

Oysco 500+D: Calcium 500 mg and vitamin D 200 int. units [contains tartrazine]

Oyst-Cal-D: Calcium 250 mg and vitamin D 125 int. units [sodium free, sugar free; contains tartrazine]
Oyst-Cal-D 500: Calcium 500 mg and vitamin D 200 int. units [sodium free, sugar free; contains tartrazine]
Tablet, chewable: Calcium 500 mg and vitamin D 100 int. units; Calcium 600 mg and vitamin D 400 int. units
Os-Cal® 500+D: Calcium 500 mg and vitamin D 400 int. units [sugar free; contains phenylalanine; light lemon flavor]
Wafer, chewable:
Cal-CYUM: Calcium 519 mg and vitamin D 150 int. units (50s) [dye free; vanilla flavor]
Chew-Cal: Calcium 333 mg and vitamin D 40 int. units (100s, 250s)

Calcium Carbonate (KAL see um KAR bun ate)

U.S. Brand Names Alcalak [OTC]; Alka-Mints® [OTC]; Calcarb 600 [OTC]; Calci-Chew® [OTC]; Calci-Mix® [OTC]; Cal-Gest [OTC]; Cal-Mint [OTC]; Caltrate® 600 [OTC]; Children's Pepto [OTC]; Chooz® [OTC]; Florical® [OTC]; Maalox® Regular Chewable [OTC]; Mylanta® Children's [OTC]; Nephro-Calci® [OTC]; Nutralox® [OTC]; Os-Cal® 500 [OTC] [DSC]; Oysco 500 [OTC]; Oyst-Cal 500 [OTC]; Rolaids® Softchews [OTC]; Titralac™ [OTC]; Tums® [OTC]; Tums® E-X [OTC]; Tums® Extra Strength Sugar Free [OTC]; Tums® Smoothies™ [OTC]; Tums® Ultra [OTC]

Canadian Brand Names Apo-Cal®; Calcite-500; Caltrate®; Caltrate® Select; Os-Cal®

Pharmacologic Category Antacid; Antidote; Calcium Salt; Electrolyte Supplement, Oral

Use As an antacid; treatment and prevention of calcium deficiency or hyperphosphatemia (eg, osteoporosis, osteomalacia, mild/moderate renal insufficiency, hypoparathyroidism, postmenopausal osteoporosis, rickets); has been used to bind phosphate

Pregnancy Implications Available evidence suggests safe use during pregnancy and breast-feeding.

Medication Safety Issues
Sound-alike/look-alike issues:
Florical® may be confused with Fiorinal®
Mylanta® may be confused with Mynatal®
Nephro-Calci® may be confused with Nephrocaps®
Os-Cal® may be confused with Asacol®

International Issues:
Remegel® [Great Britain, Ireland, Italy] may be confused with Renagel® which is a brand name for sevelamer in the U.S.

Contraindications Hypercalcemia, renal calculi, hypophosphatemia; patients with suspected digoxin toxicity

Warnings/Precautions Calcium carbonate absorption is impaired in achlorhydria (common in elderly - use alternate salt, administer with food). Administration is followed by increased gastric acid secretion within 2 hours of administration. While hypercalcemia and hypercalciuria may result when therapeutic replacement amounts are given for prolonged periods, they are most likely to occur in hypoparathyroid patients receiving high doses of vitamin D.

Adverse Reactions Well tolerated
1% to 10%:
Central nervous system: Headache
Endocrine & metabolic: Hypophosphatemia, hypercalcemia
Gastrointestinal: Constipation, laxative effect, acid rebound, nausea, vomiting, anorexia, abdominal pain, xerostomia, flatulence
Miscellaneous: Milk-alkali syndrome with very high, chronic dosing and/or renal failure (headache, nausea, irritability, and weakness or alkalosis, hypercalcemia, renal impairment)

Overdosage/Toxicology Acute single ingestions of calcium salts may produce mild gastrointestinal distress, but hypercalcemia or other toxic manifestations are extremely unlikely. Treatment is supportive.

Drug Interactions
Increased Effect/Toxicity: High doses of calcium with thiazide diuretics may result in milk-alkali syndrome and hypercalcemia; monitor response. Calcium salts may decrease T_4 absorption; separate dose from levothyroxine by at least 4 hours. Calcium acetate may potentiate digoxin toxicity.
Decreased Effect: Absorption of tetracycline, atenolol (and potentially other beta-blockers), iron, quinolone antibiotics, alendronate, sodium fluoride, and zinc absorption may be significantly decreased; space administration times. Effects of calcium channel blockers (eg, verapamil) effects may be diminished. Polystyrene sulfonate's potassium-binding ability may be reduced; avoid concurrent administration.

Ethanol/Nutrition/Herb Interactions
Ethanol: Avoid ethanol (may increase risk of osteoporosis).
Food: Food may increase calcium absorption. Calcium may decrease iron absorption. Bran, foods high in oxalates, or whole grain cereals may decrease calcium absorption.

Mechanism of Action As dietary supplement, used to prevent or treat negative calcium balance; in osteoporosis, it helps to prevent or decrease the rate of bone loss. The calcium in calcium salts moderates nerve and muscle performance and allows normal cardiac function. Also used to treat hyperphosphatemia in patients with advanced renal insufficiency by combining with dietary phosphate to form insoluble calcium phosphate, which is excreted in feces. Calcium salts as antacids neutralize gastric acidity resulting in increased gastric and duodenal bulb pH; they additionally inhibit proteolytic activity of peptic if the pH is increased >4 and increase lower esophageal sphincter tone.

Pharmacodynamics/Kinetics
Absorption: Requires vitamin D; minimal unless chronic, high doses are given; calcium is absorbed in soluble, ionized form; solubility of calcium is increased in an acid environment
Distribution: Crosses placenta; enters breast milk
Excretion: Primarily feces (as unabsorbed calcium); urine (20%)
(Continued)

Calcium Carbonate *(Continued)*

Dosage Oral (dosage is in terms of elemental calcium):
Dietary Reference Intake:
0-6 months: 210 mg/day
7-12 months: 270 mg/day
1-3 years: 500 mg/day
4-8 years: 800 mg/day
Adults, Male/Female:
9-18 years: 1300 mg/day
19-50 years: 1000 mg/day
≥51 years: 1200 mg/day
Female: Pregnancy/Lactating: Same as for Adults, Male/Female

Hypocalcemia (dose depends on clinical condition and serum calcium level): Dose expressed in mg of **elemental calcium**
Neonates: 50-150 mg/kg/day in 4-6 divided doses; not to exceed 1 g/day
Children: 45-65 mg/kg/day in 4 divided doses
Adults: 1-2 g or more/day in 3-4 divided doses

Antacid:
Children 2-5 years (24-47 lb): Elemental calcium 161 mg as needed; maximum 483 mg per 24 hours
Children 6-11 years (48-95 lb): Elemental calcium 322 mg as needed; maximum: 966 mg per 24 hours
Adults: Dosage based on acid-neutralizing capacity of specific product; generally, 1-2 tablets or 5-10 mL every 2 hours; maximum: 7000 mg calcium carbonate per 24 hours; specific product labeling should be consulted

Dietary supplementation: Adults: 500 mg to 2 g divided 2-4 times/day
Osteoporosis: Adults >51 years: 1200 mg/day
Dosing adjustment in renal impairment: Cl_{cr} <25 mL/minute: Dosage adjustments may be necessary depending on the serum calcium levels

Dietary Considerations As a dietary supplement, should be given with meals to increase absorption. May decrease iron absorption, so should be administered 1-2 hours before or after iron supplementation. Limit intake of bran, foods high in oxalates, or whole grain cereals which may decrease calcium absorption.

Maalox® Quick Dissolve 600 mg tablet contains phenylalanine 0.5 mg/tablet.
Tums® Extra Strength Sugar Free 750 mg tablet contains phenylalanine <1 mg/tablet.
Titralac™ 420 mg tablet and Titralac™ Extra Strength 750 mg tablet each contain sodium 1.1 mg/tablet.

Reference Range
Serum calcium: 8.4-10.2 mg/dL: Monitor plasma calcium levels if using calcium salts as electrolyte supplements for deficiency
Due to a poor correlation between the serum ionized calcium (free) and total serum calcium, particularly in states of low albumin or acid/base imbalances, direct measurement of ionized calcium is recommended
In low albumin states, the corrected **total** serum calcium may be estimated by:
Corrected total calcium = total serum calcium + 0.8 (4.0 - measured serum albumin)

Test Interactions Increased calcium (S); decreased magnesium

Additional Information 20 mEq calcium/g; 400 mg elemental calcium/g calcium carbonate (40% elemental calcium)

Dosage Forms
[DSC] = Discontinued product
Capsule:
Calci-Mix®: 1250 mg [equivalent to elemental calcium 500 mg]
Florical®: 364 mg [equivalent to elemental calcium 145.6 mg; contains sodium fluoride 3.75 mg]
Gum, chewing: 250 mg (30s)
Chooz®: 500 mg [equivalent to elemental calcium 200 mg; mint flavor]
Powder: 4000 mg/teaspoonful (480 g) [equivalent to 1600 mg elemental calcium/teaspoonful]
Suspension, oral: 1250 mg/5 mL (5 mL, 500 mL) [equivalent to elemental calcium 500 mg/5 mL; mint flavor]
Tablet: 1250 mg [equivalent to elemental calcium 500 mg]; 1500 mg [equivalent to elemental calcium 600 mg]
Calcarb 600, Caltrate® 600, Nephro-Calci®: 1500 mg [equivalent to elemental calcium 600 mg]
Florical®: 364 mg [equivalent to elemental calcium 145.6 mg; contains sodium fluoride 8.3 mg]
Os-Cal® 500: 1250 mg [equivalent to elemental calcium 500 mg; contains tartrazine] [DSC]
Oysco 500, Oyst-Cal 500: 1250 mg [equivalent to elemental calcium 500 mg]
Tablet, chewable: 500 mg [equivalent to elemental calcium 200 mg]; 650 mg [equivalent to elemental calcium 260 mg]; 750 mg [equivalent to elemental calcium 300 mg]
Alcalak: 420 mg [equivalent to elemental calcium 168 mg; mint flavor]
Alka-Mints®: 850 mg [equivalent to elemental calcium 340 mg; spearmint flavor]
Cal-Gest: 500 mg [equivalent to elemental calcium 200 mg; assorted flavors]
Calci-Chew®: 1250 mg [equivalent to elemental calcium 500 mg; cherry, lemon, and orange flavors]
Cal-Mint: 650 mg [equivalent to elemental calcium 260 mg; mint flavor]
Children's Pepto: 400 mg [equivalent to elemental calcium 161 mg; bubble gum or watermelon flavors]
Maalox® Regular: 600 mg [equivalent to elemental calcium 222 mg; contains phenylalanine 0.5 mg/tablet; lemon flavor]
Mylanta® Children's: 400 mg [equivalent to elemental calcium 160 mg; bubble gum flavor]
Nutralox®: 420 mg [equivalent to elemental calcium 168 mg; sugar free; mint flavor]
Os-Cal® 500: 1250 mg [equivalent to elemental calcium 500 mg; Bavarian cream flavor] [DSC]

Titralac™: 420 mg [equivalent to elemental calcium 168 mg; sugar free; contains sodium 1.1 mg/tablet; spearmint flavor]

Tums®: 500 mg [equivalent to elemental calcium 200 mg; contains tartrazine; assorted fruit and peppermint flavors]

Tums® E-X: 750 mg [equivalent to elemental calcium 300 mg; contains tartrazine; assorted fruit, cool relief mint, fresh blend, tropical assorted fruit, wintergreen, and assorted berry flavors]

Tums® Extra Strength Sugar Free: 750 mg [equivalent to elemental calcium 300 mg; sugar free; contains phenylalanine <1 mg/tablet; orange cream flavor]

Tums® Smoothies™: 750 mg [equivalent to elemental calcium 300 mg; contains tartrazine; assorted fruit, assorted tropical fruit, peppermint flavors]

Tums® Ultra®: 1000 mg [equivalent to elemental calcium 400 mg; contains tartrazine; assorted berry, assorted fruit, assorted tropical fruit, peppermint, and spearmint flavors]

Tablet, softchew:

Rolaids®: 1177 mg [equivalent to elemental calcium 471 mg; contains coconut oil and soy lecithin; vanilla creme and wild cherry flavors]

Calcium Carbonate and Magnesium Hydroxide
(KAL see um KAR bun ate & mag NEE zhum hye DROKS ide)

U.S. Brand Names Mi-Acid™ Double Strength [OTC]; Mylanta® Gelcaps® [OTC]; Mylanta® Supreme [OTC]; Mylanta® Ultra [OTC]; Rolaids® [OTC]; Rolaids® Extra Strength [OTC]

Index Terms Magnesium Hydroxide and Calcium Carbonate

Pharmacologic Category Antacid

Use Hyperacidity

Medication Safety Issues

Sound-alike/look-alike issues:

Mylanta® may be confused with Mynatal®

Dosage Adults: Oral: 2-4 tablets between meals, at bedtime, or as directed by healthcare provider

Additional Information Complete prescribing information for this medication should be consulted for additional detail.

Dosage Forms

Gelcap (Mylanta® Gelcaps®): Calcium carbonate 550 mg and magnesium hydroxide 125 mg

Liquid (Mylanta® Supreme): Calcium carbonate 400 mg and magnesium hydroxide 135 mg per 5 mL (360 mL, 720 mL) [cherry flavor]

Tablet, chewable:

Mi-Acid™ Double Strength: Calcium carbonate 700 mg and magnesium hydroxide 300 mg

Mylanta® Ultra: Calcium carbonate 700 mg and magnesium hydroxide 300 mg [cherry créme and cool mint flavors]

Rolaids®: Calcium carbonate 550 mg and magnesium hydroxide 110 mg [sodium free; contains elemental calcium 220 mg and elemental magnesium 45 mg; original (peppermint), cherry, and spearmint flavors]

Rolaids® Extra Strength: Calcium carbonate 675 mg and magnesium hydroxide 135 mg [sodium free; contains elemental calcium 271 mg and elemental magnesium 56 mg, fruit flavor contains tartrazine; cool strawberry, fresh mint, fruit, and tropical fruit punch flavors]

♦ **Calcium Carbonate, Magnesium Hydroxide, and Famotidine** see Famotidine, Calcium Carbonate, and Magnesium Hydroxide on page 685

Calcium Chloride (KAL see um KLOR ide)

Pharmacologic Category Calcium Salt; Electrolyte Supplement, Parenteral

Use Cardiac resuscitation when epinephrine fails to improve myocardial contractions, cardiac disturbances of hyperkalemia, hypocalcemia; emergent treatment of hypocalcemic tetany; treatment of hypermagnesemia

Unlabeled/Investigational Use Calcium channel blocker overdose

Pregnancy Risk Factor C

Contraindications In ventricular fibrillation during cardiac resuscitation, hypercalcemia, and in patients with risk of digitalis toxicity, renal or cardiac disease; not recommended in treatment of asystole and electromechanical dissociation; patients with suspected digoxin toxicity

Warnings/Precautions Avoid too rapid I.V. administration (<1 mL/minute) and extravasation. Use with caution in digitalized patients, respiratory failure, or acidosis. Hypercalcemia may occur in patients with renal failure, and frequent determination of serum calcium is necessary. Avoid metabolic acidosis (ie, administer only 2-3 days then change to another calcium salt).

Adverse Reactions <1% (Limited to important or life-threatening): Bradycardia, cardiac arrhythmia, coma, serum magnesium decreased, serum amylase increased, erythema, hypercalcemia, hypercalciuria, hypotension, lethargy, mania, muscle weakness, syncope, tissue necrosis, vasodilation, ventricular fibrillation

Overdosage/Toxicology Symptoms include lethargy, nausea, vomiting, and coma. Following withdrawal of the drug, treatment consists of bedrest, liberal fluid intake, reduced calcium intake, and cathartic administration. Severe hypercalcemia requires I.V. hydration and forced diuresis. Urine output should be monitored and maintained at >3 mL/kg/hour. I.V. saline and natriuretic agents (eg, furosemide) can quickly and significantly increase excretion of calcium.

Drug Interactions

Increased Effect/Toxicity: High doses of calcium with thiazide diuretics may result in milk-alkali syndrome and hypercalcemia; monitor response. Calcium may potentiate digoxin toxicity.

Decreased Effect: Effects of calcium channel blockers (eg, verapamil) effects may be diminished.

(Continued)

Calcium Chloride *(Continued)*

Stability

Do not refrigerate solutions; IVPB solutions/I.V. infusion solutions are stable for 24 hours at room temperature.

Maximum concentration in parenteral nutrition solutions: 15 mEq/L of calcium and 30 mmol/L of phosphate.

Mechanism of Action Moderates nerve and muscle performance via action potential excitation threshold regulation

Pharmacodynamics/Kinetics

Distribution: Crosses placenta; enters breast milk

Excretion: Primarily feces (as unabsorbed calcium); urine (20%)

Dosage Note: Calcium chloride has 3 times more elemental calcium than calcium gluconate. Calcium chloride is 27% elemental calcium; calcium gluconate is 9% elemental calcium. One gram of calcium chloride is equal to 270 mg of elemental calcium; one gram of calcium gluconate is equal to 90 mg of elemental calcium. Dosages are expressed in terms of the calcium chloride salt based on a solution concentration of 100 mg/mL (10%) containing 1.4 mEq (27.3 mg)/mL elemental calcium.

Cardiac arrest in the presence of hyperkalemia or hypocalcemia, magnesium toxicity: I.V.:
Infants and Children: 20 mg/kg; may repeat in 10 minutes if necessary
Adolescents and Adults: 2-4 mg/kg, repeated every 10 minutes if necessary

Calcium channel blocker overdose (unlabeled use): Adults:
I.V.: 1 g every 15-20 minutes (total of 4 doses) **or** 1 g every 2-3 minutes until clinical effect is achieved
I.V. infusion: 0.2-0.4 mL/kg/hour

Hypocalcemia: I.V.:
Children (manufacturer's recommendation): 2.7-5 mg/kg/dose every 4-6 hours
Alternative pediatric dosing: Infants and Children: 10-20 mg/kg/dose, repeat every 4-6 hours if needed
Adults: 500 mg to 1 g/dose repeated every 4-6 hours if needed

Hypocalcemic tetany: I.V.:
Neonates: Divided doses totaling approximately 170 mg/kg/24 hours
Infants and Children: 10 mg/kg over 5-10 minutes; may repeat after 6-8 hours or follow with an infusion with a maximum dose of 200 mg/kg/day; alternatively, higher doses of 35-50 mg/kg/dose repeated every 6-8 hours have been used
Adults: 1 g over 10-30 minutes; may repeat after 6 hours

Hypocalcemia secondary to citrated blood transfusion: I.V.: **Note:** Routine administration of calcium, in the absence of signs/symptoms of hypocalcemia, is generally not recommended. A number of recommendations have been published seeking to address potential hypocalcemia during massive transfusion of citrated blood; however, many practitioners recommend replacement only as guided by clinical evidence of hypocalcemia and/or serial monitoring of ionized calcium.
Neonates, Infants, and Children: Give 32 mg (0.45 mEq elemental calcium) for each 100 mL citrated blood infused
Adults: 200-500 mg per 500 mL of citrated blood (infused into another vein)

Dosing adjustment in renal impairment: Cl_{cr} <25 mL/minute: Dosage adjustments may be necessary depending on the serum calcium levels

Administration For I.V. administration only; avoid extravasation. Administer slowly (0.7-1.8 mEq per minute or between 0.5 mL and 1.5 mL per minute of calcium chloride 10%); for I.V. infusion, dilute to a maximum concentration of 20 mg/mL and infuse over 1 hour or no greater than 45-90 mg/kg/hour (0.6-1.2 mEq/kg/hour); administration via a central or deep vein is preferred; do not use scalp, small hand or foot veins for I.V. administration since severe necrosis and sloughing may occur. Monitor ECG if calcium is infused faster than 2.5 mEq/minute; **stop the infusion if the patient complains of pain or discomfort.** Warm to body temperature. If used as intraventricular injection, inject into ventricular cavity - not myocardium; **do not infuse calcium chloride in the same I.V. line as phosphate-containing solutions.**

Monitoring Parameters Serum calcium, albumin, ionized calcium

Reference Range

Serum calcium: 8.4-10.2 mg/dL

Due to a poor correlation between the serum ionized calcium (free) and total serum calcium, particularly in states of low albumin or acid/base imbalances, direct measurement of ionized calcium is recommended.

In low albumin states, the corrected **total** serum calcium may be estimated by the following equation (assuming a normal albumin of 4 g/dL).

Corrected total calcium = total serum calcium + 0.8 (4.0 - measured serum albumin)

or

Corrected calcium = measured calcium - measured albumin + 4.0

Serum/plasma chloride: 95-108 mEq/L

Test Interactions Increased calcium (S); decreased magnesium

Additional Information 14 mEq calcium/g (10 mL); 270 mg elemental calcium/g calcium chloride (27% elemental calcium)

Dosage Forms Injection, solution [preservative free]: 10% [100 mg/mL] (10 mL) [equivalent to elemental calcium 27.2 mg/mL, calcium 1.36 mEq/mL]

Calcium Citrate *(KAL see um SIT rate)*

U.S. Brand Names Cal-Citrate® 250 [OTC]; Citracal® [OTC]

Canadian Brand Names Osteocit®

Pharmacologic Category Calcium Salt

Use Antacid; treatment and prevention of calcium deficiency or hyperphosphatemia (eg, osteoporosis, osteomalacia, mild/moderate renal insufficiency, hypoparathyroidism, postmenopausal osteoporosis, rickets)

Pregnancy Risk Factor C
Medication Safety Issues
Sound-alike/look-alike issues:
Citracal® may be confused with Citrucel®
Dosage Oral: Dosage is in terms of elemental calcium
Dietary Reference Intake:
0-6 months: 210 mg/day
7-12 months: 270 mg/day
1-3 years: 500 mg/day
4-8 years: 800 mg/day
Adults, Male/Female:
9-18 years: 1300 mg/day
19-50 years: 1000 mg/day
≥51 years: 1200 mg/day
Female: Pregnancy/Lactating: Same as for Adults, Male/Female
Dietary supplement: Usual dose: 500 mg to 2 g 2-4 times/day
Additional Information Complete prescribing information for this medication should be consulted for additional detail.
Dosage Forms
Granules: 760 mg/teaspoonful (480 g)
Tablet: Elemental calcium 200 mg, 250 mg
Cal-Citrate®: Elemental calcium 250 mg
Citracal®: 950 mg [equivalent to elemental calcium 200 mg]

♦ **Calcium Disodium Edetate** see Edetate Calcium Disodium on page 566
♦ **Calcium Disodium Versenate®** see Edetate Calcium Disodium on page 566
♦ **Calcium EDTA** see Edetate Calcium Disodium on page 566

Calcium Glubionate (KAL see um gloo BYE oh nate)

U.S. Brand Names Calcionate [OTC]
Pharmacologic Category Calcium Salt
Use Dietary supplement
Medication Safety Issues
Sound-alike/look-alike issues:
Calcium glubionate may be confused with calcium gluconate
Dosage Dosage is in terms of **elemental** calcium
Dietary Reference Intake:
0-6 months: 210 mg/day
7-12 months: 270 mg/day
1-3 years: 500 mg/day
4-8 years: 800 mg/day
Adults, Male/Female:
9-18 years: 1300 mg/day
19-50 years: 1000 mg/day
≥51 years: 1200 mg/day
Female: Pregnancy/Lactating: Same as for Adults, Male/Female
Dietary supplement: Oral:
Infants <12 months: 1 teaspoonful 5 times a day; may mix with juice or formula
Children <4 years: 2 teaspoonsful 3 times a day
Children ≥4 years and Adults: 1 tablespoonful 3 times a day
Pregnant or lactating women: 1 tablespoonful 4 times a day
Dosing adjustment in renal impairment: Cl_{cr} <25 mL/minute: Dosage adjustments may be necessary depending on the serum calcium levels
Additional Information Complete prescribing information for this medication should be consulted for additional detail.
Dosage Forms
Syrup:
Calcionate: 1.8 g/5 mL (480 mL) [equivalent to elemental calcium 115 mg/5 mL; contains benzoic acid; caramel and orange flavor]

Calcium Gluconate (KAL see um GLOO koe nate)

Pharmacologic Category Calcium Salt; Electrolyte Supplement, Oral; Electrolyte Supplement, Parenteral
Additional Appendix Information
Management of Overdosages on page 2075
Use Treatment and prevention of hypocalcemia; treatment of tetany, cardiac disturbances of hyperkalemia, cardiac resuscitation when epinephrine fails to improve myocardial contractions, hypocalcemia; calcium supplementation
Unlabeled/Investigational Use Hydrofluoric acid (HF) burns; calcium channel blocker overdose
Pregnancy Risk Factor C
Pregnancy Implications Reproduction studies have not been completed.
Lactation Enters breast milk
Medication Safety Issues
Sound-alike/look-alike issues:
Calcium gluconate may be confused with calcium glubionate
Contraindications Ventricular fibrillation during cardiac resuscitation; digitalis toxicity or suspected digoxin toxicity; hypercalcemia
Warnings/Precautions Injection solution is for I.V. use only; do not inject SubQ or I.M. Avoid too rapid I.V. administration and avoid extravasation. Use with caution in digitalized patients, severe hyperphosphatemia, respiratory failure, or acidosis. May produce cardiac arrest. (Continued)

Calcium Gluconate *(Continued)*

Hypercalcemia may occur in patients with renal failure; frequent determination of serum calcium is necessary. Use caution with renal disease. Solutions may contain aluminum; toxic levels may occur following prolonged administration in premature neonates or patients with renal dysfunction.

Adverse Reactions Frequency not defined.

I.V.:

Cardiovascular: Arrhythmia, bradycardia, cardiac arrest, hypotension, vasodilation, and syncope may occur following rapid I.V. injection

Central nervous system: Sense of oppression

Gastrointestinal: Chalky taste

Local: Abscess and necrosis following I.M. administration

Neuromuscular & skeletal: Tingling sensation

Miscellaneous: Heat waves

Postmarketing and/or case reports: Calcinosis cutis

Oral: Gastrointestinal: Constipation

Overdosage/Toxicology Acute single oral ingestions of calcium salts may produce mild gastrointestinal distress, but hypercalcemia or other toxic manifestations are extremely unlikely. Symptoms of hypercalcemia include lethargy, nausea, vomiting, and coma. Treatment is supportive. Severe hypercalcemia following parenteral overdose requires I.V. hydration. Urine output should be monitored and maintained at >3 mL/kg/hour. I.V. saline and natriuretic agents (eg, furosemide) can quickly and significantly increase excretion of calcium into urine.

Drug Interactions

Increased Effect/Toxicity: Calcium salts may potentiate digoxin toxicity. Thiazide diuretics may decrease the excretion of calcium salts. Continued concomitant use can also result in metabolic alkalosis.

Decreased Effect: Bisphosphonate derivative absorption may be decreased by calcium salts. Calcium channel blockers (eg, verapamil) effects may be diminished; monitor response. Calcium salts may diminish the therapeutic effect of dobutamine. Calcium carbonate (and possibly other calcium salts) may decrease T_4 absorption; separate dose from levothyroxine by at least 4 hours. Calcium salts may decrease the absorption of phosphate supplements. Calcium salts may decrease the absorption of quinolone antibiotics with oral adminstration of both agents.

Stability

Do not refrigerate solutions. IVPB solutions/I.V. infusion solutions are stable for 24 hours at room temperature.

Standard diluent: 1 g/100 mL D_5W or NS; 2 g/100 mL D_5W or NS.

Maximum concentration in parenteral nutrition solutions is variable depending upon concentration and solubility (consult detailed reference).

Mechanism of Action As dietary supplement, used to prevent or treat negative calcium balance; in osteoporosis, it helps to prevent or decrease the rate of bone loss. The calcium in calcium salts moderates nerve and muscle performance and allows normal cardiac function.

Pharmacodynamics/Kinetics

Absorption: Requires vitamin D; calcium is absorbed in soluble, ionized form; solubility of calcium is increased in an acid environment

Distribution: Primarily in bones and teeth; crosses placenta; enters breast milk

Protein binding: Primarily albumin

Excretion: Primarily feces (as unabsorbed calcium); urine (20%)

Dosage

Adequate Intake (as elemental calcium):

0-6 months: 210 mg/day

7-12 months: 270 mg/day

1-3 years: 500 mg/day

4-8 years: 800 mg/day

9-18 years: 1300 mg/day

Adults, Male/Female:

19-50 years: 1000 mg/day

≥51 years: 1200 mg/day

Female: Pregnancy/Lactating: Same as for Adults, Male/Female

Dosage note: Calcium chloride has 3 times more elemental calcium than calcium gluconate. Calcium chloride is 27% elemental calcium; calcium gluconate is 9% elemental calcium. One gram of calcium chloride is equal to 270 mg of elemental calcium; 1 gram of calcium gluconate is equal to 90 mg of elemental calcium. The following dosages are expressed in terms of the calcium gluconate salt based on a solution concentration of 100 mg/mL (10%) containing 0.465 mEq (9.3 mg)/mL elemental calcium:

Hypocalcemia: I.V.:

Neonates: 200-800 mg/kg/day as a continuous infusion or in 4 divided doses (maximum: 1 g/dose)

Infants and Children: 200-500 mg/kg/day as a continuous infusion or in 4 divided doses (maximum: 2-3 g/dose)

Adults: 2-15 g/24 hours as a continuous infusion or in divided doses

Hypocalcemia: Oral:

Children: 200-500 mg/kg/day divided every 6 hours

Adults: 500 mg to 2 g 2-4 times/day

Hypocalcemia secondary to citrated blood infusion: I.V.: **Note:** Routine administration of calcium, in the absence of signs/symptoms of hypocalcemia, is generally not recommended. A number of recommendations have been published seeking to address potential hypocalcemia during massive transfusion of citrated blood; however, many practitioners recommend replacement only as guided by clinical evidence of hypocalcemia and/or serial monitoring of ionized calcium.

Neonates, Infants, and Children: Give 98 mg (0.45 mEq **elemental** calcium) for each 100 mL citrated blood infused

Adults: 500 mg to 1 g per 500 mL of citrated blood (infused into another vein). Single doses up to 2 g have also been recommended.

Hypocalcemic tetany: I.V.:

Neonates, Infants, and Children: 100-200 mg/kg/dose over 5-10 minutes; may repeat every 6-8 hours **or** follow with an infusion of 500 mg/kg/day

Adults: 1-3 g may be administered until therapeutic response occurs

Magnesium intoxication, cardiac arrest in the presence of hyperkalemia or hypocalcemia: I.V.:

Infants and Children: 60-100 mg/kg/dose (maximum: 3 g/dose)

Adults: 500-800 mg/dose (maximum: 3 g/dose)

Maintenance electrolyte requirements for total parenteral nutrition: I.V.: Daily requirements: Adults: 1.7-3.4 g/1000 kcal/24 hours

Calcium channel blocker overdose (unlabeled use): Adults: I.V. infusion: 10% solution: 0.6-1.2 mL/kg/hour or I.V. 0.2-0.5 ml/kg every 15-20 minutes for 4 doses (maximum: 2-3 g/dose). In life-threatening situations, 1 g has been given every 1-10 minutes until clinical effect is achieved (case reports of resistant hypotension reported use of 12-18 g total).

Dosing adjustment in renal impairment: Cl_{cr} <25 mL/minute: Dosage adjustments may be necessary depending on the serum calcium levels

Administration Not for I.M. or SubQ administration. For I.V. administration only; administer slowly (~1.5 mL calcium gluconate 10% per minute) through a small needle into a large vein in order to avoid too rapid increased in serum calcium and extravasation.

Extravasation treatment example: Hyaluronidase: Add 1 mL NS to 150 unit vial to make 150 units/mL of concentration; mix 0.1 mL of above with 0.9 mL NS in 1 mL syringe to make final concentration = 15 units/mL

Reference Range

Serum calcium: 8.4-10.2 mg/dL: Monitor plasma calcium levels if using calcium salts as electrolyte supplements for deficiency

Due to a poor correlation between the serum ionized calcium (free) and total serum calcium, particularly in states of low albumin or acid/base imbalances, direct measurement of ionized calcium is recommended

In low albumin states, the corrected **total** serum calcium may be estimated by: Corrected total calcium = total serum calcium + 0.8 (4.0 - measured serum albumin)

Test Interactions Increased calcium (S); decreased magnesium

Additional Information A topical 2.5% to 5% calcium gel for the treatment of hydrofluoric acid (HF) burns can be prepared by adding calcium gluconate to a surgical lubricant (water soluble such as K-Y® Jelly). Calcium chloride should not be used for this purpose. Use of injectable calcium gluconate (I.V., SubQ) has also been reported in the literature for the treatment of HF burns not amenable to topical treatment.

Dosage Forms

Injection, solution [preservative free]: 10% [100 mg/mL] (10 mL, 50 mL, 100 mL, 200 mL) [equivalent to elemental calcium 9 mg/mL; calcium 0.46 mEq/mL]

Powder: 347 mg/tablespoonful (480 g)

Tablet: 500 mg [equivalent to elemental calcium 45 mg]; 650 mg [equivalent to elemental calcium 58.5 mg]; 975 mg [equivalent to elemental calcium 87.75 mg]

♦ **Calcium Leucovorin** see Leucovorin on page 990

♦ **Cal-CYUM [OTC]** see Calcium and Vitamin D on page 268

♦ **Caldecort® [OTC]** see Hydrocortisone on page 852

Calfactant (kaf AKT ant)

U.S. Brand Names Infasurf®

Pharmacologic Category Lung Surfactant

Use Prevention of respiratory distress syndrome (RDS) in premature infants at high risk for RDS and for the treatment ("rescue") of premature infants who develop RDS

Prophylaxis: Therapy at birth with calfactant is indicated for premature infants <29 weeks of gestational age at significant risk for RDS. Should be administered as soon as possible, preferably within 30 minutes after birth.

Treatment: For infants ≤72 hours of age with RDS (confirmed by clinical and radiologic findings) and requiring endotracheal intubation.

Warnings/Precautions Rapidly affects oxygenation and lung compliance and should be restricted to highly supervised use in a clinical setting with immediate availability of clinicians experienced with intubation and ventilatory management of premature infants. If transient episodes of bradycardia and decreased oxygen saturation occur, discontinue the dosing procedure and initiate measures to alleviate the condition. Produces rapid improvement in lung oxygenation and compliance that may require immediate reductions in ventilator settings and FiO_2. For intratracheal administration only.

Adverse Reactions

Cardiovascular: Bradycardia (34%), cyanosis (65%)

Respiratory: Airway obstruction (39%), reflux (21%), requirement for manual ventilation (16%), reintubation (1% to 10%)

Overdosage/Toxicology There have been no known reports of overdosage. While there are no known adverse effects of excess lung surfactant, overdoses would result in overloading the lungs with an isotonic solution. Ventilation should be supported until clearance of the liquid is accomplished.

Stability Gentle swirling or agitation of the vial of suspension is often necessary for redispersion. **Do not shake.** Visible flecks of the suspension and foaming under the surface are normal. Calfactant should be stored at refrigeration (2°C to 8°C/36°F to 46°F). Warming before administration is not necessary. Unopened and unused vials of calfactant that have been warmed to room temperature can be returned to the refrigeration storage within 24 hours for future use. Repeated warming to room temperature should be avoided. Each single-use vial should be entered only once and the vial with any unused material should be discarded after the initial entry.

(Continued)

Calfactant (Continued)

Mechanism of Action Endogenous lung surfactant is essential for effective ventilation because it modifies alveolar surface tension, thereby stabilizing the alveoli. Lung surfactant deficiency is the cause of respiratory distress syndrome (RDS) in premature infants and lung surfactant restores surface activity to the lungs of these infants.

Pharmacodynamics/Kinetics No human studies of absorption, biotransformation, or excretion have been performed

Dosage Intratracheal administration **only**: Each dose is 3 mL/kg body weight at birth; should be administered every 12 hours for a total of up to 3 doses

Administration Gentle swirling or agitation of the vial is often necessary for redispersion as suspension settles during storage; do **not** shake; visible flecks in the suspension and foaming at the surface are normal; does not require reconstitution; do not dilute or sonicate.

Should be administered intratracheally through an endotracheal tube. Dose is drawn into a syringe from the single-use vial using a 20-gauge or larger needle with care taken to avoid excessive foaming. Should be administered in two aliquots of 1.5 mL/kg each. After each aliquot is instilled, the infant should be positioned with either the right or the left side dependent. Administration is made while ventilation is continued over 20-30 breaths for each aliquot, with small bursts timed only during the inspiratory cycles. A pause followed by evaluation of the respiratory status and repositioning should separate the two aliquots.

Monitoring Parameters Following administration, patients should be carefully monitored so that oxygen therapy and ventilatory support can be modified in response to changes in respiratory status.

Additional Information Each mL = 35 mg total phospholipids (including 26 mg phosphatidylcholine, of which 16 mg is desaturated phosphatidylcholine) and 0.65 protein (including 0.26 mg SP-B)

Dosage Forms
Suspension, intratracheal [preservative free; calf lung derived]:
Infasurf®: 35 mg/mL (3 mL, 6 mL)

♦ **Cal-Gest [OTC]** see Calcium Carbonate on page 269

♦ **Cal-Mint [OTC]** see Calcium Carbonate on page 269

♦ **Calmylin with Codeine (Can)** see Guaifenesin, Pseudoephedrine, and Codeine on page 820

♦ **Caltine® (Can)** see Calcitonin on page 264

♦ **Caltrate® (Can)** see Calcium Carbonate on page 269

♦ **Caltrate® 600 [OTC]** see Calcium Carbonate on page 269

♦ **Caltrate® 600+D [OTC]** see Calcium and Vitamin D on page 268

♦ **Caltrate® 600+ Soy™ [OTC]** see Calcium and Vitamin D on page 268

♦ **Caltrate® ColonHealth™ [OTC]** see Calcium and Vitamin D on page 268

♦ **Caltrate® Select (Can)** see Calcium Carbonate on page 269

♦ **Campath®** see Alemtuzumab on page 63

♦ **Campath-1H** see Alemtuzumab on page 63

♦ **Camphorated Tincture of Opium (error-prone synonym)** see Paregoric on page 1311

♦ **Campral®** see Acamprosate on page 24

♦ **Camptosar®** see Irinotecan on page 935

♦ **Camptothecin-11** see Irinotecan on page 935

♦ **Canasa™** see Mesalamine on page 1089

♦ **Cancidas®** see Caspofungin on page 302

Candesartan (kan de SAR tan)

U.S. Brand Names Atacand®
Canadian Brand Names Atacand®
Index Terms Candesartan Cilexetil
Pharmacologic Category Angiotensin II Receptor Blocker
Additional Appendix Information
Angiotensin Agents on page 1860

Use Alone or in combination with other antihypertensive agents in treating essential hypertension; treatment of heart failure (NYHA class II-IV)

Pregnancy Risk Factor C/D (2nd and 3rd trimesters)

Pregnancy Implications Candesartan should be discontinued as soon as possible when pregnancy is detected. Drugs which act directly on renin-angiotensin can cause fetal and neonatal morbidity and death. Fetal and neonatal toxicity have been reported in infants born to women treated with candesartan during pregnancy.

Lactation Enters breast milk/contraindicated

Contraindications Hypersensitivity to candesartan or any component of the formulation; hypersensitivity to other A-II receptor antagonists; bilateral renal artery stenosis; pregnancy

Warnings/Precautions [U.S. Boxed Warning]: Based on human data, drugs that act on the angiotensin system can cause injury and death to the developing fetus when used in the second and third trimesters. Angiotensin receptor blockers should be discontinued as soon as possible once pregnancy is detected. May cause hyperkalemia; avoid potassium supplementation unless specifically required by healthcare provider. Avoid use or use a smaller dose in patients who are volume depleted; correct depletion first. May be associated with deterioration of renal function and/or increases in serum creatinine, particularly in patients dependent on renin-angiotensin-aldosterone system. Use with caution in unilateral renal artery stenosis, hepatic dysfunction, pre-existing renal insufficiency, or significant aortic/mitral stenosis. Use caution when initiating in heart failure; may need to adjust dose, and/or concurrent diuretic therapy, because of candesartan-induced hypotension. Hypotension may occur during major surgery and anesthesia; use cautiously before, during, and immediately after such interventions. Although some properties may be shared between these agents, concurrent therapy with ACE inhibitor may be rational in selected patients. Safety and efficacy have not been established in children.

Adverse Reactions

Cardiovascular: Angina, hypotension (CHF 19%), MI, palpitation, tachycardia

Central nervous system: Dizziness, lightheadedness, drowsiness, headache, vertigo, anxiety, depression, somnolence, fever

Dermatologic: Angioedema, rash

Endocrine & metabolic: Hyperglycemia, hyperkalemia (CHF <1% to 6%), hypertriglyceridemia, hyperuricemia

Gastrointestinal: Dyspepsia, gastroenteritis

Genitourinary: Hematuria

Neuromuscular & skeletal: Back pain, CPK increased, myalgia, paresthesia, weakness

Renal: Serum creatinine increased (up to 13% in patients with CHF with drug discontinuation required in 6%)

Respiratory: Dyspnea, epistaxis, pharyngitis, rhinitis, upper respiratory tract infection

Miscellaneous: Diaphoresis increased

<1%, postmarketing, and/or case reports: Abnormal hepatic function, agranulocytosis, anemia, hepatitis, hyponatremia, leukopenia, neutropenia, pruritus, renal failure, renal impairment, rhinitis, sinusitis, thrombocytopenia, urticaria; rhabdomyolysis has been reported (rarely) with angiotensin-receptor antagonists

Overdosage/Toxicology Symptoms include hypotension and tachycardia. Treatment is supportive.

Drug Interactions

Cytochrome P450 Effect: Substrate of CYP2C9 (minor); **Inhibits** CYP2C8 (weak), 2C9 (weak)

Increased Effect/Toxicity: The risk of lithium toxicity may be increased by candesartan; monitor lithium levels. Concurrent use with potassium-sparing diuretics (amiloride, spironolactone, triamterene), potassium supplements, or trimethoprim (high-dose) may increase the risk of hyperkalemia.

Ethanol/Nutrition/Herb Interactions

Food: Food reduces the time to maximal concentration and increases the C_{max}.

Herb/Nutraceutical: Avoid dong quai if using for hypertension (has estrogenic activity). Avoid ephedra, yohimbe, ginseng (may worsen hypertension). Avoid garlic (may have increased antihypertensive effect).

Mechanism of Action Candesartan is an angiotensin receptor antagonist. Angiotensin II acts as a vasoconstrictor. In addition to causing direct vasoconstriction, angiotensin II also stimulates the release of aldosterone. Once aldosterone is released, sodium as well as water are reabsorbed. The end result is an elevation in blood pressure. Candesartan binds to the AT1 angiotensin II receptor. This binding prevents angiotensin II from binding to the receptor thereby blocking the vasoconstriction and the aldosterone secreting effects of angiotensin II.

Pharmacodynamics/Kinetics

Onset of action: 2-3 hours

Peak effect: 6-8 hours

Duration: >24 hours

Distribution: V_d: 0.13 L/kg

Protein binding: 99%

Metabolism: To candesartan by the intestinal wall cells

Bioavailability: 15%

Half-life elimination (dose dependent): 5-9 hours

Time to peak: 3-4 hours

Excretion: Urine (26%)

Clearance: Total body: 0.37 mL/kg/minute; Renal: 0.19 mL/kg/minute

Dosage Adults: Oral:

Hypertension: Usual dose is 4-32 mg once daily; dosage must be individualized. Blood pressure response is dose related over the range of 2-32 mg. The usual recommended starting dose of 16 mg once daily when it is used as monotherapy in patients who are not volume depleted. It can be administered once or twice daily with total daily doses ranging from 8-32 mg. Larger doses do not appear to have a greater effect and there is relatively little experience with such doses.

Congestive heart failure: Initial: 4 mg once daily; double the dose at 2-week intervals, as tolerated; target dose: 32 mg

Note: In selected cases, concurrent therapy with an ACE inhibitor may provide additional benefit.

Elderly: No initial dosage adjustment is necessary for elderly patients (although higher concentrations (C_{max}) and AUC were observed in these populations), for patients with mildly impaired renal function, or for patients with mildly impaired hepatic function.

Dosage adjustment in hepatic impairment: No initial dosage adjustment required in mild hepatic impairment. Consider initiation at lower dosages in moderate hepatic impairment (AUC increased by 145%). No data available concerning dosing in severe hepatic impairment.

Monitoring Parameters Supine blood pressure, electrolytes, serum creatinine, BUN, urinalysis, symptomatic hypotension, and tachycardia; in CHF, serum potassium during dose escalation and periodically thereafter

Additional Information May have an advantage over losartan due to minimal metabolism requirements and consequent use in mild-to-moderate hepatic impairment

Dosage Forms

Tablet, as cilexetil:

Atacand®: 4 mg, 8 mg, 16 mg, 32 mg

Candesartan and Hydrochlorothiazide
(kan de SAR tan & hye droe klor oh THYE a zide)

U.S. Brand Names Atacand HCT™
Canadian Brand Names Atacand® Plus
Index Terms Candesartan Cilexetil and Hydrochlorothiazide
Pharmacologic Category Angiotensin II Receptor Blocker Combination; Antihypertensive Agent, Combination; Diuretic, Thiazide
Use Treatment of hypertension; combination product should not be used for initial therapy
Pregnancy Risk Factor C/D (2nd and 3rd trimesters)
Dosage Oral: Adults: Replacement therapy: Combination product can be substituted for individual agents; maximum therapeutic effect would be expected within 4 weeks

Usual dosage range:
Candesartan: 16-32 mg/day, given once daily or twice daily in divided doses
Hydrochlorothiazide: 12.5-25 mg once daily
Dosage adjustment in renal impairment: Serum levels of candesartan are increased and the half-life of hydrochlorothiazide is prolonged in patients with renal impairment. Do not use if Cl_{cr} is <30 mL/minute.
Dosage adjustment in hepatic impairment: Use with caution
Elderly: No initial dosage adjustment is recommended in patients with normal renal and hepatic function; some patients may have increased sensitivity.
Additional Information Complete prescribing information for this medication should be consulted for additional detail.
Dosage Forms
Tablet:
Atacand HCT™:
16-12.5: Candesartan cilexetil 16 mg and hydrochlorothiazide 12.5 mg
32-12.5: Candesartan cilexetil 32 mg and hydrochlorothiazide 12.5 mg

♦ **Candesartan Cilexetil** see Candesartan on page 276
♦ **Candesartan Cilexetil and Hydrochlorothiazide** see Candesartan and Hydrochlorothiazide on page 278
♦ **Candistatin® (Can)** see Nystatin on page 1250
♦ **Canesten® Topical (Can)** see Clotrimazole on page 404
♦ **Canesten® Vaginal (Can)** see Clotrimazole on page 404
♦ **Cankaid® [OTC]** see Carbamide Peroxide on page 287
♦ **Capastat® Sulfate** see Capreomycin on page 280

Capecitabine (ka pe SITE a been)

U.S. Brand Names Xeloda®
Canadian Brand Names Xeloda®
Index Terms NSC-712807
Pharmacologic Category Antineoplastic Agent, Antimetabolite; Antineoplastic Agent, Antimetabolite (Pyrimidine Antagonist)
Use Treatment of metastatic colorectal cancer; adjuvant therapy of Dukes' C colon cancer; treatment of metastatic breast cancer
Pregnancy Risk Factor D
Pregnancy Implications Animal studies have demonstrated teratogenicity and fetal loss. There are no adequate and well-controlled studies in pregnant women; however, fetal harm may occur. Women of childbearing potential should avoid pregnancy.
Lactation Excretion in breast milk unknown/not recommended
Medication Safety Issues
Sound-alike/look-alike issues:
Xeloda® may be confused with Xenical®

High alert medication: The Institute for Safe Medication Practices (ISMP) includes this medication among its list of drugs which have a heightened risk of causing significant patient harm when used in error.

Contraindications Hypersensitivity to capecitabine, fluorouracil, or any component of the formulation; known deficiency of dihydropyrimidine dehydrogenase (DPD); severe renal impairment (Cl_{cr} <30 mL/minute); pregnancy

Warnings/Precautions Hazardous agent - use appropriate precautions for handling and disposal. Use with caution in patients with bone marrow suppression, ≥80 years of age, or renal or hepatic dysfunction. Patients with baseline moderate renal impairment require dose reduction. Patients with mild-to-moderate renal impairment require careful monitoring and subsequent dose reduction with any grade 2 or higher adverse event. Use with caution in patients who have received extensive pelvic radiation or alkylating therapy. Use cautiously with warfarin. Rare and unexpected severe toxicity may be attributed to dihydropyrimidine dehydrogenase (DPD) deficiency. Necrotizing enterocolitis (typhlitis) has been reported.

Capecitabine can cause severe diarrhea; median time to first occurrence is 34 days. Subsequent doses should be reduced after grade 3 or 4 diarrhea or recurrence of grade 2 diarrhea.

Hand-and-foot syndrome is characterized by numbness, dysesthesia/paresthesia, tingling, painless or painful swelling, erythema, desquamation, blistering, and severe pain. If grade 2 or 3 hand-and-foot syndrome occurs, interrupt administration of capecitabine until decreases to grade 1. Following grade 3 hand-and-foot syndrome, decrease subsequent doses of capecitabine.

There has been cardiotoxicity associated with fluorinated pyrimidine therapy. May be more common in patients with a history of coronary artery disease. **[U.S. Boxed Warning]: Capecitabine may increase the anticoagulant effects of warfarin; monitor closely.**

Safety and officacy in children <18 years of age have not been established.

Adverse Reactions Frequency listed derived from monotherapy trials.

>10%:
Cardiovascular: Edema (9% to 15%)
Central nervous system: Fatigue (16% to 42%), fever (7% to 18%), pain (12%)
Dermatologic: Palmar-plantar erythrodysesthesia (hand-and-foot syndrome) (54% to 60%; grade 3: 11% to 17%; may be dose limiting), dermatitis (27% to 37%)
Gastrointestinal: Diarrhea (47% to 57%; may be dose limiting; grade 3: 12% to 13%; grade 4: 2% to 3%), nausea (34% to 53%), vomiting (15% to 37%), abdominal pain (7% to 35%), stomatitis (22% to 25%), appetite decreased (26%), anorexia (9% to 23%), constipation (9% to 15%)
Hematologic: Lymphopenia (94%; grade 4: 14%), anemia (72% to 80%; grade 4: <1% to 1%), neutropenia (2% to 26%; grade 4: 2%), thrombocytopenia (24%; grade 4: 1%)
Hepatic: Bilirubin increased (22% to 48%; grades 3/4: 11% to 23%)
Neuromuscular & skeletal: Paresthesia (21%)
Ocular: Eye irritation (13% to 15%)
Respiratory: Dyspnea (14%)

5% to 10%:
Cardiovascular: Venous thrombosis (8%), chest pain (6%)
Central nervous system: Headache (5% to 10%), lethargy (10%), dizziness (6% to 8%), insomnia (7% to 8%), mood alteration (5%), depression (5%)
Dermatologic: Nail disorder (7%), rash (7%), skin discoloration (7%), alopecia (6%), erythema (6%)
Endocrine & metabolic: Dehydration (7%)
Gastrointestinal: Motility disorder (10%), oral discomfort (10%), dyspepsia (6% to 8%), upper GI inflammatory disorders (colorectal cancer: 8%), hemorrhage (6%), ileus (6%), taste perversion (colorectal cancer: 6%)
Neuromuscular & skeletal: Back pain (10%), weakness (10%), neuropathy (10%), myalgia (9%), arthralgia (8%), limb pain (6%)
Ocular: Abnormal vision (colorectal cancer: 5%), conjunctivitis (5%)
Respiratory: Cough (7%)
Miscellaneous: Viral infection (colorectal cancer: 5%)

<5% (Limited to important or life-threatening): Angina, ascites, asthma, atrial fibrillation, bradycardia, bronchitis, bronchopneumonia, bronchospasm, cachexia, cardiac arrest, cardiac failure, cardiomyopathy, cerebral vascular accident, cholestasis, coagulation disorder, colitis, deep vein thrombosis, diaphoresis, duodenitis, dysphagia, dysrhythmia, ECG changes, encephalopathy, epistaxis, fungal infection, gastric ulcer, gastroenteritis, hematemesis, hemoptysis, hepatic failure, hepatic fibrosis, hepatitis, hypokalemia, hypomagnesemia, hyper-/hypotension, hypersensitivity, hypertriglyceridemia, idiopathic thrombocytopenia purpura, ileus, infection, intestinal obstruction (~1%), keratoconjunctivitis, lacrimal duct stenosis, leukopenia, loss of consciousness, lymphedema, MI, myocardial ischemia, myocarditis, necrotizing enterocolitis, oral candidiasis, pericardial effusion, thrombocytopenic purpura, pancytopenia, photosensitivity reaction, pneumonia, pruritus, pulmonary embolism, radiation recall syndrome, renal impairment, respiratory distress, sedation, sepsis, skin ulceration, tachycardia, thrombophlebitis, toxic megacolon, tremor, ventricular extrasystoles

Overdosage/Toxicology Symptoms of overdose include myelosuppression, nausea, vomiting, diarrhea, and gastrointestinal irritation/bleeding. No specific antidote exists. Monitor hematologically for at least 4 weeks. Dialysis may be of benefit in reducing levels of the metabolite 5'-DFUR. Treatment is symptom-directed and supportive.

Drug Interactions
Increased Effect/Toxicity: Phenytoin and warfarin levels or effects may be increased.
Ethanol/Nutrition/Herb Interactions Food: Food reduced the rate and extent of absorption of capecitabine.
Stability Store at room temperature between 15°C and 30°C (59°F and 86°F).
Mechanism of Action Capecitabine is a prodrug of fluorouracil. It undergoes hydrolysis in the liver and tissues to form fluorouracil which is the active moiety. Fluorouracil is a fluorinated pyrimidine antimetabolite that inhibits thymidylate synthetase, blocking the methylation of deoxyuridylic acid to thymidylic acid, interfering with DNA, and to a lesser degree, RNA synthesis. Fluorouracil appears to be phase specific for the G_1 and S phases of the cell cycle.
Pharmacodynamics/Kinetics
Absorption: Rapid and extensive
Protein binding: <60%; ~35% to albumin
Metabolism:
Hepatic: Inactive metabolites: 5'-deoxy-5-fluorocytidine, 5'-deoxy-5-fluorouridine
Tissue: Active metabolite: Fluorouracil
Half-life elimination: 0.5-1 hour
Time to peak: 1.5 hours; Fluorouracil: 2 hours
Excretion: Urine (96%, 57% as α-fluoro-β-alanine); feces (<3%)
Dosage Oral:
Adults: 1250 mg/m^2 twice daily (morning and evening) for 2 weeks, every 21-28 days
Adjuvant therapy of Dukes' C colon cancer: Recommended for a total of 24 weeks (8 cycles of 2 weeks of drug administration and 1 week rest period.
Elderly: The elderly may be more sensitive to the toxic effects of fluorouracil. Insufficient data are available to provide dosage modifications.
Dosing adjustment in renal impairment:
Cl_{cr} 51-80 mL/minute: No adjustment of initial dose
Cl_{cr} 30-50 mL/minute: Administer 75% of normal dose
Cl_{cr} <30 mL/minute: Use is contraindicated
Dosing adjustment in hepatic impairment:
Mild-to-moderate impairment: No starting dose adjustment is necessary; however, carefully monitor patients
Severe hepatic impairment: Patients have not been studied
Dosage modification guidelines: See table on next page.
(Continued)

Capecitabine *(Continued)*

Refer to package labeling for modifications when administered in combination with docetaxel.

Recommended Dose Modifications

Toxicity NCI Grades	During a Course of Therapy (Monotherapy)	Dose Adjustment for Next Cycle (% of starting dose)
Grade 1	Maintain dose level	Maintain dose level
Grade 2		
1st appearance	Interrupt until resolved to grade 0-1	100%
2nd appearance	Interrupt until resolved to grade 0-1	75%
3rd appearance	Interrupt until resolved to grade 0-1	50%
4th appearance	Discontinue treatment permanently	
Grade 3		
1st appearance	Interrupt until resolved to grade 0-1	75%
2nd appearance	Interrupt until resolved to grade 0-1	50%
3rd appearance	Discontinue treatment permanently	
Grade 4		
1st appearance	Discontinue permanently **or** If physician deems it to be in the patient's best interest to continue, interrupt until resolved to grade 0-1	50%

Dietary Considerations Because current safety and efficacy data are based upon administration with food, it is recommended that capecitabine be administered with food. In all clinical trials, patients were instructed to take with water within 30 minutes after a meal.

Administration Usually administered in 2 divided doses taken 12 hours apart. Doses should be taken with water within 30 minutes after a meal.

Monitoring Parameters Renal function should be estimated at baseline to determine initial dose. During therapy, CBC with differential, hepatic function, and renal function should be monitored.

Dosage Forms Tablet: 150 mg, 500 mg

♦ **Capex™** *see* Fluocinolone *on page 721*
♦ **Capital® and Codeine** *see* Acetaminophen and Codeine *on page 31*
♦ **Capoten®** *see* Captopril *on page 281*
♦ **Capoten™ (Can)** *see* Captopril *on page 281*
♦ **Capozide®** *see* Captopril and Hydrochlorothiazide *on page 284*

Capreomycin *(kap ree oh MYE sin)*

U.S. Brand Names Capastat® Sulfate
Index Terms Capreomycin Sulfate
Pharmacologic Category Antibiotic, Miscellaneous; Antitubercular Agent
Additional Appendix Information
Angiotensin Agents *on page 1860*
Heart Failure (Systolic) *on page 2051*
Hypertension *on page 2063*
Use Treatment of tuberculosis in conjunction with at least one other antituberculosis agent
Pregnancy Risk Factor C
Pregnancy Implications Capreomycin has been shown to be teratogenic in animal studies. There are no adequate and well-controlled studies in pregnant women; use during pregnancy only if the potential benefit to the mother outweighs the possible risk to the fetus.
Lactation Excretion in breast milk unknown/use caution
Medication Safety Issues
Sound-alike/look-alike issues:
Capastat® may be confused with Cepastat®
Contraindications Hypersensitivity to capreomycin sulfate or any component of the formulation
Warnings/Precautions [U.S. Boxed Warning]: Use in patients with renal insufficiency or pre-existing auditory impairment must be undertaken with great caution, and the risk of additional eighth nerve impairment or renal injury should be weighed against the benefits to be derived from therapy. Since other parenteral antituberculous agents (eg, streptomycin) also have similar and sometimes irreversible toxic effects, particularly on eighth cranial nerve and renal function, simultaneous administration of these agents with capreomycin is not recommended. Use with nonantituberculous drugs (ie, aminoglycoside antibiotics) having ototoxic or nephrotoxic potential should be undertaken only with great caution. Use caution with renal dysfunction and in the elderly. **[U.S. Boxed Warning]: Safety in pregnant women or pediatric patients not established.**
Adverse Reactions
>10%:
Otic: Ototoxicity [subclinical hearing loss (11%), clinical loss (3%)], tinnitus
Renal: Nephrotoxicity (36%, increased BUN)
1% to 10%: Hematologic: Eosinophilia (dose related, mild)
<1% (Limited to important or life-threatening): Acute tubular necrosis; Bartter's syndrome; hypersensitivity (urticaria, rash, fever); hypokalemia; leukocytosis; pain, induration, and bleeding at injection site; thrombocytopenia (rare); vertigo

Overdosage/Toxicology Symptoms include renal failure, ototoxicity, and thrombocytopenia. Treatment is supportive.

Drug Interactions
Increased Effect/Toxicity: May increase effect/duration of nondepolarizing neuromuscular blocking agents. Additive toxicity (nephrotoxicity and ototoxicity), respiratory paralysis may occur with aminoglycosides (eg, streptomycin).

Stability Powder for injection should be stored at room temperature of 15°C to 30°C (59°F to 86°F). Dissolve powder in 2 mL of NS or SWFI; allow 2-3 minutes for dissolution. For I.V. administration, further dilute in NS 100 mL. For I.M. administration, dose <1 g may be further diluted to concentrations of 200-350 mg/mL. Following reconstitution, may store under refrigeration for up to 24 hours.

Mechanism of Action Capreomycin is a cyclic polypeptide antimicrobial. It is administered as a mixture of capreomycin IA and capreomycin IB. The mechanism of action of capreomycin is not well understood. Mycobacterial species that have become resistant to other agents are usually still sensitive to the action of capreomycin. However, significant cross-resistance with viomycin, kanamycin, and neomycin occurs.

Pharmacodynamics/Kinetics
Half-life elimination: Normal renal function: 4-6 hours
Time to peak, serum: I.M.: ~1 hour
Excretion: Urine (as unchanged drug)

Dosage I.M., I.V.:
Infants and Children: 15-30 mg/kg/day, up to 1 g/day maximum
Adults: 1 g/day (not to exceed 20 mg/kg/day) for 60-120 days, followed by 1 g 2-3 times/week
Elderly: Use with caution due to the increased potential for pre-existing renal dysfunction or impaired hearing
Dosing interval in renal impairment: Adults:
Cl_{cr} >100 mL/minute: Administer 13-15 mg/kg every 24 hours
Cl_{cr} 80-100 mL/minute: Administer 10-13 mg/kg every 24 hours
Cl_{cr} 60-80 mL/minute: Administer 7-10 mg/kg every 24 hours
Cl_{cr} 40-60 mL/minute: Administer 11-14 mg/kg every 48 hours
Cl_{cr} 20-40 mL/minute: Administer 10-14 mg/kg every 72 hours
Cl_{cr} <20 mL/minute: Administer 4-7 mg/kg every 72 hours

Administration
I.M.: Administer by deep I.M. injection into a large muscle mass.
I.V.: Administer over 60 minutes.

Monitoring Parameters Audiometric measurements and vestibular function at baseline and during therapy; renal function at baseline and weekly during therapy; serum potassium; liver function tests

Reference Range 10 mcg/mL

Dosage Forms Injection, powder for reconstitution, as sulfate: 1 g

♦ **Capreomycin Sulfate** see Capreomycin on page 280

Captopril (KAP toe pril)

U.S. Brand Names Capoten®
Canadian Brand Names Alti-Captopril; Apo-Capto®; Capoten™; Gen-Captopril; Novo-Captopril; Nu-Capto; PMS-Captopril
Index Terms ACE
Pharmacologic Category Angiotensin-Converting Enzyme (ACE) Inhibitor
Additional Appendix Information
Angiotensin Agents on page 1860
Heart Failure (Systolic) on page 2051
Hypertension on page 2063

Use Management of hypertension; treatment of congestive heart failure, left ventricular dysfunction after myocardial infarction, diabetic nephropathy

Unlabeled/Investigational Use Treatment of hypertensive crisis, rheumatoid arthritis; diagnosis of anatomic renal artery stenosis, hypertension secondary to scleroderma renal crisis; diagnosis of aldosteronism, idiopathic edema, Bartter's syndrome, postmyocardial infarction for prevention of ventricular failure; increase circulation in Raynaud's phenomenon, hypertension secondary to Takayasu's disease

Pregnancy Risk Factor C (1st trimester)/D (2nd and 3rd trimesters)

Pregnancy Implications Decreased placental blood flow, low birth weight, fetal hypotension, preterm delivery, and fetal death have been noted with the use of some ACE inhibitors (ACEIs) in animal studies. Neonatal hypotension, skull hypoplasia, anuria, renal failure, oligohydramnios (associated with fetal limb contractures, craniofacial deformities, hypoplastic lung development), prematurity, intrauterine growth retardation, and patent ductus arteriosus have been reported with the use of ACEIs, primarily in the 2nd and 3rd trimesters. The risk of neonatal toxicity has been considered less when ACEIs have been used in the 1st trimester; however, major congenital malformations have been reported. The cardiovascular and/or central nervous systems are most commonly affected. Unless alternative agents are not appropriate, ACEIs should be discontinued as soon as possible once pregnancy is detected.

Lactation Enters breast milk/not recommended (AAP rates "compatible")

Medication Safety Issues
Sound-alike/look-alike issues:
Captopril may be confused with Capitrol®, carvedilol

International issues:
Acepril® [Great Britain] may be confused with Accupril® which is a brand name for quinapril in the U.S.
Acepril®: Brand name for enalapril in Hungary and Switzerland; brand name for lisinopril in Denmark
(Continued)

Captopril (Continued)

Contraindications Hypersensitivity to captopril or any component of the formulation; angioedema related to previous treatment with an ACE inhibitor; idiopathic or hereditary angioedema; bilateral renal artery stenosis; pregnancy (2nd or 3rd trimester)

Warnings/Precautions Anaphylactic reactions can occur. Angioedema can occur at any time during treatment (especially following first dose). It may involve head and neck (potentially affecting the airway) or the intestine (presenting with abdominal pain). Prolonged monitoring may be required especially if tongue, glottis, or larynx are involved as they are associated with airway obstruction. Those with a history of airway surgery in this situation have a higher risk. Careful blood pressure monitoring with first dose (hypotension can occur especially in volume-depleted patients). **[U.S. Boxed Warning]: Based on human data, ACEIs can cause injury and death to the developing fetus when used in the second and third trimesters. ACEIs should be discontinued as soon as possible once pregnancy is detected.** Use with caution in collagen vascular diseases; valvular stenosis (particularly aortic stenosis); hyperkalemia; or before, during, or immediately after anesthesia. Avoid rapid dosage escalation which may lead to renal insufficiency. Hyperkalemia may rarely occur. Rare toxicities associated with ACE inhibitors include cholestatic jaundice (which may progress to hepatic necrosis) and neutropenia/agranulocytosis with myeloid hyperplasia. May be associated with deterioration of renal function and/or increases in serum creatinine, particularly in patients dependent on renin-angiotensin-aldosterone system. Use with caution in unilateral renal artery stenosis and pre-existing renal insufficiency; if patient has renal impairment then a baseline WBC with differential and serum creatinine should be evaluated and monitored closely during the first 3 months of therapy. Hypersensitivity reactions may be seen during hemodialysis with high-flux dialysis membranes (eg, AN69).

Use with caution and decrease dosage in patients with renal impairment (especially renal artery stenosis), severe CHF, or with coadministered diuretic therapy; experience in children is limited. Severe hypotension may occur in patients who are sodium and/or volume depleted; initiate lower doses and monitor closely when starting therapy in these patients. ACE inhibitors may be preferred agents in elderly patients with CHF and diabetes mellitus (diabetic proteinuria is reduced, minimal CNS effects, and enhanced insulin sensitivity); however, due to decreased renal function, tolerance must be carefully monitored.

Adverse Reactions

1% to 10%:

Cardiovascular: Hypotension (1% to 2.5%), tachycardia (1%), chest pain (1%), palpitation (1%)

Dermatologic: Rash (maculopapular or urticarial) (4% to 7%), pruritus (2%); in patients with rash, a positive ANA and/or eosinophilia has been noted in 7% to 10%.

Endocrine & metabolic: Hyperkalemia (1% to 11%)

Hematologic: Neutropenia may occur in up to 3.7% of patients with renal insufficiency or collagen-vascular disease.

Renal: Proteinuria (1%), serum creatinine increased, worsening of renal function (may occur in patients with bilateral renal artery stenosis or hypovolemia)

Respiratory: Cough (0.5% to 2%)

Miscellaneous: Hypersensitivity reactions (rash, pruritus, fever, arthralgia, and eosinophilia) have occurred in 4% to 7% of patients (depending on dose and renal function); dysgeusia - loss of taste or diminished perception (2% to 4%)

Frequency not defined:

Cardiovascular: Angioedema, cardiac arrest, cerebrovascular insufficiency, rhythm disturbances, orthostatic hypotension, syncope, flushing, pallor, angina, MI, Raynaud's syndrome, CHF

Central nervous system: Ataxia, confusion, depression, nervousness, somnolence

Dermatologic: Bullous pemphigus, erythema multiforme, Stevens-Johnson syndrome, exfoliative dermatitis

Endocrine & metabolic: Alkaline phosphatase increased, bilirubin increased, gynecomastia

Gastrointestinal: Pancreatitis, glossitis, dyspepsia

Genitourinary: Urinary frequency, impotence

Hematologic: Anemia, thrombocytopenia, pancytopenia, agranulocytosis

Hepatic: Jaundice, hepatitis, hepatic necrosis (rare), cholestasis, hyponatremia (symptomatic), transaminases increased

Neuromuscular & skeletal: Asthenia, myalgia, myasthenia

Ocular: Blurred vision

Renal: Renal insufficiency, renal failure, nephrotic syndrome, polyuria, oliguria

Respiratory: Bronchospasm, eosinophilic pneumonitis, rhinitis

Miscellaneous: Anaphylactoid reactions

Postmarketing and/or case reports: Alopecia, aplastic anemia, exacerbations of Huntington's disease, Guillain-Barré syndrome, hemolytic anemia, Kaposi's sarcoma, pericarditis, seizure (in premature infants), systemic lupus erythematosus. A syndrome which may include fever, myalgia, arthralgia, interstitial nephritis, vasculitis, rash, eosinophilia, and elevated ESR has been reported for captopril and other ACE inhibitors.

Overdosage/Toxicology Mild hypotension has been the only toxic effect seen with acute overdose; bradycardia may also occur. Hyperkalemia occurs even with therapeutic doses, especially in patients with renal insufficiency and those taking NSAIDs. Following initiation of essential overdose management, toxic symptom treatment and supportive treatment should be initiated. Hypotension usually responds to I.V. fluids or Trendelenburg positioning.

Drug Interactions

Cytochrome P450 Effect: Substrate of CYP2D6 (major)

Increased Effect/Toxicity: Potassium supplements, co-trimoxazole (high dose), angiotensin II receptor antagonists (candesartan, losartan, irbesartan, etc), or potassium-sparing diuretics (amiloride, spironolactone, triamterene) may result in elevated serum potassium levels when combined with captopril. CYP2D6 inhibitors may increase the levels/effects of captopril; example inhibitors include chlorpromazine, delavirdine, fluoxetine, miconazole, paroxetine, pergolide, quinidine, quinine, ritonavir, and ropinirole. ACE inhibitor effects may be increased by phenothiazines or probenecid (increases levels of captopril). ACE inhibitors may increase serum concentrations/effects of lithium. ACE inhibitors may enhance the adverse/toxic effects (nitritoid reaction) of gold sodium thiomalate.

Diuretics have additive hypotensive effects with ACE inhibitors, and hypovolemia increases the potential for adverse renal effects of ACE inhibitors. In patients with compromised renal function, coadministration with NSAIDs may result in further deterioration of renal function. Allopurinol and ACE inhibitors may cause a higher risk of hypersensitivity reaction when taken concurrently.

Decreased Effect: Aspirin (high dose) may reduce the therapeutic effects of ACE inhibitors; at low dosages this does not appear to be significant. Rifampin may decrease the effect of ACE inhibitors. Antacids may decrease the bioavailability of ACE inhibitors (may be more likely to occur with captopril); separate administration times by 1-2 hours. NSAIDs, specifically indomethacin, may reduce the hypotensive effects of ACE inhibitors. More likely to occur in low renin or volume-dependent hypertensive patients.

Ethanol/Nutrition/Herb Interactions

Food: Captopril serum concentrations may be decreased if taken with food. Long-term use of captopril may result in a zinc deficiency which can result in a decrease in taste perception.

Herb/Nutraceutical: Avoid dong quai if using for hypertension (has estrogenic activity). Avoid ephedra, yohimbe, ginseng (may worsen hypertension). Avoid garlic (may have increased antihypertensive effect).

Mechanism of Action Competitive inhibitor of angiotensin-converting enzyme (ACE); prevents conversion of angiotensin I to angiotensin II, a potent vasoconstrictor; results in lower levels of angiotensin II which causes an increase in plasma renin activity and a reduction in aldosterone secretion

Pharmacodynamics/Kinetics

Onset of action: Peak effect: Blood pressure reduction: 1-1.5 hours after dose

Duration: Dose related, may require several weeks of therapy before full hypotensive effect

Absorption: 60% to 75%; reduced 30% to 40% by food

Protein binding: 25% to 30%

Metabolism: 50%

Half-life elimination (renal and cardiac function dependent):
    Adults, healthy volunteers: 1.9 hours; Congestive heart failure: 2.06 hours; Anuria: 20-40 hours

Excretion: Urine (95%) within 24 hours

Dosage Note: Titrate dose according to patient's response; use lowest effective dose. Oral:

Infants: Initial: 0.15-0.3 mg/kg/dose; titrate dose upward to maximum of 6 mg/kg/day in 1-4 divided doses; usual required dose: 2.5-6 mg/kg/day

Children: Initial: 0.5 mg/kg/dose; titrate upward to maximum of 6 mg/kg/day in 2-4 divided doses

Older Children: Initial: 6.25-12.5 mg/dose every 12-24 hours; titrate upward to maximum of 6 mg/kg/day

Adolescents: Initial: 12.5-25 mg/dose given every 8-12 hours; increase by 25 mg/dose to maximum of 450 mg/day

Adults:
    Acute hypertension (urgency/emergency): 12.5-25 mg, may repeat as needed (may be given sublingually, but no therapeutic advantage demonstrated)
    Hypertension:
        Initial dose: 12.5-25 mg 2-3 times/day; may increase by 12.5-25 mg/dose at 1- to 2-week intervals up to 50 mg 3 times/day; maximum dose: 150 mg 3 times/day; add diuretic before further dosage increases
        Usual dose range (JNC 7): 25-100 mg/day in 2 divided doses
    Congestive heart failure:
        Initial dose: 6.25-12.5 mg 3 times/day in conjunction with cardiac glycoside and diuretic therapy; initial dose depends upon patient's fluid/electrolyte status
        Target dose: 50 mg 3 times/day
    LVD after MI: Initial dose: 6.25 followed by 12.5 mg 3 times/day; then increase to 25 mg 3 times/day during next several days and then over next several weeks to target dose of 50 mg 3 times/day
    Diabetic nephropathy: 25 mg 3 times/day; other antihypertensives often given concurrently

Dosing adjustment in renal impairment:
    Cl_{cr} 10-50 mL/minute: Administer at 75% of normal dose.
    Cl_{cr} <10 mL/minute: Administer at 50% of normal dose.
    Note: Smaller dosages given every 8-12 hours are indicated in patients with renal dysfunction; renal function and leukocyte count should be carefully monitored during therapy.
    Hemodialysis: Moderately dialyzable (20% to 50%); administer dose postdialysis or administer 25% to 35% supplemental dose.
    Peritoneal dialysis: Supplemental dose is not necessary.

Dietary Considerations Should be taken at least 1 hour before or 2 hours after eating.

Administration Unstable in aqueous solutions; to prepare solution for oral administration, mix prior to administration and use within 10 minutes.

Monitoring Parameters BUN, serum creatinine, urine dipstick for protein, complete leukocyte count, and blood pressure

Test Interactions Increased BUN, creatinine, potassium, positive Coombs' [direct]; decreased cholesterol (S); may cause false-positive results in urine acetone determinations using sodium nitroprusside reagent

Dosage Forms Tablet: 12.5 mg, 25 mg, 50 mg, 100 mg

Extemporaneous Preparations Captopril has limited stability in aqueous preparations. The addition of an antioxidant (sodium ascorbate) has been shown to increase the stability of captopril in solution; captopril (1 mg/mL) in syrup with methylcellulose is stable for 7 days stored either at 4°C or 22°C; captopril (1 mg/mL) in distilled water (no additives) is stable for 14 days if stored at 4°C and 7 days if stored at 22°C; captopril (1 mg/mL) with sodium ascorbate (5 mg/mL) in distilled water is stable for 56 days at 4°C and 11 days at 22°C. (Continued)

Captopril *(Continued)*

Captopril (0.75 mg/mL) in cherry syrup is stable for only 2 days in amber clear plastic containers stored at room temperature or under refrigeration; captopril (0.75 mg/mL) in either a 1:1 mixture of Ora-Sweet® and Ora-Plus® or a 1:1 mixture of Ora-Sweet® SF and Ora-Plus® is stable for 10 days or less depending on the storage temperature (see Allen, 1996).

Powder papers can also be made; powder papers are stable for 12 weeks when stored at room temperature

Allen LV and Erickson III MA, "Stability of Baclofen, Captopril, Diltiazem Hydrochloride, Dipyridamole, and Flecainide Acetate in Extemporaneously Compounded Oral Liquids," *Am J Health Syst Pharm*, 1996, 53:2179-84.

Nahata MC, Morosco RS, and Hipple TF, "Stability of Captopril in Three Liquid Dosage Forms," *Am J Hosp Pharm*, 1994, 51(1):95-6.

Taketomo CK, Chu SA, Cheng MH, et al, "Stability of Captopril in Powder Papers Under Three Storage Conditions," *Am J Hosp Pharm*, 1990, 47(8):1799-1801.

Captopril and Hydrochlorothiazide
(KAP toe pril & hye droe klor oh THYE a zide)

U.S. Brand Names Capozide®
Canadian Brand Names Capozide®
Index Terms Hydrochlorothiazide and Captopril
Pharmacologic Category Antihypertensive Agent, Combination
Use Management of hypertension and treatment of congestive heart failure
Pregnancy Risk Factor C/D (2nd and 3rd trimesters)
Dosage Oral: Adults: Hypertension, CHF: May be substituted for previously titrated dosages of the individual components; alternatively, may initiate as follows:
Initial: Single tablet (captopril 25 mg/hydrochlorothiazide 15 mg) taken once daily; daily dose of captopril should not exceed 150 mg; daily dose of hydrochlorothiazide should not exceed 50 mg
Additional Information Complete prescribing information for this medication should be consulted for additional detail.
Dosage Forms Tablet:
25/15: Captopril 25 mg and hydrochlorothiazide 15 mg
25/25: Captopril 25 mg and hydrochlorothiazide 25 mg
50/15: Captopril 50 mg and hydrochlorothiazide 15 mg
50/25: Captopril 50 mg and hydrochlorothiazide 25 mg

♦ **Carac™** *see* Fluorouracil *on page 725*
♦ **Carafate®** *see* Sucralfate *on page 1606*
♦ **Carapres®** *(Can) see* Clonidine *on page 399*

Carbachol *(KAR ba kole)*

U.S. Brand Names Carbastat® [DSC]; Isopto® Carbachol; Miostat®
Canadian Brand Names Isopto® Carbachol; Miostat®
Index Terms Carbacholine; Carbamylcholine Chloride
Pharmacologic Category Cholinergic Agonist; Ophthalmic Agent, Antiglaucoma; Ophthalmic Agent, Miotic
Additional Appendix Information
Glaucoma Drug Therapy *on page 2050*
Use Lowers intraocular pressure in the treatment of glaucoma; cause miosis during surgery
Pregnancy Risk Factor C
Medication Safety Issues
Sound-alike/look-alike issues:
Isopto® Carbachol may be confused with Isopto® Carpine
Dosage Adults:
Ophthalmic: Instill 1-2 drops up to 3 times/day
Intraocular: 0.5 mL instilled into anterior chamber before or after securing sutures
Additional Information Complete prescribing information for this medication should be consulted for additional detail.
Dosage Forms [DSC] = Discontinued product
Solution, intraocular (Carbastat® [DSC], Miostat®): 0.01% (1.5 mL)
Solution, ophthalmic (Isopto® Carbachol): 1.5% (15 mL); 3% (30 mL) [contains benzalkonium chloride]

♦ **Carbacholine** *see* Carbachol *on page 284*

Carbamazepine *(kar ba MAZ e peen)*

U.S. Brand Names Carbatrol®; Epitol®; Equetro™; Tegretol®; Tegretol®-XR
Canadian Brand Names Apo-Carbamazepine®; Gen-Carbamazepine CR; Mapezine®; Novo-Carbamaz; Nu-Carbamazepine; PMS-Carbamazepine; Taro-Carbamazepine Chewable; Tegretol®
Index Terms CBZ; SPD417
Pharmacologic Category Anticonvulsant, Miscellaneous
Additional Appendix Information
Anticonvulsants by Seizure Type *on page 1865*
Epilepsy *on page 2048*
Use
Carbatrol®, Tegretol®, Tegretol®-XR: Partial seizures with complex symptomatology (psychomotor, temporal lobe), generalized tonic-clonic seizures (grand mal), mixed seizure patterns, trigeminal neuralgia

Equetro™: Acute manic and mixed episodes associated with bipolar 1 disorder

Unlabeled/Investigational Use Treatment of resistant schizophrenia, ethanol withdrawal, restless leg syndrome, psychotic behavior associated with dementia, post-traumatic stress disorders

Pregnancy Risk Factor D

Pregnancy Implications Crosses the placenta. Dysmorphic facial features, cranial defects, cardiac defects, spina bifida, IUGR, and multiple other malformations reported. Epilepsy itself, number of medications, genetic factors, or a combination of these probably influence the teratogenicity of anticonvulsant therapy. Benefit:risk ratio usually favors continued use during pregnancy and breast-feeding.

Lactation Enters breast milk/not recommended (AAP rates "compatible")

Medication Safety Issues

Sound-alike/look-alike issues:

Carbatrol® may be confused with Cartrol®

Epitol® may be confused with Epinal®

Tegretol®, Tegretol®-XR may be confused with Mebaral®, Tegrin®, Toprol-XL®, Toradol®, Trental®

Contraindications Hypersensitivity to carbamazepine, tricyclic antidepressants, or any component of the formulation; bone marrow depression; with or within 14 days of MAO inhibitor use; pregnancy

Warnings/Precautions Administer carbamazepine with caution to patients with history of cardiac damage, hepatic or renal disease. **[U.S. Boxed Warning]: Potentially fatal blood cell abnormalities have been reported.** Patients with a previous history of adverse hematologic reaction to any drug may be at increased risk. Prescriptions should be written for the smallest quantity consistent with good patient care. The smallest effective dose is suggested for use in bipolar disorder to reduce the risk for overdose; high-risk patients should be monitored. Actuation of latent psychosis is possible.

Carbamazepine is not effective in absence, myoclonic, or akinetic seizures; exacerbation of certain seizure types have been seen after initiation of carbamazepine therapy in children with mixed seizure disorders. Abrupt discontinuation is not recommended in patients being treated for seizures. Dizziness or drowsiness may occur; caution should be used when performing tasks which require alertness until the effects are known. Coadministration of carbamazepine and delavirdine may lead to loss of virologic response and possible resistance. Elderly may have increased risk of SIADH-like syndrome. Carbamazepine has mild anticholinergic activity; use with caution in patients with increased intraocular pressure, or sensitivity to anticholinergic effects. Severe dermatologic reactions, including Lyell and Stevens-Johnson syndromes, although rarely reported, have resulted in fatalities. Discontinue if there are any signs of hypersensitivity.

Adverse Reactions Frequency not defined, unless otherwise specified.

Cardiovascular: Arrhythmias, AV block, bradycardia, chest pain (bipolar use), CHF, edema, hyper-/hypotension, lymphadenopathy, syncope, thromboembolism, thrombophlebitis

Central nervous system: Amnesia (bipolar use), anxiety (bipolar use), aseptic meningitis (case report), ataxia (bipolar use 15%), confusion, depression (bipolar use), dizziness (bipolar use 44%), fatigue, headache (bipolar use 22%), sedation, slurred speech, somnolence (bipolar use 32%)

Dermatologic: Alopecia, alterations in skin pigmentation, erythema multiforme, exfoliative dermatitis, photosensitivity reaction, pruritus (bipolar use 8%), purpura, rash, Stevens-Johnson syndrome, toxic epidermal necrolysis, urticaria

Endocrine & metabolic: Chills, fever, hyponatremia, syndrome of inappropriate ADH secretion (SIADH)

Gastrointestinal: Abdominal pain, anorexia, constipation, diarrhea, dyspepsia (bipolar use), gastric distress, nausea (bipolar use 29%), pancreatitis, vomiting (bipolar use 18%), xerostomia (bipolar use)

Genitourinary: Azotemia, impotence, renal failure, urinary frequency, urinary retention

Hematologic: Acute intermittent porphyria, agranulocytosis, aplastic anemia, bone marrow suppression, eosinophilia, leukocytosis, leukopenia, pancytopenia, thrombocytopenia

Hepatic: Abnormal liver function tests, hepatic failure, hepatitis, jaundice

Neuromuscular & skeletal: Back pain, pain (bipolar use 12%), peripheral neuritis, weakness

Ocular: Blurred vision, conjunctivitis, lens opacities, nystagmus

Otic: Hyperacusis, tinnitus

Miscellaneous: Diaphoresis, hypersensitivity (including multiorgan reactions, may include disorders mimicking lymphoma, eosinophilia, hepatosplenomegaly, vasculitis); infection (bipolar use 12%)

Overdosage/Toxicology Symptoms include dizziness ataxia, drowsiness, nausea, vomiting, tremor, agitation, nystagmus, urinary retention, dysrhythmias, coma, seizures, twitches, respiratory depression, and neuromuscular disturbances. Severe cardiac complications occur with very high doses. Provide general supportive care. Activated charcoal is effective at binding carbamazepine. Other treatment is supportive/symptomatic. Treatment consists of inducing emesis or gastric lavage. ECG should also be monitored to detect cardiac dysfunction. Monitor blood pressure, body temperature, pupillary reflexes, bladder function for several days following ingestion.

Drug Interactions

Cytochrome P450 Effect: Substrate of CYP2C8 (minor), 3A4 (major); **Induces** CYP1A2 (strong), 2B6 (strong), 2C8 (strong), 2C9 (strong), 2C19 (strong), 3A4 (strong)

Increased Effect/Toxicity: Carbamazepine may enhance the hepatotoxic potential of acetaminophen. Neurotoxicity may result in patients receiving lithium and carbamazepine concurrently. CYP3A4 inhibitors may increase the levels/effects of carbamazepine; example inhibitors include azole antifungals, clarithromycin, diclofenac, doxycycline, erythromycin, imatinib, isoniazid, nefazodone, nicardipine, propofol, protease inhibitors, quinidine, telithromycin, and verapamil. Carbamazepine may increase the levels/effects of phenytoin.

Decreased Effect: The levels/effects of carbamazepine may be decreased by aminoglutethimide, nafcillin, nevirapine, phenobarbital, phenytoin, and rifamycins, and other

(Continued)

Carbamazepine *(Continued)*

CYP3A4 inducers. Carbamazepine may induce its own metabolism. Carbamazepine suspension is incompatible with chlorpromazine solution and thioridazine liquid. Schedule carbamazepine suspension at least 1-2 hours apart from other liquid medicinals. Concomitant use of antimalarial drugs (chloroquine, mefloquine) with carbamazepine may reduce seizure control by lowering plasma levels.

Carbamazepine may decrease the effect of clozapine, corticosteroids, cyclosporine, delavirdine, doxycycline, ethosuximide, felbamate, felodipine, haloperidol, mebendazole, methadone, oral contraceptives, thyroid hormones, tricyclic antidepressants, and valproic acid. Carbamazepine may decrease the levels/effects of aminophylline, amiodarone, benzodiazepines, bupropion, calcium channel blockers, citalopram, clarithromycin, cyclosporine, diazepam, efavirenz, erythromycin, estrogens, fluoxetine, fluvoxamine, glimepiride, glipizide, losartan, methsuximide, mirtazapine, nateglinide, nefazodone, nevirapine, pioglitazone, promethazine, propranolol, protease inhibitors, proton pump inhibitors, ropinirole, rosiglitazone, selegiline, sertraline, sulfonamides, tacrolimus, theophylline, venlafaxine. voriconazole, warfarin, zafirlukast, and other CYP1A2, 2B6, 2C8, 2C9, 2C19, or 3A4 substrates.

Ethanol/Nutrition/Herb Interactions

Ethanol: Avoid ethanol (may increase CNS depression).

Food: Carbamazepine serum levels may be increased if taken with food. Carbamazepine serum concentration may be increased if taken with grapefruit juice; avoid concurrent use.

Herb/Nutraceutical: Avoid evening primrose (seizure threshold decreased). Avoid valerian, St John's wort, kava kava, gotu kola (may increase CNS depression).

Mechanism of Action In addition to anticonvulsant effects, carbamazepine has anticholinergic, antineuralgic, antidiuretic, muscle relaxant, antimanic, antidepressive, and antiarrhythmic properties; may depress activity in the nucleus ventralis of the thalamus or decrease synaptic transmission or decrease summation of temporal stimulation leading to neural discharge by limiting influx of sodium ions across cell membrane or other unknown mechanisms; stimulates the release of ADH and potentiates its action in promoting reabsorption of water; chemically related to tricyclic antidepressants

Pharmacodynamics/Kinetics

Absorption: Slow

Distribution: V_d: Neonates: 1.5 L/kg; Children: 1.9 L/kg; Adults: 0.59-2 L/kg

Protein binding: Carbamazepine: 75% to 90%, may be decreased in newborns; Epoxide metabolite: 50%

Metabolism: Hepatic via CYP3A4 to active epoxide metabolite; induces hepatic enzymes to increase metabolism

Bioavailability: 85%

Half-life elimination:

Carbamazepine: Initial: 18-55 hours; Multiple doses: Children: 8-14 hours; Adults: 12-17 hours

Epoxide metabolite: Initial: 25-43 hours

Time to peak, serum: Unpredictable:

Immediate release: Suspension: 1.5 hour; tablet: 4-5 hours

Extended release: Carbatrol®, Equetro™: 12-26 hours (single dose), 4-8 hours (multiple doses); Tegretol®-XR: 3-12 hours

Excretion: Urine 72% (1% to 3% as unchanged drug); feces (28%)

Dosage Dosage must be adjusted according to patient's response and serum concentrations. Administer tablets (chewable or conventional) in 2-3 divided doses daily and suspension in 4 divided doses daily. (See Additional Information for investigational oral loading dose and rectal maintenance dose information.) Oral:

Epilepsy:

Children:

<6 years: Initial: 10-20 mg/kg/day divided twice or 3 times daily as tablets or 4 times/day as suspension; increase dose every week until optimal response and therapeutic levels are achieved

Maintenance dose: Divide into 3-4 doses daily (tablets or suspension); maximum recommended dose: 35 mg/kg/day

6-12 years: Initial: 100 mg twice daily (tablets or extended release tablets) or 50 mg of suspension 4 times/day (200 mg/day); increase by up to 100 mg/day at weekly intervals using a twice daily regimen of extended release tablets or 3-4 times daily regimen of other formulations until optimal response and therapeutic levels are achieved

Maintenance: Usual: 400-800 mg/day; maximum recommended dose: 1000 mg/day

Note: Children <12 years who receive ≥400 mg/day of carbamazepine may be converted to extended release capsules (Carbatrol®) using the same total daily dosage divided twice daily

Children >12 years and Adults: Initial: 200 mg twice daily (tablets, extended release tablets, or extended release capsules) or 100 mg of suspension 4 times/day (400 mg daily); increase by up to 200 mg/day at weekly intervals using a twice daily regimen of extended release tablets or capsules, or a 3-4 times/day regimen of other formulations until optimal response and therapeutic levels are achieved; usual dose: 800-1200 mg/day

Maximum recommended doses:

Children 12-15 years: 1000 mg/day

Children >15 years: 1200 mg/day

Adults: 1600 mg/day; however, some patients have required up to 1.6-2.4 g/day

Trigeminal or glossopharyngeal neuralgia: Adults: Initial: 100 mg twice daily with food, gradually increasing in increments of 100 mg twice daily as needed

Maintenance: Usual: 400-800 mg daily in 2 divided doses; maximum dose: 1200 mg/day

Elderly: 100 mg 1-2 times daily, increase in increments of 100 mg/day at weekly intervals until therapeutic level is achieved; usual dose: 400-1000 mg/day

Bipolar disorder (Equetro™): Adults: Initial: 400 mg/day in divided doses, twice daily; may adjust by 200 mg daily increments; maximum dose: 1600 mg/day

Dietary Considerations Drug may cause GI upset, take with large amount of water or food to decrease GI upset. May need to split doses to avoid GI upset.

Administration

Suspension: Must be given on a 3-4 times/day schedule versus tablets which can be given 2-4 times/day. When carbamazepine suspension has been combined with chlorpromazine or thioridazine solutions, a precipitate forms which may result in loss of effect. Therefore, it is recommended that the carbamazepine suspension dosage form not be administered at the same time with other liquid medicinal agents or diluents. Since a given dose of suspension will produce higher peak levels than the same dose given as the tablet form, patients given the suspension should be started on lower doses and increased slowly to avoid unwanted side effects. Should be administered with meals.

Extended release capsule (Carbatrol®, Equetro™): Consists of three different types of beads: Immediate release, extended-release, and enteric release. The bead types are combined in a ratio to allow twice daily dosing. May be opened and contents sprinkled over food such as a teaspoon of applesauce; may be administered with or without food; do not crush or chew.

Extended release tablet: Should be inspected for damage. Damaged extended release tablets (without release portal) should not be administered. Should be administered with meals; swallow whole, do not crush or chew.

Monitoring Parameters CBC with platelet count, reticulocytes, serum iron, lipid panel, liver function tests, urinalysis, BUN, serum carbamazepine levels, thyroid function tests, serum sodium; ophthalmic exams (pupillary reflexes); observe patient for excessive sedation, especially when instituting or increasing therapy

Reference Range

Timing of serum samples: Absorption is slow, peak levels occur 6-8 hours after ingestion of the first dose; the half-life ranges from 8-60 hours, therefore, steady-state is achieved in 2-5 days

Therapeutic levels: 4-12 mcg/mL (SI: 17-51 µmol/L)

Toxic concentration: >15 mcg/mL; patients who require higher levels of 8-12 mcg/mL (SI: 34-51 µmol/L) should be watched closely. Side effects including CNS effects occur commonly at higher dosage levels. If other anticonvulsants are given therapeutic range is 4-8 mcg/mL.

Test Interactions May interact with some pregnancy tests; increased BUN, AST, ALT, bilirubin, alkaline phosphatase (S); decreased calcium, T_3, T_4, sodium (S)

Additional Information Investigationally, loading doses of the suspension (10 mg/kg for children <12 years of age and 8 mg/kg for children >12 years of age) were given (via NG or ND tubes followed by 5-10 mL of water to flush through tube) to PICU patients with frequent seizures/status. Five of 6 patients attained mean Cp of 4.3 mcg/mL and 7.3 mcg/mL at 1 and 2 hours postload. Concurrent enteral feeding or ileus may delay absorption.

Dosage Forms

Capsule, extended release (Carbatrol®, Equetro™): 100 mg, 200 mg, 300 mg

Suspension, oral: 100 mg/5 mL (10 mL, 450 mL)

Tegretol®: 100 mg/5 mL (450 mL) [citrus vanilla flavor]

Tablet (Epitol®, Tegretol®): 200 mg

Tablet, chewable (Tegretol®): 100 mg

Tablet, extended release (Tegretol®-XR): 100 mg, 200 mg, 400 mg

♦ **Carbamide** see Urea on page 1758

Carbamide Peroxide (KAR ba mide per OKS ide)

U.S. Brand Names Cankaid® [OTC]; Debrox® [OTC]; Dent's Ear Wax [OTC]; E•R•O [OTC]; Gly-Oxide® [OTC]; Murine® Ear Wax Removal System [OTC]; Orajel® Perioseptic® Spot Treatment [OTC]

Index Terms Urea Peroxide

Pharmacologic Category Anti-inflammatory, Locally Applied; Otic Agent, Cerumenolytic

Use Relief of minor inflammation of gums, oral mucosal surfaces, and lips including canker sores and dental irritation; emulsify and disperse ear wax

Pregnancy Risk Factor C

Dosage Children and Adults:

Oral: Inflammation/dental irritation: Solution (should not be used for >7 days): Oral preparation should not be used in children <2 years of age; apply several drops undiluted on affected area 4 times/day after meals and at bedtime; expectorate after 2-3 minutes **or** place 10 drops onto tongue, mix with saliva, swish for several minutes, expectorate

Otic:

Children <12 years: Tilt head sideways and individualize the dose according to patient size; 3 drops (range: 1-5 drops) twice daily for up to 4 days, tip of applicator should not enter ear canal; keep drops in ear for several minutes by keeping head tilted and placing cotton in ear

Children ≥12 years and Adults: Tilt head sideways and instill 5-10 drops twice daily up to 4 days, tip of applicator should not enter ear canal; keep drops in ear for several minutes by keeping head tilted and placing cotton in ear

Additional Information Complete prescribing information for this medication should be consulted for additional detail.

Dosage Forms

Solution, oral: 10% (60 mL)

Cankaid®: 10% (22 mL) [in anhydrous glycerol]

Gly-Oxide®: 10% (15 mL, 60 mL) [contains glycerin]

Orajel® Perioseptic® Spot Treatment: 15% (13.3 mL) [contains anhydrous glycerin]

Solution, otic: 6.5% (15 mL)

Debrox®: 6.5% (15 mL, 30 mL) [contains propylene glycol]

Dent's Ear Wax: 6.5% (3.7 mL) [contains glycerin]

E•R•O: 6.5% (15 mL)

Murine® Ear Wax Removal System: 6.5% (15 mL) [contains alcohol 6.3% and glycerin]

♦ **Carbamylcholine Chloride** *see* Carbachol *on page 284*

♦ **Carbastat® [DSC]** *see* Carbachol *on page 284*

♦ **Carbatrol®** *see* Carbamazepine *on page 284*

♦ **Carbaxefed DM RF [DSC]** *see* Carbinoxamine, Pseudoephedrine, and Dextromethorphan *on page 291*

♦ **Carbaxefed RF [DSC]** *see* Carbinoxamine and Pseudoephedrine *on page 290*

Carbenicillin (kar ben i SIL in)

U.S. Brand Names Geocillin®
Index Terms Carbenicillin Indanyl Sodium; Carindacillin
Pharmacologic Category Antibiotic, Penicillin
Use Treatment of serious urinary tract infections and prostatitis caused by susceptible gram-negative aerobic bacilli
Pregnancy Risk Factor B
Lactation Enters breast milk/use caution
Contraindications Hypersensitivity to carbenicillin, penicillins, or any component of the formulation
Warnings/Precautions Do not use in patients with severe renal impairment (Cl$_{cr}$ <10 mL/minute); dosage modification is required in patients with impaired renal and/or hepatic function. Use with caution in patients with history of hypersensitivity to cephalosporins.
Adverse Reactions
>10%: Gastrointestinal: Diarrhea
1% to 10%: Gastrointestinal: Nausea, bad taste, vomiting, flatulence, glossitis
<1% (Limited to important or life-threatening): Anemia, AST increased (mild), eosinophilia, epigastric distress, furry tongue, headache, hematuria, hypersensitivity reactions, hyperthermia, hypokalemia, leukopenia, LFTs increased, neutropenia, rash, thrombocytopenia, urticaria
Overdosage/Toxicology Symptoms include neuromuscular hypersensitivity and convulsions. Many beta-lactam containing antibiotics have the potential to cause neuromuscular hyperirritability or convulsive seizures. Hemodialysis may be helpful to aid in the removal of the drug from the blood, otherwise, most treatment is supportive or symptom-directed.
Drug Interactions
Increased Effect/Toxicity: Increased bleeding effects if taken with high doses of heparin or oral anticoagulants. Aminoglycosides may be synergistic against selected organisms. Penicillins may increase the exposure to methotrexate during concurrent therapy; monitor. Probenecid and disulfiram may increase levels of penicillins (carbenicillin).
Decreased Effect: Decreased effectiveness with tetracyclines. Although anecdotal reports suggest oral contraceptive efficacy could be reduced by penicillins, this has been refuted by more rigorous scientific and clinical data.
Mechanism of Action Inhibits bacterial cell wall synthesis by binding to one or more of the penicillin-binding proteins (PBPs) which in turn inhibits the final transpeptidation step of peptidoglycan synthesis in bacterial cell walls, thus inhibiting cell wall biosynthesis. Bacteria eventually lyse due to ongoing activity of cell wall autolytic enzymes (autolysins and murein hydrolases) while cell wall assembly is arrested.
Pharmacodynamics/Kinetics
Absorption: 30% to 40%
Distribution: Crosses placenta; small amounts enter breast milk; distributes into bile; low concentrations attained in CSF
Protein binding: ~50%
Half-life elimination: Children: 0.8-1.8 hours; Adults: 1-1.5 hours, prolonged to 10-20 hours with renal insufficiency
Time to peak, serum: Normal renal function: 0.5-2 hours; concentrations are inadequate for treatment of systemic infections
Excretion: Urine (~80% to 99% as unchanged drug)
Dosage
Usual dosage range:
Children: Oral: 30-50 mg/kg/day divided every 6 hours (maximum dose: 2-3 g/day)
Adults: Oral: 1-2 tablets every 6 hours
Indication-specific dosing:
Adults: Oral:
Prostatitis: 2 tablets every 6 hours
Urinary tract infections: 1-2 tablets every 6 hours
Dosing interval in renal impairment: Adults:
Cl$_{cr}$ 10-50 mL/minute: Administer 382-764 mg every 12-24 hours
Cl$_{cr}$ <10 mL/minute: Administer 382-764 mg every 24-48 hours
Moderately dialyzable (20% to 50%)
Dietary Considerations Should be taken with water on empty stomach. Sodium content of 382 mg tablet: 23 mg (1 mEq).
Administration Administer around-the-clock to promote less variation in peak and trough serum levels.

Some penicillins (eg, carbenicillin, ticarcillin and piperacillin) have been shown to inactivate aminoglycosides *in vitro*. This has been observed to a greater extent with tobramycin and gentamicin, while amikacin has shown greater stability against inactivation. Concurrent use of these agents may pose a risk of reduced antibacterial efficacy *in vivo*, particularly in the setting of profound renal impairment. However, definitive clinical evidence is lacking. If combination penicillin/aminoglycoside therapy is desired in a patient with renal dysfunction, separation of doses (if feasible), and routine monitoring of aminoglycoside levels, CBC, and clinical response should be considered.

Monitoring Parameters Renal, hepatic, and hematologic function tests
Reference Range Therapeutic: Not established; Toxic: >250 mcg/mL (SI: >660 µmol/L)

Test Interactions May interfere with urinary glucose tests using cupric sulfate (Benedict's solution, Clinitest®); false-positive urine or serum proteins.

Some penicillin derivatives may accelerate the degradation of aminoglycosides. *in vitro*, leading to a potential underestimation of aminoglycoside serum concentration.

Dosage Forms Tablet: 382 mg [contains sodium 23 mg/tablet]

♦ **Carbenicillin Indanyl Sodium** *see* Carbenicillin *on page 288*

Carbetapentane and Phenylephrine (kar bay ta PEN tane & fen il EF rin)

U.S. Brand Names L-All 12
Index Terms Phenylphrine Tannate and Carbetapentane Tannate
Pharmacologic Category Antitussive; Antitussive/Decongestant; Sympathomimetic
Use Symptomatic relief of upper respiratory tract conditions such as the common cold, bronchial asthma, and bronchitis (acute and chronic)
Pregnancy Risk Factor C
Dosage Oral:
  Children:
    2-6 years: 2.5 mL every 12 hours, not to exceed 5 mL/24 hours
    6-12 years: 5 mL every 12 hours, not to exceed 10 mL/24 hours
  Children >12 years and Adults: 5-10 mL every 12 hours, not to exceed 20 mL/24 hours
Additional Information Complete prescribing information for this medication should be consulted for additional detail.
Dosage Forms
  Suspension:
    L-All 12: Carbetapentane tannate 30 mg and phenylephrine tannate 30 mg per 5 mL (120 mL) [contains sodium benzoate and phenylalanine; strawberry flavor]

Carbetapentane and Pseudoephedrine
(kar bay ta PEN tane & soo doe e FED rin)

U.S. Brand Names Respi-Tann™
Index Terms Carbetapentane Tannate and Pseudoephedrine Tannate; Pseudoephedrine and Carbetapentane
Pharmacologic Category Antitussive/Decongestant
Use Relief of cough and congestion due to the common cold, influenza, sinusitis, or bronchitis
Pregnancy Risk Factor C
Dosage Relief of cough and congestion: Oral:
  Children:
    2-6 years: $^1/_2$ tablet or 2.5 mL suspension every 12 hours (maximum: 4 doses/24 hours)
    6-12 years: 1 tablet or 5 mL suspension every 12 hours (maximum: 4 doses/24 hours)
  Children >12 years and Adults: 2 tablets or 10 mL suspension every 12 hours (maximum: 4 doses/24 hours)
Additional Information Complete prescribing information for this medication should be consulted for additional detail.
Dosage Forms
  Suspension: Carbetapentane tannate 25 mg and pseudoephedrine tannate 75 mg per 5 mL (480 mL) [dye free; contains sodium benzoate; cherry flavor]
  Tablet, chewable: Carbetapentane tannate 25 mg and pseudoephedrine tannate 75 mg [dye free; cherry flavor]

♦ **Carbetapentane, Ephedrine, Phenylephrine, and Chlorpheniramine** *see* Chlorpheniramine, Ephedrine, Phenylephrine, and Carbetapentane *on page 351*
♦ **Carbetapentane Tannate and Pseudoephedrine Tannate** *see* Carbetapentane and Pseudoephedrine *on page 289*

Carbidopa (kar bi DOE pa)

U.S. Brand Names Lodosyn®
Pharmacologic Category Anti-Parkinson's Agent, Dopamine Agonist
Use Given with levodopa in the treatment of parkinsonism to enable a lower dosage of levodopa to be used and a more rapid response to be obtained and to decrease side effects; for details of administration and dosage, see Levodopa; has no effect without levodopa
Pregnancy Risk Factor C
Medication Safety Issues
  International issues:
    Lodosyn® may be confused with Lidosen® which is a brand name for lidocaine in Italy
Dosage Oral: Adults: 70-100 mg/day; maximum daily dose: 200 mg
Additional Information Complete prescribing information for this medication should be consulted for additional detail.
Dosage Forms Tablet: 25 mg

♦ **Carbidopa and Levodopa** *see* Levodopa and Carbidopa *on page 999*
♦ **Carbidopa, Levodopa, and Entacapone** *see* Levodopa, Carbidopa, and Entacapone *on page 1001*

Carbinoxamine (kar bi NOKS a meen)

U.S. Brand Names Palgic®
Index Terms Carbinoxamine Maleate
Pharmacologic Category Antihistamine
Use Seasonal and perennial allergic rhinitis; vasomotor rhinitis; urticaria; decrease severity of other allergic reactions
(Continued)

Carbinoxamine *(Continued)*

Pregnancy Risk Factor C

Dosage Oral (Palgic®):

Children:

>3-6 years: 2-5 mg 3-4 times/day

>6 years: 4-6 mg 3-4 times/day

Adults: 4-8 mg 3-4 times/day

Additional Information Complete prescribing information for this medication should be consulted for additional detail.

Dosage Forms

Solution, as maleate:

Palgic®: 4 mg/5 mL (480 mL) [bubble gum flavor]

Tablet, as maleate [scored]:

Palgic®: 4 mg

Carbinoxamine and Pseudoephedrine

(kar bi NOKS a meen & soo doe e FED rin)

U.S. Brand Names Andehist NR Drops [DSC]; Carbaxefed RF [DSC]; Carboxine-PSE [DSC]; Cordron-D NR [DSC]; Hydro-Tussin™-CBX; Palgic®-D; Palgic®-DS; Pediatex™-D [DSC]; Rondec® Tablets; Rondec-TR®; Sildec [DSC]

Index Terms Pseudoephedrine and Carbinoxamine

Pharmacologic Category Adrenergic Agonist Agent; Antihistamine, H₁ Blocker; Decongestant

Use Seasonal and perennial allergic rhinitis; vasomotor rhinitis

Pregnancy Risk Factor C

Dosage Oral:

Children:

Drops (Andehist NR, Carbaxefed RF, Sildec):

1-3 months: 0.25 mL 4 times/day

3-6 months: 0.5 mL 4 times/day

6-12 months: 0.75 mL 4 times/day

12-24 months: 1 mL 4 times/day

Liquid (Pediatex™-D):

1-3 months: 1.25 mL up to 4 times/day

3-6 months: 2.5 mL up to 4 times/day

6-9 months: 3.75 mL up to 4 times/day

9-18 months: 3.75-5 mL up to 4 times/day

18 months to 6 years: 5 mL 3-4 times/day

>6 years: Refer to adult dosing

Syrup (Hydro-Tussin™-CBX, Palgic®-DS):

1-3 months: 1.25 mL up to 4 times/day

3-6 months: 2.5 mL up to 4 times/day

6-9 months: 3.75 mL up to 4 times/day

9-18 months: 3.75-5 mL up to 4 times/day

18 months to 6 years: 5 mL 3-4 times/day

>6 years: Refer to adult dosing

Tablet (Rondec®): ≥6 years: Refer to adult dosing

Tablet, timed release:

6-12 years (Palgic®-D): One-half tablet every 12 hours

≥12 years (Palgic®-D, Rondec-TR®): Refer to adult dosing

Adults:

Liquid (Pediatex™-D): 10 mL 4 times/day

Syrup (Hydro-Tussin™-CBX, Palgic®-DS): 10 mL 4 times/day

Tablet (Rondec®): 1 tablet 4 times a day

Tablet, timed release (Palgic®-D, Rondec-TR®): 1 tablet every 12 hours

Additional Information Complete prescribing information for this medication should be consulted for additional detail.

Dosage Forms [DSC] = Discontinued product

Liquid:

Cordron-D NR: Carbinoxamine maleate 2 mg and pseudoephedrine hydrochloride 12.5 mg per 5 mL (480 mL) [cotton candy flavor] [DSC]

Pediatex™-D: Carbinoxamine maleate 2 mg and pseudoephedrine hydrochloride 20 mg per 5 mL (480 mL) [alcohol free, dye free, sugar free; cotton candy flavor]

Solution: Carbinoxamine maleate 2 mg and pseudoephedrine hydrochloride 25 mg per 5 mL (480 mL) [DSC]

Carboxine-PSE: Carbinoxamine maleate 2 mg and pseudoephedrine hydrochloride 20 mg per 5 mL (480 mL) [peach flavor] [DSC]

Solution, oral drops:

Andehist NR: Carbinoxamine maleate 1 mg and pseudoephedrine hydrochloride 15 mg per mL (30 mL) [alcohol and sugar free; raspberry flavor] [DSC]

Carbaxefed RF: Carbinoxamine maleate 1 mg and pseudoephedrine hydrochloride 15 mg per mL (30 mL) [alcohol free; contains sodium benzoate; cherry flavor] [DSC]

Sildec: Carbinoxamine maleate 1 mg and pseudoephedrine hydrochloride 15 mg per mL (30 mL) [raspberry flavor] [DSC]

Syrup: Carbinoxamine maleate 2 mg and pseudoephedrine hydrochloride 25 mg per 5 mL (480 mL)

Hydro-Tussin™-CBX, Palgic®-DS: Carbinoxamine maleate 2 mg and pseudoephedrine hydrochloride 25 mg per 5 mL (480 mL) [alcohol, dye, and sugar free; strawberry/pineapple flavor]

Tablet:

Rondec®: Carbinoxamine maleate 4 mg and pseudoephedrine hydrochloride 60 mg

Tablet, timed release:
Palgic®-D: Carbinoxamine maleate 8 mg and pseudoephedrine hydrochloride 80 mg [dye free]
Rondec-TR®: Carbinoxamine maleate 8 mg and pseudoephedrine hydrochloride 120 mg

♦ **Carbinoxamine, Dextromethorphan, and Pseudoephedrine** *see* Carbinoxamine, Pseudoephedrine, and Dextromethorphan *on page 291*
♦ **Carbinoxamine Maleate** *see* Carbinoxamine *on page 289*

Carbinoxamine, Pseudoephedrine, and Dextromethorphan
(kar bi NOKS a meen, soo doe e FED rin, & deks troe meth OR fan)

U.S. Brand Names Andehist DM NR Drops [DSC]; Carbaxefed DM RF [DSC]; Cordron-DM NR [DSC]; Pediatex™ DM [DSC]; Sildec-DM [DSC]; Tussafed® [DSC]
Index Terms Carbinoxamine, Dextromethorphan, and Pseudoephedrine; Dextromethorphan, Carbinoxamine, and Pseudoephedrine; Dextromethorphan, Pseudoephedrine, and Carbinoxamine; Pseudoephedrine, Carbinoxamine, and Dextromethorphan; Pseudoephedrine, Dextromethorphan, and Carbinoxamine
Pharmacologic Category Antihistamine/Decongestant/Antitussive
Use Relief of coughs and upper respiratory symptoms, including nasal congestion, associated with allergy or the common cold
Pregnancy Risk Factor C
Medication Safety Issues
Sound-alike/look-alike issues:
Tussafed® may be confused with Tussafin®
Dosage Oral:
Drops: Infants and Children:
1-3 months: 1/4 mL 4 times/day
3-6 months: 1/2 mL 4 times/day
6-12 months: 3/4 mL 4 times/day
12-24 months: 1 mL 4 times/day
Liquid (Pediatex™ DM):
Children 18 months to 6 years: 2.5 mL 4 times/day
Children 6-12 years: 5 mL 4 times/day
Children ≥12 years and Adults: 10 mL 4 times/day
Syrup (Tussafed®):
Children 18 months to 6 years: 2.5 mL 4 times/day
Children >6 years and Adults: 5 mL 4 times/day
Additional Information Complete prescribing information for this medication should be consulted for additional detail.
Dosage Forms [DSC] = Discontinued product
Liquid:
Cordron-DM NR: Carbinoxamine maleate 3 mg, pseudoephedrine hydrochloride 12.5 mg, and dextromethorphan hydrobromide 15 mg per 5 mL (480 mL) [cotton candy flavor] [DSC]
Pediatex™ DM: Carbinoxamine maleate 2 mg, pseudoephedrine hydrochloride 15 mg, and dextromethorphan hydrobromide 15 mg per 5 mL (480 mL) [alcohol free, dye free, sugar free; cotton candy flavor] [DSC]
Liquid, oral drops: Carbinoxamine maleate 1 mg, pseudoephedrine hydrochloride 15 mg, and dextromethorphan hydrobromide 4 mg per mL (30 mL) [DSC]
Andehist DM NR: Carbinoxamine maleate 1 mg, pseudoephedrine hydrochloride 15 mg, and dextromethorphan hydrobromide 4 mg per mL (30 mL) [alcohol and sugar free; grape flavor] [DSC]
Carbaxefed DM RF: Carbinoxamine maleate 1 mg, pseudoephedrine hydrochloride 15 mg, and dextromethorphan hydrobromide 4 mg per mL (30 mL) [alcohol free; grape flavor] [DSC]
Sildec-DM: Carbinoxamine maleate 1 mg, pseudoephedrine hydrochloride 15 mg, and dextromethorphan hydrobromide 4 mg per mL (30 mL) [DSC]
Syrup, oral: Carbinoxamine maleate 4 mg, pseudoephedrine hydrochloride 60 mg, and dextromethorphan hydrobromide 12.5 mg per 5 mL (480 mL) [alcohol and sugar free] [DSC]
Tussafed®: Carbinoxamine maleate 4 mg, pseudoephedrine hydrochloride 60 mg, and dextromethorphan hydrobromide 15 mg per 5 mL (480 mL) [alcohol and sugar free] [DSC]

♦ **Carbinoxamine, Pseudoephedrine, and Hydrocodone** *see* Hydrocodone, Carbinoxamine, and Pseudoephedrine *on page 851*
♦ **Carbocaine®** *see* Mepivacaine *on page 1084*
♦ **Carbolith™ (Can)** *see* Lithium *on page 1023*

Carboplatin (KAR boe pla tin)

U.S. Brand Names Paraplatin® [DSC]
Canadian Brand Names Paraplatin-AQ
Index Terms CBDCA; NSC-241240
Pharmacologic Category Antineoplastic Agent, Alkylating Agent
Use Treatment of ovarian cancer
Unlabeled/Investigational Use Lung cancer, head and neck cancer, endometrial cancer, esophageal cancer, bladder cancer, breast cancer, cervical cancer, CNS tumors, germ cell tumors, osteogenic sarcoma, and high-dose therapy with stem cell/bone marrow support
Pregnancy Risk Factor D
Lactation Excretion in breast milk unknown/contraindicated
(Continued)

Carboplatin *(Continued)*

Medication Safety Issues

Sound-alike/look-alike issues:

Carboplatin may be confused with cisplatin, oxaliplatin

Paraplatin® may be confused with Platinol®

High alert medication: The Institute for Safe Medication Practices (ISMP) includes this medication among its list of drugs which have a heightened risk of causing significant patient harm when used in error.

Contraindications
History of severe allergic reaction to cisplatin, carboplatin, other platinum-containing formulations, or any component of the formulation; pregnancy; breast-feeding

Warnings/Precautions
Hazardous agent - use appropriate precautions for handling and disposal. High doses have resulted in severe abnormalities of liver function tests. **[U.S. Boxed Warning]: Bone marrow suppression, which may be severe, and vomiting are dose related;** reduce dosage in patients with bone marrow suppression and impaired renal function. Anemia is cumulative. Clinically significant hearing loss has been reported to occur in pediatric patients when carboplatin was administered at higher than recommended doses in combination with other ototoxic agents.

[U.S. Boxed Warning]: Increased risk of allergic reactions in patients previously exposed to platinum therapy. When administered as sequential infusions, taxane derivatives (docetaxel, paclitaxel) should be administered before the platinum derivatives (carboplatin, cisplatin) to limit myelosuppression and to enhance efficacy. Loss of vision (reversible) has been reported with higher than recommended doses. The elderly (≥65 years) and patients who have previously received cisplatin have an increased incidence of peripheral neuropathy. **[U.S. Boxed Warning]: Should be administered under the supervision of an experienced cancer chemotherapy physician.**

Adverse Reactions
Percentages reported with single-agent therapy.

>10%:

Central nervous system: Pain (23%)

Endocrine & metabolic: Hyponatremia (29% to 47%), hypomagnesemia (29% to 43%), hypocalcemia (22% to 31%), hypokalemia (20% to 28%)

Gastrointestinal: Vomiting (65% to 81%), abdominal pain (17%), nausea (10% to 15%)

Hematologic: Myelosuppression (dose related and dose limiting; nadir at ~21 days; recovery by ~28 days), leukopenia (85%; grades 3/4: 15% to 26%), anemia (71% to 90%; grades 3/4: 21%), neutropenia (67%; grades 3/4: 16% to 21%), thrombocytopenia (62%; grades 3/4: 25% to 35%)

Hepatic: Alkaline phosphatase increased (24% to 37%), AST increased (15% to 19%)

Neuromuscular & skeletal: Weakness (11%)

Renal: Creatinine clearance decreased (27%), BUN increased (14% to 22%)

1% to 10%:

Central nervous system: Neurotoxicity (5%)

Dermatologic: Alopecia (2% to 3%)

Gastrointestinal: Constipation (5%), diarrhea (6%), mucositis (1%), taste dysgeusia (1%)

Hematologic: Hemorrhagic complications (5%)

Hepatic: Bilirubin increased (5%)

Local: Pain at injection site

Neuromuscular & skeletal: Peripheral neuropathy (4% to 6%; up to 10% in older and/or previously-treated patients)

Ocular: Visual disturbance (1%)

Otic: Ototoxicity (1%)

Renal: Creatinine increased (6% to 10%)

Miscellaneous: Infection (5%), hypersensitivity (2%)

<1% (Limited to important or life-threatening): Anaphylaxis, anorexia, bronchospasm, cardiac failure, cerebrovascular accident, embolism, erythema, fever, hemolytic uremic syndrome (HUS), hyper-/hypotension, malaise, necrosis (associated with extravasation), nephrotoxicity, neurotoxicity, pruritus, rash, secondary malignancies, urticaria, vision loss

Overdosage/Toxicology
Symptoms include bone marrow suppression and hepatic toxicity.

Drug Interactions

Increased Effect/Toxicity: Aminoglycosides increase risk of ototoxicity and/or nephrotoxicity. When administered as sequential infusions, observational studies indicate a potential for increased toxicity when platinum derivatives (carboplatin, cisplatin) are administered before taxane derivatives (docetaxel, paclitaxel).

Ethanol/Nutrition/Herb Interactions
Herb/Nutraceutical: Avoid black cohosh, dong quai in estrogen-dependent tumors.

Stability
Store intact vials at room temperature of 15°C to 30°C (59°F to 86°F); protect from light. Further dilution to a concentration as low as 0.5 mg/mL is stable at room temperature (25°C) for 8 hours in NS; stable at room temperature or under refrigeration for at least 9 days in D_5W, although the manufacturer states to use within 8 hours due to lack of preservative.

Powder for reconstitution: Reconstitute powder to yield a final concentration of 10 mg/mL which is stable for 5 days at room temperature (25°C). Reconstituted carboplatin 10 mg/mL should be further diluted to a final concentration of 0.5-2 mg/mL with D_5W or NS for administration.

Solution for injection: Multidose vials are stable for up to 14 days after opening when stored at room temperature.

Mechanism of Action
Carboplatin is an alkylating agent which covalently binds to DNA; possible cross-linking and interference with the function of DNA

Pharmacodynamics/Kinetics

Distribution: V_d: 16 L/kg; into liver, kidney, skin, and tumor tissue

Protein binding: 0%; platinum is 30% irreversibly bound

Metabolism: Minimally hepatic to aquated and hydroxylated compounds

Half-life elimination: Terminal: 22-40 hours; Cl_{cr} >60 mL/minute: 2.5-5.9 hours

Excretion: Urine (~60% to 90%) within 24 hours

Dosage Refer to individual protocols: **Note:** Doses for adults are usually determined by the AUC using the Calvert formula.

IVPB, I.V. infusion:
Children:
Solid tumor (unlabeled use): 300-600 mg/m² once every 4 weeks
Brain tumor (unlabeled use): 175 mg/m² weekly for 4 weeks every 6 weeks, with a 2-week recovery period between courses
Adults:
Ovarian cancer: 300-360 mg/m² every 4 weeks
Autologous BMT (unlabeled use): 1600 mg/m² (total dose) divided over 4 days
In adults, dosing is commonly calculated using the Calvert formula:
Total dose (mg) = Target AUC (mg/mL * minute) x (GFR [mL/minute] + 25)
Usual target AUCs:
Previously untreated patients: 6-8 mg/mL * minute
Previously treated patients: 4-6 mg/mL * minute
Elderly: The Calvert formula should be used to calculate dosing for elderly patients.
Intraperitoneal (unlabeled use): Adults: 200-650 mg/m² in 2 L of dialysis fluid have been administered into the peritoneum of ovarian cancer patients **or** target AUC: 5-7 mg/mL * minute
Dosage adjustment for toxicity: Platelets <50,000 cells/mm³ or ANC <500 cells/mm³: Administer 75% of dose

Dosing adjustment in renal impairment: Note: Dose determination with Calvert formula uses GFR and, therefore, inherently adjusts for renal dysfunction.
Baseline Cl$_{cr}$ 41-59 mL/minute: Initiate at 250 mg/m² and adjust subsequent doses based on bone marrow toxicity
Baseline Cl$_{cr}$ 10-40 mL/minute: Initiate at 200 mg/m² and adjust subsequent doses based on bone marrow toxicity
Baseline Cl$_{cr}$ ≤15 mL/minute: No guidelines are available.
Dosing adjustment in hepatic impairment: No guidelines are available.

Administration Infuse over 15 minutes to 24 hours. May also be administered intraperitoneally. When administered as sequential infusions, taxane derivatives (docetaxel, paclitaxel) should be administered before platinum derivatives to limit myelosuppression and to enhance efficacy.

Monitoring Parameters CBC (with differential and platelet count), serum electrolytes, creatinine clearance, liver function tests, BUN, creatinine

Dosage Forms [DSC] = Discontinued product
Injection, powder for reconstitution: 50 mg, 150 mg, 450 mg
Paraplatin®: 50 mg, 150 mg, 450 mg [DSC]
Injection, solution: 10 mg/mL (5 mL, 15 mL, 45 mL, 60 mL)
Paraplatin®: 10 mg/mL (5 mL, 15 mL, 45 mL, 60 mL) [DSC]

♦ **Carboprost** see Carboprost Tromethamine on page 293

Carboprost Tromethamine (KAR boe prost tro METH a meen)

U.S. Brand Names Hemabate®
Canadian Brand Names Hemabate®
Index Terms Carboprost; Prostaglandin F$_2$
Pharmacologic Category Abortifacient; Prostaglandin
Use Termination of pregnancy; treatment of refractory postpartum uterine bleeding
Unlabeled/Investigational Use Investigational: Hemorrhagic cystitis
Pregnancy Risk Factor C
Pregnancy Implications Teratogenic effects were not observed in animal studies. Carboprost tromethamine is not considered feticidal, but is used to terminate pregnancy due to its ability to stimulate uterine contractions. Use is not indicated if the fetus has reached a stage of viability *in utero*. Complete abortion may not be induced in ~20% of cases.
Lactation Excretion in breast milk unknown
Contraindications Hypersensitivity to carboprost tromethamine or any component of the formulation; acute pelvic inflammatory disease; active cardiac, pulmonary, renal, or hepatic dysfunction
Warnings/Precautions [U.S. Boxed Warning] Potent oxytocic agent; use with strict adherence to recommended dosing. Immediate intensive care and acute surgical facilities must be available. Transient pyrexia and increased blood pressure may be observed with treatment. Use caution with history of asthma; hypotension or hypertension; cardiovascular, adrenal, renal, or hepatic disease; anemia; jaundice; diabetes; epilepsy; or compromised uteri. Concomitant use of antiemetic and antidiarrheal agents is recommended to decrease incidence of GI side effects. Safety and efficacy have not been established in pediatric patients.
Adverse Reactions Frequency not defined. Effects due to increased smooth muscle contractility are most common.
Cardiovascular: Chest pain, flushing, hypertension, syncope, palpitations, tachycardia, tightness of chest
Central nervous system: Anxiety, chills/shivering, dizziness, drowsiness, dystonia, faintness, headache, lethargy, lightheadedness, nervousness, sleep disturbance, temperature elevation (may be drug induced or due to postabortion endometritis), vasovagal syndrome, vertigo
Dermatologic: Rash
Endocrine & metabolic: Breast tenderness, dysmenorrhea-like pain, endometritis, hot flashes, thyroid storm
Gastrointestinal: Choking sensation, diarrhea (~²/₃ patients), dry throat, epigastric pain, gagging/retching, hematemesis, nausea (~¹/₃ patients), taste alteration, thirst, throat fullness, vomiting (~²/₃ patients), xerostomia
(Continued)

Carboprost Tromethamine (Continued)

Genitourinary: Perforated uterus, posterior cervical perforation, urinary tract infection, uterine bleeding (excessive), uterine rupture, uterine sacculation

Local: Injection site pain

Neuromuscular & skeletal: Backache, leg cramps, muscular pain, paresthesia, torticollis, weakness

Ocular: Blurred vision, eye pain, eyelid twitching

Otic: Tinnitus

Respiratory: Asthma, cough, bronchospasm, dyspnea, epistaxis, hyperventilation, pulmonary edema, respiratory distress, upper respiratory tract infection, wheezing

Miscellaneous: Diaphoresis, hiccups, retained placental fragment, septic shock

Drug Interactions

Increased Effect/Toxicity: May augment activity of other oxytocic agents (concomitant use is not recommended).

Stability Store under refrigeration at 2°C to 8°C (36°F to 46°F).

Bladder irrigation: Dilute immediately prior to administration in NS; stability unknown.

Mechanism of Action Carboprost tromethamine is a prostaglandin similar to prostaglandin F_2 alpha (dinoprost) except for the addition of a methyl group at the C-15 position. This substitution produces longer duration of activity than dinoprost; carboprost stimulates uterine contractility which usually results in expulsion of the products of conception and is used to induce abortion between 13-20 weeks of pregnancy. Hemostasis at the placentation site is achieved through the myometrial contractions produced by carboprost.

Pharmacodynamics/Kinetics Excretion: Urine

Dosage I.M.: Adults:

Abortion: Initial: 250 mcg, then 250 mcg at 1.5- to 3.5-hour intervals, depending on uterine response; a 500 mcg dose may be given if uterine response is not adequate after several 250 mcg doses; do not exceed 12 mg total dose or continuous administration for >2 days

Refractory postpartum uterine bleeding: Initial: 250 mcg; if needed, may repeat at 15- to 90-minute intervals; maximum total dose: 2 mg (8 doses)

Bladder irrigation for hemorrhagic cystitis (unlabeled use): [0.1-1.0 mg/dL as solution] 50 mL instilled into bladder 4 times/day for 1 hour

Administration Do not inject I.V.; may result in bronchospasm, hypertension, vomiting, or anaphylaxis. Administer deep I.M.; rotate site if repeat injections are required.

Dosage Forms

Injection, solution:

Hemabate®: Carboprost 250 mcg and tromethamine 83 mcg per mL (1 mL) [contains benzyl alcohol]

- ♦ **Carboxine-PSE [DSC]** see Carbinoxamine and Pseudoephedrine on page 290
- ♦ **Cardene®** see NiCARdipine on page 1222
- ♦ **Cardene® I.V.** see NiCARdipine on page 1222
- ♦ **Cardene® SR** see NiCARdipine on page 1222
- ♦ **Cardizem®** see Diltiazem on page 509
- ♦ **Cardizem® CD** see Diltiazem on page 509
- ♦ **Cardizem® LA** see Diltiazem on page 509
- ♦ **Cardizem® SR (Can)** see Diltiazem on page 509
- ♦ **Cardura®** see Doxazosin on page 544
- ♦ **Cardura-1™ (Can)** see Doxazosin on page 544
- ♦ **Cardura-2™ (Can)** see Doxazosin on page 544
- ♦ **Cardura-4™ (Can)** see Doxazosin on page 544
- ♦ **Cardura® XL** see Doxazosin on page 544
- ♦ **Carimune™ NF** see Immune Globulin (Intravenous) on page 892
- ♦ **Carindacillin** see Carbenicillin on page 288
- ♦ **Carisoprodate** see Carisoprodol on page 294

Carisoprodol (kar eye soe PROE dole)

U.S. Brand Names Soma®

Canadian Brand Names Soma®

Index Terms Carisoprodate; Isobamate

Pharmacologic Category Skeletal Muscle Relaxant

Use Relief of discomfort associated with skeletal muscle condition

Pregnancy Risk Factor C

Pregnancy Implications Reproduction studies have not been conducted.

Lactation Enters breast milk (high concentrations)/not recommended

Contraindications Hypersensitivity to carisoprodol, meprobamate, or any component of the formulation; acute intermittent porphyria

Warnings/Precautions May cause CNS depression, which may impair physical or mental abilities. Effects with other sedative drugs or ethanol may be potentiated. Use with caution in patients with hepatic/renal dysfunction. Tolerance or drug dependence may result from extended use. Limit to 2-3 weeks; use caution in patients who may be prone to addiction. Idiosyncratic reactions and/or severe allergic reactions may occur. Idiosyncratic reactions occur following the initial dose and may include severe weakness, transient quadriplegia, euphoria, or vision loss (temporary). Has been associated (rarely) with seizures in patients with and without seizure history. Safety and efficacy in children <12 years of age have not been established.

Adverse Reactions Frequency not defined.

Cardiovascular: Flushing of face, hypotension (postural), syncope, tachycardia, tightness in chest

Central nervous system: Agitation, allergic fever, ataxia, depression, dizziness, drowsiness, dysarthria, headache, insomnia, irritability, lightheadedness, paradoxical CNS stimulation, seizure, vertigo

Dermatologic: Angioedema, dermatitis (allergic), erythema multiforme, fixed drug reaction, pruritus, rash, urticaria

Gastrointestinal: Nausea, epigastric distress, vomiting

Hematologic: Aplastic anemia, eosinophilia, leukopenia

Neuromuscular & skeletal: Tremor

Ocular: Blurred vision, burning eyes

Respiratory: Dyspnea

Miscellaneous: Anaphylaxis, hiccups, hypersensitivity reaction, idiosyncratic reaction (symptoms may include ataxia, dysarthria, temporary vision loss, extreme weakness, agitation, euphoria, transient quadriplegia, confusion, and/or disorientation); withdrawal symptoms (abdominal cramps, headache, nausea, seizure) may occur upon abrupt discontinuation

Overdosage/Toxicology Symptoms include CNS depression, stupor, coma, shock, and respiratory depression. Treatment is supportive following attempts to enhance drug elimination. Hypotension should be treated with I.V. fluids and/or Trendelenburg positioning. Dialyzable by peritoneal and hemodialysis.

Drug Interactions

Cytochrome P450 Effect: Substrate of CYP2C19 (major)

Increased Effect/Toxicity: CYP2C19 inhibitors may increase the levels/effects of carisoprodol; example inhibitors include delavirdine, fluconazole, fluvoxamine, gemfibrozil, isoniazid, omeprazole, and ticlopidine. Sedation may be increased with CNS depressants (benzodiazepines, phenothiazines); avoid concurrent use.

Ethanol/Nutrition/Herb Interactions Ethanol: Avoid ethanol (may increase CNS depression).

Stability Store at 20°C to 25°C (68°F to 77°F).

Mechanism of Action Precise mechanism is not yet clear, but many effects have been ascribed to its central depressant actions

Pharmacodynamics/Kinetics

Onset of action: ~30 minutes

Duration: 4-6 hours

Distribution: Crosses placenta; high concentrations enter breast milk

Metabolism: Hepatic, via CYP2C19 to active metabolite (meprobamate)

Half-life elimination: 2.4 hours; Meprobamate: 10 hours

Excretion: Urine, as metabolite

Dosage Oral: Adults: 350 mg 3-4 times/day; take last dose at bedtime

Administration Give with food to decrease GI upset.

Monitoring Parameters Look for relief of pain and/or muscle spasm and avoid excessive drowsiness.

Dosage Forms

Tablet: 350 mg

Soma®: 350 mg

Carisoprodol and Aspirin (kar eye soe PROE dole & AS pir in)

U.S. Brand Names Soma® Compound

Index Terms Aspirin and Carisoprodol

Pharmacologic Category Skeletal Muscle Relaxant

Use Skeletal muscle relaxant

Pregnancy Risk Factor C/D (full-dose aspirin in 3rd trimester)

Dosage Oral: Adults: 1-2 tablets 4 times/day

Additional Information Complete prescribing information for this medication should be consulted for additional detail.

Dosage Forms Tablet: Carisoprodol 200 mg and aspirin 325 mg

Carisoprodol, Aspirin, and Codeine
(kar eye soe PROE dole, AS pir in, and KOE deen)

U.S. Brand Names Soma® Compound w/Codeine

Index Terms Aspirin, Carisoprodol, and Codeine; Codeine, Aspirin, and Carisoprodol

Pharmacologic Category Skeletal Muscle Relaxant

Use Skeletal muscle relaxant

Restrictions C-III

Pregnancy Risk Factor C/D (full-dose aspirin in 3rd trimester)

Dosage Oral: Adults: 1 or 2 tablets 4 times/day

Additional Information Complete prescribing information for this medication should be consulted for additional detail.

Dosage Forms Tablet: Carisoprodol 200 mg, aspirin 325 mg, and codeine phosphate 16 mg

♦ **Carmol® 10 [OTC]** see Urea on page 1758

♦ **Carmol® 20 [OTC]** see Urea on page 1758

♦ **Carmol® 40** see Urea on page 1758

♦ **Carmol® Deep Cleaning** see Urea on page 1758

♦ **Carmol-HC®** see Urea and Hydrocortisone on page 1759

♦ **Carmol® Scalp** see Sulfacetamide on page 1609

Carmustine (kar MUS teen)

U.S. Brand Names BiCNu®; Gliadel®
Canadian Brand Names BiCNu®; Gliadel Wafer®
Index Terms BCNU; bis-chloronitrosourea; Carmustinum; NSC-409962; WR-139021
Pharmacologic Category Antineoplastic Agent; Antineoplastic Agent, Alkylating Agent (Nitrosourea); Antineoplastic Agent, DNA Adduct-Forming Agent; Antineoplastic Agent, DNA Binding Agent

Use

Injection: Treatment of brain tumors (glioblastoma, brainstem glioma, medulloblastoma, astrocytoma, ependymoma, and metastatic brain tumors); multiple myeloma, Hodgkin's disease, non-Hodgkin's lymphomas, melanoma, lung cancer, colon cancer

Wafer (implant): Adjunct to surgery in patients with recurrent glioblastoma multiforme; adjunct to surgery and radiation in patients with high-grade malignant glioma

Pregnancy Risk Factor D

Pregnancy Implications Carmustine can cause fetal harm if administered to a pregnant woman.

Lactation Excretion in breast milk unknown/contraindicated

Medication Safety Issues

Sound-alike/look-alike issues:

Carmustine may be confused with lomustine

High alert medication: The Institute for Safe Medication Practices (ISMP) includes this medication among its list of drugs which have a heightened risk of causing significant patient harm when used in error.

Contraindications Hypersensitivity to carmustine or any component of the formulation; myelosuppression; pregnancy

Warnings/Precautions Hazardous agent - use appropriate precautions for handling and disposal. **[U.S. Boxed Warning]: Bone marrow suppression (thrombocytopenia, leukopenia) is the major toxicity and may be delayed; monitor blood counts weekly for at least 6 weeks after administration. Myelosuppression is cumulative; consider nadir blood counts from prior dose for dosage adjustment. May cause bleeding (due to thrombocytopenia) or infections (due to neutropenia); monitor closely.** Administer with caution to patients with depressed platelet, leukocyte, or erythrocyte counts; renal or hepatic impairment. Diluent contains significant amounts of ethanol; use caution with aldehyde dehydrogenase-2 deficiency or history of "alcohol flushing syndrome."

[U.S. Boxed Warning]: Dose-related pulmonary toxicity may occur; patients receiving cumulative doses >1400 mg/m^2 are at higher risk. Baseline pulmonary function tests are recommended. **[U.S. Boxed Warning]: Delayed onset of pulmonary fibrosis has occurred up to 17 years after treatment** in children (1-16 years) who received carmustine in cumulative doses ranging from 770-1800 mg/m^2 combined with cranial radiotherapy for intracranial tumors. **[U.S. Boxed Warning]: Should be administered under the supervision of an experienced cancer chemotherapy physician.** Safety and efficacy in children have not been established.

Adverse Reactions

>10%:

Cardiovascular: Hypotension (with high dose therapy, due to the alcohol content of the diluent)

Central nervous system: Dizziness, ataxia; Wafers: Seizures (54%) postoperatively

Dermatologic: Hyperpigmentation of skin (with skin contact)

Gastrointestinal: Severe nausea and vomiting, usually begins within 2-4 hours of drug administration and lasts for 4-6 hours; dose related. Patients should receive a prophylactic antiemetic regimen.

Hematologic: Myelosuppression - cumulative, dose related, delayed, thrombocytopenia is usually more common and more severe than leukopenia

Onset (days): 7-14

Nadir (days): 21-35

Recovery (days): 42-56

Hepatic: Reversible increases in bilirubin, alkaline phosphatase, and SGOT occur in 20% to 25% of patients

Local: Pain and burning at injection site; phlebitis

Ocular: Ocular toxicities (transient conjunctival flushing and blurred vision), retinal hemorrhages

Respiratory: Interstitial fibrosis occurs in up to 50% of patients receiving a cumulative dose >1400 mg/m^2, or bone marrow transplantation doses; may be delayed up to 3 years; rare in patients receiving lower doses. A history of lung disease or concomitant bleomycin therapy may increase the risk of this reaction. Patients with forced vital capacity (FVC) or carbon monoxide diffusing capacity of the lungs (DLCO) <70% of predicted are at higher risk.

1% to 10%:

Central nervous system: Wafers: Amnesia, aphasia, ataxia, cerebral edema, confusion, convulsion, depression, diplopia, dizziness, headache, hemiplegia, hydrocephalus, insomnia, meningitis, somnolence, stupor

Dermatologic: Facial flushing, probably due to the alcohol diluent; alopecia

Gastrointestinal: Anorexia, constipation, diarrhea, stomatitis

Hematologic: Anemia

<1% (Limited to important or life-threatening): Azotemia, cerebral hemorrhage infarction (wafer formulation), dermatitis, hepatic coma, hyperpigmentation, painless jaundice, subacute hepatitis

Overdosage/Toxicology Symptoms include nausea, vomiting, thrombocytopenia, and leukopenia. There are no known antidotes and treatment is primarily symptomatic and supportive.

Drug Interactions

Increased Effect/Toxicity: Carmustine given in combination with cimetidine is reported to cause bone marrow depression. Carmustine given in combination with etoposide is reported to cause severe hepatic dysfunction with hyperbilirubinemia, ascites, and thrombocytopenia. Diluent for infusion contains alcohol; avoid concurrent use of medications that inhibit aldehyde dehydrogenase-2 or cause disulfiram-like reactions.

Stability

Injection: Store intact vials under refrigeration; vials are stable for 36 days at room temperature. Initially, dilute with 3 mL of absolute alcohol. Further dilute with SWFI (27 mL) to a concentration of 3.3 mg/mL; protect from light; may further dilute with D_5W or NS, using a non-PVC container. Solutions are stable for 8 hours at room temperature (25°C) and 24 hours under refrigeration (2°C to 8°C) and protected from light. Further dilution in D_5W or NS is stable for 8 hours at room temperature (25°C) and 48 hours under refrigeration (4°C) in glass or Excel® protected from light.

Wafer: Store at or below -20°C (-4°F); may be kept at room temperature for up to 6 hours.

Mechanism of Action Interferes with the normal function of DNA by alkylation and cross-linking the strands of DNA, and by possible protein modification

Pharmacodynamics/Kinetics

Distribution: Readily crosses blood-brain barrier producing CSF levels equal to 15% to 70% of blood plasma levels; enters breast milk; highly lipid soluble

Metabolism: Rapidly hepatic

Half-life elimination: Biphasic: Initial: 1.4 minutes; Secondary: 20 minutes (active metabolites: plasma half-life of 67 hours)

Excretion: Urine (~60% to 70%) within 96 hours; lungs (6% to 10% as CO_2)

Dosage

I.V. (refer to individual protocols):

Children: 200-250 mg/m² every 4-6 weeks as a single dose

Adults: Usual dosage (per manufacturer labeling): 150-200 mg/m² every 6 weeks as a single dose or divided into daily injections on 2 successive days

Alternative regimens:

75-120 mg/m² days 1 and 2 every 6-8 weeks **or**

50-80 mg/m² days 1,2,3 every 6-8 weeks

Primary brain cancer:

150-200 mg/m² every 6-8 weeks as a single dose **or**

75-120 mg/m² days 1 and 2 every 6-8 weeks **or**

20-65 mg/m² every 4-6 weeks **or**

0.5-1 mg/kg every 4-6 weeks **or**

40-80 mg/m²/day for 3 days every 6-8 weeks

Autologous BMT: ALL OF THE FOLLOWING DOSES ARE FATAL WITHOUT BMT

Combination therapy: Up to 300-900 mg/m²

Single-agent therapy: Up to 1200 mg/m² (fatal necrosis is associated with doses >2 g/m²)

Implantation (wafer): Adults: Recurrent glioblastoma multiforme, malignant glioma: Up to 8 wafers may be placed in the resection cavity (total dose 62.6 mg); should the size and shape not accommodate 8 wafers, the maximum number of wafers allowed should be placed

Hemodialysis: Supplemental dosing is not required

Dosing adjustment in hepatic impairment: Dosage adjustment may be necessary; however, no specific guidelines are available

Administration Injection: Significant absorption to PVC containers - should be administered in either glass or Excel® container. I.V. infusion over 1-2 hours is recommended; infusion through a free-flowing saline or dextrose infusion, or administration through a central catheter can alleviate venous pain/irritation.

High-dose carmustine: Maximum rate of infusion of ≤3 mg/m²/minute to avoid excessive flushing, agitation, and hypotension; infusions should run over at least 2 hours; some investigational protocols dictate shorter infusions.

Fatal doses if not followed by bone marrow or peripheral stem cell infusions.

Extravasation management: Elevate extremity. Inject long-acting dexamethasone (Decadron® LA) or by hyaluronidase throughout tissue with a 25- to 37-gauge needle. Apply warm, moist compresses.

Monitoring Parameters CBC with differential and platelet count, pulmonary function, liver function, and renal function tests; monitor blood pressure during administration

Wafer: Complications of craniotomy (seizures, intracranial infection, brain edema)

Additional Information Accidental skin contact may cause transient burning and brown discoloration of the skin. Delayed onset pulmonary fibrosis occurring up to 17 years after treatment has been reported in patients who received cumulative doses >1400 mg/m².

Dosage Forms

Injection, powder for reconstitution:

BiCNu®: 100 mg [packaged with 3 mL of absolute alcohol as diluent]

Wafer, implant:

Gliadel®: 7.7 mg (8s)

♦ **Carmustinum** see Carmustine on page 296

♦ **Carnitor®** see Levocarnitine on page 997

♦ **Carrington Antifungal [OTC]** see Miconazole on page 1137

Carteolol (KAR tee oh lole)

U.S. Brand Names Cartrol®; Ocupress® [DSC]
Canadian Brand Names Cartrol® Oral; Ocupress® Ophthalmic
Index Terms Carteolol Hydrochloride
Pharmacologic Category Beta Blocker With Intrinsic Sympathomimetic Activity; Ophthalmic Agent, Antiglaucoma
Additional Appendix Information
Beta-Blockers on page 1875
Glaucoma Drug Therapy on page 2050
Use Management of hypertension; treatment of chronic open-angle glaucoma and intraocular hypertension
Pregnancy Risk Factor C (manufacturer); D (2nd and 3rd trimesters - expert analysis)
Lactation Excretion in breast milk unknown/use caution
Medication Safety Issues
Sound-alike/look-alike issues:
Carteolol may be confused with carvedilol
Cartrol® may be confused with Carbatrol®
Ocupress® may be confused with Ocufen®

Contraindications Hypersensitivity to carteolol or any component of the formulation; sinus bradycardia; heart block greater than first-degree (except in patients with a functioning artificial pacemaker); cardiogenic shock; bronchial asthma, bronchospasm, or COPD; uncompensated cardiac failure; pulmonary edema; pregnancy (2nd and 3rd trimesters)

Warnings/Precautions Consider pre-existing conditions such as sick sinus syndrome before initiating. Beta-blocker therapy should not be withdrawn abruptly (particularly in patients with CAD), but gradually tapered to avoid acute tachycardia, hypertension, and/or ischemia. Use caution in patients with PVD (can aggravate arterial insufficiency), myasthenia gravis, or psychiatric disease (may cause CNS depression). Use caution with concurrent use of beta-blockers and either verapamil or diltiazem; bradycardia or heart block can occur. Use with caution in patients receiving anesthetic agents which decrease myocardial function. In general, patients with bronchospastic disease should not receive beta-blockers; if used at all, should be used cautiously with close monitoring. Use cautiously in diabetics because it can mask prominent hypoglycemic symptoms. Dosage adjustment is required in patients with renal dysfunction. Use care with anesthetic agents that decrease myocardial function. Beta-blockers with intrinsic sympathomimetic activity have not been demonstrated to be of value in CHF. Systemic absorption and adverse effects may occur with ophthalmic product, including bradycardia and/or hypotension. Should not be used alone in angle-closure glaucoma (has no effect on pupillary constriction). Adequate alpha-blockade is required prior to use of any beta-blocker for patients with untreated pheochromocytoma. Safety and efficacy have not been established in children.

Adverse Reactions
Ophthalmic:
>10%: Ocular: Conjunctival hyperemia
1% to 10%: Ocular: Anisocoria, corneal punctate keratitis, corneal staining, corneal sensitivity decreased, eye pain, vision disturbances
Systemic:
>10%:
Central nervous system: Drowsiness, insomnia
Endocrine & metabolic: Sexual ability decreased
1% to 10%:
Cardiovascular: Bradycardia, palpitation, edema, CHF, peripheral circulation reduced
Central nervous system: Mental depression
Gastrointestinal: Constipation, diarrhea, nausea, vomiting, stomach discomfort
Respiratory: Bronchospasm
Miscellaneous: Cold extremities
<1% (Limited to important or life-threatening): Arrhythmias, chest pain, confusion (especially in the elderly), depression, dyspnea, hallucinations, headache, leukopenia, nervousness, orthostatic hypotension, polyuria, psoriasiform eruption, thrombocytopenia

Overdosage/Toxicology Symptoms include cardiac disturbances, CNS toxicity, bronchospasm, hypoglycemia, and hyperkalemia. The most common cardiac symptoms include hypotension and bradycardia. Atrioventricular block, intraventricular conduction disturbances, cardiogenic shock, and asystole may occur with severe overdose, especially with membrane-depressant drugs (eg, propranolol). CNS effects include convulsions, coma, and respiratory arrest (commonly seen with propranolol and other membrane-depressant and lipid-soluble drugs). Treatment is symptomatic for seizures, hypotension, hyperkalemia, and hypoglycemia. Bradycardia and hypotension resistant to atropine, isoproterenol, or pacing may respond to glucagon. Wide QRS defects caused by membrane-depressant poisoning may respond to hypertonic sodium bicarbonate. Repeat-dose charcoal, hemoperfusion, or hemodialysis may be helpful in removal of only those beta-blockers with a small V_d, long half-life, or low intrinsic clearance (acebutolol, atenolol, nadolol, sotalol).

Drug Interactions
Cytochrome P450 Effect: Substrate of CYP2D6 (minor)
Increased Effect/Toxicity: Carteolol may increase the effects of other drugs which slow AV conduction (digoxin, verapamil, diltiazem), alpha-blockers (prazosin, terazosin), and alpha-adrenergic stimulants (epinephrine, phenylephrine). Carteolol may mask the tachycardia from hypoglycemia caused by insulin and oral hypoglycemics. In patients receiving concurrent therapy, the risk of hypertensive crisis is increased when either clonidine or the beta-blocker is withdrawn. Reserpine has been shown to enhance the effect of beta-blockers. Beta-blockers may increase the action or levels of ethanol, disopyramide, nondepolarizing muscle relaxants, and theophylline although the effects are difficult to predict.

Decreased Effect: Decreased effect of beta-blockers with aluminum salts, barbiturates, calcium salts, cholestyramine, colestipol, NSAIDs, penicillins (ampicillin), rifampin, salicylates, and sulfinpyrazone due to decreased bioavailability and plasma levels. Beta-blockers may decrease the effect of sulfonylureas (possibly hyperglycemia). Nonselective beta-blockers blunt the effect of beta-2 adrenergic agonists (albuterol).

Ethanol/Nutrition/Herb Interactions Herb/Nutraceutical: Avoid dong quai if using for hypertension (has estrogenic activity). Avoid ephedra, yohimbe, ginseng (may worsen hypertension). Avoid garlic (may have increased antihypertensive effect).

Mechanism of Action Blocks both beta₁- and beta₂-receptors and has mild intrinsic sympathomimetic activity; has negative inotropic and chronotropic effects and can significantly slow AV nodal conduction

Pharmacodynamics/Kinetics
Onset of action: Oral: 1-1.5 hours
Peak effect: 2 hours
Duration: 12 hours
Absorption: Oral: 80%
Protein binding: 23% to 30%
Metabolism: 30% to 50%
Half-life elimination: 6 hours
Excretion: Urine (as metabolites)

Dosage Adults:
Oral: 2.5 mg as a single daily dose, with a maintenance dose normally 2.5-5 mg once daily; doses >10 mg do not increase response and may in fact decrease effect.
Ophthalmic: Instill 1 drop in affected eye(s) twice daily.
Dosing interval in renal impairment: Oral:
Cl$_{cr}$ >60 mL/minute/1.73 m²: Administer every 24 hours.
Cl$_{cr}$ 20-60 mL/minute/1.73 m²: Administer every 48 hours.
Cl$_{cr}$ <20 mL/minute/1.73 m²: Administer every 72 hours.

Administration
Oral: Administer with meals.
Ophthalmic: Intended for twice daily dosing. Keep eye open and do not blink for 30 seconds after instillation. Wear sunglasses to avoid photophobic discomfort. Apply gentle pressure to lacrimal sac during and immediately following instillation (1 minute).

Monitoring Parameters Ophthalmic: Intraocular pressure; Systemic: Blood pressure, pulse, CNS status

Dosage Forms [DSC] = Discontinued product
Solution, ophthalmic, as hydrochloride: 1% (5 mL, 10 mL, 15 mL) [contains benzalkonium chloride]
Ocupress® [DSC]: 1% (5 mL, 10 mL, 15 mL) [contains benzalkonium chloride]
Tablet, as hydrochloride (Cartrol®): 2.5 mg, 5 mg

♦ **Carteolol Hydrochloride** see Carteolol on page 298
♦ **Carter's Little Pills® (Can)** see Bisacodyl on page 223
♦ **Cartia XT™** see Diltiazem on page 509
♦ **Cartrol®** see Carteolol on page 298
♦ **Cartrol® Oral (Can)** see Carteolol on page 298

Carvedilol (KAR ve dil ole)

U.S. Brand Names Coreg®; Coreg CR™
Canadian Brand Names Apo-Carvedilol®; Coreg®; Novo-Carvedilol; PMS-Carvedilol; RAN™-Carvedilol; ratio-Carvedilol
Pharmacologic Category Beta Blocker With Alpha-Blocking Activity
Additional Appendix Information
Beta-Blockers on page 1875
Heart Failure (Systolic) on page 2051
Use Mild-to-severe heart failure of ischemic or cardiomyopathic origin (usually in addition to standardized therapy); left ventricular dysfunction following myocardial infarction (MI); management of hypertension
Unlabeled/Investigational Use Angina pectoris
Pregnancy Risk Factor C (manufacturer); D (2nd and 3rd trimesters - expert analysis)
Pregnancy Implications Postimplantation losses were observed in animal studies. No data available on whether carvedilol crosses the placenta. Beta-blockers have been associated with persistent bradycardia, hypotension, and IUGR; IUGR probably related to maternal hypertension. Cases of neonatal hypoglycemia have been reported following maternal use of beta-blockers at parturition or during breast-feeding.
Lactation Excretion in breast milk unknown/not recommended
Medication Safety Issues
Sound-alike/look-alike issues:
Carvedilol may be confused with captopril, carteolol

International issues:
Talliton® [Hungary] may be confused with Talacen® which is a brand name for pentazocine/acetaminophen combination in the U.S.
Contraindications Hypersensitivity to carvedilol or any component of the formulation; decompensated cardiac failure requiring intravenous inotropic therapy; bronchial asthma or related bronchospastic conditions; second- or third-degree AV block, sick sinus syndrome, and severe bradycardia (except in patients with a functioning artificial pacemaker); cardiogenic shock; severe hepatic impairment; pregnancy (2nd and 3rd trimesters)
Warnings/Precautions Consider pre-existing conditions such as sick sinus syndrome before initiating. Initiate cautiously and monitor for possible deterioration in patient status (including symptoms of CHF). Adjustment of other medications (ACE inhibitors and/or diuretics) may be required. In severe chronic heart failure, trial patients were excluded if they had cardiac-related rales, ascites, or a serum creatinine >2.8 mg/dL. Congestive heart failure (Continued)

Carvedilol *(Continued)*

patients may experience a worsening of renal function; risks include ischemic disease, diffuse vascular disease, underlying renal dysfunction; systolic BP <100 mm Hg. Patients should be advised to avoid driving or other hazardous tasks during initiation of therapy due to the risk of syncope. Beta-blocker therapy should not be withdrawn abruptly (particularly in patients with CAD), but gradually tapered to avoid acute tachycardia, hypertension, and/or ischemia.

Manufacturer recommends discontinuation of therapy if liver injury occurs (confirmed by laboratory testing). In general, patients with bronchospastic disease should not receive beta-blockers; if used at all, should be used cautiously with close monitoring. Use caution in patients with PVD (can aggravate arterial insufficiency). Use caution with concurrent use of verapamil or diltiazem; bradycardia or heart block can occur. Use cautiously in diabetics because it can mask prominent hypoglycemic symptoms. Use with caution in patients with myasthenia gravis or psychiatric disease (may cause CNS depression). Adequate alpha-blockade is required prior to use of any beta-blocker for patients with untreated pheochromocytoma. Use care with anesthetic agents that decrease myocardial function. Safety and efficacy in children <18 years of age have not been established.

Adverse Reactions Note: Frequency ranges include data from hypertension and heart failure trials. Higher rates of adverse reactions have generally been noted in patients with CHF. However, the frequency of adverse effects associated with placebo is also increased in this population. Events occurring at a frequency > placebo in clinical trials.

>10%:
 Cardiovascular: Hypotension (9% to 20%)
 Central nervous system: Dizziness (2% to 32%), fatigue (4% to 24%)
 Endocrine & metabolic: Hyperglycemia (5% to 12%), weight gain (10% to 12%)
 Gastrointestinal: Diarrhea (1% to 12%)
 Neuromuscular & skeletal: Weakness (11%)

1% to 10%:
 Cardiovascular: Bradycardia (2% to 10%), syncope (3% to 8%), peripheral edema (1% to 7%), generalized edema (5% to 6%), angina (2% to 6%), dependent edema (4%), AV block (3%), hypertension (3%), postural hypotension (2%), palpitation
 Central nervous system: Headache (5% to 8%), fever (3%), somnolence (2%), insomnia (1% to 2%), malaise, hypoesthesia, vertigo
 Endocrine & metabolic: Alkaline phosphatase increased, gout (6%), hypercholesterolemia (4%), dehydration (2%), hyperkalemia (3%), hypervolemia (2%), hypertriglyceridemia (1%), hyperuricemia, hypoglycemia, hyponatremia
 Gastrointestinal: Nausea (2% to 9%), vomiting (6%), melena, periodontitis
 Genitourinary: Hematuria (3%), impotence
 Hematologic: Thrombocytopenia (1% to 2%), prothrombin decreased, purpura
 Hepatic: Transaminases increased
 Neuromuscular & skeletal: Back pain (2% to 7%), arthralgia (6%), myalgia (3%), muscle cramps, paresthesia (1%)
 Ocular: Blurred vision (3% to 5%), lacrimation
 Renal: BUN increased (6%), creatinine increased (3%), renal function abnormal, albuminuria, glycosuria, kidney failure
 Respiratory: Cough increased (5%), nasopharyngitis (4%), rhinitis (2%), nasal congestion (1%), sinus congestion (1%)
 Miscellaneous: Injury (3% to 6%), allergy, sudden death

<1% (Limited to important or life-threatening): Anaphylactoid reaction, anemia, aplastic anemia (rare, all events occurred in patients receiving other medications capable of causing this effect); asthma, AV block (complete), bronchospasm, bundle branch block, cholestatic jaundice, concentration decreased, convulsion, depression exacerbation, diabetes mellitus, erythema multiforme, exfoliative dermatitis, GI hemorrhage, interstitial pneumonitis, leukopenia, migraine, myocardial ischemia, neuralgia, pancytopenia, peripheral ischemia, pulmonary edema, Stevens-Johnson syndrome, toxic epidermal necrolysis, urinary incontinence

Overdosage/Toxicology Symptoms include cardiac disturbances, CNS toxicity, bronchospasm, hypoglycemia, and hyperkalemia. The most common cardiac symptoms include hypotension and bradycardia. Atrioventricular block, intraventricular conduction disturbances, cardiogenic shock, and asystole may occur with severe overdose, especially with membrane-depressant drugs (eg, propranolol). CNS effects include convulsions, coma, and respiratory arrest, commonly seen with propranolol and other membrane-depressant and lipid-soluble drugs. Treatment is symptomatic for seizures, hypotension, hyperkalemia, and hypoglycemia. For excessive bradycardia: consider atropine. Bradycardia and hypotension resistant to atropine, isoproterenol, or pacing may respond to glucagon. Wide QRS defects caused by membrane-depressant poisoning may respond to hypertonic sodium bicarbonate. Repeat-dose charcoal, hemoperfusion, or hemodialysis may be helpful in removal of only those beta-blockers with a small V_d, long half-life, or low intrinsic clearance (acebutolol, atenolol, nadolol, sotalol).

Drug Interactions
 Cytochrome P450 Effect: Substrate of CYP1A2 (minor), 2C9 (major), 2D6 (major), 2E1 (minor), 3A4 (minor)
 Increased Effect/Toxicity: CYP2C9 Inhibitors may increase the levels/effects of carvedilol; example inhibitors include delavirdine, fluconazole, gemfibrozil, ketoconazole, nicardipine, NSAIDs, sulfonamides and tolbutamide. CYP2D6 inhibitors may increase the levels/effects of carvedilol; example inhibitors include chlorpromazine, delavirdine, fluoxetine, miconazole, paroxetine, pergolide, quinidine, quinine, ritonavir, and ropinirole. Cimetidine increase the serum levels and effects of carvedilol. Carvedilol may increase the effects of other drugs which slow AV conduction (digoxin, verapamil, diltiazem) and alpha-blockers (prazosin, terazosin). Carvedilol may mask the tachycardia from hypoglycemia caused by insulin and oral hypoglycemics. SSRIs may decrease the metabolism of carvedilol.

Decreased Effect: CYP2C9 inducers may decrease the levels/effects of carvedilol; example inducers include carbamazepine, phenobarbital, phenytoin, rifampin, rifapentine, and secobarbital. Decreased antihypertensive effect of beta-blockers has occurred with concurrent NSAID or salicylate use. Beta-blockers may alter the effect of sulfonylureas. Disopyramide may exacerbate heart failure or enhance bradycardic effect of beta-blockers. Beta-blockers may counteract desired effects of beta-agonists.

Ethanol/Nutrition/Herb Interactions

Ethanol: Coreg CR™: Avoid ethanol (including prescription and over the counter medications containing ethanol). Ethanol may affect extended release properties causing a faster release; separate by at least 2 hours.

Food: Food decreases rate but not extent of absorption. Administration with food minimizes risks of orthostatic hypotension.

Herb/Nutraceutical: Avoid dong quai if using for hypertension (has estrogenic activity). Avoid ephedra, yohimbe, ginseng (may worsen hypertension). Avoid garlic (may have increased antihypertensive effect).

Stability Store at 15°C to 30°C (59°F to 86°F).

Mechanism of Action As a racemic mixture, carvedilol has nonselective beta-adrenoreceptor and alpha-adrenergic blocking activity. No intrinsic sympathomimetic activity has been documented. Associated effects in hypertensive patients include reduction of cardiac output, exercise- or beta agonist-induced tachycardia, reduction of reflex orthostatic tachycardia, vasodilation, decreased peripheral vascular resistance (especially in standing position), decreased renal vascular resistance, reduced plasma renin activity, and increased levels of atrial natriuretic peptide. In CHF, associated effects include decreased pulmonary capillary wedge pressure, decreased pulmonary artery pressure, decreased heart rate, decreased systemic vascular resistance, increased stroke volume index, and decreased right arterial pressure (RAP).

Pharmacodynamics/Kinetics

Onset of action: 1-2 hours

Peak antihypertensive effect: ~1-2 hours

Absorption: Rapid

Distribution: V_d: 115 L

Protein binding: >98%, primarily to albumin

Metabolism: Extensively hepatic, via CYP2C9, 2D6, 3A4, and 2C19 (2% excreted unchanged); three active metabolites (4-hydroxyphenyl metabolite is 13 times more potent than parent drug for beta-blockade); first-pass effect; plasma concentrations in the elderly and those with cirrhotic liver disease are 50% and 4-7 times higher, respectively

Bioavailability: Immediate release: 25% to 35%; Extended release: 85% of immediate release

Half-life elimination: 7-10 hours

Excretion: Primarily feces

Dosage Oral: Adults: Reduce dosage if heart rate drops to <55 beats/minute.

Hypertension:

Immediate release: 6.25 mg twice daily; if tolerated, dose should be maintained for 1-2 weeks, then increased to 12.5 mg twice daily. Dosage may be increased to a maximum of 25 mg twice daily after 1-2 weeks; maximum dose: 50 mg/day.

Extended release: Initial: 20 mg once daily, if tolerated, dose should be maintained for 1-2 weeks then increased to 40 mg once daily if necessary; maximum dose: 80 mg once daily

Congestive heart failure:

Immediate release: 3.125 mg twice daily for 2 weeks; if this dose is tolerated, may increase to 6.25 mg twice daily. Double the dose every 2 weeks to the highest dose tolerated by patient. (Prior to initiating therapy, other heart failure medications should be stabilized and fluid retention minimized.)

Maximum recommended dose:

Mild-to-moderate heart failure:

<85 kg: 25 mg twice daily

>85 kg: 50 mg twice daily

Severe heart failure: 25 mg twice daily

Extended release: Initial: 10 mg once daily for 2 weeks; if the dose is tolerated, increase dose to 20 mg, 40 mg, and 80 mg over successive intervals of at least 2 weeks. Maintain on lower dose if higher dose is not tolerated.

Left ventricular dysfunction following MI: **Note**: Should be initiated only after patient is hemodynamically stable and fluid retention has been minimized.

Immediate release: Initial 3.125-6.25 mg twice daily; increase dosage incrementally (ie, from 6.25-12.5 mg twice daily) at intervals of 3-10 days, based on tolerance, to a target dose of 25 mg twice daily.

Extended release: Initial: 20 mg once daily; increase dosage incrementally at intervals of 3-10 days. Target dose: 80 mg once daily.

Angina pectoris (unlabeled use): Immediate release: 25-50 mg twice daily

Conversion from immediate release to extended release (Coreg CR™):

Current dose immediate release tablets 3.125 mg twice daily: Convert to extended release capsules 10 mg once daily

Current dose immediate release tablets 6.25 mg twice daily: Convert to extended release capsules 20 mg once daily

Current dose immediate release tablets 12.5 mg twice daily: Convert to extended release capsules 40 mg once daily

Current dose immediate release tablets 25 mg twice daily: Convert to extended release capsules 80 mg once daily

Dosing adjustment in renal impairment: None necessary

Dosing adjustment in hepatic impairment: Use is contraindicated in severe liver dysfunction.

Dietary Considerations Should be taken with food to minimize the risk of orthostatic hypotension.

Administration Administer with food. Extended release capsules should not be crushed or chewed. Capsules may be opened and sprinkled on applesauce for immediate use. (Continued)

Carvedilol (Continued)

Monitoring Parameters Heart rate, blood pressure (base need for dosage increase on trough blood pressure measurements and for tolerance on standing systolic pressure 1 hour after dosing); renal studies, BUN, liver function; in patient with increase risk for developing renal dysfunction, monitor during dosage titration.

Additional Information Fluid retention during therapy should be treated with an increase in diuretic dosage.

Dosage Forms

Capsule, extended release; as phosphate:
  Coreg CR™: 10 mg, 20 mg, 40 mg, 80 mg
Tablet:
  Coreg®: 3.125 mg, 6.25 mg, 12.5 mg, 25 mg

♦ **Casodex®** *see* Bicalutamide *on page 221*

Caspofungin (kas poe FUN jin)

U.S. Brand Names Cancidas®
Canadian Brand Names Cancidas®
Index Terms Caspofungin Acetate
Pharmacologic Category Antifungal Agent, Parenteral; Echinocandin
Additional Appendix Information
  Antifungal Agents *on page 1869*
Use Treatment of invasive *Aspergillus* infections in patients who are refractory or intolerant of other therapy; treatment of candidemia and other *Candida* infections (intra-abdominal abscesses, esophageal, peritonitis, pleural space); empirical treatment for presumed fungal infections in febrile neutropenic patient
Pregnancy Risk Factor C
Pregnancy Implications There are no adequate and well-controlled studies in pregnant women. Should be used during pregnancy only if potential benefit justifies the potential risk to the fetus. Embryotoxicity has been demonstrated in animal studies.
Lactation Excretion in breast milk unknown/use caution
Contraindications Hypersensitivity to caspofungin or any component of the formulation
Warnings/Precautions Concurrent use of cyclosporine should be limited to patients for whom benefit outweighs risk, due to a high frequency of hepatic transaminase elevations observed during concurrent use. Limited data are available concerning treatment durations longer than 4 weeks.
Adverse Reactions
>10%:
  Central nervous system: Headache (up to 11%), fever (3% to 26%), chills (up to 14%)
  Endocrine & metabolic: Hypokalemia (4% to 11%)
  Hematologic: Hemoglobin decreased (1% to 12%)
  Hepatic: Serum alkaline phosphatase increased (3% to 11%), transaminases increased (up to 13%)
  Local: Infusion site reactions (2% to 12%), phlebitis/thrombophlebitis (up to 16%)
1% to 10%:
  Cardiovascular: Flushing (2% to 3%), facial edema (up to 3%), hypertension (1% to 2%), tachycardia (1% to 2%), hypotension (1%)
  Central nervous system: Dizziness (2%), pain (1% to 5%), insomnia (1%)
  Dermatologic: Rash (<1% to 6%), pruritus (1% to 3%), erythema (1% to 2%)
  Gastrointestinal: Nausea (2% to 6%), vomiting (1% to 4%), abdominal pain (1% to 4%), diarrhea (1% to 4%), anorexia (1%)
  Hematologic: Eosinophils increased (3%), neutrophils decreased (2% to 3%), WBC decreased (5% to 6%), anemia (up to 4%), platelet count decreased (2% to 3%)
  Hepatic: Bilirubin increased (3%)
  Local: Induration (up to 3%)
  Neuromuscular & skeletal: Myalgia (up to 3%), paresthesia (1% to 3%), tremor (≤2%)
  Renal: Nephrotoxicity (8%)*, proteinuria (5%), hematuria (2%), serum creatinine increased (<1% to 4%), urinary WBCs increased (up to 8%), urinary RBCs increased (1% to 4%), blood urea nitrogen increased (1%)
  *Nephrotoxicity defined as serum creatinine ≥2x baseline value or ≥1 mg/dL in patients with serum creatinine above ULN range (patients with Cl_{cr} <30 mL/minute were excluded)
  Miscellaneous: Flu-like syndrome (3%), diaphoresis (up to 3%)
<1% (Limited to important or life-threatening): Adult respiratory distress syndrome (ARDS), anaphylaxis, hepatic dysfunction, pulmonary edema, renal insufficiency; histamine-mediated reaction (including facial swelling, bronchospasm, sensation of warmth) have been reported
Overdosage/Toxicology No experience with overdosage has been reported. Caspofungin is not dialyzable. Treatment is symptomatic and supportive.
Drug Interactions
  Increased Effect/Toxicity: Concurrent administration of cyclosporine may increase caspofungin concentrations; hepatic serum transaminases may be observed.
  Decreased Effect: Caspofungin may decrease blood concentrations of tacrolimus. Dosage adjustment of caspofungin to 70 mg is required for patients on rifampin.
Stability Store vials at 2°C to 8°C (36°F to 46°F). Reconstituted solution may be stored at less than 25°C (77°F) for 1 hour prior to preparation of infusion solution. Infusion solutions may be stored at less than 25°C (77°F) and should be used within 24 hours; up to 48 hours if stored at 2°C to 8°C (36°F to 46°F).

Bring refrigerated vial to room temperature. Reconstitute vials using 0.9% sodium chloride for injection, SWFI, or bacteriostatic water for injection. Mix gently until clear solution is formed; do not use if cloudy or contains particles. Solution should be further diluted with 0.9%, 0.45%, or 0.225% sodium chloride or LR.

Mechanism of Action Inhibits synthesis of β(1,3)-D-glucan, an essential component of the cell wall of susceptible fungi. Highest activity in regions of active cell growth. Mammalian cells do not require β(1,3)-D-glucan, limiting potential toxicity.

Pharmacodynamics/Kinetics

Protein binding: 97% to albumin

Metabolism: Slowly, via hydrolysis and *N*-acetylation as well as by spontaneous degradation, with subsequent metabolism to component amino acids. Overall metabolism is extensive.

Half-life elimination: Beta (distribution): 9-11 hours; Terminal: 40-50 hours

Excretion: Urine (41% as metabolites, 1% to 9% unchanged) and feces (35% as metabolites)

Dosage I.V.:

Children: Safety and efficacy in pediatric patients have not been established

Adults: **Note:** Duration of caspofungin treatment should be determined by patient status and clinical response. Empiric therapy should be given until neutropenia resolves. In patients with positive cultures, treatment should continue until 14 days after last positive culture. In neutropenic patients, treatment should be given at least 7 days after both signs and symptoms of infection **and** neutropenia resolve.

Empiric therapy: Initial dose: 70 mg on day 1; subsequent dosing: 50 mg/day; may increase up to 70 mg/day if tolerated, but clinical response is inadequate

Invasive *Aspergillus*, candidiasis: Initial dose: 70 mg on day 1; subsequent dosing: 50 mg/day

Esophageal candidiasis: 50 mg/day; **Note:** The majority of patients studied for this indication also had oropharyngeal involvement.

Concomitant use of an enzyme inducer:

Patients receiving rifampin: 70 mg caspofungin daily

Patients receiving carbamazepine, dexamethasone, efavirenz, nevirapine, **or** phenytoin (and possibly other enzyme inducers) may require an increased daily dose of caspofungin (70 mg/day).

Elderly: The number of patients >65 years of age in clinical studies was not sufficient to establish whether a difference in response may be anticipated.

Dosage adjustment in renal impairment: No specific dosage adjustment is required; supplemental dose is not required following dialysis

Dosage adjustment in hepatic impairment:

Mild hepatic insufficiency (Child-Pugh score 5-6): No adjustment necessary

Moderate hepatic insufficiency (Child-Pugh score 7-9): 35 mg/day; initial 70 mg loading dose should still be administered in treatment of invasive infections

Severe hepatic insufficiency (Child-Pugh score >9): No clinical experience

Administration Infuse slowly, over 1 hour; monitor during infusion. Isolated cases of possible histamine-related reactions have occurred during clinical trials (rash, flushing, pruritus, facial edema).

Dosage Forms Injection, powder for reconstitution, as acetate: 50 mg [contains sucrose 39 mg], 70 mg [contains sucrose 54 mg]

- **Caspofungin Acetate** *see* Caspofungin *on page 302*
- **Castor Oil, Trypsin, and Balsam Peru** *see* Trypsin, Balsam Peru, and Castor Oil *on page 1754*
- **Cataflam®** *see* Diclofenac *on page 492*
- **Catapres®** *see* Clonidine *on page 399*
- **Catapres-TTS®** *see* Clonidine *on page 399*
- **Cathflo® Activase®** *see* Alteplase *on page 79*
- **Caverject®** *see* Alprostadil *on page 77*
- **Caverject Impulse®** *see* Alprostadil *on page 77*
- **CaviRinse™** *see* Fluoride *on page 722*
- **CB-1348** *see* Chlorambucil *on page 340*
- **CBDCA** *see* Carboplatin *on page 291*
- **CBZ** *see* Carbamazepine *on page 284*
- **CC-5013** *see* Lenalidomide *on page 984*
- **CCNU** *see* Lomustine *on page 1026*
- **2-CdA** *see* Cladribine *on page 383*
- **CDDP** *see* Cisplatin *on page 379*
- **CDX** *see* Bicalutamide *on page 221*
- **Ceclor® (Can)** *see* Cefaclor *on page 303*
- **Cecon® [OTC]** *see* Ascorbic Acid *on page 156*
- **Cedax®** *see* Ceftibuten *on page 322*
- **Cedocard®-SR (Can)** *see* Isosorbide Dinitrate *on page 945*
- **CEE** *see* Estrogens (Conjugated/Equine) *on page 631*
- **CeeNU®** *see* Lomustine *on page 1026*

Cefaclor (SEF a klor)

U.S. Brand Names Raniclor™

Canadian Brand Names Apo-Cefaclor®; Ceclor®; Novo-Cefaclor; Nu-Cefaclor; PMS-Cefaclor

Pharmacologic Category Antibiotic, Cephalosporin (Second Generation)

Additional Appendix Information

Antimicrobial Drugs of Choice *on page 1981*

Use Treatment of susceptible bacterial infections including otitis media, lower respiratory tract infections, acute exacerbations of chronic bronchitis, pharyngitis and tonsillitis, urinary tract infections, skin and skin structure infections

Pregnancy Risk Factor B

Lactation Enters breast milk/use caution

(Continued)

Cefaclor *(Continued)*

Medication Safety Issues
Sound-alike/look-alike issues:
Cefaclor may be confused with cephalexin

Contraindications
Hypersensitivity to cefaclor, any component of the formulation, or other cephalosporins

Warnings/Precautions
Modify dosage in patients with severe renal impairment. Prolonged use may result in superinfection. Use with caution in patients with a history of penicillin allergy, especially IgE-mediated reactions (eg, anaphylaxis, urticaria). Beta-lactamase-negative, ampicillin-resistant (BLNAR) strains of *H. influenzae* should be considered resistant to cefaclor. Extended release tablets are not approved for use in children <16 years of age.

Adverse Reactions
1% to 10%:
Dermatologic: Rash (maculopapular, erythematous, or morbilliform) (1% to 2%)
Gastrointestinal: Diarrhea (3%)
Genitourinary: Vaginitis (2%)
Hematologic: Eosinophilia (2%)
Hepatic: Transaminases increased (3%)
Miscellaneous: Moniliasis (2%)

<1% (Limited to important or life-threatening): Agitation, agranulocytosis, anaphylaxis, angioedema, aplastic anemia, arthralgia, cholestatic jaundice, CNS irritability, confusion, dizziness, hallucinations, hemolytic anemia, hepatitis, hyperactivity, insomnia, interstitial nephritis, nausea, nervousness, neutropenia, paresthesia, PT prolonged, pruritus, pseudomembranous colitis, seizure, serum-sickness, somnolence, Stevens-Johnson syndrome, thrombocytopenia, toxic epidermal necrolysis, urticaria, vomiting

Reactions reported with other cephalosporins: Abdominal pain, cholestasis, fever, hemorrhage, renal dysfunction, superinfection, toxic nephropathy

Overdosage/Toxicology
Symptoms include diarrhea, epigastric distress, nausea, and vomiting. Many beta-lactam antibiotics have the potential to cause neuromuscular hyperirritability or seizures. Hemodialysis may be helpful to aid in removal of the drug from the blood, but is not usually indicated; otherwise, most treatment is supportive and symptom-directed.

Drug Interactions
Increased Effect/Toxicity: Probenecid may decrease cephalosporin elimination. Furosemide, aminoglycosides when taken with cefaclor may result in additive nephrotoxicity.

Ethanol/Nutrition/Herb Interactions
Food: Cefaclor serum levels may be decreased slightly if taken with food. The bioavailability of cefaclor extended release tablets is decreased 23% and the maximum concentration is decreased 67% when taken on an empty stomach.

Stability
Store at controlled room temperature. Refrigerate suspension after reconstitution. Discard after 14 days. Do not freeze.

Mechanism of Action
Inhibits bacterial cell wall synthesis by binding to one or more of the penicillin-binding proteins (PBPs) which in turn inhibits the final transpeptidation step of peptidoglycan synthesis in bacterial cell walls, thus inhibiting cell wall biosynthesis. Bacteria eventually lyse due to ongoing activity of cell wall autolytic enzymes (autolysins and murein hydrolases) while cell wall assembly is arrested.

Pharmacodynamics/Kinetics
Absorption: Well absorbed, acid stable
Distribution: Widely throughout the body and reaches therapeutic concentration in most tissues and body fluids, including synovial, pericardial, pleural, peritoneal fluids; bile, sputum, and urine; bone, myocardium, gallbladder, skin and soft tissue; crosses placenta; enters breast milk
Protein binding: 25%
Metabolism: Partially hepatic
Half-life elimination: 0.5-1 hour; prolonged with renal impairment
Time to peak: Capsule: 60 minutes; Suspension: 45 minutes
Excretion: Urine (80% as unchanged drug)

Dosage
Usual dosage range:
Children >1 month: Oral: 20-40 mg/kg/day divided every 8-12 hours (maximum dose: 1 g/day)
Adults: Oral: 250-500 mg every 8 hours
Indication-specific dosing:
Children: Oral:
Otitis media: 40 mg/kg/day divided every 12 hours
Pharyngitis: 20 mg/kg/day divided every 12 hours
Dosing adjustment in renal impairment:
Cl$_{cr}$ 10-50 mL/minute: Administer 50% to 100% of dose
Cl$_{cr}$ <10 mL/minute: Administer 50% of dose
Hemodialysis: Moderately dialyzable (20% to 50%)

Dietary Considerations
Capsule, chewable tablet, and suspension may be taken with or without food. Raniclor™ contains phenylalanine 2.8 mg/cefaclor 125 mg.

Administration
Administer around-the-clock to promote less variation in peak and trough serum levels.
Chewable tablet: Should be chewed before swallowing; should not be swallowed whole.
Oral suspension: Shake well before using.

Monitoring Parameters
Assess patient at beginning and throughout therapy for infection; monitor for signs of anaphylaxis during first dose

Test Interactions
Positive direct Coombs', false-positive urinary glucose test using cupric sulfate (Benedict's solution, Clinitest®, Fehling's solution), false-positive serum or urine creatinine with Jaffé reaction

Dosage Forms

Capsule: 250 mg, 500 mg

Powder for oral suspension: 125 mg/5 mL (75 mL, 150 mL); 187 mg/5 mL (50 mL, 100 mL); 250 mg/5 mL (75 mL, 150 mL); 375 mg/5 mL (50 mL, 100 mL)

Tablet, chewable (Raniclor™): 125 mg [contains phenylalanine 2.8 mg; fruity flavor], 187 mg [contains phenylalanine 4.2 mg; fruity flavor]

Cefadroxil (sef a DROKS il)

U.S. Brand Names Duricef®

Canadian Brand Names Apo-Cefadroxil®; Duricef®; Novo-Cefadroxil

Index Terms Cefadroxil Monohydrate

Pharmacologic Category Antibiotic, Cephalosporin (First Generation)

Additional Appendix Information

Prevention of Bacterial Endocarditis *on page 1960*

Use Treatment of susceptible bacterial infections, including those caused by group A beta-hemolytic *Streptococcus*; prophylaxis against bacterial endocarditis in patients who are allergic to penicillin and undergoing surgical or dental procedures

Pregnancy Risk Factor B

Lactation Enters breast milk (small amounts)/use caution (AAP rates "compatible")

Contraindications Hypersensitivity to cefadroxil, any component of the formulation, or other cephalosporins

Warnings/Precautions Modify dosage in patients with severe renal impairment. Prolonged use may result in superinfection. Use with caution in patients with a history of penicillin allergy, especially IgE-mediated reactions (eg, anaphylaxis, urticaria). May cause antibiotic-associated colitis or colitis secondary to *C. difficile*.

Adverse Reactions

1% to 10%: Gastrointestinal: Diarrhea

<1% (Limited to important or life-threatening): Abdominal pain, agranulocytosis, anaphylaxis, angioedema, arthralgia, cholestasis, dyspepsia, erythema multiforme, fever, nausea, neutropenia, pruritus, pseudomembranous colitis, rash (maculopapular and erythematous), serum sickness, Stevens-Johnson syndrome, thrombocytopenia, transaminases increased, urticaria, vaginitis, vomiting

Reactions reported with other cephalosporins: Abdominal pain, aplastic anemia, BUN increased, creatinine increased, eosinophilia, hemolytic anemia, hemorrhage, pancytopenia, prothrombin time prolonged, renal dysfunction, seizure, superinfection, toxic epidermal necrolysis, toxic nephropathy

Overdosage/Toxicology After acute overdose, most agents cause only nausea, vomiting, and diarrhea, although neuromuscular hypersensitivity and seizures are possible, especially in patients with renal insufficiency. Many beta-lactam antibiotics have the potential to cause neuromuscular hyperirritability or seizures. Hemodialysis may be helpful to aid in removal of the drug from the blood, but is not usually indicated; otherwise, most treatment is supportive or symptom-directed, following GI decontamination.

Drug Interactions

Increased Effect/Toxicity: Bleeding may occur when administered with anticoagulants. Probenecid may decrease cephalosporin elimination.

Ethanol/Nutrition/Herb Interactions Food: Concomitant administration with food, infant formula, or cow's milk does **not** significantly affect absorption.

Stability Refrigerate suspension after reconstitution; discard after 14 days.

Mechanism of Action Inhibits bacterial cell wall synthesis by binding to one or more of the penicillin-binding proteins (PBPs) which in turn inhibits the final transpeptidation step of peptidoglycan synthesis in bacterial cell walls, thus inhibiting cell wall biosynthesis. Bacteria eventually lyse due to ongoing activity of cell wall autolytic enzymes (autolysins and murein hydrolases) while cell wall assembly is arrested.

Pharmacodynamics/Kinetics

Absorption: Rapid and well absorbed

Distribution: Widely throughout the body and reaches therapeutic concentrations in most tissues and body fluids, including synovial, pericardial, pleural, and peritoneal fluids; bile, sputum, and urine; bone, myocardium, gallbladder, skin and soft tissue; crosses placenta; enters breast milk

Protein binding: 20%

Half-life elimination: 1-2 hours; Renal failure: 20-24 hours

Time to peak, serum: 70-90 minutes

Excretion: Urine (>90% as unchanged drug)

Dosage

Usual dosage range: Oral:

Children: 30 mg/kg/day divided twice daily up to a maximum of 2 g/day

Adults: 1-2 g/day in 2 divided doses

Indication-specific dosing:

Prophylaxis against bacterial endocarditis:

Children: Oral: 50 mg/kg 1 hour prior to the procedure

Adults: Oral: 2 g 1 hour prior to the procedure

Dosing interval in renal impairment:

Cl_{cr} 10-25 mL/minute: Administer every 24 hours

Cl_{cr} <10 mL/minute: Administer every 36 hours

Administration Administer around-the-clock to promote less variation in peak and trough serum levels.

Monitoring Parameters Observe for signs and symptoms of anaphylaxis during first dose.

Test Interactions Positive direct Coombs', false-positive urinary glucose test using cupric sulfate (Benedict's solution, Clinitest®, Fehling's solution), false-positive serum or urine creatinine with Jaffé reaction

Dosage Forms [DSC] = Discontinued product

Capsule, as monohydrate: 500 mg

(Continued)

Cefadroxil *(Continued)*

Duricef®: 500 mg [DSC]

Powder for oral suspension, as monohydrate: 250 mg/5 mL (50 mL, 100 mL); 500 mg/5 mL (75 mL, 100 mL)

Duricef®: 250 mg/5 mL (50 mL, 100 mL); 500 mg/5 mL (75 mL, 100 mL) [contains sodium benzoate; orange-pineapple flavor]

Tablet, as monohydrate: 1 g

Duricef®: 1 g [DSC]

♦ **Cefadroxil Monohydrate** *see Cefadroxil on page 305*

Cefazolin *(sef A zoe lin)*

U.S. Brand Names Ancef®
Index Terms Cefazolin Sodium
Pharmacologic Category Antibiotic, Cephalosporin (First Generation)
Additional Appendix Information
  Animal and Human Bites *on page 1976*
  Antibiotic Treatment of Adults With Infective Endocarditis *on page 1977*
  Prevention of Bacterial Endocarditis *on page 1960*
  Prevention of Wound Infection and Sepsis in Surgical Patients *on page 1964*
Use Treatment of respiratory tract, skin and skin structure, genital, urinary tract, biliary tract, bone and joint infections, and septicemia due to susceptible gram-positive cocci (except enterococcus); some gram-negative bacilli including *E. coli*, *Proteus*, and *Klebsiella* may be susceptible; perioperative prophylaxis
Unlabeled/Investigational Use Prophylaxis against bacterial endocarditis
Pregnancy Risk Factor B
Lactation Enters breast milk (small amounts)/use caution (AAP rates "compatible")
Medication Safety Issues
  Sound-alike/look-alike issues:
    Cefazolin may be confused with cefprozil, cephalexin, cephalothin
    Kefzol® may be confused with Cefzil®
Contraindications Hypersensitivity to cefazolin sodium, any component of the formulation, or other cephalosporins
Warnings/Precautions Modify dosage in patients with severe renal impairment. Prolonged use may result in superinfection. Use with caution in patients with a history of penicillin allergy, especially IgE-mediated reactions (eg, anaphylaxis, angioedema, urticaria). May cause antibiotic-associated colitis or colitis secondary to *C. difficile*.
Adverse Reactions Frequency not defined.
  Central nervous system: Fever, seizure
  Dermatologic: Rash, pruritus, Stevens-Johnson syndrome
  Gastrointestinal: Diarrhea, nausea, vomiting, abdominal cramps, anorexia, pseudomembranous colitis, oral candidiasis
  Genitourinary: Vaginitis
  Hepatic: Transaminases increased, hepatitis
  Hematologic: Eosinophilia, neutropenia, leukopenia, thrombocytopenia, thrombocytosis
  Local: Pain at injection site, phlebitis
  Renal: BUN increased, serum creatinine increased, renal failure
  Miscellaneous: Anaphylaxis
  Reactions reported with other cephalosporins: Toxic epidermal necrolysis, abdominal pain, cholestasis, superinfection, toxic nephropathy, aplastic anemia, hemolytic anemia, hemorrhage, prothrombin time prolonged, pancytopenia
Overdosage/Toxicology Symptoms include neuromuscular hypersensitivity and convulsions, especially with renal insufficiency. Many beta-lactam antibiotics have the potential to cause neuromuscular hyperirritability or seizures. Hemodialysis may be helpful to aid in removal of the drug from the blood; otherwise, most treatment is supportive or symptom-directed.
Drug Interactions
  Increased Effect/Toxicity: High-dose probenecid decreases clearance and increases effect of cefazolin. Aminoglycosides increase nephrotoxic potential when taken with cefazolin. Cefazolin may increase the hypothrombinemic response to warfarin (due to alteration of GI microbial flora).
Stability Store intact vials at room temperature and protect from temperatures exceeding 40°C. Dilute large vial with 2.5 mL SWFI; 10 g vial may be diluted with 45 mL to yield 1 g/5 mL or 96 mL to yield 1 g/10 mL. May be injected or further dilution for I.V. administration in 50-100 mL compatible solution. Standard diluent is 1 g/50 mL D_5W or 2 g/50 mL D_5W.

Reconstituted solutions of cefazolin are light yellow to yellow. Protection from light is recommended for the powder and for the reconstituted solutions. Reconstituted solutions are stable for 24 hours at room temperature and for 10 days under refrigeration. Stability of parenteral admixture at room temperature (25°C) is 48 hours. Stability of parenteral admixture at refrigeration temperature (4°C) is 14 days.

DUPLEX™: Store at 20°C to 25°C (68°F to 77°F); excursions permitted to 15°C to 30°C (59°F to 86°F) prior to activation. Following activation, stable for 24 hours at room temperature and for 7 days under refrigeration.
Mechanism of Action Inhibits bacterial cell wall synthesis by binding to one or more of the penicillin-binding proteins (PBPs) which in turn inhibits the final transpeptidation step of peptidoglycan synthesis in bacterial cell walls, thus inhibiting cell wall biosynthesis. Bacteria eventually lyse due to ongoing activity of cell wall autolytic enzymes (autolysins and murein hydrolases) while cell wall assembly is arrested.

Pharmacodynamics/Kinetics

Distribution: Widely into most body tissues and fluids including gallbladder, liver, kidneys, bone, sputum, bile, pleural, and synovial; CSF penetration is poor; crosses placenta; enters breast milk

Protein binding: 74% to 86%

Metabolism: Minimally hepatic

Half-life elimination: 90-150 minutes; prolonged with renal impairment

Time to peak, serum: I.M.: 0.5-2 hours

Excretion: Urine (80% to 100% as unchanged drug)

Dosage

Usual dosage range: I.M., I.V.:

Children >1 month: 25-100 mg/kg/day divided every 6-8 hours; maximum: 6 g/day

Adults: 250 mg to 2 g every 6-12 (usually 8) hours, depending on severity of infection; maximum dose: 12 g/day

Indication-specific dosing:

Prophylaxis against bacterial endocarditis (unlabeled use):

Infants and Children: 25 mg/kg 30 minutes before procedure; maximum dose: 1 g

Adults: 1 g 30 minutes before procedure

Mild-to-moderate infections: Adults: 500 mg to 1 g every 6-8 hours

Mild infection with gram-positive cocci: Adults: 250-500 mg every 8 hours

Perioperative prophylaxis: Adults: 1 g given 30 minutes prior to surgery (repeat with 500 mg to 1 g during prolonged surgery); followed by 500 mg to 1 g every 6-9 hours for 24 hours postop

Pneumococcal pneumonia: Adults: 500 mg every 12 hours

Severe infection: Adults: 1-2 g every 6 hours

Prophylaxis against bacterial endocarditis (unlabeled use): Adults: 1 g 30 minutes before procedure

UTI (uncomplicated): Adults: 1 g every 12 hours

Dosing adjustment in renal impairment:

Cl_{cr} 10-30 mL/minute: Administer every 12 hours

Cl_{cr} <10 mL/minute: Administer every 24 hours

Hemodialysis: Moderately dialyzable (20% to 50%); administer dose postdialysis or administer supplemental dose of 0.5-1 g after dialysis

Peritoneal dialysis: Administer 0.5 g every 12 hours

Continuous arteriovenous or venovenous hemofiltration: Dose as for Cl_{cr} 10-30 mL/minute; removes 30 mg of cefazolin per liter of filtrate per day

Dietary Considerations Sodium content of 1 g: 48 mg (2 mEq)

Administration

I.M.: Inject deep I.M. into large muscle mass.

I.V.: Inject direct I.V. over 5 minutes. Infuse intermittent infusion over 30-60 minutes.

Some penicillins (eg, carbenicillin, ticarcillin and piperacillin) have been shown to inactivate aminoglycosides *in vitro*. This has been observed to a greater extent with tobramycin and gentamicin, while amikacin has shown greater stability against inactivation. Concurrent use of these agents may pose a risk of reduced antibacterial efficacy *in vivo*, particularly in the setting of profound renal impairment. However, definitive clinical evidence is lacking. If combination penicillin/aminoglycoside therapy is desired in a patient with renal dysfunction, separation of doses (if feasible), and routine monitoring of aminoglycoside levels, CBC, and clinical response should be considered.

Monitoring Parameters Renal function periodically when used in combination with other nephrotoxic drugs, hepatic function tests, CBC; monitor for signs of anaphylaxis during first dose

Test Interactions Positive direct Coombs', false-positive urinary glucose test using cupric sulfate (Benedict's solution, Clinitest®, Fehling's solution), false-positive serum or urine creatinine with Jaffé reaction.

Some penicillin derivatives may accelerate the degradation of aminoglycosides *in vitro*, leading to a potential underestimation of aminoglycoside serum concentration.

Dosage Forms [DSC] = Discontinued product

Infusion [premixed in D_5W]: 500 mg (50 mL); 1 g (50 mL)

Injection, powder for reconstitution: 500 mg, 1 g, 10 g, 20 g

Ancef®: 1 g; 10 g [DSC]

♦ **Cefazolin Sodium** *see* Cefazolin *on page 306*

Cefdinir (SEF di ner)

U.S. Brand Names Omnicef®

Canadian Brand Names Omnicef®

Index Terms CFDN

Pharmacologic Category Antibiotic, Cephalosporin (Third Generation)

Use Treatment of community-acquired pneumonia, acute exacerbations of chronic bronchitis, acute bacterial otitis media, acute maxillary sinusitis, pharyngitis/tonsillitis, and uncomplicated skin and skin structure infections.

Pregnancy Risk Factor B

Pregnancy Implications Teratogenic effects were not observed in animal studies. There are no adequate and well-controlled studies in pregnant women.

Lactation Excretion in breast milk unknown/use caution

Contraindications Hypersensitivity to cefdinir, any component of the formulation, other cephalosporins, or related antibiotics

Warnings/Precautions Administer cautiously to penicillin-sensitive patients, especially IgE-mediated reactions (eg, anaphylaxis, urticaria). There is evidence of partial cross-allergenicity and cephalosporins cannot be assumed to be an absolutely safe alternative to penicillin in the penicillin-allergic patient. Serum sickness-like reactions have been reported. Signs and symptoms occur after a few days of therapy and resolve a few days after drug discontinuation with no serious sequelae. Pseudomembranous colitis occurs, consider (Continued)

Cefdinir *(Continued)*

its diagnosis in patients who develop diarrhea with antibiotic use. Use caution with renal dysfunction; dose adjustment may be required.

Adverse Reactions

>10%: Gastrointestinal: Diarrhea (8% to 15%)

1% to 10%:

Central nervous system: Headache (2%)

Dermatologic: Rash (≤3%)

Gastrointestinal: Nausea (≤3%), abdominal pain (≤1%), vomiting (≤1%)

Genitourinary: Vaginal moniliasis (≤4%), urine leukocytes increased (2%), urine protein increased (1% to 2%), vaginitis (≤1%)

Hematologic: Eosinophils increased (1%)

Hepatic: Alkaline phosphatase increased (≤1%), platelets increased (1%)

Renal: Microhematuria (1%)

Miscellaneous: Lymphocytes increased (≤2%), GGT increased (1%), lactate dehydrogenase increased (≤1%), bicarbonate decreased (≤1%), lymphocytes decreased (≤1%), PMN changes (≤1%)

<1% (Limited to important or life-threatening): Allergic vasculitis, anaphylaxis, anorexia, bloody diarrhea, cardiac failure, chest pain, cholestasis, coagulation disorder, constipation, cutaneous moniliasis, disseminated intravascular coagulation (DIC), enterocolitis (acute), eosinophilic pneumonia, erythema multiforme, erythema nodosum, exfoliative dermatitis, facial edema, fulminant hepatitis, granulocytopenia, hemolytic anemia, hemorrhagic colitis, hepatic failure, hepatitis (acute), hyperkinesia, hypertension, idiopathic thrombocytopenia purpura, ileus, interstitial pneumonia (idiopathic), involuntary movement, jaundice, laryngeal edema, leukopenia, loss of consciousness, maculopapular rash, melena, MI, nephropathy, pancytopenia, pruritus, pseudomembranous colitis, renal failure (acute), respiratory failure (acute), rhabdomyolysis, serum sickness, shock, Stevens-Johnson syndrome, thrombocytopenia, toxic epidermal necrolysis, upper GI bleed, weakness, xerostomia

Reactions reported with other cephalosporins: Dizziness, fever, encephalopathy, asterixis, neuromuscular excitability, seizure, aplastic anemia, interstitial nephritis, toxic nephropathy, angioedema, hemorrhage, PT prolonged, and superinfection

Overdosage/Toxicology After acute overdose, most agents cause only nausea, vomiting, and diarrhea, although neuromuscular hypersensitivity and seizures are possible, especially in patients with renal insufficiency. Hemodialysis may be helpful to aid in the removal of the drug from the blood but not usually indicated, otherwise, most treatment is supportive or symptom-directed following GI decontamination.

Drug Interactions

Increased Effect/Toxicity: Probenecid may increase the effects of cefdinir by decreasing renal elimination (peak plasma levels of cefdinir are increased by 54% and half-life is prolonged by 50%).

Decreased Effect: Coadministration with iron or antacids reduces the rate and extent of cefdinir absorption.

Stability Capsules and unmixed powder should be stored at room temperature of 25°C (77°F). Oral suspension should be mixed with 38 mL water for the 60 mL bottle and 63 mL of water for the 120 mL bottle. After mixing, the suspension can be stored at room temperature of 25°C (77°F) for 10 days.

Mechanism of Action Inhibits bacterial cell wall synthesis by binding to one or more of the penicillin-binding proteins (PBPs) which in turn inhibits the final transpeptidation step of peptidoglycan synthesis in bacterial cell walls, thus inhibiting cell wall biosynthesis. Bacteria eventually lyse due to ongoing activity of cell wall autolytic enzymes (autolysins and murein hydrolases) while cell wall assembly is arrested.

Pharmacodynamics/Kinetics

Distribution: V_d:

Children 6 months to 12 years: 0.29-1.05 L/kg

Adults: 0.06-0.64 L/kg

Protein binding: 60% to 70%

Metabolism: Minimally hepatic

Bioavailability: Capsule: 16% to 21%; suspension 25%

Half-life elimination: 100 minutes

Excretion: Primarily urine

Dosage

Usual dosage range:

Children 6 months to 12 years: Oral: 7 mg/kg/dose twice daily or 14 mg/kg/dose once daily (maximum: 600 mg/day)

Adolescents and Adults: Oral: 300 mg twice daily or 600 mg once daily

Indication-specific dosing:

Children 6 months to 12 years: Oral:

Acute bacterial otitis media, pharyngitis/tonsillitis: 7 mg/kg/dose twice daily for 5-10 days **or** 14 mg/kg/dose once daily for 10 days (maximum: 600 mg/day)

Acute maxillary sinusitis: 7 mg/kg/dose twice daily **or** 14 mg/kg/dose once daily for 10 days (maximum: 600 mg/day)

Uncomplicated skin and skin structure infections: 7 mg/kg/dose twice daily for 10 days (maximum: 600 mg/day)

Adolescents and Adults:

Acute exacerbations of chronic bronchitis, pharyngitis/tonsillitis: 300 mg twice daily for 5-10 days **or** 600 mg once daily for 10 days

Acute maxillary sinusitis: 300 mg twice daily **or** 600 mg once daily for 10 days

Community-acquired pneumonia, uncomplicated skin and skin structure infections: 300 mg twice daily for 10 days

Dosing adjustment in renal impairment: Cl_{cr} <30 mL/minute:

Children: 7 mg/kg once daily (maximum: 300 mg/day)

Adults: 300 mg once daily

Hemodialysis removes cefdinir; recommended initial dose: 300 mg (or 7 mg/kg/dose) every other day. At the conclusion of each hemodialysis session, 300 mg (or 7 mg/kg/dose) should be given. Subsequent doses (300 mg or 7 mg/kg/dose) should be administered every other day.

Dietary Considerations Suspension contains sucrose 2.86 g/5 mL

Administration Twice daily doses should be given every 12 hours. May be taken with or without food. The suspension should be shaken well before each administration.

Monitoring Parameters Observe for signs and symptoms of anaphylaxis during first dose.

Dosage Forms
Capsule: 300 mg
Powder for oral suspension: 125 mg/5 mL (60 mL, 100 mL) [contains sodium benzoate and sucrose 2.86 g/5 mL; strawberry flavor]; 250 mg/5 mL (60 mL, 100 mL) [contains sodium benzoate and sucrose 2.86 g/5 mL; strawberry flavor]

Cefditoren (sef de TOR en)

U.S. Brand Names Spectracef™

Index Terms Cefditoren Pivoxil

Pharmacologic Category Antibiotic, Cephalosporin

Use Treatment of acute bacterial exacerbation of chronic bronchitis or community-acquired pneumonia (due to susceptible organisms including *Haemophilus influenzae*, *Haemophilus parainfluenzae*, *Streptococcus pneumoniae*-penicillin susceptible only, *Moraxella catarrhalis*); pharyngitis or tonsillitis (*Streptococcus pyogenes*); and uncomplicated skin and skin-structure infections (*Staphylococcus aureus* - not MRSA, *Streptococcus pyogenes*)

Pregnancy Risk Factor B

Pregnancy Implications Fetal toxicity and fetal loss have been reported in some animal studies. There are no adequate and well-controlled studies in pregnant women; use only if clearly needed.

Lactation Excretion in breast milk unknown/use caution

Medication Safety Issues
International issues:
Spectracef™ may be confused with Spectrocef® which is a brand name for cefotaxime in Italy

Contraindications Hypersensitivity to cefditoren, any component of the formulation, other cephalosporins, or milk protein; carnitine deficiency

Warnings/Precautions Use with caution in patients with a history of penicillin allergy, especially IgE-mediated reactions (eg, anaphylaxis, urticaria). May cause antibiotic-associated colitis or colitis secondary to *C. difficile*. Prolonged use may result in superinfection. Caution in individuals with seizure disorders. Use caution in patients with renal or hepatic impairment; modify dosage in patients with severe renal impairment. Cefditoren causes renal excretion of carnitine; do not use in patients with carnitine deficiency, not for long-term therapy due to the possible development of carnitine deficiency over time. May prolong prothrombin time; use with caution in patients with a history of bleeding disorder. Cefditoren tablets contain sodium caseinate, which may cause hypersensitivity reactions in patients with milk protein hypersensitivity; this does not affect patients with lactose intolerance. Safety and efficacy have not been established in children <12 years of age.

Adverse Reactions
>10%: Gastrointestinal: Diarrhea (11% to 15%)
1% to 10%:
Central nervous system: Headache (2% to 3%)
Endocrine & metabolic: Glucose increased (1% to 2%)
Gastrointestinal: Nausea (4% to 6%), abdominal pain (2%), dyspepsia (1% to 2%), vomiting (1%)
Genitourinary: Vaginal moniliasis (3% to 6%)
Hematologic: Hematocrit decreased (2%)
Renal: Hematuria (3%), urinary white blood cells increased (2%)
<1% (Limited to important or life-threatening): Acute renal failure, albumin decreased, allergic reaction, arthralgia, asthma, BUN increased, calcium decreased, eosinophilic pneumonia, coagulation time increased, erythema multiforme, fungal infection, hyperglycemia, interstitial pneumonia, leukopenia, leukorrhea, positive direct Coombs' test, potassium increased, pseudomembranous colitis, rash, sodium decreased, Stevens-Johnson syndrome, thrombocythemia, thrombocytopenia, toxic epidermal necrolysis, white blood cells increased/decreased

Reactions reported with other cephalosporins: Anaphylaxis, aplastic anemia, cholestasis, hemorrhage, hemolytic anemia, renal dysfunction, reversible hyperactivity, serum sickness-like reaction, toxic nephropathy

Overdosage/Toxicology Specific information not available. General symptoms of cephalosporin overdose may include nausea, vomiting, epigastric distress, diarrhea, and seizures. Treatment should be symptom-directed and supportive. Hemodialysis may be helpful (removes ~30% from circulation).

Drug Interactions
Increased Effect/Toxicity: Increased levels of cefditoren with probenecid. Prothrombin time may be prolonged with warfarin.

Ethanol/Nutrition/Herb Interactions Food: Moderate- to high-fat meals increase bioavailability and maximum plasma concentration.

Stability Store at controlled room temperature of 15°C to 30°C (59°F to 86°F). Protect from light and moisture.

Mechanism of Action Inhibits bacterial cell wall synthesis by binding to one or more of the penicillin binding proteins (PBPs) which in turn inhibits the final transpeptidation step of peptidoglycan synthesis in bacterial cell walls, thus inhibiting cell wall biosynthesis. Bacteria eventually lyse due to ongoing activity of cell wall autolytic enzymes (autolysins and murein hydrolases) while cell wall assembly is arrested.
(Continued)

Cefditoren *(Continued)*

Pharmacodynamics/Kinetics
Distribution: 9.3 ± 1.6 L

Protein binding: 88% (*in vitro*), primarily to albumin

Metabolism: Cefditoren pivoxil is hydrolyzed to cefditoren (active) and pivalate

Bioavailability: ~14% to 16%, increased by moderate to high-fat meal

Half-life elimination: 1.6 ± 0.4 hours

Time to peak: 1.5-3 hours

Excretion: Urine (as cefditoren and pivaloylcarnitine)

Dosage

Usual dosage range:

Children ≥12 years and Adults: Oral: 200-400 mg twice daily

Indication-specific dosing:

Children ≥12 years and Adults: Oral:

Acute bacterial exacerbation of chronic bronchitis: 400 mg twice daily for 10 days

Dental infections (unlabeled use): 400 mg twice daily for 10 days

Community-acquired pneumonia: 400 mg twice daily for 14 days

Pharyngitis, tonsillitis, uncomplicated skin and skin structure infections: 200 mg twice daily for 10 days

Dosage adjustment in renal impairment:

Cl_{cr} 30-49 mL/minute/1.73 m²: Maximum dose: 200 mg twice daily

Cl_{cr} <30 mL/minute/1.73 m²: Maximum dose: 200 mg once daily

End-stage renal disease: Appropriate dosing not established

Dosage adjustment in hepatic impairment:

Mild-to-moderate impairment: Adjustment not required

Severe impairment (Child-Pugh Class C): Specific guidelines not available

Dietary Considerations Cefditoren should be taken with meals. Plasma carnitine levels are decreased during therapy (39% with 200 mg dosing, 63% with 400 mg dosing); normal concentrations return within 7-10 days after treatment is discontinued.

Administration Should be administered with meals.

Monitoring Parameters Assess patient at beginning and throughout therapy for infection; monitor for signs of anaphylaxis during first dose.

Test Interactions May induce a positive direct Coomb's test. May cause a false-negative ferricyanide test. Glucose oxidase or hexokinase methods recommended for blood/plasma glucose determinations. False-positive urine glucose test when using copper reduction based assays (eg, Clinitest®).

Dosage Forms Tablet, as pivoxil: 200 mg [equivalent to cefditoren; contains sodium caseinate]

♦ **Cefditoren Pivoxil** *see Cefditoren on page 309*

Cefepime *(SEF e pim)*

U.S. Brand Names Maxipime®

Canadian Brand Names Maxipime®

Index Terms Cefepime Hydrochloride

Pharmacologic Category Antibiotic, Cephalosporin (Fourth Generation)

Additional Appendix Information

Antimicrobial Drugs of Choice *on page 1981*

Community-Acquired Pneumonia in Adults *on page 1999*

Use Treatment of uncomplicated and complicated urinary tract infections, including pyelonephritis caused by typical urinary tract pathogens; monotherapy for febrile neutropenia; uncomplicated skin and skin structure infections caused by *Streptococcus pyogenes*; moderate-to-severe pneumonia caused by pneumococcus, *Pseudomonas aeruginosa*, and other gram-negative organisms; complicated intra-abdominal infections (in combination with metronidazole). Also active against methicillin-susceptible staphylococci, *Enterobacter* sp, and many other gram-negative bacilli.

Children 2 months to 16 years: Empiric therapy of febrile neutropenia patients, uncomplicated skin/soft tissue infections, pneumonia, and uncomplicated/complicated urinary tract infections.

Pregnancy Risk Factor B

Lactation Enters breast milk/use caution

Contraindications Hypersensitivity to cefepime, any component of the formulation, or other cephalosporins

Warnings/Precautions Modify dosage in patients with severe renal impairment; prolonged use may result in superinfection; use with caution in patients with a history of penicillin or cephalosporin allergy, especially IgE-mediated reactions (eg, anaphylaxis, urticaria). May cause antibiotic-associated colitis or colitis secondary to *C. difficile*.

Adverse Reactions

>10%: Hematologic: Positive Coombs' test without hemolysis

1% to 10%:

Central nervous system: Fever (1%), headache (1%)

Dermatologic: Rash, pruritus

Gastrointestinal: Diarrhea, nausea, vomiting

Local: Pain, erythema at injection site

<1% (Limited to important or life-threatening): Agranulocytosis, anaphylactic shock, anaphylaxis, coma, encephalopathy, hallucinations, leukopenia, myoclonus, neuromuscular excitability, neutropenia, seizure, thrombocytopenia

Reactions reported with other cephalosporins: Aplastic anemia, erythema multiforme, hemolytic anemia, hemorrhage, pancytopenia, PT prolonged, renal dysfunction, Stevens-Johnson syndrome, superinfection, toxic epidermal necrolysis, toxic nephropathy, vaginitis

Overdosage/Toxicology Symptoms include neuromuscular hypersensitivity and CNS toxicity (including hallucinations, confusion, seizures, and coma). Many beta-lactam antibiotics have the potential to cause neuromuscular hyperirritability or seizures. Hemodialysis may be helpful to aid in the removal of the drug from the blood, however, most often treatment is supportive and symptom-directed.

Drug Interactions

Increased Effect/Toxicity: High-dose probenecid decreases clearance and increases effect of cefepime. Aminoglycosides increase nephrotoxic potential when taken with cefepime.

Stability Stable with normal saline, D_5W, and a variety of other solutions for 24 hours at room temperature and 7 days refrigerated.

Mechanism of Action Inhibits bacterial cell wall synthesis by binding to one or more of the penicillin-binding proteins (PBPs) which in turn inhibits the final transpeptidation step of peptidoglycan synthesis in bacterial cell walls, thus inhibiting cell wall biosynthesis. Bacteria eventually lyse due to ongoing activity of cell wall autolytic enzymes (autolysis and murein hydrolases) while cell wall assembly is arrested.

Pharmacodynamics/Kinetics

Absorption: I.M.: Rapid and complete

Distribution: V_d: Adults: 14-20 L; penetrates into inflammatory fluid at concentrations ~80% of serum levels and into bronchial mucosa at levels ~60% of those reached in the plasma; crosses blood-brain barrier

Protein binding, plasma: 16% to 19%

Metabolism: Minimally hepatic

Half-life elimination: 2 hours

Time to peak: 0.5-1.5 hours

Excretion: Urine (85% as unchanged drug)

Dosage

Usual dosage range:

Children: I.V.: 50 mg/kg every 8-12 hours

Adults: I.V.: 1-2 g every 6-12 hours

Indication-specific dosing:

Children >2 months: I.V.:

Febrile neutropenia: 50 mg/kg every 8 hours for 7-10 days

Uncomplicated skin/soft tissue infections, pneumonia, complicated/uncomplicated UTI: 50 mg/kg twice daily

Adults:

Brain abscess (Pseudomonas), meningitis (postsurgical): I.V.: 2 g every 8 hours

Hospital-acquired pneumonia (HAP): I.V.: 1-2 g every 8-12 hours (American Thoracic Society/ATS guidelines)

Monotherapy for febrile neutropenic patients: I.V: 2 g every 8 hours for 7 days or until the neutropenia resolves

Otitis externa (malignant), pneumonia: I.V.: 2 g every 12 hours

Peritonitis (spontaneous): I.V.: 2 g every 12 hours with metronidazole

Septic lateral/cavernous sinus thrombosis: I.V.: 2 g every 8-12 hours; with metronidazole for lateral

Urinary tract infections (mild to moderate) I.M., I.V.: 500-1000 mg every 12 hours

Dosing adjustment in renal impairment: Adults: Recommended maintenance schedule based on creatinine clearance (mL/minute), compared to normal dosing schedule: See table.

Cefepime Hydrochloride

Creatinine Clearance (mL/minute)	Recommended Maintenance Schedule			
>60 Normal recommended dosing schedule	500 mg every 12 hours	1 g every 12 hours	2 g every 12 hours	2 g every 8 hours
30-60	500 mg every 24 hours	1 g every 24 hours	2 g every 24 hours	2 g every 12 hours
11-29	500 mg every 24 hours	500 mg every 24 hours	1 g every 24 hours	2 g every 24 hours
<11	250 mg every 24 hours	250 mg every 24 hours	500 mg every 24 hours	1 g every 24 hours

Hemodialysis: Initial: 1 g (single dose) on day 1. Maintenance: 500 mg once daily (1 g once daily in febrile neutropenic patients). Dosage should be administered after dialysis on dialysis days.

Peritoneal dialysis: Removed to a lesser extent than hemodialysis; administer 250 mg every 48 hours

Continuous arteriovenous or venovenous hemofiltration: Dose as normal Cl_{cr} (eg, >30 mL/minute)

Administration May be administered either I.M. or I.V.

Monitoring Parameters Obtain specimen for culture and sensitivity prior to the first dose. Monitor for signs of anaphylaxis during first dose.

Test Interactions Positive direct Coombs', false-positive urinary glucose test using cupric sulfate (Benedict's solution, Clinitest®, Fehling's solution), false-positive serum or urine creatinine with Jaffé reaction, false-positive urinary proteins and steroids

Dosage Forms Injection, powder for reconstitution, as hydrochloride: 500 mg, 1 g, 2 g

♦ **Cefepime Hydrochloride** see Cefepime on page 310

Cefixime (sef IKS eem)

U.S. Brand Names Suprax®
Canadian Brand Names Suprax®
Index Terms Cefixime Trihydrate
Pharmacologic Category Antibiotic, Cephalosporin (Third Generation)
Additional Appendix Information
Antimicrobial Drugs of Choice *on page 1981*
Treatment of Sexually Transmitted Infections *on page 2007*
Use Treatment of urinary tract infections, otitis media, respiratory infections due to susceptible organisms including *S. pneumoniae* and *S. pyogenes*, *H. influenzae*, and many Enterobacteriaceae; uncomplicated cervical/urethral gonorrhea due to *N. gonorrhoeae*
Pregnancy Risk Factor B
Lactation Excretion in breast milk unknown/use caution
Medication Safety Issues
Sound-alike/look-alike issues:
Suprax® may be confused with Sporanox®, Surbex®
International issues:
Cefiton® [Portugal] may be confused with Cefotan® which is a brand name for cefotetan in the U.S.
Cefiton® [Portugal] may be confused with Ceftim® which is a brand name for ceftazidime in Italy
Cefiton® [Portugal] may be confused with Ceftin® which is a brand name for cefuroxime in the U.S.
Cefiton® [Portugal] may be confused with Lexotan® which is a brand name for bromazepam in multiple international markets
Contraindications Hypersensitivity to cefixime, any component of the formulation, or other cephalosporins
Warnings/Precautions Prolonged use may result in superinfection. Modify dosage in patients with renal impairment. Use with caution in patients with a history of penicillin allergy, especially IgE-mediated reactions (eg, anaphylaxis, urticaria). May cause antibiotic-associated colitis or colitis secondary to *C. difficile*.
Adverse Reactions
>10%: Gastrointestinal: Diarrhea (16%)
2% to 10%: Gastrointestinal: Abdominal pain, nausea, dyspepsia, flatulence, loose stools
<2% (Limited to important or life-threatening): Acute renal failure, anaphylactic/anaphylactoid reactions, angioedema, BUN increased, candidiasis, creatinine increased, dizziness, drug fever, eosinophilia, erythema multiforme, facial edema, fever, headache, hepatitis, hyperbilirubinemia, jaundice, leukopenia, neutropenia, pruritus, pseudomembranous colitis, PT prolonged, rash, seizure, serum sickness-like reaction, Stevens-Johnson syndrome, thrombocytopenia, toxic epidermal necrolysis, transaminases increased, urticaria, vaginitis, vomiting
Reactions reported with other cephalosporins: Agranulocytosis, aplastic anemia, colitis, hemolytic anemia, hemorrhage, interstitial nephritis, pancytopenia, superinfection
Overdosage/Toxicology After acute overdose, most agents cause only nausea, vomiting, and diarrhea, although neuromuscular hypersensitivity and seizures are possible, especially in patients with renal insufficiency. Many beta-lactam antibiotics have the potential to cause neuromuscular hyperirritability or seizures. Hemodialysis may be helpful to aid in removal of the drug from the blood but is not usually indicated; otherwise, most treatment is supportive or symptom-directed, following GI decontamination.
Drug Interactions
Increased Effect/Toxicity: Aminoglycosides and furosemide may be possible additives to nephrotoxicity. Probenecid increases cefixime concentration. Cefixime may increase carbamazepine. Cefixime may increase prothrombin time when administered with warfarin.
Ethanol/Nutrition/Herb Interactions Food: Delays cefixime absorption.
Stability After reconstitution, suspension may be stored for 14 days at room temperature or under refrigeration.
Mechanism of Action Inhibits bacterial cell wall synthesis by binding to one or more of the penicillin binding proteins (PBPs); which in turn inhibits the final transpeptidation step of peptidoglycan synthesis in bacterial cell walls, thus inhibiting cell wall biosynthesis. Bacteria eventually lyse due to ongoing activity of cell wall autolytic enzymes (autolysins and murein hydrolases) while cell wall assembly is arrested.
Pharmacodynamics/Kinetics
Absorption: 40% to 50%
Distribution: Widely throughout the body and reaches therapeutic concentration in most tissues and body fluids, including synovial, pericardial, pleural, peritoneal; bile, sputum, and urine; bone, myocardium, gallbladder, and skin and soft tissue
Protein binding: 65%
Half-life elimination: Normal renal function: 3-4 hours; Renal failure: Up to 11.5 hours
Time to peak, serum: 2-6 hours; delayed with food
Excretion: Urine (50% of absorbed dose as active drug); feces (10%)
Dosage
Usual dosage range:
Children ≥6 months: Oral: 8-20 mg/kg/day divided every 12-24 hours (maximum: 400 mg/day)
Children >50 kg or >12 years and Adults: Oral: 400 mg/day divided every 12-24 hours
Indication-specific dosing:
Children: Oral:
S. pyogenes infections: Treat for 10 days
Typhoid fever: 20 mg/kg/day for 10-14 days; maximum 400 mg
Adults: Oral:
S. pyogenes infections: Treat for 10 days

Typhoid fever: 20-30 mg/kg/day in 2 divided doses for 7-14 days after I.V. therapy
Uncomplicated cervical/urethral gonorrhea due to *N. gonorrhoeae:* 400 mg as a single dose
Dosing adjustment in renal impairment:
Cl$_{cr}$ 21-60 mL/minute or with renal hemodialysis: Administer 75% of the standard dose
Cl$_{cr}$ <20 mL/minute or with CAPD: Administer 50% of the standard dose
Moderately dialyzable (10%)
Dietary Considerations May be taken with food.
Administration May be administered with or without food; administer with food to decrease GI distress.
Monitoring Parameters With prolonged therapy, monitor renal and hepatic function periodically. Observe for signs and symptoms of anaphylaxis during first dose.
Test Interactions Positive direct Coombs', false-positive urinary glucose test using cupric sulfate (Benedict's solution, Clinitest®, Fehling's solution), false-positive serum or urine creatinine with Jaffé reaction
Dosage Forms
Powder for oral suspension, as trihydrate:
Suprax®: 100 mg/5 mL (50 mL, 75 mL, 100 mL) [contains sodium benzoate; strawberry flavor]

◆ **Cefixime Trihydrate** *see* Cefixime *on page 312*
◆ **Cefizox®** *see* Ceftizoxime *on page 323*
◆ **Cefotan® [DSC]** *see* Cefotetan *on page 315*
◆ **Cefotan® (Can)** *see* Cefotetan *on page 315*

Cefotaxime (sef oh TAKS eem)

U.S. Brand Names Claforan®
Canadian Brand Names Claforan®
Index Terms Cefotaxime Sodium
Pharmacologic Category Antibiotic, Cephalosporin (Third Generation)
Additional Appendix Information
Antibiotic Treatment of Adults With Infective Endocarditis *on page 1977*
Antimicrobial Drugs of Choice *on page 1981*
Community-Acquired Pneumonia in Adults *on page 1999*
Treatment of Sexually Transmitted Infections *on page 2007*
Use Treatment of susceptible infection in respiratory tract, skin and skin structure, bone and joint, urinary tract, gynecologic as well as septicemia, and documented or suspected meningitis. Active against most gram-negative bacilli (not *Pseudomonas*) and gram-positive cocci (not enterococcus). Active against many penicillin-resistant pneumococci.
Pregnancy Risk Factor B
Lactation Enters breast milk/use caution (AAP rates "compatible")
Medication Safety Issues
Sound-alike/look-alike issues:
Cefotaxime may be confused with cefoxitin, ceftizoxime, cefuroxime

International issues:
Spectrocef® [Italy] may be confused with Spectracef™ which is a brand name for cefditoren in the U.S.
Contraindications Hypersensitivity to cefotaxime, any component of the formulation, or other cephalosporins
Warnings/Precautions Modify dosage in patients with severe renal impairment. Prolonged use may result in superinfection. A potentially life-threatening arrhythmia has been reported in patients who received a rapid bolus injection via central line. Use caution in patients with colitis. Minimize tissue inflammation by changing infusion sites when needed. Use with caution in patients with a history of penicillin allergy, especially IgE-mediated reactions (eg, anaphylaxis, urticaria). May cause antibiotic-associated colitis or colitis secondary to *C. difficile.*
Adverse Reactions
1% to 10%:
Dermatologic: Rash, pruritus
Gastrointestinal: Diarrhea, nausea, vomiting, colitis
Local: Pain at injection site
<1% (Limited to important or life-threatening): Anaphylaxis, arrhythmia (after rapid I.V. injection via central catheter), BUN increased, candidiasis, creatinine increased, eosinophilia, erythema multiforme, fever, headache, interstitial nephritis, neutropenia, phlebitis, pseudomembranous colitis, Stevens-Johnson syndrome, thrombocytopenia, transaminases increased, toxic epidermal necrolysis, urticaria, vaginitis
Reactions reported with other cephalosporins: Agranulocytosis, aplastic anemia, cholestasis, hemolytic anemia, hemorrhage, pancytopenia, renal dysfunction, seizure, superinfection, toxic nephropathy.
Overdosage/Toxicology Usually well tolerated even in overdose; convulsions are possible. Many beta-lactam antibiotics have the potential to cause neuromuscular hyperirritability or seizures. Hemodialysis may be helpful to aid in removal of the drug from the blood; otherwise, most treatment is supportive or symptom-directed.
Drug Interactions
Increased Effect/Toxicity: Probenecid may decrease cephalosporin elimination resulting in increased levels. Furosemide, aminoglycosides in combination with cefotaxime may result in additive nephrotoxicity.
Stability Reconstituted solution is stable for 12-24 hours at room temperature and 7-10 days when refrigerated and for 13 weeks when frozen. For I.V. infusion in NS or D$_5$W, solution is stable for 24 hours at room temperature, 5 days when refrigerated, or 13 weeks when frozen in Viaflex® plastic containers. Thawed solutions previously of frozen premixed bags are stable for 24 hours at room temperature or 10 days when refrigerated.
(Continued)

Cefotaxime *(Continued)*

Mechanism of Action Inhibits bacterial cell wall synthesis by binding to one or more of the penicillin-binding proteins (PBPs) which in turn inhibits the final transpeptidation step of peptidoglycan synthesis in bacterial cell walls, thus inhibiting cell wall biosynthesis. Bacteria eventually lyse due to ongoing activity of cell wall autolytic enzymes (autolysins and murein hydrolases) while cell wall assembly is arrested.

Pharmacodynamics/Kinetics

Distribution: Widely to body tissues and fluids including aqueous humor, ascitic and prostatic fluids, bone; penetrates CSF best when meninges are inflamed; crosses placenta; enters breast milk

Metabolism: Partially hepatic to active metabolite, desacetylcefotaxime

Half-life elimination:

Cefotaxime: Premature neonates <1 week: 5-6 hours; Full-term neonates <1 week: 2-3.4 hours; Adults: 1-1.5 hours; prolonged with renal and/or hepatic impairment

Desacetylcefotaxime: 1.5-1.9 hours; prolonged with renal impairment

Time to peak, serum: I.M.: Within 30 minutes

Excretion: Urine (as unchanged drug and metabolites)

Dosage

Usual dosage range:

Infants and Children 1 month to 12 years <50 kg: I.M., I.V.: 50-200 mg/kg/day in divided doses every 4-6 hours

Children >12 years and Adults: I.M., I.V.: 1-2 g every 4-12 hours

Indication-specific dosing:

Infants and Children 1 month to 12 years:

Epiglottitis: I.M., I.V.: 150-200 mg/kg/day in 4 divided doses with clindamycin for 7-10 days

Meningitis: I.M., I.V.: 200 mg/kg/day in divided doses every 6 hours

Pneumonia: I.V.: 200 mg/kg/day divided every 8 hours

Sepsis: I.V.: 150 mg/kg/day divided every 8 hours

Typhoid fever: I.M., I.V.: 150-200 mg/kg/day in 3-4 divided doses (maximum: 12 g/day); fluoroquinolone resistant: 80 mg/kg/day in 3-4 divided doses (maximum: 12 g/day)

Children >12 years and Adults:

Arthritis (septic): I.V.: 1 g every 8 hours

Brain abscess, meningitis: I.V.: 2 g every 4-6 hours

Caesarean section: I.M., I.V.: 1 g as soon as the umbilical cord is clamped, then 1 g at 6- and 12-hour intervals

Epiglottitis: I.V.: 2 g every 4-8 hours

Gonorrhea: I.M.: 1 g as a single dose

Disseminated: I.V.: 1 g every 8 hours

Life-threatening infections: I.V.: 2 g every 4 hours

Liver abscess: I.V.: 1-2 g every 6 hours

Lyme disease:

Cardiac manifestations: I.V.: 2 g every 4 hours

CNS manifestations: I.V.: 2 g every 8 hours for 14-28 days

Moderate-to-severe infections: I.M., I.V.: 1-2 g every 8 hours

Orbital cellulitis: I.V.: 2 g every 4 hours

Peritonitis (spontaneous): I.V.: 2 g every 8 hours, unless life-threatening then 2 g every 4 hours

Septicemia: I.V.: 2 g every 6-8 hours

Skin and soft tissue:

Mixed, necrotizing: I.V.: 2 g every 6 hours, with metronidazole or clindamycin

Bite wounds (animal): I.V.: 2 g every 6 hours

Surgical prophylaxis: I.M., I.V.: 1 g 30-90 minutes before surgery

Uncomplicated infections: I.M., I.V.: 1 g every 12 hours

Dosing interval in renal impairment:

Cl$_{cr}$ 10-50 mL/minute: Administer every 8-12 hours

Cl$_{cr}$ <10 mL/minute: Administer every 24 hours

Hemodialysis: Moderately dialyzable

Dosing adjustment in hepatic impairment: Moderate dosage reduction is recommended in severe liver disease

Continuous arteriovenous or venovenous hemodiafiltration effects: Administer 1 g every 12 hour

Dietary Considerations Sodium content of 1 g: 50.5 mg (2.2 mEq)

Administration Can be administered IVP over 3-5 minutes or I.V. intermittent infusion over 15-30 minutes.

Monitoring Parameters Observe for signs and symptoms of anaphylaxis during first dose; CBC with differential (especially with long courses)

Test Interactions Positive direct Coombs', false-positive urinary glucose test using cupric sulfate (Benedict's solution, Clinitest®, Fehling's solution), false-positive serum or urine creatinine with Jaffé reaction

Dosage Forms

Infusion, as sodium [premixed iso-osmotic solution]:

Claforan®: 1 g (50 mL); 2 g (50 mL) [contains sodium 50.5 mg (2.2 mEq) per cefotaxime 1 g]

Injection, powder for reconstitution, as sodium: 500 mg, 1 g, 2 g, 10 g, 20 g

Claforan®: 500 mg, 1 g, 2 g, 10 g [contains sodium 50.5 mg (2.2 mEq) per cefotaxime 1 g]

♦ **Cefotaxime Sodium** *see* Cefotaxime *on page 313*

Cefotetan (SEF oh tee tan)

U.S. Brand Names Cefotan® [DSC]
Canadian Brand Names Cefotan®
Index Terms Cefotetan Disodium
Pharmacologic Category Antibiotic, Cephalosporin (Second Generation)
Additional Appendix Information
Animal and Human Bites *on page 1976*
Antimicrobial Drugs of Choice *on page 1981*
Prevention of Wound Infection and Sepsis in Surgical Patients *on page 1964*
Treatment of Sexually Transmitted Infections *on page 2007*
Use Surgical prophylaxis; intra-abdominal infections and other mixed infections; respiratory tract, skin and skin structure, bone and joint, urinary tract and gynecologic as well as septicemia; active against gram-negative enteric bacilli including *E. coli*, *Klebsiella*, and *Proteus*; less active against staphylococci and streptococci than first generation cephalosporins, but active against anaerobes including *Bacteroides fragilis*
Pregnancy Risk Factor B
Lactation Enters breast milk (small amounts)/use caution
Medication Safety Issues
Sound-alike/look-alike issues:
Cefotetan may be confused with cefoxitin, Ceftin®
Cefotan® may be confused with Ceftin®

International issues:
Cefotan® may be confused with Lexotan® which is a brand name for bromazepam in multiple international markets
Cefotan® may be confused with Cefiton® which is a brand name for cefixime in Portugal
Contraindications Hypersensitivity to cefotetan, any component of the formulation, or other cephalosporins; previous cephalosporin-associated hemolytic anemia
Warnings/Precautions Modify dosage in patients with severe renal impairment. Prolonged use may result in superinfection. Although cefotetan contains the methyltetrazolethiol side chain, bleeding has not been a significant problem. Use with caution in patients with a history of penicillin allergy, especially IgE-mediated reactions (eg, anaphylaxis, urticaria). Cefotetan has been associated with a higher risk of hemolytic anemia relative to other cephalosporins (approximately threefold); monitor carefully during use and consider cephalosporin-associated immune anemia in patients who have received cefotetan within 2-3 weeks (either as treatment or prophylaxis). May cause antibiotic-associated colitis or colitis secondary to *C. difficile*.
Adverse Reactions
1% to 10%:
Gastrointestinal: Diarrhea (1%)
Hepatic: Transaminases increased (1%)
Miscellaneous: Hypersensitivity reactions (1%)
<1%: Anaphylaxis, urticaria, rash, pruritus, pseudomembranous colitis, nausea, vomiting, eosinophilia, thrombocytosis, agranulocytosis, hemolytic anemia, leukopenia, thrombocytopenia, prolonged PT, bleeding, BUN increased, creatinine increased, nephrotoxicity, phlebitis, fever
Reactions reported with other cephalosporins: Seizure, Stevens-Johnson syndrome, toxic epidermal necrolysis, renal dysfunction, toxic nephropathy, cholestasis, aplastic anemia, hemolytic anemia, hemorrhage, pancytopenia, agranulocytosis, colitis, superinfection
Overdosage/Toxicology Symptoms include neuromuscular hypersensitivity and convulsions especially with renal insufficiency. Many beta-lactam antibiotics have the potential to cause neuromuscular hyperirritability or seizures. Hemodialysis may be helpful to aid in removal of the drug from the blood; otherwise, most treatment is supportive or symptom-directed.
Drug Interactions
Increased Effect/Toxicity: Disulfiram-like reaction may occur if ethanol is consumed by a patient taking cefotetan. Probenecid may increase cefotetan plasma levels. Cefotetan may increase risk of bleeding in patients receiving warfarin.
Ethanol/Nutrition/Herb Interactions Ethanol: Avoid ethanol (may cause a disulfiram-like reaction).
Stability Reconstituted solution is stable for 24 hours at room temperature and 96 hours when refrigerated. For I.V. infusion in NS or D₅W solution and after freezing, thawed solution is stable for 24 hours at room temperature or 96 hours when refrigerated. Frozen solution is stable for 12 weeks.
Mechanism of Action Inhibits bacterial cell wall synthesis by binding to one or more of the penicillin-binding proteins (PBPs) which in turn inhibits the final transpeptidation step of peptidoglycan synthesis in bacterial cell walls, thus inhibiting cell wall biosynthesis. Bacteria eventually lyse due to ongoing activity of cell wall autolytic enzymes (autolysins and murein hydrolases) while cell wall assembly is arrested.
Pharmacodynamics/Kinetics
Distribution: Widely to body tissues and fluids including bile, sputum, prostatic, peritoneal; low concentrations enter CSF; crosses placenta; enters breast milk
Protein binding: 76% to 90%
Half-life elimination: 3-5 hours
Time to peak, serum: I.M.: 1.5-3 hours
Excretion: Primarily urine (as unchanged drug); feces (20%)
Dosage
Usual dosage range:
Children (unlabeled use): I.M., I.V.: 20-40 mg/kg/dose every 12 hours (maximum: 6 g/day)
Adults: I.M., I.V.: 1-6 g/day in divided doses every 12 hours
Indication-specific dosing:
Children (unlabeled use):
Preoperative prophylaxis: I.M., I.V.: 40 mg/kg 30-60 minutes prior to surgery
(Continued)

Cefotetan *(Continued)*

Adolescents and Adults:

Pelvic inflammatory disease: I.V.: 2 g every 12 hours; used in combination with doxycycline

Adults:

Orbital cellulitis, odontogenic infections: I.V.: 2 g every 12 hours

Preoperative prophylaxis: I.M., I.V.: 1-2 g 30-60 minutes prior to surgery; when used for cesarean section, dose should be given as soon as umbilical cord is clamped

Urinary tract infection: I.M., I.V.: 1-2 g may be given every 24 hours

Dosing interval in renal impairment:

Cl_{cr} 10-30 mL/minute: Administer every 24 hours

Cl_{cr} <10 mL/minute: Administer every 48 hours

Hemodialysis: Dialyzable (5% to 20%); administer $^1/_4$ the usual dose every 24 hours on days between dialysis; administer $^1/_2$ the usual dose on the day of dialysis.

Continuous arteriovenous or venovenous hemodiafiltration effects: Administer 750 mg every 12 hours

Dietary Considerations Contains sodium of 80 mg (3.5 mEq) per cefotetan 1 g

Administration

I.M.: Inject deep I.M. into large muscle mass.

I.V.: Inject direct I.V. over 3-5 minutes. Infuse intermittent infusion over 30 minutes.

Monitoring Parameters Observe for signs and symptoms of anaphylaxis during first dose; monitor for signs and symptoms of hemolytic anemia, including hematologic parameters where appropriate.

Test Interactions Positive direct Coombs', false-positive urinary glucose test using cupric sulfate (Benedict's solution, Clinitest®, Fehling's solution), false-positive serum or urine creatinine with Jaffé reaction

Dosage Forms [DSC] = Discontinued product

Infusion [premixed iso-osmotic solution]: 1 g (50 mL); 2 g (50 mL) [contains sodium 80 mg/g (3.5 mEq/g)] [DSC]

Injection, powder for reconstitution: 1 g, 2 g [contains sodium 80 mg/g (3.5 mEq/g)] [DSC]

♦ **Cefotetan Disodium** *see Cefotetan on page 315*

Cefoxitin *(se FOKS i tin)*

U.S. Brand Names Mefoxin®

Index Terms Cefoxitin Sodium

Pharmacologic Category Antibiotic, Cephalosporin (Second Generation)

Additional Appendix Information

Antimicrobial Drugs of Choice *on page 1981*

Prevention of Wound Infection and Sepsis in Surgical Patients *on page 1964*

Treatment of Sexually Transmitted Infections *on page 2007*

Use Less active against staphylococci and streptococci than first generation cephalosporins, but active against anaerobes including *Bacteroides fragilis*; active against gram-negative enteric bacilli including *E. coli*, *Klebsiella*, and *Proteus*; used predominantly for respiratory tract, skin and skin structure, bone and joint, urinary tract and gynecologic as well as septicemia; surgical prophylaxis; intra-abdominal infections and other mixed infections; indicated for bacterial *Eikenella corrodens* infections

Pregnancy Risk Factor B

Lactation Enters breast milk (small amounts)/use caution (AAP rates "compatible")

Medication Safety Issues

Sound-alike/look-alike issues:

Cefoxitin may be confused with cefotaxime, cefotetan, Cytoxan®

Mefoxin® may be confused with Lanoxin®

Contraindications Hypersensitivity to cefoxitin, any component of the formulation, or other cephalosporins

Warnings/Precautions Use with caution in patients with history of colitis. Cefoxitin may increase resistance of organisms by inducing beta-lactamase. Modify dosage in patients with severe renal impairment. Prolonged use may result in superinfection. Use with caution in patients with a history of penicillin allergy, especially IgE-mediated reactions (eg, anaphylaxis, urticaria). May cause antibiotic-associated colitis or colitis secondary to *C. difficile*.

Adverse Reactions

1% to 10%: Gastrointestinal: Diarrhea

<1% (Limited to important or life-threatening): Anaphylaxis, angioedema, bone marrow suppression, BUN increased, creatinine increased, dyspnea, eosinophilia, exacerbation of myasthenia gravis, exfoliative dermatitis, fever, hemolytic anemia, hypotension, interstitial nephritis, jaundice, leukopenia, nausea, nephrotoxicity (with aminoglycosides), phlebitis, prolonged PT, pruritus, pseudomembranous colitis, rash, thrombocytopenia, thrombophlebitis, toxic epidermal necrolysis, transaminases increased, urticaria, vomiting

Reactions reported with other cephalosporins: Agranulocytosis, aplastic anemia, cholestasis, colitis, erythema multiforme, hemolytic anemia, hemorrhage, pancytopenia, renal dysfunction, seizure, serum-sickness reactions, Stevens-Johnson syndrome, superinfection, toxic nephropathy, vaginitis

Overdosage/Toxicology Symptoms include neuromuscular hypersensitivity and convulsions, especially with renal insufficiency. Many beta-lactam antibiotics have the potential to cause neuromuscular hyperirritability or seizures. Hemodialysis may be helpful to aid in removal of the drug from the blood; otherwise, most treatment is supportive or symptom-directed.

Drug Interactions

Increased Effect/Toxicity: Probenecid may decrease cephalosporin elimination. Furosemide, aminoglycosides in combination with cefoxitin may result in additive nephrotoxicity.

Stability Reconstitute vials with SWFI, bacteriostatic water for injection, NS, or D_5W. For I.V. infusion, solutions may be further diluted in NS, $D_5^1/_4NS$, $D_5^1/_2NS$, D_5NS, D_5W, $D_{10}W$, LR,

D$_5$LR, mannitol 10%, or sodium bicarbonate 5%. Reconstituted solution is stable for 6 hours at room temperature or 7 days when refrigerated; I.V. infusion in NS or D$_5$W solution is stable for 18 hours at room temperature or 48 hours when refrigerated. Premixed frozen solution, when thawed, is stable for 24 hours at room temperature or 21 days when refrigerated.

Mechanism of Action Inhibits bacterial cell wall synthesis by binding to one or more of the penicillin-binding proteins (PBPs) which in turn inhibits the final transpeptidation step of peptidoglycan synthesis in bacterial cell walls, thus inhibiting cell wall biosynthesis. Bacteria eventually lyse due to ongoing activity of cell wall autolytic enzymes (autolysins and murein hydrolases) while cell wall assembly is arrested.

Pharmacodynamics/Kinetics

Distribution: Widely to body tissues and fluids including pleural, synovial, ascitic, bile; poorly penetrates into CSF even with inflammation of the meninges; crosses placenta; small amounts enter breast milk

Protein binding: 65% to 79%

Half-life elimination: 45-60 minutes; significantly prolonged with renal impairment

Time to peak, serum: I.M.: 20-30 minutes

Excretion: Urine (85% as unchanged drug)

Dosage

Usual dosage range:

Infants >3 months and Children: I.M., I.V.: 80-160 mg/kg/day in divided doses every 4-6 hours (maximum dose: 12 g/day)

Adults: I.M., I.V.: 1-2 g every 6-8 hours (maximum dose: 12 g/day)

Note: I.M. injection is painful

Indication-specific dosing:

Infants >3 months and Children:

Mild-to-moderate infection: I.M., I.V.: 80-100 mg/kg/day in divided doses every 4-6 hours

Perioperative prophylaxis: I.V.: 30-40 mg/kg 30-60 minutes prior to surgery followed by 30-40 mg/kg/dose every 6 hours for no more than 24 hours after surgery depending on the procedure

Severe infection: I.M., I.V.: 100-160 mg/kg/day in divided doses every 4-6 hours

Adolescents and Adults:

Perioperative prophylaxis: I.M., I.V.: 1-2 g 30-60 minutes prior to surgery followed by 1-2 g every 6-8 hours for no more than 24 hours after surgery depending on the procedure

Adults:

Amnionitis, endomyometritis: I.M., I.V.: 2 g every 6-8 hours

Aspiration pneumonia, empyema, orbital cellulitis, parapharyngeal space, human bites: I.M., I.V.: 2 g every 8 hours

Liver abscess: I.V.: 1 g every 4 hours

Mycobacterium species, not MTB or MAI: I.V.: 12 g/day with amikacin

Pelvic inflammatory disease:

Inpatients: I.V.: 2 g every 6 hours **plus** doxycycline 100 mg I.V. or 100 mg orally every 12 hours until improved, followed by doxycycline 100 mg orally twice daily to complete 14 days

Outpatients: I.M.: 2 g **plus** probenecid 1 g orally as a single dose, followed by doxycycline 100 mg orally twice daily for 14 days

Dosing interval in renal impairment:

Cl$_{cr}$ 30-50 mL/minute: Administer 1-2 g every 8-12 hours

Cl$_{cr}$ 10-29 mL/minute: Administer 1-2 g every 12-24 hours

Cl$_{cr}$ 5-9 mL/minute: Administer 0.5-1 g every 12-24 hours

Cl$_{cr}$ <5 mL/minute: Administer 0.5-1 g every 24-48 hours

Hemodialysis: Moderately dialyzable (20% to 50%); administer a loading dose of 1-2 g after each hemodialysis; maintenance dose as noted above based on Cl$_{cr}$

Continuous arteriovenous or venovenous hemodiafiltration effects: Dose as for Cl$_{cr}$ 10-50 mL/minute

Dietary Considerations Sodium content of 1 g: 53 mg (2.3 mEq)

Administration

I.M.: Inject deep I.M. into large muscle mass.

I.V.: Can be administered IVP over 3-5 minutes at a maximum concentration of 100 mg/mL or I.V. intermittent infusion over 10-60 minutes at a final concentration for I.V. administration not to exceed 40 mg/mL

Monitoring Parameters Monitor renal function periodically when used in combination with other nephrotoxic drugs; observe for signs and symptoms of anaphylaxis during first dose

Test Interactions Positive direct Coombs', false-positive urinary glucose test using cupric sulfate (Benedict's solution, Clinitest®, Fehling's solution), false-positive serum or urine creatinine with Jaffé reaction

Dosage Forms

Infusion, as sodium [premixed iso-osmotic solution]: 1 g (50 mL); 2 g (50 mL) [contains sodium 53.8 mg/g (2.3 mEq/g)]

Injection, powder for reconstitution, as sodium: 1 g, 2 g, 10 g [contains sodium 53.8 mg/g (2.3 mEq/g)]

♦ **Cefoxitin Sodium** see Cefoxitin on page 316

Cefpodoxime (sef pode OKS eem)

U.S. Brand Names Vantin®

Canadian Brand Names Vantin®

Index Terms Cefpodoxime Proxetil

Pharmacologic Category Antibiotic, Cephalosporin (Third Generation)

Additional Appendix Information

Antimicrobial Drugs of Choice on page 1981

Community-Acquired Pneumonia in Adults on page 1999

(Continued)

Cefpodoxime *(Continued)*

Treatment of Sexually Transmitted Infections *on page 2007*

Use Treatment of susceptible acute, community-acquired pneumonia caused by *S. pneumoniae* or nonbeta-lactamase producing *H. influenzae*; acute uncomplicated gonorrhea caused by *N. gonorrhoeae*; uncomplicated skin and skin structure infections caused by *S. aureus* or *S. pyogenes*; acute otitis media caused by *S. pneumoniae*, *H. influenzae*, or *M. catarrhalis*; pharyngitis or tonsillitis; and uncomplicated urinary tract infections caused by *E. coli*, *Klebsiella*, and *Proteus*

Pregnancy Risk Factor B

Lactation Enters breast milk (small amounts)/use caution

Medication Safety Issues

Sound-alike/look-alike issues:

Vantin® may be confused with Ventolin®

Contraindications Hypersensitivity to cefpodoxime, any component of the formulation, or other cephalosporins

Warnings/Precautions Modify dosage in patients with severe renal impairment. Prolonged use may result in superinfection. Use with caution in patients with a history of penicillin allergy, especially IgE-mediated reactions (eg, anaphylaxis, urticaria).

Adverse Reactions

>10%:

Dermatologic: Diaper rash (12.1%)

Gastrointestinal: Diarrhea in infants and toddlers (15.4%)

1% to 10%:

Central nervous system: Headache (1.1%)

Dermatologic: Rash (1.4%)

Gastrointestinal: Diarrhea (7.2%), nausea (3.8%), abdominal pain (1.6%), vomiting (1.1% to 2.1%)

Genitourinary: Vaginal infection (3.1%)

<1% (Limited to important or life-threatening): Anaphylaxis, anxiety, appetite decreased, chest pain, cough, dizziness, epistaxis, eye itching, fatigue, fever, flatulence, flushing, fungal skin infection, hypotension, insomnia, malaise, nightmares, pruritus, pseudomembranous colitis, purpuric nephritis, salivation decreased, taste alteration, tinnitus, vaginal candidiasis, weakness

Reactions reported with other cephalosporins: Agranulocytosis, aplastic anemia, cholestasis, colitis, erythema multiforme, hemolytic anemia, hemorrhage, interstitial nephritis, toxic nephropathy, pancytopenia, renal dysfunction, seizure, serum-sickness reactions, Stevens-Johnson syndrome, superinfection, toxic epidermal necrolysis, urticaria, vaginitis

Overdosage/Toxicology After acute overdose, most agents cause only nausea, vomiting, and diarrhea, although neuromuscular hypersensitivity and seizures are possible, especially in patients with renal insufficiency. Many beta-lactam antibiotics have the potential to cause neuromuscular hyperirritability or seizures. Hemodialysis may be helpful to aid in removal of the drug from the blood but not usually indicated; otherwise, most treatment is supportive or symptom-directed, following GI decontamination.

Drug Interactions

Increased Effect/Toxicity: Probenecid may decrease cephalosporin elimination. Furosemide, aminoglycosides in combination with cefpodoxime may result in additive nephrotoxicity.

Decreased Effect: Antacids and H_2-receptor antagonists reduce absorption and serum concentration of cefpodoxime.

Ethanol/Nutrition/Herb Interactions Food: Food delays absorption; cefpodoxime serum levels may be increased if taken with food.

Stability Shake well before using. After mixing, keep suspension in refrigerator. Discard unused portion after 14 days.

Mechanism of Action Inhibits bacterial cell wall synthesis by binding to one or more of the penicillin-binding proteins (PBPs) which in turn inhibits the final transpeptidation step of peptidoglycan synthesis in bacterial cell walls, thus inhibiting cell wall biosynthesis. Bacteria eventually lyse due to ongoing activity of cell wall autolytic enzymes (autolysins and murein hydrolases) while cell wall assembly is arrested.

Pharmacodynamics/Kinetics

Absorption: Rapid and well absorbed (50%), acid stable; enhanced in the presence of food or low gastric pH

Distribution: Good tissue penetration, including lung and tonsils; penetrates into pleural fluid

Protein binding: 18% to 23%

Metabolism: De-esterified in GI tract to active metabolite, cefpodoxime

Half-life elimination: 2.2 hours; prolonged with renal impairment

Time to peak: Within 1 hour

Excretion: Urine (80% as unchanged drug) in 24 hours

Dosage

Usual dosage range:

Children 2 months to 12 years: Oral: 10 mg/kg/day divided every 12 hours (maximum dose: 400 mg/day)

Children ≥12 years and Adults: Oral: 100-400 mg every 12 hours

Indication-specific dosing:

Children 2 months to 12 years: Oral:

Acute maxillary sinusitis: 10 mg/kg/day divided every 12 hours for 10 days (maximum: 200 mg/dose)

Acute otitis media: 10 mg/kg/day divided every 12 hours (400 mg/day) for 5 days (maximum: 200 mg/dose)

Pharyngitis/tonsillitis: 10 mg/kg/day in 2 divided doses for 5-10 days (maximum: 100 mg/dose)

Children ≥12 years and Adults: Oral:

Acute community-acquired pneumonia and bacterial exacerbations of chronic bronchitis: 200 mg every 12 hours for 14 days and 10 days, respectively

Acute maxillary sinusitis: 200 mg every 12 hours for 10 days
Pharyngitis/tonsillitis: 100 mg every 12 hours for 5-10 days
Skin and skin structure: 400 mg every 12 hours for 7-14 days
Uncomplicated gonorrhea (male and female) and rectal gonococcal infections (female): 200 mg as a single dose
Uncomplicated urinary tract infection: 100 mg every 12 hours for 7 days
Dosing adjustment in renal impairment: Cl$_{cr}$ <30 mL/minute: Administer every 24 hours
Hemodialysis: Administer dose 3 times/week following hemodialysis

Dietary Considerations May be taken with food.

Administration Administer around-the-clock to promote less variation in peak and trough serum levels.

Monitoring Parameters Observe for signs and symptoms of anaphylaxis during first dose

Test Interactions Positive direct Coombs', false-positive urinary glucose test using cupric sulfate (Benedict's solution, Clinitest®, Fehling's solution), false-positive serum or urine creatinine with Jaffé reaction

Dosage Forms
Granules for oral suspension: 50 mg/5 mL (50 mL, 75 mL, 100 mL); 100 mg/5 mL (50 mL, 75 mL, 100 mL) [contains sodium benzoate; lemon creme flavor]
Tablet: 100 mg, 200 mg

♦ **Cefpodoxime Proxetil** see Cefpodoxime on page 317

Cefprozil (sef PROE zil)

U.S. Brand Names Cefzil®
Canadian Brand Namoo Cefzil®
Pharmacologic Category Antibiotic, Cephalosporin (Second Generation)
Additional Appendix Information
Community-Acquired Pneumonia in Adults on page 1999
Use Treatment of otitis media and infections involving the respiratory tract and skin and skin structure; active against methicillin-sensitive staphylococci, many streptococci, and various gram-negative bacilli including *E. coli*, some *Klebsiella*, *P. mirabilis*, *H. influenzae*, and *Moraxella*.
Pregnancy Risk Factor B
Lactation Enters breast milk/use caution (AAP rates "compatible")
Medication Safety Issues
Sound-alike/look-alike issues:
Cefprozil may be confused with cefazolin, cefuroxime
Cefzil® may be confused with Cefol®, Ceftin®, Kefzol®
Contraindications Hypersensitivity to cefprozil, any component of the formulation, or other cephalosporins
Warnings/Precautions Modify dosage in patients with severe renal impairment. Prolonged use may result in superinfection. Use with caution in patients with a history of penicillin allergy, especially IgE-mediated reactions (eg, anaphylaxis, urticaria). May cause antibiotic-associated colitis or colitis secondary to *C. difficile*.
Adverse Reactions
1% to 10%:
Central nervous system: Dizziness (1%)
Dermatologic: Diaper rash (1.5%)
Gastrointestinal: Diarrhea (2.9%), nausea (3.5%), vomiting (1%), abdominal pain (1%)
Genitourinary: Vaginitis, genital pruritus (1.6%)
Hepatic: Transaminases increased (2%)
Miscellaneous: Superinfection
<1% (Limited to important or life-threatening): Anaphylaxis, angioedema, arthralgia, BUN increased, cholestatic jaundice, confusion, creatinine increased, eosinophilia, erythema multiforme, fever, headache, hyperactivity, insomnia, leukopenia, pseudomembranous colitis, rash, serum sickness, somnolence, Stevens-Johnson syndrome, thrombocytopenia, urticaria
Reactions reported with other cephalosporins: Aagranulocytosis, aplastic anemia, colitis, hemolytic anemia, hemorrhage, interstitial nephritis, pancytopenia, renal dysfunction, seizure, superinfection, toxic epidermal necrolysis, toxic nephropathy, vaginitis
Overdosage/Toxicology After acute overdose, most agents cause only nausea, vomiting, and diarrhea, although neuromuscular hypersensitivity and seizures are possible, especially in patients with renal insufficiency. Many beta-lactam antibiotics have the potential to cause neuromuscular hyperirritability or seizures. Hemodialysis may be helpful to aid in removal of the drug from the blood but not usually indicated; otherwise, most treatment is supportive or symptom-directed, following GI decontamination.
Drug Interactions
Increased Effect/Toxicity: Probenecid may decrease cephalosporin elimination. Furosemide, aminoglycosides in combination with cefprozil may result in additive nephrotoxicity.
Ethanol/Nutrition/Herb Interactions Food: Food delays cefprozil absorption.
Mechanism of Action Inhibits bacterial cell wall synthesis by binding to one or more of the penicillin-binding proteins (PBPs) which in turn inhibits the final transpeptidation step of peptidoglycan synthesis in bacterial cell walls, thus inhibiting cell wall biosynthesis. Bacteria eventually lyse due to ongoing activity of cell wall autolytic enzymes (autolysins and murein hydrolases) while cell wall assembly is arrested.
Pharmacodynamics/Kinetics
Absorption: Well absorbed (94%)
Distribution: Low amounts enter breast milk
Protein binding: 35% to 45%
Half-life elimination: Normal renal function: 1.3 hours
Time to peak, serum: Fasting: 1.5 hours
Excretion: Urine (61% as unchanged drug)
(Continued)

Cefprozil *(Continued)*

Dosage

Usual dosage range:

Infants and Children >6 months to 12 years: Oral: 7.5-15 mg/kg/day divided every 12 hours

Children >12 years and Adults: Oral: 250-500 mg every 12 hours or 500 mg every 24 hours

Indication-specific dosing:

Infants and Children >6 months to 12 years: Oral:

Otitis media: 15 mg/kg every 12 hours for 10 days

Children 2-12 years: Oral:

Pharyngitis/tonsillitis: 7.5-15 mg/kg/day divided every 12 hours for 10 days (administer for >10 days if due to *S. pyogenes*); maximum: 1 g/day

Uncomplicated skin and skin structure infections: 20 mg/kg every 24 hours for 10 days; maximum: 1 g/day

Children >12 years and Adults: Oral:

Pharyngitis/tonsillitis: 500 mg every 24 hours for 10 days

Secondary bacterial infection of acute bronchitis or acute bacterial exacerbation of chronic bronchitis: 500 mg every 12 hours for 10 days

Uncomplicated skin and skin structure infections: 250 mg every 12 hours or 500 mg every 12-24 hours for 10 days

Dosing adjustment in renal impairment: Cl_{cr} <30 mL/minute: Reduce dose by 50%

Hemodialysis: Reduced by hemodialysis; administer dose after the completion of hemodialysis

Dietary Considerations May be taken with food. Oral suspension contains phenylalanine 28 mg/5 mL.

Administration Administer around-the-clock to promote less variation in peak and trough serum levels. Chilling the reconstituted oral suspension improves flavor (do not freeze).

Monitoring Parameters Assess patient at beginning and throughout therapy for infection; monitor for signs of anaphylaxis during first dose

Test Interactions Positive direct Coombs', false-positive urinary glucose test using cupric sulfate (Benedict's solution, Clinitest®, Fehling's solution), false-positive serum or urine creatinine with Jaffé reaction

Dosage Forms

Powder for oral suspension, as anhydrous: 125 mg/5 mL (50 mL, 75 mL, 100 mL); 250 mg/5 mL (50 mL, 75 mL, 100 mL)

Cefzil®: 125 mg/5 mL (50 mL, 75 mL, 100 mL) [contains phenylalanine 28 mg/5 mL and sodium benzoate; bubble gum flavor]; 250 mg/5 mL (50 mL, 75 mL, 100 mL) [contains phenylalanine 28 mg/5 mL and sodium benzoate; bubble gum flavor]

Tablet, as anhydrous: 250 mg, 500 mg

Cefzil®: 250 mg, 500 mg

Ceftazidime *(SEF tay zi deem)*

U.S. Brand Names Ceptaz® [DSC]; Fortaz®; Tazicef®

Canadian Brand Names Fortaz®

Pharmacologic Category Antibiotic, Cephalosporin (Third Generation)

Additional Appendix Information

Antimicrobial Drugs of Choice *on page 1981*

Use Treatment of documented susceptible *Pseudomonas aeruginosa* infection and infections due to other susceptible aerobic gram-negative organisms; empiric therapy of a febrile, granulocytopenic patient

Pregnancy Risk Factor B

Lactation Enters breast milk (small amounts)/use caution (AAP rates "compatible")

Medication Safety Issues

Sound-alike/look-alike issues:

Ceftazidime may be confused with ceftizoxime

Ceptaz® may be confused with Septra®

Tazicef® may be confused with Tazidime®

Tazidime® may be confused with Tazicef®

International issues:

Ceftim® [Italy] may be confused with Ceftin® which is a brand name for cefuroxime in the U.S.

Ceftim® [Italy] may be confused with Cefiton® which is a brand name for cefixime in Portugal

Ceftim® [Italy] may be confused with Ceftina® which is a brand name for cefalotin in Mexico

Contraindications Hypersensitivity to ceftazidime, any component of the formulation, or other cephalosporins

Warnings/Precautions Modify dosage in patients with severe renal impairment. Prolonged use may result in superinfection. Use with caution in patients with a history of penicillin allergy, especially IgE-mediated reactions (eg, anaphylaxis, urticaria). May cause antibiotic-associated colitis or colitis secondary to *C. difficile*.

Adverse Reactions

1% to 10%:

Gastrointestinal: Diarrhea (1%)

Local: Pain at injection site (1%)

Miscellaneous: Hypersensitivity reactions (2%)

<1% (Limited to important or life-threatening): Anaphylaxis, angioedema, asterixis, BUN increased, candidiasis, creatinine increased, dizziness, encephalopathy, eosinophilia, erythema multiforme, fever, headache, hemolytic anemia, hyperbilirubinemia, jaundice, leukopenia, myoclonus, nausea, neuromuscular excitability, paresthesia, phlebitis, pruritus, pseudomembranous colitis, rash, Stevens-Johnson syndrome, thrombocytosis, toxic epidermal necrolysis, transaminases increased, vaginitis, vomiting

Reactions reported with other cephalosporins: Agranulocytosis, aplastic anemia, cholestasis, colitis, hemolytic anemia, hemorrhage, interstitial nephritis, pancytopenia, prolonged PT, renal dysfunction, seizure, serum-sickness reactions, superinfection, toxic nephropathy, urticaria

Overdosage/Toxicology Symptoms include neuromuscular hypersensitivity and convulsions, especially with renal insufficiency. Many beta-lactam antibiotics have the potential to cause neuromuscular hyperirritability or seizures. Hemodialysis may be helpful to aid in removal of the drug from the blood, otherwise, most treatment is supportive or symptom-directed.

Drug Interactions

Increased Effect/Toxicity: Probenecid may decrease cephalosporin elimination. Aminoglycosides: *in vitro* studies indicate additive or synergistic effect against some strains of Enterobacteriaceae and *Pseudomonas aeruginosa*. Furosemide, aminoglycosides in combination with ceftazidime may result in additive nephrotoxicity.

Stability Reconstituted solution and I.V. infusion in NS or D_5W solution are stable for 24 hours at room temperature, 10 days when refrigerated, or 12 weeks when frozen. After freezing, thawed solution is stable for 24 hours at room temperature or 4 days when refrigerated; 96 hours under refrigeration, after mixing.

Mechanism of Action Inhibits bacterial cell wall synthesis by binding to one or more of the penicillin-binding proteins (PBPs) which in turn inhibits the final transpeptidation step of peptidoglycan synthesis in bacterial cell walls, thus inhibiting cell wall biosynthesis. Bacteria eventually lyse due to ongoing activity of cell wall autolytic enzymes (autolysins and murein hydrolases) while cell wall assembly is arrested.

Pharmacodynamics/Kinetics

Distribution: Widely throughout the body including bone, bile, skin, CSF (higher concentrations achieved when meninges are inflamed), endometrium, heart, pleural and lymphatic fluids

Protein binding: 17%

Half-life elimination: 1-2 hours, prolonged with renal impairment; Neonates <23 days: 2.2-4.7 hours

Time to peak, serum: I.M.: ~1 hour

Excretion: Urine (80% to 90% as unchanged drug)

Dosage

Usual dosage range:

Infants and Children 1 month to 12 years: I.V.: 30-50 mg/kg/dose every 8 hours (maximum dose: 6 g/day)

Adults: I.M., I.V.: 500 mg to 2 g every 8-12 hours

Indication-specific dosing:

Bacterial arthritis (gram-negative bacilli): I.V.: 1-2 g every 8 hours

Cystic fibrosis: I.V.: 30-50 mg/kg every 8 hours (maximum: 6 g/day)

Melioidosis: I.V.: 40 mg/kg every 8 hours for 10 days, followed by oral therapy with doxycycline or TMP/SMX

Otitis externa: I.V.: 2 g every 8 hours

Peritonitis (CAPD):

Anuric, intermittent: 1000-1500 mg/day

Anuric, continuous (per liter exchange): Loading dose: 250 mg; maintenance dose: 125 mg

Severe infections, including meningitis, complicated pneumonia, endophthalmitis, CNS infection, osteomyelitis, intra-abdominal and gynecological, skin and soft tissue: I.V.: 2 g every 8 hours

Dosing interval in renal impairment:

Cl_{cr} 30-50 mL/minute: Administer every 12 hours

Cl_{cr} 10-30 mL/minute: Administer every 24 hours

Cl_{cr} <10 mL/minute: Administer every 48-72 hours

Hemodialysis: Dialyzable (50% to 100%)

Continuous arteriovenous or venovenous hemodiafiltration effects: Dose as for Cl_{cr} 30-50 mL/minute

Dietary Considerations Sodium content of 1 g: 2.3 mEq

Administration Any carbon dioxide bubbles that may be present in the withdrawn solution should be expelled prior to injection. Administer around-the-clock to promote less variation in peak and trough serum levels. Ceftazidime can be administered deep I.M. into large mass muscle, IVP over 3-5 minutes, or I.V. intermittent infusion over 15-30 minutes. Do not admix with aminoglycosides in same bottle/bag. Final concentration for I.V. administration should not exceed 100 mg/mL.

Monitoring Parameters Observe for signs and symptoms of anaphylaxis during first dose

Test Interactions Positive direct Coombs', false-positive urinary glucose test using cupric sulfate (Benedict's solution, Clinitest®, Fehling's solution), false-positive serum or urine creatinine with Jaffé reaction

Additional Information With some organisms, resistance may develop during treatment (including *Enterobacter* spp and *Serratia* spp). Consider combination therapy or periodic susceptibility testing for organisms with inducible resistance.

Dosage Forms [DSC] = Discontinued product

Infusion, as sodium [premixed iso-osmotic solution] (Fortaz®): 1 g (50 mL); 2 g (50 mL)

Injection, powder for reconstitution:

Ceptaz® [DSC]: 10 g [L-arginine formulation]

Fortaz®: 500 mg, 1 g, 2 g, 6 g [contains sodium carbonate]

Tazicef®: 1 g, 2 g, 6 g [contains sodium carbonate]

Ceftibuten (sef TYE byoo ten)

U.S. Brand Names Cedax®
Pharmacologic Category Antibiotic, Cephalosporin (Third Generation)
Use Oral cephalosporin for treatment of bronchitis, otitis media, and pharyngitis/tonsillitis due to *H. influenzae* and *M. catarrhalis*, both beta-lactamase-producing and nonproducing strains, as well as *S. pneumoniae* (weak) and *S. pyogenes*
Pregnancy Risk Factor B
Lactation Excretion in breast milk unknown/use caution
Medication Safety Issues
International issues:
Cedax® may be confused with Codex which is a brand name for saccharomyces boulardii in Italy
Contraindications Hypersensitivity to ceftibuten, any component of the formulation, or other cephalosporins
Warnings/Precautions Modify dosage in patients with severe renal impairment. Prolonged use may result in superinfection. Use with caution in patients with a history of penicillin allergy, especially IgE-mediated reactions (eg, anaphylaxis, urticaria). May cause antibiotic-associated colitis or colitis secondary to *C. difficile*.
Adverse Reactions
1% to 10%:
Central nervous system: Headache (3%), dizziness (1%)
Gastrointestinal: Nausea (4%), diarrhea (3%), dyspepsia (2%), vomiting (1%), abdominal pain (1%)
Hematologic: Eosinophils increased (3%), hemoglobin decreased (2%), thrombocytosis
Hepatic: ALT increased (1%), bilirubin increased (1%)
Renal: BUN increased (4%)
<1% (Limited to important or life-threatening): Agitation, anorexia, candidiasis, constipation, creatinine increased, diaper rash, dry mouth, dyspnea, dysuria, fatigue, insomnia, irritability, leukopenia, nasal congestion, paresthesia, rash, rigors, transaminases increased, urticaria
Reactions reported with other cephalosporins: Agranulocytosis, anaphylaxis, angioedema, aplastic anemia, asterixis, candidiasis, cholestasis, colitis, encephalopathy, erythema multiforme, fever, hemolytic anemia, hemorrhage, interstitial nephritis, neuromuscular excitability, pancytopenia, paresthesia, prolonged PT, pruritus, pseudomembranous colitis, renal dysfunction, seizure, serum-sickness reactions, Stevens-Johnson syndrome, superinfection, toxic epidermal necrolysis, toxic nephropathy, vaginitis
Overdosage/Toxicology After acute overdose, most agents cause only nausea, vomiting, and diarrhea, although neuromuscular hypersensitivity and seizures are possible, especially in patients with renal insufficiency. Many beta-lactam antibiotics have the potential to cause neuromuscular hyperirritability or seizures. Hemodialysis may be helpful to aid in removal of the drug from the blood but not usually indicated; otherwise, most treatment is supportive or symptom-directed, following GI decontamination.
Drug Interactions
Increased Effect/Toxicity: High-dose probenecid decreases clearance. Aminoglycosides in combination with ceftibuten may increase nephrotoxic potential.
Stability Reconstituted suspension is stable for 14 days when refrigerated.
Mechanism of Action Inhibits bacterial cell wall synthesis by binding to one or more of the penicillin-binding proteins (PBPs) which in turn inhibits the final transpeptidation step of peptidoglycan synthesis in bacterial cell walls, thus inhibiting cell wall biosynthesis. Bacteria eventually lyse due to ongoing activity of cell wall autolytic enzymes (autolysins and murein hydrolases) while cell wall assembly is arrested.
Pharmacodynamics/Kinetics
Absorption: Rapid; food decreases peak concentrations, delays T_{max}, and lowers AUC
Distribution: V_d: Children: 0.5 L/kg; Adults: 0.21 L/kg
Half-life elimination: 2 hours
Time to peak: 2-3 hours
Excretion: Urine
Dosage
Usual dosage range:
Children <12 years: Oral: 9 mg/kg/day for 10 days (maximum dose: 400 mg/day)
Children ≥12 years and Adults: Oral: 400 mg once daily for 10 days (maximum dose: 400 mg/day)
Dosage adjustment in renal impairment:
Cl_{cr} 30-49 mL//minute: Administer 4.5 mg/kg or 200 mg every 24 hours
Cl_{cr} 5-29 mL/minute: Administer 2.25 mg/kg or 100 mg every 24 hours.
Hemodialysis: Administer 400 mg or 9 mg/kg (maximum: 400 mg) after hemodialysis
Dietary Considerations
Capsule: Take without regard to food.
Suspension: Take 2 hours before or 1 hour after meals; contains 1 g of sucrose per 5 mL
Administration Shake suspension well before use.
Monitoring Parameters Observe for signs and symptoms of anaphylaxis during first dose; with prolonged therapy, monitor renal, hepatic, and hematologic function periodically
Test Interactions Positive direct Coombs', false-positive urinary glucose test using cupric sulfate (Benedict's solution, Clinitest®, Fehling's solution), false-positive serum or urine creatinine with Jaffé reaction
Dosage Forms
Capsule:
Cedax®: 400 mg
Powder for oral suspension:
Cedax®: 90 mg/5 mL (30 mL, 60 mL, 90 mL, 120 mL) [contains sucrose 1g/5 mL and sodium benzoate; cherry flavor]

♦ **Ceftin®** *see* Cefuroxime *on page 326*

Ceftizoxime (sef ti ZOKS eem)

U.S. Brand Names Cefizox®
Canadian Brand Names Cefizox®
Index Terms Ceftizoxime Sodium
Pharmacologic Category Antibiotic, Cephalosporin (Third Generation)
Additional Appendix Information
    Antimicrobial Drugs of Choice *on page 1981*
    Treatment of Sexually Transmitted Infections *on page 2007*
Use Treatment of susceptible bacterial infections, mainly respiratory tract, skin and skin structure, bone and joint, urinary tract and gynecologic, as well as septicemia; active against many gram-negative bacilli (not *Pseudomonas*), some gram-positive cocci (not *Enterococcus*), and some anaerobes
Pregnancy Risk Factor B
Lactation Enters breast milk (small amounts)/use caution
Medication Safety Issues
    Sound-alike/look-alike issues:
        Ceftizoxime may be confused with cefotaxime, ceftazidime, cefuroxime
Contraindications Hypersensitivity to ceftizoxime, any component of the formulation, or other cephalosporins
Warnings/Precautions Modify dosage in patients with severe renal impairment. Prolonged use may result in superinfection. Use with caution in patients with a history of penicillin allergy, especially IgE-mediated reactions (eg, anaphylaxis, urticaria). May cause antibiotic-associated colitis or colitis secondary to *C. difficile*.
Adverse Reactions
    1% to 10%:
        Central nervous system: Fever
        Dermatologic: Rash, pruritus
        Hematologic: Eosinophilia, thrombocytosis
        Hepatic: Alkaline phosphatase increased, transaminases increased
        Local: Pain, burning at injection site
    <1% (Limited to important or life-threatening): Anaphylaxis, anemia, bilirubin increased, BUN increased, creatinine increased, diarrhea, injection site reactions, leukopenia, nausea, neutropenia, numbness, paresthesia, phlebitis, thrombocytopenia, vaginitis, vomiting
    Reactions reported with other cephalosporins: Agranulocytosis, angioedema, aplastic anemia, asterixis, candidiasis, cholestasis, colitis, encephalopathy, erythema multiforme, hemolytic anemia, hemorrhage, interstitial nephritis, neuromuscular excitability, pancytopenia, prolonged PT, pseudomembranous colitis, renal dysfunction, seizure, serum-sickness reactions, Stevens-Johnson syndrome, superinfection, toxic epidermal necrolysis, toxic nephropathy
Overdosage/Toxicology Symptoms include neuromuscular hypersensitivity and convulsions especially with renal insufficiency. Many beta-lactam antibiotics have the potential to cause neuromuscular hyperirritability or seizures. Hemodialysis may be helpful to aid in removal of the drug from the blood; otherwise, most treatment is supportive or symptom-directed.
Drug Interactions
    Increased Effect/Toxicity: Probenecid may decrease cephalosporin elimination. Furosemide, aminoglycosides in combination with ceftizoxime may result in additive nephrotoxicity.
Stability Reconstituted solution is stable for 24 hours at room temperature and 96 hours when refrigerated. For I.V. infusion in NS or D₅W solution is stable for 24 hours at room temperature, 96 hours when refrigerated, or 12 weeks when frozen. After freezing, thawed solution is stable for 24 hours at room temperature or 10 days when refrigerated.
Mechanism of Action Inhibits bacterial cell wall synthesis by binding to one or more of the penicillin-binding proteins (PBPs) which in turn inhibits the final transpeptidation step of peptidoglycan synthesis in bacterial cell walls, thus inhibiting cell wall biosynthesis. Bacteria eventually lyse due to ongoing activity of cell wall autolytic enzymes (autolysins and murein hydrolases) while cell wall assembly is arrested.
Pharmacodynamics/Kinetics
    Distribution: V_d: 0.35-0.5 L/kg; widely into most body tissues and fluids including gallbladder, liver, kidneys, bone, sputum, bile, pleural and synovial fluids; has good CSF penetration; crosses placenta; small amounts enter breast milk
    Protein binding: 30%
    Half-life elimination: 1.6 hours; Cl_{cr} <10 mL/minute: 25 hours
    Time to peak, serum: I.M.: 0.5-1 hour
    Excretion: Urine (as unchanged drug)
Dosage
    Usual dosage range:
        Children ≥6 months: I.M., I.V.: 150-200 mg/kg/day divided every 6-8 hours (maximum: 12 g/24 hours)
        Adults: I.M., I.V.: 1-4 g every 8-12 hours
    Indication-specific dosing:
        Adults:
            Gonococcal:
                Disseminated infection: I.M., I.V.: 1 g every 8 hours
                Uncomplicated: I.M.: 1 g as single dose
            Life-threatening infections: I.V.: 2 g every 4 hours or 4 g every 8 hours
    Dosing adjustment in renal impairment: Adults:
        Cl_{cr} 50-79 mL/minute: Administer 500-1500 mg every 8 hours.
        Cl_{cr} 5-49 mL/minute: Administer 250-1000 mg every 12 hours.
        Cl_{cr} 0-4 mL/minute: Administer 500-1000 mg every 48 hours or 250-500 mg every 24 hours.
(Continued)

Ceftizoxime *(Continued)*

Moderately dialyzable (20% to 50%)

Continuous arteriovenous hemofiltration: Dose as for Cl$_{cr}$ 10-50 mL/minute.

Dietary Considerations Sodium content of 1 g: 60 mg (2.6 mEq)

Administration
I.M.: Inject deep I.M. into large muscle mass.
I.V.: Inject direct I.V. over 3-5 minutes. Infuse intermittent infusion over 30 minutes.

Monitoring Parameters Observe for signs and symptoms of anaphylaxis during first dose

Test Interactions Positive direct Coombs', false-positive urinary glucose test using cupric sulfate (Benedict's solution, Clinitest®, Fehling's solution), false-positive serum or urine creatinine with Jaffé reaction

Dosage Forms
Infusion [premixed iso-osmotic solution]:
Cefizox®: 1 g (50 mL); 2 g (50 mL)
Injection, powder for reconstitution:
Cefizox®: 1 g, 2 g, 10 g [DSC]

♦ **Ceftizoxime Sodium** *see Ceftizoxime on page 323*

Ceftriaxone *(sef trye AKS one)*

U.S. Brand Names Rocephin®
Canadian Brand Names Rocephin®
Index Terms Ceftriaxone Sodium
Pharmacologic Category Antibiotic, Cephalosporin (Third Generation)
Additional Appendix Information
Animal and Human Bites *on page 1976*
Antibiotic Treatment of Adults With Infective Endocarditis *on page 1977*
Antimicrobial Drugs of Choice *on page 1981*
Community-Acquired Pneumonia in Adults *on page 1999*
Desensitization Protocols *on page 1913*
Treatment of Sexually Transmitted Infections *on page 2007*

Use Treatment of lower respiratory tract infections, acute bacterial otitis media, skin and skin structure infections, bone and joint infections, intra-abdominal and urinary tract infections, pelvic inflammatory disease (PID), uncomplicated gonorrhea, bacterial septicemia, and meningitis; used in surgical prophylaxis

Unlabeled/Investigational Use Treatment of chancroid, epididymitis, complicated gonococcal infections; sexually-transmitted diseases (STD); periorbital or buccal cellulitis; salmonellosis or shigellosis; atypical community-acquired pneumonia; Lyme disease; used in chemoprophylaxis for high-risk contacts and persons with invasive meningococcal disease; sexual assault

Pregnancy Risk Factor B

Lactation Enters breast milk/use caution (AAP rates "compatible")

Medication Safety Issues
Sound-alike/look-alike issues:
Rocephin® may be confused with Roferon®

Contraindications Hypersensitivity to ceftriaxone sodium, any component of the formulation, or other cephalosporins; **do not use in hyperbilirubinemic neonates**, particularly those who are premature since ceftriaxone is reported to displace bilirubin from albumin binding sites

Warnings/Precautions Modify dosage in patients with severe renal impairment. Prolonged use may result in superinfection. Use with caution in patients with a history of penicillin allergy, especially IgE-mediated reactions (eg, anaphylaxis, urticaria). May cause antibiotic-associated colitis or colitis secondary to *C. difficile*. Discontinue in patients with signs and symptoms of gallbladder disease.

Adverse Reactions
1% to 10%:
Dermatologic: Rash (2%)
Gastrointestinal: Diarrhea (3%)
Hematologic: Eosinophilia (6%), thrombocytosis (5%), leukopenia (2%)
Hepatic: Transaminases increased (3.1% to 3.3%)
Local: Pain, induration at injection site (I.V. 1%); warmth, tightness, induration (5% to 17%) following I.M. injection
Renal: BUN increased (1%)
<1% (Limited to important or life-threatening): Agranulocytosis, alkaline phosphatase increased, allergic pneumonitis, anaphylaxis, anemia, basophilia, bilirubin increased, bronchospasm, candidiasis, chills, colitis, creatinine increased, diaphoresis, dizziness, dysgeusia, flushing, gallstones, glycosuria, headache, hematuria, hemolytic anemia, jaundice, leukocytosis, lymphocytosis, lymphopenia, monocytosis, nausea, nephrolithiasis, neutropenia, phlebitis, prolonged or decreased PT, pruritus, pseudomembranous colitis, renal precipitations, renal stones, seizure, serum sickness, thrombocytopenia, urinary casts, vaginitis, vomiting
Reactions reported with other cephalosporins: Angioedema, aplastic anemia, asterixis, cholestasis, encephalopathy, erythema multiforme, hemorrhage, interstitial nephritis, neuromuscular excitability, pancytopenia, paresthesia, renal dysfunction, Stevens-Johnson syndrome, superinfection, toxic epidermal necrolysis, toxic nephropathy

Overdosage/Toxicology Symptoms include neuromuscular hypersensitivity and convulsions especially with renal insufficiency. Many beta-lactam antibiotics have the potential to cause neuromuscular hyperirritability or seizures. Hemodialysis may be helpful to aid in removal of the drug from the blood; otherwise, most treatment is supportive or symptom-directed.

Drug Interactions
Increased Effect/Toxicity: Cephalosporins may increase the anticoagulant effect of coumarin derivatives (eg, dicumarol, warfarin).

Decreased Effect: Uricosuric agents (eg, probenecid, sulfinpyrazone) may decrease the excretion of cephalosporin; monitor for toxic effects.

Stability

Powder for injection: Prior to reconstitution, store at room temperature of 25°C (77°F); protect from light.

Premixed solution (manufacturer premixed): Store at -20°C. Once thawed, solutions are stable for 3 days at room temperature of 25°C (77°F) or for 21 days refrigerated at 5°C (41°F). Do not refreeze.

Stability of reconstituted solutions:

10-40 mg/mL: Reconstituted in D_5W or NS: Stable for 2 days at room temperature of 25°C (77°F) or for 10 days when refrigerated at 5°C (41°F).

100 mg/mL:

Reconstituted in D_5W or NS: Stable for 2 days at room temperature of 25°C (77°F) or for 10 days when refrigerated at 5°C (41°F). Stable for 26 weeks when frozen at -20°C. Once thawed, solutions are stable for 2 days at room temperature of 25°C (77°F) or for 10 days when refrigerated at 5°C (41°F); does not apply to manufacturer's premixed bags. Do not refreeze.

Reconstituted in lidocaine 1% solution: Stable for 24 hours at room temperature of 25°C (77°F) or for 10 days when refrigerated at 5°C (41°F).

250-350 mg/mL: Reconstituted in D_5W, NS, lidocaine 1% solution, or SWFI: Stable for 24 hours at room temperature of 25°C (77°F) or for 3 days when refrigerated at 5°C (41°F).

Reconstitution:

I.M. injection: Vials should be reconstituted with appropriate volume of diluent (including D_5W, NS, or 1% lidocaine) to make a final concentration of 250 mg/mL or 350 mg/mL.

Volume to add to create a **250 mg/mL** solution:

250 mg vial: 0.9 mL

500 mg vial: 1.8 mL

1 g vial: 3.6 mL

2 g vial: 7.2 mL

Volume to add to create a **350 mg/mL** solution:

500 mg vial: 1.0 mL

1 g vial: 2.1 mL

2 g vial: 4.2 mL

I.V. infusion: Infusion is prepared in two stages: Initial reconstitution of powder, followed by dilution to final infusion solution.

Vials: Reconstitute powder with appropriate I.V. diluent (including SWFI, D_5W, NS) to create an initial solution of ~100 mg/mL. Recommended volume to add:

250 mg vial: 2.4 mL

500 mg vial: 4.8 mL

1 g vial: 9.6 mL

2 g vial: 19.2 mL

Note: After reconstitution of powder, further dilution into a volume of compatible solution (eg, 50-100 mL of D_5W or NS) is recommended.

Piggyback bottle: Reconstitute powder with appropriate I.V. diluent (D_5W or NS) to create a resulting solution of ~100 mg/mL. Recommended initial volume to add:

1 g bottle: 10 mL

2 g bottle: 20 mL

Note: After reconstitution, to prepare the final infusion solution, further dilution to 50 mL or 100 mL volumes with the appropriate I.V. diluent (including D_5W or NS) is recommended.

Mechanism of Action Inhibits bacterial cell wall synthesis by binding to one or more of the penicillin-binding proteins (PBPs) which in turn inhibits the final transpeptidation step of peptidoglycan synthesis in bacterial cell walls, thus inhibiting cell wall biosynthesis. Bacteria eventually lyse due to ongoing activity of cell wall autolytic enzymes (autolysins and murein hydrolases) while cell wall assembly is arrested.

Pharmacodynamics/Kinetics

Absorption: I.M.: Well absorbed

Distribution: Widely throughout the body including gallbladder, lungs, bone, bile, CSF (higher concentrations achieved when meninges are inflamed); crosses placenta; enters amniotic fluid and breast milk

Protein binding: 85% to 95%

Half-life elimination: Normal renal and hepatic function: 5-9 hours

Time to peak, serum: I.M.: 1-2 hours

Excretion: Urine (33% to 65% as unchanged drug); feces

Dosage

Usual dosage range:

Infants and Children: I.M., I.V.: 50-100 mg/kg/day in 1-2 divided doses (maximum: 4 g/day)

Adults: I.M., I.V.: 1-2 g every 12-24 hours

Indication-specific dosing:

Infants and Children:

Epiglottitis: I.M., I.V.: 50-100 mg/kg once daily for 7-10 days with clindamycin

Gonococcal infections:

Conjunctivitis, complicated (unlabeled use): I.M.:

<45 kg: 50 mg/kg in a single dose (maximum: 1 g)

>45 kg: 1 g in a single dose

Disseminated (unlabeled use): I.M., I.V.:

<45 kg: 25-50 mg/kg once daily (maximum: 1 g)

>45 kg: 1 g once daily for 7 days

Endocarditis (unlabeled use):

<45 kg: I.M., I.V.: 50 mg/kg/day every 12 hours (maximum: 2 g/day) for at least 28 days

>45 kg: I.V.: 1-2 g every 12 hours, for at least 28 days

Uncomplicated: I.M.: 125 mg in a single dose

(Continued)

Ceftriaxone (Continued)

Mild-to-moderate infections: I.M., I.V.: 50-75 mg/kg/day in 1-2 divided doses every 12-24 hours (maximum: 2 g/day); continue until at least 2 days after signs and symptoms of infection have resolved

Meningitis:

Gonococcal, complicated:

<45 kg: I.V.: 50 mg/kg/day given every 12 hours (maximum: 2 g/day); usual duration of treatment is 10-14 days

>45 kg: I.V.: 1-2 g every 12 hours; usual duration of treatment is 10-14 days

Uncomplicated: I.M., I.V.: Loading dose of 100 mg/kg (maximum: 4 g), followed by 100 mg/kg/day divided every 12-24 hours (maximum: 4 g/day); usual duration of treatment is 7-14 days

Otitis media:

Acute: I.M.: 50 mg/kg in a single dose (maximum: 1 g)

Persistent or relapsing (unlabeled use): I.M., I.V.: 50 mg/kg once daily for 3 days

Pneumonia: I.V.: 50-75 mg/kg once daily

Serious infections: I.V.: 80-100 mg/kg/day in 1-2 divided doses (maximum: 4 g/day)

STD, sexual assault (unlabeled use): I.M.: 125 mg in a single dose

Typhoid fever: I.V.: 100 mg/kg once daily (maximum 4 g)

Children >8 years (≥45 kg) and Adolescents:

Epididymitis, acute (unlabeled use): I.M.: 125 mg in a single dose

Children ≤15 years:

Chemoprophylaxis for high-risk contacts and persons with invasive meningococcal disease (unlabeled use): I.M.: 125 mg in a single dose. Children >15 years: Refer to adult dosing.

Adults:

Arthritis (septic): I.V.: 1-2 g once daily

Brain abscess and necrotizing fasciitis: I.V.: 2 g every 12 hours

Cavernous sinus thrombosis: I.V.: 1 g every 12 hours with vancomycin or linezolid

Chancroid (unlabeled use): I.M.: 250 mg as single dose

Chemoprophylaxis for high-risk contacts and persons with invasive meningococcal disease (unlabeled use): I.M.: 250 mg in a single dose

Endocarditis, acute native valve: I.V.: 2 g once daily for 2-4 weeks

Epididymitis, acute (unlabeled use) and prostatitis: I.M.: 250 mg in a single dose with doxycycline

Gonococcal infections:

Conjunctivitis, complicated (unlabeled use): I.M., I.V.: 1 g in a single dose

Disseminated (unlabeled use): I.M., I.V.: 1 g once daily for 7 days

Endocarditis (unlabeled use): I.M., I.V.: 1-2 g every 12 hours for at least 28 days

Uncomplicated: I.M.: 125-250 mg in a single dose

Lyme disease: I.V.: 2 g once daily for 14-28 days

Mastoiditis (hospitalized): I.V.: 2 g once daily; >60 years old: 1 g once daily

Meningitis: I.V.: 2 g every 12 hours for 7-14 days (longer courses may be necessary for selected organisms)

Orbital cellulitis (unlabeled use) and endophthalmitis: I.V.: 2 g once daily

Pelvic inflammatory disease: I.M.: 250 mg in a single dose

Pneumonia, community-acquired: I.V.: 2 g once daily; >65 years of age: 1 g once daily

Septic/toxic shock: I.V.: 2 g once daily; with clindamycin for toxic shock

Surgical prophylaxis: I.V.: 1 g 30 minutes to 2 hours before surgery

Syphilis: I.M., I.V.: 1 g once daily for 8-10 days

Typhoid fever: I.V.: 2-3 g once daily for 7-14 days

Dosage adjustment in renal/hepatic impairment: No adjustment necessary

Hemodialysis: Not dialyzable (0% to 5%); administer dose postdialysis

Peritoneal dialysis effects: Administer 750 mg every 12 hours

Continuous arteriovenous or venovenous hemofiltration: Removes 10 mg of ceftriaxone of liter of filtrate per day

Dietary Considerations Sodium contents: 83 mg (3.6 mEq) per ceftriaxone 1 g

Administration Do not admix with aminoglycosides in same bottle/bag.

I.M.: Inject deep I.M. into large muscle mass; a concentration of 250 mg/mL or 350 mg/mL is recommended for all vial sizes except the 250 mg size (250 mg/mL is suggested); can be diluted with 1:1 water and 1% lidocaine for I.M. administration.

I.V.: Infuse intermittent infusion over 30 minutes.

Monitoring Parameters Observe for signs and symptoms of anaphylaxis

Test Interactions Positive direct Coombs', false-positive urinary glucose test using cupric sulfate (Benedict's solution, Clinitest®, Fehling's solution), false-positive serum or urine creatinine with Jaffé reaction

Dosage Forms Note: Contains sodium 83 mg (3.6 mEq) per ceftriaxone 1 g

Infusion [premixed in dextrose]: 1 g (50 mL); 2 g (50 mL)

Injection, powder for reconstitution: 250 mg, 500 mg, 1 g, 2 g, 10 g

♦ Ceftriaxone Sodium *see* Ceftriaxone *on page 324*

Cefuroxime (se fyoor OKS eem)

U.S. Brand Names Ceftin®; Zinacef®

Canadian Brand Names Apo-Cefuroxime®; Ceftin®; ratio-Cefuroxime; Zinacef®

Index Terms Cefuroxime Axetil; Cefuroxime Sodium

Pharmacologic Category Antibiotic, Cephalosporin (Second Generation)

Additional Appendix Information

Antimicrobial Drugs of Choice *on page 1981*

Community-Acquired Pneumonia in Adults *on page 1999*

Prevention of Wound Infection and Sepsis in Surgical Patients *on page 1964*

Use Treatment of infections caused by staphylococci, group B streptococci, *H. influenzae* (type A and B), *E. coli*, *Enterobacter*, *Salmonella*, and *Klebsiella*; treatment of susceptible infections of the lower respiratory tract, otitis media, urinary tract, skin and soft tissue, bone and joint, sepsis and gonorrhea

Pregnancy Risk Factor B

Lactation Enters breast milk/use caution

Medication Safety Issues

Sound-alike/look-alike issues:

Cefuroxime may be confused with cefotaxime, cefprozil, ceftizoxime, deferoxamine

Ceftin® may be confused with Cefotan®, cefotetan, Cefzil®, Cipro®

Zinacef® may be confused with Zithromax®

International issues:

Ceftin® may be confused with Cefiton® which is a brand name for cefixime in Portugal

Ceftin® may be confused with Ceftina® which is a brand name for cefalotin in Mexico

Ceftin® may be confused with Ceftim® which is a brand name for ceftazidime in Italy

Contraindications Hypersensitivity to cefuroxime, any component of the formulation, or other cephalosporins

Warnings/Precautions Modify dosage in patients with severe renal impairment. Prolonged use may result in superinfection. Use with caution in patients with a history of penicillin allergy, especially IgE-mediated reactions (eg, anaphylaxis, urticaria). May cause antibiotic-associated colitis or colitis secondary to *C. difficile*. May be associated with increased INR, especially in nutritionally-deficient patients, prolonged treatment, hepatic or renal disease. Tablets and oral suspension are not bioequivalent (do not substitute on a mg-per-mg basis).

Adverse Reactions

1% to 10%:

Hematologic: Eosinophilia (7%), hemoglobin and hematocrit decreased (10%)

Hepatic: Transaminases increased (4%), alkaline phosphatase increased (2%)

Local: Thrombophlebitis (1.7%)

<1% (Limited to important or life-threatening): Anaphylaxis, angioedema, BUN increased, cholestasis, colitis, creatinine increased, diarrhea, dizziness, erythema multiforme, fever, GI bleeding, hemolytic anemia, headache, hepatitis, interstitial nephritis, jaundice, leukopenia, nausea, neutropenia, pain at injection site, pancytopenia, prolonged PT/INR, pseudomembranous colitis, rash, seizure, Stevens-Johnson syndrome, stomach cramps, thrombocytopenia, toxic epidermal necrolysis, vaginitis, vomiting

Reactions reported with other cephalosporins: Agranulocytosis, aplastic anemia, asterixis, colitis, encephalopathy, hemorrhage, neuromuscular excitability, serum-sickness reactions, superinfection, toxic nephropathy

Overdosage/Toxicology After acute overdose, most agents cause only nausea, vomiting, and diarrhea, although neuromuscular hypersensitivity and seizures are possible, especially in patients with renal insufficiency. Many beta-lactam antibiotics have the potential to cause neuromuscular hyperirritability or seizures. Hemodialysis may be helpful to aid in removal of the drug from the blood but not usually indicated; otherwise, most treatment is supportive or symptom-directed, following GI decontamination.

Drug Interactions

Increased Effect/Toxicity: High-dose probenecid decreases clearance. Aminoglycosides in combination with cefuroxime may result in additive nephrotoxicity.

Ethanol/Nutrition/Herb Interactions Food: Bioavailability is increased with food; cefuroxime serum levels may be increased if taken with food or dairy products.

Stability Reconstituted solution is stable for 24 hours at room temperature and 48 hours when refrigerated. I.V. infusion in NS or D_5W solution is stable for 24 hours at room temperature, 7 days when refrigerated, or 26 weeks when frozen. After freezing, thawed solution is stable for 24 hours at room temperature or 21 days when refrigerated.

Oral suspension: Store in refrigerator or at room temperature. Discard after 10 days.

Mechanism of Action Inhibits bacterial cell wall synthesis by binding to one or more of the penicillin-binding proteins (PBPs) which in turn inhibits the final transpeptidation step of peptidoglycan synthesis in bacterial cell walls, thus inhibiting cell wall biosynthesis. Bacteria eventually lyse due to ongoing activity of cell wall autolytic enzymes (autolysins and murein hydrolases) while cell wall assembly is arrested.

Pharmacodynamics/Kinetics

Absorption: Oral (cefuroxime axetil): Increases with food

Distribution: Widely to body tissues and fluids; crosses blood-brain barrier; therapeutic concentrations achieved in CSF even when meninges are not inflamed; crosses placenta; enters breast milk

Protein binding: 33% to 50%

Bioavailability: Tablet: Fasting: 37%; Following food: 52%

Half-life elimination: Adults: 1-2 hours; prolonged with renal impairment

Time to peak, serum: I.M.: ~15-60 minutes; I.V.: 2-3 minutes

Excretion: Urine (66% to 100% as unchanged drug)

Dosage Note: Cefuroxime axetil film-coated tablets and oral suspension are not bioequivalent and are not substitutable on a mg/mg basis

Usual dosage range:

Neonates: I.M., I.V.: 50-100 mg/kg/day divided every 12 hours

Children <13 years:

Oral: 20-30 mg/kg/day in 2 divided doses

I.M., I.V.: 75-150 mg/kg/day divided every 8 hours (maximum dose: 6 g/day)

Children ≥13 years and Adults:

Oral: 250-500 mg twice daily

I.M., I.V.: 750 mg to 1.5 g every 6-8 hours or 100-150 mg/kg/day in divided doses every 6-8 hours (maximum: 6 g/day)

(Continued)

Cefuroxime *(Continued)*

Indication-specific dosing:

Children ≥3 months to 12 years:

Acute bacterial maxillary sinusitis, acute otitis media, and impetigo:

Oral: Suspension: 30 mg/kg/day in 2 divided doses for 10 days (maximum dose: 1 g/day); tablet: 250 mg twice daily for 10 days

I.M., I.V.: 75-150 mg/kg/day divided every 8 hours (maximum dose: 6 g/day)

Epiglottitis: Oral: 150 mg/kg/day in 3 divided doses for 7-10 days

Pharyngitis/tonsillitis:

Oral: 20 mg/kg/day (maximum: 500 mg/day) in 2 divided doses for 10 days; tablet: 125 mg every 12 hours for 10 days

I.M., I.V.: 75-150 mg/kg day divided every 8 hours (maximum: 6 g/day)

Children ≥13 years and Adults:

Bronchitis (acute and exacerbations of chronic bronchitis):

Oral: 250-500 mg every 12 hours for 10 days

I.V.: 500-750 mg every 8 hours (complete therapy with oral dosing)

Cellulitis:

Oral: 500 mg every 12 hours

Orbital: I.V.: 1.5 g every 8 hours

Gonorrhea:

Disseminated: I.M., I.V.: 750 mg every 8 hours

Uncomplicated:

Oral: 1 g as a single dose

I.M.: 1.5 g as single dose (administer in 2 different sites with probenecid)

Lyme disease (early): Oral: 500 mg twice daily for 20 days

Pharyngitis/tonsillitis and sinusitis: Oral: 250 mg twice daily for 10 days

Pneumonia (uncomplicated): I.V.: 750 mg every 8 hours

Severe or complicated infections: I.M., I.V.: 1.5 g every 8 hours (up to 1.5 g every 6 hours in life-threatening infections)

Skin/skin structure infection (uncomplicated):

Oral: 250-500 mg every 12 hours for 10 days

I.M., I.V.: 750 mg every 8 hours

Surgical prophylaxis:

I.V.: 1.5 g 30 minutes to 1 hour prior to procedure (if procedure is prolonged can give 750 mg every 8 hours I.M.)

Open heart: I.V.: 1.5 g every 12 hours to a total of 6 g

Urinary tract infection (uncomplicated):

Oral: 125-250 mg every 12 hours for 7-10 days

I.M., I.V.: 750 mg every 8 hours

Dosing adjustment in renal impairment:

Cl$_{cr}$ 10-20 mL/minute: Administer every 12 hours

Cl$_{cr}$ <10 mL/minute: Administer every 24 hours

Hemodialysis: Dialyzable (25%)

Continuous arteriovenous or venovenous hemodiafiltration effects: Dose as for Cl$_{cr}$ 10-20 mL/minute

Dietary Considerations May be taken with food.

Zinacef®: Sodium content: 1.8 mEq (41 mg) per 750 mg

Ceftin®: Powder for oral suspension 125 mg/5 mL contains phenylalanine 11.8 mg/5 mL; 250 mg/5 mL contains phenylalanine 25.2 mg/5 mL.

Administration

Oral: Administer around-the-clock to promote less variation in peak and trough serum levels.

Oral suspension: Administer with food. Shake well before use.

I.M.: Inject deep I.M. into large muscle mass.

I.V.: Inject direct I.V. over 3-5 minutes. Infuse intermittent infusion over 15-30 minutes.

Monitoring Parameters Observe for signs and symptoms of anaphylaxis during first dose; with prolonged therapy, monitor renal, hepatic, and hematologic function periodically; monitor prothrombin time in patients at risk of prolongation during cephalosporin therapy (nutritionally-deficient, prolonged treatment, renal or hepatic disease)

Test Interactions Positive direct Coombs', false-positive urinary glucose test using cupric sulfate (Benedict's solution, Clinitest®, Fehling's solution), false-positive serum or urine creatinine with Jaffé reaction

Dosage Forms Note: Strength expressed as base

Infusion, as sodium [premixed]: 750 mg (50 mL); 1.5 g (50 mL)

Zinacef®: 750 mg (50 mL); 1.5 g (50 mL) [contains sodium 4.8 mEq (111 mg) per 750 mg]

Injection, powder for reconstitution, as sodium: 750 mg, 1.5 g, 7.5 g

Zinacef®: 750 mg, 1.5 g, 7.5 g [contains sodium 1.8 mEq (41 mg) per 750 mg]

Powder for oral suspension, as axetil:

Ceftin®: 125 mg/5 mL (100 mL) [contains phenylalanine 11.8 mg/5 mL; tutti-frutti flavor]; 250 mg/5 mL (50 mL, 100 mL) [contains phenylalanine 25.2 mg/5 mL; tutti-frutti flavor]

Tablet, as axetil: 250 mg, 500 mg

Ceftin®: 250 mg, 500 mg

♦ **Cefuroxime Axetil** *see* Cefuroxime *on page 326*

♦ **Cefuroxime Sodium** *see* Cefuroxime *on page 326*

♦ **Cefzil®** *see* Cefprozil *on page 319*

♦ **Celebrex®** *see* Celecoxib *on page 329*

Celecoxib (se le KOKS ib)

U.S. Brand Names Celebrex®
Canadian Brand Names Celebrex®
Pharmacologic Category Nonsteroidal Anti-inflammatory Drug (NSAID), COX-2 Selective
Additional Appendix Information
Nonsteroidal Anti-inflammatory Agents *on page 1894*
Sulfonamide Derivatives *on page 1897*
Use Relief of the signs and symptoms of osteoarthritis, ankylosing spondylitis, juvenile rheumatoid arthritis (JRA), and rheumatoid arthritis; management of acute pain; treatment of primary dysmenorrhea; decreasing intestinal polyps in familial adenomatous polyposis (FAP).

Canadian note: Celecoxib is only indicated for relief of symptoms of rheumatoid arthritis, osteoarthritis, and relief of acute pain in adults
Restrictions An FDA-approved medication guide must be distributed when dispensing an oral outpatient prescription (new or refill) where this medication is to be used without direct supervision of a healthcare provider. Medication guides are available at http://www.fda.gov/cder/Offices/ODS/medication_guides.htm.
Pregnancy Risk Factor C/D (3rd trimester)
Pregnancy Implications Teratogenic effects were observed in animal studies. In late pregnancy, this drug may cause premature closure of the ductus arteriosus.
Lactation Enters breast milk/not recommended
Medication Safety Issues
Sound-alike/look-alike issues:
Celebrex® may be confused with Celexa®, cerebra, Cerebyx®
Contraindications Hypersensitivity to celecoxib, sulfonamides, aspirin, other NSAIDs, or any component of the formulation; perioperative pain in the setting of coronary artery bypass surgery (CABG); pregnancy (3rd trimester)
Warnings/Precautions [U.S. Boxed Warning]: NSAIDs are associated with an increased risk of adverse cardiovascular events, including MI, and new onset or worsening of pre-existing hypertension. Risk may be increased with duration of use or pre-existing cardiovascular risk factors or disease. Carefully evaluate individual cardiovascular risk profiles prior to prescribing. Use caution with fluid retention, CHF, cerebrovascular disease, ischemic heart disease, or hypertension. Long-term cardiovascular risk in children has not been evaluated.

[U.S. Boxed Warning]: Celecoxib is contraindicated for treatment of perioperative pain in the setting of coronary artery bypass surgery (CABG). Risk of MI and stroke may be increased with use following CABG surgery.

[U.S. Boxed Warning]: NSAIDs may increase risk of gastrointestinal irritation, ulceration, bleeding, and perforation. These events may occur at any time during therapy and without warning. Use caution with a history of GI disease (bleeding or ulcers), concurrent therapy with aspirin, anticoagulants and/or corticosteroids, smoking, use of alcohol, the elderly or debilitated patients.

Use the lowest effective dose for the shortest duration of time, consistent with individual patient goals, to reduce risk of cardiovascular or GI adverse events. Alternate therapies should be considered for patients at high risk.

NSAIDs may cause serious skin adverse events including exfoliative dermatitis, Stevens-Johnson syndrome (SJS), and toxic epidermal necrolysis (TEN). Anaphylactoid reactions may occur, even without prior exposure; patients with "aspirin triad" (bronchial asthma, aspirin intolerance, rhinitis) may be at increased risk. Do not use in patients who experience bronchospasm, asthma, rhinitis, or urticaria with NSAID or aspirin therapy.

Use with caution in patients with decreased hepatic or renal function. Closely monitor patients with any abnormal LFT. Severe hepatic reactions (eg, fulminant hepatitis, liver failure) have occurred with NSAID use, rarely; discontinue if signs or symptoms of liver disease develop, or if systemic manifestations occur. Use of NSAIDs can compromise existing renal function. Renal toxicity can occur in patients with impaired renal function, dehydration, heart failure, liver dysfunction, those taking diuretics and ACE inhibitors, and the elderly. Rehydrate patient before starting therapy; monitor renal function closely. Not recommended for use in patients with advanced renal disease.

Anaphylactoid reactions may occur, even with no prior exposure to celecoxib. Use caution in patients with known or suspected deficiency of cytochrome P450 Isoenzyme 2C9.

When used for the treatment of FAP, routine monitoring and care should be continued. When used for JRA, safety and efficacy have not been established in children <2 years of age or in children <10 kg. Use caution with systemic onset JRA. Safety and efficacy have not been established for use in children for indications other than JRA.
Adverse Reactions Note: Percentages noted in adults.
>10%: Central nervous system: Headache (15.8%)
2% to 10%:
Cardiovascular: Peripheral edema (2.1%)
Central nervous system: Insomnia (2.3%), dizziness (2%)
Dermatologic: Skin rash (2.2%)
Gastrointestinal: Dyspepsia (8.8%), diarrhea (5.6%), abdominal pain (4.1%), nausea (3.5%), flatulence (2.2%)
Neuromuscular & skeletal: Back pain (2.8%)
Respiratory: Upper respiratory tract infection (8.1%), sinusitis (5%), pharyngitis (2.3%), rhinitis (2%)
Miscellaneous: Accidental injury (2.9%)
<2%, postmarketing, and/or case reports (limited to important or life-threatening): Acute renal failure, agranulocytosis, albuminuria, allergic reactions, alopecia, anaphylactoid reactions, angioedema, aplastic anemia, arthralgia, aseptic meningitis, ataxia, bronchospasm, cerebrovascular accident, CHF, colitis, conjunctivitis, cystitis, deafness, diabetes mellitus, DVT,
(Continued)

Celecoxib *(Continued)*

dyspnea, dysuria, ecchymosis, erythema multiforme, esophageal perforation, esophagitis, exfoliative dermatitis, flu-like syndrome, gangrene, gastroenteritis, gastroesophageal reflux, gastrointestinal bleeding, glaucoma, hematuria, hepatic failure, hepatitis, hypertension, hypoglycemia, hypokalemia, hyponatremia, interstitial nephritis, intestinal perforation, intracranial hemorrhage, jaundice, leukopenia, melena, migraine, myalgia, MI, neuralgia, neuropathy, pancreatitis, pancytopenia, paresthesia, photosensitivity, prostate disorder, pulmonary embolism, rash, renal calculi, sepsis, Stevens-Johnson syndrome, stomatitis, sudden death, syncope, thrombophlebitis, tinnitus, toxic epidermal necrolysis, urticaria, vaginal bleeding, vaginitis, vasculitis, ventricular fibrillation, vertigo, vomiting

Overdosage/Toxicology Doses up to 2400 mg/day for up to 10 days have been reported without serious toxicity. Symptoms may include epigastric pain, drowsiness, lethargy, nausea, and vomiting. Gastrointestinal bleeding may occur. Rare manifestations include hypertension, respiratory depression, coma, and acute renal failure. Treatment is symptomatic and supportive. Forced diuresis, hemodialysis and/or urinary alkalinization may not be useful.

Drug Interactions

Cytochrome P450 Effect: Substrate of CYP2C9 (major), 3A4 (minor); **Inhibits** CYP2C8 (moderate), 2D6 (weak)

Increased Effect/Toxicity: Fluconazole increases celecoxib concentrations twofold. Probenecid may increase the serum concentration of celecoxib. Lithium and methotrexate concentrations may be increased by celecoxib. Celecoxib may enhance the neuroexcitatory and/or seizure-potentiating effect of quinolone antibiotics. Celecoxib may be used with low-dose aspirin, however, rates of gastrointestinal bleeding may be increased with coadministration. Celecoxib may enhance the anticoagulant effect of anticoagulants. NSAIDs may increase levels/nephrotoxicity of cyclosporine. Celecoxib may increase the levels/effects of CYP2C8 substrates; example substrates include amiodarone, paclitaxel, pioglitazone, repaglinide, and rosiglitazone. CYP2C9 inhibitors may increase the levels/effects of celecoxib; example inhibitors include delavirdine, fluconazole, gemfibrozil, ketoconazole, nicardipine, NSAIDs, pioglitazone, and sulfonamides. Treprostinil may enhance the adverse/toxic effect of celecoxib; bleeding may occur.

Decreased Effect: CYP2C9 inducers may decrease the levels/effects of celecoxib; example inducers include carbamazepine, phenobarbital, phenytoin, rifampin, rifapentine, and secobarbital. Efficacy of thiazide diuretics, loop diuretics (furosemide), ACE inhibitors, beta-blockers, and hydralazine may be diminished by celecoxib. Celecoxib may decrease excretion of vancomycin and aminoglycosides; monitor levels. Bile acid sequestrants may decrease absorption of NSAIDs.

Ethanol/Nutrition/Herb Interactions

Ethanol: Avoid ethanol (increased GI irritation).

Food: Peak concentrations are delayed and AUC is increased by 10% to 20% when taken with a high-fat meal.

Herb/Nutraceutical: Avoid concomitant use with herbs possessing anticoagulation/antiplatelet properties, including alfalfa, anise, bilberry, bladderwrack, bromelain, cat's claw, celery, chamomile, coleus, cordyceps, dong quai, evening primrose oil, fenugreek, feverfew, garlic, ginger, ginkgo biloba, ginseng, grape seed, green tea, guggul, horse chestnut seed, horseradish, licorice, prickly ash, red clover, reishi, SAMe, sweet clover, turmeric, white willow

Stability Store at controlled room temperature of 25°C (77°F).

Mechanism of Action Inhibits prostaglandin synthesis by decreasing the activity of the enzyme, cyclooxygenase-2 (COX-2), which results in decreased formation of prostaglandin precursors. Celecoxib does not inhibit cyclooxygenase-1 (COX-1) at therapeutic concentrations. Celecoxib has no effect on platelets. In FAP, celecoxib reduces the number of colorectal polyps.

Pharmacodynamics/Kinetics

Distribution: V_d (apparent): 400 L

Protein binding: 97% primarily to albumin

Metabolism: Hepatic via CYP2C9; forms inactive metabolites

Bioavailability: Absolute: Unknown

Half-life elimination: 11 hours (fasted)

Time to peak: 3 hours

Excretion: Urine (27% as metabolites, <3% as unchanged drug); feces (57%)

Dosage Note: Use the lowest effective dose for the shortest duration of time, consistent with individual patient goals. Oral:

Children ≥2 years: JRA

≥10 kg to ≤25 kg: 50 mg twice daily

>25 kg: 100 mg twice daily

Adults:

Acute pain or primary dysmenorrhea: Initial dose: 400 mg, followed by an additional 200 mg if needed on day 1; maintenance dose: 200 mg twice daily as needed

Ankylosing spondylitis: 200 mg/day as a single dose or in divided doses twice daily; if no effect after 6 weeks, may increase to 400 mg/day. If no response following 6 weeks of treatment with 400 mg/day, consider discontinuation and alternative treatment.

Familial adenomatous polyposis: 400 mg twice daily

Osteoarthritis: 200 mg/day as a single dose or in divided dose twice daily

Rheumatoid arthritis: 100-200 mg twice daily

Elderly: No specific adjustment is recommended. However, the AUC in elderly patients may be increased by 50% as compared to younger subjects. Use the lowest recommended dose in patients weighing <50 kg.

Dosing adjustment in renal impairment: No specific dosage adjustment is recommended; not recommended in patients with severe renal dysfunction

Dosing adjustment in hepatic impairment: Reduced dosage is recommended (AUC may be increased by 40% to 180%); decrease dose by 50% in patients with moderate hepatic impairment (Child-Pugh class B). Not recommended for use with severe impairment.

Dietary Considerations Lower doses (200 mg twice daily) may be taken without regard to meals. Larger doses should be taken with food to improve absorption.

Administration Lower doses (200 mg twice daily) may be taken without regard to meals. Larger doses should be taken with food to improve absorption. Capsules may be swallowed whole or the entire contents emptied onto a teaspoon of cool or room temperature applesauce. The contents of the capsules sprinkled onto applesauce may be stored under refrigeration for up to 6 hours.

Monitoring Parameters CBC; occult blood loss and periodic liver function tests; monitor response (pain, range of motion, grip strength, mobility, ADL function), inflammation; observe for weight gain, edema; monitor renal function (urine output, serum BUN and creatinine); observe for bleeding, bruising; evaluate gastrointestinal effects (abdominal pain, bleeding, dyspepsia); blood pressure

FAP: Continue routine endoscopic exams

JRA: Monitor for development of abnormal coagulation tests with systemic onset JRA

Dosage Forms

Capsule:

Celebrex®: 100 mg, 200 mg, 400 mg

- **Celestone®** see Betamethasone on page 211
- **Celestone® Soluspan®** see Betamethasone on page 211
- **Celexa®** see Citalopram on page 381
- **CellCept®** see Mycophenolate on page 1181
- **Celontin®** see Methsuximide on page 1116
- **Cenestin®** see Estrogens (Conjugated A/Synthetic) on page 627
- **Cenestin (Can)** see Estrogens (Conjugated A/Synthetic) on page 627
- **Centany™** see Mupirocin on page 1179
- **Cepacol® Sore Throat [OTC]** see Benzocaine on page 204
- **Cephadyn** see Butalbital and Acetaminophen on page 259

Cephalexin (sef a LEKS in)

U.S. Brand Names Biocef®; Keflex®; Panixine DisperDose™ [DSC]

Canadian Brand Names Apo-Cephalex®; Keftab®; Novo-Lexin; Nu-Cephalex

Index Terms Cephalexin Monohydrate

Pharmacologic Category Antibiotic, Cephalosporin (First Generation)

Additional Appendix Information

Animal and Human Bites on page 1976

Prevention of Bacterial Endocarditis on page 1960

Use Treatment of susceptible bacterial infections including respiratory tract infections, otitis media, skin and skin structure infections, bone infections, and genitourinary tract infections, including acute prostatitis; alternative therapy for acute bacterial endocarditis prophylaxis

Pregnancy Risk Factor B

Pregnancy Implications Animal studies have not demonstrated fetal effects. There are no adequate and well-controlled studies in pregnant women. Use in pregnancy only if clearly needed.

Lactation Enters breast milk (small amounts)/use caution

Medication Safety Issues

Sound-alike/look-alike issues:

Cephalexin may be confused with cefaclor, cefazolin, cephalothin, ciprofloxacin

Contraindications Hypersensitivity to cephalexin, any component of the formulation, or other cephalosporins

Warnings/Precautions Modify dosage in patients with severe renal impairment; prolonged use may result in superinfection. Use with caution in patients with a history of penicillin allergy, especially IgE-mediated reactions (eg, anaphylaxis, urticaria). May cause antibiotic-associated colitis or colitis secondary to *C. difficile*.

Adverse Reactions Frequency not defined.

Central nervous system: Agitation, confusion, dizziness, fatigue, hallucinations, headache

Dermatologic: Angioedema, erythema multiforme (rare), rash, Stevens-Johnson syndrome (rare), toxic epidermal necrolysis (rare), urticaria

Gastrointestinal: Abdominal pain, diarrhea, dyspepsia, gastritis, nausea (rare), pseudomembranous colitis, vomiting (rare)

Genitourinary: Genital pruritus, genital moniliasis, vaginitis, vaginal discharge

Hematologic: Eosinophilia, hemolytic anemia, neutropenia, thrombocytopenia

Hepatic: AST/ALT increased, cholestatic jaundice (rare), transient hepatitis (rare)

Neuromuscular & skeletal: Arthralgia, arthritis, joint disorder

Renal: Interstitial nephritis (rare)

Miscellaneous: Allergic reactions, anaphylaxis

Overdosage/Toxicology Symptoms include epigastric distress, diarrhea, hematuria, nausea, and vomiting. Many beta-lactam containing antibiotics have the potential to cause neuromuscular hyperirritability or seizures. Hemodialysis may be helpful to aid in removal of the drug from blood; otherwise, treatment is supportive and symptom-directed. Activated charcoal may help reduce absorption, although GI decontamination is usually not required for doses <5-10 times normal.

Drug Interactions

Increased Effect/Toxicity: High-dose probenecid may decrease clearance of cephalexin. Aminoglycosides in combination with cephalexin may result in additive nephrotoxicity.

Decreased Effect: Antibiotics may decrease the therapeutic efficacy of the live, attenuated Ty21a strain typhoid vaccine.

Ethanol/Nutrition/Herb Interactions Food: Peak antibiotic serum concentration is lowered and delayed, but total drug absorbed is not affected. Cephalexin serum levels may be decreased if taken with food.

(Continued)

Cephalexin *(Continued)*

Stability
Capsule: Store at 15°C to 30°C (59°F to 86°F).

Powder for oral suspension: Refrigerate suspension after reconstitution; discard after 14 days.

Tablet for oral suspension (Panixine DisperDose™): Tablet must be dissolved in ~10 mL water prior to administration, and should be used immediately after dissolving.

Mechanism of Action Inhibits bacterial cell wall synthesis by binding to one or more of the penicillin-binding proteins (PBPs) which in turn inhibits the final transpeptidation step of peptidoglycan synthesis in bacterial cell walls, thus inhibiting cell wall biosynthesis. Bacteria eventually lyse due to ongoing activity of cell wall autolytic enzymes (autolysins and murein hydrolases) while cell wall assembly is arrested.

Pharmacodynamics/Kinetics
Absorption: Delayed in young children

Distribution: Widely into most body tissues and fluids, including gallbladder, liver, kidneys, bone, sputum, bile, and pleural and synovial fluids; CSF penetration is poor; crosses placenta; enters breast milk

Protein binding: 6% to 15%

Half-life elimination: Adults: 0.5-1.2 hours; prolonged with renal impairment

Time to peak, serum: ~1 hour

Excretion: Urine (80% to 100% as unchanged drug) within 8 hours

Dosage
Usual dosage range:

Children >1 year: Oral: 25-100 mg/kg/day every 6-8 hours (maximum: 4 g/day)

Adults: Oral: 250-1000 mg every 6 hours; maximum: 4 g/day

Indication-specific dosing:

Children >1 year: Oral:

Furunculosis: 25-50 mg/kg/day in 4 divided doses

Impetigo: 25 mg/kg/day in 4 divided doses

Otitis media: 75-100 mg/kg/day in 4 divided doses

Prophylaxis of bacterial endocarditis (dental, oral, respiratory tract, or esophageal procedures): 50 mg/kg 1 hour prior to procedure (maximum: 2 g)

Severe infections: 50-100 mg/kg/day in divided doses every 6-8 hours

Skin abscess: 50 mg/kg/day in 4 divided doses (maximum: 4 g)

Streptococcal pharyngitis, skin and skin structure infections: 25-50 mg/kg/day divided every 12 hours

Children >15 years and Adults: Oral:

Cellulitis and mastitis: 500 mg every 6 hours

Furunculosis/skin abscess: 250 mg 4 times/day

Prophylaxis of bacterial endocarditis (dental, oral, respiratory tract, or esophageal procedures): 2 g 1 hour prior to procedure

Streptococcal pharyngitis, skin and skin structure infections: 500 mg every 12 hours

Uncomplicated cystitis: 500 mg every 12 hours for 7-14 days

Dosing adjustment in renal impairment: Adults:

Cl_{cr} 10-50 mL/minute: 500 mg every 8-12 hours

Cl_{cr} <10: 250-500 mg every 12-24 hours

Hemodialysis: 250 mg every 12-24 hours; moderately dialyzable (20% to 50%); give dose after dialysis session

Dietary Considerations Take without regard to food. If GI distress, take with food. Panixine DisperDose™ contains phenylalanine 2.8 mg/cephalexin 125 mg.

Administration Take without regard to food. If GI distress, take with food. Give around-the-clock to promote less variation in peak and trough serum levels.

Panixine DisperDose™: Tablets should be mixed in ~10 mL of water immediately prior to administration. Drink entire solution, then rinse glass with additional water and drink contents to ensure entire dose has been taken. Tablets should not be chewed or swallowed whole.

Monitoring Parameters With prolonged therapy monitor renal, hepatic, and hematologic function periodically; monitor for signs of anaphylaxis during first dose

Test Interactions Positive direct Coombs', false-positive urinary glucose test using cupric sulfate (Benedict's solution, Clinitest®, Fehling's solution), false-positive serum or urine creatinine with Jaffé reaction, false-positive urinary proteins and steroids

Dosage Forms [DSC] = Discontinued product

Capsule: 250 mg, 500 mg

Biocef®: 500 mg

Keflex®: 250 mg, 333 mg [DSC], 500 mg, 750 mg

Powder for oral suspension: 125 mg/5 mL (100 mL, 200 mL); 250 mg/5 mL (100 mL, 200 mL)

Biocef®: 125 mg/5 mL (100 mL); 250 mg/5 mL (100 mL)

Keflex®: 125 mg/5 mL (100 mL, 200 mL); 250 mg/5 mL (100 mL, 200 mL)

Tablet, for oral suspension (Panixine DisperDose™): 125 mg [contains phenylalanine 2.8 mg; peppermint flavor], 250 mg [contains phenylalanine 5.6 mg; peppermint flavor] [DSC]

♦ **Cephalexin Monohydrate** *see* Cephalexin *on page 331*

Cephradine *(SEF ra deen)*

U.S. Brand Names Velosef®

Pharmacologic Category Antibiotic, Cephalosporin (First Generation)

Use Treatment of infections when caused by susceptible strains in respiratory, genitourinary, gastrointestinal, skin and soft tissue, bone and joint infections; treatment of susceptible gram-positive bacilli and cocci (never enterococcus); some gram-negative bacilli including *E. coli*, *Proteus*, and *Klebsiella* may be susceptible

Pregnancy Risk Factor B

Lactation Enters breast milk/use caution

Medication Safety Issues
Sound-alike/look-alike issues:
Cephradine may be confused with cephapirin
Velosef® may be confused with Vasosulf®

Contraindications Hypersensitivity to cephradine, any component of the formulation, or cephalosporins

Warnings/Precautions Use caution with renal impairment; dose adjustment required. Prolonged use may result in superinfection; use with caution in patients with a history of penicillin allergy, especially IgE-mediated reactions (eg, anaphylaxis, urticaria). May cause antibiotic-associated colitis or colitis secondary to *C. difficile*.

Adverse Reactions Frequency not defined.
Central nervous system: Dizziness
Dermatologic: Rash, pruritus
Gastrointestinal: Diarrhea, nausea, vomiting, pseudomembranous colitis
Hematologic: Leukopenia, neutropenia, eosinophilia
Neuromuscular & skeletal: Joint pain
Renal: BUN increased, creatinine increased
Reactions reported with other cephalosporins include anaphylaxis, erythema multiforme, toxic epidermal necrolysis, Stevens-Johnson syndrome, fever, headache, encephalopathy, asterixis, neuromuscular excitability, seizure, agranulocytosis, pancytopenia, aplastic anemia, hemolytic anemia, interstitial nephritis, toxic nephropathy, vaginitis, angioedema, cholestasis, hemorrhage, prolonged PT, serum-sickness reactions, superinfection

Overdosage/Toxicology Symptoms include neuromuscular hypersensitivity and convulsions especially with renal insufficiency. Many beta-lactam antibiotics have the potential to cause neuromuscular hyperirritability or seizures. Hemodialysis may be helpful to aid in removal of the drug from the blood; otherwise, most treatment is supportive or symptom-directed.

Drug Interactions
Increased Effect/Toxicity: High-dose probenecid decreases clearance of cephradine. Aminoglycosides in combination with cephradine may result in additive nephrotoxicity.

Ethanol/Nutrition/Herb Interactions Food: Food delays cephradine absorption but does not decrease extent.

Stability
Capsule: Store at controlled room temperature.
Powder for oral suspension: Store at controlled room temperature. Following reconstitution, refrigerated storage of oral suspension maintains potency for 14 days. Room temperature storage maintains potency for 7 days.

Mechanism of Action Inhibits bacterial cell wall synthesis by binding to one or more of the penicillin-binding proteins (PBPs) which in turn inhibits the final transpeptidation step of peptidoglycan synthesis in bacterial cell walls, thus inhibiting cell wall biosynthesis. Bacteria eventually lyse due to ongoing activity of cell wall autolytic enzymes (autolysins and murein hydrolases) while cell wall assembly is arrested.

Pharmacodynamics/Kinetics
Absorption: Well absorbed
Distribution: Widely into most body tissues and fluids including gallbladder, liver, kidneys, bone, sputum, bile, and pleural and synovial fluids; CSF penetration is poor; crosses placenta; enters breast milk
Protein binding: 18% to 20%
Half-life elimination: 1-2 hours; prolonged with renal impairment
Time to peak, serum: 1-2 hours
Excretion: Urine (~80% to 90% as unchanged drug) within 6 hours

Dosage
Usual dosage range:
Children ≥9 months: Oral: 25-100 mg/kg/day in divided doses every 6 or 12 hours (maximum: 4 g/day)
Adults: Oral: 250-500 mg every 6-12 hours
Indication-specific dosing:
Children ≥9 months: Oral:
Otitis media: 75-100 mg/kg/day in divided doses every 6 or 12 hours (maximum: 4 g/day)
Dosing adjustment in renal impairment: Adults:
Cl_{cr} 10-50 mL/minute: 250 mg every 6 hours
Cl_{cr} <10 mL/minute: 125 mg every 6 hours

Dietary Considerations May administer with food to decrease GI distress.

Administration Administer around-the-clock to promote less variation in peak and trough serum levels. Shake oral suspension well.

Monitoring Parameters Observe for signs and symptoms of anaphylaxis during first dose

Test Interactions Positive direct Coombs', false-positive urinary glucose test using cupric sulfate (Benedict's solution, Clinitest®, Fehling's solution), false-positive serum or urine creatinine with Jaffé reaction, false-positive urinary proteins and steroids

Dosage Forms [DSC] = Discontinued product
Capsule: 250 mg, 500 mg [DSC]
Powder for oral suspension: 250 mg/5 mL (100 mL) [fruit flavor]

♦ Ceptaz® [DSC] *see* Ceftazidime *on page 320*
♦ Cerebyx® *see* Fosphenytoin *on page 768*
♦ Ceredase® *see* Alglucerase *on page 69*
♦ Cerezyme® *see* Imiglucerase *on page 885*
♦ Ceron *see* Chlorpheniramine and Phenylephrine *on page 349*
♦ Ceron-DM *see* Chlorpheniramine, Phenylephrine, and Dextromethorphan *on page 352*
♦ Cerovel™ *see* Urea *on page 1758*
♦ Cerubidine® *see* DAUNOrubicin Hydrochloride *on page 462*
♦ Cerumenex® [DSC] *see* Triethanolamine Polypeptide Oleate-Condensate *on page 1740*
♦ Cerumenex® (Can) *see* Triethanolamine Polypeptide Oleate-Condensate *on page 1740*

- ◆ **Cervidil®** *see* Dinoprostone *on page 513*
- ◆ **C.E.S.** *see* Estrogens (Conjugated/Equine) *on page 631*
- ◆ **C.E.S.® (Can)** *see* Estrogens (Conjugated/Equine) *on page 631*
- ◆ **Cesia™** *see* Ethinyl Estradiol and Desogestrel *on page 645*
- ◆ **Cetacaine®** *see* Benzocaine, Butyl Aminobenzoate, Tetracaine, and Benzalkonium Chloride *on page 207*
- ◆ **Cetacort®** *see* Hydrocortisone *on page 852*
- ◆ **Cetafen® [OTC]** *see* Acetaminophen *on page 28*
- ◆ **Cetafen Extra® [OTC]** *see* Acetaminophen *on page 28*
- ◆ **Cetamide™ (Can)** *see* Sulfacetamide *on page 1609*
- ◆ **Ceta-Plus®** *see* Hydrocodone and Acetaminophen *on page 848*

Cetirizine (se TI ra zeen)

U.S. Brand Names Zyrtec®
Canadian Brand Names Apo-Cetirizine®; Reactine™
Index Terms Cetirizine Hydrochloride; P-071; UCB-P071
Pharmacologic Category Antihistamine
Use Perennial and seasonal allergic rhinitis and other allergic symptoms including urticaria; chronic idiopathic urticaria
Pregnancy Risk Factor B
Pregnancy Implications Cetirizine was not shown to be teratogenic in animal studies, however, adequate studies have not been conducted in pregnant women. Use during pregnancy only if clearly needed.
Lactation Enters breast milk/not recommended
Medication Safety Issues
Sound-alike/look-alike issues:
Zyrtec® may be confused with Serax®, Xanax®, Zantac®, Zyprexa®
Contraindications Hypersensitivity to cetirizine, hydroxyzine, or any component of the formulation
Warnings/Precautions Cetirizine should be used cautiously in patients with hepatic or renal dysfunction, the elderly and in nursing mothers. May cause drowsiness; use caution performing tasks which require alertness (eg, operating machinery or driving). Safety and efficacy in pediatric patients <6 months of age have not been established.
Adverse Reactions
>10%: Central nervous system: Headache (children 11% to 14%, placebo 12%), somnolence (adults 14%, children 2% to 4%)
2% to 10%:
Central nervous system: Insomnia (children 9%, adults <2%), fatigue (adults 6%), malaise (4%), dizziness (adults 2%)
Gastrointestinal: Abdominal pain (children 4% to 6%), dry mouth (adults 5%), diarrhea (children 2% to 3%), nausea (children 2% to 3%, placebo 2%), vomiting (children 2% to 3%)
Respiratory: Epistaxis (children 2% to 4%, placebo 3%), pharyngitis (children 3% to 6%, placebo 3%), bronchospasm (children 2% to 3%, placebo 2%)
<2% (Limited to important or life-threatening; as reported in adults and/or children): Aggressive reaction, anaphylaxis, angioedema, ataxia, chest pain, confusion, convulsions, depersonalization, depression, edema, fussiness, hallucinations, hemolytic anemia, hepatitis, hypertension, hypotension (severe), irritability, liver function abnormal, nervousness, ototoxicity, palpitation, paralysis, paresthesia, photosensitivity, rash, suicidal ideation, suicide, taste perversion, tongue discoloration, tongue edema, tremor, visual field defect, weakness
Overdosage/Toxicology Symptoms may include somnolence, restlessness, or irritability. Treatment is symptomatic and supportive. Cetirizine is not removed by dialysis.
Drug Interactions
Cytochrome P450 Effect: Substrate of CYP3A4 (minor)
Increased Effect/Toxicity: Increased toxicity with CNS depressants and anticholinergics.
Ethanol/Nutrition/Herb Interactions Ethanol: Avoid ethanol (may increase CNS depression).
Stability
Syrup: Store at room temperature of 15°C to 30°C (59°F to 86°F), or under refrigeration at 2°C to 8°C (36°F to 46°F).
Tablet: Store at room temperature of 15°C to 30°C (59°F to 86°F).
Mechanism of Action Competes with histamine for H_1-receptor sites on effector cells in the gastrointestinal tract, blood vessels, and respiratory tract
Pharmacodynamics/Kinetics
Onset of action: 15-30 minutes
Absorption: Rapid
Protein binding, plasma: Mean: 93%
Metabolism: Limited hepatic
Half-life elimination: 8 hours
Time to peak, serum: 1 hour
Excretion: Urine (70%); feces (10%)
Dosage Oral:
Children:
6-12 months: Chronic urticaria, perennial allergic rhinitis: 2.5 mg once daily
12 months to <2 years: Chronic urticaria, perennial allergic rhinitis: 2.5 mg once daily; may increase to 2.5 mg every 12 hours if needed
2-5 years: Chronic urticaria, perennial or seasonal allergic rhinitis: Initial: 2.5 mg once daily; may be increased to 2.5 mg every 12 hours **or** 5 mg once daily
Children ≥6 years and Adults: Chronic urticaria, perennial or seasonal allergic rhinitis: 5-10 mg once daily, depending upon symptom severity

Elderly: Initial: 5 mg once daily; may increase to 10 mg/day. **Note:** Manufacturer recommends 5 mg/day in patients ≥77 years of age.

Dosage adjustment in renal/hepatic impairment:
  Children <6 years: Cetirizine use not recommended
  Children 6-11 years: <2.5 mg once daily
  Children ≥12 and Adults:
    Cl_{cr} 11-31 mL/minute, hemodialysis, or hepatic impairment: Administer 5 mg once daily
    Cl_{cr} <11 mL/minute, not on dialysis: Cetirizine use not recommended
Dietary Considerations May be taken with or without food.
Administration May be administered with or without food.
Monitoring Parameters Relief of symptoms, sedation and anticholinergic effects
Dosage Forms
  Syrup, as hydrochloride: 5 mg/5 mL (120 mL, 480 mL) [banana-grape flavor]
  Tablet, as hydrochloride: 5 mg, 10 mg
  Tablet, chewable, as hydrochloride: 5 mg, 10 mg [grape flavor]

♦ **Cetirizine Hydrochloride** see Cetirizine on page 334

Cetrorelix (set roe REL iks)

U.S. Brand Names Cetrotide®
Canadian Brand Names Cetrotide®
Index Terms Cetrorelix Acetate
Pharmacologic Category Gonadotropin Releasing Hormone Antagonist
Use Inhibits premature luteinizing hormone (LH) surges in women undergoing controlled ovarian stimulation
Pregnancy Risk Factor X
Pregnancy Implications Animal studies have shown fetal resorption and implantation losses following administration. Resorption resulting in fetal loss would be expected if used in a pregnant woman.
Lactation Excretion in breast milk unknown/not recommended
Contraindications Hypersensitivity to cetrorelix or any component of the formulation; extrinsic peptide hormones, mannitol, gonadotropin releasing hormone (GnRH) or GnRH analogs; severe renal impairment; pregnancy
Warnings/Precautions Should only be prescribed by fertility specialists. Monitor carefully after first injection for possible hypersensitivity reactions. Use caution in women with active allergic conditions or a history of allergies; use in women with severe allergic conditions is not recommended. Pregnancy should be excluded before treatment is begun.
Adverse Reactions
  1% to 10%:
    Central nervous system: Headache (1%)
    Endocrine & metabolic: Ovarian hyperstimulation syndrome, WHO grade II or III (4%)
    Gastrointestinal: Nausea (1%)
    Hepatic: ALT, AST, GGT, and alkaline phosphatase increased (1% to 2%)
  Postmarketing and/or case reports: Severe anaphylactic reaction (cough, rash, hypotension) occurred in one patient following several months of treatment in a study not related to fertility. Congenital abnormalities and stillbirths have been reported, however, the relationship to cetrorelix treatment has not been established. Local injection site reactions (bruising, erythema, itching, pruritus, redness, swelling) have also been reported.
Overdosage/Toxicology No cases of overdose have been reported. In nonfertility studies, single doses of up to 120 mg have been well tolerated.
Drug Interactions
  Increased Effect/Toxicity: No formal studies have been performed.
  Decreased Effect: No formal studies have been performed.
Stability Store in outer carton. Once mixed, solution should be used immediately.
  0.25 mg vials: Store under refrigeration at 2°C to 8°C (36°F to 46°F).
  3 mg vials: Store at controlled room temperature at 25°C (77°F).
Mechanism of Action Competes with naturally-occurring GnRH for binding on receptors of the pituitary. This delays luteinizing hormone surge, preventing ovulation until the follicles are of adequate size.
Pharmacodynamics/Kinetics
  Onset of action: 0.25 mg dose: 2 hours; 3 mg dose: 1 hour
  Duration: 3 mg dose (single dose): 4 days
  Absorption: Rapid
  Protein binding: 86%
  Metabolism: Transformed by peptidases; cetrorelix and peptides (1-9), (1-7), (1-6), and (1-4) are found in the bile; peptide (1-4) is the predominant metabolite
  Bioavailability: 85%
  Half-life elimination: 0.25 mg dose: 5 hours; 0.25 mg multiple doses: 20.6 hours; 3 mg dose: 62.8 hours
  Time to peak: 0.25 mg dose: 1 hour; 3 mg dose: 1.5 hours
  Excretion: Feces (5% to 10% as unchanged drug and metabolites); urine (2% to 4% as unchanged drug); within 24 hours
Dosage Adults: Female: SubQ: Used in conjunction with controlled ovarian stimulation therapy using gonadotropins (FSH, HMG):
  Single-dose regimen: 3 mg given when serum estradiol levels show appropriate stimulation response, usually stimulation day 7 (range days 5-9). If hCG is not administered within 4 days, continue cetrorelix at 0.25 mg/day until hCG is administered.
  Multiple-dose regimen: 0.25 mg morning or evening of stimulation day 5, or morning of stimulation day 6; continue until hCG is administered.
  Dosing adjustment in renal impairment:
    Severe impairment: Use is contraindicated
    Mild-to-moderate impairment: No specific guidelines are available
(Continued)

Cetrorelix *(Continued)*

Dosing adjustment in hepatic impairment: No specific guidelines are available

Elderly: Not intended for use in women ≥65 years of age (Phase 2 and Phase 3 studies included women 19-40 years of age)

Administration Cetrorelix is administered by SubQ injection following proper aseptic technique procedures. Injections should be to the lower abdomen, preferably around the navel (but staying at least 1 inch from the navel). The injection site should be rotated daily. The needle should be inserted completely into the skin at a 45-degree angle.

Monitoring Parameters Ultrasound to assess follicle size

Dosage Forms Injection, powder for reconstitution: 0.25 mg, 3 mg [supplied with SWFI in prefilled syringe]

♦ **Cetrorelix Acetate** *see* Cetrorelix *on page 335*

♦ **Cetrotide®** *see* Cetrorelix *on page 335*

Cetuximab *(se TUK see mab)*

U.S. Brand Names Erbitux®
Canadian Brand Names Erbitux®
Index Terms C225; IMC-C225; NSC-714692
Pharmacologic Category Antineoplastic Agent, Monoclonal Antibody; Epidermal Growth Factor Receptor (EGFR) Inhibitor
Use Treatment of metastatic colorectal cancer; treatment of squamous cell cancer of the head and neck
Unlabeled/Investigational Use Breast cancer, tumors overexpressing EGFR
Pregnancy Risk Factor C
Pregnancy Implications Animal reproductive studies have not been conducted. There are no adequate and well-controlled studies in pregnant women. It is not known whether cetuximab can cause fetal harm or affect reproductive capacity. Because cetuximab inhibits epidermal growth factor (EGF), a component of fetal development, adverse effects on pregnancy would be expected. Cetuximab should only be given to a pregnant woman if the potential benefit justifies the potential risk to the fetus.
Lactation Excretion in breast milk is unknown/not recommended
Medication Safety Issues
Sound-alike/look-alike issues:
Cetuximab may be confused with bevacizumab
Contraindications Hypersensitivity to cetuximab, murine proteins, or any component of the formulation
Warnings/Precautions [U.S. Boxed Warning]: Severe infusion reactions have been reported in ~3% of patients (~90% with the first infusion despite the use of prophylactic antihistamines). In case of severe reaction, treatment should be stopped and permanently discontinued. Immediate treatment for anaphylactic/anaphylactoid reactions should be available during administration. Patients should be monitored for at least 1 hour following completion of infusion, or longer if a reaction occurs. Mild-to-moderate infusion reactions are managed by slowing the infusion rate and administering antihistamines.

[U.S. Boxed Warning]: Cardiopulmonary arrest has been reported in patients receiving radiation therapy in combination with cetuximab; use caution with history of coronary artery disease, CHF, and arrhythmias. Close monitoring of serum electrolytes during and after cetuximab therapy is recommended. Interstitial lung disease (ILD) has been reported; use caution with pre-existing lung disease. Dermatologic toxicities have been reported, including a 90% incidence of acneform rash (may require dose modification); sunlight may exacerbate skin reactions. Dermatologic toxicities should be treated with topical and/or oral antibiotics; topical corticosteroids are not recommended. Non-neutralizing anticetuximab antibodies were detected in 5% of evaluable patients. Safety and efficacy in children have not been established.

Adverse Reactions Except where noted, percentages reported for cetuximab monotherapy.

>10%:
Central nervous system: Malaise (48%), pain (17% to 28%), fever (5% to 27%), headache (26%)
Dermatologic: Acneform rash (76% to 90%; grades 3/4: 1% to 8%), nail disorder (16%), pruritus (11%)
Endocrine & metabolic: Hypomagnesemia (50%; grades 3/4: 10% to 15%)
Gastrointestinal: Nausea (mild to moderate 29%), weight loss (7% to 27%), constipation (26%), abdominal pain (26%), diarrhea (25%), vomiting (25%), anorexia (23%)
Neuromuscular & skeletal: Weakness (45% to 48%)
Respiratory: Dyspnea (17%), cough (11%)
Miscellaneous: Infusion reaction (19% to 21%; grades 3/4: 2% to 4%; 90% with first infusion), infection (14%)
1% to 10%:
Cardiovascular: Peripheral edema (10%), cardiopulmonary arrest (2%; with radiation therapy)
Central nervous system: Insomnia (10%), depression (7%)
Dermatologic: Alopecia (4%), skin disorder (4%)
Endocrine & metabolic: Dehydration (2% to 10%)
Gastrointestinal: Stomatitis (10%), dyspepsia (6%)
Hematologic: Anemia (9%)
Hepatic: Alkaline phosphatase increased (5% to 10%), transaminases increased (5% to 10%)
Neuromuscular & skeletal: Back pain (10%)
Ocular: Conjunctivitis (7%)
Renal: Kidney failure (2%)
Respiratory: Pulmonary embolus (1%)

Miscellaneous: Sepsis (3%)

<1% (Limited to important or life-threatening): Arrhythmia, interstitial lung disease (occurred between the fourth and eleventh doses), leukopenia, MI

Overdosage/Toxicology Single doses >500 mg/m^2 have not been tested. Treatment is symptom-directed and supportive.

Drug Interactions

Increased Effect/Toxicity: Interactions have not been evaluated in clinical trials.

Stability Store unopened vials under refrigeration at 2°C to 8°C (36°F to 46°F). Do not freeze. Reconstitution is not required. Appropriate dose should be added to empty sterile container; do not shake or dilute. Preparations in infusion containers are stable for up to 12 hours under refrigeration at 2°C to 8°C (36°F to 46°F) and up to 8 hours at controlled room temperature of 20°C to 25°C (68°F to 77°F).

Mechanism of Action Recombinant human/mouse chimeric monoclonal antibody which binds specifically to the epidermal growth factor receptor (EGFR, HER1, c-ErbB-1) and competitively inhibits the binding of epidermal growth factor (EGF) and other ligands. Binding to the EGFR blocks phosphorylation and activation of receptor-associated kinases, resulting in inhibition of cell growth, induction of apoptosis, and decreased matrix metalloproteinase and vascular endothelial growth factor production.

Pharmacodynamics/Kinetics

Distribution: V$_d$: ~2-3 L/m^2

Half-life elimination: 112 hours (range: 63-230 hours)

Dosage I.V.: Adults:

Colorectal cancer:

Initial loading dose: 400 mg/m^2 infused over 120 minutes

Maintenance dose: 250 mg/m^2 infused over 60 minutes weekly

Head and neck cancer:

Initial loading dose: 400 mg/m^2 infused over 120 minutes

Maintenance dose: 250 mg/m^2 infused over 60 minutes weekly

Note: If given in combination with radiation therapy, administer loading dose 1 week prior to initiation of radiation course. Administer weekly maintenance dose 1 hour prior to radiation for the duration of radiation therapy (6-7 weeks).

Breast cancer (unlabeled use): 50-200 mg/m^2 weekly for 6 weeks

Tumors overexpressing EGFR (unlabeled use): 5-100 mg/m^2 weekly

or

Loading dose: 100-500 mg/m^2

Maintenance dose: 5-400 mg/m^2 weekly

Dosage adjustment for toxicity:

Infusion reactions, mild to moderate (grade 1 or 2): Permanently reduce the infusion rate by 50% and continue to use prophylactic antihistamines

Infusion reactions, severe (grade 3 or 4): Immediately and permanently discontinue treatment

Skin toxicity, mild to moderate: No dosage modification required

Acneform rash, severe (grade 3 or 4):

First occurrence: Delay cetuximab infusion 1-2 weeks

If improvement, continue at 250 mg/m^2

If no improvement, discontinue therapy

Second occurrence: Delay cetuximab infusion 1-2 weeks

If improvement, continue at 200 mg/m^2

If no improvement, discontinue therapy

Third occurrence: Delay cetuximab infusion 1-2 weeks

If improvement, continue at 150 mg/m^2

If no improvement, discontinue therapy

Fourth occurrence: Discontinue therapy

Note: Dose adjustments are not recommended for severe **radiation** dermatitis.

Dosage adjustment for renal/hepatic impairment: No adjustment required.

Dietary Considerations Injection solution 2 mg/mL (50 mL) contains sodium chloride 8.48 mg/mL.

Administration Administer via I.V. Infusion; loading dose over 2 hours, weekly maintenance dose over 1 hour. Do not administer as I.V. push or bolus. Do not shake or dilute. Administer via infusion pump or syringe pump. Following the infusion, an observation period is recommended; longer observation time (following an infusion reaction) may be required. Premedication with antihistamines is recommended. The maximum infusion rate is 5 mL/minute. Administer through a low protein-binding 0.22 micrometer in-line filter. Use 0.9% NaCl to flush line at the end of infusion.

Monitoring Parameters EGF receptor expression testing should be completed prior to treatment (for colorectal cancer). Vital signs during infusion and observe for at least 1 hour postinfusion. Patients developing dermatologic toxicities should be monitored for the development of complications. Periodic monitoring of serum magnesium, calcium, and potassium are recommended to continue over an interval consistent with the half-life (8 weeks); monitor closely (during and after treatment) for cetuximab plus radiation therapy.

Additional Information Premedication with an H$_1$ antagonist (eg, diphenhydramine 50 mg I.V.) is recommended. EGFR expression is detected in nearly all patients with head and neck cancer; laboratory evidence of EGFR expression is not necessary for head and neck cancers.

Dosage Forms Injection, solution [preservative free]: 2 mg/mL (50 mL) [contains sodium chloride 8.48 mg/mL]

♦ **Cevi-Bid® [OTC]** *see* Ascorbic Acid *on page 156*

Cevimeline (se vi ME leen)

U.S. Brand Names Evoxac®
Canadian Brand Names Evoxac®
Index Terms Cevimeline Hydrochloride
Pharmacologic Category Cholinergic Agonist
Use Treatment of symptoms of dry mouth in patients with Sjögren's syndrome
Pregnancy Risk Factor C
Medication Safety Issues
Sound-alike/look-alike issues:
Evoxac® may be confused with Eurax®
Dosage Adults: Oral: 30 mg 3 times/day
   Dosage adjustment in renal/hepatic impairment: Not studied; no specific dosage adjustment is recommended
   Elderly: No specific dosage adjustment is recommended; however, use caution when initiating due to potential for increased sensitivity
Additional Information Complete prescribing information for this medication should be consulted for additional detail.
Dosage Forms Capsule, as hydrochloride: 30 mg

- **Cevimeline Hydrochloride** see Cevimeline *on page 338*
- **CFDN** see Cefdinir *on page 307*
- **CG** see Chorionic Gonadotropin (Human) *on page 363*
- **CGP-42446** see Zoledronic Acid *on page 1820*
- **CGP-57148B** see Imatinib *on page 881*
- **C-Gram [OTC]** see Ascorbic Acid *on page 156*
- **CGS-20267** see Letrozole *on page 988*
- **Chantix™** see Varenicline *on page 1777*
- **Charcadole® (Can)** see Charcoal *on page 338*
- **Charcadole®, Aqueous (Can)** see Charcoal *on page 338*
- **Charcadole® TFS (Can)** see Charcoal *on page 338*
- **Char-Caps [OTC]** see Charcoal *on page 338*

Charcoal (CHAR kole)

U.S. Brand Names Actidose-Aqua® [OTC]; Actidose® with Sorbitol [OTC]; Char-Caps [OTC]; Charcoal Plus® DS [OTC]; Charcocaps® [OTC]; EZ-Char™ [OTC]; Kerr Insta-Char® [OTC]
Canadian Brand Names Charcadole®; Charcadole®, Aqueous; Charcadole® TFS
Index Terms Activated Carbon; Activated Charcoal; Adsorbent Charcoal; Liquid Antidote; Medicinal Carbon; Medicinal Charcoal
Pharmacologic Category Antidote
Additional Appendix Information
Toxicology Information *on page 2081*
Use Emergency treatment in poisoning by drugs and chemicals; aids the elimination of certain drugs and improves decontamination of excessive ingestions of sustained-release products or in the presence of bezoars; repetitive doses have proven useful to enhance the elimination of certain drugs (eg, theophylline, phenobarbital, and aspirin); repetitive doses for gastric dialysis in uremia to adsorb various waste products; dietary supplement (digestive aid)
Pregnancy Risk Factor C
Lactation Does not enter breast milk/compatible
Medication Safety Issues
Sound-alike/look-alike issues:
Actidose® may be confused with Actos®
Contraindications Intestinal obstruction; GI tract not anatomically intact; patients at risk of hemorrhage or GI perforation; if use would increase risk and severity of aspiration; not effective for cyanide, mineral acids, caustic alkalis, organic solvents, iron, ethanol, methanol poisoning, lithium; do not use charcoal with sorbitol in patients with fructose intolerance; charcoal with sorbitol not recommended in children <1 year of age
Warnings/Precautions When using ipecac with charcoal, induce vomiting with ipecac before administering activated charcoal since charcoal adsorbs ipecac syrup. Charcoal may cause vomiting which is hazardous in petroleum distillate and caustic ingestions. If charcoal in sorbitol is administered, doses should be limited to prevent excessive fluid and electrolyte losses. Use caution with decreased peristalsis. Most effective when administered within 1 hour of ingestion for most ingestions.
Adverse Reactions Frequency not defined.
Endocrine & metabolic: Hypernatremia, hypokalemia, and hypermagnesemia may occur with coadministration of cathartics
Gastrointestinal: Vomiting (incidence may increase with sorbitol), diarrhea (with sorbitol), constipation, swelling of abdomen, bowel obstruction
Miscellaneous: Fecal discoloration (black)
Drug Interactions
Decreased Effect: Charcoal decreases the effect of ipecac syrup.
Ethanol/Nutrition/Herb Interactions Food: Do not mix with milk, ice cream, sherbet, or marmalade (may reduce charcoal's effectiveness).
Stability Adsorbs gases from air, store in closed container. Dilute powder with at least 8 mL of water per 1 g of charcoal, or mix in a charcoal to water ratio of 1:4 to 1:8. Mix to form a slurry.
Mechanism of Action Adsorbs toxic substances or irritants, thus inhibiting GI absorption; adsorbs intestinal gas; the addition of sorbitol results in hyperosmotic laxative action causing catharsis
Pharmacodynamics/Kinetics Excretion: Feces (as charcoal)

Dosage Oral:

Acute poisoning: **Note:** ~10 g of activated charcoal for each 1 g of toxin is considered adequate; this may require multiple doses. If sorbitol is also used, sorbitol dose should not exceed 1.5 g/kg. When using multiple doses of charcoal, sorbitol should be given with every other dose (not to exceed 2 doses/day).

Children: 1 g/kg as a single dose; if multiple doses are needed, additional doses can be given as 0.25 g/kg every hour or equivalent (ie, 0.5 g/kg every 2 hours) **or**

>1 year-12 years: 25-50 g as a single dose; smaller doses (10-25 g) may be used in children 1-5 years due to smaller gut lumen capacity

Children >12 years and Adults: 25-100 g as a single dose; if multiple doses are needed, additional doses may be given as 12.5 g/hour or equivalent (ie, 25 g every 2 hours)

Dietary supplement: Adult: 500-520 mg after meals; may repeat in 2 hours if needed (maximum 10 g/day)

Administration Flavoring agents (eg, chocolate) and sorbitol can enhance charcoal's palatability. If treatment includes ipecac syrup, induce vomiting prior to administration of charcoal. Often given with a laxative or cathartic; check for presence of bowel sounds before administration.

Dosage Forms

Capsule:
Char-Caps, Charcocaps®: 260 mg

Liquid:
Actidose-Aqua®: 15 g (72 mL); 25 g (120 mL); 50 g (240 mL)
Kerr Insta-Char®: 25 g (120 mL) [cherry flavor]; 50 g (240 mL) [unflavored or cherry flavor]

Liquid [with sorbitol]:
Actidose® with Sorbitol: 25 g (120 mL); 50 g (240 mL)
Kerr Insta-Char®: 25 g (120 mL); 50 g (240 mL) [cherry flavor]

Pellet:
EZ-Char™: 25 g

Powder for suspension: 30 g, 240 g

Tablet:
Charcoal Plus® DS: 250 mg

♦ **Charcoal Plus® DS [OTC]** see Charcoal on page 338
♦ **Charcocaps® [OTC]** see Charcoal on page 338
♦ **Chemet®** see Succimer on page 1604
♦ **Cheracol®** see Guaifenesin and Codeine on page 815
♦ **Cheracol® D [OTC]** see Guaifenesin and Dextromethorphan on page 816
♦ **Cheracol® Plus [OTC]** see Guaifenesin and Dextromethorphan on page 816
♦ **Cheratussin AC** see Guaifenesin and Codeine on page 815
♦ **Chew-Cal [OTC]** see Calcium and Vitamin D on page 268
♦ **CHG** see Chlorhexidine Gluconate on page 344
♦ **Chicken Pox Vaccine** see Varicella Virus Vaccine on page 1778
♦ **Chiggerex® [OTC]** see Benzocaine on page 204
♦ **Chiggertox® [OTC]** see Benzocaine on page 204
♦ **Children's Advil® Cold (Can)** see Pseudoephedrine and Ibuprofen on page 1456
♦ **Children's Dimetapp® Elixir Cold & Allergy [OTC]** see Brompheniramine and Pseudoephedrine on page 243
♦ **Children's Pepto [OTC]** see Calcium Carbonate on page 269
♦ **Children's Motion Sickness Liquid (Can)** see DimenhyDRINATE on page 511
♦ **Chirocaine® [DSC]** see Levobupivacaine on page 997
♦ **Chirocaine® (Can)** see Levobupivacaine on page 997
♦ **Chloral** see Chloral Hydrate on page 339

Chloral Hydrate (KLOR al HYE drate)

U.S. Brand Names Aquachloral® Supprettes®; Somnote™

Canadian Brand Names PMS-Chloral Hydrate

Index Terms Chloral; Hydrated Chloral; Trichloroacetaldehyde Monohydrate

Pharmacologic Category Hypnotic, Nonbenzodiazepine

Use Short-term sedative and hypnotic (<2 weeks); sedative/hypnotic for diagnostic procedures; sedative prior to EEG evaluations

Restrictions C-IV

Pregnancy Risk Factor C

Dosage

Children:

Sedation or anxiety: Oral, rectal: 5-15 mg/kg/dose every 8 hours (maximum: 500 mg/dose)

Prior to EEG: Oral, rectal: 20-25 mg/kg/dose, 30-60 minutes prior to EEG; may repeat in 30 minutes to maximum of 100 mg/kg or 2 g total

Hypnotic: Oral, rectal: 20-40 mg/kg/dose up to a maximum of 50 mg/kg/24 hours or 1 g/dose or 2 g/24 hours

Conscious sedation: Oral: 50-75 mg/kg/dose 30-60 minutes prior to procedure; may repeat 30 minutes after initial dose if needed, to a total maximum dose of 120 mg/kg or 1 g total

Adults: Oral, rectal:

Sedation, anxiety: 250 mg 3 times/day

Hypnotic: 500-1000 mg at bedtime or 30 minutes prior to procedure, not to exceed 2 g/24 hours

Discontinuation: Withdraw gradually over 2 weeks if patient has been maintained on high doses for prolonged period of time. Do not stop drug abruptly; sudden withdrawal may result in delirium.

Dosing adjustment/comments in renal impairment: Cl_{cr} <50 mL/minute: Avoid use

Hemodialysis: Dialyzable (50% to 100%); supplemental dose is not necessary

(Continued)

Chloral Hydrate *(Continued)*

Dosing adjustment/comments in hepatic impairment: Avoid use in patients with severe hepatic impairment

Additional Information Complete prescribing information for this medication should be consulted for additional detail.

Dosage Forms

Capsule (Somnote™): 500 mg

Suppository, rectal (Aquachloral® Supprettes®): 325 mg [contains tartrazine], 650 mg

Syrup: 500 mg/5 mL (480 mL) [contains sodium benzoate]

Chlorambucil (klor AM byoo sil)

U.S. Brand Names Leukeran®

Canadian Brand Names Leukeran®

Index Terms CB-1348; Chlorambucilum; Chloraminophene; Chlorbutinum; NSC-3088; WR-139013

Pharmacologic Category Antineoplastic Agent, Alkylating Agent

Use Management of chronic lymphocytic leukemia, Hodgkin's and non-Hodgkin's lymphoma; breast and ovarian carcinoma; Waldenström's macroglobulinemia, testicular carcinoma, thrombocythemia, choriocarcinoma

Pregnancy Risk Factor D

Pregnancy Implications Carcinogenic and mutagenic in humans

Lactation Excretion in breast milk unknown

Medication Safety Issues

Sound-alike/look-alike issues:

Chlorambucil may be confused with Chloromycetin®

Leukeran® may be confused with Alkeran®, leucovorin, Leukine®

High alert medication: The Institute for Safe Medication Practices (ISMP) includes this medication among its list of drugs which have a heightened risk of causing significant patient harm when used in error.

Contraindications Hypersensitivity to chlorambucil or any component of the formulation; hypersensitivity to other alkylating agents (may have cross-hypersensitivity); pregnancy

Warnings/Precautions Hazardous agent - use appropriate precautions for handling and disposal. Convulsions have been observed; use with caution in patients with seizure disorder; history of nephrotic syndrome and high pulse doses are at higher risk of seizures. **[U.S. Boxed Warning]: May cause bone marrow suppression;** reduce initial dosage if patient has received myelosuppressive or radiation therapy, or has a depressed baseline leukocyte or platelet count within the previous 4 weeks. Lymphopenia may occur. Avoid administration of live vaccines to immunocompromised patients. Rare instances of severe skin reactions (eg, erythema multiforme, Stevens-Johnson syndrome) have been reported; discontinue if a reaction occurs.

[U.S. Boxed Warning]: Affects human fertility; carcinogenic in humans and probably mutagenic and teratogenic as well; chromosomal damage has been documented. Secondary malignancies and acute myelocytic leukemia may be associated with chronic therapy. Safety and efficacy in pediatric patients have not been established.

Adverse Reactions Frequency not defined.

Central nervous system: Agitation, ataxia, confusion, focal/generalized seizures (rare), hallucinations

Dermatologic: Angioneurotic edema, erythema multiforme (rare), skin hypersensitivity, Stevens-Johnson syndrome (rare), toxic epidermal necrolysis (rare), urticaria

Endocrine & metabolic: Amenorrhea, azoospermia, chromosomal damage, infertility, sterility

Gastrointestinal: Hepatotoxicity, jaundice, diarrhea (infrequent), nausea (infrequent), stomatitis (infrequent), vomiting (infrequent)

Genitourinary: Sterile cystitis

Hematologic: Myelosuppression (common), leukemia, lymphopenia, neutropenia, secondary malignancies

Hepatic: Hepatotoxicity, jaundice

Neuromuscular & skeletal: Flaccid paresis, muscular twitching, myoclonia, neuropathy (peripheral), tremor

Respiratory: Interstitial pneumonia, pulmonary fibrosis, SIADH (rare)

Miscellaneous: Fever, secondary malignancies

Overdosage/Toxicology Symptoms include vomiting, ataxia, coma, seizures, and pancytopenia. There are no known antidotes for chlorambucil intoxication. Treatment is mainly supportive, directed at decontaminating the GI tract and controlling symptoms. Blood products may be used to treat hematologic toxicity.

Drug Interactions

Decreased Effect: Patients may experience impaired immune response to vaccines; possible infection after administration of live vaccines in patients receiving immunosuppressants.

Ethanol/Nutrition/Herb Interactions Food: Avoid acidic foods and hot foods. Avoid spices.

Stability Store in refrigerator at 2°C to 8°C (36°F to 46°F); protect from light.

Mechanism of Action Interferes with DNA replication and RNA transcription by alkylation and cross-linking the strands of DNA

Pharmacodynamics/Kinetics

Absorption: Rapid and complete

Distribution: V_d: 0.14-0.24 L/kg

Protein binding: ~99%

Metabolism: Hepatic; active metabolite, phenylacetic acid mustard

Bioavailability: Reduced 10% to 20% with food

Half-life elimination: ~1.5 hours; Phenylacetic acid mustard: 2.5 hours

Time to peak, plasma: Within 1 hour; Phenylacetic acid mustard: 1.2-2.6 hours

Excretion: Urine (15% to 60% primarily as metabolites, <1% as unchanged drug or phenylacetic acid mustard: 2.5 hours)

Dosage Oral (refer to individual protocols):

Children:

General short courses: 0.1-0.2 mg/kg/day **or** 4.5 mg/m^2/day for 3-6 weeks for remission induction (usual: 4-10 mg/day); maintenance therapy: 0.03-0.1 mg/kg/day (usual: 2-4 mg/day)

Nephrotic syndrome: 0.1-0.2 mg/kg/day every day for 5-15 weeks with low-dose prednisone

Chronic lymphocytic leukemia (CLL):

Biweekly regimen: Initial: 0.4 mg/kg/dose every 2 weeks; increase dose by 0.1 mg/kg every 2 weeks until a response occurs and/or myelosuppression occurs

Monthly regimen: Initial: 0.4 mg/kg, increase dose by 0.2 mg/kg every 4 weeks until a response occurs and/or myelosuppression occurs

Malignant lymphomas:

Non-Hodgkin's lymphoma: 0.1 mg/kg/day

Hodgkin's lymphoma: 0.2 mg/kg/day

Adults: 0.1-0.2 mg/kg/day **or**

3-6 mg/m^2/day for 3-6 weeks, then adjust dose on basis of blood counts **or**

0.4 mg/kg and increased by 0.1 mg/kg biweekly or monthly **or**

14 mg/m^2/day for 5 days, repeated every 21-28 days

Hemodialysis: Supplemental dosing is not necessary

Peritoneal dialysis: Supplemental dosing is not necessary

Administration Usually administered as a single dose; preferably on an empty stomach.

Monitoring Parameters Liver function tests, CBC, platelets, serum uric acid

Dosage Forms Tablet: 2 mg

Extemporaneous Preparations A 2 mg/mL oral suspension can be prepared by crushing sixty 2 mg tablets in a mortar and then mixing in small amounts of methylcellulose (mix in a total of 30 mL of methylcellulose). Next, add a sufficient quantity of syrup to make 60 mL of final product. Transfer to amber container. Label "shake well," "refrigerate," and "protect from light." Refrigerated stability is 7 days.

Nahata MC and Hipple TF, *Pediatric Drug Formulations*, 4th ed, Cincinnati, OH: Harvey Whitney Books Co, 2000.

Dressman JB and Poust RI, "Stability of Allopurinol and of Five Antineoplastics in Suspension," *Am J Hosp Pharm*, 1983, 40(4):616-8.

♦ **Chlorambucilum** *see* Chlorambucil *on page 340*

♦ **Chloraminophene** *see* Chlorambucil *on page 340*

Chloramphenicol (klor am FEN i kole)

U.S. Brand Names Chloromycetin® Sodium Succinate

Canadian Brand Names Chloromycetin®; Chloromycetin® Succinate; Diochloram®; Pentamycetin®

Pharmacologic Category Antibiotic, Miscellaneous

Additional Appendix Information

Antimicrobial Drugs of Choice *on page 1981*

Use Treatment of serious infections due to organisms resistant to other less toxic antibiotics or when its penetrability into the site of infection is clinically superior to other antibiotics to which the organism is sensitive; useful in infections caused by *Bacteroides*, *H. influenzae*, *Neisseria meningitidis*, *Salmonella*, and *Rickettsia*; active against many vancomycin-resistant enterococci

Pregnancy Risk Factor C

Pregnancy Implications Embryotoxic and teratogenic in animals, but there are no adequate and well-controlled studies in pregnant women. Has been shown to cross placental barrier. "Gray syndrome" has been reported in a neonate following administration to the mother during labor.

Lactation Enters breast milk/not recommended (AAP rates "of concern")

Medication Safety Issues

Sound-alike/look-alike issues:

Chloromycetin® may be confused with chlorambucil, Chlor-Trimeton®

Contraindications Hypersensitivity to chloramphenicol or any component of the formulation

Warnings/Precautions Use with caution in patients with impaired renal or hepatic function and in neonates; reduce dose with impaired liver function. Use with care in patients with glucose 6-phosphate dehydrogenase deficiency. **[U.S. Boxed Warning]: Serious and fatal blood dyscrasias have occurred after both short-term and prolonged therapy.** Should not be used when less potentially toxic agents are effective. Prolonged use may result in superinfection.

Adverse Reactions

Three (3) major toxicities associated with chloramphenicol include:

Aplastic anemia, an idiosyncratic reaction which can occur with any route of administration; usually occurs 3 weeks to 12 months after initial exposure to chloramphenicol.

Bone marrow suppression is thought to be dose related with serum concentrations >25 mcg/mL and reversible once chloramphenicol is discontinued; anemia and neutropenia may occur during the first week of therapy.

Gray syndrome is characterized by circulatory collapse, cyanosis, acidosis, abdominal distention, myocardial depression, coma, and death. Reaction appears to be associated with serum levels ≥50 mcg/mL. May result from drug accumulation in patients with impaired hepatic or renal function.

Additional adverse reactions, frequency not defined:

Central nervous system: Confusion, delirium, depression, fever, headache

Dermatologic: Angioedema, rash, urticaria

Gastrointestinal: Diarrhea, enterocolitis, glossitis, nausea, stomatitis, vomiting

Hematologic: Granulocytopenia, hypoplastic anemia, pancytopenia, thrombocytopenia

(Continued)

Chloramphenicol *(Continued)*

Ocular: Optic neuritis

Miscellaneous: Anaphylaxis, hypersensitivity reactions

Overdosage/Toxicology Symptoms include anemia, metabolic acidosis, hypotension, and hypothermia. Treatment is supportive following GI decontamination.

Drug Interactions

Cytochrome P450 Effect: Inhibits CYP2C9 (weak), 3A4 (weak)

Increased Effect/Toxicity: Chloramphenicol increases serum concentrations of chlorpropamide, phenytoin, and oral anticoagulants.

Decreased Effect: Phenobarbital and rifampin may decrease serum concentrations of chloramphenicol.

Ethanol/Nutrition/Herb Interactions Food: May decrease intestinal absorption of vitamin B_{12} may have increased dietary need for riboflavin, pyridoxine, and vitamin B_{12}.

Stability Store at room temperature prior to reconstitution. Reconstituted solutions remain stable for 30 days. Use only clear solutions. Frozen solutions remain stable for 6 months.

Mechanism of Action Reversibly binds to 50S ribosomal subunits of susceptible organisms preventing amino acids from being transferred to growing peptide chains thus inhibiting protein synthesis

Pharmacodynamics/Kinetics

Distribution: To most tissues and body fluids; readily crosses placenta; enters breast milk

CSF:blood level ratio: Normal meninges: 66%; Inflamed meninges: >66%

Protein binding: 60%

Metabolism: Extensively hepatic (90%) to inactive metabolites, principally by glucuronidation; chloramphenicol sodium succinate is hydrolyzed by esterases to active base

Half-life elimination:

Normal renal function: 1.6-3.3 hours

End-stage renal disease: 3-7 hours

Cirrhosis: 10-12 hours

Excretion: Urine (5% to 15%)

Dosage

Meningitis: I.V.: Infants >30 days and Children: 50-100 mg/kg/day divided every 6 hours

Other infections: I.V.:

Infants >30 days and Children: 50-75 mg/kg/day divided every 6 hours; maximum daily dose: 4 g/day

Adults: 50-100 mg/kg/day in divided doses every 6 hours; maximum daily dose: 4 g/day

Dosing adjustment/comments in hepatic impairment: Avoid use in severe liver impairment as increased toxicity may occur

Hemodialysis: Slightly dialyzable (5% to 20%) via hemo- and peritoneal dialysis; no supplemental doses needed in dialysis or continuous arteriovenous or veno-venous hemofiltration

Dietary Considerations May have increased dietary need for riboflavin, pyridoxine, and vitamin B_{12}. Sodium content of 1 g injection: ~52 mg (2.25 mEq).

Administration Do not administer I.M.; can be administered IVP over at least 1 minute at a concentration of 100 mg/mL, or I.V. intermittent infusion over 15-30 minutes at a final concentration for administration of ≤20 mg/mL.

Monitoring Parameters CBC with reticulocyte and platelet counts, periodic liver and renal function tests, serum drug concentration

Reference Range

Therapeutic levels:

Meningitis:

Peak: 15-25 mcg/mL; toxic concentration: >40 mcg/mL

Trough: 5-15 mcg/mL

Other infections:

Peak: 10-20 mcg/mL

Trough: 5-10 mcg/mL

Timing of serum samples: Draw levels 0.5-1.5 hours after completion of I.V. dose

Test Interactions May cause false-positive results in urine glucose tests when using cupric sulfate (Benedict's solution, Clinitest®).

Dosage Forms Injection, powder for reconstitution: 1 g [contains sodium ~52 mg/g (2.25 mEq/g)]

♦ **ChloraPrep® [OTC]** see Chlorhexidine Gluconate *on page 344*

♦ **Chlorbutinum** see Chlorambucil *on page 340*

Chlordiazepoxide *(klor dye az e POKS ide)*

U.S. Brand Names Librium®

Canadian Brand Names Apo-Chlordiazepoxide®

Index Terms Methaminodiazepoxide Hydrochloride

Pharmacologic Category Benzodiazepine

Additional Appendix Information

Benzodiazepines *on page 1874*

Use Management of anxiety disorder or for the short-term relief of symptoms of anxiety; withdrawal symptoms of acute alcoholism; preoperative apprehension and anxiety

Restrictions C-IV

Pregnancy Risk Factor D

Lactation Enters breast milk/not recommended

Medication Safety Issues

Sound-alike/look-alike issues:

Librium® may be confused with Librax®

Contraindications Hypersensitivity to chlordiazepoxide or any component of the formulation (cross-sensitivity with other benzodiazepines may also exist); narrow-angle glaucoma; pregnancy

Warnings/Precautions Active metabolites with extended half-lives may lead to delayed accumulation and adverse effects. Use with caution in elderly or debilitated patients, pediatric patients, patients with hepatic disease (including alcoholics) or renal impairment, patients with respiratory disease or impaired gag reflex, patients with porphyria.

Parenteral administration should be avoided in comatose patients or shock. Adequate resuscitative equipment/personnel should be available, and appropriate monitoring should be conducted at the time of injection and for several hours following administration. The parenteral formulation should be diluted for I.M. administration with the supplied diluent only. This diluent should not be used when preparing the drug for intravenous administration.

Causes CNS depression (dose related) resulting in sedation, dizziness, confusion, or ataxia which may impair physical and mental capabilities. Patients must be cautioned about performing tasks which require mental alertness (eg, operating machinery or driving). Use with caution in patients receiving other CNS depressants or psychoactive agents (lithium, phenothiazines). Effects with other sedative drugs or ethanol may be potentiated. Benzodiazepines have been associated with falls and traumatic injury and should be used with extreme caution in patients who are at risk of these events (especially the elderly).

Use caution in patients with depression, particularly if suicidal risk may be present. Use with caution in patients with a history of drug dependence. Benzodiazepines have been associated with dependence and acute withdrawal symptoms on discontinuation or reduction in dose. Acute withdrawal, including seizures, may be precipitated in patients after administration of flumazenil to patients receiving long-term benzodiazepine therapy.

Benzodiazepines have been associated with anterograde amnesia. Paradoxical reactions, including hyperactive or aggressive behavior have been reported with benzodiazepines, particularly in adolescent/pediatric or psychiatric patients. Does not have analgesic, antidepressant, or antipsychotic properties.

Adverse Reactions
>10%:
Central nervous system: Drowsiness, fatigue, ataxia, lightheadedness, memory impairment, dysarthria, irritability
Dermatologic: Rash
Endocrine & metabolic: Libido decreased, menstrual disorders
Gastrointestinal: Xerostomia, salivation decreased, appetite increased or decreased, weight gain/loss
Genitourinary: Micturition difficulties
1% to 10%:
Cardiovascular: Hypotension
Central nervous system: Confusion, dizziness, disinhibition, akathisia
Dermatologic: Dermatitis
Endocrine & metabolic: Libido increased
Gastrointestinal: Salivation increased
Genitourinary: Sexual dysfunction, incontinence
Neuromuscular & skeletal: Rigidity, tremor, muscle cramps
Otic: Tinnitus
Respiratory: Nasal congestion
<1% (Limited to important or life-threatening): Photosensitivity

Overdosage/Toxicology Symptoms include hypotension, respiratory depression, coma, hypothermia, and cardiac arrhythmias. Treatment for benzodiazepine overdose is supportive. Flumazenil has been shown to selectively block the binding of benzodiazepines to CNS receptors, resulting in a reversal of benzodiazepine-induced CNS depression. Respiratory depression may not be reversed.

Drug Interactions
Cytochrome P450 Effect: Substrate of CYP3A4 (major)
Increased Effect/Toxicity: Chlordiazepoxide potentiates the CNS depressant effects of opioid analgesics, barbiturates, phenothiazines, ethanol, antihistamines, MAO inhibitors, sedative-hypnotics, and cyclic antidepressants. CYP3A4 inhibitors may increase the levels/effects of chlordiazepoxide; example inhibitors include azole antifungals, clarithromycin, diclofenac, doxycycline, erythromycin, imatinib, isoniazid, nefazodone, nicardipine, propofol, protease inhibitors, quinidine, telithromycin, and verapamil.
Decreased Effect: CYP3A4 inducers may decrease the levels/effects of chlordiazepoxide; example inducers include aminoglutethimide, carbamazepine, nafcillin, nevirapine, phenobarbital, phenytoin, and rifamycins.

Ethanol/Nutrition/Herb Interactions
Ethanol: Avoid ethanol (may increase CNS depression).
Food: Serum concentrations/effects may be increased with grapefruit juice, but unlikely because of high oral bioavailability of chlordiazepoxide.
Herb/Nutraceutical: Avoid valerian, St John's wort, kava kava, gotu kola (may increase CNS depression).

Stability Injection: Prior to reconstitution, store under refrigeration and protect from light. Solution should be used immediately following reconstitution.

I.M. use: Reconstitute by adding 2 mL of provided diluent; agitate gently until dissolved. Provided diluent is **not** for I.V. use.
I.V. use: Reconstitute by adding 5 mL NS or SWFI; agitate gently until dissolved; **do not administer this dilution I.M.**

Mechanism of Action Binds to stereospecific benzodiazepine receptors on the postsynaptic GABA neuron at several sites within the central nervous system, including the limbic system, reticular formation. Enhancement of the inhibitory effect of GABA on neuronal excitability results by increased neuronal membrane permeability to chloride ions. This shift in chloride ions results in hyperpolarization (a less excitable state) and stabilization.

Pharmacodynamics/Kinetics
Distribution: V_d: 3.3 L/kg; crosses placenta; enters breast milk
Protein binding: 90% to 98%
Metabolism: Extensively hepatic to desmethyldiazepam (active and long-acting)
(Continued)

Chlordiazepoxide *(Continued)*

Half-life elimination: 6.6-25 hours; End-stage renal disease: 5-30 hours; Cirrhosis: 30-63 hours

Time to peak, serum: Oral: Within 2 hours; I.M.: Results in lower peak plasma levels than oral

Excretion: Urine (minimal as unchanged drug)

Dosage

Children:

<6 years: Not recommended

>6 years: Anxiety: Oral, I.M.: 0.5 mg/kg/24 hours divided every 6-8 hours

Adults:

Anxiety:

Oral: 15-100 mg divided 3-4 times/day

I.M., I.V.: Initial: 50-100 mg followed by 25-50 mg 3-4 times/day as needed

Preoperative anxiety: I.M.: 50-100 mg prior to surgery

Ethanol withdrawal symptoms: Oral, I.V.: 50-100 mg to start, dose may be repeated in 2-4 hours as necessary to a maximum of 300 mg/24 hours

Note: Up to 300 mg may be given I.M. or I.V. during a 6-hour period, but not more than this in any 24-hour period.

Dosing adjustment in renal impairment: Cl_{cr} <10 mL/minute: Administer 50% of dose

Hemodialysis: Not dialyzable (0% to 5%)

Dosing adjustment/comments in hepatic impairment: Avoid use

Administration

I.M.: Administer by deep I.M. injection slowly into the upper outer quadrant of the gluteus muscle. Use only the diluent provided for I.M. use. Solutions made with SWFI or NS cause pain with I.M. administration.

I.V.: Administer slowly over at least 1 minute. Do not use the diluent provided for I.M. use. Air bubbles form during reconstitution.

Monitoring Parameters Respiratory and cardiovascular status, mental status, check for orthostasis

Reference Range Therapeutic: 0.1-3 mcg/mL (SI: 0-10 µmol/L); Toxic: >23 mcg/mL (SI: >77 µmol/L)

Additional Information Abrupt discontinuation after sustained use (generally >10 days) may cause withdrawal symptoms.

Dosage Forms

Capsule, as hydrochloride: 5 mg, 10 mg, 25 mg

Injection, powder for reconstitution, as hydrochloride: 100 mg [diluent contains benzyl alcohol, polysorbate 80, and propylene glycol]

♦ **Chlordiazepoxide and Amitriptyline Hydrochloride** *see* Amitriptyline and Chlordiazepoxide *on page 103*

♦ **Chlordiazepoxide and Clidinium** *see* Clidinium and Chlordiazepoxide *on page 388*

Chlordiazepoxide and Methscopolamine

(klor dye az e POKS ide & meth skoe POL a meen)

U.S. Brand Names Librax® *[reformulation]* [DSC]

Index Terms Methscopolamine Nitrate and Chlordiazepoxide Hydrochloride

Pharmacologic Category Anticholinergic Agent; Benzodiazepine

Use Adjunctive treatment of peptic ulcer; treatment of irritable bowel syndrome, acute enterocolitis

Restrictions C-IV

Pregnancy Risk Factor C

Medication Safety Issues

Librax® formulation may be cause for confusion:

In November 2004, Valeant Pharmaceuticals licensed the Librax® trademark to Victory Pharmaceuticals. Subsequently, the product was reformulated to contain chlordiazepoxide and methscopolamine. In January 2006, Valeant Pharmaceuticals began redistributing the original formulation of Librax®, containing clidinium and chlordiazepoxide. Victory Pharmaceuticals has discontinued their product. **Note:** The formulation of Librax® distributed in Canada (Valeant Canada Ltd) always contained clidinium and chlordiazepoxide.

Dosage Oral: Peptic ulcer, irritable bowel syndrome, acute enterocolitis:

Adults: 1-2 capsules 3-4 times/day; adjust dose based on individual response

Elderly: Initial dose should not exceed 2 capsules/day; adjust dose as tolerated

Additional Information Complete prescribing information for this medication should be consulted for additional detail.

Dosage Forms Capsule: Chlordiazepoxide hydrochloride 5 mg and methscopolamine nitrate 2.5 mg [DSC]

♦ **Chlorethazine** *see* Mechlorethamine *on page 1061*

♦ **Chlorethazine Mustard** *see* Mechlorethamine *on page 1061*

Chlorhexidine Gluconate (klor HEKS i deen GLOO koe nate)

U.S. Brand Names Avagard™ [OTC]; BactoShield® CHG [OTC]; Betasept® [OTC]; ChloraPrep® [OTC]; Dyna-Hex® [OTC]; Hibiclens® [OTC]; Hibistat® [OTC]; Operand® Chlorhexidine Gluconate [OTC]; Peridex®; PerioChip®; PerioGard®

Canadian Brand Names Hibidil® 1:2000; ORO-Clense

Index Terms CHG; 3M™ Avagard™ [OTC]

Pharmacologic Category Antibiotic, Oral Rinse; Antibiotic, Topical

Use Skin cleanser for surgical scrub, cleanser for skin wounds, preoperative skin preparation, germicidal hand rinse, and as antibacterial dental rinse. Chlorhexidine is active against gram-positive and gram-negative organisms, facultative anaerobes, aerobes, and yeast.

Orphan drug: Peridex®: Oral mucositis with cytoreductive therapy when used for patients undergoing bone marrow transplant

Pregnancy Risk Factor B

Medication Safety Issues

Sound-alike/look-alike issues:

Peridex® may be confused with Precedex™

Dosage Adults:

Oral rinse (Peridex®, PerioGard®):

Floss and brush teeth, completely rinse toothpaste from mouth and swish 15 mL (one capful) undiluted oral rinse around in mouth for 30 seconds, then expectorate. Caution patient not to swallow the medicine and instruct not to eat for 2-3 hours after treatment. (Cap on bottle measures 15 mL.)

Treatment of gingivitis: Oral prophylaxis: Swish for 30 seconds with 15 mL chlorhexidine, then expectorate; repeat twice daily (morning and evening). Patient should have a re-evaluation followed by a dental prophylaxis every 6 months.

Periodontal chip: One chip is inserted into a periodontal pocket with a probing pocket depth ≥5 mm. Up to 8 chips may be inserted in a single visit. Treatment is recommended every 3 months in pockets with a remaining depth ≥5 mm. If dislodgment occurs 7 days or more after placement, the subject is considered to have had the full course of treatment. If dislodgment occurs within 48 hours, a new chip should be inserted. The chip biodegrades completely and does not need to be removed. Patients should avoid dental floss at the site of PerioChip® insertion for 10 days after placement because flossing might dislodge the chip.

Insertion of periodontal chip: Pocket should be isolated and surrounding area dried prior to chip insertion. The chip should be grasped using forceps with the rounded edges away from the forceps. The chip should be inserted into the periodontal pocket to its maximum depth. It may be maneuvered into position using the tips of the forceps or a flat instrument.

Cleanser:

Surgical scrub: Scrub 3 minutes and rinse thoroughly, wash for an additional 3 minutes

Hand sanitizer (Avagard™): Dispense 1 pumpful in palm of one hand; dip fingertips of opposite hand into solution and work it under nails. Spread remainder evenly over hand and just above elbow, covering all surfaces. Repeat on other hand. Dispense another pumpful in each hand and reapply to each hand up to the wrist. Allow to dry before gloving.

Hand wash: Wash for 15 seconds and rinse

Hand rinse: Rub 15 seconds and rinse

Additional Information Complete prescribing information for this medication should be consulted for additional detail.

Dosage Forms

Chip, for periodontal pocket insertion (PerioChip®): 2.5 mg

Liquid, topical [surgical scrub]:

Avagard™: 1% (500 mL) [contains ethyl alcohol and moisturizers]

BactoShield® CHG: 2% (120 mL, 480 mL, 750 mL, 1000 mL, 3800 mL); 4% (120 mL, 480 mL, 750 mL, 1000 mL, 3800 mL) [contains isopropyl alcohol]

Betasept®: 4% (120 mL, 240 mL, 480 mL, 960 mL, 3840 mL) [contains isopropyl alcohol]

ChloraPrep®: 2% (0.67 mL, 1.5 mL, 3 mL, 10.5 mL) [contains isopropyl alcohol 70%; prefilled applicator]

Dyna-Hex®: 2% (120 mL, 960 mL, 3840 mL); 4% (120 mL, 960 mL, 3840 mL)

Hibiclens®: 4% (15 mL, 120 mL, 240 mL, 480 mL, 960 mL, 3840 mL) [contains isopropyl alcohol]

Operand® Chlorhexidine Gluconate: 2% (120 mL); 4% (120 mL, 240 mL, 480 mL, 960 mL, 3840 mL) [contains isopropyl alcohol]

Liquid, oral rinse: 0.12% (480 mL)

Peridex®: 0.12% (480 mL) [contains alcohol 11.6%]

PerioGard®: 0.12% (480 mL) [contains alcohol 11.6%; mint flavor]

Pad [prep pad] (Hibistat®): 0.5% (50s) [contains isopropyl alcohol]

Sponge/Brush (BactoShield® CHG): 4% per sponge/brush [contains isopropyl alcohol]

♦ **Chlormeprazine** see Prochlorperazine on page 1429

♦ **Chlor-Mes-D** see Chlorpheniramine, Phenylephrine, and Methscopolamine on page 353

♦ **2-Chlorodeoxyadenosine** see Cladribine on page 383

♦ **Chloromag®** see Magnesium Chloride on page 1046

♦ **Chloromycetin® (Can)** see Chloramphenicol on page 341

♦ **Chloromycetin® Sodium Succinate** see Chloramphenicol on page 341

♦ **Chloromycetin® Succinate (Can)** see Chloramphenicol on page 341

♦ **Chlorophyllin Copper Complex Sodium, Papain, and Urea** see Chlorophyllin, Papain, and Urea on page 345

Chlorophyllin, Papain, and Urea (KLOR oh fil in, pa PAY in, & yoor EE a)

U.S. Brand Names Allanfil 405; Allanfil Spray; Panafil®; Panafil® SE; Ziox™ [DSC]; Ziox 405™

Index Terms Chlorophyllin Copper Complex Sodium, Papain, and Urea; Papain, Urea, and Chlorophyllin; Urea, Chlorophyllin, and Papain

Pharmacologic Category Enzyme, Topical Debridement

Use Treatment of acute and chronic lesions, such as varicose, diabetic decubitus ulcers, burns, postoperative wounds, pilonidal cyst wounds, carbuncles, and miscellaneous traumatic or infected wounds

Medication Safety Issues

Sound-alike/look-alike issues:

Ziox™ may be confused with Zyvox™

Dosage Topical: Adults: Apply with each dressing change; daily or twice daily dressing changes are preferred, but may be every 2-3 days. Cover with dressing following application

(Continued)

Chlorophyllin, Papain, and Urea *(Continued)*

Ointment: Apply ¹/₈" thickness over the wound with clean applicator.

Spray: Completely cover the wound site so that the wound is not visible.

Additional Information Complete prescribing information for this medication should be consulted for additional detail.

Dosage Forms

Emulsion [spray]:

Panafil® SE: Copper chlorophyllin complex sodium 0.5%, papain ≥405,900 units/g, and urea 10% (34 mL)

Ointment: Copper chlorophyllin complex sodium 0.5%, papain ≥521,700 units/g, and urea 10% (30 g)

Allanfil 405, Panafil®: Chlorophyllin copper complex sodium 0.5%, papain ≥405,900 units/g, and urea 10% (6 g, 30 g)

Ziox™: Chlorophyllin copper complex sodium 0.5%, papain ≥521,700 units/g, and urea 10% (3.5 g [single-dose packets], 30 g) [DSC]

Ziox 405™: Copper chlorophyllin complex sodium 0.5%, papain ≥405,900 units/g, and urea 10% (3.5 g [single-dose packets], 30 g)

Solution [spray]:

Allanfil, Panafil®: Copper chlorophyllin complex sodium 0.5%, papain ≥405,900 units/g, and urea 10% (33 mL)

Chloroprocaine *(klor oh PROE kane)*

U.S. Brand Names Nesacaine®; Nesacaine®-MPF

Canadian Brand Names Nesacaine®-CE

Index Terms Chloroprocaine Hydrochloride

Pharmacologic Category Local Anesthetic

Use Infiltration anesthesia and peripheral and epidural anesthesia

Pregnancy Risk Factor C

Pregnancy Implications Animal reproduction studies have not been conducted. Local anesthetics rapidly cross the placenta and may cause varying degrees of maternal, fetal, and neonatal toxicity. Close maternal and fetal monitoring (heart rate and electronic fetal monitoring advised) are required during obstetrical use. Maternal hypotension has resulted from regional anesthesia. Positioning the patient on her left side and elevating the legs may help. Epidural, paracervical, or pudendal anesthesia may alter the forces of parturition through changes in uterine contractility or maternal expulsive efforts. The use of some local anesthetic drugs during labor and delivery may diminish muscle strength and tone for the first day or two of life. Administration as a paracervical block is not recommended with toxemia of pregnancy, fetal distress, or prematurity. Administration of a paracervical block early in pregnancy has resulted in maternal seizures and cardiovascular collapse. Fetal bradycardia and acidosis also have been reported. Fetal depression has occurred following unintended fetal intracranial injection while administering a paracervical and/or pudendal block.

Lactation Excretion in breast milk unknown/use caution

Medication Safety Issues

Sound-alike/look-alike issues:

Nesacaine® may be confused with Neptazane®

Contraindications Hypersensitivity to chloroprocaine, other ester type anesthetics, or any component of the formulation; myasthenia gravis; do not use for subarachnoid administration

Warnings/Precautions Use with caution in patients with hepatic impairment. **Do not use solutions containing preservatives for caudal or epidural block.** Local anesthetics have been associated with rare occurrences of sudden respiratory arrest, seizures, and cardiac arrest. A test dose is recommended prior to epidural administration.

Adverse Reactions

Frequency not defined.

Cardiovascular: Bradycardia, cardiac arrest, hypotension, ventricular arrhythmia

Central nervous system: Anxiety, dizziness, restlessness, tinnitus, unconsciousness

Dermatologic: Angioneurotic edema, erythema, pruritus, urticaria

Ocular: Blurred vision

Respiratory: Respiratory arrest

Miscellaneous: Allergic reactions, anaphylactoid reactions

<1% (Limited to important or life-threatening): Seizure (0.1%)

Overdosage/Toxicology Symptoms may include anxiety, blurred vision, bradyarrhythmias, CNS depression, dizziness, drowsiness, metabolic acidosis, methemoglobinemia, restlessness, seizures, and tremors. Treatment is symptomatic and supportive. Termination of anesthesia by pneumatic tourniquet inflation should be attempted when chloroprocaine is administered by infiltration or regional injection.

Drug Interactions

Decreased Effect: The para-aminobenzoic acid metabolite of chloroprocaine may decrease the efficacy of sulfonamide antibiotics.

Stability Store at 15°C to 30°C (59°F to 86°F); protect from light and freezing. Dilute with NS. To prepare 1:200,000 epinephrine-chloroprocaine HCl injection, add 0.1 mL of a 1:1000 epinephrine injection to 20 mL of preservative free chloroprocaine. Discard Nesacaine®-MPF following single use.

Mechanism of Action Chloroprocaine HCl is benzoic acid, 4-amino-2-chloro-2-(diethylamino) ethyl ester monohydrochloride. Chloroprocaine is an ester-type local anesthetic, which stabilizes the neuronal membranes and prevents initiation and transmission of nerve impulses thereby affecting local anesthetic actions. Local anesthetics including chloroprocaine, reversibly prevent generation and conduction of electrical impulses in neurons by decreasing the transient increase in permeability to sodium. The differential sensitivity generally depends on the size of the fiber; small fibers are more sensitive than larger fibers and require a longer period for recovery. Sensory pain fibers are usually blocked first, followed by fibers that transmit sensations of temperature, touch, and deep pressure. High concentrations block sympathetic somatic sensory and somatic motor fibers. The spread of anesthesia depends upon the distribution of the solution. This is primarily dependent on the volume of drug injected.

Pharmacodynamics/Kinetics
Onset of action: 6-12 minutes
Duration: 30-60 minutes
Distribution: V_d: Depends upon route of administration; high concentrations found in highly perfused organs such as liver, lungs, heart, and brain
Metabolism: Plasma cholinesterases
Excretion: Urine

Dosage Dosage varies with anesthetic procedure, the area to be anesthetized, the vascularity of the tissues, depth of anesthesia required, degree of muscle relaxation required, and duration of anesthesia; range.

Children >3 years (normally developed): Maximum dose (without epinephrine): 11 mg/kg; for infiltration, concentrations of 0.5% to 1% are recommended; for nerve block, concentrations of 1% to 1.5% are recommended

Adults:
Maximum single dose (without epinephrine): 11 mg/kg; maximum dose: 800 mg
Maximum single dose (with epinephrine): 14 mg/kg; maximum dose: 1000 mg
Infiltration and peripheral nerve block:
Mandibular: 2%: 2-3 mL; total dose 40-60 mg
Infraorbital: 2%: 0.5-1 mL; total dose 10-20 mg
Brachial plexus: 2%; 30-40 mL; total dose 600-800 mg
Digital (without epinephrine): 1%; 3-4 mL; total dose: 30-40 mg
Pudendal: 2%; 10 mL each side; total dose: 400 mg
Paracervical: 1%; 3 mL per each of four sites
Caudal block: Preservative-free: 2% or 3%: 15-25 mL; may repeat at 40-60 minute intervals
Lumbar epidural block: Preservative-free: 2% or 3%: 2-2.5 mL per segment; usual total volume: 15-25 mL; may repeat with doses that are 2-6 mL less than initial dose every 40-50 minutes.

Administration Before injecting, withdraw syringe plunger to ensure injection is not into vein or artery.

Monitoring Parameters Cardiovascular and respiratory status; mental status

Dosage Forms
Injection, solution, as hydrochloride (Nesacaine®): 1% (30 mL); 2% (30 mL) [contains disodium EDTA and methylparaben]
Injection, solution, as hydrochloride [preservative free] (Nesacaine®-MPF): 2% (20 mL); 3% (20 mL)

◆ **Chloroprocaine Hydrochloride** see Chloroprocaine on page 346

Chloroquine (KLOR oh kwin)

U.S. Brand Names Aralen®
Canadian Brand Names Aralen®; Novo-Chloroquine
Index Terms Chloroquine Phosphate
Pharmacologic Category Aminoquinoline (Antimalarial)
Additional Appendix Information
Malaria Treatment on page 2003
Use Suppression or chemoprophylaxis of malaria; treatment of uncomplicated or mild-to-moderate malaria; extraintestinal amebiasis
Unlabeled/Investigational Use Rheumatoid arthritis; discoid lupus erythematosus
Pregnancy Risk Factor C
Pregnancy Implications There are no adequate and well-controlled studies using chloroquine during pregnancy. However, based on clinical experience and because malaria infection in pregnant women may be more severe than in nonpregnant women, chloroquine prophylaxis may be considered in areas of chloroquine-sensitive P. falciparum malaria. Pregnant women should be advised not to travel to areas of P. falciparum resistance to chloroquine.
Lactation Enters breast milk/not recommended (AAP considers "compatible")
Medication Safety Issues
International issues:
Aralen® may be confused with Oralon® which is a brand name for povidone-iodine in Japan
Aralen® may be confused with Paralen® which is a brand name for acetaminophen in the Czech Republic
Contraindications Hypersensitivity to chloroquine or any component of the formulation; retinal or visual field changes
Warnings/Precautions Use with caution in patients with liver disease, G6PD deficiency, alcoholism or in conjunction with hepatotoxic drugs. May exacerbate psoriasis or porphyria. Retinopathy (irreversible) has occurred with long or high-dose therapy; discontinue drug if any abnormality in the visual field or if muscular weakness develops during treatment. Use caution in patients with pre-existing auditory damage; discontinue immediately if hearing defects are noted. Use caution in patients with seizure disorders.
Adverse Reactions Frequency not defined.
Cardiovascular: Hypotension (rare), ECG changes (rare; including T-wave inversion), cardiomyopathy
Central nervous system: Fatigue, personality changes, headache, psychosis, seizure, delirium, depression
Dermatologic: Pruritus, hair bleaching, pleomorphic skin eruptions, lichen planus eruptions, alopecia, mucosal pigmentary changes (blue-black), photosensitivity
Gastrointestinal: Nausea, diarrhea, vomiting, anorexia, stomatitis, abdominal cramps
Hematologic: Aplastic anemia, agranulocytosis (reversible), neutropenia, thrombocytopenia
(Continued)

Chloroquine *(Continued)*

Neuromuscular & skeletal: Rare cases of myopathy, neuromyopathy, proximal muscle atrophy, and depression of deep tendon reflexes have been reported

Ocular: Retinopathy (including irreversible changes in some patients long-term or high-dose therapy), blurred vision

Otic: Nerve deafness, tinnitus, hearing reduced (risk increased in patients with pre-existing auditory damage)

Overdosage/Toxicology Symptoms of overdose include headache, visual changes, cardiovascular collapse, shock, seizures, abdominal cramps, vomiting, cyanosis, methemoglobinemia, leukopenia, and respiratory and cardiac arrest. Following initial measures (immediate GI decontamination), treatment is supportive and symptomatic.

Drug Interactions

Cytochrome P450 Effect: Substrate (major) of CYP2D6, 3A4; **Inhibits** CYP2D6 (moderate)

Increased Effect/Toxicity: Chloroquine may increase the levels/effects of dextromethorphan, fluoxetine, lidocaine, mirtazapine, nefazodone, paroxetine, risperidone, ritonavir, thioridazine, tricyclic antidepressants, venlafaxine, and other CYP2D6 substrates. Chloroquine may increase the levels/effects of cyclosporine. The levels/effects of chloroquine may be increased by azole antifungals, chlorpromazine, cimetidine, clarithromycin, delavirdine, diclofenac, doxycycline, erythromycin, fluoxetine, imatinib, isoniazid, miconazole, nefazodone, nicardipine, paroxetine, pergolide, propofol, protease inhibitors, quinidine, quinine, ritonavir, ropinirole, telithromycin, verapamil, and other CYP2D6 or 3A4 inhibitors.

Decreased Effect: Chloroquine levels may be decreased by antacids or kaolin. Chloroquine may decrease ampicillin and/or praziquantel levels. Chloroquine may decrease the levels/effects of CYP2D6 prodrug substrates; example prodrug substrates include codeine, hydrocodone, oxycodone, and tramadol. The levels/effects of chloroquine may be decreased by aminoglutethimide, carbamazepine, nafcillin, nevirapine, phenobarbital, phenytoin, rifamycins, and other CYP3A4 inducers.

Ethanol/Nutrition/Herb Interactions Ethanol: Avoid ethanol (may increase GI irritation).

Stability Store tablets at 25°C (77°F); excursions permitted at 15°C to 30°C (59°F to 86°F).

Mechanism of Action Binds to and inhibits DNA and RNA polymerase; interferes with metabolism and hemoglobin utilization by parasites; inhibits prostaglandin effects; chloroquine concentrates within parasite acid vesicles and raises internal pH resulting in inhibition of parasite growth; may involve aggregates of ferriprotoporphyrin IX acting as chloroquine receptors causing membrane damage; may also interfere with nucleoprotein synthesis

Pharmacodynamics/Kinetics

Duration: Small amounts may be present in urine months following discontinuation of therapy

Absorption: Oral: Rapid (~89%)

Distribution: Widely in body tissues (eg, eyes, heart, kidneys, liver, lungs) where retention prolonged; crosses placenta; enters breast milk

Metabolism: Partially hepatic

Half-life elimination: 3-5 days

Time to peak, serum: 1-2 hours

Excretion: Urine (~70% as unchanged drug); acidification of urine increases elimination

Dosage Oral:

Suppression or prophylaxis of malaria:

Children: Administer 5 mg base/kg/week on the same day each week (not to exceed 300 mg base/dose); begin 1-2 weeks prior to exposure; continue for 4-6 weeks after leaving endemic area; if suppressive therapy is not begun prior to exposure, double the initial loading dose to 10 mg base/kg and administer in 2 divided doses 6 hours apart, followed by the usual dosage regimen

Adults: 500 mg/week (300 mg base) on the same day each week; begin 1-2 weeks prior to exposure; continue for 4-6 weeks after leaving endemic area; if suppressive therapy is not begun prior to exposure, double the initial loading dose to 1 g (600 mg base) and administer in 2 divided doses 6 hours apart, followed by the usual dosage regimen

Acute attack:

Children: 10 mg/kg (base) on day 1, followed by 5 mg/kg (base) 6 hours later and 5 mg/kg (base) on days 2 and 3

Adults: 1 g (600 mg base) on day 1, followed by 500 mg (300 mg base) 6 hours later, followed by 500 mg (300 mg base) on days 2 and 3

Extraintestinal amebiasis:

Children: 10 mg/kg (base) once daily for 2-3 weeks (up to 300 mg base/day)

Adults: 1 g/day (600 mg base) for 2 days followed by 500 mg/day (300 mg base) for at least 2-3 weeks

Rheumatoid arthritis, lupus erythematosus (unlabeled uses): Adults: 250 mg (150 mg base) once daily; reduce dosage following maximal response (taper to discontinue after response in lupus); generally requires 3-6 weeks

Note: Not considered first-line agent.

Dosing adjustment in renal impairment: Cl_{cr} <10 mL/minute: Administer 50% of dose

Hemodialysis: Minimally removed by hemodialysis

Dietary Considerations May be taken with meals to decrease GI upset.

Administration Chloroquine phosphate tablets have also been mixed with chocolate syrup or enclosed in gelatin capsules to mask the bitter taste.

Monitoring Parameters Periodic CBC, examination for muscular weakness, and ophthalmologic examination in patients receiving prolonged therapy

Dosage Forms

Tablet, as phosphate: 250 mg [equivalent to 150 mg base]; 500 mg [equivalent to 300 mg base]

Aralen®: 500 mg [equivalent to 300 mg base]

Extemporaneous Preparations A 10 mg chloroquine base/mL suspension is made by pulverizing two Aralen® 500 mg phosphate = 300 mg base/tablet, levigating with sterile water, and adding by geometric proportion, a significant amount of the cherry syrup and levigating until a uniform mixture is obtained; qs ad to 60 mL with cherry syrup, stable for up to 4 weeks when stored in the refrigerator or at a temperature of 29°C

Mirochnick M, Barnett E, Clarke DF, et al, "Stability of Chloroquine in an Extemporaneously Prepared Suspension Stored at Three Temperatures," *Pediatr Infect Dis J*, 1994, 13(9):827-8.

♦ **Chloroquine Phosphate** see Chloroquine on page 347

Chlorothiazide (klor oh THYE a zide)

U.S. Brand Names Diuril®
Canadian Brand Names Diuril®
Pharmacologic Category Diuretic, Thiazide
Additional Appendix Information
Sulfonamide Derivatives on page 1897
Use Management of mild-to-moderate hypertension; adjunctive treatment of edema
Pregnancy Risk Factor C (manufacturer); D (expert analysis)
Medication Safety Issues
International issues:
Diuril® may be confused with Duorol® which is a brand name for acetaminophen in Spain
Dosage Note: The manufacturer states that I.V. and oral dosing are equivalent. Some clinicians may use lower I.V. doses, however, because of chlorothiazide's poor oral absorption. I.V. dosing in infants and children has not been well established.

Infants <6 months:
Oral: 20-40 mg/kg/day in 2 divided doses (maximum dose: 375 mg/day)
I.V. (unlabeled): 2-8 mg/kg/day in 2 divided doses; doses up to 20 mg/kg/day have been used (anecdotal reports)
Infants >6 months and Children:
Oral: 10-20 mg/kg/day in 2 divided doses (maximum dose: 375 mg/day in children <2 years or 1 g/day in children 2-12 years)
I.V. (unlabeled): 4 mg/kg/day in 1-2 divided doses; doses up to 20 mg/kg/day have been used (anecdotal reports)
Adults:
Hypertension: Oral: 500-2000 mg/day divided in 1-2 doses (manufacturer labeling); doses of 125-500 mg/day have also been recommended
Edema: Oral, I.V.: 250-1000 mg once or twice daily; intermittent treatment (eg, therapy on alternative days) may be appropriate for some patients. Maximum daily dose: 1000 mg (ACC/AHA 2005 Heart Failure Guidelines)
Elderly: Oral: 500 mg once daily **or** 1 g 3 times/week
Dosage adjustment in renal impairment: Cl$_{cr}$ <10 mL/minute: Avoid use. Ineffective with low GFR (Aronoff G, 2002)
Note: ACC/AHA 2005 Heart Failure Guidelines suggest that thiazides lose their efficacy when Cl$_{cr}$ <40 mL/minute
Additional Information Complete prescribing information for this medication should be consulted for additional detail.
Dosage Forms
Injection, powder for reconstitution, as sodium: 500 mg
Suspension, oral: 250 mg/5 mL (237 mL) [contains alcohol 0.5% and benzoic acid]
Tablet: 250 mg, 500 mg

♦ **Chlorpheniramine, Acetaminophen, and Pseudoephedrine** see Acetaminophen, Chlorpheniramine, and Pseudoephedrine on page 35

Chlorpheniramine and Acetaminophen
(klor fen IR a meen & a seet a MIN oh fen)

U.S. Brand Names Coricidin HBP® Cold and Flu [OTC]
Index Terms Acetaminophen and Chlorpheniramine
Pharmacologic Category Antihistamine/Analgesic
Use Symptomatic relief of congestion, headache, aches and pains of colds and flu
Dosage Adults: Oral: 2 tablets every 4 hours
Additional Information Complete prescribing information for this medication should be consulted for additional detail.
Dosage Forms Tablet: Chlorpheniramine maleate 2 mg and acetaminophen 325 mg

Chlorpheniramine and Phenylephrine (klor fen IR a meen & fen il EF rin)

U.S. Brand Names Acitred® Cold and Allergy [OTC] *[reformulation]*; AllanTan Pediatric; AlleRx™ Suspension; Ceron; C-Phen; Dallergy-JR®; Dec-Chlorphen; Ed A-Hist; NoHist; PD-Hist-D; PediaTan™D; Phenabid®; Relera; Rescon-Jr; Rondec®; R-Tanna; Rynatan®; Rynatan® Pediatric Suspension; Sildec PE
Index Terms Chlorpheniramine Maleate and Phenylephrine Hydrochloride; Chlorpheniramine Tannate and Phenylephrine Tannate; Phenylephrine and Chlorpheniramine
Pharmacologic Category Antihistamine/Decongestant Combination
Use Temporary relief of upper respiratory conditions such as nasal congestion, runny nose, and sneezing due to the common cold, hay fever, or allergic or vasomotor rhinitis
Pregnancy Risk Factor C
Medication Safety Issues
Sound-alike/look-alike issues:
Rynatan® may be confused with Rynatuss®
Dosage Antihistamine/decongestant: Oral:
Children:
6-12 months: Rondec® Drops: 0.75 mL 1 times/day
(Continued)

Chlorpheniramine and Phenylephrine *(Continued)*

1-2 years: Rondec® Drops: 1 mL 4 times/day

2-6 years:
Allerx™: 1.25 -2.5 mL every 12 hours
Dallergy-JR® suspension: 2.5 mL every 12 hours
Rondec® Syrup: 1.25 mL every 4-6 hours; maximum 7.5 mL/24 hours
Rynatan® Suspension: 2.5 -5 mL every 12 hours

6-12 years:
Allerx™: 2.5- 5 mL every 12 hours
Dallergy-JR®: One capsule every 12 hours; maximum 2 capsules/24 hours
Dallergy-JR® suspension: 5 mL every 12 hours
Ed A-Hist™: One-half caplet every 12 hours
Rondec® Syrup: 2.5 mL every 4-6 hours; maximum 15 mL/24 hours
Rynatan® Suspension: 5-10 mL every 12 hours

≥12 years: Refer to adult dosing.

Adults:
Allerx™: 15 mL every 12 hours
Dallergy-JR®: Two capsules every 12 hours; maximum 4 capsules/24 hours
Dallergy-JR® suspension: 10 mL every 12 hours
Ed A-Hist™: One caplet every 12 hours
R-Tanna: 1-2 tablets every 12 hours
Rondec® Syrup: 5 mL every 4-6 hours; maximum 30 mL/24 hours
Rynatan® Tablet: 1-2 tablets every 12 hours

Additional Information Complete prescribing information for this medication should be consulted for additional detail.

Dosage Forms

Caplet, prolonged release:
Ed A-Hist®, NoHist, Relera: Chlorpheniramine maleate 8 mg and phenylephrine hydrochloride 20 mg

Capsule, extended release:
Dallergy-JR®: Chlorpheniramine maleate 4 mg and phenylephrine hydrochloride 20 mg

Capsule, timed release:
Phenabid®: Chlorpheniramine maleate 8 mg and phenylephrine hydrochloride 20 mg [dye free, sugar free]

Liquid:
Ed A-Hist®: Chlorpheniramine maleate 4 mg and phenylephrine hydrochloride 10 mg per 5 mL (480 mL) [sugar free; grape flavor]

Liquid, oral [drops]:
C-Phen, PD-Hist-D: Chlorpheniramine maleate 1 mg and phenylephrine hydrochloride 3.5 mg per mL (30 mL) [alcohol free, sugar free; bubblegum flavor]
Ceron, Sildec PE: Chlorpheniramine maleate 1 mg and phenylephrine hydrochloride 3.5 mg per mL (30 mL) [raspberry flavor]
Dec-Chlorphen: Chlorpheniramine maleate 1 mg and phenylephrine hydrochloride 3.5 mg per mL (30 mL) [alcohol free, sugar free; grape flavor]
Rondec®: Chlorpheniramine maleate 1 mg and phenylephrine hydrochloride 3.5 mg per mL (30 mL) [alcohol free, sugar free; bubble gum flavor]

Suspension, oral: Chlorpheniramine tannate 4.5 mg and phenylephrine tannate 5 mg per 5 mL (480 mL)
AllanTan Pediatric: Chlorpheniramine tannate 4.5 mg and phenylephrine tannate 5 mg per 5 mL (473 mL)
AlleRx™: Chlorpheniramine tannate 3 mg and phenylephrine tannate 7.5 per 5 mL (480 mL) [contains benzoic acid; raspberry flavor]
Dallergy-JR®: Chlorpheniramine tannate 4 mg and phenylephrine tannate 20 mg per 5 mL (480 mL) [contains sodium benzoate; peaches and cream flavor]
PediaTan™D: Chlorpheniramine tannate 8 mg and phenylephrine tannate 10 mg per 5 mL (480 mL) [sugar free; contains sodium benzoate; bubblegum flavor]
Rynatan® Pediatric Suspension: Chlorpheniramine tannate 4.5 mg and phenylephrine tannate 5 mg per 5 mL (480 mL) [contains benzoic acid and tartrazine; strawberry flavor]

Syrup:
C-Phen, Rondec®: Chlorpheniramine maleate 4 mg and phenylephrine hydrochloride 12. 5 mg per 5 mL (120 mL, 480 mL) [alcohol free, sugar free; bubble gum flavor]
Ceron, Sildec PE: Chlorpheniramine maleate 4 mg and phenylephrine hydrochloride 12. 5 mg per 5 mL (480 mL) [raspberry flavor]
PD-Hist-D: Chlorpheniramine maleate 4 mg and phenylephrine hydrochloride 12. 5 mg per 5 mL (480 mL)[alcohol free, sugar free; bubblegum flavor]

Tablet:
Actifed® Cold and Allergy, Sudafed PE® Sinus and Allergy: Chlorpheniramine maleate 4 mg and phenylephrine hydrochloride 10 mg
R-Tanna, Rynatan®: Chlorpheniramine tannate 9 mg and phenylephrine tannate 25 mg

Tablet, sustained release:
Rescon-Jr: Chlorpheniramine maleate 4 mg and phenylephrine hydrochloride 20 mg

---

Chlorpheniramine and Pseudoephedrine

(klor fen IR a meen & soo doe e FED rin)

U.S. Brand Names Allerest® Maximum Strength Allergy and Hay Fever [OTC]; A.R.M® [OTC]; Chlor-Trimeton® Allergy D [OTC] [DSC]; Deconamine®; Deconamine® SR; Dicel™; Dynahist-ER Pediatric®; Histade™; Histex™; Kronofed-A®; Kronofed-A®-Jr; LoHist-D; Pedia-Care® Cold and Allergy [OTC] [DSC]; QDALL®; Sudafed® Sinus & Allergy [OTC]; Sudal® 12; Triaminic® Cold and Allergy [OTC] [DSC]

Canadian Brand Names Triaminic® Cold & Allergy

Index Terms Chlorpheniramine Maleate and Pseudoephedrine Hydrochloride; Chlorpheniramine Tannate and Pseudoephedrine Tannate; Pseudoephedrine and Chlorpheniramine

Pharmacologic Category Alpha/Beta Agonist; Antihistamine

Use Relief of nasal congestion associated with the common cold, hay fever, and other allergies, sinusitis, eustachian tube blockage, and vasomotor and allergic rhinitis

Pregnancy Risk Factor C

Medication Safety Issues
Sound-alike/look-alike issues:
Allerest® may be confused with Sinarest®
Chlor-Trimeton® may be confused with Chloromycetin®
Sudafed® may be confused with Sufenta®

Dosage General dosing guidelines; consult specific product labeling. Rhinitis/decongestant:
Oral:
Children:
2-6 years:
Chlorpheniramine maleate 1 mg and pseudoephedrine hydrochloride 15 mg every 4-6 hours
Chlorpheniramine tannate 4.5 mg and pseudoephedrine tannate 75 mg: 2.5-5 mL every 12 hours (maximum: 10 mL/24 hours)
6-12 years: Chlorpheniramine maleate 2 mg and pseudoephedrine hydrochloride 30 mg every 4-6 hours (immediate release products)
Children ≥12 years and Adults:
Chlorpheniramine maleate 4 mg and pseudoephedrine hydrochloride 60 mg every 4-6 hours (immediate release products)
Chlorpheniramine tannate 4.5 mg and pseudoephedrine tannate 75 mg: 10-20 mL every 12 hours (maximum: 40 mL/24 hours)
Deconamine® SR, Kronofed-A®: Chlorpheniramine maleate 8 mg and pseudoephedrine hydrochloride 120 mg every 12 hours

Additional Information Complete prescribing information for this medication should be consulted for additional detail.

Dosage Forms [DSC] = Discontinued product
Caplet:
A.R.M.®: Chlorpheniramine maleate 4 mg and pseudoephedrine hydrochloride 60 mg
Capsule, extended release: Chlorpheniramine maleate 8 mg and pseudoephedrine hydrochloride 120 mg
Dynahist-ER Pediatric®: Chlorpheniramine maleate 4 mg and pseudoephedrine hydrochloride 60 mg
Histade™: Chlorpheniramine maleate 12 mg and pseudoephedrine hydrochloride 120 mg
QDALL®: Chlorpheniramine maleate 12 mg and pseudoephedrine hydrochloride 100 mg
Capsule, sustained release: Chlorpheniramine maleate 8 mg and pseudoephedrine hydrochloride 120 mg
Deconamine® SR, Kronofed-A®: Chlorpheniramine maleate 8 mg and pseudoephedrine hydrochloride 120 mg
Kronofed-A®-Jr: Chlorpheniramine maleate 4 mg and pseudoephedrine hydrochloride 60 mg
Liquid:
Histex™: Chlorpheniramine maleate 2 mg and pseudoephedrine sulfate 30 mg per 5 mL (480 mL) [peach flavor]
PediaCare® Cold and Allergy: Chlorpheniramine maleate 1 mg and pseudoephedrine sulfate 15 mg per 5 mL (120 mL) [alcohol free; contains sodium benzoate; bubble gum flavor] [DSC]
Triaminic® Cold and Allergy: Chlorpheniramine maleate 1 mg and pseudoephedrine sulfate 15 mg per 5 mL (120 mL) [contains benzoic acid; orange flavor] [DSC]
Suspension:
Dicel™: Chlorpheniramine tannate 5 mg and pseudoephedrine tannate 75 mg per 5 mL (480 mL) [contains sodium benzoate; strawberry banana flavor]
Syrup: Chlorpheniramine maleate 2 mg and pseudoephedrine hydrochloride 30 mg per 5 mL (480 mL)
Deconamine®: Chlorpheniramine maleate 2 mg and pseudoephedrine sulfate 30 mg per 5 mL (480 mL) [alcohol free, dye free; contains sodium benzoate; grape flavor]
LoHist-D: Chlorpheniramine maleate 2 mg and pseudoephedrine hydrochloride 30 mg per 5 mL (480 mL) [alcohol free, dye free; peach flavor]
Tablet: Chlorpheniramine maleate 4 mg and pseudoephedrine hydrochloride 60 mg
Allerest® Maximum Strength Allergy and Hay Fever: Chlorpheniramine maleate 2 mg and pseudoephedrine hydrochloride 30 mg
Chlor-Trimeton® Allergy D [DSC], Sudafed® Sinus & Allergy: Chlorpheniramine maleate 4 mg and pseudoephedrine hydrochloride 60 mg
Deconamine®: Chlorpheniramine maleate 4 mg and pseudoephedrine hydrochloride 60 mg [dye free] [DSC]
Tablet, chewable:
Sudal® 12: Chlorpheniramine polisterex (maleate) 4 mg and pseudoephedrine polistirex (as hydrochloride) 30 mg [contains phenylalanine 25 mg/tablet; grape flavor]

Chlorpheniramine, Ephedrine, Phenylephrine, and Carbetapentane
(klor fen IR a meen, e FED rin, fen il EF rin, & kar bay ta PEN tane)

U.S. Brand Names Rynatuss®; Rynatuss® Pediatric [DSC]; Tetra Tannate Pediatric

Index Terms Carbetapentane, Ephedrine, Phenylephrine, and Chlorpheniramine; Ephedrine, Chlorpheniramine, Phenylephrine, and Carbetapentane; Phenylephrine, Ephedrine, Chlorpheniramine, and Carbetapentane

Pharmacologic Category Antihistamine/Decongestant/Antitussive

Use Symptomatic relief of cough with a decongestant and an antihistamine

Pregnancy Risk Factor C
(Continued)

Chlorpheniramine, Ephedrine, Phenylephrine, and Carbetapentane *(Continued)*

Medication Safety Issues
Sound-alike/look-alike issues:
Rynatuss® may be confused with Rynatan®

Dosage Oral:
Children:
<2 years: Titrate dose individually
2-6 years: 2.5-5 mL every 12 hours
>6 years: 5-10 mL every 12 hours
Adults: 1-2 tablets every 12 hours

Additional Information
Complete prescribing information for this medication should be consulted for additional detail.

Dosage Forms
Suspension:
Rynatuss® Pediatric [DSC], Tetra Tannate Pediatric: Carbetapentane tannate 30 mg, ephedrine tannate 5 mg, phenylephrine tannate 5 mg, and chlorpheniramine tannate 4 mg per 5 mL (240 mL, 480 mL) [contains tartrazine and benzoic acid; strawberry flavor]
Tablet:
Rynatuss®: Carbetapentane tannate 60 mg, ephedrine tannate 10 mg, phenylephrine tannate 10 mg, and chlorpheniramine tannate 5 mg

♦ **Chlorpheniramine, Hydrocodone, Phenylephrine, Acetaminophen, and Caffeine** *see* Hydrocodone, Chlorpheniramine, Phenylephrine, Acetaminophen, and Caffeine *on page 852*

♦ **Chlorpheniramine Maleate and Hydrocodone Bitartrate** *see* Hydrocodone and Chlorpheniramine *on page 849*

♦ **Chlorpheniramine Maleate and Phenylephrine Hydrochloride** *see* Chlorpheniramine and Phenylephrine *on page 349*

♦ **Chlorpheniramine Maleate and Pseudoephedrine Hydrochloride** *see* Chlorpheniramine and Pseudoephedrine *on page 350*

♦ **Chlorpheniramine Maleate, Dihydrocodeine Bitartrate, and Phenylephrine Hydrochloride** *see* Dihydrocodeine, Chlorpheniramine, and Phenylephrine *on page 506*

♦ **Chlorpheniramine Maleate, Pseudoephedrine Hydrochloride, and Dextromethorphan Hydrobromide** *see* Chlorpheniramine, Pseudoephedrine, and Dextromethorphan *on page 355*

Chlorpheniramine, Phenylephrine, and Dextromethorphan
(klor fen IR a meen, fen il EF rin, & deks troe meth OR fan)

U.S. Brand Names Ceron-DM; Coldtuss DR [DSC]; Corfen DM; C-Phen DM; Dec-Chlorphen DM; De-Chlor DM; De-Chlor DR; Dex PC; PD-Cof; Phenabid DM®; Rondec®-DM; Sildec PE-DM; Statuss™ DM; Tri-Vent™ DPC

Index Terms Dextromethorphan, Chlorpheniramine, and Phenylephrine; Phenylephrine, Chlorpheniramine, and Dextromethorphan

Pharmacologic Category Antihistamine/Decongestant/Antitussive

Use Temporary relief of cough and upper respiratory symptoms associated with allergies or the common cold

Pregnancy Risk Factor C

Dosage Oral: Relief of cough and cold symptoms:
Children:
6-12 months (Rondec®-DM drops): 0.75 mL 4 times/day
1-2 years (Rondec®-DM drops): 1 mL 4 times/day
2-6 years:
Rondec®-DM syrup: 1.25 mL every 4-6 hours (maximum: 7.5 mL/24 hours)
Tri-Vent™ DPC: 2.5 mL every 6 hours (maximum: 10 mL/24 hours)
6-12 years:
Rondec®-DM syrup: 2.5 mL every 4-6 hours (maximum: 15 mL/24 hours)
Tri-Vent™ DPC: 5 mL every 6 hours (maximum: 20 mL/24 hours)
Children ≥12 years and Adults:
Rondec®-DM syrup: 5 mL every 4-6 hours (maximum: 30 mL/24 hours)
Tri-Vent™ DPC: 10 mL every 6 hours (maximum: 40 mL/24 hours)

Additional Information Complete prescribing information for this medication should be consulted for additional detail.

Dosage Forms
[DSC] = Discontinued product
Liquid:
Corfen DM: Chlorpheniramine maleate 4 mg, phenylephrine hydrochloride 10 mg, and dextromethorphan hydrobromide 15 mg per 5 mL (480 mL) [grape flavor]
De-Chlor DM: Chlorpheniramine maleate 2 mg, phenylephrine hydrochloride 10 mg, and dextromethorphan hydrobromide 15 mg per 5 mL (480 mL) [strawberry flavor]
De-Chlor DR: Chlorpheniramine maleate 2 mg, phenylephrine hydrochloride 6 mg, and dextromethorphan hydrobromide 15 mg per 5 mL (480 mL) [strawberry flavor]
Liquid, oral [drops]:
Ceron-DM, C-Phen DM, Sildec PE-DM: Chlorpheniramine maleate 1 mg, phenylephrine hydrochloride 3.5 mg, and dextromethorphan hydrobromide 3 mg per 1 mL (30 mL) [grape flavor]
Dec-Chlorphen DM, PD-Cof: Chlorpheniramine maleate 1 mg, phenylephrine hydrochloride 3.5 mg, and dextromethorphan hydrobromide 3 mg per 1 mL (30 mL) [alcohol free, sugar free; grape flavor]
Rondec® DM: Chlorpheniramine maleate 1 mg, phenylephrine hydrochloride 3.5 mg, and dextromethorphan hydrobromide 3 mg per 1 mL (30 mL)

Syrup:

Ceron-DM: Chlorpheniramine maleate 4 mg, phenylephrine hydrochloride 12.5 mg, and dextromethorphan hydrobromide 15 mg per 5 mL (480 mL) [grape flavor]

C-Phen DM: Chlorpheniramine maleate 4 mg, phenylephrine hydrochloride 12.5 mg, and dextromethorphan hydrobromide 15 mg per 5 mL (120 mL, 480 mL) [grape flavor]

Coldtuss DR: Chlorpheniramine maleate 4 mg, phenylephrine hydrochloride 6 mg, and dextromethorphan hydrobromide 15 mg per 5 mL (480 mL) [strawberry flavor] [DSC]

Dec-Chlorphen DM: Chlorpheniramine maleate 4 mg, phenylephrine hydrochloride 12.5 mg, and dextromethorphan hydrobromide 15 mg per 5 mL (480 mL) [alcohol free, sugar free; grape flavor]

Dex PC: Chlorpheniramine maleate 2 mg, phenylephrine hydrochloride 6 mg, and dextromethorphan hydrobromide 15 mg per 5 mL (480 mL) [strawberry flavor]

Rondec®-DM: Chlorpheniramine maleate 4 mg, phenylephrine hydrochloride 12.5 mg, and dextromethorphan hydrobromide 15 mg per 5 mL (120 mL, 480 mL) [alcohol free, sugar free; grape flavor]

Sildec PE-DM: Chlorpheniramine maleate 4 mg, phenylephrine hydrochloride 12.5 mg, and dextromethorphan hydrobromide 15 mg per 5 mL (480 mL) [grape flavor]

Statuss™: DM: Chlorpheniramine maleate 2 mg, phenylephrine hydrochloride 10 mg, and dextromethorphan hydrobromide 15 mg per 5 mL (480 mL) [alcohol free, sugar free; raspberry flavor]

Tri-Vent™ DPC: Chlorpheniramine maleate 2 mg, phenylephrine hydrochloride 6 mg, and dextromethorphan hydrobromide 15 mg per 5 mL (480 mL) [alcohol free; contains sodium benzoate; strawberry flavor]

Tablet, timed release:

Phenabid DM®: Chlorpheniramine maleate 8 mg, phenylephrine hydrochloride 20 mg, and dextromethorphan hydrobromide 30 mg [dye free, sugar free]

Chlorpheniramine, Phenylephrine, and Methscopolamine
(klor fen IR a meen, fen il EF rin, & meth skoe POL a meen)

U.S. Brand Names aeroKid™; AH-Chew®; AH-Chew II; Chlor-Mes-D; Dallergy®; Dehistine; Drize®-R [DSC]; Duradyl®; Durahist™ PE; Extendryl; Extendryl JR; Extendryl SR; Hista-Vent® DA; OMNIhist® II L.A.; PCM; PCM Allergy; Ralix; Rescon® MX

Index Terms Methscopolamine Nitrate, Chlorpheniramine Maleate, and Phenylephrine Hydrochloride; Phenylephrine Tannate, Chlorpheniramine Tannate, and Methscopolamine Nitrate

Pharmacologic Category Antihistamine/Decongestant/Anticholinergic

Use Treatment of upper respiratory symptoms such as respiratory congestion, allergic rhinitis, vasomotor rhinitis, sinusitis, and allergic skin reactions of urticaria and angioedema

Pregnancy Risk Factor C

Dosage

Children 6-11 years: Relief of respiratory symptoms: Oral:

aeroKid™: 2.5-5 mL every 4 hours

Ah-Chew® suspension: 2.5-5 mL every 12 hours

Dallergy®, Durahist™ PE, OMNIhist® II L.A., Rescon® MX: One-half caplet/tablet every 12 hours

Duradryl® syrup, Extendryl syrup: 2.5-5 mL, may repeat up to every 4 hours depending on age and body weight

Extendryl chewable tablet: One tablet every 4 hours; do not exceed 4 doses in 24 hours

Extendryl JR: One capsule every 12 hours

Children ≥12 years and Adults: Relief of respiratory symptoms: Oral: **Note:** If disturbances in urination occur in patients without renal impairment, medication should be discontinued for 1-2 days and should then be restarted at a lower dose

aeroKid™: 5-10 mL every 3-4 hours

Ah-Chew® suspension: 5-10 mL every 12 hours

Dallergy®, Durahist™ PE, Extendryl SR, OMNIhist® II L.A., Rescon® MX: One capsule/tablet every 12 hours

Duradryl® syrup, Extendryl syrup: 5-10 mL every 3-4 hours (4 times/day)

Extendryl: 1-2 chewable tablets every 4 hours

Elderly: Use with caution, may have increased adverse reactions

Dosage adjustment in renal impairment: Use is not recommended

Additional Information Complete prescribing information for this medication should be consulted for additional detail.

Dosage Forms [DSC] = Discontinued product

Caplet, extended release:

Dallergy®: Chlorpheniramine maleate 12 mg, phenylephrine hydrochloride 20 mg, and methscopolamine nitrate 2.5 mg

Capsule, extended release:

Extendryl JR: Chlorpheniramine maleate 4 mg, phenylephrine hydrochloride 10 mg, and methscopolamine nitrate 1.25 mg

Liquid:

Chlor-Mes-D: Chlorpheniramine maleate 2 mg, phenylephrine hydrochloride 10 mg, and methscopolamine nitrate 0.625 mg per 5 mL (480 mL)

Suspension:

Ah-Chew®: Chlorpheniramine tannate [equivalent to chlorpheniramine maleate 2 mg], phenylephrine tannate [equivalent to phenylephrine hydrochloride 10 mg], and methscopalamine nitrate 1.5 mg per 5 mL (120 mL) [grape flavor]

Syrup:

aeroKid™: Chlorpheniramine maleate 4 mg, phenylephrine hydrochloride 10 mg, and methscopolamine nitrate 1.25 mg per 5 mL (120 mL, 480 mL) [blue raspberry flavor]

Dallergy®: Chlorpheniramine maleate 2 mg, phenylephrine hydrochloride 10 mg, and methscopolamine nitrate 0.625 mg per 5 mL (480 mL)

Dehistine: Chlorpheniramine maleate 2 mg, phenylephrine hydrochloride 10 mg, and methscopolamine nitrate 1.25 mg per 5 mL (480 mL) [root beer flavor]

(Continued)

Chlorpheniramine, Phenylephrine, and Methscopolamine
(Continued)

Duradryl®: Chlorpheniramine maleate 2 mg, phenylephrine hydrochloride 10 mg, and methscopolamine nitrate 1.25 mg per 5 mL (480 mL) [contains sodium benzoate; cherry flavor]

Extendryl: Chlorpheniramine maleate 2 mg, phenylephrine hydrochloride 10 mg, and methscopolamine nitrate 1.25 mg per 5 mL (480 mL) [contains sodium benzoate; root beer flavor]

Tablet [scored]:

Dallergy®: Chlorpheniramine maleate 4 mg, phenylephrine hydrochloride 10 mg, and methscopolamine nitrate 1.25 mg

Tablet, chewable:

AH-Chew®: Chlorpheniramine maleate 2 mg, phenylephrine hydrochloride 10 mg, and methscopolamine nitrate 1.25 mg [grape flavor] [DSC]

AH-Chew II: Chlorpheniramine maleate 2 mg, phenylephrine hydrochloride 15 mg, and methscopolamine nitrate 1.25 mg [grape flavor]

Extendryl: Chlorpheniramine maleate 2 mg, phenylephrine hydrochloride 10 mg, and methscopolamine nitrate 1.25 mg [root beer flavor]

PCM: Chlorpheniramine maleate 2 mg, phenylephrine hydrochloride 10 mg, and methscopolamine nitrate 1.25 mg

Tablet, extended release: Chlorpheniramine maleate 8 mg, phenylephrine hydrochloride 20 mg, and methscopolamine nitrate 2.5 mg

Drize®-R: Chlorpheniramine maleate 8 mg, phenylephrine hydrochloride 20 mg, and methscopolamine nitrate 2.5 mg [dye free; scored] [DSC]

Durahist™ PE: Chlorpheniramine maleate 8 mg, phenylephrine hydrochloride 20 mg, and methscopolamine nitrate 1.25 mg [scored]

Extendryl SR: Chlorpheniramine maleate 8 mg, phenylephrine hydrochloride 20 mg, and methscopolamine nitrate 2.5 mg

Hista-Vent® DA: Chlorpheniramine maleate 8 mg, phenylephrine hydrochloride 20 mg, and methscopolamine nitrate 2.5 mg [scored]

PCM Allergy: Chlorpheniramine maleate 12 mg, phenylephrine hydrochloride 20 mg, and methscopolamine nitrate 2.5 mg

Tablet, long acting [scored]:

OMNIhist® II L.A.: Chlorpheniramine maleate 8 mg, phenylephrine hydrochloride 25 mg, and methscopolamine nitrate 2.5 mg

Rescon® MX: Chlorpheniramine maleate 8 mg, phenylephrine hydrochloride 40 mg, and methscopolamine nitrate 2.5 mg

Tablet, sustained release:

Ralix: Chlorpheniramine maleate 8 mg, phenylephrine hydrochloride 40 mg, and methscopolamine nitrate 2 mg

Chlorpheniramine, Phenylephrine, and Phenyltoloxamine
(klor fen IR a meen, fen il EF rin, & fen il tole LOKS a meen)

U.S. Brand Names Comhist®; Nalex®-A

Index Terms Phenylephrine, Chlorpheniramine, and Phenyltoloxamine; Phenyltoloxamine, Chlorpheniramine, and Phenylephrine

Pharmacologic Category Antihistamine/Decongestant Combination

Use Symptomatic relief of rhinitis and nasal congestion due to colds or allergy

Pregnancy Risk Factor C

Dosage Oral:

Children:

2-6 years: Nalex®-A liquid: 1.25-2.5 mL every 4-6 hours

6-12 years:

Nalex®-A liquid: 5 mL every 4-6 hours

Nalex®-A tablet: ½ tablet 2-3 times/day

Children >12 years and Adults:

Nalex®-A liquid: 10 mL every 4-6 hours

Nalex®-A tablet: 1 tablet 2-3 times/day

Additional Information Complete prescribing information for this medication should be consulted for additional detail.

Dosage Forms

Liquid (Nalex®-A): Chlorpheniramine maleate 2.5 mg, phenylephrine hydrochloride 5 mg, and phenyltoloxamine citrate 7.5 mg per 5 mL (480 mL) [alcohol free, sugar free; cotton candy flavor]

Tablet (Comhist®): Chlorpheniramine maleate 2 mg, phenylephrine hydrochloride 10 mg, and phenyltoloxamine citrate 25 mg

Tablet, prolonged release (Nalex®-A): Chlorpheniramine maleate 4 mg, phenylephrine hydrochloride 20 mg, and phenyltoloxamine citrate 40 mg

Chlorpheniramine, Phenylephrine, Codeine, and Potassium Iodide
(klor fen IR a meen, fen il EF rin, KOE deen, & poe TASS ee um EYE oh dide)

U.S. Brand Names Pediacof® [DSC]

Index Terms Codeine, Chlorpheniramine, Phenylephrine, and Potassium Iodide; Phenylephrine, Chlorpheniramine, Codeine, and Potassium Iodide; Potassium Iodide, Chlorpheniramine, Phenylephrine, and Codeine

Pharmacologic Category Antihistamine/Decongestant/Antitussive/Expectorant

Use Symptomatic relief of rhinitis, nasal congestion and cough due to colds or allergy

Restrictions C-V

Dosage Children 6 months to 12 years: 1.25-10 mL every 4-6 hours

Additional Information Complete prescribing information for this medication should be consulted for additional detail.

Dosage Forms Syrup: Chlorpheniramine maleate 0.75 mg, phenylephrine hydrochloride 2.5 mg, codeine phosphate 5 mg, and potassium iodide 75 mg per 5 mL (480 mL) [contains alcohol 5% and sodium benzoate; raspberry flavor] [DSC]

♦ **Chlorpheniramine, Pseudoephedrine, and Acetaminophen** *see* Acetaminophen, Chlorpheniramine, and Pseudoephedrine *on page 35*

Chlorpheniramine, Pseudoephedrine, and Codeine
(klor fen IR a meen, soo doe e FED rin, & KOE deen)

U.S. Brand Names Dihistine® DH

Index Terms Codeine, Chlorpheniramine, and Pseudoephedrine; Pseudoephedrine, Chlorpheniramine, and Codeine

Pharmacologic Category Antihistamine/Decongestant/Antitussive

Use Temporary relief of cough associated with minor throat or bronchial irritation or nasal congestion due to common cold, allergic rhinitis, or sinusitis

Restrictions C-V

Pregnancy Risk Factor C

Dosage Oral:

Children:

25-50 lb: 1.25-2.5 mL every 4-6 hours, up to 4 doses in 24-hour period

50-90 lb: 2.5-5 mL every 4-6 hours, up to 4 doses in 24-hour period

Adults: 10 mL every 4-6 hours, up to 4 doses in 24-hour period

Additional Information Complete prescribing information for this medication should be consulted for additional detail.

Dosage Forms

Elixir: Chlorpheniramine maleate 2 mg, pseudoephedrine hydrochloride 30 mg, and codeine phosphate 10 mg per 5 mL (120 mL, 480 mL)

Dihistine® DH: Chlorpheniramine maleate 2 mg, pseudoephedrine hydrochloride 30 mg, and codeine phosphate 10 mg per 5 mL (120 mL, 480 mL) [contains alcohol; grape flavor]

Chlorpheniramine, Pseudoephedrine, and Dextromethorphan
(klor fen IR a meen, soo doe e FED rin, & deks troe meth OR fan)

U.S. Brand Names Dicel™ DM; DuraTan™ Forte; Kidkare Cough and Cold [OTC]; PediaCare® Multi-Symptom Cold [OTC] [DSC]; PediaCare® NightRest Cough and Cold [OTC] [DSC]; Rescon DM [OTC]; Robitussin® Pediatric Night Relief [OTC] [DSC]; Tanafed DMX™; Triaminic® Cold and Cough [OTC] [DSC]; Triaminic® Night Time Cough and Cold [OTC] [DSC]; Vicks® Children's NyQuil® [OTC] [DSC]; Vicks® Pediatric 44®m [OTC] [DSC]

Index Terms Chlorpheniramine Maleate, Pseudoephedrine Hydrochloride, and Dextromethorphan Hydrobromide; Chlorpheniramine Tannate, Pseudoephedrine Tannate, and Dextromethorphan Tannate; Dexchlorpheniramine Tannate, Pseudoephedrine Tannate, and Dextromethorphan Tannate; Dextromethorphan, Chlorpheniramine, and Pseudoephedrine; Pseudoephedrine, Chlorpheniramine, and Dextromethorphan

Pharmacologic Category Antihistamine/Decongestant/Antitussive

Use Temporarily relieves nasal congestion, runny nose, cough, and sneezing due to the common cold, hay fever, or allergic rhinitis

Pregnancy Risk Factor C

Dosage General dosing guidelines; consult specific product labeling. Relief of cold symptoms: Oral:

Children:

2-6 years:

Dexchlorpheniramine tannate 2.5 mg, pseudoephedrine tannate 75 mg, and dextromethorphan tannate 25 mg (Tanafed DMX™): 2.5-5 mL every 12 hours (maximum: 10 mL/24 hours)

Dexchlorpheniramine tannate 3.5 mg, pseudoephedrine tannate 45 mg, and dextromethorphan tannate 30 mg (DuraTan™ Forte): 1.25-2.5 mL every 12 hours (maximum: 5 mL/24 hours)

6-12 years:

Chlorpheniramine maleate 1 mg, pseudoephedrine 15 mg, and dextromethorphan hydrobromide 7.5 mg per 5 mL: 10 mL every 6 hours

Chlorpheniramine maleate 1 mg, pseudoephedrine 15 mg, and dextromethorphan hydrobromide 5 mg per tablet or 5 mL: 2 tablets or 10 mL every 4-6 hours (maximum: 4 doses/24 hours)

Chlorpheniramine maleate 2 mg, pseudoephedrine 30 mg, and dextromethorphan hydrobromide 10 mg per tablet or 5 mL (Rescon DM): 5 mL every 4-6 hours (maximum: 4 doses/24 hours)

Dexchlorpheniramine tannate 2.5 mg, pseudoephedrine tannate 75 mg, and dextromethorphan tannate 25 mg (Tanafed DMX™): 5-10 mL every 12 hours (maximum: 20 mL/24 hours)

Dexchlorpheniramine tannate 3.5 mg, pseudoephedrine tannate 45 mg, and dextromethorphan tannate 30 mg (DuraTan™ Forte): 2.5-5 mL every 12 hours (maximum: 10 mL/24 hours)

>12 years: Refer to adult dosing

Adults:

Chlorpheniramine maleate 1 mg, pseudoephedrine 15 mg, and dextromethorphan hydrobromide 7.5 mg per 5 mL: 20 mL every 6 hours

Chlorpheniramine maleate 2 mg, pseudoephedrine 30 mg, and dextromethorphan hydrobromide 10 mg per tablet or 5 mL (Rescon DM): 10 mL every 4-6 hours (maximum: 4 doses/24 hours)

(Continued)

Chlorpheniramine, Pseudoephedrine, and Dextromethorphan
(Continued)

Dexchlorpheniramine tannate 2.5 mg, pseudoephedrine tannate 75 mg, and dextromethorphan tannate 25 mg (Tanafed DMX™): 10-20 mL every 12 hours (maximum: 40 mL/24 hours)

Dexchlorpheniramine tannate 3.5 mg, pseudoephedrine tannate 45 mg, and dextromethorphan tannate 30 mg (DuraTan™ Forte): 5-15 mL every 12 hours (maximum: 30 mL/24 hours)

Additional Information Complete prescribing information for this medication should be consulted for additional detail.

Dosage Forms [DSC] = Discontinued product

Liquid: Chlorpheniramine maleate 1 mg, pseudoephedrine hydrochloride 15 mg, and dextromethorphan hydrobromide 5 mg per 5 mL (120 mL)

Kidkare Cough and Cold: Chlorpheniramine maleate 1 mg, pseudoephedrine hydrochloride 15 mg, and dextromethorphan hydrobromide 5 mg per 5 mL (120 mL)

PediaCare® Multi-Symptom Cold: Chlorpheniramine maleate 1 mg, pseudoephedrine hydrochloride 15 mg, and dextromethorphan hydrobromide 5 mg per 5 mL (120 mL) [contains sodium benzoate; cherry flavor] [DSC]

PediaCare® NightRest Cough and Cold: Chlorpheniramine maleate 1 mg, pseudoephedrine hydrochloride 15 mg, and dextromethorphan hydrobromide 7.5 mg per 5 mL (120 mL) [contains sodium benzoate; cherry flavor] [DSC]

Rescon DM: Chlorpheniramine maleate 2 mg, pseudoephedrine hydrochloride 30 mg, and dextromethorphan hydrobromide 10 mg per 5 mL (120 mL, 480 mL) [dye free; cherry flavor]

Triaminic® Cold and Cough: Chlorpheniramine maleate 1 mg, pseudoephedrine hydrochloride 15 mg, and dextromethorphan hydrobromide 5 mg per 5 mL (120 mL) [contains sodium 10 mg/5 mL and benzoic acid; cherry flavor] [DSC]

Triaminic® Night Time Cough and Cold: Chlorpheniramine maleate 1 mg, pseudoephedrine hydrochloride 15 mg, and dextromethorphan hydrobromide 7.5 mg per 5 mL (120 mL, 240 mL) [contains sodium 7.5 mg/5 mL and benzoic acid; grape flavor] [DSC]

Vicks® Pediatric 44®m: Chlorpheniramine maleate 2 mg, pseudoephedrine hydrochloride 30 mg, and dextromethorphan hydrobromide 15 mg per 15 mL (120 mL) [contains sodium 30 mg/15 mL and sodium benzoate; cherry flavor] [DSC]

Vicks® Children's NyQuil®: Chlorpheniramine maleate 2 mg, pseudoephedrine hydrochloride 30 mg, and dextromethorphan hydrobromide 15 mg per 15 mL (120 mL) [contains sodium 71 mg/15 mL; cherry flavor] [DSC]

Suspension:

Dicel™ DM: Chlorpheniramine tannate 5 mg, pseudoephedrine tannate 75 mg, and dextromethorphan tannate 25 mg per 5 mL (480 mL) [contains sodium benzoate; cotton candy flavor]

DuraTan™ Forte: Dexchlorpheniramine tannate 3.5 mg, pseudoephedrine tannate 45 mg, and dextromethorphan tannate 30 mg per 5 mL (480 mL) [contains sodium benzoate; grape flavor]

Tanafed DMX™: Dexchlorpheniramine tannate 2.5 mg, pseudoephedrine tannate 75 mg, and dextromethorphan tannate 25 mg (120 mL, 480 mL) [contains sodium benzoate; cotton candy flavor]

Syrup:

Robitussin® Pediatric Night Relief: Chlorpheniramine maleate 1 mg, pseudoephedrine hydrochloride 15 mg, and dextromethorphan hydrobromide 7.5 mg per 5 mL (120 mL) [contains sodium benzoate; fruit punch flavor] [DSC]

Tablet, chewable:

PediaCare® Multi-Symptom Cold: Chlorpheniramine maleate 1 mg, pseudoephedrine hydrochloride 15 mg, and dextromethorphan hydrobromide 5 mg [contains phenylalanine 8.4 mg/tablet; cherry flavor] [DSC]

♦ **Chlorpheniramine Tannate and Phenylephrine Tannate** *see* Chlorpheniramine and Phenylephrine *on page 349*

♦ **Chlorpheniramine Tannate and Pseudoephedrine Tannate** *see* Chlorpheniramine and Pseudoephedrine *on page 350*

♦ **Chlorpheniramine Tannate, Pseudoephedrine Tannate, and Dextromethorphan Tannate** *see* Chlorpheniramine, Pseudoephedrine, and Dextromethorphan *on page 355*

ChlorproMAZINE (klor PROE ma zeen)

Canadian Brand Names Largactil®; Novo-Chlorpromazine

Index Terms Chlorpromazine Hydrochloride; CPZ

Pharmacologic Category Antipsychotic Agent, Typical, Phenothiazine

Additional Appendix Information

Antipsychotic Agents *on page 1872*

Use Control of mania; treatment of schizophrenia; control of nausea and vomiting; relief of restlessness and apprehension before surgery; acute intermittent porphyria; adjunct in the treatment of tetanus; intractable hiccups; combativeness and/or explosive hyperexcitable behavior in children 1-12 years of age and in short-term treatment of hyperactive children

Unlabeled/Investigational Use Management of psychotic disorders

Pregnancy Risk Factor C

Lactation Enters breast milk/not recommended (AAP rates "of concern")

Medication Safety Issues

Sound-alike/look-alike issues:

ChlorproMAZINE may be confused with chlorproPAMIDE, clomiPRAMINE, prochlorperazine, promethazine

Thorazine® may be confused with thiamine, thioridazine

Contraindications Hypersensitivity to chlorpromazine or any component of the formulation (cross-reactivity between phenothiazines may occur); severe CNS depression; coma

Warnings/Precautions Safety in children <6 months of age has not been established; use with caution in patients with seizures, bone marrow suppression, or severe liver disease

Significant hypotension may occur, especially when the drug is administered parenterally; injection contains sulfites which may cause allergic reaction

Tardive dyskinesia: Prevalence rate may be 40% in elderly; development of the syndrome and the irreversible nature are proportional to duration and total cumulative dose over time. May be reversible if diagnosed early in therapy.

Extrapyramidal reactions are more common in elderly with up to 50% developing these reactions after 60 years of age. Drug-induced **Parkinson's syndrome** occurs often. **Akathisia** is the most common extrapyramidal symptom in elderly.

Increased confusion, memory loss, psychotic behavior, and agitation frequently occur as a consequence of anticholinergic effects

Orthostatic hypotension is due to alpha-receptor blockade, the elderly are at greater risk for orthostatic hypotension

Antipsychotic associated sedation in nonpsychotic patients is extremely unpleasant due to feelings of depersonalization, derealization, and dysphoria

Life-threatening arrhythmias have occurred at therapeutic doses of antipsychotics

Adverse Reactions Frequency not defined.

Cardiovascular: Postural hypotension, tachycardia, dizziness, nonspecific QT changes

Central nervous system: Drowsiness, dystonias, akathisia, pseudoparkinsonism, tardive dyskinesia, neuroleptic malignant syndrome, seizure

Dermatologic: Photosensitivity, dermatitis, skin pigmentation (slate gray)

Endocrine & metabolic: Lactation, breast engorgement, false-positive pregnancy test, amenorrhea, gynecomastia, hyper- or hypoglycemia

Gastrointestinal: Xerostomia, constipation, nausea

Genitourinary: Urinary retention, ejaculatory disorder, impotence

Hematologic: Agranulocytosis, eosinophilia, leukopenia, hemolytic anemia, aplastic anemia, thrombocytopenic purpura

Hepatic: Jaundice

Ocular: Blurred vision, corneal and lenticular changes, epithelial keratopathy, pigmentary retinopathy

Overdosage/Toxicology Symptoms include deep sleep, coma, extrapyramidal symptoms, abnormal involuntary muscle movements, and hypotension. Following initiation of essential overdose management, toxic symptom treatment and supportive treatment should be initiated. Hypotension usually responds to I.V. fluids or Trendelenburg positioning. If unresponsive to these measures, the use of a parenteral inotrope may be required. Seizures commonly respond to diazepam (I.V. 5-10 mg bolus in adults every 15 minutes if needed up to a total of 30 mg; I.V. 0.25-0.4 mg/kg/dose up to a total of 10 mg in children) or to phenytoin or phenobarbital; critical cardiac arrhythmias often respond to I.V. phenytoin (15 mg/kg up to 1 g), while other antiarrhythmics can be used. Neuroleptics often cause extrapyramidal symptoms (eg, dystonic reactions) requiring management with anticholinergic agents such as benztropine mesylate I.V. 1-2 mg (adults) may be effective. These agents are generally effective within 2-5 minutes.

Drug Interactions

Cytochrome P450 Effect: Substrate of CYP1A2 (minor), 2D6 (major), 3A4 (minor); **Inhibits** CYP2D6 (strong), 2E1 (weak)

Increased Effect/Toxicity: The levels/effects of chlorpromazine may be increased by delavirdine, fluoxetine, miconazole, paroxetine, pergolide, quinidine, quinine, ritonavir, ropinirole, and other CYP2D6 inhibitors. Effects on CNS depression may be additive when chlorpromazine is combined with CNS depressants (opioid analgesics, ethanol, barbiturates, cyclic antidepressants, antihistamines, or sedative-hypnotics). Chlorpromazine may increase the levels/effects of amphetamines, selected beta-blockers, dextromethorphan, fluoxetine, lidocaine, mirtazapine, nefazodone, paroxetine, risperidone, ritonavir, thioridazine, tricyclic antidepressants, and venlafaxine and other CYP2D6 substrates. Chlorpromazine may increase the effects/toxicity of anticholinergics, antihypertensives, lithium (rare neurotoxicity), trazodone, or valproic acid. Concurrent use with TCA may produce increased toxicity or altered therapeutic response. Chloroquine and propranolol may increase chlorpromazine concentrations. Hypotension may occur when chlorpromazine is combined with epinephrine. May increase the risk of arrhythmia when combined with antiarrhythmics, cisapride, pimozide, sparfloxacin, or other drugs which prolong QT interval. Metoclopramide may increase risk of extrapyramidal symptoms (EPS). Acetylcholinesterase inhibitors (central) may increase the risk of antipsychotic-related EPS.

Decreased Effect: Chlorpromazine may decrease the levels/effects of CYP2D6 prodrug substrates; example prodrug substrates include codeine, hydrocodone, oxycodone, and tramadol. Phenothiazines inhibit the ability of bromocriptine to lower serum prolactin concentrations. Benztropine (and other anticholinergics) may inhibit the therapeutic response to chlorpromazine and excess anticholinergic effects may occur. Antihypertensive effects of guanethidine and guanadrel may be inhibited by chlorpromazine. Chlorpromazine may inhibit the antiparkinsonian effect of levodopa. Chlorpromazine and possibly other low potency antipsychotics may reverse the pressor effects of epinephrine.

Ethanol/Nutrition/Herb Interactions

Ethanol: Avoid ethanol (may increase CNS depression).

Herb/Nutraceutical: Avoid St John's wort (may decrease chlorpromazine levels, increase photosensitization, or enhance sedative effect). Avoid dong quai (may enhance photosensitization). Avoid kava kava, gotu kola, valerian (may increase CNS depression).

Stability Injection: Protect from light. A slightly yellowed solution does not indicate potency loss, but a markedly discolored solution should be discarded. Diluted injection (1 mg/mL) with NS and stored in 5 mL vials remains stable for 30 days.

Mechanism of Action Chlorpromazine is an aliphatic phenothiazine antipsychotic which blocks postsynaptic mesolimbic dopaminergic receptors in the brain; exhibits a strong alpha-adrenergic blocking effect and depresses the release of hypothalamic and hypophyseal hormones; believed to depress the reticular activating system, thus affecting basal metabolism, body temperature, wakefulness, vasomotor tone, and emesis

(Continued)

ChlorproMAZINE (Continued)

Pharmacodynamics/Kinetics

Onset of action: I.M.: 15 minutes; Oral: 30-60 minutes

Absorption: Rapid

Distribution: V_d: 20 L/kg; crosses the placenta; enters breast milk

Protein binding: 92% to 97%

Metabolism: Extensively hepatic to active and inactive metabolites

Bioavailability: 20%

Half-life, biphasic: Initial: 2 hours; Terminal: 30 hours

Excretion: Urine (<1% as unchanged drug) within 24 hours

Dosage

Children ≥6 months:

Schizophrenia/psychoses:

Oral: 0.5-1 mg/kg/dose every 4-6 hours; older children may require 200 mg/day or higher

I.M., I.V.: 0.5-1 mg/kg/dose every 6-8 hours

<5 years (22.7 kg): Maximum: 40 mg/day

5-12 years (22.7-45.5 kg): Maximum: 75 mg/day

Nausea and vomiting:

Oral: 0.5-1 mg/kg/dose every 4-6 hours as needed

I.M., I.V.: 0.5-1 mg/kg/dose every 6-8 hours

<5 years (22.7 kg): Maximum: 40 mg/day

5-12 years (22.7-45.5 kg): Maximum: 75 mg/day

Adults:

Schizophrenia/psychoses:

Oral: Range: 30-2000 mg/day in 1-4 divided doses, initiate at lower doses and titrate as needed; usual dose: 400-600 mg/day; some patients may require 1-2 g/day

I.M., I.V.: Initial: 25 mg, may repeat (25-50 mg) in 1-4 hours, gradually increase to a maximum of 400 mg/dose every 4-6 hours until patient is controlled; usual dose: 300-800 mg/day

Intractable hiccups: Oral, I.M.: 25-50 mg 3-4 times/day

Nausea and vomiting:

Oral: 10-25 mg every 4-6 hours

I.M., I.V.: 25-50 mg every 4-6 hours

Elderly: Behavioral symptoms associated with dementia: Initial: 10-25 mg 1-2 times/day; increase at 4- to 7-day intervals by 10-25 mg/day. Increase dose intervals (bid, tid, etc) as necessary to control behavior response or side effects; maximum daily dose: 800 mg; gradual increases (titration) may prevent some side effects or decrease their severity.

Dosing comments in renal impairment: Hemodialysis: Not dialyzable (0% to 5%)

Dosing adjustment/comments in hepatic impairment: Avoid use in severe hepatic dysfunction

Administration Note: Avoid skin contact with oral solution or injection solution; may cause contact dermatitis.

I.V.: Direct or intermittent infusion: Infuse 1 mg or portion thereof over 1 minute.

Monitoring Parameters Vital signs; lipid profile, fasting blood glucose/Hgb A_{1c}; BMI; mental status; abnormal involuntary movement scale (AIMS); extrapyramidal symptoms (EPS)

Reference Range

Therapeutic: 50-300 ng/mL (SI: 157-942 nmol/L)

Toxic: >750 ng/mL (SI: >2355 nmol/L); serum concentrations poorly correlate with expected response

Test Interactions False-positives for phenylketonuria, amylase, uroporphyrins, urobilinogen. May cause false-positive pregnancy test.

Dosage Forms

Injection, solution, as hydrochloride: 25 mg/mL (1 mL, 2 mL)

Tablet, as hydrochloride: 10 mg, 25 mg, 50 mg, 100 mg, 200 mg

♦ **Chlorpromazine Hydrochloride** see ChlorproMAZINE on page 356

ChlorproPAMIDE (klor PROE pa mide)

U.S. Brand Names Diabinese®

Canadian Brand Names Apo-Chlorpropamide®; Novo-Propamide

Pharmacologic Category Antidiabetic Agent, Sulfonylurea

Additional Appendix Information

Hyperglycemia- or Hypoglycemia-Causing Drugs on page 2057

Sulfonamide Derivatives on page 1897

Use Management of blood sugar in type 2 diabetes mellitus (noninsulin dependent, NIDDM)

Unlabeled/Investigational Use Neurogenic diabetes insipidus

Pregnancy Risk Factor C

Medication Safety Issues

Sound-alike/look-alike issues:

ChlorproPAMIDE may be confused with chlorproMAZINE

Diabinese® may be confused with DiaBeta®, Dialume®

Dosage Oral: The dosage of chlorpropamide is variable and should be individualized based upon the patient's response

Initial dose:

Adults: 250 mg/day in mild-to-moderate diabetes in middle-aged, stable diabetic

Elderly: 100-125 mg/day in older patients

Subsequent dosages may be increased or decreased by 50-125 mg/day at 3- to 5-day intervals

Maintenance dose: 100-250 mg/day; severe diabetics may require 500 mg/day; avoid doses >750 mg/day

Dosing adjustment/comments in renal impairment: Cl_{cr} <50 mL/minute: Avoid use

Hemodialysis: Removed with hemoperfusion

Peritoneal dialysis: Supplemental dose is not necessary

Dosing adjustment in hepatic Impairment: Dosage reduction is recommended. Conservative initial and maintenance doses are recommended in patients with liver impairment because chlorpropamide undergoes extensive hepatic metabolism.

Additional Information Complete prescribing information for this medication should be consulted for additional detail.

Dosage Forms Tablet: 100 mg, 250 mg

Chlorthalidone (klor THAL i done)

U.S. Brand Names Thalitone®

Canadian Brand Names Apo-Chlorthalidone®

Index Terms Hygroton

Pharmacologic Category Diuretic, Thiazide

Additional Appendix Information
Heart Failure (Systolic) *on page 2051*
Sulfonamide Derivatives *on page 1897*

Use Management of mild-to-moderate hypertension when used alone or in combination with other agents; treatment of edema associated with congestive heart failure or nephrotic syndrome. Recent studies have found chlorthalidone effective in the treatment of isolated systolic hypertension in the elderly.

Pregnancy Risk Factor B (manufacturer); D (expert analysis)

Dosage Oral:
Children (nonapproved): 2 mg/kg/dose 3 times/week or 1-2 mg/kg/day
Adults:
Hypertension: 25-100 mg/day or 100 mg 3 times/week; usual dosage range (JNC 7): 12.5-25 mg/day
Edema: Initial: 50-100 mg/day or 100 mg on alternate days; maximum dose: 200 mg/day
Heart failure-associated edema: 12.5-25 mg once daily; maximum daily dose: 100 mg (ACC/AHA 2005 Heart Failure Guidelines)
Elderly: Initial: 12.5-25 mg/day or every other day; there is little advantage to using doses >25 mg/day

Dosage adjustment in renal impairment: Cl_{cr} <10 mL/minute: Avoid use. Ineffective with low GFR (Aronoff G, 2002)

Note: ACC/AHA 2005 Heart Failure Guidelines suggest that thiazides lose their efficacy when Cl_{cr} <40 mL/minute

Additional Information Complete prescribing information for this medication should be consulted for additional detail.

Dosage Forms
Tablet: 25 mg, 50 mg, 100 mg
Thalitone®: 15 mg

♦ **Chlorthalidone and Atenolol** *see* Atenolol and Chlorthalidone *on page 169*

♦ **Chlorthalidone and Clonidine** *see* Clonidine and Chlorthalidone *on page 401*

♦ **Chlor-Trimeton® Allergy D [OTC] [DSC]** *see* Chlorpheniramine and Pseudoephedrine *on page 350*

♦ **Chlor-Tripolon ND® (Can)** *see* Loratadine and Pseudoephedrine *on page 1034*

Chlorzoxazone (klor ZOKS a zone)

U.S. Brand Names Parafon Forte® DSC

Canadian Brand Names Parafon Forte®; Strifon Forte®

Pharmacologic Category Skeletal Muscle Relaxant

Use Symptomatic treatment of muscle spasm and pain associated with acute musculoskeletal conditions

Pregnancy Risk Factor C

Lactation Excretion in breast milk unknown/not recommended

Medication Safety Issues
Sound-alike/look-alike issues:
Parafon Forte® may be confused with Fam-Pren Forte

Contraindications Hypersensitivity to chlorzoxazone or any component of the formulation; impaired liver function

Adverse Reactions Frequency not defined.
Central nervous system: Dizziness, drowsiness, lightheadedness, paradoxical stimulation, malaise
Dermatologic: Rash, petechiae, ecchymoses (rare), angioneurotic edema
Gastrointestinal: Nausea, vomiting, stomach cramps
Genitourinary: Urine discoloration
Hepatic: Liver dysfunction
Miscellaneous: Anaphylaxis (very rare)

Overdosage/Toxicity Symptoms include nausea, vomiting, diarrhea, drowsiness, dizziness, headache, absent tendon reflexes, and hypotension. Treatment is supportive following attempts to enhance drug elimination. Hypotension should be treated with I.V. fluids and/or Trendelenburg positioning. Dialysis and hemoperfusion and osmotic diuresis have all been useful in reducing serum drug concentrations. Patients should be observed for possible relapses due to incomplete gastric emptying.

Drug Interactions
Cytochrome P450 Effect: Substrate of CYP1A2 (minor), 2A6 (minor), 2D6 (minor), 2E1 (major), 3A4 (minor); **Inhibits** CYP2E1 (weak), 3A4 (weak)
Increased Effect/Toxicity: Effects of CNS depressants may be increased by chlorzoxazone. CYP2E1 inhibitors may increase the levels/effects of chlorzoxazone; example inhibitors include disulfiram, isoniazid, and miconazole. Disulfiram and isoniazid may increase chlorzoxazone concentration; monitor.
(Continued)

Chlorzoxazone *(Continued)*

Ethanol/Nutrition/Herb Interactions Ethanol: Avoid ethanol (may increase CNS depression).

Mechanism of Action Acts on the spinal cord and subcortical levels by depressing polysynaptic reflexes

Pharmacodynamics/Kinetics
Onset of action: ~1 hour
Duration: 6-12 hours
Absorption: Readily absorbed
Metabolism: Extensively hepatic via glucuronidation
Excretion: Urine (as conjugates)

Dosage Oral:
Children: 20 mg/kg/day or 600 mg/m^2/day in 3-4 divided doses
Adults: 250-500 mg 3-4 times/day up to 750 mg 3-4 times/day

Monitoring Parameters Periodic liver functions tests

Dosage Forms
Caplet (Parafon Forte® DSC): 500 mg
Tablet: 250 mg, 500 mg

♦ **Cholecalciferol and Alendronate** *see* Alendronate and Cholecalciferol *on page 67*

Cholestyramine Resin *(koe LES teer a meen REZ in)*

U.S. Brand Names Prevalite®; Questran®; Questran® Light
Canadian Brand Names Novo-Cholamine; Novo-Cholamine Light; PMS-Cholestyramine; Questran®; Questran® Light Sugar Free
Pharmacologic Category Antilipemic Agent, Bile Acid Sequestrant
Additional Appendix Information
Hyperlipidemia Management *on page 2058*
Lipid-Lowering Agents *on page 1887*
Use Adjunct in the management of primary hypercholesterolemia; pruritus associated with elevated levels of bile acids; diarrhea associated with excess fecal bile acids; binding toxicologic agents; pseudomembraneous colitis
Pregnancy Risk Factor C
Pregnancy Implications Cholestyramine is not absorbed systemically, but may interfere with vitamin absorption; therefore, regular prenatal supplementation may not be adequate. There are no studies in pregnant women; use with caution.
Lactation Does not enter breast milk/use caution
Contraindications Hypersensitivity to bile acid sequestering resins or any component of the formulation; complete biliary obstruction; bowel obstruction
Warnings/Precautions Use with caution in patients with constipation (GI dysfunction) and patients with phenylketonuria (Questran® Light contains aspartame). Overdose may result in GI obstruction. Not to be taken simultaneously with many other medicines (decreased absorption). Treat any diseases contributing to hypercholesterolemia first. May interfere with fat-soluble vitamins (A, D, E, K) and folic acid. Chronic use may be associated with bleeding problems (especially in high doses).

Adverse Reactions
>10%: Gastrointestinal: Constipation, heartburn, nausea, vomiting, stomach pain
1% to 10%:
Central nervous system: Headache
Gastrointestinal: Belching, bloating, diarrhea
<1% (Limited to important or life-threatening): Gallstones or pancreatitis, GI bleeding, hyperchloremic acidosis, hypoprothrombinemia (secondary to vitamin K deficiency), peptic ulcer, steatorrhea or malabsorption syndrome

Overdosage/Toxicology Symptoms include GI obstruction. Treatment is supportive.

Drug Interactions
Decreased Effect:
Cholestyramine can reduce the absorption of numerous medications when used concurrently. Give other medications 1 hour before or 4-6 hours after giving cholestyramine. Medications which may be affected include HMG-CoA reductase inhibitors, thiazide diuretics, propranolol (and potentially other beta-blockers), corticosteroids, thyroid hormones, digoxin, valproic acid, NSAIDs, loop diuretics, sulfonylureas, troglitazone (and potentially other agents in this class).
Warfarin and other oral anticoagulants: Hypoprothrombinemic effects may be reduced by cholestyramine. Separate administration times (as detailed above) and monitor INR closely when initiating or discontinuing.

Ethanol/Nutrition/Herb Interactions
Food: Cholestyramine (especially high doses or long-term therapy) may decrease the absorption of folic acid, calcium, and iron.
Herb/Nutraceutical: Cholestyramine (especially high doses or long-term therapy) may decrease the absorption of fat-soluble vitamins (vitamins A, D, E, and K).

Stability Store powder at controlled room temperature of 15°C to 30°C (59°F to 86°F). Mix contents of 1 packet or 1 level scoop of powder with 4-6 oz of beverage. Allow to stand 1-2 minutes prior to mixing. May also be mixed with highly-fluid soups, cereals, applesauce, etc. Suspension may be used for up to 48 hours after refrigeration.

Mechanism of Action Forms a nonabsorbable complex with bile acids in the intestine, releasing chloride ions in the process; inhibits enterohepatic reuptake of intestinal bile salts and thereby increases the fecal loss of bile salt-bound low density lipoprotein cholesterol

Pharmacodynamics/Kinetics
Onset of action: Peak effect: 21 days
Absorption: None
Excretion: Feces (as insoluble complex with bile acids)

Dosage Oral (dosages are expressed in terms of anhydrous resin):
    Children: 240 mg/kg/day in 3 divided doses; need to titrate dose depending on indication
    Adults: 4 g 1-2 times/day to a maximum of 24 g/day and 6 doses/day
    Dialysis: Not removed by hemo- or peritoneal dialysis; supplemental doses not necessary with dialysis or continuous arteriovenous or venovenous hemofiltration

Dietary Considerations Supplementation of vitamins A, D, E, and K, folic acid, and iron may be required with high-dose, long-term therapy.
    Questran® Light contains phenylalanine 16.8 g/5 g powder.
    Prevalite® contains phenylalanine 14.1 g/5.5 g powder.

Administration Mix powder with water or other fluid prior to administration; not to be taken in dry form. Suspension should not be sipped or held in mouth for prolonged periods (may cause tooth discoloration or enamel decay).

Test Interactions Increased prothrombin time; decreased cholesterol (S), iron (B)

Dosage Forms
    Powder for oral suspension: 4 g of resin/5 g of powder (5 g packets, 210 g can) [contains phenylalanine 14 mg/5 g]; 4 g of resin/5.7 g of powder (5.7 g packets, 240 g can) [light formulation]; 4 g of resin/9 g of powder (9 g packets, 378 g can)
    Prevalite®: 4 g of resin/5.5 g of powder (5.5 g packets, 231 g can) [contains phenylalanine 14.1 mg/5.5 g; orange flavor]
    Questran®: 4 g of resin/9 g of powder (9 g packets, 378 g can)
    Questran® Light: 4 g of resin/6.4 g of powder (5 g packets, 268 g can) [contains phenylalanine 28.1 mg/6.4 g]

Choline Magnesium Trisalicylate (KOE leen mag NEE zhum trye sa LIS i late)

U.S. Brand Names Trilisate® [DSC]
Index Terms Tricosal
Pharmacologic Category Salicylate
Additional Appendix Information
    Salicylates *on page 2080*
Use Management of osteoarthritis, rheumatoid arthritis, and other arthritis; acute painful shoulder
Pregnancy Risk Factor C/D (3rd trimester)
Pregnancy Implications Animal reproduction studies have not been conducted. Due to the known effects of other salicylates (closure of ductus arteriosus), use during late pregnancy should be avoided.
Lactation Enters breast milk/use caution
Contraindications Hypersensitivity to salicylates, other nonacetylated salicylates, other NSAIDs, or any component of the formulation; bleeding disorders; pregnancy (3rd trimester)
Warnings/Precautions Salicylate salts may not inhibit platelet aggregation and, therefore, should not be substituted for aspirin in the prophylaxis of thrombosis. Use with caution in patients with impaired renal function, dehydration, erosive gastritis, asthma, or peptic ulcer. Discontinue use 1 week prior to surgical procedures. Children and teenagers who have or are recovering from chickenpox or flu-like symptoms should not use this product. Changes in behavior (along with nausea and vomiting) may be an early sign of Reye's syndrome; patients should be instructed to contact their healthcare provider if these occur.

Elderly are a high-risk population for adverse effects from NSAIDs. As many as 60% of elderly can develop peptic ulceration and/or hemorrhage asymptomatically. Use lowest effective dose for shortest period possible. Tinnitus or impaired hearing may indicate toxicity. Tinnitus may be a difficult and unreliable indication of toxicity due to age-related hearing loss or eighth cranial nerve damage. CNS adverse effects may be observed in the elderly at lower doses than younger adults.

Adverse Reactions
    <20%:
        Gastrointestinal: Nausea, vomiting, diarrhea, heartburn, dyspepsia, epigastric pain, constipation
        Otic: Tinnitus
    <2%:
        Central nervous system: Headache, lightheadedness, dizziness, drowsiness, lethargy
        Otic: Hearing impairment
    <1%: Anorexia, asthma, BUN and creatinine increased, bruising, confusion, duodenal ulceration, dysgeusia, edema, epistaxis, erythema multiforme, esophagitis, hallucinations, hearing loss (irreversible), hepatic enzymes increased, gastric ulceration, occult bleeding, pruritus, rash, weight gain

Overdosage/Toxicology Symptoms include tinnitus, vomiting, acute renal failure, hyperthermia, irritability, seizures, coma, and metabolic acidosis. For acute ingestions, determine serum salicylate levels 6 hours after ingestion. The "Done" nomogram may be helpful for estimating the severity of aspirin poisoning and directing treatment using serum salicylate levels. Treatment can also be based upon symptomatology.

Drug Interactions
    Increased Effect/Toxicity: Choline magnesium trisalicylate may increase the hypoprothrombinemic effect of warfarin.
    Decreased Effect: Antacids may decrease choline magnesium trisalicylate absorption/salicylate concentrations.

Ethanol/Nutrition/Herb Interactions
    Ethanol: Avoid ethanol (may enhance gastric mucosal irritation).
    Food: May decrease the rate but not the extent of oral absorption.
    Herb/Nutraceutical: Avoid cat's claw, dong quai, evening primrose, feverfew, garlic, ginger, ginkgo, red clover, horse chestnut, green tea, ginseng (all have additional antiplatelet activity). Limit curry powder, paprika, licorice, Benedictine liqueur, prunes, raisins, tea, and gherkins; may cause salicylate accumulation. These foods contain 6 mg salicylate/100 g.

Stability Store at controlled room temperature of 15°C to 30°C (59°F to 86°F).
(Continued)

Choline Magnesium Trisalicylate (Continued)

Mechanism of Action Inhibits prostaglandin synthesis; acts on the hypothalamus heat-regulating center to reduce fever; blocks the generation of pain impulses

Pharmacodynamics/Kinetics

Onset of action: Peak effect: ~2 hours

Absorption: Stomach and small intestines

Distribution: Readily into most body fluids and tissues; crosses placenta; enters breast milk

Half-life elimination (dose dependent): Low dose: 2-3 hours; High dose: 30 hours

Time to peak, serum: ~2 hours

Dosage Oral (based on total salicylate content):

Children <37 kg: 50 mg/kg/day given in 2 divided doses; 2250 mg/day for heavier children

Adults: 500 mg to 1.5 g 2-3 times/day **or** 3 g at bedtime; usual maintenance dose: 1-4.5 g/day

Elderly: 750 mg 3 times/day

Dosing adjustment/comments in renal impairment: Avoid use in severe renal impairment

Dietary Considerations Take with food or large volume of water or milk to minimize GI upset. Liquid may be mixed with fruit juice just before drinking. Hypermagnesemia resulting from magnesium salicylate; avoid or use with caution in renal insufficiency.

Administration Liquid may be mixed with fruit juice just before drinking. Do not administer with antacids. Take with a full glass of water and remain in an upright position for 15-30 minutes after administration.

Monitoring Parameters Serum magnesium with high dose therapy or in patients with impaired renal function; serum salicylate levels, renal function, hearing changes or tinnitus, abnormal bruising, weight gain and response (ie, pain)

Reference Range Salicylate blood levels for anti-inflammatory effect: 150-300 mcg/mL; analgesia and antipyretic effect: 30-50 mcg/mL

Test Interactions False-negative results for glucose oxidase urinary glucose tests (Clinistix®); false-positives using the cupric sulfate method (Clinitest®); also, interferes with Gerhardt test (urinary ketone analysis), VMA determination; 5-HIAA, xylose tolerance test, and T_3 and T_4; increased PBI

Dosage Forms

Liquid: 500 mg/5 mL (240 mL) [choline salicylate 293 mg and magnesium salicylate 362 mg per 5 mL; cherry cordial flavor]

Tablet: 500 mg [choline salicylate 293 mg and magnesium salicylate 362 mg]; 750 mg [choline salicylate 440 mg and magnesium salicylate 544 mg]; 1000 mg [choline salicylate 587 mg and magnesium salicylate 725 mg]

Chondroitin Sulfate and Sodium Hyaluronate
(kon DROY tin SUL fate & SOW de um hye al yoor ON ate)

U.S. Brand Names Viscoat®

Index Terms Sodium Hyaluronate and Chondroitin Sulfate

Pharmacologic Category Ophthalmic Agent, Viscoelastic

Use Surgical aid in anterior segment procedures; protects corneal endothelium and coats intraocular lens thus protecting it

Pregnancy Risk Factor C

Contraindications Hypersensitivity to hyaluronate

Warnings/Precautions Product is extracted from avian tissues and contains minute amounts of protein; potential risks of hypersensitivity may exist. Intraocular pressure may be elevated as a result of pre-existing glaucoma; compromised outflow; or by operative procedures and sequelae, including enzymatic zonulysis, absence of an iridectomy, trauma to filtration structures, and by blood and lenticular remnants in the anterior chamber. Monitor IOP, especially during the immediate postoperative period.

Adverse Reactions 1% to 10%: Ocular: Intraocular pressure increased

Stability Store at 2°C to 8°C (36°F to 46°F); do not freeze.

Mechanism of Action Functions as a tissue lubricant and is thought to play an important role in modulating the interactions between adjacent tissues

Pharmacodynamics/Kinetics

Absorption: Intravitreous injection: Diffusion occurs slowly

Excretion: By Canal of Schlemm

Dosage Carefully introduce (using a 27-gauge needle or cannula) into anterior chamber after thoroughly cleaning the chamber with a balanced salt solution

Administration May inject prior to or following delivery of the crystalline lens. Instillation prior to lens delivery provides additional protection to corneal endothelium, protecting it from possible damage arising from surgical instrumentation. May also be used to coat intraocular lens and tips of surgical instruments prior to implantation surgery. May inject additional solution during anterior segment surgery to fully maintain the solution lost during surgery. At the end of surgery, remove solution by thoroughly irrigating with a balanced salt solution.

Test Interactions False-negative results for Clinistix® urine test; false-positive results with Clinitest®

Dosage Forms Solution, ophthalmic: Sodium chondroitin 4% and sodium hyaluronate 3% (0.5 mL)

- ◆ **Chooz®** [OTC] see Calcium Carbonate on page 269
- ◆ **Choriogonadotropin Alfa** see Chorionic Gonadotropin (Recombinant) on page 364

Chorionic Gonadotropin (Human)
(kor ee ON ik goe NAD oh troe pin, HYU man)

U.S. Brand Names Novarel®; Pregnyl®
Canadian Brand Names Humegon®; Pregnyl®; Profasi® HP
Index Terms CG; hCG
Pharmacologic Category Gonadotropin; Ovulation Stimulator
Use Induces ovulation and pregnancy in anovulatory, infertile females; treatment of hypogonadotropic hypogonadism, prepubertal cryptorchidism; spermatogenesis induction with follitropin alfa
Pregnancy Risk Factor X
Pregnancy Implications Teratogenic effects (forelimb, CNS) have been noted in animal studies at doses intended to induce superovulation (used in combination with gonadotropin). Testicular tumors in otherwise healthy men have been reported when treating secondary infertility.
Lactation Excretion in breast milk unknown/use caution
Contraindications Hypersensitivity to chorionic gonadotropin or any component of the formulation; precocious puberty; prostatic carcinoma or similar neoplasms; pregnancy
Warnings/Precautions Use with caution in asthma, seizure disorders, migraine, cardiac or renal disease. **Not** effective in the treatment of obesity. Safety and efficacy in children <4 years of age have not been established.

Cryptorchidism: May induce precocious puberty in children being treated for cryptorchidism; discontinue if signs of precocious puberty occur.

Ovulation induction: For use by infertility specialists. May cause ovarian hyperstimulation syndrome (OHSS); if severe, treatment should be discontinued and patient should be hospitalized. OHSS results in a rapid (<24 hours to 7 days) accumulation of fluid in the peritoneal cavity, thorax, and possibly the pericardium, which may become more severe if pregnancy occurs; monitor for ovarian enlargement. Use may lead to multiple births, arterial thromboembolism, enlargement or rupture of pre-existing ovarian cysts.

Adverse Reactions Frequency not defined.
Cardiovascular: Edema
Central nervous system: Depression, fatigue, headache, irritability, restlessness
Endocrine & metabolic: Gynecomastia, precocious puberty
Local: Injection site reaction
Miscellaneous: Hypersensitivity reaction (local or systemic)

Drug Interactions
Increased Effect/Toxicity: No data reported
Decreased Effect: No data reported

Stability Following reconstitution with the provided diluent, solutions are stable for 30-60 days, depending on the specific preparation, when stored at 2°C to 15°C.
Mechanism of Action Luteinizing hormone obtained from the urine of pregnant women. Stimulates production of gonadal steroid hormones by causing production of androgen by the testes; as a substitute for luteinizing hormone (LH) to stimulate ovulation

Pharmacodynamics/Kinetics
Half-life elimination: Biphasic: Initial: 11 hours; Terminal: 23 hours
Excretion: Urine

Dosage I.M.:
Children: Various regimens:
Prepubertal cryptorchidism:
4000 units 3 times/week for 3 weeks **or**
5000 units every second day for 4 injections **or**
500 units 3 times/week for 4-6 weeks **or**
15 injections of 500-1000 units given over 6 weeks

Hypogonadotropic hypogonadism: Male:
500-1000 units 3 times/week for 3 weeks, followed by the same dose twice weekly for 3 weeks **or**
4000 units 3 times/week for 6-9 months, then reduce dosage to 2000 units 3 times/week for additional 3 months

Adults:
Induction of ovulation: Female: 5000-10,000 units one day following last dose of menotropins
Spermatogenesis induction associated with hypogonadotropic hypogonadism: Male: Treatment regimens vary (range: 1000-2000 units 2-3 times a week). Administer hCG until serum testosterone levels are normal (may require 2-3 months of therapy), then may add follitropin alfa or menopausal gonadotropin if needed to induce spermatogenesis; continue hCG at the dose required to maintain testosterone levels.

Administration I.M. administration only
Monitoring Parameters
Male: Serum testosterone levels, semen analysis
Female: Ultrasound and/or estradiol levels to assess follicle development; ultrasound to assess number and size of follicles; ovulation (basal body temperature, serum progestin level, menstruation, sonography)
Reference Range Depends on application and methodology; <3 mIU/mL (SI: <3 units/L) usually normal (nonpregnant)
Dosage Forms
Injection, powder for reconstitution: 10,000 units [packaged with diluent; diluent contains benzyl alcohol and mannitol]
Novarel®: 10,000 units [packaged with diluent; diluent contains benzyl alcohol and mannitol]
Pregnyl®: 10,000 units [packaged with diluent; diluent contains benzyl alcohol]

Chorionic Gonadotropin (Recombinant)
(kor ee ON ik goe NAD oh troe pin ree KOM be nant)

U.S. Brand Names Ovidrel®
Canadian Brand Names Ovidrel®
Index Terms Choriogonadotropin Alfa; r-hCG
Pharmacologic Category Gonadotropin; Ovulation Stimulator
Use As part of an assisted reproductive technology (ART) program, induces ovulation in infertile females who have been pretreated with follicle stimulating hormones (FSH); induces ovulation and pregnancy in infertile females when the cause of infertility is functional
Pregnancy Risk Factor X
Pregnancy Implications Ectopic pregnancy, premature labor, postpartum fever, and spontaneous abortion have been reported in clinical trials. Congenital abnormalities have also been observed, however, the incidence is similar during natural conception.
Lactation Excretion in breast milk unknown/use caution
Contraindications Hypersensitivity to hCG preparations or any component of the formulation; primary ovarian failure; uncontrolled thyroid or adrenal dysfunction; uncontrolled organic intracranial lesion (ie, pituitary tumor); abnormal uterine bleeding, ovarian cyst or enlargement of undetermined origin; sex hormone dependent tumors; pregnancy
Warnings/Precautions For use by infertility specialists. May cause ovarian hyperstimulation syndrome (OHSS); if severe, treatment should be discontinued and patient should be hospitalized. OHSS results in a rapid (<24 hours to 7 days) accumulation of fluid in the peritoneal cavity, thorax, and possibly the pericardium, which may become more severe if pregnancy occurs; monitor for ovarian enlargement. Use may lead to multiple births. Risk of arterial thromboembolism with hCG products. Safety and efficacy in pediatric and geriatric patients have not been established.
Adverse Reactions
2% to 10%:
Endocrine & metabolic: Ovarian cyst (3%), ovarian hyperstimulation (<2% to 3%)
Gastrointestinal: Abdominal pain (3% to 4%), nausea (3%), vomiting (3%)
Local: Injection site: Pain (8%), bruising (3% to 5%), reaction (<2% to 3%), inflammation (<2% to 2%)
Miscellaneous: Postoperative pain (5%)
<2% (Limited to important or life-threatening): Abdominal enlargement, albuminuria, back pain, breast pain, cardiac arrhythmia, cervical carcinoma, cervical lesion, cough, diarrhea, dizziness, dysuria, ectopic pregnancy, emotional lability, fever, flatulence, genital herpes, genital moniliasis, headache, heart murmur, hiccups, hot flashes, hyperglycemia, insomnia, intermenstrual bleeding, leukocytosis, leukorrhea, malaise, paresthesia, pharyngitis, pruritus, rash, upper respiratory tract infection, urinary incontinence, urinary tract infection, vaginal hemorrhage, vaginitis
In addition, the following have been reported with menotropin therapy: Adnexal torsion, hemoperitoneum, mild-to-moderate ovarian enlargement, pulmonary and vascular complications. Ovarian neoplasms have also been reported (rare) with multiple drug regimens used for ovarian induction (relationship not established).
Overdosage/Toxicology Information not reported
Drug Interactions
Increased Effect/Toxicity: Specific drug interaction studies have not been conducted.
Decreased Effect: Specific drug interaction studies have not been conducted.
Stability
Powder for reconstitution: Store in original package under refrigeration or at room temperature of 2°C to 25°C (36°F to 77°F). Protect from light. Mix vial with 1 mL sterile water for injection. Gently mix by rotating vial to dissolve powder; do not shake. Use immediately following reconstitution.
Prefilled syringe: Prior to dispensing, store at 2°C to 8°C (36°F to 46°F). Patient may store at 25°C (77°F) for up to 30 days. Protect from light.
Mechanism of Action Luteinizing hormone analogue produced by recombinant DNA techniques; stimulates rupture of the ovarian follicle once follicular development has occurred.
Pharmacodynamics/Kinetics
Distribution: V_d: 5.9 ± 1 L
Bioavailability: 40%
Half-life elimination: Initial: 4 hours; Terminal: 29 hours
Time to peak: 12-24 hours
Excretion: Urine (10% of dose)
Dosage SubQ:
Adults: Female:
Assisted reproductive technologies (ART) and ovulation induction: 250 mcg given 1 day following the last dose of follicle stimulating agent. Use only after adequate follicular development has been determined. Hold treatment when there is an excessive ovarian response.
Elderly: Safety and efficacy have not been established
Dosage adjustment in renal impairment: Safety and efficacy have not been established
Dosage adjustment in hepatic impairment: Safety and efficacy have not been established
Administration For SubQ use only; inject into stomach area.
Monitoring Parameters Ultrasound and/or estradiol levels to assess follicle development; ultrasound to assess number and size of follicles; ovulation (basal body temperature, serum progestin level, menstruation, sonography)
Test Interactions May interfere with interpretation of pregnancy tests; may cross-react with radioimmunoassay of luteinizing hormone and other gonadotropins
Additional Information Clinical studies have shown r-hCG to be clinically and statistically equivalent to urinary-derived hCG products.

Dosage Forms [DSC] = Discontinued product
Injection, powder for reconstitution: 285 mcg [packaged with 1 mL SWFI, delivers 250 mcg r-hCG following reconstitution] [DSC]
Injection, solution: 257.5 mcg/0.515 mL (0.515 mL) [prefilled syringe; delivers 250 mcg r-hCG/0.5 mL]

♦ **Chronovera® (Can)** *see* Verapamil *on page 1784*
♦ **CI-1008** *see* Pregabalin *on page 1418*
♦ **Cialis®** *see* Tadalafil *on page 1629*

Ciclesonide (sye KLES oh nide)

U.S. Brand Names Omnaris™
Pharmacologic Category Corticosteroid, Nasal
Use Management of seasonal and perennial allergic rhinitis
Pregnancy Risk Factor C
Pregnancy Implications Teratogenic effects were reported in some, but not all animal studies. There are no adequate and well-controlled studies in pregnant women. The extent of intranasal absorption of ciclesonide systemically is low but variable; use during pregnancy with caution. Hypoadrenalism may occur in infants born to mothers receiving corticosteroids during pregnancy.
Lactation Excretion in breast milk unknown/use caution
Medication Safety Issues
International issues:
Omnaris™ is the U.S. brand name for ciclesonide **Intranasal** formulation; Alvesco® is the brand name for ciclesonide available in Australia and Great Britain which is an **oral inhalation** formulation
Contraindications Hypersensitivity to ciclesonide or any component of the formulation
Warnings/Precautions May cause hypercorticism or suppression of hypothalamic-pituitary-adrenal (HPA) axis, particularly in younger children or in patients receiving high doses for prolonged periods. HPA axis suppression may lead to adrenal crisis. Withdrawal and discontinuation of a corticosteroid should be done slowly and carefully. Particular care is required when patients are transferred from systemic corticosteroids to inhaled products due to possible adrenal insufficiency or withdrawal from steroids, including an increase in allergic symptoms. Patients receiving >20 mg per day of prednisone (or equivalent) may be most susceptible. Fatalities have occurred due to adrenal insufficiency in asthmatic patients during and after transfer from systemic corticosteroids to aerosol steroids; aerosol steroids do **not** provide the systemic steroid needed to treat patients having trauma, surgery, or infections.

Bronchospasm may occur with wheezing after inhalation; if this occurs stop steroid and treat with a fast-acting bronchodilator. Supplemental steroids (oral or parenteral) may be needed during stress or severe asthma attacks. Not to be used in status asthmaticus or for the relief of acute bronchospasm. Corticosteroid use may cause psychiatric disturbances, including depression, euphoria, insomnia, mood swings, and personality changes. Pre-existing psychiatric conditions may be exacerbated by corticosteroid use. Prolonged use of corticosteroids may also increase the incidence of secondary infection, mask acute infection (including fungal infections), prolong or exacerbate viral infections, or limit response to vaccines. Exposure to chickenpox should be avoided; corticosteroids should not be used to treat ocular herpes simplex. Corticosteroids should not be used for cerebral malaria. Close observation is required in patients with latent tuberculosis and/or TB reactivity; restrict use in active TB (only in conjunction with antituberculosis treatment). Prolonged treatment with corticosteroids has been associated with the development of Kaposi's sarcoma (case reports); if noted, discontinuation of therapy should be considered.

Use with caution in patients with thyroid disease, hepatic impairment, renal impairment, cardiovascular disease, diabetes, glaucoma, cataracts, myasthenia gravis, patients at risk for osteoporosis, patients at risk for seizures, or GI diseases (diverticulitis, peptic ulcer, ulcerative colitis) due to perforation risk. Use caution following acute MI (corticosteroids have been associated with myocardial rupture). Because of the risk of adverse effects, systemic corticosteroids should be used cautiously in the elderly in the smallest possible effective dose for the shortest duration. Avoid nasal corticosteroid use in patients with recent nasal septal ulcers, nasal surgery or nasal trauma until healing has occurred.

Orally-inhaled and intranasal corticosteroids may cause a reduction in growth velocity in pediatric patients (~1 centimeter per year [range 0.3-1.8 cm per year] and related to dose and duration of exposure). To minimize the systemic effects of orally-inhaled and intranasal corticosteroids, each patient should be titrated to the lowest effective dose. Growth should be routinely monitored in pediatric patients. Safety and efficacy have not been established in children <12 years of age.
Adverse Reactions
1% to 10%:
Central nervous system: Headache (6%)
Otic: Ear pain (2%)
Respiratory: Epistaxis (5%), nasopharyngitis (4%), nasal discomfort
<1% (Limited to important or life-threatening): Local infection
Overdosage/Toxicology No data available; acute overdose unlikely due to low systemic bioavailability. Excessive doses over prolonged periods may result in systemic hypercorticolism. In those cases, discontinuation of ciclesonide should be done slowly and treatment should be symptom-directed and supportive.
Drug Interactions
Cytochrome P450 Effect: Substrate (minor) of CYP3A4, 2D6
Increased Effect/Toxicity: Ciclesonide effects are increased by ketoconazole.
Stability Store at 15°C to 30°C (59°F to 86°F); do not freeze. Use within 4 months after opening aluminum pouch.
(Continued)

Ciclesonide *(Continued)*

Mechanism of Action Ciclesonide is a nonhalogenated, glucocorticoid prodrug that is hydrolyzed to the pharmacologically active metabolite des-ciclesonide following intranasal application. Des-ciclesonide has a high affinity for the glucocorticoid receptor and exhibits anti-inflammatory activity. The precise mechanism in allergic rhinitis is unknown; however, the mechanism of action for all topical corticosteroids is believed to be a combination of three important properties — anti-inflammatory activity, immunosuppressive properties, and antiproliferative actions.

Pharmacodynamics/Kinetics

Onset of action: 24-48 hours; further improvement observed over 1-2 weeks in seasonal allergic rhinitis or 5 weeks in perennial allergic rhinitis

Absorption: Intranasal: Minimal systemic absorption

Protein binding: ≥99%

Metabolism: Ciclesonide hydrolyzed to active metabolite, des-ciclesonide via esterases in nasal mucosa; further metabolism via hepatic CYP3A4 and 2D6

Bioavailability: <1%

Excretion: Feces (~66%); urine (≤20%)

Dosage Intranasal: Children ≥12 years and Adults: Rhinitis: 2 sprays (50 mcg/spray) per nostril once daily; maximum: 200 mcg/day

Administration Intranasal: Shake bottle gently before using. Prime pump prior to first use (press 8 times until fine mist appears) or if spray has not been used in 4 consecutive days (press 1 time or until a fine mist appears). Blow nose to clear nostrils. Insert applicator into nostril, keeping bottle upright, and close off the other nostril. Breathe in through nose. While inhaling, press pump to release spray. Avoid spraying directly onto the nasal septum. Nasal applicator may be removed and rinsed with warm water to clean. Discard after the "discard by" date or after labeled number of doses has been used, even if bottle is not completely empty.

Monitoring Parameters Growth (adolescents) and signs/symptoms of HPA axis suppression/adrenal insufficiency

Dosage Forms

Suspension, intranasal [spray]:

Omnaris™: 50 mcg/inhalation (12.5 g) [120 metered doses]

Ciclopirox *(sye kloe PEER oks)*

U.S. Brand Names Loprox®; Penlac®

Canadian Brand Names Loprox®; Penlac®; Stieprox®

Index Terms Ciclopirox Olamine

Pharmacologic Category Antifungal Agent, Topical

Use

Cream/suspension: Treatment of tinea pedis (athlete's foot), tinea cruris (jock itch), tinea corporis (ringworm), cutaneous candidiasis, and tinea versicolor (pityriasis)

Gel: Treatment of tinea pedis (athlete's foot), tinea corporis (ringworm); seborrheic dermatitis of the scalp

Lacquer (solution): Topical treatment of mild-to-moderate onychomycosis of the fingernails and toenails due to *Trichophyton rubrum* (not involving the lunula) and the immediately-adjacent skin

Shampoo: Treatment of seborrheic dermatitis of the scalp

Pregnancy Risk Factor B

Medication Safety Issues

Sound-alike/look-alike issues:

Loprox® may be confused with Lonox®

Dosage Topical:

Children >10 years and Adults: Tinea pedis, tinea cruris, tinea corporis, cutaneous candidiasis, and tinea versicolor: Cream/suspension: Apply twice daily, gently massage into affected areas; if no improvement after 4 weeks of treatment, re-evaluate the diagnosis.

Children ≥12 years and Adults: Onychomycosis of the fingernails and toenails: Lacquer (solution): Apply to adjacent skin and affected nails daily (as a part of a comprehensive management program for onychomycosis). Remove with alcohol every 7 days.

Children >16 years and Adults:

Tinea pedis, tinea corporis: Gel: Apply twice daily, gently massage into affected areas and surrounding skin; if no improvement after 4 weeks of treatment, re-evaluate diagnosis

Seborrheic dermatitis of the scalp:

Gel: Apply twice daily, gently massage into affected areas and surrounding skin; if no improvement after 4 weeks of treatment, re-evaluate diagnosis.

Shampoo: Apply ~5 mL (1 teaspoonful) to wet hair; lather, and leave in place ~3 minutes; rinse. May use up to 10 mL for longer hair. Repeat twice weekly for 4 weeks; allow a minimum of 3 days between applications.

Dosage Forms

Cream, as olamine: 0.77% (15 g, 30 g, 90 g)

Loprox®: 0.77% (15 g, 30 g, 90 g)

Gel:

Loprox®: 0.77% (30 g, 45 g, 100 g)

Shampoo:

Loprox®: 1% (120 mL)

Solution, topical [nail lacquer]:

Penlac®: 8% (6.6 mL)

Suspension, topical, as olamine: 0.77% (30 mL, 60 mL)

Loprox®: 0.77% (30 mL, 60 mL)

♦ **Ciclopirox Olamine** *see* Ciclopirox *on page 366*

♦ **Cidecin** *see* Daptomycin *on page 452*

Cidofovir (si DOF o veer)

U.S. Brand Names Vistide®

Pharmacologic Category Antiviral Agent

Use Treatment of cytomegalovirus (CMV) retinitis in patients with acquired immunodeficiency syndrome (AIDS). **Note:** Should be administered with probenecid.

Pregnancy Risk Factor C

Pregnancy Implications Cidofovir was shown to be teratogenic and embryotoxic in animal studies, some at doses which also produced maternal toxicity. Reduced testes weight and hypospermia were also noted in animal studies. There are no adequate and well-controlled studies in pregnant women; use during pregnancy only if the potential benefit to the mother outweighs the possible risk to the fetus. Women of childbearing potential should use effective contraception during therapy and for 1 month following treatment. Males should use a barrier contraceptive during therapy and for 3 months following treatment.

Lactation Excretion in breast milk unknown/contraindicated

Contraindications Hypersensitivity to cidofovir; history of clinically-severe hypersensitivity to probenecid or other sulfa-containing medications; serum creatinine >1.5 mg/dL; Cl_{cr} <55 mL/minute; urine protein ≥100 mg/dL (≥2+ proteinuria); use with or within 7 days of nephrotoxic agents; direct intraocular injection

Warnings/Precautions [U.S. Boxed Warning]: Dose-dependent nephrotoxicity requires dose adjustment or discontinuation if changes in renal function occur during therapy (eg, proteinuria, glycosuria, decreased serum phosphate, uric acid or bicarbonate, and elevated creatinine). Neutropenia has been reported; monitor counts during therapy. Cases of ocular hypotony have also occurred; monitor intraocular pressure. Monitor for signs of metabolic acidosis. Safety and efficacy have not been established in children or the elderly. Administration must be accompanied by oral probenecid and intravenous saline prehydration. Prepare admixtures in a class two laminar flow hood, wearing protective gear; dispose of cidofovir as directed. **[U.S. Boxed Warning]: Indicated only for CMV retinitis treatment in HIV patients; possibly carcinogenic based on animal data.**

Adverse Reactions

>10%:
Central nervous system: Chills, fever, headache, pain
Dermatologic: Alopecia, rash
Gastrointestinal: Nausea, vomiting, diarrhea, anorexia
Hematologic: Anemia, neutropenia
Neuromuscular & skeletal: Weakness
Ocular: Intraocular pressure decreased, iritis, ocular hypotony, uveitis
Renal: Creatinine increased, proteinuria, renal toxicity
Respiratory: Cough, dyspnea
Miscellaneous: Infection, oral moniliasis, serum bicarbonate decreased

1% to 10%:
Renal: Fanconi syndrome
Respiratory: Pneumonia

<1%: Hepatic failure, metabolic acidosis, pancreatitis

Frequency not defined (limited to important or life-threatening reactions):
Cardiovascular: Cardiomyopathy, cardiovascular disorder, CHF, edema, postural hypotension, shock, syncope, tachycardia
Central nervous system: Agitation, amnesia, anxiety, confusion, convulsion, dizziness, hallucinations, insomnia, malaise, vertigo
Dermatologic: Photosensitivity reaction, skin discoloration, urticaria
Endocrine & metabolic: Adrenal cortex insufficiency
Gastrointestinal: Abdominal pain, aphthous stomatitis, colitis, constipation, dysphagia, fecal incontinence, gastritis, GI hemorrhage, gingivitis, melena, proctitis, splenomegaly, stomatitis, tongue discoloration
Genitourinary: Urinary incontinence
Hematologic: Hypochromic anemia, leukocytosis, leukopenia, lymphadenopathy, lymphoma-like reaction, pancytopenia, thrombocytopenia, thrombocytopenic purpura
Hepatic: Hepatomegaly, hepatosplenomegaly, jaundice, liver function tests abnormal, liver damage, liver necrosis
Local: Injection site reaction
Neuromuscular & skeletal: Tremor
Ocular: Amblyopia, blindness, cataract, conjunctivitis, corneal lesion, diplopia, vision abnormal
Otic: Hearing loss
Miscellaneous: Allergic reaction, sepsis

Overdosage/Toxicology Hemodialysis and hydration may reduce drug plasma concentrations. Probenecid may assist in decreasing active tubular secretion.

Drug Interactions

Increased Effect/Toxicity: Drugs with nephrotoxic potential (eg, amphotericin B, aminoglycosides, foscarnet, and I.V. pentamidine) should not be used with or within 7 days of cidofovir therapy. Due to concomitant probenecid administration, temporarily discontinue or decrease zidovudine dose by 50% on the day of cidofovir administration only.

Stability Store at controlled room temperature 20°C to 25°C (68°F to 77°F). Dilute dose in NS 100 mL prior to infusion. Store admixtures under refrigeration for ≤24 hours. Cidofovir infusion admixture should be administered within 24 hours of preparation at room temperature or refrigerated. Admixtures should be allowed to equilibrate to room temperature prior to use.

Mechanism of Action Cidofovir is converted to cidofovir diphosphate which is the active intracellular metabolite; cidofovir diphosphate suppresses CMV replication by selective inhibition of viral DNA synthesis. Incorporation of cidofovir into growing viral DNA chain results in reductions in the rate of viral DNA synthesis.

Pharmacodynamics/Kinetics The following pharmacokinetic data is based on a combination of cidofovir administered with probenecid:
Distribution: V_d: 0.54 L/kg; does not cross significantly into CSF
(Continued)

Cidofovir (Continued)

Protein binding: <6%
Metabolism: Minimal; phosphorylation occurs intracellularly
Half-life elimination, plasma: ~2.6 hours
Excretion: Urine

Dosage Adults:
Induction: 5 mg/kg I.V. over 1 hour once weekly for 2 consecutive weeks
Maintenance: 5 mg/kg over 1 hour once every other week

Note: Administer with probenecid 2 g orally 3 hours prior to each cidofovir dose and 1 g at 2 hours and 8 hours after completion of the infusion (total: 4 g)

Hydrate with 1 L of 0.9% NS I.V. prior to cidofovir infusion; a second liter may be administered over a 1- to 3-hour period immediately following infusion, if tolerated

Dosing adjustment in renal impairment:
Changes in renal function during therapy: If the creatinine increases by 0.3-0.4 mg/dL, reduce the cidofovir dose to 3 mg/kg; discontinue therapy for increases ≥0.5 mg/dL or development of ≥3+ proteinuria

Pre-existing renal impairment: Use is contraindicated with serum creatinine >1.5 mg/dL, Cl$_{cr}$ <55 mL/minute, or urine protein ≥100 mg/dL (≥2+ proteinuria)

Administration For I.V. infusion only. Infuse over 1 hour. Hydrate with 1 L of 0.9% NS I.V. prior to cidofovir infusion. A second liter may be administered over a 1- to 3-hour period immediately following infusion, if tolerated.

Monitoring Parameters Renal function (Cr, BUN, UAs) within 48 hours of each dose, LFTs, WBCs; intraocular pressure and visual acuity, signs and symptoms of uveitis/iritis

Dosage Forms Injection, solution [preservative free]: 75 mg/mL (5 mL)

Cilostazol (sil OH sta zol)

U.S. Brand Names Pletal®
Canadian Brand Names Pletal®
Index Terms OPC-13013
Pharmacologic Category Antiplatelet Agent; Phosphodiesterase Enzyme Inhibitor
Use Symptomatic management of peripheral vascular disease, primarily intermittent claudication
Unlabeled/Investigational Use Treatment of acute coronary syndromes and for graft patency improvement in percutaneous coronary interventions with or without stenting
Pregnancy Risk Factor C
Pregnancy Implications In animal studies, abnormalities of the skeletal, renal and cardiovascular system were increased. In addition, the incidence of stillbirth and decreased birth weights were increased.
Lactation Excretion in breast milk unknown/not recommended
Medication Safety Issues
Sound-alike/look-alike issues:
Pletal® may be confused with Plendil®
Contraindications Hypersensitivity to cilostazol or any component of the formulation; heart failure (of any severity)
Warnings/Precautions Use with caution in patients receiving other platelet aggregation inhibitors or in patients with thrombocytopenia. Discontinue therapy if thrombocytopenia or leukopenia occur, progression to agranulocytosis (reversible) has been reported when cilostazol was not immediately stopped. When cilostazol and clopidogrel are used concurrently, manufacturer recommends checking bleeding times. Withhold for at least 4-6 half-lives prior to elective surgical procedures. Use with caution in patients receiving CYP3A4 inhibitors (eg, ketoconazole or erythromycin) or CYP2C19 inhibitors (eg, omeprazole). **[U.S. Boxed Warning]: Heart disease (of any severity)**; use with caution in severe underlying heart disease. Use caution in moderate-to-severe hepatic impairment. Use cautiously in severe renal impairment (Cl$_{cr}$ <25 mL/minute). Safety and efficacy in pediatric patients have not been established.

Adverse Reactions
>10%:
Central nervous system: Headache (27% to 34%)
Gastrointestinal: Abnormal stools (12% to 15%), diarrhea (12% to 19%)
Respiratory: Rhinitis (7% to 12%)
Miscellaneous: Infection (10% to 14%)
2% to 10%:
Cardiovascular: Peripheral edema (7% to 9%), palpitation (5% to 10%), tachycardia (4%)
Central nervous system: Dizziness (9% to 10%), vertigo (up to 3%)
Gastrointestinal: Dyspepsia (6%), nausea (6% to 7%), abdominal pain (4% to 5%), flatulence (2% to 3%)
Neuromuscular & skeletal: Back pain (6% to 7%), myalgia (2% to 3%)
Respiratory: Pharyngitis (7% to 10%), cough (3% to 4%)
<2% (Limited to important or life-threatening): Agranulocytosis, anemia, asthma, atrial fibrillation, atrial flutter, blindness, bursitis, cardiac arrest, cerebral infarction/ischemia, cholelithiasis, colitis, CHF, cystitis, diabetes mellitus, duodenal ulcer, duodenitis, esophageal hemorrhage, esophagitis, extradural hematoma, gout, granulocytopenia, hemorrhage, hepatic dysfunction, hypotension, leukopenia, myocardial infarction/ischemia, neuralgia, nodal arrhythmia, periodontal abscess, peptic ulcer, pneumonia, polycythemia, postural hypotension, QT$_c$ prolongation, rectal hemorrhage, retinal hemorrhage, retroperitoneal hemorrhage, Stevens-Johnson syndrome, subdural hematoma, supraventricular tachycardia, syncope, thrombocytopenia, thrombosis, torsade de pointes, ventricular tachycardia

Overdosage/Toxicology Experience with overdosage in humans is limited. Headache, diarrhea, hypotension, tachycardia and/or cardiac arrhythmias may occur. Treatment is symptomatic and supportive. Hemodialysis is unlikely to be of value. In some animal models, high-dose or long-term administration was associated with a variety of cardiovascular lesions, including endocardial hemorrhage, hemosiderin deposition and left ventricular fibrosis, coronary arteritis, and periarteritis.

Drug Interactions

Cytochrome P450 Effect: Substrate of CYP1A2 (minor), 2C19 (minor), 2D6 (minor), 3A4 (major)

Increased Effect/Toxicity: Cilostazol serum concentrations may be increased by antifungal agents (midazole), macrolide antibiotics, and omeprazole. Increased concentrations of cilostazol may be anticipated during concurrent therapy with other inhibitors of CYP3A4 (eg, clarithromycin, diclofenac, doxycycline, erythromycin, imatinib, isoniazid, nefazodone, nicardipine, propofol, protease inhibitors, quinidine, telithromycin, and verapamil) or inhibitors of CYP2C19 (eg, delavirdine, fluconazole, fluvoxamine, gemfibrozil, isoniazid, omeprazole, and ticlopidine). Aspirin-induced inhibition of platelet aggregation is potentiated by concurrent cilostazol. Concurrent use of drotrecogin alfa, NSAIDs, or treprostinil may cause increased bleeding.

Ethanol/Nutrition/Herb Interactions Food: Taking cilostazol with a high-fat meal may increase peak concentration by 90%. Avoid concurrent ingestion of grapefruit juice due to the potential to inhibit CYP3A4.

Mechanism of Action Cilostazol and its metabolites are inhibitors of phosphodiesterase III. As a result, cyclic AMP is increased leading to reversible inhibition of platelet aggregation and vasodilation. Other effects of phosphodiesterase III inhibition include increased cardiac contractility, accelerated AV nodal conduction, increased ventricular automaticity, heart rate, and coronary blood flow.

Pharmacodynamics/Kinetics

Onset of action: 2-4 weeks; may require up to 12 weeks

Protein binding: 97% to 98%

Metabolism: Hepatic via CYP3A4 (primarily), 1A2, 2C19, and 2D6, at least one metabolite has significant activity

Half-life elimination: 11-13 hours

Excretion: Urine (74%) and feces (20%) as metabolites

Dosage Adults: Oral: 100 mg twice daily taken at least one-half hour before or 2 hours after breakfast and dinner; dosage should be reduced to 50 mg twice daily during concurrent therapy with inhibitors of CYP3A4 or CYP2C19 (see Drug Interactions)

Dietary Considerations It is best to take cilostazol 30 minutes before or 2 hours after meals.

Dosage Forms

Tablet: 50 mg, 100 mg

Pletal®: 50 mg, 100 mg

♦ **Ciloxan®** see Ciprofloxacin *on page 372*

Cimetidine (sye MET i deen)

U.S. Brand Names Tagamet® [DSC]; Tagamet® HB 200 [OTC]

Canadian Brand Names Apo-Cimetidine®; Gen-Cimetidine; Novo-Cimetidine; Nu-Cimet; PMS-Cimetidine; Tagamet® HB

Pharmacologic Category Histamine H_2 Antagonist

Use Short-term treatment of active duodenal ulcers and benign gastric ulcers; long-term prophylaxis of duodenal ulcer; gastric hypersecretory states; gastroesophageal reflux; prevention of upper GI bleeding in critically-ill patients; labeled for OTC use for prevention or relief of heartburn, acid indigestion, or sour stomach

Unlabeled/Investigational Use Part of a multidrug regimen for *H. pylori* eradication to reduce the risk of duodenal ulcer recurrence

Pregnancy Risk Factor B

Pregnancy Implications Teratogenic events were not observed in animal studies.

Lactation Enters breast milk/not recommended

Medication Safety Issues

Sound-alike/look-alike issues:

Cimetidine may be confused with simethicone

Contraindications Hypersensitivity to cimetidine, any component of the formulation, or other H_2 antagonists

Warnings/Precautions Reversible confusional states, usually clearing within 3-4 days after discontinuation, have been linked to use. Increased age (>50 years) and renal or hepatic impairment are thought to be associated. Dosage should be adjusted in renal/hepatic impairment or in patients receiving drugs metabolized through the P450 system. Rapid intravenous administration has been associated with rare cases of arrhythmia and/or hypotension.

Over the counter (OTC) cimetidine should not be taken by individuals experiencing painful swallowing, vomiting with blood, or bloody or black stools; medical attention should be sought. A physician should be consulted prior to use when pain in the stomach, shoulder, arms or neck is present; if heartburn has occurred for >3 months; or if unexplained weight loss, or nausea and vomiting occur. Frequent wheezing, shortness of breath, lightheadedness, or sweating, especially with chest pain or heartburn, should also be reported. Consultation of a healthcare provider should occur by patients if also taking theophylline, phenytoin, or warfarin; if heartburn or stomach pain continues or worsens; or if use is required for >14 days. Symptoms of GI distress may be associated with a variety of conditions; symptomatic response to H_2 antagonists does not rule out the potential for significant pathology (eg, malignancy). OTC cimetidine is not approved for use in patients <12 years of age.

Adverse Reactions

1% to 10%:

Central nervous system: Headache (2% to 4%), dizziness (1%), somnolence (1%), agitation

Endocrine & metabolic: Gynecomastia (<1% to 4%)

Gastrointestinal: Diarrhea (1%)

Frequency not defined:

Cardiovascular: AV block, bradycardia, hypotension, tachycardia, vasculitis

(Continued)

Cimetidine *(Continued)*

Central nervous system: Confusion, fever

Dermatologic: Alopecia, erythema multiforme, exfoliative dermatitis, Stevens-Johnson syndrome, toxic epidermal necrolysis, rash

Endocrine & metabolic: Edema of the breasts, sexual ability decreased

Gastrointestinal: Nausea, pancreatitis, vomiting

Hematologic: Agranulocytosis, aplastic anemia, hemolytic anemia (immune-based), neutropenia, pancytopenia, thrombocytopenia

Hepatic: AST/ALT increased, hepatic fibrosis (case report)

Neuromuscular & skeletal: Arthralgia, myalgia, polymyositis

Renal: Creatinine increased, interstitial nephritis

Miscellaneous: Anaphylaxis, pneumonia (causal relationship not established)

Overdosage/Toxicology Reported ingestions of up to 20 g have resulted in transient side effects seen with recommended doses. Reports of ingestions up to 40 g have documented severe CNS depression, including unresponsiveness. Treatment is symptom-directed and supportive. Animal data suggests that ventilation assistance and beta-blocker treatment may be effective in managing the possible respiratory depression and tachycardia, respectively.

Drug Interactions

Cytochrome P450 Effect: Inhibits CYP1A2 (moderate), 2C9 (weak), 2C19 (moderate), 2D6 (moderate), 2E1 (weak), 3A4 (moderate)

Increased Effect/Toxicity: Cimetidine may increase the levels/effects of aminophylline, amphetamines, selected beta-blockers, selected benzodiazepines, calcium channel blockers, cyclosporine, dextromethorphan, dofetilide, ergot derivatives, lidocaine, meperidine, metformin, methsuximide, metronidazole, mexiletine, mirtazapine, moricizine, nateglinide, nefazodone, paroxetine (and other SSRIs), phenytoin, procainamide, propafenone, propranolol, quinidine, quinolone antibiotics, risperidone, ritonavir, ropinirole, sildenafil (and other PDE-5 inhibitors), sulfonylureas, tacrine, tacrolimus, theophylline, thioridazine, triamterene, tricyclic antidepressants, trifluoperazine, venlafaxine, and other CYP1A2, 2C19, or 2D6 substrates.

Cimetidine increases warfarin's effect in a dose-related manner. Cimetidine increases carmustine's myelotoxicity; avoid concurrent use.

Decreased Effect: Cimetidine may decrease the levels/effects of CYP2D6 prodrug substrates (eg, codeine, hydrocodone, oxycodone, and tramadol). Ketoconazole, fluconazole, itraconazole (especially capsule) decrease serum concentration; avoid concurrent use with H_2 antagonists. Absorption of delavirdine and atazanavir may be decreased; avoid concurrent use of delavirdine with H_2 antagonists.

Ethanol/Nutrition/Herb Interactions

Ethanol: Avoid ethanol (may enhance gastric mucosal irritation).

Food: Cimetidine may increase serum caffeine levels if taken with caffeine. Cimetidine peak serum levels may be decreased if taken with food.

Herb/Nutraceutical: St John's wort may decrease cimetidine levels.

Stability

Tablet: Store between 15°C and 30°C (59°F to 86°F); protect from light.

Solution for injection/infusion: Intact vials should be stored at room temperature, between 15°C and 30°C (59°F to 86°F); protect from light. May precipitate from solution upon exposure to cold, but can be redissolved by warming without degradation.

Stability at room temperature:

Prepared bags: 7 days

Premixed bags: Manufacturer expiration dating and out of overwrap stability: 15 days

Stable in parenteral nutrition solutions for up to 7 days when protected from light.

Mechanism of Action Competitive inhibition of histamine at H_2 receptors of the gastric parietal cells resulting in reduced gastric acid secretion, gastric volume and hydrogen ion concentration reduced

Pharmacodynamics/Kinetics

Onset of action: 1 hour

Duration: 4-8 hours

Absorption: Rapid

Distribution: Crosses placenta; enters breast milk

Protein binding: 20%

Metabolism: Partially hepatic, forms metabolites

Bioavailability: 60% to 70%

Half-life elimination: Neonates: 3.6 hours; Children: 1.4 hours; Adults: Normal renal function: 2 hours

Time to peak, serum: Oral: 1-2 hours

Excretion: Primarily urine (48% as unchanged drug); feces (some)

Dosage

Children: Oral, I.M., I.V.: 20-40 mg/kg/day in divided doses every 6 hours

Children ≥12 years and Adults: Oral: Heartburn, acid indigestion, sour stomach (OTC labeling): 200 mg up to twice daily; may take 30 minutes prior to eating foods or beverages expected to cause heartburn or indigestion

Adults:

Short-term treatment of active ulcers:

Oral: 300 mg 4 times/day or 800 mg at bedtime or 400 mg twice daily for up to 8 weeks

Note: Higher doses of 1600 mg at bedtime for 4 weeks may be beneficial for a subpopulation of patients with larger duodenal ulcers (>1 cm defined endoscopically) who are also heavy smokers (≥1 pack/day).

I.M., I.V.: 300 mg every 6 hours or 37.5 mg/hour by continuous infusion; I.V. dosage should be adjusted to maintain an intragastric pH ≥5

Prevention of upper GI bleed in critically-ill patients: 50 mg/hour by continuous infusion; I.V. dosage should be adjusted to maintain an intragastric pH ≥5

Note: Reduce dose by 50% if Cl_{cr} <30 mL/minute; treatment >7 days has not been evaluated.

Duodenal ulcer prophylaxis: Oral: 400 mg at bedtime

Gastric hypersecretory conditions: Oral, I.M., I.V.: 300-600 mg every 6 hours; dosage not to exceed 2.4 g/day

Gastroesophageal reflux disease: Oral: 400 mg 4 times/day or 800 mg twice daily for 12 weeks

Helicobacter pylori eradication (unlabeled use): 400 mg twice daily; requires combination therapy with antibiotics

Dosing adjustment/interval in renal impairment: Children and Adults:

Cl_{cr} 10-50 mL/minute: Administer 50% of normal dose

Cl_{cr} 10-50 mL/minute: Administer 50% of normal dose

Cl_{cr} <10 mL/minute: Administer 25% of normal dose

Hemodialysis: Slightly dialyzable (5% to 20%); administer after dialysis

Dosing adjustment/comments in hepatic impairment: Usual dose is safe in mild liver disease but use with caution and in reduced dosage in severe liver disease; increased risk of CNS toxicity in cirrhosis suggested by enhanced penetration of CNS

Administration

Oral: Administer with meals so that the drug's peak effect occurs at the proper time (peak inhibition of gastric acid secretion occurs at 1 and 3 hours after dosing in fasting subjects and approximately 2 hours in nonfasting subjects; this correlates well with the time food is no longer in the stomach offering a buffering effect)

Injection: May be administered as a slow I.V. push or preferably as an I.V. intermittent or I.V. continuous infusion. Administer each 300 mg (or fraction thereof) over a minimum of 5 minutes when giving I.V. push. Rapid intravenous administration has been associated with rare cases of arrhythmia and/or hypotension. Give intermittent infusion over 15-30 minutes for each 300 mg dose. Intermittent infusions are administered over 15-30 minutes at a final concentration not to exceed 6 mg/mL; for patients with an active bleed, preferred method of administration is continuous infusion.

Monitoring Parameters CBC, gastric pH, occult blood with GI bleeding; monitor renal function to correct dose.

Dosage Forms [DSC] = Discontinued product

Infusion, as hydrochloride [premixed in NS]: 300 mg (50 mL)

Injection, solution, as hydrochloride: 150 mg/mL (2 mL, 8 mL) [8 mL size contains benzyl alcohol]

Liquid, oral, as hydrochloride: 300 mg/5 mL (240 mL, 480 mL) [contains alcohol 2.8%; mint-peach flavor]

Tablet: 200 mg [OTC], 300 mg, 400 mg, 800 mg

Tagamet®: 300 mg, 400 mg [DSC]

Tagamet® HB 200: 200 mg

Cinacalcet (sin a KAL cet)

U.S. Brand Names Sensipar™

Index Terms AMG 073; Cinacalcet Hydrochloride

Pharmacologic Category Calcimimetic

Use Treatment of secondary hyperparathyroidism in dialysis patients; treatment of hypercalcemia in patients with parathyroid carcinoma

Unlabeled/Investigational Use Primary hyperparathyroidism

Pregnancy Risk Factor C

Pregnancy Implications In animal studies, there were no teratogenic effects seen. There are no adequate or well-controlled studies in pregnant women.

Lactation Excretion in breast milk unknown/not recommended

Contraindications Hypersensitivity to cinacalcet or any component of the formulation

Warnings/Precautions If hypocalcemia develops during treatment, consider initiating treatment or temporarily withholding cinacalcet. Use caution in patients with a seizure disorder. Adynamic bone disease may develop if iPTH levels are suppressed (<100 pg/mL). Chronic kidney disease patients with hyperparathyroidism not requiring dialysis may be at increased risk for developing hypocalcemia. Use caution in patients with hepatic impairment. Safety and efficacy have not been established in pediatric patients.

Adverse Reactions

>10%:

Endocrine & metabolic: Hypocalcemia

Gastrointestinal: Nausea (31%), vomiting (27%), diarrhea (21%)

Neuromuscular & skeletal: Myalgia (15%)

1% to 10%:

Cardiovascular: Hypertension (7%)

Central nervous system: Dizziness (10%), seizure (1%)

Endocrine & metabolic: Testosterone decreased

Gastrointestinal: Anorexia (6%)

Neuromuscular & skeletal: Weakness (7%), chest pain (6%)

Overdosage/Toxicology Overdose may cause hypocalcemia. Signs and symptoms may include paresthesias, myalgias, cramping, tetany, and seizures. Treatment is symptom-directed and supportive. Cinacalcet is not removed by dialysis.

Drug Interactions

Cytochrome P450 Effect: Substrate of CYP1A2, 2D6, 3A4; **Inhibits** CYP2D6

Increased Effect/Toxicity: Cinacalcet increases levels of amitriptyline and nortriptyline. Ketoconazole may increase cinacalcet levels.

Ethanol/Nutrition/Herb Interactions Food: Food increases bioavailability.

Stability Store at 25°C (77°F).

Mechanism of Action Increases the sensitivity of the calcium-sensing receptor on the parathyroid gland.

Pharmacodynamics/Kinetics

Distribution: V_d: 1000 L

Protein binding: 93% to 97%

Metabolism: Hepatic via CYP3A4, 2D6, 1A2; forms inactive metabolites

Half-life elimination: Terminal: 30-40 hours

(Continued)

Cinacalcet *(Continued)*

Time to peak, plasma: Nadir in iPTH levels: 2-6 hours postdose

Excretion: Urine 80% (as metabolites); feces 15%

Dosage Oral: Adults: **Do not titrate dose more frequently than every 2-4 weeks.**

Secondary hyperparathyroidism: Initial: 30 mg once daily (maximum daily dose: 180 mg); increase dose incrementally (60 mg, 90 mg, 120 mg, 180 mg once daily) as necessary to maintain iPTH level between 150-300 pg/mL.

Parathyroid carcinoma: Initial: 30 mg twice daily (maximum daily dose: 360 mg daily as 90 mg 4 times/day); increase dose incrementally (60 mg twice daily, 90 mg twice daily, 90 mg 4 times/day) as necessary to normalize serum calcium levels.

Elderly: No adjustment required; refer to adult dosing

Dosage adjustment for hypocalcemia:

If serum calcium >7.5 mg/dL but <8.4 mg/dL **or** if hypocalcemia symptoms occur: Use calcium-containing phosphate binders and/or vitamin D to raise calcium levels.

If serum calcium <7.5 mg/dL **or** if hypocalcemia symptoms occur and the dose of vitamin D cannot be increased: Discontinue cinacalcet until serum calcium ≥8 mg/dL or symptoms of hypocalcemia resolve. Reinitiate cinacalcet at the next lowest dose.

If iPTH <150-300 pg/mL: Reduce dose or discontinue cinacalcet and/or vitamin D.

Dosage adjustment in renal impairment: No adjustment required.

Dosage adjustment in hepatic impairment: Patients with moderate to severe dysfunction have an increased exposure to cinacalcet and increased half-life.

Dietary Considerations Take with food. May be taken with vitamin D and/or phosphate binders.

Administration Administer with food. Do not break tablet; should be taken whole.

Monitoring Parameters

Hyperparathyroidism: Serum calcium levels prior to initiation and within a week of initiation or dosage adjustment; iPTH should be measured 1-4 weeks after initiation or dosage adjustment. After the maintenance dose is established, monthly calcium and phosphorus levels and iPTH every 1-3 months are required.

Parathyroid carcinoma: Serum calcium levels prior to initiation and within a week of initiation or dosage adjustment; once maintenance dose is established, obtain serum calcium level every 2 months.

Reference Range Chronic kidney disease: Goal iPTH: 150-300 pg/mL

Dosage Forms Tablet: 30 mg, 60 mg, 90 mg

♦ **Cinacalcet Hydrochloride** *see Cinacalcet on page 371*

♦ **Cipralex® (Can)** *see Escitalopram on page 613*

♦ **Cipro®** *see Ciprofloxacin on page 372*

♦ **Cipro® XL (Can)** *see Ciprofloxacin on page 372*

♦ **Ciprodex®** *see Ciprofloxacin and Dexamethasone on page 376*

Ciprofloxacin (sip roe FLOKS a sin)

U.S. Brand Names Ciloxan®; Cipro®; Cipro® XR; Proquin® XR

Canadian Brand Names Apo-Ciprofloxx®; Ciloxan®; Cipro®; Cipro® XL; CO Ciprofloxacin; Gen-Ciprofloxacin; Novo-Ciprofloxacin; PMS-Ciprofloxacin; RAN™-Ciprofloxacin; ratio-Ciprofloxacin; Rhoxal-ciprofloxacin; Sandoz-Ciprofloxacin; Taro-Ciprofloxacin

Index Terms Ciprofloxacin Hydrochloride

Pharmacologic Category Antibiotic, Ophthalmic; Antibiotic, Quinolone

Additional Appendix Information

Antimicrobial Drugs of Choice *on page 1981*

Community-Acquired Pneumonia in Adults *on page 1999*

Desensitization Protocols *on page 1913*

Prevention of Wound Infection and Sepsis in Surgical Patients *on page 1964*

Treatment of Sexually Transmitted Infections *on page 2007*

Tuberculosis *on page 2010*

Use

Children: Complicated urinary tract infections and pyelonephritis due to *E. coli*. **Note:** Although effective, ciprofloxacin is not the drug of first choice in children.

Children and adults: To reduce incidence or progression of disease following exposure to aerolized *Bacillus anthracis*. Ophthalmologically, for superficial ocular infections (corneal ulcers, conjunctivitis) due to susceptible strains

Adults: Treatment of the following infections when caused by susceptible bacteria: Urinary tract infections; acute uncomplicated cystitis in females; chronic bacterial prostatitis; lower respiratory tract infections (including acute exacerbations of chronic bronchitis); acute sinusitis; skin and skin structure infections; bone and joint infections; complicated intra-abdominal infections (in combination with metronidazole); infectious diarrhea; typhoid fever due to *Salmonella typhi* (eradication of chronic typhoid carrier state has not been proven); uncomplicated cervical and urethra gonorrhea (due to *N. gonorrhoeae*); nosocomial pneumonia; empirical therapy for febrile neutropenic patients (in combination with piperacillin)

Unlabeled/Investigational Use Acute pulmonary exacerbations in cystic fibrosis (children); cutaneous/gastrointestinal/oropharyngeal anthrax (treatment, children and adults); disseminated gonococcal infection (adults); chancroid (adults); prophylaxis to *Neisseria meningitidis* following close contact with an infected person; empirical therapy (oral) for febrile neutropenia in low-risk cancer patients; infectious diarrhea (children)

Pregnancy Risk Factor C

Pregnancy Implications Ciprofloxacin crosses the placenta and concentrates in amniotic fluid; maternal serum levels may be decreased during pregnancy. Reports of arthropathy (observed in immature animals and reported rarely in humans) have limited the use of fluoroquinolones in pregnancy. According to the FDA, the Teratogen Information System concluded that therapeutic doses during pregnancy are unlikely to produce substantial teratogenic risk, but data are insufficient to say that there is no risk. In general, reports of exposure have been limited to short durations of therapy in the first trimester. When considering treatment for life-threatening infection and/or prolonged duration of therapy (such as in anthrax), the potential risk to the fetus must be balanced against the severity of the potential illness.

Lactation Enters breast milk/not recommended (AAP rates "compatible")

Medication Safety Issues
Sound-alike/look-alike issues:
Ciprofloxacin may be confused with cephalexin
Ciloxan® may be confused with cinoxacin, Cytoxan®
Cipro® may be confused with Ceftin®

Contraindications Hypersensitivity to ciprofloxacin, any component of the formulation, or other quinolones; concurrent administration of tizanidine

Warnings/Precautions CNS stimulation may occur (tremor, restlessness, confusion, and very rarely hallucinations or seizures). Use with caution in patients with known or suspected CNS disorder. Potential for seizures, although very rare, may be increased with concomitant NSAID therapy. Use with caution in individuals at risk of seizures. Prolonged use may result in superinfection. Tendon inflammation and/or rupture have been reported with ciprofloxacin and other quinolone antibiotics. Risk may be increased with concurrent corticosteroids, particularly in the elderly. Discontinue at first sign of tendon inflammation or pain. Adverse effects, including those related to joints and/or surrounding tissues, are increased in pediatric patients and therefore, ciprofloxacin should not be considered as drug of choice in children (exception is anthrax treatment). Rare cases of peripheral neuropathy may occur.

Severe hypersensitivity reactions, including anaphylaxis, have occurred with quinolone therapy. Quinolones may exacerbate myasthenia gravis, use with caution (rare, potentially life-threatening weakness of respiratory muscles may occur). Use caution in renal impairment. Avoid excessive sunlight; may cause moderate-to-severe phototoxicity reactions.

Ciprofloxacin is a potent inhibitor of CYP1A2. Coadministration of drugs which depend on this pathway may lead to substantial increases in serum concentrations and adverse effects.

Adverse Reactions
1% to 10%:
Central nervous system: Neurologic events (children 2%, includes dizziness, insomnia, nervousness, somnolence); fever (children 2%); headache (I.V. administration); restlessness (I.V. administration)
Dermatologic: Rash (children 2%, adults 1%)
Gastrointestinal: Nausea (children/adults 3%); diarrhea (children 5%, adults 2%); vomiting (children 5%, adults 1%); abdominal pain (children 3%, adults <1%); dyspepsia (children 3%)
Hepatic: ALT/AST increased (adults 1%)
Local: Injection site reactions (I.V. administration)
Respiratory: Rhinitis (children 3%)
<1% (Limited to important or life-threatening): Abnormal gait, acute renal failure, agitation, agranulocytosis, albuminuria, allergic reactions, anaphylactic shock, anaphylaxis, anemia, angina pectoris, angioedema, anorexia, anosmia, arthralgia, ataxia, atrial flutter, bone marrow depression (life-threatening), breast pain, bronchospasm, candidiasis, candiduria, cardiopulmonary arrest, cerebral thrombosis, chills, cholestatic jaundice, chromatopsia, confusion, constipation, crystalluria (particularly in alkaline urine), cylindruria, delirium, depersonalization, depression, diarrhea, drowsiness, dyspepsia (adults), dysphagia, dyspnea, edema, eosinophilia, erythema multiforme, erythema nodosum, exfoliative dermatitis, fever (adults), fixed eruption, flatulence, gastrointestinal bleeding, hallucinations, headache (oral), hematuria, hemolytic anemia, hepatic failure, hepatic necrosis, hyperesthesia, hyperglycemia, hyperpigmentation, hyper-/hypotension, hypertonia, insomnia, interstitial nephritis, intestinal perforation, irritability, jaundice, joint pain, laryngeal edema, lightheadedness, lymphadenopathy, malaise, manic reaction, methemoglobinemia, MI, migraine, moniliasis, myalgia, myasthenia gravis, myoclonus, nephritis, nightmares, nystagmus, orthostatic hypotension, palpitation, pancreatitis, pancytopenia (life-threatening or fatal), paranoia, paresthesia, peripheral neuropathy, petechia, photosensitivity, prolongation of PT/INR, pseudomembranous colitis, psychosis, pulmonary edema, renal calculi, seizure; serum cholesterol, glucose, triglycerides increased; serum sickness-like reactions, Stevens-Johnson syndrome, syncope, tachycardia, taste loss, tendon rupture, tendonitis, thrombophlebitis, tinnitus, torsade de pointes, toxic epidermal necrolysis (Lyell's syndrome), tremor, twitching, urethral bleeding, vaginal candidiasis, vaginitis, vasculitis, ventricular ectopy, visual disturbance, weakness

Overdosage/Toxicology Symptoms include acute renal failure and seizures. Treatment is supportive and should include adequate hydration and renal function monitoring. Magnesium- or calcium-containing antacids may be given to decrease absorption of oral ciprofloxacin. Only a small amount of ciprofloxacin (<10%) is removed from the body after hemodialysis or peritoneal dialysis.

Drug Interactions
Cytochrome P450 Effect: Inhibits CYP1A2 (strong), 3A4 (weak)
Increased Effect/Toxicity: Ciprofloxacin may increase serum levels of tizanidine; concurrent administration is contraindicated. Ciprofloxacin may increase the effects/toxicity of caffeine, CYP1A2 substrates (eg, aminophylline, fluvoxamine, mexiletine, mirtazapine, ropinirole, tizanidine, and trifluoperazine), glyburide, methotrexate, ropivacaine, theophylline, and warfarin. Headache has been observed with concomitant pentoxifylline therapy. Concomitant use with corticosteroids may increase the risk of tendon rupture. Concomitant use with foscarnet or NSAIDs may increase the risk of seizures. Probenecid may increase ciprofloxacin levels.
Decreased Effect: Concurrent administration of metal cations, including most antacids, oral electrolyte supplements, quinapril, sucralfate, some didanosine formulations (pediatric powder for oral suspension), other highly-buffered oral drugs, and sevelamer may decrease quinolone absorption; separate doses. Ciprofloxacin may decrease phenytoin levels.
(Continued)

Ciprofloxacin *(Continued)*

Ethanol/Nutrition/Herb Interactions

Food: Food decreases rate, but not extent, of absorption. Ciprofloxacin serum levels may be decreased if taken with dairy products or calcium-fortified juices. Ciprofloxacin may increase serum caffeine levels if taken with caffeine.

Enteral feedings may decrease plasma concentrations of ciprofloxacin probably by >30% inhibition of absorption. Ciprofloxacin should not be administered with enteral feedings. The feeding would need to be discontinued for 1-2 hours prior to and after ciprofloxacin administration. Nasogastric administration produces a greater loss of ciprofloxacin bioavailability than does nasoduodenal administration.

Herb/Nutraceutical: Avoid dong quai, St John's wort (may also cause photosensitization).

Stability

Injection:

Premixed infusion: Store between 5°C to 25°C (41°F to 77°F); avoid freezing. Protect from light.

Vial: Store between 5°C to 30°C (41°F to 86°F); avoid freezing. Protect from light. May be diluted with NS, D$_5$W, SWFI, D$_{10}$W, D$_5$^{1}/$_4$NS, D$_5$^{1}/$_2$NS, LR. Diluted solutions of 0.5-2 mg/mL are stable for up to 14 days refrigerated or at room temperature.

Ophthalmic solution/ointment: Store at 36°F to 77°F (2°C to 25°C); protect from light.

Microcapsules for oral suspension: Prior to reconstitution, store below 25°C (77°F); protect from freezing. Following reconstitution, store below 30°C (86°F) for up to 14 days; protect from freezing.

Tablet:

Immediate release: Store below 30°C (86°F).

Extended release: Store at room temperature of 15°C to 30°C (59°F to 86°F).

Mechanism of Action Inhibits DNA-gyrase in susceptible organisms; inhibits relaxation of supercoiled DNA and promotes breakage of double-stranded DNA

Pharmacodynamics/Kinetics

Absorption: Oral: Immediate release tablet: Rapid (~50% to 85%)

Distribution: V$_d$: 2.1-2.7 L/kg; tissue concentrations often exceed serum concentrations especially in kidneys, gallbladder, liver, lungs, gynecological tissue, and prostatic tissue; CSF concentrations: 10% of serum concentrations (noninflamed meninges), 14% to 37% (inflamed meninges); crosses placenta; enters breast milk

Protein binding: 20% to 40%

Metabolism: Partially hepatic; forms 4 metabolites (limited activity)

Half-life elimination: Children: 2.5 hours; Adults: Normal renal function: 3-5 hours

Time to peak: Oral:

Immediate release tablet: 0.5-2 hours

Extended release tablet: Cipro® XR: 1-2.5 hours, Proquin® XR: 3.5-8.7 hours

Excretion: Urine (30% to 50% as unchanged drug); feces (15% to 43%)

Dosage Note: Extended release tablets and immediate release formulations are not interchangeable. Unless otherwise specified, oral dosing reflects the use of immediate release formulations.

Usual dosage ranges:

Children (see Warnings/Precautions):

Oral: 20-30 mg/kg/day in 2 divided doses; maximum dose: 1.5 g/day

I.V.: 20-30 mg/kg/day divided every 12 hours; maximum dose: 800 mg/day

Adults:

Oral: 250-750 mg every 12 hours

I.V.: 200-400 mg every 12 hours

Indication-specific dosing:

Children:

Anthrax:

Inhalational (postexposure prophylaxis):

Oral: 15 mg/kg/dose every 12 hours for 60 days; maximum: 500 mg/dose

I.V.: 10 mg/kg/dose every 12 hours for 60 days; do **not** exceed 400 mg/dose (800 mg/day)

Cutaneous (treatment, CDC guidelines): Oral: 10-15 mg/kg every 12 hours for 60 days (maximum: 1 g/day); amoxicillin 80 mg/kg/day divided every 8 hours is an option for completion of treatment after clinical improvement. **Note:** In the presence of systemic involvement, extensive edema, lesions on head/neck, refer to I.V. dosing for treatment of inhalational/gastrointestinal/oropharyngeal anthrax.

Inhalational/gastrointestinal/oropharyngeal (treatment, CDC guidelines): I.V.: Initial: 10-15 mg/kg every 12 hours for 60 days (maximum: 500 mg/dose); switch to oral therapy when clinically appropriate; refer to adult dosing for notes on combined therapy and duration

Bacterial conjunctivitis: See adult dosing

Corneal ulcer: See adult dosing

Cystic fibrosis (unlabeled use):

Oral: 40 mg/kg/day divided every 12 hours administered following 1 week of I.V. therapy has been reported in a clinical trial; total duration of therapy: 10-21 days

I.V.: 30 mg/kg/day divided every 8 hours for 1 week, followed by oral therapy, has been reported in a clinical trial

Urinary tract infection (complicated) or pyelonephritis:

Oral: 20-30 mg/kg/day in 2 divided doses (every 12 hours) for 10-21 days; maximum: 1.5 g/day

I.V.: 6-10 mg/kg every 8 hours for 10-21 days (maximum: 400 mg/dose)

Adults:

Anthrax:

Inhalational (postexposure prophylaxis):

Oral: 500 mg every 12 hours for 60 days

I.V.: 400 mg every 12 hours for 60 days

Cutaneous (treatment, CDC guidelines): Oral: Immediate release formulation: 500 mg every 12 hours for 60 days. **Note:** In the presence of systemic involvement, extensive edema, lesions on head/neck, refer to I.V. dosing for treatment of inhalational/gastrointestinal/oropharyngeal anthrax

Inhalational/gastrointestinal/oropharyngeal (treatment, CDC guidelines): I.V.: 400 mg every 12 hours. **Note:** Initial treatment should include two or more agents predicted to be effective (per CDC recommendations). Agents suggested for use in conjunction with ciprofloxacin or doxycycline include rifampin, vancomycin, imipenem, penicillin, ampicillin, chloramphenicol, clindamycin, and clarithromycin. May switch to oral antimicrobial therapy when clinically appropriate. Continue combined therapy for 60 days.

Bacterial conjunctivitis:
Ophthalmic solution: Instill 1-2 drops in eye(s) every 2 hours while awake for 2 days and 1-2 drops every 4 hours while awake for the next 5 days
Ophthalmic ointment: Apply a ½" ribbon into the conjunctival sac 3 times/day for the first 2 days, followed by a ½" ribbon applied twice daily for the next 5 days

Bone/joint infections:
Oral: 500-750 mg twice daily for 4-6 weeks, depending on severity and susceptibility
I.V.: Mild to moderate: 400 mg every 12 hours for 4-6 weeks; Severe/complicated: 400 mg every 8 hours for 4-6 weeks

Chancroid (CDC guidelines): Oral: 500 mg twice daily for 3 days

Corneal ulcer: Ophthalmic solution: Instill 2 drops into affected eye every 15 minutes for the first 6 hours, then 2 drops into the affected eye every 30 minutes for the remainder of the first day. On day 2, instill 2 drops into the affected eye hourly. On days 3-14, instill 2 drops into affected eye every 4 hours. Treatment may continue after day 14 if re-epithelialization has not occurred.

Febrile neutropenia (with piperacillin): I.V.: 400 mg every 8 hours for 7-14 days

Gonococcal infections:
Urethral/cervical gonococcal infections: Oral: 250-500 mg as a single dose (CDC recommends concomitant doxycycline or azithromycin due to developing resistance; avoid use in Asian or Western Pacific travelers)
Disseminated gonococcal infection (CDC guidelines): Oral: 500 mg twice daily to complete 7 days of therapy (initial treatment with ceftriaxone 1 g I.M./I.V. daily for 24-48 hours after improvement begins)

Infectious diarrhea: Oral:
Salmonella: 500 mg twice daily for 5-7 days
Shigella: 500 mg twice daily for 3 days
Traveler's diarrhea: Mild: 750 mg for one dose; Severe: 500 mg twice daily for 3 days
Vibrio cholerae: 1 g for one dose

Intra-abdominal (in combination with metronidazole):
Oral: 500 mg every 12 hours for 7-14 days
I.V.: 400 mg every 12 hours for 7-14 days

Lower respiratory tract, skin/skin structure infections:
Oral: 500-750 mg twice daily for 7-14 days depending on severity and susceptibility
I.V.: Mild to moderate: 400 mg every 12 hours for 7-14 days; Severe/complicated: 400 mg every 8 hours for 7-14 days

Nosocomial pneumonia: I.V.: 400 mg every 8 hours for 10-14 days

Prostatitis (chronic, bacterial):
Oral: 500 mg every 12 hours for 28 days
I.V.: 400 mg every 12 hours for 28 days

Sinusitis (acute):
Oral: 500 mg every 12 hours for 10 days
I.V.: 400 mg every 12 hours for 10 days

Typhoid fever: Oral: 500 mg every 12 hours for 10 days

Urinary tract infection:
Acute uncomplicated: Oral: Immediate release formulation: 250 mg every 12 hours for 3 days; Extended release formulation (Cipro® XR, Proquin® XR): 500 mg every 24 hours for 3 days
Acute uncomplicated pyelonephritis: Oral: Extended release formulation (Cipro® XR): 1000 mg every 24 hours for 7-14 days
Mild to moderate:
Oral: Immediate release formulation: 250 mg every 12 hours for 7-14 days
I.V.: 200 mg every 12 hours for 7-14 days
Severe/complicated:
Oral:
Immediate release formulation: 500 mg every 12 hours for 7-14 days
Extended release formulation (Cipro® XR): 1000 mg every 24 hours for 7-14 days
I.V.: 400 mg every 12 hours for 7-14 days

Elderly: No adjustment needed in patients with normal renal function

Dosing adjustment in renal impairment: Adults:
Cl_{cr} 30-50 mL/minute: Oral: 250-500 mg every 12 hours
Cl_{cr} <30 mL/minute: Acute uncomplicated pyelonephritis or complicated UTI: Oral: Extended release formulation: 500 mg every 24 hours
Cl_{cr} 5-29 mL/minute:
Oral: 250-500 mg every 18 hours
I.V.: 200-400 mg every 18-24 hours
Dialysis: Only small amounts of ciprofloxacin are removed by hemo- or peritoneal dialysis (<10%); usual dose: Oral: 250-500 mg every 24 hours following dialysis
Continuous arteriovenous or venovenous hemodiafiltration effects: Administer 200-400 mg I.V. every 12 hours

Dietary Considerations
Food: Drug may cause GI upset; take without regard to meals (manufacturer prefers that immediate release tablet is taken 2 hours after meals). Extended release tablet may be
(Continued)

Ciprofloxacin *(Continued)*

taken with meals that contain dairy products (calcium content <800 mg), but not with dairy products alone.

Dairy products, calcium-fortified juices, oral multivitamins, and mineral supplements: Absorption of ciprofloxacin is decreased by divalent and trivalent cations. The manufacturer states that the usual dietary intake of calcium (including meals which include dairy products) has not been shown to interfere with ciprofloxacin absorption. Immediate release ciprofloxacin and Cipro® XR may be taken 2 hours before or 6 hours after, and Proquin® XR may be taken 4 hours before or 6 hours after, any of these products.

Caffeine: Patients consuming regular large quantities of caffeinated beverages may need to restrict caffeine intake if excessive cardiac or CNS stimulation occurs.

Administration

Oral: May administer with food to minimize GI upset; avoid antacid use; maintain proper hydration and urine output. Administer immediate release ciprofloxacin and Cipro® XR at least 2 hours before or 6 hours after, and Proquin® XR at least 4 hours before or 6 hours after antacids or other products containing calcium, iron, or zinc (including dairy products or calcium-fortified juices). Separate oral administration from drugs which may impair absorption (see Drug Interactions).

Oral suspension: Should not be administered through feeding tubes (suspension is oil-based and adheres to the feeding tube). Patients should avoid chewing on the microcapsules.

Nasogastric/orogastric tube: Crush immediate-release tablet and mix with water. Flush feeding tube before and after administration. Hold tube feedings at least 1 hour before and 2 hours after administration.

Tablet, extended release: Do not crush, split, or chew. May be administered with meals containing dairy products (calcium content <800 mg), but not with dairy products alone. Proquin® XR should be administered with a main meal of the day; evening meal is preferred.

Parenteral: Administer by slow I.V. infusion over 60 minutes to reduce the risk of venous irritation (burning, pain, erythema, and swelling); final concentration for administration should not exceed 2 mg/mL.

Monitoring Parameters Patients receiving concurrent ciprofloxacin, theophylline, or cyclosporine should have serum levels monitored; CBC, renal and hepatic function during prolonged therapy

Reference Range Therapeutic: 2.6-3 mcg/mL; Toxic: >5 mcg/mL

Test Interactions Some quinolones may produce a false-positive urine screening result for opiates using commercially-available immunoassay kits. This has been demonstrated most consistently for levofloxacin and ofloxacin, but other quinolones have shown cross-reactivity in certain assay kits. Confirmation of positive opiate screens by more specific methods should be considered.

Additional Information Although the systemic use of ciprofloxacin is only FDA approved in children for the treatment of complicated UTI and postexposure treatment of inhalation anthrax, use of the fluoroquinolones in pediatric patients is increasing. Current recommendations by the American Academy of Pediatrics note that the systemic use of these agents in children should be restricted to infections caused by multidrug resistant pathogens with no safe or effective alternative, and when parenteral therapy is not feasible or other oral agents are not available.

Dosage Forms

Infusion [premixed in D₅W]:

Cipro®: 200 mg (100 mL); 400 mg (200 mL) [latex free]

Injection, solution: 10 mg/mL (20 mL, 40 mL)

Cipro®: 10 mg/mL (20 mL, 40 mL)

Microcapsules for suspension, oral:

Cipro®: 250 mg/5 mL (100 mL); 500 mg/5 mL (100 mL) [strawberry flavor]

Ointment, ophthalmic; as hydrochloride:

Ciloxan®: 3.33 mg/g [0.3% base] (3.5 g)

Solution, ophthalmic, as hydrochloride: 3.5 mg/mL (2.5 mL, 5mL, 10 mL) [0.3% base]

Ciloxin®: 3.5 mg/mL (2.5 mL, 5mL, 10 mL) [0.3% base; contains benzalkonium chloride]

Tablet: 250 mg, 500 mg, 750 mg

Cipro®: 250 mg, 500 mg, 750 mg

Tablet, extended release:

Cipro® XR: 500 mg [equivalent to ciprofloxacin hydrochloride 287.5 mg and ciprofloxacin base 212.6 mg]; 1000 mg [equivalent to ciprofloxacin hydrochloride 574.9 mg and ciprofloxacin base 425.2 mg]

Proquin® XR: 500 mg

Tablet, extended release [dose pack]:

Proquin® XR: 500 mg (3s)

Ciprofloxacin and Dexamethasone

(sip roe FLOKS a sin & deks a METH a sone)

U.S. Brand Names Ciprodex®

Canadian Brand Names Ciprodex®

Index Terms Ciprofloxacin Hydrochloride and Dexamethasone; Dexamethasone and Ciprofloxacin

Pharmacologic Category Antibiotic/Corticosteroid, Otic

Use Treatment of acute otitis media in pediatric patients with tympanostomy tubes or acute otitis externa in children and adults

Pregnancy Risk Factor C

Dosage Otic:

Children: Acute otitis media in patients with tympanostomy tubes or acute otitis externa: Instill 4 drops into affected ear(s) twice daily for 7 days

Adults: Acute otitis externa: Instill 4 drops into affected ear(s) twice daily for 7 days

Additional Information Complete prescribing information for this medication should be consulted for additional detail.

Dosage Forms Suspension, otic: Ciprofloxacin 0.3% and dexamethasone 0.1% (7.5 mL) [contains benzalkonium chloride]

Ciprofloxacin and Hydrocortisone
(sip roe FLOKS a sin & hye droe KOR ti sone)

U.S. Brand Names Cipro® HC

Canadian Brand Names Cipro® HC

Index Terms Ciprofloxacin Hydrochloride and Hydrocortisone; Hydrocortisone and Ciprofloxacin

Pharmacologic Category Antibiotic/Corticosteroid, Otic

Use Treatment of acute otitis externa, sometimes known as "swimmer's ear"

Dosage Children >1 year of age and Adults: Otic: The recommended dosage for all patients is three drops of the suspension in the affected ear twice daily for 7 days; twice-daily dosing schedule is more convenient for patients than that of existing treatments with hydrocortisone, which are typically administered three or four times a day; a twice-daily dosage schedule may be especially helpful for parents and caregivers of young children

Additional Information Complete prescribing information for this medication should be consulted for additional detail.

Dosage Forms Suspension, otic: Ciprofloxacin hydrochloride 0.2% and hydrocortisone 1% (10 mL) [contains benzyl alcohol]

♦ **Ciprofloxacin Hydrochloride** see Ciprofloxacin on page 372

♦ **Ciprofloxacin Hydrochloride and Dexamethasone** see Ciprofloxacin and Dexamethasone on page 376

♦ **Ciprofloxacin Hydrochloride and Hydrocortisone** see Ciprofloxacin and Hydrocortisone on page 377

♦ **Cipro® HC** see Ciprofloxacin and Hydrocortisone on page 377

♦ **Cipro® XR** see Ciprofloxacin on page 372

Cisapride (SIS a pride)

U.S. Brand Names Propulsid®

Pharmacologic Category Gastrointestinal Agent, Prokinetic

Use Treatment of nocturnal symptoms of gastroesophageal reflux disease (GERD); has demonstrated effectiveness for gastroparesis, refractory constipation, and nonulcer dyspepsia

Restrictions In U.S., available via limited-access protocol only (1-800-JANSSEN).

Pregnancy Risk Factor C

Medication Safety Issues
Sound-alike/look-alike issues:
Propulsid® may be confused with propranolol

Dosage Oral:
Children: 0.15-0.3 mg/kg/dose 3-4 times/day; maximum: 10 mg/dose
Adults: Initial: 10 mg 4 times/day at least 15 minutes before meals and at bedtime; in some patients the dosage will need to be increased to 20 mg to obtain a satisfactory result

Additional Information Complete prescribing information for this medication should be consulted for additional detail.

Cisatracurium (sis a tra KYOO ree um)

U.S. Brand Names Nimbex®

Canadian Brand Names Nimbex®

Index Terms Cisatracurium Besylate

Pharmacologic Category Neuromuscular Blocker Agent, Nondepolarizing

Additional Appendix Information
Neuromuscular Blocking Agents on page 1890

Use Adjunct to general anesthesia to facilitate endotracheal intubation and to relax skeletal muscles during surgery; to facilitate mechanical ventilation in ICU patients; does not relieve pain or produce sedation

Pregnancy Risk Factor B

Lactation Excretion in breast milk unknown/use caution

Medication Safety Issues
Sound-alike/look-alike issues:
Nimbex® may be confused with Revox®

High alert medication: The Institute for Safe Medication Practices (ISMP) includes this medication among its list of drugs which have a heightened risk of causing significant patient harm when used in error.

Contraindications Hypersensitivity to cisatracurium besylate or any component of the formulation

Warnings/Precautions Certain clinical conditions may result in potentiation or antagonism of neuromuscular blockade:
Potentiation: Electrolyte abnormalities, severe hyponatremia, severe hypocalcemia, severe hypokalemia, hypermagnesemia, neuromuscular diseases, acidosis, acute intermittent porphyria, renal failure, hepatic failure
Antagonism: Alkalosis, hypercalcemia, demyelinating lesions, peripheral neuropathies, diabetes mellitus
Increased sensitivity in patients with myasthenia gravis, Eaton-Lambert syndrome; resistance in burn patients (>30% of body) for period of 5-70 days postinjury; resistance in patients with
(Continued)

Cisatracurium *(Continued)*

muscle trauma, denervation, immobilization, infection. Cross-sensitivity with other neuromuscular-blocking agents may occur; use extreme caution in patients with previous anaphylactic reactions.

Adverse Reactions <1%: Effects are minimal and transient, bradycardia and hypotension, flushing, pruritus, rash, bronchospasm, acute quadriplegic myopathy syndrome (prolonged use), myositis ossificans (prolonged use)

Overdosage/Toxicology Symptoms include respiratory depression and cardiovascular collapse. Neostigmine 1-3 mg slow I.V. in adults (0.5 mg in children) antagonizes the neuromuscular blockade, and should be administered with or immediately after atropine 1-1.5 mg I.V. push (adults). This may be especially useful in the presence of bradycardia.

Drug Interactions

Increased Effect/Toxicity: Increased effects are possible with aminoglycosides, beta-blockers, clindamycin, calcium channel blockers, halogenated anesthetics, imipenem, ketamine, lidocaine, loop diuretics (furosemide), macrolides (case reports), magnesium sulfate, procainamide, quinidine, quinolones, tetracyclines, and vancomycin. May increase risk of myopathy when used with high-dose corticosteroids for extended periods.

Decreased Effect: Effect of nondepolarizing neuromuscular blockers may be reduced by carbamazepine (chronic use), corticosteroids (also associated with myopathy - see increased effect), phenytoin (chronic use), sympathomimetics, and theophylline.

Stability Refrigerate intact vials at 2°C to 8°C/36°F to 46°F; use vials within 21 days upon removal from the refrigerator to room temperature (25°C to 77°F). Dilutions of 0.1-0.2 mg/mL in 0.9% sodium chloride or dextrose 5% in water are stable for up to 24 hours at room temperature.

Mechanism of Action Blocks neural transmission at the myoneural junction by binding with cholinergic receptor sites

Pharmacodynamics/Kinetics

Onset of action: I.V.: 2-3 minutes

Peak effect: 3-5 minutes

Duration: Recovery begins in 20-35 minutes when anesthesia is balanced; recovery is attained in 90% of patients in 25-93 minutes

Metabolism: Undergoes rapid nonenzymatic degradation in the bloodstream (Hofmann elimination), additional metabolism occurs via ester hydrolysis; some active metabolites

Half-life elimination: 22-29 minutes

Dosage I.V. (not to be used I.M.):

Operating room administration:

Infants 1-23 months: 0.15 mg/kg over 5-10 seconds during either halothane or opioid anesthesia

Children 2-12 years: Intubating doses: 0.1-0.15 mg/kg over 5-15 seconds during either halothane or opioid anesthesia. (**Note:** When given during stable opioid/nitrous oxide/oxygen anesthesia, 0.1 mg/kg produces maximum neuromuscular block in an average of 2.8 minutes and clinically effective block for 28 minutes.)

Adults: Intubating doses: 0.15-0.2 mg/kg as component of propofol/nitrous oxide/oxygen induction-intubation technique. (**Note:** May produce generally good or excellent conditions for tracheal intubation in 1.5-2 minutes with clinically effective duration of action during propofol anesthesia of 55-61 minutes.); initial dose after succinylcholine for intubation: 0.1 mg/kg; maintenance dose: 0.03 mg/kg 40-60 minutes after initial dose, then at ~20-minute intervals based on clinical criteria

Children ≥2 years and Adults: Continuous infusion: After an initial bolus, a diluted solution can be given by continuous infusion for maintenance of neuromuscular blockade during extended surgery; adjust the rate of administration according to the patient's response as determined by peripheral nerve stimulation. An initial infusion rate of 3 mcg/kg/minute may be required to rapidly counteract the spontaneous recovery of neuromuscular function; thereafter, a rate of 1-2 mcg/kg/minute should be adequate to maintain continuous neuromuscular block in the 89% to 99% range in most pediatric and adult patients. Consider reduction of the infusion rate by 30% to 40% when administering during stable isoflurane, enflurane, sevoflurane, or desflurane anesthesia. Spontaneous recovery from neuromuscular blockade following discontinuation of infusion of cisatracurium may be expected to proceed at a rate comparable to that following single bolus administration.

Intensive care unit administration: Follow the principles for infusion in the operating room. At initial signs of recovery from bolus dose, begin the infusion at a dose of 3 mcg/kg/minute and adjust rates accordingly; dosage ranges of 0.5-10 mcg/kg/minute have been reported. If patient is allowed to recover from neuromuscular blockade, readministration of a bolus dose may be necessary to quickly re-establish neuromuscular block prior to reinstituting the infusion. See table.

Cisatracurium Besylate Infusion Chart

Drug Delivery Rate (mcg/kg/min)	Infusion Rate (mL/kg/min) 0.1 mg/mL (10 mg/100 mL)	Infusion Rate (mL/kg/min) 0.4 mg/mL (40 mg/100 mL)
1	0.01	0.0025
1.5	0.015	0.00375
2	0.02	0.005
3	0.03	0.0075
5	0.05	0.0125

Dosing adjustment in renal impairment: Because slower times to onset of complete neuromuscular block were observed in renal dysfunction patients, extending the interval between the administration of cisatracurium and intubation attempt may be required to achieve adequate intubation conditions.

Administration Administer I.V. only; the use of a peripheral nerve stimulator will permit the most advantageous use of cisatracurium, minimize the possibility of overdosage or underdosage and assist in the evaluation of recovery

Give undiluted as a bolus injection; not for I.M. injection, too much tissue irritation; continuous administration requires the use of an infusion pump

Monitoring Parameters Vital signs (heart rate, blood pressure, respiratory rate)

Additional Information Cisatracurium is classified as an intermediate-duration neuromuscular-blocking agent. It does not appear to have a cumulative effect on the duration of blockade. Neuromuscular-blocking potency is 3 times that of atracurium; maximum block is up to 2 minutes longer than for equipotent doses of atracurium.

Dosage Forms

Injection, solution: 2 mg/mL (5 mL); 10 mg/mL (20 mL)

Injection, solution: 2 mg/mL (10 mL) [contains benzyl alcohol]

♦ **Cisatracurium Besylate** *see* Cisatracurium *on page 377*

Cisplatin (SIS pla tin)

U.S. Brand Names Platinol®-AQ [DSC]

Index Terms CDDP

Pharmacologic Category Antineoplastic Agent, Alkylating Agent

Use Treatment of bladder, testicular, and ovarian cancer

Unlabeled/Investigational Use Treatment of head and neck, breast, gastric, lung, esophageal, cervical, prostate and small cell lung cancer; Hodgkin's and non-Hodgkin's lymphoma; neuroblastoma; sarcomas, myeloma, melanoma, mesothelioma, and osteosarcoma

Pregnancy Risk Factor D

Pregnancy Implications Animal studies have demonstrated teratogenicity and embryotoxicity. There are no adequate and well-controlled studies in pregnant women. Women of childbearing potential should be advised to avoid pregnancy. If used in pregnancy, or if patient becomes pregnant during treatment, the patient should be apprised of potential hazard to the fetus.

Lactation Enters breast milk/contraindicated

Medication Safety Issues

Sound-alike/look-alike issues:

Cisplatin may be confused with carboplatin

Platinol®-AQ may be confused with Paraplatin®, Patanol®, Plaquenil®

High alert medication: The Institute for Safe Medication Practices (ISMP) includes this medication among its list of drugs which have a heightened risk of causing significant patient harm when used in error.

Doses >100 mg/m^2 once every 3-4 weeks are rarely used and should be verified with the prescriber.

Contraindications Hypersensitivity to cisplatin, other platinum-containing compounds, or any component of the formulation (anaphylactic-like reactions have been reported); pre-existing renal insufficiency; myelosuppression; hearing impairment; pregnancy

Warnings/Precautions Hazardous agent - use appropriate precautions for handling and disposal. **[U.S. Boxed Warning]: Doses >100 mg/m^2 once every 3-4 weeks are rarely used and should be verified with the prescriber.** Patients should receive adequate hydration, with or without diuretics, prior to and for 24 hours after cisplatin administration. Reduce dosage in renal impairment. **[U.S. Boxed Warning]: Cumulative renal toxicity may be severe.** Elderly patients may be more susceptible to nephrotoxicity and peripheral neuropathy; select dose cautiously and monitor closely. **[U.S. Boxed Warnings]: Dose-related toxicities include myelosuppression, nausea, and vomiting. Ototoxicity, especially pronounced in children, is manifested by tinnitus or loss of high frequency hearing and occasionally, deafness.** Severe and possibly irreversible neuropathies may occur with higher than recommended doses or more frequent regimen. Serum electrolytes, particularly magnesium and potassium, should be monitored and replaced as needed during and after cisplatin therapy. When administered as sequential infusions, taxane derivatives (docetaxel, paclitaxel) should be administered before platinum derivatives (carboplatin, cisplatin). **[U.S. Boxed Warnings]: Anaphylactic-like reactions have been reported; may be managed with epinephrine, corticosteroids, and/or antihistamines. Should be administered under the supervision of an experienced cancer chemotherapy physician.**

Adverse Reactions

>10%:

Central nervous system: Neurotoxicity: Peripheral neuropathy is dose- and duration-dependent.

Dermatologic: Mild alopecia

Gastrointestinal: Nausea and vomiting (76% to 100%)

Hematologic: Myelosuppression (25% to 30%; mild with moderate doses, mild to moderate with high-dose therapy)

WBC: Mild

Platelets: Mild

Onset: 10 days

Nadir: 14-23 days

Recovery: 21-39 days

Hepatic: Liver enzymes increased

Renal: Nephrotoxicity (acute renal failure and chronic renal insufficiency)

Otic: Ototoxicity (10% to 30%; manifested as high frequency hearing loss; ototoxicity is especially pronounced in children)

1% to 10%:

Gastrointestinal: Diarrhea

Local: Tissue irritation

(Continued)

Cisplatin *(Continued)*

<1% (Limited to important or life-threatening): Anaphylactic reaction, arrhythmias, blurred vision, bradycardia, cerebral blindness, hemolytic anemia, liver enzymes increased, mild alopecia, mouth sores, optic neuritis, papilledema

BMT:

Central nervous system: Peripheral and autonomic neuropathy, ototoxicity

Endocrine & metabolic: Hypokalemia, hypomagnesemia

Gastrointestinal: Highly emetogenic

Hematologic: Myelosuppression

Renal: Acute renal failure, increased serum creatinine, azotemia

Miscellaneous: Transient pain at tumor, transient autoimmune disorders

Overdosage/Toxicology Symptoms of overdose include severe myelosuppression, intractable nausea and vomiting, kidney and liver failure, deafness, ocular toxicity, and neuritis. Overdose may be fatal. There is no known antidote. Hemodialysis appears to have little effect. Treatment is symptom-directed and supportive.

Drug Interactions

Increased Effect/Toxicity: Cisplatin and ethacrynic acid have resulted in severe ototoxicity in animals. Delayed bleomycin elimination with decreased glomerular filtration rate. When administered as sequential infusions, observational studies indicate a potential for increased toxicity when platinum derivatives (carboplatin, cisplatin) are administered before taxane derivatives (docetaxel, paclitaxel).

Decreased Effect: Sodium thiosulfate and amifostine theoretically inactivate drug systemically; have been used clinically to reduce systemic toxicity with administration of cisplatin.

Ethanol/Nutrition/Herb Interactions Herb/Nutraceutical: Avoid black cohosh, dong quai in estrogen-dependent tumors.

Stability

Store intact vials at room temperature of 15°C to 25°C (59°F to 77°F); protect from light. Do not refrigerate solution, a precipitate may form. Further dilution **stability is dependent on the chloride ion concentration** and should be mixed in solutions of NS (at least 0.3% NaCl). Further dilutions in NS, $D_5/0.45\%$ NaCl or D_5/NS to a concentration of 0.05-2 mg/mL are stable for 72 hours at 4°C to 25°C. The infusion solution should have a final sodium chloride concentration ≥0.2%.

After initial entry into the vial, solution is stable for 28 days protected from light or for at least 7 days under fluorescent room light at room temperature.

Standard I.V. dilution: Dose/250-1000 mL NS, D_5/NS, or $D_5/0.45\%$ NaCl

Mechanism of Action Inhibits DNA synthesis by the formation of DNA cross-links; denatures the double helix; covalently binds to DNA bases and disrupts DNA function; may also bind to proteins; the *cis*-isomer is 14 times more cytotoxic than the *trans*-isomer; both forms cross-link DNA but cis-platinum is less easily recognized by cell enzymes and, therefore, not repaired. Cisplatin can also bind two adjacent guanines on the same strand of DNA producing intrastand cross-linking and breakage.

Pharmacodynamics/Kinetics

Distribution: I.V.: Rapidly into tissue; high concentrations in kidneys, liver, ovaries, uterus, and lungs

Protein binding: >90%

Metabolism: Nonenzymatic; inactivated (in both cell and bloodstream) by sulfhydryl groups; covalently binds to glutathione and thiosulfate

Half-life elimination: Initial: 20-30 minutes; Beta: 60 minutes; Terminal: ~24 hours; Secondary half-life: 44-73 hours

Excretion: Urine (>90%); feces (10%)

Dosage Refer to individual protocols. **VERIFY ANY CISPLATIN DOSE EXCEEDING 100 mg/ m² PER COURSE.**

Children (unlabeled uses):

Intermittent dosing schedule: 37-75 mg/m² once every 2-3 weeks or 50-100 mg/m² over 4-6 hours, once every 21-28 days

Daily dosing schedule: 15-20 mg/m²/day for 5 days every 3-4 weeks

Osteogenic sarcoma or neuroblastoma: 60-100 mg/m² on day 1 every 3-4 weeks

Recurrent brain tumors: 60 mg/m² once daily for 2 consecutive days every 3-4 weeks

Bone marrow/blood cell transfusion: Continuous Infusion: High dose: 55 mg/m²/day for 72 hours; total dose = 165 mg/m²

Adults:

Advanced bladder cancer: 50-70 mg/m² every 3-4 weeks

Head and neck cancer (unlabeled use): 100-120 mg/m² every 3-4 weeks

Malignant pleural mesothelioma in combination with pemetrexed: 75 mg/m² on day 1 of each 21-day cycle; see Pemetrexed monograph for additional details

Metastatic ovarian cancer: 75-100 mg/m² every 3-4 weeks

Intraperitoneal: Cisplatin has been administered intraperitoneal with systemic sodium thiosulfate for ovarian cancer; doses up to 90-270 mg/m² have been administered and retained for 4 hours before draining

Testicular cancer: 10-20 mg/m²/day for 5 days repeated every 3-4 weeks

Dosing adjustment in renal impairment: The manufacturer(s) recommend that repeat courses of cisplatin should not be given until serum creatinine is <1.5 mg/100 mL and/or BUN is <25 mg/100 mL. There is no FDA-approved renal dosing adjustment guideline; the following guidelines have been used by some clinicians:

Kintzel, 1995:

Cl_{cr} 46-60 mL/minute: Reduce dose by 25%

Cl_{cr} 31-45 mL/minute: Reduce dose by 50%

Cl_{cr} <30 mL/minute: Consider use of alternative drug

Aronoff, 1999:

Cl_{cr} 10-50 mL/minute: Administer 75% of dose

Cl_{cr} <10 mL/minute: Administer 50% of dose

Hemodialysis: Partially cleared by hemodialysis; administer dose posthemodialysis

CAPD effects: Unknown

CAVH effects: Unknown

Dietary Considerations Sodium content: 9 mg/mL (equivalent to 0.9% sodium chloride solution)

Administration Pretreatment hydration with 1-2 L of fluid is recommended prior to cisplatin administration; adequate hydration and urinary output (>100 mL/hour) should be maintained for 24 hours after administration.

I.V.: Rate of administration has varied from a 15- to 120-minute infusion, 1 mg/minute infusion, 6- to 8-hour infusion, 24-hour infusion, or per protocol; maximum rate of infusion of 1 mg/minute in patients with CHF.

Monitoring Parameters Renal function (serum creatinine, BUN, Cl_{cr}); electrolytes (particularly magnesium, calcium, potassium) before and within 48 hours after cisplatin therapy; audiography (baseline and prior to each subsequent dose), neurologic exam (with high dose); liver function tests periodically, CBC with differential and platelet count; urine output, urinalysis

Dosage Forms [DSC] = Discontinued product

Injection, solution: 1 mg/mL (50 mL, 100 mL, 200 mL)

Platinol®-AQ: 1 mg/mL (50 mL, 100 mL) [contains sodium 9 mg/mL] [DSC]

♦ **13-*cis*-Retinoic Acid** *see* Isotretinoin *on page 948*

Citalopram (sye TAL oh pram)

U.S. Brand Names Celexa®

Canadian Brand Names Apo-Citalopram®; Celexa®; CO Citalopram; Dom-Citalopram; Gen-Citalopram; Novo-Citalopram; PHL-Citalopram; PMS-Citalopram; RAN™-Citalopram; ratio-Citalopram; Rhoxal-citalopram; Sandoz-Citalopram

Index Terms Citalopram Hydrobromide; Nitalapram

Pharmacologic Category Antidepressant, Selective Serotonin Reuptake Inhibitor

Additional Appendix Information

Antidepressant Agents *on page 1866*

Selective Serotonin Reuptake Inhibitors (SSRIs) Pharmacokinetics *on page 1896*

Use Treatment of depression

Unlabeled/Investigational Use Treatment of dementia, smoking cessation, ethanol abuse, obsessive-compulsive disorder (OCD) in children, diabetic neuropathy

Restrictions An FDA-approved medication guide concerning the use of antidepressants in children and teenagers must be distributed when dispensing an outpatient prescription (new or refill) where this medication is to be used without direct supervision of a healthcare provider. Medication guides are available at http://www.fda.gov/cder/Offices/ODS/medication_guides.htm. Dispense to parents or guardians of children and teenagers receiving this medication.

Pregnancy Risk Factor C

Pregnancy Implications Teratogenic effects have been observed in animal studies. Nonteratogenic effects including respiratory distress, cyanosis, apnea, seizures, temperature instability, feeding difficulty, vomiting, hypoglycemia, hypo- or hypertonia, hyper-reflexia, jitteriness, irritability, constant crying, and tremor have been reported in the neonate immediately following delivery after exposure late in the third trimester. Exposure to SSRIs late in pregnancy has also been associated with persistent pulmonary hypertension of the newborn (PPHN). Adverse effects may be due to toxic effects of SSRI or drug discontinuation. In some cases, effects may present clinically as serotonin syndrome. There are no adequate and well-controlled studies in pregnant women. Use during pregnancy only if the potential benefit to the mother outweighs the possible risk to the fetus. If treatment during pregnancy is required, consider tapering therapy during the third trimester.

Lactation Enters breast milk/contraindicated

Medication Safety Issues

Sound-alike/look-alike issues:

Celexa® may be confused with Celebrex®, Cerebra®, Cerebyx®, Zyprexa®

Contraindications Hypersensitivity to citalopram or any component of the formulation; hypersensitivity or other adverse sequelae during therapy with other SSRIs; concomitant use with MAO inhibitors or within 2 weeks of discontinuing MAO inhibitors

Warnings/Precautions [U.S. Boxed Warning]: Antidepressants increase the risk of suicidal thinking and behavior in children and adolescents with major depressive disorder (MDD) and other depressive disorders; consider risk prior to prescribing. All patients must be closely monitored for clinical worsening, suicidality, or unusual changes in behavior, especially during the initiation of therapy or following an increase or decrease in dosage. When used in children, the child's family or caregiver should be instructed to closely observe the patient and communicate condition with healthcare provider. A medication guide should be dispensed with each prescription. **Citalopram is not FDA approved for use in children.**

The possibility of a suicide attempt is inherent in major depression and may persist until remission occurs. Use caution in high-risk patients. Worsening depression and severe abrupt suicidality that are not part of the presenting symptoms may require discontinuation or modification of drug therapy. The patient's family or caregiver should be alerted to monitor patients for the emergence of suicidality and associated behaviors (such as agitation, irritability, hostility, impulsivity, and hypomania) and call healthcare provider.

May worsen psychosis in some patients or precipitate a shift to mania or hypomania in patients with bipolar disorder. Patients presenting with depressive symptoms should be screened for bipolar disorder. Monotherapy in patients with bipolar disorder should be avoided. **Citalopram is not FDA approved for the treatment of bipolar depression.**

The potential for severe reaction exists when used with MAO inhibitors, SSRIs/SNRIs or triptans; serotonin syndrome (hyperthermia, muscular rigidity, mental status changes/agitation, autonomic instability) may occur. Concurrent use with MAO inhibitors is contraindicated. May increase the risks associated with electroconvulsive therapy. Has a low potential to impair cognitive or motor performance; caution operating hazardous machinery or driving. (Continued)

Citalopram *(Continued)*

Use with caution in patients with hepatic or renal dysfunction, in elderly patients, concomitant CNS depressants, and pregnancy (high doses of citalopram have been associated with teratogenicity in animals). Use caution with concomitant use of NSAIDs, ASA, or other drugs that affect coagulation; the risk of bleeding is potentiated. May cause hyponatremia/SIADH. May cause or exacerbate sexual dysfunction. Upon discontinuation of citalopram therapy, gradually taper dose. If intolerable symptoms occur following a decrease in dosage or upon discontinuation of therapy, then resuming the previous dose with a more gradual taper should be considered.

Adverse Reactions

>10%:

Central nervous system: Somnolence, insomnia

Gastrointestinal: Nausea, xerostomia

Miscellaneous: Diaphoresis

<10%:

Central nervous system: Anxiety, anorexia, agitation, yawning

Dermatologic: Rash, pruritus

Endocrine & metabolic: Sexual dysfunction

Gastrointestinal: Diarrhea, dyspepsia, vomiting, abdominal pain, weight gain

Neuromuscular & skeletal: Tremor, arthralgia, myalgia

Respiratory: Cough, rhinitis, sinusitis

<1%, Postmarketing, and/or case reports (limited to important or life-threatening): Acute renal failure, anaphylaxis, angioedema, delirium, dyskinesia, epidermal necrolysis, erythema multiforme, hemolytic anemia, hepatic necrosis, neuroleptic malignant syndrome (NMS), pancreatitis, priapism, QT prolonged, rhabdomyolysis, serotonin syndrome, SIADH, ventricular arrhythmia, torsade de pointes, withdrawal syndrome

Overdosage/Toxicology Symptoms include dizziness, nausea, vomiting, sweating, tremor, somnolence, and sinus tachycardia. Rare symptoms have included amnesia, confusion, coma, seizures, hyperventilation, and ECG changes (including QT_c prolongation, ventricular arrhythmia, and torsade de pointes). Management is supportive.

Drug Interactions

Cytochrome P450 Effect: Substrate of CYP2C19 (major), 2D6 (minor), 3A4 (major); **Inhibits** CYP1A2 (weak), 2B6 (weak), 2C19 (weak), 2D6 (weak)

Increased Effect/Toxicity: Citalopram should not be used with nonselective MAO inhibitors (phenelzine, isocarboxazid) or other drugs with MAO inhibition (linezolid); fatal reactions have been reported. Wait 2 weeks after stopping an MAO inhibitor before starting citalopram. Concurrent selegiline has been associated with mania, hypertension, or serotonin syndrome (risk may be reduced relative to nonselective MAO inhibitors).

CYP2C19 inhibitors may increase the levels/effects of citalopram; example inhibitors include delavirdine, fluconazole, fluvoxamine, gemfibrozil, isoniazid, omeprazole, and ticlopidine. CYP3A4 inhibitors may increase the levels/effects of citalopram; example inhibitors include azole antifungals, clarithromycin, diclofenac, doxycycline, erythromycin, imatinib, isoniazid, nefazodone, nicardipine, propofol, protease inhibitors, quinidine, telithromycin, and verapamil.

Combined use of SSRIs and amphetamines, buspirone, meperidine, nefazodone, serotonin agonists (such as sumatriptan), sibutramine, other SSRIs/SNRIs, sympathomimetics, ritonavir, tramadol, and venlafaxine may increase the risk of serotonin syndrome. Risk of hyponatremia may increase with concurrent use of loop diuretics (bumetanide, furosemide, torsemide). Citalopram may increase the hypoprothrombinemic response to warfarin. Concomitant use of citalopram and NSAIDs, aspirin, or other drugs affecting coagulation has been associated with an increased risk of bleeding; monitor.

Combined use of sumatriptan (and other serotonin agonists) may result in toxicity; weakness, hyper-reflexia, and incoordination have been observed with sumatriptan and SSRIs. In addition, concurrent use may theoretically increase the risk of serotonin syndrome; includes sumatriptan, naratriptan, rizatriptan, and zolmitriptan.

Decreased Effect: CYP2C19 inducers may decrease the levels/effects of citalopram; example inducers include aminoglutethimide, carbamazepine, phenytoin, and rifampin. Cyproheptadine may inhibit the effects of serotonin reuptake inhibitors. CYP3A4 inducers may decrease the levels/effects of citalopram; example inducers include aminoglutethimide, carbamazepine, nafcillin, nevirapine, phenobarbital, phenytoin, and rifamycins.

Ethanol/Nutrition/Herb Interactions

Ethanol: Avoid ethanol (may increase CNS depression).

Herb/Nutraceutical: Avoid valerian, St John's wort, SAMe, kava kava, and gotu kola (may increase CNS depression).

Stability Store below 25°C.

Mechanism of Action A bicyclic phthalane derivative, citalopram selectively inhibits serotonin reuptake in the presynaptic neurons

Pharmacodynamics/Kinetics

Distribution: V_d: 12 L/kg

Protein binding, plasma: ~80%

Metabolism: Extensively hepatic, primarily via CYP3A4 and 2C19; forms metabolites, N-demethylcitalopram (DCT) and didemethylcitalopram (DDCT) which are ~ eight times less potent than citalopram

Bioavailability: 80%

Half-life elimination: 24-48 hours (average: 35 hours); doubled with hepatic impairment

Time to peak, serum: 1-6 hours, average within 4 hours

Excretion: Urine (Citalopram 10% and DCT 5%)

Note: Clearance was decreased, while AUC and half-life were significantly increased in elderly patients and in patients with hepatic impairment. Mild-to-moderate renal impairment may reduce clearance (17%) and prolong half-life of citalopram. No pharmacokinetic information is available concerning patients with severe renal impairment.

Dosage Oral:
Children and Adolescents: OCD (unlabeled use): 10-40 mg/day
Adults: Depression: Initial: 20 mg/day, generally with an increase to 40 mg/day; doses of more than 40 mg are not usually necessary. Should a dose increase be necessary, it should occur in 20 mg increments at intervals of no less than 1 week. Maximum dose: 60 mg/day; reduce dosage in elderly or those with hepatic impairment.

Dietary Considerations May be taken without regard to food.

Monitoring Parameters Monitor patient periodically for symptom resolution; mental status for depression, suicidal ideation (especially at the beginning of therapy or when doses are increased or decreased), anxiety, social functioning, mania, panic attacks; akathisia

Dosage Forms
Solution, oral: 10 mg/5 mL (240 mL)
Celexa®: 10 mg/5 mL (240 mL) [alcohol free, sugar free; peppermint flavor]
Tablet: 10 mg, 20 mg, 40 mg
Celexa®: 10 mg, 20 mg, 40 mg

♦ **Citalopram Hydrobromide** *see* Citalopram *on page 381*

♦ **Citracal® [OTC]** *see* Calcium Citrate *on page 272*

♦ **Citrate of Magnesia** *see* Magnesium Citrate *on page 1046*

♦ **Citric Acid and Potassium Citrate** *see* Potassium Citrate and Citric Acid *on page 1398*

Citric Acid, Sodium Citrate, and Potassium Citrate
(SIT rik AS id, SOW dee um SIT rate, & poe TASS ee um SIT rate)

U.S. Brand Names Cytra-3; Polycitra®; Polycitra®-LC

Index Terms Potassium Citrate, Citric Acid, and Sodium Citrate; Sodium Citrate, Citric Acid, and Potassium Citrate

Pharmacologic Category Alkalinizing Agent, Oral

Use Conditions where long-term maintenance of an alkaline urine is desirable as in control and dissolution of uric acid and cystine calculi of the urinary tract

Pregnancy Risk Factor Not established

Dosage Oral:
Children: 5-15 mL diluted in water after meals and at bedtime
Adults: 15-30 mL diluted in water after meals and at bedtime

Additional Information Complete prescribing information for this medication should be consulted for additional detail.

Dosage Forms Note: Equivalent to potassium 1 mEq/mL, sodium 1 mEq/mL, and bicarbonate 2 mEq/mL
Solution, oral:
Cytra-3: Citric acid 334 mg, sodium citrate 500 mg, and potassium citrate 550 mg per 5 mL (480 mL) [alcohol free, sugar free; contains sodium benzoate; raspberry flavor]
Polycitra®-LC: Citric acid 334 mg, sodium citrate 500 mg, and potassium citrate 550 mg per 5 mL (480 mL) [alcohol free, sugar free]
Syrup, oral (Polycitra®): Citric acid 334 mg, sodium citrate 500 mg, and potassium citrate 550 mg per 5 mL (480 mL) [alcohol free]

♦ **Citroma® [OTC]** *see* Magnesium Citrate *on page 1046*

♦ **Citro-Mag® (Can)** *see* Magnesium Citrate *on page 1046*

♦ **Citrovorum Factor** *see* Leucovorin *on page 990*

♦ **CL-118,532** *see* Triptorelin *on page 1750*

♦ **Cl-719** *see* Gemfibrozil *on page 787*

♦ **CL-825** *see* Pentostatin *on page 1342*

♦ **CL-184116** *see* Porfimer *on page 1391*

Cladribine (KLA dri been)

U.S. Brand Names Leustatin®

Canadian Brand Names Leustatin®

Index Terms 2-CdA; 2-Chlorodeoxyadenosine; NSC-105014

Pharmacologic Category Antineoplastic Agent, Antimetabolite; Antineoplastic Agent, Antimetabolite (Purine Antagonist)

Use Treatment of hairy cell leukemia

Unlabeled/Investigational Use Treatment of chronic lymphocytic leukemia (CLL), chronic myelogenous leukemia (CML), non-Hodgkin's lymphomas, progressive multiple sclerosis

Pregnancy Risk Factor D

Pregnancy Implications Teratogenic effects and fetal mortality were observed in animal studies. There are no adequate and well-controlled studies in pregnant women. Women of childbearing potential should avoid becoming pregnant.

Lactation Excretion in breast milk unknown/not recommended

Medication Safety Issues
Sound-alike/look-alike issues:
Cladribine may be confused with clofarabine
Leustatin® may be confused with lovastatin

High alert medication: The Institute for Safe Medication Practices (ISMP) includes this medication among its list of drugs which have a heightened risk of causing significant patient harm when used in error.

Contraindications Hypersensitivity to cladribine or any component of the formulation

Warnings/Precautions Hazardous agent - use appropriate precautions for handling and disposal. [U.S. Boxed Warnings]: **Dose-dependent, reversible myelosuppression will occur; use with caution in patients with pre-existing hematologic or immunologic abnormalities. Neurologic toxicity has been reported, usually with higher doses, but may occur at normal doses. Acute renal toxicity has been reported with high doses;**
(Continued)

Cladribine *(Continued)*

use caution when administering with other nephrotoxic agents. Use caution with renal or hepatic impairment. Fever may occur, with or without neutropenia. Use caution in patients with high tumor burden; tumor lysis syndrome may occur. **[U.S. Boxed Warning]: Should be administered under the supervision of an experienced cancer chemotherapy physician.** Safety and efficacy in children have not been established.

Adverse Reactions

>10%:

Central nervous system: Fever (69%; ≥104°F: 11%), fatigue (11% to 45%), headache (7% to 22%)

Dermatologic: Rash (10% to 27%)

Gastrointestinal: Nausea (28%), appetite decreased (17%), vomiting (13%)

Hematologic: Myelosuppression, common, dose limiting (nadir: 5-10 days, recovery: 4-8 weeks); neutropenia (70%); anemia (37%); thrombocytopenia (12%)

Local: Injection site reactions (9% to 19%)

Respiratory: Abnormal breath sounds (11%)

Miscellaneous: Infection (28%)

1% to 10%:

Cardiovascular: Edema (6%), tachycardia (6%), thrombosis (2%)

Central nervous system: Dizziness (9%), chills (9%), insomnia (7%), malaise (5% to 7%), pain (6%)

Dermatologic: Purpura (10%), petechiae (8%), pruritus (6%), erythema (6%)

Gastrointestinal: Diarrhea (10%), constipation (9%), abdominal pain (6%)

Local: Phlebitis (2%)

Neuromuscular & skeletal: Weakness (9%), myalgia (7%), arthralgia (5%)

Respiratory: Cough (7% to 10%), abnormal chest sounds (9%), dyspnea (7%), epistaxis (5%)

Miscellaneous: Diaphoresis (9%)

<1% (Limited to important or life-threatening): Aplastic anemia, bilirubin increased, hemolytic anemia, hypereosinophilia, myelodysplastic syndrome, neurologic toxicity, opportunistic infections, pancytopenia, paraparesis, pneumonia, polyneuropathy (with high doses), pulmonary interstitial infiltrates, quadriplegia (reported at high doses); renal dysfunction (with high doses), Stevens-Johnson syndrome, toxic epidermal necrolysis, transaminases increased, tumor lysis syndrome, urticaria

Overdosage/Toxicology High doses are associated with irreversible neurologic toxicity, nephrotoxicity, and severe bone marrow suppression. Treatment is symptom-directed and supportive.

Ethanol/Nutrition/Herb Interactions Ethanol: Avoid ethanol (due to GI irritation).

Stability Store intact vials under refrigeration 2°C to 8°C (36°F to 46°F); protect from light. Dilutions in 500 mL NS are stable for 72 hours. Stable in PVC containers for 24 hours at room temperature of 15°C to 30°C (59°F to 86°F) and 7 days in Pharmacia Deltec® cassettes. Dilute in 500 mL; dilute to a total volume of 100 mL for 7-day infusion. Solutions for 7-day infusion should be prepared in bacteriostatic NS. The manufacturer recommends filtering with a 0.22 micron filter when preparing 7-day infusions.

Mechanism of Action A purine nucleoside analogue; prodrug which is activated via phosphorylation by deoxycytidine kinase to a 5'-triphosphate derivative. This active form incorporates into DNA to result in the breakage of DNA strand and shutdown of DNA synthesis. This also results in a depletion of nicotinamide adenine dinucleotide and adenosine triphosphate (ATP). Cladribine is cell-cycle nonspecific.

Pharmacodynamics/Kinetics

Absorption: Oral: 55%; SubQ: 100%; Rectal: 20%

Distribution: V_d: 4.52 ± 2.82 L/kg

Protein binding: 20%

Metabolism: Hepatic; 5'-triphosphate moiety-active

Half-life elimination: Biphasic: Alpha: 25 minutes; Beta: 6.7 hours; Terminal, mean: Normal renal function: 5.4 hours

Excretion: Urine (18% to 44%)

Clearance: Estimated systemic: 640 mL/hour/kg

Dosage I.V.: Refer to individual protocols.

Children (unlabeled use): Acute leukemias: 6.2-7.5 mg/m²/day continuous infusion for days 1-5; maximum tolerated dose was 8.9 mg/m²/day.

Adults:

Hairy cell leukemia: Continuous infusion:

0.09 mg/kg/day days 1-7; may be repeated every 28-35 days **or**

3.4 mg/m²/day SubQ days 1-7 (unlabeled dose)

Chronic lymphocytic leukemia (unlabeled use): Continuous infusion:

0.1 mg/kg/day days 1-7 **or**

0.028-0.14 mg/kg/day as a 2-hour infusion days 1-5

Chronic myelogenous leukemia (unlabeled use): 15 mg/m²/day as a 1-hour infusion days 1-5; if no response, increase dose to 20 mg/m²/day in the second course.

Administration I.V.: Administer as a 1- to 2-hour infusion or by continuous infusion

Monitoring Parameters CBC with differential, renal and hepatic function; monitor for fever

Periodic assessment of peripheral blood counts, particularly during the first 4-8 weeks post-treatment, is recommended to detect the development of anemia, neutropenia, and thrombocytopenia and for early detection of any potential sequelae (eg, infection or bleeding)

Dosage Forms Injection, solution [preservative free]: 1 mg/mL (10 mL)

♦ **Claforan**® *see* Cefotaxime *on page 313*

♦ **Claravis**™ *see* Isotretinoin *on page 948*

♦ **Clarinex**® *see* Desloratadine *on page 475*

♦ **Clarinex-D**® **12 Hour** *see* Desloratadine and Pseudoephedrine *on page 476*

♦ **Clarinex-D**® **24 Hour** *see* Desloratadine and Pseudoephedrine *on page 476*

♦ Claripel™ *see* Hydroquinone *on page 859*

Clarithromycin (kla RITH roe mye sin)

U.S. Brand Names Biaxin®; Biaxin® XL
Canadian Brand Names Biaxin®; Biaxin® XL; ratio-Clarithromycin
Pharmacologic Category Antibiotic, Macrolide
Additional Appendix Information
  Antimicrobial Drugs of Choice *on page 1981*
  Community-Acquired Pneumonia in Adults *on page 1999*
  Helicobacter pylori Treatment *on page 2056*
  Prevention of Bacterial Endocarditis *on page 1960*
  USPHS / IDSA Guidelines for the Prevention of Opportunistic Infections in Persons Infected With HIV *on page 1966*

Use
  Children:
    Acute otitis media (*H. influenzae, M. catarrhalis,* or *S. pneumoniae*)
    Community-acquired pneumonia due to susceptible *Mycoplasma pneumoniae, S. pneumoniae,* or *Chlamydia pneumoniae* (TWAR)
    Pharyngitis/tonsillitis, acute maxillary sinusitis, uncomplicated skin/skin structure infections, and mycobacterial infections
    Prevention of disseminated mycobacterial infections due to MAC disease in patients with advanced HIV infection
  Adults:
    Pharyngitis/tonsillitis due to susceptible *S. pyogenes*
    Acute maxillary sinusitis and acute exacerbation of chronic bronchitis due to susceptible *H. influenzae, M. catarrhalis,* or *S. pneumoniae*
    Community-acquired pneumonia due to susceptible *H. influenzae, H. parainfluenzae, Mycoplasma pneumoniae, S. pneumoniae,* or *Chlamydia pneumoniae* (TWAR)
    Uncomplicated skin/skin structure infections due to susceptible *S. aureus, S. pyogenes*
    Disseminated mycobacterial infections due to *M. avium* or *M. intracellulare*
    Prevention of disseminated mycobacterial infections due to *M. avium* complex (MAC) disease (eg, patients with advanced HIV infection)
    Duodenal ulcer disease due to *H. pylori* in regimens with other drugs including amoxicillin and lansoprazole or omeprazole, ranitidine bismuth citrate, bismuth subsalicylate, tetracycline, and/or an H_2 antagonist

Unlabeled/Investigational Use Pertussis (CDC guidelines); alternate antibiotic for prophylaxis of bacterial endocarditis in patients who are allergic to penicillin and undergoing surgical or dental procedures (ACC/AHA guidelines)

Pregnancy Risk Factor C

Pregnancy Implications There are no adequate and well-controlled studies in pregnant women. Due to adverse fetal effects reported in animal studies, the manufacturer recommends that clarithromycin not be used in a pregnant woman unless there are no alternatives to therapy.

Lactation Excretion in breast milk unknown/use caution

Medication Safety Issues
  Sound-alike/look-alike issues:
    Clarithromycin may be confused with erythromycin

Contraindications Hypersensitivity to clarithromycin, erythromycin, or any macrolide antibiotic; use with ergot derivatives, pimozide, cisapride

Warnings/Precautions Dosage adjustment required with severe renal impairment, decreased dosage or prolonged dosing interval may be appropriate. Antibiotic-associated colitis has been reported with use of clarithromycin. Macrolides (including clarithromycin) have been associated with rare QT prolongation and ventricular arrhythmias, including torsade de pointes. Use caution in patients with coronary artery disease. Avoid use of extended release tablets (Biaxin® XL) in patients with known stricture/narrowing of the GI tract. Safety and efficacy in children <6 months of age have not been established.

Adverse Reactions
  1% to 10%:
    Central nervous system: Headache (adults and children 2%)
    Dermatologic: Rash (children 3%)
    Gastrointestinal: Abnormal taste (adults 3% to 7%), diarrhea (adults 3% to 6%; children 6%), vomiting (children 6%), nausea (adults 3%), abdominal pain (adults 2%; children 3%), dyspepsia 2%
    Hepatic: Prothrombin time increased (1%)
    Renal: BUN increased (4%)
  <1% (Limited to important or life-threatening): *Clostridium difficile* colitis, alkaline phosphatase increased, anaphylaxis, anorexia, anxiety, behavioral changes, bilirubin increased, confusion, disorientation, GGT increased, glossitis, hallucinations, hearing loss (reversible), hepatic dysfunction, hepatic failure, hepatitis, hypoglycemia, insomnia, interstitial nephritis, jaundice, leukopenia, manic behavior, neutropenia, oral moniliasis, pancreatitis, psychosis, QT prolongation, seizure, serum creatinine increased, Stevens-Johnson syndrome, stomatitis, tinnitus, tongue discoloration, tooth discoloration, torsade de pointes, toxic epidermal necrolysis, transaminases increased, tremor, urticaria, ventricular tachycardia, ventricular arrhythmia, vertigo

Overdosage/Toxicology Symptoms include nausea, vomiting, diarrhea, prostration, reversible pancreatitis, hearing loss with or without tinnitus, or vertigo. Treatment includes symptomatic and supportive care. Dialysis not likely to benefit.

Drug Interactions
  Cytochrome P450 Effect: Substrate of CYP3A4 (major); **Inhibits** CYP1A2 (weak), 3A4 (strong)
  Increased Effect/Toxicity: Avoid concomitant use of the following with clarithromycin due to increased risk of malignant arrhythmias: Cisapride, gatifloxacin, moxifloxacin, pimozide, (Continued)

Clarithromycin *(Continued)*

sparfloxacin, thioridazine. Other agents that prolong the QT_c interval, including type Ia (eg, quinidine) and type III antiarrhythmic agents, and selected antipsychotic agents (eg, thioridazine) should be used with extreme caution.

Clarithromycin is a strong CYP3A4 inhibitor, and may increase the levels/effects of alfentanil (and possibly other opioid analgesics), selected benzodiazepines, calcium channel blockers, cyclosporine, eletriptan, eplerenone, mirtazapine, nateglinide, nefazodone, quinidine, sildenafil (and other PDE-5 inhibitors), sirolimus, SSRIs, tacrolimus, venlafaxine, and other CYP3A4 substrates. Selected benzodiazepines (midazolam, triazolam), cisapride, ergot alkaloids, selected HMG-CoA reductase inhibitors (lovastatin and simvastatin), and pimozide are generally contraindicated with strong CYP3A4 inhibitors. When used with strong CYP3A4 inhibitors, dosage adjustment/limits are recommended for sildenafil and other PDE-5 inhibitors; refer to individual monographs.

The effects of warfarin have been potentiated by clarithromycin. Clarithromycin serum concentrations may be increased by amprenavir (and possibly other protease inhibitors). Digoxin serum levels may be increased by clarithromycin; digoxin toxicity and potentially fatal arrhythmias have been reported; monitor digoxin levels. Fluconazole increases clarithromycin levels and AUC by ~25%. Peak levels (but not AUC) of zidovudine may be increased; other studies suggest levels may be decreased.

The levels/effects of clarithromycin may be increased by azole antifungals, diclofenac, doxycycline, erythromycin, imatinib, isoniazid, nefazodone, nicardipine, propofol, protease inhibitors, quinidine, telithromycin, verapamil, and other CYP3A4 inhibitors.

Decreased Effect: Therapeutic effect of clopidogrel may be decreased by clarithromycin. Peak levels (but not AUC) of zidovudine may be increased; other studies suggest levels may be decreased. The levels/effects of clarithromycin may be decreased by aminoglutethimide, carbamazepine, nafcillin, nevirapine, phenobarbital, phenytoin, rifamycins, and other CYP3A4 inducers.

Ethanol/Nutrition/Herb Interactions

Food: Immediate release: Food delays rate, but not extent of absorption; Extended release: Food increases clarithromycin AUC by ~30% relative to fasting conditions.

Herb/Nutraceutical: St John's wort may decrease clarithromycin levels.

Stability Store tablets and granules for oral suspension at controlled room temperature. Reconstituted oral suspension should not be refrigerated because it might gel; microencapsulated particles of clarithromycin in suspension is stable for 14 days when stored at room temperature

Mechanism of Action Exerts its antibacterial action by binding to 50S ribosomal subunit resulting in inhibition of protein synthesis. The 14-OH metabolite of clarithromycin is twice as active as the parent compound against certain organisms.

Pharmacodynamics/Kinetics

Absorption: Immediate release: Rapid; food delays rate, but not extent of absorption

Distribution: Widely into most body tissues except CNS

Protein binding: 42% to 50%

Metabolism: Partially hepatic via CYP3A4; converted to 14-OH clarithromycin (active metabolite)

Bioavailability: 50%

Half-life elimination: Immediate release: Clarithromycin: 3-7 hours; 14-OH-clarithromycin: 5-9 hours

Time to peak: Immediate release: 2-3 hours

Excretion: Primarily urine (20% to 40% as unchanged drug; additional 10% to 15% as metabolite)

Clearance: Approximates normal GFR

Dosage

Usual dosage range:

Children ≥6 months: Oral: 7.5 mg/kg every 12 hours (maximum: 500 mg/dose)

Adults: Oral: 250-500 mg every 12 hours **or** 1000 mg (two 500 mg extended release tablets) once daily for 7-14 days

Indication-specific dosing:

Children: Oral:

Community-acquired pneumonia, sinusitis, bronchitis, skin infections: 15 mg/kg/day divided every 12 hours for 10 days

Endocarditis, prophylaxis (unlabeled use): 15 mg/kg 1 hour before procedure (maximum: 500 mg)

Mycobacterial infection (prevention and treatment): 7.5 mg/kg (up to 500 mg) twice daily. **Note:** Safety of clarithromycin for MAC not studied in children <20 months.

Pertussis (unlabeled use; CDC guidelines):

Children 1-5 months: 15 mg/kg/day divided every 12 hours for 7 days

Children ≥6 months: 15 mg/kg/day divided every 12 hours for 7 days (maximum: 1 g/day)

Adults: Oral:

Acute exacerbation of chronic bronchitis:

M. catarrhalis and *S. pneumoniae*: 250 mg every 12 hours for 7-14 days **or** 1000 mg (two 500 mg extended release tablets) once daily for 7 days

H. influenzae: 500 mg every 12 hours for 7-14 days or 1000 mg (two 500 mg extended release tablets) once daily for 7 days

H. parainfluenzae: 500 mg every 12 hours for 7 days or 1000 mg (two 500 mg extended release tablets) once daily for 7 days

Acute maxillary sinusitis: 500 mg every 12 hours **or** 1000 mg (two 500 mg extended release tablets) once daily for 14 days

Endocarditis, prophylaxis (unlabeled use): 500 mg 1 hour prior to procedure

Mycobacterial infection (prevention and treatment): 500 mg twice daily (use with other antimycobacterial drugs, eg, ethambutol or rifampin)

Peptic ulcer disease: Eradication of *Helicobacter pylori*: Dual or triple combination regimens with bismuth subsalicylate, amoxicillin, an H_2-receptor antagonist, or proton-pump inhibitor: 500 mg every 8-12 hours for 10-14 days

Pertussis (unlabeled use; CDC guidelines): 500 mg twice daily for 7 days

Pharyngitis, tonsillitis: 250 mg every 12 hours for 10 days

Pneumonia:

C. pneumoniae, M. pneumoniae, and *S. pneumoniae*: 250 mg every 12 hours for 7-14 days **or** 1000 mg (two 500 mg extended release tablets) once daily for 7 days

H. influenzae: 250 mg every 12 hours for 7 days **or** 1000 mg (two 500 mg extended release tablets) once daily for 7 days

Skin and skin structure infection, uncomplicated: 250 mg every 12 hours for 7-14 days

Elderly: Pharmacokinetics are similar to those in younger adults; may have age-related reductions in renal function; monitor and adjust dose if necessary

Dosing adjustment in renal impairment:

Cl_{cr} <30 mL/minute: Half the normal dose or double the dosing interval

In combination with ritonavir:

Cl_{cr} 30-60 mL/minute: Decrease clarithromycin dose by 50%

Cl_{cr} <30 mL/minute: Decrease clarithromycin dose by 75%

Dosing adjustment in hepatic impairment: No dosing adjustment is needed as long as renal function is normal

Dietary Considerations Clarithromycin immediate release tablets and oral solution may be given with or without meals. May be taken with milk. Biaxin® XL should be taken with food.

Administration Clarithromycin immediate release tablets and oral solution may be given with or without meals. Give every 12 hours rather than twice daily to avoid peak and trough variation.

Biaxin® XL: Should be given with food. Do not crush or chew extended release tablet.

Dosage Forms

Granules for oral suspension:

Biaxin®: 125 mg/5 mL (50 mL, 100 mL); 250 mg/5 mL (50 mL, 100 mL) [fruit punch flavor]

Tablet:

Biaxin®: 250 mg, 500 mg

Tablet, extended release:

Biaxin® XL: 500 mg

- **Clarithromycin, Lansoprazole, and Amoxicillin** *see* Lansoprazole, Amoxicillin, and Clarithromycin *on page 979*
- **Claritin® (Can)** *see* Loratadine *on page 1033*
- **Claritin® 24 Hour Allergy [OTC]** *see* Loratadine *on page 1033*
- **Claritin-D® 12-Hour [OTC]** *see* Loratadine and Pseudoephedrine *on page 1034*
- **Claritin-D® 24-Hour [OTC]** *see* Loratadine and Pseudoephedrine *on page 1034*
- **Claritin® Extra (Can)** *see* Loratadine and Pseudoephedrine *on page 1034*
- **Claritin® Hives Relief [OTC]** *see* Loratadine *on page 1033*
- **Claritin® Kids (Can)** *see* Loratadine *on page 1033*
- **Claritin® Liberator (Can)** *see* Loratadine and Pseudoephedrine *on page 1034*
- **Clarus™ (Can)** *see* Isotretinoin *on page 948*
- **Clavulanic Acid and Amoxicillin** *see* Amoxicillin and Clavulanate Potassium *on page 112*
- **Clavulin® (Can)** *see* Amoxicillin and Clavulanate Potassium *on page 112*
- **Clear Eyes® ACR [OTC]** *see* Naphazoline *on page 1198*
- **Clear Eyes® Extra Relief [OTC]** *see* Naphazoline *on page 1198*

Clemastine (KLEM as teen)

U.S. Brand Names Dayhist® Allergy [OTC]; Tavist® Allergy [OTC]

Index Terms Clemastine Fumarate

Pharmacologic Category Antihistamine

Use Perennial and seasonal allergic rhinitis and other allergic symptoms including urticaria

Pregnancy Risk Factor B

Lactation Enters breast milk/not recommended

Contraindications Hypersensitivity to clemastine or any component of the formulation; narrow-angle glaucoma

Warnings/Precautions Safety and efficacy have not been established in children <6 years of age. Use caution with bladder neck obstruction, symptomatic prostate hypertrophy, asthmatic attacks, stenosing peptic ulcer, increased intraocular pressure, hyperthyroidism, cardiovascular disease, hypertension, and in the elderly. May cause drowsiness; use caution in performing tasks which require alertness.

Adverse Reactions Frequency not defined.

Cardiovascular: Palpitations, hypotension, tachycardia

Central nervous system: Dyscoordination, sedation, somnolence slight to moderate, sleepiness, confusion, restlessness, nervousness, insomnia, irritability, fatigue, headache, dizziness increased

Dermatologic: Rash, photosensitivity

Gastrointestinal: Diarrhea, nausea, xerostomia, epigastric distress, vomiting, constipation

Genitourinary: Urinary frequency, difficult urination, urinary retention

Hematologic: Hemolytic anemia, thrombocytopenia, agranulocytosis

Ocular: Blurred vision

Otic: Tinnitus

Respiratory: Thickening of bronchial secretions

Miscellaneous: Anaphylaxis

Overdosage/Toxicology Symptoms include anemia, metabolic acidosis, hypotension, and hypothermia. There is no specific treatment for an antihistamine overdose, however, clinical toxicity is mostly due to anticholinergic effects. For anticholinergic overdose with severe

(Continued)

Clemastine (Continued)

life-threatening symptoms, physostigmine 1-2 mg (0.5 mg or 0.02 mg/kg for children) slow I.V. may be given to reverse these effects.

Drug Interactions

Cytochrome P450 Effect: Inhibits CYP2D6 (weak), 3A4 (weak)

Increased Effect/Toxicity: CNS depressants may increase the degree of sedation and respiratory depression with antihistamines. May increase the absorption of digoxin. Central and/or peripheral anticholinergic syndrome can occur when administered with amantadine, rimantadine, narcotic analgesics, phenothiazines and other antipsychotics (especially with high anticholinergic activity), tricyclic antidepressants, quinidine, disopyramide, procainamide, and antihistamines.

Decreased Effect: May increase gastric degradation of levodopa and decrease the amount of levodopa absorbed by delaying gastric emptying. Therapeutic effects of cholinergic agents (tacrine, donepezil) and neuroleptics may be antagonized.

Ethanol/Nutrition/Herb Interactions Ethanol: Avoid ethanol (may increase CNS depression).

Mechanism of Action Competes with histamine for H_1-receptor sites on effector cells in the gastrointestinal tract, blood vessels, and respiratory tract

Pharmacodynamics/Kinetics

Onset of action: Peak effect: Therapeutic: 5-7 hours

Duration: 8-16 hours

Absorption: Almost complete

Metabolism: Hepatic

Excretion: Urine

Dosage Oral:

Infants and Children <6 years: 0.05 mg/kg/day as **clemastine base** or 0.335-0.67 mg/day clemastine fumarate (0.25-0.5 mg base/day) divided into 2 or 3 doses; maximum daily dosage: 1.34 mg (1 mg base)

Children 6-12 years: 0.67-1.34 mg clemastine fumarate (0.5-1 mg base) twice daily; do not exceed 4.02 mg/day (3 mg/day base)

Children ≥12 years and Adults:

1.34 mg clemastine fumarate (1 mg base) twice daily to 2.68 mg (2 mg base) 3 times/day; do not exceed 8.04 mg/day (6 mg base)

OTC labeling: 1.34 mg clemastine fumarate (1 mg base) twice daily; do not exceed 2 mg base/24 hours

Elderly: Lower doses should be considered in patients >60 years

Monitoring Parameters Look for a reduction of rhinitis, urticaria, eczema, pruritus, or other allergic symptoms

Dosage Forms

Syrup, as fumarate [prescription formulation]: 0.67 mg/5 mL (120 mL) [0.5 mg base/5 mL; contains alcohol 5.5%; citrus flavor]

Tablet, as fumarate: 1.34 mg [1 mg base; OTC], 2.68 mg [2 mg base; prescription formulation]

Dayhist® Allergy, Tavist® Allergy: 1.34 mg [1 mg base]

- ♦ **Clemastine Fumarate** see Clemastine on page 387
- ♦ **Clenia™** see Sulfur and Sulfacetamide on page 1618
- ♦ **Cleocin®** see Clindamycin on page 389
- ♦ **Cleocin HCl®** see Clindamycin on page 389
- ♦ **Cleocin Pediatric®** see Clindamycin on page 389
- ♦ **Cleocin Phosphate®** see Clindamycin on page 389
- ♦ **Cleocin T®** see Clindamycin on page 389

Clidinium and Chlordiazepoxide (kli DI nee um & klor dye az e POKS ide)

U.S. Brand Names Librax® [original formulation]

Canadian Brand Names Apo-Chlorax®; Librax®

Index Terms Chlordiazepoxide and Clidinium

Pharmacologic Category Antispasmodic Agent, Gastrointestinal; Benzodiazepine

Use Adjunct treatment of peptic ulcer; treatment of irritable bowel syndrome

Pregnancy Risk Factor D

Medication Safety Issues

Sound-alike/look-alike issues:

Librax® may be confused with Librium®

Librax® formulation may be cause for confusion:

In November 2004, Valeant Pharmaceuticals licensed the Librax® trademark to Victory Pharmaceuticals. Subsequently, the product was reformulated to contain chlordiazepoxide and methscopolamine. In January 2006, Valeant Pharmaceuticals began redistributing the original formulation of Librax®, containing clidinium and chlordiazepoxide. Victory Pharmaceuticals has discontinued their product. **Note:** The formulation of Librax® distributed in Canada (Valeant Canada Ltd) always contained clidinium and chlordiazepoxide.

Dosage Oral: 1-2 capsules 3-4 times/day, before meals or food and at bedtime

Additional Information Complete prescribing information for this medication should be consulted for additional detail.

Dosage Forms Capsule: Clidinium bromide 2.5 mg and chlordiazepoxide hydrochloride 5 mg

- ♦ **Climara®** see Estradiol on page 620
- ♦ **ClimaraPro®** see Estradiol and Levonorgestrel on page 624
- ♦ **Clindagel®** see Clindamycin on page 389
- ♦ **ClindaMax™** see Clindamycin on page 389

Clindamycin (klin da MYE sin)

U.S. Brand Names Cleocin®; Cleocin HCl®; Cleocin Pediatric®; Cleocin Phosphate®; Cleocin T®; Clindagel®; ClindaMax™; Clindesse™; Clindets®; Evoclin™

Canadian Brand Names Alti-Clindamycin; Apo-Clindamycin®; Clindamycin Injection, USP; Clindoxyl®; Dalacin® C; Dalacin® T; Dalacin® Vaginal; Novo-Clindamycin; Taro-Clindamycin

Index Terms Clindamycin Hydrochloride; Clindamycin Palmitate; Clindamycin Phosphate

Pharmacologic Category Antibiotic, Lincosamide; Topical Skin Product, Acne

Additional Appendix Information
Animal and Human Bites *on page 1976*
Antimicrobial Drugs of Choice *on page 1981*
Community-Acquired Pneumonia in Adults *on page 1999*
Malaria Treatment *on page 2003*
Prevention of Bacterial Endocarditis *on page 1960*
Prevention of Wound Infection and Sepsis in Surgical Patients *on page 1964*
Treatment of Sexually Transmitted Infections *on page 2007*
USPHS / IDSA Guidelines for the Prevention of Opportunistic Infections in Persons Infected With HIV *on page 1966*

Use Treatment against aerobic and anaerobic streptococci (except enterococci), most staphylococci, *Bacteroides* sp and *Actinomyces*; bacterial vaginosis (vaginal cream, vaginal suppository); pelvic inflammatory disease (I.V.); topically in treatment of severe acne; vaginally for *Gardnerella vaginalis*

Unlabeled/Investigational Use May be useful in PCP; alternate treatment for toxoplasmosis

Pregnancy Risk Factor B

Lactation Enters breast milk/compatible

Medication Safety Issues
Sound-alike/look-alike issues:
Cleocin® may be confused with bleomycin, Clinoril®, Lincocin®

Contraindications Hypersensitivity to clindamycin or any component of the formulation; previous pseudomembranous colitis; regional enteritis, ulcerative colitis

Warnings/Precautions Dosage adjustment may be necessary in patients with severe hepatic dysfunction. **[U.S. Boxed Warning]: Can cause severe and possibly fatal colitis.** Discontinue drug if significant diarrhea, abdominal cramps, or passage of blood and mucus occurs. Vaginal products may weaken latex or rubber condoms, or contraceptive diaphragms. Barrier contraceptives are not recommended concurrently or for 3-5 days (depending on the product) following treatment. Some dosage forms contain benzyl alcohol or tartrazine. Use caution in atopic patients.

Adverse Reactions
Systemic:
>10%: Gastrointestinal: Diarrhea, abdominal pain
1% to 10%:
Cardiovascular: Hypotension
Dermatologic: Urticaria, rash, Stevens-Johnson syndrome
Gastrointestinal: Pseudomembranous colitis, nausea, vomiting
Local: Thrombophlebitis, sterile abscess at I.M. injection site
Miscellaneous: Fungal overgrowth, hypersensitivity
<1% (Limited to important or life-threatening): Granulocytopenia, neutropenia, polyarthritis, renal dysfunction (rare), thrombocytopenia
Topical:
>10%: Dermatologic: Dryness, burning, itching, scaliness, erythema, or peeling of skin (lotion, solution); oiliness (gel, lotion)
1% to 10%: Central nervous system: Headache
<1% (Limited to important or life-threatening): Pseudomembranous colitis, nausea, vomiting, diarrhea (severe), abdominal pain, folliculitis, hypersensitivity reactions
Vaginal:
>10%: Genitourinary: Fungal vaginosis, vaginitis or vulvovaginal pruritus (from *Candida albicans*)
1% to 10%:
Central nervous system: Back pain, headache
Gastrointestinal: Constipation, diarrhea
Genitourinary: Urinary tract infection
Respiratory: Nasopharyngitis
Miscellaneous: Fungal infection
<1% (Limited to important or life-threatening): Atrophic vaginitis, bladder infection, bladder spasm, cervical dysplasia, diarrhea, dizziness, epistaxis, erythema, fever, hypersensitivity, hyperthyroidism, local edema, menstrual disorder, nausea, pain, palpable lymph node, pruritus, pyelonephritis, pyrexia, rash, sciatica, stomach cramps, upper respiratory urticaria, uterine cervical disorder, uterine spasm, vaginal burning, vertigo, vomiting, vulvar erythema, vulvar laceration, wheezing

Overdosage/Toxicology Following GI decontamination, symptoms include diarrhea, nausea, and vomiting. Treatment is supportive.

Drug Interactions
Increased Effect/Toxicity: Increased duration of neuromuscular blockade when given in conjunction with tubocurarine and pancuronium.

Ethanol/Nutrition/Herb Interactions
Food: Peak concentrations may be delayed with food.
Herb/Nutraceutical: St John's wort may decrease clindamycin levels.

Stability
Capsule: Store at room temperature of 20°C to 25°C (68°F to 77°F).
Cream: Store at room temperature.
Foam: Store at room temperature of 20°C to 25°C (68°F to 77°F); avoid fire, flame, or smoking during or following application.
Gel: Store at room temperature.
(Continued)

389

Clindamycin *(Continued)*

Clindagel®: Do not store in direct sunlight.

I.V.: Infusion solution in NS or D$_5$W solution is stable for 16 days at room temperature.

Lotion: Store at room temperature of 20°C to 25°C (68°F to 77°F).

Oral solution: Do not refrigerate reconstituted oral solution (it will thicken); following reconstitution, oral solution is stable for 2 weeks at room temperature of 20°C to 25°C (68°F to 77°F).

Ovule: Store at room temperature of 15°C to 30°C (68°F to 77°F).

Pledget: Store at room temperature.

Topical solution: Store at room temperature of 20°C to 25°C (68°F to 77°F).

Mechanism of Action Reversibly binds to 50S ribosomal subunits preventing peptide bond formation thus inhibiting bacterial protein synthesis; bacteriostatic or bactericidal depending on drug concentration, infection site, and organism

Pharmacodynamics/Kinetics

Absorption: Topical: ~10%; Oral: Rapid (90%)

Distribution: High concentrations in bone and urine; no significant levels in CSF, even with inflamed meninges; crosses placenta; enters breast milk

Metabolism: Hepatic

Bioavailability: Topical: <1%

Half-life elimination: Neonates: Premature: 8.7 hours; Full-term: 3.6 hours; Adults: 1.6-5.3 hours (average: 2-3 hours)

Time to peak, serum: Oral: Within 60 minutes; I.M.: 1-3 hours

Excretion: Urine (10%) and feces (~4%) as active drug and metabolites

Dosage

Usual dosage ranges:

Infants and Children:

Oral: 8-20 mg/kg/day as hydrochloride; 8-25 mg/kg/day as palmitate in 3-4 divided doses (minimum dose of palmitate: 37.5 mg 3 times/day)

I.M., I.V.:

<1 month: 15-20 mg/kg/day

>1 month: 20-40 mg/kg/day in 3-4 divided doses

Adults:

Oral: 150-450 mg/dose every 6-8 hours; maximum dose: 1.8 g/day

I.M., I.V.: 1.2-1.8 g/day in 2-4 divided doses; maximum dose: 4.8 g/day

Indication-specific dosing:

Children:

Anthrax: I.V.: 7.5 mg/kg every 6 hours

Babesiosis: Oral: 20-40 mg/kg/day divided every 8 hours for 7 days plus quinine

Orofacial infections: 8-25 mg/kg in 3-4 equally divided doses

Prevention of bacterial endocarditis (unlabeled use):

Oral: 20 mg/kg 1 hour before procedure with no follow-up dose needed

I.V.: 20 mg/kg within 30 minutes before procedure

Children ≥12 years and Adults:

Acne vulgaris: Topical:

Gel, pledget, lotion, solution: Apply a thin film twice daily

Foam (Evoclin™): Apply once daily

Adults:

Amnionitis: I.V.: 450-900 mg every 8 hours

Anthrax: I.V.: 900 mg every 8 hours with ciprofloxacin or doxycycline

Babesiosis:

Oral: 600 mg 3 times/day for 7 days with quinine

I.V.: 1.2 g twice daily

Bacterial vaginosis: Intravaginal:

Suppositories: Insert one ovule (100 mg clindamycin) daily into vagina at bedtime for 3 days

Cream:

Cleocin®: One full applicator inserted intravaginally once daily before bedtime for 3 or 7 consecutive days in nonpregnant patients or for 7 consecutive days in pregnant patients

Clindesse™: One full applicator inserted intravaginally as a single dose at anytime during the day in nonpregnant patients

Bite wounds (canine): Oral: 300 mg 4 times/day with a fluoroquinolone

Gangrenous myositis: I.V.: 900 mg every 8 hours with penicillin G

Group B streptococcus (neonatal prophylaxis): I.V.: 900 mg every 8 hours until delivery

Orofacial/parapharyngeal space infections:

Oral: 150-450 mg every 6 hours for 7 days, maximum 1.8 g/day

I.V.: 600-900 mg every 8 hours

Pelvic inflammatory disease: I.V.: 900 mg every 8 hours with gentamicin 2 mg/kg, then 1.5 mg/kg every 8 hours; continue after discharge with doxycycline 100 mg twice daily to complete 14 days of total therapy

***Pneumocystis jiroveci* pneumonia (unlabeled use):**

Oral: 300-450 mg 4 times/day with primaquine

I.M., I.V.: 1200-2400 mg/day with pyrimethamine or 600 mg 4 times/day with primaquine

Prevention of bacterial endocarditis (unlabeled use):

Oral: 600 mg 1 hour before procedure with no follow-up dose needed

I.V.: 600 mg within 30 minutes before procedure

Toxic shock syndrome: I.V.: 900 mg every 8 hours with penicillin G or ceftriaxone

Toxoplasmosis (unlabeled use): Oral, I.V.: 600 mg every 6 hours with pyrimethamine and folinic acid

Dosing adjustment in hepatic impairment: Adjustment recommended in patients with severe hepatic disease

Dietary Considerations May be taken with food.

Administration
I.M.: Deep I.M. sites, rotate sites; do not exceed 600 mg in a single injection.

Intravaginal:
Cream: Insertion should be as far as possible into the vagina without causing discomfort.

Ovule: The foil should be removed; if the applicator is used for insertion, it should be washed for additional use.

I.V.: **Never administer as bolus**; administer by I.V. intermittent infusion over at least 10-60 minutes, at a rate **not** to exceed 30 mg/minute (not exceed 1200 mg/hour); final concentration for administration should not exceed 18 mg/mL.

Oral: Administer with a full glass of water to minimize esophageal ulceration; give around-the-clock to promote less variation in peak and trough serum levels.

Topical foam: Dispense directly into cap or onto a cool surface; do not dispense directly into hands.

Monitoring Parameters Observe for changes in bowel frequency. Monitor for colitis and resolution of symptoms. During prolonged therapy monitor CBC, liver and renal function tests periodically.

Dosage Forms Note: Strength is expressed as base

Capsule, as hydrochloride: 150 mg, 300 mg
Cleocin HCl®: 75 mg [contains tartrazine], 150 mg [contains tartrazine], 300 mg

Cream, vaginal, as phosphate:
Cleocin®: 2% (40 g) [contains benzyl alcohol and mineral oil; packaged with 7 disposable applicators]
Clindesse™: 2% (5 g) [contains mineral oil; prefilled single disposable applicator]

Foam, topical, as phosphate (Evoclin™): 1% (50 g, 100 g) [contains ethanol 58%]

Gel, topical, as phosphate: 1% [10 mg/g] (30 g, 60 g)
Cleocin T®: 1% [10 mg/g] (30 g, 60 g)
Clindagel®: 1% [10 mg/g] (40 mL, 75 mL)
ClindaMax™: 1% (30 g, 60 g)

Granules for oral solution, as palmitate (Cleocin Pediatric®): 75 mg/5 mL (100 mL) [cherry flavor]

Infusion, as phosphate [premixed in D₅W] (Cleocin Phosphate®): 300 mg (50 mL); 600 mg (50 mL); 900 mg (50 mL)

Injection, solution, as phosphate (Cleocin Phosphate®): 150 mg/mL (2 mL, 4 mL, 6 mL, 60 mL) [contains benzyl alcohol and disodium edetate 0.5 mg]

Lotion, as phosphate (Cleocin T®, ClindaMax™): 1% [10 mg/mL] (60 mL)

Pledgets, topical: 1% (60s) [contains alcohol]
Cleocin T®: 1% (60s) [contains isopropyl alcohol 50%]
Clindets®: 1% (69s) [contains isopropyl alcohol 52%]

Solution, topical, as phosphate (Cleocin T®): 1% [10 mg/mL] (30 mL, 60 mL) [contains isopropyl alcohol 50%]

Suppository (ovule), vaginal, as phosphate (Cleocin®): 100 mg (3s) [contains oleaginous base; single reusable applicator]

Clindamycin and Tretinoin (klin da MYE sin & TRET i noyn)

U.S. Brand Names Ziana™
Index Terms Clindamycin Phosphate and Tretinoin; Tretinoin and Clindamycin
Pharmacologic Category Acne Products; Retinoic Acid Derivative; Topical Skin Product; Topical Skin Product, Acne
Use Treatment of acne vulgaris
Pregnancy Risk Factor C
Dosage Topical: Children ≥12 years and Adults: Apply pea-size amount to entire face once daily at bedtime
Dosage Forms
Gel, topical:
Ziana™: Clindamycin phosphate 1.2% and tretinoin 0.025% (2 g, 30 g, 60 g)

♦ **Clindamycin Hydrochloride** see Clindamycin on page 389
♦ **Clindamycin Injection, USP (Can)** see Clindamycin on page 389
♦ **Clindamycin Palmitate** see Clindamycin on page 389
♦ **Clindamycin Phosphate** see Clindamycin on page 389
♦ **Clindamycin Phosphate and Tretinoin** see Clindamycin and Tretinoin on page 391
♦ **Clindesse™** see Clindamycin on page 389
♦ **Clindets®** see Clindamycin on page 389
♦ **Clindoxyl® (Can)** see Clindamycin on page 389
♦ **Clinoril®** see Sulindac on page 1618

Clobetasol (kloe BAY ta sol)

U.S. Brand Names Clobevate®; Clobex®; Cormax®; Embeline™ [DSC]; Embeline™ E [DSC]; Olux®; Temovate®; Temovate E®
Canadian Brand Names Clobex®; Dermovate®; Gen-Clobetasol; Novo-Clobetasol; Taro-Clobetasol
Index Terms Clobetasol Propionate
Pharmacologic Category Corticosteroid, Topical
Additional Appendix Information
Corticosteroids on page 1879
Use Short-term relief of inflammation of moderate-to-severe corticosteroid-responsive dermatoses (very high potency topical corticosteroid)
Pregnancy Risk Factor C
(Continued)

Clobetasol (Continued)

Medication Safety Issues
International issues:
Clobex® may be confused with Codex® which is a brand name for saccharomyces boulardii in Italy

Dosage Topical: Discontinue when control achieved; if improvement not seen within 2 weeks, reassessment of diagnosis may be necessary.

Children <12 years: Use is not recommended
Children ≥12 years and Adults:
Oral mucosal inflammation, dental (unlabeled use): Cream: Apply twice daily for up to 2 weeks (maximum dose: 50 g/week); discontinue application when control is achieved; if no improvement is seen, reassessment of diagnosis may be necessary
Steroid-responsive dermatoses:
Cream, emollient cream, gel, ointment: Apply twice daily for up to 2 weeks (maximum dose: 50 g/week)
Foam, solution: Apply to affected scalp twice daily for up to 2 weeks (maximum dose: 50 g/week or 50 mL/week)
Mild-to-moderate plaque-type psoriasis of nonscalp areas: Foam: Apply to affected area twice daily for up to 2 weeks (maximum dose: 50 g/week); do not apply to face or intertriginous areas
Children ≥16 years and Adults: Moderate-to-severe plaque-type psoriasis: Emollient cream, lotion: Apply twice daily for up to 2 weeks, has been used for up to 4 weeks when application is <10% of body surface area; use with caution (maximum dose: 50 g/week)
Children ≥18 years and Adults:
Moderate-to-severe plaque-type psoriasis: Spray: Apply by spraying directly onto affected area twice daily; should be gently rubbed into skin. Should be used for not longer than 4 weeks; treatment beyond 2 weeks should be limited to localized lesions which have not improved sufficiently. Total dose should not exceed 50 g/week or 59 mL/week.
Scalp psoriasis: Shampoo: Apply thin film to dry scalp once daily; leave in place for 15 minutes, then add water, lather; rinse thoroughly
Steroid-responsive dermatoses: Lotion: Apply twice daily for up to 2 weeks (maximum dose: 50 g/week)

Additional Information Complete prescribing information for this medication should be consulted for additional detail.

Dosage Forms [DSC] = Discontinued product
Cream, as propionate: 0.05% (15 g, 30 g, 45 g, 60 g)
Cormax®: 0.05% (30 g)
Embeline™ [DSC], Temovate®: 0.05% (15 g, 30 g, 45 g, 60 g)
Cream, as propionate [in emollient base]: 0.05% (15 g, 30 g, 60 g)
Embeline™ E: 0.05% (15 g, 30 g, 60 g) [DSC]
Temovate E®: 0.05% (15 g [DSC], 30 g, 60 g)
Foam, topical, as propionate [for scalp application] (Olux®): 0.05% (50 g, 100 g) [contains ethanol 60%]
Gel, as propionate: 0.05% (15 g, 30 g, 60 g)
Clobevate®, Embeline™ [DSC]: 0.05% (15 g, 30 g, 60 g)
Temovate®: 0.05% (15 g [DSC], 30 g, 60 g)
Lotion, as propionate (Clobex®): 0.05% (30 mL, 59 mL)
Ointment, as propionate: 0.05% (15 g, 30 g, 45 g, 60 g)
Cormax®: 0.05% (15 g, 45 g)
Embeline™: 0.05% (15 g, 30 g, 45 g, 60 g) [DSC]
Temovate®: 0.05% (15 g, 30 g, 45 g [DSC], 60 g)
Shampoo, as propionate:
Clobex®: 0.05% (120 mL) [contains alcohol]
Solution, topical, as propionate [for scalp application]: 0.05% (25 mL, 50 mL)
Cormax®, Embeline™ [DSC], Temovate®: 0.05% (25 mL, 50 mL) [contains isopropyl alcohol 40%]
Spray, topical, as propionate (Clobex®): 0.05% (60 mL) [contains alcohol]

♦ **Clobetasol Propionate** see Clobetasol on page 391
♦ **Clobevate®** see Clobetasol on page 391
♦ **Clobex®** see Clobetasol on page 391

Clocortolone (kloe KOR toe lone)

U.S. Brand Names Cloderm®
Canadian Brand Names Cloderm®
Index Terms Clocortolone Pivalate
Pharmacologic Category Corticosteroid, Topical
Additional Appendix Information
Corticosteroids on page 1879
Use Inflammation of corticosteroid-responsive dermatoses (intermediate-potency topical corticosteroid)
Pregnancy Risk Factor C
Medication Safety Issues
Sound-alike/look-alike issues:
Cloderm® may be confused with Clocort®

International issues:
Cloderm®: Brand name for clotrimazole in Germany

Dosage Adults: Apply sparingly and gently; rub into affected area from 1-4 times/day. Therapy should be discontinued when control is achieved; if no improvement is seen, reassessment of diagnosis may be necessary.
Dosage Forms Cream, as pivalate: 0.1% (15 g, 45 g, 90 g)

♦ **Clocortolone Pivalate** *see* Clocortolone *on page 392*
♦ **Cloderm**® *see* Clocortolone *on page 392*

Clofarabine (klo FARE a been)

U.S. Brand Names Clolar™
Index Terms Clofarex; NSC606869
Pharmacologic Category Antineoplastic Agent, Antimetabolite (Purine Antagonist)
Use Treatment of relapsed or refractory acute lymphoblastic leukemia
Unlabeled/Investigational Use Adults: Relapsed and refractory acute myeloid leukemia (AML), chronic myeloid leukemia (CML) in blast phase, acute lymphocytic leukemia (ALL), myelodysplastic syndrome
Pregnancy Risk Factor D
Pregnancy Implications Teratogenic effects were observed in animal studies. There are no adequate or well-controlled studies in pregnant women. Women of childbearing potential should be advised to use effective contraception and avoid becoming pregnant during therapy.
Lactation Excretion in breast milk unknown/not recommended
Medication Safety Issues
High alert medication: The Institute for Safe Medication Practices (ISMP) includes this medication among its list of drugs which have a heightened risk of causing significant patient harm when used in error.
Contraindications Hypersensitivity to clofarabine or any component of the formulation
Warnings/Precautions Hazardous agent - use appropriate precautions for handling and disposal. Tumor lysis syndrome may occur. Cytokine release may develop into systemic inflammatory response syndrome (SIRS)/capillary leak syndrome, and organ dysfunction; discontinuation of clofarabine should be considered with the presentation of SIRS or capillary leak syndrome. Safety and efficacy have not been established with renal or hepatic dysfunction; use with caution. Safety and efficacy in pediatric patients <1 year of age or adults >21 years have not been established.
Adverse Reactions
>10%:
Cardiovascular: Pericardial effusion (35%), tachycardia (34%), hypotension (29%), left ventricular systolic dysfunction (27%), edema (20%), flushing (18%), hypertension (11%)
Central nervous system: Headache (46%), pyrexia (41%), fatigue (36%) anxiety (22%), pain (19%), dizziness (16%), depression (11%), irritability (11%), lethargy (1%)
Dermatologic: Pruritus (47%), dermatitis (41%), petechiae (29%), erythema (18%), palmar-plantar erythrodysesthesia syndrome (13%), oral candidiasis (13%), cellulitis (11%)
Gastrointestinal: Vomiting (83%), nausea (75%), diarrhea (53%), abdominal pain (36%), anorexia (30%), constipation (21%), mucosal inflammation (18%), gingival bleeding (15%), sore throat (14%), appetite decreased (11%)
Genitourinary: Hematuria (17%)
Hematologic: Febrile neutropenia (57%)
Hepatic: ALT increased (44%), AST increased (38%), bilirubin increased (15%), hepatomegaly (15%), jaundice (15%)
Neuromuscular & skeletal: Rigors (38%), pain in limb (29%), myalgia (14%), back pain (13%), arthralgia (11%)
Respiratory: Epistaxis (31%), cough (19%), respiratory distress (14%), dyspnea (13%)
Miscellaneous: Infection (85%), injection site pain (14%), staphylococcal infection (13%), herpes simplex (11%)
1% to 10%:
Central nervous system: Somnolence (10%)
Gastrointestinal: Weight gain (10%)
Genitourinary: Creatinine increased (6%)
Neuromuscular & skeletal: Tremor (10%)
Respiratory: Pleural effusion (10%), pneumonia (10%), systemic inflammatory response syndrome (SIRS)/capillary leak syndrome
Miscellaneous: Transfusion reaction (10%), bacteremia (10%)
Overdosage/Toxicology No known overdoses have been reported; treatment should be symptom directed and supportive.
Drug Interactions
Increased Effect/Toxicity: None known
Decreased Effect: None known
Stability Store undiluted and diluted solutions at room temperature of 15°C to 30°C (59°F to 86°F). Clofarabine should be diluted with 100-500 mL NS or D_5W; manufacturer recommends the product be filtered through a 0.2 micrometer filter before dilution. Solutions diluted in 100-500 mL of D_5W or NS are stable for 24 hours at room temperature.
Mechanism of Action Clofarabine, a purine (deoxyadenosine) nucleoside analog, is metabolized to clofarabine 5'-triphosphate. Clofarabine 5'-triphosphate decreases cell replication and repair as well as causing cell death. To decrease cell replication and repair, clofarabine 5'-triphosphate competes with deoxyadenosine triphosphate for the enzymes ribonucleotide reductase and DNA polymerase. Cell replication is decreased when clofarabine 5'-triphosphate inhibits ribonucleotide reductase from reacting with deoxyadenosine triphosphate to produce deoxynucleotide triphosphate which is needed for DNA synthesis. Cell replication is also decreased when clofarabine 5'-triphosphate competes with DNA polymerase for incorporation into the DNA chain; when done during the repair process, cell repair is affected. To cause cell death, clofarabine 5'-triphosphate alters the mitochondrial membrane by releasing proteins, an inducing factor and cytochrome C.
Pharmacodynamics/Kinetics
Distribution: V_d: 172 L/m^2
Protein binding: 47%
(Continued)

Clofarabine *(Continued)*

Metabolism: Intracellular by deoxycytidine kinase and mono- and diphosphokinases to active metabolite clofarabine 5'-triphosphate

Half-life elimination: ~5.2 hours

Excretion: Urine (49% to 60% unchanged)

Dosage I.V.: Children and Adults 1-21 years: ALL: 52 mg/m^2/day days 1 through 5; repeat every 2-6 weeks

Dosage adjustment in renal/hepatic impairment: Safety not established; use with caution

Administration I.V. infusion: Over 2 hours. Continuous I.V. fluids are encouraged to decrease adverse events and tumor lysis effects. Hypotension may be a sign of capillary leak syndrome or systemic inflammatory response syndrome (SIRS). Discontinue if the patient becomes hypotensive during administration. Retreatment should only be considered if the hypotension is not related to capillary leak syndrome or SIRS.

Monitoring Parameters Blood pressure, cardiac function, and respiratory status during infusion; periodic CBC with platelet count (increase frequency in patients who develop cytopenias); liver and kidney function during 5 days of clofarabine administration; signs and symptoms of tumor lysis syndrome and cytokine release syndrome (tachypnea, tachycardia, hypotension, pulmonary edema); hydration status

Additional Information The use of prophylactic steroids (hydrocortisone 100 mg/m^2 on days 1-3) may be of benefit in preventing signs of SIRS or capillary leak syndrome; allopurinol may be used if hyperuricemia is anticipated. Dosage should be based on BSA, calculated based upon height and weight prior to each cycle.

Dosage Forms Injection, solution [preservative free]: 1 mg/mL (20 mL)

♦ **Clofarex** *see* Clofarabine *on page 393*

♦ **Clolar**™ *see* Clofarabine *on page 393*

♦ **Clomid**® *see* ClomiPHENE *on page 394*

ClomiPHENE *(KLOE mi feen)*

U.S. Brand Names Clomid®; Serophene®

Canadian Brand Names Clomid®; Milophene®; Serophene®

Index Terms Clomiphene Citrate

Pharmacologic Category Ovulation Stimulator

Use Treatment of ovulatory failure in patients desiring pregnancy

Unlabeled/Investigational Use Male infertility

Pregnancy Risk Factor X

Lactation Excretion in breast milk unknown/contraindicated

Medication Safety Issues
Sound-alike/look-alike issues:
ClomiPHENE may be confused with clomiPRAMINE, clonidine
Clomid® may be confused with clonidine
Serophene® may be confused with Sarafem™

Contraindications Hypersensitivity to clomiphene citrate or any of its components; liver disease; abnormal uterine bleeding; enlargement or development of ovarian cyst; uncontrolled thyroid or adrenal dysfunction in the presence of an organic intracranial lesion such as pituitary tumor; pregnancy

Warnings/Precautions Use with caution in patients unusually sensitive to pituitary gonadotropins (eg, polycystic ovary disease). Multiple pregnancies, blurring or other visual symptoms, ovarian hyperstimulation syndrome, and abdominal pain can occur.

Adverse Reactions
>10%: Endocrine & metabolic: Hot flashes, ovarian enlargement
1% to 10%:
Cardiovascular: Thromboembolism
Central nervous system: Mental depression, headache
Endocrine & metabolic: Breast enlargement (males), breast discomfort (females), abnormal menstrual flow, ovarian cyst formation, ovarian enlargement, premenstrual syndrome, uterine fibroid enlargement
Gastrointestinal: Distention, bloating, nausea, vomiting
Hepatic: Hepatotoxicity
Ocular: Blurring of vision, diplopia, floaters, after-images, phosphenes, photophobia, scotoma
<1% (Limited to important or life-threatening): Alopecia (reversible), polyuria

Drug Interactions
Decreased Effect: Decreased response when used with danazol. Decreased estradiol response when used with clomiphene.

Stability Protect from light.

Mechanism of Action Induces ovulation by stimulating the release of pituitary gonadotropins

Pharmacodynamics/Kinetics
Metabolism: Undergoes enterohepatic recirculation
Half-life elimination: 5-7 days
Excretion: Primarily feces; urine (small amounts)

Dosage Adults: Oral:
Male (infertility): 25 mg/day for 25 days with 5 days rest, or 100 mg every Monday, Wednesday, Friday

Female (ovulatory failure): 50 mg/day for 5 days (first course); start the regimen on or about the fifth day of cycle. The dose should be increased only in those patients who do not ovulate in response to cyclic 50 mg Clomid®. A low dosage or duration of treatment course is particularly recommended if unusual sensitivity to pituitary gonadotropin is suspected, such as in patients with polycystic ovary syndrome.

If ovulation does not appear to occur after the first course of therapy, a second course of 100 mg/day (two 50 mg tablets given as a single daily dose) for 5 days should be given. This course may be started as early as 30 days after the previous one after precautions are taken to exclude the presence of pregnancy. Increasing the dosage or duration of therapy beyond 100 mg/day for 5 days is not recommended. The majority of patients who are going to ovulate will do so after the first course of therapy. If ovulation does not occur after 3 courses of therapy, further treatment is not recommended and the patient should be re-evaluated. If 3 ovulatory responses occur, but pregnancy has not been achieved, further treatment is not recommended. If menses does not occur after an ovulatory response, the patient should be re-evaluated. Long-term cyclic therapy is not recommended beyond a total of about 6 cycles.

Reference Range FSH and LH are expected to peak 5-9 days after completing clomiphene; ovulation assessed by basal body temperature or serum progesterone 2 weeks after last clomiphene dose

Test Interactions Clomiphene may increase levels of serum thyroxine and thyroxine-binding globulin (TBG)

Dosage Forms Tablet, as citrate: 50 mg

♦ **Clomiphene Citrate** see ClomiPHENE on page 394

ClomiPRAMINE (kloe MI pra meen)

U.S. Brand Names Anafranil®

Canadian Brand Names Anafranil®; Apo-Clomipramine®; CO Clomipramine; Gen-Clomipramine

Index Terms Clomipramine Hydrochloride

Pharmacologic Category Antidepressant, Tricyclic (Tertiary Amine)

Additional Appendix Information
Antidepressant Agents on page 1866

Use Treatment of obsessive-compulsive disorder (OCD)

Unlabeled/Investigational Use Depression, panic attacks, chronic pain

Restrictions An FDA-approved medication guide concerning the use of antidepressants in children and teenagers must be distributed when dispensing an outpatient prescription (new or refill) where this medication is to be used without direct supervision of a healthcare provider. Medication guides are available at http://www.fda.gov/cder/Offices/ODS/medication_guides.htm. Dispense to parents or guardians of children and teenagers receiving this medication.

Pregnancy Risk Factor C

Pregnancy Implications There are no adequate and well-controlled studies in pregnant women. Withdrawal symptoms (including dizziness, nausea, vomiting, headache, malaise, sleep disturbance, hyperthermia, and/or irritability) have been observed in neonates whose mothers took clomipramine up to delivery. Use in pregnancy only if the benefits to the mother outweigh the potential risks to the fetus.

Lactation Enters breast milk/contraindicated (AAP rates "of concern")

Medication Safety Issues
Sound-alike/look-alike issues:
ClomiPRAMINE may be confused with chlorproMAZINE, clomiPHENE, desipramine, Norpramin®
Anafranil® may be confused with alfentanil, enalapril, nafarelin

Contraindications Hypersensitivity to clomipramine, other tricyclic agents, or any component of the formulation; use of MAO inhibitors within 14 days; use in a patient during the acute recovery phase of MI

Warnings/Precautions [U.S. Boxed Warning]: Antidepressants increase the risk of suicidal thinking and behavior in children and adolescents with major depressive disorder (MDD) and other depressive disorders; consider risk prior to prescribing. All patients must be closely monitored for clinical worsening, suicidality, or unusual changes in behavior, especially during the initiation of therapy or following an increase or decrease in dosage. When used in children, the child's family or caregiver should be instructed to closely observe the patient and communicate condition with healthcare provider. A medication guide should be dispensed with each prescription. **Clomipramine is FDA approved for the treatment of OCD in children ≥10 years of age.**

The possibility of a suicide attempt is inherent in major depression and may persist until remission occurs. Use caution in high-risk patients. Worsening depression and severe abrupt suicidality that are not part of the presenting symptoms may require discontinuation or modification of drug therapy. The patient's family or caregiver should be alerted to monitor patients for the emergence of suicidality and associated behaviors (such as agitation, irritability, hostility, impulsivity, and hypomania) and notify the healthcare provider.

May worsen psychosis in some patients or precipitate a shift to mania or hypomania in patients with bipolar disorder. Patients presenting with depressive symptoms should be screened for bipolar disorder. Monotherapy in patients with bipolar disorder should be avoided. **Clomipramine is not FDA approved for bipolar depression.**

May cause seizures (relationship to dose and/or duration of therapy) - do not exceed maximum doses. Use caution in patients with a previous seizure disorder or condition predisposing to seizures such as brain damage, alcoholism, or concurrent therapy with other drugs which lower the seizure threshold. May increase the risks associated with electroconvulsive therapy. Has been associated with a high incidence of sexual dysfunction. Weight gain may occur.

(Continued)

ClomiPRAMINE *(Continued)*

The degree of sedation, anticholinergic effects, and conduction abnormalities are high relative to other antidepressants. Clomipramine often causes drowsiness/sedation, resulting in impaired performance of tasks requiring alertness (eg, operating machinery or driving). Sedative effects may be additive with other CNS depressants and/or ethanol. The risk of orthostasis is moderate to high relative to other antidepressants. Use with caution in patients with a history of cardiovascular disease (including previous MI, stroke, tachycardia, or conduction abnormalities). Use with caution in patients with urinary retention, benign prostatic hyperplasia, narrow-angle glaucoma, xerostomia, visual problems, constipation, or a history of bowel obstruction.

Consider discontinuing, when possible, prior to elective surgery. Therapy should not be abruptly discontinued in patients receiving high doses for prolonged periods. Use with caution in hyperthyroid patients or those receiving thyroid supplementation. Use with caution in patients with hepatic or renal dysfunction and in elderly patients.

Adverse Reactions
>10%:
Central nervous system: Dizziness, drowsiness, headache, insomnia, nervousness
Endocrine & metabolic: Libido changes
Gastrointestinal: Xerostomia, constipation, appetite increased, nausea, weight gain, dyspepsia, anorexia, abdominal pain
Neuromuscular & skeletal: Fatigue, tremor, myoclonus
Miscellaneous: Diaphoresis increased
1% to 10%:
Cardiovascular: Hypotension, palpitation, tachycardia
Central nervous system: Confusion, hypertonia, sleep disorder, yawning, speech disorder, abnormal dreaming, paresthesia, memory impairment, anxiety, twitching, coordination impaired, agitation, migraine, depersonalization, emotional lability, flushing, fever
Dermatologic: Rash, pruritus, dermatitis
Gastrointestinal: Diarrhea, vomiting
Genitourinary: Difficult urination
Ocular: Blurred vision, eye pain
<1% (Limited to important or life-threatening): Alopecia, galactorrhea, hyperacusis, marrow depression, photosensitivity, reflux, seizure, SIADH

Overdosage/Toxicology Symptoms include agitation, confusion, hallucinations, urinary retention, hypothermia, hypotension, tachycardia, ventricular tachycardia, seizures, and coma. Following initiation of essential overdose management, toxic symptoms should be treated. Sodium bicarbonate is indicated when the QRS interval is >0.10 seconds or the QT_c is >0.42 seconds. Ventricular arrhythmias and ECG abnormalities (eg, QRS widening) often respond to systemic alkalinization (sodium bicarbonate 0.5-2 mEq/kg I.V.) and/or phenytoin 15-20 mg/kg (adults). Arrhythmias unresponsive to this therapy may respond to lidocaine 1 mg/kg I.V. followed by a titrated infusion. Physostigmine (1-2 mg slow I.V. for adults or 0.5 mg slow I.V. for children) may be indicated in reversing life-threatening cardiac arrhythmias. Seizures usually respond to diazepam I.V. boluses (5-10 mg for adults up to 30 mg or 0.25-0.4 mg/kg/dose for children up to 10 mg/dose). If seizures are unresponsive or recur, phenytoin or phenobarbital may be required.

Drug Interactions
Cytochrome P450 Effect: Substrate of CYP1A2 (major), 2C19 (major), 2D6 (major), 3A4 (minor); **Inhibits** CYP2D6 (moderate)
Increased Effect/Toxicity: The levels/effects of clomipramine may be increased by amiodarone, chlorpromazine, ciprofloxacin, delavirdine, fluconazole, fluoxetine, fluvoxamine, gemfibrozil, isoniazid, ketoconazole, miconazole, norfloxacin, ofloxacin, omeprazole, paroxetine, pergolide, quinidine, quinine, ritonavir, rofecoxib, ropinirole, ticlopidine, and other CYP1A2, 2C19, or 2D6 inhibitors. Clomipramine may increase the levels/effects of amphetamines, selected beta-blockers, dextromethorphan, fluoxetine, lidocaine, mirtazapine, nefazodone, paroxetine, risperidone, ritonavir, thioridazine, tricyclic antidepressants, venlafaxine, and other CYP2D6 substrates.

Clomipramine increases the effects of amphetamines, anticholinergics, lithium, other CNS depressants (sedatives, hypnotics, ethanol) chlorpropamide, tolazamide, phenothiazines, and warfarin. When used with MAO inhibitors or other serotonergic drugs, serotonin syndrome may occur. Serotonin syndrome has also been reported with ritonavir (rare). Pressor response to I.V. epinephrine, norepinephrine, and phenylephrine may be enhanced in patients receiving TCAs. (**Note:** Effect is unlikely with epinephrine or levonordefrin dosages typically administered as infiltration in combination with local anesthetics.) Combined use of beta-agonists or drugs which prolong QT_c (including quinidine, procainamide, disopyramide, cisapride, sparfloxacin, gatifloxacin, moxifloxacin) with TCAs may predispose patients to cardiac arrhythmias.
Decreased Effect: The levels/effects of clomipramine may be decreased by aminoglutethimide, carbamazepine, phenobarbital, phenytoin, rifampin, and other CYP1A2 or 2C19 inducers. Clomipramine may decrease the levels/effects of CYP2D6 prodrug substrates (eg, codeine, hydrocodone, oxycodone, tramadol). Clomipramine inhibits the antihypertensive response to bethanidine, clonidine, debrisoquin, guanadrel, guanethidine, guanabenz, and guanfacine. Cholestyramine and colestipol may decrease the absorption of clomipramine.

Ethanol/Nutrition/Herb Interactions
Ethanol: Avoid ethanol (may increase CNS depression).
Food: Serum concentrations/toxicity may be increased by grapefruit juice.
Herb/Nutraceutical: Avoid valerian, St John's wort, SAMe, kava kava.
Mechanism of Action Clomipramine appears to affect serotonin uptake while its active metabolite, desmethylclomipramine, affects norepinephrine uptake
Pharmacodynamics/Kinetics
Absorption: Rapid
Metabolism: Hepatic to desmethylclomipramine (active); extensive first-pass effect
Half-life elimination: 20-30 hours

Dosage Oral: Initial:
Children:
    <10 years: Safety and efficacy have not been established.
    ≥10 years: OCD: 25 mg/day; gradually increase, as tolerated, to a maximum of 3 mg/kg/
    day or 200 mg/day (whichever is smaller)
Adults: OCD: 25 mg/day and gradually increase, as tolerated, to 100 mg/day the first 2
weeks, may then be increased to a total of 250 mg/day maximum
Monitoring Parameters Pulse rate and blood pressure prior to and during therapy; ECG/
cardiac status in older adults and patients with cardiac disease
Test Interactions Increased glucose
Dosage Forms Capsule, as hydrochloride: 25 mg, 50 mg, 75 mg

♦ **Clomipramine Hydrochloride** see ClomiPRAMINE on page 395
♦ **Clonapam (Can)** see Clonazepam on page 397

Clonazepam (kloe NA ze pam)

U.S. Brand Names Klonopin®
Canadian Brand Names Alti-Clonazepam; Apo-Clonazepam®; Clonapam; CO Clonazepam;
Gen-Clonazepam; Klonopin®; Novo-Clonazepam; Nu-Clonazepam; PMS-Clonazepam;
Rho®-Clonazepam; Rivotril®; Sandoz-Clonazepam
Pharmacologic Category Benzodiazepine
Additional Appendix Information
Anticonvulsants by Seizure Type on page 1865
Benzodiazepines on page 1874
Epilepsy on page 2048
Use Alone or as an adjunct in the treatment of petit mal variant (Lennox-Gastaut), akinetic, and
myoclonic seizures; petit mal (absence) seizures unresponsive to succimides; panic disorder
with or without agoraphobia
Unlabeled/Investigational Use Restless legs syndrome; neuralgia; multifocal tic disorder;
parkinsonian dysarthria; bipolar disorder; adjunct therapy for schizophrenia
Restrictions C-IV
Pregnancy Risk Factor D
Pregnancy Implications Clonazepam was shown to be teratogenic in some animal studies.
Clonazepam crosses the placenta. Benzodiazepine use during pregnancy is associated with
increased risk of congenital malformations. Nonteratogenic effects (including neonatal flac-
cidity, respiratory and feeding problems, and withdrawal symptoms) during the postnatal
period have also been reported with benzodiazepine use. Epilepsy itself, number of medica-
tions, genetic factors, or a combination of these probably influence the teratogenicity of
anticonvulsant therapy.
Lactation Enters breast milk/not recommended
Medication Safety Issues
Sound-alike/look-alike issues:
Clonazepam may be confused with clofazimine, clonidine, clorazepate, clozapine, lorazepam
Klonopin® may be confused with clofazimine, clonidine, clorazepate, clozapine, lorazepam
Contraindications Hypersensitivity to clonazepam or any component of the formulation
(cross-sensitivity with other benzodiazepines may exist); significant liver disease;
narrow-angle glaucoma; pregnancy
Warnings/Precautions Use with caution in elderly or debilitated patients, patients with
hepatic disease (including alcoholics), or renal impairment. Use with caution in patients with
respiratory disease or impaired gag reflex or ability to protect the airway from secretions
(salivation may be increased). Worsening of seizures may occur when added to patients with
multiple seizure types. Concurrent use with valproic acid may result in absence status.
Monitoring of CBC and liver function tests has been recommended during prolonged therapy.

Causes CNS depression (dose related) resulting in sedation, dizziness, confusion, or ataxia
which may impair physical and mental capabilities. Patients must be cautioned about
performing tasks which require mental alertness (eg, operating machinery or driving). Use
with caution in patients receiving other CNS depressants or psychoactive agents. Effects with
other sedative drugs or ethanol may be potentiated. Benzodiazepines have been associated
with falls and traumatic injury and should be used with extreme caution in patients who are at
risk of these events (especially the elderly).

Use caution in patients with depression, particularly if suicidal risk may be present. Use with
caution in patients with a history of drug dependence. Benzodiazepines have been associated with dependence and acute withdrawal symptoms, including seizures, on discontinuation or reduction in dose. Acute withdrawal, including seizures, may be precipitated in
patients after administration of flumazenil to patients receiving long-term benzodiazepine
therapy.

Benzodiazepines have been associated with anterograde amnesia. Paradoxical reactions,
including hyperactive or aggressive behavior, have been reported with benzodiazepines,
particularly in adolescent/pediatric or psychiatric patients. Does not have analgesic, antidepressant, or antipsychotic properties.
Adverse Reactions Reactions reported in patients with seizure and/or panic disorder.
Frequency not defined.

Cardiovascular: Edema (ankle or facial), palpitation
Central nervous system: Amnesia, ataxia (seizure disorder ~30%; panic disorder 5%),
behavior problems (seizure disorder ~25%), coma, confusion, depression, dizziness,
drowsiness (seizure disorder ~50%), emotional lability, fatigue, fever, hallucinations, headache, hypotonia, hysteria, insomnia, intellectual ability reduced, memory disturbance,
nervousness; paradoxical reactions (including aggressive behavior, agitation, anxiety,
excitability, hostility, irritability, nervousness, nightmares, sleep disturbance, vivid dreams);
psychosis, slurred speech, somnolence (panic disorder 37%), suicidal attempt, vertigo
(Continued)

Clonazepam *(Continued)*

Dermatologic: Hair loss, hirsutism, skin rash

Endocrine & metabolic: Dysmenorrhea, libido increased/decreased

Gastrointestinal: Abdominal pain, anorexia, appetite increased/decreased, coated tongue, constipation, dehydration, diarrhea, gastritis, gum soreness, nausea, weight changes (loss/gain), xerostomia

Genitourinary: Colpitis, dysuria, ejaculation delayed, enuresis, impotence, micturition frequency, nocturia, urinary retention, urinary tract infection

Hematologic: Anemia, eosinophilia, leukopenia, thrombocytopenia

Hepatic: Alkaline phosphatase increased (transient), hepatomegaly, transaminases increased (transient)

Neuromuscular & skeletal: Choreiform movements, coordination abnormal, dysarthria, muscle pain, muscle weakness, myalgia, tremor

Ocular: Blurred vision, eye movements abnormal, diplopia, nystagmus

Respiratory: Chest congestion, cough, bronchitis, hypersecretions, pharyngitis, respiratory depression, respiratory tract infection, rhinitis, rhinorrhea, shortness of breath, sinusitis

Miscellaneous: Allergic reaction, aphonia, dysdiadochokinesis, encopresis, "glassy-eyed" appearance, hemiparesis, lymphadenopathy

Overdosage/Toxicology May produce somnolence, confusion, ataxia, diminished reflexes, or coma. Treatment for benzodiazepine overdose is supportive. Flumazenil has been shown to selectively block the binding of benzodiazepines to CNS receptors, resulting in a reversal of benzodiazepine-induced CNS depression, but not respiratory depression.

Drug Interactions

Cytochrome P450 Effect: Substrate of CYP3A4 (major)

Increased Effect/Toxicity: Combined use of clonazepam and valproic acid has been associated with absence seizures. Clonazepam potentiates the CNS depressant effects of opioid analgesics, barbiturates, phenothiazines, ethanol, antihistamines, MAO inhibitors, sedative-hypnotics, and cyclic antidepressants. CYP3A4 inhibitors may increase the levels/effects of clonazepam; example inhibitors include azole antifungals, clarithromycin, diclofenac, doxycycline, erythromycin, imatinib, isoniazid, nefazodone, nicardipine, propofol, protease inhibitors, quinidine, telithromycin, and verapamil.

Decreased Effect: The combined use of clonazepam and valproic acid has been associated with absence seizures. CYP3A4 inducers may decrease the levels/effects of clonazepam; example inducers include aminoglutethimide, carbamazepine, nafcillin, nevirapine, phenobarbital, phenytoin, and rifamycins.

Ethanol/Nutrition/Herb Interactions

Ethanol: Avoid ethanol (may increase CNS depression).

Food: Clonazepam serum concentration is unlikely to be increased by grapefruit juice because of clonazepam's high oral bioavailability.

Herb/Nutraceutical: St John's wort may decrease clonazepam levels. Avoid valerian, St John's wort, kava kava, gotu kola (may increase CNS depression).

Mechanism of Action The exact mechanism is unknown, but believed to be related to its ability to enhance the activity of GABA; suppresses the spike-and-wave discharge in absence seizures by depressing nerve transmission in the motor cortex

Pharmacodynamics/Kinetics

Onset of action: 20-60 minutes

Duration: Infants and young children: 6-8 hours; Adults: ≤12 hours

Absorption: Well absorbed

Distribution: Adults: V_d: 1.5-4.4 L/kg

Protein binding: 85%

Metabolism: Extensively hepatic via glucuronide and sulfate conjugation

Half-life elimination: Children: 22-33 hours; Adults: 19-50 hours

Time to peak, serum: 1-3 hours; Steady-state: 5-7 days

Excretion: Urine (<2% as unchanged drug); metabolites excreted as glucuronide or sulfate conjugates

Dosage Oral:

Children <10 years or 30 kg: Seizure disorders:

Initial daily dose: 0.01-0.03 mg/kg/day (maximum: 0.05 mg/kg/day) given in 2-3 divided doses; increase by no more than 0.5 mg every third day until seizures are controlled or adverse effects seen

Usual maintenance dose: 0.1-0.2 mg/kg/day divided 3 times/day, not to exceed 0.2 mg/kg/day

Adults:

Burning mouth syndrome (dental use): 0.25-3 mg/day in 2 divided doses, in morning and evening

Seizure disorders:

Initial daily dose not to exceed 1.5 mg given in 3 divided doses; may increase by 0.5-1 mg every third day until seizures are controlled or adverse effects seen (maximum: 20 mg/day)

Usual maintenance dose: 0.05-0.2 mg/kg; do not exceed 20 mg/day

Panic disorder: 0.25 mg twice daily; increase in increments of 0.125-0.25 mg twice daily every 3 days; target dose: 1 mg/day (maximum: 4 mg/day)

Discontinuation of treatment: To discontinue, treatment should be withdrawn gradually. Decrease dose by 0.125 mg twice daily every 3 days until medication is completely withdrawn.

Elderly: Initiate with low doses and observe closely

Hemodialysis: Supplemental dose is not necessary

Administration Orally-disintegrating tablet: Open pouch and peel back foil on the blister; do not push tablet through foil. Use dry hands to remove tablet and place in mouth. May be swallowed with or without water. Use immediately after removing from package.

Monitoring Parameters CBC, liver function tests; observe patient for excess sedation, respiratory depression

Reference Range Relationship between serum concentration and seizure control is not well established

Timing of serum samples; Peak serum levels occur 1-3 hours after oral ingestion; the half-life is 20-40 hours; therefore, steady-state occurs in 5-7 days

Therapeutic levels: 20-80 ng/mL; Toxic concentration: >80 ng/mL

Additional Information Ethosuximide or valproic acid may be preferred for treatment of absence (petit mal) seizures. Clonazepam-induced behavioral disturbances may be more frequent in mentally handicapped patients. Abrupt discontinuation after sustained use (generally >10 days) may cause withdrawal symptoms. Flumazenil, a competitive benzodiazepine antagonist at the CNS receptor site, reverses benzodiazepine-induced CNS depression.

Dosage Forms

Tablet: 0.5 mg, 1 mg, 2 mg

Tablet, orally disintegrating [wafer]: 0.125 mg, 0.25 mg, 0.5 mg, 1 mg, 2 mg

Extemporaneous Preparations A 0.1 mg/mL oral suspension has been made using five 2 mg tablets, purified water USP (10 ml), and methylcellulose 1% (qs ad 100 mL). The expected stability of this preparation is 2 weeks if stored under refrigeration; shake well before use.

Nahata MC and Hipple TF, *Pediatric Drug Formulations*, 2nd ed, Cincinnati, OH: Harvey Whitney Books Co, 1992.

Clonidine (KLON i deen)

U.S. Brand Names Catapres®; Catapres-TTS®; Duraclon™

Canadian Brand Names Apo-Clonidine®; Carapres®; Dixarit®; Novo-Clonidine; Nu-Clonidine

Index Terms Clonidine Hydrochloride

Pharmacologic Category Alpha$_2$-Adrenergic Agonist

Additional Appendix Information

Hypertension *on page 2063*

Use Management of mild-to-moderate hypertension; either used alone or in combination with other antihypertensives

Orphan drug: Duraclon™: For continuous epidural administration as adjunctive therapy with intraspinal opiates for treatment of cancer pain in patients tolerant to or unresponsive to intraspinal opiates

Unlabeled/Investigational Use Heroin or nicotine withdrawal; severe pain; dysmenorrhea; vasomotor symptoms associated with menopause; ethanol dependence; prophylaxis of migraines; glaucoma; diabetes-associated diarrhea; Impulse control disorder, attention-deficit/hyperactivity disorder (ADHD), clozapine-induced sialorrhea

Pregnancy Risk Factor C

Pregnancy Implications Clonidine crosses the placenta. Caution should be used with this drug due to the potential of rebound hypertension with abrupt discontinuation.

Lactation Enters breast milk/not recommended

Medication Safety Issues

Sound-alike/look-alike issues:

Clonidine may be confused with Clomid®, clomiPHENE, clonazepam, clozapine, Klonopin™, quinidine

Catapres® may be confused with Cataflam®, Cetapred®, Combipres®

Transdermal patch may contain conducting metal (eg, aluminum); remove patch prior to MRI.

Contraindications Hypersensitivity to clonidine hydrochloride or any component of the formulation

Warnings/Precautions Gradual withdrawal is needed (over 1 week for oral, 2-4 days with epidural) if drug needs to be stopped. Patients should be instructed about abrupt discontinuation (causes rapid increase in BP and symptoms of sympathetic overactivity). In patients on both a beta-blocker and clonidine where withdrawal of clonidine is necessary, withdraw the beta-blocker first and several days before clonidine. Then slowly decrease clonidine.

Use with caution in patients with severe coronary insufficiency; conduction disturbances; recent MI, CVA, or chronic renal insufficiency. Caution in sinus node dysfunction. Discontinue within 4 hours of surgery then restart as soon as possible after. Clonidine injection should be administered via a continuous epidural infusion device. **[U.S. Boxed Warning]: Epidural clonidine is not recommended for perioperative, obstetrical, or postpartum pain.** It is not recommended for use in patients with severe cardiovascular disease or hemodynamic instability. In all cases, the epidural may lead to cardiovascular instability (hypotension, bradycardia). Transdermal patch may contain conducting metal (eg, aluminum); remove patch prior to MRI. Due to the potential for altered electrical conductivity, remove transdermal patch before cardioversion or defibrillation. Clonidine cause significant CNS depression and xerostomia. Caution in patients with pre-existing CNS disease or depression. Elderly may be at greater risk for CNS depressive effects, favoring other agents in this population.

Adverse Reactions Incidence of adverse events is not always reported.

>10%:

Central nervous system: Drowsiness (35% oral, 12% transdermal), dizziness (16% oral, 2% transdermal)

Dermatologic: Transient localized skin reactions characterized by pruritus, and erythema (15% to 50% transdermal)

Gastrointestinal: Dry mouth (40% oral, 25% transdermal)

Neuromuscular & skeletal: Weakness (10% transdermal)

1% to 10%:

Cardiovascular: Orthostatic hypotension (3% oral)

Central nervous system: Headache (1% oral, 5% transdermal), sedation (3% transdermal), fatigue (6% transdermal), lethargy (3% transdermal), insomnia (2% transdermal), nervousness (3% oral, 1% transdermal), mental depression (1% oral)

Dermatologic: Rash (1% oral), allergic contact sensitivity (5% transdermal), localized vesiculation (7%), hyperpigmentation (5% at application site), edema (3%), excoriation (3%),

(Continued)

Clonidine *(Continued)*

burning (3%), throbbing, blanching (1%), papules (1%), and generalized macular rash (1%) has occurred in patients receiving transdermal clonidine.

Endocrine & metabolic: Sodium and water retention, sexual dysfunction (3% oral, 2% transdermal), impotence (3% oral, 2% transdermal), weakness (10% transdermal)

Gastrointestinal: Nausea (5% oral, 1% transdermal), vomiting (5% oral), anorexia and malaise (1% oral), constipation (10% oral, 1% transdermal), dry throat (2% transdermal), taste disturbance (1% transdermal), weight gain (1% oral)

Genitourinary: Nocturia (1% oral)

Hepatic: Liver function test (mild abnormalities, 1% oral)

Miscellaneous: Withdrawal syndrome (1% oral)

<1% (Limited to important or life-threatening): Abdominal pain, agitation, alopecia, angioedema, AV block, behavioral changes, blurred vision, bradycardia, chest pain, CHF, contact dermatitis (transdermal), CVA, delirium, depression, dryness of eyes, ECG abnormalities, ethanol sensitivity increased, gynecomastia, hallucinations, hepatitis, localized hypo- or hyperpigmentation (transdermal), nightmares, orthostatic symptoms, pseudo-obstruction, rash, Raynaud's phenomenon, syncope, tachycardia, thrombocytopenia, urinary retention, urticaria, vomiting, withdrawal syndrome

Overdosage/Toxicology Symptoms include bradycardia, CNS depression, hypothermia, diarrhea, respiratory depression, and apnea. Treatment is primarily supportive and symptomatic. Hypotension usually responds to I.V. fluids or Trendelenburg positioning. Naloxone may be utilized in treating CNS depression and/or apnea and should be given I.V. 0.4-2 mg, with repeated doses as needed, or as an infusion.

Drug Interactions

Increased Effect/Toxicity: Concurrent use with antipsychotics (especially low potency), opioid analgesics, or nitroprusside may produce additive hypotensive effects. Clonidine may decrease the symptoms of hypoglycemia with oral hypoglycemic agents or insulin. Alcohol, barbiturates, and other CNS depressants may have additive CNS effects when combined with clonidine. Epidural clonidine may prolong the sensory and motor blockade of local anesthetics. Clonidine may increase cyclosporine (and perhaps tacrolimus) serum concentrations. Beta-blockers may potentiate bradycardia in patients receiving clonidine and may increase the rebound hypertension of withdrawal. Tricyclic antidepressants may also enhance the hypertensive response associated with abrupt clonidine withdrawal.

Decreased Effect: Tricyclic antidepressants (TCAs) antagonize the hypotensive effects of clonidine.

Ethanol/Nutrition/Herb Interactions

Ethanol: Avoid ethanol (may increase CNS depression).

Herb/Nutraceutical: Avoid dong quai if using for hypertension (has estrogenic activity). Avoid ephedra, yohimbe, ginseng (may worsen hypertension). Avoid valerian, St John's wort, kava kava, gotu kola (may increase CNS depression).

Mechanism of Action Stimulates alpha$_2$-adrenoceptors in the brain stem, thus activating an inhibitory neuron, resulting in reduced sympathetic outflow from the CNS, producing a decrease in peripheral resistance, renal vascular resistance, heart rate, and blood pressure; epidural clonidine may produce pain relief at spinal presynaptic and postjunctional alpha$_2$-adrenoceptors by preventing pain signal transmission; pain relief occurs only for the body regions innervated by the spinal segments where analgesic concentrations of clonidine exist

Pharmacodynamics/Kinetics

Onset of action: Oral: 0.5-1 hour; Transdermal: Initial application: 2-3 days

Duration: 6-10 hours

Distribution: V_d: Adults: 2.1 L/kg; highly lipid soluble; distributes readily into extravascular sites

Protein binding: 20% to 40%

Metabolism: Extensively hepatic to inactive metabolites; undergoes enterohepatic recirculation

Bioavailability: 75% to 95%

Half-life elimination: Adults: Normal renal function: 6-20 hours; Renal impairment: 18-41 hours

Time to peak: 2-4 hours

Excretion: Urine (65%, 32% as unchanged drug); feces (22%)

Dosage

Children:

Oral:

Hypertension: Initial: 5-10 mcg/kg/day in divided doses every 8-12 hours; increase gradually at 5- to 7-day intervals to 25 mcg/kg/day in divided doses every 6 hours; maximum: 0.9 mg/day

Clonidine tolerance test (test of growth hormone release from pituitary): 0.15 mg/m^2 or 4 mcg/kg as single dose

ADHD (unlabeled use): Initial: 0.05 mg/day; increase every 3-7 days by 0.05 mg/day to 3-5 mcg/kg/day given in divided doses 3-4 times/day (maximum dose: 0.3-0.4 mg/day)

Epidural infusion: Pain management: Reserved for patients with severe intractable pain, unresponsive to other analgesics or epidural or spinal opiates: Initial: 0.5 mcg/kg/hour; adjust with caution, based on clinical effect

Adults:

Oral:

Acute hypertension (urgency): Initial 0.1-0.2 mg; may be followed by additional doses of 0.1 mg every hour, if necessary, to a maximum total dose of 0.6 mg.

Unlabeled route of administration: Sublingual clonidine 0.1-0.2 mg twice daily may be effective in patients unable to take oral medication

Hypertension: Initial dose: 0.1 mg twice daily (maximum recommended dose: 2.4 mg/day); usual dose range (JNC 7): 0.1-0.8 mg/day in 2 divided doses

Nicotine withdrawal symptoms: 0.1 mg twice daily to maximum of 0.4 mg/day for 3-4 weeks

Transdermal: Hypertension: Apply once every 7 days; for initial therapy start with 0.1 mg and increase by 0.1 mg at 1- to 2-week intervals (dosages >0.6 mg do not improve efficacy); usual dose range (JNC 7): 0.1-0.3 mg once weekly

Note: If transitioning from oral to transdermal therapy, overlap oral regimen for 1-2 days; transdermal route takes 2-3 days to achieve therapeutic effects.

Conversion from oral to transdermal:
Day 1: Place Catapres-TTS® 1; administer 100% of oral dose.
Day 2: Administer 50% of oral dose.
Day 3: Administer 25% of oral dose.
Day 4: Patch remains, no further oral supplement necessary.

Epidural infusion: Pain management: Starting dose: 30 mcg/hour; titrate as required for relief of pain or presence of side effects; minimal experience with doses >40 mcg/hour; should be considered an adjunct to intraspinal opiate therapy

Elderly: Initial: 0.1 mg once daily at bedtime, increase gradually as needed

Dosing adjustment in renal impairment: Cl_{cr} <10 mL/minute: Administer 50% to 75% of normal dose initially

Dialysis: Not dialyzable (0% to 5%) via hemo- or peritoneal dialysis; supplemental dose not necessary

Dietary Considerations Hypertensive patients may need to decrease sodium and calories in diet.

Administration
Oral: Do not discontinue clonidine abruptly. if needed, gradually reduce dose over 2-4 days to avoid rebound hypertension

Transdermal patch: Patches should be applied weekly at bedtime to a clean, hairless area of the upper outer arm or chest. Rotate patch sites weekly. Redness under patch may be reduced if a topical corticosteroid spray is applied to the area before placement of the patch.

Monitoring Parameters Blood pressure, standing and sitting/supine, mental status, heart rate

Reference Range Therapeutic: 1-2 ng/mL (SI: 4.4-8.7 nmol/L)

Additional Information Transdermal clonidine should only be used in patients unable to take oral medication. The transdermal product is much more expensive than oral clonidine and produces no better therapeutic effects.

Dosage Forms
Injection, epidural solution, as hydrochloride [preservative free] (Duraclon™): 100 mcg/mL (10 mL); 500 mcg/mL (10 mL)
Patch, transdermal [once-weekly patch]:
Catapres-TTS®-1: 0.1 mg/24 hours (4s)
Catapres-TTS®-2: 0.2 mg/24 hours (4s)
Catapres-TTS®-3: 0.3 mg/24 hours (4s)
Tablet, as hydrochloride (Catapres®): 0.1 mg, 0.2 mg, 0.3 mg

Clonidine and Chlorthalidone (KLON i deen & klor THAL i done)

U.S. Brand Names Clorpres®; Combipres® [DSC]
Index Terms Chlorthalidone and Clonidine
Pharmacologic Category Antihypertensive Agent, Combination
Use Management of mild-to-moderate hypertension
Pregnancy Risk Factor C
Medication Safety Issues
Sound-alike/look-alike issues:
Combipres® may be confused with Catapres®
Dosage Oral: 1 tablet 1-2 times/day; maximum: 0.6 mg clonidine and 30 mg chlorthalidone
Additional Information Complete prescribing information for this medication should be consulted for additional detail.
Dosage Forms Tablet:
0.1: Clonidine hydrochloride 0.1 mg and chlorthalidone 15 mg
0.2: Clonidine hydrochloride 0.2 mg and chlorthalidone 15 mg
0.3: Clonidine hydrochloride 0.3 mg and chlorthalidone 15 mg

♦ **Clonidine Hydrochloride** *see* Clonidine *on page 399*

Clopidogrel (kloh PID oh grel)

U.S. Brand Names Plavix®
Canadian Brand Names Plavix®
Index Terms Clopidogrel Bisulfate
Pharmacologic Category Antiplatelet Agent
Use Reduces rate of atherothrombotic events (myocardial infarction, stroke, vascular deaths) in patients with recent MI or stroke, or established peripheral arterial disease; reduces rate of atherothrombotic events in patients with unstable angina or non-ST-segment elevation acute coronary syndromes (unstable angina and non-ST-segment elevation MI) managed medically or through PCI (with or without stent) or CABG; reduces rate of death and atherothrombotic events in patients with ST-segment elevation MI (STEMI) managed medically
Unlabeled/Investigational Use In aspirin-allergic patients, prevention of coronary artery bypass graft closure (saphenous vein)
Pregnancy Risk Factor B
Pregnancy Implications Teratogenic effects were not observed in animal studies. Use during pregnancy only if clearly needed.
Lactation Excretion in breast milk unknown/not recommended
Medication Safety Issues
Sound-alike/look-alike issues:
Plavix® may be confused with Elavil®, Paxil®
(Continued)

Clopidogrel (Continued)

Contraindications Hypersensitivity to clopidogrel or any component of the formulation; active pathological bleeding such as PUD or intracranial hemorrhage; coagulation disorders

Warnings/Precautions Use with caution in patients who may be at risk of increased bleeding, including patients with peptic ulcer disease, trauma, or surgery. Consider discontinuing 5 days before elective surgery (except in patients with cardiac stents that have not completed their full course of dual antiplatelet therapy; AHA/ACC/SCAI/ACS/ADA Science Advisory provides recommendations). Use caution in concurrent treatment with other antiplatelet drugs; bleeding risk is increased. Use with caution in patients with severe liver or renal disease (experience is limited). Cases of thrombotic thrombocytopenic purpura (usually occurring within the first 2 weeks of therapy) have been reported; urgent plasmapheresis is required. Safety and efficacy have not been established in pediatric patients.

Adverse Reactions As with all drugs which may affect hemostasis, bleeding is associated with clopidogrel. Hemorrhage may occur at virtually any site. Risk is dependent on multiple variables, including the concurrent use of multiple agents which alter hemostasis and patient susceptibility.

>10%: Gastrointestinal: The overall incidence of gastrointestinal events (including abdominal pain, vomiting, dyspepsia, gastritis, and constipation) has been documented to be 27% compared to 30% in patients receiving aspirin.

3% to 10%:

Cardiovascular: Chest pain (8%), edema (4%), hypertension (4%)

Central nervous system: Headache (3% to 8%), dizziness (2% to 6%), depression (4%), fatigue (3%), general pain (6%)

Dermatologic: Rash (4%), pruritus (3%)

Endocrine & metabolic: Hypercholesterolemia (4%)

Gastrointestinal: Abdominal pain (2% to 6%), dyspepsia (2% to 5%), diarrhea (2% to 5%), nausea (3%)

Genitourinary: Urinary tract infection (3%)

Hematologic: Bleeding (major 4%; minor 5%), purpura (5%), epistaxis (3%)

Hepatic: Liver function test abnormalities (<3%; discontinued in 0.11%)

Neuromuscular & skeletal: Arthralgia (6%), back pain (6%)

Respiratory: Dyspnea (5%), rhinitis (4%), bronchitis (4%), cough (3%), upper respiratory infection (9%)

Miscellaneous: Flu-like syndrome (8%)

1% to 3%:

Cardiovascular: Atrial fibrillation, cardiac failure, palpitation, syncope

Central nervous system: Fever, insomnia, vertigo, anxiety

Dermatologic: Eczema

Endocrine & metabolic: Gout, hyperuricemia

Gastrointestinal: Constipation, GI hemorrhage, vomiting

Genitourinary: Cystitis

Hematologic: Hematoma, anemia

Neuromuscular & skeletal: Arthritis, leg cramps, neuralgia, paresthesia, weakness

Ocular: Cataract, conjunctivitis

<1% (Limited to important or life-threatening): Acute liver failure, agranulocytosis, allergic reaction, anaphylactoid reaction, angioedema, aplastic anemia, bilirubinemia, bronchospasm, bullous eruption, confusion, erythema multiforme, fatty liver, fever, granulocytopenia, hallucination, hematuria, hemoptysis, hemothorax, hepatitis, hypersensitivity, hypochromic anemia, interstitial pneumonitis, intracranial hemorrhage (0.4%), ischemic necrosis, leukopenia, lichen planus, maculopapular rash, menorrhagia, neutropenia (0.05%), ocular hemorrhage, pancreatitis, pancytopenia, pulmonary hemorrhage, purpura, retroperitoneal bleeding, serum sickness, Stevens-Johnson syndrome, stomatitis, taste disorder, thrombocytopenia, thrombotic thrombocytopenic purpura (TTP), toxic epidermal necrolysis, urticaria, vasculitis

Overdosage/Toxicology Symptoms of acute toxicity include vomiting, prostration, difficulty breathing, and gastrointestinal hemorrhage. Only one case of overdose with clopidogrel has been reported to date; no symptoms were reported with this case and no specific treatments were required. Based on its pharmacology, platelet transfusions may be an appropriate treatment when attempting to reverse the effects of clopidogrel. After decontamination, treatment is symptomatic and supportive.

Drug Interactions

Cytochrome P450 Effect: Substrate (minor) of CYP1A2, 3A4; **Inhibits** CYP2C9 (weak)

Increased Effect/Toxicity: Anticoagulants, antiplatelet agents, drotrecogin alfa, NSAIDs, salicylates, thrombolytics, and treprostinil may increase the risk of bleeding with concurrent use. Rifampin may increase the effects of clopidogrel (monitor).

Decreased Effect: Atorvastatin may attenuate the effects of clopidogrel; monitor. CYP3A4-inhibiting macrolide antibiotics may attenuate the effects of clopidogrel (including clarithromycin, erythromycin, and troleandomycin); monitor.

Ethanol/Nutrition/Herb Interactions Herb/Nutraceutical: Avoid cat's claw, dong quai, evening primrose, feverfew, garlic, ginger, ginkgo, red clover, horse chestnut, green tea, ginseng (all have additional antiplatelet activity).

Stability Store at 25°C (77°F); excursions permitted to 15°C to 3°C (59°F to 86°F).

Mechanism of Action Blocks the ADP receptors, which prevent fibrinogen binding at that site and thereby reduce the possibility of platelet adhesion and aggregation

Pharmacodynamics/Kinetics

Onset of action: Inhibition of platelet aggregation detected: 2 hours after 300 mg administered; after second day of treatment with 50-100 mg/day

Peak effect: 50-100 mg/day: Bleeding time: 5-6 days; Platelet function: 3-7 days

Absorption: Well absorbed

Protein binding: Parent drug: 98%; metabolite: 94%

Metabolism: Extensively hepatic via hydrolysis; biotransformation primarily to carboxyl acid derivative (inactive). The active metabolite that inhibits platelet aggregation has not been isolated.

Half-life elimination: ~8 hours
Time to peak, serum: ~1 hour
Excretion: Urine (50%); feces (46%)

Dosage Oral: Adults:

Recent MI, recent stroke, or established arterial disease: 75 mg once daily

Non-ST-segment elevation acute coronary syndrome: Initial: 300 mg loading dose, followed by 75 mg once daily (in combination with aspirin 75-325 mg once daily). **Note:** A loading dose of 600 mg has been used in some investigations; limited research exists comparing the two doses.

Note: Drug-eluting stents: Duration of clopidogrel (in combination with aspirin): Ideally 12 months following drug-eluting stent placement in patients not at high risk for bleeding; at a minimum, 1-, 3-, and 6 months for bare metal, sirolimus, and paclitaxel stents, respectively, for uninterrupted therapy.

ST-segment elevation MI: 75 mg once daily (in combination with aspirin 75-162 mg/day) . CLARITY used a 300 mg loading dose of clopidogrel. The duration of therapy was <28 days (usually until hospital discharge).

Prevention of coronary artery bypass graft closure (saphenous vein): Aspirin-allergic patients (unlabeled use): Loading dose: 300 mg 6 hours following procedure; maintenance: 50-100 mg/day

Dosing adjustment in renal Impairment and elderly: None necessary

Dietary Considerations May be taken without regard to meals.

Monitoring Parameters Signs of bleeding; hemoglobin and hematocrit periodically

Dosage Forms
Tablet:
Plavix®: 75 mg

♦ **Clopidogrel Bisulfate** see Clopidogrel on page 401

Clorazepate (klor AZ e pate)

U.S. Brand Names Tranxene® SD™; Tranxene® SD™-Half Strength; Tranxene® T-Tab®
Canadian Brand Names Apo-Clorazepate®; Novo-Clopate
Index Terms Clorazepate Dipotassium; Tranxene T-Tab®
Pharmacologic Category Benzodiazepine
Additional Appendix Information
Benzodiazepines on page 1874
Epilepsy on page 2048
Use Treatment of generalized anxiety disorder; management of ethanol withdrawal; adjunct anticonvulsant in management of partial seizures
Restrictions C-IV
Pregnancy Risk Factor D
Lactation Excretion in breast milk unknown/not recommended
Medication Safety Issues
Sound-alike/look-alike issues:
Clorazepate may be confused with clofibrate, clonazepam
Contraindications Hypersensitivity to clorazepate or any component of the formulation (cross-sensitivity with other benzodiazepines may exist); narrow-angle glaucoma; pregnancy
Warnings/Precautions Not recommended for use in patients <9 years of age or patients with depressive or psychotic disorders. Use with caution in elderly or debilitated patients, patients with hepatic disease (including alcoholics), or renal impairment. Active metabolites with extended half-lives may lead to delayed accumulation and adverse effects. Use with caution in patients with respiratory disease or impaired gag reflex. Avoid use in patients with sleep apnea.

Causes CNS depression (dose related) resulting in sedation, dizziness, confusion, or ataxia which may impair physical and mental capabilities. Patients must be cautioned about performing tasks which require mental alertness (eg, operating machinery or driving). Use with caution in patients receiving other CNS depressants or psychoactive agents. Effects with other sedative drugs or ethanol may be potentiated. Benzodiazepines have been associated with falls and traumatic injury and should be used with extreme caution in patients who are at risk of these events (especially the elderly).

Use caution in patients with depression, particularly if suicidal risk may be present. Use with caution in patients with a history of drug dependence. Benzodiazepines have been associated with dependence and acute withdrawal symptoms on discontinuation or reduction in dose. Acute withdrawal, including seizures, may be precipitated in patients after administration of flumazenil to patients receiving long-term benzodiazepine therapy.

Benzodiazepines have been associated with anterograde amnesia. Paradoxical reactions, including hyperactive or aggressive behavior, have been reported with benzodiazepines, particularly in adolescent/pediatric or psychiatric patients. Does not have analgesic, antidepressant, or antipsychotic properties.

Adverse Reactions Frequency not defined.
Cardiovascular: Hypotension
Central nervous system: Drowsiness, fatigue, ataxia, lightheadedness, memory impairment, insomnia, anxiety, headache, depression, slurred speech, confusion, nervousness, dizziness, irritability
Dermatologic: Rash
Endocrine & metabolic: Libido decreased
Gastrointestinal: Xerostomia, constipation, diarrhea, salivation decreased, nausea, vomiting, appetite increased or decreased
Neuromuscular & skeletal: Dysarthria, tremor
Ocular: Blurred vision, diplopia
Overdosage/Toxicology May produce somnolence, confusion, ataxia, diminished reflexes, and coma. Treatment for benzodiazepine overdose is supportive. Mechanical ventilation is
(Continued)

Clorazepate *(Continued)*

rarely required. Flumazenil has been shown to selectively block the binding of benzodiazepines to CNS receptors, resulting in a reversal of benzodiazepine-induced CNS depression, but not respiratory depression.

Drug Interactions

Cytochrome P450 Effect: Substrate of CYP3A4 (major)

Increased Effect/Toxicity: Clorazepate potentiates the CNS depressant effects of opioid analgesics, barbiturates, phenothiazines, ethanol, antihistamines, MAO inhibitors, sedative-hypnotics, and cyclic antidepressants. CYP3A4 inhibitors may increase the levels/effects of clorazepate; example inhibitors include azole antifungals, clarithromycin, diclofenac, doxycycline, erythromycin, imatinib, isoniazid, nefazodone, nicardipine, propofol, protease inhibitors, quinidine, telithromycin, and verapamil.

Decreased Effect: CYP3A4 inducers may decrease the levels/effects of clorazepate; example inducers include aminoglutethimide, carbamazepine, nafcillin, nevirapine, phenobarbital, phenytoin, and rifamycins.

Ethanol/Nutrition/Herb Interactions

Ethanol: Avoid ethanol (may increase CNS depression).

Food: Serum concentrations/toxicity may be increased by grapefruit juice.

Herb/Nutraceutical: Avoid valerian, St John's wort, kava kava, gotu kola (may increase CNS depression).

Mechanism of Action Binds to stereospecific benzodiazepine receptors on the postsynaptic GABA neuron at several sites within the central nervous system, including the limbic system, reticular formation. Enhancement of the inhibitory effect of GABA on neuronal excitability results by increased neuronal membrane permeability to chloride ions. This shift in chloride ions results in hyperpolarization (a less excitable state) and stabilization.

Pharmacodynamics/Kinetics

Onset of action: 1-2 hours

Duration: Variable, 8-24 hours

Distribution: Crosses placenta; appears in urine

Metabolism: Rapidly decarboxylated to desmethyldiazepam (active) in acidic stomach prior to absorption; hepatically to oxazepam (active)

Half-life elimination: Adults: Desmethyldiazepam: 48-96 hours; Oxazepam: 6-8 hours

Time to peak, serum: ~1 hour

Excretion: Primarily urine

Dosage Oral:

Children 9-12 years: Anticonvulsant: Initial: 3.75-7.5 mg/dose twice daily; increase dose by 3.75 mg at weekly intervals, not to exceed 60 mg/day in 2-3 divided doses

Children >12 years and Adults: Anticonvulsant: Initial: Up to 7.5 mg/dose 2-3 times/day; increase dose by 7.5 mg at weekly intervals, not to exceed 90 mg/day

Adults:

Anxiety:

Regular release tablets (Tranxene® T-Tab®): 7.5-15 mg 2-4 times/day

Sustained release (Tranxene® SD): 11.25 or 22.5 mg once daily at bedtime

Ethanol withdrawal: Initial: 30 mg, then 15 mg 2-4 times/day on first day; maximum daily dose: 90 mg; gradually decrease dose over subsequent days

Monitoring Parameters Respiratory and cardiovascular status, excess CNS depression

Reference Range Therapeutic: 0.12-1 mcg/mL (SI: 0.36-3.01 μmol/L)

Test Interactions Decreased hematocrit; abnormal liver and renal function tests

Additional Information Abrupt discontinuation after sustained use (generally >10 days) may cause withdrawal symptoms.

Dosage Forms

Tablet, as dipotassium: 3.75 mg, 7.5 mg, 15 mg

Tranxene® SD™: 22.5 mg [once daily]

Tranxene® SD™-Half Strength: 11.25 mg [once daily]

Tranxene® T-Tab®: 3.75 mg, 7.5 mg, 15 mg

♦ **Clorazepate Dipotassium** *see* Clorazepate *on page 403*

♦ **Clorpres®** *see* Clonidine and Chlorthalidone *on page 401*

♦ **Clotrimaderm (Can)** *see* Clotrimazole *on page 404*

Clotrimazole *(kloe TRIM a zole)*

U.S. Brand Names Cruex® Cream [OTC]; Gyne-Lotrimin® 3 [OTC]; Lotrimin® AF Athlete's Foot Cream [OTC]; Lotrimin® AF Athlete's Foot Solution [OTC]; Lotrimin® AF Jock Itch Cream [OTC]; Mycelex®; Mycelex®-7 [OTC]; Mycelex® Twin Pack [OTC]

Canadian Brand Names Canesten® Topical; Canesten® Vaginal; Clotrimaderm; Trivagizole-3®

Pharmacologic Category Antifungal Agent, Oral Nonabsorbed; Antifungal Agent, Topical; Antifungal Agent, Vaginal

Additional Appendix Information

Treatment of Sexually Transmitted Infections *on page 2007*

USPHS / IDSA Guidelines for the Prevention of Opportunistic Infections in Persons Infected With HIV *on page 1966*

Use Treatment of susceptible fungal infections, including oropharyngeal candidiasis, dermatophytoses, superficial mycoses, and cutaneous candidiasis, as well as vulvovaginal candidiasis; limited data suggest that clotrimazole troches may be effective for prophylaxis against oropharyngeal candidiasis in neutropenic patients

Pregnancy Risk Factor B (topical); C (troches)

Lactation Excretion in breast milk unknown

Medication Safety Issues

Sound-alike/look-alike issues:

Clotrimazole may be confused with co-trimoxazole

Lotrimin® may be confused with Lotrisone®, Otrivin®

Mycelex® may be confused with Myoflex®

International issues:

Cloderm®: Brand name for clocortolone in the United States

Canesten® [multiple international markets] may be confused with Cenestin® which is a brand name for estrogens (conjugated a/synthetic) in the U.S.

Canesten® [multiple international markets]: Brand name for fluconazole in Great Britain

Mycelex® may be confused with Mucolex® which is a brand name for carbocysteine in Ireland, Portugal, and Thailand; a brand name for guaifenesin in Hong Kong

Contraindications Hypersensitivity to clotrimazole or any component of the formulation

Warnings/Precautions Clotrimazole should not be used for treatment of systemic fungal infection. Safety and effectiveness of clotrimazole lozenges (troches) in children <3 years of age have not been established. When using topical formulation, avoid contact with eyes.

Adverse Reactions

Oral:

>10%: Hepatic: Abnormal liver function tests

1% to 10%:

Gastrointestinal: Nausea and vomiting may occur in patients on clotrimazole troches

Local: Mild burning, irritation, stinging to skin or vaginal area

Vaginal:

1% to 10%: Genitourinary: Vulvar/vaginal burning

<1% (Limited to important or life-threatening): Burning or itching of penis of sexual partner; polyuria; vulvar itching, soreness, edema, or discharge

Drug Interactions

Cytochrome P450 Effect: Inhibits CYP1A2 (weak), 2A6 (weak), 2B6 (weak), 2C8 (weak), 2C9 (weak), 2C19 (weak), 2D6 (weak), 2E1 (weak), 3A4 (moderate)

Increased Effect/Toxicity: Clotrimazole may increase the levels/effects of selected benzodiazepines, calcium channel blockers, cisapride, cyclosporine, ergot derivatives, selected HMG-CoA reductase inhibitors, mesoridazine, mirtazapine, nateglinide, nefazodone, pimozide, quinidine, sildenafil (and other PDE-5 inhibitors), tacrolimus, thioridazine, venlafaxine, and other CYP3A4 substrates.

Mechanism of Action Binds to phospholipids in the fungal cell membrane altering cell wall permeability resulting in loss of essential intracellular elements

Pharmacodynamics/Kinetics

Absorption: Topical: Negligible through intact skin

Time to peak, serum:

Oral topical (troche): Salivary levels occur within 3 hours following 30 minutes of dissolution time

Vaginal cream: High vaginal levels: 8-24 hours

Vaginal tablet: High vaginal levels: 1-2 days

Excretion: Feces (as metabolites)

Dosage

Children >3 years and Adults:

Oral:

Prophylaxis: 10 mg troche dissolved 3 times/day for the duration of chemotherapy or until steroids are reduced to maintenance levels

Treatment: 10 mg troche dissolved slowly 5 times/day for 14 consecutive days

Topical (cream, solution): Apply twice daily; if no improvement occurs after 4 weeks of therapy, re-evaluate diagnosis

Children >12 years and Adults:

Vaginal:

Cream:

1%: Insert 1 applicatorful vaginal cream daily (preferably at bedtime) for 7 consecutive days

2%: Insert 1 applicatorful vaginal cream daily (preferably at bedtime) for 3 consecutive days

Tablet: Insert 100 mg/day for 7 days or 500 mg single dose

Topical (cream, solution): Apply to affected area twice daily (morning and evening) for 7 consecutive days

Administration

Oral (troche): Allow to dissolve slowly over 15-30 minutes.

Topical: Avoid contact with eyes. For external use only. Apply sparingly. Protect hands with latex gloves. Do not use occlusive dressings.

Monitoring Parameters Periodic liver function tests during oral therapy with clotrimazole troche

Dosage Forms

Combination pack (Mycelex®-7): Vaginal tablet 100 mg (7s) and vaginal cream 1% (7 g)

Cream, topical: 1% (15 g, 30 g, 45 g)

Cruex®: 1% (15 g)

Lotrimin® AF Athlete's Foot: 1% (12 g, 24 g)

Lotrimin® AF Jock Itch: 1% (12 g)

Cream, vaginal: 2% (21 g)

Mycelex®-7: 1% (45 g)

Solution, topical: 1% (10 mL, 30 mL)

Lotrimin® AF Athlete's Foot: 1% (10 mL)

Tablet, vaginal (Gyne-Lotrimin® 3): 200 mg (3s)

Troche (Mycelex®): 10 mg

♦ **Clotrimazole and Betamethasone** see Betamethasone and Clotrimazole on page 214

Clozapine (KLOE za peen)

U.S. Brand Names Clozaril®; FazaClo®
Canadian Brand Names Apo-Clozapine®; Clozaril®; Gen-Clozapine
Pharmacologic Category Antipsychotic Agent, Atypical
Additional Appendix Information
Antipsychotic Agents *on page 1872*
Use Treatment-refractory schizophrenia; to reduce risk of recurrent suicidal behavior in schizophrenia or schizoaffective disorder
Unlabeled/Investigational Use Schizoaffective disorder, bipolar disorder, childhood psychosis, severe obsessive-compulsive disorder
Restrictions Patient-specific registration is required to dispense clozapine. Monitoring systems for individual clozapine manufacturers are independent. If a patient is switched from one brand/manufacturer of clozapine to another, the patient must be entered into a new registry (must be completed by the prescriber and delivered to the dispensing pharmacy). Healthcare providers, including pharmacists dispensing clozapine, should verify the patient's hematological status and qualification to receive clozapine with all existing registries. The manufacturer of Clozaril® requests that healthcare providers submit all WBC/ANC values following discontinuation of therapy to the Clozaril National Registry for all nonrechallengable patients until WBC is ≥3500/mm^3 and ANC is ≥2000/mm^3.
Pregnancy Risk Factor B
Pregnancy Implications Teratogenic effects were not seen in animal studies; however, there are no adequate and well-controlled studies in pregnant women. Use during pregnancy only if clearly needed.
Lactation Enters breast milk/not recommended (AAP rates "of concern")
Medication Safety Issues
Sound-alike/look-alike issues:
Clozapine may be confused with clofazimine, clonidine, Klonopin®
Clozaril® may be confused with Clinoril®, Colazal®
Contraindications Hypersensitivity to clozapine or any component of the formulation; history of agranulocytosis or granulocytopenia with clozapine; uncontrolled epilepsy, severe central nervous system depression or comatose state; paralytic ileus; myeloproliferative disorders or use with other agents which have a well-known risk of agranulocytosis or bone marrow suppression
Warnings/Precautions [U.S. Boxed Warning]: Patients with dementia-related behavioral disorders treated with atypical antipsychotics are at an increased risk of death compared to placebo. An increased incidence of cerebrovascular adverse events (including fatalities) has been reported in elderly patients with dementia-related psychosis. Risk may be increased by dehydration; use caution with concurrent diuretics. Clozapine is not approved for this indication.

[U.S. Boxed Warning]: Significant risk of agranulocytosis, potentially life-threatening. Therapy should not be initiated in patients with WBC <3500 cells/mm^3 or ANC <2000 cells/mm^3 or history of myeloproliferative disorder. WBC testing should occur periodically on an on-going basis (see prescribing information for monitoring details) to ensure that acceptable WBC/ANC counts are maintained. Initial episodes of moderate leukopenia or granulopoietic suppression confer up to a 12-fold increased risk for subsequent episodes of agranulocytosis. WBCs must be monitored weekly for at least 4 weeks after therapy discontinuation or until WBC is ≥3500/mm^3 and ANC is ≥2000/mm^3. Use with caution in patients receiving other marrow suppressive agents. Eosinophilia has been reported to occur with clozapine and may require temporary or permanent interruption of therapy. Due to the significant risk of agranulocytosis, it is strongly recommended that a patient must fail at least two trials of other primary medications for the treatment of schizophrenia (of adequate dose and duration) before initiating therapy with clozapine.

Cognitive and/or motor impairment (sedation) is common with clozapine, resulting in impaired performance of tasks requiring alertness (eg, operating machinery or driving); use caution in patients receiving general anesthesia. **[U.S. Boxed Warning]: Seizures have been associated with clozapine use in a dose-dependent manner;** use with caution in patients at risk of seizures, including those with a history of seizures, head trauma, brain damage, alcoholism, or concurrent therapy with medications which may lower seizure threshold. Has been associated with benign, self-limiting fever (<100.4°F, usually within first 3 weeks). However, clozapine may also be associated with severe febrile reactions, including neuroleptic malignant syndrome (NMS). Clozapine's potential for extrapyramidal symptoms (including tardive dyskinesia) appears to be extremely low.

Deep vein thrombosis, myocarditis, pericarditis, pericardial effusion, cardiomyopathy, and CHF have also been associated with clozapine. **[U.S. Boxed Warning]: Fatalities due to myocarditis have been reported; highest risk in the first month of therapy, however, later cases also reported.** Clozapine should be discontinued in patients with confirmed cardiomyopathy unless benefit clearly outweighs risk. Rare cases of thromboembolism, including pulmonary embolism and stroke resulting in fatalities, have been associated with clozapine.

May cause anticholinergic effects; use with caution in patients with urinary retention, benign prostatic hyperplasia, narrow-angle glaucoma, xerostomia, visual problems, constipation, or history of bowel obstruction. May cause hyperglycemia; in some cases may be extreme and associated with ketoacidosis, hyperosmolar coma, or death. Use with caution in patients with diabetes or other disorders of glucose regulation; monitor for worsening of glucose control. Use with caution in patients with hepatic disease or impairment; hepatitis has been reported as a consequence of therapy.

Use caution with cardiovascular or renal disease. **[U.S. Boxed Warning]: May cause orthostatic hypotension (with or without syncope)** and tachycardia; use with caution in patients at risk of hypotension or in patients where transient hypotensive episodes would be poorly tolerated (cardiovascular disease or cerebrovascular disease). Concurrent use with benzodiazepines may increase the risk of severe cardiopulmonary reactions.

The possibility of a suicide attempt is inherent in psychotic illness or bipolar disorder; use caution in high-risk patients during initiation of therapy. Prescriptions should be written for the smallest quantity consistent with good patient care.

Medication should not be stopped abruptly; taper off over 1-2 weeks. If conditions warrant abrupt discontinuation (leukopenia, myocarditis, cardiomyopathy), monitor patient for psychosis and cholinergic rebound (headache, nausea, vomiting, diarrhea). Significant weight gain has been observed with antipsychotic therapy; incidence varies with product. Elderly patients are more susceptible to adverse effects (including agranulocytosis, cardiovascular, anticholinergic, and tardive dyskinesia). Safety and efficacy have not been established in children.

Adverse Reactions

>10%:

Cardiovascular: Tachycardia (25%)

Central nervous system: Drowsiness (39% to 46%), dizziness (19% to 27%), insomnia (2% to 20%)

Gastrointestinal: Constipation (14% to 25%), weight gain (4% to 31%), sialorrhea (31% to 48%), nausea/vomiting (3% to 17%)

1% to 10%:

Cardiovascular: Angina (1%), ECG changes (1%), hypertension (4%), hypotension (9%), syncope (6%)

Central nervous system: Akathisia (3%), seizure (3%), headache (7%), nightmares (4%), akinesia (4%), confusion (3%), myoclonic jerks (1%), restlessness (4%), agitation (4%), lethargy (1%), ataxia (1%), slurred speech (1%), depression (1%), anxiety (1%)

Dermatologic: Rash (2%)

Gastrointestinal: Abdominal discomfort/heartburn (4% to 14%), anorexia (1%), diarrhea (2%), xerostomia (6%), throat discomfort (1%)

Genitourinary: Urinary abnormalities (eg, abnormal ejaculation, retention, urgency, incontinence; 1% to 2%)

Hematologic: Eosinophilia (1%), leukopenia, leukocytosis, agranulocytosis (1%)

Hepatic: Liver function tests abnormal (1%)

Neuromuscular & skeletal: Tremor (6%), hypokinesia (4%), rigidity (3%), hyperkinesia (1%), weakness (1%), pain (1%), spasm (1%)

Ocular: Visual disturbances (5%)

Respiratory: Dyspnea (1%), nasal congestion (1%)

Miscellaneous: Diaphoresis increased, fever, tongue numbness (1%)

<1%, postmarketing, and/or case reports (limited to important or life-threatening): Amentia, amnesia, anemia, arrhythmia (atrial or ventricular), aspiration, blurred vision, bradycardia, bronchitis, cardiomyopathy (usually dilated), cataplexy, CHF, cholestasis, cyanosis, delusions, diabetes mellitus, difficult urination, edema, erythema multiforme, ESR increased, fecal impaction, gastroenteritis, granulocytopenia, hallucinations, hematemesis, hepatitis, hypercholesterolemia (rare), hyperglycemia, hypertriglyceridemia (rare), hyponatremia, hypothermia, impotence, interstitial nephritis (acute), intestinal obstruction, jaundice, loss of speech, MI, myasthenia syndrome, myocarditis, narrow-angle glaucoma, neuroleptic malignant syndrome, palpitations, pancreatitis (acute), paralytic ileus, Parkinsonism, pericardial effusion, pericarditis, phlebitis, pleural effusion, pneumonia, priapism, pulmonary embolism, rhabdomyolysis, rectal bleeding, salivary gland swelling, sepsis, status epilepticus, stroke, Stevens-Johnson syndrome, tardive dyskinesia, thrombocytopenia, thrombocytosis, thromboembolism, thrombophlebitis, vasculitis, wheezing

Overdosage/Toxicology

Symptoms include altered states of consciousness (delirium, drowsiness, coma), tachycardia, hypotension, hypersalivation, and respiratory depression. Aspiration pneumonia and cardiac arrhythmias have also been reported. Fatal overdose generally at >2500 mg. Following initiation of essential overdose management, toxic symptom treatment and supportive treatment should be initiated. Hypotension usually responds to I.V. fluids or Trendelenburg positioning. If unresponsive to these measures, the use of a parenteral inotrope may be required. Seizures commonly respond to diazepam (I.V. 5-10 mg bolus in adults every 15 minutes, if needed, up to a total of 30 mg; I.V. 0.25-0.4 mg/kg/dose up to a total of 10 mg in children), or to phenytoin or phenobarbital. Critical cardiac arrhythmias often respond to I.V. phenytoin (15 mg/kg up to 1 g), while other antiarrhythmics can be used. Neuroleptics often cause extrapyramidal symptoms (eg, dystonic reactions) requiring management with anticholinergic agents such as benztropine mesylate I.V. 1-2 mg (adults) may be effective. These agents are generally effective within 2-5 minutes.

Drug Interactions

Cytochrome P450 Effect: Substrate of CYP1A2 (major), 2A6 (minor), 2C9 (minor), 2C19 (minor), 2D6 (minor), 3A4 (minor); Inhibits CYP1A2 (weak), 2C9 (weak), 2C19 (weak), 2D6 (moderate), 2E1 (weak), 3A4 (weak)

Increased Effect/Toxicity: May potentiate anticholinergic and hypotensive effects of other drugs. Benzodiazepines in combination with clozapine may produce respiratory depression and hypotension, especially during the first few weeks of therapy. May potentiate effect/toxicity of risperidone. Clozapine serum concentrations may be increased by inhibitors of CYP1A2; example inhibitors include ciprofloxacin, fluvoxamine, ketoconazole, norfloxacin, ofloxacin, and rofecoxib. Clozapine may increase the levels/effects of amphetamines, selected beta-blockers, substrates; example substrates include dextromethorphan, fluoxetine, lidocaine, mirtazapine, nefazodone, paroxetine, risperidone, ritonavir, thioridazine, tricyclic antidepressants, venlafaxine, and other CYP2D6 substrates. Sedative effects may be additive with other CNS depressants (eg, ethanol, barbiturates, benzodiazepines, opioid analgesics, and other sedatives). Metoclopramide may increase risk of extrapyramidal symptoms (EPS). Acetylcholinesterase inhibitors (central) may increase the risk of antipsychotic-related EPS. Citalopram may increase the levels/effects of clozapine. Omeprazole may alter the concentrations/effects of clozapine.

Decreased Effect: Clozapine may decrease the levels/effects of CYP2D6 prodrug substrates; example prodrug substrates include codeine, hydrocodone, oxycodone, and (Continued)

Clozapine *(Continued)*

tramadol. The levels/effects of clozapine may be decreased by carbamazepine, phenobarbital, primidone, rifampin, and other CYP1A2 inducers. Clozapine may reverse the pressor effect of epinephrine (avoid in treatment of drug-induced hypotension). Omeprazole may alter the concentrations/effects of clozapine.

Ethanol/Nutrition/Herb Interactions
Ethanol: Avoid ethanol (may increase CNS depression).
Herb/Nutraceutical: St John's wort may decrease clozapine levels. Avoid kava kava, gotu kola, valerian, St John's wort (may increase CNS depression).

Stability Dispensed in "clozapine patient system" packaging. Store at controlled room temperature. FazaClo™: Protect from moisture; do not remove from package until ready to use.

Mechanism of Action Clozapine (dibenzodiazepine antipsychotic) exhibits weak antagonism of D_1, D_2, D_3, and D_5 dopamine receptor subtypes, but shows high affinity for D_4; in addition, it blocks the serotonin (5HT$_2$), alpha-adrenergic, histamine H_1, and cholinergic receptors

Pharmacodynamics/Kinetics
Protein binding: 97% to serum proteins
Metabolism: Extensively hepatic; forms metabolites with limited or no activity
Bioavailability: 12% to 81% (not affected by food)
Half-life elimination: Steady state: 12 hours (range: 4-66 hours)
Time to peak: 2.5 hours (range: 1-6 hours)
Excretion: Urine (~50%) and feces (30%) with trace amounts of unchanged drug

Dosage Oral:
Children and Adolescents: Childhood psychosis (unlabeled use): Initial: 25 mg/day; increase to a target dose of 25-400 mg/day

Adults:
Schizophrenia: Initial: 12.5 mg once or twice daily; increased, as tolerated, in increments of 25-50 mg/day to a target dose of 300-450 mg/day after 2-4 weeks; may require doses as high as 600-900 mg/day
Reduce risk of suicidal behavior: Initial: 12.5 mg once or twice daily; increased, as tolerated, in increments of 25-50 mg/day to a target dose of 300-450 mg/day after 2-4 weeks; median dose is ~300 mg/day (range: 12.5-900 mg)
Elderly: Schizophrenia: Dose selection and titration should be cautious

Termination of therapy: If dosing is interrupted for ≥48 hours, therapy must be reinitiated at 12.5-25 mg/day; may be increased more rapidly than with initial titration, unless cardiopulmonary arrest occurred during initial titration.
In the event of planned termination of clozapine, gradual reduction in dose over a 1- to 2-week period is recommended. If conditions warrant abrupt discontinuation (leukopenia), monitor patient for psychosis and cholinergic rebound (headache, nausea, vomiting, diarrhea).
Patients discontinued on clozapine therapy due to WBC <2000/mm^3 or ANC <1000/mm^3 should not be restarted on clozapine.

Dosage adjustment for toxicity:
Moderate leukopenia or granulocytopenia (WBC <3000/mm^3 and/or ANC <1500/mm^3): Discontinue therapy; may rechallenge patient when WBC is >3500/mm^3 and ANC is >2000/mm^3. **Note:** Patient is at greater risk for developing agranulocytosis.
Severe leukopenia or granulocytopenia (WBC <2000/mm^3 and/or ANC <1000/mm^3): Discontinue therapy and do not rechallenge patient.

Dietary Considerations May be taken without regard to food. Fazaclo™ contains phenylalanine 1.75 mg per 25 mg tablet and phenylalanine 6.96 mg per 100 mg tablet.

Administration Orally-disintegrating tablet: Should be removed from foil blister by peeling apart (do not push tablet through the foil). Remove immediately prior to use. Place tablet in mouth and allow to dissolve; swallow with saliva. If dosing requires splitting tablet, throw unused portion away.

Monitoring Parameters Mental status, ECG, WBC (see below), vital signs, fasting lipid profile and fasting blood glucose/Hgb A$_{1c}$ (prior to treatment, at 3 months, then annually; BMI, personal/family history of obesity; waist circumference (weight should be assessed prior to treatment, at 4 weeks, 8 weeks, 12 weeks, and then at quarterly intervals. Consider titrating to a different antipsychotic agent for a weight gain ≥5% of the initial weight); blood pressure; abnormal involuntary movement scale (AIMS).

WBC and ANC should be obtained at baseline and at least weekly for the first 6 months of continuous treatment. If counts remain acceptable (WBC ≥3500/mm^3, ANC ≥2000/mm^3) during this time period, then they may be monitored every other week for the next 6 months. If WBC/ANC continue to remain within these acceptable limits after the second 6 months of therapy, monitoring can be decreased to every 4 weeks. (**Note:** The decease in monitoring to every 4 weeks is applicable in the United States. Blood monitoring requirements related to the use of clozapine have not changed in Canada. If clozapine is discontinued, a weekly WBC should be conducted for an additional 4 weeks or until WBC is ≥3500/mm^3 and ANC is ≥2000/mm^3. If clozapine therapy is interrupted due to moderate leukopenia, weekly WBC/ANC monitoring is required for 12 months in patients restarted on clozapine treatment. If therapy is interrupted for reasons other than leukopenia/granulocytopenia, the 6-month time period for initiation of biweekly WBCs may need to be reset. This determination depends upon the treatment duration, the length of the break in therapy, and whether or not an abnormal blood event occurred.

Consult full prescribing information for determination of appropriate WBC/ANC monitoring interval (http://www.clozaril.com/index.jsp).

Dosage Forms
Tablet: 12.5 mg, 25 mg, 100 mg
Clozaril®: 25 mg, 100 mg
Tablet, orally disintegrating (FazaClo®): 25 mg [contains phenylalanine 1.75 mg; mint flavor], 100 mg [contains phenylalanine 6.96 mg; mint flavor]

♦ **Clozaril®** *see* Clozapine *on page 406*
♦ **CMA-676** *see* Gemtuzumab Ozogamicin *on page 790*

- ◆ **CMV-IGIV** *see* Cytomegalovirus Immune Globulin (Intravenous-Human) *on page 441*
- ◆ **CNJ-016™** *see* Vaccinia Immune Globulin (Intravenous) *on page 1762*
- ◆ **CoActifed® (Can)** *see* Triprolidine, Pseudoephedrine, and Codeine *on page 1750*
- ◆ **Coagulant Complex Inhibitor** *see* Anti-inhibitor Coagulant Complex *on page 137*
- ◆ **Coagulation Factor VIIa** *see* Factor VIIa (Recombinant) *on page 678*
- ◆ **CO Alendronate (Can)** *see* Alendronate *on page 65*
- ◆ **CO Azithromycin (Can)** *see* Azithromycin *on page 186*
- ◆ **CO Bicalutamide (Can)** *see* Bicalutamide *on page 221*

Cocaine (koe KANE)

Index Terms Cocaine Hydrochloride
Pharmacologic Category Local Anesthetic
Use Topical anesthesia for mucous membranes
Restrictions C-II
Pregnancy Risk Factor C/X (nonmedicinal use)
Lactation Enters breast milk/contraindicated
Contraindications Hypersensitivity to cocaine or any component of the topical solution; ophthalmologic anesthesia (causing sloughing of the corneal epithelium); pregnancy (nonmedicinal use)
Warnings/Precautions For topical use only. Limit to office and surgical procedures only. Resuscitative equipment and drugs should be immediately available when any local anesthetic is used. Debilitated, elderly patients, acutely ill patients, and children should be given reduced doses consistent with their age and physical status. Use caution in patients with severely traumatized mucosa and sepsis in the region of the proposed application. Use with caution in patients with cardiovascular disease or a history of cocaine abuse. In patients being treated for cardiovascular complication of cocaine abuse, avoid beta-blockers for treatment.
Adverse Reactions
>10%:
  Central nervous system: CNS stimulation
  Gastrointestinal: Loss of taste perception
  Respiratory: Rhinitis, nasal congestion
  Miscellaneous: Loss of smell
1% to 10%:
  Cardiovascular: Heart rate (decreased) with low doses, tachycardia with moderate doses, hypertension, cardiomyopathy, cardiac arrhythmia, myocarditis, QRS prolongation, Raynaud's phenomenon, cerebral vasculitis, thrombosis, fibrillation (atrial), flutter (atrial), sinus bradycardia, CHF, pulmonary hypertension, sinus tachycardia, tachycardia (supraventricular), arrhythmia (ventricular), vasoconstriction
  Central nervous system: Fever, nervousness, restlessness, euphoria, excitation, headache, psychosis, hallucinations, agitation, seizure, slurred speech, hyperthermia, dystonic reactions, cerebral vascular accident, vasculitis, clonic-tonic reactions, paranoia, sympathetic storm
  Dermatologic: Skin infarction, pruritus, madarosis
  Gastrointestinal: Nausea, anorexia, colonic ischemia, spontaneous bowel perforation
  Genitourinary: Priapism, uterine rupture
  Hematologic: Thrombocytopenia
  Neuromuscular & skeletal: Chorea (extrapyramidal), paresthesia, tremor, fasciculations
  Ocular: Mydriasis (peak effect at 45 minutes; may last up to 12 hours), sloughing of the corneal epithelium, ulceration of the cornea, iritis, chemosis
  Renal: Myoglobinuria, necrotizing vasculitis
  Respiratory: Tachypnea, nasal mucosa damage (when snorting), hyposmia, bronchiolitis obliterans organizing pneumonia
  Miscellaneous: "Washed-out" syndrome
Overdosage/Toxicology Symptoms include anxiety, excitement, confusion, nausea, vomiting, headache, rapid pulse, irregular respiration, delirium, fever, seizures, respiratory arrest, hallucinations, dilated pupils, muscle spasms, sensory aberrations, and cardiac arrhythmias. Fatal dose: Oral: 500 mg to 1.2 g; severe toxic effects have occurred with doses as low as 20 mg. Since no specific antidote for cocaine exists, serious toxic effects are treated symptomatically. Maintain airway and respiration. Attempt delay of absorption (if ingested) with activated charcoal, gastric lavage or emesis. Seizures are treated with diazepam while propranolol or labetalol may be useful for life-threatening arrhythmias, agitation, and/or hypertension.
Drug Interactions
  Cytochrome P450 Effect: **Substrate** of CYP3A4 (major); **Inhibits** CYP2D6 (strong), 3A4 (weak)
  Increased Effect/Toxicity: Cocaine may increase the levels/effects of CYP2D6 substrates (eg, amphetamines, selected beta-blockers, dextromethorphan, fluoxetine, lidocaine, mirtazapine, nefazodone, paroxetine, risperidone, ritonavir, thioridazine, tricyclic antidepressants, venlafaxine). Increased toxicity with MAO inhibitors. Use with epinephrine may cause extreme hypertension and/or cardiac arrhythmias. CYP3A4 inhibitors may increase the levels/effects of cocaine (eg, azole antifungals, clarithromycin, diclofenac, doxycycline, erythromycin, imatinib, isoniazid, nefazodone, nicardipine, propofol, protease inhibitors, quinidine, telithromycin, verapamil).
Stability Store in well closed, light-resistant containers.
Mechanism of Action Ester local anesthetic blocks both the initiation and conduction of nerve impulses by decreasing the neuronal membrane's permeability to sodium ions, which results in inhibition of depolarization with resultant blockade of conduction; interferes with the uptake of norepinephrine by adrenergic nerve terminals producing vasoconstriction
Pharmacodynamics/Kinetics Following topical administration to mucosa:
  Onset of action: ~1 minute
  Peak effect: ~5 minutes
  (Continued)

Cocaine *(Continued)*

Duration (dose dependent): ≥30 minutes; cocaine metabolites may appear in urine of neonates up to 5 days after birth due to maternal cocaine use shortly before birth

Absorption: Well absorbed through mucous membranes; limited by drug-induced vasoconstriction; enhanced by inflammation

Distribution: Enters breast milk

Metabolism: Hepatic; major metabolites are ecgonine methyl ester and benzoyl ecgonine

Half-life elimination: 75 minutes

Excretion: Primarily urine (<10% as unchanged drug and metabolites)

Dosage Topical application (ear, nose, throat, bronchoscopy): Dosage depends on the area to be anesthetized, tissue vascularity, technique of anesthesia, and individual patient tolerance; the lowest dose necessary to produce adequate anesthesia should be used; concentrations of 1% to 10% are used (not to exceed 1 mg/kg). Use reduced dosages for children, elderly, or debilitated patients.

Administration Topical: Use only on mucous membranes of the oral, laryngeal, and nasal cavities. Do not use on extensive areas of broken skin.

Monitoring Parameters Vital signs

Reference Range Therapeutic: 100-500 ng/mL (SI: 330 nmol/L); Toxic: >1000 ng/mL (SI: >3300 nmol/L)

Additional Information Cocaine intoxication of infants who are receiving breast milk from their mothers abusing cocaine has been reported.

Dosage Forms

Powder, as hydrochloride: 1 g, 5 g, 25 g

Solution, topical, as hydrochloride: 4% [40 mg/mL] (4 mL, 10 mL); 10% [100 mg/mL] (4 mL, 10 mL)

♦ **Cocaine Hydrochloride** *see Cocaine on page 409*

♦ **CO Ciprofloxacin (Can)** *see Ciprofloxacin on page 372*

♦ **CO Citalopram (Can)** *see Citalopram on page 381*

♦ **CO Clomipramine (Can)** *see ClomiPRAMINE on page 395*

♦ **CO Clonazepam (Can)** *see Clonazepam on page 397*

Codeine *(KOE deen)*

Canadian Brand Names Codeine Contin®

Index Terms Codeine Phosphate; Codeine Sulfate; Methylmorphine

Pharmacologic Category Analgesic, Opioid; Antitussive

Additional Appendix Information

Narcotic Agonists *on page 1888*

Use Treatment of mild-to-moderate pain; antitussive in lower doses; dextromethorphan has equivalent antitussive activity but has much lower toxicity in accidental overdose

Restrictions C-II

Pregnancy Risk Factor C/D (prolonged use or high doses at term)

Lactation Enters breast milk/use caution (AAP rates "compatible")

Medication Safety Issues

Sound-alike/look-alike issues:

Codeine may be confused with Cardene®, Cophene®, Cordran®, iodine, Lodine®

Contraindications Hypersensitivity to codeine or any component of the formulation; pregnancy (prolonged use or high doses at term)

Warnings/Precautions

Use with caution in patients with hypersensitivity reactions to other phenanthrene derivative opioid agonists (morphine, hydrocodone, hydromorphone, levorphanol, oxycodone, oxymorphone); respiratory diseases including asthma, emphysema, COPD, adrenal insufficiency, biliary tract impairment, CNS depression/coma, head trauma, morbid obesity, prostatic hyperplasia, urinary stricture, thyroid dysfunction, or severe liver or renal insufficiency; some preparations contain sulfites which may cause allergic reactions; tolerance or drug dependence may result from extended use. May obscure diagnosis or clinical course of patients with acute abdominal conditions. May cause CNS depression, which may impair physical or mental abilities; patients must be cautioned about performing tasks which require mental alertness (eg, operating machinery or driving). May cause hypotension; use with caution in patients with hypovolemia, cardiovascular disease (including acute MI), or drugs which may exaggerate hypotensive effects (including phenothiazines or general anesthetics).

Not recommended for use for cough control in patients with a productive cough; not recommended as an antitussive for children <2 years of age; the elderly and debilitated patients may be particularly susceptible to adverse effects of narcotics

Not approved for I.V. administration (although this route has been used clinically). If given intravenously, must be given slowly and the patient should be lying down. Rapid intravenous administration of narcotics may increase the incidence of serious adverse effects, in part due to limited opportunity to assess response prior to administration of the full dose. Access to respiratory support should be immediately available.

Concurrent use of agonist/antagonist analgesics may precipitate withdrawal symptoms and/or reduced analgesic efficacy in patients following prolonged therapy with mu opioid agonists. Abrupt discontinuation following prolonged use may also lead to withdrawal symptoms.

Adverse Reactions

Frequency not defined: AST/ALT increased

>10%:

Central nervous system: Drowsiness

Gastrointestinal: Constipation

1% to 10%:

Cardiovascular: Tachycardia or bradycardia, hypotension

Central nervous system: Dizziness, lightheadedness, false feeling of well being, malaise, headache, restlessness, paradoxical CNS stimulation, confusion
Dermatologic: Rash, urticaria
Gastrointestinal: Dry mouth, anorexia, nausea, vomiting
Genitourinary: Urination decreased, ureteral spasm
Hepatic: LFTs increased
Local: Burning at injection site
Neuromuscular & skeletal: Weakness
Ocular: Blurred vision
Respiratory: Dyspnea
Miscellaneous: Histamine release
<1% (Limited to important or life-threatening): Convulsions, hallucinations, insomnia, mental depression, nightmares

Overdosage/Toxicology Symptoms include CNS and respiratory depression, gastrointestinal cramping, and constipation. Treatment includes naloxone 2 mg I.V. (0.01 mg/kg for children), with repeat administration as necessary, up to a total of 10 mg.

Drug Interactions

Cytochrome P450 Effect: Substrate of CYP2D6 (major), 3A4 (minor); **Inhibits** CYP2D6 (weak)

Increased Effect/Toxicity: May cause severely increased toxicity of codeine when taken with CNS depressants, phenothiazines, tricyclic antidepressants, other opioid analgesics, guanabenz, MAO inhibitors, and neuromuscular blockers.

Decreased Effect: CYP2D6 inhibitors may decrease the effects of codeine. Example inhibitors include chlorpromazine, delavirdine, fluoxetine, miconazole, paroxetine, pergolide, quinidine, quinine, ritonavir, and ropinirole. Decreased effect with cigarette smoking.

Ethanol/Nutrition/Herb Interactions

Ethanol: Avoid or limit ethanol (may increase CNS depression).
Herb/Nutraceutical: St John's wort may decrease codeine levels. Avoid valerian, St John's wort, kava kava, gotu kola (may increase CNS depression).

Stability Store injection between 15°C to 30°C; avoid freezing. Do not use if injection is discolored or contains a precipitate. Protect injection from light.

Mechanism of Action Binds to opiate receptors in the CNS, causing inhibition of ascending pain pathways, altering the perception of and response to pain; causes cough supression by direct central action in the medulla; produces generalized CNS depression

Pharmacodynamics/Kinetics

Onset of action: Oral: 0.5-1 hour; I.M.: 10-30 minutes
Peak effect: Oral: 1-1.5 hours; I.M.: 0.5-1 hour
Duration: 4-6 hours
Absorption: Oral: Adequate
Distribution: Crosses placenta; enters breast milk
Protein binding: 7%
Metabolism: Hepatic to morphine (active)
Half-life elimination: 2.5-3.5 hours
Excretion: Urine (3% to 16% as unchanged drug, norcodeine, and free and conjugated morphine)

Dosage Note: These are guidelines and do not represent the maximum doses that may be required in all patients. Doses should be titrated to pain relief/prevention. Doses >1.5 mg/kg body weight are not recommended.

Analgesic:
Children: Oral, I.M., SubQ: 0.5-1 mg/kg/dose every 4-6 hours as needed; maximum: 60 mg/dose
Adults:
Oral: 30 mg every 4-6 hours as needed; patients with prior opiate exposure may require higher initial doses. Usual range: 15-120 mg every 4-6 hours as needed
Oral, controlled release formulation (Codeine Contin®, not available in U.S.): 50-300 mg every 12 hours. **Note:** A patient's codeine requirement should be established using prompt release formulations; conversion to long acting products may be considered when chronic, continuous treatment is required. Higher dosages should be reserved for use only in opioid-tolerant patients.
I.M., SubQ: 30 mg every 4-6 hours as needed; patients with prior opiate exposure may require higher initial doses. Usual range: 15-120 mg every 4-6 hours as needed; more frequent dosing may be needed
Antitussive: Oral (for nonproductive cough):
Children: 1-1.5 mg/kg/day in divided doses every 4-6 hours as needed: Alternative dose according to age:
2-6 years: 2.5-5 mg every 4-6 hours as needed; maximum: 30 mg/day
6-12 years: 5-10 mg every 4-6 hours as needed; maximum: 60 mg/day
Adults: 10-20 mg/dose every 4-6 hours as needed; maximum: 120 mg/day

Dosing adjustment in renal impairment:
Cl_{cr} 10-50 mL/minute: Administer 75% of dose
Cl_{cr} <10 mL/minute: Administer 50% of dose

Dosing adjustment in hepatic impairment: Probably necessary in hepatic insufficiency

Administration Not approved for I.V. administration (although this route has been used clinically). If given intravenously, must be given slowly and the patient should be lying down. Rapid intravenous administration of narcotics may increase the incidence of serious adverse effects, in part due to limited opportunity to assess response prior to administration of the full dose. Access to respiratory support should be immediately available.

Monitoring Parameters Pain relief, respiratory and mental status, blood pressure, heart rate

Reference Range Therapeutic: Not established; Toxic: >1.1 mcg/mL

Test Interactions Some quinolones may produce a false-positive urine screening result for opiates using commercially-available immunoassay kits. This has been demonstrated most consistently for levofloxacin and ofloxacin, but other quinolones have shown cross-reactivity in certain assay kits. Confirmation of positive opiate screens by more specific methods should be considered.

(Continued)

Codeine *(Continued)*

Dosage Forms [CAN] = Canadian brand name
Injection, as phosphate: 15 mg/mL (2 mL); 30 mg/mL (2 mL) [contains sodium metabisulfite]
Tablet, as phosphate: 30 mg, 60 mg
Tablet, as sulfate: 15 mg, 30 mg, 60 mg
Tablet, controlled release (Codeine Contin®) [CAN]: 50 mg, 100 mg, 150 mg, 200 mg [not available in U.S.]

♦ **Codeine and Acetaminophen** *see* Acetaminophen and Codeine *on page 31*
♦ **Codeine and Guaifenesin** *see* Guaifenesin and Codeine *on page 815*
♦ **Codeine and Promethazine** *see* Promethazine and Codeine *on page 1437*
♦ **Codeine, Aspirin, and Carisoprodol** *see* Carisoprodol, Aspirin, and Codeine *on page 295*
♦ **Codeine, Chlorpheniramine, and Pseudoephedrine** *see* Chlorpheniramine, Pseudoephedrine, and Codeine *on page 355*
♦ **Codeine, Chlorpheniramine, Phenylephrine, and Potassium Iodide** *see* Chlorpheniramine, Phenylephrine, Codeine, and Potassium Iodide *on page 354*
♦ **Codeine Contin® (Can)** *see* Codeine *on page 410*
♦ **Codeine, Guaifenesin, and Pseudoephedrine** *see* Guaifenesin, Pseudoephedrine, and Codeine *on page 820*
♦ **Codeine Phosphate** *see* Codeine *on page 410*
♦ **Codeine, Promethazine, and Phenylephrine** *see* Promethazine, Phenylephrine, and Codeine *on page 1438*
♦ **Codeine, Pseudoephedrine, and Triprolidine** *see* Triprolidine, Pseudoephedrine, and Codeine *on page 1750*
♦ **Codeine Sulfate** *see* Codeine *on page 410*
♦ **Codeine, Triprolidine, and Pseudoephedrine** *see* Triprolidine, Pseudoephedrine, and Codeine *on page 1750*
♦ **Codiclear® DH** *see* Hydrocodone and Guaifenesin *on page 849*
♦ **Cod Liver Oil** *see* Vitamin A and Vitamin D *on page 1794*
♦ **CO Fluoxetine (Can)** *see* Fluoxetine *on page 727*
♦ **Cogentin®** *see* Benztropine *on page 208*
♦ **Co-Gesic®** *see* Hydrocodone and Acetaminophen *on page 848*
♦ **CO Glimepiride (Can)** *see* Glimepiride *on page 797*
♦ **Cognex®** *see* Tacrine *on page 1625*
♦ **CO Ipra-Sal (Can)** *see* Ipratropium and Albuterol *on page 934*
♦ **Colace® [OTC]** *see* Docusate *on page 533*
♦ **Colace® (Can)** *see* Docusate *on page 533*
♦ **Colax-C® (Can)** *see* Docusate *on page 533*
♦ **Colazal®** *see* Balsalazide *on page 194*
♦ **ColBenemid** *see* Colchicine and Probenecid *on page 414*

Colchicine *(KOL chi seen)*

Pharmacologic Category Colchicine
Use Treatment of acute gouty arthritis attacks and prevention of recurrences of such attacks
Unlabeled/Investigational Use Primary biliary cirrhosis; management of familial Mediterranean fever; pericarditis
Pregnancy Risk Factor C (oral); D (parenteral)
Lactation Enters breast milk/use caution (AAP rates "compatible")
Medication Safety Issues
    High alert medication: The Institute for Safe Medication Practices (ISMP) includes this medication among its list of drugs which have a heightened risk of causing significant patient harm when used in error.
Contraindications Hypersensitivity to colchicine or any component of the formulation; severe renal, gastrointestinal, hepatic, or cardiac disorders; blood dyscrasias; pregnancy (parenteral)
Warnings/Precautions Use with caution in debilitated patients or elderly patients; use caution in patients with mild-to-moderate cardiac, GI, renal, or liver disease. Severe local irritation can occur following SubQ or I.M. administration. Dosage reduction is recommended in patients who develop weakness or gastrointestinal symptoms (anorexia, diarrhea, nausea, vomiting) related to drug therapy.

Intravenous: Use only with extreme caution; potential for serious, life-threatening complications. Should not be administered to patients with renal insufficiency, hepatobiliary obstruction, patients >70 years of age, or recent oral colchicine use. Should be reserved for hospitalized patients who are under the care of a physician experienced in the use of intravenous colchicine.
Adverse Reactions
    >10%: Gastrointestinal: Nausea, vomiting, diarrhea, abdominal pain
    1% to 10%:
        Dermatologic: Alopecia
        Gastrointestinal: Anorexia
    <1% (Limited to important or life-threatening): Agranulocytosis, aplastic anemia, arrhythmia (with intravenous administration), bone marrow suppression, hepatotoxicity
Overdosage/Toxicology Symptoms include nausea, vomiting, abdominal pain, shock, kidney damage, muscle weakness, burning in throat, watery to bloody diarrhea, hypotension, anuria, cardiovascular collapse, delirium, and convulsions. Treatment includes gastric lavage and measures to prevent shock, hemodialysis or peritoneal dialysis. Atropine and morphine may relieve abdominal pain.

Drug Interactions

Cytochrome P450 Effect: Substrate of CYP3A4 (major); **Induces** CYP2C8 (weak), 2C9 (weak), 2E1 (weak), 3A4 (weak)

Increased Effect/Toxicity: Concurrent use of cyclosporine with colchicine may increase toxicity of colchicine. CYP3A4 inhibitors may increase the levels/effects of colchicine (example inhibitors include azole antifungals, diclofenac, doxycycline, imatinib, isoniazid, nefazodone, nicardipine, propofol, protease inhibitors, quinidine, and verapamil. Macrolide antibiotics (clarithromycin, erythromycin, troleandomycin) and telithromycin may decrease the metabolism of colchicine resulting in severe colchicine toxicity; avoid, if possible. Verapamil may increase colchicine toxicity (especially nephrotoxicity).

Ethanol/Nutrition/Herb Interactions

Ethanol: Avoid ethanol.

Food: Cyanocobalamin (vitamin B_{12}): Malabsorption of the substrate. May result in macrocytic anemia or neurologic dysfunction.

Herb/Nutraceutical: Vitamin B_{12} absorption may be decreased by colchicine.

Stability Protect tablets from light.

Mechanism of Action Decreases leukocyte motility, decreases phagocytosis in joints and lactic acid production, thereby reducing the deposition of urate crystals that perpetuates the inflammatory response

Pharmacodynamics/Kinetics

Onset of action: Oral: Pain relief: ~12 hours if adequately dosed

Distribution: Concentrates in leukocytes, kidney, spleen, and liver; does not distribute in heart, skeletal muscle, and brain

Protein binding: 10% to 31%

Metabolism: Partially hepatic via deacetylation

Half-life elimination: 12-30 minutes; End-stage renal disease: 45 minutes

Time to peak, serum: Oral: 0.5-2 hours, declining for the next 2 hours before increasing again due to enterohepatic recycling

Excretion: Primarily feces; urine (10% to 20%)

Dosage

Familial Mediterranean fever (unlabeled use): Prophylaxis: Oral:

Children:

≤5 years: 0.5 mg/day

>5 years: 1-1.5 mg/day in 2-3 divided doses

Adults: 1-2 mg daily in divided doses (occasionally reduced to 0.6 mg/day in patients with GI intolerance)

Gouty arthritis: Adults:

Prophylaxis of acute attacks: Oral: 0.6 mg twice daily; initial and/or subsequent dosage may be decreased (ie, 0.6 mg once daily) in patients at risk of toxicity or in those who are intolerant (including weakness, loose stools, or diarrhea); range: 0.6 mg every other day to 0.6 mg 3 times/day

Acute attacks:

Oral: Initial: 0.6-1.2 mg, followed by 0.6 every 1-2 hours; some clinicians recommend a maximum of 3 doses; more aggressive approaches have recommended a maximum dose of up to 6 mg. Wait at least 3 days before initiating another course of therapy

I.V.: Initial: 1-2 mg, then 0.5 mg every 6 hours until response, not to exceed total dose of 4 mg. If pain recurs, it may be necessary to administer additional daily doses. The amount of colchicine administered intravenously in an acute treatment period (generally ~1 week) should not exceed a total dose of 4 mg. Do not administer more colchicine by any route for at least 7 days after a full course of I.V. therapy.

Note: Many experts would avoid use because of potential for serious, life-threatening complications. Should not be administered to patients with renal insufficiency, hepatobiliary obstruction, patients >70 years of age, or recent oral colchicine use. Should be reserved for hospitalized patients who are under the care of a physician experienced in the use of intravenous colchicine.

Surgery: Gouty arthritis, prophylaxis of recurrent attacks: Adults: Oral: 0.6 mg/day or every other day; patients who are to undergo surgical procedures may receive 0.6 mg 3 times/day for 3 days before and 3 days after surgery

Primary biliary cirrhosis (unlabeled use): Adults: Oral: 0.6 mg twice daily

Pericarditis (unlabeled use): Adults: Oral: 0.6 mg twice daily

Elderly: Reduce maintenance/prophylactic dose by 50% in individuals >70 years

Dosing adjustment in renal impairment: Gouty arthritis, acute attacks: Oral: Specific dosing recommendations not available from the manufacturer:

Prophylaxis:

Cl_{cr} 35-49 mL/minute: 0.6 mg once daily

Cl_{cr} 10-34 mL/minute: 0.6 mg every 2-3 days

Cl_{cr} <10 mL/minute: Avoid chronic use of colchicine. Use in serious renal impairment is contraindicated by the manufacturer.

Treatment: Cl_{cr} <10 mL/minute: Use in serious renal impairment is contraindicated by the manufacturer. If a decision is made to use colchicine, decrease dose by 75%.

Peritoneal dialysis: Supplemental dose is not necessary

Dosage adjustment in hepatic impairment: Avoid in hepatobiliary dysfunction and in patients with hepatic disease.

Dietary Considerations May need to supplement with vitamin B_{12}.

Administration

I.V.: Injection should be made over 2-5 minutes into tubing of free-flowing I.V. with compatible fluid. Do not administer I.M. or SubQ; severe local irritation can occur following SubQ or I.M. administration. Extravasation can cause tissue irritation.

Tablet: Administer orally with water and maintain adequate fluid intake.

Monitoring Parameters CBC and renal function test

Test Interactions May cause false-positive results in urine tests for erythrocytes or hemoglobin

Dosage Forms

Injection, solution: 0.5 mg/mL (2 mL)

Tablet: 0.6 mg

Colchicine and Probenecid (KOL chi seen & proe BEN e sid)

Index Terms ColBenemid; Probenecid and Colchicine
Pharmacologic Category Anti-inflammatory Agent; Antigout Agent; Uricosuric Agent
Use Treatment of chronic gouty arthritis when complicated by frequent, recurrent acute attacks of gout
Pregnancy Risk Factor C
Dosage Adults: Oral: 1 tablet daily for 1 week, then 1 tablet twice daily thereafter
Additional Information Complete prescribing information for this medication should be consulted for additional detail.
Dosage Forms Tablet: Colchicine 0.5 mg and probenecid 0.5 g

◆ **Coldcough PD** see Dihydrocodeine, Chlorpheniramine, and Phenylephrine on page 506

◆ **Coldmist DM** see Guaifenesin, Pseudoephedrine, and Dextromethorphan on page 821

◆ **Coldtuss DR [DSC]** see Chlorpheniramine, Phenylephrine, and Dextromethorphan on page 352

Colesevelam (koh le SEV a lam)

U.S. Brand Names WelChol®
Canadian Brand Names WelChol®
Pharmacologic Category Antilipemic Agent, Bile Acid Sequestrant
Additional Appendix Information
Hyperlipidemia Management on page 2058
Lipid-Lowering Agents on page 1887
Use Adjunctive therapy to diet and exercise in the management of elevated LDL in primary hypercholesterolemia (Fredrickson type IIa) when used alone or in combination with an HMG-CoA reductase inhibitor
Pregnancy Risk Factor B
Pregnancy Implications There are no adequate and well-controlled studies in pregnant women; use only in pregnancy if clearly needed.
Lactation Excretion in breast milk unknown
Contraindications Hypersensitivity to colesevelam or any component of the formulation; bowel obstruction
Warnings/Precautions Use caution in treating patients with serum triglyceride levels >300 mg/dL (may cause increased levels). Use caution in dysphagia, swallowing disorders, severe GI motility disorders, major GI tract surgery, and in patients susceptible to fat-soluble vitamin deficiencies. Minimal effects are seen on HDL-C and triglyceride levels. Secondary causes of hypercholesterolemia should be excluded before initiation. Safety and efficacy have not been established in pediatric patients.
Adverse Reactions
>10%: Gastrointestinal: Constipation (11%)
2% to 10%:
Gastrointestinal: Dyspepsia (8%)
Neuromuscular & skeletal: Weakness (4%), myalgia (2%)
Respiratory: Pharyngitis (3%)
Overdosage/Toxicology Systemic toxicity is low since the drug is not absorbed.
Drug Interactions
Decreased Effect: The absorption of thyroid supplements may be reduced by colesevelam (may be noted by elevation in TSH). Separate administration times by least 1 hour before or 4 hours after dose and monitor TSH levels during concurrent therapy. The absorption of corticosteroids, diuretics, ezetimibe, fibric acid derivatives, methotrexate, niacin, NSAIDs, raloxifene, tetracyclines, and thiazolidinediones may be reduced by concurrent colesevelam. Separate administration times by at least 1 hour before or 4 hours after dose. The absorption of amiodarone may also be reduced by concurrent colesevelam and close monitoring is recommended.

A number of medications, including digoxin, HMG-CoA reductase inhibitors (atorvastatin, lovastatin, simvastatin), metoprolol, quinidine, valproic acid, verapamil, or warfarin absorption have been specifically evaluated and were not found to be significantly affected with concurrent administration.
Stability Store at room temperature. Protect from moisture.
Mechanism of Action Colesevelam binds bile acids including glycocholic acid in the intestine, impeding their reabsorption. Increases the fecal loss of bile salt-bound LDL-C
Pharmacodynamics/Kinetics
Onset of action: Peak effect: Therapeutic: ~2 weeks
Absorption: Insignificant
Excretion: Urine (0.05%) after 1 month of chronic dosing
Dosage Adult: Oral:
Monotherapy: 3 tablets twice daily with meals or 6 tablets once daily with a meal; maximum dose: 7 tablets/day
Combination therapy with an HMG-CoA reductase inhibitor: 4-6 tablets daily; maximum dose: 6 tablets/day
Dosage adjustment in renal impairment: No recommendations made
Dosage adjustment in hepatic impairment: No recommendations made
Elderly: No recommendations made
Dietary Considerations Should be taken with meal(s) and a liquid. Follow dietary guidelines.
Administration Administer with meal(s) and a liquid. Make sure patient understands dietary guidelines.

Monitoring Parameters Serum cholesterol, LDL, and triglyceride levels should be obtained before initiating treatment and periodically thereafter (in accordance with NCEP guidelines)

Dosage Forms
Tablet, as hydrochloride:
WelChol®: 625 mg

♦ **Colestid®** *see* Colestipol *on page 415*

Colestipol (koe LES ti pole)

U.S. Brand Names Colestid®
Canadian Brand Names Colestid®
Index Terms Colestipol Hydrochloride
Pharmacologic Category Antilipemic Agent, Bile Acid Sequestrant
Additional Appendix Information
Hyperlipidemia Management *on page 2058*
Lipid-Lowering Agents *on page 1887*
Use Adjunct in management of primary hypercholesterolemia; regression of arteriolosclerosis; relief of pruritus associated with elevated levels of bile acids; possibly used to decrease plasma half-life of digoxin in toxicity
Pregnancy Risk Factor C
Lactation Not recommended
Contraindications Hypersensitivity to bile acid sequestering resins or any component of the formulation; bowel obstruction
Warnings/Precautions Not to be taken simultaneously with many other medicines (decreased absorption) Avoid in patients with high triglycerides, GI dysfunction (constipation); fecal impaction may occur; hemorrhoids may be worsened. May be associated with increased bleeding tendency as a result of hypothrombinemia secondary to vitamin K deficiency; may cause depletion of vitamins A, D, and E, and folic acid.
Adverse Reactions
>10%: Gastrointestinal: Constipation
1% to 10%:
Central nervous system: Headache, dizziness, anxiety, vertigo, drowsiness, fatigue
Gastrointestinal: Abdominal pain and distention, belching, flatulence, nausea, vomiting, diarrhea
<1% (Limited to important or life-threatening): Cholecystitis, cholelithiasis, dyspnea breath, gallstones, GI bleeding, malabsorption syndrome, peptic ulceration
Overdosage/Toxicology Symptoms include GI obstruction, nausea, and GI distress. Treatment is supportive.
Drug Interactions
Decreased Effect: Colestipol can reduce the absorption of numerous medications when used concurrently. Give other medications 1 hour before or 4 hours after giving colestipol. Medications which may be affected include HMG-CoA reductase inhibitors, thiazide diuretics, propranolol (and potentially other beta-blockers), corticosteroids, thyroid hormones, digoxin, valproic acid, NSAIDs, loop diuretics, sulfonylureas, troglitazone (and potentially other agents in this class - pioglitazone and rosiglitazone).

Warfarin and other oral anticoagulants: Absorption is reduced by cholestyramine and may also be reduced by colestipol. Separate administration times (as detailed above).
Mechanism of Action Binds with bile acids to form an insoluble complex that is eliminated in feces; it thereby increases the fecal loss of bile acid-bound low density lipoprotein cholesterol
Pharmacodynamics/Kinetics
Absorption: None
Excretion: Feces
Dosage Adults: Oral:
Granules: 5-30 g/day given once or in divided doses 2-4 times/day; initial dose: 5 g 1-2 times/day; increase by 5 g at 1- to 2-month intervals
Tablets: 2-16 g/day; initial dose: 2 g 1-2 times/day; increase by 2 g at 1- to 2-month intervals
Dietary Considerations Granules, orange flavor, contain phenylalanine 18.2 mg/7.5 g.
Administration Dry powder should be added to at least 90 mL of liquid and stirred until completely mixed; other drugs should be administered at least 1 hour before or 4 hours after colestipol
Test Interactions Increased prothrombin time; decreased cholesterol (S)
Dosage Forms
Granules, as hydrochloride:
5 g/7.5 g packet (30s, 90s) [unflavored]
5 g/7.5 g (300 g, 500 g) [unflavored]
5 g/7.5 g packet (60s) [contains phenylalanine 18.2 mg/7.5 g; orange flavor]
5 g/7.5 g (450 g) [contains phenylalanine 18.2 mg/7.5 g; orange flavor]
Tablet, as hydrochloride: 1 g

♦ **Colestipol Hydrochloride** *see* Colestipol *on page 415*
♦ **CO Levetiracetam (Can)** *see* Levetiracetam *on page 995*

Colistimethate (koe lis ti METH ate)

U.S. Brand Names Coly-Mycin® M
Canadian Brand Names Coly-Mycin® M
Index Terms Colistimethate Sodium
Pharmacologic Category Antibiotic, Miscellaneous
Use Treatment of infections due to sensitive strains of certain gram-negative bacilli which are resistant to other antibacterials or in patients allergic to other antibacterials
Unlabeled/Investigational Use Used as inhalation in the prevention of *Pseudomonas aeruginosa* respiratory tract infections in immunocompromised patients, and used as inhalation
(Continued)

Colistimethate *(Continued)*

adjunct agent for the treatment of *P. aeruginosa* infections in patients with cystic fibrosis and other seriously ill or chronically ill patients

Pregnancy Risk Factor C

Contraindications Hypersensitivity to colistimethate or any component of the formulation

Warnings/Precautions Use with caution in patients with pre-existing renal disease

Adverse Reactions 1% to 10%:
Central nervous system: Vertigo, slurring of speech
Dermatologic: Urticaria
Gastrointestinal: GI upset
Respiratory: Respiratory arrest
Renal: Nephrotoxicity

Drug Interactions
Increased Effect/Toxicity: Other nephrotoxic drugs, neuromuscular blocking agents.

Stability Freshly prepare any infusion and use for no longer than 24 hours.

Mechanism of Action Hydrolyzed to colistin, which acts as a cationic detergent which damages the bacterial cytoplasmic membrane causing leaking of intracellular substances and cell death

Pharmacodynamics/Kinetics
Distribution: Widely, except for CNS, synovial, pleural, and pericardial fluids
Half-life elimination: 1.5-8 hours; Anuria: ≤2-3 days
Time to peak: ~2 hours
Excretion: Primarily urine (as unchanged drug)

Dosage Children and Adults:
I.M., I.V.: 2.5-5 mg/kg/day in 2-4 divided doses
Inhalation: 50-75 mg in NS (3-4 mL total) via nebulizer 2-3 times/day
Dosing interval in renal impairment: Adults:
S_{cr} 0.7-1.2 mg/dL: 100-125 mg 2-4 times/day
S_{cr} 1.3-1.5 mg/dL: 75-115 mg twice daily
S_{cr} 1.6-2.5 mg/dL: 66-150 mg once or twice daily
S_{cr} 2.6-4 mg/dL: 100-150 mg every 36 hours

Administration
Parenteral: Reconstitute vial with 2 mL SWFI resulting in a concentration of 75 mg colistin/mL; swirl gently to avoid frothing. Administer by I.M., direct I.V. injection over 3-10 minutes, intermittent infusion over 30 minutes, or by continuous I.V. infusion. For continuous I.V. infusion, one-half of the total daily dose is administered by direct I.V. injection over 3-10 minutes followed 1-2 hours later by the remaining one-half of the total daily dose diluted in a compatible I.V. solution infused over 22-23 hours. The final concentration for administration should be based on the patient's fluid needs.
Inhalation: Further dilute dose to a total volume of 3-4 mL in NS and administer via nebulizer. If patient is on a ventilator, place medicine in a T-piece at the midinspiratory circuit of the ventilator.

Dosage Forms Injection, powder for reconstitution: 150 mg

♦ **Colistimethate Sodium** *see* Colistimethate *on page 415*
♦ **Colistin, Neomycin, Hydrocortisone, and Thonzonium** *see* Neomycin, Colistin, Hydrocortisone, and Thonzonium *on page 1211*
♦ **Collagen** *see* Collagen Hemostat *on page 416*
♦ **Collagen Absorbable Hemostat** *see* Collagen Hemostat *on page 416*

Collagenase *(KOL la je nase)*

U.S. Brand Names Santyl®
Pharmacologic Category Enzyme, Topical Debridement
Use Promotes debridement of necrotic tissue in dermal ulcers and severe burns
Orphan drug: Injection: Treatment of Peyronie's disease; treatment of Dupytren's disease
Pregnancy Risk Factor C
Dosage Topical: Apply once daily (or more frequently if the dressing becomes soiled)
Additional Information Complete prescribing information for this medication should be consulted for additional detail.
Dosage Forms Ointment: 250 units/g (15 g, 30 g)

Collagen Hemostat *(KOL la jen HEE moe stat)*

U.S. Brand Names Avitene®; Avitene® Flour; Avitene® Ultrafoam; Avitene® UltraWrap™; EndoAvitene®; Helistat®; Helitene®; Instat™; Instat™ MCH; SyringeAvitene™
Index Terms Collagen; Collagen Absorbable Hemostat; MCH; Microfibrillar Collagen Hemostat
Pharmacologic Category Hemostatic Agent
Use Adjunct to hemostasis when control of bleeding by ligature is ineffective or impractical
Medication Safety Issues
Sound-alike/look-alike issues:
Avitene® may be confused with Ativan®
Over 100 reports of paralysis or other neural deficits have been received by the FDA, attributable to collagen hemostat-associated neuronal impingement
Dosage Apply dry directly to source of bleeding; remove excess material after ~10-15 minutes
Additional Information Complete prescribing information for this medication should be consulted for additional detail.
Dosage Forms
Pad (Instat™) [bovine derived]: 1 inch x 2 inch (24s); 3 inch x 4 inch (24s)
Powder:
Avitene® Flour [microfibrillar product, bovine derived]: 0.5 g, 1 g, 5 g

Helitene® [bovine derived]: 0.5 g, 1 g
Instat™ MCH [microfibrillar product, bovine derived]: 0.5 g, 1 g
SyringeAvitene™ [microfibrillar product, bovine derived, prefilled syringe]: 1 g
Sheet:
  Avitene® [microfibrillar product, bovine derived, nonwoven web]: 35 mm x 35 mm (1s); 70
    mm x 35 mm (6s, 12s); 70 mm x 70 mm (6s, 12s)
  EndoAvitene® [microfibrillar product, bovine derived, preloaded applicator]: 5 mm diameter
    (6s); 10 mm diameter (6s)
Sponge:
  Avitene® Ultrafoam [microfibrillar product, bovine derived]: 2 cm x 6.25 cm x 7 mm (12s); 8
    cm x 6.25 cm x 1 cm (6s); 8 cm x 12.5 cm x 1 cm (6s); 8 cm x 12.5 cm x 3 mm (6s)
  Avitene® UltraWrap™ [microfibrillar product, bovine derived]: 8 cm x 12.5 cm (6s)
  Helistat® [bovine derived]: 0.5 inch x 1 inch x 7 mm (18s) [packaged as 3 strips of 6
    sponges]; 3 inch x 4 inch x 5 inch (10s)

♦ **Colocort®** see Hydrocortisone on page 852
♦ **CO Lovastatin (Can)** see Lovastatin on page 1040
♦ **Coly-Mycin® M** see Colistimethate on page 415
♦ **Coly-Mycin® S** see Neomycin, Colistin, Hydrocortisone, and Thonzonium on page 1211
♦ **Colyte®** see Polyethylene Glycol-Electrolyte Solution on page 1387
♦ **Colyte™ (Can)** see Polyethylene Glycol-Electrolyte Solution on page 1387
♦ **Combantrin™ (Can)** see Pyrantel Pamoate on page 1459
♦ **CombiPatch®** see Estradiol and Norethindrone on page 624
♦ **Combipres® [DSC]** see Clonidine and Chlorthalidone on page 401
♦ **Combivent®** see Ipratropium and Albuterol on page 934
♦ **Combivir®** see Zidovudine and Lamivudine on page 1815
♦ **Combunox™** see Oxycodone and Ibuprofen on page 1290
♦ **CO Meloxicam (Can)** see Meloxicam on page 1072
♦ **Comhist®** see Chlorpheniramine, Phenylephrine, and Phenyltoloxamine on page 354
♦ **CO Mirtazapine (Can)** see Mirtazapine on page 1152
♦ **Commit® [OTC]** see Nicotine on page 1223
♦ **Compazine** see Prochlorperazine on page 1429
♦ **Compazine® (Can)** see Prochlorperazine on page 1429
♦ **Compound E** see Cortisone on page 420
♦ **Compound F** see Hydrocortisone on page 852
♦ **Compound S** see Zidovudine on page 1812
♦ **Compound S, Abacavir, and Lamivudine** see Abacavir, Lamivudine, and Zidovudine on page 19
♦ **Compoz® Nighttime Sleep Aid [OTC]** see DiphenhydrAMINE on page 515
♦ **Compro™** see Prochlorperazine on page 1429
♦ **Comtan®** see Entacapone on page 585
♦ **Comtrex® Flu Therapy Day/Night [OTC]** see Acetaminophen, Chlorpheniramine, and Pseudoephedrine on page 35
♦ **Comtrex® Flu Therapy Nighttime [OTC]** see Acetaminophen, Chlorpheniramine, and Pseudoephedrine on page 35
♦ **Comtrex® Non-Drowsy Cold and Cough Relief [OTC] [DSC]** see Acetaminophen, Dextromethorphan, and Pseudoephedrine on page 35
♦ **Comtrex® Sore Throat Maximum Strength [OTC]** see Acetaminophen on page 28
♦ **Comvax®** see Haemophilus b Conjugate and Hepatitis B Vaccine on page 823
♦ **Conceptrol® [OTC]** see Nonoxynol 9 on page 1239
♦ **Concerta®** see Methylphenidate on page 1119
♦ **Congestac® [OTC]** see Guaifenesin and Pseudoephedrine on page 819

Conivaptan (koe NYE vap tan)

U.S. Brand Names Vaprisol®
Index Terms Conivaptan Hydrochloride; YM087
Pharmacologic Category Vasopressin Antagonist
Use Treatment of euvolemic hyponatremia in hospitalized patients
Pregnancy Risk Factor C
Pregnancy Implications Animal studies indicate that conivaptan accumulates in the placenta (2.2-fold relative to maternal plasma); systemic exposure to fetus is likely. No teratogenic effects have been observed in animal studies; however, these studies have shown decreased neonatal viability and delayed growth and development at doses lower than those required for therapeutic efficacy. There are no adequate and well-controlled studies in pregnant women. Use only if benefit outweighs risk.
Lactation Excretion in breast milk unknown/use caution
Contraindications Hypersensitivity to conivaptan or any component of the formulation; use in hypovolemic hyponatremia; concurrent use with strong CYP3A4 inhibitors (eg, ketoconazole, itraconazole, ritonavir, indinavir, and clarithromycin)
Warnings/Precautions Monitor closely for rate of serum sodium increase and neurological status; overly rapid serum sodium correction (>12 mEq/L/24 hours) can lead to permanent neurological damage. Discontinue use if rate of serum sodium increase is undesirable; may reinitiate infusion (at reduced dose) if hyponatremia persists in the absence of neurological symptoms typically associated with rapid sodium rise. Use with caution in patients with hepatic and renal impairment. Safety and efficacy in pediatric patients, or patients with underlying heart failure, have not been established.
Adverse Reactions
>10%:
Central nervous system: Headache (12%)
(Continued)

Conivaptan (Continued)

Local: Injection site reactions including pain, erythema, phlebitis, swelling (53%)

1% to 10%:

Cardiovascular: Hypertension (6%), phlebitis (5%), atrial fibrillation (3%), hypotension (3%; orthostatic 6%)

Central nervous system: Fever (4%), confusion (4%), insomnia (3%), pain (2%)

Dermatologic: Erythema (3%)

Endocrine & metabolic: Hypokalemia (10%), hyper-/hypoglycemia (3%), hypomagnesemia (2%), hyponatremia (3%)

Gastrointestinal: Vomiting (7%), diarrhea (6%), constipation (5%), dry mouth (4%), nausea (4%), dehydration (2%), oral candidiasis (2%)

Genitourinary: Urinary tract infection (3%)

Hematologic: Anemia (4%)

Renal: Polyuria (5% to 6%), hematuria (2%)

Respiratory: Pneumonia (3%)

Miscellaneous: Thirst (10%)

Overdosage/Toxicology No specific overdose information available. Doses of up to 120 mg/day for 2 days have been evaluated, with no additional toxicity other than an expected increased incidence of hypotension and thirst. Treatment should be symptom-directed and supportive.

Drug Interactions

Cytochrome P450 Effect: Substrate of CYP3A4 (major); **Inhibits** CYP3A4 (strong)

Increased Effect/Toxicity: Conivaptan may increase the levels/effects of CYP3A4 substrates (eg, benzodiazepines, calcium channel blockers, clarithromycin, cyclosporine, erythromycin, estrogens, mirtazapine, nateglinide, nefazodone, nevirapine, protease inhibitors, tacrolimus, and venlafaxine) and digoxin. CYP3A4 inhibitors may increase the levels/effects of conivaptan; example inhibitors include ketoconazole, itraconazole, ritonavir, indinavir, and clarithromycin. Concurrent use of conivaptan and strong CYP3A4 inhibitors is contraindicated.

Decreased Effect: CYP3A4 inducers may decrease the levels/effects of conivaptan; example inducers include aminoglutethimide, carbamazepine, nafcillin, nevirapine, phenobarbital, phenytoin, and rifamycins.

Stability Store ampuls in original cardboard container at 15°C to 30°C (59°F to 86°F); protect from light. Dilute loading dose of 20 mg in 100 mL D_5W and continuous infusion dose of 20-40 mg in 250 mL D_5W. After dilution, infusion bag (final concentration of 0.08-0.2 mg/mL) is stable at room temperature for 24 hours.

Mechanism of Action Conivaptan is an arginine vasopressin (AVP) receptor antagonist with affinity for AVP receptor subtypes V_{1A} and V_2. The antidiuretic action of AVP is mediated through activation of the V_2 receptor, which functions to regulate water and electrolyte balance at the level of the collecting ducts in the kidney. Serum levels of AVP are commonly elevated in euvolemic or hypervolemic hyponatremia, which results in the dilution of serum sodium and the relative hyponatremic state. Antagonism of the V_2 receptor by conivaptan promotes the excretion of free water (without loss of serum electrolytes) resulting in net fluid loss, increased urine output, decreased urine osmolality, and subsequent restoration of normal serum sodium levels.

Pharmacodynamics/Kinetics

Protein binding: 99%

Metabolism: Hepatic via CYP3A4 to four minimally-active metabolites

Half-life elimination: 6.7-8.6 hours

Excretion: Feces (83%); urine (12%)

Dosage I.V.: Adults:

Loading dose: 20 mg infused over 30 minutes, followed by continuous infusion of 20 mg over 24 hours

Maintenance: 20 mg/day as continuous infusion over 24 hours; may titrate to maximum of 40 mg/day if serum sodium not rising sufficiently; total duration of therapy not to exceed 4 days

Administration For intravenous use only; do not administer undiluted; infuse into large veins and change infusion site every 24 hours to minimize vascular irritation

Monitoring Parameters Rate of serum sodium increase, urine output

Dosage Forms

Injection, solution:

Vaprisol®: 5 mg/mL (4 mL) [single-use ampul; contains propylene glycol and ethanol]

♦ **Conivaptan Hydrochloride** see Conivaptan on page 417

♦ **Conjugated Estrogen and Methyltestosterone** see Estrogens (Esterified) and Methyltestosterone on page 637

♦ **CO Norfloxacin (Can)** see Norfloxacin on page 1241

♦ **Constulose** see Lactulose on page 971

♦ **Contac® Cold [OTC] [DSC]** see Pseudoephedrine on page 1454

♦ **Contac® Cold 12 Hour Relief Non Drowsy (Can)** see Pseudoephedrine on page 1454

♦ **Contac® Cold and Sore Throat, Non Drowsy, Extra Strength (Can)** see Acetaminophen and Pseudoephedrine on page 33

♦ **Contac® Cold-Chest Congestion, Non Drowsy, Regular Strength (Can)** see Guaifenesin and Pseudoephedrine on page 819

♦ **Contac® Complete (Can)** see Acetaminophen, Dextromethorphan, and Pseudoephedrine on page 35

♦ **Contac® Cough, Cold and Flu Day & Night™ (Can)** see Acetaminophen, Dextromethorphan, and Pseudoephedrine on page 35

♦ **ControlRx™** see Fluoride on page 722

♦ **CO Paroxetine (Can)** see Paroxetine on page 1314

♦ **Copaxone®** see Glatiramer Acetate on page 796

♦ **Copegus®** see Ribavirin on page 1503

- **Copolymer-1** *see* Glatiramer Acetate *on page 796*
- **CO Pravastatin (Can)** *see* Pravastatin *on page 1409*
- **CO Ranitidine (Can)** *see* Ranitidine *on page 1485*
- **Cordarone®** *see* Amiodarone *on page 97*
- **Cordran®** *see* Flurandrenolide *on page 733*
- **Cordran® SP** *see* Flurandrenolide *on page 733*
- **Cordron-D NR [DSC]** *see* Carbinoxamine and Pseudoephedrine *on page 290*
- **Cordron-DM NR [DSC]** *see* Carbinoxamine, Pseudoephedrine, and Dextromethorphan *on page 291*
- **Coreg®** *see* Carvedilol *on page 299*
- **Coreg CR™** *see* Carvedilol *on page 299*
- **Corfen DM** *see* Chlorpheniramine, Phenylephrine, and Dextromethorphan *on page 352*
- **Corgard®** *see* Nadolol *on page 1187*
- **Coricidin HBP® Chest Congestion and Cough [OTC]** *see* Guaifenesin and Dextromethorphan *on page 816*
- **Coricidin HBP® Cold and Flu [OTC]** *see* Chlorpheniramine and Acetaminophen *on page 349*
- **Corlopam®** *see* Fenoldopam *on page 691*
- **Cormax®** *see* Clobetasol *on page 391*
- **Coronex® (Can)** *see* Isosorbide Dinitrate *on page 945*
- **Correctol® Tablets [OTC]** *see* Bisacodyl *on page 223*
- **Cortaid® Intensive Therapy [OTC]** *see* Hydrocortisone *on page 852*
- **Cortaid® Maximum Strength [OTC]** *see* Hydrocortisone *on page 852*
- **Cortaid® Sensitive Skin [OTC]** *see* Hydrocortisone *on page 852*
- **Cortamed® (Can)** *see* Hydrocortisone *on page 852*
- **Cortef®** *see* Hydrocortisone *on page 852*
- **Cortenema® (Can)** *see* Hydrocortisone *on page 852*
- **Corticool® [OTC]** *see* Hydrocortisone *on page 852*

Corticorelin (kor ti koe REL in)

U.S. Brand Names Acthrel®
Index Terms Corticorelin Ovine Triflutate; Human Corticotrophin-Releasing Hormone, Analogue; Ovine Corticotrophin-Releasing Hormone
Pharmacologic Category Diagnostic Agent, ACTH-Dependent Hypercortisolism
Use Diagnostic test used in adrenocorticotropic hormone (ACTH)-dependent Cushing's syndrome to differentiate between pituitary and ectopic production of ACTH
Pregnancy Risk Factor C
Pregnancy Implications Reproduction studies have not been conducted.
Lactation Excretion in breast milk unknown/use caution
Medication Safety Issues
Sound-alike/look-alike issues:
Acthrel® may be confused with Acthar®
Corticorelin may be confused with corticotropin
Contraindications Hypersensitivity to corticorelin or any component of the formulation
Warnings/Precautions Use with caution in pediatric patients; safety and efficacy has not been established (limited data). Use caution in patients with previous reactions to sheep products (lanolin). Doses administered as a bolus or in excess of recommendations have been associated with hypotension, transient tachycardia, dyspnea, chest tightness, loss of consciousness. and asystole. Infusion over 30 seconds may reduce the potential for these effects. Use of heparin to maintain I.V. patency is not recommended; may increase risk of hypotension. False negative responses may occur in 5% to 10% of patients.
Adverse Reactions
>10%: Cardiovascular: Flushing (face, neck and upper chest, 16%)
1% to 10%:
Gastrointestinal: Metallic taste (transient, 5%)
Respiratory: Dyspnea (urge to inspire, 6%)
<1% (Limited to important or life-threatening): Hypotension (severe), seizure
Overdosage/Toxicology Symptoms include tachycardia, dyspnea, chest tightness, flushing (prolonged), hypotension, and asystole. Treatment is symptom-directed and supportive.
Drug Interactions
Increased Effect/Toxicity: Corticorelin administration with heparin has been implicated in a case of severe hypotension (mechanism and confidence level unknown).
Decreased Effect: Corticorelin response may be decreased via a decreased plasma ACTH level. Other corticosteroids would theoretically exhibit this same blunting effect, secondary to suppression of the hypothalamic-pituitary-adrenal axis mechanism in normal patients.
Stability
Store powder for injection under refrigeration at 2°C to 8°C (36°F to 46°F); protect from light. For I.V. infusion, reconstitute with 2 mL NS resulting in a 50 mcg/mL solution. **Do not shake vial; roll to dissolve.** Reconstituted solution is stable for 8 hours under refrigeration; discard unused solution.
Mechanism of Action Stimulates adrenocorticotropic hormone (ACTH) release from anterior pituitary. ACTH stimulates the adrenal cortex to produce cortisol.
Pharmacodynamics/Kinetics
Onset: I.V.: Plasma ACTH level increases 2 minutes after injection; plasma cortisol level increases within 10 minutes after injection
Duration: I.V.: Plasma ACTH and cortisol levels remain elevated for up to 2 hours
Time to peak, plasma: ACTH: 15-60 minutes; cortisol: 30-120 minutes; both levels show a dose-dependent, biphasic response with a second lower peak 2-3 hours after injection
(Continued)

Corticorelin *(Continued)*

Dosage I.V.: Adults: Testing pituitary corticotrophin function: 1 mcg/kg; dosages >100 mcg have been associated with an increase in adverse effects

Note: Venous blood samples should be drawn 15 minutes before and immediately prior to corticorelin administration to determine baseline ACTH and cortisol. At 15-, 30-, and 60 minutes after administration, venous blood samples should be drawn again to determine response. **Basal and peak responses differ depending on AM or PM administration; therefore, any repeat evaluations are recommended to be done at the same time of day as initial testing.**

Administration Administer I.V. over 30-60 seconds. Use of heparin to maintain patency is not recommended.

Reference Range

High basal plasma ACTH and cortisol (20-40 mcg/dL) resulting in **increased** plasma ACTH and cortisol after administration of test indicates **ACTH-dependent disease of pituitary origin.**

High basal plasma ACTH (may be very high) and cortisol (20-40 mcg/dL) resulting in **little to no change** in plasma ACTH and cortisol after administration of test indicates **ACTH-dependent syndrome of ectopic origin.**

Dosage Forms

Injection, powder for reconstitution, as trifluoroacetate:

Acthrel®: 100 mcg [ovine derived; contains lactose 10 mg]

♦ **Corticorelin Ovine Triflutate** *see Corticorelin on page 419*

♦ **Cortifoam®** *see Hydrocortisone on page 852*

♦ **Cortifoam™ (Can)** *see Hydrocortisone on page 852*

♦ **Cortimyxin® (Can)** *see Neomycin, Polymyxin B, and Hydrocortisone on page 1212*

♦ **Cortisol** *see Hydrocortisone on page 852*

Cortisone *(KOR ti sone)*

Index Terms Compound E; Cortisone Acetate

Pharmacologic Category Corticosteroid, Systemic

Additional Appendix Information

Corticosteroids *on page 1879*

Use Management of adrenocortical insufficiency

Pregnancy Risk Factor D

Lactation Enters breast milk/use caution

Medication Safety Issues

Sound-alike/look-alike issues:

Cortisone may be confused with Cortizone®

Contraindications Hypersensitivity to cortisone acetate or any component of the formulation; serious infections, except septic shock or tuberculous meningitis; administration of live virus vaccines; pregnancy

Warnings/Precautions Use with caution in patients with thyroid disease, hepatic impairment, renal impairment, cardiovascular disease, diabetes, glaucoma, cataracts, myasthenia gravis, patients at risk for osteoporosis, patients at risk for seizures, or GI diseases (diverticulitis, peptic ulcer, ulcerative colitis) due to perforation risk. Use caution following acute MI (corticosteroids have been associated with myocardial rupture). Because of the risk of adverse effects, systemic corticosteroids should be used cautiously in the elderly in the smallest possible effective dose for the shortest duration. May affect growth velocity; growth should be routinely monitored in pediatric patients. Withdraw therapy with gradual tapering of dose.

May cause hypercorticism or suppression of hypothalamic-pituitary-adrenal (HPA) axis, particularly in younger children or in patients receiving high doses for prolonged periods. HPA axis suppression may lead to adrenal crisis. Withdrawal and discontinuation of a corticosteroid should be done slowly and carefully. Particular care is required when patients are transferred from systemic corticosteroids to inhaled products due to possible adrenal insufficiency or withdrawal from steroids, including an increase in allergic symptoms. Patients receiving >20 mg per day of prednisone (or equivalent) may be most susceptible. Fatalities have occurred due to adrenal insufficiency in asthmatic patients during and after transfer from systemic corticosteroids to aerosol steroids; aerosol steroids do not provide the systemic steroid needed to treat patients having trauma, surgery, or infections.

Acute myopathy has been reported with high dose corticosteroids, usually in patients with neuromuscular transmission disorders; may involve ocular and/or respiratory muscles; monitor creatine kinase; recovery may be delayed. Corticosteroid use may cause psychiatric disturbances, including depression, euphoria, insomnia, mood swings, and personality changes. Pre-existing psychiatric conditions may be exacerbated by corticosteroid use. Prolonged use of corticosteroids may also increase the incidence of secondary infection, mask acute infection (including fungal infections), prolong or exacerbate viral infections, or limit response to vaccines. Exposure to chickenpox should be avoided; corticosteroids should not be used to treat ocular herpes simplex. Corticosteroids should not be used for cerebral malaria. Close observation is required in patients with latent tuberculosis and/or TB reactivity; restrict use in active TB (only in conjunction with antituberculosis treatment). Prolonged treatment with corticosteroids has been associated with the development of Kaposi's sarcoma (case reports); if noted, discontinuation of therapy should be considered.

Adverse Reactions

>10%:

Central nervous system: Insomnia, nervousness

Gastrointestinal: Increased appetite, indigestion

1% to 10%:

Dermatologic: Hirsutism

Endocrine & metabolic: Diabetes mellitus

Neuromuscular & skeletal: Arthralgia

Ocular: Cataracts, glaucoma

Respiratory: Epistaxis

<1% (Limited to important or life-threatening): Alkalosis, Cushing's syndrome, delirium, edema, euphoria, fractures, hallucinations, hypersensitivity reactions, hypertension, hypokalemia, muscle wasting, myalgia, osteoporosis, pancreatitis, peptic ulcer, pituitary-adrenal axis suppression, pseudotumor cerebri, psychoses, seizure, skin atrophy, ulcerative esophagitis

Overdosage/Toxicology When consumed in excessive quantities for prolonged periods, systemic hypercorticism and adrenal suppression may occur; in those cases, discontinuation and withdrawal of the corticosteroid should be done judiciously. Cushingoid changes from continued administration of large doses results in moon face, central obesity, striae, hirsutism, acne, ecchymoses, hypertension, osteoporosis, myopathy, sexual dysfunction, diabetes, hyperlipidemia, peptic ulcer, increased susceptibility to infection, and electrolyte and fluid imbalance.

Drug Interactions

Increased Effect/Toxicity: Estrogens may increase cortisone effects. Cortisone may increase ulcerogenic potential of NSAIDs, and may increase potassium deletion due to diuretics.

Decreased Effect: Enzyme inducers (barbiturates, phenytoin, rifampin) may decrease cortisone effects. Effect of live virus vaccines may be decreased. Anticholinesterase agents may decrease effect of cortisone.

Cortisone may decrease effects of warfarin and salicylates.

Ethanol/Nutrition/Herb Interactions Food: Limit caffeine intake.

Mechanism of Action Decreases inflammation by suppression of migration of polymorphonuclear leukocytes and reversal of increased capillary permeability

Pharmacodynamics/Kinetics

Onset of action: Peak effect: Oral: ~2 hours; I.M.: 20-48 hours

Duration: 30-36 hours

Absorption: Slow

Distribution: Muscles, liver, skin, intestines, and kidneys; crosses placenta; enters breast milk

Metabolism: Hepatic to inactive metabolites

Half-life elimination: 0.5-2 hours; End-stage renal disease: 3.5 hours

Excretion: Urine and feces

Dosage If possible, administer glucocorticoids before 9 AM to minimize adrenocortical suppression; dosing depends upon the condition being treated and the response of the patient. **Note:** Supplemental doses may be warranted during times of stress in the course of withdrawing therapy.

Children:

Anti-inflammatory or immunosuppressive: Oral: 2.5-10 mg/kg/day **or** 20-300 mg/m^2/day in divided doses every 6-8 hours

Physiologic replacement: Oral: 0.5-0.75 mg/kg/day **or** 20-25 mg/m^2/day in divided doses every 8 hours

Adults:

Anti-inflammatory or immunosuppressive: Oral: 25-300 mg/day in divided doses every 12-24 hours

Physiologic replacement: Oral: 25-35 mg/day

Hemodialysis: Supplemental dose is not necessary

Peritoneal dialysis: Supplemental dose is not necessary

Dietary Considerations May need diet with increased potassium, pyridoxine, vitamin C, vitamin D, folate, calcium, and phosphorus and decreased sodium; may be taken with food to decrease GI distress.

Administration Insoluble in water.

Dosage Forms Tablet, as acetate: 25 mg

♦ **Cortisone Acetate** see Cortisone on page 420

♦ **Cortisporin® Cream** see Neomycin, Polymyxin B, and Hydrocortisone on page 1212

♦ **Cortisporin® Ointment** see Bacitracin, Neomycin, Polymyxin B, and Hydrocortisone on page 192

♦ **Cortisporin® Ophthalmic** see Neomycin, Polymyxin B, and Hydrocortisone on page 1212

♦ **Cortisporin® Otic** see Neomycin, Polymyxin B, and Hydrocortisone on page 1212

♦ **Cortisporin®-TC** see Neomycin, Colistin, Hydrocortisone, and Thonzonium on page 1211

♦ **Cortisporin® Topical Ointment (Can)** see Bacitracin, Neomycin, Polymyxin B, and Hydrocortisone on page 192

♦ **Cortizone®-10 Maximum Strength [OTC]** see Hydrocortisone on page 852

♦ **Cortizone®-10 Plus Maximum Strength [OTC]** see Hydrocortisone on page 852

♦ **Cortizone®-10 Quick Shot [OTC]** see Hydrocortisone on page 852

♦ **Cortrosyn®** see Cosyntropin on page 422

♦ **Corvert®** see Ibutilide on page 876

♦ **CO Simvastatin (Can)** see Simvastatin on page 1567

♦ **Cosmegen®** see Dactinomycin on page 444

♦ **Cosopt®** see Dorzolamide and Timolol on page 542

♦ **CO Sotalol (Can)** see Sotalol on page 1592

♦ **CO Sumatriptan (Can)** see Sumatriptan on page 1620

Cosyntropin (koe sin TROE pin)

U.S. Brand Names Cortrosyn®
Canadian Brand Names Cortrosyn®
Index Terms Synacthen; Tetracosactide
Pharmacologic Category Diagnostic Agent
Use Diagnostic test to differentiate primary adrenal from secondary (pituitary) adrenocortical insufficiency
Pregnancy Risk Factor C
Lactation Excretion in breast milk unknown/use caution
Medication Safety Issues
Sound-alike/look-alike issues:
Cortrosyn® may be confused with Cotazym®
Contraindications Hypersensitivity to cosyntropin or any component of the formulation
Warnings/Precautions Use with caution in patients with pre-existing allergic disease or a history of allergic reactions to corticotropin.
Adverse Reactions Frequency not defined.
Cardiovascular: Bradycardia, hypertension, peripheral edema, tachycardia
Dermatologic: Rash
Local: Whealing with redness at the injection site
Miscellaneous: Anaphylaxis, hypersensitivity reaction
Stability Powder for injection: Store at controlled room temperature of 15°C to 30°C (59°F to 86°F).

I.M.: Reconstitute cosyntropin 0.25 mg with NS 1 mL.
I.V. push: Reconstitute cosyntropin 0.25 mg with NS 2-5 mL.
I.V. infusion: Mix in NS or D_5W. Stable for 12 hours at room temperature; stable for 21 days under refrigeration.
Mechanism of Action Stimulates the adrenal cortex to secrete adrenal steroids (including hydrocortisone, cortisone), androgenic substances, and a small amount of aldosterone
Pharmacodynamics/Kinetics Time to peak, serum: I.M., IVP: ~1 hour; plasma cortisol levels rise in healthy individuals within 5 minutes
Dosage
Adrenocortical insufficiency: I.M., I.V. (over 2 minutes): Peak plasma cortisol concentrations usually occur 45-60 minutes after cosyntropin administration
Children <2 years: 0.125 mg
Children >2 years and Adults: 0.25-0.75 mg
When greater cortisol stimulation is needed, an I.V. infusion may be used:
Children >2 years and Adults: 0.25 mg administered at 0.04 mg/hour over 6 hours
Administration Administer I.V. doses over 2 minutes
Reference Range Normal baseline cortisol; increase in serum cortisol after cosyntropin injection of >7 mcg/dL or peak response >18 mcg/dL; plasma cortisol concentrations should be measured immediately before and exactly 30 minutes after a dose
Test Interactions Decreased effect: Spironolactone, hydrocortisone, cortisone, etomidate
Additional Information Each 0.25 mg of cosyntropin is equivalent to 25 units of corticotropin. Patient should not receive corticosteroids or spironolactone the day prior and the day of the test.
Dosage Forms Injection, powder for reconstitution: 0.25 mg

♦ **Cotazym® (Can)** see Pancrelipase on page 1302
♦ **CO Temazepam (Can)** see Temazepam on page 1640
♦ **CO Terbinafine (Can)** see Terbinafine on page 1648
♦ **Co-Trimoxazole** see Sulfamethoxazole and Trimethoprim on page 1613
♦ **Coughcold HCM** see Hydrocodone and Pseudoephedrine on page 851
♦ **Coumadin®** see Warfarin on page 1800
♦ **Covan® (Can)** see Triprolidine, Pseudoephedrine, and Codeine on page 1750
♦ **Covera® (Can)** see Verapamil on page 1784
♦ **Covera-HS®** see Verapamil on page 1784
♦ **Coversyl® (Can)** see Perindopril Erbumine on page 1346
♦ **Co-Vidarabine** see Pentostatin on page 1342
♦ **Coviracil** see Emtricitabine on page 576
♦ **Cozaar®** see Losartan on page 1037
♦ **CP358774** see Erlotinib on page 606
♦ **C-Phen** see Chlorpheniramine and Phenylephrine on page 349
♦ **C-Phen DM** see Chlorpheniramine, Phenylephrine, and Dextromethorphan on page 352
♦ **CPM** see Cyclophosphamide on page 428
♦ **CPT-11** see Irinotecan on page 935
♦ **CPZ** see ChlorproMAZINE on page 356
♦ **Crantex LA** see Guaifenesin and Phenylephrine on page 818
♦ **Creon®** see Pancrelipase on page 1302
♦ **Creon® 5 (Can)** see Pancrelipase on page 1302
♦ **Creon® 10 (Can)** see Pancrelipase on page 1302
♦ **Creon® 20 (Can)** see Pancrelipase on page 1302
♦ **Creon® 25 (Can)** see Pancrelipase on page 1302
♦ **Crestor®** see Rosuvastatin on page 1537
♦ **Crinone®** see Progesterone on page 1433
♦ **Critic-Aid Skin Care® [OTC]** see Zinc Oxide on page 1817
♦ **Crixivan®** see Indinavir on page 899
♦ **Crolom®** see Cromolyn on page 423

♦ **Cromoglycic Acid** *see Cromolyn on page 423*

Cromolyn (KROE moe lin)

U.S. Brand Names Crolom®; Gastrocrom®; Intal®; NasalCrom® [OTC]; Opticrom®
Canadian Brand Names Apo-Cromolyn®; Intal®; Nalcrom®; Nu-Cromolyn; Opticrom®
Index Terms Cromoglycic Acid; Cromolyn Sodium; Disodium Cromoglycate; DSCG
Pharmacologic Category Mast Cell Stabilizer
Additional Appendix Information
Asthma *on page 2029*
Use
Inhalation: May be used as an adjunct in the prophylaxis of allergic disorders, including asthma; prevention of exercise-induced bronchospasm
Nasal: Prevention and treatment of seasonal and perennial allergic rhinitis
Oral: Systemic mastocytosis
Ophthalmic: Treatment of vernal keratoconjunctivitis, vernal conjunctivitis, and vernal keratitis
Unlabeled/Investigational Use Oral: Food allergy, treatment of inflammatory bowel disease
Pregnancy Risk Factor B
Pregnancy Implications No data available on whether cromolyn crosses the placenta or clinical effects on the fetus. Available evidence suggests safe use during pregnancy.
Lactation Excretion in breast milk unknown/use caution
Medication Safety Issues
Sound-alike/look-alike issues:
Intal® may be confused with Endal®
NasalCrom® may be confused with Nasacort®, Nasalide®
Contraindications Hypersensitivity to cromolyn or any component of the formulation; acute asthma attacks
Warnings/Precautions Severe anaphylactic reactions may occur rarely; cromolyn is a prophylactic drug with no benefit for acute situations; caution should be used when withdrawing the drug or tapering the dose as symptoms may reoccur; use with caution in patients with a history of cardiac arrhythmias. Transient burning or stinging may occur with ophthalmic use. Dosage of oral product should be decreased with hepatic or renal dysfunction.
Adverse Reactions
Inhalation: >10%: Gastrointestinal: Unpleasant taste in mouth
Nasal:
>10%: Respiratory: Increase in sneezing, burning, stinging, or irritation inside of nose
1% to 10%:
Central nervous system: Headache
Gastrointestinal: Unpleasant taste
Respiratory: Hoarseness, cough, postnasal drip
<1% (Limited to important or life-threatening): Anaphylactic reactions, epistaxis
Ophthalmic: Frequency not defined:
Ocular: Conjunctival injection, dryness around the eye, edema, eye irritation, immediate hypersensitivity reactions, itchy eyes, puffy eyes, styes, rash, watery eyes
Respiratory: Dyspnea
Systemic: Frequency not defined:
Cardiovascular: Angioedema, chest pain, edema, flushing, palpitation, premature ventricular contractions, tachycardia
Central nervous system: Anxiety, behavior changes, convulsions, depression, dizziness, fatigue, hallucinations, headache, irritability, insomnia, lethargy, migraine, nervousness, hypoesthesia, postprandial lightheadedness, psychosis
Dermatologic: Erythema, photosensitivity, pruritus, purpura, rash, urticaria
Gastrointestinal: Abdominal pain, constipation, diarrhea, dyspepsia, dysphagia, esophagospasm, flatulence, glossitis, nausea, stomatitis, unpleasant taste, vomiting
Genitourinary: Dysuria, urinary frequency
Hematologic: Neutropenia, pancytopenia, polycythemia
Hepatic: Liver function test abnormal
Local: Burning
Neuromuscular & skeletal: Arthralgia, leg stiffness, leg weakness, myalgia, paresthesia
Otic: Tinnitus
Respiratory: Dyspnea, pharyngitis
Miscellaneous: Lupus erythematosus
Overdosage/Toxicology Symptoms include bronchospasm, laryngeal edema, and dysuria.
Stability Store at room temperature of 15°C to 30°C (59°F to 86°F); protect from light. Do not use oral solution if solution becomes discolored or forms a precipitate.
Mechanism of Action Prevents the mast cell release of histamine, leukotrienes and slow-reacting substance of anaphylaxis by inhibiting degranulation after contact with antigens
Pharmacodynamics/Kinetics
Onset: Response to treatment:
Nasal spray: May occur at 1-2 weeks
Ophthalmic: May be seen within a few days; treatment for up to 6 weeks is often required
Oral: May occur within 2-6 weeks
Absorption:
Inhalation: ~8% reaches lungs upon inhalation; well absorbed
Oral: <1% of dose absorbed
Half-life elimination: 80-90 minutes
Time to peak, serum: Inhalation: ~15 minutes
Excretion: Urine and feces (equal amounts as unchanged drug); exhaled gases (small amounts)
(Continued)

Cromolyn (Continued)

Dosage

Oral:

Systemic mastocytosis:

Children 2-12 years: 100 mg 4 times/day; not to exceed 40 mg/kg/day; given $\frac{1}{2}$ hour prior to meals and at bedtime

Children >12 years and Adults: 200 mg 4 times/day; given $\frac{1}{2}$ hour prior to meals and at bedtime; if control of symptoms is not seen within 2-3 weeks, dose may be increased to a maximum 40 mg/kg/day

Food allergy and inflammatory bowel disease (unlabeled use):

Children <2 years: Not recommended

Children 2-12 years: Initial dose: 100 mg 4 times/day; may double the dose if effect is not satisfactory within 2-3 weeks; not to exceed 40 mg/kg/day

Children >12 years and Adults: Initial dose: 200 mg 4 times/day; may double the dose if effect is not satisfactory within 2-3 weeks; up to 400 mg 4 times/day

Note: Once desired effect is achieved, dose may be tapered to lowest effective dose

Inhalation:

For chronic control of asthma, taper frequency to the lowest effective dose (ie, 4 times/day to 3 times/day to twice daily): **Note:** Not effective for immediate relief of symptoms in acute asthmatic attacks; must be used at regular intervals for 2-4 weeks to be effective.

Nebulization solution: Children >2 years and Adults: Initial: 20 mg 4 times/day; usual dose: 20 mg 3-4 times/day

Metered spray:

Children 5-12 years: Initial: 2 inhalations 4 times/day; usual dose: 1-2 inhalations 3-4 times/day

Children ≥12 years and Adults: Initial: 2 inhalations 4 times/day; usual dose: 2-4 inhalations 3-4 times/day

Prevention of allergen- or exercise-induced bronchospasm: Administer 10-15 minutes prior to exercise or allergen exposure but no longer than 1 hour before:

Nebulization solution: Children >2 years and Adults: Single dose of 20 mg

Metered spray: Children >5 years and Adults: Single dose of 2 inhalations

Ophthalmic: Children >4 years and Adults: 1-2 drops in each eye 4-6 times/day

Nasal: Allergic rhinitis (treatment and prophylaxis): Children ≥2 years and Adults: 1 spray into each nostril 3-4 times/day; may be increased to 6 times/day (symptomatic relief may require 2-4 weeks)

Dosage adjustment in renal/hepatic impairment: Specific guidelines not available; consider lower dose of oral product.

Dietary Considerations Oral: Should be taken at least 30 minutes before meals.

Administration

Oral solution: Open ampul and squeeze contents into glass of water; stir well; administer at least 30 minutes before meals and at bedtime

Oral inhalation: Shake canister gently before use; do not immerse canister in water.

Nasal inhalation: Clear nasal passages by blowing nose prior to use.

Monitoring Parameters Periodic pulmonary function tests

Dosage Forms

Aerosol, for oral inhalation, as sodium (Intal®): 800 mcg/inhalation (8.1 g) [112 metered inhalations; 56 doses], (14.2 g) [200 metered inhalations; 100 doses]

Solution for nebulization, as sodium (Intal®): 20 mg/2 mL (60s, 120s)

Solution, intranasal, as sodium [spray] (NasalCrom®): 40 mg/mL (13 mL, 26 mL) [5.2 mg/inhalation; contains benzalkonium chloride]

Solution, ophthalmic, as sodium (Crolom®, Opticrom®): 4% (10 mL) [contains benzalkonium chloride]

Solution, oral, as sodium (Gastrocrom®): 100 mg/5 mL (96s)

♦ **Cromolyn Sodium** see Cromolyn on page 423

Crotamiton (kroe TAM i tonn)

U.S. Brand Names Eurax®

Pharmacologic Category Scabicidal Agent

Use Treatment of scabies (*Sarcoptes scabiei*) and symptomatic treatment of pruritus

Pregnancy Risk Factor C

Pregnancy Implications Animal reproduction studies have not been conducted; use during pregnancy only if clearly needed.

Lactation Excretion in breast milk unknown

Medication Safety Issues

Sound-alike/look-alike issues:

Eurax® may be confused with Efudex®, Eulexin®, Evovac™, Serax®, Urex®

International issues:

Eurax® may be confused with Urex® which is a brand name for furosemide in Australia

Contraindications Hypersensitivity to crotamiton or any component of the formulation; patients who manifest a primary irritation response to topical medications

Warnings/Precautions Avoid contact with face, eyes, mucous membranes, and urethral meatus; do not apply to acutely inflamed or raw skin; for external use only

Adverse Reactions Frequency not defined. Topical:

Dermatologic: Contact dermatitis, pruritus, rash

Local: Local irritation

Miscellaneous: Allergic sensitivity reactions, warm sensation

Overdosage/Toxicology Symptoms of ingestion include burning sensation in mouth; irritation of the buccal, esophageal and gastric mucosa, nausea, vomiting, and abdominal pain. There is no specific antidote. General measures to eliminate the drug and reduce its absorption, combined with symptomatic treatment, are recommended.

Stability Store at room temperature.

Mechanism of Action Crotamiton has scabicidal activity against *Sarcoptes scabiei*; mechanism of action unknown

Dosage Topical:

Scabicide: Children and Adults: Wash thoroughly and scrub away loose scales, then towel dry; apply a thin layer and massage drug onto skin of the entire body from the neck to the toes (with special attention to skin folds, creases, and interdigital spaces). Repeat application in 24 hours. Take a cleansing bath 48 hours after the final application. Treatment may be repeated after 7-10 days if live mites are still present.

Pruritus: Massage into affected areas until medication is completely absorbed; repeat as necessary

Administration For external use only. Shake lotion well before using. Avoid contact with face, eyes, mucous membranes, and urethral meatus.

Dosage Forms

Cream: 10% (60 g)

Lotion: 10% (60 mL, 480 mL)

♦ **Cruex®** **Cream [OTC]** *see* Clotrimazole *on page 404*

♦ **Cryselle™** *see* Ethinyl Estradiol and Norgestrel *on page 663*

♦ **Crystalline Penicillin** *see* Penicillin G (Parenteral/Aqueous) *on page 1333*

♦ **Crystal Violet** *see* Gentian Violet *on page 796*

♦ **CsA** *see* CycloSPORINE *on page 431*

♦ **CTLA-4lg** *see* Abatacept *on page 21*

♦ **CTX** *see* Cyclophosphamide *on page 428*

♦ **Cubicin®** *see* Daptomycin *on page 452*

♦ **Culturelle® [OTC]** *see* Lactobacillus *on page 969*

♦ **Cuprimine®** *see* Penicillamine *on page 1330*

♦ **Cutivate®** *see* Fluticasone *on page 738*

♦ **Cutivate™ (Can)** *see* Fluticasone *on page 738*

♦ **CyA** *see* CycloSPORINE *on page 431*

Cyanocobalamin (sye an oh koe BAL a min)

U.S. Brand Names Nascobal®; Twelve Resin-K

Index Terms Vitamin B_{12}

Pharmacologic Category Vitamin, Water Soluble

Use Treatment of pernicious anemia; vitamin B_{12} deficiency due to dietary deficiencies or malabsorption diseases, inadequate secretion of intrinsic factor, and inadequate utilization of B_{12} (eg, during neoplastic treatment); increased B_{12} requirements due to pregnancy, thyrotoxicosis, hemorrhage, malignancy, liver or kidney disease

Pregnancy Risk Factor A/C (dose exceeding RDA recommendation); C (intranasal)

Lactation Enters breast milk/compatible

Contraindications Hypersensitivity to cyanocobalamin, cobalt, or any component of the formulation

Warnings/Precautions I.M./SubQ routes are used to treat pernicious anemia; oral and intranasal administration are not indicated until hematologic remission and no signs of nervous system involvement. Treatment of severe vitamin B_{12} megaloblastic anemia may result in thrombocytosis and severe hypokalemia, sometimes fatal, due to intracellular potassium shift upon anemia resolution. Vitamin B_{12} deficiency masks signs of polycythemia vera; use caution in other conditions where folic acid or vitamin B_{12} administration alone might mask true diagnosis, despite hematologic response. Vitamin B_{12} deficiency for >3 months results in irreversible degenerative CNS lesions; neurologic manifestations will not be prevented with folic acid unless vitamin B_{12} is also given. Spinal cord degeneration might also occur when folic acid used as a substitute for vitamin B_{12} in anemia prevention. Use caution in Leber's disease patients; B_{12} treatment may result in rapid optic atrophy. Some parenteral products contain aluminum; use caution in patients with impaired renal function and neonates. Some parenteral products contain benzyl alcohol; use caution in neonates. Avoid intravenous route; anaphylactic shock has occurred. Intradermal test dose of vitamin B_{12} is recommended for any patient suspected of cyanocobalamin sensitivity prior to intranasal or injectable administration.

Adverse Reactions Frequency not defined.

Cardiovascular: CHF, peripheral vascular disorder, peripheral vascular thrombosis

Central nervous system: Anxiety, dizziness, headache, hypoesthesia, incoordination, pain, nervousness

Dermatologic: Itching, urticaria, exanthema (transient)

Gastrointestinal: Diarrhea, dyspepsia, glossitis, nausea, sore throat, vomiting

Hematologic: Polycythemia vera

Neuromuscular & skeletal: Abnormal gait, arthritis, back pain, myalgia, paresthesia, weakness

Respiratory: Dyspnea, pulmonary edema, rhinitis

Miscellaneous: Anaphylaxis (parenteral) and infection

Drug Interactions

Decreased Effect: Cyanocobalamin effect may be decreased with concurrent chloramphenicol.

Ethanol/Nutrition/Herb Interactions Ethanol: Heavy consumption >2 weeks may impair vitamin B_{12} absorption.

Stability Injection: Clear pink to red solutions are stable at room temperature. Protect from light.

Intranasal spray: Store at 15°C to 30°C (59°F to 86°F); do not freeze. Protect from light.

Mechanism of Action Coenzyme for various metabolic functions, including fat and carbohydrate metabolism and protein synthesis, used in cell replication and hematopoiesis

(Continued)

Cyanocobalamin *(Continued)*

Pharmacodynamics/Kinetics

Absorption: Oral: Variable from the terminal ileum; requires the presence of calcium and gastric "intrinsic factor" to transfer the compound across the intestinal mucosa

Distribution: Principally stored in the liver and bone marrow, also stored in the kidneys and adrenals

Protein binding: Transcobalamins

Metabolism: Converted in tissues to active coenzymes, methylcobalamin and deoxyadenosylcobalamin; undergoes some enterohepatic recycling

Bioavailability: Intranasal solution: 6.1% (relative to I.M.)

Dosage

Adequate intake:

Children:

0-6 months: 0.4 mcg/day

7-12 months: 0.5 mcg/day

Recommended intake:

Children:

1-3 years: 0.9 mcg/day

4-8 years: 1.2 mcg/day

9-13 years: 1.8 mcg/day

Children >14 years and Adults: 2.4 mcg/day

Pregnancy: 2.6 mcg/day

Lactation: 2.8 mcg/day

Vitamin B$_{12}$ deficiency:

I.M., deep SubQ:

Children (dosage not well established): 0.2 mcg/kg for 2 days, followed by 1000 mcg/day for 2-7 days, followed by 100 mcg/week for one month; for malabsorptive causes of B$_{12}$ deficiency, monthly maintenance doses of 100 mcg have been recommended **or** as an alternative 100 mcg/day for 10-15 days, then once or twice weekly for several months

Adults: Initial: 30 mcg/day for 5-10 days; maintenance: 100-200 mcg/month

Intranasal: Adults: 500 mcg in one nostril once weekly

Oral: Adults: 250 mcg/day

Pernicious anemia: I.M., deep SubQ (administer concomitantly with folic acid if needed, 1 mg/day for 1 month):

Children: 30-50 mcg/day for 2 or more weeks (to a total dose of 1000-5000 mcg), then follow with 100 mcg/month as maintenance dosage

Adults: 100 mcg/day for 6-7 days; if improvement, administer same dose on alternate days for 7 doses, then every 3-4 days for 2-3 weeks; once hematologic values have returned to normal, maintenance dosage: 100 mcg/month. **Note:** Alternative dosing of 1000 mcg/day for 5 days (followed by 500-1000 mcg/month) has been used.

Hematologic remission (without evidence of nervous system involvement): Adults:

Intranasal: 500 mcg in one nostril once weekly

Oral: 1000-2000 mcg/day

I.M., SubQ: 100-1000 mcg/month

Schilling test: Adults: I.M.: 1000 mcg

Dietary Considerations Strict vegetarian diets(eg, without eggs or dairy products) may result in vitamin B$_{12}$ deficiency.

Administration

I.M./SubQ: I.M. or deep SubQ are preferred routes of administration

Intranasal: Nasal spray: Prior to initial dose, activate (prime) spray nozzle by pumping unit quickly and firmly until first appearance of spray, then prime twice more. The unit must be reprimed once immediately before each subsequent use. Administer 1 hour before or after ingestion of hot foods/liquids.

I.V.: Not recommended due to rapid elimination

Oral: Not recommended due to variable absorption; however, oral therapy of 1000-2000 mcg/day has been effective for anemia if I.M./SubQ routes refused or not tolerated.

Monitoring Parameters Vitamin B$_{12}$, hematocrit, reticulocyte count, folate and iron levels should be obtained prior to treatment; vitamin B$_{12}$ and peripheral blood counts should be monitored 1 month after beginning treatment, then every 3-6 months thereafter.

Megaloblastic anemia: In addition to normal hematological parameters, serum potassium and platelet counts should be monitored during therapy

Reference Range Normal range of serum B$_{12}$ is 150-750 pg/mL; this represents 0.1% of total body content. Metabolic requirements are 2-5 mcg/day; years of deficiency required before hematologic and neurologic signs and symptoms are seen. Occasional patients with significant neuropsychiatric abnormalities may have no hematologic abnormalities and normal serum cobalamin levels, 200 pg/mL (SI: >150 pmol/L), or more commonly between 100-200 pg/mL (SI: 75-150 pmol/L).

Test Interactions Methotrexate, pyrimethamine, and most antibiotics invalidate folic acid and vitamin B$_{12}$ diagnostic blood assays

Dosage Forms

Injection, solution: 1000 mcg/mL (1 mL, 10 mL, 30 mL) [may contain benzyl alcohol and/or aluminum]

Lozenge [OTC]: 100 mcg, 250 mcg, 500 mcg

Solution, intranasal [spray]:

Nascobal®: 500 mcg/0.1 mL actuation (2.3 mL) [contains benzalkonium chloride; delivers 8 doses]

Tablet [OTC]: 50 mcg, 100 mcg, 250 mcg, 500 mcg, 1000 mcg, 5000 mcg

Twelve Resin-K: 1000 mcg [may be used as oral, sublingual, or buccal]

Tablet, extended release [OTC]: 1000 mcg, 1500 mcg

Tablet, sublingual [OTC]: 2500 mcg

♦ **Cyanocobalamin, Folic Acid, and Pyridoxine** *see* Folic Acid, Cyanocobalamin, and Pyridoxine *on page 750*

♦ **Cyclen®** **(Can)** *see* Ethinyl Estradiol and Norgestimate *on page 660*

♦ **Cyclessa®** *see* Ethinyl Estradiol and Desogestrel *on page 645*

Cyclobenzaprine (sye kloe BEN za preen)

U.S. Brand Names Flexeril®

Canadian Brand Names Apo-Cyclobenzaprine®; Flexeril®; Flexitec; Gen-Cyclobenzaprine; Novo-Cycloprine; Nu-Cyclobenzaprine

Index Terms Cyclobenzaprine Hydrochloride

Pharmacologic Category Skeletal Muscle Relaxant

Use Treatment of muscle spasm associated with acute painful musculoskeletal conditions

Pregnancy Risk Factor B

Lactation Excretion in breast milk unknown/not recommended

Medication Safety Issues

Sound-alike/look-alike issues:

Cyclobenzaprine may be confused with cycloSERINE, cyproheptadine

Flexeril® may be confused with Floxin®

Contraindications Hypersensitivity to cyclobenzaprine or any component of the formulation; do not use concomitantly or within 14 days of MAO Inhibitors; hyperthyroidism; congestive heart failure; arrhythmias; acute recovery phase of MI

Warnings/Precautions Cyclobenzaprine shares the toxic potentials of the tricyclic antidepressants and the usual precautions of tricyclic antidepressant therapy should be observed; use with caution in patients with urinary hesitancy, angle-closure glaucoma, hepatic impairment, or in the elderly. Do not use concomitantly or within 14 days after MAO inhibitors; combination may cause hypertensive crisis, severe convulsions. Safety and efficacy have not been established in patients <15 years of age.

Adverse Reactions

>10%:

Central nervous system: Drowsiness (29% to 39%), dizziness (1% to 11%)

Gastrointestinal: Xerostomia (21% to 32%)

1% to 10%:

Central nervous system: Fatigue (1% to 6%), confusion (1% to 3%), headache (1% to 3%), irritability (1% to 3%), mental acuity decreased (1% to 3%), nervousness (1% to 3%)

Gastrointestinal: Abdominal pain (1% to 3%), constipation (1% to 3%), diarrhea (1% to 3%), dyspepsia (1% to 3%), nausea (1% to 3%)

Neuromuscular & skeletal: Muscle weakness (1% to 3%)

Ocular: Blurred vision (1% to 3%)

Respiratory: Pharyngitis (1% to 3%)

<1% (Limited to important or life-threatening): Ageusia, agitation, anaphylaxis, angioedema, anorexia, arrhythmia, cholestasis, diplopia, facial edema, gastritis, hallucinations, hepatitis (rare), hypertonia, hypotension, insomnia, jaundice, liver function tests abnormal, malaise, palpitation, paresthesia, pruritus, psychosis, rash, seizure, tachycardia, thinking abnormal, tinnitus, tongue edema, tremor, urinary frequency, urinary retention, urticaria, vertigo, vomiting

Overdosage/Toxicology Symptoms include difficulty breathing, drowsiness, syncope, seizures, tachycardia, hallucinations, and vomiting. Following initiation of essential overdose management, toxic symptoms should be treated. Ventricular arrhythmias often respond to systemic alkalinization (sodium bicarbonate 0.5-2 mEq/kg I.V.) and/or phenytoin 15-20 mg/kg (adults). Arrhythmias unresponsive to this therapy may respond to lidocaine 1 mg/kg I.V. followed by a titrated infusion. Physostigmine (1-2 mg I.V. slowly for adults or 0.5 mg I.V. slowly for children) may be indicated in reversing life-threatening cardiac arrhythmias. Seizures usually respond to diazepam I.V. boluses (5-10 mg for adults up to 30 mg, or 0.25-0.4 mg/kg/dose for children up to 10 mg/dose). If seizures are unresponsive or recur, phenytoin or phenobarbital may be required.

Drug Interactions

Cytochrome P450 Effect: Substrate of CYP1A2 (major), 2D6 (minor); 3A4 (minor)

Increased Effect/Toxicity: CYP1A2 inhibitors may increase the levels/effects of cyclobenzaprine; example inhibitors include ciprofloxacin, fluvoxamine, ketoconazole, norfloxacin, ofloxacin, and rofecoxib. Because of cyclobenzaprine's similarities to the tricyclic antidepressants, there may be additive toxicities and side effects similar to tricyclic antidepressants. Cyclobenzaprine's toxicity may also be additive with other agents with anticholinergic properties. Cyclobenzaprine may enhance effects of CNS depressants. Do not use concomitantly or within 14 days of MAO inhibitors. Tramadol may increase risk of seizure; effect seen with tricyclic antidepressants and tramadol.

Decreased Effect: Cyclobenzaprine may decrease effect of guanethidine; effect seen with tricyclic antidepressants and guanethidine

Ethanol/Nutrition/Herb Interactions

Ethanol: Avoid ethanol (may increase CNS depression).

Herb/Nutraceutical: Avoid valerian, kava kava, gotu kola (may increase CNS depression).

Stability Store at room temperature 25°C (77°F); excursions permitted to 15°C to 30°C (59°F to 86°F).

Mechanism of Action Centrally-acting skeletal muscle relaxant pharmacologically related to tricyclic antidepressants; reduces tonic somatic motor activity influencing both alpha and gamma motor neurons

Pharmacodynamics/Kinetics

Onset of action: ~1 hour

Duration: 12-24 hours

Absorption: Complete

Metabolism: Hepatic via CYP3A4, 1A2, and 2D6; may undergo enterohepatic recirculation

Bioavailability: 33% to 55%

Half-life elimination: 18 hours (range: 8-37 hours)

Time to peak, serum: 3-8 hours

Excretion: Urine (as inactive metabolites); feces (as unchanged drug)

(Continued)

Cyclobenzaprine *(Continued)*

Dosage Oral: **Note:** Do not use longer than 2-3 weeks

Adults: Initial: 5 mg 3 times/day; may increase to 10 mg 3 times/day if needed

Elderly: 5 mg 3 times/day; plasma concentration and incidence of adverse effects are increased in the elderly; dose should be titrated slowly

Dosage adjustment in hepatic impairment:

Mild: 5 mg 3 times/day; use with caution and titrate slowly

Moderate to severe: Use not recommended

Dosage Forms

Tablet, as hydrochloride: 5 mg, 10 mg

Flexeril®: 5 mg, 10 mg

- ◆ **Cyclobenzaprine Hydrochloride** *see* Cyclobenzaprine *on page 427*
- ◆ **Cyclocort® [DSC]** *see* Amcinonide *on page 88*
- ◆ **Cyclocort® (Can)** *see* Amcinonide *on page 88*
- ◆ **Cyclogyl®** *see* Cyclopentolate *on page 428*
- ◆ **Cyclomen® (Can)** *see* Danazol *on page 447*
- ◆ **Cyclomydril®** *see* Cyclopentolate and Phenylephrine *on page 428*

Cyclopentolate *(sye kloe PEN toe late)*

U.S. Brand Names AK-Pentolate® [DSC]; Cyclogyl®; Cylate®

Canadian Brand Names Cyclogyl®; Diopentolate®

Index Terms Cyclopentolate Hydrochloride

Pharmacologic Category Anticholinergic Agent, Ophthalmic

Additional Appendix Information

Cycloplegic Mydriatics *on page 1882*

Use Diagnostic procedures requiring mydriasis and cycloplegia

Pregnancy Risk Factor C

Dosage Ophthalmic:

Neonates and Infants: **Note:** Cyclopentolate and phenylephrine combination formulation is the preferred agent for use in neonates and infants due to lower cyclopentolate concentration and reduced risk for systemic reactions

Children: Instill 1 drop of 0.5%, 1%, or 2% in eye followed by 1 drop of 0.5% or 1% in 5 minutes, if necessary

Adults: Instill 1 drop of 1% followed by another drop in 5 minutes; 2% solution in heavily pigmented iris

Additional Information Complete prescribing information for this medication should be consulted for additional detail.

Dosage Forms [DSC] = Discontinued product

Solution, ophthalmic, as hydrochloride: 1% (2 mL, 15 mL)

AK-Pentolate® [DSC], Cylate®: 1% (2 mL, 15 mL) [contains benzalkonium chloride]

Cyclogyl®: 0.5% (15 mL); 1% (2 mL, 5 mL, 15 mL); 2% (2 mL, 5 mL, 15 mL) [contains benzalkonium chloride]

Cyclopentolate and Phenylephrine *(sye kloe PEN toe late & fen il EF rin)*

U.S. Brand Names Cyclomydril®

Index Terms Phenylephrine and Cyclopentolate

Pharmacologic Category Ophthalmic Agent, Antiglaucoma

Use Induce mydriasis greater than that produced with cyclopentolate HCl alone

Pregnancy Risk Factor C

Dosage Ophthalmic: Neonates, Infants, Children, and Adults: Instill 1 drop into the eye every 5-10 minutes, for up to 3 doses, approximately 40-50 minutes before the examination

Additional Information Complete prescribing information for this medication should be consulted for additional detail.

Dosage Forms Solution, ophthalmic: Cyclopentolate hydrochloride 0.2% and phenylephrine hydrochloride 1% (2 mL, 5 mL) [contains benzalkonium chloride]

- ◆ **Cyclopentolate Hydrochloride** *see* Cyclopentolate *on page 428*

Cyclophosphamide *(sye kloe FOS fa mide)*

U.S. Brand Names Cytoxan®

Canadian Brand Names Cytoxan®; Procytox®

Index Terms CPM; CTX; CYT; Neosar; NSC-26271

Pharmacologic Category Antineoplastic Agent, Alkylating Agent

Use

Oncologic: Treatment of Hodgkin's and non-Hodgkin's lymphoma, Burkitt's lymphoma, chronic lymphocytic leukemia (CLL), chronic myelocytic leukemia (CML), acute myelocytic leukemia (AML), acute lymphocytic leukemia (ALL), mycosis fungoides, multiple myeloma, neuroblastoma, retinoblastoma, rhabdomyosarcoma, Ewing's sarcoma; breast, testicular, endometrial, ovarian, and lung cancers, and in conditioning regimens for bone marrow transplantation

Nononcologic: Prophylaxis of rejection for kidney, heart, liver, and bone marrow transplants, severe rheumatoid disorders, nephrotic syndrome, Wegener's granulomatosis, idiopathic pulmonary hemosideroses, myasthenia gravis, multiple sclerosis, systemic lupus erythematosus, lupus nephritis, autoimmune hemolytic anemia, idiopathic thrombocytic purpura (ITP), macroglobulinemia, and antibody-induced pure red cell aplasia

Pregnancy Risk Factor D

Lactation Enters breast milk/contraindicated

Medication Safety Issues

Sound-alike/look-alike issues:

Cyclophosphamide may be confused with cycloSPORINE, ifosfamide

Cytoxan® may be confused with cefoxitin, Centoxin®, Ciloxan®, cytarabine, CytoGam®, Cytosar®, Cytosar-U®, Cytotec®

High alert medication: The Institute for Safe Medication Practices (ISMP) includes this medication among its list of drugs which have a heightened risk of causing significant patient harm when used in error.

Contraindications Hypersensitivity to cyclophosphamide or any component of the formulation; pregnancy

Warnings/Precautions Hazardous agent - use appropriate precautions for handling and disposal. Dosage adjustment may be needed for renal or hepatic failure. Hemorrhagic cystitis may occur; increased hydration and frequent voiding is recommended. Immunosuppression may occur; monitor for infections. May cause cardiotoxicity (CHF, usually with higher doses); may potentiate the cardiotoxicity of anthracyclines. May impair fertility; interferes with oogenesis and spermatogenesis. Secondary malignancies (usually delayed) have been reported

Adverse Reactions

>10%:

Dermatologic: Alopecia (40% to 60%) but hair will usually regrow although it may be a different color and/or texture. Hair loss usually begins 3-6 weeks after the start of therapy.

Endocrine & metabolic: Fertility: May cause sterility; interferes with oogenesis and spermatogenesis; may be irreversible in some patients; gonadal suppression (amenorrhea)

Gastrointestinal: Nausea and vomiting, usually beginning 6-10 hours after administration; anorexia, diarrhea, mucositis, and stomatitis are also seen

Genitourinary: Severe, potentially fatal acute hemorrhagic cystitis (7% to 40%)

Hematologic: Thrombocytopenia and anemia are less common than leukopenia

Onset: 7 days

Nadir: 10-14 days

Recovery: 21 days

1% to 10%:

Cardiovascular: Facial flushing

Central nervous system: Headache

Dermatologic: Skin rash

Renal: SIADH may occur, usually with doses >50 mg/kg (or 1 g/m^2); renal tubular necrosis, which usually resolves with discontinuation of the drug, is also reported

Respiratory: Nasal congestion occurs when I.V. doses are administered too rapidly; patients experience runny eyes, rhinorrhea, sinus congestion, and sneezing during or immediately after the infusion.

<1% (Limited to important or life-threatening): High-dose therapy may cause cardiac dysfunction manifested as CHF; cardiac necrosis or hemorrhagic myocarditis has occurred rarely, but may be fatal. Interstitial pneumonitis and pulmonary fibrosis are occasionally seen with high doses. Cyclophosphamide may also potentiate the cardiac toxicity of anthracyclines. Other adverse reactions include anaphylactic reactions, darkening of skin/fingernails, dizziness, hemorrhagic colitis, hemorrhagic ureteritis, hepatotoxicity, hyperuricemia, hypokalemia, jaundice, malaise, neutrophilic eccrine hidradenitis, radiation recall, renal tubular necrosis, secondary malignancy (eg, bladder carcinoma), SAIDH, Stevens-Johnson syndrome, toxic epidermal necrolysis, weakness.

BMT:

Cardiovascular: Heart failure, cardiac necrosis, pericardial tamponade

Endocrine & metabolic: Hyponatremia

Hematologic: Methemoglobinemia

Gastrointestinal: Severe nausea and vomiting

Miscellaneous: Hemorrhagic cystitis, secondary malignancy

Overdosage/Toxicology Symptoms include myelosuppression, alopecia, nausea, and vomiting. Treatment is symptom-directed and supportive. Cyclophosphamide is moderately dialyzable (20% to 50%).

Drug Interactions

Cytochrome P450 Effect: Substrate of CYP2A6 (minor), 2B6 (major), 2C9 (minor), 2C19 (minor), 3A4 (major); **Inhibits** CYP3A4 (weak); **Induces** CYP2B6 (weak), 2C8 (weak), 2C9 (weak)

Increased Effect/Toxicity: Allopurinol may cause an increase in bone marrow depression and may result in significant elevations of cyclophosphamide cytotoxic metabolites. CYP2B6 inducers may increase the levels/effects of acrolein (the active metabolite of cyclophosphamide); example inducers include carbamazepine, nevirapine, phenobarbital, phenytoin, and rifampin. CYP3A4 inducers may increase the levels/effects of acrolein (the active metabolite of cyclophosphamide); example inducers include aminoglutethimide, carbamazepine, nafcillin, nevirapine, phenobarbital, phenytoin, and rifamycins. Etanercept may enhance the adverse effects of cyclophosphamide. Cyclophosphamide reduces serum pseudocholinesterase concentrations and may prolong the neuromuscular blocking activity of succinylcholine and mivacurium.

Decreased Effect: Cyclophosphamide may decrease the absorption of digoxin tablets. CYP2B6 inhibitors may decrease the levels/effects of acrolein (the active metabolite of cyclophosphamide); example inhibitors include desipramine, paroxetine, and sertraline. CYP3A4 inhibitors may decrease the levels/effects of acrolein (the active metabolite of cyclophosphamide); example inhibitors include azole antifungals, ciprofloxacin, clarithromycin, diclofenac, doxycycline, erythromycin, imatinib, isoniazid, nefazodone, nicardipine, propofol, protease inhibitors, quinidine, and verapamil.

Ethanol/Nutrition/Herb Interactions Herb/Nutraceutical: Avoid black cohosh, dong quai in estrogen-dependent tumors.

Stability Store intact vials of powder at room temperature of 15°C to 30°C (59°F to 86°F). Reconstitute vials with sterile water, normal saline, or 5% dextrose to a concentration of 20 mg/mL. Reconstituted solutions are stable for 24 hours at room temperature and 6 days (Continued)

Cyclophosphamide (Continued)

under refrigeration at 2°C to 8°C (36°F to 46°F). Further dilutions in D5W or NS are stable for 24 hours at room temperature and 6 days at refrigeration.

Mechanism of Action Cyclophosphamide is an alkylating agent that prevents cell division by cross-linking DNA strands and decreasing DNA synthesis. It is a cell cycle phase nonspecific agent. Cyclophosphamide also possesses potent immunosuppressive activity. Cyclophosphamide is a prodrug that must be metabolized to active metabolites in the liver.

Pharmacodynamics/Kinetics

Absorption: Oral: Well absorbed

Distribution: V_d: 0.48-0.71 L/kg; crosses placenta; crosses into CSF (not in high enough concentrations to treat meningeal leukemia)

Protein binding: 10% to 60%

Metabolism: Hepatic to active metabolites acrolein, 4-aldophosphamide, 4-hydroperoxy-cyclophosphamide, and nor-nitrogen mustard

Bioavailability: >75%

Half-life elimination: 3-12 hours

Time to peak, serum: Oral: ~1 hour

Excretion: Urine (<30% as unchanged drug, 85% to 90% as metabolites)

Dosage Refer to individual protocols

Children:

SLE: I.V.: 500-750 mg/m² every month; maximum dose: 1 g/m²

JRA/vasculitis: I.V.: 10 mg/kg every 2 weeks

Children and Adults:

Oral: 50-100 mg/m²/day as continuous therapy or 400-1000 mg/m² in divided doses over 4-5 days as intermittent therapy

I.V.:

Single doses: 400-1800 mg/m² (30-50 mg/kg) per treatment course (1-5 days) which can be repeated at 2-4 week intervals

Continuous daily doses: 60-120 mg/m² (1-2.5 mg/kg) per day

Autologous BMT: IVPB: 50 mg/kg/dose x 4 days or 60 mg/kg/dose for 2 days; total dose is usually divided over 2-4 days

Nephrotic syndrome: Oral: 2-3 mg/kg/day every day for up to 12 weeks when corticosteroids are unsuccessful

Dosing adjustment in renal impairment: A large fraction of cyclophosphamide is eliminated by hepatic metabolism

Some authors recommend no dose adjustment unless severe renal insufficiency (Cl_{cr} <20 mL/minute)

Cl_{cr} >10 mL/minute: Administer 100% of normal dose

Cl_{cr} <10 mL/minute: Administer 75% of normal dose

Hemodialysis: Moderately dialyzable (20% to 50%); administer dose posthemodialysis

CAPD effects: Unknown

CAVH effects: Unknown

Dosing adjustment in hepatic impairment: The pharmacokinetics of cyclophosphamide are not significantly altered in the presence of hepatic insufficiency. No dosage adjustments are recommended.

Dietary Considerations Tablets should be administered during or after meals.

Administration Administer I.P., intrapleurally, IVPB, or continuous I.V. infusion; may also be administered slow IVP in doses ≤1 g.

I.V. infusions may be administered over 1-24 hours

Doses >500 mg to approximately 2 g may be administered over 20-30 minutes

To minimize bladder toxicity, increase normal fluid intake during and for 1-2 days after cyclophosphamide dose. Most adult patients will require a fluid intake of at least 2 L/day. High-dose regimens should be accompanied by vigorous hydration with or without mesna therapy.

Oral: Tablets are not scored and should not be cut or crushed. To minimize the risk of bladder irritation, do not administer tablets at bedtime.

Monitoring Parameters CBC with differential and platelet count, BUN, UA, serum electrolytes, serum creatinine

Additional Information In patients with CYP2B6 G516T variant allele, cyclophosphamide metabolism is markedly increased; metabolism is not influenced by CYP2C9 and CYP2C19 isotypes.

Dosage Forms

Injection, powder for reconstitution:

Cytoxan®: 500 mg, 1 g, 2 g [contains mannitol 75 mg per cyclophosphamide 100 mg]

Tablet: 25 mg, 50 mg

Cytoxan®: 25 mg, 50 mg

Extemporaneous Preparations A 2 mg/mL oral elixir was stable for 14 days when refrigerated when made as follows: Reconstitute a 200 mg vial with aromatic elixir, withdraw the solution, and add sufficient aromatic elixir to make a final volume of 100 mL (store in amber glass container).

Brook D, Davis RE, and Bequette RJ, "Chemical Stability of Cyclophosphamide in Aromatic Elixir U.S.P.," Am J Health Syst Pharm, 1973, 30:618-20.

CycloSERINE (sye kloe SER een)

U.S. Brand Names Seromycin®

Pharmacologic Category Antibiotic, Miscellaneous; Antitubercular Agent

Additional Appendix Information

Antimicrobial Drugs of Choice on page 1981

Tuberculosis on page 2010

Use Adjunctive treatment in pulmonary or extrapulmonary tuberculosis

Unlabeled/Investigational Use Treatment of Gaucher's disease

Pregnancy Risk Factor C

Lactation Enters breast milk/compatible

Medication Safety Issues
Sound-alike/look-alike issues:
CycloSERINE may be confused with cyclobenzaprine, cycloSPORINE

Contraindications Hypersensitivity to cycloserine or any component of the formulation

Warnings/Precautions Epilepsy, depression, severe anxiety, psychosis, severe renal insufficiency, chronic alcoholism

Adverse Reactions Frequency not defined.
Cardiovascular: Cardiac arrhythmia
Central nervous system: Drowsiness, headache, dizziness, vertigo, seizure, confusion, psychosis, paresis, coma
Dermatologic: Rash
Endocrine & metabolic: Vitamin B_{12} deficiency
Hematologic: Folate deficiency
Hepatic: Liver enzymes increased
Neuromuscular & skeletal: Tremor

Overdosage/Toxicology Symptoms include confusion, agitation, CNS depression, psychosis, coma, and seizures. Decontaminate with activated charcoal. Can be hemodialyzed. Management is supportive. Administer pyridoxine 100-300 mg/day to reduce neurotoxic effects. Acute toxicity can occur with ingestions >1 g, chronic toxicity can occur with ingestions >500 mg/day.

Drug Interactions
Increased Effect/Toxicity: Alcohol, isoniazid, and ethionamide increase toxicity of cycloserine. Cycloserine inhibits the hepatic metabolism of phenytoin and may increase risk of epileptic seizures.

Ethanol/Nutrition/Herb Interactions
Ethanol: Avoid ethanol (may increase CNS depression).
Food: May increase vitamin B_{12} and folic acid dietary requirements.

Mechanism of Action Inhibits bacterial cell wall synthesis by competing with amino acid (D-alanine) for incorporation into the bacterial cell wall; bacteriostatic or bactericidal

Pharmacodynamics/Kinetics
Absorption: ~70% to 90%
Distribution: Widely to most body fluids and tissues including CSF, breast milk, bile, sputum, lymph tissue, lungs, and ascitic, pleural, and synovial fluids; crosses placenta
Half-life elimination: Normal renal function: 10 hours
Metabolism: Hepatic
Time to peak, serum: 3-4 hours
Excretion: Urine (60% to 70% as unchanged drug) within 72 hours; feces (small amounts); remainder metabolized

Dosage Some neurotoxic effects may be relieved or prevented by concomitant administration of pyridoxine

Tuberculosis: Oral:
Children: 10-20 mg/kg/day in 2 divided doses up to 1000 mg/day for 18-24 months
Adults: Initial: 250 mg every 12 hours for 14 days, then administer 500 mg to 1 g/day in 2 divided doses for 18-24 months (maximum daily dose: 1 g)
Dosing interval in renal impairment:
Cl_{cr} 10-50 mL/minute: Administer every 24 hours
Cl_{cr} <10 mL/minute: Administer every 36-48 hours

Dietary Considerations May be taken with food; may increase vitamin B_{12} and folic acid dietary requirements.

Monitoring Parameters Periodic renal, hepatic, hematological tests, and plasma cycloserine concentrations

Reference Range Toxicity is greatly increased at levels >30 mcg/mL

Dosage Forms Capsule: 250 mg

♦ **Cyclosporin A** see CycloSPORINE on page 431

CycloSPORINE (SYE kloe spor een)

U.S. Brand Names Gengraf®; Neoral®; Restasis®; Sandimmune®
Canadian Brand Names Neoral®; Rhoxal-cyclosporine; Sandimmune® I.V.; Sandoz-Cyclosporine
Index Terms CsA; CyA; Cyclosporin A
Pharmacologic Category Immunosuppressant Agent
Use Prophylaxis of organ rejection in kidney, liver, and heart transplants, has been used with azathioprine and/or corticosteroids; severe, active rheumatoid arthritis (RA) not responsive to methotrexate alone; severe, recalcitrant plaque psoriasis in nonimmunocompromised adults unresponsive to or unable to tolerate other systemic therapy

Ophthalmic emulsion (Restasis®): Increase tear production when suppressed tear production is presumed to be due to keratoconjunctivitis sicca-associated ocular inflammation (in patients not already using topical anti-inflammatory drugs or punctal plugs)

Unlabeled/Investigational Use Short-term, high-dose cyclosporine as a modulator of multi-drug resistance in cancer treatment; allogenic bone marrow transplants for prevention and treatment of graft-versus-host disease; also used in some cases of severe autoimmune disease (eg, SLE, myasthenia gravis) that are resistant to corticosteroids and other therapy; focal segmental glomerulosclerosis

Pregnancy Risk Factor C

Pregnancy Implications Reproductive toxicity has been observed in animal studies; mutagenic and teratogenic effects were not observed in the standard test systems following oral administration. In humans, cyclosporine crosses the placenta. Based on clinical use, premature births and low birth weight were consistently observed. Use only if the benefit to the mother outweighs the possible risks to the fetus.

(Continued)

CycloSPORINE (Continued)

A pregnancy registry has been established for pregnant women taking immunosuppressants following any solid organ transplant (National Transplantation Pregnancy Registry, Temple University, 877-955-6877).

Lactation Enters breast milk/not recommended

Medication Safety Issues

Sound-alike/look-alike issues:

CycloSPORINE may be confused with cyclophosphamide, Cyklokapron®, cycloSERINE

CycloSPORINE modified (Neoral®, Gengraf®) may be confused with cycloSPORINE non-modified (Sandimmne®)

Gengraf® may be confused with Prograf®

Neoral® may be confused with Neurontin®, Nizoral®

Sandimmune® may be confused with Sandostatin®

Contraindications Hypersensitivity to cyclosporine or any component of the formulation. Rheumatoid arthritis and psoriasis: Abnormal renal function, uncontrolled hypertension, malignancies. Concomitant treatment with PUVA or UVB therapy, methotrexate, other immunosuppressive agents, coal tar, or radiation therapy are also contraindications for use in patients with psoriasis. Ophthalmic emulsion is contraindicated in patients with active ocular infections.

Warnings/Precautions [U.S. Boxed Warning]: Use caution with other potentially nephrotoxic drugs. Increased risk of lymphomas and other malignancies. **[U.S. Boxed Warning]: Increased risk of infection. [U.S. Boxed Warning]: May cause hypertension.** Use caution when changing dosage forms. **[U.S. Boxed Warning]: Cyclosporine (modified) has increased bioavailability as compared to cyclosporine (non-modified) and cannot be used interchangeably without close monitoring.** Monitor cyclosporine concentrations closely following the addition, modification, or deletion of other medications; live, attenuated vaccines may be less effective; use should be avoided.

Transplant patients: To be used initially with corticosteroids. May cause significant hyperkalemia and hyperuricemia, seizures (particularly if used with high dose corticosteroids), and encephalopathy. Make dose adjustments based on cyclosporine blood concentrations. **[U.S. Boxed Warning]: Adjustment of dose should only be made under the direct supervision of an experienced physician.** Anaphylaxis has been reported with I.V. use; reserve for patients who cannot take oral form.

Psoriasis: Patients should avoid excessive sun exposure; safety and efficacy in children <18 years of age have not been established. **[U.S. Boxed Warning]: Risk of skin cancer may be increased with a history of PUVA and possibly methotrexate or other immunosuppressants, UVB, coal tar, or radiation.**

Rheumatoid arthritis: Safety and efficacy for use in juvenile rheumatoid arthritis have not been established. If receiving other immunosuppressive agents, radiation or UV therapy, concurrent use of cyclosporine is not recommended.

Ophthalmic emulsion: Safety and efficacy have not been established in patients <16 years of age.

Products may contain corn oil, castor oil, ethanol, or propylene glycol; injection also contains Cremophor® EL (polyoxyethylated castor oil), which has been associated with rare anaphylactic reactions.

Adverse Reactions Adverse reactions reported with systemic use, including rheumatoid arthritis, psoriasis, and transplantation (kidney, liver, and heart). Percentages noted include the highest frequency regardless of indication/dosage. Frequencies may vary for specific conditions or formulation.

>10%:

Cardiovascular: Hypertension (8% to 53%), edema (5% to 14%)

Central nervous system: Headache (2% to 25%)

Dermatologic: Hirsutism (21% to 45%), hypertrichosis (5% to 19%)

Endocrine & metabolic: Triglycerides increased (15%), female reproductive disorder (9% to 11%)

Gastrointestinal: Nausea (23%), diarrhea (3% to 13%), gum hyperplasia (2% to 16%), abdominal discomfort (<1% to 15%), dyspepsia (2% to 12%)

Neuromuscular & skeletal: Tremor (7% to 55%), paresthesia (1% to 11%), leg cramps/muscle contractions (2% to 12%)

Renal: Renal dysfunction/nephropathy (10% to 38%), creatinine increased (16% to ≥50%)

Respiratory: Upper respiratory infection (1% to 14%)

Miscellaneous: Infection (3% to 25%)

1% to 10%:

Cardiovascular: Chest pain (4% to 6%), arrhythmia (2% to 5%), abnormal heart sounds, cardiac failure, flushes (<1% to 5%), MI, peripheral ischemia

Central nervous system: Dizziness (8%), pain (6%), convulsions (1% to 5%), insomnia (4%), psychiatric events (4% to 5%), pain (3% to 4%), depression (1% to 6%), migraine (2% to 3%), anxiety, confusion, fever, hypoesthesia, emotional lability, impaired concentration, lethargy, malaise, nervousness, paranoia, somnolence, vertigo

Dermatologic: Purpura (3% to 4%), acne (1% to 6%), brittle fingernails, hair breaking, abnormal pigmentation, angioedema, cellulitis, dermatitis, dry skin, eczema, folliculitis, keratosis, pruritus, rash, skin disorder, skin malignancies, urticaria

Endocrine & metabolic: Gynecomastia (<1% to 4%), menstrual disorder (1% to 3%), breast fibroadenosis, breast pain, hyper-/hypoglycemia, diabetes mellitus, goiter, hot flashes, hyperkalemia, hyperuricemia, libido increased/decreased

Gastrointestinal: Vomiting (2% to 10%), flatulence (5%), gingivitis (up to 4%), cramps (up to 4%), anorexia, constipation, dry mouth, dysphagia, enanthema, eructation, esophagitis, gastric ulcer, gastritis, gastroenteritis, gastrointestinal bleeding (upper), gingival bleeding, glossitis, mouth sores, peptic ulcer, pancreatitis, swallowing difficulty, salivary gland enlargement, taste perversion, tongue disorder, tooth disorder, weight loss/gain

Genitourinary: Leukorrhea (1%), abnormal urine, micturition increased, micturition urgency, nocturia, polyuria, pyelonephritis, urinary incontinence, uterine hemorrhage

Hematologic: Leukopenia (<1% to 6%), anemia, bleeding disorder, clotting disorder, platelet disorder, red blood cell disorder, thrombocytopenia

Hepatic: Hepatotoxicity (<1% to 7%), hyperbilirubinemia

Neuromuscular & skeletal: Arthralgia (1% to 6%), bone fracture, joint dislocation, joint pain, muscle pain, myalgia, neuropathy, stiffness, synovial cyst, tendon disorder, tingling, weakness

Ocular: Abnormal vision, cataract, conjunctivitis, eye pain, visual disturbance

Otic: Deafness, hearing loss, tinnitus, vestibular disorder

Renal: BUN increased, hematuria, renal abscess

Respiratory: Sinusitis (<1% to 7%), bronchospasm (up to 5%), cough (3% to 5%), pharyngitis (3% to 5%), dyspnea (1% to 5%), rhinitis (up to 5%), abnormal chest sounds, epistaxis, respiratory infection, pneumonia (up to 1%)

Miscellaneous: Flu-like syndrome (8% to 10%), lymphoma (<1% to 6% reported in transplant), abscess, allergic reactions, bacterial infection, carcinoma, diaphoresis increased, fungal infection, herpes simplex, herpes zoster, hiccups, lymphadenopathy, moniliasis, night sweats, tonsillitis, viral infection

Postmarketing and/or case reports (any indication): Anaphylaxis/anaphylactoid reaction (possibly associated with Cremophor® EL vehicle in injection formulation), benign intracranial hypertension, cholesterol increased, death (due to renal deterioration), encephalopathy, gout, hyperbilirubinemia, hyperkalemia, hypomagnesemia (mild), impaired consciousness, neurotoxicity, papilloedema, pulmonary edema (noncardiogenic), uric acid increased

Ophthalmic emulsion (Restasis®):

>10%: Ocular: Burning (17%)

1% to 10%: Ocular: Hyperemia (conjunctival 5%), eye pain, pruritus, stinging

Overdosage/Toxicology Symptoms of overdose include hepatotoxicity, nephrotoxicity, nausea, vomiting, tremor. CNS secondary to direct action of the drug may not be reflected in serum concentrations, may be more predictable by renal magnesium loss. Forced emesis may be beneficial if done within 2 hours of ingestion of oral cyclosporine. Treatment is symptom-directed and supportive. Cyclosporine is not dialyzable.

Drug Interactions

Cytochrome P450 Effect: Substrate of CYP3A4 (major); **Inhibits** CYP2C9 (weak), 3A4 (moderate)

Increased Effect/Toxicity: The levels/effects of cyclosporine may be increased by allopurinol, amiodarone, azole antifungals, clarithromycin, colchicine, diclofenac, doxycycline, erythromycin, imatinib, isoniazid, metoclopramide, nefazodone, nicardipine, norfloxacin, octreotide, oral contraceptives (hormonal), propofol, protease inhibitors, quinidine, quinupristin/dalfopristin, telithromycin, verapamil, and other CYP3A4 inhibitors. Cyclosporine may increase the levels/effects of sirolimus. Cyclosporine may increase the levels/effects of selected benzodiazepines, calcium channel blockers, cisapride, ergot alkaloids, selected HMG-CoA reductase inhibitors, mesoridazine, mirtazapine, nateglinide, nefazodone, pimozide, quinidine, sildenafil (and other PDE-5 inhibitors), tacrolimus, thioridazine, venlafaxine, and other CYP3A4 substrates. Drugs that enhance nephrotoxicity of cyclosporine include ACE inhibitors, aminoglycosides, amphotericin B, acyclovir, cimetidine, ketoconazole, lovastatin, melphalan, NSAIDs, ranitidine, and trimethoprim and sulfamethoxazole. Cyclosporine increases toxicity of digoxin, methotrexate, nifedipine. Fibric acid derivatives may increase the risk of renal dysfunction and may alter CSA concentrations. Concurrent therapy with sirolimus may increase the risk of HUS/TTP/TMA. Cyclosporine may increase the serum concentration of bosentan. Cyclosporine may decrease the clearance of colchicine. Systemic corticosteroids may increase the serum concentration of cyclosporine (reported with methylprednisolone). Cyclosporine may increase the serum concentration of systemic corticosteroids. Convulsions have been reported with high-dose methylprednisolone.

Decreased Effect: Isoniazid and ticlopidine decrease cyclosporine concentrations. The levels/effects of cyclosporine may be decreased by aminoglutethimide, carbamazepine, nafcillin, nevirapine, phenobarbital, phenytoin, rifamycins, and other CYP3A4 inducers. Orlistat may decrease absorption of cyclosporine; avoid concomitant use. Vaccination may be less effective; avoid use of live vaccines during therapy. Sulfasalazine and sulfinpyrazone may decrease cyclosporine levels.

Ethanol/Nutrition/Herb Interactions

Food: Grapefruit juice increases absorption; unsupervised use should be avoided.

Herb/Nutraceutical: Avoid St John's wort; as an enzyme inducer, it may increase the metabolism of and decrease plasma levels of cyclosporine; organ rejection and graft loss have been reported. Avoid cat's claw, echinacea (have immunostimulant properties).

Stability

Capsule: Store at controlled room temperature.

Injection: Store at controlled room temperature; do not refrigerate. Ampuls should be protected from light. Stability of injection of parenteral admixture at room temperature (25°C) is 6 hours in PVC; 24 hours in Excel®, PAB® containers, or glass.

Sandimmune® injection: Injection should be further diluted [1 mL (50 mg) of concentrate in 20-100 mL of D₅W or NS] for administration by intravenous infusion.

Ophthalmic emulsion: Store at 15°C to 25°C (59°F to 77°F). Vials are single-use; discard immediately following administration.

Oral solution: Store at controlled room temperature; do not refrigerate. Use within 2 months after opening; should be mixed in glass containers.

Neoral® oral solution: Orange juice, apple juice; avoid changing diluents frequently; mix thoroughly and drink at once.

Sandimmune® oral solution: Milk, chocolate milk, orange juice; avoid changing diluents frequently; mix thoroughly and drink at once.

Mechanism of Action Inhibition of production and release of interleukin II and inhibits interleukin II-induced activation of resting T-lymphocytes.

(Continued)

CycloSPORINE *(Continued)*

Pharmacodynamics/Kinetics

Absorption:

Ophthalmic emulsion: Serum concentrations not detectable.

Oral:

Cyclosporine (non-modified): Erratic and incomplete; dependent on presence of food, bile acids, and GI motility; larger oral doses are needed in pediatrics due to shorter bowel length and limited intestinal absorption

Cyclosporine (modified): Erratic and incomplete; increased absorption, up to 30% when compared to cyclosporine (non-modified); less dependent on food, bile acids, or GI motility when compared to cyclosporine (non-modified)

Distribution: Widely in tissues and body fluids including the liver, pancreas, and lungs; crosses placenta; enters breast milk

V_{dss}: 4-6 L/kg in renal, liver, and marrow transplant recipients (slightly lower values in cardiac transplant patients; children <10 years have higher values)

Protein binding: 90% to 98% to lipoproteins

Metabolism: Extensively hepatic via CYP3A4; forms at least 25 metabolites; extensive first-pass effect following oral administration

Bioavailability: Oral:

Cyclosporine (non-modified): Dependent on patient population and transplant type (<10% in adult liver transplant patients and as high as 89% in renal transplant patients); bioavailability of Sandimmune® capsules and oral solution are equivalent; bioavailability of oral solution is ~30% of the I.V. solution

Children: 28% (range: 17% to 42%); gut dysfunction common in BMT patients and oral bioavailability is further reduced

Cyclosporine (modified): Bioavailability of Neoral® capsules and oral solution are equivalent:

Children: 43% (range: 30% to 68%)

Adults: 23% greater than with cyclosporine (non-modified) in renal transplant patients; 50% greater in liver transplant patients

Half-life elimination: Oral: May be prolonged in patients with hepatic impairment and shorter in pediatric patients due to the higher metabolism rate

Cyclosporine (non-modified): Biphasic: Alpha: 1.4 hours; Terminal: 19 hours (range: 10-27 hours)

Cyclosporine (modified): Biphasic: Terminal: 8.4 hours (range: 5-18 hours)

Time to peak, serum: Oral:

Cyclosporine (non-modified): 2-6 hours; some patients have a second peak at 5-6 hours

Cyclosporine (modified): Renal transplant: 1.5-2 hours

Excretion: Primarily feces; urine (6%, 0.1% as unchanged drug and metabolites)

Dosage Neoral®/Genraf® and Sandimmune® are not bioequivalent and cannot be used interchangeably.

Children: Transplant: Refer to adult dosing; children may require, and are able to tolerate, larger doses than adults.

Adults:

Newly-transplanted patients: Adjunct therapy with corticosteroids is recommended. Initial dose should be given 4-12 hours prior to transplant or may be given postoperatively; adjust initial dose to achieve desired plasma concentration

Oral: Dose is dependent upon type of transplant and formulation:

Cyclosporine (modified):

Renal: 9 ± 3 mg/kg/day, divided twice daily

Liver: 8 ± 4 mg/kg/day, divided twice daily

Heart: 7 ± 3 mg/kg/day, divided twice daily

Cyclosporine (non-modified): Initial dose: 15 mg/kg/day as a single dose (range 14-18 mg/kg); lower doses of 10-14 mg/kg/day have been used for renal transplants. Continue initial dose daily for 1-2 weeks; taper by 5% per week to a maintenance dose of 5-10 mg/kg/day; some renal transplant patients may be dosed as low as 3 mg/kg/day

Note: When using the non-modified formulation, cyclosporine levels may increase in liver transplant patients when the T-tube is closed; dose may need decreased

I.V.: Cyclosporine (non-modified): Manufacturer's labeling: Initial dose: 5-6 mg/kg/day as a single dose ($1/3$ the oral dose), infused over 2-6 hours; use should be limited to patients unable to take capsules or oral solution; patients should be switched to an oral dosage form as soon as possible

Note: Many transplant centers administer cyclosporine as "divided dose" infusions (in 2-3 doses/day) or as a continuous (24-hour) infusion; dosages range from 3-7.5 mg/kg/day. Specific institutional protocols should be consulted.

Conversion to cyclosporine (modified) from cyclosporine (non-modified): Start with daily dose previously used and adjust to obtain preconversion cyclosporine trough concentration. Plasma concentrations should be monitored every 4-7 days and dose adjusted as necessary, until desired trough level is obtained. When transferring patients with previously poor absorption of cyclosporine (non-modified), monitor trough levels at least twice weekly (especially if initial dose exceeds 10 mg/kg/day); high plasma levels are likely to occur.

Rheumatoid arthritis: Oral: Cyclosporine (modified): Initial dose: 2.5 mg/kg/day, divided twice daily; salicylates, NSAIDs, and oral glucocorticoids may be continued (refer to Drug Interactions); dose may be increased by 0.5-0.75 mg/kg/day if insufficient response is seen after 8 weeks of treatment; additional dosage increases may be made again at 12 weeks (maximum dose: 4 mg/kg/day). Discontinue if no benefit is seen by 16 weeks of therapy.

Note: Increase the frequency of blood pressure monitoring after each alteration in dosage of cyclosporine. Cyclosporine dosage should be decreased by 25% to 50% in patients with no history of hypertension who develop sustained hypertension during therapy and, if hypertension persists, treatment with cyclosporine should be discontinued.

Psoriasis: Oral: Cyclosporine (modified): Initial dose: 2.5 mg/kg/day, divided twice daily; dose may be increased by 0.5 mg/kg/day if insufficient response is seen after 4 weeks of treatment. Additional dosage increases may be made every 2 weeks if needed (maximum dose: 4 mg/kg/day). Discontinue if no benefit is seen by 6 weeks of therapy. Once patients are adequately controlled, the dose should be decreased to the lowest effective dose. Doses lower than 2.5 mg/kg/day may be effective. Treatment longer than 1 year is not recommended.

Note: Increase the frequency of blood pressure monitoring after each alteration in dosage of cyclosporine. Cyclosporine dosage should be decreased by 25% to 50% in patients with no history of hypertension who develop sustained hypertension during therapy and, if hypertension persists, treatment with cyclosporine should be discontinued.

Focal segmental glomerulosclerosis (unlabeled use): Initial: 3 mg/kg/day divided every 12 hours

Autoimmune diseases (unlabeled use): 1-3 mg/kg/day

Keratoconjunctivitis sicca: Ophthalmic (Restasis®): Children ≥16 years and Adults: Instill 1 drop in each eye every 12 hours

Dosage adjustment in renal impairment: For severe psoriasis:

Serum creatinine levels ≥25% above pretreatment levels: Take another sample within 2 weeks; if the level remains ≥25% above pretreatment levels, decrease dosage of cyclosporine (modified) by 25% to 50%. If two dosage adjustments do not reverse the increase in serum creatinine levels, treatment should be discontinued.

Serum creatinine levels ≥50% above pretreatment levels: Decrease cyclosporine dosage by 25% to 50%. If two dosage adjustments do not reverse the increase in serum creatinine levels, treatment should be discontinued.

Hemodialysis: Supplemental dose is not necessary.

Peritoneal dialysis: Supplemental dose is not necessary.

Dosage adjustment in hepatic impairment: Probably necessary; monitor levels closely

Dietary Considerations Administer this medication consistently with relation to time of day and meals. Avoid grapefruit juice.

Administration

Oral solution: Do not administer liquid from plastic or styrofoam cup. May dilute Neoral® oral solution with orange juice or apple juice. May dilute Sandimmune® oral solution with milk, chocolate milk, or orange juice. Avoid changing diluents frequently. Mix thoroughly and drink at once. Use syringe provided to measure dose. Mix in a glass container and rinse container with more diluent to ensure total dose is taken. Do not rinse syringe before or after use (may cause dose variation).

I.V.: The manufacturer recommends that following dilution, intravenous admixture be administered over 2-6 hours. However, many transplant centers administer as divided doses (2-3 doses/day) or as a 24-hour continuous infusion. Discard solution after 24 hours. Anaphylaxis has been reported with I.V. use; reserve for patients who cannot take oral form. Patients should be under continuous observation for at least the first 30 minutes of the infusion, and should be monitored frequently thereafter. Maintain patent airway; other supportive measures and agents for treating anaphylaxis should be present when I.V. drug is given.

Ophthalmic emulsion: Prior to use, invert vial several times to obtain a uniform emulsion. Remove contact lenses prior to instillation of drops; may be reinserted 15 minutes after administration. May be used with artificial tears; allow 15 minute interval between products.

Monitoring Parameters Monitor blood pressure and serum creatinine after any cyclosporine dosage changes or addition, modification, or deletion of other medications. Monitor plasma concentrations periodically.

Transplant patients: Cyclosporine trough levels, serum electrolytes, renal function, hepatic function, blood pressure, lipid profile

Psoriasis therapy: Baseline blood pressure, serum creatinine (2 levels each), BUN, CBC, serum magnesium, potassium, uric acid, lipid profile. Biweekly monitoring of blood pressure, complete blood count, and levels of BUN, uric acid, potassium, lipids, and magnesium during the first 3 months of treatment for psoriasis. Monthly monitoring is recommended after this initial period. Also evaluate any atypical skin lesions prior to therapy. Increase the frequency of blood pressure monitoring after each alteration in dosage of cyclosporine. Cyclosporine dosage should be decreased by 25% to 50% in patients with no history of hypertension who develop sustained hypertension during therapy and, if hypertension persists, treatment with cyclosporine should be discontinued.

Rheumatoid arthritis: Baseline blood pressure, and serum creatinine (2 levels each); serum creatinine every 2 weeks for first 3 months, then monthly if patient is stable. Increase the frequency of blood pressure monitoring after each alteration in dosage of cyclosporine. Cyclosporine dosage should be decreased by 25% to 50% in patients with no history of hypertension who develop sustained hypertension during therapy and, if hypertension persists, treatment with cyclosporine should be discontinued.

Reference Range Reference ranges are method dependent and specimen dependent; use the same analytical method consistently

Method-dependent and specimen-dependent: Trough levels should be obtained:

Oral: 12-18 hours after dose (chronic usage)

I.V.: 12 hours after dose or immediately prior to next dose

Therapeutic range: Not absolutely defined, dependent on organ transplanted, time after transplant, organ function and CsA toxicity:

General range of 100-400 ng/mL

Toxic level: Not well defined, nephrotoxicity may occur at any level

Test Interactions Specific whole blood, HPLC assay for cyclosporine may be falsely elevated if sample is drawn from the same line through which dose was administered (even if flush has been administered and/or dose was given hours before).

Additional Information Cyclosporine (modified): Refers to the capsule dosage formulation of cyclosporine in an aqueous dispersion (previously referred to as "microemulsion"). Cyclosporine (modified) has increased bioavailability as compared to cyclosporine (non-modified) and cannot be used interchangeably without close monitoring.

Dosage Forms

Capsule, soft gel, modified: 25 mg, 100 mg [contains castor oil, ethanol]

Gengraf®: 25 mg, 100 mg [contains ethanol, castor oil, propylene glycol]

Neoral®: 25 mg, 100 mg [contains dehydrated ethanol, corn oil, castor oil, propylene glycol]

(Continued)

CycloSPORINE *(Continued)*

Capsule, soft gel, non-modified (Sandimmune®): 25 mg, 100 mg [contains dehydrated ethanol, corn oil]

Emulsion, ophthalmic [preservative free, single-use vial] (Restasis®): 0.05% (0.4 mL) [contains glycerin, castor oil, polysorbate 80, carbomer 1342; 32 vials/box]

Injection, solution, non-modified (Sandimmune®): 50 mg/mL (5 mL) [contains Cremophor® EL (polyoxyethylated castor oil), ethanol]

Solution, oral, modified:

Gengraf®: 100 mg/mL (50 mL) [contains castor oil, propylene glycol]

Neoral®: 100 mg/mL (50 mL) [contains dehydrated ethanol, corn oil, castor oil, propylene glycol]

Solution, oral, non-modified (Sandimmune®): 100 mg/mL (50 mL) [contains olive oil, ethanol]

◆ **Cyklokapron**® *see* Tranexamic Acid *on page 1722*
◆ **Cylate**® *see* Cyclopentolate *on page 428*
◆ **Cylex**® **[OTC]** *see* Benzocaine *on page 204*
◆ **Cymbalta**® *see* Duloxetine *on page 562*

Cyproheptadine (si proe HEP ta deen)

Index Terms Cyproheptadine Hydrochloride; Periactin

Pharmacologic Category Antihistamine

Use Perennial and seasonal allergic rhinitis and other allergic symptoms including urticaria

Unlabeled/Investigational Use Appetite stimulation, blepharospasm, cluster headaches, migraine headaches, Nelson's syndrome, pruritus, schizophrenia, spinal cord damage associated spasticity, and tardive dyskinesia

Pregnancy Risk Factor B

Lactation Excretion in breast milk unknown/contraindicated

Medication Safety Issues

Sound-alike/look-alike issues:

Cyproheptadine may be confused with cyclobenzaprine

Periactin may be confused with Perative®, Percodan®, Persantine®

Contraindications Hypersensitivity to cyproheptadine or any component of the formulation; narrow-angle glaucoma; bladder neck obstruction; acute asthmatic attack; stenosing peptic ulcer; GI tract obstruction; concurrent use of MAO inhibitors; avoid use in premature and term newborns due to potential association with SIDS

Warnings/Precautions Do not use in neonates, safety and efficacy have not been established in children <2 years of age; symptomatic prostate hypertrophy; antihistamines are more likely to cause dizziness, excessive sedation, syncope, toxic confusion states, and hypotension in the elderly. In case reports, cyproheptadine has promoted weight gain in anorexic adults, though it has not been specifically studied in the elderly. All cases of weight loss or decreased appetite should be adequately assessed.

Adverse Reactions

>10%:

Central nervous system: Slight to moderate drowsiness

Respiratory: Thickening of bronchial secretions

1% to 10%:

Central nervous system: Dizziness, fatigue, headache, nervousness

Gastrointestinal: Abdominal pain, appetite stimulation, diarrhea, nausea, xerostomia

Neuromuscular & skeletal: Arthralgia

Respiratory: Pharyngitis

<1% (Limited to important or life-threatening): Bronchospasm, CNS stimulation, depression, epistaxis, hemolytic anemia, hepatitis, leukopenia, sedation, seizure, thrombocytopenia

Overdosage/Toxicology Symptoms include CNS depression or stimulation, dry mouth, flushed skin, fixed and dilated pupils, and apnea. There is no specific treatment for an antihistamine overdose, however, clinical toxicity is mostly due to anticholinergic effects. Anticholinesterase inhibitors may be useful by reducing acetylcholinesterase. Anticholinesterase inhibitors include physostigmine, neostigmine, pyridostigmine, and edrophonium. For anticholinergic overdose with severe life-threatening symptoms, physostigmine 1-2 mg (0.5 mg or 0.02 mg/kg for children) slow I.V. may be given to reverse these effects.

Drug Interactions

Increased Effect/Toxicity: Cyproheptadine may potentiate the effect of CNS depressants. MAO inhibitors may cause hallucinations when taken with cyproheptadine.

Ethanol/Nutrition/Herb Interactions Ethanol: Avoid ethanol (may increase CNS sedation).

Mechanism of Action A potent antihistamine and serotonin antagonist, competes with histamine for H_1-receptor sites on effector cells in the gastrointestinal tract, blood vessels, and respiratory tract

Pharmacodynamics/Kinetics

Absorption: Completely

Metabolism: Almost completely hepatic

Excretion: Urine (>50% primarily as metabolites); feces (~25%)

Dosage Oral:

Children:

Allergic conditions: 0.25 mg/kg/day or 8 mg/m²/day in 2-3 divided doses **or**

2-6 years: 2 mg every 8-12 hours (not to exceed 12 mg/day)

7-14 years: 4 mg every 8-12 hours (not to exceed 16 mg/day)

Migraine headaches: 4 mg 2-3 times/day

Children ≥12 years and Adults: Spasticity associated with spinal cord damage: 4 mg at bedtime; increase by a 4 mg dose every 3-4 days; average daily dose: 16 mg in divided doses; not to exceed 36 mg/day

Children >13 years and Adults: Appetite stimulation (anorexia nervosa): 2 mg 4 times/day; may be increased gradually over a 3-week period to 8 mg 4 times/day

Adults:
Allergic conditions: 4-20 mg/day divided every 8 hours (not to exceed 0.5 mg/kg/day)
Cluster headaches: 4 mg 4 times/day
Migraine headaches: 4-8 mg 3 times/day

Dosage adjustment in hepatic impairment: Reduce dosage in patients with significant hepatic dysfunction

Test Interactions Diagnostic antigen skin test results may be suppressed; false positive serum TCA screen

Additional Information May stimulate appetite. In case reports, cyproheptadine has promoted weight gain in anorexic adults.

Dosage Forms
Syrup, as hydrochloride: 2 mg/5 mL (473 mL) [contains alcohol 5%; mint flavor]
Tablet, as hydrochloride: 4 mg

- ◆ **Cyproheptadine Hydrochloride** *see* Cyproheptadine *on page 436*
- ◆ **Cystadane®** *see* Betaine *on page 211*
- ◆ **Cystagon®** *see* Cysteamine *on page 437*

Cysteamine (sis TEE a meen)

U.S. Brand Names Cystagon®
Index Terms Cysteamine Bitartrate
Pharmacologic Category Anticystine Agent; Urinary Tract Product
Use Orphan drug: Treatment of nephropathic cystinosis
Pregnancy Risk Factor C
Dosage Oral: Initiate therapy with ¼ to ⅙ of maintenance dose; titrate slowly upward over 4-6 weeks. **Note:** Dosage may be increased if cystine levels are <1 nmol/½ cystine/mg protein, although intolerance and incidence of adverse events may be increased.

Children <12 years: Maintenance: 1.3 g/m²/day or 60 mg/kg/day divided into 4 doses (maximum dose: 1.95 g/m²/day or 90 mg/kg/day)
Children >12 years and Adults (>110 lb): 2 g/day in 4 divided doses; maximum dose: 1.95 g/m²/day or 90 mg/kg/day

Additional Information Complete prescribing information for this medication should be consulted for additional detail.

Dosage Forms Capsule: 50 mg, 150 mg

- ◆ **Cysteamine Bitartrate** *see* Cysteamine *on page 437*
- ◆ **Cystistat®** (Can) *see* Hyaluronate and Derivatives *on page 841*
- ◆ **Cystospaz®** *see* Hyoscyamine *on page 866*
- ◆ **Cystospaz-M®** [DSC] *see* Hyoscyamine *on page 866*
- ◆ **CYT** *see* Cyclophosphamide *on page 428*
- ◆ **Cytadren®** *see* Aminoglutethimide *on page 95*

Cytarabine (sye TARE a been)

U.S. Brand Names Cytosar-U®
Canadian Brand Names Cytosar®
Index Terms Arabinosylcytosine; Ara-C; Cytarabine Hydrochloride; Cytosine Arabinosine Hydrochloride; NSC-63878
Pharmacologic Category Antineoplastic Agent, Antimetabolite; Antineoplastic Agent, Antimetabolite (Purine Antagonist)
Use Treatment of acute myeloid leukemia (AML), acute lymphocytic leukemia (ALL), chronic myelocytic leukemia (CML; blast phase), and lymphomas; prophylaxis and treatment of meningeal leukemia
Pregnancy Risk Factor D
Pregnancy Implications Cytarabine is teratogenic in animal studies. Limb and ear defects have been noted in case reports when cytarabine has been used during pregnancy. The following have also been noted in the neonate: Pancytopenia, WBC depression, electrolyte abnormalities, prematurity, low birth weight, decreased hematocrit or platelets. Risk to the fetus is decreased if therapy is avoided during the 1st trimester; however, women of child-bearing potential should be advised of the potential risks.
Lactation Excretion in breast milk unknown/not recommended
Medication Safety Issues
Sound-alike/look-alike issues:
Cytarabine may be confused with Cytadren®, Cytosar®, Cytoxan®, vidarabine
Cytosar-U® may be confused with cytarabine, Cytovene®, Cytoxan®, Neosar®

High alert medication: The Institute for Safe Medication Practices (ISMP) includes this medication among its list of drugs which have a heightened risk of causing significant patient harm when used in error.

Contraindications Hypersensitivity to cytarabine or any component of the formulation
Warnings/Precautions Hazardous agent - use appropriate precautions for handling and disposal. **[U.S. Boxed Warning]: Potent myelosuppressive agent;** use with caution in patients with prior bone marrow suppression; monitor for signs of febrile neutropenia. High-dose regimens are associated with CNS, gastrointestinal, ocular (prophylaxis with ophthalmic corticosteroid drops is recommended), pulmonary toxicities and cardiomyopathy. Use with caution in patients with impaired renal (high dose cytarabine) and hepatic function; may be at higher risk for CNS toxicities; dosage adjustments may be required. Tumor lysis syndrome and subsequent hyperuricemia may occur with high dose cytarabine; monitor, consider allopurinol and hydrate accordingly. Cytarabine syndrome is characterized by fever, myalgia, bone pain, chest pain, maculopapular rash, conjunctivitis, and malaise, and may occur 6-12 hours following administration; may be managed with corticosteroids. There have been reports of acute pancreatitis in patients receiving continuous infusion and in patients
(Continued)

Cytarabine *(Continued)*

previously treated with L-asparaginase. **[U.S. Boxed Warning]: Should be administered under the supervision of an experienced cancer chemotherapy physician.** Some products may contain benzyl alcohol; do not use products containing benzyl alcohol or products reconstituted with bacteriostatic diluent intrathecally or for high-dose cytarabine regimens.

Adverse Reactions Note: Frequencies not defined; CNS, gastrointestinal, ocular and pulmonary toxicities are more common with high-dose cytarabine regimens.

More frequent:

Central nervous system: Fever (>80%)

Dermatologic: Alopecia, rash

Gastrointestinal: Nausea, vomiting, diarrhea, mucositis, anal inflammation, anal ulceration, anorexia; GI effects may be more pronounced with divided I.V. bolus doses than with continuous infusion

Hematologic: Myelosuppression, neutropenia (onset: 1-7 days; nadir [biphasic]: 7-9 days and at 15-24 days; recovery [biphasic]: 9-12 and at 24-34 days), thrombocytopenia (onset: 5 days; nadir: 12-15 days; recovery 15-25 days), anemia, leukopenia, megaloblastosis, reticulocytes decreased, bleeding

Hepatic: Hepatic dysfunction, transaminases increased (acute)

Local: Thrombophlebitis

Ocular: Tearing, ocular pain, foreign body sensation, photophobia, and blurred vision may occur with high-dose therapy; ophthalmic corticosteroids or 0.9% NaCl usually prevents or relieves the condition

Less frequent:

Cardiovascular: Chest pain, pericarditis

Central nervous system: Dizziness, headache, somnolence, confusion, malaise, neural toxicity, neuritis; a severe cerebellar toxicity occurs in about 8% of patients receiving a high dose (>36-48 g/m^2/cycle); it is irreversible or fatal in about 1%

Dermatologic: Skin freckling, itching, pruritus, ulceration, urticaria, pain, erythema, and skin sloughing of the palmar and plantar surfaces may occur with high-dose therapy. Prophylactic topical steroids and/or skin moisturizers may be useful.

Gastrointestinal: Abdominal pain, bowel necrosis, esophageal irritation, esophagitis, pancreatitis, sore throat

Genitourinary: Urinary retention

Hepatic: Jaundice

Local: Injection site cellulitis

Neuromuscular & skeletal: Myalgia, bone pain

Ocular: Conjunctivitis

Renal: Renal dysfunction

Respiratory: Syndrome of sudden respiratory distress, including tachypnea, hypoxemia, interstitial and alveolar infiltrates progressing to pulmonary edema, pneumonia, dyspnea

Miscellaneous: Allergic edema, anaphylaxis, sepsis

Infrequent and/or case reports: Amylase increased, aseptic meningitis, cardiomegaly, cardiomyopathy (in combination with cyclophosphamide), cardiopulmonary arrest, cerebral dysfunction, coma, corneal toxicity, desquamation, exanthematous pustulosis, gastrointestinal ulceration, hemorrhagic conjunctivitis, hyperbilirubinemia, lipase increased, liver abscess, liver damage, necrotizing colitis, paralysis (intrathecal and I.V. combination therapy), peritonitis, personality changes, pneumatosis cystoides intestinalis, pulmonary edema, rhabdomyolysis, veno-occlusive liver disease

Adverse events associated with intrathecal cytarabine administration: Dysphagia, accessory nerve paralysis, diplopia, cough, hoarseness, aphonia, blindness (with concurrent systemic chemotherapy and cranial irradiation), fever, nausea, necrotizing leukoencephalopathy (with concurrent cranial irradiation, I.T. methotrexate, and I.T. hydrocortisone), neurotoxicity, paraplegia, vomiting

Overdosage/Toxicology Doses of 4.5 g/m^2 every 12 hours for 12 doses (total of 54 g/m^2) have resulted in irreversible CNS toxicity and death. Symptoms of overdose include myelosuppression, megaloblastosis, nausea, vomiting, respiratory distress, and pulmonary edema. A syndrome of sudden respiratory distress progressing to pulmonary edema and cardiomegaly has been reported following high doses. Treatment is symptom-directed and supportive.

Drug Interactions

Decreased Effect: Decreased effect of flucytosine; decreases digoxin oral tablet absorption.

Stability

Powder for reconstitution: Store intact vials of powder at room temperature 15°C to 30°C (59°F to 86°F). Reconstitute with bacteriostatic water for injection. Reconstituted solutions are stable for up to 8 days at room temperature.

Solution: Prior to dilution, store at room temperature, 15°C to 30°C (59°F to 86°F); protect from light. Do not refrigerate solution; precipitate may form.

Further dilution in D$_5$W or NS is stable for 8 days at room temperature (25°C). Intrathecal solutions in 3-20 mL lactated Ringer's are stable for 7 days at room temperature (30°C); however, should be used within 24 hours due to sterility concerns.

Reconstitute powder with bacteriostatic water for injection, bacteriostatic 0.9% NaCl.

For I.T. use: Reconstitute with preservative free diluent.

For I.V. infusion: Dilute in 250-1000 mL 0.9% NaCl or D$_5$W.

Note: Solutions containing bacteriostatic agents should not be used for the preparation of either high doses or intrathecal doses of cytarabine; may be used for I.M., SubQ, and low-dose (100-200 mg/m^2) I.V. solution.

Mechanism of Action Inhibition of DNA synthesis. Cytosine gains entry into cells by a carrier process, and then must be converted to its active compound, aracytidine triphosphate. Cytosine is a purine analog and is incorporated into DNA; however, the primary action is inhibition of DNA polymerase resulting in decreased DNA synthesis and repair. The degree of cytotoxicity correlates linearly with incorporation into DNA; therefore, incorporation into the

DNA is responsible for drug activity and toxicity. Cytarabine is specific for the S phase of the cell cycle.

Pharmacodynamics/Kinetics

Distribution: V_d: Total body water; widely and rapidly since it enters the cells readily; crosses blood-brain barrier with CSF levels of 40% to 50% of plasma level

Metabolism: Primarily hepatic; metabolized by deoxycytidine kinase and other nucleotide kinases to aracytidine triphosphate (active); about 86% to 96% of dose is metabolized to inactive uracil arabinoside

Half-life elimination: Initial: 7-20 minutes; Terminal: 0.5-2.6 hours

Excretion: Urine (~80% as metabolites) within 24-36 hours

Dosage Refer to individual protocols. Children and Adults:

Remission induction:

I.V.: 100-200 mg/m²/day for 5-10 days; a second course, beginning 2-4 weeks after the initial therapy, may be required in some patients.

or 100 mg/m² every 12 hours for 7 days

I.T.: 5-75 mg/m² every 2-7 days until CNS findings normalize; or age-based dosing:

<1 year of age: 20 mg

1-2 years of age: 30 mg

2-3 years of age: 50 mg

>3 years of age: 75 mg

Remission maintenance:

I.V.: 70-200 mg/m²/day for 2-5 days at monthly intervals

I.M., SubQ: 1-1.5 mg/kg single dose for maintenance at 1- to 4-week intervals

High-dose therapies:

Doses as high as 1-3 g/m² have been used for refractory or secondary leukemias or refractory non-Hodgkin's lymphoma.

Doses of 1-3 g/m² every 12 hours for up to 12 doses have been used for leukemia

Bone marrow transplant: 1.5 g/m² continuous infusion over 48 hours

Dosage adjustment in renal impairment: There is no FDA-approved renal dosing adjustment guideline; the following guidelines have been used by some clinicians:

Aronoff, 1999 (Cytarabine 100-200 mg/m²): Do not adjust based on renal function

Kintzel, 1995 (High-dose cytarabine 1-3 g/m²):

Cl_{cr} 46-60 mL/minute: Administer 60% of dose

Cl_{cr} 31-45 mL/minute: Administer 50% of dose

Cl_{cr} <30 mL/minute: Consider use of alternative drug

Hemodialysis: Supplemental dose is not necessary.

Peritoneal dialysis: Supplemental dose is not necessary.

Dosage adjustment in hepatic impairment: Dose may need to be adjusted in patients with liver failure since cytarabine is partially detoxified in the liver. There is no FDA-approved hepatic dosing adjustment guideline; the following guideline has been used by some clinicians: Koren, 1992 (dose level not specified): Bilirubin >34 micromol/L: Administer 50% of dose and elevate subsequent doses with lack of toxicity

Administration May be administered I.M., I.T., or SubQ at a concentration not to exceed 100 mg/mL. When administered via I.V. infusion, infuse over 1-3 hours or as a continuous infusion.

Monitoring Parameters Liver function tests, CBC with differential and platelet count, serum creatinine, BUN, serum uric acid

Additional Information I.V. doses ≥1.5 g/m² may produce conjunctivitis which can be ameliorated with prophylactic use of corticosteroid (0.1% dexamethasone) eye drops. Dexamethasone eye drops should be administered at 1-2 drops every 6 hours during and for 2-7 days after cytarabine is done.

Dosage Forms

Injection, powder for reconstitution: 100 mg, 500 mg, 1 g, 2 g

Injection, solution: 20 mg/mL (5 mL, 25 mL, 50 mL); 100 mg/mL (20 mL)

♦ **Cytarabine Hydrochloride** see Cytarabine on page 437

Cytarabine (Liposomal) (sye TARE a been lip po SOE mal)

U.S. Brand Names DepoCyt®

Canadian Brand Names DepoCyt®

Pharmacologic Category Antineoplastic Agent, Antimetabolite

Use Treatment of neoplastic (lymphomatous) meningitis

Pregnancy Risk Factor D

Pregnancy Implications Cytarabine may cause fetal harm if a pregnant woman is exposed systemically.

Lactation Excretion in breast milk unknown/not recommended

Medication Safety Issues

Sound-alike/look-alike issues:

Cytarabine may be confused with Cytadren®, Cytosar®, Cytoxan®, vidarabine

DepoCyt® may be confused with Depoject®

High alert medication: The Institute for Safe Medication Practices (ISMP) includes this medication among its list of drugs which have a heightened risk of causing significant patient harm when used in error.

Contraindications Hypersensitivity to cytarabine or any component of the formulation; active meningeal infection; pregnancy

Warnings/Precautions Hazardous agent - use appropriate precautions for handling and disposal. **[U.S. Boxed Warning]: Chemical arachnoiditis (nausea, vomiting , headache, fever) occurs commonly; may be fatal if untreated. The incidence and severity of chemical arachnoiditis is reduced by coadministration with dexamethasone.** May cause neurotoxicity (including myelopathy), which may lead to permanent neurologic deficit. Blockage to CSF flow may increase the risk of neurotoxicity. Monitor for neurotoxicity; reduce subsequent doses; discontinue with persistent neurotoxicity. The risk of adverse events,
(Continued)

Cytarabine (Liposomal) *(Continued)*

including neurotoxicity, is increased with concurrent radiation therapy or systemic chemotherapy. **[U.S. Boxed Warning]: Should be administered under the supervision of an experienced cancer chemotherapy physician.** Safety and efficacy in pediatric patients have not been established.

Adverse Reactions

>10%:

Central nervous system: Headache (28%), confusion (14%), somnolence (12%), fever (11%), pain (11%); chemical arachnoiditis is commonly observed, and may include neck pain, neck rigidity, headache, fever, nausea, vomiting, and back pain; may occur in up to 100% of cycles without dexamethasone prophylaxis; incidence is reduced to 33% when dexamethasone is used concurrently

Gastrointestinal: Vomiting (12%), nausea (11%)

Neuromuscular & skeletal: Weakness (19%)

1% to 10%:

Cardiovascular: Peripheral edema (7%)

Gastrointestinal: Constipation (7%)

Genitourinary: Incontinence (3%)

Hematologic: Neutropenia (9%), thrombocytopenia (8%), anemia (1%)

Neuromuscular & skeletal: Back pain (7%), abnormal gait (4%)

1% (Limited to important or life-threatening): Anaphylaxis, blindness, cranial nerve palsies, deafness, encephalopathy, hemiplegia, hydrocephalus, infectious meningitis, myelopathy, neck pain, peripheral neuropathy, seizure, somnolence, visual disturbance

Overdosage/Toxicology No overdosage with liposomal cytarabine has been reported. See Cytarabine *on page 437* for toxicology related to systemic administration. Overdose would likely result in severe chemical arachnoiditis, including encephalopathy; coadministration of dexamethasone should be continued. Exchange of CSF with isotonic saline may be considered; treatment is otherwise symptom-directed and supportive.

Drug Interactions

Increased Effect/Toxicity: No formal studies of interactions with other medications have been conducted. The limited systemic exposure minimizes the potential for interaction between liposomal cytarabine and other medications.

Decreased Effect: No formal studies of interactions with other medications have been conducted. The limited systemic exposure minimizes the potential for interaction between liposomal cytarabine and other medications.

Stability Store under refrigeration (2°C to 8°C). Protect from freezing and avoid aggressive agitation. Solutions should be used within 4 hours of withdrawal from the vial. Particles may settle in diluent over time, and may be resuspended by gentle agitation or inversion of the vial.

Mechanism of Action This is a sustained-release formulation of the active ingredient cytarabine, which acts through inhibition of DNA synthesis; cell cycle-specific for the S phase of cell division; cytosine gains entry into cells by a carrier process, and then must be converted to its active compound; cytosine acts as an analog and is incorporated into DNA; however, the primary action is inhibition of DNA polymerase resulting in decreased DNA synthesis and repair; degree of its cytotoxicity correlates linearly with its incorporation into DNA; therefore, incorporation into the DNA is responsible for drug activity and toxicity

Pharmacodynamics/Kinetics

Absorption: Systemic exposure following intrathecal administration is negligible since transfer rate from CSF to plasma is slow

Metabolism: In plasma to ara-U (inactive)

Half-life elimination, CSF: 100-263 hours

Time to peak, CSF: Intrathecal: ~5 hours

Excretion: Primarily urine (as metabolites - ara-U)

Dosage Note: Patients should be started on dexamethasone 4 mg twice daily (oral or I.V.) for 5 days, beginning on the day of liposomal cytarabine injection.

Adults:

Induction: 50 mg intrathecally every 14 days for a total of 2 doses (weeks 1 and 3)

Consolidation: 50 mg intrathecally every 14 days for 3 doses (weeks 5, 7, and 9), followed by an additional dose at week 13

Maintenance: 50 mg intrathecally every 28 days for 4 doses (weeks 17, 21, 25, and 29)

If drug-related neurotoxicity develops, the dose should be reduced to 25 mg. If toxicity persists, treatment with liposomal cytarabine should be discontinued.

Administration For intrathecal use only. Dose should be removed from vial immediately before administration (must be administered within 4 hours of removal). An in-line filter should **not** be used. Administer directly into the CSF via an intraventricular reservoir or by direct injection into the lumbar sac. Injection should be made slowly (over 1-5 minutes). Patients should lie flat for 1 hour after lumbar puncture.

Monitoring Parameters Monitor closely for signs of an immediate reaction; neurotoxicity

Test Interactions Since cytarabine liposomes are similar in appearance to WBCs, care must be taken in interpreting CSF examinations in patients receiving liposomal cytarabine

Dosage Forms

Injection, suspension [preservative free]:

Depocyt®: 10 mg/mL (5 mL)

♦ **CytoGam®** *see* Cytomegalovirus Immune Globulin (Intravenous-Human) *on page 441*

Cytomegalovirus Immune Globulin (Intravenous-Human)
(sye toe meg a low VYE rus i MYUN GLOB yoo lin in tra VEE nus HYU man)

U.S. Brand Names CytoGam®
Index Terms CMV-IGIV
Pharmacologic Category Immune Globulin
Use Prophylaxis of cytomegalovirus (CMV) disease associated with kidney, lung, liver, pancreas, and heart transplants; concomitant use with ganciclovir should be considered in organ transplants (other than kidney) from CMV seropositive donors to CMV seronegative recipients
Unlabeled/Investigational Use Adjunct therapy in the treatment of CMV disease in immuno-compromised patients
Pregnancy Risk Factor C
Pregnancy Implications Reproduction studies have not been conducted.
Lactation Excretion in breast milk unknown
Medication Safety Issues
Sound-alike/look-alike issues:
CytoGam® may be confused with Cytoxan®, Gamimune® N
Contraindications Hypersensitivity to CMV-IGIV, other immunoglobulins, or any component of the formulation; immunoglobulin A deficiency
Warnings/Precautions Monitor for anaphylactic reactions during infusion. May theoretically transmit blood-borne viruses. Use with caution in patients with renal insufficiency, diabetes mellitus, patients >65 years of age, volume depletion, sepsis, paraproteinemia, or patients on concomitant nephrotoxic drugs. Stabilized with sucrose and albumin, contains no preservative.
Adverse Reactions
<6%:
Cardiovascular: Flushing
Central nervous system: Chills, fever
Gastrointestinal: Nausea, vomiting
Neuromuscular & skeletal: Arthralgia, back pain, muscle cramps
Respiratory: Wheezing
<1%: Blood pressure decreased
Postmarketing and/or case reports: Acute renal failure, acute tubular necrosis, AMS, anaphylactic shock, angioneurotic edema, anuria, BUN increase, oliguria, osmotic nephrosis, proximal tubular nephropathy, serum creatinine increased
Overdosage/Toxicology Symptoms related to volume overload would be expected to occur with overdose. Treatment is symptom-directed and supportive.
Drug Interactions
Decreased Effect: Decreased effect of live vaccines may be seen if given within 3 months of IGIV administration. Defer vaccination or revaccinate.
Stability Store between 2°C and 8°C (35.6°F and 46.4°F). Use reconstituted product within 6 hours; do not admix with other medications; do not use if turbid. Do not shake vials. Dilution is not recommended. Infusion with other products is not recommended.
Mechanism of Action CMV-IGIV is a preparation of immunoglobulin G derived from pooled healthy blood donors with a high titer of CMV antibodies; administration provides a passive source of antibodies against cytomegalovirus
Dosage I.V.: Adults:
Kidney transplant:
Initial dose (within 72 hours of transplant): 150 mg/kg/dose
2-, 4-, 6-, and 8 weeks after transplant: 100 mg/kg/dose
12 and 16 weeks after transplant: 50 mg/kg/dose
Liver, lung, pancreas, or heart transplant:
Initial dose (within 72 hours of transplant): 150 mg/kg/dose
2-, 4-, 6-, and 8 weeks after transplant: 150 mg/kg/dose
12 and 16 weeks after transplant: 100 mg/kg/dose
Severe CMV pneumonia (unlabeled): Various regimens have been used, including 400 mg/kg CMV-IGIV in combination with ganciclovir on days 1, 2, 7, or 8, followed by 200 mg/kg CMV-IGIV on days 14 and 21
Elderly: Use with caution in patients >65 years of age, may be at increased risk of renal insufficiency
Dosage adjustment in renal impairment: Use with caution; specific dosing adjustments are not available. Infusion rate should be the minimum practical; do not exceed 180 mg/kg/hour.
Administration Administer through an I.V. line containing an in-line filter (pore size 15 micron) using an infusion pump. Do not mix with other infusions; do not use if turbid. Begin infusion within 6 hours of entering vial, complete infusion within 12 hours.

Infuse at 15 mg/kg/hour. If no adverse reactions occur within 30 minutes, may increase rate to 30 mg/kg/hour. If no adverse reactions occur within the second 30 minutes, may increase rate to 60 mg/kg/hour; maximum rate of infusion: 75 mL/hour. When infusing subsequent doses, may decrease titration interval from 30 minutes to 15 minutes. If patient develops nausea, back pain, or flushing during infusion, slow the rate or temporarily stop the infusion. Discontinue if blood pressure drops or in case of anaphylactic reaction.
Monitoring Parameters Vital signs (throughout infusion), flushing, chills, muscle cramps, back pain, fever, nausea, vomiting, wheezing, decreased blood pressure, or anaphylaxis; renal function and urine output
Dosage Forms Injection, solution [preservative free]: 50 mg ± 10 mg/mL (50 mL) [contains human albumin and sucrose]

- **Cytomel®** see Liothyronine on page 1020
- **Cytosar® (Can)** see Cytarabine on page 437
- **Cytosar-U®** see Cytarabine on page 437
- **Cytosine Arabinosine Hydrochloride** see Cytarabine on page 437

- **Cytotec®** *see* Misoprostol *on page 1154*
- **Cytovene®** *see* Ganciclovir *on page 779*
- **Cytoxan®** *see* Cyclophosphamide *on page 428*
- **Cytra-2** *see* Sodium Citrate and Citric Acid *on page 1579*
- **Cytra-3** *see* Citric Acid, Sodium Citrate, and Potassium Citrate *on page 383*
- **Cytra-K** *see* Potassium Citrate and Citric Acid *on page 1398*
- **Cēpacol® Dual Action Maximum Strength [OTC]** *see* Dyclonine *on page 565*
- **D2E7** *see* Adalimumab *on page 47*
- **D-3-Mercaptovaline** *see* Penicillamine *on page 1330*
- **d4T** *see* Stavudine *on page 1599*
- **DAB₃₈₉IL-2** *see* Denileukin Diftitox *on page 471*

Dacarbazine (da KAR ba zeen)

U.S. Brand Names DTIC-Dome®
Canadian Brand Names DTIC®
Index Terms DIC; Dimethyl Triazeno Imidazole Carboxamide; DTIC; Imidazole Carboxamide; Imidazole Carboxamide Dimethyltriazene; WR-139007
Pharmacologic Category Antineoplastic Agent, Alkylating Agent (Triazene)
Use Treatment of malignant melanoma, Hodgkin's disease, soft-tissue sarcomas, fibrosarcomas, rhabdomyosarcoma, islet cell carcinoma, medullary carcinoma of the thyroid, and neuroblastoma
Pregnancy Risk Factor C
Lactation Excretion in breast milk unknown/not recommended
Medication Safety Issues
Sound-alike/look-alike issues:
Dacarbazine may be confused with Dicarbosil®, procarbazine

High alert medication: The Institute for Safe Medication Practices (ISMP) includes this medication among its list of drugs which have a heightened risk of causing significant patient harm when used in error.

Contraindications Hypersensitivity to dacarbazine or any component of the formulation
Warnings/Precautions Hazardous agent - use appropriate precautions for handling and disposal. **[U.S. Boxed Warnings]: Bone marrow suppression is a common toxicity; monitor closely. Hepatotoxicity with hepatocellular necrosis and hepatic vein thrombosis has been reported,** usually with combination chemotherapy, but may occur with dacarbazine alone. The half-life is increased in patients with renal and/or hepatic impairment; use caution, monitor for toxicity and consider dosage reduction. Anaphylaxis may occur. Extravasation may result in tissue damage and pain. **[U.S. Boxed Warnings]: May be carcinogenic and/or teratogenic. Should be administered under the supervision of an experienced cancer chemotherapy physician.**
Adverse Reactions
>10%:
Gastrointestinal: Nausea and vomiting (>90%), can be severe and dose limiting; nausea and vomiting decrease on successive days when dacarbazine is given daily for 5 days; diarrhea
Hematologic: Myelosuppression, leukopenia, thrombocytopenia - dose limiting
Onset: 5-7 days
Nadir: 7-10 days
Recovery: 21-28 days
Local: Pain on infusion, may be minimized by administration through a central line, or by administration as a short infusion (eg, 1-2 hours as opposed to bolus injection)
1% to 10%:
Dermatologic: Alopecia, rash, photosensitivity
Gastrointestinal: Anorexia, metallic taste
Miscellaneous: Flu-like syndrome (fever, myalgia, malaise)
<1% (Limited to important or life-threatening): Anaphylactic reactions, diarrhea (following high-dose bolus injection), eosinophilia, headache, hepatic necrosis, hepatic vein occlusion, liver enzymes increased (transient), paresthesia
Overdosage/Toxicology Symptoms include myelosuppression and diarrhea. There are no known antidotes and treatment is primarily symptomatic and supportive.
Drug Interactions
Cytochrome P450 Effect: Substrate (major) of CYP1A2, 2E1
Increased Effect/Toxicity: CYP1A2 inhibitors may increase the levels/effects of dacarbazine; example inhibitors include ciprofloxacin, fluvoxamine, ketoconazole, norfloxacin, ofloxacin, and rofecoxib. CYP2E1 inhibitors may increase the levels/effects of dacarbazine; example inhibitors include disulfiram, isoniazid, and miconazole.
Decreased Effect: CYP1A2 inducers may decrease the levels/effects of dacarbazine; example inducers include aminoglutethimide, carbamazepine, phenobarbital, and rifampin. Patients may experience impaired immune response to vaccines; possible infection after administration of live vaccines in patients receiving immunosuppressants.
Ethanol/Nutrition/Herb Interactions
Ethanol: Avoid ethanol (due to GI irritation).
Herb/Nutraceutical: Avoid dong quai, St John's wort (may also cause photosensitization).
Stability Store intact vials under refrigeration (2°C to 8°C) and protect from light; vials are stable for 4 weeks at room temperature. Reconstituted solution is stable for 24 hours at room temperature (20°C) and 96 hours under refrigeration (4°C). Solutions for infusion (in D₅W or NS) are stable for 24 hours at room temperature and protected from light. Decomposed drug turns pink.
The manufacturer recommends reconstituting 100 mg and 200 mg vials with 9.9 mL and 19.7 mL SWFI, respectively, to a concentration of 10 mg/mL; some institutions use different standard dilutions (eg, 20 mg/mL).

Standard I.V. dilution: Dilute in 250-1000 mL D_5W or NS.

Mechanism of Action Alkylating agent which appears to form methylcarbonium ions that attack nucleophilic groups in DNA; cross-links strands of DNA resulting in the inhibition of DNA, RNA, and protein synthesis, the exact mechanism of action is still unclear.

Pharmacodynamics/Kinetics

Onset of action: I.V.: 18-24 days

Distribution: V_d: 0.6 L/kg, exceeding total body water; suggesting binding to some tissue (probably liver)

Protein binding: 5%

Metabolism: Extensively hepatic; hepatobiliary excretion is probably of some importance; metabolites may also have an antineoplastic effect

Half-life elimination: Biphasic: Initial: 20-40 minutes; Terminal: 5 hours

Excretion: Urine (~30% to 50% as unchanged drug)

Dosage Refer to individual protocols. Some dosage regimens include:

Intra-arterial: 50-400 mg/m² for 5-10 days

I.V.:

Hodgkin's disease, ABVD: 375 mg/m² days 1 and 15 every 4 weeks **or** 100 mg/m²/day for 5 days

Metastatic melanoma (alone or in combination with other agents): 150-250 mg/m² days 1-5 every 3-4 weeks

Metastatic melanoma: 850 mg/m² every 3 weeks

High dose: Bone marrow/blood cell transplantation: I.V.: 1-3 g/m²; maximum dose as a single agent: 3.38 g/m²; generally combined with other high-dose chemotherapeutic drugs

Dosage adjustment in renal/hepatic impairment: No guidelines exist for adjustment

Administration Infuse over 30-60 minutes; rapid infusion may cause severe venous irritation.

Extravasation management: Local pain, burning sensation, and irritation at the injection site may be relieved by local application of hot packs. If extravasation occurs, apply cold packs. Protect exposed tissue from light following extravasation.

Monitoring Parameters CBC with differential, liver function

Dosage Forms

Injection, powder for reconstitution: 100 mg, 200 mg, 500 mg

DTIC-Dome®: 200 mg

Daclizumab (dac KLYE zue mab)

U.S. Brand Names Zenapax®

Canadian Brand Names Zenapax®

Pharmacologic Category Immunosuppressant Agent

Use Part of an immunosuppressive regimen (including cyclosporine and corticosteroids) for the prophylaxis of acute organ rejection in patients receiving renal transplant

Unlabeled/Investigational Use Graft-versus-host disease; prevention of organ rejection after heart transplant

Pregnancy Risk Factor C

Pregnancy Implications Animal reproduction studies have not been conducted. Generally, IgG molecules cross the placenta. Do not use during pregnancy unless the potential benefit to the mother outweighs the possible risk to the fetus. Women of childbearing potential should use effective contraception before, during, and for 4 months following treatment.

Lactation Excretion in breast milk unknown/use caution

Contraindications Hypersensitivity to daclizumab or any component of the formulation

Warnings/Precautions Only physicians experienced in immunosuppressive therapy and management of organ transplant patients should prescribe daclizumab. Manage patients receiving the drug in facilities equipped and staffed with adequate laboratory and supportive medical resources. Readministration of daclizumab after an initial course of therapy has not been studied in humans. The potential risks of such readministration, specifically those associated with immunosuppression or the occurrence of anaphylaxis/anaphylactoid reactions, are not known. **[U.S. Boxed Warning]: Should be administered under the supervision of a physician experienced in immunosuppressive therapy.**

Adverse Reactions Although reported adverse events are frequent, when daclizumab is compared with placebo the incidence of adverse effects is similar between the two groups. Many of the adverse effects reported during clinical trial use of daclizumab may be related to the patient population, transplant procedure, and concurrent transplant medications. Diarrhea, fever, postoperative pain, pruritus, respiratory tract infection, urinary tract infection, and vomiting occurred more often in children than adults.

≥5%:

Cardiovascular: Chest pain, edema, hyper-/hypotension, tachycardia, thrombosis

Central nervous system: Dizziness, fatigue, fever, headache, insomnia, pain, post-traumatic pain, tremor

Dermatologic: Acne, cellulitis, wound healing impaired

Gastrointestinal: Abdominal distention, abdominal pain, constipation, diarrhea, dyspepsia, epigastric pain, nausea, pyrosis, vomiting

Genitourinary: Dysuria

Hematologic: Bleeding

Neuromuscular & skeletal: Back pain, musculoskeletal pain

Renal: Oliguria, renal tubular necrosis

Respiratory: Cough, dyspnea, pulmonary edema

Miscellaneous: Lymphocele, wound infection

≥2% to <5%:

Central nervous system: Anxiety, depression, shivering

Dermatologic: Hirsutism, pruritus, rash

Endocrine & metabolic: Dehydration, diabetes mellitus, fluid overload

Gastrointestinal: Flatulence, gastritis, hemorrhoids

Genitourinary: Urinary retention, urinary tract bleeding

Local: Application site reaction

(Continued)

Daclizumab *(Continued)*

Neuromuscular & skeletal: Arthralgia, leg cramps, myalgia, weakness

Ocular: Vision blurred

Renal: Hydronephrosis, renal damage, renal insufficiency

Respiratory: Atelectasis, congestion, hypoxia, pharyngitis, pleural effusion, rales, rhinitis

Miscellaneous: Night sweats, prickly sensation, diaphoresis

<1% (Limited to important or life-threatening): Severe hypersensitivity reactions (rare): Anaphylaxis, bronchospasm, cardiac arrest, cytokine release syndrome, hypotension, laryngeal edema, pulmonary edema, pruritus, urticaria

Overdosage/Toxicology Overdose has not been reported.

Drug Interactions

Increased Effect/Toxicity: The combined use of daclizumab, cyclosporine, mycophenolate mofetil, and corticosteroids has been associated with an increased mortality in a population of cardiac transplant recipients, particularly in patients who received antilymphocyte globulin and in patients with severe infections.

Stability Refrigerate vials at 2°C to 8°C (36°F to 46°F). Do not shake or freeze; protect undiluted solution against direct sunlight. Dose should be further diluted in 50 mL 0.9% sodium chloride solution. When mixing, gently invert bag to avoid foaming; do not shake. Do not use if solution is discolored. Diluted solution is stable for 24 hours at 4°C or for 4 hours at room temperature. Do not mix with other medications or infuse other medications through same I.V. line.

Mechanism of Action Daclizumab is a chimeric (90% human, 10% murine) monoclonal IgG antibody produced by recombinant DNA technology. Daclizumab inhibits immune reactions by binding and blocking the alpha-chain of the interleukin-2 receptor (CD25) located on the surface of activated lymphocytes.

Pharmacodynamics/Kinetics

Distribution: V_d:

Adults: Central compartment: 0.031 L/kg; Peripheral compartment: 0.043 L/kg

Children: Central compartment: 0.067 L/kg; Peripheral compartment: 0.047 L/kg

Half-life elimination (estimated): Adults: Terminal: 20 days; Children: 13 days

Dosage Daclizumab is used adjunctively with other immunosuppressants (eg, cyclosporine, corticosteroids, mycophenolate mofetil, and azathioprine): I.V.:

Children: Use same weight-based dose as adults

Adults:

Immunoprophylaxis against acute renal allograft rejection: 1 mg/kg infused over 15 minutes within 24 hours before transplantation (day 0), then every 14 days for 4 additional doses

Treatment of graft-versus-host disease (unlabeled use, limited data): 0.5-1.5 mg/kg, repeat same dosage for transient response. Repeat doses have been administered 11-48 days following the initial dose.

Prevention of organ rejection after heart transplant (unlabeled use): 1 mg/kg up to a maximum of 100 mg; administer within 12 hours after heart transplant and on days 8, 22, 36, and 50 post-transplant

Dosage adjustment in renal impairment: No adjustment needed.

Dosage adjustment in hepatic impairment: No data available for patients with severe impairment.

Administration For I.V. administration following dilution. Daclizumab solution should be administered within 4 hours of preparation if stored at room temperature; infuse over a 15-minute period via a peripheral or central vein.

Dosage Forms Injection, solution [preservative free]: 5 mg/mL (5 mL)

♦ **Dacogen**™ *see* Decitabine *on page 463*

♦ **DACT** *see* Dactinomycin *on page 444*

Dactinomycin *(dak ti noe MYE sin)*

U.S. Brand Names Cosmegen®

Canadian Brand Names Cosmegen®

Index Terms ACT; Act-D; Actinomycin; Actinomycin Cl; Actinomycin D; DACT; NSC-3053

Pharmacologic Category Antineoplastic Agent, Antibiotic

Use Treatment of testicular tumors, melanoma, gestational trophoblastic neoplasm, Wilms' tumor, neuroblastoma, retinoblastoma, rhabdomyosarcoma, uterine sarcomas, Ewing's sarcoma, Kaposi's sarcoma, sarcoma botryoides, and soft tissue sarcoma

Pregnancy Risk Factor D

Pregnancy Implications Animal studies have demonstrated teratogenic effects and fetal loss There are no adequate and well-controlled studies in pregnant women. Women of childbearing potential are advised not to become pregnant. Use only when potential benefit justifies potential risk to the fetus.

Lactation Excretion in breast milk unknown/contraindicated

Medication Safety Issues

Sound-alike/look-alike issues:

Dactinomycin may be confused with daptomycin, DAUNOrubicin

Actinomycin may be confused with Achromycin

High alert medication: The Institute for Safe Medication Practices (ISMP) includes this medication among its list of drugs which have a heightened risk of causing significant patient harm when used in error.

Contraindications Hypersensitivity to dactinomycin or any component of the formulation; patients with concurrent or recent chickenpox or herpes zoster; avoid in infants <6 months of age

Warnings/Precautions [U.S. Boxed Warnings]: Hazardous agent - use appropriate precautions for handling and disposal. Dactinomycin is extremely irritating to tissues and must be administered I.V.; if extravasation occurs during I.V. use, severe damage to soft tissues will occur. Avoid inhalation of vapors or contact with skin, mucous

membrane, or eyes; avoid exposure during pregnancy. Dosage is usually expressed in **MICRO**grams, **NOT** milligrams, and must be calculated on the basis of body surface area (BSA) in obese or edematous adult patients. Dactinomycin potentiates the effects of radiation therapy; use with caution in patients who have received radiation therapy; reduce dosages in patients who are receiving dactinomycin and radiation therapy simultaneously; combination with radiation therapy may result in increased GI toxicity and myelosuppression. Avoid dactinomycin use within 2 months of radiation treatment for right-sided Wilms' tumor, may increase the risk of hepatotoxicity. Toxic effects may be delayed in onset (2-4 days following a course of treatment) and may require 1-2 weeks to reach maximum severity. Avoid administration of live vaccines. Use caution in hepatobiliary dysfunction; may cause veno-occlusive liver disease, increased risk in children <4 years of age. Long-term observation of cancer survivors is recommended due to the potential for secondary primary tumors following treatment with radiation and antineoplastic agents. **[U.S. Boxed Warning]: Should be administered under the supervision of an experienced cancer chemotherapy physician.**

Adverse Reactions Frequency not defined.

Central nervous system: Fatigue, fever, lethargy, malaise

Dermatologic: Acne, alopecia (reversible), cheilitis; increased pigmentation, sloughing, or erythema of previously irradiated skin; skin eruptions

Endocrine & metabolic: Growth retardation, hypocalcemia

Gastrointestinal: Abdominal pain, anorexia, diarrhea, dysphagia, esophagitis, GI ulceration, mucositis, nausea, pharyngitis, proctitis, stomatitis, vomiting

Hematologic: Agranulocytosis, anemia, aplastic anemia, leukopenia, pancytopenia, reticulocytopenia, thrombocytopenia, myelosuppression (onset: 7 days, nadir: 14-21 days, recovery: 21-28 days)

Hepatic: Ascites, hepatic failure, hepatitis, hepatomegaly, hepatotoxicity, liver function test abnormality, veno-occlusive disease

Local: Erythema, edema, epidermolysis, pain, tissue necrosis, and ulceration (following extravasation)

Neuromuscular & skeletal: Myalgia

Renal: Renal function abnormality

Respiratory: Pneumonitis

Miscellaneous: Anaphylactoid reaction, infection

Overdosage/Toxicology Symptoms include nausea, vomiting, diarrhea, depression, GI ulceration, mucositis, severe myelosuppression, skin disorders (eg, exanthema, desquamation, epidermolysis), stomatitis, veno-occlusive disease, acute renal failure and fatality. Treatment is symptom-directed and supportive. Toxic effects may not be apparent until 2-4 days after a treatment course (peak after 1-2 weeks).

Drug Interactions

Increased Effect/Toxicity: Administration of live vaccines during treatment with dactinomycin should be avoided.

Stability Store at controlled room temperature of 15°C to 30°C (59°F to 86°F); protect from light and humidity. Dilute with 1.1 mL of preservative-free SWI to yield a final concentration of 500 mcg/mL. Solutions in 50 mL D$_5$W or NS are stable for 24 hours at room temperature. Do not use preservative diluent, as precipitation may occur. Cellulose ester membrane filters should not be used during preparation.

Mechanism of Action Binds to the guanine portion of DNA intercalating between guanine and cytosine base pairs inhibiting DNA and RNA synthesis and protein synthesis

Pharmacodynamics/Kinetics

Distribution: High concentrations found in bone marrow and tumor cells, submaxillary gland, liver, and kidney; crosses placenta; poor CSF penetration

Metabolism: Hepatic, minimal

Half-life elimination: ~36 hours

Time to peak, serum: I.V.: 2-5 minutes

Excretion: Bile (50%); feces (14%); urine (~10% as unchanged drug)

Dosage Refer to individual protocols:

Note: Medication orders for dactinomycin are commonly written in MICROgrams (eg, 150 mcg) although many regimens list the dose in MILLIgrams (eg, mg/kg or mg/m^2). One-time doses for >1000 mcg, or multiple-day doses for >500 mcg/day are not common. The dose intensity per 2-week cycle for adults and children should not exceed 15 mcg/kg/day for 5 days or 400-600 mcg/m^2/day for 5 days. Some practitioners recommend calculation of the dosage for obese or edematous adult patients on the basis of body surface area in an effort to relate dosage to lean body mass.

Children >6 months: I.V.: Usual dose: 15 mcg/kg/day **or** 400-600 mcg/m^2/day for 5 days every 3-6 weeks

Wilms' tumor, rhabdomyosarcoma, Ewing's sarcoma: 15 mcg/kg/day for 5 days (in various combination regimens and schedules)

Adults: I.V.:

Usual doses:

2.5 mg/m^2 in divided doses over 1 week, repeated every 2 weeks **or**

0.75-2 mg/m^2 every 1-4 weeks **or**

400-600 mcg/m^2/day for 5 days, repeated every 3-6 weeks

Testicular cancer: 1000 mcg/m^2 on day 1 (as part of a combination chemotherapy regimen)

Gestational trophoblastic neoplasm: 12 mcg/kg/day for 5 days **or** 500 mcg days 1 and 2 (as part of a combination chemotherapy regimen)

Wilms' tumor, Ewing's sarcoma: 15 mcg/kg/day for 5 days (in various combination regimens and schedules)

Elderly: Elderly patients are at increased risk of myelosuppression; dosing should begin at the low end of the dosing range.

Dosage adjustment in renal impairment: No adjustment required

Administration Do not administer I.M. or SubQ. Administer by slow I.V. push or infuse over 10-15 minutes. Avoid extravasation. Do not filter with cellulose ester membrane filters.

Monitoring Parameters CBC with differential and platelet count, liver function tests, and renal function tests

Test Interactions May interfere with bioassays of antibacterial drug levels

(Continued)

Dactinomycin (Continued)

Dosage Forms
Injection, powder for reconstitution:
Cosmegen®: 0.5 mg [contains mannitol 20 mg]

- ◆ **DAD** see Mitoxantrone on page 1157
- ◆ **Dakin's Solution** see Sodium Hypochlorite Solution on page 1579
- ◆ **Dalacin® C (Can)** see Clindamycin on page 389
- ◆ **Dalacin® T (Can)** see Clindamycin on page 389
- ◆ **Dalacin® Vaginal (Can)** see Clindamycin on page 389
- ◆ **Dallergy®** see Chlorpheniramine, Phenylephrine, and Methscopolamine on page 353
- ◆ **Dallergy-JR®** see Chlorpheniramine and Phenylephrine on page 349
- ◆ **Dalmane®** see Flurazepam on page 733
- ◆ **d-Alpha-Gems™ [OTC]** see Vitamin E on page 1794
- ◆ **d-Alpha Tocopherol** see Vitamin E on page 1794

Dalteparin (dal TE pa rin)

U.S. Brand Names Fragmin®
Canadian Brand Names Fragmin®
Pharmacologic Category Low Molecular Weight Heparin
Additional Appendix Information
Anticoagulants, Injectable on page 1864

Use Prevention of deep vein thrombosis which may lead to pulmonary embolism, in patients requiring abdominal surgery who are at risk for thromboembolism complications (eg, patients >40 years of age, obesity, patients with malignancy, history of deep vein thrombosis or pulmonary embolism, and surgical procedures requiring general anesthesia and lasting >30 minutes); prevention of DVT in patients undergoing hip-replacement surgery; patients immobile during an acute illness; acute treatment of unstable angina or non-Q-wave myocardial infarction; prevention of ischemic complications in patients on concurrent aspirin therapy

Unlabeled/Investigational Use Active treatment of deep vein thrombosis

Pregnancy Risk Factor B

Pregnancy Implications Multiple-dose vials contain benzyl alcohol (avoid in pregnant women due to association with fetal syndrome in premature infants).

Lactation Excretion in breast milk unknown/use caution

Contraindications Hypersensitivity to dalteparin or any component of the formulation; thrombocytopenia associated with a positive *in vitro* test for antiplatelet antibodies in the presence of dalteparin; hypersensitivity to heparin or pork products; patients with active major bleeding; patients with unstable angina or non-Q-wave MI undergoing regional anesthesia; not for I.M. or I.V. use

Warnings/Precautions Use with caution in patients with pre-existing thrombocytopenia, recent childbirth, subacute bacterial endocarditis, peptic ulcer disease, pericarditis or pericardial effusion, liver or renal function impairment, recent lumbar puncture, vasculitis, concurrent use of aspirin (increased bleeding risk), previous hypersensitivity to heparin, heparin-associated thrombocytopenia. Monitor platelet count closely. Rare thrombocytopenia may occur. Consider discontinuation of dalteparin in any patient developing significant thrombocytopenia. Rare cases of thrombocytopenia with thrombosis have occurred. Use caution in patients with congenital or drug-induced thrombocytopenia or platelet defects. If thromboembolism develops despite dalteparin prophylaxis, dalteparin should be discontinued and appropriate treatment should be initiated.

Use with caution in patients with known hypersensitivity to methylparaben or propylparaben. Monitor patient closely for signs or symptoms of bleeding. Certain patients are at increased risk of bleeding. Risk factors include bacterial endocarditis; congenital or acquired bleeding disorders; active ulcerative or angiodysplastic GI diseases; severe uncontrolled hypertension; hemorrhagic stroke; or use shortly after brain, spinal, or ophthalmology surgery; in patient treated concomitantly with platelet inhibitors; recent GI bleeding; thrombocytopenia or platelet defects; severe liver disease; hypertensive or diabetic retinopathy; or in patients undergoing invasive procedures.

Use with caution in patients with severe renal failure (has not been studied). Safety and efficacy in pediatric patients have not been established. Rare cases of thrombocytopenia with thrombosis have occurred. Multidose vials contain benzyl alcohol and should not be used in pregnant women. In neonates, large amounts of benzyl alcohol (>100 mg/kg/day) have been associated with fatal toxicity (gasping syndrome). Heparin can cause hyperkalemia by affecting aldosterone. Similar reactions could occur with LMWHs. Monitor for hyperkalemia. Do **not** administer intramuscularly.

[U.S. Boxed Warning]: Patients with recent or anticipated neuraxial anesthesia (epidural or spinal anesthesia) are at risk of spinal or epidural hematoma and subsequent paralysis. Consider risk versus benefit prior to neuraxial anesthesia. Risk is increased by concomitant agents which may alter hemostasis, as well as traumatic or repeated epidural or spinal puncture. Patient should be observed closely for bleeding if dalteparin is administered during or immediately following diagnostic lumbar puncture, epidural anesthesia, or spinal anesthesia.

Adverse Reactions
1% to 10%:
Hematologic: Bleeding (3% to 5%), wound hematoma (0.1% to 3%)
Local: Pain at injection site (up to 12%), injection site hematoma (0.2% to 7%)
<1% (Limited to important or life-threatening): Allergic reaction (fever, pruritus, rash, injection site reaction, bullous eruption), anaphylactoid reaction, gastrointestinal bleeding, injection site hematoma, operative site bleeding, skin necrosis, thrombocytopenia (including heparin-induced thrombocytopenia). Spinal or epidural hematomas can occur following neuraxial anesthesia or spinal puncture, resulting in paralysis. Risk is increased in patients

with indwelling epidural catheters or concomitant use of other drugs affecting hemostasis, osteoporosis (3-6 month use).

Drug Interactions

Increased Effect/Toxicity: The risk of bleeding with dalteparin may be increased by drugs which affect platelet function (eg, aspirin, NSAIDs, dipyridamole, ticlopidine, clopidogrel), oral anticoagulants, and thrombolytic agents. Although the risk of bleeding may be increased during concurrent warfarin therapy, dalteparin is commonly continued during the initiation of warfarin therapy to assure anticoagulation and to protect against possible transient hypercoagulability.

Ethanol/Nutrition/Herb Interactions Herb/Nutraceutical: Avoid cat's claw, dong quai, evening primrose, garlic, ginseng (all have additional antiplatelet activity).

Stability Store at temperatures 20°C to 25°C (68°F to 77°F).

Mechanism of Action Low molecular weight heparin analog with a molecular weight of 4000-6000 daltons; the commercial product contains 3% to 15% heparin with a molecular weight <3000 daltons, 65% to 78% with a molecular weight of 3000-8000 daltons and 14% to 26% with a molecular weight >8000 daltons; while dalteparin has been shown to inhibit both factor Xa and factor IIa (thrombin), the antithrombotic effect of dalteparin is characterized by a higher ratio of antifactor Xa to antifactor IIa activity (ratio = 4)

Pharmacodynamics/Kinetics

Onset of action: 1-2 hours

Duration: >12 hours

Half-life elimination (route dependent): 2-5 hours

Time to peak, serum: 4 hours

Dosage Adults: SubQ:

Abdominal surgery:

Low-to-moderate DVT risk: 2500 int. units 1-2 hours prior to surgery, then once daily for 5-10 days postoperatively

High DVT risk: 5000 int. units 1-2 hours prior to surgery and then once daily for 5-10 days postoperatively

Patients undergoing total hip surgery: **Note:** Three treatment options are currently available. Dose is given for 5-10 days, although up to 14 days of treatment have been tolerated in clinical trials:

Postoperative start:

Initial: 2500 int. units 4-8 hours* after surgery

Maintenance: 5000 int. units once daily; start at least 6 hours after postsurgical dose

Preoperative (starting day of surgery):

Initial: 2500 int. units within 2 hours before surgery

Adjustment: 2500 int. units 4-8 hours* after surgery

Maintenance: 5000 int. units once daily; start at least 6 hours after postsurgical dose

Preoperative (starting evening prior to surgery):

Initial: 5000 int. units 10-14 hours before surgery

Adjustment: 5000 int. units 4-8 hours* after surgery

Maintenance: 5000 int. units once daily, allowing 24 hours between doses.

*Dose may be delayed if hemostasis is not yet achieved.

Unstable angina or non-Q-wave myocardial infarction: 120 int. units/kg body weight (maximum dose: 10,000 int. units) every 12 hours for 5-8 days with concurrent aspirin therapy. Discontinue dalteparin once patient is clinically stable.

Immobility during acute illness: 5000 int. units once daily

Dosing adjustment in renal impairment: Half-life is increased in patients with chronic renal failure, use with caution, accumulation can be expected; specific dosage adjustments have not been recommended

Dosing adjustment in hepatic impairment: Use with caution in patients with hepatic insufficiency; specific dosage adjustments have not been recommended

Administration For deep SubQ injection only. May be injected in a U-shape to the area surrounding the navel, the upper outer side of the thigh, or the upper outer quadrangle of the buttock. Apply pressure to injection site; do not massage. Use thumb and forefinger to lift a fold of skin when injecting dalteparin to the navel area or thigh. Insert needle at a 45- to 90-degree angle. The entire length of needle should be inserted. Do not expel air bubble from fixed-dose syringe prior to injection. Air bubble (and extra solution, if applicable) may be expelled from graduated syringes.

Administration once daily beginning prior to surgery and continuing 5-10 days after surgery prevents deep vein thrombosis in patients at risk for thromboembolic complications. For unstable angina or non-Q-wave myocardial infarction, dalteparin is administered every 12 hours until the patient is stable (5-8 days).

Monitoring Parameters Periodic CBC including platelet count; stool occult blood tests; monitoring of PT and PTT is not necessary

Additional Information Multidose vial contains 14 mg/mL benzyl alcohol.

Dosage Forms

Injection, solution [multidose vial]: Antifactor Xa 10,000 int. units per 1 mL (9.5 mL) [contains benzyl alcohol]; antifactor Xa 25,000 units per 1 mL (3.8 mL) [contains benzyl alcohol]

Injection, solution [preservative free; prefilled syringe]: Antifactor Xa 2500 int. units per 0.2 mL (0.2 mL); antifactor Xa 5000 int. units per 0.2 mL (0.2 mL); antifactor Xa 7500 int. units per 0.3 mL (0.3 mL); antifactor Xa 10,000 int. units per 1 mL (1 mL)

♦ **Damason-P®** see Hydrocodone and Aspirin on page 849

Danazol (DA na zole)

U.S. Brand Names Danocrine® [DSC]

Canadian Brand Names Cyclomen®; Danocrine®

Pharmacologic Category Androgen

Use Treatment of endometriosis, fibrocystic breast disease, and hereditary angioedema

Pregnancy Risk Factor X

(Continued)

Danazol (Continued)

Pregnancy Implications Pregnancy should be ruled out prior to treatment using a sensitive test (beta subunit test, if available). Nonhormonal contraception should be used during therapy. May cause androgenic effects to the female fetus; clitoral hypertrophy, labial fusion, urogenital sinus defect, vaginal atresia, and ambiguous genitalia have been reported.

Lactation Enters breast milk/contraindicated

Medication Safety Issues
Sound-alike/look-alike issues:
Danazol may be confused with Dantrium®
Danocrine® may be confused with Dacriose®

Contraindications Hypersensitivity to danazol or any component of the formulation; undiagnosed genital bleeding; pregnancy; breast-feeding; porphyria; markedly impaired hepatic, renal, or cardiac function

Warnings/Precautions Use with caution in patients with seizure disorders, migraine, or conditions influenced by edema. **[U.S. Boxed Warning]: Thromboembolism, thrombotic, and thrombophlebitic events have been reported (including life-threatening or fatal strokes). [U.S. Boxed Warning]: Peliosis hepatis and benign hepatic adenoma have been reported with long-term use. [U.S. Boxed Warning]: May cause benign intracranial hypertension.** Breast cancer should be ruled out prior to treatment for fibrocystic breast disease. May increase risk of atherosclerosis and coronary artery disease. May cause nonreversible androgenic effects. **[U.S. Boxed Warning]: Pregnancy must be ruled out prior to treatment.** Safety and efficacy in pediatric patients have not been established.

Adverse Reactions Frequency not defined.
Cardiovascular: Benign intracranial hypertension (rare), edema, flushing, hypertension
Central nervous system: Anxiety (rare), chills (rare), convulsions (rare), depression, dizziness, emotional lability, fainting, fever (rare), Guillain-Barré syndrome, headache, nervousness, sleep disorders, tremor
Dermatologic: Acne, hair loss, mild hirsutism, maculopapular rash, papular rash, petechial rash, pruritus, purpuric rash, seborrhea, Stevens-Johnson syndrome (rare), photosensitivity (rare), urticaria, vesicular rash
Endocrine & metabolic: Amenorrhea (which may continue post therapy), breast size reduction, clitoris hypertrophy, glucose intolerance, HDL decreased, LDL increased, libido changes, nipple discharge, menstrual disturbances (spotting, altered timing of cycle), semen abnormalities (changes in volume, viscosity, sperm count/motility), spermatogenesis reduction
Gastrointestinal: Appetite changes (rare), bleeding gums (rare), constipation, gastroenteritis, nausea, pancreatitis (rare), vomiting, weight gain
Genitourinary: Vaginal dryness, vaginal irritation, pelvic pain
Hematologic: Eosinophilia, erythrocytosis (reversible), leukocytosis, leukopenia, platelet count increased, polycythemia, RBC increased, thrombocytopenia
Hepatic: Cholestatic jaundice, hepatic adenoma, jaundice, liver enzymes (elevated), malignant tumors (after prolonged use), peliosis hepatis
Neuromuscular & skeletal: Back pain, carpal tunnel syndrome (rare), CPK abnormalities, extremity pain, joint lockup, joint pain, joint swelling, muscle cramps, neck pain, paresthesia, spasms, weakness
Ocular: Cataracts (rare), visual disturbances
Renal: Hematuria
Respiratory: Nasal congestion (rare)
Miscellaneous: Voice change (hoarseness, sore throat, instability, deepening of pitch), diaphoresis

Drug Interactions
Cytochrome P450 Effect: Inhibits CYP3A4 (weak)
Increased Effect/Toxicity: Danazol may increase serum levels of carbamazepine, cyclosporine, tacrolimus, and warfarin leading to toxicity; dosage adjustment may be needed; monitor. Concomitant use of danazol and HMG-CoA reductase inhibitors may lead to severe myopathy or rhabdomyolysis. Danazol may enhance the glucose-lowering effect of hypoglycemic agents.
Decreased Effect: Danazol may decrease effectiveness of hormonal contraceptives. Nonhormonal birth control methods are recommended.

Ethanol/Nutrition/Herb Interactions Food: Delays time to peak; high-fat meal increases plasma concentration

Stability Store at controlled room temperature of 15°C to 30°C (59°F to 86°F).

Mechanism of Action Suppresses pituitary output of follicle-stimulating hormone and luteinizing hormone that causes regression and atrophy of normal and ectopic endometrial tissue; decreases rate of growth of abnormal breast tissue; reduces attacks associated with hereditary angioedema by increasing levels of C4 component of complement

Pharmacodynamics/Kinetics
Onset of action: Therapeutic: ~4 weeks
Metabolism: Extensively hepatic, primarily to 2-hydroxymethylethisterone
Half-life elimination: 4.5 hours (variable)
Time to peak, serum: Within 2 hours
Excretion: Urine

Dosage Adults: Oral:
Female: Endometriosis: Initial: 200-400 mg/day in 2 divided doses for mild disease; individualize dosage. Usual maintenance dose: 800 mg/day in 2 divided doses to achieve amenorrhea and rapid response to painful symptoms. Continue therapy uninterrupted for 3-6 months (up to 9 months).
Female: Fibrocystic breast disease: Range: 100-400 mg/day in 2 divided doses
Male/Female: Hereditary angioedema: Initial: 200 mg 2-3 times/day; after favorable response, decrease the dosage by 50% or less at intervals of 1-3 months or longer if the frequency of attacks dictates. If an attack occurs, increase the dosage by up to 200 mg/day.

Monitoring Parameters Signs and symptoms of intracranial hypertension (papilledema, headache, nausea, vomiting), lipoproteins, androgenic changes, hepatic function

Test Interactions Testosterone, androstenedione, dehydroepiandrosterone

Dosage Forms [DSC] = Discontinued product
Capsule: 50 mg, 100 mg, 200 mg
Danocrine®: 50 mg, 100 mg, 200 mg [DSC]

♦ **Danocrine® [DSC]** see Danazol on page 447
♦ **Danocrine® (Can)** see Danazol on page 447
♦ **Dantrium®** see Dantrolene on page 449

Dantrolene (DAN troe leen)

U.S. Brand Names Dantrium®
Canadian Brand Names Dantrium®
Index Terms Dantrolene Sodium
Pharmacologic Category Skeletal Muscle Relaxant
Use Treatment of spasticity associated with spinal cord injury, stroke, cerebral palsy, or multiple sclerosis; treatment of malignant hyperthermia
Unlabeled/Investigational Use Neuroleptic malignant syndrome (NMS)
Pregnancy Risk Factor C
Lactation Excretion in breast milk unknown/not recommended
Medication Safety Issues
Sound-alike/look-alike issues:
Dantrium® may be confused with danazol, Daraprim®
Contraindications Active hepatic disease; should not be used where spasticity is used to maintain posture or balance
Warnings/Precautions Use with caution in patients with impaired cardiac function or impaired pulmonary function. **[U.S. Boxed Warning]: Has potential for hepatotoxicity.** Overt hepatitis has been most frequently observed between the third and twelfth month of therapy. Hepatic injury appears to be greater in females and in patients >35 years of age.
Adverse Reactions
>10%:
Central nervous system: Drowsiness, dizziness, lightheadedness, fatigue
Dermatologic: Rash
Gastrointestinal: Diarrhea (mild), vomiting
Neuromuscular & skeletal: Muscle weakness
1% to 10%:
Cardiovascular: Pleural effusion with pericarditis
Central nervous system: Chills, fever, headache, insomnia, nervousness, mental depression
Gastrointestinal: Diarrhea (severe), constipation, anorexia, stomach cramps
Ocular: Blurred vision
Respiratory: Respiratory depression
<1% (Limited to important or life-threatening): Confusion, hepatic necrosis, hepatitis, seizure
Overdosage/Toxicology Symptoms include CNS depression, hypotension, nausea, and vomiting. For decontamination, lavage/activated charcoal with cathartic; do not use ipecac. Hypotension can be treated with isotonic I.V. fluids with the patient placed in the Trendelenburg position. Dopamine or norepinephrine can be given if hypotension is refractory to the above therapy.
Drug Interactions
Cytochrome P450 Effect: Substrate of CYP3A4 (major)
Increased Effect/Toxicity: Increased toxicity with estrogens (hepatotoxicity), CNS depressants (sedation), MAO inhibitors, phenothiazines, clindamycin (increased neuromuscular blockade), verapamil (hyperkalemia and cardiac depression), warfarin, clofibrate, and tolbutamide. CYP3A4 inhibitors may increase the levels/effects of dantrolene; example inhibitors include azole antifungals, clarithromycin, diclofenac, doxycycline, erythromycin, imatinib, isoniazid, nefazodone, nicardipine, propofol, protease inhibitors, quinidine, telithromycin, and verapamil.
Decreased Effect: CYP3A4 inducers may decrease the levels/effects of dantrolene; example inducers include aminoglutethimide, carbamazepine, nafcillin, nevirapine, phenobarbital, phenytoin, and rifamycins.
Ethanol/Nutrition/Herb Interactions
Ethanol: Avoid ethanol (may increase CNS depression).
Herb/Nutraceutical: Avoid valerian, St John's wort, kava kava, gotu kola (may increase CNS depression).
Stability Reconstitute vial by adding 60 mL of sterile water for injection USP (**not bacteriostatic water for injection**). Protect from light. Use within 6 hours; avoid glass bottles for I.V. infusion.
Mechanism of Action Acts directly on skeletal muscle by interfering with release of calcium ion from the sarcoplasmic reticulum; prevents or reduces the increase in myoplasmic calcium ion concentration that activates the acute catabolic processes associated with malignant hyperthermia
Pharmacodynamics/Kinetics
Absorption: Oral: Slow and incomplete
Metabolism: Hepatic
Half-life elimination: 8.7 hours
Excretion: Feces (45% to 50%); urine (25% as unchanged drug and metabolites)
Dosage
Spasticity: Oral:
Children: Initial: 0.5 mg/kg/dose twice daily, increase frequency to 3-4 times/day at 4- to 7-day intervals, then increase dose by 0.5 mg/kg to a maximum of 3 mg/kg/dose 2-4 times/day up to 400 mg/day
(Continued)

Dantrolene (Continued)

Adults: 25 mg/day to start, increase frequency to 2-4 times/day, then increase dose by 25 mg every 4-7 days to a maximum of 100 mg 2-4 times/day or 400 mg/day

Malignant hyperthermia: Children and Adults:
Preoperative prophylaxis:
Oral: 4-8 mg/kg/day in 4 divided doses, begin 1-2 days prior to surgery with last dose 3-4 hours prior to surgery
I.V.: 2.5 mg/kg ~1¼ hours prior to anesthesia and infused over 1 hour with additional doses as needed and individualized
Crisis: I.V.: 2.5 mg/kg; may repeat dose up to cumulative dose of 10 mg/kg; if physiologic and metabolic abnormalities reappear, repeat regimen
Postcrisis follow-up: Oral: 4-8 mg/kg/day in 4 divided doses for 1-3 days; I.V. dantrolene may be used when oral therapy is not practical; individualize dosage beginning with 1 mg/kg or more as the clinical situation dictates
Neuroleptic malignant syndrome (unlabeled use): I.V.: 1 mg/kg; may repeat dose up to maximum cumulative dose of 10 mg/kg, then switch to oral dosage
Administration I.V.: Therapeutic or emergency dose can be administered with rapid continuous I.V. push. Follow-up doses should be administered over 2-3 minutes.
Monitoring Parameters Motor performance should be monitored for therapeutic outcomes; nausea, vomiting, and liver function tests should be monitored for potential hepatotoxicity; intravenous administration requires cardiac monitor and blood pressure monitor
Dosage Forms
Capsule, as sodium: 25 mg, 50 mg, 100 mg
Dantrium®: 25 mg, 50 mg, 100 mg
Injection, powder for reconstitution, as sodium:
Dantrium®: 20 mg [contains mannitol 3 g]
Extemporaneous Preparations A 5 mg/mL suspension may be made by adding five 100 mg capsules to a citric acid solution (150 mg citric acid powder in 10 mL water) and then adding syrup to a total volume of 100 mL; stable 2 days in refrigerator
Nahata MC and Hipple TF, *Pediatric Drug Formulations*, 1st ed, Cincinnati, OH: Harvey Whitney Books Co, 1990.

♦ **Dantrolene Sodium** see Dantrolene on page 449
♦ **Dapcin** see Daptomycin on page 452

Dapiprazole (DA pi pray zole)

U.S. Brand Names Rēv-Eyes™
Index Terms Dapiprazole Hydrochloride
Pharmacologic Category Alpha₁ Blocker, Ophthalmic
Use Reverse dilation due to drugs (adrenergic or parasympathomimetic) after eye exams
Pregnancy Risk Factor B
Dosage Adults: Ophthalmic: Instill 2 drops followed 5 minutes later by an additional 2 drops into the conjunctiva of each eye; should not be used more frequently than once a week in the same patient
Additional Information Complete prescribing information for this medication should be consulted for additional detail.
Dosage Forms Powder, ophthalmic, as hydrochloride: 25 mg [contains benzalkonium chloride; 0.5% solution when mixed with supplied diluent]

♦ **Dapiprazole Hydrochloride** see Dapiprazole on page 450

Dapsone (DAP sone)

U.S. Brand Names Aczone™
Index Terms Diaminodiphenylsulfone
Pharmacologic Category Antibiotic, Miscellaneous; Topical Skin Product, Acne
Additional Appendix Information
Antimicrobial Drugs of Choice on page 1981
Sulfonamide Derivatives on page 1897
USPHS / IDSA Guidelines for the Prevention of Opportunistic Infections in Persons Infected With HIV on page 1966
Use Treatment of leprosy and dermatitis herpetiformis (infections caused by *Mycobacterium leprae*); treatment of acne vulgaris
Unlabeled/Investigational Use Prophylaxis of toxoplasmosis in severely-immunocompromised patients; alternative agent for *Pneumocystis carinii* pneumonia prophylaxis (monotherapy) and treatment (in combination with trimethoprim)
Pregnancy Risk Factor C
Pregnancy Implications There are no adequate and well-controlled studies in pregnant women. Use during pregnancy when the benefit to the mother outweighs the potential risk to the fetus.
Lactation Enters breast milk/not recommended (AAP rates "compatible")
Medication Safety Issues
Sound-alike/look-alike issues:
Dapsone may be confused with Diprosone®
Contraindications Hypersensitivity to dapsone or any component of the formulation
Warnings/Precautions Use with caution in patients with severe anemia, G6PD, methemoglobin reductase or hemoglobin M deficiency; hypersensitivity to other sulfonamides; aplastic anemia, agranulocytosis and other severe blood dyscrasias have resulted in death; monitor carefully; serious dermatologic reactions (including toxic epidermal necrolysis) are rare but potential occurrences; sulfone reactions may also occur as potentially fatal hypersensitivity reactions; these, but not leprosy reactional states, require drug discontinuation. Safety and

efficacy of topical dapsone has not been adequately evaluated in patient with G6PD deficiency or in patients <12 years of age.

Adverse Reactions

>10%: Hematologic: Hemolysis (dose related; seen in patients with and without G6PD deficiency), hemoglobin decrease (1-2 g/dL - almost all patients), reticulocyte increase (2% to 12%), methemoglobinemia, red cell life span shortened

Frequency not defined.

Cardiovascular: Tachycardia

Central nervous system: Fever, headache, insomnia, psychosis, tonic-clonic movement (topical), vertigo

Dermatologic: Bullous and exfoliative dermatitis, erythema nodosum, exfoliative dermatitis (oral), morbilliform and scarlatiniform reactions, phototoxicity (oral), Stevens-Johnson syndrome, toxic epidural necrolysis, urticaria

Endocrine & metabolic: Hypoalbuminemia (without proteinuria), male infertility

Gastrointestinal: Abdominal pain (oral, topical), nausea, pancreatitis (oral, topical), vomiting

Hematologic: Agranulocytosis, anemia, leukopenia, pure red cell aplasia (case report)

Hepatic: Cholestatic jaundice, hepatitis

Neuromuscular & skeletal: Drug-induced lupus erythematosus, lower motor neuron toxicity (prolonged therapy), peripheral neuropathy (rare, nonleprosy patients)

Ocular: Blurred vision

Otic: Tinnitus

Renal: Albuminuria, nephrotic syndrome, renal papillary necrosis

Respiratory: Interstitial pneumonitis, pharyngitis (topical), pulmonary eosinophilia

Miscellaneous: Infectious mononucleosis-like syndrome (rash, fever, lymphadenopathy, hepatic dysfunction)

Overdosage/Toxicology Symptoms include nausea, vomiting, confusion, hyperexcitability, seizures, cyanosis, hemolysis, methemoglobinemia, sulfhemoglobinemia, metabolic acidosis, hallucinations, and hepatitis. Following decontamination, methylene blue 1-2 mg/kg I.V. is the treatment of choice if MHb level is >15%; may repeat every 6-8 hours for 2-3 days if needed. If hemolysis is present, give I.V. fluids and alkalinize urine to prevent acute tubular necrosis.

Drug Interactions

Cytochrome P450 Effect: Substrate of CYP2C8 (minor), 2C9 (major), 2C19 (minor), 2E1 (minor), 3A4 (major)

Increased Effect/Toxicity: Folic acid antagonists (methotrexate) may increase the risk of hematologic reactions of dapsone; probenecid decreases dapsone excretion; trimethoprim with dapsone may increase toxic effects of both drugs. CYP2C9 Inhibitors may increase the levels/effects of dapsone; example inhibitors include delavirdine, fluconazole, gemfibrozil, ketoconazole, nicardipine, NSAIDs, sulfonamides and tolbutamide. CYP3A4 inhibitors may increase the levels/effects of dapsone; example inhibitors include azole antifungals, clarithromycin, diclofenac, doxycycline, erythromycin, imatinib, isoniazid, nefazodone, nicardipine, propofol, protease inhibitors, quinidine, telithromycin, and verapamil.

Decreased Effect: CYP2C9 Inducers may decrease the levels/effects of dapsone; example inducers include carbamazepine, phenobarbital, phenytoin, rifampin, rifapentine, and secobarbital.CYP3A4 inducers may decrease the levels/effects of dapsone; example inducers include aminoglutethimide, carbamazepine, efavirenz, fosphenytoin, nafcillin, nevirapine, oxcarbazine, phenobarbital, phenytoin, primidone, and rifamycins. Didanosine (except enteric coated capsules) may decrease absorption of dapsone.

Ethanol/Nutrition/Herb Interactions Herb/Nutraceutical: St John's wort may decrease dapsone levels.

Stability

Gel: Store at 20°C to 25°C (68°F to 76°F); protect from freezing; protect from light. Keep tube in original box.

Tablet: Store at 20°C to 25°C (68°F to 76°F); protect from light.

Mechanism of Action Competitive antagonist of para-aminobenzoic acid (PABA) and prevents normal bacterial utilization of PABA for the synthesis of folic acid

Pharmacodynamics/Kinetics

Absorption:

Oral: Well absorbed

Topical: ~1% of the absorption of 100 mg tablet

Distribution: V_d: 1.5 L/kg; throughout total body water and present in all tissues, especially liver and kidney

Metabolism: Hepatic; forms metabolite

Half-life elimination: 30 hours (range: 10-50 hours)

Excretion: Urine (~85%)

Dosage Oral:

Leprosy:

Children: 1-2 mg/kg/24 hours, up to a maximum of 100 mg/day

Adults: 50-100 mg/day for 3-10 years

Dermatitis herpetiformis: Adults: Start at 50 mg/day, increase to 300 mg/day, or higher to achieve full control, reduce dosage to minimum level as soon as possible

Pneumocystis carinii pneumonia (unlabeled use):

Prophylaxis:

Children >1 month: 2 mg/kg/day once daily (maximum dose: 100 mg/day) or 4 mg/kg/dose once weekly (maximum dose: 200 mg)

Adults: 100 mg/day

Treatment: Adults: 100 mg/day in combination with trimethoprim (15-20 mg/kg/day) for 21 days

Topical: Acne vulgaris: Children ≥12 years and Adults: Apply pea-sized amount twice daily

Dosing in renal impairment: No specific guidelines are available

Dietary Considerations Do not administer with antacids, alkaline foods, or drugs.

(Continued)

Dapsone *(Continued)*

Administration
Oral: May give with meals if GI upset occurs.

Topical: Apply to clean, dry skin; rub in completely. Wash hands after application.

Monitoring Parameters
Check G6PD levels prior to initiation

Oral: Monitor patients for signs of jaundice and hemolysis; CBC weekly for first month, monthly for 6 months and semiannually thereafter.

Topical: For patients at risk of anemia, monitor with CBC, reticulocyte counts at baseline and routinely thereafter.

Dosage Forms
Gel, topical (Aczone™): 5% (30 g)

Tablet: 25 mg, 100 mg

Extemporaneous Preparations
One report indicated that dapsone may not be well absorbed when administered to children as suspensions made from pulverized tablets

Mirochnick M, Clarke D, Brenn A, et al, "Low Serum Dapsone Concentrations in Children Receiving an Extemporaneously Prepared Oral Formulation," [Abstract Th B 365], APS-SPR, Baltimore, MD: 1992.

Jacobus Pharmaceutical Company (609) 921-7447 makes a 2 mg/mL proprietary liquid formulation available under an IND for the prophylaxis of *Pneumocystis carinii* pneumonia

♦ **Daptacel®** *see* Diphtheria, Tetanus Toxoids, and Acellular Pertussis Vaccine *on page 521*

Daptomycin (DAP toe mye sin)

U.S. Brand Names
Cubicin®

Index Terms
Cidecin; Dapcin; LY146032

Pharmacologic Category
Antibiotic, Cyclic Lipopeptide

Additional Appendix Information
Antimicrobial Drugs of Choice *on page 1981*

Use
Treatment of complicated skin and skin structure infections caused by susceptible aerobic Gram-positive organisms; *Staphylococcus aureus* bacteremia, including right-sided infective endocarditis caused by MSSA or MRSA

Unlabeled/Investigational Use
Treatment of severe infections caused by MRSA or VRE

Pregnancy Risk Factor
B

Pregnancy Implications
Teratogenic effects were not observed in animal studies. There are no adequate and well-controlled studies in pregnant women; use in pregnancy only if clearly needed.

Lactation
Excretion in breast milk unknown/use caution

Medication Safety Issues
Sound-alike/look-alike issues:

Daptomycin may be confused with dactinomycin

Contraindications
Hypersensitivity to daptomycin or any component of the formulation

Warnings/Precautions
May be associated with an increased incidence of myopathy; discontinue in patients with signs and symptoms of myopathy in conjunction with an increase in CPK (>5 times ULN or 1000 units/L) or in asymptomatic patients with a CPK ≥10 times ULN. Myopathy may occur more frequently at dose and/or frequency in excess of recommended dosages. Use caution in patients receiving other drugs associated with myopathy (eg, HMG-CoA reductase inhibitors). Not indicated for the treatment of pneumonia (poor lung penetration). Use caution in renal impairment (dosage adjustment required). Symptoms suggestive of peripheral neuropathy have been observed with treatment; monitor for new-onset or worsening neuropathy. Superinfection by resistant strains and/or pseudomembranous colitis may be associated with use. Safety and efficacy in patients <18 years of age have not been established.

Adverse Reactions
>10%:

Cardiovascular: Anemia (2% to 13%)

Gastrointestinal: Diarrhea (5% to 12%), vomiting (3% to 12%), constipation (6% to 11%)

1% to 10%:

Cardiovascular: Peripheral edema (7%), chest pain (7%), hypertension (1% to 6%), hypotension (2% to 5%)

Central nervous system: Insomnia (5% to 9%), headache (5% to7%), fever (2% to 7%), dizziness (2% to 6%), anxiety (5%)

Dermatologic: Rash (4% to 7%), pruritus (3% to 6%), erythema (5%)

Endocrine & metabolic: Hypokalemia (9%), hyperkalemia (5%), hyperphosphatemia (3%)

Gastrointestinal: Nausea (6% to 10%), abdominal pain (6%), dyspepsia (1% to 4%), loose stool (4%), GI hemorrhage (2%)

Genitourinary: Urinary tract infection (2% to 7%)

Hematologic: INR increased (2%), eosinophilia (2%)

Hepatic: Transaminases increased (2% to 3%), alkaline phosphatase increased (2%)

Local: Injection site reaction (3% to 6%)

Neuromuscular & skeletal: CPK increased (3% to 9%), limb pain (2% to 9%), back pain (7%), weakness (5%), arthralgia (1% to 3%)

Renal: Renal failure (2% to 3%)

Respiratory: Pharyngolaryngeal pain (8%), pleural effusion (6%), cough (3%), pneumonia (3%), dyspnea (2% to 3%)

Miscellaneous: Osteomyelitis (6%), bacteremia (5%), diaphoresis (5%), sepsis (5%), infection (fungal, 2% to 3%)

<1% (Limited to important or life-threatening): Anaphylaxis, appetite decreased, arthralgia, atrial fibrillation, atrial flutter, cardiac arrest, dyskinesia, dysphagia, eczema, electrolyte disturbance, eosinophilia, erythema (truncal), eye irritation, fatigue, flatulence, flushing, GI discomfort, gingival pain, hallucination, hives, hypomagnesemia, hypersensitivity, hypoesthesia, jaundice, jitteriness, LDH increased, leukocytosis, lymphadenopathy, mental status

change, muscle cramps, muscle weakness, myalgia, osteomyelitis, paresthesia, protein-uria, prothrombin time prolonged, rhabdomyolysis, rigors, serum bicarbonate increased, stomatitis, supraventricular arrhythmia, taste disturbance, thrombocytopenia, thrombocy-themia, tinnitus, vertigo, vision blurred, xerostomia

Overdosage/Toxicology Treatment is symptomatic and supportive; hemodialysis removes approximately 15% in 4 hours.

Drug Interactions

Increased Effect/Toxicity: No clinically-significant interactions have been identified.

Stability Store under refrigeration at 2°C to 8°C (36°F to 46°F). Reconstitute vial with 10 mL NS. Should be further diluted following reconstitution in an appropriate volume of NS. Do not shake or agitate vial vigorously. Reconstituted solution (either in vial or in infusion bag) is stable for a cumulative time of 12 hours at room temperature and 48 hours if refrigerated (2°C to 8°C).

Mechanism of Action Daptomycin binds to components of the cell membrane of susceptible organisms and causes rapid depolarization, inhibiting intracellular synthesis of DNA, RNA, and protein. Daptomycin is bactericidal in a concentration-dependent manner.

Pharmacodynamics/Kinetics

Distribution: 0.1 L/kg

Protein binding: 90% to 93%; 84% to 88% in patients with Cl_{cr}<30 mL/minute

Half-life elimination: 8-9 hours (up to 28 hours in renal impairment)

Excretion: Urine (78%; primarily as unchanged drug); feces (6%)

Dosage I.V.: Adults:

Skin and soft tissue: 4 mg/kg once daily for 7-14 days

Bacteremia, right-sided endocarditis caused by MSSA or MRSA: 6 mg/kg once daily for 2-6 weeks

Dosage adjustment in renal impairment: Cl_{cr} <30 mL/minute:

Skin and soft tissue infections: 4 mg/kg every 48 hours

Staphylococcal bacteremia: 6 mg/kg every 48 hours

Hemodialysis (administer after hemodialysis) and/or CAPD: Dose as in Cl_{cr} <30 mL/minute

Dosage adjustment in hepatic impairment: No adjustment required for mild-to-moderate impairment (Child-Pugh Class A or B); not evaluated in severe hepatic impairment

Administration Infuse over 30 minutes.

Monitoring Parameters Monitor signs and symptoms of infection. CPK should be monitored at least weekly during therapy; more frequent monitoring if current or prior statin therapy, unexplained CPK increases, and/or renal impairment. Monitor for muscle pain or weakness, especially if noted in distal extremities.

Reference Range

Trough concentrations at steady-state:

4 mg/kg once daily: 5.9 ± 1.6 mcg/mL

6 mg/kg once daily: 6.7 ± 1.6 mcg/mL

Note: Trough concentrations are not predictive of efficacy/toxicity. Drug exhibits concentration-dependent bactericidal activity, so C_{max}:MIC ratios may be a more useful parameter.

Test Interactions Daptomycin may cause false prolongation of the PT and increase of INR with certain reagents. This appears to be a dose-dependent phenomenon. Therefore, it is recommended to obtain blood samples immediately prior to next daptomycin dose (eg, trough). If PT/INR elevated, clinicians should repeat PT/INR and evaluate for other causes of hypocoagulation.

Dosage Forms

Injection, powder for reconstitution:

Cubicin®: 500 mg

♦ **Daraprim®** see Pyrimethamine on page 1464

Darbepoetin Alfa (dar be POE e tin AL fa)

U.S. Brand Names Aranesp®

Canadian Brand Names Aranesp®

Index Terms Erythropoiesis Stimulating Protein

Pharmacologic Category Colony Stimulating Factor; Growth Factor; Recombinant Human Erythropoietin

Use Treatment of anemia associated with chronic renal failure (CRF), including patients on dialysis (ESRD) and patients not on dialysis; anemia associated with chemotherapy for nonmyeloid malignancies

Pregnancy Risk Factor C

Pregnancy Implications There are no adequate and well-controlled studies in pregnant women. Darbepoetin alfa should be used in a pregnant woman only if potential benefit justifies the potential risk to the fetus.

Lactation Excretion in breast milk unknown/use caution

Medication Safety Issues

Sound-alike/look-alike issues:

Darbepoetin alfa may be confused with epoetin alfa

Contraindications Hypersensitivity to darbepoetin or any component of the formulation; uncontrolled hypertension

Warnings/Precautions Erythropoietic therapies may be associated with an increased risk of cardiovascular and/or neurologic events. Darbepoetin alfa should be managed carefully; avoid hemoglobin increases >1 g/dL in any 2-week period, and do not exceed a target level of 12 g/dL. Prior to and during therapy, iron stores must be evaluated. Supplemental iron is recommended if serum ferritin <100 mcg/mL or serum transferrin saturation <20%. In cancer patients, the risk of thrombotic events (eg, pulmonary emboli, thrombophlebitis, thrombosis) was increased by erythropoietic therapy.

Use with caution in patients with hypertension or with a history of seizures; hypertensive encephalopathy and seizures have been reported. If hypertension is difficult to control, reduce or hold darbepoetin alpha. **Not** recommended for acute correction of severe anemia

(Continued)

Darbepoetin Alfa *(Continued)*

or as a substitute for transfusion. Consider discontinuing in patients who receive a renal transplant.

Prior to treatment, correct or exclude deficiencies of vitamin B_{12} and/or folate, as well as other factors which may impair erythropoiesis (aluminum toxicity, inflammatory conditions, infections). Poor response should prompt evaluation of these potential factors, as well as possible malignant processes, occult blood loss, hemolysis, and/or bone marrow fibrosis. Pure red cell aplasia (PRCA) with associated neutralizing antibodies to erythropoietin has been reported, predominantly in patients with CRF. Patients with loss of response to darbepoetin alfa should be evaluated. Discontinue treatment in patients with PRCA secondary to neutralizing antibodies to erythropoietin.

Due to the delayed onset of erythropoiesis, darbepoetin is of no value in the acute treatment of anemia. Safety and efficacy in patients with underlying hematologic diseases have not been established, including porphyria, thalassemia, hemolytic anemia, and sickle cell disease. Potentially serious allergic reactions have been reported. Do not shake solution; vigorous shaking may denature darbepoetin alfa, rendering it biologically inactive. Safety and efficacy (as initial treatment) in children have not been established; children >1 year of age with CRF have been converted from epoetin alfa to darbepoetin.

Adverse Reactions
>10%:
   Cardiovascular: Hypertension (4% to 23%), hypotension (22%), edema (21%), peripheral edema (11%)
   Central nervous system: Fatigue (9% to 33%), fever (4% to 19%), headache (12% to 16%), dizziness (8% to 14%)
   Gastrointestinal: Diarrhea (16% to 22%), constipation (5% to 18%), vomiting (2% to 15%), nausea (14%), abdominal pain (12%)
   Neuromuscular & skeletal: Myalgia (8% to 21%), arthralgia (11% to 13%)
   Respiratory: Upper respiratory infection (14%), dyspnea (2% to 12%)
   Miscellaneous: Infection (27%)
1% to 10%:
   Cardiovascular: Arrhythmia (10%), angina/chest pain (6% to 8%), fluid overload (6%), CHF (6%), thrombosis (6%), MI (2%)
   Central nervous system: Seizure (≤1%), stroke (1%), TIA (1%)
   Dermatologic: Pruritus (8%), rash (7%)
   Endocrine & metabolic: Dehydration (3% to 5%)
   Local: Vascular access thrombosis (8%), injection site pain (7%), vascular access hemorrhage (6%), vascular access infection (6%)
   Neuromuscular & skeletal: Limb pain (10%), back pain (8%), weakness (5%)
   Respiratory: Cough (10%), bronchitis (6%), pneumonia (3%), pulmonary embolism (1%)
   Miscellaneous: Death (7% to 10 %; similar to placebo), flu-like syndrome (6%)
Postmarketing and/or case reports: Deep vein thrombosis, pure red cell aplasia, severe anemia (with or without other cytopenias), thromboembolism, thrombophlebitis

Overdosage/Toxicology The maximum amount of darbepoetin has not been determined. However, cardiovascular and neurologic adverse events have been correlated to excessive and/or rapid rise in hemoglobin. Phlebotomy may be performed if clinically indicated.

Ethanol/Nutrition/Herb Interactions Ethanol: Should be avoided due to adverse effects on erythropoiesis.

Stability Store at 2°C to 8°C (36°F to 46°F). Do not freeze or shake. Protect from light. Do not dilute or administer with other solutions.

Mechanism of Action Induces erythropoiesis by stimulating the division and differentiation of committed erythroid progenitor cells; induces the release of reticulocytes from the bone marrow into the bloodstream, where they mature to erythrocytes. There is a dose response relationship with this effect. This results in an increase in reticulocyte counts followed by a rise in hematocrit and hemoglobin levels. When administered SubQ or I.V., darbepoetin's half-life is ~3 times that of epoetin alfa concentrations.

Pharmacodynamics/Kinetics
Onset of action: Increased hemoglobin levels not generally observed until 2-6 weeks after initiating treatment
Absorption: SubQ: Slow
Distribution: V_d: 0.06 L/kg
Bioavailability: CRF: SubQ: ~37% (range: 30% to 50%)
Half-life elimination: CRF: Terminal: I.V.: 21 hours, SubQ: 49 hours; cancer: SubQ: 74 hours
   Note: Half-life is ~3 times as long as epoetin alfa
Time to peak: SubQ: CRF: 34 hours (range: 24-72 hours); Cancer: 90 hours (range: 71-123 hours)

Dosage Adults:
Anemia associated with CRF: I.V., SubQ: Initial: 0.45 mcg/kg once weekly; titrate to response; some patients may respond to doses given once every 2 weeks
   Unlabeled dosing:
      Every 2-weeks: 0.75 mcg/kg every 2 weeks (Toto, 2004)
      or
      Every 4-weeks: 0.75 mcg/kg every 2 weeks; once titrated, multiply dose by 2 and give every 4 weeks (Jadoul, 2004).
   Dosage adjustment:
      Inadequate response: Increase dose by ~25% (not more frequently than once a month) for hemoglobin increase <1 g/dL after 4 weeks
      Excessive response:
         Decrease dose by ~25% when hemoglobin increases >1 g/dL in any 2-week period **or** hemoglobin increases and approaches 12 g/dL in any 2-week period
         Hold dose, then decrease dose by ~25% when hemoglobin increases despite previous dose decrease (hold until hemoglobin decreases)
Anemia associated with chemotherapy: SubQ: Initial: 2.25 mcg/kg once weekly; with inadequate response after 6 weeks: 4.5 mcg/kg once weekly
   or
   500 mcg once every 3 weeks

Unlabeled dosing:
Every 2 weeks:
Initial: 200 mcg every 2 weeks; inadequate response: 300 mcg every 2 weeks (Thames, 2003)
or
Initial: 3 mcg/kg every 2 weeks; inadequate response: 5 mcg/kg every 2 weeks (Vadhan-Raj, 2003)
or
Every 3 weeks (front load): Initial:
4.5 mcg/kg every week until desired Hgb obtained; maintenance: 4.5 mcg/kg (or titrated dose) every 3 weeks (Hesketh, 2004)
or
Initial: 325 mcg every week until desired Hgb obtained; maintenance: 325 mcg every 3 weeks (Hesketh, 2004)
Dosage adjustment: Titration may be required to limit rises of Hgb to <1 g/dL over any 2-week interval and to reach a hemoglobin concentration not to exceed 12 g/dL.
Inadequate response: Increase dose up to 4.5 mcg/kg when hemoglobin increase <1 g/dL after 4-6 weeks
Excessive response:
Decrease dose by ~40% when hemoglobin increases >1 g/dL in any 2-week period **or** hemoglobin exceeds 11 g/dL in any 2-week period
Hold dose, then decrease dose by ~40% when hemoglobin increases despite previous dose decrease (hold until hemoglobin decreases) **or** when hemoglobin ≥13 g/dL (hold until hemoglobin ≤12 g/dL)
Conversion from epoetin alfa to darbepoetin alfa: See table.

Conversion From Epoetin Alfa to Darbepoetin Alfa

Previous Dosage of Epoetin Alfa (units/week)	Children Darbepoetin Alfa Dosage (mcg/week)	Adults Darbepoetin Alfa Dosage (mcg/week)	Adults Darbepoetin Alfa Dosage (mcg/every 2 weeks)
<1500	Not established	6.25	12.5
1500-2499	6.25	6.25	12.5
2500-4999	10	12.5	25
5000-10,999	20	25	50
11,000-17,999	40	40	80
18,000-33,999	60	60	120
34,000-89,999	100	100	200
≥90,000	200	200	400

Note: In patients receiving epoetin alfa 2-3 times per week, darbepoetin alfa is administered once weekly. In patients receiving epoetin alfa once weekly, darbepoetin alfa is administered once every 2 weeks.

Dosage adjustment in renal impairment: Dosage requirements for patients with chronic renal failure who do not require dialysis may be lower than in dialysis patients. Monitor patients closely during the time period in which a dialysis regimen is initiated, dosage requirement may increase.

Dietary Considerations Supplemental iron intake may be required in patients with low iron stores.

Administration May be administered by SubQ or I.V. injection. The I.V. route is recommended in hemodialysis patients. Do not shake; vigorous shaking may denature darbepoetin alfa, rendering it biologically inactive. Do not dilute or administer in conjunction with other drug solutions. Discard any unused portion of the vial; do not pool unused portions.

Monitoring Parameters Hemoglobin (weekly until maintenance dose established and after dosage changes; monitor at regular intervals once hemoglobin is stabilized); iron stores (prior to and during therapy); blood pressure

Dosage Forms [DSC] = Discontinued product
Injection, solution [preservative free; contains human albumin 2.5 mg/mL; single-dose vial]:
Aranesp®: 25 mcg/mL (1 mL); 40 mcg/mL (1 mL); 60 mcg/mL (1 mL); 100 mcg/mL (1 mL); 150 mcg/0.75 mL (0.75 mL); 200 mcg/mL (1 mL); 300 mcg/mL (1 mL)
Injection, solution [preservative free; contains human albumin 2.5 mg/mL; prefilled syringe]:
Aranesp®: 25 mcg/0.42 mL (0.42 mL); 40 mcg/0.4 mL (0.4 mL); 60 mcg/0.3 mL (0.3 mL); 100 mcg/0.5 mL (0.5 mL); 150 mcg/0.3 mL (0.3 mL); 200 mcg/0.4 mL (0.4 mL); 300 mcg/0.6 mL (0.6 mL); 500 mcg/mL (1 mL) [DSC]
Injection, solution [preservative free; contains polysorbate 80; prefilled syringe]:
Aranesp®: 500 mcg/mL (1 mL)

Darifenacin (dar i FEN a sin)

U.S. Brand Names Enablex®
Canadian Brand Names Enablex®
Index Terms Darifenacin Hydrobromide; UK-88,525
Pharmacologic Category Anticholinergic Agent
Use Management of symptoms of bladder overactivity (urge incontinence, urgency, and frequency)
Pregnancy Risk Factor C
Pregnancy Implications Teratogenic effects and developmental delay were observed in some animal studies. There are no adequate and well-controlled studies in pregnant women; should be used only if potential benefit outweighs possible risk to the fetus.
(Continued)

Darifenacin *(Continued)*

Lactation Excretion in breast milk unknown/use caution

Contraindications Hypersensitivity to darifenacin or any component of the formulation; uncontrolled narrow-angle glaucoma; urinary retention, paralytic ileus, GI or GU obstruction

Warnings/Precautions Use with caution with hepatic impairment; dosage limitation is required in moderate hepatic impairment (Child-Pugh Class B). Not recommended for use in severe hepatic impairment (Child-Pugh Class C). Use with caution in patients with clinically-significant bladder outlet obstruction or prostatic hyperplasia (nonobstructive).Use caution in patients with decreased GI motility, constipation, hiatal hernia, reflux esophagitis, and ulcerative colitis. Use caution in patients with myasthenia gravis. In patients with controlled narrow-angle glaucoma, darifenacin should be used with extreme caution and only when the potential benefit outweighs risks of treatment. Safety and efficacy have not been established in pediatric patients.

Adverse Reactions

>10%: Gastrointestinal: Xerostomia (19% to 35%), constipation (15% to 21%)

1% to 10%:

Cardiovascular: Hypertension, peripheral edema

Central nervous system: Headache (7%), dizziness (1% to 2%)

Gastrointestinal: Dyspepsia (3% to 8%), abdominal pain (2% to 4%), nausea (2% to 4%), diarrhea (1% to 2%), vomiting, weight gain

Genitourinary: Urinary tract infection (4% to 5%), urinary retention, urinary tract disorder, vaginitis

Neuromuscular & skeletal: Weakness (2% to 3%), arthralgia, back pain

Ocular: Dry eyes (2%), abnormal vision

Respiratory: Bronchitis, pharyngitis, rhinitis, sinusitis

Miscellaneous: Flu-like syndrome (<1% to 3%), accidental injury (<1% to 3%)

Overdosage/Toxicology Doses of up to 75 mg have been used in clinical trials, with abnormal vision as the primary adverse event. Overdose may result in severe antimuscarinic effects. Treatment should be symptom-directed and supportive. ECG monitoring is recommended.

Drug Interactions

Cytochrome P450 Effect: Substrate of CYP2D6 (minor), CYP3A4 (major); **Inhibits** CYP2D6 (moderate), 3A4 (weak)

Increased Effect/Toxicity: Adverse anticholinergic effects may be additive with other anticholinergic agents (includes tricyclic antidepressants, antihistamines, and phenothiazines). Coadministration with pramlintide may result an additive reduction in gut motility. Darifenacin may increase the levels/effects of CYP2D6 substrates; example substrates include amphetamines, selected beta-blockers, dextromethorphan, fluoxetine, lidocaine, mirtazapine, nefazodone, paroxetine, risperidone, ritonavir, thioridazine, tricyclic antidepressants, and venlafaxine. CYP3A4 inhibitors may increase the levels/effects of darifenacin; example inhibitors include azole antifungals, clarithromycin, diclofenac, doxycycline, erythromycin, imatinib, isoniazid, nefazodone, nicardipine, propofol, protease inhibitors, quinidine, telithromycin, and verapamil.

Decreased Effect: Darifenacin may decrease the levels/effects of CYP2D6 prodrug substrates; example prodrug substrates include codeine, hydrocodone, oxycodone, and tramadol. CYP3A4 inducers may decrease the levels/effects of darifenacin; example inducers include aminoglutethimide, carbamazepine, nafcillin, nevirapine, phenobarbital, phenytoin, and rifamycins. Concomitant use with acetylcholinesterase inhibitors may reduce the therapeutic efficacy of darifenacin.

Stability Store at 25°C (77°F); excursions permitted to 15°C to 30°C (59°F to 86°F). Protect from light.

Mechanism of Action Selective antagonist of the M3 muscarinic (cholinergic) receptor subtype. Blockade of the receptor limits bladder contractions, reducing the symptoms of bladder irritability/overactivity (urge incontinence, urgency and frequency).

Pharmacodynamics/Kinetics

Distribution: V_{dss}: 163 L

Protein binding: 98%

Metabolism: Hepatic, via CYP3A4 (major) and CYP2D6 (minor)

Bioavailability: 15% to 19%

Half-life elimination: 13-19 hours

Time to peak, plasma: 7 hours

Excretion: As metabolites (inactive); urine (60%), feces (40%)

Dosage Oral: Adults: Initial: 7.5 mg once daily. If response is not adequate after a minimum of 2 weeks, dosage may be increased to 15 mg once daily.

Dosage adjustment with concomitant potent CYP3A4 inhibitors: Daily dosage should not exceed 7.5 mg/day

Dosage adjustment in renal impairment: No adjustment required.

Dosage adjustment in hepatic impairment:

Moderate impairment (Child-Pugh Class B): Daily dosage should not exceed 7.5 mg/day

Severe impairment (Child-Pugh Class C): Has not been evaluated; use is not recommended

Dietary Considerations May be taken without regard to meals, with or without food.

Administration Tablet should be taken with liquid and swallowed whole; do not chew, crush or split tablet. May be taken without regard to food.

Dosage Forms Tablet, extended release: 7.5 mg, 15 mg

♦ **Darifenacin Hydrobromide** *see* Darifenacin *on page 455*

Darunavir (dar OO na veer)

U.S. Brand Names Prezista™
Index Terms Darunavir Ethanolate; TMC-114
Pharmacologic Category Antiretroviral Agent, Protease Inhibitor
Additional Appendix Information
 Antiretroviral Therapy for HIV Infection: Adults and Adolescents *on page 1988*
 Management of Healthcare Worker Exposures to HBV, HCV, and HIV *on page 1941*
Use Treatment of HIV-1 infections in combination with ritonavir and other antiretroviral agents; limited to highly treatment-experienced or multiprotease inhibitor-resistant patients
Pregnancy Risk Factor B
Pregnancy Implications It is not known if darunavir crosses the human placenta. No teratogenicity has been demonstrated in animal studies. However, there are no adequate and well-controlled studies in pregnant women. Pregnancy and protease inhibitors are both associated with an increased risk of hyperglycemia. Glucose levels should be closely monitored. Women receiving estrogen (as hormonal contraception or replacement therapy) have an increased incidence of rash. Alternative forms of contraception may be needed. Health professionals are encouraged to contact the antiretroviral pregnancy registry to monitor outcomes of pregnant women exposed to antiretroviral medications (1-800-258-4263 or www.APRegistry.com).
Lactation Excretion in breast milk unknown/not recommended
Contraindications Hypersensitivity to darunavir or any component of the formulation; concurrent therapy with cisapride, dihydroergotamine, ergonovine, ergotamine, methylergonovine, midazolam, pimozide, triazolam or any other major CYP3A4 substrates
Warnings/Precautions Coadministration with ritonavir is required. Use with caution in patients taking strong CYP3A4 inhibitors, moderate or strong CYP3A4 inducers and major CYP3A4 substrates (see drug interactions); consider alternative agents that avoid or lessen the potential for CYP-mediated interactions. Use with caution in patients with hepatic impairment, including active chronic hepatitis; consider interruption or discontinuation with worsening hepatic function. May cause fat redistribution (buffalo hump, increased abdominal girth, breast engorgement, facial atrophy). Immune reconstitution syndrome, including inflammatory responses to indolent infections, has been associated with antiretroviral therapy; additional evaluation and treatment may be required. May increase cholesterol and/or triglycerides. Protease inhibitors have been associated with glucose dysregulation; use caution in diabetic patients. Use with caution in patients with sulfonamide allergy or hemophilia. Darunavir has been associated with dermatological adverse effects, including rash, erythema multiforme, and Stevens-Johnson syndrome (sometimes accompanied by fever and elevated transaminases). Treatment history and resistance data should guide use of darunavir with ritonavir. Safety and efficacy have not been established in children or treatment-naive patients.
Adverse Reactions As a class, protease inhibitors potentially cause dyslipidemias which includes elevated cholesterol and triglycerides and a redistribution of body fat centrally to cause increased abdominal girth, buffalo hump, facial atrophy, and breast enlargement. These agents also cause hyperglycemia. Frequency of adverse events is reported for darunavir/ritonavir where incidence was greater than in the comparator protease inhibitor group. See also Ritonavir monograph.
 >10%:
  Gastrointestinal: Nausea (18%), amylase increased (11% to 17%)
  Hematologic: Neutropenia (7% to 12%)
  Respiratory: Nasopharyngitis (14%)
 2% to 10%:
  Central nervous system: Headache (1% to 4%)
  Dermatologic: Rash (7%)
  Endocrine & metabolic: Hypercholesterolemia (≥240 mg/dL: 8% to 9%), hypoglycemia (2% to 4%), hypocalcemia (up to 4%), hyponatremia (1% to 3%), hypernatremia (up to 2%)
  Gastrointestinal: Lipase increased (6% to 9%), diarrhea (2% to 3%), vomiting (2%), abdominal pain (1% to 2%), constipation (<1% to 2%)
  Hematologic: Thromboplastin time increased (4% to 8%), hypoalbuminemia (3% to 4%), prothrombin time increased (1% to 4%), thrombocytopenia (3%)
  Hepatic: Alkaline phosphatase increased (3% to 5%)
 <2% (Limited to important or life-threatening): Abdominal distention, acute renal failure, allergic dermatitis, alopecia, anorexia, anxiety, appetite decreased, arthralgia, confusion, cough, dermatitis medicamentosa, diabetes, disorientation, dyspepsia, dyspnea, erythema multiforme, extremity pain, fat redistribution (eg, buffalo hump, increased abdominal girth, breast engorgement, facial atrophy), fatigue, fever, flatulence, folliculitis, gynecomastia, hiccups, hypercholesterolemia, hyperhidrosis, hyperlipidemia, hypertension, hyperthermia, hypoesthesia, hyponatremia, irritability, lipoatrophy, maculopapular rash, memory impairment, MI, mood changes, myalgia, nephrolithiasis, night sweats, nightmare, obesity, osteopenia, osteoporosis, paresthesia, peripheral edema, peripheral neuropathy, polydipsia, polyuria, renal insufficiency, rigors, skin inflammation, somnolence, Stevens-Johnson syndrome, tachycardia, toxic skin eruption, transient ischemic attack, vertigo, weakness, xerostomia
Overdosage/Toxicology Information on overdose is limited. Single doses of up to 3200 mg darunavir have been well tolerated in healthy subjects. Treatment is symptom-directed and supportive. Unabsorbed drug may be removed via emesis, lavage, or activated charcoal. Dialysis not likely to benefit.
Drug Interactions
 Cytochrome P450 Effect: Substrate of CYP3A4 (major)
 Increased Effect/Toxicity: Listed interactions include interactions resulting from coadministration with ritonavir. Refer to Ritonavir monograph for additional interaction concerns.
  The serum concentrations of darunavir may be increased by ritonavir. This combination is recommended to enhance the effect ("boost") darunavir. Darunavir/ritonavir may
(Continued)

457

Darunavir *(Continued)*

increase the levels/effects of CYP3A4 substrates. Darunavir/ritonavir may increase the toxicity of benzodiazepines; concurrent use of midazolam and triazolam is specifically contraindicated. Darunavir may increase serum concentrations of cisapride, increasing the risk of malignant arrhythmias; use is contraindicated. Toxicity of pimozide is significantly increased by darunavir/ritonavir; concurrent use is contraindicated. Darunavir/ritonavir may increase serum concentrations/toxicity of several antiarrhythmic agents, including amiodarone, quinidine, and systemic lidocaine. Darunavir/ritonavir may also increase serum concentrations/effects of calcium channel blockers, immunosuppressants (cyclosporine, sirolimus, tacrolimus), inhaled corticosteroids, trazodone and warfarin; use reduced dose of trazodone, monitor INR with warfarin, and monitor for adrenal suppression with steroids.

Serum concentrations of HMG-CoA reductase inhibitors (atorvastatin, pravastatin, lovastatin, simvastatin) may be increased by darunavir/ritonavir, increasing the risk of myopathy/rhabdomyolysis. Lovastatin and simvastatin are not recommended. Use lowest possible dose of atorvastatin and pravastatin. Serum concentrations of rifabutin may be increased by darunavir/ritonavir; dosage adjustment of rifabutin is required. The toxicity of ergot alkaloids (dihydroergotamine, ergotamine, ergonovine, methylergonovine) is increased by darunavir; concurrent use is contraindicated. The serum concentrations of sildenafil, tadalafil, and vardenafil may be increased by darunavir/ritonavir; dose adjustment and limitations related to ritonavir coadministration must be recognized. Darunavir/ritonavir may increase serum concentrations of clarithromycin. Use with caution and adjust dose of clarithromycin during concurrent therapy in renally impaired patients. Ketoconazole may increase the serum levels of darunavir, while darunavir/ritonavir may increase the levels of ketoconazole; monitor.

Decreased Effect: CYP3A4 inducers may decrease the levels/effects of darunavir. Example inducers include aminoglutethimide, carbamazepine, nafcillin, nevirapine, phenobarbital, phenytoin, and rifamycins. Rifampin may decrease serum concentrations of darunavir; concurrent use of rifampin is not recommended. Darunavir/ritonavir may decrease the serum concentrations of ethinyl estradiol; nonhormonal contraception recommended. The effect of methadone may be reduced by darunavir (dosage increase of methadone may be required). Serum concentrations of darunavir may be decreased by lopinavir/ritonavir or saquinavir (hard gel cap); concurrent therapy not recommended. Darunavir may decrease the levels/effects of sertraline or paroxetine.

Ethanol/Nutrition/Herb Interactions
Food: Bioavailability is increased with a high-fat meal.
Herb/nutraceutical: St John's wort may decrease the plasma levels of darunavir (concomitant use not recommended).

Stability Store at 15°C to 30°C (59°F to 86°F).

Mechanism of Action Darunavir binds to the HIV-1 protease activity site and inhibits the activity of the enzyme. HIV protease is required for the cleavage of viral Gag-Pol polyprotein precursors into individual functional proteins found in infectious HIV. Inhibition prevents cleavage of these polyproteins, resulting in the formation of immature, noninfectious viral particles.

Pharmacodynamics/Kinetics All kinetic parameters derived in the presence of ritonavir coadministration.
Absorption: Increased 30% with food
Protein binding: 95%
Metabolism: Hepatic, via CYP3A4 to minimally-active metabolites
Bioavailability: 82% (with ritonavir)
Half-life elimination: 15 hours (with ritonavir)
Time to peak, plasma: 2.5-4 hours
Excretion: Feces (~80%, 41% as unchanged drug); urine (~14%, 8% as unchanged drug)

Dosage Oral: Adults: 600 mg twice daily with meals
Note: Coadministration with ritonavir (100 mg twice daily) is required.

Dosage adjustment in renal impairment: No adjustment required for mild-to-moderate impairment. No data available for use in severe renal failure.
Dosage adjustment in hepatic impairment: No data available for use in hepatic impairment

Dietary Considerations Absorption increased with food. Take with meals.

Administration Administer with food (bioavailability is increased). Coadministration with ritonavir is required.

Monitoring Parameters Viral load, CD4, serum glucose

Dosage Forms
Tablet:
Prezista™: 300 mg

- ◆ **Darunavir Ethanolate** *see* Darunavir *on page 457*
- ◆ **Darvocet A500™** *see* Propoxyphene and Acetaminophen *on page 1445*
- ◆ **Darvocet-N® 50** *see* Propoxyphene and Acetaminophen *on page 1445*
- ◆ **Darvocet-N® 100** *see* Propoxyphene and Acetaminophen *on page 1445*
- ◆ **Darvon®** *see* Propoxyphene *on page 1444*
- ◆ **Darvon® Compound [DSC]** *see* Propoxyphene, Aspirin, and Caffeine *on page 1446*
- ◆ **Darvon-N®** *see* Propoxyphene *on page 1444*

Dasatinib *(da SA ti nib)*

U.S. Brand Names Sprycel™
Index Terms BMS-354825; NSC-732517
Pharmacologic Category Antineoplastic Agent, Tyrosine Kinase Inhibitor
Use Treatment of chronic myelogenous leukemia (CML); treatment of Philadelphia chromosome-positive (Ph+) acute lymphoblastic leukemia (ALL)
Pregnancy Risk Factor D

Lactation Excretion in breast milk unknown/not recommended

Medication Safety Issues

High alert medication: The Institute for Safe Medication Practices (ISMP) includes this medication among its list of drugs which have a heightened risk of causing significant patient harm when used in error.

Contraindications Hypersensitivity to dasatinib or any component of the formulation; pregnancy

Warnings/Precautions Hazardous agent - use appropriate precautions for handling and disposal. Severe bone marrow suppression (thrombocytopenia, neutropenia, anemia) is associated with treatment; the incidence of myelosuppression is higher in patients with advanced CML and Ph+ ALL. Severe hemorrhages (including CNS, GI) may occur due to thrombocytopenia. Use caution with patients taking anticoagulants or medications interfering with platelet function; not studied in clinical trials. Fluid retention, including pleural and pericardial effusions, severe ascites, severe pulmonary edema, and generalized edema were reported. Use caution in patients where fluid accumulation may be poorly tolerated, such as in cardiovascular disease (CHF or hypertension) and pulmonary disease. May prolong QT interval; use caution in patients at risk for QT prolongation, including patients with pre-existing QT interval prolongation; patients taking antiarrhythmic medications or other medications that lead to QT prolongation or potassium-wasting diuretics; patients with cumulative high-dose anthracycline therapy, and conditions which cause hypokalemia or hypomagnesemia. Correct hypokalemia and hypomagnesemia prior to initiation of therapy. Use caution with hepatic impairment; patients with ALT and/or AST >2.5 times the upper limit of normal (ULN) and total bilirubin >2 times the ULN were excluded from clinical trials. Safety and efficacy in children have not been established.

Adverse Reactions

≥10%:

Cardiovascular: Fluid retention (14% to 50%), superficial edema (36%), chest pain (13%), arrhythmia (11%)

Central nervous system: Headache (40%), fatigue (39%), fever (39%), pain (26%), dizziness (14%), chills (11%)

Dermatologic: Rash (35%), pruritus (11%)

Endocrine & metabolic: Hypophosphatemia (grades 3/4: 11% to 23%), hypocalcemia (grades 3/4 : 2% to 20%)

Gastrointestinal: Diarrhea (49%; grades 3/4: 5%), nausea (34%), abdominal pain (25%), vomiting (22%), anorexia (19%), mucositis/stomatitis (16%), gastrointestinal hemorrhage (14%; grades 3/4: 7%), constipation (14%), weight loss (14%), abdominal distention (11%), weight gain (11%)

Hematologic: Neutropenia (grades 3/4: 49% to 83%), thrombocytopenia (grades 3/4: 48% to 83%), anemia (grades 3/4: 18% to 70%), hemorrhage (40%; grades 3/4: 10%)

Hepatic: ALT increased (grades 3/4: 1% to 11%)

Neuromuscular & skeletal: Musculoskeletal pain (39%), arthralgia (19%), weakness (19%), neuropathy (including peripheral; 13%), myalgia (12%)

Respiratory: Dyspnea (32%; grades 3/4: 6%), cough (28%), upper respiratory tract infection/inflammation (26%), pleural effusion (22%; grades 3/4: 5%), pneumonia (11%)

Miscellaneous: Infection (34%; grades 3/4: 7%)

1% to <10%:

Cardiovascular: Generalized edema (5%), CHF/cardiac dysfunction (4%; grades 3/4: 2%), pericardial effusion (4%; grades 3/4: 1%), angina, cardiomegaly, flushing, hyper-/hypotension, MI, palpitations, syncope

Central nervous system: CNS bleeding (2%), affect lability, anxiety, confusion, depression, insomnia, malaise, seizure, somnolence, vertigo

Dermatologic: Acne, alopecia, dermatitis, dry skin, hyperhydrosis, nail disorder, photosensitivity, pigmentation disorder, urticaria

Endocrine & metabolic: Gynecomastia, hyperuricemia, libido decreased

Gastrointestinal: Anal fissure, colitis, dyspepsia, dysphagia, enterocolitis, gastritis, oral soft tissue disorder, taste perversion

Genitourinary: Polyuria, renal failure

Hematologic: Febrile neutropenia (9%; grades 3/4: 8%), contusion, pancytopenia

Hepatic: AST increased (grades 3/4: 1% to 8%), bilirubin increased (grades 3/4: <1% to 8%), ascites (1%; grades 3/4: 1%)

Neuromuscular & skeletal: Creatine phosphokinase increased, muscle inflammation, muscle weakness, musculoskeletal stiffness, tremor, troponin increased

Ocular: Conjunctivitis, periorbital edema, xerophthalmia

Otic: Tinnitus

Renal: Serum creatinine increased (grades 3/4: up to 2%)

Respiratory: Pulmonary edema (4%; grades 3/4: 1%), pulmonary hypertension (1%), asthma, lung infiltration, pneumonitis

Miscellaneous: Herpes virus infection, sepsis, tumor lysis syndrome

<1% (Limited to important or life-threatening): Acute coronary syndrome, acute febrile neutrophilic dermatosis, acute respiratory distress syndrome, amnesia, bronchospasm, bullous conditions, cerebrovascular accident, cholecystitis, cholestasis, coagulopathy, esophagitis, hand-foot syndrome, hepatitis, hypersensitivity, hypoalbuminemia, ileus, livedo reticularis, menstrual irregularities myocarditis, pancreatitis, panniculitis, pericarditis, platelet aggregation abnormal, proteinuria, pure red cell aplasia, QT$_c$ prolongation, reversible posterior leukoencephalopathy syndrome, rhabdomyolysis, skin ulcer, temperature intolerance, tendonitis, TIA, ventricular tachycardia, upper gastrointestinal ulcer

Overdosage/Toxicology A single-dose of 200 mg was well tolerated without symptoms or laboratory abnormalities. Treatment is symptom-directed and supportive.

Drug Interactions

Cytochrome P450 Effect: Substrate of CYP3A4 (major); **Inhibits** CYP3A4 (weak)

Increased Effect/Toxicity:

The levels/effects of dasatinib may be increased by azole antifungals, clarithromycin, diclofenac, doxycycline, erythromycin, imatinib, isoniazid, nefazodone, nicardipine, (Continued)

Dasatinib *(Continued)*

propofol, protease inhibitors, quinidine, telithromycin, verapamil, and other CYP3A4 inhibitors. Concurrent use of dasatinib with other drugs which may prolong QT_c interval may increase the risk of potentially-fatal arrhythmias. Anticoagulants and antiplatelet agents may increase the risk of bleeding.

Decreased Effect: The levels/effects of dasatinib may be decreased by aminoglutethimide, carbamazepine, nafcillin, nevirapine, phenobarbital, phenytoin, rifamycins, and other CYP3A4 inducers. Antacids, H_2 blockers and proton pump inhibitors may decrease the absorption of dasatinib.

Ethanol/Nutrition/Herb Interactions Herb/Nutraceutical: Avoid St John's wort (may increase metabolism and decrease dasatinib plasma concentration).

Stability Store at 15°C to 30°C (59°F to 86°F).

Mechanism of Action BCR-ABL tyrosine kinase inhibitor; targets most imatinib-resistant BCR-ABL mutations (except the T315I and F317V mutants) by distinctly binding to ABL-kinase. Kinase inhibition halts proliferation of leukemia cells. Also inhibits SRC family (including SRC, LKC, YES, FYN); c-KIT, EPHA2 and platelet derived growth factor receptor (PDGFRβ)

Pharmacodynamics/Kinetics

Distribution: 2505 L

Protein binding: Dasatinib: 96%; metabolite: 93%

Metabolism: Hepatic; metabolized by CYP3A4 (primarily), flavin-containing mono-oxygenase-3 (FOM-3) and uridine diphosphate-glucuronosyltransferase (UGT) to an active metabolite and other inactive metabolites (the active metabolite plays only a minor role in the pharmacology of dasatinib)

Half-life elimination: Terminal: 3-5 hours

Time to peak, plasma: 0.5-6 hours

Excretion: Feces (85%, 19% as unchanged drug); urine (4%, 0.1% as unchanged drug)

Dosage Oral: Adults: CML, Ph+ ALL: 70 mg twice daily

Note: Dose reductions are likely to be needed when dasatinib is administered concomitantly with a strong CYP3A4 inhibitor (an alternate medication for CYP3A4 enzyme inhibitors should be investigated first); in the event that dasatinib must be administered concomitantly with a potent enzyme inhibitor, consider reducing dasatinib to 20-40 mg daily with careful monitoring. Likewise, concomitant administration with CYP3A4 inducers may require increased dasatinib doses, with careful monitoring; (alternatives to the enzyme inducing agent should be utilized first.) See Drug Interactions for examples of CYP3A4 inhibitors and inducers.

Dosage adjustment for toxicity: Dose increases or reductions should be made in 20 mg increments (per dose) or as follows:

Hematologic toxicity:

Chronic phase CML: For ANC <0.5 x 10^9/L and/or platelets <50 x 10^9/L, withhold treatment until ANC ≥1 x 10^9/L and platelets ≥50 x 10^9/L; then resume treatment at the original starting dose. If platelets <25 x 10^9/L and/or recurrence of ANC <0.5 x 10^9/L for >7 days, withhold treatment until ANC ≥1 x 10^9/L and platelets ≥50 x 10^9/L; then resume treatment at 50 mg twice daily (2nd episode) or 40 mg twice daily (3rd episode)

Accelerated or blast phase CML and Ph+ ALL: For ANC <0.5 x 10^9/L and/or platelets <10 x 10^9/L, if cytopenia unrelated to leukemia, withhold treatment until ANC ≥1 x 10^9/L and platelets ≥20 x 10^9/L; then resume treatment at the original starting dose. If cytopenia recurs, withhold treatment until ANC ≥1 x 10^9/L and platelets ≥20 x 10^9/L; then resume treatment at 50 mg twice daily (2nd episode) or 40 mg twice daily (3rd episode). For cytopenias related to leukemia (confirm with marrow aspirate or biopsy), consider dose escalation to 100 mg twice daily with careful monitoring.

Nonhematologic toxicity: Withhold treatment until toxicity improvement or resolution; if appropriate, resume treatment at a reduced dose based on the event severity.

Dietary Considerations May be taken without regard to food.

Administration Administer twice daily, in the morning and evening. May be taken without regard to food. Do not break, crush, or chew tablets.

Monitoring Parameters CBC with differential (weekly for 2 months, then monthly); bone marrow biopsy; liver function tests, electrolytes including calcium, phosphorus, magnesium; monitor for fluid retention; ECG monitoring if at risk for QT_c prolongation

Additional Information In clinical trials, dasatinib was continued until disease progression or until the patient no longer tolerated treatment. Patients who did not achieve hematologic or cytogenetic response at 70 mg twice daily were allowed to escalate the dose to 90 mg twice daily (chronic phase CML) or 100 mg twice daily (advanced phase CML and Ph+ ALL)

Dosage Forms

Tablet:

Sprycel™: 20 mg, 50 mg, 70 mg

♦ **Daunomycin** *see* DAUNOrubicin Hydrochloride *on page 462*

DAUNOrubicin Citrate (Liposomal)

(daw noe ROO bi sin SI trate lip po SOE mal)

U.S. Brand Names DaunoXome®

Pharmacologic Category Antineoplastic Agent, Anthracycline

Use First-line cytotoxic therapy for advanced HIV-associated Kaposi's sarcoma

Pregnancy Risk Factor D

Lactation Excretion in breast milk unknown/not recommended

Medication Safety Issues

Sound-alike/look-alike issues:

DAUNOrubicin may be confused with dactinomycin, DOXOrubicin, epirubicin, idarubicin

Liposomal formulations (DaunoXome®) may be confused with conventional formulations (Adriamycin PFS®, Adriamycin RDF®, Cerubidine®, Rubex®)

High alert medication: The Institute for Safe Medication Practices (ISMP) includes this medication among its list of drugs which have a heightened risk of causing significant patient harm when used in error.

Contraindications Hypersensitivity to daunorubicin or any component of the formulation; pregnancy

Warnings/Precautions Hazardous agent - use appropriate precautions for handling and disposal. Daunorubicin is associated with a dose-related cardiac toxicity. The risk of similar toxicity with liposome-encapsulated daunorubicin is not certain. **[U.S. Boxed Warnings]: Monitor cardiac function regularly; especially in patients with previous therapy with high cumulative doses of anthracyclines, cyclophosphamide, or thoracic radiation, or who have pre-existing cardiac disease. May cause bone marrow suppression. Use caution with liver impairment; dosage reduction is recommended. The lipid component is associated with infusion-related reactions (back pain, flushing, chest tightness) usually within the first 5 minutes of infusion; monitor, interrupt infusion and resume at reduced infusion rate. Should be administered under the supervision of an experienced cancer chemotherapy physician.**

Adverse Reactions
>10%:
Dermatologic: Alopecia (reversible)
Gastrointestinal: Mild nausea or vomiting occurs in 50% of patients within the first 24 hours; esophagitis or stomatitis may occur 3-7 days after administration, but is not as severe as that caused by doxorubicin
Time course for nausea/vomiting: Onset: 1-3 hours; Duration: 4-24 hours
Genitourinary: Discoloration of urine (red)
Miscellaneous: Allergic reactions (24%)
1% to 10%:
Cardiovascular: CHF; maximum lifetime dose: Refer to Warnings/Precautions
Dermatologic: Darkening or redness of skin
Endocrine & metabolic: Hyperuricemia
Gastrointestinal: GI ulceration, diarrhea
Hematologic: Myelosuppressive: Dose-limiting toxicity; occurs in all patients; leukopenia is more significant than thrombocytopenia
WBC: Severe
Platelets: Severe
Onset (days): 7
Nadir (days): 14
Recovery (days): 21-28
Local: **Vesicant chemotherapy**
<1% (Limited to important or life-threatening): Elevation in serum bilirubin, AST, and alkaline phosphatase; myocarditis; pericarditis

Overdosage/Toxicology Symptoms of acute overdose are increased severity of the observed dose-limiting toxicities of therapeutic doses, such as myelosuppression (especially granulocytopenia), fatigue, nausea, and vomiting. Treatment is symptomatic.

Drug Interactions
Decreased Effect: Patients may experience impaired immune response to vaccines; possible infection after administration of live vaccines in patients receiving immunosuppressants.

Stability Store intact vials under refrigeration (2°C to 8°C/36°F to 46°F). Reconstitute liposomal daunorubicin 1:1 with 5% dextrose injection before administration. Must not be mixed with saline, bacteriostatic agents such as benzyl alcohol, or any other solution. Store reconstituted solution for a maximum of 6 hours. Do not freeze and protect from light. Do not use an in-line filter for intravenous infusion.

Mechanism of Action Liposomes have been shown to penetrate solid tumors more effectively, possibly because of their small size and longer circulation time. Once in tissues, daunorubicin is released. Daunorubicin inhibits DNA and RNA synthesis by intercalation between DNA base pairs and by steric obstruction; and intercalates at points of local uncoiling of the double helix. Although the exact mechanism is unclear, it appears that direct binding to DNA (intercalation) and inhibition of DNA repair (topoisomerase II inhibition) result in blockade of DNA and RNA synthesis and fragmentation of DNA.

Pharmacodynamics/Kinetics
Distribution: V_d: 3-6.4 L
Metabolism: Similar to daunorubicin, but metabolite plasma levels are low
Half-life elimination: Distribution: 4.4 hours; Terminal: 3-5 hours
Excretion: Primarily feces; some urine
Clearance, plasma: 17.3 mL/minute

Dosage Refer to individual protocols. Adults: I.V.:
20-40 mg/m^2 every 2 weeks
100 mg/m^2 every 3 weeks
Dosing adjustment in renal impairment: Serum creatinine >3 mg/dL: Administer 50% of normal dose
Dosing adjustment in hepatic impairment:
Bilirubin 1.2-3 mg/dL: Administer 75% of normal dose
Bilirubin >3 mg/dL: Administer 50% of normal dose

Administration Infuse over 1 hour; do not mix with other drugs. **Extravasation management:** Infiltration can cause severe inflammation, tissue necrosis, and ulceration. If the drug is infiltrated, consult institutional policy, apply ice to the area, and elevate the limb.

Monitoring Parameters Observe patient closely and monitor chemical and laboratory tests extensively. Evaluate cardiac, renal, and hepatic function. Repeat blood counts prior to each dose and withhold if the absolute granulocyte count is <750 cells/mm^3. Monitor serum uric acid levels.

Dosage Forms Injection, solution [preservative free]: 2 mg/mL (25 mL) [contains sucrose 2125 mg/25 mL]

DAUNOrubicin Hydrochloride (daw noe ROO bi sin hye droe KLOR ide)

U.S. Brand Names Cerubidine®
Canadian Brand Names Cerubidine®
Index Terms Daunomycin; DNR; NSC-82151; Rubidomycin Hydrochloride
Pharmacologic Category Antineoplastic Agent, Anthracycline
Use Treatment of acute lymphocytic (ALL) and nonlymphocytic (ANLL) leukemias
Pregnancy Risk Factor D
Pregnancy Implications May cause fetal harm when administered to a pregnant woman. Animal studies have shown an increased incidence of fetal abnormalities.
Lactation Excretion in breast milk unknown/not recommended
Medication Safety Issues
Sound-alike/look-alike issues:
DAUNOrubicin may be confused with dactinomycin, DOXOrubicin, epirubicin, idarubicin
Conventional formulations (Cerubidine®) may be confused with liposomal formulations (DaunoXome®, Doxil®)

High alert medication: The Institute for Safe Medication Practices (ISMP) includes this medication among its list of drugs which have a heightened risk of causing significant patient harm when used in error.
Contraindications Hypersensitivity to daunorubicin or any component of the formulation; congestive heart failure or arrhythmias; previous therapy with high cumulative doses of daunorubicin and/or doxorubicin; pre-existing bone marrow suppression; pregnancy
Warnings/Precautions Hazardous agent - use appropriate precautions for handling and disposal. Use with caution in patients who have received radiation therapy; reduce dosage in patients who are receiving radiation therapy simultaneously. **[U.S. Boxed Warnings: Use caution with renal impairment or in the presence of hepatic dysfunction; dosage reduction is recommended. Potent vesicant; if extravasation occurs, severe tissue damage leading to ulceration and necrosis, and pain may occur. For I.V. use only. Severe bone marrow suppression may occur.**

[U.S. Boxed Warning]: May cause cumulative, dose-related myocardial toxicity (concurrent or delayed). Total cumulative dose should take into account previous or concomitant treatment with cardiotoxic agents or irradiation of chest. The incidence of irreversible myocardial toxicity increases as the total cumulative (lifetime) dosages approach:
550 mg/m^2 in adults
400 mg/m^2 in adults receiving chest radiation
300 mg/m^2 in children >2 years of age
Although the risk increases with cumulative dose, irreversible cardiotoxicity may occur at any dose level. Patients with pre-existing heart disease, hypertension, concurrent administration of other antineoplastic agents, prior or concurrent chest irradiation, advanced age; and infants and children are at increased risk. Monitor left ventricular (LV) function (baseline and periodic).

[U.S. Boxed Warning]: Should be administered under the supervision of an experienced cancer chemotherapy physician].
Adverse Reactions
>10%:
Cardiovascular: Transient ECG abnormalities (supraventricular tachycardia, S-T wave changes, atrial or ventricular extrasystoles); generally asymptomatic and self-limiting. CHF, dose related, may be delayed for 7-8 years after treatment.
Dermatologic: Alopecia, radiation recall
Gastrointestinal: Mild nausea or vomiting, stomatitis
Genitourinary: Discoloration of urine (red)
Hematologic: Myelosuppression, primarily leukopenia; thrombocytopenia and anemia
Onset: 7 days
Nadir: 10-14 days
Recovery: 21-28 days
1% to 10%:
Dermatologic: Skin "flare" at injection site; discoloration of saliva, sweat, or tears
Endocrine & metabolic: Hyperuricemia
Gastrointestinal: Abdominal pain, GI ulceration, diarrhea
<1% (Limited to important or life-threatening): Anaphylactoid reaction, bilirubin increased, hepatitis, infertility; local (cellulitis, pain, thrombophlebitis at injection site); MI, myocarditis, nail banding, onycholysis, pericarditis, pigmentation of nailbeds, skin rash, sterility, systemic hypersensitivity (including urticaria, pruritus, angioedema, dysphagia, dyspnea); transaminases increased

Overdosage/Toxicology Symptoms include myelosuppression, nausea, vomiting, and stomatitis. There are no known antidotes. Treatment is primarily symptomatic and supportive.
Drug Interactions
Decreased Effect: Patients may experience impaired immune response to vaccines; possible infection after administration of live vaccines in patients receiving immunosuppressants.
Ethanol/Nutrition/Herb Interactions Ethanol: Avoid ethanol (due to GI irritation).
Stability Store intact vials at room temperature and protect from light. Dilute vials with 4 mL SWFI for a final concentration of 5 mg/mL. May further dilute in 100 mL D$_5$W or NS. Reconstituted solution is stable for 4 days at 15°C to 25°C. Further dilution in D$_5$W, LR, or NS is stable at room temperature (25°C) for up to 4 weeks if protected from light.
Mechanism of Action Inhibition of DNA and RNA synthesis by intercalation between DNA base pairs and by steric obstruction. Daunomycin intercalates at points of local uncoiling of the double helix. Although the exact mechanism is unclear, it appears that direct binding to DNA (intercalation) and inhibition of DNA repair (topoisomerase II inhibition) result in blockade of DNA and RNA synthesis and fragmentation of DNA.

Pharmacodynamics/Kinetics

Distribution: Many body tissues, particularly the liver, kidneys, lung, spleen, and heart; not into CNS; crosses placenta; V_d: 40 L/kg

Metabolism: Primarily hepatic to daunorubicinol (active), then to inactive aglycones, conjugated sulfates, and glucuronides

Half-life elimination: Distribution: 2 minutes; Elimination: 14-20 hours; Terminal: 18.5 hours; Daunorubicinol plasma half-life: 24-48 hours

Excretion: Feces (40%); urine (~25% as unchanged drug and metabolites)

Dosage I.V. (refer to individual protocols):

Children: **Note:** Cumulative dose should not exceed 300 mg/m² in children >2 years; maximum cumulative doses for younger children are unknown.

ALL combination therapy: Remission induction: 25-45 mg/m² on day 1 every week for 4 cycles **or** 30-45 mg/m²/day for 3 days

AML combination therapy: Induction: I.V. continuous infusion: 30-60 mg/m²/day on days 1-3 of cycle

Note: In children <2 years or <0.5 m², daunorubicin should be based on weight - mg/kg: 1 mg/kg per protocol with frequency dependent on regimen employed

Adults: **Note:** Cumulative dose should not exceed 550 mg/m² in adults without risk factors for cardiotoxicity and should not exceed 400 mg/m² in adults receiving chest irradiation.

Range: 30-60 mg/m²/day for 3-5 days, repeat dose in 3-4 weeks

AML: Single agent induction: 60 mg/m²/day for 3 days; repeat every 3-4 weeks

AML: Combination therapy induction: 45 mg/m²/day for 3 days of the first course of induction therapy; subsequent courses: Every day for 2 days

ALL combination therapy: 45 mg/m²/day for 3 days

Dosing adjustment in renal impairment:
Cl_cr <10 mL/minute: Administer 75% of normal dose
S_cr >3 mg/dL: Administer 50% of normal dose

Dosing adjustment in hepatic impairment:
Serum bilirubin 1.2-3 mg/dL or AST 60-180 int. units: Reduce dose to 75%
Serum bilirubin 3.1-5 mg/dL or AST >180 int. units: Reduce dose to 50%
Serum bilirubin >5 mg/dL: Omit use

Administration Not for I.M. or SubQ administration. Administer as slow I.V. push over 1-5 minutes into the tubing of a rapidly infusing I.V. solution of D₅W or NS or dilute in 100 mL of D₅W or NS and infuse over 15-30 minutes.

Monitoring Parameters CBC with differential and platelet count, liver function test, ECG, left ventricular ejection function (echocardiography [Echo] or radionuclide angiography [RNA]), renal function test

Dosage Forms
Injection, powder for reconstitution: 20 mg, 50 mg
Cerubidine®: 20 mg
Injection, solution: 5 mg/mL (4 mL, 10 mL)

♦ **DaunoXome®** see DAUNOrubicin Citrate (Liposomal) on page 460
♦ **1-Day™ [OTC]** see Tioconazole on page 1691
♦ **Dayhist® Allergy [OTC]** see Clemastine on page 387
♦ **Daypro®** see Oxaprozin on page 1279
♦ **Daytrana™** see Methylphenidate on page 1119
♦ **dCF** see Pentostatin on page 1342
♦ **DDAVP®** see Desmopressin on page 476
♦ **ddC** see Zalcitabine on page 1807
♦ **ddl** see Didanosine on page 496
♦ **1-Deamino-8-D-Arginine Vasopressin** see Desmopressin on page 476
♦ **Debrox® [OTC]** see Carbamide Peroxide on page 287
♦ **Deca-Durabolin® (Can)** see Nandrolone on page 1197
♦ **Decavac™** see Diphtheria and Tetanus Toxoid on page 519
♦ **Dec-Chlorphen** see Chlorpheniramine and Phenylephrine on page 349
♦ **Dec-Chlorphen DM** see Chlorpheniramine, Phenylephrine, and Dextromethorphan on page 352
♦ **De-Chlor DM** see Chlorpheniramine, Phenylephrine, and Dextromethorphan on page 352
♦ **De-Chlor DR** see Chlorpheniramine, Phenylephrine, and Dextromethorphan on page 352

Decitabine (de SYE ta been)

U.S. Brand Names Dacogen™
Index Terms 5-Aza-2'-deoxycytidine; 5-AzaC; NSC-127716
Pharmacologic Category Antineoplastic Agent, Antimetabolite (Pyrimidine)
Use Treatment of myelodysplastic syndrome (MDS)
Unlabeled/Investigational Use Treatment of acute myelogenous leukemia (AML), chronic myelogenous leukemia (CML), sickle cell anemia
Pregnancy Risk Factor D
Pregnancy Implications Teratogenic effects, decreased fetal weight, and increased fetal deaths were observed in animal studies. There are no adequate and well-controlled studies in pregnant women. Women of childbearing potential should be advised to avoid pregnancy during treatment. In addition, males should be advised to avoid fathering a child while on decitabine therapy and for 2 months after treatment.
Lactation Excretion in breast milk unknown/not recommended
Medication Safety Issues
High alert medication: The Institute for Safe Medication Practices (ISMP) includes this medication among its list of drugs which have a heightened risk of causing significant patient harm when used in error.
Contraindications Hypersensitivity to decitabine or any component of the formulation
(Continued)

Decitabine *(Continued)*

Warnings/Precautions Hazardous agent - use appropriate precautions for handling and disposal. The dose-limiting toxicity is bone marrow suppression; worsening neutropenia is common in first two treatment cycles and may not correlate with progression of underlying MDS; may require growth factor support. Not studied in hepatic and renal disease; use caution. Safety and efficacy in children have not been established.

Adverse Reactions
>10%:
Cardiovascular: Peripheral edema (25%), pallor (23%), edema (18%), cardiac murmur (16%)
Central nervous system: Pyrexia (6% to 53%), headache (28%), insomnia (28%), dizziness (18%), pain (13%), confusion (12%), lethargy (12%), anxiety (11%), hypoesthesia (11%)
Dermatologic: Petechiae (39%), bruising (22%), rash (19%), erythema (14%), cellulitis (12%), lesions (11%), pruritus (11%)
Endocrine & metabolic: Hyperglycemia (33%), hypoalbuminemia (7% to 24%), hypomagnesemia (24%), hypokalemia (22%), hyperkalemia (13%), hyponatremia (13%)
Gastrointestinal: Nausea (42%), constipation (35%), diarrhea (34%), vomiting (25%), anorexia (16%), appetite decreased (16%), abdominal pain (5% to 14%), oral mucosal petechiae (13%), stomatitis (12%), dyspepsia (12%)
Hematologic: Neutropenia (90%; recovery 28-50 days), thrombocytopenia (89%), anemia (82%), febrile neutropenia (29%), leukopenia (28%), lymphadenopathy (12%)
Hepatic: Hyperbilirubinemia (14%), alkaline phosphatase increased (11%)
Local: Tenderness (11%)
Neuromuscular & skeletal: Rigors (22%), arthralgia (20%), limb pain (19%), back pain (17%)
Respiratory: Cough (40%), pneumonia (22%), pharyngitis (16%), lung crackles (14%)
5% to 10%:
Cardiovascular: Chest discomfort (7%), facial swelling (6%), hypotension (6%)
Central nervous system: Malaise (5%)
Dermatologic: Alopecia (8%), urticaria (6%)
Endocrine & metabolic: Hyperuricemia (10%), LDH increased (8%), bicarbonate increased (6%), dehydration (6%), hypochloremia (6%), bicarbonate decreased (5%), hypoproteinemia (5%)
Gastrointestinal: Gingival bleeding (8%), hemorrhoids (8%), loose stools (7%), tongue ulceration (7%), dysphagia (6%), oral candidiasis (6%), lip ulceration (5%), abdominal distension (5%), gastroesophageal reflux (5%), glossodynia (5%)
Genitourinary: Urinary tract infection (7%), dysuria (6%), polyuria (5%)
Hematologic: Hematoma (5%), thrombocythemia (5%), bacteremia (5%)
Hepatic: Ascites (10%), AST increased (10%), hypobilirubinemia (5%)
Local: Catheter infection (8%), catheter site erythema (5%), catheter site pain (5%), injection site swelling (5%)
Neuromuscular & skeletal: Falling (8%), chest wall pain (7%), musculoskeletal discomfort (6%), crepitation (5%), myalgia (5%)
Ocular: Blurred vision (5%)
Respiratory: Breath sounds diminished (10%), hypoxia (10%), rales (8%), pulmonary edema (6%), postnasal drip (5%), sinusitis (5%)
Miscellaneous: Candidal infection (10%), staphylococcal infection (7%), transfusion reaction (7%)
<5% (Limited to important or life-threatening): Anaphylactic reaction, atrial fibrillation, bronchopulmonary aspergillosis, cardiomyopathy, cardiorespiratory failure, catheter site hemorrhage, chest pain, CHF, cholecystitis, dyspnea, fungal infection, gastrointestinal hemorrhage, hemoptysis, hypersensitivity, intracranial hemorrhage, MI, peridiverticular abscess, pseudomonal lung infection, pulmonary embolism, pulmonary infiltrates, pulmonary mass, renal failure, respiratory arrest, respiratory tract infection, sepsis, splenomegaly, supraventricular tachycardia, urethral hemorrhage, weakness

Overdosage/Toxicology Higher doses are associated with increased and prolonged myelosuppression. Treatment is symptom-directed and supportive.

Stability Store vials at 15°C to 30°C (59°F to 86°F). Vials should be reconstituted with 10 mL SWFI to a concentration of 5 mg/mL. Further dilute with 50-250 mL NS, D_5W, or lactated Ringer's to a final concentration of 0.1-1 mg/mL. Solutions not administered within 15 minutes of preparation should be prepared with cold (2°C to 8°C [36°F to 46°F]) infusion solutions. Solutions diluted for infusion may be stored for up to 7 hours under refrigeration at 2°C to 8°C (36°F to 46°F) if prepared with cold infusion fluids.

Mechanism of Action After phosphorylation, decitabine is incorporated into DNA and inhibits DNA methyltransferase causing hypomethylation and subsequent cell death.

Pharmacodynamics/Kinetics
Protein binding: <1%
Half-life elimination: ~30 minutes

Dosage Adults:
MDS: I.V.: 15 mg/m² over 3 hours every 8 hours (45 mg/m²/day) for 3 days (135 mg/m²/cycle) every 6 weeks. Treatment is recommended for at least 4 cycles and may continue until the patient no longer continues to benefit.
AML (investigational use): I.V.:
5-15 mg/m² over 1 hour daily, 5 days/week for 2 weeks (5 days on, 2 days off, 5 days on; 10 doses total) every 6 weeks
or
15 mg/m² over 1 hour daily for 10 days every 6 weeks
CML (investigational use): I.V.:
10-15 mg/m² over 1 hour daily, 5 days/week for 2 weeks (5 days on, 2 days off, 5 days on; 10 doses total) every 6 weeks
or
50-100 mg/m² over 6 hours every 12 hours for 5 days every 4-8 weeks
Sickle cell anemia (investigational use): I.V., SubQ: 0.15-0.3 mg/kg/day over 2 minutes 5 days/week for 2 weeks (5 days on, 2 days off, 5 days on; 10 doses total) every 6 weeks

Dosage adjustment for toxicity:
For delayed hematologic recovery (ANC ≥1000/mm^3 and platelets ≥50,000/mm^3):
Greater than 6 weeks but less than 8 weeks: Delay dose for up to 2 weeks and temporarily reduce dose to 11 mg/m^2 every 8 hours (33 mg/m^2/day) for 3 days
Greater than 8 weeks but less than 10 weeks: Assess for disease progression; if no disease progression, delay dose for up to 2 weeks and reduce dose to 11 mg/m^2 every 8 hours (33 mg/m^2/day) for 3 days; maintain or increase dose with subsequent cycles if clinically indicated
Temporarily hold treatment until resolution for any of the following nonhematologic toxicities:
Serum creatinine ≥2 mg/dL
SGPT, bilirubin ≥2 times ULN
Active or uncontrolled infection
Administration Infuse over 1-6 hours. Premedication with antiemetics is recommended.
Monitoring Parameters CBC and platelets with each cycle, more frequently if needed; liver enzymes; serum creatinine
Dosage Forms
Injection, powder for reconstitution:
Dacogen™: 50 mg

♦ **Declomycin®** see Demeclocycline on page 469
♦ **Deconamine®** see Chlorpheniramine and Pseudoephedrine on page 350
♦ **Deconamine® SR** see Chlorpheniramine and Pseudoephedrine on page 350
♦ **Deconsal® II** see Guaifenesin and Phenylephrine on page 818
♦ **Deep Sea [OTC]** see Sodium Chloride on page 1576

Deferasirox (de FER a sir ox)

U.S. Brand Names Exjade®
Index Terms ICL670
Pharmacologic Category Antidote; Chelating Agent
Use Treatment of chronic iron overload due to blood transfusions
Pregnancy Risk Factor B
Pregnancy Implications Teratogenic effects were not observed in animal studies. There are no adequate and well-controlled studies in pregnant women. Use during pregnancy only if clearly needed.
Lactation Excretion in breast milk unknown/use caution
Contraindications Hypersensitivity to deferasirox or any component of the formulation
Warnings/Precautions Dose-related elevations in serum creatinine have been reported; monitor and consider dose reduction, interruption, or discontinuation. May cause proteinuria; closely monitor. Hepatitis and elevated transaminases have been reported; monitor LFTs and consider dose modifications. May cause skin rash (dose-related); mild-to-moderate rashes may resolve without treatment interruption; for severe rash, interrupt and consider restarting at a lower dose with dose escalation and oral steroids. Auditory or ocular disturbances have been reported; monitor and consider dose reduction or treatment interruption. Use caution with hepatic impairment. Do not combine with other iron chelation therapies; safety of combinations has not been established. Safety and efficacy in children <2 years of age have not been established.
Adverse Reactions
>10%:
Central nervous system: Fever (19%), headache (16%)
Gastrointestinal: Abdominal pain (8% to 14%), diarrhea (12%), nausea (11%)
Renal: Serum creatinine increased (2% to 38%), proteinuria (19%)
Respiratory: Cough (14%), nasopharyngitis (13%), pharyngolaryngeal pain (11%)
Miscellaneous: Influenza (11%)
1% to 10%:
Central nervous system: Fatigue (6%)
Dermatologic: Rash (8% to 11%), urticaria (4%)
Gastrointestinal: Vomiting (10%)
Hepatic: ALT increased (6% to 8%), transaminitis (4%)
Neuromuscular & skeletal: Arthralgia (7%), back pain (6%)
Otic: Ear infection (5%)
Respiratory: Respiratory tract infection (10%), bronchitis (9%), pharyngitis (8%), acute tonsillitis (6%), rhinitis (6%)
<1% (Limited to important or life-threatening): Hearing loss (including high frequency), hepatic transaminases increased, hepatitis, maculopathy, purpura, visual disturbance
Overdosage/Toxicology Single doses of up to 80 mg/kg have been tolerated with incidences of nausea and diarrhea. In case of overdose, induce vomiting and gastric lavage.
Drug Interactions
Decreased Effect: Aluminum-containing antacids may decrease absorption of deferasirox.
Stability Store at room temperature between 15°C and 30°C (59°F and 86°F). Protect from moisture.
Mechanism of Action Selectively binds iron, forming a complex which is excreted primarily through the feces.
Pharmacodynamics/Kinetics
Distribution: Adults: 14 L
Protein binding: 99% to serum albumin
Metabolism: Hepatic via glucuronidation by UGT1A1 and UGT1A3; minor oxidation by CYP450; undergoes enterohepatic recirculation
Bioavailability: 70%
Half-life elimination: 8-16 hours
Time to peak, plasma: 1-4 hours
Excretion: Feces (84%), urine (6% to 8%)
(Continued)

Deferasirox (Continued)

Dosage Oral: Children ≥2 years and Adults:

Initial: 20 mg/kg daily (calculate dose to nearest whole tablet)

Maintenance: Adjust dose every 3-6 months based on serum ferritin levels; increase by 5-10 mg/kg/day (calculate dose to nearest whole tablet); titrate. Maximum dose: 30 mg/kg/day; hold dose for serum ferritin <500 mcg/L. **Note:** Consider dose reduction or interruption for hearing loss or visual disturbances.

Dosage adjustment in renal impairment: Consider dose reduction, interruption, or discontinuation with serum creatinine elevation.

Dosage adjustment in hepatic impairment: Consider dose adjustment or discontinuation for severe elevations in liver function tests.

Dietary Considerations Bioavailability increased variably when taken with food; take on empty stomach 30 minutes before a meal.

Administration Do not chew or swallow whole tablets. Take at same time each day on an empty stomach, 30 minutes before food. Disperse tablets in water, orange juice, or apple juice (use 3.5 ounces for total doses <1 g; 7 ounces for doses ≥1 g); stir to form suspension and drink entire contents. Rinse remaining residue with more fluid; drink. Do not take simultaneously with aluminum-containing antacids.

Monitoring Parameters

CBC with differential, serum creatinine, urine protein, liver function tests, and serum ferritin monthly; baseline and annual auditory and ophthalmic function

Additional Information Deferasirox has a low affinity for binding with zinc and copper, may cause variable decreases in the serum concentration of these trace minerals.

Dosage Forms Tablet, for oral suspension: 125 mg, 250 mg, 500 mg

Deferoxamine (de fer OKS a meen)

U.S. Brand Names Desferal®

Canadian Brand Names Desferal®; PMS-Deferoxamine

Index Terms Deferoxamine Mesylate

Pharmacologic Category Antidote

Additional Appendix Information

Management of Overdosages *on page 2075*

Use Acute iron intoxication or when clinical signs of significant iron toxicity exist; chronic iron overload secondary to multiple transfusions

Unlabeled/Investigational Use Removal of corneal rust rings following surgical removal of foreign bodies; diagnosis or treatment of aluminum induced toxicity associated with chronic kidney disease (CKD)

Pregnancy Risk Factor C

Pregnancy Implications Skeletal anomalies and delayed ossification were observed in some but not all animal studies. Toxic amounts of iron or deferoxamine have not been noted to cross the placenta. In case of acute toxicity, treatment during pregnancy should not be withheld.

Lactation Excretion in breast milk unknown/use caution

Medication Safety Issues

Sound-alike/look-alike issues:

Deferoxamine may be confused with cefuroxime

Desferal® may be confused with desflurane, Dexferrum®, Disophrol®

International issues:

Desferal® may be confused with Deseril® which is a brand name for methysergide in multiple international markets

Contraindications Hypersensitivity to deferoxamine or any component of the formulation; patients with severe renal disease and anuria; primary hemochromatosis

Warnings/Precautions Use with caution in patients with pyelonephritis; may increase susceptibility to *Yersinia enterocolitica*. Ocular and auditory disturbances and growth retardation (children only), have been reported following prolonged administration. Has been associated with adult respiratory distress syndrome (ARDS) following excessively high-dose treatment of acute intoxication. Caution must be used in performing tasks which require alertness (eg, operating machinery or driving). Patients should be informed that urine may have a reddish color.

Adverse Reactions Frequency not defined.

Cardiovascular: Flushing, hypotension, tachycardia, shock, edema

Central nervous system: Fever, dizziness, neuropathy, seizure, exacerbation of aluminum-related encephalopathy (dialysis), headache

Dermatologic: Angioedema, rash, urticaria

Endocrine & metabolic: Growth retardation (children), hypocalcemia

Gastrointestinal: Abdominal discomfort, abdominal pain, diarrhea, nausea, vomiting

Genitourinary: Dysuria

Hematologic: Thrombocytopenia, leukopenia

Local: Injection site: Burning, crust, edema, erythema, eschar, induration, infiltration, irritation, pain, pruritus, swelling, vesicles

Neuromuscular & skeletal: Arthralgia, leg cramps, myalgia, paresthesias

Ocular: Acuity decreased, blurred vision, dichromatopsia, visual loss, scotoma, visual field defects, optic neuritis, cataracts, retinal pigmentary abnormalities, night blindness

Otic: Hearing loss, tinnitus

Renal: Renal impairment, urine discoloration (vin-rose color)

Respiratory: Acute respiratory distress syndrome, asthma

Miscellaneous: Anaphylaxis, hypersensitivity reaction, infections (*Yersinia*, mucormycosis)

Overdosage/Toxicology Symptoms include aphasia, agitation, CNS depression, coma, bradycardia, acute renal failure, headache, hypotension, nausea, pallor, transient vision loss, and tachycardia. Treatment is symptomatic and supportive. Desferoxamine is dialyzable.

Drug Interactions

Increased Effect/Toxicity: May cause loss of consciousness or coma when administered with prochlorperazine. Concomitant treatment with vitamin C (>500 mg/day) has been associated with cardiac impairment.

Stability Prior to reconstitution, do not store above 25°C (77°F). Reconstitute using sterile water for injection to a final solution of 100 mg/mL (for I.V. administration). Following reconstitution, may be stored at room temperature for 7 days; protect from light. Do not refrigerate reconstituted solution.

Mechanism of Action Complexes with trivalent ions (ferric ions) to form ferrioxamine, which are removed by the kidneys

Pharmacodynamics/Kinetics

Absorption: I.M.: Erratic

Metabolism: Hepatic; binds with iron to form ferrioxamine

Half-life elimination: Parent drug: 6.1 hours; Ferrioxamine: 5.8 hours

Excretion: Urine (as unchanged drug and ferrioxamine)

Dosage

Acute iron toxicity: **Note:** I.V. route is used when severe toxicity is evidenced by systemic symptoms (coma, shock, metabolic acidosis, or severe gastrointestinal bleeding) or potentially severe intoxications (serum iron level >500 mcg/dL). When severe symptoms are not present, the I.M. route may be preferred (per manufacturer); however, the use of deferoxamine in situations where the serum iron concentration is <500 mcg/dL or when severe toxicity is not evident is a subject of some clinical debate.

Children:

    I.M.: 90 mg/kg/dose every 8 hours (maximum: 6 g/24 hours)

    I.V.: 15 mg/kg/hour (maximum: 6 g/24 hours)

Adults: I.M., I.V.: Initial: 1000 mg, may be followed by 500 mg every 4 hours for up to 2 doses; subsequent doses of 500 mg have been administered every 4-12 hours

    Maximum recommended dose: 6 g/day (per manufacturer, however, higher doses have been administered)

Chronic iron overload:

Children: SubQ: 20-40 mg/kg/day over 8-12 hours (maximum: 1000-2000 mg/day)

Adults:

    I.M., I.V.: 500-1000 mg/day I.M.; in addition, 2000 mg should be given I.V. with each unit of blood transfused (administer separately from blood); maximum: 6 g/day

    SubQ: 1-2 g every day over 8-24 hours

Diagnosis of aluminum induced toxicity with CKD (unlabeled use): Children and Adults: I.V.: Test dose: 5 mg/kg during the last hour of dialysis if serum aluminum levels are 60-200 mcg/L and there are clinical signs/symptoms of toxicity. Do not use if aluminum serum levels are >200 mcg/L

Treatment of aluminum toxicity with CKD (unlabeled use): Children and Adults: I.V.: 5-10 mg/kg 4-6 hours before dialysis. Administer every 7-10 days with 3-4 dialysis procedures between doses. Do not use if aluminum serum levels are >200 mcg/L .

Dosing adjustment in renal impairment: Cl_{cr} <10 mL/minute: Administer 50% of dose

Dietary Considerations Vitamin C supplements may need to be limited. The manufacturer recommends a maximum of 200 mg/day in adults (given in divided doses) and avoiding use in patients with heart failure.

Administration

I.V.: Urticaria, hypotension, and shock have occurred following rapid I.V. administration; limiting infusion rate to 15mg/kg/hour may help avoid infusion-related adverse effects.

Acute iron toxicity: The manufacturer states that the I.M. route is preferred; however, the I.V. route is generally preferred in patients with severe toxicity (ie, patients in shock). For the first 1000 mg, infuse at 15 mg/kg/hour (although rates up to 40-50 mg/kg/hour have been given in patients with massive iron intoxication). Subsequent doses may be given over 4-12 hours; maximum I.V. rate (per manufacturer): 15 mg/kg/hour.

Diagnosis or treatment of aluminum induced toxicity with CKD: Administer dose over 1 hour

SubQ: When administered for chronic iron overload, daily dose should be given over 8-24 hours using portable pump.

Monitoring Parameters Serum iron; ophthalmologic exam (fundoscopy, slit-lamp exam) and audiometry with chronic therapy; growth and body weight in children (every 3 months)

Dialysis patients: Serum aluminum (yearly; every 3 months in patients on aluminum-containing medications)

Aluminum-induced bone disease: Serum aluminum 2 days following test dose; test is considered positive if serum aluminum increases ≥50 mcg/L

Reference Range

Iron, serum: Normal: 50-150 mcg/dL; levels >500 mcg/dL associated with toxicity. Consider treatment with symptomatic patients with levels ≥350 mcg/dL; toxicity cannot be excluded with serum iron levels <350 mcg/dL

Aluminum, serum: <20 mcg/L recommended baseline level in dialysis patients

Test Interactions TIBC may be falsely elevated with high serum iron concentrations or deferoxamine therapy.

Dosage Forms Injection, powder for reconstitution, as mesylate: 500 mg, 2 g

◆ **Deferoxamine Mesylate** see Deferoxamine on page 466

◆ **Dehistine** see Chlorpheniramine, Phenylephrine, and Methscopolamine on page 353

◆ **Dehydral® (Can)** see Methenamine on page 1106

◆ **Dehydrobenzperidol** see Droperidol on page 559

◆ **Delatestryl®** see Testosterone on page 1653

Delavirdine (de la VIR deen)

U.S. Brand Names Rescriptor®
Canadian Brand Names Rescriptor®
Index Terms U-90152S
Pharmacologic Category Antiretroviral Agent, Reverse Transcriptase Inhibitor (Non-nucleoside)
Additional Appendix Information
Antiretroviral Therapy for HIV Infection: Adults and Adolescents *on page 1988*
Management of Healthcare Worker Exposures to HBV, HCV, and HIV *on page 1941*
Use Treatment of HIV-1 infection in combination with at least two additional antiretroviral agents
Pregnancy Risk Factor C
Pregnancy Implications It is not known if delavirdine crosses the human placenta. Delavirdine was shown to be teratogenic in some animal studies. There are no adequate and well-controlled studies in pregnant women. Health professionals are encouraged to contact the antiretroviral pregnancy registry to monitor outcomes of pregnant women exposed to antiretroviral medications (1-800-258-4263 or www.APRegistry.com).
Lactation Excretion in breast milk unknown/contraindicated
Contraindications Hypersensitivity to delavirdine or any component of the formulation; concurrent use of alprazolam, cisapride, ergot alkaloids, midazolam, pimozide, rifampin, or triazolam
Warnings/Precautions Delavirdine may interact with many medications; careful review is required. Use with caution in patients with hepatic or renal dysfunction; due to rapid emergence of resistance, delavirdine should not be used as monotherapy; cross-resistance may be conferred to other non-nucleoside reverse transcriptase inhibitors, although potential for cross-resistance with protease inhibitors is low. Long-term effects of delavirdine are not known. Immune reconstitution syndrome may develop resulting in the occurrence of an inflammatory response to an indolent or residual opportunistic infection; further evaluation and treatment may be required. Safety and efficacy have not been established in children. Rash, which occurs frequently, may require discontinuation of therapy; usually occurs within 1-3 weeks and lasts <2 weeks. Most patients may resume therapy following a treatment interruption.

Adverse Reactions
Frequency of adverse reactions reported from occurrence in clinical trials with delavirdine when used as part of combination antiretroviral therapy.

>10%:
Central nervous system: Headache (19% to 20%), depressive symptoms (10% to 15%), fever (4% to 12%)
Dermatologic: Rash (16% to 32%)
Gastrointestinal: Nausea (20% to 25%), vomiting (3% to 11%)
1% to 10%:
Central nervous system: Anxiety (6% to 8%)
Endocrine & metabolic: Transaminases increased (2% to 5%), amylase increased (3%), bilirubin increased (2%)
Gastrointestinal: Diarrhea, vomiting, abdominal pain (4% to 6%)
Hematologic: Prothrombin time increased (2%), hemoglobin decreased (1% to 3%)
Respiratory: Bronchitis (6% to 8%)
Frequency not defined (limited to important or life threatening): Abscess, adenopathy, alkaline phosphatase increased, allergic reaction, angioedema, anorexia, arrhythmia, bloody stool, bone pain, bruising, cardiac insufficiency, cardiac rate abnormal, cardiomyopathy, chest congestion, cognitive impairment, colitis, confusion, conjunctivitis, dermal leukocytoclastic vasculitis, desquamation, diverticulitis, dyspnea, emotional lability, eosinophilia, erythema multiforme, fecal incontinence, fungal dermatitis, gamma glutamyl transpeptidase increased, gastroenteritis, gastrointestinal bleeding, granulocytosis, gum hemorrhage, hallucination, hematuria, hepatomegaly, hyperglycemia, hyperkalemia, hypertension, hypertriglyceridemia, hyperuricemia, hypocalcemia, hyponatremia, hypophosphatemia, infection, jaundice, kidney pain, leukopenia, lipase increased, menstrual irregularities, moniliasis (oral/vaginal), pancreatitis, pancytopenia, paralysis, peripheral vascular disorder, pneumonia, postural hypotension, purpura, redistribution of body fat, renal calculi, serum creatinine increased, spleen disorder, Stevens-Johnson syndrome, tetany, thrombocytopenia, urinary tract infection, vertigo
Postmarketing and/or case reports: Acute renal failure, hemolytic anemia, hepatic failure, immune reconstitution syndrome, rhabdomyolysis

Overdosage/Toxicology Human reports of overdose with delavirdine are not available. GI decontamination and supportive measures are recommended, dialysis is unlikely to be of benefit in removing the drug since it is extensively metabolized by the liver and is highly protein bound.

Drug Interactions
Cytochrome P450 Effect: Substrate of CYP2D6 (minor), 3A4 (major); **Inhibits** CYP1A2 (weak), 2C9 (strong), 2C19 (strong), 2D6 (strong), 3A4 (strong)
Increased Effect/Toxicity: Delavirdine has been reported to increase the serum concentrations of amprenavir, indinavir, nelfinavir, ritonavir, saquinavir, inhaled corticosteroids, and trazodone. Dose reduction of indinavir, saquinavir, and trazodone should be considered. Plasma concentrations of delavirdine may be increased by fluoxetine and ketoconazole. Clarithromycin, rifabutin, and methadone serum concentrations may be increased by delavirdine.

Delavirdine may increase the levels/effects of CYP2C9, 2C19, or 2D6 substrates. Example substrates include amiodarone, amphetamines, selected beta-blockers, bosentan, citalopram, dapsone, dextromethorphan, diazepam, fluoxetine, glimepiride, glipizide, lidocaine, methsuximide, nateglinide, nefazodone, paroxetine, phenytoin, pioglitazone, propranolol, risperidone, ritonavir, rosiglitazone, sertraline, thioridazine, tricyclic antidepressants, venlafaxine, and warfarin.

Delavirdine may increase the levels/effects of CYP3A4 substrates. Example substrates include benzodiazepines, calcium channel blockers, cisapride, cyclosporine, mirtazapine, nateglinide, nefazodone, sildenafil (and other PDE-5 inhibitors), tacrolimus, and venlafaxine. Concomitant use with alprazolam, cisapride, ergot alkaloids, midazolam, pimozide, or triazolam is contraindicated. Use with lovastatin or simvastatin is not recommended.

Decreased Effect: Antacids, histamine-2 receptor antagonists, or proton pump inhibitors (omeprazole, lansoprazole) may reduce the absorption of delavirdine. Separate administration of didanosine buffered tablets or antacids and delavirdine by 1 hour. Concomitant use with histamine-2 receptor antagonists, omeprazole, or lansoprazole is not recommended.

Decreased delavirdine concentrations may occur when used with amprenavir, nelfinavir, or rifamycin derivatives. Delavirdine decreases plasma concentrations of didanosine and didanosine may decrease plasma concentrations of delavirdine. Separate administration of didanosine buffered tablets and delavirdine by 1 hour. Concomitant use with rifampin is contraindicated.

Delavirdine may decrease the levels/effects of CYP2D6 prodrug substrates. Example prodrug substrates include codeine, hydrocodone, oxycodone, and tramadol. CYP3A4 inducers may decrease the levels/effects of delavirdine. Example inducers include aminoglutethimide, carbamazepine, nafcillin, nevirapine, phenobarbital, phenytoin, and rifamycins. Carbamazepine, phenobarbital, phenytoin and rifamycins should not be coadministered with delavirdine. Dexamethasone may decrease the plasma concentrations of delavirdine.

Ethanol/Nutrition/Herb Interactions Herb/Nutraceutical: Delavirdine serum concentration may be decreased by St John's wort; avoid concurrent use.

Stability Store at 20°C to 25°C (68°F to 77°F); protect from humidity.

Mechanism of Action Delavirdine binds directly to reverse transcriptase, blocking RNA-dependent and DNA-dependent DNA polymerase activities

Pharmacodynamics/Kinetics

Absorption: Rapid

Distribution: Low concentration in saliva and semen; CSF 0.4% concurrent plasma concentration

Protein binding: ~98%, primarily albumin

Metabolism: Hepatic via CYP3A4 and 2D6 (**Note:** May reduce CYP3A activity and inhibit its own metabolism.)

Bioavailability: Tablet: 85% as tablet; ~100% as oral slurry

Half-life elimination: 5.8 hours (range: 2-11 hours)

Time to peak, plasma: 1 hour

Excretion: Urine (51%, <5% as unchanged drug); feces (44%); nonlinear kinetics exhibited

Dosage Adolescents ≥16 years and Adults: Oral: 400 mg 3 times/day

Dietary Considerations May be taken without regard to food.

Administration Patients with achlorhydria should take the drug with an acidic beverage; antacids and delavirdine should be separated by 1 hour. A dispersion of delavirdine may be prepared by adding four 100 mg tablets to at least 3 oz of water. Allow to stand for a few minutes and stir until uniform dispersion. Drink immediately. Rinse glass and mouth, then swallow the rinse to ensure total dose administered. The 200 mg tablets should be taken intact.

Monitoring Parameters Liver function tests if administered with saquinavir

Additional Information Potential compliance problems, frequency of administration, and adverse effects should be discussed with patients before initiating therapy to help prevent the emergence of resistance.

Dosage Forms Tablet, as mesylate: 100 mg, 200 mg

Extemporaneous Preparations A dispersion of delavirdine may be prepared by adding four 100 mg tablets to at least 3 oz of water; allow to stand for a few minutes and stir until uniform dispersion; drink immediately; rinse glass and mouth following ingestion to ensure total dose administered

◆ **Delestrogen®** see Estradiol on page 620

◆ **Delfen® [OTC]** see Nonoxynol 9 on page 1239

◆ **Delta-9-tetrahydro-cannabinol** see Dronabinol on page 558

◆ **Delta-9 THC** see Dronabinol on page 558

◆ **Deltacortisone** see PredniSONE on page 1416

◆ **Deltadehydrocortisone** see PredniSONE on page 1416

◆ **Deltahydrocortisone** see PrednisoLONE on page 1413

◆ **Demadex®** see Torsemide on page 1712

Demeclocycline (dem e kloe SYE kleen)

U.S. Brand Names Declomycin®

Canadian Brand Names Declomycin®

Index Terms Demeclocycline Hydrochloride; Demethylchlortetracycline

Pharmacologic Category Antibiotic, Tetracycline Derivative

Use Treatment of susceptible bacterial infections (acne, gonorrhea, pertussis and urinary tract infections) caused by both gram-negative and gram-positive organisms

Unlabeled/Investigational Use Treatment of chronic syndrome of inappropriate secretion of antidiuretic hormone (SIADH)

Pregnancy Risk Factor D

Pregnancy Implications Tetracyclines cross the placenta and enter fetal circulation; may cause permanent discoloration of teeth if used during the last half of pregnancy. Related

(Continued)

Demeclocycline *(Continued)*

antibiotics have been associated with mutagenesis, embryotoxicity, and oncogenic activity in animals.

Lactation Enters breast milk/not recommended (AAP rates tetracycline "compatible")

Contraindications Hypersensitivity to demeclocycline, tetracyclines, or any component of the formulation; children <8 years of age; concomitant use with methoxyflurane; pregnancy

Warnings/Precautions Photosensitivity reactions occur frequently with this drug; avoid prolonged exposure to sunlight and do not use tanning equipment. Use of tetracyclines during tooth development may cause permanent discoloration of the teeth and enamel, hypoplasia and retardation of skeletal development and bone growth with risk being the greatest for children <4 years and those receiving high doses. Use caution in patients with renal or hepatic impairment (eg, elderly); dosage modification required in patients with renal impairment. May act as an antianabolic agent and increase BUN. Pseudotumor cerebri has been reported with tetracycline use (usually resolves with discontinuation). Outdated drug can cause nephropathy; superinfection possible.

Adverse Reactions Frequency not defined.

Cardiovascular: Pericarditis

Central nervous system: Bulging fontanels (infants), dizziness, headache, pseudotumor cerebri (adults)

Dermatologic: Angioneurotic edema, erythema multiforme, erythematous rash, maculopapular rash, photosensitivity, pigmentation of skin, Stevens-Johnson syndrome (rare), urticaria

Endocrine & metabolic: Discoloration of thyroid gland (brown/black), nephrogenic diabetes insipidus

Gastrointestinal: Anorexia, diarrhea, dysphagia, enterocolitis, esophageal ulcerations, glossitis, nausea, pancreatitis, vomiting

Genitourinary: Balanitis

Hematologic: Eosinophilia, neutropenia, hemolytic anemia, thrombocytopenia

Hepatic: Hepatitis (rare), hepatotoxicity (rare), liver enzymes increased, liver failure (rare)

Neuromuscular & skeletal: Myasthenic syndrome, polyarthralgia, tooth discoloration (children <8 years, rarely in adults)

Ocular: Visual disturbances

Otic: Tinnitus

Renal: Acute renal failure

Respiratory: Pulmonary infiltrates

Miscellaneous: Anaphylaxis, anaphylactoid purpura, lupus-like syndrome, systemic lupus erythematosus exacerbation

Overdosage/Toxicology Treatment is supportive.

Drug Interactions

Increased Effect/Toxicity: Methoxyflurane anesthesia may cause fatal nephrotoxicity; retinoic acid derivatives may increase adverse and toxic effects; warfarin may result in increased anticoagulation; methotrexate levels may be increased

Decreased Effect: Antacid preparations containing calcium, magnesium, aluminum bismuth, or sodium bicarbonate may decrease tetracycline absorption; bile acid sequestrants, quinapril (magnesium-containing formulation), iron, or zinc may also decrease absorption; penicillin decrease therapeutic effect of tetracyclines. Although anecdotal reports suggest oral contraceptive efficacy could be reduced by tetracyclines, this has been refuted by more rigorous scientific and clinical data.

Ethanol/Nutrition/Herb Interactions

Food: Demeclocycline serum levels may be decreased if taken with food.

Herb/Nutraceutical: Avoid dong quai, St John's wort (may also cause photosensitization).

Stability Tetracyclines form toxic products when outdated or when exposed to light, heat, or humidity (Fanconi-like syndrome).

Mechanism of Action Inhibits protein synthesis by binding with the 30S and possibly the 50S ribosomal subunit(s) of susceptible bacteria; may also cause alterations in the cytoplasmic membrane; inhibits the action of ADH in patients with chronic SIADH

Pharmacodynamics/Kinetics

Onset of action: SIADH: Several days

Absorption: ~50% to 80%; reduced by food and dairy products

Protein binding: 41% to 50%

Metabolism: Hepatic (small amounts) to inactive metabolites; undergoes enterohepatic recirculation

Half-life elimination: 10-17 hours

Time to peak, serum: 3-6 hours

Excretion: Urine (42% to 50% as unchanged drug)

Dosage Oral:

Children ≥8 years: 8-12 mg/kg/day divided every 6-12 hours

Adults: 150 mg 4 times/day or 300 mg twice daily

SIADH (unlabeled use): 900-1200 mg/day or 13-15 mg/kg/day divided every 6-8 hours initially, then decrease to 600-900 mg/day

Dosing adjustment/comments in renal/hepatic impairment: Should be avoided in patients with renal/hepatic dysfunction

Dietary Considerations Should be taken 1 hour before or 2 hours after food or milk with plenty of fluid.

Administration Administer 1 hour before or 2 hours after food or milk with plenty of fluid.

Monitoring Parameters CBC, renal and hepatic function

Test Interactions May interfere with tests for urinary glucose (false-negative urine glucose using Clinistix®, Tes-Tape®)

Dosage Forms Tablet, as hydrochloride: 150 mg, 300 mg

♦ **Demeclocycline Hydrochloride** *see* Demeclocycline *on page 469*

♦ **Demerol®** *see* Meperidine *on page 1081*

♦ **4-Demethoxydaunorubicin** *see* Idarubicin *on page 878*

♦ **Demethylchlortetracycline** *see Demeclocycline on page 469*
♦ **Demser®** *see Metyrosine on page 1134*
♦ **Demulen® [DSC]** *see Ethinyl Estradiol and Ethynodiol Diacetate on page 648*
♦ **Demulen® 30 (Can)** *see Ethinyl Estradiol and Ethynodiol Diacetate on page 648*
♦ **Denavir®** *see Penciclovir on page 1329*

Denileukin Diftitox (de ni LOO kin DIF ti toks)

U.S. Brand Names ONTAK®
Index Terms DAB$_{389}$IL-2; NSC-714744
Pharmacologic Category Antineoplastic Agent, Miscellaneous
Use Treatment of persistent or recurrent cutaneous T-cell lymphoma whose malignant cells express the CD25 component of the IL-2 receptor
Pregnancy Risk Factor C
Pregnancy Implications Animal reproduction studies have not been conducted. There are no adequate and well-controlled studies in pregnant women. Should be given to a pregnant woman only if clearly needed
Lactation Excretion in breast milk unknown/contraindicated
Medication Safety Issues
High alert medication: The Institute for Safe Medication Practices (ISMP) includes this medication among its list of drugs which have a heightened risk of causing significant patient harm when used in error.
Contraindications Hypersensitivity to denileukin diftitox, diphtheria toxin, interleukin-2, or any component of the formulation
Warnings/Precautions Hazardous agent - use appropriate precautions for handling and disposal. Acute hypersensitivity reactions, including anaphylaxis, may occur; most events (eg, hypotension, back pain, dyspnea, vasodilation, rash, chest pain, tachycardia, dysphagia, syncope) occur during or within 24 hours of infusion; with ~50% occurring on the day 1, regardless of treatment cycle. Denileukin diftitox has been associated with a potentially-severe, delayed-onset vascular leak syndrome, which may be severe. The onset of symptoms (hypotension, edema, hypoalbuminemia) of vascular leak syndrome usually occurred within the first 2 weeks of infusion and may persist or worsen after cessation of denileukin diftitox. Use caution in patients with pre-existing cardiovascular disease. Pre-existing low serum albumin levels (<3 g/dL) may predict or predispose to vascular leak syndrome. Immunogenicity may develop; patients with antibodies have a two- to threefold increase in clearance. The presence of antibodies does not correlate with risk for hypersensitivity/infusion related reactions. Denileukin diftitox may impair immune function. Loss of visual acuity with loss of color vision (with or without retinal pigment mottling) has been reported. Use with caution in patients >65 years of age; adverse events (anemia, anorexia, confusion, hypotension, rash, nausea/vomiting) occur more frequently. Safety and efficacy in children have not been established. **[U.S. Boxed Warning]: Should be administered under the supervision of an experienced cancer chemotherapy physician.**
Adverse Reactions
>10%:
Cardiovascular: Edema (47%; grade 3 and 4, 15%), hypotension (36%), chest pain (24%), vasodilation (22%), tachycardia (12%)
Central nervous system: Fever/chills (81%; grade 3 and 4, 22%), headache (26%), pain (48%; grade 3 and 4, 13%), dizziness (22%), nervousness (11%)
Dermatologic: Rash (34%; grade 3 and 4, 13%), pruritus (20%)
Endocrine & metabolic: Hypoalbuminemia (83%; grade 3 and 4, 14%), hypocalcemia (17%), weight loss (14%)
Gastrointestinal: Nausea/vomiting (64%; grade 3 and 4, 14%), anorexia (36%), diarrhea (29%)
Hematologic: Lymphocyte count decreased (34%), anemia (18%)
Hepatic: Transaminases increased (61%; grade 3 and 4, 15%)
Neuromuscular & skeletal: Weakness (66%; grade 3 and 4, 22%), myalgia (17%), paresthesia (13%)
Respiratory: Dyspnea (29%; grade 3 and 4, 14%), cough increased (26%), pharyngitis (17%), rhinitis (13%)
Miscellaneous: Flu-like syndrome (91%; beginning several hours to days following infusion), hypersensitivity (69%; reactions are variable, but may include hypotension, back pain, dyspnea, vasodilation, rash, chest pain, tachycardia, dysphagia, syncope, or anaphylaxis), infection (48%; grade 3 and 4, 24%), vascular leak syndrome (27%; characterized by hypotension, edema, or hypoalbuminemia; the syndrome usually developed within the first 2 weeks of infusion; 6% of patients who developed this syndrome required hospitalization; the symptoms may persist or even worsen despite cessation of denileukin diftitox)
1% to 10%:
Cardiovascular: Thrombotic events (7%), hypertension (6%), arrhythmia (6%), MI (1%)
Central nervous system: Insomnia (9%), confusion (9%)
Endocrine & metabolic: Dehydration (9%), hypokalemia (6%), hyperthyroidism (<5%), hypothyroidism (<5%)
Gastrointestinal: Constipation (9%), dyspepsia (7%), dysphagia (6%), oral ulcer (<5%), pancreatitis (<5%)
Hematologic: Thrombocytopenia (8%), leukopenia (6%)
Local: Injection site reaction (8%), anaphylaxis (1%)
Neuromuscular & skeletal: Arthralgia (8%)
Renal: Hematuria (10%), albuminuria (10%), pyuria (10%), creatinine increased (7%), acute renal insufficiency (<5%)
Respiratory: Lung disorder (8%)
Miscellaneous: Anaphylaxis (1%), diaphoresis decreased (10%)
Postmarketing and/or case reports: Toxic epidermal necrolysis, visual loss
(Continued)

Denileukin Diftitox *(Continued)*

Overdosage/Toxicology Although there is no human experience in overdose, dose-limiting toxicities include nausea, vomiting, fever, chills and persistent weakness. Treatment is supportive and symptom-directed. Fluid balance and hepatic and renal function should be closely monitored.

Stability Store frozen at or below -10°C (14°F); cannot be refrozen. Must be brought to room temperature (25°C or 77°F) before preparing the dose. Do **not** heat vials. Thaw in refrigerator for not >24 hours or at room temperature for 1-2 hours. Avoid vigorous agitation. Solution may be mixed by gentle swirling. Dilute with NS to a concentration of ≥15 mcg/mL; the concentration must be ≥15 mcg/mL during all steps of preparation. This solution should be used within 6 hours. Add drug to the empty sterile I.V. bag first, then add NS. Do **not** use glass syringes or containers.

Mechanism of Action Denileukin diftitox is a fusion protein (a combination of amino acid sequences from diphtheria toxin and interleukin-2) which selectively delivers the cytotoxic activity of diphtheria toxin to targeted cells. It interacts with the high-affinity IL-2 receptor on the surface of malignant cells to inhibit intracellular protein synthesis, rapidly leading to cell death.

Pharmacodynamics/Kinetics
Distribution: V_d: 0.06-0.08 L/kg
Metabolism: Hepatic via proteolytic degradation (animal studies)
Half-life elimination: Distribution: 2-5 minutes; Terminal: 70-80 minutes

Dosage Adults: I.V.: 9 or 18 mcg/kg/day days 1 through 5 every 21 days

Administration For I.V. use only. Infuse over at least 15 minutes. Should not be given as a rapid I.V. bolus. Discontinue or reduce infusion rate for infusion related reactions. There is no clinical experience with prolonged infusions (>80 minutes). Do not administer through an in-line filter. Consider premedication with antipyretics, antihistamines, and antiemetics.

Monitoring Parameters Baseline CD25 expression (on malignant cells); CBC, blood chemistry panel, renal and hepatic function tests as well as a serum albumin level; these tests should be done prior to initiation of therapy and repeated at weekly intervals during therapy. During the infusion, the patient should be monitored for symptoms of an acute hypersensitivity reaction. After infusion, the patient should be monitored for the development of a delayed vascular leak syndrome (usually in the first 2 weeks), including careful monitoring of weight, blood pressure, and serum albumin.

Additional Information Formulation includes polysorbate 20.

Dosage Forms
Injection, solution [frozen]:
ONTAK®: 150 mcg/mL (2 mL) [contains EDTA]

♦ **Denta 5000 Plus** see Fluoride *on page 722*
♦ **DentaGel** see Fluoride *on page 722*
♦ **Dentapaine [OTC]** see Benzocaine *on page 204*
♦ **Dent's Ear Wax [OTC]** see Carbamide Peroxide *on page 287*
♦ **Dent's Extra Strength Toothache [OTC]** see Benzocaine *on page 204*
♦ **Dent's Maxi-Strength Toothache [OTC]** see Benzocaine *on page 204*
♦ **2'-Deoxycoformycin** see Pentostatin *on page 1342*
♦ **Deoxycoformycin** see Pentostatin *on page 1342*
♦ **Depacon®** see Valproic Acid and Derivatives *on page 1767*
♦ **Depade®** see Naltrexone *on page 1195*
♦ **Depakene®** see Valproic Acid and Derivatives *on page 1767*
♦ **Depakote®** see Valproic Acid and Derivatives *on page 1767*
♦ **Depakote® ER** see Valproic Acid and Derivatives *on page 1767*
♦ **Depakote® Sprinkle** see Valproic Acid and Derivatives *on page 1767*
♦ **Depen®** see Penicillamine *on page 1330*
♦ **DepoCyt®** see Cytarabine (Liposomal) *on page 439*
♦ **DepoDur™** see Morphine Sulfate *on page 1171*
♦ **Depo®-Estradiol** see Estradiol *on page 620*
♦ **Depo-Medrol®** see MethylPREDNISolone *on page 1122*
♦ **Depo-Prevera® (Can)** see MedroxyPROGESTERone *on page 1065*
♦ **Depo-Provera®** see MedroxyPROGESTERone *on page 1065*
♦ **Depo-Provera® Contraceptive** see MedroxyPROGESTERone *on page 1065*
♦ **depo-subQ provera 104™** see MedroxyPROGESTERone *on page 1065*
♦ **Depotest® 100 (Can)** see Testosterone *on page 1653*
♦ **Depo®-Testosterone** see Testosterone *on page 1653*
♦ **Deprenyl** see Selegiline *on page 1552*
♦ **DermaFungal [OTC]** see Miconazole *on page 1137*
♦ **Dermagran® [OTC]** see Aluminum Hydroxide *on page 83*
♦ **Dermagran® AF [OTC]** see Miconazole *on page 1137*
♦ **Dermamycin® [OTC]** see DiphenhydrAMINE *on page 515*
♦ **Dermarest Dricort® [OTC]** see Hydrocortisone *on page 852*
♦ **Dermarest® Insect Bite [OTC]** see DiphenhydrAMINE *on page 515*
♦ **Dermarest® Plus [OTC]** see DiphenhydrAMINE *on page 515*
♦ **Dermarest® Skin Correction Cream Plus [OTC]** see Hydroquinone *on page 859*
♦ **Derma-Smoothe/FS®** see Fluocinolone *on page 721*
♦ **Dermatop®** see Prednicarbate *on page 1413*
♦ **Dermazene®** see Iodoquinol and Hydrocortisone *on page 931*
♦ **Dermazole (Can)** see Miconazole *on page 1137*
♦ **Dermoplast® Antibacterial [OTC]** see Benzocaine *on page 204*
♦ **Dermoplast® Pain Relieving [OTC]** see Benzocaine *on page 204*

+ **Dermovate® (Can)** *see* Clobetasol *on page 391*
+ **Dermtex® HC [OTC]** *see* Hydrocortisone *on page 852*
+ **Desferal®** *see* Deferoxamine *on page 466*
+ **Desiccated Thyroid** *see* Thyroid *on page 1676*

Desipramine (des IP ra meen)

U.S. Brand Names Norpramin®
Canadian Brand Names Alti-Desipramine; Apo-Desipramine®; Norpramin®; Nu-Desipramine; PMS-Desipramine
Index Terms Desipramine Hydrochloride; Desmethylimipramine Hydrochloride
Pharmacologic Category Antidepressant, Tricyclic (Secondary Amine)
Additional Appendix Information
    Antidepressant Agents *on page 1866*
Use Treatment of depression
Unlabeled/Investigational Use Analgesic adjunct in chronic pain; peripheral neuropathies; substance-related disorders (eg, cocaine withdrawal); attention-deficit/hyperactivity disorder (ADHD); depression in children ≤12 years of age
Restrictions An FDA-approved medication guide concerning the use of antidepressants in children and teenagers must be distributed when dispensing an outpatient prescription (new or refill) where this medication is to be used without direct supervision of a healthcare provider. Medication guides are available at http://www.fda.gov/cder/Offices/ODS/medication_guides.htm. Dispense to parents or guardians of children and teenagers receiving this medication.
Pregnancy Risk Factor C
Lactation Enters breast milk/not recommended (AAP rates "of concern")
Medication Safety Issues
    Sound-alike/look-alike issues:
        Desipramine may be confused with clomiPRAMINE, deserpidine, diphenhydrAMINE, disopyramide, imipramine, nortriptyline
        Norpramin® may be confused with clomiPRAMINE, imipramine, Norpace®, nortriptyline, Tenormin®

    International issues:
        Norpramin®: Brand name for omeprazole in Spain
Contraindications Hypersensitivity to desipramine, drugs of similar chemical class, or any component of the formulation; use of MAO inhibitors within 14 days; use in a patient during the acute recovery phase of MI; concurrent use of thioridazine
Warnings/Precautions [U.S. Boxed Warning]: Antidepressants increase the risk of suicidal thinking and behavior in children and adolescents with major depressive disorder (MDD) and other depressive disorders; consider risk prior to prescribing. All patients must be closely monitored for clinical worsening, suicidality, or unusual changes in behavior, especially during the initiation of therapy or following an increase or decrease in dosage. When used in children, the child's family or caregiver should be instructed to closely observe the patient and communicate condition with healthcare provider. A medication guide should be dispensed with each prescription. **Desipramine is FDA approved for the treatment of depression in adolescents.**

The possibility of a suicide attempt is inherent in major depression and may persist until remission occurs. Use caution in high-risk patients. Worsening depression and severe abrupt suicidality that are not part of the presenting symptoms may require discontinuation or modification of drug therapy. The patient's family or caregiver should be alerted to monitor patients for the emergence of suicidality and associated behaviors (such as agitation, irritability, hostility, impulsivity, and hypomania) and notify healthcare provider.

May worsen psychosis in some patients or precipitate a shift to mania or hypomania in patients with bipolar disorder. Patients presenting with depressive symptoms should be screened for bipolar disorder. Monotherapy in patients with bipolar disorder should be avoided. **Desipramine is not FDA approved for the treatment of bipolar depression.**

The degree of anticholinergic blockade produced by this agent is low relative to other cyclic antidepressants - however, caution should be used in patients with urinary retention, benign prostatic hyperplasia, narrow-angle glaucoma, xerostomia, visual problems, constipation, or a history of bowel obstruction. The degree of sedation and conduction disturbances with desipramine are low relative to other antidepressants. However, desipramine may cause drowsiness/sedation, resulting in impaired performance of tasks requiring alertness (eg, operating machinery or driving). Sedative effects may be additive with other CNS depressants and/or ethanol. The risk of orthostasis is moderate relative to other antidepressants. Use with caution in patients with a history of cardiovascular disease (including previous MI, stroke, tachycardia, or conduction abnormalities).

Consider discontinuing, when possible, prior to elective surgery. Therapy should not be abruptly discontinued in patients receiving high doses for prolonged periods. May lower seizure threshold - use caution in patients with a previous seizure disorder or condition predisposing to seizures such as brain damage, alcoholism, or concurrent therapy with other drugs which lower the seizure threshold. May increase the risks associated with electroconvulsive therapy. Use with caution in hyperthyroid patients or those receiving thyroid supplementation. Use with caution in patients with hepatic or renal dysfunction and in elderly patients.
Adverse Reactions Frequency not defined.
    Cardiovascular: Arrhythmias, edema, flushing, heart block, hyper-/hypotension, MI, palpitation, stroke, tachycardia
    Central nervous system: Agitation, anxiety, ataxia, confusion, delirium, disorientation, dizziness, drowsiness, drug fever, exacerbation of psychosis, extrapyramidal symptoms, fatigue, hallucinations, headache, hypomania, incoordination, insomnia, nervousness, parkinsonian syndrome, restlessness, seizure
(Continued)

Desipramine *(Continued)*

Dermatologic: Alopecia, itching, petechiae, photosensitivity, skin rash, urticaria

Endocrine & metabolic: Breast enlargement, galactorrhea, hyper-/hypoglycemia, impotence, libido changes, SIADH

Gastrointestinal: Abdominal cramps, anorexia, black tongue, constipation, decreased lower esophageal sphincter tone may cause GE reflux, diarrhea, heartburn, nausea, paralytic ileus, stomatitis, unpleasant taste, vomiting, weight gain/loss, xerostomia

Genitourinary: Difficult urination, polyuria, sexual dysfunction, testicular edema, urinary retention

Hematologic: Agranulocytosis, eosinophilia, purpura, thrombocytopenia

Hepatic: Cholestatic jaundice, hepatitis, liver enzymes increased

Neuromuscular & skeletal: Fine muscle tremor, numbness, paresthesia of extremities, peripheral neuropathy, tingling, weakness

Ocular: Blurred vision, disturbances of accommodation, intraocular pressure increased, mydriasis

Otic: Tinnitus

Miscellaneous: Allergic reaction, diaphoresis (excessive)

Overdosage/Toxicology Symptoms include severe hypotension, agitation, confusion, hypo-/hyperthermia, hypotension (severe), urinary retention, CNS depression, coma, cyanosis, dry mucous membranes, cardiac arrhythmias, seizures, changes in ECG (particularly in QRS axis and width), transient visual hallucinations, stupor, and muscle rigidity. Treatment is supportive and symptom-directed. Initiate gastric decontamination (emesis is contraindicated) and ECG monitoring immediately; monitor for a minimum of 6 hours. Sodium bicarbonate is indicated when the QRS interval is ≥0.10 seconds or the QT_c is >0.42 seconds. Ventricular arrhythmias and ECG changes (eg, QRS widening) often respond with concurrent systemic alkalinization (sodium bicarbonate 0.5-2 mEq/kg I.V.). Arrhythmias unresponsive to phenytoin 15-20 mg/kg (adults) may respond to lidocaine 1 mg/kg I.V. followed by a titrated infusion. Physostigmine (1-2 mg slow I.V. for adults or 0.5 mg slow I.V. for children) may be indicated in reversing life-threatening cardiac arrhythmias. Seizures usually respond to diazepam I.V. boluses (5-10 mg for adults up to 30 mg or 0.25-0.4 mg/kg/dose for children up to 10 mg/dose). If seizures are unresponsive or recur, phenytoin or phenobarbital may be required. Dialysis and diuresis have not been proven beneficial.

Drug Interactions

Cytochrome P450 Effect: Substrate of CYP1A2 (minor), 2D6 (major); **Inhibits** CYP2A6 (moderate), 2B6 (moderate), 2D6 (moderate), 2E1 (weak), 3A4 (moderate)

Increased Effect/Toxicity: Desipramine increases the effects of amphetamines, anticholinergics, other CNS depressants (sedatives, hypnotics, or ethanol), chlorpropamide, tolazamide, and warfarin. When used with MAO inhibitors, or other serotonin modulators (eg, SSRIs), enhanced serotonergic effects, including serotonin syndrome may occur. Concurrent use with sibutramine is contraindicated. Serotonin syndrome has also been reported with ritonavir (rare). The levels/effects of desipramine may be increased by chlorpromazine, delavirdine, fluoxetine, miconazole, paroxetine, pergolide, quinidine, quinine, ritonavir, ropinirole, and other CYP2D6 inhibitors.

Cimetidine, grapefruit juice, indinavir, methylphenidate, diltiazem, and verapamil may increase the serum concentration of TCAs. Use of lithium with a TCA may increase the risk for neurotoxicity. Phenothiazines may increase concentration of some TCAs and TCAs may increase concentration of phenothiazines. Pressor response to I.V. epinephrine, norepinephrine, and phenylephrine may be enhanced in patients receiving TCAs. (**Note:** Effect is unlikely with epinephrine or levonordefrin dosages typically administered as infiltration in combination with local anesthetics.) Combined use of beta-agonists or drugs which prolong QT_c (including quinidine, procainamide, disopyramide, cisapride, sparfloxacin, gatifloxacin, moxifloxacin) with TCAs may predispose patients to cardiac arrhythmias.

Desipramine may increase the levels/effects of selected benzodiazepines, bupropion, calcium channel blockers, cisapride, dexmedetomidine, dextromethorphan, ergot derivatives, ifosfamide, fluoxetine, selected HMG-CoA reductase inhibitors, lidocaine, mesoridazine, mirtazapine, nateglinide, nefazodone, paroxetine, pimozide, promethazine, propofol, quinidine, risperidone, ritonavir, selegiline, sertraline, sildenafil (and other PDE-5 inhibitors), tacrolimus, thioridazine, tricyclic antidepressants, venlafaxine, and other CYP2A6, 2B6, 2D6, or 3A4 substrates.

Decreased Effect: Desipramine may decrease the levels/effects of CYP2D6 prodrug substrates (eg, codeine, hydrocodone, oxycodone, tramadol). Desipramine's serum levels/effect may be decreased by carbamazepine, cholestyramine, colestipol, phenobarbital, and rifampin. Desipramine may inhibit the antihypertensive effect of clonidine, guanadrel, or methyldopa.

Ethanol/Nutrition/Herb Interactions

Ethanol: Avoid ethanol (may increase CNS depression).

Food: Grapefruit juice may inhibit the metabolism of some TCAs and clinical toxicity may result.

Herb/Nutraceutical: Avoid valerian, St John's wort, SAMe, kava kava (may increase risk of serotonin syndrome and/or excessive sedation).

Mechanism of Action Traditionally believed to increase the synaptic concentration of norepinephrine (and to a lesser extent, serotonin) in the central nervous system by inhibition of its reuptake by the presynaptic neuronal membrane. However, additional receptor effects have been found including desensitization of adenyl cyclase, down regulation of beta-adrenergic receptors, and down regulation of serotonin receptors.

Pharmacodynamics/Kinetics

Onset of action: 1-3 weeks; Maximum antidepressant effect: >2 weeks

Absorption: Well absorbed

Metabolism: Hepatic

Half-life elimination: Adults: 7-60 hours

Time to peak, plasma: 4-6 hours

Excretion: Urine (70%)

Dosage Oral (dose is generally administered at bedtime):
Children 6-12 years: Depression (unlabeled use): 10-30 mg/day or 1-3 mg/kg/day in divided doses; do not exceed 5 mg/kg/day
Adolescents: Depression: Initial: 25-50 mg/day; gradually increase to 100 mg/day in single or divided doses (maximum: 150 mg/day)
Adults:
Depression: Initial: 75 mg/day in divided doses; increase gradually to 150-200 mg/day in divided or single dose (maximum: 300 mg/day)
Cocaine withdrawal (unlabeled use): 50-200 mg/day in divided or single dose
Elderly: Depression: Initial dose: 10-25 mg/day; increase by 10-25 mg every 3 days for inpatients and every week for outpatients if tolerated; usual maintenance dose: 75-100 mg/day, but doses up to 150 mg/day may be necessary
Hemodialysis/peritoneal dialysis: Supplemental dose is not necessary

Monitoring Parameters Monitor blood pressure and pulse rate prior to and during initial therapy evaluate mental status; monitor weight; ECG in older adults and those patients with cardiac disease; blood levels are useful for therapeutic monitoring

Reference Range
Plasma levels do not always correlate with clinical effectiveness
Timing of serum samples: Draw trough just before next dose
Therapeutic: 50-300 ng/mL
In elderly patients the response rate is greatest with steady-state plasma concentrations >115 ng/mL
Possible toxicity: >300 ng/mL
Toxic: >1000 ng/mL

Additional Information Less sedation and anticholinergic effects than with amitriptyline or imipramine

Dosage Forms Tablet, as hydrochloride: 10 mg, 25 mg, 50 mg, 75 mg, 100 mg, 150 mg

♦ **Desipramine Hydrochloride** *see* Desipramine *on page 473*
♦ **Desitin® [OTC]** *see* Zinc Oxide *on page 1817*
♦ **Desitin® Creamy [OTC]** *see* Zinc Oxide *on page 1817*

Desloratadine (des lor AT a deen)

U.S. Brand Names Clarinex®
Canadian Brand Names Aerius®
Pharmacologic Category Antihistamine, Nonsedating
Use Relief of nasal and non-nasal symptoms of seasonal allergic rhinitis (SAR) and perennial allergic rhinitis (PAR); treatment of chronic idiopathic urticaria (CIU)
Pregnancy Risk Factor C
Pregnancy Implications There are no adequate and well-controlled studies in pregnant women. Use during pregnancy only if clearly needed.
Lactation Enters breast milk/not recommended
Contraindications Hypersensitivity to desloratadine, loratadine, or any component of the formulation
Warnings/Precautions Dose should be adjusted in patients with liver or renal impairment. Use with caution in patients known to be slow metabolizers of desloratadine (incidence of side effects may be increased). RediTabs® contain phenylalanine. Safety and efficacy have not been established for children <6 months of age.

Adverse Reactions
>10%: Central nervous system: Headache (14%)
1% to 10%:
Central nervous system: Fatigue (2% to 5%), somnolence (2%), dizziness (4%)
Endocrine & metabolic: Dysmenorrhea (2%)
Gastrointestinal: Xerostomia (3%), nausea (5%), dyspepsia (3%)
Neuromuscular & skeletal: Myalgia (2% to 3%)
Respiratory: Pharyngitis (3% to 4%)
Postmarketing and/or case reports: Anaphylaxis, bilirubin increased, dyspnea, edema, hypersensitivity reactions, liver enzymes increased, palpitation, pruritus, rash, tachycardia, urticaria

Overdosage/Toxicology Information is limited to doses studied during clinical trials (up to 45 mg/day). Symptoms included somnolence, and small increases in heart rate and QT_c interval (not clinically significant). In the event of an overdose, treatment should be symptom-directed and supportive. Desloratadine and its metabolite are not removed by hemodialysis.

Drug Interactions
Increased Effect/Toxicity: With concurrent use of desloratadine and erythromycin or ketoconazole, the C_{max} and AUC of desloratadine and its metabolite are increased; however, no clinically-significant changes in the safety profile of desloratadine were observed in clinical studies.
Ethanol/Nutrition/Herb Interactions Food: Does not affect bioavailability.
Stability Syrup, tablet, orally-disintegrating tablet: Store at 25°C (77°F); excursions permitted between 15°C to 30°C (59°F to 86°F). Protect from moisture and excessive heat (85°F). Use orally-disintegrating tablet immediately after opening blister package. Syrup should be protected from light.
Mechanism of Action Desloratadine, a major metabolite of loratadine, is a long-acting tricyclic antihistamine with selective peripheral histamine H_1 receptor antagonistic activity and additional anti-inflammatory properties.

Pharmacodynamics/Kinetics
Protein binding: Desloratadine: 82% to 87%; 3-hydroxydesloratadine: 85% to 89%
Metabolism: Hepatic to active metabolite, 3-hydroxydesloratadine (specific enzymes not identified); undergoes glucuronidation. Decreased in slow metabolizers of desloratadine. Not expected to affect or be affected by medications metabolized by CYP with normal doses.
(Continued)

Desloratadine *(Continued)*

Half-life elimination: 27 hours
Time to peak: 3 hours
Excretion: Urine and feces (as metabolites)

Dosage Oral:
Children:
6-11 months: 1 mg once daily
12 months to 5 years: 1.25 mg once daily
6-11 years: 2.5 mg once daily
Children ≥12 years and Adults: 5 mg once daily

Dosage adjustment in renal/hepatic impairment:
Children: Not established
Adults: 5 mg every other day

Dietary Considerations May be taken with or without food. Orally-disintegrating tablets contain phenylalanine.

Administration May be taken with or without food.
RediTabs® should be placed on the tongue; tablet will disintegrate immediately. May be taken with or without water.
Syrup: A commercially-available measuring dropper or syringe calibrated to deliver 2 mL or 2.5 mL should be used to administer age-appropriate doses in children.

Dosage Forms
Syrup (Clarinex®): 0.5 mg/mL (120 mL, 480 mL) [bubble gum flavor]
Tablet (Clarinex®): 5 mg
Tablet, orally disintegrating (Clarinex® RediTabs®): 2.5 mg [contains phenylalanine 1.28 mg/tablet; tutti-frutti flavor]; 5 mg [contains phenylalanine 2.55 mg/tablet; tutti-frutti flavor]

Desloratadine and Pseudoephedrine

(des lor AT a deen & soo doe e FED rin)

U.S. Brand Names Clarinex-D® 12 Hour; Clarinex-D® 24 Hour
Index Terms Pseudoephedrine and Desloratadine
Pharmacologic Category Antihistamine/Decongestant Combination, Nonsedating
Use Relief of symptoms of seasonal allergic rhinitis, in children ≥12 years of age and adults
Pregnancy Risk Factor C

Dosage Oral: Children ≥12 years and Adults:
Clarinex-D® 12 Hour: One tablet twice daily
Clarinex-D® 24 Hour: One tablet daily

Dosage adjustment in renal impairment:
Clarinex-D® 12 Hour: Not recommended
Clarinex-D® 24 Hour: One tablet every other day
Dosage adjustment in hepatic impairment: Not recommended

Additional Information Complete prescribing information for this medication should be consulted for additional detail.

Dosage Forms Tablet, variable release:
Clarinex-D® 12 Hour: Desloratadine 2.5 mg [immediate release] and pseudoephedrine 120 mg [extended release]
Clarinex-D® 24 Hour: Desloratadine 5 mg [immediate release] and pseudoephedrine 240 mg [extended release]

◆ **Desmethylimipramine Hydrochloride** *see Desipramine on page 473*

Desmopressin *(des moe PRES in)*

U.S. Brand Names DDAVP®; Stimate™
Canadian Brand Names Apo-Desmopressin®; DDAVP®; Minirin®; Octostim®
Index Terms 1-Deamino-8-D-Arginine Vasopressin; Desmopressin Acetate
Pharmacologic Category Antihemophilic Agent; Hemostatic Agent; Vasopressin Analog, Synthetic
Use
Injection: Treatment of diabetes insipidus; control of bleeding in hemophilia A, and mild-to-moderate classic von Willebrand disease (type I)
Tablet, nasal solution: Treatment of diabetes insipidus; primary nocturnal enuresis
Pregnancy Risk Factor B
Lactation Excretion in breast milk unknown/use caution
Contraindications Hypersensitivity to desmopressin or any component of the formulation; moderate to severe renal impairment (Cl$_{cr}$<50 mL/minute)
Warnings/Precautions Fluid intake should be adjusted downward in the elderly and very young patients to decrease the possibility of water intoxication and hyponatremia. Avoid overhydration especially when drug is used for its hemostatic effect. Use may rarely lead to extreme decreases in plasma osmolality, resulting in seizures and coma. Use caution with cystic fibrosis or other conditions associated with fluid and electrolyte imbalance due to potential hyponatremia. Use caution with coronary artery insufficiency or hypertensive cardiovascular disease; may increase or decrease blood pressure leading to changes in heart rate. Consider switching from nasal to intravenous solution if changes in the nasal mucosa (scarring, edema) occur leading to unreliable absorption. Use caution in patients predisposed to thrombus formation; thrombotic events (acute cerebrovascular thrombosis, acute myocardial infarction) have occurred (rare). Injection is not for use in hemophilia B, severe classic von Willebrand disease (type IIB), or in patients with factor VIII antibodies. In general, the injection is also not recommended for use in patients with ≤5% factor VIII activity level, although it may be considered in selected patients with activity levels between 2% and 5%. Some patients may demonstrate a change in response after long-term therapy (>6 months) characterized as decreased response or a shorter duration of response.

Adverse Reactions Frequency not defined (may be dose or route related).

Cardiovascular: Acute cerebrovascular thrombosis, acute MI, blood pressure increased/
decreased, chest pain, edema, facial flushing, palpitation

Central nervous system: Agitation, chills, coma, dizziness, headache, insomnia, somnolence

Dermatologic: Rash

Endocrine & metabolic: Hyponatremia, water intoxication

Gastrointestinal: Abdominal cramps, dyspepsia, nausea, sore throat, vomiting

Genitourinary: Balanitis, vulval pain

Local: Injection: Burning pain, erythema, and swelling at the injection site

Ocular: Conjunctivitis, eye edema, lacrimation disorder

Respiratory: Cough, epistaxis, nasal congestion, rhinitis

Miscellaneous: Allergic reactions (rare), anaphylaxis (rare)

Overdosage/Toxicology Symptoms include drowsiness, headache, confusion, anuria, and water intoxication. In case of overdose, decrease or discontinue desmopressin.

Drug Interactions

Increased Effect/Toxicity: Chlorpropamide, fludrocortisone may increase ADH response.

Decreased Effect: Demeclocycline and lithium may decrease ADH response.

Ethanol/Nutrition/Herb Interactions Ethanol: Avoid ethanol (may decrease antidiuretic effect).

Stability

DDAVP®:

Tablet, nasal spray: Store at controlled room temperature of 20°C to 25°C (68°F to 77°F). Keep nasal spray in upright position.

Rhinal tube: Store refrigerated at 2°C to 8°C (36°F to 46°F). May store at room temperature for up to 3 weeks.

Injection: Store refrigerated at 2°C to 8°C (36°F to 46°F). Dilute in 10-50 mL NS for I.V. infusion (10 mL for children ≤10 kg; 50 mL for adults and children >10 kg).

Stimate™: Store refrigerated at 2°C to 8°C (36°F to 46°F). May store at room temperature for up to 3 weeks.

Mechanism of Action Enhances reabsorption of water in the kidneys by increasing cellular permeability of the collecting ducts; possibly causes smooth muscle constriction with resultant vasoconstriction; raises plasma levels of von Willebrand factor and factor VIII

Pharmacodynamics/Kinetics

Intranasal administration:

Onset of increased factor VIII activity: 30 minutes (dose related)

Peak effect 1.5 hours

Bioavailability: 3.2%

I.V. infusion:

Onset of increased factor VIII activity: 30 minutes (dose related)

Peak effect: 1.5-2 hours

Half-life elimination: Terminal: 3 hours (up to 9 hours in renal dysfunction)

Excretion: Urine

Oral tablet:

Onset of action: ADH: ~1 hour

Peak effect: 4-7 hours

Bioavailability: 5% compared to intranasal; 0.16% compared to I.V.

Half-life elimination: 1.5-2.5 hours

Dosage

Children:

Diabetes insipidus:

Intranasal (using 100 mcg/mL nasal solution): 3 months to 12 years: Initial: 5 mcg/day (0.05 mL/day) divided 1-2 times/day; range: 5-30 mcg/day (0.05-0.3 mL/day) divided 1-2 times/day; adjust morning and evening doses separately for an adequate diurnal rhythm of water turnover; doses <10 mcg should be administered using the rhinal tube system

Oral: ≥4 years: Initial: 0.05 mg twice daily; total daily dose should be increased or decreased as needed to obtain adequate antidiuresis (range: 0.1-1.2 mg divided 2-3 times/day)

Hemophilia A and von Willebrand disease (type I):

I.V.: >3 months: 0.3 mcg/kg by slow infusion; may repeat dose if needed; begin 30 minutes before procedure

Intranasal: ≥11 months: Refer to adult dosing.

Nocturnal enuresis:

Intranasal (using 100 mcg/mL nasal solution): ≥6 years: Initial: 20 mcg (0.2 mL) at bedtime; range: 10-40 mcg; it is recommended that ½ of the dose be given in each nostril. **Note:** The nasal spray pump can only deliver doses of 10 mcg (0.1 mL) or multiples of 10 mcg (0.1 mL); if doses other than this are needed, the rhinal tube delivery system is preferred. For 10 mcg dose, administer in one nostril.

Oral: 0.2 mg at bedtime; dose may be titrated up to 0.6 mg to achieve desired response. Patients previously on intranasal therapy can begin oral tablets 24 hours after the last intranasal dose.

Children ≥12 years and Adults:

Diabetes insipidus:

I.V., SubQ: 2-4 mcg/day (0.5-1 mL) in 2 divided doses or 1/10 of the maintenance intranasal dose

Intranasal (using 100 mcg/mL nasal solution): 10-40 mcg/day (0.1-0.4 mL) divided 1-3 times/day; adjust morning and evening doses separately for an adequate diurnal rhythm of water turnover. **Note:** The nasal spray pump can only deliver doses of 10 mcg (0.1 mL) or multiples of 10 mcg (0.1 mL); if doses other than this are needed, the rhinal tube delivery system is preferred.

Oral: Initial: 0.05 mg twice daily; total daily dose should be increased or decreased as needed to obtain adequate antidiuresis (range: 0.1-1.2 mg divided 2-3 times/day)

Hemophilia A and mild to moderate von Willebrand disease (Type I):

I.V.: 0.3 mcg/kg by slow infusion, begin 30 minutes before procedure

(Continued)

Desmopressin *(Continued)*

Intranasal: Using high concentration spray (1.5 mg/mL): <50 kg: 150 mcg (1 spray); >50 kg: 300 mcg (1 spray each nostril); repeat use is determined by the patient's clinical condition and laboratory work; if using preoperatively, administer 2 hours before surgery

Dosage adjustment in renal impairment: Cl_{cr} <50 mL/minute: Use is contraindicated

Administration

I.V.: Infuse over 15-30 minutes

Intranasal:

DDAVP®: Nasal pump spray: Delivers 0.1 mL (10 mcg); for other doses which are not multiples, use rhinal tube. DDAVP® Nasal spray delivers fifty 10 mcg doses. For 10 mcg dose, administer in one nostril. Any solution remaining after 50 doses should be discarded. Pump must be primed prior to first use.

DDAVP® Rhinal tube: Insert top of dropper into tube (arrow marked end) in downward position. Squeeze dropper until solution reaches desired calibration mark. Disconnect dropper. Grasp the tube ¾ inch from the end and insert tube into nostril until the fingertips reach the nostril. Place opposite end of tube into the mouth (holding breath). Tilt head back and blow with a strong, short puff into the nostril (for very young patients, an adult should blow solution into the child's nose). Reseal dropper after use.

Monitoring Parameters Blood pressure and pulse should be monitored during I.V. infusion.

Diabetes insipidus: Fluid intake, urine volume, specific gravity, plasma and urine osmolality, serum electrolytes

Hemophilia A: Factor VIII coagulant activity, factor VIII ristocetin cofactor activity, and factor VIII antigen levels, aPTT

von Willebrand disease: Factor VIII coagulant activity, factor VIII ristocetin cofactor activity, and factor VIII von Willebrand antigen levels, bleeding time

Nocturnal enuresis: Serum electrolytes if used for >7 days

Additional Information 10 mcg of desmopressin acetate is equivalent to 40 int. units

Dosage Forms

Injection, solution, as acetate (DDAVP®): 4 mcg/mL (1 mL, 10 mL)

Solution, intranasal, as acetate (DDAVP®): 100 mcg/mL (2.5 mL) [with rhinal tube]

Solution, intranasal, as acetate [spray]: 100 mcg/mL (5 mL) [delivers 10 mcg/spray]

DDAVP®: 100 mcg/mL (5 mL) [delivers 10 mcg/spray]

Stimate™: 1.5 mg/mL (2.5 mL) [delivers 150 mcg/spray]

Tablet, as acetate (DDAVP®): 0.1 mg, 0.2 mg

♦ **Desmopressin Acetate** *see Desmopressin on page 476*

♦ **Desocort® (Can)** *see Desonide on page 478*

♦ **Desogen®** *see Ethinyl Estradiol and Desogestrel on page 645*

♦ **Desogestrel and Ethinyl Estradiol** *see Ethinyl Estradiol and Desogestrel on page 645*

♦ **Desonate™** *see Desonide on page 478*

Desonide *(DES oh nide)*

U.S. Brand Names Desonate™; DesOwen®; LoKara™; Verdeso™

Canadian Brand Names Desocort®; PMS-Desonide

Pharmacologic Category Corticosteroid, Topical

Additional Appendix Information

Corticosteroids *on page 1879*

Use Adjunctive therapy for inflammation in acute and chronic corticosteroid responsive dermatosis (low potency corticosteroid); mild-to-moderate atopic dermatitis

Pregnancy Risk Factor C

Dosage Topical:

Corticosteroid responsive dermatoses: Children and Adults: Therapy should be discontinued when control is achieved. If no improvement is seen within 2 weeks, reassessment of diagnosis may be necessary.

Cream, ointment: Apply 2-4 times/day sparingly

Lotion: Apply 2-3 times/day sparingly

Atopic dermatitis: Children ≥3 months and Adults: Aerosol, gel: Apply 2 times/day sparingly. Therapy should be discontinued when control is achieved. If no improvement is seen within 4 weeks, reassessment of diagnosis may be necessary.

Additional Information Complete prescribing information for this medication should be consulted for additional detail.

Dosage Forms

Aerosol, topical [foam]:

Verdeso®: 0.05% (50 g, 100 g)

Cream, topical: 0.05% (15 g, 60 g)

DesOwen®: 0.05% (15 g, 60 g, 90 g)

Gel, topical [aqueous]:

Desonate™: 0.05% (15 g, 30 g, 60g)

Lotion, topical: 0.05% (60 mL, 120 mL)

DesOwen®, LoKara™: 0.05% (60 mL, 120 mL)

Ointment, topical: 0.05% (15 g, 60 g)

DesOwen®: 0.05% (15 g, 60 g)

♦ **DesOwen®** *see Desonide on page 478*

Desoximetasone (des oks i MET a sone)

U.S. Brand Names Topicort®; Topicort®-LP
Canadian Brand Names Taro-Desoximetasone; Topicort®
Pharmacologic Category Corticosteroid, Topical
Additional Appendix Information
  Corticosteroids *on page 1879*
Use Relieves inflammation and pruritic symptoms of corticosteroid-responsive dermatosis (intermediate- to high-potency topical corticosteroid)
Pregnancy Risk Factor C
Medication Safety Issues
  Sound-alike/look-alike issues:
    Desoximetasone may be confused with dexamethasone
    Topicort® may be confused with Topic®
Dosage Desoximetasone is a potent fluorinated topical corticosteroid. Therapy should be discontinued when control is achieved; if no improvement is seen, reassessment of diagnosis may be necessary.

  Cream, gel: Children and Adults: Apply a thin film to affected area twice daily
  Ointment: Children ≥10 years and Adults: Apply a thin film to affected area twice daily
Additional Information Complete prescribing information for this medication should be consulted for additional detail.
Dosage Forms
  Cream, topical: 0.25% (15 g, 60 g); 0.05% (15 g, 60 g)
    Topicort®: 0.25% (15 g, 60 g)
    Topicort®-LP: 0.05% (15 g, 60 g)
  Gel, topical (Topicort®): 0.05% (15 g, 60 g) [contains alcohol 20%]
  Ointment, topical (Topicort®): 0.25% (15 g, 60 g)

- ◆ **Desoxyephedrine Hydrochloride** *see* Methamphetamine *on page 1104*
- ◆ **Desoxyn®** *see* Methamphetamine *on page 1104*
- ◆ **Desoxyphenobarbital** *see* Primidone *on page 1422*
- ◆ **Desyrel® [DSC]** *see* Trazodone *on page 1727*
- ◆ **Desyrel® (Can)** *see* Trazodone *on page 1727*
- ◆ **Detane® [OTC]** *see* Benzocaine *on page 204*
- ◆ **Detemir Insulin** *see* Insulin Detemir *on page 910*
- ◆ **Detrol®** *see* Tolterodine *on page 1705*
- ◆ **Detrol® LA** *see* Tolterodine *on page 1705*

Dexamethasone (deks a METH a sone)

U.S. Brand Names Dexamethasone Intensol™; DexPak® TaperPak®; Maxidex®
Canadian Brand Names Apo-Dexamethasone®; Dexasone®; Diodex®; Maxidex®; PMS-Dexamethasone
Index Terms Dexamethasone Sodium Phosphate
Pharmacologic Category Anti-inflammatory Agent; Anti-inflammatory Agent, Ophthalmic; Antiemetic; Corticosteroid, Ophthalmic; Corticosteroid, Otic; Corticosteroid, Systemic
Additional Appendix Information
  Corticosteroids *on page 1879*
Use
  Systemic: Primarily as an anti-inflammatory or immunosuppressant agent in the treatment of a variety of diseases including those of allergic, dermatologic, endocrine, hematologic, inflammatory, neoplastic, nervous system, renal, respiratory, rheumatic, and autoimmune origin; may be used in management of cerebral edema, septic shock, chronic swelling, as a diagnostic agent, diagnosis of Cushing's syndrome, antiemetic
  Ophthalmic: Treatment of palpebral and bulbar conjunctivitis; corneal injury from chemical, radiation, thermal burns, or foreign body penetration
  Otic: Treatment of inflammation of external auditory meatus; treatment of edema associated with infective otitis externa
Unlabeled/Investigational Use Dexamethasone suppression test: General indicator consistent with depression and/or suicide
Pregnancy Risk Factor C
Pregnancy Implications Teratogenic effects have been observed in animal studies. Dexamethasone has been used in patients with premature labor (26-34 weeks gestation) to stimulate fetal lung maturation. Crosses the placenta; transient leukocytosis reported. Available evidence suggests safe use during pregnancy.
Lactation Enters breast milk/use caution
Medication Safety Issues
  Sound-alike/look-alike issues:
    Dexamethasone may be confused with desoximetasone
    Decadron® may be confused with Percodan®
    Maxidex® may be confused with Maxzide®
Contraindications Hypersensitivity to dexamethasone or any component of the formulation; systemic fungal infections; cerebral malaria; ophthalmic use in viral (active ocular herpes simplex), fungal, or tuberculosis diseases of the eye
Warnings/Precautions Use with caution in patients with thyroid disease, hepatic impairment, renal impairment, cardiovascular disease, diabetes, glaucoma, cataracts, myasthenia gravis, patients at risk for osteoporosis, patients at risk for seizures, or GI diseases (diverticulitis, peptic ulcer, ulcerative colitis) due to perforation risk. Use caution following acute MI (corticosteroids have been associated with myocardial rupture). Because of the risk of adverse effects, systemic corticosteroids should be used cautiously in the elderly in the smallest
(Continued)

Dexamethasone *(Continued)*

possible effective dose for the shortest duration. May affect growth velocity; growth should be routinely monitored in pediatric patients. Withdraw therapy with gradual tapering of dose.

May cause hypercorticism or suppression of hypothalamic-pituitary-adrenal (HPA) axis, particularly in younger children or in patients receiving high doses for prolonged periods. HPA axis suppression may lead to adrenal crisis. Withdrawal and discontinuation of a corticosteroid should be done slowly and carefully. Particular care is required when patients are transferred from systemic corticosteroids to inhaled products due to possible adrenal insufficiency or withdrawal from steroids, including an increase in allergic symptoms. Patients receiving >20 mg per day of prednisone (or equivalent) may be most susceptible. Fatalities have occurred due to adrenal insufficiency in asthmatic patients during and after transfer from systemic corticosteroids to aerosol steroids; aerosol steroids do not provide the systemic steroid needed to treat patients having trauma, surgery, or infections. Dexamethasone does not provide adequate mineralocorticoid activity in adrenal insufficiency (may be employed as a single dose while cortisol assays are performed). The lowest possible dose should be used during treatment; discontinuation and/or dose reductions should be gradual.

Acute myopathy has been reported with high dose corticosteroids, usually in patients with neuromuscular transmission disorders; may involve ocular and/or respiratory muscles; monitor creatine kinase; recovery may be delayed. Corticosteroid use may cause psychiatric disturbances, including depression, euphoria, insomnia, mood swings, and personality changes. Pre-existing psychiatric conditions may be exacerbated by corticosteroid use. Prolonged use of corticosteroids may also increase the incidence of secondary infection, mask acute infection (including fungal infections), prolong or exacerbate viral infections, or limit response to vaccines. Exposure to chickenpox should be avoided; corticosteroids should not be used to treat ocular herpes simplex. Corticosteroids should not be used for cerebral malaria. Close observation is required in patients with latent tuberculosis and/or TB reactivity; restrict use in active TB (only in conjunction with antituberculosis treatment). Prolonged treatment with corticosteroids has been associated with the development of Kaposi's sarcoma (case reports); if noted, discontinuation of therapy should be considered.

Adverse Reactions Frequency not defined.

Cardiovascular: Arrhythmia, bradycardia, cardiac arrest, cardiomyopathy, CHF, circulatory collapse, edema, hypertension, myocardial rupture (post-MI), syncope, thromboembolism, vasculitis

Central nervous system: Depression, emotional instability, euphoria, headache, intracranial pressure increased, insomnia, malaise, mood swings, neuritis, personality changes, pseudotumor cerebri (usually following discontinuation), psychic disorders, seizure, vertigo

Dermatologic: Acne, allergic dermatitis, alopecia, angioedema, bruising, dry skin, erythema, fragile skin, hirsutism, hyper-/hypopigmentation, hypertrichosis, perianal pruritus (following I.V. injection), petechiae, rash, skin atrophy, skin test reaction impaired, striae, urticaria, wound healing impaired

Endocrine & metabolic: Adrenal suppression, carbohydrate tolerance decreased, Cushing's syndrome, diabetes mellitus, glucose intolerance decreased, growth suppression (children), hyperglycemia, hypokalemic alkalosis, menstrual irregularities, negative nitrogen balance, pituitary-adrenal axis suppression, protein catabolism, sodium retention

Gastrointestinal: Abdominal distention, appetite increased, gastrointestinal hemorrhage, gastrointestinal perforation, nausea, pancreatitis, peptic ulcer, ulcerative esophagitis, weight gain

Genitourinary: Altered (increased or decreased) spermatogenesis

Hepatic: Hepatomegaly, transaminases increased

Local: Postinjection flare (intra-articular use), thrombophlebitis

Neuromuscular & skeletal: Arthropathy, aseptic necrosis (femoral and humoral heads), fractures, muscle mass loss, myopathy (particularly in conjunction with neuromuscular disease or neuromuscular-blocking agents), neuropathy, osteoporosis, parasthesia, tendon rupture, vertebral compression fractures, weakness

Ocular: Cataracts, exophthalmos, glaucoma, intraocular pressure increased

Renal: Glucosuria

Respiratory: Pulmonary edema

Miscellaneous: Abnormal fat deposition, anaphylactoid reaction, anaphylaxis, avascular necrosis, diaphoresis, hiccups, hypersensitivity, impaired wound healing, infections, Kaposi's sarcoma, moon face, secondary malignancy

Overdosage/Toxicology
Symptoms include moon face, central obesity, hypertension, psychosis, hallucinations, diabetes, hyperlipidemia, peptic ulcer, increased susceptibility to infection, electrolyte and fluid imbalance. When consumed in excessive quantities, systemic hypercorticism and adrenal suppression may occur; in those cases, discontinuation and withdrawal of the corticosteroid should be done judiciously.

Drug Interactions

Cytochrome P450 Effect: Substrate of CYP3A4 (minor); **Induces** CYP2A6 (weak), 2B6 (weak), 2C8 (weak), 2C9 (weak), 3A4 (weak)

Increased Effect/Toxicity: Aprepitant, azole antifungals, calcium channel blockers (nondihydropyridine), cyclosporine, estrogens, and macrolides may increase the serum levels of corticosteroids. Antacids may increase the absorption of corticosteroids, separate administration by 2 hours. Corticosteroids may increase the serum levels of cyclosporine.

Concurrent use of nonsteroidal anti-inflammatory drugs (NSAIDs) and salicylates with corticosteroids may lead to an increased incidence of gastrointestinal adverse effects. Concurrent use with anticholinergic agents may lead to severe weakness in patients with myasthenia gravis. Concurrent use of fluoroquinolone antibiotics may increase the risk of tendon rupture, particularly in elderly patients (overall incidence rare). Concurrent use of neuromuscular-blocking agents with corticosteroids may increase the risk of myopathy. The concurrent use of thalidomide with corticosteroids may increase the risk of selected adverse effects (toxic epidermal necrolysis and DVT). Concurrent use with cyclosporine may increase cyclosporine levels. Concurrent use of ophthalmic NSAIDs may enhance the toxic effects of ophthalmic dexamethasone. The use of live vaccines is contraindicated in immunosuppressed patients (may increase the risk of vaccinal infection). In patients receiving high doses of systemic corticosteroids for ≥14 days, wait at least 1 month between discontinuing steroid therapy and administering immunization.

Decreased Effect: Bile acid sequestrants may reduce the absorption of corticosteroids; separate administration by 2 hours. Aminoglutethimide, barbiturates, primidone, and rifamycins may reduce the serum levels/effects of dexamethasone. Serum concentrations of isoniazid and phenytoin may be decreased by corticosteroids. Corticosteroids may lead to a reduction in warfarin effect. Corticosteroids may suppress the response to vaccinations.

Ethanol/Nutrition/Herb Interactions

Ethanol: Avoid ethanol (may enhance gastric mucosal irritation).

Food: Dexamethasone interferes with calcium absorption. Limit caffeine.

Herb/Nutraceutical: Avoid cat's claw, echinacea (have immunostimulant properties).

Stability

Injection solution: Store at room temperature; protect from light and freezing.

Stability of injection of parenteral admixture at room temperature (25°C): 24 hours

Stability of injection of parenteral admixture at refrigeration temperature (4°C): 2 days; protect from light and freezing.

Injection should be diluted in 50-100 mL NS or D_5W.

Mechanism of Action Decreases inflammation by suppression of neutrophil migration, decreased production of inflammatory mediators, and reversal of increased capillary permeability; suppresses normal immune response. Dexamethasone's mechanism of antiemetic activity is unknown.

Pharmacodynamics/Kinetics

Onset of action: Acetate: Prompt

Duration of metabolic effect: 72 hours; acetate is a long-acting repository preparation

Metabolism: Hepatic

Half-life elimination: Normal renal function: 1.8-3.5 hours; Biological half-life: 36-54 hours

Time to peak, serum: Oral: 1-2 hours; I.M.: ~8 hours

Excretion: Urine and feces

Dosage Refer to individual protocols.

Children:

Antiemetic (prior to chemotherapy): I.V.: 10 mg/m² (initial dose) followed by 5 mg/m² every 6 hours as needed **or** 5-20 mg given 15-30 minutes before treatment

Anti-inflammatory immunosuppressant: Oral, I.M., I.V.: 0.08-0.3 mg/kg/day **or** 2.5-10 mg/m²/day in divided doses every 6-12 hours

Extubation or airway edema: Oral, I.M., I.V.: 0.5-2 mg/kg/day in divided doses every 6 hours beginning 24 hours prior to extubation and continuing for 4-6 doses afterwards

Cerebral edema: I.V.: Loading dose: 1-2 mg/kg/dose as a single dose; maintenance: 1-1.5 mg/kg/day (maximum: 16 mg/day) in divided doses every 4-6 hours, taper off over 1-6 weeks

Bacterial meningitis in infants and children >2 months: I.V.: 0.6 mg/kg/day in 4 divided doses every 6 hours for the first 4 days of antibiotic treatment; start dexamethasone at the time of the first dose of antibiotic

Physiologic replacement: Oral, I.M., I.V.: 0.03-0.15 mg/kg/day **or** 0.6-0.75 mg/m²/day in divided doses every 6-12 hours

Adults:

Antiemetic:

Prophylaxis: Oral, I.V.: 10-20 mg 15-30 minutes before treatment on each treatment day

Continuous infusion regimen: Oral or I.V.: 10 mg every 12 hours on each treatment day

Mildly emetogenic therapy: Oral, I.M., I.V.: 4 mg every 4-6 hours

Delayed nausea/vomiting: Oral: 4-10 mg 1-2 times/day for 2-4 days **or**

8 mg every 12 hours for 2 days; then

4 mg every 12 hours for 2 days **or**

20 mg 1 hour before chemotherapy; then

10 mg 12 hours after chemotherapy; then

8 mg every 12 hours for 4 doses; then

4 mg every 12 hours for 4 doses

Anti-inflammatory:

Oral, I.M., I.V. (injections should be given as sodium phosphate): 0.75-9 mg/day in divided doses every 6-12 hours

Intra-articular, intralesional, or soft tissue (as sodium phosphate): 0.4-6 mg/day

Ophthalmic:

Solution: Instill 1-2 drops into conjunctival sac every hour during the day and every other hour during the night; gradually reduce dose to every 3-4 hours, then to 3-4 times/day

Suspension: Instill 1-2 drops into conjunctival sac up to 4-6 times per day; may use hourly in severe disease; taper prior to discontinuation

Otic: Instill 3-4 drops 2-3 times a day; reduce dose gradually prior to discontinuation

Multiple myeloma: Oral, I.V.: 40 mg/day, days 1 to 4, 9 to 12, and 17 to 20, repeated every 4 weeks (alone or as part of a regimen)

Cerebral edema: I.V. 10 mg stat, 4 mg I.M./I.V. every 6 hours until response is maximized, then switch to oral regimen, then taper off if appropriate; dosage may be reduced after 24 days and gradually discontinued over 5-7 days

Extubation or airway edema: Oral, I.M., I.V. (injections should be given as sodium phosphate): 0.5-2 mg/kg/day in divided doses every 6 hours beginning 24 hours prior to extubation and continuing for 4-6 doses afterwards

Dexamethasone suppression test (depression/suicide indicator) (unlabeled use): Oral: 1 mg at 11 PM, draw blood at 8 AM the following day for plasma cortisol determination

Cushing's syndrome, diagnostic: Oral: 1 mg at 11 PM, draw blood at 8 AM; greater accuracy for Cushing's syndrome may be achieved by the following:

Dexamethasone 0.5 mg by mouth every 6 hours for 48 hours (with 24-hour urine collection for 17-hydroxycorticosteroid excretion)

(Continued)

Dexamethasone *(Continued)*

Differentiation of Cushing's syndrome due to ACTH excess from Cushing's due to other causes: Oral: Dexamethasone 2 mg every 6 hours for 48 hours (with 24-hour urine collection for 17-hydroxycorticosteroid excretion)

Multiple sclerosis (acute exacerbation): 30 mg/day for 1 week, followed by 4-12 mg/day for 1 month

Physiological replacement: Oral, I.M., I.V. (should be given as sodium phosphate): 0.03-0.15 mg/kg/day **or** 0.6-0.75 mg/m²/day in divided doses every 6-12 hours

Treatment of shock:

Addisonian crisis/shock (ie, adrenal insufficiency/responsive to steroid therapy): I.V. (given as sodium phosphate): 4-10 mg as a single dose, which may be repeated if necessary

Unresponsive shock (ie, unresponsive to steroid therapy): I.V. (given as sodium phosphate): 1-6 mg/kg as a single I.V. dose or up to 40 mg initially followed by repeat doses every 2-6 hours while shock persists

Hemodialysis: Supplemental dose is not necessary

Peritoneal dialysis: Supplemental dose is not necessary

Dietary Considerations May be taken with meals to decrease GI upset. May need diet with increased potassium, pyridoxine, vitamin C, vitamin D, folate, calcium, and phosphorus.

Administration

Oral: Administer with meals to decrease GI upset.

I.V.: Administer as a 5-10 minute bolus; rapid injection is associated with a high incidence of perianal discomfort.

Ophthalmic: Remove soft contact lenses prior to using solutions containing benzalkonium chloride. Do not touch tip of container to eye.

Otic: Use ophthalmic solution for otic administration. Instill directly into aural canal or may pack canal with gauze saturated with solution. Keep wick moist and remove after 12-24 hours.

Monitoring Parameters Hemoglobin, occult blood loss, serum potassium, and glucose; intraocular pressure (with use >6 weeks)

Reference Range Dexamethasone suppression test, overnight: 8 AM cortisol <6 mcg/100 mL (dexamethasone 1 mg); plasma cortisol determination should be made on the day after giving dose

Additional Information Effects of inhaled/intranasal steroids on growth have been observed in the absence of laboratory evidence of HPA axis suppression, suggesting that growth velocity is a more sensitive indicator of systemic corticosteroid exposure in pediatric patients than some commonly used tests of HPA axis function. The long-term effects of this reduction in growth velocity associated with orally-inhaled and intranasal corticosteroids, including the impact on final adult height, are unknown. The potential for "catch up" growth following discontinuation of treatment with inhaled corticosteroids has not been adequately studied.

Withdrawal/tapering of therapy: Corticosteroid tapering following short-term use is limited primarily by the need to control the underlying disease state; tapering may be accomplished over a period of days. Following longer-term use, tapering over weeks to months may be necessary to avoid signs and symptoms of adrenal insufficiency and to allow recovery of the HPA axis. Testing of HPA axis responsiveness may be of value in selected patients. Subtle deficits in HPA response may persist for months after discontinuation of therapy, and may require supplemental dosing during periods of acute illness or surgical stress.

Dosage Forms [DSC] = Discontinued product

Elixir, as base: 0.5 mg/5 mL (240 mL)

Injection, solution, as sodium phosphate: 4 mg/mL (1 mL, 5 mL, 30 mL); 10 mg/mL (10 mL)

Injection, solution, as sodium phosphate [preservative free]: 10 mg/mL (1 mL)

Solution, ophthalmic, as sodium phosphate: 0.1% (5 mL)

Solution, oral: 0.5 mg/5 mL (500 mL)

Solution, oral concentrate:

Dexamethasone Intensol™: 1 mg/mL (30 mL) [contains alcohol 30%]

Suspension, ophthalmic:

Maxidex®: 0.1% (5 mL; 15 mL [DSC]) [contains benzalkonium chloride]

Tablet [scored]: 0.5 mg, 0.75 mg, 1 mg, 1.5 mg, 2 mg, 4 mg, 6 mg

DexPak® TaperPak®: 1.5 mg [51 tablets on taper dose card]

- ♦ **Dexamethasone and Ciprofloxacin** *see* Ciprofloxacin and Dexamethasone *on page 376*
- ♦ **Dexamethasone and Tobramycin** *see* Tobramycin and Dexamethasone *on page 1700*
- ♦ **Dexamethasone Intensol™** *see* Dexamethasone *on page 479*
- ♦ **Dexamethasone, Neomycin, and Polymyxin B** *see* Neomycin, Polymyxin B, and Dexamethasone *on page 1211*
- ♦ **Dexamethasone Sodium Phosphate** *see* Dexamethasone *on page 479*
- ♦ **Dexasone® (Can)** *see* Dexamethasone *on page 479*

Dexbrompheniramine and Pseudoephedrine
(deks brom fen EER a meen & soo doe e FED rin)

U.S. Brand Names Drixoral® Cold & Allergy [OTC]

Canadian Brand Names Drixoral®

Index Terms Pseudoephedrine and Dexbrompheniramine

Pharmacologic Category Antihistamine/Decongestant Combination

Use Relief of symptoms of upper respiratory mucosal congestion in seasonal and perennial nasal allergies, acute rhinitis, rhinosinusitis and eustachian tube blockage

Pregnancy Risk Factor B

Dosage Children >12 years and Adults: Oral: 1 timed release tablet every 12 hours, may require 1 tablet every 8 hours

Additional Information Complete prescribing information for this medication should be consulted for additional detail.

Dosage Forms Tablet, sustained action: Dexbrompheniramine maleate 6 mg and pseudoe-phedrine sulfate 120 mg

Dexchlorpheniramine (deks klor fen EER a meen)

Index Terms Dexchlorpheniramine Maleate
Pharmacologic Category Antihistamine
Use Perennial and seasonal allergic rhinitis and other allergic symptoms including urticaria
Pregnancy Risk Factor B
Dosage Oral:
  Children:
    2-5 years: 0.5 mg every 4-6 hours (do not use timed release)
    6-11 years: 1 mg every 4-6 hours or 4 mg timed release at bedtime
  Adults: 2 mg every 4-6 hours or 4-6 mg timed release at bedtime or every 8-10 hours
Additional Information Complete prescribing information for this medication should be consulted for additional detail.
Dosage Forms
  Syrup, as maleate: 2 mg/5 mL (480 mL, 3840 mL) [contains alcohol 6%; orange flavor]
  Tablet, sustained action, as maleate: 4 mg, 6 mg

Dexchlorpheniramine and Pseudoephedrine
(deks klor fen EER a meen & soo doe e FED rin)

U.S. Brand Names Duotan PD; Tanafed DP™
Index Terms Pseudoephedrine Tannate and Dexchlorpheniramine Tannate
Pharmacologic Category Alpha/Beta Agonist; Antihistamine
Use Relief of nasal congestion associated with the common cold, hay fever, and other aller-gies, sinusitis, and vasomotor and allergic rhinitis
Pregnancy Risk Factor C
Dosage Oral: Rhinitis/decongestant: Dexchlorpheniramine tannate 2.5 mg and pseudoephed-rine tannate 75 mg per 5 mL:

  Children:
    2-6 years: 2.5-5 mL every 12 hours (maximum: 10 mL/24 hours)
    6-12 years: 5-10 mL every 12 hours (maximum: 20 mL/24 hours)
    Children ≥12 years and Adults: 10-20 mL every 12 hours (maximum: 40 mL/24 hours)
Additional Information Complete prescribing information for this medication should be consulted for additional detail.
Dosage Forms Suspension: Dexchlorpheniramine tannate 2.5 mg and pseudoephedrine tannate 75 mg per 5 mL (120 mL, 480 mL) [contains sodium benzoate; strawberry-banana flavor]

♦ **Dexchlorpheniramine Maleate** *see Dexchlorpheniramine on page 483*
♦ **Dexchlorpheniramine Tannate, Pseudoephedrine Tannate, and Dextromethorphan Tannate** *see Chlorpheniramine, Pseudoephedrine, and Dextromethorphan on page 355*
♦ **Dexedrine®** *see Dextroamphetamine on page 486*
♦ **Dexferrum®** *see Iron Dextran Complex on page 939*
♦ **Dexiron™ (Can)** *see Iron Dextran Complex on page 939*

Dexmedetomidine (deks MED e toe mi deen)

U.S. Brand Names Precedex™
Canadian Brand Names Precedex™
Index Terms Dexmedetomidine Hydrochloride
Pharmacologic Category Alpha$_2$-Adrenergic Agonist; Sedative
Use Sedation of initially intubated and mechanically ventilated patients during treatment in an intensive care setting; duration of infusion should not exceed 24 hours
Unlabeled/Investigational Use Unlabeled uses include premedication prior to anesthesia induction with thiopental; relief of pain and reduction of opioid dose following laparoscopic tubal ligation; as an adjunct anesthetic in ophthalmic surgery; treatment of shivering; premed-ication to attenuate the cardiostimulatory and postanesthetic delirium of ketamine
Pregnancy Risk Factor C
Lactation Excretion in breast milk unknown/use caution
Medication Safety Issues
  Sound-alike/look-alike issues:
    Precedex™ may be confused with Peridex®
Contraindications Hypersensitivity to dexmedetomidine or any component of the formulation; use outside of an intensive care setting
Warnings/Precautions Should be administered only by persons skilled in management of patients in intensive care setting. Patients should be continuously monitored. Episodes of bradycardia, hypotension, and sinus arrest have been associated with dexmedetomidine. Use caution in patients with heart block, severe ventricular dysfunction, hypovolemia, diabetes, chronic hypertension, and elderly. Use with caution in patients receiving vasodila-tors or drugs which decrease heart rate. If medical intervention is required, treatment may include stopping or decreasing the infusion; increasing the rate of I.V. fluid administration, use of pressor agents, and elevation of the lower extremities. Transient hypertension has been primarily observed during the dose in association with the initial peripheral vasocon-strictive effects of dexmedetomidine. Treatment of this is not generally necessary; however, reduction of infusion rate may be desirable.
Adverse Reactions
  >10%:
    Cardiovascular: Hypotension (30%)
    Gastrointestinal: Nausea (11%)
  (Continued)

Dexmedetomidine *(Continued)*

1% to 10%:
Cardiovascular: Bradycardia (8%), atrial fibrillation (7%)
Central nervous system: Pain (3%)
Hematologic: Anemia (3%), leukocytosis (2%)
Renal: Oliguria (2%)
Respiratory: Hypoxia (6%), pulmonary edema (2%), pleural effusion (3%)
Miscellaneous: Infection (2%), thirst (2%)

Overdosage/Toxicology In reports of overdosages where the blood concentration was 13 times the upper boundary of the therapeutic range, first degree AV block and second degree heart block occurred. No hemodynamic compromise was noted with AV block and heart block resolved spontaneously within one minute. Two patients who received a 2 mcg/kg loading dose over 10 minutes experienced bradycardia and/or hypotension. One patient who received a loading dose of undiluted dexmedetomidine (19.4 mcg/kg) had cardiac arrest and was successfully resuscitated.

Drug Interactions

Cytochrome P450 Effect: Substrate of CYP2A6 (major); **Inhibits** CYP1A2 (weak), 2C9 (weak), 2D6 (strong), 3A4 (weak)

Increased Effect/Toxicity: The levels/effects of dexmedetomidine may be increased by isoniazid, methoxsalen, miconazole, and other CYP2A6 inhibitors. Dexmedetomidine may increase the levels/effects of amphetamines, selected beta-blockers, dextromethorphan, fluoxetine, lidocaine, mirtazapine, nefazodone, paroxetine, risperidone, ritonavir, thioridazine, tricyclic antidepressants, venlafaxine, and other CYP2D6 substrates. Hypotension and/or bradycardia may be increased by vasodilators and heart rate-lowering agents.

Decreased Effect: Dexmedetomidine may decrease the levels/effects of CYP2D6 prodrug substrates; example prodrug substrates include codeine, hydrocodone, oxycodone, and tramadol.

Mechanism of Action Selective alpha$_2$-adrenoceptor agonist with sedative properties; alpha$_1$ activity was observed at high doses or after rapid infusions

Pharmacodynamics/Kinetics
Onset of action: Rapid
Distribution: V$_{ss}$: Approximately 118 L; rapid
Protein binding: 94%
Metabolism: Hepatic via glucuronidation and CYP2A6
Half-life elimination: 6 minutes; Terminal: 2 hours
Excretion: Urine (95%); feces (4%)

Dosage Individualized and titrated to desired clinical effect
Adults: I.V.: Solution must be diluted prior to administration. Initial: Loading infusion of 1 mcg/kg over 10 minutes, followed by a maintenance infusion of 0.2-0.7 mcg/kg/hour; not indicated for infusions lasting >24 hours
Elderly (>65 years of age): Dosage reduction may need to be considered. No specific guidelines available. Dose selections should be cautious, at the low end of dosage range; titration should be slower, allowing adequate time to evaluate response.
Dosage adjustment in hepatic impairment: Dosage reduction may need to be considered. No specific guidelines available.

Administration Administer using a controlled infusion device. Must be diluted in 0.9% sodium chloride solution to achieve the required concentration prior to administration. Advisable to use administration components made with synthetic or coated natural rubber gaskets. Parenteral products should be inspected visually for particulate matter and discoloration prior to administration.

Monitoring Parameters Level of sedation, heart rate, respiration, rhythm, blood pressure
Dosage Forms Injection, solution [preservative free]: 100 mcg/mL (2 mL)

♦ **Dexmedetomidine Hydrochloride** *see* Dexmedetomidine *on page 483*

Dexmethylphenidate *(dex meth il FEN i date)*

U.S. Brand Names Focalin®; Focalin® XR
Index Terms Dexmethylphenidate Hydrochloride
Pharmacologic Category Central Nervous System Stimulant
Use Treatment of attention-deficit/hyperactivity disorder (ADHD)
Restrictions C-II
Pregnancy Risk Factor C
Dosage Treatment of ADHD: Oral:
Children ≥6 years: Patients not currently taking methylphenidate:
Tablet: Initial: 2.5 mg twice daily; dosage may be adjusted in increments of 2.5-5 mg at weekly intervals (maximum dose: 20 mg/day); doses should be taken at least 4 hours apart
Capsule: Initial: 5 mg/day; dosage may be adjusted in increments of 5 mg/day at weekly intervals (maximum dose: 20 mg/day)
Adults: Patients not currently taking methylphenidate:
Tablet: Initial: 2.5 mg twice daily; dosage may be adjusted in increments of 2.5-5 mg at weekly intervals (maximum dose: 20 mg/day); doses should be taken at least 4 hours apart
Capsule: Initial: 10 mg/day; dosage may be adjusted in increments of 10 mg/day at weekly intervals (maximum dose: 20 mg/day)
Conversion to dexmethylphenidate from methylphenidate: Tablet, capsule: Initial: Half the total daily dose of racemic methylphenidate (maximum dexmethylphenidate dose: 20 mg/day)
Conversion from dexmethylphenidate immediate release to dexmethylphenidate extended release: When changing from Focalin® tablets to Focalin® XR capsules, patients may be switched to the same daily dose using Focalin® XR (maximum dose: 20 mg/day)

Dose reductions and discontinuation: Reduce dose or discontinue in patients with paradoxical aggravation of symptoms. Discontinue if no improvement is seen after one month of treatment.

Dosage adjustment in renal impairment: No data available. However, considering extensive metabolism to inactive compounds, renal insufficiency expected to have minimal effect on kinetics of dexmethylphenidate.
Dosage adjustment in renal impairment: No data available.
Additional Information Complete prescribing information for this medication should be consulted for additional detail.
Dosage Forms
Capsule, extended release:
Focalin® XR: 5 mg, 10 mg, 15 mg, 20 mg [bimodal release]
Tablet, as hydrochloride
Focalin®: 2.5 mg, 5 mg, 10 mg

♦ **Dexmethylphenidate Hydrochloride** see Dexmethylphenidate on page 484
♦ **DexPak® TaperPak®** see Dexamethasone on page 479

Dexpanthenol (deks PAN the nole)

U.S. Brand Names Panthoderm® [OTC]
Index Terms Pantothenyl Alcohol
Pharmacologic Category Gastrointestinal Agent, Stimulant; Topical Skin Product
Use Prophylactic use to minimize paralytic ileus; treatment of postoperative distention; topical to relieve itching and to aid healing of minor dermatoses
Pregnancy Risk Factor C
Dosage
Children and Adults: Relief of itching and aid in skin healing: Topical: Apply to affected area 1-2 times/day
Adults:
Prevention of postoperative ileus: I.M.: 250-500 mg stat, repeat in 2 hours, followed by doses every 6 hours until danger passes
Paralytic ileus: I.M.: 500 mg stat, repeat in 2 hours, followed by doses every 6 hours, if needed
Additional Information Complete prescribing information for this medication should be consulted for additional detail.
Dosage Forms
Cream, topical: 2% (30 g, 60 g)
Injection, solution: 250 mg/mL (2 mL)

♦ **Dex PC** see Chlorpheniramine, Phenylephrine, and Dextromethorphan on page 352

Dexrazoxane (deks ray ZOKS ane)

U.S. Brand Names Zinecard®
Canadian Brand Names Zinecard®
Index Terms ICRF-187
Pharmacologic Category Cardioprotectant
Use Reduction of the incidence and severity of cardiomyopathy associated with doxorubicin administration in women with metastatic breast cancer who have received a cumulative doxorubicin dose of 300 mg/m^2 and who would benefit from continuing therapy with doxorubicin. It is not recommended for use with the initiation of doxorubicin therapy.
Pregnancy Risk Factor C
Medication Safety Issues
Sound-alike/look-alike issues:
Zinecard® may be confused with Gemzar®
Dosage Adults: I.V.: A 10:1 ratio of dexrazoxane:doxorubicin (500 mg/m^2 dexrazoxane: 50 mg/m^2 doxorubicin)
Dosage adjustment in renal impairment: Moderate-to-severe (Cl$_{cr}$ <40 mL/minute): A 5:1 ratio (250 mg/m^2 dexrazoxane: 50 mg/m^2 doxorubicin).
Dosage adjustment in hepatic impairment: Since doxorubicin dosage is reduced in hyperbilirubinemia, a proportional reduction in dexrazoxane dosage is recommended (maintain ratio of 10:1).
Additional Information Complete prescribing information for this medication should be consulted for additional detail.
Dosage Forms Injection, powder for reconstitution: 250 mg, 500 mg [10 mg/mL when reconstituted]

Dextran (DEKS tran)

U.S. Brand Names Gentran®; LMD®
Canadian Brand Names Gentran®
Index Terms Dextran 40; Dextran 70; Dextran, High Molecular Weight; Dextran, Low Molecular Weight
Pharmacologic Category Plasma Volume Expander
Use Blood volume expander used in treatment of shock or impending shock when blood or blood products are not available; dextran 40 is also used as a priming fluid in cardiopulmonary bypass and for prophylaxis of venous thrombosis and pulmonary embolism in surgical procedures associated with a high risk of thromboembolic complications
Pregnancy Risk Factor C
Medication Safety Issues
Sound-alike/look-alike issues:
Dextran may be confused with Dexatrim®, Dexodrine®
(Continued)

Dextran *(Continued)*

Dosage I.V. (requires an infusion pump): Dose and infusion rate are dependent upon the patient's fluid status and must be individualized:

Volume expansion/shock:
Children (Dextran 40 or 70): Total dose should not exceed 20 mL/kg during first 24 hours
Adults:
Dextran 40: 500-1000 mL at a rate of 20-40 mL/minute (maximum: 20 mL/kg/day for first 24 hours); 10 mL/kg/day thereafter; therapy should not be continued beyond 5 days
Dextran 70: 500-1000 mL at a rate of 20-40 mL/minute (maximum: 20 mL/kg/day for first 24 hours)

Pump prime (Dextran 40): Varies with the volume of the pump oxygenator; generally, the 10% solution is added in a dose of 1-2 g/kg

Prophylaxis of venous thrombosis/pulmonary embolism (Dextran 40): Begin during surgical procedure and give 50-100 g on the day of surgery; an additional 50 g (500 mL) should be administered every 2-3 days during the period of risk (up to 2 weeks postoperatively); usual maximum infusion rate for nonemergency use: 4 mL/minute

Dosing in renal and/or hepatic impairment: Use with extreme caution

Additional Information Complete prescribing information for this medication should be consulted for additional detail.

Dosage Forms
Infusion [premixed in D₅W; high molecular weight]: 6% Dextran 70 (500 mL)
Infusion [premixed in D₅W; low molecular weight] (Gentran®, LMD®): 10% Dextran 40 (500 mL)
Infusion [premixed in D₁₀W; high molecular weight]: 32% Dextran 70 (500 mL)
Infusion [premixed in NS; high molecular weight] (Gentran®): 6% Dextran 70 (500 mL)
Infusion [premixed in NS; low molecular weight] (Gentran®, LMD®): 10% Dextran (500 mL)

♦ **Dextran 40** *see Dextran on page 485*
♦ **Dextran 70** *see Dextran on page 485*

Dextran 1 *(DEKS tran won)*

U.S. Brand Names Promit® [DSC]
Pharmacologic Category Plasma Volume Expander
Use Prophylaxis of serious anaphylactic reactions to I.V. infusion of dextran
Pregnancy Risk Factor C
Medication Safety Issues
Sound-alike/look-alike issues:
Dextran may be confused with Dexatrim®, Dexedrine®

Dosage I.V. (time between dextran 1 and dextran solution should not exceed 15 minutes):
Children: 0.3 mL/kg 1-2 minutes before I.V. infusion of dextran
Adults: 20 mL 1-2 minutes before I.V. infusion of dextran

Additional Information Complete prescribing information for this medication should be consulted for additional detail.

Dosage Forms
[DSC] = Discontinued product
Injection, solution:
Promit®: 150 mg/mL (20 mL) [DSC]

♦ **Dextran, High Molecular Weight** *see Dextran on page 485*
♦ **Dextran, Low Molecular Weight** *see Dextran on page 485*

Dextroamphetamine *(deks troe am FET a meen)*

U.S. Brand Names Dexedrine®; Dextrostat®
Canadian Brand Names Dexedrine®
Index Terms Dextroamphetamine Sulfate
Pharmacologic Category Stimulant
Use Narcolepsy; attention-deficit/hyperactivity disorder (ADHD)
Unlabeled/Investigational Use Exogenous obesity; depression; abnormal behavioral syndrome in children (minimal brain dysfunction)
Restrictions C-II
Pregnancy Risk Factor C
Medication Safety Issues
Sound-alike/look-alike issues:
Dexedrine® may be confused with dextran, Excedrin®

Dosage Oral:
Children:
Narcolepsy: 6-12 years: Initial: 5 mg/day; may increase at 5 mg increments in weekly intervals until side effects appear (maximum dose: 60 mg/day)
ADHD:
3-5 years: Initial: 2.5 mg/day given every morning; increase by 2.5 mg/day in weekly intervals until optimal response is obtained; usual range: 0.1-0.5 mg/kg/dose every morning with maximum of 40 mg/day
≥6 years: 5 mg once or twice daily; increase in increments of 5 mg/day at weekly intervals until optimal response is obtained; usual range: 0.1-0.5 mg/kg/dose every morning (5-20 mg/day) with maximum of 40 mg/day
Children >12 years and Adults:
Narcolepsy: Initial: 10 mg/day, may increase at 10 mg increments in weekly intervals until side effects appear; maximum: 60 mg/day
Exogenous obesity (unlabeled use): 5-30 mg/day in divided doses of 5-10 mg 30-60 minutes before meals

Additional Information Complete prescribing information for this medication should be consulted for additional detail.

Dosage Forms [DSC] = Discontinued product

Capsule, sustained release, as sulfate: 5 mg, 10 mg, 15 mg

Dexedrine® Spansule®: 5 mg, 10 mg, 15 mg

Tablet, as sulfate: 5 mg, 10 mg

Dexedrine®: 5 mg [contains tartrazine] [DSC]

Dextrostat®: 5 mg, 10 mg [contains tartrazine]

Dextroamphetamine and Amphetamine

(deks troe am FET a meen & am FET a meen)

U.S. Brand Names Adderall®; Adderall XR®

Canadian Brand Names Adderall XR®

Index Terms Amphetamine and Dextroamphetamine

Pharmacologic Category Stimulant

Use Attention-deficit/hyperactivity disorder (ADHD); narcolepsy

Restrictions C-II

Pregnancy Risk Factor C

Medication Safety Issues

Sound-alike/look-alike issues:

Adderall® may be confused with Inderal®

Dosage Oral: **Note:** Use lowest effective individualized dose; administer first dose as soon as awake

ADHD:

Children: <3 years: Not recommended

Children: 3-5 years (Adderall®): Initial 2.5 mg/day given every morning; increase daily dose in 2.5 mg increments at weekly intervals until optimal response is obtained (maximum dose: 40 mg/day given in 1-3 divided doses); use intervals of 4-6 hours between additional doses

Children: ≥6 years:

Adderall®: Initial: 5 mg 1-2 times/day; increase daily dose in 5 mg increments at weekly intervals until optimal response is obtained (usual maximum dose: 40 mg/day given in 1-3 divided doses); use intervals of 4-6 hours between additional doses

Adderall XR®: 5-10 mg once daily in the morning; if needed, may increase daily dose in 5-10 mg increments at weekly intervals (maximum dose: 30 mg/day)

Adolescents 13-17 years (Adderall XR®): 10 mg once daily in the morning; maybe increased to 20 mg/day after 1 week if symptoms are not controlled; higher doses (up to 60 mg/day) have been evaluated; however, there is not adequate evidence that higher doses afford additional benefit.

Adults (Adderall XR®): Initial: 20 mg once daily in the morning; higher doses (up to 60 mg once daily) have been evaluated; however, there is not adequate evidence that higher doses afforded additional benefit

Narcolepsy (Adderall®):

Children: 6-12 years: Initial: 5 mg/day; increase daily dose in 5 mg at weekly intervals until optimal response is obtained (maximum dose: 60 mg/day given in 1-3 divided doses with intervals of 4-6 hours between doses)

Children >12 years and Adults: Initial: 10 mg/day; increase daily dose in 10 mg increments at weekly intervals until optimal response is obtained (maximum dose: 60 mg/day given in 1-3 divided doses with intervals of 4-6 hours between doses)

Additional Information Complete prescribing information for this medication should be consulted for additional detail.

Dosage Forms

Capsule, extended release (Adderall XR®):

5 mg [dextroamphetamine sulfate 1.25 mg, dextroamphetamine saccharate 1.25 mg, amphetamine aspartate monohydrate 1.25 mg, amphetamine sulfate 1.25 mg (equivalent to amphetamine base 3.1 mg)]

10 mg [dextroamphetamine sulfate 2.5 mg, dextroamphetamine saccharate 2.5 mg, amphetamine aspartate monohydrate 2.5 mg, amphetamine sulfate 2.5 mg (equivalent to amphetamine base 6.3 mg)]

15 mg [dextroamphetamine sulfate 3.75 mg, dextroamphetamine saccharate 3.75 mg, amphetamine aspartate monohydrate 3.75 mg, amphetamine sulfate 3.75 mg (equivalent to amphetamine base 9.4 mg)]

20 mg [dextroamphetamine sulfate 5 mg, dextroamphetamine saccharate 5 mg, amphetamine aspartate monohydrate 5 mg, amphetamine sulfate 5 mg (equivalent to amphetamine base 12.5 mg)]

25 mg [dextroamphetamine sulfate 6.25 mg, dextroamphetamine saccharate 6.25 mg, amphetamine aspartate monohydrate 6.25 mg, amphetamine sulfate 6.25 mg (equivalent to amphetamine base 15.6 mg)]

30 mg [dextroamphetamine sulfate 7.5 mg, dextroamphetamine saccharate 7.5 mg, amphetamine aspartate monohydrate 7.5 mg, amphetamine sulfate 7.5 mg (equivalent to amphetamine base 18.8 mg)]

Tablet (Adderall®):

5 mg [dextroamphetamine sulfate 1.25 mg, dextroamphetamine saccharate 1.25 mg, amphetamine aspartate 1.25 mg, amphetamine sulfate 1.25 mg (equivalent to amphetamine base 3.13 mg)]

7.5 mg [dextroamphetamine 1.875 mg, dextroamphetamine saccharate 1.875 mg, amphetamine aspartate 1.875 mg, amphetamine sulfate 1.875 mg (equivalent to amphetamine base 4.7 mg)]

10 mg [dextroamphetamine sulfate 2.5 mg, dextroamphetamine saccharate 2.5 mg, amphetamine aspartate 2.5 mg, amphetamine sulfate 2.5 mg (equivalent to amphetamine base 6.3 mg)]

(Continued)

Dextroamphetamine and Amphetamine *(Continued)*

12.5 mg [dextroamphetamine sulfate 3.125 mg, dextroamphetamine saccharate 3.125 mg, amphetamine aspartate 3.125 mg, amphetamine sulfate 3.125 mg (equivalent to amphetamine base 7.8 mg)]

15 mg [dextroamphetamine sulfate 3.75 mg, dextroamphetamine saccharate 3.75 mg, amphetamine aspartate 3.75 mg, amphetamine sulfate 3.75 mg (equivalent to amphetamine base 9.4 mg)]

20 mg [dextroamphetamine sulfate 5 mg, dextroamphetamine saccharate 5 mg, amphetamine aspartate 5 mg, amphetamine sulfate 5 mg (equivalent to amphetamine base 12.6 mg)]

30 mg [dextroamphetamine sulfate 7.5 mg, dextroamphetamine saccharate 7.5 mg, amphetamine aspartate 7.5 mg, amphetamine sulfate 7.5 mg (equivalent to amphetamine base 18.8 mg)]

- ◆ **Dextroamphetamine Sulfate** *see* Dextroamphetamine *on page 486*
- ◆ **Dextromethorphan, Acetaminophen, and Pseudoephedrine** *see* Acetaminophen, Dextromethorphan, and Pseudoephedrine *on page 35*
- ◆ **Dextromethorphan and Guaifenesin** *see* Guaifenesin and Dextromethorphan *on page 816*
- ◆ **Dextromethorphan and Promethazine** *see* Promethazine and Dextromethorphan *on page 1437*
- ◆ **Dextromethorphan and Pseudoephedrine** *see* Pseudoephedrine and Dextromethorphan *on page 1455*
- ◆ **Dextromethorphan, Carbinoxamine, and Pseudoephedrine** *see* Carbinoxamine, Pseudoephedrine, and Dextromethorphan *on page 291*
- ◆ **Dextromethorphan, Chlorpheniramine, and Phenylephrine** *see* Chlorpheniramine, Phenylephrine, and Dextromethorphan *on page 352*
- ◆ **Dextromethorphan, Chlorpheniramine, and Pseudoephedrine** *see* Chlorpheniramine, Pseudoephedrine, and Dextromethorphan *on page 355*
- ◆ **Dextromethorphan, Guaifenesin, and Pseudoephedrine** *see* Guaifenesin, Pseudoephedrine, and Dextromethorphan *on page 821*
- ◆ **Dextromethorphan, Pseudoephedrine, and Carbinoxamine** *see* Carbinoxamine, Pseudoephedrine, and Dextromethorphan *on page 291*
- ◆ **Dextropropoxyphene** *see* Propoxyphene *on page 1444*
- ◆ **Dextrostat®** *see* Dextroamphetamine *on page 486*
- ◆ **DFMO** *see* Eflornithine *on page 573*
- ◆ **DHAD** *see* Mitoxantrone *on page 1157*
- ◆ **DHAQ** *see* Mitoxantrone *on page 1157*
- ◆ **DHE** *see* Dihydroergotamine *on page 507*
- ◆ **D.H.E. 45®** *see* Dihydroergotamine *on page 507*
- ◆ **DHPG Sodium** *see* Ganciclovir *on page 779*
- ◆ **DHT™ [DSC]** *see* Dihydrotachysterol *on page 508*
- ◆ **DHT™ Intensol™ [DSC]** *see* Dihydrotachysterol *on page 508*
- ◆ **Diabeta** *see* GlyBURIDE *on page 803*
- ◆ **DiabetAid™ Antifungal Foot Bath [OTC]** *see* Miconazole *on page 1137*
- ◆ **Diabetic Tussin C®** *see* Guaifenesin and Codeine *on page 815*
- ◆ **Diabetic Tussin® DM [OTC]** *see* Guaifenesin and Dextromethorphan *on page 816*
- ◆ **Diabetic Tussin® DM Maximum Strength [OTC]** *see* Guaifenesin and Dextromethorphan *on page 816*
- ◆ **Diabetic Tussin® EX [OTC]** *see* Guaifenesin *on page 814*
- ◆ **Diabinese®** *see* ChlorproPAMIDE *on page 358*
- ◆ **Diaβeta®** *see* GlyBURIDE *on page 803*
- ◆ **Diaminocyclohexane Oxalatoplatinum** *see* Oxaliplatin *on page 1277*
- ◆ **Diaminodiphenylsulfone** *see* Dapsone *on page 450*
- ◆ **Diamode [OTC]** *see* Loperamide *on page 1027*
- ◆ **Diamox® (Can)** *see* AcetaZOLAMIDE *on page 37*
- ◆ **Diamox® Sequels®** *see* AcetaZOLAMIDE *on page 37*
- ◆ **Diarr-Eze (Can)** *see* Loperamide *on page 1027*
- ◆ **Diastat®** *see* Diazepam *on page 488*
- ◆ **Diastat® AcuDial™** *see* Diazepam *on page 488*
- ◆ **Diastat® Rectal Delivery System (Can)** *see* Diazepam *on page 488*
- ◆ **Diazemuls® (Can)** *see* Diazepam *on page 488*

Diazepam *(dye AZ e pam)*

U.S. Brand Names Diastat®; Diastat® AcuDial™; Diazepam Intensol®; Valium®
Canadian Brand Names Apo-Diazepam®; Diastat®; Diastat® Rectal Delivery System; Diazemuls®; Novo-Dipam®; Valium®
Pharmacologic Category Benzodiazepine
Additional Appendix Information
Benzodiazepines *on page 1874*
Use Management of anxiety disorders, ethanol withdrawal symptoms; skeletal muscle relaxant; treatment of convulsive disorders
Rectal gel: Management of selected, refractory epilepsy patients on stable regimens of antiepileptic drugs (AEDs) requiring intermittent use of diazepam to control episodes of increased seizure activity
Unlabeled/Investigational Use Panic disorders; preoperative sedation, light anesthesia, amnesia
Restrictions C-IV

Pregnancy Risk Factor D

Pregnancy Implications Teratogenic effects have been reported in animal studies. In humans, diazepam crosses the placenta. An increased risk of fetal malformations has been associated with diazepam and other minor tranquilizers; epilepsy itself may also increase the risk. Hypotonia, hypothermia, withdrawal symptoms, respiratory and feeding difficulties have reported in the infant following use maternal use of benzodiazepines near time of delivery.

Lactation Enters breast milk/contraindicated (AAP rates "of concern")

Medication Safety Issues
Sound-alike/look-alike issues:
Diazepam may be confused with diazoxide, Ditropan®, lorazepam
Valium® may be confused with Valcyte™

Contraindications Hypersensitivity to diazepam or any component of the formulation (cross-sensitivity with other benzodiazepines may exist); narrow-angle glaucoma; not for use in children <6 months of age (oral); pregnancy

Warnings/Precautions Diazepam has been associated with increasing the frequency of grand mal seizures. Withdrawal has also been associated with an increase in the seizure frequency. Use with caution with drugs which may decrease diazepam metabolism. Use with caution in elderly or debilitated patients, patients with hepatic disease (including alcoholics), or renal impairment. Active metabolites with extended half-lives may lead to delayed accumulation and adverse effects. Use with caution in patients with respiratory disease or impaired gag reflex.

Acute hypotension, muscle weakness, apnea, and cardiac arrest have occurred with parenteral administration. Acute effects may be more prevalent in patients receiving concurrent barbiturates, narcotics, or ethanol. Appropriate resuscitative equipment and qualified personnel should be available during administration and monitoring. Avoid use of the injection in patients with shock, coma, or acute ethanol intoxication. Intra-arterial injection or extravasation of the parenteral formulation should be avoided. Parenteral formulation contains propylene glycol, which has been associated with toxicity when administered in high dosages. Administration of rectal gel should only be performed by individuals trained to recognize characteristic seizure activity and monitor response.

Causes CNS depression (dose-related) resulting in sedation, dizziness, confusion, or ataxia which may impair physical and mental capabilities. Patients must be cautioned about performing tasks which require mental alertness (eg, operating machinery or driving). Use with caution in patients receiving other CNS depressants or psychoactive agents. Effects with other sedative drugs or ethanol may be potentiated. The dosage of narcotics should be reduced by approximately 1/3 when diazepam is added. Benzodiazepines have been associated with falls and traumatic injury and should be used with extreme caution in patients who are at risk of these events (especially the elderly).

Use caution in patients with depression, particularly if suicidal risk may be present. Use with caution in patients with a history of drug dependence. Benzodiazepines have been associated with dependence and acute withdrawal symptoms on discontinuation or reduction in dose. Acute withdrawal, including seizures, may be precipitated in patients after administration of flumazenil to patients receiving long-term benzodiazepine therapy.

Diazepam has been associated with anterograde amnesia. Paradoxical reactions, including hyperactive or aggressive behavior, have been reported with benzodiazepines, particularly in adolescent/pediatric or psychiatric patients. Does not have analgesic, antidepressant, or antipsychotic properties.

Rectal gel: Safety and efficacy have not been established in children <2 years of age.
Oral: Safety and efficacy have not been established in children <6 months of age.
Injection: Safety and efficacy have not been established in children <30 days of age. Solution for injection may contain sodium benzoate, benzyl alcohol, or benzoic acid. Large amounts have been associated with "gasping syndrome" in neonates.

Adverse Reactions Frequency not defined. Adverse reactions may vary by route of administration.

Cardiovascular: Hypotension, vasodilatation
Central nervous system: Agitation, amnesia, anxiety, ataxia, confusion, depression, dizziness, drowsiness, emotional lability, euphoria, fatigue, headache, incoordination, insomnia, memory impairment, paradoxical excitement or rage, seizure, slurred speech, somnolence, vertigo
Dermatologic: Rash
Endocrine & metabolic: Libido changes
Gastrointestinal: Constipation, diarrhea, nausea, salivation changes
Genitourinary: Incontinence, urinary retention
Hepatic: Jaundice
Local: Phlebitis, pain with injection
Neuromuscular & skeletal: Dysarthria, tremor, weakness
Ocular: Blurred vision, diplopia
Respiratory: Apnea, asthma, respiratory rate decreased

Overdosage/Toxicology Symptoms include somnolence, confusion, coma, hypoactive reflexes, dyspnea, hypotension, slurred speech, and impaired coordination. Treatment for benzodiazepine overdose is supportive. Rarely is mechanical ventilation required. Flumazenil has been shown to selectively block the binding of benzodiazepines to CNS receptors, resulting in a reversal of benzodiazepine-induced CNS depression, but not respiratory depression.

Drug Interactions
Cytochrome P450 Effect: Substrate of CYP1A2 (minor), 2B6 (minor), 2C9 (minor), 2C19 (major), 3A4 (major); **Inhibits** CYP2C19 (weak), 3A4 (weak)
Increased Effect/Toxicity: Diazepam potentiates the CNS depressant effects of opioid analgesics, barbiturates, phenothiazines, ethanol, antihistamines, MAO inhibitors, sedative-hypnotics, and cyclic antidepressants. CYP2C19 inhibitors may increase the levels/effects of diazepam; example inhibitors include delavirdine, fluconazole, fluvoxamine, gemfibrozil, isoniazid, omeprazole, and ticlopidine. CYP3A4 inhibitors may increase the
(Continued)

Diazepam *(Continued)*

levels/effects of diazepam; example inhibitors include azole antifungals, clarithromycin, diclofenac, doxycycline, erythromycin, imatinib, isoniazid, nefazodone, nicardipine, propofol, protease inhibitors, quinidine, telithromycin, and verapamil. Calcium channel blockers, nondihydropyridine (diltiazem, verapamil) may decrease the metabolism, via CYP isoenzymes, of diazepam. Benzodiazepines may enhance the adverse/toxic effect of clozapine.

Decreased Effect: CYP2C19 inducers may decrease the levels/effects of diazepam; example inducers include aminoglutethimide, carbamazepine, phenytoin, and rifampin. CYP3A4 inducers may decrease the levels/effects of diazepam; example inducers include aminoglutethimide, carbamazepine, nafcillin, nevirapine, phenobarbital, phenytoin, and rifamycins.

Ethanol/Nutrition/Herb Interactions

Ethanol: Avoid ethanol (may increase CNS depression).

Food: Diazepam serum levels may be increased if taken with food. Diazepam effect/toxicity may be increased by grapefruit juice; avoid concurrent use.

Herb/Nutraceutical: St John's wort may decrease diazepam levels. Avoid valerian, St John's wort, kava kava, gotu kola (may increase CNS depression).

Stability

Protect parenteral dosage form from light. Potency is retained for up to 3 months when kept at room temperature. Most stable at pH 4-8; hydrolysis occurs at pH <3. Per manufacturer, do not mix I.V. product with other medications.

Rectal gel: Store at 25°C (77°F); excursion permitted to 15°C to 30°C (59°F to 86°F).

Mechanism of Action

Binds to stereospecific benzodiazepine receptors on the postsynaptic GABA neuron at several sites within the central nervous system, including the limbic system, reticular formation. Enhancement of the inhibitory effect of GABA on neuronal excitability results by increased neuronal membrane permeability to chloride ions. This shift in chloride ions results in hyperpolarization (a less excitable state) and stabilization.

Pharmacodynamics/Kinetics

I.V.: Status epilepticus:

Onset of action: Almost immediate

Duration: 20-30 minutes

Absorption: Oral: 85% to 100%, more reliable than I.M.

Protein binding: 98%

Metabolism: Hepatic

Half-life elimination: Parent drug: Adults: 20-50 hours; increased half-life in neonates, elderly, and those with severe hepatic disorders; Active major metabolite (desmethyldiazepam): 50-100 hours; may be prolonged in neonates

Dosage Oral absorption is more reliable than I.M.

Children:

Conscious sedation for procedures: Oral: 0.2-0.3 mg/kg (maximum: 10 mg) 45-60 minutes prior to procedure

Sedation/muscle relaxant/anxiety:

Oral: 0.12-0.8 mg/kg/day in divided doses every 6-8 hours

I.M., I.V.: 0.04-0.3 mg/kg/dose every 2-4 hours to a maximum of 0.6 mg/kg within an 8-hour period if needed

Status epilepticus:

Infants 30 days to 5 years: I.V.: 0.05-0.3 mg/kg/dose given over 2-3 minutes, every 15-30 minutes to a maximum total dose of 5 mg; repeat in 2-4 hours as needed **or** 0.2-0.5 mg/dose every 2-5 minutes to a maximum total dose of 5 mg

>5 years: I.V.: 0.05-0.3 mg/kg/dose given over 2-3 minutes every 15-30 minutes to a maximum total dose of 10 mg; repeat in 2-4 hours as needed **or** 1 mg/dose given over 2-3 minutes, every 2-5 minutes to a maximum total dose of 10 mg

Rectal: 0.5 mg/kg, then 0.25 mg/kg in 10 minutes if needed (prepare dose using parenteral formulation)

Anticonvulsant (acute treatment): Rectal gel:

Children <2 years: Safety and efficacy have not been studied

Children 2-5 years: 0.5 mg/kg

Children 6-11 years: 0.3 mg/kg

Children ≥12 years: 0.2 mg/kg

Note: Dosage should be rounded upward to the next available dose, 2.5, 5, 7.5, 10, 12.5, 15, 17.5, and 20 mg/dose; dose may be repeated in 4-12 hours if needed; do not use for more than 5 episodes per month or more than one episode every 5 days

Adolescents: Conscious sedation for procedures:

Oral: 10 mg

I.V.: 5 mg, may repeat with ½ dose if needed

Adults:

Anticonvulsant (acute treatment): Rectal gel: 0.2 mg/kg

Note: Dosage should be rounded upward to the next available dose, 2.5, 5, 7.5, 10, 12.5, 15, 17.5, and 20 mg/dose; dose may be repeated in 4-12 hours if needed; do not use for more than 5 episodes per month or more than one episode every 5 days.

Anxiety/sedation/skeletal muscle relaxant:

Oral: 2-10 mg 2-4 times/day

I.M., I.V.: 2-10 mg, may repeat in 3-4 hours if needed

Sedation in the ICU patient: I.V.: 0.03-0.1 mg/kg every 30 minutes to 6 hours

Status epilepticus: I.V.: 5-10 mg every 10-20 minutes, up to 30 mg in an 8-hour period; may repeat in 2-4 hours if necessary

Rapid tranquilization of agitated patient (administer every 30-60 minutes): Oral: 5-10 mg; average total dose for tranquilization: 20-60 mg

Elderly:

Anticonvulsant: Rectal gel: Due to the increased half-life in elderly and debilitated patients, consider reducing dose.

Anxiety: Oral: Initial: 1-2 mg 1-2 times/day; increase gradually as needed, rarely need to use >10 mg/day (watch for hypotension and excessive sedation)

Skeletal muscle relaxant. Oral: Initial: 2-5 mg 2-4 times/day

Hemodialysis: Not dialyzable (0% to 5%); supplemental dose is not necessary

Dosing adjustment in hepatic impairment: Reduce dose by 50% in cirrhosis and avoid in severe/acute liver disease

Administration Intensol® should be diluted before use.

In children, do not exceed 1-2 mg/minute IVP; adults 5 mg/minute.

Rectal gel: Prior to administration, confirm that prescribed dose is visible and correct, and that the green "ready" band is visible. Patient should be positioned on side (facing person responsible for monitoring), with top leg bent forward. Insert rectal tip (lubricated) into rectum and push in plunger gently over 3 seconds. Remove tip of rectal syringe after 3 additional seconds. Buttocks should be held together for 3 seconds after removal. Dispose of syringe appropriately.

Monitoring Parameters Respiratory, cardiovascular, and mental status; check for orthostasis

Reference Range Therapeutic: Diazepam: 0.2-1.5 mcg/mL (SI: 0.7-5.3 μmol/L); N-desmethyldiazepam (nordiazepam): 0.1-0.5 mcg/mL (SI: 0.35-1.8 μmol/L)

Test Interactions False-negative urinary glucose determinations when using Clinistix® or Diastix®

Additional Information Diazepam does not have any analgesic effects.

Diastat®AcuDial™: When dispensing, consult package information for directions on setting patient's dose; confirm green "ready" band is visible prior to dispensing product.

Dosage Forms

Gel, rectal:

Diastat®: Pediatric rectal tip [4.4 cm]: 5 mg/mL (2.5 mg, 5 mg) [contains ethyl alcohol 10%, sodium benzoate, benzyl alcohol 1.5%; twin pack]

Diastat® AcuDial™ delivery system:

10 mg: Pediatric/adult rectal tip [4.4 cm]: 5 mg/mL (delivers set doses of 5 mg, 7.5 mg, and 10 mg) [contains ethyl alcohol 10%, sodium benzoate, benzyl alcohol 1.5%; twin pack]

20 mg: Adult rectal tip [6 cm]: 5 mg/mL (delivers set doses of 10 mg, 12.5 mg, 15 mg, 17.5 mg, and 20 mg) [contains ethyl alcohol 10%, sodium benzoate, benzyl alcohol 1.5%; twin pack]

Injection, solution: 5 mg/mL (2 mL, 10 mL) [may contain benzyl alcohol, sodium benzoate, benzoic acid]

Solution, oral: 5 mg/5 mL (5 mL, 500 mL) [wintergreen-spice flavor]

Solution, oral concentrate:

Diazepam Intensol®: 5 mg/mL (30 mL)

Tablet: 2 mg, 5 mg, 10 mg

Valium®: 2 mg, 5 mg, 10 mg

♦ **Diazepam Intensol®** see Diazepam on page 488

Diazoxide (dye az OKS ide)

U.S. Brand Names Hyperstat® [DSC]; Proglycem®

Canadian Brand Names Proglycem®

Pharmacologic Category Antihypertensive; Antihypoglycemic Agent

Additional Appendix Information

Hypertension on page 2063

Use

Oral: Hypoglycemia related to islet cell adenoma, carcinoma, hyperplasia, or adenomatosis, nesidioblastosis, leucine sensitivity, or extrapancreatic malignancy

I.V.: Severe hypertension

Pregnancy Risk Factor C

Medication Safety Issues

Sound-alike/look-alike issues:

Diazoxide may be confused with diazepam, Dyazide®

Hyperstat® may be confused with Nitrostat®

Dosage

Hypertension: Children and Adults: I.V.: 1-3 mg/kg up to a maximum of 150 mg in a single injection; repeat dose in 5-15 minutes until blood pressure adequately reduced; repeat administration at intervals of 4-24 hours; monitor the blood pressure closely; do not use longer than 10 days

Hyperinsulinemic hypoglycemia: Oral: **Note:** Use lower dose listed as initial dose

Newborns and Infants: 8-15 mg/kg/day in divided doses every 8-12 hours

Children and Adults: 3-8 mg/kg/day in divided doses every 8-12 hours

Dosing adjustment in renal impairment: None

Dialysis: Elimination is not enhanced via hemo- or peritoneal dialysis; supplemental dose is not necessary

Additional Information Complete prescribing information for this medication should be consulted for additional detail.

Dosage Forms [DSC] = Discontinued product

Capsule:

Proglycem®: 50 mg [not available in the U.S.]

Injection, solution:

Hyperstat®: 15 mg/mL (20 mL) [DSC]

Suspension, oral:

Proglycem®: 50 mg/mL (30 mL) [contains alcohol 7.25%; chocolate-mint flavor]

♦ **Dibenzyline®** see Phenoxybenzamine on page 1355

♦ **DIC** see Dacarbazine on page 442

♦ **Dicel™** see Chlorpheniramine and Pseudoephedrine on page 350

♦ **Dicel™ DM** see Chlorpheniramine, Pseudoephedrine, and Dextromethorphan on page 355

♦ **Dichloralphenazone, Acetaminophen, and Isometheptene** see Acetaminophen, Isometheptene, and Dichloralphenazone on page 36

♦ **Dichloralphenazone, Isometheptene, and Acetaminophen** *see* Acetaminophen, Isometheptene, and Dichloralphenazone *on page 36*

♦ **6,7-Dichloro-1,5-Dihydroimidazo [2,1b] quinazolin-2(3H)-one Monohydrochloride** *see* Anagrelide *on page 128*

Dichlorodifluoromethane and Trichloromonofluoromethane
(dye klor oh dye flor oh METH ane & tri klor oh mon oh flor oh METH ane)

U.S. Brand Names Fluori-Methane®

Index Terms Trichloromonofluoromethane and Dichlorodifluoromethane

Pharmacologic Category Analgesic, Topical

Use Management of pain associated with injections

Dosage Invert bottle over treatment area approximately 12" away from site of application; open dispenseal spring valve completely, allowing liquid to flow in a stream from the bottle. The rate of spraying is approximately 10 cm/second and should be continued until entire muscle has been covered.

Additional Information Complete prescribing information for this medication should be consulted for additional detail.

Dosage Forms Aerosol, topical: Dichlorodifluoromethane 15% and trichloromonofluoromethane 85% (103 mL) [contains chlorofluorocarbons]

♦ **Dichysterol** *see* Dihydrotachysterol *on page 508*

Diclofenac (dye KLOE fen ak)

U.S. Brand Names Cataflam®; Solaraze®; Voltaren®; Voltaren Ophthalmic®; Voltaren®-XR

Canadian Brand Names Apo-Diclo®; Apo-Diclo Rapide®; Apo-Diclo SR®; Cataflam®; Novo-Difenac; Novo-Difenac K; Novo-Difenac-SR; Nu-Diclo; Nu-Diclo-SR; Pennsaid®; PMS-Diclofenac; PMS-Diclofenac SR; Riva-Diclofenac; Riva-Diclofenac-K; Voltaren®; Voltaren Ophtha®; Voltaren Rapide®

Index Terms Diclofenac Potassium; Diclofenac Sodium

Pharmacologic Category Nonsteroidal Anti-inflammatory Drug (NSAID); Nonsteroidal Anti-inflammatory Drug (NSAID), Ophthalmic; Nonsteroidal Anti-inflammatory Drug (NSAID), Oral

Additional Appendix Information
Nonsteroidal Anti-inflammatory Agents *on page 1894*

Use
Immediate release: Ankylosing spondylitis; primary dysmenorrhea; acute and chronic treatment of rheumatoid arthritis, osteoarthritis

Delayed-release tablets: Acute and chronic treatment of rheumatoid arthritis, osteoarthritis, ankylosing spondylitis

Extended-release tablets: Chronic treatment of osteoarthritis, rheumatoid arthritis

Ophthalmic solution: Postoperative inflammation following cataract extraction; temporary relief of pain and photophobia in patients undergoing corneal refractive surgery

Topical gel: Actinic keratosis (AK) in conjunction with sun avoidance

Unlabeled/Investigational Use Juvenile rheumatoid arthritis

Restrictions An FDA-approved medication guide must be distributed when dispensing an oral outpatient prescription (new or refill) where this medication is to be used without direct supervision of a healthcare provider. Medication guides are available at http://www.fda.gov/cder/Offices/ODS/medication_guides.htm.

Pregnancy Risk Factor B (topical); C (oral)/D (3rd trimester)

Pregnancy Implications Safety and efficacy in pregnant women have not been established. Exposure late in pregnancy may lead to premature closure of the ductus arteriosus and may inhibit uterine contractions.

Lactation Excretion in breast milk unknown/not recommended

Medication Safety Issues
Sound-alike/look-alike issues:
Diclofenac may be confused with Diflucan®, Duphalac®
Cataflam® may be confused with Catapres®
Voltaren® may be confused with tramadol, Ultram®, Verelan®

Contraindications Hypersensitivity to diclofenac, aspirin, other NSAIDs, or any component of the formulation; perioperative pain in the setting of coronary artery bypass surgery (CABG); pregnancy (3rd trimester)

Warnings/Precautions [U.S. Boxed Warning]: NSAIDs are associated with an increased risk of adverse cardiovascular events, including MI, stroke, and new onset or worsening of pre-existing hypertension. Risk may be increased with duration of use or pre-existing cardiovascular risk factors or disease. Carefully evaluate individual cardiovascular risk profiles prior to prescribing. Use caution with fluid retention, CHF, or hypertension. Concurrent administration of ibuprofen, and potentially other nonselective NSAIDs, may interfere with aspirin's cardioprotective effect.

Use of NSAIDs can compromise existing renal function. Renal toxicity can occur in patient with impaired renal function, dehydration, heart failure, liver dysfunction, those taking diuretics and ACEI, and the elderly. Rehydrate patient before starting therapy. Monitor renal function closely. Not recommended for use in patients with advanced renal disease.

[U.S. Boxed Warning]: NSAIDs may increase risk of gastrointestinal irritation, ulceration, bleeding, and perforation. These events may occur at any time during therapy and without warning. Use caution with a history of GI disease (bleeding or ulcers), concurrent therapy with aspirin, anticoagulants and/or corticosteroids, smoking, use of alcohol, the elderly or debilitated patients.

Use the lowest effective dose for the shortest duration of time, consistent with individual patient goals, to reduce risk of cardiovascular or GI adverse events. Alternate therapies should be considered for patients at high risk.

NSAIDs may cause serious skin adverse events including exfoliative dermatitis, Stevens-Johnson syndrome (SJS), and toxic epidermal necrolysis (TEN). Anaphylactoid reactions may occur, even without prior exposure; patients with "aspirin triad" (bronchial asthma, aspirin intolerance, rhinitis) may be at increased risk. Do not use in patients who experience bronchospasm, asthma, rhinitis, or urticaria with NSAID or aspirin therapy.

Use with caution in patients with decreased hepatic function. Closely monitor patients with any abnormal LFT. Severe hepatic reactions (eg, fulminant hepatitis, liver failure) have occurred with NSAID use, rarely; discontinue if signs or symptoms of liver disease develop, or if systemic manifestations occur.

The elderly are at increased risk for adverse effects (especially peptic ulceration, CNS effects, renal toxicity) from NSAIDs even at low doses.

Withhold for at least 4-6 half-lives prior to surgical or dental procedures. Safety and efficacy have not been established in children.

Topical gel should not be applied to the eyes, open wounds, infected areas, or to exfoliative dermatitis. Monitor patients for 1 year following application of ophthalmic drops for corneal refractive procedures. Patients using ophthalmic drops should not wear soft contact lenses. Ophthalmic drops may slow/delay healing or prolong bleeding time following surgery.

Adverse Reactions

>10%:

Local: Application site reactions (gel): Pruritus (31% to 52%), rash (35% to 46%), contact dermatitis (19% to 33%), dry skin (25% to 27%), pain (15% to 26%), exfoliation (6% to 24%), paresthesia (8% to 20%)

Ocular: Ophthalmic drops (incidence may be dependent upon indication): Lacrimation (30%), keratitis (28%), elevated IOP (15%), transient burning/stinging (15%)

1% to 10%:

Central nervous system: Headache (7%), dizziness (3%)

Dermatologic: Pruritus (1% to 3%), rash (1% to 3%)

Endocrine & metabolic: Fluid retention (1% to 3%)

Gastrointestinal: Abdominal cramps (3% to 9%), abdominal pain (3% to 9%), constipation (3% to 9%), diarrhea (3% to 9%), flatulence (3% to 9%), indigestion (3% to 9%), nausea (3% to 9%), abdominal distention (1% to 3%), peptic ulcer/GI bleed (0.6% to 2%)

Hepatic: ALT/AST increased (2%)

Local: Application site reactions (gel): Edema (4%)

Ocular: Ophthalmic drops: Abnormal vision, acute elevated IOP, blurred vision, conjunctivitis, corneal deposits, corneal edema, corneal opacity, corneal lesions, discharge, eyelid swelling, injection, iritis, irritation, itching, lacrimation disorder, ocular allergy

Otic: Tinnitus (1% to 3%)

<1% (Limited to important or life-threatening): Oral dosage forms: Acute renal failure, agranulocytosis, allergic purpura, alopecia, anaphylactoid reactions, anaphylaxis, angioedema, aplastic anemia, aseptic meningitis, asthma, bullous eruption, cirrhosis, CHF, eosinophilia, erythema multiforme major, GI hemorrhage, hearing loss, hemolytic anemia, hepatic necrosis, hepatitis, hepatorenal syndrome, interstitial nephritis, jaundice, laryngeal edema, leukopenia, nephrotic syndrome, pancreatitis, papillary necrosis, photosensitivity, purpura, Stevens-Johnson syndrome, swelling of lips and tongue, thrombocytopenia, urticaria, visual changes, vomiting

Overdosage/Toxicology Symptoms include acute renal failure, vomiting, drowsiness, and leukocytosis. Management of nonsteroidal anti-inflammatory drug (NSAID) intoxication is primarily supportive and symptomatic. Fluid therapy is commonly effective in managing hypotension that may occur following an acute NSAID overdose, except when due to acute blood loss.

Drug Interactions

Cytochrome P450 Effect: Substrate (minor) of CYP1A2, 2B6, 2C8, 2C9, 2C19, 2D6, 3A4; **Inhibits** CYP1A2 (moderate), 2C9 (weak), 2E1 (weak), 3A4 (strong)

Increased Effect/Toxicity: Increased toxicity of digoxin, methotrexate, cyclosporine, lithium, insulin, sulfonylureas, potassium-sparing diuretics, warfarin, and aspirin. Diclofenac may increase the levels/effects of aminophylline, selected benzodiazepines, calcium channel blockers, cyclosporine, fluvoxamine, mexiletine, mirtazapine, nateglinide, nefazodone, ropinirole, sildenafil (and other PDE-5 inhibitors), tacrolimus, theophylline, trifluoperazine, venlafaxine, and other CYP1A2 or 3A4 substrates. Selected benzodiazepines (midazolam and triazolam), cisapride, ergot alkaloids, selected HMG-CoA reductase inhibitors (lovastatin and simvastatin), mesoridazine, pimozide, and thioridazine are generally contraindicated with strong CYP3A4 inhibitors. When used with strong CYP3A4 inhibitors, dosage adjustment/limits are recommended for sildenafil and other PDE-5 inhibitors; refer to individual monographs. Concomitant use with fluoroquinolones may rarely increase risk of seizure.

Decreased Effect: Decreased effect of diclofenac with aspirin. Decreased effect of thiazides, furosemide. NSAIDs may decrease the antihypertensive effect of ACE inhibitors, angiotensin antagonists, beta-blockers, or hydralazine. Cholestyramine (and other bile acid sequestrants) may decrease the absorption of NSAIDs; separate by at least 2 hours.

Ethanol/Nutrition/Herb Interactions

Ethanol: Avoid ethanol (may enhance gastric mucosal irritation).

Herb/Nutraceutical: Avoid alfalfa, anise, bilberry, bladderwrack, bromelain, cat's claw, celery, coleus, cordyceps, dong quai, evening primrose, feverfew, fenugreek, garlic, ginger, ginkgo biloboa, red clover, horse chestnut, grapeseed, green tea, ginseng, guggul, horse chestnut seed, horseradish, licorice, prickly ash, red clover, reishi, SAMe, sweet clover, turmeric, white willow (all have additional antiplatelet activity).

Stability Store below 30°C (86°F). Protect from moisture; store in tight container.

Mechanism of Action Inhibits prostaglandin synthesis by decreasing the activity of the enzyme, cyclooxygenase, which results in decreased formation of prostaglandin precursors. Mechanism of action for the treatment of AK has not been established.

(Continued)

Diclofenac *(Continued)*

Pharmacodynamics/Kinetics

Onset of action: Cataflam® is more rapid than sodium salt (Voltaren®) because it dissolves in the stomach instead of the duodenum

Absorption: Topical gel: 10%

Protein binding: 99% to albumin

Metabolism: Hepatic to several metabolites

Half-life elimination: 2 hours

Time to peak, serum: Cataflam®: ~1 hour; Voltaren®: ~2 hours

Excretion: Urine (65%); feces (35%)

Dosage Adults:

Oral:

Analgesia/primary dysmenorrhea: Starting dose: 50 mg 3 times/day; maximum dose: 150 mg/day

Rheumatoid arthritis: 150-200 mg/day in 2-4 divided doses (100 mg/day of sustained release product)

Osteoarthritis: 100-150 mg/day in 2-3 divided doses (100-200 mg/day of sustained release product)

Ankylosing spondylitis: 100-125 mg/day in 4-5 divided doses

Ophthalmic:

Cataract surgery: Instill 1 drop into affected eye 4 times/day beginning 24 hours after cataract surgery and continuing for 2 weeks

Corneal refractive surgery: Instill 1-2 drops into affected eye within the hour prior to surgery, within 15 minutes following surgery, and then continue for 4 times/day, up to 3 days

Topical: Apply gel to lesion area twice daily for 60-90 days

Dosage adjustment in renal impairment: Not recommended in patients with advanced renal disease

Dosage adjustment in hepatic impairment: No specific dosing recommendations

Elderly: No specific dosing recommendations; elderly may demonstrate adverse effects at lower doses than younger adults, and >60% may develop asymptomatic peptic ulceration with or without hemorrhage; monitor renal function

Dietary Considerations May be taken with food to decrease GI distress.

Diclofenac potassium = Cataflam®; potassium content: 5.8 mg (0.15 mEq) per 50 mg tablet

Administration

Oral: Do not crush tablets. Administer with food or milk to avoid gastric distress. Take with full glass of water to enhance absorption.

Ophthalmic: Wait at least 5 minutes before administering other types of eye drops.

Topical gel: Cover lesion with gel and smooth into skin gently. Do not cover lesion with occlusive dressings or apply sunscreens, cosmetics, or other medications to affected area.

Monitoring Parameters Monitor CBC, liver enzymes; monitor urine output and BUN/serum creatinine; occult blood loss, hemoglobin, hematocrit

Dosage Forms [DSC] = Discontinued product

Gel, as sodium:

Solaraze®: 30 mg/g (50 g)

Solution, ophthalmic, as sodium:

Voltaren Ophthalmic®: 0.1% (2.5 mL, 5 mL)

Tablet, as potassium: 50 mg

Cataflam®: 50 mg

Tablet, delayed release, enteric coated, as sodium: 50 mg, 75 mg

Voltaren®: 25 mg [DSC], 50 mg [DSC], 75 mg

Tablet, extended release, as sodium: 100 mg

Voltaren®-XR: 100 mg

Diclofenac and Misoprostol (dye KLOE fen ak & mye soe PROST ole)

U.S. Brand Names Arthrotec®

Canadian Brand Names Arthrotec®

Index Terms Misoprostol and Diclofenac

Pharmacologic Category Nonsteroidal Anti-inflammatory Drug (NSAID), Oral; Prostaglandin

Use The diclofenac component is indicated for the treatment of osteoarthritis and rheumatoid arthritis; the misoprostol component is indicated for the prophylaxis of NSAID-induced gastric and duodenal ulceration

Restrictions An FDA-approved medication guide must be distributed when dispensing an oral outpatient prescription (new or refill) where this medication is to be used without direct supervision of a h ealthcare provider. Medication guides are available at http://www.fda.gov/cder/Offices/ODS/medication_guides.htm.

Pregnancy Risk Factor X

Dosage Oral:

Adults:

Arthrotec® 50:

Osteoarthritis: 1 tablet 2-3 times/day

Rheumatoid arthritis: 1 tablet 3-4 times/day

For both regimens, if not tolerated by patient, the dose may be reduced to 1 tablet twice daily

Arthrotec® 75:

Patients who cannot tolerate full daily Arthrotec® 50 regimens: 1 tablet twice daily

Note: The use of these tablets may not be as effective at preventing GI ulceration

Elderly: No specific dosage adjustment is recommended; may require reduced dosage due to lower body weight; monitor renal function

Dosage adjustment in renal impairment: Not recommended in patients with advanced renal disease. In renal insufficiency, diclofenac should be used with caution due to potential detrimental effects on renal function, and misoprostol dosage reduction may be required if adverse effects occur (misoprostol is renally eliminated).

Additional Information Complete prescribing information for this medication should be consulted for additional detail.

Dosage Forms Tablet: Diclofenac sodium 50 mg and misoprostol 200 mcg; diclofenac sodium 75 mg and misoprostol 200 mcg

♦ **Diclofenac Potassium** see Diclofenac on page 492

♦ **Diclofenac Sodium** see Diclofenac on page 492

Dicloxacillin (dye kloks a SIL in)

Canadian Brand Names Dycill®; Pathocil®

Index Terms Dicloxacillin Sodium

Pharmacologic Category Antibiotic, Penicillin

Use Treatment of systemic infections such as pneumonia, skin and soft tissue infections, and osteomyelitis caused by penicillinase-producing staphylococci

Pregnancy Risk Factor B

Lactation Excretion in breast milk unknown (probably similar to penicillin G)

Contraindications Hypersensitivity to dicloxacillin, penicillin, or any component of the formulation

Warnings/Precautions Monitor PT if patient concurrently on warfarin; elimination of drug is slow in neonates; use with caution in patients allergic to cephalosporins

Adverse Reactions
1% to 10%: Gastrointestinal: Nausea, diarrhea, abdominal pain

<1% (Limited to important or life-threatening): Agranulocytosis, eosinophilia, hemolytic anemia, hepatotoxicity, hypersensitivity, interstitial nephritis, leukopenia, neutropenia, prolonged PT, pseudomembranous colitis, rash (maculopapular to exfoliative), seizure with extremely high doses and/or renal failure, serum sickness-like reactions, thrombocytopenia, vaginitis, vomiting

Overdosage/Toxicology Symptoms of penicillin overdose include neuromuscular hypersensitivity (agitation, hallucinations, asterixis, encephalopathy, confusion, seizures) and electrolyte imbalance (with potassium or sodium salts), especially in renal failure. Hemodialysis may be helpful to aid in removal of the drug from the blood, otherwise, most treatment is supportive or symptom-directed.

Drug Interactions
Cytochrome P450 Effect: Induces CYP3A4 (weak)
Increased Effect/Toxicity: Disulfiram, probenecid may increase penicillin levels. Penicillins may increase the exposure to methotrexate during concurrent therapy; monitor.
Decreased Effect: Although anecdotal reports suggest oral contraceptive efficacy could be reduced by penicillins, this has been refuted by more rigorous scientific and clinical data. Decreased effect of (warfarin) anticoagulants.

Ethanol/Nutrition/Herb Interactions Food: Decreases drug absorption rate; decreases drug serum concentration.

Mechanism of Action Inhibits bacterial cell wall synthesis by binding to one or more of the penicillin binding proteins (PBPs) which in turn inhibits the final transpeptidation step of peptidoglycan synthesis in bacterial cell walls, thus inhibiting cell wall biosynthesis. Bacteria eventually lyse due to ongoing activity of cell wall autolytic enzymes (autolysins and murein hydrolases) while cell wall assembly is arrested.

Pharmacodynamics/Kinetics
Absorption: 35% to 76%; rate and extent reduced by food
Distribution: Throughout body with highest concentrations in kidney and liver; CSF penetration is low; crosses placenta; enters breast milk
Protein binding: 96%
Half-life elimination: 0.6-0.8 hour; slightly prolonged with renal impairment
Time to peak, serum: 0.5-2 hours
Excretion: Feces; urine (56% to 70% as unchanged drug); prolonged in neonates

Dosage
Usual dosage range:
Newborns: Use not recommended
Children <40 kg: Oral: 12.5-100 mg/kg/day divided every 6 hours
Children >40 kg: Oral: 125-250 mg every 6 hours
Adults: Oral: 125-1000 mg every 6 hours

Indication-specific dosing:
Children: Oral:
Furunculosis: 25-50 mg/kg/day divided every 6 hours
Osteomyelitis: 50-100 mg/kg/day in divided doses every 6 hours
Adults: Oral:
Erysipelas, furunculosis, mastitis, otitis externa, septic bursitis, skin abscess: 500 mg every 6 hours
Impetigo: 250 mg every 6 hours
Prosthetic joint (long-term suppression therapy): 250 mg twice daily
Staphylococcus aureus, methicillin susceptible infection if no I.V. access: 500-1000 mg every 6-8 hours

Dosage adjustment in renal impairment: Not necessary
Hemodialysis: Not dialyzable (0% to 5%); supplemental dosage not necessary
Peritoneal dialysis: Supplemental dosage not necessary
Continuous arteriovenous or venovenous hemofiltration: Supplemental dosage not necessary

Dietary Considerations Administer on an empty stomach 1 hour before or 2 hours after meals. Sodium content of 250 mg capsule: 13 mg (0.6 mEq).

Administration Administer 1 hour before or 2 hours after meals. Administer around-the-clock to promote less variation in peak and trough serum levels.
(Continued)

Dicloxacillin *(Continued)*

Monitoring Parameters Monitor prothrombin time if patient concurrently on warfarin; monitor for signs of anaphylaxis during first dose

Test Interactions False-positive urine and serum proteins; false-positive in uric acid, urinary steroids; may interfere with urinary glucose tests using cupric sulfate (Benedict's solution, Clinitest®); may inactivate aminoglycosides *in vitro*

Dosage Forms Capsule: 250 mg, 500 mg

♦ **Dicloxacillin Sodium** *see Dicloxacillin on page 495*

Dicyclomine *(dye SYE kloe meen)*

U.S. Brand Names Bentyl®

Canadian Brand Names Bentylol®; Formulex®; Lomine; Riva-Dicyclomine

Index Terms Dicyclomine Hydrochloride; Dicycloverine Hydrochloride

Pharmacologic Category Anticholinergic Agent

Use Treatment of functional disturbances of GI motility such as irritable bowel syndrome

Unlabeled/Investigational Use Urinary incontinence

Pregnancy Risk Factor B

Medication Safety Issues
Sound-alike/look-alike issues:
Dicyclomine may be confused with diphenhydrAMINE, doxycycline, dyclonine
Bentyl® may be confused with Aventyl®, Benadryl®, Bontril®, Cantil®, Proventil®, Trental®

Dosage
Oral:
Infants >6 months: 5 mg/dose 3-4 times/day
Children: 10 mg/dose 3-4 times/day
Adults: Begin with 80 mg/day in 4 equally divided doses, then increase up to 160 mg/day
I.M. **(should not be used I.V.):** Adults: 80 mg/day in 4 divided doses (20 mg/dose)

Additional Information Complete prescribing information for this medication should be consulted for additional detail.

Dosage Forms
Capsule, as hydrochloride: 10 mg
Injection, solution, as hydrochloride: 10 mg/mL (2 mL)
Syrup, as hydrochloride: 10 mg/5 mL (480 mL)
Tablet, as hydrochloride: 20 mg

♦ **Dicyclomine Hydrochloride** *see Dicyclomine on page 496*
♦ **Dicycloverine Hydrochloride** *see Dicyclomine on page 496*
♦ **Di-Dak-Sol** *see Sodium Hypochlorite Solution on page 1579*

Didanosine *(dye DAN oh seen)*

U.S. Brand Names Videx®; Videx® EC

Canadian Brand Names Videx®; Videx® EC

Index Terms ddl; Dideoxyinosine

Pharmacologic Category Antiretroviral Agent, Reverse Transcriptase Inhibitor (Nucleoside)

Additional Appendix Information
Antiretroviral Therapy for HIV Infection: Adults and Adolescents *on page 1988*
Management of Healthcare Worker Exposures to HBV, HCV, and HIV *on page 1941*

Use Treatment of HIV infection; always to be used in combination with at least two other antiretroviral agents

Pregnancy Risk Factor B

Pregnancy Implications Cases of fatal and nonfatal lactic acidosis, with or without pancreatitis, have been reported in pregnant women. It is not known if pregnancy itself potentiates this known side effect; however, pregnant women may be at increased risk of lactic acidosis and liver damage. Hepatic enzymes and electrolytes should be monitored frequently during the 3rd trimester of pregnancy. Use during pregnancy only if the potential benefit to the mother outweighs the potential risk of this complication. Didanosine has been shown to cross the placenta. Preliminary information from the antiretroviral pregnancy registry note an increased risk of birth defects with 1st trimester exposure compared to exposure later in pregnancy; no pattern of defects have been noted. Pharmacokinetics are not significantly altered during pregnancy; dose adjustments are not needed. The Perinatal HIV Guidelines Working Group considers didanosine to be an alternative NRTI in dual nucleoside combination regimens; use with stavudine only if no other alternatives are available. Health professionals are encouraged to contact the antiretroviral pregnancy registry to monitor outcomes of pregnant women exposed to antiretroviral medications (1-800-258-4263 or www.APRegistry.com).

Lactation Excretion in breast milk unknown/contraindicated

Medication Safety Issues
Sound-alike/look-alike issues:
Videx® may be confused with Lidex®

Contraindications Hypersensitivity to didanosine or any component of the formulation

Warnings/Precautions [U.S. Boxed Warning]: Pancreatitis (sometimes fatal) has been reported; incidence is dose related. Risk factors for developing pancreatitis may include a previous history of the condition, concurrent cytomegalovirus or *Mycobacterium avium-intracellulare* infection, renal impairment, advanced age, and concomitant use of stavudine, pentamidine, or hydroxyurea. Discontinue didanosine if clinical signs of pancreatitis occur. **[U.S. Boxed Warning]: Lactic acidosis, symptomatic hyperlactatemia, and severe hepatomegaly with steatosis (sometimes fatal) have occurred with antiretroviral nucleoside analogues, including didanosine.** Hepatotoxicity may occur even in the absence of marked transaminase elevations; suspend therapy in any patient developing clinical/laboratory findings which suggest hepatotoxicity. Pregnant women may be at increased risk of lactic acidosis and liver damage.

Peripheral neuropathy occurs in ~20% of patients receiving the drug. If symptomatic, discontinue therapy; after resolution of symptoms, reinitiation of therapy at a reduced dose may be tolerated. Permanently discontinue if neuropathy recurs. Retinal changes (including retinal depigmentation) and optic neuritis have been reported in adults and children using didanosine. Patients should undergo retinal examination every 6-12 months. Use with caution in patients with decreased hepatic function, phenylketonuria, sodium-restricted diets, or with edema, CHF, or hyperuricemia. Use caution in renal impairment; dose reduction recommended for Cl$_{cr}$ <60 mL/minute. May cause redistribution of fat (eg, buffalo hump, peripheral wasting with increased abdominal girth, cushingoid appearance). Patients may develop immune reconstitution syndrome resulting in the occurrence of an inflammatory response to an indolent or residual opportunistic infection; further evaluation and treatment may be required. Didanosine delayed release capsules are indicated for once-daily use. Safety and efficacy of didanosine delayed release capsules in children have not been established.

Adverse Reactions As reported in monotherapy studies; risk of toxicity may increase when combined with other agents.

>10%:
Gastrointestinal: Diarrhea (19% to 28%), amylase increased (15% to 17%), abdominal pain (7% to 13%)
Neuromuscular & skeletal: Peripheral neuropathy (17% to 20%)

1% to 10%:
Dermatologic: Rash/pruritus (7% to 9%)
Endocrine & metabolic: Uric acid increased (2% to 3%)
Gastrointestinal: Pancreatitis (1% to 7% dose dependent); patients >65 years of age had a higher frequency of pancreatitis than younger patients
Hepatic: AST/ALT increased (6% to 9%), alkaline phosphatase increased (1% to 4%)

Postmarketing and/or reports: Acute renal impairment, alopecia, anaphylactoid reaction, anemia, anorexia, arthralgia, chills/fever, diabetes mellitus, dry eyes, dyspepsia, flatulence, granulocytopenia, hepatic steatosis, hepatitis, hyper-/hypoglycemia, hyperlactatemia (symptomatic), hypersensitivity, immune reconstitution syndrome, lactic acidosis/hepatomegaly, leukopenia, lipodystrophy, liver failure, myalgia, myopathy, optic neuritis, pain, parotid gland enlargement, retinal depigmentation, rhabdomyolysis, seizure, sialoadenitis, thrombocytopenia, weakness, xerostomia

Overdosage/Toxicology Chronic overdose may cause pancreatitis, peripheral neuropathy, diarrhea, hyperuricemia, and hepatic impairment. There is no known antidote for didanosine overdose. Treatment is symptom-directed and supportive. Didanosine is not removed via peritoneal dialysis, but some clearance occurs with hemodialysis.

Drug Interactions
Increased Effect/Toxicity: Concomitant administration of other drugs which have the potential to cause peripheral neuropathy or pancreatitis may increase the risk of these toxicities. Allopurinol may increase didanosine concentration; avoid concurrent use. Ganciclovir may increase didanosine concentration; monitor. Coadministration with ribavirin, tenofovir, hydroxyurea or stavudine may increase exposure to didanosine and/or its active metabolite increasing the risk of hepatic decompensation (or other signs of mitochondrial toxicity), including pancreatitis, lactic acidosis, and peripheral neuropathy; monitor closely and suspend therapy if signs or symptoms of toxicity are noted. Additionally, concomitant tenofovir administration has been associated with hyperglycemia, decreased CD4 cell counts, and reduced virologic response.

Decreased Effect: Didanosine buffered tablets and pediatric oral solution may decrease absorption of dapsone, quinolones or tetracyclines (administer 2 hours prior to didanosine buffered formulations). Didanosine should be held during PCP treatment with pentamidine. Didanosine may decrease levels of indinavir and atazanavir. Drugs whose absorption depends on the level of acidity in the stomach such as ketoconazole, itraconazole, and dapsone should be administered at least 2 hours prior to the buffered formulations of didanosine (not affected by delayed release capsules). Methadone may decrease didanosine concentrations.

Ethanol/Nutrition/Herb Interactions
Ethanol: Avoid ethanol (increases risk of pancreatitis).
Food: Decreases AUC and C$_{max}$. Didanosine serum levels may be decreased by 55% if taken with food.

Stability Delayed release capsules should be stored in tightly closed bottles at 15°C to 30°C (59°F to 86°F). Unreconstituted powder should be stored at 15°C to 30°C (59°F to 86°F). Reconstituted pediatric solution is stable for 30 days if refrigerated.
Videx® pediatric powder: Add 100 mL or 200 mL distilled water to the 2 g or 4 g container, respectively, to achieve a 20 mg/mL solution. Immediately mix the resulting solution with an equal volume of Mylanta® Maximum Strength (or equivalent) to achieve a final concentration of 10 mg/mL.

Mechanism of Action Didanosine, a purine nucleoside (adenosine) analog and the deamination product of dideoxyadenosine (ddA), inhibits HIV replication *in vitro* in both T cells and monocytes. Didanosine is converted within the cell to the mono-, di-, and triphosphates of ddA. These ddA triphosphates act as substrate and inhibitor of HIV reverse transcriptase substrate and inhibitor of HIV reverse transcriptase thereby blocking viral DNA synthesis and suppressing HIV replication.

Pharmacodynamics/Kinetics
Absorption: Subject to degradation by acidic pH of stomach; some formulations are buffered to resist acidic pH; ≤50% reduction in peak plasma concentration is observed in presence of food. Delayed release capsules contain enteric-coated beadlets which dissolve in the small intestine.
Distribution: V$_d$: Children: 35.6 L/m^2; Adults: 1.08 L/kg
Protein binding: <5%
(Continued)

Didanosine *(Continued)*

Metabolism: Has not been evaluated in humans; studies conducted in dogs show extensive metabolism with allantoin, hypoxanthine, xanthine, and uric acid being the major metabolites found in urine

Bioavailability: 42%

Half-life elimination:

Children and Adolescents: 0.8 hour

Adults: Normal renal function: 1.5 hours; active metabolite, ddATP, has an intracellular half-life >12 hours *in vitro*; Renal impairment: 2.5-5 hours

Time to peak: Delayed release capsules: 2 hours; Powder for suspension: 0.25-1.5 hours

Excretion: Urine (~55% as unchanged drug)

Clearance: Total body: Averages 800 mL/minute

Dosage Treatment of HIV infection: Oral (administer on an empty stomach):

Children: Pediatric powder for oral solution (Videx®):

2 weeks to 8 months: 100 mg/m² twice daily is recommended by the manufacturer; 50 mg/m² may be considered in infants 2 weeks to 4 months

>8 months: 120 mg/m² twice daily; dosing range: 90-150 mg/m² twice daily; patients with CNS disease may require higher dose

Adolescents and Adults: Dosing based on patient weight:

Pediatric powder for oral solution (Videx®):

<60 kg: 125 mg twice daily or 250 mg once daily

≥60 kg: 200 mg twice daily or 400 mg once daily

Delayed release capsule (Videx® EC):

<60 kg: 250 mg once daily

≥60 kg: 400 mg once daily

Elderly patients have a higher frequency of pancreatitis (10% versus 5% in younger patients); monitor renal function and dose accordingly

Dosing adjustment with tenofovir (delayed release capsules; based on tenofovir product labeling): Adults:

<60 kg and Cl$_{cr}$ ≥60 mL/minute: 200 mg once daily

≥60 kg and Cl$_{cr}$ ≥60 mL/minute: 250 mg once daily

Dosage adjustment in renal impairment: Adults: Dosing based on patient weight, creatinine clearance, and dosage form: See table.

Recommended Dose (mg) of Didanosine by Body Weight - Adults

Creatinine Clearance (mL/min)	≥60 kg		<60 kg	
	Powder for Oral Solution	Delayed Release Capsule	Powder for Oral Solution	Delayed Release Capsule
≥60	400 mg daily or 200 mg twice daily	400 mg daily	250 mg daily or 125 mg twice daily	250 mg daily
30-59	200 mg daily or 100 mg twice daily	200 mg daily	150 mg daily or 75 mg twice daily	125 mg daily
10-29	150 mg daily	125 mg daily	100 mg daily	125 mg daily
<10	100 mg daily	125 mg daily	75 mg daily	See Note.

Note: Not suitable for use in patients <60 kg with Cl$_{cr}$ <10 mL/minute; use alternate formulation.

Patients requiring hemodialysis or CAPD: Dose per Cl$_{cr}$ <10 mL/minute. No didanosine removed via CAPD.

Hemodialysis: Minimal amount of dose (≤7%) removed by hemodialysis; no supplemental dosing necessary

Dosing adjustment in hepatic impairment: Should be considered; monitor for toxicity

Dietary Considerations Videx® EC: Take on an empty stomach; administer at least 1 hour before or 2 hours after eating

Administration Pediatric powder for oral solution: Prior to dispensing, the powder should be mixed with purified water USP to an initial concentration of 20 mg/mL and then further diluted with an appropriate antacid suspension to a final mixture of 10 mg/mL. Shake well prior to use.

Monitoring Parameters Serum potassium, uric acid, creatinine; hemoglobin, CBC with neutrophil and platelet count, CD4 cells; viral load; liver function tests, amylase; weight gain; perform dilated retinal exam every 6 months

Additional Information A high rate of early virologic nonresponse was observed when didanosine, lamivudine, and tenofovir were used as the initial regimen in treatment-naive patients. Use of this combination is not recommended; patients currently on this regimen should be closely monitored for modification of therapy. Early virologic failure was also observed with tenofovir and didanosine delayed release capsules, plus either efavirenz or nevirapine; use caution in treatment-naive patients with high baseline viral loads.

Dosage Forms

Capsule, delayed release: 200 mg, 250 mg, 400 mg

Videx® EC: 125 mg, 200 mg, 250 mg, 400 mg

Powder for oral solution, pediatric:

Videx®: 2 g, 4 g [makes 10 mg/mL solution after final mixing]

♦ **Dideoxycytidine** *see* Zalcitabine *on page 1807*

♦ **Dideoxyinosine** *see* Didanosine *on page 496*

♦ **Didronel**® *see* Etidronate Disodium *on page 665*

Diethylpropion (dye eth il PROE pee on)

U.S. Brand Names Tenuate® [DSC]; Tenuate® Dospan® [DSC]
Canadian Brand Names Tenuate®; Tenuate® Dospan®
Index Terms Amfepramone; Diethylpropion Hydrochloride
Pharmacologic Category Anorexiant
Use Short-term adjunct in a regimen of weight reduction based on exercise, behavioral modification, and caloric reduction in the management of exogenous obesity for patients with an initial body mass index ≥30 kg/m² or ≥27 kg/m² in the presence of other risk factors (diabetes, hypertension)
Unlabeled/Investigational Use Migraine
Restrictions C-IV
Pregnancy Risk Factor B
Dosage Adults: Oral:
  Tablet: 25 mg 3 times/day before meals or food
  Tablet, controlled release: 75 mg at midmorning
Additional Information Complete prescribing information for this medication should be consulted for additional detail.
Dosage Forms [DSC] = Discontinued product
  Tablet, as hydrochloride: 25 mg
    Tenuate®: 25 mg [DSC]
  Tablet, controlled release, as hydrochloride: 75 mg
    Tenuate® Dospan®: 75 mg [DSC]

♦ **Diethylpropion Hydrochloride** *see* Diethylpropion *on page 499*

Difenoxin and Atropine (dye fen OKS in & A troe peen)

U.S. Brand Names Motofen®
Index Terms Atropine and Difenoxin
Pharmacologic Category Antidiarrheal
Use Treatment of diarrhea
Restrictions C-IV
Pregnancy Risk Factor C
Dosage Adults: Oral: Initial: 2 tablets (each tablet contains difenoxin hydrochloride 1 mg and atropine sulfate 0.025 mg), then 1 tablet after each loose stool; 1 tablet every 3-4 hours, up to 8 tablets in a 24-hour period; if no improvement after 48 hours, continued administration is not indicated
Additional Information Complete prescribing information for this medication should be consulted for additional detail.
Dosage Forms Tablet: Difenoxin hydrochloride 1 mg and atropine sulfate 0.025 mg

♦ **Differin®** *see* Adapalene *on page 49*
♦ **Differin® XP (Can)** *see* Adapalene *on page 49*

Diflorasone (dye FLOR a sone)

U.S. Brand Names ApexiCon™; ApexiCon™ E; Florone®; Psorcon® e™ [DSC]
Canadian Brand Names Florone®; Psorcon®
Index Terms Diflorasone Diacetate
Pharmacologic Category Corticosteroid, Topical
Additional Appendix Information
  Corticosteroids *on page 1879*
Use Relieves inflammation and pruritic symptoms of corticosteroid-responsive dermatosis (high to very high potency topical corticosteroid)

  Maxiflor®: High potency topical corticosteroid
  Psorcon®: Very high potency topical corticosteroid
Pregnancy Risk Factor C
Medication Safety Issues
  Sound-alike/look-alike issues:
    Psorcon® may be confused with Proscar®, ProSom®, Psorion®

  International issues:
    Florone® may be confused with Fluoron® which is a brand name for fluorine in Canada
    Florone® may be confused with Flogene® which is a brand name for fentiazac in Italy and a brand name for piroxicam in Brazil
Dosage Topical: Apply ointment sparingly 1-3 times/day; apply cream sparingly 2-4 times/day. Therapy should be discontinued when control is achieved; if no improvement is seen, reassessment of diagnosis may be necessary.
Dosage Forms [DSC] = Discontinued product
  Cream, as diacetate: 0.05% (15 g, 30 g, 60 g)
    ApexiCon™ E, Florone®: 0.05% (30 g, 60 g)
    Psorcon® e™: 0.05% (15 g, 30 g, 60 g) [DSC]
  Ointment, as diacetate: 0.05% (15 g, 30 g, 60 g)
    ApexiCon™: 0.05% (30 g, 60 g)
    Psorcon® e™: 0.05% (15 g, 30 g, 60 g) [DSC]

♦ **Diflorasone Diacetate** *see* Diflorasone *on page 499*
♦ **Diflucan®** *see* Fluconazole *on page 712*

Diflunisal (dye FLOO ni sal)

U.S. Brand Names Dolobid® [DSC]
Canadian Brand Names Apo-Diflunisal®; Novo-Diflunisal; Nu-Diflunisal
Pharmacologic Category Nonsteroidal Anti-inflammatory Drug (NSAID), Oral
Additional Appendix Information
  Nonsteroidal Anti-inflammatory Agents *on page 1894*
Use Management of inflammatory disorders usually including rheumatoid arthritis and osteoarthritis; can be used as an analgesic for treatment of mild to moderate pain
Restrictions An FDA-approved medication guide must be distributed when dispensing an oral outpatient prescription (new or refill) where this medication is to be used without direct supervision of a healthcare provider. Medication guides are available at http://www.fda.gov/cder/Offices/ODS/medication_guides.htm.
Pregnancy Risk Factor C (1st and 2nd trimesters)/D (3rd trimester)
Pregnancy Implications Teratogenic effects have been documented in animal studies. However, known effects of NSAIDs suggest the potential for premature ductus arteriosus closure, particularly in late pregnancy. There are no adequate and well-controlled studies in pregnant women.
Lactation Enters breast milk/not recommended
Medication Safety Issues
  Sound-alike/look-alike issues:
    Dolobid® may be confused with Slo-Bid®
Contraindications Hypersensitivity to diflunisal, aspirin, other NSAIDs, or any component of the formulation; perioperative pain in the setting of coronary artery bypass surgery (CABG); pregnancy (3rd trimester)
Warnings/Precautions [U.S. Boxed Warning]: NSAIDs are associated with an increased risk of adverse cardiovascular events, including MI, stroke, and new onset or worsening of pre-existing hypertension. Risk may be increased with duration of use or pre-existing cardiovascular risk-factors or disease. Carefully evaluate individual cardiovascular risk profiles prior to prescribing. Use caution with fluid retention, CHF, or hypertension. Concurrent administration of ibuprofen, and potentially other nonselective NSAIDs, may interfere with aspirin's cardioprotective effect.

[U.S. Boxed Warning]: NSAIDs may increase risk of gastrointestinal irritation, ulceration, bleeding, and perforation. Use caution with a history of GI disease (bleeding or ulcers), concurrent therapy with aspirin, anticoagulants and/or corticosteroids, smoking, use of alcohol, the elderly or debilitated patients.

Use of NSAIDs can compromise existing renal function. Diflunisal is not recommended for patients with advanced renal disease. Use with caution in patients with decreased hepatic function.

Use the lowest effective dose for the shortest duration of time, consistent with individual patient goals, to reduce risk of cardiovascular or GI adverse events.

NSAIDs may cause serious skin adverse events including exfoliative dermatitis, Stevens-Johnson syndrome (SJS), and toxic epidermal necrolysis (TEN). Do not use in patients who experience bronchospasm, asthma, rhinitis, or urticaria with NSAID or aspirin therapy.

A hypersensitivity syndrome has been reported; monitor for constitutional symptoms and cutaneous findings; other organ dysfunction may be involved.

Diflunisal is a derivative of acetylsalicylic acid and therefore may be associated with Reye's syndrome. Withhold for at least 4-6 half-lives prior to surgical or dental procedures. Safety and efficacy have not been established in children <12 years of age.
Adverse Reactions
  1% to 10%:
    Central nervous system: Headache (3% to 9%), dizziness (1% to 3%), insomnia (1% to 3%), somnolence (1% to 3%), fatigue (1% to 3%)
    Dermatologic: Rash (3% to 9%)
    Gastrointestinal: Nausea (3% to 9%), dyspepsia (3% to 9%), GI pain (3% to 9%), diarrhea (3% to 9%), constipation (1% to 3%), flatulence (1% to 3%), vomiting (1% to 3%), GI ulceration
    Otic: Tinnitus (1% to 3%)
  <1% (Limited to important or life-threatening): Acute anaphylactic reaction, agranulocytosis, allergic reactions, angioedema, anorexia, blurred vision, bronchospasm, confusion, chest pain, cholestasis, cystitis, depression, diaphoresis, disorientation, dry mucous membranes, dyspnea, dysuria, edema, eructation, erythema multiforme, esophagitis, exfoliative dermatitis, flushing, gastritis, GI bleeding, GI perforation, hallucinations, hearing decreased, hearing loss, hematuria, hemolytic anemia, hepatitis, hypersensitivity syndrome, hypersensitivity vasculitis, interstitial nephritis, itching, jaundice, mental depression, muscle cramps, necrotizing fasciitis, nephrotic syndrome, nervousness, palpitations, paresthesia, peptic ulcer, peripheral neuropathy, photosensitivity, proteinuria, pruritus, renal impairment, renal failure, seizure, Stevens-Johnson syndrome, stomatitis, syncope, tachycardia, thrombocytopenia, toxic epidermal necrolysis, trembling, urticaria, vasculitis, vertigo, weakness, wheezing
Overdosage/Toxicology Symptoms include drowsiness, nausea, vomiting, hyperventilation, tachycardia, tinnitus, stupor, coma, renal failure, and leukocytosis. Management of nonsteroidal anti-inflammatory drug (NSAID) intoxication is primarily supportive and symptomatic. Fluid therapy is commonly effective in managing hypotension that may occur following an acute NSAID overdose, except when due to acute blood loss.
Drug Interactions
  Increased Effect/Toxicity: Diflunisal may increase effect/toxicity of anticoagulants (bleeding), antiplatelet agents (bleeding), aminoglycosides, biphosphonates (GI irritation),

corticosteroids (GI irritation), cyclosporine (nephrotoxicity), lithium, methotrexate, pemetrexed, treprostinil (bleeding), vancomycin. Concomitant use with fluoroquinolones may
rarely increase risk of seizure.

Decreased Effect: May reduce effect of some diuretics and antihypertensive effect of ACE
inhibitors, angiotensin II inhibitors, beta-blockers, and hydralazine. Cholestyramine and
colestipol may reduce absorption of diflunisal; separate by at least 2 hours. Salicylates'
antiplatelet effect may be reduced.

Ethanol/Nutrition/Herb Interactions
Ethanol: Avoid ethanol (may enhance gastric mucosal irritation).
Herb/Nutraceutical: Avoid alfalfa, anise, bilberry, bladderwrack, bromelain, cat's claw, celery,
coleus, cordyceps, dong quai, evening primrose, feverfew, fenugreek, garlic, ginger,
ginkgo biloboa, red clover, horse chestnut, grapeseed, green tea, ginseng, guggul, horse
chestnut seed, horseradish, licorice, prickly ash, red clover, reishi, SAMe, sweet clover,
turmeric, white willow (all have additional antiplatelet activity).

Mechanism of Action Inhibits prostaglandin synthesis by decreasing the activity of the
enzyme, cyclooxygenase, which results in decreased formation of prostaglandin precursors

Pharmacodynamics/Kinetics
Onset of action: Analgesic: ~1 hour; maximal effect: 2-3 hours
Duration: 8-12 hours
Absorption: Well absorbed
Protein binding: >99%
Distribution: Enters breast milk
Metabolism: Extensively hepatic; metabolic pathways are saturable
Half-life elimination: 8-12 hours; prolonged with renal impairment
Time to peak, serum: 2-3 hours
Excretion: Urine (~3% as unchanged drug, 90% as glucuronide conjugates) within 72-96
hours

Dosage Adults: Oral:
Mild-to-moderate pain: Initial: 500-1000 mg followed by 250-500 mg every 8-12 hours;
maximum daily dose: 1.5 g
Arthritis: 500-1000 mg/day in 2 divided doses; maximum daily dose: 1.5 g
Dosing adjustment in renal impairment: Use with caution; Cl$_{cr}$ <50 mL/minute: Administer
50% of normal dose (Aronoff, 1998)
Hemodialysis: No supplement required
CAPD: No supplement require
CAVH: Dose for GFR 10-50

Dietary Considerations Should be taken with food to decrease GI distress.

Administration Tablet should be swallowed whole; do not crush or chew.

Test Interactions Falsely elevated increase in serum salicylate levels

Additional Information Diflunisal is a salicylic acid derivative which is chemically different
than aspirin and is not metabolized to salicylic acid. It is not considered a salicylate. Diflunisal
500 mg is equal in analgesic efficacy to aspirin 650 mg, acetaminophen 650 mg, and
acetaminophen 650 mg/propoxyphene napsylate 100 mg, but has a longer duration of effect
(8-12 hours). Not recommended as an antipyretic. Not found to be clinically useful to treat
fever; at doses ≥2 g/day, platelets are reversibly inhibited in function. Diflunisal is uricosuric at
500-750 mg/day; causes less GI and renal toxicity than aspirin and other NSAIDs; fecal blood
loss is $\frac{1}{2}$ that of aspirin at 2.6 g/day.

Dosage Forms [DSC] = Discontinued product
Tablet: 500 mg
Dolobid®: 250 mg, 500 mg [DSC]

◆ **Digibind®** see Digoxin Immune Fab on page 504
◆ **DigiFab™** see Digoxin Immune Fab on page 504
◆ **Digitek®** see Digoxin on page 501

Digoxin (di JOKS in)

U.S. Brand Names Digitek®; Lanoxicaps®; Lanoxin®
Canadian Brand Names Digoxin CSD; Lanoxicaps®; Lanoxin®; Novo-Digoxin; Pediatric
Digoxin CSD
Pharmacologic Category Antiarrhythmic Agent, Class IV; Cardiac Glycoside
Additional Appendix Information
Heart Failure (Systolic) on page 2051
Use Treatment of congestive heart failure and to slow the ventricular rate in tachyarrhythmias
such as atrial fibrillation, atrial flutter, and supraventricular tachycardia (paroxysmal atrial
tachycardia); cardiogenic shock
Pregnancy Risk Factor C
Lactation Enters breast milk (small amounts)/compatible
Medication Safety Issues
Sound-alike/look-alike issues:
Digoxin may be confused with Desoxyn®, doxepin
Lanoxin® may be confused with Lasix®, Levoxyl®, Levsinex®, Lomotil®, Lonox®, Mefoxin®,
Xanax®

International issues:
Dilacor®: Brand name for diltiazem in the U.S.; brand name for verapamil in Brazil; brand
name for barnidipine in Argentina
Lanoxin® may be confused with Lemoxin® which is a brand bane for cefuroxime in Mexico
Lanoxin® may be confused with Limoxin® which is a brand name for amoxicillin in Mexico
Contraindications Hypersensitivity to digoxin or any component of the formulation; hypersensitivity to cardiac glycosides (another may be tried); history of toxicity; ventricular tachycardia
or fibrillation; idiopathic hypertrophic subaortic stenosis; constrictive pericarditis; amyloid
disease; second- or third-degree heart block (except in patients with a functioning artificial
pacemaker); Wolff-Parkinson-White syndrome and atrial fibrillation concurrently
(Continued)

Digoxin *(Continued)*

Warnings/Precautions Use with caution in patients with hypoxia, myxedema, hypothyroidism, acute myocarditis; patients with incomplete AV block (Stokes-Adams attack) may progress to complete block with digitalis drug administration; use with caution in patients with acute myocardial infarction, severe pulmonary disease, advanced heart failure, idiopathic hypertrophic subaortic stenosis, Wolff-Parkinson-White syndrome, sick-sinus syndrome (bradyarrhythmias), amyloid heart disease, and constrictive cardiomyopathies; adjust dose with renal impairment and when verapamil, quinidine or amiodarone are added to a patient on digoxin; elderly and neonates may develop exaggerated serum/tissue concentrations due to age-related alterations in clearance and pharmacodynamic differences; exercise will reduce serum concentrations of digoxin due to increased skeletal muscle uptake; recent studies indicate photopsia, chromatopsia and decreased visual acuity may occur even with therapeutic serum drug levels; reduce or hold dose 1-2 days before elective electrical cardioversion

Adverse Reactions Incidence not always reported.

Cardiovascular: Heart block; first-, second- (Wenckebach), or third-degree heart block; asystole; atrial tachycardia with block; AV dissociation; accelerated junctional rhythm; ventricular tachycardia or ventricular fibrillation; PR prolongation; ST segment depression

Central nervous system: Visual disturbances (blurred or yellow vision), headache (3.2%), dizziness (4.9%), apathy, confusion, mental disturbances (4.1%), anxiety, depression, delirium, hallucinations, fever

Dermatologic: Maculopapular rash (1.6%); erythematous, scarlatiniform, papular, vesicular, or bullous rash; urticaria; pruritus; facial, angioneurotic, or laryngeal edema; shedding of fingernails or toenails; alopecia

Gastrointestinal: Nausea (3.2%), vomiting (1.6%), diarrhea (3.2%), abdominal pain

Neuromuscular & skeletal: Weakness

<1% (Limited to important or life-threatening): Abdominal pain, anorexia, eosinophilia, gynecomastia, hemorrhagic necrosis of the intestines, increased plasma estrogen and decreased serum luteinizing hormone in men and postmenopausal women and decreased plasma testosterone in men, intestinal ischemia, palpitation, sexual dysfunction, thrombocytopenia, unifocal or multiform ventricular premature contractions (especially bigeminy or trigeminy), vaginal cornification

Any arrhythmia seen in a child on digoxin should be considered as digoxin toxicity. The gastrointestinal and central nervous system symptoms are not frequently seen in children.

Overdosage/Toxicology Symptoms of acute overdose include vomiting, hyperkalemia, sinus bradycardia, S-A arrest and AV block are common, ventricular tachycardia, and fibrillation. Symptoms of chronic intoxication include visual disturbances, weakness, sinus bradycardia, atrial fibrillation with slowed ventricular response, and ventricular arrhythmias. After GI decontamination, treat hyperkalemia if >5.5 mEq/L with sodium bicarbonate and glucose with insulin or Kayexalate®. Treat bradycardia or heart block with atropine or pacemaker and other arrhythmias with conventional antiarrhythmics. Use Digibind® for severe hyperkalemia, symptomatic arrhythmias unresponsive to other drugs, and for prophylactic treatment in massive overdose.

Drug Interactions

Cytochrome P450 Effect: Substrate of CYP3A4 (minor)

Increased Effect/Toxicity: Beta-blocking agents (propranolol), verapamil, and diltiazem may have additive effects on heart rate. Carvedilol has additive effects on heart rate and inhibits the metabolism of digoxin. Digoxin levels may be increased by amiodarone (reduce digoxin dose 50%), bepridil, cyclosporine, diltiazem, indomethacin, itraconazole, some macrolides (erythromycin, clarithromycin), methimazole, propafenone, propylthiouracil, quinidine (reduce digoxin dose 33% to 50% on initiation), tetracyclines, and verapamil. Moricizine may increase the toxicity of digoxin (mechanism undefined). Spironolactone may interfere with some digoxin assays, but may also increase blood levels directly. Succinylcholine administration to patients on digoxin has been associated with an increased risk of arrhythmias. Rare cases of acute digoxin toxicity have been associated with parenteral calcium (bolus) administration. The following medications have been associated with increased digoxin blood levels which appear to be of limited clinical significance: Famciclovir, flecainide, ibuprofen, fluoxetine, nefazodone, cimetidine, famotidine, ranitidine, omeprazole, trimethoprim.

Decreased Effect: Amiloride and spironolactone may reduce the inotropic response to digoxin. Cholestyramine, colestipol, kaolin-pectin, and metoclopramide may reduce digoxin absorption. Levothyroxine (and other thyroid supplements) may decrease digoxin blood levels. Penicillamine has been associated with reductions in digoxin blood levels The following reported interactions appear to be of limited clinical significance: Aminoglutethimide, aminosalicylic acid, aluminum-containing antacids, sucralfate, sulfasalazine, neomycin, ticlopidine.

Ethanol/Nutrition/Herb Interactions

Food: Digoxin peak serum levels may be decreased if taken with food. Meals containing increased fiber (bran) or foods high in pectin may decrease oral absorption of digoxin.

Herb/Nutraceutical: Avoid ephedra (risk of cardiac stimulation). Avoid natural licorice (causes sodium and water retention and increases potassium loss).

Stability Protect elixir and injection from light.

Mechanism of Action

Congestive heart failure: Inhibition of the sodium/potassium ATPase pump which acts to increase the intracellular sodium-calcium exchange to increase intracellular calcium leading to increased contractility

Supraventricular arrhythmias: Direct suppression of the AV node conduction to increase effective refractory period and decrease conduction velocity - positive inotropic effect, enhanced vagal tone, and decreased ventricular rate to fast atrial arrhythmias. Atrial fibrillation may decrease sensitivity and increase tolerance to higher serum digoxin concentrations.

Pharmacodynamics/Kinetics

Onset of action: Oral: 1-2 hours; I.V.: 5-30 minutes

Peak effect: Oral: 2-8 hours; I.V.: 1-4 hours

Duration: Adults: 3-4 days both forms

Absorption: By passive nonsaturable diffusion in the upper small intestine; food may delay, but does not affect extent of absorption

Distribution:

Normal renal function: 6-7 L/kg

V_d: Extensive to peripheral tissues, with a distinct distribution phase which lasts 6-8 hours; concentrates in heart, liver, kidney, skeletal muscle, and intestines. Heart/serum concentration is 70:1. Pharmacologic effects are delayed and do not correlate well with serum concentrations during distribution phase.

Hyperthyroidism: Increased V_d

Hyperkalemia, hyponatremia: Decreased digoxin distribution to heart and muscle

Hypokalemia: Increased digoxin distribution to heart and muscles

Concomitant quinidine therapy: Decreased V_d

Chronic renal failure: 4-6 L/kg

Decreased sodium/potassium ATPase activity - decreased tissue binding

Neonates, full-term: 7.5-10 L/kg

Children: 16 L/kg

Adults: 7 L/kg, decreased with renal disease

Protein binding: 30%; in uremic patients, digoxin is displaced from plasma protein binding sites

Metabolism: Via sequential sugar hydrolysis in the stomach or by reduction of lactone ring by intestinal bacteria (in ~10% of population, gut bacteria may metabolize up to 40% of digoxin dose); metabolites may contribute to therapeutic and toxic effects of digoxin; metabolism is reduced with CHF

Bioavailability: Oral (formulation dependent): Elixir: 75% to 85%; Tablet: 70% to 80%

Half-life elimination (age, renal and cardiac function dependent):

Neonates: Premature: 61-170 hours; Full-term: 35-45 hours

Infants: 18-25 hours

Children: 35 hours

Adults: 38-48 hours

Adults, anephric: 4-6 days

Half-life elimination: Parent drug: 38 hours; Metabolites: Digoxigenin: 4 hours; Monodigitoxoside: 3-12 hours

Time to peak, serum: Oral: ~1 hour

Excretion: Urine (50% to 70% as unchanged drug)

Dosage When changing from oral (tablets or liquid) or I.M. to I.V. therapy, dosage should be reduced by 20% to 25%. Refer to the following: See table.

Dosage Recommendations for Digoxin

Age	Total Digitalizing Dose[2] (mcg/kg[1])		Daily Maintenance Dose[3] (mcg/kg[1])	
	P.O.	I.V. or I.M.	P.O.	I.V. or I.M.
Preterm infant[1]	20-30	15-25	5-7.5	4-6
Full-term infant[1]	25-35	20-30	6-10	5-8
1 mo - 2 y[1]	35-60	30-50	10-15	7.5-12
2-5 y[1]	30-40	25-35	7.5-10	6-9
5-10 y[1]	20-35	15-30	5-10	4-8
>10 y[1]	10-15	8-12	2.5-5	2-3
Adults	0.75-1.5 mg	0.5-1 mg	0.125-0.5 mg	0.1-0.4 mg

[1]Based on lean body weight and normal renal function for age. Decrease dose in patients with ↓ renal function; digitalizing dose often not recommended in infants and children.

[2]Give one-half of the total digitalizing dose (TDD) in the initial dose, then give one-quarter of the TDD in each of two subsequent doses at 8- to 12-hour intervals. Obtain ECG 6 hours after each dose to assess potential toxicity.

[3]Divided every 12 hours in infants and children <10 years of age. Given once daily to children >10 years of age and adults.

Dosing adjustment/interval in renal impairment:

Cl_{cr} 10-50 mL/minute: Administer 25% to 75% of dose or every 36 hours

Cl_{cr} <10 mL/minute: Administer 10% to 25% of dose or every 48 hours

Reduce loading dose by 50% in ESRD

Hemodialysis: Not dialyzable (0% to 5%)

Dietary Considerations Maintain adequate amounts of potassium in diet to decrease risk of hypokalemia (hypokalemia may increase risk of digoxin toxicity).

Administration

I.M.: Inject no more than 2 mL per injection site. May cause intense pain.

I.V.: May be administered undiluted or diluted fourfold in D_5W, NS, or SWFI for direct injection. Less than fourfold dilution may lead to drug precipitation. Inject slowly over ≥5 minutes.

Monitoring Parameters

When to draw serum digoxin concentrations: Digoxin serum concentrations are monitored because digoxin possesses a narrow therapeutic serum range; the therapeutic endpoint is difficult to quantify and digoxin toxicity may be life-threatening. Digoxin serum levels should be drawn **at least 4 hours after an intravenous dose** and **at least 6 hours after an oral dose (optimally 12-24 hours after a dose).**

Initiation of therapy:

If a loading dose is given: Digoxin serum concentration may be drawn within 12-24 hours after the initial loading dose administration. Levels drawn this early may confirm the relationship of digoxin plasma levels and response but are of little value in determining maintenance doses.

If a loading dose is not given: Digoxin serum concentration should be obtained after 3-5 days of therapy.

(Continued)

Digoxin *(Continued)*

Maintenance therapy:

Trough concentrations should be followed just prior to the next dose or at a minimum of 4 hours after an I.V. dose and at least 6 hours after an oral dose.

Digoxin serum concentrations should be obtained within 5-7 days (approximate time to steady-state) after any dosage changes. Continue to obtain digoxin serum concentrations 7-14 days after any change in maintenance dose. **Note:** In patients with end-stage renal disease, it may take 15-20 days to reach steady-state.

Additionally, patients who are receiving potassium-depleting medications such as diuretics, should be monitored for potassium, magnesium, and calcium levels.

Digoxin serum concentrations should be obtained whenever any of the following conditions occur:

Questionable patient compliance or to evaluate clinical deterioration following an initial good response

Changing renal function

Suspected digoxin toxicity

Initiation or discontinuation of therapy with drugs (amiodarone, quinidine, verapamil) which potentially interact with digoxin; if quinidine therapy is started; digoxin levels should be drawn within the first 24 hours after starting quinidine therapy, then 7-14 days later or empirically skip one day's digoxin dose and decrease the daily dose by 50%

Any disease changes (hypothyroidism)

Heart rate and rhythm should be monitored along with periodic ECGs to assess both desired effects and signs of toxicity

Follow closely (especially in patients receiving diuretics or amphotericin) for decreased serum potassium and magnesium or increased calcium, all of which predispose to digoxin toxicity

Assess renal function

Be aware of drug interactions

Observe patients for noncardiac signs of toxicity, confusion, and depression

Reference Range

Digoxin therapeutic serum concentrations:

Congestive heart failure: 0.5-0.8 ng/mL

Arrhythmias: 0.8-2 ng/mL

Adults: <0.5 ng/mL; probably indicates underdigitalization unless there are special circumstances

Toxic: >2.5 ng/mL

Digoxin-like immunoreactive substance (DLIS) may cross-react with digoxin immunoassay. DLIS has been found in patients with renal and liver disease, congestive heart failure, neonates, and pregnant women (3rd trimester).

Dosage Forms

Capsule:

Lanoxicaps®: 100 mcg, 200 mcg [contains ethyl alcohol]

Injection, solution: 250 mcg/mL (1 mL, 2 mL)

Lanoxin®: 250 mcg/mL (2 mL) [contains alcohol 10% and propylene glycol 40%]

Injection, solution [pediatric]: 100 mcg/mL (1 mL)

Solution, oral: 50 mcg/mL (2.5 mL, 5 mL, 60 mL)

Tablet: 125 mcg, 250 mcg

Digitek®, Lanoxin®: 125 mcg, 250 mcg

♦ **Digoxin CSD (Can)** *see Digoxin on page 501* *see Digoxin on page 501*

Digoxin Immune Fab (di JOKS in i MYUN fab)

U.S. Brand Names Digibind®; DigiFab™

Canadian Brand Names Digibind®

Index Terms Antidigoxin Fab Fragments, Ovine

Pharmacologic Category Antidote

Additional Appendix Information

Management of Overdosages *on page 2075*

Use Treatment of life-threatening or potentially life-threatening digoxin intoxication, including:

- acute digoxin ingestion (ie, >10 mg in adults or >4 mg in children)
- chronic ingestions leading to steady-state digoxin concentrations >6 ng/mL in adults or >4 ng/mL in children
- manifestations of digoxin toxicity due to overdose (life-threatening ventricular arrhythmias, progressive bradycardia, second- or third-degree heart block not responsive to atropine, serum potassium >5 mEq/L in adults or >6 mEq in children)

Pregnancy Risk Factor C

Pregnancy Implications Animal reproduction studies have not been conducted. Safety and efficacy in pregnant women have not been established. Use during pregnancy only if clearly needed.

Lactation Excretion in breast milk unknown/use caution

Contraindications Hypersensitivity to sheep products or any component of the formulation

Warnings/Precautions Use with caution in renal or cardiac failure; allergic reactions possible (sheep product)-skin testing not routinely recommended; epinephrine should be immediately available, Fab fragments may be eliminated more slowly in patients with renal failure, heart failure may be exacerbated as digoxin level is reduced; total serum digoxin concentration may rise precipitously following administration of Digibind®, but this will be almost entirely bound to the Fab fragment and not able to react with receptors in the body; Digibind® will interfere with digitalis immunoassay measurements - this will result in clinically misleading serum digoxin concentrations until the Fab fragment is eliminated from the body (several days to >1 week after Digibind® administration). Hypokalemia has been reported to occur following reversal of digitalis intoxication as has exacerbation of underlying heart failure.

Serum digoxin levels drawn prior to therapy may be difficult to evaluate if 6-8 hours have not elapsed after the last dose of digoxin (time to equilibration between serum and tissue); redigitalization should not be initiated until Fab fragments have been eliminated from the body, which may occur over several days or greater than a week in patients with impaired renal function.

Adverse Reactions Frequency not defined.

Cardiovascular: Effects (due to withdrawal of digitalis) include exacerbation of low cardiac output states and CHF, rapid ventricular response in patients with atrial fibrillation; postural hypotension

Endocrine & metabolic: Hypokalemia

Local: Phlebitis

Miscellaneous: Allergic reactions, serum sickness

Overdosage/Toxicology Symptoms include delayed serum sickness. Treatment of serum sickness includes acetaminophen, histamine$_1$ and possibly histamine$_2$ blockers and corticosteroids.

Drug Interactions

Increased Effect/Toxicity: Digoxin: Following administration of digoxin immune Fab, serum digoxin levels are markedly increased due to bound complexes (may be clinically misleading, since bound complex cannot interact with receptors)

Stability Should be refrigerated (2°C to 8°C). Reconstitute by adding 4 mL sterile water, resulting in 10 mg/mL for I.V. infusion. The reconstituted solution may be further diluted with NS to a convenient volume (eg, 1 mg/mL). Reconstituted solutions should be used within 4 hours if refrigerated. For very small doses, vial can be reconstituted by adding an additional 36 mL of sterile isotonic saline, to achieve a final concentration of 1 mg/mL.

Mechanism of Action Digoxin immune antigen-binding fragments (Fab) are specific antibodies for the treatment of digitalis intoxication in carefully selected patients; binds with molecules of digoxin or digitoxin and then is excreted by the kidneys and removed from the body

Pharmacodynamics/Kinetics

Onset of action: I.V.: Improvement in 2-30 minutes for toxicity

Half-life elimination: 15-20 hours; prolonged with renal impairment

Excretion: Urine; undetectable amounts within 5-7 days

Dosage Each vial of Digibind® 38 mg or DigiFab™ 40 mg will bind ~0.5 mg of digoxin or digitoxin.

Estimation of the dose is based on the body burden of digitalis. This may be calculated if the amount ingested is known or the postdistribution serum drug level is known (round dose to the nearest whole vial). See table.

Digoxin Immune Fab

Tablets Ingested (0.25 mg)	Fab Dose (vials)
5	2
10	4
25	10
50	20
75	30
100	40
150	60
200	80

Fab dose based on serum drug level postdistribution:

Digoxin: No. of vials = level (ng/mL) x body weight (kg) divided by 100

Digitoxin: No. of vials = digitoxin (ng/mL) x body weight (kg) divided by 1000

If neither amount ingested nor drug level are known, dose empirically as follows:

For acute toxicity: 20 vials, administered in 2 divided doses to decrease the possibility of a febrile reaction, and to avoid fluid overload in small children.

For chronic toxicity: 6 vials; for infants and small children (≤20 kg), a single vial may be sufficient

Administration Continuous I.V. infusion over ≥30 minutes is preferred. May give by bolus injection if cardiac arrest is imminent. Small doses (infants/small children) may be administered using tuberculin syringe. Stopping the infusion and restarting at a slower rate may help if infusion-related reactions occur.

Monitoring Parameters Serum potassium, serum digoxin concentration prior to first dose of digoxin immune Fab; **digoxin levels will greatly increase with digoxin immune Fab use and are not an accurate determination of body stores**; standard digoxin concentration measurements may be misleading until Fab fragments are eliminated from the body.

Patients with renal failure should be monitored for a prolonged period for reintoxication with digoxin following the rerelease of bound digoxin into the blood.

Test Interactions Digoxin immune Fab interferes with digitalis immunoassay test leading to misleading digoxin serum concentrations until the Fab fragments are eliminated from the body. If possible, take digoxin serum levels prior to the administration of digoxin immune Fab; keeping in mind the time the last dose of digoxin was taken.

Dosage Forms Injection, powder for reconstitution:

Digibind®: 38 mg

DigiFab™: 40 mg

♦ **Dihematoporphyrin Ether** see Porfimer on page 1391

♦ **Dihistine® DH** see Chlorpheniramine, Pseudoephedrine, and Codeine on page 355

Dihydrocodeine, Aspirin, and Caffeine
(dye hye droe KOE deen, AS pir in, & KAF een)

U.S. Brand Names Synalgos®-DC
Index Terms Dihydrocodeine Compound
Pharmacologic Category Analgesic, Opioid
Use Management of mild to moderate pain that requires relaxation
Restrictions C-III
Pregnancy Risk Factor B/D (prolonged use or high doses at term)
Medication Safety Issues
Sound-alike/look-alike issues:
Synalgos®-DC may be confused with Synagis®
Dosage
Adults: Oral: 1-2 capsules every 4-6 hours as needed for pain
Elderly: Initial dosing should be cautious (low end of adult dosing range)
Additional Information Complete prescribing information for this medication should be consulted for additional detail.
Dosage Forms Capsule: Dihydrocodeine bitartrate 16 mg, aspirin 356.4 mg, and caffeine 30 mg

---

Dihydrocodeine, Chlorpheniramine, and Phenylephrine
(dye hye droe KOE deen, klor fen IR a meen, & fen il EF rin)

U.S. Brand Names Baltussin; Coldcough PD; Pancof®-PD
Index Terms Chlorpheniramine Maleate, Dihydrocodeine Bitartrate, and Phenylephrine Hydrochloride; Phenylephrine, Chlorpheniramine, and Dihydrocodeine
Pharmacologic Category Antihistamine; Antihistamine/Decongestant/Antitussive; Antitussive; Decongestant
Use Symptomatic relief of cough and congestion associated with the upper respiratory tract
Restrictions C-III/C-V
Pregnancy Risk Factor C
Dosage Cough and congestion: Oral:
Children 2-6 years (Pancof®-PD): 1.25-2.5 mL every 4-6 hours as needed (maximum: 10 mL/24 hours)
Children 6-12 years:
Baltussin: 2.5 mL every 4-6 hours as needed
Pancof®-PD: 2.5-5 mL every 4-6 hours as needed (maximum: 20 mL/24 hours)
Children ≥12 years and adults:
Baltussin: 5 mL every 4-6 hours as needed
Pancof®-PD: 5-10 mL every 4-6 hours as needed (maximum: 40 mL/24 hours)
Additional Information Complete prescribing information for this medication should be consulted for additional detail.
Dosage Forms
Liquid (Pancof®-PD): Dihydrocodeine bitartrate 3 mg, chlorpheniramine maleate 2 mg, and phenylephrine hydrochloride 7.5 mg per 5 mL (120 mL) [alcohol free, sugar free; grape flavor; C-V]
Syrup:
Baltussin: Dihydrocodeine bitartrate 3 mg, chlorpheniramine maleate 5 mg, and phenylephrine hydrochloride 20 mg per 5 mL (480 mL) [alcohol free, sugar free; fruit flavor; C-III]
Coldcough PD: Dihydrocodeine bitartrate 3 mg, chlorpheniramine maleate 2 mg, and phenylephrine hydrochloride 7.5 mg per 5 mL (120 mL) [alcohol free, sugar free; grape flavor; C-V]

♦ **Dihydrocodeine Compound** see Dihydrocodeine, Aspirin, and Caffeine on page 506

Dihydrocodeine, Pseudoephedrine, and Guaifenesin
(dye hye droe KOE deen, soo doe e FED rin, & gwye FEN e sin)

U.S. Brand Names DiHydro-GP; Hydro-Tussin™ EXP; Pancof®-EXP
Index Terms Guaifenesin, Dihydrocodeine, and Pseudoephedrine; Pseudoephedrine Hydrochloride, Guaifenesin, and Dihydrocodeine Bitartrate
Pharmacologic Category Antitussive/Decongestant/Expectorant
Use Temporary relief of cough and congestion associated with upper respiratory tract infections and allergies
Pregnancy Risk Factor C
Dosage Oral: Cough/congestion (Hydro-Tussin™ EXP, Pancof®-EXP):
Children:
2-6 years: 1.25-2.5 mL every 4-6 hours as needed
6-12 years: 2.5-5 mL every 4-6 hours as needed
Children ≥12 years and Adults: 5-10 mL every 4-6 hours as needed
Additional Information Complete prescribing information for this medication should be consulted for additional detail.
Dosage Forms Syrup:
DiHydro-GP: Dihydrocodeine bitartrate 7.5 mg, pseudoephedrine hydrochloride 15 mg, and guaifenesin 100 mg per 5 mL (480 mL) [vanilla flavor]
Hydro-Tussin™ EXP, Pancof®-EXP: Dihydrocodeine bitartrate 7.5 mg, pseudoephedrine hydrochloride 15 mg, and guaifenesin 100 mg per 5 mL (480 mL) [alcohol free, dye free, sugar free]

Dihydroergotamine (dye hye droe er GOT a meen)

U.S. Brand Names D.H.E. 45®; Migranal®
Canadian Brand Names Migranal®
Index Terms DHE; Dihydroergotamine Mesylate
Pharmacologic Category Antimigraine Agent; Ergot Derivative
Use Treatment of migraine headache with or without aura; injection also indicated for treatment of cluster headaches
Unlabeled/Investigational Use Adjunct for DVT prophylaxis for hip surgery, for orthostatic hypotension, xerostomia secondary to antidepressant use, and pelvic congestion with pain
Pregnancy Risk Factor X
Pregnancy Implications Dihydroergotamine is oxytocic and should not be used during pregnancy.
Lactation May be excreted in breast milk/contraindicated
Contraindications Hypersensitivity to dihydroergotamine or any component of the formulation; high-dose aspirin therapy; uncontrolled hypertension, ischemic heart disease, angina pectoris, history of MI, silent ischemia, or coronary artery vasospasm including Prinzmetal's angina; hemiplegic or basilar migraine; peripheral vascular disease; sepsis; severe hepatic or renal dysfunction; following vascular surgery; avoid use within 24 hours of sumatriptan, zolmitriptan, other serotonin agonists, or ergot-like agents; avoid during or within 2 weeks of discontinuing MAO inhibitors; ergot alkaloids are contraindicated with potent inhibitors of CYP3A4 (includes protease inhibitors, azole antifungals, and some macrolide antibiotics); pregnancy
Warnings/Precautions [U.S. Boxed Warning]: Ergot alkaloids are contraindicated with potent inhibitors of CYP3A4 (includes protease inhibitors, azole antifungals, and some macrolide antibiotics). Do not give to patients with risk factors for CAD until a cardiovascular evaluation has been performed; if evaluation is satisfactory, the healthcare provider should administer the first dose and cardiovascular status should be periodically evaluated. May cause vasospastic reactions; persistent vasospasm may lead to gangrene or death in patients with compromised circulation. Discontinue if signs of vasoconstriction develop. Rare reports of increased blood pressure in patients without history of hypertension. Rare reports of adverse cardiac events (acute MI, life-threatening arrhythmias, death) have been reported following use of the injection. Cerebral hemorrhage, subarachnoid hemorrhage, and stroke have also occurred following use of the injection. Not for prolonged use. Pleural and peritoneal fibrosis have been reported with prolonged daily use. Cardiac valvular fibrosis has also been associated with ergot alkaloids. Safety and efficacy in pediatric patients have not been established.

Adverse Reactions
>10%: Nasal spray: Respiratory: Rhinitis (26%)
1% to 10%: Nasal spray:
Central nervous system: Dizziness (4%), somnolence (3%)
Endocrine & metabolic: Hot flashes (1%)
Gastrointestinal: Nausea (10%), taste disturbance (8%), vomiting (4%), diarrhea (2%)
Local: Application site reaction (6%)
Neuromuscular & skeletal: Weakness (1%), stiffness (1%)
Respiratory: Pharyngitis (3%)
<1% (Limited to important or life-threatening): Injection and nasal spray: Cerebral hemorrhage, coronary artery vasospasm, hypertension, MI, paresthesia, peripheral cyanosis, peripheral ischemia, rash, stroke, subarachnoid hemorrhage, ventricular fibrillation, ventricular tachycardia. Pleural and retroperitoneal fibrosis have been reported following prolonged use of the injection; cardiac valvular fibrosis has been associated with ergot alkaloids.
Overdosage/Toxicology Symptoms include peripheral ischemia, paresthesia, headache, nausea, and vomiting. Activated charcoal is effective at binding certain chemicals; this is especially true for ergot alkaloids.
Drug Interactions
Cytochrome P450 Effect: Substrate of CYP3A4 (major); **Inhibits** CYP3A4 (weak)
Increased Effect/Toxicity: CYP3A4 inhibitors may increase the levels/effects of dihydroergotamine; example inhibitors include azole antifungals, clarithromycin, diclofenac, doxycycline, erythromycin, imatinib, isoniazid, nefazodone, nicardipine, propofol, protease inhibitors, quinidine, telithromycin, and verapamil. Ergot alkaloids are contraindicated with potent CYP3A4 inhibitors. Dihydroergotamine may increase the effects of 5-HT$_1$ agonists (eg, sumatriptan), MAO inhibitors, sibutramine, and other serotonin agonists (serotonin syndrome). Severe vasoconstriction may occur when peripheral vasoconstrictors or beta-blockers are used in patients receiving ergot alkaloids; concurrent use is contraindicated.
Decreased Effect: Effects of dihydroergotamine may be diminished by antipsychotics, metoclopramide. Antianginal effects of nitrates may be reduced by ergot alkaloids.
Stability
Injection: Store below 25°C (77°F); do not refrigerate or freeze. Protect from heat and light.
Nasal spray: Prior to use, store below 25°C (77°F); do not refrigerate or freeze. Once spray applicator has been prepared, use within 8 hours; discard any unused solution.
Mechanism of Action Ergot alkaloid alpha-adrenergic blocker directly stimulates vascular smooth muscle to vasoconstrict peripheral and cerebral vessels; also has effects on serotonin receptors
Pharmacodynamics/Kinetics
Onset of action: 15-30 minutes
Duration: 3-4 hours
Distribution: V$_d$: 14.5 L/kg
Protein binding: 93%
Metabolism: Extensively hepatic
Half-life elimination: 1.3-3.9 hours
Time to peak, serum: I.M.: 15-30 minutes
(Continued)

Dihydroergotamine *(Continued)*

Excretion: Primarily feces; urine (10% mostly as metabolites)

Dosage Adults:

I.M., SubQ: 1 mg at first sign of headache; repeat hourly to a maximum dose of 3 mg total; maximum dose: 6 mg/week

I.V.: 1 mg at first sign of headache; repeat hourly up to a maximum dose of 2 mg total; maximum dose: 6 mg/week

Intranasal: 1 spray (0.5 mg) of nasal spray should be administered into each nostril; if needed, repeat after 15 minutes, up to a total of 4 sprays. **Note:** Do not exceed 3 mg (6 sprays) in a 24-hour period and no more than 8 sprays in a week.

Elderly: Patients >65 years of age were not included in controlled clinical studies

Dosing adjustment in renal impairment: Contraindicated in severe renal impairment

Dosing adjustment in hepatic impairment: Dosage reductions are probably necessary but specific guidelines are not available; contraindicated in severe hepatic dysfunction

Administration Prior to administration of nasal spray, the nasal spray applicator must be primed (pumped 4 times); in order to let the drug be absorbed through the skin in the nose, patients should not inhale deeply through the nose while spraying or immediately after spraying; for best results, treatment should be initiated at the first symptom or sign of an attack; however, nasal spray can be used at any stage of a migraine attack

Reference Range Minimum concentration for vasoconstriction is reportedly 0.06 ng/mL

Dosage Forms

Injection, solution, as mesylate (D.H.E. 45®): 1 mg/mL (1 mL) [contains ethanol 94%]

Solution, intranasal spray, as mesylate (Migranal®): 4 mg/mL [0.5 mg/spray] (1 mL) [contains caffeine 10 mg/mL]

♦ **Dihydroergotamine Mesylate** *see Dihydroergotamine on page 507*

♦ **Dihydroergotoxine** *see Ergoloid Mesylates on page 604*

♦ **Dihydrogenated Ergot Alkaloids** *see Ergoloid Mesylates on page 604*

♦ **DiHydro-GP** *see Dihydrocodeine, Pseudoephedrine, and Guaifenesin on page 506*

♦ **Dihydrohydroxycodeinone** *see Oxycodone on page 1286*

♦ **Dihydromorphinone** *see Hydromorphone on page 856*

Dihydrotachysterol *(dye hye droe tak ISS ter ole)*

U.S. Brand Names DHT™ [DSC]; DHT™ Intensol™ [DSC]; Hytakerol® [DSC]

Canadian Brand Names Hytakerol®

Index Terms Dichysterol

Pharmacologic Category Vitamin D Analog

Use Treatment of hypocalcemia associated with hypoparathyroidism; prophylaxis of hypocalcemic tetany following thyroid surgery

Pregnancy Risk Factor A/D (dose exceeding RDA recommendation)

Dosage Oral:

Hypoparathyroidism:

Infants and young Children: Initial: 1-5 mg/day for 4 days, then 0.1-0.5 mg/day

Older Children and Adults: Initial: 0.8-2.4 mg/day for several days followed by maintenance doses of 0.2-1 mg/day

Nutritional rickets: 0.5 mg as a single dose or 13-50 mcg/day until healing occurs

Renal osteodystrophy: Maintenance: 0.25-0.6 mg/24 hours adjusted as necessary to achieve normal serum calcium levels and promote bone healing

Additional Information Complete prescribing information for this medication should be consulted for additional detail.

Dosage Forms [DSC] = Discontinued product

Capsule (Hytakerol®): 0.125 mg [contains sesame oil] [DSC]

Solution, oral concentrate (DHT™ Intensol™): 0.2 mg/mL (30 mL) [contains alcohol 20%] [DSC]

Tablet (DHT™): 0.125 mg, 0.2 mg, 0.4 mg [DSC]

♦ **Dihydroxyanthracenedione Dihydrochloride** *see Mitoxantrone on page 1157*

♦ **1,25 Dihydroxycholecalciferol** *see Calcitriol on page 266*

♦ **Dihydroxydeoxynorvinkaleukoblastine** *see Vinorelbine on page 1791*

♦ **Diiodohydroxyquin** *see Iodoquinol on page 930*

♦ **Dilacor® XR** *see Diltiazem on page 509*

♦ **Dilantin®** *see Phenytoin on page 1361*

♦ **Dilatrate®-SR** *see Isosorbide Dinitrate on page 945*

♦ **Dilaudid®** *see Hydromorphone on page 856*

♦ **Dilaudid-HP®** *see Hydromorphone on page 856*

♦ **Dilaudid-HP-Plus® (Can)** *see Hydromorphone on page 856*

♦ **Dilaudid® Sterile Powder (Can)** *see Hydromorphone on page 856*

♦ **Dilaudid-XP® (Can)** *see Hydromorphone on page 856*

Diloxanide Furoate *(dye LOKS ah nide FYOOR oh ate)*

U.S. Brand Names Furamide®

Pharmacologic Category Amebicide

Use Treatment of amebiasis (asymptomatic cyst passers)

Restrictions Not commercially available in U.S.

Additional Information Complete prescribing information for this medication should be consulted for additional detail.

♦ **Diltia XT®** *see Diltiazem on page 509*

Diltiazem (dil TYE a zem)

U.S. Brand Names Cardizem®; Cardizem® CD; Cardizem® LA; Cartia XT™; Dilacor® XR; Diltia XT®; Dilt-XR; Taztia XT™; Tiazac®

Canadian Brand Names Alti-Diltiazem CD; Apo-Diltiaz®; Apo-Diltiaz CD®; Apo-Diltiaz® Injectable; Apo-Diltiaz SR®; Cardizem®; Cardizem® CD; Cardizem® SR; Diltiazem HCl ER®; Diltiazem Hydrochloride Injection; Gen-Diltiazem; Gen-Diltiazem CD; Med-Diltiazem; Novo-Diltiazem; Novo-Diltiazem-CD; Novo-Diltiazem HCl ER; Nu-Diltiaz; Nu-Diltiaz-CD; ratio-Diltiazem CD; Rhoxal-diltiazem CD; Rhoxal-diltiazem SR; Rhoxal-diltiazem T; Sandoz-Diltiazem CD; Sandoz-Diltiazem T; Syn-Diltiazem®; Tiazac®; Tiazac® XC

Index Terms Diltiazem Hydrochloride

Pharmacologic Category Calcium Channel Blocker

Additional Appendix Information
Calcium Channel Blockers *on page 1878*
Hypertension *on page 2063*

Use
Oral: Essential hypertension; chronic stable angina or angina from coronary artery spasm
Injection: Atrial fibrillation or atrial flutter; paroxysmal supraventricular tachycardia (PSVT)

Unlabeled/Investigational Use Investigational: Therapy of Duchenne muscular dystrophy

Pregnancy Risk Factor C

Pregnancy Implications Teratogenic and embryotoxic effects have been demonstrated in small animals.

Lactation Enters breast milk/not recommended (AAP considers "compatible")

Medication Safety Issues
Sound-alike/look-alike issues:
Diltiazem may be confused with Dilantin®
Cardizem® may be confused with Cardene®, Cardene SR®, Cardizem CD®, Cardizem SR®, cardlem
Cartia XT™ may be confused with Procardia XL®
Tiazac® may be confused with Tigan®, Ziac®

Significant differences exist between oral and I.V. dosing. Use caution when converting from one route of administration to another.

International issues:
Cardizem® may be confused with Cardem® which is a brand name for celiprolol in Spain
Cartia XT™ may be confused with Cartia® which is a brand name for aspirin in multiple international markets
Dilacor®: Brand name for digoxin in Serbia, a brand name for verapamil in Brazil, and a brand name for barnidipine in Argentina
Tiazac® may be confused with Tazac® which is a brand name for nizatidine in Australia

Contraindications Hypersensitivity to diltiazem or any component of the formulation; sick sinus syndrome; second- or third-degree AV block (except in patients with a functioning artificial pacemaker); hypotension (systolic <90 mm Hg); acute MI and pulmonary congestion

Warnings/Precautions Increased angina and/or MI has occurred with initiation or dosage titration of calcium channel blockers. Can cause first-degree AV block or sinus bradycardia; other conduction abnormalities are rare. The most common side effect is peripheral edema; occurs within 2-3 weeks of starting therapy. Symptomatic hypotension with or without syncope can rarely occur; blood pressure must be lowered at a rate appropriate for the patient's clinical condition. Concomitant use with beta-blockers or digoxin can result in conduction disturbances. Avoid concurrent I.V. use of diltiazem and a beta-blocker. Use caution in left ventricular dysfunction (can exacerbate condition). Use with caution with hypertrophic cardiomyopathy. Use with caution in hepatic or renal dysfunction.

Adverse Reactions Note: Frequencies represent ranges for various dosage forms. Patients with impaired ventricular function and/or conduction abnormalities may have higher incidence of adverse reactions.

>10%:
Cardiovascular: Edema (2% to 15%)
Central nervous system: Headache (5% to 12%)
2% to 10%:
Cardiovascular: AV block (first degree 2% to 8%), edema (lower limb, 2% to 8%), pain (6%), bradycardia (2% to 6%), hypotension (<2% to 4%), vasodilation (2% to 3%), extrasystoles (2%), flushing (1% to 2%), palpitation (1% to 2%)
Central nervous system: Dizziness (3% to 10%), nervousness (2%)
Dermatologic: Rash (1% to 4%)
Endocrine & metabolic: Gout (1% to 2%)
Gastrointestinal: Dyspepsia (1% to 6%), constipation (<2% to 4%), vomiting (2%), diarrhea (1% to 2%)
Local: Injection site reactions: Burning, itching (4%)
Neuromuscular & skeletal: Weakness (1% to 4%), myalgia (2%)
Respiratory: Rhinitis (<2% to 10%), pharyngitis (2% to 6%), dyspnea (1% to 6%), bronchitis (1% to 4%), sinus congestion (1% to 2%)
<2% (Limited to important or life-threatening): Alkaline phosphatase increased, allergic reaction, amblyopia, amnesia, arrhythmia, AV block (second or third degree), bundle branch block, CHF, depression, dysgeusia, extrapyramidal symptoms, gingival hyperplasia, hemolytic anemia, petechiae, photosensitivity, SGOT increased, SGPT increased, Stevens-Johnson syndrome, syncope, tachycardia, thrombocytopenia, tremor, toxic epidermal necrolysis

Overdosage/Toxicology
Primary cardiac symptoms of calcium blocker overdose include hypotension and bradycardia. Hypotension is caused by peripheral vasodilation, myocardial depression, and bradycardia. Bradycardia results from sinus bradycardia, second- or third-degree atrioventricular block, or sinus arrest with junctional rhythm. Intraventricular conduction is usually not affected, so QRS duration is normal (verapamil prolongs the PR interval and bepridil
(Continued)

Diltiazem *(Continued)*

prolongs the QT interval and may cause ventricular arrhythmias, including torsade de pointes).

Noncardiac symptoms include confusion, stupor, nausea, vomiting, metabolic acidosis, and hyperglycemia. Following initial gastric decontamination, if possible, repeated calcium administration may promptly reverse depressed cardiac contractility (but not sinus node depression or peripheral vasodilation). Glucagon, epinephrine, and inamrinone (amrinone) may treat refractory hypotension. Glucagon and epinephrine also increase the heart rate (outside the U.S., 4-aminopyridine may be available as an antidote). Dialysis and hemoperfusion are not effective in enhancing elimination, although repeat-dose activated charcoal may serve as an adjunct with sustained-release preparations.

In a few reported cases, overdose with calcium channel blockers has been associated with hypotension and bradycardia, initially refractory to atropine, but becoming more responsive to this agent when larger doses (approaching 1 g/hour for more than 24 hours) of calcium chloride were administered.

Drug Interactions

Cytochrome P450 Effect: Substrate of CYP2C9 (minor), 2D6 (minor), 3A4 (major); **Inhibits** CYP2C9 (weak), 2D6 (weak), 3A4 (moderate)

Increased Effect/Toxicity: Diltiazem effects may be additive with amiodarone, beta-blockers, or digoxin, which may lead to bradycardia, other conduction delays, and decreased cardiac output. The levels/effects of diltiazem may be increased by azole antifungals, clarithromycin, diclofenac, doxycycline, erythromycin, imatinib, isoniazid, nefazodone, nicardipine, propofol, protease inhibitors, quinidine, telithromycin, verapamil, and other CYP3A4 inhibitors.

Diltiazem may increase the levels/effects of selected benzodiazepines, calcium channel blockers, cisapride, cyclosporine, ergot alkaloids, selected HMG-CoA reductase inhibitors, mesoridazine, mirtazapine, nateglinide, nefazodone, pimozide, quinidine, sildenafil (and other PDE-5 inhibitors), tacrolimus, thioridazine, venlafaxine, and other CYP3A4 substrates. Blood pressure-lowering effects may be additive with sildenafil, tadalafil, and vardenafil (use caution).

Decreased Effect: Levels/effects of diltiazem may be decreased by aminoglutethimide, carbamazepine, nafcillin, nevirapine, phenobarbital, phenytoin, rifamycins, and other CYP3A4 inducers.

Ethanol/Nutrition/Herb Interactions

Ethanol: Avoid ethanol (may increase risk of hypotension or vasodilation).

Food: Diltiazem serum levels may be elevated if taken with food. Serum concentrations were not altered by grapefruit juice in small clinical trials.

Herb/Nutraceutical: St John's wort may decrease diltiazem levels. Avoid dong quai if using for hypertension (has estrogenic activity). Avoid ephedra (may worsen arrhythmia or hypertension). Avoid yohimbe, ginseng (may worsen hypertension). Avoid garlic (may have increased antihypertensive effect).

Stability

Capsule, tablet: Store at controlled room temperature.

Solution for injection: Store in refrigerator at 2°C to 8°C (36°F to 46°F). May be stored at room temperature for up to 1 month; do not freeze. Following dilution with $D_5$1/2NS, D_5W, or NS, solution is stable for 24 hours at room temperature or under refrigeration.

Mechanism of Action Inhibits calcium ion from entering the "slow channels" or select voltage-sensitive areas of vascular smooth muscle and myocardium during depolarization, producing a relaxation of coronary vascular smooth muscle and coronary vasodilation; increases myocardial oxygen delivery in patients with vasospastic angina

Pharmacodynamics/Kinetics

Onset of action: Oral: Immediate release tablet: 30-60 minutes

Absorption: 70% to 80%

Distribution: V_d: 3-13 L/kg; enters breast milk

Protein binding: 70% to 80%

Metabolism: Hepatic; extensive first-pass effect; following single I.V. injection, plasma concentrations of N-monodesmethyldiltiazem and desacetyldiltiazem are typically undetectable; however, these metabolites accumulate to detectable concentrations following 24-hour constant rate infusion. N-monodesmethyldiltiazem appears to have 20% of the potency of diltiazem; desacetyldiltiazem is about 25% to 50% as potent as the parent compound.

Bioavailability: Oral: ~40%

Half-life elimination: Immediate release tablet: 3-4.5 hours, may be prolonged with renal impairment

Time to peak, serum: Immediate release tablet: 2-4 hours

Excretion: Urine and feces (primarily as metabolites)

Dosage Adults:

Oral:

Angina:

Capsule, extended release (Cardizem® CD, Cartia XT™, Dilacor® XR, Diltia XT®, Tiazac®): Initial: 120-180 mg once daily (maximum dose: 480 mg/day)

Tablet, extended release (Cardizem® LA): 180 mg once daily; may increase at 7- to 14-day intervals (maximum recommended dose: 360 mg/day)

Tablet, immediate release (Cardizem®): Usual starting dose: 30 mg 4 times/day; usual range: 180-360 mg/day

Hypertension:

Capsule, extended release (Cardizem® CD, Cartia XT™, Dilacor® XR, Diltia XT®, Tiazac®): Initial: 180-240 mg once daily; dose adjustment may be made after 14 days; usual dose range (JNC 7): 180-420 mg/day; Tiazac®: usual dose range: 120-540 mg/day

Capsule, sustained release: Initial: 60-120 mg twice daily; dose adjustment may be made after 14 days; usual range: 240-360 mg/day

Tablet, extended release (Cardizem® LA): Initial: 180-240 mg once daily; dose adjustment may be made after 14 days; usual dose range (JNC 7): 120-540 mg/day

Note: Elderly: Patients ≥60 years may respond to a lower initial dose (ie, 120 mg once daily using extended release capsule)

I.V.: Atrial fibrillation, atrial flutter, PSVT:

Initial bolus dose: 0.25 mg/kg actual body weight over 2 minutes (average adult dose: 20 mg)

Repeat bolus dose (may be administered after 15 minutes if the response is inadequate.): 0.35 mg/kg actual body weight over 2 minutes (average adult dose: 25 mg)

Continuous infusion (requires an infusion pump; infusions >24 hours or infusion rates >15 mg/hour are not recommended.): Initial infusion rate of 10 mg/hour; rate may be increased in 5 mg/hour increments up to 15 mg/hour as needed; some patients may respond to an initial rate of 5 mg/hour.

If diltiazem injection is administered by continuous infusion for >24 hours, the possibility of decreased diltiazem clearance, prolonged elimination half-life, and increased diltiazem and/or diltiazem metabolite plasma concentrations should be considered.

Conversion from I.V. diltiazem to oral diltiazem: Start oral approximately 3 hours after bolus dose.

Oral dose (mg/day) is approximately equal to [rate (mg/hour) x 3 + 3] x 10.

3 mg/hour = 120 mg/day
5 mg/hour = 180 mg/day
7 mg/hour = 240 mg/day
11 mg/hour = 360 mg/day

Dosing comments in renal/hepatic impairment: Use with caution as extensively metabolized by the liver and excreted in the kidneys and bile.

Dialysis: Not removed by hemo- or peritoneal dialysis; supplemental dose is not necessary.

Administration

Oral: Do not crush long acting dosage forms.

Tiazac®: Capsules may be opened and sprinkled on a spoonful of applesauce. Applesauce should be swallowed without chewing, followed by drinking a glass of water.

I.V.: Bolus doses given over 2 minutes with continuous ECG and blood pressure monitoring. Continuous infusion should be via infusion pump.

Monitoring Parameters Liver function tests, blood pressure, ECG

Dosage Forms

Capsule, extended release, as hydrochloride [once-daily dosing]: 120 mg, 180 mg, 240 mg, 300 mg, 360 mg, 420 mg

Cardizem® CD: 120 mg, 180 mg, 240 mg, 300 mg, 360 mg

Cartia XT™: 120 mg, 180 mg, 240 mg, 300 mg

Dilacor® XR, Dilt-XR, Diltia XT®: 120 mg, 180 mg, 240 mg

Taztia XT™: 120 mg, 180 mg, 240 mg, 300 mg, 360 mg

Tiazac®: 120 mg, 180 mg, 240 mg, 300 mg, 360 mg, 420 mg

Capsule, sustained release, as hydrochloride [twice-daily dosing]: 60 mg, 90 mg, 120 mg

Injection, solution, as hydrochloride: 5 mg/mL (5 mL, 10 mL, 25 mL)

Injection, powder for reconstitution, as hydrochloride:

Cardizem®: 25 mg

Tablet, as hydrochloride: 30 mg, 60 mg, 90 mg, 120 mg

Cardizem®: 30 mg, 60 mg, 90 mg, 120 mg

Tablet, extended release, as hydrochloride:

Cardizem® LA: 120 mg, 180 mg, 240 mg, 300 mg, 360 mg, 420 mg

Extemporaneous Preparations A 12 mg/mL oral liquid preparation made from tablets (regular, not sustained release) and 3 different vehicles (cherry syrup, a 1:1 mixture of Ora-Sweet® and Ora-Plus®, or a 1:1 mixture of Ora-Sweet® SF and Ora-Plus®) was stable for 60 days when stored in amber plastic prescription bottles in the dark at room temperature (25°C) or under refrigeration (5°C); grind sixteen 90 mg tablets in a mortar into a fine powder; add 10 mL of the vehicle and mix well to form a uniform paste; mix while adding the vehicle in geometric proportions to almost 120 mL; transfer to a calibrated bottle and qs ad with vehicle to 120 mL; label "shake well" and "protect from light".

Allen LV and Erickson MA, "Stability of Baclofen, Captopril, Diltiazem Hydrochloride, Dipyridamole, and Flecainide Acetate in Extemporaneously Compounded Oral Liquids," *Am J Health Syst Pharm,* 1996, 53(18):2179-84.

♦ **Diltiazem HCl ER® (Can)** see Diltiazem *on page 509*

♦ **Diltiazem Hydrochloride** see Diltiazem *on page 509*

♦ **Diltiazem Hydrochloride Injection (Can)** see Diltiazem *on page 509*

♦ **Dilt-XR** see Diltiazem *on page 509*

DimenhyDRINATE (dye men HYE dri nate)

U.S. Brand Names Dramamine® [OTC]; TripTone® [OTC] [DSC]

Canadian Brand Names Apo-Dimenhydrinate®; Children's Motion Sickness Liquid; Dinate®; Gravol®; Jamp® Travel Tablet; Nauseatol; Novo-Dimenate; SAB-Dimenhydrinate

Pharmacologic Category Antihistamine

Use Treatment and prevention of nausea, vertigo, and vomiting associated with motion sickness

Dosage forms available in Canada (not available in the U.S.), including parenteral formulations and suppositories, are also approved for the treatment of postoperative nausea and vomiting and treatment of radiation sickness.

Unlabeled/Investigational Use Treatment of Meniere's disease

Pregnancy Risk Factor B

Medication Safety Issues

Sound-alike/look-alike issues:

DimenhyDRINATE may be confused with diphenhydrAMINE

(Continued)

DimenhyDRINATE *(Continued)*

Dosage Oral:
Children:
2-5 years: 12.5-25 mg every 6-8 hours, maximum: 75 mg/day
6-12 years: 25-50 mg every 6-8 hours, maximum: 150 mg/day
Adults: 50-100 mg every 4-6 hours, not to exceed 400 mg/day
Gravol® L/A (not available in the U.S.): 75-150 mg every 8-12 hours, up to a maximum of five 75 mg caplets or three 100 mg caplets in 24 hours

Additional formulations/uses (approved in Canada) for parenteral/suppository formulations (not available in U.S.):
I.M., I.V., rectal: Adults:
Postoperative nausea and vomiting: 50-100 mg administered 30-60 minutes prior to radiation therapy; may be repeated as needed up to a maximum of 400 mg in 24 hours
Radiation sickness: 50-100 mg administered 30-60 minutes prior to radiation therapy. May be repeated as needed up to a maximum of 400 mg in 24 hours

Additional Information Complete prescribing information for this medication should be consulted for additional detail.

Dosage Forms [CAN] = Canadian brand name
Caplet (TripTone®): 50 mg [DSC]
Capsule, softgel (Gravol®) [CAN]: 50 mg [not available in the U.S.]
Capsule, long-acting (Gravol® L/A) [CAN]: 75 mg, 100 mg [not available in the U.S.]
Injection, solution:
Gravol® I.M. [CAN]: 50 mg/mL (1 mL, 5 mL) [not available in the U.S.]
Gravol® I.V. [CAN]: 10 mg/mL (5 mL) [not available in the U.S.]
Solution, oral (Gravol® [CAN], Children's Motion Sickness [CAN]): 3 mg/mL (75 mL) [not available in the U.S.]
Suppository, rectal (Gravol® [CAN], Sab-Dimenhydrinate [CAN]): 75 mg, 100 mg [not available in the U.S.]
Tablet:
Dinate® [CAN], Jamp® Travel Tablet [CAN], Nauseatol® [CAN]: 50 mg
Dramamine®: 50 mg
Gravol® Filmkote Jr [CAN]: 25 mg [not available in the U.S.]
Gravol® Filmkote [CAN]: 50 mg [not available in the U.S.]
Tablet, chewable:
Dramamine®: 50 mg [contains phenylalanine 1.5 mg/tablet and tartrazine; orange flavor]
Gravol® Chewable for Children [CAN]: 25 mg [not available in the U.S.]
Gravol® Chewable for Adults [CAN]: 50 mg [not available in the U.S.]

Dimercaprol *(dye mer KAP role)*

U.S. Brand Names BAL in Oil®
Index Terms BAL; British Anti-Lewisite; Dithioglycerol
Pharmacologic Category Antidote
Additional Appendix Information
Management of Overdosages *on page 2075*
Use Antidote to gold, arsenic (except arsine), and mercury poisoning (except nonalkyl mercury); adjunct to edetate calcium disodium in lead poisoning; possibly effective for antimony, bismuth, chromium, copper, nickel, tungsten, or zinc
Pregnancy Risk Factor C
Contraindications Hepatic insufficiency (unless due to arsenic poisoning); do not use on iron, cadmium, or selenium poisoning
Warnings/Precautions Potentially a nephrotoxic drug, use with caution in patients with oliguria or glucose 6-phosphate dehydrogenase deficiency; keep urine alkaline to protect kidneys; administer all injections deep I.M. at different sites
Adverse Reactions
>10%:
Cardiovascular: Hypertension, tachycardia (dose related)
Central nervous system: Headache
1% to 10%: Gastrointestinal: Nausea, vomiting
<1% (Limited to important or life-threatening): Abscess formation, blepharospasm, burning eyes; burning sensation of the lips, mouth, throat, and penis; convulsions, dysuria, fever, increased PT, myalgia, nephrotoxicity, nervousness, pain at the injection site, paresthesia, salivation, thrombocytopenia, transient neutropenia
Drug Interactions
Increased Effect/Toxicity: Toxic complexes with iron, cadmium, selenium, or uranium.
Stability Do not mix in the same syringe with edetate calcium disodium.
Mechanism of Action Sulfhydryl group combines with ions of various heavy metals to form relatively stable, nontoxic, soluble chelates which are excreted in urine
Pharmacodynamics/Kinetics
Distribution: To all tissues including the brain
Metabolism: Rapidly hepatic to inactive metabolites
Time to peak, serum: 0.5-1 hour
Excretion: Urine
Dosage Children and Adults: Deep I.M.:
Arsenic, mercury, and gold poisoning: 3 mg/kg every 4-6 hours for 2 days, then every 12 hours for 7-10 days or until recovery (initial dose may be up to 5 mg if severe poisoning)
Lead poisoning (in conjunction with calcium EDTA): For symptomatic acute encephalopathy or blood level >100 mcg/dL: 4-5 mg/kg every 4 hours for 3-5 days
Administration Administer deep I.M. only; keep urine alkaline to protect renal function
Test Interactions Iodine ^{131}I thyroidal uptake values may be decreased
Dosage Forms Injection, oil: 100 mg/mL (3 mL) [contains benzyl benzoate and peanut oil]

♦ **Dimetapp® 12-Hour Non-Drowsy Extentabs® [OTC] [DSC]** *see* Pseudoephedrine *on page 1454*

♦ **Dimetapp® Decongestant Infant [OTC] [DSC]** *see* Pseudoephedrine *on page 1454*

♦ **Dimetapp® Infant Decongestant Plus Cough [OTC] [DSC]** *see* Pseudoephedrine and Dextromethorphan *on page 1455*

♦ **β,β-Dimethylcysteine** *see* Penicillamine *on page 1330*

♦ **Dimethyl Triazeno Imidazole Carboxamide** *see* Dacarbazine *on page 442*

♦ **Dinate® (Can)** *see* DimenhyDRINATE *on page 511*

Dinoprostone (dye noe PROST one)

U.S. Brand Names Cervidil®; Prepidil®; Prostin E$_2$®
Canadian Brand Names Cervidil®; Prepidil®; Prostin E$_2$®
Index Terms PGE$_2$; Prostaglandin E$_2$
Pharmacologic Category Abortifacient; Prostaglandin
Use
Gel: Promote cervical ripening in patients at or near term in whom there is a medical or obstetrical indication for the induction of labor
Suppositories: Terminate pregnancy from 12th through 20th week of gestation; evacuate uterus in cases of missed abortion or intrauterine fetal death up to 28 weeks of gestation; manage benign hydatidiform mole (nonmetastatic gestational trophoblastic disease)
Vaginal insert: Initiation and/or continuation of cervical ripening in patients at or near term in whom there is a medical or obstetrical indication for the induction of labor
Pregnancy Risk Factor C
Pregnancy Implications Skeletal anomalies and embryotoxicity have been observed in animal studies. Although these effects would not be expected in humans when administered after the period of organogenesis, a sustained increase in uterine tone may have increased risks of adverse events to the fetus.

Fetal distress without corresponding maternal uterine hyperstimulation was observed in 3% to 4% of infants exposed to Cervidil® *in utero*. No adverse effects on physical or psychomotor function were observed in a 3 year follow-up study of exposed infants. Abnormal fetal heart rates were observed in 17% of infants exposed to Prepidil® gel *in utero*. Deceleration, intrauterine fetal sepsis, fetal depression and fetal acidosis have also been reported with administration of the gel.

When used for termination of pregnancy, dinoprostone is not considered feticidal, but is used to terminate pregnancy due to its ability to stimulate uterine contractions; do not use if fetus has reached the stage of viability.
Lactation Excretion in breast milk unknown
Medication Safety Issues
Sound-alike/look-alike issues:
Prepidil® may be confused with Bepridil®

International issues:
Cervidil®: Brand name for gemeprost in Italy
Contraindications
Gel, vaginal insert: Hypersensitivity to prostaglandins or any component of the formulation; fetal distress (suspicion or clinical evidence unless delivery is imminent); unexplained vaginal bleeding during this pregnancy; strong suspicion of marked cephalopelvic disproportion; patients in whom oxytocic drugs are contraindicated or when prolonged contraction of the uterus may be detrimental to fetal safety or uterine integrity (including previous cesarean section or major uterine surgery); >6 previous term pregnancies; patients already receiving oxytocic drugs; hyperactive or hypotonic uterine patterns; when vaginal delivery is not indicated (vasa previa, active herpes genitalia); obstetrical emergencies when surgical intervention would be favorable
Suppository: Hypersensitivity to dinoprostone or any component of the formulation; acute pelvic inflammatory disease; active cardiac, pulmonary, renal or hepatic disease
Warnings/Precautions [U.S. Boxed Warning]: Dinoprostone should be used only by medically-trained personnel in a hospital.

Gel, vaginal insert: Use caution with ruptured membranes; nonvertex or nonsingleton pregnancy; previous uterine hypertony; glaucoma; history of asthma. Vaginal insert must be removed prior to administration of oxytocin; in case of hyperstimulation or if labor begins; fetal or maternal distress; and prior to amniotomy.

Suppository: Transient pyrexia and decreased blood pressure may be observed with treatment. Use caution with history of asthma; hypotension or hypertension; cardiovascular, renal, or hepatic disease; anemia; jaundice; diabetes; epilepsy; compromised uteri; cervicitis, endocervical infections or acute vaginitis. Measures should be taken to ensure complete abortion. Commercially available suppositories should not be used for extemporaneous preparation of any other dosage form of drug. Do not use for cervical ripening or other indications in patients with term pregnancy.
Adverse Reactions
Gel:
1% to 10%:
Central nervous system: Fever (1%)
Gastrointestinal: GI upset (6%)
Genitourinary: Abnormal uterine contractions (7%), warm feeling in vagina (2%)
Neuromuscular & skeletal: Back pain (3%)
Postmarketing and/or case reports: Amnionitis, premature rupture of membranes, uterine rupture (with intracervical administration)

Suppository:
Frequency not defined:
Cardiovascular: Arrhythmia, chest pain, chest tightness, hypotension, syncope
Central nervous system: Chills, dizziness, fever, headache, shivering, tension
(Continued)

Dinoprostone *(Continued)*

Dermatologic: Rash, skin discoloration

Endocrine & metabolic: Breast tenderness, endometritis, hot flashes

Gastrointestinal: Dehydration, diarrhea, nausea, vomiting

Genitourinary: uterine rupture, urinary retention, vaginal pain, vaginismus, vaginitis, vulvitis

Neuromuscular & skeletal: Arthralgia, backache, joint inflammation/pain (new or exacerbated), leg cramps (nocturnal), muscle cramp/pain, myalgia, paresthesia, stiff neck, tremor, weakness

Ocular: Blurred vision, eye pain

Otic: Hearing impairment

Respiratory: Cough, dyspnea, laryngitis, pharyngitis, wheezing

Miscellaneous: Diaphoresis

Postmarketing and/or case reports: MI

Vaginal insert:

1% to 10%: Genitourinary: Uterine hyperstimulation *without* fetal distress (2% to 5%), uterine hyperstimulation *with* fetal distress (3%)

<1% (Limited to important or life-threatening): Abdominal pain, diarrhea, fever, nausea, uterine rupture, vomiting

Overdosage/Toxicology Uterine hyperstimulation with or without fetal distress may be observed. Beta-adrenergic agents may be used for increased uterine activity. Treatment may also include changing of maternal position and oxygen administration; remove vaginal insert if in place.

Drug Interactions

Increased Effect/Toxicity: Dinoprostone may increase the effect of oxytocin; wait 6-12 hours after dinoprostone gel administration or at least 30 minutes after removal of vaginal insert before initiating oxytocin.

Stability

Cervical gel should be stored under refrigeration 2°C to 8°C (36°F to 46°F).

Suppositories must be kept frozen; store in freezer not above -20°C (-4°F).

Vaginal insert should be stored in freezer between -20°C and -10°C (-4°F and 14°F).

Mechanism of Action A synthetic prostaglandin E_2 abortifacient that stimulates uterine contractions similar to those seen during natural labor. Prostaglandin E_2 plays a role in cervical ripening, which allows the fetus to pass through the birth canal.

Pharmacodynamics/Kinetics

Onset of action (uterine contractions): Vaginal suppository: Within 10 minutes

Duration: Vaginal insert: 0.3 mg/hour over 12 hours; Vaginal suppository: Up to 2-3 hours

Absorption: Vaginal suppository: Slow

Metabolism: In many tissues including lungs, liver, and kidney

Half-life elimination: 2.5-5 minutes

Time to peak, plasma: Gel: 30-45 minutes

Excretion: Primarily urine; feces (small amounts)

Dosage Females of reproductive age:

Abortifacient: Vaginal suppository: Insert 20 mg (1 suppository) high in vagina, repeat at 3- to 5-hour intervals until abortion occurs; continued administration for longer than 2 days is not advisable

Cervical ripening:

Endocervical gel: Using catheter supplied with gel, insert 0.5 mg into the cervical canal. May repeat every 6 hours if needed. Maximum cumulative dose: 1.5 mg/24 hours

Vaginal insert: Insert 10 mg transversely into the posterior fornix of the vagina (to be removed at the onset of active labor or after 12 hours)

Administration

Endocervical gel: Bring to room temperature just prior to use. Do not force the warming process (eg, water bath, microwave). Avoid contact with skin while handling; wash hands thoroughly with soap and water after administration. For cervical ripening, patient should be supine in the dorsal position. The appropriate catheter length should be based on degree of effacement; 20 mm for no effacement; 10 mm if 50% effaced. Patient should remain supine for 15-30 minutes following administration.

Vaginal insert: One vaginal insert is placed transversely in the posterior fornix of the vagina immediately after removal from its foil package. Patients should remain in the recumbent position for 2 hours after insertion, but thereafter may be ambulatory. Do not use without retrieval system. Product does not need warmed prior to use. A water miscible lubricant may be used to facilitate insertion (avoid excessive use of lubricant). Ensure complete removal of system at completion of therapy.

Vaginal suppository: Bring to room temperature just prior to use. Patient should remain supine for 10 minutes following insertion.

Monitoring Parameters

Gel, insert: Fetal heart rate and uterine activity

Suppository: Confirmation of fetal death

Dosage Forms

Gel, endocervical (Prepidil®): 0.5 mg/3 g syringe [each package contains a 10 mm and 20 mm shielded catheter]

Insert, vaginal (Cervidil®): 10 mg [releases 0.3 mg/hour]

Suppository, vaginal (Prostin E_2®): 20 mg

- **Diocaine® (Can)** *see* Proparacaine *on page 1440*
- **Diocarpine (Can)** *see* Pilocarpine *on page 1368*
- **Diochloram® (Can)** *see* Chloramphenicol *on page 341*
- **Diocto® [OTC]** *see* Docusate *on page 533*
- **Dioctyl Calcium Sulfosuccinate** *see* Docusate *on page 533*
- **Dioctyl Sodium Sulfosuccinate** *see* Docusate *on page 533*
- **Diodex® (Can)** *see* Dexamethasone *on page 479*
- **Diodoquin® (Can)** *see* Iodoquinol *on page 930*

- **Diogent®** (Can) *see* Gentamicin *on page 793*
- **Diomycin®** (Can) *see* Erythromycin *on page 609*
- **Dioncphrine®** (Can) *see* Phenylephrine *on page 1358*
- **Diopentolate®** (Can) *see* Cyclopentolate *on page 428*
- **Diopred®** (Can) *see* PrednisoLONE *on page 1413*
- **Dioptic's Atropine Solution (Can)** *see* Atropine *on page 176*
- **Dioptimyd®** (Can) *see* Sulfacetamide and Prednisolone *on page 1610*
- **Dioptrol®** (Can) *see* Neomycin, Polymyxin B, and Dexamethasone *on page 1211*
- **Diosulf™** (Can) *see* Sulfacetamide *on page 1609*
- **Diotame®** [OTC] *see* Bismuth *on page 224*
- **Diotrope®** (Can) *see* Tropicamide *on page 1752*
- **Diovan®** *see* Valsartan *on page 1771*
- **Diovan HCT®** *see* Valsartan and Hydrochlorothiazide *on page 1773*
- **Diovol®** (Can) *see* Aluminum Hydroxide and Magnesium Hydroxide *on page 85*
- **Diovol® Ex (Can)** *see* Aluminum Hydroxide and Magnesium Hydroxide *on page 85*
- **Diovol Plus®** (Can) *see* Aluminum Hydroxide, Magnesium Hydroxide, and Simethicone *on page 85*
- **Dipentum®** *see* Olsalazine *on page 1262*
- **Diphen®** [OTC] *see* DiphenhydrAMINE *on page 515*
- **Diphen® AF** [OTC] *see* DiphenhydrAMINE *on page 515*
- **Diphenhist** [OTC] *see* DiphenhydrAMINE *on page 515*

DiphenhydrAMINE (dye fen HYE dra meen)

U.S. Brand Names Aler-Cap [OTC]; Aler-Dryl [OTC]; Aler-Tab [OTC]; AllerMax® [OTC]; Altaryl [OTC]; Banophen® [OTC]; Banophen® Anti-Itch [OTC]; Benadryl® Allergy [OTC]; Benadryl® Children's Allergy [OTC]; Benadryl® Children's Allergy Fastmelt® [OTC]; Benadryl® Dye-Free Allergy [OTC]; Benadryl® Injection; Benadryl® Itch Stopping [OTC]; Benadryl® Itch Stopping Extra Strength [OTC]; Compoz® Nighttime Sleep Aid [OTC]; Dermamycin® [OTC]; Dermarest® Insect Bite [OTC]; Dermarest® Plus [OTC]; Diphen® [OTC]; Diphen® AF [OTC]; Diphenhist [OTC]; Dytan™; Genahist® [OTC]; Hydramine® [OTC]; Nytol® Quick Caps [OTC]; Nytol® Quick Gels [OTC]; Q-Dryl [OTC]; Quenalin [OTC]; Siladryl® Allergy [OTC]; Siladryl® DAS [OTC]; Silphen® [OTC]; Simply Sleep® [OTC]; Sleep-ettes D [OTC]; Sleepinal® [OTC]; Sominex® [OTC]; Sominex® Maximum Strength [OTC]; Triaminic® Thin Strips™ Cough and Hunny Nose [OTC]; Twilite® [OTC]; Unisom® Maximum Strength SleepGels® [OTC]

Canadian Brand Names Allerdryl®; Allernix; Benadryl®; Nytol®; Nytol® Extra Strength; PMS-Diphenhydramine; Simply Sleep®

Index Terms Diphenhydramine Citrate; Diphenhydramine Hydrochloride; Diphenhydramine Tannate

Pharmacologic Category Antihistamine

Additional Appendix Information

Contrast Media Reactions, Premedication for Prophylaxis *on page 2036*

Use Symptomatic relief of allergic symptoms caused by histamine release which include nasal allergies and allergic dermatosis; can be used for mild nighttime sedation; prevention of motion sickness and as an antitussive; has antinauseant and topical anesthetic properties; treatment of antipsychotic-induced extrapyramidal symptoms

Pregnancy Risk Factor B

Lactation Enters breast milk/contraindicated

Medication Safety Issues

Sound-alike/look-alike issues:

DiphenhydrAMINE may be confused with desipramine, dicyclomine, dimenhyDRINATE

Benadryl® may be confused with benazepril, Bentyl®, Benylin®, Caladryl®

Contraindications Hypersensitivity to diphenhydramine or any component of the formulation; acute asthma; not for use in neonates

Warnings/Precautions Causes sedation, caution must be used in performing tasks which require alertness (eg, operating machinery or driving). Sedative effects of CNS depressants or ethanol are potentiated. Use with caution in patients with angle-closure glaucoma, pyloroduodenal obstruction (including stenotic peptic ulcer), urinary tract obstruction (including bladder neck obstruction and symptomatic prostatic hypertrophy), hyperthyroidism, increased intraocular pressure, and cardiovascular disease (including hypertension and tachycardia). Diphenhydramine has high sedative and anticholinergic properties, so it may not be considered the antihistamine of choice for prolonged use in the elderly. May cause paradoxical excitation in pediatric patients, and can result in hallucinations, coma, and death in overdose. Some preparations contain sodium bisulfite; syrup formulations may contain alcohol. Some preparations contain soy protein; patients with soy protein or peanut allergies should avoid.

Adverse Reactions Frequency not defined.

Cardiovascular: Hypotension, palpitation, tachycardia

Central nervous system: Sedation, sleepiness, dizziness, disturbed coordination, headache, fatigue, nervousness, paradoxical excitement, insomnia, euphoria, confusion

Dermatologic: Photosensitivity, rash, angioedema, urticaria

Gastrointestinal: Nausea, vomiting, diarrhea, abdominal pain, xerostomia, appetite increase, weight gain, dry mucous membranes, anorexia

Genitourinary: Urinary retention, urinary frequency, difficult urination

Hematologic: Hemolytic anemia, thrombocytopenia, agranulocytosis

Neuromuscular & skeletal: Tremor, paresthesia

Ocular: Blurred vision

Respiratory: Thickening of bronchial secretions

Overdosage/Toxicology Symptoms include CNS stimulation or depression. Overdose may result in death in infants and children. There is no specific treatment for antihistamine overdose, however, clinical toxicity is mostly due to anticholinergic effects. Anticholinesterase *(Continued)*

DiphenhydrAMINE *(Continued)*

inhibitors (eg, physostigmine, neostigmine, pyridostigmine, or edrophonium) may be useful by reducing acetylcholinesterase. For anticholinergic overdose with severe life-threatening symptoms, physostigmine 1-2 mg (0.5 mg or 0.02 mg/kg for children) slow I.V. may be given to reverse these effects.

Drug Interactions

Cytochrome P450 Effect: Inhibits CYP2D6 (moderate)

Increased Effect/Toxicity: Diphenhydramine may increase the levels/effects of amphetamines, selected beta-blockers, dextromethorphan, fluoxetine, lidocaine, mirtazapine, nefazodone, paroxetine, risperidone, ritonavir, thioridazine, tricyclic antidepressants, venlafaxine and other CYP2D6 substrates. CNS depressants may increase the degree of sedation and respiratory depression with diphenhydramine. May increase the absorption of digoxin. Central and/or peripheral anticholinergic syndrome can occur when administered with amantadine, rimantadine, opioid analgesics, phenothiazines and other antipsychotics (especially with high anticholinergic activity), tricyclic antidepressants, quinidine, disopyramide, procainamide, and antihistamines. Syrup should not be given to patients taking drugs that can cause disulfiram reactions (ie, metronidazole, chlorpropamide) due to high alcohol content.

Decreased Effect: Diphenhydramine may decrease the levels/effects of CYP2D6 prodrug substrates; example prodrug substrates include codeine, hydrocodone, oxycodone, and tramadol. May increase gastric degradation of levodopa and decrease the amount of levodopa absorbed by delaying gastric emptying. Therapeutic effects of cholinergic agents (tacrine, donepezil) and neuroleptics may be antagonized.

Ethanol/Nutrition/Herb Interactions

Ethanol: Avoid ethanol (may increase CNS depression).

Herb/Nutraceutical: Avoid valerian, St John's wort, kava kava, gotu kola (may increase CNS depression).

Stability Protect injection from light.

Mechanism of Action Competes with histamine for H_1-receptor sites on effector cells in the gastrointestinal tract, blood vessels, and respiratory tract; anticholinergic and sedative effects are also seen

Pharmacodynamics/Kinetics

Onset of action: Maximum sedative effect: 1-3 hours

Duration: 4-7 hours

Protein binding: 78%

Metabolism: Extensively hepatic; smaller degrees in pulmonary and renal systems; significant first-pass effect

Bioavailability: Oral: 40% to 60%

Half-life elimination: 2-8 hours; Elderly: 13.5 hours

Time to peak, serum: 2-4 hours

Excretion: Urine (as unchanged drug)

Dosage

Children:

Oral, I.M., I.V.:

Treatment of moderate to severe allergic reactions: 5 mg/kg/day or 150 mg/m²/day in divided doses every 6-8 hours, not to exceed 300 mg/day

Minor allergic rhinitis or motion sickness:

2 to <6 years: 6.25 mg every 4-6 hours; maximum: 37.5 mg/day

6 to <12 years: 12.5-25 mg every 4-6 hours; maximum: 150 mg/day

≥12 years: 25-50 mg every 4-6 hours; maximum: 300 mg/day

Night-time sleep aid: 30 minutes before bedtime:

2 to <12 years: 1 mg/kg/dose; maximum: 50 mg/dose

≥12 years: 50 mg

Oral: Antitussive:

2 to <6 years: 6.25 mg every 4 hours; maximum 37.5 mg/day

6 to <12 years: 12.5 mg every 4 hours; maximum 75 mg/day

≥12 years: 25 mg every 4 hours; maximum 150 mg/day

I.M., I.V.: Treatment of dystonic reactions: 0.5-1 mg/kg/dose

Adults:

Oral: 25-50 mg every 6-8 hours

Minor allergic rhinitis or motion sickness: 25-50 mg every 4-6 hours; maximum: 300 mg/day

Moderate to severe allergic reactions: 25-50 mg every 4 hours, not to exceed 400 mg/day

Nighttime sleep aid: 50 mg at bedtime

I.M., I.V.: 10-50 mg in a single dose every 2-4 hours, not to exceed 400 mg/day

Dystonic reaction: 50 mg in a single dose; may repeat in 20-30 minutes if necessary

Topical: For external application, not longer than 7 days

Dietary Considerations Tablet:

Chewable, as hydrochloride: Contains phenylalanine 4.2 mg per 12.5 mg tablet

Chewable, as tannate: Contains phenylalanine 1.5 mg per 25 mg tablet

Orally-disintegrating, as citrate: Contains phenylalanine 4.5 mg per 19 mg [equivalent to diphenhydramine hydrochloride 12.5 mg] tablet; contains soy protein isolate (contraindicated in patients with soy protein allergies; use caution in peanut allergic individuals, ~10% are estimated to also have soy protein allergies)

Monitoring Parameters Relief of symptoms, mental alertness

Reference Range

Antihistamine effects at levels >25 ng/mL

Drowsiness at levels 30-40 ng/mL

Mental impairment at levels >60 ng/mL

Therapeutic: Not established

Toxic: >0.1 mcg/mL

Test Interactions May suppress the wheal and flare reactions to skin test antigens

Additional Information Its use as a sleep aid is discouraged due to its anticholinergic effects.

Dosage Forms

Caplet, as hydrochloride: 25 mg, 50 mg

Aler-Dryl, AllerMax®, Compoz® Nighttime Sleep Aid, Sleep-ettes D, Sominex® Maximum Strength, Twilite®: 50 mg

Simply Sleep®, Nytol® Quick Caps: 25 mg

Capsule, as hydrochloride: 25 mg, 50 mg

Aler-Cap, Banophen®, Benadryl® Allergy, Diphen®, Diphenhist, Genahist®, Q-Dryl: 25 mg

Sleepinal®: 50 mg

Capsule, softgel, as hydrochloride: 50 mg

Benadryl® Dye-Free Allergy: 25 mg [dye-free]

Compoz® Nighttime Sleep Aid, Nytol® Quick Gels, Sleepinal®, Unisom® Maximum Strength SleepGels®: 50 mg

Captab, as hydrochloride (Diphenhist®): 25 mg

Cream, as hydrochloride: 2% (30 g) [contains zinc acetate 0.1%]

Banophen® Anti-Itch: 2% (30 g) [contains zinc acetate 0.1%]

Benadryl® Itch Stopping: 1% (30 g) [contains zinc acetate 0.1%]

Benadryl® Itch Stopping Extra Strength: 2% (30 g) [contains zinc acetate 0.1%]

Diphenhist®: 2% (30 g) [contains zinc acetate 0.1%]

Elixir, as hydrochloride:

Altaryl: 12.5 mg/5 mL (120 mL, 480 mL, 3840 mL) [cherry flavor]

Banophen®: 12.5 mg/5 mL (120 mL)

Diphen AF: 12.5 mg/5 mL (120 mL, 240 mL, 480 mL) [alcohol free; cherry flavor]

Q-Dryl: 12.5 mg/5 mL (480 mL) [alcohol free]

Gel, topical, as hydrochloride:

Benadryl® Itch Stopping Extra Strength: 2% (120 mL)

Dermarest® Plus: 2% (28 g, 42 g) [contains menthol 1%]

Injection, solution, as hydrochloride: 50 mg/mL (1 mL)

Benadryl®: 50 mg/mL (1 mL, 10 mL)

Liquid, as hydrochloride:

AllerMax®: 12.5 mg/5 mL (120 mL)

Benadryl® Allergy: 12.5 mg/5 mL (120 mL, 240 mL) [alcohol free; contains sodium benzoate; cherry flavor]

Benadryl® Dye-Free Allergy: 12.5 mg/5 mL (120 mL) [alcohol free, dye free, sugar free; contains sodium benzoate; bubble gum flavor]

Genahist®: 12.5 mg/5 mL (120 mL) [alcohol free, sugar free; contains sodium benzoate; cherry flavor]

Hydramine®: 12.5 mg/5 mL (120 mL, 480 mL) [alcohol free]

Q-Dryl: 12.5 mg/5 mL (120 mL) [alcohol free; cherry flavor]

Quenalin: 12.5 mg/5 mL (120 mL) [fruit flavor]

Siladryl® Allergy: 12.5 mg/5 mL (120 mL, 240 mL, 480 mL) [alcohol free, sugar free; black cherry flavor]

Siladryl® DAS: 12.5 mg/5 mL (120 mL) [alcohol free, dye free, sugar free; black cherry flavor]

Liquid, topical, as hydrochloride [stick] (Benadryl® Itch Stopping Extra Strength): 2% (14 mL) [contains zinc acetate 0.1% and alcohol]

Solution, oral, as hydrochloride:

Banophen®: 12.5 mg/5mL (480 mL) [sugar free]

Diphenhist: 12.5 mg/5 mL (120 mL, 480 mL) [alcohol free; contains sodium benzoate]

Solution, topical, as hydrochloride [spray]:

Benadryl® Itch Stopping Extra Strength: 2% (60 mL) [contains zinc acetate 0.1% and alcohol]

Dermamycin®, Dermarest® Insect Bite: 2% (60 mL) [contains menthol 1%]

Strips, oral, as hydrochloride (Triaminic® Thin Strips™ Cough and Runny Nose): 12. 5 mg (16s) [grape flavor]

Suspension, as tannate: 25 mg/5 mL (120 mL)

Dytan™: 25 mg/5 mL (120 mL) [strawberry flavor]

Syrup, as hydrochloride (Silphen® Cough): 12.5 mg/5 mL (120 mL, 240 mL, 480 mL) [contains alcohol; 5%; strawberry flavor]

Tablet, as hydrochloride: 25 mg, 50 mg

Aler-Tab, Benadryl® Allergy, Genahist®, Sleepinal®, Sominex®: 25 mg

Tablet, chewable, as hydrochloride (Benadryl® Children's Allergy): 12.5 mg [contains phenylalanine 4.2 mg/tablet; grape flavor]

Tablet, chewable, as tannate (Dytan™): 25 mg [contains phenylalanine; strawberry flavor]

Tablet, orally disintegrating, as citrate (Benadryl® Children's Allergy Fastmelt®): 19 mg [equivalent to diphenhydramine hydrochloride 12.5 mg; contains phenylalanine 4.5 mg/tablet and soy protein isolate; cherry flavor]

♦ **Diphenhydramine and Acetaminophen** see Acetaminophen and Diphenhydramine on page 31

Diphenhydramine and Pseudoephedrine

(dye fen HYE dra meen & soo doe e FED rin)

U.S. Brand Names Benadryl® Children's Allergy and Cold Fastmelt™ [OTC]; Benadryl-D™ Allergy and Sinus Fastmelt™ [OTC]; Benadryl-D™ Children's Allergy and Sinus [OTC]

Index Terms Pseudoephedrine and Diphenhydramine

Pharmacologic Category Antihistamine/Decongestant Combination

Use Relief of symptoms of upper respiratory mucosal congestion in seasonal and perennial nasal allergies, acute rhinitis, rhinosinusitis, and eustachian tube blockage

Medication Safety Issues

Sound-alike/look-alike issues:

Benadryl® may be confused with benazepril, Bentyl®, Benylin®, Caladryl®

Dosage Based on **pseudoephedrine** component:

Adults: Oral: 60 mg every 4-6 hours, maximum 240 mg/day

(Continued)

Diphenhydramine and Pseudoephedrine *(Continued)*

Additional Information Complete prescribing information for this medication should be consulted for additional detail.

Dosage Forms
Liquid:
Benadryl-D™ Children's Allergy and Sinus: Diphenhydramine hydrochloride 12.5 mg and pseudoephedrine hydrochloride 30 mg per 5 mL [alcohol free, sugar free; contains sodium 10 mg/5 mL and sodium benzoate; grape flavor]
Tablet, quick dissolving:
Benadryl® Children's Allergy and Cold Fastmelt™, Benadryl-D™ Allergy and Sinus Fastmelt™: Diphenhydramine citrate 19 mg [equivalent to diphenhydramine hydrochloride 12.5 mg] and pseudoephedrine 30 mg [contains phenylalanine 4.6 mg/tablet; cherry flavor]

♦ **Diphenhydramine Citrate** *see* DiphenhydrAMINE *on page 515*

♦ **Diphenhydramine Hydrochloride** *see* DiphenhydrAMINE *on page 515*

♦ **Diphenhydramine Tannate** *see* DiphenhydrAMINE *on page 515*

Diphenoxylate and Atropine *(dye fen OKS i late & A troe peen)*

U.S. Brand Names Lomotil®; Lonox®
Canadian Brand Names Lomotil®
Index Terms Atropine and Diphenoxylate
Pharmacologic Category Antidiarrheal
Use Treatment of diarrhea
Restrictions C-V
Pregnancy Risk Factor C
Pregnancy Implications Teratogenic effects were not noted in animal studies; decreased maternal weight, fertility and litter sizes were observed. There are no adequate and well-controlled studies in pregnant women.
Lactation Enters breast milk/use caution
Medication Safety Issues
Sound-alike/look-alike issues:
Lomotil® may be confused with Lamictal®, Lamisil®, lamotrigine, Lanoxin®, Lasix®, ludiomil
Lonox® may be confused with Lanoxin®, Loprox®

International issues:
Lomotil® may be confused with Lemesil® which is a brand name for nimesulide in Greece
Lonox® may be confused with Flomox® which is a brand of cefcapene in Japan

Contraindications Hypersensitivity to diphenoxylate, atropine, or any component of the formulation; obstructive jaundice; diarrhea associated with pseudomembranous enterocolitis or enterotoxin-producing bacteria; not for use in children <2 years of age

Warnings/Precautions Use in conjunction with fluid and electrolyte therapy when appropriate. In case of severe dehydration or electrolyte imbalance, withhold diphenoxylate/atropine treatment until corrective therapy has been initiated. Inhibiting peristalsis may lead to fluid retention in the intestine aggravating dehydration and electrolyte imbalance. Reduction of intestinal motility may be deleterious in diarrhea resulting from *Shigella, Salmonella*, toxigenic strains of *E. coli*, and pseudomembranous enterocolitis associated with broad-spectrum antibiotics; use is not recommended.

Use with caution in children. Younger children may be predisposed to toxicity; signs of atropinism may occur even at recommended doses, especially in patients with Down syndrome. Overdose in children may result in severe respiratory depression, coma, and possibly permanent brain damage.

Use caution with acute ulcerative colitis, hepatic or renal dysfunction. If there is no response with 48 hours, this medication is unlikely to be effective and should be discontinued; if chronic diarrhea is not improved symptomatically within 10 days at maximum dosage, control is unlikely with further use. Physical and psychological dependence have been reported with higher than recommended dosing.

Adverse Reactions Frequency not defined.
Cardiovascular: Tachycardia
Central nervous system: Confusion, depression, dizziness, drowsiness, euphoria, flushing, headache, hyperthermia, lethargy, malaise, restlessness, sedation
Dermatologic: Angioneurotic edema, dry skin, pruritus, urticaria
Gastrointestinal: Abdominal discomfort, anorexia, gum swelling, nausea, pancreatitis, paralytic ileus, toxic megacolon, vomiting
Genitourinary: Urinary retention
Neuromuscular & skeletal: Numbness
Miscellaneous: Anaphylaxis

Overdosage/Toxicology Symptoms of overdose include drowsiness, hypotension, blurred vision, flushing, dry mouth, and miosis. Administration of activated charcoal will reduce bioavailability of diphenoxylate. Naloxone may be used to counteract respiratory depression which may occur as late as 30 hours after ingestion. Adults may be given naloxone 0.4-2 mg I.V., with repeat administration as necessary up to a total of 10 mg; can also be used to reverse toxic effects of the opiate. Children may be given naloxone 0.01 mg/kg I.V. initially, with subsequent dose of 0.1 mg/kg (may also be administered I.M. or SubQ in divided doses if necessary). For anticholinergic overdose with severe life-threatening symptoms, physostigmine 1-2 mg SubQ or I.V. slowly, may be given to reverse these effects (adult dose). Monitor for at least 48 hours.

Drug Interactions
Increased Effect/Toxicity: Pramlintide: Pramlintide may enhance the anticholinergic effect of anticholinergics; additive effects on reduced GI motility may occur.
Ethanol/Nutrition/Herb Interactions Ethanol: Avoid ethanol (may increase CNS depression).

Mechanism of Action Diphenoxylate inhibits excessive GI motility and GI propulsion; commercial preparations contain a subtherapeutic amount of atropine to discourage abuse

Pharmacodynamics/Kinetics

Atropine: See Atropine monograph.

Diphenoxylate:

Onset of action: Antidiarrheal: 45-60 minutes

Duration: Antidiarrheal: 3-4 hours

Absorption: Well absorbed

Metabolism: Extensively hepatic via ester hydrolysis to diphenoxylic acid (active)

Half-life elimination: Diphenoxylate: 2.5 hours; Diphenoxylic acid: 12-14 hours

Time to peak, serum: 2 hours

Excretion: Primarily feces (49% as unchanged drug and metabolites); urine (~14%, <1% as unchanged drug)

Dosage Oral:

Children 2-12 years (use with caution in young children due to variable responses): Liquid: Diphenoxylate 0.3-0.4 mg/kg/day in 4 divided doses until control achieved (maximum: 10 mg/day), then reduce dose as needed; some patients may be controlled on doses as low as 25% of the initial daily dose

Adults: Diphenoxylate 5 mg 4 times/day until control achieved (maximum: 20 mg/day), then reduce dose as needed; some patients may be controlled on doses of 5 mg/day

Administration If there is no response within 48 hours of continuous therapy, this medication is unlikely to be effective and should be discontinued; if chronic diarrhea is not improved symptomatically within 10 days at maximum dosage, control is unlikely with further use. Use of the liquid preparation is recommended in children <13 years of age; use plastic dropper provided when measuring liquid.

Monitoring Parameters Watch for signs of atropinism (dryness of skin and mucous membranes, tachycardia, thirst, flushing); monitor number and consistency of stools; observe for signs of toxicity, fluid and electrolyte loss, hypotension, and respiratory depression

Dosage Forms

Solution, oral: Diphenoxylate hydrochloride 2.5 mg and atropine sulfate 0.025 mg per 5 mL (5 mL, 10 mL, 60 mL)

Lomotil®: Diphenoxylate hydrochloride 2.5 mg and atropine sulfate 0.025 mg per 5 mL (60 mL) [contains alcohol 15%; cherry flavor]

Tablet: Diphenoxylate hydrochloride 2.5 mg and atropine sulfate 0.025 mg

Lomotil®, Lonox®: Diphenoxylate hydrochloride 2.5 mg and atropine sulfate 0.025 mg

♦ **Diphenylhydantoin** see Phenytoin on page 1361

Diphtheria and Tetanus Toxoid (dif THEER ee a & TET a nus TOKS oyd)

U.S. Brand Names Decavac™

Canadian Brand Names Td Adsorbed

Index Terms DT; Td; Tetanus and Diphtheria Toxoid

Pharmacologic Category Toxoid

Additional Appendix Information

Immunization Recommendations on page 1929

Use

Diphtheria and tetanus toxoids adsorbed for pediatric use (DT): Infants and children through 6 years of age: Active immunity against diphtheria and tetanus when pertussis vaccine is contraindicated

Tetanus and diphtheria toxoids adsorbed for adult use (Td) (Decavac™): Children ≥7 years of age and Adults: Active immunity against diphtheria and tetanus; tetanus prophylaxis in wound management

Pregnancy Risk Factor C

Pregnancy Implications The Advisory Committee on Immunization Practices (ACIP) recommends booster injections for previously vaccinated pregnant women who have not had Td vaccination within the past 10 years. Pregnant women who are not immunized or are only partially immunized should complete the primary series.

Lactation Excretion in breast milk unknown/use caution

Contraindications Hypersensitivity to diphtheria, tetanus toxoid, or any component of the formulation

Warnings/Precautions Do not confuse pediatric diphtheria and tetanus (DT) with adult tetanus and diphtheria (Td). Immediate treatment for anaphylactic/anaphylactoid reaction should be available during administration. Patients with a history of severe local reaction (Arthus-type) or temperature of >39.4°C (103°F) following a previous dose should not be given further routine or emergency doses of Td more frequently than every 10 years. Continue use with caution if Guillain-Barré syndrome occurs within 6 weeks of prior tetanus toxoid. For I.M. administration; use caution with history of bleeding disorders or anticoagulant therapy. Defer administration during moderate or severe illness (with or without fever) or during outbreaks of poliomyelitis. Immune response may be decreased in immunocompromised patients. Safety and efficacy of DT have not been established in children <6 weeks of age; Td should be administered to children ≥7 years of age and adults.

Adverse Reactions All serious adverse reactions must be reported to the U.S. Department of Health and Human Services (DHHS) Vaccine Adverse Event Reporting System (VAERS) 1-800-822-7967.

>10%: Local: Injection site (adolescents and adults): Pain (81% to 85%), redness (5% to 21%), swelling (10% to 16%)

Frequency not defined; reactions reported with adult and pediatric preparations

Cardiovascular: EEG disturbances

Central nervous system: Brachial neuritis, Guillain-Barré syndrome, dizziness, paresthesia, seizure

Dermatologic: Rash

Gastrointestinal: Nausea, vomiting

Local: Injection site: Persistent nodules; local reactions (erythema, cellulitis, swelling)

(Continued)

Diphtheria and Tetanus Toxoid *(Continued)*

Neuromuscular & skeletal: Arthralgia, myalgia

Miscellaneous: Allergic/anaphylactic reactions, Arthus-type hypersensitivity reaction (severe local reaction starting 2-8 hours after injection)

Note: Other neurological conditions reported in temporal association with vaccine administration have not been demonstrated to be causally related to the vaccine. These have included demyelinating CNS diseases, mononeuropathies, and encephalopathy.

Drug Interactions

Decreased Effect: The effect of the vaccine may be decreased by immunosuppressant medications or therapies (antimetabolites, alkylating agents, cytotoxic drugs, corticosteroids, irradiation); consider deferring vaccination for 3 months after immunosuppressant therapy is discontinued

Stability Store at 2°C to 8°C (35°F to 46°F); do not freeze. Discard if product has been frozen.

Dosage I.M.:

Infants and Children ≤6 years (DT): Primary immunization:

6 weeks to 1 year: Three 0.5 mL doses at least 4 weeks apart; administer a reinforcing dose 6-12 months after the third injection

1-6 years: Two 0.5 mL doses at least 4 weeks apart; reinforcing dose 6-12 months after second injection; if final dose is given after seventh birthday, use adult preparation

4-6 years (booster immunization): 0.5 mL; not necessary if the fourth dose was given after fourth birthday; routinely administer booster doses at 10-year intervals with the adult preparation

Children ≥7 years and Adults (Td):

Primary immunization: Patients previously not immunized should receive 2 primary doses of 0.5 mL each, given at an interval of 4-6 weeks; third (reinforcing) dose of 0.5 mL 6-12 months later

Booster immunization: 0.5 mL every 10 years; to be given to children 11-12 years of age if at least 5 years have elapsed since last dose of toxoid containing vaccine. Subsequent routine doses are not recommended more often than every 10 years. The ACIP prefers Tdap for use in adolescents 11-18 years; refer to Diphtheria and Tetanus Toxoids and Acellular Pertussis Vaccine monograph for additional information.

Tetanus prophylaxis in wound management; use of tetanus toxoid (Td) and/or tetanus immune globulin (TIG) depends upon the number of prior tetanus toxoid doses and type of wound: See table.

Tetanus Prophylaxis in Wound Management

Number of Prior Tetanus Toxoid Doses	Clean, Minor Wounds		All Other Wounds	
	Td[1]	TIG[2]	Td[1]	TIG[2]
Unknown or <3	Yes	No	Yes	Yes
≥3[3]	No[4]	No	No[5]	No

[1]Adult tetanus and diphtheria toxoids; use pediatric preparations (DT or DTP) if the patient is <7 years old.

[2]Tetanus immune globulin.

[3]If only three doses of fluid tetanus toxoid have been received, a fourth dose of toxoid, preferably an adsorbed toxoid, should be given.

[4]Yes, if >10 years since last dose.

[5]Yes, if >5 years since last dose.

Adapted from Report of the Committee on Infectious Diseases, American Academy of Pediatrics, Elk Grove Village, IL: American Academy of Pediatrics, 1986.

Administration For I.M. administration; prior to use, shake suspension well

Td: Administer in the deltoid muscle; do not inject in the gluteal area

DT: Administer in the anterolateral aspect of the thigh or the deltoid muscle; do not inject in the gluteal area

For patients at risk of hemorrhage following intramuscular injection, the ACIP recommends "it should be administered intramuscularly if, in the opinion of the physician familiar with the patients bleeding risk, the vaccine can be administered with reasonable safety by this route. If the patient receives antihemophilia or other similar therapy, intramuscular vaccination can be scheduled shortly after such therapy is administered. A fine needle (23 gauge or smaller) can be used for the vaccination and firm pressure applied to the site (without rubbing) for at least 2 minutes. The patient should be instructed concerning the risk of hematoma from the injection."

Additional Information Pediatric dosage form should only be used in patients ≤6 years of age. Federal law requires that the date of administration, the vaccine manufacturer, lot number of vaccine, and the administering person's name, title, and address be entered into the patient's permanent medical record.

Since protective tetanus and diphtheria antibodies decline with age, only 28% of persons >70 years of age in the U.S. are believed to be immune to tetanus, and most of the tetanus-induced deaths occur in people >60 years of age, it is advisable to offer Td especially to the elderly concurrent with their influenza and other immunization programs if history of vaccination is unclear; boosters should be given at 10-year intervals; earlier for wounds

DT contains higher proportions of diphtheria toxoid than Td.

Dosage Forms

Injection, suspension, adult:

Decavac™: Diphtheria 2 Lf units and tetanus 5 Lf units per 0.5 mL (0.5 mL) [latex free prefilled syringe; contains thimerosal]

Injection, suspension, pediatric [preservative free]: Diphtheria 6.7 Lf units and tetanus 5 Lf units per 0.5 mL (0.5 mL)

♦ **Diphtheria and Tetanus Toxoids and Acellular Pertussis Adsorbed, Hepatitis B (Recombinant) and Inactivated Poliovirus Vaccine Combined** *see* Diphtheria, Tetanus Toxoids, Acellular Pertussis, Hepatitis B (Recombinant), and Poliovirus (Inactivated) Vaccine *on page 521*

♦ **Diphtheria CRM$_{197}$ Protein** *see* Pneumococcal Conjugate Vaccine (7-Valent) *on page 1382*

♦ **Diphtheria CRM$_{197}$ Protein Conjugate** *see* Haemophilus b Conjugate Vaccine *on page 824*

Diphtheria, Tetanus Toxoids, Acellular Pertussis, Hepatitis B (Recombinant), and Poliovirus (Inactivated) Vaccine
(dif THEER ee a, TET a nus TOKS oyds, ay CEL yoo lar per TUS sis, hep a TYE tis bee ree KOM be nant, & POE lee oh VYE rus, in ak ti VAY ted vak SEEN)

U.S. Brand Names Pediarix™
Canadian Brand Names Pediarix™
Index Terms Diphtheria and Tetanus Toxoids and Acellular Pertussis Adsorbed, Hepatitis B (Recombinant) and Inactivated Poliovirus Vaccine Combined
Pharmacologic Category Vaccine
Use Combination vaccine for the active immunization against diphtheria, tetanus, pertussis, hepatitis B virus (all known subtypes), and poliomyelitis (caused by poliovirus types 1, 2, and 3)
Pregnancy Risk Factor C
Dosage I.M.: Children:
Immunization: 0.5 mL; repeat in 6-8 week intervals (preferably 8-week intervals) for a total of 3 doses. Vaccination usually begins at 2 months, but may be started as early as 6 weeks of age.
Use in children previously vaccinated with one or more component, and who are also scheduled to receive all vaccine components:
Hepatitis B vaccine: Infants born of HB$_s$Ag-negative mothers who received 1 dose of hepatitis B vaccine at birth may be given Pediarix™ (safety data limited); use in infants who received more than 1 dose of hepatitis B vaccine has not been studied. Infants who received 1 or more doses of hepatitis B vaccine (recombinant) may be given Pediarix™ to complete the hepatitis B series (safety and efficacy not established).
Diphtheria and tetanus toxoids, and acellular pertussis vaccine (DTaP): Infants previously vaccinated with 1 or 2 doses of Infanrix® may use Pediarix™ to complete the first 3 doses of the series (safety and efficacy not established); use of Pediarix™ to complete DTaP vaccination started with products other than Infanrix® is not recommended.
Inactivated polio vaccine (IPV): Infants previously vaccinated with 1 or 2 doses of IPV may use Pediarix™ to complete the first 3 doses of the series (safety and efficacy not established).
Additional Information Complete prescribing information for this medication should be consulted for additional detail.
Dosage Forms Injection, suspension [single-dose]: Diphtheria toxoid 25 Lf, tetanus toxoid 10 Lf, inactivated PT 25 mcg, FHA 25 mcg, pertactin 8 mcg, HB$_s$Ag 10 mcg, poliovirus type 1 40 DU, poliovirus type 2 8 DU, and poliovirus type 3 32 DU per 0.5 mL [contains neomycin sulfate ≤0.05 ng/0.5 mL, polymyxin B ≤0.01 ng/0.5 mL, and yeast protein ≤5%; packaged in vials or prefilled syringes; the needleless prefilled syringes contain dry natural latex rubber in the tip cap and plunger]

Diphtheria, Tetanus Toxoids, and Acellular Pertussis Vaccine
(dif THEER ee a, TET a nus TOKS oyds & ay CEL yoo lar per TUS sis vak SEEN)

U.S. Brand Names Adacel™; Boostrix®; Daptacel®; Infanrix®; Tripedia®
Canadian Brand Names Adacel™
Index Terms DTaP; dTpa; Tdap; Tetanus Toxoid, Reduced Diphtheria Toxoid, and Acellular Pertussis, Adsorbed
Pharmacologic Category Toxoid
Additional Appendix Information
Immunization Recommendations *on page 1929*
Use
Daptacel®, Infanrix®, Tripedia® (DTaP): Active immunization against diphtheria, tetanus, and pertussis from age 6 weeks through 6 years of age (prior to seventh birthday)
Adacel™, Boostrix® (Tdap): Active booster immunization against diphtheria, tetanus, and pertussis
Pregnancy Risk Factor C
Pregnancy Implications
Animal reproduction studies have not been conducted. It is not known whether the vaccine can cause fetal harm when administered to a pregnant woman or can affect reproductive capacity. Daptacel®, Infanrix®, and Tripedia® are not recommended for use in a pregnant woman or any patient ≥7 years of age. Although pregnancy itself is generally not considered a contraindication to Tdap (Adacel™, Boostrix®) vaccination, Td is preferred to Tdap when vaccination cannot be delayed during pregnancy. In order to help prevent pertussis exposure among infants, the use of Adacel™, is recommended in women of childbearing potential prior to pregnancy. Due to lack of information with Tdap, a pregnancy registry has been established for women who may become exposed to Boostrix® (888-825-5249) or Adacel™ (800-822-2463) while pregnant.
Medication Safety Issues
Carefully review product labeling to prevent inadvertent administration of Tdap when DTaP is indicated. Tdap contains lower amounts of diphtheria toxoid and some pertussis antigens than DTaP.
Tdap is not indicated for use in children <10 years of age
DTaP is not indicated for use in persons ≥7 years of age
Guidelines are available in case of inadvertent administration of these products; refer to ACIP recommendations, February 2006 available at http://www.cdc.gov/mmwr/preview/mmwrhtml/rr55e223a1.htm
(Continued)

Diphtheria, Tetanus Toxoids, and Acellular Pertussis Vaccine
(Continued)

Note:

DTaP: Diphtheria and tetanus toxoids and acellular pertussis vaccine

DTP: Diphtheria and tetanus toxoids and pertussis vaccine (unspecified pertussis antigens)

DTwP: Diphtheria and tetanus toxoids and whole-cell pertussis vaccine (no longer available on U.S. market)

Tdap: Tetanus toxoid, reduced diphtheria toxoid, and acellular pertussis vaccine

Contraindications Hypersensitivity to diphtheria, tetanus toxoids, pertussis, or any component of the formulation; history of any of the following effects from previous administration of pertussis-containing vaccine — progressive neurologic disorder, including infantile spasms, uncontrolled epilepsy or progressive epilepsy (postpone until condition stabilized); encephalopathy occurring within 7 days of administration and not attributable to another cause

Warnings/Precautions Defer administration during moderate or severe illness (with or without fever). Carefully consider use in patients with history of any of the following effects from previous administration of whole-cell DTP or acellular pertussis vaccine: Fever ≥105°F (40.5°C) within 48 hours of unknown cause; seizures with or without fever occurring within 3 days; persistent, inconsolable crying episodes lasting ≥3 hours and occurring within 48 hours; shock or collapse within 48 hours. Carefully consider use in patients with history of Guillain-Barré syndrome occurring within 6 weeks of a vaccine containing tetanus toxoid. Td or Tdap vaccines and emergency doses of Td vaccine should not be given more frequently than every 10 years in patients who have experienced a serious Arthus-type hypersensitivity reaction following a prior use of tetanus toxoid.

Use caution in patients with coagulation disorders (including thrombocytopenia) where intramuscular injections should not be used. Patients who are immunocompromised may have reduced response; may be used in patients with HIV infection. Defer immunization during outbreaks of poliomyelitis. Use caution in patients with history of seizure disorder, progressive neurologic disease, or conditions predisposing to seizures; ACIP and APP guidelines recommend deferring immunization until health status can be assessed and condition stabilized. Products may contain thimerosal; packaging may contain natural latex rubber. Immediate treatment for anaphylactic/anaphylactoid reaction should be available during vaccine use.

Adacel™ is formulated with the same antigens found in Daptacel®, but with reduced quantities of tetanus and pertussis. Booster doses of Td are generally recommended every 10 years, however, intervals as short as 2 years may used among healthcare providers, adults in contact with infants, or others in settings with increased risk for pertussis, including during pertussis outbreaks. Adacel™ is only approved to replace a single booster dose of Td; subsequent doses should use other tetanus-containing vaccines such as Td or tetanus toxoid. May be used in adults with history of pertussis. In addition to routine booster immunization, the ACIP also recommends the use of Adacel™ in adults with close contact to infants <12 months of age. Vaccination should be done >2 weeks prior to expected contact or in women of childbearing potential, prior to pregnancy. The ACIP also recommends the use of Adacel™ in healthcare providers with direct patient contact. Safety and efficacy have not been established in children <11 years or adults ≥65 years of age.

Boostrix® is formulated with the same antigens found in Infanrix®, but in reduced quantities. Safety and efficacy have not been established in patients <7 years or >18 years of age. Use of Adacel™ or Boostrix® in the primary immunization series or to complete the primary series has not been evaluated.

Daptacel®, Infanrix®, Tripedia®: Safety and efficacy in children <6 weeks of age or ≥7 years of age have not been established.

Adverse Reactions All serious adverse reactions must be reported to the U.S. Department of Health and Human Services (DHHS) Vaccine Adverse Event Reporting System (VAERS) 1-800-822-7967.

Daptacel®, Infanrix®, Tripedia® (incidence of erythema, swelling, and fever increases with successive doses):

Frequency not defined:

Central nervous system: Drowsiness, fever

Gastrointestinal: Appetite decreased, vomiting

Local: Pain, redness, swelling, tenderness

Miscellaneous: Prolonged or persistent crying, refusal to play

Postmarketing and/or case reports: Allergic reaction, anaphylactic reactions, cellulitis, cyanosis, diarrhea, ear pain, encephalopathy, erythema, hypersensitivity, hypotonia, hypotonic-hyporesponsive episode, idiopathic thrombocytopenic purpura, infantile spasm, injection site reaction (abscess, cellulitis, mass, nodule, rash), intussusception, irritability, limb swelling, lymphadenopathy, nausea, pruritus, rash, respiratory tract infection, seizure, screaming, somnolence, sudden infant death syndrome, thrombocytopenia, urticaria

Adacel™, Boostrix®: Note: Ranges presented, actual percent varies by product and age group

>10%:

Central nervous system: Fatigue, tiredness (24% to 37%; grade 3/severe: 1% to 4%), headache (34% to 44%; grade 3/severe: 2% to 4%), chills (8% to 15%; severe: <1%)

Gastrointestinal: Gastrointestinal symptoms, includes abdominal pain, diarrhea, nausea and/or vomiting (3% to 26%; grade 3/severe: ≤3%)

Local: Injection site pain (66% to 78%; grade 3/severe: 1% to 5%), arm circumference increased (28%; >40 mm: 0.5%), redness (21% to 25%; ≥50 mm: 2% to 4%), swelling (21%; ≥50 mm: 3%)

Neuromuscular & skeletal: Body aches/muscle weakness (22% to 30%; severe: 1%), soreness/swollen joints (9% to 11%; severe: <1%)

1% to 10%:

Central nervous system: Fever ≥38°C (≥100.4°F: 1% to 5%)

Dermatologic: Rash (2% to 3%)

Miscellaneous: Lymph node swelling (7%; severe: <1%)

Postmarketing and/or case reports: Arthralgia, back pain, bruising, diabetes mellitus, encephalitis, exanthema, facial palsy, Henoch-Schönlein purpura, injection site reaction (induration, inflammation, mass, nodule, warmth), limb swelling (extensive), lymphadenitis, lymphadenopathy, myalgia, myocarditis, nerve compression, paresthesia, pruritus, seizure, sterile abscess, urticaria

Additional adverse reactions associated with diphtheria, tetanus, and/or pertussis antigens: Arthus hypersensitivity, brachial neuritis, GBS, peripheral/central mononeuropathies

Drug Interactions

Increased Effect/Toxicity: Increased bleeding/bruising with anticoagulants.

Decreased Effect: Vaccine effect may be decreased with corticosteroids and immunosuppressant agents. Consider deferring vaccine for 1 month after agent is discontinued.

Stability Refrigerate at 2°C to 8°C (35°F to 46°F); do not freeze.

Mechanism of Action Promotes active immunity to diphtheria, tetanus, and pertussis by inducing production of specific antibodies.

Dosage

Primary immunization: Children 6 weeks to <7 years. I.M.: **Note:** Whenever possible, the same product should be used for all doses. Interruption of recommended schedule does not require starting the series over; a delay between doses should not interfere with final immunity.

Daptacel®: 0.5 mL per dose, total of 4 doses administered as follows (data insufficient to recommend a fifth dose):

Three doses, usually given at 2-, 4-, and 6 months of age; may be given as early as 6 weeks of age and repeated every 6-8 weeks

Fourth dose: Given at ~15-20 months of age, but at least 6 months after third dose

Infanrix®, Tripedia®: 0.5 mL per dose, total of 5 doses administered as follows:

Three doses, usually given at 2-, 4-, and 6 months of age; may be given as early as 6 weeks of age and repeated every 4-8 weeks

Fourth dose: Given at ~15-20 months of age, but at least 6 months after third dose

Fifth dose: Given at 5-6 years of age, prior to starting school or kindergarten; if the fourth dose is given at ≥4 years of age, the fifth dose may be omitted

Booster immunization:

ACIP recommendations:

Adolescents 11-18 years: I.M.: 0.5 mL. A single dose of Tdap should be given instead of Td in adolescents who have completed the recommended childhood DTP/DTaP series and have not received Td or Tdap; preferred age of vaccination with Tdap is 11-12 years. Adolescents who received Td but not Tdap and who have completed the recommended childhood DTP/DTaP series are encouraged to receive Tdap; an interval of at least 5 years between Td and Tdap is recommended, but lesser intervals may be used if the benefit outweighs the risk.

Adults 19-64 years (Adacel™): I.M.: 0.5 mL. A single dose should be given instead of Td in adults if they received their last dose of Td ≥10 years previous. Shorter intervals (as short as 2 years) may used among healthcare providers, adults in contact with infants, or others in settings with increased risk for pertussis, including during pertussis outbreaks. Adacel™ should only be used to replace a single booster dose of Td.

Manufacturer's labeling:

Children 10-18 years (Boostrix®): I.M.: 0.5 mL as a single dose, administered 5 years after last dose of DTwP or DTaP vaccine.

Children ≥11 years and Adults ≤64 years (Adacel™): I.M.: 0.5 mL as a single dose, administered 5 years after last dose of DTwP or DTaP vaccine.

Wound management: Adacel™ (in patients 11-64 years of age) or Boostrix® (in patients 10-18 years of age) may be used as an alternative to Td vaccine when a tetanus toxoid-containing vaccine is needed for wound management, and in whom the pertussis component is also indicated. Td vaccine is the preferred agent in children ≥7 years and adults.

ACIP recommendations: ACIP prefers Tdap for adolescents 11-18 years requiring a tetanus toxoid product and who were vaccinated against tetanus ≥5 years earlier. Adolescents who completed the primary 3 dose series containing tetanus toxoid <5 years earlier are protected against tetanus and do not need a tetanus toxoid vaccine as part of wound management. The ACIP prefers Adacel™ for use in adults <65 years requiring a tetanus toxoid product and who were vaccinated against tetanus ≥5 years earlier if they have not previously received Tdap.

Administration Shake suspension well.

Adacel™, Boostrix®: Administer only I.M. in deltoid muscle of upper arm.

Daptacel®, Infanrix®, Tripedia®: Administer only I.M. in anterolateral aspect of thigh or deltoid muscle of upper arm.

For patients at risk of hemorrhage following intramuscular injection, the ACIP recommends "it should be administered intramuscularly if, in the opinion of the physician familiar with the patients bleeding risk, the vaccine can be administered with reasonable safety by this route. If the patient receives antihemophilia or other similar therapy, intramuscular vaccination can be scheduled shortly after such therapy is administered. A fine needle (23 gauge or smaller) can be used for the vaccination and firm pressure applied to the site (without rubbing) for at least 2 minutes. The patient should be instructed concerning the risk of hematoma from the injection."

Additional Information DTaP may be given for the fourth and fifth doses in children who started immunization with DTP vaccine. In patients who cannot be given pertussis vaccine, DT for pediatric use should be given to complete the series.

TriHIBit® is Tripedia® vaccine used to reconstitute ActHIB® (*Haemophilus* b conjugate) vaccine. The combination can be used for the DTaP dose given at 15-18 months when Tripedia® was used for the initial doses and a primary series of HIB vaccine has been given. (Continued)

Diphtheria, Tetanus Toxoids, and Acellular Pertussis Vaccine *(Continued)*

Adacel™ is formulated with the same antigens found in Daptacel® but with reduced quantities of pertussis and tetanus. It is intended for use as a booster dose in children and adults, 11-64 years of age, and **not** for primary immunization.

Boostrix® is formulated with the same antigens found in Infanrix® but in reduced quantities. It is intended for use as a booster dose in children 10-18 years, and is **not** for primary immunization.

The ACIP considers Adacel™ and Boostrix® to be interchangeable when administered to adolescents for childhood vaccination.

Acetaminophen or ibuprofen may reduce or prevent fever; the child's medical record should document that the small risk of postvaccination seizure and the benefits of the pertussis vaccination were discussed with the patient; parents or guardians should be questioned prior to administration of vaccine as to any adverse reactions from previous dose. Provide Vaccine Information Materials, as required by National Childhood Vaccine Injury Act of 1986, prior to immunization.

Federal law requires that the date of administration, the vaccine manufacturer, lot number of vaccine, and the administering person's name, title and address be entered into the patient's permanent medical record.

Dosage Forms Injection, suspension:

Adacel™: Diphtheria 2 Lf units, tetanus 5 Lf units, and acellular pertussis 2.5 mcg per 0.5 mL (0.5 mL) [vial stopper is latex free]

Boostrix®: Diphtheria 2.5 Lf units, tetanus 5 Lf units, and acellular pertussis 8 mcg per 0.5 mL (0.5 mL) [available in vial and prefilled syringe; preservative free; contains polysorbate 80; syringe cap and rubber plunger contain natural latex rubber]

Daptacel®: Diphtheria 15 Lf units, tetanus 5 Lf units, and acellular pertussis 10 mcg per 0.5 mL (0.5 mL) [vial stopper contains natural latex rubber]

Infanrix®: Diphtheria 25 Lf units, tetanus 10 Lf units, and acellular pertussis 25 mcg per 0.5 mL (0.5 mL) [available in vial and prefilled syringe; contains polysorbate 80; syringe cap and rubber plunger contain natural latex rubber]

Tripedia®: Diphtheria 6.7 Lf units, tetanus 5 Lf units, and acellular pertussis 46.8 mcg per 0.5 mL (7.5 mL) [contains polysorbate 80 and trace amounts of thimerosal; vial stopper contains natural latex rubber]

Note: Tripedia® vaccine is also used to reconstitute ActHIB® to prepare TriHIBit® vaccine (diphtheria, tetanus toxoids, and acellular pertussis and *Haemophilus influenzae* b conjugate vaccine combination)

Diphtheria, Tetanus Toxoids, and Acellular Pertussis Vaccine and *Haemophilus influenzae* b Conjugate Vaccine

(dif THEER ee a, TET a nus TOKS oyds & ay CEL yoo lar per TUS sis vak SEEN & hem OF fi lus in floo EN za bee KON joo gate vak SEEN)

U.S. Brand Names TriHIBit®

Index Terms *Haemophilus influenzae* b Conjugate Vaccine and Diphtheria, Tetanus Toxoids, and Acellular Pertussis Vaccine

Pharmacologic Category Toxoid; Vaccine, Inactivated Bacteria

Use Active immunization of children 15-18 months of age for prevention of diphtheria, tetanus, pertussis, and invasive disease caused by *H. influenzae* type b

Dosage Children >15 months of age: I.M.: 0.5 mL (as part of a general vaccination schedule; see individual vaccines). Vaccine should be used within 30 minutes of reconstitution.

Additional Information Complete prescribing information for this medication should be consulted for additional detail.

Dosage Forms Injection, suspension: 5 Lf units tetanus toxoid, 6.7 Lf units diphtheria toxoid, 46.8 mcg pertussis antigens, and 10 mcg *H. influenzae* type b purified capsular polysaccharide per 0.5 mL (0.5 mL) [The combination of Tripedia® vaccine used to reconstitute ActHIB® forms TriHIBit®]

♦ **Diphtheria Toxoid Conjugate** *see Haemophilus b Conjugate Vaccine on page 824*

♦ **Dipivalyl Epinephrine** *see Dipivefrin on page 524*

Dipivefrin (dye PI ve frin)

U.S. Brand Names Propine®

Canadian Brand Names Ophtho-Dipivefrin™; PMS-Dipivefrin; Propine®

Index Terms Dipivalyl Epinephrine; Dipivefrin Hydrochloride; DPE

Pharmacologic Category Alpha/Beta Agonist; Ophthalmic Agent, Antiglaucoma; Ophthalmic Agent, Vasoconstrictor

Additional Appendix Information

Glaucoma Drug Therapy *on page 2050*

Use Reduces elevated intraocular pressure in chronic open-angle glaucoma; also used to treat ocular hypertension, low tension, and secondary glaucomas

Pregnancy Risk Factor B

Dosage Adults: Ophthalmic: Instill 1 drop every 12 hours into the eyes

Additional Information Complete prescribing information for this medication should be consulted for additional detail.

Dosage Forms Solution, ophthalmic, as hydrochloride: 0.1% (5 mL, 10 mL, 15 mL) [contains benzalkonium chloride]

Propine®: 0.1% (5 mL [DSC], 10 mL, 15 mL) [contains benzalkonium chloride]

♦ **Dipivefrin Hydrochloride** *see Dipivefrin on page 524*

♦ **Diprivan®** see Propofol on page 1441
♦ **Diprolene®** see Betamethasone on page 211
♦ **Diprolene® AF** see Betamethasone on page 211
♦ **Diprolene® Glycol (Can)** see Betamethasone on page 211
♦ **Dipropylacetic Acid** see Valproic Acid and Derivatives on page 1767
♦ **Diprosone® (Can)** see Betamethasone on page 211

Dipyridamole (dye peer ID a mole)

U.S. Brand Names Persantine®
Canadian Brand Names Apo-Dipyridamole FC®; Persantine®
Pharmacologic Category Antiplatelet Agent; Vasodilator
Use
    Oral: Used with warfarin to decrease thrombosis in patients after artificial heart valve replacement
    I.V.: Diagnostic agent in CAD
Pregnancy Risk Factor B
Pregnancy Implications Teratogenic effects were not observed in animal studies.
Lactation Enters breast milk/use caution
Medication Safety Issues
    Sound-alike/look-alike issues:
        Dipyridamole may be confused with disopyramide
        Persantine® may be confused with Periactin®, Permitil®
Contraindications Hypersensitivity to dipyridamole or any component of the formulation
Warnings/Precautions Use caution in patients with hypotension and severe cardiac disease. Use caution in patients on other antiplatelet agents or anticoagulation. Severe adverse reactions have occurred rarely with I.V. administration. Use the I.V. form with caution in patients with bronchospastic disease or unstable angina. Have aminophylline ready in case of urgency or emergency with I.V. use. Safety and efficacy in children <12 years of age have not been established.
Adverse Reactions
    Oral:
    >10%: Dizziness (14%)
    1% to 10%:
        Central nervous system: Headache (2%)
        Dermatologic: Rash (2%)
        Gastrointestinal: Abdominal distress (6%)
    Frequency not defined: Diarrhea, vomiting, flushing, pruritus, angina pectoris, liver dysfunction
    Postmarketing and/or case reports: Alopecia, arthritis, cholelithiasis, dyspepsia, fatigue, hepatitis, hypersensitivity reaction, hypotension, larynx edema, malaise, myalgia, nausea, palpitation, paresthesia, tachycardia, thrombocytopenia
    I.V.:
    >10%:
        Cardiovascular: Exacerbation of angina pectoris (20%)
        Central nervous system: Dizziness (12%), headache (12%)
    1% to 10%:
        Cardiovascular: Hypotension (5%), hypertension (2%), blood pressure lability (2%), ECG abnormalities (ST-T changes, extrasystoles; 5% to 8%), pain (3%), tachycardia (3%)
        Central nervous system: Flushing (3%), fatigue (1%)
        Gastrointestinal: Nausea (5%)
        Neuromuscular & skeletal: Paresthesia (1%)
        Respiratory: Dyspnea (3%)
    <1% (Limited to important or life-threatening): Abdominal pain, abnormal coordination, allergic reaction (pruritus, rash, urticaria), appetite increased, arrhythmia (ventricular tachycardia, bradycardia, AV block, SVT, atrial fibrillation, asystole), arthralgia, asthenia, back pain, breast pain, bronchospasm, cardiomyopathy, cough, depersonalization, diaphoresis, dry mouth, dysgeusia, dyspepsia, dysphagia, earache, ECG abnormalities (unspecified), edema, eructation, flatulence, hypertonia, hyperventilation, injection site reaction, intermittent claudication leg cramping, malaise, MI, myalgia, orthostatic hypotension, palpitation, perineal pain, pharyngitis, pleural pain, renal pain, rhinitis, rigor, syncope, tenesmus, thirst, tinnitus, tremor, vertigo, vision abnormalities, vomiting
Overdosage/Toxicology Symptoms include hypotension and peripheral vasodilation. Dialysis is not effective. Treatment includes fluids and vasopressors although hypotension is often transient.
Drug Interactions
    Increased Effect/Toxicity: Adenosine blood levels and pharmacologic effects are increased with dipyridamole; consider reduced doses of adenosine.
    Decreased Effect: Decreased vasodilation from I.V. dipyridamole when given to patients taking theophylline. Theophylline may reduce the pharmacologic effects of dipyridamole (hold theophylline preparations for 36-48 hours before dipyridamole facilitated stress test). Dipyridamole may counteract effect of cholinesterase inhibitor and may aggravate myasthenia gravis.
Ethanol/Nutrition/Herb Interactions Herb/Nutraceutical: Avoid cat's claw, dong quai, evening primrose, feverfew, garlic, ginger, ginkgo, red clover, horse chestnut, green tea, ginseng (all have additional antiplatelet activity).
Stability I.V.: Store between 15°C to 25°C (59°F to 77°F). Do not freeze, protect from light. Prior to administration, dilute to a ≥1:2 ratio in NS, 1/2NS, or D$_5$W. Total volume should be ~20-50 mL.
Mechanism of Action Inhibits the activity of adenosine deaminase and phosphodiesterase, which causes an accumulation of adenosine, adenine nucleotides, and cyclic AMP; these mediators then inhibit platelet aggregation and may cause vasodilation; may also stimulate release of prostacyclin or PGD$_2$; causes coronary vasodilation
(Continued)

Dipyridamole *(Continued)*

Pharmacodynamics/Kinetics
Absorption: Readily, but variable
Distribution: Adults: V_d: 2-3 L/kg
Protein binding: 91% to 99%
Metabolism: Hepatic
Half-life elimination: Terminal: 10-12 hours
Time to peak, serum: 2-2.5 hours
Excretion: Feces (as glucuronide conjugates and unchanged drug)

Dosage
Oral: Children ≥12 years and Adults: Adjunctive therapy for prophylaxis of thromboembolism with cardiac valve replacement: 75-100 mg 4 times/day
I.V.: Adults: Evaluation of coronary artery disease: 0.14 mg/kg/minute for 4 minutes; maximum dose: 60 mg

Dietary Considerations
Should be taken with water 1 hour before meals.

Administration
I.V.: Infuse diluted solution over 4 minutes; following dipyridamole infusion, inject thallium-201 within 5 minutes. **Note:** Aminophylline should be available for urgent/emergent use; dosing of 50-100 mg (range: 50-250 mg) IVP over 30-60 seconds.
Tablet: Administer with water 1 hour before meals.

Monitoring Parameters
Blood pressure, heart rate, ECG (stress test)

Dosage Forms
Injection, solution: 5 mg/mL (2 mL, 10 mL)
Tablet: 25 mg, 50 mg, 75 mg
Persantine®: 25 mg, 50 mg, 75 mg

Extemporaneous Preparations
A 10 mg/mL oral suspension has been made using four 25 mg tablets and purified water USP qs ad to 10 mL; expected stability is 3 days. Dipyridamole 10 mg/mL was stable for up to 60 days at 5°C and 25°C in 1:1 mixtures of Ora-Sweet® and Ora-Plus®, Ora-Sweet® SF and Ora-Plus® and in cherry syrup
Allen LV and Erickson III MA, "Stability of Baclofen, Captopril, Diltiazem, Hydrochloride, Dipyridamole, and Flecainide Acetate in Extemporaneously Compounded Oral Liquids," *Am J Health Syst Pharm*, 1996, 53:2179-84.
Nahata MC and Hipple TF, *Pediatric Drug Formulations*, 2nd ed, Cincinnati, OH: Harvey Whitney Books Co, 1992.

♦ **Dipyridamole and Aspirin** see Aspirin and Dipyridamole *on page 163*

Dirithromycin *(dye RITH roe mye sin)*

U.S. Brand Names
Dynabac® [DSC]

Pharmacologic Category
Antibiotic, Macrolide

Use
Treatment of mild to moderate upper and lower respiratory tract infections due to *Moraxella catarrhalis*, *Streptococcus pneumoniae*, *Legionella pneumophila*, *H. influenzae*, or *S. pyogenes*, ie, acute exacerbation of chronic bronchitis, secondary bacterial infection of acute bronchitis, community-acquired pneumonia, pharyngitis/tonsillitis, and uncomplicated infections of the skin and skin structure due to *Staphylococcus aureus*

Pregnancy Risk Factor
C

Medication Safety Issues
Sound-alike/look-alike issues:
Dynabac® may be confused with Dynacin®, DynaCirc®, Dynapen®

Dosage
Adults: Oral: 500 mg once daily for 5-14 days (14 days required for treatment of community-acquired pneumonia due to *Legionella*, *Mycoplasma*, or *S. pneumoniae*; 10 days is recommended for treatment of *S. pyogenes* pharyngitis/tonsillitis)

Dosing adjustment in renal impairment: None necessary
Dosing adjustment in hepatic impairment: None needed in mild dysfunction; not studied in moderate to severe dysfunction

Additional Information
Complete prescribing information for this medication should be consulted for additional detail.

Dosage Forms
[DSC] = Discontinued product
Tablet, enteric coated: 250 mg [DSC]

♦ **Disalicylic Acid** see Salsalate *on page 1544*
♦ **Disodium Cromoglycate** see Cromolyn *on page 423*
♦ **Disodium Thiosulfate Pentahydrate** see Sodium Thiosulfate *on page 1584*
♦ ***d*-Isoephedrine Hydrochloride** see Pseudoephedrine *on page 1454*

Disopyramide *(dye soe PEER a mide)*

U.S. Brand Names
Norpace®; Norpace® CR

Canadian Brand Names
Norpace®; Rythmodan®; Rythmodan®-LA

Index Terms
Disopyramide Phosphate

Pharmacologic Category
Antiarrhythmic Agent, Class Ia

Use
Suppression and prevention of unifocal and multifocal atrial and premature, ventricular premature complexes, coupled ventricular tachycardia; effective in the conversion of atrial fibrillation, atrial flutter, and paroxysmal atrial tachycardia to normal sinus rhythm and prevention of the recurrence of these arrhythmias after conversion by other methods

Unlabeled/Investigational Use
Hypertrophic obstructive cardiomyopathy (HOCM)

Pregnancy Risk Factor
C

Lactation
Enters breast milk/compatible

Medication Safety Issues
Sound-alike/look-alike issues:
Disopyramide may be confused with desipramine, dipyridamole

Norpace® may be confused with Norpramin®

Contraindications Hypersensitivity to disopyramide or any component of the formulation; cardiogenic shock; pre-existing second- or third-degree heart block (except in patients with a functioning artificial pacemaker); congenital QT syndrome; sick sinus syndrome

Warnings/Precautions Monitor and adjust dose to prevent QT_c prolongation. Avoid concurrent use with other medications that prolong QT interval or decrease myocardial contractility. Correct hypokalemia before initiating therapy; may worsen toxicity. Watch for proarrhythmic effects. **[U.S. Boxed Warning]: In the Cardiac Arrhythmia Suppression Trial (CAST), recent (>6 days but <2 years ago) myocardial infarction patients with asymptomatic, nonlife-threatening ventricular arrhythmias did not benefit and may have been harmed by attempts to suppress the arrhythmia with flecainide or encainide. An increased mortality or nonfatal cardiac arrest rate (7.7%) was seen in the active treatment group compared with patients in the placebo group (3%). The applicability of the CAST results to other populations is unknown. Antiarrhythmic agents should be reserved for patients with life-threatening ventricular arrhythmias.** May precipitate or exacerbate CHF. Due to significant anticholinergic effects, do not use in patients with urinary retention, BPH, glaucoma, or myasthenia gravis. Reduce dosage in renal or hepatic impairment. The extended release form is not recommended for Cl_{cr} <40 mL/minute. In patients with atrial fibrillation or flutter, block the AV node before initiating. Use caution in Wolff-Parkinson-White syndrome or bundle branch block. Monitor closely for hypotension during the initiation of therapy.

Adverse Reactions The most common adverse effects are related to cholinergic blockade. The most serious adverse effects of disopyramide are hypotension and CHF.

>10%:
Gastrointestinal: Xerostomia (32%), constipation (11%)
Genitourinary: Urinary hesitancy (14% to 23%)

1% to 10%:
Cardiovascular: CHF, hypotension, cardiac conduction disturbance, edema, syncope, chest pain
Central nervous system: Fatigue, headache, malaise, dizziness, nervousness
Dermatologic: Rash, generalized dermatoses, pruritus
Endocrine & metabolic: Hypokalemia, elevated cholesterol, elevated triglycerides
Gastrointestinal: Dry throat, nausea, abdominal distension, flatulence, abdominal bloating, anorexia, diarrhea, vomiting, weight gain
Genitourinary: Urinary retention, urinary frequency, urinary urgency, impotence (1% to 3%)
Neuromuscular & skeletal: Muscle weakness, muscular pain
Ocular: Blurred vision, dry eyes
Respiratory: Dyspnea

<1% (Limited to important or life-threatening): Agranulocytosis, AV block, cholestatic jaundice, depression, dysuria, creatinine increased, gynecomastia, hepatotoxicity, hypoglycemia, BUN increased, insomnia, new or worsened arrhythmia (proarrhythmic effect), paresthesia, psychotic reaction, respiratory distress, thrombocytopenia, transaminases increased. Rare cases of lupus have been reported (generally in patients previously receiving procainamide), peripheral neuropathy, psychosis, toxic cutaneous blisters.

Overdosage/Toxicology Has a low toxic therapeutic ratio and may easily produce fatal intoxication (acute toxic dose: 1 g in adults). Symptoms include sinus bradycardia, sinus node arrest or asystole; PR, QRS, or QT interval prolongation; torsade de pointes (polymorphous ventricular tachycardia) and depressed myocardial contractility; depressed myocardium, along with alpha-adrenergic or ganglionic blockade, may result in hypotension and pulmonary edema. Other effects are anticholinergic (dry mouth, dilated pupils, and delirium) as well as seizures, coma and respiratory arrest.

Treatment is primarily symptomatic and effects usually respond to conventional therapies (fluids, positioning, vasopressors, anticonvulsants, antiarrhythmics). **Note:** Do not use other type Ia or Ic antiarrhythmic agents to treat ventricular tachycardia. Sodium bicarbonate may treat wide QRS intervals or hypotension. Markedly impaired conduction or high degree AV block, unresponsive to bicarbonate, indicates consideration of a pacemaker.

Drug Interactions
Cytochrome P450 Effect: Substrate of CYP3A4 (major)
Increased Effect/Toxicity: Disopyramide may increase the effects/toxicity of anticholinergics, beta-blockers, flecainide, procainamide, quinidine, or propafenone. Digoxin and quinidine serum concentrations may be increased by disopyramide.

CYP3A4 inhibitors may increase the levels/effects of disopyramide. Example inhibitors include azole antifungals, clarithromycin, diclofenac, doxycycline, erythromycin, imatinib, isoniazid, nefazodone, nicardipine, propofol, protease inhibitors, quinidine, telithromycin, and verapamil.

Disopyramide effect/toxicity may be additive with drugs which may prolong the QT interval - amiodarone, amitriptyline, bepridil, cisapride (use is contraindicated), disopyramide, erythromycin, haloperidol, imipramine, pimozide, quinidine, sotalol, and thioridazine. In addition concurrent use with sparfloxacin, gatifloxacin, and moxifloxacin may result in additional prolongation of the QT interval; concurrent use is contraindicated.
Decreased Effect: CYP3A4 inducers may decrease the levels/effects of disopyramide; example inducers include aminoglutethimide, carbamazepine, nafcillin, nevirapine, phenobarbital, phenytoin, and rifamycins.

Ethanol/Nutrition/Herb Interactions
Ethanol: Avoid ethanol (may increase CNS depression).
Herb/Nutraceutical: St John's wort may decrease disopyramide levels. Avoid ephedra (may worsen arrhythmia).

Stability Extemporaneously prepared suspension is stable for 4 weeks refrigerated.
Mechanism of Action Class Ia antiarrhythmic: Decreases myocardial excitability and conduction velocity; reduces disparity in refractory between normal and infarcted myocardium; possesses anticholinergic, peripheral vasoconstrictive, and negative inotropic effects
Pharmacodynamics/Kinetics
Onset of action: 0.5-3.5 hours
(Continued)

Disopyramide *(Continued)*

Duration: 1.5-8.5 hours

Absorption: 60% to 83%

Protein binding (concentration dependent): 20% to 60%

Metabolism: Hepatic to inactive metabolites

Half-life elimination: Adults: 4-10 hours; prolonged with hepatic or renal impairment

Excretion: Urine (40% to 60% as unchanged drug); feces (10% to 15%)

Dosage Oral:

Children:

<1 year: 10-30 mg/kg/24 hours in 4 divided doses

1-4 years: 10-20 mg/kg/24 hours in 4 divided doses

4-12 years: 10-15 mg/kg/24 hours in 4 divided doses

12-18 years: 6-15 mg/kg/24 hours in 4 divided doses

Adults:

<50 kg: 100 mg every 6 hours or 200 mg every 12 hours (controlled release)

>50 kg: 150 mg every 6 hours or 300 mg every 12 hours (controlled release); if no response, increase to 200 mg every 6 hours. Maximum dose required for patients with severe refractory ventricular tachycardia is 400 mg every 6 hours.

Hypertrophic obstructive cardiomyopathy (unlabeled use): Initial: Controlled release: 200 mg twice daily. If symptoms do not improve, increase by 100 mg/day at 2-week intervals to a maximum daily dose of 600 mg.

Elderly: Dose with caution, starting at the lower end of dosing range

Dosing adjustment in renal impairment: 100 mg (nonsustained release) given at the following intervals, based on creatinine clearance (mL/minute):

Cl_{cr} 30-40 mL/minute: Administer every 8 hours

Cl_{cr} 15-30 mL/minute: Administer every 12 hours

Cl_{cr} <15 mL/minute: Administer every 24 hours

or alter the dose as follows:

Cl_{cr} 30-<40 mL/minute: Reduce dose 50%

Cl_{cr} 15-30 mL/minute: Reduce dose 75%

Dialysis: Not dialyzable (0% to 5%) by hemo- or peritoneal methods; supplemental dose is not necessary.

Dosing interval in hepatic impairment: 100 mg every 6 hours or 200 mg every 12 hours (controlled release)

Dietary Considerations Should be taken on an empty stomach.

Administration Do not break or chew controlled release capsules. Administer around-the-clock to Administer around-the-clock rather than 4 times/day (ie, 12-6-12-6, not 9-1-5-9) to promote less variation in peak and trough serum levels

Monitoring Parameters ECG, blood pressure, urinary retention, CNS anticholinergic effects (confusion, agitation, hallucinations, etc)

Reference Range

Therapeutic concentration:

Atrial arrhythmias: 2.8-3.2 mcg/mL

Ventricular arrhythmias 3.3-7.5 mcg/mL

Toxic concentration: >7 mcg/mL

Dosage Forms

Capsule (Norpace®): 100 mg, 150 mg

Capsule, controlled release (Norpace® CR): 100 mg, 150 mg

Extemporaneous Preparations Extemporaneous suspensions in cherry syrup (1 mg/mL and 10 mg/mL) are stable for 4 weeks in amber glass bottles stored at 5°C, 30°C, or at room temperature; shake well before use; do not use extended release capsules for this suspension

Mathur LK, Lai PK, and Shively CD, "Stability of Disopyramide Phosphate in Cherry Syrup," *Am J Hosp Pharm*, 1982, 39(2):309-10.

♦ **Disopyramide Phosphate** *see* Disopyramide *on page 526*

Disulfiram *(dye SUL fi ram)*

U.S. Brand Names Antabuse®

Pharmacologic Category Aldehyde Dehydrogenase Inhibitor

Use Management of chronic alcoholism

Pregnancy Risk Factor C

Medication Safety Issues

Sound-alike/look-alike issues:

Disulfiram may be confused with Diflucan®

Antabuse® may be confused with Anturane®

Dosage Adults: Oral: Do not administer until the patient has abstained from ethanol for at least 12 hours

Initial: 500 mg/day as a single dose for 1-2 weeks; maximum daily dose is 500 mg

Average maintenance dose: 250 mg/day; range: 125-500 mg; duration of therapy is to continue until the patient is fully recovered socially and a basis for permanent self control has been established; maintenance therapy may be required for months or even years

Additional Information Complete prescribing information for this medication should be consulted for additional detail.

Dosage Forms Tablet: 250 mg

♦ **Dithioglycerol** *see* Dimercaprol *on page 512*

♦ **Dithranol** *see* Anthralin *on page 132*

♦ **Ditropan®** *see* Oxybutynin *on page 1285*

♦ **Ditropan® XL** *see* Oxybutynin *on page 1285*

♦ **Diuril®** *see* Chlorothiazide *on page 349*

♦ **Divalproex Sodium** *see* Valproic Acid and Derivatives *on page 1767*

- **Dixarit® (Can)** *see* Clonidine *on page 399*
- **5071-1DL(6)** *see* Megestrol *on page 1071*
- **dl-Alpha Tocopherol** *see* Vitamin E *on page 1794*
- **4-DMDR** *see* Idarubicin *on page 878*
- **DMSA** *see* Succimer *on page 1604*
- **DNA-Derived Humanized Monoclonal Antibody** *see* Alemtuzumab *on page 63*
- **DNase** *see* Dornase Alfa *on page 541*
- **DNR** *see* DAUNOrubicin Hydrochloride *on page 462*
- **Doan's® [OTC]** *see* Magnesium Salicylate *on page 1051*
- **Doan's® Extra Strength [OTC]** *see* Magnesium Salicylate *on page 1051*

DOBUTamine (doe BYOO ta meen)

Canadian Brand Names Dobutamine Injection, USP; Dobutrex®
Index Terms Dobutamine Hydrochloride
Pharmacologic Category Adrenergic Agonist Agent
Additional Appendix Information
    Hemodynamic Support, Intravenous *on page 1885*
Use Short-term management of patients with cardiac decompensation
Unlabeled/Investigational Use Positive inotropic agent for use in myocardial dysfunction of sepsis
Pregnancy Risk Factor B
Lactation Excretion in breast milk unknown
Medication Safety Issues
    Sound-alike/look-alike issues:
        DOBUTamine may be confused with DOPamine
Contraindications Hypersensitivity to dobutamine or sulfites (some contain sodium metabisulfate), or any component of the formulation; idiopathic hypertrophic subaortic stenosis (IHSS)
Warnings/Precautions May increase heart rate. Patients with atrial fibrillation may experience an increase in ventricular response. An increase in blood pressure is more common, but occasionally a patient may become hypotensive. May exacerbate ventricular ectopy. If needed, correct hypovolemia first to optimize hemodynamics. Ineffective in the presence of mechanical obstruction such as severe aortic stenosis. Use caution post-MI (can increase myocardial oxygen demand). Use cautiously in the elderly starting at lower end of the dosage range.
Adverse Reactions Incidence of adverse events is not always reported.

    Cardiovascular: Increased heart rate, increased blood pressure, increased ventricular ectopic activity, hypotension, premature ventricular beats (5%, dose related), anginal pain (1% to 3%), nonspecific chest pain (1% to 3%), palpitation (1% to 3%)
    Central nervous system: Fever (1% to 3%), headache (1% to 3%), paresthesia
    Endocrine & metabolic: Slight decrease in serum potassium
    Gastrointestinal: Nausea (1% to 3%)
    Hematologic: Thrombocytopenia (isolated cases)
    Local: Phlebitis, local inflammatory changes and pain from infiltration, cutaneous necrosis (isolated cases)
    Neuromuscular & skeletal: Mild leg cramps
    Respiratory: Dyspnea (1% to 3%)
Overdosage/Toxicology Symptoms include fatigue, nervousness, tachycardia, hypertension, and arrhythmias. Reduce rate of administration or discontinue infusion until condition stabilizes.
Drug Interactions
    Increased Effect/Toxicity: General anesthetics (eg, halothane or cyclopropane) and usual doses of dobutamine have resulted in ventricular arrhythmias in animals. Bretylium and may potentiate dobutamine's effects. Beta-blockers (nonselective ones) may increase hypertensive effect; avoid concurrent use. Cocaine may cause malignant arrhythmias. Guanethidine, MAO inhibitors, methyldopa, reserpine, and tricyclic antidepressants can increase the pressor response to sympathomimetics.
    Decreased Effect: Beta-adrenergic blockers may decrease effect of dobutamine and increase risk of severe hypotension.
Stability Remix solution every 24 hours. Store reconstituted solution under refrigeration for 48 hours or 6 hours at room temperature. Pink discoloration of solution indicates slight oxidation but **no** significant loss of potency.

    Stability of parenteral admixture at room temperature (25°C): 48 hours; at refrigeration (4°C): 7 days.
    Standard adult diluent: 250 mg/500 mL D_5W; 500 mg/500 mL D_5W.
Mechanism of Action Stimulates beta$_1$-adrenergic receptors, causing increased contractility and heart rate, with little effect on beta$_2$- or alpha-receptors
Pharmacodynamics/Kinetics
    Onset of action: I.V.: 1-10 minutes
        Peak effect: 10-20 minutes
    Metabolism: In tissues and hepatically to inactive metabolites
    Half-life elimination: 2 minutes
    Excretion: Urine (as metabolites)
Dosage Administration requires the use of an infusion pump; I.V. infusion:
    Neonates: 2-15 mcg/kg/minute, titrate to desired response
    Children and Adults: 2.5-20 mcg/kg/minute; maximum: 40 mcg/kg/minute, titrate to desired response. See table on next page.
    (Continued)

DOBUTamine *(Continued)*

Infusion Rates of Various Dilutions of Dobutamine

Desired Delivery Rate (mcg/kg/min)	Infusion Rate (mL/kg/min)	
	500 mcg/mL[1]	1000 mcg/mL[2]
2.5	0.005	0.0025
5.0	0.01	0.005
7.5	0.015	0.0075
10.0	0.02	0.01
12.5	0.025	0.0125
15.0	0.03	0.015

[1]500 mg per liter or 250 mg per 500 mL of diluent.
[2]1000 mg per liter or 250 mg per 250 mL of diluent.

Administration Use infusion device to control rate of flow; administer into large vein. Do not administer through same I.V. line as heparin, hydrocortisone sodium succinate, cefazolin, or penicillin.

To prepare for infusion:

$$\frac{6 \times \text{weight (kg)} \times \text{desired dose (mcg/kg/min)}}{\text{I.V. infusion rate (mL/h)}} = \begin{array}{l} \text{mg of drug to be added to} \\ \text{100 mL of I.V. fluid} \end{array}$$

Monitoring Parameters Blood pressure, ECG, heart rate, CVP, RAP, MAP, urine output; if pulmonary artery catheter is in place, monitor CI, PCWP, and SVR; also monitor serum potassium

Additional Information Dobutamine lowers central venous pressure and wedge pressure but has little effect on pulmonary vascular resistance.

Dobutamine therapy should be avoided in patients with stable heart failure due to an increase in mortality. In patients with intractable heart failure, dobutamine may be used as a short-term infusion to provide symptomatic benefit. It is not known whether short-term dobutamine therapy in end-stage heart failure has any outcome benefit.

Dobutamine infusion during echocardiography is used as a cardiovascular stress. Wall motion abnormalities developing with increasing doses of dobutamine may help to identify ischemic and/or hibernating myocardium.

Dosage Forms

Infusion, as hydrochloride [premixed in dextrose]: 1 mg/mL (250 mL, 500 mL); 2 mg/mL (250 mL); 4 mg/mL (250 mL)

Injection, solution, as hydrochloride: 12.5 mg/mL (20 mL, 40 mL, 100 mL) [contains sodium bisulfite]

♦ **Dobutamine Hydrochloride** *see* DOBUTamine *on page 529*
♦ **Dobutamine Injection, USP (Can)** *see* DOBUTamine *on page 529*
♦ **Dobutrex® (Can)** *see* DOBUTamine *on page 529*

Docetaxel *(doe se TAKS el)*

U.S. Brand Names Taxotere®
Canadian Brand Names Taxotere®
Index Terms NSC-628503; RP-6976
Pharmacologic Category Antineoplastic Agent, Natural Source (Plant) Derivative
Use Treatment of breast cancer; locally-advanced or metastatic nonsmall cell lung cancer (NSCLC); hormone refractory, metastatic prostate cancer; advanced gastric adenocarcinoma; locally-advanced squamous cell head and neck cancer
Unlabeled/Investigational Use Investigational: Treatment of pancreatic cancer, ovarian cancer, soft tissue sarcoma, and melanoma
Pregnancy Risk Factor D
Pregnancy Implications Animal studies have demonstrated embryotoxicity, fetal toxicity, and maternal toxicity. There are no adequate and well-controlled studies in pregnant women; however, fetal harm may occur. Women of childbearing potential should avoid becoming pregnant. A pregnancy registry is available for all cancers diagnosed during pregnancy at Cooper Health (856-757-7876).
Lactation Excretion in breast milk unknown/contraindicated
Medication Safety Issues
Sound-alike/look-alike issues:
Taxotere® may be confused with Taxol®

High alert medication: The Institute for Safe Medication Practices (ISMP) includes this medication among its list of drugs which have a heightened risk of causing significant patient harm when used in error.
Contraindications Hypersensitivity to docetaxel or any component of the formulation; prior hypersensitivity to medications containing polysorbate 80; pre-existing bone marrow suppression (neutrophils <1500 cells/mm^3); pregnancy
Warnings/Precautions Hazardous agent - use appropriate precautions for handling and disposal. **[U.S. Boxed Warnings]: Use caution in hepatic disease; avoid use in patients with bilirubin exceeding upper limit of normal (ULN) or AST and/or ALT >1.5 times ULN in conjunction with alkaline phosphatase >2.5 times ULN; patients with abnormal liver function are at increased risk of treatment-related adverse events. Severe hypersensitivity reactions characterized by hypotension, bronchospasms, anaphylaxis, or minor reactions characterized by generalized rash/erythema may occur. Fluid retention syndrome characterized by pleural effusions, ascites, edema, and weight gain (2-15 kg) has also been reported.** The incidence and severity of the syndrome increase sharply at

cumulative doses ≥400 mg/m². Patients should be premedicated with a corticosteroid to prevent hypersensitivity reactions and fluid retention; severity is reduced with dexamethasone premedication starting one day prior to docetaxel administration.

[U.S. Boxed Warning]: Patients with abnormal liver function, those receiving higher doses, and patients with nonsmall cell lung cancer and a history of prior treatment with platinum derivatives who receive docetaxel doses higher than 100 mg/m³ are at higher risk for treatment-related mortality.

Neutropenia is the dose-limiting toxicity; however, this rarely results in treatment delays and prophylactic colony stimulating factors have not been routinely used. Patients with increased liver function tests experienced more episodes of neutropenia with a greater number of severe infections. **[U.S. Boxed Warning]: Patients with an absolute neutrophil count <1500 cells/mm³ should not receive docetaxel.** When administered as sequential infusions, taxane derivatives (docetaxel, paclitaxel) should be administered before platinum derivatives (carboplatin, cisplatin) to limit myelosuppression and to enhance efficacy.

Cutaneous reactions including erythema and desquamation have been reported; may require dose reduction. Dosage adjustment is recommended with severe neurosensory symptoms (paresthesia, dysesthesia, pain). **[U.S. Boxed Warning]: Should be administered under the supervision of an experienced cancer chemotherapy physician.** Safety and efficacy in children <16 years of age have not been established.

Adverse Reactions Percentages reported for docetaxel monotherapy; frequency may vary depending on diagnosis, dose, liver function, prior treatment, and premedication. The incidence of adverse events was usually higher in patients with elevated liver function tests.

>10%:
Cardiovascular: Fluid retention (13% to 60%; dose dependent)
Central nervous system: Neurosensory events (20% to 58%; including neuropathy), fever (31% to 35%), neuromotor events (16%)
Dermatologic: Alopecia (56% to 76%), cutaneous events (20% to 48%), nail disorder (11% to 41%)
Gastrointestinal: Stomatitis (19% to 53%, severe 1% to 8%), diarrhea (23% to 43%; severe: 5% to 6%), nausea (34% to 42%), vomiting (22% to 23%)
Hematologic: Neutropenia (84% to 99%; grade 4: 75% to 86%; onset: 4-7 days, nadir: 5-9 days, recovery: 21 days; dose dependent), leukopenia (84% to 99%; grade 4: 32% to 44%), anemia (8% to 94%; dose dependent), thrombocytopenia (8% to 14%; grade 4: 1%; dose dependent), febrile neutropenia (6% to 12%; dose dependent)
Hepatic: Transaminases increased (4% to 19%)
Neuromuscular and skeletal: Weakness (53% to 66%; severe 13% to 18%), myalgia (3% to 23%)
Respiratory: Pulmonary events (41%)
Miscellaneous: Infection (1% to 34%; dose dependent), hypersensitivity (1% to 21%; with premedication 15%)
1% to 10%:
Cardiovascular: Hypotension (3%)
Dermatologic: Rash/erythema (2%)
Gastrointestinal: Taste perversion (6%)
Hepatic: Bilirubin increased (9%), alkaline phosphatase increased (4% to 7%)
Local: Infusion-site reactions (4%, including hyperpigmentation, inflammation, redness, dryness, phlebitis, extravasation, swelling of the vein)
Neuromuscular and skeletal: Arthralgia (3% to 9%)
Ocular: Epiphora associated with canalicular stenosis (up to 77% with weekly administration; up to 1% with every-3-week administration)
<1% (Limited to important or life-threatening): Abdominal pain, acute myeloid leukemia (AML), acute respiratory distress syndrome (ARDS), anaphylactic shock, angina, ascites, atrial fibrillation, atrial flutter, bleeding episodes, bronchospasm, cardiac tamponade, chest pain, chest tightness, colitis, conjunctivitis, constipation, cutaneous lupus erythematosus, deep vein thrombosis, dehydration, drug fever, duodenal ulcer, dyspnea, dysrhythmia, ECG abnormalities, erythema multiforme, esophagitis, gastrointestinal hemorrhage, gastrointestinal obstruction, gastrointestinal perforation, hand and foot syndrome, hearing loss, heart failure, hepatitis, hypertension, ileus, interstitial pneumonia, ischemic colitis, lacrimal duct obstruction, loss of consciousness (transient), MI, neutropenic enterocolitis, ototoxicity, pain, pleural effusion, pruritus, pulmonary edema, pulmonary embolism, pulmonary fibrosis, radiation pneumonitis, radiation recall, renal insufficiency, seizure, sinus tachycardia, Stevens-Johnson syndrome, syncope, toxic epidermal necrolysis, tachycardia, thrombophlebitis, visual disturbances (transient)

Overdosage/Toxicology Symptoms may include bone marrow suppression, severe neutropenia, peripheral neural toxicity, paresthesia, weakness, cutaneous reactions and mucositis. Growth factor support should be administered immediately; treatment is otherwise symptom-directed and supportive.

Drug Interactions
Cytochrome P450 Effect: Substrate of CYP3A4 (major); **Inhibits** CYP3A4 (weak)
Increased Effect/Toxicity: CYP3A4 inhibitors may increase the levels/effects of docetaxel; example inhibitors include azole antifungals, clarithromycin, diclofenac, doxycycline, erythromycin, imatinib, isoniazid, nefazodone, nicardipine, propofol, protease inhibitors, quinidine, telithromycin, and verapamil. When administered as sequential infusions, observational studies indicate a potential for increased toxicity when platinum derivatives (carboplatin, cisplatin) are administered before taxane derivatives (docetaxel, paclitaxel).
Decreased Effect: CYP3A4 inducers may decrease the levels/effects of docetaxel; example inducers include aminoglutethimide, carbamazepine, nafcillin, nevirapine, phenobarbital, phenytoin, and rifamycins.

Ethanol/Nutrition/Herb Interactions
Ethanol: Avoid ethanol (due to GI irritation).
Herb/Nutraceutical: St John's wort may decrease docetaxel levels.

Stability Intact vials should be stored at 2°C to 25°C (36°F to 77°F) and protected from light. Freezing does not adversely affect the product. If refrigerated, vials should be stored at room (Continued)

Docetaxel *(Continued)*

temperature for approximately 5 minutes before using. Vials should be diluted with 13% (w/w) ethanol/water (provided with the drug) to a final concentration of 10 mg/mL. Do not shake. The solution should be further diluted in 250-1000 mL of NS or D_5W to a final concentration of 0.3-0.9 mg/mL and dispensed in a non-PVC container.

Diluted solutions in the vial are stable for 8 hours at room temperature or under refrigeration. Solutions diluted for infusion in D_5W or NS are stable for up to 4 weeks at room temperature of 15°C to 25°C (59°F to 77°F) in polyolefin containers; however, the manufacturer recommends use within 4 hours.

Mechanism of Action Docetaxel promotes the assembly of microtubules from tubulin dimers, and inhibits the depolymerization of tubulin which stabilizes microtubules in the cell. This results in inhibition of DNA, RNA, and protein synthesis. Most activity occurs during the M phase of the cell cycle.

Pharmacodynamics/Kinetics Exhibits linear pharmacokinetics at the recommended dosage range

Distribution: Extensive extravascular distribution and/or tissue binding; V_d: 80-90 L/m^2, V_{dss}: 113 L (mean steady state)

Protein binding: >94%, primarily to alpha$_1$-acid glycoprotein, albumin, and lipoproteins

Metabolism: Hepatic; oxidation via CYP3A4 to metabolites

Half-life elimination: Terminal: 11 hours

Excretion: Feces (75%, <8% as unchanged drug); urine (6%); ~80% within 48 hours

Clearance: Total body: Mean: 21 L/hour/m^2

Dosage Children ≥16 years and Adults: I.V. infusion: Refer to individual protocols:

Breast cancer:

Locally-advanced or metastatic: 60-100 mg/m^2 every 3 weeks; patients initially started at 60 mg/m^2 who do not develop toxicity may tolerate higher doses

Operable, node-positive (adjuvant treatment): 75 mg/m^2 every 3 weeks for 6 courses

Nonsmall cell lung cancer: 75 mg/m^2 every 3 weeks

Prostate cancer: 75 mg/m^2 every 3 weeks; prednisone (5 mg twice daily) is administered continuously

Gastric adenocarcinoma: 75 mg/m^2 every 3 weeks (in combination with cisplatin and fluorouracil)

Head and neck cancer: 75 mg/m^2 every 3 weeks (in combination with cisplatin and fluorouracil) for 4 cycles,followed by radiation therapy

Dosing adjustment for toxicity:

Note: Toxicity includes febrile neutropenia, neutrophils ≤500/mm^3 for >1 week, severe or cumulative cutaneous reactions; in nonsmall cell lung cancer, this may also include platelets <25,000/mm^3 and other grade 3/4 nonhematologic toxicities.

Breast cancer: Patients dosed initially at 100 mg/m^2; reduce dose to 75 mg/m^2; **Note:** If the patient continues to experience these adverse reactions, the dosage should be reduced to 55 mg/m^2 or therapy should be discontinued

Breast cancer, adjuvant treatment: TAC regimen should be administered when neutrophils are ≥1500 cells/mm^3. Patients experiencing febrile neutropenia should receive G-CSF in all subsequent cycles. Patients continuing to experience febrile neutropenia or patients experiencing severe/cumulative cutaneous reactions or moderate neurosensory effects (signs/symptoms) should receive a reduced dose (60 mg/m^2) of docetaxel. Patients who experience grade 3 or 4 stomatitis should also receive a reduced dose (60 mg/m^2) of docetaxel. Discontinue therapy in patients continuing to experience these reactions after dosage reduction.

Nonsmall cell lung cancer:

Monotherapy: Patients dosed initially at 75 mg/m^2 should have dose held until toxicity is resolved, then resume at 55 mg/m^2; discontinue patients who develop ≥ grade 3 peripheral neuropathy

Combination therapy (with cisplatin): Patients dosed initially at 75 mg/m^2 should have the docetaxel dosage reduced to 65 mg/m^2 in subsequent cycles; if further adjustment is required, dosage may be reduced to 50 mg/m^2

Prostate cancer: Reduce dose to 60 mg/m^2; discontinue therapy if adverse reactions persist at lower dose

Gastric cancer, head and neck cancer: **Note:** Cisplatin may require dose reductions/ therapy delays for peripheral neuropathy, ototoxicity, and/or nephrotoxicity. Patients experiencing febrile neutropenia, documented infection with neutropenia or neutropenia >7 days should receive G-CSF in all subsequent cycles. For neutropenic complications despite G-CSF use, further reduce dose to 60 mg/m^2. Neutropenic complications in subsequent cycles should be further dose reduced to 45 mg/m^2. Patients who experience grade 4 thrombocytopenia should receive a dose reduction from 75 mg/m^2 to 60 mg/m^2. Discontinue therapy for persistent toxicities.

Gastrointestinal toxicity for docetaxel in combination with cisplatin and fluorouracil for treatment of gastric cancer or head and neck cancer:

Diarrhea, grade 3:

First episode: Reduce fluorouracil dose by 20%

Second episode: Reduce docetaxel dose by 20%

Diarrhea, grade 4:

First episode: Reduce fluorouracil and docetaxel doses by 20%

Second episode: Discontinue treatment

Stomatitis, grade 3:

First episode: Reduce fluorouracil dose by 20%

Second episode: Discontinue fluorouracil for all subsequent cycles

Third episode: Reduce docetaxel dose by 20%

Stomatitis, grade 4:

First episode: Discontinue fluorouracil for all subsequent cycles

Second episode: Reduce docetaxel dose by 20%

Dosing adjustment in hepatic impairment: Total bilirubin greater than the ULN, or AST/ALT >1.5 times ULN concomitant with alkaline phosphatase >2.5 times ULN: Docetaxel **generally should not be administered**.

Hepatic impairment dosing adjustment specific for treatment of gastric adenocarcinoma:
AST/ALT >2.5 to ≤5 times ULN and alkaline phosphatase ≤2.5 times ULN: Decrease docetaxel dose by 20%
AST/ALT >1.5 to ≤5 times ULN and alkaline phosphatase >2.5 to ≤5 times ULN: Decrease docetaxel dose by 20%
AST/ALT >5 times ULN and /or alkaline phosphatase >5 times ULN: Discontinue docetaxel

Administration Administer I.V. infusion over 1-hour through nonsorbing (nonpolyvinylchloride) tubing; in-line filter is not necessary. **Note:** Premedication with corticosteroids for 1-5 days, beginning the day before docetaxel administration, is recommended to prevent hypersensitivity reactions and pulmonary/peripheral edema (see Additional Information).

Monitoring Parameters CBC with differential, liver function tests, bilirubin, alkaline phosphatase, renal function; monitor for hypersensitivity reactions, fluid retention, epiphora, and canalicular stenosis

Additional Information Premedication with oral corticosteroids is recommended to decrease the incidence and severity of fluid retention and severity of hypersensitivity reactions. Dexamethasone 8-10 mg orally twice daily for 3-5 days, starting the day before docetaxel administration, is usually recommended. When prednisone is part of the antineoplastic regimen (eg, prostate cancer), the prednisone is sometimes withheld on the days dexamethasone is administered.

Dosage Forms

Injection, solution [concentrate]:
Taxotere®: 20 mg/0.5 mL (0.5 mL, 2 mL) [contains Polysorbate 80®; diluent contains ethanol 13%]

Docosanol (doe KOE san ole)

U.S. Brand Names Abreva® [OTC]
Index Terms Behenyl Alcohol; n-Docosanol
Pharmacologic Category Antiviral Agent, Topical
Use Treatment of herpes simplex of the face or lips
Dosage Children ≥12 years and Adults: Topical: Apply 5 times/day to affected area of face or lips. Start at first sign of cold sore or fever blister and continue until healed.
Additional Information Complete prescribing information for this medication should be consulted for additional detail.
Dosage Forms Cream: 10% (2 g)

Docusate (DOK yoo sate)

U.S. Brand Names Colace® [OTC]; Diocto® [OTC]; Docusoft-S™ [OTC]; DOK™ [OTC]; DOS® [OTC]; D-S-S® [OTC]; Dulcolax® Stool Softener [OTC]; Enemeez® [OTC]; Fleet® Sof-Lax® [OTC]; Genasoft® [OTC]; Phillips'® Stool Softener Laxative [OTC]; Silace [OTC]; Surfak® [OTC]
Canadian Brand Names Apo-Docusate-Sodium®; Colace®; Colax-C®; Novo-Docusate Calcium; Novo-Docusate Sodium; PMS-Docusate Calcium; PMS-Docusate Sodium; Regulex®; Selax®; Soflax™
Index Terms Dioctyl Calcium Sulfosuccinate; Dioctyl Sodium Sulfosuccinate; Docusate Calcium; Docusate Potassium; Docusate Sodium; DOSS; DSS
Pharmacologic Category Stool Softener
Additional Appendix Information
Laxatives, Classification and Properties on page 1886
Use Stool softener in patients who should avoid straining during defecation and constipation associated with hard, dry stools; prophylaxis for straining (Valsalva) following myocardial infarction. A safe agent to be used in elderly; some evidence that doses <200 mg are ineffective; stool softeners are unnecessary if stool is well hydrated or "mushy" and soft; shown to be ineffective used long-term.
Unlabeled/Investigational Use Ceruminolytic
Pregnancy Risk Factor C
Medication Safety Issues
Sound-alike/look-alike issues:
Docusate may be confused with Doxinate®
Colace® may be confused with Calan®
Surfak® may be confused with Surbex®
Dosage Docusate salts are interchangeable; the amount of sodium or calcium per dosage unit is clinically insignificant

Infants and Children <3 years: Oral: 10-40 mg/day in 1-4 divided doses
Children: Oral:
3-6 years: 20-60 mg/day in 1-4 divided doses
6-12 years: 40-150 mg/day in 1-4 divided doses
Adolescents and Adults: Oral: 50-500 mg/day in 1-4 divided doses
Older Children and Adults: Rectal: Add 50-100 mg of docusate liquid to enema fluid (saline or water); administer as retention or flushing enema

Ceruminolytic (unlabeled use): Intra-aural: Administer 1 mL of docusate sodium in 2 mL syringes; if no clearance in 15 minutes, irrigate with 50-100 mL normal saline (this method is 80% effective)
Additional Information Complete prescribing information for this medication should be consulted for additional detail.
Dosage Forms
Capsule, as calcium (Surfak®): 240 mg
(Continued)

Docusate *(Continued)*

Capsule, as sodium: 100 mg, 250 mg
  Colace®: 50 mg [contains sodium 3 mg], 100 mg [contains sodium 5 mg]
  Docusoft-S™: 100 mg [contains sodium 5 mg]
  DOK™, Genasoft®: 100 mg
  DOS®, D-S-S®: 100 mg, 250 mg
  Dulcolax® Stool Softener: 100 mg [contains sodium 5 mg]
  Phillips'® Stool Softener Laxative: 100 mg [contains sodium 5.2 mg]
Enema, rectal, as sodium (Enemeez®): 283 mg/5 mL 5 mL
Gelcap, as sodium (Fleet® Sof-Lax®): 100 mg
Liquid, as sodium: 150 mg/15 mL (480 mL)
  Colace®: 150 mg/15 mL (30 mL) [contains sodium 1 mg/mL]
  Diocto®: 150 mg/15 mL (480 mL) [vanilla flavor]
  Silace: 150 mg/15 mL (480 mL) [lemon-vanilla flavor]
Syrup, as sodium: 60 mg/15 mL (480 mL)
  Colace®, Diocto®: 60 mg/15 mL (480 mL) [alcohol free, sugar free; contains sodium 36 mg/5 mL]
  Silace: 20 mg/5 mL (480 mL) [peppermint flavor]

Docusate and Senna *(DOK yoo sate & SEN na)*

U.S. Brand Names Peri-Colace® [OTC]; Senokot-S® [OTC]; SenoSol™-SS [OTC]
Index Terms Senna and Docusate; Senna-S
Pharmacologic Category Laxative, Stimulant; Stool Softener
Additional Appendix Information
  Laxatives, Classification and Properties *on page 1886*
Use Short-term treatment of constipation
Unlabeled/Investigational Use Evacuate the colon for bowel or rectal examinations; management/prevention of opiate-induced constipation
Medication Safety Issues
  Sound-alike/look-alike issues:
    Senokot® may be confused with Depakote®
Dosage Oral: Constipation: OTC ranges:
  Children:
    2-6 years: Initial: 4.3 mg sennosides plus 25 mg docusate ($^1/_2$ tablet) once daily (maximum: 1 tablet twice daily)
    6-12 years: Initial: 8.6 mg sennosides plus 50 mg docusate (1 tablet) once daily (maximum: 2 tablets twice daily)
  Children ≥12 years and Adults: Initial: 2 tablets (17.2 mg sennosides plus 100 mg docusate) once daily (maximum: 4 tablets twice daily)
  Elderly: Consider half the initial dose in older, debilitated patients
Additional Information Complete prescribing information for this medication should be consulted for additional detail.
Dosage Forms
  Tablet: Docusate sodium 50 mg and sennosides 8.6 mg
    Peri-Colace®: Docusate sodium 50 mg and sennosides 8.6 mg
    Senokot-S®: Docusate sodium 50 mg and sennosides 8.6 mg [sugar free; contains sodium 4 mg/tablet]
    SenoSol™-SS: Docusate sodium 50 mg and sennosides 8.6 mg [contains sodium 3 mg/tablet]

♦ **Docusate Calcium** *see Docusate on page 533*
♦ **Docusate Potassium** *see Docusate on page 533*
♦ **Docusate Sodium** *see Docusate on page 533*
♦ **Docusoft-S™ [OTC]** *see Docusate on page 533*

Dofetilide *(doe FET il ide)*

U.S. Brand Names Tikosyn®
Canadian Brand Names Tikosyn®
Pharmacologic Category Antiarrhythmic Agent, Class III
Use Maintenance of normal sinus rhythm in patients with chronic atrial fibrillation/atrial flutter of longer than 1-week duration who have been converted to normal sinus rhythm; conversion of atrial fibrillation and atrial flutter to normal sinus rhythm
Restrictions Tikosyn® is only available to prescribers and hospitals that have confirmed their participation in a designated Tikosyn® Education Program. The program provides comprehensive education about the importance of in-hospital treatment initiation and individualized dosing.

T.I.P.S. is the Tikosyn® In Pharmacy System designated to allow retail pharmacies to stock and dispense Tikosyn® once they have been enrolled. A participating pharmacy must confirm receipt of the T.I.P.S. program materials and educate its pharmacy staff about the procedures required to fill an outpatient prescription for Tikosyn®. The T.I.P.S. enrollment form is available at www.tikosyn.com. Tikosyn® is only available from a special mail order pharmacy, and enrolled retail pharmacies. Pharmacists must verify that the hospital/prescriber is a confirmed participant before Tikosyn® is provided. For participant verification, the pharmacist may call 1-800-788-7353 or use the web site located at www.tikosynlist.com. Further details and directions on the program are provided at www.tikosyn.com.

Dofetilide therapy must be initiated/adjusted in a hospital setting with proper monitoring under the guidance of experienced personnel.
Pregnancy Risk Factor C
Pregnancy Implications Dofetilide has been shown to adversely affect *in utero* growth, organogenesis, and survival of rats and mice. There are no adequate and well-controlled

studies in pregnant women. Dofetilide should be used with extreme caution in pregnant women and in women of childbearing age only when the benefit to the patient unequivocally justifies the potential risk to the fetus.

Lactation Excretion in breast milk unknown/not recommended

Contraindications Hypersensitivity to dofetilide or any component of the formulation; patients with congenital or acquired long QT syndromes, do not use if a baseline QT interval or QT_c is >440 msec (500 msec in patients with ventricular conduction abnormalities); severe renal impairment (estimated Cl_{cr} <20 mL/minute); concurrent use with verapamil, cimetidine, hydrochlorothiazide (alone or in combinations), trimethoprim (alone or in combination with sulfamethoxazole), itraconazole, ketoconazole, prochlorperazine, or megestrol; baseline heart rate <50 beats/minute; other drugs that prolong QT intervals (phenothiazines, cisapride, bepridil, tricyclic antidepressants, sparfloxacin, gatifloxacin, moxifloxacin; hypokalemia or hypomagnesemia; concurrent amiodarone, clarithromycin, or erythromycin

Warnings/Precautions **[U.S. Boxed Warning]: Must be initiated (or reinitiated) in a setting with continuous monitoring and staff familiar with the recognition and treatment of life-threatening arrhythmias. Patients must be monitored with continuous ECG for a minimum of 3 days,** or for a minimum of 12 hours after electrical or pharmacological cardioversion to normal sinus rhythm, whichever is greater. Patients should be readmitted for continuous monitoring if dosage is later increased.

Reserve for patients who are highly symptomatic with atrial fibrillation/atrial flutter; torsade de pointes significantly increases with doses >500 mcg twice daily; hold Class Ia or Class II antiarrhythmics for at least three half-lives prior to starting dofetilide; use in patients on amiodarone therapy only if serum amiodarone level is <0.3 mg/L or if amiodarone was stopped for >3 months previously; correct hypokalemia or hypomagnesemia before initiating dofetilide and maintain within normal limits during treatment. Risk of hypokalemia and/or hypomagnesemia may be increased by potassium-depleting diuretics, increasing the risk of torsade de pointes. Concurrent use with other drugs known to prolong QT_c interval is not recommended.

Patients with sick sinus syndrome or with second or third-degree heart block should not receive dofetilide unless a functional pacemaker is in place. Defibrillation threshold is reduced in patients with ventricular tachycardia or ventricular fibrillation undergoing implantation of a cardioverter-defibrillator device. Safety and efficacy in children (<18 years of age) have not been established. Use with caution in renal impairment; not recommended in patients receiving drugs which may compete for renal secretion via cationic transport. Use with caution in patients with severe hepatic impairment.

Adverse Reactions
Supraventricular arrhythmia patients (incidence > placebo)

>10%: Central nervous system: Headache (11%)

2% to 10%:

Central nervous system: Dizziness (8%), insomnia (4%)

Cardiovascular: Ventricular tachycardia (2.6% to 3.7%), chest pain (10%), torsade de pointes (3.3% in CHF patients and 0.9% in patients with a recent MI; up to 10.5% in patients receiving doses in excess of those recommended). Torsade de pointes occurs most frequently within the first 3 days of therapy.

Dermatologic: Rash (3%)

Gastrointestinal: Nausea (5%), diarrhea (3%), abdominal pain (3%)

Neuromuscular & skeletal: Back pain (3%)

Respiratory: Dyspnea (6%), respiratory tract infection (7%)

Miscellaneous: Flu syndrome (4%)

<2% (Limited to important or life-threatening): Angioedema, AV block (0.4% to 1.5%), bundle branch block, cardiac arrest, facial paralysis, flaccid paralysis, heart block, hepatotoxicity, MI, paralysis, paresthesia, stroke, syncope, ventricular fibrillation (0% to 0.4%)

Overdosage/Toxicology The major dose-related toxicity is torsade de pointes. Treatment should be symptomatic and supportive. Watch for excessive prolongation of the QT interval in overdose situations. Continuous cardiac monitoring is necessary. A charcoal slurry is helpful when given early (15 minutes) after the overdose. Isoproterenol infusion into anesthetized dogs with cardiac pacing has been shown to correct atrial and ventricular effective refractory periods caused by dofetilide. General treatment measures, override pacing, and magnesium therapy appear to be effective in the management of dofetilide-induced torsade de pointes.

Drug Interactions
Cytochrome P450 Effect: Substrate of CYP3A4 (minor)

Increased Effect/Toxicity: Dofetilide concentrations are increased by cimetidine, verapamil, hydrochlorothiazide, ketoconazole, and trimethoprim (concurrent use of these agents is contraindicated). Dofetilide levels may also be increased by renal cationic transport inhibitors (including triamterene, metformin, amiloride, and megestrol). Diuretics and other drugs which may deplete potassium and/or magnesium (aminoglycoside antibiotics, amphotericin, cyclosporine) may increase dofetilide's toxicity (torsade de pointes); concurrent use of hydrochlorothiazide is contraindicated. Use of QT_c-prolonging agents (including bepridil, cisapride, clarithromycin, erythromycin, tricyclic antidepressants, phenothiazines, sparfloxacin, gatifloxacin, moxifloxacin) is contraindicated. Itraconazole may decrease the metabolism of dofetilide (concurrent use is contraindicated).

Ethanol/Nutrition/Herb Interactions Herb/Nutraceutical: St John's wort may decrease dofetilide levels. Avoid ephedra (may worsen arrhythmia).

Mechanism of Action Vaughan Williams Class III antiarrhythmic activity. Blockade of the cardiac ion channel carrying the rapid component of the delayed rectifier potassium current. Dofetilide has no effect on sodium channels, adrenergic alpha-receptors, or adrenergic beta-receptors. It increases the monophasic action potential duration due to delayed repolarization. The increase in the QT interval is a function of prolongation of both effective and functional refractory periods in the His-Purkinje system and the ventricles. Changes in cardiac conduction velocity and sinus node function have not been observed in patients with or without structural heart disease. PR and QRS width remain the same in patients with pre-existing heart block and or sick sinus syndrome.

(Continued)

Dofetilide *(Continued)*

Pharmacodynamics/Kinetics

Absorption: >90%

Distribution: V_d: 3 L/kg

Protein binding: 60% to 70%

Metabolism: Hepatic via CYP3A4, but low affinity for it; metabolites formed by N-dealkylation and N-oxidation

Bioavailability: >90%

Half-life elimination: 10 hours

Time to peak: Fasting: 2-3 hours

Excretion: Urine (80%, 80% as unchanged drug, 20% as inactive or minimally active metabolites); renal elimination consists of glomerular filtration and active tubular secretion via cationic transport system

Dosage Adults: Oral:

Note: QT or QT_c must be determined prior to first dose. If QT_c >440 msec (>500 msec in patients with ventricular conduction abnormalities), dofetilide is contraindicated (see Contraindications and Warnings/Precautions).

Initial: 500 mcg orally twice daily. Initial dosage must be adjusted in patients with estimated Cl_{cr} <60 mL/minute (see Dosage Adjustment in Renal Impairment). Dofetilide may be initiated at lower doses than recommended based on physician discretion.

Modification of dosage in response to initial dose: QT_c interval should be measured 2-3 hours after the initial dose. If the QT_c >15% of baseline, or if the QT_c is >500 msec (550 msec in patients with ventricular conduction abnormalities) dofetilide should be adjusted. If the starting dose is 500 mcg twice daily, then adjust to 250 mcg twice daily. If the starting dose was 250 mcg twice daily, then adjust to 125 mcg twice daily. If the starting dose was 125 mcg twice daily then adjust to 125 mcg every day.

Continued monitoring for doses 2-5: QT_c interval must be determined 2-3 hours after each subsequent dose of dofetilide for in-hospital doses 2-5. If the measured QT_c is >500 msec (550 msec in patients with ventricular conduction abnormalities) at any time, dofetilide should be discontinued.

Chronic therapy (following the 5th dose):

QT or QT_c and creatinine clearance should be evaluated every 3 months. If QT_c >500 msec (>550 msec in patients with ventricular conduction abnormalities), dofetilide should be discontinued.

Dosage adjustment in renal impairment:

Cl_{cr} >60 mL/minute: Administer 500 mcg twice daily.

Cl_{cr} 40-60 mL/minute: Administer 250 mcg twice daily.

Cl_{cr} 20-39 mL/minute: Administer 125 mcg twice daily.

Cl_{cr} <20 mL/minute: Contraindicated in this group.

Dosage adjustment in hepatic impairment: No dosage adjustments required in Child-Pugh Class A and B. Patients with severe hepatic impairment were not studied.

Elderly: No specific dosage adjustments are recommended based on age, however, careful assessment of renal function is particularly important in this population.

Administration Do not open capsules.

Monitoring Parameters ECG monitoring with attention to QT_c and occurrence of ventricular arrhythmias, baseline serum creatinine and changes in serum creatinine. Check serum potassium and magnesium levels if on medications where these electrolyte disturbances can occur, or if patient has a history of hypokalemia or hypomagnesemia. QT or QT_c must be monitored at specific times prior to the first dose and during the first 3 days of therapy. Thereafter, QT or QT_c and creatinine clearance must be evaluated at 3-month intervals.

Dosage Forms Capsule: 125 mcg, 250 mcg, 500 mcg

♦ **Dofus [OTC]** *see Lactobacillus on page 969*

♦ **DOK™ [OTC]** *see Docusate on page 533*

Dolasetron *(dol A se tron)*

U.S. Brand Names Anzemet®

Canadian Brand Names Anzemet®

Index Terms Dolasetron Mesylate; MDL 73,147EF

Pharmacologic Category Antiemetic; Selective 5-HT$_3$ Receptor Antagonist

Use Prevention of nausea and vomiting associated with emetogenic cancer chemotherapy; prevention of postoperative nausea and vomiting; treatment of postoperative nausea and vomiting (injectable form only).

Note: In Canada, the use of dolasetron is contraindicated for all uses in children <18 years of age or in the treatment of postoperative nausea and vomiting in adults. These are not labeled contraindications in the U.S.

Pregnancy Risk Factor B

Pregnancy Implications

Teratogenic effects were not observed in animal studies. There are no adequate and well-controlled studies in pregnant women.

Lactation Excretion in breast milk unknown/use caution

Medication Safety Issues

Sound-alike/look-alike issues:

Anzemet® may be confused with Aldomet® and Avandamet™

Dolasetron may be confused with granisetron, ondansetron, palonosetron

Contraindications Hypersensitivity to dolasetron or any component of the formulation

Note: In Canada, the use of dolasetron is contraindicated for all uses in children <18 years of age or in the treatment of postoperative nausea and vomiting in adults. These are not labeled contraindications in the U.S.

Warnings/Precautions Dolasetron should be administered with caution in patients with congenital QT syndrome or other risk factors for QT prolongation (eg, medications known to prolong QT interval, electrolyte abnormalities, and cumulative high dose anthracycline therapy). Use with caution in patients allergic to other 5-HT$_3$ receptor antagonists; cross-reactivity has been reported. **For chemotherapy, should be used on a scheduled basis, not on an "as needed" (PRN) basis,** since data support the use of this drug only in the prevention of nausea and vomiting (due to antineoplastic therapy) and not in the rescue of nausea and vomiting. Not intended for treatment of nausea and vomiting or for chronic continuous therapy. Safety and efficacy in children <2 years of age have not been established.

Adverse Reactions Adverse events may vary according to indication

>10%:
  Central nervous system: Headache (7% to 24%)
  Gastrointestinal: Diarrhea (2% to 12%)
1% to 10%:
  Cardiovascular: Bradycardia (5%), hypotension (5%), hypertension (2% to 3%), tachycardia (2% to 3%)
  Central nervous system: Dizziness (1% to 6%), fatigue (3% to 6%), fever (3% to 5%), chills/shivering (1% to 2%), sedation (2%)
  Dermatological: Pruritus (3% to 4%)
  Gastrointestinal: Dyspepsia (2% to 3%), abdominal pain (3%)
  Hepatic: Abnormal hepatic function (4%)
  Neuromuscular & skeletal: Pain (3%)
  Renal: Oliguria (1% to 3%), urinary retention (2%)
<1% (Limited to important or life-threatening): Abnormal vision, abnormal dreaming, acute renal failure, anaphylactic reaction, anemia, anorexia, arrhythmia, ataxia, bronchospasm, cardiac arrest, confusion, constipation, diaphoresis increased, dyspnea, dysuria, edema, epistaxis, GGT increased, hematuria, hyperbilirubinemia, ischemia (peripheral), local injection site reaction, MI, pancreatitis, photophobia, polyuria; prolonged P-R, QRS, and QT$_c$ intervals; prothrombin time increased, purpura/hematoma, rash, sleep disorder, syncope, taste perversion, thrombocytopenia, thrombophlebitis/phlebitis, tinnitus, urticaria

Overdosage/Toxicology In animal toxicity studies, doses 6.3-12.6 times the recommended human dose (based upon surface area) were lethal. Symptoms of acute poisoning included tremors, depression, and convulsions. There is no known specific antidote for dolasetron. Patients with suspected overdose should be managed with supportive therapy.

Drug Interactions

Cytochrome P450 Effect: Substrate (minor) of CYP2C9, 3A4; **Inhibits** CYP2D6 (weak)

Increased Effect/Toxicity: Due to reports of profound hypotension during concomitant therapy with ondansetron, the manufacturer of apomorphine contraindicates its use with all 5-HT$_3$ antagonists. Use caution with QT$_c$-prolonging agents (includes but may not be limited to amitriptyline, bepridil, disopyramide, erythromycin, haloperidol, imipramine, quinidine, pimozide, procainamide, sotalol, and thioridazine); effect/toxicity of dolasetron and other QT$_c$-prolonging agents may be increased

Decreased Effect: Blood levels of active metabolite are decreased during coadministration of rifampin.

Ethanol/Nutrition/Herb Interactions Herb/Nutraceutical: St John's wort may decrease dolasetron levels.

Stability Store intact vials and tablets at room temperature; protect from light. A 20 mg/mL solution in syringes is stable for 8 months at room temperature. Dilute in 50-100 mL of a compatible solution (ie, 0.9% NS, D$_5$W, D$_5$½NS, D$_5$LR, LR, and 10% mannitol injection). Solutions diluted for infusion are stable at room temperature for 24 hours or under refrigeration for 48 hours.

Mechanism of Action Selective serotonin receptor (5-HT$_3$) antagonist, blocking serotonin both peripherally (primary site of action) and centrally at the chemoreceptor trigger zone

Pharmacodynamics/Kinetics

Absorption: Rapid and complete

Distribution: 5.8 L/kg

Protein binding: Hydrodolasetron: 69% to 77% (50% bound to alpha$_1$-acid glycoprotein)

Metabolism: Hepatic; reduction by carbonyl reductase to hydrodolasetron (active metabolite); further metabolized by CYP3A and flavin monooxygenase

Bioavailability: 75%

Half-life elimination: Dolasetron: 10 minutes; hydrodolasetron: Adults: 6-8 hours; Children: 4-6 hours

Time to peak, plasma: I.V.: 0.6 hours; Oral: 1 hour

Excretion: Urine ~67% (53% to 61% as active metabolite hydrodolasetron); feces ~33%

Dosage Note: In Canada, the use of dolasetron is contraindicated in children <18 years of age or in the treatment of postoperative nausea and vomiting in adults. These are not labeled contraindications in the U.S.

Nausea and vomiting prophylaxis, chemotherapy-induced (including initial and repeat courses):
  Children 2-16 years:
    Oral: 1.8 mg/kg within 1 hour before chemotherapy; maximum: 100 mg/dose
    I.V.: 1.8 mg/kg ~30 minutes before chemotherapy; maximum: 100 mg/dose
  Adults:
    Oral: 100 mg single dose 1 hour prior to chemotherapy
    I.V.: 1.8 mg/kg or 100 mg 30 minutes prior to chemotherapy
Prevention of postoperative nausea and vomiting:
  Children 2-16 years:
    Oral: 1.2 mg/kg within 2 hours before surgery; maximum: 100 mg/dose
    I.V.: 0.35 mg/kg (maximum: 12.5 mg) ~15 minutes before stopping anesthesia
  Adults:
    Oral: 100 mg within 2 hours before surgery
    I.V.: 12.5 mg ~15 minutes before stopping anesthesia
Treatment of postoperative nausea and vomiting: I.V. (only):
  Children: 0.35 mg/kg (maximum: 12.5 mg) as soon as needed
  Adults: 12.5 mg as soon as needed
(Continued)

Dolasetron *(Continued)*

Dosing adjustment for elderly, renal/hepatic impairment: No dosage adjustment is recommended

Administration I.V. injection may be given either undiluted IVP over 30 seconds or diluted in 50 mL of compatible fluid and infused over 15 minutes. Line should be flushed, prior to and after, dolasetron administration. Dolasetron injection may be diluted in apple or apple-grape juice and taken orally; this dilution is stable for 2 hours at room temperature.

Monitoring Parameters Liver function tests, blood pressure and pulse, and ECG in patients with cardiovascular disease

Additional Information Efficacy of dolasetron, for chemotherapy treatment, is enhanced with concomitant administration of dexamethasone 20 mg (increases complete response by 10% to 20%). Oral administration of the intravenous solution is equivalent to tablets. A single I.V. dose of dolasetron mesylate (1.8 or 2.4 mg/kg) has comparable safety and efficacy to a single 32 mg I.V. dose of ondansetron in patients receiving cisplatin chemotherapy.

Dosage Forms

Injection, solution, as mesylate:
Anzemet®: 20 mg/mL (0.625 mL) [single-use Carpuject® or vial]; 20 mg/mL (5 mL) [single-use vial]; 20 mg/mL (25 mL) [multidose vial]

Tablet, as mesylate:
Anzemet®: 50 mg, 100 mg

◆ **Dolasetron Mesylate** *see Dolasetron on page 536*
◆ **Dolgic® LQ** *see Butalbital, Acetaminophen, and Caffeine on page 259*
◆ **Dolgic® Plus** *see Butalbital, Acetaminophen, and Caffeine on page 259*
◆ **Dolobid® [DSC]** *see Diflunisal on page 500*
◆ **Dologesic®** *see Acetaminophen and Phenyltoloxamine on page 32*
◆ **Dolophine®** *see Methadone on page 1100*
◆ **Dom-Citalopram (Can)** *see Citalopram on page 381*
◆ **Domeboro® [OTC]** *see Aluminum Sulfate and Calcium Acetate on page 86*
◆ **Dome Paste Bandage** *see Zinc Gelatin on page 1817*
◆ **Dom-Fenofibrate Supra (Can)** *see Fenofibrate on page 689*
◆ **Dom-Mefenamic Acid (Can)** *see Mefenamic Acid on page 1068*
◆ **Dom-Methimazole (Can)** *see Methimazole on page 1108*
◆ **Dom-Sumatriptan (Can)** *see Sumatriptan on page 1620*
◆ **Dom-Topiramate (Can)** *see Topiramate on page 1707*

Donepezil *(doh NEP e zil)*

U.S. Brand Names Aricept®; Aricept® ODT
Canadian Brand Names Aricept®; Aricept® RDT
Index Terms E2020
Pharmacologic Category Acetylcholinesterase Inhibitor (Central)
Use Treatment of mild, moderate, or severe dementia of the Alzheimer's type
Unlabeled/Investigational Use Attention-deficit/hyperactivity disorder (ADHD), behavioral syndromes in dementia
Pregnancy Risk Factor C
Pregnancy Implications Teratogenic effects were not observed in animal studies. There are no adequate and well-controlled studies in pregnant women.
Lactation Excretion in breast milk unknown/not recommended
Medication Safety Issues
Sound-alike/look-alike issues:
Aricept® may be confused with AcipHex®, Ascriptin®, and Azilect®
Contraindications Hypersensitivity to donepezil, piperidine derivatives, or any component of the formulation
Warnings/Precautions Cholinesterase inhibitors may have vagotonic effects which may cause bradycardia and/or heart block with or without a history of cardiac disease; syncopal episodes have been associated with donepezil. Use with caution with sick sinus syndrome or other supraventricular cardiac conduction abnormalities, with seizures, COPD, or asthma. Use with caution in patients at risk of ulcer disease (eg, previous history or NSAID use), or in patients with bladder outlet obstruction. May cause diarrhea, nausea, and/or vomiting, which may be dose-related. Safety and efficacy in children have not been established.
Adverse Reactions
>10%:
Central nervous system: Insomnia (5% to 14%)
Gastrointestinal: Nausea (5% to 19%), diarrhea (8% to 15%)
Miscellaneous: Accident (7% to 13%), infection (11%)
1% to 10%:
Cardiovascular: Hypertension (3%), chest pain (2%), hemorrhage (2%), syncope (2%), hypotension, atrial fibrillation, bradycardia, ECG abnormal, edema, heart failure, hot flashes, peripheral edema, vasodilation
Central nervous system: Headache (4% to 10%), pain (3% to 9%), fatigue (3% to 8%), dizziness (2% to 8%), abnormal dreams (3% to 8%), depression (2% to 3%), hostility (3%), nervousness (3%), hallucinations (3%), confusion (2%), emotional lability (2%), personality disorder (2%), fever (2%), somnolence (2%), abnormal crying, aggression, agitation, anxiety, aphasia, delusions, irritability, restlessness, seizure
Dermatologic: Bruising (4% to 5%), eczema (3%), pruritus, rash, skin ulcer, urticaria
Endocrine & metabolic: Dehydration (2%), hyperlipemia (2%), libido increased
Gastrointestinal: Anorexia (3% to 8%), vomiting (3% to 8%), weight loss (3%), abdominal pain, constipation, dyspepsia, fecal incontinence, gastroenteritis, GI bleeding, bloating, epigastric pain, toothache

Genitourinary: Urinary frequency (2%), urinary incontinence (2%), hematuria, glycosuria, nocturia, UTI

Hematologic: Anemia

Hepatic: Alkaline phosphatase increased

Neuromuscular & skeletal: Muscle cramps (3% to 8%), back pain (3%), CPK increased (3%), arthritis (2%), ataxia, bone fracture, gait abnormal, lactate dehydrogenase increased, paresthesia, tremor, weakness

Ocular: Blurred vision, cataract, eye irritation

Respiratory: Cough increased, dyspnea, bronchitis, pharyngitis, pneumonia, sore throat

Miscellaneous: Diaphoresis, fungal infection, flu symptoms, wandering

<1%, postmarketing, and/or case reports (limited to important or life-threatening): Abscess, breast fibroadenosis, cellulitis, cerebrovascular accident, CHF, cholecystitis, conjunctival hemorrhage, conjunctivitis, deep vein thrombosis, diabetes mellitus, diverticulitis, ear pain, eosinophilia, fibrocystic breast, gastrointestinal ulcer, glaucoma, goiter, heart block, hemolytic anemia, hepatitis, hostility, hyperglycemia, hypertonia, hypokalemia, hypokinesia, hyponatremia, hypoxia, intracranial hemorrhage, jaundice, LFTs increased, MI, neuroleptic malignant syndrome, pancreatitis, pleurisy, pulmonary collapse, pulmonary congestion, pyelonephritis, renal failure, retinal hemorrhage, SVT, thrombocythemia, thrombocytopenia, tongue edema, transient ischemic attack, vision abnormal

Overdosage/Toxicology Donepezil can cause cholinergic crisis characterized by severe nausea, vomiting, salivation, sweating, bradycardia, hypotension, cardiovascular collapse, and convulsions. Increased muscle weakness is a possibility and may result in death if respiratory muscles are involved. The effectiveness of dialysis is unknown.

Tertiary anticholinergics, such as atropine, may be used as an antidote. I.V. atropine sulfate titrated to effect is recommended, with an initial dose of 1-2 mg I.V., and with subsequent doses based on clinical response. Atypical blood pressure and heart rate increases have been reported with other cholinomimetics when coadministered with quaternary anticholinergics (eg, glycopyrrolate). Implement general supportive measures.

Drug Interactions

Cytochrome P450 Effect: Substrate (minor) of CYP2D6, 3A4

Increased Effect/Toxicity: A synergistic effect may be seen with concurrent administration of succinylcholine or cholinergic agonists (bethanechol). Cholinesterase inhibitors may enhance the bradycardic effects of beta-blockers.

Decreased Effect: Anticholinergic agents (benztropine) may inhibit the effects of donepezil. Acetylcholinesterase inhibitors (central) may increase the risk of antipsychotic-related extrapyramidal symptoms. Acetylcholinesterase inhibitors may diminish the neuromuscular-blocking effects of nondepolarizing blockers.

Ethanol/Nutrition/Herb Interactions Herb/Nutraceutical: St John's wort may decrease donepezil levels. Gingko biloba may increase adverse effects/toxicity of acetylcholinesterase inhibitors.

Stability Store at 15°C to 30°C (59°F to 86°F).

Mechanism of Action Alzheimer's disease is characterized by cholinergic deficiency in the cortex and basal forebrain, which contributes to cognitive deficits. Donepezil reversibly and noncompetitively inhibits centrally-active acetylcholinesterase, the enzyme responsible for hydrolysis of acetylcholine. This appears to result in increased concentrations of acetylcholine available for synaptic transmission in the central nervous system.

Pharmacodynamics/Kinetics

Absorption: Well absorbed

Protein binding: 96%, primarily to albumin (75%) and α_1-acid glycoprotein (21%)

Metabolism: Extensively to four major metabolites (two are active) via CYP2D6 and 3A4; undergoes glucuronidation

Bioavailability: 100%

Half-life elimination: 70 hours; time to steady-state: 15 days

Time to peak, plasma: 3-4 hours

Excretion: Urine 57% (17% as unchanged drug); feces 15%

Dosage Oral:

Children: ADHD (unlabeled use): 5 mg/day

Adults: Dementia of Alzheimer's type: Initial: 5 mg/day at bedtime; may increase to 10 mg/day at bedtime after 4-6 weeks

Dietary Considerations May take with or without food.

Administration Aricept® ODT: Allow tablet to dissolve completely on tongue and follow with water.

Monitoring Parameters Behavior, mood, bowel function, cognitive function, general function (eg, activities of daily living)

Dosage Forms

Tablet, as hydrochloride:

Aricept®: 5 mg, 10 mg

Tablet, orally disintegrating, as hydrochloride:

Aricept® ODT: 5 mg, 10 mg

♦ **Donnatal®** see Hyoscyamine, Atropine, Scopolamine, and Phenobarbital on page 868

♦ **Donnatal Extentabs®** see Hyoscyamine, Atropine, Scopolamine, and Phenobarbital on page 868

DOPamine (DOE pa meen)

Index Terms Dopamine Hydrochloride; Intropin

Pharmacologic Category Adrenergic Agonist Agent

Additional Appendix Information

Hemodynamic Support, Intravenous on page 1885

Use Adjunct in the treatment of shock (eg, MI, open heart surgery, renal failure, cardiac decompensation) which persists after adequate fluid volume replacement

(Continued)

DOPamine *(Continued)*

Unlabeled/Investigational Use Symptomatic bradycardia or heart block unresponsive to atropine or pacing

Pregnancy Risk Factor C

Lactation Excretion in breast milk unknown

Medication Safety Issues

Sound-alike/look-alike issues:

DOPamine may be confused with DOBUTamine, Dopram®

Contraindications Hypersensitivity to sulfites (commercial preparation contains sodium bisulfite); pheochromocytoma; ventricular fibrillation

Warnings/Precautions Use with caution in patients with cardiovascular disease or cardiac arrhythmias or patients with occlusive vascular disease. Correct hypovolemia and electrolytes when used in hemodynamic support. May cause increases in HR and arrhythmia. Avoid infiltration - may cause severe tissue necrosis. Use with caution in post-MI patients.

Adverse Reactions Frequency not defined.

Most frequent:

Cardiovascular: Ectopic beats, tachycardia, anginal pain, palpitation, hypotension, vasoconstriction

Central nervous system: Headache

Gastrointestinal: Nausea and vomiting

Respiratory: Dyspnea

Infrequent:

Cardiovascular: Aberrant conduction, bradycardia, widened QRS complex, ventricular arrhythmia (high dose), gangrene (high dose), hypertension

Central nervous system: Anxiety

Endocrine & metabolic: Piloerection, serum glucose increased (usually not above normal limits)

Local: Extravasation of dopamine can cause tissue necrosis and sloughing of surrounding tissues

Ocular: Intraocular pressure increased, dilated pupils

Renal: Azotemia, polyuria

Overdosage/Toxicology Symptoms include severe hypertension, cardiac arrhythmias, and acute renal failure. **Important:** Antidote for peripheral ischemia: To prevent sloughing and necrosis in ischemic areas, the area should be infiltrated as soon as possible with 10-15 mL of saline solution containing 5-10 mg of Regitine (brand of phentolamine), an adrenergic blocking agent. A syringe with a fine hypodermic needle should be used, and the solution liberally infiltrated throughout the ischemic area. Sympathetic blockade with phentolamine causes immediate and conspicuous local hyperemic changes if the area is infiltrated within 12 hours. Therefore, phentolamine should be given as soon as possible after the extravasation is noted.

Drug Interactions

Increased Effect/Toxicity: Dopamine's effects are prolonged and intensified by MAO inhibitors, alpha- and beta-adrenergic blockers, cocaine, general anesthetics, methyldopa, phenytoin, reserpine, and TCAs.

Decreased Effect: Tricyclic antidepressants may have a decreased effect when coadministered with dopamine. Guanethidine's hypotensive effects may only be partially reversed; may need to use a direct-acting sympathomimetic.

Stability Protect from light; solutions that are darker than slightly yellow should not be used.

Mechanism of Action Stimulates both adrenergic and dopaminergic receptors, lower doses are mainly dopaminergic stimulating and produce renal and mesenteric vasodilation, higher doses also are both dopaminergic and beta$_1$-adrenergic stimulating and produce cardiac stimulation and renal vasodilation; large doses stimulate alpha-adrenergic receptors

Pharmacodynamics/Kinetics

Children: Dopamine has exhibited nonlinear kinetics in children; with medication changes, may not achieve steady-state for ~1 hour rather than 20 minutes

Onset of action: Adults: 5 minutes

Duration: Adults: <10 minutes

Metabolism: Renal, hepatic, plasma; 75% to inactive metabolites by monoamine oxidase and 25% to norepinephrine

Half-life elimination: 2 minutes

Excretion: Urine (as metabolites)

Clearance: Neonates: Varies and appears to be age related; clearance is more prolonged with combined hepatic and renal dysfunction

Dosage I.V. infusion (administration requires the use of an infusion pump):

Neonates: 1-20 mcg/kg/minute continuous infusion, titrate to desired response.

Children: 1-20 mcg/kg/minute, maximum: 50 mcg/kg/minute continuous infusion, titrate to desired response.

Adults: 1-5 mcg/kg/minute up to 20 mcg/kg/minute, titrate to desired response (maximum: 50 mcg/kg/minute). Infusion may be increased by 1-4 mcg/kg/minute at 10- to 30-minute intervals until optimal response is obtained.

If dosages >20-30 mcg/kg/minute are needed, a more direct-acting pressor may be more beneficial (ie, epinephrine, norepinephrine).

The hemodynamic effects of dopamine are dose dependent:

Low-dose: 1-3 mcg/kg/minute, increased renal blood flow and urine output

Intermediate-dose: 3-10 mcg/kg/minute, increased renal blood flow, heart rate, cardiac contractility, and cardiac output

High-dose: >10 mcg/kg/minute, alpha-adrenergic effects begin to predominate, vasoconstriction, increased blood pressure

Administration Administer into large vein to prevent the possibility of extravasation (central line administration); monitor continuously for free flow; use infusion device to control rate of flow; administration into an umbilical arterial catheter is not recommended; when discontinuing the infusion, gradually decrease the dose of dopamine (sudden discontinuation may cause hypotension).

To prepare for infusion:

$$\frac{6 \times \text{weight (kg)} \times \text{desired dose (mcg/kg/min)}}{\text{I.V. infusion rate (mL/h)}} = \frac{\text{mg of drug to be added to}}{100 \text{ mL of I.V. fluid}}$$

Extravasation management: Due to short half-life, withdrawal of drug is often only necessary treatment. Use phentolamine as antidote. Mix 5 mg with 9 mL of NS; inject a small amount of this dilution into extravasated area. Blanching should reverse immediately. Monitor site. If blanching should recur, additional injections of phentolamine may be needed.

Monitoring Parameters Blood pressure, ECG, heart rate, CVP, RAP, MAP, urine output; if pulmonary artery catheter is in place, monitor CI, PCWP, SVR, and PVR

Additional Information Dopamine is most frequently used for treatment of hypotension because of its peripheral vasoconstrictor action. In this regard, dopamine is often used together with dobutamine and minimizes hypotension secondary to dobutamine-induced vasodilation. Thus, pressure is maintained by increased cardiac output (from dobutamine) and vasoconstriction (by dopamine). It is critical neither dopamine nor dobutamine be used in patients in the absence of correcting any hypovolemia as a cause of hypotension.

Low-dose dopamine is often used in the intensive care setting for presumed beneficial effects on renal function. However, there is no clear evidence that low-dose dopamine confers any renal or other benefit. Indeed, dopamine may act on dopamine receptors in the carotid bodies causing chemoreflex suppression. In patients with heart failure, dopamine may inhibit breathing and cause pulmonary shunting. Both these mechanisms would act to decrease minute ventilation and oxygen saturation. This could potentially be deleterious in patients with respiratory compromise and patients being weaned from ventilators.

Dosage Forms

Infusion, as hydrochloride [premixed in D_5W]: 0.8 mg/mL (250 mL, 500 mL); 1.6 mg/mL (250 mL, 500 mL); 3.2 mg/mL (250 mL)

Injection, solution, as hydrochloride: 40 mg/mL (5 mL, 10 mL); 80 mg/mL (5 mL); 160 mg/mL (5 mL) [contains sodium metabisulfite]

- **Dopamine Hydrochloride** see DOPamine on page 539
- **Dopram**® see Doxapram on page 543
- **Doral**® see Quazepam on page 1466

Dornase Alfa (DOOR nase AL fa)

U.S. Brand Names Pulmozyme®
Canadian Brand Names Pulmozyme™
Index Terms DNase; Recombinant Human Deoxyribonuclease
Pharmacologic Category Enzyme
Use Management of cystic fibrosis patients to reduce the frequency of respiratory infections that require parenteral antibiotics, and to improve pulmonary function
Unlabeled/Investigational Use Treatment of chronic bronchitis
Pregnancy Risk Factor B
Lactation Excretion in breast milk unknown
Contraindications Hypersensitivity to dornase alfa, Chinese hamster ovary cell products (eg, epoetin alfa), or any component of the formulation
Warnings/Precautions No clinical trials have been conducted to demonstrate safety and effectiveness of dornase in children <5 years of age, in patients with pulmonary function <40% of normal, or in patients for longer treatment periods >12 months; no data exists regarding safety during lactation
Adverse Reactions
>10%:
Cardiovascular: Chest pain
Respiratory: Pharyngitis
Miscellaneous: Voice alteration
1% to 10%:
Dermatologic: Rash
Ocular: Conjunctivitis
Respiratory: Laryngitis, cough, dyspnea, hemoptysis, rhinitis, hoarse throat, wheezing
Stability Must be stored in the refrigerator at 2°C to 8°C (36°F to 46°F) and protected from strong light. Should not be exposed to room temperature for a total of 24 hours.
Mechanism of Action The hallmark of cystic fibrosis lung disease is the presence of abundant, purulent airway secretions composed primarily of highly polymerized DNA. The principal source of this DNA is the nuclei of degenerating neutrophils, which is present in large concentrations in infected lung secretions. The presence of this DNA produces a viscous mucous that may contribute to the decreased mucociliary transport and persistent infections that are commonly seen in this population. Dornase alfa is a deoxyribonuclease (DNA) enzyme produced by recombinant gene technology. Dornase selectively cleaves DNA, thus reducing mucous viscosity and as a result, airflow in the lung is improved and the risk of bacterial infection may be decreased.
Pharmacodynamics/Kinetics
Onset of action: Nebulization: Enzyme levels are measured in sputum in ~15 minutes
Duration: Rapidly declines
Dosage Inhalation:
Children >3 months to Adults: 2.5 mg once daily through selected nebulizers; experience in children <5 years is limited
Patients unable to inhale or exhale orally throughout the entire treatment period may use Pari-Baby™ nebulizer. Some patients may benefit from twice daily administration.
Administration Nebulization: Should not be diluted or mixed with any other drugs in the nebulizer, this may inactivate the drug
Dosage Forms Solution for nebulization: 1 mg/mL (2.5 mL)

- **Doryx**® see Doxycycline on page 555

Dorzolamide (dor ZOLE a mide)

U.S. Brand Names Trusopt®
Canadian Brand Names Trusopt®
Index Terms Dorzolamide Hydrochloride
Pharmacologic Category Carbonic Anhydrase Inhibitor; Ophthalmic Agent, Antiglaucoma
Additional Appendix Information
Glaucoma Drug Therapy *on page 2050*
Use Lowers intraocular pressure in patients with ocular hypertension or open-angle glaucoma
Pregnancy Risk Factor C
Dosage Children and Adults: Reduction of intraocular pressure: Instill 1 drop in the affected eye(s) 3 times/day
Additional Information Complete prescribing information for this medication should be consulted for additional detail.
Dosage Forms [DSC] = Discontinued product
Solution, ophthalmic, as hydrochloride:
Trusopt®: 2% (5 mL [DSC]; 10 mL) [contains benzalkonium chloride]

Dorzolamide and Timolol (dor ZOLE a mide & TYE moe lole)

U.S. Brand Names Cosopt®
Canadian Brand Names Cosopt®; Preservative-Free Cosopt®
Index Terms Timolol and Dorzolamide
Pharmacologic Category Beta-Adrenergic Blocker, Nonselective; Carbonic Anhydrase Inhibitor; Ophthalmic Agent, Antiglaucoma
Use Reduction of intraocular pressure in patients with ocular hypertension or open-angle glaucoma
Pregnancy Risk Factor C
Dosage Ophthalmic: Children ≥2 years and Adults: Instill 1 drop in affected eye(s) twice daily
Additional Information Complete prescribing information for this medication should be consulted for additional detail.
Dosage Forms [DSC] = Discontinued product
Solution, ophthalmic:
Cosopt®: Dorzolamide hydrochloride 2% (as base) and timolol maleate 0.5% (as base) (5 mL [DSC]; 10 mL) [contains benzalkonium chloride]

- ◆ **Dorzolamide Hydrochloride** *see Dorzolamide on page 542*
- ◆ **DOS® [OTC]** *see Docusate on page 533*
- ◆ **DOSS** *see Docusate on page 533*
- ◆ **Dostinex®** *see Cabergoline on page 263*
- ◆ **Dovobet® (Can)** *see Calcipotriene and Betamethasone on page 264*
- ◆ **Dovonex®** *see Calcipotriene on page 264*

Doxacurium (doks a KYOO ri um)

U.S. Brand Names Nuromax®
Index Terms Doxacurium Chloride
Pharmacologic Category Neuromuscular Blocker Agent, Nondepolarizing
Additional Appendix Information
Neuromuscular Blocking Agents *on page 1890*
Use Adjunct to general anesthesia to facilitate endotracheal intubation and to relax skeletal muscles during surgery; to facilitate mechanical ventilation in ICU patients; does not relieve pain or produce sedation; the characteristics of this agent make it especially useful in procedures requiring careful maintenance of hemodynamic stability for prolonged periods
Pregnancy Risk Factor C
Medication Safety Issues
Sound-alike/look-alike issues:
Doxacurium may be confused with doxapram, DOXOrubicin

High alert medication: The Institute for Safe Medication Practices (ISMP) includes this medication among its list of drugs which have a heightened risk of causing significant patient harm when used in error.
Contraindications Hypersensitivity to doxacurium or any component of the formulation
Warnings/Precautions Use with caution in the elderly, effects and duration are more variable; product contains benzyl alcohol, use with caution in newborns; use with caution in patients with renal or hepatic impairment; certain clinical conditions may result in potentiation or antagonism of neuromuscular blockade:
Potentiation: Electrolyte abnormalities, severe hyponatremia, severe hypocalcemia, severe hypokalemia, hypermagnesemia, neuromuscular diseases, acidosis, acute intermittent porphyria, renal failure, hepatic failure
Antagonism: Alkalosis, hypercalcemia, demyelinating lesions, peripheral neuropathies, diabetes mellitus
Increased sensitivity in patients with myasthenia gravis, Eaton-Lambert syndrome; resistance in burn patients (>30% of body) for period of 5-70 days postinjury; resistance in patients with muscle trauma, denervation, immobilization, infection; does not counteract bradycardia produced by anesthetics/vagal stimulation. Cross-sensitivity with other neuromuscular-blocking agents may occur; use extreme caution in patients with previous anaphylactic reactions. **[U.S. Boxed Warning]: Should be administered by adequately trained individuals familiar with its use.**
Adverse Reactions <1% (Limited to important or life-threatening): Acute quadriplegic myopathy syndrome (prolonged use), diplopia, fever, hypotension, myositis ossificans (prolonged

use), respiratory insufficiency and apnea, skeletal muscle weakness, urticaria, wheezing; **produces little, if any, histamine release**

Overdosage/Toxicology Overdosage is manifested by prolonged neuromuscular blockage. Treatment is supportive. Reverse blockade with neostigmine, pyridostigmine, or edrophonium.

Drug Interactions

Increased Effect/Toxicity: Increased effects are possible with aminoglycosides, beta-blockers, clindamycin, calcium channel blockers, halogenated anesthetics, imipenem, ketamine, lidocaine, loop diuretics (furosemide), macrolides (case reports), magnesium sulfate, procainamide, quinidine, quinolones, tetracyclines, and vancomycin. May increase risk of myopathy when used with high- dose corticosteroids for extended periods.

Decreased Effect: Effect of nondepolarizing neuromuscular blockers may be reduced by carbamazepine (chronic use), corticosteroids (also associated with myopathy - see increased effect), phenytoin (chronic use), sympathomimetics, and theophylline.

Stability Stable for 24 hours at room temperature when diluted, up to 0.1 mg/mL in dextrose 5% or normal saline.

Mechanism of Action Prevents depolarization of muscle membrane and subsequent muscle contraction by acting as a competitive antagonist to acetylcholine at the alpha subunits of the nicotinic cholinergic receptors on the motor endplates in skeletal muscle, also interferes with the mobilization of acetylcholine presynaptically; the neuromuscular blockade can be pharmacologically reversed with an anticholinesterase agent (neostigmine, edrophonium, pyridostigmine)

Pharmacodynamics/Kinetics

Onset of action: 5-11 minutes

Duration: 30 minutes (range: 12-54 minutes)

Protein binding: 30%

Excretion: Primarily urine and feces (as unchanged drug); recovery time prolonged in elderly

Dosage Administer I.V.; dose to effect; doses will vary due to interpatient variability; use ideal body weight for obese patients

Surgery:

Children >2 years: Initial: 0.03-0.05 mg/kg followed by maintenance doses of 0.005-0.01 mg/kg after 30-45 minutes

Adults: 0.05-0.08 mg/kg with thiopental/narcotic or 0.025 mg/kg after initial dose of succinylcholine for intubation; initial maintenance dose of 0.005-0.01 mg/kg after 100-160 minutes followed by repeat doses every 30-45 minutes

Pretreatment/priming: 10% of intubating dose given 3-5 minutes before initial dose

ICU: 0.05 mg/kg bolus followed by 0.025 mg/kg every 2-3 hours or 0.25-0.75 mcg/kg/minute once initial recovery from bolus dose observed

Dosing adjustment in renal impairment: Reduce initial dose and titrate carefully as duration may be prolonged

Administration May be given rapid I.V. injection undiluted or via a continuous infusion using an infusion pump; use infusion solutions within 24 hours of preparation

Monitoring Parameters Blockade is monitored with a peripheral nerve stimulator, should also evaluate ECG, blood pressure, and heart rate

In the ICU setting, prolonged paralysis and generalized myopathy, following discontinuation of agent, may be minimized by appropriately monitoring degree of blockade.

Additional Information Doxacurium is a long-acting nondepolarizing neuromuscular blocker with virtually no cardiovascular side effects. Characteristics of this agent make it especially useful in procedures requiring careful maintenance of hemodynamic stability for prolonged periods; reduce dosage in renal or hepatic impairment. It does not relieve pain or produce sedation. It does not appear to have a cumulative effect on duration of blockade.

Dosage Forms Injection, solution, as chloride: 1 mg/mL (5 mL) [contains benzyl alcohol]

♦ **Doxacurium Chloride** see Doxacurium on page 542

Doxapram (DOKS a pram)

U.S. Brand Names Dopram®

Index Terms Doxapram Hydrochloride

Pharmacologic Category Respiratory Stimulant; Stimulant

Use Respiratory and CNS stimulant for respiratory depression secondary to anesthesia, drug-induced CNS depression; acute hypercapnia secondary to COPD

Pregnancy Risk Factor B

Medication Safety Issues

Sound-alike/look-alike issues:

Doxapram may be confused with doxacurium, doxazosin, doxepin, Doxinate®, DOXOrubicin

Dopram® may be confused with DOPamine

Dosage

Respiratory depression following anesthesia:

Intermittent injection: Initial: 0.5-1 mg/kg; may repeat at 5-minute intervals (only in patients who demonstrate initial response); maximum total dose: 2 mg/kg

I.V. infusion: Initial: 5 mg/minute until adequate response or adverse effects seen; decrease to 1-3 mg/minute; maximum total dose: 4 mg/kg

Drug-induced CNS depression:

Intermittent injection: Initial: Priming dose of 1-2 mg/kg, repeat after 5 minutes; may repeat at 1-2 hour intervals (until sustained consciousness); maximum: 3 g/day. May repeat in 24 hours if necessary.

I.V. infusion: Initial: Priming dose of 1-2 mg/kg, repeat after 5 minutes. If no response, wait 1-2 hours and repeat. If some stimulation is noted, initiate infusion at 1-3 mg/minute (depending on size of patient/depth of CNS depression); suspend infusion if patient begins to awaken. Infusion should not be continued for >2 hours. May reinstitute infusion

(Continued)

Doxapram *(Continued)*

as described above, including bolus, after rest interval of 30 minutes to 2 hours; maximum: 3 g/day

Acute hypercapnia secondary to COPD: I.V. infusion: Initial: Initiate infusion at 1-2 mg/minute (depending on size of patient/depth of CNS depression); may increase to maximum rate of 3 mg/minute; infusion should not be continued for >2 hours. Monitor arterial blood gases prior to initiation of infusion and at 30-minute intervals during the infusion (to identify possible development of acidosis/CO_2 retention). Additional infusions are not recommended (per manufacturer).

Additional Information Complete prescribing information for this medication should be consulted for additional detail.

Dosage Forms Injection, solution, as hydrochloride: 20 mg/mL (20 mL) [contains benzyl alcohol]

♦ **Doxapram Hydrochloride** *see* Doxapram *on page 543*

Doxazosin *(doks AY zoe sin)*

U.S. Brand Names Cardura®; Cardura® XL

Canadian Brand Names Alti-Doxazosin; Apo-Doxazosin®; Cardura-1™; Cardura-2™; Cardura-4™; Gen-Doxazosin; Novo-Doxazosin

Index Terms Doxazosin Mesylate

Pharmacologic Category Alpha₁ Blocker

Use Treatment of hypertension alone or in conjunction with diuretics, ACE inhibitors, beta blockers, or calcium antagonists; treatment of urinary outflow obstruction and/or obstructive and irritative symptoms associated with benign prostatic hyperplasia (BPH), particularly useful in patients with troublesome symptoms who are unable or unwilling to undergo invasive procedures, but who require rapid symptomatic relief; can be used in combination with finasteride

Pregnancy Risk Factor C

Pregnancy Implications Some studies demonstrated embryolethality resulting from doxazosin exposure during organogenesis. Delayed postnatal development was also noted. There are no adequate and well-controlled studies in pregnant women. Use only if benefit outweighs risk.

Lactation Excretion in breast milk unknown/not recommended

Medication Safety Issues
Sound-alike/look-alike issues:
Doxazosin may be confused with doxapram, doxepin, DOXOrubicin
Cardura® may be confused with Cardene®, Cordarone®, Cordran®, Coumadin®, K-Dur®, Ridaura®

Contraindications Hypersensitivity to quinazolines (prazosin, terazosin), doxazosin, or any component of the formulation

Warnings/Precautions Can cause significant orthostatic hypotension and syncope, especially with first dose; anticipate a similar effect if therapy is interrupted for a few days, if dosage is rapidly increased, or if another antihypertensive drug (particularly vasodilators) or a PDE5 inhibitor is introduced. Discontinue if symptoms of angina occur or worsen. Patients should be cautioned about performing hazardous tasks when starting new therapy or adjusting dosage upward. Prostate cancer should be ruled out before starting for BPH. Use with caution in mild to moderate hepatic impairment; not recommended in severe dysfunction. Intraoperative floppy iris syndrome has been observed in cataract surgery patients who were on or were previously treated with alpha₁ blockers. Causality has not been established and there appears to be no benefit in discontinuing alpha blocker therapy prior to surgery. Safety and efficacy in children have not been established.

The extended release formulation consists of drug within a nondeformable matrix; following drug release/absorption, the matrix/shell is expelled in the stool. The use of nondeformable products in patients with known stricture/narrowing of the GI tract has been associated with symptoms of obstruction. Use caution in patients with increased GI retention (eg, chronic constipation) as doxazosin exposure may be increased. Extended release formulation is not approved for the treatment of hypertension.

Adverse Reactions Note: Type and frequency of adverse reactions reflect combined data from trials with immediate release and extended release products.

>10%: Central nervous system: Dizziness (5% to 19%), headache (5% to 14%)

1% to 10%:
Cardiovascular: Orthostatic hypotension (dose related; 0.3% up to 2%), edema (3% to 4%), hypotension (2%), palpitation (1% to 2%), chest pain (1% to 2%), arrhythmia (1%), syncope (2%), flushing (1%)
Central nervous system: Fatigue (8% to 12%), somnolence (1% to 5%), nervousness (2%), pain (2%), vertigo (2% to 4%), insomnia (1%), anxiety (1%), paresthesia (1%), movement disorder (1%), ataxia (1%), hypertonia (1%), depression (1%)
Dermatologic: Rash (1%), pruritus (1%)
Endocrine & metabolic: Sexual dysfunction (2%)
Gastrointestinal: Abdominal pain (2%), diarrhea (2%), dyspepsia (1% to 2%), nausea (1% to 3%), xerostomia (1% to 2%), constipation (1%), flatulence (1%)
Genitourinary: Urinary tract infection (1%), impotence (1%), polyuria (2%), incontinence (1%)
Neuromuscular & skeletal: Back pain (2% to 3%), weakness (1% to 7%), arthritis (1%), muscle weakness (1%), myalgia (≤1%), muscle cramps (1%)
Ocular: Abnormal vision (1% to 2%), conjunctivitis (1%)
Otic: Tinnitus (1%)
Respiratory: Respiratory tract infection (5%), rhinitis (3%), dyspnea (1% to 3%), respiratory disorder (1%), epistaxis (1%)
Miscellaneous: Diaphoresis increased (1%), flu-like syndrome (1%)

<1% (Limited to important or life-threatening): Abnormal thinking, agitation, allergic reaction, amnesia, angina, anorexia, bradycardia, breast pain, bronchospasm, cataplexy, cerebrovascular accident, cholestasis, confusion, depersonalization, emotional lability, enuresis, fecal incontinence, fever, gastroenteritis, gout, hematuria, hepatitis, hypoesthesia, hypokalemia, infection, intraoperative floppy iris syndrome (cataract surgery),jaundice, leukopenia, liver function tests increased, lymphadenopathy, MI, micturition abnormality, migraine, neutropenia, nocturia, pallor, paranoia, paresis, paresthesia, parosmia, peripheral ischemia, priapism,purpura, renal calculus, rigors stroke, syncope, systemic lupus erythematosus, tachycardia, thrombocytopenia, vomiting

Overdosage/Toxicology Symptoms include severe hypotension, drowsiness, and tachycardia. Hypotension usually responds to I.V. fluids, Trendelenburg positioning, or a parenteral vasoconstrictor. Treatment is primarily supportive and symptomatic. Lavage, activated charcoal and fluids have shown to be effective. Dialysis not likely to benefit.

Drug Interactions
    Increased Effect/Toxicity: Increased hypotensive effect with beta-blockers, diuretics, ACE inhibitors, calcium channel blockers, other antihypertensive medications, sildenafil (use with extreme caution at a dose ≤25 mg), tadalafil, and vardenafil.

Ethanol/Nutrition/Herb Interactions Herb/Nutraceutical: Avoid dong quai if using for hypertension (has estrogenic activity). Avoid ephedra, yohimbe, ginseng (may worsen hypertension). Avoid saw palmetto when used for BPH (due to limited experience with this combination). Avoid garlic (may have increased antihypertensive effect).

Mechanism of Action
Hypertension: Competitively inhibits postsynaptic alpha1-adrenergic receptors which results in vasodilation of veins and arterioles and a decrease in total peripheral resistance and blood pressure; ~50% as potent on a weight by weight basis as prazosin.

DPH. Competitively inhibits postsynaptic alpha$_1$-adrenergic receptors in prostatic stromal and bladder neck tissues. This reduces the sympathetic tone-induced urethral stricture causing BPH symptoms.

Pharmacodynamics/Kinetics Not significantly affected by increased age
Duration: >24 hours
Protein binding: Extended release: 98%
Metabolism: Extensively hepatic to active metabolites; primarily via CYP3A4; secondary pathways involve CYP2D6 and 2C19
Bioavailability: Extended release relative to immediate release: 54% to 59%
Half-life elimination: 15-22 hours
Time to peak, serum: Immediate release: 2-3 hours; extended release: 8-9 hours
Excretion: Feces (63% primarily as metabolites); urine (9%)

Dosage Oral: Adults:
Immediate release: 1 mg once daily in morning or evening; may be increased to 2 mg once daily. Thereafter titrate upwards, if needed, over several weeks, balancing therapeutic benefit with doxazosin-induced postural hypotension. In the elderly, initiate at 0.5 mg once daily
    Hypertension: Maximum dose: 16 mg/day
    BPH: Goal: 4-8 mg/day; maximum dose: 8 mg/day
Extended release: BPH: 4 mg once daily with breakfast; titrate based on response and tolerability every 3-4 weeks to maximum recommended dose of 8 mg/day
    Reinitiation of therapy: If therapy is discontinued for several days, restart at 4 mg dose and titrate as before.
    Conversion to extended release from immediate release: Initiate with 4 mg once daily; omit final evening dose of immediate release prior to starting morning dosing with extended release product.
Dosing adjustment in hepatic impairment: Use with caution in mild-to-moderate hepatic dysfunction. Do not use with severe impairment.

Dietary Considerations Cardura® XL: Take with morning meal.

Administration Cardura ® XL: Tablets should be swallowed whole; do not crush, chew, or divide.

Monitoring Parameters Blood pressure, standing and sitting/supine; syncope may occur usually within 90 minutes of the initial dose

Additional Information First-dose hypotension occurs less frequently with doxazosin as compared to prazosin; this may be due to its slower onset of action.

Dosage Forms
Tablet: 1 mg, 2 mg, 4 mg, 8 mg
    Cardura®: 1 mg, 2 mg, 4 mg, 8 mg
Tablet, extended release:
    Cardura® XL: 4 mg, 8 mg

♦ **Doxazosin Mesylate** see Doxazosin on page 544

Doxepin (DOKS e pin)

U.S. Brand Names Prudoxin™; Sinequan® [DSC]; Zonalon®
Canadian Brand Names Apo-Doxepin®; Novo-Doxepin; Sinequan®; Zonalon®
Index Terms Doxepin Hydrochloride
Pharmacologic Category Antidepressant, Tricyclic (Tertiary Amine); Topical Skin Product
Additional Appendix Information
Antidepressant Agents on page 1866
Use
Oral: Depression
Topical: Short-term (<8 days) management of moderate pruritus in adults with atopic dermatitis or lichen simplex chronicus
Unlabeled/Investigational Use Analgesic for certain chronic and neuropathic pain; anxiety
Restrictions An FDA-approved medication guide concerning the use of antidepressants in children and teenagers must be distributed when dispensing an outpatient prescription (new (Continued)

Doxepin *(Continued)*

or refill) where this medication is to be used without direct supervision of a healthcare provider. Medication guides are available at http://www.fda.gov/cder/Offices/ODS/medication_guides.htm. Dispense to parents or guardians of children and teenagers receiving this medication.

Pregnancy Risk Factor B (cream); C (all other forms)

Pregnancy Implications Teratogenic effects were not observed in animal studies; however, there are no adequate and well-controlled studies in pregnant women. Use during pregnancy only if clearly needed.

Lactation Enters breast milk/not recommended (AAP rates "of concern")

Medication Safety Issues

Sound-alike/look-alike issues:

Doxepin may be confused with digoxin, doxapram, doxazosin, Doxidan®, doxycycline

Sinequan® may be confused with saquinavir, Serentil®, Seroquel®, Singulair®

Zonalon® may be confused with Zone-A Forte®

International issues:

Doxal® [Finland] may be confused with Doxil® which is a brand name for doxorubicin in the U.S.

Doxal® [Finland]: Brand name for doxycycline in Austria; brand name for pyridoxine/thiamine in Brazil

Contraindications Hypersensitivity to doxepin, drugs from similar chemical class, or any component of the formulation; narrow-angle glaucoma; urinary retention; use of MAO inhibitors within 14 days; use in a patient during acute recovery phase of MI

Warnings/Precautions [U.S. Boxed Warning]: Antidepressants increase the risk of suicidal thinking and behavior in children and adolescents with major depressive disorder (MDD) and other depressive disorders; consider risk prior to prescribing. All patients must be closely monitored for clinical worsening, suicidality, or unusual changes in behavior, especially during the initiation of therapy or following an increase or decrease in dosage. When used in children, the child's family or caregiver should be instructed to closely observe the patient and communicate condition with healthcare provider. A medication guide should be dispensed with each prescription. **Doxepin is approved for treatment of depression in adolescents.**

The possibility of a suicide attempt is inherent in major depression and may persist until remission occurs. Use caution in high-risk patients. Worsening depression and severe abrupt suicidality that are not part of the presenting symptoms may require discontinuation or modification of drug therapy. The patient's family or caregiver should be alerted to monitor patients for the emergence of suicidality and associated behaviors (such as agitation, irritability, hostility, impulsivity, and hypomania) and call healthcare provider.

May worsen psychosis in some patients or precipitate a shift to mania or hypomania in patients with bipolar disorder. Patients presenting with depressive symptoms should be screened for bipolar disorder. Monotherapy in patients with bipolar disorder should be avoided. **Doxepin is not FDA approved for the treatment of bipolar depression.**

The risks of sedative and anticholinergic effects are high relative to other antidepressant agents. Doxepin frequently causes sedation, which may result in impaired performance of tasks requiring alertness (eg, operating machinery or driving). Sedative effects may be additive with other CNS depressants and/or ethanol. Also use caution in patients with benign prostatic hyperplasia, xerostomia, visual problems, constipation, or history of bowel obstruction.

May cause orthostatic hypotension or conduction disturbances (risks are moderate relative to other antidepressants). Use with caution in patients with a history of cardiovascular disease (including previous MI, stroke, tachycardia, or conduction abnormalities). Consider discontinuation, when possible, prior to elective surgery. Therapy should not be abruptly discontinued in patients receiving high doses for prolonged periods.

Use caution in patients with a previous seizure disorder or condition predisposing to seizures such as brain damage, alcoholism, or concurrent therapy with other drugs which lower the seizure threshold. Use with caution in hyperthyroid patients or those receiving thyroid supplementation. Use with caution in patients with hepatic or renal dysfunction and in elderly patients.

Cream formulation is for external use only (not for ophthalmic, vaginal, or oral use). Do not use occlusive dressings. Use for >8 days may increase risk of contact sensitization. Doxepin is significantly absorbed following topical administration; plasma levels may be similar to those achieved with oral administration.

Adverse Reactions

Oral: Frequency not defined.

Cardiovascular: Hyper-/hypotension, tachycardia

Central nervous system: Drowsiness, dizziness, headache, disorientation, ataxia, confusion, seizure

Dermatologic: Alopecia, photosensitivity, rash, pruritus

Endocrine & metabolic: Breast enlargement, galactorrhea, SIADH, blood sugar increased/decreased, libido increased/decreased

Gastrointestinal: Xerostomia, constipation, vomiting, indigestion, anorexia, aphthous stomatitis, nausea, unpleasant taste, weight gain, diarrhea, trouble with gums, lower esophageal sphincter tone decrease may cause GE reflux

Genitourinary: Urinary retention, testicular edema

Hematologic: Agranulocytosis, leukopenia, eosinophilia, thrombocytopenia, purpura

Neuromuscular & skeletal: Weakness, tremor, numbness, paresthesia, extrapyramidal symptoms, tardive dyskinesia

Ocular: Blurred vision

Otic: Tinnitus

Miscellaneous: Diaphoresis (excessive), allergic reactions

Topical:
>10%:
  Central nervous system: Drowsiness (22%)
  Dermatologic: Stinging/burning (23%)
1% to 10%:
  Cardiovascular: Edema (1%)
  Central nervous system: Dizziness (2%), emotional changes (2%)
  Gastrointestinal: Xerostomia (10%), taste alteration (2%)
<1% (Limited to important or life-threatening): Contact dermatitis, tongue numbness, anxiety

Overdosage/Toxicology Symptoms include confusion, hallucinations, seizures, urinary retention, hypothermia, hypotension, tachycardia, and cyanosis. Following initiation of essential overdose management, toxic symptoms should be treated. Sodium bicarbonate is indicated when the QRS interval is >0.10 seconds or the QT_c interval is >0.42 seconds. Ventricular arrhythmias often respond to systemic alkalinization with or without phenytoin 15-20 mg/kg (adults) (sodium bicarbonate 0.5-2 mEq/kg I.V.). Arrhythmias unresponsive to this therapy may respond to lidocaine 1 mg/kg I.V. followed by a titrated infusion. Physostigmine (1-2 mg slow I.V. for adults or 0.5 mg slow I.V. for children) may be indicated in reversing life-threatening cardiac arrhythmias. Seizures usually respond to diazepam I.V. boluses (5-10 mg for adults up to 30 mg or 0.25-0.4 mg/kg/dose for children up to 10 mg/dose). If seizures are unresponsive or recur, phenytoin or phenobarbital may be required.

Drug Interactions
  Cytochrome P450 Effect: Substrate (major) of CYP1A2, 2D6, 3A4
    Increased Effect/Toxicity: Doxepin increases the effects of amphetamines, anticholinergics, other CNS depressants (sedatives, hypnotics, or ethanol), chlorpropamide, tolazamide, and warfarin. When used with MAO inhibitors, hyperpyrexia, hypertension, tachycardia, confusion, seizures, and **deaths have been reported** (serotonin syndrome). Serotonin syndrome has also been reported with ritonavir (rare).

      CYP1A2 inhibitors may increase the levels/effects of doxepin; example inhibitors include ciprofloxacin, fluvoxamine, ketoconazole, norfloxacin, ofloxacin, and rofecoxib. CYP2D6 inhibitors may increase the levels/effects of doxepin; example inhibitors include chlorpromazine, delavirdine, fluoxetine, miconazole, paroxetine, pergolide, quinidine, quinine, ritonavir, and ropinirole. CYP3A4 inhibitors may increase the levels/effects of doxepin. Example inhibitors include azole antifungals, clarithromycin, diclofenac, doxycycline, erythromycin, imatinib, isoniazid, nefazodone, nicardipine, propofol, protease inhibitors, quinidine, telithromycin, and verapamil. Cimetidine, grapefruit juice, indinavir, methylphenidate, diltiazem, and verapamil may increase the serum concentrations of TCAs. Use of lithium with a TCA may increase the risk for neurotoxicity. Phenothiazines may increase concentration of some TCAs and TCAs may increase concentration of phenothiazines.

      Pressor response to I.V. epinephrine, norepinephrine, and phenylephrine may be enhanced in patients receiving TCAs (**Note:** Effect is unlikely with epinephrine or levonordefrin dosages typically administered as infiltration in combination with local anesthetics). Combined use of beta-agonists or drugs which prolong QT_c (including quinidine, procainamide, disopyramide, cisapride, sparfloxacin, gatifloxacin, moxifloxacin) with TCAs may predispose patients to cardiac arrhythmias.

    Decreased Effect: CYP1A2 inducers may decrease the levels/effects of doxepin; example inducers include aminoglutethimide, carbamazepine, phenobarbital, and rifampin. Doxepin inhibits the antihypertensive response to bethanidine, clonidine, debrisoquin, guanadrel, guanethidine, guanabenz, and guanfacine. Cholestyramine and colestipol may bind TCAs and reduce their absorption. CYP3A4 inducers may decrease the levels/effects of doxepin; example inducers include aminoglutethimide, carbamazepine, nafcillin, nevirapine, phenobarbital, phenytoin, and rifamycins.

Ethanol/Nutrition/Herb Interactions
  Ethanol: Avoid ethanol (may increase CNS depression).
  Food: Grapefruit juice may inhibit the metabolism of some TCAs and clinical toxicity may result.
  Herb/Nutraceutical: Avoid valerian, St John's wort, SAMe, kava kava (may increase risk of serotonin syndrome and/or excessive sedation).

Stability Protect from light.

Mechanism of Action Increases the synaptic concentration of serotonin and norepinephrine in the central nervous system by inhibition of their reuptake by the presynaptic neuronal membrane

Pharmacodynamics/Kinetics
  Onset of action: Peak effect: Antidepressant: Usually >2 weeks; Anxiolytic: may occur sooner
  Absorption: Following topical application, plasma levels may be similar to those achieved with oral administration
  Distribution: Crosses placenta; enters breast milk
  Protein binding: 80% to 85%
  Metabolism: Hepatic; metabolites include desmethyldoxepin (active)
  Half-life elimination: Adults: 6-8 hours
  Excretion: Urine

Dosage
  Oral: Topical: Burning mouth syndrome (dental use): Cream: Apply 3-4 times daily
  Oral (entire daily dose may be given at bedtime):
    Depression or anxiety:
      Children (unlabeled use): 1-3 mg/kg/day in single or divided doses
      Adolescents: Initial: 25-50 mg/day in single or divided doses; gradually increase to 100 mg/day
      Adults: Initial: 25-150 mg/day at bedtime or in 2-3 divided doses; may gradually increase up to 300 mg/day; single dose should not exceed 150 mg; select patients may respond to 25-50 mg/day
      Elderly: Use a lower dose and adjust gradually
    Chronic urticaria, angioedema, nocturnal pruritus: Adults and Elderly: 10-30 mg/day
  Dosing adjustment in hepatic impairment: Use a lower dose and adjust gradually
(Continued)

Doxepin *(Continued)*

Topical: Pruritus: Adults and Elderly: Apply a thin film 4 times/day with at least 3- to 4-hour interval between applications; not recommended for use >8 days. **Note:** Low-dose (25-50 mg) oral administration has also been used to treat pruritus, but systemic effects are increased.

Administration

Oral: Do not mix oral concentrate with carbonated beverages (physically incompatible).

Topical: Apply thin film to affected area; use of occlusive dressings is not recommended.

Monitoring Parameters Monitor blood pressure and pulse rate prior to and during initial therapy; monitor mental status, weight; ECG in older adults; adverse effects may be increased if topical formulation is applied to >10% of body surface area

Reference Range Proposed therapeutic concentration (doxepin plus desmethyldoxepin): 110-250 ng/mL. Toxic concentration (doxepin plus desmethyldoxepin): >500 ng/mL. Utility of serum level monitoring is controversial.

Test Interactions Increased glucose

Dosage Forms [DSC] = Discontinued product

Capsule, as hydrochloride: 10 mg, 25 mg, 50 mg, 75 mg, 100 mg, 150 mg

Sinequan®: 10 mg, 25 mg, 50 mg, 75 mg, 100 mg, 150 mg [DSC]

Cream, as hydrochloride:

Prudoxin™: 5% (45 g) [contains benzyl alcohol]

Zonalon®: 5% (30 g, 45 g) [contains benzyl alcohol]

Solution, oral concentrate, as hydrochloride (Sinequan®): 10 mg/mL (120 mL)

Sinequan®: 10 mg/mL (120 mL) [DSC]

♦ **Doxepin Hydrochloride** *see Doxepin on page 545*

Doxercalciferol *(doks er kal si fe FEER ole)*

U.S. Brand Names Hectorol®

Canadian Brand Names Hectorol®

Index Terms 1α-Hydroxyergocalciferol

Pharmacologic Category Vitamin D Analog

Use Treatment of secondary hyperparathyroidism in patients with chronic kidney disease

Pregnancy Risk Factor B

Pregnancy Implications Reproduction in animals (usual and high dose) do not reveal teratogenic or fetotoxic effects.

Lactation Excretion in breast milk unknown/not recommended

Contraindications Hypersensitivity to any component of the formulation; history of hypercalcemia or evidence of vitamin D toxicity

Warnings/Precautions Other forms of vitamin D should be discontinued when doxercalciferol is started. Overdose from vitamin D may lead to progressive hypercalcemia and needs to be avoided. Careful dosage titration and monitoring can minimize risk. Hyperphosphatemia exacerbates secondary hyperparathyroidism, diminishing the effect of doxercalciferol. Hyperphosphatemia should be corrected before initiating therapy. Use with caution in patients with hepatic impairment. Injection is intended for I.V. use only. Safety and efficacy have not been established in pediatric patients.

Adverse Reactions

Note: As reported in dialysis patients.

>10%:

Cardiovascular: Edema (34%)

Central nervous system: Headache (28%), malaise (28%), dizziness (12%)

Gastrointestinal: Nausea/vomiting (24%)

Respiratory: Dyspnea (12%)

1% to 10%:

Cardiovascular: Bradycardia (7%)

Central nervous system: Sleep disorder (3%)

Dermatologic: Pruritus (8%)

Gastrointestinal: Anorexia (5%), constipation (3%), dyspepsia (5%), weight gain (5%)

Neuromuscular & skeletal: Arthralgia (5%)

Miscellaneous: Abscess (3%)

Overdosage/Toxicology Doxercalciferol, in excess, can cause hypercalcemia, hypercalciuria, hyperphosphatemia, and oversuppression of PTH secretion. Following withdrawal of the drug and calcium supplements, hypercalcemia treatment consists of a low calcium diet and monitoring. Adjustments of calcium in the dialysis bath can also be made if necessary. When calcium levels normalize, doxercalciferol can be restarted. Reduce each dose by at least 2.5 mcg. Monitor serum calcium levels closely.

Signs and symptoms of early hypercalcemia include: Anorexia, bone pain, constipation, headache, metallic taste, muscle pain, nausea, somnolence, vomiting, weakness, xerostomia

Signs and symptoms of late hypercalcemia include: Albuminuria, anorexia, apathy, AST/ALT increased, BUN increased, cardiac arrhythmias, conjunctivitis (calcific), dehydration, ectopic calcification, growth arrested, hypercholesterolemia, hypertension, hyperthermia, libido decreased, nocturia, pancreatitis, photophobia, polydipsia, polyuria, pruritus, psychosis (rare), rhinorrhea, sensory disturbances, urinary tract infections, weight loss

Drug Interactions

Increased Effect/Toxicity: Doxercalciferol toxicity may be increased by concurrent use of other vitamin D supplements or magnesium-containing antacids and supplements.

Decreased Effect: Absorption of doxercalciferol is reduced with mineral oil and cholestyramine.

Stability Store at controlled room temperature of 15°C to 30°C (59°F to 86°F). Protect injection from light.

Mechanism of Action Doxercalciferol is metabolized to the active form of vitamin D. The active form of vitamin D controls the intestinal absorption of dietary calcium, the tubular reabsorption of calcium by the kidneys, and in conjunction with PTH, the mobilization of calcium from the skeleton.

Pharmacodynamics/Kinetics

Metabolism: Hepatic via CYP27

Half-life elimination: Active metabolite: 32-37 hours; up to 96 hours

Dosage

Oral:

Dialysis patients: Dose should be titrated to lower iPTH to 150-300 pg/mL; dose is adjusted at 8-week intervals (maximum dose: 20 mcg 3 times/week)

Initial dose: iPTH >400 pg/mL: 10 mcg 3 times/week at dialysis

Dose titration:

iPTH level decreased by 50% and >300 pg/mL: Dose can be increased to 12.5 mcg 3 times/week for 8 more weeks; this titration process can continue at 8-week intervals; each increase should be by 2.5 mcg/dose

iPTH level 150-300 pg/mL: Maintain current dose

iPTH level <100 pg/mL: Suspend doxercalciferol for 1 week; resume at a reduced dose; decrease each dose (not weekly dose) by at least 2.5 mcg

Predialysis patients: Dose should be titrated to lower iPTH to 35-70 pg/mL with stage 3 disease or to 70-110 pg/mL with stage 4 disease: Dose may be adjusted at 2-week intervals (maximum dose: 3.5 mcg/day)

Initial dose: 1 mcg/day

Dose titration:

iPTH level >70 pg/mL with stage 3 disease or >110 pg/mL with stage 4 disease: Increase dose by 0.5 mcg every 2 weeks as necessary

iPTH level 35-70 pg/mL with stage 3 disease or 70-110 pg/mL with stage 4 disease: Maintain current dose

iPTH level is <35 pg/mL with stage 3 disease or <70 pg/mL with stage 4 disease: Suspend doxercalciferol for 1 week, then resume at a reduced dose (at least 0.5 mcg lower)

I.V.:

Dialysis patients: Dose should be titrated to lower iPTH to 150-300 pg/mL; dose is adjusted at 8-week intervals (maximum dose: 18 mcg/week)

Initial dose: iPTH level >400 pg/mL: 4 mcg 3 times/week after dialysis, administered as a bolus dose

Dose titration:

iPTH level decreased by <50% and >300 pg/mL: Dose can be increased by 1-2 mcg at 8-week intervals, as necessary

iPTH level decreased by >50% and >300 pg/mL: Maintain current dose

iPTH level 150-300 pg/mL: Maintain the current dose

iPTH level <100 pg/mL: Suspend doxercalciferol for 1 week; resume at a reduced dose (at least 1 mcg lower)

Dietary Considerations Based on serum levels, dietary phosphorus may be restricted and/or controlled with calcium-based phosphorus binders. The daily combined calcium intake (dietary and calcium based phosphate binder) should be 1.5-2 g. Additional vitamin D supplements and magnesium-containing antacids should be avoided. Capsules contain coconut oil.

Monitoring Parameters

Dialysis patients: Before initiating, check iPTH, serum calcium and phosphorus. Check weekly thereafter until stable. Serum iPTH, calcium, phosphorus, and alkaline phosphatase should be monitored.

Predialysis patients: iPTH, serum calcium and phosphorus every 2 weeks for 3 months following initiation and dose adjustments, then monthly for 3 months, then every 3 months

Reference Range Serum calcium times phosphorus product should be >55 mg^2/dL^2 with chronic kidney disease

Target range by stage of chronic kidney disease:

Stage 3:

GFR 30-59 mL/minute: iPTH 35-70 pg/mL

Serum phosphorus: 2.7-4.6 mg/dL

Stage 4:

GFR 15-29 mL/minute: iPTH 70-110 pg/mL

Serum phosphorus: 2.7-4.6 mg/dL

Stage 5:

GFR <15 mL/minute or dialysis: iPTH 150-300 pg/mL

Serum phosphorus: 3.5-5.5 mg/dL

Dosage Forms

Capsule, softgel:

Hectorol®: 0.5 mcg, 2.5 mcg [contains coconut oil]

Injection, solution:

Hectorol®: 2 mcg/mL (2 mL) [contains disodium edetate]

◆ **Doxidan® [OTC]** see Bisacodyl on page 223
◆ **Doxil®** see DOXOrubicin (Liposomal) on page 552

DOXOrubicin (doks oh ROO bi sin)

U.S. Brand Names Adriamycin PFS®; Adriamycin RDF®; Rubex®

Canadian Brand Names Adriamycin®

Index Terms ADR (error-prone abbreviation); Adria; Doxorubicin Hydrochloride; Hydroxydaunomycin Hydrochloride; Hydroxyldaunorubicin Hydrochloride; NSC-123127

Pharmacologic Category Antineoplastic Agent, Anthracycline

Use Treatment of leukemias, lymphomas, multiple myeloma, osseous and nonosseous sarcomas, mesotheliomas, germ cell tumors of the ovary or testis, and carcinomas of the head and neck, thyroid, lung, breast, stomach, pancreas, liver, ovary, bladder, prostate, uterus, neuroblastoma and Wilms' tumor.

Pregnancy Risk Factor D

(Continued)

DOXOrubicin *(Continued)*

Pregnancy Implications Advise patients to avoid becoming pregnant (females) and to avoid causing pregnancy (males).

Lactation Enters breast milk/contraindicated

Medication Safety Issues

Sound-alike/look-alike issues:

DOXOrubicin may be confused with dactinomycin, DAUNOrubicin, doxacurium, doxapram, doxazosin, epirubicin, idarubicin

Adriamycin PFS® may be confused with achromycin, Aredia®, Idamycin®

Rubex® may be confused with Revex®, Robaxin®

Conventional formulations (Adriamycin PFS®, Adriamycin RDF®, Rubex®) may be confused with liposomal formulations (DaunoXome®, Doxil®)

High alert medication: The Institute for Safe Medication Practices (ISMP) includes this medication among its list of drugs which have a heightened risk of causing significant patient harm when used in error.

ADR is an error-prone abbreviation

International issues:

Doxil® may be confused with Doxal® which is a brand name for doxepin in Finland, a brand name for doxycycline in Austria, and a brand name for pyridoxine/thiamine combination in Brazil

Rubex®: Brand name for ascorbic acid in Ireland

Contraindications Hypersensitivity to doxorubicin or any component of the formulation; congestive heart failure or arrhythmias; previous therapy with high cumulative doses of doxorubicin and/or daunorubicin; pre-existing bone marrow suppression; pregnancy

Warnings/Precautions Hazardous agent - use appropriate precautions for handling and disposal. Total dose should not exceed 550 mg/m^2 or 450 mg/m^2 in patients with previous or concomitant treatment with daunorubicin, cyclophosphamide, or irradiation of the cardiac region. **[U.S. Boxed Warning]: Irreversible myocardial toxicity may occur** as total dosage approaches 550 mg/m^2. A baseline cardiac evaluation (ECG, LVEF, +/- ECHO) is recommended, especially in patients with risk factors for increased cardiac toxicity and in pediatric patients. Pediatric patients are at increased risk for delayed cardiotoxicity. **[U.S. Boxed Warnings]: Reduce dose in patients with impaired hepatic function; severe myelosuppression is also possible. Secondary acute myelogenous leukemia may occur following treatment.**

[U.S. Boxed Warnings]: I.V. use only. Doxorubicin is a potent vesicant; if extravasation occurs, severe tissue damage leading to ulceration and necrosis, and pain may occur. Should be administered under the supervision of an experienced cancer chemotherapy physician.

Adverse Reactions

>10%:

Cardiovascular: Transient ECG abnormalities (supraventricular tachycardia, S-T wave changes, atrial or ventricular extrasystoles); generally asymptomatic and self-limiting. CHF, dose related, may be delayed for 7-8 years after treatment. Cumulative dose, mediastinal/pericardial radiation therapy, cardiovascular disease, age, and use of cyclophosphamide (or other cardiotoxic agents) all increase the risk.

Recommended maximum cumulative doses:

No risk factors: 550 mg/m^2

Concurrent radiation: 450 mg/m^2

Note: Regardless of cumulative dose, if the left ventricular ejection fraction is <30% to 40%, the drug is usually not given.

Dermatologic: Alopecia

Gastrointestinal: Acute nausea and vomiting (21% to 55%), mucositis, ulceration, and necrosis of the colon, anorexia, and diarrhea, stomatitis, esophagitis

Genitourinary: Discoloration of urine (red)

Hematologic: Myelosuppression, leukopenia (75%), dose-limiting toxicity

WBC: Moderate

Platelets: Moderate

Onset (days): 7

Nadir (days): 10-14

Recovery (days): 21-28

Local: **Vesicant chemotherapy**

1% to 10%:

Cardiovascular: Acute: Arrhythmias, heart block, pericarditis-myocarditis, facial flushing; Delayed: CHF (related to cumulative dose; usually a maximum total lifetime dose of 450-550 mg/m^2; possibly higher if given by continuous infusion)

Dermatologic: Hyperpigmentation of nail beds, erythematous streaking along the vein if administered rapidly

Endocrine & metabolic: Hyperuricemia

<1% (Limited to important or life-threatening):

Pediatric patients may be at increased risk of later neoplastic disease, particularly acute myeloid leukemia (pediatric patients). Prepubertal growth failure may result from intensive chemotherapy regimens.

Radiation recall: Noticed in patients who have had prior irradiation; reactions include redness, warmth, erythema, and dermatitis in the radiation port. Can progress to severe desquamation and ulceration. Occurs 5-7 days after doxorubicin administration; local therapy with topical corticosteroids and cooling have given the best relief.

Overdosage/Toxicology Symptoms include myelosuppression, nausea, vomiting, and myocardial toxicity.

Drug Interactions

Cytochrome P450 Effect: Substrate (major) of CYP2D6, 3A4; **Inhibits** CYP2B6 (moderate), 2D6 (weak), 3A4 (weak)

Increased Effect/Toxicity: Allopurinol may enhance the antitumor activity of doxorubicin (animal data only). Cyclosporine may increase doxorubicin levels, enhancing hematologic toxicity or may induce coma or seizures. Cyclophosphamide enhances the cardiac toxicity of doxorubicin by producing additional myocardial cell damage. Mercaptopurine increases doxorubicin toxicities. Streptozocin greatly enhances leukopenia and thrombocytopenia. Verapamil alters the cellular distribution of doxorubicin and may result in increased cell toxicity by inhibition of the P-glycoprotein pump. Paclitaxel reduces doxorubicin clearance and increases toxicity if administered prior to doxorubicin. High doses of progesterone enhance toxicity (neutropenia and thrombocytopenia).

Doxorubicin may increase the levels/effects of bupropion, promethazine, propofol, selegiline, sertraline, and other CYP2B6 substrates. The levels/effects of doxorubicin may be increased by azole antifungals, chlorpromazine, clarithromycin, delavirdine, diclofenac, doxycycline, erythromycin, fluoxetine, imatinib, isoniazid, miconazole, nefazodone, nicardipine, paroxetine, pergolide, propofol, protease inhibitors, quinidine, quinine, ritonavir, ropinirole, telithromycin, verapamil and other inhibitors of CYP2D6 or 3A4. Based on mouse studies, cardiotoxicity may be enhanced by verapamil. Concurrent therapy with actinomycin-D may result in recall pneumonitis following radiation.

Decreased Effect: The levels/effects of doxorubicin may be decreased by aminoglutethimide, carbamazepine, nafcillin, nevirapine, phenobarbital, phenytoin, rifamycins, and other CYP3A4 inducers. Doxorubicin may decrease plasma levels and effectiveness of digoxin. Doxorubicin may decrease the antiviral activity of zidovudine.

Ethanol/Nutrition/Herb Interactions Herb/Nutraceutical: St John's wort may decrease doxorubicin levels. Avoid black cohosh, dong quai in estrogen-dependent tumors.

Stability Store intact vials of solution under refrigeration (2°C to 8°C) and protect from light; store intact vials of lyophilized powder at room temperature (15°C to 30°C). Reconstitute lyophilized powder with NS to a final concentration of 2 mg/mL. Reconstituted vials are stable for 7 days at room temperature (25°C) and 15 days under refrigeration (5°C) when protected from light. Infusions are stable for 48 hours at room temperature (25°C) when protected from light. Solutions diluted in 50-1000 mL D_5W or NS are stable for 48 hours at room temperature (25°C) when protected from light.

Unstable in solutions with a pH <3 or >7.

Mechanism of Action Inhibition of DNA and RNA synthesis by intercalation between DNA base pairs by inhibition of topoisomerase II and by steric obstruction. Doxorubicin intercalates at points of local uncoiling of the double helix. Although the exact mechanism is unclear, it appears that direct binding to DNA (intercalation) and inhibition of DNA repair (topoisomerase II inhibition) result in blockade of DNA and RNA synthesis and fragmentation of DNA. Doxorubicin is also a powerful iron chelator; the iron-doxorubicin complex can bind DNA and cell membranes and produce free radicals that immediately cleave the DNA and cell membranes.

Pharmacodynamics/Kinetics

Absorption: Oral: Poor (<50%)

Distribution: V_d: 25 L/kg; to many body tissues, particularly liver, spleen, kidney, lung, heart; does not distribute into the CNS; crosses placenta

Protein binding, plasma: 70%

Metabolism: Primarily hepatic to doxorubicinol (active), then to inactive aglycones, conjugated sulfates, and glucuronides

Half-life elimination:
Distribution: 10 minutes
Elimination: Doxorubicin: 1-3 hours; Metabolites: 3-3.5 hours
Terminal: 17-30 hours
Male: 54 hours; Female: 35 hours

Excretion: Feces (~40% to 50% as unchanged drug); urine (~3% to 10% as metabolites, 1% doxorubicinol, <1% Adriamycin aglycones, and unchanged drug)
Clearance: Male: 113 L/hour; Female: 44 L/hour

Dosage Refer to individual protocols. I.V.:
Children:
35-75 mg/m² as a single dose, repeat every 21 days **or**
20-30 mg/m² once weekly **or**
60-90 mg/m² given as a continuous infusion over 96 hours every 3-4 weeks
Adults: Usual or typical dose: 60-75 mg/m² as a single dose, repeat every 21 days **or** other dosage regimens like 20-30 mg/m²/day for 2-3 days, repeat in 4 weeks **or** 20 mg/m² once weekly

Dosing adjustment in renal impairment:
Adjustments are not required.
Hemodialysis effects: Supplemental dose is not necessary.

Dosing adjustment in hepatic impairment:
ALT/AST 2-3 times ULN: Administer 75% of dose
ALT/AST >3 times ULN **or** bilirubin 1.2-3 mg/dL (20-51 µmol/L): Administer 50% of dose
Bilirubin 3.1-5 mg/dL (51-85 µmol/L): Administer 25% of dose
Bilirubin >5 mg/dL (85 µmol/L): Do not administer

Administration Administer I.V. push over 1-2 minutes, IVPB over 15-60 minutes, or continuous infusion.

Monitoring Parameters CBC with differential and platelet count, cardiac and liver function tests

Dosage Forms
Injection, powder for reconstitution, as hydrochloride: 10 mg, 20 mg, 50 mg [contains lactose]
Adriamycin RDF®: 10 mg, 20 mg, 50 mg, 150 mg [contains lactose; rapid dissolution formula]
Rubex®: 50 mg, 100 mg [contains lactose]
Injection, solution, as hydrochloride [preservative free]: 2 mg/mL (5 mL, 10 mL, 25 mL, 100 mL)
Adriamycin PFS® [preservative free]: 2 mg/mL (5 mL, 10 mL, 25 mL, 37.5 mL, 100 mL)

♦ **Doxorubicin Hydrochloride** see DOXOrubicin on page 549

♦ **Doxorubicin Hydrochloride (Liposomal)** *see* DOXOrubicin (Liposomal) *on page 552*

DOXOrubicin (Liposomal) (doks oh ROO bi sin lip pah SOW mal)

U.S. Brand Names Doxil®
Canadian Brand Names Caelyx®
Index Terms Doxorubicin Hydrochloride (Liposomal)
Pharmacologic Category Antineoplastic Agent, Anthracycline
Use Treatment of AIDS-related Kaposi's sarcoma, breast cancer, ovarian cancer, solid tumors
Pregnancy Risk Factor D
Pregnancy Implications Advise patients to avoid becoming pregnant (females) and to avoid causing pregnancy (males).
Lactation Excretion in breast milk unknown/contraindicated
Medication Safety Issues
Sound-alike/look-alike issues:
DOXOrubicin may be confused with dactinomycin, DAUNOrubicin, doxacurium, doxapram, doxazosin, epirubicin, idarubicin
Doxil® may be confused with Doxy®, Paxil®
Liposomal formulations (Doxil®) may be confused with conventional formulations (Adriamycin PFS®, Adriamycin RDF®, Cerubidine®, Rubex®).

High alert medication: The Institute for Safe Medication Practices (ISMP) includes this medication among its list of drugs which have a heightened risk of causing significant patient harm when used in error.

Liposomal formulations of doxorubicin should NOT be substituted for doxorubicin hydrochloride on a mg-per-mg basis.
Contraindications Hypersensitivity to doxorubicin, other anthracyclines, or any component of the formulation; breast-feeding, pregnancy
Warnings/Precautions Hazardous agent - use appropriate precautions for handling and disposal.

[U.S. Boxed Warning]: Doxorubicin is associated with dose-related myocardial damage leading to congestive heart failure. Doxorubicin and liposomal doxorubicin should be used cautiously in patients with high cumulative doses of anthracyclines, anthracenediones, and cyclophosphamide. Caution should also be used in patients with previous thoracic radiation or who have pre-existing cardiac disease. Total dose should not exceed 550 mg/m^2 or 400 mg/m^2 in patients with previous or concomitant treatment (with daunorubicin, cyclophosphamide, or irradiation of the cardiac region); irreversible myocardial toxicity may occur as total dosage approaches 550 mg/m^2. Symptoms of anthracycline-induced CHF and/or cardiomyopathy may be delayed in onset (up to 7-8 years in some cases). I.V. use only. **[U.S. Boxed Warnings]: Reduce dose in patients with impaired hepatic function; severe myelosuppression is also possible. Acute infusion reactions may occur, some may be serious/life-threatening. Liposomal formulations of doxorubicin should NOT be substituted for doxorubicin hydrochloride on a mg-per-mg basis.**

Hand-foot syndrome (palmar-plantar erythrodysesthesia) has been reported in up to 51% of patients with ovarian cancer (and significantly lower frequency in patients with Kaposi's sarcoma). May occur early in treatment, but is usually seen after 2-3 treatment cycles. Dosage modification may be required. In severe cases, treatment discontinuation may be required. **[U.S. Boxed Warning]: Should be administered under the supervision of an experienced cancer chemotherapy physician.**
Adverse Reactions
>10%:
Cardiovascular: Peripheral edema (up to 11%)
Central nervous system: Fever (8% to 12%), headache (up to 11%), pain (up to 21%)
Dermatologic: Alopecia (9% to 19%); palmar-plantar erythrodysesthesia/hand-foot syndrome (up to 51% in ovarian cancer, 4% in Kaposi's sarcoma), rash (up to 29% in ovarian cancer, up to 5% in Kaposi's sarcoma)
Gastrointestinal: Stomatitis (5% to 41%), vomiting (8% to 33%), nausea (18% to 46%), mucositis (up to 14%), constipation (up to 30%), anorexia (up to 20%), diarrhea (5% to 21%), dyspepsia (up to 12%), intestinal obstruction (up to 11%)
Hematologic: Myelosuppression, neutropenia (12% to 62%), leukopenia (36%), thrombocytopenia (13% to 65%), anemia (6% to 74%)
Onset: 7 days
Nadir: 10-14 days
Recovery: 21-28 days
Neuromuscular & skeletal: Weakness (7% to 40%), back pain (up to 12%)
Respiratory: Pharyngitis (up to 16%), dyspnea (up to 15%)
1% to 10%:
Cardiovascular: Cardiac arrest, chest pain, edema, hypotension, pallor, tachycardia, vasodilation
Central nervous system: Agitation, anxiety, chills, confusion, depression, dizziness, emotional lability, insomnia, somnolence, vertigo
Dermatologic: Acne, dry skin (6%), dermatitis, furunculosis, maculopapular rash, pruritus, rash, skin discoloration, vesiculobullous rash
Endocrine & metabolic: Dehydration, hyperbilirubinemia, hyperglycemia, hypocalcemia, hypokalemia, hyponatremia
Gastrointestinal: Abdomen enlarged, ascites, cachexia, dyspepsia, dysphagia, esophagitis, flatulence, gingivitis, glossitis, ileus, mouth ulceration, rectal bleeding, taste perversion, weight loss, xerostomia
Genitourinary: Cystitis, dysuria, leukorrhea, pelvic pain, polyuria, urinary incontinence, urinary tract infection, urinary urgency, vaginal bleeding
Hematologic: Ecchymosis, hemolysis, prothrombin time increased
Hepatic: ALT increased
Local: Thrombophlebitis

Neuromuscular & skeletal: Arthralgia, hypertonia, myalgia, neuralgia, neuritis (peripheral), neuropathy, paresthesia (up to 10%), pathological fracture,

Ocular: Conjunctivitis, dry eyes, retinitis

Otic: Ear pain

Renal: Albuminuria, hematuria

Respiratory: Apnea, cough increased (up to 10%), epistaxis, pleural effusion, pneumonia, rhinitis, sinusitis

Miscellaneous: Allergic reaction; infusion-related reactions (bronchospasm, chest tightness, chills, dyspnea, facial edema, flushing, headache, herpes simplex/zoster, hypotension, pruritus); moniliasis, diaphoresis

<1% (Limited to important or life-threatening): Abscess, acute brain syndrome, abnormal vision, anaphylactic or anaphylactoid reaction, asthma, blindness, bone pain, BUN increased, bundle branch block, cardiomegaly, cellulitis, colitis, creatinine increased, cryptococcosis, diabetes mellitus, erythema multiforme, erythema nodosum, eosinophilia, eye pain, flu-like syndrome, glucosuria, heart arrest, hematuria, hemiplegia, hemorrhage, hepatic failure, hepatitis, hepatosplenomegaly, hypercalcemia, hyperkalemia, hypernatremia, hyperuricemia, hyperventilation, hypoglycemia, hypokinesia, hypolipidemia, hypomagnesemia, hyponatremia, hypophosphatemia, hypoproteinemia, hypothermia, injection site hemorrhage, injection site pain, jaundice, ketosis, lactic dehydrogenase increased, kidney failure, lymphadenopathy, lymphangitis, migraine, myositis, optic neuritis, otitis media, palpitation, pancreatitis, pericardial effusion, petechia, pleural effusion, pneumothorax, radiation injury, sclerosing cholangitis, seizure, sepsis, skin necrosis, skin ulcer, syncope, thrombophlebitis, thromboplastin decreased, thrombosis, tinnitus, urticaria, visual field defect, ventricular arrhythmia, weight gain

Overdosage/Toxicology Symptoms include increased mucositis, leukopenia, and thrombocytopenia. In acute overdose, the severely myelosuppressed patient should be hospitalized and treated with antibiotics, hematopoietic growth factors, platelet and granulocyte transfusions. Mucositis should be treated symptomatically.

Drug Interactions

Cytochrome P450 Effect: Substrate (major) of CYP2D6, 3A4; **Inhibits** CYP2B6 (moderate), 2D6 (weak), 3A4 (weak)

Increased Effect/Toxicity: Allopurinol may enhance the antitumor activity of doxorubicin (animal data only). Cyclosporine may increase doxorubicin levels, enhancing hematologic toxicity or may induce coma or seizures. Cyclophosphamide enhances the cardiac toxicity of doxorubicin by producing additional myocardial cell damage. Mercaptopurine increases doxorubicin toxicities. Streptozocin greatly enhances leukopenia and thrombocytopenia. Verapamil alters the cellular distribution of doxorubicin and may result in increased cell toxicity by inhibition of the P-glycoprotein pump. Paclitaxel reduces doxorubicin clearance and increases toxicity if administered prior to doxorubicin. High doses of progesterone enhance toxicity (neutropenia and thrombocytopenia).

Doxorubicin may increase the levels/effects of bupropion, promethazine, propofol, selegiline, sertraline, and other CYP2B6 substrates. The levels/effects of doxorubicin may be increased by azole antifungals, chlorpromazine, clarithromycin, delavirdine, diclofenac, doxycycline, erythromycin, fluoxetine, imatinib, isoniazid, miconazole, nefazodone, nicardipine, paroxetine, pergolide, propofol, protease inhibitors, quinidine, quinine, ritonavir, ropinirole, telithromycin, verapamil and other inhibitors of CYP2D6 or 3A4. Based on mouse studies, cardiotoxicity may be enhanced by verapamil. Concurrent therapy with actinomycin-D may result in recall pneumonitis following radiation.

Decreased Effect: The levels/effects of doxorubicin may be decreased by aminoglutethimide, carbamazepine, nafcillin, nevirapine, phenobarbital, phenytoin, rifamycins, and other CYP3A4 inducers. Doxorubicin may decrease plasma levels and effectiveness of digoxin. Doxorubicin may decrease the antiviral activity of zidovudine.

Ethanol/Nutrition/Herb Interactions

Ethanol: Avoid ethanol (due to GI irritation).

Herb/Nutraceutical: St John's wort may decrease doxorubicin levels. Avoid black cohosh, dong quai in estrogen-dependent tumors.

Stability Store intact vials of solution under refrigeration (2°C to 8°C); avoid freezing. Prolonged freezing may adversely affect liposomal drug products, however, short-term freezing (<1 month) does not appear to have a deleterious effect.

Doses Doxil® ≤90 mg must be diluted in 250 mL of D_5W prior to administration. Doses >90 mg should be diluted in 500 mL D_5W. Diluted doxorubicin hydrochloride liposome injection may be refrigerated at 2°C to 8°C or at room temperature; administer within 24 hours. **Do not use with in-line filters.**

Mechanism of Action Doxorubicin inhibits DNA and RNA synthesis by intercalating between DNA base pairs causing steric obstruction and inhibits topoisomerase-II at the point of DNA cleavage. Doxorubicin is also a powerful iron chelator. The iron-doxorubicin complex can bind DNA and cell membranes, producing free hydroxyl (OH) radicals that cleave DNA and cell membranes. Active throughout entire cell cycle.

Pharmacodynamics/Kinetics

Distribution: V_{dss}: 2.8 L/m^2

Protein binding, plasma: Unknown; nonliposomal doxorubicin 70%

Half-life elimination: Terminal: Distribution: 4.7-5.2 hours, Elimination: 44-55 hours

Metabolism: Hepatic and in plasma to doxorubicinol and the sulfate and glucuronide conjugates of 4-demethyl,7-deoxyaglycones

Excretion: Urine (5% as doxorubicin or doxorubicinol)

Clearance: Mean: 0.041 $L/hour/m^2$

Dosage Refer to individual protocols. **Liposomal formulations of doxorubicin should NOT be substituted for doxorubicin hydrochloride on a mg-per-mg basis.**

AIDS-KS patients: I.V.: 20 mg/m^2/dose once every 3 weeks

Breast cancer (unlabeled use): I.V.: 20-80 mg/m^2/dose every 8 weeks has been studied in a limited number of phase I/II trials

Ovarian cancer: I.V.: 50 mg/m^2/dose every 4 weeks

Solid tumors (unlabeled use): I.V.: 50-60 mg/m^2/dose every 3-4 weeks

(Continued)

DOXOrubicin (Liposomal) (Continued)

See table: "Recommended Dose Modification Guidelines"

Recommended Dose Modification Guidelines

Toxicity Grade	Dose Adjustment
HAND FOOT SYNDROME (HFS)	
1 (Mild erythema, swelling, or desquamation not interfering with daily activities)	Redose unless patient has experienced previous Grade 3 or 4 toxicity. If so, delay up to 2 weeks and decrease dose by 25%; return to original dosing interval.
2 (Erythema, desquamation, or swelling interfering with, but not precluding, normal physical activities; small blisters or ulcerations <2 cm in diameter)	Delay dosing up to 2 weeks or until resolved to Grade 0-1. If after 2 weeks there is no resolution, liposomal doxorubicin should be discontinued. Otherwise, if no prior Grade 3-4 HFS, continue treatment at previous dose and dosage interval. If a prior Grade 3-4 HFS has occurred, continue prior dosage interval, but decrease dose by 25%.
3 (Blistering, ulceration, or swelling interfering with walking or normal daily activities; cannot wear regular clothing)	Delay dosing up to 2 weeks or until resolved to Grade 0-1. Decrease dose by 25% and return to original dosing interval; if after 2 weeks there is no resolution, liposomal doxorubicin should be discontinued.
4 (Diffuse or local process causing infectious complications, or a bedridden state or hospitalization)	Delay dosing up to 2 weeks or until resolved to Grade 0-1. Decrease dose by 25% and return to original dosing interval. If after 2 weeks there is no resolution, liposomal doxorubicin should be discontinued.
STOMATITIS	
1 (Painless ulcers, erythema, or mild soreness)	Redose unless patient has experienced previous Grade 3 or 4 toxicity. If so, delay up to 2 weeks and decrease by 25%. Return to original dosing interval.
2 (Painful erythema, edema, or ulcers, but can eat)	Delay dosing up to 2 weeks or until resolved to Grade 0-1. If after 2 weeks there is no resolution, liposomal doxorubicin should be discontinued. Otherwise, if not prior Grade 3-4 stomatitis, continue treatment at previous dose and dosage interval. If prior Grade 3-4 toxicity, continue treatment with previous dosage interval, but decrease dose by 25%.
3 (Painful erythema, edema, or ulcers, but cannot eat)	Delay dosing up to 2 weeks or until resolved to Grade 0-1. Decrease dose by 25% and return to original dosing interval. If after 2 weeks there is no resolution, liposomal doxorubicin should be discontinued.
4 (Requires parenteral or enteral support)	Delay dosing up to 2 weeks or until resolved to Grade 0-1. Decrease dose by 25% and return to original dosing interval. If after 2 weeks there is no resolution, liposomal doxorubicin should be discontinued.

Dosing adjustment in hepatic impairment:

ALT/AST 2-3 times ULN: Administer 75% of dose

ALT/AST >3 times ULN **or** bilirubin 1.2-3 mg/dL (20-51 µmol/L): Administer 50% of dose

Bilirubin 3.1-5 mg/dL (51-85 µmol/L): Administer 25% of dose

Bilirubin >5 mg/dL (85 µmol/L): Do not administer

See table: "Hematological Toxicity"

Hematological Toxicity

Grade	ANC	Platelets	Modification
1	1500-1900	75,000-150,000	Resume treatment with no dose reduction.
2	1000-<1500	50,000-<75,000	Wait until ANC ≥1500 and platelets ≥75,000; redose with no dose reduction.
3	500-999	25,000-<50,000	Wait until ANC ≥1500 and platelets ≥75,000; redose with no dose reduction.
4	<500	<25,000	Wait until ANC ≥1500 and platelets ≥75,000; redose at 25% dose reduction or continue full dose with cytokine support.

Administration Administer IVPB over 60 minutes; manufacturer recommends administering at initial rate of 1 mg/minute to minimize risk of infusion reactions until the absence of a reaction has been established, then increase the infusion rate for completion over 1 hour. **Do not administer I.M. or SubQ. Do not use with in-line filters.** Avoid extravasation associated with severe ulceration and soft tissue necrosis. Flush with 5-10 mL of D_5W solution before and after drug administration, incompatible with heparin flushes. Monitor for local erythematous streaking along vein and/or facial flushing (may indicate rapid infusion rate).

Monitoring Parameters CBC with differential and platelet count, liver function tests

Cardiac function should be carefully monitored; echocardiography, MUGA scan may be used during therapy. Endomyocardial biopsy is the most definitive test for anthracycline myocardial injury.

Dosage Forms Injection, solution, as hydrochloride: 2 mg/mL (10 mL, 25 mL)

♦ **Doxy-100®** see Doxycycline on page 555

♦ **Doxycin (Can)** see Doxycycline on page 555

Doxycycline (doks i SYE kleen)

U.S. Brand Names Adoxa®; Doryx®; Doxy-100®; Monodox®; Oracea™; Periostat®; Vibramycin®; Vibra-Tabs®

Canadian Brand Names Apo-Doxy®; Apo-Doxy Tabs®; Doxycin; Doxytec; Novo-Doxylin; Nu-Doxycycline; Periostat®; Vibra-Tabs®

Index Terms Doxycycline Calcium; Doxycycline Hyclate; Doxycycline Monohydrate

Pharmacologic Category Antibiotic, Tetracycline Derivative

Additional Appendix Information
Animal and Human Bites *on page 1976*
Antimicrobial Drugs of Choice *on page 1981*
Community-Acquired Pneumonia in Adults *on page 1999*
Malaria Treatment *on page 2003*
Prevention of Wound Infection and Sepsis in Surgical Patients *on page 1964*
Treatment of Sexually Transmitted Infections *on page 2007*

Use Principally in the treatment of infections caused by susceptible *Rickettsia, Chlamydia,* and *Mycoplasma*; alternative to mefloquine for malaria prophylaxis; treatment for syphilis, uncomplicated *Neisseria gonorrhoeae, Listeria, Actinomyces israelii,* and *Clostridium* infections in penicillin-allergic patients; used for community-acquired pneumonia and other common infections due to susceptible organisms; anthrax due to *Bacillus anthracis,* including inhalational anthrax (postexposure); treatment of infections caused by uncommon susceptible gram-negative and gram-positive organisms including *Borrelia recurrentis, Ureaplasma urealyticum, Haemophilus ducreyi, Yersinia pestis, Francisella tularensis, Vibrio cholerae, Campylobacter fetus, Brucella* spp, *Bartonella bacilliformis,* and *Calymmatobacterium granulomatis*; treatment of inflammatory lesions associated with rosacea

Unlabeled/Investigational Use Sclerosing agent for pleural effusion injection; vancomycin-resistant enterococci (VRE)

Pregnancy Risk Factor D

Pregnancy Implications Exposure during the last half or pregnancy causes permanent yellow-gray-brown discoloration of the teeth. Tetracyclines also form a complex in bone-forming tissue, leading to a decreased fibula growth rate when given to premature infants.

According to the FDA, the Teratogen Information System concluded that therapeutic doses during pregnancy are unlikely to produce substantial teratogenic risk, but data are insufficient to say that there is no risk. In general, reports of exposure have been limited to short durations of therapy in the first trimester. When considering treatment for life-threatening infection and/or prolonged duration of therapy (such as in anthrax), the potential risk to the fetus must be balanced against the severity of the potential illness.

Lactation Enters breast milk/not recommended

Medication Safety Issues
Sound-alike/look-alike issues:
Doxycycline may be confused with dicyclomine, doxepin, doxylamine
Doxy-100® may be confused with Doxil®
Monodox® may be confused with Maalox®

Contraindications Hypersensitivity to doxycycline, tetracycline or any component of the formulation; children <8 years of age, except in treatment of anthrax (including inhalational anthrax postexposure prophylaxis); severe hepatic dysfunction; pregnancy

Warnings/Precautions Do not use during pregnancy - use of tetracyclines during tooth development may cause permanent discoloration of the teeth and enamel hypoplasia; prolonged use may result in superinfection, including oral or vaginal candidiasis; photosensitivity reaction may occur with this drug; avoid prolonged exposure to sunlight or tanning equipment. Anti-anabolic effects of tetracyclines can increase BUN leading to significant renal dysfunction and hepatotoxicity in patients with pre-existing renal impairment. Autoimmune syndromes have been reported; if symptomatic conduct LFT and discontinue drug. Tetracyclines have been associated with pseudotumor cerebri. Avoid in children ≤8 years of age.

Additional specific warnings: Periostat®: Effectiveness has not been established in patients with coexistent oral candidiasis; use with caution in patients with a history or predisposition to oral candidiasis. Oracea™: Should not be used for the treatment or prophylaxis of bacterial infections, since the lower dose of drug per capsule may be subefficacious and promote resistance.

Adverse Reactions Frequency not defined.
Cardiovascular: Intracranial hypertension, pericarditis
Dermatologic: Angioneurotic edema, exfoliative dermatitis (rare), photosensitivity, rash, skin hyperpigmentation, urticaria
Endocrine & metabolic: Brown/black discoloration of thyroid gland (no dysfunction reported)
Gastrointestinal: Anorexia, diarrhea, dysphagia, enterocolitis, esophagitis (rare), esophageal ulcerations (rare), glossitis, inflammatory lesions in anogenital region, oral (mucosal) pigmentation, tooth discoloration (children)
Hematologic: Eosinophilia, hemolytic anemia, neutropenia, thrombocytopenia
Renal: BUN increased (dose related)
Miscellaneous: Anaphylactoid purpura, anaphylaxis, bulging fontanels (infants), SLE exacerbation
Note: Adverse effects in clinical trials with Periostat® occurring at a frequency more than 1% greater than placebo included nausea, dyspepsia, joint pain, diarrhea, menstrual cramp, and pain.

Overdosage/Toxicology Symptoms include nausea, anorexia, and diarrhea. Following GI decontamination, care is supportive only. Fluid support may be required for hypotension.

Drug Interactions
Cytochrome P450 Effect: Substrate of CYP3A4 (major); **Inhibits** CYP3A4 (moderate)
Increased Effect/Toxicity: Increased digoxin toxicity when taken with digoxin. Increased prothrombin time with warfarin. Doxycycline may increase the levels/effects of selected
(Continued)

Doxycycline *(Continued)*

benzodiazepines, calcium channel blockers, cyclosporine, mirtazapine, nateglinide, nefazodone, quinidine, sildenafil (and other PDE-5 inhibitors), tacrolimus, venlafaxine, and other CYP3A4 substrates. Selected benzodiazepines (midazolam, triazolam), cisapride, ergot alkaloids, selected HMG-CoA reductase inhibitors (lovastatin and simvastatin), mesoridazine, pimozide, and thioridazine are generally contraindicated with strong CYP3A4 inhibitors. When used with strong CYP3A4 inhibitors, dosage adjustment/limits are recommended

Decreased Effect: Decreased levels of doxycycline may occur when taken with antacids containing aluminum, calcium, or magnesium. Decreased levels when taken with iron, bismuth subsalicylate, barbiturates, sucralfate, didanosine, and quinapril. Concurrent use of tetracycline and Penthrane® has been reported to result in fatal renal toxicity. Although anecdotal reports suggest oral contraceptive efficacy could be reduced by tetracyclines, this has been refuted by more rigorous scientific and clinical data. The levels/effects of doxycycline may be decreased by include aminoglutethimide, carbamazepine, nafcillin, nevirapine, phenobarbital, phenytoin, rifamycins, and other CYP3A4 inducers.

Ethanol/Nutrition/Herb Interactions

Ethanol: Chronic ethanol ingestion may reduce the serum concentration of doxycycline.

Food: Doxycycline serum levels may be slightly decreased if taken with food or milk. Administration with iron or calcium may decrease doxycycline absorption. May decrease absorption of calcium, iron, magnesium, zinc, and amino acids.

Herb/Nutraceutical: St John's wort may decrease doxycycline levels. Avoid dong quai, St John's wort (may also cause photosensitization).

Stability

Capsule, tablet: Store at controlled room temperature 15°C to 30°C (59°F to 86°F); protect from light

I.V. infusion: Following reconstitution with sterile water for injection, dilute to a final concentration of 0.1-1 mg/mL using a compatible solution. Solutions for I.V. infusion may be prepared using 0.9% sodium chloride, D₅W, Ringer's injection, lactated Ringer's, D₅LR. Protect from light. Stability varies based on solution.

Mechanism of Action Inhibits protein synthesis by binding with the 30S and possibly the 50S ribosomal subunit(s) of susceptible bacteria; may also cause alterations in the cytoplasmic membrane

Periostat® capsules (proposed mechanism): Has been shown to inhibit collagenase activity *in vitro*. Also has been noted to reduce elevated collagenase activity in the gingival crevicular fluid of patients with periodontal disease. Systemic levels do not reach inhibitory concentrations against bacteria.

Pharmacodynamics/Kinetics

Absorption: Oral: Almost complete

Distribution: Widely into body tissues and fluids including synovial, pleural, prostatic, seminal fluids, and bronchial secretions; saliva, aqueous humor, and CSF penetration is poor; readily crosses placenta; enters breast milk

Protein binding: 90%

Metabolism: Not hepatic; partially inactivated in GI tract by chelate formation

Half-life elimination: 12-15 hours (usually increases to 22-24 hours with multiple doses); End-stage renal disease: 18-25 hours

Time to peak, serum: 1.5-4 hours

Excretion: Feces (30%); urine (23%)

Dosage

Usual dosage range:

Children ≥8 years (<45 kg): Oral, I.V.: 2-5 mg/kg/day in 1-2 divided doses, not to exceed 200 mg/day

Children >8 years (>45 kg) and Adults: Oral, I.V.: 100-200 mg/day in 1-2 divided doses

Indication-specific dosing:

Children:

Anthrax: Doxycycline should be used in children if antibiotic susceptibility testing, exhaustion of drug supplies, or allergic reaction preclude use of penicillin or ciprofloxacin. For treatment, the consensus recommendation does not include a loading dose for doxycycline.

Inhalational (postexposure prophylaxis) (MMWR, 2001, 50:889-893): Oral, I.V. (use oral route when possible):

≤8 years: 2.2 mg/kg every 12 hours for 60 days

>8 years and ≤45 kg: 2.2 mg/kg every 12 hours for 60 days

>8 years and >45 kg: 100 mg every 12 hours for 60 days

Cutaneous (treatment): Oral: See dosing for "Inhalational (postexposure prophylaxis)"

Note: In the presence of systemic involvement, extensive edema, and/or lesions on head/neck, doxycycline should initially be administered I.V.

Inhalational/gastrointestinal/oropharyngeal (treatment): I.V.: Refer to dosing for inhalational anthrax (postexposure prophylaxis); switch to oral therapy when clinically appropriate

Note: Initial treatment should include two or more agents predicted to be effective (per CDC recommendations). Agents suggested for use in conjunction with doxycycline or ciprofloxacin include rifampin, vancomycin, imipenem, penicillin, ampicillin, chloramphenicol, clindamycin, and clarithromycin. May switch to oral antimicrobial therapy when clinically appropriate. Continue combined therapy for 60 days

Adults:

Anthrax:

Inhalational (postexposure prophylaxis): Oral, I.V. (use oral route when possible): 100 mg every 12 hours for 60 days (*MMWR*, 2001, 50:889-93); **Note:** Preliminary recommendation, FDA review and update is anticipated.

Cutaneous (treatment): Oral: 100 mg every 12 hours for 60 days. **Note:** In the presence of systemic involvement, extensive edema, lesions on head/neck, refer to I.V. dosing for treatment of inhalational/gastrointestinal/oropharyngeal anthrax

Inhalational/gastrointestinal/oropharyngeal (treatment): I.V.: Initial: 100 mg every 12 hours; switch to oral therapy when clinically appropriate; some recommend initial loading dose of 200 mg, followed by 100 mg every 8-12 hours (*JAMA*, 1997, 278:399-411). **Note:** Initial treatment should include two or more agents predicted to be effective (per CDC recommendations). Agents suggested for use in conjunction with doxycycline or ciprofloxacin include rifampin, vancomycin, imipenem, penicillin, ampicillin, chloramphenicol, clindamycin, and clarithromycin. May switch to oral antimicrobial therapy when clinically appropriate. Continue combined therapy for 60 days

Brucellosis: Oral: 100 mg twice daily for 6 weeks with rifampin or streptomycin

Chlamydial infections, uncomplicated: Oral: 100 mg twice daily for ≥7 days

Community-acquired pneumonia, bronchitis: Oral, I.V.: 100 mg twice daily

Endometritis, salpingitis, parametritis, or peritonitis: I.V.: 100 mg twice daily with cefoxitin 2 g every 6 hours for 4 days and for ≥48 hours after patient improves; then continue with oral therapy 100 mg twice daily to complete a 10- to 14-day course of therapy

Gonococcal infection, acute (PID) in combination with another antibiotic: I.V.: 100 mg every 12 hours until improved, followed by 100 mg orally twice daily to complete 14 days

Lyme disease, Q fever, or Tularemia: Oral: 100 mg twice daily for 14-21 days

Periodontitis: Oral (Periostat®): 20 mg twice daily as an adjunct following scaling and root planing; may be administered for up to 9 months. Safety beyond 12 months of treatment and efficacy beyond 9 months of treatment have not been established.

Rickettsial disease or erlichiosis: Oral, I.V.: 100 mg twice daily for 7-14 days

Rosacea: (Oracea™): Oral: 40 mg once daily in the morning

Sclerosing agent for pleural effusion Injection (unlabeled use): Irrigation: 500 mg as a single dose in 30-50 mL of NS or SWI

Syphilis:

Early syphilis: Oral, I.V.: 200 mg/day in divided doses for 14 days

Late syphilis: Oral, I.V.: 200 mg/day in divided doses for 28 days

Yersinia pestis (plague): Oral: 100 mg twice daily for 10 days

Vibrio cholerae: Oral: 300 mg as a single dose

Dosing adjustment in renal impairment: No adjustment necessary

Dialysis: Not dialyzable; 0% to 5% by hemo- and peritoneal methods or by continuous arteriovenous or venovenous hemofiltration: No supplemental dosage necessary

Dietary Considerations

Tetracyclines (in general): Take with food if gastric irritation occurs. While administration with food may decrease GI absorption of doxycycline by up to 20%, administration on an empty stomach is not recommended due to GI intolerance. Of currently available tetracyclines, doxycycline has the least affinity for calcium.

Oracea™: Take on an empty stomach 1 hour before or 2 hours after meals.

Doryx® 75 mg and 100 mg tablets contain sodium 4.5 mg and 6 mg, respectively.

Administration

Oral: May give with meals to decrease GI upset. Capsule and tablet: Administer with at least 8 ounces of water and have patient sit up for at least 30 minutes after taking to reduce the risk of esophageal irritation and ulceration.

Oracea™: Take on an empty stomach 1 hour before or 2 hours after meals.

I.V.: Infuse I.V. doxycycline over 1-4 hours; avoid extravasation

Test Interactions False elevations of urine catecholamine levels; false-negative urine glucose using Clinistix®, Tes-Tape®

Dosage Forms [DSC] = Discontinued product. **Note:** Strength expressed as base.

Capsule, as hyclate: 50 mg, 100 mg

Vibramycin®: 100 mg

Capsule, as monohydrate: 50 mg, 100 mg

Monodox®: 50 mg, 100 mg

Capsule, variable release:

Oracea™: 40 mg [30 mg (immediate-release) and 10 mg (delayed-release)]

Injection, powder for reconstitution, as hyclate: 100 mg

Doxy-100®: 100 mg

Powder for oral suspension, as monohydrate:

Vibramycin®: 25 mg/5 mL (60 mL) [raspberry flavor]

Syrup, as calcium:

Vibramycin®: 50 mg/5 mL (480 mL) [contains sodium metabisulfite; raspberry-apple flavor]

Tablet, as hyclate: 20 mg, 100 mg

Periostat®: 20 mg

Vibra-Tabs®: 100 mg

Tablet, as monohydrate: 50 mg, 75 mg, 100 mg

Adoxa®: 50 mg, 75 mg, 100 mg

Adoxa® Pak™ 1/75 [unit-dose pack]: 75 mg (31s)

Adoxa® Pak™ 1/100 [unit-dose pack]: 100 mg (31s)

Adoxa® Pak™ 1/150 [unit-dose pack]: 150 mg (30s)

Adoxa® Pak™ 2/100 [unit-dose pack]: 100 mg (60s)

Tablet, delayed-release coated pellets, as hyclate:

Doryx®: 75 mg [contains sodium 4.5 mg (0.196 mEq)], 100 mg [contains sodium 6 mg (0.261 mEq)]

Extemporaneous Preparations If liquid doxycycline is unavailable for the treatment of anthrax, emergency doses may be prepared for children using the tablets.

Crush one 100 mg tablet and grind into a fine powder. Mix with 4 teaspoons of food or drink (lowfat milk, chocolate milk, chocolate pudding, or apple juice). Appropriate dose may be taken from this mixture. Mixture may be stored for up to 24 hours. Dairy mixtures should be refrigerated; apple juice may be stored at room temperature.

(Continued)

Doxycycline (Continued)

U.S. Food and Drug Administration, Center for Drug Evaluation and Research, "How to Prepare Emergency Dosages of Doxycycline at Home for Infants and Children," April 25, 2003, viewable at http://www.fda.gov/cder/drug/infopage/penG_doxy/doxy-cyclinePeds.htm, last accessed May 8, 2003.

- ◆ **Doxycycline Calcium** see Doxycycline on page 555
- ◆ **Doxycycline Hyclate** see Doxycycline on page 555
- ◆ **Doxycycline Monohydrate** see Doxycycline on page 555
- ◆ **Doxytec (Can)** see Doxycycline on page 555
- ◆ **DPA** see Valproic Acid and Derivatives on page 1767
- ◆ **DPE** see Dipivefrin on page 524
- ◆ **D-Penicillamine** see Penicillamine on page 1330
- ◆ **DPH** see Phenytoin on page 1361
- ◆ **DPM™ [OTC]** see Urea on page 1758
- ◆ **Dramamine® [OTC]** see DimenhyDRINATE on page 511
- ◆ **Dramamine® Less Drowsy Formula [OTC]** see Meclizine on page 1063
- ◆ **Dried Smallpox Vaccine** see Smallpox Vaccine on page 1573
- ◆ **Drinex [OTC]** see Acetaminophen, Chlorpheniramine, and Pseudoephedrine on page 35
- ◆ **Drisdol®** see Ergocalciferol on page 603
- ◆ **Dristan® N.D. (Can)** see Acetaminophen and Pseudoephedrine on page 33
- ◆ **Dristan® N.D., Extra Strength (Can)** see Acetaminophen and Pseudoephedrine on page 33
- ◆ **Dritho-Scalp®** see Anthralin on page 132
- ◆ **Drituss DM** see Guaifenesin and Dextromethorphan on page 816
- ◆ **Drixoral® (Can)** see Dexbrompheniramine and Pseudoephedrine on page 482
- ◆ **Drixoral® Cold & Allergy [OTC]** see Dexbrompheniramine and Pseudoephedrine on page 482
- ◆ **Drixoral® ND (Can)** see Pseudoephedrine on page 1454
- ◆ **Drize®-R [DSC]** see Chlorpheniramine, Phenylephrine, and Methscopolamine on page 353

Dronabinol (droe NAB i nol)

U.S. Brand Names Marinol®
Canadian Brand Names Marinol®
Index Terms Delta-9-tetrahydro-cannabinol; Delta-9 THC; Tetrahydrocannabinol; THC
Pharmacologic Category Antiemetic; Appetite Stimulant
Use Chemotherapy-associated nausea and vomiting refractory to other antiemetic(s); AIDS-related anorexia
Unlabeled/Investigational Use Cancer-related anorexia
Restrictions C-III
Pregnancy Risk Factor C
Lactation Enters breast milk/contraindicated
Medication Safety Issues
Sound-alike/look-alike issues:
Dronabinol may be confused with droperidol
Contraindications Hypersensitivity to dronabinol, cannabinoids, sesame oil, or any component of the formulation, or marijuana; should be avoided in patients with a history of schizophrenia
Warnings/Precautions Use with caution in patients with heart disease, hepatic disease, or seizure disorders. Reduce dosage in patients with severe hepatic impairment. May cause additive CNS effects with sedatives, hypnotics or other psychoactive agents; patients must be cautioned about performing tasks which require mental alertness (eg, operating machinery or driving).

May have potential for abuse; drug is psychoactive substance in marijuana; use caution in patients with a history of substance abuse or potential. May cause withdrawal symptoms upon abrupt discontinuation. Use with caution in patients with mania, depression, or schizophrenia; careful psychiatric monitoring is recommended. Use caution in elderly; they are more sensitive to adverse effects.

Adverse Reactions Frequency not always specified.
>1%:
Cardiovascular: Palpitations, tachycardia, vasodilation/facial flushing
Central nervous system: Euphoria (8% to 24%, dose related), abnormal thinking (3% to 10%), dizziness (3% to 10%), paranoia (3% to 10%), somnolence (3% to 10%), amnesia, anxiety, ataxia, confusion, depersonalization, hallucination
Gastrointestinal: Abdominal pain (3% to 10%), nausea (3% to 10%), vomiting (3% to 10%)
Neuromuscular & skeletal: Weakness
<1% (Limited to important or life-threatening): Conjunctivitis, depression, diarrhea, fatigue, fecal incontinence, flushing, hypotension, myalgia, nightmares, seizure, speech difficulties, tinnitus, vision difficulties
Overdosage/Toxicology Symptoms may include tachycardia, hyper- or hypotension, behavioral disturbances, lethargy, panic reactions, seizures or motor incoordination. Benzodiazepines may be helpful for agitative behavior; Trendelenburg position and hydration may be helpful for hypotensive effects. For other manifestations, treatment should be symptom-directed and supportive.
Drug Interactions
Increased Effect/Toxicity: Sedative effects may be additive with CNS depressants (includes barbiturates, opioid analgesics, and other sedative agents). Use in combination with phenothiazines (prochlorperazine) may result in additive or synergistic effects (as antiemetics), but sedation must be monitored.

Ethanol/Nutrition/Herb Interactions
Ethanol: Avoid ethanol (may increase CNS depression).
Food: Administration with high-lipid meals may increase absorption.
Herb/Nutraceutical: St John's wort may decrease dronabinol levels.

Stability Store under refrigeration (or in a cool environment) between 8°C and 15°C (46°F and 59°F). Protect from freezing.

Mechanism of Action Unknown, may inhibit endorphins in the brain's emetic center, suppress prostaglandin synthesis, and/or inhibit medullary activity through an unspecified cortical action. Some pharmacologic effects appear to involve sympathomimetic activity; tachyphylaxis to some effect (eg, tachycardia) may occur, but appetite-stimulating effects do not appear to wane over time. Antiemetic activity may be due to effect on cannabinoid receptors (CB1) within the central nervous system.

Pharmacodynamics/Kinetics
Onset of action: Within 1 hour
Peak effect: 2-4 hours
Duration: 24 hours (appetite stimulation)
Absorption: Oral: 90% to 95%; 10% to 20% of dose gets into systemic circulation
Distribution: V_d: 10 L/kg; dronabinol is highly lipophilic and distributes to adipose tissue
Protein binding: 97% to 99%
Metabolism: Hepatic to at least 50 metabolites, some of which are active; 11-hydroxy-delta-9-tetrahydrocannabinol (11-OH-THC) is the major metabolite; extensive first-pass effect
Half-life elimination: Dronabinol: 25-36 hours (terminal); Dronabinol metabolites: 44-59 hours
Time to peak, serum: 0.5-4 hours
Excretion: Feces (50% as unconjugated metabolites, 5% as unchanged drug); urine (10% to 15% as acid metabolites and conjugates)

Dosage Refer to individual protocols. Oral:
Antiemetic: Children and Adults: 5 mg/m² 1-3 hours before chemotherapy, then 5 mg/m²/dose every 2-4 hours after chemotherapy for a total of 4-6 doses/day; increase doses in increments of 2.5 mg/m² to a maximum of 15 mg/m²/dose.
Appetite stimulant: Adults: Initial: 2.5 mg twice daily (before lunch and dinner); titrate up to a maximum of 20 mg/day.

Dietary Considerations Capsules contain sesame oil.

Monitoring Parameters CNS effects, heart rate, blood pressure, behavioral profile

Reference Range Antinauseant effects: 5-10 ng/mL

Test Interactions Decreased FSH, LH, growth hormone, and testosterone

Dosage Forms
Capsule, gelatin:
Marinol®: 2.5 mg, 5 mg, 10 mg [contains sesame oil]

Droperidol (droe PER i dole)

U.S. Brand Names Inapsine®
Canadian Brand Names Droperidol Injection, USP
Index Terms Dehydrobenzperidol
Pharmacologic Category Antiemetic; Antipsychotic Agent, Typical
Use Antiemetic in surgical and diagnostic procedures; preoperative medication in patients when other treatments are ineffective or inappropriate
Pregnancy Risk Factor C
Pregnancy Implications Crosses the placenta
Lactation Excretion in breast milk unknown
Medication Safety Issues
Sound-alike/look-alike issues:
Droperidol may be confused with dronabinol
Inapsine® may be confused with Nebcin®
Contraindications Hypersensitivity to droperidol or any component of the formulation; known or suspected QT prolongation, including congenital long QT syndrome (prolonged QT_c is defined as >440 msec in males or >450 msec in females)
Warnings/Precautions May alter cardiac conduction. **[U.S. Boxed Warning]: Cases of QT prolongation and torsade de pointes, including some fatal cases, have been reported.** Use extreme caution in patients with bradycardia (<50 bpm), cardiac disease, concurrent MAOI therapy, Class I and Class III antiarrhythmics or other drugs known to prolong QT interval, and electrolyte disturbances (hypokalemia or hypomagnesemia), including concomitant drugs which may alter electrolytes (diuretics).

Use with caution in patients with seizures, bone marrow suppression, or severe liver disease. May be sedating, use with caution in disorders where CNS depression is a feature. Caution in patients with hemodynamic instability, predisposition to seizures, subcortical brain damage, renal or respiratory disease. Esophageal dysmotility and aspiration have been associated with antipsychotic use - use with caution in patients at risk of pneumonia (ie, Alzheimer's disease). Caution in breast cancer or other prolactin-dependent tumors (may elevate prolactin levels). May alter temperature regulation or mask toxicity of other drugs due to antiemetic effects. May cause orthostatic hypotension - use with caution in patients at risk of this effect or those who would tolerate transient hypotensive episodes (cerebrovascular disease, cardiovascular disease, or other medications which may predispose). Significant hypotension may occur; injection contains benzyl alcohol; injection also contains sulfites which may cause allergic reaction.

May cause anticholinergic effects (confusion, agitation, constipation, xerostomia, blurred vision, urinary retention). Therefore, they should be used with caution in patients with decreased gastrointestinal motility, urinary retention, BPH, xerostomia, or visual problems. Conditions which also may be exacerbated by cholinergic blockade include narrow-angle glaucoma (screening is recommended) and worsening of myasthenia gravis. Relative to other neuroleptics, droperidol has a low potency of cholinergic blockade.
(Continued)

Droperidol *(Continued)*

May cause extrapyramidal symptoms, including pseudoparkinsonism, acute dystonic reactions, akathisia, and tardive dyskinesia (risk of these reactions is high relative to other neuroleptics). May be associated with neuroleptic malignant syndrome (NMS) or pigmentary retinopathy. Safety in children <6 months of age has not been established.

Adverse Reactions

>10%:

Cardiovascular: QT_c prolongation (dose dependent)

Central nervous system: Restlessness, anxiety, extrapyramidal symptoms, dystonic reactions, pseudoparkinsonian signs and symptoms, tardive dyskinesia, seizure, altered central temperature regulation, sedation, drowsiness

Endocrine & metabolic: Swelling of breasts

Gastrointestinal: Weight gain, constipation

1% to 10%:

Cardiovascular: Hypotension (especially orthostatic), tachycardia, abnormal T waves with prolonged ventricular repolarization, hypertension

Central nervous system: Hallucinations, persistent tardive dyskinesia, akathisia

Gastrointestinal: Nausea, vomiting

Genitourinary: Dysuria

<1% (Limited to important or life-threatening): Adynamic ileus, agranulocytosis, alopecia, arrhythmia, cholestatic jaundice, heat stroke, hyperpigmentation, laryngospasm, leukopenia, neuroleptic malignant syndrome (NMS), obstructive jaundice, photosensitivity (rare), priapism, rash, respiratory depression, retinal pigmentation, tardive dystonia, torsade de pointes, urinary retention, ventricular tachycardia, visual acuity decreased (may be irreversible)

Overdosage/Toxicology Symptoms include hypotension, tachycardia, hallucinations, and extrapyramidal symptoms. Prolonged QT interval, seizures, and arrhythmias have been reported. Following initiation of essential overdose management, toxic symptom and supportive treatment should be initiated. Hypotension usually responds to I.V. fluids or Trendelenburg positioning. If unresponsive to these measures, the use of a parenteral inotrope may be required (eg, norepinephrine 0.1-0.2 mcg/kg/minute titrated to response). Seizures commonly respond to diazepam (I.V. 5-10 mg bolus in adults every 15 minutes, if needed, up to a total of 30 mg; I.V. 0.25-0.4 mg/kg/dose up to a total of 10 mg in children) or to phenytoin or phenobarbital. Arrhythmia management is per ACLS protocols (**Note:** Potential for QT prolongation and/or torsade de pointes). Neuroleptics often cause extrapyramidal symptoms (eg, dystonic reactions) requiring management with diphenhydramine 1-2 mg/kg (adults), up to a maximum of 50 mg I.M. or slow I.V. push, followed by a maintenance dose for 48-72 hours. When these reactions are unresponsive to diphenhydramine, anticholinergic agents such as benztropine mesylate I.V. 1-2 mg (adults) may be effective. These agents are generally effective within 2-5 minutes.

Drug Interactions

Increased Effect/Toxicity: Droperidol in combination with certain forms of conduction anesthesia may produce peripheral vasodilatation and hypotension. Droperidol and CNS depressants will likely have additive CNS effects. Droperidol and cyclobenzaprine may have an additive effect on prolonging the QT interval. Use caution with other agents known to prolong QT interval (Class I or Class III antiarrhythmics, some quinolone antibiotics, cisapride, some phenothiazines, pimozide, tricyclic antidepressants). Potassium- or magnesium-depleting agents (diuretics, aminoglycosides, amphotericin B, cyclosporine) may increase risk of arrhythmias. Metoclopramide may increase risk of extrapyramidal symptoms (EPS). Acetylcholinesterase inhibitors (central) may increase the risk of antipsychotic-related EPS.

Stability Droperidol ampuls/vials should be stored at room temperature and protected from light. Solutions diluted in NS or D_5W are stable at room temperature for up to 7 days.

Mechanism of Action Droperidol is a butyrophenone antipsychotic; antiemetic effect is a result of blockade of dopamine stimulation of the chemoreceptor trigger zone. Other effects include alpha-adrenergic blockade, peripheral vascular dilation, and reduction of the pressor effect of epinephrine resulting in hypotension and decreased peripheral vascular resistance; may also reduce pulmonary artery pressure

Pharmacodynamics/Kinetics

Onset of action: Peak effect: Parenteral: ~30 minutes

Duration: Parenteral: 2-4 hours, may extend to 12 hours

Absorption: I.M.: Rapid

Distribution: Crosses blood-brain barrier and placenta

V_d: Children: ~0.25-0.9 L/kg; Adults: ~2 L/kg

Protein binding: Extensive

Metabolism: Hepatic, to *p*-fluorophenylacetic acid, benzimidazolone, *p*-hydroxypiperidine

Half-life elimination: Adults: 2.3 hours

Excretion: Urine (75%, <1% as unchanged drug); feces (22%, 11% to 50% as unchanged drug)

Dosage Titrate carefully to desired effect

Children 2-12 years: Nausea and vomiting: I.M., I.V.: 0.05-0.06 mg/kg (maximum initial dose: 0.1 mg/kg); additional doses may be repeated to achieve effect; administer additional doses with caution

Adults: Nausea and vomiting: I.M., I.V.: Initial: 2.5 mg; additional doses of 1.25 mg may be administered to achieve desired effect; administer additional doses with caution

Administration Administer I.M. and/or I.V.; according to the manufacturer, I.V. push administration should be slow (generally regarded as 2-5 minutes); however, many clinicians administer I.V. doses rapidly (over 30-60 seconds) in an effort to reduce the incidence of EPS. The effect, if any, of rapid administration on QT prolongation is unclear. For I.V. infusion, dilute in 50-100 mL NS or D_5W; ECG monitoring for 2-3 hours after administration is recommended regardless of rate of infusion.

Monitoring Parameters To identify QT prolongation, a 12-lead ECG prior to use is recommended; continued ECG monitoring for 2-3 hours following administration is recommended. Vital signs; lipid profile, fasting blood glucose/Hgb A_{1c}, serum magnesium and potassium;

BMI; mental status, abnormal involuntary movement scale (AIMS); observe for dystonias, extrapyramidal side effects, and temperature changes

Additional Information Does not possess analgesic effects; has little or no amnesic properties.

Dosage Forms Injection, solution: 2.5 mg/mL (1 mL, 2 mL)

♦ **Droperidol Injection, USP (Can)** *see* Droperidol *on page 559*

♦ **Drospirenone and Ethinyl Estradiol** *see* Ethinyl Estradiol and Drospirenone *on page 646*

Drotrecogin Alfa (dro TRE coe jin AL fa)

U.S. Brand Names Xigris®
Canadian Brand Names Xigris®
Index Terms Activated Protein C, Human, Recombinant; Drotrecogin Alfa, Activated; Protein C (Activated), Human, Recombinant
Pharmacologic Category Protein C (Activated)
Additional Appendix Information
APACHE II Scoring System *on page 1836*
Use Reduction of mortality from severe sepsis (associated with organ dysfunction) in adults at high risk of death (eg, APACHE II score ≥25)
Unlabeled/Investigational Use Purpura fulminans
Pregnancy Risk Factor C
Lactation Excretion in breast milk unknown/not recommended
Contraindications Hypersensitivity to drotrecogin alfa or any component of the formulation; active internal bleeding; recent hemorrhagic stroke (within 3 months); severe head trauma (within 2 months); recent intracranial or intraspinal surgery (within 2 months); intracranial neoplasm or mass lesion; evidence of cerebral herniation; presence of an epidural catheter; trauma with an increased risk of life-threatening bleeding
Warnings/Precautions Increases risk of bleeding; careful evaluation of risks and benefit is required prior to initiation (see Contraindications). Bleeding risk is increased in patients receiving concurrent therapeutic heparin, oral anticoagulants, glycoprotein IIb/IIIa antagonists, platelet aggregation inhibitors, or aspirin at a dosage of >650 mg/day (within 7 days). In addition, an increased bleeding risk is associated with prolonged INR (>3.0), gastrointestinal bleeding (within 6 weeks), decreased platelet count (<30,000/mm³), thrombolytic therapy (within 3 days), recent ischemic stroke (within 3 months), intracranial AV malformation or aneurysm, known platelet diathesis, severe hepatic disease (chronic), or other condition where bleeding is a significant hazard or difficult to manage due to its location. Discontinue if significant bleeding occurs (may consider continued use after stabilization). Treatment interruption required for invasive procedures. During treatment, aPTT cannot be used to assess coagulopathy (PT/INR not affected).

Efficacy not established in adult patients at a low risk of death. Patients with pre-existing nonsepsis-related medical conditions with a poor prognosis (anticipated survival <28 days), HIV-infected patients with a CD4 count ≤50 cells/mm³, chronic dialysis patients, pre-existing hypercoagulable conditions, and patients who had received bone marrow, liver, lung, pancreas, or small bowel transplants were excluded from the clinical trial which established benefit. In addition, patients with a high body weight (>135 kg) were not evaluated. Safety and efficacy have not been established in pediatric patients.

Adverse Reactions As with all drugs which may affect hemostasis, bleeding is the major adverse effect associated with drotrecogin alfa. Hemorrhage may occur at virtually any site. Risk is dependent on multiple variables, including the dosage administered, concurrent use of multiple agents which alter hemostasis, and patient predisposition.

>10%:
Dermatologic: Bruising
Gastrointestinal: Gastrointestinal bleeding
1% to 10%: Hematologic: Bleeding (serious 2.4% during infusion vs 3.5% during 28-day study period; individual events listed as <1%)
<1% (Limited to important or life-threatening): Gastrointestinal hemorrhage, genitourinary bleeding, immune reaction (antibody production), intracranial hemorrhage (0.2%; frequencies up to 2% noted in a previous trial without placebo control), intrathoracic hemorrhage, retroperitoneal bleeding, skin/soft tissue bleeding

Overdosage/Toxicology There has been no reported experience with overdose. Hemorrhagic complications are likely consequences of overdose. Treatment is supportive including immediate interruption of the infusion and monitoring for hemorrhagic complications. There is no known antidote.

Drug Interactions
Increased Effect/Toxicity: Concurrent use of antiplatelet agents, including aspirin (>650 mg/day, recent use within 7 days), cilostazol, clopidogrel, dipyridamole, ticlopidine, NSAIDs, or glycoprotein IIb/IIIa antagonists (recent use within 7 days) may increase risk of bleeding. Concurrent use of low molecular weight heparins or heparin at therapeutic rates of infusion may increase the risk of bleeding. However, the use of low-dose prophylactic heparin does not appear to affect safety. Recent use of thrombolytic agents (within 3 days) may increase the risk of bleeding. Recent use of warfarin (within 7 days or elevation of INR ≥3) may increase the risk of bleeding. Other drugs which interfere with coagulation may increase risk of bleeding (including antithrombin III, danaparoid, direct thrombin inhibitors).
Ethanol/Nutrition/Herb Interactions Herb/Nutraceutical: Recent use/intake of herbs with anticoagulant or antiplatelet activity (including cat's claw, feverfew, garlic, ginkgo, ginseng, and horse chestnut seed) may increase the risk of bleeding.
Stability Store vials under refrigeration at 2°C to 8°C (36°F to 46°F). Protect from light. Do not freeze. Reconstitute 5 mg vials with 2.5 mL and 20 mg vials with 10 mL sterile water for injection (resultant solution ~2 mg/mL). Must be further diluted (within 3 hours of reconstitution) in 0.9% sodium chloride, typically to a concentration between 100 mcg/mL and 200 mcg/mL when using infusion pump and between 100 mcg/mL and 1000 mcg/mL when infused via syringe pump. Although product information states administration must be completed within
(Continued)

Drotrecogin Alfa *(Continued)*

12 hours of preparation, additional studies (data on file, Lilly Research Laboratories) show that the final solution is stable for 14 hours at 15°C to 30°C (59°F to 86°F). If not used immediately, a prepared solution may be stored in the refrigerator for up to 12 hours. The total expiration time (refrigeration and administration) should be ≤24 hours from time of preparation.

Mechanism of Action Inhibits factors Va and VIIIa, limiting thrombotic effects. Additional *in vitro* data suggest inhibition of plasminogen activator inhibitor-1 (PAF-1) resulting in profibrinolytic activity, inhibition of macrophage production of tumor necrosis factor, blocking of leukocyte adhesion, and limitation of thrombin-induced inflammatory responses. Relative contribution of effects on the reduction of mortality from sepsis is not completely understood.

Pharmacodynamics/Kinetics

Duration: Plasma nondetectable within 2 hours of discontinuation

Metabolism: Inactivated by endogenous plasma protease inhibitors; mean clearance: 40 L/hour; increased with severe sepsis (~50%)

Half-life elimination: 1.6 hours

Dosage I.V.:

Children and Adults: Purpura fulminans (unlabeled use): 24 mcg/kg/hour

Adults: Sepsis: 24 mcg/kg/hour for a total of 96 hours; stop infusion **immediately** if clinically-important bleeding is identified

Dosage adjustment in renal impairment: No specific adjustment recommended.

Administration Infuse separately from all other medications. Only dextrose, normal saline, dextrose/saline combinations, and lactated Ringer's solution may be infused through the same line. May administer via infusion pump. Administration of prepared solution must be completed within 12 hours of preparation. Suspend administration for 2 hours prior to invasive procedures or other procedure with significant bleeding risk; may continue treatment immediately following uncomplicated, minimally-invasive procedures, but delay for 12 hours after major invasive procedures/surgery.

Monitoring Parameters Monitor for signs and symptoms of bleeding, hemoglobin/hematocrit, PT/INR, platelet count

Test Interactions May interfere with one-stage coagulation assays based on the aPTT (such as factor VIII, IX, and XI assays).

Additional Information Prepared by recombinant DNA technology in human cell line

Dosage Forms Injection, powder for reconstitution [preservative free]: 5 mg [contains sucrose 31.8 mg], 20 mg [contains sucrose 124.9 mg]

- ◆ **Drotrecogin Alfa, Activated** *see* Drotrecogin Alfa *on page 561*
- ◆ **Droxia®** *see* Hydroxyurea *on page 863*
- ◆ **Dryvax®** *see* Smallpox Vaccine *on page 1573*
- ◆ **DSCG** *see* Cromolyn *on page 423*
- ◆ **D-Ser(Buᵗ)⁶,Azgly¹⁰-LHRH** *see* Goserelin *on page 810*
- ◆ **DSS** *see* Docusate *on page 533*
- ◆ **D-S-S® [OTC]** *see* Docusate *on page 533*
- ◆ **DT** *see* Diphtheria and Tetanus Toxoid *on page 519*
- ◆ **DTaP** *see* Diphtheria, Tetanus Toxoids, and Acellular Pertussis Vaccine *on page 521*
- ◆ **DTIC** *see* Dacarbazine *on page 442*
- ◆ **DTIC® (Can)** *see* Dacarbazine *on page 442*
- ◆ **DTIC-Dome®** *see* Dacarbazine *on page 442*
- ◆ **DTO (error-prone abbreviation)** *see* Opium Tincture *on page 1269*
- ◆ **dTpa** *see* Diphtheria, Tetanus Toxoids, and Acellular Pertussis Vaccine *on page 521*
- ◆ **D-Trp(6)-LHRH** *see* Triptorelin *on page 1750*
- ◆ **Duetact™** *see* Pioglitazone and Glimepiride *on page 1374*
- ◆ **Dulcolax® [OTC]** *see* Bisacodyl *on page 223*
- ◆ **Dulcolax® (Can)** *see* Bisacodyl *on page 223*
- ◆ **Dulcolax® Milk of Magnesia [OTC]** *see* Magnesium Hydroxide *on page 1047*
- ◆ **Dulcolax® Stool Softener [OTC]** *see* Docusate *on page 533*
- ◆ **Dull-C® [OTC]** *see* Ascorbic Acid *on page 156*

Duloxetine *(doo LOX e teen)*

U.S. Brand Names Cymbalta®

Index Terms Duloxetine Hydrochloride; LY248686; (+)-(S)-N-Methyl-γ-(1-naphthyloxy)-2-thiophenepropylamine Hydrochloride

Pharmacologic Category Antidepressant, Serotonin/Norepinephrine Reuptake Inhibitor

Additional Appendix Information

Antidepressant Agents *on page 1866*

Use Treatment of major depressive disorder; management of pain associated with diabetic neuropathy

Unlabeled/Investigational Use Treatment of stress incontinence; management of chronic pain syndromes; management of fibromyalgia

Restrictions An FDA-approved medication guide concerning the use of antidepressants in children and teenagers must be distributed when dispensing an outpatient prescription (new or refill) where this medication is to be used without direct supervision of a healthcare provider. Medication guides are available at http://www.fda.gov/cder/Offices/ODS/medication_guides.htm. Dispense to parents or guardians of children and teenagers receiving this medication.

Pregnancy Risk Factor C

Pregnancy Implications Decreased fetal weight and behavioral effects have been reported in animal studies. Nonteratogenic effects including respiratory distress, cyanosis, apnea, seizures, temperature instability, feeding difficulty, vomiting, hypoglycemia, hypo- or hypertonia, hyper-reflexia, jitteriness, irritability, constant crying, and tremor have been reported in the neonate immediately following delivery after exposure late in the third trimester. Exposure to SSRIs late in pregnancy has also been associated with persistent pulmonary hypertension of the newborn (PPHN). Adverse effects may be due to toxic effects of SNRI or drug discontinuation. In some cases, effects may present clinically as serotonin syndrome. There are no adequate and well-controlled studies in pregnant women. Use during pregnancy only if the potential benefit to the mother outweighs the possible risk to the fetus. If treatment during pregnancy is required, consider tapering therapy during the third trimester.

Lactation Enters breast milk/not recommended

Medication Safety Issues
Sound-alike/look-alike issues:
Duloxetine may be confused with fluoxetine.

Contraindications Hypersensitivity to duloxetine or any component of the formulation; concomitant use or within 2 weeks of MAO inhibitors; uncontrolled narrow angle glaucoma

Warnings/Precautions [U.S. Boxed Warning]: Antidepressants increase the risk of suicidal thinking and behavior in children and adolescents with major depressive disorder (MDD) and other depressive disorders; consider risk prior to prescribing. All patients must be closely monitored for clinical worsening, suicidality, or unusual changes in behavior, especially during the initiation of therapy or following an increase or decrease in dosage. When used in children, the child's family or caregiver should be instructed to closely observe the patient and communicate condition with healthcare provider. A medication guide should be dispensed with each prescription. **Duloxetine is not FDA approved for use in children.**

The possibility of a suicide attempt is inherent in major depression and may persist until remission occurs. Use caution in high-risk patients. Worsening depression and severe abrupt suicidality that are not part of the presenting symptoms may require discontinuation or modification of drug therapy. The patient's family or caregiver should be alerted to monitor patients for the emergence of suicidality and associated behaviors (such as agitation, irritability, hostility, impulsivity, and hypomania) and call healthcare provider.

May worsen psychosis in some patients or precipitate a shift to mania or hypomania in patients with bipolar disorder. Patients presenting with depressive symptoms should be screened for bipolar disorder. Monotherapy in patients with bipolar disorder should be avoided. **Duloxetine is not FDA approved for the treatment of bipolar depression.**

Duloxetine may cause increased urinary resistance; advise patient to report symptoms of urinary hesitation/difficulty. Has a low potential to impair cognitive or motor performance. Use caution with a previous seizure disorder or condition predisposing to seizures such as brain damage or alcoholism. May cause hepatotoxicity; avoid use in patients with substantial alcohol intake, evidence of chronic liver disease, or hepatic impairment. Use with caution in patients with controlled narrow angle glaucoma. May cause or exacerbate sexual dysfunction. Use caution with renal impairment or with concomitant CNS depressants.

A potential exists for severe reactions when used with MAO inhibitors, SSRIs/SNRIs or triptans; serotonin syndrome (hyperthermia, muscular rigidity, mental status changes/agitation, autonomic instability) may occur. Use caution during concurrent therapy with other drugs which lower the seizure threshold.

Upon discontinuation of duloxetine therapy, gradually taper dose. If intolerable symptoms occur following a decrease in dosage or upon discontinuation of therapy, then resuming the previous dose with a more gradual taper should be considered. May increase the risks associated with electroconvulsive therapy. Consider discontinuing, when possible, prior to elective surgery.

Adverse Reactions
>10%:
Central nervous system: Somnolence (7% to 15%), dizziness (6% to 14%), headache (13%), insomnia (8% to 11%)
Gastrointestinal: Nausea (14% to 22%), xerostomia (5% to 15%), diarrhea (8% to 13%), constipation (5% to 11%)
1% to 10%:
Cardiovascular: Palpitations (1%)
Central nervous system: Fatigue (2% to 10%), anxiety (3%), fever (1% to 2%), hypoesthesia (1%), irritability (1%), lethargy (1%), nervousness (1%), nightmares (1%), restlessness (1%), sleep disorder (1%), vertigo (1%), yawning (1%)
Dermatologic: Hyperhydrosis (6%), pruritus (1%), rash (1%)
Endocrine & metabolic: Libido decreased (3% to 6%), orgasm abnormality (3% to 4%), hot flushes (2%), anorgasmia (1%), hypoglycemia (1%)
Gastrointestinal: Appetite decreased (3% to 8%), vomiting (5% to 6%), dyspepsia (4%), loose stools (2% to 3%), weight loss (1% to 2%), gastritis (1%)
Genitourinary: Erectile dysfunction (1% to 4%), ejaculation delayed (3%), ejaculatory dysfunction (3%), pollakiuria (1% to 3%), dysuria (1%), urinary symptoms (hesitancy, obstructive symptoms; 1%)
Hepatic: Transaminases increased: Occasionally associated with hyperbilirubinemia and/or increased alkaline phosphatase (1%)
Neuromuscular & skeletal: Muscle cramp (4% to 5%), weakness (2% to 4%), myalgia (1% to 3%), tremor (1% to 3%), muscle tightness (1%), muscle twitching (1%), rigors (1%)
Ocular: Blurred vision (4%)
Respiratory: Nasopharyngitis (7% to 9%), cough (3% to 6%), pharyngolaryngeal pain (1% to 3%)
Miscellaneous: Diaphoresis increased (6%), night sweats (1%)
<1% (Limited to important or life-threatening): Abdominal pain, acne, agitation, alopecia, anaphylactic reaction, anemia, angioneurotic edema, aphthous stomatitis, ataxia, atrial fibrillation, bilirubin increased, bloody stools, bruxism, bundle branch block, CHF, cholesterol increased, colitis, dehydration, diplopia, disorientation, diverticulitis, dysarthria, dyslipidemia, dysphagia, ecchymosis, eczema, edema (peripheral), eructation, erythema,
(Continued)

Duloxetine *(Continued)*

esophageal stenosis, facial edema, flu-like syndrome, gastric emptying impaired, gastric irritation, gastric ulcer, gingivitis, glaucoma, hepatic steatosis, hepatitis, hypercholesterolemia, hyperlipidemia, hypertensive crisis, hypertriglyceridemia, hyponatremia, irritable bowel syndrome, jaundice, keroconjunctivitis sicca, leukopenia, lymphadenopathy, macular degeneration, maculopathy, malaise, mania, melena, MI, micturation urgency, mood swings, muscle weakness, nephropathy, nocturia, oropharyngeal edema, orthostatic hypotension, phlebitis, photopsia, photosensitivity, retinal detachment, seizure, Stevens-Johnson syndrome, stomatitis, suicide, syncope, tachycardia, thirst, thrombocytopenia, urinary retention, urticaria, visual disturbance, weight increased; withdrawal syndrome (including headache, dizziness, nightmares, irritability, paresthesia, and/or vomiting)

Drug Interactions

Cytochrome P450 Effect: Substrate (major) of CYP1A2, 2D6; **inhibits** CYP2D6 (moderate)

Increased Effect/Toxicity: Hyperpyrexia, hypertension, tachycardia, confusion, seizures, and deaths have been reported with MAO inhibitors (serotonin syndrome); this combination is contraindicated. Avoid use of linezolid (due to MAO activity). Duloxetine may increase serum concentrations of thioridazine, which has been associated with the development of malignant ventricular arrhythmias. Serum levels/effects of tricyclic antidepressants may be increased by duloxetine.

Concurrent use of duloxetine with buspirone, meperidine, moclobemide, nefazodone, SSRIs/SNRIs, serotonin agonists (eg, triptans), sibutramine, tramadol and trazodone and venlafaxine may cause serotonin syndrome; avoid concurrent use. Concurrent use of selegiline with SSRIs has been reported to cause serotonin syndrome (less than with nonselective MAO inhibitors).

CYP1A2 and CYP2D6 inhibitors may increase the levels/effects of duloxetine. Example inhibitors include amiodarone, chlorpromazine, ciprofloxacin, delavirdine, fluvoxamine, fluoxetine, ketoconazole, miconazole, norfloxacin, ofloxacin, paroxetine, pergolide, quinidine, quinine, rofecoxib, ritonavir, and ropinirole.

Decreased Effect: CYP1A2 inducers may decrease the levels/effects of duloxetine. Example inducers include aminoglutethimide, carbamazepine, phenobarbital, and rifampin.

Ethanol/Nutrition/Herb Interactions

Ethanol: Avoid ethanol (may increase CNS depression and/or hepatotoxic potential of duloxetine).

Herb/Nutraceutical: Avoid valerian, St John's wort, SAMe, kava kava, and gotu kola (may increase CNS depression).

Stability Store at 25°C (77°F); excursions permitted to 15°C to 30°C (59°F to 86°F)

Mechanism of Action Duloxetine is a potent inhibitor of neuronal serotonin and norepinephrine reuptake and a weak inhibitor of dopamine reuptake. Duloxetine has no significant activity for muscarinic cholinergic, H_1-histaminergic, or alpha$_2$-adrenergic receptors. Duloxetine does not possess MAO-inhibitory activity.

Pharmacodynamics/Kinetics

Absorption: Well absorbed, 2-hour delay in absorption after ingestion

Distribution: 1640 L

Protein binding: >90%

Metabolism: Hepatic, via CYP1A2 and CYP2D6; forms multiple metabolites (inactive)

Half-life elimination: 12 hours (range 8-17 hours)

Time to peak: 6 hours

Excretion: As metabolites; urine (70%), feces (20%)

Dosage Oral:

Adults:

Treatment of major depressive disorder: Initial: 40-60 mg/day; dose may be divided (ie, 20 or 30 mg twice daily) or given as a single daily dose of 60 mg; maximum dose: 60 mg/day

Management of diabetic neuropathy: 60 mg once daily; lower initial doses may be considered in patients where tolerability is a concern and/or renal impairment is present

Management of chronic pain syndromes (unlabeled use): 60 mg once daily

Management of fibromyalgia (unlabeled use): 60 mg twice daily

Management of stress incontinence (unlabeled use): 40 mg twice daily

Elderly:

Treatment of major depressive disorder: Initial dose: 20 mg 1-2 times/day; increase to 40-60 mg/day as a single daily dose or in divided doses

Other indications: Refer to adult dosing

Dosage adjustment in renal impairment: Not recommended for use in Cl_{cr} <30 mL/minute or ESRD; in mild-moderate impairment, lower initial doses may be considered with titration guided by response and tolerability

Dosage adjustment in hepatic impairment: Not recommended for use in hepatic impairment

Dietary Considerations May be taken without regard to meals.

Administration Capsule should be swallowed whole; do not break open or crush.

Monitoring Parameters Blood pressure should be regularly monitored, especially in patients with a high baseline blood pressure; mental status for depression, suicidal ideation (especially at the beginning of therapy or when doses are increased or decreased), anxiety, social functioning, mania, panic attacks

Dosage Forms Capsule: 20 mg, 30 mg, 60 mg [contains enteric coated pellets]

- ◆ **Duloxetine Hydrochloride** *see* Duloxetine *on page 562*
- ◆ **Duocaine™** *see* Lidocaine and Bupivacaine *on page 1014*
- ◆ **DuoNeb™** *see* Ipratropium and Albuterol *on page 934*
- ◆ **Duotan PD** *see* Dexchlorpheniramine and Pseudoephedrine *on page 483*
- ◆ **DuP 753** *see* Losartan *on page 1037*

- **Durabolin®** **(Can)** *see* Nandrolone *on page 1197*
- **Duraclon**™ *see* Clonidine *on page 399*
- **Duradrin®** *see* Acetaminophen, Isometheptene, and Dichloralphenazone *on page 36*
- **Duradyl®** *see* Chlorpheniramine, Phenylephrine, and Methscopolamine *on page 353*
- **Duragesic®** *see* Fentanyl *on page 693*
- **Durahist**™ **PE** *see* Chlorpheniramine, Phenylephrine, and Methscopolamine *on page 353*
- **Duralith®** **(Can)** *see* Lithium *on page 1023*
- **Duramorph®** *see* Morphine Sulfate *on page 1171*
- **DuraTan**™ **Forte** *see* Chlorpheniramine, Pseudoephedrine, and Dextromethorphan *on page 355*
- **Duratuss®** *see* Guaifenesin and Phenylephrine *on page 818*
- **Duratuss® DM** *see* Guaifenesin and Dextromethorphan *on page 816*
- **Duratuss® GP** *see* Guaifenesin and Phenylephrine *on page 818*
- **Duricef®** *see* Cefadroxil *on page 305*
- **Durolane®** **(Can)** *see* Hyaluronate and Derivatives *on page 841*

Dutasteride (doo TAS teer ide)

U.S. Brand Names Avodart™
Canadian Brand Names Avodart™
Pharmacologic Category 5 Alpha-Reductase Inhibitor
Use Treatment of symptomatic benign prostatic hyperplasia (BPH)
Unlabeled/Investigational Use Treatment of male patterned baldness
Pregnancy Risk Factor X
Dosage Oral: Adults: Male: 0.5 mg once daily
  Dosage adjustment in renal impairment: No adjustment required
  Dosage adjustment in hepatic impairment: Use caution; no specific adjustments recommended
Additional Information Complete prescribing information for this medication should be consulted for additional detail.
Dosage Forms Capsule, softgel: 0.5 mg

- **Duvoid®** **(Can)** *see* Bethanechol *on page 216*
- **DW286** *see* Gemifloxacin *on page 788*
- **Dyazide®** *see* Hydrochlorothiazide and Triamterene *on page 847*
- **Dycill®** **(Can)** *see* Dicloxacillin *on page 495*

Dyclonine (DYE kloe neen)

U.S. Brand Names Cēpacol® Dual Action Maximum Strength [OTC]; Sucrets® [OTC]
Index Terms Dyclonine Hydrochloride
Pharmacologic Category Local Anesthetic, Oral
Use Temporary relief of pain associated with oral mucosa
Medication Safety Issues
  Sound-alike/look-alike issues:
    Dyclonine may be confused with dicyclomine
Dosage Oral:
  Lozenge: Children ≥2 years and Adults: One lozenge every 2 hours as needed (maximum: 10 lozenges/day)
  Spray:
    Children ≥3-12 years: 1-3 sprays, up to 4 times a day
    Children ≥12 years and Adults: 1-4 sprays, up to 4 times a day
Additional Information Complete prescribing information for this medication should be consulted for additional detail.
Dosage Forms
  Lozenge, as hydrochloride (Sucrets®): 1.2 mg [children's cherry flavor]; 2 mg [wild cherry and assorted flavors]; 3 mg [vapor black cherry and wintergreen flavors]
  Spray, oral, as hydrochloride (Cēpacol® Dual Action Maximum Strength): 0.1% (120 mL) [contains glycerin 33%; cherry, honey lemon and cool menthol flavors]

- **Dyclonine Hydrochloride** *see* Dyclonine *on page 565*
- **Dynabac® [DSC]** *see* Dirithromycin *on page 526*
- **Dynacin®** *see* Minocycline *on page 1149*
- **DynaCirc® [DSC]** *see* Isradipine *on page 950*
- **DynaCirc® (Can)** *see* Isradipine *on page 950*
- **DynaCirc® CR** *see* Isradipine *on page 950*
- **Dyna-Hex® [OTC]** *see* Chlorhexidine Gluconate *on page 344*
- **Dynahist-ER Pediatric®** *see* Chlorpheniramine and Pseudoephedrine *on page 350*
- **Dynex** *see* Guaifenesin and Pseudoephedrine *on page 819*
- **Dyrenium®** *see* Triamterene *on page 1737*
- **Dytan**™ *see* DiphenhydrAMINE *on page 515*
- **7E3** *see* Abciximab *on page 22*
- **E2020** *see* Donepezil *on page 538*
- **EarSol® HC** *see* Hydrocortisone *on page 852*
- **Easprin®** *see* Aspirin *on page 160*
- **Ebixa® (Can)** *see* Memantine *on page 1076*

Echothiophate Iodide (ek oh THYE oh fate EYE oh dide)

U.S. Brand Names Phospholine Iodide®
Index Terms Ecostigmine Iodide
Pharmacologic Category Acetylcholinesterase Inhibitor; Ophthalmic Agent, Antiglaucoma; Ophthalmic Agent, Miotic
Additional Appendix Information
Glaucoma Drug Therapy *on page 2050*
Use Used as miotic in treatment of chronic, open-angle glaucoma; may be useful in specific cases of angle-closure glaucoma (postiridectomy or where surgery refused/contraindicated); postcataract surgery-related glaucoma; accommodative esotropia
Pregnancy Risk Factor C
Dosage Ophthalmic:
  Children: Accommodative esotropia:
    Diagnosis: Instill 1 drop (0.125%) once daily into both eyes at bedtime for 2-3 weeks
    Treatment: Usual dose: Instill 1 drop of 0.06% once daily or 0.125% every other day (maximum: 0.125% daily). **Note:** Use lowest concentration and frequency which gives satisfactory response; if necessary, doses >0.125% daily may be used for short periods of time.
  Adults: Open-angle or secondary glaucoma:
    Initial: Instill 1 drop (0.03%) twice daily into eyes with 1 dose just prior to bedtime
    Maintenance: Some patients have been treated with 1 dose daily or every other day
    Conversion from other ophthalmic agents: If IOP control was unsatisfactory, patients may be expected to require higher doses of echothiophate (eg, ≥0.06%); however, patients should be initially started on the 0.03% strength for a short period to better tolerance.
Additional Information Complete prescribing information for this medication should be consulted for additional detail.
Dosage Forms
  Powder for reconstitution, ophthalmic: 6.25 mg [0.125%]
    Phospholine Iodide®: 6.25 mg [0.125%] (5 mL) [packaged with sterile diluent containing mannitol]

♦ **EC-Naprosyn®** *see* Naproxen *on page 1199*
♦ ***E. coli* Asparaginase** *see* Asparaginase *on page 157*

Econazole (e KONE a zole)

U.S. Brand Names Spectazole®
Canadian Brand Names Ecostatin®; Spectazole™
Index Terms Econazole Nitrate
Pharmacologic Category Antifungal Agent, Topical
Use Topical treatment of tinea pedis (athlete's foot), tinea cruris (jock itch), tinea corporis (ringworm), tinea versicolor, and cutaneous candidiasis
Pregnancy Risk Factor C
Dosage Children and Adults: Topical:
  Tinea pedis, tinea cruris, tinea corporis, tinea versicolor: Apply sufficient amount to cover affected areas once daily
  Cutaneous candidiasis: Apply sufficient quantity twice daily (morning and evening)
  Duration of treatment: Candidal infections and tinea cruris, versicolor, and corporis should be treated for 2 weeks and tinea pedis for 1 month; occasionally, longer treatment periods may be required
Additional Information Complete prescribing information for this medication should be consulted for additional detail.
Dosage Forms Cream, topical, as nitrate: 1% (15 g, 30 g, 85 g)

♦ **Econazole Nitrate** *see* Econazole *on page 566*
♦ **Econopred® Plus** *see* PrednisoLONE *on page 1413*
♦ **Ecostatin® (Can)** *see* Econazole *on page 566*
♦ **Ecostigmine Iodide** *see* Echothiophate Iodide *on page 566*
♦ **Ecotrin® [OTC]** *see* Aspirin *on page 160*
♦ **Ecotrin® Low Strength [OTC]** *see* Aspirin *on page 160*
♦ **Ecotrin® Maximum Strength [OTC]** *see* Aspirin *on page 160*
♦ **Ectosone (Can)** *see* Betamethasone *on page 211*
♦ **Ed A-Hist®** *see* Chlorpheniramine and Phenylephrine *on page 349*
♦ **Edathamil Disodium** *see* Edetate Disodium *on page 568*
♦ **Edecrin®** *see* Ethacrynic Acid *on page 642*

Edetate Calcium Disodium (ED e tate KAL see um dye SOW dee um)

U.S. Brand Names Calcium Disodium Versenate®
Index Terms CaEDTA; Calcium Disodium Edetate; Calcium EDTA; EDTA (Calcium Disodium)
Pharmacologic Category Chelating Agent
Use Treatment of symptomatic acute and chronic lead poisoning or for symptomatic patients with high blood lead levels; used as an aid in the diagnosis of lead poisoning; possibly useful in poisoning by zinc, manganese, and certain heavy radioisotopes
Pregnancy Risk Factor B
Medication Safety Issues
Sound-alike look-alike issues:
  Edetate calcium disodium (CaEDTA) may be confused with edetate disodium (Na₂EDTA). CDC recommends that edetate disodium should **never** be used for chelation therapy in

children. Fatal hypocalcemia may result if edetate disodium is used for chelation therapy instead of edetate calcium disodium.

Contraindications Severe renal disease, anuria

Warnings/Precautions [U.S. Boxed Warning]: Use with extreme caution in patients with lead encephalopathy and cerebral edema. In these patients, I.V. infusion has been associated with lethal increase in intracranial pressure; I.M. injection is preferred.

Edetate calcium disodium is potentially nephrotoxic; renal tubular acidosis and fatal nephrosis may occur, especially with high doses; ECG changes may occur during therapy; do not exceed recommended daily dose. If anuria, increasing proteinuria, or hematuria occurs during therapy, discontinue calcium EDTA. Minimize nephrotoxicity by adequate hydration, establishment of good urine output, avoidance of excessive doses, and limitation of continuous administration to ≤5 days.

Exercise caution in the ordering, dispensing, and administration of this EDTA product. Edetate calcium disodium (CaEDTA) may be confused with edetate disodium (Na$_2$EDTA). CDC recommends that edetate disodium should never be used for chelation therapy in children. Fatal hypocalcemia may result if edetate disodium is used for chelation therapy instead of edetate calcium disodium.

Adverse Reactions Frequency not defined.
Cardiovascular: Arrhythmias, ECG changes, hypotension
Central nervous system: Chills, fever, headache
Dermatologic: Cheilosis, skin lesions
Endocrine & metabolic: Hypercalcemia
Gastrointestinal: Anorexia, GI upset, nausea, vomiting
Hematologic: Anemia, bone marrow suppression (transient)
Hepatic: Liver function test increased (mild)
Local: Thrombophlebitis following I.V. infusion (when concentration >5 mg/mL), pain at injection site following I.M. injection
Neuromuscular & skeletal: Arthralgia, numbness, tremor, paresthesia
Ocular: Lacrimation
Renal: Renal tubular necrosis, microscopic hematuria, proteinuria
Respiratory: Nasal congestion, sneezing
Miscellaneous: Zinc deficiency

Drug Interactions
Decreased Effect: Do not use simultaneously with zinc insulin preparations; do not mix in the same syringe with dimercaprol.

Stability Dilute with 0.9% sodium chloride or D$_5$W.

Mechanism of Action Calcium is displaced by divalent and trivalent heavy metals, forming a nonionizing soluble complex that is excreted in urine

Pharmacodynamics/Kinetics
Onset of action: Chelation of lead: I.V.: 1 hour
Absorption: I.M., SubQ: Well absorbed
Distribution: Into extracellular fluid; minimal CSF penetration
Half-life elimination, plasma: I.M.: 1.5 hours; I.V.: 20 minutes
Excretion: Urine (as metal chelates or unchanged drug); decreased GFR decreases elimination

Dosage Several regimens have been recommended:
Diagnosis of lead poisoning: Mobilization test (not recommended by AAP guidelines): I.M., I.V.:
Children: 500 mg/m^2/dose (maximum dose: 1 g) as a single dose or divided into 2 doses
Adults: 500 mg/m^2/dose
Note: Urine is collected for 24 hours after first EDTA dose and analyzed for lead content; if the ratio of mcg of lead in urine to mg calcium EDTA given is >1, then test is considered positive; for convenience, an 8-hour urine collection may be done after a single 50 mg/kg I.M. (maximum dose: 1 g) or 500 mg/m^2 I.V. dose; a positive test occurs if the ratio of lead excretion to mg calcium EDTA >0.5-0.6.
Treatment of lead poisoning: Children and Adults (each regimen is specific for route):
Symptoms of lead encephalopathy and/or blood lead level >70 mcg/dL: Treat 5 days; give in conjunction with dimercaprol; wait a minimum of 2 days with no treatment before considering a repeat course:
I.M.: 250 mg/m^2/dose every 4 hours
I.V.: 50 mg/kg/day as 24-hour continuous I.V. infusion **or** 1-1.5 g/m^2 I.V. as either an 8- to 24-hour infusion or divided into 2 doses every 12 hours
Symptomatic lead poisoning **without** encephalopathy **or** asymptomatic with blood lead level >70 mcg/dL: Treat 3-5 days; treatment with dimercaprol is recommended until the blood lead level concentration <50 mcg/dL:
I.M.: 167 mg/m^2 every 4 hours
I.V.: 1 g/m^2 as an 8- to 24-hour infusion or divided every 12 hours
Asymptomatic **children** with blood lead level 45-69 mcg/dL: I.V.: 25 mg/kg/day for 5 days as an 8- to 24-hour infusion or divided into 2 doses every 12 hours
Depending upon the blood lead level, additional courses may be necessary; repeat at least 2-4 days and preferably 2-4 weeks apart
Adults with lead nephropathy: An alternative dosing regimen reflecting the reduction in renal clearance is based upon the serum creatinine. Refer to the following:
Dose of Ca EDTA based on serum creatinine:
S$_{cr}$ ≤2 mg/dL: 1 g/m^2/day for 5 days*
S$_{cr}$ 2-3 mg/dL: 500 mg/m^2/day for 5 days*
S$_{cr}$ 3-4 mg/dL: 500 mg/m^2/dose every 48 hours for 3 doses*
S$_{cr}$ >4 mg/dL: 500 mg/m^2/week*
*Repeat these regimens monthly until lead excretion is reduced toward normal.

Administration For intermittent I.V. infusion, administer the dose I.V. over at least 1 hour in asymptomatic patients, 2 hours in symptomatic patients; for I.V. continuous infusion, dilute to 2-4 mg/mL in D$_5$W or NS and infuse over at least 8 hours, usually over 12-24 hours; for I.M.
(Continued)

Edetate Calcium Disodium *(Continued)*

injection, 1 mL of 1% procaine hydrochloride may be added to each mL of EDTA calcium to minimize pain at injection site

Monitoring Parameters BUN, creatinine, urinalysis, I & O, and ECG during therapy; intravenous administration requires a cardiac monitor, blood and urine lead concentrations

Test Interactions If calcium EDTA is given as a continuous I.V. infusion, stop the infusion for at least 1 hour before blood is drawn for lead concentration to avoid a falsely elevated value

Dosage Forms Injection, solution: 200 mg/mL (5 mL)

Edetate Disodium *(ED e tate dye SOW dee um)*

U.S. Brand Names Endrate®

Index Terms Edathamil Disodium; EDTA (Disodium); Na2EDTA; Sodium Edetate

Pharmacologic Category Chelating Agent

Use Emergency treatment of hypercalcemia; control digitalis-induced cardiac dysrhythmias (ventricular arrhythmias)

Pregnancy Risk Factor C

Medication Safety Issues

Sound-alike look-alike issues:

Edetate disodium (Na_2EDTA) may be confused with edetate calcium disodium (CaEDTA). CDC recommends that edetate disodium should **never** be used for chelation therapy in children. Fatal hypocalcemia may result if edetate disodium is used for chelation therapy instead of edetate calcium disodium.

Contraindications Severe renal failure or anuria

Warnings/Precautions Use of this drug is recommended only when the severity of the clinical condition justifies the aggressive measures associated with this type of therapy; use with caution in patients with renal dysfunction, intracranial lesions, seizure disorders, coronary or peripheral vascular disease

Exercise caution in the ordering, dispensing, and administration of this EDTA product. Edetate disodium (Na_2EDTA) may be confused with edetate calcium disodium (CaEDTA). CDC recommends that edetate disodium should never be used for chelation therapy in children. Fatal hypocalcemia may result if edetate disodium is used for chelation therapy instead of edetate calcium disodium.

Adverse Reactions Rapid I.V. administration or excessive doses may cause a sudden drop in serum calcium concentration which may lead to hypocalcemic tetany, seizure, arrhythmia, and death from respiratory arrest. Do **not** exceed recommended dosage and rate of administration.

1% to 10%: Gastrointestinal: Nausea, vomiting, abdominal cramps, diarrhea

<1% (Limited to important or life-threatening): Acute tubular necrosis, anemia, arrhythmia, back pain, chills, death from respiratory arrest, dermatologic lesions, eruptions, fever, headache, hypokalemia, hypomagnesemia, muscle cramps, nephrotoxicity, pain at the site of injection, paresthesia may occur, seizure, tetany, thrombophlebitis, transient hypotension

Overdosage/Toxicology Symptoms include hypotension, dysrhythmias, tetany, and seizures. Treatment includes immediate I.V. calcium salts for hypocalcemia-related adverse reactions. Replace calcium cautiously in patients on digitalis.

Drug Interactions

Increased Effect/Toxicity: Increased effect of insulin (edetate disodium may decrease blood glucose concentrations and reduce insulin requirements in diabetic patients treated with insulin).

Mechanism of Action Chelates with divalent or trivalent metals to form a soluble complex that is then eliminated in urine

Pharmacodynamics/Kinetics

Metabolism: None

Half-life elimination: 20-60 minutes

Time to peak: I.V.: 24-48 hours

Excretion: Following chelation: Urine (95%); chelates within 24-48 hours

Dosage Hypercalcemia: I.V.:

Children: 40-70 mg/kg/day slow infusion over 3-4 hours or more to a maximum of 3 g/24 hours; administer for 5 days and allow 5 days between courses of therapy

Adults: 50 mg/kg/day over 3 or more hours to a maximum of 3 g/24 hours; a suggested regimen of 5 days followed by 2 days without drug and repeated courses up to 15 total doses

Digitalis-induced arrhythmias: Children and Adults: 15 mg/kg/hour (maximum dose: 60 mg/kg/day) as continuous infusion

Dietary Considerations Sodium content of 1 g: 5.4 mEq

Administration Parenteral: I.V.: Must be diluted before I.V. use in D_5W or NS to a maximum concentration of 30 mg/mL (3%) and infused over at least 3 hours; avoid extravasation; not for I.M. use

Monitoring Parameters Cardiac function (ECG monitoring); blood pressure during infusion; renal function should be assessed before and during therapy; monitor calcium, magnesium, and potassium levels; cardiac monitor required

Dosage Forms Injection, solution: 150 mg/mL (20 mL)

♦ **Edex**® *see* Alprostadil *on page 77*

Edrophonium (ed roe FOE nee um)

U.S. Brand Names Enlon®; Reversol®
Canadian Brand Names Enlon®; Tensilon®
Index Terms Edrophonium Chloride
Pharmacologic Category Antidote; Cholinergic Agonist; Diagnostic Agent
Use Diagnosis of myasthenia gravis; differentiation of cholinergic crises from myasthenia crises; reversal of nondepolarizing neuromuscular blockers; adjunct treatment of respiratory depression caused by curare overdose
Pregnancy Risk Factor C
Lactation Excretion in breast milk unknown
Contraindications Hypersensitivity to edrophonium, sulfites, or any component of the formulation; GI or GU obstruction
Warnings/Precautions Use with caution in patients with bronchial asthma and those receiving a cardiac glycoside; atropine sulfate should always be readily available as an antagonist. Overdosage can cause cholinergic crisis which may be fatal. I.V. atropine should be readily available for treatment of cholinergic reactions.
Adverse Reactions Frequency not defined.

Cardiovascular: Arrhythmias (especially bradycardia), AV block, cardiac arrest, decreased carbon monoxide, flushing, hypotension, nodal rhythm, nonspecific ECG changes, syncope, tachycardia

Central nervous system: Convulsions, dizziness, drowsiness, dysarthria, dysphonia, headache, loss of consciousness

Dermatologic: Skin rash, thrombophlebitis (I.V.), urticaria

Gastrointestinal: Diarrhea, dysphagia, flatulence, hyperperistalsis, nausea, salivation, stomach cramps, vomiting

Genitourinary: Urinary urgency

Neuromuscular & skeletal: Arthralgias, fasciculations, muscle cramps, spasms, weakness

Ocular: Lacrimation, small pupils

Respiratory: Bronchiolar constriction, bronchospasm, dyspnea, bronchial secretions increased, laryngospasm, respiratory arrest, respiratory depression, respiratory muscle paralysis

Miscellaneous: Allergic reactions, anaphylaxis, diaphoresis increased

Overdosage/Toxicology Symptoms of overdose include muscle weakness, nausea, vomiting, miosis, bronchospasm, and respiratory paralysis. Maintain an adequate airway. For muscarinic symptoms, the antidote is atropine 0.4-0.5 mg I.V. repeated every 3-10 minutes (initial doses as high as 1.2 mg have been administered). Skeletal muscle effects of edrophonium are not alleviated by atropine.

Drug Interactions

Increased Effect/Toxicity: Digoxin may enhance bradycardia potential of edrophonium. Effects of succinylcholine, decamethonium, nondepolarizing muscle relaxants (eg, pancuronium, vecuronium) are prolonged by edrophonium. I.V. acetazolamide, neostigmine, physostigmine, and acute muscle weakness may increase the effects of edrophonium.

Decreased Effect: Atropine, nondepolarizing muscle relaxants, procainamide, and quinidine may antagonize the effects of edrophonium.

Mechanism of Action Inhibits destruction of acetylcholine by acetylcholinesterase. This facilitates transmission of impulses across myoneural junction and results in increased cholinergic responses such as miosis, increased tonus of intestinal and skeletal muscles, bronchial and ureteral constriction, bradycardia, and increased salivary and sweat gland secretions.

Pharmacodynamics/Kinetics

Onset of action: I.M.: 2-10 minutes; I.V.: 30-60 seconds

Duration: I.M.: 5-30 minutes; I.V.: 10 minutes

Distribution: V_d: Adults: 1.1 L/kg

Half-life elimination: Adults: 1.2-2.4 hours; Anephric patients: 2.4-4.4 hours

Excretion: Adults: Primarily urine (67%)

Dosage Usually administered I.V., however, if not possible, I.M. or SubQ may be used:

Infants:

I.M.: 0.5-1 mg

I.V.: Initial: 0.1 mg, followed by 0.4 mg if no response; total dose = 0.5 mg

Children:

Diagnosis: Initial: 0.04 mg/kg over 1 minute followed by 0.16 mg/kg if no response, to a maximum total dose of 5 mg for children <34 kg, or 10 mg for children >34 kg **or**

Alternative dosing (manufacturer's recommendation):

≤34 kg: 1 mg; if no response after 45 seconds, repeat dosage in 1 mg increments every 30-45 seconds, up to a total of 5 mg

>34 kg: 2 mg; if no response after 45 seconds, repeat dosage in 1 mg increments every 30-45 seconds, up to a total of 10 mg

I.M.:

<34 kg: 1 mg

>34 kg: 5 mg

Titration of oral anticholinesterase therapy: 0.04 mg/kg once given 1 hour after oral intake of the drug being used in treatment; if strength improves, an increase in neostigmine or pyridostigmine dose is indicated

Adults:

Diagnosis:

I.V.: 2 mg test dose administered over 15-30 seconds; 8 mg given 45 seconds later if no response is seen; test dose may be repeated after 30 minutes

I.M.: Initial: 10 mg; if no cholinergic reaction occurs, administer 2 mg 30 minutes later to rule out false-negative reaction

Titration of oral anticholinesterase therapy: 1-2 mg given 1 hour after oral dose of anticholinesterase; if strength improves, an increase in neostigmine or pyridostigmine dose is indicated

(Continued)

Edrophonium *(Continued)*

Reversal of nondepolarizing neuromuscular blocking agents (neostigmine with atropine usually preferred): I.V.: 10 mg over 30-45 seconds; may repeat every 5-10 minutes up to 40 mg

Termination of paroxysmal atrial tachycardia: I.V. rapid injection: 5-10 mg

Differentiation of cholinergic from myasthenic crisis: I.V.: 1 mg; may repeat after 1 minute. **Note:** Intubation and controlled ventilation may be required if patient has cholinergic crisis

Dosing adjustment in renal impairment: Dose may need to be reduced in patients with chronic renal failure

Administration Edrophonium is administered by direct I.V. injection; see Dosage

Monitoring Parameters Pre- and postinjection strength (cranial musculature is most useful); heart rate, respiratory rate, blood pressure

Test Interactions Increased aminotransferase [ALT (SGPT)/AST (SGOT)] (S), amylase (S)

Additional Information Atropine should be administered along with edrophonium when reversing the effects of nondepolarizing agents to antagonize the cholinergic effects at the muscarinic receptors, especially bradycardia. It is important to recognize the difference in dose for diagnosis of myasthenia gravis versus reversal of muscle relaxant, a much larger dose is needed for desired effect of reversal of muscle paralysis.

Dosage Forms Injection, solution, as chloride:
Enlon®: 10 mg/mL (15 mL) [contains sodium sulfite]
Reversol®: 10 mg/mL (10 mL) [contains sodium sulfite]

Edrophonium and Atropine *(ed roe FOE nee um & A troe peen)*

U.S. Brand Names Enlon-Plus™

Index Terms Atropine Sulfate and Edrophonium Chloride; Edrophonium Chloride and Atropine Sulfate

Pharmacologic Category Anticholinergic Agent; Antidote; Cholinergic Agonist

Use Reversal of nondepolarizing neuromuscular blockers; adjunct treatment of respiratory depression caused by curare overdose

Pregnancy Risk Factor C

Dosage I.V.: Adults: Reversal of neuromuscular blockade: 0.05 mL/kg given over 45-60 seconds. The dose delivered is 0.5-1 mg/kg of edrophonium and 0.007-0.015 mg/kg of atropine. An edrophonium dose of 1 mg/kg should rarely be exceeded. **Note:** Monitor closely for bradyarrhythmias. Have atropine on hand in case needed.

Dosage adjustment in renal impairment: Adjustment not required.

Dosage adjustment in hepatic impairment: Adjustment not required.

Additional Information Complete prescribing information for this medication should be consulted for additional detail.

Dosage Forms Injection, solution, as chloride: Edrophonium 10 mg/mL and atropine 0.14 mg/mL (5 mL, 15 mL) [contains sodium sulfite]

♦ **Edrophonium Chloride** *see Edrophonium on page 569*
♦ **Edrophonium Chloride and Atropine Sulfate** *see Edrophonium and Atropine on page 570*
♦ **EDTA (Calcium Disodium)** *see Edetate Calcium Disodium on page 566*
♦ **EDTA (Disodium)** *see Edetate Disodium on page 568*
♦ **E.E.S.®** *see Erythromycin on page 609*
♦ **EES® (Can)** *see Erythromycin on page 609*

Efalizumab *(e fa li ZOO mab)*

U.S. Brand Names Raptiva®

Index Terms Anti-CD11a; hu1124

Pharmacologic Category Immunosuppressant Agent; Monoclonal Antibody

Use Treatment of chronic moderate-to-severe plaque psoriasis in patients who are candidates for systemic therapy or phototherapy

Pregnancy Risk Factor C

Pregnancy Implications Reproduction studies have not been conducted. A decreased ability to mount an antibody response was observed in the offspring of female mice who received efalizumab during toxicity studies. There are no adequate and well-controlled studies in pregnant women. Healthcare providers are encouraged to enroll patients who may become pregnant during therapy or within 6 weeks of discontinuing treatment in the Raptiva® registry (877-727-8482).

Lactation Excretion in breast milk unknown/not recommended

Contraindications Hypersensitivity to efalizumab or any component of the formulation

Warnings/Precautions May result in increased susceptibility to infections or reactivation of latent infection; use caution with chronic infections, history of recurrent infection, or the elderly. Avoid administration to patients with clinically important infection. Discontinue therapy if serious infection develops. Thrombocytopenia has been reported (rare) and may require treatment; discontinue if thrombocytopenia develops. Hemolytic anemia, which may occur after 4-6 months of treatment, has been reported; discontinue if signs and symptoms of hemolytic anemia occur. Use caution in patients at high risk for malignancy or history of malignancy; effects of efalizumab on the development of malignancies is unknown. Psoriasis and/or arthritis may worsen with efalizumab treatment or following discontinuation (rare). First-dose reactions have been reported; a lower, conditioning dose is recommended to reduce the incidence and severity of reactions. Concomitant use with other immunosuppressant agents is not recommended. Produced in a Chinese hamster cell medium. Safety and efficacy in pediatric patients or patients with renal or hepatic impairment have not been established.

Adverse Reactions
>10%:
Central nervous system: Headache (32%), chills (13%)
Gastrointestinal: Nausea (11%)
Hematologic: Lymphocytosis (40%), leukocytosis (26%)
Miscellaneous: First-dose reaction (29%, described as chills, fever, headache, myalgia, and nausea occurring within 2 days of the first injection; percent reported in patients receiving a 1 mg/kg dose; severity decreased with 0.7 mg/kg dose); infection (29%, serious infection <1%)
1% to 10%:
Cardiovascular: Peripheral edema (1% to 2%)
Central nervous system: Pain (10%), fever (7%)
Dermatologic: Acne (4%), psoriasis (1% to 2%), urticaria (1%)
Hepatic: Alkaline phosphatase elevated (4%)
Neuromuscular & skeletal: Myalgia (8%), back pain (4%), arthralgia (1% to 2%), weakness (1% to 2%)
Miscellaneous: Antibodies to efalizumab (6%); hypersensitivity reaction, including asthma, dyspnea, angioedema, urticaria, or maculopapular rash (8%); flu-like syndrome (7%)
<1% (Limited to important or life-threatening): Arthritis, aseptic meningitis, asthma, bacterial sepsis (with seeding of distant sites); bronchiolitis obliterans, drug eruption (allergic), erythema multiforme, hemolytic anemia (immune mediated), inflammatory arthritis, idiopathic hepatitis, interstitial pneumonitis, laryngospasm, malignancies, necrotizing fasciitis, photoallergic dermatitis, photosensitivity, pneumonia (severe with neutropenia); serious psoriasis events (include erythrodermic, guttate, and pustular subtypes); psoriatic arthritis, serum sickness-like reaction, sialadenitis, sensorineural hearing loss, thrombocytopenia (immune mediated), toxic epidermal necrolysis, transverse myelitis, tuberculous pneumonia

Overdosage/Toxicology Limited data. Severe vomiting reported in one patient receiving 10 mg/kg intravenously. In case of overdose, monitor for 24-48 hours.

Drug Interactions
Increased Effect/Toxicity: Concurrent use of immunosuppressants may increase risk of infection.
Decreased Effect: Note: Formal drug interaction studies have not been conducted. Acellular, live, and live-attenuated vaccines should not be administered during therapy.

Stability Powder should be stored under refrigeration at 2°C to 8°C (36°F to 46°F) and protected from light. Slowly inject 1.3 mL of the provided diluent into vial. Gently swirl to mix; do not shake. Following reconstitution, solution should be stored at room temperature and used within 8 hours. Discard unused solution.

Mechanism of Action Efalizumab is a recombinant monoclonal antibody which binds to CD11a, a subunit of leukocyte function antigen-1 (LFA-1) found on leukocytes. By binding to CD11a, efalizumab blocks multiple T-cell mediated responses involved in the pathogenesis of psoriatic plaques.

Pharmacodynamics/Kinetics
Onset: Reduction of CD11a expression and free CD11a-binding sites seen 1-2 days after the first dose; time to steady state serum concentration: 4 weeks
Response to therapy (75% reduction from baseline of PASI score): Observed after 12 weeks
Duration: CD11a expression was ~74% of baseline at 5-13 weeks after discontinuing dose; free CD11a binding sites were at ~86% of baseline at 8-13 weeks following discontinuation; response to therapy (75% reduction from baseline PASI score) continued 1-2 months after discontinuation
Bioavailability: SubQ: 50%
Excretion: Time to eliminate (at steady state): 25 days (range: 13-35 days)

Dosage SubQ: Adults: Psoriasis: Initial: 0.7 mg/kg, followed by weekly dose of 1 mg/kg (maximum: 200 mg/dose)

Administration For SubQ injection in the abdomen, buttocks, thigh, or upper arm

Monitoring Parameters Platelet counts (at least monthly at the start of treatment, every 3 months as therapy continues); signs of infection; worsening of psoriasis

Test Interactions Increased lymphocytes (related to mechanism of action)

Dosage Forms Injection, powder for reconstitution: 150 mg [contains sucrose 123.2 mg/vial; delivers 125 mg/1.25 mL; packaged with prefilled syringe containing sterile water for injection]

Efavirenz (e FAV e renz)

U.S. Brand Names Sustiva®
Canadian Brand Names Sustiva®
Pharmacologic Category Antiretroviral Agent, Reverse Transcriptase Inhibitor (Non-nucleoside)
Additional Appendix Information
Antiretroviral Therapy for HIV Infection: Adults and Adolescents *on page 1988*
Management of Healthcare Worker Exposures to HBV, HCV, and HIV *on page 1941*
Use Treatment of HIV-1 infections in combination with at least two other antiretroviral agents
Pregnancy Risk Factor D
Pregnancy Implications Teratogenic effects have been observed in Primates receiving efavirenz. Severe CNS defects have been reported in infants following efavirenz exposure in the first trimester. Pregnancy should be avoided and alternate therapy should be considered in women of childbearing potential. Women of childbearing potential should undergo pregnancy testing prior to initiation of efavirenz. Barrier contraception should be used in combination with other (hormonal) methods of contraception. If therapy with efavirenz is administered during pregnancy, avoid use during the first trimester. Health professionals are encouraged to contact the antiretroviral pregnancy registry to monitor outcomes of pregnant women exposed to antiretroviral medications (1-800-258-4263 or www.APRegistry.com).
(Continued)

Efavirenz *(Continued)*

Lactation Excretion is breast milk unknown/contraindicated

Contraindications Clinically-significant hypersensitivity to efavirenz or any component of the formulation; concurrent use of cisapride, midazolam, triazolam, voriconazole, or ergot alkaloids (includes dihydroergotamine, ergotamine, ergonovine, methylergonovine)

Warnings/Precautions Do not use as single-agent therapy; avoid pregnancy; women of childbearing potential should undergo pregnancy testing prior to initiation of therapy; use caution with other agents metabolized by cytochrome P450 isoenzyme 3A4 (see Contraindications); use caution with history of mental illness/drug abuse (predisposition to psychological reactions); may cause CNS and psychiatric symptoms, which include impaired concentration, dizziness or drowsiness (avoid potentially hazardous tasks such as driving or operating machinery if these effects are noted); serious psychiatric side effects have been associated with efavirenz, including severe depression, suicide, paranoia, and mania; discontinue if severe rash (involving blistering, desquamation, mucosal involvement or fever) develops. Children are more susceptible to development of rash; prophylactic antihistamines may be used. Caution in patients with known or suspected hepatitis B or C infection (monitoring of liver function is recommended); hepatic impairment. Persistent elevations of serum transaminases >5 times the upper limit of normal should prompt evaluation - benefit of continued therapy should be weighed against possible risk of hepatotoxicity. Concomitant use with St John's wort is not recommended.

Adverse Reactions

>10%:

> Central nervous system: Dizziness* (2% to 28%), depression (1% to 16%), insomnia (6% to 16%), anxiety (1% to 11%), pain* (1% to 13%)
>
> Dermatologic: Rash* (NCI grade 1: 9% to 11%, NCI grade 2: 15% to 32%, NCI grade 3 or 4: <1%); 26% experienced new rash vs 17% in control groups; up to 46% of pediatric patients experience rash (median onset: 8 days)
>
> Endocrine & metabolic: HDL increased (25% to 35%), total cholesterol increased (20% to 40%)
>
> Gastrointestinal: Diarrhea* (3% to 14%), nausea* (2% to 12%)

1% to 10%:

> Central nervous system: Impaired concentration (2% to 8%), headache* (2% to 7%), somnolence (2% to 7%), fatigue (2% to 7%), abnormal dreams (1% to 6%), nervousness (2% to 6%), severe depression (1%), hallucinations (1%)
>
> Dermatologic: Pruritus (1% to 9%)
>
> Gastrointestinal: Vomiting* (6% to 7%), dyspepsia (3%), abdominal pain (1% to 3%), anorexia (1% to 2%)
>
> Miscellaneous: Diaphoresis increased (1% to 2%)

*Adverse effect reported in ≥10% of patients 3-16 years of age

<1% (Limited to important or life-threatening): Aggressive reaction, agitation, allergic reaction, body fat accumulation/redistribution, convulsions, liver failure, manic reaction, neuropathy, paranoid reaction, Stevens-Johnson syndrome, suicide, visual abnormality

Overdosage/Toxicology Increased central nervous system symptoms and involuntary muscle contractions have been reported in accidental overdose. Treatment is supportive. Activated charcoal may enhance elimination. Dialysis is unlikely to remove the drug.

Drug Interactions

Cytochrome P450 Effect: Substrate (major) of CYP2B6, 3A4; **Inhibits** CYP2C9 (moderate), 2C19 (moderate), 3A4 (moderate); **Induces** CYP2B6 (weak), 3A4 (strong)

Increased Effect/Toxicity: Coadministration with medications metabolized by these enzymes may lead to increased concentration-related effects. Cisapride, midazolam, triazolam, and ergot alkaloids may result in life-threatening toxicities; concurrent use is contraindicated. May increase (or decrease) effect of warfarin. Efavirenz may increase the levels/effects of CYP2C9 substrates; example substrates include bosentan, dapsone, fluoxetine, glimepiride, glipizide, losartan, montelukast, nateglinide, paclitaxel, phenytoin, warfarin, and zafirlukast. CYP2C19 substrates: Efavirenz may increase the levels/effects of CYP2C19 substrates; example substrates include citalopram, diazepam, methsuximide, phenytoin, propranolol, and sertraline. Efavirenz may alter the levels/effects of CYP3A4 substrates; example substrates include benzodiazepines, calcium channel blockers, ergot derivatives, mirtazapine, nateglinide, nefazodone, tacrolimus, and venlafaxine.

Decreased Effect: CYP2B6 inducers may decrease the levels/effects of efavirenz; example inducers include carbamazepine, nevirapine, phenobarbital, phenytoin, and rifampin. St John's wort may decrease serum concentrations of efavirenz. Concentrations of atazanavir, indinavir, and/or lopinavir may be reduced; dosage adjustments required. Concentrations of saquinavir may be decreased (use as sole protease inhibitor is not recommended). Serum concentrations of methadone may be decreased; monitor for withdrawal. May decrease (or increase) effect of warfarin. Serum concentrations of sertraline may be decreased by efavirenz. CYP3A4 inducers may decrease the levels/effects of efavirenz; example inducers include aminoglutethimide, carbamazepine, nafcillin, nevirapine, phenobarbital, phenytoin, and rifamycins. Voriconazole serum levels may be reduced by efavirenz (concurrent use is contraindicated). Efavirenz may alter the levels/effects of CYP3A4 substrates; example substrates include benzodiazepines, calcium channel blockers, ergot derivatives, mirtazapine, nateglinide, nefazodone, tacrolimus, and venlafaxine.

Ethanol/Nutrition/Herb Interactions

Ethanol: Avoid ethanol (hepatic and CNS adverse effects).

Food: Avoid high-fat meals (increase the absorption of efavirenz).

Herb/Nutraceutical: St John's wort may decrease efavirenz serum levels. Avoid concurrent use.

Stability Store below 25°C (77°F).

Mechanism of Action As a non-nucleoside reverse transcriptase inhibitor, efavirenz has activity against HIV-1 by binding to reverse transcriptase. It consequently blocks the RNA-dependent and DNA-dependent DNA polymerase activities including HIV-1 replication. It does not require intracellular phosphorylation for antiviral activity.

Pharmacodynamics/Kinetics
Absorption: Increased by fatty meals
Distribution: CSF concentrations exceed free fraction in serum
Protein binding: >99%, primarily to albumin
Metabolism: Hepatic via CYP3A4 and 2B6; may induce its own metabolism
Half-life elimination: Single dose: 52-76 hours; Multiple doses: 40-55 hours
Time to peak: 3-8 hours
Excretion: Feces (16% to 41% primarily as unchanged drug); urine (14% to 34% as metabolites)

Dosage Oral: Dosing at bedtime is recommended to limit central nervous system effects; should not be used as single-agent therapy

Children ≥3 years: Dosage is based on body weight
10 kg to <15 kg: 200 mg once daily
15 kg to <20 kg: 250 mg once daily
20 kg to <25 kg: 300 mg once daily
25 kg to <32.5 kg: 350 mg once daily
32.5 kg to <40 kg: 400 mg once daily
≥40 kg: 600 mg once daily
Adults: 600 mg once daily

Dosing adjustment in renal impairment: None recommended
Dosing comments in hepatic impairment: Limited clinical experience, use with caution
Dietary Considerations Should be taken on an empty stomach.
Administration Administer on an empty stomach. Capsules may be opened and added to liquids or small amounts of food.
Monitoring Parameters Serum transaminases (discontinuation of treatment should be considered for persistent elevations greater than five times the upper limit of normal), cholesterol, triglycerides, signs and symptoms of infection
Test Interactions False-positive test for cannabinoids have been reported when the CEDIA DAU Multilevel THC assay is used. False-positive results with other assays for cannabinoids have not been observed.
Additional Information Efavirenz oral solution is available only through an expanded access (compassionate use) program. Enrollment information may be obtained by calling 1-877-372-7097.

Early virologic failure was observed with tenofovir and didanosine delayed release capsules, plus either efavirenz or nevirapine; use caution in treatment-naive patients with high baseline viral loads.

Dosage Forms
Capsule: 50 mg, 100 mg, 200 mg
Tablet: 600 mg

Efavirenz, Emtricitabine, and Tenofovir
(e FAV e renz, em trye SYE ta been, & te NOE fo veer)

U.S. Brand Names Atripla™
Index Terms Emtricitabine, Efavirenz, and Tenofovir; Tenofovir Disoproxil Fumarate, Efavirenz, and Emtricitabine
Pharmacologic Category Antiretroviral Agent, Reverse Transcriptase Inhibitor (Non-nucleoside); Antiretroviral Agent, Reverse Transcriptase Inhibitor (Nucleoside); Antiretroviral Agent, Reverse Transcriptase Inhibitor (Nucleotide)
Additional Appendix Information
Antiretroviral Therapy for HIV Infection: Adults and Adolescents *on page 1988*
Management of Healthcare Worker Exposures to HBV, HCV, and HIV *on page 1941*
Use Treatment of HIV infection
Pregnancy Risk Factor D
Dosage Oral: Adults: One tablet once daily to be taken on an empty stomach (at bedtime is recommended).
Dosage adjustment in renal impairment: Moderate-to-severe renal impairment (Cl_{cr} <50 mL/minute): Use not recommended
Additional Information Complete prescribing information for this medication should be consulted for additional detail.
Dosage Forms
Tablet:
Atripla™: Efavirenz 600 mg, emtricitabine 200 mg, and tenofovir disoproxil fumarate 300 mg

♦ **Effer-K™** *see* Potassium Bicarbonate and Potassium Citrate *on page 1396*
♦ **Effexor®** *see* Venlafaxine *on page 1781*
♦ **Effexor® XR** *see* Venlafaxine *on page 1781*
♦ **Eflone® [DSC]** *see* Fluorometholone *on page 724*

Eflornithine (ee FLOR ni theen)

U.S. Brand Names Vaniqa™
Canadian Brand Names Vaniqa™
Index Terms DFMO; Eflornithine Hydrochloride
Pharmacologic Category Antiprotozoal; Topical Skin Product
Use Cream: Females ≥12 years: Reduce unwanted hair from face and adjacent areas under the chin
Orphan status: Injection: Treatment of meningoencephalitic stage of *Trypanosoma brucei gambiense* infection (sleeping sickness)
Pregnancy Risk Factor C
(Continued)

Eflornithine *(Continued)*

Pregnancy Implications There are no adequate and well-controlled studies of topical eflornithine cream in pregnant women. The potential benefits to the mother versus the possible risks to the fetus should be considered prior to use.

Lactation Excretion in breast milk unknown/use caution

Medication Safety Issues
Sound-alike/look-alike issues:
Vaniqa™ may be confused with Viagra®

Contraindications Hypersensitivity to eflornithine or any component of the formulation

Warnings/Precautions
Injection: For I.V. use only; not for I.M. administration. Must be diluted before use; frequent monitoring for myelosuppression should be done; use with caution in patients with a history of seizures and in patients with renal impairment; serial audiograms should be obtained; due to the potential for relapse, patients should be followed up for at least 24 months

Cream: For topical use by females only; discontinue if hypersensitivity occurs; safety and efficacy in children <12 years has not been studied

Adverse Reactions
Injection:
>10%: Hematologic (reversible): Anemia (55%), leukopenia (37%), thrombocytopenia (14%)
1% to 10%:
Central nervous system: Seizures (may be due to the disease) (8%), dizziness
Dermatologic: Alopecia
Gastrointestinal: Vomiting, diarrhea
Hematologic: Eosinophilia
Otic: Hearing impairment
<1% (Limited to important or life-threatening): Abdominal pain, anorexia, facial edema, headache, weakness

Topical:
>10%: Dermatologic: Acne (11% to 21%), pseudofolliculitis barbae (5% to 15%)
1% to 10%:
Central nervous system: Headache (4% to 5%), dizziness (1%), vertigo (0.3% to 1%)
Dermatologic: Pruritus (3% to 4%), burning skin (2% to 4%), tingling skin (1% to 4%), dry skin (2% to 3%), rash (1% to 3%), facial edema (0.3% to 3%), alopecia (1% to 2%), skin irritation (1% to 2%), erythema (up to 2%), ingrown hair (0.3% to 2%), folliculitis (up to 1%)
Gastrointestinal: Dyspepsia (2%), anorexia (0.7% to 2%)
<1% (Limited to important or life-threatening): Bleeding skin, cheilitis, contact dermatitis, herpes simplex, lip swelling, nausea, numbness, rosacea, weakness

Overdosage/Toxicology There is no known antidote. Treatment is supportive. In mice and rats CNS depression, seizures, and death have occurred. Overdose with the topical product is not expected due to low percutaneous penetration.

Drug Interactions
Increased Effect/Toxicity: Cream: Possible interactions with other topical products have not been studied.
Decreased Effect: Cream: Possible interactions with other topical products have not been studied.

Stability
Injection: Must be diluted before use and used within 24 hours of preparation.
Cream: Store at controlled room temperature 25°C (77°F); do not freeze.

Mechanism of Action Eflornithine exerts antitumor and antiprotozoal effects through specific, irreversible ("suicide") inhibition of the enzyme ornithine decarboxylase (ODC). ODC is the rate-limiting enzyme in the biosynthesis of putrescine, spermine, and spermidine, the major polyamines in nucleated cells. Polyamines are necessary for the synthesis of DNA, RNA, and proteins and are, therefore, necessary for cell growth and differentiation. Although many microorganisms and higher plants are able to produce polyamines from alternate biochemical pathways, all mammalian cells depend on ornithine decarboxylase to produce polyamines. Eflornithine inhibits ODC and rapidly depletes animal cells of putrescine and spermidine; the concentration of spermine remains the same or may even increase. Rapidly dividing cells appear to be most susceptible to the effects of eflornithine. Topically, the inhibition of ODC in the skin leads to a decreased rate of hair growth.

Pharmacodynamics/Kinetics
Absorption: Topical: <1%
Half-life elimination: I.V.: 3-3.5 hours; Topical: 8 hours
Excretion: Primarily urine (as unchanged drug)

Dosage
Children ≥12 years and Adults: Females: Topical: Apply thin layer of cream to affected areas of face and adjacent chin twice daily, at least 8 hours apart
Adults: I.V. infusion: 100 mg/kg/dose given every 6 hours (over at least 45 minutes) for 14 days
Dosing adjustment in renal impairment: Injection: Dose should be adjusted although no specific guidelines are available

Administration
I.V.: Administered I.V. only; infuse over 45 minutes. Not for I.M. administration.
Cream: Apply thin layer of eflornithine cream to affected areas of face and adjacent chin area twice daily, at least 8 hours apart. Rub in thoroughly. Hair removal techniques must still be continued; wait at least 5 minutes after removing hair to apply cream. Do not wash affected area for at least 8 hours following application.

Monitoring Parameters CBC with platelet counts

Dosage Forms
Cream, topical, as hydrochloride: 13.9% (30 g)
Injection, solution, as hydrochloride: 200 mg/mL (100 mL) [orphan drug status]

♦ **Eflornithine Hydrochloride** *see* Eflornithine *on page 573*
♦ **Eformoterol and Budesonide** *see* Budesonide and Formoterol *on page 247*

- **Efudex®** see Fluorouracil on page 725
- **E-Gems®** [OTC] see Vitamin E on page 1794
- **E-Gems Elite®** [OTC] see Vitamin E on page 1794
- **E-Gems Plus®** [OTC] see Vitamin E on page 1794
- **EHDP** see Etidronate Disodium on page 665
- **Elaprase™** see Idursulfase on page 879
- **Elavil** see Amitriptyline on page 101
- **Eldepryl®** see Selegiline on page 1552
- **Eldopaque®** [OTC] see Hydroquinone on page 859
- **Eldopaque®** (Can) see Hydroquinone on page 859
- **Eldopaque Forte®** see Hydroquinone on page 859
- **Eldoquin®** [OTC] see Hydroquinone on page 859
- **Eldoquin®** (Can) see Hydroquinone on page 859
- **Eldoquin Forte®** see Hydroquinone on page 859
- **Electrolyte Lavage Solution** see Polyethylene Glycol-Electrolyte Solution on page 1387
- **Elestat™** see Epinastine on page 589
- **Elestrin™** see Estradiol on page 620

Eletriptan (el e TRIP tan)

U.S. Brand Names Relpax®
Canadian Brand Names Relpax®
Index Terms Eletriptan Hydrobromide
Pharmacologic Category Antimigraine Agent; Serotonin 5-HT$_{1B, 1D}$ Receptor Agonist
Additional Appendix Information
Antimigraine Drugs: 5-HT$_1$ Receptor Agonists on page 1871
Use Acute treatment of migraine, with or without aura
Pregnancy Risk Factor C
Pregnancy Implications There are no adequate and well-controlled studies in pregnant women; use during pregnancy only if the potential benefit to the mother outweighs the possible risk to the fetus. Teratogenic effects were observed in animal studies.
Lactation Enters breast milk/use caution
Contraindications Hypersensitivity to eletriptan or any component of the formulation; ischemic heart disease or signs or symptoms of ischemic heart disease (including Prinzmetal's angina, angina pectoris, MI, silent myocardial ischemia); cerebrovascular syndromes (including strokes, transient ischemic attacks); peripheral vascular syndromes (including ischemic bowel disease); uncontrolled hypertension; use within 24 hours of ergotamine derivatives; use within 24 hours of another 5-HT$_1$ agonist; use within 72 hours of potent CYP3A4 inhibitors; management of hemiplegic or basilar migraine; prophylactic treatment of migraine; severe hepatic impairment
Warnings/Precautions Eletriptan is indicated only in patients ≥18 years of age with a clear diagnosis of migraine headache. If a patient does not respond to the first dose, the diagnosis of migraine should be reconsidered. Do not give to patients with risk factors for CAD until a cardiovascular evaluation has been performed; if evaluation is satisfactory, the healthcare provider should administer the first dose and cardiovascular status should be periodically evaluated. Cardiac events (coronary artery vasospasm, transient ischemia, MI, ventricular tachycardia/fibrillation, cardiac arrest, and death), cerebral/subarachnoid hemorrhage, stroke, peripheral vascular ischemia, and colonic ischemia have been reported with 5-HT$_1$ agonist administration. Significant elevation in blood pressure, including hypertensive crisis, has also been reported on rare occasions in patients with and without a history of hypertension. Use with caution with mild to moderate hepatic impairment. Symptoms of agitation, confusion, hallucinations, hyperreflexia, myoclonus, shivering, and tachycardia (serotonin syndrome) may occur with concomitant proserotonergic drugs (ie, SSRIs/SNRIs or triptans) or agents which reduce eletriptan's metabolism. Concurrent use of serotonin precursors (eg, tryptophan) is not recommended. Safety and efficacy in pediatric patients have not been established.
Adverse Reactions
1% to 10%:
Cardiovascular: Chest pain/tightness (1% to 4%; placebo 1%), palpitation
Central nervous system: Dizziness (3% to 7%; placebo 3%), somnolence (3% to 7%; placebo 4%), headache (3% to 4%; placebo 3%), chills, pain, vertigo
Gastrointestinal: Nausea (4% to 8%; placebo 5%), xerostomia (2% to 4%, placebo 2%), dysphagia (1% to 2%), abdominal pain/discomfort (1% to 2%; placebo 1%), dyspepsia (1% to 2%; placebo 1%)
Neuromuscular & skeletal: Weakness (4% to 10%), paresthesia (3% to 4%), back pain, hypertonia, hypoesthesia
Respiratory: Pharyngitis
Miscellaneous: Diaphoresis
<1% (Limited to important or life-threatening): Agitation, allergic reaction, angina, arrhythmia, ataxia, confusion, constipation, CPK increased, depersonalization, depression, diarrhea, dreams (abnormal), dyspnea, edema, emotional lability, esophagitis, euphoria, hyperesthesia, hyperkinesia, hypertension, impotence, incoordination, insomnia, lacrimation disorder, liver function tests abnormal, myalgia, myasthenia, nervousness, peripheral vascular disorder, photophobia, polyuria, pruritus, rash, salivation increased, shock, speech disorder, stupor, tachycardia, taste perversion, thrombophlebitis, tinnitus, tongue edema, tremor, urinary frequency, vasospasm, vision abnormal
Overdosage/Toxicology Hypertension or more serious cardiovascular symptoms may occur. Clinical and electrocardiographic monitoring needed for at least 20 hours even if patient is asymptomatic. Treatment is symptom-directed and supportive.
(Continued)

Eletriptan *(Continued)*

Drug Interactions

Cytochrome P450 Effect: Substrate of CYP3A4 (major)

Increased Effect/Toxicity: CYP3A4 inhibitors increase serum concentration and half-life of eletriptan; do not use eletriptan within 72 hours of potent CYP3A4 inhibitors (eg, azole antifungals, clarithromycin, diclofenac, doxycycline, erythromycin, imatinib, isoniazid, nefazodone, nicardipine, propofol, protease inhibitors, quinidine, telithromycin, verapamil). Ergot-containing drugs prolong vasospastic reactions; do not use within 24 hours of eletriptan. SSRIs/SNRIs or other serotonin agonists may increase symptoms of hyper-reflexia, weakness, and incoordination.

Ethanol/Nutrition/Herb Interactions Food: High-fat meal increases bioavailability.

Stability Store at 25°C (77°F); excursions permitted to 15°C to 30°C (59°F to 86°F).

Mechanism of Action Selective agonist for serotonin (5-HT$_{1B}$, 5-HT$_{1D}$, 5-HT$_{1F}$ receptors) in cranial arteries; causes vasoconstriction and reduce sterile inflammation associated with antidromic neuronal transmission correlating with relief of migraine

Pharmacodynamics/Kinetics

Absorption: Well absorbed

Distribution: V$_d$: 138 L

Protein binding: ~85%

Metabolism: Hepatic via CYP3A4; forms one metabolite (active)

Bioavailability: ~50%, increased with high-fat meal

Half-life elimination: 4 hours (Elderly: 4.4-5.7 hours); Metabolite: ~13 hours

Time to peak, plasma: 1.5-2 hours

Dosage Oral: Adults: Acute migraine: 20-40 mg; if the headache improves but returns, dose may be repeated after 2 hours have elapsed since first dose; maximum 80 mg/day.

Note: If the first dose is ineffective, diagnosis needs to be re-evaluated. Safety of treating >3 headaches/month has not been established.

Dosage adjustment in renal impairment: No dosing adjustment needed; monitor for increased blood pressure

Dosage adjustment in hepatic impairment:
Mild to moderate impairment: No adjustment necessary
Severe impairment: Use is contraindicated

Dosage Forms Tablet, as hydrobromide: 20 mg, 40 mg [as base]

♦ **Eletriptan Hydrobromide** *see* Eletriptan *on page 575*
♦ **Elidel®** *see* Pimecrolimus *on page 1369*
♦ **Eligard®** *see* Leuprolide *on page 991*
♦ **Elimite®** *see* Permethrin *on page 1348*
♦ **Elipten** *see* Aminoglutethimide *on page 95*
♦ **Elitek™** *see* Rasburicase *on page 1490*
♦ **Elixophyllin®** *see* Theophylline Salts *on page 1664*
♦ **Elixophyllin-GG®** *see* Theophylline and Guaifenesin *on page 1663*
♦ **ElixSure™ IB [OTC]** *see* Ibuprofen *on page 873*
♦ **Ellence®** *see* Epirubicin *on page 592*
♦ **Elmiron®** *see* Pentosan Polysulfate Sodium *on page 1342*
♦ **Elocom® (Can)** *see* Mometasone Furoate *on page 1165*
♦ **Elocon®** *see* Mometasone Furoate *on page 1165*
♦ **Eloxatin®** *see* Oxaliplatin *on page 1277*
♦ **Elspar®** *see* Asparaginase *on page 157*
♦ **Eltor® (Can)** *see* Pseudoephedrine *on page 1454*
♦ **Eltroxin® (Can)** *see* Levothyroxine *on page 1007*
♦ **Embeline™ [DSC]** *see* Clobetasol *on page 391*
♦ **Embeline™ E [DSC]** *see* Clobetasol *on page 391*
♦ **Emcyt®** *see* Estramustine *on page 626*
♦ **Emend®** *see* Aprepitant *on page 144*
♦ **Emko® [OTC] [DSC]** *see* Nonoxynol 9 *on page 1239*
♦ **EMLA®** *see* Lidocaine and Prilocaine *on page 1015*
♦ **Emo-Cort® (Can)** *see* Hydrocortisone *on page 852*
♦ **Emsam®** *see* Selegiline *on page 1552*

Emtricitabine *(em trye SYE ta been)*

U.S. Brand Names Emtriva®

Canadian Brand Names Emtriva®

Index Terms BW524W91; Coviracil; FTC

Pharmacologic Category Antiretroviral Agent, Reverse Transcriptase Inhibitor (Nucleoside)

Additional Appendix Information
Antiretroviral Therapy for HIV Infection: Adults and Adolescents *on page 1988*
Management of Healthcare Worker Exposures to HBV, HCV, and HIV *on page 1941*

Use Treatment of HIV infection in combination with at least two other antiretroviral agents

Unlabeled/Investigational Use Hepatitis B (with HIV coinfection)

Pregnancy Risk Factor B

Pregnancy Implications Cases of fatal and nonfatal lactic acidosis, with or without pancreatitis, have been reported in pregnant women receiving reverse transcriptase inhibitors. It is not known if pregnancy itself potentiates this known side effect; however, pregnant women may be at increased risk of lactic acidosis and liver damage. Hepatic enzymes and electrolytes should be monitored frequently during the 3rd trimester of pregnancy. There are no studies of emtricitabine during pregnancy. The Perinatal HIV Guidelines Working Group considers emtricitabine to be an alternative NRTI in dual nucleoside combination regimens.

Health professionals are encouraged to contact the antiretroviral pregnancy registry to monitor outcomes of pregnant women exposed to antiretroviral medications (1-800-258-4263 or www.APRegistry.com).

Lactation Excretion in breast milk unknown/not recommended

Contraindications Hypersensitivity to emtricitabine or any component of the formulation

Warnings/Precautions [U.S. Boxed Warning]: Lactic acidosis, severe hepatomegaly, and hepatic failure have occurred rarely with emtricitabine (similar to other nucleoside analogues). Some cases have been fatal; stop treatment if lactic acidosis or hepatotoxicity occur. Prior liver disease, obesity, extended duration of therapy, and female gender may represent risk factors for severe hepatic reactions. Testing for hepatitis B is recommended prior to the initiation of therapy; **[U.S. Boxed Warnings]: Hepatitis B may be exacerbated following discontinuation of emtricitabine; not indicated for treatment of chronic hepatitis B; safety and efficacy in HIV/HBV coinfected patients not established.** Immune reconstitution syndrome may develop resulting in the occurrence of an inflammatory response to an indolent or residual opportunistic infection; further evaluation and treatment may be required. Use caution in patients with renal impairment (dosage adjustment required). Safety and efficacy in children ≤3 years of age have not been established.

Adverse Reactions Clinical trials were conducted in patients receiving other antiretroviral agents, and it is not possible to correlate frequency of adverse events with emtricitabine alone. The range of frequencies of adverse events is generally comparable to comparator groups, with the exception of hyperpigmentation, which occurred more frequently in patients receiving emtricitabine. Unless otherwise noted, percentages are as reported in adults.

>10%:
Central nervous system: Dizziness (4% to 25%), headache (13% to 22%), fever (children 18%), insomnia (7% to 16%), abnormal dreams (2% to 11%)
Dermatologic: Hyperpigmentation (adults 2% to 4%; children 32%; primarily of palms and/or soles but may include tongue, arms, lip and nails; generally mild and nonprogressive without associated local reactions such as pruritus or rash); rash (17% to 30%; includes pruritus, maculopapular rash, vesiculobullous rash, pustular rash, and allergic reaction)
Gastrointestinal: Diarrhea (adults 23%; children 20%), vomiting (adults 9%; children 23%), nausea (13% to 18%), abdominal pain (8% to 14%), gastroenteritis (children 11%)
Neuromuscular & skeletal: Weakness (12% to 16%), CPK increased (11% to 12%)
Otic: Otitis media (children 23%)
Respiratory: Cough (adults 14%; children 28%), rhinitis (adults 12% to 18%; children 20%), pneumonia (children 15%)
Miscellaneous: Infection (children 44%)

1% to 10%:
Central nervous system: Depression (6% to 9%), neuropathy/neuritis (4%)
Endocrine & metabolic: Serum triglycerides increased (9% to 10%), disordered glucose homeostasis (2% to 3%), serum amylase increased (adults 2% to 5%; children 9%), serum lipase increased (≤1%)
Gastrointestinal: Dyspepsia (4% to 8%)
Hematologic: Anemia (children: 7%)
Hepatic: Transaminases increased (2% to 6%), bilirubin increased (1%)
Neuromuscular & skeletal: Myalgia (4% to 6%), paresthesia (5% to 6%), arthralgia (3% to 5%)

Overdosage/Toxicology Treatment is supportive and symptom-directed. Approximately 30% of a dose is removed by hemodialysis.

Drug Interactions
Increased Effect/Toxicity: Concomitant use of ribavirin with or without interferon alfa and nucleoside analogues may increase the risk of developing hepatic decompensation or other signs of mitochondrial toxicity, including pancreatitis or lactic acidosis. .

Ethanol/Nutrition/Herb Interactions Food: Food decreases peak plasma concentrations, but does not alter the extent of absorption or overall systemic exposure.

Stability Store capsules at 15°C to 30°C (59°F to 86°F). Solution should be stored under refrigeration at 2°C to 8°C (36°F to 46°F). Once dispensed, may be stored at 15°C to 30°C (59°F to 86°F) if used within 3 months.

Mechanism of Action Nucleoside reverse transcriptase inhibitor; emtricitabine is a cytosine analogue which is phosphorylated intracellularly to emtricitabine 5'-triphosphate which interferes with HIV viral RNA dependent DNA polymerase resulting in inhibition of viral replication.

Pharmacodynamics/Kinetics
Absorption: Rapid, extensive
Protein binding: <4%
Metabolism: Limited, via oxidation and conjugation (not via CYP isoenzymes)
Bioavailability: Capsule: 93%; solution: 75%
Half-life elimination: Normal renal function: Adults: 10 hours; children: 5-18 hours
Time to peak, plasma: 1-2 hours
Excretion: Urine (86% primarily as unchanged drug, 13% as metabolites); feces (14%)

Dosage Oral:
Children: 3 months to 17 years:
Capsule: Children >33 kg: 200 mg once daily
Solution: 6 mg/kg once daily; maximum: 240 mg/day
Adults:
Capsule: 200 mg once daily
Solution: 240 mg once daily
Dosage adjustment in renal impairment: Adults (consider similar adjustments in children):
Cl_{cr} 30-49 mL/minute: Capsule: 200 mg every 48 hours; solution: 120 mg every 24 hours
Cl_{cr} 15-29 mL/minute: Capsule: 200 mg every 72 hours; solution: 80 mg every 24 hours
Cl_{cr} <15 mL/minute (including hemodialysis patients): Capsule: 200 mg every 96 hours; solution: 60 mg every 24 hours; administer after dialysis on dialysis days
Dosage adjustment in hepatic impairment: No adjustment required.

Dietary Considerations May be taken with or without food.

Administration May be administered with or without food.

(Continued)

Emtricitabine *(Continued)*

Monitoring Parameters Viral load, CD4, liver function tests; hepatitis B testing is recommended prior to initiation of therapy

Dosage Forms
    Capsule: 200 mg
    Solution: 10 mg/mL (170 mL) [cotton candy flavor]

Emtricitabine and Tenofovir *(em trye SYE ta been & te NOE fo veer)*

U.S. Brand Names Truvada®
Canadian Brand Names Truvada®
Index Terms Tenofovir and Emtricitabine
Pharmacologic Category Antiretroviral Agent, Reverse Transcriptase Inhibitor (Nucleoside); Antiretroviral Agent, Reverse Transcriptase Inhibitor (Nucleotide)
Additional Appendix Information
    Antiretroviral Therapy for HIV Infection: Adults and Adolescents *on page 1988*
    Management of Healthcare Worker Exposures to HBV, HCV, and HIV *on page 1941*
Use Treatment of HIV infection in combination with other antiretroviral agents
Pregnancy Risk Factor B
Dosage Adults: Oral: One tablet (emtricitabine 200 mg and tenofovir 300 mg) once daily
    Dosage adjustment in renal impairment:
        Cl$_{cr}$ 30-49 mL/minute: Increase interval to every 48 hours.
        Cl$_{cr}$ <30 mL/minute or hemodialysis: Not recommended.
Additional Information Complete prescribing information for this medication should be consulted for additional detail.
Dosage Forms Tablet: Emtricitabine 200 mg and tenofovir disoproxil fumarate 300 mg

- ◆ **Emtricitabine, Efavirenz, and Tenofovir** *see* Efavirenz, Emtricitabine, and Tenofovir *on page 573*
- ◆ **Emtriva®** *see* Emtricitabine *on page 576*
- ◆ **ENA 713** *see* Rivastigmine *on page 1526*
- ◆ **Enablex®** *see* Darifenacin *on page 455*

Enalapril *(e NAL a pril)*

U.S. Brand Names Vasotec®
Canadian Brand Names Vasotec®
Index Terms Enalaprilat; Enalapril Maleate
Pharmacologic Category Angiotensin-Converting Enzyme (ACE) Inhibitor
Additional Appendix Information
    Angiotensin Agents *on page 1860*
    Heart Failure (Systolic) *on page 2051*
Use Management of mild to severe hypertension; treatment of congestive heart failure, left ventricular dysfunction after myocardial infarction
Unlabeled/Investigational Use
    Unlabeled: Hypertensive crisis, diabetic nephropathy, rheumatoid arthritis, diagnosis of anatomic renal artery stenosis, hypertension secondary to scleroderma renal crisis, diagnosis of aldosteronism, idiopathic edema, Bartter's syndrome, postmyocardial infarction for prevention of ventricular failure
    Investigational: Severe congestive heart failure in infants, neonatal hypertension, acute pulmonary edema
Pregnancy Risk Factor C (1st trimester)/D (2nd and 3rd trimesters)
Pregnancy Implications Decreased placental blood flow, low birth weight, fetal hypotension, preterm delivery, and fetal death have been noted with the use of some ACE inhibitors (ACEIs) in animal studies. Neonatal hypotension, skull hypoplasia, anuria, renal failure, oligohydramnios (associated with fetal limb contractures, craniofacial deformities, hypoplastic lung development), prematurity, intrauterine growth retardation, and patent ductus arteriosus have been reported with the use of ACEIs, primarily in the 2nd and 3rd trimesters. The risk of neonatal toxicity has been considered less when ACEIs have been used in the 1st trimester; however, major congenital malformations have been reported. The cardiovascular and/or central nervous systems are most commonly affected. Unless alternative agents are not appropriate, ACEIs should be discontinued as soon as possible once pregnancy is detected.
Lactation Enters breast milk/not recommended (AAP rates "compatible")
Medication Safety Issues
    Sound-alike/look-alike issues:
        Enalapril may be confused with Anafranil®, Elavil®, Eldepryl®, nafarelin, ramipril

    Significant differences exist between oral and I.V. dosing. Use caution when converting from one route of administration to another.

    International issues:
        Acepril® [Hungary, Switzerland] may be confused with Accupril® which is a brand name for quinapril in the U.S.
        Acepril®: Brand name for lisinopril in Denmark; brand name for captopril in Great Britain
        Nacor® [Spain] may be confused with Niacor® which is a brand name for niacin in the U.S.
Contraindications Hypersensitivity to enalapril or enalaprilat; angioedema related to previous treatment with an ACE inhibitor; patients with idiopathic or hereditary angioedema; bilateral renal artery stenosis; pregnancy (2nd and 3rd trimesters)
Warnings/Precautions Anaphylactic reactions can occur. Angioedema can occur at any time during treatment (especially following first dose). It may involve head and neck (potentially affecting the airway) or the intestine (presenting with abdominal pain). Prolonged monitoring may be required especially if tongue, glottis, or larynx are involved as they are associated with airway obstruction. Those with a history of airway surgery in this situation have a higher

risk. Careful blood pressure monitoring with first dose (hypotension can occur especially in volume-depleted patients). **[U.S. Boxed Warning]: Based on human data, ACEIs can cause injury and death to the developing fetus when used in the second and third trimesters. ACEIs should be discontinued as soon as possible once pregnancy is detected.** Dosage adjustment needed in renal impairment. Use with caution in hypovolemia; collagen vascular diseases; valvular stenosis (particularly aortic stenosis); hyperkalemia; or before, during, or immediately after anesthesia. Avoid rapid dosage escalation which may lead to renal insufficiency.

Rare toxicities associated with ACE inhibitors include cholestatic jaundice (which may progress to hepatic necrosis) and neutropenia/agranulocytosis with myeloid hyperplasia. Hyperkalemia may rarely occur. May be associated with deterioration of renal function and/or increases in serum creatinine, particularly in patients dependent on renin-angiotensin-aldosterone system. Use with caution in unilateral renal artery stenosis and pre-existing renal insufficiency; if patient has renal impairment then a baseline WBC with differential and serum creatinine should be evaluated and monitored closely during the first 3 months of therapy. Hypersensitivity reactions may be seen during hemodialysis with high-flux dialysis membranes (eg, AN69).

Adverse Reactions Note: Frequency ranges include data from hypertension and heart failure trials. Higher rates of adverse reactions have generally been noted in patients with CHF. However, the frequency of adverse effects associated with placebo is also increased in this population.

1% to 10%:
Cardiovascular: Hypotension (0.9% to 6.7%), chest pain (2%), syncope (0.5% to 2%), orthostasis (2%), orthostatic hypotension (2%)
Central nervous system: Headache (2% to 5%), dizziness (4% to 8%), fatigue (2% to 3%)
Dermatologic: Rash (1.5%)
Gastrointestinal: Abnormal taste, abdominal pain, vomiting, nausea, diarrhea, anorexia, constipation
Neuromuscular & skeletal: Weakness
Renal: Serum creatinine increased (0.2% to 20%), worsening of renal function (in patients with bilateral renal artery stenosis or hypovolemia)
Respiratory: Bronchitis, cough, dyspnea

<1% (Limited to important or life-threatening): Agranulocytosis, alopecia, angina pectoris, angioedema, ataxia, bronchospasm, cardiac arrest, cerebral vascular accident, depression, erythema multiforme, exfoliative dermatitis, giant cell arteritis, gynecomastia, hallucinations, hemolysis with G6PD, Henoch-Schönlein purpura, hepatitis, ileus, impotence, jaundice, lichen-form reaction, MI, neutropenia, ototoxicity, pancreatitis, paresthesia, pemphigus, pemphigus foliaceus, photosensitivity, psychosis, pulmonary edema, sicca syndrome, Stevens-Johnson syndrome, systemic lupus erythematosus, toxic epidermal necrolysis, toxic pustuloderma, vertigo. Worsening of renal function may occur in patients with bilateral renal artery stenosis or in hypovolemic patients. A syndrome which may include fever, myalgia, arthralgia, interstitial nephritis, vasculitis, rash, eosinophilia and positive ANA, and elevated ESR has been reported for enalapril and other ACE inhibitors.

Overdosage/Toxicology Mild hypotension has been the only toxic effect seen with acute overdose. Bradycardia may also occur. Hyperkalemia occurs even with therapeutic doses, especially in patients with renal insufficiency, and those taking NSAIDs. Following initiation of essential overdose management, toxic symptom and supportive treatment should be initiated. Hypotension usually responds to I.V. fluids or Trendelenburg positioning.

Drug Interactions
Cytochrome P450 Effect: Substrate of CYP3A4 (major)
Increased Effect/Toxicity: Potassium supplements, co-trimoxazole (high dose), angiotensin II receptor antagonists (eg, candesartan, losartan, irbesartan), or potassium-sparing diuretics (amiloride, spironolactone, triamterene) may result in elevated serum potassium levels when combined with enalapril. ACE inhibitor effects may be increased by phenothiazines or probenecid (increases levels of captopril). ACE inhibitors may increase serum concentrations/effects of lithium.

Diuretics have additive hypotensive effects with ACE inhibitors, and hypovolemia increases the potential for adverse renal effects of ACE inhibitors. In patients with compromised renal function, coadministration with NSAIDs may result in further deterioration of renal function. Allopurinol and ACE inhibitors may cause a higher risk of hypersensitivity reaction when taken concurrently.

Decreased Effect: Aspirin (high dose) may reduce the therapeutic effects of ACE inhibitors; at low dosages this does not appear to be significant. Antacids may decrease the bioavailability of ACE inhibitors (may be more likely to occur with captopril); separate administration times by 1-2 hours. NSAIDs may reduce the hypotense effects of ACE inhibitors. More likely to occur in low renin or volume-dependent hypertensive patients. CYP3A4 inducers may decrease the levels/effects of enalapril; example inducers include aminoglutethimide, carbamazepine, nafcillin, nevirapine, phenobarbital, phenytoin, and rifamycins.

Ethanol/Nutrition/Herb Interactions Herb/Nutraceutical: St John's wort may decrease enalapril levels. Avoid dong quai if using for hypertension (has estrogenic activity). Avoid ephedra, yohimbe, ginseng (may worsen hypertension). Avoid natural licorice (causes sodium and water retention and increases potassium loss). Avoid garlic (may have increased antihypertensive effect).

Stability Enalaprilat: Clear, colorless solution which should be stored at <30°C. I.V. is 24 hours at room temperature in D_5W or NS.

Mechanism of Action Competitive inhibitor of angiotensin-converting enzyme (ACE); prevents conversion of angiotensin I to angiotensin II, a potent vasoconstrictor; results in lower levels of angiotensin II which causes an increase in plasma renin activity and a reduction in aldosterone secretion

Pharmacodynamics/Kinetics
Onset of action: Oral: ~1 hour
Duration: Oral: 12-24 hours
Absorption: Oral: 55% to 75%
(Continued)

Enalapril *(Continued)*

Protein binding: 50% to 60%

Metabolism: Prodrug, undergoes hepatic biotransformation to enalaprilat

Half-life elimination:
Enalapril: Adults: Healthy: 2 hours; Congestive heart failure: 3.4-5.8 hours
Enalaprilat: Infants 6 weeks to 8 months old: 6-10 hours; Adults: 35-38 hours

Time to peak, serum: Oral: Enalapril: 0.5-1.5 hours; Enalaprilat (active): 3-4.5 hours

Excretion: Urine (60% to 80%); some feces

Dosage Use lower listed initial dose in patients with hyponatremia, hypovolemia, severe congestive heart failure, decreased renal function, or in those receiving diuretics.

Oral: **Enalapril:** Children 1 month to 16 years: Hypertension: Initial: 0.08 mg/kg (up to 5 mg) once daily; adjust dosage based on patient response; doses >0.58 mg/kg (40 mg) have not been evaluated in pediatric patients

Investigational: Congestive heart failure: Initial oral doses of **enalapril:** 0.1 mg/kg/day increasing as needed over 2 weeks to 0.5 mg/kg/day have been used in infants

Investigational: Neonatal hypertension: I.V. doses of **enalaprilat:** 5-10 mcg/kg/dose administered every 8-24 hours have been used; monitor patients carefully; select patients may require higher doses

Adults:
Oral: **Enalapril:**
Hypertension: 2.5-5 mg/day then increase as required, usually at 1- to 2-week intervals; usual dose range (JNC 7): 2.5-40 mg/day in 1-2 divided doses. **Note:** Initiate with 2.5 mg if patient is taking a diuretic which cannot be discontinued. May add a diuretic if blood pressure cannot be controlled with enalapril alone.

Heart failure: Initial: 2.5 mg once or twice daily (usual range: 5-40 mg/day in 2 divided doses). Titrate slowly at 1- to 2-week intervals. Target dose: 10-20 mg twice daily (ACC/AHA 2005 Heart Failure Guidelines)

Asymptomatic left ventricular dysfunction: 2.5 mg twice daily, titrated as tolerated to 20 mg/day

I.V.: **Enalaprilat:**
Hypertension: 1.25 mg/dose, given over 5 minutes every 6 hours; doses as high as 5 mg/dose every 6 hours have been tolerated for up to 36 hours. **Note:** If patients are concomitantly receiving diuretic therapy, begin with 0.625 mg I.V. over 5 minutes; if the effect is not adequate after 1 hour, repeat the dose and administer 1.25 mg at 6-hour intervals thereafter; if adequate, administer 0.625 mg I.V. every 6 hours.

Heart failure: Avoid I.V. administration in patients with unstable heart failure or those suffering acute myocardial infarction.

Conversion from I.V. to oral therapy if not concurrently on diuretics: 5 mg once daily; subsequent titration as needed; if concurrently receiving diuretics and responding to 0.625 mg I.V. every 6 hours, initiate with 2.5 mg/day.

Dosing adjustment in renal impairment:
Oral: Enalapril:
Cl$_{cr}$ 30-80 mL/minute: Administer 5 mg/day titrated upwards to maximum of 40 mg.
Cl$_{cr}$ <30 mL/minute: Administer 2.5 mg day; titrated upward until blood pressure is controlled.
For heart failure patients with sodium <130 mEq/L or serum creatinine >1.6 mg/dL, initiate dosage with 2.5 mg/day, increasing to twice daily as needed. Increase further in increments of 2.5 mg/dose at >4-day intervals to a maximum daily dose of 40 mg.

I.V.: Enalaprilat:
Cl$_{cr}$ >30 mL/minute: Initiate with 1.25 mg every 6 hours and increase dose based on response.
Cl$_{cr}$ <30 mL/minute: Initiate with 0.625 mg every 6 hours and increase dose based on response.

Hemodialysis: Moderately dialyzable (20% to 50%); administer dose postdialysis (eg, 0.625 mg I.V. every 6 hours) or administer 20% to 25% supplemental dose following dialysis; Clearance: 62 mL/minute.

Peritoneal dialysis: Supplemental dose is not necessary, although some removal of drug occurs.

Dosing adjustment in hepatic impairment: Hydrolysis of enalapril to enalaprilat may be delayed and/or impaired in patients with severe hepatic impairment, but the pharmacodynamic effects of the drug do not appear to be significantly altered; no dosage adjustment.

Dietary Considerations Limit salt substitutes or potassium-rich diet.

Administration Administer direct IVP over at least 5 minutes or dilute up to 50 mL and infuse; discontinue diuretic, if possible, for 2-3 days before beginning enalapril therapy

Monitoring Parameters Blood pressure, renal function, WBC, serum potassium; blood pressure monitor required during intravenous administration

Test Interactions Positive Coombs' [direct]; may cause false-positive results in urine acetone determinations using sodium nitroprusside reagent

Dosage Forms
Injection, solution, as enalaprilat: 1.25 mg/mL (1 mL, 2 mL) [contains benzyl alcohol]
Tablet, as maleate (Vasotec®): 2.5 mg, 5 mg, 10 mg, 20 mg

Extemporaneous Preparations
An enalapril oral suspension (0.2 mg/mL) has been made using one 2.5 mg tablet and 12.5 mL sterile water; stability unknown; suspension should be used immediately and the remaining amount discarded

Young TE and Mangum OB, "Neofax®, '95: A Manual of Drugs Used in Neonatal Care," 8th ed, Columbus, OH: Ross Products Division, Abbott Laboratories, 1995, 85.

An enalapril oral suspension (1 mg/mL) has been made using 20 mg tablets and mL Bicitra®. Add 50 mL Bicitra® to a polyethylene terephthalate (PET) bottle containing ten 20 mg tablets and shake for at least 2 minutes. Let concentrate stand for 60 minutes. Following the 60-minute hold time, shake the concentration for an additional minute. Add 150 mL Bicitra® to the concentrate and shake the suspension to disperse the ingredients. The

suspension should refrigerated at 2°C to 8°C (36°F to 46°F); it can be stored for up to 30 days. Shake suspension well before use.
Package labeling, Merck & Co, Inc, issued October 2000.

Enalapril and Felodipine (e NAL a pril & fe LOE di peen)

U.S. Brand Names Lexxel®
Canadian Brand Names Lexxel®
Index Terms Felodipine and Enalapril
Pharmacologic Category Antihypertensive Agent, Combination
Use Treatment of hypertension, however, not indicated for initial treatment of hypertension; replacement therapy in patients receiving separate dosage forms (for patient convenience); when monotherapy with one component fails to achieve desired antihypertensive effect, or when dose-limiting adverse effects limit upward titration of monotherapy
Pregnancy Risk Factor C/D (2nd and 3rd trimesters)
Dosage Oral:
 Adults: Enalapril 5-20 mg and felodipine 2.5-10 mg once daily
 Elderly: Initial dose of felodipine is 2.5 mg daily
Additional Information Complete prescribing information for this medication should be consulted for additional detail.
Dosage Forms Tablet, extended release:
 Enalapril maleate 5 mg and felodipine 2.5 mg
 Enalapril maleate 5 mg and felodipine 5 mg

Enalapril and Hydrochlorothiazide
(e NAL a pril & hye droe klor oh THYE a zide)

U.S. Brand Names Vaseretic®
Canadian Brand Names Vaseretic®
Index Terms Hydrochlorothiazide and Enalapril
Pharmacologic Category Antihypertensive Agent, Combination
Use Treatment of hypertension
Pregnancy Risk Factor C/D (2nd and 3rd trimesters)
Dosage Oral: Adults: Enalapril 5-10 mg and hydrochlorothiazide 12.5-25 mg once daily (maximum: 20 mg/day [enalapril]; 50 mg/day [hydrochlorothiazide])
Additional Information Complete prescribing information for this medication should be consulted for additional detail.
Dosage Forms Tablet:
 5-12.5: Enalapril maleate 5 mg and hydrochlorothiazide 12.5 mg
 10-25: Enalapril maleate 10 mg and hydrochlorothiazide 25 mg

♦ **Enalaprilat** see Enalapril on page 578
♦ **Enalapril Maleate** see Enalapril on page 578
♦ **Enbrel®** see Etanercept on page 641
♦ **Encare®** [OTC] see Nonoxynol 9 on page 1239
♦ **Encort™** see Hydrocortisone on page 852
♦ **EndaCof** see Hydrocodone and Guaifenesin on page 849
♦ **EndaCof-XP** see Hydrocodone and Guaifenesin on page 849
♦ **Endantadine® (Can)** see Amantadine on page 86
♦ **EndoAvitene®** see Collagen Hemostat on page 416
♦ **Endocet®** see Oxycodone and Acetaminophen on page 1289
♦ **Endodan®** see Oxycodone and Aspirin on page 1289
♦ **Endo®-Levodopa/Carbidopa (Can)** see Levodopa and Carbidopa on page 999
♦ **Endrate®** see Edetate Disodium on page 568
♦ **Enduron® [DSC]** see Methyclothiazide on page 1116
♦ **Enduron® (Can)** see Methyclothiazide on page 1116
♦ **Enemeez®** [OTC] see Docusate on page 533

Enfuvirtide (en FYOO vir tide)

U.S. Brand Names Fuzeon®
Canadian Brand Names Fuzeon®
Index Terms T-20
Pharmacologic Category Antiretroviral Agent, Fusion Protein Inhibitor
Additional Appendix Information
 Antiretroviral Therapy for HIV Infection: Adults and Adolescents on page 1988
 Management of Healthcare Worker Exposures to HBV, HCV, and HIV on page 1941
Use Treatment of HIV-1 infection in combination with other antiretroviral agents in treatment-experienced patients with evidence of HIV-1 replication despite ongoing antiretroviral therapy
Pregnancy Risk Factor B
Pregnancy Implications Teratogenic effects were not observed in animal studies, however, there are no adequate and well-controlled studies in pregnant women. An antiretroviral registry has been established to monitor maternal and fetal outcomes in women receiving antiretroviral drugs. Physicians are encouraged to register patients at 1-800-258-4263 or www.APRegistry.com.
Lactation Excretion in breast milk unknown/contraindicated
Contraindications Hypersensitivity to enfuvirtide or any component of the formulation
Warnings/Precautions Monitor closely for signs/symptoms of pneumonia; associated with an increased incidence during clinical trials, particularly in patients with a low CD4 cell count,
(Continued)

Enfuvirtide *(Continued)*

high initial viral load, I.V. drug use, smoking, or a history of lung disease. May cause hypersensitivity reactions (symptoms may include rash, fever, nausea, vomiting, hypotension, and elevated transaminases). In addition, local injection site reactions are common. An inflammatory response to indolent or residual opportunistic infections (immune reconstitution syndrome) has occurred with antiretroviral therapy; further investigation is warranted. Safety and efficacy have not been established in children <6 years of age.

Adverse Reactions
>10%:
Central nervous system: Fatigue (20%), insomnia (11%)
Gastrointestinal: Diarrhea (32%), nausea (23%)
Local: Injection site reactions (98%; may include pain, erythema, induration, pruritus, ecchymosis, nodule or cyst formation)
1% to 10%:
Dermatologic: Folliculitis (2%)
Gastrointestinal: Triglycerides increased (9%), weight loss (7%), constipation (4%), abdominal pain (4%), appetite decreased (3%), pancreatitis (3%), anorexia (2%), xerostomia (2%)
Hematologic: Eosinophilia (2% to 8%)
Hepatic: Transaminases increased (4%, grade 4: 1%)
Local: Injection site infection (1%)
Neuromuscular & skeletal: CPK increased (3% to 7%), limb pain (3%), myalgia (3%)
Ocular: Conjunctivitis (2%)
Respiratory: Sinusitis (6%), cough (4%), pneumonia (3%)
Miscellaneous: Infections (4% to 6%), herpes simplex (4%), flu-like syndrome (2%), lymphadenopathy (2%)
<1% (Limited to important or life-threatening): Abacavir hypersensitivity worsening, amylase increased, angina, anxiety, depression, GGT increased, glomerulonephritis, Guillain-Barré syndrome, hepatic steatosis, hyperglycemia; hypersensitivity reactions (symptoms may include rash, fever, nausea, vomiting, hypotension, and transaminase increases); insomnia, lipase increased, lymphadenopathy, neutropenia, peripheral neuropathy, pneumonopathy, renal failure, renal insufficiency, respiratory distress, sepsis, sixth nerve palsy, suicide attempt, taste disturbances, thrombocytopenia, toxic hepatitis, tubular necrosis, weakness

Overdosage/Toxicology No clinical experience in overdosage. Treatment is symptom-directed and supportive.

Drug Interactions
Increased Effect/Toxicity: No significant interactions identified.
Decreased Effect: No significant interactions identified.

Stability Store powder at 15°C to 30°C (59°F to 86°F). Reconstitute with 1.1 mL SWFI. Tap vial for 10 seconds and roll gently to ensure contact with diluent. Allow to stand until solution is completed. May require up to 45 minutes to form solution. Reconstituted solutions should be refrigerated and must be used within 24 hours.

Mechanism of Action Binds to the first heptad-repeat (HR1) in the gp41 subunit of the viral envelope glycoprotein. Inhibits the fusion of HIV-1 virus with CD4 cells by blocking the conformational change in gp41 required for membrane fusion and entry into CD4 cells

Pharmacodynamics/Kinetics
Distribution: V_d: 5.5 L
Protein binding: 92%
Metabolism: Proteolytic hydrolysis (CYP isoenzymes do not appear to contribute to metabolism)
Clearance: Adults: 24.8 mL/hour/kg
Bioavailability: 84% ± 16%
Half-life elimination: 3.8 hours
Time to peak: 4-8 hours

Dosage SubQ:
Children 6-16 years: 2 mg/kg twice daily (maximum dose: 90 mg twice daily)
Adolescents ≥16 years and Adults: 90 mg twice daily
Dosage adjustment in renal impairment: No dosage adjustment required
Dosage adjustment in hepatic impairment: No dosage adjustment required

Administration Inject subcutaneously into upper arm, abdomen, or anterior thigh. Do not inject into moles, scar tissue, bruises, or the navel. Rotate injection site; give injections at a site different from the preceding injection site; do not inject into any site where an injection site reaction is evident.

Dosage Forms Injection, powder for reconstitution [preservative free]:
Fuzeon®: 108 mg [90 mg/mL following reconstitution; available in convenience kit of 60 vials, SWFI, syringes, alcohol wipes, patient instructions]

♦ **ENG** *see Etonogestrel on page 668*
♦ **Engerix-B®** *see Hepatitis B Vaccine on page 835*
♦ **Engerix-B® and Havrix®** *see Hepatitis A Inactivated and Hepatitis B (Recombinant) Vaccine on page 832*
♦ **Enhanced-potency Inactivated Poliovirus Vaccine** *see Poliovirus Vaccine (Inactivated) on page 1385*
♦ **Enjuvia™** *see Estrogens (Conjugated B/Synthetic) on page 629*
♦ **Enlon®** *see Edrophonium on page 569*
♦ **Enlon-Plus™** *see Edrophonium and Atropine on page 570*

Enoxaparin (ee noks a PA rin)

U.S. Brand Names Lovenox®
Canadian Brand Names Enoxaparin Injection; Lovenox®; Lovenox® HP
Index Terms Enoxaparin Sodium
Pharmacologic Category Low Molecular Weight Heparin
Additional Appendix Information
Anticoagulants, Injectable *on page 1864*
Use
DVT treatment (acute): Inpatient treatment (patients with and without pulmonary embolism) and outpatient treatment (patients without pulmonary embolism)

DVT prophylaxis: Following hip or knee replacement surgery, abdominal surgery, or in medical patients with severely-restricted mobility during acute illness in patients at risk of thromboembolic complications

Note: High-risk patients include those with one or more of the following risk factors: >40 years of age, obesity, general anesthesia lasting >30 minutes, malignancy, history of deep vein thrombosis or pulmonary embolism

Unstable angina and non-Q-wave myocardial infarction (to prevent ischemic complications)

Unlabeled/Investigational Use Prophylaxis and treatment of thromboembolism in children
Pregnancy Risk Factor B
Pregnancy Implications There are no adequate and well-controlled studies using enoxaparin in pregnant women. Animal studies have not shown teratogenic or fetotoxic effects. Postmarketing reports include congenital abnormalities (cause and effect not established) and also fetal death when used in pregnant women. In addition, prosthetic valve thrombosis, including fatal cases, has been reported in pregnant women receiving enoxaparin as thromboprophylaxis. Multiple dose vials contain benzyl alcohol; use caution in pregnant women.
Lactation Excretion in breast milk unknown/use caution
Medication Safety Issues
Sound-alike/look-alike issues:
Lovenox® may be confused with Lotronex®, Protonix®

High alert medication: The Institute for Safe Medication Practices (ISMP) includes this medication among its list of drugs which have a heightened risk of causing significant patient harm when used in error.

International issues:
Lovenox® may be confused with Lotanax® which is a brand name for terfenadine in the Czech Republic

Contraindications Hypersensitivity to enoxaparin, heparin, or any component of the formulation; thrombocytopenia associated with a positive *in vitro* test for antiplatelet antibodies in the presence of enoxaparin; hypersensitivity to pork products; active major bleeding; not for I.M. or I.V. use
Warnings/Precautions
[U.S. Boxed Warning]: Patients with recent or anticipated neuraxial anesthesia (epidural or spinal anesthesia) are at risk of spinal or epidural hematoma and subsequent paralysis. Consider risk versus benefit prior to neuraxial anesthesia; risk is increased by concomitant agents which may alter hemostasis, as well as traumatic or repeated epidural or spinal puncture. Patient should be observed closely for bleeding if enoxaparin is administered during or immediately following diagnostic lumbar puncture, epidural anesthesia, or spinal anesthesia.

Do not administer intramuscularly. Not recommended for thromboprophylaxis in patients with prosthetic heart valves (especially pregnant women). Not to be used interchangeably (unit for unit) with heparin or any other low molecular weight heparins. Use caution in patients with history of heparin-induced thrombocytopenia. Monitor patient closely for signs or symptoms of bleeding. Certain patients are at increased risk of bleeding. Risk factors include bacterial endocarditis; congenital or acquired bleeding disorders; active ulcerative or angiodysplastic GI diseases; severe uncontrolled hypertension; hemorrhagic stroke; use shortly after brain, spinal, or ophthalmology surgery; patients treated concomitantly with platelet inhibitors; recent GI bleeding; thrombocytopenia or platelet defects; severe liver disease; hypertensive or diabetic retinopathy; or in patients undergoing invasive procedures. Monitor platelet count closely. Rare cases of thrombocytopenia have occurred. Manufacturer recommends discontinuation of therapy if platelets are <100,000/mm³. Rare cases of thrombocytopenia with thrombosis have occurred. Use caution in patients with congenital or drug-induced thrombocytopenia or platelet defects. Risk of bleeding may be increased in women <45 kg and in men <57 kg. Use caution in patients with renal failure; dosage adjustment needed if Cl_{cr} <30 mL/minute. Safety and efficacy in pediatric patients have not been established. Use with caution in the elderly (delayed elimination may occur). Heparin can cause hyperkalemia by affecting aldosterone. Similar reactions could occur with LMWHs. Monitor for hyperkalemia. Multiple-dose vials contain benzyl alcohol (use caution in pregnant women). In neonates, large amounts of benzyl alcohol (>100 mg/kg/day) have been associated with fatal toxicity (gasping syndrome).

Adverse Reactions As with all anticoagulants, bleeding is the major adverse effect of enoxaparin. Hemorrhage may occur at virtually any site. Risk is dependent on multiple variables. At the recommended doses, single injections of enoxaparin do not significantly influence platelet aggregation or affect global clotting time (ie, PT or aPTT).

1% to 10%:
Central nervous system: Fever (5% to 8%), confusion, pain
Dermatologic: Erythema, bruising
Gastrointestinal: Nausea (3%), diarrhea
Hematologic: Hemorrhage (5% to 13%), thrombocytopenia (2%), hypochromic anemia (2%)
Hepatic: ALT/AST increased
(Continued)

Enoxaparin *(Continued)*

Local: Injection site hematoma (9%), local reactions (irritation, pain, ecchymosis, erythema)

<1% (Limited to important or life-threatening): Allergic reaction, anaphylactoid reaction, eczematous plaques, hyperlipidemia, hypersensitivity cutaneous vasculitis, hypertriglyceridemia, itchy erythematous patches. pruritus, purpura, skin necrosis, thrombocytosis, urticaria, vesicobullous rash. Retroperitoneal or intracranial bleed (some fatal). Spinal or epidural hematomas can occur following neuraxial anesthesia or spinal puncture, resulting in paralysis. Risk is increased in patients with indwelling epidural catheters or concomitant use of other drugs affecting hemostasis. Cases of heparin-induced thrombocytopenia with thrombosis (some complicated by organ infarction, limb ischemia, or death) have been reported. Prosthetic valve thrombosis, including fatal cases, has been reported in pregnant women receiving enoxaparin as thromboprophylaxis.

Overdosage/Toxicology Symptoms of overdose include hemorrhage. Protamine sulfate has been used to reverse effects (protamine 1 mg neutralizes enoxaparin 1 mg). Monitor aPTT 2-4 hours after first infusion; consider readministration of protamine (50% of original dose). **Note:** Anti-Xa activity is never completely neutralized (maximum of 60% to 75%). Avoid overdose of protamine.

Drug Interactions

Increased Effect/Toxicity: Risk of bleeding with enoxaparin may be increased with thrombolytic agents, oral anticoagulants (warfarin), drugs which affect platelet function (eg, aspirin, NSAIDs, dipyridamole, ticlopidine, clopidogrel, and IIb/IIIa antagonists). Although the risk of bleeding may be increased during concurrent therapy with warfarin, enoxaparin is commonly continued during the initiation of warfarin therapy to assure anticoagulation and to protect against possible transient hypercoagulability. Some cephalosporins and penicillins may block platelet aggregation, theoretically increasing the risk of bleeding.

Ethanol/Nutrition/Herb Interactions Herb/Nutraceutical: Avoid cat's claw, dong quai, evening primrose, feverfew, garlic, ginger, ginkgo, red clover, horse chestnut, green tea, ginseng (all have additional antiplatelet activity).

Stability Store at 15°C to 25°C (59°F to 77°F); do not freeze.

Mechanism of Action Standard heparin consists of components with molecular weights ranging from 4000-30,000 daltons with a mean of 16,000 daltons. Heparin acts as an anticoagulant by enhancing the inhibition rate of clotting proteases by antithrombin III impairing normal hemostasis and inhibition of factor Xa. Low molecular weight heparins have a small effect on the activated partial thromboplastin time and strongly inhibit factor Xa. Enoxaparin is derived from porcine heparin that undergoes benzylation followed by alkaline depolymerization. The average molecular weight of enoxaparin is 4500 daltons which is distributed as (≤20%) 2000 daltons (≥68%) 2000-8000 daltons, and (≤15%) >8000 daltons. Enoxaparin has a higher ratio of antifactor Xa to antifactor IIa activity than unfractionated heparin.

Pharmacodynamics/Kinetics

Onset of action: Peak effect: SubQ: Antifactor Xa and antithrombin (antifactor IIa): 3-5 hours

Duration: 40 mg dose: Antifactor Xa activity: ~12 hours

Metabolism: Hepatic, to lower molecular weight fragments (little activity)

Protein binding: Does not bind to heparin binding proteins

Half-life elimination, plasma: 2-4 times longer than standard heparin, independent of dose; based on anti-Xa activity: 4.5-7 hours

Excretion: Urine (40% of dose; 10% as active fragments)

Dosage SubQ:

Infants and Children (unlabeled use):

Infants <2 months: Initial:

Prophylaxis: 0.75 mg/kg every 12 hours

Treatment: 1.5 mg/kg every 12 hours

Infants >2 months and Children ≤18 years: Initial:

Prophylaxis: 0.5 mg/kg every 12 hours

Treatment: 1 mg/kg every 12 hours

Maintenance: See **Dosage Titration** table:

Enoxaparin Pediatric Dosage Titration

Antifactor Xa	Dose Titration	Time to Repeat Antifactor Xa Level
<0.35 units/mL	Increase dose by 25%	4 h after next dose
0.35-0.49 units/mL	Increase dose by 10%	4 h after next dose
0.5-1 unit/mL	Keep same dosage	Next day, then 1 wk later, then monthly (4 h after dose)
1.1-1.5 units/mL	Decrease dose by 20%	Before next dose
1.6-2 units/mL	Hold dose for 3 h and decrease dose by 30%	Before next dose, then 4 h after next dose
>2 units/mL	Hold all doses until antifactor Xa is 0.5 units/mL, then decrease dose by 40%	Before next dose and every 12 h until antifactor Xa <0.5 units/mL

Modified from Monagle P, Michelson AD, Bovill E, et al, "Antithrombotic Therapy in Children," *Chest*, 2001, 119:344S-70S.

Adults:

DVT prophylaxis:

Hip replacement surgery:

Twice-daily dosing: 30 mg twice daily, with initial dose within 12-24 hours after surgery, and every 12 hours until risk of DVT has diminished or the patient is adequately anticoagulated on warfarin.

Once-daily dosing: 40 mg once daily, with initial dose within 9-15 hours before surgery, and daily until risk of DVT has diminished or the patient is adequately anticoagulated on warfarin.

Knee replacement surgery: 30 mg twice daily, with initial dose within 12-24 hours after surgery, and every 12 hours until risk of DVT has diminished (usually 7-10 days).

Abdominal surgery: 40 mg once daily, with initial dose given 2 hours prior to surgery; continue until risk of DVT has diminished (usual 7-10 days).

Medical patients with severely-restricted mobility during acute illness: 40 mg once daily; continue until risk of DVT has diminished

DVT treatment (acute): **Note:** Start warfarin within 72 hours and continue enoxaparin until INR is between 2.0 and 3.0 (usually 7 days).

Inpatient treatment (with or without pulmonary embolism): 1 mg/kg/dose every 12 hours or 1.5 mg/kg once daily.

Outpatient treatment (without pulmonary embolism): 1 mg/kg/dose every 12 hours.

Unstable angina or non-Q-wave MI: 1 mg/kg twice daily in conjunction with oral aspirin therapy (100-325 mg once daily); continue until clinical stabilization (a minimum of at least 2 days)

Elderly: Increased incidence of bleeding with doses of 1.5 mg/kg/day or 1 mg/kg every 12 hours; injection-associated bleeding and serious adverse reactions are also increased in the elderly. Careful attention should be paid to elderly patients <45 kg.

Dosing adjustment in renal impairment: SubQ:

Cl_{cr} ≥30 mL/minute: No specific adjustment recommended (per manufacturer); monitor closely for bleeding

Cl_{cr} <30 mL/minute:

DVT prophylaxis in abdominal surgery, hip replacement, knee replacement, or in medical patients during acute illness: 30 mg once daily

DVT treatment (inpatient or outpatient treatment in conjunction with warfarin): 1 mg/kg once daily

Unstable angina, non-Q-wave MI (with ASA): 1 mg/kg once daily

Dialysis: Enoxaparin has not been FDA approved for use in dialysis patients. It's elimination is primarily via the renal route. Serious bleeding complications have been reported with use in patients who are dialysis dependent or have severe renal failure. LMWH administration at fixed doses without monitoring has greater unpredictable anticoagulant effects in patients with chronic kidney disease. If used, dosages should be reduced and anti-Xa activity frequently monitored, as accumulation may occur with repeated doses. Many clinicians would not use enoxaparin in this population especially without timely anti-Xa activity assay results.

Hemodialysis: Supplemental dose is not necessary.

Peritoneal dialysis: Significant drug removal is unlikely based on physiochemical characteristics.

Administration Should be administered by deep SubQ injection to the left or right anterolateral and left or right posterolateral abdominal wall. To avoid loss of drug from the 30 mg and 40 mg syringes, do not expel the air bubble from the syringe prior to injection. In order to minimize bruising, do not rub injection site. An automatic injector (Lovenox EasyInjector™) is available with the 30 mg and 40 mg syringes to aid the patient with self-injections. **Note:** Enoxaparin is available in 100 mg/mL and 150 mg/mL concentrations.

Monitoring Parameters Platelets, occult blood, and anti-Xa activity, if available; the monitoring of PT and/or aPTT is not necessary

Dosage Forms

Injection, solution, as sodium [graduated prefilled syringe; preservative free]: 60 mg/0.6 mL (0.6 mL); 80 mg/0.8 mL (0.8 mL); 100 mg/mL (1 mL); 120 mg/0.8 mL (0.8 mL); 150 mg/mL (1 mL)

Injection, solution, as sodium [multidose vial]: 100 mg/mL (3 mL) [contains benzyl alcohol]

Injection, solution, as sodium [prefilled syringe; preservative free]: 30 mg/0.3 mL (0.3 mL); 40 mg/0.4 mL (0.4 mL)

♦ **Enoxaparin Injection (Can)** see Enoxaparin on page 583
♦ **Enoxaparin Sodium** see Enoxaparin on page 583
♦ **Enpresse™** see Ethinyl Estradiol and Levonorgestrel on page 653

Entacapone (en TA ka pone)

U.S. Brand Names Comtan®
Canadian Brand Names Comtan®
Pharmacologic Category Anti-Parkinson's Agent, COMT Inhibitor
Additional Appendix Information
Parkinson's Agents on page 1895
Use Adjunct to levodopa/carbidopa therapy in patients with idiopathic Parkinson's disease who experience "wearing-off" symptoms at the end of a dosing interval
Pregnancy Risk Factor C
Pregnancy Implications Not recommended
Lactation Excretion in breast milk unknown/use caution
Contraindications Hypersensitivity to entacapone or any of component of the formulation
Warnings/Precautions Patient should not be treated concomitantly with entacapone and a nonselective MAO inhibitor. Orthostatic hypotension may be increased in patients on dopaminergic therapy in Parkinson's disease.
Adverse Reactions
>10%:
Gastrointestinal: Nausea (14%)
Neuromuscular & skeletal: Dyskinesia (25%), placebo (15%)
1% to 10%:
Cardiovascular: Orthostatic hypotension (4.3%), syncope (1.2%)
(Continued)

Entacapone (Continued)

Central nervous system: Dizziness (8%), fatigue (6%), hallucinations (4%), anxiety (2%), somnolence (2%), agitation (1%)

Dermatologic: Purpura (2%)

Gastrointestinal: Diarrhea (10%), abdominal pain (8%), constipation (6%), vomiting (4%), dry mouth (3%), dyspepsia (2%), flatulence (2%), gastritis (1%), taste perversion (1%)

Genitourinary: Brown-orange urine discoloration (10%)

Neuromuscular & skeletal: Hyperkinesia (10%), hypokinesia (9%), back pain (4%), weakness (2%)

Respiratory: Dyspnea (3%)

Miscellaneous: Diaphoresis increased (2%), bacterial infection (1%)

<1% (Limited to important or life-threatening): Hyperpyrexia and confusion (resembling neuroleptic malignant syndrome), pulmonary fibrosis, retroperitoneal fibrosis, rhabdomyolysis

Overdosage/Toxicology There have been no reported cases of intentional or accidental overdose with this drug. COMT inhibition by entacapone treatment is dose dependent.

Drug Interactions

Cytochrome P450 Effect: Inhibits CYP1A2 (weak), 2A6 (weak), 2C9 (weak), 2C19 (weak), 2D6 (weak), 2E1 (weak), 3A4 (weak)

Increased Effect/Toxicity: Entacapone may decrease the metabolism and increase the side effects of COMT substrates (eg, apomorphine, bitolterol, dobutamine, dopamine, epinephrine, norepinephrine, isoproterenol, isoetharine, and methyldopa). Effects on mental status may be additive with other CNS depressants; includes barbiturates, benzodiazepines, TCAs, antipsychotics, ethanol, opioid analgesics, and other sedative-hypnotics. Concurrent use of nonselective MAO inhibitors with entacapone may increase the risk of cardiovascular side effects; selective MAO inhibitors (eg, selegiline) appear to pose limited risk.

Ethanol/Nutrition/Herb Interactions Ethanol: Avoid ethanol (may increase CNS adverse effects).

Mechanism of Action Entacapone is a reversible and selective inhibitor of catechol-O-methyltransferase (COMT). When entacapone is taken with levodopa, the pharmacokinetics are altered, resulting in more sustained levodopa serum levels compared to levodopa taken alone. The resulting levels of levodopa provide for increased concentrations available for absorption across the blood-brain barrier, thereby providing for increased CNS levels of dopamine, the active metabolite of levodopa.

Pharmacodynamics/Kinetics

Onset of action: Rapid

Peak effect: 1 hour

Absorption: Rapid

Distribution: I.V.: V_{dss}: 20 L

Protein binding: 98%, primarily to albumin

Metabolism: Isomerization to the *cis*-isomer, followed by direct glucuronidation of the parent and *cis*-isomer

Bioavailability: 35%

Half-life elimination: B phase: 0.4-0.7 hours; Y phase: 2.4 hours

Time to peak, serum: 1 hour

Excretion: Feces (90%); urine (10%)

Dosage Oral: Adults: 200 mg with each dose of levodopa/carbidopa, up to a maximum of 8 times/day (maximum daily dose: 1600 mg/day). To optimize therapy, the dosage of levodopa may need reduced or the dosing interval may need extended. Patients taking levodopa ≥800mg/day or who had moderate-to-severe dyskinesias prior to therapy required an average decrease of 25% in the daily levodopa dose.

Dosage adjustment in hepatic impairment: Treat with caution and monitor carefully; AUC and C_{max} can be possibly doubled

Dietary Considerations May be taken with or without food.

Administration Always administer in association with levodopa/carbidopa; can be combined with both the immediate and sustained release formulations of levodopa/carbidopa. Can be taken with or without food. Should not be abruptly withdrawn from patient's therapy due to significant worsening of symptoms.

Monitoring Parameters Signs and symptoms of Parkinson's disease; liver function tests, blood pressure, patient's mental status

Dosage Forms Tablet: 200 mg

♦ **Entacapone, Carbidopa, and Levodopa** *see* Levodopa, Carbidopa, and Entacapone *on page 1001*

Entecavir (en TE ka veer)

U.S. Brand Names Baraclude™

Pharmacologic Category Antiretroviral Agent, Reverse Transcriptase Inhibitor (Nucleoside)

Use Treatment of chronic hepatitis B infection in adults with evidence of active viral replication and either evidence of persistent transaminase elevations or histologically-active disease

Pregnancy Risk Factor C

Pregnancy Implications Teratogenic effects have been observed in animal studies. There are no adequate and well-controlled studies in pregnant women. Use only if benefit outweighs risk. Pregnant women taking entecavir should enroll in the pregnancy registry by calling 1-800-258-4263.

Lactation Excretion in breast milk unknown/contraindicated

Contraindications Hypersensitivity to entecavir or any component of the formulation

Warnings/Precautions [U.S. Boxed Warning]: **Lactic acidosis and severe hepatomegaly with steatosis have been reported.** [U.S. Boxed Warning]: **Exacerbation of hepatitis B may occur upon discontinuation.** Monitor liver function several months after stopping treatment; reinitiation of antihepatitis B therapy may be required. Use caution in patients with renal impairment or in patients receiving concomitant therapy which may reduce renal function; entecavir dosage may need to be adjusted. Cross-resistance may develop in patients failing previous therapy with lamivudine. Entecavir does not exhibit any clinically-relevant activity against human immunodeficiency virus (HIV type 1). Safety and efficacy in pediatric patients and liver transplant patients have not been established.

Adverse Reactions
>10%: Hepatic: Alanine aminotransferase increased (2% to 12%)
1% to 10%:
  Central nervous system: Headache (2% to 4%), fatigue (1% to 3%)
  Endocrine & metabolic: Hyperglycemia (2%)
  Gastrointestinal: Lipase increased (7% to 8%), amylase increased (2% to 3%), diarrhea (≤1%), dyspepsia (≤1%)
  Hepatic: Aspartate aminotransferase increased (5%), bilirubin increased (2% to 3%)
  Renal: Hematuria (9%), glycosuria (4%), creatinine increased (1% to 2%),
<1% (Limited to important or life-threatening): Dizziness, hypoalbuminemia, insomnia, nausea, somnolence, thrombocytopenia, vomiting

Overdosage/Toxicology There have been limited reports of healthy subjects receiving single doses up to 40 mg or multiple doses up to 20 mg/day for 14 days with no adverse effects. Treatment should be symptom-directed and supportive. Hemodialysis (4 hours) will remove approximately 13% of dose.

Drug Interactions
Increased Effect/Toxicity:
  Concomitant use of ribavirin with or without interferon alfa and nucleoside analogues may increase the risk of developing hepatic decompensation or other signs of mitochondrial toxicity, including pancreatitis or lactic acidosis. Gancyclovir/valgancyclovir may increase the adverse effects/toxicity (eg, hematologic) of nucleoside reverse transcriptase inhibitors.

Ethanol/Nutrition/Herb Interactions
Food: Food delays absorption and reduces AUC by 20%.

Stability Store at 15°C to 30°C (59°F to 86°F). Protect oral solution from light.

Mechanism of Action Entecavir is intracellularly phosphorylated to guanosine triphosphate which competes with natural substrates to effectively inhibit hepatitis B viral polymerase; enzyme inhibition blocks reverse transcriptase activity thereby reducing viral DNA synthesis.

Pharmacodynamics/Kinetics
Distribution: Extensive (V_d in excess of body water)
Protein binding: 13%
Metabolism: Minor hepatic glucuronide/sulfate conjugation
Half-life elimination: Terminal: 5-6 days, accumulation: 24 hours
Time to peak, plasma: 0.5-1.5 hours
Excretion: Urine (60% to 70% as unchanged drug)

Dosage Oral: Adolescents ≥16 years and Adults:
Nucleoside treatment naive: 0.5 mg daily
Lamivudine-resistant viremia (or known lamivudine-resistant mutations): 1 mg daily
Dosage adjustment in renal impairment: Cl_{cr} <50 mL/minute (including hemodialysis/CAPD):
  Cl_{cr} 30-49 mL/minute: Administer 50% of usual dose
  Cl_{cr} 10-29 mL/minute: Administer 30% of usual dose
  Cl_{cr} <10 mL/minute (including dialysis): Administer 10% of usual dose; administer after hemodialysis

Dietary Considerations Take on an empty stomach (2 hours before or after a meal).

Administration Administer on an empty stomach. Do not dilute or mix oral solution with water or other beverages; use calibrated oral dosing syringe. Oral solution and tablet are bioequivalent on a mg-to-mg basis.

Monitoring Parameters Liver function tests, renal function

Dosage Forms
Oral solution: 0.05 mg/mL (210 mL) [orange flavor]
Tablet: 0.5 mg, 1 mg

♦ **Enterex® Glutapak-10® [OTC]** see Glutamine on page 803
♦ **Entex® [DSC]** see Guaifenesin and Phenylephrine on page 818
♦ **Entex® ER [DSC]** see Guaifenesin and Phenylephrine on page 818
♦ **Entex® LA [DSC]** see Guaifenesin and Phenylephrine on page 818
♦ **Entex® LA (Can)** see Guaifenesin and Pseudoephedrine on page 819
♦ **Entex® PSE** see Guaifenesin and Pseudoephedrine on page 819
♦ **Entocort® (Can)** see Budesonide on page 244
♦ **Entocort® EC** see Budesonide on page 244
♦ **Entrophen® (Can)** see Aspirin on page 160
♦ **Entsol® [OTC]** see Sodium Chloride on page 1576
♦ **Enulose** see Lactulose on page 971
♦ **Enzone®** see Pramoxine and Hydrocortisone on page 1409
♦ **Eperbel-S** see Belladonna, Phenobarbital, and Ergotamine on page 201

Ephedrine (e FED rin)

U.S. Brand Names Pretz-D® [OTC]
Index Terms Ephedrine Sulfate
Pharmacologic Category Alpha/Beta Agonist
Additional Appendix Information
  Contrast Media Reactions, Premedication for Prophylaxis on page 2036
Use Treatment of bronchial asthma, nasal congestion, acute bronchospasm, idiopathic orthostatic hypotension, hypotension induced by spinal anesthesia
Pregnancy Risk Factor C
Lactation Enters breast milk/not recommended
(Continued)

Ephedrine *(Continued)*

Medication Safety Issues
Sound-alike/look-alike issues:
Ephedrine may be confused with Epifrin®, epinephrine

Contraindications Hypersensitivity to ephedrine or any component of the formulation; cardiac arrhythmias; angle-closure glaucoma; concurrent use of other sympathomimetic agents

Warnings/Precautions Blood volume depletion should be corrected before ephedrine therapy is instituted; use caution in patients with unstable vasomotor symptoms, diabetes, hyperthyroidism, prostatic hyperplasia, a history of seizures or those on other sympathomimetic agents; also use caution in the elderly and those patients with cardiovascular disorders such as coronary artery disease, arrhythmias, and hypertension. Ephedrine may cause hypertension resulting in intracranial hemorrhage. Long-term use may cause anxiety and symptoms of paranoid schizophrenia. Avoid as a bronchodilator; generally not used as a bronchodilator since new beta₂ agents are less toxic. Use with caution in the elderly, since it crosses the blood-brain barrier and may cause confusion.

Adverse Reactions Frequency not defined.
Cardiovascular: Arrhythmias, chest pain, elevation or depression of blood pressure, hypertension, palpitation, tachycardia, unusual pallor
Central nervous system: Agitation, anxiety, apprehension, CNS stimulating effects, dizziness, excitation, fear, headache hyperactivity, insomnia, irritability, nervousness, restlessness, tension
Gastrointestinal: Anorexia, GI upset, nausea, vomiting, xerostomia
Genitourinary: Painful urination
Neuromuscular & skeletal: Trembling, tremor (more common in the elderly), weakness
Respiratory: Dyspnea
Miscellaneous: Diaphoresis increased

Overdosage/Toxicology Symptoms include dysrhythmias, CNS excitation, respiratory depression, vomiting, and convulsions. There is no specific antidote for ephedrine intoxication and the bulk of the treatment is supportive. Hyperactivity and agitation usually respond to reduced sensory input; however, with extreme agitation, haloperidol (2-5 mg I.M. for adults) may be required. Hyperthermia is best treated with external cooling measures; or when severe or unresponsive, muscle paralysis with pancuronium may be needed. Hypertension is usually transient and generally does not require treatment unless severe. For diastolic blood pressures >110 mm Hg, a nitroprusside infusion should be initiated. Seizures usually respond to diazepam I.V. and/or phenytoin maintenance regimens.

Drug Interactions
Increased Effect/Toxicity: Increased (toxic) cardiac stimulation with other sympathomimetic agents, theophylline, cardiac glycosides, or general anesthetics. Increased blood pressure with atropine or MAO inhibitors.

Decreased Effect: Alpha- and beta-adrenergic blocking agents decrease ephedrine vasopressor effects.

Ethanol/Nutrition/Herb Interactions Herb/Nutraceutical: Avoid ephedra, yohimbe (may cause CNS stimulation).

Stability Protect all dosage forms from light.

Mechanism of Action Releases tissue stores of epinephrine and thereby produces an alpha- and beta-adrenergic stimulation; longer-acting and less potent than epinephrine

Pharmacodynamics/Kinetics
Onset of action: Oral: Bronchodilation: 0.25-1 hour
Duration: Oral: 3-6 hours
Distribution: Crosses placenta; enters breast milk
Metabolism: Minimally hepatic
Half-life elimination: 2.5-3.6 hours
Excretion: Urine (60% to 77% as unchanged drug) within 24 hours

Dosage
Children:
Oral, SubQ: 3 mg/kg/day or 25-100 mg/m²/day in 4-6 divided doses every 4-6 hours
I.M., slow I.V. push: 0.2-0.3 mg/kg/dose every 4-6 hours
Adults:
Oral: 25-50 mg every 3-4 hours as needed
I.M., SubQ: 25-50 mg, parenteral adult dose should not exceed 150 mg in 24 hours
I.M.: Hypotension induced by anesthesia: 25 mg
I.V.: 5-25 mg/dose slow I.V. push repeated after 5-10 minutes as needed, then every 3-4 hours not to exceed 150 mg/24 hours
Nasal spray:
Children 6-12 years: 1-2 sprays into each nostril, not more frequently than every 4 hours
Children ≥12 years and Adults: 2-3 sprays into each nostril, not more frequently than every 4 hours

Monitoring Parameters Injection solution: Monitor blood pressure, pulse

Test Interactions Can cause a false-positive amphetamine EMIT assay

Dosage Forms
Capsule, as sulfate: 25 mg
Injection, solution, as sulfate: 50 mg/mL (1 mL, 10 mL)
Solution, intranasal spray, as sulfate (Pretz-D®): 0.25% (50 mL)

♦ **Ephedrine, Chlorpheniramine, Phenylephrine, and Carbetapentane** see Chlorpheniramine, Ephedrine, Phenylephrine, and Carbetapentane *on page 351*

♦ **Ephedrine Sulfate** see Ephedrine *on page 587*

♦ **Epidermal Thymocyte Activating Factor** see Aldesleukin *on page 59*

♦ **Epifoam®** see Pramoxine and Hydrocortisone *on page 1409*

Epinastine (ep i NAS teen)

U.S. Brand Names Elestat™
Index Terms Epinastine Hydrochloride
Pharmacologic Category Antihistamine, H₁ Blocker, Ophthalmic
Use Treatment of allergic conjunctivitis
Pregnancy Risk Factor C
Pregnancy Implications Teratogenic effects were not observed in animal studies. There are no adequate and well-controlled studies in pregnant women.
Lactation Excretion in breast milk unknown/use caution
Contraindications Hypersensitivity to epinastine or any component of the formulation
Warnings/Precautions Contains benzalkonium chloride; contact lenses should be removed prior to use. Not for the treatment of contact lens irritation. Safety and efficacy in children <3 years of age have not been established.
Adverse Reactions 1% to 10%:
Central nervous system: Headache (1% to 3%)
Ocular: Burning sensation, folliculosis, hyperemia, pruritus
Respiratory: Cough (1% to 3%), pharyngitis (1% to 3%), rhinitis (1% to 3%), sinusitis (1% to 3%)
Miscellaneous: Infection (10%; defined as cold symptoms and upper respiratory infection)
Stability Store at controlled room temperature of 15°C to 25°C (59°F to 77°F). Keep tightly closed.
Mechanism of Action Selective H₁-receptor antagonist; inhibits release of histamine from the mast cell
Pharmacodynamics/Kinetics
Onset: 3-5 minutes
Duration: 8 hours
Absorption: Low systemic absorption following topical application
Distribution: Does not cross blood-brain barrier
Protein binding: 64%
Metabolism: <10% metabolized
Half-life elimination: 12 hours
Excretion: I.V.: Urine (55%); feces (30%)
Dosage Ophthalmic: Allergic conjunctivitis: Children ≥3 years and Adults: Instill 1 drop into each eye twice daily; continue throughout period of exposure, even in the absence of symptoms
Administration For ophthalmic use only; avoid touching tip of applicator to eye or other surfaces. Contact lenses should be removed prior to application, may be reinserted after 10 minutes. Do not wear contact lenses if eyes are red.
Dosage Forms Solution, ophthalmic, as hydrochloride: 0.05% (5 mL) [contains benzalkonium chloride]

♦ **Epinastine Hydrochloride** see Epinastine on page 589

Epinephrine (ep i NEF rin)

U.S. Brand Names Adrenalin®; EpiPen®; EpiPen® Jr; Primatene® Mist [OTC]; Raphon [OTC]; S2® [OTC]; Twinject™
Canadian Brand Names Adrenalin®; EpiPen®; EpiPen® Jr; Twinject™
Index Terms Adrenaline; Epinephrine Bitartrate; Epinephrine Hydrochloride; Racepinephrine
Pharmacologic Category Alpha/Beta Agonist; Antidote
Additional Appendix Information
Bronchodilators on page 1877
Glaucoma Drug Therapy on page 2050
Hemodynamic Support, Intravenous on page 1885
Use Treatment of bronchospasms, bronchial asthma, nasal congestion, viral croup, anaphylactic reactions, cardiac arrest; added to local anesthetics to decrease systemic absorption of local anesthetics and increase duration of action; decrease superficial hemorrhage
Unlabeled/Investigational Use ACLS guidelines: Ventricular fibrillation (VF) or pulseless ventricular tachycardia (VT) unresponsive to initial defibrillatory shocks; pulseless electrical activity, asystole, hypotension unresponsive to volume resuscitation; symptomatic bradycardia or hypotension unresponsive to atropine or pacing; inotropic support
Pregnancy Risk Factor C
Pregnancy Implications Crosses the placenta. Reported association with malformations in 1 study; may be secondary to severe maternal disease.
Lactation Excretion in breast milk unknown
Medication Safety Issues
Sound-alike/look-alike issues:
Epinephrine may be confused with ephedrine
Epifrin® may be confused with ephedrine, EpiPen®
EpiPen® may be confused with Epifrin®

Medication errors have occurred due to confusion with epinephrine products expressed as ratio strengths (eg, 1:1000 vs 1:10,000).
Epinephrine 1:1000 = 1 mg/mL and is most commonly used SubQ.
Epinephrine 1:10,000 = 0.1 mg/mL and is used I.V.

International issues:
EpiPen® may be confused with Epigen® which is a brand name for glycyrrhizinic acid in Mexico
EpiPen® may be confused with Epopen® which is a brand name for epoetin alfa in Spain
Contraindications Hypersensitivity to epinephrine or any component of the formulation; cardiac arrhythmias; angle-closure glaucoma
(Continued)

Epinephrine (Continued)

Warnings/Precautions Use with caution in elderly patients, patients with diabetes mellitus, cardiovascular diseases (angina, tachycardia, myocardial infarction), thyroid disease, or cerebral arteriosclerosis, Parkinson's; some products contain sulfites as preservatives. Rapid I.V. infusion may cause death from cerebrovascular hemorrhage or cardiac arrhythmias. Oral inhalation of epinephrine is **not** the preferred route of administration. Avoid topical application where reduced perfusion could lead to ischemic tissue damage (eg, penis, ears, digits).

Adverse Reactions Frequency not defined.

Cardiovascular: Angina, cardiac arrhythmia, chest pain, flushing, hypertension, increased myocardial oxygen consumption, pallor, palpitation, sudden death, tachycardia (parenteral), vasoconstriction, ventricular ectopy

Central nervous system: Anxiety, dizziness, headache, insomnia, lightheadedness, nervousness, restlessness

Gastrointestinal: Dry throat, nausea, vomiting, xerostomia

Genitourinary: Acute urinary retention in patients with bladder outflow obstruction

Neuromuscular & skeletal: Trembling, weakness

Ocular: Allergic lid reaction, burning, eye pain, ocular irritation, precipitation of or exacerbation of narrow-angle glaucoma, transient stinging

Renal: Decreased renal and splanchnic blood flow

Respiratory: Dyspnea, wheezing

Miscellaneous: Diaphoresis increased

Overdosage/Toxicology Symptoms include arrhythmias, unusually large pupils, pulmonary edema, renal failure, metabolic acidosis; and hypertension, which may result in subarachnoid hemorrhage and hemiplegia. There is no specific antidote for epinephrine intoxication and the bulk of treatment is supportive. Hyperactivity and agitation usually respond to reduced sensory input; however, with extreme agitation, haloperidol (2-5 mg I.M. for adults) may be required. Hyperthermia is best treated with external cooling measures; or when severe or unresponsive, muscle paralysis with pancuronium may be needed. Hypertension is usually transient and generally does not require treatment unless severe. For diastolic blood pressures >110 mm Hg, a nitroprusside infusion should be initiated. Seizures usually respond to diazepam I.V. and/or phenytoin maintenance regimens.

Drug Interactions

Increased Effect/Toxicity: Increased cardiac irritability if administered concurrently with halogenated inhalation anesthetics, beta-blocking agents, or alpha-blocking agents.

Decreased Effect: Decreased bronchodilation with β-blockers. Decreases antihypertensive effects of methyldopa or guanethidine.

Ethanol/Nutrition/Herb Interactions Herb/Nutraceutical: Avoid ephedra, yohimbe (may cause CNS stimulation).

Stability

Epinephrine is sensitive to light and air; protection from light is recommended. Oxidation turns drug pink, then a brown color. **Solutions should not be used if they are discolored or contain a precipitate.**

Adrenalin®: Store between 15°C to 25°C (59°F to 77°F); do not freeze. Protect from light. The 1:1000 solution should be discarded 30 days after initial use.

Raphon: Store between 2°C to 25°C (36°F to 77°F). Refrigerate after opening.

Twinject™: Store between 20°C to 25°C (68°F to 77°F); do not freeze or refrigerate. Protect from light.

Stability of injection of parenteral admixture at room temperature (25°C) or refrigeration (4°C) is 24 hours.

Standard I.V. diluent: 1 mg/250 mL NS.

Preparation of adult I.V. infusion: Dilute 1 mg in 250 mL of D_5W or NS (4 mcg/mL). Administer at an initial rate of 1 mcg/minute and increase to desired effects. At 20 mcg/minute pure alpha effects occur.

S2®: Dilution not required when administered via hand-nebulizer; dilute with NS 3-5 mL if using jet nebulizer

Mechanism of Action Stimulates alpha-, beta$_1$-, and beta$_2$-adrenergic receptors resulting in relaxation of smooth muscle of the bronchial tree, cardiac stimulation, and dilation of skeletal muscle vasculature; small doses can cause vasodilation via beta$_2$-vascular receptors; large doses may produce constriction of skeletal and vascular smooth muscle

Pharmacodynamics/Kinetics

Onset of action: Bronchodilation: SubQ: ~5-10 minutes; Inhalation: ~1 minute

Distribution: Crosses placenta

Metabolism: Taken up into the adrenergic neuron and metabolized by monoamine oxidase and catechol-o-methyltransferase; circulating drug hepatically metabolized

Excretion: Urine (as inactive metabolites, metanephrine, and sulfate and hydroxy derivatives of mandelic acid, small amounts as unchanged drug)

Dosage

Neonates: Cardiac arrest: I.V.: 0.01-0.03 mg/kg (0.1-0.3 mL/kg of **1:10,000** solution) every 3-5 minutes as needed. Although I.V. route is preferred, may consider administration of doses up to 0.1 mg/kg through the endotracheal tube until I.V. access established; dilute intratracheal doses to 1-2 mL with normal saline.

Infants and Children:

Asystole/pulseless arrest, bradycardia, VT/VF (after failed defibrillations):

I.V., I.O.: 0.01 mg/kg (0.1 mL/kg of **1:10,000** solution) every 3-5 minutes as needed (maximum: 1 mg)

Intratracheal: 0.1 mg/kg (0.1 mL/kg of **1:1000** solution) every 3-5 minutes (maximum: 10 mg)

Continuous I.V. infusion: 0.1-1 mcg/kg/minute; doses <0.3 mcg/kg/minute generally produce β-adrenergic effects and higher doses generally produce α-adrenergic vasoconstriction; titrate dosage to desired effect

Bronchodilator: SubQ: 0.01 mg/kg (0.01 mL/kg of **1:1000**) (single doses not to exceed 0.5 mg) every 20 minutes for 3 doses

Nebulization: 1-3 inhalations up to every 3 hours using solution prepared with 10 drops of 1:100

Children <4 years: S2® (racepinephrine, OTC labeling): Croup: 0.05 mL/kg (max 0.5 mL/dose); dilute in NS 3 mL. Administer over ~15 minutes; do not administer more frequently than every 2 hours.

Inhalation: Children ≥4 years: Primatene® Mist: Refer to Adults dosing.

Decongestant: Children ≥6 years: Refer to Adults dosing

Hypersensitivity reaction:

SubQ, I.V.: 0.01 mg/kg every 20 minutes; larger doses or continuous infusion may be needed for some anaphylactic reactions

Self-administration following severe allergic reactions (eg, insect stings, food): **Note:** World Health Organization (WHO) and Anaphylaxis Canada recommend the availability of 1 dose for every 10-20 minutes of travel time to a medical emergency facility:

Twinject™: SubQ, I.M.:

Children 15-30 kg: 0.15 mg

Children >30 kg: 0.3 mg

Epipen® Jr: I.M.: Children <30 kg: 0.15 mg

Epipen®: I.M.: Children ≥30 kg: 0.3 mg

Adults:

Asystole/pulseless arrest, bradycardia, VT/VF:

I.V., I.O.: 1 mg every 3-5 minutes; if this approach fails, higher doses of epinephrine (up to 0.2 mg/kg) may be indicated for treatment of specific problems (eg, beta-blocker or calcium channel blocker overdose)

Intratracheal: Administer 2-2.5 mg for VF or pulseless VT if I.V./I.O. access is delayed or cannot be established; dilute in 5-10 mL NS or distilled water. **Note:** Absorption is greater with distilled water, but causes more adverse effects on PaO_2.

Bradycardia (symptomatic) or hypotension (not responsive to atropine or pacing): I.V. infusion: 2-10 mcg/minute; titrate to desired effect

Bronchodilator:

SubQ: 0.3-0.5 mg **(1:1000)** every 20 minutes for 3 doses

Nebulization: 1-3 inhalations up to every 3 hours using solution prepared with 10 drops of the **1:100** product

S2® (racepinephrine, OTC labeling): 0.5 mL (~10 drops). Dose may be repeated not more frequently than very 3-4 hours if needed. Solution should be diluted if using jet nebulizer.

Inhalation: Primatene® Mist (OTC labeling): One inhalation, wait at least 1 minute; if relieved, may use once more. Do not use again for at least 3 hours.

Decongestant: Intranasal: Apply 1:1000 locally as drops or spray or with sterile swab

Hypersensitivity reaction:

SubQ, I.M.: 0.3-0.5 mg (1:1000) every 15-20 minutes if condition requires (I.M route is preferred)

I.V.: 0.1 mg (1:10,000) over 5 minutes. May infuse at 1-4 mcg/minute to prevent the need to repeat injections frequently.

Self-administration following severe allergic reactions (eg, insect stings, food): **Note:** The World Health Organization (WHO) and Anaphylaxis Canada recommend the availability of one dose for every 10 to 20 minutes of travel time to a medical emergency facility. More than 2 doses should only be administered under direct medical supervision.

Twinject™: SubQ, I.M.: 0.3 mg

Epipen®: I.M.: 0.3 mg

Administration Central line administration only. I.V. infusions require an infusion pump. Epinephrine solutions for injection can be administered SubQ, I.M., I.V., I.O.; I.M. administration into the buttocks should be avoided.

Inhalation: S2®: Administer over ~15 minutes; must be diluted if using jet nebulizer.

Intratracheal: Dilute in NS or distilled water. Absorption is greater with distilled water, but causes more adverse effects on PaO_2. Pass catheter beyond tip of tracheal tube, stop compressions, spray drug quickly down tube. Follow immediately with several quick insufflations and continue chest compressions.

Extravasation management: Use phentolamine as antidote. Mix 5 mg with 9 mL of NS. Inject a small amount of this dilution into extravasated area. Blanching should reverse immediately. Monitor site. If blanching should recur, additional injections of phentolamine may be needed.

Monitoring Parameters Pulmonary function, heart rate, blood pressure, site of infusion for blanching, extravasation; cardiac monitor and blood pressure monitor required. If using to treat hypotension, assess intravascular volume and support as needed.

Reference Range Therapeutic: 31-95 pg/mL (SI: 170-520 pmol/L)

Test Interactions Increased bilirubin (S), catecholamines (U), glucose, uric acid (S)

Additional Information

Twinject® and EpiPen® are not interchangeable due to packaging considerations.

Dosage Forms

Aerosol for oral inhalation:

Primatene® Mist: 0.22 mg/inhalation (15 mL, 22.5 mL) [contains CFCs]

Injection, solution [prefilled auto injector]:

EpiPen®: 0.3 mg/0.3 mL [1:1000] (2 mL) [contains sodium metabisulfite; available as single unit or in double-unit pack with training unit]

EpiPen® Jr: 0.15 mg/0.3 mL [1:2000] (2 mL) [contains sodium metabisulfite; available as single unit or in double-unit pack with training unit]

Twinject™: 0.15 mg/0.15 mL [1:1000] (1.1 mL) [contains sodium bisulfite; two 0.15 mg doses per injector]; 0.3 mg/0.3 mL [1:1000] (1.1 mL) [contains sodium bisulfite; two 0.3 mg doses per injector]

Injection, solution, as hydrochloride: 0.1 mg/mL [1:10,000] (10 mL); 1 mg/mL [1:1000] (1 mL) [products may contain sodium metabisulfite]

Adrenalin®: 1 mg/mL [1:1000] (1 mL, 30 mL) [contains sodium bisulfite]

(Continued)

Epinephrine *(Continued)*

Solution for oral inhalation, as hydrochloride:
Adrenalin®: 1% [10 mg/mL, 1:100] (7.5 mL) [contains sodium bisulfite]
Solution for oral inhalation [racepinephrine]:
S2®: 2.25% (0.5 mL, 15 mL) [as d-epinephrine 1.125% and l-epinephrine 1.125%; contains metabisulfites]
Solution, topical [racepinephrine]:
Raphon: 2.25% (15 mL) [as d-epinephrine 1.125% and l-epinephrine 1.125%; contains metabisulfites]

- ♦ **Epinephrine and Lidocaine** *see* Lidocaine and Epinephrine *on page 1014*
- ♦ **Epinephrine Bitartrate** *see* Epinephrine *on page 589*
- ♦ **Epinephrine Hydrochloride** *see* Epinephrine *on page 589*
- ♦ **EpiPen®** *see* Epinephrine *on page 589*
- ♦ **EpiPen® Jr** *see* Epinephrine *on page 589*
- ♦ **Epipodophyllotoxin** *see* Etoposide *on page 670*
- ♦ **EpiQuin™ Micro** *see* Hydroquinone *on page 859*

Epirubicin *(ep i ROO bi sin)*

U.S. Brand Names Ellence®
Canadian Brand Names Ellence®; Pharmorubicin®
Index Terms Epirubicin Hydrochloride; NSC-256942; Pidorubicin; Pidorubicin Hydrochloride
Pharmacologic Category Antineoplastic Agent, Anthracycline
Use Adjuvant therapy for primary breast cancer
Pregnancy Risk Factor D
Pregnancy Implications Teratogenic effects and embryotoxicity were noted in animal studies. There are no adequate and well-controlled studies in pregnant women. If a pregnant woman is treated with epirubicin, or if a woman becomes pregnant while receiving this drug, she should be informed of the potential hazard to the fetus. Women of childbearing potential should be advised to avoid becoming pregnant. Men undergoing treatment should use effective contraception.
Lactation Excretion in breast milk unknown/contraindicated
Medication Safety Issues
Sound-alike/look-alike issues:
Epirubicin may be confused with DOXOrubicin, DAUNOrubicin, idarubicin
Ellence® may be confused with Elase®

High alert medication: The Institute for Safe Medication Practices (ISMP) includes this medication among its list of drugs which have a heightened risk of causing significant patient harm when used in error.

Contraindications Hypersensitivity to epirubicin or any component of the formulation, other anthracyclines, or anthracenediones; previous anthracycline treatment up to maximum cumulative dose; severe myocardial insufficiency; severe arrhythmias; recent myocardial infarction; severe hepatic dysfunction; baseline neutrophil count 1500 cells/mm^3; pregnancy

Warnings/Precautions Hazardous agent - use appropriate precautions for handling and disposal.

[U.S. Boxed Warning]: Potential cardiotoxicity, particularly in patients who have received prior anthracyclines, prior or concomitant radiotherapy to the mediastinal/pericardial area, or who have pre-existing cardiac disease, may occur. Acute toxicity (primarily arrhythmias) and delayed toxicity (CHF) have been described. Delayed toxicity usually develops late in the course of therapy or within 2-3 months after completion, however, events with an onset of several months to years after termination of treatment have been described. The risk of delayed cardiotoxicity increases more steeply with cumulative doses >900 mg/m^2, and this dose should be exceeded only with extreme caution. (The risk of CHF is ~0.9% at a cumulative dose of 550 mg/m^2, ~1.6% at a cumulative dose of 700 mg/m^2, and ~3.3% at a cumulative dose of 900 mg/m^2.) Toxicity may be additive with other anthracyclines or anthracenediones, and may be increased in pediatric patients. Regular monitoring of LVEF and discontinuation at the first sign of impairment is recommended especially in patients with cardiac risk factors or impaired cardiac function.

[U.S. Boxed Warning]: Myelosuppression (severe) may occur; neutropenia is the dose-limiting toxicity; severe thrombocytopenia or anemia may occur. Thrombophlebitis and thromboembolic phenomena (including pulmonary embolism) have occurred.

[U.S. Boxed Warning]: Reduce dosage and use with caution in mild-to-moderate hepatic impairment or in severe renal dysfunction (serum creatinine >5 mg/dL). May cause tumor lysis syndrome or radiation recall. **[U.S. Boxed Warnings]: Treatment with anthracyclines may increase the risk of secondary leukemias. For I.V. administration only, severe local tissue necrosis will result if extravasation occurs.** Women ≥70 years of age should be especially monitored for toxicity; women of childbearing age should be advised to avoid becoming pregnant. **[U.S. Boxed Warning]: Should be administered under the supervision of an experienced cancer chemotherapy physician.** Safety and efficacy in children have not been established.

Adverse Reactions Percentages reported as part of combination chemotherapy regimens.
>10%:
Central nervous system: Lethargy (1% to 46%)
Dermatologic: Alopecia (69% to 96%)
Endocrine & metabolic: Amenorrhea (69% to 72%), hot flashes (5% to 39%)
Gastrointestinal: Nausea/vomiting (83% to 92%), mucositis (9% to 59%), diarrhea (7% to 25%)
Hematologic: Leukopenia (50% to 80%; grades 3/4: 2% to 59%), neutropenia (54% to 80%; grades 3/4: 11% to 67%; nadir: 10-14 days; recovery: 21 days), anemia (13% to 72%; grades 3/4: 6%), thrombocytopenia (5% to 49%; grades 3/4: 5%)

Local: Injection site reactions (3% to 20%)

Ocular: Conjunctivitis (1% to 15%)

Miscellaneous: Infection (15% to 21%)

1% to 10%:

Cardiovascular: CHF (0.4% to 1.5%), decreased LVEF (asymptomatic) (1% to 2%); recommended maximum cumulative dose: 900 mg/m^2

Central nervous system: Fever (1% to 5%)

Dermatologic: Rash (1% to 9%), skin changes (1% to 5%)

Gastrointestinal: Anorexia (2% to 3%)

Hematologic: Neutropenic fever (grades 3/4: 6%)

<1%, postmarketing, case reports, and/or frequency not defined: Acute lymphoid leukemia; acute myelogenous leukemia (0.3% at 3 years, 0.5% at 5 years, 0.6% at 8 years); anaphylaxis, atrioventricular block, bradycardia, bundle-branch block, cardiomyopathy, ECG abnormalities, hypersensitivity, myelodysplastic syndrome, photosensitivity, premature menopause, premature ventricular contractions, pulmonary embolism, radiation recall, sinus tachycardia, skin and nail hyperpigmentation, ST-T wave changes (nonspecific), tachyarrhythmias, thromboembolism, thrombophlebitis, transaminases increased, urticaria, ventricular tachycardia

Overdosage/Toxicology Symptoms of overdose are generally extensions of known cytotoxic effects, including myelosuppression, mucositis, gastrointestinal bleeding, lactic acidosis, multiple organ failure, and death. Treatment is symptom-directed and supportive; consider growth factor support and antimicrobial coverage. Patients should be followed long-term for delayed-onset CHF.

Drug Interactions

Increased Effect/Toxicity: Cimetidine may increase the levels/effects of epirubicin. Bevacizumab and trastuzumab may enhance the cardiotoxic effects of epirubicin.

Ethanol/Nutrition/Herb Interactions

Ethanol: Avoid ethanol (due to GI irritation).

Herb/Nutraceutical: Avoid black cohosh, dong quai in estrogen-dependent tumors.

Stability Store intact vials of solution under refrigeration at 2°C to 8°C (36°F to 46°F). Store intact vials of lyophilized powder at room temperature 15°C to 30°C (59°F to 86°F). Protect from light. Reconstitute lyophilized powder with SWFI to a final concentration of 2 mg/mL. May administer undiluted for IVP or dilute in 50-250 mL NS or D$_5$W for infusion. Reconstituted solutions and solutions for infusion are stable for 24 hours when stored at 2°C to 8°C (36°F to 46°F).

Mechanism of Action Epirubicin is an anthracycline antibiotic; known to inhibit DNA and RNA synthesis by steric obstruction after intercalating between DNA base pairs; active throughout entire cell cycle. Intercalation triggers DNA cleavage by topoisomerase II, resulting in cytocidal activity. Also inhibits DNA helicase, and generates cytotoxic free radicals.

Pharmacodynamics/Kinetics

Distribution: V$_{ss}$ 21-27 L/kg

Protein binding: 77% to albumin

Metabolism: Extensively via hepatic and extrahepatic (including RBCs) routes

Half-life elimination: Triphasic; Mean terminal: 33 hours

Excretion: Feces (34% to 35%); urine (20% to 27%)

Dosage Adults: I.V.: 100-120 mg/m^2 once every 3-4 weeks **or** 50-60 mg/m^2 days 1 and 8 every 3-4 weeks

Breast cancer:

CEF-120: 60 mg/m^2 on days 1 and 8 every 28 days for 6 cycles

FEC-100: 100 mg/m^2 on day 1 every 21 days for 6 cycles

Note: Note: Patients receiving 120 mg/m^2/cycle as part of combination therapy should also receive prophylactic therapy with sulfamethoxazole/trimethoprim or a fluoroquinolone.

Dosage modifications:

Delay day 1 dose until platelets are ≥100,000/mm^3, ANC ≥1500/mm^3, and nonhematologic toxicities have recovered to ≤grade 1

Reduce day 1 dose in subsequent cycles to 75% of previous day 1 dose if patient experiences nadir platelet counts <50,000/mm^3, ANC <250/mm^3, neutropenic fever, or grade 3/4 nonhematologic toxicity during the previous cycle

For divided doses (day 1 and day 8), reduce day 8 dose to 75% of day 1 dose if platelet counts are 75,000-100,000/mm^3 and ANC is 1000-1499/mm^3; omit day 8 dose if platelets are <75,000/mm^3, ANC <1000/mm^3, or grade 3/4 nonhematologic toxicity

Dosage adjustment in bone marrow dysfunction: Heavily-treated patients, patients with pre-existing bone marrow depression or neoplastic bone marrow infiltration: Lower starting doses (75-90 mg/m^2) should be considered.

Elderly: Plasma clearance of epirubicin in elderly female patients was noted to be reduced by 35%. Although no initial dosage reduction is specifically recommended, particular care should be exercised in monitoring toxicity and adjusting subsequent dosage in elderly patients (particularly females >70 years of age).

Dosage adjustment in renal impairment: Severe renal impairment (serum creatinine >5 mg/dL): Lower doses should be considered

Dosage adjustment in hepatic impairment:

Bilirubin 1.2-3 mg/dL or AST 2-4 times the upper limit of normal: 50% of recommended starting dose

Bilirubin >3 mg/dL or AST >4 times the upper limit of normal: 25% of recommended starting dose

Severe hepatic impairment: Use is contraindicated

Administration I.V.: Infuse over 15-20 minutes or slow I.V. push (for lower doses [due to dose modification or organ dysfunction]) over 3-10 minutes

Monitoring Parameters Monitor injection site during infusion for possible extravasation or local reactions; CBC with differential and platelet count, liver function tests, renal function, ECG, and left ventricular ejection fraction. Monitor during therapy for potential cardiotoxicity with ECHO or with MUGA scans (patients with higher cumulative doses).

(Continued)

Epirubicin *(Continued)*

Dosage Forms
Injection, powder for reconstitution, as hydrochloride, [preservative free]: 50 mg, 200 mg [contains lactose]

Injection, solution, as hydrochloride [preservative free]:
Ellence®: 2 mg/mL (25 mL, 100 mL)

♦ **Epirubicin Hydrochloride** *see* Epirubicin *on page 592*
♦ **Epitol®** *see* Carbamazepine *on page 284*
♦ **Epival® I.V. (Can)** *see* Valproic Acid and Derivatives *on page 1767*
♦ **Epivir®** *see* Lamivudine *on page 971*
♦ **Epivir-HBV®** *see* Lamivudine *on page 971*

Eplerenone *(e PLER en one)*

U.S. Brand Names Inspra™
Pharmacologic Category Diuretic, Potassium-Sparing; Selective Aldosterone Blocker
Use Treatment of hypertension (may be used alone or in combination with other antihypertensive agents); treatment of CHF following acute MI
Pregnancy Risk Factor B
Pregnancy Implications No teratogenic effects were seen in animal studies, however, there are no adequate and well-controlled studies in pregnant women. Use during pregnancy only if the potential benefit to the mother outweighs the possible risk to the fetus.
Lactation Excretion in breast milk unknown/not recommended
Medication Safety Issues
Sound-alike/look-alike issues:
Inspra™ may be confused with Spiriva®
Contraindications Hypersensitivity to eplerenone or any component of the formulation; serum potassium >5.5 mEq/L; Cl_{cr} ≤30 mL/minute; concomitant use of strong CYP3A4 inhibitors (see Drug Interactions for details)

The following additional contraindications apply to patients with hypertension: Type 2 diabetes mellitus (noninsulin dependent, NIDDM) with microalbuminuria; serum creatinine >2.0 mg/dL in males or >1.8 mg/dL in females; Cl_{cr} <50 mL/minute; concomitant use with potassium supplements or potassium-sparing diuretics
Warnings/Precautions Dosage adjustment needed for patients on moderate CYP3A4 inhibitors (see drug interactions for details). Monitor closely for hyperkalemia; increases in serum potassium were dose related during clinical trials and rates of hyperkalemia also increased with declining renal function. Safety and efficacy have not been established in pediatric patients or in patients with severe hepatic impairment. Use with caution in CHF patients post-MI with diabetes.
Adverse Reactions
>10%: Endocrine & metabolic: Hypertriglyceridemia (1% to 15%, dose related)
1% to 10%:
Central nervous system: Dizziness (3%), fatigue (2%)
Endocrine & metabolic: Breast pain (males <1% to 1%), creatinine increased (6% in CHF), gynecomastia (males <1% to 1%), hyponatremia (2%, dose related), hypercholesterolemia (<1% to 1%); hyperkalemia (mild-to-moderate hypertension <1%; left ventricular dysfunction ~6% had serum potassium ≥6 mEq/L)
Gastrointestinal: Diarrhea (2%), abdominal pain (1%)
Genitourinary: Abnormal vaginal bleeding (<1% to 2%)
Renal: Albuminuria (1%)
Respiratory: Cough (2%)
Miscellaneous: Flu-like syndrome (2%)
<1% (Limited to important or life-threatening): BUN increased, liver function tests increased, serum creatinine increased, uric acid increased
Overdosage/Toxicology Cases of human overdose have not been reported; hypotension or hyperkalemia would be expected. Treatment should be symptom-directed and supportive. Eplerenone is not removed by hemodialysis; binds extensively to charcoal.
Drug Interactions
Cytochrome P450 Effect: Substrate of CYP3A4 (major)
Increased Effect/Toxicity: ACE inhibitors, angiotensin II receptor antagonists, NSAIDs, potassium supplements, and potassium-sparing diuretics increase the risk of hyperkalemia; concomitant use with potassium supplements and potassium-sparing diuretics is contraindicated; monitor potassium levels with ACE inhibitors and angiotensin II receptor antagonists. Potent CYP3A4 inhibitors (eg, itraconazole, ketoconazole) lead to fivefold increase in eplerenone; concurrent use is contraindicated. Less potent CYP3A4 inhibitors (eg, erythromycin, fluconazole, saquinavir, verapamil) lead to approximately twofold increase in eplerenone; starting dose should be decreased to 25 mg/day. Although interaction studies have not been conducted, monitoring of lithium levels is recommended.
Decreased Effect: NSAIDs may decrease the antihypertensive effects of eplerenone. CYP3A4 inducers may decrease the levels/effects of eplerenone; example inducers include aminoglutethimide, carbamazepine, nafcillin, nevirapine, phenobarbital, phenytoin, and rifamycins.
Ethanol/Nutrition/Herb Interactions
Food: Grapefruit juice increases eplerenone AUC ~25%.
Herb/Nutraceutical: St John's wort decreases eplerenone AUC ~30%.
Stability Store at controlled room temperature of 25°C (77°F).
Mechanism of Action Aldosterone increases blood pressure primarily by inducing sodium reabsorption. Eplerenone reduces blood pressure by blocking aldosterone binding at mineralocorticoid receptors found in the kidney, heart, blood vessels and brain.
Pharmacodynamics/Kinetics
Distribution: V_d: 43-90 L

Protein binding: ~50%; primarily to alpha$_1$-acid glycoproteins

Metabolism: Primarily hepatic via CYP3A4; metabolites inactive

Half-life elimination: 4-6 hours

Time to peak, plasma: 1.5 hours; may take up to 4 weeks for full therapeutic effect

Excretion: Urine (67%; <5% as unchanged drug), feces (32%)

Dosage Oral: Adults:

Hypertension: Initial: 50 mg once daily; may increase to 50 mg twice daily if response is not adequate; may take up to 4 weeks for full therapeutic response. Doses >100 mg/day are associated with increased risk of hyperkalemia and no greater therapeutic effect.

Concurrent use with moderate CYP3A4 inhibitors: Initial: 25 mg once daily

Congestive heart failure (post-MI): Initial: 25 mg once daily; dosage goal: titrate to 50 mg once daily within 4 weeks, as tolerated

Dosage adjustment per serum potassium concentrations for CHF:

<5.0 mEq/L:

Increase dose from 25 mg every other day to 25 mg daily **or**

Increase dose from 25 mg daily to 50 mg daily

5.0-5.4 mEq/L: No adjustment needed

5.5-5.9 mEq/L:

Decrease dose from 50 mg daily to 25 mg daily **or**

Decrease dose from 25 mg daily to 25 mg every other day **or**

Decrease does from 25 mg every other day to withhold medication

≥6.0 mEq/L: Withhold medication until potassium <5.5 mEq/L, then restart at 25 mg every other day

Dosage adjustment in renal impairment:

Patients with hypertension with Cl$_{cr}$ <50 mL/minute or serum creatinine >2.0 mg/dL in males or >1.8 mg/dL in females: Use is contraindicated; risk of hyperkalemia increases with declining renal function

Patients with CHF post-MI: Use with caution

Dosage adjustment in hepatic impairment: No dosage adjustment needed for mild-to-moderate impairment; safety and efficacy not established for severe impairment

Dietary Considerations May be taken with or without food. Do not use salt substitutes containing potassium.

Administration May be administered with or without food.

Monitoring Parameters Blood pressure; serum potassium (levels monitored every 2 weeks for the first 1-2 months, then monthly in clinical trials); renal function

Dosage Forms Tablet: 25 mg, 50 mg

♦ **EPO** *see* Epoetin Alfa *on page 595*

Epoetin Alfa (e POE e tin AL fa)

U.S. Brand Names Epogen®; Procrit®

Canadian Brand Names Eprex®

Index Terms EPO; Erythropoietin; NSC-724223; rHuEPO-α

Pharmacologic Category Colony Stimulating Factor

Use Treatment of anemia related to HIV therapy, chronic renal failure, antineoplastic therapy (for nonmyeloid malignancies); reduction of allogeneic blood transfusion for elective, noncardiac, nonvascular surgery

Unlabeled/Investigational Use Anemia associated with rheumatic disease; hypogenerative anemia of Rh hemolytic disease; sickle cell anemia; acute renal failure; Gaucher's disease; Castleman's disease; paroxysmal nocturnal hemoglobinuria; anemia of critical illness (limited documentation); anemia of prematurity

Pregnancy Risk Factor C

Pregnancy Implications Epoetin alfa has been shown to have adverse effects (decreased weight gain, delayed development, delayed ossification) in animal studies. Studies suggest that rHuEPO-α does not cross the human placenta. Based on case reports, treatment with rHuEPO-α may be an option in pregnant women with ESRD on dialysis. Amenorrheic premenopausal women should be cautioned that menstruation may resume following treatment with rHuEPO-α and contraception should be considered if pregnancy is to be avoided.

Lactation Excretion in breast milk unknown/use caution

Medication Safety Issues

Sound-alike/look-alike issues:

Epoetin alfa may be confused with darbepoetin alfa

International issues:

Epopen® [Spain] may be confused with EpiPen® which is a brand name for epinephrine in the U.S.

Contraindications Hypersensitivity to erythropoietin, albumin (human) or mammalian cell-derived products, or any component of the formulation; uncontrolled hypertension

Warnings/Precautions Use caution with history of seizures or hypertension; blood pressure should be controlled prior to start of therapy and monitored closely throughout treatment. Excessive rate of rise of hematocrit may be possibly associated with the exacerbation of hypertension or seizures; decrease the epoetin dose if the hemoglobin increase exceeds 1 g/dL in any 2-week period. Use caution in patients at risk for thrombosis or with history of cardiovascular disease. Increased mortality has been observed when aggressive dosing is used in CHF or anginal patients undergoing hemodialysis. Multidose vials contain benzyl alcohol; do not use in premature infants.

Pure red cell aplasia (PRCA) with neutralizing antibodies to erythropoietin has been reported in patients treated with recombinant products; may occur more in patients with CRF. Patients should be evaluated for any loss of effect to therapy and treatment discontinued with evidence of PRCA. Response to therapy may be limited by multiple factors; refer to Additional Information for details.

Prior to and during therapy, iron stores must be evaluated; iron supplementation should be given during therapy. Use caution with porphyria, exacerbation of porphyria has been (Continued)

Epoetin Alfa (Continued)

reported in patients with chronic renal failure. Not recommended for acute correction of severe anemia or as a substitute for transfusion. Safety and efficacy in children <1 month of age have not been established.

Adverse Reactions

>10%:

Cardiovascular: Hypertension (5% to 24%), edema (6% to 17%)

Central nervous system: Fever (29% to 51%), dizziness (<7% to 21%), insomnia (13% to 21%), headache (10% to 19%)

Dermatologic: Pruritus (14% to 22%), skin pain (4% to 18%), rash (≤16%)

Gastrointestinal: Nausea (11% to 58%), constipation (42% to 53%), vomiting (8% to 29%), diarrhea (9% to 21%), dyspepsia (7% to 11%)

Genitourinary: Urinary tract infection (3% to 12%)

Local: Injection site reaction (<10% to 29%)

Neuromuscular & skeletal: Arthralgia (11%), paresthesia (11%)

Respiratory: Cough (18%), congestion (15%), dyspnea (13% to 14%), upper respiratory infection (11%)

1% to 10%:

Cardiovascular: Deep vein thrombosis (3% to 10%)

Central nervous system: Seizure (1% to 3%)

Local: Clotted vascular access (7%)

<1% (Limited to important or life-threatening): Allergic reaction, anemia (severe; with or without other cytopenias), CVA, flu-like syndrome, hyperkalemia, hypersensitivity reactions, hypertensive encephalopathy, microvascular thrombosis, MI, myalgia, neutralizing antibodies, pulmonary embolism, pure red cell aplasia, thrombophlebitis, tachycardia, thrombosis, TIA, urticaria

Overdosage/Toxicology Symptoms include erythrocytosis and polycythemia. Doses of up to 1500 units/kg 3 times a week for 3-4 weeks have been administered to adults. Phlebotomy may be indicated for polycythemia; treatment is otherwise symptom-directed and supportive.

Stability

Vials should be stored at 2°C to 8°C (36°F to 46°F); **do not freeze or shake**.

Single-dose 1 mL vial contains no preservative: Use one dose per vial. Do not re-enter vial; discard unused portions.

Single-dose vials (except 40,000 units/mL vial) are stable for 2 weeks at room temperature.

Single-dose 40,000 units/mL vial is stable for 1 week at room temperature.

Multidose 1 mL or 2 mL vial contains preservative. Store at 2°C to 8°C after initial entry and between doses. Discard 21 days after initial entry.

Multidose vials (with preservative) are stable for 1 week at room temperature.

Prefilled syringes containing the 20,000 units/mL formulation with preservative are stable for 6 weeks refrigerated (2°C to 8°C).

Dilutions of 1:10 and 1:20 (1 part epoetin:19 parts sodium chloride) are stable for 18 hours at room temperature.

Prior to SubQ administration, preservative free solutions may be mixed with bacteriostatic NS containing benzyl alcohol 0.9% in a 1:1 ratio. Dilutions of 1:10 in $D_{10}W$ with human albumin 0.05% or 0.1% are stable for 24 hours.

Mechanism of Action Induces erythropoiesis by stimulating the division and differentiation of committed erythroid progenitor cells; induces the release of reticulocytes from the bone marrow into the bloodstream, where they mature to erythrocytes. There is a dose response relationship with this effect. This results in an increase in reticulocyte counts followed by a rise in hematocrit and hemoglobin levels.

Pharmacodynamics/Kinetics

Onset of action: Several days

Peak effect: 2-3 weeks

Distribution: V_d: 9 L; rapid in the plasma compartment; concentrated in liver, kidneys, and bone marrow

Metabolism: Some degradation does occur

Bioavailability: SubQ: ~21% to 31%; intraperitoneal epoetin: 3% (a few patients)

Half-life elimination: Cancer: SubQ: 16-67 hours; Chronic renal failure: 4-13 hours

Time to peak, serum: Chronic renal failure: 5-13 hours

Excretion: Feces (majority); urine (small amounts, 10% unchanged in normal volunteers)

Dosage

Chronic renal failure patients: I.V., SubQ:

Children: Initial dose: 50 units/kg 3 times/week

Adults: Initial dose: 50-100 units/kg 3 times/week

Dose adjustment: Children and Adults: Reduce dose by 25% when hemoglobin approaches 12 g/dL **or** hemoglobin increases 1 g/dL in any 2-week period. Increase dose by 25% if hemoglobin does not increase by 2 g/dL after 8 weeks of therapy (with adequate iron stores, may increase dose by 25% if hemoglobin increase <1 g/dL over 4 weeks) and hemoglobin is below suggested target range. Suggested target hemoglobin range: 10-12 g/dL. Do not increase dose more frequently than at 4-week intervals.

Maintenance dose: Individualize to target range; limit additional dosage increases to every 4 weeks (or longer)

Dialysis patients: Median dose:

Children: 167 units/kg/week (hemodialysis) **or** 76 units/kg/week (peritoneal dialysis)

Adults: 75 units/kg 3 times/week

Nondialysis patients:

Children: Dosing range: 50-250 units/kg 1-3 times/week

Adults: Median dose: 75-150 units/kg/week

Zidovudine-treated, HIV-infected patients (patients with erythropoietin levels >500 mU/mL are **unlikely** to respond): I.V., SubQ:

Children: Initial dose: Reported dosing range: 50-400 units/kg 2-3 times/week

Adults: 100 units/kg 3 times/week for 8 weeks. **Dose adjustment:** Increase dose by 50-100 units/kg 3 times/week if response is not satisfactory in terms of reducing transfusion requirements or increasing hemoglobin after 8 weeks of therapy. Evaluate response every 4-8 weeks thereafter and adjust the dose accordingly by 50-100 units/kg increments 3 times/week. If patient has not responded satisfactorily to a 300 unit/kg dose 3 times/week, a response to higher doses is unlikely. Stop dose if hemoglobin exceeds 13 g/dL and resume treatment at a 25% dose reduction when hemoglobin drops to 12 g/dL.

Cancer patient on chemotherapy: Treatment of patients with erythropoietin levels >200 mU/mL is **not recommended**

Children: I.V.: 600 units/kg once weekly (maximum: 40,000 units)

Adults: SubQ: Initial dose: 150 units/kg 3 times/week or 40,000 units once weekly; commonly used doses range from 10,000 units 3 times/week to 40,000-60,000 units once weekly.

Dose adjustment: Children and Adults: If response is not satisfactory after a sufficient period of evaluation (8 weeks of 3 times/week and 4 weeks of once-weekly therapy), the dose may be increased every 4 weeks (or longer) up to 300 units/kg 3 times/week, **or** when dosed weekly, increased all at once to 60,000 units weekly (adults) or 900 units/kg/ week; maximum 60,000 units (pediatrics). If patient does not respond, a response to higher doses is unlikely. Stop dose if hemoglobin exceeds 13 g/dL and resume treatment at a 25% dose reduction when hemoglobin drops to 12 g/dL; reduce dose by 25% if hemoglobin increases by 1 g/dL in any 2-week period, or if hemoglobin approaches 12 g/ dL.

Alternative dose (unlabeled dosing): Adults: SubQ: Initial dose: 60,000 units once weekly for 8 weeks. **Dose adjustment:** If patient does not respond, a response to higher doses is unlikely. If response is adequate (hemoglobin increases >2 g/dL after 8 weeks), begin maintenance dose of 120,000 units, to be given once every 3 weeks. During any point of initial or maintenance therapy, if the hemoglobin increases 1.3 g/dL in a 2-week period, decrease dose to 40,000 units once weekly. Stop dose if hemoglobin exceeds 15 g/dL and resume treatment at 20,000 units once-weekly when hemoglobin drops to 13 g/dL (Patton, 2003).

Surgery patients: Prior to initiating treatment, obtain a hemoglobin to establish that is >10 mg/dL or ≤13 mg/dL: Adults: SubQ: Initial dose: 300 units/kg/day for 10 days before surgery, on the day of surgery, and for 4 days after surgery

Alternative dose: 600 units/kg in once weekly doses (21, 14, and 7 days before surgery) plus a fourth dose on the day of surgery

Anemia of critical illness (unlabeled use): Adults: SubQ: 40,000 units once weekly

Anemia of prematurity (unlabeled use): Infants: I.V., SubQ: Dosing range: 500-1250 units/kg/ week; commonly used dose: 250 units/kg 3 times/week; supplement with oral iron therapy 3-8 mg/kg/day

Dosage adjustment in renal impairment:

Hemodialysis: Supplemental dose is not necessary.

Peritoneal dialysis: Supplemental dose is not necessary.

Administration SubQ, I.M. (I.V. not recommended unless on hemodialysis; I.V. administration may require up to 40% more drug as SubQ/I.M. administration to achieve the same therapeutic result)

Patients with CRF on dialysis: I.V. route preferred; may be administered I.V. bolus into the venous line after dialysis.

Patients with CRF not on dialysis: May be administered I.V. or SubQ

Monitoring Parameters Blood pressure; hematocrit/hemoglobin, CBC with differential and platelets, transferring saturation and ferritin

Suggested tests to be monitored and their frequency: See table.

Test	Initial Phase Frequency	Maintenance Phase Frequency
Hematocrit/hemoglobin	2 x/week	2-4 x/month
Blood pressure	3 x/week	3 x/week
Serum ferritin	Monthly	Quarterly
Transferrin saturation	Monthly	Quarterly
Serum chemistries including CBC with differential, creatinine, blood urea nitrogen, potassium, phosphorous	Regularly per routine	Regularly per routine

Hematocrit should be determined twice weekly until stabilization within the target range (30% to 36%), and twice weekly for at least 2-6 weeks after a dose increase. It may take 6-8 weeks to begin to see an effect and may take 16 weeks to see full therapeutic effect.

Reference Range Guidelines should be based on the following figure or published literature Guidelines for estimating appropriateness of endogenous EPO levels for varying levels of anemia via the EIA assay method: See figure on next page. The reference range for erythropoietin in serum, for subjects with normal hemoglobin and hematocrit, is 4.1-22.2 mU/mL by the EIA method. Erythropoietin levels are typically inversely related to hemoglobin (and hematocrit) levels in anemias not attributed to impaired erythropoietin production.

Zidovudine-treated HIV patients: Available evidence indicates patients with endogenous serum erythropoietin levels >500 mU/mL are unlikely to respond

Cancer chemotherapy patients: Treatment of patients with endogenous serum erythropoietin levels >200 mU/mL is not recommended

Serum EPO levels can be ordered routinely from clinical chemistry (red top serum separator tube).

Additional Information Due to the delayed onset of erythropoiesis (7-10 days to increase reticulocyte count; 2-6 weeks to increase hemoglobin), erythropoietin is of no value in the acute treatment of anemia.

Professional Services:

Amgen (Epogen®): 1-800-772-6436

Ortho Biotech (Procrit®): 1-800-325-7504

(Continued)

Epoetin Alfa *(Continued)*

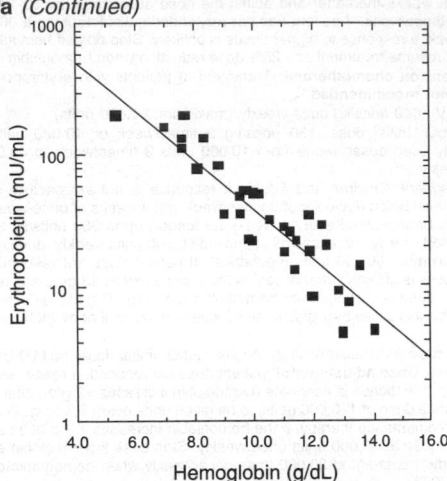

Factors Limiting Response to Epoetin Alfa

Factor	Mechanism
Iron deficiency	Limits hemoglobin synthesis
Blood loss/hemolysis	Counteracts epoetin alfa-stimulated erythropoiesis
Infection/inflammation	Inhibits iron transfer from storage to bone marrow
	Suppresses erythropoiesis through activated macrophages
Aluminum overload	Inhibits iron incorporation into heme protein
Bone marrow replacement Hyperparathyroidism Metastatic, neoplastic	Limits bone marrow volume
Folic acid/vitamin B_{12} deficiency	Limits hemoglobin synthesis
Patient compliance	Self-administered epoetin alfa or iron therapy

Reimbursement Assistance:
Amgen: 1-800-272-9376
Ortho Biotech: 1-800-553-3851

Dosage Forms

Injection, solution [preservative free]: 2000 units/mL (1 mL); 3000 units/mL (1 mL); 4000 units/mL (1 mL); 10,000 units/mL (1 mL); 40,000 units/mL (1 mL) [contains human albumin]

Injection, solution [with preservative]: 10,000 units/mL (2 mL); 20,000 units/mL (1 mL) [contains human albumin and benzyl alcohol]

♦ **Epogen®** *see* Epoetin Alfa *on page 595*

Epoprostenol (e poe PROST en ole)

U.S. Brand Names Flolan®

Canadian Brand Names Flolan®

Index Terms Epoprostenol Sodium; PGI_2; PGX; Prostacyclin

Pharmacologic Category Prostaglandin

Use Treatment of idiopathic pulmonary arterial hypertension [IPAH]; pulmonary hypertension associated with the scleroderma spectrum of disease [SSD] in NYHA Class III and Class IV patients who do not respond adequately to conventional therapy

Restrictions Orders for epoprostenol are distributed by two sources in the United States. Information on orders or reimbursement assistance may be obtained from either Accredo Health, Inc (1-800-935-6526) or TheraCom, Inc (1-877-356-5264).

Pregnancy Risk Factor B

Pregnancy Implications Teratogenic effects were not reported in animal studies. There are no adequate and well-controlled studies in pregnant women. Pregnant women with IPAH are encouraged to avoid pregnancy.

Lactation Excretion in breast milk unknown/use caution

Contraindications Hypersensitivity to epoprostenol or to structurally-related compounds; chronic use in patients with CHF due to severe left ventricular systolic dysfunction; patients who develop pulmonary edema during dose initiation

Warnings/Precautions Abrupt interruptions or large sudden reductions in dosage may result in rebound pulmonary hypertension; some patients with primary pulmonary hypertension have developed pulmonary edema during dose ranging, which may be associated with pulmonary veno-occlusive disease; during chronic use, unless contraindicated, anticoagulants should be coadministered to reduce the risk of thromboembolism. Clinical studies of epoprostenol in pulmonary hypertension did not include sufficient numbers of patients ≥65 years of age to substantiate its safety and efficacy in the geriatric population. As a result, in general, dose selection for an elderly patient should be cautious usually starting at the low end of the dosing range.

Adverse Reactions

Note: Adverse events reported during dose initiation and escalation include flushing (58%), headache (49%), nausea/vomiting (32%), hypotension (16%), anxiety/nervousness/agitation (11%), chest pain (11%); abdominal pain, back pain, bradycardia, diaphoresis, dizziness, dyspepsia, dyspnea, hypoesthesia/paresthesia, musculoskeletal pain, and tachycardia are also reported. The following adverse events have been reported during chronic administration for IPAH. Although some may be related to the underlying disease state, anxiety, diarrhea, flu-like syndrome, flushing, headache, jaw pain, nausea, nervousness, and vomiting are clearly contributed to epoprostenol.

>10%:

Cardiovascular: Chest pain (67%), palpitation (63%), flushing (42%), tachycardia (35%), arrhythmia (27%), hemorrhage (19%), bradycardia (15%)

Central nervous system: Dizziness (83%), headache (83%), chills/fever/sepsis/flu-like syndrome (25%), anxiety/nervousness/tremor (21%)

Gastrointestinal: Nausea/vomiting (67%), diarrhea (37%)

Genitourinary: Weight loss (27%)

Local: Injection site reactions: Infection (21%), pain (13%)

Neuromuscular & skeletal: Weakness (87%), jaw pain (54%), myalgia (44%), musculoskeletal pain (35%; predominantly involving legs and feet), hypoesthesia/hyperparesthesia/paresthesia (12%)

Respiratory: Dyspnea (90%)

1% to 10%:

Cardiovascular: Supraventricular tachycardia (8%), cerebrovascular accident (4%)

Central nervous system: Convulsion (4%)

Dermatologic: Rash (10%; conventional therapy 13%), pruritus (4%)

Endocrine & metabolic: Hypokalemia (6%)

Gastrointestinal: Constipation (6%), weight gain (6%)

Neuromuscular & skeletal: Arthralgia (6%)

Ocular: Amblyopia (8%), vision abnormality (4%)

Respiratory: Epistaxis (4%), pleural effusion (4%)

<1% (Limited to important or life-threatening): Anemia, ascites, hypersplenism, hyperthyroidism, pancytopenia, splenomegaly, thrombocytopenia

Overdosage/Toxicology
Symptoms include headache, hypotension, tachycardia, nausea, vomiting, diarrhea, and flushing. If any of these symptoms occur, the infusion rate should be reduced until symptoms subside. If symptoms do not subside, consider drug discontinuation. Fatal cases of hypoxemia, hypotension, and respiratory arrest have been reported. Long-term overdose may lead to high output cardiac failure. failure.

Drug Interactions

Increased Effect/Toxicity: The hypotensive effects of epoprostenol may be exacerbated by other vasodilators, diuretics, or by using acetate in dialysis fluids. Patients treated with anticoagulants (heparins, warfarin, thrombin inhibitors) or antiplatelet agents (ticlopidine, clopidogrel, IIb/IIIa antagonists, aspirin) and epoprostenol should be monitored for increased bleeding risk.

Stability Prior to use, store vials at 15°C to 25°C (59°F to 77°F); do not freeze. Protect from light. Reconstitute with provided sterile diluent. Following reconstitution, solution must be stored under refrigeration at 2°C to 8°C (36°F to 46°F) if not used immediately; do not freeze. Protect from light. Discard if refrigerated for >48 hours. See table. During use, a single reservoir of solution may be used at room temperature for a total duration of 8 hours, or used with a cold pouch for administration up to 24 hours. Cold packs should be changed every 12 hours.

Preparation of Epoprostenol Infusion

To make 100 mL of solution with concentration:	Directions
3000 ng/mL	Dissolve one 0.5 mg vial with 5 mL supplied diluent, withdraw 3 mL, and add to sufficient diluent to make a total of 100 mL.
5000 ng/mL	Dissolve one 0.5 mg vial with 5 mL supplied diluent, withdraw entire vial contents, and add a sufficient volume of diluent to make a total of 100 mL.
10,000 ng/mL	Dissolve two 0.5 mg vials each with 5 mL supplied diluent, withdraw entire vial contents, and add a sufficient volume of diluent to make a total of 100 mL.
15,000 ng/mL	Dissolve one 1.5 mg vial with 5 mL supplied diluent, withdraw entire vial contents, and add a sufficient volume of diluent to make a total of 100 mL.

Mechanism of Action Epoprostenol is also known as prostacyclin and PGI_2. It is a strong vasodilator of all vascular beds. In addition, it is a potent endogenous inhibitor of platelet aggregation. The reduction in platelet aggregation results from epoprostenol's activation of intracellular adenylate cyclase and the resultant increase in cyclic adenosine monophosphate concentrations within the platelets. Additionally, it is capable of decreasing thrombogenesis and platelet clumping in the lungs by inhibiting platelet aggregation.

Pharmacodynamics/Kinetics

Metabolism: Rapidly hydrolyzed; subject to some enzymatic degradation; forms one active metabolite and 13 inactive metabolites

Half-life elimination: 6 minutes

Excretion: Urine (84%); feces (4%)

Dosage Children (unlabeled use) and Adults; I.V.: Initial: 1-2 ng/kg/minute, increase dose in increments of 1-2 ng/kg/minute every 15 minutes or longer until dose-limiting side effects are noted or tolerance limit to epoprostenol is observed

(Continued)

Epoprostenol *(Continued)*

Dose adjustment:

Increase dose in 1-2 ng/kg/minute increments at intervals of at least 15 minutes if symptoms persist or recur following improvement. In clinical trials, dosing increases occurred at intervals of 24-48 hours.

Decrease dose in 2 ng/kg/minute decrements at intervals of at least 15 minutes in case of dose-limiting pharmacologic events. Avoid abrupt withdrawal or sudden large dose reductions.

Lung transplant: In patients receiving lung transplants, epoprostenol was tapered after the initiation of cardiopulmonary bypass.

Administration The ambulatory infusion pump should be small and lightweight, be able to adjust infusion rates in 2 ng/kg/minute increments, have occlusion, end of infusion, and low battery alarms, have ± 6% accuracy of the programmed rate, and have positive continuous or pulsatile pressure with intervals ≤3 minutes between pulses. The reservoir should be made of polyvinyl chloride, polypropylene, or glass. The infusion pump used in the most recent clinical trial was CADD-1 HFX 5100 (Pharmacia Deltec).

Monitoring Parameters Monitor for improvements in pulmonary function, decreased exertional dyspnea, fatigue, syncope and chest pain, pulmonary vascular resistance, pulmonary arterial pressure and quality of life. In addition, the pump device and catheters should be monitored frequently to avoid "system" related failure. Monitor arterial pressure; assess all vital functions. Hypoxia, flushing, and tachycardia may indicate overdose.

Dosage Forms Injection, powder for reconstitution, as sodium: 0.5 mg, 1.5 mg [provided with 50 mL sterile diluent]

♦ **Epoprostenol Sodium** *see* Epoprostenol *on page 598*

♦ **Eprex® (Can)** *see* Epoetin Alfa *on page 595*

Eprosartan *(ep roe SAR tan)*

U.S. Brand Names Teveten®

Canadian Brand Names Teveten®

Pharmacologic Category Angiotensin II Receptor Blocker

Additional Appendix Information

Angiotensin Agents *on page 1860*

Use Treatment of hypertension; may be used alone or in combination with other antihypertensives

Pregnancy Risk Factor C (1st trimester); D (2nd and 3rd trimesters)

Pregnancy Implications Discontinue as soon as possible when pregnancy is detected. Drugs that act directly on renin-angiotensin can cause fetal and neonatal morbidity and death. Adverse effects to the fetus appear to be limited to the 2nd and 3rd trimesters.

Lactation Not recommended

Contraindications Hypersensitivity to eprosartan or any component of the formulation; sensitivity to other A-II receptor antagonists; bilateral renal artery stenosis; pregnancy

Warnings/Precautions [U.S. Boxed Warning]: Based on human data, drugs that act on the angiotensin system can cause injury and death to the developing fetus when used in the second and third trimesters. Angiotensin receptor blockers should be discontinued as soon as possible once pregnancy is detected. May cause hyperkalemia; avoid potassium supplementation unless specifically required by healthcare provider. Avoid use or use a smaller dose in patients who are volume depleted; correct depletion first. May be associated with deterioration of renal function and/or increases in serum creatinine, particularly in patients dependent on renin-angiotensin-aldosterone system. Use with caution in unilateral renal artery stenosis and pre-existing renal insufficiency; significant aortic/mitral stenosis. Safety and efficacy not established in pediatric patients.

Adverse Reactions

1% to 10%:

Central nervous system: Fatigue (2%), depression (1%)

Endocrine & metabolic: Hypertriglyceridemia (1%)

Gastrointestinal: Abdominal pain (2%)

Genitourinary: Urinary tract infection (1%)

Respiratory: Upper respiratory tract infection (8%), rhinitis (4%), pharyngitis (4%), cough (4%)

Miscellaneous: Viral infection (2%), injury (2%)

<1% (Limited to important or life-threatening): Abnormal ECG, angina, arthritis, asthma, ataxia, bradycardia, BUN increased, creatinine increased, eczema, edema, esophagitis, ethanol intolerance, gingivitis, gout, hypotension, influenza-like symptoms, leg cramps, leukopenia, maculopapular rash, migraine, neuritis, neutropenia, orthostasis, palpitation, paresthesia, peripheral ischemia, purpura, renal calculus, somnolence, tachycardia, tendonitis, thrombocytopenia, tinnitus, tremor, urinary incontinence, vertigo; rhabdomyolysis has been reported (rarely) with angiotensin-receptor antagonists.

Overdosage/Toxicology The most likely manifestations of overdose would be hypotension and tachycardia. Initiate supportive care for symptomatic hypotension.

Drug Interactions

Cytochrome P450 Effect: Inhibits CYP2C9 (weak)

Increased Effect/Toxicity: Eprosartan may increase risk of lithium toxicity. May increase risk of hyperkalemia with potassium-sparing diuretics (eg, amiloride, potassium, spironolactone, triamterene), potassium supplements, or high doses of trimethoprim.

Ethanol/Nutrition/Herb Interactions Herb/Nutraceutical: Avoid dong quai if using for hypertension (has estrogenic activity). Avoid ephedra, yohimbe, ginseng (may worsen hypertension). Avoid garlic (may have increased antihypertensive effect).

Mechanism of Action Angiotensin II is formed from angiotensin I in a reaction catalyzed by angiotensin-converting enzyme (ACE, kininase II). Angiotensin II is the principal pressor agent of the renin-angiotensin system, with effects that include vasoconstriction, stimulation of synthesis and release of aldosterone, cardiac stimulation, and renal reabsorption of sodium. Eprosartan blocks the vasoconstrictor and aldosterone-secreting effects of angiotensin II by selectively blocking the binding of angiotensin II to the AT1 receptor in many tissues, such as vascular smooth muscle and the adrenal gland. Its action is therefore independent of the pathways for angiotensin II synthesis. Blockade of the renin-angiotensin system with ACE inhibitors, which inhibit the biosynthesis of angiotensin II from angiotensin I, is widely used in the treatment of hypertension. ACE inhibitors also inhibit the degradation of bradykinin, a reaction also catalyzed by ACE. Because eprosartan does not inhibit ACE (kininase II), it does not affect the response to bradykinin. Whether this difference has clinical relevance is not yet known. Eprosartan does not bind to or block other hormone receptors or ion channels known to be important in cardiovascular regulation.

Pharmacodynamics/Kinetics
Protein binding: 98%
Metabolism: Minimally hepatic
Bioavailability: 300 mg dose: 13%
Half-life elimination: Terminal: 5-9 hours
Time to peak, serum: Fasting: 1-2 hours
Excretion: Feces (90%); urine (7%, mostly as unchanged drug)
Clearance: 7.9 L/hour

Dosage Adults: Oral: Dosage must be individualized; can administer once or twice daily with total daily doses of 400-800 mg. Usual starting dose is 600 mg once daily as monotherapy in patients who are euvolemic. Limited clinical experience with doses >800 mg.
Dosage adjustment in renal impairment: No starting dosage adjustment is necessary; however, carefully monitor the patient
Dosage adjustment in hepatic impairment: No starting dosage adjustment is necessary; however, carefully monitor the patient
Elderly: No starting dosage adjustment is necessary; however, carefully monitor the patient
Dosage Forms Tablet: 400 mg, 600 mg

Eprosartan and Hydrochlorothiazide
(ep roe SAR tan & hye droe klor oh THYE a zide)

U.S. Brand Names Teveten® HCT
Canadian Brand Names Teveten® HCT; Teveten® Plus
Index Terms Eprosartan Mesylate and Hydrochlorothiazide; Hydrochlorothiazide and Eprosartan
Pharmacologic Category Angiotensin II Receptor Blocker Combination; Antihypertensive Agent, Combination; Diuretic, Thiazide
Use Treatment of hypertension (not indicated for initial treatment)
Pregnancy Risk Factor C/D (2nd and 3rd trimesters)
Dosage Oral: Adults: Dose is individualized (combination substituted for individual components)
Usual recommended dose: Eprosartan 600 mg/hydrochlorothiazide 12.5 mg once daily (maximum dose: Eprosartan 600 mg/hydrochlorothiazide 25 mg once daily)
Dosage adjustment in renal impairment: Initial dose adjustments not recommended by manufacturer; carefully monitor patient. Hydrochlorothiazide is ineffective in patients with Cl$_{cr}$ <30 mL/minute.
Dosage adjustment in hepatic impairment: Initial dose adjustments not recommended by manufacturer; carefully monitor patient.
Additional Information Complete prescribing information for this medication should be consulted for additional detail.
Dosage Forms Tablet:
600 mg/12.5 mg: Eprosartan 600 mg and hydrochlorothiazide 12.5 mg
600 mg/25 mg: Eprosartan 600 mg and hydrochlorothiazide 25 mg

♦ **Eprosartan Mesylate and Hydrochlorothiazide** see Eprosartan and Hydrochlorothiazide on page 601
♦ **Epsilon Aminocaproic Acid** see Aminocaproic Acid on page 93
♦ **Epsom Salts** see Magnesium Sulfate on page 1052
♦ **EPT** see Teniposide on page 1645
♦ **Eptacog Alfa (Activated)** see Factor VIIa (Recombinant) on page 678

Eptifibatide (ep TIF i ba tide)

U.S. Brand Names Integrilin®
Canadian Brand Names Integrilin®
Index Terms Intrifiban
Pharmacologic Category Antiplatelet Agent, Glycoprotein IIb/IIIa Inhibitor
Additional Appendix Information
Glycoprotein Antagonists on page 1884
Use Treatment of patients with acute coronary syndrome (unstable angina/non-Q wave myocardial infarction [UA/NQMI]), including patients who are to be managed medically and those undergoing percutaneous coronary intervention (PCI including angioplasty, intracoronary stenting)
Pregnancy Risk Factor B
Pregnancy Implications Teratogenic effects were not observed in animal studies.
Lactation Excretion in breast milk unknown/use caution
Contraindications Hypersensitivity to eptifibatide or any component of the product; active abnormal bleeding or a history of bleeding diathesis within the previous 30 days; history of CVA within 30 days or a history of hemorrhagic stroke; severe hypertension (systolic blood pressure >200 mm Hg or diastolic blood pressure >110 mm Hg) not adequately controlled on antihypertensive therapy; major surgery within the preceding 6 weeks; current or planned administration of another parenteral GP IIb/IIIa inhibitor; thrombocytopenia; dependency on renal dialysis
(Continued)

Eptifibatide *(Continued)*

Warnings/Precautions Bleeding is the most common complication. Most major bleeding occurs at the arterial access site where the cardiac catheterization was done. When bleeding can not be controlled with pressure, discontinue infusion and heparin. Use caution in patients with hemorrhagic retinopathy or with other drugs that affect hemostasis. Concurrent use with thrombolytics has not been established as safe. Minimize other procedures including arterial and venous punctures, I.M. injections, nasogastric tubes, etc. Prior to sheath removal, the aPTT or ACT should be checked (do not remove unless aPTT is <45 seconds or the ACT <150 seconds). Use caution in renal dysfunction (estimated Cl$_{cr}$ <50 mL/minute); dosage adjustment required. Safety and efficacy in pediatric patients have not been determined.

Adverse Reactions Bleeding is the major drug-related adverse effect. Access site is often primary source of bleeding complications. Incidence of bleeding is also related to heparin intensity. Patients weighing <70 kg may have an increased risk of major bleeding.

>10%: Hematologic: Bleeding (major: 1% to 11%; minor: 3% to 14%; transfusion required: 2% to 13%)

1% to 10%:
Cardiovascular: Hypotension (up to 7%)
Hematologic: Thrombocytopenia (1% to 3%)
Local: Injection site reaction

<1% (Limited to important or life-threatening): Acute profound thrombocytopenia, anaphylaxis, fatal bleeding events, GI hemorrhage, intracranial hemorrhage (0.5% to 0.7%), pulmonary hemorrhage, stroke

Overdosage/Toxicology Two cases of human overdosage have been reported. Neither case was eventful and were not associated with major bleeding. Symptoms of overdose in animal studies include loss of righting reflex, dyspnea, ptosis, decreased muscle tone, and petechial hemorrhages. Dialysis may be beneficial.

Drug Interactions

Increased Effect/Toxicity: Eptifibatide effect may be increased by other drugs which affect hemostasis include thrombolytics, oral anticoagulants, NSAIDs, dipyridamole, heparin, low molecular weight heparins, ticlopidine, and clopidogrel. Avoid concomitant use of other IIb/IIIa inhibitors. Cephalosporins which contain the MTT side chain may theoretically increase the risk of hemorrhage. Use with aspirin and heparin may increase bleeding over aspirin and heparin alone. However, aspirin and heparin were used concurrently in the majority of patients in the major clinical studies of eptifibatide. Antiplatelet agents (eg, eptifibatide) may enhance the adverse/toxic effect of drotrecogin alfa; bleeding may occur.

Ethanol/Nutrition/Herb Interactions Herb/Nutraceutical: Avoid alfalfa, anise, bilberry, bladderwrack, bromelain, cat's claw, celery, coleus, cordyceps, dong quai, evening primrose oil, fenugreek, feverfew, garlic, ginger, ginkgo biloba, ginseng (American), ginseng (Panax), ginseng (Siberian), grape seed, green tea, guggul, horse chestnut seed, horseradish, licorice, prickly ash, red clover, reishi, same (s-adenosylmethionine), sweet clover, turmeric, and white willow (all have additional antiplatelet activity).

Stability Vials should be stored refrigerated at 2°C to 8°C (36°F to 46°F). Vials can be kept at room temperature for 2 months. Protect from light until administration. Do not use beyond the expiration date. Discard any unused portion left in the vial.

Mechanism of Action Eptifibatide is a cyclic heptapeptide which blocks the platelet glycoprotein IIb/IIIa receptor, the binding site for fibrinogen, von Willebrand factor, and other ligands. Inhibition of binding at this final common receptor reversibly blocks platelet aggregation and prevents thrombosis.

Pharmacodynamics/Kinetics

Onset of action: Within 1 hour
Duration: Platelet function restored ~4 hours following discontinuation
Protein binding: ~25%
Half-life elimination: 2.5 hours
Excretion: Primarily urine (as eptifibatide and metabolites); significant renal impairment may alter disposition of this compound
Clearance: Total body: 55-58 mL/kg/hour; Renal: ~50% of total in healthy subjects

Dosage I.V.: Adults:

Acute coronary syndrome: Bolus of 180 mcg/kg (maximum: 22.6 mg) over 1-2 minutes, begun as soon as possible following diagnosis, followed by a continuous infusion of 2 mcg/kg/minute (maximum: 15 mg/hour) until hospital discharge or initiation of CABG surgery, up to 72 hours. Concurrent aspirin and heparin therapy (target aPTT 50-70 seconds) are recommended.

Percutaneous coronary intervention (PCI) with or without stenting: Bolus of 180 mcg/kg (maximum: 22.6 mg) administered immediately before the initiation of PCI, followed by a continuous infusion of 2 mcg/kg/minute (maximum: 15 mg/hour). A second 180 mcg/kg bolus (maximum: 22.6 mg) should be administered 10 minutes after the first bolus. Infusion should be continued until hospital discharge or for up to 18-24 hours, whichever comes first. Concurrent aspirin (160-325 mg 1-24 hours before PCI and daily thereafter) and heparin therapy (ACT 200-300 seconds during PCI) are recommended. Heparin infusion after PCI is discouraged. In patients who undergo coronary artery bypass graft surgery, discontinue infusion prior to surgery.

Elderly: No dosing adjustment for the elderly appears to be necessary; adjust carefully to renal function.

Dosing adjustment in renal impairment: Dialysis is a contraindication to use.

Note: The Cockroft-Gault equation using actual body weight sould be used to estimate renal function.

Acute coronary syndrome: Cl$_{cr}$ <50 mL/minute: Use 180 mcg/kg bolus (maximum: 22.6 mg) and 1 mcg/kg/minute infusion (maximum: 7.5 mg/hour)
Percutaneous coronary intervention (PCI) with or without stenting: Cl$_{cr}$ <50 mL/minute: Use 180 mcg/kg bolus (maximum: 22.6 mg) administered immediately before the initiation of PCI and followed by a continuous infusion of 1 mcg/kg/minute (maximum: 7.5 mg/hour).

A second 180 mcg/kg (maximum: 22.6 mg) bolus should be administered 10 minutes after the first bolus.

Administration Do not shake vial. Visually inspect for discoloration or particulate matter prior to administration. The bolus dose should be withdrawn from the 10 mL vial into a syringe and administered by I.V. push over 1-2 minutes. Begin continuous infusion immediately following bolus administration, administered directly from the 100 mL vial. The 100 mL vial should be spiked with a vented infusion set.

Monitoring Parameters Coagulation parameters, signs/symptoms of excessive bleeding. Laboratory tests at baseline and monitoring during therapy: hematocrit and hemoglobin, platelet count, serum creatinine, PT/aPTT (maintain aPTT between 50-70 seconds unless PCI is to be performed), and ACT with PCI (maintain ACT between 200-300 seconds during PCI).

Assess sheath insertion site and distal pulses of affected leg every 15 minutes for the first hour and then every 1 hour for the next 6 hours. Arterial access site care is important to prevent bleeding. Care should be taken when attempting vascular access that only the anterior wall of the femoral artery is punctured, avoiding a Seldinger (through and through) technique for obtaining sheath access. Femoral vein sheath placement should be avoided unless needed. While the vascular sheath is in place, patients should be maintained on complete bed rest with the head of the bed at a 30° angle and the affected limb restrained in a straight position.

Observe patient for mental status changes, hemorrhage, assess nose and mouth mucous membranes, puncture sites for oozing, ecchymosis and hematoma formation, and examine urine, stool and emesis for presence of occult or frank blood; gentle care should be provided when removing dressings.

Dosage Forms Injection, solution: 0.75 mg/mL (100 mL); 2 mg/mL (10 mL, 100 mL)

- ◆ **Epzicom™** *see* Abacavir and Lamivudine *on page 19*
- ◆ **Equagesic®** *see* Aspirin and Meprobamate *on page 164*
- ◆ **Equanil** *see* Meprobamate *on page 1085*
- ◆ **Equetro™** *see* Carbamazepine *on page 284*
- ◆ **Eraxis™** *see* Anidulafungin *on page 131*
- ◆ **Erbitux®** *see* Cetuximab *on page 336*

Ergocalciferol (er goe kal SIF e role)

U.S. Brand Names Calciferol™; Drisdol®
Canadian Brand Names Drisdol®; Ostoforte®
Index Terms Activated Ergosterol; Viosterol; Vitamin D$_2$
Pharmacologic Category Vitamin D Analog
Use Treatment of refractory rickets, hypophosphatemia, hypoparathyroidism; dietary supplement
Pregnancy Risk Factor A/C (dose exceeding RDA recommendation)
Medication Safety Issues
Sound-alike/look-alike issues:
Calciferol™ may be confused with calcitriol
Drisdol® may be confused with Drysol™
Dosage Oral dosing is preferred; I.M. therapy required with GI, liver, or biliary disease associated with malabsorption

Dietary supplementation (each 1 mcg = 40 int. units):
Infants and Children: 5 mcg/day (200 int. units/day)
Adults:
18-50 years: 5 mcg/day (200 int. units/day)
51-70 years: 10 mcg/day (400 int. units/day)
Elderly >70 years: 15 mcg/day (600 int. units/day)
Renal failure:
Children: 100-1000 mcg/day (4000-40,000 int. units)
Adults: 500 mcg/day (20,000 int. units)
Hypoparathyroidism:
Children: 1.25-5 mg/day (50,000-200,000 int. units) and calcium supplements
Adults: 625 mcg to 5 mg/day (25,000-200,000 int. units) and calcium supplements
Vitamin D-dependent rickets:
Children: 75-125 mcg/day (3000-5000 int. units); maximum: 1500 mcg/day
Adults: 250 mcg to 1.5 mg/day (10,000-60,000 int. units)
Nutritional rickets and osteomalacia:
Children and Adults (with normal absorption): 25-125 mcg/day (1000-5000 int. units)
Children with malabsorption: 250-625 mcg/day (10,000-25,000 int. units)
Adults with malabsorption: 250-7500 mcg (10,000-300,000 int. units)
Vitamin D-resistant rickets:
Children: Initial: 1000-2000 mcg/day (40,000-80,000 int. units) with phosphate supplements; daily dosage is increased at 3- to 4-month intervals in 250-500 mcg (10,000-20,000 int. units) increments
Adults: 250-1500 mcg/day (10,000-60,000 int. units) with phosphate supplements
Familial hypophosphatemia: 10,000-80,000 int. units daily plus 1-2 g/day elemental phosphorus
Osteoporosis prophylaxis: Adults:
51-70 years: 400 int. units/day
>70 years: 600 int. units/day
Maximum daily dose: 2000 int. units/day
Additional Information Complete prescribing information for this medication should be consulted for additional detail.
Dosage Forms [DSC] = Discontinued product
Capsule (Drisdol®): 50,000 int. units [1.25 mg; contains tartrazine and soybean oil] (Continued)

Ergocalciferol *(Continued)*

Injection, solution (Calciferol™): 500,000 int. units/mL [12.5 mg/mL] (1 mL) [contains sesame oil] [DSC]

Liquid, drops (Calciferol™, Drisdol®): 8000 int. units/mL [200 mcg/mL] (60 mL) [OTC]

Ergoloid Mesylates (ER goe loid MES i lates)

Canadian Brand Names Hydergine®

Index Terms Dihydroergotoxine; Dihydrogenated Ergot Alkaloids; Hydergine [DSC]

Pharmacologic Category Ergot Derivative

Use Treatment of cerebrovascular insufficiency in primary progressive dementia, Alzheimer's dementia, and senile onset

Pregnancy Risk Factor C

Dosage Adults: Oral: 1 mg 3 times/day up to 4.5-12 mg/day; up to 6 months of therapy may be necessary

Additional Information Complete prescribing information for this medication should be consulted for additional detail.

Dosage Forms

Tablet: 1 mg

Tablet, sublingual: 1 mg

- ◆ **Ergomar®** *see* Ergotamine *on page 605*
- ◆ **Ergometrine Maleate** *see* Ergonovine *on page 604*

Ergonovine (er goe NOE veen)

U.S. Brand Names Ergotrate®

Index Terms Ergometrine Maleate; Ergonovine Maleate

Pharmacologic Category Ergot Derivative

Use Prevention and treatment of postpartum and postabortion hemorrhage caused by uterine atony or subinvolution

Unlabeled/Investigational Use Diagnostically to identify Prinzmetal's angina

Pregnancy Implications Administration causes hyperstimulation of the uterus and may cause uterine tetany, decreased uteroplacental blood flow, uterine rupture, cervical and perineal lacerations, amniotic fluid embolism, and possible trauma to the infant. Ergonovine is used in the third stage of labor for the prevention and treatment of postpartum hemorrhage; use is contraindicated during pregnancy.

Contraindications Hypersensitivity to ergonovine or any component of the formulation; ergot alkaloids are contraindicated with potent inhibitors of CYP3A4 (includes protease inhibitors, azole antifungals, and some macrolide antibiotics); induction of labor, threatened spontaneous abortion, pregnancy

Warnings/Precautions Use with caution in patients with sepsis, heart disease, hypertension, venoatrial shunts, mitral valve stenosis, obliterative vascular disease, or with hepatic or renal impairment. Restore uterine responsiveness in calcium-deficient patients who do not respond to ergonovine by I.V. calcium administration. Avoid prolonged use; discontinue if ergotism develops. Pleural and peritoneal fibrosis have been reported with prolonged daily use. Cardiac valvular fibrosis has also been associated with ergot alkaloids.

Adverse Reactions Frequency not defined.

Cardiovascular: Hypertension, MI, shock

Gastrointestinal: Nausea, vomiting

Miscellaneous: Allergic reactions, ergotism

Overdosage/Toxicology Diarrhea, headache, nausea, uterine cramping and vomiting have been reported following overdose of ergot alkaloids. Encephalopathy, feeding intolerance, hypertension, hypoxemia, peripheral circulatory disturbances, retinal hemorrhage, seizures, and oliguria have been reported following inadvertent administration to the neonate. Cardiac ischemia, MI, severe chest pain or death may occur in patients with coronary artery disease. Treatment should be symptom directed and supportive. Nitroglycerin may be used to treat cardiac ischemia; diazepam or phenytoin may be used to treat convulsions. Chlorpromazine 15 mg may be used for hypertension. Dialysis and diuresis have not been established as effective.

Drug Interactions

Cytochrome P450 Effect: Substrate of CYP3A4 (major)

Increased Effect/Toxicity: CYP3A4 inhibitors may increase the levels/effects of ergonovine; example inhibitors include azole antifungals, clarithromycin, diclofenac, doxycycline, erythromycin, imatinib, isoniazid, nefazodone, nicardipine, propofol, protease inhibitors, quinidine, telithromycin, troleandomycin, and verapamil. Ergot alkaloids are contraindicated with potent CYP3A4 inhibitors. Ergonovine may increase the effects of MAO inhibitors, sibutramine, and other serotonin modulators (eg, 5-HT$_{1D}$ receptor agonists, buspirone, SSRIs, TCAs, nefazodone, and trazodone). Severe vasoconstriction may occur when peripheral vasoconstrictors or beta-blockers are used in patients receiving ergot alkaloids; concurrent use is contraindicated.

Decreased Effect: Effects of ergonovine may be diminished by antipsychotics, metoclopramide. Antianginal effects of nitrates may be reduced by ergot alkaloids.

Stability

Injection: Store at <46°F; protect from light. May store at room temperature for up to 60 days. Do not use if discoloration occurs.

Tablet: Store at controlled room temperature of 15°C to 30°C (59°F to 86°F).

Mechanism of Action Similar smooth muscle actions as seen with ergotamine; however, it affects primarily uterine smooth muscles producing sustained contractions and thereby shortens the third stage of labor.

Pharmacodynamics/Kinetics

Onset of action: I.M.: ~2-5 minutes; Oral: 6-15 minutes

Duration: I.M.: Uterine effect: 3 hours; I.V.: ~45 minutes; Oral: 3 hours

Absorption: Oral: Rapid

Metabolism: Hepatic

Half-life elimination: I.V.: 120 minutes

Excretion: Primarily feces; urine

Dosage Adults:

I.M., I.V. (I.V. should be reserved for emergency use only): 0.2 mg, may repeat dose in 2-4 hours if needed

Oral, SL:

Immediate post-partum: 0.2 mg (usually given I.M. or I.V)

Late post-partum: 0.2-0.4 mg every 6-12 hours until danger of uterine atony has passed (usually ~48 hours)

Administration I.V. doses should be administered over a period of not <1 minute. Dilute in NS to 5 mL for I.V. administration. Oral tablets may also be administered sublingually.

Monitoring Parameters Blood pressure, pulse, uterine response; cramping, if severe, may justify a need for dose reduction (oral)

Dosage Forms

Injection, as maleate:

Ergotrate®: 0.2 mg/mL (1 mL)

Tablet, as maleate:

Ergotrate®: 0.2 mg

♦ **Ergonovine Maleate** see Ergonovine on page 604

Ergotamine (er GOT a meen)

U.S. Brand Names Ergomar®

Index Terms Ergotamine Tartrate

Pharmacologic Category Antimigraine Agent; Ergot Derivative

Use Abort or prevent vascular headaches, such as migraine, migraine variants, or so-called "histaminic cephalalgia"

Pregnancy Risk Factor X

Pregnancy Implications May cause prolonged constriction of the uterine vessels and/or increased myometrial tone leading to reduced placental blood flow. This has contributed to fetal growth retardation in animals.

Lactation Enters breast milk/not recommended

Contraindications Hypersensitivity to ergotamine or any component of the formulation; peripheral vascular disease; hepatic or renal disease; coronary artery disease; hypertension; sepsis; ergot alkaloids are contraindicated with strong inhibitors of CYP3A4 (includes protease inhibitors, azole antifungals, and some macrolide antibiotics); pregnancy

Warnings/Precautions Avoid prolonged administration or excessive dosage because of the danger of ergotism (intense vasoconstriction), gangrene, cardiac valvular fibrosis, retroperitoneal and/or pleuropulmonary fibrosis. Patients who take ergotamine for extended periods of time may experience withdrawal symptoms and rebound headache when ergotamine is discontinued. May be harmful due to reduction in cerebral blood flow; may precipitate angina, myocardial infarction, or aggravate intermittent claudication; therefore, not considered a drug of choice in the elderly.

[U.S. Boxed Warning]: Concomitant use with medications considered to be "strong" CYP3A4 inhibitors has been associated with acute ergot toxicity; use caution with inhibitors of CYP3A4 enzymes.

Adverse Reactions Frequency not defined.

Cardiovascular: Absence of pulse, bradycardia, cardiac valvular fibrosis, cyanosis, edema, ECG changes, gangrene, hypertension, ischemia, precordial distress and pain, tachycardia, vasospasm

Central nervous system: Vertigo

Dermatologic: Itching

Gastrointestinal: Nausea, vomiting

Genitourinary: Retroperitoneal fibrosis

Neuromuscular & skeletal: Muscle pain, numbness, paresthesia, weakness

Respiratory: Pleuropulmonary fibrosis

Miscellaneous: Cold extremities

Overdosage/Toxicology Symptoms include vasospastic effects, nausea, vomiting, lassitude, impaired mental function, hypotension, hypertension, unconsciousness, seizures, shock, and death. Treatment includes general supportive therapy, gastric lavage, or induction of emesis, and saline cathartic, Keep extremities warm. Activated charcoal is effective at binding certain chemicals, this is especially true for ergot alkaloids. Treatment is symptomatic, with heparin and vasodilators (nitroprusside). Use vasodilators with caution to avoid exaggerating any pre-existing hypotension.

Drug Interactions

Cytochrome P450 Effect: Substrate of CYP3A4 (major); Inhibits CYP3A4 (weak)

Increased Effect/Toxicity: CYP3A4 inhibitors may increase the levels/effects of ergotamine; example inhibitors include azole antifungals, clarithromycin, diclofenac, doxycycline, erythromycin, imatinib, isoniazid, nefazodone, nicardipine, propofol, protease inhibitors, quinidine, telithromycin, troleandomycin, and verapamil. Ergot alkaloids are contraindicated with strong CYP3A4 inhibitors. Ergotamine may increase the effects of 5-HT₁ agonists (eg, sumatriptan), MAO inhibitors, sibutramine, and other serotonin agonists (serotonin syndrome). Severe vasoconstriction may occur when peripheral vasoconstrictors or beta-blockers are used in patients receiving ergot alkaloids; concurrent use is contraindicated.

Decreased Effect: Effects of ergotamine may be diminished by antipsychotics, metoclopramide. Antianginal effects of nitrates may be reduced by ergot alkaloids.

(Continued)

Ergotamine *(Continued)*

Ethanol/Nutrition/Herb Interactions Food: Avoid tea, cola, and coffee (caffeine may increase GI absorption of ergotamine). Grapefruit juice may cause increased blood levels of ergotamine, leading to increased toxicity.

Stability Store sublingual tablet at room temperature. Protect from light and heat.

Mechanism of Action Has partial agonist and/or antagonist activity against tryptaminergic, dopaminergic and alpha-adrenergic receptors depending upon their site; is a highly active uterine stimulant; it causes constriction of peripheral and cranial blood vessels and produces depression of central vasomotor centers

Pharmacodynamics/Kinetics

Absorption: Oral: Erratic; enhanced by caffeine coadministration

Metabolism: Extensively hepatic

Time to peak, serum: 0.5-3 hours

Half-life elimination: 2 hours

Excretion: Feces (90% as metabolites)

Dosage Sublingual: One tablet under tongue at first sign, then 1 tablet every 30 minutes if needed; maximum dose: 3 tablets/24 hours, 5 tablets/week

Administration Do not crush sublingual tablets.

Dosage Forms Tablet, sublingual: Ergotamine tartrate 2 mg

♦ **Ergotamine Tartrate** *see* Ergotamine *on page 605*

♦ **Ergotamine Tartrate, Belladonna, and Phenobarbital** *see* Belladonna, Phenobarbital, and Ergotamine *on page 201*

♦ **Ergotrate®** *see* Ergonovine *on page 604*

Erlotinib *(er LOE tye nib)*

U.S. Brand Names Tarceva®

Canadian Brand Names Tarceva®

Index Terms CP358774; Erlotinib Hydrochloride; NSC-718781; OSI-774; R 14-15

Pharmacologic Category Antineoplastic Agent, Tyrosine Kinase Inhibitor; Epidermal Growth Factor Receptor (EGFR) Inhibitor

Use Treatment of refractory advanced or metastatic nonsmall cell lung cancer (NSCLC); pancreatic cancer (first-line therapy in combination with gemcitabine)

Unlabeled/Investigational Use Treatment of advanced or metastatic breast cancer, colorectal cancer, head and neck tumors, ovarian cancer, and renal cell cancer

Pregnancy Risk Factor D

Pregnancy Implications Animal studies have demonstrated fetal harm and abortion. There are no well-controlled studies in pregnant women. Women of childbearing potential should be advised to avoid pregnancy; adequate contraception is recommended during treatment and for 2 weeks after treatment has been completed.

Lactation Excretion in breast milk unknown/not recommended

Medication Safety Issues

Sound-alike/look-alike issues:

Erlotinib may be confused with gefitinib

High alert medication: The Institute for Safe Medication Practices (ISMP) includes this medication among its list of drugs which have a heightened risk of causing significant patient harm when used in error.

Contraindications Hypersensitivity to erlotinib or any component of the formulation; pregnancy

Warnings/Precautions Hazardous agent - use appropriate precautions for handling and disposal. Rare, sometimes fatal, pulmonary toxicity (interstitial pneumonia, interstitial lung disease, obliterative bronchiolitis, pulmonary fibrosis) has occurred; an interruption of therapy should occur with unexplained pulmonary symptoms (dyspnea, cough, and fever); use caution in hepatic or severe renal impairment. Use caution with cardiovascular disease; MI, CVA, and microangiopathic hemolytic anemia with thrombocytopenia have been noted in patients receiving concomitant erlotinib and gemcitabine. Elevated INR and bleeding events have been reported; use caution with concomitant anticoagulant therapy. Safety and efficacy in pediatric patients have not been established.

Adverse Reactions Percentages as reported with monotherapy; frequency of adverse event with combination chemotherapy (gemcitabine) noted where applicable

>10%:

Cardiovascular: Edema (37% combination)

Central nervous system: Fatigue (14% to 55%; 73% combination), pyrexia (36% combination), anxiety (21%), headache (17%), depression (16%; 19% combination), dizziness (15% combination), insomnia (12%; 15% combination)

Dermatologic: Acneiform rash (50% to 88%; grade 3/4: 9%), pruritus (13% to 55%), dry skin (12% to 35%), erythema (18%), alopecia (14% combination)

Gastrointestinal: Diarrhea (30% to 56%; grade 3/4: 6%), anorexia (23% to 52%), nausea (11% to 33%; 60% combination), vomiting (23%; 42% combination), mucositis (17% to 18%), glossodynia (18%), stomatitis (17%; 22% combination), xerostomia (17%), pain (14%), flatulence (13% combination), constipation (12%; 31% combination), dyspepsia (12%; 17% combination), dysphagia (12%), weight loss (12%; 39% combination), abnormal taste (11%), abdominal pain (11%; 46% combination)

Hepatic: ALT increased (4%; combination grade 2: 31%, grade 3: 13%, grade 4: <1%), AST increased (combination grade 2: 24%, grade 3: 10%, grade 4 <1%), hyperbilirubinemia (20%; combination grade 2: 17%, grade 3: 10%, grade 4: <1%)

Neuromuscular & skeletal: Bone pain (25% combination), myalgia (21% combination), arthralgia (14%), neuropathy (13% combination), rigors (12% combination), paresthesia (11%)

Ocular: Conjunctivitis (12%; <1% combination), keratoconjunctivitis sicca (12%)

Respiratory: Dyspnea (21% to 41%), cough (16% to 33%)

Miscellaneous: Infection (24%; 39% combination)

1% to 10%:

Cardiovascular (reported with combination chemotherapy): Deep venous thrombosis (4%), arrhythmia, cerebrovascular accidents (including cerebral hemorrhage), MI, myocardial ischemia, syncope

Gastrointestinal (reported with combination chemotherapy): Ileus, pancreatitis

Hematologic (reported with combination chemotherapy): Hemolytic anemia, microangiopathic hemolytic anemia with thrombocytopenia

Ocular: Keratitis (6%; <1% combination)

Renal (reported with combination chemotherapy): Renal insufficiency

Respiratory: Pneumonitis (6%)

<1% (Limited to important or life-threatening): Corneal ulcerations, epistaxis, gastrointestinal bleeding, interstitial lung disease-related events, rash (acneiform; sparing prior radiation field)

Overdosage/Toxicology Single doses of up to 1000 mg in healthy patients and 1600 mg in cancer patients have been tolerated. Repeated doses of 200 mg twice daily in healthy subjects were poorly tolerated after a few days. Specific overdose-related toxicities include diarrhea, rash, and liver transaminase elevation. Overdose management should include withdrawal of erlotinib, and symptom-directed and supportive treatment.

Drug Interactions

Cytochrome P450 Effect: Substrate of CYP1A2 (minor), 3A4 (major)

Increased Effect/Toxicity: Ketoconazole and CYP3A4 inhibitors may increase erlotinib levels/effects; example inhibitors include azole antifungals, clarithromycin, diclofenac, doxycycline, erythromycin, imatinib, isoniazid, nefazodone, nicardipine, propofol, protease inhibitors, quinidine, telithromycin, and verapamil.

Decreased Effect: Rifamycins and CYP3A4 inducers may decrease erlotinib levels/effects; example inducers include aminoglutethimide, carbamazepine, nafcillin, nevirapine, phenobarbital, and phenytoin. Erlotinib may decrease the absorption of digoxin tablets.

Ethanol/Nutrition/Herb Interactions

Food: Erlotinib bioavailability is increased with food.

Herb/Nutraceutical: Avoid St John's wort (may increase metabolism and decrease erlotinib concentrations).

Stability Store at room temperature between 15°C and 30°C (59°F and 86°F).

Mechanism of Action The mechanism of erlotinib's antitumor action is not fully characterized. The drug is known to inhibit overall epidermal growth factor receptor (HER1/EGFR)-tyrosine kinase. Active competitive inhibition of adenosine triphosphate inhibits downstream signal transduction of ligand dependent HER1/EGFR activation.

Pharmacodynamics/Kinetics

Absorption: Oral: 60% on an empty stomach; ~100% on a full stomach

Distribution: 94-232 L

Protein binding: 92% to 95%, albumin and α_1-acid glycoprotein

Metabolism: Hepatic, CYP3A4 (major), CYP1A1 (minor), CYP1A2 (minor), and CYP1C (minor)

Bioavailability: 100% when given with food; 60% without food

Half-life elimination: 24-36 hours

Time to peak, plasma: 1-7 hours

Excretion: Primarily as metabolites: Feces (83%); urine (8%)

Dosage Oral: Adults: **Note:** Treatment should continue until disease progression or unacceptable toxicity occurs

NSCLC: 150 mg/day

Pancreatic cancer: 100 mg/day in combination with gemcitabine

Note: Dose reductions are more likely to be needed when erlotinib is administered concomitantly with strong CYP3A4 inhibitors. Dose reduction (if required) should be done in increments of 50 mg. Likewise, the CYP3A4 inducers may require increased doses; doses >150 mg/day should be considered with rifampin (see Drug Interactions for examples of CYP3A4 inhibitors and inducers).

Dosage adjustment for toxicity: Patients experiencing poorly-tolerated diarrhea or a severe skin reaction may benefit from a brief therapy interruption. Patients experiencing acute onset (or worsening) of pulmonary symptoms should have therapy interrupted and be evaluated for drug-induced interstitial lung disease.

Dosage adjustment in renal impairment: No adjustment required.

Dosage adjustment in hepatic impairment: Dose reduction or interruption should be considered if liver function changes are severe.

Administration The manufacturer recommends administration on an empty stomach (at least 1 hour before or 2 hours after the ingestion of food) even though this reduces drug absorption by approximately 40%. Administration after a meal results in nearly 100% absorption.

Monitoring Parameters Periodic liver function tests (asymptomatic increases in liver enzymes have occurred)

Dosage Forms

Tablet:

Tarceva®: 25 mg, 100 mg, 150 mg

♦ **Erlotinib Hydrochloride** *see* Erlotinib *on page 606*

♦ **Ertaczo™** *see* Sertaconazole *on page 1557*

Ertapenem (er ta PEN em)

U.S. Brand Names Invanz®

Canadian Brand Names Invanz®

Index Terms Ertapenem Sodium; L-749,345; MK0826

Pharmacologic Category Antibiotic, Carbapenem

Additional Appendix Information

Antimicrobial Drugs of Choice *on page 1981*

Community-Acquired Pneumonia in Adults *on page 1999*

(Continued)

Ertapenem *(Continued)*

Use Treatment of the following moderate-severe infections: Complicated intra-abdominal infections, complicated skin and skin structure infections (including diabetic foot infections without osteomyelitis), complicated UTI (including pyelonephritis), acute pelvic infections, and community-acquired pneumonia. Prophylaxis of surgical site infection following elective colorectal surgery. Antibacterial coverage includes aerobic gram-positive organisms, aerobic gram-negative organisms, anaerobic organisms.

Note: Methicillin-resistant *Staphylococcus*, *Enterococcus* spp, penicillin-resistant strains of *Streptococcus pneumoniae*, beta-lactamase-positive strains of *Haemophilus influenzae* are **resistant** to ertapenem, as are most *Pseudomonas aeruginosa*.

Pregnancy Risk Factor B

Pregnancy Implications Developmental prenatal toxicity was not observed in animal studies; decreased fetal weight was observed. There are no adequate and well-controlled studies in pregnant women. Use only if clearly needed. Ertapenem is approved for use in postpartum endomyometritis, septic abortion, and postsurgical gynecologic infections.

Lactation Enters breast milk/use caution

Medication Safety Issues
Sound-alike/look-alike issues:
Invanz® may be confused with Avinza™

Contraindications Hypersensitivity to ertapenem, other carbapenems, or any component of the formulation; anaphylactic reactions to beta-lactam antibiotics. If using intramuscularly, known hypersensitivity to local anesthetics of the amide type (lidocaine is the diluent).

Warnings/Precautions Use caution with renal impairment. Dosage adjustment required in patients with moderate-to-severe renal dysfunction; elderly patients often require lower doses (based upon renal function). Prolonged use may result in superinfection, including pseudomembranous colitis. Has been associated with CNS adverse effects, including confusional states and seizures; use caution with CNS disorders (eg, brain lesions, history of seizures, or renal impairment). Serious hypersensitivity reactions, including anaphylaxis, have been reported (some without a history of previous allergic reactions to beta-lactams). Doses for I.M. administration are mixed with lidocaine; consult Lidocaine *on page 1010* information for associated Warnings/Precautions. Safety and efficacy have not been established in children <3 months of age.

Adverse Reactions Note: Percentages reported in adults.
1% to 10%:
Cardiovascular: Swelling/edema (3%), chest pain (1% to 2%), hypertension (1% to 2%), hypotension (1% to 2%), tachycardia (1% to 2%)
Central nervous system: Headache (6% to 7%), altered mental status (ie, agitation, confusion, disorientation, decreased mental acuity, changed mental status, somnolence, stupor) (3% to 5%), fever (2% to 5%), insomnia (3%), dizziness (2%), fatigue (1%), anxiety (1%)
Dermatologic: Rash (2% to 3%), pruritus (1% to 2%), erythema (1% to 2%), wound complication (3%)
Gastrointestinal: Diarrhea (9% to 10%), nausea (6% to 9%), abdominal pain (4%), vomiting (4%), constipation (3% to 4%), acid regurgitation (1% to 2%), dyspepsia (1%), oral candidiasis (≤1%)
Genitourinary: Vaginitis (1% to 3%), dysuria (1%), proteinuria
Hematologic: Platelet count increased (3% to 7%), leukopenia (1% to 2%), neutrophils decreased (1% to 2%), prothrombin time increased (1% to 2%)
Hepatic: Hepatic enzyme increased (5% to 9%), alkaline phosphatase increase (3% to 7%)
Local: Infused vein complications (5% to 7%), phlebitis/thrombophlebitis (2%), extravasation (1% to 2%)
Neuromuscular & skeletal: Leg pain (≤1%), weakness (1%)
Respiratory: Atelectasis (3%), dyspnea (1% to 3%), cough (1% to 2%), pharyngitis (1%), rales/rhonchi (1%), respiratory distress (≤1%)
<1% (limited to important or life-threatening): Abdominal abscess, aggressive behavior, anaphylactoid reactions, anaphylaxis, anorexia, arrhythmia, asthma, asystole, atrial fibrillation, bicarbonate (serum) decreased, bilirubin (direct and indirect) increased, bladder dysfunction, bradycardia, bronchoconstriction, BUN increased, *C. difficile*-associated diarrhea, cardiac arrest, cerebrovascular accident, cholelithiasis, dehydration, depression, desquamation, duodenitis, dysphagia, epistaxis, esophagitis, flank pain, fungal rash, gastritis, gastrointestinal hemorrhage, hallucinations, heart failure, heart murmur, hematochezia, hematoma, hematuria, hemoptysis, hypoesthesia, hypoxemia, ileus, jaundice, lung infiltrate, monocytes increased, necrosis, oliguria/anuria, pancreatitis, paresthesia, pelvic abscess, pharyngeal discomfort, pleural effusion, pleuritic pain, pollakiuria, pseudomembranous colitis, PTT increased, pulmonary congestion, pulmonary embolism, pyloric stenosis, renal insufficiency, seizure (0.5%), sodium (serum) increased, spasm, stoma complications, stomatitis, subdural hemorrhage, syncope, tremor, urinary retention, urticaria, ventricular tachycardia, vertigo, weight loss, wheezing

Overdosage/Toxicology Treatment is symptom-directed and supportive. Ertapenem is removed by hemodialysis (plasma clearance increased by 30% following 4-hour session).

Drug Interactions
Increased Effect/Toxicity: Probenecid may increase serum concentrations of ertapenem; use caution.
Decreased Effect: Ertapenem may decrease valproic acid serum concentrations to subtherapeutic levels; monitor. Antibiotics may decrease effectiveness of the Ty21a live, attenuated typhoid vaccine; delay vaccination for >24 hours after administration of antibiotic

Stability Before reconstitution store at ≤25°C (77°F).
I.M.: Reconstitute 1 g vial with 3.2 mL of 1% lidocaine HCl injection (without epinephrine). Shake well. Use within 1 hour after preparation.
I.V.: Reconstitute 1 g vial with 10 mL of water for injection, 0.9% sodium chloride injection, or bacteriostatic water for injection. Shake well. For adults, transfer dose to 50 mL of 0.9% sodium chloride injection; for children, dilute dose with NS to a final concentration ≤20 mg/mL.

Reconstituted I.V. solution may be stored at room temperature and must be used within 6 hours **or** refrigerated, stored for up to 24 hours and used within 4 hours after removal from refrigerator. Do not freeze.

Mechanism of Action Inhibits bacterial cell wall synthesis by binding to one or more of the penicillin binding proteins; which in turn inhibits the final transpeptidation step of peptidoglycan synthesis in bacterial cell walls, thus inhibiting cell wall biosynthesis. Bacteria eventually lyse due to ongoing activity of cell wall autolytic enzymes (autolysins and murein hydrolases) while cell wall assembly is arrested.

Pharmacodynamics/Kinetics

Absorption: I.M.: Almost complete

Distribution: V_{dss}:

Children 3 months to 12 years: 0.2 L/kg

Children 13-17 years: 0.16 L/kg

Adults: 0.12 L/kg

Protein binding (concentration dependent): 85% at 300 mcg/mL, 95% at <100 mcg/mL

Metabolism: Non-CYP-mediated hydrolysis to inactive metabolite

Bioavailability: I.M.: ~90%

Half-life elimination:

Children 3 months to 12 years: 2.5 hours

Children ≥13 years and Adults: 4 hours

Time to peak: I.M.: ~2.3 hours

Excretion: Urine (80% as unchanged drug and metabolite); feces (10%)

Dosage

Usual dosage ranges:

Children 3 months to 12 years: I.M., I.V.: 15 mg/kg twice daily (maximum: 1 g/day)

Children >13 years and Adults: I.M., I.V.: 1 g/day

Indication-specific dosing:

Children 3 months to 12 years: I.M., I.V.:

Community-acquired pneumonia, urinary tract infections/pyelonephritis: 15 mg/kg twice daily (maximum: 1 g/day); duration of total antibiotic treatment: 10-14 days (**Note:** Duration includes possible switch to appropriate oral therapy after at least 3 days of parenteral treatment, once clinical improvement demonstrated.)

Intra-abdominal infection: 15 mg/kg twice daily (maximum: 1 g/day) for 5-14 days

Pelvic infections (acute): 15 mg/kg twice daily (maximum: 1 g/day) for 3-10 days

Skin and skin structure infections: 15 mg/kg twice daily (maximum: 1 g/day) for 7-14 days

Children ≥13 years and Adults: I.M., I.V.:

Community-acquired pneumonia, urinary tract infections/pyelonephritis: 1 g/day; duration of total antibiotic treatment: 10-14 days (**Note:** Duration includes possible switch to appropriate oral therapy after at least 3 days of parenteral treatment, once clinical improvement demonstrated.)

Intra-abdominal infection: 1 g/day for 5-14 days

Pelvic infections (acute): 1 g/day for 3-10 days

Skin and skin structure infections (including diabetic foot infections): 1 g/day for 7-14 days

Adults: I.V.:

Prophylaxis of surgical site following colorectal surgery: 1 g given 1 hour preoperatively

Dosage adjustment in renal impairment:

Children: No data available for pediatric patients with renal insufficiency.

Adults: $Cl_{cr} \leq 30$ mL/minute/1.73 m^2 and ESRD: 500 mg/day

Hemodialysis: Adults: When the daily dose is given within 6 hours prior to hemodialysis, a supplementary dose of 150 mg is required following hemodialysis.

Dosage adjustment in hepatic impairment: Adjustments cannot be recommended (lack of experience and research in this patient population).

Dietary Considerations Sodium content: 137 mg (~6 mEq) per gram of ertapenem

Administration

I.M.: Avoid injection into a blood vessel. Make sure patient does not have an allergy to lidocaine or another anesthetic of the amide type. Administer by deep I.M. injection into a large muscle mass (eg, gluteal muscle or lateral part of the thigh). Do not administer I.M. preparation or drug reconstituted for I.M. administration intravenously.

I.V.: Infuse over 30 minutes

Monitoring Parameters Periodic renal, hepatic, and hematopoietic assessment during prolonged therapy; neurological assessment

Dosage Forms Injection, powder for reconstitution: 1 g [contains sodium 137 mg/g (~6 mEq/g)]

♦ **Ertapenem Sodium** see Ertapenem on page 607

♦ **Erwinase® (Can)** see Asparaginase on page 157

♦ **Erwinia Asparaginase** see Asparaginase on page 157

♦ **Erybid™ (Can)** see Erythromycin on page 609

♦ **Eryc®** see Erythromycin on page 609

♦ **Eryderm®** see Erythromycin on page 609

♦ **Erygel®** see Erythromycin on page 609

♦ **EryPed®** see Erythromycin on page 609

♦ **Ery-Tab®** see Erythromycin on page 609

♦ **Erythrocin®** see Erythromycin on page 609

Erythromycin (er ith roe MYE sin)

U.S. Brand Names Akne-Mycin®; A/T/S®; E.E.S.®; Eryc®; Eryderm®; Erygel®; EryPed®; Ery-Tab®; Erythrocin®; PCE®; Romycin®; Staticin® [DSC]; Theramycin Z®; T-Stat® [DSC] (Continued)

Erythromycin *(Continued)*

Canadian Brand Names Apo-Erythro Base®; Apo-Erythro E-C®; Apo-Erythro-ES®; Apo-Erythro-S®; Diomycin®; EES®; Erybid™; Eryc®; Novo-Rythro Estolate; Novo-Rythro Ethylsuccinate; Nu-Erythromycin-S; PCE®; PMS-Erythromycin; Sans Acne®

Index Terms Erythromycin Base; Erythromycin Ethylsuccinate; Erythromycin Lactobionate; Erythromycin Stearate

Pharmacologic Category Acne Products; Antibiotic, Macrolide; Antibiotic, Ophthalmic; Antibiotic, Topical; Topical Skin Product; Topical Skin Product, Acne

Additional Appendix Information
Animal and Human Bites *on page 1976*
Antimicrobial Drugs of Choice *on page 1981*
Community-Acquired Pneumonia in Adults *on page 1999*
Prevention of Wound Infection and Sepsis in Surgical Patients *on page 1964*
Treatment of Sexually Transmitted Infections *on page 2007*

Use
Systemic: Treatment of susceptible bacterial infections including *S. pyogenes,* some *S. pneumoniae,* some *S. aureus, M. pneumoniae, Legionella pneumophila,* diphtheria, pertussis, *Chlamydia,* erythrasma, *N. gonorrhoeae, E. histolytica,* syphilis and nongono-coccal urethritis, and *Campylobacter* gastroenteritis; used in conjunction with neomycin for decontaminating the bowel
Ophthalmic: Treatment of superficial eye infections involving the conjunctiva or cornea; neonatal ophthalmia
Topical: Treatment of acne vulgaris

Unlabeled/Investigational Use Systemic: Treatment of gastroparesis, chancroid; preoperative gut sterilization

Pregnancy Risk Factor B

Lactation Enters breast milk/use caution (AAP considers "compatible")

Medication Safety Issues
Sound-alike/look-alike issues:
Erythromycin may be confused with azithromycin, clarithromycin, Ethmozine®
Akne-Mycin® may be confused with AK-Mycin®
E.E.S.® may be confused with DES®
Eryc® may be confused with Emcyt®, Ery-Tab®
Ery-Tab® may be confused with Eryc®
Erythrocin® may be confused with Ethmozine®

Contraindications Hypersensitivity to erythromycin or any component of the formulation
Systemic: Concomitant use with pimozide or cisapride

Warnings/Precautions Systemic: Use caution with hepatic impairment with or without jaundice has occurred, it may be accompanied by malaise, nausea, vomiting, abdominal colic, and fever; discontinue use if these occur. Use caution with other medication relying on CYP3A4 metabolism; high potential for drug interactions exists. May cause pseudomembranous colitis; observe for superinfections. Use in infants has been associated with infantile hypertrophic pyloric stenosis (IHPS). Macrolides have been associated with rare QT$_c$ prolongation and ventricular arrhythmias, including torsade de pointes. Use caution in elderly patients, as risk of adverse events may be increased. Use caution in myasthenia gravis patients; erythromycin may aggravate muscular weakness.

Adverse Reactions Frequency not defined. Incidence may vary with formulation.
Systemic:
Cardiovascular: QT$_c$ prolongation, torsade de pointes, ventricular arrhythmia, ventricular tachycardia
Central nervous system: Seizure
Dermatitis: Pruritus, rash
Gastrointestinal: Abdominal pain, anorexia, diarrhea, infantile hypertrophic pyloric stenosis, nausea, pancreatitis, pseudomembranous colitis, vomiting
Hepatic: Cholestatic jaundice (most common with estolate), hepatitis, liver function tests abnormal
Local: Phlebitis at the injection site, thrombophlebitis
Neuromuscular & skeletal: Weakness
Otic: Hearing loss
Miscellaneous: Allergic reactions, anaphylaxis, hypersensitivity reactions, urticaria
Topical: 1% to 10%: Dermatologic: Erythema, desquamation, dryness, pruritus

Overdosage/Toxicology Symptoms include nausea, vomiting, and diarrhea. Treatment is symptom-directed and supportive. Erythromycin is not dialyzable.

Drug Interactions
Cytochrome P450 Effect: Substrate of CYP2B6 (minor), 3A4 (major); **Inhibits** CYP1A2 (weak), 3A4 (moderate)
Increased Effect/Toxicity: Agents that prolong the QT$_c$ interval, including type Ia (eg, quinidine) and type III antiarrhythmic agents, and selected antipsychotic agents (eg, thioridazine) should be used with extreme caution or are contraindicated with erythromycin (eg, pimozide, cisapride). Concurrent use of ergot alkaloids with erythromycin is not recommended.

Erythromycin is a moderate CYP3A4 inhibitor, and may increase the levels/effects of azole antifungals, alfentanil (and possibly other opioid analgesics), selected benzodiazepines, calcium channel blockers, corticosteroids, cyclosporine, eletriptan, eplerenone, mirtazapine, repaglinide, nefazodone, quinidine, sildenafil (and other PDE-5 inhibitors), SSRIs, tacrolimus, venlafaxine, and other CYP3A4 substrates. Selected benzodiazepines (midazolam, triazolam), cisapride, ergot alkaloids, selected HMG-CoA reductase inhibitors (lovastatin and simvastatin), and pimozide are generally contraindicated with strong CYP3A4 inhibitors. When used with strong CYP3A4 inhibitors, dosage adjustment/limits are recommended for sildenafil and other PDE-5 inhibitors; refer to individual monographs. The effects of warfarin have been potentiated by erythromycin.

The levels/effects of erythromycin may be increased by azole antifungals, clarithromycin, diclofenac, doxycycline, imatinib, isoniazid, nefazodone, nicardipine, propofol, quinidine, telithromycin, verapamil, and other CYP3A4 inhibitors.

Decreased Effect: Erythromycin may decrease the serum concentrations of zafirlukast. Erythromycin may antagonize the therapeutic effects of clindamycin and lincomycin. Antiplatelet efficacy of clopidogrel may be attenuated by erythromycin. The levels/effects of erythromycin may be decreased by aminoglutethimide, carbamazepine, nafcillin, nevirapine, phenobarbital, phenytoin, rifamycins, and other CYP3A4 inducers.

Ethanol/Nutrition/Herb Interactions

Ethanol: Avoid ethanol (may decrease absorption of erythromycin or enhance ethanol effects).

Food: Erythromycin serum levels may be altered if taken with food (formulation"dependent).

Herb/Nutraceutical: St John's wort may decrease erythromycin levels.

Stability

Injection:

Store unreconstituted vials at 15°C to 30°C (59°F to 86°F). Erythromycin lactobionate should be reconstituted with sterile water for injection without preservatives to avoid gel formation. The reconstituted solution is stable for 2 weeks when refrigerated or for 8 hours at room temperature.

Erythromycin I.V. infusion solution is stable at pH 6-8. Stability of lactobionate is pH dependent. I.V. form has the longest stability in 0.9% sodium chloride (NS) and should be prepared in this base solution whenever possible. Do not use D_5W as a diluent unless sodium bicarbonate is added to solution. If I.V. must be prepared in D_5W, 0.5 mL of the 8.4% sodium bicarbonate solution should be added per each 100 mL of D_5W.

Stability of parenteral admixture at room temperature (25°C) and at refrigeration temperature (4°C) is 24 hours.

Standard diluent: 500 mg/250 mL D_5W/NS; 750 mg/250 mL D_5W/NS; 1 g/250 mL D_5W/NS.

Oral suspension:

Granules: Prior to mixing, store at <30°C (<86°F). After mixing, store under refrigeration and use within 10 days.

Powder: Refrigerate to preserve taste. Erythromycin ethylsuccinate may be stored at room temperature if used within 14 days. EryPed® drops should be used within 35 days following reconstitution. May store at room temperature or under refrigeration.

Tablet and capsule formulations: Store at <30°C (<86°F).

Topical and ophthalmic formulations: Store at room temperature.

Mechanism of Action Inhibits RNA-dependent protein synthesis at the chain elongation step; binds to the 50S ribosomal subunit resulting in blockage of transpeptidation

Pharmacodynamics/Kinetics

Absorption: Oral: Variable but better with salt forms than with base form; 18% to 45%; ethylsuccinate may be better absorbed with food

Distribution:

Relative diffusion from blood into CSF: Minimal even with inflammation

CSF:blood level ratio: Normal meninges: 2% to 13%; Inflamed meninges: 7% to 25%

Protein binding: Base: 73% to 81%

Metabolism: Demethylation primarily via hepatic CYP3A4

Half-life elimination: Peak: 1.5-2 hours; End-stage renal disease: 5-6 hours

Time to peak, serum: Base: 4 hours; Ethylsuccinate: 0.5-2.5 hours; delayed with food due to differences in absorption

Excretion: Primarily feces; urine (2% to 15% as unchanged drug)

Dosage Note: Due to differences in absorption, 400 mg erythromycin ethylsuccinate produces the same serum levels as 250 mg erythromycin base or stearate.

Usual dosage range:

Neonates: Ophthalmic: Prophylaxis of neonatal gonococcal or chlamydial conjunctivitis: 0.5-1 cm ribbon of ointment should be instilled into each conjunctival sac

Infants and Children:

Oral:

Base: 30-50 mg/kg/day in 2-4 divided doses; maximum: 2 g/day

Ethylsuccinate: 30-50 mg/kg/day in 2-4 divided doses; maximum: 3.2 g/day

Stearate: 30-50 mg/kg/day in 2-4 divided doses; maximum: 2 g/day

I.V.: Lactobionate: 15-50 mg/kg/day divided every 6 hours, not to exceed 4 g/day

Children and Adults:

Ophthalmic: Instill ½" (1.25 cm) 2-6 times/day depending on the severity of the infection

Topical: Acne: Apply over the affected area twice daily after the skin has been thoroughly washed and patted dry

Adults:

Oral:

Base: 250-500 mg every 6-12 hours; maximum 4 g/day

Ethylsuccinate: 400-800 mg every 6-12 hours; maximum: 4 g/day

I.V.: Lactobionate: 15-20 mg/kg/day divided every 6 hours or 500 mg to 1 g every 6 hours, or given as a continuous infusion over 24 hours; maximum: 4 g/24 hours

Indication-specific dosing:

Children:

***Bartonella sp* infections (bacillary angiomatosis [BA], peliosis hepatitis [PH]) (unlabeled use):** Oral: 40 mg/kg/day (ethylsuccinate) in 4 divided doses (maximum: 2 g/day) for 3 months (BA) or 4 months (PH)

Conjunctivitis, neonatal *(C. trachomatis):* Oral: 50 mg/kg/day (base or ethylsuccinate) in 4 divided doses for 14 days

Mild/moderate infection: Oral: 30-50 mg/kg/day in divided doses every 6-12 hours

Pertussis: Oral: 40-50 mg/kg/day in 4 divided doses for 14 days; maximum 2 g/day (not preferred agent for infants <1 month due to IHPS)

Pharyngitis, tonsillitis (streptococcal): Oral: 20 mg (base)/kg/day or 40 mg (ethylsuccinate)/kg/day in 2 divided doses for 10 days. **Note:** No longer preferred therapy due to increased organism resistance.

(Continued)

Erythromycin *(Continued)*

Pneumonia *(C. trachomatis):* Oral: 50 mg/kg/day (base or ethylsuccinate) in 4 divided doses for 14-21 days

Preop bowel preparation: Oral: 20 mg (base)/kg at 1, 2, and 11 PM on the day before surgery combined with mechanical cleansing of the large intestine and oral neomycin

Severe infection: I.V.: 15-50 mg/kg/day; maximum: 4 g/day

Adults:

Bartonella sp infections (bacillary angiomatosis [BA], peliosis hepatitis [PH]) (unlabeled use): Oral: 500 mg (base) 4 times/day for 3 months (BA) or 4 months (PH)

Chancroid (unlabeled use): Oral: 500 mg (base) 3 times/day for 7 days; Note: Not a preferred agent; isolates with intermediate resistance have been documented

Gastrointestinal prokinetic (unlabeled use): I.V.: 200 mg initially followed by 250 mg (base) orally 3 times/day 30 minutes before meals. Lower dosages have been used in some trials.

Granuloma inguinale *(K. granulomatis)* (unlabeled use): Oral: 500 mg (base) 4 times/day for 21 days

Legionnaires' disease: Oral: 1.6-4 g (ethylsuccinate)/day or 1-4 g (base)/day in divided doses for 21 days. **Note:** No longer preferred therapy and only used in nonhospitalized patients.

Lymphogranuloma venereum: Oral: 500 mg (base) 4 times/day for 21 days

Nongonococcal urethritis (including coinfection with *C. trachomatis*): Oral: 500 mg (base) 4 times/day for 7 days or 800 mg (ethylsuccinate) 4 times/day for 7 days. **Note:** May use 250 mg (base) or 400 mg (ethylsuccinate) 4 times/day for 14 days if gastrointestinal intolerance.

Pelvic inflammatory disease: I.V.: 500 mg every 6 hours for 3 days, followed by 1000 mg (base)/day orally in 2-4 divided doses for 7 days. **Note:** Not recommended therapy per current treatment guidelines.

Pertussis: Oral: 500 mg (base) every 6 hours for 14 days

Preop bowel preparation (unlabeled use): Oral: 1 g erythromycin base at 1, 2, and 11 PM on the day before surgery combined with mechanical cleansing of the large intestine and oral neomycin

Syphilis, primary: Oral: 48-64 g (ethylsuccinate) or 30-40 g (base) in divided doses over 10-15 days. **Note:** Not recommended therapy per current treatment guidelines.

Dosage adjustment in renal impairment: Dialysis: Slightly dialyzable (5% to 20%); no supplemental dosage necessary in hemo- or peritoneal dialysis or in continuous arteriovenous or venovenous hemofiltration

Dietary Considerations

Systemic: Drug may cause GI upset; may take with food.

E.E.S.® granules for oral suspension contain sodium 25.9 mg (1.1 mEq)/5 mL

EryPed® powder for oral suspension contains sodium 117.5 mg (5.1 mEq)/5 mL; powder for oral suspension (drops) contains sodium 58.8 mg (2.6 mEq)/dropperful dose

Administration

Oral: Do not crush enteric coated drug product. GI upset, including diarrhea, is common. May be administered with food to decrease GI upset. Do not give with milk or acidic beverages.

I.V.: Infuse 1 g over 20-60 minutes. I.V. infusion may be very irritating to the vein. If phlebitis/pain occurs with used dilution, consider diluting further (eg, 1:5) if fluid status of the patient will tolerate, or consider administering in larger available vein. The addition of lidocaine or bicarbonate does not decrease the irritation of erythromycin infusions.

Ophthalmic: Avoid contact of tip of ophthalmic ointment tube with affected eye

Test Interactions False-positive urinary catecholamines

Dosage Forms [DSC] = Discontinued product; [CAN] = Canadian brand name; **Note:** Strength expressed as base

Capsule, delayed release, enteric-coated pellets, as base: 250 mg
    Eryc®: 250 mg
Gel, topical: 2% (30 g, 60 g)
    A/T/S®: 2% (30 g) [contains alcohol 92%]
    Erygel®: 2% (30 g, 60 g) [contains alcohol 92%]
Granules for oral suspension, as ethylsuccinate:
    E.E.S.®: 200 mg/5 mL (100 mL, 200 mL) [contains sodium 25.9 mg (1.1 mEq)/5 mL; cherry flavor]
Injection, powder for reconstitution, as lactobionate:
    Erythrocin®: 500 mg, 1 g
Ointment, ophthalmic: 0.5% [5 mg/g] (1 g, 3.5 g)
    Romycin®: 0.5% [5 mg/g] (3.5 g)
Ointment, topical:
    Akne-Mycin®: 2% (25 g)
Powder for oral suspension, as ethylsuccinate:
    EryPed®: 200 mg/5 mL (100 mL, 200 mL) [contains sodium 117.5 mg (5.1 mEq)/5 mL; fruit flavor]; 400 mg/5 mL (100 mL, 200 mL) [contains sodium 117.5 mg (5.1 mEq)/5 mL; banana flavor]
Powder for oral suspension, as ethylsuccinate [drops]:
    EryPed®: 100 mg/2.5 mL (50 mL) [contains sodium 58.8 mg (2.6 mEq)/dropperful; fruit flavor]
Solution, topical: 2% (60 mL)
    A/T/S®: 2% (60 mL) [contains alcohol 66%]
    Eryderm®, T-Stat® [DSC], Theramycin Z®: 2% (60 mL) [contain alcohol]
    Sans acne [CAN]: 2% (60 mL) [contains ethyl alcohol 44%; not available in U.S.]
    Staticin®: 1.5% (60 mL) [DSC]
Suspension, oral, as ethylsuccinate: 200 mg/5 mL (480 mL); 400 mg/5 mL (480 mL)
    E.E.S.®: 200 mg/5 mL (100 mL, 480 mL) [fruit flavor]; 400 mg/5 mL (100 mL, 480 mL) [orange flavor]
Swab (T-Stat® [DSC]): 2% (60s)
Tablet, as base: 250 mg, 500 mg

Tablet, as base [polymer-coated particles]:
PCE®: 333 mg, 500 mg
Tablet, as ethylsuccinate: 400 mg
E.E.S.®: 400 mg
Tablet, as stearate: 250 mg, 500 mg
Erythrocin®: 250 mg, 500 mg
Tablet, chewable, as ethylsuccinate:
EryPed®: 200 mg [fruit flavor] [DSC]
Tablet, delayed release, enteric coated, as base:
Ery-Tab®: 250 mg, 333 mg, 500 mg

Erythromycin and Benzoyl Peroxide
(er ith roe MYE sin & BEN zoe il per OKS ide)

U.S. Brand Names Benzamycin®; Benzamycin® Pak
Index Terms Benzoyl Peroxide and Erythromycin
Pharmacologic Category Acne Products; Topical Skin Product, Acne
Use Topical control of acne vulgaris
Pregnancy Risk Factor C
Dosage Apply twice daily, morning and evening
Additional Information Complete prescribing information for this medication should be consulted for additional detail.
Dosage Forms
Gel, topical: Erythromycin 30 mg and benzoyl peroxide 50 mg per g (23g, 47g)
Benzamycin®: Erythromycin 30 mg and benzoyl peroxide 50 mg per g (47 g) [contains alcohol 20%]
Benzamycin® Pak: Erythromycin 30 mg and benzoyl peroxide 50 mg per 0.8 g packet (60s) [supplied with diluent containing alcohol]

Erythromycin and Sulfisoxazole (er ith roe MYE sin & sul fi SOKS a zole)

U.S. Brand Names Pediazole® [DSC]
Canadian Brand Names Pediazole®
Index Terms Sulfisoxazole and Erythromycin
Pharmacologic Category Antibiotic, Macrolide; Antibiotic, Macrolide Combination; Antibiotic, Sulfonamide Derivative
Use Treatment of susceptible bacterial infections of the upper and lower respiratory tract, otitis media in children caused by susceptible strains of *Haemophilus influenzae*, and many other infections in patients allergic to penicillin
Pregnancy Risk Factor C
Medication Safety Issues
Sound-alike/look-alike issues:
Pediazole® may be confused with Pediapred®
Dosage Oral (dosage recommendation is based on the product's erythromycin content):
Children ≥2 months: 50 mg/kg/day erythromycin and 150 mg/kg/day sulfisoxazole in divided doses every 6 hours; not to exceed 2 g erythromycin/day or 6 g sulfisoxazole/day for 10 days
Adults >45 kg: 400 mg erythromycin and 1200 mg sulfisoxazole every 6 hours
Dosing adjustment in renal impairment (sulfisoxazole must be adjusted in renal impairment):
Cl$_{cr}$ 10-50 mL/minute: Administer every 8-12 hours
Cl$_{cr}$ <10 mL/minute: Administer every 12-24 hours
Additional Information Complete prescribing information for this medication should be consulted for additional detail.
Dosage Forms [DSC] = Discontinued product
Powder for oral suspension: Erythromycin ethylsuccinate 200 mg and sulfisoxazole acetyl 600 mg per 5 mL (100 mL, 200 mL)
Pediazole®: Erythromycin ethylsuccinate 200 mg and sulfisoxazole acetyl 600 mg per 5 mL (100 mL, 150 mL, 200 mL) [strawberry-banana flavor] [DSC]

♦ **Erythromycin Base** *see* Erythromycin *on page 609*
♦ **Erythromycin Ethylsuccinate** *see* Erythromycin *on page 609*
♦ **Erythromycin Lactobionate** *see* Erythromycin *on page 609*
♦ **Erythromycin Stearate** *see* Erythromycin *on page 609*
♦ **Erythropoiesis Stimulating Protein** *see* Darbepoetin Alfa *on page 453*
♦ **Erythropoietin** *see* Epoetin Alfa *on page 595*

Escitalopram (es sye TAL oh pram)

U.S. Brand Names Lexapro®
Canadian Brand Names Cipralex®
Index Terms Escitalopram Oxalate; Lu-26-054; S-Citalopram
Pharmacologic Category Antidepressant, Selective Serotonin Reuptake Inhibitor
Additional Appendix Information
Antidepressant Agents *on page 1866*
Selective Serotonin Reuptake Inhibitors (SSRIs) Pharmacokinetics *on page 1896*
Use Treatment of major depressive disorder; generalized anxiety disorders (GAD)
Restrictions An FDA-approved medication guide concerning the use of antidepressants in children and teenagers must be distributed when dispensing an outpatient prescription (new or refill) where this medication is to be used without direct supervision of a healthcare
(Continued)

Escitalopram *(Continued)*

provider. Medication guides are available at http://www.fda.gov/cder/Offices/ODS/medication_guides.htm. Dispense to parents or guardians of children and teenagers receiving this medication.

Pregnancy Risk Factor C

Pregnancy Implications Teratogenic effects have been reported in animal studies. Nonteratogenic effects including respiratory distress, cyanosis, apnea, seizures, temperature instability, feeding difficulty, vomiting, hypoglycemia, hypo- or hypertonia, hyper-reflexia, jitteriness, irritability, constant crying, and tremor have been reported in the neonate immediately following delivery after exposure late in the third trimester. Exposure to SSRIs late in pregnancy has also been associated with persistent pulmonary hypertension of the newborn (PPHN). Adverse effects may be due to toxic effects of SSRI or drug discontinuation. In some cases, effects may present clinically as serotonin syndrome. There are no adequate and well-controlled studies in pregnant women. Use during pregnancy only if the potential benefit to the mother outweighs the possible risk to the fetus. If treatment during pregnancy is required, consider tapering therapy during the third trimester.

Lactation Enters breast milk/not recommended

Contraindications Hypersensitivity to escitalopram, citalopram, or any component of the formulation; concomitant use or within 2 weeks of MAO inhibitors

Warnings/Precautions   [U.S. Boxed Warning]: Antidepressants increase the risk of suicidal thinking and behavior in children and adolescents with major depressive disorder (MDD) and other depressive disorders; consider risk prior to prescribing. All patients must be closely monitored for clinical worsening, suicidality, or unusual changes in behavior, especially during the initiation of therapy or following an increase or decrease in dosage. When used in children, the child's family or caregiver should be instructed to closely observe the patient and communicate condition with healthcare provider. A medication guide should be dispensed with each prescription. Escitalopram is not FDA approved for use in children

The possibility of a suicide attempt is inherent in major depression and may persist until remission occurs. Use caution in high-risk patients. Worsening depression and severe abrupt suicidality that are not part of the presenting symptoms may require discontinuation or modification of drug therapy. The patient's family or caregiver should be alerted to monitor patients for the emergence of suicidality and associated behaviors (such as agitation, irritability, hostility, impulsivity, and hypomania) and call healthcare provider.

May worsen psychosis in some patients or precipitate a shift to mania or hypomania in patients with bipolar disorder. Patients presenting with depressive symptoms should be screened for bipolar disorder. Monotherapy in patients with bipolar disorder should be avoided. Escitalopram is not FDA approved for the treatment of bipolar depression.

The potential for a severe reaction exists when used with MAO inhibitors, SSRIs/SNRIs or triptans; serotonin syndrome (hyperthermia, muscular rigidity, mental status changes/agitation, autonomic instability) may occur. Concurrent use with MAO inhibitors is contraindicated. May increase the risks associated with electroconvulsive therapy. Has a low potential to impair cognitive or motor performance; caution operating hazardous machinery or driving.

Use caution with a previous seizure disorder or condition predisposing to seizures such as brain damage, alcoholism, or concurrent therapy with other drugs which lower the seizure threshold. May cause hyponatremia/SIADH. May cause or exacerbate sexual dysfunction. Use caution with renal or liver impairment; concomitant CNS depressants; pregnancy (high doses of citalopram has been associated with teratogenicity in animals). Use caution with concomitant use of NSAIDs, ASA, or other drugs that affect coagulation; the risk of bleeding is potentiated.

Upon discontinuation of escitalopram therapy, gradually taper dose. If intolerable symptoms occur following a decrease in dosage or upon discontinuation of therapy, then resuming the previous dose with a more gradual taper should be considered.

Adverse Reactions

>10%:
- Central nervous system: Headache (24%), somnolence (6% to 13%), insomnia (9% to 12%)
- Gastrointestinal: Nausea (15%)
- Genitourinary: Ejaculation disorder (9% to 14%)

1% to 10%:
- Cardiovascular: Chest pain, hypertension, palpitation
- Central nervous system: Dizziness (5%), fatigue (5% to 8%), dreaming abnormal, concentration impaired, fever, irritability, lethargy, lightheadedness, migraine, vertigo, yawning
- Dermatologic: Rash
- Endocrine & metabolic: Libido decreased (3% to 7%), anorgasmia (2% to 6%), hot flashes, menstrual cramps, menstrual disorder
- Gastrointestinal: Diarrhea (8%), xerostomia (6% to 9%), appetite decreased (3%), constipation (3% to 5%), indigestion (3%), abdominal pain (2%), abdominal cramps, appetite increased, flatulence, gastroenteritis, gastroesophageal reflux, heartburn, toothache, vomiting, weight gain/loss
- Genitourinary: Impotence (3%), urinary tract infection, urinary frequency
- Neuromuscular & skeletal: Arthralgia, limb pain, muscle cramp, myalgia, neck/shoulder pain, paresthesia, tremor
- Ocular: Blurred vision
- Otic: Earache, tinnitus
- Respiratory: Rhinitis (5%), sinusitis (3%), bronchitis, cough, nasal or sinus congestion, sinus headache
- Miscellaneous: Diaphoresis (4% to 5%), flu-like syndrome (5%), allergy

<1% (Limited to important or life-threatening): Acute renal failure, aggression, akathisia, allergic reaction, anaphylaxis, anemia, angioedema, anxiety attack, apathy, atrial fibrillation, auditory hallucination, bilirubin increased, bradycardia, carbohydrate craving, chest tightness, choreoathetosis, confusion, decreased prothrombin, delirium, depersonalization,

depression aggravated, depression, dyskinesia, ecchymosis, ECG abnormal, emotional lability, epidermal necrolysis, erythema multiforme, excitability, grand mal seizure, hallucination, hemolytic anemia, hepatic necrosis, hepatitis, hypercholesterolemia, hyperglycemia, hyper-reflexia, malaise, muscle contractions (involuntary), muscle weakness, nystagmus, pancreatitis, panic reaction, priapism, prolactinemia, pulmonary embolism, QT prolonged, rhabdomyolysis, serotonin syndrome, SIADH, spontaneous abortion, suicidal tendency, suicide attempt, syncope, tachycardia, taste alteration, thrombocytopenia, thrombosis, tics, torsade de pointes, ventricular arrhythmia, vision abnormal, visual disturbance, weakness, withdrawal syndrome

Overdosage/Toxicology Treatment should be symptom-directed and supportive.

Drug Interactions

Cytochrome P450 Effect: Substrate (major) of CYP2C19, 3A4; **Inhibits** CYP2D6 (weak)

Increased Effect/Toxicity: Escitalopram should not be used with nonselective MAO inhibitors (phenelzine, isocarboxazid) or other drugs with MAO inhibition (linezolid); fatal reactions have been reported. Wait 2 weeks after stopping an MAO inhibitor before starting escitalopram. Concurrent selegiline has been associated with mania, hypertension, or serotonin syndrome (risk may be reduced relative to nonselective MAO inhibitors).

CYP2C19 inhibitors may increase the levels/effects of imipramine; example inhibitors include delavirdine, fluconazole, fluvoxamine, gemfibrozil, isoniazid, omeprazole, and ticlopidine. CYP3A4 inhibitors may increase the levels/effects of escitalopram; example inhibitors include azole antifungals, clarithromycin, diclofenac, doxycycline, erythromycin, imatinib, isoniazid, nefazodone, nicardipine, propofol, protease inhibitors, quinidine, telithromycin, and verapamil.

Combined use of SSRIs and buspirone, meperidine, moclobemide, nefazodone, other SSRIs/SNRIs, tramadol, trazodone, triptans and venlafaxine may increase the risk of serotonin syndrome. Escitalopram increases serum levels/effects of CYP2D6 substrates (tricyclic antidepressants). Escitalopram may increase desipramine levels.

Combined use of sumatriptan (and other serotonin agonists) may result in toxicity; weakness, hyper-reflexia, and incoordination have been observed with sumatriptan and SSRIs. In addition, concurrent use may theoretically increase the risk of serotonin syndrome; includes sumatriptan, naratriptan, rizatriptan, and zolmitriptan.

Concomitant use of escitalopram and NSAIDs, aspirin, or other drugs affecting coagulation has been associated with an increased risk of bleeding; monitor.

Decreased Effect: CYP2C19 inducers may decrease the levels/effects of imipramine; example inducers include aminoglutethimide, carbamazepine, phenytoin, and rifampin. CYP3A4 inducers may decrease the levels/effects of escitalopram; example inducers include aminoglutethimide, carbamazepine, nafcillin, nevirapine, phenobarbital, phenytoin, and rifamycins.

Ethanol/Nutrition/Herb Interactions

Ethanol: Avoid ethanol (may increase CNS depression).

Herb/Nutraceutical: Avoid valerian, St John's wort, SAMe, kava kava, and gotu kola (may increase CNS depression).

Stability Store at 25°C (77°F).

Mechanism of Action Escitalopram is the S-enantiomer of the racemic derivative citalopram, which selectively inhibits the reuptake of serotonin with little to no effect on norepinephrine or dopamine reuptake. It has no or very low affinity for 5-HT$_{1-7}$, alpha- and beta-adrenergic, D$_{1-5}$, H$_{1-3}$, M$_{1-5}$, and benzodiazepine receptors. Escitalopram does not bind or has low affinity for Na$^+$, K$^+$, Cl$^-$, and Ca^{++} ion channels.

Pharmacodynamics/Kinetics

Protein binding: 56% to plasma proteins

Metabolism: Hepatic via CYP2C19 and 3A4 to an active metabolite, S-desmethylcitalopram (S-DCT; 1/7 the activity); S-DCT is metabolized to S-didesmethylcitalopram (S-DDCT; active; 1/27 the activity) via CYP2D6

Half-life elimination: Escitalopram: 27-32 hours; S-desmethylcitalopram: 59 hours

Time to peak: Escitalopram: 5 ± 1.5 hours; S-desmethylcitalopram: 14 hours

Excretion: Urine (Escitalopram: 8%; S-DCT: 10%)

Clearance: Total body: 37-40 L/hour; Renal: Escitalopram: 2.7 L/hour; S-desmethylcitalopram: 6.9 L/hour

Dosage Oral:

Adults: Depression, GAD: Initial: 10 mg/day; dose may be increased to 20 mg/day after at least 1 week

Elderly: 10 mg/day; bioavailability and half-life are increased by 50% in the elderly

Dosage adjustment in renal impairment:

Mild-to-moderate impairment: No dosage adjustment needed

Severe impairment: Cl$_{cr}$ <20 mL/minute: Use caution

Dosage adjustment in hepatic impairment: 10 mg/day

Dietary Considerations May be taken with or without food.

Administration Administer once daily (morning or evening), with or without food.

Monitoring Parameters Mental status for depression, suicidal ideation (especially at the beginning of therapy or when doses are increased or decreased), anxiety, social functioning, mania, panic attacks; akathisia

Additional Information The tablet and oral solution dosage forms are bioequivalent. Clinically, escitalopram 20 mg is equipotent to citalopram 40 mg. Do not coadminister with citalopram.

Dosage Forms

Solution, oral: 1 mg/mL (240 mL) [peppermint flavor]

Tablet: 5 mg, 10 mg, 20 mg

Note: Cipralex® [CAN] is available only in 10 mg and 20 mg strengths.

♦ **Escitalopram Oxalate** see Escitalopram on page 613

♦ **Esclim®** see Estradiol on page 620

♦ **Eserine® (Can)** see Physostigmine on page 1365

♦ **Eserine Salicylate** *see* Physostigmine *on page 1365*
♦ **Esgic**® *see* Butalbital, Acetaminophen, and Caffeine *on page 259*
♦ **Esgic-Plus**™ *see* Butalbital, Acetaminophen, and Caffeine *on page 259*
♦ **Eskalith**® **[DSC]** *see* Lithium *on page 1023*
♦ **Eskalith CR**® **[DSC]** *see* Lithium *on page 1023*

Esmolol (ES moe lol)

U.S. Brand Names Brevibloc®
Canadian Brand Names Brevibloc®
Index Terms Esmolol Hydrochloride
Pharmacologic Category Antiarrhythmic Agent, Class II; Beta Blocker, Beta₁ Selective
Additional Appendix Information
Beta-Blockers *on page 1875*
Hypertension *on page 2063*
Use Treatment of supraventricular tachycardia (SVT) and atrial fibrillation/flutter (control ventricular rate); treatment of tachycardia and/or hypertension (especially intraoperative or postoperative); treatment of noncompensatory sinus tachycardia
Unlabeled/Investigational Use In children, for SVT and postoperative hypertension
Pregnancy Risk Factor C (manufacturer); D (2nd and 3rd trimesters - expert analysis)
Pregnancy Implications Teratogenic effects are not noted in animal studies. Fetal bradycardia can occur when administered in the 3rd trimester of pregnancy or at delivery.
Lactation Excretion in breast milk unknown/use with caution
Medication Safety Issues
Sound-alike/look-alike issues:
Esmolol may be confused with Osmitrol®
Brevibloc® may be confused with bretylium, Brevital®, Bumex®, Buprenex®
Contraindications Hypersensitivity to esmolol or any component of the formulation; sinus bradycardia; heart block greater than first degree (except in patients with a functioning artificial pacemaker); cardiogenic shock; bronchial asthma (relative); uncompensated cardiac failure; hypotension; pregnancy (2nd and 3rd trimesters)
Warnings/Precautions Consider pre-existing conditions such as sick sinus syndrome before initiating. Hypotension is common; patients need close blood pressure monitoring. Administer cautiously in compensated heart failure and monitor for a worsening of the condition. Use caution in patients with PVD (can aggravate arterial insufficiency). Use caution with concurrent use of beta-blockers and either verapamil or diltiazem; bradycardia or heart block can occur. Avoid concurrent I.V. use of both agents. Use beta-blockers cautiously in patients with bronchospastic disease; monitor pulmonary status closely. Use cautiously in diabetics because it can mask prominent hypoglycemic symptoms. Use with caution in patients with myasthenia gravis and psychiatric disease (may cause CNS depression). Use caution in patients with renal dysfunction (active metabolite retained). Adequate alpha-blockade is required prior to use of any beta-blocker for patients with untreated pheochromocytoma. Beta-blocker therapy should not be withdrawn abruptly (particularly in patients with CAD), but gradually tapered to avoid acute tachycardia, hypertension, and/or ischemia. Do not use in the treatment of hypertension associated with vasoconstriction related to hypothermia. Concentrations >10 mcg/mL or infusion into small veins or through a butterfly catheter should be avoided (can cause thrombophlebitis). Extravasation can lead to skin necrosis and sloughing. Safety and efficacy have not been established in children.
Adverse Reactions
>10%:
Cardiovascular: Asymptomatic hypotension (dose related: 25% to 38%), symptomatic hypotension (dose related: 12%)
Miscellaneous: Diaphoresis (10%)
1% to 10%:
Cardiovascular: Peripheral ischemia (1%)
Central nervous system: Dizziness (3%), somnolence (3%), confusion (2%), headache (2%), agitation (2%), fatigue (1%)
Gastrointestinal: Nausea (7%), vomiting (1%)
Local: Pain on injection (8%), infusion site reaction
<1% (Limited to important or life-threatening): Alopecia, bronchospasm, chest pain, CHF, depression, dyspnea, edema, exfoliative dermatitis, heart block, infusion site reactions, paresthesia, pruritus, pulmonary edema, rigors, seizure, severe bradycardia/asystole (rare), skin necrosis (from extravasation), syncope, thrombophlebitis, urinary retention
Overdosage/Toxicology Symptoms include hypotension, bradycardia, bronchospasm, congestive heart failure, and heart block. Initially, a decrease/discontinuation of the esmolol infusion and administration of fluids may be the best treatment for hypotension. Sympathomimetics (eg, epinephrine or dopamine), glucagon, or an anticholinergic or a pacemaker can be used to treat the toxic bradycardia, asystole, and/or hypotension. Bradycardia and hypotension resistant to atropine, isoproterenol, or pacing may respond to glucagon. Wide QRS defects caused by membrane-depressant poisoning may respond to hypertonic sodium bicarbonate. Repeat-dose charcoal, hemoperfusion, or hemodialysis may be helpful in removal of only those beta-blockers with a small V_d, long half-life, or low intrinsic clearance (acebutolol, atenolol, nadolol, sotalol).
Drug Interactions
Increased Effect/Toxicity: Anticholinesterase inhibitors, amiodarone, cardia glycosides dipyridamole (I.V.) increase bradycardia; beta blockers increase alpha₁ blockers orthostasis, alpha/beta agonists (direct acting) vasopressor effects, alpha₂ agonists rebound hypertension when withdrawn. Beta-blockers may enhance the hypoglycemia and mask most symptoms of hypoglycemia in patients on insulin or sulfonylureas. Calcium channel blockers increase hypotension
Decreased Effect: Alpha₂ agonists decrease the effectiveness of beta blockers (beta₁ selective). NSAIDs may diminish the antihypertensive effects of beta blockers.

Stability Clear, colorless to light yellow solution which should be stored at 15°C to 30°C (59°F to 85°F); do not freeze. Protect from excessive heat.

Stability of parenteral admixture at room temperature (25°C) is 24 hours.

Mechanism of Action Class II antiarrhythmic: Competitively blocks response to beta$_1$-adrenergic stimulation with little or no effect of beta$_2$-receptors except at high doses, no intrinsic sympathomimetic activity, no membrane stabilizing activity

Pharmacodynamics/Kinetics

Onset of action: Beta-blockade: I.V.: 2-10 minutes (quickest when loading doses are administered)

Duration of hemodynamic effects: 10-30 minutes; prolonged following higher cumulative doses, extended duration of use

Protein binding: 55%

Metabolism: In blood by red blood cell esterases

Half-life elimination: Adults: 9 minutes; elimination of metabolite decreases with end stage renal disease

Excretion: Urine (~69% as metabolites, 2% unchanged drug)

Dosage I.V. infusion requires an infusion pump (must be adjusted to individual response and tolerance):

Children:

SVT (unlabeled use): A limited amount of information regarding esmolol use in pediatric patients is currently available. Some centers have utilized doses of 100-500 mcg/kg given over 1 minute for control of supraventricular tachycardias.

Postoperative hypertension (unlabeled use): Loading doses of 500 mcg/kg/minute over 1 minute with maximal doses of 50-250 mcg/kg/minute (mean = 173) have been used in addition to nitroprusside to treat postoperative hypertension after coarctation of aorta repair.

Adults:

Intraoperative tachycardia and/or hypertension (immediate control): Initial bolus: 80 mg (~1 mg/kg) over 30 seconds, followed by a 150 mcg/kg/minute infusion, if necessary. Adjust infusion rate as needed to maintain desired heart rate and/or blood pressure, up to 300 mcg/kg/minute.

For control of postoperative hypertension, as many as one-third of patients may require higher doses (250-300 mcg/kg/minute) to control blood pressure; the safety of doses >300 mcg/kg/minute has not been studied.

Supraventricular tachycardia or gradual control of postoperative tachycardia/hypertension: Loading dose: 500 mcg/kg over 1 minute; follow with a 50 mcg/kg/minute infusion for 4 minutes; response to this initial infusion rate may be a rough indication of the responsiveness of the ventricular rate.

Infusion may be continued at 50 mcg/kg/minute or, if the response is inadequate, titrated upward in 50 mcg/kg/minute increments (increased no more frequently than every 4 minutes) to a maximum of 200 mcg/kg/minute.

To achieve more rapid response, following the initial loading dose and 50 mcg/kg/minute infusion, rebolus with a second 500 mcg/kg loading dose over 1 minute, and increase the maintenance infusion to 100 mcg/kg/minute for 4 minutes. If necessary, a third (and final) 500 mcg/kg loading dose may be administered, prior to increasing to an infusion rate of 150 mcg/kg/minute. After 4 minutes of the 150 mcg/kg/minute infusion, the infusion rate may be increased to a maximum rate of 200 mcg/kg/minute (without a bolus dose).

Usual dosage range (SVT): 50-200 mcg/kg/minute with average dose of 100 mcg/kg/minute.

Guidelines for transfer to oral therapy (beta blocker, calcium channel blocker):

Infusion should be reduced by 50% 30 minutes following the first dose of the alternative agent

Manufacturer suggests following the second dose of the alternative drug, patient's response should be monitored and if control is adequate for the first hours, esmolol may be discontinued.

Dialysis: Not removed by hemo- or peritoneal dialysis; supplemental dose is not necessary.

Administration Infusions must be administered with an infusion pump. The concentrate (250 mg/mL ampul) is **not** for direct I.V. injection, but rather must first be diluted to a final concentration of 10 mg/mL (ie, 2.5 g in 250 mL or 5 g in 500 mL). Concentrations >10 mg/mL or infusion into small veins or through a butterfly catheter should be avoided (can cause thrombophlebitis). Decrease or discontinue infusion if hypotension or congestive heart failure occur. Medication port of premixed bags should be used to withdraw only the initial bolus, if necessary (not to be used for withdrawal of additional bolus doses).

Monitoring Parameters Blood pressure, heart rate, MAP, ECG, respiratory rate, I.V. site; cardiac monitor and blood pressure monitor required

Test Interactions Increases cholesterol (S), glucose

Dosage Forms

Infusion [premixed in sodium chloride; preservative free]:
Brevibloc®: 2000 mg (100 mL) [20 mg/mL; double strength]; 2500 mg (250 mL) [10 mg/mL]

Injection, solution, as hydrochloride: 10 mg/mL (10 mL) [premixed in sodium chloride]
Brevibloc®: 10 mg/mL (10 mL) [alcohol free; premixed in sodium chloride]; 20 mg/mL (5 mL, 100 mL) [alcohol free; double strength; premixed in sodium chloride]; 250 mg/mL (10 mL) [contains alcohol 25%, propylene glycol 25%; concentrate]

♦ **Esmolol Hydrochloride** *see* Esmolol *on page 616*

Esomeprazole (es oh ME pray zol)

U.S. Brand Names Nexium®
Canadian Brand Names Nexium®
Index Terms Esomeprazole Magnesium; Esomeprazole Sodium
Pharmacologic Category Proton Pump Inhibitor; Substituted Benzimidazole
Additional Appendix Information
  Helicobacter pylori Treatment *on page 2056*
Use
  Oral: Short-term (4-8 weeks) treatment of erosive esophagitis; maintaining symptom resolution and healing of erosive esophagitis; treatment of symptomatic gastroesophageal reflux disease (GERD); as part of a multidrug regimen for *Helicobacter pylori* eradication in patients with duodenal ulcer disease (active or history of within the past 5 years); prevention of gastric ulcers in patients at risk (age ≥60 years and/or history of gastric ulcer) associated with continuous NSAID therapy; long-term treatment of pathological hypersecretory conditions including Zollinger-Ellison syndrome
  I.V.: Short-term (≤10 days) treatment of gastroesophageal reflux disease (GERD) when oral therapy is not possible or appropriate
Pregnancy Risk Factor B
Pregnancy Implications Teratogenic effects were not observed in animal studies. However, there are no adequate and well-controlled studies in pregnant women. Congenital abnormalities have been reported sporadically following omeprazole use during pregnancy.
Lactation Excretion in breast milk unknown/not recommended
Contraindications Hypersensitivity to esomeprazole, substituted benzimidazoles (ie, lansoprazole, omeprazole, pantoprazole, rabeprazole), or any component of the formulation
Warnings/Precautions Relief of symptoms does not preclude the presence of a gastric malignancy. Atrophic gastritis (by biopsy) has been noted with long-term omeprazole therapy; this may also occur with esomeprazole. No reports of enterochromaffin-like (ECL) cell carcinoids, dysplasia, or neoplasia have occurred. Severe liver dysfunction may require dosage reductions. Safety and efficacy in children <12 years of age have not been established.
Adverse Reactions Unless otherwise specified, percentages represent adverse reactions identified in clinical trials evaluating the intravenous formulation.

  >10%: Central nervous system: Headache (I.V. 11%; oral 4% to 8%)
  1% to 10%:
    Central nervous system: Dizziness (3%)
    Dermatologic: Pruritus (≤1%)
    Gastrointestinal: Flatulence (10%), nausea (I.V. 6%; oral 2%), abdominal pain (6%; oral 3% to 4%), diarrhea (4%), xerostomia (I.V. 4%; oral ≥1%), dyspepsia (<1% to 6%), constipation (3%)
    Local: Injection site reaction (2%)
    Respiratory: Sinusitis (I.V. 2%; oral <1%), respiratory infection (1%)
  <1%, postmarketing, and/or case reports (limited to important or life-threatening): Acne, aggression, agitation, agranulocytosis, albuminuria, alkaline phosphatase increased, allergic reactions, alopecia, anaphylactic reaction/shock, angioedema, anorexia, apathy, arthralgia, arthritis exacerbation, arthropathy, asthenia, asthma exacerbation, benign polyps/nodules, bilirubinemia, blurred vision, bronchospasm, candidiasis (GI and genital), cervical lymphadenopathy, chest pain, confusion, conjunctivitis, cough, cramps, creatinine increased, cystitis, depression, dermatitis, duodenitis, dysmenorrhea, dysphagia, dyspnea, dysuria, earache, edema (including facial, peripheral and tongue), epigastric pain, epistaxis, eructation, erythema multiforme, erythematous rash, esophageal varices, fatigue, fever, fibromyalgia syndrome, flu-like syndrome, flushing, fungal infection, gastroenteritis, GI dysplasia, glycosuria, goiter, gynecomastia, hallucinations, hematuria, hepatic encephalopathy, hepatic failure, hepatitis, hernia, hiccups, hot flushes, hyperhidrosis, hypertension, hypertonia, hyperuricemia, hypoesthesia, hyponatremia, impotence, insomnia, interstitial nephritis, jaundice, larynx edema, leukocytosis, leukopenia, maculopapular rash, malaise, micturition increased, migraine, muscular weakness, myalgia, nervousness, otitis media, pain, pancreatitis, pancytopenia, paresthesia, parosmia, pharyngitis, photosensitivity, polymyalgia rheumatica, polyuria, pruritus ani, rash, rhinitis, rigors, serum gastrin increased, skin irritation, somnolence, Stevens-Johnson syndrome, stomatitis, tachycardia, taste disturbances, thirst, thrombocytopenia, thyroid-stimulating hormone increased, tinnitus, total bilirubin increased, toxic epidermal necrolysis, transaminases increased, tremor, urticaria, vaginitis, vertigo, visual field defects, vitamin B_{12} deficiency, vomiting, weight changes
Overdosage/Toxicology Doses up to 2400 mg have been reported. Symptoms of overdose may include confusion, drowsiness, blurred vision, tachycardia, nausea, sweating, headache, or xerostomia. Treatment is symptom-directed and supportive; not dialyzable.
Drug Interactions
  Cytochrome P450 Effect: Substrate of CYP2C19 (major), 3A4 (minor); **Inhibits** CYP2C19 (moderate)
  Increased Effect/Toxicity: Esomeprazole and omeprazole may increase the levels of carbamazepine, HMG-CoA reductase inhibitors, methotrexate, and CYP2C19 substrates, including benzodiazepines metabolized by oxidation (eg, diazepam, midazolam, triazolam)
  Decreased Effect: CYP2C19 inducers may decrease the levels/effects of esomeprazole; example inducers include aminoglutethimide, carbamazepine, phenytoin, and rifampin. Proton pump inhibitors may decrease the absorption of atazanavir, indinavir, iron salts, itraconazole, and ketoconazole.
Ethanol/Nutrition/Herb Interactions Food: Absorption is decreased by 43% to 53% when taken with food.
Stability
  Capsule: Store at 15°C to 30°C (59°F to 86°F). Keep container tightly closed.
  Powder for injection: Store at 15°C to 30°C (59°F to 86°F). Protect from light.
    For I.V. injection: Reconstitute powder with 5 mL NS.

For I.V. infusion: Initially reconstitute powder with 5 mL of NS, LR, or D₅W, then further dilute to a final volume of 50 mL.

Following reconstitution, solution for injection prepared in NS, and solution for infusion prepared in NS or LR should be used within 12 hours. Following reconstitution, solution for infusion prepared in D₅W should be used within 6 hours. Refrigeration is not required following reconstitution.

Mechanism of Action Proton pump inhibitor suppresses gastric acid secretion by inhibition of the H⁺/K⁺-ATPase in the gastric parietal cell

Pharmacodynamics/Kinetics

Distribution: V_{dss}: 16 L

Protein binding: 97%

Metabolism: Hepatic via CYP2C19 and 3A4 enzymes to hydroxy, desmethyl, and sulfone metabolites (all inactive)

Bioavailability: 90% with repeat dosing

Half-life elimination: 1-1.5 hours

Time to peak: 1.5 hours

Excretion: Urine (80%); feces (20%)

Dosage

Adolescents 12-17 years: Oral: GERD: 20-40 mg once daily for up to 8 weeks

Adults:

Oral:

Erosive esophagitis (healing): Initial: 20-40 mg once daily for 4-8 weeks; if incomplete healing, may continue for an additional 4-8 weeks; maintenance: 20 mg once daily

Symptomatic GERD: 20 mg once daily for 4 weeks; may continue an additional 4 weeks if symptoms persist

Helicobacter pylori eradication: 40 mg once daily for 10 days; requires combination therapy

Prevention of NSAID-induced gastric ulcers: 20-40 mg once daily for up to 6 months

Pathological hypersecretory conditions (Zollinger-Ellison syndrome): 40 mg twice daily; adjust regimen to individual patient needs; doses up to 240 mg/day have been administered

I.V.: GERD: 20 mg or 40 mg once daily for ≤10 days; change to oral therapy as soon as appropriate

Elderly: No dosage adjustment needed

Dosage adjustment in renal impairment: No dosage adjustment needed

Dosage adjustment in hepatic impairment:

Mild-to-moderate hepatic impairment (Child-Pugh Class A or B): No dosage adjustment needed

Severe hepatic impairment (Child-Pugh Class C): Dose should not exceed 20 mg/day

Dietary Considerations Take at least 1 hour before meals; best if taken before breakfast. The contents of the capsule may be mixed in applesauce or water; pellets also remain intact when exposed to orange juice, apple juice, and yogurt.

Administration

Oral: Capsule should be swallowed whole and taken at least 1 hour before eating (best if taken before breakfast). For patients with difficulty swallowing, open capsule and mix contents with 1 tablespoon of applesauce. Swallow immediately; mixture should not be chewed or warmed. The mixture should not be stored for future use.

I.V.: May be administered by injection (≥3 minutes) or infusion (10-30 minutes). Flush line prior to and after administration with NS, LR, or D₅W.

Nasogastric tube: Open capsule and place intact granules into a 60 mL syringe; mix with 50 mL of water. Replace plunger and shake vigorously for 15 seconds. Ensure that no granules remain in syringe tip. Do not administer if pellets dissolve or disintegrate. Use immediately after preparation. After administration, flush nasogastric tube with additional water.

Monitoring Parameters Susceptibility testing recommended in patients who fail *H. pylori* eradication regimen (esomeprazole, clarithromycin, and amoxicillin)

Additional Information Esomeprazole is the S-isomer of omeprazole.

Dosage Forms Note: Strength expressed as base

Capsule, delayed release, as magnesium:

Nexium®: 20 mg, 40 mg

Injection, powder for reconstitution, as sodium:

Nexium®: 20 mg, 40 mg [contains edetate sodium]

♦ **Esomeprazole Magnesium** *see* Esomeprazole *on page 618*

♦ **Esomeprazole Sodium** *see* Esomeprazole *on page 618*

♦ **Esoterica® Regular [OTC]** *see* Hydroquinone *on page 859*

♦ **Estalis® (Can)** *see* Estradiol and Norethindrone *on page 624*

♦ **Estalis-Sequi® (Can)** *see* Estradiol and Norethindrone *on page 624*

Estazolam (es TA zoe lam)

U.S. Brand Names ProSom®

Pharmacologic Category Benzodiazepine

Additional Appendix Information

Benzodiazepines *on page 1874*

Use Short-term management of insomnia

Restrictions C-IV

Pregnancy Risk Factor X

Medication Safety Issues

Sound-alike/look-alike issues:

ProSom® may be confused with PhosLo®, Proscar®, Pro-Sof® Plus, Prozac®, Psorcon®

Dosage Adults: Oral: 1 mg at bedtime, some patients may require 2 mg; start at doses of 0.5 mg in debilitated or small elderly patients

(Continued)

Estazolam *(Continued)*

Dosing adjustment in hepatic impairment: May be necessary

Additional Information Complete prescribing information for this medication should be consulted for additional detail.

Dosage Forms Tablet: 1 mg, 2 mg

♦ **Ester-E™ [OTC]** *see Vitamin E on page 1794*

♦ **Esterified Estrogen and Methyltestosterone** *see Estrogens (Esterified) and Methyltestosterone on page 637*

♦ **Esterified Estrogens** *see Estrogens (Esterified) on page 635*

♦ **Estrace®** *see Estradiol on page 620*

♦ **Estraderm®** *see Estradiol on page 620*

Estradiol *(es tra DYE ole)*

U.S. Brand Names Alora®; Climara®; Delestrogen®; Depo®-Estradiol; Elestrin™; Esclim®; Estrace®; Estraderm®; Estrasorb™; Estring®; EstroGel®; Femring™; Femtrace®; Gynodiol®; Menostar™; Vagifem®; Vivelle®; Vivelle-Dot®

Canadian Brand Names Climara®; Depo®-Estradiol; Estrace®; Estraderm®; Estradot®; Estring®; EstroGel®; Menostar™; Oesclim®; Sandoz-Estradiol Derm 50; Sandoz-Estradiol Derm 75; Sandoz-Estradiol Derm 100; Vagifem®

Index Terms Estradiol Acetate; Estradiol Cypionate; Estradiol Hemihydrate; Estradiol Transdermal; Estradiol Valerate

Pharmacologic Category Estrogen Derivative

Use Treatment of moderate-to-severe vasomotor symptoms associated with menopause; treatment of vulvar and vaginal atrophy; hypoestrogenism (due to hypogonadism, castration, or primary ovarian failure); prostatic cancer (palliation), breast cancer (palliation), osteoporosis (prophylaxis); abnormal uterine bleeding due to hormonal imbalance; postmenopausal urogenital symptoms of the lower urinary tract (urinary urgency, dysuria)

Pregnancy Risk Factor X

Pregnancy Implications Estrogens are not indicated for use during pregnancy or immediately postpartum. Increased risk of fetal reproductive tract disorders and other birth defects have been observed with diethylstilbestrol (DES); do not use during pregnancy.

Lactation Enters breast milk/use caution

Medication Safety Issues

Sound-alike/look-alike issues:

Alora® may be confused with Aldara™

Estraderm® may be confused with Testoderm®

International issues:

Vivelle®: Brand name for ethinyl estradiol and norgestimate in Austria

Estring® may be confused with Estrena® [Finland]

Estrena® [Finland] may be confused with estrone in the U.S.

Transdermal patch may contain conducting metal (eg, aluminum); remove patch prior to MRI.

Contraindications Hypersensitivity to estradiol or any component of the formulation; undiagnosed abnormal vaginal bleeding; history of or current thrombophlebitis or venous thromboembolic disorders (including DVT, PE); active or recent (within 1 year) arterial thromboembolic disease (eg, stroke, MI); carcinoma of the breast, except in appropriately selected patients being treated for metastatic disease; estrogen-dependent tumor; hepatic dysfunction or disease; porphyria; pregnancy

Warnings/Precautions

Cardiovascular-related considerations: **[U.S. Boxed Warning]: Estrogens with or without progestin should not be used to prevent coronary heart disease.** Use caution with cardiovascular disease or dysfunction. May increase the risks of hypertension, myocardial infarction (MI), stroke, pulmonary emboli (PE), and deep vein thrombosis; incidence of these effects was shown to be significantly increased in postmenopausal women using conjugated equine estrogens (CEE) in combination with medroxyprogesterone acetate (MPA). Nonfatal MI, PE, and thrombophlebitis have also been reported in males taking high doses of CEE (eg, for prostate cancer). Estrogen compounds are generally associated with lipid effects such as increased HDL-cholesterol and decreased LDL-cholesterol. Triglycerides may also be increased; use with caution in patients with familial defects of lipoprotein metabolism. Whenever possible, estrogens should be discontinued at least 4 weeks prior to and for 2 weeks following elective surgery associated with an increased risk of thromboembolism or during periods of prolonged immobilization.

Neurological considerations: **[U.S. Boxed Warning]: The risk of dementia may be increased in postmenopausal women;** increased incidence was observed in women ≥65 years of age taking CEE alone or in combination with MPA.

Cancer-related considerations: **[U.S. Boxed Warning]: Unopposed estrogens may increase the risk of endometrial carcinoma in postmenopausal women.** Estrogens may exacerbate endometriosis. Malignant transformation of residual endometrial implants has been reported posthysterectomy with estrogen only therapy. Consider adding a progestin in women with residual endometriosis posthysterectomy. Estrogens may increase the risk of breast cancer. An increased risk of invasive breast cancer was observed in postmenopausal women using CEE in combination with MPA; a smaller increase in risk was seen with estrogen therapy alone in observational studies. An increase in abnormal mammograms has also been reported with estrogen and progestin therapy. Estrogen use may lead to severe hypercalcemia in patients with breast cancer and bone metastases; discontinue estrogen if hypercalcemia occurs.

Estrogens may cause retinal vascular thrombosis; discontinue permanently if papilledema or retinal vascular lesions are observed on examination. Use with caution in patients with diseases which may be exacerbated by fluid retention, including asthma, epilepsy, migraine, diabetes or renal dysfunction. Use with caution in patients with a history of severe hypocalcemia, SLE, hepatic hemangiomas, porphyria, endometriosis, and gallbladder disease. Use caution with history of cholestatic jaundice associated with past estrogen use or pregnancy. Safety and efficacy in pediatric patients have not been established. Prior to puberty, estrogens may cause premature closure of the epiphyses, premature breast development in girls or gynecomastia in boys. Vaginal bleeding and vaginal cornification may also be induced in girls.

Before prescribing estrogen therapy to postmenopausal women, the risks and benefits must be weighed for each patient. Women should be informed of these risks and benefits, as well as possible effects of progestin when added to estrogen therapy. Estrogens with or without progestin should be used for shortest duration possible consistent with treatment goals. Conduct periodic risk:benefit assessments.

When used solely for prevention of osteoporosis in women at significant risk, nonestrogen treatment options should be considered. When used solely for the treatment of vulvar and vaginal atrophy, topical vaginal products should be considered. Use caution applying topical products to severely atrophic vaginal mucosa. Absorption of the topical emulsion (Estrasorb™) and topical gel (Elestrin™) is increased by application of sunscreen; do not apply sunscreen within close proximity of estradiol. Application of EstroGel® with sunscreen has not been evaluated. Transdermal patch may contain conducting metal (eg, aluminum); remove patch prior to MRI.

Adverse Reactions Frequency not defined. Some adverse reactions observed with estrogen and/or progestin combination therapy.

Cardiovascular: DVT, edema, hypertension, MI, stroke, venous thromboembolism

Central nervous system: Anxiety, dementia, dizziness, epilepsy exacerbation, headache, irritability, mental depression, migraine, mood disturbances, nervousness

Dermatologic: Angioedema, chloasma, erythema multiforme, erythema nodosum, hemorrhagic eruption, hirsutism, loss of scalp hair, melasma, rash, pruritus, urticaria

Endocrine & metabolic: Breast cancer, breast enlargement, breast tenderness, fibrocystic breast changes, HDL-cholesterol increased, galactorrhea, glucose intolerance, hypocalcemia, LDL-cholesterol decreased, libido changes, nipple pain, serum triglycerides/phospholipids increased, thyroid-binding globulin increased, total thyroid hormone (T_4) increased, vaginal discharge, vaginitis

Gastrointestinal: Abdominal cramps, abdominal pain, bloating, cholecystitis, cholelithiasis, diarrhea, flatulence, gallbladder disease, nausea, pancreatitis, vomiting, weight gain/loss

Genitourinary: Alterations in frequency and flow of menses, cervical secretion changes, endometrial cancer, endometrial hyperplasia, Pap smear suspicious, uterine leiomyomata size increased, vaginal candidiasis

    Vaginal: Trauma from applicator insertion may occur in women with severely atrophic vaginal mucosa

Hematologic: Aggravation of porphyria, antithrombin III and antifactor Xa decreased, fibrinogen levels increased, platelet aggregability increased, platelet count increased, prothrombin increased; factors VII, VIII, IX, X increased

Hepatic: Cholestatic jaundice, hepatic hemangioma enlargement

Local: Thrombophlebitis

    Transdermal patches: Burning, erythema, irritation

Neuromuscular & skeletal: Arthralgia, back pain, chorea, leg cramps

Ocular: Contact lens intolerance, corneal curvature steepening, retinal vascular thrombosis

Respiratory: Asthma exacerbation, pulmonary thromboembolism

Miscellaneous: Anaphylactoid/anaphylactic reactions

Postmarketing and/or case reports: Liver function tests increased (rare), leg pain

Overdosage/Toxicology Symptoms include fluid retention, jaundice, thrombophlebitis, nausea, and vomiting. Toxicity is unlikely following single exposures of excessive doses. Treatment following emesis and charcoal administration should be supportive and symptomatic.

Drug Interactions

    Cytochrome P450 Effect: Substrate of CYP1A2 (major), 2A6 (minor), 2B6 (minor), 2C9 (minor), 2C19 (minor), 2D6 (minor), 2E1 (minor), 3A4 (major); **Inhibits** CYP1A2 (weak), 2C8 (weak); **Induces** CYP3A4 (weak)

    Increased Effect/Toxicity: Estradiol with hydrocortisone increases corticosteroid toxic potential. Anticoagulants and estradiol increase the potential for thromboembolic events. Estrogen derivatives may enhance the hepatotoxic effect of cyclosporine. Estrogen derivatives may increase the serum concentration of cyclosporine.

    Decreased Effect: CYP1A2 inducers may decrease the levels/effects of estradiol; example inducers include aminoglutethimide, carbamazepine, phenobarbital, and rifampin. CYP3A4 inducers may decrease the levels/effects of estradiol; example inducers include aminoglutethimide, carbamazepine, nafcillin, nevirapine, phenobarbital, phenytoin, and rifamycins. Estrogen derivatives may diminish the therapeutic effect of thyroid products.

Ethanol/Nutrition/Herb Interactions

    Ethanol: Avoid ethanol (routine use increases estrogen level and risk of breast cancer). Ethanol may also increase the risk of osteoporosis.

    Food: Folic acid absorption may be decreased

    Herb/Nutraceutical: St John's wort may decrease levels. Herbs with estrogenic properties may enhance the adverse/toxic effect of estrogen derivatives; examples include alfalfa, black cohosh, bloodroot, hops, kudzu, licorice, red clover, saw palmetto, soybean, thyme, wild yam, yucca.

Mechanism of Action Estrogens are responsible for the development and maintenance of the female reproductive system and secondary sexual characteristics. Estradiol is the principle intracellular human estrogen and is more potent than estrone and estriol at the receptor level; it is the primary estrogen secreted prior to menopause. Following menopause, estrone and estrone sulfate are more highly produced. Estrogens modulate the pituitary secretion of gonadotropins, luteinizing hormone, and follicle-stimulating hormone through a negative feedback system; estrogen replacement reduces elevated levels of these hormones in postmenopausal women.

(Continued)

Estradiol *(Continued)*

Pharmacodynamics/Kinetics

Absorption: Oral, topical: Well absorbed

Protein binding: 37% to sex hormone-binding globulin; 61% to albumin

Metabolism: Hepatic via oxidation and conjugation in GI tract; hydroxylated via CYP3A4 to metabolites; first-pass effect; enterohepatic recirculation; reversibly converted to estrone and estriol

Excretion: Primarily urine (as metabolites estrone and estriol); feces (small amounts)

Dosage All dosage needs to be adjusted based upon the patient's response

Oral:

Prostate cancer (androgen-dependent, inoperable, progressing): 10 mg 3 times/day for at least 3 months

Breast cancer (inoperable, progressing in appropriately selected patients): 10 mg 3 times/day for at least 3 months

Osteoporosis prophylaxis in postmenopausal females: 0.5 mg/day in a cyclic regimen (3 weeks on and 1 week off)

Female hypoestrogenism (due to hypogonadism, castration, or primary ovarian failure): 1-2 mg/day; titrate as necessary to control symptoms using minimal effective dose for maintenance therapy

Moderate-to-severe vasomotor symptoms associated with menopause: 1-2 mg/day, adjusted as necessary to limit symptoms; administration should be cyclic (3 weeks on, 1 week off). Patients should be re-evaluated at 3- to 6-month intervals to determine if treatment is still necessary.

I.M.:

Prostate cancer: Valerate: ≥30 mg or more every 1-2 weeks

Moderate-to-severe vasomotor symptoms associated with menopause:

Cypionate: 1-5 mg every 3-4 weeks

Valerate: 10-20 mg every 4 weeks

Female hypoestrogenism (due to hypogonadism):

Cypionate: 1.5-2 mg monthly

Valerate: 10-20 mg every 4 weeks

Topical:

Emulsion: Moderate-to-severe vasomotor symptoms associated with menopause: 3.84 g applied once daily in the morning

Gel: Moderate-to-severe vasomotor symptoms associated with menopause, vulvar and vaginal atrophy:

Elestrin™: 0.87g/day applied at the same time each day

EstroGel®: 1.25 g/day applied at the same time each day

Transdermal: Indicated dose may be used continuously in patients without an intact uterus. May be given continuously or cyclically (3 weeks on, 1 week off) in patients with an intact uterus **(exception - Menostar™, see specific dosing instructions)**. When changing patients from oral to transdermal therapy, start transdermal patch 1 week after discontinuing oral hormone (may begin sooner if symptoms reappear within 1 week):

Once-weekly patch:

Moderate to severe vasomotor symptoms associated with menopause (Climara®): Apply 0.025 mg/day patch once weekly. Adjust dose as necessary to control symptoms. Patients should be re-evaluated at 3- to 6-month intervals to determine if treatment is still necessary.

Osteoporosis prophylaxis in postmenopausal women:

Climara®: Apply patch once weekly; minimum effective dose 0.025 mg/day; adjust response to therapy by biochemical markers and bone mineral density

Menostar™: Apply patch once weekly. In women with a uterus, also administer a progestin for 14 days every 6-12 months

Twice-weekly patch:

Moderate-to-severe vasomotor symptoms associated with menopause, vulvar/vaginal atrophy, female hypogonadism: Titrate to lowest dose possible to control symptoms, adjusting initial dose after the first month of therapy; re-evaluate therapy at 3- to 6-month intervals to taper or discontinue medication:

Alora®, Esclim®, Estraderm®, Vivelle-Dot®: Apply 0.05 mg patch twice weekly

Vivelle®: Apply 0.0375 mg patch twice weekly

Prevention of osteoporosis in postmenopausal women:

Alora®, Vivelle®, Vivelle-Dot®: Apply 0.025 mg patch twice weekly, increase dose as necessary

Estraderm®: Apply 0.05 mg patch twice weekly

Vaginal cream: Vulvar and vaginal atrophy: Insert 2-4 g/day intravaginally for 2 weeks, then gradually reduce to ½ the initial dose for 2 weeks, followed by a maintenance dose of 1 g 1-3 times/week

Vaginal ring:

Postmenopausal vaginal atrophy, urogenital symptoms: Estring®: 2 mg intravaginally; following insertion, ring should remain in place for 90 days

Moderate-to-severe vasomotor symptoms associated with menopause: vulvar/vaginal atrophy: Femring™: 0.05 mg intravaginally; following insertion, ring should remain in place for 3 months; dose may be increased to 0.1 mg if needed

Vaginal tablets: Atrophic vaginitis: Vagifem®: Initial: Insert 1 tablet once daily for 2 weeks; maintenance: Insert 1 tablet twice weekly; attempts to discontinue or taper medication should be made at 3- to 6-month intervals

Dosing adjustment in hepatic impairment:

Mild-to-moderate liver impairment: Dosage reduction of estrogens is recommended

Severe liver impairment: **Not recommended**

Dietary Considerations Ensure adequate calcium and vitamin D intake when used for the prevention of osteoporosis.

Administration

Injection formulation: Intramuscular use only

Emulsion: Apply to clean, dry skin while in a sitting position. Contents of two pouches (total 3.48 g) are to be applied individually, once daily in the morning. Apply contents of first pouch to left thigh; massage into skin of left thigh and calf until thoroughly absorbed (~3 minutes). Apply excess from both hands to the buttocks. Apply contents of second pouch to the right thigh; massage into skin of right thigh and calf until thoroughly absorbed (~3 minutes). Apply excess from both hands to buttocks. Wash hands with soap and water. Allow skin to dry before covering legs with clothing. Do not apply to other areas of body. Do not apply to red or irritated skin.

Gel: Apply to clean, dry, unbroken skin at the same time each day. Allow to dry for 5 minutes prior to dressing. Gel is flammable; avoid fire or flame until dry. After application, wash hands with soap and water. Prior to the first use, pump must be primed. Do not apply gel to breast.

Elestrin™: Apply to upper arm and shoulder area using two fingers to spread gel. Apply after bath or shower; allow at least 2 hours between applying gel and going swimming. Wait at least 25 minutes before applying sunscreen to application area. Do not apply sunscreen to application area for ≥7 days (may increase absorption of gel).

EstroGel®: Apply gel to the arm, from the wrist to the shoulder. Spread gel as thinly as possible over one arm.

Transdermal patch: Aerosol topical corticosteroids applied under the patch may reduce allergic reactions. Do not apply transdermal system to breasts, but place on trunk of body (preferably abdomen). Rotate application sites allowing a 1-week interval between applications at a particular site. Do not apply to oily, damaged or irritated skin; avoid waistline or other areas where tight clothing may rub the patch off. Apply patch immediately after removing from protective pouch. In general, if patch falls off, the same patch may be reapplied or a new system may be used for the remainder of the dosing interval. Swimming, bathing or showering are not expected to affect use of the patch. Note the following exceptions:

Estraderm®: Do not apply to an area exposed to direct sunlight.

Menostar™: Swimming, bathing, or wearing patch while in a sauna have not been studied; adhesion of patch may be decreased or delivery of estradiol may be affected. Remove patch slowly after use to avoid skin irritation. If any adhesive remains on the skin after removal, first allow skin to dry for 15 minutes, then gently rub area with an oil-based cream or lotion. If patch falls off, a new patch should be applied for the remainder of the dosing interval.

Vaginal ring: Exact positioning is not critical for efficacy, however, patient should not feel anything once inserted. In case of discomfort, ring should be pushed further into vagina. If ring is expelled prior to 90 days, it may be rinsed off and reinserted.

Monitoring Parameters Yearly physical examination that includes blood pressure and Papanicolaou smear, breast exam, mammogram. Monitor for signs of endometrial cancer in female patients with uterus. Adequate diagnostic measures, including endometrial sampling, if indicated, should be performed to rule out malignancy in all cases of undiagnosed abnormal vaginal bleeding. Monitor for loss of vision, sudden onset of proptosis, diplopia, migraine; signs and symptoms of thromboembolic disorders; glycemic control in diabetics; lipid profiles in patients being treated for hyperlipidemias; thyroid function in patients on thyroid hormone replacement therapy.

When using Menostar™ in a woman with a uterus, endometrial sampling is recommended at yearly intervals or when clinically indicated.

Menopausal symptoms: Assess need for therapy at 3- to 6-month intervals

Prevention of osteoporosis: Bone density measurement

Reference Range

Children: <10 pg/mL (SI: <37 pmol/L)

Male: 10-50 pg/mL (SI: 37-184 pmol/L)

Female:

Premenopausal: 30-400 pg/mL (SI: 110-1468 pmol/L)

Postmenopausal: 0-30 pg/mL (SI: 0-110 pmol/L)

Test Interactions Pathologist should be advised of estrogen/progesterone therapy when specimens are submitted. Reduced response to metyrapone test.

Dosage Forms

Cream, vaginal:

Estrace®: 0.1 mg/g (12 g) [refill]; 0.1 mg/g (42.5 g) [packaged with applicator]

Emulsion, topical, as hemihydrate:

Estrasorb™: 2.5 mg/g (56s) [each pouch contains 4.35 mg estradiol hemihydrate; contents of two pouches delivers estradiol 0.05 mg/day]

Gel, topical:

Elestrin™: 0.06% (144 g) [pump; delivers estradiol 0.52 mg/0.87 g; 100 actuations]

EstroGel®: 0.06% (93 g) [pump; delivers estradiol 0.75 mg/1.25 g; 64 actuations]

Injection, oil, as cypionate:

Depo®-Estradiol: 5 mg/mL (5 mL) [contains chlorobutanol; in cottonseed oil]

Injection, oil, as valerate:

Delestrogen®:

10 mg/mL (5 mL) [contains chlorobutanol; in sesame oil]

20 mg/mL (5 mL) [contains benzyl alcohol; in castor oil]

40 mg/mL (5 mL) [contains benzyl alcohol; in castor oil]

Ring, vaginal, as base:

Estring®: 2 mg [total estradiol 2 mg; releases 7.5 mcg/day over 90 days] (1s)

Ring, vaginal, as acetate:

Femring™: 0.05 mg [total estradiol 12.4 mg; releases 0.05 mg/day over 3 months] (1s); 0.1 mg [total estradiol 24.8 mg; releases 0.1 mg/day over 3 months] (1s)

Tablet, oral, as acetate:

Femtrace®: 0.45 mg, 0.9 mg, 1.8 mg

Tablet, oral, micronized: 0.5 mg, 1 mg, 2 mg

Estrace®: 0.5 mg, 1 mg, 2 mg [2 mg tablets contain tartrazine]

Gynodiol®: 0.5 mg, 1 mg, 1.5 mg, 2 mg

Tablet, vaginal, as base:

Vagifem®: 25 mcg [contains lactose]

(Continued)

Estradiol *(Continued)*

Transdermal system: 0.025 mg/24 hours [once-weekly patch] (4s); 0.0375 mg/24 hours (4s) [once-weekly patch]; 0.05 mg/24 hours (4s) [once-weekly patch]; 0.06 mg/24 hours (4s) [once-weekly patch]; 0.075 mg/24 hours [once-weekly patch]; 0.1 mg/24 hours [once-weekly patch]

Alora® [twice-weekly patch]:
0.025 mg/24 hours [9 cm^2, total estradiol 0.77 mg] (8s)
0.05 mg/24 hours [18 cm^2, total estradiol 1.5 mg] (8s, 24s)
0.075 mg/24 hours [27 cm^2, total estradiol 2.3 mg] (8s)
0.1 mg/24 hours [36 cm^2, total estradiol 3.1 mg] (8s)

Climara® [once-weekly patch]:
0.025 mg/24 hours [6.5 cm^2, total estradiol 2.04 mg] (4s)
0.0375 mg/24 hours [9.375 cm^2, total estradiol 2.85 mg] (4s)
0.05 mg/24 hours [12.5 cm^2, total estradiol 3.8 mg] (4s)
0.06 mg/24 hours [15 cm^2, total estradiol 4.55 mg] (4s)
0.075 mg/24 hours [18.75 cm^2, total estradiol 5.7 mg] (4s)
0.1 mg/24 hours [25 cm^2, total estradiol 7.6 mg] (4s)

Esclim® [twice-weekly patch]:
0.025 mg/day [11 cm^2, total estradiol 5 mg] (8s)
0.0375 mg/day [16.5 cm^2, total estradiol 7.5 mg] (8s)
0.05 mg/day [22 cm^2, total estradiol 10 mg] (8s)
0.075 mg/day [33 cm^2, total estradiol 15 mg] (8s)
0.1 mg/day [44 cm^2, total estradiol 20 mg] (8s)

Estraderm® [twice-weekly patch]:
0.05 mg/24 hours [10 cm^2, total estradiol 4 mg] (8s)
0.1 mg/24 hours [20 cm^2, total estradiol 8 mg] (8s)

Menostar™ [once-weekly patch]: 0.014 mg/24 hours [3.25 cm^2, total estradiol 1 mg] (4s)

Vivelle® [twice-weekly patch]:
0.05 mg/24 hours [14.5 cm^2, total estradiol 4.33 mg] (8s)
0.1 mg/24 hours [29 cm^2, total estradiol 8.66 mg] (8s)

Vivelle-Dot® [twice-weekly patch]:
0.025 mg/day [2.5 cm^2, total estradiol 0.39 mg] (8s)
0.0375 mg/day [3.75 cm^2, total estradiol 0.585 mg] (8s)
0.05 mg/day [5 cm^2, total estradiol 0.78 mg] (8s)
0.075 mg/day [7.5 cm^2, total estradiol 1.17 mg] (8s)
0.1 mg/day [10 cm^2, total estradiol 1.56 mg] (8s)

♦ **Estradiol Acetate** *see Estradiol on page 620*

Estradiol and Levonorgestrel (es tra DYE ole & LEE voe nor jes trel)

U.S. Brand Names ClimaraPro®
Index Terms Levonorgestrel and Estradiol
Pharmacologic Category Estrogen and Progestin Combination
Use Women with an intact uterus: Treatment of moderate-to-severe vasomotor symptoms associated with menopause; prevention of postmenopausal osteoporosis
Medication Safety Issues
Transdermal patch may contain conducting metal (eg, aluminum); remove patch prior to MRI.
Dosage Topical: Adult females with an intact uterus: Treatment of moderate-to-severe vaso-motor symptoms associated with menopause or prevention of postmenopausal osteoporosis:
Estradiol 0.045 mg/levonorgestrel 0.015 mg: Apply one patch weekly
Additional Information Complete prescribing information for this medication should be consulted for additional detail.
Dosage Forms Transdermal system: Estradiol 0.045 mg/24 hours and levonorgestrel 0.015 mg/24 hours (4s) [once-weekly patch; 22 cm^2; contains estradiol 4.4 mg and levonorgestrel 1.39 mg]

Estradiol and Norethindrone (es tra DYE ole & nor eth IN drone)

U.S. Brand Names Activella®; CombiPatch®
Canadian Brand Names Estalis®; Estalis-Sequi®
Index Terms Norethindrone and Estradiol
Pharmacologic Category Estrogen and Progestin Combination
Use Women with an intact uterus:
Tablet: Treatment of moderate-to-severe vasomotor symptoms associated with menopause; treatment of vulvar and vaginal atrophy; prophylaxis for postmenopausal osteoporosis
Transdermal patch: Treatment of moderate-to-severe vasomotor symptoms associated with menopause; treatment of vulvar and vaginal atrophy; treatment of hypoestrogenism due to hypogonadism, castration, or primary ovarian failure
Pregnancy Risk Factor X
Pregnancy Implications Estrogens/progestins should not be used during pregnancy.

Estrogens: Increased risk of fetal reproductive tract disorders and other birth defects; do not use during pregnancy.
Progestins: Associated with fetal genital abnormalities when used during the 1st trimester; not recommended for use during pregnancy.
Lactation Enters breast milk/use caution
Medication Safety Issues
Transdermal patch may contain conducting metal (eg, aluminum); remove patch prior to MRI.
Contraindications Hypersensitivity to estrogens, progestins, or any components; carcinoma of the breast; estrogen-dependent tumor; undiagnosed abnormal vaginal bleeding; history of or current thrombophlebitis or venous thromboembolic disorders (including DVT, PE); active

or recent (within 1 year) arterial thromboembolic disease (eg, stroke, MI); hysterectomy; hepatic dysfunction or disease; pregnancy

Warnings/Precautions

Cardiovascular-related considerations: Estrogens with or without progestin should not be used to prevent coronary heart disease. Use caution with cardiovascular disease or dysfunction. May increase the risks of hypertension, myocardial infarction (MI), stroke, pulmonary emboli (PE), and deep vein thrombosis; incidence of these effects was shown to be significantly increased in postmenopausal women using conjugated equine estrogens (CEE) in combination with medroxyprogesterone acetate (MPA). Nonfatal MI, PE, and thrombophlebitis have also been reported in males taking high doses of CEE (eg, for prostate cancer). Estrogen compounds are generally associated with lipid effects such as increased HDL-cholesterol and decreased LDL-cholesterol. Triglycerides may also be increased; use with caution in patients with familial defects of lipoprotein metabolism. Whenever possible, combination hormonal contraceptives should be discontinued at least 4 weeks prior to and for 2 weeks following elective surgery associated with an increased risk of thromboembolism or during periods of prolonged immobilization.

Neurological considerations: The risk of dementia may be increased in postmenopausal women; increased incidence was observed in women ≥65 years of age taking CEE alone or in combination with MPA.

Cancer-related considerations: Unopposed estrogens may increase the risk of endometrial carcinoma in postmenopausal women. Estrogens may exacerbate endometriosis. Malignant transformation of residual endometrial implants has been reported posthysterectomy with estrogen only therapy. Estrogens may increase the risk of breast cancer. An increased risk of invasive breast cancer was observed in postmenopausal women using CEE in combination with MPA; a smaller increase in risk was seen with estrogen therapy alone in observational studies. An increase in abnormal mammograms has also been reported with estrogen and progestin therapy. Estrogen use may lead to severe hypercalcemia in patients with breast cancer and bone metastases; discontinue estrogen if hypercalcemia occurs.

Estrogens may cause retinal vascular thrombosis; discontinue permanently if papilledema or retinal vascular lesions are observed on examination. Use with caution in patients with diseases which may be exacerbated by fluid retention, including asthma, epilepsy, migraine, diabetes or renal dysfunction. Use with caution in patients with a history of severe hypocalcemia, SLE, hepatic hemangiomas, porphyria, endometriosis, and gallbladder disease. Use caution with history of cholestatic jaundice associated with past estrogen use or pregnancy. Safety and efficacy in pediatric patients have not been established.

Before prescribing estrogen therapy to postmenopausal women, the risks and benefits must be weighed for each patient. Women should be informed of these risks and benefits, as well as possible effects of progestin when added to estrogen therapy. Estrogens with or without progestin should be used for shortest duration possible consistent with treatment goals. Conduct periodic risk:benefit assessments.

When used solely for prevention of osteoporosis in women at significant risk, nonestrogen treatment options should be considered. When used solely for the treatment of vulvar and vaginal atrophy, topical vaginal products should be considered.

Transdermal patch may contain conducting metal (eg, aluminum); remove patch prior to MRI.

Adverse Reactions Frequency not defined.

Cardiovascular: Altered blood pressure, cardiovascular accident, edema, venous thromboembolism

Central nervous system: Dizziness, fatigue, headache, insomnia, mental depression, migraine, nervousness

Dermatologic: Chloasma, erythema multiforme, erythema nodosum, hemorrhagic eruption, hirsutism, itching, loss of scalp hair, melasma, pruritus, skin rash

Endocrine & metabolic: Breast enlargement, breast tenderness, breast pain, libido (changes in)

Gastrointestinal: Abdominal pain, bloating, changes in appetite, flatulence, gallbladder disease, nausea, pancreatitis, vomiting, weight gain/loss

Genitourinary: Alterations in frequency and flow of menses, changes in cervical secretions, cystitis-like syndrome, premenstrual-like syndrome, size of uterine leiomyomata increased, vaginal candidiasis, vaginitis

Hematologic: Aggravation of porphyria

Hepatic: Cholestatic jaundice

Local: Application site reaction (transdermal patch)

Neuromuscular & skeletal: Arthralgia, back pain, chorea, myalgia, weakness

Ocular: Contact lens intolerance, corneal curvature steepening

Respiratory: Pharyngitis, pulmonary thromboembolism, rhinitis

Miscellaneous: Allergic reactions, carbohydrate intolerance, flu-like syndrome

Drug Interactions

Cytochrome P450 Effect:

Estradiol: **Substrate** of CYP1A2 (major), 2A6 (minor), 2B6 (minor), 2C9 (minor), 2C19 (minor), 2D6 (minor), 2E1 (minor), 3A4 (major); **Inhibits** CYP1A2 (weak), 2C8 (weak); **Induces** CYP3A4 (weak)

Norethindrone: **Substrate** of CYP3A4 (major); **Induces** CYP2C19 (weak)

Ethanol/Nutrition/Herb Interactions

Ethanol: Avoid ethanol (routine use increases estrogen level and risk of breast cancer). Ethanol may also increase the risk of osteoporosis.

Food: Folic acid absorption may be decreased

Herb/Nutraceutical: St John's wort may decrease estradiol levels. Avoid black cohosh, dong quai (has estrogenic activity). Avoid red clover, saw palmetto, ginseng.

Pharmacodynamics/Kinetics

Activella®:

Bioavailability: Estradiol: 50%; Norethindrone: 100%

Half-life elimination: Estradiol: 12-14 hours; Norethindrone: 8-11 hours

Time to peak: Estradiol: 5-8 hours

(Continued)

Estradiol and Norethindrone *(Continued)*

Dosage Adults:
Oral (Activella®): 1 tablet daily
Transdermal patch (CombiPatch®):
Continuous combined regimen: Apply one patch twice weekly
Continuous sequential regimen: Apply estradiol-only patch for first 14 days of cycle, followed by one CombiPatch® applied twice weekly for the remaining 14 days of a 28-day cycle
Transdermal patch, combination pack (product-specific dosing for Canadian formulation):
Estalis®: Continuous combined regimen: Apply a new patch twice weekly during a 28-day cycle
Estalis-Sequi®: Continuous sequential regimen: Apply estradiol-only patch (Vivelle®) for first 14 days, followed by one Estalis® patch applied twice weekly during the last 14 days of a 28-day cycle
Note: In women previously receiving oral estrogens, initiate upon reappearance of menopausal symptoms following discontinuation of oral therapy.

Administration Transdermal patch: Apply to clean dry skin. Do not apply transdermal patch to breasts; apply to lower abdomen, avoiding waistline. Rotate application sites.

Monitoring Parameters Yearly physical examination that includes blood pressure and Papanicolaou smear, breast exam, mammogram. Monitor for signs of endometrial cancer. Adequate diagnostic measures, including endometrial sampling, if indicated, should be performed to rule out malignancy in all cases of undiagnosed abnormal vaginal bleeding. Monitor for loss of vision, sudden onset of proptosis, diplopia, migraine; signs and symptoms of thromboembolic disorders; glycemic control in diabetics; lipid profiles in patients being treated for hyperlipidemias; thyroid function in patients on thyroid hormone replacement therapy.
Menopausal symptoms: Assess need for therapy at 3- to 6-month intervals
Prevention of osteoporosis: Bone density measurement

Dosage Forms [CAN] = Canadian brand name
Combination pack (Estalis-Sequi® [CAN; not available in U.S.]):
140/50:
Transdermal system (Vivelle®): Estradiol 50 mcg per day (4s) [14.5 sq cm; total estradiol 4.33 mg]
Transdermal system (Estalis®): Norethindrone acetate 140 mcg and estradiol 50 mcg per day (4s) [9 sq cm; total norethindrone acetate 2.7 mg, total estradiol 0.62 mg; not available in U.S.]
250/50:
Transdermal system (Vivelle®): Estradiol 50 mcg per day (4s) [14.5 sq cm; total estradiol 4.33 mg]
Transdermal system (Estalis®): Norethindrone acetate 250 mcg and estradiol 50 mcg per day (4s) [16 sq cm; total norethindrone acetate 4.8 mg, total estradiol 0.51 mg; not available in U.S.]
Tablet (Activella®): Estradiol 1 mg and norethindrone acetate 0.5 mg (28s)
Transdermal system:
CombiPatch®:
0.05/0.14: Estradiol 0.05 mg and norethindrone acetate 0.14 mg per day (8s) [9 sq cm]
0.05/0.25: Estradiol 0.05 mg and norethindrone acetate 0.25 mg per day (8s) [16 sq cm]
Estalis® [CAN]:
140/50: Norethindrone acetate 140 mcg and estradiol 50 mcg per day (8s) [9 sq cm; total norethindrone acetate 2.7 mg, total estradiol 0.62 mg; not available in U.S.]
250/50 Norethindrone acetate 250 mcg and estradiol 50 mcg per day (8s) [16 sq cm; total norethindrone acetate 4.8 mg, total estradiol 0.51 mg; not available in U.S.]

♦ **Estradiol Cypionate** *see Estradiol on page 620*
♦ **Estradiol Hemihydrate** *see Estradiol on page 620*
♦ **Estradiol Transdermal** *see Estradiol on page 620*
♦ **Estradiol Valerate** *see Estradiol on page 620*
♦ **Estradot® (Can)** *see Estradiol on page 620*

Estramustine *(es tra MUS teen)*

U.S. Brand Names Emcyt®
Canadian Brand Names Emcyt®
Index Terms Estramustine Phosphate Sodium; NSC-89199
Pharmacologic Category Antineoplastic Agent, Alkylating Agent; Antineoplastic Agent, Hormone; Antineoplastic Agent, Hormone (Estrogen/Nitrogen Mustard)
Use Palliative treatment of prostatic carcinoma (progressive or metastatic)
Pregnancy Risk Factor C
Lactation Excretion in breast milk unknown/contraindicated
Medication Safety Issues
Sound-alike/look-alike issues:
Emcyt® may be confused with Eryc®

High alert medication: The Institute for Safe Medication Practices (ISMP) includes this medication among its list of drugs which have a heightened risk of causing significant patient harm when used in error.

Contraindications Hypersensitivity to estramustine or any component, estradiol or nitrogen mustard; active thrombophlebitis or thromboembolic disorders

Warnings/Precautions Hazardous agent - use appropriate precautions for handling and disposal. Glucose tolerance may be decreased; use with caution in patients with diabetes; elevated blood pressure may occur; exacerbation of peripheral edema or congestive heart disease may occur; use with caution in patients with impaired liver function, renal insufficiency, metabolic bone diseases, or history of cardiovascular disease (eg, thrombophlebitis, thrombosis, or thromboembolic disease). Patients with prostate cancer and osteoblastic metastases should have their calcium monitored regularly. Allergic reactions and angioedema have been reported with use.

Adverse Reactions

>10%:

Cardiovascular: Edema

Endocrine & metabolic: Sodium retention, libido decreased, breast tenderness, breast enlargement

Gastrointestinal: Diarrhea, nausea

Hematologic: Thrombocytopenia

Respiratory: Dyspnea

1% to 10%:

Cardiovascular: Myocardial infarction

Central nervous system: Insomnia, lethargy

Gastrointestinal: Anorexia, flatulence, vomiting

Hematologic: Leukopenia

Local: Thrombophlebitis

Neuromuscular & skeletal: Leg cramps

Respiratory: Pulmonary embolism

<1% (Limited to important or life-threatening): Allergic reactions, anemia, angioedema, cardiac arrest, gynecomastia

Overdosage/Toxicology Symptoms include nausea, vomiting, and myelosuppression. There are no known antidotes. Treatment is primarily symptomatic and supportive.

Drug Interactions

Decreased Effect: Milk products and calcium-rich foods/drugs may impair the oral absorption of estramustine phosphate sodium.

Ethanol/Nutrition/Herb Interactions Food: Estramustine serum levels may be decreased if taken with dairy products.

Stability Refrigerate at 2°C to 8°C (36°F to 46°F). Capsules may be stored outside of refrigerator for up to 24-48 hours without affecting potency.

Mechanism of Action Mechanism is not completely clear. It appears to bind to microtubule proteins, preventing normal tubulin function. The antitumor effect may be due solely to an estrogenic effect. Estramustine causes a marked decrease in plasma testosterone and an increase in estrogen levels.

Pharmacodynamics/Kinetics

Absorption: Oral: 75%

Metabolism:

GI tract: Initial dephosphorylation

Hepatic: Oxidation and hydrolysis; metabolites include estramustine, estrone, estradiol, nitrogen mustard

Half-life elimination: Terminal: 20-24 hours

Time to peak, serum: 2-3 hours

Excretion: Feces (2.9% to 4.8% as unchanged drug)

Dosage Refer to individual protocols.

Oral: 10-16 mg/kg/day (14 mg/kg/day is most common) or 140 mg 4 times/day (some patients have been maintained for >3 years on therapy)

Dietary Considerations Should be taken at least 1 hour before or 2 hours after eating.

Administration Administer on an empty stomach, at least 1 hour before or 2 hours after eating.

Monitoring Parameters Serum calcium, liver function tests

Dosage Forms Capsule, as phosphate sodium: 140 mg

♦ **Estramustine Phosphate Sodium** see Estramustine on page 626

♦ **Estrasorb™** see Estradiol on page 620

♦ **Estratab® (Can)** see Estrogens (Esterified) on page 635

♦ **Estratest®** see Estrogens (Esterified) and Methyltestosterone on page 637

♦ **Estratest® H.S.** see Estrogens (Esterified) and Methyltestosterone on page 637

♦ **Estring®** see Estradiol on page 620

♦ **EstroGel®** see Estradiol on page 620

♦ **Estrogenic Substances, Conjugated** see Estrogens (Conjugated/Equine) on page 631

Estrogens (Conjugated A/Synthetic)
(ES troe jenz, KON joo gate ed, aye, sin THET ik)

U.S. Brand Names Cenestin®

Canadian Brand Names Cenestin

Pharmacologic Category Estrogen Derivative

Use Treatment of moderate-to-severe vasomotor symptoms of menopause; treatment of vulvar and vaginal atrophy

Pregnancy Implications Use during pregnancy is contraindicated.

Lactation Enters breast milk/use caution

Medication Safety Issues

Sound-alike/look-alike issues:

Cenestin® may be confused with Senexon®

International issues:

Cenestin® may be confused with Canesten® which is a brand name for clotrimazole in multiple international markets and a brand name for fluconazole in Great Britain

Contraindications Hypersensitivity to estrogens or any component of the formulation; undiagnosed abnormal vaginal bleeding; history of or current thrombophlebitis or venous thromboembolic disorders (including DVT, PE); active or recent (within 1 year) arterial thromboembolic disease (eg, stroke, MI); carcinoma of the breast; estrogen-dependent tumor; hepatic dysfunction or disease; pregnancy

(Continued)

Estrogens (Conjugated A/Synthetic) *(Continued)*

Warnings/Precautions

Cardiovascular-related considerations: **[U.S. Boxed Warning]: Estrogens with or without progestin should not be used to prevent coronary heart disease.** Use caution with cardiovascular disease or dysfunction. May increase the risks of hypertension, myocardial infarction (MI), stroke, pulmonary emboli (PE), and deep vein thrombosis; incidence of these effects was shown to be significantly increased in postmenopausal women using conjugated equine estrogens (CEE) in combination with medroxyprogesterone acetate (MPA). Nonfatal MI, PE, and thrombophlebitis have also been reported in males taking high doses of CEE (eg, for prostate cancer). Estrogen compounds are generally associated with lipid effects such as increased HDL-cholesterol and decreased LDL-cholesterol. Triglycerides may also be increased; use with caution in patients with familial defects of lipoprotein metabolism. Whenever possible, estrogens should be discontinued at least 4 weeks prior to and for 2 weeks following elective surgery associated with an increased risk of thromboembolism or during periods of prolonged immobilization.

Neurological considerations: **[U.S. Boxed Warning]: The risk of dementia may be increased in postmenopausal women;** increased incidence was observed in women ≥65 years of age taking CEE alone or in combination with MPA.

Cancer-related considerations: **[U.S. Boxed Warning]: Unopposed estrogens may increase the risk of endometrial carcinoma in postmenopausal women.** Estrogens may exacerbate endometriosis. Malignant transformation of residual endometrial implants has been reported posthysterectomy with estrogen only therapy. Consider adding a progestin in women with residual endometriosis posthysterectomy. Estrogens may increase the risk of breast cancer. An increased risk of invasive breast cancer was observed in postmenopausal women using CEE in combination with MPA; a smaller increase in risk was seen with estrogen therapy alone in observational studies. An increase in abnormal mammograms has also been reported with estrogen and progestin therapy. Estrogen use may lead to severe hypercalcemia in patients with breast cancer and bone metastases; discontinue estrogen if hypercalcemia occurs.

Estrogens may cause retinal vascular thrombosis; discontinue permanently if papilledema or retinal vascular lesions are observed on examination. Use with caution in patients with diseases which may be exacerbated by fluid retention, including asthma, epilepsy, migraine, diabetes or renal dysfunction. Use with caution in patients with a history of severe hypocalcemia, SLE, hepatic hemangiomas, porphyria, endometriosis, and gallbladder disease. Use caution with history of cholestatic jaundice associated with past estrogen use or pregnancy. Safety and efficacy in pediatric patients have not been established. Prior to puberty, estrogens may cause premature closure of the epiphyses, premature breast development in girls or gynecomastia in boys. Vaginal bleeding and vaginal cornification may also be induced in girls.

Before prescribing estrogen therapy to postmenopausal women, the risks and benefits must be weighed for each patient. Women should be informed of these risks and benefits, as well as possible effects of progestin when added to estrogen therapy. Estrogens with or without progestin should be used for shortest duration possible consistent with treatment goals. Conduct periodic risk:benefit assessments.

When used solely for prevention of osteoporosis in women at significant risk, nonestrogen treatment options should be considered. When used solely for the treatment of vulvar and vaginal atrophy, topical vaginal products should be considered.

Adverse Reactions

>10%:
Central nervous system: Headache (11% to 68%), dizziness (11%), pain (11%)
Endocrine & metabolic: Breast pain (29%), endometrial thickening (19%), metrorrhagia (14%)
Gastrointestinal: Abdominal pain (9% to 28%), nausea (9% to 18%)
Neuromuscular & skeletal: Paresthesia (8% to 33%), back pain (14%)
Respiratory: Upper respiratory tract infection (13%)
Miscellaneous: Infection (2% to 14%)

1% to 10%:
Central nervous system: Anxiety (6%), fever (1%)
Gastrointestinal: Dyspepsia (10%), vomiting (7%), constipation (6%), diarrhea (6%), weight gain (6%)
Genitourinary: Vaginitis (8%)
Neuromuscular & skeletal: Leg cramps (10%), hypertonia (6%)
Respiratory: Rhinitis (6% to 8%), cough (6%)

In addition, the following have been reported with estrogen and/or progestin therapy:
Cardiovascular: Edema, hypertension, MI, stroke, venous thromboembolism
Central nervous system: Epilepsy exacerbation, irritability, mental depression, migraine, mood disturbances, nervousness
Dermatologic: Angioedema, chloasma, erythema multiforme, erythema nodosum, hemorrhagic eruption, hirsutism, melasma, pruritus, rash, scalp hair loss, urticaria
Endocrine & metabolic: Breast cancer, breast enlargement, breast tenderness, glucose tolerance impaired, HDL-cholesterol increased, hyper-/hypocalcemia, LDL-cholesterol decreased, libido changes, serum triglycerides/phospholipids increased, thyroid-binding globulin increased, total thyroid hormone (T$_4$) increased
Gastrointestinal: Abdominal cramps, bloating, cholecystitis, cholelithiasis, gallbladder disease, pancreatitis, weight gain/loss
Genitourinary: Alterations in frequency and flow of menses, cervical secretion changes, endometrial cancer, endometrial hyperplasia, uterine leiomyomata size increased, vaginal candidiasis
Hematologic: Aggravation of porphyria, antithrombin III and antifactor Xa decreased, fibrinogen levels increased, platelet aggregability and platelet count increased; prothrombin and factors VII, VIII, IX, X increased
Hepatic: Cholestatic jaundice, hepatic hemangiomas enlarged

Neuromuscular & skeletal: Arthralgias, chorea, leg cramps

Local: Thrombophlebitis

Ocular: Contact lens intolerance, corneal curvature steepening, retinal vascular thrombosis

Respiratory: Asthma exacerbation, pulmonary thromboembolism

Miscellaneous: Anaphylactoid/anaphylactic reactions, carbohydrate intolerance

Overdosage/Toxicology Symptoms include nausea and vomiting; withdrawal bleeding may occur in females. Toxicity is unlikely following single exposures of excessive doses, any treatment following emesis and charcoal administration should be supportive and symptomatic.

Drug Interactions

Cytochrome P450 Effect: Based on estradiol and estrone: **Substrate** of CYP1A2 (major), 2A6 (minor), 2B6 (minor), 2C9 (minor), 2C19 (minor), 2D6 (minor), 2E1 (minor), 3A4 (major); **Inhibits** CYP1A2 (weak); **Induces** CYP3A4 (weak)

Increased Effect/Toxicity: Anticoagulants increase the potential for thromboembolic events. Estrogens may enhance the effects of hydrocortisone and prednisone. Estrogen derivatives may enhance the hepatotoxic effect of cyclosporine. Estrogen derivatives may increase the serum concentration of cyclosporine.

Decreased Effect: CYP1A2 inducers may decrease the levels/effects of estrogens; example inducers include aminoglutethimide, carbamazepine, phenobarbital, and rifampin. CYP3A4 inducers may decrease the levels/effects of estrogen; example inducers include aminoglutethimide, carbamazepine, nafcillin, nevirapine, phenobarbital, phenytoin, and rifamycins. Estrogen derivatives may diminish the therapeutic effect of thyroid products.

Ethanol/Nutrition/Herb Interactions

Ethanol: Avoid ethanol (routine use increases estrogen level and risk of breast cancer).

Food: Grapefruit juice may increase estrogen levels, leading to increased adverse effects.

Herb/Nutraceutical: St John's wort may decrease levels. Herbs with estrogenic properties may enhance the adverse/toxic effect of estrogen derivatives; examples include alfalfa, black cohosh, bloodroot, hops, kudzu, licorice, red clover, saw palmetto, soybean, thyme, wild yam, yucca.

Stability Store at room temperature of 25°C (77°F).

Mechanism of Action Conjugated A/synthetic estrogens contain a mixture of 9 synthetic estrogen substances, including sodium estrone sulfate, sodium equilin sulfate, sodium 17 alpha-dihydroequilin, sodium 17 alpha-estradiol and sodium 17 beta-dihydroequilin. Estrogens are responsible for the development and maintenance of the female reproductive system and secondary sexual characteristics. Estradiol is the principle intracellular human estrogen and is more potent than estrone and estriol at the receptor level; it is the primary estrogen secreted prior to menopause. Following menopause, estrone and estrone sulfate are more highly produced. Estrogens modulate the pituitary secretion of gonadotropins, luteinizing hormone, and follicle-stimulating hormone through a negative feedback system; estrogen replacement reduces elevated levels of these hormones in postmenopausal women.

Pharmacodynamics/Kinetics

Absorption: Well absorbed over a period of several hours

Protein-binding: Sex hormone-binding globulin (SHBG) and albumin

Metabolism: Hepatic via CYP3A4; estradiol is converted to estrone and estriol; also undergoes enterohepatic recirculation; estrone sulfate is the main metabolite in postmenopausal women

Excretion: Urine (primarily estriol, also as estradiol, estrone, and conjugates)

Dosage The lowest dose that will control symptoms should be used; medication should be discontinued as soon as possible. Oral:

Adults:

Moderate-to-severe vasomotor symptoms: 0.45 mg/day; may be titrated up to 1.25 mg/day. Attempts to discontinue medication should be made at 3- to 6-month intervals.

Vulvar and vaginal atrophy: 0.3 mg/day

Elderly: Refer to adult dosing. A higher incidence of stroke and invasive breast cancer were observed in women >75 years in a WHI substudy using conjugated equine estrogen.

Monitoring Parameters Yearly physical examination that includes blood pressure and Papanicolaou smear, breast exam, mammogram. Monitor for signs of endometrial cancer in female patients with uterus. Adequate diagnostic measures, including endometrial sampling, if indicated, should be performed to rule out malignancy in all cases of undiagnosed abnormal vaginal bleeding. Monitor for loss of vision, sudden onset of proptosis, diplopia, migraine; signs and symptoms of thromboembolic disorders; glycemic control in diabetics; lipid profiles in patients being treated for hyperlipidemias; thyroid function in patients on thyroid hormone replacement therapy.

Menopausal symptoms: Assess need for therapy at 3- to 6-month intervals

Test Interactions Pathologist should be advised of estrogen/progesterone therapy when specimens are submitted. Reduced response to metyrapone test observed with conjugated estrogens (equine).

Additional Information Not biologically equivalent to conjugated estrogens from equine source. Contains 9 unique estrogenic compounds (equine source contains at least 10 active estrogenic compounds).

Dosage Forms Tablet: 0.3 mg, 0.45 mg, 0.625 mg, 0.9 mg, 1.25 mg

Estrogens (Conjugated B/Synthetic)

(ES troe jenz, KON joo gate ed, bee, sin THET ik)

U.S. Brand Names Enjuvia™

Pharmacologic Category Estrogen Derivative

Use Treatment of moderate-to-severe vasomotor symptoms of menopause

Pregnancy Implications Use during pregnancy is contraindicated.

Lactation Enters breast milk/use caution

Contraindications Hypersensitivity to estrogens or any component of the formulation; undiagnosed abnormal vaginal bleeding; history of or current thrombophlebitis or venous (Continued)

Estrogens (Conjugated B/Synthetic) *(Continued)*

thromboembolic disorders (including DVT, PE); active or recent (within 1 year) arterial thromboembolic disease (eg, stroke, MI); carcinoma of the breast; estrogen-dependent tumor; hepatic dysfunction or disease; pregnancy

Warnings/Precautions

Cardiovascular-related considerations: **[U.S. Boxed Warning]: Estrogens with or without progestin should not be used to prevent coronary heart disease.** Use caution with cardiovascular disease or dysfunction. May increase the risks of hypertension, myocardial infarction (MI), stroke, pulmonary emboli (PE), and deep vein thrombosis; incidence of these effects was shown to be significantly increased in postmenopausal women using conjugated equine estrogens (CEE) in combination with medroxyprogesterone acetate (MPA). Nonfatal MI, PE, and thrombophlebitis have also been reported in males taking high doses of CEE (eg, for prostate cancer). Estrogen compounds are generally associated with lipid effects such as increased HDL-cholesterol and decreased LDL-cholesterol. Triglycerides may also be increased; use with caution in patients with familial defects of lipoprotein metabolism. Whenever possible, estrogens should be discontinued at least 4 weeks prior to and for 2 weeks following elective surgery associated with an increased risk of thromboembolism or during periods of prolonged immobilization.

Neurological considerations: **[U.S. Boxed Warning]: The risk of dementia may be increased in postmenopausal women;** increased incidence was observed in women ≥65 years of age taking CEE alone or in combination with MPA.

Cancer-related considerations: **[U.S. Boxed Warning]: Unopposed estrogens may increase the risk of endometrial carcinoma in postmenopausal women.** Estrogens may exacerbate endometriosis. Malignant transformation of residual endometrial implants has been reported posthysterectomy with estrogen only therapy. Consider adding a progestin in women with residual endometriosis posthysterectomy. Estrogens may increase the risk of breast cancer. An increased risk of invasive breast cancer was observed in postmenopausal women using CEE in combination with MPA; a smaller increase in risk was seen with estrogen therapy alone in observational studies; An increase in abnormal mammograms has also been reported with estrogen and progestin therapy. Estrogen use may lead to severe hypercalcemia in patients with breast cancer and bone metastases; discontinue estrogen if hypercalcemia occurs.

Estrogens may cause retinal vascular thrombosis; discontinue permanently if papilledema or retinal vascular lesions are observed on examination. Use with caution in patients with diseases which may be exacerbated by fluid retention, including asthma, epilepsy, migraine, diabetes or renal dysfunction. Use with caution in patients with a history of severe hypocalcemia, SLE, hepatic hemangiomas, porphyria, endometriosis, and gallbladder disease. Use caution with history of cholestatic jaundice associated with past estrogen use or pregnancy. Safety and efficacy in pediatric patients have not been established. Prior to puberty, estrogens may cause premature closure of the epiphyses, premature breast development in girls or gynecomastia in boys. Vaginal bleeding and vaginal cornification may also be induced in girls.

Before prescribing estrogen therapy to postmenopausal women, the risks and benefits must be weighed for each patient. Women should be informed of these risks and benefits, as well as possible effects of progestin when added to estrogen therapy. Estrogens with or without progestin should be used for shortest duration possible consistent with treatment goals. Conduct periodic risk:benefit assessments.

Adverse Reactions

>10%:

Central nervous system: Headache (15% to 25%), pain (10% to 19%)
Endocrine & metabolic: Breast pain (up to 14%)
Gastrointestinal: Abdominal pain (4% to 15%), nausea (7% to 12%)

1% to 10%:

Central nervous system: Dizziness (1% to 7%)
Endocrine & metabolic: Dysmenorrhea (1% to 8%)
Gastrointestinal: Flatulence (4% to 7%)
Genitourinary: Vaginitis (2% to 7%)
Neuromuscular & skeletal: Paresthesia (up to 6%)
Respiratory: Bronchitis (up to 7%), rhinitis (4% to 7%), sinusitis (3% to 7%)
Miscellaneous: Flu-like syndrome (4% to 7%)

In addition, the following have been reported with estrogen and/or progestin therapy:

Cardiovascular: Edema, hypertension, MI, stroke, venous thromboembolism
Central nervous system: Epilepsy exacerbation, irritability, mental depression, migraine, mood disturbances, nervousness
Dermatologic: Angioedema, chloasma, erythema multiforme, erythema nodosum, hemorrhagic eruption, hirsutism, loss of scalp hair, melasma, pruritus, rash, urticaria
Endocrine & metabolic: Breast cancer, breast enlargement, breast tenderness, HDL-cholesterol increased, hyper-/hypocalcemia, impaired glucose tolerance, LDL-cholesterol decreased, libido (changes in), serum triglycerides/phospholipids increased, thyroid-binding globulin increased, total thyroid hormone (T_4) increased
Gastrointestinal: Abdominal cramps, bloating, cholecystitis, cholelithiasis, gallbladder disease, pancreatitis, weight gain/loss
Genitourinary: Alterations in frequency and flow of menses, changes in cervical secretions, endometrial cancer, endometrial hyperplasia, increased size of uterine leiomyomata, vaginal candidiasis
Hematologic: Aggravation of porphyria; antithrombin III and antifactor Xa decreased; fibrinogen levels increased; platelet aggregability and platelet count increased; prothrombin and factors VII, VIII, IX, X increased
Hepatic: Cholestatic jaundice, hepatic hemangiomas enlarged
Local: Thrombophlebitis
Neuromuscular & skeletal: Arthralgias, chorea, leg cramps
Ocular: Contact lens intolerance, corneal curvature steepening, retinal vascular thrombosis

Respiratory: Asthma exacerbation, pulmonary thromboembolism
Miscellaneous: Anaphylactoid/anaphylactic reactions, carbohydrate intolerance

Overdosage/Toxicology Symptoms include nausea and vomiting; withdrawal bleeding may occur in females. Toxicity is unlikely following single exposures of excessive doses, any treatment following emesis and charcoal administration should be supportive and symptomatic.

Drug Interactions

Cytochrome P450 Effect: Based on estradiol and estrone: **Substrate** of CYP1A2 (major), 2A6 (minor), 2B6 (minor), 2C9 (minor), 2C19 (minor), 2D6 (minor), 2E1 (minor), 3A4 (major); **Inhibits** CYP1A2 (weak); **Induces** CYP3A4 (weak)

Increased Effect/Toxicity: Anticoagulants increase the potential for thromboembolic events. Estrogens may enhance the effects of hydrocortisone and prednisone. Estrogen derivatives may enhance the hepatotoxic effect of cyclosporine. Estrogen derivatives may increase the serum concentration of cyclosporine.

Decreased Effect: CYP1A2 inducers may decrease the levels/effects of estrogens; example inducers include aminoglutethimide, carbamazepine, phenobarbital, and rifampin. CYP3A4 inducers may decrease the levels/effects of estrogen; example inducers include aminoglutethimide, carbamazepine, nafcillin, nevirapine, phenobarbital, phenytoin, and rifamycins. Estrogen derivatives may diminish the therapeutic effect of thyroid products.

Ethanol/Nutrition/Herb Interactions

Ethanol: Avoid ethanol (routine use increases estrogen level and risk of breast cancer).
Food: Grapefruit juice may increase estrogen levels, leading to increased adverse effects.
Herb/Nutraceutical: St John's wort may decrease levels. Herbs with estrogenic properties may enhance the adverse/toxic effect of estrogen derivatives; examples include alfalfa, black cohosh, bloodroot, hops, kudzu, licorice, red clover, saw palmetto, soybean, thyme, wild yam, and yucca.

Stability Store at room temperature of 25°C (77°F).

Mechanism of Action Conjugated B/synthetic estrogens contain a mixture of 10 synthetic estrogen substances, including sodium estrone sulfate, sodium equilin sulfate, sodium 17-alpha-dihydroequilin, sodium 17-alpha-estradiol, and sodium 17-beta-dihydroequilin. Estrogens are responsible for the development and maintenance of the female reproductive system and secondary sexual characteristics. Estradiol is the principle intracellular human estrogen and is more potent than estrone and estriol at the receptor level; it is the primary estrogen secreted prior to menopause. Following menopause, estrone and estrone sulfate are more highly produced. Estrogens modulate the pituitary secretion of gonadotropins, luteinizing hormone, and follicle-stimulating hormone through a negative feedback system; estrogen replacement reduces elevated levels of these hormones in postmenopausal women.

Pharmacodynamics/Kinetics

Absorption: Well absorbed over a period of several hours
Protein-binding: Sex hormone-binding globulin (SHBG) and albumin
Metabolism: Hepatic via CYP3A4; estradiol is converted to estrone and estriol; also undergoes enterohepatic recirculation; estrone sulfate is the main metabolite in postmenopausal women
Excretion: Urine (primarily estriol, also as estradiol, estrone, and conjugates)

Dosage The lowest dose that will control symptoms should be used; medication should be discontinued as soon as possible. Oral:
Adults: Moderate-to-severe vasomotor symptoms associated with menopause: 0.3 mg/day; may be titrated up to 1.25 mg/day. Attempts to discontinue medication should be made at 3- to 6-month intervals.
Elderly: A higher incidence of stroke and invasive breast cancer were observed in women >75 years in a WHI substudy using conjugated equine estrogen.

Monitoring Parameters Yearly physical examination that may include blood pressure and Papanicolaou smear, breast exam, mammogram. Monitor for signs of endometrial cancer in female patients with uterus. Adequate diagnostic measures, including endometrial sampling, if indicated, should be performed to rule out malignancy in all cases of undiagnosed abnormal vaginal bleeding. Monitor for loss of vision, sudden onset of proptosis, diplopia, migraine; signs and symptoms of thromboembolic disorders; glycemic control in diabetics; lipid profiles in patients being treated for hyperlipidemias; thyroid function in patients on thyroid hormone replacement therapy.

Test Interactions Pathologist should be advised of estrogen/progesterone therapy when specimens are submitted. Reduced response to metyrapone test observed with conjugated estrogens (equine).

Additional Information Not biologically equivalent to conjugated estrogens from equine source. Contains 10 unique estrogenic compounds (equine source contains at least 10 active estrogenic compounds).

Dosage Forms
Tablet:
Enjuvia™: 0.3 mg, 0.45 mg, 0.625 mg, 1.25 mg

Estrogens (Conjugated/Equine) (ES troe jenz KON joo gate ed, EE kwine)

U.S. Brand Names Premarin®
Canadian Brand Names C.E.S.®; Premarin®
Index Terms CEE; C.E.S.; Estrogenic Substances, Conjugated
Pharmacologic Category Estrogen Derivative
Use Treatment of moderate-to-severe vasomotor symptoms associated with menopause; treatment of vulvar and vaginal atrophy; hypoestrogenism (due to hypogonadism, castration, or primary ovarian failure); prostatic cancer (palliation); breast cancer (palliation); osteoporosis (prophylaxis, postmenopausal women at significant risk only); abnormal uterine bleeding
Unlabeled/Investigational Use Uremic bleeding
Pregnancy Implications Use during pregnancy is contraindicated.
Lactation Enters breast milk/use caution
(Continued)

Estrogens (Conjugated/Equine) *(Continued)*

Medication Safety Issues
Sound-alike/look-alike issues:
Premarin® may be confused with Primaxin®, Provera®, Remeron®

Contraindications Hypersensitivity to estrogens or any component of the formulation; undiagnosed abnormal vaginal bleeding; history of or current thrombophlebitis or venous thromboembolic disorders (including DVT, PE); active or recent (within 1 year) arterial thromboembolic disease (eg, stroke, MI); carcinoma of the breast (except in appropriately selected patients being treated for metastatic disease); estrogen-dependent tumor; hepatic dysfunction or disease; pregnancy

Warnings/Precautions
Cardiovascular-related considerations: **[U.S. Boxed Warning]: Estrogens with or without progestin should not be used to prevent coronary heart disease.** Use caution with cardiovascular disease or dysfunction. May increase the risks of hypertension, myocardial infarction (MI), stroke, pulmonary emboli (PE), and deep vein thrombosis; incidence of these effects was shown to be significantly increased in postmenopausal women using conjugated equine estrogens (CEE) in combination with medroxyprogesterone acetate (MPA). Nonfatal MI, PE, and thrombophlebitis have also been reported in males taking high doses of CEE (eg, for prostate cancer). Estrogen compounds are generally associated with lipid effects such as increased HDL-cholesterol and decreased LDL-cholesterol. Triglycerides may also be increased; use with caution in patients with familial defects of lipoprotein metabolism. Whenever possible, estrogens should be discontinued at least 4 weeks prior to and for 2 weeks following elective surgery associated with an increased risk of thromboembolism or during periods of prolonged immobilization.

Neurological considerations: **[U.S. Boxed Warning]: The risk of dementia may be increased in postmenopausal women;** increased incidence was observed in women ≥65 years of age taking CEE alone or in combination with MPA.

Cancer-related considerations: **[U.S. Boxed Warning]: Unopposed estrogens may increase the risk of endometrial carcinoma in postmenopausal women.** Estrogens may exacerbate endometriosis. Malignant transformation of residual endometrial implants has been reported posthysterectomy with estrogen only therapy. Consider adding a progestin in women with residual endometriosis posthysterectomy. Estrogens may increase the risk of breast cancer. An increased risk of invasive breast cancer was observed in postmenopausal women using CEE in combination with MPA; a smaller increase in risk was seen with estrogen therapy alone in observational studies. An increase in abnormal mammograms has also been reported with estrogen and progestin therapy. Estrogen use may lead to severe hypercalcemia in patients with breast cancer and bone metastases; discontinue estrogen if hypercalcemia occurs.

Estrogens may cause retinal vascular thrombosis; discontinue permanently if papilledema or retinal vascular lesions are observed on examination. Use with caution in patients with diseases which may be exacerbated by fluid retention, including asthma, epilepsy, migraine, diabetes or renal dysfunction. Use with caution in patients with a history of severe hypocalcemia, SLE, hepatic hemangiomas, porphyria, endometriosis, and gallbladder disease. Use caution with history of cholestatic jaundice associated with past estrogen use or pregnancy. Safety and efficacy in pediatric patients have not been established. Prior to puberty, estrogens may cause premature closure of the epiphyses, premature breast development in girls or gynecomastia in boys. Vaginal bleeding and vaginal cornification may also be induced in girls.

Before prescribing estrogen therapy to postmenopausal women, the risks and benefits must be weighed for each patient. Women should be informed of these risks and benefits, as well as possible effects of progestin when added to estrogen therapy. Estrogens with or without progestin should be used for shortest duration possible consistent with treatment goals. Conduct periodic risk:benefit assessments.

When used solely for prevention of osteoporosis in women at significant risk, nonestrogen treatment options should be considered. When used solely for the treatment of vulvar and vaginal atrophy, topical vaginal products should be considered. Use caution applying topical products to severely atrophic vaginal mucosa.

Adverse Reactions
Note: Percentages reported in postmenopausal women.

>10%:
Central nervous system: Headache (26% to 32%; placebo 28%)
Endocrine & metabolic: Breast pain (7% to 12%; placebo 9%)
Gastrointestinal: Abdominal pain (15% to 17%)
Genitourinary: Vaginal hemorrhage (2% to 14%)
Neuromuscular & skeletal: Back pain (13% to 14%)

1% to 10%:
Central nervous system: Nervousness (2% to 5%)
Endocrine & metabolic: Leukorrhea (4% to 7%)
Gastrointestinal: Flatulence (6% to 7%)
Genitourinary: Vaginitis (5% to 7%), vaginal moniliasis (5% to 6%)
Neuromuscular & skeletal: Weakness (7% to 8%), leg cramps (3% to 7%)

In addition, the following have been reported with estrogen and/or progestin therapy:
Cardiovascular: Edema, hypertension, MI, stroke, venous thromboembolism
Central nervous system: Dizziness, epilepsy exacerbation, headache, irritability, mental depression, migraine, mood disturbances, nervousness
Dermatologic: Angioedema, chloasma, erythema multiforme, erythema nodosum, hemorrhagic eruption, hirsutism, loss of scalp hair, melasma, pruritus, rash, urticaria
Endocrine & metabolic: Breast cancer, breast enlargement, breast tenderness, libido (changes in), increased thyroid-binding globulin, increased total thyroid hormone (T$_4$), increased serum triglycerides/phospholipids, increased HDL-cholesterol, decreased LDL-cholesterol, impaired glucose tolerance, hypercalcemia, hypocalcemia

Gastrointestinal: Abdominal cramps, bloating, cholecystitis, cholelithiasis, gallbladder disease, nausea, pancreatitis, vomiting, weight gain/loss

Genitourinary: Alterations in frequency and flow of menses, changes in cervical secretions, endometrial cancer, endometrial hyperplasia, increased size of uterine leiomyomata, vaginal candidiasis

Hematologic: Aggravation of porphyria, decreased antithrombin III and antifactor Xa, increased levels of fibrinogen, increased platelet aggregability and platelet count; increased prothrombin and factors VII, VIII, IX, X

Hepatic: Cholestatic jaundice, hepatic hemangiomas enlarged

Neuromuscular & skeletal: Arthralgias, chorea, leg cramps

Local: Thrombophlebitis

Ocular: Contact lens intolerance, corneal curvature steepening, retinal vascular thrombosis

Respiratory: Asthma exacerbation, pulmonary thromboembolism

Miscellaneous: Anaphylactoid/anaphylactic reactions, carbohydrate intolerance

Overdosage/Toxicology Toxicity is unlikely following single exposures of excessive doses. Effects noted after large doses include headache, nausea, and vomiting. Bleeding may occur in females. Treatment following emesis and charcoal administration should be supportive and symptomatic.

Drug Interactions

Cytochrome P450 Effect:

Based on estradiol and estrone: **Substrate** of CYP1A2 (major), 2A6 (minor), 2B6 (minor), 2C9 (minor), 2C19 (minor), 2D6 (minor), 2E1 (minor), 3A4 (major); Inhibits CYP1A2 (weak), 2C8 (weak); Induces CYP3A4 (weak)

Increased Effect/Toxicity: Hydrocortisone taken with estrogen may cause corticosteroid-induced toxicity. Increased potential for thromboembolic events with anticoagulants. Estrogen derivatives may enhance the hepatotoxic effect of cyclosporine. Estrogen derivatives may increase the serum concentration of cyclosporine.

Decreased Effect: CYP1A2 inducers may decrease the levels/effects of estrogens; example inducers include aminoglutethimide, carbamazepine, phenobarbital, and rifampin. CYP3A4 inducers may decrease the levels/effects of estrogens; example inducers include aminoglutethimide, carbamazepine, nafcillin, nevirapine, phenobarbital, phenytoin, and rifamycins. Estrogen derivatives may diminish the therapeutic effect of thyroid products.

Ethanol/Nutrition/Herb Interactions

Ethanol: Avoid ethanol (routine use increases estrogen level and risk of breast cancer). Ethanol may also increase the risk of osteoporosis.

Food: Folic acid absorption may be decreased.

Herb/Nutraceutical: St John's wort may decrease levels. Herbs with estrogenic properties may enhance the adverse/toxic effect of estrogen derivatives; examples include alfalfa, black cohosh, bloodroot, hops, kudzu, licorice, red clover, saw palmetto, soybean, thyme, wild yam, yucca.

Stability

Injection: Refrigerate at 2°C to 8°C (36°F to 46°F) prior to reconstitution. Reconstitute using provided diluent; do not shake violently. Following reconstitution, solution may be stored under refrigeration for up to 60 days. Do not use if darkening or precipitation occurs.

Tablets, vaginal cream: Store at room temperature (25°C).

Mechanism of Action Conjugated estrogens contain a mixture of estrone sulfate, equilin sulfate, 17 alpha-dihydroequilin, 17 alpha-estradiol and 17 beta-dihydroequilin. Estrogens are responsible for the development and maintenance of the female reproductive system and secondary sexual characteristics. Estradiol is the principle intracellular human estrogen and is more potent than estrone and estriol at the receptor level; it is the primary estrogen secreted prior to menopause. Following menopause, estrone and estrone sulfate are more highly produced. Estrogens modulate the pituitary secretion of gonadotropins, luteinizing hormone, and follicle-stimulating hormone through a negative feedback system; estrogen replacement reduces elevated levels of these hormones in postmenopausal women.

Pharmacodynamics/Kinetics

Absorption: Well absorbed

Metabolism: Hepatic via CYP3A4; estradiol is converted to estrone and estriol; also undergoes enterohepatic recirculation; estrone sulfite is the main metabolite in postmenopausal women

Excretion: Urine (primarily estriol, also as estradiol, estrone, and conjugates

Dosage Adults:

Male: Androgen-dependent prostate cancer palliation: Oral: 1.25-2.5 mg 3 times/day

Female:

Prevention of postmenopausal osteoporosis: Oral: Initial: 0.3 mg/day cyclically* or daily, depending on medical assessment of patient. Dose may be adjusted based on bone mineral density and clinical response. The lowest effective dose should be used.

Moderate to severe vasomotor symptoms associated with menopause: Oral: Initial: 0.3 mg/day, cyclically* or daily, depending on medical assessment of patient. The lowest dose that will control symptoms should be used. Medication should be discontinued as soon as possible.

Vulvar and vaginal atrophy:

Oral: Initial: 0.3 mg/day; the lowest dose that will control symptoms should be used. May be given cyclically* or daily, depending on medical assessment of patient. Medication should be discontinued as soon as possible.

Vaginal cream: Intravaginal: ½ to 2 g/day given cyclically*

Abnormal uterine bleeding:

Acute/heavy bleeding:

Oral (unlabeled route): 1.25 mg, may repeat every 4 hours for 24 hours, followed by 1.25 mg once daily for 7-10 days

I.M., I.V.: 25 mg, may repeat in 6-12 hours if needed

Note: Treatment should be followed by a low-dose oral contraceptive; medroxyprogesterone acetate along with or following estrogen therapy can also be given

Nonacute/lesser bleeding: Oral (unlabeled route): 1.25 mg once daily for 7-10 days

(Continued)

Estrogens (Conjugated/Equine) *(Continued)*

Female hypogonadism: Oral: 0.3-0.625 mg/day given cyclically*; dose may be titrated in 6- to 12-month intervals; progestin treatment should be added to maintain bone mineral density once skeletal maturity is achieved.

Female castration, primary ovarian failure: Oral: 1.25 mg/day given cyclically*; adjust according to severity of symptoms and patient response. For maintenance, adjust to the lowest effective dose.

*Cyclic administration: Either 3 weeks on, 1 week off **or** 25 days on, 5 days off

Male and Female:

Breast cancer palliation, metastatic disease in selected patients: Oral: 10 mg 3 times/day for at least 3 months

Uremic bleeding (unlabeled use): I.V.: 0.6 mg/kg/day for 5 days

Elderly: Refer to Adults dosing; a higher incidence of stroke and invasive breast cancer was observed in women >75 years in a WHI substudy.

Dietary Considerations Ensure adequate calcium and vitamin D intake when used for the prevention of osteoporosis. Powder for reconstitution for injection (25 mg) contains lactose 200 mg.

Administration

Injection: May also be administered intramuscularly; when administered I.V., drug should be administered slowly to avoid the occurrence of a flushing reaction

Oral tablet, vaginal cream: Administer at bedtime to minimize adverse effects.

Monitoring Parameters Yearly physical examination that includes blood pressure and Papanicolaou smear, breast exam, mammogram. Monitor for signs of endometrial cancer in female patients with uterus. Adequate diagnostic measures, including endometrial sampling, if indicated, should be performed to rule out malignancy in all cases of undiagnosed abnormal vaginal bleeding. Monitor for loss of vision, sudden onset of proptosis, diplopia, migraine; signs and symptoms of thromboembolic disorders; glycemic control in diabetics; lipid profiles in patients being treated for hyperlipidemias; thyroid function in patients on thyroid hormone replacement therapy.

Menopausal symptoms: Assess need for therapy at 3- to 6-month intervals

Prevention of osteoporosis: Bone density measurement

Reference Range

Children: <10 mcg/24 hours (SI: <35 µmol/day) (values at Mayo Medical Laboratories)

Adults:

Male: 15-40 mcg/24 hours (SI: 52-139 µmol/day)

Female:

Menstruating: 15-80 mcg/24 hours (SI: 52-277 µmol/day)

Postmenopausal: <20 mcg/24 hours (SI: <69 µmol/day)

Test Interactions Pathologist should be advised of estrogen/progesterone therapy when specimens are submitted. Reduced response to metyrapone test.

Dosage Forms

Cream, vaginal: 0.625 mg/g (42.5 g)

Injection, powder for reconstitution: 25 mg [contains lactose 200 mg; diluent contains benzyl alcohol]

Tablet: 0.3 mg, 0.45 mg, 0.625 mg, 0.9 mg, 1.25 mg

Estrogens (Conjugated/Equine) and Medroxyprogesterone

(ES troe jenz KON joo gate ed/EE kwine & me DROKS ee proe JES te rone)

U.S. Brand Names Premphase®; Prempro™

Canadian Brand Names Premphase®; Premplus®; Prempro™

Index Terms Medroxyprogesterone and Estrogens (Conjugated); MPA and Estrogens (Conjugated)

Pharmacologic Category Estrogen and Progestin Combination

Use Women with an intact uterus: Treatment of moderate-to-severe vasomotor symptoms associated with menopause; treatment of atrophic vaginitis; osteoporosis (prophylaxis)

Medication Safety Issues

Sound-alike/look-alike issues:

Premphase® may be confused with Prempro™

Prempro™ may be confused with Premphase®

Dosage Oral: Adults:

Treatment of moderate-to-severe vasomotor symptoms associated with menopause or treatment of atrophic vaginitis in females with an intact uterus. (The lowest dose that will control symptoms should be used; medication should be discontinued as soon as possible):

Premphase®: One maroon conjugated estrogen 0.625 mg tablet daily on days 1 through 14 and one light blue conjugated estrogen 0.625 mg/MPA 5 mg tablet daily on days 15 through 28; re-evaluate patients at 3- and 6-month intervals to determine if treatment is still necessary; monitor patients for signs of endometrial cancer; rule out malignancy if unexplained vaginal bleeding occurs

Prempro™: One conjugated estrogen 0.3 mg/MPA 1.5 mg tablet daily; re-evaluate at 3-and 6-month intervals to determine if therapy is still needed; dose may be increased to a maximum of one conjugated estrogen 0.625 mg/MPA 5 mg tablet daily in patients with bleeding or spotting, once malignancy has been ruled out

Osteoporosis prophylaxis in females with an intact uterus:

Premphase®: One maroon conjugated estrogen 0.625 tablet daily on days 1 through 14 and one light blue conjugated estrogen 0.625 mg/MPA 5 mg tablet daily on days 15 through 28; monitor patients for signs of endometrial cancer; rule out malignancy if unexplained vaginal bleeding occurs

Prempro™: One conjugated estrogen 0.3 mg/MPA 1.5 mg tablet daily; dose may be increased to one conjugated estrogen 0.625 mg/MPA 5 mg tablet daily; in patients with bleeding or spotting, once malignancy has been ruled out

Elderly: Refer to adult dosing; a higher incidence of stroke and invasive breast cancer was observed in women >75 years in a WHI substudy.

Additional Information Complete prescribing information for this medication should be consulted for additional detail.

Dosage Forms Tablet:

Premphase® [therapy pack contains 2 separate tablet formulations]: Conjugated estrogens 0.625 mg [14 maroon tablets] and conjugated estrogen 0.625 mg/medroxyprogesterone acetate 5 mg [14 light blue tablets] (28s)

Prempro™:

0.3/1.5: Conjugated estrogens 0.3 mg and medroxyprogesterone acetate 1.5 mg (28s)

0.45/1.5: Conjugated estrogens 0.45 mg and medroxyprogesterone acetate 1.5 mg (28s)

0.625/2.5: Conjugated estrogens 0.625 mg and medroxyprogesterone acetate 2.5 mg (28s)

0.625/5: Conjugated estrogens 0.625 mg and medroxyprogesterone acetate 5 mg (28s)

Estrogens (Esterified) (ES troe jenz, es TER i fied)

U.S. Brand Names Menest®

Canadian Brand Names Estratab®; Menest®

Index Terms Esterified Estrogens

Pharmacologic Category Estrogen Derivative

Use Treatment of moderate to severe vasomotor symptoms associated with menopause; treatment of vulvar and vaginal atrophy; hypoestrogenism (due to hypogonadism, castration, or primary ovarian failure); prostatic cancer (palliation); breast cancer (palliation); osteoporosis (prophylaxis, in women at significant risk only)

Pregnancy Risk Factor X

Pregnancy Implications Increased risk of fetal reproductive tract disorders and other birth defects; do not use during pregnancy.

Lactation Enters breast milk/use caution

Medication Safety Issues

Sound-alike/look-alike issues:

Estratab® may be confused with Estratest®, Estratest® H.S.

Contraindications Hypersensitivity to estrogens or any component of the formulation; undiagnosed abnormal vaginal bleeding; history of or current thrombophlebitis or venous thromboembolic disorders (including DVT, PE); active or recent (within 1 year) arterial thromboembolic disease (eg, stroke, MI); carcinoma of the breast, except in appropriately selected patients being treated for metastatic disease; estrogen-dependent tumor; hepatic dysfunction or disease; pregnancy

Warnings/Precautions

Cardiovascular-related considerations: **[U.S. Boxed Warning]: Estrogens with or without progestin should not be used to prevent coronary heart disease.** Use caution with cardiovascular disease or dysfunction. May increase the risks of hypertension, myocardial infarction (MI), stroke, pulmonary emboli (PE), and deep vein thrombosis; incidence of these effects was shown to be significantly increased in postmenopausal women using conjugated equine estrogens (CEE) in combination with medroxyprogesterone acetate (MPA). Nonfatal MI, PE, and thrombophlebitis have also been reported in males taking high doses of CEE (eg, for prostate cancer). Estrogen compounds are generally associated with lipid effects such as increased HDL-cholesterol and decreased LDL-cholesterol. Triglycerides may also be increased; use with caution in patients with familial defects of lipoprotein metabolism. Whenever possible, estrogens should be discontinued at least 4 weeks prior to and for 2 weeks following elective surgery associated with an increased risk of thromboembolism or during periods of prolonged immobilization.

Neurological considerations: **[U.S. Boxed Warning]: The risk of dementia may be increased in postmenopausal women;** increased incidence was observed in women ≥65 years of age taking CEE alone or in combination with MPA.

Cancer-related considerations: **[U.S. Boxed Warning]: Unopposed estrogens may increase the risk of endometrial carcinoma in postmenopausal women.** Estrogens may exacerbate endometriosis. Malignant transformation of residual endometrial implants has been reported post-hysterectomy with estrogen only therapy. Consider adding a progestin in women with residual endometriosis post-hysterectomy. Estrogens may increase the risk of breast cancer. An increased risk of invasive breast cancer was observed in postmenopausal women using CEE in combination with MPA; a smaller increase in risk was seen with estrogen therapy alone in observational studies. An increase in abnormal mammograms has also been reported with estrogen and progestin therapy. Estrogen use may lead to severe hypercalcemia in patients with breast cancer and bone metastases; discontinue estrogen if hypercalcemia occurs.

Estrogens may cause retinal vascular thrombosis; discontinue permanently if papilledema or retinal vascular lesions are observed on examination. Use with caution in patients with diseases which may be exacerbated by fluid retention, including asthma, epilepsy, migraine, diabetes or renal dysfunction. Use with caution in patients with a history of severe hypocalcemia, SLE, hepatic hemangiomas, porphyria, endometriosis, and gallbladder disease. Use caution with history of cholestatic jaundice associated with past estrogen use or pregnancy. Safety and efficacy in pediatric patients have not been established. Prior to puberty, estrogens may cause premature closure of the epiphyses, premature breast development in girls or gynecomastia in boys. Vaginal bleeding and vaginal cornification may also be induced in girls.

Before prescribing estrogen therapy to postmenopausal women, the risks and benefits must be weighed for each patient. Women should be informed of these risks and benefits, as well as possible effects of progestin when added to estrogen therapy. Estrogens with or without progestin should be used for shortest duration possible consistent with treatment goals. Conduct periodic risk:benefit assessments.

(Continued)

Estrogens (Esterified) *(Continued)*

When used solely for prevention of osteoporosis in women at significant risk, nonestrogen treatment options should be considered. When used solely for the treatment of vulvar and vaginal atrophy, topical vaginal products should be considered.

Adverse Reactions

Cardiovascular: Edema, hypertension, venous thromboembolism

Central nervous system: Dizziness, headache, mental depression, migraine

Dermatologic: Chloasma, erythema multiforme, erythema nodosum, hemorrhagic eruption, hirsutism, loss of scalp hair, melasma

Endocrine & metabolic: Breast enlargement, breast tenderness, libido (changes in), increased thyroid-binding globulin, increased total thyroid hormone (T_4), increased serum triglycerides/phospholipids, increased HDL-cholesterol, decreased LDL-cholesterol, impaired glucose tolerance, hypercalcemia

Gastrointestinal: Abdominal cramps, bloating, cholecystitis, cholelithiasis, gallbladder disease, nausea, pancreatitis, vomiting, weight gain/loss

Genitourinary: Alterations in frequency and flow of menses, changes in cervical secretions, endometrial cancer, increased size of uterine leiomyomata, vaginal candidiasis

Hematologic: Aggravation of porphyria, decreased antithrombin III and antifactor Xa, increased levels of fibrinogen, increased platelet aggregability and platelet count; increased prothrombin and factors VII, VIII, IX, X

Hepatic: Cholestatic jaundice

Neuromuscular & skeletal: Chorea

Ocular: Contact lens intolerance, corneal curvature steepening

Respiratory: Pulmonary thromboembolism

Miscellaneous: Carbohydrate intolerance

Overdosage/Toxicology

Toxicity is unlikely following single exposures of excessive doses. Effects noted after large doses include headache, nausea, and vomiting. Bleeding may occur in females. Treatment following emesis and charcoal administration should be supportive and symptomatic.

Drug Interactions

Cytochrome P450 Effect: Based on estrone: **Substrate** of CYP1A2 (major), 2B6 (minor), 2C9 (minor), 2E1 (minor), 3A4 (major)

Increased Effect/Toxicity: Hydrocortisone taken with estrogen may cause corticosteroid-induced toxicity. Increased potential for thromboembolic events with anticoagulants. Estrogen derivatives may enhance the hepatotoxic effect of cyclosporine. Estrogen derivatives may increase the serum concentration of cyclosporine.

Decreased Effect: CYP1A2 inducers may decrease the levels/effects of estrogens; example inducers include aminoglutethimide, carbamazepine, phenobarbital, and rifampin. CYP3A4 inducers may decrease the levels/effects of estrogens; example inducers include aminoglutethimide, carbamazepine, nafcillin, nevirapine, phenobarbital, phenytoin, and rifamycins. Estrogen derivatives may diminish the therapeutic effect of thyroid products.

Ethanol/Nutrition/Herb Interactions

Ethanol: Avoid ethanol (routine use increases estrogen level and risk of breast cancer). Ethanol may also increase the risk of osteoporosis.

Food: Folic acid absorption may be decreased.

Herb/Nutraceutical: St John's wort may decrease levels. Herbs with estrogenic properties may enhance the adverse/toxic effect of estrogen derivatives; examples include alfalfa, black cohosh, bloodroot, hops, kudzu, licorice, red clover, saw palmetto, soybean, thyme, wild yam, yucca.

Stability

Store below 30°C (86°F). Protect from moisture.

Mechanism of Action

Esterified estrogens contain a mixture of estrogenic substances; the principle component is estrone. Preparations contain 75% to 85% sodium estrone sulfate and 6% to 15% sodium equilin sulfate such that the total is not <90%. Estrogens are responsible for the development and maintenance of the female reproductive system and secondary sexual characteristics. Estradiol is the principle intracellular human estrogen and is more potent than estrone and estriol at the receptor level; it is the primary estrogen secreted prior to menopause. In males and following menopause in females, estrone and estrone sulfate are more highly produced. Estrogens modulate the pituitary secretion of gonadotropins, luteinizing hormone, and follicle-stimulating hormone through a negative feedback system; estrogen replacement reduces elevated levels of these hormones.

Pharmacodynamics/Kinetics

Absorption: Readily

Metabolism: Rapidly hepatic to estrone sulfate, conjugated and unconjugated metabolites; first-pass effect

Excretion: Urine (as unchanged drug and as glucuronide and sulfate conjugates)

Dosage

Oral: Adults:

Prostate cancer (palliation): 1.25-2.5 mg 3 times/day

Female hypogonadism: 2.5-7.5 mg of estrogen daily for 20 days followed by a 10-day rest period. Administer cyclically (3 weeks on and 1 week off). If bleeding does not occur by the end of the 10-day period, repeat the same dosing schedule; the number of courses is dependent upon the responsiveness of the endometrium. If bleeding occurs before the end of the 10-day period, begin an estrogen-progestin cyclic regimen of 2.5-7.5 mg esterified estrogens daily for 20 days. During the last 5 days of estrogen therapy, give an oral progestin. If bleeding occurs before regimen is concluded, discontinue therapy and resume on the fifth day of bleeding.

Moderate to severe vasomotor symptoms associated with menopause: 1.25 mg/day administered cyclically (3 weeks on and 1 week off). If patient has not menstruated within the last 2 months or more, cyclic administration is started arbitrary. If the patient is menstruating, cyclical administration is started on day 5 of the bleeding. For short-term use only and should be discontinued as soon as possible. Re-evaluate at 3- to 6-month intervals for tapering or discontinuation of therapy.

Atopic vaginitis and kraurosis vulvae: 0.3 to ≥1.25 mg/day, depending on the tissue response of the individual patient. Administer cyclically. For short-term use only and should be discontinued as soon as possible. Re-evaluate at 3- to 6-month intervals for tapering or discontinuation of therapy.

Breast cancer (palliation): 10 mg 3 times/day for at least 3 months

Osteoporosis in postmenopausal women: Initial: 0.3 mg/day and increase to a maximum daily dose of 1.25 mg/day; initiate therapy as soon as possible after menopause; cyclically or daily, depending on medical assessment of patient. Monitor patients with an intact uterus for signs of endometrial cancer; rule out malignancy if unexplained vaginal bleeding occurs

Female castration and primary ovarian failure: 1.25 mg/day, cyclically. Adjust dosage upward or downward, according to the severity of symptoms and patient response. For maintenance, adjust dosage to lowest level that will provide effective control.

Elderly: Refer to Adults dosing. A higher incidence of stroke and invasive breast cancer were observed in women >75 years in a WHI substudy using conjugated equine estrogen.

Dosing adjustment in hepatic impairment:
Mild to moderate liver impairment: Dosage reduction of estrogens is recommended
Severe liver impairment: **Not recommended**

Dietary Considerations Should be taken with food at same time each day. Ensure adequate calcium and vitamin D intake when used for the prevention of osteoporosis.

Monitoring Parameters Yearly physical examination that includes blood pressure and Papanicolaou smear, breast exam, mammogram. Monitor for signs of endometrial cancer in female patients with uterus. Adequate diagnostic measures, including endometrial sampling, if indicated, should be performed to rule out malignancy in all cases of undiagnosed abnormal vaginal bleeding. Monitor for loss of vision, sudden onset of proptosis, diplopia, migraine; signs and symptoms of thromboembolic disorders; glycemic control in diabetics; lipid profiles in patients being treated for hyperlipidemias; thyroid function in patients on thyroid hormone replacement therapy.

Menopausal symptoms: Assess need for therapy at 3- to 6-month intervals
Prevention of osteoporosis: Bone density measurement

Test Interactions Pathologist should be advised of estrogen/progesterone therapy when specimens are submitted. Reduced response to metyrapone test.

Dosage Forms Tablet: 0.3 mg, 0.625 mg, 1.25 mg, 2.5 mg

Estrogens (Esterified) and Methyltestosterone
(ES troe jenz es TER i fied & meth il tes TOS te rone)

U.S. Brand Names Estratest®; Estratest® H.S.; Syntest D.S.; Syntest H.S.

Canadian Brand Names Estratest®

Index Terms Conjugated Estrogen and Methyltestosterone; Esterified Estrogen and Methyltestosterone

Pharmacologic Category Estrogen and Progestin Combination

Use Vasomotor symptoms of menopause

Pregnancy Risk Factor X

Medication Safety Issues
Sound-alike/look-alike issues:
Estratest® may be confused with Eskalith®, Estratab®, Estratest® H.S.
Estratest® H.S. may be confused with Eskalith®, Estratab®, Estratest®

Dosage Adults: Female: Oral: Lowest dose that will control symptoms should be chosen, normally given 3 weeks on and 1 week off

Additional Information Complete prescribing information for this medication should be consulted for additional detail.

Dosage Forms Tablet:
Estratest®: Esterified estrogen 1.25 mg and methyltestosterone 2.5 mg [contains sodium benzoate]
Estratest® H.S.: Esterified estrogen 0.625 mg and methyltestosterone 1.25 mg [contains sodium benzoate]
Syntest D.S.: Esterified estrogen 1.25 mg and methyltestosterone 2.5 mg
Syntest H.S.: Esterified estrogen 0.625 mg and methyltestosterone 1.25 mg

---

Estropipate (ES troe pih pate)

U.S. Brand Names Ogen®; Ortho-Est®

Canadian Brand Names Ogen®

Index Terms Ortho Est; Piperazine Estrone Sulfate

Pharmacologic Category Estrogen Derivative

Use Treatment of moderate to severe vasomotor symptoms associated with menopause; treatment of vulvar and vaginal atrophy; hypoestrogenism (due to hypogonadism, castration, or primary ovarian failure); osteoporosis (prophylaxis, in women at significant risk only)

Pregnancy Risk Factor X

Pregnancy Implications Increased risk of fetal reproductive tract disorders and other birth defects; do not use during pregnancy.

Lactation Enters breast milk/use caution

Contraindications Hypersensitivity to estrogens or any component of the formulation; undiagnosed abnormal vaginal bleeding; history of or current thrombophlebitis or venous thromboembolic disorders (including DVT, PE); active or recent (within 1 year) arterial thromboembolic disease (eg, stroke, MI); carcinoma of the breast, except in appropriately selected patients being treated for metastatic disease; estrogen-dependent tumor; hepatic dysfunction or disease; pregnancy

Warnings/Precautions
Cardiovascular-related considerations: **[U.S. Boxed Warning]: Estrogens with or without progestin should not be used to prevent coronary heart disease.** Use caution with cardiovascular disease or dysfunction. May increase the risks of hypertension, myocardial infarction (MI), stroke, pulmonary emboli (PE), and deep vein thrombosis; incidence of these (Continued)

Estropipate *(Continued)*

effects was shown to be significantly increased in postmenopausal women using conjugated equine estrogens (CEE) in combination with medroxyprogesterone acetate (MPA). Nonfatal MI, PE, and thrombophlebitis have also been reported in males taking high doses of CEE (eg, for prostate cancer). Estrogen compounds are generally associated with lipid effects such as increased HDL-cholesterol and decreased LDL-cholesterol. Triglycerides may also be increased; use with caution in patients with familial defects of lipoprotein metabolism. Whenever possible, estrogens should be discontinued at least 4 weeks prior to and for 2 weeks following elective surgery associated with an increased risk of thromboembolism or during periods of prolonged immobilization.

Neurological considerations: [U.S. Boxed Warning]: **The risk of dementia may be increased in postmenopausal women;** increased incidence was observed in women ≥65 years of age taking CEE alone or in combination with MPA.

Cancer-related considerations: [U.S. Boxed Warning]: **Unopposed estrogens may increase the risk of endometrial carcinoma in postmenopausal women.** Estrogens may exacerbate endometriosis. Malignant transformation of residual endometrial implants has been reported post-hysterectomy with estrogen only therapy. Consider adding a progestin in women with residual endometriosis post-hysterectomy. Estrogens may increase the risk of breast cancer. An increased risk of invasive breast cancer was observed in postmenopausal women using CEE in combination with MPA; a smaller increase in risk was seen with estrogen therapy alone in observational studies. An increase in abnormal mammograms has also been reported with estrogen and progestin therapy. Estrogen use may lead to severe hypercalcemia in patients with breast cancer and bone metastases; discontinue estrogen if hypercalcemia occurs.

Estrogens may cause retinal vascular thrombosis; discontinue permanently if papilledema or retinal vascular lesions are observed on examination. Use with caution in patients with diseases which may be exacerbated by fluid retention, including asthma, epilepsy, migraine, diabetes or renal dysfunction. Use with caution in patients with a history of severe hypocalcemia, SLE, hepatic hemangiomas, porphyria, endometriosis, and gallbladder disease. Use caution with history of cholestatic jaundice associated with past estrogen use or pregnancy. Safety and efficacy in pediatric patients have not been established. Prior to puberty, estrogens may cause premature closure of the epiphyses, premature breast development in girls or gynecomastia in boys. Vaginal bleeding and vaginal cornification may also be induced in girls.

Before prescribing estrogen therapy to postmenopausal women, the risks and benefits must be weighed for each patient. Women should be informed of these risks and benefits, as well as possible effects of progestin when added to estrogen therapy. Estrogens with or without progestin should be used for shortest duration possible consistent with treatment goals. Conduct periodic risk:benefit assessments.

When used solely for prevention of osteoporosis in women at significant risk, nonestrogen treatment options should be considered. When used solely for the treatment of vulvar and vaginal atrophy, topical vaginal products should be considered.

Adverse Reactions Frequency not defined.
Cardiovascular: Edema, hypertension, venous thromboembolism
Central nervous system: Dizziness, headache, mental depression, migraine
Dermatologic: Chloasma, erythema multiforme, erythema nodosum, hemorrhagic eruption, hirsutism, loss of scalp hair, melasma
Endocrine & metabolic: Breast enlargement, breast tenderness, libido (changes in), increased thyroid-binding globulin, increased total thyroid hormone (T_4), increased serum triglycerides/phospholipids, increased HDL-cholesterol, decreased LDL-cholesterol, impaired glucose tolerance, hypercalcemia
Gastrointestinal: Abdominal cramps, bloating, cholecystitis, cholelithiasis, gallbladder disease, nausea, pancreatitis, vomiting, weight gain/loss
Genitourinary: Alterations in frequency and flow of menses, changes in cervical secretions, endometrial cancer, increased size of uterine leiomyomata, vaginal candidiasis
Hematologic: Aggravation of porphyria, decreased antithrombin III and antifactor Xa, increased levels of fibrinogen, increased platelet aggregability and platelet count; increased prothrombin and factors VII, VIII, IX, X
Hepatic: Cholestatic jaundice
Neuromuscular & skeletal: Chorea
Ocular: Ocular: Contact lens intolerance, corneal curvature steepening
Respiratory: Pulmonary thromboembolism
Miscellaneous: Carbohydrate intolerance

Overdosage/Toxicology Toxicity is unlikely following single exposures of excessive doses. Effects noted after large doses include headache, nausea, and vomiting. Bleeding may occur in females. Treatment following emesis and charcoal administration should be supportive and symptomatic.

Drug Interactions
Cytochrome P450 Effect: Based on estrone: **Substrate** of CYP1A2 (major), 2B6 (minor), 2C9 (minor), 2E1 (minor), 3A4 (major)
Increased Effect/Toxicity: Hydrocortisone taken with estrogen may cause corticosteroid-induced toxicity. Increased potential for thromboembolic events with anticoagulants. Estrogen derivatives may enhance the hepatotoxic effect of cyclosporine. Estrogen derivatives may increase the serum concentration of cyclosporine.
Decreased Effect: CYP1A2 inducers may decrease the levels/effects of estrogens; example inducers include aminoglutethimide, carbamazepine, phenobarbital, and rifampin. CYP3A4 inducers may decrease the levels/effects of estrogens; example inducers include aminoglutethimide, carbamazepine, nafcillin, nevirapine, phenobarbital, phenytoin, and rifamycins. Estrogen derivatives may diminish the therapeutic effect of thyroid products.

Ethanol/Nutrition/Herb Interactions
Ethanol: Routine use increases estrogen level and risk of breast cancer; avoid ethanol. Ethanol may also increase the risk of osteoporosis.

Food: Folic acid absorption may be decreased.

Herb/Nutraceutical: St John's wort may decrease levels. Herbs with estrogenic properties may enhance the adverse/toxic effect of estrogen derivatives; examples include alfalfa, black cohosh, bloodroot, hops, kudzu, licorice, red clover, saw palmetto, soybean, thyme, wild yam, yucca.

Stability Tablet: Store below 25°C (77°F).

Mechanism of Action Estrogens are responsible for the development and maintenance of the female reproductive system and secondary sexual characteristics. Estradiol is the principle intracellular human estrogen and is more potent than estrone and estriol at the receptor level; it is the primary estrogen secreted prior to menopause. In males and following menopause in females, estrone and estrone sulfate are more highly produced. Estrogens modulate the pituitary secretion of gonadotropins, luteinizing hormone, and follicle-stimulating hormone through a negative feedback system; estrogen replacement reduces elevated levels of these hormones. Estropipate is prepared from purified crystalline estrone that has been solubilized as the sulfate and stabilized with piperazine.

Pharmacodynamics/Kinetics
Absorption: Well absorbed
Metabolism: Hepatic and in target tissues; first-pass effect

Dosage Adults:
Oral:
Moderate to severe vasomotor symptoms associated with menopause: Usual dosage range: 0.75-6 mg estropipate daily; use the lowest dose and regimen that will control symptoms, and discontinue as soon as possible. Attempt to discontinue or taper medication at 3- to 6-month intervals. If a patient with vasomotor symptoms has not menstruated within the last ≥2 months, start the cyclic administration arbitrarily. If the patient has menstruated, start cyclic administration on day 5 of bleeding.

Female hypogonadism: 1.5-9 mg estropipate daily for the first 3 weeks, followed by a rest period of 8-10 days; use the lowest dose and regimen that will control symptoms. Repeat if bleeding does not occur by the end of the rest period. The duration of therapy necessary to produce the withdrawal bleeding will vary according to the responsiveness of the endometrium. If satisfactory withdrawal bleeding does not occur, give an oral progestin in addition to estrogen during the third week of the cycle.

Female castration or primary ovarian failure: 1.5-9 mg estropipate daily for the first 3 weeks of a theoretical cycle, followed by a rest period of 8-10 days; use the lowest dose and regimen that will control symptoms

Osteoporosis prophylaxis: 0.75 mg estropipate daily for 25 days of a 31-day cycle

Atrophic vaginitis or kraurosis vulvae: 0.75-6 mg estropipate daily; administer cyclically. Use the lowest dose and regimen that will control symptoms; discontinue as soon as possible.

Elderly: Refer to Adults dosing. A higher incidence of stroke and invasive breast cancer were observed in women >75 years in a WHI substudy using conjugated equine estrogen.

Dosing adjustment in hepatic impairment:
Mild to moderate liver impairment: Dosage reduction of estrogens is recommended
Severe liver impairment: **Not recommended**

Dietary Considerations Ensure adequate calcium and vitamin D intake when used for the prevention of osteoporosis.

Monitoring Parameters Yearly physical examination that includes blood pressure and Papanicolaou smear, breast exam, mammogram. Monitor for signs of endometrial cancer in female patients with uterus. Adequate diagnostic measures, including endometrial sampling, if indicated, should be performed to rule out malignancy in all cases of undiagnosed abnormal vaginal bleeding. Monitor for loss of vision, sudden onset of proptosis, diplopia, migraine; signs and symptoms of thromboembolic disorders; glycemic control in diabetics; lipid profiles in patients being treated for hyperlipidemias; thyroid function in patients on thyroid hormone replacement therapy.
Menopausal symptoms: Assess need for therapy at 3- to 6-month intervals
Prevention of osteoporosis: Bone density measurement

Test Interactions Pathologist should be advised of estrogen/progesterone therapy when specimens are submitted. Reduced response to metyrapone test.

Dosage Forms
Tablet: 0.625 mg [estropipate 0.75 mg]; 1.25 mg [estropipate 1.5 mg]; 2.5 mg [estropipate 3 mg]
Ogen®: 0.625 mg [estropipate 0.75 mg]; 1.25 mg [estropipate 1.5 mg]; 2.5 mg [estropipate 3 mg]
Ortho-Est®: 0.625 mg [estropipate 0.75 mg]; 1.25 mg [estropipate 1.5 mg]

♦ **Estrostep® Fe** see Ethinyl Estradiol and Norethindrone on page 655

Eszopiclone (es zoe PIK lone)

U.S. Brand Names Lunesta™
Pharmacologic Category Hypnotic, Nonbenzodiazepine
Use Treatment of insomnia
Restrictions C-IV
Pregnancy Risk Factor C
Pregnancy Implications No evidence of teratogenicity in animal models (high dose). There are no adequate or well-controlled studies in pregnant women; use only if clearly needed.
Lactation Excretion in breast milk unknown/use caution
Medication Safety Issues
Sound-alike/look-alike issues:
Lunesta™ may be confused with Neulasta®
Contraindications Hypersensitivity to eszopiclone or any component of the formulation
Warnings/Precautions Symptomatic treatment of insomnia should be initiated only after careful evaluation of potential causes of sleep disturbance. Tolerance did not develop over 6 (Continued)

Eszopiclone *(Continued)*

months of use. Use with caution in patients with depression or a history of drug dependence. Abrupt discontinuance may lead to withdrawal symptoms. Use with caution in patients receiving other CNS depressants or psychoactive medications. Hypnotics/sedatives have been associated with abnormal thinking and behavior changes including decreased inhibition, aggression, bizarre behavior, agitation, hallucinations, and depersonalization. These changes may occur unpredictably and may indicate previously unrecognized psychiatric disorders; evaluate appropriately. Amnesia may occur. May impair physical and mental capabilities. Use caution in patients with respiratory compromise, hepatic dysfunction, elderly or those taking strong CYP3A4 inhibitors. Because of the rapid onset of action, administer immediately prior to bedtime or after the patient has gone to bed and is having difficulty falling asleep. Safety and efficacy in children have not been established.

Adverse Reactions

>10%:
    Central nervous system: Headache (15% to 21%)
    Gastrointestinal: Unpleasant taste (8% to 34%)

1% to 10%:
    Cardiovascular: Chest pain, peripheral edema
    Central nervous system: Somnolence (8% to 10%), dizziness (5% to 7%), hallucinations (1% to 3%), anxiety (1% to 3%), nervousness (up to 5%), confusion (up to 3%), depression (1% to 4%), abnormal dreams (1% to 3%), migraine
    Dermatologic: Rash (3% to 4%), pruritus (1% to 4%)
    Endocrine & metabolic: Libido decreased (up to 3%), dysmenorrhea (up to 3%), gynecomastia (males up to 3%)
    Gastrointestinal: Xerostomia (3% to 7%), dyspepsia (5% to 6%), nausea (5%), diarrhea (2% to 4%), vomiting (up to 3%)
    Genitourinary: Urinary tract infection (up to 3%)
    Neuromuscular & skeletal: Neuralgia (up to 3%)
    Miscellaneous: Infection (5% to 10%), viral infection (3%)

<1% (Limited to important or life-threatening): Agitation, allergic reaction, arthritis, arthrosis, asthma, ataxia, breast neoplasm, cellulitis, cholelithiasis, colitis, conjunctivitis, contact dermatitis, cystitis, difficulty concentrating, dyspnea, dysphagia, dysuria, epistaxis, erythema multiforme, euphoria, facial edema, fever, furunculosis, gastritis, gout, heat stroke, hematuria, hepatitis, hepatomegaly, herpes zoster, hyperacusis, hypertension, hypertonia, hypoesthesia, incoordination, kidney calculus, liver damage, melena, memory impairment, myasthenia, myopathy, neuritis, neuropathy, neurosis, photophobia, photosensitivity, pyelonephritis, rectal hemorrhage, reflexes decreased, stomach ulcer, stupor, thrombophlebitis, tinnitus, tongue edema, ulcerative stomatitis, uterine hemorrhage, urethritis, vaginal hemorrhage, vertigo, vesiculobullous rash

Overdosage/Toxicology Overdose symptoms range from somnolence to coma. Treatment is symptom-directed and supportive. Flumazenil may be useful.

Drug Interactions

Cytochrome P450 Effect: Substrate of CYP2E1 (minor), 3A4 (major)

Increased Effect/Toxicity: CYP3A4 inhibitors may increase the levels/effects of eszopiclone; example inhibitors include azole antifungals, clarithromycin, diclofenac, doxycycline, erythromycin, imatinib, isoniazid, nefazodone, nicardipine, propofol, protease inhibitors, quinidine, telithromycin, and verapamil. Concurrent use with olanzapine may lead to decreased psychomotor function.

Decreased Effect: CYP3A4 inducers may decrease the levels/effects of eszopiclone; example inducers include aminoglutethimide, carbamazepine, nafcillin, nevirapine, phenobarbital, phenytoin, and rifampins.

Ethanol/Nutrition/Herb Interactions

Ethanol: Use caution with concurrent use. Effects are additive and may decrease psychomotor function.

Food: Onset of action may be reduced if taken with or immediately after a heavy meal.

Herb/Nutraceutical: Avoid valerian, St John's wort, kava kava, gotu kola (may increase CNS depression).

Stability Store at 15°C to 30°C (59°F to 86°F).

Mechanism of Action May interact with GABA-receptor complexes at binding domains located close to or allosterically coupled to benzodiazepine receptors.

Pharmacodynamics/Kinetics

Absorption: Rapid; high-fat/heavy meal may delay absorption
Protein binding: 52% to 59%
Metabolism: Hepatic via oxidation and demethylation (CYP2E1, 3A4); 2 primary metabolites; one with activity less than parent.
Half-life elimination: 6 hours; Elderly (≥65 years): ~9 hours
Time to peak, plasma: 1 hour
Excretion: Urine (75%, primarily as metabolites; <10% as parent drug)

Dosage Oral:

Adults: Insomnia: Initial: 2 mg before bedtime (maximum dose: 3 mg)
    Concurrent use with strong CYP3A4 inhibitor: 1 mg before bedtime; if needed, dose may be increased to 2 mg

Elderly:
    Difficulty **falling** asleep: Initial: 1 mg before bedtime; maximum dose: 2 mg
    Difficulty **staying** asleep: 2 mg before bedtime

Dosage adjustment in renal impairment: None required

Dosage adjustment in hepatic impairment:
    Mild-to-moderate: Use with caution; dosage adjustment unnecessary
    Severe: Maximum dose: 2 mg

Dietary Considerations Avoid taking after a heavy meal; may delay onset.

Administration Because of the rapid onset of action, eszopiclone should be administered immediately prior to bedtime or after the patient has gone to bed and is having difficulty falling asleep. Do not take with, or immediately following, a high-fat meal; do not crush or break tablet.

Dosage Forms Tablet: 1 mg, 2 mg, 3 mg

♦ **ETAF** *see* Aldesleukin *on page 59*

Etanercept (et a NER sept)

U.S. Brand Names Enbrel®
Canadian Brand Names Enbrel®
Pharmacologic Category Antirheumatic, Disease Modifying; Tumor Necrosis Factor (TNF) Blocking Agent
Use Treatment of moderately- to severely-active rheumatoid arthritis (RA); moderately- to severely-active polyarticular juvenile rheumatoid arthritis (JRA) in patients with inadequate response to at least one disease-modifying antirheumatic drug; psoriatic arthritis; active ankylosing spondylitis (AS); moderate-to-severe chronic plaque psoriasis
Pregnancy Risk Factor B
Pregnancy Implications Developmental toxicity studies performed in animals have revealed no evidence of harm to the fetus. There are no studies in pregnant women; this drug should be used during pregnancy only if clearly needed. A pregnancy registry has been established to monitor outcomes of women exposed to etanercept during pregnancy (877-311-8972).
Lactation Excretion in breast milk unknown/not recommended
Contraindications Hypersensitivity to etanercept or any component of the formulation; patients with sepsis (mortality may be increased); active infections (including chronic or local infection)
Warnings/Precautions Serious and potentially fatal rare infections, including reactivation of hepatitis or cases of tuberculosis have been reported. Discontinue administration if patient develops a serious infection. Caution should be exercised when considering the use in patients with chronic infection, history of recurrent infection, or predisposition to infection (such as poorly-controlled diabetes). Do not give to patients with an active chronic or localized infection. Patients who develop a new infection while undergoing treatment should be monitored closely. If a patient develops a serious infection, therapy should be discontinued. Patients should be brought up to date with all immunizations before initiating therapy. Live vaccines should not be given concurrently. Patients with a significant exposure to varicella virus should temporarily discontinue etanercept. Treatment with varicella zoster immune globulin should be considered.

Impact on the development and course of malignancies is not fully defined. As compared to the general population, an increased risk of lymphoma has been noted in clinical trials; however, rheumatoid arthritis has been previously associated with an increased rate of lymphoma. Etanercept is not recommended for use in patients with Wegener's granulomatosis who are receiving immunosuppressive therapy. Treatment may result in the formation of autoimmune antibodies; cases of autoimmune disease have not been described. Non-neutralizing antibodies to etanercept may also be formed. Rarely, a reversible lupus-like syndrome has occurred. Safety and efficacy have not been established in children <4 years of age.

Use caution in patients with pre-existing or recent-onset demyelinating CNS disorders; cases of optic neuritis, demyelinating disease and/or seizures have been reported. Use caution in patients with CHF; has been associated with worsening and new-onset CHF. Use caution in patients with a history of significant hematologic abnormalities; has been associated with pancytopenia and aplastic anemia (rare). Discontinue if significant hematologic abnormalities are confirmed.

Should not be used in combination with anakinra, unless no satisfactory alternatives exist, and then only with extreme caution. Some dosage forms may contain dry natural rubber (latex).
Adverse Reactions
>10%:
  Central nervous system: Headache (17%)
  Local: Injection site reaction (14% to 37%; erythema, itching, pain or swelling)
  Respiratory: Respiratory tract infection (upper, 20% to 29%), rhinitis (12%)
  Miscellaneous: Infection (35%), positive ANA (11%), positive antidouble-stranded DNA antibodies (15% by RIA, 3% by *Crithidia luciliae* assay)
≥3% to 10%:
  Central nervous system: Dizziness (7%)
  Dermatologic: Rash (5%)
  Gastrointestinal: Abdominal pain (5%), dyspepsia (4%), nausea (9%), vomiting (3%)
  Neuromuscular & skeletal: Weakness (5%)
  Respiratory: Pharyngitis (7%), respiratory disorder (5%), sinusitis (3%), cough (6%)
<3% (Limited to important or life-threatening): Abscess, adenopathy, anemia, angioedema, aplastic anemia, appendicitis, bursitis, cerebral ischemia, chest pain, cholecystitis, CHF, coagulopathy, deep vein thrombosis; demyelinating CNS disorders (suggestive of multiple sclerosis, transverse myelitis, or optic neuritis); depression, fever, flushing, flu-like syndrome, hepatitis (autoimmune), hydrocephalus (with normal pressure), infections (bacterial, fungal, protozoal, viral), interstitial lung disease, intestinal perforation, leukopenia, lupus-like syndrome, lymphadenopathy, malignancies (including lymphoma), membranous glomerulopathy, MI, mouth ulcer, multiple sclerosis, myocardial ischemia, neutropenia, optic neuritis, pancreatitis, pancytopenia, paresthesia, polymyositis, pruritus, pulmonary disease, ocular inflammation, pulmonary embolism, renal calculus, sarcoidosis, seizure, stroke, thrombocytopenia, thrombophlebitis, transaminases increased, tuberculosis, urinary tract infection, urticaria, vasculitis (cutaneous), weight gain
Pediatric patients (JRA): The percentages of patients reporting abdominal pain (17%) and vomiting (13%) were higher than in adult RA. Two patients developed varicella infection associated with aseptic meningitis which resolved without complications (see Warnings/
(Continued)

Etanercept *(Continued)*

Precautions). Other severe reactions included gastroenteritis, depression, cutaneous ulcer, esophagitis/gastritis, group A streptococcal septic shock, and wound infections.

Overdosage/Toxicology No dose-limiting toxicities have been observed during clinical trials. Single I.V. doses up to 60 mg/m^2 have been administered to healthy volunteers in an endotoxemia study, without evidence of dose-limiting toxicities.

Drug Interactions

Increased Effect/Toxicity: Abatacept and anakinra may increase the risk of infection. Cyclophosphamide may increase the risk of noncutaneous solid malignancy. Etanercept may increase the risk of vaccinal infection (live organism vaccine).

Decreased Effect: Etanercept may decrease the effect of killed organism or component vaccines.

Ethanol/Nutrition/Herb Interactions Herb/Nutraceutical: Echinacea may decrease the therapeutic effects of etanercept (avoid concurrent use).

Stability Store prefilled syringes at 2°C to 8°C (36°F to 46°F); protect from light; do not freeze or shake. Powder for reconstitution must be refrigerated at 2°C to 8°C (36°F to 46°F). Do not freeze. Reconstitute lyophilized powder aseptically with 1 mL sterile bacteriostatic water for injection, USP (supplied); swirl gently, do not shake. Do not filter reconstituted solution during preparation or administration. Reconstituted vials of etanercept should be administered as soon as possible after reconstitution. If not administered immediately after reconstitution, etanercept may be stored in the vial at 2°C to 8°C (36°F to 46°F) for up to 14 days.

Mechanism of Action Etanercept is a recombinant DNA-derived protein composed of tumor necrosis factor receptor (TNFR) linked to the Fc portion of human IgG1. Etanercept binds tumor necrosis factor (TNF) and blocks its interaction with cell surface receptors. TNF plays an important role in the inflammatory processes and the resulting joint pathology of rheumatoid arthritis (RA), polyarticular-course juvenile arthritis (JRA), ankylosing spondylitis (AS), and plaque psoriasis.

Pharmacodynamics/Kinetics

Onset of action: ~2-3 weeks; RA: 1-2 weeks

Half-life elimination: RA: SubQ: 72-132 hours

Time to peak: RA: SubQ: 35-103 hours

Excretion: Clearance: Children: 45.9 mL/hour/m^2; Adults: 89 mL/hour (52 mL/hour/m^2)

Dosage SubQ:

Children 4-17 years: Juvenile rheumatoid arthritis:

Once-weekly dosing (patients weighing <31 kg or ≥63 kg): 0.8 mg/kg (maximum: 50 mg/dose) once weekly

Twice-weekly dosing (patients weighing 31-62 kg): 0.4 mg/kg (maximum: 25 mg/dose) twice weekly (individual doses should be separated by 72-96 hours)

Adults:

Rheumatoid arthritis, psoriatic arthritis, ankylosing spondylitis:

Once-weekly dosing: 50 mg once weekly

Twice weekly dosing: 25 mg given twice weekly (individual doses should be separated by 72-96 hours)

Plaque psoriasis:

Initial: 50 mg twice weekly, 3-4 days apart (starting doses of 25 or 50 mg once weekly have also been used successfully); maintain initial dose for 3 months

Maintenance dose: 50 mg weekly

Elderly: Refer to adult dosing. Although greater sensitivity of some elderly patients cannot be ruled out, no overall differences in safety or effectiveness were observed.

Administration Administer subcutaneously. Rotate injection sites. New injections should be given at least one inch from an old site and never into areas where the skin is tender, bruised, red, or hard. **Note:** If the physician determines that it is appropriate, patients may self-inject after proper training in injection technique.

Powder for reconstitution: Follow package instructions carefully for reconstitution. The maximum amount injected at any single site should not exceed 25 mg.

Solution for injection: May be allowed to reach room temperature prior to injection.

Dosage Forms

Injection, powder for reconstitution:

Enbrel®: 25 mg [contains sucrose; diluent contains benzyl alcohol]

Injection, solution:

Enbrel®: 50 mg/mL (0.98 mL) [contains sucrose; packaging may contain dry natural rubber (latex)]

♦ **Ethacrynate Sodium** see Ethacrynic Acid *on page 642*

Ethacrynic Acid *(eth a KRIN ik AS id)*

U.S. Brand Names Edecrin®

Canadian Brand Names Edecrin®

Index Terms Ethacrynate Sodium

Pharmacologic Category Diuretic, Loop

Use Management of edema associated with congestive heart failure; hepatic cirrhosis or renal disease; short-term management of ascites due to malignancy, idiopathic edema, and lymphedema

Pregnancy Risk Factor B

Medication Safety Issues

Sound-alike/look-alike issues:

Edecrin® may be confused with Eulexin®, Ecotrin®

Dosage I.V. formulation should be diluted in D$_5$W or NS (1 mg/mL) and infused over several minutes.

Children: Oral: 1 mg/kg/dose once daily; increase at intervals of 2-3 days as needed, to a maximum of 3 mg/kg/day.

Adults:
  Oral: 50-200 mg/day in 1-2 divided doses; may increase in increments of 25-50 mg at
    intervals of several days; doses up to 200 mg twice daily may be required with severe,
    retractory edema.
  I.V.: 0.5-1 mg/kg/dose (maximum: 100 mg/dose); repeat doses not routinely recom-
    mended; however, if indicated, repeat doses every 8-12 hours.
  Dosing adjustment/comments in renal impairment: Cl_{cr} <10 mL/minute: Avoid use.
  Dialysis: Not removed by hemo- or peritoneal dialysis; supplemental dose is not necessary.
Additional Information Complete prescribing information for this medication should be
  consulted for additional detail.
Dosage Forms
  Injection, powder for reconstitution, as ethacrynate sodium: 50 mg
  Tablet: 25 mg

Ethambutol (e THAM byoo tole)

U.S. Brand Names Myambutol®
Canadian Brand Names Etibi®
Index Terms Ethambutol Hydrochloride
Pharmacologic Category Antitubercular Agent
Additional Appendix Information
  Antimicrobial Drugs of Choice *on page 1981*
  Desensitization Protocols *on page 1913*
  Tuberculosis *on page 2010*
  USPHS / IDSA Guidelines for the Prevention of Opportunistic Infections in Persons Infected
    With HIV *on page 1966*
Use Treatment of tuberculosis and other mycobacterial diseases in conjunction with other
  antituberculosis agents
Pregnancy Risk Factor C
Pregnancy Implications There are no adequate and well-controlled studies in pregnant
  women; teratogenic effects have been seen in animals. Ethambutol has been used safely
  during pregnancy.
Lactation Enters breast milk/use caution (AAP considers "compatible")
Medication Safety Issues
  Sound-alike/look-alike issues:
    Myambutol® may be confused with Nembutal®
Contraindications Hypersensitivity to ethambutol or any component of the formulation; optic
  neuritis; use in children, unconscious patients, or any other patient who may be unable to
  discern and report visual changes
Warnings/Precautions May cause optic neuritis, resulting in decreased visual acuity or other
  vision changes. Discontinue promptly in patients with changes in vision, color blindness, or
  visual defects (effects normally reversible, but reversal may require up to a year). Use only in
  children whose visual acuity can accurately be determined and monitored (not recommended
  for use in children <13 years of age unless the benefit outweighs the risk). Dosage modifica-
  tion is required in patients with renal insufficiency. Hepatic toxicity has been reported,
  possibly due to concurrent therapy.
Adverse Reactions Frequency not defined.
  Cardiovascular: Myocarditis, pericarditis
  Central nervous system: Headache, confusion, disorientation, malaise, mental confusion,
    fever, dizziness, hallucinations
  Dermatologic: Rash, pruritus, dermatitis, exfoliative dermatitis
  Endocrine & metabolic: Acute gout or hyperuricemia
  Gastrointestinal: Abdominal pain, anorexia, nausea, vomiting
  Hematologic: Leukopenia, thrombocytopenia, eosinophilia, neutropenia, lymphadenopathy
  Hepatic: Abnormal LFTs, hepatotoxicity (possibly related to concurrent therapy), hepatitis
  Neuromuscular & skeletal: Peripheral neuritis, arthralgia
  Ocular: Optic neuritis; symptoms may include decreased acuity, scotoma, color blindness, or
    visual defects (usually reversible with discontinuation, irreversible blindness has been
    described)
  Renal: Nephritis
  Respiratory: Infiltrates (with or without eosinophilia), pneumonitis
  Miscellaneous: Anaphylaxis, anaphylactoid reaction; hypersensitivity syndrome (rash, eosin-
    ophilia, and organ-specific inflammation)
Overdosage/Toxicology Symptoms include decreased visual acuity, anorexia, joint pain,
  and numbness of the extremities. Following GI decontamination, treatment is supportive.
Drug Interactions
  Decreased Effect: Decreased absorption with aluminum hydroxide. Avoid concurrent
    administration of aluminum-containing antacids for at least 4 hours following ethambutol.
Stability Store at controlled room temperature of 20°C to 25°C (68°F to 77°F).
Mechanism of Action Suppresses mycobacteria multiplication by interfering with RNA
  synthesis
Pharmacodynamics/Kinetics
  Absorption: ~80%
  Distribution: Widely throughout body; concentrated in kidneys, lungs, saliva, and red blood
    cells
    Relative diffusion from blood into CSF: Adequate with or without inflammation (exceeds
      usual MICs)
    CSF:blood level ratio: Normal meninges: 0%; Inflamed meninges: 25%
  Protein binding: 20% to 30%
  Metabolism: Hepatic (20%) to inactive metabolite
  Half-life elimination: 2.5-3.6 hours; End-stage renal disease: 7-15 hours
  Time to peak, serum: 2-4 hours
  Excretion: Urine (~50%) and feces (20%) as unchanged drug
  (Continued)

Ethambutol *(Continued)*

Dosage Oral:

Treatment of tuberculosis: **Note:** Used as part of a multidrug regimen. Treatment regimens consist of an initial 2 month phase, followed by a continuation phase of 4 or 7 additional months; frequency of dosing may differ depending on phase of therapy.

Children:

Daily therapy: 15-20 mg/kg/day (maximum: 1 g/day)

Twice weekly directly observed therapy (DOT): 50 mg/kg (maximum: 4 g/dose)

Adults (suggested doses by lean body weight):

Daily therapy: 15-25 mg/kg

40-55 kg: 800 mg

56-75 kg: 1200 mg

76-90 kg: 1600 mg (maximum dose regardless of weight)

Twice weekly directly observed therapy (DOT): 50 mg/kg

40-55 kg: 2000 mg

56-75 kg: 2800 mg

76-90 kg: 4000 mg (maximum dose regardless of weight)

Three times/week DOT: 25-30 mg/kg (maximum: 2.5 g)

40-55 kg: 1200 mg

56-75 kg: 2000 mg

76-90 kg: 2400 mg (maximum dose regardless of weight)

Disseminated *Mycobacterium avium* complex (MAC) in patients with advanced HIV infection: 15 mg/kg ethambutol in combination with azithromycin 600 mg daily

Dosing interval in renal impairment:

Cl_{cr} 10-50 mL/minute: Administer every 24-36 hours

Cl_{cr} <10 mL/minute: Administer every 48 hours

Hemodialysis: Slightly dialyzable (5% to 20%); Administer dose postdialysis

Peritoneal dialysis: Dose for Cl_{cr} <10 mL/minute

Continuous arteriovenous or venovenous hemofiltration: Administer every 24-36 hours

Dietary Considerations May be taken with food as absorption is not affected, may cause gastric irritation.

Monitoring Parameters Baseline and periodic (monthly) visual testing (each eye individually, as well as both eyes tested together) in patients receiving >15 mg/kg/day; baseline and periodic renal, hepatic, and hematopoietic tests

Dosage Forms Tablet, as hydrochloride: 100 mg, 400 mg

♦ **Ethambutol Hydrochloride** *see* Ethambutol *on page 643*

♦ **Ethamolin®** *see* Ethanolamine Oleate *on page 644*

♦ **Ethanoic Acid** *see* Acetic Acid *on page 38*

Ethanolamine Oleate (ETH a nol a meen OH lee ate)

U.S. Brand Names Ethamolin®

Index Terms Monoethanolamine

Pharmacologic Category Sclerosing Agent

Use Orphan drug: Sclerosing agent used for bleeding esophageal varices

Pregnancy Risk Factor C

Medication Safety Issues

Sound-alike/look-alike issues:

Ethamolin® may be confused with ethanol

Contraindications Hypersensitivity to agent or oleic acid

Warnings/Precautions Fatal anaphylactic shock has been reported following administration; use with caution and decrease doses in patients with significant liver dysfunction (Child class C), with concomitant cardiorespiratory disease, or in the elderly or critically-ill

Adverse Reactions

1% to 10%:

Central nervous system: Pyrexia (1.8%)

Gastrointestinal: Esophageal ulcer (2%), esophageal stricture (1.3%)

Respiratory: Pleural effusion (2%), pneumonia (1.2%)

Miscellaneous: Retrosternal pain (1.6%)

<1% (Limited to important or life-threatening): Acute renal failure, anaphylaxis, esophagitis, injection necrosis, perforation

Overdosage/Toxicology Anaphylaxis and severe intramural necrosis can occur after administration of larger than normal volumes. Treatment is supportive with epinephrine, corticosteroids, fluids, and pressors.

Mechanism of Action Derived from oleic acid and similar in physical properties to sodium morrhuate; however, the exact mechanism of the hemostatic effect used in endoscopic injection sclerotherapy is not known. Intravenously injected ethanolamine oleate produces a sterile inflammatory response resulting in fibrosis and occlusion of the vein; a dose-related extravascular inflammatory reaction occurs when the drug diffuses through the venous wall. Autopsy results indicate that variceal obliteration occurs secondary to mural necrosis and fibrosis. Thrombosis appears to be a transient reaction.

Dosage Adults: 1.5-5 mL per varix, up to 20 mL total or 0.4 mL/kg for a 50 kg patient; doses should be decreased in patients with severe hepatic dysfunction and should receive less than recommended maximum dose

Administration Use care to use acceptable technique to avoid necrosis

Dosage Forms Injection, solution: 5% [50 mg/mL] (2 mL) [contains benzyl alcohol]

♦ **EtheDent™** *see* Fluoride *on page 722*

♦ **Ethezyme™** *see* Papain and Urea *on page 1309*

♦ **Ethezyme™ 830** *see* Papain and Urea *on page 1309*

Ethinyl Estradiol and Desogestrel

(ETH in il es tra DYE ole & des oh JES trel)

U.S. Brand Names Apri®; Cesia™; Cyclessa®; Desogen®; Kariva™; Mircette®; Ortho-Cept®; Reclipsen™; Solia®; Velivet™

Canadian Brand Names Cyclessa®; Linessa®; Marvelon®; Ortho Cept®

Index Terms Desogestrel and Ethinyl Estradiol; Ortho Cept

Pharmacologic Category Contraceptive; Estrogen and Progestin Combination

Use Prevention of pregnancy

Unlabeled/Investigational Use Treatment of hypermenorrhea (menorrhagia); pain associated with endometriosis; dysmenorrhea; dysfunctional uterine bleeding

Pregnancy Risk Factor X

Medication Safety Issues

Sound-alike/look-alike issues:

Ortho-Cept® may be confused with Ortho-Cyclen®

Dosage Oral: Adults: Female: Contraception:

Schedule 1 (Sunday starter): Dose begins on first Sunday after onset of menstruation; if the menstrual period starts on Sunday, take first tablet that very same day. **With a Sunday start, an additional method of contraception should be used until after the first 7 days of consecutive administration.**

For 21-tablet package: Dosage is 1 tablet daily for 21 consecutive days, followed by 7 days off of the medication; a new course begins on the 8th day after the last tablet is taken.

For 28-tablet package: Dosage is 1 tablet daily without interruption.

Schedule 2 (Day 1 starter): Dose starts on first day of menstrual cycle taking 1 tablet daily.

For 21-tablet package: Dosage is 1 tablet daily for 21 consecutive days, followed by 7 days off of the medication; a new course begins on the 8th day after the last tablet is taken.

For 28-tablet package: Dosage is 1 tablet daily without interruption.

If all doses have been taken on schedule and one menstrual period is missed, continue dosing cycle. If two consecutive menstrual periods are missed, pregnancy test is required before new dosing cycle is started.

Missed doses **monophasic formulations** (refer to package insert for complete information):

One dose missed: Take as soon as remembered or take 2 tablets next day

Two consecutive doses missed in the first 2 weeks: Take 2 tablets as soon as remembered or 2 tablets next 2 days. **An additional method of contraception should be used for 7 days after missed dose.**

Two consecutive doses missed In week 3 or three consecutive doses missed at any time:

Schedule 1 (Sunday starter): Continue to take 1 tablet daily until Sunday, then discard the rest of the pack, and a new pack is started that same day.

Schedule 2 (Day 1 starter): Current pack should be discarded, and a new pack started that same day. **An additional method of contraception should be used for 7 days after missed dose.**

Missed doses **biphasic/triphasic formulations** (refer to package insert for complete information):

One dose missed: Take as soon as remembered or take 2 tablets next day.

Two consecutive doses missed in week 1 or week 2 of the pack: Take 2 tablets as soon as remembered and 2 tablets the next day. Resume taking 1 tablet daily until the pack is empty. **An additional method of contraception should be used for 7 days after a missed dose.**

Two consecutive doses missed in week 3 of the pack; **an additional method of contraception must be used for 7 days after a missed dose**:

Schedule 1 (Sunday starter): Take 1 tablet every day until Sunday. Discard the remaining pack and start a new pack of pills on the same day.

Schedule 2 (Day 1 starter): Discard the remaining pack and start a new pack the same day.

Three or more consecutive doses missed; **an additional method of contraception must be used for 7 days after a missed dose**:

Schedule 1 (Sunday starter): Take 1 tablet every day until Sunday; on Sunday, discard the pack and start a new pack.

Schedule 2 (Day 1 starter): Discard the remaining pack and begin new pack of tablets starting on the same day.

Dosage adjustment in renal impairment: Specific guidelines not available; use with caution and monitor blood pressure closely. Consider other forms of contraception.

Dosage adjustment in hepatic impairment: Contraindicated in patients with hepatic impairment

Additional Information Complete prescribing information for this medication should be consulted for additional detail.

Dosage Forms

Tablet, low-dose formulations:

Kariva™:

Day 1-21: Ethinyl estradiol 0.02 mg and desogestrel 0.15 mg [21 white tablets]

Day 22-23: 2 inactive light green tablets

Day 24-28: Ethinyl estradiol 0.01 mg [5 light blue tablets] (28s)

Mircette®:

Day 1-21: Ethinyl estradiol 0.02 mg and desogestrel 0.15 mg [21 white tablets]

Day 22-23: 2 inactive green tablets

Day 24-28: Ethinyl estradiol 0.01 mg [5 yellow tablets] (28s)

Tablet, monophasic formulations:

Apri® 28: Ethinyl estradiol 0.03 mg and desogestrel 0.15 mg [21 rose tablets and 7 white inactive tablets] (28s)

Desogen®, Reclipsen™, Solia™: Ethinyl estradiol 0.03 mg and desogestrel 0.15 mg [21 white tablets and 7 green inactive tablets] (28s)

Ortho-Cept® 28: Ethinyl estradiol 0.03 mg and desogestrel 0.15 mg [21 orange tablets and 7 green inactive tablets] (28s)

(Continued)

Ethinyl Estradiol and Desogestrel *(Continued)*

Tablet, triphasic formulations:

Cesia™, Cyclessa®:

Day 1-7:Ethinyl estradiol 0.025 mg and desogestrel 0.1 mg [7 light yellow tablets]

Day 8-14: Ethinyl estradiol 0.025 mg and desogestrel 0.125 mg [7 orange tablets]

Day 14-21: Ethinyl estradiol 0.025 mg and desogestrel 0.15 mg [7 red tablets]

Day 21-28: 7 green inactive tablets (28s)

Velivet™:

Day 1-7: Ethinyl estradiol 0.025 mg and desogestrel 0.1 mg [7 beige tablets]

Day 8-14: Ethinyl estradiol 0.025 mg and desogestrel 0.125 mg [7 orange tablets]

Day 14-21: Ethinyl estradiol 0.025 mg and desogestrel 0.15 mg [7 pink tablets]

Day 21-28: 7 white inactive tablets (28s)

Ethinyl Estradiol and Drospirenone

(ETH in il es tra DYE ole & droh SPYE re none)

U.S. Brand Names Yasmin®; Yaz

Canadian Brand Names Yasmin®

Index Terms Drospirenone and Ethinyl Estradiol

Pharmacologic Category Contraceptive; Estrogen and Progestin Combination

Use Prevention of pregnancy; treatment of premenstrual dysphoric disorder (PMDD) in women choosing to use an oral contraceptive

Unlabeled/Investigational Use Treatment of hypermenorrhea (menorrhagia); pain associated with endometriosis; dysmenorrhea; dysfunctional uterine bleeding

Pregnancy Risk Factor X

Pregnancy Implications In general, the use of oral contraceptives when inadvertently taken early in pregnancy have not been associated with teratogenic effects. Esophageal atresia was reported in one infant with a single-cycle exposure to ethinyl estradiol and drospirenone *in utero* (association not known). Pregnancy should be ruled out prior to treatment and discontinued if pregnancy occurs. Due to increased risk of thromboembolism postpartum, do not start oral contraceptives earlier than 4-6 weeks following delivery. Hormonal contraceptives may be less effective in obese patients. An increase in oral contraceptive failure was noted in women with a BMI >27.3. Similar findings were noted in patients weighing ≥90 kg (198 lb) using the contraceptive patch.

Lactation Enters breast milk/not recommended

Contraindications Hypersensitivity to ethinyl estradiol, drospirenone, or to any component of the formulation; history of or current thrombophlebitis or venous thromboembolic disorders (including DVT, PE); active or recent (within 1 year) arterial thromboembolic disease (eg, stroke, MI); cerebral vascular disease, coronary artery disease, severe hypertension, valvular heart disease with thrombogenic complications; diabetes with vascular involvement; headache with focal neurological symptoms; known or suspected breast carcinoma, endometrial cancer, estrogen-dependent neoplasms, undiagnosed abnormal genital bleeding; renal insufficiency, hepatic dysfunction or tumor, adrenal insufficiency, cholestatic jaundice of pregnancy, jaundice with prior oral contraceptive use; heavy smoking (≥15 cigarettes/day) in patients >35 years of age; pregnancy

Warnings/Precautions Oral contraceptives do not protect against HIV infection or other sexually-transmitted diseases. **[U.S. Boxed Warning]: The risk of cardiovascular side effects increases in women who smoke cigarettes, especially those who are >35 years of age; women who use oral contraceptives should be strongly advised not to smoke.** Oral contraceptives may lead to increased risk of myocardial infarction, use with caution in patients with risk factors for coronary artery disease. May increase the risk of thromboembolism. Whenever possible, combination hormonal contraceptives should be discontinued at least 4 weeks prior to and for 2 weeks following elective surgery associated with an increased risk of thromboembolism or during periods of prolonged immobilization. Oral contraceptives may have a dose-related risk of vascular disease, hypertension, and gallbladder disease. Women with hypertension should be encouraged to use another form of contraception. The use of combination hormonal contraceptives has been associated with a slight increase in frequency of breast cancer, however, studies are not consistent. Combination hormonal contraceptives may cause glucose intolerance or effect serum triglyceride and lipoprotein levels. Retinal thrombosis has been reported (rarely) with oral contraceptive use. Use with caution in patients with conditions that may be aggravated by fluid retention, depression, or patients with history of migraine. Not for use prior to menarche.

The minimum dosage combination of estrogen/progestin that will effectively treat the individual patient should be used.

Drospirenone has antimineralocorticoid activity that may lead to hyperkalemia in patients with renal insufficiency, hepatic dysfunction, or adrenal insufficiency. Use caution with medications that may increase serum potassium.

Adverse Reactions

>1%:

Central nervous system: Depression, dizziness, emotional lability, fever, headache, migraine, nervousness, pain

Dermatologic: Acne, pruritus, rash

Endocrine & metabolic: Amenorrhea, breast pain, dysmenorrhea, hyperlipidemia, intermenstrual bleeding, libido decreased, menstrual irregularities

Gastrointestinal: Abdomen enlarged, abdominal pain, diarrhea, dyspepsia, gastroenteritis, nausea, tooth disorder, vomiting, weight gain

Genitourinary: Cystitis, leukorrhea, papanicolaou smear suspicious, pelvic pain, UTI, vaginal moniliasis, vaginitis

Neuromuscular & skeletal: Back pain, extremity pain, weakness

Respiratory: Bronchitis, cough, pharyngitis, rhinitis, sinusitis, upper respiratory infection

Miscellaneous: Allergic reaction, flu-like syndrome, infection

Adverse reactions reported with other oral contraceptives: Appetite changes, antithrombin III decreased, arterial thromboembolism, benign liver tumors, breast changes, Budd-Chiari syndrome, carbohydrate intolerance, cataracts, cerebral hemorrhage, cerebral thrombosis, cervical changes, change in corneal curvature (steepening), cholestatic jaundice, colitis, contact lens intolerance, decreased lactation (postpartum), deep vein thrombosis, diplopia, edema, erythema multiforme, erythema nodosum; factors VII, VIII, IX, X increased; folate serum concentrations decreased, gallbladder disease, glucose intolerance, hemolytic uremic syndrome, hemorrhagic eruption, hepatic adenomas, hirsutism, hypercalcemia, hyperglycemia, hypertension, melasma, mesenteric thrombosis, MI, papilledema, platelet aggregability increased, porphyria, premenstrual syndrome, proptosis, prothrombin increased, pulmonary thromboembolism, renal function impairment, retinal thrombosis, sex hormone-binding globulin increased, thrombophlebitis, thyroid-binding globulin increased, total thyroid hormone (T_4) increased, triglycerides/phospholipids increased, vaginal candidiasis

Overdosage/Toxicology May cause nausea; withdrawal bleeding may occur in females. Due to the antimineralocorticoid properties of drospirenone, monitor potassium and sodium serum concentrations and monitor for evidence of metabolic acidosis.

Drug Interactions
Cytochrome P450 Effect:
Ethinyl estradiol: **Substrate** of CYP2C9 (minor), 3A4 (major), 3A5-7 (minor); **Inhibits** CYP1A2 (weak), 2B6 (weak), 2C8 (weak), 2C19 (weak), 3A4 (weak)
Drospirenone: **Substrate** of CYP3A4 (minor); **Inhibits** CYP1A2 (weak), 2C9 (weak), 2C19 (weak), 3A4 (weak)

Increased Effect/Toxicity: ACE inhibitors, aldosterone antagonists, angiotensin II receptor antagonists, heparin, NSAIDs (when taken daily, long term), and potassium salts increase risk of hyperkalemia with concomitant use. Ethinyl estradiol may increase plasma concentrations of cyclosporine, prednisolone, and selegiline. Oral contraceptives may increase (or decrease) the effects of coumarin derivatives. Drospirenone may of the risk of systemic acidosis when used with ammonium chloride.

Decreased Effect: Acitretin may diminish the therapeutic effect of progestins; contraceptive failure is possible. Oral contraceptives may decrease the plasma concentration of lamotrigine and morphine. Aminoglutethimide, anticonvulsants (carbamazepine, felbamate, oxcarbazepine, phenobarbital, phenytoin, topiramate), aprepitant, rifampin, and protease inhibitors (except atazanavir, tipranavir) may increase metabolism leading to decreased effect of oral contraceptives. Griseofulvin may diminish the therapeutic effect of contraceptive (progestins). Oral contraceptives may decrease (or increase) the effects of coumarin derivatives. Modafinil and topiramate may decrease the serum concentration of oral contraceptive (estrogens). Barbiturates and protease inhibitors (except atazanavir, tipranavir) may diminish the therapeutic effect of estrogen and progestin contraceptives.

Ethanol/Nutrition/Herb Interactions
Food: CNS effects of caffeine may be enhanced if oral contraceptives are used concurrently with caffeine. Grapefruit juice increases ethinyl estradiol concentrations; clinical implications are unclear.
Herb/Nutraceutical: St John's wort may decrease levels. Herbs with estrogenic properties may enhance the adverse/toxic effect of estrogen derivatives; examples include alfalfa, black cohosh, bloodroot, hops, kudzu, licorice, red clover, saw palmetto, soybean, thyme, wild yam, yucca. Herbs with progestogenic properties may enhance the adverse/toxic effect of progestins; examples include bloodroot, chasteberry, damiana, oregano, yucca.

Stability Store at 25°C (77°F).

Mechanism of Action Combination oral contraceptives inhibit ovulation via a negative feedback mechanism on the hypothalamus, which alters the normal pattern of gonadotropin secretion of a follicle-stimulating hormone (FSH) and luteinizing hormone by the anterior pituitary. The follicular phase FSH and midcycle surge of gonadotropins are inhibited. In addition, oral contraceptives produce alterations in the genital tract, including changes in the cervical mucus, rendering it unfavorable for sperm penetration even if ovulation occurs. Changes in the endometrium may also occur, producing an unfavorable environment for nidation. Oral contraceptive drugs may alter the tubal transport of the ova through the fallopian tubes. Progestational agents may also alter sperm fertility. Drospirenone is a spironolactone analogue with antimineralocorticoid and antiandrogenic activity.

Pharmacodynamics/Kinetics
Distribution: Drospirenone: 4 L/kg; Ethinyl estradiol: 4-5 L/kg
Protein binding: Drospirenone: Serum proteins (excluding sex hormone-binding globulin and corticosteroid-binding globulin): 97%; Ethinyl estradiol: ~98%
Metabolism: Drospirenone: To inactive metabolites, minor metabolism hepatically via CYP3A4; Ethinyl estradiol: Hepatic via CYP3A4; forms metabolites; undergoes enterohepatic circulation
Bioavailability: Drospirenone: 76%; Ethinyl estradiol: 40%
Half-life elimination: Drospirenone: 30 hours; Ethinyl estradiol: ~ 24 hours
Time to peak: 1-3 hours
Excretion: Drospirenone, ethinyl estradiol: Urine and feces

Dosage Oral: Adults: Female: Contraception (Yasmin®, Yaz), PMDD (Yaz): Dosage is 1 tablet daily for 28 consecutive days. Dose should be taken at the same time each day, either after the evening meal or at bedtime. Dosing may be started on the first day of menstrual period (Day 1 starter) or on the first Sunday after the onset of the menstrual period (Sunday starter).

Day 1 starter: Dose starts on first day of menstrual cycle taking 1 tablet daily.

Sunday starter: Dose begins on first Sunday after onset of menstruation; if the menstrual period starts on Sunday, take first tablet that very same day. **With a Sunday start, an additional method of contraception should be used until after the first 7 days of consecutive administration.**

If all doses have been taken on schedule and one menstrual period is missed, continue dosing cycle. If two consecutive menstrual periods are missed, pregnancy test is required before new dosing cycle is started.

If doses have been missed during the first 3 weeks and the menstrual period is missed, pregnancy should be ruled out prior to continuing treatment.

(Continued)

Ethinyl Estradiol and Drospirenone *(Continued)*

Missed doses (monophasic formulations) (refer to package insert for complete information):

One dose missed: Take as soon as remembered or take 2 tablets next day

Two consecutive doses missed in the first 2 weeks: Take 2 tablets as soon as remembered or 2 tablets next 2 days. **An additional method of contraception should be used for 7 days after missed dose.**

Two consecutive doses missed in week 3 or three consecutive doses missed at any time: **An additional method of contraception must be used for 7 days after a missed dose.**

Day 1 starter: Current pack should be discarded, and a new pack should be started that same day.

Sunday starter: Continue dose of 1 tablet daily until Sunday, then discard the rest of the pack, and a new pack should be started that same day.

Any number of doses missed in week 4: Continue taking one pill each day until pack is empty; no back-up method of contraception is needed

Dosage adjustment in renal impairment: Contraindicated in patients with renal dysfunction (Cl_{cr} ≤50 mL/minute)

Dosage adjustment in hepatic impairment: Contraindicated in patients with hepatic dysfunction

Administration To be taken at the same time each day, either after the evening meal or at bedtime

Monitoring Parameters Before starting therapy, a physical exam with reference to the breasts and pelvis are recommended, including a Papanicolaou smear. Exam may be deferred if appropriate; pregnancy should be ruled out prior to use. Monitor patient closely for loss of vision, sudden onset of proptosis, diplopia, migraine; blood pressure; signs and symptoms of thromboembolic disorders; signs or symptoms of depression; glycemic control in diabetics; lipid profiles in patients being treated for hyperlipidemias; serum potassium in high-risk patients and those on medications with potassium-retaining properties. Adequate diagnostic measures, including endometrial sampling, if indicated, should be performed to rule out malignancy in all cases of undiagnosed abnormal vaginal bleeding.

Additional Information The World Health Organization (WHO) has issued revised management recommendations for missed combined oral contraceptive pills. Refer to the following reference for a complete presentation and discussion of the guidelines:

Faculty of Family Planning and Reproductive Health Care Clinical Effectiveness Unit, "Faculty Statement from the CEU on a New Publication: WHO Selected Practice Recommendations for Contraceptive Use Update. Missed Pills: New Recommendations," *J Fam Plann Reprod Health Care*, 2005, 31(2):153-5.

Dosage Forms
Tablet:
Yasmin®: Ethinyl estradiol 0.03 mg and drospirenone 3 mg [21 yellow active tablets and 7 white inactive tablets] (28s)
Yaz: Ethinyl estradiol 0.02 mg and drospirenone 3 mg [24 light pink tablets and 4 white inactive tablets] (28s)

Ethinyl Estradiol and Ethynodiol Diacetate
(ETH in il es tra DYE ole & e thye noe DYE ole dye AS e tate)

U.S. Brand Names Demulen® [DSC]; Kelnor™; Zovia™
Canadian Brand Names Demulen® 30
Index Terms Ethynodiol Diacetate and Ethinyl Estradiol
Pharmacologic Category Contraceptive; Estrogen and Progestin Combination
Use Prevention of pregnancy
Unlabeled/Investigational Use Treatment of hypermenorrhea (menorrhagia); pain associated with endometriosis; dysmenorrhea; dysfunctional uterine bleeding
Pregnancy Risk Factor X
Pregnancy Implications Pregnancy should be ruled out prior to treatment and discontinued if pregnancy occurs. In general, the use of combination hormonal contraceptives when inadvertently taken early in pregnancy have not been associated with teratogenic effects. Due to increased risk of thromboembolism postpartum, combination hormonal contraceptives should not be started earlier than 4-6 weeks following delivery. Hormonal contraceptives may be less effective in obese patients. An increase in oral contraceptive failure was noted in women with a BMI >27.3. Similar findings were noted in patients weighing ≥90 kg (198 lb) using the contraceptive patch.
Lactation Enters breast milk/not recommended (AAP rates "compatible")
Medication Safety Issues
Sound-alike/look-alike issues:
Demulen® may be confused with Dalmane®, Demerol®
Contraindications Hypersensitivity to ethinyl estradiol, ethynodiol diacetate, or any component of the formulation; history of or current thrombophlebitis or venous thromboembolic disorders (including DVT, PE); active or recent (within 1 year) arterial thromboembolic disease (eg, stroke, MI); cerebral vascular disease, coronary artery disease, valvular heart disease with complications, severe hypertension; diabetes mellitus with vascular involvement; severe headache with focal neurological symptoms; known or suspected breast carcinoma, endometrial cancer, estrogen-dependent neoplasms, undiagnosed abnormal genital bleeding; hepatic dysfunction or tumor, cholestatic jaundice of pregnancy, jaundice with prior combination hormonal contraceptive use; major surgery with prolonged immobilization; heavy smoking (≥15 cigarettes/day) in patients >35 years of age; pregnancy
Warnings/Precautions Combination hormonal contraceptives do not protect against HIV infection or other sexually-transmitted diseases. **[U.S. Boxed Warning]: The risk of cardiovascular side effects increases in women who smoke cigarettes, especially those who are >35 years of age; women who use combination hormonal contraceptives should be**

strongly advised not to smoke. Combination hormonal contraceptives may lead to increased risk of myocardial infarction, use with caution in patients with risk factors for coronary artery disease. May increase the risk of thromboembolism. Whenever possible, combination hormonal contraceptives should be discontinued at least 4 weeks prior to and for 2 weeks following elective surgery associated with an increased risk of thromboembolism or during periods of prolonged immobilization. Combination hormonal contraceptives may have a dose-related risk of vascular disease, hypertension, and gallbladder disease. Women with hypertension or renal disease should be encouraged to use a nonhormonal form of contraception. The use of combination hormonal contraceptives has been associated with a slight increase in frequency of breast cancer, however, studies are not consistent. Combination hormonal contraceptives may cause glucose intolerance or effect serum triglyceride and lipoprotein levels. Retinal thrombosis has been reported (rarely). Use caution with conditions that may be aggravated by fluid retention, depression, or history of migraine. Not for use prior to menarche.

The minimum dosage combination of estrogen/progestin that will effectively treat the individual patient should be used. New patients should be started on products containing ≤0.035 mg of estrogen per tablet.

Adverse Reactions Frequency not defined.

Cardiovascular: Arterial thromboembolism, cerebral hemorrhage, cerebral thrombosis, edema, hypertension, mesenteric thrombosis, MI

Central nervous system: Depression, dizziness, headache, migraine, nervousness, premenstrual syndrome, stroke

Dermatologic: Acne, erythema multiforme, erythema nodosum, hirsutism, loss of scalp hair, melasma (may persist), rash (allergic)

Endocrine & metabolic: Amenorrhea, breakthrough bleeding, breast enlargement, breast secretion, breast tenderness, carbohydrate intolerance, lactation decreased (postpartum), glucose tolerance decreased, libido changes, menstrual flow changes, sex hormone-binding globulins (SHBG) increased, spotting, temporary infertility (following discontinuation), thyroid-binding globulin increased, triglycerides increased

Gastrointestinal: Abdominal cramps, appetite changes, bloating, cholestasis, colitis, gallbladder disease, jaundice, nausea, vomiting, weight gain/loss

Genitourinary: Cervical erosion changes, cervical secretion changes, cystitis-like syndrome, vaginal candidiasis, vaginitis

Hematologic: Antithrombin III decreased, folate levels decreased, hemolytic uremic syndrome, norepinephrine induced platelet aggregability increased, porphyria, prothrombin increased; factors VII, VIII, IX, and X increased

Hepatic: Benign liver tumors, Budd-Chiari syndrome, cholestatic jaundice, hepatic adenomas

Local: Thrombophlebitis

Ocular: Cataracts, change in corneal curvature (steepening), contact lens intolerance, optic neuritis, retinal thrombosis

Renal: Impaired renal function

Respiratory: Pulmonary thromboembolism

Miscellaneous: Hemorrhagic eruption

Overdosage/Toxicology Toxicity is unlikely following single exposures of excessive doses. Treatment following emesis and charcoal administration should be supportive and symptomatic.

Drug Interactions

Cytochrome P450 Effect: Ethinyl estradiol: **Substrate** of CYP2C9 (minor), 3A4 (major), 3A5-7 (minor); **Inhibits** CYP1A2 (weak), 2B6 (weak), 2C8 (weak), 2C19 (weak), 3A4 (weak)

Increased Effect/Toxicity: Acetaminophen and ascorbic acid may increase plasma levels of estrogen component. Atorvastatin and indinavir increase plasma levels of combination hormonal contraceptives. Combination hormonal contraceptives increase the plasma levels of alprazolam, chlordiazepoxide, cyclosporine, diazepam, prednisolone, selegiline, theophylline, tricyclic antidepressants. Combination hormonal contraceptives may increase (or decrease) the effects of coumarin derivatives.

Decreased Effect: CYP3A4 inducers may decrease the levels/effects of ethinyl estradiol; example inducers include aminoglutethimide, carbamazepine, nafcillin, nevirapine, phenobarbital, phenytoin, and rifamycins. Combination hormonal contraceptives may decrease plasma levels of acetaminophen, clofibric acid, lorazepam, morphine, oxazepam, salicylic acid, temazepam. Contraceptive effect decreased by acitretin, aminoglutethimide, amprenavir, anticonvulsants, griseofulvin, lopinavir, nelfinavir, penicillins (effect not consistent), rifampin, ritonavir, tetracyclines (effect not consistent). Combination hormonal contraceptives may decrease (or increase) the effects of coumarin derivatives. Aprepitant, modafinil, and topiramate may decrease the serum concentration of oral contraceptive (estrogens). Oral contraceptive (estrogens) may decrease the serum concentration of lamotrigine.

Ethanol/Nutrition/Herb Interactions

Food: CNS effects of caffeine may be enhanced if combination hormonal contraceptives are used concurrently with caffeine. Grapefruit juice increases ethinyl estradiol concentrations and would be expected to increase progesterone serum levels as well; clinical implications are unclear.

Herb/Nutraceutical: St John's wort may decrease levels. Herbs with estrogenic properties may enhance the adverse/toxic effect of estrogen derivatives; examples include alfalfa, black cohosh, bloodroot, hops, kudzu, licorice, red clover, saw palmetto, soybean, thyme, wild yam, yucca. Herbs with progestogenic properties may enhance the adverse/toxic effect of progestins; examples include bloodroot, chasteberry, damiana, oregano, yucca.

Stability Store at controlled room temperature of 25°C (77°F).

Mechanism of Action Combination hormonal contraceptives inhibit ovulation via a negative feedback mechanism on the hypothalamus, which alters the normal pattern of gonadotropin secretion of a follicle-stimulating hormone (FSH) and luteinizing hormone by the anterior pituitary. The follicular phase FSH and midcycle surge of gonadotropins are inhibited. In addition, combination hormonal contraceptives produce alterations in the genital tract, including changes in the cervical mucus, rendering it unfavorable for sperm penetration even (Continued)

Ethinyl Estradiol and Ethynodiol Diacetate *(Continued)*

if ovulation occurs. Changes in the endometrium may also occur, producing an unfavorable environment for nidation. Combination hormonal contraceptive drugs may alter the tubal transport of the ova through the fallopian tubes. Progestational agents may also alter sperm fertility.

Pharmacodynamics/Kinetics
Ethynodiol diacetate (converted to norethindrone)
Metabolism: Hepatic conjugation
Half-life elimination: Terminal: 5-14 hours

Dosage Oral: Adults: Female: Contraception:
Schedule 1 (Sunday starter): Dose begins on first Sunday after onset of menstruation; if the menstrual period starts on Sunday, take first tablet that very same day. **With a Sunday start, an additional method of contraception should be used until after the first 7 days of consecutive administration.**
For 21-tablet package: 1 tablet/day for 21 consecutive days, followed by 7 days off of the medication; a new course begins on the 8th day after the last tablet is taken.
For 28-tablet package: 1 tablet/day without interruption.
Schedule 2 (Day 1 starter): Dose starts on first day of menstrual cycle taking 1 tablet daily.
For 21-tablet package: 1 tablet/day for 21 consecutive days, followed by 7 days off of the medication; a new course begins on the 8th day after the last tablet is taken.
For 28-tablet package: 1 tablet/day without interruption.
If all doses have been taken on schedule and one menstrual period is missed, continue dosing cycle. If two consecutive menstrual periods are missed, pregnancy test is required before new dosing cycle is started.
Missed doses **monophasic formulations** (refer to package insert for complete information):
One dose missed: Take as soon as remembered or take 2 tablets next day
Two consecutive doses missed in the first 2 weeks: Take 2 tablets as soon as remembered or 2 tablets next 2 days. **An additional method of contraception should be used for 7 days after missed dose.**
Two consecutive doses missed in week 3 or three consecutive doses missed at any time: **An additional method of contraception should be used for 7 days after missed dose:**
Schedule 1 (Sunday starter): Continue dose of 1 tablet daily until Sunday, then discard the rest of the pack, and a new pack should be started that same day.
Schedule 2 (Day 1 starter): Current package should be discarded, and a new pack should be started that same day.

Dosage adjustment in renal impairment: Specific guidelines not available; use with caution and monitor blood pressure closely. Consider other forms of contraception.

Dosage adjustment in hepatic impairment: Contraindicated in patients with hepatic impairment

Dietary Considerations Should be taken with food at same time each day.

Administration Administer at the same time each day.

Monitoring Parameters Before starting therapy, a physical exam with reference to the breasts and pelvis are recommended, including a Papanicolaou smear. Exam may be deferred if appropriate; pregnancy should be ruled out prior to use. Monitor patient closely for loss of vision, sudden onset of proptosis, diplopia, migraine; blood pressure; signs and symptoms of thromboembolic disorders; signs or symptoms of depression; glycemic control in diabetics; lipid profiles in patients being treated for hyperlipidemias. Adequate diagnostic measures, including endometrial sampling, if indicated, should be performed to rule out malignancy in all cases of undiagnosed abnormal vaginal bleeding.

Additional Information The World Health Organization (WHO) has issued revised management recommendations for missed combined oral contraceptive pills. Refer to the following reference for a complete presentation and discussion of the guidelines:
Faculty of Family Planning and Reproductive Health Care Clinical Effectiveness Unit, "Faculty Statement from the CEU on a New Publication: WHO Selected Practice Recommendations for Contraceptive Use Update. Missed Pills: New Recommendations," *J Fam Plann Reprod Health Care*, 2005, 31(2):153-5.

Dosage Forms [DSC] = Discontinued products
Tablet, monophasic formulations:
Demulen® 1/35-28: Ethinyl estradiol 0.035 mg and ethynodiol diacetate 1 mg [21 white tablets and 7 blue inactive tablets] (28s) [DSC]
Kelnor™ 1/35: Ethinyl estradiol 0.035 mg and ethynodiol diacetate 1 mg [21 light yellow tablets and 7 white inactive tablets] (28s)
Zovia™ 1/35-28: Ethinyl estradiol 0.035 mg and ethynodiol diacetate 1 mg [21 light pink tablets and 7 white inactive tablets] (28s)
Zovia™ 1/50-28: Ethinyl estradiol 0.05 mg and ethynodiol diacetate 1 mg [21 pink tablets and 7 white inactive tablets] (28s)

Ethinyl Estradiol and Etonogestrel
(ETH in il es tra DYE ole & et oh noe JES trel)

U.S. Brand Names NuvaRing®
Canadian Brand Names NuvaRing®
Index Terms Etonogestrel and Ethinyl Estradiol
Pharmacologic Category Contraceptive; Estrogen and Progestin Combination
Use Prevention of pregnancy
Unlabeled/Investigational Use Treatment of hypermenorrhea (menorrhagia); pain associated with endometriosis; dysmenorrhea; dysfunctional uterine bleeding
Pregnancy Risk Factor X
Pregnancy Implications Pregnancy should be ruled out prior to treatment and discontinued if pregnancy occurs. In general, the use of combination hormonal contraceptives, when inadvertently used early in pregnancy, have not been associated with teratogenic effects. Due to

increased risk of thromboembolism postpartum, do not start earlier than 4-6 weeks following delivery. Hormonal contraceptives may be less effective in obese patients. An increase in oral contraceptive failure was noted in women with a BMI >27.3. Similar findings were noted in patients weighing ≥90 kg (198 lb) using the contraceptive patch.

Lactation Enters breast milk/not recommended (AAP rates "compatible")

Contraindications Hypersensitivity to ethinyl estradiol, etonogestrel, or any component of the formulation; history of or current thrombophlebitis or venous thromboembolic disorders (including DVT, PE); active or recent (within 1 year) arterial thromboembolic disease (eg, stroke, MI); major surgery with prolonged immobilization, cerebral vascular disease, coronary artery disease, valvular heart disease with complications, severe hypertension; diabetes mellitus with vascular involvement; severe headache with focal neurological symptoms; known or suspected breast carcinoma, endometrial cancer, estrogen-dependent neoplasms, undiagnosed abnormal genital bleeding; hepatic dysfunction or tumor, cholestatic jaundice of pregnancy, jaundice with prior combination hormonal contraceptive use; heavy smoking (≥15 cigarettes/day) in patients >35 years of age; conditions which make the vagina susceptible to irritation or ulceration; pregnancy

Warnings/Precautions Combination hormonal contraceptive agents do not protect against HIV infection or other sexually-transmitted diseases. **[U.S. Boxed Warning]: The risk of cardiovascular side effects increases in women who smoke cigarettes, especially those who are >35 years of age; women who use combination hormonal contraceptives should be strongly advised not to smoke.** May lead to increased risk of myocardial infarction, use with caution in patients with risk factors for coronary artery disease. May increase the risk of thromboembolism. Whenever possible, combination hormonal contraceptives should be discontinued at least 4 weeks prior to and for 2 weeks following elective surgery associated with an increased risk of thromboembolism or during periods of prolonged immobilization. May have a dose-related risk of vascular disease, hypertension, and gallbladder disease. Women with hypertension or renal disease should be encouraged to use another form of contraception. The use of combination hormonal contraceptives has been associated with a slight increase in frequency of breast cancer, however, studies are not consistent. Combination hormonal contraceptives may cause glucose intolerance or effect serum triglyceride and lipoprotein levels. Retinal thrombosis has been reported (rarely). Use caution with conditions that may be aggravated by fluid retention, depression, or history of migraine. Not for use prior to menarche.

Vaginally-administered combination hormonal contraceptive agents may have a similar adverse effects associated with oral contraceptive products. In order to reduce some of the possible risks, the minimum dosage combination of estrogen/progestin that will effectively treat the individual patient should be used.

Adverse Reactions Adverse reactions associated with oral combination hormonal contraceptive agents are also likely to appear with vaginally-administered products (frequency difficult to anticipate). Refer to oral contraceptive monographs for additional information.

5% to 14%:

    Central nervous system: Headache

    Gastrointestinal: Nausea, weight gain

    Genitourinary: Leukorrhea, vaginitis

    Respiratory: Sinusitis, upper respiratory tract infection

Frequency not defined:

    Central nervous system: Emotional lability

    Genitourinary: Bleeding irregularities, coital problems, device expulsion, foreign body sensation, toxic shock syndrome (in some cases associated with tampon use), vaginal discomfort

Overdosage/Toxicology Overdose with the vaginal ring is not likely. If broken, the ring will not release higher doses of hormonal agents. In the event of overdose, treatment should be symptom-directed and supportive.

Drug Interactions

Cytochrome P450 Effect:

    Ethinyl estradiol: **Substrate** of CYP2C9 (minor), 3A4 (major), 3A5-7 (minor); **Inhibits** CYP1A2 (weak), 2B6 (weak), 2C8 (weak), 2C19 (weak), 3A4 (weak)

    Etonogestrel: **Substrate** of CYP3A4 (minor)

Increased Effect/Toxicity: Acetaminophen and ascorbic acid may increase plasma levels of estrogen component. Atorvastatin and indinavir increase plasma levels of combination hormonal contraceptives. Combination hormonal contraceptives increase the plasma levels of alprazolam, chlordiazepoxide, cyclosporine, diazepam, prednisolone, selegiline, theophylline, tricyclic antidepressants. Combination hormonal contraceptives may increase (or decrease) the effects of coumarin derivatives.

Decreased Effect: Combination hormonal contraceptives may decrease plasma levels of acetaminophen, clofibric acid, lorazepam, morphine, oxazepam, salicylic acid, temazepam. Contraceptive effect decreased by acitretin, aminoglutethimide, amprenavir, anticonvulsants, griseofulvin, lopinavir, nelfinavir, nevirapine, penicillins (effect not consistent), rifampin, ritonavir, tetracyclines (effect not consistent). Combination hormonal contraceptives may decrease (or increase) the effects of coumarin derivatives. Aprepitant, modafinil, and topiramate may decrease the serum concentration of oral contraceptive (estrogens). Oral contraceptive (estrogens) may decrease the serum concentration of lamotrigine.

Ethanol/Nutrition/Herb Interactions

Food: CNS effects of caffeine may be enhanced if combination hormonal contraceptives are used concurrently with caffeine. Grapefruit juice increases ethinyl estradiol concentrations and would be expected to increase progesterone serum levels as well; clinical implications are unclear.

Herb/Nutraceutical: St John's wort may decrease levels. Herbs with estrogenic properties may enhance the adverse/toxic effect of estrogen derivatives; examples include alfalfa, black cohosh, bloodroot, hops, kudzu, licorice, red clover, saw palmetto, soybean, thyme, wild yam, yucca. Herbs with progestogenic properties may enhance the adverse/toxic effect of progestins; examples include bloodroot, chasteberry, damiana, oregano, yucca.

(Continued)

Ethinyl Estradiol and Etonogestrel *(Continued)*

Stability Prior to dispensing, store under refrigeration, 2°C to 8°C (36°F to 46°F). After dispensing, may be stored at room temperature of 25°C (77°F) for up to 4 months. Avoid direct sunlight or temperatures >30°C (86°F).

Mechanism of Action Combination hormonal contraceptives inhibit ovulation via a negative feedback mechanism on the hypothalamus, which alters the normal pattern of gonadotropin secretion of a follicle-stimulating hormone (FSH) and luteinizing hormone by the anterior pituitary. The follicular phase FSH and midcycle surge of gonadotropins are inhibited. In addition, combination hormonal contraceptives produce alterations in the genital tract, including changes in the cervical mucus, rendering it unfavorable for sperm penetration even if ovulation occurs. Changes in the endometrium may also occur, producing an unfavorable environment for nidation. Combination hormonal contraceptive drugs may alter the tubal transport of the ova through the fallopian tubes. Progestational agents may also alter sperm fertility.

Pharmacodynamics/Kinetics

Duration: Serum levels (contraceptive effectiveness) decrease after 3 weeks of continuous use

Absorption: Ethinyl estradiol and etonogestrel: Rapid
Tampons do not interfere with absorption.

Protein binding:
Ethinyl estradiol: 98%, primarily to albumin
Etonogestrel: 32% to sex hormone-binding globulin (SHBG) and 66% to albumin; SHBG capacity is affected by plasma ethinyl estradiol levels

Metabolism:
Ethinyl estradiol: Hepatic via CYP3A4; forms metabolites (weak estrogenic activity)
Etonogestrel: Hepatic via CYP3A4; forms metabolites (activity not known)

Bioavailability: Ethinyl estradiol: ~56% Etonogestrel: 100%

Half-life elimination: Ethinyl estradiol: 45 hours; Etonogestrel: 29 hours

Excretion: Ethinyl estradiol and etonogestrel: Urine, bile, and feces

Dosage Vaginal: Adults: Female: Contraception: One ring, inserted vaginally and left in place for 3 consecutive weeks, then removed for 1 week. A new ring is inserted 7 days after the last was removed (even if bleeding is not complete) and should be inserted at approximately the same time of day the ring was removed the previous week.

Initial treatment should begin as follows (pregnancy should always be ruled out first):

No hormonal contraceptive use in the past month: Using the first day of menstruation as "Day 1," insert the ring on or prior to "Day 5," even if bleeding is not complete. **An additional form of contraception should be used for the following 7 days.***

Switching from combination oral contraceptive: Ring can be inserted on any day within 7 days after the last **active** tablet in the cycle was taken and no later than the first day a new cycle of tablets would begin. Additional forms of contraception are not needed.

Switching from progestin-only contraceptive: **An additional form of contraception should be used for the following 7 days with any of the following.***

If previously using a progestin-only mini-pill, insert the ring on any day of the month; do not skip days between the last pill and insertion of the ring.

If previously using an implant, insert the ring on the same day of implant removal.

If previously using a progestin-containing IUD, insert the ring on day of IUD removal.

If previously using a progestin injection, insert the ring on the day the next injection would be given.

Following complete 1st trimester abortion: Insert ring within the first five days of abortion. If not inserted within five days, follow instructions for "No hormonal contraceptive use within the past month" and instruct patient to use a nonhormonal contraceptive in the interim.

Following delivery or 2nd trimester abortion: Insert ring 4 weeks postpartum (in women who are not breast-feeding) or following 2nd trimester abortion. **An additional form of contraception should be used for the following 7 days.***

If the ring is accidentally removed from the vagina at anytime during the 3-week period of use, it may be rinsed with cool or lukewarm water (not hot) and reinserted as soon as possible. If the ring is not reinserted within three hours, contraceptive effectiveness will be decreased. **An additional form of contraception should be used until the ring has been in place for 7 consecutive days.***

If the ring has been removed for longer than 1 week, pregnancy must be ruled out prior to restarting therapy. **An additional form of contraception should be used for the following 7 days.***

If the ring has been left in place for >3 weeks, a new ring should be inserted following a 1-week (ring-free) interval. Pregnancy must be ruled out prior to insertion and **an additional form of contraception should be used for the following 7 days.***

Disconnected ring: In the event the ring disconnects at the weld joint, discard and replace with a new ring.

***Note:** Diaphragms may interfere with proper ring placement, and therefore, are not recommended for use as an additional form of contraception.

Dosage adjustment in renal impairment: Specific guidelines not available; use with caution and monitor blood pressure closely. Consider other forms of contraception.

Dosage adjustment in hepatic impairment: Contraindicated in patients with hepatic impairment

Administration Vaginal: Wash hands and remove ring from protective pouch (keep pouch for later ring disposal). Press sides of ring together between thumb and index finger and insert folded ring into vagina. Specific placement is not required for ring to be effective, but ring should be inserted far enough into the vagina as to be comfortable. To remove, hook index finger around rim and pull out. Vaginal ring **cannot** be disposed of in the toilet. New rings should be inserted at approximately the same time of day the ring was removed the previous week. If the ring accidentally falls out, it may be rinsed with cool or warm (not hot) water and replaced. However, it must be replaced within 3 hours. Refer to dosing if ring is out of place for >3 hours. Tampons do not interfere with the effectiveness of the ring; caution should be used when removing tampon not to remove ring. The ring may interfere with correct placement of diaphragms; diaphragms should not be used as a back-up method of contraception.

Monitoring Parameters Before starting therapy, a physical exam with reference to the breasts and pelvis are recommended, including a Papanicolaou smear. Exam may be deferred if appropriate; pregnancy should be ruled out prior to use. Monitor patient closely for loss of vision, sudden onset of proptosis, diplopia, migraine; blood pressure; signs and symptoms of thromboembolic disorders; signs or symptoms of depression; glycemic control in diabetics; lipid profiles in patients being treated for hyperlipidemias. Adequate diagnostic measures, including endometrial sampling, if indicated, should be performed to rule out malignancy in all cases of undiagnosed abnormal vaginal bleeding.

Dosage Forms Ring, vaginal: Ethinyl estradiol 0.015 mg/day and etonogestrel 0.12 mg/day (1s) [3-week duration]

Ethinyl Estradiol and Levonorgestrel
(ETH in il es tra DYE ole & LEE voe nor jes trel)

U.S. Brand Names Alesse®; Aviane™; Enpresse™; Jolessa™; Lessina™; Levlen®; Levlite™; Levora®; Lutera™; Nordette®; Portia™; Quasense™; Seasonale®; Seasonique™; Sronyx™; Tri-Levlen®; Triphasil®; Trivora®

Canadian Brand Names Alesse®; Min-Ovral®; Triphasil®; Triquilar®

Index Terms Levonorgestrel and Ethinyl Estradiol

Pharmacologic Category Contraceptive; Estrogen and Progestin Combination

Use Prevention of pregnancy; postcoital contraception

Unlabeled/Investigational Use Treatment of hypermenorrhea (menorrhagia); pain associated with endometriosis; dysmenorrhea; dysfunctional uterine bleeding

Pregnancy Risk Factor X

Medication Safety Issues
Sound-alike/look-alike issues:
Alesse® may be confused with Aleve®
Nordette® may be confused with Nicorette®
PREVEN® may be confused with Prevnar®
Seasonale® may be confused with Seasonique™
Seasonique™ may be confused with Seasonale®
Tri-Levlen® may be confused with Trilafon®
Triphasil® may be confused with Tri-Norinyl®

Dosage Oral: Adults: Female:
Contraception, 28-day cycle:
Schedule 1 (Sunday starter): Dose begins on first Sunday after onset of menstruation; if the menstrual period starts on Sunday, take first tablet that very same day. With a Sunday start, an additional method of contraception should be used until after the first 7 days of consecutive administration:
For 21-tablet package: 1 tablet/day for 21 consecutive days, followed by 7 days off of the medication; a new course begins on the 8th day after the last tablet is taken
For 28-tablet package: 1 tablet/day without interruption
Schedule 2 (Day 1 starter): Dose starts on first day of menstrual cycle taking 1 tablet/day:
For 21-tablet package: 1 tablet/day for 21 consecutive days, followed by 7 days off of the medication; a new course begins on the 8th day after the last tablet is taken
For 28-tablet package: 1 tablet/day without interruption
If all doses have been taken on schedule and one menstrual period is missed, continue dosing cycle. If two consecutive menstrual periods are missed, pregnancy test is required before new dosing cycle is started.
Missed doses **monophasic formulations** (refer to package insert for complete information):
One dose missed: Take as soon as remembered or take 2 tablets next day
Two consecutive doses missed in the first 2 weeks: Take 2 tablets as soon as remembered or 2 tablets next 2 days. An additional method of contraception should be used for 7 days after missed dose.
Two consecutive doses missed in week 3 or three consecutive doses missed at any time: An additional method of contraception must be used for 7 days after a missed dose:
Schedule 1 (Sunday starter): Continue dose of 1 tablet daily until Sunday, then discard the rest of the pack, and a new pack should be started that same day.
Schedule 2 (Day 1 starter): Current pack should be discarded, and a new pack should be started that same day.
Missed doses **biphasic/triphasic formulations** (refer to package insert for complete information):
One dose missed: Take as soon as remembered or take 2 tablets next day.
Two consecutive doses missed in week 1 or week 2 of the pack: Take 2 tablets as soon as remembered and 2 tablets the next day. Resume taking 1 tablet daily until the pack is empty. An additional method of contraception should be used for 7 days after a missed dose.
Two consecutive doses missed in week 3 of the pack: An additional method of contraception must be used for 7 days after a missed dose.
Schedule 1 (Sunday starter): Take 1 tablet every day until Sunday. Discard the remaining pack and start a new pack of pills on the same day.
Schedule 2 (Day 1 starter): Discard the remaining pack and start a new pack the same day.
Three or more consecutive doses missed: An additional method of contraception must be used for 7 days after a missed dose.
Schedule 1 (Sunday starter): Take 1 tablet every day until Sunday; on Sunday, discard the pack and start a new pack.
Schedule 2 (Day 1 starter): Discard the remaining pack and begin new pack of tablets starting on the same day.

(Continued)

Ethinyl Estradiol and Levonorgestrel *(Continued)*

Contraception, 91-day cycle (extended cycle regimen): Dose begins on first Sunday after onset of menstruation; if the menstrual period starts on Sunday, take first tablet that very same day. An additional method of contraception should be used until after the first 7 days of consecutive administration:

Seasonale®: One active tablet/day for 84 consecutive days, followed by 1 inactive tablet/day for 7 days; if all doses have been taken on schedule and one menstrual period is missed, pregnancy should be ruled out prior to continuing therapy.

Seasonique™: One active tablet/day for 84 consecutive days, followed by 1 low dose estrogen tablet/day for 7 days; if all doses have been taken on schedule and one menstrual period is missed, pregnancy should be ruled out prior to continuing therapy.

Missed doses:

One dose missed: Take as soon as remembered or take 2 tablets the next day

Two consecutive doses missed: Take 2 tablets as soon as remembered or 2 tablets the next 2 days. An additional nonhormonal method of contraception should be used for 7 consecutive days after the missed dose.

Three or more consecutive doses missed: Do not take the missed doses; continue taking 1 tablet/day until pack is complete. Bleeding may occur during the following week. An additional nonhormonal method of contraception should be used for 7 consecutive days after the missed dose.

Any number of pills during week 13: Throw away the missed pills and keep taking scheduled pills until the pack is finished. A back-up method of contraception is not needed

Dosage adjustment in renal impairment: Specific guidelines not available; use with caution and monitor blood pressure closely. Consider other forms of contraception.

Dosage adjustment in hepatic impairment: Contraindicated in patients with hepatic impairment

Additional Information Complete prescribing information for this medication should be consulted for additional detail.

Dosage Forms

Tablet, low-dose formulations:

Alesse® 28: Ethinyl estradiol 0.02 mg and levonorgestrel 0.1 mg [21 pink tablets and 7 light green inactive tablets] (28s)

Aviane™ 28: Ethinyl estradiol 0.02 mg and levonorgestrel 0.1 mg [21 orange tablets and 7 light green inactive tablets] (28s)

Lessina™ 28, Levlite™ 28: Ethinyl estradiol 0.02 mg and levonorgestrel 0.1 mg [21 pink tablets and 7 white inactive tablets] (28s)

Lutera™, Sronyx™: Ethinyl estradiol 0.02 mg and levonorgestrel 0.1 mg [21 white tablets and 7 peach inactive tablets] (28s)

Tablet, monophasic formulations:

Levlen® 28: Ethinyl estradiol 0.03 mg and levonorgestrel 0.15 mg [21 light orange tablets and 7 pink inactive tablets] (28s)

Levora® 28: Ethinyl estradiol 0.03 mg and levonorgestrel 0.15 mg [21 white tablets and 7 peach inactive tablets] (28s)

Nordette® 28: Ethinyl estradiol 0.03 mg and levonorgestrel 0.15 mg [21 light orange tablets and 7 pink inactive tablets] (28s)

Portia™ 28: Ethinyl estradiol 0.03 mg and levonorgestrel 0.15 mg [21 pink tablets and 7 white inactive tablets] (28s)

Tablet, monophasic formulations [extended cycle regimen]:

Jolessa™, Seasonale®: Ethinyl estradiol 0.03 mg and levonorgestrel 0.15 mg [84 pink tablets and 7 white inactive tablets] (91s)

Quasense™: Ethinyl estradiol 0.03 mg and levonorgestrel 0.15 mg [84 white tablets and 7 peach inactive tablets] (91s)

Seasonique™: Ethinyl estradiol 0.03 mg and levonorgestrel 0.15 mg [84 light blue-green tablets] and ethinyl estradiol 0.01 mg [7 yellow tablets] (91s)

Tablet, triphasic formulations:

Enpresse™:

Day 1-6: Ethinyl estradiol 0.03 mg and levonorgestrel 0.05 mg [6 pink tablets]

Day 7-11: Ethinyl estradiol 0.04 mg and levonorgestrel 0.075 mg [5 white tablets]

Day 12-21: Ethinyl estradiol 0.03 mg and levonorgestrel 0.125 mg [10 orange tablets]

Day 22-28: 7 light green inactive tablets (28s)

Tri-Levlen® 28, Triphasil® 28:

Day 1-6: Ethinyl estradiol 0.03 mg and levonorgestrel 0.05 mg [6 brown tablets]

Day 7-11: Ethinyl estradiol 0.04 mg and levonorgestrel 0.075 mg [5 white tablets]

Day 12-21: Ethinyl estradiol 0.03 mg and levonorgestrel 0.125 mg [10 light yellow tablets]

Day 22-28: 7 light green inactive tablets (28s)

Trivora® 28:

Day 1-6: Ethinyl estradiol 0.03 mg and levonorgestrel 0.05 mg [6 blue tablets]

Day 7-11: Ethinyl estradiol 0.04 mg and levonorgestrel 0.075 mg [5 white tablets]

Day 12-21: Ethinyl estradiol 0.03 mg and levonorgestrel 0.125 mg [10 pink tablets]

Day 22-28: 7 peach inactive tablets (28s)

◆ **Ethinyl Estradiol and NGM** *see* Ethinyl Estradiol and Norgestimate *on page 660*

Ethinyl Estradiol and Norelgestromin
(ETH in il es tra DYE ole & nor el JES troe min)

U.S. Brand Names Ortho Evra®
Canadian Brand Names Evra®
Index Terms Norelgestromin and Ethinyl Estradiol; Ortho-Evra
Pharmacologic Category Contraceptive; Estrogen and Progestin Combination
Use Prevention of pregnancy
Pregnancy Risk Factor X
Medication Safety Issues
  Transdermal patch may contain conducting metal (eg, aluminum); remove patch prior to MRI.
Dosage Topical: Adults: Female:
  Contraception: Apply one patch each week for 3 weeks (21 total days); followed by one week
    that is patch-free. Each patch should be applied on the same day each week ("patch
    change day") and only one patch should be worn at a time. No more than 7 days should
    pass during the patch-free interval.
    Schedule 1 (Sunday starter): Dose begins on first Sunday after onset of menstruation; if
      the menstrual period starts on Sunday, apply one patch that very same day. **With a
      Sunday start, an additional method of contraception (nonhormonal) should be
      used until after the first 7 days of consecutive administration.** Each patch change
      will then occur on Sunday.
    Schedule 2 (Day 1 starter): Dose starts on first day of menstrual cycle, applying one patch
      during the first 24 hours of menstrual cycle. No back-up method of contraception is
      needed as long as the patch is applied on the first day of cycle. Each patch change will
      then occur on that same day of the week.

  Additional dosing considerations:
  No bleeding during patch-free week/missed menstrual period: If patch has been applied as
    directed, continue treatment on usual "patch change day". If used correctly, no bleeding
    during patch-free week does not necessarily indicate pregnancy. However, if no withdrawal
    bleeding occurs for 2 consecutive cycles, pregnancy should be ruled out. If patch has not
    been applied as directed, and one menstrual period is missed, pregnancy should be ruled
    out prior to continuing treatment.
  If a patch becomes partially or completely detached for <24 hours: Try to reapply to same
    place, or replace with a new patch immediately. Do not reapply if patch is no longer sticky,
    if it is sticking to itself or another surface, or if it has material sticking to it.
  If a patch becomes partially or completely detached for >24 hours (or time period is
    unknown): Apply a new patch and use this day of the week as the new "patch change day"
    from this point on. **An additional method of contraception (nonhormonal) should be
    used until after the first 7 days of consecutive administration.**
  Switching from oral contraceptives: Apply first patch on the first day of withdrawal bleeding. If
    there is no bleeding within 5 days of taking the last active tablet, pregnancy must first be
    ruled out. If patch is applied later than the first day of bleeding, **an additional method of
    contraception (nonhormonal) should be used until after the first 7 days of consecu-
    tive administration**
  Use after childbirth: Therapy should not be started <4 weeks after childbirth. Pregnancy
    should be ruled out prior to treatment if menstrual periods have not restarted. **An addi-
    tional method of contraception (nonhormonal) should be used until after the first 7
    days of consecutive administration.**
  Use after abortion or miscarriage: Therapy may be started immediately if abortion/miscar-
    riage occur within the first trimester. If therapy is not started within 5 days, follow instruc-
    tions for first time use. If abortion/miscarriage occur during the second trimester, therapy
    should not be started for at least 4 weeks. Follow directions for use after childbirth.
  Dosage adjustment in renal impairment: Specific guidelines not available; use with caution
    and monitor blood pressure closely. Consider other forms of contraception.
  Dosage adjustment in hepatic impairment: Contraindicated in patients with hepatic impair-
    ment
Additional Information Complete prescribing information for this medication should be
  consulted for additional detail.
Dosage Forms [CAN] = Canadian brand name
  Note: The formulation available in Canada differs from the U.S. product in both composition
    and the manufacturing process (although delivery rates appear similar).

  Patch, transdermal:
    Ortho Evra®: Ethinyl estradiol 0.75 mg and norelgestromin 6 mg [releases ethinyl estradiol
      20 mcg and norelgestromin 150 mcg per day] (1s, 3s)
    Evra® [CAN]: Ethinyl estradiol 0.6 mg and norelgestromin 6 mg [releases ethinyl estradiol
      20 mcg and norelgestromin 150 mcg per day] (1s, 3s) [Not available in U.S.]

Ethinyl Estradiol and Norethindrone
(ETH in il es tra DYE ole & nor eth IN drone)

U.S. Brand Names Aranelle™; Brevicon®; Estrostep® Fe; Femcon™ Fe; femhrt®; Junel™;
  Junel™ Fe; Leena™; Loestrin®; Loestrin® 24 Fe; Loestrin® Fe; Microgestin™; Microgestin™
  Fe; Modicon®; Necon® 0.5/35; Necon® 1/35; Necon® 7/7/7; Necon® 10/11; Norinyl® 1+35;
  Nortrel™; Nortrel™ 7/7/7; Ortho-Novum®; Ovcon®; Tri-Norinyl®
Canadian Brand Names Brevicon® 0.5/35; Brevicon® 1/35; FemHRT®; Loestrin® 1.5/30;
  Minestrin™ 1/20; Ortho® 0.5/35; Ortho® 1/35; Ortho® 7/7/7; Select® 1/35; Synphasic®
Index Terms Norethindrone Acetate and Ethinyl Estradiol; Ortho Novum
Pharmacologic Category Contraceptive; Estrogen and Progestin Combination
Use Prevention of pregnancy; treatment of acne; moderate to severe vasomotor symptoms
  associated with menopause; prevention of osteoporosis (in women at significant risk only)
  (Continued)

Ethinyl Estradiol and Norethindrone *(Continued)*

Unlabeled/Investigational Use Treatment of hypermenorrhea (menorrhagia); pain associated with endometriosis, dysmenorrhea; dysfunctional uterine bleeding

Pregnancy Risk Factor X

Pregnancy Implications Pregnancy should be ruled out prior to treatment and discontinued if pregnancy occurs. In general, the use of combination hormonal contraceptives when inadvertently taken early in pregnancy have not been associated with teratogenic effects. Due to increased risk of thromboembolism postpartum, combination hormonal contraceptives should not be started earlier than 4-6 weeks following delivery. Hormonal contraceptives may be less effective in obese patients. An increase in oral contraceptive failure was noted in women with a BMI >27.3. Similar findings were noted in patients weighing ≥90 kg (198 lb) using the contraceptive patch.

Lactation Enters breast milk/not recommended

Medication Safety Issues

Sound-alike/look-alike issues:

femhrt® may be confused with Femara®

Modicon® may be confused with Mylicon®

Norinyl® may be confused with Nardil®

Tri-Norinyl® may be confused with Triphasil®

International issues:

Notrel™ may be confused with Nostril® which is a brand name for chlorhexidine and cetrimonium in France

Contraindications Hypersensitivity to ethinyl estradiol, norethindrone, norethindrone acetate, or any component of the formulation; history of current thrombophlebitis or venous thromboembolic disorders (including DVT, PE); active or recent (within 1 year) arterial thromboembolic disease (eg, stroke, MI); cerebral vascular disease, coronary artery disease, severe hypertension; diabetes mellitus with vascular involvement; severe headache with focal neurological symptoms; known or suspected breast carcinoma, endometrial cancer, estrogen-dependent neoplasms, undiagnosed abnormal genital bleeding; hepatic dysfunction or tumor, cholestatic jaundice of pregnancy, jaundice with prior combination hormonal contraceptive use; major surgery with prolonged immobilization; heavy smoking (≥15 cigarettes/day) in patients >35 years of age; pregnancy

Warnings/Precautions

Cardiovascular-related considerations: Use caution with cardiovascular disease or dysfunction. Combination estrogen/progestin therapy has been associated with an increased risk of cardiovascular disease, which may be dose related. May increase the risks of hypertension, myocardial infarction (MI), stroke, pulmonary emboli (PE), and deep vein thrombosis; incidence of these effects was shown to be significantly increased in postmenopausal women using conjugated equine estrogens (CEE) in combination with medroxyprogesterone acetate (MPA). Nonfatal MI, PE, and thromboembolism have also been reported in males taking high doses of CEE (eg, for prostate cancer). An increased risk of MI has been noted with use of combination hormonal contraceptives, primarily in women with underlying risk factors. The risk of cardiovascular events increases in women who smoke cigarettes, especially those who are >35 years of age; women who use combination hormonal contraceptives should be strongly advised not to smoke. Women with hypertension or renal disease should be encouraged to use another form of contraception. Estrogen compounds are generally associated with lipid effects such as increased HDL-cholesterol and decreased LDL-cholesterol. Triglycerides may also be increased; use with caution in patients with familial defects of lipoprotein metabolism. Estrogens with or without progestin should not be used to prevent coronary heart disease in postmenopausal women. Whenever possible, combination hormonal contraceptives should be discontinued at least 4 weeks prior to and for 2 weeks following elective surgery associated with an increased risk of thromboembolism or during periods of prolonged immobilization.

Cancer-related considerations: Estrogens may increase the risk of breast cancer. The use of combination hormonal contraceptives has been associated with a slight increase in frequency of breast cancer, however studies are not consistent. An increased risk of invasive breast cancer was observed in postmenopausal women using CEE in combination with MPA; a smaller increase in risk was seen with estrogen therapy alone in observational studies. An increase in abnormal mammograms has also been reported with estrogen and progestin therapy in postmenopausal women. Unopposed estrogens may increase the risk of endometrial carcinoma in postmenopausal women. Estrogens may exacerbate endometriosis. Malignant transformation of residual endometrial implants has been reported post-hysterectomy with estrogen only therapy. Consider adding a progestin in women with residual endometriosis post-hysterectomy. Estrogen use may lead to severe hypercalcemia in postmenopausal patients with breast cancer and bone metastases; discontinue estrogen if hypercalcemia occurs.

Use with caution in patients with diseases which may be exacerbated by fluid retention, including asthma, epilepsy, migraine, or diabetes. Use with caution in patients with a history of severe hypocalcemia, SLE, hepatic hemangiomas, porphyria, endometriosis, and gallbladder disease. Use caution with history of cholestatic jaundice associated with past estrogen use or pregnancy.

Estrogens may cause retinal vascular thrombosis. Discontinue pending examination in cases of sudden partial or complete vision loss, sudden onset of proptosis, diplopia, or migraine; discontinue permanently if papilledema or retinal vascular lesions are observed on examination.

Combination hormonal contraceptives do not protect against HIV infection or other sexually-transmitted diseases. The minimum dosage combination of estrogen/progestin that will effectively treat the individual patient should be used. New patients should be started on products containing ≤0.035 mg of estrogen per tablet. When used for acne, use only in females ≥15 years, who also desire combination hormonal contraceptive therapy, are unresponsive to topical treatments, and have no contraindications to combination hormonal contraceptive use. Not for use prior to menarche.

The risk of dementia may be increased in postmenopausal women; increased incidence was observed in women ≥65 years of age taking CEE alone or in combination with MPA. Before prescribing estrogen therapy to postmenopausal women, the risks and benefits must be weighed for each patient. Women should be informed of these risks and benefits, as well as possible effects of progestin when added to estrogen therapy. Estrogens with or without progestin should be used for shortest duration possible consistent with treatment goals. Conduct periodic risk:benefit assessments. When used solely for prevention of osteoporosis in women at significant risk, nonestrogen treatment options should be considered.

Adverse Reactions As reported with oral contraceptive agents. Frequency not defined.

Cardiovascular: Arterial thromboembolism, cerebral hemorrhage, cerebral thrombosis, edema, hypertension, mesenteric thrombosis, MI

Central nervous system: Depression, dizziness, headache, migraine, nervousness, premenstrual syndrome, stroke

Dermatologic: Acne, erythema multiforme, erythema nodosum, hirsutism, loss of scalp hair, melasma (may persist), rash (allergic)

Endocrine & metabolic: Amenorrhea, breakthrough bleeding, breast enlargement, breast secretion, breast tenderness, carbohydrate intolerance, lactation decreased (postpartum), glucose tolerance decreased, libido changes, menstrual flow changes, sex hormone-binding globulins (SHBG) increased, spotting, temporary infertility (following discontinuation), thyroid-binding globulin increased, triglycerides increased

Gastrointestinal: Abdominal cramps, appetite changes, bloating, cholestasis, colitis, gallbladder disease, jaundice, nausea, vomiting, weight gain/loss

Genitourinary: Cervical erosion changes, cervical secretion changes, cystitis-like syndrome, vaginal candidiasis, vaginitis

Hematologic: Antithrombin III decreased, folate levels decreased, hemolytic uremic syndrome, norepinephrine induced platelet aggregability increased, porphyria, prothrombin increased; factors VII, VIII, IX, and X increased

Hepatic: Benign liver tumors, Budd-Chiari syndrome, cholestatic jaundice, hepatic adenomas

Local: Thrombophlebitis

Ocular: Cataracts, change in corneal curvature (steepening), contact lens intolerance, optic neuritis, retinal thrombosis

Renal: Impaired renal function

Respiratory: Pulmonary thromboembolism

Miscellaneous: Hemorrhagic eruption

Drug Interactions

Cytochrome P450 Effect:

Ethinyl estradiol: **Substrate** of CYP2C9 (minor), 3A4 (major), 3A5-7 (minor); **Inhibits** CYP1A2 (weak), 2B6 (weak), 2C8 (weak), 2C19 (weak), 3A4 (weak)

Norethindrone: **Substrate** of CYP3A4 (major); Induces CYP2C19 (weak)

Increased Effect/Toxicity: Acetaminophen and ascorbic acid may increase plasma levels of estrogen component. Atorvastatin and indinavir increase plasma levels of combination hormonal contraceptives. Combination hormonal contraceptives increase the plasma levels of alprazolam, chlordiazepoxide, cyclosporine, diazepam, prednisolone, selegiline, theophylline, tricyclic antidepressants. Combination hormonal contraceptives may increase (or decrease) the effects of coumarin derivatives.

Decreased Effect: CYP3A4 inducers may decrease the levels/effects of ethinyl estradiol and norethindrone; example inducers include aminoglutethimide, carbamazepine, nafcillin, nevirapine, phenobarbital, phenytoin, and rifamycins. Combination hormonal contraceptives may decrease plasma levels of acetaminophen, clofibric acid, lorazepam, morphine, oxazepam, salicylic acid, temazepam. Contraceptive effect decreased by acitretin, aminoglutethimide, amprenavir, anticonvulsants, griseofulvin, lopinavir, nelfinavir, penicillins (effect not consistent), rifampin, ritonavir, tetracyclines (effect not consistent), troglitazone. Oral contraceptives may decrease (or increase) the effects of coumarin derivatives. Aprepitant, modafinil, and topiramate may decrease the serum concentration of oral contraceptive (estrogens). Oral contraceptive (estrogens) may decrease the serum concentration of lamotrigine.

Ethanol/Nutrition/Herb Interactions

Ethanol: Routine use increases estrogen level and risk of breast cancer; avoid ethanol. Ethanol may also increase the risk of osteoporosis.

Food: CNS effects of caffeine may be enhanced if combination hormonal contraceptives are used concurrently with caffeine. Grapefruit juice increases ethinyl estradiol concentrations and would be expected to increase progesterone serum levels as well; clinical implications are unclear. Norethindrone absorption is increased by 27% following administration with food.

Herb/Nutraceutical: St John's wort may decrease levels. Herbs with estrogenic properties may enhance the adverse/toxic effect of estrogen derivatives; examples include alfalfa, black cohosh, bloodroot, hops, kudzu, licorice, red clover, saw palmetto, soybean, thyme, wild yam, yucca. Herbs with progestogenic properties may enhance the adverse/toxic effect of progestins; examples include bloodroot, chasteberry, damiana, oregano, yucca.

Stability Store at controlled room temperature of 25°C (77°F).

Estrostep®: Protect from light.

Mechanism of Action Combination oral contraceptives inhibit ovulation via a negative feedback mechanism on the hypothalamus, which alters the normal pattern of gonadotropin secretion of a follicle-stimulating hormone (FSH) and luteinizing hormone by the anterior pituitary. The follicular phase FSH and midcycle surge of gonadotropins are inhibited. In addition, combination hormonal contraceptives produce alterations in the genital tract, including changes in the cervical mucus, rendering it unfavorable for sperm penetration even if ovulation occurs. Changes in the endometrium may also occur, producing an unfavorable environment for nidation. Combination hormonal contraceptive drugs may alter the tubal transport of the ova through the fallopian tubes. Progestational agents may also alter sperm fertility.

(Continued)

Ethinyl Estradiol and Norethindrone *(Continued)*

In postmenopausal women, exogenous estrogen is used to replace decreased endogenous production. The addition of progestin reduces the incidence of endometrial hyperplasia and risk of endometrial cancer in women with an intact uterus.

Pharmacodynamics/Kinetics

Norethindrone: See individual monograph.

Ethinyl estradiol:

Absorption: Rapid

Bioavailability: 43% to 55%

Distribution: V_d: 2-4 L/kg

Protein binding: >95% to albumin

Metabolism: Hepatic via oxidation and conjugation in GI tract; hydroxylated via CYP3A4 to metabolites; first-pass effect; enterohepatic recirculation; reversibly converted to estrone and estriol

Half-life elimination: 19-24 hours

Excretion: Urine (as estradiol, estrone, and estriol); feces

Dosage Oral:

Adolescents ≥15 years and Adults: Female: Acne: Estrostep®: Refer to dosing for contraception

Adults: Female:

Moderate-to-severe vasomotor symptoms associated with menopause: Initial: femhrt® 0.5/2.5: 1 tablet daily; patient should be re-evaluated at 3- to 6-month intervals to determine if treatment is still necessary; patient should be maintained at the lowest effective dose

Prevention of osteoporosis: Initial: femhrt® 0.5/2.5: 1 tablet daily; patient should be maintained on the lowest effective dose

Contraception:

Schedule 1 (Sunday starter): Dose begins on first Sunday after onset of menstruation; if the menstrual period starts on Sunday, take first tablet that very same day. With a Sunday start, an additional method of contraception should be used until after the first 7 days of consecutive administration.

For 21-tablet package: Dosage is 1 tablet daily for 21 consecutive days, followed by 7 days off of the medication; a new course begins on the 8th day after the last tablet is taken.

For 28-tablet package: Dosage is 1 tablet daily without interruption.

Schedule 2 (Day 1 starter): Dose starts on first day of menstrual cycle taking 1 tablet daily.

For 21-tablet package: Dosage is 1 tablet daily for 21 consecutive days, followed by 7 days off of the medication; a new course begins on the 8th day after the last tablet is taken.

For 28-tablet package: Dosage is 1 tablet daily without interruption.

If all doses have been taken on schedule and one menstrual period is missed, continue dosing cycle. If two consecutive menstrual periods are missed, pregnancy test is required before new dosing cycle is started.

Missed doses **monophasic formulations** (refer to package insert for complete information):

One dose missed: Take as soon as remembered or take 2 tablets next day Two consecutive doses missed in the first 2 weeks: Take 2 tablets as soon as remembered or 2 tablets next 2 days. An additional method of contraception should be used for 7 days after missed dose.

Two consecutive doses missed in week 3 or three consecutive doses missed at any time: An additional method of contraception must be used for 7 days after a missed dose.

Schedule 1 (Sunday starter): Continue dose of 1 tablet until Sunday, then discard the rest of the pack, and a new pack should be started that same day.

Schedule 2 (Day 1 starter): Current pack should be discarded, and a new pack should be started that same day.

Missed doses **biphasic/triphasic formulations** (refer to package insert for complete information):

One dose missed: Take as soon as remembered or take 2 tablets next day.

Two consecutive doses missed in week 1 or week 2 of the pack: Take 2 tablets as soon as remembered and 2 tablets the next day. Resume taking 1 tablet daily until the pack is empty. An additional method of contraception should be used for 7 days after a missed dose.

Two consecutive doses missed in week 3 of the pack: An additional method of contraception must be used for 7 days after a missed dose.

Schedule 1 (Sunday Starter): Take 1 tablet every day until Sunday. Discard the remaining pack and start a new pack of pills on the same day.

Schedule 2 (Day 1 starter): Discard the remaining pack and start a new pack the same day.

Three or more consecutive doses missed: An additional method of contraception must be used for 7 days after a missed dose.

Schedule 1 (Sunday Starter): Take 1 tablet every day until Sunday; on Sunday, discard the pack and start a new pack.

Schedule 2 (Day 1 Starter): Discard the remaining pack and begin new pack of tablets starting on the same day.

Dosage adjustment in renal impairment: Specific guidelines not available; use with caution and monitor blood pressure closely. Consider other forms of contraception.

Dosage adjustment in hepatic impairment: Contraindicated in patients with hepatic impairment.

Dietary Considerations Should be taken at same time each day. May be taken with or without food. Ensure adequate calcium and vitamin D intake when used for the prevention of osteoporosis.

Administration Administer at the same time each day.

Monitoring Parameters Before starting therapy, a physical exam with reference to the breasts and pelvis are recommended, including a Papanicolaou smear. Exam may be deferred if appropriate; pregnancy should be ruled out prior to use. Monitor patient closely for loss of vision, sudden onset of proptosis, diplopia, migraine; blood pressure; signs and symptoms of thromboembolic disorders; signs or symptoms of depression; glycemic control in diabetics; lipid profiles in patients being treated for hyperlipidemias; thyroid function in patients on thyroid hormone replacement therapy. Adequate diagnostic measures, including endometrial sampling, if indicated, should be performed to rule out malignancy in all cases of undiagnosed abnormal vaginal bleeding.

Menopausal symptoms: Assess need for therapy at 3- to 6-month intervals

Prevention of osteoporosis: Bone density measurement

Test Interactions Increased prothrombin and factors VII, VIII, IX, X; increased platelet aggregability, thyroid-binding globulin, total thyroid hormone (T_4), serum triglycerides/phospholipids; decreased antithrombin III, serum folate concentration; pathologist should be advised of estrogen/progesterone therapy when specimens are submitted

Additional Information Norethindrone acetate 1 mg is equivalent to ethinyl estradiol 2.8 mcg.

The World Health Organization (WHO) has issued revised management recommendations for missed combined oral contraceptive pills. Refer to the following reference for a complete presentation and discussion of the guidelines:

Faculty of Family Planning and Reproductive Health Care Clinical Effectiveness Unit, "Faculty Statement from the CEU on a New Publication: WHO Selected Practice Recommendations for Contraceptive Use Update. Missed Pills: New Recommendations," *J Fam Plann Reprod Health Care*, 2005, 31(2):153-5.

Dosage Forms

Tablet:

femhrt® 1/5: Ethinyl estradiol 5 mcg and norethindrone acetate 1 mg [white tablets]

femhrt® 0.5/2.5: Ethinyl estradiol 2.5 mcg and norethindrone acetate 0.5 mg [white tablets]

Tablet, monophasic formulations:

Brevicon®: Ethinyl estradiol 0.035 mg and norethindrone 0.5 mg [21 blue tablets and 7 orange inactive tablets] (28s)

Junel™ 21 1/20: Ethinyl estradiol 0.02 mg and norethindrone acetate 1 mg [yellow tablets] (21s)

Junel™ 21 1.5/30: Ethinyl estradiol 0.03 mg and norethindrone acetate 1.5 mg [pink tablets] (21s)

Junel™ Fe 1/20: Ethinyl estradiol 0.02 mg and norethindrone acetate 1 mg [21 yellow tablets] and ferrous fumarate 75 mg [7 brown tablets] (28s)

Junel™ Fe 1.5/30: Ethinyl estradiol 0.03 mg and norethindrone acetate 1.5 mg [21 pink tablets] and ferrous fumarate 75 mg [7 brown tablets] (28s)

Loestrin® 21 1/20, Microgestin™ 1/20: Ethinyl estradiol 0.02 mg and norethindrone acetate 1 mg [white tablets] (21s)

Loestrin® 21 1.5/30, Microgestin™ 1.5/30: Ethinyl estradiol 0.03 mg and norethindrone acetate 1.5 mg [green tablets] (21s)

Loestrin® 24 Fe: 1/20: Ethinyl estradiol 0.02 mg and norethindrone acetate 1 mg [24 white tablets] and ferrous fumarate 75 mg [4 brown tablets] (28s)

Loestrin® Fe 1/20, Microgestin™ Fe 1/20: Ethinyl estradiol 0.02 mg and norethindrone acetate 1 mg [21 white tablets] and ferrous fumarate 75 mg [7 brown tablets] (28s)

Loestrin® Fe 1.5/30, Microgestin™ Fe 1.5/30: Ethinyl estradiol 0.03 mg and norethindrone acetate 1.5 mg [21 green tablets] and ferrous fumarate 75 mg [7 brown tablets] (28s)

Modicon® 28: Ethinyl estradiol 0.035 mg and norethindrone 0.5 mg [21 white tablets and 7 green inactive tablets] (28s)

Necon® 0.5/35-28: Ethinyl estradiol 0.035 mg and norethindrone 0.5 mg [21 light yellow tablets and 7 white inactive tablets] (28s)

Necon® 1/35-28: Ethinyl estradiol 0.035 mg and norethindrone 1 mg [21 dark yellow tablets and 7 white inactive tablets] (28s)

Norinyl® 1+35: Ethinyl estradiol 0.035 mg and norethindrone 1 mg [21 yellow-green tablets and 7 orange inactive tablets] (28s)

Nortrel™ 0.5/35 mg:

Ethinyl estradiol 0.035 mg and norethindrone 0.5 mg [light yellow tablets] (21s)

Ethinyl estradiol 0.035 mg and norethindrone 0.5 mg [21 light yellow tablets and 7 white inactive tablets] (28s)

Nortrel™ 1/35 mg:

Ethinyl estradiol 0.035 mg and norethindrone 1 mg [yellow tablets] (21s)

Ethinyl estradiol 0.035 mg and norethindrone 1 mg [21 yellow tablets and 7 white inactive tablets] (28s)

Ortho-Novum® 1/35 28: Ethinyl estradiol 0.035 mg and norethindrone 1 mg [21 peach tablets and 7 green inactive tablets] (28s)

Ovcon® 35 21-day: Ethinyl estradiol 0.035 mg and norethindrone 0.4 mg [peach tablets] (21s)

Ovcon® 35 28-day: Ethinyl estradiol 0.035 mg and norethindrone 0.4 mg [21 peach tablets and 7 green inactive tablets] (28s)

Ovcon® 50: Ethinyl estradiol 0.05 mg and norethindrone 1 mg [21 yellow tablets and 7 green inactive tablets] (28s)

Tablet, chewable, monophasic formulations:

Femcon™ Fe: Ethinyl estradiol 0.035 mg and norethindrone 0.4 mg [21 white tablets and 7 brown inactive tablets] (28s) [spearmint flavor]

Tablet, biphasic formulations:

Necon® 10/11-28:

Day 1-10: Ethinyl estradiol 0.035 mg and norethindrone 0.5 mg [10 light yellow tablets]

Day 11-21: Ethinyl estradiol 0.035 mg and norethindrone 1 mg [11 dark yellow tablets]

Day 22-28: 7 white inactive tablets (28s)

Ortho-Novum® 10/11-28:

Day 1-10: Ethinyl estradiol 0.035 mg and norethindrone 0.5 mg [10 white tablets]

(Continued)

Ethinyl Estradiol and Norethindrone *(Continued)*

Day 11-21: Ethinyl estradiol 0.035 mg and norethindrone 1 mg [11 peach tablets]
Day 22-28: 7 green inactive tablets (28s)

Tablet, triphasic formulations:
Aranelle™:
Day 1-7: Ethinyl estradiol 0.035 mg and norethindrone 0.5 mg [7 light yellow tablets]
Day 8-16: Ethinyl estradiol 0.035 mg and norethindrone 1 mg [9 white tablets]
Day 17-21: Ethinyl estradiol 0.035 mg and norethindrone 0.5 mg [5 light yellow tablets]
Day 22-28: 7 peach inactive tablets (28s)

Estrostep® Fe:
Day 1-5: Ethinyl estradiol 0.02 mg and norethindrone acetate 1 mg [5 white triangular tablets]
Day 6-12: Ethinyl estradiol 0.03 mg and norethindrone acetate 1 mg [7 white square tablets]
Day 13-21: Ethinyl estradiol 0.035 mg and norethindrone acetate 1 mg [9 white round tablets]
Day 22-28: Ferrous fumarate 75 mg [7 brown tablets] (28s)

Leena™:
Day 1-7: Ethinyl estradiol 0.035 mg and norethindrone 0.5 mg [7 light blue tablets]
Day 8-16: Ethinyl estradiol 0.035 mg and norethindrone 1 mg [9 light yellow-green tablets]
Day 17-21: Ethinyl estradiol 0.035 mg and norethindrone 0.5 mg [5 light blue tablets]
Day 22-28: 7 orange inactive tablets (28s)

Necon® 7/7/7, Ortho-Novum® 7/7/7 28:
Day 1-7: Ethinyl estradiol 0.035 mg and norethindrone 0.5 mg [7 white tablets]
Day 8-14: Ethinyl estradiol 0.035 mg and norethindrone 0.75 mg [7 light peach tablets]
Day 15-21: Ethinyl estradiol 0.035 mg and norethindrone 1 mg [7 peach tablets]
Day 22-28: 7 green inactive tablets (28s)

Nortrel™ 7/7/7 28:
Day 1-7: Ethinyl estradiol 0.035 mg and norethindrone 0.5 mg [7 light yellow tablets]
Day 8-14: Ethinyl estradiol 0.035 mg and norethindrone 0.75 mg [7 blue tablets]
Day 15-21: Ethinyl estradiol 0.035 mg and norethindrone 1 mg [7 peach tablets]
Day 22-28: 7 white inactive tablets (28s)

Ortho-Novum® 7/7/7 28:
Day 1-7: Ethinyl estradiol 0.035 mg and norethindrone 0.5 mg [7 white tablets]
Day 8-14: Ethinyl estradiol 0.035 mg and norethindrone 0.75 mg [7 light peach tablets]
Day 15-21: Ethinyl estradiol 0.035 mg and norethindrone 1 mg [7 peach tablets]
Day 22-28: 7 green inactive tablets (28s)

Tri-Norinyl® 28:
Day 1-7: Ethinyl estradiol 0.035 mg and norethindrone 0.5 mg [7 blue tablets]
Day 8-16: Ethinyl estradiol 0.035 mg and norethindrone 1 mg [9 yellow-green tablets]
Day 17-21: Ethinyl estradiol 0.035 mg and norethindrone 0.5 mg [5 blue tablets]
Day 22-28: 7 orange inactive tablets (28s)

Ethinyl Estradiol and Norgestimate
(ETH in il es tra DYE ole & nor JES ti mate)

U.S. Brand Names MonoNessa™; Ortho-Cyclen®; Ortho Tri-Cyclen®; Ortho Tri-Cyclen® Lo; Previfem™; Sprintec™; TriNessa™; Tri-Previfem™; Tri-Sprintec™

Canadian Brand Names Cyclen®; Tri-Cyclen®; Tri-Cyclen® Lo

Index Terms Ethinyl Estradiol and NGM; Norgestimate and Ethinyl Estradiol; Ortho Cyclen; Ortho Tri Cyclen

Pharmacologic Category Contraceptive; Estrogen and Progestin Combination

Use Prevention of pregnancy; treatment of acne

Unlabeled/Investigational Use Treatment of hypermenorrhea (menorrhagia); pain associated with endometriosis; dysmenorrhea; dysfunctional uterine bleeding

Pregnancy Risk Factor X

Pregnancy Implications Pregnancy should be ruled out prior to treatment and discontinued if pregnancy occurs. In general, the use of combination hormonal contraceptives when inadvertently taken early in pregnancy have not been associated with teratogenic effects. Due to increased risk of thromboembolism postpartum, combination hormonal contraceptives should not be started earlier than 4-6 weeks following delivery. Hormonal contraceptives may be less effective in obese patients. An increase in oral contraceptive failure was noted in women with a BMI >27.3. Similar findings were noted in patients weighing ≥90 kg (198 lb) using the contraceptive patch.

Lactation Enters breast milk/not recommended (AAP rates "compatible")

Medication Safety Issues
Sound-alike/look-alike issues:
Ortho-Cyclen® may be confused with Ortho-Cept®

Contraindications Hypersensitivity to ethinyl estradiol, norgestimate, or any component of the formulation; history of or current thrombophlebitis or venous thromboembolic disorders (including DVT, PE); active or recent (within 1 year) arterial thromboembolic disease (eg, stroke, MI); cerebral vascular disease, coronary artery disease, valvular heart disease with complications, severe hypertension; severe headache with focal neurological symptoms; known or suspected breast carcinoma, endometrial cancer, estrogen-dependent neoplasms, undiagnosed abnormal genital bleeding; hepatic dysfunction or tumor, cholestatic jaundice of pregnancy, jaundice with prior combination hormonal contraceptive use; heavy smoking (≥15 cigarettes/day) in patients >35 years of age; pregnancy

Warnings/Precautions Combination hormonal contraceptives do not protect against HIV infection or other sexually-transmitted diseases. **[U.S. Boxed Warning]: The risk of cardiovascular side effects increases in women who smoke cigarettes, especially those who are >35 years of age; women who use combination hormonal contraceptives should be strongly advised not to smoke.** Combination hormonal contraceptives may lead to increased risk of myocardial infarction, use with caution in patients with risk factors for coronary artery disease. May increase the risk of thromboembolism. Whenever possible, combination hormonal contraceptives should be discontinued at least 4 weeks prior to and for 2 weeks following elective surgery associated with an increased risk of thromboembolism or during periods of prolonged immobilization. Combination hormonal contraceptives may have a dose-related risk of vascular disease, hypertension, and gallbladder disease. Women with hypertension or renal disease should be encouraged to use a nonhormonal form of contraception. The use of combination hormonal contraceptives has been associated with a slight increase in frequency of breast cancer, however, studies are not consistent. Combination hormonal contraceptives may cause glucose intolerance or effect serum triglyceride and lipoprotein levels. Retinal thrombosis has been reported (rarely). Use caution with conditions that may be aggravated by fluid retention, depression, or history of migraine. Not for use prior to menarche.

The minimum dosage combination of estrogen/progestin that will effectively treat the individual patient should be used. New patients should be started on products containing ≤0.035 mg of estrogen per tablet.

Acne: For use only in females ≥15 years, who also desire combination hormonal contraceptive therapy, are unresponsive to topical treatments, and have no contraindications to combination hormonal contraceptive use.

Adverse Reactions Frequency not defined.

Cardiovascular: Arterial thromboembolism, cerebral hemorrhage, cerebral thrombosis, edema, hypertension, mesenteric thrombosis, MI

Central nervous system: Depression, dizziness, headache, migraine, nervousness, premenstrual syndrome, stroke

Dermatologic: Acne, erythema multiforme, erythema nodosum, hirsutism, loss of scalp hair, melasma (may persist), rash (allergic)

Endocrine & metabolic: Amenorrhea, breakthrough bleeding, breast enlargement, breast secretion, breast tenderness, carbohydrate intolerance, lactation decreased (postpartum), glucose tolerance decreased, libido changes, menstrual flow changes, sex hormone-binding globulins (SHBG) increased, spotting, temporary infertility (following discontinuation), thyroid-binding globulin increased, triglycerides increased

Gastrointestinal: Abdominal cramps, appetite changes, bloating, cholestasis, colitis, gallbladder disease, jaundice, nausea, vomiting, weight gain/loss

Genitourinary: Cervical erosion changes, cervical secretion changes, cystitis-like syndrome, vaginal candidiasis, vaginitis

Hematologic: Antithrombin III decreased, folate levels decreased, hemolytic uremic syndrome, norepinephrine induced platelet aggregability increased, porphyria, prothrombin increased; factors VII, VIII, IX, and X increased

Hepatic: Benign liver tumors, Budd-Chiari syndrome, cholestatic jaundice, hepatic adenomas

Local: Thrombophlebitis

Ocular: Cataracts, change in corneal curvature (steepening), contact lens intolerance, optic neuritis, retinal thrombosis

Renal: Impaired renal function

Respiratory: Pulmonary thromboembolism

Miscellaneous: Hemorrhagic eruption

Overdosage/Toxicology Toxicity is unlikely following single exposures of excessive doses. May cause withdrawal bleeding in females. Treatment following emesis and charcoal administration should be supportive and symptomatic.

Drug Interactions

Cytochrome P450 Effect: Ethinyl estradiol: **Substrate** of CYP2C9 (minor), 3A4 (major), 3A5-7 (minor); **Inhibits** CYP1A2 (weak), 2B6 (weak), 2C8 (weak), 2C19 (weak), 3A4 (weak)

Increased Effect/Toxicity: Acetaminophen and ascorbic acid may increase plasma levels of estrogen component. Atorvastatin and indinavir increase plasma levels of combination hormonal contraceptives. Combination hormonal contraceptives increase the plasma levels of alprazolam, chlordiazepoxide, cyclosporine, diazepam, prednisolone, selegiline, theophylline, tricyclic antidepressants. Combination hormonal contraceptives may increase (or decrease) the effects of coumarin derivatives.

Decreased Effect: CYP3A4 inducers may decrease the levels/effects of ethinyl estradiol; example inducers include aminoglutethimide, carbamazepine, nafcillin, nevirapine, phenobarbital, phenytoin, and rifamycins. Combination hormonal contraceptives may decrease plasma levels of acetaminophen, clofibric acid, lorazepam, morphine, oxazepam, salicylic acid, temazepam. Contraceptive effect decreased by acitretin, aminoglutethimide, amprenavir, anticonvulsants, griseofulvin, lopinavir, nelfinavir, nevirapine, penicillins (effect not consistent), rifampin, ritonavir, tetracyclines (effect not consistent). Combination hormonal contraceptives may decrease (or increase) the effects of coumarin derivatives. Aprepitant, modafinil, and topiramate may decrease the serum concentration of oral contraceptive (estrogens). Oral contraceptive (estrogens) may decrease the serum concentration of lamotrigine.

Ethanol/Nutrition/Herb Interactions

Food: CNS effects of caffeine may be enhanced if combination hormonal contraceptives are used concurrently with caffeine. Grapefruit juice increases ethinyl estradiol concentrations and would be expected to increase progesterone serum levels as well; clinical implications are unclear.

Herb/Nutraceutical: St John's wort may decrease levels. Herbs with estrogenic properties may enhance the adverse/toxic effect of estrogen derivatives; examples include alfalfa, black cohosh, bloodroot, hops, kudzu, licorice, red clover, saw palmetto, soybean, thyme, wild yam, yucca. Herbs with progestogenic properties may enhance the adverse/toxic effect of progestins; examples include bloodroot, chasteberry, damiana, oregano, yucca.

Stability Store at controlled room temperature of 25°C (77°F).

Mechanism of Action Combination hormonal contraceptives inhibit ovulation via a negative feedback mechanism on the hypothalamus, which alters the normal pattern of gonadotropin secretion of a follicle-stimulating hormone (FSH) and luteinizing hormone by the anterior

(Continued)

Ethinyl Estradiol and Norgestimate *(Continued)*

pituitary. The follicular phase FSH and midcycle surge of gonadotropins are inhibited. In addition, combination hormonal contraceptives produce alterations in the genital tract, including changes in the cervical mucus, rendering it unfavorable for sperm penetration even if ovulation occurs. Changes in the endometrium may also occur, producing an unfavorable environment for nidation. Combination hormonal contraceptive drugs may alter the tubal transport of the ova through the fallopian tubes. Progestational agents may also alter sperm fertility.

Pharmacodynamics/Kinetics
Norgestimate:
Absorption: Well absorbed

Protein binding: To albumin and sex hormone-binding globulin (SHBG); SHBG capacity is affected by plasma ethinyl estradiol levels

Metabolism: Hepatic; forms 17-deacetylnorgestimate (major active metabolite) and other metabolites

Half-life elimination: 17-deacetylnorgestimate: 12-30 hours

Excretion: Urine and feces

Dosage Oral:
Children ≥15 years and Adults: Female: Acne (Ortho Tri-Cyclen®): Refer to dosing for contraception

Adults: Female:

Contraception:

Schedule 1 (Sunday starter): Dose begins on first Sunday after onset of menstruation; if the menstrual period starts on Sunday, take first tablet that very same day. **With a Sunday start, an additional method of contraception should be used until after the first 7 days of consecutive administration.**

For 21-tablet package: Dosage is 1 tablet daily for 21 consecutive days, followed by 7 days off of the medication; a new course begins on the 8th day after the last tablet is taken.

For 28-tablet package: Dosage is 1 tablet daily without interruption.

Schedule 2 (Day 1 starter): Dose starts on first day of menstrual cycle taking 1 tablet daily.

For 21-tablet package: Dosage is 1 tablet daily for 21 consecutive days, followed by 7 days off of the medication; a new course begins on the 8th day after the last tablet is taken.

For 28-tablet package: Dosage is 1 tablet daily without interruption.

If all doses have been taken on schedule and one menstrual period is missed, continue dosing cycle. If two consecutive menstrual periods are missed, pregnancy test is required before new dosing cycle is started.

Missed doses **monophasic formulations** (refer to package insert for complete information):

One dose missed: Take as soon as remembered or take 2 tablets next day

Two consecutive doses missed in the first 2 weeks: Take 2 tablets as soon as remembered or 2 tablets next 2 days. **An additional method of contraception should be used for 7 days after missed dose.**

Two consecutive doses missed in week 3 or three consecutive doses missed at any time: **An additional method of contraception must be used for 7 days after a missed dose:**

Schedule 1 (Sunday starter): Continue dose of 1 tablet daily until Sunday, then discard the rest of the pack, and a new pack should be started that same day.

Schedule 2 (Day 1 starter): Current pack should be discarded, and a new pack should be started that same day.

Missed doses **biphasic/triphasic formulations** (refer to package insert for complete information):

One dose missed: Take as soon as remembered or take 2 tablets next day.

Two consecutive doses missed in week 1 or week 2 of the pack: Take 2 tablets as soon as remembered and 2 tablets the next day. Resume taking 1 tablet daily until the pack is empty. **An additional method of contraception must be used for 7 days after a missed dose.**

Two consecutive doses missed in week 3 of the pack. **An additional method of contraception must be used for 7 days after a missed dose.**

Schedule 1 (Sunday starter): Take 1 tablet every day until Sunday. Discard the remaining pack and start a new pack of pills on the same day.

Schedule 2 (Day 1 starter): Discard the remaining pack and start a new pack the same day.

Three or more consecutive doses missed. **An additional method of contraception must be used for 7 days after a missed dose.**

Schedule 1 (Sunday starter): Take 1 tablet every day until Sunday; on Sunday, discard the pack and start a new pack.

Schedule 2 (Day 1 starter): Discard the remaining pack and begin new pack of tablets starting on the same day.

Dosage adjustment in renal impairment: Specific guidelines not available; use with caution and monitor blood pressure closely. Consider other forms of contraception.

Dosage adjustment in hepatic impairment: Contraindicated in patients with hepatic impairment.

Dietary Considerations Should be taken at same time each day.

Administration Administer at the same time each day.

Monitoring Parameters Before starting therapy, a physical exam with reference to the breasts and pelvis are recommended, including a Papanicolaou smear. Exam may be deferred if appropriate; pregnancy should be ruled out prior to use. Monitor patient closely for loss of vision, sudden onset of proptosis, diplopia, migraine; blood pressure; signs and symptoms of thromboembolic disorders; signs or symptoms of depression; glycemic control in diabetics; lipid profiles in patients being treated for hyperlipidemias. Adequate diagnostic measures, including endometrial sampling, if indicated, should be performed to rule out malignancy in all cases of undiagnosed abnormal vaginal bleeding

Additional Information The World Health Organization (WHO) has issued revised management recommendations for missed combined oral contraceptive pills. Refer to the following reference for a complete presentation and discussion of the guidelines:

Faculty of Family Planning and Reproductive Health Care Clinical Effectiveness Unit, "Faculty Statement from the CEU on a New Publication: WHO Selected Practice Recommendations for Contraceptive Use Update. Missed Pills: New Recommendations," *J Fam Plann Reprod Health Care*, 2005, 31(2):153-5.

Dosage Forms
Tablet, monophasic formulations:
MonoNessa™, Ortho-Cyclen®: Ethinyl estradiol 0.035 mg and norgestimate 0.25 mg [21 blue tablets and 7 green inactive tablets] (28s)
Previfem™: Ethinyl estradiol 0.035 mg and norgestimate 0.25 mg [21 blue tablets and 7 teal inactive tablets] (28s)
Sprintec™: Ethinyl estradiol 0.035 mg and norgestimate 0.25 mg [21 blue tablets and 7 white inactive tablets] (28s)
Tablet, triphasic formulations:
Ortho Tri-Cyclen®, TriNessa™:
Day 1-7: Ethinyl estradiol 0.035 mg and norgestimate 0.18 mg [7 white tablets]
Day 8-14: Ethinyl estradiol 0.035 mg and norgestimate 0.215 mg [7 light blue tablets]
Day 15-21: Ethinyl estradiol 0.035 mg and norgestimate 0.25 mg [7 blue tablets]
Day 22-28: 7 green inactive tablets (28s)
Tri-Previfem™:
Day 1-7: Ethinyl estradiol 0.035 mg and norgestimate 0.18 mg [7 white tablets]
Day 8-14: Ethinyl estradiol 0.035 mg and norgestimate 0.215 mg [7 light blue tablets]
Day 15-21: Ethinyl estradiol 0.035 mg and norgestimate 0.25 mg [7 blue tablets]
Day 22-28: 7 teal inactive tablets (28s)
Tri-Sprintec™:
Day 1-7: Ethinyl estradiol 0.035 mg and norgestimate 0.18 mg [7 gray tablets]
Day 8-14: Ethinyl estradiol 0.035 mg and norgestimate 0.215 mg [7 light blue tablets]
Day 15-21: Ethinyl estradiol 0.035 mg and norgestimate 0.25 mg [7 blue tablets]
Day 22-28: 7 white inactive tablets (28s)
Ortho Tri-Cyclen® Lo:
Day 1-7: Ethinyl estradiol 0.025 mg and norgestimate 0.18 mg [7 white tablets]
Day 8-14: Ethinyl estradiol 0.025 mg and norgestimate 0.215 mg [7 light blue tablets]
Day 15-21: Ethinyl estradiol 0.025 mg and norgestimate 0.25 mg [7 dark blue tablets]
Day 22-28: 7 green inactive tablets (28s)

Ethinyl Estradiol and Norgestrel (ETH in il es tra DYE ole & nor JES trel)

U.S. Brand Names Cryselle™; Lo/Ovral®; Low-Ogestrel®; Ogestrel®
Canadian Brand Names Ovral®
Index Terms Morning After Pill; Norgestrel and Ethinyl Estradiol
Pharmacologic Category Contraceptive; Estrogen and Progestin Combination
Use Prevention of pregnancy; postcoital contraceptive or "morning after" pill
Unlabeled/Investigational Use Treatment of hypermenorrhea (menorrhagia); pain associated with endometriosis; dysmenorrhea; dysfunctional uterine bleeding
Pregnancy Risk Factor X
Dosage Oral: Adults: Female:
Contraception:
Schedule 1 (Sunday starter): Dose begins on first Sunday after onset of menstruation; if the menstrual period starts on Sunday, take first tablet that very same day. **With a Sunday start, an additional method of contraception should be used until after the first 7 days of consecutive administration.**
For 21-tablet package: Dosage is 1 tablet daily for 21 consecutive days, followed by 7 days off of the medication; a new course begins on the 8th day after the last tablet is taken.
For 28-tablet package: Dosage is 1 tablet daily without interruption.
Schedule 2 (Day 1 starter): Dose starts on first day of menstrual cycle taking 1 tablet daily.
For 21-tablet package: Dosage is 1 tablet daily for 21 consecutive days, followed by 7 days off of the medication; a new course begins on the 8th day after the last tablet is taken.
For 28-tablet package: Dosage is 1 tablet daily without interruption.
If all doses have been taken on schedule and one menstrual period is missed, continue dosing cycle. If two consecutive menstrual periods are missed, pregnancy test is required before new dosing cycle is started.
Missed doses **monophasic formulations** (refer to package insert for complete information):
One dose missed: Take as soon as remembered or take 2 tablets next day
Two consecutive doses missed in the first 2 weeks: Take 2 tablets as soon as remembered or 2 tablets next 2 days. **An additional method of contraception should be used for 7 days after missed dose.**
Two consecutive doses missed in week 3 or three consecutive doses missed at any time:
Schedule 1 (Sunday starter): Continue to take 1 tablet daily until Sunday, then discard the rest of the pack, and a new pack is started that same day.
Schedule 2 (Day 1 starter): Current pack should be discarded, and a new pack started that same day. **An additional method of contraception should be used for 7 days after missed dose.**
Postcoital contraception:
Ethinyl estradiol 0.03 mg and norgestrel 0.3 mg formulation: 4 tablets within 72 hours of unprotected intercourse and 4 tablets 12 hours after first dose
Ethinyl estradiol 0.05 mg and norgestrel 0.5 mg formulation: 2 tablets within 72 hours of unprotected intercourse and 2 tablets 12 hours after first dose
Dosage adjustment in renal impairment: Specific guidelines not available; use with caution and monitor blood pressure closely. Consider other forms of contraception.
(Continued)

663

Ethinyl Estradiol and Norgestrel *(Continued)*

Dosage adjustment in hepatic impairment: Contraindicated in patients with hepatic impairment.

Additional Information Complete prescribing information for this medication should be consulted for additional detail.

Dosage Forms

Tablet, monophasic formulations:

Crysselle™: Ethinyl estradiol 0.03 mg and norgestrel 0.3 mg [21 white tablets and 7 light green inactive tablets] (28s)

Low-Ogestrel® 28: Ethinyl estradiol 0.03 mg and norgestrel 0.3 mg [21 white tablets and 7 peach inactive tablets] (28s)

Lo/Ovral® 28: Ethinyl estradiol 0.03 mg and norgestrel 0.3 mg [21 white tablets and 7 pink inactive tablets] (28s)

Ogestrel® 28: Ethinyl estradiol 0.05 mg and norgestrel 0.5 mg [21 white tablets and 7 peach inactive tablets] (28s)

♦ **Ethiofos** *see Amifostine on page 89*

Ethionamide (e thye on AM ide)

U.S. Brand Names Trecator®
Canadian Brand Names Trecator®
Pharmacologic Category Antitubercular Agent
Additional Appendix Information
Antimicrobial Drugs of Choice *on page 1981*
Tuberculosis *on page 2010*
Use Treatment of tuberculosis and other mycobacterial diseases, in conjunction with other antituberculosis agents, when first-line agents have failed or resistance has been demonstrated
Pregnancy Risk Factor C
Pregnancy Implications Ethionamide crosses the placenta; teratogenic effects were observed in animal studies. Use during pregnancy is not recommended.
Lactation Excretion in breast milk unknown/use caution
Contraindications Hypersensitivity to ethionamide or any component of the formulation; severe hepatic impairment
Warnings/Precautions Use with caution in patients with diabetes mellitus; use with caution in patients receiving cycloserine or isoniazid. Use caution when switching patients from the sugar-coated tablet formulation (Trecator®-SC) to film-coated tablet (Trecator®); the dosage may need retitrated in order to avoid intolerance.
Adverse Reactions Frequency not defined.
Cardiovascular: Postural hypotension
Central nervous system: Depression, dizziness, drowsiness, headache, psychiatric disturbances, restlessness, seizure
Dermatologic: Acne, alopecia, photosensitivity, purpura, rash
Endocrine & metabolic: Gynecomastia, hypoglycemia, hypothyroidism or goiter, pellagra-like syndrome
Gastrointestinal: Abdominal pain, anorexia, diarrhea, excessive salivation, metallic taste, nausea, stomatitis, vomiting, weight loss
Genitourinary: Impotence
Hematologic: Thrombocytopenia
Hepatic: Hepatitis, jaundice, liver function tests increased
Neuromuscular & skeletal: Peripheral neuritis, weakness (common)
Ocular: Blurred vision, diplopia, optic neuritis
Respiratory: Olfactory disturbances
Miscellaneous: Hypersensitivity reaction
Overdosage/Toxicology Symptoms include peripheral neuropathy, anorexia, and joint pain. Following GI decontamination, treatment is supportive. Pyridoxine may be given to prevent peripheral neuropathy.
Ethanol/Nutrition/Herb Interactions
Ethanol: Avoid excessive ethanol ingestion; psychotic reaction may occur.
Mechanism of Action Inhibits peptide synthesis
Pharmacodynamics/Kinetics
Absorption: Rapid, complete
Distribution: Crosses placenta; V_d: 93.5 L
Protein binding: ~30%
Metabolism: Extensively hepatic to active and inactive metabolites
Bioavailability: 80%
Half-life elimination: 2-3 hours
Time to peak, serum: 1 hour
Excretion: Urine (<1% as unchanged drug; as active and inactive metabolites)
Dosage Oral:
Children: 15-20 mg/kg/day in 2-3 divided doses, not to exceed 1 g/day
Adults: 15-20 mg/kg/day; initiate dose at 250 mg/day for 1-2 days, then increase to 250 mg twice daily for 1-2 days, with gradual increases to highest tolerated dose; average adult dose: 750 mg/day (maximum: 1 g/day in 3-4 divided doses)
Dosing adjustment in renal impairment: Cl_{cr} <30 mL/minute: 250-500 mg/day
Dietary Considerations Healthcare provider may recommend an increase in dietary intake of pyridoxine to prevent neurotoxic effects of ethionamide. Avoid alcohol.
Administration Neurotoxic effects may be relieved by the administration of pyridoxine (6-100 mg daily, lower doses are more common). May be taken with or without meals. Gastrointestinal adverse effects may be decreased by administration at bedtime, decreased dose, or giving antiemetics.

Monitoring Parameters Initial and periodic serum ALT and AST; ophthalmic exams; thyroid function

Additional Information Neurotoxic effects may be relieved by the administration of pyridoxine.

Dosage Forms Tablet: 250 mg

◆ **Ethmozine**® *see Moricizine on page 1169*

Ethosuximide (eth oh SUKS i mide)

U.S. Brand Names Zarontin®
Canadian Brand Names Zarontin®
Pharmacologic Category Anticonvulsant, Succinimide
Additional Appendix Information
  Anticonvulsants by Seizure Type *on page 1865*
  Epilepsy *on page 2048*
Use Management of absence (petit mal) seizures
Medication Safety Issues
  Sound-alike/look-alike issues:
    Ethosuximide may be confused with methsuximide
    Zarontin® may be confused with Xalatan®, Zantac®, Zaroxolyn®
Dosage Oral:
  Children 3-6 years: Initial: 250 mg/day; increase every 4-7 days; usual maintenance dose: 20 mg/kg/day; maximum dose: 1.5 g/day in divided doses
  Children >6 years and Adults: Initial: 500 mg/day; increase by 250 mg as needed every 4-7 days, up to 1.5 g/day in divided doses; usual maintenance dose for most pediatric patients is 20 mg/kg/day.
  Dosing comment in renal/hepatic dysfunction: Use with caution.
Additional Information Complete prescribing information for this medication should be consulted for additional detail.
Dosage Forms
  Capsule: 250 mg
    Zarontin®: 250 mg
  Syrup: 250 mg/5 mL (473 mL)
    Zarontin®: 250 mg/5 mL [contains sodium benzoate; raspberry flavor]

◆ **ETH-Oxydose**™ *see Oxycodone on page 1286*
◆ **Ethoxynaphthamido Penicillin Sodium** *see Nafcillin on page 1190*
◆ **Ethyl Aminobenzoate** *see Benzocaine on page 204*
◆ **Ethyl Esters of Omega-3 Fatty Acids** *see Omega-3-Acid Ethyl Esters on page 1264*
◆ **Ethynodiol Diacetate and Ethinyl Estradiol** *see Ethinyl Estradiol and Ethynodiol Diacetate on page 648*
◆ **Ethyol**® *see Amifostine on page 89*
◆ **Etibi**® **(Can)** *see Ethambutol on page 643*

Etidronate Disodium (e ti DROE nate dye SOW dee um)

U.S. Brand Names Didronel®
Canadian Brand Names Didronel®; Gen-Etidronate
Index Terms EHDP; Sodium Etidronate
Pharmacologic Category Bisphosphonate Derivative
Use Symptomatic treatment of Paget's disease; prevention and treatment of heterotopic ossification due to spinal cord injury or after total hip replacement
Unlabeled/Investigational Use Postmenopausal osteoporosis
Pregnancy Risk Factor C
Medication Safety Issues
  Sound-alike/look-alike issues:
    Etidronate may be confused with etidocaine, etomidate, etretinate
Dosage Oral: Adults:
  Paget's disease:
    Initial: 5-10 mg/kg/day (not to exceed 6 months) or 11-20 mg/kg/day (not to exceed 3 months). Doses >20 mg/kg/day are **not** recommended.
    Retreatment: Initiate only after etidronate-free period ≥90 days. Monitor patients every 3-6 months. Retreatment regimens are the same as for initial treatment.
  Heterotopic ossification:
    Caused by spinal cord injury: 20 mg/kg/day for 2 weeks, then 10 mg/kg/day for 10 weeks; total treatment period: 12 weeks
    Complicating total hip replacement: 20 mg/kg/day for 1 month preoperatively then 20 mg/kg/day for 3 months postoperatively; total treatment period is 4 months
  Postmenopausal osteoporosis (unlabeled use): Oral: 400 mg/day for 2 weeks, followed by 13-week period with no etidronate, then repeat cycle. Maintain adequate calcium and vitamin D intake during the entire 15-week treatment cycle
  Dosing adjustment in renal impairment: Use with caution; specific guidelines are not available, however consider dose reduction.
Additional Information Complete prescribing information for this medication should be consulted for additional detail.
Dosage Forms Tablet: 200 mg, 400 mg

Etodolac (ee toe DOE lak)

U.S. Brand Names Lodine® [DSC]; Lodine® XL [DSC]
Canadian Brand Names Apo-Etodolac®; Lodine®; Utradol™
Index Terms Etodolic Acid
Pharmacologic Category Nonsteroidal Anti-inflammatory Drug (NSAID), Oral
Additional Appendix Information
  Nonsteroidal Anti-inflammatory Agents *on page 1894*
Use Acute and long-term use in the management of signs and symptoms of osteoarthritis; rheumatoid arthritis and juvenile rheumatoid arthritis; management of acute pain
Restrictions An FDA-approved medication guide must be distributed when dispensing an oral outpatient prescription (new or refill) where this medication is to be used without direct supervision of a healthcare provider. Medication guides are available at http://www.fda.gov/cder/Offices/ODS/medication_guides.htm.
Pregnancy Risk Factor C/D (3rd trimester)
Lactation Excretion in breast milk unknown/not recommended
Medication Safety Issues
  Sound-alike/look-alike issues:
    Lodine® may be confused with codeine, iodine, Iopidine®, Lopid®
Contraindications Hypersensitivity to etodolac, aspirin, other NSAIDs, or any component of the formulation; perioperative pain in the setting of coronary artery bypass surgery (CABG); pregnancy
Warnings/Precautions [U.S. Boxed Warning]: NSAIDs are associated with an increased risk of adverse cardiovascular events, including MI, stroke, and new onset or worsening of pre-existing hypertension. Risk may be increased with duration of use or pre-existing cardiovascular risk-factors or disease. Carefully evaluate individual cardiovascular risk profiles prior to prescribing. Use caution with fluid retention, CHF, or hypertension. Concurrent administration of ibuprofen, and potentially other nonselective NSAIDs, may interfere with aspirin's cardioprotective effect.

[U.S. Boxed Warning]: NSAIDs may increase risk of gastrointestinal irritation, ulceration, bleeding, and perforation. These events may occur at any time during therapy and without warning. Use caution with a history of GI disease (bleeding or ulcers), concurrent therapy with aspirin, anticoagulants and/or corticosteroids, smoking, use of alcohol, the elderly or debilitated patients.

Use of NSAIDs can compromise existing renal function. Renal toxicity can occur in patient with impaired renal function, dehydration, heart failure, liver dysfunction, those taking diuretics and ACE inhibitors and the elderly. Rehydrate patient before starting therapy. Monitor renal function closely. Etodolac is not recommended for patients with advanced renal disease.

Use the lowest effective dose for the shortest duration of time, consistent with individual patient goals, to reduce risk of cardiovascular or GI adverse events. Alternate therapies should be considered for patients at high risk.

NSAIDs may cause serious skin adverse events including exfoliative dermatitis, Stevens-Johnson syndrome (SJS), and toxic epidermal necrolysis (TEN). Anaphylactoid reactions may occur, even without prior exposure; patients with "aspirin triad" (bronchial asthma, aspirin intolerance, rhinitis) may be at increased risk. Do not use in patients who experience bronchospasm, asthma, rhinitis, or urticaria with NSAID or aspirin therapy.

Use with caution in patients with decreased hepatic function. Closely monitor patients with any abnormal LFT. Severe hepatic reactions (eg, fulminant hepatitis, liver failure) have occurred with NSAID use, rarely; discontinue if signs or symptoms of liver disease develop, or if systemic manifestations occur. The elderly are at increased risk for adverse effects (especially peptic ulceration, CNS effects, renal toxicity) from NSAIDs even at low doses.

Withhold for at least 4-6 half-lives prior to surgical or dental procedures. Safety and efficacy have not been established in children.

Use of extended release product consisting of a nondeformable matrix should be avoided in patients with stricture/narrowing of the GI tract; symptoms of obstruction have been associated with nondeformable products.

Adverse Reactions
1% to 10%:
  Central nervous system: Dizziness (3% to 9 %), chills/fever (1% to 3%), depression (1% to 3%), nervousness (1% to 3%)
  Dermatologic: Rash (1% to 3%), pruritus (1% to 3%)
  Gastrointestinal: Abdominal cramps (3% to 9%), nausea (3% to 9%), vomiting (1% to 3%), dyspepsia (10%), diarrhea (3% to 9%), constipation (1% to 3%), flatulence (3% to 9%), melena (1% to 3%), gastritis (1% to 3%)
  Genitourinary: Dysuria (1% to 3%)
  Neuromuscular & skeletal: Weakness (3% to 9%)
  Ocular: Blurred vision (1% to 3%)
  Otic: Tinnitus (1% to 3%)
  Renal: Polyuria (1% to 3%)
  <1% (Limited to important or life-threatening): Agranulocytosis, allergic reaction, allergic/necrotizing vasculitis, alopecia, anaphylactic/anaphylactoid reactions, anemia, angioedema, anorexia, arrhythmia, aseptic meningitis, asthma, bleeding time increased, CHF, confusion, conjunctivitis, CVA, cystitis, duodenitis, dyspnea, ecchymosis, edema, erythema multiforme, esophagitis (+/- stricture or cardiospasm), exfoliative dermatitis, GI ulceration, hallucinations, headache, hearing decreased, hematemesis, hematuria, hepatic failure, hepatitis, hyperglycemia (in controlled diabetics), hyperpigmentation, hypertension, infection, insomnia, interstitial nephritis, irregular uterine bleeding, jaundice, LFTs increased, leukopenia, MI, palpitations, pancreatitis, pancytopenia, paresthesia, peptic ulcer (+/- bleeding/perforation), peripheral neuropathy, photophobia, photosensitivity,

pulmonary infiltration (eosinophilia), rectal bleeding, renal calculus, renal failure, renal insufficiency, shock, Stevens-Johnson syndrome, syncope, thrombocytopenia, toxic epidermal necrolysis, ulcerative stomatitis, urticaria, vesiculobullous rash, renal papillary necrosis, visual disturbances

Overdosage/Toxicology Symptoms include acute renal failure, vomiting, drowsiness, and leukocytosis. Management of nonsteroidal anti-inflammatory drug (NSAID) intoxication is primarily supportive and symptomatic. Fluid therapy is commonly effective in managing hypotension that may occur following an acute NSAID overdose, except when due to acute blood loss. Emesis and/or activated charcoal and/or osmotic cathartic may be considered when overdoses are large (5-10 times usual dose) or recent (within 4 hours). Diuresis, urine alkalinization, hemodialysis, and hemoperfusion are not likely to be useful.

Drug Interactions

    Increased Effect/Toxicity: Etodolac may increase effect/toxicity of anticoagulants (bleeding), antiplatelet agents (bleeding), aminoglycosides, biphosphonates (GI irritation), corticosteroids (GI irritation), cyclosporine (nephrotoxicity), lithium, methotrexate, pemetrexed, treprostinil (bleeding), vancomycin. Concomitant use with fluoroquinolones may rarely increase risk of seizure.

    Decreased Effect: May reduce effect of some diuretics and antihypertensive effect of beta-blockers, ACE inhibitors, angiotensin II inhibitors, hydralazine, verapamil. Cholestyramine and colestipol may reduce absorption of etodolac. Salicylates' antiplatelet effect may be reduced.

Ethanol/Nutrition/Herb Interactions

    Ethanol: Avoid ethanol (may enhance gastric mucosal irritation).

    Food: Etodolac peak serum levels may be decreased if taken with food.

    Herb/Nutraceutical: Avoid alfalfa, anise, bilberry, bladderwrack, bromelain, cat's claw, celery, coleus, cordyceps, dong quai, evening primrose, feverfew, fenugreek, garlic, ginger, ginkgo biloba, red clover, horse chestnut, grapeseed, green tea, ginseng, guggul, horse chestnut seed, horseradish, licorice, prickly ash, red clover, reishi, SAMe, sweet clover, turmeric, white willow (all have additional antiplatelet activity).

Stability Store at 20°C to 25°C (68°F to 77°F). Protect from moisture.

Mechanism of Action Inhibits prostaglandin synthesis by decreasing the activity of the enzyme, cyclooxygenase, which results in decreased formation of prostaglandin precursors

Pharmacodynamics/Kinetics

    Onset of action: Analgesic: 2-4 hours; Maximum anti-inflammatory effect: A few days

    Absorption: ≥80%

    Distribution: V_d:

        Immediate release: Adults:0.4 L/kg

        Extended release: Adults: 0.57 L/kg; Children (6-16 years): 0 .08 L/kg

    Protein binding: ≥99%, primarily albumin

    Metabolism: Hepatic

    Half-life elimination: Terminal: Adults: 5-8 hours

        Extended release: Children (6-16 years): 12 hours

    Time to peak, serum:

        Immediate release: Adults: 1-2 hours

        Extended release: Extended release: 5-7 hours, increased 1.4-3.8 hours with food

    Excretion: Urine 73% (1% unchanged); feces 16%

Dosage Note: For chronic conditions, response is usually observed within 2 weeks.

    Children 6-16 years: Oral: Juvenile rheumatoid arthritis (Lodine® XL):

        20-30 kg: 400 mg once daily

        31-45 kg: 600 mg once daily

        46-60 kg: 800 mg once daily

        >60 kg: 1000 mg once daily

    Adults: Oral:

        Acute pain: 200-400 mg every 6-8 hours, as needed, not to exceed total daily doses of 1000 mg

        Rheumatoid arthritis, osteoarthritis: 400 mg 2 times/day **or** 300 mg 2-3 times/day **or** 500 mg 2 times/day (doses >1000 mg/day have not been evaluated)

        Lodine® XL: 400-1000 mg once daily

    Elderly: Refer to adult dosing; in patients ≥65 years, no dosage adjustment required based on pharmacokinetics. The elderly are more sensitive to antiprostaglandin effects and may need dosage adjustments.

    Dosage adjustment in renal impairment:

        Mild to moderate: No adjustment required

        Severe: Use not recommended; use with caution

        Hemodialysis: Not removed

    Dosage adjustment in hepatic impairment: No adjustment required.

Dietary Considerations May be taken with food to decrease GI distress.

Monitoring Parameters Monitor CBC and chemistry profile, liver enzymes; in patients with an increased risk for renal failure (CHF or decreased renal function, taking ACE inhibitors or diuretics, elderly), monitor urine output and BUN/serum creatinine

Test Interactions False-positive for urinary bilirubin and ketone

Dosage Forms [DSC] = Discontinued product

    Capsule: 200 mg, 300 mg

        Lodine®: 200 mg, 300 mg [DSC]

    Tablet: 400 mg, 500 mg

    Tablet, extended release (Lodine® XL): 400 mg, 500 mg [DSC]

♦ **Etodolic Acid** see Etodolac on page 666

Etomidate (e TOM i date)

U.S. Brand Names Amidate®
Canadian Brand Names Amidate®
Pharmacologic Category General Anesthetic
Use Induction and maintenance of general anesthesia
Unlabeled/Investigational Use Sedation for diagnosis of seizure foci
Pregnancy Risk Factor C
Medication Safety Issues
Sound-alike/look-alike issues:
Etomidate may be confused with etidronate
Contraindications Hypersensitivity to etomidate or any component of the formulation
Warnings/Precautions Consider exogenous corticosteroid replacement in patients under-
going severe stress
Adverse Reactions
>10%:
Gastrointestinal: Nausea, vomiting on emergence from anesthesia
Local: Pain at injection site (30% to 80%)
Neuromuscular & skeletal: Myoclonus (33%), transient skeletal movements, uncontrolled
eye movements
1% to 10%: Hiccups
<1% (Limited to important or life-threatening): Apnea, arrhythmia, bradycardia, decreased
cortisol synthesis, hypertension, hyperventilation, hypotension, hypoventilation, laryngo-
spasm, tachycardia
Overdosage/Toxicology Symptoms include respiratory arrest and coma. Treatment is
supportive.
Drug Interactions
Increased Effect/Toxicity: Fentanyl decreases etomidate elimination. Verapamil may
increase the anesthetic and respiratory depressant effects of etomidate.
Stability Store at room temperature.
Mechanism of Action Ultrashort-acting nonbarbiturate hypnotic (benzylimidazole) used for
the induction of anesthesia; chemically, it is a carboxylated imidazole which produces a rapid
induction of anesthesia with minimal cardiovascular effects; produces EEG burst suppression
at high doses
Pharmacodynamics/Kinetics
Onset of action: 30-60 seconds
Peak effect: 1 minute
Duration: 3-5 minutes; terminated by redistribution
Distribution: V_d: 2-4.5 L/kg
Protein binding: 76%;
Metabolism: Hepatic and plasma esterases
Half-life elimination: Terminal: 2.6 hours
Dosage Children >10 years and Adults: I.V.: Initial: 0.2-0.6 mg/kg over 30-60 seconds for
induction of anesthesia; maintenance: 5-20 mcg/kg/minute
Administration Administer I.V. push over 30-60 seconds. Solution is highly irritating; avoid
administration into small vessels; in some cases, preadministration of lidocaine may be
considered.
Monitoring Parameters Cardiac monitoring and blood pressure required
Additional Information Etomidate decreases cerebral metabolism and cerebral blood flow
while maintaining perfusion pressure. Premedication with opioids or benzodiazepines can
decrease myoclonus. Etomidate can enhance somatosensory evoked potential recordings.
Dosage Forms Injection, solution: 2 mg/mL (10 mL, 20 mL) [contains propylene glycol 35% v/v]

Etonogestrel (e toe noe JES trel)

U.S. Brand Names Implanon™
Index Terms ENG; 3-Keto-desogestrel
Use Prevention of pregnancy; for use in women who request long-acting (up to 3 years)
contraception
Restrictions Only healthcare providers who have undergone training in the insertion and
removal procedures will be able to order Implanon™.
Pregnancy Implications Teratogenic effects were not observed in animal studies. Not for
use during pregnancy; remove implant if pregnancy is detected. Ovulation may return within 1
week of implant removal; alternate forms of contraception may be required. In a multicenter
clinical trial, 11 out of 46 women no longer using contraception became pregnant between 1
and 18 weeks following removal of the implant. Do not insert <21 days postpartum. Women
weighing >130% of their ideal body weight were not included in clinical studies. With oral
combination hormonal contraceptives, an increase in contraceptive failure was noted in
women with a BMI >27.3. Similar findings were noted in patients weighing ≥90 kg (198 lb)
using the contraceptive patch.

Lactation Enters breast milk/use caution
Contraindications Hypersensitivity to etonogestrel or any component of the formulation;
undiagnosed abnormal uterine bleeding; active hepatic disease or malignant tumors; active
thrombophlebitis or thromboembolic disorders (current or history of); known or suspected
carcinoma of the breast; concomitant use with chronic potent hepatic enzyme inducers;
pregnancy
Warnings/Precautions Use does not protect against HIV infection or other sexually-transmitted diseases. Improper insertion may lead to unintended pregnancy or may
cause difficult or impossible removal. Failure to properly remove may lead to infertility,

ectopic pregnancy, or continued adverse reactions. Menstrual bleeding patterns are likely to be altered; patients should be counseled prior to implant insertion. Abnormal bleeding should be evaluated as required to exclude pathologic conditions or pregnancy. Ectopic pregnancy (rare) may occur more commonly than in women using no contraception. Etonogestrel serum levels and contraceptive efficacy may be significantly decreased by potent hepatic enzyme inducers. The manufacturer does not recommend use in women chronically taking hepatic enzyme inducers. Use caution in overweight women; women >130% of ideal body weight were not included in clinical studies. Use caution with renal disease.

Additional warnings based on combination hormonal (estrogen and progestin) contraceptives: The risk of cardiovascular side effects increases in women who smoke cigarettes, especially those who are >35 years of age; women who use combination hormonal contraceptives should be strongly advised not to smoke. Combination hormonal contraceptives may lead to increased risk of myocardial infarction; use with caution in patients with risk factors for coronary artery disease. May increase the risk of thromboembolism (also reported with etonogestrel). Whenever possible, combination hormonal contraceptives should be discontinued at least 4 weeks prior to and for 2 weeks following elective surgery associated with an increased risk of thromboembolism or during periods of prolonged immobilization. Combination hormonal contraceptives may have a dose-related risk of vascular disease, hypertension, and gallbladder disease. Women with hypertension or renal disease should be encouraged to use another form of contraception. The use of combination hormonal contraceptives has been associated with a slight increase in frequency of breast cancer; however, studies are not consistent. Combination hormonal contraceptives may cause glucose intolerance or effect serum triglyceride and lipoprotein levels. Retinal thrombosis has been reported (rarely). Use caution with conditions that may be aggravated by fluid retention, depression, or history of migraine. Not for use prior to menarche.

Adverse Reactions

>10%:
Central nervous system: Headache (25%)
Dermatologic: Acne (14%)
Endocrine & metabolic: Infrequent menstrual bleeding (<3 episodes/90 days: 34%), amenorrhea (no bleeding in 90 days: 22%), prolonged menstrual bleeding (lasting >14 days: 18%), breast pain (13%), menstrual bleeding irregularities requiring discontinuation (11%)
Gastrointestinal: Weight gain (14%), abdominal pain (11%)
Genitourinary: Vaginitis (15%)
Respiratory: Upper respiratory tract infection (13%), pharyngitis (11%)

5% to 10%:
Central nervous system: Dizziness (7%), emotional lability (7%), depression (6%), nervousness (6%), pain (6%)
Endocrine & metabolic: Dysmenorrhea (7%), frequent menstrual bleeding (>5 episodes/90 days: 7%)
Gastrointestinal: Nausea (6%)
Genitourinary: Leukorrhea (10%)
Local: Insertion site pain (5%)
Neuromuscular & skeletal: Back pain (7%)
Respiratory: Sinusitis (6%)
Miscellaneous: Flu-like syndrome (8%)

<5% (Limited to important or life-threatening): Allergic reaction, alopecia, anorexia, anxiety, appetite increased, arthralgia, asthma, breast discharge, breast enlargement, breast fibroadenosis, cervical smear test positive, constipation, coughing, crying, diarrhea, dyspepsia, dysuria, edema, fatigue, fever, flatulence, gastritis, hot flushes, hypertension, hypoesthesia, injection site reaction, insomnia, lactation nonpuerperal, libido decreased, migraine, myalgia, otitis media, ovarian cyst, pelvic cramping, premenstrual tension, pruritus, rash, rhinitis, sexual function abnormal, skeletal pain, somnolence, vaginal discomfort, varicose vein, vision abnormal, vomiting, weakness, weight loss

Overdosage/Toxicology Other rod or contraceptive implants should be removed prior to insertion. Remove implant in case of overdose. Treatment should be symptomatic and supportive.

Drug Interactions

Cytochrome P450 Effect: Substrate of CYP3A4 (minor)

Increased Effect/Toxicity: Progestins may enhance the hepatotoxic effect of cyclosporine. Progestins may increase the serum concentration of cyclosporine. Progestin contraceptives may increase the serum concentration of selegiline. Progestin contraceptives may diminish the anticoagulant effect of coumarin derivatives. In contrast, enhanced anticoagulant effects have also been noted with some products.

Decreased Effect: Specific drug interaction studies have not been conducted with strong CYP3A4 inducers; however, strong CYP3A4 inducers may increase the metabolism of etonogestrel. Chronic use of these agents is not recommended with the etonogestrel implant. Felbamate, griseofulvin, retinoic acid, and retinoids may decrease the serum concentration of progestin contraceptives. Progestin contraceptives may diminish the anticoagulant effect of coumarin derivatives. In contrast, enhanced anticoagulant effects have also been noted with some products.

Ethanol/Nutrition/Herb Interactions

Herb/Nutraceutical: St John's wort (an enzyme inducer) may decrease serum levels of etonogestrel. Concomitant use is not recommended. Bloodroot, chasteberry, damiana, oregano, and yucca may enhance the adverse/toxic effect of progestins.

Stability Store at controlled room temperature 15°C to 30°C (59°F to 86°F); protect from light

Mechanism of Action Etonogestrel is the active metabolite of desogestrel. It prevents pregnancy by suppressing ovulation, increasing the viscosity of cervical mucous, and inhibiting endometrial proliferation.

Pharmacodynamics/Kinetics

Onset of action: Serum levels sufficient to inhibit ovulation: ≤8 hours of implant
Duration: Implant: Each rod maintains etonogestrel levels sufficient to inhibit ovulation for 3 years
(Continued)

Etonogestrel *(Continued)*

Distribution: V_d: 201 L

Protein binding: Albumin (66%) and sex hormone binding globulin (32%)

Metabolism: Hepatic via CYP3A4; forms metabolites (activity not known)

Bioavailability: Implant: 100%

Half-life, elimination: 25 hours

Excretion: Urine (primarily); feces

Dosage

Children: Not for use prior to menarche.

Adults: Contraception: Subdermal: Implant 1 rod in the inner side of the upper, nondominant arm. Remove no later than 3 years after the date of insertion. After ruling out pregnancy, timing of insertion is based on the patient's contraceptive history:

No hormonal contraceptives within the past month: Insert between days 1 through 5 of menstruation, even if woman is still bleeding

Switching from combination hormonal contraceptive:

Oral tablet: Insert anytime within 7 days after the last active tablet

Vaginal ring: Insert anytime during the 7-day ring-free period

Transdermal system: Insert anytime during the 7-day patch-free period

Switching from a progestin-only contraceptive:

Oral pill: Any day during the month; do not skip days between the last pill and implant insertion

Implant: Insert on same day as removal of implant

IUD: Insert on same day as removal of IUD

Injection: Insert on day next injection is due

First trimester abortion or miscarriage: Insert immediately. If not inserted within first 5 days follow directions for "no hormonal contraception within the past month"

Following delivery or second trimester abortion: May insert between 21 and 28 days (if not exclusively breast-feeding) or after 4 weeks (if exclusively breast-feeding). Patients should use a second form of contraception for the first 7 days if insertion occurs at >4 weeks.

Note: If following above insertion schedule, no back-up contraception needed. If deviating, use back-up method for 7 days postinsertion.

Elderly: Not for use after menopause

Dosage adjustment in renal impairment: Use with caution; formal studies have not been conducted

Dosage adjustment in hepatic impairment: Use is contraindicated

Administration Subdermal: For insertion under local anesthesia by healthcare providers trained in the insertion and removal procedure. Rod must be palpable after insertion. Deep insertion may require surgery to remove. If rod is impalpable, ultrasound should be used to locate the rod; MRI may also be useful if ultrasound is not successful. A pressure bandage should be applied and left in place for 24 hours after insertion to decrease bruising; a small bandage placed over the insertion site should remain in place for 3-5 days.

Monitoring Parameters Before starting therapy, a physical exam with reference to the breasts and pelvis are recommended, including a Papanicolaou smear. Exam may be deferred if appropriate; pregnancy should be ruled out prior to use. Monitor patient closely for loss of vision, sudden onset of proptosis, diplopia, migraine; blood pressure; signs and symptoms of thromboembolic disorders; signs or symptoms of depression; glycemic control in diabetics; lipid profiles in patients being treated for hyperlipidemias. Adequate diagnostic measures, including endometrial sampling, if indicated, should be performed to rule out malignancy in all cases of undiagnosed abnormal vaginal bleeding.

Reference Range Etonogestrel: A release rate of 25-30 mcg/day is required to inhibit ovulation

Test Interactions

Sex hormone-binding globulin: Serum concentrations may be decreased for first 6 months following implantation.

Thyroxine: Serum concentrations may be slightly decreased initially.

Additional Information For subdermal insertion by healthcare providers trained on the insertion and removal procedure. For use in women who request long-acting (up to 3 years) contraception. A User Card (to give to the patient), consent form (to keep on file), and a medication guide (for the patient) are provided with the device.

The rod releases etonogestrel at a rate of 60-70 mcg/day, decreasing to 35-45 mcg/day after the first year, 30-40 mcg/day after the second year, and 25-30 mcg/day at the end of the third year. Following removal of rod, levels decrease rapidly and are less than the level of detection within 1 week.

Dosage Forms

Rod, subdermal:

Implanon™: 68 mg [latex free]

♦ **Etonogestrel and Ethinyl Estradiol** *see* Ethinyl Estradiol and Etonogestrel *on page 650*

♦ **Etopophos**® *see* Etoposide Phosphate *on page 673*

Etoposide (e toe POE side)

U.S. Brand Names Toposar®; VePesid®

Canadian Brand Names VePesid®

Index Terms Epipodophyllotoxin; VP-16; VP-16-213

Pharmacologic Category Antineoplastic Agent, Podophyllotoxin Derivative

Use Treatment of refractory testicular tumors; treatment of small cell lung cancer

Unlabeled/Investigational Use Treatment of lymphomas, acute nonlymphocytic leukemia (ANLL); lung, bladder, and prostate carcinoma; hepatoma, rhabdomyosarcoma, uterine carcinoma, neuroblastoma, mycosis fungoides, Kaposi's sarcoma, histiocytosis, gestational trophoblastic disease, Ewing's sarcoma, Wilms' tumor, brain tumors

Pregnancy Risk Factor D

Pregnancy Implications Animal studies have demonstrated teratogenicity and fetal loss. There are no adequate and well-controlled studies in pregnant women. Women of child-bearing potential should be advised to avoid pregnancy.

Lactation Enters breast milk/contraindicated

Medication Safety Issues
Sound-alike/look-alike issues:
Etoposide may be confused with teniposide
VePesid® may be confused with Versed

High alert medication: The Institute for Safe Medication Practices (ISMP) includes this medication among its list of drugs which have a heightened risk of causing significant patient harm when used in error.

Contraindications Hypersensitivity to etoposide or any component of the formulation; pregnancy

Warnings/Precautions Hazardous agent - use appropriate precautions for handling and disposal. **[U.S. Boxed Warning]: Severe myelosuppression with resulting infection or bleeding may occur.** Treatment should be withheld for platelets <50,000/mm³ or absolute neutrophil count (ANC) <500/mm³. May cause anaphylactic reaction manifested by chills, fever, tachycardia, bronchospasm, dyspnea, and hypotension. In children, the use of concentrations higher than recommended were associated with higher rates of anaphylactic-like reactions. Infusion should be interrupted and medications for the treatment of anaphylaxis should be available for immediate use. Must be diluted; do not give I.V. push, infuse over at least 30-60 minutes; hypotension is associated with rapid infusion. Dosage should be adjusted in patients with hepatic or renal impairment. **[U.S. Boxed Warning]: Should be administered under the supervision of an experienced cancer chemotherapy physician.** Injectable formula contains polysorbate 80; do not use in premature infants. May contain benzyl alcohol; do not use in newborn infants.

Adverse Reactions
>10%:
Dermatologic: Alopecia (8% to 66%)
Endocrine & metabolic: Ovarian failure (38%), amenorrhea
Gastrointestinal: Nausea/vomiting (31% to 43%), anorexia (10% to 13%), diarrhea (1% to 13%), mucositis/esophagitis (with high doses)
Hematologic: Leukopenia (60% to 91%; grade 4: 3% to 17%; onset: 5-7 days; nadir: 7-14 days; recovery: 21-28 days), thrombocytopenia (22% to 41%; grades 3/4: 1% to 20%; nadir 9-16 days), anemia (up to 33%)

1% to 10%:
Cardiovascular: Hypotension (1% to 2%; due to rapid infusion)
Gastrointestinal: Stomatitis (1% to 6%), abdominal pain (up to 2%)
Hepatic: Hepatic toxicity (up to 3%)
Neuromuscular & skeletal: Peripheral neuropathy (1% to 2%)
Miscellaneous: Anaphylactic-like reaction (I.V. infusion: 1% to 2%; including chills, fever, tachycardia, bronchospasm, dyspnea)

<1% (Limited to important or life-threatening): Anovulatory cycles, back pain; blindness (transient, cortical); CHF, constipation, cough, cyanosis, diaphoresis, dysphagia, erythema; extravasation (induration, necrosis, swelling); facial swelling, fatigue, fever, headache, hepatic toxicity, hepatitis, hyperpigmentation, hypersensitivity, hypersensitivity-associated apnea, hypomenorrhea, interstitial pneumonitis, laryngospasm, maculo-papular rash, malaise, metabolic acidosis, MI, optic neuritis, perivasculitis, pruritus, pulmonary fibrosis, radiation-recall dermatitis, rash, seizure, somnolence, Stevens-Johnson syndrome, tachycardia, taste perversion, thrombophlebitis, tongue swelling, toxic epidermal necrolysis, urticaria, weakness

BMT:
Cardiovascular: Hypotension (infusion-related)
Dermatologic: Skin lesions resembling Stevens-Johnson syndrome, alopecia
Endocrine & metabolic: Metabolic acidosis
Gastrointestinal: Severe nausea and vomiting, mucositis
Hepatic: Hepatitis
Miscellaneous: Secondary malignancy, ethanol intoxication

Overdosage/Toxicology Symptoms include bone marrow depression, leukopenia, thrombocytopenia, nausea, and vomiting. Treatment is symptom-directed and supportive.

Drug Interactions
Cytochrome P450 Effect: Substrate of CYP1A2 (minor), 2E1 (minor), 3A4 (major); **Inhibits** CYP2C9 (weak), 3A4 (weak)

Increased Effect/Toxicity: Cyclosporine may increase the levels of etoposide; consider reducing the dose of etoposide by 50%. Etoposide may increase the effects/toxicity of warfarin. CYP3A4 inhibitors may increase the levels/effects of etoposide; example inhibitors include azole antifungals, clarithromycin, diclofenac, doxycycline, erythromycin, imatinib, isoniazid, nefazodone, nicardipine, propofol, protease inhibitors, quinidine, telithromycin, and verapamil.

Decreased Effect: Barbiturates and phenytoin may decrease the levels/effects of etoposide; monitor. CYP3A4 inducers may decrease the levels/effects of etoposide; example inducers include aminoglutethimide, carbamazepine, nafcillin, nevirapine, phenobarbital, phenytoin, and rifamycins.

Ethanol/Nutrition/Herb Interactions
Ethanol: Avoid ethanol (may increase GI irritation).
Herb/Nutraceutical: Avoid concurrent St John's wort; may decrease etoposide levels.

Stability
Store intact vials of injection at 15°C to 30°C (59°F to 86°F). Protect from light. Store oral capsules at 2°C to 8°C (36°F to 46°F).
Etoposide should be diluted to a concentration of 0.2-0.4 mg/mL in D₅W or NS for administration. Diluted solutions have concentration-dependent stability; more concentrated solutions have shorter stability times. Precipitation may occur with concentrations >0.4 mg/mL.

(Continued)

Etoposide *(Continued)*

Solutions for infusion, at room temperature, in D_5W or NS in polyvinyl chloride, the concentration is stable as follows:

0.2 mg/mL: 96 hours

0.4 mg/mL: 24 hours

Etoposide injection contains polysorbate 80 which may cause leaching of diethylhexyl phthalate (DEHP), a plasticizer contained in polyvinyl chloride (PVC) bags and tubing. Higher concentrations and longer storage time after preparation in PVC bags may increase DEHP leaching. Preparation in glass or polyolefin containers will minimize patient exposure to DEHP.

Etoposide injection diluted for oral use to 10 mg/mL in NS may be stored for 22 days in plastic oral syringes at room temperature. Mix with orange juice, apple juice, or lemonade to a concentration of ≤0.4 mg/mL, and use within a 3-hour period.

Mechanism of Action Etoposide has been shown to delay transit of cells through the S phase and arrest cells in late S or early G_2 phase. The drug may inhibit mitochondrial transport at the NADH dehydrogenase level or inhibit uptake of nucleosides into HeLa cells. It is a topoisomerase II inhibitor and appears to cause DNA strand breaks. Etoposide does not inhibit microtubular assembly.

Pharmacodynamics/Kinetics

Absorption: Oral: 25% to 75%; significant inter- and intrapatient variation

Distribution: Average V_d: 7-17 L/m^2; poor penetration across the blood-brain barrier; CSF concentrations <10% of plasma concentrations

Protein binding: 94% to 97%

Metabolism: Hepatic to hydroxy acid and cislactone metabolites

Bioavailability: Oral: ~50% (range 25% to 75%)

Half-life elimination: Terminal: 4-11 hours; Children: Normal renal/hepatic function: 6-8 hours

Time to peak, serum: Oral: 1-1.5 hours

Excretion:

Children: Urine (≤55% as unchanged drug)

Adults: Urine (42% to 67%; 8% to 35% as unchanged drug) within 24 hours; feces (up to 44%)

Dosage Refer to individual protocols:

Children (unlabeled uses): I.V.: 60-120 mg/m^2/day for 3-5 days every 3-6 weeks

AML:

Remission induction: 150 mg/m^2/day for 2-3 days for 2-3 cycles

Intensification or consolidation: 250 mg/m^2/day for 3 days, courses 2-5

Brain tumor: 150 mg/m^2/day on days 2 and 3 of treatment course

Neuroblastoma: 100 mg/m^2/day over 1 hour on days 1-5 of cycle; repeat cycle every 4 weeks

BMT conditioning regimen used in patients with rhabdomyosarcoma or neuroblastoma: I.V. continuous infusion: 160 mg/m^2/day for 4 days

Conditioning regimen for allogenic BMT: 60 mg/kg/dose as a single dose

Adults:

Small cell lung cancer (in combination with other approved chemotherapeutic drugs):

Oral: Due to poor bioavailability, oral doses should be twice the I.V. dose, rounded to the nearest 50 mg given once daily

I.V.: 35 mg/m^2/day for 4 days or 50 mg/m^2/day for 5 days every 3-4 weeks

IVPB: 60-100 mg/m^2/day for 3 days (with cisplatin)

CIV: 500 mg/m^2 over 24 hours every 3 weeks

Testicular cancer (in combination with other approved chemotherapeutic drugs):

IVPB: 50-100 mg/m^2/day for 5 days repeated every 3-4 weeks

I.V.: 100 mg/m^2 every other day for 3 doses repeated every 3-4 weeks

BMT/relapsed leukemia (unlabeled uses): I.V.: 2.4-3.5 g/m^2 or 25-70 mg/kg administered over 4-36 hours

Dosing adjustment in renal impairment:

Manufacturer recommended guidelines:

Cl_{cr} 15-50 mL/minute: Administer 75% of normal dose

Cl_{cr} <15 mL minute: Data not available, consider further dose reductions

Aronoff, 1999:

Cl_{cr} 10-50 mL/minute: Administer 75% of normal dose

Cl_{cr} <10 mL minute: Administer 50% of normal dose

Hemodialysis: Supplemental dose is not necessary

Peritoneal dialysis: Supplemental dose is not necessary

CAPD effects: Unknown

CAVH effects: Dose for Cl_{cr} 10-50 mL/minute (Aronoff, 1999)

Dosing adjustment in hepatic impairment: There is no FDA-approved hepatic dosing adjustment guideline. The following adjustments have been used by some clinicians:

Donelli, 1998: Liver dysfunction may reduce the metabolism and increase the toxicity of etoposide. Normal doses of I.V. etoposide should be given to patients with liver dysfunction (dose reductions may result in subtherapeutic concentrations); however, use caution with concomitant liver dysfunction (severe) and renal dysfunction as the decreased metabolic clearance cannot be compensated by increased renal clearance.

King, 2001: Bilirubin 2.5-5.2 mg/dL or ALT or AST >180 units/L: Reduce dose by 50%

Koren, 1992: Bilirubin 2.5-5.1 mg/dL or AST >180 units/L: Reduce dose by 50%

Perry, 1982:

Bilirubin 1.5-3 mg/dL or AST 60-180 units/L: Reduce dose by 50%

Bilirubin >3 mg/dL or AST >180 units/L: Do not administer

Administration

Oral: Doses ≤400 mg/day as a single once daily dose; doses >400 mg should be given in 2-4 divided doses. If necessary, the injection may be used for oral administration.

I.V.: As a bolus or 24-hour continuous infusion; bolus infusions are usually administered over at least 45-60 minutes. Infusion of doses in ≤30 minutes greatly increases the risk of hypotension. Etoposide injection contains polysorbate 80 which may cause leaching of diethylhexyl phthalate (DEHP), a plasticizer contained in polyvinyl chloride (PVC) tubing.

Administration through non-PVC (low sorbing) tubing will minimize patient exposure to DEHP. Concentrations >0.4 mg/mL are very unstable and may precipitate within a few minutes. For large doses, where dilution to ≤0.4 mg/mL is not feasible, consideration should be given to slow infusion of the undiluted drug through a running normal saline, dextrose or saline/dextrose infusion; or use of etoposide phosphate. Etoposide solutions of 0.1-0.4 mg/mL may be filtered through a 0.22 micron filter without damage to the filter or significant loss of drug.

Monitoring Parameters CBC with differential, platelet count, and hemoglobin, vital signs (blood pressure), bilirubin, and renal function tests

Dosage Forms

Capsule, softgel:
VePesid®: 50 mg

Injection, solution: 20 mg/mL (5 mL, 25 mL, 50 mL)
Toposar®: 20 mg/mL (5 mL, 25 mL, 50 mL) [contains alcohol 33% and polysorbate 80]

Etoposide Phosphate (e toe POE side FOS fate)

U.S. Brand Names Etopophos®

Pharmacologic Category Antineoplastic Agent, Podophyllotoxin Derivative

Use Treatment of refractory testicular tumors; treatment of small cell lung cancer

Pregnancy Risk Factor D

Pregnancy Implications Animal studies have demonstrated teratogenicity and fetal loss. There are no adequate and well-controlled studies in pregnant women. Women of child-bearing potential should be advised to avoid pregnancy.

Lactation Enters breast milk/contraindicated

Medication Safety Issues

Sound-alike/look-alike issues:

Etoposide may be confused with teniposide

Etoposide phosphate is a prodrug of etoposide and is rapidly converted in the plasma to etoposide. To avoid confusion or dosing errors, **dosage should be expressed as the desired etoposide dose,** not as the etoposide phosphate dose (eg, etoposide phosphate equivalent to ____ mg etoposide).

High alert medication: The Institute for Safe Medication Practices (ISMP) includes this medication among its list of drugs which have a heightened risk of causing significant patient harm when used in error.

Contraindications Hypersensitivity to etoposide, etoposide phosphate, or any component of the formulation; pregnancy

Warnings/Precautions Hazardous agent - use appropriate precautions for handling and disposal. **[U.S. Boxed Warning]: Severe myelosuppression with resulting infection or bleeding may occur.** Treatment should be withheld for platelets <50,000/mm^3 or absolute neutrophil count (ANC) <500/mm^3. May cause anaphylactic reaction manifested by chills, fever, tachycardia, bronchospasm, dyspnea, and hypotension (higher concentrations were associated with higher rates of reactions in children). Infusion should be interrupted and medications for the treatment of anaphylaxis should be available for immediate use. Dosage should be adjusted in patients with hepatic or renal impairment. Doses of etoposide phosphate >175mg/m^2 have not been evaluated. Use caution in elderly patients (may be more likely to develop severe myelosuppression and/or GI effects. **[U.S. Boxed Warning]: Should be administered under the supervision of an experienced cancer chemotherapy physician.** Safety and efficacy in children have not been established.

Adverse Reactions Refer to Etoposide monograph *on page 670* for details.

Overdosage/Toxicology Refer to Etoposide monograph *on page 670* for details.

Drug Interactions

Cytochrome P450 Effect: Substrate of CYP1A2 (minor), 2E1 (minor), 3A4 (major); **Inhibits** CYP2C9 (weak), 3A4 (weak)

Increased Effect/Toxicity: Cyclosporine may increase the levels of etoposide; consider reducing the dose of etoposide by 50%. Etoposide may increase the effects/toxicity of warfarin. CYP3A4 inhibitors may increase the levels/effects of etoposide; example inhibitors include azole antifungals, clarithromycin, diclofenac, doxycycline, erythromycin, imatinib, isoniazid, nefazodone, nicardipine, propofol, protease inhibitors, quinidine, telithromycin, and verapamil.

Decreased Effect: Barbiturates and phenytoin may decrease the levels/effects of etoposide; monitor. CYP3A4 inducers may decrease the levels/effects of etoposide; example inducers include aminoglutethimide, carbamazepine, nafcillin, nevirapine, phenobarbital, phenytoin, and rifamycins.

Ethanol/Nutrition/Herb Interactions

Ethanol: Avoid ethanol (may increase GI irritation).

Herb/Nutraceutical: St John's wort may decrease etoposide levels.

Stability Store intact vials of injection under refrigeration 2°C to 8°C (36°F to 46°F). Protect from light. Reconstitute vials with 5 mL or 10 mL SWI, D$_5$W, NS, bacteriostatic SWI, or bacteriostatic NS to a concentration of 20 mg/mL or 10 mg/mL etoposide equivalent. These solutions may be administered without further dilution or may be diluted in 50-500 mL of D$_5$W or NS to a concentration as low as 0.1 mg/mL.

Reconstituted etoposide phosphate is stable refrigerated at 2°C to 8°C (36°F to 47°F) for 7 days. Undiluted solutions are stable for 24 hours at room temperature of 20°C to 25°C (68°F to 77°F) when reconstituted with SWI, D$_5$W or NS; and stable for 48 hours at room temperature when reconstituted with bacteriostatic SWI or NS. Further diluted solutions are stable at room temperature 20°C to 25°C (68°F to 77°F) or under refrigeration 2°C to 8°C (36°F to 47°F) for up to 24 hours.

Mechanism of Action Etoposide phosphate is converted *in vivo* to the active moiety, etoposide, by dephosphorylation. Etoposide inhibits mitotic activity; inhibits cells from entering prophase; inhibits DNA synthesis. Initially thought to be mitotic inhibitors similar to podophyllotoxin, but actually have no effect on microtubule assembly. However, later shown to induce

(Continued)

Etoposide Phosphate *(Continued)*

DNA strand breakage and inhibition of topoisomerase II (an enzyme which breaks and repairs DNA); etoposide acts in late S or early G2 phases.

Pharmacodynamics/Kinetics

Distribution: Average V_d: 7-17 L/m^2; poor penetration across blood-brain barrier; concentrations in CSF being <10% that of plasma

Protein binding: 94% to 97%

Metabolism:

Etoposide phosphate: Rapidly and completely converted to etoposide in plasma

Etoposide: Hepatic to hydroxy acid and cislactone metabolites

Half-life elimination: Terminal: 4-11 hours; Children: Normal renal/hepatic function: 6-8 hours

Excretion: Urine (as unchanged drug and metabolites); feces (2% to 16%)

Children: I.V.: Urine (≤55% as unchanged drug)

Dosage Refer to individual protocols. Adults: **Note:** Etoposide phosphate is a prodrug of etoposide, doses should be expressed as the desired **ETOPOSIDE** dose; **not** as the etoposide phosphate dose. (eg, etoposide phosphate equivalent to _____ mg etoposide).

Small cell lung cancer (in combination with other approved chemotherapeutic drugs): I.V.: Etoposide 35 mg/m^2/day for 4 days to 50 mg/m^2/day for 5 days. Courses are repeated at 3- to 4-week intervals after adequate recovery from any toxicity.

Testicular cancer (in combination with other approved chemotherapeutic agents): I.V.: Etoposide 50-100 mg/m^2/day on days 1-5 to 100 mg/m^2/day on days 1, 3, and 5. Courses are repeated at 3- to 4-week intervals after adequate recovery from any toxicity.

Dosage adjustment in renal impairment:

Manufacturer recommended guidelines:

Cl_{cr} 15-50 mL/minute: Administer 75% of normal dose

Cl_{cr} <15 mL minute: Data are available; consider further dose reductions

Aronoff, 1999:

Cl_{cr} 10-50 mL/minute: Administer 75% of normal dose

Cl_{cr} <10 mL minute: Administer 50% of normal dose

Hemodialysis: Supplemental dose is not necessary

Peritoneal dialysis: Supplemental dose is not necessary

CAPD effects: Unknown

CAVH effects: Dose for Cl_{cr} 10-50 mL/minute (Aronoff, 1999)

Dosage adjustment in hepatic impairment:

Bilirubin 1.5-3 mg/dL or AST 60-180 units: Reduce dose by 50%

Bilirubin 3-5 mg/dL or AST >180 units: Reduce by 75%

Bilirubin >5 mg/dL: Do not administer

Administration Infuse over 5-210 minutes.

Monitoring Parameters CBC with differential, platelet count, bilirubin, renal function

Additional Information Etoposide phosphate 113.5 mg is equivalent to etoposide 100 mg. Dosages should always be expressed, and calculated, as the desired **etoposide** dose.

Dosage Forms Injection, powder for reconstitution, as base: 100 mg

- **Etrafon®** **(Can)** *see* Amitriptyline and Perphenazine *on page 103*
- **Eudal®-SR** *see* Guaifenesin and Pseudoephedrine *on page 819*
- **Euflex®** **(Can)** *see* Flutamide *on page 737*
- **Euflexxa™** *see* Hyaluronate and Derivatives *on page 841*
- **Euglucon®** **(Can)** *see* GlyBURIDE *on page 803*
- **Eulexin®** *see* Flutamide *on page 737*
- **Eurax®** *see* Crotamiton *on page 424*
- **Everone® 200 (Can)** *see* Testosterone *on page 1653*
- **Evista®** *see* Raloxifene *on page 1480*
- **Evoclin™** *see* Clindamycin *on page 389*
- **Evoxac®** *see* Cevimeline *on page 338*
- **Evra®** **(Can)** *see* Ethinyl Estradiol and Norelgestromin *on page 655*
- **Exactacain™** *see* Benzocaine, Butamben, and Tetracaine *on page 207*
- **Excedrin® Extra Strength [OTC]** *see* Acetaminophen, Aspirin, and Caffeine *on page 34*
- **Excedrin® Migraine [OTC]** *see* Acetaminophen, Aspirin, and Caffeine *on page 34*
- **Excedrin® P.M. [OTC]** *see* Acetaminophen and Diphenhydramine *on page 31*
- **ExeClear** *see* Hydrocodone and Guaifenesin *on page 849*
- **ExeCof-XP** *see* Hydrocodone and Guaifenesin *on page 849*
- **ExeFen-PD** *see* Guaifenesin and Phenylephrine *on page 818*
- **Exelderm®** *see* Sulconazole *on page 1609*
- **Exelon®** *see* Rivastigmine *on page 1526*

Exemestane *(ex e MES tane)*

U.S. Brand Names Aromasin®

Canadian Brand Names Aromasin®

Pharmacologic Category Antineoplastic Agent, Aromatase Inactivator

Use Treatment of advanced breast cancer in postmenopausal women whose disease has progressed following tamoxifen therapy; adjuvant treatment of postmenopausal estrogen receptor-positive early breast cancer following 2-3 years of tamoxifen (for a total of 5 years of adjuvant therapy)

Pregnancy Risk Factor D

Pregnancy Implications Exemestane has been associated with prolonged gestation, abnormal or difficult labor, increased resorption, reduced number of live fetuses, decreased fetal weight, and retarded ossification in rats. It is not indicated for premenopausal women, but if exposure occurred during pregnancy, risk to the fetus and potential risk for loss of the pregnancy should be discussed.

Lactation Excretion in breast milk unknown/use caution

Contraindications Hypersensitivity to exemestane or any component of the formulation; pregnancy

Warnings/Precautions Hazardous agent - use appropriate precautions for handling and disposal. Exemestane should not be administered concurrently with estrogen-containing drugs; not recommended for use in premenopausal women.

Adverse Reactions

>10%:

Cardiovascular: Hypertension (5% to 15%)

Central nervous system: Fatigue (8% to 22%), insomnia (11% to 14%), pain (13%), headache (7% to 13%), depression (6% to 13%)

Dermatological: Hyperhidrosis (4% to 18%), alopecia (15%)

Endocrine & metabolic: Hot flashes (13% to 21%)

Gastrointestinal: Nausea (9% to 18%), abdominal pain (6% to 11%)

Hepatic: Alkaline phosphatase increased (14% to 15%)

Neuromuscular & skeletal: Arthralgia (15% to 29%)

1% to 10%:

Cardiovascular: Edema (6% to 7%); cardiac ischemic events (2%: MI, angina, myocardial ischemia); chest pain

Central nervous system: Dizziness (8% to 10%), anxiety (4% to 10%), fever (5%), confusion, hypoesthesia

Dermatologic: Dermatitis (8%), itching, rash

Endocrine & metabolic: Weight gain (8%)

Gastrointestinal: Diarrhea (4% to 10%), vomiting (7%), anorexia (6%), constipation (5%), appetite increased (3%), dyspepsia

Genitourinary: Urinary tract infection

Hepatic: Bilirubin increased (5% to 7%)

Neuromuscular & skeletal: Back pain (9%), limb pain (9%), osteoarthritis (6%), weakness (6%), osteoporosis (5%), pathological fracture (4%), paresthesia (3%), carpal tunnel syndrome (2%), cramps (2%)

Ocular: Visual disturbances (5%)

Renal: Creatinine increased (6%)

Respiratory: Dyspnea (10%), cough (6%), bronchitis, pharyngitis, rhinitis, sinusitis, upper respiratory infection

Miscellaneous: Influenza-like symptoms (6%), diaphoresis (6%), lymphedema, infection

<1% (Limited to important or life-threatening): Cardiac failure, endometrial hyperplasia, GGT increased, neuropathy, osteochondrosis, thromboembolism, transaminases increased, trigger finger, uterine polyps

A dose-dependent decrease in sex hormone-binding globulin has been observed with daily doses of 25 mg or more. Serum luteinizing hormone and follicle-stimulating hormone levels have increased with this medicine.

Overdosage/Toxicology In case of overdose, treatment should be symptom-directed and supportive. Mice given 3200 mg/kg as a single dose died. This would be equivalent to 640 times the recommended human dose on a mg/m^2 basis. Rats and dogs died at higher single doses equivalent to 2000-4000 times the recommended human dose on a mg/m^2 basis.

Drug Interactions

Cytochrome P450 Effect: Substrate of CYP3A4 (major)

Decreased Effect: CYP3A4 inducers may decrease the levels/effects of exemestane; example inducers include aminoglutethimide, carbamazepine, efavirenz, fosphenytoin, nafcillin, nevirapine, oxcarbazepine, pentobarbital, phenobarbital, phenytoin, primidone, rifabutin, rifampin, and rifapentine; adjustment required with potent inducers.

Ethanol/Nutrition/Herb Interactions

Food: Plasma levels increased by 40% when exemestane was taken with a fatty meal.

Herb/Nutraceutical: St John's wort may decrease exemestane levels. Avoid black cohosh, dong quai in estrogen-dependent tumors.

Stability Store at 25°C (77°F)

Mechanism of Action Exemestane is an irreversible, steroidal aromatase inactivator. It prevents conversion of androgens to estrogens by tying up the enzyme aromatase. In breast cancers where growth is estrogen-dependent, this medicine will lower circulating estrogens.

Pharmacodynamics/Kinetics

Absorption: Rapid and moderate (~42%) following oral administration; absorption increases ~40% following high-fat meal

Distribution: Extensive

Protein binding: 90%, primarily to albumin and α_1-acid glycoprotein

Metabolism: Extensively hepatic; oxidation (CYP3A4) of methylene group, reduction of 17-keto group with formation of many secondary metabolites; metabolites are inactive

Half-life elimination: 24 hours

Time to peak: Women with breast cancer: 1.2 hours

Excretion: Urine (<1% as unchanged drug, 39% to 45% as metabolites); feces (36% to 48%)

Dosage Adults: Oral: 25 mg once daily

Dosage adjustment with CYP3A4 inducers: 50 mg once daily when used with potent inducers (eg, rifampin, phenytoin)

Dosing adjustment in renal/hepatic impairment: Safety of chronic doses has not been studied

Dietary Considerations Take after a meal; patients on aromatase inhibitor therapy should receive vitamin D and calcium supplements.

Administration Administer after a meal.

Dosage Forms Tablet: 25 mg

Exenatide (ex EN a tide)

U.S. Brand Names Byetta™
Index Terms AC002993; Exendin-4; LY2148568
Pharmacologic Category Antidiabetic Agent, Incretin Mimetic
Use Management (adjunctive) of type 2 diabetes mellitus (noninsulin dependent, NIDDM)
Pregnancy Risk Factor C
Pregnancy Implications There are no adequate and well-controlled studies in pregnant women. Decreased fetal and neonatal growth and adverse skeletal effects were observed in animal studies. Insulin is the drug of choice for the control of diabetes in pregnancy. Exenatide should be used only if potential benefit outweighs possible risk.
Lactation Excretion in breast milk unknown/use caution
Contraindications Hypersensitivity to exenatide or any component of the formulation; type 1 diabetes; diabetic ketoacidosis
Warnings/Precautions Mechanism requires the presence of insulin, therefore use in type 1 diabetes (insulin dependent, IDDM) or diabetic ketoacidosis is not recommended; it is not a substitute for insulin in insulin requiring patients. Should be used as an adjunct to diet and exercise in patients previously treated with a sulfonylurea, metformin, or a combination of these agents. Concurrent use with other hypoglycemic agents and/or insulin therapy has not been evaluated. May increase the risk of hypoglycemia in patients receiving sulfonylurea therapy (risk of hypoglycemia was not increased when added to metformin monotherapy). Risk of hypoglycemia is related to the dosage of both exenatide and the sulfonylurea.

Exenatide is frequently associated with gastrointestinal adverse effects and is not recommended for use in patients with gastroparesis or severe gastrointestinal disease. Gastrointestinal effects may be dose-related and may decrease in frequency/severity with gradual titration and continued use. Use may be associated with the development of anti-exenatide antibodies; low titers are not associated with a loss of efficacy, however high titers (observed in 6% of patients in clinical studies) may result in an attenuation of response. May be associated with weight loss (due to reduced intake) independent of the change in hemoglobin A_{1c}. Not recommended in severe renal impairment (Cl_{cr} <30 mL/minute). Safety and efficacy have not been established in children.

Adverse Reactions
>10%:
    Endocrine & metabolic: Hypoglycemia (with concurrent sulfonylurea therapy 14% to 36%; frequency similar to placebo with metformin therapy)
    Gastrointestinal: Nausea (44%), vomiting (13%), diarrhea (13%)
    Miscellaneous: Anti-exenatide antibodies (low titers 38%, high titers 6%)
1% to 10%:
    Central nervous system: Dizziness (9%), headache (9%)
    Endocrine & metabolic: Appetite decreased
    Gastrointestinal: Dyspepsia (6%), GERD
    Neuromuscular & skeletal: Weakness
    Miscellaneous: Feeling jittery (9%), diaphoresis increased

Drug Interactions
    Decreased Effect: Note: Due to its effects on gastric emptying, exenatide may reduce the rate and extent of absorption of orally-administered drugs. Should be used with caution in patients receiving medications which increase rapid absorption from the gastrointestinal tract. Administration of medications 1 hour prior to the use of exenatide has been recommended by the manufacturer when optimal drug absorption and peak levels are important to the overall therapeutic effect (such as with antibiotics and/or oral contraceptives).
Ethanol/Nutrition/Herb Interactions Ethanol: Caution with ethanol (may cause hypoglycemia)
Stability Store under refrigeration at 2°C to 8°C (36°F to 46°F); do not freeze (discard if freezing occurs). Protect from light. Pen should be discarded 30 days after initial use.
Mechanism of Action Exenatide is an analog of the hormone incretin (glucagon-like peptide 1 or GLP-1) which increases insulin secretion, increases B-cell growth/replication, slows gastric emptying, and may decrease food intake. When added to sulfonylureas and/or metformin, it results in additional lowering of hemoglobin A_{1c} by approximately 0.5% to 1%.
Pharmacodynamics/Kinetics
    Distribution: V_d: 28.3 L
    Metabolism: Minimal systemic metabolism; proteolytic degradation may occur following glomerular filtration
    Half-life elimination: 2.4 hours
    Time to peak, plasma: SubQ: 2.1 hours
    Excretion: Urine (majority of dose)
Dosage SubQ: Adults: Initial: 5 mcg twice daily within 60 minutes prior to a meal (morning and evening); after 1 month, may be increased to 10 mcg twice daily (based on response)
    Dosage adjustment in renal impairment:
        Cl_{cr} ≥30 mL/minute: No adjustment necessary
        Cl_{cr} <30 mL/minute: Not recommended
Administration Should be administered subcutaneously in the upper arm, thigh, or abdomen. Administer within 60 minutes prior to a meal (morning and evening). Set up each new pen before the first use by priming it. See pen user manual for further details. Dial the dose into the dose window before each administration.
Monitoring Parameters Serum glucose, hemoglobin A_{1c}, and renal function
Additional Information A dosing strategy which employs progressive dose escalation of exenatide (initiating at 0.02 mcg/kg 3 times daily and increasing in increments of 0.02 mcg/kg every 3 days) has been described, limiting the frequency and severity of gastrointestinal adverse effects. The complexity of this regimen may limit its clinical application.

In animal models, exenatide has been a useful adjunctive therapy when added to immunotherapy protocols, resulting in recovery of beta cell function and sustained remission.

Dosage Forms Injection, solution [prefilled pen]: 250 mcg/mL (1.2 mL [provides 5 mcg/dose]; 2.4 mL [provides 10 mcg/dose])

♦ **Exendin-4** see Exenatide on page 676
♦ **ExeTuss** see Guaifenesin and Phenylephrine on page 818
♦ **ExeTuss-GP** see Guaifenesin and Phenylephrine on page 818
♦ **Exjade®** see Deferasirox on page 465
♦ **Exsel® [DSC]** see Selenium Sulfide on page 1555
♦ **Extendryl** see Chlorpheniramine, Phenylephrine, and Methscopolamine on page 353
♦ **Extendryl® HC** see Hydrocodone and Guaifenesin on page 849
♦ **Extendryl JR** see Chlorpheniramine, Phenylephrine, and Methscopolamine on page 353
♦ **Extendryl SR** see Chlorpheniramine, Phenylephrine, and Methscopolamine on page 353
♦ **Extraneal®** see Icodextrin on page 877
♦ **Exubera®** see Insulin Inhalation on page 911
♦ **EYE001** see Pegaptanib on page 1319
♦ **Eyestil (Can)** see Hyaluronate and Derivatives on page 841
♦ **EZ-Char™ [OTC]** see Charcoal on page 338

Ezetimibe (ez ET i mibe)

U.S. Brand Names Zetia™
Canadian Brand Names Ezetrol®
Pharmacologic Category Antilipemic Agent, 2-Azetidinone
Additional Appendix Information
Hyperlipidemia Management on page 2058
Lipid-Lowering Agents on page 1887
Use Use in combination with dietary therapy for the treatment of primary hypercholesterolemia (as monotherapy or in combination with HMG-CoA reductase inhibitors); homozygous sitosterolemia; homozygous familial hypercholesterolemia (in combination with atorvastatin or simvastatin); mixed hyperlipidemia (in combination with fenofibrate)
Pregnancy Risk Factor C
Pregnancy Implications Safety and efficacy have not been established; use during pregnancy only if the potential benefit to the mother outweighs the possible risk to the fetus.
Lactation Excretion in breast milk unknown/not recommended
Medication Safety Issues
Sound-alike/look-alike issues:
Zetia™ may be confused with Zestril®
Contraindications Hypersensitivity to ezetimibe or any component of the formulation
Warnings/Precautions Secondary causes of hyperlipidemia should be ruled out prior to therapy. Use caution with renal or mild hepatic impairment; not recommended for use with moderate or severe hepatic impairment. Use of ezetimibe and fenofibrate (160 mg daily) may increase rate of cholecystectomy. Safety and efficacy have not been established in patients <10 years of age.
Adverse Reactions
1% to 10%:
Cardiovascular: Chest pain (3%), dizziness (3%), fatigue (2%)
Central nervous system: Headache (8%)
Gastrointestinal: Diarrhea (3% to 4%), abdominal pain (3%)
Neuromuscular & skeletal: Arthralgia (4%)
Respiratory: Sinusitis (4% to 5%), pharyngitis (2% to 3%, placebo 2%)
Postmarketing and/or case reports: Anaphylaxis, cholecystitis, cholelithiasis, CPK increased, hepatitis, hypersensitivity reactions (including angioedema and rash), myalgia, myopathy, nausea, pancreatitis, rhabdomyolysis, thrombocytopenia, transaminases increased, urticaria
Overdosage/Toxicology Doses of up to 50 mg/day were well-tolerated. Treatment should be symptom-directed and supportive.
Drug Interactions
Increased Effect/Toxicity: Cyclosporine may increase plasma levels of ezetimibe. Fibric acid derivatives may increase serum concentrations of ezetimibe. Ezetimibe may increase serum levels of cyclosporine.
Decreased Effect: Bile acid sequestrants may decrease ezetimibe bioavailability; administer ezetimibe ≥2 hours before or ≥4 hours after bile acid sequestrants.
Stability Store at controlled room temperature of 15°C to 30°C (59°F to 86°F). Protect from moisture.
Mechanism of Action Inhibits absorption of cholesterol at the brush border of the small intestine via the sterol transporter, Niemann-Pick C1-Like 1 (NPC1L1). This leads to a decreased delivery of cholesterol to the liver, reduction of hepatic cholesterol stores and an increased clearance of cholesterol from the blood; decreases total C, LDL-cholesterol (LDL-C), ApoB, and triglycerides (TG) while increasing HDL-cholesterol (HDL-C).
Pharmacodynamics/Kinetics
Protein binding: >90% to plasma proteins
Metabolism: Undergoes conjugation in the small intestine and liver; forms metabolite (active); may undergo enterohepatic recycling
Bioavailability: Variable
Half-life elimination: 22 hours (ezetimibe and metabolite)
Time to peak, plasma: 4-12 hours
Excretion: Feces (78%, 69% as ezetimibe); urine (11%, 9% as metabolite)
Dosage Oral:
Hyperlipidemias: Children ≥10 years and Adults: 10 mg/day
Sitosterolemia: Adults: 10 mg/day
Elderly: Refer to Adults dosing
(Continued)

Ezetimibe *(Continued)*

Dosage adjustment in renal impairment: Bioavailability increased with severe impairment; no dosing adjustment recommended

Dosage adjustment in hepatic impairment: Bioavailability increased with hepatic impairment

Mild impairment (Child-Pugh score 5-6): No dosing adjustment necessary

Moderate to severe impairment (Child-Pugh score 7-15): Use of ezetimibe not recommended

Dietary Considerations May be taken without regard to meals. Before initiation of therapy, patients should be placed on a standard cholesterol-lowering diet for 6 weeks and the diet should be continued during drug therapy.

Administration May be administered without regard to meals. May be taken at the same time as HMG-CoA reductase inhibitors. Administer ≥2 hours before or ≥4 hours after bile acid sequestrants.

Monitoring Parameters Total cholesterol profile prior to therapy, and when clinically indicated and/or periodically thereafter. When used in combination with fenofibrate, monitor LFTs and signs and symptoms of cholelithiasis.

Additional Information When studied in combination with fenofibrate for mixed hyperlipidemia, the dose of fenofibrate was 160 mg daily.

Dosage Forms Tablet: 10 mg [capsule shaped]

Ezetimibe and Simvastatin (ez ET i mibe & SIM va stat in)

U.S. Brand Names Vytorin®

Pharmacologic Category Antilipemic Agent, 2-Azetidinone; Antilipemic Agent, HMG-CoA Reductase Inhibitor

Use Used in combination with dietary modification for the treatment of primary hypercholesterolemia and homozygous familial hypercholesterolemia

Pregnancy Risk Factor X

Dosage Oral: Adults:

Homozygous familial hypercholesterolemia: Ezetimibe 10 mg and simvastatin 40 mg once daily or ezetimibe 10 mg and simvastatin 80 mg once daily in the evening. Dosing range: Ezetimibe 10 mg and simvastatin 10-80 mg once daily.

Hyperlipidemias: Initial: Ezetimibe 10 mg and simvastatin 20 mg once daily in the evening

Patients who require less aggressive reduction in LDL-C: Initial: Ezetimibe 10 mg and simvastatin 10 mg once daily

Patients who require >55% reduction in LDL-C: Initial: Ezetimibe 10 mg and simvastatin 40 mg once daily

Dosage adjustment with concomitant medications:

Amiodarone or verapamil: Dose should not exceed ezetimibe 10 mg and simvastatin 20 mg once daily.

Danazol or cyclosporine: Patient must first demonstrate tolerance to simvastatin ≥5 mg once daily. Dose should not exceed ezetimibe 10 mg and simvastatin 10 mg once daily.

Gemfibrozil: Although concurrent use is not recommended by manufacturer, dose should not exceed ezetimibe 10 mg and simvastatin 10 mg once daily.

Dosage adjustment in renal impairment: Dosage adjustment unnecessary in mild to moderate renal dysfunction. In severe dysfunction, start only if patient tolerates 5 mg daily of simvastatin; monitor closely.

Dosage adjustment in hepatic impairment: Dosage adjustment unnecessary in mild hepatic dysfunction.

Additional Information Complete prescribing information for this medication should be consulted for additional detail.

Dosage Forms Tablet:

10/10: Ezetimibe 10 mg and simvastatin 10 mg

10/20: Ezetimibe 10 mg and simvastatin 20 mg

10/40: Ezetimibe 10 mg and simvastatin 40 mg

10/80: Ezetimibe 10 mg and simvastatin 80 mg

♦ **Ezetrol® (Can)** *see* Ezetimibe *on page 677*

♦ **E•R•O [OTC]** *see* Carbamide Peroxide *on page 287*

♦ **F₃T** *see* Trifluridine *on page 1741*

♦ **Fabrazyme®** *see* Agalsidase Beta *on page 53*

♦ **Factive®** *see* Gemifloxacin *on page 788*

Factor VIIa (Recombinant) (FAK ter SEV en aye ree KOM be nant)

U.S. Brand Names NovoSeven®

Canadian Brand Names Niastase®

Index Terms Coagulation Factor VIIa; Eptacog Alfa (Activated); rFVIIa

Pharmacologic Category Antihemophilic Agent; Blood Product Derivative

Use Treatment of bleeding episodes and prevention of bleeding in surgical interventions in patients with hemophilia A or B with inhibitors to factor VIII or factor IX and in patients with congenital factor VII deficiency

Pregnancy Risk Factor C

Pregnancy Implications Animal studies have demonstrated fetal loss, but no evidence of teratogenic effects. There are no adequate and well-controlled studies in pregnant women. Use only if the potential benefit justifies the potential risk to the fetus.

Lactation Excretion in breast milk unknown/compatible

Medication Safety Issues

Sound-alike/look-alike issues:

NovoSeven® may be confused with Novacet®

Contraindications Hypersensitivity to factor VII or any component of the formulation; hypersensitivity to mouse, hamster, or bovine proteins

Warnings/Precautions Patients should be monitored for signs and symptoms of activation of the coagulation system or thrombosis. Thrombotic events may be increased in patients with disseminated intravascular coagulation (DIC), advanced atherosclerotic disease, sepsis, crush injury, or concomitant treatment with prothrombin complex concentrates. Decreased dosage or discontinuation is warranted in confirmed DIC. Efficacy with prolonged infusions and data evaluating this agent's long-term adverse effects are limited.

Adverse Reactions

1% to 10%:
    Cardiovascular: Hypertension
    Central nervous system: Fever
    Hematologic: Hemorrhage, decreased plasma fibrinogen
    Neuromuscular & skeletal: Hemarthrosis

<1% (Limited to important or life-threatening): Abnormal renal function, allergic reaction, anaphylactic reaction, arterial thrombosis, arthrosis, bradycardia, cerebral infarction and/or ischemia, coagulation disorder, consumptive coagulopathy, decreased therapeutic response, deep vein thrombosis, disseminated intravascular coagulation (DIC), edema, fibrinolysis increased, gastrointestinal bleeding, headache, hypersensitivity, hypotension, injection site reactions, intracranial hemorrhage, localized phlebitis, MI, myocardial ischemia, pain, pneumonia, prothrombin decreased, pruritus, pulmonary embolism, purpura, rash, splenic hematoma, thrombophlebitis, thrombosis, vomiting

Overdosage/Toxicology Experience with human overdose is limited. An increased risk of thrombotic events may occur. Treatment is symptomatic and supportive.

Stability Store under refrigeration at 2°C to 8°C (36°F to 46°F). Protect from light. Prior to reconstitution, bring vials to room temperature. Reconstitute each vial to a final concentration of 0.6 mg/mL as follows:
    1.2 mg vial: 2.2 mL sterile water
    2.4 mg vial: 4.3 mL sterile water
    4.8 mg vial: 8.5 mL sterile water

Add diluent along wall of vial; do not inject directly into powder. Gently swirl until dissolved. Reconstituted solutions may be stored at room temperature or under refrigeration, but must be infused within 3 hours of reconstitution. Do not freeze reconstituted solutions. Do not store reconstituted solutions in syringes.

Mechanism of Action Recombinant factor VIIa, a vitamin K-dependent glycoprotein, promotes hemostasis by activating the extrinsic pathway of the coagulation cascade. It replaces deficient activated coagulation factor VII, which complexes with tissue factor and may activate coagulation factor X to Xa and factor IX to IXa. When complexed with other factors, coagulation factor Xa converts prothrombin to thrombin, a key step in the formation of a fibrin-platelet hemostatic plug.

Pharmacodynamics/Kinetics

Distribution: V_d: 103 mL/kg (78-139)
Half-life elimination: 2.3 hours (1.7-2.7)
Excretion: Clearance: 33 mL/kg/hour (27-49)

Dosage Children and Adults: I.V. administration only: Hemophilia A or B with inhibitors:
Bleeding episodes: 90 mcg/kg every 2 hours until hemostasis is achieved or until the treatment is judged ineffective. The dose and interval may be adjusted based upon the severity of bleeding and the degree of hemostasis achieved. For patients experiencing severe bleeds, dosing should be continued at 3- to 6-hour intervals after hemostasis has been achieved and the duration of dosing should be minimized.

Surgical interventions: 90 mcg/kg immediately before surgery, repeat at 2-hour intervals for the duration of surgery. Continue every 2 hours for 48 hours, then every 2-6 hours until healed for minor surgery; continue every 2 hours for 5 days, then every 4 hours until healed for major surgery.

Congenital factor VII deficiency: Bleeding episodes and surgical interventions: 15-30 mcg/kg every 4-6 hours until hemostasis. Doses as low as 10 mcg/kg have been effective.

Dietary Considerations Contains sodium 0.44 mEq/mg rFVIIa

Administration I.V. administration only; bolus over 2-5 minutes; administer within 3 hours after reconstitution

Monitoring Parameters Monitor for evidence of hemostasis; although the prothrombin time, aPTT, and factor VII clotting activity have no correlation with achieving hemostasis, these parameters may be useful as adjunct tests to evaluate efficacy and guide dose or interval adjustments

Dosage Forms Injection, powder for reconstitution [preservative free]: 1.2 mg, 2.4 mg, 4.8 mg [latex free; contains sodium 0.44 mEq/mg rFVIIa, polysorbate 80]

- ♦ **Factor VIII (Human)** see Antihemophilic Factor (Human) on page 133
- ♦ **Factor VIII (Human)** see Antihemophilic Factor/von Willebrand Factor Complex (Human) on page 136
- ♦ **Factor VIII (Recombinant)** see Antihemophilic Factor (Recombinant) on page 135

Factor IX (FAK ter nyne)

U.S. Brand Names AlphaNine® SD; BeneFix®; Mononine®
Canadian Brand Names BeneFix®; Immunine® VH; Mononine®
Pharmacologic Category Antihemophilic Agent; Blood Product Derivative
Use Control bleeding in patients with factor IX deficiency (hemophilia B or Christmas disease)
Pregnancy Risk Factor C
Contraindications Hypersensitivity to mouse protein (Mononine®), hamster protein (BeneFix®), or any component of the formulation
Warnings/Precautions Use with caution in patients with liver dysfunction; some products prepared from pooled human plasma - the risk of viral transmission is not totally eradicated; monitor patients who receive repeated doses twice daily with PTT and level of factor being replaced (eg, IX). Observe closely for signs or symptoms of intravascular coagulation or (Continued)

Factor IX *(Continued)*

thrombosis. Caution should be exercised when administering to patients with liver disease, postoperatively, neonates, or patients at risk of thromboembolic phenomena or disseminated intravascular coagulation because of the potential risk of thromboembolic complications.

AlphaNine® SD, Mononine® contain **nondetectable levels of factors II, VII, and X** (<0.0025 units per factor IX unit using standard coagulation assays) and are, therefore, **NOT INDICATED** for replacement therapy of any of these clotting factors.

BeneFix®, Mononine® are **NOT INDICATED** in the treatment or reversal of coumarin-induced anticoagulation or in a hemorrhagic state caused by hepatitis-induced lack of production of liver dependent coagulation factors.

Adverse Reactions Frequency not defined.

Cardiovascular: Angioedema, cyanosis, flushing, hypotension, tightness in chest, tightness in neck, thrombosis (following high dosages because of presence of activated clotting factors)

Central nervous system: Fever, headache, chills, somnolence, dizziness, drowsiness, light-headedness

Dermatologic: Urticaria, rash

Gastrointestinal: Nausea, vomiting, abnormal taste

Hematologic: Disseminated intravascular coagulation (DIC)

Local: Injection site discomfort

Neuromuscular & skeletal: Tingling

Respiratory: Dyspnea, laryngeal edema, allergic rhinitis

Miscellaneous: Transient fever (following rapid administration), anaphylaxis, burning sensation in jaw/skull

Overdosage/Toxicology Symptoms include disseminated intravascular coagulation (DIC).

Drug Interactions

Increased Effect/Toxicity: Do not coadminister with aminocaproic acid; may increase risk for thrombosis.

Stability When stored at refrigerator temperature, 2°C to 8°C (36°F to 46°F), coagulation factor IX is stable for the period indicated by the expiration date on its label. Avoid freezing which may damage container for the diluent.

AlphaNine® SD: May also be stored at ≤30°C (≤86°F) for up to 3 months.

BeneFix®: May also be stored at ≤25°C (≤77°F) for up to 6 months.

Mononine®: May also be stored at ≤30°C (≤86°F) for up to 1 month. When reconstituted to ~100 int. units/mL, infusion rate should be up to 225 units/minute (2 mL/minute).

Stability of parenteral admixture at room temperature (25°C): 3 hours

Mechanism of Action Replaces deficient clotting factor IX; concentrate of factor IX; hemophilia B, or Christmas disease, is an X-linked inherited disorder of blood coagulation characterized by insufficient or abnormal synthesis of the clotting protein factor IX. Factor IX is a vitamin K-dependent coagulation factor which is synthesized in the liver. Factor IX is activated by factor XIa in the intrinsic coagulation pathway. Activated factor IX (IXa), in combination with factor VII:C activates factor X to Xa, resulting ultimately in the conversion of prothrombin to thrombin and the formation of a fibrin clot. The infusion of exogenous factor IX to replace the deficiency present in hemophilia B temporarily restores hemostasis.

Pharmacodynamics/Kinetics Half-life elimination: IX component: 23-31 hours

Dosage Dosage is expressed in units of factor IX activity and must be individualized. I.V. only:

Formula for units required to raise blood level %:

AlphaNine® SD, Mononine®: Children and Adults:

Number of Factor IX Units Required = body weight (in kg) x desired Factor IX level increase (% normal) x 1 unit/kg

For example, for a 100% level a patient who has an actual level of 20%: Number of Factor IX Units needed = 70 kg x 80% x 1 Unit/kg = 5600 Units

BeneFix®:

Children <15 years:

Number of Factor IX Units Required = body weight (in kg) x desired Factor IX level increase (% normal) x 1.4 units/kg

Adults:

Number of Factor IX Units Required = body weight (in kg) x desired Factor IX level increase (% normal) x 1.2 units/kg

Guidelines: As a general rule, the level of factor IX required for treatment of different conditions is listed below:

Minor spontaneous hemorrhage, prophylaxis:

Desired levels of factor IX for hemostasis: 15% to 25%

Initial loading dose to achieve desired level: 20-30 units/kg

Frequency of dosing: Every 12-24 hours if necessary

Duration of treatment: 1-2 days

Moderate hemorrhage:

Desired levels of factor IX for hemostasis: 25% to 50%

Initial loading dose to achieve desired level: 25-50 units/kg

Frequency of dosing: Every 12-24 hours

Duration of treatment: 2-7 days

Major hemorrhage:

Desired levels of factor IX for hemostasis: >50%

Initial loading dose to achieve desired level: 30-50 units/kg

Frequency of dosing: Every 12-24 hours, depending on half-life and measured factor IX levels (after 3-5 days, maintain at least 20% activity)

Duration of treatment: 7-10 days, depending upon nature of insult

Surgery:

Desired levels of factor IX for hemostasis: 50% to 100%

Initial loading dose to achieve desired level: 50-100 units/kg

Frequency of dosing: Every 12-24 hours, depending on half-life and measured factor IX levels

Duration of treatment: 7-10 days, depending upon nature of insult

Administration Solution should be infused at room temperature

I.V. administration only: Should be infused **slowly**: The rate of administration should be determined by the response and comfort of the patient.

Mononine®: Intravenous dosage administration rates of up to 225 units/minute (~2 mL/minute) have been regularly tolerated without incident. **Infuse at a rate not exceeding 2 mL/minute**.

Monitoring Parameters Levels of factors IX, PTT

Reference Range Average normal factor IX levels are 50% to 150%; patients with severe hemophilia will have levels <1%, often undetectable. Moderate forms of the disease have levels of 1% to 10% while some mild cases may have 11% to 49% of normal factor IX.

Maintain factor IX plasma level at least 20% until hemostasis achieved after acute joint or muscle bleeding

In preparation for and following surgery:

Level to prevent spontaneous hemorrhage: 5%

Minimum level for hemostasis following trauma and surgery: 30% to 50%

Severe hemorrhage: >60%

Major surgery: ≥50% prior to procedure, 30% to 50% for several days after surgery, and >20% for 10-14 days thereafter

Dosage Forms Injection, powder for reconstitution (**Note:** Exact potency labeled on each vial):

AlphaNine® SD [human derived; solvent detergent treated; virus filtered; contains nondetectable of factors II, VII, X; supplied with diluent]

BeneFix® [recombinant formulation; supplied with diluent]

Mononine® [human derived; monoclonal antibody purified; contains nondetectable levels of factors II, VII, X; supplied with diluent]

Factor IX Complex (Human) (FAK ter nyne KOM pleks HYU man)

U.S. Brand Names Bebulin® VH; Konyne® 80; Profilnine® SD; Proplex® T

Index Terms Prothrombin Complex Concentrate

Pharmacologic Category Antihemophilic Agent; Blood Product Derivative

Use

Control bleeding in patients with factor IX deficiency (hemophilia B or Christmas disease)

Note: Factor IX concentrate containing **only** factor IX is also available and preferable for this indication.

Prevention/control of bleeding in hemophilia A patients with inhibitors to factor VIII

Prevention/control of bleeding in patients with factor VII deficiency

Emergency correction of the coagulopathy of warfarin excess in critical situations.

Pregnancy Risk Factor C

Contraindications Liver disease with signs of intravascular coagulation or fibrinolysis, not for use in factor VII deficiencies, patients undergoing elective surgery

Warnings/Precautions Use with caution in patients with liver dysfunction. Prepared from pooled human plasma - the risk of viral transmission is not totally eradicated. Thromboembolic complications rarely occur; more likely to occur during postoperative period or in patients with risk factors. Treatment should stop if respiratory distress or any changes in blood pressure or pulse rate occur.

Adverse Reactions

1% to 10%:

Central nervous system: Fever, headache, chills

Neuromuscular & skeletal: Tingling

Miscellaneous: Following rapid administration: Transient fever

<1% (Limited to important or life-threatening): Disseminated intravascular coagulation (DIC), flushing, nausea, somnolence, thrombosis following high dosages because of presence of activated clotting factors, tightness in chest, tightness in neck, urticaria, vomiting

Overdosage/Toxicology Symptoms include disseminated intravascular coagulation (DIC).

Drug Interactions

Increased Effect/Toxicity: Do not coadminister with aminocaproic acid; may increase risk for thrombosis.

Stability When stored at refrigerator temperature, 2°C to 8°C (36°F to 46°F), coagulation factor IX is stable for the period indicated by the expiration date on its label. Avoid freezing which may damage container for the diluent. Once diluted should be used promptly; stable for up to 3 hours.

For reconstitution, refer to instructions for individual products. Diluent and factor IX complex should come to room temperature before combining. Diluent vial should be inverted over concentrate vial. After diluent is pulled, disconnect. The provided filter needle should be used to withdraw concentrate. Remove needle and attach to infusion set or replace needle for infusion.

Mechanism of Action Replaces deficient clotting factor including factor X; hemophilia B, or Christmas disease, is an X-linked recessively inherited disorder of blood coagulation characterized by insufficient or abnormal synthesis of the clotting protein factor IX. Factor IX is a vitamin K-dependent coagulation factor which is synthesized in the liver. Factor IX is activated by factor XIa in the intrinsic coagulation pathway. Activated factor IX (IXa), in combination with factor VII:C activates factor X to Xa, resulting ultimately in the conversion of prothrombin to thrombin and the formation of a fibrin clot. The infusion of exogenous factor IX to replace the deficiency present in hemophilia B temporarily restores hemostasis.

Pharmacodynamics/Kinetics

Half-life elimination:

VII component: Initial: 4-6 hours; Terminal: 22.5 hours

IX component: 24 hours

(Continued)

Factor IX Complex (Human) *(Continued)*

Dosage Children and Adults: Dosage is expressed in units of factor IX activity and must be individualized. I.V. only:

Formula for units required to raise blood level %:

Total blood volume (mL blood/kg) = 70 mL/kg (adults), 80 mL/kg (children)

Plasma volume = total blood volume (mL) x [1 - Hct (in decimals)]

For example, for a 70 kg adult with a Hct = 40%: Plasma volume = [70 kg x 70 mL/kg] x [1 - 0.4] = 2940 mL

To calculate number of units needed to increase level to desired range (highly individualized and dependent on patient's condition): Number of units = desired level increase [desired level - actual level] x plasma volume (in mL)

For example, for a 100% level in the above patient who has an actual level of 20%: Number of units needed = [1 (for a 100% level) - 0.2] x 2940 mL = 2352 units

As a general rule, the level of factor IX required for treatment of different conditions is listed below:

Minor Spontaneous Hemorrhage, Prophylaxis:

Desired levels of factor IX for hemostasis: 15% to 25%

Initial loading dose to achieve desired level: <20-30 units/kg

Frequency of dosing: Once; repeated in 24 hours if necessary

Duration of treatment: Once; repeated if necessary

Major Trauma or Surgery:

Desired levels of factor IX for hemostasis: 25% to 50%

Initial loading dose to achieve desired level: <75 units/kg

Frequency of dosing: Every 18-30 hours, depending on half-life and measured factor IX levels

Duration of treatment: Up to 10 days, depending upon nature of insult

Factor VIII inhibitor patients: 75 units/kg/dose; may be given every 6-12 hours

Anticoagulant overdosage: I.V.: 15 units/kg

Administration I.V. administration only; should be infused **slowly**. Rate should not exceed 2 mL/minute for Bebulin® VH, 3 mL/minute for Proplex® T, or 10 mL/minute for Profilnine® SD.

Monitoring Parameters Levels of factors being replaced (eg, VII or IX), PT, PTT

Reference Range Average normal factor VII and factor IX levels are 50% to 150%; patients with severe hemophilia will have levels <1%, often undetectable. Moderate forms of the disease have levels of 1% to 10% while some mild cases may have 11% to 49% of normal factor IX.

Maintain factor IX plasma level at least 20% until hemostasis achieved after acute joint or muscle bleeding

In preparation for and following surgery:

Level to prevent spontaneous hemorrhage: 5%

Minimum level for hemostasis following trauma and surgery: 30% to 50%

Severe hemorrhage: >60%

Major surgery: >60% prior to procedure, 30% to 50% for several days after surgery, and >20% for 7-10 days thereafter

Dosage Forms Injection, powder for reconstitution (**Note:** Exact potency labeled on each vial):

Bebulin® VH [single-dose vial; vapor heated; supplied with sterile water for injection]

Profilnine® SD [single-dose vial; solvent detergent treated]

Proplex® T [single-dose vial; heat treated; supplied with sterile water for injection]

♦ **Factrel**® *see* Gonadorelin *on page 809*

Famciclovir *(fam SYE kloe veer)*

U.S. Brand Names Famvir®

Canadian Brand Names Famvir®

Pharmacologic Category Antiviral Agent

Additional Appendix Information

Treatment of Sexually Transmitted Infections *on page 2007*

Use Treatment of acute herpes zoster (shingles); treatment and suppression of recurrent episodes of genital herpes in immunocompetent patients; treatment of herpes labialis (cold sores) in immunocompetent patients; treatment of recurrent mucocutaneous/genital herpes simplex in HIV-infected patients

Pregnancy Risk Factor B

Pregnancy Implications Teratogenic effects were not observed in animal studies. There are no adequate and well-controlled studies in pregnant women. Use only if benefit outweighs risk. A registry has been established for women exposed to famciclovir during pregnancy (888-669-6682).

Lactation Excretion in breast milk unknown/use caution

Contraindications Hypersensitivity to famciclovir, penciclovir, or any component of the formulation

Warnings/Precautions Has not been studied in immunocompromised patients or patients with ophthalmic or disseminated zoster. Dosage adjustment is required in patients with renal insufficiency. Tablets contain lactose; do not use with galactose intolerance, severe lactase deficiency, or glucose-galactose malabsorption syndromes. Safety and efficacy have not been established in children <18 years of age.

Adverse Reactions

Note: Frequencies vary with dose and duration. Single-dose treatment (herpes labialis) was associated only with headache (10%), diarrhea (2%), fatigue (1%), and dysmenorrhea (1%).

>10%:

Central nervous system: Headache (17% to 39%)

Gastrointestinal: Nausea (7% to 13%)

1% to 10%:
Central nervous system: Fatigue (4% to 6%), migraine (1% to 3%)
Dermatologic: Pruritus (1% to 4%), rash (<1% to 3%)
Endocrine and metabolic: Dysmenorrhea (up to 8%)
Gastrointestinal: Diarrhea (5% to 9%), flatulence (2% to 5%), vomiting (1% to 5%), abdominal pain (1% to 8%)
Hematologic: Neutropenia (3%), leukopenia (1%)
Hepatic: Transaminases increased (2% to 3%), bilirubin increased (2%)
Neuromuscular & skeletal: Paresthesia (1% to 3%)
Postmarketing and/or case reports: Confusion, delirium, disorientation, dizziness, erythema multiforme, hallucinations, jaundice, somnolence, thrombocytopenia, urticaria

Overdosage/Toxicology Supportive and symptomatic care is recommended. Hemodialysis may enhance elimination of penciclovir.

Ethanol/Nutrition/Herb Interactions Food: Rate of absorption and/or conversion to penciclovir and peak concentration are reduced with food, but bioavailability is not affected.

Stability Store at controlled room temperature.

Mechanism of Action Famciclovir undergoes rapid biotransformation to the active compound, penciclovir, which is phosphorylated by viral thymidine kinase in HSV-1, HSV-2, and VZV-infected cells to a monophosphate form; this is then converted to penciclovir triphosphate and competes with deoxyguanosine triphosphate to inhibit HSV-2 polymerase (eg, herpes viral DNA synthesis/replication is selectively inhibited)

Pharmacodynamics/Kinetics
Absorption: Food decreases maximum peak concentration and delays time to peak; AUC remains the same
Distribution: V_{dss}: 0.91-1.25 L/kg
Protein binding: ≤20%
Metabolism: Rapidly deacetylated and oxidized to penciclovir; not via CYP
Bioavailability: 69% to 85%
Half-life elimination: Penciclovir: 2-3 hours (10, 20, and 7 hours in HSV-1, HSV-2, and VZV-infected cells, respectively); prolonged with renal impairment
Time to peak: 0.9 hours; C_{max} and T_{max} are decreased and prolonged with noncompensated hepatic impairment
Excretion: Urine (73% primarily as penciclovir); feces (27%)

Dosage Adults: Oral:
Acute herpes zoster: 500 mg every 8 hours for 7 days (**Note:** Initiate therapy within 72 hours of rash onset.)
Recurrent genital herpes simplex in immunocompetent patients:
Initial: 1000 mg twice daily for 1 day (**Note:** initiate therapy within 6 hours of symptoms/lesions.)
Suppressive therapy: 250 mg twice daily for up to 1 year
Recurrent herpes labialis (cold sores): 1500 mg as a single dose; initiate therapy at first sign or symptom such as tingling, burning, or itching (initiated within 1 hour in clinical studies)
Recurrent mucocutaneous/genital herpes simplex in HIV patients: 500 mg twice daily for 7 days

Dosing interval in renal impairment:
Herpes zoster:
Cl_{cr} 40-59 mL/minute: Administer 500 mg every 12 hours
Cl_{cr} 20-39 mL/minute: Administer 500 mg every 24 hours
Cl_{cr} <20 mL/minute: Administer 250 mg every 24 hours
Hemodialysis: Administer 250 mg after each dialysis session.
Recurrent genital herpes: Treatment (single day regimen):
Cl_{cr} 40-59 mL/minute: Administer 500 mg every 12 hours for 1 day
Cl_{cr} 20-39 mL/minute: Administer 500 mg as a single dose
Cl_{cr} <20 mL/minute: Administer 250 mg as a single dose
Hemodialysis: Administer 250 mg as a single dose after dialysis session.
Recurrent genital herpes: Suppression:
Cl_{cr} 20-39 mL/minute: Administer 125 mg every 12 hours
Cl_{cr} <20 mL/minute: Administer 125 mg every 24 hours
Hemodialysis: Administer 125 mg after each dialysis session.
Recurrent herpes labialis: Treatment (single dose regimen):
Cl_{cr} 40-59 mL/minute: Administer 750 mg as a single dose
Cl_{cr} 20-39 mL/minute: Administer 500 mg as a single dose
Cl_{cr} <20 mL/minute: Administer 250 mg as a single dose
Hemodialysis: Administer 250 mg as a single dose after dialysis session.
Recurrent orolabial or genital herpes in HIV-infected patients:
Cl_{cr} 20-39 mL/minute: Administer 500 mg every 12 hours
Cl_{cr} <20 mL/minute: Administer 250 mg every 24 hours
Hemodialysis: Administer 250 mg after each dialysis session.

Dietary Considerations May be taken with food or on an empty stomach

Monitoring Parameters Periodic CBC during long-term therapy

Additional Information Most effective for herpes zoster if therapy is initiated within 48 hours of initial lesion. Resistance may occur by alteration of thymidine kinase, resulting in loss of or reduced penciclovir phosphorylation (cross-resistance occurs between acyclovir and famciclovir). When treatment for herpes labialis is initiated within 1 hour of symptom onset, healing time is reduced by ~2 days.

Dosage Forms Tablet: 125 mg, 250 mg, 500 mg [contains lactose]

Famotidine (fa MOE ti deen)

U.S. Brand Names Pepcid®; Pepcid® AC [OTC]
Canadian Brand Names Apo-Famotidine®; Apo-Famotidine® Injectable; Famotidine Omega; Gen-Famotidine; Novo-Famotidine; Nu-Famotidine; Pepcid®; Pepcid® AC; Pepcid® I.V.; ratio-Famotidine; Riva-Famotidine; Ulcidine
(Continued)

Famotidine *(Continued)*

Pharmacologic Category Histamine H_2 Antagonist

Use Therapy and treatment of duodenal ulcer, gastric ulcer, control gastric pH in critically-ill patients, symptomatic relief in gastritis, gastroesophageal reflux, active benign ulcer, and pathological hypersecretory conditions

OTC labeling: Relief of heartburn, acid indigestion, and sour stomach

Unlabeled/Investigational Use Part of a multidrug regimen for *H. pylori* eradication to reduce the risk of duodenal ulcer recurrence

Pregnancy Risk Factor B

Pregnancy Implications Crosses the placenta; insufficient data concerning effects on the fetus

Lactation Enters breast milk/not recommended

Contraindications Hypersensitivity to famotidine, other H_2 antagonists, or any component of the formulation

Warnings/Precautions Modify dose in patients with renal impairment; chewable tablets contain phenylalanine; multidose vials contain benzyl alcohol

OTC labeling: When used for self-medication, patients should be instructed not to use if they have difficulty swallowing, have vomiting with blood, or bloody or black stools. Not for use with other acid reducers.

Adverse Reactions

Note: Agitation and vomiting have been reported in up to 14% of pediatric patients <1 year of age.

1% to 10%:

Central nervous system: Dizziness (1%), headache (5%)

Gastrointestinal: Constipation (1%), diarrhea (2%)

<1% (Limited to important or life-threatening): Abdominal discomfort, acne, agranulocytosis, allergic reaction, alopecia, anaphylaxis, angioedema, anorexia, arrhythmia, AST/ALT increased, bradycardia, bronchospasm, BUN/creatinine increased, drowsiness, fatigue, fever, hypertension, insomnia, jaundice, neutropenia, palpitation, paresthesia, proteinuria, pruritus, psychic disturbances, rash, seizure, tachycardia, thrombocytopenia, toxic epidermal necrolysis, urticaria, vomiting, weakness

Overdosage/Toxicology Symptoms include hypotension, tachycardia, vomiting, and drowsiness. Treatment is symptomatic and supportive.

Drug Interactions

Decreased Effect: Decreased serum levels of ketoconazole and itraconazole (reduced absorption).

Ethanol/Nutrition/Herb Interactions

Ethanol: Avoid ethanol (may cause gastric mucosal irritation).

Food: Famotidine bioavailability may be increased if taken with food.

Stability

Oral:

Powder for oral suspension: Prior to mixing, dry powder should be stored at room temperature of 25°C (77°F). Reconstituted oral suspension is stable for 30 days at room temperature; do not freeze.

Tablet: Store at 20°C (77°F); excursions permitted between 15°C to 30°C (59°F to 86°F). Protect from moisture.

I.V.:

Solution for injection: Prior to use, store at 2°C to 8°C (36°F to 46°F). If solution freezes, allow to solubilize at room temperature.

I.V. push: Dilute famotidine with NS (or another compatible solution) to a total of 5-10 mL (some centers also administer undiluted). Following reconstitution, solutions for I.V. push should be used immediately, or may be stored in refrigerator and used within 48 hours.

Infusion: Dilute with D_5W 100 mL or another compatible solution. Following reconstitution, solutions for infusion are stable for 7 days at room temperature.

Solution for injection, premixed bags: Store at room temperature of 25°C (77°F). Avoid excessive heat.

Mechanism of Action Competitive inhibition of histamine at H_2 receptors of the gastric parietal cells, which inhibits gastric acid secretion

Pharmacodynamics/Kinetics

Onset of action: GI: Oral: Within 1-3 hour

Duration: 10-12 hours

Protein binding: 15% to 20%

Bioavailability: Oral: 40% to 50%

Half-life elimination: Injection, oral suspension, tablet: 2.5-3.5 hours; prolonged with renal impairment; Oliguria: 20 hours

Time to peak, serum: Oral: ~1-3 hours

Excretion: Urine (as unchanged drug)

Dosage

Children: Treatment duration and dose should be individualized

Peptic ulcer: 1-16 years:

Oral: 0.5 mg/kg/day at bedtime or divided twice daily (maximum dose: 40 mg/day); doses of up to 1 mg/kg/day have been used in clinical studies

I.V.: 0.25 mg/kg every 12 hours (maximum dose: 40 mg/day); doses of up to 0.5 mg/kg have been used in clinical studies

GERD: Oral:

<3 months: 0.5 mg/kg once daily

3-12 months: 0.5 mg/kg twice daily

1-16 years: 1 mg/kg/day divided twice daily (maximum dose: 40 mg twice daily); doses of up to 2 mg/kg/day have been used in clinical studies

Children ≥12 years and Adults: Heartburn, indigestion, sour stomach: OTC labeling: Oral: 10-20 mg every 12 hours; dose may be taken 15-60 minutes before eating foods known to cause heartburn

Adults:
Duodenal ulcer: Oral: Acute therapy: 40 mg/day at bedtime for 4-8 weeks; maintenance therapy: 20 mg/day at bedtime
Helicobacter pylori eradication (unlabeled use): 40 mg once daily; requires combination therapy with antibiotics
Gastric ulcer: Oral: Acute therapy: 40 mg/day at bedtime
Hypersecretory conditions: Oral: Initial: 20 mg every 6 hours, may increase in increments up to 160 mg every 6 hours
GERD: Oral: 20 mg twice daily for 6 weeks
Esophagitis and accompanying symptoms due to GERD: Oral: 20 mg or 40 mg twice daily for up to 12 weeks
Patients unable to take oral medication: I.V.: 20 mg every 12 hours

Dosing adjustment in renal impairment: Cl_{cr} <50 mL/minute: Manufacturer recommendation: Administer 50% of dose or increase the dosing interval to every 36-48 hours (to limit potential CNS adverse effects).
Dietary Considerations Phenylalanine content: Pepcid® AC chewable: Each 10 mg tablet contains phenylalanine 1.4 mg
Administration
Oral:
Suspension: Shake vigorously before use. May be taken with or without food.
Tablet: May be taken with or without food.
I.V.:
I.V. push: Inject over at least 2 minutes
Solution for infusion: Administer over 15-30 minutes
Dosage Forms [DSC] = Discontinued product
Gelcap:
Pepcid® AC: 10 mg [DSC]
Infusion [premixed in NS]: 20 mg (50 mL)
Pepcid®: 20 mg (50 mL)
Injection, solution: 10 mg/mL (4 mL, 20 mL)
Pepcid®: 10 mg/mL (20 mL) [contains benzyl alcohol]
Injection, solution [preservative free]: 10 mg/mL (2 mL)
Pepcid®: 10 mg/mL (2 mL)
Powder for oral suspension:
Pepcid®: 40 mg/5 mL (50 mL) [contains sodium benzoate; cherry-banana-mint flavor]
Tablet: 10 mg [OTC], 20 mg, 40 mg
Pepcid®: 20 mg, 40 mg
Pepcid® AC: 10 mg, 20 mg
Tablet, chewable:
Pepcid® AC: 10 mg [contains phenylalanine 1.4 mg/tablet; mint flavor]

Famotidine, Calcium Carbonate, and Magnesium Hydroxide
(fa MOE ti deen, KAL see um KAR bun ate, & mag NEE zhum hye DROKS ide)

U.S. Brand Names Pepcid® Complete [OTC]
Canadian Brand Names Pepcid® Complete [OTC]
Index Terms Calcium Carbonate, Magnesium Hydroxide, and Famotidine; Magnesium Hydroxide, Famotidine, and Calcium Carbonate
Pharmacologic Category Antacid; Histamine H_2 Antagonist
Use Relief of heartburn due to acid indigestion
Contraindications Hypersensitivity to famotidine or other H_2 antagonists, calcium carbonate, magnesium hydroxide, or any component of the formulation. See individual agents for additional information.
Warnings/Precautions See individual agents.
Adverse Reactions See individual agents.
Drug Interactions
Increased Effect/Toxicity: See individual agents.
Decreased Effect: See individual agents.
Stability Store at 25°C to 30°C (77°F to 86°F). Protect from moisture.
Mechanism of Action
Famotidine: H_2 antagonist
Calcium carbonate: Antacid
Magnesium hydroxide: Antacid
Pharmacodynamics/Kinetics See individual agents.
Dosage Children ≥12 years and Adults: Relief of heartburn due to acid indigestion: Oral: Pepcid® Complete: 1 tablet as needed; no more than 2 tablets in 24 hours; do **not** swallow whole, chew tablet completely before swallowing; do not use for longer than 14 days (see Additional Information for dosing ranges for individual ingredients)
Additional Information Presented in dosage field is the specific OTC labeling for the indicated product. Dosing ranges of the individual ingredients include:

Adults:
Famotidine: Duodenal/gastric ulcer: 40 mg/day at bedtime
Calcium carbonate: Antacid: ≤3 g/day of elemental calcium
Magnesium hydroxide: Antacid: Approximately ≤5 g/day of magnesium hydroxide
Healthcare providers should also refer to the individual monographs for more specific information.
Dosage Forms Tablet, chewable: Famotidine 10 mg, calcium carbonate 800 mg, and magnesium hydroxide 165 mg [berry blend and mint flavors]

♦ **Famotidine Omega (Can)** see Famotidine on page 683
♦ **Famvir®** see Famciclovir on page 682
♦ **Fansidar®** see Sulfadoxine and Pyrimethamine on page 1611

♦ **Fareston**® *see* Toremifene *on page 1711*

♦ **Faslodex**® *see* Fulvestrant *on page 772*

♦ **Fasturtec**® **(Can)** *see* Rasburicase *on page 1490*

Fat Emulsion (fat e MUL shun)

U.S. Brand Names Intralipid®; Liposyn® III

Canadian Brand Names Intralipid®; Liposyn® II

Index Terms Intravenous Fat Emulsion

Pharmacologic Category Caloric Agent

Use Source of calories and essential fatty acids for patients requiring parenteral nutrition of extended duration

Pregnancy Risk Factor C

Lactation Excretion in breast milk unknown/compatible

Contraindications Hypersensitivity to fat emulsion or any component of the formulation; severe egg or legume (soybean) allergies; pathologic hyperlipidemia, lipoid nephrosis pancreatitis with hyperlipemia

Warnings/Precautions Use caution in patients with severe liver damage, pulmonary disease, anemia, or blood coagulation disorder; use with caution in jaundiced, premature, and low birth weight children. Some formulations may contain aluminum which may accumulate following prolonged administration in renally-impaired patients. Due to immature renal function, premature neonates are at higher risk of accumulation/toxicity from aluminum. To avoid hyperlipidemia and/or fat deposition, do not exceed recommended daily doses. Monitor by appropriate laboratory evaluation (eg, triglycerides).

[U.S. Boxed Warning]: Deaths have been reported in preterm infants in association with fat emulsion infusion; fat accumulation in the lungs has been noted on autopsy. Infusion rate should not exceed 1g fat/kg in four hours; strict monitoring of metabolic tolerance and elimination of infused fat from the circulation must occur. Allow lipemia to resolve between daily infusions.

Adverse Reactions Frequency not defined.

Cardiovascular: Chest pain, cyanosis, flushing

Central nervous system: Dizziness, headache

Endocrine & metabolic: Hyperlipemia, hypertriglyceridemia

Gastrointestinal: Diarrhea, nausea, vomiting

Hematologic: Hypercoagulability, thrombocytopenia in neonates (rare)

Hepatic: Hepatomegaly, pancreatitis

Local: Thrombophlebitis

Respiratory: Dyspnea

Miscellaneous: Brown pigment deposition in the reticuloendothelial system (significance unknown), diaphoresis, sepsis

Overdosage/Toxicology Too rapid administration results in fluid or fat overloading, causing dilution of serum electrolytes, overhydration, pulmonary edema, impaired pulmonary diffusion capacity, or metabolic acidosis. Treatment is supportive.

Stability May be stored at room temperature. Do not store partly used bottles for later use. Do not use if emulsion appears to be oiling out.

Mechanism of Action Essential for normal structure and function of cell membranes

Pharmacodynamics/Kinetics

Metabolism: Undergoes lipolysis to free fatty acids which are utilized by reticuloendothelial cells

Half-life elimination: 0.5-1 hour

Dosage Fat emulsion should not exceed 60% of the total daily calories

Premature Infants: Initial dose: 0.25-0.5 g/kg/day, increase by 0.25-0.5 g/kg/day to a maximum of 3 g/kg/day depending on needs/nutritional goals; limit to 1 g/kg/day if on phototherapy; maximum rate of infusion: 0.15 g/kg/hour (0.75 mL/kg/hour of 20% solution)

Infants and Children: Initial dose: 0.5-1 g/kg/day, increase by 0.5 g/kg/day to a maximum of 3 g/kg/day depending on needs/nutritional goals; maximum rate of infusion: 0.25 g/kg/hour (1.25 mL/kg/hour of 20% solution)

Adolescents and Adults: Initial dose: 1 g/kg/day, increase by 0.5-1 g/kg/day to a maximum of 2.5 g/kg/day of 10% and 3 g/kg/day of 20% depending on needs/nutritional goals; maximum rate of infusion: 0.25 g/kg/hour (1.25 mL/kg/hour of 20% solution); do not exceed 50 mL/hour (20%) or 100 mL/hour (10%)

Prevention of essential fatty acid deficiency (8% to 10% of total caloric intake): 0.5-1 g/kg/24 hours

Children: 5-10 mL/kg/day at 0.1 mL/minute then up to 100 mL/hour

Adults: 500 mL (10%) twice weekly at rate of 1 mL/minute for 30 minutes, then increase to 42 mL/hour (500 mL over 12 hours)

Note: At the onset of therapy, the patient should be observed for any immediate allergic reactions such as dyspnea, cyanosis, and fever; slower initial rates of infusion may be used for the first 10-15 minutes of the infusion (eg, 0.1 mL/minute of 10% or 0.05 mL/minute of 20% solution)

Administration May be simultaneously infused with amino acid dextrose mixtures by means of Y-connector located near infusion site. The 10% isotonic solution which has 1.1 cal/mL (10%) and may be administered peripherally; the 20% (2 cal/mL) is not recommended for use in low birth weight infants.

Monitoring Parameters Serum triglycerides; before initiation of therapy and at least weekly during therapy. Frequent (some advise daily) platelet counts should be performed in neonatal patients receiving parenteral lipids.

Dosage Forms Injection, emulsion [soybean oil]:

Intralipid®: 10% [100 mg/mL] (100 mL, 250 mL, 500 mL); 20% [200 mg/mL] (50 mL, 100 mL, 250 mL, 500 mL, 1000 mL); 30% [300 mg/mL] (500 mL)

Liposyn® III: 10% [100 mg/mL] (200 mL, 500 mL); 20% [200 mg/mL] (200 mL, 500 mL); 30% [300 mg/mL] (500 mL)

♦ **FazaClo**® *see Clozapine on page 406*
♦ **5-FC** *see Flucytosine on page 714*
♦ **FC1157a** *see Toremifene on page 1711*
♦ **Feiba VH** *see Anti-inhibitor Coagulant Complex on page 137*
♦ **Feiba VH Immuno (Can)** *see Anti-inhibitor Coagulant Complex on page 137*

Felbamate (FEL ba mate)

U.S. Brand Names Felbatol®
Pharmacologic Category Anticonvulsant, Miscellaneous
Additional Appendix Information
  Epilepsy *on page 2048*
Use Not as a first-line antiepileptic treatment; only in those patients who respond inadequately to alternative treatments and whose epilepsy is so severe that a substantial risk of aplastic anemia and/or liver failure is deemed acceptable in light of the benefits conferred by its use. Patient must be fully advised of risk and provide signed written informed consent. Felbamate can be used as either monotherapy or adjunctive therapy in the treatment of partial seizures (with and without generalization) and in adults with epilepsy.
  Orphan drug: Adjunctive therapy in the treatment of partial and generalized seizures associated with Lennox-Gastaut syndrome in children
Restrictions A patient "informed consent" form should be completed and signed by the patient and physician. Copies are available from Wallace Pharmaceuticals by calling 609-655-6147.
Pregnancy Risk Factor C
Dosage Anticonvulsant:
  Monotherapy: Children >14 years and Adults:
    Initial: 1200 mg/day in divided doses 3 or 4 times/day; titrate previously untreated patients under close clinical supervision, increasing the dosage in 600 mg increments every 2 weeks to 2400 mg/day based on clinical response and thereafter to 3600 mg/day as clinically indicated
    Conversion to monotherapy: Initiate at 1200 mg/day in divided doses 3 or 4 times/day, reduce the dosage of the concomitant anticonvulsant(s) by 20% to 33% at the initiation of felbamate therapy; at week 2, increase the felbamate dosage to 2400 mg/day while reducing the dosage of the other anticonvulsant(s) up to an additional 33% of their original dosage; at week 3, increase the felbamate dosage up to 3600 mg/day and continue to reduce the dosage of the other anticonvulsant(s) as clinically indicated
  Adjunctive therapy: Children with Lennox-Gastaut and ages 2-14 years:
    Week 1:
      Felbamate: 15 mg/kg/day divided 3-4 times/day
      Concomitant anticonvulsant(s): Reduce original dosage by 20% to 30%
    Week 2:
      Felbamate: 30 mg/kg/day divided 3-4 times/day
      Concomitant anticonvulsant(s): Reduce original dosage up to an additional 33%
    Week 3:
      Felbamate: 45 mg/kg/day divided 3-4 times/day
      Concomitant anticonvulsant(s): Reduce dosage as clinically indicated
  Adjunctive therapy: Children >14 years and Adults:
    Week 1:
      Felbamate: 1200 mg/day initial dose
      Concomitant anticonvulsant(s): Reduce original dosage by 20% to 33%
    Week 2:
      Felbamate: 2400 mg/day (therapeutic range)
      Concomitant anticonvulsant(s): Reduce original dosage by up to an additional 33%
    Week 3:
      Felbamate: 3600 mg/day (therapeutic range)
      Concomitant anticonvulsant(s): Reduce original dosage as clinically indicated

  Dosage adjustment in renal impairment: Use caution; reduce initial and maintenance doses by 50% (half-life prolonged by 9-15 hours)
Additional Information Complete prescribing information for this medication should be consulted for additional detail.
Dosage Forms [DSC] = Discontinued product
  Suspension, oral:
    Felbatol®: 600 mg/5 mL (240 mL, 960 mL)
  Tablet:
    Felbatol®: 400 mg; 600 mg [DSC]

♦ **Felbatol**® *see Felbamate on page 687*
♦ **Feldene**® *see Piroxicam on page 1378*

Felodipine (fe LOE di peen)

U.S. Brand Names Plendil®
Canadian Brand Names Plendil®; Renedil®
Pharmacologic Category Calcium Channel Blocker
Additional Appendix Information
  Calcium Channel Blockers *on page 1878*
Use Treatment of hypertension
Pregnancy Risk Factor C
Pregnancy Implications Potentially, calcium channel blockers may prolong labor. There are no adequate or well-controlled studies in pregnant women.
Lactation Excretion in breast milk unknown/not recommended
  (Continued)

Felodipine (Continued)

Medication Safety Issues

Sound-alike/look-alike issues:

Plendil® may be confused with Isordil®, pindolol, Pletal®, Prilosec®, Prinivil®

Contraindications Hypersensitivity to felodipine, any component of the formulation, or other calcium channel blocker

Warnings/Precautions Increased angina and/or MI has occurred with initiation or dosage titration of calcium channel blockers. Use caution in patients with heart failure and/or hypertrophic cardiomyopathy. Elderly patients and patients with hepatic impairment should start off with a lower dose. Peripheral edema is the most common side effect (occurs within 2-3 weeks of starting therapy). May cause reflex tachycardia. Symptomatic hypotension with or without syncope can rarely occur; blood pressure must be lowered at a rate appropriate for the patient's clinical condition. Use caution in hepatic impairment. Safety and efficacy in children have not been established. Dosage titration should occur after 14 days on a given dose.

Adverse Reactions

>10%: Central nervous system: Headache (11% to 15%)

2% to 10%: Cardiovascular: Peripheral edema (2% to 17%), tachycardia (0.4% to 2.5%), flushing (4% to 7%)

<1% (Limited to important or life-threatening): Angina, angioedema, anxiety, arrhythmia, CHF, CVA, libido decreased, depression, dizziness, gingival hyperplasia, dyspnea, dysuria, gynecomastia, hypotension, impotence, insomnia, irritability, leukocytoclastic vasculitis, MI, nervousness, paresthesia, somnolence, syncope, urticaria, vomiting

Overdosage/Toxicology Primary cardiac symptoms of calcium blocker overdose include hypotension and bradycardia. Hypotension is caused by peripheral vasodilation, myocardial depression, and bradycardia. Bradycardia results from sinus bradycardia, second- or third-degree atrioventricular block, or sinus arrest with junctional rhythm. Intraventricular conduction is usually not affected so QRS duration is normal (verapamil prolongs the PR interval and bepridil prolongs the QT interval and may cause ventricular arrhythmias, including torsade de pointes).

Noncardiac symptoms include confusion, stupor, nausea, vomiting, metabolic acidosis and hyperglycemia. Following initial gastric decontamination, if possible, repeated calcium administration may promptly reverse depressed cardiac contractility (but not sinus node depression or peripheral vasodilation). Glucagon, epinephrine, and inamrinone (amrinone) may treat refractory hypotension. Glucagon and epinephrine also increase the heart rate (outside the U.S., 4-aminopyridine may be available as an antidote). Dialysis and hemoperfusion are not effective in enhancing elimination, although repeat-dose activated charcoal may serve as an adjunct with sustained-release preparations.

In a few reported cases, overdose with calcium channel blockers has been associated with hypotension and bradycardia, initially refractory to atropine, but becoming more responsive to this agent when larger doses (approaching 1 g/hour for more than 24 hours) of calcium chloride were administered.

Drug Interactions

Cytochrome P450 Effect: Substrate of CYP3A4 (major); **Inhibits** CYP2C8 (moderate), 2C9 (weak), 2D6 (weak), 3A4 (weak)

Increased Effect/Toxicity: Felodipine may increase the levels/effects of CYP2C8 substrates; example substrates include amiodarone, paclitaxel, pioglitazone, repaglinide, and rosiglitazone. CYP3A4 inhibitors may increase the levels/effects of felodipine; example inhibitors include azole antifungals, clarithromycin, diclofenac, doxycycline, erythromycin, imatinib, isoniazid, nefazodone, nicardipine, propofol, protease inhibitors, quinidine, telithromycin, and verapamil. Beta-blockers may have increased pharmacokinetic or pharmacodynamic interactions with felodipine. Cyclosporine increases felodipine's serum concentration. Blood pressure-lowering effects may be additive with sildenafil, tadalafil, and vardenafil (use caution). Felodipine may increase tacrolimus serum levels (monitor).

Decreased Effect: Felodipine may decrease pharmacologic actions of theophylline. Calcium may reduce the calcium channel blocker's effects, particularly hypotension. Felodipine may decrease pharmacologic actions of theophylline. CYP3A4 inducers may decrease the levels/effects of felodipine; example inducers include aminoglutethimide, carbamazepine, nafcillin, nevirapine, phenobarbital, phenytoin, and rifamycins.

Ethanol/Nutrition/Herb Interactions

Ethanol: Increases felodipine's absorption; watch for a greater hypotensive effect.

Food: Increased therapeutic and vasodilator side effects, including severe hypotension and myocardial ischemia, may occur if felodipine is taken with grapefruit juice; avoid concurrent use. High-fat/carbohydrate meals will increase C_{max} by 60%; grapefruit juice will increase C_{max} by twofold.

Herb/Nutraceutical: St John's wort may decrease felodipine levels. Avoid dong quai if using for hypertension (has estrogenic activity). Avoid ephedra, yohimbe, ginseng (may worsen hypertension). Avoid garlic (may have increased antihypertensive effect).

Mechanism of Action Inhibits calcium ions from entering the "slow channels" or select voltage-sensitive areas of vascular smooth muscle and myocardium during depolarization, producing a relaxation of coronary vascular smooth muscle and coronary vasodilation; increases myocardial oxygen delivery in patients with vasospastic angina

Pharmacodynamics/Kinetics

Onset of action: Antihypertensive: 2-5 hours

Duration of antihypertensive effect: 24 hours

Absorption: 100%; Absolute: 20% due to first-pass effect

Protein binding: >99%

Metabolism: Hepatic; CYP3A4 substrate (major); extensive first-pass effect

Half-life elimination: Immediate release: 11-16 hours

Excretion: Urine (70% as metabolites); feces 10%

Dosage

Adults: Oral: 2.5-10 mg once daily; usual initial dose: 5 mg; increase by 5 mg at 2-week intervals, as needed, to a maximum of 20 mg/day

Usual dose range (JNC 7) for hypertension: 2.5-20 mg once daily
Elderly: Begin with 2.5 mg/day
Dosing adjustment/comments in hepatic impairment: Initial: 2.5 mg/day; monitor blood pressure
Dietary Considerations Should be taken without food.
Administration Do not crush or chew extended release tablets; swallow whole.
Additional Information Felodipine maintains renal and mesenteric blood flow during hemor-rhagic shock in animals.
Dosage Forms Tablet, extended release: 2.5 mg, 5 mg, 10 mg

♦ **Felodipine and Enalapril** see Enalapril and Felodipine on page 581
♦ **Femara®** see Letrozole on page 988
♦ **Femcon™ Fe** see Ethinyl Estradiol and Norethindrone on page 655
♦ **femhrt®** see Ethinyl Estradiol and Norethindrone on page 655
♦ **FemHRT® (Can)** see Ethinyl Estradiol and Norethindrone on page 655
♦ **Femilax™ [OTC]** see Bisacodyl on page 223
♦ **Femiron® [OTC]** see Ferrous Fumarate on page 702
♦ **Fem-Prin® [OTC]** see Acetaminophen, Aspirin, and Caffeine on page 34
♦ **Femring™** see Estradiol on page 620
♦ **Femstat® One (Can)** see Butoconazole on page 260
♦ **Femtrace®** see Estradiol on page 620

Fenofibrate (fen oh FYE brate)

U.S. Brand Names Antara™; Lipofen™; Lofibra™; TriCor®; Triglide™
Canadian Brand Names Apo-Fenofibrate®; Apo-Feno-Micro®; Dom-Fenofibrate Supra; Gen-Fenofibrate Micro; Lipidil EZ®; Lipidil Micro®; Lipidil Supra®; Novo-Fenofibrate; Nu-Fenofibrate; PHL-Fenofibrate Supra; PMS-Fenofibrate Micro; PMS-Fenofibrate Supra; ratio-Fenofibrate MC; TriCor®
Index Terms Procetofene; Proctofene
Pharmacologic Category Antilipemic Agent, Fibric Acid
Additional Appendix Information
  Hyperlipidemia Management on page 2058
  Lipid-Lowering Agents on page 1887
Use Adjunct to dietary therapy for the treatment of adults with elevations of serum triglyceride levels (types IV and V hyperlipidemia); adjunct to dietary therapy for the reduction of low density lipoprotein cholesterol (LDL-C), total cholesterol (total-C), triglycerides, and apolipo-protein B (apo B) in adult patients with primary hypercholesterolemia or mixed dyslipidemia (Fredrickson types IIa and IIb)
Pregnancy Risk Factor C
Pregnancy Implications Animal studies have shown embryocidal and teratogenic effect. There are no adequate and well-controlled studies in pregnant women. Use should be avoided, if possible, in pregnant women since the neonatal glucuronide conjugation pathways are immature.
Lactation Excretion in breast milk unknown/not recommended
Contraindications Hypersensitivity to fenofibrate or any component of the formulation; hepatic dysfunction including primary biliary cirrhosis and unexplained persistent liver func-tion abnormalities; severe renal dysfunction; pre-existing gallbladder disease
Warnings/Precautions Hepatic transaminases can become significantly elevated (dose-related); hepatocellular, chronic active, and cholestatic hepatitis have been reported. Regular monitoring of liver function tests is required. May cause cholelithiasis. Use caution with warfarin; adjustments in warfarin therapy may be required. Use caution with HMG-CoA reductase inhibitors (may lead to myopathy, rhabdomyolysis). Therapy should be withdrawn if an adequate response is not obtained after 2 months of therapy at the maximal daily dose. May cause mild to moderate decreases in hemoglobin, hematocrit and WBC upon initiation of therapy which usually stabilizes with long-term therapy. Rare hypersensitivity reactions may occur. Dose adjustment is required for renal impairment and elderly patients. Safety and efficacy in children have not been established.
Adverse Reactions
  >10%: Hepatic: ALT/AST increased (3% to 13%)
  1% to 10%:
    Gastrointestinal: Abdominal pain (5%), constipation (2%)
    Neuromuscular & skeletal: Back pain (3%)
    Respiratory: Respiratory disorder (6%), rhinitis (2%)

  Frequency not defined:
    Cardiovascular: Angina pectoris, arrhythmia, atrial fibrillation, cardiovascular disorder, chest pain, coronary artery disorder, edema, electrocardiogram abnormality, extrasys-toles, hyper-/hypotension, MI, palpitation, peripheral edema, peripheral vascular disorder, phlebitis, tachycardia, varicose veins, vasodilatation
    Central nervous system: Anxiety, depression, dizziness, fever, headache, insomnia, malaise, nervousness, neuralgia, pain, somnolence, vertigo
    Dermatologic: Acne, alopecia, bruising, contact dermatitis, eczema, fungal dermatitis, maculopapular rash, nail disorder, photosensitivity reaction, pruritus, skin ulcer, Stevens-Johnson syndrome, toxic epidermal necrolysis, urticaria
    Endocrine & metabolic: Diabetes mellitus, gout, gynecomastia, hypoglycemia, hyperuri-cemia, libido decreased
    Gastrointestinal: Anorexia, appetite increased, colitis, diarrhea, dry mouth, duodenal ulcer, dyspepsia, eructation, esophagitis, flatulence, gastroenteritis, gastritis, gastrointestinal disorder, nausea, peptic ulcer, rectal disorder, rectal hemorrhage, tooth disorder, vomiting, weight gain/loss
    Genitourinary: Cystitis, dysuria, prostatic disorder, libido decreased, pregnancy (unin-tended), urinary frequency, urolithiasis, vaginal moniliasis
(Continued)

Fenofibrate *(Continued)*

Hematologic: Agranulocytosis, anemia, eosinophilia, leukopenia, lymphadenopathy, thrombocytopenia

Hepatic: Cholelithiasis, cholecystitis, creatine phosphokinase increased, fatty liver deposits, liver function tests abnormal

Neuromuscular & skeletal: Arthralgia, arthritis, arthrosis, bursitis, hypertonia, joint disorder, leg cramps, muscle pain, myalgia, myasthenia, myopathy, myositis, paresthesia, rhabdomyolysis, tenderness, tenosynovitis, weakness

Ocular: Abnormal vision, amblyopia, cataract, conjunctivitis, eye disorder, refraction disorder

Otic: Ear pain, otitis media

Renal: Creatinine increased, kidney function abnormality

Respiratory: Asthma, bronchitis, cough increased, dyspnea, laryngitis, pharyngitis, pneumonia, sinusitis

Miscellaneous: Allergic reaction, cyst, diaphoresis, hernia, herpes simplex, herpes zoster, hypersensitivity reaction, infection

Overdosage/Toxicology Symptoms include nausea, vomiting, diarrhea, and GI distress. Treatment is supportive. Hemodialysis has no effect on removal of fenofibric acid from the plasma.

Drug Interactions

Cytochrome P450 Effect: Substrate of CYP3A4 (minor); **Inhibits** CYP2A6 (weak), 2C8 (moderate), 2C9 (moderate), 2C19 weak

Increased Effect/Toxicity: Fenofibrate may increase the effects of sulfonylureas and warfarin. Concurrent use of fenofibrate with HMG-CoA reductase inhibitors may increase the risk of myopathy and rhabdomyolysis. Ezetimibe's serum concentration may be increased with concurrent use. Fenofibrate may increase the levels/effects of CYP2C8 substrates (example substrates include amiodarone, paclitaxel, pioglitazone, repaglinide, and rosiglitazone). Fenofibrate may increase the levels/effects of CYP2C9 substrates (example substrates include bosentan, dapsone, fluoxetine, glimepiride, glipizide, losartan, montelukast, nateglinide, paclitaxel, phenytoin, warfarin, and zafirlukast).

Decreased Effect: Bile acid sequestrants may decrease absorption of fenofibrate (separate administration).

Stability Store at 15°C to 30°C (59°F to 86°F). Protect from moisture.

Mechanism of Action Fenofibric acid is believed to increase VLDL catabolism by enhancing the synthesis of lipoprotein lipase; as a result of a decrease in VLDL levels, total plasma triglycerides are reduced by 30% to 60%; modest increase in HDL occurs in some hypertriglyceridemic patients

Pharmacodynamics/Kinetics

Absorption: Increased when taken with meals

Distribution: Widely to most tissues

Protein binding: >99%

Metabolism: Tissue and plasma via esterases to active form, fenofibric acid; undergoes inactivation by glucuronidation hepatically or renally

Half-life elimination: Fenofibric acid: Mean: 20 hours (range: 10-35 hours)

Time to peak: 3-8 hours

Excretion: Urine (60% as metabolites); feces (25%); hemodialysis has no effect on removal of fenofibric acid from plasma

Dosage Oral:

Adults:

Hypertriglyceridemia: Initial:

Antara™: 43-130 mg/day

Lipofen™: 50-150 mg/day; maximum dose: 150 mg/day

Lofibra™: 67 mg/day with meals, up to 200 mg/day

TriCor®: 48 mg/day, up to 145 mg/day

Triglide™: 50-160 mg/day

Hypercholesterolemia or mixed hyperlipidemia:

Antara™: 130 mg/day

Lipofen™: 150 mg/day

Lofibra™: 200 mg/day with meals

TriCor®: 145 mg/day

Triglide™: 160 mg/day

Elderly: Initial:

Antara™: 43 mg/day

Lipofen™: 50 mg/day

Lofibra™: 67 mg/day

TriCor®: 48 mg/day

Triglide™: 50 mg/day

Dosage adjustment/interval in renal impairment: Monitor renal function and lipid panel before adjusting. Decrease dose or increase dosing interval for patients with renal failure:

Initial:

Antara™: 43 mg/day

Lipofen™: 50 mg/day

Lofibra™: 67 mg/day

TriCor®: 48 mg/day

Triglide™: 50 mg/day

Dietary Considerations

Lofibra™: Take with meals.

Antara™, Lipofen™, TriCor®, Triglide™: May be taken with or without food.

Administration 6-8 weeks of therapy is required to determine efficacy.

Lofibra™: Administer with meals.

Antara™, Lipofen™, TriCor®, Triglide™: May be administered with or without food.

Monitoring Parameters Periodic blood counts during first year of therapy. Total cholesterol, LDL-C, triglycerides, and HDL-C should be measured periodically; If only marginal changes are noted in 6-8 weeks, the drug should be discontinued. Monitor LFTs regularly and discontinue therapy if levels remain >3 times normal limits.

Dosage Forms [DSC] = Discontinued product
Capsule:
Lipofen™: 50 mg, 100 mg, 150 mg
Capsule [micronized]: 67 mg, 134 mg, 200 mg
Antara™: 43 mg, 87 mg [DSC], 130 mg
Lofibra™: 67 mg, 134 mg, 200 mg
Tablet: 54 mg, 160 mg
TriCor®: 48 mg, 145 mg
Triglide™: 50 mg, 160 mg

Fenoldopam (fe NOL doe pam)

U.S. Brand Names Corlopam®
Canadian Brand Names Corlopam®
Index Terms Fenoldopam Mesylate
Pharmacologic Category Dopamine Agonist
Additional Appendix Information
Hypertension *on page 2063*
Use Treatment of severe hypertension (up to 48 hours in adults), including in patients with renal compromise; short-term (up to 4 hours) blood pressure reduction in pediatric patients
Pregnancy Risk Factor B
Pregnancy Implications Fetal harm was not observed in animal studies; however, safety and efficacy have not been established for use during pregnancy. Use during pregnancy only if clearly needed. Fetal heart rate monitoring is recommended.
Lactation Excretion in breast milk unknown/use caution
Contraindications Hypersensitivity of fenoldopam or any component of the formulation
Warnings/Precautions Use caution in patients with glaucoma or intraocular hypertension. A dose-related tachycardia can occur, especially at infusion rates >0.1 mcg/kg/minute. Use caution in angina patients (can increase myocardial oxygen demand with tachycardia). Close monitoring of blood pressure is necessary (hypotension can occur). Monitor for hypokalemia at intervals of 6 hours during infusion. For continuous infusion only (no bolus doses). The effects of hemodialysis on the pharmacokinetics of fenoldopam have not been evaluated. Use caution with increased intracranial pressure. Contains sulfites; may cause allergic reaction in susceptible individuals.
Adverse Reactions Frequency not always defined.
Cardiovascular: Angina, asymptomatic T wave flattening on ECG, chest pain, edema, facial flushing (>5%), fibrillation (atrial), flutter (atrial), hypotension (>5%), tachycardia
Central nervous system: Dizziness, headache (>5%)
Endocrine & metabolic: Hypokalemia
Gastrointestinal: Abdominal pain/fullness, diarrhea, nausea (>5%), vomiting, xerostomia
Local: Injection site reactions
Ocular: Intraocular pressure (increased), blurred vision
Hepatic: Increases in portal pressure in cirrhotic patients
Drug Interactions
Increased Effect/Toxicity: Concurrent acetaminophen may increase fenoldopam levels (30% to 70%). Beta-blockers increase the risk of hypotension; avoid concurrent use. If used concurrently with beta-blockers, close monitoring is recommended.
Stability Store at 2°C to 30°C (35°F to 86°F). Must be diluted prior to infusion. Final dilution for children is 60 mcg/mL and for adults is 40 mcg/mL. Following dilution, store at room temperature and use solution within 24 hours.
Mechanism of Action A selective postsynaptic dopamine agonist (D_1-receptors) which exerts hypotensive effects by decreasing peripheral vasculature resistance with increased renal blood flow, diuresis, and natriuresis; 6 times as potent as dopamine in producing renal vasodilitation; has minimal adrenergic effects
Pharmacodynamics/Kinetics
Onset of action: I.V.: 10 minutes
Duration: I.V.: 1 hour
Distribution: V_d: 0.6 L/kg
Half-life elimination: I.V.: Children: 3-5 minutes; Adults: ~5 minutes
Metabolism: Hepatic via methylation, glucuronidation, and sulfation; the 8-sulfate metabolite may have some activity; extensive first-pass effect
Excretion: Urine (90%); feces (10%)
Dosage I.V.: Hypertension, severe:
Children: Initial: 0.2 mcg/kg/minute; may be increased to dosages of 0.3-0.5 mcg/kg/minute every 20-30 minutes (maximum dose: 0.8 mcg/kg/minute); limited to short-term (4 hours) use
Adults: Initial: 0.1-0.3 mcg/kg/minute (lower initial doses may be associated with less reflex tachycardia); may be increased in increments of 0.05-0.1 mcg/kg/minute every 15 minutes until target blood pressure is reached; the maximal infusion rate reported in clinical studies was 1.6 mcg/kg/minute

Dosing adjustment in renal impairment: None required
Dosing adjustment in hepatic impairment: None published
Administration For I.V. infusion using an infusion pump.
Monitoring Parameters Blood pressure, heart rate, ECG, renal/hepatic function tests
Reference Range Mean plasma fenoldopam levels after a 2 hour infusion (at 0.5 mcg/kg/minute) and a 100 mg dose is approximately 13 ng/mL and 50 ng/mL
Additional Information Suitable for use in patients whose condition is unstable or rapidly changing because the effects of the drug are predictable and easily reversible; it has been found to safely control blood pressure in patients with a variety of pre-existing conditions including kidney disease, liver disease, and heart failure. (Clinical benefit other than blood pressure reduction has not been established.) In none of these situations does the dose need (Continued)

Fenoldopam *(Continued)*

to be adjusted, minimizing the risk of drug overdose in patients with these conditions. The drug is quickly metabolized into inactive substances before it is excreted; therefore, there are no toxic chemicals derived from the drug. Unlike the situation with some other intravenous antihypertensives, the adult patient does not need an arterial line for blood pressure monitoring; a blood pressure cuff is sufficient to monitor blood pressure lowering. Since the drug induces natriuresis, diuresis, and increased creatinine clearance, it may have an advantage over nitroprusside, especially in patients with severe renal insufficiency and in volume overloaded patients.

Dosage Forms Injection, solution: 10 mg/mL (1 mL, 2 mL) [contains sodium metabisulfite and propylene glycol]

♦ **Fenoldopam Mesylate** *see* Fenoldopam *on page 691*

Fenoprofen *(fen oh PROE fen)*

U.S. Brand Names Nalfon®
Canadian Brand Names Nalfon®
Index Terms Fenoprofen Calcium
Pharmacologic Category Nonsteroidal Anti-inflammatory Drug (NSAID), Oral
Additional Appendix Information
Nonsteroidal Anti-inflammatory Agents *on page 1894*
Use Symptomatic treatment of acute and chronic rheumatoid arthritis and osteoarthritis; relief of mild to moderate pain
Restrictions An FDA-approved medication guide must be distributed when dispensing an oral outpatient prescription (new or refill) where this medication is to be used without direct supervision of a healthcare provider. Medication guides are available at http://www.fda.gov/cder/Offices/ODS/medication_guides.htm.
Pregnancy Risk Factor C/D (3rd trimester)
Lactation Enters breast milk/not recommended
Medication Safety Issues
Sound-alike/look-alike issues:
Fenoprofen may be confused with flurbiprofen
Nalfon® may be confused with Naldecon®
Contraindications Hypersensitivity to fenoprofen, aspirin, or other NSAIDs, or any component of the formulation; perioperative pain in the setting of coronary artery bypass surgery (CABG); significant renal dysfunction; pregnancy (3rd trimester)
Warnings/Precautions [U.S. Boxed Warning]: NSAIDs are associated with an increased risk of adverse cardiovascular events, including MI, stroke, and new onset or worsening of pre-existing hypertension. Risk may be increased with duration of use or pre-existing cardiovascular risk-factors or disease. Carefully evaluate individual cardiovascular risk profiles prior to prescribing. Use caution with fluid retention, CHF, or hypertension. Concurrent administration of ibuprofen, and potentially other nonselective NSAIDs, may interfere with aspirin's cardioprotective effect.

Use of NSAIDs can compromise existing renal function. Renal toxicity can occur in patient with impaired renal function, dehydration, heart failure, liver dysfunction, those taking diuretics and ACEI, and the elderly. Rehydrate patient before starting therapy. Monitor renal function closely. Not recommended for use in patients with advanced renal disease.

[U.S. Boxed Warning]: NSAIDs may increase risk of gastrointestinal irritation, ulceration, bleeding, and perforation. These events may occur at any time during therapy and without warning. Use caution with a history of GI disease (bleeding or ulcers), concurrent therapy with aspirin, anticoagulants and/or corticosteroids, smoking, use of alcohol, the elderly or debilitated patients.

Use the lowest effective dose for the shortest duration of time, consistent with individual patient goals, to reduce risk of cardiovascular or GI adverse events. Alternate therapies should be considered for patients at high risk.

NSAIDs may cause serious skin adverse events including exfoliative dermatitis, Stevens-Johnson syndrome (SJS), and toxic epidermal necrolysis (TEN). Anaphylactoid reactions may occur, even without prior exposure; patients with "aspirin triad" (bronchial asthma, aspirin intolerance, rhinitis) may be at increased risk. Do not use in patients who experience bronchospasm, asthma, rhinitis, or urticaria with NSAID or aspirin therapy.

Use with caution in patients with decreased hepatic function. Closely monitor patients with any abnormal LFT. Severe hepatic reactions (eg, fulminant hepatitis, liver failure) have occurred with NSAID use, rarely; discontinue if signs or symptoms of liver disease develop, or if systemic manifestations occur.

The elderly are at increased risk for adverse effects (especially peptic ulceration, CNS effects, renal toxicity) from NSAIDs even at low doses.

Withhold for at least 4-6 half-lives prior to surgical or dental procedures. Safety and efficacy have not been established in children.

Adverse Reactions
>10%:
Central nervous system: Dizziness (7% to 15%), somnolence (9% to 15%)
Gastrointestinal: Abdominal cramps (2% to 4%), heartburn, indigestion, nausea (8% to 14%), dyspepsia (10% to 14%), flatulence (14%), anorexia (14%), constipation (7% to 14%), occult blood in stool (14%), vomiting (3% to 14%), diarrhea (2% to 14%)
1% to 10%:
Central nervous system: Headache (9%)
Dermatologic: Itching
Endocrine & metabolic: Fluid retention

<1% (Limited to important or life-threatening): Agranulocytosis, anemia, angioedema, arrhythmia, bone marrow depression, CHF, dyspnea, erythema multiforme, GI ulceration, hemolytic anemia, hepatitis, hypertension, leukopenia, polyuria, renal failure (acute), Stevens-Johnson syndrome, thrombocytopenia, tachycardia, toxic epidermal necrolysis

Overdosage/Toxicology Symptoms include acute renal failure, vomiting, drowsiness, and leukocytosis. Management of nonsteroidal anti-inflammatory drug (NSAID) intoxication is primarily supportive and symptomatic. Fluid therapy is commonly effective in managing hypotension that may occur following an acute NSAID overdose, except when due to acute blood loss.

Drug Interactions

Increased Effect/Toxicity: Increased effect/toxicity of phenytoin, sulfonamides, sulfonylureas, salicylates, and oral anticoagulants. Serum concentration/toxicity of methotrexate may be increased. Concomitant use with fluoroquinolones may rarely increase risk of seizure.

Decreased Effect: Decreased effect with phenobarbital. Thiazide efficacy (diuretic and antihypertensive effect) may be reduced (indomethacin may reduce this efficacy and it may be anticipated with any NSAID). NSAIDs may decrease the antihypertensive effect of ACE inhibitors, angiotensin antagonists, beta-blockers, or hydralazine. Cholestyramine (and other bile acid sequestrants) may decrease the absorption of NSAIDs; separate by at least 2 hours. Salicylates' antiplatelet effect may be reduced.

Ethanol/Nutrition/Herb Interactions

Ethanol: Avoid ethanol (may enhance gastric mucosal irritation).

Food: Fenoprofen peak serum levels may be decreased if taken with food.

Herb/Nutraceutical: Avoid alfalfa, anise, bilberry, bladderwrack, bromelain, cat's claw, celery, coleus, cordyceps, dong quai, evening primrose, feverfew, fenugreek, garlic, ginger, ginkgo biloboa, red clover, horse chestnut, grapeseed, green tea, ginseng, guggul, horse chestnut seed, horseradish, licorice, prickly ash, red clover, reishi, SAMe, sweet clover, turmeric, white willow (all have additional antiplatelet activity).

Mechanism of Action Inhibits prostaglandin synthesis by decreasing the activity of the enzyme, cyclooxygenase, which results in decreased formation of prostaglandin precursors

Pharmacodynamics/Kinetics

Onset of action: A few days

Absorption: Rapid, 80%

Distribution: Does not cross the placenta

Protein binding: 99%

Metabolism: Extensively hepatic

Half-life elimination: 2.5-3 hours

Time to peak, serum: ~2 hours

Excretion: Urine (2% to 5% as unchanged drug); feces (small amounts)

Dosage Adults: Oral:

Rheumatoid arthritis: 300-600 mg 3-4 times/day up to 3.2 g/day

Mild to moderate pain: 200 mg every 4-6 hours as needed

Dosage adjustment in renal impairment: Not recommended in patients with advanced renal disease

Dietary Considerations May be taken with food to decrease GI distress.

Administration Do not crush tablets. Swallow whole with a full glass of water. Take with food to minimize stomach upset.

Monitoring Parameters Monitor CBC, liver enzymes; monitor urine output and BUN/serum creatinine in patients receiving diuretics

Reference Range Therapeutic: 20-65 mcg/mL (SI: 82-268 μmol/L)

Test Interactions Increased chloride (S), increased sodium (S)

Dosage Forms

Capsule, as calcium (Nalfon®): 200 mg, 300 mg

Tablet, as calcium: 600 mg

♦ **Fenoprofen Calcium** see Fenoprofen on page 692

Fentanyl (FEN ta nil)

U.S. Brand Names Actiq®; Duragesic®; Fentora™; Ionsys™; Sublimaze®

Canadian Brand Names Actiq®; Duragesic®; Fentanyl Citrate Injection, USP

Index Terms Fentanyl Citrate; Fentanyl Hydrochloride; OTFC (Oral Transmucosal Fentanyl Citrate)

Pharmacologic Category Analgesic, Opioid; General Anesthetic

Additional Appendix Information

Narcotic Agonists on page 1888

Use

Injection: Sedation, relief of pain, preoperative medication, adjunct to general or regional anesthesia

Iontophoretic transdermal system (Ionsys™): Short-term in-hospital management of acute postoperative pain

Transdermal patch (eg, Duragesic®): Management of moderate-to-severe chronic pain

Transmucosal lozenge (eg, Actiq®), buccal tablet (Fentora™): Management of breakthrough cancer pain

Restrictions C-II

An FDA-approved medication guide for buccal tablet (Fentora™) and transmucosal lozenge (eg, Actiq®) must be distributed when dispensing an outpatient prescription (new or refill) where this medication is to be used without direct supervision of a healthcare provider. Medication guides are available at http://www.fda.gov/cder/Offices/ODS/medication_guides.htm

Pregnancy Risk Factor C/D (prolonged use or high doses at term)

(Continued)

Fentanyl *(Continued)*

Pregnancy Implications Fentanyl crosses the placenta and has been used safely during labor. Chronic use during pregnancy has shown detectable serum levels in the newborn with mild opioid withdrawal (case report). Transdermal patch, transmucosal lozenge, and buccal tablet (Fentora™) are not recommended for analgesia during labor and delivery.

Lactation Enters breast milk/not recommended (AAP rates "compatible")

Medication Safety Issues

Sound-alike/look-alike issues:

Fentanyl may be confused with alfentanil, sufentanil

Dosing of transdermal fentanyl patches may be confusing. Transdermal fentanyl patches should always be prescribed in mcg/hour, not size.

New patch dosage form of Duragesic®-12 actually delivers 12.5 mcg/hour of fentanyl. Use caution, as orders may be written as "Duragesic 12.5" which can be erroneously interpreted as a 125 mcg dose.

Iontophoretic transdermal system (Ionsys™) may contain conducting metal (eg, aluminum); remove patch prior to MRI. Transdermal patch (eg, Duragesic®) does not contain any metal-based compounds; however, the printed ink used to indicate strength on the outer surface of the patch does contain titanium dioxide, but the amount is minimal.

Contraindications Hypersensitivity to fentanyl or any component of the formulation; increased intracranial pressure; severe respiratory disease or depression including acute asthma (unless patient is mechanically ventilated); paralytic ileus; severe liver or renal insufficiency; pregnancy (prolonged use or high doses near term)

Iontophoretic transdermal system (Ionsys™): Hypersensitivity to fentanyl, cetylpyridinium chloride (eg, Cepacol®) or any component of Ionsys™ system

Transmucosal buccal tablets (Fentora™), lozenges (eg, Actiq®), and/or transdermal patches (eg, Duragesic®) are recommended for use only in patients who are opioid-tolerant. Patients are considered opioid-tolerant if they are taking at least 60 mg oral morphine/day, 30 mg oral oxycodone/day, 8 mg oral hydromorphone/day, 25 mcg transdermal fentanyl/hour, or an equivalent dose of another opioid for ≥1 week. Transmucosal buccal tablets (Fentora™), lozenges (eg, Actiq®), and transdermal patches (eg, Duragesic®) are not for use in acute pain, mild pain, intermittent pain, or postoperative pain management.

Warnings/Precautions An opioid-containing analgesic regimen should be tailored to each patient's needs and based upon the type of pain being treated (acute versus chronic), the route of administration, degree of tolerance for opioids (naive versus chronic user), age, weight, and medical condition. The optimal analgesic dose varies widely among patients. Doses should be titrated to pain relief/prevention. When using with other CNS depressants, reduce dose of one or both agents. Fentanyl shares the toxic potentials of opiate agonists, and precautions of opiate agonist therapy should be observed; use with caution in patients with bradycardia; rapid I.V. infusion may result in skeletal muscle and chest wall rigidity leading to respiratory distress and/or apnea, bronchoconstriction, laryngospasm; inject slowly over 3-5 minutes. Tolerance or drug dependence may result from extended use. Use caution in patients with a history of drug dependence or abuse. The elderly may be particularly susceptible to the CNS depressant and constipating effects of narcotics. Use extreme caution in patients with COPD or other chronic respiratory conditions. Use caution with head injuries, morbid obesity, or hepatic dysfunction. Concurrent use of agonist/antagonist analgesics may precipitate withdrawal symptoms and/or reduced analgesic efficacy in patients following prolonged therapy with mu opioid agonists. Abrupt discontinuation following prolonged use may also lead to withdrawal symptoms.

Transmucosal: Lozenge (eg, Actiq®), buccal tablet (Fentora™): **[U.S. Boxed Warning]: Do not substitute Fentora™ on a mcg-per-mcg basis when converting from transmucosal lozenge to buccal tablet. Buccal tablet has higher bioavailability. [U.S. Boxed Warning]: Should be used only for the care of opioid-tolerant cancer patients. [U.S. Boxed Warning]: Buccal tablet and lozenge contain an amount of medication that can be fatal to children.** Keep all units out of the reach of children and discard any open units properly. Safety and efficacy have not been established in children <16 years of age for the lozenge and <18 years of age for the buccal tablet.

Transdermal patches (eg, Duragesic®): **[U.S. Boxed Warning]: Serious or life-threatening hypoventilation may occur, even in opioid-tolerant patients.** Serum fentanyl concentrations may increase approximately one-third for patients with a body temperature of 40°C secondary to a temperature-dependent increase in fentanyl release from the patch and increased skin permeability. Avoid exposure of application site to direct external heat sources. Patients who experience adverse reactions should be monitored for at least 24 hours after removal of the patch. Transdermal patch does not contain any metal-based compounds; the printed ink used to indicate strength on the outer surface of the patch does contain titanium dioxide but the amount is minimal; adverse events have not been reported while wearing during an MRI. **[U.S. Boxed Warning]: Safety and efficacy of transdermal patch have been limited to children ≥2 years of age who are opioid tolerant.**

Iontophoretic transdermal system (Ionsys™): **[U.S. Boxed Warning]: Should only be used for the treatment of hospitalized patients. To avoid overdose, the patient should be the only one to activate the system. Unintended exposure to fentanyl hydrogel could lead to absorption of fatal dose; hydrogel should not come in contact with fingers or mouth.** Should be used only in patients who are able to understand and follow instructions to operate the system. Use caution in patients who have high frequency hearing impairment. Remove prior to MRI procedure, cardioversion, or defibrillation. May interfere with radiographic image or CAT scan. Patients on chronic opioids or with a history of opioid abuse may require higher analgesic doses than Ionsys™ is able to provide. Prior to patient's hospital discharge, the system must be removed and disposed of. **[U.S. Boxed Warning]: A significant amount of fentanyl remains in the iontophoretic transdermal system and requires proper removal and disposal to avoid misuse, abuse, or diversion.** Safety and efficacy of iontophoretic transdermal system have not been established in children <18 years of age.

Adverse Reactions
>10%:
Cardiovascular: Hypotension, bradycardia
Central nervous system: CNS depression, confusion, drowsiness, sedation
Gastrointestinal: Nausea, vomiting, constipation, xerostomia
Local: Application-site reaction (iontophoretic system 14%)
Neuromuscular & skeletal: Chest wall rigidity (high dose I.V.), weakness
Ocular: Miosis
Respiratory: Respiratory depression
Miscellaneous: Diaphoresis

1% to 10%:
Cardiovascular: Cardiac arrhythmia, edema, orthostatic hypotension, hypertension, syncope, tachycardia
Central nervous system: Abnormal dreams, abnormal thinking, agitation, amnesia, anxiety, dizziness, euphoria, fatigue, fever, hallucinations, headache, insomnia, nervousness, paranoid reaction
Dermatologic: Erythema, papules, pruritus (iontophoretic system 6%), rash
Gastrointestinal: Abdominal pain, anorexia, biliary tract spasm, diarrhea, dyspepsia, flatulence, ileus
Genitourinary: Urinary retention (iontophoretic transdermal system 3%)
Hematologic: Anemia
Local: Application site reactions (buccal tablet)
Neuromuscular & skeletal: Abnormal coordination, abnormal gait, back pain, paresthesia, rigors, tremor
Respiratory: Apnea, bronchitis, dyspnea, hemoptysis, hypoxia, pharyngitis, rhinitis, sinusitis, upper respiratory infection
Miscellaneous: Hiccups, flu-like syndrome, speech disorder

<1% (Limited to important or life-threatening): Amblyopia, anorgasmia, aphasia, bradycardia, bronchospasm, circulatory depression, CNS excitation or delirium, convulsions, dental caries (Actiq®), depersonalization, dysesthesia, ejaculatory difficulty, exfoliative dermatitis, gum line erosion (Actiq®), hyper-/hypotonia, laryngospasm, paradoxical dizziness, physical and psychological dependence with prolonged use, stertorous breathing, stupor, tachycardia, tooth loss (Actiq®), urinary tract spasm, urticaria, vertigo

Overdosage/Toxicology Symptoms of overdose include CNS depression, respiratory depression, and miosis; muscle and chest wall rigidity (may require nondepolarizing skeletal muscle relaxant). Treatment is symptom-directed and supportive. If overdose from transdermal patch (eg, Duragesic®), remove system from patient's skin. Naloxone, 2 mg I.V. with repeat administration as necessary up to a total of 10 mg, can also be used to reverse toxic effects of the opiate. Use of an opioid antagonist can precipitate withdrawal in opioid-tolerant patients. Patients who experience adverse reactions during use of transdermal patch (eg, Duragesic®) should be monitored for at least 24 hours after removal of the patch.

Drug Interactions
Cytochrome P450 Effect: Substrate of CYP3A4 (major); **Inhibits** CYP3A4 (weak)
Increased Effect/Toxicity: Increased sedation with CNS depressants. Potential for serotonin syndrome if combined with other serotonergic drugs. Fentanyl may enhance the serotonergic effects of SSRIs and sibutramine. CYP3A4 inhibitors may increase the levels/effects of fentanyl; potentially fatal respiratory depression may occur when a potent inhibitor is used in a patient receiving chronic fentanyl (eg, transdermal patch); example inhibitors include azole antifungals, clarithromycin, diclofenac, doxycycline, erythromycin, imatinib, isoniazid, nefazodone, nicardipine, propofol, protease inhibitors, quinidine, telithromycin, and verapamil. Antipsychotic agents (phenothiazines) may increase hypotension. Protease inhibitors may increase effects of fentanyl.
Decreased Effect: Ammonium chloride may decrease the duration of opioid's analgesia. CYP3A4 inducers (including carbamazepine, phenytoin, phenobarbital, rifampin) may decrease serum levels of fentanyl by increasing metabolism. Pegvisomant effect may be decreased.

Ethanol/Nutrition/Herb Interactions
Ethanol: Avoid ethanol (may increase CNS depression).
Food: Glucose may cause hyperglycemia.
Herb/Nutraceutical: St John's wort may decrease fentanyl levels. Avoid valerian, St John's wort, kava kava, gotu kola (may increase CNS depression).

Stability
Injection formulation: Store at controlled room temperature of 15°C to 25°C (59°F to 86°F). Protect from light.
Iontophoretic transdermal system: Store at 15°C to 30°C (59°F to 86°F).
Transdermal patch: Do not store above 25°C (77°F).
Transmucosal (buccal tablets, lozenges): Store at controlled room temperature of 15°C to 30°C (59°F to 86°F). Protect from freezing and moisture.

Mechanism of Action Binds with stereospecific receptors at many sites within the CNS, increases pain threshold, alters pain reception, inhibits ascending pain pathways

Pharmacodynamics/Kinetics
Onset of action: Analgesic: I.M.: 7-15 minutes; I.V.: Almost immediate; Transmucosal: 5-15 minutes
Peak effect: Transmucosal: Analgesic: 15-30 minutes
Duration: I.M.: 1-2 hours; I.V.: 0.5-1 hour; Transmucosal: Related to blood level; respiratory depressant effect may last longer than analgesic effect
Absorption:
Transmucosal, buccal tablet: Rapid, ~50% from the buccal mucosa; remaining 50% swallowed with saliva and slowly absorbed from GI tract
Transmucosal, lozenge: Rapid, ~25% from the buccal mucosa; 75% swallowed with saliva and slowly absorbed from GI tract
Iontophoretic transdermal system (Ionsys™): Fentanyl levels continue to rise for 5 minutes after the completion of each 10-minute dose
Distribution: Highly lipophilic, redistributes into muscle and fat
(Continued)

Fentanyl *(Continued)*

Protein binding: 80% to 85%

Metabolism: Hepatic, primarily via CYP3A4

Bioavailability: Total (transmucosal and GI absorption): Buccal: 65% (range: 45% to 85%); Lozenge: 47% (range: 37% to 57%)

Half-life elimination:

I.V.: 2-4 hours

Iontophoretic transdermal system (Ionsys™): 11 hours

Transdermal patch: 17 hours (half-life is influenced by absorption rate)

Transmucosal: Lozenge: 7 hours; Buccal tablet: 100-200 mcg: 3-4 hours, 400-800 mcg: 11-12 hours

Time to peak: Buccal tablet: 46 minutes; Lozenge: ~91 minutes; Transdermal patch: 24-72 hours

Excretion: Urine (primarily as metabolites, <7% to 10% as unchanged drug)

Dosage Note: These are guidelines and do not represent the maximum doses that may be required in all patients. Doses should be titrated to pain relief/prevention. Monitor vital signs routinely. Single I.M. doses have a duration of 1-2 hours, single I.V. doses last 0.5-1 hour.

Sedation for minor procedures/analgesia:

Children 1-12 years:

Sedation for minor procedures/analgesia: I.M., I.V.: 1-2 mcg/kg/dose; may repeat at 30- to 60-minute intervals. **Note:** Children 18-36 months of age may require 2-3 mcg/kg/dose

Continuous sedation/analgesia: Initial I.V. bolus: 1-2 mcg/kg; then 1-3 mcg/kg/hour to a maximum dose of 5 mcg/kg/hour

Children >12 years and Adults: I.V.: 25-50 mcg; may repeat every 3-5 minutes to desired effect or adverse event; maximum dose of 500 mcg/4 hours; higher doses are used for major procedures

Surgery: Adults:

Premedication: I.M., slow I.V.: 25-100 mcg/dose 30-60 minutes prior to surgery

Adjunct to regional anesthesia: Slow I.V.: 25-100 mcg/dose over 1-2 minutes. **Note:** An I.V. should be in place with regional anesthesia so the I.M. route is rarely used but still maintained as an option in the package labeling.

Adjunct to general anesthesia: Slow I.V.:

Low dose: 0.5-2 mcg/kg/dose depending on the indication. For example, 0.5 mcg/kg will provide analgesia or reduce the amount of propofol needed for laryngeal mask airway insertion with minimal respiratory depression. However, to blunt the hemodynamic response to intubation 2 mcg/kg is often necessary.

Moderate dose: Initial: 2-15 mcg/kg/dose; Maintenance (bolus or infusion): 1-2 mcg/kg/hour. Discontinuing fentanyl infusion 30-60 minutes prior to the end of surgery will usually allow adequate ventilation upon emergence from anesthesia. For "fast-tracking" and early extubation following major surgery, total fentanyl doses are limited to 10-15 mcg/kg.

High dose: **Note:** High-dose (20-50 mcg/kg/dose) fentanyl is rarely used, but is still maintained in the package labeling.

Acute pain management: Adults:

Severe: I.M, I.V.: 50-100 mcg/dose every 1-2 hours as needed; patients with prior opiate exposure may tolerate higher initial doses

Patient-controlled analgesia (PCA): I.V.: Usual concentration: 10 mcg/mL

Demand dose: Usual: 10 mcg; range: 10-50 mcg

Lockout interval: 5-8 minutes

Mechanically-ventilated patients (based on 70 kg patient): Slow I.V.: 0.35-1.5 mcg/kg every 30-60 minutes as needed; infusion: 0.7-10 mcg/kg/hour

Iontophoretic transdermal system: 40 mcg per activation on-demand (maximum: 6 doses/hour). **Note:** Patient's pain should be controlled prior to initiating system. Instruct patient how to operate system. Only the patient should initiate system. Each system operates for 24 hours or until 80 doses have been administered, whichever comes first.

Breakthrough cancer pain: For patients who are tolerant to and currently receiving opioid therapy for persistent cancer pain; dosing should be individually titrated to provide adequate analgesia with minimal side effects. Dose titration should be done if patient requires more than 1 dose/breakthrough pain episode for several consecutive episodes. Patients experiencing >4 breakthrough pain episodes/day should have the dose of their long-term opioid re-evaluated.

Children ≥16 years and Adults: Lozenge: Initial dose: 200 mcg; the second dose may be started 15 minutes after completion of the first dose. Consumption should be limited to ≤4 units/day.

Adults: Buccal tablet (Fentora™): Initial dose: 100 mcg; a second 100 mcg dose, if needed, may be started 30 minutes after the start of the first dose.

Dose titration, if required, should be done using multiples of the 100 mcg tablets. Patient can take two 100 mcg tablets (one on each side of mouth). If that dose is not successful, can use four 100 mcg tablets (two on each side of mouth). If titration requires >400 mcg/dose, then use 200 mcg tablets.

Conversion from lozenge to buccal tablet (Fentora™):

Lozenge dose 200-400 mcg, then buccal tablet 100 mcg

Lozenge dose 600-800 mcg, then buccal tablet 200 mcg

Lozenge dose 1200 mcg, then buccal tablet 400 mcg

Note: Four 100 mcg buccal tablets deliver approximately 12% and 13% higher values of C_{max} and AUC, respectively, compared to one 400 mcg buccal tablet. To prevent confusion, patient should only have one strength available at a time. Using more than four buccal tablets at a time has not been studied.

Elderly >65 years: Transmucosal lozenge (eg, Actiq®): Dose should be reduced to 2.5-5 mcg/kg

Chronic pain management: Children ≥2 years and Adults (opioid-tolerant patients): Transdermal patch (eg, Duragesic®):

Initial: To convert patients from oral or parenteral opioids to transdermal patch, a 24-hour analgesic requirement should be calculated (based on prior opiate use). Using the tables, the appropriate initial dose can be determined. The initial fentanyl dosage may be approximated from the 24-hour morphine dosage and titrated to minimize adverse effects and provide analgesia. With the initial application, the absorption of transdermal fentanyl requires several hours to reach plateau; therefore transdermal fentanyl is inappropriate for management of acute pain. Change patch every 72 hours.

Conversion from continuous infusion of fentanyl: In patients who have adequate pain relief with a fentanyl infusion, fentanyl may be converted to transdermal dosing at a rate equivalent to the intravenous rate. A two-step taper of the infusion to be completed over 12 hours has been recommended (Kornick, 2001) after the patch is applied. The infusion is decreased to 50% of the original rate six hours after the application of the first patch, and subsequently discontinued twelve hours after application.

Titration: Short-acting agents may be required until analgesic efficacy is established and/or as supplements for "breakthrough" pain. The amount of supplemental doses should be closely monitored. Appropriate dosage increases may be based on daily supplemental dosage using the ratio of 45 mg/24 hours of oral morphine to a 12.5 mcg/hour increase in fentanyl dosage.

Frequency of adjustment: The dosage should not be titrated more frequently than every 3 days after the initial dose or every 6 days thereafter. Patients should wear a consistent fentanyl dosage through two applications (6 days) before dosage increase based on supplemental opiate dosages can be estimated.

Frequency of application: The majority of patients may be controlled on every 72-hour administration; however, a small number of patients require every 48-hour administration.

Dose conversion guidelines for transdermal fentanyl[1] (see tables below and on next page).

Recommended Initial Duragesic® Dose Based Upon Daily Oral Morphine Dose[1]

Oral 24-Hour Morphine (mg/d)	Duragesic® Dose (mcg/h)
60-134[2]	25
135-224	50
225-314	75
315-404	100
405-494	125
495-584	150
585-674	175
675-764	200
765-854	225
855-944	250
945-1034	275
1035-1124	300

[1]The table should NOT be used to convert from transdermal fentanyl (eg, Duragesic®) to other opioid analgesics. Rather, following removal of the patch, titrate the dose of the new opioid until adequate analgesia is achieved.
[2]Pediatric patients initiating therapy on a 25 mcg/hour Duragesic® system should be opioid-tolerant and receiving at least 60 mg oral morphine equivalents per day.

Dosing Conversion Guidelines[1,2]

Current Analgesic	Daily Dosage (mg/day)			
Morphine (I.M./I.V.)	10-22	23-37	38-52	53-67
Oxycodone (oral)	30-67	67.5-112	112.5-157	157.5-202
Oxycodone (I.M./I.V.)	15-33	33.1-56	56.1-78	78.1-101
Codeine (oral)	150-447	448-747	748-1047	1048-1347
Hydromorphone (oral)	8-17	17.1-28	28.1-39	39.1-51
Hydromorphone (I.V.)	1.5-3.4	3.5-5.6	5.7-7.9	8-10
Meperidine (I.M.)	75-165	166-278	279-390	391-503
Methadone (oral)	20-44	45-74	75-104	105-134
Methadone (I.M.)	10-22	23-37	38-52	53-67
Fentanyl transdermal recommended dose (mcg/h)	**25 mcg/h**	**50 mcg/h**	**75 mcg/h**	**100 mcg/h**

[1]The table should NOT be used to convert from transdermal fentanyl (eg, Duragesic®) to other opioid analgesics. Rather, following removal of the patch, titrate the dose of the new opioid until adequate analgesia is achieved.

[2] Duragesic® product insert, Janssen Pharmaceutica, Feb 2005.

(Continued)

Fentanyl *(Continued)*

Opioid Analgesics Initial Oral Dosing Commonly Used for Severe Pain

Drug	Equianalgesic Dose (mg)		Initial Oral Dose	
	Oral[1]	Parenteral[2]	Children (mg/kg)	Adults (mg)
Buprenorphine	—	0.4	—	—
Butorphanol	—	2	—	—
Hydromorphone	7.5	1.5	0.06	4-8
Levorphanol	4 (acute) 1 (chronic)	2 (acute) 1 (chronic)	0.04	2-4
Meperidine	300	75	Not Recommended	
Methadone	10	5	0.2	0.2
Morphine	30	10	0.3	15-30
Nalbuphine	—	10	—	—
Pentazocine	50	30	—	—
Oxycodone	20	—	0.3	10-20
Oxymorphone	1	—	—	—

From "Principles of Analgesic Use in the Treatment of Acute Pain and Cancer Pain," *Am Pain Soc*, Fifth Ed.

[1]Elderly: Starting dose should be lower for this population group

[2]Standard parenteral doses for acute pain in adults; can be used to doses for I.V. infusions and repeated small I.V. boluses. Single I.V. boluses, use half the I.M. dose. Children >6 months: I.V. dose = parenteral equianalgesic dose x weight (kg)/100

Dosing adjustment in hepatic impairment: Actiq®: Although fentanyl kinetics may be altered in hepatic disease, Actiq® can be used successfully in the management of breakthrough cancer pain. Doses should be titrated to reach clinical effect with careful monitoring of patients with severe hepatic disease.

Dietary Considerations Transmucosal lozenge contains 2 g sugar per unit.

Administration

I.V.: Muscular rigidity may occur with rapid I.V. administration.

Transdermal patch (eg, Duragesic®): Apply to nonirritated and nonirradiated skin, such as chest, back, flank, or upper arm. Do not shave skin; hair at application site should be clipped. Prior to application, clean site with clear water and allow to dry completely. Do not use damaged or cut patches; a rapid release of fentanyl and increased systemic absorption may occur. Firmly press in place and hold for 30 seconds. Change patch every 72 hours. Do **not** use soap, alcohol, or other solvents to remove transdermal gel if it accidentally touches skin; use copious amounts of water. Avoid exposing application site to external heat sources (eg, heating pad, electric blanket, heat lamp, hot tub).

Iontophoretic transdermal system: System should be tested and applied by healthcare professional. The sticker on the back of the pouch is intended for use by the registered nurse. The sticker should be removed and applied to the Ionsys™ system with a date and time of application so that subsequent healthcare providers will know when the system expires (24 hours after application). Apply to intact, nonirritated, nonirradiated skin on chest or upper outer arm. Do not apply to scarred, burned, or tattooed areas. Any excessive hair at application site should be clipped; do not shave. Remove clear, plastic release liner before placement on skin. Avoid pulling on red tab. To administer a dose, the patient must press the button twice firmly within 3 seconds. An audible tone (beep) indicates the start of the delivery of the dose; red light remains on throughout the 10-minute dosing period. Each system operates for 24 hours or until 80 doses have been used (whichever comes first). Rotate site if another system is required after the first one is finished. Do not touch sticky side of system or the gels. If the hydrogel (where fentanyl is housed) becomes separated from the delivery system during removal, use gloves or tweezers to remove the hydrogel from skin. Do not use soap, alcohol, or other solvents to remove the hydrogel as they can increase absorption of fentanyl. Once a system has been removed, the same system can not be reapplied. Contains metal; remove prior to MRi procedure, cardioversion, or defibrillation.

Lozenge: Foil overwrap should be removed just prior to administration. Place the unit in mouth and allow it to dissolve. Do not chew. Lozenge may be moved from one side of the mouth to the other. The unit should be consumed over a period of 15 minutes. Handle should be removed after it is consumed or if patient has achieved an adequate response and/or shows signs of respiratory depression.

Buccal tablet: Patient should not open blister until ready to administer. The blister backing should be peeled back to expose the tablet; tablet should not be pushed out through the blister. Immediately use tablet once removed from blister. Place entire tablet in the buccal cavity (above a rear molar, between the upper cheek and gum). Tablet should not be broken, sucked, chewed, or swallowed. Should dissolve in about 14-25 minutes when left between the cheek and the gum. If remnants remain they may be swallowed with water.

Monitoring Parameters Respiratory and cardiovascular status, blood pressure, heart rate; signs of misuse, abuse, or addiction

Transdermal patch: Monitor for 24 hours after application of first dose

Additional Information Fentanyl is 50-100 times as potent as morphine; morphine 10 mg I.M. is equivalent to fentanyl 0.1-0.2 mg I.M.; fentanyl has less hypotensive effects than morphine due to lack of histamine release. However, fentanyl may cause rigidity with high doses. If the patient has required high-dose analgesia or has used for a prolonged period (~7 days), taper dose to prevent withdrawal; monitor for signs and symptoms of withdrawal.

Iontophoretic transdermal system: Pharmacist should test before dispensing for patient. Without opening pouch, pharmacist should locate button side, find button and firmly press and release button twice within 3 seconds. Listen for a single audible tone (beep) confirming that the system is functional. The pharmacist should sign the front of the pouch after performing the functionality test.

Four minutes after the functional test, the system will beep for 15 seconds indicating that it is not in contact with skin. Open by cutting on dotted line of pouch, remove and discard plastic liner covering adhesive. Do not pull on red tab while removing. Press system firmly in place with sticky side down, on skin for at least 15 seconds. Make sure all sides of outer edge stick to skin. May tape sides down if they loosen; don't tape over button or red light. To determine the number of doses delivered, the red light will flash between doses in one second pulses to indicate the approximate number of doses that have been administered up to the present time. Each flash indicates up to 5 doses have been administered: One flash 1-5 doses; two flashes 6-10 doses; three flashes 11-15 doses; four flashes 16-20 doses, continuing up to 16 flashes (76-80 doses).

To dispose of system, wear gloves and pull the red tab to separate the bottom from the top. Fold the bottom in half with the sticky side facing in and flush down the toilet (needs to be witnessed by second healthcare provider). Dispose of top section according to hospital procedures for batteries.

Transmucosal (oral lozenge): Disposal of lozenge units: After consumption of a complete unit, the handle may be disposed of in a trash container that is out of the reach of children. For a partially-consumed unit, or a unit that still has any drug matrix remaining on the handle, the handle should be placed under hot running tap water until the drug matrix has dissolved. Special child-resistant containers are available to temporarily store partially consumed units that cannot be disposed of immediately.

Transdermal patch (Duragesic®): Upon removal of the patch, ~17 hours are required before serum concentrations fall to 50% of their original values. Opioid withdrawal symptoms are possible. Gradual downward titration (potentially by the sequential use of lower-dose patches) is recommended. Keep transdermal patch (both used and unused) out of the reach of children. Do **not** use soap, alcohol, or other solvents to remove transdermal gel if it accidentally touches skin as they may increase transdermal absorption, use copious amounts of water. Avoid exposure of direct external heat sources (eg, heating pads, electric blankets, heat lamps, saunas, hot tubs, heated water beds) to application site.

Dosage Forms

Infusion [premixed in NS]: 0.05 mg (10 mL); 1 mg (100 mL); 1.25 mg (250 mL); 2 mg (100 mL); 2.5 mg (250 mL)

Injection, solution [preservative free]: 0.05 mg/mL (2 mL, 5 mL, 10 mL, 20 mL, 30 mL, 50 mL)

Sublimaze®: 0.05 mg/mL (2 mL, 5 mL, 10 mL, 20 mL)

Lozenge, oral [transmucosal]: 200 mcg, 400 mcg, 600 mcg, 800 mcg, 1200 mcg, 1600 mcg

Actiq®: 200 mcg, 400 mcg, 600 mcg, 800 mcg, 1200 mcg, 1600 mcg [mounted on a plastic radiopaque handle; contains sugar 2 g/unit; raspberry flavor]

Tablet, for buccal application:

Fentora™: 100 mcg, 200 mcg, 400 mcg, 600 mcg, 800 mcg

Transdermal system, topical: 25 mcg/hour [6.25 cm²] (5s); 50 mcg/hour [12.5 cm²] (5s); 75 mcg/hour [18.75 cm²]; 100 mcg/hour [25 cm²] (5s)

Duragesic®: 12 [delivers 12.5 mcg/hour; 5 cm²; contains alcohol 0.1 mL/10 cm²] (5s); 25 [delivers 25 mcg/hour; 10 cm²; contains alcohol 0.1 mL/10 cm²] (5s); 50 [delivers 50 mcg/hour; 20 cm²; contains alcohol 0.1 mL/10 cm²] (5s); 75 [delivers 75 mcg/hour; 30 cm²; contains alcohol 0.1 mL/10 cm²] (5s); 100 [delivers 100 mcg/hour; 40 cm²; contains alcohol 0.1 mL/10 cm²] (5s)

Transdermal iontophoretic system, topical:

Ionsys™: Fentanyl 40 mcg/dose [80 doses/patch; contains 3-volt lithium battery]

♦ **Fentanyl Citrate** *see* Fentanyl *on page 693*

♦ **Fentanyl Citrate Injection, USP (Can)** *see* Fentanyl *on page 693*

♦ **Fentanyl Hydrochloride** *see* Fentanyl *on page 693*

♦ **Fentora™** *see* Fentanyl *on page 693*

♦ **Feosol® [OTC]** *see* Ferrous Sulfate *on page 704*

♦ **Feostat® [OTC] [DSC]** *see* Ferrous Fumarate *on page 702*

♦ **Feratab® [OTC]** *see* Ferrous Sulfate *on page 704*

♦ **Fer-Gen-Sol [OTC]** *see* Ferrous Sulfate *on page 704*

♦ **Fergon® [OTC]** *see* Ferrous Gluconate *on page 703*

♦ **Fer-In-Sol® [OTC]** *see* Ferrous Sulfate *on page 704*

♦ **Fer-In-Sol® (Can)** *see* Ferrous Sulfate *on page 704*

♦ **Fer-Iron® [OTC]** *see* Ferrous Sulfate *on page 704*

♦ **Fermalac (Can)** *see* Lactobacillus *on page 969*

♦ **Ferodan™ (Can)** *see* Ferrous Sulfate *on page 704*

♦ **Fero-Grad 500® [OTC]** *see* Ferrous Sulfate and Ascorbic Acid *on page 705*

♦ **Ferretts [OTC]** *see* Ferrous Fumarate *on page 702*

♦ **Ferrex 150 [OTC]** *see* Polysaccharide-Iron Complex *on page 1390*

♦ **Ferric (III) Hexacyanoferrate (II)** *see* Ferric Hexacyanoferrate *on page 701*

Ferric Gluconate (FER ik GLOO koe nate)

U.S. Brand Names Ferrlecit®

Canadian Brand Names Ferrlecit®

Index Terms Sodium Ferric Gluconate

Pharmacologic Category Iron Salt

Use Repletion of total body iron content in patients with iron-deficiency anemia who are undergoing hemodialysis in conjunction with erythropoietin therapy

Pregnancy Risk Factor B

(Continued)

Ferric Gluconate *(Continued)*

Pregnancy Implications There are no well-controlled studies available. Should be used in pregnancy only when the potential benefit to the mother clearly outweighs the potential risk to the fetus.

Lactation Excretion in breast milk unknown/use caution

Medication Safety Issues
Sound-alike/look-alike issues:
Ferrlecit® may be confused with Ferralet®

Contraindications Hypersensitivity to ferric gluconate or any component of the formulation; use in any anemia not caused by iron deficiency; iron overload

Warnings/Precautions Potentially serious hypersensitivity reactions may occur. Fatal immediate hypersensitivity reactions have occurred with other iron carbohydrate complexes. Avoid rapid administration. Flushing and transient hypotension may occur. May augment hemodialysis-induced hypotension. Use with caution in elderly patients. Use only in patients with documented iron deficiency; caution with hemoglobinopathies or other refractory anemias. Safety and efficacy in children <6 years of age have not been established. Contains benzyl alcohol; do not use in neonates. Administration rate should not exceed 2.1 mg/minute.

Adverse Reactions
Cardiovascular: Angina, bradycardia, chest pain, edema, hyper-/hypotension, hypervolemia, MI, pulmonary edema, syncope, tachycardia, thrombosis, vasodilation
Central nervous system: Agitation, chills, dizziness, fatigue, fever, headache, insomnia, malaise, pain, somnolence
Dermatologic: Pruritus, rash
Endocrine & metabolic: Hyper-/hypokalemia, hypoglycemia
Gastrointestinal: Abdominal pain, anorexia, diarrhea, dyspepsia, epigastric pain, eructation, flatulence, melena, nausea, vomiting
Genitourinary: Urinary tract infection
Hematologic: Abnormal erythrocytes, leukocytosis, lymphadenopathy
Local: Injection site reactions, injection site pain
Neuromuscular & skeletal: Arthralgia, back pain, cramps, groin pain, leg cramps, myalgia, paresthesia, rigors, weakness
Ocular: Blurred vision, conjunctivitis
Respiratory: Cough, dyspnea, pneumonia, rhinitis, upper respiratory infection
Miscellaneous: Carcinoma, diaphoresis increased, flu-like syndrome, hypersensitivity reactions, infection, sepsis
Postmarketing and/or case reports: Dry mouth, epigastric pain, groin pain, hemorrhage, hypertonia, nervousness

Overdosage/Toxicology Serum iron levels >300 mcg/dL may indicate iron poisoning. Initially, symptoms include abdominal pain, diarrhea, and/or vomiting and may progress to pallor, cyanosis, lassitude, drowsiness, acidosis and cardiovascular collapse. Treatment is generally symptom-directed and supportive

Drug Interactions
Decreased Effect: Ferric gluconate injection may decrease the absorption of oral iron.

Stability Store at 20°C to 25°C (68°F to 77°F). Do not freeze. For I.V. infusion, dilute 10 mL ferric gluconate in 0.9% sodium chloride (children: 25 mL NS; adults: 100 mL NS); use immediately after dilution.

Mechanism of Action Supplies a source to elemental iron necessary to the function of hemoglobin, myoglobin and specific enzyme systems; allows transport of oxygen via hemoglobin

Pharmacodynamics/Kinetics Half-life elimination: Bound: 1 hour

Dosage I.V.: Repletion of iron in hemodialysis patients:
Children ≥6 years: 1.5 mg/kg of elemental iron (maximum: 125 mg/dose) diluted in NS 25 mL, administered over 60 minutes at 8 sequential dialysis sessions
Adults: 125 mg elemental iron per 10 mL (either by I.V. infusion or slow I.V. injection). Most patients will require a cumulative dose of 1 g elemental iron over approximately 8 sequential dialysis treatments to achieve a favorable response.
Note: A test dose of 2 mL diluted in NS 50 mL administered over 60 minutes was previously recommended (not in current manufacturer labeling). Doses >125 mg are associated with increased adverse events.

Administration
I.V.: Adults: May be diluted prior to administration; avoid rapid administration. Infusion rate should not exceed 2.1 mg/minute. If administered undiluted, infuse slowly at a rate of up to 12.5 mg/minute.

Monitoring Parameters Hemoglobin and hematocrit, serum ferritin, iron saturation; vital signs

NKF K/DOQI guidelines recommend that iron status should be monitored monthly during initiation through the percent transferrin saturation (TSAT) and serum ferritin.

Reference Range CKD patients should have sufficient iron to achieve and maintain hemoglobin of 11-12 g/dL. To achieve and maintain this target Hgb, sufficient iron should be administered to maintain a TSAT of 20%, and a serum ferritin level >100 ng/mL (nondialysis chronic kidney disease and peritoneal dialysis chronic kidney disease) or serum ferritin level >200 ng/mL (hemodialysis chronic kidney disease).

Test Interactions Serum or transferrin bound iron levels may be falsely elevated if assessed within 24 hours of ferric gluconate administration. Serum ferritin levels may be falsely elevated for 5 days after ferric gluconate administration.

Dosage Forms
Injection, solution:
Ferrlecit®: Elemental iron 12.5 mg/mL (5 mL) [contains benzyl alcohol and sucrose 20%]

Ferric Hexacyanoferrate (FER ik hex a SYE an oh fer ate)

U.S. Brand Names Radiogardase™
Index Terms Ferric (III) Hexacyanoferrate (II); Insoluble Prussian Blue; Prussian Blue
Pharmacologic Category Antidote
Use Treatment of known or suspected internal contamination with radioactive cesium and/or radioactive or nonradioactive thallium
Pregnancy Risk Factor C
Pregnancy Implications Ferric hexacyanoferrate is not absorbed from the gastrointestinal tract and reproduction studies have not been conducted. Cesium-137 crosses the placenta; in one case, reported levels were equal in the mother and the neonate. Thallium also crosses the placenta; fetal death, failure to thrive, and alopecia in the neonate have been reported. Toxicity from exposure to thallium or radioactive cesium is expected to be greater than the risk of toxicity to ferric hexacyanoferrate. Oligospermia or azoospermia has been reported following whole body radiation in doses >1 Gy of cesium-137.
Lactation Excretion in breast milk unknown/not recommended
Contraindications None known
Warnings/Precautions Ferric hexacyanoferrate increases the rate of elimination of thallium and cesium; it does not treat complications of radiation exposure. Supportive treatment for radiation toxicity should be given concomitantly. Use caution with decreased gastric motility; constipation should be avoided to prevent increased radiation absorption from the gastrointestinal tract. Use caution with pre-existing cardiac arrhythmias or electrolyte imbalances. Patients should be instructed to minimize radiation exposure to others. Additional decontamination and/or treatment may be needed if exposure to other radioactive isotopes is known or suspected.
Adverse Reactions
>10%: Gastrointestinal: Constipation (24%)
1% to 10%: Endocrine & metabolic: Hypokalemia (7%)
Frequency not defined: Gastrointestinal: Gastric distress, fecal discoloration (blue)
Overdosage/Toxicology Effects of overdose are not known. Severe constipation, GI obstruction,or severe electrolyte depletion may be expected.
Ethanol/Nutrition/Herb Interactions Food: May increase effectiveness by stimulating bile secretion and thereby increasing the amount of cesium or thallium available to bind with ferric hexacyanoferrate. May bind with essential nutrients.
Stability Store in the dark at controlled room temperature of 15°C to 30°C (59°F to 86°F).
Mechanism of Action Binds to cesium and thallium isotopes in the gastrointestinal tract following their ingestion or excretion in the bile; reduces their gastrointestinal reabsorption (enterohepatic circulation)
Pharmacodynamics/Kinetics
Absorption: Ferric hexacyanoferrate: Oral: None
Half-life elimination:
Cesium-137: Effective: Adults: 80 days, decreased by 69% with ferric hexacyanoferrate; adolescents: 62 days, decreased by 46% with ferric hexacyanoferrate; children: 42 days, decreased by 43% with ferric hexacyanoferrate
Nonradioactive thallium: Biological: 8-10 days; with ferric hexacyanoferrate: 3 days
Excretion:
Cesium-137: Without ferric hexacyanoferrate: Urine (~80%); feces (~20%)
Thallium: Without ferric hexacyanoferrate: Fecal to urine excretion ration: 2:1
Ferric hexacyanoferrate: Feces (99%, unchanged)
Dosage Oral: Internal contamination with radioactive cesium and/or radioactive or nonradioactive thallium:
Children 2-12 years: 1 g 3 times/day; treatment should begin as soon as possible following exposure, but is also effective if therapy is delayed
Children >12 years and Adults: 3 g 3 times/day; treatment should begin as soon as possible following exposure, but is also effective if therapy is delayed
Note: Cesium exposure: Once internal radioactivity is substantially decreased, dosage may be reduced to 1-2 g 3 times/day to improve gastrointestinal tolerance
Elderly: Refer to Adults dosing
Dosage adjustment in renal impairment: Studies have not been conducted; however, ferric hexacyanoferrate is not renally eliminated.
Dosage adjustment in hepatic impairment: Studies have not been conducted; however, effectiveness may be decreased due to decreased bile excretion of cesium and thallium.
Dietary Considerations Take with food to stimulate excretion of cesium or thallium. A high-fiber diet or fiber laxative is recommended to avoid constipation.
Administration Capsules may be opened and mixed with bland food or liquid (instruct patients that mouth and teeth may become blue). Administer with food to stimulate excretion of cesium or thallium. Increase dietary fiber or take with fiber laxative to decrease constipation.
Monitoring Parameters
Bowel movements; CBC and electrolytes weekly
Baseline cesium and/or thallium exposure (whole body counting and/or bioassay, feces or urine sample); urine and fecal cesium and/or thallium weekly during therapy; residual whole body radioactivity after 30 days of treatment
Additional Information Detailed treatment information should be reported to the manufacturer; contact the manufacturer or the complete prescribing information for data collection forms. In case of thallium intoxication, elimination of thallium may also be increased by: Induced emesis followed by intubation and lavage; forced diuresis if urinary excretion is <1 mg/24 hours; charcoal hemoperfusion during the first 48 hours following ingestion; hemodialysis
Dosage Forms Capsule: 0.5 g

♦ **Ferrlecit®** see Ferric Gluconate on page 699
♦ **Ferro-Sequels® [OTC]** see Ferrous Fumarate on page 702

Ferrous Fumarate (FER us FYOO ma rate)

U.S. Brand Names Femiron® [OTC]; Feostat® [OTC] [DSC]; Ferretts [OTC]; Ferro-Sequels® [OTC]; Hemocyte® [OTC]; Ircon® [OTC]; Nephro-Fer® [OTC]

Canadian Brand Names Palafer®

Index Terms Iron Fumarate

Pharmacologic Category Iron Salt

Use Prevention and treatment of iron-deficiency anemias

Pregnancy Risk Factor A

Medication Safety Issues
Sound-alike/look-alike issues:
Feostat® may be confused with Feosol®

Contraindications Hypersensitivity to iron salts or any component of the formulation; hemochromatosis, hemolytic anemia

Warnings/Precautions Avoid in patients with peptic ulcer, enteritis, or ulcerative colitis. Administration of iron for >6 months should be avoided except in patients with continuous bleeding or menorrhagia. Anemia in the elderly is often caused by "anemia of chronic disease" or associated with inflammation rather than blood loss. Iron stores are usually normal or increased, with a serum ferritin >50 ng/mL and a decreased total iron binding capacity. Hence, the "anemia of chronic disease" is not secondary to iron deficiency but the inability of the reticuloendothelial system to reclaim available iron stores. Avoid in patients receiving frequent blood transfusions Avoid use in premature infants until the vitamin E stores, deficient at birth, are replenished. **[U.S. Boxed Warning]: Severe iron toxicity may occur in overdose, particularly when ingested by children; iron is a leading cause of fatal poisoning in children; store out of children's reach and in child-resistant containers.**

Adverse Reactions
>10%: Gastrointestinal: Stomach cramping, constipation, nausea, vomiting, dark stools
1% to 10%:
Gastrointestinal: Heartburn, diarrhea, staining of teeth
Genitourinary: Discoloration of urine
<1% (Limited to important or life-threatening): Contact irritation

Overdosage/Toxicology Symptoms include acute GI irritation, erosion of GI mucosa, hepatic and renal impairment, coma, hematemesis, lethargy, and acidosis. Due to severe toxicity, serum iron ≥300 mcg/mL requires treatment. Following treatment for fluid losses, metabolic acidosis, and shock, a severe iron overdose may be treated with deferoxamine. Deferoxamine may be administered I.V. (80 mg/kg over 24 hours) or I.M. (40-90 mg/kg every 8 hours). The usual toxic dose of elemental iron is ≥35 mg/kg.

Drug Interactions
Increased Effect/Toxicity: Concurrent administration of ≥200 mg vitamin C per 30 mg elemental iron increases absorption of oral iron.
Decreased Effect: Absorption of oral preparation of iron and tetracyclines are decreased when both of these drugs are given together. Absorption of fluoroquinolones, levodopa, methyldopa, and penicillamine may be decreased due to formation of a ferric ion-quinoline complex. Concurrent administration of antacids, H₂ blockers (cimetidine), or proton pump inhibitors may decrease iron absorption. Response to iron therapy may be delayed by chloramphenicol.

Ethanol/Nutrition/Herb Interactions Food: Cereals, dietary fiber, tea, coffee, eggs, and milk may decrease absorption.

Stability Iron is a leading cause of fatal poisoning in children. Store out of children's reach and in child-resistant containers.

Mechanism of Action Replaces iron found in hemoglobin, myoglobin, and enzymes; allows the transportation of oxygen via hemoglobin

Pharmacodynamics/Kinetics
Onset of action: Hematologic response: Oral, parenteral iron salts: ~3-10 days
Peak effect: Reticulocytosis: 5-10 days; hemoglobin values increase within 2-4 weeks
Absorption: Iron is absorbed in the duodenum and upper jejunum; in persons with normal serum iron stores, 10% of an oral dose is absorbed, this is increased to 20% to 30% in persons with inadequate iron stores. Food and achlorhydria will decrease absorption.
Protein binding: To serum transferrin
Excretion: Urine, sweat, sloughing of intestinal mucosa, and menses

Dosage Oral (dose expressed in terms of elemental iron):
Children:
Severe iron-deficiency anemia: 4-6 mg Fe/kg/day in 3 divided doses
Mild to moderate iron deficiency anemia: 3 mg Fe/kg/day in 1-2 divided doses
Prophylaxis: 1-2 mg Fe/kg/day
Adults:
Iron deficiency: 60-100 mg twice daily up to 60 mg 2 times/day
Prophylaxis: 60-100 mg/day
To avoid GI upset, start with a single daily dose and increase by 1 tablet/day each week or as tolerated until desired daily dose is achieved
Elderly: 200 mg 3-4 times/day

Dietary Considerations Should be taken with water or juice on an empty stomach; may be administered with food to prevent irritation; however, not with cereals, dietary fiber, tea, coffee, eggs, or milk.
Elemental iron content of ferrous fumarate: 33%

Administration Administer 2 hours prior to or 4 hours after antacids.

Reference Range
Serum iron:
Male: 75-175 mcg/dL (SI: 13.4-31.3 µmol/L)
Female: 65-165 mcg/dL (SI: 11.6-29.5 µmol/L)
Total iron binding capacity: 230-430 mcg/dL
Transferrin: 204-360 mg/dL

Percent transferrin saturation: 20% to 50%
Iron levels >300 mcg/dL can be considered toxic, should be treated as an overdose

Dosage Forms [DSC] = Discontinued product

Tablet: 324 mg [elemental iron 106 mg]

Femiron®: 63 mg [elemental iron 20 mg]

Ferretts: 325 mg [elemental iron 106 mg]

Hemocyte®: 324 mg [elemental iron 106 mg]

Ircon®: 200 mg [elemental iron 66 mg]

Nephro-Fer®: 350 mg [elemental iron 115 mg; contains tartrazine]

Tablet, chewable (Feostat®): 100 mg [elemental iron 33 mg; chocolate flavor] [DSC]

Tablet, timed release (Ferro-Sequels®): 150 mg [elemental iron 50 mg; contains docusate sodium and sodium benzoate]

Ferrous Gluconate (FER us GLOO koe nate)

U.S. Brand Names Fergon® [OTC]

Canadian Brand Names Apo-Ferrous Gluconate®; Novo-Ferrogluc

Index Terms Iron Gluconate

Pharmacologic Category Iron Salt

Use Prevention and treatment of iron-deficiency anemias

Pregnancy Risk Factor A

Contraindications Hypersensitivity to iron salts or any component of the formulation; hemochromatosis, hemolytic anemia

Warnings/Precautions Avoid in patients with peptic ulcer, enteritis, or ulcerative colitis. Administration of iron for >6 months should be avoided except in patients with continuous bleeding or menorrhagia. Anemia in the elderly is often caused by "anemia of chronic disease" or associated with inflammation rather than blood loss. Iron stores are usually normal or increased, with a serum ferritin >50 ng/mL and a decreased total iron binding capacity. Hence, the "anemia of chronic disease" is not secondary to iron deficiency but the inability of the reticuloendothelial system to reclaim available iron stores. Avoid in patients receiving frequent blood transfusions Avoid use in premature infants until the vitamin E stores, deficient at birth, are replenished. **[U.S. Boxed Warning]: Severe iron toxicity may occur in overdose, particularly when ingested by children; iron is a leading cause of fatal poisoning in children; store out of children's reach and in child-resistant containers.**

Adverse Reactions

>10%: Gastrointestinal: Stomach cramping, constipation, nausea, vomiting, dark stools

1% to 10%:

Gastrointestinal: Heartburn, diarrhea, staining of teeth

Genitourinary: Discoloration of urine

<1% (Limited to important or life-threatening): Contact irritation

Overdosage/Toxicology Symptoms include acute GI irritation, erosion of GI mucosa, hepatic and renal impairment, coma, hematemesis, lethargy, and acidosis. Due to severe toxicity, serum iron ≥300 mcg/mL requires treatment. Following treatment for fluid losses, metabolic acidosis, and shock, a severe iron overdose may be treated with deferoxamine. Deferoxamine may be administered I.V. (80 mg/kg over 24 hours) or I.M. (40-90 mg/kg every 8 hours). The usual toxic dose of elemental iron is ≥35 mg/kg.

Drug Interactions

Increased Effect/Toxicity: Concurrent administration of ≥200 mg vitamin C per 30 mg elemental iron increases absorption of oral iron.

Decreased Effect: Absorption of oral preparation of iron and tetracyclines are decreased when both of these drugs are given together. Absorption of fluoroquinolones, levodopa, methyldopa, and penicillamine may be decreased due to formation of a ferric ion-quinolone complex. Concurrent administration of antacids, H_2 blockers (cimetidine), or proton pump inhibitors may decrease iron absorption. Response to iron therapy may be delayed by chloramphenicol.

Ethanol/Nutrition/Herb Interactions Food: Cereals, dietary fiber, tea, coffee, eggs, and milk may decrease absorption.

Stability Iron is a leading cause of fatal poisoning in children. Store out of children's reach and in child-resistant containers.

Mechanism of Action Replaces iron found in hemoglobin, myoglobin, and enzymes; allows the transportation of oxygen via hemoglobin

Pharmacodynamics/Kinetics Onset of action: Hematologic response: Oral: 3-10 days; peak reticulocytosis occurs in 5-10 days, and hemoglobin values increase in ~2-4 weeks

Dosage Oral **(dose expressed in terms of elemental iron):**

Children:

Severe iron-deficiency anemia: 4-6 mg Fe/kg/day in 3 divided doses

Mild to moderate iron deficiency anemia: 3 mg Fe/kg/day in 1-2 divided doses

Prophylaxis: 1-2 mg Fe/kg/day

Adults:

Iron deficiency: 60 mg twice daily up to 60 mg 4 times/day

Prophylaxis: 60 mg/day

Dietary Considerations Should be taken with water or juice on an empty stomach; may be administered with food to prevent irritation; however, not with cereals, dietary fiber, tea, coffee, eggs, or milk.

Elemental iron content of ferrous gluconate: 12%

Administration Administer 2 hours before or 4 hours after antacids. Administration of iron preparations to premature infants with vitamin E deficiency may cause increased red cell hemolysis and hemolytic anemia, therefore, vitamin E deficiency should be corrected if possible.

Monitoring Parameters Serum iron, total iron binding capacity, reticulocyte count, hemoglobin

(Continued)

Ferrous Gluconate *(Continued)*

Reference Range Therapeutic: Male: 75-175 mcg/dL (SI: 13.4-31.3 µmol/L); Female: 65-165 mcg/dL (SI: 11.6-29.5 µmol/L); serum iron level >300 mcg/dL usually requires treatment of overdose due to severe toxicity

Test Interactions False-positive for blood in stool by the guaiac test

Dosage Forms
  Tablet: 246 mg [elemental iron 28 mg]; 300 mg [elemental iron 34 mg]; 325 mg [elemental iron 36 mg]
  Fergon®: 240 mg [elemental iron 27 mg]

Ferrous Sulfate *(FER us SUL fate)*

U.S. Brand Names Feosol® [OTC]; Feratab® [OTC]; Fer-Gen-Sol [OTC]; Fer-In-Sol® [OTC]; Fer-Iron™ [OTC]; Slow FE® [OTC]

Canadian Brand Names Apo-Ferrous Sulfate®; Fer-In-Sol®; Ferodan™

Index Terms FeSO₄; Iron Sulfate

Pharmacologic Category Iron Salt

Use Prevention and treatment of iron-deficiency anemias

Pregnancy Risk Factor A

Medication Safety Issues
  Sound-alike/look-alike issues:
    Feosol® may be confused with Feostat®, Fer-In-Sol®
    Fer-In-Sol® may be confused with Feosol®
    Slow FE® may be confused with Slow-K®

Contraindications Hypersensitivity to iron salts or any component of the formulation; hemochromatosis, hemolytic anemia

Warnings/Precautions Avoid in patients with peptic ulcer, enteritis, or ulcerative colitis. Administration of iron for >6 months should be avoided except in patients with continuous bleeding or menorrhagia. Anemia in the elderly is often caused by "anemia of chronic disease" or associated with inflammation rather than blood loss. Iron stores are usually normal or increased, with a serum ferritin >50 ng/mL and a decreased total iron binding capacity. Hence, the "anemia of chronic disease" is not secondary to iron deficiency but the inability of the reticuloendothelial system to reclaim available iron stores. Avoid in patients receiving frequent blood transfusions Avoid use in premature infants until the vitamin E stores, deficient at birth, are replenished. **[U.S. Boxed Warning]: Severe iron toxicity may occur in overdose, particularly when ingested by children; iron is a leading cause of fatal poisoning in children; store out of children's reach and in child-resistant containers.**

Adverse Reactions
  >10%: Gastrointestinal: GI irritation, epigastric pain, nausea, dark stools, vomiting, stomach cramping, constipation
  1% to 10%:
    Gastrointestinal: Heartburn, diarrhea
    Genitourinary: Discoloration of urine
    Miscellaneous: Liquid preparations may temporarily stain the teeth
  <1% (Limited to important or life-threatening): Contact irritation

Overdosage/Toxicology Symptoms include acute GI irritation, erosion of GI mucosa, hepatic and renal impairment, coma, hematemesis, lethargy, and acidosis. Due to severe toxicity, serum iron ≥300 mcg/mL requires treatment. Following treatment for fluid losses, metabolic acidosis, and shock, a severe iron overdose may be treated with deferoxamine. Deferoxamine may be administered I.V. (80 mg/kg over 24 hours) or I.M. (40-90 mg/kg every 8 hours). The usual toxic dose of elemental iron is ≥35 mg/kg.

Drug Interactions
  Increased Effect/Toxicity: Concurrent administration of ≥200 mg vitamin C per 30 mg elemental iron increases absorption of oral iron.
  Decreased Effect: Absorption of oral preparation of iron and tetracyclines are decreased when both of these drugs are given together. Absorption of fluoroquinolones, levodopa, methyldopa, and penicillamine may be decreased due to formation of a ferric ion-quinolone complex. Concurrent administration of antacids, H₂ blockers (cimetidine), or proton pump inhibitors may decrease iron absorption. Response to iron therapy may be delayed by chloramphenicol.

Ethanol/Nutrition/Herb Interactions Food: Cereals, dietary fiber, tea, coffee, eggs, and milk may decrease absorption.

Stability Iron is a leading cause of fatal poisoning in children. Store out of children's reach and in child-resistant containers.

Mechanism of Action Replaces iron, found in hemoglobin, myoglobin, and other enzymes; allows the transportation of oxygen via hemoglobin

Pharmacodynamics/Kinetics
  Onset of action: Hematologic response: Oral: ~3-10 days
    Peak effect: Reticulocytosis: 5-10 days; hemoglobin increases within 2-4 weeks
  Absorption: Iron is absorbed in the duodenum and upper jejunum; in persons with normal serum iron stores, 10% of an oral dose is absorbed; this is increased to 20% to 30% in persons with inadequate iron stores. Food and achlorhydria will decrease absorption
  Protein binding: To transferrin
  Excretion: Urine, sweat, sloughing of the intestinal mucosa, and menses

Dosage Oral:
  Children **(dose expressed in terms of elemental iron):**
    Severe iron-deficiency anemia: 4-6 mg Fe/kg/day in 3 divided doses
    Mild to moderate iron deficiency anemia: 3 mg Fe/kg/day in 1-2 divided doses
    Prophylaxis: 1-2 mg Fe/kg/day up to a maximum of 15 mg/day

Adults (dose expressed in terms of ferrous sulfate):
Iron deficiency: 300 mg twice daily up to 300 mg 4 times/day or 250 mg (extended release) 1-2 times/day
Prophylaxis: 300 mg/day

Dietary Considerations Should be taken with water or juice on an empty stomach; may be administered with food to prevent irritation; however, not with cereals, dietary fiber, tea, coffee, eggs, or milk.
Elemental iron content of iron salts in ferrous sulfate is 20% (ie, 300 mg ferrous sulfate is equivalent to 60 mg ferrous iron)

Administration Administer ferrous sulfate 2 hours prior to, or 4 hours after antacids

Monitoring Parameters Serum iron, total iron binding capacity, reticulocyte count, hemoglobin

Reference Range
Serum iron:
Male: 75-175 mcg/dL (SI: 13.4-31.3 µmol/L)
Female: 65-165 mcg/dL (SI: 11.6-29.5 µmol/L)
Total iron binding capacity: 230-430 mcg/dL
Transferrin: 204-360 mg/dL
Percent transferrin saturation: 20% to 50%

Test Interactions False-positive for blood in stool by the guaiac test

Dosage Forms
Elixir: 220 mg/5 mL (480 mL) [elemental iron 44 mg/5 mL; contains alcohol]
Liquid, oral drops: 75 mg/0.6 mL (50 mL) [elemental iron 15 mg/0.6 mL]
Fer-Gen-Sol: 75 mg/0.6 mL (50 mL) [elemental iron 15 mg/0.6 mL]
Fer-In-Sol®: 75 mg/0.6 mL (50 mL) [elemental iron 15 mg/0.6 mL; contains alcohol 0.2% and sodium bisulfite]
Fer-Iron®: 75 mg/0.6 mL (50 mL) [elemental iron 15 mg/0.6 mL]
Tablet: 324 mg [elemental iron 65 mg]; 325 mg [elemental iron 65 mg]
Feratab®: 300 mg [elemental iron 60 mg]
Tablet, exsiccated (Feosol®): 200 mg [elemental iron 65 mg]
Tablet, exsiccated, timed release (Slow FE®): 160 mg [elemental iron 50 mg]

Ferrous Sulfate and Ascorbic Acid (FER us SUL fate & a SKOR bik AS id)

U.S. Brand Names Fero-Grad 500® [OTC]; Vitelle™ Irospan® [OTC] [DSC]
Index Terms Ascorbic Acid and Ferrous Sulfate; Iron Sulfate and Vitamin C
Pharmacologic Category Iron Salt; Vitamin
Use Treatment of iron deficiency in nonpregnant adults; treatment and prevention of iron deficiency in pregnant adults
Dosage Adults: Oral: 1 tablet daily
Additional Information Complete prescribing information for this medication should be consulted for additional detail.
Dosage Forms [DSC] = Discontinued product
Capsule, extended release (Vitelle™ Irospan®): Ferrous sulfate [elemental iron 65 mg] and ascorbic acid 150 mg [DSC]
Tablet, controlled release (Fero-Grad 500®): Ferrous sulfate 525 mg [elemental iron 105 mg] and ascorbic acid 500 mg
Tablet, extended release (Vitelle™ Irospan®): Ferrous sulfate [elemental iron 65 mg] and ascorbic acid 150 mg [DSC]

♦ **Fertinorm® H.P. (Can)** see Urofollitropin on page 1759
♦ **FeSO₄** see Ferrous Sulfate on page 704
♦ **FeverALL® [OTC]** see Acetaminophen on page 28

Fexofenadine (feks oh FEN a deen)

U.S. Brand Names Allegra®
Canadian Brand Names Allegra®
Index Terms Fexofenadine Hydrochloride
Pharmacologic Category Antihistamine, Nonsedating
Use Relief of symptoms associated with seasonal allergic rhinitis; treatment of chronic idiopathic urticaria
Pregnancy Risk Factor C
Pregnancy Implications Decreased fetal weight gain and survival were observed in animal studies. There are no adequate and well-controlled studies in pregnant women; use during pregnancy only if potential benefit to mother outweighs possible risk to fetus.
Lactation Excretion in breast milk unknown/use caution (AAP rates "compatible")
Medication Safety Issues
Sound-alike/look-alike issues:
Allegra® may be confused with Viagra®

International issues:
Allegra® may be confused with Allegro® which is a brand name for frovatriptan in Germany; a brand name for fluticasone in Israel
Contraindications Hypersensitivity to fexofenadine or any component of the formulation
Warnings/Precautions Safety and efficacy in children <6 months of age have not been established.
Adverse Reactions
>10%:
Central nervous system: Headache (5% to 11%)
Gastrointestinal: Vomiting (children 6 months to 5 years): 4% to 12%
(Continued)

Fexofenadine *(Continued)*

1% to 10%:

Central nervous system: Somnolence (1% to 3%), dizziness (2%), drowsiness (2%), pain (2%), fatigue (1%)

Endocrine & metabolic: Dysmenorrhea (2%)

Gastrointestinal: Dyspepsia (1% to 5%), diarrhea (3% to 4%), nausea (2%)

Neuromuscular & skeletal: Myalgia (3%), back pain (2% to 3%)

Otic: Otitis media (2%)

Respiratory: Upper respiratory tract infection (4%), cough (2% to 4%), nasopharyngitis (2%)

Miscellaneous: Viral infection (3%)

<1% (Limited to important or life-threatening): Hypersensitivity reactions (anaphylaxis, angioedema, dyspnea, flushing, pruritus, rash, urticaria); insomnia, nervousness, sleep disorders, paroniria

Overdosage/Toxicology Symptoms may include: dizziness, drowsiness, and xerostomia. Not effectively removed by hemodialysis. Doses up to 690 mg twice daily were administered for 1 month without significant adverse effects. Treatment is symptom-directed and supportive.

Drug Interactions

Cytochrome P450 Effect: Substrate of CYP3A4 (minor); **Inhibits** CYP2D6 (weak)

Increased Effect/Toxicity: Anticholinergics, CNS depressants may have increased adverse/toxic effects. Verapamil increases levels/effects of fexofenadine.

Decreased Effect: Acetylcholinesterase inhibitors (central) may decrease the adverse effects of fexofenadine. Acetylcholinesterase inhibitor, betahistine may be less effective. Pramlintide may increase the adverse GI effects of fexofenadine. Rifampin decreases levels/effects of fexofenadine.

Ethanol/Nutrition/Herb Interactions

Ethanol: Avoid ethanol (although limited with fexofenadine, may increase risk of sedation).

Food: Fruit juice (apple, grapefruit, orange) may decrease bioavailability of fexofenadine by ~36%.

Herb/Nutraceutical: St John's wort may decrease fexofenadine levels.

Stability Store at controlled room temperature of 20°C to 25°C (68°F to 77°F). Protect from excessive moisture.

Mechanism of Action Fexofenadine is an active metabolite of terfenadine and like terfenadine it competes with histamine for H_1-receptor sites on effector cells in the gastrointestinal tract, blood vessels and respiratory tract; it appears that fexofenadine does not cross the blood brain barrier to any appreciable degree, resulting in a reduced potential for sedation

Pharmacodynamics/Kinetics

Onset of action: 60 minutes

Duration: Antihistaminic effect: ≥12 hours

Protein binding: 60% to 70%, primarily albumin and alpha$_1$-acid glycoprotein

Metabolism: Minimal (~5%)

Half-life elimination: 14.4 hours

Time to peak, serum: ~2.6 hours

Excretion: Feces (~80%) and urine (~11%) as unchanged drug

Dosage Oral:

Chronic idiopathic urticaria: Children 6 months to <2 years: 15 mg twice daily

Chronic idiopathic urticaria, seasonal allergic rhinitis:

Children 2-11 years: 30 mg twice daily

Children ≥12 years and Adults: 60 mg twice daily **or** 180 mg once daily

Elderly: Starting dose: 60 mg once daily; adjust for renal impairment

Dosing adjustment in renal impairment: Cl_{cr} <80 mL/minute:

Children 6 months to <2 years: Initial: 15 mg once daily

Children 2-11 years: Initial: 30 mg once daily

Children ≥12 years and Adults: Initial: 60 mg once daily

Administration Administer with water only; do not administer with fruit juices. Shake suspension well before use.

Monitoring Parameters Relief of symptoms

Dosage Forms

Suspension:

Allegra®: 6 mg/mL (300 mL) [raspberry cream]

Tablet, as hydrochloride: 30 mg, 60 mg, 180 mg

Allegra®: 30 mg, 60 mg, 180 mg

Fexofenadine and Pseudoephedrine

(feks oh FEN a deen & soo doe e FED rin)

U.S. Brand Names Allegra-D® 12 Hour; Allegra-D® 24 Hour

Canadian Brand Names Allegra-D®

Index Terms Pseudoephedrine and Fexofenadine

Pharmacologic Category Antihistamine/Decongestant Combination

Use Relief of symptoms associated with seasonal allergic rhinitis in adults and children ≥12 years of age

Pregnancy Risk Factor C

Medication Safety Issues

Sound-alike/look-alike issues:

Allegra-D® may be confused with Viagra®

Dosage Oral: Children ≥12 years and Adults:

Allegra-D® 12 Hour: One tablet twice daily

Allegra-D® 24 Hour: One tablet once daily

Dosage adjustment in renal impairment:
Allegra-D® 12 Hour: Cl$_{cr}$ <80 mL/minute (based on fexofenadine component): One tablet once daily
Allegra-D® 24 Hour: Avoid use.

Additional Information Complete prescribing information for this medication should be consulted for additional detail.

Dosage Forms Tablet, extended release:
Allegra-D® 12 Hour: Fexofenadine hydrochloride 60 mg [immediate release] and pseudoephedrine hydrochloride 120 mg [extended release]
Allegra-D® 24 Hour: Fexofenadine hydrochloride 180 mg [immediate release] and pseudoephedrine hydrochloride 240 mg [extended release]

♦ **Fexofenadine Hydrochloride** see Fexofenadine on page 705
♦ **Fiberall®** see Psyllium on page 1458
♦ **Fibro-XL [OTC]** see Psyllium on page 1458
♦ **Fibro-Lax [OTC]** see Psyllium on page 1458

Filgrastim (fil GRA stim)

U.S. Brand Names Neupogen®
Canadian Brand Names Neupogen®
Index Terms G-CSF; Granulocyte Colony Stimulating Factor; NSC-614629
Pharmacologic Category Colony Stimulating Factor
Use Stimulation of granulocyte production in chemotherapy-induced neutropenia (nonmyeloid malignancies, acute myeloid leukemia, and bone marrow transplantation); severe chronic neutropenia (SCN); patients undergoing peripheral blood progenitor cell (PBPC) collection
Unlabeled/Investigational Use Treatment of anemia in myelodysplastic syndrome; treatment of drug-induced (nonchemotherapy) agranulocytosis in the elderly
Pregnancy Risk Factor C
Pregnancy Implications Animal studies have demonstrated adverse effects and fetal loss. Filgrastim has been shown to cross the placenta in humans. There are no adequate and well-controlled studies in pregnant women. Use only if potential benefit to mother justifies risk to the fetus.
Lactation Excretion in breast milk unknown/use caution
Medication Safety Issues
Sound-alike/look-alike issues:
Neupogen® may be confused with Epogen®, Neumega®, Nutramigen®
Contraindications Hypersensitivity to filgrastim, E. coli-derived proteins, or any component of the formulation
Warnings/Precautions Do not use filgrastim in the period 24 hours before to 24 hours after administration of cytotoxic chemotherapy because of the potential sensitivity of rapidly dividing myeloid cells to cytotoxic chemotherapy. May potentially act as a growth factor for any tumor type, particularly myeloid malignancies; precaution should be exercised in the usage of filgrastim in any malignancy with myeloid characteristics. Safety and efficacy have not been established with patients receiving radiation therapy, or with chemotherapy associated with delayed myelosuppression (eg, nitrosoureas, mitomycin C).

Allergic-type reactions (rash, urticaria, wheezing, dyspnea, tachycardia and/or hypotension) have occurred with first or later doses. Reactions tended to occur more frequently with intravenous administration and within 30 minutes of administration. Rare cases of splenic rupture or adult respiratory distress syndrome have been reported in association with filgrastim; patients must be instructed to report left upper quadrant pain or shoulder tip pain or respiratory distress. Use caution in patients with sickle cell diseases; sickle cell crises have been reported following filgrastim therapy. Cytogenetic abnormalities, transformation to AML and MDS have been observed in patients treated with filgrastim for congenital neutropenia; a longer duration of treatment and poorer ANC response appear to increase the risk. The packaging of some forms may contain latex.

Adverse Reactions
>10%:
Central nervous system: Fever (12%)
Dermatologic: Petechiae (17%), rash (12%)
Gastrointestinal: Splenomegaly (severe chronic neutropenia: 30%; rare in other patients)
Hepatic: Alkaline phosphatase increased (21%)
Neuromuscular & skeletal: Bone pain (22% to 33%), commonly in the lower back, posterior iliac crest, and sternum
Respiratory: Epistaxis (9% to 15%)
1% to 10%:
Cardiovascular: Hyper-/hypotension (4%), S-T segment depression (3%), myocardial infarction/arrhythmias (3%)
Central nervous system: Headache (7%)
Gastrointestinal: Nausea (10%), vomiting (7%), peritonitis (2%)
Hematologic: Leukocytosis (2%)
Miscellaneous: Transfusion reaction (10%)
<1% (Limited to important or life-threatening): Adult respiratory distress syndrome, allergic reactions, alopecia, arthralgia, capillary leak syndrome, cerebral hemorrhage, cutaneous vasculitis, dyspnea, edema (facial), erythema nodosum, hematuria, hepatomegaly, hypersensitivity reaction, injection site reaction, osteoporosis, pericarditis, proteinuria, psoriasis exacerbation, renal insufficiency, splenic rupture, tachycardia, transient supraventricular arrhythmia, thrombophlebitis, urticaria, wheezing
Overdosage/Toxicology No clinical adverse effects have been seen with high doses producing ANC >10,000/mm^3. Filgrastim discontinuation should result in a 50% decrease in circulating neutrophils within 1-2 days and a return to pretreatment levels in 1-7 days.
Stability Intact vials and prefilled syringes should be stored under refrigeration at 2°C to 8°C (36°F to 46°F) and protected from direct sunlight. Filgrastim should be protected from
(Continued)

Filgrastim *(Continued)*

freezing and temperatures >30°C to avoid aggregation. If inadvertently frozen, thaw in a refrigerator and use within 24 hours; do not use if frozen >24 hours or frozen more than once. Do not shake.

Filgrastim vials and prefilled syringes are stable for 7 days at 9°C to 30°C (47°F to 86°F).

Undiluted filgrastim is stable for 24 hours at 15°C to 30°C and for 2 weeks at 2°C to 8°C (36°F to 46°F) in tuberculin syringes.

Do not dilute with saline at any time; product may precipitate. Filgrastim may be diluted with D_5W or with D_5W with albumin for I.V. infusion administration (5-15 mcg/mL; minimum concentration is 5 mcg/mL). This diluted solution is stable for 7 days at 2°C to 8°C (36°F to 46°F). Dilution to <5 mcg/mL is not recommended. Concentrations 5-15 mcg/mL require addition of albumin (final concentration of 2 mg/mL) to prevent absorption to plastics.

Mechanism of Action Stimulates the production, maturation, and activation of neutrophils; filgrastim activates neutrophils to increase both their migration and cytotoxicity.

Pharmacodynamics/Kinetics

Onset of action: ~24 hours; plateaus in 3-5 days

Duration: ANC decreases by 50% within 2 days after discontinuing filgrastim; white counts return to the normal range in 4-7 days; peak plasma levels can be maintained for up to 12 hours

Absorption: SubQ: 100%

Distribution: V_d: 150 mL/kg; no evidence of drug accumulation over a 11- to 20-day period

Metabolism: Systemically degraded

Half-life elimination: 1.8-3.5 hours

Time to peak, serum: SubQ: 2-8 hours

Dosage Refer to individual protocols.

Dosing, even in morbidly obese patients, should be based on actual body weight. Rounding doses to the nearest vial size often enhances patient convenience and reduces costs without compromising clinical response.

Children and Adults:

Chemotherapy-induced neutropenia: SubQ, I.V.: 5 mcg/kg/day; doses may be increased by 5 mcg/kg according to the duration and severity of the neutropenia; continue for up to 14 days or until the ANC reaches 10,000/mm³

Bone marrow transplantation: SubQ, I.V.: 10 mcg/kg/day; adjust the dose according to the duration and severity of neutropenia; recommended steps based on neutrophil response:

When ANC >1000/mm³ for 3 consecutive days: Reduce filgrastim dose to 5 mcg/kg/day

If ANC remains >1000/mm³ for 3 more consecutive days: Discontinue filgrastim

If ANC decreases to <1000/mm³: Resume at 5 mcg/kg/day

If ANC decreases <1000/mm³ during the 5 mcg/kg/day dose, increase filgrastim to 10 mcg/kg/day and follow the above steps

Peripheral blood progenitor cell (PBPC) collection: SubQ: 10 mcg/kg daily in donors, usually for 6-7 days. Begin at least 4 days before the first leukopheresis and continue until the last leukopheresis; consider dose adjustment for WBC >100,000/mm³

Severe chronic neutropenia: SubQ:

Congenital: 6 mcg/kg twice daily; adjust the dose based on ANC and clinical response

Idiopathic/cyclic: 5 mcg/kg/day; adjust the dose based on ANC and clinical response

Anemia in myelodysplastic syndrome (unlabeled use - in combination with epoetin): SubQ: 0.3-3 mcg/kg daily **or** 30-150 mcg daily **or** 1-2 mcg/kg 2-3 times weekly

Elderly: Refer to adult dosing.

Drug-induced agranulocytosis (nonchemotherapy) in the elderly (unlabeled use): SubQ: 300 mcg daily until ANC >1500/mm³

Dietary Considerations Solution for injection contains sodium 0.035 mg/mL and sorbitol.

Administration May be administered undiluted by SubQ injection. May also be administered by I.V. bolus over 15-30 minutes in D_5W, or by continuous SubQ or I.V. infusion. Do not administer earlier than 24 hours after or in the 24 hours prior to cytotoxic chemotherapy.

Monitoring Parameters CBC with differential prior to treatment and twice weekly during filgrastim treatment for chemotherapy-induced neutropenia (3 times a week following marrow transplantation). For severe chronic neutropenia, monitor CBC twice weekly during the first month of therapy and for 2 weeks following dose adjustments; monthly thereafter.

Reference Range No clinical benefit seen with ANC >10,000/mm³

Test Interactions May interfere with bone imaging studies; increased hematopoietic activity of the bone marrow may appear as transient positive bone imaging changes

Additional Information

Reimbursement Hotline: 1-800-272-9376

Professional Services [Amgen]: 1-800-77-AMGEN

Dosage Forms

Injection, solution [preservative free]:

Neupogen®: 300 mcg/mL (1 mL, 1.6 mL) [vial; contains sodium 0.035 mg/mL and sorbitol]

Injection, solution [preservative free]:

Neupogen®: 600 mcg/mL (0.5 mL, 0.8 mL) [prefilled Singleject® syringe; contains sodium 0.035 mg/mL and sorbitol; needle cover contains latex]

♦ **Finacea®** *see Azelaic Acid on page 184*

Finasteride *(fi NAS teer ide)*

U.S. Brand Names Propecia®; Proscar®

Canadian Brand Names Propecia®; Proscar®

Pharmacologic Category 5 Alpha-Reductase Inhibitor

Use

Propecia®: Treatment of male pattern hair loss in **men only**. Safety and efficacy were demonstrated in men between 18-41 years of age.

Proscar®: Treatment of symptomatic benign prostatic hyperplasia (BPH); can be used in combination with an alpha blocker, doxazosin

Unlabeled/Investigational Use Adjuvant monotherapy after radical prostatectomy in the treatment of prostatic cancer; female hirsutism

Pregnancy Risk Factor X

Pregnancy Implications Abnormalities of external male genitalia were reported in animal studies. Pregnant women are advised to avoid contact with crushed or broken tablets.

Lactation Excretion in breast milk unknown/contraindicated

Medication Safety Issues
Sound-alike/look-alike issues:
Proscar® may be confused with ProSom®, Prozac®, Psorcon®

High alert medication: The Institute for Safe Medication Practices (ISMP) includes this medication among its list of drugs which have a heightened risk of causing significant patient harm when used in error.

Contraindications Hypersensitivity to finasteride or any component of the formulation; pregnancy; not for use in children

Warnings/Precautions Hazardous agent - use appropriate precautions for handling and disposal. A minimum of 6 months of treatment may be necessary to determine whether an individual will respond to finasteride. Use with caution in those patients with hepatic dysfunction. Carefully monitor patients with a large residual urinary volume or severely diminished urinary flow for obstructive uropathy. These patients may not be candidates for finasteride therapy.

Adverse Reactions Note: "Combination therapy" refers to finasteride and doxazosin.
>10%:
Endocrine & metabolic: Impotence (19%; combination therapy 23%), libido decreased (10%; combination therapy 12%)
Neuromuscular & skeletal: Weakness (5%; combination therapy 17%)
1% to 10%:
Cardiovascular: Postural hypotension (9%; combination therapy 18%), edema (1%; combination therapy 3%)
Central nervous system: Dizziness (7%; combination therapy 23%), somnolence (2%; combination therapy 3%)
Genitourinary: Ejaculation disturbances (7%; combination therapy 14%), decreased volume of ejaculate
Endocrine & metabolic: Gynecomastia (2%)
Respiratory: Dyspnea (1%; combination therapy 2%), rhinitis (1%; combination therapy 2%)
<1%, postmarketing and/or case reports: Hypersensitivity (pruritus, rash, urticaria, swelling of face/lips); breast tenderness, breast enlargement, breast cancer (males), prostate cancer (high grade), testicular pain

Drug Interactions
Cytochrome P450 Effect: Substrate of CYP3A4 (minor)

Ethanol/Nutrition/Herb Interactions
Herb/Nutraceutical: St John's wort may decrease finasteride levels. Avoid saw palmetto (concurrent use has not been adequately studied).

Stability Store below 30°C (86°F). Protect from light.

Mechanism of Action Finasteride is a competitive inhibitor of both tissue and hepatic 5-alpha reductase. This results in inhibition of the conversion of testosterone to dihydrotestosterone and markedly suppresses serum dihydrotestosterone levels

Pharmacodynamics/Kinetics
Onset of action: 3-6 months of ongoing therapy
Duration:
After a single oral dose as small as 0.5 mg: 65% depression of plasma dihydrotestosterone levels persists 5-7 days
After 6 months of treatment with 5 mg/day: Circulating dihydrotestosterone levels are reduced to castrate levels without significant effects on circulating testosterone; levels return to normal within 14 days of discontinuation of treatment
Distribution: V_{dss}: 76 L
Protein binding: 90%
Metabolism: Hepatic via CYP3A4; two active metabolites (<20% activity of finasteride)
Bioavailability: Mean: 63%
Half-life elimination, serum: Elderly: 8 hours; Adults: 6 hours (3-16)
Time to peak, serum: 2-6 hours
Excretion: Feces (57%) and urine (39%) as metabolites

Dosage Oral: Adults:
Male:
Benign prostatic hyperplasia (Proscar®): 5 mg/day as a single dose; clinical responses occur within 12 weeks to 6 months of initiation of therapy; long-term administration is recommended for maximal response
Male pattern baldness (Propecia®): 1 mg daily
Female hirsutism (unlabeled use): 5 mg/day
Dosing adjustment in renal impairment: No dosage adjustment is necessary
Dosing adjustment in hepatic impairment: Use with caution in patients with liver function abnormalities because finasteride is metabolized extensively in the liver

Administration Administration with food may delay the rate and reduce the extent of oral absorption. Women of childbearing age should not touch or handle broken tablets.

Monitoring Parameters Objective and subjective signs of relief of benign prostatic hyperplasia, including improvement in urinary flow, reduction in symptoms of urgency, and relief of difficulty in micturition

Dosage Forms
Tablet: 5 mg
Propecia®: 1 mg
Proscar®: 5 mg

- ◆ **Fioricet®** *see* Butalbital, Acetaminophen, and Caffeine *on page 259*
- ◆ **Fiorinal®** *see* Butalbital, Aspirin, and Caffeine *on page 260*
- ◆ **First® Testosterone** *see* Testosterone *on page 1653*
- ◆ **First® Testosterone MC** *see* Testosterone *on page 1653*
- ◆ **Fisalamine** *see* Mesalamine *on page 1089*
- ◆ **Fish Oil** *see* Omega-3-Acid Ethyl Esters *on page 1264*
- ◆ **FK506** *see* Tacrolimus *on page 1626*
- ◆ **Flagyl®** *see* Metronidazole *on page 1132*
- ◆ **Flagyl ER®** *see* Metronidazole *on page 1132*
- ◆ **Flagyl® I.V. RTU™** *see* Metronidazole *on page 1132*
- ◆ **Flamazine® (Can)** *see* Silver Sulfadiazine *on page 1567*
- ◆ **Flarex®** *see* Fluorometholone *on page 724*

Flavoxate (fla VOKS ate)

U.S. Brand Names Urispas®
Canadian Brand Names Apo-Flavoxate®; Urispas®
Index Terms Flavoxate Hydrochloride
Pharmacologic Category Antispasmodic Agent, Urinary
Use Antispasmodic to provide symptomatic relief of dysuria, nocturia, suprapubic pain, urgency, and incontinence due to detrusor instability and hyper-reflexia in elderly with cystitis, urethritis, urethrocystitis, urethrotrigonitis, and prostatitis
Pregnancy Risk Factor B
Medication Safety Issues
Sound-alike/look-alike issues:
Flavoxate may be confused with fluvoxamine
Urispas® may be confused with Urised®
Dosage Children >12 years and Adults: Oral: 100-200 mg 3-4 times/day; reduce the dose when symptoms improve
Additional Information Complete prescribing information for this medication should be consulted for additional detail.
Dosage Forms Tablet, as hydrochloride: 100 mg

- ◆ **Flavoxate Hydrochloride** *see* Flavoxate *on page 710*

Flecainide (fle KAY nide)

U.S. Brand Names Tambocor™
Canadian Brand Names Apo-Flecainide®; Tambocor™
Index Terms Flecainide Acetate
Pharmacologic Category Antiarrhythmic Agent, Class Ic
Use Prevention and suppression of documented life-threatening ventricular arrhythmias (eg, sustained ventricular tachycardia); controlling symptomatic, disabling supraventricular tachycardias in patients without structural heart disease in whom other agents fail
Pregnancy Risk Factor C
Lactation Enters breast milk/compatible
Medication Safety Issues
Sound-alike/look-alike issues:
Flecainide may be confused with fluconazole
Tambocor™ may be confused with tamoxifen
Contraindications Hypersensitivity to flecainide or any component of the formulation; pre-existing second- or third-degree AV block or with right bundle branch block when associated with a left hemiblock (bifascicular block) (except in patients with a functioning artificial pacemaker); cardiogenic shock; coronary artery disease (based on CAST study results); concurrent use of ritonavir or amprenavir
Warnings/Precautions [U.S. Boxed Warning]: In the Cardiac Arrhythmia Suppression Trial (CAST), recent (>6 days but <2 years ago) myocardial infarction patients with asymptomatic, nonlife-threatening ventricular arrhythmias did not benefit and may have been harmed by attempts to suppress the arrhythmia with flecainide or encainide. An increased mortality or nonfatal cardiac arrest rate (7.7%) was seen in the active treatment group compared with patients in the placebo group (3%). The applicability of the CAST results to other populations is unknown. The risks of class 1C agents and the lack of improved survival make use in patients without life-threatening arrhythmias generally unacceptable. Not recommended for patients with chronic atrial fibrillation; may have proarrhythmic effects. When treating atrial flutter, 1:1 atrioventricular conduction may occur; pre-emptive negative chronotropic therapy (eg, digoxin, beta-blockers) may lower the risk. Pre-existing hypokalemia or hyperkalemia should be corrected before initiation (can alter drug's effect). A worsening or new arrhythmia may occur (proarrhythmic effect). Use caution in heart failure (may precipitate or exacerbate CHF). Dose-related increases in PR, QRS, and QT intervals occur. Use with caution in sick sinus syndrome or with permanent pacemakers or temporary pacing wires (can increase endocardial pacing thresholds). Cautious use in significant hepatic impairment.
Adverse Reactions
>10%:
Central nervous system: Dizziness (19% to 30%)
Ocular: Visual disturbances (16%)
Respiratory: Dyspnea (~10%)
1% to 10%:
Cardiovascular: Palpitations (6%), chest pain (5%), edema (3.5%), tachycardia (1% to 3%), proarrhythmic (4% to 12%), sinus node dysfunction (1.2%), syncope

Central nervous system: Headache (4% to 10%), fatigue (8%), nervousness (5%) additional symptoms occurring at a frequency between 1% and 3%: fever, malaise, hypoesthesia, paresis, ataxia, vertigo, somnolence, tinnitus, anxiety, insomnia, depression

Dermatologic: Rash (1% to 3%)

Gastrointestinal: Nausea (9%), constipation (1%), abdominal pain (3%), anorexia (1% to 3%), diarrhea (0.7% to 3%)

Neuromuscular & skeletal: Tremor (5%), weakness (5%), paresthesia (1%)

Ocular: Diplopia (1% to 3%), blurred vision

<1% (Limited to important or life-threatening): Alopecia, alters pacing threshold, amnesia, angina, AV block, bradycardia, bronchospasm, CHF, corneal deposits, depersonalization, euphoria, exfoliative dermatitis, granulocytopenia, heart block, increased P-R, leukopenia, metallic taste, neuropathy, paradoxical increase in ventricular rate in atrial fibrillation/flutter, paresthesia, photophobia, pneumonitis, pruritus, QRS duration, swollen lips/tongue/mouth, tardive dyskinesia, thrombocytopenia, urinary retention, urticaria, ventricular arrhythmia

Overdosage/Toxicology Has a narrow therapeutic index; severe toxicity may occur slightly above the therapeutic range, especially if combined with other antiarrhythmic drugs. An acute single ingestion of twice the daily therapeutic dose is life-threatening. Symptoms include increased PR, QRS, and QT intervals; amplitude of the T wave, AV block, bradycardia, hypotension, ventricular arrhythmias (monomorphic or polymorphic ventricular tachycardia), and asystole. Other symptoms include dizziness, blurred vision, headache, and GI upset. Treatment is supportive, using conventional treatment (fluids, positioning, anticonvulsants, antiarrhythmics). **Note:** Type Ia antiarrhythmic agents should not be used to treat cardiotoxicity caused by type Ic antiarrhythmics. Sodium bicarbonate may reverse QRS prolongation, bradycardia, and hypotension. Ventricular pacing may be needed. Hemodialysis is only of possible benefit for tocainide or flecainide overdose in patients with renal failure.

Drug Interactions

Cytochrome P450 Effect: Substrate of CYP1A2 (minor), 2D6 (major); **Inhibits** CYP2D6 (weak)

Increased Effect/Toxicity: CYP2D6 inhibitors may increase the levels/effects of flecainide; example inhibitors include chlorpromazine, delavirdine, fluoxetine, miconazole, paroxetine, pergolide, quinidine, quinine, ritonavir, and ropinirole. Flecainide concentrations may be increased by amiodarone (reduce flecainide 25% to 33%), and propranolol. Beta-adrenergic blockers, disopyramide, verapamil may enhance flecainide's negative inotropic effects. Alkalinizing agents (ie, high-dose antacids, cimetidine, carbonic anhydrase inhibitors, sodium bicarbonate) may decrease flecainide clearance, potentially increasing toxicity. Propranolol blood levels are increased by flecainide.

Decreased Effect: Smoking and acid urine increase flecainide clearance.

Ethanol/Nutrition/Herb Interactions Food: Clearance may be decreased in patients following strict vegetarian diets due to urinary pH ≥8. Dairy products (milk, infant formula, yogurt) may interfere with the absorption of flecainide in infants; there is one case report of a neonate (GA 34 weeks PNA >6 days) who required extremely large doses of oral flecainide when administered every 8 hours with feedings ("milk feeds"); changing the feedings from "milk feeds" to 5% glucose feeds alone resulted in a doubling of the flecainide serum concentration and toxicity.

Mechanism of Action Class Ic antiarrhythmic; slows conduction in cardiac tissue by altering transport of ions across cell membranes; causes slight prolongation of refractory periods; decreases the rate of rise of the action potential without affecting its duration; increases electrical stimulation threshold of ventricle, His-Purkinje system; possesses local anesthetic and moderate negative inotropic effects

Pharmacodynamics/Kinetics

Absorption: Oral: Rapid

Distribution: Adults: V_d: 5-13.4 L/kg

Protein binding: Alpha$_1$ glycoprotein: 40% to 50%

Metabolism: Hepatic

Bioavailability: 85% to 90%

Half-life elimination: Infants: 11-12 hours; Children: 8 hours; Adults: 7-22 hours, increased with congestive heart failure or renal dysfunction; End-stage renal disease: 19-26 hours

Time to peak, serum: ~1.5-3 hours

Excretion: Urine (80% to 90%, 10% to 50% as unchanged drug and metabolites)

Dosage Oral:

Children:

Initial: 3 mg/kg/day or 50-100 mg/m^2/day in 3 divided doses

Usual: 3-6 mg/kg/day or 100-150 mg/m^2/day in 3 divided doses; up to 11 mg/kg/day or 200 mg/m^2/day for uncontrolled patients with subtherapeutic levels

Adults:

Life-threatening ventricular arrhythmias:

Initial: 100 mg every 12 hours

Increase by 50-100 mg/day (given in 2 doses/day) every 4 days; maximum: 400 mg/day. Use of higher initial doses and more rapid dosage adjustments has resulted in an increased incidence of proarrhythmic events and congestive heart failure, particularly during the first few days. Do not use a loading dose. Use very cautiously in patients with history of congestive heart failure or myocardial infarction.

Prevention of paroxysmal supraventricular arrhythmias in patients with disabling symptoms but no structural heart disease:

Initial: 50 mg every 12 hours

Increase by 50 mg twice daily at 4-day intervals; maximum: 300 mg/day.

Dosing adjustment in severe renal impairment: Cl$_{cr}$ <35 mL/minute: Decrease initial dose to 50 mg every 12 hours; increase doses at intervals >4 days monitoring ECG levels closely.

Dialysis: Not dialyzable (0% to 5%) via hemo- or peritoneal dialysis; no supplemental dose necessary.

Dosing adjustment/comments in hepatic impairment: Monitoring of plasma levels is recommended because of significantly increased half-life.

(Continued)

Flecainide (Continued)

When transferring from another antiarrhythmic agent, allow for 2-4 half-lives of the agent to pass before initiating flecainide therapy.

Administration Administer around-the-clock to promote less variation in peak and trough serum levels

Monitoring Parameters ECG, blood pressure, pulse, periodic serum concentrations, especially in patients with renal or hepatic impairment

Reference Range Therapeutic: 0.2-1 mcg/mL; pediatric patients may respond at the lower end of the recommended therapeutic range

Dosage Forms Tablet, as acetate: 50 mg, 100 mg, 150 mg

Extemporaneous Preparations A 5 mg/mL suspension compounded from tablets and an oral flavored commercially available diluent (Roxane®) was stable for up to 45 days when stored at 5°C or 25°C in amber glass bottles. Flecainide 20 mg/mL was found stable for up to 60 days at 5°C and 25°C in a 1:1 preparation of Ora-Sweet® and Ora-Plus®, in Ora-Sweet® SF and Ora-Plus® and in cherry syrup

Allen LV and Erickson III MA, "Stability of Baclofen, Captopril, Diltiazem, Hydrochloride, Dipyridamole, and Flecainide Acetate in Extemporaneously Compounded Oral Liquids," *Am J Health Syst Pharm*, 53:2179-84.

Wiest DB, Garner SS, and Pagacz LR, "Stability of Flecainide Acetate in an Extemporaneously Compounded Oral Suspension," *Am J Hosp Pharm*, 1992, 49(6):1467-70.

- ♦ **Flecainide Acetate** *see Flecainide on page 710*
- ♦ **Fleet® Bisacodyl Enema [OTC]** *see Bisacodyl on page 223*
- ♦ **Fleet® Sof-Lax® [OTC]** *see Docusate on page 533*
- ♦ **Fleet® Stimulant Laxative [OTC]** *see Bisacodyl on page 223*
- ♦ **Flexbumin** *see Albumin on page 55*
- ♦ **Flexeril®** *see Cyclobenzaprine on page 427*
- ♦ **Flexitec (Can)** *see Cyclobenzaprine on page 427*
- ♦ **Flextra 650** *see Acetaminophen and Phenyltoloxamine on page 32*
- ♦ **Flextra-DS** *see Acetaminophen and Phenyltoloxamine on page 32*
- ♦ **Flolan®** *see Epoprostenol on page 598*
- ♦ **Flomax®** *see Tamsulosin on page 1633*
- ♦ **Flomax® CR (Can)** *see Tamsulosin on page 1633*
- ♦ **Flonase®** *see Fluticasone on page 738*
- ♦ **Flora-Q™ [OTC]** *see Lactobacillus on page 969*
- ♦ **Florazole® ER (Can)** *see Metronidazole on page 1132*
- ♦ **Florical® [OTC]** *see Calcium Carbonate on page 269*
- ♦ **Florinef®** *see Fludrocortisone on page 717*
- ♦ **Florone®** *see Diflorasone on page 499*
- ♦ **Flovent® Diskus® (Can)** *see Fluticasone on page 738*
- ♦ **Flovent® HFA** *see Fluticasone on page 738*
- ♦ **Floxin®** *see Ofloxacin on page 1254*
- ♦ **Floxin Otic Singles** *see Ofloxacin on page 1254*
- ♦ **Fluarix®** *see Influenza Virus Vaccine on page 906*
- ♦ **Flubenisolone** *see Betamethasone on page 211*
- ♦ **Flucaine®** *see Proparacaine and Fluorescein on page 1441*

Fluconazole (floo KOE na zole)

U.S. Brand Names Diflucan®

Canadian Brand Names Apo-Fluconazole®; Diflucan®; Fluconazole Injection; Fluconazole Omega; Gen-Fluconazole; GMD-Fluconazole; Novo-Fluconazole; Riva-Fluconazole

Pharmacologic Category Antifungal Agent, Oral; Antifungal Agent, Parenteral

Additional Appendix Information
Antifungal Agents *on page 1869*
Treatment of Sexually Transmitted Infections *on page 2007*
USPHS / IDSA Guidelines for the Prevention of Opportunistic Infections in Persons Infected With HIV *on page 1966*

Use Treatment of candidiasis (vaginal, oropharyngeal, esophageal, urinary tract infections, peritonitis, pneumonia, and systemic infections); cryptococcal meningitis; antifungal prophylaxis in allogeneic bone marrow transplant recipients

Pregnancy Risk Factor C

Pregnancy Implications When used in high doses, fluconazole is teratogenic in animal studies. Following exposure during the first trimester, case reports have noted similar malformations in humans when used in higher doses (400 mg/day) over extended periods of time. Use of lower doses (150 mg as a single dose or 200 mg/day) may have less risk; however, additional data is needed. Use during pregnancy only if the potential benefit to the mother outweighs any potential risk to the fetus.

Lactation Enters breast/not recommended (AAP rates "compatible")

Medication Safety Issues
Sound-alike/look-alike issues:
Fluconazole may be confused with flecainide
Diflucan® may be confused with diclofenac, Diprivan®, disulfiram

International issues:
Canesten® [Great Britain]: Brand name for clotrimazole in multiple international markets

Contraindications Hypersensitivity to fluconazole, other azoles, or any component of the formulation; concomitant administration with cisapride

Warnings/Precautions Should be used with caution in patients with renal and hepatic dysfunction or previous hepatotoxicity from other azole derivatives. Patients who develop abnormal liver function tests during fluconazole therapy should be monitored closely and discontinued if symptoms consistent with liver disease develop. Use caution in patients at risk of proarrhythmias.

Adverse Reactions Frequency not always defined.

Cardiovascular: Angioedema, pallor, QT prolongation, torsade de pointes

Central nervous system: Headache (2% to 13%), seizure, dizziness

Dermatologic: Rash (2%), alopecia, toxic epidermal necrolysis, Stevens-Johnson syndrome

Endocrine & metabolic: Hypercholesterolemia, hypertriglyceridemia, hypokalemia

Gastrointestinal: Nausea (4% to 7%), vomiting (2%), abdominal pain (2% to 6%), diarrhea (2% to 3%), taste perversion, dyspepsia

Hematologic: Agranulocytosis, leukopenia, neutropenia, thrombocytopenia

Hepatic: Hepatic failure (rare), hepatitis, cholestasis, jaundice, increased ALT/AST, increased alkaline phosphatase

Respiratory: Dyspnea

Miscellaneous: Anaphylactic reactions (rare)

Overdosage/Toxicology Symptoms include decreased lacrimation, salivation, respiration, GI motility, urinary incontinence, and cyanosis. Treatment includes supportive measures. A 3-hour hemodialysis will remove 50% of the drug.

Drug Interactions

Cytochrome P450 Effect: Inhibits CYP1A2 (weak), 2C9 (strong), 2C19 (strong), 3A4 (moderate)

Increased Effect/Toxicity: Concurrent use of fluconazole with cisapride is contraindicated due to the potential for malignant arrhythmias. Fluconazole may increase the levels/effects of amiodarone, selected benzodiazepines, bosentan, calcium channel blockers, citalopram, cyclosporine, dapsone, diazepam, fluoxetine, glimepiride, glipizide, losartan, methosuximide, mirtazapine, montelukast, nateglinide, nefazodone, paclitaxel, phenytoin, propranolol, sertraline, sildenafil (and other PDE-5 inhibitors), tacrolimus, venlafaxine, warfarin, zafirlukast, and other substrates of CYP2C9, 2C19, and 3A4.

Decreased Effect: Rifampin decreases concentrations of fluconazole.

Stability

Powder for oral suspension: Store dry powder at ≤30°C (86°F). Following reconstitution, store at 5°C to 30°C (41°F to 86°F). Discard unused portion after 2 weeks. Do not freeze.

Injection: Store injection in glass at 5°C to 30°C (41°F to 86°F). Store injection in Viaflex® at 5°C to 25°C (41°F to 77°F). Do not freeze. Do not unwrap unit until ready for use.

Mechanism of Action Interferes with cytochrome P450 activity, decreasing ergosterol synthesis (principal sterol in fungal cell membrane) and inhibiting cell membrane formation

Pharmacodynamics/Kinetics

Distribution: Widely throughout body with good penetration into CSF, eye, peritoneal fluid, sputum, skin, and urine

Relative diffusion blood into CSF: Adequate with or without inflammation (exceeds usual MICs)

CSF:blood level ratio: Normal meninges: 70% to 80%; Inflamed meninges: >70% to 80%

Protein binding, plasma: 11% to 12%

Bioavailability: Oral: >90%

Half-life elimination: Normal renal function: ~30 hours

Time to peak, serum: Oral: 1-2 hours

Excretion: Urine (80% as unchanged drug)

Dosage The daily dose of fluconazole is the same for oral and I.V. administration

Usual dosage ranges:

Neonates: First 2 weeks of life, especially premature neonates: Same dose as older children every 72 hours

Children: Loading dose: 6-12 mg/kg; maintenance: 3-12 mg/kg/day; duration and dosage depends on severity of infection

Adults: 200-400 mg/day; duration and dosage depends on severity of infection

Indication-specific dosing:

Children:

Candidiasis:

Oropharyngeal: Loading dose: 6 mg/kg; maintenance: 3 mg/kg/day for 2 weeks

Esophageal: Loading dose: 6 mg/kg; maintenance: 3-12 mg/kg/day for 21 days and at least 2 weeks following resolution of symptoms

Systemic infection: 6 mg/kg every 12 hours for 28 days

Meningitis, cryptococcal: Loading dose: 12 mg/kg; maintenance: 6-12 mg/kg/day for 10-12 weeks following negative CSF culture; relapse suppression: 6 mg/kg/day

Adults:

Candidiasis:

Candidemia, primary therapy, non-neutropenic: 400-800 mg/day for 14 days after last positive blood culture and resolution of signs/symptoms

Alternate therapy: 800 mg/day with amphotericin B for 4-7 days followed by 800 mg/day for 14 days after last positive blood culture and resolution of signs/symptoms

Candidemia, secondary, neutropenic: 6-12 mg/kg/day for 14 days after last positive blood culture and resolution of signs/symptoms

Chronic, disseminated: 6 mg/kg/day for 3-6 months

Oropharyngeal (long-term suppression): 200 mg/day; chronic therapy is recommended in immunocompromised patients with history of oropharyngeal candidiasis (OPC)

Osteomyelitis: 6 mg/kg/day for 6-12 months

Esophageal: 200 mg on day 1, then 100-200 mg/day for 2-3 weeks after clinical improvement

Prophylaxis in bone marrow transplant: 400 mg/day; begin 3 days before onset of neutropenia and continue for 7 days after neutrophils >1000 cells/mm^3

Urinary: 200 mg/day for 1-2 weeks

Vaginal: 150 mg as a single dose

(Continued)

Fluconazole *(Continued)*

Coccidiomycosis: 400 mg/day; doses of 800-1000 mg/day have been used for meningeal disease; usual duration of therapy ranges from 3-6 months for primary uncomplicated infections and up to 1 year for pulmonary (chronic and diffuse) infection

Endocarditis, prosthetic valve, early: 6-12 mg/kg/day for 6 weeks after valve replacement

Endophthalmitis: 6-12 mg/kg/day or 400-800 mg/day for 6-12 weeks after surgical intervention. **Note:** *C. krusei* and *C. galbrata* infection acquired exogenously should be treated with voriconazole.

Meningitis, cryptococcal: 400-800 mg/day for 10-12 weeks or with flucytosine 100-150 mg/day for 6 weeks; maintenance: 200-400 mg/day

Pneumonia, cryptococcal (mild-to-moderate): 200-400 mg/day for 6-12 months (life-long in HIV-positive patients)

Dosing adjustment/interval in renal impairment:
No adjustment for vaginal candidiasis single-dose therapy
For multiple dosing, administer usual load then adjust daily doses
Cl_{cr} ≤50 mL/minute (no dialysis): Administer 50% of recommended dose or administer every 48 hours.
Hemodialysis: 50% is removed by hemodialysis; administer 100% of daily dose (according to indication) after each dialysis treatment.
Continuous arteriovenous or venovenous hemofiltration: Dose as for Cl_{cr} 10-50 mL/minute.

Dietary Considerations Take with or without regard to food.

Administration
I.V.: Infuse over approximately 1-2 hours; do not exceed 200 mg/hour
Oral: May be administred with or without food

Monitoring Parameters Periodic liver function tests (AST, ALT, alkaline phosphatase) and renal function tests, potassium

Dosage Forms
Infusion [premixed in sodium chloride or dextrose]: 200 mg (100 mL); 400 mg (200 mL)
Diflucan® [premixed in sodium chloride or dextrose]: 200 mg (100 mL); 400 mg (200 mL)
Powder for oral suspension: 10 mg/mL (35 mL); 40 mg/mL (35 mL)
Diflucan®: 10 mg/mL (35 mL); 40 mg/mL (35 mL) [contains sodium benzoate; orange flavor]
Tablet: 50 mg, 100 mg, 150 mg, 200 mg
Diflucan®: 50 mg, 100 mg, 150 mg, 200 mg

♦ **Fluconazole Injection (Can)** *see* Fluconazole *on page 712*
♦ **Fluconazole Omega (Can)** *see* Fluconazole *on page 712*

Flucytosine *(floo SYE toe seen)*

U.S. Brand Names Ancobon®
Canadian Brand Names Ancobon®
Index Terms 5-FC; 5-Fluorocytosine; 5-Flurocytosine
Pharmacologic Category Antifungal Agent, Oral
Additional Appendix Information
Antifungal Agents *on page 1869*
Use Adjunctive treatment of systemic fungal infections (eg, septicemia, endocarditis, UTI, meningitis, or pulmonary) caused by susceptible strains of *Candida* or *Cryptococcus*
Pregnancy Risk Factor C
Pregnancy Implications Teratogenic in some animal studies, however, there are no adequate and well-controlled studies in pregnant women.
Lactation Excretion in breast milk unknown/not recommended
Medication Safety Issues
Sound-alike/look-alike issues:
Flucytosine may be confused with fluorouracil
Ancobon® may be confused with Oncovin®

High alert medication: The Institute for Safe Medication Practices (ISMP) includes this medication among its list of drugs which have a heightened risk of causing significant patient harm when used in error.

Contraindications Hypersensitivity to flucytosine or any component of the formulation
Warnings/Precautions [U.S. Boxed Warning]: Use with extreme caution in patients with renal dysfunction; dosage adjustment required. Avoid use as monotherapy; resistance rapidly develops. Use with caution in patients with bone marrow depression; patients with hematologic disease or who have been treated with radiation or drugs that suppress the bone marrow may be at greatest risk. Bone marrow toxicity can be irreversible. **[U.S. Boxed Warning]: Closely monitor hematologic, renal, and hepatic status.** Hepatotoxicity and bone marrow toxicity appear to be dose related; monitor levels closely and adjust dose accordingly. Safety and efficacy in children have not been established.

Adverse Reactions Frequency not defined.
Cardiovascular: Cardiac arrest, myocardial toxicity, ventricular dysfunction, chest pain
Central nervous system: Ataxia, confusion, dizziness, drowsiness, fatigue, hallucinations, headache, parkinsonism, psychosis, pyrexia, sedation, seizure, vertigo
Dermatologic: Rash, photosensitivity, pruritus, toxic epidermal necrolysis, urticaria
Endocrine & metabolic: Hypoglycemia, hypokalemia
Gastrointestinal: Abdominal pain, diarrhea, dry mouth, duodenal ulcer, hemorrhage, loss of appetite, nausea, ulcerative colitis, vomiting
Hematologic: Agranulocytosis, anemia, aplastic anemia, eosinophilia, leukopenia, pancytopenia, thrombocytopenia
Hepatic: Acute hepatic injury, bilirubin increased, hepatic dysfunction, jaundice, liver enzymes increased
Neuromuscular & skeletal: Paresthesia, peripheral neuropathy, weakness

Otic: Hearing loss

Renal: Azotemia, BUN increased, crystalluria, renal failure, serum creatinine increased

Respiratory: Dyspnea, respiratory arrest

Miscellaneous: Allergic reaction

Overdosage/Toxicology Symptoms include nausea, vomiting, diarrhea, hepatitis, and bone marrow suppression. Monitor hematologic, renal, and hepatic parameters frequently. Treatment is symptom-directed and supportive. Removed by hemodialysis.

Drug Interactions

Decreased Effect: Cytarabine may decrease levels/effects of flucytosine.

Ethanol/Nutrition/Herb Interactions Food: Food decreases the rate, but not the extent of absorption.

Stability Store at room temperature of 15°C to 30°C (59°F to 86°F); protect from light.

Mechanism of Action Penetrates fungal cells and is converted to fluorouracil which competes with uracil interfering with fungal RNA and protein synthesis

Pharmacodynamics/Kinetics

Absorption: 76% to 89%

Distribution: Into CSF, aqueous humor, joints, peritoneal fluid, and bronchial secretions; V_d: 0.6 L/kg

Protein binding: 3% to 4%

Metabolism: Minimally hepatic; deaminated, possibly via gut bacteria, to 5-fluorouracil

Half-life elimination:

Normal renal function: 2-5 hours

Anuria: 85 hours (range: 30-250)

End stage renal disease: 75-200 hours

Time to peak, serum: ~1-2 hours

Excretion: Urine (>90% as unchanged drug)

Dosage

Usual dosage ranges: Children (unlabeled use) and Adults: Oral: 50-150 mg/kg/day in divided doses every 6 hours

Indication-specific dosing:

Children (unlabeled use) and Adults:

Endocarditis: Oral: 25-37.5 mg/kg 4 times/day (with amphotericin B) for at least 6 weeks after valve replacement

Meningoencephalitis, cryptococcal: Induction: Oral: 100 mg/kg/day (with amphotericin B) divided every 6 hours for 2 weeks; if clinical improvement, may discontinue both amphotericin and flucytosine and follow with an extended course of fluconazole; alternatively, may continue flucytosine for 6-10 weeks (with amphotericin B) without conversion to fluconazole treatment

Pneumonia, cryptococcal: HIV positive: Oral: 100-150 mg/kg/day for 10 weeks (with fluconazole 400 mg/day)

Dosing interval in renal impairment: Use lower initial dose:

Cl_{cr} 20-40 mL/minute: Administer 37.5 mg/kg every 12 hours

Cl_{cr} 10-20 mL/minute: Administer 37.5 mg/kg every 24 hours

Cl_{cr} <10 mL/minute: Administer 37.5 mg/kg every 24-48 hours, but monitor drug concentrations frequently

Hemodialysis: Dialyzable (50% to 100%); administer dose posthemodialysis

Peritoneal dialysis: Adults: Administer 0.5-1 g every 24 hours

Continuous arteriovenous or venovenous hemodiafiltration effects: Change dosing frequency to every 12-24 hours (monitor serum concentrations and adjust)

Administration Administer around-the-clock to promote less variation in peak and trough serum levels. To avoid nausea and vomiting, administer a few capsules at a time over 15 minutes until full dose is taken.

Monitoring Parameters

Pretreatment: Electrolytes (especially potassium), CBC with differential, BUN, renal function, blood culture

During treatment: CBC with differential, and LFTs (eg, alkaline phosphatase, AST/ALT) frequently, serum flucytosine concentration, renal function

Reference Range

Therapeutic: Trough: 25-50 mcg/mL; peak: 50-100 mcg/mL; peak levels should not exceed 100 mcg/mL to avoid toxic bone marrow depressive and hepatic effects

Trough: Draw just prior to dose administration

Peak: Draw 2 hours after an oral dose administration

Test Interactions Flucytosine causes markedly false elevations in serum creatinine values when the Ektachem® analyzer is used. The Jaffé reaction is recommended for determining serum creatinine.

Dosage Forms Capsule: 250 mg, 500 mg

Extemporaneous Preparations Flucytosine oral liquid has been prepared by using the contents of ten 500 mg capsules triturated in a mortar and pestle with a small amount of distilled water; the mixture was transferred to a 500 mL volumetric flask; the mortar was rinsed several times with a small amount of distilled water and the fluid added to the flask; sufficient distilled water was added to make a total volume of 500 mL of a 10 mg/mL liquid; oral liquid was stable for 70 days when stored in glass or plastic prescription bottles at 4°C or for up to 14 days at room temperature.

Wintermeyer SM and Nahata MC, "Stability of Flucytosine in an Extemporaneously Compounded Oral Liquid," *Am J Health Syst Pharm,* 1996, 53:407-9.

♦ **Fludara®** *see* Fludarabine *on page 716*

Fludarabine (floo DARE a been)

U.S. Brand Names Fludara®
Canadian Brand Names Beneflur®; Fludara®
Index Terms Fludarabine Phosphate; NSC-312887
Pharmacologic Category Antineoplastic Agent, Antimetabolite (Purine Antagonist)
Use
I.V.: Treatment of chronic lymphocytic leukemia (CLL) (including refractory CLL); non-Hodgkin's lymphoma in adults
Oral (formulation not available in U.S.): Approved in Canada for treatment of CLL
Unlabeled/Investigational Use Treatment of non-Hodgkin's lymphoma and acute leukemias in pediatric patients; reduced-intensity conditioning regimens prior to allogeneic hematopoietic stem cell transplantation (generally administered in combination with busulfan and antithymocyte globulin or lymphocyte immune globulin, or in combination with melphalan and alemtuzumab)
Pregnancy Risk Factor D
Pregnancy Implications Teratogenic effects were observed in animal studies. Women of childbearing potential should be advised to avoid becoming pregnant.
Lactation Excretion in breast milk unknown/contraindicated
Medication Safety Issues
Sound-alike/look-alike issues:
Fludarabine may be confused with floxuridine, Flumadine®
Fludara® may be confused with FUDR®

High alert medication: The Institute for Safe Medication Practices (ISMP) includes this medication among its list of drugs which have a heightened risk of causing significant patient harm when used in error.

Contraindications Hypersensitivity of fludarabine or any component of the formulation; decompensated hemolytic anemia; breast-feeding, pregnancy
Warnings/Precautions Hazardous agent - use appropriate precautions for handling and disposal. Use with caution with renal insufficiency, patients with a fever, documented infection, or pre-existing hematological disorders (particularly granulocytopenia) or in patients with pre-existing central nervous system disorder (epilepsy), spasticity, or peripheral neuropathy. **[U.S. Boxed Warnings]: Higher doses are associated with severe neurologic toxicity (blindness, coma, death); similar toxicity was reported rarely at recommended doses. Life-threatening (and sometimes fatal) autoimmune hemolytic anemia has occurred; monitor closely for hemolysis. Severe bone marrow suppression may occur;** severe myelosuppression (trilineage bone marrow hypoplasia/aplasia) has been reported (rare); the duration of significant cytopenias in these cases may be prolonged (up to 1 year). May cause tumor lysis syndrome; risk is increased in patients with large tumor burden prior to treatment. Patients receiving blood products should only receive irradiated blood products due to the potential for transfusion related GVHD. **[U.S. Boxed Warnings]: Do not use in combination with pentostatin; may lead to severe, even fatal pulmonary toxicity. Should be administered under the supervision of an experienced cancer chemotherapy physician.**
Adverse Reactions
>10%:
Cardiovascular: Edema (8% to 19%)
Central nervous system: Fever (60% to 69%), fatigue (10% to 38%), pain (20% to 22%), chills (11% to 19%)
Dermatologic: Rash (15%)
Gastrointestinal: Nausea/vomiting (mild: 31% to 36%), anorexia (7% to 34%), diarrhea (13% to 15%), gastrointestinal bleeding (3% to 13%)
Genitourinary: Urinary tract infection (2% to 15%)
Hematologic: Myelosuppression (nadir: 10-14 days; recovery: 5-7 weeks; dose-limiting toxicity), anemia (60%), neutropenia (grade 4: 59%; nadir: ~13 days), thrombocytopenia (50% to 55%; nadir: ~16 days)
Neuromuscular & skeletal: Weakness (9% to 65%), myalgia (4% to 16%), paresthesia (4% to 12%)
Ocular: Visual disturbance (3% to 15%)
Respiratory: Cough (10% to 44%), pneumonia (16% to 22%), dyspnea (9% to 22%), upper respiratory infection (2% to 16%)
Miscellaneous: Infection (33% to 44%), diaphoresis (1% to 13%)
1% to 10%:
Cardiovascular: Angina (≤6%), CHF (≤3%), arrhythmia (≤3%), cerebrovascular accident (≤3%), MI (≤3%), supraventricular tachycardia (≤3%), deep vein thrombosis (1% to 3%), phlebitis (1% to 3%), aneurysm (≤1%), transient ischemic attack (≤1%)
Central nervous system: Malaise (6% to 8%), headache (≤3%), sleep disorder (1% to 3%), cerebellar syndrome (≤1%), depression (≤1%), mentation impaired (≤1%)
Dermatologic: Alopecia (≤3%), pruritus (1% to 3%), seborrhea (≤1%)
Endocrine & metabolic: Hyperglycemia (1% to 6%), dehydration (≤1%)
Gastrointestinal: Stomatitis (≤9%), esophagitis (≤3%), constipation (1% to 3%), mucositis (≤2%), dysphagia (≤1%)
Genitourinary: Dysuria (3% to 4%), hesitancy (≤3%)
Hematologic: Hemorrhage (≤1%)
Hepatic: Cholelithiasis (≤3%), liver function tests abnormal (1% to 3%), liver failure (≤1%)
Neuromuscular & skeletal: Osteoporosis (≤2%), arthralgia (≤1%)
Otic: Hearing loss (2% to 6%)
Renal: Hematuria (2% to 3%), renal failure (≤1%), renal function test abnormal (≤1%), proteinuria (≤1%)
Respiratory: Pharyngitis (≤9%), allergic pneumonitis (≤6%), hemoptysis (1% to 6%), sinusitis (≤5%), bronchitis (≤1%), epistaxis (≤1%), hypoxia (≤1%)
Miscellaneous: Anaphylaxis (≤1%), tumor lysis syndrome (1%)

<1% (Limited to important or life-threatening): Agitation, ARDS, autoimmune hemolytic anemia, blurred vision, bone marrow fibrosis, coma, confusion, diplopia, eosinophilia, hemorrhagic cystitis, interstitial pneumonitis, metabolic acidosis, opportunistic infection, pancytopenia, pericardial effusion, peripheral neuropathy, photophobia (primarily with high doses), pulmonary fibrosis, pulmonary hemorrhage, pulmonary infiltrate, respiratory failure, trilineage bone marrow aplasia, trilineage bone marrow hypoplasia, urate crystalluria, wrist drop

Also observed: Neurologic syndrome characterized by cortical blindness, coma, and paralysis [36% at doses >96 mg/m^2 for 5-7 days; <0.2% at doses <125 mg/m^2/cycle (onset of neurologic symptoms may be delayed for 3-4 weeks)]

Overdosage/Toxicology High doses of fludarabine are associated with bone marrow depression including severe neutropenia and thrombocytopenia; irreversible central nervous system toxicity with delayed blindness, coma, and death has occurred. Discontinue drug; treatment is symptom-directed and supportive.

Drug Interactions

Increased Effect/Toxicity: Combined use with pentostatin may lead to severe, even fatal, pulmonary toxicity.

Ethanol/Nutrition/Herb Interactions Ethanol: Avoid ethanol (due to GI irritation).

Stability

I.V.: Store intact vials under refrigeration at 2°C to 8°C (36°F to 46°F). Reconstituted vials are stable for 16 days at room temperature of 15°C to 30°C (59°F to 86°F) or refrigerated. Solutions diluted in saline or dextrose are stable for 48 hours at room temperature or under refrigeration. Reconstitute vials with SWI, NS, or D$_5$W to a concentration of 10-25 mg/mL; standard I.V. dilution: 50-100 mL D$_5$W or NS.

Tablet (formulation not available in U.S.): Store between 15°C to 30°C (59°F to 86°F); should be kept within packaging until use.

Mechanism of Action Fludarabine inhibits DNA synthesis by inhibition of DNA polymerase, ribonucleotide reductase and DNA primase.

Pharmacodynamics/Kinetics

Distribution: V$_d$: 38-96 L/m^2; widely with extensive tissue binding

Metabolism: I.V.: Fludarabine phosphate is rapidly dephosphorylated to 2-fluoro-vidarabine, which subsequently enters tumor cells and is phosphorylated by deoxycytidine kinase to the active triphosphate derivative; rapidly dephosphorylated in the serum

Bioavailability: 75%

Half-life elimination: 2-fluoro-vidarabine: 9 hours

Excretion: Urine (60%, 23% as 2-fluoro-vidarabine) within 24 hours

Dosage

I.V.:

Children (unlabeled use):

Acute leukemia: 10 mg/m^2 bolus over 15 minutes followed by continuous infusion of 30.5 mg/m^2/day for 5 days **or**

10.5 mg/m^2 bolus over 15 minutes followed by 30.5 mg/m^2/day for 48 hours

Solid tumors: 9 mg/m^2 bolus followed by 27 mg/m^2/day continuous infusion for 5 days

Adults:

Chronic lymphocytic leukemia: 25 mg/m^2/day for 5 days every 28 days

Non-hodgkin's lymphoma: Loading dose: 20 mg/m^2 followed by 30 mg/m^2/day for 48 hours

Reduced-intensity conditioning regimens prior to allogeneic hematopoietic stem cell transplantation (unlabeled use): 120-150 mg/m^2 administered in divided doses over 4-5 days

Oral: Adults: **Note:** Formulation available in Canada; not available in U.S.:

CLL: 40 mg/m^2 once daily for 5 days every 28 days

Dosing in renal impairment:

Cl$_{cr}$ 30-70 mL/minute:

U.S. product labeling: Reduce dose by 20%

Canadian product labeling: Reduce dose by 50%

Cl$_{cr}$ <30 mL/minute: Not recommended

Administration

I.V.: Usually administered as a 15- to 30-minute infusion; continuous infusions are occasionally used

Oral: Tablet (formulation not available in U.S.) may be administered with or without food; should be swallowed whole; do not chew, break, or crush.

Monitoring Parameters CBC with differential, platelet count, AST, ALT, creatinine, serum albumin, uric acid

Dosage Forms [CAN] = Canadian brand name

Injection, powder for reconstitution, as phosphate: 50 mg

Tablet, as phosphate [CAN]: 10 mg [not available in U.S.]

♦ **Fludarabine Phosphate** *see* Fludarabine *on page 716*

Fludrocortisone (floo droe KOR ti sone)

U.S. Brand Names Florinef®

Canadian Brand Names Florinef®

Index Terms 9α-Fluorohydrocortisone Acetate; Fludrocortisone Acetate; Fluohydrisone Acetate; Fluohydrocortisone Acetate

Pharmacologic Category Corticosteroid, Systemic

Additional Appendix Information

Corticosteroids *on page 1879*

Use Partial replacement therapy for primary and secondary adrenocortical insufficiency in Addison's disease; treatment of salt-losing adrenogenital syndrome

Pregnancy Risk Factor C

Lactation Excretion in breast milk unknown

(Continued)

Fludrocortisone *(Continued)*

Medication Safety Issues

Sound-alike/look-alike issues:

Florinef® may be confused with Fiorinal®

Contraindications Hypersensitivity to fludrocortisone or any component of the formulation; systemic fungal infections

Warnings/Precautions May cause hypercorticism or suppression of hypotha-lamic-pituitary-adrenal (HPA) axis, particularly in younger children or in patients receiving high doses for prolonged periods. HPA axis suppression may lead to adrenal crisis. With-drawal and discontinuation of a corticosteroid should be done slowly and carefully. Fludrocor-tisone is primarily a mineralocorticoid agonist, but may also inhibit the HPA axis. May increase risk of infection and/or limit response to vaccinations; close observation is required in patients with latent tuberculosis and/or TB reactivity. Restrict use in active TB (only in conjunction with antituberculosis treatment). Use with caution in patients with sodium reten-tion and potassium loss, hepatic impairment, myocardial infarction, osteoporosis, and/or renal impairment. Use with caution in the elderly. Withdraw therapy with gradual tapering of dose. Safety and efficacy have not been established in children.

Adverse Reactions Frequency not defined.

Cardiovascular: Hypertension, edema, CHF

Central nervous system: Convulsions, headache, dizziness

Dermatologic: Acne, rash, bruising

Endocrine & metabolic: Hypokalemic alkalosis, suppression of growth, hyperglycemia, HPA suppression

Gastrointestinal: Peptic ulcer

Neuromuscular & skeletal: Muscle weakness

Ocular: Cataracts

Miscellaneous: Diaphoresis, anaphylaxis (generalized)

Overdosage/Toxicology Symptoms include hypertension, edema, hypokalemia, and exces-sive weight gain. When consumed in excessive quantities, systemic hypercorticism and adrenal suppression may occur; in those cases, discontinuation and withdrawal of the corti-costeroid should be done judiciously.

Drug Interactions

Decreased Effect: Anticholinesterases effects are antagonized. Decreased corticosteroid effects by rifampin, barbiturates, and hydantoins. May decrease salicylate levels.

Mechanism of Action Promotes increased reabsorption of sodium and loss of potassium from renal distal tubules

Pharmacodynamics/Kinetics

Absorption: Rapid and complete

Protein binding: 42%

Metabolism: Hepatic

Half-life elimination, plasma: 30-35 minutes; Biological: 18-36 hours

Time to peak, serum: ~1.7 hours

Dosage Oral:

Infants and Children: 0.05-0.1 mg/day

Adults: 0.1-0.2 mg/day with ranges of 0.1 mg 3 times/week to 0.2 mg/day

Addison's disease: Initial: 0.1 mg/day; if transient hypertension develops, reduce the dose to 0.05 mg/day. Preferred administration with cortisone (10-37.5 mg/day) or hydrocorti-sone (10-30 mg/day).

Salt-losing adrenogenital syndrome: 0.1-0.2 mg/day

Dietary Considerations Systemic use of mineralocorticoids/corticosteroids may require a diet with increased potassium, vitamins A, B₆, C, D, folate, calcium, zinc, and phosphorus, and decreased sodium. With fludrocortisone, a decrease in dietary sodium is often not required as the increased retention of sodium is usually the desired therapeutic effect.

Administration Administration in conjunction with a glucocorticoid is preferable

Monitoring Parameters Monitor blood pressure and signs of edema when patient is on chronic therapy; very potent mineralocorticoid with high glucocorticoid activity; monitor serum electrolytes, serum renin activity, and blood pressure; monitor for evidence of infection; stop treatment if a significant increase in weight or blood pressure, edema, or cardiac enlargement occurs

Additional Information In patients with salt-losing forms of congenital adrenogenital syndrome, use along with cortisone or hydrocortisone. Fludrocortisone 0.1 mg has sodium retention activity equal to DOCA® 1 mg.

Dosage Forms Tablet, as acetate: 0.1 mg

♦ **Fludrocortisone Acetate** *see Fludrocortisone on page 717*

♦ **FluLaval™** *see Influenza Virus Vaccine on page 906*

♦ **Flumadine®** *see Rimantadine on page 1513*

Flumazenil *(FLOO may ze nil)*

U.S. Brand Names Romazicon®

Canadian Brand Names Anexate®; Flumazenil Injection; Flumazenil Injection, USP; Romazicon®

Pharmacologic Category Antidote

Additional Appendix Information

Management of Overdosages *on page 2075*

Use Benzodiazepine antagonist; reverses sedative effects of benzodiazepines used in conscious sedation and general anesthesia; treatment of benzodiazepine overdose

Pregnancy Risk Factor C

Pregnancy Implications Teratogenic effects were not seen in animal studies. Embryocidal effects were seen at large doses. There are no adequate or well-controlled studies in preg-nant women. Use only if clearly needed.

Lactation Excretion in breast milk unknown/use caution

Contraindications Hypersensitivity to flumazenil, benzodiazepines, or any component of the formulation; patients given benzodiazepines for control of potentially life-threatening conditions (eg, control of intracranial pressure or status epilepticus); patients who are showing signs of serious cyclic-antidepressant overdosage

Warnings/Precautions [U.S. Boxed Warning]: Benzodiazepine reversal may result in seizures in some patients. Patients who may develop seizures include patients on benzodiazepines for long-term sedation, tricyclic antidepressant overdose patients, concurrent major sedative-hypnotic drug withdrawal, recent therapy with repeated doses of parenteral benzodiazepines, myoclonic jerking or seizure activity prior to flumazenil administration. Flumazenil does not reverse respiratory depression/hypoventilation or cardiac depression. Resedation occurs more frequently in patients where a large single dose or cumulative dose of a benzodiazepine is administered along with a neuromuscular blocking agent and multiple anesthetic agents. Flumazenil should be used with caution in the intensive care unit because of increased risk of unrecognized benzodiazepine dependence in such settings. Should not be used to diagnose benzodiazepine-induced sedation. Reverse neuromuscular blockade before considering use. Flumazenil does not antagonize the CNS effects of other GABA agonists (such as ethanol, barbiturates, or general anesthetics); nor does it reverse narcotics. Use with caution in patients with a history of panic disorder; may provoke panic attacks. Use caution in drug and ethanol-dependent patients; these patients may also be dependent on benzodiazepines. Not recommended for treatment of benzodiazepine dependence. Use with caution in head injury patients. Use caution in patients with mixed drug overdoses; toxic effects of other drugs taken may emerge once benzodiazepine effects are reversed. Flumazenil does not consistently reverse amnesia; patient may not recall verbal instructions after procedure. Use caution in severe hepatic dysfunction and in patients relying on a benzodiazepine for seizure control. Safety and efficacy have not been established in children >1 year of age.

Adverse Reactions

>10%: Gastrointestinal: Vomiting, nausea

1% to 10%:

Cardiovascular: Palpitations

Central nervous system: Headache, anxiety, nervousness, insomnia, abnormal crying, euphoria, depression, agitation, dizziness, emotional lability, ataxia, depersonalization, increased tears, dysphoria, paranoia, fatigue, vertigo

Endocrine & metabolic: Hot flashes

Gastrointestinal: Xerostomia

Local: Pain at injection site

Neuromuscular & skeletal: Tremor, weakness, paresthesia

Ocular: Abnormal vision, blurred vision

Respiratory: Dyspnea, hyperventilation

Miscellaneous: Diaphoresis

<1% (Limited to important or life-threatening): Bradycardia, chest pain, confusion, fear, generalized convulsions, hypertension, junctional tachycardia, panic attacks, tachycardia, ventricular tachycardia, withdrawal syndrome

Overdosage/Toxicology Excessively high doses may cause anxiety, agitation, increased muscle tone, hyperesthesia and seizures.

Drug Interactions

Increased Effect/Toxicity: Flumazenil reverses the effects of these nonbenzodiazepine hypnotics (zaleplon, zolpidem, zopiclone).

Stability Store at 15°C to 30°C (59°F to 86°F). For I.V. use only. Once drawn up in the syringe or mixed with solution use within 24 hours. Discard any unused solution after 24 hours.

Mechanism of Action Competitively inhibits the activity at the benzodiazepine recognition site on the GABA/benzodiazepine receptor complex. Flumazenil does not antagonize the CNS effect of drugs affecting GABA-ergic neurons by means other than the benzodiazepine receptor (ethanol, barbiturates, general anesthetics) and does not reverse the effects of opioids

Flumazenil

Pediatric Dosage (further studies needed)	
Pediatric dosage for reversal of conscious sedation and general anesthesia:	
Initial dose	0.01 mg/kg over 15 seconds (maximum: 0.2 mg)
Repeat doses (maximum: 4 doses)	0.005-0.01 mg/kg (maximum: 0.2 mg) repeated at 1-minute intervals
Maximum total cumulative dose	1 mg or 0.05 mg/kg (whichever is lower)
Adult Dosage	
Adult dosage for reversal of conscious sedation and general anesthesia:	
Initial dose	0.2 mg intravenously over 15 seconds
Repeat doses	If desired level of consciousness is not obtained, 0.2 mg may be repeated at 1-minute intervals.
Maximum total cumulative dose	1 mg (usual dose: 0.6-1 mg) **In the event of resedation:** Repeat doses may be given at 20-minute intervals with maximum of 1 mg/dose and 3 mg/hour.
Adult dosage for suspected benzodiazepine overdose:	
Initial dose	0.2 mg intravenously over 30 seconds; if the desired level of consciousness is not obtained, 0.3 mg can be given over 30 seconds
Repeat doses	0.5 mg over 30 seconds repeated at 1-minute intervals
Maximum total cumulative dose	3 mg (usual dose 1-3 mg) Patients with a partial response at 3 mg may require additional titration up to a total dose of 5 mg. If a patient has not responded 5 minutes after cumulative dose of 5 mg, the major cause of sedation is not likely due to benzodiazepines. **In the event of resedation:** May repeat doses at 20-minute intervals with maximum of 1 mg/dose and 3 mg/hour.

(Continued)

Flumazenil *(Continued)*

Pharmacodynamics/Kinetics
Onset of action: 1-3 minutes; 80% response within 3 minutes
Peak effect: 6-10 minutes
Duration: Resedation: ~1 hour; duration related to dose given and benzodiazepine plasma concentrations; reversal effects of flumazenil may wear off before effects of benzodiazepine
Distribution: Initial V_d: 0.5 L/kg; V_{dss} 0.77-1.6 L/kg
Protein binding: 40% to 50%
Metabolism: Hepatic; dependent upon hepatic blood flow
Half-life elimination: Adults: Alpha: 7-15 minutes; Terminal: 41-79 minutes
Excretion: Feces; urine (0.2% as unchanged drug)

Dosage
Children and Adults: I.V.: See table on previous page.

Resedation: Repeated doses may be given at 20-minute intervals as needed; repeat treatment doses of 1 mg (at a rate of 0.5 mg/minute) should be given at any time and no more than 3 mg should be given in any hour. After intoxication with high doses of benzodiazepines, the duration of a single dose of flumazenil is not expected to exceed 1 hour; if desired, the period of wakefulness may be prolonged with repeated low intravenous doses of flumazenil, or by an infusion of 0.1-0.4 mg/hour. Most patients with benzodiazepine overdose will respond to a cumulative dose of 1-3 mg and doses >3 mg do not reliably produce additional effects. Rarely, patients with a partial response at 3 mg may require additional titration up to a total dose of 5 mg. **If a patient has not responded 5 minutes after receiving a cumulative dose of 5 mg, the major cause of sedation is not likely to be due to benzodiazepines.**

Elderly: No differences in safety or efficacy have been reported. However, increased sensitivity may occur in some elderly patients.

Dosing in renal impairment: Not significantly affected by renal failure (Cl_{cr} <10 mL/minute) or hemodialysis beginning 1 hour after drug administration

Dosing in hepatic impairment: Initial dose of flumazenil used for initial reversal of benzodiazepine effects is not changed; however, subsequent doses in liver disease patients should be reduced in size or frequency

Administration I.V.: Administer in freely-running I.V. into large vein. Inject over 15 seconds for conscious sedation and general anesthesia and over 30 seconds for overdose.

Monitoring Parameters Monitor patients for return of sedation or respiratory depression

Dosage Forms Injection, solution: 0.1 mg/mL (5 mL, 10 mL) [contains edetate sodium]

♦ **Flumazenil Injection (Can)** see Flumazenil on page 718

♦ **Flumazenil Injection, USP (Can)** see Flumazenil on page 718

♦ **fluMist®** see Influenza Virus Vaccine on page 906

Flunisolide *(floo NISS oh lide)*

U.S. Brand Names AeroBid®; AeroBid®-M; Aerospan™; Nasarel®
Canadian Brand Names Alti-Flunisolide; Apo-Flunisolide®; Nasalide®; PMS-Flunisolide; Rhinalar®
Pharmacologic Category Corticosteroid, Inhalant (Oral); Corticosteroid, Nasal
Additional Appendix Information
Asthma on page 2029
Use Steroid-dependent asthma; nasal solution is used for seasonal or perennial rhinitis
Pregnancy Risk Factor C
Medication Safety Issues
Sound-alike/look-alike issues:
Flunisolide may be confused with Flumadine®, fluocinonide
Nasarel® may be confused with Nizoral®
Dosage Note: AeroBid® and Aerospan™ are not interchangeable; dosing changes when switching from one to another.
Oral Inhalation: Asthma:
AeroBid®:
Children 6-15 years: 2 inhalations twice daily (morning and evening); up to 4 inhalations/day
Children ≥16 years and Adults: 2 inhalations twice daily (morning and evening); up to 8 inhalations/day maximum
Aerospan™:
Children 6-11 years: 1 inhalation twice daily; up to 4 inhalations/day
Children ≥12 years and Adults: 2 inhalations twice daily; up to 8 inhalations/day
Intranasal: Rhinitis:
Children 6-14 years: 1 spray each nostril 3 times daily **or** 2 sprays in each nostril twice daily; not to exceed 4 sprays/day in each nostril (200 mcg/day)
Children ≥15 years and Adults: 2 sprays each nostril twice daily (morning and evening); may increase to 2 sprays 3 times daily; maximum dose: 8 sprays/day in each nostril (400 mcg/day)
Additional Information Complete prescribing information for this medication should be consulted for additional detail.
Dosage Forms
Aerosol for oral inhalation:
AeroBid®: 250 mcg/actuation (7 g) [100 metered inhalations; contains CFCs]
AeroBid®-M: 250 mcg/actuation (7 g) [100 metered inhalations; contains CFCs; menthol flavor]

Aerospan™: 80 mcg/actuation (5.1 g) [60 metered inhalations; CFC free]; 80 mcg/actuation (8.9 g) [120 metered inhalations; CFC free]
Solution, intranasal [spray]: 29 mcg/actuation (25 mL) [200 sprays]
Nasarel®: 29 mcg/actuation (25 mL) [200 sprays; contains benzalkonium chloride]

Fluocinolone (floo oh SIN oh lone)

U.S. Brand Names Capex™; Derma-Smoothe/FS®; Retisert™; Synalar®
Canadian Brand Names Capex™; Derma-Smoothe/FS®; Synalar®
Index Terms Fluocinolone Acetonide
Pharmacologic Category Corticosteroid, Ophthalmic; Corticosteroid, Topical
Additional Appendix Information
Corticosteroids *on page 1879*
Use Relief of susceptible inflammatory dermatosis [low, medium, high potency topical corticosteroid]; psoriasis of the scalp; atopic dermatitis in children ≥2 years of age
Ocular implant (Retisert™): Treatment of chronic, noninfectious uveitis affecting the posterior segment of the eye.
Pregnancy Risk Factor C
Medication Safety Issues
Sound-alike/look-alike issues:
Fluocinolone may be confused with fluocinonide
Dosage
Children ≥2 years: Topical: Atopic dermatitis (Derma-Smoothe/FS®): Moisten skin; apply to affected area twice daily; do not use for longer than 4 weeks
Children and Adults: Topical: Corticosteroid-responsive dermatoses: Cream, ointment, solution: Apply a thin layer to affected area 2-4 times/day; may use occlusive dressings to manage psoriasis or recalcitrant conditions
Adults:
Topical:
Atopic dermatitis (Derma-Smoothe/FS®): Apply thin film to affected area 3 times/day
Inflammatory and pruritic manifestations (dental use): Apply to oral lesion 4 times/day , after meals and at bedtime
Scalp psoriasis (Derma-Smoothe/FS®): Massage thoroughly into wet or dampened hair/scalp; cover with shower cap. Leave on overnight (or for at least 4 hours). Remove by washing hair with shampoo and rinsing thoroughly.
Seborrheic dermatitis of the scalp (Capex™): Apply no more than 1 ounce to scalp once daily; work into lather and allow to remain on scalp for ~5 minutes. Remove from hair and scalp by rinsing thoroughly with water.
Ocular implant: Chronic uveitis: One silicone-encased tablet (0.59 mg) surgically implanted into the posterior segment of the eye is designed to release 0.6 mcg/day, decreasing over 30 days to a steady-state release rate of 0.3-0.4 mcg/day for 30 months. Recurrence of uveitis denotes depletion of tablet, requiring reimplantation.
Additional Information Complete prescribing information for this medication should be consulted for additional detail.
Dosage Forms
Cream, as acetonide: 0.01% (15 g, 60 g); 0.025% (15 g, 60 g)
Synalar®: 0.025% (15 g, 60 g)
Oil, as acetonide:
Derma-Smoothe/FS® [eczema oil]: 0.01% (120 mL) [contains peanut oil]
Derma-Smoothe/FS® [scalp oil]: 0.01% (120 mL) [contains peanut oil; packaged with shower caps]
Ointment, as acetonide (Synalar®): 0.025% (15 g, 60 g)
Shampoo, as acetonide (Capex™): 0.01% (120 mL)
Solution, as acetonide: 0.01% (60 mL)
Synalar®: 0.01% (20 mL, 60 mL)
Tablet, ocular implant, as acetonide (Retisert™): 0.59 mg [enclosed in silicone elastomer]

♦ **Fluocinolone Acetonide** *see* Fluocinolone *on page 721*

Fluocinolone, Hydroquinone, and Tretinoin
(floo oh SIN oh lone, HYE droe kwin one, & TRET i noyn)

U.S. Brand Names Tri-Luma™
Index Terms Hydroquinone, Fluocinolone Acetonide, and Tretinoin; Tretinoin, Fluocinolone Acetonide, and Hydroquinone
Pharmacologic Category Corticosteroid, Topical; Depigmenting Agent; Retinoic Acid Derivative
Use Short-term treatment of moderate to severe melasma of the face
Pregnancy Risk Factor C
Dosage Topical: Adults: Melasma: Apply a thin film once daily to hyperpigmented areas of melasma (including 1/2 inch of normal-appearing surrounding skin). Apply 30 minutes prior to bedtime; not indicated for use beyond 8 weeks. Do not use occlusive dressings.
Dosage Forms Cream, topical: Hydroquinone 4%, tretinoin 0.05%, fluocinolone acetonide 0.01% (30 g) [contains sodium metabisulfite]

Fluocinonide (floo oh SIN oh nide)

U.S. Brand Names Lidex®; Lidex-E®; Vanos™
Canadian Brand Names Lidemol®; Lidex®; Lyderm®; Tiamol®; Topsyn®
Pharmacologic Category Corticosteroid, Topical
Additional Appendix Information
Corticosteroids *on page 1879*
(Continued)

Fluocinonide *(Continued)*

Use Anti-inflammatory, antipruritic; treatment of plaque-type psoriasis (up to 10% of body surface area) [high-potency topical corticosteroid]

Pregnancy Risk Factor C

Medication Safety Issues
Sound-alike/look-alike issues:
Fluocinonide may be confused with flunisolide, fluocinolone
Lidex® may be confused with Lasix®, Videx®, Wydase®

Dosage
Children and Adults: Pruritus and inflammation: Topical (0.5% cream): Apply thin layer to affected area 2-4 times/day depending on the severity of the condition. Therapy should be discontinued when control is achieved; if no improvement is seen, reassessment of diagnosis may be necessary.

Children ≥12 years and Adults: Plaque-type psoriasis (Vanos™): Topical (0.1% cream): Apply a thin layer once or twice daily to affected areas (limited to <10% of body surface area). **Note:** Not recommended for use >2 consecutive weeks or >60 g/week total exposure. Discontinue when control is achieved.

Additional Information Complete prescribing information for this medication should be consulted for additional detail.

Dosage Forms
Cream, anhydrous, emollient (Lidex®): 0.05% (15 g, 30 g, 60 g)
Cream, aqueous, emollient (Lidex-E®): 0.05% (15 g, 30 g, 60 g)
Cream (Vanos™): 0.1% (30 g, 60 g)
Gel (Lidex®): 0.05% (15 g, 30 g, 60 g)
Ointment (Lidex®): 0.05% (15 g, 30 g, 60 g)
Solution (Lidex®): 0.05% (60 mL) [contains alcohol 35%]

♦ **Fluohydrisone Acetate** *see* Fludrocortisone *on page 717*
♦ **Fluohydrocortisone Acetate** *see* Fludrocortisone *on page 717*
♦ **Fluor-I-Strip®** *see* Fluorescein Sodium *on page 722*
♦ **Fluor-I-Strip-AT®** *see* Fluorescein Sodium *on page 722*
♦ **Fluoracaine®** *see* Proparacaine and Fluorescein *on page 1441*
♦ **Fluor-A-Day** *see* Fluoride *on page 722*
♦ **Fluorescein and Proparacaine** *see* Proparacaine and Fluorescein *on page 1441*

Fluorescein Sodium *(FLURE e seen SOW dee um)*

U.S. Brand Names AK-Fluor; Angiscein®; Fluorescite®; Fluorets®; Fluor-I-Strip®; Fluor-I-Strip-AT®; Ful-Glo®

Canadian Brand Names Fluorescite®

Index Terms Soluble Fluorescein

Pharmacologic Category Diagnostic Agent

Use Demonstrates defects of corneal epithelium; diagnostic aid in ophthalmic angiography

Pregnancy Risk Factor C (topical); X (parenteral)

Dosage
Ophthalmic:
Solution: Instill 1-2 drops of 2% solution and allow a few seconds for staining; wash out excess with sterile water or irrigating solution
Strips: Moisten strip with sterile water. Place moistened strip at the fornix into the lower cul-de-sac close to the punctum. For best results, patient should close lid tightly over strip until desired amount of staining is obtained. Patient should blink several times after application.
Removal of foreign bodies, sutures or tonometry (Fluress®): Instill 1 or 2 drops (single instillations) into each eye before operating
Deep ophthalmic anesthesia (Fluress®): Instill 2 drops into each eye every 90 seconds up to 3 doses
Injection: Prior to use, perform intradermal skin test; have epinephrine 1:1000, an antihistamine, and oxygen available
Children: 3.5 mg/lb (7.5 mg/kg) injected rapidly into antecubital vein
Adults: 500-750 mg injected rapidly into antecubital vein

Additional Information Complete prescribing information for this medication should be consulted for additional detail.

Dosage Forms
Injection, solution:
AK-Fluor, Fluorescite®: 10% (5 mL); 25% (2 mL)
Angiscein®: 10% (5 mL)
Strip, ophthalmic:
Fluorets®, Fluor-I-Strip-AT®: 1 mg
Fluor-I-Strip®: 9 mg
Ful-Glo®: 0.6 mg

♦ **Fluorescite®** *see* Fluorescein Sodium *on page 722*
♦ **Fluorets®** *see* Fluorescein Sodium *on page 722*

Fluoride *(FLOR ide)*

U.S. Brand Names ACT® [OTC]; ACT® Plus [OTC]; ACT® x2™ [OTC]; CaviRinse™; ControlRx®; Denta 5000 Plus; DentaGel; EtheDent™; Fluor-A-Day; Fluorigard® [OTC]; Fluorinse®; Flura-Drops®; Gel-Kam® [OTC]; Gel-Kam® Rinse; Just for Kids™ [OTC]; Lozi-Flur™; Luride®; Luride® Lozi-Tab®; NeutraCare®; NeutraGard® [OTC]; NeutraGard® Advanced; NeutraGard® Plus; Omnii Gel™ [OTC]; Pediaflor® [DSC]; PerioMed™; Pharmaflur®; Pharmaflur® 1.1; Phos-Flur®; Phos-Flur® Rinse [OTC]; PreviDent®; PreviDent® 5000 Plus™; StanGard®; StanGard® Perio; Stop®; Thera-Flur-N®

Canadian Brand Names Fluor-A-Day; Fluotic®

Index Terms Acidulated Phosphate Fluoride; Sodium Fluoride; Stannous Fluoride

Pharmacologic Category Nutritional Supplement

Use Prevention of dental caries

Pregnancy Risk Factor C

Medication Safety Issues
Sound-alike/look-alike issues:
Luride® may be confused with Lortab®
Phos-Flur® may be confused with PhosLo®
Thera-Flur-N® may be confused with Thera-Flu®

International issues:
Fluorex® [France] may be confused with Flarex® which is a brand name for fluorometholone in the U.S.

Contraindications Hypersensitivity to fluoride, tartrazine, or any component of the formulation; when fluoride content of drinking water exceeds 0.7 ppm; low sodium or sodium-free diets; do not use 1 mg tablets in children <3 years of age or when drinking water fluoride content is ≥0.3 ppm; do not use 1 mg/5 mL rinse (as supplement) in children <6 years of age

Warnings/Precautions Prolonged ingestion with excessive doses may result in dental fluorosis and osseous changes; do **not** exceed recommended dosage; some products contain tartrazine

Adverse Reactions <1% (Limited to important or life-threatening): Discoloration of teeth, rash, nausea, vomiting

Overdosage/Toxicology Symptoms include hypersalivation, salty or soapy taste, epigastric pain, nausea, vomiting, diarrhea, rash, muscle weakness, tremor, seizures, cardiac failure, respiratory arrest, shock, and death. The fatal dose not known. Treatment consists of gastric lavage with $CaCl_2$ or $Ca(OH)_2$ solution. Administer a large quantity of milk at frequent intervals. $Al(OH)_3$ may also bind the fluoride ion.

Drug Interactions
Decreased Effect: Decreased effect/absorption with magnesium-, aluminum-, and calcium-containing products.

Stability Store in tight plastic containers (not glass).

Mechanism of Action Promotes remineralization of decalcified enamel; inhibits the cariogenic microbial process in dental plaque; increases tooth resistance to acid dissolution

Pharmacodynamics/Kinetics
Absorption: Oral: Rapid and complete; sodium fluoride, other soluble fluoride salts; calcium, iron, or magnesium may delay absorption
Distribution: 50% of fluoride is deposited in teeth and bone after ingestion; topical application works superficially on enamel and plaque; crosses placenta; enters breast milk
Excretion: Urine and feces

Dosage Oral:
The recommended daily dose of oral fluoride supplement (mg), based on fluoride ion content (ppm) in drinking water (2.2 mg of sodium fluoride is equivalent to 1 mg of fluoride ion): See table.

Fluoride Ion

Fluoride Content of Drinking Water	Daily Dose, Oral (mg)
<0.3 ppm	
Birth - 6 mo	None
6 mo - 3 y	0.25
3-6 y	0.5
6-16 y	1
0.3-0.6 ppm	
Birth - 6 mo	None
6 mo - 3 y	None
3-6 y	0.25
6-16 y	0.5

Adapted from Recommended Dosage Schedule of The American Dental Association, The American Academy of Pediatric Dentistry, and The American Academy of Pediatrics

Cream: Children ≥6 years and Adults: Brush teeth with cream once daily regardless of fluoride content of drinking water

Dental rinse or gel:
Children 6-12 years: 5-10 mL rinse or apply to teeth and spit daily after brushing
Adults: 10 mL rinse or apply to teeth and spit daily after brushing
PreviDent® rinse: Children >6 years and Adults: Once weekly, rinse 10 mL vigorously around and between teeth for 1 minute, then spit; this should be done preferably at bedtime, after thoroughly brushing teeth; for maximum benefit, do not eat, drink, or rinse mouth for at least 30 minutes after treatment; do not swallow
Fluorinse®: Children >6 years and Adults: Once weekly, vigorously swish 5-10 mL in mouth for 1 minute, then spit
Lozenge (Lozi-Flur™): Adults: One lozenge daily regardless of fluoride content of drinking water

Dietary Considerations Do not administer with milk; do **not** allow eating or drinking for 30 minutes after use.

Dosage Forms [DSC] = Discontinued product
Cream, oral, as sodium [toothpaste]: 1.1% (51 g) [fluoride 2.5 mg/dose]
Denta 5000 Plus: 1.1% (51g) [fluoride 2.5 mg/dose; spearmint flavor]
EtheDent™: 1.1% (51g) [fluoride 2.5 mg/dose]
(Continued)

Fluoride *(Continued)*

Gel-drops, as sodium fluoride (Thera-Flur-N®): 1.1% (24 mL) [fluoride 0.5%; neutral pH; no artificial color or flavor]

Gel, topical, as acidulated phosphate fluoride (Phos-Flur®): 1.1% (60 g) [fluoride 0.5%; cherry and mint flavors]

Gel, topical, as sodium fluoride: 1.1% (56 g) [fluoride 2 mg/dose]
DentaGel, EtheDent™: 1.1% (56 g) [fluoride 2 mg/dose; fresh mint flavor]
NeutraCare®: 1.1% (60 g) [neutral pH; grape and mint flavors]
NeutraGard® Advanced: 1.1% (60 g) [cinnamon and mint flavors]
PreviDent®: 1.1% (60 g) [fluoride 2 mg/dose; berry, cherry, and mint flavors]

Gel, topical, as stannous fluoride:
Gel-Kam®: 0.4% (129 g) [bubble gum, cinnamon, fruit/berry, and mint flavors]
Just for Kids™: 0.4% (122 g) [bubble gum, fruit punch, and grapey grape flavors]
Omnii Gel™: 0.4% (122 g) [cinnamon, grape, natural, mint, and raspberry flavors]
StanGard®: 0.4% (122 g) [bubble gum, cherry, mint, and raspberry flavors]
Stop®: 0.4% (120 g) [bubble gum, cinnamon, grape, and mint flavors]

Lozenge, as sodium (Lozi-Flur™): 2.21 mg [fluoride 1 mg; cherry flavor]

Paste, oral, as sodium [toothpaste] (ControlRx®): 1.1% (56 g) [vanilla mint flavor]

Solution, oral drops, as sodium: 1.1 mg/mL (50 mL) [fluoride 0.5 mg/mL]
Flura-Drops®: 0.55 mg/drop (24 mL) [fluoride 0.25 mg/drop; dye free, sugar free]
Luride®: 1.1 mg/mL (50 mL) [fluoride 0.5 mg/mL; sugar free]
Pediaflor®: 1.1 mg/mL (50 mL) [fluoride 0.5 mg/mL; contains alcohol <0.5%; sugar free; cherry flavor] [DSC]

Solution, oral rinse, as sodium:
ACT®: 0.05% (530 mL) [fluoride 0.02%; bubble gum, cinnamon (contains tartrazine), and mint flavors]
ACT® Plus: 0.05% (530 mL) [fluoride 0.02%; alcohol free; icy cool mint flavor]
ACT® x2™: 0.5% (530 mL) [fluoride 0.02%; contains alcohol 11%; icy cool mint and spearmint flavors]
CaviRinse™: 0.2% (240 mL) [mint flavor]
Fluorigard®: 0.05% (480 mL) [alcohol free, sugar free; contains sodium benzoate and tartrazine; mint flavor]
Fluorinse®: 0.2% (480 mL) [alcohol free; cinnamon and mint flavors]
NeutraGard®: 0.05% (480 mL) [neutral pH; mint and tropical blast flavors]
NeutraGard® Plus: 0.2% (480 mL) [neutral pH; mint and tropical blast flavors]
Phos-Flur®: 0.44% (500 mL) [bubble gum, cherry, grape, and mint flavors]
PreviDent®: 0.2% (250 mL) [contains alcohol; mint flavor]

Solution, oral rinse concentrate, as stannous fluoride:
Gel-Kam®: 0.63% (300 mL) [fluoride 0.1%/dose; cinnamon and mint flavors]
PerioMed™: 0.63% (284 mL) [fluoride 7 mg/30 mL; alcohol free; cinnamon, mint and tropical fruit flavors]
StanGard® Perio: 0.63% (284 mL) [mint flavor]

Tablet, chewable, as sodium: 0.5 mg [fluoride 0.25 mg]; 1.1 mg [fluoride 0.5 mg]; 2.2 mg [fluoride 1 mg]
EtheDent™:
0.55 mg [fluoride 0.25 mg; sugar free; contains aspartame; vanilla flavor]
1.1 mg [fluoride 0.5 mg; sugar free; contains aspartame; grape flavor]
2.2 mg [fluoride 1 mg; sugar free; contains aspartame; cherry flavor]
Fluor-A-Day:
0.56 mg [fluoride 0.25 mg; raspberry flavor]
1.1 mg [fluoride 0.5 mg; raspberry flavor]
2.21 mg [fluoride 1 mg; raspberry flavor]
Luride® Lozi-Tab®:
0.55 mg [fluoride 0.25 mg; sugar free; vanilla flavor]
1.1 mg [fluoride 0.5 mg; sugar free; grape flavor]
2.2 mg [fluoride 1 mg; sugar free; cherry flavor]
Pharmaflur®: 2.2 mg [fluoride 1 mg; dye free, sugar free; cherry flavor]
Pharmaflur® 1.1: 1.1 mg [fluoride 0.5 mg; dye free, sugar free; grape flavor]

♦ **Fluorigard®** **[OTC]** *see* Fluoride *on page 722*
♦ **Fluori-Methane®** *see* Dichlorodifluoromethane and Trichloromonofluoromethane *on page 492*
♦ **Fluorinse®** *see* Fluoride *on page 722*
♦ **5-Fluorocytosine** *see* Flucytosine *on page 714*
♦ **9α-Fluorohydrocortisone Acetate** *see* Fludrocortisone *on page 717*

Fluorometholone *(flure oh METH oh lone)*

U.S. Brand Names Eflone® [DSC]; Flarex®; Fluor-Op® [DSC]; FML®; FML® Forte
Canadian Brand Names Flarex®; FML®; FML Forte®; PMS-Fluorometholone
Pharmacologic Category Corticosteroid, Ophthalmic
Use Treatment of steroid-responsive inflammatory conditions of the eye
Pregnancy Risk Factor C
Pregnancy Implications The extent of systemic absorption is not known. Use with caution in pregnant women.
Lactation Excretion in breast milk unknown/use caution
Medication Safety Issues
International issues:
Flarex® may be confused with Flurets® which is a brand name for sodium fluoride in Australia
Flarex® may be confused with Fluarix® which is a brand name for influenza virus vaccine in the U.S. and in numerous international markets
Flarex® may be confused with Fluorex® which is a brand name for sodium fluoride in France

Fluor Op® may be confused with Fluoron® which is a brand name for fluorine in Canada

Contraindications Hypersensitivity to fluorometholone or any component of the formulation; viral diseases of the cornea and conjunctiva (including epithelial herpes simplex keratitis, vaccinia and varicella); mycobacterial or fungal infections of the eye; untreated eye infections which may be masked/enhanced by a steroid

Warnings/Precautions Not recommended in children <2 years of age. Prolonged use may result in glaucoma, elevated intraocular pressure, or other ocular damage. May exacerbate severity of viral infections, use caution in patients with history of herpes simplex. Re-evaluate after 2 days if symptoms have not improved. May delay healing following cataract surgery. Some products contain sulfites.

Adverse Reactions
Ocular: Anterior uveitis, burning upon application, cataract formation, conjunctival hyperemia, conjunctivitis, corneal ulcers, glaucoma with optic nerve damage, perforation of the globe, secondary ocular infection (bacterial, fungal, viral), intraocular pressure elevation, visual acuity and field defects, keratitis, mydriasis, stinging upon application, delayed wound healing
Miscellaneous: Systemic hypercorticoidism (rare) and taste perversion have also been reported

Overdosage/Toxicology When consumed in high doses over prolonged periods, systemic hypercorticism and adrenal suppression may occur; in those cases, discontinuation of the corticosteroid should be done judiciously.

Stability Store at room temperature.

Mechanism of Action Decreases inflammation by suppression of migration of polymorphonuclear leukocytes and reversal of increased capillary permeability

Pharmacodynamics/Kinetics Absorption: Into aqueous humor with slight systemic absorption

Dosage Children >2 years and Adults: Ophthalmic: Re-evaluate therapy if improvement is not seen within 2 days; use care not to discontinue prematurely; in chronic conditions, gradually decrease dosing frequency prior to discontinuing treatment
Ointment: Apply small amount (~½ inch ribbon) to conjunctival sac every 4 hours in severe cases; 1-3 times/day in mild to moderate cases
Solution: Instill 1-2 drops into conjunctival sac every hour during day, every 2 hours at night until favorable response is obtained, then use 1 drop every 4 hours; for mild to moderate inflammation, instill 1-2 drops into conjunctival sac 2-4 times/day

Monitoring Parameters Intraocular pressure in patients with glaucoma or when used for ≥10 days; presence of secondary infections (including the development of fungal infections and exacerbation of viral infections)

Dosage Forms [DSC] = Discontinued product
Ointment, ophthalmic, as base (FML®): 0.1% (3.5 g)
Suspension, ophthalmic, as base: 0.1% (5 mL, 10 mL, 15 mL)
Fluor-Op®: 0.1% (5 mL, 10 mL, 15 mL) [contains benzalkonium chloride and polyvinyl alcohol] [DSC]
FML®: 0.1% (5 mL, 10 mL, 15 mL) [contains benzalkonium chloride]
FML® Forte: 0.25% (2 mL, 5 mL, 10 mL, 15 mL) [contains benzalkonium chloride]
Suspension, ophthalmic, as acetate:
Eflone®: 0.1% (5 mL, 10 mL) [DSC]
Flarex®: 0.1% (5 mL, 10 mL) [contains benzalkonium chloride]

♦ **Fluorometholone and Sulfacetamide** see Sulfacetamide Sodium and Fluorometholone on page 1610
♦ **Fluor-Op® [DSC]** see Fluorometholone on page 724
♦ **Fluoroplex®** see Fluorouracil on page 725

Fluorouracil (flure oh YOOR a sil)

U.S. Brand Names Adrucil®; Carac™; Efudex®; Fluoroplex®
Canadian Brand Names Efudex®
Index Terms 5-Fluorouracil; FU; 5-FU
Pharmacologic Category Antineoplastic Agent, Antimetabolite (Pyrimidine Antagonist)
Use Treatment of carcinomas of the breast, colon, head and neck, pancreas, rectum, or stomach; topically for the management of actinic or solar keratoses and superficial basal cell carcinomas
Pregnancy Risk Factor D (injection); X (topical)
Pregnancy Implications There are no adequate and well-controlled studies in pregnant women, however, fetal defects and miscarriages have been reported following use of topical and intravenous products. Use is contraindicated during pregnancy.
Lactation Excretion in breast milk unknown/not recommended
Medication Safety Issues
Sound-alike/look-alike issues:
Fluorouracil may be confused with flucytosine
Efudex® may be confused with Efidac (Efidac 24®), Eurax®

High alert medication: The Institute for Safe Medication Practices (ISMP) includes this medication among its list of drugs which have a heightened risk of causing significant patient harm when used in error.

International issues:
Carac™ may be confused with Carace® which is a brand name for lisinopril in Ireland and Great Britain
Contraindications Hypersensitivity to fluorouracil or any component of the formulation; dihydropyrimidine dehydrogenase (DPD) enzyme deficiency; pregnancy
Warnings/Precautions Hazardous agent - use appropriate precautions for handling and disposal. Use with caution in patients with impaired kidney or liver function. The drug should be discontinued if intractable vomiting or diarrhea, precipitous falls in leukocyte or platelet counts, stomatitis, hemorrhage, or myocardial ischemia occurs. Use with caution in patients
(Continued)

Fluorouracil (Continued)

who have had high-dose pelvic radiation or previous use of alkylating agents. Palmar-plantar erythrodysesthesia (hand-foot) syndrome has been associated with use. Safety and efficacy have not been established in pediatric patients.

Administration to patients with a genetic deficiency of dihydropyrimidine dehydrogenase (DPD) has been associated with increased toxicity following administration (diarrhea, neutropenia, and neurotoxicity). Systemic toxicity normally associated with parenteral administration has also been associated with topical use, particularly in patients with DPD. Discontinue if symptoms of DPD occur. **[U.S. Boxed Warning]: Should be administered under the supervision of an experienced cancer chemotherapy physician.**

Avoid topical application to mucous membranes due to potential for local inflammation and ulceration. The use of occlusive dressings with topical preparations may increase the severity of inflammation in nearby skin areas. Avoid exposure to ultraviolet rays during and immediately following therapy.

Adverse Reactions Toxicity depends on route and duration of infusion.

>10%:

Dermatologic: Dermatitis, pruritic maculopapular rash, alopecia

Gastrointestinal (route and schedule dependent): Heartburn, nausea, vomiting, anorexia, stomatitis, esophagitis, anorexia, stomatitis, diarrhea

Emetic potential:
<1000 mg: Moderately low (10% to 30%)
≥1000 mg: Moderate (30% to 60%)

Hematologic: Leukopenia; Myelosuppressive (tends to be more pronounced in patients receiving bolus dosing of FU):
WBC: Moderate
Platelets: Mild to moderate
Onset (days): 7-10
Nadir (days): 14
Recovery (days): 21

Local: **Irritant chemotherapy**

1% to 10%:
Dermatologic: Dry skin
Gastrointestinal: GI ulceration

<1% (Limited to important or life-threatening): Cardiac enzyme abnormalities, chest pain, coagulopathy, dyspnea, ECG changes similar to ischemic changes, hepatotoxicity; hyperpigmentation of nailbeds, face, hands, and veins used in infusion; hypotension, palmar-plantar syndrome (hand-foot syndrome), photosensitization

Cerebellar ataxia, headache, somnolence, ataxia are seen primarily in intracarotid arterial infusions for head and neck tumors.

Topical: Note: Systemic toxicity normally associated with parenteral administration (including neutropenia, neurotoxicity, and gastrointestinal toxicity) has been associated with topical use particularly in patients with a genetic deficiency of dihydropyrimidine dehydrogenase (DPD).

Overdosage/Toxicology Symptoms include myelosuppression, nausea, vomiting, diarrhea, and alopecia. No specific antidote exists. Monitor hematologically for at least 4 weeks. Treatment is supportive.

Drug Interactions

Increased Effect/Toxicity: Fluorouracil may increase effects of warfarin.

Ethanol/Nutrition/Herb Interactions

Ethanol: Avoid ethanol (due to GI irritation).

Herb/Nutraceutical: Avoid black cohosh, dong quai in estrogen-dependent tumors.

Stability

Injection: Store intact vials at room temperature and protect from light; slight discoloration does not usually denote decomposition. Dilute in 50-1000 mL NS, D_5W, or bacteriostatic NS for infusion. If exposed to cold, a precipitate may form; **gentle** heating to 60°C will dissolve the precipitate without impairing the potency; solutions in 50-1000 mL NS or D_5W, or undiluted solutions in syringes are stable for 72 hours at room temperature.

Topical: Store at controlled room temperature of 15°C to 30°C (59°F to 86°F).

Mechanism of Action A pyrimidine antimetabolite that interferes with DNA synthesis by blocking the methylation of deoxyuridylic acid; fluorouracil inhibits thymidylate synthetase (TS), or is incorporated into RNA. The reduced folate cofactor is required for tight binding to occur between the 5-FdUMP and TS.

Pharmacodynamics/Kinetics

Duration: ~3 weeks

Distribution: V_d: ~22% of total body water; penetrates extracellular fluid, CSF, and third space fluids (eg, pleural effusions and ascitic fluid)

Metabolism: Hepatic (90%); via a dehydrogenase enzyme; FU must be metabolized to be active

Bioavailability: <75%, erratic and undependable

Half-life elimination: Biphasic: Initial: 6-20 minutes; two metabolites, FdUMP and FUTP, have prolonged half-lives depending on the type of tissue

Excretion: Lung (large amounts as CO_2); urine (5% as unchanged drug) in 6 hours

Dosage Adults:

Refer to individual protocols:
I.V. bolus: 500-600 mg/m² every 3-4 weeks **or** 425 mg/m² on days 1-5 every 4 weeks

Continuous I.V. infusion: 1000 mg/m²/day for 4-5 days every 3-4 weeks **or**
2300-2600 mg/m² on day 1 every week **or**
300-400 mg/m²/day **or**
225 mg/m²/day for 5-8 weeks (with radiation therapy)

Actinic keratoses: Topical:
Carac™: Apply thin film to lesions once daily for up to 4 weeks, as tolerated

Efudex®: Apply to lesions twice daily for 2-4 weeks; complete healing may not be evident for 1-2 months following treatment

Fluoroplex®: Apply to lesions twice daily for 2-6 weeks

Superficial basal cell carcinoma: Topical: Efudex® 5%: Apply to affected lesions twice daily for 3-6 weeks; treatment may be continued for up to 10-12 weeks

Dosage adjustment for renal impairment: Hemodialysis: Administer dose following hemodialysis.

Dosage adjustment for hepatic impairment: Bilirubin >5 mg/dL: Omit use.

Dietary Considerations Increase dietary intake of thiamine.

Administration

I.V.: I.V. bolus as a slow push or short (5-15 minutes) bolus infusion, or as a continuous infusion. Doses >1000 mg/m² are usually administered as a 24-hour infusion. Toxicity may be reduced by giving the drug as a constant infusion. Bolus doses may be administered by slow IVP or IVPB.

Note: I.V. formulation may be given orally mixed in water, grape juice, or carbonated beverage. It is generally best to drink undiluted solution, then rinse the mouth. CocaCola® has been recommended as the "best chaser" for oral fluorouracil.

Topical: Apply 10 minutes after washing, rinsing, and drying the affected area. Apply using fingertip (wash hands immediately after application) or nonmetal applicator. Do not cover area with an occlusive dressing. Wash hands immediately after topical application of the 5% cream. Topical preparations are for external use only; not for ophthalmic, oral, or intravaginal use.

Monitoring Parameters CBC with differential and platelet count, renal function tests, liver function tests

Dosage Forms

Cream, topical:
Carac™: 0.5% (30 g)
Efudex®: 5% (25 g, 40 g)
Fluoroplex®: 1% (30 g) [contains benzyl alcohol]
Injection, solution: 50 mg/mL (10 mL, 20 mL, 50 mL, 100 mL)
Adrucil®: 50 mg/mL (10 mL, 50 mL, 100 mL)
Solution, topical (Efudex®): 2% (10 mL); 5% (10 mL)

♦ 5-Fluorouracil *see Fluorouracil on page 725*
♦ Fluotic® (Can) *see Fluoride on page 722*

Fluoxetine (floo OKS e teen)

U.S. Brand Names Prozac®; Prozac® Weekly™; Sarafem®

Canadian Brand Names Alti-Fluoxetine; Apo-Fluoxetine®; BCI-Fluoxetine; CO Fluoxetine; FXT; Gen-Fluoxetine; Novo-Fluoxetine; Nu-Fluoxetine; PMS-Fluoxetine; Prozac®; Rhoxal-fluoxetine; Sandoz-Fluoxetine

Index Terms Fluoxetine Hydrochloride

Pharmacologic Category Antidepressant, Selective Serotonin Reuptake Inhibitor

Additional Appendix Information

Antidepressant Agents *on page 1866*
Selective Serotonin Reuptake Inhibitors (SSRIs) Pharmacokinetics *on page 1896*

Use Treatment of major depressive disorder (MDD); treatment of binge-eating and vomiting in patients with moderate-to-severe bulimia nervosa; obsessive-compulsive disorder (OCD); premenstrual dysphoric disorder (PMDD); panic disorder with or without agoraphobia

Unlabeled/Investigational Use Selective mutism

Restrictions An FDA-approved medication guide concerning the use of antidepressants in children and teenagers must be distributed when dispensing an outpatient prescription (new or refill) where this medication is to be used without direct supervision of a healthcare provider. Medication guides are available at http://www.fda.gov/cder/Offices/ODS/medication_guides.htm. Dispense to parents or guardians of children and teenagers receiving this medication.

Pregnancy Risk Factor C

Pregnancy Implications Fluoxetine crosses the placenta. Nonteratogenic effects including respiratory distress, cyanosis, apnea, seizures, temperature instability, feeding difficulty, vomiting, hypoglycemia, hypo- or hypertonia, hyper-reflexia, jitteriness, irritability, constant crying, and tremor have been reported in the neonate immediately following delivery after exposure to SSRIs late in the third trimester. Exposure to SSRIs late in pregnancy has also been associated with persistent pulmonary hypertension of the newborn (PPHN). Adverse effects may be due to toxic effects of SSRI or drug discontinuation. In some cases, effects may present clinically as serotonin syndrome. There are no adequate and well-controlled studies in pregnant women. Use during pregnancy only if the potential benefit to the mother outweighs the possible risk to the fetus. If treatment during pregnancy is required, consider tapering SSRI therapy during the third trimester.

Lactation Enters breast milk/not recommended (AAP rates "of concern")

Medication Safety Issues

Sound-alike/look-alike issues:
Fluoxetine may be confused with duloxetine, fluvastatin, fluvoxamine
Prozac® may be confused with Prilosec®, Proscar®, ProSom®, ProStep®
Sarafem® may be confused with Serophene®

International issues:
Fluoxin® [Czech Republic and Romania] may be confused with Floxin® which is a brand name for ofloxacin in the U.S.
Prozac® may be confused with Prazac® a brand of prazosin in Denmark
Reneuron® [Spain] may be confused with Remeron® a brand of mirtazapine in the U.S.

Contraindications Hypersensitivity to fluoxetine or any component of the formulation; patients currently receiving MAO inhibitors, pimozide, or thioridazine

(Continued)

Fluoxetine *(Continued)*

Note: MAO inhibitor therapy must be stopped for 14 days before fluoxetine is initiated. Treatment with MAO inhibitors, thioridazine, or mesoridazine should not be initiated until 5 weeks after the discontinuation of fluoxetine.

Warnings/Precautions   [U.S. Boxed Warning]: Antidepressants increase the risk of suicidal thinking and behavior in children and adolescents with major depressive disorder (MDD) and other depressive disorders; consider risk prior to prescribing. All patients must be closely monitored for clinical worsening, suicidality, or unusual changes in behavior, especially during the initiation of therapy or following an increase or decrease in dosage. When used in children, the child's family or caregiver should be instructed to closely observe the patient and communicate condition with healthcare provider. A medication guide should be dispensed with each prescription. **Fluoxetine is FDA approved for the treatment of OCD in children ≥7 years of age and MDD in children ≥8 years of age.**

The possibility of a suicide attempt is inherent in major depression and may persist until remission occurs. Use caution in high-risk patients. Worsening depression and severe abrupt suicidality that are not part of the presenting symptoms may require discontinuation or modification of drug therapy. The patient's family or caregiver should be alerted to monitor patients for the emergence of suicidality and associated behaviors (such as agitation, irritability, hostility, impulsivity, and hypomania) and call healthcare provider.

May worsen psychosis in some patients or precipitate a shift to mania or hypomania in patients with bipolar disorder. Patients presenting with depressive symptoms should be screened for bipolar disorder. Monotherapy in patients with bipolar disorder should be avoided. **Fluoxetine is not FDA approved for the treatment of bipolar depression.** May cause insomnia, anxiety, nervousness or anorexia. Use with caution in patients where weight loss is undesirable. May impair cognitive or motor performance; caution operating hazardous machinery or driving.

The potential for severe reactions exists when used with MAO inhibitors, SSRIs/SNRIs or triptans; serotonin syndrome (hyperthermia, muscular rigidity, mental status changes/agitation, autonomic instability) may occur. Concurrent use with MAO inhibitors is contraindicated. Fluoxetine may elevate plasma levels of thioridazine and increase the risk of QT_c interval prolongation. This may lead to serious ventricular arrhythmias such as torsade de pointes-type arrhythmias and sudden death. Fluoxetine use has been associated with occurrences of significant rash and allergic events, including vasculitis, lupus-like syndrome, laryngospasm, anaphylactoid reactions, and pulmonary inflammatory disease. Discontinue if underlying cause of rash cannot be identified.

Use caution in patients with a previous seizure disorder or condition predisposing to seizures such as brain damage, alcoholism, or concurrent therapy with other drugs which lower the seizure threshold. Use with caution in patients with hepatic or renal dysfunction and in elderly patients. May cause hyponatremia/SIADH. May increase the risks associated with electroconvulsive treatment. Use with caution in patients at risk of bleeding or receiving concurrent anticoagulant therapy - may cause impairment in platelet function. Use caution with history of MI or unstable heart disease; use in these patients is limited. May alter glycemic control in patients with diabetes. Due to the long half-life of fluoxetine and its metabolites, the effects and interactions noted may persist for prolonged periods following discontinuation. May cause or exacerbate sexual dysfunction. Discontinuation symptoms (eg, dysphoric mood, irritability, agitation, confusion, anxiety, insomnia, hypomania) may occur upon abrupt discontinuation. Taper dose when discontinuing therapy.

Adverse Reactions Percentages listed for adverse effects as reported in placebo-controlled trials and were generally similar in adults and children; actual frequency may be dependent upon diagnosis and in some cases the range presented may be lower than or equal to placebo for a particular disorder.

>10%:
  Central nervous system: Insomnia (10% to 33%), headache (21%), anxiety (6% to 15%), nervousness (8% to 14%), somnolence (5% to 17%)
  Endocrine & metabolic: Libido decreased (1% to 11%)
  Gastrointestinal: Nausea (12% to 29%), diarrhea (8% to 18%), anorexia (4% to 11%), xerostomia (4% to 12%)
  Neuromuscular & skeletal: Weakness (7% to 21%), tremor (3% to 13%)
  Respiratory: Pharyngitis (3% to 11%), yawn (<1% to 11%)
1% to 10%:
  Cardiovascular: Vasodilation (1% to 5%), fever (2%), chest pain, hemorrhage, hypertension, palpitation
  Central nervous system: Dizziness (9%), dream abnormality (1% to 5%), thinking abnormality (2%), agitation, amnesia, chills, confusion, emotional lability, sleep disorder
  Dermatologic: Rash (2% to 6%), pruritus (4%)
  Endocrine & metabolic: Ejaculation abnormal (<1% to 7%), impotence (<1% to 7%)
  Gastrointestinal: Dyspepsia (6% to 10%), constipation (5%), flatulence (3%), vomiting (3%), weight loss (2%), appetite increased, taste perversion, weight gain
  Genitourinary: Urinary frequency
  Ocular: Vision abnormal (2%)
  Otic: Ear pain, tinnitus
  Respiratory: Sinusitis (1% to 6%)
  Miscellaneous: Flu-like syndrome (3% to 10%), diaphoresis (2% to 8%)
<1% (Limited to important or life-threatening): Allergies, alopecia, anaphylactoid reactions, angina, arrhythmia, asthma, cataract, CHF, cholelithiasis, cholestatic jaundice, colitis, dyskinesia, dysphagia, eosinophilic pneumonia, erythema nodosum, esophagitis, euphoria, exfoliative dermatitis, extrapyramidal symptoms (rare), gout, hallucinations, hepatic failure/necrosis, hemorrhage, hyperprolactinemia, hyponatremia (possibly in association with SIADH), immune-related hemolytic anemia, laryngospasm, lupus-like syndrome, MI, neuroleptic malignant syndrome (NMS), optic neuritis, pancreatitis, pancytopenia, photosensitivity reaction, postural hypotension, priapism, pulmonary embolism, pulmonary fibrosis, pulmonary hypertension, QT prolongation, renal failure, serotonin

syndrome, Stevens-Johnson syndrome, syncope, thrombocytopenia, thrombocytopenic purpura, vasculitis, ventricular tachycardia (including torsade de pointes)

Overdosage/Toxicology Among 633 adult patients who overdosed on fluoxetine alone, 34 resulted in a fatal outcome. Symptoms include ataxia, sedation, coma, and ECG abnormalities (QT prolongation, torsade de pointes). Respiratory depression may occur, especially with coingestion of alcohol or other drugs. Seizures rarely occur. Treatment is symptom-directed and supportive. Forced diuresis and dialysis are not likely to benefit.

Drug Interactions

Cytochrome P450 Effect: Substrate of CYP1A2 (minor), 2B6 (minor), 2C9 (major), 2C19 (minor), 2D6 (major), 2E1 (minor), 3A4 (minor); **Inhibits** CYP1A2 (moderate), 2B6 (weak), 2C9 (weak), 2C19 (moderate), 2D6 (strong), 3A4 (weak)

Increased Effect/Toxicity: Fluoxetine should not be used with nonselective MAO inhibitors (phenelzine, isocarboxazid) or other drugs with MAO inhibition (linezolid); fatal reactions have been reported. Wait 5 weeks after stopping fluoxetine before starting a nonselective MAO inhibitor and 2 weeks after stopping an MAO inhibitor before starting fluoxetine. Concurrent selegiline has been associated with mania, hypertension, or serotonin syndrome (risk may be reduced relative to nonselective MAO inhibitors).

Due to potential QT_c interval prolongation, concomitant use of pimozide is contraindicated. Fluoxetine may inhibit the metabolism of thioridazine, resulting in increased plasma levels and increasing the risk of QT_c interval prolongation. This may lead to serious ventricular arrhythmias, such as torsade de pointes-type arrhythmias and sudden death. Do not use together. Wait at least 5 weeks after discontinuing fluoxetine prior to starting thioridazine.

Fluoxetine may increase the levels/effects of aminophylline, amphetamines, selected beta-blockers, citalopram, dextromethorphan, diazepam, fluvoxamine, lidocaine, mexiletine, methsuximide, mirtazapine, nefazodone, paroxetine, phenytoin, propranolol, risperidone, ritonavir, ropinirole, sertraline, theophylline, thioridazine, tricyclic antidepressants, trifluoperazine, venlafaxine, and other substrates of CYP1A2, 2C19, or 2D6.

Combined use of SSRIs and amphetamines, buspirone, meperidine, nefazodone, serotonin agonists (such as sumatriptan), sibutramine, other SSRIs/SNRIs, sympathomimetics, ritonavir, tramadol, and venlafaxine may increase the risk of serotonin syndrome. Combined use of sumatriptan (and other serotonin agonists) may result in toxicity; weakness, hyper-reflexia, and incoordination have been observed with sumatriptan and SSRIs. In addition, concurrent use may theoretically increase the risk of serotonin syndrome.

Concurrent lithium may increase risk of neurotoxicity, and lithium levels may be increased. Risk of hyponatremia may increase with concurrent use of loop diuretics (bumetanide, furosemide, torsemide). Fluoxetine may increase the hypoprothrombinemic response to warfarin. Concomitant use of fluoxetine and NSAIDs, aspirin, or other drugs affecting coagulation has been associated with an increased risk of bleeding; monitor.

The levels/effects of fluoxetine may be increased by chlorpromazine, delavirdine, fluconazole, gemfibrozil, ketoconazole, miconazole, nicardipine, NSAIDs, paroxetine, pergolide, quinidine, quinine, ritonavir, sulfonamides, ropinirole, tolbutamide, and other CYP2C9 or 2D6 inhibitors.

Decreased Effect: The levels/effects of fluoxetine may be decreased by carbamazepine, phenobarbital, phenytoin, rifampin, rifapentine, secobarbital and other CYP2C9 inducers. Fluoxetine may decrease the levels/effects of CYP2D6 prodrug substrates (eg, codeine, hydrocodone, oxycodone, tramadol). Cyproheptadine may inhibit the effects of serotonin reuptake inhibitors. Lithium levels may be decreased by fluoxetine (in addition to reports of increased lithium levels).

Ethanol/Nutrition/Herb Interactions

Ethanol: Avoid ethanol (may increase CNS depression). Depressed patients should avoid/limit intake.

Herb/Nutraceutical: Avoid valerian, St John's wort, kava kava, gotu kola (may increase CNS depression).

Stability All dosage forms should be stored at controlled room temperature of 15°C to 30°C (50°F to 86°F). Oral liquid should be dispensed in a light-resistant container.

Mechanism of Action Inhibits CNS neuron serotonin reuptake; minimal or no effect on reuptake of norepinephrine or dopamine; does not significantly bind to alpha-adrenergic, histamine, or cholinergic receptors

Pharmacodynamics/Kinetics

Onset of action: Depression: ≥4 weeks; OCD: ≥5 weeks

Absorption: Well absorbed; delayed 1-2 hours with weekly formulation

Distribution: 12-43 L/kg

Protein binding: 95% to albumin and alpha$_1$ glycoprotein

Metabolism: Hepatic, via CYP2C19 and 2D6, to norfluoxetine (activity equal to fluoxetine)

Half-life elimination: Adults:

Parent drug: 1-3 days (acute), 4-6 days (chronic), 7.6 days (cirrhosis)

Metabolite (norfluoxetine): 9.3 days (range: 4-16 days), 12 days (cirrhosis)

Time to peak, serum: 6-8 hours

Excretion: Urine (10% as norfluoxetine, 2.5% to 5% as fluoxetine)

Note: Weekly formulation results in greater fluctuations between peak and trough concentrations of fluoxetine and norfluoxetine compared to once-daily dosing (24% daily/164% weekly; 17% daily/43% weekly, respectively). Trough concentrations are 76% lower for fluoxetine and 47% lower for norfluoxetine than the concentrations maintained by 20 mg once-daily dosing. Steady-state fluoxetine concentrations are ~50% lower following the once-weekly regimen compared to 20 mg once daily. Average steady-state concentrations of once-daily dosing were highest in children ages 6 to <13 (fluoxetine 171 ng/mL; norfluoxetine 195 ng/mL), followed by adolescents ages 13 to <18 (fluoxetine 86 ng/mL; norfluoxetine 113 ng/mL); concentrations were considered to be within the ranges reported in adults (fluoxetine 91-302 ng/mL; norfluoxetine 72-258 ng/mL).

Dosage Oral: **Note:** Upon discontinuation of fluoxetine therapy, gradually taper dose. If intolerable symptoms occur following a dose reduction, consider resuming the previously prescribed dose and/or decrease dose at a more gradual rate.

(Continued)

Fluoxetine *(Continued)*

Children:

Depression: 8-18 years: 10-20 mg/day; lower-weight children can be started at 10 mg/day, may increase to 20 mg/day after 1 week if needed

OCD: 7-18 years: Initial: 10 mg/day; in adolescents and higher-weight children, dose may be increased to 20 mg/day after 2 weeks. Range: 10-60 mg/day

Selective mutism (unlabeled use):

<5 years: No dosing information available

5-18 years: Initial: 5-10 mg/day; titrate upwards as needed (usual maximum dose: 60 mg/day)

Adults: 20 mg/day in the morning; may increase after several weeks by 20 mg/day increments; maximum: 80 mg/day; doses >20 mg may be given once daily or divided twice daily. **Note:** Lower doses of 5-10 mg/day have been used for initial treatment.

Usual dosage range:

Bulimia nervosa: 60-80 mg/day

Depression: 20-40 mg/day; patients maintained on Prozac® 20 mg/day may be changed to Prozac® Weekly™ 90 mg/week, starting dose 7 days after the last 20 mg/day dose

OCD: 40-80 mg/day

Panic disorder: Initial: 10 mg/day; after 1 week, increase to 20 mg/day; may increase after several weeks; doses >60 mg/day have not been evaluated

PMDD (Sarafem™): 20 mg/day continuously, **or** 20 mg/day starting 14 days prior to menstruation and through first full day of menses (repeat with each cycle)

Elderly: Depression: Some patients may require an initial dose of 10 mg/day with dosage increases of 10 and 20 mg every several weeks as tolerated; should not be taken at night unless patient experiences sedation

Dosing adjustment in renal impairment:

Single dose studies: Pharmacokinetics of fluoxetine and norfluoxetine were similar among subjects with all levels of impaired renal function, including anephric patients on chronic hemodialysis

Chronic administration: Additional accumulation of fluoxetine or norfluoxetine may occur in patients with severely impaired renal function

Hemodialysis: Not removed by hemodialysis; use of lower dose or less frequent dosing is not usually necessary.

Dosing adjustment in hepatic impairment: Elimination half-life of fluoxetine is prolonged in patients with hepatic impairment; a lower or less frequent dose of fluoxetine should be used in these patients

Cirrhosis patients: Administer a lower dose or less frequent dosing interval

Compensated cirrhosis without ascites: Administer 50% of normal dose

Dietary Considerations May be taken with or without food.

Monitoring Parameters Mental status for depression, suicidal ideation, anxiety, social functioning, mania, panic attacks; akathisia; sleep

Reference Range Therapeutic levels have not been well established

Therapeutic: Fluoxetine: 100-800 ng/mL (SI: 289-2314 nmol/L); Norfluoxetine: 100-600 ng/mL (SI: 289-1735 nmol/L)

Toxic: Fluoxetine plus norfluoxetine: >2000 ng/mL

Additional Information ECG may reveal S-T segment depression; not shown to be teratogenic in rodents; 15-60 mg/day, buspirone and cyproheptadine, may be useful in treatment of sexual dysfunction during treatment with a selective serotonin reuptake inhibitor.

Weekly capsules are a delayed release formulation containing enteric-coated pellets of fluoxetine hydrochloride, equivalent to 90 mg fluoxetine. Therapeutic equivalence of weekly formulation with daily formulation for delaying time to relapse has not been established.

Dosage Forms [DSC] = Discontinued product

Capsule, as hydrochloride: 10 mg, 20 mg, 40 mg

Prozac®: 10 mg, 20 mg, 40 mg

Sarafem®: 10 mg, 20 mg

Capsule, delayed release, as hydrochloride (Prozac® Weekly™): 90 mg

Solution, oral, as hydrochloride (Prozac®): 20 mg/5 mL (120 mL) [contains alcohol 0.23% and benzoic acid; mint flavor]

Tablet, as hydrochloride: 10 mg, 20 mg

Prozac® [scored]: 10 mg [DSC]

Extemporaneous Preparations A 20 mg capsule may be mixed with 4 oz of water, apple juice, or Gatorade® to provide a solution that is stable for 14 days under refrigeration

♦ **Fluoxetine and Olanzapine** *see Olanzapine and Fluoxetine on page 1259*
♦ **Fluoxetine Hydrochloride** *see Fluoxetine on page 727*

Fluoxymesterone *(floo oks i MES te rone)*

U.S. Brand Names Halotestin®

Pharmacologic Category Androgen

Use Replacement of endogenous testicular hormone; in females, palliative treatment of breast cancer

Unlabeled/Investigational Use Stimulation of erythropoiesis, angioneurotic edema

Restrictions C-III

Pregnancy Risk Factor X

Lactation Excretion in breast milk unknown/contraindicated

Medication Safety Issues

Sound-alike/look-alike issues:

Halotestin® may be confused with Haldol®, haloperidol, halothane

Contraindications Hypersensitivity to fluoxymesterone or any component of the formulation; serious cardiac disease, liver or kidney disease; pregnancy

Warnings/Precautions May accelerate bone maturation without producing compensatory gain in linear growth in children; in prepubertal children perform radiographic examination of the hand and wrist every 6 months to determine the rate of bone maturation and to assess the effect of treatment on the epiphyseal centers

Adverse Reactions

>10%:
Male: Priapism
Female: Menstrual problems (amenorrhea), virilism, breast soreness
Cardiovascular: Edema
Dermatologic: Acne

1% to 10%:
Male: Prostatic carcinoma, hirsutism (increase in pubic hair growth), impotence, testicular atrophy
Cardiovascular: Edema
Gastrointestinal: GI irritation, nausea, vomiting
Genitourinary: Prostatic hyperplasia
Hepatic: Hepatic dysfunction

<1% (Limited to important or life-threatening): Cholestatic hepatitis, hepatic necrosis, leukopenia, polycythemia

Overdosage/Toxicology Symptoms include abnormal liver function tests and water retention.

Drug Interactions

Increased Effect/Toxicity: Fluoxymesterone may suppress clotting factors II, V, VII, and X; therefore, bleeding may occur in patients on anticoagulant therapy May elevate cyclosporine serum levels. May enhance hypoglycemic effect of insulin therapy; may decrease blood glucose concentrations and insulin requirements in patients with diabetes. Lithium may potentiate EPS and other CNS effect. May potentiate the effects of narcotics including respiratory depression

Decreased Effect: May decrease barbiturate levels and fluphenazine effectiveness.

Stability Protect from light.

Mechanism of Action Synthetic androgenic anabolic hormone responsible for the normal growth and development of male sex hormones and development of male sex organs and maintenance of secondary sex characteristics; synthetic testosterone derivative with significant androgen activity; stimulates RNA polymerase activity resulting in an increase in protein production; increases bone development; halogenated derivative of testosterone with up to 5 times the activity of methyltestosterone

Pharmacodynamics/Kinetics
Absorption: Rapid
Protein binding: 98%
Metabolism: Hepatic; enterohepatic recirculation
Half-life elimination: 10-100 minutes
Excretion: Urine (90%)

Dosage Adults: Oral:
Male:
Hypogonadism: 5-20 mg/day
Delayed puberty: 2.5-20 mg/day for 4-6 months
Female: Inoperable breast carcinoma: 10-40 mg/day in divided doses for 1-3 months

Monitoring Parameters In prepubertal children, perform radiographic examination of the hand and wrist every 6 months

Test Interactions Decreased levels of thyroxine-binding globulin; decreased total T_4 serum levels; increased resin uptake of T_3 and T_4

Dosage Forms [DSC] = Discontinued product
Tablet: 10 mg
Halotestin®: 2 mg, 5 mg, 10 mg [contains tartrazine; 10 mg tablet DSC]

Fluphenazine (floo FEN a zeen)

U.S. Brand Names Prolixin® [DSC]; Prolixin Decanoate®

Canadian Brand Names Apo-Fluphenazine®; Apo-Fluphenazine Decanoate®; Modecate®; Modecate® Concentrate; PMS-Fluphenazine Decanoate

Index Terms Fluphenazine Decanoate

Pharmacologic Category Antipsychotic Agent, Typical, Phenothiazine

Additional Appendix Information
Antipsychotic Agents on page 1872

Use Management of manifestations of psychotic disorders and schizophrenia; depot formulation may offer improved outcome in individuals with psychosis who are nonadherent with oral antipsychotics

Unlabeled/Investigational Use Pervasive developmental disorder

Pregnancy Risk Factor C

Lactation Enters breast milk/not recommended

Medication Safety Issues
Sound-alike/look-alike issues:
Prolixin® may be confused with Proloprim®

International issues:
Prolixin® may be confused with Prolixan® which is a brand name for azapropazone in multiple international markets

Contraindications Hypersensitivity to fluphenazine or any component of the formulation (cross-reactivity between phenothiazines may occur); severe CNS depression; coma; subcortical brain damage; blood dyscrasias; hepatic disease

Warnings/Precautions Safety in children <6 months of age has not been established. May be sedating, use with caution in disorders where CNS depression is a feature. Use with caution in Parkinson's disease. Caution in patients with hemodynamic instability; bone marrow suppression; predisposition to seizures; severe cardiac, renal, or respiratory disease. Esophageal dysmotility and aspiration have been associated with antipsychotic use - use (Continued)

Fluphenazine *(Continued)*

with caution in patients at risk of pneumonia (ie, Alzheimer's disease). Caution in breast cancer or other prolactin-dependent tumors (may elevate prolactin levels). May alter temperature regulation or mask toxicity of other drugs due to antiemetic effects. May alter cardiac conduction; life-threatening arrhythmias have occurred with therapeutic doses of phenothiazines. Hypotension may occur, particularly with I.M. administration. May cause orthostatic hypotension - use with caution in patients at risk of this effect or those who would tolerate transient hypotensive episodes (cerebrovascular disease, cardiovascular disease, or other medications which may predispose). Adverse effects of depot injections may be prolonged.

Phenothiazines may cause anticholinergic effects (confusion, agitation, constipation, xerostomia, blurred vision, urinary retention). Therefore, they should be used with caution in patients with decreased gastrointestinal motility, urinary retention, BPH, xerostomia, or visual problems. Conditions which also may be exacerbated by cholinergic blockade include narrow-angle glaucoma (screening is recommended) and worsening of myasthenia gravis. Relative to other antipsychotics, fluphenazine has a low potency of cholinergic blockade.

May cause extrapyramidal reactions, including pseudoparkinsonism, acute dystonic reactions, akathisia and tardive dyskinesia (risk of these reactions is high relative to other antipsychotics). May be associated with neuroleptic malignant syndrome (NMS) or pigmentary retinopathy.

Adverse Reactions Frequency not defined.

Cardiovascular: Tachycardia, fluctuations in blood pressure, hyper-/hypotension, arrhythmia, edema

Central nervous system: Parkinsonian symptoms, akathisia, dystonias, tardive dyskinesia, dizziness, hyper-reflexia, headache, cerebral edema, drowsiness, lethargy, restlessness, excitement, bizarre dreams, EEG changes, depression, seizure, NMS, altered central temperature regulation

Dermatologic: Dermatitis, eczema, erythema, itching, photosensitivity, rash, seborrhea, skin pigmentation, urticaria

Endocrine & metabolic: Changes in menstrual cycle, breast pain, amenorrhea, galactorrhea, gynecomastia, libido (changes in), elevated prolactin, SIADH

Gastrointestinal: Weight gain, loss of appetite, salivation, xerostomia, constipation, paralytic ileus, laryngeal edema

Genitourinary: Ejaculatory disturbances, impotence, polyuria, bladder paralysis, enuresis

Hematologic: Agranulocytosis, leukopenia, thrombocytopenia, nonthrombocytopenic purpura, eosinophilia, pancytopenia

Hepatic: Cholestatic jaundice, hepatotoxicity

Neuromuscular & skeletal: Trembling of fingers, SLE, facial hemispasm

Ocular: Pigmentary retinopathy, cornea and lens changes, blurred vision, glaucoma

Respiratory: Nasal congestion, asthma

Overdosage/Toxicology Symptoms include deep sleep, hypotension, hypertension, dystonia, seizures, extrapyramidal symptoms, and respiratory failure. Following initiation of essential overdose management, toxic symptom and supportive treatment should be initiated. Hypotension usually responds to I.V. fluids or Trendelenburg positioning. If unresponsive to these measures, the use of a parenteral inotrope may be required. Seizures commonly respond to diazepam (I.V. 5-10 mg bolus in adults every 15 minutes, if needed, up to a total of 30 mg; I.V. 0.25-0.4 mg/kg/dose up to a total of 10 mg in children) or to phenytoin or phenobarbital. Cardiac arrhythmias often respond to I.V. lidocaine while other antiarrhythmics can be used. Neuroleptics often cause extrapyramidal symptoms (eg, dystonic reactions) requiring management with anticholinergic agents such as benztropine mesylate I.V. 1-2 mg (adults) may be effective. These agents are generally effective within 2-5 minutes.

Drug Interactions

Cytochrome P450 Effect: Substrate of CYP2D6 (major); **Inhibits** CYP1A2 (weak), 2C9 (weak), 2D6 (weak), 2E1 (weak)

Increased Effect/Toxicity: CYP2D6 inhibitors may increase the levels/effects of fluphenazine; example inhibitors include chlorpromazine, delavirdine, fluoxetine, miconazole, paroxetine, pergolide, quinidine, quinine, ritonavir, and ropinirole. Effects on CNS depression may be additive when fluphenazine is combined with CNS depressants (opioid analgesics, ethanol, barbiturates, cyclic antidepressants, antihistamines, sedative-hypnotics). Fluphenazine may increase the effects/toxicity of anticholinergics, antihypertensives, lithium (rare neurotoxicity), trazodone, or valproic acid. Concurrent use with TCA may produce increased toxicity or altered therapeutic response. Chloroquine and propranolol may increase chlorpromazine concentrations. Hypotension may occur when fluphenazine is combined with epinephrine. May increase the risk of arrhythmia when combined with antiarrhythmics, cisapride, pimozide, sparfloxacin, or other drugs which prolong QT interval. Metoclopramide may increase risk of extrapyramidal symptoms (EPS). Acetylcholinesterase inhibitors (central) may increase the risk of antipsychotic-related EPS.

Decreased Effect: Phenothiazines inhibit the activity of guanethidine, guanadrel, levodopa, and bromocriptine. Barbiturates and cigarette smoking may enhance the hepatic metabolism of fluphenazine. Fluphenazine and possibly other low potency antipsychotics may reverse the pressor effects of epinephrine.

Ethanol/Nutrition/Herb Interactions

Ethanol: Avoid ethanol (may increase CNS depression).

Herb/Nutraceutical: Avoid dong quai, St John's wort (may also cause photosensitization). Avoid kava kava, gotu kola, valerian, St John's wort (may increase CNS depression).

Stability Avoid freezing. Protect all dosage forms from light. Clear or slightly yellow solutions may be used. Should be dispensed in amber or opaque vials/bottles. Solutions may be diluted or mixed with fruit juices or other liquids, but must be administered immediately after mixing. Do not prepare bulk dilutions or store bulk dilutions.

Mechanism of Action Fluphenazine is a piperazine phenothiazine antipsychotic which blocks postsynaptic mesolimbic dopaminergic D_1 and D_2 receptors in the brain; depresses the release of hypothalamic and hypophyseal hormones; believed to depress the reticular activating system thus affecting basal metabolism, body temperature, wakefulness, vasomotor tone, and emesis

Pharmacodynamics/Kinetics
Onset of action: I.M., SubQ (derivative dependent): Hydrochloride salt: ~1 hour
Peak effect: Neuroleptic: Decanoate: 48-96 hours
Duration: Hydrochloride salt: 6-8 hours; Decanoate: 24-72 hours
Absorption: Oral: Erratic and variable
Distribution: Crosses placenta; enters breast milk
Protein binding: 91% and 99%
Metabolism: Hepatic
Half-life elimination (derivative dependent): Hydrochloride: 33 hours; Decanoate: 163-232 hours
Excretion: Urine (as metabolites)

Dosage
Children: Oral: Childhood-onset pervasive developmental disorder (unlabeled use): 0.04 mg/kg/day
Adults: Psychoses:
Oral: 0.5-10 mg/day in divided doses at 6- to 8-hour intervals; some patients may require up to 40 mg/day
I.M.: 2.5-10 mg/day in divided doses at 6- to 8-hour intervals (parenteral dose is $^1/_3$ to $^1/_2$ the oral dose for the hydrochloride salts)
I.M. (decanoate): 12.5 mg every 2 weeks
Conversion from hydrochloride to decanoate I.M. 0.5 mL (12.5 mg) decanoate every 3 weeks is approximately equivalent to 10 mg hydrochloride/day

Hemodialysis: Not dialyzable (0% to 5%)
Administration Avoid contact of oral solution or injection with skin (contact dermatitis). Oral liquid should be diluted in the following **only**: Water, saline, homogenized milk, carbonated orange beverages, pineapple, apricot, prune, orange, tomato, and grapefruit juices. Do **not** dilute in beverages containing caffeine, tannics, or pectinate. Watch for hypotension when administering I.M.
Monitoring Parameters Vital signs; lipid profile, fasting blood glucose/Hgb A_{1c}; BMI; mental status, abnormal involuntary movement scale (AIMS), extrapyramidal symptoms (EPS)
Reference Range Therapeutic: 0.3-3 ng/mL (SI: 0.6-6.0 nmol/L); correlation of serum concentrations and efficacy is controversial; most often dosed to best response
Additional Information Less sedative and hypotensive effects than chlorpromazine.
Dosage Forms [DSC] = Discontinued product
Elixir, as hydrochloride (Prolixin®): 2.5 mg/5 mL (60 mL) [contains alcohol 14% and sodium benzoate] [DSC]
Injection, oil, as decanoate: 25 mg/mL (5 mL) [may contain benzyl alcohol, sesame oil]
Prolixin Decanoate®: 25 mg/mL (5 mL) [contains benzyl alcohol, sesame oil]
Injection, solution, as hydrochloride (Prolixin® [DSC]): 2.5 mg/mL (10 mL)
Solution, oral concentrate, as hydrochloride (Prolixin®): 5 mg/mL (120 mL) [contains alcohol 14%] [DSC]
Tablet, as hydrochloride: 1 mg, 2.5 mg, 5 mg, 10 mg
Prolixin®: 1 mg, 2.5 mg, 5 mg [contains tartrazine], 10 mg [DSC]

♦ **Fluphenazine Decanoate** see Fluphenazine on page 731
♦ **Flura-Drops®** see Fluoride on page 722

Flurandrenolide (flure an DREN oh lide)

U.S. Brand Names Cordran®; Cordran® SP
Canadian Brand Names Cordran®
Index Terms Flurandrenolone
Pharmacologic Category Corticosteroid, Topical
Additional Appendix Information
Corticosteroids on page 1879
Use Inflammation of corticosteroid-responsive dermatoses [medium potency topical corticosteroid]
Pregnancy Risk Factor C
Medication Safety Issues
Sound-alike/look-alike issues:
Cordran® may be confused with Cardura®, codeine, Cordarone®
Dosage Topical: Therapy should be discontinued when control is achieved; if no improvement is seen, reassessment of diagnosis may be necessary.
Children:
Ointment, cream: Apply sparingly 1-2 times/day
Tape: Apply once daily
Adults: Cream, lotion, ointment: Apply sparingly 2-3 times/day
Dosage Forms
Cream, emulsified, as base (Cordran® SP): 0.025% (30 g, 60 g); 0.05% (15 g, 30 g, 60 g)
Lotion (Cordran®): 0.05% (15 mL, 60 mL)
Ointment (Cordran®): 0.025% (30 g, 60 g); 0.05% (15 g, 30 g, 60 g)
Tape, topical [roll] (Cordran®): 4 mcg/cm^2 (7.5 cm x 60 cm, 7.5 cm x 200 cm)

♦ **Flurandrenolone** see Flurandrenolide on page 733

Flurazepam (flure AZ e pam)

U.S. Brand Names Dalmane®
Canadian Brand Names Apo-Flurazepam®; Dalmane®; Som Pam
Index Terms Flurazepam Hydrochloride
Pharmacologic Category Hypnotic, Benzodiazepine
Additional Appendix Information
Benzodiazepines on page 1874
(Continued)

Flurazepam *(Continued)*

Use Short-term treatment of insomnia

Restrictions C-IV

Pregnancy Risk Factor X

Pregnancy Implications An increased risk of fetal malformations has been associated with maternal use of other benzodiazepines during the 1st trimester of pregnancy. Neonatal depression has been observed specifically following exposure to flurazepam when used maternally for 10 consecutive days prior to delivery. Serum levels of N-desalkylflurazepam were measurable in the infant during the first 4 days of life. Use of flurazepam during pregnancy is contraindicated.

Lactation Excretion in breast milk unknown/not recommended

Medication Safety Issues
Sound-alike/look-alike issues:
Flurazepam may be confused with temazepam
Dalmane® may be confused with Demulen®, Dialume®

Contraindications Hypersensitivity to flurazepam or any component of the formulation (cross-sensitivity with other benzodiazepines may exist); narrow-angle glaucoma; pregnancy

Warnings/Precautions Use with caution in elderly or debilitated patients, patients with hepatic disease (including alcoholics), or renal impairment. Use with caution in patients with respiratory disease, or impaired gag reflex. Avoid use in patients with sleep apnea.

Causes CNS depression (dose-related); patients must be cautioned about performing tasks which require mental alertness (eg, operating machinery or driving). Use with caution in patients receiving other CNS depressants or psychoactive agents. Benzodiazepines have been associated with falls and traumatic injury and should be used with extreme caution in patients who are at risk of these events (especially the elderly).

Use caution in patients with depression, particularly if suicidal risk may be present. Use with caution in patients with a history of drug dependence. Benzodiazepines have been associated with dependence and acute withdrawal symptoms on discontinuation or reduction in dose (may occur after as little as 10 days of use).

As a hypnotic, should be used only after evaluation of potential causes of sleep disturbance. Failure of sleep disturbance to resolve after 7-10 days may indicate psychiatric or medical illness. A worsening of insomnia or the emergence of new abnormalities of thought or behavior may represent unrecognized psychiatric or medical illness and requires immediate and careful evaluation.

Benzodiazepines have been associated with anterograde amnesia. Paradoxical reactions have been reported, particularly in adolescent/pediatric or psychiatric patients. Does not have analgesic, antidepressant, or antipsychotic properties.

Safety and efficacy have not been established in children <15 years of age.

Adverse Reactions Frequency not defined.
Cardiovascular: Chest pain, flushing, hypotension, palpitation
Central nervous system: Apprehension, ataxia, confusion, depression, dizziness, drowsiness, euphoria, faintness, falling, hallucinations, hangover effect, headache, irritability, lightheadedness, memory impairment, nervousness, paradoxical reactions, restlessness, slurred speech, staggering, talkativeness
Dermatologic: Pruritus, rash
Gastrointestinal: Bitter taste, constipation, diarrhea, GI pain, heartburn, increased/decreased appetite, increased/excessive salivation, nausea, upset stomach, vomiting, weight gain/loss, xerostomia
Hematologic: Granulocytopenia, leukopenia
Hepatic: Alkaline phosphatase increased, cholestatic jaundice, SGOT/SGPT increased, total bilirubin increased
Neuromuscular & skeletal: Body/joint pain, dysarthria, reflex slowing, weakness
Ocular: Blurred vision, burning eyes, difficulty focusing
Respiratory: Apnea, dyspnea
Miscellaneous: Diaphoresis, drug dependence

Overdosage/Toxicology Symptoms of overdose include respiratory depression, disorientation, hypoactive reflexes, lethargy, unsteady gait, severe sedation, and hypotension. Flumazenil has been shown to selectively block the binding of benzodiazepines to CNS receptors, resulting in a short-term reversal of benzodiazepine-induced CNS depression; caution, may induce seizures with chronic benzodiazepine ingestion. Respiratory depression may not be reversed. Gastric lavage may be useful, administer I.V. fluids and maintain adequate airway. Treatment is otherwise symptom-directed and supportive.

Drug Interactions
Cytochrome P450 Effect: Substrate of CYP3A4 (major); **Inhibits** CYP2E1 (weak)
Increased Effect/Toxicity: CYP3A4 inhibitors may increase the levels/effects of flurazepam; example inhibitors include azole antifungals, clarithromycin, diclofenac, doxycycline, erythromycin, imatinib, isoniazid, nefazodone, nicardipine, propofol, protease inhibitors, quinidine, telithromycin, and verapamil. Serum levels and response to flurazepam may be increased by cimetidine, clozapine, CNS depressants, diltiazem, disulfiram, digoxin, ethanol, fluconazole, fluoxetine, fluvoxamine, grapefruit juice, labetalol, levodopa, loxapine, metoprolol, metronidazole, nelfinavir, omeprazole, and valproic acid.
Decreased Effect: CYP3A4 inducers may decrease the levels/effects of flurazepam; example inducers include aminoglutethimide, carbamazepine, nafcillin, nevirapine, phenobarbital, phenytoin, and rifamycins.

Ethanol/Nutrition/Herb Interactions
Ethanol: Avoid ethanol (may increase CNS depression).
Food: Serum levels and response to flurazepam may be increased by grapefruit juice, but unlikely because of flurazepam's high oral bioavailability.
Herb/Nutraceutical: Avoid valerian, St John's wort, kava kava, gotu kola (may increase CNS depression).

Stability Store at 15°C to 30°C (59°F to 86°F).

Mechanism of Action Binds to stereospecific benzodiazepine receptors on the postsynaptic GABA neuron at several sites within the central nervous system, including the limbic system, reticular formation. Enhancement of the inhibitory effect of GABA on neuronal excitability results by increased neuronal membrane permeability to chloride ions. This shift in chloride ions results in hyperpolarization (a less excitable state) and stabilization.

Pharmacodynamics/Kinetics
Onset of action: Hypnotic: 15-20 minutes
Peak effect: 3-6 hours
Duration: 7-8 hours
Metabolism: Hepatic to N-desalkylflurazepam (active) and N-hydroxyethylflurazepam
Half-life elimination:
Flurazepam: 2.3 hours
N-desalkylflurazepam:
Adults: Single dose: 74-90 hours; Multiple doses: 111-113 hours
Elderly (61-85 years): Single dose: 120-160 hours; Multiple doses: 126-158 hours
Excretion: Urine: N-hydroxyethylflurazepam (22% to 55%); N-desalkylflurazepam (<1%)

Dosage Oral:
Children: Insomnia:
<15 years: Dose not established
≥15 years: 15 mg at bedtime
Adults: Insomnia: 15-30 mg at bedtime
Elderly: Insomnia: Oral: 15 mg at bedtime; avoid use if possible

Administration Give 30 minutes to 1 hour before bedtime on an empty stomach with full glass of water. May be taken with food if GI distress occurs.

Monitoring Parameters Respiratory and cardiovascular status

Reference Range Therapeutic: 0-4 ng/mL (SI: 0-9 nmol/L); Metabolite N-desalkylflurazepam: 20-110 ng/mL (SI: 43-240 nmol/L); Toxic: >0.12 mcg/mL

Dosage Forms
Capsule, as hydrochloride: 15 mg, 30 mg
Dalmane®: 15 mg, 30 mg

♦ **Flurazepam Hydrochloride** see Flurazepam on page 733

Flurbiprofen (flure BI proe fen)

U.S. Brand Names Ansaid® [DSC]; Ocufen®
Canadian Brand Names Alti-Flurbiprofen; Ansaid®; Apo-Flurbiprofen®; Froben®; Froben-SR®; Novo-Flurprofen; Nu-Flurprofen; Ocufen®
Index Terms Flurbiprofen Sodium
Pharmacologic Category Nonsteroidal Anti-inflammatory Drug (NSAID), Ophthalmic; Nonsteroidal Anti-inflammatory Drug (NSAID), Oral
Additional Appendix Information
Nonsteroidal Anti-inflammatory Agents on page 1894
Use
Oral: Treatment of rheumatoid arthritis and osteoarthritis
Ophthalmic: Inhibition of intraoperative miosis
Restrictions An FDA-approved medication guide must be distributed when dispensing an oral outpatient prescription (new or refill) where this medication is to be used without direct supervision of a healthcare provider. Medication guides are available at http://www.fda.gov/cder/Offices/ODS/medication_guides.htm.
Pregnancy Risk Factor C/D (3rd trimester)
Pregnancy Implications Teratogenic effects were not observed in animal studies, however, adequate and well-controlled studies have not been conducted in pregnant women. Exposure late in pregnancy may lead to premature closure of the ductus arteriosus.
Lactation Enters breast milk/not recommended
Medication Safety Issues
Sound-alike/look-alike issues:
Flurbiprofen may be confused with fenoprofen
Ansaid® may be confused with Asacol®, Axid®
Ocufen® may be confused with Ocuflox®, Ocupress®
Contraindications Hypersensitivity to flurbiprofen, aspirin, other NSAIDs, or any component of the formulation; perioperative pain in the setting of coronary artery bypass surgery (CABG); dendritic keratitis; pregnancy (3rd trimester)
Warnings/Precautions [U.S. Boxed Warning]: NSAIDs are associated with an increased risk of adverse cardiovascular events, including MI, stroke, and new onset or worsening of pre-existing hypertension. Risk may be increased with duration of use or pre-existing cardiovascular risk-factors or disease. Carefully evaluate individual cardiovascular risk profiles prior to prescribing. Use caution with fluid retention, CHF, or hypertension. Concurrent administration of ibuprofen, and potentially other nonselective NSAIDs, may interfere with aspirin's cardioprotective effect.

Use of NSAIDs can compromise existing renal function. Renal toxicity can occur in patient with impaired renal function, dehydration, heart failure, liver dysfunction, those taking diuretics and ACEI, and the elderly. Rehydrate patient before starting therapy. Monitor renal function closely. Not recommended for use in patients with advanced renal disease.

[U.S. Boxed Warning]: NSAIDs may increase risk of gastrointestinal irritation, ulceration, bleeding, and perforation. These events may occur at any time during therapy and without warning. Use caution with a history of GI disease (bleeding or ulcers), concurrent therapy with aspirin, anticoagulants and/or corticosteroids, smoking, use of alcohol, the elderly or debilitated patients.

Use the lowest effective dose for the shortest duration of time, consistent with individual patient goals, to reduce risk of cardiovascular or GI adverse events. Alternate therapies should be considered for patients at high risk.
(Continued)

Flurbiprofen *(Continued)*

NSAIDs may cause serious skin adverse events including exfoliative dermatitis, Stevens-Johnson syndrome (SJS), and toxic epidermal necrolysis (TEN). Anaphylactoid reactions may occur, even without prior exposure; patients with "aspirin triad" (bronchial asthma, aspirin intolerance, rhinitis) may be at increased risk. Do not use in patients who experience bronchospasm, asthma, rhinitis, or urticaria with NSAID or aspirin therapy.

Use with caution in patients with decreased hepatic function. Closely monitor patients with any abnormal LFT. Severe hepatic reactions (eg, fulminant hepatitis, liver failure) have occurred with NSAID use, rarely; discontinue if signs or symptoms of liver disease develop, or if systemic manifestations occur.

The elderly are at increased risk for adverse effects (especially peptic ulceration, CNS effects, renal toxicity) from NSAIDs even at low doses.

Withhold for at least 4-6 half-lives prior to surgical or dental procedures. Safety and efficacy have not been established in children.

Adverse Reactions
Ophthalmic: Frequency not defined: Ocular: Slowing of corneal wound healing, mild ocular stinging, itching and burning, ocular irritation, fibrosis, miosis, mydriasis, bleeding tendency increased

Oral:

>1%:

Cardiovascular: Edema

Central nervous system: Amnesia, anxiety, depression, dizziness, headache, insomnia, malaise, nervousness, somnolence, vertigo

Dermatologic: Rash

Gastrointestinal: Abdominal pain, constipation, diarrhea, dyspepsia, flatulence, GI bleeding, nausea, vomiting, weight changes

Hepatic: Liver enzymes increased

Neuromuscular & skeletal: Reflexes increased, tremor, weakness

Ocular: Vision changes

Otic: Tinnitus

Respiratory: Rhinitis

<1% (Limited to important or life-threatening): Anaphylactic reaction, anemia, angioedema, asthma, bruising, cerebrovascular ischemia, CHF, confusion, eczema, eosinophilia, epistaxis, exfoliative dermatitis, fever, gastric/peptic ulcer, hematocrit decreased, hematuria, hemoglobin decreased, hepatitis, hypertension, hyperuricemia, interstitial nephritis, jaundice, leukopenia, paresthesia, parosmia, photosensitivity, pruritus, purpura, renal failure, stomatitis, thrombocytopenia, toxic epidermal necrolysis, urticaria, vasodilation

Overdosage/Toxicology Symptoms include apnea, metabolic acidosis, coma, nystagmus, leukocytosis, and renal failure. Management of nonsteroidal anti-inflammatory drug (NSAID) intoxication is primarily supportive and symptomatic. Fluid therapy is commonly effective in managing hypotension that may occur following an acute NSAID overdose, except when due to acute blood loss. Seizures tend to be very short-lived and often do not require drug treatment, although recurrent seizures should be treated with I.V. diazepam. Since many of NSAIDs undergo enterohepatic cycling, multiple doses of charcoal may be needed to reduce the potential for delayed toxicities.

Drug Interactions
Cytochrome P450 Effect: Substrate of CYP2C9 (minor); **Inhibits** CYP2C9 (strong)

Increased Effect/Toxicity: Flurbiprofen may increase cyclosporine, digoxin, lithium, and methotrexate serum concentrations. The renal adverse effects of ACE inhibitors may be potentiated by NSAIDs. Corticosteroids may increase the risk of GI ulceration. Flurbiprofen may increase the levels/effects of CYP2C9 substrates; example substrates include bosentan, dapsone, fluoxetine, glimepiride, glipizide, losartan, montelukast, nateglinide, paclitaxel, phenytoin, warfarin, and zafirlukast. Concomitant use with fluoroquinolones may rarely increase risk of seizure.

Decreased Effect:
Ophthalmic: When used with concurrent administration of flurbiprofen, acetylcholine chloride and carbachol have been shown to be ineffective. Reports of acetylcholine chloride and carbachol being ineffective when used with flurbiprofen.

Oral: NSAIDs may decrease the antihypertensive effect of ACE inhibitors, angiotensin antagonists, beta-blockers, or hydralazine. Cholestyramine (and other bile acid sequestrants) may decrease the absorption of NSAIDs; separate by at least 2 hours. Salicylates' antiplatelet effect may be reduced.

Ethanol/Nutrition/Herb Interactions
Ethanol: Avoid ethanol (may enhance gastric mucosal irritation).

Food: Food may decrease the rate but not the extent of absorption.

Herb/Nutraceutical: Avoid alfalfa, anise, bilberry, bladderwrack, bromelain, cat's claw, celery, coleus, cordyceps, dong quai, evening primrose, feverfew, fenugreek, garlic, ginger, ginkgo biloba, red clover, horse chestnut, grapeseed, green tea, ginseng, guggul, horse chestnut seed, horseradish, licorice, prickly ash, red clover, reishi, SAMe, sweet clover, turmeric, white willow (all have additional antiplatelet activity).

Mechanism of Action Inhibits prostaglandin synthesis by decreasing the activity of the enzyme, cyclooxygenase, which results in decreased formation of prostaglandin precursors

Pharmacodynamics/Kinetics
Onset of action: ~1-2 hours

Distribution: V_d: 0.12 L/kg

Protein binding: 99%, primarily albumin

Metabolism: Hepatic via CYP2C9; forms metabolites such as 4-hydroxy-flurbiprofen (inactive)

Half-life elimination: 5.7 hours

Time to peak: 1.5 hours

Excretion: Urine (primarily as metabolites)

Dosage
Oral:
Rheumatoid arthritis and osteoarthritis: 200-300 mg/day in 2-, 3-, or 4 divided doses; do not administer more than 100 mg for any single dose; maximum: 300 mg/day
Dental: Management of postoperative pain: 100 mg every 12 hours
Ophthalmic: Instill 1 drop every 30 minutes, beginning 2 hours prior to surgery (total of 4 drops in each affected eye)
Dosage adjustment in renal impairment: Not recommended in patients with advanced renal disease
Dietary Considerations Tablet may be taken with food, milk, or antacid to decrease GI effects.
Administration Tablet: Take with a full glass of water.
Dosage Forms [DSC] = Discontinued product
Solution, ophthalmic, as sodium (Ocufen®): 0.03% (2.5 mL) [contains thimerosal]
Tablet: 50 mg, 100 mg
Ansaid®: 50 mg, 100 mg [DSC]

♦ **Flurbiprofen Sodium** see Flurbiprofen on page 735
♦ **5-Flurocytosine** see Flucytosine on page 714

Flutamide (FLOO ta mide)

U.S. Brand Names Eulexin®
Canadian Brand Names Apo-Flutamide®; Euflex®; Eulexin®; Novo-Flutamide
Index Terms Niftolid; NSC-147834; 4'-Nitro-3'-Trifluoromethylisobutyrantide; SCH 13521
Pharmacologic Category Antineoplastic Agent, Antiandrogen
Use Treatment of metastatic prostatic carcinoma in combination therapy with LHRH agonist analogues
Unlabeled/Investigational Use Female hirsutism
Pregnancy Risk Factor D
Lactation Excretion in breast milk unknown/not recommended
Medication Safety Issues
Sound-alike/look-alike issues:
Flutamide may be confused with Flumadine®, thalidomide
Eulexin® may be confused with Edecrin®, Eurax®
Contraindications Hypersensitivity to flutamide or any component of the formulation; severe hepatic impairment; pregnancy
Warnings/Precautions Hazardous agent - use appropriate precautions for handling and disposal. **[U.S. Boxed Warning]: Hospitalization and, rarely, death due to liver failure has been reported in patients taking flutamide.** Elevated serum transaminase levels, jaundice, hepatic encephalopathy, and acute hepatic failure have been reported. Product labeling states flutamide is not for use in women, particularly for nonlife-threatening conditions. In some patients, the toxicity reverses after discontinuation of therapy. About 50% of the cases occur within the first 3 months of treatment. Serum transaminase levels should be measured prior to starting treatment, monthly for 4 months, and periodically thereafter. Liver function tests should be obtained at the first suggestion of liver dysfunction (nausea, vomiting, abdominal pain, fatigue, anorexia, "flu-like" symptoms, hyperbilirubinuria, jaundice, or right upper quadrant tenderness). Flutamide should be immediately discontinued any time a patient has jaundice, and/or an ALT level greater than twice the upper limit of normal. Flutamide should not be used in patients whose ALT values are greater than twice the upper limit of normal.

Patients with glucose-6 phosphate dehydrogenase deficiency or hemoglobin M disease or smokers are at risk of toxicities associated with aniline exposure, including methemoglobinemia, hemolytic anemia, and cholestatic jaundice. Monitor methemoglobin levels.
Adverse Reactions
>10%:
Endocrine & metabolic: Gynecomastia, hot flashes, breast tenderness, galactorrhea (9% to 42%); impotence; decreased libido; tumor flare
Gastrointestinal: Nausea, vomiting (11% to 12%)
Hepatic: Increased AST (SGOT) and LDH levels, transient, mild
1% to 10%:
Cardiovascular: Hypertension (1%), edema
Central nervous system: Drowsiness, confusion, depression, anxiety, nervousness, headache, dizziness, insomnia
Dermatologic: Pruritus, ecchymosis, photosensitivity
Gastrointestinal: Anorexia, increased appetite, constipation, indigestion, upset stomach (4% to 6%); diarrhea
Hematologic: Anemia (6%), leukopenia (3%), thrombocytopenia (1%)
Neuromuscular & skeletal: Weakness (1%)
Miscellaneous: Herpes zoster
<1% (Limited to important or life-threatening): Hepatic failure, hepatitis, hypersensitivity pneumonitis, jaundice, malignant breast neoplasm (male), MI, pulmonary embolism, sulfhemoglobinemia, thrombophlebitis, yellow discoloration of the urine
Overdosage/Toxicology Symptoms include hypoactivity, ataxia, anorexia, vomiting, slow respirations, and lacrimation. Induce vomiting. Management is supportive. There is no benefit from dialysis.
Drug Interactions
Cytochrome P450 Effect: Substrate (major) of CYP1A2, 3A4; **Inhibits** CYP1A2 (weak)
Increased Effect/Toxicity: CYP1A2 inhibitors may increase the levels/effects of flutamide; example inhibitors include ciprofloxacin, fluvoxamine, ketoconazole, lomefloxacin, ofloxacin, and rofecoxib. CYP3A4 inhibitors may increase the levels/effects of flutamide;
(Continued)

Flutamide (Continued)

example inhibitors include azole antifungals, clarithromycin, diclofenac, doxycycline, erythromycin, imatinib, isoniazid, nefazodone, nicardipine, propofol, protease inhibitors, quinidine, telithromycin, and verapamil. Warfarin effects may be increased.

Decreased Effect: CYP1A2 inducers may decrease the levels/effects of flutamide; example inducers include aminoglutethimide, carbamazepine, phenobarbital, and rifampin. CYP3A4 inducers may decrease the levels/effects of flutamide; example inducers include aminoglutethimide, carbamazepine, nafcillin, nevirapine, phenobarbital, phenytoin, and rifamycins.

Ethanol/Nutrition/Herb Interactions
Food: No effect on bioavailability of flutamide.
Herb/Nutraceutical: St John's wort may decrease flutamide levels.

Stability Store at room temperature.

Mechanism of Action Nonsteroidal antiandrogen that inhibits androgen uptake or inhibits binding of androgen in target tissues

Pharmacodynamics/Kinetics
Absorption: Oral: Rapid and complete
Protein binding: Parent drug: 94% to 96%; 2-hydroxyflutamide: 92% to 94%
Metabolism: Extensively hepatic to more than 10 metabolites, primarily 2-hydroxyflutamide (active)
Half-life elimination: 5-6 hours (2-hydroxyflutamide)
Excretion: Primarily urine (as metabolites)

Dosage Oral: Adults:
Prostatic carcinoma: 250 mg 3 times/day; alternatively, once-daily doses of 0.5-1.5 g have been used (unlabeled dosing)
Female hirsutism (unlabeled use): 250 mg daily

Administration Usually administered orally in 3 divided doses; contents of capsule may be opened and mixed with applesauce, pudding, or other soft foods; mixing with a beverage is not recommended

Monitoring Parameters Serum transaminase levels should be measured prior to starting treatment and should be repeated monthly for the first 4 months of therapy, and periodically thereafter. LFTs should be checked at the first sign or symptom of liver dysfunction (eg, nausea, vomiting, abdominal pain, fatigue, anorexia, flu-like symptoms, hyperbilirubinuria, jaundice, or right upper quadrant tenderness). Other parameters include tumor reduction, testosterone/estrogen, and phosphatase serum levels.

Dosage Forms Capsule: 125 mg

Fluticasone (floo TIK a sone)

U.S. Brand Names Cutivate®; Flonase®; Flovent® HFA
Canadian Brand Names Cutivate™; Flonase®; Flovent® Diskus®; Flovent® HFA
Index Terms Fluticasone Propionate
Pharmacologic Category Corticosteroid, Inhalant (Oral); Corticosteroid, Nasal; Corticosteroid, Topical; Corticosteroid, Topical (Medium Potency)

Additional Appendix Information
Asthma on page 2029
Corticosteroids on page 1879

Use
Inhalation: Maintenance treatment of asthma as prophylactic therapy. It is also indicated for patients requiring oral corticosteroid therapy for asthma to assist in total discontinuation or reduction of total oral dose
Intranasal: Management of seasonal and perennial allergic rhinitis and nonallergic rhinitis
Topical: Relief of inflammation and pruritus associated with corticosteroid-responsive dermatoses; atopic dermatitis

Pregnancy Risk Factor C

Pregnancy Implications There are no adequate and well-controlled studies using inhaled fluticasone in pregnant women. Oral corticosteroid use has shown animals to be more prone to teratogenic effects than humans. Due to the natural increase in corticosteroid production during pregnancy, most women may require a lower steroid dose; use with caution.

Lactation Excretion in breast milk unknown/use caution

Medication Safety Issues
Sound-alike/look-alike issues:
Cutivate® may be confused with Ultravate®

International issues:
Allegra® [Israel] may be confused with Allegra® which is a brand name for fexofenadine in the U.S.
Allegro®: Brand name for frovatriptan in Germany
Flovent® may be confused with Flogen® which is a brand name for naproxen in Mexico

Contraindications Hypersensitivity to fluticasone or any component of the formulation; primary treatment of status asthmaticus or acute bronchospasm
Topical: Do not use if infection is present at treatment site, in the presence of skin atrophy, or for the treatment of rosacea or perioral dermatitis

Warnings/Precautions May cause hypercorticism or suppression of hypothalamic-pituitary-adrenal (HPA) axis, particularly in younger children or in patients receiving high doses for prolonged periods. HPA axis suppression may lead to adrenal crisis. Withdrawal and discontinuation of a corticosteroid should be done slowly and carefully. Particular care is required when patients are transferred from systemic corticosteroids to inhaled products due to possible adrenal insufficiency or withdrawal from steroids, including an increase in allergic symptoms. Patients receiving >20 mg per day of prednisone (or equivalent) may be most susceptible. Concurrent use of ritonavir (and potentially other strong inhibitors of CYP3A4) may increase fluticasone levels and effects on HPA suppression. Fatalities have occurred due to adrenal insufficiency in asthmatic patients during and after transfer from systemic corticosteroids to aerosol steroids; aerosol steroids do **not** provide the systemic steroid needed to treat patients having trauma, surgery, or infections.

Bronchospasm may occur with wheezing after inhalation; if this occurs stop steroid and treat with a fast-acting bronchodilator. Supplemental steroids (oral or parenteral) may be needed during stress or severe asthma attacks. Corticosteroid use may cause psychiatric disturbances, including depression, euphoria, insomnia, mood swings, and personality changes. Pre-existing psychiatric conditions may be exacerbated by corticosteroid use. Prolonged use of corticosteroids may also increase the incidence of secondary infection, mask acute infection (including fungal infections), prolong or exacerbate viral infections, or limit response to vaccines. Exposure to chickenpox should be avoided; corticosteroids should not be used to treat ocular herpes simplex. Corticosteroids should not be used for cerebral malaria. Close observation is required in patients with latent tuberculosis and/or TB reactivity; restrict use in active TB (only in conjunction with antituberculosis treatment). Rare cases of vasculitis (Churg-Strauss syndrome) or other eosinophilic conditions can occur. Prolonged treatment with corticosteroids has been associated with the development of Kaposi's sarcoma (case reports); if noted, discontinuation of therapy should be considered.

Use with caution in patients with thyroid disease, hepatic impairment, renal impairment, cardiovascular disease, diabetes, glaucoma, cataracts, myasthenia gravis, patients at risk for osteoporosis, patients at risk for seizures, or GI diseases (diverticulitis, peptic ulcer, ulcerative colitis) due to perforation risk. Use caution following acute MI (corticosteroids have been associated with myocardial rupture). Because of the risk of adverse effects, systemic corticosteroids should be used cautiously in the elderly in the smallest possible effective dose for the shortest duration. Avoid nasal corticosteroid use in patients with recent nasal septal ulcers, nasal surgery or nasal trauma until healing has occurred.

Orally-inhaled and intranasal corticosteroids may cause a reduction in growth velocity in pediatric patients (~1 centimeter per year [range 0.3-1.8 cm per year] and related to dose and duration of exposure). To minimize the systemic effects of orally-inhaled and intranasal corticosteroids, each patient should be titrated to the lowest effective dose. Growth should be routinely monitored in pediatric patients.

Inhalation: Not to be used in status asthmaticus or for the relief of acute bronchospasm. Flovent® Diskus® [CAN] contain lactose; very rare anaphylactic reactions have been reported in patients with severe milk protein allergy. There have been reports of systemic corticosteroid withdrawal symptoms (eg, joint/muscle pain, lassitude, depression) when withdrawing oral inhalation therapy.

Topical: May also cause suppression of HPA axis, especially when used on large areas of the body, denuded areas, for prolonged periods of time or with an occlusive dressing. Pediatric patients may be more susceptible to systemic toxicity.

Adverse Reactions

>10%:

Central nervous system: Headache (5% to 16%)

Respiratory: Upper respiratory tract infection (16% to 18%)

1% to 10%:

Cardiovascular: Chest symptoms (1% to 3%)

Central nervous system (all 1% to 3%): Dizziness, fever, migraine, pain

Dermatologic: Dry skin (7%), skin burning/stinging (2% to 5%), pruritus (3%), skin irritation (3%), viral skin infection (1% to 3%), exacerbation of eczema (2%), excoriation (2%), dryness (1%), numbness of fingers (1%)

Gastrointestinal: Nausea/vomiting (3% to 5%); all others (1% to 3%): abdominal pain, diarrhea, dyspepsia, gastrointestinal infection (viral), gastrointestinal discomfort/pain, hyposalivation

Genitourinary: Urinary tract infection (1% to 3%)

Neuromuscular & skeletal (all 1% to 3%): Musculoskeletal pain, muscle pain, muscle stiffness/tightness/rigidity

Respiratory: Throat irritation (8% to 10%), pharyngitis (6% to 8%), epistaxis (6% to 7%), sinusitis/sinus infection (4% to 7%), asthma symptoms (3% to 7%), cough (4% to 6%), bronchitis (1% to 6%), hoarseness/dysphonia (2% to 6%), upper respiratory tract inflammation (2% to 5%), nasal burning/irritation (2% to 3%), blood in nasal mucous (1% to 3%), runny nose (1% to 3%), rhinitis (1% to 3%), throat infection (1% to 3%), rhinorrhea/postnasal drip (1% to 3%), nasal sinus disorder (1% to 3%), laryngitis (1% to 3%)

Miscellaneous: Oral candidiasis (2% to 5%), aches and pains (1% to 3%), flu-like syndrome (1% to 3%)

<1%, postmarketing and/or case reports: Aggression, agitation, anaphylaxis/anaphylactoid reactions, angioedema, anxiety, aphonia, arthralgia, asthma exacerbation, anxiety, blurred vision, bronchospasm (immediate and delayed), cataracts, chest tightness, Churg-Strauss syndrome, conjunctivitis, contusion, Cushingoid features, cutaneous hypersensitivity, depression, dry throat, dry/irritated eyes, dyspnea, ecchymoses, edema (face and tongue), eosinophilia, fatigue, glaucoma, growth velocity reduction in children/adolescents, hoarseness, HPA axis suppression, hyperactivity/irritability (primarily children), hyperglycemia, hypersensitivity reactions (immediate and delayed), intraocular pressure increased, malaise, nasal septal perforation (rare), nasal ulcer, oropharyngeal edema, osteoporosis, paradoxical bronchospasm, pneumonia, rash, restlessness, sleep disorder, smell alterations, sore throat, taste perversion, urticaria, voice changes, weight gain, wheezing

Reported with other topical corticosteroids (in decreasing order of occurrence): Irritation, folliculitis, acneiform eruptions, hypopigmentation, perioral dermatitis, allergic contact dermatitis, secondary infection, skin atrophy, striae, miliaria, pustular psoriasis from chronic plaque psoriasis

Overdosage/Toxicology When consumed in excessive quantities, systemic hypercorticism and adrenal suppression may occur; in those cases, discontinuation and withdrawal of the corticosteroid should be done judiciously.

(Continued)

Fluticasone *(Continued)*

Drug Interactions

Cytochrome P450 Effect: Substrate of CYP3A4 (major)

Increased Effect/Toxicity: CYP3A4 inhibitors: May increase the levels/effects of fluticasone; example inhibitors include azole antifungals, clarithromycin, diclofenac, doxycycline, erythromycin, imatinib, isoniazid, nefazodone, nicardipine, propofol, protease inhibitors, quinidine, telithromycin, and verapamil. Ritonavir may increase serum levels (due to CYP3A4 inhibition) and the potential for steroid-related adverse effects (eg, Cushing syndrome, adrenal suppression).

The addition of salmeterol has been demonstrated to improve response to inhaled corticosteroids (as compared to increasing steroid dosage).

Ethanol/Nutrition/Herb Interactions Herb/Nutraceutical: In theory, St John's wort may decrease serum levels of fluticasone by inducing CYP3A4 isoenzymes.

Stability

Nasal spray: Store between 4°C to 30°C (39°F to 86°F).

Oral inhalation: Flovent®, Flovent® HFA: Store at 15°C to 30°C (59°F to 86°F). Store with mouthpiece down.

Powder for oral inhalation: Flovent® Diskus® [CAN]: Store between 2°C to 30°C in a dry place away from direct frost, heat, or sunlight. Do not store in a damp environment (eg, bathroom).

Topical, cream: Store at 15°C to 30°C (59°F to 86°F).

Cutivate® lotion: Store at 15°C to 30°C (59°F to 86°F); do not refrigerate.

Cutivate® cream, ointment: Store at 2°C to 30°C (36°F to 86°F).

Mechanism of Action Fluticasone belongs to a new group of corticosteroids which utilizes a fluorocarbothioate ester linkage at the 17 carbon position; extremely potent vasoconstrictive and anti-inflammatory activity; has a weak HPA inhibitory potency when applied topically, which gives the drug a high therapeutic index. The effectiveness of inhaled fluticasone is due to its direct local effect. The mechanism of action for all topical corticosteroids is believed to be a combination of three important properties: anti-inflammatory activity, immunosuppressive properties, and antiproliferative actions.

Pharmacodynamics/Kinetics

Onset: Flovent® HFA: Maximal benefit may take 1-2 weeks or longer

Absorption:

Topical cream: 5% (increased with inflammation)

Oral inhalation: Absorbed systemically (DISKUS®: ~18%) primarily via lungs, minimal GI absorption (<1%) due to presystemic metabolism

Distribution: 4.2 L/kg

Protein binding: 91%

Metabolism: Hepatic via CYP3A4 to 17β-carboxylic acid (negligible activity)

Bioavailability: Nasal: ≤2%; Oral inhalation: (~18% to 21%)

Excretion: Feces (as parent drug and metabolites); urine (<5% as metabolites)

Dosage

Children:

Asthma: Inhalation, oral:

Flovent® HFA:

Children 4-11 years: 88 mcg twice daily

Children ≥12 years: Refer to Adults dosing.

Note: NIH Asthma Guidelines (administer in divided doses twice daily):

"Low" dose: 88-176 mcg/day

"Medium" dose: 176-440 mcg/day

"High" dose: >440 mcg/day

Flovent® Diskus® [CAN]:

Children 4-16 years: Usual starting dose: 50-100 mcg twice daily; may increase to 200 mcg twice daily in patients not adequately controlled; titrate to the lowest effective dose once asthma stability is achieved

Children ≥16 years: Refer to Adults dosing.

Corticosteroid-responsive dermatoses: Topical: Children ≥3 months: Cream: Apply sparingly to affected area twice daily. If no improvement is seen within 2 weeks, reassessment of diagnosis may be necessary. **Note:** Safety and efficacy of treatment >4 weeks duration have not been established.

Atopic dermatitis: Topical:

Children ≥3 months: Cream: Apply sparingly to affected area 1-2 times/day. If no improvement is seen within 2 weeks, reassessment of diagnosis may be necessary.

Children ≥1 year: Lotion: Apply sparingly to affected area once daily

Note: Safety and efficacy of treatment >4 weeks duration have not been established.

Rhinitis: Intranasal: Children ≥4 years and Adolescents: Initial: 1 spray (50 mcg/spray) per nostril once daily; patients not adequately responding or patients with more severe symptoms may use 2 sprays (100 mcg) per nostril. Depending on response, dosage may be reduced to 100 mcg daily. Total daily dosage should not exceed 2 sprays in each nostril (200 mcg)/day. Dosing should be at regular intervals.

Adults:

Asthma: Inhalation, oral: **Note:** Titrate to the lowest effective dose once asthma stability is achieved

Flovent® HFA: Manufacturers labeling: Dosing based on previous therapy

Bronchodilator alone: Recommended starting dose: 88 mcg twice daily; highest recommended dose: 440 mcg twice daily

Inhaled corticosteroids: Recommended starting dose: 88-220 mcg twice daily; highest recommended dose: 440 mcg twice daily; a higher starting dose may be considered in patients previously requiring higher doses of inhaled corticosteroids

Oral corticosteroids: Recommended starting dose:

Flovent® HFA: 440 mcg twice daily

Highest recommended dose: 880 mcg twice daily; starting dose is patient dependent. In patients on chronic oral corticosteroids therapy, reduce prednisone dose no faster than 2.5-5 mg/day on a weekly basis; begin taper after 1 week of fluticasone therapy

NIH Asthma Guidelines (administer in divided doses twice daily).
"Low" dose: 88-264 mcg/day
"Medium" dose: 264-660 mcg/day
"High" dose: >660 mcg/day

Flovent® Diskus® [CAN]:
Mild asthma: 100-250 mcg twice daily
Moderate asthma: 250-500 mcg twice daily
Severe asthma: 500 mcg twice daily; may increase to 1000 mcg twice daily in very severe patients requiring high doses of corticosteroids

Corticosteroid-responsive dermatoses: Topical: Cream, lotion, ointment: Apply sparingly to affected area twice daily. If no improvement is seen within 2 weeks, reassessment of diagnosis may be necessary

Atopic dermatitis: Topical: Cream, lotion: Apply sparingly to affected area once or twice daily. If no improvement is seen within 2 weeks, reassessment of diagnosis may be necessary

Rhinitis: Intranasal: Initial: 2 sprays (50 mcg/spray) per nostril once daily; may also be divided into 100 mcg twice a day. After the first few days, dosage may be reduced to 1 spray per nostril once daily for maintenance therapy. Dosing should be at regular intervals.

Elderly: No differences in safety have been observed in the elderly when compared to younger patients. Based on current data, no dosage adjustment is needed based on age.

Dosage adjustment in hepatic impairment: Fluticasone is primarily cleared in the liver. Fluticasone plasma levels may be increased in patients with hepatic impairment, use with caution; monitor.

Dietary Considerations Flovent® Diskus® [CAN] contains lactose; very rare anaphylactic reactions have been reported with Flovent® Rotadisk® in patients with severe milk protein allergy.

Administration

Aerosol inhalation: Flovent® HFA: Shake container thoroughly before using. Take 3-5 deep breaths. Use inhaler on inspiration. Allow 1 full minute between inhalations. Rinse mouth with water after use to reduce aftertaste and incidence of candidiasis. Inhaler must be primed before first use, when not used for 7 days, or if dropped. To prime the first time, release 4 sprays into air; shake well before each spray and spray away from face. If dropped or not used for 7 days, prime by releasing a single test spray. Discard after 120 actuations; do not use "float" test to determine contents.

Nasal spray: Shake bottle gently before using. Prime pump prior to first use (press 6 times until fine spray appears). Blow nose to clear nostrils. Insert applicator into nostril, keeping bottle upright, and close off the other nostril. Breathe in through nose. While inhaling, press pump to release spray. Nasal applicator may be removed and rinsed with warm water to clean. Discard after labeled number of doses has been used, even if bottle is not completely empty.

Powder for oral inhalation: Flovent® Diskus® [CAN]: Do not use with a spacer device. Do not exhale into Diskus®. Do not wash or take apart. Use in horizontal position.

Topical cream, lotion, ointment: Apply sparingly in a thin film. Rub in lightly. Unless otherwise directed by healthcare professional, do not use with occlusive dressing; do not use on children's skin covered by diapers or plastic pants.

Monitoring Parameters Growth (adolescents and children); signs/symptoms of HPA axis suppression/adrenal insufficiency; possible eosinophilic conditions (including Churg-Strauss syndrome); FEV_1, peak flow, and/or other pulmonary function tests; asthma symptoms

Additional Information Effects of inhaled/intranasal steroids on growth have been observed in the absence of laboratory evidence of HPA axis suppression, suggesting that growth velocity is a more sensitive indicator of systemic corticosteroid exposure in pediatric patients than some commonly used tests of HPA axis function. The long-term effects of this reduction in growth velocity associated with orally-inhaled and intranasal corticosteroids, including the impact on final adult height, are unknown. The potential for "catch up" growth following discontinuation of treatment with inhaled corticosteroids has not been adequately studied. The product labeling notes that intranasal administration was not associated with a statistically-significant reduction in growth velocity (based on a small study conducted over 1 year).

In the United States, dosage for the metered dose inhaler (Flovent® HFA) is expressed as the amount of drug which leaves the actuator and is delivered to the patient. This differs from other countries, which express the dosage as the amount of drug which leaves the valve.

Dosage Forms [CAN] = Canadian brand name
Aerosol for oral inhalation, as propionate [CFC free]:
Flovent® HFA: 44 mcg/inhalation (10.6 g) [120 metered doses]
Flovent® HFA: 110 mcg/inhalation (12 g) [120 metered doses]
Flovent® HFA: 220 mcg/inhalation (12 g) [120 metered doses]
Cream, as propionate: 0.05% (15 g, 30 g, 60 g)
Cutivate®: 0.05% (15 g, 30 g, 60 g)
Lotion, as propionate:
Cutivate®: 0.05% (60 mL)
Ointment, as propionate: 0.005% (15 g, 30 g, 60 g)
Cutivate®: 0.005% (15 g, 30 g, 60 g)
Powder for oral inhalation, as propionate [prefilled blister pack]:
Flovent® Diskus® [CAN]: 50 mcg (28s, 60s) [contains lactose] [not available in the U.S.]
Flovent® Diskus® [CAN]: 100 mcg (28s, 60s) [contains lactose] [not available in the U.S.]
Flovent® Diskus® [CAN]: 250 mcg (28s, 60s) [contains lactose] [not available in the U.S.]
Flovent® Diskus® [CAN]: 500 mcg (28s, 60s) [contains lactose] [not available in the U.S.]
Suspension, intranasal spray, as propionate: 50 mcg/inhalation (16 g) [120 metered doses]
Flonase®: 50 mcg/inhalation (16 g) [120 metered doses]

Fluticasone and Salmeterol (floo TIK a sone & sal ME te role)

U.S. Brand Names Advair Diskus®; Advair® HFA

Canadian Brand Names Advair Diskus®

Index Terms Fluticasone Propionate and Salmeterol Xinafoate; Salmeterol and Fluticasone

Pharmacologic Category Beta$_2$-Adrenergic Agonist; Corticosteroid, Inhalant (Oral)

Use Maintenance treatment of asthma; maintenance treatment of COPD associated with chronic bronchitis

Restrictions An FDA-approved medication guide must be distributed when dispensing an outpatient prescription (new or refill) where this medication is to be used without direct supervision of a healthcare provider. Medication guides are available at http://www.fda.gov/cder/Offices/ODS/medication_guides.htm.

Pregnancy Risk Factor C

Pregnancy Implications There are no adequate and well-controlled studies of fluticasone and/or salmeterol in pregnant women. Use only during pregnancy if the potential benefit to the mother outweighs the potential risk to the fetus.

Lactation

Fluticasone: Excretion in breast milk unknown/use caution

Salmeterol: Enters breast milk/use caution

Medication Safety Issues

Sound-alike/look-alike issues:

Advair may be confused with Advicor®

Contraindications Hypersensitivity to fluticasone, salmeterol, or any component of the formulation; status asthmaticus; acute episodes of asthma or COPD

Warnings/Precautions

Asthma treatment: Long-acting beta$_2$ agonists may increase the risk of asthma-related deaths. In a large, randomized clinical trial (SMART, 2006), salmeterol was associated with an increase in asthma-related deaths (when added to usual asthma therapy); risk may be greater in African-American patients versus Caucasians. Should only be used as adjuvant therapy in patients not adequately controlled on inhaled corticosteroids or whose disease requires two maintenance therapies. Salmeterol is not meant to relieve acute asthmatic symptoms, should not be initiated in patients with significantly worsening or acutely deteriorating asthma, and is not a substitute for inhaled or oral corticosteroids. Short-acting beta$_2$ agonist should be used for acute symptoms and symptoms occurring between treatments. Corticosteroids should not be stopped or reduced when salmeterol is initiated. During the initiation of salmeterol watch for signs of worsening asthma. Patients must be instructed to seek medical attention in cases where acute symptoms are not relieved or a previous level of response is diminished. The need to increase frequency of use may indicate deterioration of asthma, and treatment must not be delayed.

Concurrent diseases: Use caution in patients with cardiovascular disease (eg, arrhythmia, hypertension, or CHF), seizure disorders, diabetes, ocular disease, thyroid disease, osteoporosis, gastrointestinal disease, hepatic impairment, renal impairment, myasthenia gravis, osteoporosis, or hypokalemia. Beta agonists may cause elevation in blood pressure, heart rate, CNS stimulation/excitation, increase risk of arrhythmia, increase serum glucose, decrease serum potassium.

Adverse events: Salmeterol should not be used more than twice daily; do not exceed recommended dose; do not use with other long-acting beta$_2$ agonists; serious adverse events, have been associated with excessive use of inhaled sympathomimetics. There have been reports of laryngeal spasm, irritation, swelling (stridor, choking) with use. Rarely, paradoxical bronchospasm may occur with use of inhaled bronchodilating agents; this should be distinguished from inadequate response. Powder for oral inhalation contains lactose; very rare anaphylactic reactions have been reported in patients with severe milk protein allergy. Immediate hypersensitivity reactions (urticaria, angioedema, rash, bronchospasm) have been reported. Rare cases of vasculitis (Churg-Strauss syndrome) have been reported with fluticasone use. Glaucoma, increased intraocular pressure, and cataracts have occurred with fluticasone inhalation; consider routine eye exams in chronic users. Local yeast infections (eg, oral pharyngeal candidiasis) may occur. Corticosteroid use may cause psychiatric manifestations, including depression, euphoria, insomnia, mood swings, and personality changes. Pre-existing psychiatric conditions may be exacerbated by corticosteroid use.

Adrenal suppression: Fluticasone may cause hypercorticism or suppression of hypothalamic-pituitary-adrenal (HPA) axis, particularly in younger children or in patients receiving high doses for prolonged periods. Withdrawal and discontinuation of a corticosteroid should be done slowly and carefully. Particular care is required when patients are transferred from systemic corticosteroids to inhaled products. Patients receiving >20 mg per day of prednisone (or equivalent) may be most susceptible. Concurrent use of ritonavir (or potentially other strong inhibitors of CYP3A4) may increase fluticasone levels and effects on HPA suppression. Fatalities have occurred due to adrenal insufficiency in asthmatic patients during and after transfer from systemic corticosteroids to aerosol steroids; aerosol steroids do not provide the systemic steroid needed to treat patients having trauma, surgery, or infections. Do not use this product to transfer patients from oral corticosteroid therapy.

Immune system: Prolonged use of corticosteroids may also increase the incidence of secondary infection, mask acute infection (including fungal infections), prolong or exacerbate viral infections, or limit response to vaccines. Exposure to chickenpox should be avoided; corticosteroids should not be used to treat ocular herpes simplex. Corticosteroids should not be used for cerebral malaria. Close observation is required in patients with latent tuberculosis and/or TB reactivity; restrict use in active TB (only in conjunction with antituberculosis treatment).

Growth: Orally-inhaled and intranasal corticosteroids may cause a reduction in growth velocity in pediatric patients (~1 centimeter per year [range 0.3-1.8 cm per year]) and related to dose and duration of exposure). To minimize the systemic effects of orally-inhaled and intranasal corticosteroids, each patient should be titrated to the lowest effective dose. Growth should be routinely monitored in pediatric patients.

There have been reports of systemic corticosteroid withdrawal symptoms (eg, joint/muscle pain, lassitude, depression) when withdrawing oral inhalation therapy. Advair Diskus®: Safety and efficacy have not been established in children <4 years of age. Advair® HFA: Safety and efficacy have not been established in children <12 years of age.

Adverse Reactions Percentages reported in patients with asthma; also see individual agents:

>10%:
  Central nervous system: Headache (12% to 21%)
  Respiratory: Upper respiratory tract infection (16% to 27%), pharyngitis (9% to 13%)

>3% to 10%:
  Central nervous system: Dizziness (1% to 4%)
  Gastrointestinal: Nausea/vomiting (4% to 6%), diarrhea (2% to 4%), pain/discomfort (1% to 4%), oral candidiasis (1% to 4%)
  Neuromuscular & skeletal: Musculoskeletal pain (2% to 7%)
  Respiratory: Bronchitis (2% to 8%), upper respiratory tract inflammation (4% to 7%), cough (3% to 6%), sinusitis (4% to 5%), hoarseness/dysphonia (1% to 5%), viral respiratory tract infection (4%), epistaxis (1% to 4%)

1% to 3%:
  Cardiovascular: Arrhythmia, chest symptoms, fluid retention, MI, palpitation, syncope, tachycardia
  Central nervous system: Compressed nerve syndromes, hypnagogic effects, migraine, pain, sleep disorders, tremor
  Dermatologic: Dermatitis, dermatosis, eczema, hives, skin flakiness, urticaria, viral skin infection
  Endocrine & metabolic: Hypothyroidism
  Gastrointestinal: Appendicitis, constipation, dental discomfort/pain, gastrointestinal infection, gastrointestinal signs and symptoms (nonspecified), hemorrhoids, oral discomfort/pain, oral erythema/rash, oral ulcerations, unusual taste, viral GI Infection (0% to 3%), weight gain
  Genitourinary: Urinary tract infection
  Hematologic: Contusions/hematomas, lymphatic signs and symptoms (nonspecified)
  Hepatic: Abnormal liver function tests
  Neuromuscular & skeletal: Arthralgia, articular rheumatism, bone/cartilage disorders, bone pain, cramps, fractures, muscle injuries, muscle spasm, muscle stiffness, tightness/rigidity
  Ocular: Conjunctivitis, edema, eye redness, keratitis, xerophthalmia
  Otic: Ear signs and symptoms (nonspecified)
  Respiratory: Blood in nasal mucosa, congestion, ear/nose/throat infection, laryngitis, lower respiratory tract infection, lower respiratory signs and symptoms (nonspecified), nasal irritation, nasal signs and symptoms (nonspecified), nasal sinus disorders, pneumonia, rhinitis, rhinorrhea/post nasal drip, sneezing, wheezing
  Miscellaneous: Allergies/allergic reactions, bacterial infection, burns, candidiasis (0% to 3%), diaphoresis, sweat/sebum disorders, viral infection, wounds and lacerations

Postmarketing and/or case reports: Asthma exacerbation (serious and some fatal), abdominal pain, agitation, aggression, anaphylactic reaction, angioedema, aphonia, back pain, bronchospasm and immediate bronchospasm, cataracts, chest congestion, chest tightness, choking, contact dermatitis, contusions, Cushing syndrome, Cushingoid features, depression, dysmenorrhea, dyspepsia, dyspnea, earache, ecchymoses, eosinophilic conditions, glaucoma, growth velocity reduction in children/adolescents, hypercorticism, hyperglycemia, hypersensitivity reaction (immediate and delayed), hypertension, hypokalemia, hypothyroidism, influenza, intraocular pressure increased, laryngeal spasm/irritation, irregular menstruation, myositis, osteoporosis, pallor, paresthesia, paradoxical tracheitis, paranasal sinus pain, photodermatitis, PID, rash, restlessness, stridor, syncope, throat soreness/irritation, vaginal candidiasis, vaginitis, vulvovaginitis, rare cases of vasculitis (Churg-Strauss syndrome), ventricular tachycardia, xerostomia

Overdosage/Toxicology Symptoms of overdose include tachycardia, tremor, hypertension, angina, and seizures. Hypokalemia also may occur. Cardiac arrest and death may be associated with abuse of beta-agonist bronchodilators. Treatment includes immediate discontinuation and symptomatic and supportive therapies. Cautious use of beta-adrenergic blocking agents may be considered in severe cases. Cardiac monitoring is recommended.

Drug Interactions
  Cytochrome P450 Effect: Fluticasone: **Substrate** of CYP3A4 (major); Salmeterol: **Substrate** of CYP3A4 (major)
  Increased Effect/Toxicity: CYP3A4 inhibitors may increase the levels/effects of fluticasone and salmeterol; example inhibitors include amprenavir, atazanavir, clarithromycin, delavirdine, diclofenac, fosamprenavir, imatinib, indinavir, isoniazid, itraconazole, ketoconazole, miconazole, nefazodone, nelfinavir, nicardipine, propofol, quinidine, ritonavir, and telithromycin. Atomoxetine may enhance the tachycardia effect of beta$_2$-agonists. Protease inhibitors may decrease the metabolism, via CYP isoenzymes, of corticosteroids (orally inhaled); examples include amprenavir, atazanavir, fosamprenavir, indinavir, lopinavir, nelfinavir, ritonavir, and saquinavir; **exception** is tipranavir. Sympathomimetics may enhance the adverse/toxic effect of salmeterol. Antifungal agents (imidazole) may decrease the metabolism, via CYP isoenzymes, of corticosteroids (orally inhaled).
  Decreased Effect: Beta$_2$-agonists may diminish the bradycardia effect of beta-blockers (beta$_1$ selective). Beta-blockers (nonselective) may diminish the bronchodilator effect of beta$_2$-agonists.

Stability
  Advair Diskus®: Store at 20°C to 25°C (68°F to 77°F). Store in a dry place out of direct heat or sunlight. Diskus® device should be discarded 1 month after removal from foil pouch, or when dosing indicator reads "zero," whichever comes first. Device is not reusable.
  Advair® HFA: Store at 15°C to 30°C (59°F to 86°F). Store with mouthpiece down. Discard after 120 inhalations. Device is not reusable.
  (Continued)

Fluticasone and Salmeterol *(Continued)*

Mechanism of Action Combination of fluticasone (corticosteroid) and salmeterol (long-acting beta$_2$ agonist) designed to improve pulmonary function and control over what is produced by either agent when used alone. Because fluticasone and salmeterol act locally in the lung, plasma levels do not predict therapeutic effect.

Fluticasone: The mechanism of action for all topical corticosteroids is believed to be a combination of three important properties: Anti-inflammatory activity, immunosuppressive properties, and antiproliferative actions. Fluticasone has extremely potent vasoconstrictive and anti-inflammatory activity.

Salmeterol: Relaxes bronchial smooth muscle by selective action on beta$_2$-receptors with little effect on heart rate

Pharmacodynamics/Kinetics See individual agents.

Duration: 12 hours

Dosage Oral inhalation: **Note:** Do not use to transfer patients from systemic corticosteroid therapy.

COPD: Adults: Advair Diskus®: Fluticasone 250 mcg/salmeterol 50 mcg twice daily, 12 hours apart. **Note:** This is the maximum dose.

Asthma:

Children 4-11 years: Advair Diskus®: Fluticasone 100 mcg/salmeterol 50 mcg twice daily, 12 hours apart. **Note:** This is the maximum dose.

Children ≥12 and Adults:

Advair Diskus®: One inhalation twice daily, morning and evening, 12 hours apart
Maximum dose: Fluticasone 500 mcg/salmeterol 50 mcg per inhalation

Advair® HFA: Two inhalations twice daily, morning and evening, 12 hours apart
Maximum dose: Fluticasone 230 mcg/salmeterol 21 mcg per inhalation

Note: Initial dose prescribed should be based upon previous dose of inhaled-steroid asthma therapy. Dose should be increased after 2 weeks if adequate response is not achieved. Patients should be titrated to lowest effective dose once stable. Each suggestion below specifies the product strength to use; remember to **use 1 inhalation for Diskus® and 2 inhalations for HFA.**

Patients not currently on inhaled corticosteroids:

Advair Diskus®: Fluticasone 100 mcg/salmeterol 50 mcg **or** fluticasone 250 mcg/salmeterol 50 mcg

Advair® HFA: Fluticasone 45 mcg/salmeterol 21 mcg **or** fluticasone 115 mcg/salmeterol 21 mcg

Patients currently using inhaled beclomethasone dipropionate:

≤160 mcg/day: Advair Diskus®: Fluticasone 100 mcg/salmeterol 50 mcg **or** Advair® HFA: Fluticasone 45 mcg/salmeterol 21 mcg

320 mcg/day: Advair Diskus®:Fluticasone 250 mcg/salmeterol 50 mcg **or** Advair® HFA: Fluticasone 115 mcg/salmeterol 21 mcg

640 mcg/day: Advair Diskus®: Fluticasone 500 mcg/salmeterol 50 mcg **or** Advair® HFA: Fluticasone 230 mcg/salmeterol 21 mcg

Patients currently using inhaled budesonide:

≤400 mcg/day: Advair Diskus®: Fluticasone 100 mcg/salmeterol 50 mcg **or** Advair® HFA: Fluticasone 45 mcg/salmeterol 21 mcg

800-1200 mcg/day: Advair Diskus®: Fluticasone 250 mcg/salmeterol 50 mcg **or** Advair® HFA: Fluticasone 115 mcg/salmeterol 21mcg

1600 mcg/day: Advair Diskus®: Fluticasone 500 mcg/salmeterol 50 mcg **or** Advair® HFA: Fluticasone 230 mcg/salmeterol 21 mcg

Patients currently using inhaled flunisolide CFC aerosol:

≤1000 mcg/day: Advair Diskus®: Fluticasone 100 mcg/salmeterol 50 mcg **or** Advair® HFA: Fluticasone 45 mcg/salmeterol 21 mcg

1250-2000 mcg/day: Advair Diskus®: Fluticasone 250 mcg/salmeterol 50 mcg **or** Advair® HFA: Fluticasone 115 mcg/salmeterol 21 mcg

Patients currently using inhaled fluticasone HFA aerosol:

≤176 mcg/day: Advair Diskus®: Fluticasone 100 mcg/salmeterol 50 mcg **or** Advair® HFA: Fluticasone 45 mcg/salmeterol 21 mcg

440 mcg/day: Advair Diskus®: Fluticasone 250 mcg/salmeterol 50 mcg **or** Advair® HFA: Fluticasone 115 mcg/salmeterol 21 mcg

660-880 mcg/day: Advair Diskus®: Fluticasone 500 mcg/salmeterol 50 mcg **or** Advair® HFA: Fluticasone 230 mcg/salmeterol 21 mcg

Patients currently using inhaled fluticasone propionate powder:

≤200 mcg/day: Advair Diskus®: Fluticasone 100 mcg/salmeterol 50 mcg **or** Advair® HFA: Fluticasone 45 mcg/salmeterol 21 mcg

500 mcg/day: Advair Diskus®: Fluticasone 250 mcg/salmeterol 50 mcg **or** Advair® HFA: Fluticasone 115 mcg/salmeterol 21 mcg

1000 mcg/day: Advair Diskus®: Fluticasone 500 mcg/salmeterol 50 mcg **or** Advair® HFA: Fluticasone 230 mcg/salmeterol 21 mcg

Patients currently using inhaled mometasone furoate powder:

220 mcg/day: Advair Diskus®: Fluticasone 100 mcg/salmeterol 50 mcg **or** Advair® HFA: Fluticasone 45 mcg/salmeterol 21 mcg

440 mcg/day: Advair Diskus®: Fluticasone 250 mcg/salmeterol 50 mcg **or** Advair® HFA: Fluticasone 115 mcg/salmeterol 21 mcg

880 mcg/day: Advair Diskus®: Fluticasone 500 mcg/salmeterol 50 mcg **or** Advair® HFA: Fluticasone 230 mcg/salmeterol 21 mcg

Patients currently using inhaled triamcinolone acetonide:

≤1000 mcg/day: Advair Diskus®: Fluticasone 100 mcg/salmeterol 50 mcg **or** Advair® HFA: Fluticasone 45 mcg/salmeterol 21 mcg

1100-1600 mcg/day: Advair Diskus®: Fluticasone 250 mcg/salmeterol 50 mcg **or** Advair® HFA: Fluticasone 115 mcg/salmeterol 21 mcg

Elderly: No differences in safety or effectiveness have been seen in studies of patients ≥65 years of age. However, increased sensitivity may be seen in the elderly. Use with caution in patients with concomitant cardiovascular disease.

Dosage adjustment in renal impairment: Specific guidelines are not available
Dosage adjustment in hepatic impairment: Fluticasone is cleared by hepatic metabolism. No dosing adjustment suggested. Use with caution in patients with impaired liver function.
Dietary Considerations Advair Diskus® powder for oral inhalation contains lactose; very rare anaphylactic reactions have been reported in patients with severe milk protein allergy.
Administration Advair® HFA: Shake well for 5 seconds before each spray; Prime with 4 test sprays (into air and away from face) before using for the first time. If canister is dropped or not used for >4 weeks, prime with 2 sprays. Patient must keep track of the number of uses. Throw away canister after 120 inhalations. Do not spray in eyes. Rinse mouth with water after use to reduce risk of oral candidiasis.
Monitoring Parameters FEV$_1$, peak flow, and/or other pulmonary function tests; blood pressure, heart rate; CNS stimulation; serum glucose, serum potassium. Monitor for increased use of short-acting beta$_2$-agonist inhalers; may be marker of a deteriorating asthma condition. The growth of pediatric patients receiving inhaled corticosteroids should be monitored routinely (eg, via stadiometry).
Additional Information Effects of inhaled/intranasal steroids on growth have been observed in the absence of laboratory evidence of HPA axis suppression, suggesting that growth velocity is a more sensitive indicator of systemic corticosteroid exposure in pediatric patients than some commonly used tests of HPA axis function. The long-term effects of this reduction in growth velocity associated with orally-inhaled and intranasal corticosteroids, including the impact on final adult height, are unknown. The potential for "catch up" growth following discontinuation of treatment with inhaled corticosteroids has not been adequately studied.

Advair® HFA: Salmeterol (base) 21 mcg is equivalent to 30.45 mcg of salmeterol xinafoate.

Dosage Forms
Aerosol, for oral inhalation:
    Advair® HFA:
        45/21: Fluticasone propionate 45 mcg and salmeterol xinafoate 30.45 mcg (12 g) [120 metered inhalations]
        115/21: Fluticasone propionate 115 mcg and salmeterol xinafoate 30.45 mcg (12 g) [120 metered inhalations]
        230/21: Fluticasone propionate 230 mcg and salmeterol xinafoate 30.45 mcg (12 g) [120 metered inhalations]
Powder, for oral inhalation:
    Advair Diskus®:
        100/50: Fluticasone propionate 100 mcg and salmeterol xinafoate 50 mcg (28s, 60s) [contains lactose; chlorofluorocarbon free]
        250/50: Fluticasone propionate 250 mcg and salmeterol xinafoate 50 mcg (28s, 60s) [contains lactose; chlorofluorocarbon free]
        500/50: Fluticasone propionate 500 mcg and salmeterol xinafoate 50 mcg (28s, 60s) [contains lactose; chlorofluorocarbon free]

♦ **Fluticasone Propionate** see Fluticasone on page 738
♦ **Fluticasone Propionate and Salmeterol Xinafoate** see Fluticasone and Salmeterol on page 742

Fluvastatin (FLOO va sta tin)

U.S. Brand Names Lescol®; Lescol® XL
Canadian Brand Names Lescol®; Lescol® XL
Pharmacologic Category Antilipemic Agent, HMG-CoA Reductase Inhibitor
Additional Appendix Information
    Hyperlipidemia Management on page 2058
    Lipid-Lowering Agents on page 1887
Use To be used as a component of multiple risk factor intervention in patients at risk for atherosclerosis vascular disease due to hypercholesterolemia

Adjunct to dietary therapy to reduce elevated total cholesterol (total-C), LDL-C, triglyceride, and apolipoprotein B (apo-B) levels and to increase HDL-C in primary hypercholesterolemia and mixed dyslipidemia (Fredrickson types IIa and IIb); to slow the progression of coronary atherosclerosis in patients with coronary heart disease; reduce risk of coronary revascularization procedures in patients with coronary heart disease
Pregnancy Risk Factor X
Pregnancy Implications Cholesterol biosynthesis may be important in fetal development. Contraindicated in pregnancy. Administer to women of childbearing potential only when conception is highly unlikely and patients have been informed of potential hazards.
Lactation Enters breast milk/contraindicated
Medication Safety Issues
    Sound-alike/look-alike issues:
        Fluvastatin may be confused with fluoxetine
Contraindications Hypersensitivity to fluvastatin or any component of the formulation; active liver disease; unexplained persistent elevations of serum transaminases; pregnancy; breast-feeding
Warnings/Precautions Secondary causes of hyperlipidemia should be ruled out prior to therapy. Liver function must be monitored by periodic laboratory assessment. Rhabdomyolysis with acute renal failure has occurred with fluvastatin and other HMG-CoA reductase inhibitors. Risk may be increased with concurrent use of other drugs which may cause rhabdomyolysis (including gemfibrozil, fibric acid derivatives, or niacin at doses ≥1 g/day). Temporarily discontinue in any patient experiencing markedly elevated CPK levels, myopathy, or an acute/serious condition predisposing to renal failure secondary to rhabdomyolysis. Use with caution in patients with advanced age, these patients are predisposed to myopathy. Use caution in patients with previous liver disease or heavy ethanol use. Use caution in (Continued)

Fluvastatin *(Continued)*

patients with concurrent medications or conditions which reduce steroidogenesis. Safety and efficacy in children <10 years of age have not been established.

Adverse Reactions As reported with fluvastatin capsules; in general, adverse reactions reported with fluvastatin extended release tablet were similar, but the incidence was less.

1% to 10%:
Central nervous system: Headache (9%), fatigue (3%), insomnia (3%)
Gastrointestinal: Dyspepsia (8%), diarrhea (5%), abdominal pain (5%), nausea (3%)
Genitourinary: Urinary tract infection (2%)
Neuromuscular & skeletal: Myalgia (5%)
Respiratory: Sinusitis (3%), bronchitis (2%)

<1% (Limited to important or life-threatening) including additional class-related events (not necessarily reported with fluvastatin therapy): Alopecia, anaphylaxis, angioedema, arthralgia, arthritis, cataracts, cholestatic jaundice, cirrhosis, CPK increased (>10x normal), depression, dermatomyositis, dyspnea, eosinophilia, erectile dysfunction, erythema multi-forme, ESR increased, facial paresis, fatty liver, fever, fulminant hepatic necrosis, gyneco-mastia, hemolytic anemia, hepatitis, hepatoma, hypersensitivity reaction, impotence, leukopenia, memory loss, muscle cramps, myopathy, nodules, ophthalmoplegia, pancrea-titis, paresthesia, peripheral nerve palsy, peripheral neuropathy, photosensitivity, polymy-algia rheumatica, positive ANA, pruritus, psychic disturbance, purpura, rash, renal failure (secondary to rhabdomyolysis), rhabdomyolysis, skin discoloration, Stevens-Johnson syndrome, systemic lupus erythematosus-like syndrome, taste alteration, thrombocyto-penia, thyroid dysfunction, toxic epidermal necrolysis, transaminases increased, tremor, urticaria, vasculitis, vertigo

Overdosage/Toxicology GI complaints and elevated SGOT and SGPT have been reported following large doses of the extended release tablets. In case of overdose, treatment should be symptom-directed and supportive; dialyzability is not known, but given high protein binding not likely to benefit.

Drug Interactions

Cytochrome P450 Effect: Substrate of CYP2C9 (major), 2C8 (minor), 2D6 (minor), 3A4 (minor); **Inhibits** CYP1A2 (weak), 2C8 (weak), 2C9 (moderate), 2D6 (weak), 3A4 (weak)

Increased Effect/Toxicity: Fibric acid derivatives may increase the risk of myopathy and rhabdomyolysis. Fluvastatin levels/effects may be increased by omeprazole, phenytoin, fluconazole, NSAIDs, sulfonamides, or other CYP2C9 inhibitors. The anticoagulant effect of warfarin may be increased by fluvastatin. Cholestyramine effect may be additive with fluvastatin if administration times are separated. Fluvastatin may increase the levels/effects of fluoxetine, glimepiride, glipizide, and other CYP2C9 substrates.

Decreased Effect: Administration of cholestyramine at the same time with fluvastatin reduces absorption and clinical effect of fluvastatin. Separate administration times by at least 4 hours. Rifampin and rifabutin may decrease fluvastatin blood levels.

Ethanol/Nutrition/Herb Interactions

Ethanol: Avoid excessive ethanol consumption (due to potential hepatic effects).
Food: Reduces rate but not the extent of absorption. Red yeast rice contains an estimated 2.4 mg lovastatin per 600 mg rice.

Stability Store at 15°C to 30°C (59°F to 86°F). Protect from light.

Mechanism of Action Acts by competitively inhibiting 3-hydroxy-3-methylglutaryl-coenzyme A (HMG-CoA) reductase, the enzyme that catalyzes the reduction of HMG-CoA to mevalo-nate; this is an early rate-limiting step in cholesterol biosynthesis. HDL is increased while total, LDL and VLDL cholesterols, apolipoprotein B, and plasma triglycerides are decreased.

Pharmacodynamics/Kinetics

Onset: Peak effect: Maximal LDL-C reductions achieved within 4 weeks
Distribution: V_d: 0.35 L/kg
Protein binding: >98%
Metabolism: To inactive and active metabolites (oxidative metabolism via CYP2C9 [75%], 2C8 [~5%], and 3A4 [~20%] isoenzymes); active forms do not circulate systemically; extensive (saturable) first-pass hepatic extraction
Bioavailability: Absolute: Capsule: 24%; Extended release tablet: 29%
Half-life elimination: Capsule: <3 hours; Extended release tablet: 9 hours
Time to peak: Capsule: 1 hour; Extended release tablet: 3 hours
Excretion: Feces (90%): urine (5%)

Dosage

Adolescents 10-16 years: Oral: Heterozygous familial hypercholesterolemia: Initial: 20 mg once daily; may increase every 6 weeks based on tolerability and response to a maximum recommended dose of 80 mg/day, given in 2 divided doses (immediate release capsule) or as a single daily dose (extended release tablet)

Note: Indicated only for adjunctive therapy when diet alone cannot reduce LDL-C below 190 mg/dL, or 160 mg/dL (with cardiovascular risk factors). Female patients must be 1 year postmenarche.

Adults: Oral:
Patients requiring ≥25% decrease in LDL-C: 40 mg capsule once daily in the evening, 80 mg extended release tablet once daily (anytime), or 40 mg capsule twice daily
Patients requiring <25% decrease in LDL-C: Initial: 20 mg capsule once daily in the evening; may increase based on tolerability and response to a maximum recommended dose of 80 mg/day, given in 2 divided doses (immediate release capsule) or as a single daily dose (extended release tablet)

Dosage adjustment in renal impairment: Less than 6% excreted renally; no dosage adjust-ment needed with mild-to-moderate renal impairment; use with caution in severe impair-ment

Dosage adjustment in hepatic impairment: Levels may accumulate in patients with liver disease (increased AUC and C_{max}); use caution with severe hepatic impairment or heavy ethanol ingestion; contraindicated in active liver disease or unexplained transaminase elevations; decrease dose and monitor effects carefully in patients with hepatic insuffi-ciency

Elderly: No dosage adjustment necessary based on age

Dietary Considerations Generally, patients should be placed on a standard cholesterol-lowering diet and other lifestyle modifications for 3-6 months prior to the initiation of drug therapy. The diet should be continued during drug therapy. However, for patients with advanced risk factors (eg, known coronary heart disease), drug therapy may be initiated concurrently with diet modification. May be taken without regard to meals. Red yeast rice contains an estimated 2.4 mg lovastatin per 600 mg rice.

Administration Patient should be placed on a standard cholesterol-lowering diet before and during treatment; fluvastatin may be taken without regard to meals; adjust dosage as needed in response to periodic lipid determinations during the first 4 weeks after a dosage change; lipid-lowering effects are additive when fluvastatin is combined with a bile-acid binding resin or niacin, however, it must be administered at least 2 hours following these drugs. Do not break, chew, or crush extended release tablets; do not open capsules.

Monitoring Parameters Obtain baseline LFTs and total cholesterol profile; repeat tests at 12 weeks after initiation of therapy or elevation in dose, and periodically thereafter. Monitor LDL-C at intervals no less than 4 weeks.

Dosage Forms
Capsule (Lescol®): 20 mg, 40 mg
Tablet, extended release (Lescol® XL): 80 mg

♦ **Fluviral S/F® (Can)** *see* Influenza Virus Vaccine *on page 906*
♦ **Fluvirin®** *see* Influenza Virus Vaccine *on page 906*

Fluvoxamine (floo VOKS a meen)

Canadian Brand Names Alti-Fluvoxamine; Apo-Fluvoxamine®; Luvox®; Novo-Fluvoxamine; Nu-Fluvoxamine; PMS-Fluvoxamine; Rhoxal-fluvoxamine; Sandoz-Fluvoxamine

Index Terms Luvox

Pharmacologic Category Antidepressant, Selective Serotonin Reuptake Inhibitor

Additional Appendix Information
Antidepressant Agents *on page 1866*
Selective Serotonin Reuptake Inhibitors (SSRIs) Pharmacokinetics *on page 1896*

Use Treatment of obsessive-compulsive disorder (OCD) in children ≥8 years of age and adults

Unlabeled/Investigational Use Treatment of major depression; panic disorder; anxiety disorders in children

Restrictions An FDA-approved medication guide concerning the use of antidepressants in children and teenagers must be distributed when dispensing an outpatient prescription (new or refill) where this medication is to be used without direct supervision of a healthcare provider. Medication guides are available at http://www.fda.gov/cder/Offices/ODS/medication_guides.htm. Dispense to parents or guardians of children and teenagers receiving this medication.

Pregnancy Risk Factor C

Pregnancy Implications Nonteratogenic effects including respiratory distress, cyanosis, apnea, seizures, temperature instability, feeding difficulty, vomiting, hypoglycemia, hypo- or hypertonia, hyper-reflexia, jitteriness, irritability, constant crying, and tremor have been reported in the neonate immediately following delivery after exposure to SSRIs late in the third trimester. Exposure to SSRIs late in pregnancy has also been associated with persistent pulmonary hypertension of the newborn (PPHN). Adverse effects may be due to toxic effects of SSRI or drug discontinuation. In some cases, effects may present clinically as serotonin syndrome. There are no adequate and well-controlled studies in pregnant women. Use during pregnancy only if the potential benefit to the mother outweighs the possible risk to the fetus. If treatment during pregnancy is required, consider tapering therapy during the third trimester.

Lactation Enters breast milk/not recommended (AAP rates "of concern")

Medication Safety Issues
Sound-alike/look-alike issues:
Fluvoxamine may be confused with flavoxate, fluoxetine
Luvox may be confused with Lasix®, Levoxyl®

Contraindications Hypersensitivity to fluvoxamine or any component of the formulation; concurrent use with alosetron, pimozide, thioridazine, tizanidine, mesoridazine, or cisapride; use of MAO inhibitors within 14 days

Warnings/Precautions [U.S. Boxed Warning]: Antidepressants increase the risk of suicidal thinking and behavior in children and adolescents with major depressive disorder (MDD) and other depressive disorders; consider risk prior to prescribing. All patients must be closely monitored for clinical worsening, suicidality, or unusual changes in behavior, especially during the initiation of therapy or following an increase or decrease in dosage. When used in children, the child's family or caregiver should be instructed to closely observe the patient and communicate condition with healthcare provider. A medication guide should be dispensed with each prescription. **Fluvoxamine is FDA approved for the treatment of OCD in children ≥8 years of age.**

The possibility of a suicide attempt is inherent in major depression and may persist until remission occurs. Use caution in high-risk patients. Worsening depression and severe abrupt suicidality that are not part of the presenting symptoms may require discontinuation or modification of drug therapy. The patient's family or caregiver should be alerted to monitor patients for the emergence of suicidality and associated behaviors (such as agitation, irritability, hostility, impulsivity, and hypomania) and call healthcare provider.

May worsen psychosis in some patients or precipitate a shift to mania or hypomania in patients with bipolar disorder. Patients presenting with depressive symptoms should be screened for bipolar disorder. Monotherapy in patients with bipolar disorder should be avoided. **Fluvoxamine is not FDA approved for the treatment of bipolar depression.**
(Continued)

747

Fluvoxamine (Continued)

The potential for severe reaction exits when used with MAO inhibitors, SSRIs/SNRIs or triptans; serotonin syndrome (hyperthermia, muscular rigidity, mental status changes/agitation, autonomic instability) may occur. Concurrent use with MAO inhibitors is contraindicated. Fluvoxamine has a low potential to impair cognitive or motor performance; caution operating hazardous machinery or driving. Use caution in patients with a previous seizure disorder or condition predisposing to seizures such as brain damage, alcoholism, or concurrent therapy with other drugs which lower the seizure threshold.

May increase the risks associated with electroconvulsive therapy. Use with caution in patients with hepatic or renal dysfunction and in elderly patients. May cause hyponatremia/SIADH. Use with caution in patients with renal insufficiency or other concurrent illness (cardiovascular disease). Use with caution in patients at risk of bleeding or receiving concurrent anticoagulant therapy, although not consistently noted, fluvoxamine may cause impairment in platelet function. May cause or exacerbate sexual dysfunction.

Adverse Reactions

>10%:

Central nervous system: Headache, somnolence, insomnia, nervousness, dizziness

Gastrointestinal: Nausea, diarrhea, xerostomia

Neuromuscular & skeletal: Weakness

1% to 10%:

Cardiovascular: Palpitations

Central nervous system: Mania, hypomania, vertigo, abnormal thinking, agitation, anxiety, malaise, amnesia, yawning, hypertonia, CNS stimulation, depression

Endocrine & metabolic: Decreased libido

Gastrointestinal: Abdominal pain, vomiting, dyspepsia, constipation, abnormal taste, anorexia, flatulence, weight gain

Genitourinary: Delayed ejaculation, impotence, anorgasmia, urinary frequency, urinary retention

Neuromuscular & skeletal: Tremors

Ocular: Blurred vision

Respiratory: Dyspnea

Miscellaneous: Diaphoresis

<1% (Limited to important or life-threatening): Acne, agranulocytosis, akinesia with fever, alopecia, anaphylaxis, anemia, angina, angioedema, aplastic anemia, ataxia, bradycardia, delayed menstruation, dermatitis, dry skin, dysuria, extrapyramidal reactions, Henoch-Schönlein purpura, hepatitis, lactation, leukocytosis, neuropathy, nocturia, pancreatitis, seizure, serotonin syndrome, SIADH, Stevens-Johnson syndrome, thrombocytopenia, torsade de pointes, toxic epidermal necrolysis, transaminases increased, urticaria, vasculitis, ventricular tachycardia

Overdosage/Toxicology

Symptoms include nausea, vomiting, somnolence, hypotension, hypokalemia, tachycardia, respiratory distress, and coma. Other symptoms reported in overdose (single- or multiple-drug ingestion) include bradycardia, ECG abnormalities, seizures, tremor, diarrhea, and increased reflexes. A specific antidote does not exist. Treatment is supportive. Although vomiting has not been extensive in overdose to date, patients should be monitored for fluid and electrolyte loss, and appropriate replacement therapy instituted when necessary.

Drug Interactions

Cytochrome P450 Effect: Substrate (major) of CYP1A2, 2D6; **Inhibits** CYP1A2 (strong), 2B6 (weak), 2C9 (weak), 2C19 (strong), 2D6 (weak), 3A4 (weak)

Increased Effect/Toxicity: Fluvoxamine should not be used with nonselective MAO inhibitors (phenelzine, isocarboxazid) and drugs with MAO inhibitor properties (linezolid); fatal reactions have been reported. Wait 2 weeks after stopping an MAO inhibitor before starting fluvoxamine. Concurrent selegiline has been associated with mania, hypertension, or serotonin syndrome (risk may be reduced relative to nonselective MAO inhibitors).

Fluvoxamine may inhibit the metabolism of thioridazine or mesoridazine, resulting in increased plasma levels and increasing the risk of QT_c interval prolongation. This may lead to serious ventricular arrhythmias, such as torsade de pointes-type arrhythmias and sudden death. Do not use together. Wait at least 5 weeks after discontinuing fluvoxamine prior to starting thioridazine. Fluvoxamine may increase the levels/effects of aminophylline, citalopram, diazepam, mexiletine, mirtazapine, methsuximide, phenytoin, propranolol, ropinirole, sertraline, theophylline, trifluoperazine and other substrates of CYP1A2 or 2C19. Fluvoxamine may increase the concentrations of alosetron and tizanidine; concurrent use is not recommended.

The levels/effects of fluvoxamine may be increased by amphetamines, selected beta-blockers, chlorpromazine, ciprofloxacin, delavirdine, fluoxetine, ketoconazole, miconazole, norfloxacin, ofloxacin, paroxetine, pergolide, quinidine, quinine, ritonavir, rofecoxib, ropinirole, and other CYP1A2 or 2D6 inhibitors.

Combined use of SSRIs and amphetamines, buspirone, meperidine, nefazodone, serotonin agonists (such as sumatriptan), sibutramine, other SSRIs/SNRIs, sympathomimetics, ritonavir, tramadol, and venlafaxine may increase the risk of serotonin syndrome. Combined use of sumatriptan (and other serotonin agonists) may result in toxicity; weakness, hyper-reflexia, and incoordination have been observed with sumatriptan and SSRIs. In addition, concurrent use may theoretically increase the risk of serotonin syndrome; includes sumatriptan, naratriptan, rizatriptan, and zolmitriptan.

Concurrent lithium may increase risk of nephrotoxicity. Risk of hyponatremia may increase with concurrent use of loop diuretics (bumetanide, furosemide, torsemide). Fluvoxamine may increase the hypoprothrombinemic response to warfarin. Concomitant use of fluvoxamine and NSAIDs, aspirin, or other drugs affecting coagulation has been associated with an increased risk of bleeding; monitor.

Decreased Effect: The levels/effects of fluvoxamine may be decreased by aminoglutethimide, carbamazepine, phenobarbital, rifampin, and other CYP1A2 inducers. Cyproheptadine, a serotonin antagonist, may inhibit the effects of serotonin reuptake inhibitors (fluvoxamine); monitor for altered antidepressant response.

Ethanol/Nutrition/Herb Interactions

Ethanol: Avoid ethanol. Depressed patients should avoid/limit intake.

Food: The bioavailability of melatonin has been reported to be increased by fluvoxamine.

Herb/Nutraceutical: Avoid valerian, St John's wort, SAMe, kava kava (may increase risk of serotonin syndrome and/or excessive sedation).

Stability Protect from high humidity and store at controlled room temperature 15°C to 30°C (59°F to 86°F). Dispense in tight containers.

Mechanism of Action Inhibits CNS neuron serotonin uptake; minimal or no effect on reuptake of norepinephrine or dopamine; does not significantly bind to alpha-adrenergic, histamine or cholinergic receptors

Pharmacodynamics/Kinetics

Absorption: Steady-state plasma concentrations have been noted to be 2-3 times higher in children than those in adolescents; female children demonstrated a significantly higher AUC than males

Distribution: V_d: ~25 L/kg

Protein binding: ~80%, primarily to albumin

Metabolism: Hepatic

Bioavailability: 53%; not significantly affected by food

Half-life elimination: ~15 hours

Time to peak, plasma: 3-8 hours

Excretion: Urine

Dosage Oral: **Note:** When total daily dose exceeds 50 mg, the dose should be given in 2 divided doses:

Children 8-17 years: Initial: 25 mg at bedtime; adjust in 25 mg increments at 4- to 7-day intervals, as tolerated, to maximum therapeutic benefit: Range: 50-200 mg/day

Maximum: Children: 8-11 years: 200 mg/day, adolescents: 300 mg/day; lower doses may be effective in female versus male patients

Adults: Initial: 50 mg at bedtime; adjust in 50 mg increments at 4- to 7-day intervals; usual dose range: 100-300 mg/day; divide total daily dose into 2 doses; administer larger portion at bedtime

Elderly: Reduce dose, titrate slowly

Dosage adjustment in hepatic impairment: Reduce dose, titrate slowly

Monitoring Parameters Mental status for depression, suicidal ideation, anxiety, social functioning, mania, panic attacks; akathisia, weight gain or loss, nutritional intake, sleep

Dosage Forms Tablet: 25 mg, 50 mg, 100 mg

♦ **Fluzone®** *see* Influenza Virus Vaccine *on page 906*

♦ **FML®** *see* Fluorometholone *on page 724*

♦ **FML® Forte** *see* Fluorometholone *on page 724*

♦ **FML Forte® (Can)** *see* Fluorometholone *on page 724*

♦ **FML-S®** *see* Sulfacetamide Sodium and Fluorometholone *on page 1610*

♦ **Focalin®** *see* Dexmethylphenidate *on page 484*

♦ **Focalin® XR** *see* Dexmethylphenidate *on page 484*

♦ **Foille® [OTC]** *see* Benzocaine *on page 204*

♦ **Folacin** *see* Folic Acid *on page 749*

♦ **Folacin, Vitamin B₁₂, and Vitamin B₆** *see* Folic Acid, Cyanocobalamin, and Pyridoxine *on page 750*

♦ **Folate** *see* Folic Acid *on page 749*

♦ **Folbee** *see* Folic Acid, Cyanocobalamin, and Pyridoxine *on page 750*

♦ **Folgard® [OTC]** *see* Folic Acid, Cyanocobalamin, and Pyridoxine *on page 750*

♦ **Folgard RX 2.2® [DSC]** *see* Folic Acid, Cyanocobalamin, and Pyridoxine *on page 750*

Folic Acid (FOE lik AS id)

Canadian Brand Names Apo-Folic®

Index Terms Folacin; Folate; Pteroylglutamic Acid

Pharmacologic Category Vitamin, Water Soluble

Use Treatment of megaloblastic and macrocytic anemias due to folate deficiency; dietary supplement to prevent neural tube defects

Pregnancy Risk Factor A

Pregnancy Implications Folic acid requirements are increased during pregnancy; a deficiency may result in fetal harm.

Lactation Enters breast milk/compatible

Medication Safety Issues

Sound-alike/look-alike issues:

Folic acid may be confused with folinic acid

Contraindications Hypersensitivity to folic acid or any component of the formulation

Warnings/Precautions Not appropriate for monotherapy with pernicious, aplastic, or normocytic anemias when anemia is present with vitamin B₁₂ deficiency. Doses >0.1 mg/day may obscure pernicious anemia with continuing irreversible nerve damage progression. Resistance to treatment may occur with depressed hematopoiesis, alcoholism, deficiencies of other vitamins. Injection contains benzyl alcohol (1.5%) as preservative (use care in administration to neonates).

Adverse Reactions Frequency not defined.

Allergic reaction, bronchospasm, flushing (slight), malaise (general), pruritus, rash

Drug Interactions

Decreased Effect: Folic acid may decrease phenytoin concentrations. Folic acid may diminish the therapeutic effect of raltitrexed.

(Continued)

Folic Acid *(Continued)*

Stability Do not use with oxidizing and reducing agents or heavy metal ions.

Mechanism of Action Folic acid is necessary for formation of a number of coenzymes in many metabolic systems, particularly for purine and pyrimidine synthesis; required for nucleoprotein synthesis and maintenance in erythropoiesis; stimulates WBC and platelet production in folate deficiency anemia

Pharmacodynamics/Kinetics
Onset of effect: Peak effect: Oral: 0.5-1 hour
Absorption: Proximal part of small intestine

Dosage
Oral, I.M., I.V., SubQ: Anemia:
Infants: 0.1 mg/day
Children <4 years: Up to 0.3 mg/day
Children >4 years and Adults: 0.4 mg/day
Pregnant and lactating women: 0.8 mg/day
Oral:
RDA: Expressed as dietary folate equivalents:
Children:
1-3 years: 150 mcg/day
4-8 years: 200 mcg/day
9-13 years: 300 mcg/day
Children ≥14 years and Adults: 400 mcg/day
Elderly: Vitamin B_{12} deficiency must be ruled out before initiating folate therapy due to frequency of combined nutritional deficiencies: RDA requirements (1999): 400 mcg/day (0.4 mg) minimum
Prevention of neural tube defects:
Females of childbearing potential: 400 mcg/day
Females at high risk or with family history of neural tube defects: 4 mg/day

Dietary Considerations As of January 1998, the FDA has required manufacturers of enriched flour, bread, corn meal, pasta, rice and other grain products to add folic acid to their products. The intent is to help decrease the risk of neural tube defects by increasing folic acid intake. Other foods which contain folic acid include dark green leafy vegetables, citrus fruits and juices, and lentils.

Administration Oral preferred, but may also be administered by deep I.M., SubQ, or I.V. injection

Reference Range Therapeutic: 0.005-0.015 mcg/mL

Test Interactions Falsely low serum concentrations may occur with the *Lactobacillus casei* assay method in patients on anti-infectives (eg, tetracycline)

Additional Information The RDA for folic acid is presented as dietary folate equivalents (DFE). DFE adjusts for the difference in bioavailability of folic acid from food as compared to dietary supplements.

Dosage Forms
Injection, solution, as sodium folate: 5 mg/mL (10 mL) [contains benzyl alcohol]
Tablet: 0.4 mg, 0.8 mg, 1 mg

Extemporaneous Preparations A 1 mg/mL folic acid solution may be prepared by crushing fifty 1 mg tablets. Dissolve in a small amount of distilled water, then add sufficient distilled water to make a final volume of 50 mL. Adjust the pH to 8 with sodium hydroxide. It is stable for 42 days at room temperature.

Nahata MC and Hipple TF, *Pediatric Drug Formulations*, Harvey Whitney Books Company, 1992.

Folic Acid, Cyanocobalamin, and Pyridoxine
(FOE lik AS id, sye an oh koe BAL a min, & peer i DOKS een)

U.S. Brand Names AllanFol RX; Folbee; Folgard® [OTC]; Folgard RX 2.2® [DSC]; Foltx®; Tricardio B

Index Terms Cyanocobalamin, Folic Acid, and Pyridoxine; Folacin, Vitamin B_{12}, and Vitamin B_6; Pyridoxine, Folic Acid, and Cyanocobalamin

Pharmacologic Category Vitamin

Use Nutritional supplement in end-stage renal failure, dialysis, hyperhomocysteinemia, homocystinuria, malabsorption syndromes, dietary deficiencies

Dosage Oral: Adults: 1 tablet daily

Additional Information Complete prescribing information for this medication should be consulted for additional detail.

Dosage Forms [DSC] = Discontinued product
Tablet: Folic acid 0.8 mg, cyanocobalamin 1000 mcg, and pyridoxine hydrochloride 50 mg
AllanFol RX: Folic acid 2.2 mg, cyanocobalamin 1000 mcg, and pyridoxine hydrochloride 25 mg
Folbee: Folic acid 2.5 mg, cyanocobalamin 1000 mcg, and pyridoxine hydrochloride 25 mg [dye free, lactose free, and sugar free]
Folgard®: Folic acid 0.8 mg, cyanocobalamin 115 mcg, and pyridoxine hydrochloride 10 mg
Folgard RX 2.2®: Folic acid 2.2 mg, cyanocobalamin 500 mcg, and pyridoxine hydrochloride 25 mg [DSC]
Foltx®: Folic acid 2.5 mg, cyanocobalamin 2000 mcg, and pyridoxine hydrochloride 25 mg
Tricardio B: Folic acid 0.4 mg, cyanocobalamin 250 mcg, and pyridoxine hydrochloride 25 mg

♦ **Folinic Acid** *see* Leucovorin *on page 990*
♦ **Follicle-Stimulating Hormone, Human** *see* Urofollitropin *on page 1759*
♦ **Follicle Stimulating Hormone, Recombinant** *see* Follitropin Alfa *on page 751*
♦ **Follicle Stimulating Hormone, Recombinant** *see* Follitropin Beta *on page 753*
♦ **Follistim® AQ** *see* Follitropin Beta *on page 753*
♦ **Follistim® AQ Cartridge** *see* Follitropin Beta *on page 753*

Follitropin Alfa (foe li TRO pin AL fa)

U.S. Brand Names Gonal-f®; Gonal-f® RFF
Canadian Brand Names Gonal-f®; Gonal-f® Pen
Index Terms Follicle Stimulating Hormone, Recombinant; FSH; rFSH-alpha; rhFSH-alpha
Pharmacologic Category Gonadotropin; Ovulation Stimulator
Use
Gonal-f®: Ovulation induction in patients in whom the cause of infertility is functional and not caused by primary ovarian failure; development of multiple follicles with Assisted Reproductive Technology (ART); spermatogenesis induction
Gonal-f® RFF: Ovulation induction in patients in whom the cause of infertility is functional and not caused by primary ovarian failure; development of multiple follicles with ART

Pregnancy Risk Factor X
Pregnancy Implications Ectopic pregnancy, congenital abnormalities, spontaneous abortion, and multiple births have been reported. The incidence of congenital abnormality may be slightly higher after ART than with spontaneous conception; higher incidence may be related to parenteral characteristics (maternal age, sperm characteristics).
Lactation Excretion in breast milk unknown/not recommended
Contraindications Hypersensitivity to follitropins or any component of the formulation; high levels of FSH indicating primary gonadal failure (ovarian or testicular); uncontrolled thyroid or adrenal dysfunction; tumor of the ovary, breast, uterus, hypothalamus, testis, or pituitary gland; abnormal vaginal bleeding of undetermined origin; ovarian cysts or enlargement not due to polycystic ovary syndrome; pregnancy
Warnings/Precautions These medications should only be used by physicians who are thoroughly familiar with infertility problems and their management. To minimize risks, use only at the lowest effective dose. Monitor ovarian response with serum estradiol and vaginal ultrasound on a regular basis.

Ovarian enlargement which may be accompanied by abdominal distention or abdominal pain, occurs in ~20% of those treated with urofollitropin and hCG, and generally regresses without treatment within 2-3 weeks. If ovaries are abnormally enlarged on the last day of treatment, withhold hCG to reduce the risk of ovarian hyperstimulation syndrome (OHSS). OHSS is reported in about 7% of patients; it is characterized by severe ovarian enlargement, abdominal pain/distention, nausea, vomiting, diarrhea, dyspnea, and oliguria, and may be accompanied by ascites, pleural effusion, hypovolemia, electrolyte imbalance, hemoperitoneum, and thromboembolic events. If hyperstimulation occurs, stop treatment and hospitalize patient. This syndrome develops rapidly within 24 hours to several days and generally occurs during the 7-10 days immediately following treatment. Hemoconcentration associated with fluid loss into the abdominal cavity has occurred and should be assessed by fluid intake & output, weight, hematocrit, serum & urinary electrolytes, urine specific gravity, BUN and creatinine, and abdominal girth. Determinations should be performed daily or more often if the need arises. Treatment is primarily symptomatic and consists of bed rest, fluid and electrolyte replacement and analgesics. The ascitic, pleural and pericardial fluids should not be removed unless needed to relieve symptoms of cardiopulmonary distress.

Serious pulmonary conditions (atelectasis, acute respiratory distress syndrome and exacerbation of asthma) have been reported. Thromboembolic events, both in association with and separate from ovarian hyperstimulation syndrome, have been reported.

Multiple births may result from the use of these medications, including triplet and quintuplet gestations. Advise patient of the potential risk of multiple births before starting the treatment.
Adverse Reactions Percentage may vary by indication, product formulation
>10%:
Central nervous system: Headache
Endocrine & metabolic: Ovarian cyst
Gastrointestinal: Abdomen enlarged, abdominal pain, nausea
Miscellaneous: Upper respiratory infection
1% to 10%:
Central nervous system: Dizziness, emotional lability, fever, malaise, migraine, pain
Dermatologic: Acne
Endocrine & metabolic: Breast pain, cervix lesion, hot flashes, intermenstrual bleeding, menstrual disorder, ovarian disorder, ovarian hyperstimulation
Gastrointestinal: Constipation, diarrhea, dyspepsia, flatulence, pelvic pain, stomatitis (ulcerative), toothache, vomiting, weight gain
Genitourinary: Cystitis, leukorrhea, micturition frequency, urinary tract infection, uterine hemorrhage, vaginal hemorrhage
Local: Injection site bruising, edema, inflammation, pain, reaction
Neuromuscular & skeletal: Back pain
Respiratory: Cough, flu-like symptoms, pharyngitis, rhinitis, sinusitis
Miscellaneous: Infection, moniliasis
Postmarketing, case reports, or events reported with gonadotropins: Adnexal torsion, anaphylactoid reactions, hemoperitoneum, hypersensitivity reactions, ovarian enlargement, pulmonary complications, vascular complications
Overdosage/Toxicology Aside from possible ovarian hyperstimulation and multiple gestations, little is known concerning the consequences of an acute overdose. Treatment is symptom-directed and supportive.
Stability
Gonal-f®: Store powder refrigerated or at room temperature of 2°C to 25°C (36°F to 77°F). Protect from light. Dissolve the contents of vial by slowly injecting provided diluent; do not shake. If bubbles appear, allow to settle prior to use. Final concentration: 600 int. units/mL. Following reconstitution, multidose vials may be stored under refrigeration or at room temperature for up to 28 days. Protect from light.
Gonal-f® RFF:
Powder: Store at room temperature or under refrigeration of 2°C to 25°C (36°F to 77°F). Protect from light. Dissolve contents of one or more vials using diluent provided in
(Continued)

Follitropin Alfa *(Continued)*

prefilled syringe. (Total concentration should not exceed 450 int. units/mL.) Slowly inject diluent into vial, and gently rotate vial until powder is dissolved; do not shake vial. If bubbles appear, allow to settle prior to use. Use immediately after reconstitution.

Solution: Prior to dispensing, store under refrigeration at 2°C to 8°C (36°F to 46°F). Upon dispensing, patient may store under refrigeration until product expiration date or at room temperature of 20°C to 25°C (68°F to 77°F) for up to 1 month. Do not freeze. Protect from light. After first use, discard unused portion after 28 days.

Mechanism of Action Follitropin alfa is a human FSH preparation of recombinant DNA origin. Follitropins stimulate ovarian follicular growth in women who do not have primary ovarian failure, and stimulate spermatogenesis in men with hypogonadotrophic hypogonadism. FSH is required for normal follicular growth, maturation, gonadal steroid production, and spermatogenesis.

Pharmacodynamics/Kinetics

Onset of action: Peak effect:

Spermatogenesis, median: 6.8-12.4 months (range 2.7-15.7 months)

Follicle development: Within cycle

Absorption: I.M., SubQ: Absorption rate is slower than the elimination rate

Distribution: Mean V_d: 10 L with *in vitro* fertilization/embryo transfer patients

Bioavailability: ~66% to 76% in healthy female volunteers

Half-life elimination:

I.M.:50 hours in healthy female volunteers

SubQ: 24 hours in healthy female volunteers; 32 hours with *in vitro* fertilization/embryo transfer patients; 32-41 hours in healthy male volunteers

Time to peak: In healthy volunteers:

Females: SubQ: 8-16 hours; I.M.: 25 hours

Males: SubQ: 11-20 hours

Excretion: Clearance: I.V.: 0.6 L/hour in healthy female volunteers

Dosage Adults: **Note:** Dose should be individualized. Use the lowest dose consistent with the expectation of good results. Over the course of treatment, doses may vary depending on individual patient response.

Gonal-f®, Gonal-f® RFF: Female:

Ovulation induction: SubQ: Initial: 75 int. units/day; incremental dose adjustments of up to 37.5 int. units may be considered after 14 days; further dose increases of the same magnitude can be made, if necessary, every 7 days (maximum dose: 300 int. units/day). If response to follitropin is appropriate, hCG is given 1 day following the last dose. Withhold hCG if serum estradiol is >2000 pg/mL, if the ovaries are abnormally enlarged, or if abdominal pain occurs. In general, therapy should not exceed 35 days.

ART: SubQ: Initiate therapy with follitropin alfa in the early follicular phase (cycle day 2 or day 3) at a dose of 150 int. units/day, until sufficient follicular development is attained. In most cases, therapy should not exceed 10 days. In patients ≥35 years whose endogenous gonadotropin levels are suppressed, initiate follitropin alfa at a dose of 225 int. units/day. Continue treatment until adequate follicular development is indicated as determined by ultrasound in combination with measurement of serum estradiol levels. Consider adjustments to dose after 5 days based on the patient's response; adjust subsequent dosage every 3-5 days by ≤75-150 int. units additionally at each adjustment. Doses >450 int. units/day are not recommended. Once adequate follicular development is evident, administer hCG to induce final follicular maturation in preparation for oocyte. Withhold hCG if the ovaries are abnormally enlarged.

Gonal-f®: Male: Spermatogenesis induction: SubQ: Therapy should begin with hCG pretreatment until serum testosterone is in normal range, then 150 int. units 3 times/week with hCG 3 times/week; continue with lowest dose needed to induce spermatogenesis (maximum dose: 300 int. units 3 times/week); may be given for up to 18 months

Administration Gonal-f®, Gonal-f® RFF: Administer SubQ. Contents of multidose vials should be administered using the calibrated syringes provided by the manufacturer. Do not shake solution; allow any bubbles to settle prior to administration.

Monitoring Parameters Monitor sufficient follicular maturation. This may be directly estimated by sonographic visualization of the ovaries and endometrial lining or measuring serum estradiol levels. The combination of both ultrasonography and measurement of estradiol levels is useful for monitoring for the growth and development of follicles and timing hCG administration.

The clinical evaluation of estrogenic activity (changes in vaginal cytology and changes in appearance and volume of cervical mucus) provides an indirect estimate of the estrogenic effect upon the target organs and, therefore, it should only be used adjunctively with more direct estimates of follicular development (ultrasonography and serum estradiol determinations).

The clinical confirmation of ovulation is obtained by direct and indirect indices of progesterone production. The indices most generally used are: rise in basal body temperature, increase in serum progesterone, and menstruation following the shift in basal body temperature.

Monitor for signs and symptoms of OHSS for at least 2 weeks following hCG administration.

Spermatogenesis: Monitor serum testosterone levels, sperm count

Additional Information The currently available recombinant follitropin products are structurally identical to native follicle-stimulating hormone. The "alpha" and "beta" nomenclature refers to their differences in purification and order of marketing. Follitropin alpha was marketed first, followed by follitropin beta. RFF for the Gonal-f® product signifies "revised formula female."

Dosage Forms

Injection, powder for reconstitution [rDNA origin]:

Gonal-f®: 450 int. units [contains sucrose 30 mg; packaged with diluent and calibrated syringes; diluent contains benzyl alcohol]

Gonal-f® RFF: 75 int. units [contains sucrose 30 mg; packaged with diluent in prefilled syringe]

Injection, solution [rDNA origin]:

Gonal-f® RFF: 300 int. units/0.5 mL (0.5 mL) [contains sucrose 60 mg/mL]; 450 int. units/0.75 mL (0.75 mL) [contains sucrose 60 mg/mL]; 900 int. units/1.5 mL (1.5 mL) [contains sucrose 60 mg/mL]

Follitropin Beta (foe li TRO pin BAY ta)

U.S. Brand Names Follistim® AQ; Follistim® AQ Cartridge

Canadian Brand Names Puregon®

Index Terms Follicle Stimulating Hormone, Recombinant; FSH; rFSH-beta; rhFSH-beta

Pharmacologic Category Gonadotropin; Ovulation Stimulator

Use Ovulation induction in patients in whom the cause of infertility is functional and not caused by primary ovarian failure; development of multiple follicles with Assisted Reproductive Technology (ART)

Pregnancy Risk Factor X

Pregnancy Implications Ectopic pregnancy, congenital abnormalities, and multiple births have been reported. The incidence of congenital abnormality may be slightly higher after ART than with spontaneous conception; higher incidence may be related to parenteral characteristics (maternal age, sperm characteristics).

Lactation Excretion in breast milk unknown/not recommended

Contraindications Hypersensitivity to follitropins or any component of the formulation; high levels of FSH indicating primary ovarian failure; uncontrolled thyroid or adrenal dysfunction; tumor of the ovary, breast, uterus, hypothalamus, or pituitary gland; abnormal vaginal bleeding of undetermined origin; ovarian cysts or enlargement not due to polycystic ovary syndrome; pregnancy

Warnings/Precautions These medications should only be used by physicians who are thoroughly familiar with infertility problems and their management. To minimize risks, use only at the lowest effective dose. Monitor ovarian response with serum estradiol and vaginal ultrasound on a regular basis.

Ovarian enlargement which may be accompanied by abdominal distention or abdominal pain, occurs in ~20% of those treated with urofollitropin and hCG, and generally regresses without treatment within 2-3 weeks. If ovaries are abnormally enlarged on the last day of treatment, withhold hCG to reduce the risk of ovarian hyperstimulation syndrome (OHSS). OHSS is reported in about 6% of patients; it is characterized by severe ovarian enlargement, abdominal pain/distention, nausea, vomiting, diarrhea, dyspnea, and oliguria, and may be accompanied by ascites, pleural effusion, hypovolemia, electrolyte imbalance, hemoperitoneum, and thromboembolic events. If hyperstimulation occurs, stop treatment and hospitalize patient. This syndrome develops rapidly within 24 hours to several days and generally occurs during the 7-10 days immediately following treatment. Hemoconcentration associated with fluid loss into the abdominal cavity has occurred and should be assessed by fluid intake & output, weight, hematocrit, serum & urinary electrolytes, urine specific gravity, BUN and creatinine, and abdominal girth. Determinations should be performed daily or more often if the need arises. Treatment is primarily symptomatic and consists of bed rest, fluid and electrolyte replacement and analgesics. The ascitic, pleural and pericardial fluids should not be removed unless needed to relieve symptoms of cardiopulmonary distress.

Serious pulmonary conditions (atelectasis, acute respiratory distress syndrome and exacerbation of asthma) have been reported. Thromboembolic events, both in association with and separate from ovarian hyperstimulation syndrome, have been reported.

Multiple births may result from the use of these medications, including triplet and quintuplet gestations. Advise patient of the potential risk of multiple births before starting the treatment.

Adverse Reactions Percentage may vary by indication, product formulation

>10%:

Endocrine & metabolic: Breast pain

Gastrointestinal: Abdominal pain, flatulence, nausea

Miscellaneous: Miscarriage

1% to 10%:

Central nervous system: Headache

Endocrine & metabolic: Ovarian hyperstimulation syndrome, ovarian pain

Gastrointestinal: Abdomen enlarged, constipation

Local: Injection site reaction

Neuromuscular & skeletal: Back pain

Respiratory: Sinusitis, upper respiratory tract infection

Postmarketing, case reports, or events reported with gonadotropins: Acute respiratory distress syndrome, adnexal torsion, arterial occlusions, atelectasis, breast tenderness, chills, dizziness, dry skin, dyspnea, erythema, febrile reaction, fever, flu-like syndrome, hair loss, cerebral vascular occlusion, hemoperitoneum, hives, joint pain, malaise, musculoskeletal ache, ovarian neoplasm, pulmonary embolism, rash, tachycardia, tachypnea

Overdosage/Toxicology Aside from possible ovarian hyperstimulation and multiple gestations, little is known concerning the consequences of an acute overdose. Treatment is symptom-directed and supportive.

Stability Prior to dispensing, store refrigerated at 2°C to 8°C (36°F to 46°F). After dispensed, may be stored under refrigeration or ≤25°C (77°F) for up to 3 months. Once cartridge is pierced, must be stored in refrigerator and used within 28 days. Do not freeze. Protect from light.

Mechanism of Action Follitropin beta is a human FSH preparation of recombinant DNA origin. Follitropins stimulate ovarian follicular growth in women who do not have primary ovarian failure. FSH is required for normal follicular growth, maturation, gonadal steroid production, and spermatogenesis.

Pharmacodynamics/Kinetics

Onset of action: Peak effect; Follicle development: Within cycle

(Continued)

Follitropin Beta *(Continued)*

Absorption: I.M.: 76%; SubQ: 78%

Distribution: 8 L

Half-life elimination: I.M.: 44 hours (single dose), 27-30 hours (multiple doses); SubQ: 33 hours (single dose)

Time to peak: SubQ: 13 hours

Dosage Adults: Female: **Note:** Dose should be individualized. Use the lowest dose consistent with the expectation of good results. Over the course of treatment, doses may vary depending on individual patient response.

Ovulation induction:

Follistim® AQ: I.M., SubQ: Stepwise approach: Initiate therapy with 75 int. units/day for up to 14 days. Increase by 37.5 int. units at weekly intervals until follicular growth or serum estradiol levels indicate an adequate response. The maximum (individualized) daily dose that has been safely used for ovulation induction in patients during clinical trials is 300 int. units. If response to follitropin is appropriate, hCG is given 1 day following the last dose. Withhold hCG if the ovaries are abnormally enlarged, or if abdominal pain occurs.

Follistim® AQ Cartridge: SubQ: Stepwise approach: Initiate therapy with 75 int. units/day for up to 7 days. Increase by 25 or 50 int. units at weekly intervals until follicular growth or serum estradiol levels indicate an adequate response. The maximum (individualized) daily dose that has been safely used for ovulation induction in patients during clinical trials is 175 int. units. If response to follitropin is appropriate, hCG is given 1 day following the last dose. Withhold hCG if the ovaries are abnormally enlarged, or if abdominal pain occurs. See **"Note"** for dosage adjustment for this product.

ART:

Follistim® AQ: I.M., SubQ: A starting dose of 150-225 int. units is recommended for at least the first 4 days of treatment. The dose may be adjusted for the individual patient based upon their ovarian response. The usual maintenance dose was 75-300 int. units for 6-12 days; 375-600 int. units in patients who were poor responders. The maximum daily dose used in clinical studies is 600 int. units. When a sufficient number of follicles of adequate size are present, the final maturation of the follicles is induced by administering hCG Oocyte retrieval is performed 34-36 hours later. Withhold hCG in cases where the ovaries are abnormally enlarged on the last day of follitropin beta therapy.

Follistim® AQ Cartridge: SubQ: A starting dose of 150-225 int. units is recommended for at least the first 5 days of treatment. The dose may be adjusted for the individual patient based upon their ovarian response. The maximum daily dose used in clinical studies is 450 int. units. When a sufficient number of follicles of adequate size are present, the final maturation of the follicles is induced by administering hCG. Oocyte retrieval is performed 34-36 hours later. Withhold hCG in cases where the ovaries are abnormally enlarged on the last day of follitropin beta therapy. See **"Note"** for dosage adjustment for this product.

Note: Dose adjustment for Follistim® AQ Cartridge: When administered using the Follistim Pen®, the Follistim® AQ Cartridge delivers 18% more follitropin beta when compared to dissolved lyophilized follitropin beta administered by a conventional syringe. If the above starting doses were previously used when administering a recombinant lyophilized gonadotropin product via a conventional syringe, lower starting and maintenance doses should be considered when switching to Follistim® AQ Cartridge. The following dose conversion may be used:

Follistim® AQ Dosing Conversion

Dose Administered Using Powder for Solution/Conventional Syringe	Follistim® AQ Dose Administered Using Follistim Pen®
75 int. units	50 int. units
150 int. units	125 int. units
225 int. units	175 int. units
300 int. units	250 int. units
375 int. units	300 int. units
450 int. units	375 int. units

Administration

Follistim® AQ: Administered by I.M. or SubQ injection

Follistim® AQ Cartridge: Follistim® AQ cartridge may be administered only by SubQ injection using the Follistim Pen® which can be set to deliver the appropriate dose.

Monitoring Parameters Monitor sufficient follicular maturation. This may be directly estimated by sonographic visualization of the ovaries and endometrial lining or measuring serum estradiol levels. The combination of both ultrasonography and measurement of estradiol levels is useful for monitoring for the growth and development of follicles and timing hCG administration.

The clinical evaluation of estrogenic activity (changes in vaginal cytology and changes in appearance and volume of cervical mucus) provides an indirect estimate of the estrogenic effect upon the target organs and, therefore, it should only be used adjunctively with more direct estimates of follicular development (ultrasonography and serum estradiol determinations).

The clinical confirmation of ovulation is obtained by direct and indirect indices of progesterone production. The indices most generally used are: rise in basal body temperature, increase in serum progesterone, and menstruation following the shift in basal body temperature.

Monitor for signs and symptoms of OHSS for at least 2 weeks following hCG administration.

Additional Information The currently available recombinant follitropin products are structurally identical to native follicle-stimulating hormone. The "alpha" and "beta" nomenclature refers to their differences in purification and order of marketing. Follitropin alpha was marketed first, followed by follitropin beta.

Dosage Forms

Injection, solution [rDNA origin]:

Follistim® AQ Cartridge:

175 int. units/0.21 mL (0.21 mL) [delivers 150 int. units; contains benzyl alcohol and sucrose; may contain trace amounts of neomycin or streptomycin]

350 int. units/0.42 mL (0.42 mL) [delivers 300 int. units; contains benzyl alcohol and sucrose; may contain trace amounts of neomycin or streptomycin]

650 int. units/0.78 mL (0.78 mL) [delivers 600 int. units; contains benzyl alcohol and sucrose; may contain trace amounts of neomycin or streptomycin]

975 int. units/1.17 mL (1.17 mL) [delivers 900 int. units; contains benzyl alcohol and sucrose; may contain trace amounts of neomycin or streptomycin]

Injection, solution [rDNA origin; single-dose]:

Follistim® AQ:

75 int. units/0.5 mL (0.5mL) [contains sucrose; may contain trace amounts of neomycin or streptomycin]

150 int. units/0.5 mL (0.5 mL) [contains sucrose; may contain trace amounts of neomycin or streptomycin]

♦ **Foltx®** see Folic Acid, Cyanocobalamin, and Pyridoxine *on page 750*

Fomepizole (foe ME pi zole)

U.S. Brand Names Antizol®
Index Terms 4-Methylpyrazole; 4-MP
Pharmacologic Category Antidote
Use *Orphan drug:* Treatment of methanol or ethylene glycol poisoning alone or in combination with hemodialysis
Unlabeled/Investigational Use Known or suspected propylene glycol toxicity
Pregnancy Risk Factor C
Pregnancy Implications Reproduction studies have not been conducted; use in pregnant women only if the benefits clearly outweigh the risks.
Lactation Excretion in breast milk unknown/not recommended
Contraindications Documented serious hypersensitivity reaction to fomepizole or other pyrazoles; hypersensitivity to any component of the formulation
Warnings/Precautions Should not be given undiluted or by bolus injection; fomepizole is metabolized in the liver and excreted in the urine, use caution with hepatic or renal impairment; hemodialysis should be used in patients with renal failure, significant or worsening metabolic acidosis, or ethylene glycol/methanol levels ≥50 mg/dL; monitor and manage adverse events of intoxication (respiratory distress syndrome, visual disturbances, hypocalcemia); safety and efficacy in pediatric patients have not been established
Adverse Reactions

>10%:

Central nervous system: Headache (14%)

Gastrointestinal: Nausea (11%)

1% to 10% (≤3% unless otherwise noted):

Cardiovascular: Bradycardia, facial flush, hypotension, phlebosclerosis, shock, tachycardia

Central nervous system: Dizziness (6%), increased drowsiness (6%), agitation, anxiety, lightheadedness, seizure, vertigo

Dermatologic: Rash

Endocrine & metabolic: Increased liver function tests

Gastrointestinal: Bad/metallic taste (6%), abdominal pain, decreased appetite, diarrhea, heartburn, vomiting

Hematologic: Anemia, disseminated intravascular coagulation (DIC), eosinophilia, lymphangitis

Local: Application site reaction, inflammation at the injection site, pain during injection, phlebitis

Neuromuscular & skeletal: Backache

Ocular: Nystagmus, transient blurred vision, visual disturbances

Renal: Anuria

Respiratory: Abnormal smell, hiccups, pharyngitis

Miscellaneous: Multiorgan failure, speech disturbances

<1% (Limited to important or life-threatening): Mild allergic reactions (mild rash, eosinophilia)
Overdosage/Toxicology Nausea, dizziness, and vertigo were noted in healthy volunteers receiving 3-6 times the recommended dose. Dose-dependent CNS effects were short-lived in most subjects, but lasted up to 30 hours in one subject. Because fomepizole is dialyzable, dialysis may be useful in overdosage treatment.
Ethanol/Nutrition/Herb Interactions Ethanol: Ethanol decreases the rate of fomepizole elimination by ~50%; conversely, fomepizole decreases the rate of elimination of ethanol by ~40%.
Stability Prior to administration, dilute in at least 100 mL 0.9% sodium chloride or dextrose 5% water for injection; diluted solution is stable for at least 24 hours when stored refrigerated or at room temperature. Although, it is chemically and physically stable when diluted as recommended, sterile precautions should be observed because diluents generally do not contain preservatives.

After dilution, do not use beyond 24 hours. Fomepizole solidifies at temperatures <25°C (77°F). If the fomepizole solution has become solid in the vial, the solution should carefully be warmed by running the vial under warm water or by holding in the hand. Solidification does not affect the efficacy, safety, or stability of the drug.
Mechanism of Action Fomepizole competitively inhibits alcohol dehydrogenase, an enzyme which catalyzes the metabolism of ethanol, ethylene glycol, and methanol to their toxic metabolites. Ethylene glycol is metabolized to glycoaldehyde, then oxidized to glycolate, glyoxylate, and oxalate. Glycolate and oxalate are responsible for metabolic acidosis and (Continued)

Fomepizole *(Continued)*

renal damage. Methanol is metabolized to formaldehyde, then oxidized to formic acid. Formic acid is responsible for metabolic acidosis and visual disturbances.

Pharmacodynamics/Kinetics
Onset of effect: Peak effect: Maximum: 1.5-2 hours
Absorption: Oral: Readily absorbed
Distribution: V_d: 0.6-1.02 L/kg; rapidly into total body water
Protein binding: Negligible
Metabolism: Hepatic to 4-carboxypyrazole (80% to 85% of dose), 4-hydroxymethylpyrazole, and their N-glucuronide conjugates; following multiple doses, induces its own metabolism via CYP oxidases after 30-40 hours
Half-life elimination: Has not been calculated; varies with dose
Excretion: Urine (1% to 3.5% as unchanged drug and metabolites)

Dosage Adults: Ethylene glycol and methanol toxicity: I.V.: A loading dose of 15 mg/kg should be administered, followed by doses of 10 mg/kg every 12 hours for 4 doses, then 15 mg/kg every 12 hours thereafter until ethylene glycol levels have been reduced <20 mg/dL and patient is asymptomatic with normal pH

Dosage adjustment in renal impairment: Fomepizole and its metabolites are excreted in the urine; dialysis should be considered in addition to fomepizole in the case of renal failure, significant or worsening metabolic acidosis, or a measured ethylene glycol level of ≥50 mg/dL. Patients should be dialyzed to correct metabolic abnormalities and to lower the ethylene glycol level <50 mg/dL; fomepizole is dialyzable and the frequency of dosing should be increased to every 4 hours during hemodialysis
Fomepizole is dialyzable and the frequency of dosing should be increased to every 4 hours during hemodialysis
Dose at the beginning of hemodialysis:
If <6 hours since last fomepizole dose: Do not administer dose
If ≥6 hours since last fomepizole dose: Administer next scheduled dose
Dosing during hemodialysis: Dose every 4 hours
Dosing at the time hemodialysis is complete, based on time between last dose and the end of hemodialysis:
<1 hour: Do not administer dose at the end of hemodialysis
1-3 hours: Administer 1/2 of next scheduled dose
>3 hours: Administer next scheduled dose
Maintenance dose when off hemodialysis: Give next scheduled dose 12 hours from last dose administered.

Dosage adjustment in hepatic impairment: Fomepizole is metabolized in the liver; specific dosage adjustments have not been determined in patients with hepatic impairment

Administration The appropriate dose of fomepizole should be drawn from the vial with a syringe and injected into at least 100 mL of sterile 0.9% sodium chloride injection or dextrose 5% injection. All doses should be administered as a slow intravenous infusion (IVPB) over 30 minutes.

Monitoring Parameters Fomepizole plasma levels should be monitored; response to fomepizole; monitor plasma/urinary ethylene glycol or methanol levels, urinary oxalate (ethylene glycol), plasma/urinary osmolality, renal/hepatic function, serum electrolytes, arterial blood gases; anion and osmolar gaps, resolution of clinical signs and symptoms of ethylene glycol or methanol intoxication

Reference Range
Fomepizole: Concentrations 100-300 µmol/L (8.2-24.6 mg/L) should result in enzyme inhibition of alcohol dehydrogenase
Ethylene glycol: Lethal dose is ~1.4 mL/kg
Methanol: Lethal dose is ~1-2 mL/kg

Additional Information Alternate therapies, including ethanol and hemodialysis, are difficult to use in children. Fomepizole's affinity for alcohol dehydrogenase is 8000 times greater than ethanol.

Dosage Forms Injection, solution [preservative free]: 1 g/mL (1.5 mL)

Fomivirsen *(foe MI vir sen)*

U.S. Brand Names Vitravene™ [DSC]
Canadian Brand Names Vitravene™
Index Terms Fomivirsen Sodium
Pharmacologic Category Antiviral Agent, Ophthalmic
Use Local treatment of cytomegalovirus (CMV) retinitis in patients with acquired immunodeficiency syndrome who are intolerant or insufficiently responsive to other treatments for CMV retinitis or when other treatments for CMV retinitis are contraindicated
Pregnancy Implications Studies have not been conducted in pregnant women. Should be used in pregnancy only when potential benefit to the mother outweighs the potential risk to the fetus.
Lactation Excretion in breast milk unknown/contraindicated
Contraindications Hypersensitivity to fomivirsen or any component
Warnings/Precautions For ophthalmic use via intravitreal injection only. Uveitis occurs frequently, particularly during induction dosing. Do not use in patients who have received intravenous or intravitreal cidofovir within 2-4 weeks (risk of exaggerated inflammation is increased). Patients should be monitored for CMV disease in the contralateral eye and/or extraocular disease. Commonly increases intraocular pressure - monitoring is recommended.
Adverse Reactions
5% to 10%:
Central nervous system: Fever, headache
Gastrointestinal: Abdominal pain, diarrhea, nausea, vomiting
Hematologic: Anemia
Neuromuscular & skeletal: Asthenia

Ocular: Uveitis, abnormal vision, anterior chamber inflammation, blurred vision, cataract, conjunctival hemorrhage, decreased visual acuity, loss of color vision, eye pain, increased intraocular pressure, photophobia, retinal detachment, retinal edema, retinal hemorrhage, retinal pigment changes, vitreitis

Respiratory: Pneumonia, sinusitis

Miscellaneous: Systemic CMV, sepsis, infection

2% to 5%:

Cardiovascular: Chest pain

Central nervous system: Confusion, depression, dizziness, neuropathy, pain

Endocrine & metabolic: Dehydration

Gastrointestinal: Abnormal LFTs, pancreatitis, anorexia, weight loss

Hematologic: Thrombocytopenia, lymphoma

Neuromuscular & skeletal: Back pain, cachexia

Ocular: Application site reaction, conjunctival hyperemia, conjunctivitis, corneal edema, decreased peripheral vision, eye irritation, keratic precipitates, optic neuritis, photopsia, retinal vascular disease, visual field defect, vitreous hemorrhage, vitreous opacity

Renal: Kidney failure

Respiratory: Bronchitis, dyspnea, cough

Miscellaneous: Allergic reaction, flu-like syndrome, diaphoresis (increased)

Stability Store between 2°C to 25°C (35°F to 77°F). Protect from excessive heat or light.

Mechanism of Action Inhibits synthesis of viral protein by binding to mRNA which blocks replication of cytomegalovirus through an antisense mechanism

Pharmacodynamics/Kinetics Pharmacokinetic studies have not been conducted in humans. In animal models, the drug is cleared from the eye after 7-10 days. It is metabolized by sequential nucleotide removal, with a small amount of the radioactivity from a dose appearing in the urine.

Dosage Adults: Intravitreal injection: Induction: 330 mcg (0.05 mL) every other week for 2 doses, followed by maintenance dose of 330 mcg (0.05 mL) every 4 weeks

If progression occurs during maintenance, a repeat of the induction regimen may be attempted to establish resumed control. Unacceptable inflammation during therapy may be managed by temporary interruption, provided response has been established. Topical corticosteroids have been used to reduce inflammation.

Administration Administered by intravitreal injection following application of standard topical and/or local anesthetics and antibiotics.

Monitoring Parameters Immediately after injection, light perception and optic nerve head perfusion should be monitored. Anterior chamber paracentesis may be necessary if perfusion is not complete within 7-10 minutes after injection. Subsequent patient evaluation should include monitoring for contralateral CMV infection or extraocular CMV disease, and intraocular pressure prior to each injection.

Additional Information Because the mechanism of action of fomivirsen is different than other antiviral agents active against CMV, fomivirsen may be active against isolates resistant to ganciclovir, foscarnet, or cidofovir. The converse may also be true.

Dosage Forms [DSC] = Discontinued product

Injection, solution, intravitreal, as sodium: 6.6 mg/mL (0.25 mL) [DSC]

♦ **Fomivirsen Sodium** *see* Fomivirsen *on page 756*

Fondaparinux (fon da PARE i nuks)

U.S. Brand Names Arixtra®

Canadian Brand Names Arixtra®

Index Terms Fondaparinux Sodium

Pharmacologic Category Factor Xa Inhibitor

Additional Appendix Information

Anticoagulants, Injectable *on page 1864*

Use Prophylaxis of deep vein thrombosis (DVT) in patients undergoing surgery for hip replacement, knee replacement, hip fracture (including extended prophylaxis following hip fracture surgery), or abdominal surgery (in patients at risk for thromboembolic complications); treatment of acute pulmonary embolism (PE); treatment of acute DVT without PE

Unlabeled/Investigational Use Prophylaxis of DVT in patients with a history of heparin-induced thrombocytopenia (HIT)

Pregnancy Risk Factor B

Pregnancy Implications Reproductive animal studies have not shown fetal harm. Based on case reports, small amounts of fondaparinux have been detected in the umbilical cord following multiple doses during pregnancy. There are no adequate and well-controlled studies in pregnant women; use only if clearly needed.

Lactation Excretion in breast milk unknown/use caution

Contraindications Hypersensitivity to fondaparinux or any component of the formulation; severe renal impairment (Cl$_{cr}$ <30 mL/minute); body weight <50 kg (prophylaxis); active major bleeding; bacterial endocarditis; thrombocytopenia associated with a positive *in vitro* test for antiplatelet antibody in the presence of fondaparinux

Warnings/Precautions [U.S. Boxed Warning]: Patients with recent or anticipated neuraxial anesthesia (epidural or spinal anesthesia) are at risk of spinal or epidural hematoma and subsequent paralysis. Not to be used interchangeably (unit-for-unit) with heparin, low molecular weight heparins (LMWHs), or heparinoids. Use caution in patients with moderate renal dysfunction (Cl$_{cr}$ 30-50 mL/minute). Discontinue if severe dysfunction or labile function develops.

Use caution in congenital or acquired bleeding disorders; active ulcerative or angiodysplastic gastrointestinal disease; hemorrhagic stroke; shortly after brain, spinal, or ophthalmologic surgery; or in patients taking platelet inhibitors. Risk of major bleeding may be increased if initial dose is administered earlier then recommended (initiation recommended at 6-8 hours following surgery). Discontinue agents that may enhance the risk of hemorrhage if possible. If thrombocytopenia occurs discontinue fondaparinux. Use caution in the elderly, patients with a
(Continued)

Fondaparinux *(Continued)*

history of heparin-induced thrombocytopenia, patients with a bleeding diathesis, uncontrolled hypertension, recent gastrointestinal ulceration, diabetic retinopathy, and hemorrhage. Use caution in patients <50 kg who are being treated for DVT/PE. Safety and efficacy in pediatric patients have not been established.

Adverse Reactions As with all anticoagulants, bleeding is the major adverse effect. Hemorrhage may occur at any site. Risk appears increased by a number of factors including renal dysfunction, age (>75 years), and weight (<50 kg).

>10%:
    Central nervous system: Fever (4% to 14%)
    Gastrointestinal: Nausea (11%)
    Hematologic: Anemia (20%)
1% to 10%:
    Cardiovascular: Edema (9%), hypotension (4%), confusion (3%)
    Central nervous system: Insomnia (5%), dizziness (4%), headache (2% to 5%), pain (2%)
    Dermatologic: Rash (8%), purpura (4%), bullous eruption (3%)
    Endocrine & metabolic: Hypokalemia (1% to 4%)
    Gastrointestinal: Constipation (5% to 9%), vomiting (6%), diarrhea (3%), dyspepsia (2%)
    Genitourinary: Urinary tract infection (4%), urinary retention (3%)
    Hematologic: Moderate thrombocytopenia (50,000-100,000/mm³: 3%), major bleeding (1% to 3%), minor bleeding (2% to 4%), hematoma (3%); risk of major bleeding increased as high as 5% in patients receiving initial dose <6 hours following surgery
    Hepatic: SGOT increased (2%), SGPT increased (3%)
    Local: Injection site reaction (bleeding, rash, pruritus)
    Miscellaneous: Wound drainage increased (5%)
<1% (Limited to important or life-threatening): Hepatic enzymes increased, severe thrombocytopenia (<50,000/mm³)

Overdosage/Toxicology Treatment is symptom-directed and supportive. Hemodialysis may increase clearance by 20%.

Drug Interactions
Increased Effect/Toxicity: Anticoagulants, antiplatelet agents, drotrecogin alfa, NSAIDs, salicylates, and thrombolytic agents may enhance the anticoagulant effect and/or increase the risk of bleeding.

Ethanol/Nutrition/Herb Interactions Herb/Nutraceutical: Avoid alfalfa, anise, bilberry, bladderwrack, bromelain, cat's claw, celery, coleus, cordyceps, dong quai, evening primrose oil, fenugreek, feverfew, garlic, ginger, ginkgo biloba, ginseng (American/Panax/Siberian), grape seed, green tea, guggul, horse chestnut seed, horseradish, licorice, prickly ash, red clover, reishi, sweet clover, turmeric, white willow (all possess anticoagulant or antiplatelet activity and as such, may enhance the anticoagulant effects of fondaparinux).

Stability Store at 15°C to 30°C (59°F to 86°F).

Mechanism of Action Fondaparinux is a synthetic pentasaccharide that causes an antithrombin III-mediated selective inhibition of factor Xa. Neutralization of factor Xa interrupts the blood coagulation cascade and inhibits thrombin formation and thrombus development.

Pharmacodynamics/Kinetics
Absorption: Rapid and complete
Distribution: V_d: 7-11 L; mainly in blood
Protein binding: ≥94% to antithrombin III
Bioavailability: 100%
Half-life elimination: 17-21 hours; prolonged with worsening renal impairment
Time to peak: 2-3 hours
Excretion: Urine (as unchanged drug); decreased clearance in patients <50 kg

Dosage SubQ: Adults:
DVT prophylaxis: Adults ≥50 kg: 2.5 mg once daily. **Note:** Initiate dose after hemostasis has been established, 6-8 hours postoperatively.
DVT prophylaxis with history of HIT (unlabeled use): 2.5 mg once daily
    Usual duration: 5-9 days (up to 10 days following abdominal surgery or up to 11 days following hip replacement or knee replacement)
    Extended prophylaxis is recommended following hip fracture surgery (has been tolerated for up to 32 days).
Acute DVT/PE treatment: **Note:** Concomitant treatment with warfarin sodium should be initiated as soon as possible, usually within 72 hours:
    <50 kg: 5 mg once daily
    50-100 kg: 7.5 mg once daily
    >100 kg: 10 mg once daily
    Usual duration: 5-9 days (has been administered up to 26 days)
Dosage adjustment in renal impairment:
    Cl$_{cr}$ 30-50 mL/minute: Use caution
    Cl$_{cr}$ <30 mL/minute: Contraindicated

Administration Do not administer I.M.; for SubQ administration only. Do not mix with other injections or infusions. Do not expel air bubble from syringe before injection. Administer according to recommended regimen; early initiation (before 6 hours after surgery) has been associated with increased bleeding.

Monitoring Parameters Periodic monitoring of CBC, serum creatinine, occult blood testing of stools recommended. Antifactor Xa activity of fondaparinux can be measured by the assay if fondaparinux is used as the calibrator. PT and aPTT are insensitive measures of fondaparinux activity.

Test Interactions International standards of heparin or LMWH are not the appropriate calibrators for antifactor Xa activity of fondaparinux.

Dosage Forms Injection, solution, as sodium [preservative free]: 2.5 mg/0.5 mL (0.5 mL); 5 mg/0.4 mL (0.4 mL); 7.5 mg/0.6 mL (0.6 mL); 10 mg/0.8 mL (0.8 mL) [prefilled syringe]

♦ **Fondaparinux Sodium** *see* Fondaparinux *on page 757*
♦ **Foradil® (Can)** *see* Formoterol *on page 759*
♦ **Foradil® Aerolizer™** *see* Formoterol *on page 759*

Formoterol (for MOH te rol)

U.S. Brand Names Foradil® Aerolizer™
Canadian Brand Names Foradil®; Oxeze® Turbuhaler®
Index Terms Formoterol Fumarate
Pharmacologic Category Beta₂-Adrenergic Agonist

Additional Appendix Information
Bronchodilators *on page 1877*

Use Maintenance treatment of asthma and prevention of bronchospasm in patients ≥5 years of age with reversible obstructive airway disease, including patients with symptoms of nocturnal asthma, who require regular treatment with inhaled, short-acting beta₂-agonists; maintenance treatment of bronchoconstriction in patients with COPD; prevention of exercise-induced bronchospasm in patients ≥5 years of age

Note: Oxeze® is also approved in Canada for acute relief of symptoms ("on demand" treatment) in patients ≥6 years of age.

Restrictions An FDA-approved medication guide must be distributed when dispensing an outpatient prescription (new or refill) where this medication is to be used without direct supervision of a healthcare provider. Medication guides are available at http://www.fda.gov/cder/Offices/ODS/medication_guides.htm.

Pregnancy Risk Factor C

Pregnancy Implications When given orally to rats throughout organogenesis, formoterol caused delayed ossification and decreased fetal weight, but no malformations. There were no adverse events when given to pregnant rats in late pregnancy. Doses used were ≥70 times the recommended daily inhalation dose in humans. There are no adequate and well-controlled studies in pregnant women. Use only if benefit outweighs risk to the fetus. Beta agonists interfere with uterine contractility so use during labor only if benefit outweighs risk to the fetus.

Lactation Excretion in breast milk unknown/use caution

Medication Safety Issues
Sound-alike/look-alike issues:
Foradil® may be confused with Toradol®
Foradil® capsules for inhalation are for administration via Aerolizer™ inhaler and are not for oral use.

International issues:
Foradil® may be confused with Theradol® which is a brand name for tramadol in the Netherlands

Contraindications Hypersensitivity to adrenergic amines, formoterol, or any component of the formulation

Note: The approved U.S. labeling lists the need for acute bronchodilation as a contraindication; however, a formulation (Oxeze®) is approved for acute treatment in other countries (ie, Canada).

Warnings/Precautions [U.S. Boxed Warning]: Long-acting beta₂-agonists may increase the risk of asthma-related deaths. Formoterol should only be used as adjuvant therapy in patients not adequately controlled on other asthma medications (eg, low-to-medium dose inhaled corticosteroids) or whose disease warrants initiation of two maintenance therapies. Optimize anti-inflammatory treatment before initiating maintenance treatment with formoterol. Do not use as a component of chronic therapy without an anti-inflammatory agent. Corticosteroids should not be stopped or reduced at formoterol initiation. Patients using inhaled, short acting beta₂-agonists should be instructed to discontinue routine use of these medications prior to beginning treatment; short-acting agents should be reserved for symptomatic relief of acute symptoms. Patient must be instructed to seek medical attention in cases where acute symptoms are not relieved by rapid-onset beta-agonist or when a previous level of response is diminished. Treatment must not be delayed. Rarely, paradoxical bronchospasm may occur with use of inhaled bronchodilating agents; this should be distinguished from inadequate response.

Acute episodes should be treated with rapid-onset beta₂ agonist. The approved U.S. labeling states that formoterol is not meant to relieve acute asthmatic symptoms. Although, a formulation of formoterol (Oxeze®) is approved for acute treatment outside the U.S. (eg, Canada).

Immediate hypersensitivity reactions (urticaria, angioedema, rash, bronchospasm) have been reported. Do not exceed recommended dose; serious adverse events (including serious asthma exacerbations and fatalities) have been associated with excessive use of inhaled sympathomimetics. Beta₂-agonists may increase risk of arrhythmias, decrease serum potassium, prolong QT$_c$ interval, or increase serum glucose. These effects may be exacerbated in hypoxemia. Use caution in patients with cardiovascular disease (arrhythmia or hypertension or CHF), seizures, diabetes, glaucoma, hyperthyroidism, or hypokalemia. Beta agonists may cause elevation in blood pressure and heart rate, and result in CNS stimulation/excitation. Powder for oral inhalation contains lactose; very rare anaphylactic reactions have been reported in patients with severe milk protein allergy. Safety and efficacy have not been established in children <5 years of age.

Adverse Reactions
>10%: Miscellaneous: Viral infection (17%)
1% to 10%:
Cardiovascular: Chest pain (2%)
Central nervous system: Anxiety (2%), dizziness (2%), fever (2%), insomnia (2%), dysphonia (1%)
Dermatologic: Rash (1%)
Gastrointestinal: Abdominal pain, dyspepsia, gastroenteritis, nausea, xerostomia (1%)
Respiratory: Asthma exacerbation (age 5-12 years: 5% to 6%; age >12 years: <4%), bronchitis (5%), infection (3% to 7%), pharyngitis (4%), sinusitis (3%), dyspnea (2%), tonsillitis (1%)
(Continued)

Formoterol *(Continued)*

<1% (Limited to important or life-threatening): Anaphylactic reactions (severe hypotension/angioedema), angina, arrhythmia, hyperglycemia, hypertension, hypokalemia, metabolic acidosis

Overdosage/Toxicology Symptoms of overdose include tachycardia, tremor, hypertension, angina, and seizures. Hypokalemia also may occur. Cardiac arrest and death may be associated with abuse of beta-agonist bronchodilators. Treatment includes immediate discontinuation and symptomatic and supportive therapies. Cautious use of beta-adrenergic blocking agents may be considered in severe cases.

Drug Interactions
  Cytochrome P450 Effect: Substrate (minor) of CYP2A6, 2C9, 2C19, 2D6
  Increased Effect/Toxicity: Sympathomimetics may enhance the adverse/toxic effects of formoterol. Atomoxetine may increase the tachycardia of formoterol.
  Decreased Effect: Formoterol may decrease the bradycardic effect of beta-blockers (beta₁ selective). Beta-blockers (nonselective) may decrease the bronchodilatory effect of beta₂-agonists.

Stability Prior to dispensing, store in refrigerator at 2°C to 8°C (36°F to 46°F). After dispensing, store at room temperature at 20°C to 25°C (68°F to 77°F). Protect from heat and moisture. Capsules should always be stored in the blister and only removed immediately before use. Always check expiration date. Use within 4 months of purchase date or product expiration date, whichever comes first.

Mechanism of Action Relaxes bronchial smooth muscle by selective action on beta₂ receptors with little effect on heart rate. Formoterol has a long-acting effect.

Pharmacodynamics/Kinetics
  Onset: Within 3 minutes
    Peak effect: 80% of peak effect within 15 minutes
  Duration: Improvement in FEV_1 observed for 12 hours in most patients
  Absorption: Rapidly into plasma
  Protein binding: 61% to 64% *in vitro* at higher concentrations than achieved with usual dosing
  Metabolism: Hepatic via direct glucuronidation and O-demethylation; CYP2D6, CYP2C8/9, CYP2C19, CYP2A6 involved in O-demethylation
  Half-life elimination: ~10-14 hours
  Time to peak: Maximum improvement in FEV_1 in 1-3 hours
  Excretion:
    Children 5-12 years: Urine (7% to 9% as direct glucuronide metabolites, 6% as unchanged drug)
    Adults: Urine (15% to 18% as direct glucuronide metabolites, 10% as unchanged drug)

Dosage
  Asthma maintenance treatment: Children ≥5 years and Adults: Inhalation: 12 mcg capsule every 12 hours
    Oxeze® (CAN): **Note:** Not labeled for use in the U.S.: Children ≥6 years and Adults: Inhalation: 6 mcg or 12 mcg every 12 hours. Maximum dose: Children: 24 mcg/day; Adults: 48 mcg/day
  Prevention of exercise-induced bronchospasm: Children ≥5 years and Adults: Inhalation: 12 mcg capsule at least 15 minutes before exercise on an "as needed" basis; additional doses should not be used for another 12 hours. **Note:** If already using for asthma maintenance then should not use additional doses for exercise-induced bronchospasm.
    Oxeze® (CAN): **Note:** Not labeled for use in the U.S.: Children ≥6 years and Adults: Inhalation: 6 mcg or 12 mcg at least 15 minutes before exercise.
  COPD maintenance treatment: Adults: Inhalation: 12 mcg capsule every 12 hours

  Additional indication for Oxeze® (approved in Canada): Acute ("on demand") relief of bronchoconstriction: Children ≥12 years and Adults: 6 mcg or 12 mcg as a single dose (maximum dose: 72 mcg in any 24-hour period). The prolonged use of high dosages (48 mcg/day for ≥3 consecutive days) may be a sign of suboptimal control, and should prompt the re-evaluation of therapy.

Administration Remove capsule from foil blister **immediately** before use. Place capsule in the capsule-chamber in the base of the Aerolizer™ Inhaler. Must only use the Aerolizer™ Inhaler. Press both buttons **once only** and then release. Keep inhaler in a level, horizontal position. Exhale fully. Do not exhale into inhaler. Tilt head slightly back and inhale (rapidly, steadily, and deeply). Hold breath as long as possible. If any powder remains in capsule, exhale and inhale again. Repeat until capsule is empty. Throw away empty capsule; do not leave in inhaler. Do not use a spacer with the Aerolizer™ Inhaler. Always keep capsules and inhaler dry.

Monitoring Parameters FEV_1, peak flow, and/or other pulmonary function tests; blood pressure, heart rate; CNS stimulation; serum glucose, serum potassium

Dosage Forms [CAN] = Canadian brand name
  Powder for oral inhalation, as fumarate:
    Foradil® Aerolizer™ [capsule]: 12 mcg (12s, 60s) [contains lactose 25 mg]
    Oxeze® Turbuhaler® [CAN]: 6 mcg/inhalation [delivers 60 metered doses; contains lactose 600 mcg/dose]; 12 mcg/inhalation [delivers 60 metered doses; contains lactose 600 mcg/dose] [not available in the U.S.]

◆ **Formoterol Fumarate** *see* Formoterol *on page 759*
◆ **Formoterol Fumarate Dehydrate and Budesonide** *see* Budesonide and Formoterol *on page 247*
◆ **Formulation R™ [OTC]** *see* Phenylephrine *on page 1358*
◆ **Formulex® (Can)** *see* Dicyclomine *on page 496*
◆ **5-Formyl Tetrahydrofolate** *see* Leucovorin *on page 990*
◆ **Fortamet®** *see* Metformin *on page 1098*
◆ **Fortaz®** *see* Ceftazidime *on page 320*
◆ **Forteo™** *see* Teriparatide *on page 1652*
◆ **Fortical®** *see* Calcitonin *on page 264*

♦ **Fortovase®** [DSC] *see* Saquinavir *on page 1546*
♦ **Fortovase®** (Can) *see* Saquinavir *on page 1546*
♦ **Fosamax®** *see* Alendronate *on page 65*
♦ **Fosamax Plus D™** *see* Alendronate and Cholecalciferol *on page 67*

Fosamprenavir (FOS am pren a veer)

U.S. Brand Names Lexiva®
Canadian Brand Names Telzir®
Index Terms Fosamprenavir Calcium; GW433908G
Pharmacologic Category Antiretroviral Agent, Protease Inhibitor
Additional Appendix Information
Antiretroviral Therapy for HIV Infection: Adults and Adolescents *on page 1988*
Management of Healthcare Worker Exposures to HBV, HCV, and HIV *on page 1941*
Use Treatment of HIV infections in combination with at least two other antiretroviral agents
Pregnancy Risk Factor C
Pregnancy Implications It is not known if amprenavir crosses the human placenta. There are no adequate and well-controlled studies in pregnant women. Pregnancy and protease inhibitors are both associated with an increased risk of hyperglycemia. Glucose levels should be closely monitored. Health professionals are encouraged to contact the antiretroviral pregnancy registry to monitor outcomes of pregnant women exposed to antiretroviral medications (1-800-258-4263 or www.APRegistry.com).
Lactation Excretion in breast milk unknown/contraindicated
Medication Safety Issues
Sound-alike/look-alike issues:
Lexiva® may be confused with Levitra®
Contraindications Hypersensitivity to fosamprenavir, amprenavir, or any component of the formulation; concurrent therapy with cisapride, ergot derivatives, midazolam, pimozide, and triazolam; flecainide and propafenone contraindicated with concomitant ritonavir therapy
Warnings/Precautions Use with caution in patients taking strong CYP3A4 inhibitors, moderate or strong CYP3A4 inducers and major CYP3A4 substrates (see drug interactions); consider alternative agents that avoid or lessen the potential for CYP-mediated interactions.

Use with caution in patients with diabetes mellitus, sulfonamide allergy, or hemophilia. Use caution with hepatic impairment or underlying hepatitis B or C. Redistribution of fat may occur (eg, buffalo hump, peripheral wasting, cushingoid appearance). Dosage adjustment is required for combination therapies (ritonavir and/or efavirenz); in addition, the risk of hyperlipidemia may be increased during concurrent therapy. Stevens-Johnson reactions have occurred; discontinue therapy in severe or dermatologic reactions or when a moderate rash is accompanied by systemic symptoms. Immune reconstitution syndrome may develop resulting in the occurrence of an inflammatory response to an indolent or residual opportunistic infection; further evaluation and treatment may be necessary. Safety and efficacy in children have not been established.

Adverse Reactions Incidence data is compiled from use of fosamprenavir with and without concurrent ritonavir in combination with other antiretrovirals.
>10%:
Central nervous system: Headache (19% to 27%), fatigue (9% to 18%), depression (8% to 11%)
Dermatologic: Rash (17% to 35%; moderate to severe reactions 3% to 8%)
Gastrointestinal: Diarrhea (34% to 52%), nausea (20% to 39%), vomiting (10% to 20%), abdominal pain (5% to 11%)
1% to 10%:
Central nervous system: Oral paresthesia (<1% to 10%)
Dermatologic: Pruritus (7% to 8%)
Endocrine & metabolic: Hypertriglyceridemia (up to 11%), serum lipase increased (5% to 8%), hyperglycemia (<1% to 2%)
Hematologic: Neutropenia (3%)
Hepatic: Transaminases increased (4% to 8%)
<1% (Limited to important or life-threatening): Fat redistribution, immune reconstitution syndrome, Stevens-Johnson syndrome
Overdosage/Toxicology Treatment is symptom-directed and supportive. Benefit of dialysis is unknown.
Drug Interactions
Cytochrome P450 Effect: As amprenavir: **Substrate** of CYP2C9 (minor), 3A4 (major); **Inhibits** CYP2C19 (weak), 3A4 (strong)
Increased Effect/Toxicity: Concurrent use of cisapride, midazolam, pimozide, quinidine, or triazolam is contraindicated. Concurrent use of ergot alkaloids (dihydroergotamine, ergotamine, ergonovine, methylergonovine) with amprenavir is also contraindicated (may cause vasospasm and peripheral ischemia). Concurrent use of oral solution with disulfiram or metronidazole is contraindicated, due to the risk of propylene glycol toxicity.

Serum concentrations of orally-inhaled corticosteroids, trazodone, and some antiarrhythmics (eg, amiodarone, bepridil, lidocaine, and quinidine) may be increased, potentially leading to toxicity; when amprenavir is coadministered with ritonavir, flecainide and propafenone are contraindicated. HMG-CoA reductase inhibitors serum concentrations may be increased by amprenavir, increasing the risk of myopathy/rhabdomyolysis; lovastatin and simvastatin are not recommended; fluvastatin and pravastatin may be safer alternatives.

Amprenavir may increase the levels/effects of selected benzodiazepines (midazolam and triazolam are contraindicated), calcium channel blockers, cyclosporine, eplerenone, fentanyl, mirtazapine, nateglinide, nefazodone, quinidine, sildenafil (and other PDE-5 inhibitors), tacrolimus, venlafaxine, and other CYP3A4 substrates. When used with strong CYP3A4 inhibitors, dosage adjustment/limits are recommended for sildenafil and other PDE-5 inhibitors; refer to individual monographs.
(Continued)

Fosamprenavir *(Continued)*

Concurrent therapy with ritonavir may result in increased serum concentrations: dosage adjustment is recommended. Clarithromycin, indinavir, nelfinavir may increase serum concentrations of amprenavir.

Decreased Effect: CYP3A4 inducers may decrease the levels/effects of amprenavir; example inducers include aminoglutethimide, carbamazepine, nafcillin, nevirapine, phenobarbital, phenytoin, and rifamycins. Serum concentrations of estrogen (oral contraceptives) may be decreased, use alternative (nonhormonal) forms of contraception. Serum concentrations of delavirdine may be decreased by amprenavir; may lead to loss of virologic response and possible resistance; concomitant use of amprenavir with delavirdine is not recommended. Efavirenz and nevirapine may decrease serum concentrations of amprenavir (dosing for combinations not established). Avoid St John's wort (may lead to subtherapeutic concentrations of amprenavir). Effect of amprenavir may be diminished when administered with methadone (consider alternative antiretroviral); in addition, effect of methadone may be reduced (dosage increase may be required). Antacids and H_2-blockers may impair absorption of fosamprenavir, leading to reduced serum levels of amprenavir; separate doses.

Ethanol/Nutrition/Herb Interactions Herb/Nutraceutical: Amprenavir serum concentration may be decreased by St John's wort; avoid concurrent use.

Stability Store at 15°C to 30°C (59°F to 86°F).

Mechanism of Action Fosamprenavir is rapidly and almost completely converted to amprenavir by cellular phosphatases *in vivo*. Amprenavir binds to the active site of HIV protease activity and inhibits cleavage of viral polyprotein precursors (eg, Gag and Gag-Pol) into individual functional proteins found in infectious HIV. Inhibition prevents cleavage of these polyproteins, resulting in the formation of immature, noninfectious viral particles.

Pharmacodynamics/Kinetics
Absorption: 63%
Bioavailability: Not established; food does not have a significant effect on absorption
Protein-binding: 90%
Half-Life elimination: 7.7 hours (amprenavir)
Time to peak, plasma: 1.5-4 hours (median: 2.5 hours)
Metabolism: Fosamprenavir is rapidly and almost completely converted to amprenavir by cellular phosphatases in gut epithelium; amprenavir is hepatically metabolized via CYP isoenzymes (primarily CYP3A4)
Excretion: Feces (75%); urine (14% as metabolites; <1% as unchanged drug)

Dosage Oral: Adults: HIV infection:
Antiretroviral therapy-naive patients:
Unboosted regimen: 1400 mg twice daily (without ritonavir)
Ritonavir-boosted regimens:
Once-daily regimen: Fosamprenavir 1400 mg plus ritonavir 200 mg once daily
Twice-daily regimen: Fosamprenavir 700 mg plus ritonavir 100 mg twice daily
Protease inhibitor-experienced patients: Fosamprenavir 700 mg plus ritonavir 100 mg twice daily. **Note:** Once-daily administration is not recommended in protease inhibitor-experienced patients.
Combination therapy with efavirenz (ritonavir-boosted regimen):
Once-daily regimen: Fosamprenavir 1400 mg daily plus ritonavir 300 mg once daily
Twice-daily regimen: No dosage adjustment recommended for twice-daily regimen
Combination therapy with nevirapine (ritonavir-boosted regimen): Fosamprenavir 700 mg plus ritonavir 100 mg twice daily

Dosage adjustment in renal impairment: No dosage adjustment required.
Dosage adjustment in hepatic impairment: Note: No recommendations are available for dosage adjustment in patients with any degree of liver impairment receiving ritonavir and fosamprenavir.
Mild-to-moderate impairment (Child-Pugh score 5-8): Reduce dosage of fosamprenavir to 700 mg twice daily (without concurrent ritonavir)
Severe impairment: Use is not recommended

Dietary Considerations May be taken with or without food.

Dosage Forms [CAN] = Canadian brand name
Tablet, as calcium:
Lexiva®: 700 mg
Suspension, oral, as calcium:
Telzir® [CAN]: 50 mg/mL (225 mL) [not available in the U.S.]

♦ **Fosamprenavir Calcium** *see Fosamprenavir on page 761*

♦ **Fosavance (Can)** *see Alendronate and Cholecalciferol on page 67*

Foscarnet *(fos KAR net)*

U.S. Brand Names Foscavir®
Canadian Brand Names Foscavir®
Index Terms PFA; Phosphonoformate; Phosphonoformic Acid
Pharmacologic Category Antiviral Agent
Additional Appendix Information
USPHS / IDSA Guidelines for the Prevention of Opportunistic Infections in Persons Infected With HIV *on page 1966*
Use
Treatment of mucotaneous herpes virus infections suspected to be caused by acyclovir-resistant (HSV, VZV) or ganciclovir-resistant (CMV) strains; this occurs almost exclusively in immunocompromised persons (eg, with advanced AIDS) who have received prolonged treatment for a herpes virus infection
Treatment of CMV retinitis in persons with AIDS
Unlabeled/Investigational Use Other CMV infections (eg, colitis, esophagitis, neurological disease)

Pregnancy Risk Factor C

Pregnancy Implications Associated with an increase in skeletal anomalies in animal studies. There are no adequate and well controlled studies in pregnant women. A single case report of use during the third trimester with normal infant outcome was observed. Monitoring of amniotic fluid volumes by ultrasound is recommended weekly after 20 weeks of gestation to detect oligohydramnios.

Lactation Excretion in breast milk unknown/contraindicated

Contraindications Hypersensitivity to foscarnet or any component of the formulation; Cl_{cr} <0.4 mL/minute/kg during therapy

Warnings/Precautions Hazardous agent - use appropriate precautions for handling and disposal. **[U.S. Boxed Warning]: Indicated only for immunocompromised patients with CMV retinitis and mucocutaneous acyclovir-resistant HSV infection. [U.S. Boxed Warning]: Renal impairment occurs to some degree in the majority of patients treated with foscarnet;** usually reversible within 1 week following dose adjustment or discontinuation of therapy. Renal function should be closely monitored. Adequate hydration may reduce the risk of nephrotoxicity; the manufacturer makes specific recommendations regarding this (see Administration).

Imbalance of serum electrolytes or minerals occurs in at least 15% of patients (hypocalcemia, low ionized calcium, hypophosphatemia, hypomagnesemia, or hypokalemia). Correct electrolytes before initiating therapy. Use caution when administering other medications that cause electrolyte imbalances. Patients who experience signs or symptoms of an electrolyte imbalance should be assessed immediately. **[U.S. Boxed Warning]: Seizures related to plasma electrolyte/mineral imbalance may occur;** incidence has been reported in up to 10% of AIDS patients. Risk factors for seizures include impaired baseline renal function and low total serum calcium. May cause anemia and granulocytopenia. Foscarnet has been shown to be mutagenic in animal studies. Foscarnet is deposited in teeth and bone of young, growing animals; it has adversely affected tooth enamel development in rats. Safety and efficacy in children have not been established.

Adverse Reactions

>10%:

Central nervous system: Fever (65%), headache (26%)

Endocrine & metabolic: Hypokalemia (16% to 48%), hypocalcemia (15% to 30%), hypomagnesemia (15% to 30%), hypophosphatemia (8% to 26%)

Gastrointestinal: Nausea (47%), diarrhea (30%), vomiting (26%)

Hematologic: Anemia (33%), granulocytopenia (17%)

Renal: Abnormal renal function/decreased creatinine clearance (27%)

1% to 10%:

Cardiovascular: Chest pain (1% to 5%), edema (1% to 5%), facial edema (1% to 5%), flushing (1% to 5%), hyper-/hypotension (1% to 5%), palpitation (1% to 5%), sinus tachycardia, first degree AV block, nonspecific ST-T segment changes

Central nervous system: Seizure (10%), fatigue (>5%), malaise (>5%), dizziness (>5%), hypoesthesia (>5%), depression (>5%), confusion (>5%), anxiety (≥5%), aphasia (1% to 5%), ataxia (1% to 5%), dementia (1% to 5%), meningitis (1% to 5%), stupor (1% to 5%), insomnia (1% to 5%), somnolence (1% to 5%), nervousness (1% to 5%), amnesia (1% to 5%), agitation (1% to 5%), aggressiveness (1% to 5%), hallucination (1% to 5%)

Dermatologic: Rash (>5%), pruritus (1% to 5%), skin ulceration (1% to 5%), seborrhea (1% to 5%), erythematous rash, maculopapular rash, skin discoloration

Endocrine & metabolic: Hyperphosphatemia (6%), acidosis (1% to 5%), hyponatremia (1% to 5%)

Gastrointestinal: Anorexia (>5%), abdominal pain (>5%), constipation (1% to 5%), dysphasia (1% to 5%), dyspepsia (1% to 5%), flatulence (1% to 5%), melena (1% to 5%), pancreatitis (1% to 5%), rectal hemorrhage (1% to 5%), taste perversion (1% to 5%), ulcerative stomatitis (1% to 5%), weight loss (1% to 5%), xerostomia (1% to 5%)

Genitourinary: Urinary retention (1% to 5%), dysuria (1% to 5%), nocturia (1% to 5%)

Hematologic: Leukopenia (≥5%), thrombocytopenia (1% to 5%), thrombosis (1% to 5%), lymphadenopathy (1% to 5%)

Local: Injection site pain

Neuromuscular & skeletal: Paresthesia (>5%), involuntary muscle contractions (>5%), rigors (>5%), neuropathy (peripheral; >5%), weakness (>5%), arthralgia (1% to 5%), back pain (1% to 5%), leg cramps (1% to 5%), myalgia (1% to 5%), tremor (1% to 5%)

Ocular: Vision abnormalities (>5%), conjunctivitis (1% to 5%), eye pain (1% to 5%)

Renal: Acute renal failure (1% to 5%), albuminuria (1% to 5%), BUN increased (1% to 5%), polyuria (1% to 5%), urinary tract infection (1% to 5%)

Respiratory: Cough (>5%), dyspnea (≥5%), bronchospasm (1% to 5%), hemoptysis (1% to 5%), pharyngitis (1% to 5%), pneumonia (1% to 5%), pneumothorax (1% to 5%), rhinitis (1% to 5%), sinusitis (1% to 5%), stridor (1% to 5%)

Miscellaneous: Sepsis (>5%), diaphoresis (increased), flu-like syndrome (1% to 5%), infection (1% to 5%), thirst (1% to 5%)

<1% (Limited to important or life-threatening): Amylase increased, cardiac arrest, coma, creatinine phosphokinase increased, dehydration, diabetes insipidus (usually nephrogenic), erythema multiforme, hematuria, hypoproteinemia, muscle weakness, myopathy, myositis, neutropenia, pancytopenia, QT_c prolongation, renal calculus, rhabdomyolysis, Stevens-Johnson syndrome, syndrome of inappropriate antidiuretic hormone (SIADH), toxic epidermal necrolysis, ventricular arrhythmia, vesiculobullous eruptions

Overdosage/Toxicology Overdoses, up to 20 times the recommended dose, have been observed. Symptoms of overdose include seizures, renal dysfunction, perioral or limb paresthesia, and electrolyte disturbances including hypocalcemia and hypophosphatemia. Treatment is symptom-directed and supportive. Hydration and monitoring for electrolyte abnormalities are necessary. Hemodialysis may be helpful for foscarnet removal.

Drug Interactions

Increased Effect/Toxicity: Concurrent use with ciprofloxacin (or other fluoroquinolone) increases seizure potential. Ciprofloxacin may enhance the neuroexcitatory effect of foscarnet. Foscarnet may enhance the neurotoxic (peripheral) effect of zalcitabine. Nephrotoxic drugs (amphotericin B, I.V. pentamidine, aminoglycosides, etc) should be avoided, if possible, to (Continued)

Foscarnet *(Continued)*

minimize additive renal risk with foscarnet. Concurrent use of pentamidine also increases the potential for hypocalcemia. Protease inhibitors (ritonavir, saquinavir) have been associated with an increased risk of renal impairment during concurrent use of foscarnet. QT_c-prolonging agents may enhance the adverse/toxic effect of foscarnet. Foscarnet may enhance the QT_c-prolonging effect of thioridazine.

Stability Foscarnet injection is a clear, colorless solution; it should be stored at room temperature and protected from temperatures >40°C and from freezing. Diluted solution is stable for 24 hours at room temperature or under refrigeration.

Foscarnet should be diluted in D_5W or NS. For peripheral line administration, foscarnet **must** be diluted to ≤12 mg/mL with D_5W or NS. For central line administration, foscarnet may be administered undiluted.

Mechanism of Action Pyrophosphate analogue which acts as a noncompetitive inhibitor of many viral RNA and DNA polymerases as well as HIV reverse transcriptase. Similar to ganciclovir, foscarnet is a virostatic agent. Foscarnet does not require activation by thymidine kinase.

Pharmacodynamics/Kinetics

Distribution: Up to 28% of cumulative I.V. dose may be deposited in bone

Metabolism: Biotransformation does not occur

Half-life elimination: ~3 hours

Excretion: Urine (≤28% as unchanged drug)

Dosage

CMV retinitis: I.V.:

Induction treatment: 60 mg/kg/dose every 8 hours **or** 90 mg/kg every 12 hours for 14-21 days

Maintenance therapy: 90-120 mg/kg/day as a single infusion

Herpes simplex infections (acyclovir-resistant): Induction: I.V.: 40 mg/kg/dose every 8-12 hours for 14-21 days

Dosage adjustment in renal impairment:

Induction and maintenance dosing schedules based on creatinine clearance (mL/minute/kg): See tables.

Induction Dosing of Foscarnet in Patients With Abnormal Renal Function

Cl_{cr} (mL/min/kg)	HSV Equivalent to 40 mg/kg q12h	HSV Equivalent to 40 mg/kg q8h	CMV Equivalent to 60 mg/kg q8h	CMV Equivalent to 90 mg/kg q12h
<0.4	Not recommended	Not recommended	Not recommended	Not recommended
≥0.4-0.5	20 mg/kg every 24 hours	35 mg/kg every 24 hours	50 mg/kg every 24 hours	50 mg/kg every 24 hours
>0.5-0.6	25 mg/kg every 24 hours	40 mg/kg every 24 hours	60 mg/kg every 24 hours	60 mg/kg every 24 hours
>0.6-0.8	35 mg/kg every 24 hours	25 mg/kg every 12 hours	40 mg/kg every 12 hours	80 mg/kg every 24 hours
>0.8-1.0	20 mg/kg every 12 hours	35 mg/kg every 12 hours	50 mg/kg every 12 hours	50 mg/kg every 12 hours
>1.0-1.4	30 mg/kg every 12 hours	30 mg/kg every 8 hours	45 mg/kg every 8 hours	70 mg/kg every 12 hours
>1.4	40 mg/kg every 12 hours	40 mg/kg every 8 hours	60 mg/kg every 8 hours	90 mg/kg every 12 hours

Maintenance Dosing of Foscarnet in Patients With Abnormal Renal Function

Cl_{cr} (mL/min/kg)	CMV Equivalent to 90 mg/kg q24h	CMV Equivalent to 120 mg/kg q24h
<0.4	Not recommended	Not recommended
≥0.4-0.5	50 mg/kg every 48 hours	65 mg/kg every 48 hours
>0.5-0.6	60 mg/kg every 48 hours	80 mg/kg every 48 hours
>0.6-0.8	80 mg/kg every 48 hours	105 mg/kg every 48 hours
>0.8-1.0	50 mg/kg every 24 hours	65 mg/kg every 24 hours
>1.0-1.4	70 mg/kg every 24 hours	90 mg/kg every 24 hours
>1.4	90 mg/kg every 24 hours	120 mg/kg every 24 hours

Hemodialysis:

Foscarnet is highly removed by hemodialysis (30% in 4 hours HD)

Doses of 50 mg/kg/dose posthemodialysis have been found to produce similar serum concentrations as doses of 90 mg/kg twice daily in patients with normal renal function

Doses of 60-90 mg/kg/dose loading dose (posthemodialysis) followed by 45 mg/kg/dose posthemodialysis (3 times/week) with the monitoring of weekly plasma concentrations to maintain peak plasma concentrations in the range of 400-800 μMolar has been recommended by some clinicians

Continuous arteriovenous or venovenous hemodiafiltration effects: Dose as for Cl_{cr} 10-50 mL/minute

Administration Foscarnet is administered by intravenous infusion, using an infusion pump, at a rate not exceeding 1 mg/kg/minute. Undiluted (24 mg/mL) solution can be administered without further dilution when using a central venous catheter for infusion. For peripheral vein administration, the solution **must** be diluted to a final concentration **not to exceed** 12 mg/mL. The manufacturer recommends 750-1000 mL of NS or D_5W be administered prior to first infusion. With subsequent infusions of 90-120 mg/kg, this volume would be repeated. If the dose were 40-60 mg/kg, then the volume could be reduced to 500 mL. After the first dose, the hydration fluid should be administered concurrently with foscarnet.

Monitoring Parameters 24 hour creatinine clearance at baseline and periodically thereafter. During induction therapy: obtain complete blood counts, and electrolytes (including serum creatinine, calcium, magnesium, potassium and phosphorus) twice weekly and then one weekly during maintenance therapy: More frequent monitoring may be required in some patients. Check hydration status before and after infusion.

Additional Information CMV retinitis maintenance treatment may be discontinued if immune reconstitution occurs as a result of ART.

Dosage Forms
Injection, solution: 24 mg/mL (250 mL, 500 mL)
Foscavir®: 24 mg/mL (500 mL)

♦ **Foscavir**® see Foscarnet on page 762

Fosfomycin (fos foe MYE sin)

U.S. Brand Names Monurol™
Canadian Brand Names Monurol™
Index Terms Fosfomycin Tromethamine
Pharmacologic Category Antibiotic, Miscellaneous
Additional Appendix Information
Antimicrobial Drugs of Choice on page 1981
Use Single oral dose in the treatment of uncomplicated urinary tract infections in women due to susceptible strains of *E. coli* and *Enterococcus*; may have an advantage over other agents since it maintains high concentration in the urine for up to 48 hours
Unlabeled/Investigational Use Multiple doses have been investigated for complicated urinary tract infections in men
Pregnancy Risk Factor B
Lactation Enters breast milk/not recommended
Medication Safety Issues
Sound-alike/look-alike issues:
Monurol™ may be confused with Monopril®
Adverse Reactions
1% to 10%:
Central nervous system: Headache (47%), dizziness (1%)
Dermatologic: Rash (1%)
Gastrointestinal: Diarrhea (2% to 10%), nausea (4%), epigastric discomfort (1%), abdominal pain
Genitourinary: Vaginitis
Neuromuscular & skeletal: Weakness (1%)
<1% (Limited to important or life-threatening): Angioedema, aplastic anemia, anorexia, cholestasis, drowsiness, fatigue, hepatic necrosis, jaundice, optic neuritis, paresthesia, pruritus, vomiting, somnolence, toxic megacolon
Overdosage/Toxicology Symptomatic and supportive treatment is recommended in the event of an overdose.
Drug Interactions
Decreased Effect: Antacids or calcium salts may cause precipitate formation and decrease fosfomycin absorption. Increased gastrointestinal motility due to metoclopramide may lower fosfomycin tromethamine serum concentrations and urinary excretion. This drug interaction possibly could be extrapolated to other medications which increase gastrointestinal motility.
Stability Store at 15°C to 30°C (59°F to 86°F).
Mechanism of Action As a phosphoric acid derivative, fosfomycin inhibits bacterial wall synthesis (bactericidal) by inactivating the enzyme, pyruvyl transferase, which is critical in the synthesis of cell walls by bacteria; the tromethamine salt is preferable to the calcium salt due to its superior absorption
Pharmacodynamics/Kinetics
Absorption: Well absorbed
Distribution: V_d: 2 L/kg; high concentrations in urine; well into other tissues; crosses maximally into CSF with inflamed meninges
Protein binding: <3%
Bioavailability: 34% to 58%
Half-life elimination: 4-8 hours; Cl_{cr} <10 mL/minute: 50 hours
Time to peak, serum: 2 hours
Excretion: Urine (as unchanged drug); high urinary levels (100 mcg/mL) persist for >48 hours
Dosage Adults: Oral:
Female: Uncomplicated UTI: Single dose of 3 g in 4 oz of water
Male:
Complicated UTI (unlabeled): 3 g every 2-3 days for 3 doses
Prostatitis (unlabeled): 3 g every 3 days for a total of 21 days
Dosing adjustment in renal impairment: Decrease dose; 80% removed by dialysis, repeat dose after dialysis
Dosing adjustment in hepatic impairment: No dosage decrease needed
Administration Always mix with water before ingesting; do not administer in its dry form; pour contents of envelope into 90-120 mL of water (not hot), stir to dissolve and take immediately
Monitoring Parameters Signs and symptoms of urinary tract infection; urine culture plus sensitivity
Additional Information Many gram-positive and gram-negative organisms such as staphylococci, pneumococci, *E. coli*, *Salmonella*, *Shigella*, *H. influenzae*, *Neisseria* spp, and some strains of *P. aeruginosa*, indole-negative *Proteus*, and *Providencia* are inhibited. *B. fragilis*, and anaerobic gram-negative cocci are resistant.
Dosage Forms Powder, as tromethamine: 3 g

♦ **Fosfomycin Tromethamine** see Fosfomycin on page 765

Fosinopril (foe SIN oh pril)

U.S. Brand Names Monopril®

Canadian Brand Names Apo-Fosinopril®; Monopril®; Novo-Fosinopril; ratio-Fosinopril; Riva-Fosinopril

Index Terms Fosinopril Sodium

Pharmacologic Category Angiotensin-Converting Enzyme (ACE) Inhibitor

Additional Appendix Information
Angiotensin Agents *on page 1860*
Heart Failure (Systolic) *on page 2051*

Use Treatment of hypertension, either alone or in combination with other antihypertensive agents; treatment of congestive heart failure, left ventricular dysfunction after myocardial infarction

Pregnancy Risk Factor C (1st trimester)/D (2nd and 3rd trimesters)

Pregnancy Implications Decreased placental blood flow, low birth weight, fetal hypotension, preterm delivery, and fetal death have been noted with the use of some ACE inhibitors (ACEIs) in animal studies. Neonatal hypotension, skull hypoplasia, anuria, renal failure, oligohydramnios (associated with fetal limb contractures, craniofacial deformities, hypoplastic lung development), prematurity, intrauterine growth retardation, and patent ductus arteriosus have been reported with the use of ACEIs, primarily in the 2nd and 3rd trimesters. The risk of neonatal toxicity has been considered less when ACEIs have been used in the 1st trimester; however, major congenital malformations have been reported. The cardiovascular and/or central nervous systems are most commonly affected. Unless alternative agents are not appropriate, ACEIs should be discontinued as soon as possible once pregnancy is detected.

Lactation Enters breast milk/not recommended

Medication Safety Issues
Sound-alike/look-alike issues:
Fosinopril may be confused with lisinopril
Monopril® may be confused with Accupril®, minoxidil, moexipril, Monoket®, Monurol™, ramipril

Contraindications Hypersensitivity to fosinopril or any component of the formulation; angioedema related to previous treatment with an ACE inhibitor; idiopathic or hereditary angioedema; bilateral renal artery stenosis; pregnancy (2nd and 3rd trimesters)

Warnings/Precautions Anaphylactic reactions can occur. Angioedema can occur at any time during treatment (especially following first dose). It may involve head and neck (potentially affecting the airway) or the intestine (presenting with abdominal pain). Prolonged monitoring may be required especially if tongue, glottis, or larynx are involved as they are associated with airway obstruction. Those with a history of airway surgery in this situation have a higher risk. Careful blood pressure monitoring (hypotension can occur especially in volume-depleted patients). **[U.S. Boxed Warning]: Based on human data, ACEIs can cause injury and death to the developing fetus when used in the second and third trimesters. ACEIs should be discontinued as soon as possible once pregnancy is detected.** Dosage adjustment needed in severe renal impairment (Cl$_{cr}$ <10 mL/minute). Use with caution in hypovolemia; collagen vascular diseases; valvular stenosis (particularly aortic stenosis); hyperkalemia; or before, during, or immediately after anesthesia. Avoid rapid dosage escalation which may lead to renal insufficiency. Rare toxicities associated with ACE inhibitors include cholestatic jaundice (which may progress to hepatic necrosis) and neutropenia/agranulocytosis with myeloid hyperplasia. Hyperkalemia may rarely occur. May be associated with deterioration of renal function and/or increases in serum creatinine, particularly in patients dependent on renin-angiotensin-aldosterone system. Use with caution in unilateral renal artery stenosis and pre-existing renal insufficiency; if patient has renal impairment then a baseline WBC with differential and serum creatinine should be evaluated and monitored closely during the first 3 months of therapy. Hypersensitivity reactions may be seen during hemodialysis with high-flux dialysis membranes (eg, AN69). Safety and efficacy have not been established in children <6 years of age.

Adverse Reactions Note: Frequency ranges include data from hypertension and heart failure trials. Higher rates of adverse reactions have generally been noted in patients with CHF. However, the frequency of adverse effects associated with placebo is also increased in this population.

>10%: Central nervous system: Dizziness (1.6% to 11.9%)
1% to 10%:
Cardiovascular: Orthostatic hypotension (1.4% to 1.9%), palpitation (1.4%)
Central nervous system: Dizziness (1% to 2%; up to 12% in CHF patients), headache (3.2%), fatigue (1% to 2%)
Endocrine & metabolic: Hyperkalemia (2.6%)
Gastrointestinal: Diarrhea (2.2%), nausea/vomiting (1.2% to 2.2%)
Hepatic: Transaminases increased
Neuromuscular & skeletal: Musculoskeletal pain (<1% to 3.3%), noncardiac chest pain (<1% to 2.2%), weakness (1.4%)
Renal: Increased serum creatinine, worsening of renal function (in patients with bilateral renal artery stenosis or hypovolemia)
Respiratory: Cough (2.2% to 9.7%)
Miscellaneous: Upper respiratory infection (2.2%)
>1% but ≤ frequency in patients receiving placebo: Sexual dysfunction, fever, flu-like syndrome, dyspnea, rash, headache, insomnia
<1% (Limited to important or life-threatening): Anaphylactoid reaction, angina, angioedema, arthralgia, bronchospasm, cerebral infarction, cerebrovascular accident, gout, hepatitis, hepatomegaly, myalgia, MI, pancreatitis, paresthesia, photosensitivity, pleuritic chest pain, pruritus, rash, renal insufficiency, shock, sudden death, syncope, TIA, tinnitus, urticaria, vertigo. In a small number of patients, a symptom complex of cough, bronchospasm, and eosinophilia has been observed with fosinopril.
Other events reported with ACE inhibitors: Acute renal failure, agranulocytosis, anemia, aplastic anemia, bullous pemphigus, cardiac arrest, eosinophilic pneumonitis, exfoliative

dermatitis, gynecomastia, hemolytic anemia, hepatic failure, jaundice, neutropenia, pancytopenia, Stevens-Johnson syndrome, symptomatic hyponatremia, thrombocytopenia. In addition, a syndrome which may include fever, myalgia, arthralgia, interstitial nephritis, vasculitis, rash, eosinophilia and positive ANA, and elevated ESR has been reported for other ACE inhibitors.

Overdosage/Toxicology Mild hypotension has been the only toxic effect seen with acute overdose. Bradycardia may also occur; hyperkalemia occurs even with therapeutic doses, especially in patients with renal insufficiency and those taking NSAIDs. Following initiation of essential overdose management, toxic symptom and supportive treatment should be initiated. Hypotension usually responds to I.V. fluids or Trendelenburg positioning.

Drug Interactions

Increased Effect/Toxicity: Potassium supplements, co-trimoxazole (high dose), angiotensin II receptor antagonists (eg, candesartan, losartan, irbesartan), or potassium-sparing diuretics (amiloride, spironolactone, triamterene) may result in elevated serum potassium levels when combined with fosinopril. ACE inhibitor effects may be increased by phenothiazines or probenecid (increases levels of captopril). ACE inhibitors may increase serum concentrations/effects of lithium. ACE inhibitors may enhance the adverse/toxic effects (nitritoid reaction) of gold sodium thiomalate.

Diuretics have additive hypotensive effects with ACE inhibitors, and hypovolemia increases the potential for adverse renal effects of ACE inhibitors. In patients with compromised renal function, coadministration with NSAIDs may result in further deterioration of renal function. Allopurinol and ACE inhibitors may cause a higher risk of hypersensitivity reaction when taken concurrently.

Decreased Effect: Aspirin (high dose) may reduce the therapeutic effects of ACE inhibitors; at low dosages this does not appear to be significant. Rifampin may decrease the effect of ACE inhibitors. Antacids may decrease the bioavailability of ACE inhibitors (may be more likely to occur with captopril); separate administration times by 1-2 hours. NSAIDs, specifically indomethacin, may reduce the hypotensive effects of ACE inhibitors. More likely to occur in low renin or volume dependent hypertensive patients.

Ethanol/Nutrition/Herb Interactions Herb/Nutraceutical: Avoid dong quai if using for hypertension (has estrogenic activity). Avoid ephedra, garlic, yohimbe, ginseng (may worsen hypertension).

Stability Store at 25°C (77°F); excursions permitted to 15°C to 30°C (59°F to 86°F). Protect from moisture by keeping bottle tightly closed.

Mechanism of Action Competitive inhibitor of angiotensin-converting enzyme (ACE); prevents conversion of angiotensin I to angiotensin II, a potent vasoconstrictor; results in lower levels of angiotensin II which causes an increase in plasma renin activity and a reduction in aldosterone secretion; a CNS mechanism may also be involved in hypotensive effect as angiotensin II increases adrenergic outflow from CNS; vasoactive kallikreins may be decreased in conversion to active hormones by ACE inhibitors, thus reducing blood pressure

Pharmacodynamics/Kinetics

Onset of action: 1 hour

Duration: 24 hours

Absorption: 36%

Protein binding: 95%

Metabolism: Prodrug, hydrolyzed to its active metabolite fosinoprilat by intestinal wall and hepatic esterases

Bioavailability: 36%

Half-life elimination, serum (fosinoprilat): 12 hours

Time to peak, serum: ~3 hours

Excretion: Urine and feces (as fosinoprilat and other metabolites in roughly equal proportions, 45% to 50%)

Dosage Oral:

Children >50 kg: Hypertension: Initial: 5-10 mg once daily

Adults:

Hypertension: Initial: 10 mg/day; most patients are maintained on 20-40 mg/day. May need to divide the dose into two if trough effect is inadequate; discontinue the diuretic, if possible 2-3 days before initiation of therapy; resume diuretic therapy carefully, if needed.

Heart failure: Initial: 10 mg/day (5 mg if renal dysfunction present) and increase, as needed, to a maximum of 40 mg once daily over several weeks; usual dose: 20-40 mg/day. If hypotension, orthostasis, or azotemia occur during titration, consider decreasing concomitant diuretic dose, if any.

Dosing adjustment/comments in renal impairment: None needed since hepatobiliary elimination compensates adequately diminished renal elimination.

Hemodialysis: Moderately dialyzable (20% to 50%)

Dietary Considerations Should not take a potassium salt supplement without the advice of healthcare provider.

Monitoring Parameters Blood pressure (supervise for at least 2 hours after the initial dose or any increase for significant orthostasis); serum potassium, creatinine, BUN, WBC

Test Interactions Positive Coombs' [direct]; may cause false-positive results in urine acetone determinations using sodium nitroprusside reagent

Dosage Forms

Tablet, as sodium: 10 mg, 20 mg, 40 mg

Monopril®: 10 mg, 20 mg, 40 mg

♦ **Fosinopril Sodium** see Fosinopril on page 766

Fosphenytoin (FOS fen i toyn)

U.S. Brand Names Cerebyx®
Canadian Brand Names Cerebyx®
Index Terms Fosphenytoin Sodium
Pharmacologic Category Anticonvulsant, Hydantoin
Additional Appendix Information
Fosphenytoin and Phenytoin *on page 1883*
Use Used for the control of generalized convulsive status epilepticus and prevention and treatment of seizures occurring during neurosurgery; indicated for short-term parenteral administration when other means of phenytoin administration are unavailable, inappropriate or deemed less advantageous (the safety and effectiveness of fosphenytoin in this use has not been systematically evaluated for more than 5 days)
Pregnancy Risk Factor D
Pregnancy Implications Fosphenytoin is the prodrug of phenytoin. Refer to Phenytoin *on page 1361* for additional information.
Lactation Excretion in breast milk unknown/not recommended
Medication Safety Issues
Sound-alike/look-alike issues:
Cerebyx® may be confused with Celebrex®, Celexa™, Cerezyme®
Contraindications Hypersensitivity to phenytoin, other hydantoins, or any component of the formulation; patients with sinus bradycardia, sinoatrial block, second- and third-degree AV block, or Adams-Stokes syndrome; occurrence of rash during treatment (should not be resumed if rash is exfoliative, purpuric, or bullous); treatment of absence seizures
Warnings/Precautions Doses of fosphenytoin are expressed as their phenytoin sodium equivalent (PE). Antiepileptic drugs should not be abruptly discontinued. Hypotension may occur, especially after I.V. administration at high doses and high rates of administration. Administration of phenytoin has been associated with atrial and ventricular conduction depression and ventricular fibrillation. Careful cardiac monitoring is needed when administering I.V. loading doses of fosphenytoin. Acute hepatotoxicity associated with a hypersensitivity syndrome characterized by fever, skin eruptions, and lymphadenopathy has been reported to occur within the first 2 months of treatment. Discontinue if skin rash or lymphadenopathy occurs. Use with caution in patients with hypotension, severe myocardial insufficiency, diabetes mellitus, porphyria, hypoalbuminemia, hypothyroidism, fever, or hepatic or renal dysfunction.
Adverse Reactions The more important adverse clinical events caused by the I.V. use of fosphenytoin or phenytoin are cardiovascular collapse and/or central nervous system depression. Hypotension can occur when either drug is administered rapidly by the I.V. route. Do not exceed a rate of 150 mg phenytoin equivalent/minute when administering fosphenytoin.

The adverse clinical events most commonly observed with the use of fosphenytoin in clinical trials were nystagmus, dizziness, pruritus, paresthesia, headache, somnolence, and ataxia. Paresthesia and pruritus were seen more often following fosphenytoin (versus phenytoin) administration and occurred more often with I.V. fosphenytoin than with I.M. administration. These events were dose- and rate-related (doses ≥15 mg/kg at a rate of 150 mg/minute). These sensations, generally described as itching, burning, or tingling are usually not at the infusion site. The location of the discomfort varied with the groin mentioned most frequently. The paresthesia and pruritus were transient events that occurred within several minutes of the start of infusion and generally resolved within 10 minutes after completion of infusion.

Transient pruritus, tinnitus, nystagmus, somnolence, and ataxia occurred 2-3 times more often at doses ≥15 mg/kg and rates ≥150 mg/minute.

I.V. administration (maximum dose/rate):
>10%:
Central nervous system: Nystagmus, dizziness, somnolence, ataxia
Dermatologic: Pruritus
1% to 10%:
Cardiovascular: Hypotension, vasodilation, tachycardia
Central nervous system: Stupor, incoordination, paresthesia, extrapyramidal syndrome, tremor, agitation, hypoesthesia, dysarthria, vertigo, brain edema, headache
Gastrointestinal: Nausea, tongue disorder, dry mouth, vomiting
Neuromuscular & skeletal: Pelvic pain, muscle weakness, back pain
Ocular: Diplopia, amblyopia
Otic: Tinnitus, deafness
Miscellaneous: Taste perversion
I.M. administration (substitute for oral phenytoin):
1% to 10%:
Central nervous system: Nystagmus, tremor, ataxia, headache, incoordination, somnolence, dizziness, paresthesia, reflexes decreased
Dermatologic: Pruritus
Gastrointestinal: Nausea, vomiting
Hematologic/lymphatic: Ecchymosis
Neuromuscular & skeletal: Muscle weakness
<1% (Limited to important or life-threatening): Acidosis, acute hepatic failure, acute hepatotoxicity, alkalosis, anemia, atrial flutter, bundle branch block, cardiac arrest, cardiomegaly, cerebral hemorrhage, cerebral infarct, CHF, cyanosis, dehydration, hyperglycemia, hyperkalemia, hypertension, hypochromic anemia, hypokalemia, hypophosphatemia, ketosis, leukocytosis, leukopenia, lymphadenopathy, palpitation, postural hypotension, pulmonary embolus, QT interval prolongation, sinus bradycardia, syncope, thrombocytopenia, thrombophlebitis, ventricular extrasystoles
Overdosage/Toxicology Signs and symptoms include unsteady gait, tremors, hyperglycemia, chorea (extrapyramidal), gingival hyperplasia, gynecomastia, myoglobinuria, nephrotic syndrome, slurred speech, mydriasis, myoclonus, confusion, encephalopathy, hyperthermia, drowsiness, nausea, hypothermia, fever, hypotension, respiratory depression,

hyper-reflexia, coma, systemic lupus erythematosus (SLE), ophthalmoplegia; as well as, leukopenia, neutropenia, agranulocytosis, and granulocytopenia. Treatment for hypotension is supportive. Treat with I.V. fluids and Trendelenburg positioning. Seizures may be controlled with lorazepam or diazepam 5-10 mg (0.25-0.4 mg/kg in children); intravenous albumin (25 g every 6 hours) has been used to increase the bound fraction of drug. Multiple dosing of activated charcoal may be effective. Peritoneal dialysis, diuresis, hemodialysis, hemoperfusion, and plasmapheresis are of little value.

Drug Interactions

Cytochrome P450 Effect: As phenytoin: **Substrate** of CYP2C9 (major), 2C19 (major), 3A4 (minor); **Induces** CYP2B6 (strong), 2C8 (strong), 2C9 (strong), 2C19 (strong), 3A4 (strong)

Increased Effect/Toxicity: The sedative effects of phenytoin may be additive with other CNS depressants including ethanol, barbiturates, sedatives, antidepressants, opioid analgesics, and benzodiazepines. Selected anticonvulsants (felbamate, gabapentin, and topiramate) have been reported to increase phenytoin levels/effects. In addition, serum phenytoin concentrations may be increased by allopurinol, amiodarone, calcium channel blockers (including diltiazem and nifedipine), cimetidine, disulfiram, methylphenidate, metronidazole, omeprazole, selective serotonin reuptake inhibitors (SSRIs), ticlopidine, tricyclic antidepressants, trazodone, and trimethoprim. Case reports indicate ciprofloxacin may increase or decrease serum phenytoin concentrations.

The levels/effects of phenytoin may be increased by delavirdine, fluconazole, fluvoxamine, gemfibrozil, isoniazid, ketoconazole, nicardipine, NSAIDs, omeprazole, pioglitazone, sulfonamides, ticlopidine, and other CYP2C9 or 2C19 inhibitors.

Phenytoin enhances the conversion of primidone to phenobarbital resulting in elevated phenobarbital serum concentrations. Concurrent use of acetazolamide with phenytoin may result in an increased risk of osteomalacia. Concurrent use of phenytoin and lithium has resulted in lithium intoxication. Valproic acid (and sulfisoxazole) may displace phenytoin from binding sites; valproic acid may increase, decrease, or have no effect on phenytoin serum concentrations. Phenytoin transiently increased the response to warfarin initially; this is followed by an inhibition of the hypoprothrombinemic response. Phenytoin may enhance the hepatotoxic potential of acetaminophen overdoses. Concurrent use of dopamine and intravenous phenytoin may lead to an increased risk of hypotension.

Decreased Effect: Phenytoin may enhance the metabolism of estrogen and/or oral contraceptives, decreasing their clinical effect; an alternative method of contraception should be considered. Phenytoin may increase the metabolism of anticonvulsants including barbiturates, carbamazepine, ethosuximide, felbamate, lamotrigine, tiagabine, topiramate, and zonisamide. Valproic acid may increase, decrease, or have no effect on phenytoin serum concentrations. Phenytoin may also decrease the serum concentrations/effects of some antiarrhythmics (disopyramide, propafenone, quinidine, quetiapine) and tricyclic antidepressants may be reduced by phenytoin. Phenytoin may enhance the metabolism of doxycycline, decreasing its clinical effect; higher dosages may be required. Phenytoin may increase the metabolism of chloramphenicol or itraconazole.

Phenytoin may decrease the levels/effects of amiodarone, benzodiazepines, bupropion, calcium channel blockers, carbamazepine, citalopram, clarithromycin, cyclosporine, efavirenz, erythromycin, estrogens, fluoxetine, glimepiride, glipizide, losartan, methsuximide, mirtazapine, nateglinide, nefazodone, nevirapine, phenytoin, pioglitazone, promethazine, propranolol, protease inhibitors, proton pump inhibitors, rosiglitazone, selegiline, sertraline, sulfonamides, tacrolimus, venlafaxine. voriconazole, warfarin, zafirlukast, and other CYP2B6, 2C8, 2C9, 2C19, or 3A4 substrates.

The levels/effects of phenytoin may be decreased by aminoglutethimide, carbamazepine, phenobarbital, rifampin, rifapentine, secobarbital, and other CYP2C8/9 or 2C19 inducers. Clozapine and vigabatrin may reduce phenytoin serum concentrations. Case reports indicate ciprofloxacin may increase or decrease serum phenytoin concentrations. Dexamethasone may decrease serum phenytoin concentrations. Replacement of folic acid has been reported to increase the metabolism of phenytoin, decreasing its serum concentrations and/or increasing seizures.

Initially, phenytoin increases the response to warfarin; this is followed by a decrease in response to warfarin. Phenytoin may inhibit the anti-Parkinson effect of levodopa. The duration of neuromuscular blockade from neuromuscular-blocking agents may be decreased by phenytoin. Phenytoin may enhance the metabolism of methadone resulting in methadone withdrawal. Phenytoin may decrease serum levels/effects of digitalis glycosides, theophylline, and thyroid hormones.

Several chemotherapeutic agents have been associated with a decrease in serum phenytoin levels; includes cisplatin, bleomycin, carmustine, methotrexate, and vinblastine. Enzyme-inducing anticonvulsant therapy may reduce the effectiveness of some chemotherapy regimens (specifically in ALL). Teniposide and methotrexate may be cleared more rapidly in these patients.

Ethanol/Nutrition/Herb Interactions

Ethanol:
Acute use: Avoid or limit ethanol (inhibits metabolism of phenytoin); watch for sedation.
Chronic use: Avoid or limit ethanol (stimulates metabolism of phenytoin).

Stability Refrigerate at 2°C to 8°C (36°F to 46°F). Do not store at room temperature for more than 48 hours. Do not use vials that develop particulate matter. Must be diluted to concentrations 1.5-25 mg PE/mL, in normal saline or D_5W, for I.V. infusion.

Mechanism of Action Diphosphate ester salt of phenytoin which acts as a water soluble prodrug of phenytoin; after administration, plasma esterases convert fosphenytoin to phosphate, formaldehyde and phenytoin as the active moiety; phenytoin works by stabilizing neuronal membranes and decreasing seizure activity by increasing efflux or decreasing influx of sodium ions across cell membranes in the motor cortex during generation of nerve impulses

Pharmacodynamics/Kinetics Also refer to Phenytoin monograph for additional information.
(Continued)

Fosphenytoin *(Continued)*

Protein binding: Fosphenytoin: 95% to 99% to albumin; can displace phenytoin and increase free fraction (up to 30% unbound) during the period required for conversion of fosphenytoin to phenytoin

Metabolism: Fosphenytoin is rapidly converted via hydrolysis to phenytoin; phenytoin is metabolized in the liver and forms metabolites

Bioavailability: I.M.: Fosphenytoin: 100%

Half-life elimination:

Fosphenytoin: 15 minutes

Phenytoin: Variable (mean: 12-29 hours); kinetics of phenytoin are saturable

Time to peak: Conversion to phenytoin: Following I.V. administration (maximum rate of administration): 15 minutes; following I.M. administration, peak phenytoin levels are reached in 3 hours

Excretion: Phenytoin: Urine (as inactive metabolites)

Dosage The dose, concentration, and infusion rates for fosphenytoin are expressed as phenytoin sodium equivalents (PE); fosphenytoin should always be prescribed and dispensed in phenytoin sodium equivalents (PE)

Infants and Children (unlabeled use): I.V.:

Loading dose: 10-20 mg PE/kg for the treatment of generalized convulsive status epilepticus

Maintenance dosing: Phenytoin dosing guidelines in pediatric patients are used when dosing fosphenytoin using doses in PE equal to the phenytoin doses (ie, phenytoin 1 mg = fosphenytoin 1 PE); maintenance doses may be started 8-12 hours after a loading dose

Adults:

Status epilepticus: I.V.: Loading dose: 15-20 mg PE/kg I.V. administered at 100-150 mg PE/minute

Nonemergent loading and maintenance dosing: I.V. or I.M.:

Loading dose: 10-20 mg PE/kg I.V. or I.M. (maximum I.V. rate: 150 mg PE/minute)

Initial daily maintenance dose: 4-6 mg PE/kg/day I.V. or I.M.

I.M. or I.V. substitution for oral phenytoin therapy: May be substituted for oral phenytoin sodium at the same total daily dose; however, Dilantin® capsules are ~90% bioavailable by the oral route; phenytoin, supplied as fosphenytoin, is 100% bioavailable by both the I.M. and I.V. routes; for this reason, plasma phenytoin concentrations may increase when I.M. or I.V. fosphenytoin is substituted for oral phenytoin sodium therapy; in clinical trials I.M. fosphenytoin was administered as a single daily dose utilizing either 1 or 2 injection sites; some patients may require more frequent dosing

Dosing adjustments in renal/hepatic impairment: Phenytoin clearance may be substantially reduced in cirrhosis and plasma level monitoring with dose adjustment advisable; free phenytoin levels should be monitored closely in patients with renal or hepatic disease or in those with hypoalbuminemia; furthermore, fosphenytoin clearance to phenytoin may be increased without a similar increase in phenytoin in these patients leading to increase frequency and severity of adverse events

Dietary Considerations Provides phosphate 0.0037 mmol/mg PE fosphenytoin

Administration

I.M.: May be administered as a single daily dose using either 1 or 2 injection sites.

I.V.: Rates of infusion:

Children: 1-3 mg PE/kg/minute

Adults: Should not exceed 150 mg PE/minute

Monitoring Parameters Continuous blood pressure, ECG, and respiratory function monitoring with loading dose and for 10-20 minutes following infusion; vital signs, CBC, liver function tests, plasma level monitoring (plasma levels should not be measured until conversion to phenytoin is complete, ~2 hours after an I.V. infusion or ~4 hours after an I.M. injection)

Reference Range

Therapeutic: 10-20 mcg/mL (SI: 40-79 µmol/L); toxicity is measured clinically, and some patients require levels outside the suggested therapeutic range

Toxic: 30-50 mcg/mL (SI: 120-200 µmol/L)

Lethal: >100 mcg/mL (SI: >400 µmol/L)

Manifestations of toxicity:

Nystagmus: 20 mcg/mL (SI: 79 µmol/L)

Ataxia: 30 mcg/mL (SI: 118.9 µmol/L)

Decreased mental status: 40 mcg/mL (SI: 159 µmol/L)

Coma: 50 mcg/mL (SI: 200 µmol/L)

Peak serum phenytoin level after a 375 mg I.M. fosphenytoin dose in healthy males: 5.7 mcg/mL

Peak serum fosphenytoin levels and phenytoin levels after a 1.2 g infusion (I.V.) in healthy subjects over 30 minutes were 129 mcg/mL and 17.2 mcg/mL respectively

Test Interactions Increased glucose, alkaline phosphatase (S); decreased thyroxine (S), calcium (S); serum sodium increased in overdose setting

Additional Information 1.5 mg fosphenytoin is approximately equivalent to 1 mg phenytoin. Equimolar fosphenytoin dose is 375 mg (75 mg/mL solution) to phenytoin 250 mg (50 mg/mL).

Dosage Forms Injection, solution, as sodium: 75 mg/mL [equivalent to phenytoin sodium 50 mg/mL] (2 mL, 10 mL)

◆ **Fosphenytoin Sodium** *see* Fosphenytoin *on page 768*

◆ **Fragmin®** *see* Dalteparin *on page 446*

◆ **Froben® (Can)** *see* Flurbiprofen *on page 735*

◆ **Froben-SR® (Can)** *see* Flurbiprofen *on page 735*

◆ **Frova®** *see* Frovatriptan *on page 771*

Frovatriptan (froe va TRIP tan)

U.S. Brand Names Frova®
Index Terms Frovatriptan Succinate
Pharmacologic Category Antimigraine Agent; Serotonin 5-HT$_{1B, 1D}$ Receptor Agonist
Additional Appendix Information
Antimigraine Drugs: 5-HT$_1$ Receptor Agonists *on page 1871*
Use Acute treatment of migraine with or without aura in adults
Pregnancy Risk Factor C
Pregnancy Implications There are no adequate and well-controlled studies using frovatriptan in pregnant women. Use only if potential benefit to the mother outweighs the potential risk to the fetus.
Lactation Excretion in breast milk unknown/use caution
Medication Safety Issues
International issues:
Allegro® [Germany] may be confused with Allegra® which is a brand name for fexofenadine in the U.S.
Allegro®: Brand name for fluticasone in Israel
Contraindications Hypersensitivity to frovatriptan or any component of the formulation; patients with ischemic heart disease or signs or symptoms of ischemic heart disease (including Prinzmetal's angina, angina pectoris, myocardial infarction, silent myocardial ischemia); cerebrovascular syndromes (including strokes, transient ischemic attacks); peripheral vascular syndromes (including ischemic bowel disease); uncontrolled hypertension; use within 24 hours of ergotamine derivatives; use within 24 hours of another 5-HT$_1$ agonist; management of hemiplegic or basilar migraine; prophylactic treatment of migraine; severe hepatic impairment
Warnings/Precautions Not intended for migraine prophylaxis, or treatment of cluster headaches, hemiplegic or basilar migraines.Cardiac events (coronary artery vasospasm, transient ischemia, MI, ventricular tachycardia/fibrillation, cardiac arrest, and death), cerebral/subarachnoid hemorrhage, stroke, peripheral vascular ischemia, and colonic ischemia have been reported with 5-HT$_1$ agonist administration. May cause vasospastic reactions resulting in colonic, peripheral, or coronary ischemia. Do not give to patients with risk factors for CAD until a cardiovascular evaluation has been performed; if evaluation is satisfactory, the healthcare provider should administer the first dose and cardiovascular status should be periodically evaluated. Significant elevation in blood pressure, including hypertensive crisis, has also been reported on rare occasions in patients using other 5-HT$_{1D}$ agonists with and without a history of hypertension. Symptoms of agitation, confusion, hallucinations, hyperreflexia, myoclonus, shivering, and tachycardia (serotonin syndrome) may occur with concomitant proserotonergic drugs (ie, SSRIs/SNRIs or triptans) or agents which reduce frovatriptan's metabolism. Safety and efficacy in pediatric patients have not been established
Adverse Reactions
1% to 10%:
Cardiovascular: Chest pain (2%), flushing (4%), palpitation (1%)
Central nervous system: Dizziness (8%), fatigue (5%), headache (4%), hot or cold sensation (3%), anxiety (1%), dysesthesia (1%), hypoesthesia (1%), insomnia (1%), pain (1%)
Gastrointestinal: Hyposalivation (3%), dyspepsia (2%), abdominal pain (1%), diarrhea (1%), vomiting (1%)
Neuromuscular & skeletal: Paresthesia (4%), skeletal pain (3%)
Ocular: Visual abnormalities (1%)
Otic: Tinnitus (1%)
Respiratory: Rhinitis (1%), sinusitis (1%)
Miscellaneous: Diaphoresis (1%)
<1% (Limited to important or life-threatening): Abnormal dreaming, abnormal gait, abnormal lacrimation, abnormal reflexes, abnormal urine, agitation, amnesia, arthralgia, arthrosis, ataxia, back pain, bradycardia, bullous eruption, cheilitis, confusion, conjunctivitis, constipation, dehydration, depersonalization, depression, dysphagia, dyspnea, earache, ECG changes, emotional lability, epistaxis, eructation, esophagospasm, euphoria, eye pain, fever, gastroesophageal reflux, hiccup, hot flushes, hyperacusis, hyperesthesia, hypertonia, hyperventilation, hypocalcemia, hypoglycemia, hypotonia, impaired concentration, involuntary muscle contractions, laryngitis, leg cramps, malaise, micturition, muscle weakness, myalgia, nervousness, nocturia, peptic ulcer, personality disorder, pharyngitis, polyuria, pruritus, purpura, renal pain, rigors, saliva increased, salivary gland pain, speech disorder, stomatitis, syncope, tachycardia, taste perversion, thirst, tongue paralysis, toothache, tremor, unspecified pain, urinary frequency, vertigo, weakness
Overdosage/Toxicology Single oral doses up to 100 mg have been reported without adverse effects. Treatment should be supportive and symptomatic. Monitor for at least 48 hours or until signs and symptoms subside. It is not known if hemodialysis or peritoneal dialysis is effective.
Drug Interactions
Cytochrome P450 Effect: Substrate of CYP1A2 (minor)
Increased Effect/Toxicity: The effects of frovatriptan may be increased by estrogen derivatives and propranolol. Ergot derivatives may increase the effects of frovatriptan (do not use within 24 hours of each other). SSRIs/SNRIs may exhibit additive toxicity with frovatriptan or other serotonin agonists (eg, antidepressants, dextromethorphan, tramadol) leading to serotonin syndrome.
Ethanol/Nutrition/Herb Interactions Food: Food does not affect frovatriptan bioavailability.
Stability Store at room temperature of 25°C (77°F). Protect from moisture and light.
Mechanism of Action Selective agonist for serotonin (5-HT$_{1B}$ and 5-HT$_{1D}$ receptor) in cranial arteries to cause vasoconstriction and reduces sterile inflammation associated with antidromic neuronal transmission correlating with relief of migraine.
Pharmacodynamics/Kinetics
Distribution: Male: 4.2 L/kg; Female: 3.0 L/kg
Protein binding: 15%
(Continued)

Frovatriptan *(Continued)*

Metabolism: Primarily hepatic via CYP1A2
Bioavailability: 20% to 30%
Half-life elimination: 26 hours
Time to peak: 2-4 hours
Excretion: Feces (62%); urine (32%)

Dosage Oral: Adults: Migraine: 2.5 mg; if headache recurs, a second dose may be given if first dose provided some relief and at least 2 hours have elapsed since the first dose (maximum daily dose: 7.5 mg)

Dosage adjustment in renal impairment: No adjustment necessary

Dosage adjustment in hepatic impairment: No adjustment necessary in mild to moderate hepatic impairment; use with caution in severe impairment

Administration Administer with fluids.

Dosage Forms Tablet, as base: 2.5 mg

♦ **Frovatriptan Succinate** *see* Frovatriptan *on page 771*
♦ **Frusemide** *see* Furosemide *on page 773*
♦ **FSH** *see* Follitropin Alfa *on page 751*
♦ **FSH** *see* Follitropin Beta *on page 753*
♦ **FSH** *see* Urofollitropin *on page 1759*
♦ **FTC** *see* Emtricitabine *on page 576*
♦ **FU** *see* Fluorouracil *on page 725*
♦ **5-FU** *see* Fluorouracil *on page 725*
♦ **Ful-Glo®** *see* Fluorescein Sodium *on page 722*

Fulvestrant *(fool VES trant)*

U.S. Brand Names Faslodex®
Index Terms ICI-182,780; Zeneca 182,780; ZM-182,780
Pharmacologic Category Antineoplastic Agent, Estrogen Receptor Antagonist
Use Treatment of hormone receptor positive metastatic breast cancer in postmenopausal women with disease progression following antiestrogen therapy.
Unlabeled/Investigational Use Endometriosis; uterine bleeding
Pregnancy Risk Factor D
Pregnancy Implications Antiestrogenic compounds have been associated with embryotoxicity, abnormalities in fetal development, and failure to maintain pregnancy in animal models. Approved for use only in postmenopausal women.
Lactation Excretion in breast milk unknown/contraindicated
Contraindications Hypersensitivity to fulvestrant or any component of the formulation; contraindications to I.M. injections (bleeding diatheses, thrombocytopenia, or therapeutic anticoagulation); pregnancy
Warnings/Precautions Use caution in hepatic impairment.
Adverse Reactions
>10%:
Cardiovascular: Vasodilation (18%)
Central nervous system: Pain (19%), headache (15%)
Endocrine & metabolic: Hot flushes (19% to 24%)
Gastrointestinal: Nausea (26%), vomiting (13%), constipation (13%), diarrhea (12%), abdominal pain (12%)
Local: Injection site reaction (11%)
Neuromuscular & skeletal: Weakness (23%), bone pain (16%), back pain (14%)
Respiratory: Pharyngitis (16%), dyspnea (15%)
1% to 10%:
Cardiovascular: Edema (9%), chest pain (7%)
Central nervous system: Dizziness (7%), insomnia (7%), paresthesia (6%), fever (6%), depression (6%), anxiety (5%)
Dermatologic: Rash (7%)
Gastrointestinal: Anorexia (9%), weight gain (1% to 2%)
Genitourinary: Pelvic pain (10%), urinary tract infection (6%), vaginitis (2% to 3%)
Hematologic: Anemia (5%)
Neuromuscular and skeletal: Arthritis (3%)
Respiratory: Cough (10%)
Miscellaneous: Diaphoresis increased (5%)
<1% (limited to important or life-threatening): Angioedema, hypersensitivity reactions, leukopenia, myalgia, thrombosis, urticaria, vaginal bleeding, vertigo
Overdosage/Toxicology No specific experience in overdose. Treatment is supportive.
Drug Interactions
Cytochrome P450 Effect: Substrate of CYP3A4 (minor)
Stability Store under refrigeration at 2°C to 8°C (36°F to 46°F).
Mechanism of Action Steroidal compound which competitively binds to estrogen receptors on tumors and other tissue targets, producing a nuclear complex that decreases DNA synthesis and inhibits estrogen effects. Fulvestrant has no estrogen-receptor agonist activity. Causes down-regulation of estrogen receptors and inhibits tumor growth.
Pharmacodynamics/Kinetics
Duration: I.M.: Plasma levels maintained for at least 1 month
Distribution: V_d: 3-5 L/kg
Protein binding: 99%
Metabolism: Hepatic via multiple pathways (CYP3A4 substrate, relative contribution to metabolism unknown)
Bioavailability: Oral: Poor
Half-life elimination: ~40 days
Time to peak, plasma: I.M.: 7-9 days

Excretion: Feces (>90%); urine (<1%)

Dosage I.M.: Adults (postmenopausal women): 250 mg at 1-month intervals

Dosage adjustment in renal impairment: No adjustment required.

Dosage adjustment in hepatic impairment: Use in moderate to severe hepatic impairment has not been evaluated; use caution.

Administration I.M. injection into a relatively large muscle (ie, buttock); do not administer I.V., SubQ, or intra-arterially. May be administered as a single 5 mL injection or two concurrent 2.5 mL injections.

Dosage Forms Injection, solution: 50 mg/mL (2.5 mL, 5 mL) [prefilled syringe; contains alcohol, benzyl alcohol, benzyl stearate, castor oil]

♦ **Fungi-Guard [OTC]** *see* Tolnaftate *on page 1704*

♦ **Fungizone® (Can)** *see* Amphotericin B (Conventional) *on page 116*

♦ **Fungoid® Tincture [OTC]** *see* Miconazole *on page 1137*

♦ **Furadantin®** *see* Nitrofurantoin *on page 1233*

♦ **Furamide®** *see* Diloxanide Furoate *on page 508*

♦ **Furazosin** *see* Prazosin *on page 1411*

Furosemide (fyoor OH se mide)

U.S. Brand Names Lasix®

Canadian Brand Names Apo-Furosemide®; Furosemide Injection, USP; Furosemide Special; Lasix®; Lasix® Special; Novo-Semide

Index Terms Frusemide

Pharmacologic Category Diuretic, Loop

Additional Appendix Information

Heart Failure (Systolic) *on page 2051*

Hemodynamic Support, Intravenous *on page 1885*

Sulfonamide Derivatives *on page 1897*

Use Management of edema associated with congestive heart failure and hepatic or renal disease; alone or in combination with antihypertensives in treatment of hypertension

Pregnancy Risk Factor C

Pregnancy Implications Crosses the placenta. Increased fetal urine production, electrolyte disturbances reported. Generally, use of diuretics during pregnancy is avoided due to risk of decreased placental perfusion.

Lactation Enters breast milk/use caution

Medication Safety Issues

Sound-alike/look-alike issues:

Furosemide may be confused with torsemide

Lasix® may be confused with Esidrix®, Lanoxin®, Lidex®, Lomotil®, Luvox®, Luxiq®

International issues:

Urex® [Australia] may be confused with Eurax® which is a brand name for crotamiton in the U.S.

Urex® [Australia]: Brand name for methenamine in the U.S.

Contraindications Hypersensitivity to furosemide, any component, or sulfonylureas; anuria; patients with hepatic coma or in states of severe electrolyte depletion until the condition improves or is corrected

Warnings/Precautions Loop diuretics are potent diuretics; excess amounts can lead to profound diuresis with fluid and electrolyte loss; close medical supervision and dose evaluation are required. Watch for and correct electrolyte disturbances; adjust dose to avoid dehydration. In cirrhosis, avoid electrolyte and acid/base imbalances that might lead to hepatic encephalopathy. Coadministration of antihypertensives may increase the risk of hypotension.

Monitor fluid status and renal function in an attempt to prevent oliguria, azotemia, and reversible increases in BUN and creatinine; close medical supervision of aggressive diuresis required. Rapid I.V. administration, renal impairment, excessive doses, and concurrent use of other ototoxins is associated with ototoxicity. Asymptomatic hyperuricemia has been reported with use.

Chemical similarities are present among sulfonamides, sulfonylureas, carbonic anhydrase inhibitors, thiazides, and loop diuretics (except ethacrynic acid). Use in patients with sulfonylurea allergy is specifically contraindicated in product labeling, however, a risk of cross-reaction exists in patients with allergy to any of these compounds; avoid use when previous reaction has been severe. Discontinue if signs of hypersensitivity are noted.

Adverse Reactions Frequency not defined.

Cardiovascular: Acute hypotension, chronic aortitis, necrotizing angiitis, orthostatic hypotension, thrombophlebitis, sudden death from cardiac arrest (with I.V. or I.M. administration)

Central nervous system: Blurred vision, dizziness, fever, headache, lightheadedness, restlessness, vertigo, xanthopsia

Dermatologic: Cutaneous vasculitis, erythema multiforme, exfoliative dermatitis, photosensitivity, pruritus, purpura, rash, urticaria

Endocrine & metabolic: Gout, hyperglycemia, hyperuricemia, hypocalcemia, hypochloremia, hypokalemia, hypomagnesemia, hyponatremia, metabolic alkalosis

Gastrointestinal: Anorexia, constipation, cramping, diarrhea, intrahepatic cholestatic jaundice, ischemia hepatitis, nausea, oral and gastric irritation, pancreatitis, vomiting

Genitourinary: Urinary bladder spasm, urinary frequency

Hematologic: Agranulocytosis (rare), anemia, aplastic anemia (rare), hemolytic anemia, leukopenia, purpura, thrombocytopenia

Neuromuscular & skeletal: Muscle spasm, paresthesia, weakness

Otic: Hearing impairment (reversible or permanent with rapid I.V. or I.M. administration), reversible deafness (with rapid I.V. or I.M. administration), tinnitus

Renal: Allergic interstitial nephritis, fall in glomerular filtration rate and renal blood flow (due to overdiuresis), glycosuria, transient rise in BUN, vasculitis

(Continued)

Furosemide *(Continued)*

Miscellaneous: Anaphylaxis (rare), exacerbate or activate systemic lupus erythematosus

Overdosage/Toxicology Symptoms include electrolyte imbalance, volume depletion, hypotension, dehydration, hypokalemia and hypochloremic alkalosis. Following GI decontamination, treatment is supportive. Hypotension responds to fluids and Trendelenburg position.

Drug Interactions

Increased Effect/Toxicity: Furosemide-induced hypokalemia may predispose to digoxin toxicity and may increase the risk of arrhythmia with drugs which may prolong QT interval, including type Ia and type III antiarrhythmic agents, cisapride, and some quinolones (sparfloxacin, gatifloxacin, and moxifloxacin). The risk of toxicity from lithium and salicylates (high dose) may be increased by loop diuretics. Hypotensive effects and/or adverse renal effects of ACE inhibitors and NSAIDs are potentiated by furosemide-induced hypovolemia. The effects of peripheral adrenergic-blocking drugs or ganglionic blockers may be increased by furosemide.

Furosemide may increase the risk of ototoxicity with other ototoxic agents (aminoglycosides, cis-platinum), especially in patients with renal dysfunction. Synergistic diuretic effects occur with thiazide-type diuretics. Diuretics tend to be synergistic with other antihypertensive agents, and hypotension may occur.

Decreased Effect: Indomethacin, aspirin, phenobarbital, phenytoin, and NSAIDs may reduce natriuretic and hypotensive effects of furosemide. Colestipol, cholestyramine, and sucralfate may reduce the effect of furosemide; separate administration by 2 hours. Furosemide may antagonize the effect of skeletal muscle relaxants (tubocurarine). Glucose tolerance may be decreased by furosemide, requiring an adjustment in the dose of hypoglycemic agents. Metformin may decrease furosemide concentrations.

Ethanol/Nutrition/Herb Interactions

Food: Furosemide serum levels may be decreased if taken with food.

Herb/Nutraceutical: Avoid dong quai if using for hypertension (has estrogenic activity). Avoid ephedra, yohimbe, ginseng (may worsen hypertension). Limit intake of natural licorice. Avoid garlic (may have increased antihypertensive effect).

Stability Furosemide injection should be stored at controlled room temperature and protected from light. Exposure to light may cause discoloration; do not use furosemide solutions if they have a yellow color. Furosemide solutions are unstable in acidic media, but very stable in basic media Refrigeration may result in precipitation or crystallization, however, resolubilization at room temperature or warming may be performed without affecting the drug's stability. I.V. infusion solution mixed in NS or D_5W solution is stable for 24 hours at room temperature. May also be diluted for infusion 1-2 mg/mL (maximum: 10 mg/mL) over 10-15 minutes (following infusion rate parameters).

Mechanism of Action Inhibits reabsorption of sodium and chloride in the ascending loop of Henle and distal renal tubule, interfering with the chloride-binding cotransport system, thus causing increased excretion of water, sodium, chloride, magnesium, and calcium

Pharmacodynamics/Kinetics

Onset of action: Diuresis: Oral: 30-60 minutes; I.M.: 30 minutes; I.V.: ~5 minutes

Peak effect: Oral: 1-2 hours

Duration: Oral: 6-8 hours; I.V.: 2 hours

Absorption: Oral: 60% to 67%

Protein binding: >98%

Metabolism: Minimally hepatic

Half-life elimination: Normal renal function: 0.5-1.1 hours; End-stage renal disease: 9 hours

Excretion: Urine (Oral: 50%, I.V.: 80%) within 24 hours; feces (as unchanged drug); nonrenal clearance prolonged in renal impairment

Dosage

Infants and Children:

Oral: 1-2 mg/kg/dose increased in increments of 1 mg/kg/dose with each succeeding dose until a satisfactory effect is achieved to a maximum of 6 mg/kg/dose no more frequently than 6 hours.

I.M., I.V.: 1 mg/kg/dose, increasing by each succeeding dose at 1 mg/kg/dose at intervals of 6-12 hours until a satisfactory response up to 6 mg/kg/dose.

Adults:

Oral: 20-80 mg/dose initially increased in increments of 20-40 mg/dose at intervals of 6-8 hours; usual maintenance dose interval is twice daily or every day; may be titrated up to 600 mg/day with severe edematous states.

Hypertension (JNC 7): 20-80 mg/day in 2 divided doses

I.M., I.V.: 20-40 mg/dose, may be repeated in 1-2 hours as needed and increased by 20 mg/dose until the desired effect has been obtained. Usual dosing interval: 6-12 hours; for acute pulmonary edema, the usual dose is 40 mg I.V. over 1-2 minutes. If not adequate, may increase dose to 80 mg. **Note:** ACC/AHA 2005 guidelines for chronic congestive heart failure recommend a maximum single dose of 160-200 mg.

Continuous I.V. infusion: Initial I.V. bolus dose 20-40 mg, followed by continuous I.V. infusion doses of 10-40 mg/hour. If urine output is <1 mL/kg/hour, double as necessary to a maximum of 80-160 mg/hour. The risk associated with higher infusion rates (80-160 mg/hour) must be weighed against alternative strategies. **Note:** ACC/AHA 2005 guidelines for chronic congestive heart failure recommend 40 mg I.V. load, then 10-40 mg/hour infusion.

Refractory heart failure: Oral, I.V.: Doses up to 8 g/day have been used.

Elderly: Oral, I.M., I.V.: Initial: 20 mg/day; increase slowly to desired response.

Dosing adjustment/comments in renal impairment: Acute renal failure: High doses (up to 1-3 g/day - oral/I.V.) have been used to initiate desired response; avoid use in oliguric states.

Dialysis: Not removed by hemo- or peritoneal dialysis; supplemental dose is not necessary.

Dosing adjustment/comments in hepatic disease: Diminished natriuretic effect with increased sensitivity to hypokalemia and volume depletion in cirrhosis; monitor effects, particularly with high doses.

Dietary Considerations May cause a potassium loss; potassium supplement or dietary changes may be required. Administer on an empty stomach. May be administered with food or milk if GI distress occurs. Do not mix with acidic solutions.

Administration

I.V.: I.V. injections should be given slowly. In adults, undiluted direct I.V. injections may be administered at a rate of 40 mg over 1-2 minutes; maximum rate of administration for IVPB or continuous infusion: 4 mg/minute. In children, a maximum rate of 0.5 mg/kg/minute has been recommended.

Oral: May be taken with or without food.

Monitoring Parameters Monitor weight and I & O daily; blood pressure, orthostasis, serum electrolytes, renal function; in high doses, monitor hearing

Dosage Forms

Injection, solution: 10 mg/mL (2 mL, 4 mL, 8 mL, 10 mL)

Solution, oral: 10 mg/mL (60 mL, 120 mL) [orange flavor]; 40 mg/5 mL (5 mL, 500 mL) [pineapple-peach flavor]

Tablet (Lasix®): 20 mg, 40 mg, 80 mg

- ♦ **Furosemide Injection, USP (Can)** *see Furosemide on page 773*
- ♦ **Furosemide Special (Can)** *see Furosemide on page 773*
- ♦ **Fuzeon®** *see Enfuvirtide on page 581*
- ♦ **FVIII/vWF** *see Antihemophilic Factor/von Willebrand Factor Complex (Human) on page 136*
- ♦ **FXT (Can)** *see Fluoxetine on page 727*
- ♦ **GAA** *see Alglucosidase Alfa on page 70*

Gabapentin (GA ba pen tin)

U.S. Brand Names Neurontin®

Canadian Brand Names Apo-Gabapentin®; BCI-Gabapentin; Gen-Gabapentin; Neurontin®; Novo-Gabapentin; Nu-Gabapentin; PMS-Gabapentin

Pharmacologic Category Anticonvulsant, Miscellaneous

Additional Appendix Information

Anticonvulsants by Seizure Type *on page 1865*

Epilepsy *on page 2048*

Use Adjunct for treatment of partial seizures with and without secondary generalized seizures in patients >12 years of age with epilepsy; adjunct for treatment of partial seizures in pediatric patients 3-12 years of age; management of postherpetic neuralgia (PHN) in adults

Unlabeled/Investigational Use Social phobia; chronic pain

Pregnancy Risk Factor C

Pregnancy Implications Animal studies have documented teratogenic effects. There are no adequate and well-controlled studies in pregnant women. Use during pregnancy only if the potential benefit to the mother outweighs the potential risk to the fetus.

Lactation Enters breast milk/use caution

Medication Safety Issues .

Sound-alike/look-alike issues:

Neurontin® may be confused with Neoral®, Noroxin®

Contraindications Hypersensitivity to gabapentin or any component of the formulation

Warnings/Precautions Avoid abrupt withdrawal, may precipitate seizures; use cautiously in patients with severe renal dysfunction; male rat studies demonstrated an association with pancreatic adenocarcinoma (clinical implication unknown). May cause CNS depression, which may impair physical or mental abilities. Patients must be cautioned about performing tasks which require mental alertness (eg, operating machinery or driving). Effects with other sedative drugs or ethanol may be potentiated. Pediatric patients (3-12 years of age) have shown increased incidence of CNS-related adverse effects, including emotional lability, hostility, thought disorder, and hyperkinesia. Safety and efficacy in children <3 years of age have not been established.

Adverse Reactions As reported in patients >12 years of age, unless otherwise noted in children (3-12 years)

>10%:

Central nervous system: Somnolence (20%; children 8%), dizziness (17% to 28%; children 3%), ataxia (13%), fatigue (11%)

Miscellaneous: Viral infection (children 11%)

1% to 10%:

Cardiovascular: Peripheral edema (2% to 8%), vasodilatation (1%)

Central nervous system: Fever (children 10%), hostility (children 8%), emotional lability (children 4%), fatigue (children 3%), headache (3%), ataxia (3%), abnormal thinking (2% to 3%; children 2%), amnesia (2%), depression (2%), dysarthria (2%), nervousness (2%), abnormal coordination (1% to 2%), twitching (1%), hyperesthesia (1%)

Dermatologic: Pruritus (1%), rash (1%)

Endocrine & metabolic: Hyperglycemia (1%)

Gastrointestinal: Diarrhea (6%), nausea/vomiting (3% to 4%; children 8%), abdominal pain (3%), weight gain (adults and children 2% to 3%), dyspepsia (2%), flatulence (2%), dry throat (2%), xerostomia (2% to 5%), constipation (2% to 4%), dental abnormalities (2%), appetite stimulation (1%)

Genitourinary: Impotence (2%)

Hematologic: Leukopenia (1%), decreased WBC (1%)

Neuromuscular & skeletal: Tremor (7%), weakness (6%), hyperkinesia (children 3%), abnormal gait (2%), back pain (2%), myalgia (2%), fracture (1%)

Ocular: Nystagmus (8%), diplopia (1% to 6%), blurred vision (3% to 4%), conjunctivitis (1%)

Otic: Otitis media (1%)

Respiratory: Rhinitis (4%), bronchitis (children 3%), respiratory infection (children 3%), pharyngitis (1% to 3%), cough (2%)

Miscellaneous: Infection (5%)

(Continued)

Gabapentin *(Continued)*

Postmarketing and additional clinical reports (limited to important or life-threatening): Acute renal failure, anemia, angina, angioedema, aphasia, arrhythmias (various), aspiration pneumonia, blindness, bradycardia, bronchospasm, cerebrovascular accident, CNS tumors, coagulation defect, colitis, Cushingoid appearance, dyspnea, encephalopathy, facial paralysis, fecal incontinence, glaucoma, glycosuria, heart block, hearing loss, hematemesis, hematuria, hemiplegia, hemorrhage, hepatitis, hepatomegaly, hyper-/hypotension, hyperlipidemia, hyper-/hypothyroidism, hyper-/hypoventilation, gastroenteritis, heart failure, leukocytosis, liver function tests increased, local myoclonus, lymphadenopathy, lymphocytosis, meningismus, MI, migraine, nephrosis, nerve palsy, non-Hodgkin's lymphoma, ovarian failure, pulmonary thrombosis, pericardial rub, pulmonary embolus, pericardial effusion, pericarditis, pancreatitis, peptic ulcer, purpura, paresthesia, palpitation, peripheral vascular disorder, pneumonia, psychosis, renal stone, retinopathy, skin necrosis, status epilepticus, subdural hematoma, syncope, tachycardia, thrombocytopenia, thrombophlebitis

Overdosage/Toxicology Acute oral overdoses up to 49 g have been reported; double vision, slurred speech, drowsiness, lethargy, and diarrhea were observed. Patients recovered with supportive care. Decontaminate using lavage/activated charcoal with cathartic. Multiple dosing of activated charcoal may be useful. Hemodialysis may be useful.

Drug Interactions

Increased Effect/Toxicity: Sedative effects may be additive with CNS depressants; includes ethanol, barbiturates, opioid analgesics, and other sedative agents; monitor for increased effect

Ethanol/Nutrition/Herb Interactions

Ethanol: Avoid ethanol (may increase CNS depression).

Food: Does not change rate or extent of absorption.

Herb/Nutraceutical: Avoid evening primrose (seizure threshold decreased). Avoid valerian, St John's wort, kava kava, gotu kola (may increase CNS depression).

Stability Store at 25°C (77°F); excursions permitted to 15°C to 30°C (59°F to 86°F).

Mechanism of Action Gabapentin is structurally related to GABA. However, it does not bind to $GABA_A$ or $GABA_B$ receptors, and it does not appear to influence synthesis or uptake of GABA. High affinity gabapentin binding sites have been located throughout the brain; these sites correspond to the presence of voltage-gated calcium channels specifically possessing the alpha-2-delta-1 subunit. This channel appears to be located presynaptically, and may modulate the release of excitatory neurotransmitters which participate in epileptogenesis and nociception.

Pharmacodynamics/Kinetics

Absorption: 50% to 60% from proximal small bowel by L-amino transport system

Distribution: V_d: 0.6-0.8 L/kg

Protein binding: <3%

Bioavailability: Inversely proportional to dose due to saturable absorption:

900 mg/day: 60%

1200 mg/day: 47%

2400 mg/day: 34%

3600 mg/day: 33%

4800 mg/day: 27%

Half-life elimination: 5-7 hours; anuria 132 hours; during dialysis 3.8 hours

Excretion: Proportional to renal function; urine (as unchanged drug)

Dosage Oral:

Children: Anticonvulsant:

3-12 years: Initial: 10-15 mg/kg/day in 3 divided doses; titrate to effective dose over ~3 days; dosages of up to 50 mg/kg/day have been tolerated in clinical studies

3-4 years: Effective dose: 40 mg/kg/day in 3 divided doses

≥5-12 years: Effective dose: 25-35 mg/kg/day in 3 divided doses

See "Note" in Adults dosing.

Children >12 years and Adults:

Anticonvulsant: Initial: 300 mg 3 times/day; if necessary the dose may be increased up to 1800 mg/day. Doses of up to 2400 mg/day have been tolerated in long-term clinical studies; up to 3600 mg/day has been tolerated in short-term studies.

Note: If gabapentin is discontinued or if another anticonvulsant is added to therapy, it should be done slowly over a minimum of 1 week

Pain (unlabeled use): 300-1800 mg/day given in 3 divided doses has been the most common dosage range

Adults: Postherpetic neuralgia or neuropathic pain: Day 1: 300 mg, Day 2: 300 mg twice daily, Day 3: 300 mg 3 times/day; dose may be titrated as needed for pain relief (range: 1800-3600 mg/day, daily doses >1800 mg do not generally show greater benefit)

Elderly: Studies in elderly patients have shown a decrease in clearance as age increases. This is most likely due to age-related decreases in renal function; dose reductions may be needed.

Dosing adjustment in renal impairment: Children ≥12 years and Adults: See table.

Hemodialysis: Dialyzable

Gabapentin Dosing Adjustments in Renal Impairment

Creatinine Clearance (mL/min)	Daily Dose Range
≥60	300-1200 mg tid
>30-59	200-700 mg bid
>15-29	200-700 mg daily
15[1]	100-300 mg daily
Hemodialysis[2]	125-350 mg

[1]Cl_{cr}<15 mL/minute: Reduce daily dose in proportion to creatinine clearance.

[2]Single supplemental dose administered after each 4 hours of hemodialysis

Dietary Considerations May be taken without regard to meals.

Administration Administer first dose on first day at bedtime to avoid somnolence and dizziness. Dosage must be adjusted for renal function; when given 3 times daily, the maximum time between doses should not exceed 12 hours.

Monitoring Parameters Monitor serum levels of concomitant anticonvulsant therapy

Test Interactions False positives have been reported with the Ames N-Multistix SG® dipstick test for urine protein

Dosage Forms

Capsule: 100 mg, 300 mg, 400 mg

    Neurontin®: 100 mg, 300 mg, 400 mg

Solution, oral:

    Neurontin®: 250 mg/5 mL (480 mL) [cool strawberry anise flavor]

Tablet: 100 mg, 300 mg, 400 mg, 600 mg, 800 mg

    Neurontin®: 600 mg, 800 mg

Extemporaneous Preparations A 100 mg/mL suspension was stable for 91 days when refrigerated or 56 days when kept at room temperature when compounded as follows:

Triturate sixty-seven 300 mg tablets in a mortar, reduce to a fine powder, then add a small amount of one of the following vehicles to make a paste; then add the remaining vehicle in small quantities while mixing:

Vehicle 1. Methylcellulose 1% (100 mL) and Simple Syrup N.F. (100 mL) mixed together in a graduate, **or**

Vehicle 2. Ora-Sweet® (100 mL) and Ora-Plus® (100 mL) mixed together in a graduate

Shake well before using and keep in refrigerator

Nahata MC, Morosco RS, and Hipple TF, *Stability of Gabapentin in Extemporaneously Prepared Suspensions at Two Temperatures*, American Society of Health System Pharmacists Midyear Meeting, December 7-11, 1997.

♦ **Gabitril**® *see Tiagabine on page 1679*

Galantamine (ga LAN ta mccn)

U.S. Brand Names Razadyne™; Razadyne™ ER; Reminyl® [DSC]

Canadian Brand Names Reminyl®; Reminyl® ER

Index Terms Galantamine Hydrobromide

Pharmacologic Category Acetylcholinesterase Inhibitor (Central)

Use Treatment of mild-to-moderate dementia of Alzheimer's disease

Pregnancy Risk Factor B

Pregnancy Implications In animal studies, there was a slight increased in the incident of skeletal variations when given during organogenesis. Adequate, well-controlled studies in pregnant women do not exist. Should be used in pregnancy only if benefit outweighs potential risk to the fetus.

Lactation Excretion in breast milk unknown/not recommended

Medication Safety Issues

Sound-alike/look-alike issues:

Razedyne™ may be confused with Rozerem™

Reminyl® may be confused with Amaryl®

Due to patient safety concerns regarding prescribing and dispensing errors between Reminyl® and Amaryl®, Reminyl® (galantamine) is being renamed to Razadyne™ (immediate-release) and Razadyne™ ER (extended-release). The brand name Reminyl® was discontinued with the July, 2005 distribution of Razadyne™.

Contraindications Hypersensitivity to galantamine or any component of the formulation; severe liver dysfunction (Child-Pugh score 10-15); severe renal dysfunction (Cl_{cr} <9 mL/minute)

Warnings/Precautions Use caution in patients with supraventricular conduction delays (without a functional pacemaker in place) or patients taking medicines that slow conduction through SA or AV node. Use caution in peptic ulcer disease(or in patients at risk); seizure disorder; asthma; COPD; mild to moderate liver dysfunction; moderate renal dysfunction. May cause bladder outflow obstruction. May exaggerate neuromuscular blockade effects of succinylcholine and like agents. Safety and efficacy in children have not been established.

Adverse Reactions

>10%: Gastrointestinal: Nausea (6% to 24%), vomiting (4% to 13%), diarrhea (6% to 12%)

1% to 10%:

Cardiovascular: Bradycardia (2% to 3%), syncope (0.4% to 2.2%: dose related), chest pain (≥1%)

Central nervous system: Dizziness (9%), headache (8%), depression (7%), fatigue (5%), insomnia (5%), somnolence (4%)

Gastrointestinal: Anorexia (7% to 9%), weight loss (5% to 7%), abdominal pain (5%), dyspepsia (5%), flatulence (≥1%)

Genitourinary: Urinary tract infection (8%), hematuria (<1% to 3%), incontinence (≥1%)

Hematologic: Anemia (3%)

Neuromuscular & skeletal: Tremor (3%)

Respiratory: Rhinitis (4%)

<1% (Limited to important or life-threatening): Aggression, alkaline phosphatase increased, aphasia, apraxia, ataxia, atrial fibrillation, AV block, bundle branch block, convulsions, dehydration, delirium, diverticulitis, dysphagia, epistaxis, esophageal perforation, fever, gastrointestinal bleeding, heart failure, hyper-/hypokinesia, hypokalemia, hypotension, malaise, melena, MI, palpitation, paranoid reaction, paresthesia, paroniria, postural hypotension, purpura, QT prolongation, rectal hemorrhage, renal calculi, renal failure (due to dehydration), stroke, suicide, supraventricular tachycardia, T-wave inversion, thrombocytopenia, TIA, ventricular tachycardia, vertigo, weakness

Overdosage/Toxicology Symptoms of overdose may include bradycardia, collapse, convulsions, defecation, gastrointestinal cramping, hypotension, lacrimation, muscle fasciculations, muscle weakness, QT prolongation, respiratory depression, salivation, severe nausea, sweating, torsade de pointes, urination, ventricular tachycardia, vomiting. Treatment is (Continued)

Galantamine *(Continued)*

symptom-directed and supportive. Atropine may be used as an antidote; initial dose 0.5-1 mg I.V. and titrate to effect. An atypical response in blood pressure and heart rate has been reported. Effects of hemodialysis are unknown.

Drug Interactions

Cytochrome P450 Effect: Substrate (minor) of CYP2D6, 3A4

Increased Effect/Toxicity: Succinylcholine: increased neuromuscular blockade. Amiodarone, beta-blockers without ISA activity, diltiazem, verapamil may increase bradycardia. NSAIDs increase risk of peptic ulcer. Other CYP3A4 inhibitors and other CYP2D6 inhibitors increase levels of galantamine. Concurrent cholinergic agents may have synergistic effects. Digoxin may lead to AV block. Acetylcholinesterase inhibitors (central) may increase the risk of antipsychotic-related extrapyramidal symptoms.

Decreased Effect: Anticholinergic agents are antagonized by galantamine. CYP inducers may decrease galantamine levels.

Ethanol/Nutrition/Herb Interactions

Ethanol: Avoid ethanol (may increase CNS adverse events).

Herb/Nutraceutical: St John's wort may decrease galantamine serum levels; avoid concurrent use.

Stability Store at 15°C to 30°C (59°F to 86°F). Do not freeze oral solution; protect from light.

Mechanism of Action Centrally-acting cholinesterase inhibitor (competitive and reversible). It elevates acetylcholine in cerebral cortex by slowing the degradation of acetylcholine. Modulates nicotinic acetylcholine receptor to increase acetylcholine from surviving presynaptic nerve terminals. May increase glutamate and serotonin levels.

Pharmacodynamics/Kinetics

Duration: 3 hours; maximum inhibition of erythrocyte acetylcholinesterase ~40% at 1 hour post 8 mg oral dose; levels return to baseline at 30 hours

Absorption: Rapid and complete

Distribution: 175 L; levels in the brain are 2-3 times higher than in plasma

Protein binding: 18%

Metabolism: Hepatic; linear, CYP2D6 and 3A4; metabolized to epigalanthaminone and galanthaminone both of which have acetylcholinesterase inhibitory activity 130 times less than galantamine

Bioavailability: ~90%

Half-life elimination: 7 hours

Time to peak: Immediate release: 1 hour (2.5 hours with food); extended release: 4.5-5 hours

Excretion: Urine (25%)

Dosage Oral: Adults:

Note: Oral solution and tablet should be taken with breakfast and dinner; capsule should be taken with breakfast. If therapy is interrupted for ≥3 days, restart at the lowest dose and increase to current dose.

Immediate release tablet or solution: Mild-to-moderate dementia of Alzheimer's: Initial: 4 mg twice a day for 4 weeks; if tolerated, increase to 8 mg twice daily for ≥4 weeks; if tolerated, increase to 12 mg twice daily

Range: 16-24 mg/day in 2 divided doses

Extended-release capsule: Initial: 8 mg once daily for 4 weeks; if tolerated, increase to 16 mg once daily for ≥4 weeks; if tolerated, increase to 24 mg once daily

Range: 16-24 mg once daily

Conversion to galantamine from other cholinesterase inhibitors: Patients experiencing poor tolerability with donepezil or rivastigmine should wait until side effects subside or allow a 7-day washout period prior to beginning galantamine. Patients not experiencing side effects with donepezil or rivastigmine may begin galantamine therapy the day immediately following discontinuation of previous therapy (Morris, 2001).

Elderly: No dosage adjustment needed

Dosage adjustment in renal impairment:

Moderate renal impairment: Maximum dose: 16 mg/day.

Severe renal dysfunction (Cl$_{cr}$ <9 mL/minute): Use is not recommended

Dosage adjustment in hepatic impairment:

Moderate liver dysfunction (Child-Pugh score 7-9): Maximum dose: 16 mg/day

Severe liver dysfunction (Child-Pugh score 10-15): Use is not recommended

Dietary Considerations

Administration with food is preferred, but not required; should be taken with breakfast and dinner (tablet or solution) or with breakfast (capsule).

Administration Oral: Administer solution or tablet with breakfast and dinner; administer extended release capsule with breakfast. If therapy is interrupted for ≥3 days, restart at the lowest dose and increase to current dose. If using oral solution, mix dose with 3-4 ounces of any nonalcoholic beverage; mix well and drink immediately.

Monitoring Parameters Mental status

Dosage Forms

Capsule, extended release, as hydrobromide (Razadyne™ ER): 8 mg, 16 mg, 24 mg [contains gelatin]

Solution, oral, as hydrobromide (Razadyne™): 4 mg/mL (100 mL) [with calibrated pipette]

Tablet, as hydrobromide (Razadyne™): 4 mg, 8 mg, 12 mg

♦ **Galantamine Hydrobromide** *see* Galantamine *on page 777*

♦ **Gamimune® N (Can)** *see* Immune Globulin (Intravenous) *on page 892*

♦ **Gamma Benzene Hexachloride** *see* Lindane *on page 1016*

♦ **Gamma E-Gems® [OTC]** *see* Vitamin E *on page 1794*

♦ **Gamma-E Plus [OTC]** *see* Vitamin E *on page 1794*

♦ **Gammagard® Liquid** *see* Immune Globulin (Intravenous) *on page 892*

♦ **Gammagard® S/D** *see* Immune Globulin (Intravenous) *on page 892*

♦ **Gamma Globulin** *see* Immune Globulin (Intramuscular) *on page 891*

♦ **Gamma Hydroxybutyric Acid** *see* Sodium Oxybate *on page 1580*

♦ **Gammaphos** *see* Amifostine *on page 89*
♦ **Gammar®-P I.V.** *see* Immune Globulin (Intravenous) *on page 892*
♦ **GammaSTAN™ S/D** *see* Immune Globulin (Intramuscular) *on page 891*
♦ **Gamunex®** *see* Immune Globulin (Intravenous) *on page 892*

Ganciclovir (gan SYE kloe veer)

U.S. Brand Names Cytovene®; Vitrasert®
Canadian Brand Names Cytovene®; Vitrasert®
Index Terms DHPG Sodium; GCV Sodium; Nordeoxyguanosine
Pharmacologic Category Antiviral Agent
Additional Appendix Information
USPHS / IDSA Guidelines for the Prevention of Opportunistic Infections in Persons Infected With HIV *on page 1966*
Use
Parenteral: Treatment of CMV retinitis in immunocompromised individuals, including patients with acquired immunodeficiency syndrome; prophylaxis of CMV infection in transplant patients
Oral: Alternative to the I.V. formulation for maintenance treatment of CMV retinitis in immunocompromised patients, including patients with AIDS, in whom retinitis is stable following appropriate induction therapy and for whom the risk of more rapid progression is balanced by the benefit associated with avoiding daily I.V. infusions.
Implant: Treatment of CMV retinitis
Unlabeled/Investigational Use May be given in combination with foscarnet in patients who relapse after monotherapy with either drug
Pregnancy Risk Factor C
Lactation Excretion in breast milk unknown/contraindicated
Medication Safety Issues
Sound-alike/look-alike issues:
Cytovene® may be confused with Cytosar®, Cytosar-U®
Contraindications Hypersensitivity to ganciclovir, acyclovir, or any component of the formulation; absolute neutrophil count <500/mm³; platelet count <25,000/mm³
Warnings/Precautions Hazardous agent - use appropriate precautions for handling and disposal. **[U.S. Boxed Warning]: Granulocytopenia, anemia, and thrombocytopenia may occur.** Dosage adjustment or interruption of ganciclovir therapy may be necessary in patients with neutropenia and/or thrombocytopenia and patients with impaired renal function. Use with extreme caution in children since long-term safety has not been determined and **[U.S. Boxed Warning]: Animal studies have demonstrated carcinogenic and teratogenic effects, and inhibition of spermatogenesis;** contraceptive precautions for female and male patients need to be followed during and for at least 90 days after therapy with the drug; take care to administer only into veins with good blood flow. **[U.S. Boxed Warning]: Indicated only for treatment of CMV retinitis in the immunocompromised patient and CMV prevention in transplant patients at risk.**
Adverse Reactions
>10%:
Central nervous system: Fever (38% to 48%)
Dermatologic: Rash (15% oral, 10% I.V.)
Gastrointestinal: Abdominal pain (17% to 19%), diarrhea (40%), nausea (25%), anorexia (15%), vomiting (13%)
Hematologic: Anemia (20% to 25%), leukopenia (30% to 40%)
1% to 10%:
Central nervous system: Confusion, neuropathy (8% to 9%), headache (4%)
Dermatologic: Pruritus (5%)
Hematologic: Thrombocytopenia (6%), neutropenia with ANC <500/mm³ (5% oral, 14% I.V.)
Neuromuscular & skeletal: Paresthesia (6% to 10%), weakness (6%)
Ocular: Retinal detachment (8% oral, 11% I.V.; relationship to ganciclovir not established)
Miscellaneous: Sepsis (4% oral, 15% I.V.)
<1% (Limited to important or life-threatening): Alopecia, arrhythmia, ataxia, bronchospasm, coma, dyspnea, encephalopathy, eosinophilia, exfoliative dermatitis, extrapyramidal symptoms, hemorrhage, nervousness, pancytopenia, psychosis, renal failure, seizure, SIADH, Stevens-Johnson syndrome, torsade de pointes, urticaria, visual loss
Overdosage/Toxicology Symptoms include neutropenia, vomiting, hypersalivation, bloody diarrhea, cytopenia, and testicular atrophy. Treatment is supportive. Hemodialysis removes 50% of drug. Hydration may be of some benefit.
Drug Interactions
Increased Effect/Toxicity: Immunosuppressive agents may increase hematologic toxicity of ganciclovir. Imipenem/cilastatin may increase seizure potential. Oral ganciclovir increases blood levels of zidovudine, although zidovudine decreases steady-state levels of ganciclovir. Since both drugs have the potential to cause neutropenia and anemia, some patients may not tolerate concomitant therapy with these drugs at full dosage. Didanosine levels are increased with concurrent ganciclovir. Other nephrotoxic drugs (eg, amphotericin and cyclosporine) may have additive nephrotoxicity with ganciclovir.
Decreased Effect: A decrease in blood levels of ganciclovir AUC may occur when used with didanosine.
Stability Intact vials should be stored at room temperature and protected from temperatures >40°C Reconstitute powder with unpreserved sterile water **not** bacteriostatic water because parabens may cause precipitation; dilute in 250-1000 mL D₅W or NS to a concentration ≤10 mg/mL for Infusion.
Reconstituted solution is stable for 12 hours at room temperature, however, conflicting data indicates that reconstituted solution is stable for 60 days under refrigeration (4°C). Stability of
(Continued)

Ganciclovir *(Continued)*

parenteral admixture at room temperature (25°C) and at refrigeration temperature (4°C) is 5 days.

Mechanism of Action Ganciclovir is phosphorylated to a substrate which competitively inhibits the binding of deoxyguanosine triphosphate to DNA polymerase resulting in inhibition of viral DNA synthesis

Pharmacodynamics/Kinetics

Distribution: V_d: 15.26 L/1.73 m^2; widely to all tissues including CSF and ocular tissue

Protein binding: 1% to 2%

Bioavailability: Oral: Fasting: 5%; Following food: 6% to 9%; Following fatty meal: 28% to 31%

Half-life elimination: 1.7-5.8 hours; prolonged with renal impairment; End-stage renal disease: 5-28 hours

Excretion: Urine (80% to 99% as unchanged drug)

Dosage

CMV retinitis: Slow I.V. infusion (dosing is based on total body weight):

Children >3 months and Adults:

Induction therapy: 5 mg/kg/dose every 12 hours for 14-21 days followed by maintenance therapy

Maintenance therapy: 5 mg/kg/day as a single daily dose for 7 days/week or 6 mg/kg/day for 5 days/week

CMV retinitis: Oral: 1000 mg 3 times/day with food **or** 500 mg 6 times/day with food

Prevention of CMV disease in patients with advanced HIV infection and normal renal function: Oral: 1000 mg 3 times/day with food

Prevention of CMV disease in transplant patients: Same initial and maintenance dose as CMV retinitis except duration of initial course is 7-14 days; duration of maintenance therapy is dependent on clinical condition and degree of immunosuppression

Intravitreal implant: One implant for 5- to 8-month period; following depletion of ganciclovir, as evidenced by progression of retinitis, implant may be removed and replaced

Elderly: Refer to adult dosing; in general, dose selection should be cautious, reflecting greater frequency of organ impairment

Dosing adjustment in renal impairment:

I.V. (Induction):

Cl_{cr} 50-69 mL/minute: Administer 2.5 mg/kg/dose every 12 hours

Cl_{cr} 25-49 mL/minute: Administer 2.5 mg/kg/dose every 24 hours

Cl_{cr} 10-24 mL/minute: Administer 1.25 mg/kg/dose every 24 hours

Cl_{cr} <10 mL/minute: Administer 1.25 mg/kg/dose 3 times/week following hemodialysis

I.V. (Maintenance):

Cl_{cr} 50-69 mL/minute: Administer 2.5 mg/kg/dose every 24 hours

Cl_{cr} 25-49 mL/minute: Administer 1.25 mg/kg/dose every 24 hours

Cl_{cr} 10-24 mL/minute: Administer 0.625 mg/kg/dose every 24 hours

Cl_{cr} <10 mL/minute: Administer 0.625 mg/kg/dose 3 times/week following hemodialysis

Oral:

Cl_{cr} 50-69 mL/minute: Administer 1500 mg/day or 500 mg 3 times/day

Cl_{cr} 25-49 mL/minute: Administer 1000 mg/day or 500 mg twice daily

Cl_{cr} 10-24 mL/minute: Administer 500 mg/day

Cl_{cr} <10 mL/minute: Administer 500 mg 3 times/week following hemodialysis

Hemodialysis effects: Dialyzable (50%) following hemodialysis; administer dose postdialysis. During peritoneal dialysis, dose as for Cl_{cr} <10 mL/minute. During continuous arteriovenous or venovenous hemofiltration, administer 2.5 mg/kg/dose every 24 hours.

Dietary Considerations Sodium content of 500 mg vial: 46 mg

Administration Oral: Should be administered with food.

I.V.: Should not be administered by I.M., SubQ, or rapid IVP; administer by slow I.V. infusion over at least 1 hour

Monitoring Parameters CBC with differential and platelet count, serum creatinine, ophthalmologic exams

Dosage Forms [DSC] = Discontinued product

Capsule: 250 mg, 500 mg

Cytovene®: 250 mg, 500 mg [DSC]

Implant, intravitreal (Vitrasert®): 4.5 mg [released gradually over 5-8 months]

Injection, powder for reconstitution, as sodium (Cytovene®): 500 mg

♦ **Ganidin NR** *see* Guaifenesin *on page 814*

Ganirelix *(ga ni REL ix)*

Canadian Brand Names Orgalutran®

Index Terms Ganirelix Acetate

Pharmacologic Category Gonadotropin Releasing Hormone Antagonist

Use Inhibits premature luteinizing hormone (LH) surges in women undergoing controlled ovarian hyperstimulation in fertility clinics.

Pregnancy Risk Factor X

Pregnancy Implications Fetal resorption occurred in pregnant rats and rabbits. These effects are results of hormonal alterations and could result in fetal loss in humans. The drug should not be used in pregnant women.

Lactation Excretion in breast milk unknown/not recommended

Medication Safety Issues

International issues:

Antagon®: Brand name for astemizole in Mexico; brand name for ranitidine in Brazil

Contraindications Hypersensitivity to ganirelix or any component of the formulation; hypersensitivity to gonadotropin-releasing hormone or any other analog; known or suspected pregnancy

Warnings/Precautions Should only be prescribed by fertility specialists. The packaging contains natural rubber latex (may cause allergic reactions). Pregnancy must be excluded before starting medication.

Adverse Reactions

1% to 10%:

Central nervous system: Headache (3%)

Endocrine & metabolic: Ovarian hyperstimulation syndrome (2%)

Gastrointestinal: Abdominal pain (5%), nausea (1%)

Genitourinary: Vaginal bleeding (2%)

Local: Injection site reaction (1%)

<1% (Limited to important or life-threatening): Congenital abnormalities

Overdosage/Toxicology No reports of human overdosage.

Drug Interactions

Increased Effect/Toxicity: No formal studies have been performed.

Decreased Effect: No formal studies have been performed.

Stability Store at controlled room temperature of 15°C to 30°C (59°F to 86°F).

Mechanism of Action Competitively blocks the gonadotropin-release hormone receptors on the pituitary gonadotroph and transduction pathway. This suppresses gonadotropin secretion and luteinizing hormone secretion preventing ovulation until the follicles are of adequate size.

Pharmacodynamics/Kinetics

Absorption: SubQ: Rapid

Distribution: Mean V_d: 43.7 L

Protein binding: 81.9%

Metabolism: Hepatic to two primary metabolites (1-4 and 1-6 peptide)

Bioavailability: 91.1%

Half-life elimination: 16.2 hours

Time to peak: 1.1 hours

Excretion: Feces (75%) within 288 hours; urine (22%) within 24 hours

Dosage Adult: SubQ: 250 mcg/day during the mid-to-late phase after initiating follicle-stimulating hormone on day 2 or 3 of cycle. Treatment should be continued daily until the day of chorionic gonadotropin administration.

Monitoring Parameters Ultrasound to assess the follicle's size

Dosage Forms Injection, solution, as acetate: 250 mcg/0.5 mL [prefilled glass syringe with 27-gauge x ½ inch needle]

♦ **Ganirelix Acetate** see Ganirelix on page 780

♦ **Gani-Tuss DM NR** see Guaifenesin and Dextromethorphan on page 816

♦ **Gani-Tuss® NR** see Guaifenesin and Codeine on page 815

♦ **Gantrisin®** see SulfiSOXAZOLE on page 1617

♦ **GAR-936** see Tigecycline on page 1685

♦ **Garamycin® (Can)** see Gentamicin on page 793

♦ **Gardasil®** see Papillomavirus (Types 6, 11, 16, 18) Recombinant Vaccine on page 1310

♦ **Gastrocrom®** see Cromolyn on page 423

Gatifloxacin (gat i FLOKS a sin)

U.S. Brand Names Tequin® [DSC]; Zymar™

Canadian Brand Names Tequin®; Zymar™

Pharmacologic Category Antibiotic, Ophthalmic; Antibiotic, Quinolone

Additional Appendix Information

Antimicrobial Drugs of Choice on page 1981

Community-Acquired Pneumonia in Adults on page 1999

Prevention of Wound Infection and Sepsis in Surgical Patients on page 1964

Tuberculosis on page 2010

Use

Oral, I.V.: Treatment of the following infections when caused by susceptible bacteria: Acute bacterial exacerbation of chronic bronchitis; acute sinusitis; community-acquired pneumonia including pneumonia caused by multidrug-resistant *S. pneumoniae* (MDRSP); uncomplicated skin and skin structure infection; uncomplicated urinary tract infections (cystitis); complicated urinary tract infections; pyelonephritis; uncomplicated urethral and cervical gonorrhea; acute, uncomplicated rectal infections in women caused by gonorrhea

Ophthalmic: Bacterial conjunctivitis

Pregnancy Risk Factor C

Pregnancy Implications Reports of arthropathy (observed in immature animals and reported rarely in humans) have limited the use of fluoroquinolones during pregnancy. Gatifloxacin has been shown to be fetotoxic in animal studies. There are no adequate and well-controlled studies in pregnant women. Based on limited data, quinolones are not expected to be a major human teratogen. Although quinolone antibiotics should not be used as first-line agents during pregnancy, when considering treatment for life-threatening infection and/or prolonged duration of therapy, the potential risk to the fetus must be balanced against the severity of the potential illness.

Lactation Excretion in breast milk unknown/use caution

Contraindications Hypersensitivity to gatifloxacin, other quinolone antibiotics, or any component of the formulation; diabetes mellitus

Warnings/Precautions Use with caution in patients with significant bradycardia or acute myocardial ischemia. May prolong QT interval (concentration related). Use caution in patients with known prolongation of QT interval, uncorrected hypokalemia, or concurrent administration of other medications known to prolong the QT interval (including Class Ia and Class III antiarrhythmics, cisapride, erythromycin, antipsychotics, and tricyclic antidepressants). May cause increased CNS stimulation, increased intracranial pressure, convulsions, or psychosis. Use with caution in individuals at risk of seizures. Potential for seizures, although very rare, may be increased with concomitant NSAID therapy. Discontinue in patients who experience significant CNS adverse effects. Use caution in renal dysfunction (dosage adjustment (Continued)

Gatifloxacin *(Continued)*

required) and in severe hepatic insufficiency (no data available). Serious disruptions in glucose regulation (including hyperglycemia and severe hypoglycemia) may occur, usually (but not always) in patients with diabetes. Other risk factors for glucose dysregulation include advanced age, renal insufficiency, and use of concurrent medications which alter glucose utilization. Hypoglycemia may be more prevalent in the initial 3 days of therapy while a greater risk of hyperglycemia may be present after the initial 3 days (particularly days 4-10). Monitor closely and discontinue if hyper- or hypoglycemia occur. Tendon inflammation and/or rupture has been reported with this and other quinolone antibiotics. Discontinue at first signs or symptoms of tendon or pain. Quinolones may exacerbate myasthenia gravis. May cause peripheral neuropathy (rare); discontinue if symptoms of sensory or sensorimotor neuropathy occur.

Severe hypersensitivity reactions, including anaphylaxis, have occurred with quinolone therapy. Prolonged use may result in superinfection; pseudomembranous colitis may occur and should be considered in all patients who present with diarrhea. Do not inject ophthalmic solution subconjunctivally or introduce directly into the anterior chamber of the eye.

Safety and efficacy for ophthalmic use have not been established in children <1 year of age. Safety and efficacy for systemic use have not been established in patients <18 years of age.

Adverse Reactions

Systemic therapy:

3% to 10%:

Central nervous system: Headache (3%), dizziness (3%)

Gastrointestinal: Nausea (8%), diarrhea (4%)

Genitourinary: Vaginitis (6%)

Local: Injection site reactions (5%)

0.1% to ≤3%: Abdominal pain, abnormal dreams, abnormal vision, agitation, alkaline phosphatase increased, allergic reaction, anorexia, anxiety, arthralgia, back pain, chest pain, chills, confusion, constipation, diaphoresis, dry skin, dyspepsia, dyspnea, dysuria, electrolyte abnormalities, facial edema, fever, flatulence, gastritis, glossitis, hematuria, hyperglycemia, hypertension, insomnia, leg cramps, mouth ulceration, nervousness, neutropenia, oral candidiasis, palpitation, paresthesia, peripheral edema, pharyngitis, pruritus, rash, serum amylase increased, serum bilirubin increased, serum transaminases increased, somnolence, stomatitis, taste perversion, thirst, tinnitus, tremor, weakness, vasodilation, vertigo, vomiting

<0.1% (Limited to important or life-threatening): Abnormal thinking, acute renal failure, anaphylactic reaction, angioneurotic edema, arthritis, asthenia, ataxia, bone pain, bradycardia, breast pain, bronchospasm, cheilitis, colitis, cyanosis, depersonalization, depression, diabetes mellitus, dysphagia, ear pain, ecchymosis, edema, epistaxis, ethanol intolerance, euphoria, eye pain, gastrointestinal hemorrhage, gingivitis, halitosis, hallucination, hematemesis, hematuria, hepatitis, hostility, hyperesthesia, hyperglycemia (severe; including nonketotic hyperglycemia), hypertonia, hyperventilation, hypoglycemia (severe; including hypoglycemic coma), increased INR, increased prothrombin time, lymphadenopathy, maculopapular rash, metrorrhagia, migraine, myalgia, myasthenia, neck pain, nonketotic hyperglycemia, pancreatitis, panic attacks, paranoia, parosmia, peripheral neuropathy, photophobia, pseudomembranous colitis, psychosis, ptosis, rectal hemorrhage, seizure, severe hyper-/hypoglycemia, Stevens-Johnson syndrome, stress, syncope, tachycardia, taste disturbance, tendon rupture, rupture, thrombocytopenia, torsade de pointes, tongue edema, vesiculobullous rash

Ophthalmic therapy:

5% to 10%: Ocular: Conjunctival irritation, keratitis, lacrimation increased, papillary conjunctivitis

1% to 4%:

Central nervous system: Headache

Gastrointestinal: Taste disturbance

Ocular: Chemosis, conjunctival hemorrhage, discharge, dry eye, edema, irritation, pain, visual acuity decreased

Overdosage/Toxicology

Potential symptoms of overdose include CNS excitation, seizures, QT prolongation, and arrhythmias (including torsade de pointes). Monitor by continuous ECG in the event of an overdose. Management is supportive and symptomatic. The drug is not removed by dialysis.

Drug Interactions

Increased Effect/Toxicity: Gatifloxacin may increase the effects/toxicity of hypoglycemic agents and warfarin. Concomitant use with corticosteroids may increase the risk of tendon rupture. Concomitant use with other QT_c-prolonging agents (eg, Class Ia and Class III antiarrhythmics, erythromycin, cisapride, antipsychotics, and cyclic antidepressants) may result in arrhythmias, such as torsade de pointes. Probenecid may increase gatifloxacin levels. Atypical antipsychotics and protease inhibitors may cause hyperglycemia; use with caution and monitor. Concomitant use with NSAIDs may rarely increase risk of seizure.

Decreased Effect: Concurrent administration of metal cations, including most antacids (not calcium carbonate), oral electrolyte supplements, quinapril, sucralfate, some didanosine formulations (pediatric powder for oral suspension), and other highly-buffered oral drugs, may decrease quinolone levels; separate doses.

Ethanol/Nutrition/Herb Interactions

Ethanol: Caution with ethanol (may cause hypoglycemia).

Herb/Nutraceutical: Avoid dong quai, St John's wort (may also cause photosensitization); caution with chromium, garlic, gymnema (may cause hypoglycemia).

Stability

Ophthalmic solution: Store between 15°C to 25°C (59°F to 77°F); do not freeze.

Solution for injection: Store at 25°C (77°F); do not freeze. Single-use vials must be diluted to a concentration of 2 mg/mL prior to administration. May be diluted with D_5W, NS, D_5NS, D_5LR, 5% sodium bicarbonate, or Plasma-Lyte® 56/D_5W, or $D_5$1/2NS with 20 mEq KCl. Do not dilute with SWFI (a hypotonic solution results). Following dilution, stable for 14 days when stored between 20°C to 25°C or 2° to 8°C. Diluted solutions (except those prepared in 5% sodium bicarbonate) may also be frozen for up to 6 months when stored at -25°C to -10°C (-13°F to 14°F). Solutions may then be thawed at room temperature and should be used within 14 days (store between 20°C to 25°C or 2°C to 8°C); do not refreeze.

Tablet: Store at 25°C (77°F).

Mechanism of Action Gatifloxacin is a DNA gyrase inhibitor, and also inhibits topoisomerase IV. DNA gyrase (topoisomerase II) is an essential bacterial enzyme that maintains the superhelical structure of DNA. DNA gyrase is required for DNA replication and transcription, DNA repair, recombination, and transposition; inhibition is bactericidal.

Pharmacodynamics/Kinetics

Absorption: Oral: Well absorbed; Ophthalmic: Not measurable

Distribution: V_d: 1.5-2.0 L/kg; concentrates in alveolar macrophages and lung parenchyma

Protein binding: 20%

Metabolism: Only 1%; no interaction with CYP

Bioavailability: 96%

Half-life elimination: 7.1-13.9 hours; ESRD/CAPD: 30-40 hours

Time to peak: Oral: 1 hour

Excretion: Urine (70% as unchanged drug, <1% as metabolites); feces (5%)

Dosage

Usual dosage range:

Adults: Oral, I.V.: 400 mg once daily

Indication-specific dosing:

Children ≥1 year and Adults:

Bacterial conjunctivitis: Ophthalmic:

Days 1 and 2: Instill 1 drop into affected eye(s) every 2 hours while awake (maximum: 8 times/day)

Days 3-7: Instill 1 drop into affected eye(s) up to 4 times/day while awake

Adults: Oral, I.V.:

Acute bacterial exacerbation of chronic bronchitis: 400 mg every 24 hours for 5 days

Acute sinusitis: 400 mg every 24 hours for 10 days

Community-acquired pneumonia (including atypical organisms): 400 mg every 24 hours for 7-14 days

Pyelonephritis (acute): 400 mg every 24 hours for 7-10 days

Skin/skin structure infections (uncomplicated): 400 mg every 24 hours for 7-10 days

Traveler's diarrhea (unlabeled use): 400 mg once daily for 3 days

Urinary tract infections:

Complicated: 400 mg every 24 hours for 7-10 days

Uncomplicated, cystitis: 400 mg single dose or 200 mg every 24 hours for 3 days

Urethral gonorrhea in men (uncomplicated), cervical or rectal gonorrhea in women and pharyngitis (gonococcal): 400 mg single dose

Elderly: No dosage adjustment is required based on age, however, assessment of renal function is particularly important in this population.

Dosage adjustment in renal impairment: Creatinine clearance <40 mL/minute (or patients on hemodialysis/CAPD) should receive an initial dose of 400 mg, followed by a subsequent dose of 200 mg every 24 hours. Patients receiving single-dose or 3-day therapy for appropriate indications do not require dosage adjustment. Administer after hemodialysis.

Dosage adjustment in hepatic impairment: No dosage adjustment is required in mild-moderate hepatic disease. No data are available in severe hepatic impairment (Child-Pugh Class C).

Dietary Considerations May take tablets with or without food, milk, or calcium supplements. Gatifloxacin should be taken 4 hours before supplements (including multivitamins) containing iron, zinc, or magnesium.

Administration

Oral: May be administered with or without food, milk, or calcium supplements. Gatifloxacin should be taken 4 hours before supplements (including multivitamins) containing iron, zinc, or magnesium.

I.V.: For I.V. infusion only. Concentrated injection (10 mg/mL) must be diluted to 2 mg/mL prior to administration. No further dilution is required for premixed 100 mL and 200 mL solutions. Infuse over 60 minutes. Avoid rapid or bolus infusions.

Monitoring Parameters WBC, signs of infection; signs or symptoms of hypo-/hyperglycemia

Test Interactions Some quinolones may produce a false-positive urine screening result for opiates using commercially-available immunoassay kits. This has been demonstrated most consistently for levofloxacin and ofloxacin, but other quinolones have shown cross-reactivity in certain assay kits. Confirmation of positive opiate screens by more specific methods should be considered.

Dosage Forms [DSC] = Discontinued product

Injection, infusion [premixed in D_5W]:

Tequin®: 200 mg (100 mL), 400 mg (200 mL) [DSC]

Injection, solution [preservative free]:

Tequin®: 10 mg/mL (40 mL) [DSC]

Solution, ophthalmic:

Zymar™: 0.3% (2.5 mL, 5 mL) [contains benzalkonium chloride]

Tablet:

Tequin®: 200 mg, 400 mg [DSC]

Tequin® Teq-paq™ [unit-dose pack]: 400 mg (5s) [DSC]

♦ **Gaviscon® Extra Strength [OTC]** see Aluminum Hydroxide and Magnesium Carbonate on page 84

♦ **Gaviscon® Liquid [OTC]** see Aluminum Hydroxide and Magnesium Carbonate on page 84

♦ **Gaviscon® Tablet [OTC]** see Aluminum Hydroxide and Magnesium Trisilicate on page 85

♦ **G-CSF** see Filgrastim on page 707

♦ **G-CSF (PEG Conjugate)** see Pegfilgrastim on page 1321

♦ **GCV Sodium** see Ganciclovir on page 779

Gefitinib (ge Fl tye nib)

U.S. Brand Names IRESSA®
Index Terms NSC-715055; ZD1839
Pharmacologic Category Antineoplastic Agent, Tyrosine Kinase Inhibitor
Use

U.S. labeling: Treatment of locally advanced or metastatic nonsmall cell lung cancer after failure of platinum-based and docetaxel therapies. Treatment is limited to patients who are benefiting or have benefited from treatment with gefitinib.

Note: Due to the lack of improved survival data from clinical trials of gefitinib, and in response to positive survival data with another EGFR inhibitor, physicians are advised to use other treatment options in advanced nonsmall cell lung cancer patients following one or two prior chemotherapy regimens when they are refractory/intolerant to their most recent regimen.

Canada labeling: Approved indication is limited to NSCLC patients with epidermal growth factor receptor (EGFR) expression status positive or unknown.

Restrictions As of September 15, 2005, distribution will be limited to patients enrolled in the Iressa Access Program. Under this program, access to gefitinib will be limited to the following groups:

Patients who are currently receiving and benefitting from gefitinib (IRESSA®)

Patients who have previously received and benefited from gefitinib (IRESSA®)

Previously-enrolled patients or new patients in non-Investigational New Drug (IND) clinical trials involving gefitinib (IRESSA®) if these protocols were approved by an IRB prior to June 17, 2005

New patients may also receive Iressa if the manufacturer (AstraZeneca) decides to make it available under IND, and the patients meet the criteria for enrollment under the IND

Additional information on the IRESSA® Access Program, including enrollment forms, may be obtained by calling AstraZeneca at 1-800-601-8933 or via the web at www.Iressa-access.com

Pregnancy Risk Factor D
Pregnancy Implications Animal studies have demonstrated fetal harm; there are no well-controlled studies in pregnant women. The risk of fetal harm should be carefully weighed. Women of childbearing potential should be advised to avoid pregnancy.
Lactation Excretion in breast milk unknown/not recommended
Medication Safety Issues

Sound-alike/look-alike issues:

Gefitinib may be confused with erlotinib

High alert medication: The Institute for Safe Medication Practices (ISMP) includes this medication among its list of drugs which have a heightened risk of causing significant patient harm when used in error.

Contraindications Hypersensitivity to gefitinib or any component of the formulation; pregnancy

Warnings/Precautions Rare, sometimes fatal, pulmonary toxicity (eg, alveolitis, interstitial pneumonia, pneumonitis) has occurred. Therapy should be interrupted in patients with acute onset or worsening pulmonary symptoms; discontinue gefitinib if interstitial pneumonitis is confirmed. Use caution in hepatic or severe renal impairment. May cause hepatic injury and elevation of transaminases; discontinue if elevations/changes are severe. Interruption of therapy may be required in patients with poorly tolerated diarrhea or adverse skin reactions. Eye pain should be promptly evaluated and therapy may be interrupted based on appropriate medical evaluation; may be re-initiated following resolution of symptoms and eye changes. Safety and efficacy in pediatric patients have not been established.

Adverse Reactions

>10%:

Dermatologic: Rash (43% to 54%), acne (25% to 33%), dry skin (13% to 26%)

Gastrointestinal: Diarrhea (48% to 76%), nausea (13% to 18%), vomiting (9% to 12%)

1% to 10%:

Cardiovascular: Peripheral edema (2%)

Dermatologic: Pruritus (8% to 9%)

Gastrointestinal: Anorexia (7% to 10%), weight loss (3% to 5%), mouth ulceration (1%)

Neuromuscular & skeletal: Weakness (4% to 6%)

Ocular: Amblyopia (2%), conjunctivitis (1%)

Respiratory: Dyspnea (2%), interstitial lung disease (1% to 2%)

<1%: Aberrant eyelash growth, angioedema, corneal erosion and membrane sloughing, epistaxis, erythema multiforme, eye pain, hematuria, hemorrhage, ocular hemorrhaging, ocular ischemia, pancreatitis, toxic epidermal necrolysis, urticaria

Postmarketing and/or case reports: CNS hemorrhage and death were reported in clinical trials of pediatric patients with primary CNS tumors

Overdosage/Toxicology No specific overdose-related toxicities reported; Overdose management may be symptom-based and supportive.

Drug Interactions

Cytochrome P450 Effect: Substrate of CYP3A4 (major); **Inhibits** CYP2C19 (weak), 2D6 (weak)

Increased Effect/Toxicity: Gefitinib may increase the effects of warfarin. CYP3A4 inhibitors may increase the levels/effects of gefitinib; example inhibitors include azole antifungals, clarithromycin, diclofenac, doxycycline, erythromycin, imatinib, isoniazid, nefazodone, nicardipine, propofol, protease inhibitors, quinidine, telithromycin, and verapamil.

Decreased Effect: Gefitinib effects may be decreased by H₂-receptor blockers and sodium bicarbonate. CYP3A4 inducers may decrease the levels/effects of gefitinib; example inducers include aminoglutethimide, carbamazepine, nafcillin, nevirapine, phenobarbital, phenytoin, and rifamycins.

Ethanol/Nutrition/Herb Interactions Food: Grapefruit juice may increase serum gefitinib concentrations; St John's wort may decrease serum gefitinib concentrations.

Stability Store tablets at controlled room temperature of 20°C to 25°C (68°F to 77°F).

Mechanism of Action The mechanism of antineoplastic action is not fully understood. Gefitinib inhibits tyrosine kinases (TK) associated with transmembrane cell surface receptors found on both normal and cancer cells. One such receptor is epidermal growth factor receptor. TK activity appears to be vitally important to cell proliferation and survival.

Pharmacodynamics/Kinetics
Absorption: Oral: slow
Distribution: I.V.: 1400 L
Protein binding: 90%, albumin and alpha$_1$-acid glycoprotein
Metabolism: Hepatic, primarily via CYP3A4; forms metabolites
Bioavailability: 60%
Half-life elimination: I.V.: 48 hours
Time to peak, plasma: Oral: 3-7 hours
Excretion: Feces (86%); urine (<4%)

Dosage Note: In response to the lack of improved survival data from the ISEL trial, AstraZeneca has temporarily suspended promotion of this drug.
Oral: Adults: 250 mg/day; consider 500 mg/day in patients receiving effective CYP3A4 inducers (eg, rifampin, phenytoin)
Dosage adjustment in renal/hepatic impairment: No adjustment necessary
Dosage adjustment for toxicity: Consider interruption of therapy in any patient with evidence of pulmonary decompensation or severe hepatic injury; discontinuation may be required if toxicity is confirmed. Poorly tolerated diarrhea or adverse skin reactions may be managed by a brief interruption of therapy (up to 14 days), followed by reinitiation of therapy at 250 mg/day. Eye pain should be promptly evaluated and therapy may be interrupted based on appropriate medical evaluation; may be reinitiated following resolution of symptoms and eye changes.

Dietary Considerations Food does not affect gefitinib absorption.

Administration May administer with or without food.
For patients unable to swallow tablets or for administration via NG tube: Tablets may be dispersed in noncarbonated drinking water. Drop whole tablet (do not crush) into $^1/_2$ glass of water; stir until tablet is dispersed (~10 minutes). Drink immediately. Rinse with $^1/_2$ glass of water and drink.

Monitoring Parameters Periodic liver function tests (asymptomatic increases in liver enzymes have occurred)

Dosage Forms Tablet: 250 mg

Gelatin, Pectin, and Methylcellulose
(JEL a tin, PEK tin, & meth il SEL yoo lose)

Index Terms Methylcellulose, Gelatin, and Pectin; Pectin, Gelatin, and Methylcellulose
Pharmacologic Category Topical Skin Product
Use Temporary relief from minor oral irritations
Dosage Press small dabs into place until the involved area is coated with a thin film; do not try to spread onto area; may be used as often as needed
Additional Information Complete prescribing information for this medication should be consulted for additional detail.

♦ **Gel-Kam® [OTC]** see Fluoride on page 722
♦ **Gel-Kam® Rinse** see Fluoride on page 722
♦ **Gelucast®** see Zinc Gelatin on page 1817
♦ **Gelusil® [OTC]** see Aluminum Hydroxide, Magnesium Hydroxide, and Simethicone on page 85
♦ **Gelusil® (Can)** see Aluminum Hydroxide, Magnesium Hydroxide, and Simethicone on page 85
♦ **Gelusil® Extra Strength (Can)** see Aluminum Hydroxide and Magnesium Hydroxide on page 85

Gemcitabine (jem SITE a been)

U.S. Brand Names Gemzar®
Canadian Brand Names Gemzar®
Index Terms Gemcitabine Hydrochloride; NSC-613327
Pharmacologic Category Antineoplastic Agent, Antimetabolite (Pyrimidine Antagonist)
Use Treatment of metastatic breast cancer; locally-advanced or metastatic nonsmall cell lung cancer (NSCLC) or pancreatic cancer; advanced, relapsed ovarian cancer
Unlabeled/Investigational Use Treatment of bladder cancer, acute leukemia
Pregnancy Risk Factor D
Pregnancy Implications Embryotoxicity and fetal malformations (cleft palate, incomplete ossification, fused pulmonary artery, absence of gallbladder) have been reported in animal studies. There are no adequate and well-controlled studies in pregnant women. If patient becomes pregnant, she should be informed of risks.
Lactation Excretion in breast milk unknown/not recommended
Medication Safety Issues
Sound-alike/look-alike issues:
Gemzar® may be confused with Zinecard®

High alert medication: The Institute for Safe Medication Practices (ISMP) includes this medication among its list of drugs which have a heightened risk of causing significant patient harm when used in error.
Contraindications Hypersensitivity to gemcitabine or any component of the formulation; pregnancy
Warnings/Precautions Hazardous agent - use appropriate precautions for handling and disposal. Prolongation of the infusion time >60 minutes and more frequent than weekly
(Continued)

785

Gemcitabine (Continued)

dosing have been shown to increase toxicity. Gemcitabine can suppress bone marrow function (leukopenia, thrombocytopenia and anemia); myelosuppression is usually the dose-limiting toxicity. Gemcitabine may cause fever in the absence of clinical infection. Pulmonary toxicity has occurred; discontinue if severe.

Hemolytic uremic syndrome has been reported; monitor for evidence of microangiopathic hemolysis (elevation of bilirubin or LDH, reticulocytosis, severe thrombocytopenia, and/or renal failure); use with caution in patients with pre-existing renal impairment. Serious hepatotoxicity has been reported. Use caution with hepatic impairment (history of cirrhosis, hepatitis, or alcoholism) or in patients with hepatic metastases; may lead to exacerbation of hepatic impairment. Use caution with concurrent radiation therapy; radiation toxicity has been reported with concurrent and nonconcurrent administration; may have radiosensitizing activity when gemcitabine and radiation therapy are given ≤7 days apart; optimum regimen for combination therapy has not been determined for all tumor types. Use caution in the elderly; clearance is affected by age. Efficacy in children has not been established

Adverse Reactions

>10%:

Cardiovascular: Peripheral edema (20%), edema (13%)

Central nervous system: Pain (10% to 48%), fever (30% to 41%), somnolence (5% to 11%)

Dermatologic: Rash (24% to 30%), alopecia (15% to 18%), pruritus (13%)

Gastrointestinal: Nausea/vomiting (64% to 71%; grades 3/4: 1% to 13%), constipation (10% to 31%), diarrhea (19% to 30%), stomatitis (10% to 14%)

Hematologic: Anemia (65% to 73%; grade 4: 1% to 3%), leukopenia (62% to 71%; grade 4: ≤1%), neutropenia (61% to 63%; grade 4: 6% to 7%), thrombocytopenia (24% to 47%; grade 4: ≤1%), hemorrhage (4% to 17%; grades 3/4: <1% to 2%); myelosuppression is the dose-limiting toxicity

Hepatic: Transaminases increased (67% to 78%; grades 3/4: 1% to 12%), alkaline phosphatase increased (55% to 77%; grades 3/4: 2% to 16%), bilirubin increased (13% to 26%; grades 3/4: <1% to 6%)

Renal: Proteinuria (10% to 45%; grades 3/4: <1%), hematuria (13% to 35%; grades 3/4: <1%), BUN increased (8% to 16%; grades 3/4: 0%)

Respiratory: Dyspnea (6% to 23%)

Miscellaneous: Flu-like syndrome (19%), infection (8% to 16%; grades 3/4: <1% to 2%)

1% to 10%:

Local: Injection site reactions (4%)

Neuromuscular & skeletal: Paresthesia (2% to 10%)

Renal: Creatinine increased (2% to 8%)

Respiratory: Bronchospasm (<2%)

<1% (Limited to important or life-threatening; reported with single-agent use or with combination therapy, all reported rarely): Adult respiratory distress syndrome, anaphylactoid reaction, anorexia, arrhythmias, bullous skin eruptions, cellulitis, cerebrovascular accident, CHF, chills, cough, desquamation, diaphoresis, gangrene, GGT increased, headache, hemolytic uremic syndrome (HUS), hepatotoxic reaction (rare), hypertension, insomnia, interstitial pneumonitis, liver failure, malaise, MI, peripheral vasculitis, petechiae, pulmonary edema, pulmonary fibrosis, radiation recall, renal failure, respiratory failure, rhinitis, sepsis, supraventricular arrhythmia, weakness

Overdosage/Toxicology Symptoms include myelosuppression, paresthesias, and severe rash. These were the principle effects seen when a single dose, as high as 5,700 mg/m^2, was administered by I.V. infusion over 30 minutes every 2 weeks. Monitor blood counts. Treatment is symptom-directed and supportive.

Drug Interactions

Increased Effect/Toxicity: Gemcitabine may increase the levels/effects of fluorouracil. Gemcitabine may enhance the adverse pulmonary effects of bleomycin.

Ethanol/Nutrition/Herb Interactions Ethanol: Avoid ethanol (due to GI irritation).

Stability Store intact vials at room temperature of 20°C to 25°C (68°F to 77°F). Reconstitute the 200 mg vial with preservative free 0.9% NaCl 5 mL or the 1000 mg vial with preservative free 0.9% NaCl 25 mL. Resulting solution is 38 mg/mL. Dilute with 50-500 mL 0.9% sodium chloride injection or D$_5$W to concentrations as low as 0.1 mg/mL. Reconstituted vials are stable for up to 35 days and infusion solutions diluted in 0.9% sodium chloride are stable up to 7 days at 23°C when protected from light ; however, the manufacturer recommends use within 24 hours for both reconstituted vials and infusion solutions. Do not refrigerate.

Mechanism of Action A pyrimidine antimetabolite that inhibits DNA synthesis by inhibition of DNA polymerase and ribonucleotide reductase, specific for the S-phase of the cycle. Gemcitabine is phosphorylated intracellularly by deoxycytidine kinase to gemcitabine monophosphate, which is further phosphorylated to active metabolites gemcitabine diphosphate and gemcitabine triphosphate. Gemcitabine diphosphate inhibits DNA synthesis by inhibiting ribonucleotide reductase; gemcitabine triphosphate incorporates into DNA and inhibits DNA polymerase.

Pharmacodynamics/Kinetics

Distribution: Infusions <70 minutes: 50 L/m^2; Long infusion times: 370 L/m^2

Protein binding: Low

Metabolism: Metabolized intracellularly by nucleoside kinases to the active diphosphate (dFdCDP) and triphosphate (dFdCTP) nucleoside metabolites

Half-life elimination:

Gemcitabine: Infusion time ≤1 hour: 42-94 minutes; infusion time 3-4 hours: 4-10.5 hours

Metabolite (gemcitabine triphosphate), terminal phase: 1.7-19.4 hours

Time to peak, plasma: 30 minutes after completion of infusion

Excretion: Urine (92% to 98%; primarily as inactive uracil metabolite); feces (<1%)

Dosage Refer to individual protocols. **Note**: Prolongation of the infusion time >60 minutes and administration more frequently than once weekly have been shown to increase toxicity. I.V.: Pancreatic cancer: Initial: 1000 mg/m^2 weekly for up to 7 weeks followed by 1 week rest; then weekly for 3 weeks out of every 4 weeks.

Dose adjustment: Patients who complete an entire cycle of therapy may have the dose in subsequent cycles increased by 25% as long as the absolute granulocyte count (AGC) nadir is >1500 x 10^6/L, platelet nadir is >100,000 x 10^6/L, and nonhematologic toxicity is less than WHO Grade 1. If the increased dose is tolerated (with the same parameters) the dose in subsequent cycles may again be increased by 20%.

Nonsmall cell lung cancer:
1000 mg/m^2 days 1, 8, and 15; repeat cycle every 28 days
or
1250 mg/m^2 days 1 and 8; repeat cycle every 21 days
Breast cancer: 1250 mg/m^2 days 1 and 8; repeat cycle every 21 days
Ovarian cancer: 1000 mg/m^2 days 1 and 8; repeat cycle every 21 days
Bladder cancer (unlabeled use):
I.V.: 1000 mg/m^2 once weekly for 3 weeks; repeat cycle every 4 weeks
Intravesicular instillation: 2000 mg (in 100 mL NS; retain for 1 hour) twice weekly for 3 weeks; repeat cycle every 4 weeks (for at least 2 cycles)

Dosing adjustment for toxicity:
Pancreatic cancer: Hematologic toxicity:
AGC ≥1000 x 10^6/L and platelet count ≥100,000 x 10^6/L: Administer 100% of full dose
AGC 500-999 x 10^6/L or platelet count 50,000-90,000 x 10^6/L: Administer 75% of full dose
AGC <500 x 10^6/L or platelet count <50,000 x 10^6/L: Hold dose
Nonsmall cell lung cancer:
Hematologic toxicity: Refer to guidelines for pancreatic cancer. Cisplatin dosage may also need adjusted.
Severe (grades 3 or 4) nonhematologic toxicity (except alopecia, nausea and vomiting): Hold or decrease dose by 50%.
Breast cancer:
Hematologic toxicity: Adjustments based on granulocyte and platelet counts on day 8:
AGC ≥1200 x 10^6/L and platelet count >75,000 x 10^6/L: Administer 100% of full dose
AGC 1000-1199 x 10^6/L or platelet count 50,000-75,000 x 10^6/L: Administer 75% of full dose
AGC 700-999 x 10^6/L and platelet count ≥50,000 x 10^6/L: Administer 50% of full dose
AGC <700 x 10^6/L or platelet count <50,000 x 10^6/L: Hold dose
Severe (grades 3 or 4) nonhematologic toxicity (except alopecia, nausea, and vomiting): Hold or decrease dose by 50%. Paclitaxel dose may also need adjusted.
Ovarian cancer:
Hematologic toxicity: Adjustments based on granulocyte and platelet counts on day 8:
AGC ≥1500 x 10^6/L and platelet count ≥100,000 x 10^6/L: Administer 100% of full dose
AGC 1000-1499 x 10^6/L and/or platelet count 75,000-99,999 x 10^6/L: Administer 50% of full dose
AGC <1000 x 10^6/L and/or platelet count <75,000 x 10^6/L: Hold dose
Severe (grades 3 or 4) nonhematologic toxicity (except nausea and vomiting): Hold or decrease dose by 50%. Carboplatin dose may also need adjusted.
Dose adjustment for subsequent cycles:
AGC < 500 x 10^6/L for >5 days, AGC <100 x 10^6/L for >3 days, febrile neutropenia, platelet count <25,000 x 10^6/L, cycle delay >1 week due to toxicity: Reduce gemcitabine to 800 mg/m2 on days 1 and 8.
For recurrence of any of the above toxicities after initial dose reduction: Administer gemcitabine 800 mg/m^2 on day 1 only for the subsequent cycle

Dosing adjustment in renal/hepatic impairment: Use with caution; gemcitabine has not been studied in patients with significant renal or hepatic dysfunction

Administration Infuse over 30 minutes. **Note:** Prolongation of the infusion time >60 minutes has been shown to increase toxicity. Gemcitabine is being investigated in clinical trials for fixed dose rate (FDR) infusion administration at doses from 1000 mg/m^2 to 2200 mg/m^2 at a rate of 10 mg/m^2/minute. Prolonged infusion times increase the accumulation of the active metabolite, gemcitabine triphosphate. Patients who receive gemcitabine FDR experience more grade 3/4 hematologic toxicity.

Monitoring Parameters CBC with differential and platelet count (prior to each dose); hepatic and renal function (prior to initiation of therapy and periodically, thereafter); monitor electrolytes, including potassium, magnesium, and calcium (when in combination therapy with cisplatin)

Dosage Forms
Injection, powder for reconstitution:
Gemzar®: 200 mg, 1 g

♦ **Gemcitabine Hydrochloride** *see* Gemcitabine *on page 785*

Gemfibrozil (jem FI broe zil)

U.S. Brand Names Lopid®
Canadian Brand Names Apo-Gemfibrozil®; Gen-Gemfibrozil; GMD-Gemfibrozil; Lopid®; Novo-Gemfibrozil; Nu-Gemfibrozil; PMS-Gemfibrozil
Index Terms CI-719
Pharmacologic Category Antilipemic Agent, Fibric Acid
Additional Appendix Information
Hyperlipidemia Management *on page 2058*
Lipid-Lowering Agents *on page 1887*
Use Treatment of hypertriglyceridemia in types IV and V hyperlipidemia for patients who are at greater risk for pancreatitis and who have not responded to dietary intervention
Pregnancy Risk Factor C
Lactation Excretion in breast milk unknown/contraindicated
(Continued)

Gemfibrozil (Continued)

Medication Safety Issues
Sound-alike/look-alike issues:
Lopid® may be confused with Levbid®, Lodine®, Lorabid®, Slo-bid™

Contraindications Hypersensitivity to gemfibrozil or any component of the formulation; significant hepatic or renal dysfunction; primary biliary cirrhosis; pre-existing gallbladder disease

Warnings/Precautions Abnormal elevation of AST, ALT, LDH, bilirubin, and alkaline phosphatase has occurred; if no appreciable triglyceride or cholesterol lowering effect occurs after 3 months, the drug should be discontinued; not useful for type I hyperlipidemia; myositis may be more common in patients with poor renal function

Adverse Reactions
>10%: Gastrointestinal: Dyspepsia (20%)
1% to 10%:
Central nervous system: Fatigue (4%), vertigo (2%), headache (1%)
Dermatologic: Eczema (2%), rash (2%)
Gastrointestinal: Abdominal pain (10%), diarrhea (7%), nausea/vomiting (3%), constipation (1%)
<1% (Limited to important or life-threatening): Alopecia, anaphylaxis, angioedema, bone marrow hypoplasia, cataracts, cholelithiasis, cholecystitis, depression, dermatomyositis/polymyositis, drug-induced lupus-like syndrome, eosinophilia, exfoliative dermatitis, hypokalemia, impotence, intracranial hemorrhage, jaundice, laryngeal edema, leukopenia, myasthenia, myopathy, nephrotoxicity, pancreatitis, paresthesia, peripheral neuritis, photosensitivity, positive ANA, rash, Raynaud's phenomenon, retinal edema, rhabdomyolysis, seizure, syncope, thrombocytopenia, urticaria, vasculitis

Overdosage/Toxicology Symptoms include abdominal pain, diarrhea, nausea, and vomiting. Following GI decontamination, treatment is supportive.

Drug Interactions
Cytochrome P450 Effect: Substrate of CYP3A4 (minor); **Inhibits** CYP1A2 (moderate), 2C8 (strong), 2C9 (strong), 2C19 (strong)

Increased Effect/Toxicity: Gemfibrozil may potentiate the effects of bexarotene (avoid concurrent use), sulfonylureas (including glyburide, chlorpropamide), and warfarin. HMG-CoA reductase inhibitors (atorvastatin, fluvastatin, lovastatin, pravastatin, simvastatin) may increase the risk of myopathy and rhabdomyolysis. The manufacturer warns against the concurrent use of lovastatin (if unavoidable, limit lovastatin to <20 mg/day). Combination therapy with statins has been used in some patients with resistant hyperlipidemias (with great caution). Gemfibrozil may increase the serum concentration of repaglinide (resulting in severe, prolonged hypoglycemia); the addition of itraconazole may augment the effects of gemfibrozil on repaglinide (consider alternative therapy). Gemfibrozil may increase the levels/effects of aminophylline, amiodarone, bosentan, citalopram, dapsone, diazepam, fluoxetine, fluvoxamine, glimepiride, glipizide, losartan, methsuximide, mexiletine, mirtazapine, montelukast, nateglinide, paclitaxel, phenytoin, pioglitazone, propranolol, repaglinide, ropinirole, rosiglitazone, sertraline, theophylline, trifluoperazine, warfarin, zafirlukast, and other substrates of CYP1A2, 2C8, 2C9, or 2C19.

Decreased Effect: Cyclosporine's blood levels may be reduced during concurrent therapy. Rifampin may decrease gemfibrozil blood levels.

Ethanol/Nutrition/Herb Interactions Ethanol: Avoid ethanol to decrease triglycerides.

Mechanism of Action The exact mechanism of action of gemfibrozil is unknown, however, several theories exist regarding the VLDL effect; it can inhibit lipolysis and decrease subsequent hepatic fatty acid uptake as well as inhibit hepatic secretion of VLDL; together these actions decrease serum VLDL levels; increases HDL-cholesterol; the mechanism behind HDL elevation is currently unknown

Pharmacodynamics/Kinetics
Onset of action: May require several days
Absorption: Well absorbed
Protein binding: 99%
Metabolism: Hepatic via oxidation to two inactive metabolites; undergoes enterohepatic recycling
Half-life elimination: 1.4 hours
Time to peak, serum: 1-2 hours
Excretion: Urine (70% primarily as conjugated drug); feces (6%)

Dosage Adults: Oral: 1200 mg/day in 2 divided doses, 30 minutes before breakfast and dinner
Hemodialysis: Not removed by hemodialysis; supplemental dose is not necessary

Dietary Considerations Before initiation of therapy, patients should be placed on a standard cholesterol-lowering diet for 3-6 months and the diet should be continued during drug therapy.

Monitoring Parameters Serum cholesterol, LFTs

Dosage Forms Tablet: 600 mg

Gemifloxacin (je mi FLOKS a sin)

U.S. Brand Names Factive®
Index Terms DW286; Gemifloxacin Mesylate; LA 20304a; SB-265805
Pharmacologic Category Antibiotic, Quinolone
Additional Appendix Information
Community-Acquired Pneumonia in Adults on page 1999
Use Treatment of acute exacerbation of chronic bronchitis; treatment of community-acquired pneumonia, including pneumonia caused by multidrug-resistant strains of S. pneumoniae (MDRSP)
Unlabeled/Investigational Use Acute sinusitis, uncomplicated urinary tract infection
Pregnancy Risk Factor C
Pregnancy Implications There are no adequate and well-controlled studies in pregnant women. Reports of arthropathy (observed in immature animals and reported rarely in

humans) have limited the use of fluoroquinolones in pregnancy. Reversible fetal growth retardation was observed with gemifloxacin in some animal studies. Based on limited data, quinolones are not expected to be a major human teratogen. Although quinolone antibiotics should not be used as first-line agents during pregnancy, when considering treatment for life-threatening infection and/or prolonged duration of therapy, the potential risk to the fetus must be balanced against the severity of the potential illness.

Lactation Excretion in breast milk unknown/not recommended

Contraindications Hypersensitivity to gemifloxacin, other fluoroquinolones, or any component of the formulation

Warnings/Precautions Fluoroquinolones may prolong QT_c interval; avoid use of gemifloxacin in patients with a history of QT_c prolongation, uncorrected hypokalemia, hypomagnesemia, or concurrent administration of other medications known to prolong the QT interval (including Class Ia and Class III antiarrhythmics, cisapride, erythromycin, antipsychotics, and tricyclic antidepressants). Use with caution in patients with significant bradycardia or acute myocardial ischemia. Use with caution in individuals at risk of seizures (CNS disorders or concurrent therapy with medications which may lower seizure threshold). Potential for seizures, although very rare, may be increased with concomitant NSAID therapy. Discontinue in patients who experience significant CNS adverse effects (dizziness, hallucinations, suicidal ideation or actions). Use caution in renal dysfunction; dosage adjustment required for $Cl_{cr} \leq 40$ mL/minute.

Severe hypersensitivity reactions, including anaphylaxis, have occurred with quinolone therapy. If an allergic reaction occurs (itching, urticaria, dyspnea or facial edema, loss of consciousness, tingling, cardiovascular collapse), discontinue drug immediately. May cause mild-to-moderate maculopapular rash, usually 8-10 days after treatment initiation; risk factors may include age <40 years, female gender (including postmenopausal women on HRT), and treatment duration >7 days; discontinue therapy if rash develops. Avoid excessive sunlight; may rarely cause moderate-to-severe phototoxicity reactions similar to ciprofloxacin. Prolonged use may result in superinfection; pseudomembranous colitis may occur and should be considered in all patients who present with diarrhea. Tendon inflammation and/or rupture has been reported with other quinolone antibiotics; risk may increase with concurrent corticosteroids, particularly in the elderly. Discontinue at first sign of tendon inflammation or pain. Peripheral neuropathy has been linked to the use of quinolones; these cases were rare. Experience with quinolones in immature animals has resulted in permanent arthropathy. Safety and effectiveness in pediatric patients (<18 years of age) have not been established.

Adverse Reactions
1% to 10%:
Central nervous system: Headache (1%), dizziness (1%)
Dermatologic: Rash (3%)
Endocrine & metabolic: Hyperkalemia (1%)
Gastrointestinal: Diarrhea (4%), nausea (3%), abdominal pain (1%), vomiting (1%)
Hematologic: Thrombocythemia (1%), neutropenia/neutrophilia (1%)
Hepatic: Transaminases increased (1% to 2%), GGT increased (1%)
Neuromuscular & skeletal: CPK increased (1%)
<1% (Limited to important or life-threatening): Alkaline phosphatase increased, anemia, anorexia, arthralgia, asthenia, back pain, bilirubin increased, BUN increased, constipation, cramps (leg), dermatitis, dry mouth, dyspepsia, dyspnea, eczema, eosinophilia, fatigue, flatulence, flushing, fungal infection, gastritis, gastroenteritis, genital moniliasis, granulocytopenia, hematocrit increased, hemoglobin increased, hot flashes, hyperglycemia, hyper-/hypocalcemia, hypoalbuminemia, hyponatremia, insomnia, leukopenia, moniliasis, myalgia, nervousness, pharyngitis, photosensitivity, pneumonia, pruritus, pseudomembranous colitis, QT_c prolongation, serum creatinine increased, somnolence, taste perversion, thrombocytopenia, tremor, urticaria, vaginitis, vertigo, vision abnormal
Important adverse effects reported with other agents in this drug class include (not reported for gemifloxacin): Agranulocytosis, allergic reactions, aplastic anemia, CNS stimulation, hemolytic anemia, hepatic necrosis/failure, hepatitis, hypersensitivity, jaundice, pain, pancytopenia, peripheral neuropathy, pneumonitis (eosinophilic), seizure, sensori-motor-axonal neuropathy (paresthesia, hypoesthesias, dysesthesias, weakness), serum sickness, severe dermatologic reactions (toxic epidermal necrolysis, Stevens-Johnson syndrome), tendon rupture, thrombotic thrombocytopenia purpura, torsade de pointes, vasculitis

Overdosage/Toxicology Based on animal data, acute toxicity may manifest as ataxia, lethargy, tremor and/or seizures. Treatment is symptom-directed and supportive; 20% to 30% removed by hemodialysis.

Drug Interactions
Increased Effect/Toxicity: Gemifloxacin may increase the effects/toxicity of glyburide and warfarin. Concomitant use with corticosteroids may increase the risk of tendon rupture. Concomitant use with other QT_c-prolonging agents (eg, Class Ia and Class III antiarrhythmics, erythromycin, cisapride, antipsychotics, and cyclic antidepressants) may result in arrhythmias, such as torsade de pointes. Probenecid may increase gemifloxacin levels. Concomitant use with NSAIDs may rarely increase risk of seizure.
Decreased Effect: Concurrent administration of metal cations, including most antacids, oral electrolyte supplements, quinapril, sucralfate, some didanosine formulations (pediatric powder for oral suspension), and other highly-buffered oral drugs, may decrease quinolone levels; separate doses. Gemifloxacin may diminish the therapeutic effect of the live, attenuated Ty21a strain of typhoid vaccine.

Ethanol/Nutrition/Herb Interactions Herb/Nutraceutical: Avoid dong quai, St John's wort (may also cause photosensitization).

Stability Store at 15°C to 30°C (59°F to 86°F). Protect from light.

Mechanism of Action Gemifloxacin is a DNA gyrase inhibitor and also inhibits topoisomerase IV. DNA gyrase (topoisomerase IV) is an essential bacterial enzyme that maintains the superhelical structure of DNA. DNA gyrase is required for DNA replication and transcription, DNA repair, recombination, and transposition; bactericidal

Pharmacodynamics/Kinetics
Absorption: Well absorbed from the GI tract
(Continued)

Gemifloxacin (Continued)

Distribution: V$_{dss}$: 4.2 L/kg

Bioavailability: 71%

Metabolism: Hepatic (minor); forms metabolites (CYP isoenzymes are not involved)

Time to peak, plasma: 0.5-2 hours

Protein binding: 60% to 70%

Half-life elimination: 7 hours (range 4-12 hours)

Excretion: Feces (61%); urine (36%)

Dosage

Usual dosage range:

Adults: Oral: 320 mg once daily

Indication-specific dosing:

Adults: Oral:

Acute exacerbations of chronic bronchitis: 320 mg once daily for 5 days

Community-acquired pneumonia (mild to moderate): 320 mg once daily for 7 days

Sinusitis (unlabeled use): 320 mg once daily for 10 days

Elderly: Refer to Adults dosing.

Dosage adjustment in renal impairment: Cl$_{cr}$ ≤40 mL/minute (or patients on hemodialysis/CAPD): 160 mg once daily (administer dose following hemodialysis)

Dosage adjustment in hepatic impairment: No adjustment required.

Dietary Considerations May take tablets with or without food, milk, or calcium supplements. Gemifloxacin should be taken 3 hours before or 2 hours after supplements (including multivitamins) containing iron, zinc, or magnesium.

Administration May be administered with or without food, milk, or calcium supplements. Gemifloxacin should be taken 3 hours before or 2 hours after supplements (including multivitamins) containing iron, zinc, or magnesium.

Monitoring Parameters WBC, signs/symptoms of infection, renal function

Dosage Forms

Tablet:

Factive®: 320 mg

♦ **Gemifloxacin Mesylate** see Gemifloxacin on page 788

Gemtuzumab Ozogamicin (gem TOO zoo mab oh zog a MY sin)

U.S. Brand Names Mylotarg®

Canadian Brand Names Mylotarg®

Index Terms CMA-676; NSC-720568

Pharmacologic Category Antineoplastic Agent, Monoclonal Antibody

Use Treatment of relapsed CD33 positive acute myeloid leukemia (AML) in patients ≥60 years of age who are not candidates for cytotoxic chemotherapy

Unlabeled/Investigational Use Salvage therapy for acute promyelocytic leukemia (APL), relapsed/ refractory CD33 positive acute myeloid leukemia in children and adults <60 years

Pregnancy Risk Factor D

Pregnancy Implications Animal studies have demonstrated teratogenic effects, fetal loss, and maternal toxicity. There are no adequate and well-controlled studies in pregnant women. May cause fetal harm when administered to a pregnant woman. Women of childbearing potential should avoid becoming pregnant while receiving treatment.

Lactation Excretion in breast milk unknown/not recommended

Medication Safety Issues

High alert medication: The Institute for Safe Medication Practices (ISMP) includes this medication among its list of drugs which have a heightened risk of causing significant patient harm when used in error.

Contraindications Hypersensitivity to gemtuzumab ozogamicin, calicheamicin derivatives, or any component of the formulation; patients with anti-CD33 antibody; pregnancy

Warnings/Precautions Hazardous agent - use appropriate precautions for handling and disposal.

[U.S. Boxed Warning]: Gemtuzumab has been associated with severe veno-occlusive disease or hepatotoxicity. Risk may be increased by combination chemotherapy, previous hepatic disease, or hematopoietic stem cell transplant.

[U.S. Boxed Warning]: Infusion-related reactions may be severe (including anaphylaxis, pulmonary edema, or ARDS). Infusion-related events are common, generally reported to occur with the first dose after the end of the 2-hour intravenous infusion. These symptoms usually resolved after 2-4 hours with a supportive therapy of acetaminophen, diphenhydramine, and intravenous fluids. Other severe and potentially fatal infusion related pulmonary events (including dyspnea, pulmonary infiltrates, pleural effusions, noncardiogenic pulmonary edema, pulmonary insufficiency and hypoxia) have been reported infrequently. Symptomatic intrinsic lung disease or high peripheral blast counts may increase the risk of severe reactions. Fewer infusion-related events were observed after the second dose. Postinfusion reactions (may include fever, chills, hypotension, or dyspnea) may occur during the first 24 hours after administration. Consider discontinuation in patients who develop severe infusion-related reactions.

[U.S. Boxed Warning]: Severe myelosuppression occurs in all patients at recommended dosages. Use caution in patients with renal and hepatic impairment. Tumor lysis syndrome may occur as a consequence of leukemia treatment, adequate hydration and prophylactic allopurinol must be instituted prior to use. Other methods to lower WBC <30,000 cells/mm^3 may be considered (hydroxyurea or leukapheresis) to minimize the risk of tumor lysis syndrome, and/or severe infusion reactions. **[U.S. Boxed Warnings]: Should be**

administered under the supervision of an experienced cancer chemotherapy physician. Safety and efficacy have not been established in combination with other chemotherapy agents, in pediatric patients, patients with poor performance status, or in patients with organ dysfunction.

Adverse Reactions Percentages established in adults ≥60 years of age. **Note:** A postinfusion symptom complex (fever, chills, less commonly hypertension, and/or dyspnea) may occur within 24 hours of administration; the incidence of infusion-related events decreases with repeat administration.

>10%:
  Cardiovascular: Peripheral edema (19%), hypotension (18%), hypertension (17%), tachycardia (11%)
  Central nervous system: Fever (78%), chills (64%), headache (27%), pain (18%), insomnia (11%)
  Dermatologic: Petechiae (19%), rash (18%), bruising (11%)
  Endocrine & metabolic: Hypokalemia (24%), hyperglycemia (11%)
  Gastrointestinal: Nausea (63%), vomiting (53%), diarrhea (30%), anorexia (27%), abdominal pain (26%), constipation (23%), stomatitis/mucositis (22%)
  Hematologic: Neutropenia (grades 3/4: 98%; median recovery 40.5 days), lymphopenia (grades 3/4: 93%), thrombocytopenia (49%; grades 3/4: 48%; median recovery 39 days), hemoglobin decreased (grades 3/4: 50%), leukopenia (grades 3/4: 43%), anemia (22%, grades 3/4: 12%)
  Hepatic: Abnormal liver function tests (20%; grade 3/4: 7%), LDH increased (18%), hyperbilirubinemia (11%)
  Local: Local reaction (17%)
  Neuromuscular & skeletal: Weakness (36%), back pain (12%)
  Respiratory: Dyspnea (26%), epistaxis (24%; grade 3/4: 3%), cough (18%), pneumonia (13%)
  Miscellaneous: Sepsis (25%), neutropenic fever (19%), cutaneous herpes simplex (18%),
1% to 10%:
  Central nervous system: Anxiety (10%), depression (10%), dizziness (10%), cerebral hemorrhage (2%), intracranial hemorrhage (1%)
  Dermatologic: Pruritus (4%)
  Endocrine & metabolic: Hypocalcemia (10%), hypophosphatemia (6%) hypomagnesemia (3%)
  Gastrointestinal: Dyspepsia (8%), gingival hemorrhage (5%)
  Genitourinary: Vaginal hemorrhage (5%), vaginal bleeding 2%, hematuria (grade 3/4: 1%)
  Hematologic: Hemorrhage (9%), disseminated intravascular coagulation (DIC) (1%)
  Hepatic: Alkaline phosphatase increased (10%), PT/PTT increased, veno-occlusive disease (5% to 10%; up to 20% in relapsed patients; higher frequency in patients with prior history of subsequent hematopoietic stem cell transplant)
  Neuromuscular & skeletal: Arthralgia (10%), myalgia (3%)
  Respiratory: Pharyngitis (10%), rhinitis (7%), hypoxia (5%)
  Miscellaneous: Infection (10%)
  <1% (Limited to important or life-threatening): Acute respiratory distress syndrome, anaphylaxis, gastrointestinal hemorrhage, hepatic failure, hepatosplenomegaly, hypersensitivity reactions, jaundice, noncardiogenic pulmonary edema, pulmonary hemorrhage, renal impairment, renal failure, renal failure secondary to tumor lysis syndrome

Overdosage/Toxicology Symptoms are unknown. Closely monitor vital signs and blood counts. Treatment is symptom-directed and supportive. Gemtuzumab ozogamicin is not dialyzable.

Drug Interactions
  Increased Effect/Toxicity: Monoclonal antibodies may increase the risk for allergic reactions to gemtuzumab due to the presence of HACA antibodies

Ethanol/Nutrition/Herb Interactions Ethanol: Avoid ethanol (due to GI irritation).

Stability Light sensitive; protect from light. The infusion container should be placed in a UV protectant bag immediately after preparation. Store vials under refrigeration 2°C to 8°C (36°F to 46°F). Reconstituted solutions may be stored for up to 2 hours at room temperature or under refrigeration. Following dilution, solutions are stable for up to 16 hours at room temperature. Administration requires 2 hours; therefore, the maximum elapsed time from initial reconstitution to completion of infusion should be 20 hours.

Reconstitution: Prepare in a darkened room with the lights in the biologic safety cabinet turned **off**. Allow to warm to room temperature prior to reconstitution. Reconstitute vial with sterile water for injection. Final concentration of 1 mg/mL. Dilute in 100 mL of 0.9% sodium chloride injection.

Mechanism of Action Antibody to CD33 antigen. Binding results in internalization of the antibody-antigen complex. Following internalization, the calicheamicin derivative is released inside the myeloid cell. The calicheamicin derivative binds to DNA resulting in double strand breaks and cell death. Pluripotent stem cells and nonhematopoietic cells are not affected.

Pharmacodynamics/Kinetics
  Distribution: V_{ss}: Adults: Initial dose: 21 L; Repeat dose: 10 L
  Half-life elimination: Total calicheamicin: Initial: 41-45 hours, Repeat dose: 60-64 hours; Unconjugated: 100-143 hours (no change noted in repeat dosing)
  Time to peak, plasma: Immediate; higher concentrations observed after repeat dose

Dosage I.V.:
  Children: **Note:** Patients should receive diphenhydramine (1 mg/kg) 1 hour prior to infusion and acetaminophen 15 mg/kg 1 hour prior to infusion and every 4 hours for 2 additional doses.
    AML (unlabeled use): 4-9 mg/m² infused over 2 hours every 2 weeks for a total of 1-3 doses per treatment course. Patients received the second and third doses and/or dose escalation if no dose-limiting toxicities were observed. (**Note:** Higher incidences of liver toxicities were observed in children at the 9 mg/m² dose level.)
      or
    Children <3 years: 0.2 mg/kg infused over 2 hours every 2 weeks for a total of 2 doses
(Continued)

Gemtuzumab Ozogamicin *(Continued)*

Children ≥3 years: 6 mg/m^2 infused over 2 hours every 2 weeks for a total of 2 doses

Adults: **Note:** Patients should receive diphenhydramine 50 mg orally and acetaminophen 650-1000 mg orally 1 hour prior to administration of each dose. Acetaminophen dosage should be repeated as needed every 4 hours for 2 additional doses. Pretreatment with methylprednisolone may ameliorate infusion-related symptoms.

AML:

≥60 years: 9 mg/m^2 infused over 2 hours. A full treatment course is a total of 2 doses administered with 14 days between doses. Full hematologic recovery is not necessary for administration of the second dose. There has been only limited experience with repeat courses of gemtuzumab ozogamicin.

<60 years (unlabeled use): 9 mg/m^2 infused over 2 hours. A full treatment course is a total of 2 doses administered with 14 days between doses.

APL (unlabeled use): 6 mg/m^2 infused over 2 hours. A full treatment course is a total of 2 doses administered with 15 days between doses.

Dosage adjustment in renal impairment: No recommendation (not studied)

Dosage adjustment in hepatic impairment: No recommendation (not studied)

Administration Do not administer as I.V. push or bolus. Administer via I.V. infusion, over at least 2 hours. Use of a low protein-binding (0.2-1.2 micron) in-line filter is recommended. Protect from light during infusion. Premedication with acetaminophen and diphenhydramine should be administered prior to each infusion.

Monitoring Parameters Monitor vital signs during the infusion and for 4 hours following the infusion. Monitor for signs/symptoms of postinfusion reaction. Monitor electrolytes, LFTs, CBC with differential, and platelet counts frequently. Monitor for signs and symptoms of hepatitis reaction (weight gain, right upper quadrant abdominal pain, hepatomegaly, ascites).

Test Interactions None known

Dosage Forms

Injection, powder for reconstitution:

Mylotarg®: 5 mg

- ♦ **Gemzar®** *see* Gemcitabine *on page 785*
- ♦ **Genac® [OTC]** *see* Triprolidine and Pseudoephedrine *on page 1749*
- ♦ **Gen-Acebutolol (Can)** *see* Acebutolol *on page 27*
- ♦ **Genaced™ [OTC]** *see* Acetaminophen, Aspirin, and Caffeine *on page 34*
- ♦ **Gen-Acyclovir (Can)** *see* Acyclovir *on page 44*
- ♦ **Genahist® [OTC]** *see* DiphenhydrAMINE *on page 515*
- ♦ **Gen-Alendronate (Can)** *see* Alendronate *on page 65*
- ♦ **Gen-Alprazolam (Can)** *see* Alprazolam *on page 75*
- ♦ **Gen-Amilazide (Can)** *see* Amiloride and Hydrochlorothiazide *on page 93*
- ♦ **Gen-Amiodarone (Can)** *see* Amiodarone *on page 97*
- ♦ **Gen-Amoxicillin (Can)** *see* Amoxicillin *on page 110*
- ♦ **Gen-Anagrelide (Can)** *see* Anagrelide *on page 128*
- ♦ **Genapap™ [OTC]** *see* Acetaminophen *on page 28*
- ♦ **Genapap™ Children [OTC]** *see* Acetaminophen *on page 28*
- ♦ **Genapap™ Extra Strength [OTC]** *see* Acetaminophen *on page 28*
- ♦ **Genapap™ Infant [OTC]** *see* Acetaminophen *on page 28*
- ♦ **Genapap™ Sinus Maximum Strength [OTC]** *see* Acetaminophen and Pseudoephedrine *on page 33*
- ♦ **Genaphed® [OTC]** *see* Pseudoephedrine *on page 1454*
- ♦ **Genasec™ [OTC]** *see* Acetaminophen and Phenyltoloxamine *on page 32*
- ♦ **Genasoft® [OTC]** *see* Docusate *on page 533*
- ♦ **Gen-Atenolol (Can)** *see* Atenolol *on page 167*
- ♦ **Genaton Tablet [OTC]** *see* Aluminum Hydroxide and Magnesium Trisilicate *on page 85*
- ♦ **Genatuss DM® [OTC]** *see* Guaifenesin and Dextromethorphan *on page 816*
- ♦ **Gen-Azathioprine (Can)** *see* Azathioprine *on page 183*
- ♦ **Gen-Baclofen (Can)** *see* Baclofen *on page 193*
- ♦ **Gen-Beclo (Can)** *see* Beclomethasone *on page 198*
- ♦ **Gen-Budesonide AQ (Can)** *see* Budesonide *on page 244*
- ♦ **Gen-Buspirone (Can)** *see* BusPIRone *on page 256*
- ♦ **Gen-Captopril (Can)** *see* Captopril *on page 281*
- ♦ **Gen-Carbamazepine CR (Can)** *see* Carbamazepine *on page 284*
- ♦ **Gen-Cimetidine (Can)** *see* Cimetidine *on page 369*
- ♦ **Gen-Ciprofloxacin (Can)** *see* Ciprofloxacin *on page 372*
- ♦ **Gen-Citalopram (Can)** *see* Citalopram *on page 381*
- ♦ **Gen-Clobetasol (Can)** *see* Clobetasol *on page 391*
- ♦ **Gen-Clomipramine (Can)** *see* ClomiPRAMINE *on page 395*
- ♦ **Gen-Clonazepam (Can)** *see* Clonazepam *on page 397*
- ♦ **Gen-Clozapine (Can)** *see* Clozapine *on page 406*
- ♦ **Gen-Combo Sterinebs (Can)** *see* Ipratropium and Albuterol *on page 934*
- ♦ **Gen-Cyclobenzaprine (Can)** *see* Cyclobenzaprine *on page 427*
- ♦ **Gen-Diltiazem (Can)** *see* Diltiazem *on page 509*
- ♦ **Gen-Diltiazem CD (Can)** *see* Diltiazem *on page 509*
- ♦ **Gen-Divalproex (Can)** *see* Valproic Acid and Derivatives *on page 1767*
- ♦ **Gen-Doxazosin (Can)** *see* Doxazosin *on page 544*
- ♦ **Genebs [OTC]** *see* Acetaminophen *on page 28*
- ♦ **Genebs Extra Strength [OTC]** *see* Acetaminophen *on page 28*
- ♦ **Generlac** *see* Lactulose *on page 971*
- ♦ **Gen-Etidronate (Can)** *see* Etidronate Disodium *on page 665*

- **Gen-Famotidine (Can)** *see* Famotidine *on page 683*
- **Gen-Fenofibrate Micro (Can)** *see* Fenofibrate *on page 689*
- **Genfiber® [OTC]** *see* Psyllium *on page 1458*
- **Gen-Fluconazole (Can)** *see* Fluconazole *on page 712*
- **Gen-Fluoxetine (Can)** *see* Fluoxetine *on page 727*
- **Gen-Gabapentin (Can)** *see* Gabapentin *on page 775*
- **Gen-Gemfibrozil (Can)** *see* Gemfibrozil *on page 787*
- **Gen-Glybe (Can)** *see* GlyBURIDE *on page 803*
- **Gengraf®** *see* CycloSPORINE *on page 431*
- **Gen-Hydroxychloroquine (Can)** *see* Hydroxychloroquine *on page 862*
- **Gen-Hydroxyurea (Can)** *see* Hydroxyurea *on page 863*
- **Gen-Indapamide (Can)** *see* Indapamide *on page 898*
- **Gen-Ipratropium (Can)** *see* Ipratropium *on page 932*
- **Gen-Lamotrigine (Can)** *see* Lamotrigine *on page 974*
- **Gen-Levothyroxine (Can)** *see* Levothyroxine *on page 1007*
- **Gen-Lovastatin (Can)** *see* Lovastatin *on page 1040*
- **Gen-Medroxy (Can)** *see* MedroxyPROGESTERone *on page 1065*
- **Gen-Meloxicam (Can)** *see* Meloxicam *on page 1072*
- **Gen-Metformin (Can)** *see* Metformin *on page 1098*
- **Gen-Minocycline (Can)** *see* Minocycline *on page 1149*
- **Gen-Mirtazapine (Can)** *see* Mirtazapine *on page 1152*
- **Gen-Nabumetone (Can)** *see* Nabumetone *on page 1185*
- **Gen-Naproxen EC (Can)** *see* Naproxen *on page 1199*
- **Gen-Nitro (Can)** *see* Nitroglycerin *on page 1234*
- **Gen-Nizatidine (Can)** *see* Nizatidine *on page 1238*
- **Gen-Nortriptyline (Can)** *see* Nortriptyline *on page 1243*
- **Genoptic® [DSC]** *see* Gentamicin *on page 793*
- **Genotropin®** *see* Somatropin *on page 1586*
- **Genotropin Miniquick®** *see* Somatropin *on page 1586*
- **Gen-Oxybutynin (Can)** *see* Oxybutynin *on page 1285*
- **Gen-Paroxetine (Can)** *see* Paroxetine *on page 1314*
- **Gen-Pindolol (Can)** *see* Pindolol *on page 1371*
- **Gen-Piroxicam (Can)** *see* Piroxicam *on page 1378*
- **Genpril® [OTC]** *see* Ibuprofen *on page 873*
- **Gen-Ranidine (Can)** *see* Ranitidine *on page 1485*
- **Gen-Salbutamol (Can)** *see* Albuterol *on page 57*
- **Gen-Selegiline (Can)** *see* Selegiline *on page 1552*
- **Gen-Sertraline (Can)** *see* Sertraline *on page 1557*
- **Gen-Simvastatin (Can)** *see* Simvastatin *on page 1567*
- **Gen-Sotalol (Can)** *see* Sotalol *on page 1592*
- **Gen-Sumatriptan (Can)** *see* Sumatriptan *on page 1620*
- **Gentak®** *see* Gentamicin *on page 793*

Gentamicin (jen ta MYE sin)

U.S. Brand Names Genoptic® [DSC]; Gentak®
Canadian Brand Names Alcomicin®; Diogent®; Garamycin®; Gentamicin Injection, USP; SAB-Gentamicin
Index Terms Gentamicin Sulfate
Pharmacologic Category Antibiotic, Aminoglycoside; Antibiotic, Ophthalmic; Antibiotic, Topical
Additional Appendix Information
  Aminoglycoside Dosing and Monitoring *on page 1858*
  Antibiotic Treatment of Adults With Infective Endocarditis *on page 1977*
  Antimicrobial Drugs of Choice *on page 1981*
  Prevention of Bacterial Endocarditis *on page 1960*
  Prevention of Wound Infection and Sepsis in Surgical Patients *on page 1964*
  Treatment of Sexually Transmitted Infections *on page 2007*
Use Treatment of susceptible bacterial infections, normally gram-negative organisms including *Pseudomonas*, *Proteus*, *Serratia*, and gram-positive *Staphylococcus*; treatment of bone infections, respiratory tract infections, skin and soft tissue infections, as well as abdominal and urinary tract infections, endocarditis, and septicemia; used topically to treat superficial infections of the skin or ophthalmic infections caused by susceptible bacteria; prevention of bacterial endocarditis prior to dental or surgical procedures
Pregnancy Risk Factor C (ophthalmic, topical); C/D (injection; varies per manufacturer)
Lactation Enters breast milk (small amounts)/use caution (AAP rates "compatible")
Medication Safety Issues
  Sound-alike/look-alike issues:
    Gentamicin may be confused with kanamycin
    Garamycin® may be confused with kanamycin, Terramycin®
Contraindications Hypersensitivity to gentamicin or other aminoglycosides
Warnings/Precautions [U.S. Boxed Warning]: Aminoglycosides may cause neurotoxicity and/or nephrotoxicity; usual risk factors include pre-existing renal impairment, concomitant neuro-/nephrotoxic medications, advanced age and dehydration. Ototoxicity may be directly proportional to the amount of drug given and the duration of treatment; tinnitus or vertigo are indications of vestibular injury and impending hearing loss; renal damage is usually reversible. May cause neuromuscular blockade and respiratory paralysis; especially when given soon after anesthesia or muscle relaxants.
(Continued)

Gentamicin *(Continued)*

Not intended for long-term therapy due to toxic hazards associated with extended administration; use caution in pre-existing renal insufficiency, vestibular or cochlear impairment, myasthenia gravis, hypocalcemia, conditions which depress neuromuscular transmission. Dosage modification required in patients with impaired renal function. Prolonged use may result in superinfection, including pseudomembranous colitis.

Adverse Reactions

>10%:

Central nervous system: Neurotoxicity (vertigo, ataxia)

Neuromuscular & skeletal: Gait instability

Otic: Ototoxicity (auditory), ototoxicity (vestibular)

Renal: Nephrotoxicity, decreased creatinine clearance

1% to 10%:

Cardiovascular: Edema

Dermatologic: Skin itching, reddening of skin, rash

<1% (Limited to important or life-threatening): Agranulocytosis, allergic reaction, dyspnea, granulocytopenia, photosensitivity, pseudomotor cerebri, thrombocytopenia

Overdosage/Toxicology Symptoms include ototoxicity, nephrotoxicity, and neuromuscular toxicity. Serum level monitoring is recommended. The treatment of choice, following a single acute overdose, appears to be the maintenance of urine output of at least 3 mL/kg/hour. Dialysis is of questionable value in enhancing aminoglycoside elimination. If required, hemodialysis is preferred over peritoneal dialysis in patients with normal renal function. Careful hydration may be all that is required to promote diuresis and therefore enhance the drug's elimination. Chelation with penicillins is experimental.

Drug Interactions

Increased Effect/Toxicity: Penicillins, cephalosporins, amphotericin B, loop diuretics may increase nephrotoxic potential. Aminoglycosides may potentiate the effects of neuromuscular blocking agents.

Stability

Gentamicin is a colorless to slightly yellow solution which should be stored between 2°C to 30°C, but refrigeration is not recommended.

I.V. infusion solutions mixed in NS or D_5W solution are stable for 24 hours at room temperature and refrigeration.

Premixed bag: Manufacturer expiration date.

Out of overwrap stability: 30 days.

Mechanism of Action Interferes with bacterial protein synthesis by binding to 30S and 50S ribosomal subunits in a defective bacterial cell membrane

Pharmacodynamics/Kinetics

Absorption:

Intramuscular: Rapid and complete

Oral: None

Distribution: Primarily into extracellular fluid (highly hydrophilic); crosses placenta and excreted in breast milk; high concentration in the renal cortex; minimal penetration to ocular tissues via I.V. route

V_d: Increased by edema, ascites, fluid overload; decreased with dehydration

Neonates: 0.4-0.6 L/kg

Children: 0.3-0.35 L/kg

Adults: 0.2-0.3 L/kg

Relative diffusion from blood into CSF: Minimal even with inflammation

CSF:blood level ratio: Normal meninges: Nil; Inflamed meninges: 10% to 30%

Protein binding: <30%

Half-life elimination:

Infants: <1 week: 3-11.5 hours; 1 week to 6 months: 3-3.5 hours

Adults: 1.5-3 hours; End-stage renal disease: 36-70 hours

Time to peak, serum: I.M.: 30-90 minutes; I.V.: 30 minutes after 30-minute infusion

Excretion: Urine (as unchanged drug)

Clearance: Directly related to renal function

Dosage Note: Dosage Individualization is **critical** because of the low therapeutic index.

Use of ideal body weight (IBW) for determining the mg/kg/dose appears to be more accurate than dosing on the basis of total body weight (TBW). In morbid obesity, dosage requirement may best be estimated using a dosing weight of IBW + 0.4 (TBW - IBW).

Initial and periodic plasma drug levels (eg, peak and trough with conventional dosing) should be determined, particularly in critically-ill patients with serious infections or in disease states known to significantly alter aminoglycoside pharmacokinetics (eg, cystic fibrosis, burns, or major surgery).

Usual dosage ranges:

Infants and Children <5 years: I.M., I.V.: 2.5 mg/kg/dose every 8 hours*

Children ≥5 years: I.M., I.V.: 2-2.5 mg/kg/dose every 8 hours*

*Note: Higher individual doses and/or more frequent intervals (eg, every 6 hours) may be required in selected clinical situations (cystic fibrosis) or serum levels document the need

Children and Adults:

Intrathecal: 4-8 mg/day

Ophthalmic:

Ointment: Instill 1/2" (1.25 cm) 2-3 times/day to every 3-4 hours

Solution: Instill 1-2 drops every 2-4 hours, up to 2 drops every hour for severe infections

Topical: Apply 3-4 times/day to affected area

Adults: I.M., I.V.:

Conventional: 1-2.5 mg/kg/dose every 8-12 hours; to ensure adequate peak concentrations early in therapy, higher initial dosage may be considered in selected patients when extracellular water is increased (edema, septic shock, postsurgical, or trauma)

Once daily: 4-7 mg/kg/dose once daily; some clinicians recommend this approach for all patients with normal renal function; this dose is at least as efficacious with similar, if not less, toxicity than conventional dosing

Indication-specific dosing:

Neonates: I.V.:

Meningitis:

0-7 days of age: <2000 g: 2.5 mg/kg every 18-24 hours; >2000 g: 2.5 mg/kg every 12 hours

8-28 days of age: <2000 g: 2.5 mg/kg every 8-12 hours; >2000 g: 2.5 mg/kg every 8 hours

Children and Adults: I.M., I.V.:

Brucellosis: 240 mg (I.M.) daily or 5 mg/kg (I.V.) daily for 7 days; either regimen recommended in combination with doxycycline

Cholangitis: 4-6 mg/kg once daily with ampicillin

Diverticulitis (complicated): 1.5-2 mg/kg every 8 hours (with ampicillin and metronidazole)

Endocarditis prophylaxis: Dental, oral, upper respiratory procedures, GI/GU procedures: 1.5 mg/kg with ampicillin (50 mg/kg) 30 minutes prior to procedure

Endocarditis or synergy (for Gram-positive infections): 1 mg/kg every 8 hours (with ampicillin)

Meningitis:

(Enterococcus sp or Pseudomonas aeruginosa): Loading dose 2 mg/kg, then 1.7 mg/kg/dose every 8 hours (administered with another bacteriocidal drug)

Listeria: 5-7 mg/kg/day (with penicillin) for 1 week

Pelvic inflammatory disease: Loading dose: 2 mg/kg, then 1.5 mg/kg every 8 hours
Alternate therapy: 4.5 mg/kg once daily

Plague (Yersinia pestis): Treatment: 5 mg/kg/day, followed by postexposure prophylaxis with doxycycline

Pneumonia, hospital- or ventilator-associated: 7 mg/kg/day (with antipseudomonal beta-lactam or carbapenem)

Tularemia: 5 mg/kg/day divided every 8 hours for 1-2 weeks

Urinary tract infection: 1.5 mg/kg/dose every 8 hours

Dosing interval in renal impairment:

Conventional dosing:

Cl$_{cr}$ ≥60 mL/minute: Administer every 8 hours

Cl$_{cr}$ 40-60 mL/minute: Administer every 12 hours

Cl$_{cr}$ 20-40 mL/minute: Administer every 24 hours

Cl$_{cr}$ <20 mL/minute: Loading dose, then monitor levels

High-dose therapy: Interval may be extended (eg, every 48 hours) in patients with moderate renal impairment (Cl$_{cr}$ 30-59 mL/minute) and/or adjusted based on serum level determinations.

Hemodialysis: Dialyzable; removal by hemodialysis: 30% removal of aminoglycosides occurs during 4 hours of HD; administer dose after dialysis and follow levels

Removal by continuous ambulatory peritoneal dialysis (CAPD):

Administration via CAPD fluid:

Gram-negative infection: 4-8 mg/L (4-8 mcg/mL) of CAPD fluid

Gram-positive infection (eg, synergy): 3-4 mg/L (3-4 mcg/mL) of CAPD fluid

Administration via I.V., I.M. route during CAPD: Dose as for Cl$_{cr}$ <10 mL/minute and follow levels

Removal via continuous arteriovenous or venovenous hemofiltration: Dose as for Cl$_{cr}$ 10-40 mL/minute and follow levels

Dosing adjustment/comments in hepatic disease: Monitor plasma concentrations

Dietary Considerations Calcium, magnesium, potassium: Renal wasting may cause hypocalcemia, hypomagnesemia, and/or hypokalemia.

Administration

I.M.: Administer by deep I.M. route if possible. Slower absorption and lower peak concentrations, probably due to poor circulation in the atrophic muscle, may occur following I.M. injection; in paralyzed patients, suggest I.V. route.

Ophthalmic: Administer any other ophthalmics 10 minutes before or after gentamicin preparations.

Some penicillins (eg, carbenicillin, ticarcillin and piperacillin) have been shown to inactivate aminoglycosides in vitro. This has been observed to a greater extent with tobramycin and gentamicin, while amikacin has shown greater stability against inactivation. Concurrent use of these agents may pose a risk of reduced antibacterial efficacy in vivo, particularly in the setting of profound renal impairment. However, definitive clinical evidence is lacking. If combination penicillin/aminoglycoside therapy is desired in a patient with renal dysfunction, separation of doses (if feasible), and routine monitoring of aminoglycoside levels, CBC, and clinical response should be considered.

Monitoring Parameters Urinalysis, urine output, BUN, serum creatinine; hearing should be tested before, during, and after treatment; particularly in those at risk for ototoxicity or who will be receiving prolonged therapy (>2 weeks)

Some penicillin derivatives may accelerate the degradation of aminoglycosides in vitro. This may be clinically-significant for certain penicillin (ticarcillin, piperacillin, carbenicillin) and aminoglycoside (gentamicin, tobramycin) combination therapy in patients with significant renal impairment. Close monitoring of aminoglycoside levels is warranted.

Reference Range

Timing of serum samples: Draw peak 30 minutes after 30-minute infusion has been completed or 1 hour after I.M. injection; draw trough immediately before next dose

Sample size: 0.5-2 mL blood (red top tube) or 0.1-1 mL serum (separated)

Therapeutic levels:

Peak:

Serious infections: 6-8 mcg/mL (12-17 μmol/L)

Life-threatening infections: 8-10 mcg/mL (17-21 μmol/L)

Urinary tract infections: 4-6 mcg/mL

(Continued)

Gentamicin *(Continued)*

Synergy against gram-positive organisms: 3-5 mcg/mL

Trough:

Serious infections: 0.5-1 mcg/mL

Life-threatening infections: 1-2 mcg/mL

The American Thoracic Society (ATS) recommends trough levels of <1 mcg/mL for patients with hospital-acquired pneumonia.

Obtain drug levels after the third dose unless renal dysfunction/toxicity suspected

Test Interactions

Some penicillin derivatives may accelerate the degradation of aminoglycosides *in vitro*, leading to a potential underestimation of aminoglycoside serum concentration.

Dosage Forms [DSC] = Discontinued product

Cream, topical, as sulfate: 0.1% (15 g, 30 g)

Infusion, as sulfate [premixed in NS]: 40 mg (50 mL); 60 mg (50 mL, 100 mL); 70 mg (50 mL); 80 mg (50 mL, 100 mL); 90 mg (100 mL); 100 mg (50 mL, 100 mL); 120 mg (100 mL)

Injection, solution, as sulfate [ADD-Vantage® vial]: 10 mg/mL (6 mL, 8 mL, 10 mL)

Injection, solution, as sulfate: 40 mg/mL (2 mL, 20 mL) [may contain sodium metabisulfite]

Injection, solution, pediatric, as sulfate: 10 mg/mL (2 mL) [may contain sodium metabisulfite]

Injection, solution, as sulfate [preservative free]: 10 mg/mL (2 mL)

Ointment, ophthalmic, as sulfate (Gentak®): 0.3% [3 mg/g] (3.5 g)

Ointment, topical, as sulfate: 0.1% (15 g, 30 g)

Solution, ophthalmic, as sulfate: 0.3% (5 mL, 15 mL) [contains benzalkonium chloride]

Genoptic®: 0.3% (1 mL) [contains benzalkonium chloride] [DSC]

Gentak®: 0.3% (5 mL; 15 mL [DSC]) [contains benzalkonium chloride]

- ◆ **Gentamicin and Prednisolone** *see* Prednisolone and Gentamicin *on page 1416*
- ◆ **Gentamicin Injection, USP (Can)** *see* Gentamicin *on page 793*
- ◆ **Gentamicin Sulfate** *see* Gentamicin *on page 793*
- ◆ **Gen-Tamoxifen (Can)** *see* Tamoxifen *on page 1631*
- ◆ **Gen-Temazepam (Can)** *see* Temazepam *on page 1640*
- ◆ **Gen-Terbinafine (Can)** *see* Terbinafine *on page 1648*
- ◆ **Gentex LA** *see* Guaifenesin and Phenylephrine *on page 818*

Gentian Violet *(JEN shun VYE oh let)*

Index Terms Crystal Violet; Methylrosaniline Chloride

Pharmacologic Category Antibiotic, Topical; Antifungal Agent, Topical

Use Treatment of cutaneous or mucocutaneous infections caused by *Candida albicans* and other superficial skin infections

Pregnancy Risk Factor C

Dosage Children and Adults: Topical: Apply 0.5% to 2% locally with cotton to lesion 2-3 times/day for 3 days, do not swallow and avoid contact with eyes

Dosage Forms Solution, topical: 1% (30 mL); 2% (30 mL)

- ◆ **Gen-Ticlopidine (Can)** *see* Ticlopidine *on page 1683*
- ◆ **Gen-Timolol (Can)** *see* Timolol *on page 1687*
- ◆ **Gen-Tizanidine (Can)** *see* Tizanidine *on page 1695*
- ◆ **Gentlax® (Can)** *see* Bisacodyl *on page 223*
- ◆ **Gen-Topiramate (Can)** *see* Topiramate *on page 1707*
- ◆ **Gentran®** *see* Dextran *on page 485*
- ◆ **Gen-Trazodone (Can)** *see* Trazodone *on page 1727*
- ◆ **Gen-Triazolam (Can)** *see* Triazolam *on page 1738*
- ◆ **Gen-Verapamil (Can)** *see* Verapamil *on page 1784*
- ◆ **Gen-Verapamil SR (Can)** *see* Verapamil *on page 1784*
- ◆ **Gen-Warfarin (Can)** *see* Warfarin *on page 1800*
- ◆ **Geocillin®** *see* Carbenicillin *on page 288*
- ◆ **Geodon®** *see* Ziprasidone *on page 1818*
- ◆ **Geref® Diagnostic** *see* Sermorelin Acetate *on page 1556*
- ◆ **German Measles Vaccine** *see* Rubella Virus Vaccine (Live) *on page 1540*
- ◆ **GF196960** *see* Tadalafil *on page 1629*
- ◆ **GG** *see* Guaifenesin *on page 814*
- ◆ **GHB** *see* Sodium Oxybate *on page 1580*
- ◆ **GI87084B** *see* Remifentanil *on page 1493*
- ◆ **Gilphex TR®** *see* Guaifenesin and Phenylephrine *on page 818*
- ◆ **Gladase®** *see* Papain and Urea *on page 1309*
- ◆ **Glargine Insulin** *see* Insulin Glargine *on page 911*

Glatiramer Acetate *(gla TIR a mer AS e tate)*

U.S. Brand Names Copaxone®

Canadian Brand Names Copaxone®

Index Terms Copolymer-1

Pharmacologic Category Biological, Miscellaneous

Use Treatment of relapsing-remitting type multiple sclerosis; studies indicate that it reduces the frequency of attacks and the severity of disability; appears to be most effective for patients with minimal disability

Pregnancy Risk Factor B

Pregnancy Implications There are no adequate and well-controlled studies in pregnant women. Use in pregnancy only if clearly necessary.

Lactation Excretion in breast milk unknown/use caution

Medication Safety Issues

Sound-alike/look-alike issues:

Copaxone® may be confused with Compazine®

Contraindications Previous hypersensitivity to any component of the copolymer formulation, glatiramer acetate, or mannitol

Warnings/Precautions For SubQ use only, **not for I.V. administration**. Glatiramer acetate is antigenic, and may possibly lead to the induction of untoward host responses. Systemic postinjection reactions occur in a substantial percentage of patients (~10% in premarketing studies). Safety and efficacy have not been established in patients <18 years of age.

Adverse Reactions Reported in >2% of patients in placebo-controlled trials:

>10%:

Cardiovascular: Chest pain (21%), vasodilation (27%), palpitation (17%)

Central nervous system: Pain (28%), vasodilation (27%), anxiety (23%)

Dermatologic: Pruritus (18%), rash (18%), diaphoresis (15%)

Gastrointestinal: Nausea (22%), diarrhea (12%)

Local: Injection site reactions: Pain (73%), erythema (66%), inflammation (49%), pruritus (40%), mass (27%), induration (13%), welt (11%)

Neuromuscular & skeletal: Weakness (41%), arthralgia (24%), hypertonia (22%), back pain (16%)

Respiratory: Dyspnea (19%), rhinitis (14%)

Miscellaneous: Infection (50%), flu-like syndrome (19%), lymphadenopathy (12%)

1% to 10%:

Cardiovascular: Peripheral edema (7%), facial edema (6%), edema (3%), tachycardia (5%), hypertension (1%), syncope (5%)

Central nervous system: Fever (8%), vertigo (6%), migraine (5%), agitation (4%), chills (4%), confusion (2%), nervousness (2%), speech disorder (2%), abnormal dreams (1%), emotional lability (1%), stupor (1%)

Dermatologic: Bruising (8%), erythema (4%), urticaria (4%), skin nodule (2%), eczema, pustular rash, skin atrophy

Endocrine & metabolic: Dysmenorrhea (6%), amenorrhea (1%), menorrhagia (1%), vaginal hemorrhage (1%)

Gastrointestinal: Anorexia (8%), vomiting (6%), gastrointestinal disorder (5%), gastroenteritis (3%), weight gain (3%), oral moniliasis (1%), ulcerative stomatitis (1%), salivary gland enlargement

Genitourinary: Urinary urgency (10%), vaginal moniliasis (8%), hematuria (1%), impotence (1%)

Local: Injection site reactions: Hemorrhage (5%), urticaria (5%), edema (1%), atrophy (1%), abscess (1%), hypersensitivity (1%)

Neuromuscular & skeletal: Tremor (7%), foot drop (3%)

Ocular: Eye disorder (4%), nystagmus (2%), visual field defect (1%)

Otic: Ear pain (7%)

Respiratory: Bronchitis (9%), laryngismus (5%)

Miscellaneous: Neck pain (8%), bacterial infection (5%), herpes simplex (4%), cyst (2%), herpes zoster

<1% (Limited to important or life-threatening): Anaphylactoid reaction, angina, angioedema, aphasia, arrhythmia, blindness, carcinoma (breast, bladder, lung), cardiomyopathy, cholecystitis, cholelithiasis, cirrhosis, coma, CHF, corneal ulcer, esophageal ulcer, esophagitis, ethanol intolerance, gastrointestinal hemorrhage, GI carcinoma, glaucoma, gout, hallucinations, hematemesis, hepatitis, hepatomegaly, hypotension, leukopenia, lupus erythematosus, mania, meningitis, MI, neuralgia, optic neuritis, pancreatitis, pancytopenia, paraplegia, pericardial effusion, photosensitivity, postural hypotension, priapism, pulmonary embolism, rash, renal failure, rheumatoid arthritis, seizure, sepsis, serum sickness, splenomegaly, stomatitis, stroke, suicide attempt, thrombocytopenia, thrombosis

Overdosage/Toxicology Well tolerated; no serious toxicities can be anticipated.

Stability Store in refrigerator at 2°C to 8°C (36°F to 46°F); excursions to room temperature for up to 1 week do not have a negative impact on potency.

Mechanism of Action Glatiramer is a mixture of random polymers of four amino acids; L-alanine, L-glutamic acid, L-lysine and L-tyrosine, the resulting mixture is antigenically similar to myelin basic protein, which is an important component of the myelin sheath of nerves; glatiramer is thought to suppress T-lymphocytes specific for a myelin antigen, it is also proposed that glatiramer interferes with the antigen-presenting function of certain immune cells opposing pathogenic T-cell function

Pharmacodynamics/Kinetics

Distribution: Small amounts of intact and partial hydrolyzed drug enter lymphatic circulation

Metabolism: SubQ: Large percentage hydrolyzed locally

Dosage Adults: SubQ: 20 mg daily

Administration For SubQ administration in the arms, abdomen, hips or thighs. Bring to room temperature prior to use.

Dosage Forms Injection, solution [preservative free]: 20 mg/mL (1 mL) [prefilled syringe; contains mannitol; packaged with alcohol pads]

♦ **Gleevec**® see Imatinib on page 881

♦ **Gliadel**® see Carmustine on page 296

♦ **Gliadel Wafer**® (Can) see Carmustine on page 296

♦ **Glibenclamide** see GlyBURIDE on page 803

Glimepiride (GLYE me pye ride)

U.S. Brand Names Amaryl®

Canadian Brand Names Amaryl®; CO Glimepiride; Novo-Glimepiride; ratio-Glimepiride; Rhoxal-glimepiride; Sandoz-Glimepiride

(Continued)

Glimepiride *(Continued)*

Pharmacologic Category Antidiabetic Agent, Sulfonylurea

Additional Appendix Information
Diabetes Mellitus Management, Adults *on page 2040*
Hyperglycemia- or Hypoglycemia-Causing Drugs *on page 2057*
Sulfonamide Derivatives *on page 1897*

Use Management of type 2 diabetes mellitus (noninsulin dependent, NIDDM) as an adjunct to diet and exercise to lower blood glucose; may be used in combination with metformin or insulin in patients whose hyperglycemia cannot be controlled by diet and exercise in conjunction with a single oral hypoglycemic agent

Pregnancy Risk Factor C

Pregnancy Implications Abnormal blood glucose levels are associated with a higher incidence of congenital abnormalities. Insulin is the drug of choice for the control of diabetes mellitus during pregnancy.

Lactation Excretion in breast milk unknown/contraindicated

Medication Safety Issues
Sound-alike/look-alike issues:
Glimepiride may be confused with glipiZIDE
Amaryl® may be confused with Altace®, Amerge®, Reminyl®

Contraindications Hypersensitivity to glimepiride, any component of the formulation, or sulfonamides; diabetic ketoacidosis (with or without coma)

Warnings/Precautions All sulfonylurea drugs are capable of producing severe hypoglycemia. Hypoglycemia is more likely to occur when caloric intake is deficient, after severe or prolonged exercise, when ethanol is ingested, or when more than one glucose-lowering drug is used. It is also more likely in elderly patients, malnourished patients and in patients with impaired renal or hepatic function; use with caution.

Chemical similarities are present among sulfonamides, sulfonylureas, carbonic anhydrase inhibitors, thiazides, and loop diuretics (except ethacrynic acid). Use in patients with sulfonamide allergy is specifically contraindicated in product labeling, however, a risk of cross-reaction exists in patients with allergy to any of these compounds; avoid use when previous reaction has been severe.

Product labeling states oral hypoglycemic drugs may be associated with an increased cardiovascular mortality as compared to treatment with diet alone or diet plus insulin. Data to support this association are limited, and several studies, including a large prospective trial (UKPDS) have not supported an association.

It may be necessary to discontinue therapy and administer insulin if the patient is exposed to stress (fever, trauma, infection, surgery). Safety and efficacy have not been established in children.

Adverse Reactions
1% to 10%:
Central nervous system: Dizziness (2%), headache (2%)
Endocrine & metabolic: Hypoglycemia (1% to 2%)
Gastrointestinal: Nausea (1%)
Neuromuscular & skeletal: Weakness (2%)
<1% or frequency not defined: Agranulocytosis, anorexia, aplastic anemia, cholestatic jaundice, constipation, diarrhea, disulfiram-like reaction, diuretic effect, edema, epigastric fullness, gastrointestinal pain, erythema, heartburn, hemolytic anemia, hepatitis, hypoglycemia, hyponatremia, leukopenia, liver function tests abnormal, nausea, pancytopenia, photosensitivity, porphyria cutanea tarda, pruritus, rash (morbilliform or maculopapular), SIADH, thrombocytopenia, urticaria, vasculitis (allergic), visual accommodation changes (early treatment), vomiting

Overdosage/Toxicology Symptoms include low blood sugar, tingling of lips and tongue, nausea, yawning, confusion, agitation, tachycardia, sweating, convulsions, stupor, and coma. Intoxications with sulfonylureas can cause hypoglycemia and are best managed with glucose administration (orally for milder hypoglycemia or by injection in more severe forms). Patients should be monitored for a minimum of 24-48 hours after ingestion.

Drug Interactions
Cytochrome P450 Effect: Substrate of CYP2C9 (major)
Increased Effect/Toxicity: CYP2C9 inhibitors may increase the levels/effects of glimepiride; example inhibitors include delavirdine, ketoconazole, nicardipine, NSAIDs, sulfonamides, and tolbutamide. Beta-blockers, chloramphenicol, cimetidine, fibric acid derivatives, fluconazole, pegvisomant, salicylates, sulfonamides, and tricyclic antidepressants may increase the hypoglycemic effects of glimepiride. Glimepiride may increase effects of cyclosporine. Sulfonylureas may induce a disulfiram-like reaction with ethanol.
Decreased Effect: CYP2C9 inducers may decrease the levels/effects of glimepiride; example inducers include carbamazepine, phenobarbital, phenytoin, rifampin, rifapentine, and secobarbital. There may be a decreased effect of glimepiride with corticosteroids, estrogens, oral contraceptives, thiazide and other diuretics, phenothiazines, NSAIDs, thyroid products, nicotinic acid, isoniazid, sympathomimetics, urinary alkalinizers, and charcoal. **Note:** However, pooled data did **not** demonstrate drug interactions with calcium channel blockers, estrogens, NSAIDs, HMG-CoA reductase inhibitors, sulfonamides, or thyroid hormone.

Ethanol/Nutrition/Herb Interactions
Ethanol: Caution with ethanol (may cause hypoglycemia).
Herb/Nutraceutical: Caution with chromium, garlic, gymnema (may cause hypoglycemia).

Mechanism of Action Stimulates insulin release from the pancreatic beta cells; reduces glucose output from the liver; insulin sensitivity is increased at peripheral target sites

Pharmacodynamics/Kinetics
Onset of action: Peak effect: Blood glucose reductions: 2-3 hours
Duration: 24 hours
Absorption: 100%; delayed when given with food
Distribution: V_d: 8.8 L

Protein binding: >99.5%

Metabolism: Hepatic oxidation via CYP2C9 to M1 metabolite (~33% activity of parent compound); further oxidative metabolism to inactive M2 metabolite

Half-life elimination: 5-9 hours

Time to peak, plasma: 2-3 hours

Excretion: Urine (60%, 80% to 90% M1 and M2); feces (40%, 70% M1 and M2)

Dosage Oral:

Children 10-18 years (unlabeled use): Initial: 1 mg once daily; maintenance: 1-4 mg once daily

Adults: Initial: 1-2 mg once daily, administered with breakfast or the first main meal; usual maintenance dose: 1-4 mg once daily; after a dose of 2 mg once daily, increase in increments of 2 mg at 1- to 2-week intervals based upon the patient's blood glucose response to a maximum of 8 mg once daily. If inadequate response to maximal dose, combination therapy with metformin may be considered.

Combination with insulin therapy (fasting glucose level for instituting combination therapy is in the range of >150 mg/dL in plasma or serum depending on the patient): initial recommended dose: 8 mg once daily with the first main meal

After starting with low-dose insulin, upward adjustments of insulin can be done approximately weekly as guided by frequent measurements of fasting blood glucose. Once stable, combination-therapy patients should monitor their capillary blood glucose on an ongoing basis, preferably daily.

Conversion from therapy with long half-life agents: Observe patient carefully for 1-2 weeks when converting from a longer half-life agent (eg, chlorpropamide) to glimepiride due to overlapping hypoglycemic effects.

Dosing adjustment/comments in renal impairment: Cl_{cr} <22 mL/minute: Initial starting dose should be 1 mg and dosage increments should be based on fasting blood glucose levels

Dosing adjustment in hepatic impairment: No data available

Elderly: Initial: 1 mg/day; dose titration and maintenance dosing should be conservative to avoid hypoglycemia

Dietary Considerations Administer with breakfast or the first main meal of the day. Dietary modification based on ADA recommendations is a part of therapy. Decreases blood glucose concentration. Hypoglycemia may occur. Must be able to recognize symptoms of hypoglycemia (palpitations, sweaty palms, lightheadedness).

Administration Administer once daily with breakfast or first main meal of the day. Patients who are NPO may need to have their dose held to avoid hypoglycemia.

Monitoring Parameters Urine for glucose and ketones; monitor for signs and symptoms of hypoglycemia (fatigue, excessive hunger, profuse sweating, numbness of extremities), fasting blood glucose, hemoglobin A_{1c}, fructosamine

Reference Range Target range: Adults:

Fasting blood glucose: <120 mg/dL

Glycosylated hemoglobin: <7%

Dosage Forms

Tablet: 1 mg, 2 mg, 4 mg

Amaryl®: 1 mg, 2 mg, 4 mg

- ◆ **Glimepiride and Pioglitazone** see Pioglitazone and Glimepiride on page 1374
- ◆ **Glimepiride and Pioglitazone Hydrochloride** see Pioglitazone and Glimepiride on page 1374
- ◆ **Glimepiride and Rosiglitazone Maleate** see Rosiglitazone and Glimepiride on page 1536

GlipiZIDE (GLIP i zide)

U.S. Brand Names Glucotrol®; Glucotrol® XL

Index Terms Glydiazinamide

Pharmacologic Category Antidiabetic Agent, Sulfonylurea

Additional Appendix Information

Hyperglycemia- or Hypoglycemia-Causing Drugs on page 2057

Sulfonamide Derivatives on page 1897

Use Management of type 2 diabetes mellitus (noninsulin dependent, NIDDM)

Pregnancy Risk Factor C

Pregnancy Implications Crosses the placenta. Abnormal blood glucose levels are associated with a higher incidence of congenital abnormalities. Insulin is the drug of choice for the control of diabetes mellitus during pregnancy. If glipizide is used during pregnancy, discontinue and change to insulin at least 1 month prior to delivery to decrease prolonged hypoglycemia in the neonate.

Lactation Excretion in breast milk unknown/not recommended

Medication Safety Issues

Sound-alike/look-alike issues:

GlipiZIDE may be confused with glimepiride, glyBURIDE

Glucotrol® may be confused with Glucophage®, Glucotrol® XL, glyBURIDE

Glucotrol® XL may be confused with Glucotrol®

Contraindications Hypersensitivity to glipizide or any component of the formulation, other sulfonamides; type 1 diabetes mellitus (insulin dependent, IDDM)

Warnings/Precautions All sulfonylurea drugs are capable of producing severe hypoglycemia. Hypoglycemia is more likely to occur when caloric intake is deficient, after severe or prolonged exercise, when ethanol is ingested, or when more than one glucose-lowering drug is used. It is also more likely in elderly patients, malnourished patients and in patients with impaired renal or hepatic function; use with caution.

Chemical similarities are present among sulfonamides, sulfonylureas, carbonic anhydrase inhibitors, thiazides, and loop diuretics (except ethacrynic acid). Use in patients with sulfonamide allergy is specifically contraindicated in product labeling, however, a risk of (Continued)

GlipiZIDE *(Continued)*

cross-reaction exists in patients with allergy to any of these compounds; avoid use when previous reaction has been severe.

Product labeling states oral hypoglycemic drugs may be associated with an increased cardiovascular mortality as compared to treatment with diet alone or diet plus insulin. Data to support this association are limited, and several studies, including a large prospective trial (UKPDS) have not supported an association.

Use with caution in patients with severe hepatic disease. It may be necessary to discontinue therapy and administer insulin if the patient is exposed to stress (fever, trauma, infection, surgery). Safety and efficacy have not been established in children.

Avoid use of extended release tablets (Glucotrol® XL) in patients with known stricture/narrowing of the GI tract.

Adverse Reactions Frequency not defined.

Cardiovascular: Edema, syncope

Central nervous system: Anxiety, depression, dizziness, headache, insomnia, nervousness

Dermatologic: Rash, urticaria, photosensitivity, pruritus

Endocrine & metabolic: Hypoglycemia, hyponatremia, SIADH (rare)

Gastrointestinal: Anorexia, nausea, vomiting, diarrhea, epigastric fullness, constipation, heartburn, flatulence

Hematologic: Blood dyscrasias, aplastic anemia, hemolytic anemia, bone marrow suppression, thrombocytopenia, agranulocytosis

Hepatic: Cholestatic jaundice, hepatic porphyria

Neuromuscular & skeletal: Arthralgia, leg cramps, myalgia, tremor

Ocular: Blurred vision

Renal: Diuretic effect (minor)

Miscellaneous: Diaphoresis, disulfiram-like reaction

Postmarketing and/or case reports: Abdominal pain

Overdosage/Toxicology Symptoms include low blood sugar, tingling of lips and tongue, nausea, yawning, confusion, agitation, tachycardia, sweating, convulsions, stupor, and coma. Intoxications with sulfonylureas can cause hypoglycemia and are best managed with glucose administration (orally for milder hypoglycemia or by injection in more severe forms).

Drug Interactions

Cytochrome P450 Effect: Substrate of 2C8/9 (major)

Increased Effect/Toxicity: CYP2C8/9 inhibitors may increase the levels/effects of glipizide; example inhibitors include delavirdine, fluconazole, gemfibrozil, ketoconazole, nicardipine, NSAIDs, pioglitazone, and sulfonamides. Increased effects/hypoglycemic effects of glipizide with H_2 antagonists, anticoagulants, androgens, cimetidine, salicylates, tricyclic antidepressants, probenecid, MAO inhibitors, methyldopa, digitalis glycosides, and urinary acidifiers.

Decreased Effect: CYP2C8/9 inducers may decrease the levels/effects of glipizide; example inducers include carbamazepine, phenobarbital, phenytoin, rifampin, rifapentine, and secobarbital. Decreased effect of glipizide with beta-blockers, cholestyramine, hydantoins, thiazide diuretics, urinary alkalinizers, and charcoal.

Ethanol/Nutrition/Herb Interactions

Ethanol: Caution with ethanol (may cause hypoglycemia or rare disulfiram reaction).

Food: A delayed release of insulin may occur if glipizide is taken with food. Immediate release tablets should be administered 30 minutes before meals to avoid erratic absorption.

Herb/Nutraceutical: Caution with chromium, garlic, gymnema (may cause hypoglycemia).

Mechanism of Action Stimulates insulin release from the pancreatic beta cells; reduces glucose output from the liver; insulin sensitivity is increased at peripheral target sites

Pharmacodynamics/Kinetics

Onset of action: Peak effect: Blood glucose reductions: 1.5-2 hours

Duration: 12-24 hours

Absorption: Delayed with food

Protein binding: 92% to 99%

Metabolism: Hepatic with metabolites

Half-life elimination: 2-4 hours

Excretion: Urine (60% to 80%, 91% to 97% as metabolites); feces (11%)

Dosage Oral (allow several days between dose titrations): Adults: Initial: 5 mg/day; adjust dosage at 2.5-5 mg daily increments as determined by blood glucose response at intervals of several days.

Immediate release tablet: Maximum recommended once-daily dose: 15 mg; maximum recommended total daily dose: 40 mg

Extended release tablet (Glucotrol® XL): Maximum recommended dose: 20 mg

When transferring from insulin to glipizide:

Current insulin requirement ≤20 units: Discontinue insulin and initiate glipizide at usual dose

Current insulin requirement >20 units: Decrease insulin by 50% and initiate glipizide at usual dose; gradually decrease insulin dose based on patient response. Several days should elapse between dosage changes.

Elderly: Initial: 2.5 mg/day; increase by 2.5-5 mg/day at 1- to 2-week intervals

Dosing adjustment/comments in renal impairment: Cl_{cr} <10 mL/minute: Some investigators recommend not using

Dosing adjustment in hepatic impairment: Initial dosage should be 2.5 mg/day

Dietary Considerations Take immediate release tablets 30 minutes before meals; extended release tablets should be taken with breakfast. Dietary modification based on ADA recommendations is a part of therapy. Decreases blood glucose concentration. Hypoglycemia may occur. Must be able to recognize symptoms of hypoglycemia (palpitations, sweaty palms, lightheadedness).

Administration Administer immediate release tablets 30 minutes before a meal to achieve greatest reduction in postprandial hyperglycemia. Extended release tablets should be given with breakfast. Patients who are NPO may need to have their dose held to avoid hypoglycemia.

Monitoring Parameters Urine for glucose and ketones; monitor for signs and symptoms of hypoglycemia (fatigue, excessive hunger, profuse sweating, numbness of extremities), fasting blood glucose, hemoglobin A_{1c}, fructosamine

Reference Range Target range: Adults:
Fasting blood glucose: <120 mg/dl
Glycosylated hemoglobin: <7%

Dosage Forms
Tablet (Glucotrol®): 5 mg, 10 mg
Tablet, extended release: 5 mg, 10 mg
Glucotrol® XL: 2.5 mg, 5 mg, 10 mg

Glipizide and Metformin (GLIP i zide & met FOR min)

U.S. Brand Names Metaglip™

Index Terms Glipizide and Metformin Hydrochloride; Metformin and Glipizide

Pharmacologic Category Antidiabetic Agent, Biguanide; Antidiabetic Agent, Sulfonylurea

Use Initial therapy for management of type 2 diabetes mellitus (noninsulin dependent, NIDDM) when hyperglycemia cannot be managed with diet and exercise alone. Second-line therapy for management of type 2 diabetes (NIDDM) when hyperglycemia cannot be managed with a sulfonylurea or metformin along with diet and exercise.

Pregnancy Risk Factor C

Pregnancy Implications See individual agents.

Lactation Excretion in breast milk unknown/not recommended

Contraindications See individual agents.

Warnings/Precautions See individual agents.

Adverse Reactions Also see individual agents.
>10%:
Central nervous system: Headache (12%)
Endocrine & metabolic: Hypoglycemia (8% to 13%)
Gastrointestinal: Diarrhea (2% to 18%)
1% to 10%:
Cardiovascular: Hypertension (3%)
Central nervous system: Dizziness (2% to 5%)
Gastrointestinal: Nausea/vomiting (<1% to 8%), abdominal pain (6%)
Neuromuscular & skeletal: Musculoskeletal pain (8%)
Renal: Urinary tract infection (1%)
Respiratory: Upper respiratory tract infection (8% to 10%)

Overdosage/Toxicology See individual agents.

Drug Interactions
Cytochrome P450 Effect: Glipizide: **Substrate** of 2C8/9 (major)
Increased Effect/Toxicity: See individual agents.
Decreased Effect: See individual agents.

Ethanol/Nutrition/Herb Interactions See individual agents.

Stability Store at room temperature of 15°C to 30°C (59°F to 86°F).

Mechanism of Action See individual agents.
The combination of glipizide and metformin is used to improve glycemic control in patients with type 2 diabetes mellitus (noninsulin dependent, NIDDM) by using two different, but complementary, mechanisms of action.

Pharmacodynamics/Kinetics See individual agents.

Dosage Oral:
Adults:
Type 2 diabetes, first-line therapy: Initial: Glipizide 2.5 mg/metformin 250 mg once daily with a meal. Dose adjustment: Increase dose by 1 tablet/day every 2 weeks, up to a maximum of glipizide 10 mg/metformin 1000 mg daily
Patients with fasting plasma glucose (FPG) 280-320 mg/dL: Consider glipizide 2.5 mg/metformin 500 mg twice daily. Dose adjustment: Increase dose by 1 tablet/day every 2 weeks, up to a maximum of glipizide 10 mg/metformin 2000 mg daily in divided doses
Type 2 diabetes, second-line therapy: Glipizide 2.5 mg/metformin 500 mg **or** glipizide 5 mg/metformin 500 mg twice daily with morning and evening meals; starting dose should not exceed current daily dose of glipizide (or sulfonylurea equivalent) or metformin. Dose adjustment: Titrate dose in increments of no more than glipizide 5 mg/metformin 500 mg, up to a maximum dose of glipizide 20 mg/metformin 2000 mg daily.
Elderly: Conservative doses are recommended in the elderly due to potentially decreased renal function; **do not titrate to maximum dose**; should not be used in patients ≥80 years unless renal function is verified as normal

Dosage adjustment in renal impairment: Risk of lactic acidosis increases with degree of renal impairment, contraindicated in renal disease or renal dysfunction (**see** Contraindications)

Dosage adjustment in hepatic impairment: Use should be avoided; liver disease is a risk factor for the development of lactic acidosis during metformin therapy.

Dietary Considerations May cause GI upset; should be taken with food to decrease GI upset. Dietary modification based on ADA recommendations is a part of therapy. Decreases blood glucose concentration. Hypoglycemia may occur. Must be able to recognize symptoms of hypoglycemia (palpitations, sweaty palms, lightheadedness). Monitor for signs and symptoms of vitamin B_{12} deficiency. Monitor for signs and symptoms of folic acid deficiency.

Administration All doses should be administered with a meal. Twice-daily dosing should be administered with the morning and evening meals. Patients who are anorexic or NPO may need to have their dose held to avoid hypoglycemia.

Monitoring Parameters Signs and symptoms of hypoglycemia, urine (glucose and ketones), FPG, Hb A_{1c}, and fructosamine. Initial and periodic monitoring of hematologic parameters (eg, hemoglobin/hematocrit and red blood cell indices) and renal function should be (Continued)

Glipizide and Metformin *(Continued)*

performed. Monitor at least annually once patient is on maintenance therapy. While megaloblastic anemia has been rarely seen with metformin, if suspected, vitamin B_{12} deficiency should be excluded.

Reference Range Target range: Adults: Fasting blood glucose: <120 mg/dL; glycosylated hemoglobin: <7%

Dosage Forms
Tablet: 2.5/250: Glipizide 2.5 mg and metformin hydrochloride 250 mg; 2.5/500: Glipizide 2.5 mg and metformin hydrochloride 500 mg; 5/500: Glipizide 5 mg and metformin hydrochloride 500 mg
Metaglip™ 2.5/250: Glipizide 2.5 mg and metformin hydrochloride 250 mg
Metaglip™ 2.5/500: Glipizide 2.5 mg and metformin hydrochloride 500 mg
Metaglip™ 5/500: Glipizide 5 mg and metformin hydrochloride 500 mg

♦ **Glipizide and Metformin Hydrochloride** *see Glipizide and Metformin on page 801*

♦ **Glivec** *see Imatinib on page 881*

♦ **Gln** *see Glutamine on page 803*

♦ **GlucaGen**® *see Glucagon on page 802*

♦ **GlucaGen® Diagnostic Kit** *see Glucagon on page 802*

♦ **GlucaGen® HypoKit™** *see Glucagon on page 802*

Glucagon *(GLOO ka gon)*

U.S. Brand Names GlucaGen®; GlucaGen® Diagnostic Kit; GlucaGen® HypoKit™; Glucagon Diagnostic Kit [DSC]; Glucagon Emergency Kit

Index Terms Glucagon Hydrochloride

Pharmacologic Category Antidote; Diagnostic Agent

Additional Appendix Information
Management of Overdosages *on page 2075*

Use Management of hypoglycemia; diagnostic aid in radiologic examinations to temporarily inhibit GI tract movement

Unlabeled/Investigational Use Used with some success as a cardiac stimulant in management of severe cases of beta-adrenergic blocking agent overdosage; treatment of myocardial depression due to calcium channel blocker overdose

Pregnancy Risk Factor B

Lactation Excretion in breast milk unknown/compatible

Medication Safety Issues
Sound-alike/look-alike issues:
Glucagon may be confused with Glaucon®

Contraindications Hypersensitivity to glucagon or any component of the formulation; insulinoma; pheochromocytoma

Warnings/Precautions Use caution with prolonged fasting, starvation, adrenal insufficiency or chronic hypoglycemia; levels of glucose stores in liver may be decreased. Following response to therapy, oral carbohydrates should be administered to prevent hypoglycemia.

Adverse Reactions Frequency not defined.
Cardiovascular: Hypotension (up to 2 hours after GI procedures), hypertension, tachycardia
Gastrointestinal: Nausea, vomiting (high incidence with rapid administration of high doses)
Miscellaneous: Hypersensitivity reactions, anaphylaxis

Overdosage/Toxicology Symptoms include hypokalemia, nausea and vomiting, inhibition of GI tract motility, decreased blood pressure, tachycardia

Drug Interactions
Increased Effect/Toxicity: Oral anticoagulant: Hypoprothrombinemic effects may be increased possibly with bleeding; effect seen with glucagon doses of 50 mg administered over 1-2 days

Ethanol/Nutrition/Herb Interactions Ethanol depletes glycogen stores.

Stability Prior to reconstitution, store at controlled room temperature of 20°C to 25°C (69°F to 77°F); do not freeze. Reconstitute powder for injection by adding 1 mL of sterile diluent to a vial containing 1 unit of the drug, to provide solutions containing 1 mg of glucagon/mL. Gently roll vial to dissolve. If dose to be administered is <2 mg of the drug, then use only the diluent provided by the manufacturer. If >2 mg, use sterile water for injection. Use immediately after reconstitution. May be kept at 5°C for up to 48 hours if necessary.

Mechanism of Action Stimulates adenylate cyclase to produce increased cyclic AMP, which promotes hepatic glycogenolysis and gluconeogenesis, causing a raise in blood glucose levels

Pharmacodynamics/Kinetics
Onset of action: Peak effect: Blood glucose levels: Parenteral:
I.V.: 5-20 minutes
I.M.: 30 minutes
SubQ: 30-45 minutes
Duration: Hyperglycemia: 60-90 minutes
Metabolism: Primarily hepatic; some inactivation occurring renally and in plasma
Half-life elimination, plasma: 3-10 minutes

Dosage
Hypoglycemia or insulin shock therapy: I.M., I.V., SubQ:
Children <20 kg: 0.5 mg or 20-30 mcg/kg/dose; repeated in 20 minutes as needed
Children ≥20 kg and Adults: 1 mg; may repeat in 20 minutes as needed
Note: If patient fails to respond to glucagon, I.V. dextrose must be given.
Beta-blocker overdose, calcium channel blocker overdose (unlabeled use): Adults: I.V.: 5-10 mg over 1 minutes followed by an infusion of 1-10 mg/hour. The following has also been reported for beta-blocker overdose: 3-10 mg or initially 0.5-5 mg bolus followed by continuous infusion 1-5 mg/hour
Diagnostic aid: Adults: I.M., I.V.: 0.25-2 mg 10 minutes prior to procedure

Dietary Considerations Administer carbohydrates to patient as soon as possible after response to treatment.

Administration I.V.: Bolus may be associated with nausea and vomiting. Continuous infusions may be used in beta-blocker overdose/toxicity.

Monitoring Parameters Blood pressure, blood glucose, heart rate

Additional Information 1 unit = 1 mg

Dosage Forms Injection, powder for reconstitution, as hydrochloride:
GlucaGen®: 1 mg [equivalent to 1 unit; contains lactose 107 mg]
GlucaGen® Diagnostic Kit: 1 mg [equivalent to 1 unit; contains lactose 107 mg; packaged with sterile water]
GlucaGen® HypoKit™: 1 mg [equivalent to 1 unit; contains lactose 107 mg; packaged with prefilled syringe containing sterile water]
Glucagon®: 1 mg [equivalent to 1 unit; contains lactose 49 mg]
Glucagon Diagnostic Kit, Glucagon Emergency Kit: 1 mg [equivalent to 1 unit; contains lactose 49 mg; packaged with diluent syringe containing glycerin 12 mg/mL and water for injection]

+ **Glucagon Diagnostic Kit [DSC]** *see* Glucagon *on page 802*
+ **Glucagon Emergency Kit** *see* Glucagon *on page 802*
+ **Glucagon Hydrochloride** *see* Glucagon *on page 802*
+ **Glucocerebrosidase** *see* Alglucerase *on page 69*
+ **GlucoNorm® (Can)** *see* Repaglinide *on page 1494*
+ **Glucophage®** *see* Metformin *on page 1098*
+ **Glucophage® XR** *see* Metformin *on page 1098*
+ **Glucotrol®** *see* GlipiZIDE *on page 799*
+ **Glucotrol® XL** *see* GlipiZIDE *on page 799*
+ **Glucovance®** *see* Glyburide and Metformin *on page 805*
+ **Glu-K® [OTC]** *see* Potassium Gluconate *on page 1399*
+ **Glulisine Insulin** *see* Insulin Glulisine *on page 911*
+ **Glumetza™** *see* Metformin *on page 1098*
+ **Glumetza® (Can)** *see* Metformin *on page 1098*

Glutamine (GLOO ta meen)

U.S. Brand Names Enterex® Glutapak-10® [OTC]; NutreStore™; Resource® GlutaSolve® [OTC]; Sympt-X [OTC]; Sympt-X G.I. [OTC]

Index Terms Gln; L-Glutamine

Pharmacologic Category Amino Acid

Use Treatment of short bowel syndrome when used in combination with nutritional support and growth hormone therapy; a medical food used to promote GI tract healing and nutritional supplementation with GI disorders, HIV/AIDS, cancer, and other critical illnesses

Pregnancy Risk Factor C

Dosage Oral: Adults:
Nutritional supplement (Enterex® Glutapak-10®, Resource® GlutaSolve®, Sympt-X, Sympt-X G.I.): Average dose: 10 g 3 times/day; dosing range: 5-30 g/day
Short bowel syndrome (NutreStore™): 30 g/day administered as 5 g 6 times/day (every 2-3 hours while awake) for up to 16 weeks; to be used in combination with growth hormone and nutritional support

Additional Information Complete prescribing information for this medication should be consulted for additional detail.

Dosage Forms Powder for oral solution:
Enterex® Glutapak-10®: 10 g/packet (50s)
NutreStore™: 5 g/packet
Resource® GlutaSolve®: 15 g/packet (56s)
Sympt-X, Sympt-X G.I.: 10 g/packet (60s)

+ **Glybenclamide** *see* GlyBURIDE *on page 803*
+ **Glybenzcyclamide** *see* GlyBURIDE *on page 803*

GlyBURIDE (GLYE byoor ide)

U.S. Brand Names Diaβeta®; Glynase® PresTab®; Micronase®

Canadian Brand Names Albert® Glyburide; Apo-Glyburide®; Diaβeta®; Euglucon®; Gen-Glybe; Novo-Glyburide; Nu-Glyburide; PMS-Glyburide; ratio-Glyburide; Sandoz-Glyburide

Index Terms Diabeta; Glibenclamide; Glybenclamide; Glybenzcyclamide

Pharmacologic Category Antidiabetic Agent, Sulfonylurea

Additional Appendix Information
Diabetes Mellitus Management, Adults *on page 2040*
Hyperglycemia- or Hypoglycemia-Causing Drugs *on page 2057*
Sulfonamide Derivatives *on page 1897*

Use Management of type 2 diabetes mellitus (noninsulin dependent, NIDDM)

Unlabeled/Investigational Use Alternative to insulin in women for the treatment of gestational diabetes (11-33 weeks gestation)

Pregnancy Risk Factor C

Pregnancy Implications Glyburide was not found to significantly cross the placenta *in vitro*. Studies have shown glyburide to be an acceptable alternative to insulin when treatment is needed for gestational diabetes. However, one retrospective study comparing glyburide to insulin noted an increased risk of preeclampsia in women taking glyburide and a higher rate of phototherapy in neonates. Insulin is the drug of choice for the control of diabetes mellitus during pregnancy.

Lactation Does not enter breast milk/ use caution
(Continued)

GlyBURIDE (Continued)

Medication Safety Issues

Sound-alike/look-alike issues:

GlyBURIDE may be confused with glipiZIDE, Glucotrol®

Diaβeta® may be confused with Diabinese®, Zebeta®

Micronase® may be confused with microK®, miconazole, Micronor®

Contraindications Hypersensitivity to glyburide, any component of the formulation, or other sulfonamides; type 1 diabetes mellitus (insulin dependent, IDDM), diabetic ketoacidosis with or without coma

Warnings/Precautions All sulfonylurea drugs are capable of producing severe hypoglycemia. Hypoglycemia is more likely to occur when caloric intake is deficient, after severe or prolonged exercise, when ethanol is ingested, or when more than one glucose-lowering drug is used. It is also more likely in elderly patients, malnourished patients and in patients with impaired renal or hepatic function; use with caution.

Elderly: Rapid and prolonged hypoglycemia (>12 hours) despite hypertonic glucose injections have been reported; age and hepatic and renal impairment are independent risk factors for hypoglycemia; dosage titration should be made at weekly intervals.

Chemical similarities are present among sulfonamides, sulfonylureas, carbonic anhydrase inhibitors, thiazides, and loop diuretics (except ethacrynic acid). Use in patients with sulfonamide allergy is specifically contraindicated in product labeling, however, a risk of cross-reaction exists in patients with allergy to any of these compounds; avoid use when previous reaction has been severe.

Product labeling states oral hypoglycemic drugs may be associated with an increased cardiovascular mortality as compared to treatment with diet alone or diet plus insulin. Data to support this association are limited, and several studies, including a large prospective trial (UKPDS) have not supported an association.

It may be necessary to discontinue therapy and administer insulin if the patient is exposed to stress (fever, trauma, infection, surgery). Safety and efficacy have not been established in children.

Adverse Reactions Frequency not defined.

Central nervous system: Headache, dizziness

Dermatologic: Pruritus, rash, urticaria, photosensitivity reaction

Endocrine & metabolic: Hypoglycemia, hyponatremia (SIADH reported with other sulfonylureas)

Gastrointestinal: Nausea, epigastric fullness, heartburn, constipation, diarrhea, anorexia

Genitourinary: Nocturia

Hematologic: Leukopenia, thrombocytopenia, hemolytic anemia, aplastic anemia, bone marrow suppression, agranulocytosis

Hepatic: Cholestatic jaundice, hepatitis

Neuromuscular & skeletal: Arthralgia, paresthesia

Ocular: Blurred vision

Renal: Diuretic effect (minor)

Overdosage/Toxicology Symptoms include severe hypoglycemia, seizures, cerebral damage, tingling of lips and tongue, nausea, yawning, confusion, agitation, tachycardia, sweating, convulsions, stupor, and coma. Intoxications with sulfonylureas can cause hypoglycemia and are best managed with glucose administration (orally for milder hypoglycemia or by injection in more severe forms).

Drug Interactions

Cytochrome P450 Effect: Inhibits CYP2C8 (weak), 3A4 (weak)

Increased Effect/Toxicity: Increased hypoglycemic effects of glyburide may occur with oral anticoagulants (warfarin), phenytoin, other hydantoins, salicylates, NSAIDs, sulfonamides, and beta-blockers. Ethanol ingestion may cause disulfiram reactions.

Decreased Effect: Thiazides and other diuretics, corticosteroids may decrease effectiveness of glyburide.

Ethanol/Nutrition/Herb Interactions

Ethanol: Caution with ethanol (may cause hypoglycemia).

Herb/Nutraceutical: Caution with chromium, garlic, gymnema (may cause hypoglycemia).

Mechanism of Action Stimulates insulin release from the pancreatic beta cells; reduces glucose output from the liver; insulin sensitivity is increased at peripheral target sites

Pharmacodynamics/Kinetics

Onset of action: Serum insulin levels begin to increase 15-60 minutes after a single dose

Duration: ≤24 hours

Protein binding, plasma: >99%

Metabolism: To one moderately active and several inactive metabolites

Half-life elimination: 5-16 hours; may be prolonged with renal or hepatic impairment

Time to peak, serum: Adults: 2-4 hours

Excretion: Feces (50%) and urine (50%) as metabolites

Dosage Oral:

Adults:

Initial: 2.5-5 mg/day, administered with breakfast or the first main meal of the day. In patients who are more sensitive to hypoglycemic drugs, start at 1.25 mg/day.

Increase in increments of no more than 2.5 mg/day at weekly intervals based on the patient's blood glucose response

Maintenance: 1.25-20 mg/day given as single or divided doses; maximum: 20 mg/day

Elderly: Initial: 1.25-2.5 mg/day, increase by 1.25-2.5 mg/day every 1-3 weeks

Micronized tablets (Glynase® PresTab®): Adults:

Initial: 1.5-3 mg/day, administered with breakfast or the first main meal of the day in patients who are more sensitive to hypoglycemic drugs, start at 0.75 mg/day. Increase in increments of no more than 1.5 mg/day in weekly intervals based on the patient's blood glucose response.

Maintenance: 0.75-12 mg/day given as a single dose or in divided doses. Some patients (especially those receiving >6 mg/day) may have a more satisfactory response with twice-daily dosing.

Dosing adjustment/comments in renal impairment: Cl_{cr} <50 mL/minute: **Not recommended**

Dosing adjustment in hepatic impairment: Use conservative initial and maintenance doses and avoid use in severe disease

Dietary Considerations Should be taken with meals at the same time each day. Dietary modification based on ADA recommendations is a part of therapy. Decreases blood glucose concentration. Hypoglycemia may occur. Must be able to recognize symptoms of hypoglycemia (palpitations, sweaty palms, lightheadedness).

Administration Administer with meals at the same time each day. Patients who are anorexic or NPO may need to have their dose held to avoid hypoglycemia.

Monitoring Parameters Signs and symptoms of hypoglycemia, fasting blood glucose, hemoglobin A_{1c}

Reference Range Target range: Adults:

Fasting blood glucose: <120 mg/dL

Glycosylated hemoglobin: <7%

Dosage Forms [DSC] = Discontinued product

Tablet (Diaβeta®, Micronase®): 1.25 mg, 2.5 mg, 5 mg

Tablet, micronized: 1.5 mg, 3 mg, 6 mg

Glynase® PresTab®: 1.5 mg [DSC], 3 mg, 6 mg

Glyburide and Metformin (GLYE byoor ide & met FOR min)

U.S. Brand Names Glucovance®

Index Terms Glyburide and Metformin Hydrochloride; Metformin and Glyburide

Pharmacologic Category Antidiabetic Agent, Biguanide; Antidiabetic Agent, Sulfonylurea

Use Initial therapy for management of type 2 diabetes mellitus (noninsulin dependent, NIDDM). Second-line therapy for management of type 2 diabetes (NIDDM) when hyperglycemia cannot be managed with a sulfonylurea or metformin; combination therapy with a thiazolidinedione may be required to achieve additional control.

Pregnancy Risk Factor B (manufacturer); C (expert analysis)

Pregnancy Implications See individual agents.

Lactation No data available/use caution

Contraindications Hypersensitivity to glyburide or other sulfonamides, metformin, or any component of the formulation; renal disease or renal dysfunction (serum creatinine ≥1.5 mg/dL in males or ≥1.4 mg/dL in females, or abnormal creatinine clearance which may also result from conditions such as cardiovascular collapse, acute myocardial infarction, and septicemia); acute or chronic metabolic acidosis with or without coma (including diabetic ketoacidosis); congestive heart failure requiring pharmacologic treatment

Note: Temporarily discontinue in patients undergoing radiologic studies in which intravascular iodinated contrast materials are utilized.

Warnings/Precautions Age, hepatic and renal impairment are independent risk factors for hypoglycemia. Use with caution in patients with hepatic impairment, malnourished or debilitated conditions, or adrenal or pituitary insufficiency. Use caution in patients with renal impairment.

[U.S. Boxed Warning]: Lactic acidosis is a rare, but potentially severe consequence of therapy with metformin. Withhold therapy in hypoxemia, dehydration, or sepsis. The risk of lactic acidosis is increased in any patient with CHF requiring pharmacologic management. This risk is particularly high during acute or unstable CHF because of the risk of hypoperfusion and hypoxemia. Metformin is substantially excreted by the kidney. The risk of accumulation and lactic acidosis increases with the degree of impairment of renal function. Patients with renal function below the limit of normal for their age should not receive metformin. In elderly patients, renal function should be monitored regularly; should not be used in any patient ≥80 years of age unless measurement of creatinine clearance verifies normal renal function. Use of concomitant medications that may affect renal function (ie, affect tubular secretion) may also affect metformin disposition. Metformin should be suspended in patients with dehydration and/or prerenal azotemia. Therapy should be suspended for any surgical procedures (resume only after normal intake resumed and normal renal function is verified).Intravascular iodinated contrast materials used for radiologic studies are associated with alteration of renal function and may increase risk of lactic acidosis. Discontinue Glucovance® at the time of or prior to the procedure and withhold for 48 hours subsequent to the procedure; reinstitute only after renal function has been re-evaluated and found to be normal.

Chemical similarities are present among sulfonamides, sulfonylureas, carbonic anhydrase inhibitors, thiazides, and loop diuretics (except ethacrynic acid). Use in patients with sulfonamide allergy is specifically contraindicated in product labeling, however a risk of cross-reaction exists in patients with allergy to any of these compounds; avoid use when previous reaction has been severe.

Product labeling states oral hypoglycemic drugs may be associated with an increased cardiovascular mortality as compared to treatment with diet alone or diet plus insulin. Data to support this association are limited, and several studies, including a large prospective trial (UKPDS), have not supported an association.

Adverse Reactions See individual agents.

Overdosage/Toxicology See individual agents.

(Continued)

Glyburide and Metformin *(Continued)*

Drug Interactions
Increased Effect/Toxicity: See individual agents.

Decreased Effect: See individual agents.

Ethanol/Nutrition/Herb Interactions
Ethanol: May cause hypoglycemia; incidence of lactic acidosis may be increased; a disulfiram-like reaction characterized by flushing, headache, nausea, vomiting, sweating, or tachycardia has been reported with sulfonylureas; avoid or limit use.

Food: Metformin decreases absorption of vitamin B_{12}. Metformin decreases absorption of folic acid.

Stability
Store at 25°C (77°F).

Mechanism of Action
See individual agents.

The combination of glyburide and metformin is used to improve glycemic control in patients with type 2 diabetes mellitus by using two different, but complementary, mechanisms of action.

Pharmacodynamics/Kinetics
Glucovance®:

Bioavailability: 18% with 2.5 mg glyburide/500 mg metformin dose; 7% with 5 mg glyburide/500 mg metformin dose; bioavailability is greater than that of Micronase® brand of glyburide and therefore not bioequivalent

Time to peak: 2.75 hours when taken with food

Glyburide: See Glyburide monograph.

Metformin: This component of Glucovance® is bioequivalent to metformin coadministration with glyburide.

Dosage Note:
Dose must be individualized. Dosages expressed as glyburide/metformin components.

Adults: Oral:

Initial therapy (no prior treatment with sulfonylurea or metformin): 1.25 mg/250 mg once daily with a meal; patients with Hb A_{1c} >9% or fasting plasma glucose (FPG) >200 mg/dL may start with 1.25 mg/250 mg twice daily

Dosage may be increased in increments of 1.25 mg/250 mg, at intervals of not less than 2 weeks; maximum daily dose: 10 mg/2000 mg (limited experience with higher doses)

Previously treated with a sulfonylurea or metformin alone: Initial: 2.5 mg/500 mg or 5 mg/500 mg twice daily; increase in increments no greater than 5 mg/500 mg; maximum daily dose: 20 mg/2000 mg

When switching patients previously on a sulfonylurea and metformin together, do not exceed the daily dose of glyburide (or glyburide equivalent) or metformin.

Note: May combine with a thiazolidinedione in patients with an inadequate response to glyburide/metformin therapy (risk of hypoglycemia may be increased).

Elderly: Oral: Conservative doses are recommended in the elderly due to potentially decreased renal function; **do not titrate to maximum dose**; should not be used in patients ≥80 years of age unless renal function is verified as normal

Dosage adjustment in renal impairment: Risk of lactic acidosis increases with degree of renal impairment; contraindicated in renal disease or renal dysfunction (see Contraindications)

Dosage adjustment in hepatic impairment: Use conservative initial and maintenance doses and avoid use in severe hepatic disease

Dietary Considerations
May cause GI upset; take with food to decrease GI upset. Dietary modification based on ADA recommendations is a part of therapy. Decreases blood glucose concentration. Hypoglycemia may occur. Must be able to recognize symptoms of hypoglycemia (palpitations, sweaty palms, lightheadedness). Monitor for signs and symptoms of vitamin B_{12} deficiency. Monitor for signs and symptoms of folic acid deficiency.

Administration
All doses should be administered with a meal. Twice-daily dosing should be administered with the morning and evening meals. Patients who are anorexic or NPO may need to have their dose held to avoid hypoglycemia.

Monitoring Parameters
Signs and symptoms of hypoglycemia, urine for glucose and ketones, FPG, Hb A_{1c}, and fructosamine. Initial and periodic monitoring of hematologic parameters (eg, hemoglobin/hematocrit and red blood cell indices) and renal function should be performed. Monitor at least annually once patient is on maintenance therapy. While megaloblastic anemia has been rarely seen with metformin, if suspected, vitamin B_{12} deficiency should be excluded.

Reference Range
Target range: Adults: Fasting blood glucose: <120 mg/dL; glycosylated hemoglobin: <7%

Dosage Forms
Tablet:

1.25 mg/250 mg: Glyburide 1.25 mg and metformin hydrochloride 250 mg

2.5 mg/500 mg: Glyburide 2.5 mg and metformin hydrochloride 500 mg

5 mg/500 mg: Glyburide 5 mg and metformin hydrochloride 500 mg

♦ **Glyburide and Metformin Hydrochloride** *see* Glyburide and Metformin *on page 805*

♦ **Glycerol Guaiacolate** *see* Guaifenesin *on page 814*

♦ **Glyceryl Trinitrate** *see* Nitroglycerin *on page 1234*

♦ **GlycoLax™** *see* Polyethylene Glycol 3350 *on page 1387*

♦ **Glycon (Can)** *see* Metformin *on page 1098*

Glycopyrrolate (glye koe PYE roe late)

U.S. Brand Names Robinul®; Robinul® Forte
Canadian Brand Names Glycopyrrolate Injection, USP
Index Terms Glycopyrronium Bromide
Pharmacologic Category Anticholinergic Agent
Use Inhibit salivation and excessive secretions of the respiratory tract preoperatively; reversal of neuromuscular blockade; control of upper airway secretions; adjunct in treatment of peptic ulcer
Pregnancy Risk Factor B
Pregnancy Implications
Teratogenic effects were not observed in animal studies. Small amounts of glycopyrrolate cross the human placenta.
Lactation Excretion in breast milk unknown/use caution
Contraindications Hypersensitivity to glycopyrrolate or any component of the formulation; severe ulcerative colitis, toxic megacolon complicating ulcerative colitis, paralytic ileus, obstructive disease of GI tract, intestinal atony in the elderly or debilitated patient; unstable cardiovascular status in acute hemorrhage; narrow-angle glaucoma; acute hemorrhage; tachycardia; obstructive uropathy; myasthenia gravis
Warnings/Precautions Use caution in elderly, patients with autonomic neuropathy, hepatic or renal disease, ulcerative colitis may predispose megacolon, hyperthyroidism, CAD, CHF, arrhythmias, tachycardia, BPH, or hiatal hernia with reflux. Use of anticholinergics in gastric ulcer treatment may cause a delay in gastric emptying due to antral statis. May cause drowsiness, eye sensitivity to light, or blurred vision; caution should be used when performing tasks which require mental alertness, such as driving. The risk of heat stroke with this medication may be increased during exercise or hot weather. Infants, patients with Down syndrome, and children with spastic paralysis or brain damage may be hypersensitive to antimuscarine effects. Injection contains benzyl alcohol (associated with gasping syndrome in neonates). Not recommended for use in children <12 years of age for the management of peptic ulcer or <16 years for preanesthetic use.
Adverse Reactions Frequency not defined. **Note:** Includes adverse effects which may occur as an extension of the pharmacologic action of anticholinergics (including glycopyrrolate) and adverse effects reported postmarketing with glycopyrrolate.
Cardiovascular: Arrhythmias, cardiac arrest, heart block, hyper-/hypotension, malignant hyperthermia, palpitation, QT_c interval prolongation, tachycardia
Central nervous system: Confusion, dizziness, drowsiness, excitement, headache, insomnia, nervousness, seizures
Dermatologic: Dry skin, pruritus, sensitivity to light increased
Endocrine & metabolic: Lactation suppression
Gastrointestinal: Bloated feeling, constipation, loss of taste, nausea, vomiting, xerostomia
Genitourinary: Impotence, urinary hesitancy, urinary retention
Local: Irritation at injection site
Neuromuscular & skeletal: Weakness
Ocular: Blurred vision, cycloplegia, mydriasis, ocular tension increased, photophobia, sensitivity to light increased
Respiratory: Respiratory depression
Miscellaneous: Anaphylactoid reactions, diaphoresis decreased, hypersensitivity reactions
Overdosage/Toxicology
Symptoms of overdose include blurred vision, urinary retention, tachycardia, and absent bowel sounds. For peripheral adverse effects, a quaternary ammonium anticholinesterase, such as neostigmine methylsulfate, may be given I.V. in increments of 0.25 mg in adults; may repeat every 5-10 minutes (up to a maximum of 2.5 mg) based upon decrease in heart rate and return of bowel sounds. For overdose exhibiting CNS symptoms (eg, excitement, restlessness, convulsions, psychotic behavior), physostigmine 0.5-2 mg I.V. slowly, may be given and repeated as necessary, up to 5 mg. Proportionally smaller doses should be used for pediatric patients. Artificial respiration should be given to individuals experiencing a neuromuscular or curare-like effect which could lead to muscular weakness or possible paralysis. Additional care should be symptomatic and supportive.
Drug Interactions
Increased Effect/Toxicity: Effects of other anticholinergic agents or medications with anticholinergic activity may be increased by glycopyrrolate. Severity of potassium chloride induced gastrointestinal lesions (when potassium is given in a wax matrix formulation, eg, Klor-Con®) may be increased by glycopyrrolate. Pramlinitide may enhance the anticholinergic effects of anticholinergics (effects are specific to the GI tract).
Stability Store at 20°C to 25°C (68°F to 77°F).
Mechanism of Action Blocks the action of acetylcholine at parasympathetic sites in smooth muscle, secretory glands, and the CNS
Pharmacodynamics/Kinetics
Onset of action: Oral: 50 minutes; I.M.: 15-30 minutes; I.V.: ~1 minute
Peak effect: Oral: ~1 hour; I.M.: 30-45 minutes
Duration: Vagal effect: 2-3 hours; Inhibition of salivation: Up to 7 hours; Anticholinergic: Oral: 8-12 hours
Absorption: Oral: Poor and erratic
Distribution: V_d: 0.2-0.62 L/kg
Metabolism: Hepatic (minimal)
Bioavailability: ~10%
Half-life elimination: Infants: 22-130 minutes; Children 19-99 minutes; Adults: ~30-75 minutes
Excretion: Urine (as unchanged drug, I.M.: 80%, I.V.: 85%); bile (as unchanged drug)
Dosage
Children:
Reduction of secretions (preanesthetic):
Oral: 40-100 mcg/kg/dose 3-4 times/day
(Continued)

Glycopyrrolate *(Continued)*

I.M., I.V.: 4-10 mcg/kg/dose every 3-4 hours; maximum: 0.2 mg/dose or 0.8 mg/24 hours

Intraoperative: I.V.: 4 mcg/kg not to exceed 0.1 mg; repeat at 2- to 3-minute intervals as needed

Preoperative: I.M.:
  <2 years: 4-9 mcg/kg 30-60 minutes before procedure
  >2 years: 4 mcg/kg 30-60 minutes before procedure

Children and Adults: Reverse neuromuscular blockade: I.V.: 0.2 mg for each 1 mg of neostigmine or 5 mg of pyridostigmine administered or 5-15 mg glycopyrrolate with 25-70 mcg/kg of neostigmine or 0.1-0.3 mg/kg of pyridostigmine (agents usually administered simultaneously, but glycopyrrolate may be administered first if bradycardia is present)

Adults:
  Reduction of secretions:
    Intraoperative: I.V.: 0.1 mg repeated as needed at 2- to 3-minute intervals
    Preoperative: I.M.: 4 mcg/kg 30-60 minutes before procedure
  Peptic ulcer:
    Oral: 1-2 mg 2-3 times/day
    I.M., I.V.: 0.1-0.2 mg 3-4 times/day

Administration For I.V. administration, glycopyrrolate may also be administered via the tubing of a running I.V. infusion of a compatible solution; may be administered in the same syringe with neostigmine or pyridostigmine.

Monitoring Parameters Heart rate; anticholinergic effects; bowel sounds

Dosage Forms [DSC] = Discontinued product

Injection, solution: 0.2 mg/mL (1 mL, 2 mL, 5 mL, 20 mL)
  Robinul®: 0.2 mg/mL (1 mL, 2 mL, 5 mL; 20 mL [DSC]) [contains benzoyl alcohol]
Tablet: 1 mg, 2 mg
  Robinul®: 1 mg
  Robinul® Forte: 2 mg

- ♦ **Glycopyrrolate Injection, USP (Can)** *see* Glycopyrrolate *on page 807*
- ♦ **Glycopyrronium Bromide** *see* Glycopyrrolate *on page 807*
- ♦ **Glydiazinamide** *see* GlipiZIDE *on page 799*
- ♦ **Glynase® PresTab®** *see* GlyBURIDE *on page 803*
- ♦ **Gly-Oxide® [OTC]** *see* Carbamide Peroxide *on page 287*
- ♦ **Glyquin®** *see* Hydroquinone *on page 859*
- ♦ **Glyquin-XM™** *see* Hydroquinone *on page 859*
- ♦ **Glyquin® XM (Can)** *see* Hydroquinone *on page 859*
- ♦ **Glyset®** *see* Miglitol *on page 1146*
- ♦ **GM-CSF** *see* Sargramostim *on page 1548*
- ♦ **GMD-Azithromycin (Can)** *see* Azithromycin *on page 186*
- ♦ **GMD-Fluconazole (Can)** *see* Fluconazole *on page 712*
- ♦ **GMD-Gemfibrozil (Can)** *see* Gemfibrozil *on page 787*
- ♦ **GMD-Sertraline (Can)** *see* Sertraline *on page 1557*
- ♦ **GnRH** *see* Gonadorelin *on page 809*
- ♦ **GnRH Agonist** *see* Histrelin *on page 839*
- ♦ **Gold Bond® Antifungal [OTC] [DSC]** *see* Tolnaftate *on page 1704*

Gold Sodium Thiomalate (gold SOW dee um thye oh MAL ate)

U.S. Brand Names Aurolate®

Canadian Brand Names Myochrysine®

Pharmacologic Category Gold Compound

Use Treatment of progressive rheumatoid arthritis

Pregnancy Risk Factor C

Lactation Enters breast milk/compatible (monitor closely)

Contraindications Hypersensitivity to gold compounds or any component of the formulation; systemic lupus erythematosus; history of blood dyscrasias; congestive heart failure, exfoliative dermatitis, colitis

Warnings/Precautions Frequent monitoring of patients for signs and symptoms of toxicity will prevent serious adverse reactions; NSAIDs and corticosteroids may be discontinued after initiating gold therapy; must not be injected I.V.

[U.S. Boxed Warning]: Explain the possibility of adverse reactions before initiating therapy; signs of gold toxicity include decrease in hemoglobin, leukocytes, granulocytes, and platelets; proteinuria, hematuria, pigmentation, pruritus, stomatitis or persistent diarrhea, rash, metallic taste; advise patient to report any symptoms of toxicity; use with caution in patients with liver or renal disease

Adverse Reactions

>10%:
  Dermatologic: Itching, rash
  Gastrointestinal: Stomatitis, gingivitis, glossitis
  Ocular: Conjunctivitis
1% to 10%:
  Dermatologic: Urticaria, alopecia
  Hematologic: Eosinophilia, leukopenia, thrombocytopenia
  Renal: Proteinuria, hematuria
<1% (Limited to important or life-threatening): Agranulocytosis, anemia, angioedema, aplastic anemia, dysphagia, GI hemorrhage, hepatotoxicity, interstitial pneumonitis, metallic taste, peripheral neuropathy, ulcerative enterocolitis

Overdosage/Toxicology Symptoms include hematuria, proteinuria, fever, nausea, vomiting, and diarrhea. For mild gold poisoning, dimercaprol 2.5 mg/kg 4 times/day for 2 days, or for more severe forms of gold intoxication, dimercaprol 3-5 mg/kg every 4 hours for 2 days should be initiated. Then after 2 days, the initial dose should be repeated twice daily on the third day, and once daily thereafter for 10 days. Other chelating agents have been used with some success.

Drug Interactions
  Increased Effect/Toxicity: ACE inhibitors may enhance the adverse/toxic effects (nitritoid reaction) of gold sodium thiomalate.
  Decreased Effect: Penicillamine and acetylcysteine may decrease effect of gold sodium thiomalate.

Stability Should not be used if solution is darker than pale yellow.

Mechanism of Action Unknown, may decrease prostaglandin synthesis or may alter cellular mechanisms by inhibiting sulfhydryl systems

Pharmacodynamics/Kinetics
  Onset of action: Delayed; may require up to 3 months
  Half-life elimination: 5 days; may be prolonged with multiple doses
  Time to peak, serum: 4-6 hours
  Excretion: Urine (60% to 90%); feces (10% to 40%)

Dosage I.M.:
  Children: Initial: Test dose of 10 mg is recommended, followed by 1 mg/kg/week for 20 weeks; maintenance: 1 mg/kg/dose at 2- to 4-week intervals thereafter for as long as therapy is clinically beneficial and toxicity does not develop. Administration for 2-4 months is usually required before clinical improvement is observed.
  Adults: 10 mg first week; 25 mg second week; then 25-50 mg/week until 1 g cumulative dose has been given; if improvement occurs without adverse reactions, administer 25-50 mg every 2-3 weeks for 2-20 weeks, then every 3-4 weeks indefinitely
  Dosing adjustment in renal impairment:
    Cl_{cr} 50-80 mL/minute: Administer 50% of normal dose
    Cl_{cr} <50 mL/minute: Avoid use

Administration Deep I.M. injection into the upper outer quadrant of the gluteal region addition of 0.1 mL of 1% lidocaine to each injection may reduce the discomfort associated with I.M. administration

Monitoring Parameters Signs and symptoms of gold toxicity, CBC with differential and platelet count, urinalysis

Reference Range Gold: Normal: 0-0.1 mcg/mL (SI: 0-0.0064 µmol/L); Therapeutic: 1-3 mcg/mL (SI: 0.06-0.18 µmol/L); Urine: <0.1 mcg/24 hour

Additional Information Approximately 50% gold

Dosage Forms Injection, solution: 50 mg/mL (1 mL, 10 mL) [contains benzyl alcohol]

♦ **GoLYTELY**® see Polyethylene Glycol-Electrolyte Solution on page 1387

Gonadorelin (goe nad oh RELL in)

U.S. Brand Names Factrel®
Canadian Brand Names Lutrepulse™
Index Terms GnRH; Gonadorelin Acetate; Gonadorelin Hydrochloride; Gonadotropin Releasing Hormone; LHRH; LRH; Luteinizing Hormone Releasing Hormone
Pharmacologic Category Diagnostic Agent; Gonadotropin
Use Evaluation of functional capacity and response of gonadotrophic hormones; evaluate abnormal gonadotropin regulation as in precocious puberty and delayed puberty.
  Orphan drug: Lutrepulse®: Induction of ovulation in females with hypothalamic amenorrhea
Pregnancy Risk Factor B
Lactation Excretion in breast milk unknown
Medication Safety Issues
  Sound-alike/look-alike issues:
    Gonadorelin may be confused with gonadotropin, guanadrel
    Factrel® may be confused with Sectral®
    Gonadotropin may be confused with gonadorelin
Contraindications Hypersensitivity to gonadorelin or any component of the formulation; women with any condition that could be exacerbated by pregnancy; patients who have ovarian cysts or causes of anovulation other than those of hypothalamic origin; any condition that may worsened by reproductive hormones
Warnings/Precautions Hypersensitivity and anaphylactic reactions have occurred following multiple-dose administration; multiple pregnancy is a possibility; use with caution in women in whom pregnancy could worsen pre-existing conditions (eg, pituitary prolactinemia). Multiple pregnancy is a possibility with Lutrepulse®.
Adverse Reactions 1% to 10%: Local: Pain at injection site
Overdosage/Toxicology Symptoms include abdominal discomfort, nausea, headache, and flushing. Treatment is symptomatic.
Drug Interactions
  Increased Effect/Toxicity: Increased levels/effect with androgens, estrogens, progestins, glucocorticoids, spironolactone, and levodopa.
  Decreased Effect: Decreased levels/effect with oral contraceptives, digoxin, phenothiazines, and dopamine antagonists.
Stability
  Factrel®: Prepare immediately prior to use. After reconstitution, store at room temperature and use within 1 day. Discard unused portion.
  Lutrepulse®: Store at room temperature. Reconstitute with diluent immediately prior to use and transfer to plastic reservoir. The solution will supply 90 minute pulsatile doses for 7 consecutive days (Lutrepulse® pump).
Mechanism of Action Stimulates the release of luteinizing hormone (LH) from the anterior pituitary gland
Pharmacodynamics/Kinetics
  Onset of action: Peak effect: Maximal LH release: ~20 minutes
  Duration: 3-5 hours
  (Continued)

Gonadorelin *(Continued)*

Half-life elimination: 4 minutes

Dosage

Diagnostic test: Children >12 years and Female Adults: I.V., SubQ hydrochloride salt: 100 mcg administered in women during early phase of menstrual cycle (day 1-7)

Primary hypothalamic amenorrhea: Female Adults: I.V.: 5 mcg every 90 minutes via Lutrepulse® pump kit at treatment intervals of 21 days (pump will pulsate every 90 minutes for 7 days)

Administration

Factrel®: Dilute in 3 mL of normal saline; administer I.V. push over 30 seconds

Lutrepulse®: A presterilized reservoir bag with the infusion catheter set supplied with the kit should be filled with the reconstituted solution and administered I.V. using the Lutrepulse® pump. Set the pump to deliver 25-50 mL of solution, based upon the dose, over a pulse period of 1 minute and at a pulse frequency of 90 minutes.

Monitoring Parameters LH, FSH

Dosage Forms Injection, powder for reconstitution, as hydrochloride: 100 mcg [diluent contains benzyl alcohol]

- ◆ **Gonadorelin Acetate** *see* Gonadorelin *on page 809*
- ◆ **Gonadorelin Hydrochloride** *see* Gonadorelin *on page 809*
- ◆ **Gonadotropin Releasing Hormone** *see* Gonadorelin *on page 809*
- ◆ **Gonal-f®** *see* Follitropin Alfa *on page 751*
- ◆ **Gonal-f® Pen (Can)** *see* Follitropin Alfa *on page 751*
- ◆ **Gonal-f® RFF** *see* Follitropin Alfa *on page 751*
- ◆ **Goody's® Extra Strength Headache Powder [OTC]** *see* Acetaminophen, Aspirin, and Caffeine *on page 34*
- ◆ **Goody's® Extra Strength Pain Relief [OTC]** *see* Acetaminophen, Aspirin, and Caffeine *on page 34*
- ◆ **Goody's PM® [OTC]** *see* Acetaminophen and Diphenhydramine *on page 31*
- ◆ **Gordon Boro-Packs [OTC]** *see* Aluminum Sulfate and Calcium Acetate *on page 86*
- ◆ **Gormel® [OTC]** *see* Urea *on page 1758*

Goserelin *(GOE se rel in)*

U.S. Brand Names Zoladex®

Canadian Brand Names Zoladex®; Zoladex® LA

Index Terms D-Ser(Bu^t)^6,Azgly^{10}-LHRH; Goserelin Acetate; ICI-118630; NSC-606864

Pharmacologic Category Gonadotropin Releasing Hormone Agonist

Use Palliative treatment of advanced breast cancer and carcinoma of the prostate; treatment of endometriosis, including pain relief and reduction of endometriotic lesions; endometrial thinning agent as part of treatment for dysfunctional uterine bleeding

Pregnancy Risk Factor X (endometriosis, endometrial thinning); D (advanced breast cancer)

Pregnancy Implications Goserelin has been found to be teratogenic and increases pregnancy loss in animal studies. Women of childbearing potential should avoid pregnancy. Pregnancy must be ruled out prior to treatment. Use of nonhormonal contraception should be used during therapy and following discontinuation until the return of menses (or for at least 12 weeks).

Lactation Enters breast milk/contraindicated

Contraindications Hypersensitivity to goserelin or any component of the formulation; pregnancy (or potential to become pregnant); breast-feeding

Warnings/Precautions Hazardous agent - use appropriate precautions for handling and disposal. Transient worsening of signs and symptoms (tumor flare) may develop during the first few weeks of treatment. Urinary tract obstruction or spinal cord compression have been reported when used for prostate cancer; closely observe patients for weakness, paresthesias, and urinary tract obstruction in first few weeks of therapy. Decreased bone density has been reported in women and may be irreversible; use caution if other risk factors are present; evaluate and institute preventative treatment if necessary. Rare cases of pituitary apoplexy (frequently secondary to pituitary adenoma) have been observed with leuprolide administration (onset from 1 hour to usually <2 weeks); may present as sudden headache, vomiting, visual or mental status changes, and infrequently cardiovascular collapse; immediate medical attention required. Safety and efficacy have not been established in pediatric patients.

Adverse Reactions Percentages reported in males with prostatic carcinoma and females with endometriosis using the 1-month implant:

>10%:

Central nervous system: Headache (female 75%, male 1% to 5%), emotional lability (female 60%), depression (female 54%, male 1% to 5%), pain (female 17%, male 8%), insomnia (female 11%, male 5%)

Endocrine & metabolic: Hot flashes (female 96%, male 62%), sexual dysfunction (21%), erections decreased (18%), libido decreased (female 61%), breast enlargement (female 18%)

Genitourinary: Lower urinary symptoms (male 13%), vaginitis (75%), dyspareunia (female 14%)

Miscellaneous: Diaphoresis (female 45%, male 6%); infection (female 13%)

1% to 10%:

Cardiovascular: CHF (male 5%), arrhythmia, cerebrovascular accident, hypertension, MI, peripheral vascular disorder, chest pain, palpitation, tachycardia, edema

Central nervous system: Lethargy (male 8%), dizziness (female 6%, male 5%), abnormal thinking, anxiety, chills, fever, malaise, migraine, somnolence

Dermatologic: Rash (female >1%, male 6%), alopecia, bruising, dry skin, skin discoloration

Endocrine & metabolic: Breast pain (female 7%), breast swelling/tenderness (male 1% to 5%), dysmenorrhea, gout, hyperglycemia

Gastrointestinal: Anorexia (female >1%, male 5%), nausea (male 5%), constipation, diarrhea, flatulence, dyspepsia, ulcer, vomiting, weight increased, xerostomia

Genitourinary: Renal insufficiency, urinary frequency, urinary obstruction, urinary tract infection, vaginal hemorrhage

Hematologic: Anemia, hemorrhage

Neuromuscular & skeletal: Arthralgia, bone mineral density decreased (female; ~4% decrease in 6 months), joint disorder, paresthesia

Ocular: Amblyopia, dry eyes

Respiratory: Upper respiratory tract infection (male 7%), COPD (male 5%), pharyngitis (female 5%), bronchitis, cough, epistaxis, rhinitis, sinusitis

Miscellaneous: Allergic reaction

Postmarketing and/or case reports: Pituitary apoplexy

Overdosage/Toxicology Treatment is symptomatic.

Stability Zoladex® should be stored at room temperature not to exceed 25°C or 77°F. Protect from light; should be dispensed in a lightproof bag.

Mechanism of Action Goserelin is a synthetic analog of luteinizing-hormone-releasing hormone (LHRH). Following an initial increase in luteinizing hormone (LH) and follicle stimulating hormone (FSH), chronic administration of goserelin results in a sustained suppression of pituitary gonadotropins. Serum testosterone falls to levels comparable to surgical castration. The exact mechanism of this effect is unknown, but may be related to changes in the control of LH or down-regulation of LH receptors.

Pharmacodynamics/Kinetics Note: Data reported using the 1-month implant.

Absorption: SubQ: Rapid and can be detected in serum in 10 minutes

Distribution: V_d: Male: 44.1 L; Female: 20.3 L

Time to peak, serum: SubQ: Male: 12-15 days, Female: 8-22 days

Half-life elimination: SubQ: Male: ~4 hours, Female: ~2 hours; Renal impairment: Male: 12 hours

Excretion: Urine (90%)

Dosage SubQ: Adults:

Prostate cancer:

Monthly implant: 3.6 mg injected into upper abdomen every 28 days

3-month implant: 10.8 mg injected into the upper abdominal wall every 12 weeks

Breast cancer, endometriosis, endometrial thinning: Monthly implant: 3.6 mg injected into upper abdomen every 28 days

Note: For breast cancer, treatment may continue indefinitely; for endometriosis, it is recommended that duration of treatment not exceed 6 months. Only 1-2 doses are recommended for endometrial thinning.

Dosing adjustment in renal/hepatic impairment: No adjustment is necessary

Administration Subcutaneous implant: Insert the hypodermic needle into the subcutaneous fat. Do not try to aspirate with the goserelin syringe. If the needle is in a large vessel, blood will immediately appear in the syringe chamber. Change the direction of the needle so it parallels the abdominal wall. Push the needle in until the barrel hub touches the patient's skin. Fully depress the plunger to discharge. Withdraw needle and bandage the site. Confirm discharge by ensuring tip of the plunger is visible within the tip of the needle.

Test Interactions Serum alkaline phosphatase, serum acid phosphatase, serum testosterone, serum LH and FSH, serum estradiol

Dosage Forms

Injection, solution, 1-month implant [disposable syringe; single-dose]: 3.6 mg [with 16-gauge hypodermic needle]

Injection, solution, 3-month implant [disposable syringe; single-dose]: 10.8 mg [with 14-gauge hypodermic needle]

- ◆ **Goserelin Acetate** see Goserelin on page 810
- ◆ **GP 47680** see Oxcarbazepine on page 1282
- ◆ **GR38032R** see Ondansetron on page 1267
- ◆ **Gramicidin, Neomycin, and Polymyxin B** see Neomycin, Polymyxin B, and Gramicidin on page 1212

Granisetron (gra NI se tron)

U.S. Brand Names Kytril®

Canadian Brand Names Kytril®

Index Terms BRL 43694

Pharmacologic Category Antiemetic; Selective 5-HT$_3$ Receptor Antagonist

Use Prophylaxis of nausea and vomiting associated with emetogenic chemotherapy and radiation therapy, (including total body irradiation and fractionated abdominal radiation); prophylaxis and treatment of postoperative nausea and vomiting (PONV)

Generally **not** recommended for treatment of existing chemotherapy-induced emesis (CIE) or for prophylaxis of nausea from agents with a low emetogenic potential.

Pregnancy Risk Factor B

Pregnancy Implications There are no adequate or well-controlled studies in pregnant women. Teratogenic effects were not observed in animal studies. Injection (1 mg/mL strength) contains benzyl alcohol which may cross the placenta. Use only if benefit exceeds the risk.

Lactation Excretion in breast milk unknown/use caution

Medication Safety Issues

Sound-alike/look-alike issues:

Granisetron may be confused with dolasetron, ondansetron, palonosetron

Contraindications Previous hypersensitivity to granisetron, other 5-HT$_3$ receptor antagonists, or any component of the formulation

Warnings/Precautions For chemotherapy-related emesis, **granisetron should be used on a scheduled basis, not on an "as needed" (PRN) basis**, since data support the use of this drug in the prevention of nausea and vomiting and not in the rescue of nausea and vomiting. (Continued)

811

Granisetron *(Continued)*

Granisetron should be used only in the first 24-48 hours of receiving chemotherapy or radiation. Data do not support any increased efficacy of granisetron in delayed nausea and vomiting.

Use with caution in patients allergic to other 5-HT$_3$ receptor antagonists; cross-reactivity has been reported. Routine prophylaxis for PONV is not recommended in patients with little expectation of nausea and vomiting postoperatively. In patients where nausea and vomiting must be avoided postoperatively, administer to all patients even when expected incidence of nausea and vomiting is low. Use caution following abdominal surgery or in chemotherapy-induced nausea and vomiting; may mask progressive ileus or gastric distention. Safety and efficacy in children <2 years of age have not been established. Injection contains benzyl alcohol (1 mg/mL) and should not be used in neonates.

Adverse Reactions
>10%:
    Central nervous system: Headache (9% to 21%)
    Gastrointestinal: Constipation (3% to 18%)
    Neuromuscular & skeletal: Weakness (5% to 18%)
1% to 10%:
    Cardiovascular: Hypertension (1% to 2%)
    Central nervous system: Pain (10%), fever (3% to 9%), dizziness (4% to 5%), insomnia (<2% to 5%), somnolence (1% to 4%), anxiety (2%), agitation (<2%), CNS stimulation (<2%)
    Dermatologic: Rash (1%)
    Gastrointestinal: Diarrhea (3% to 9%), abdominal pain (4% to 6%), dyspepsia (3% to 6%), taste perversion (2%)
    Hepatic: Liver enzymes increased (5% to 6%)
    Renal: Oliguria (2%)
    Respiratory: Cough (2%)
    Miscellaneous: Infection (3%)
<1% (Limited to important or life-threatening): Agitation, allergic reactions; anaphylaxis (including hypotension, dyspnea, urticaria); angina, arrhythmias, atrial fibrillation, extrapyramidal syndrome, hot flashes, hypotension, hypersensitivity, syncope

Overdosage/Toxicology
Overdoses of up to 38.5 mg have been reported without symptoms or with only slight headache. In the event of an overdose, treatment should be symptomatic and supportive.

Drug Interactions
Cytochrome P450 Effect: Substrate of CYP3A4 (minor)
Increased Effect/Toxicity: Granisetron may enhance the hypotensive effect of apomorphine.

Ethanol/Nutrition/Herb Interactions
Herb/Nutraceutical: St John's wort may decrease granisetron levels.

Stability
I.V.: Store at 15°C to 30°C (59°F to 86°F). Stable when mixed in NS or D$_5$W for 7 days under refrigeration and for 3 days at room temperature. Protect from light. Do not freeze vials.
Oral: Store tablet or oral solution at 15°C to 30°C (59°F to 86°F). Protect from light.

Mechanism of Action
Selective 5-HT$_3$-receptor antagonist, blocking serotonin, both peripherally on vagal nerve terminals and centrally in the chemoreceptor trigger zone

Pharmacodynamics/Kinetics
Duration: Generally up to 24 hours
Absorption: Tablets and oral solution are bioequivalent
Distribution: V$_d$: 2-4 L/kg; widely throughout body
Protein binding: 65%
Metabolism: Hepatic via N-demethylation, oxidation, and conjugation; some metabolites may have 5-HT$_3$ antagonist activity
Half-life elimination: Terminal: 5-9 hours
Excretion: Urine (12% as unchanged drug, 48% to 49% as metabolites); feces (34% to 38% as metabolites)

Dosage
Oral: Adults:
    Prophylaxis of chemotherapy-related emesis: 2 mg once daily up to 1 hour before chemotherapy or 1 mg twice daily; the first 1 mg dose should be given up to 1 hour before chemotherapy.
    Prophylaxis of radiation therapy-associated emesis: 2 mg once daily given 1 hour before radiation therapy.
I.V.:
    Children ≥2 years and Adults: Prophylaxis of chemotherapy-related emesis:
        Within U.S.: 10 mcg/kg/dose (maximum: 1 mg/dose) given 30 minutes prior to chemotherapy; for some drugs (eg, carboplatin, cyclophosphamide) with a later onset of emetic action, 10 mcg/kg every 12 hours may be necessary
        Outside U.S.: 40 mcg/kg/dose (or 3 mg/dose); maximum: 9 mg/24 hours
        Breakthrough: Granisetron has not been shown to be effective in terminating nausea or vomiting once it occurs and should not be used for this purpose.
    Adults: PONV:
        Prevention: 1 mg given undiluted over 30 seconds; administer before induction of anesthesia or immediately before reversal of anesthesia
        Treatment: 1 mg given undiluted over 30 seconds

Dosing interval in renal impairment: No dosage adjustment required.
Dosing interval in hepatic impairment: Kinetic studies in patients with hepatic impairment showed that total clearance was approximately halved, however, standard doses were very well tolerated, and dose adjustments are not necessary.

Administration
Oral: Doses should be given up to 1 hour prior to initiation of chemotherapy/radiation
I.V.: Administer I.V. push over 30 seconds or as a 5-10 minute-infusion

Prevention of PONV: Administer before induction of anesthesia or immediately before reversal of anesthesia.

Treatment of PONV: Administer undiluted over 30 seconds.

Dosage Forms
Injection, solution: 1 mg/mL (1 mL, 4 mL) [contains benzyl alcohol]
Injection, solution [preservative free]: 0.1 mg/mL (1 mL)
Solution, oral: 2 mg/10 mL (30 mL) [contains sodium benzoate; orange flavor]
Tablet: 1 mg

- ◆ **Granulex®** see Trypsin, Balsam Peru, and Castor Oil on page 1754
- ◆ **Granulocyte Colony Stimulating Factor** see Filgrastim on page 707
- ◆ **Granulocyte Colony Stimulating Factor (PEG Conjugate)** see Pegfilgrastim on page 1321
- ◆ **Granulocyte-Macrophage Colony Stimulating Factor** see Sargramostim on page 1548
- ◆ **Gravol® (Can)** see DimenhyDRINATE on page 511
- ◆ **Grifulvin® V** see Griseofulvin on page 813

Griseofulvin (gri see oh FUL vin)

U.S. Brand Names Grifulvin® V; Gris-PEG®
Index Terms Griseofulvin Microsize; Griseofulvin Ultramicrosize
Pharmacologic Category Antifungal Agent, Oral
Additional Appendix Information
Antifungal Agents on page 1869
Use Treatment of susceptible tinea infections of the skin, hair, and nails
Pregnancy Risk Factor C
Lactation Excretion in breast milk unknown
Medication Safety Issues
Sound-alike/look-alike issues:
Fulvicin® may be confused with Furacin®
Contraindications Hypersensitivity to griseofulvin or any component of the formulation; severe liver disease; porphyria (interferes with porphyrin metabolism)
Warnings/Precautions Safe use in children ≤2 years of age has not been established; during long-term therapy, periodic assessment of hepatic, renal, and hematopoietic functions should be performed; may cause fetal harm when administered to pregnant women; avoid exposure to intense sunlight to prevent photosensitivity reactions; hypersensitivity cross reaction between penicillins and griseofulvin is possible
Adverse Reactions Frequency not defined.
Central nervous system: Headache, fatigue, dizziness, insomnia, mental confusion
Dermatologic: Rash (most common), urticaria (most common), photosensitivity, erythema multiforme, angioneurotic edema (rare)
Gastrointestinal: Nausea, vomiting, epigastric distress, diarrhea, GI bleeding
Genitourinary: Menstrual irregularities (rare)
Hematologic: Leukopenia, granulocytopenia
Neuromuscular & skeletal: Paresthesia (rare)
Renal: Hepatotoxicity, proteinuria, nephrosis
Miscellaneous: Oral thrush, drug-induced lupus-like syndrome (rare)
Overdosage/Toxicology Symptoms include lethargy, vertigo, blurred vision, nausea, vomiting, and diarrhea. Following GI decontamination, treatment is supportive.
Drug Interactions
Cytochrome P450 Effect: Induces CYP1A2 (weak), 2C8 (weak), 2C9 (weak), 3A4 (weak)
Increased Effect/Toxicity: Increased toxicity with ethanol, may cause tachycardia and flushing.
Decreased Effect: Barbiturates may decrease levels. Decreased warfarin activity. Decreased oral contraceptive effectiveness.
Ethanol/Nutrition/Herb Interactions
Ethanol: Avoid ethanol (may increase CNS depression). Ethanol will cause "disulfiram"-type reaction consisting of flushing, headache, nausea, and in some patients, vomiting and chest and/or abdominal pain.
Food: Griseofulvin concentrations may be increased if taken with food, especially with high-fat meals.
Mechanism of Action Inhibits fungal cell mitosis at metaphase; binds to human keratin making it resistant to fungal invasion
Pharmacodynamics/Kinetics
Absorption: Ultramicrosize griseofulvin absorption is almost complete; absorption of microsize griseofulvin is variable (25% to 70% of an oral dose); enhanced by ingestion of a fatty meal (GI absorption of ultramicrosize is ~1.5 times that of microsize)
Distribution: Crosses placenta
Metabolism: Extensively hepatic
Half-life elimination: 9-22 hours
Excretion: Urine (<1% as unchanged drug); feces; perspiration
Dosage Oral:
Children >2 years:
Microsize: 10-20 mg/kg/day in single or 2 divided doses. In the treatment of tinea capitis, higher dosages (20-25 mg/kg/day for 8-12 weeks) have been recommended by some authors (unlabeled).
Ultramicrosize: >2 years: 5-10 mg/kg/day in single or 2 divided doses. In the treatment of tinea capitis, higher dosages (15 mg/kg/day for 8-12 weeks) have been recommended by some authors (unlabeled).
Adults:
Microsize: 500-1000 mg/day in single or divided doses
Ultramicrosize: 330-375 mg/day in single or divided doses; doses up to 750 mg/day have been used for infections more difficult to eradicate such as tinea unguium
(Continued)

Griseofulvin *(Continued)*

Duration of therapy depends on the site of infection:
Tinea corporis: 2-4 weeks
Tinea capitis: 4-6 weeks or longer (up to 8-12 weeks)
Tinea pedis: 4-8 weeks
Tinea unguium: 3-6 months or longer

Administration Oral: Administer with a fatty meal (peanuts or ice cream) to increase absorption, or with food or milk to avoid GI upset

Monitoring Parameters Periodic renal, hepatic, and hematopoietic function tests

Test Interactions False-positive urinary VMA levels

Dosage Forms
Suspension, oral, microsize (Grifulvin® V): 125 mg/5 mL (120 mL) [contains alcohol 0.2%]
Tablet, microsize (Grifulvin® V): 500 mg
Tablet, ultramicrosize: 125 mg, 250 mg, 330 mg
Gris-PEG®: 125 mg, 250 mg

♦ **Griseofulvin Microsize** *see* Griseofulvin *on page 813*
♦ **Griseofulvin Ultramicrosize** *see* Griseofulvin *on page 813*
♦ **Gris-PEG®** *see* Griseofulvin *on page 813*
♦ **Guaicon DM [OTC]** *see* Guaifenesin and Dextromethorphan *on page 816*
♦ **Guaicon DMS [OTC]** *see* Guaifenesin and Dextromethorphan *on page 816*
♦ **Guaifed®** *see* Guaifenesin and Phenylephrine *on page 818*
♦ **Guaifed-PD®** *see* Guaifenesin and Phenylephrine *on page 818*
♦ **Guaifen-C** *see* Guaifenesin and Codeine *on page 815*

Guaifenesin *(gwye FEN e sin)*

U.S. Brand Names Allfen Jr; Diabetic Tussin® EX [OTC]; Ganidin NR; Guiatuss™ [OTC]; Humibid® *e* [OTC] [DSC]; Humibid® Maximum Strength; Iophen NR; Mucinex® [OTC]; Organ-1 NR; Organidin® NR; Phanasin® [OTC]; Phanasin® Diabetic Choice [OTC]; Q-Tussin [OTC]; Robitussin® [OTC]; Scot-Tussin® Expectorant [OTC]; Siltussin DAS [OTC]; Siltussin SA [OTC]; Tussin [OTC]; Vicks® Casero™ [OTC]; XPECT™ [OTC]

Canadian Brand Names Balminil Expectorant; Benylin® E Extra Strength; Koffex Expectorant; Robitussin®

Index Terms GG; Glycerol Guaiacolate

Pharmacologic Category Expectorant

Use Help loosen phlegm and thin bronchial secretions to make coughs more productive

Pregnancy Risk Factor C

Lactation Excretion in breast milk unknown/use caution

Medication Safety Issues
Sound-alike/look-alike issues:
Guaifenesin may be confused with guanfacine
Mucinex® may be confused with Mucomyst®
Naldecon® may be confused with Nalfon®

International issues:
Mucolex® [Hong Kong] may be confused with Mycelex® which is a brand name for clotrimazole in the U.S.

Contraindications Hypersensitivity to guaifenesin or any component of the formulation

Warnings/Precautions Not for persistent cough such as occurs with smoking, asthma, chronic bronchitis, or emphysema or cough accompanied by excessive secretions. When used for self-medication (OTC), contact healthcare provider if needed for >7 days or for a cough with a fever, rash, or persistent headache.

Adverse Reactions Frequency not defined.
Central nervous system: Dizziness, drowsiness, headache
Dermatologic: Rash
Endocrine & metabolic: Uric acid levels decreased
Gastrointestinal: Nausea, vomiting, stomach pain

Postmarketing and/or case reports: Kidney stone formation (with consumption of large quantities)

Overdosage/Toxicology Symptoms include vomiting, lethargy, coma, and respiratory depression. Treatment is supportive.

Mechanism of Action Thought to act as an expectorant by irritating the gastric mucosa and stimulating respiratory tract secretions, thereby increasing respiratory fluid volumes and decreasing mucus viscosity

Pharmacodynamics/Kinetics
Absorption: Well absorbed
Half-life elimination: ~1 hour
Excretion: Urine (as unchanged drug and metabolites)

Dosage Oral:
Children:
6 months to 2 years: 25-50 mg every 4 hours, not to exceed 300 mg/day
2-5 years: 50-100 mg every 4 hours, not to exceed 600 mg/day
6-11 years: 100-200 mg every 4 hours, not to exceed 1.2 g/day
Children >12 years and Adults: 200-400 mg every 4 hours to a maximum of 2.4 g/day
Extended release tablet: 600-1200 mg every 12 hours, not to exceed 2.4 g/day

Dietary Considerations
Diabetic Tussin® EX contains phenylalanine 8.4 mg/5 mL.
Vicks® Casero™ contains phenylalanine 5.5 mg/12.5 mL and sodium 32 mg/12.5 mL.

Administration Do not crush, chew, or break extended release tablets; administer with a full glass of water

Test Interactions Possible color interference with determination of 5-HIAA and VMA; discontinue for 49 hours prior to test

Dosage Forms [DSC] = Discontinued product
Liquid: 100 mg/5 mL (120 mL, 480 mL)
    Diabetic Tussin EX®: 100 mg/5 mL (120 mL) [alcohol free, sugar free, dye free; contains phenylalanine 8.4 mg/5 mL]
    Ganidin NR: 100 mg/5 mL (480 mL) [raspberry flavor]
    Iophen NR: 100 mg/5 mL (480 mL)
    Organidin® NR: 100 mg/5 mL (480 mL) [contains sodium benzoate; raspberry flavor]
    Q-Tussin: 100 mg/5 mL (120 mL, 240 mL, 480 mL, 3840 mL) [alcohol free; cherry flavor]
    Siltussin DAS: 100 mg/5 mL (120 mL) [alcohol free, dye free, sugar free; strawberry flavor]
Syrup: 100 mg/5 mL (120 mL, 480 mL)
    Guiatuss™: 100 mg/5 mL (120 mL, 480 mL) [alcohol free; fruit-mint flavor]
    Phanasin®: 100 mg/5 mL (120 mL, 240 mL) [alcohol free, sugar free; mint flavor]
    Phanasin® Diabetic Choice: 100 mg/5 mL (120 mL) [alcohol free, sugar free; mint flavor]
    Robitussin®: 100 mg/5 mL (5 mL, 10 mL, 15 mL, 30 mL, 120 mL, 240 mL, 480 mL) [alcohol free; contains sodium benzoate]
    Scot-Tussin® Expectorant: 100 mg/5 mL (120 mL) [alcohol free, dye free, sugar free; contains benzoic acid; grape flavor]
    Siltussin SA: 100 mg/5 mL (120 mL, 240 mL, 480 mL) [alcohol free, sugar free; strawberry flavor]
    Tussin: 100 mg/5 mL (120 mL, 240 mL)
    Vicks® Casero™: 100 mg/6.25 mL (120 mL, 480 mL) [contains phenylalanine 5.5 mg/12.5 mL, sodium 32 mg/12.5 mL, and sodium benzoate; honey menthol flavor]
Syrup, oral drops (Phanasin®): 50 mg/mL (50 mL) [alcohol free, sugar free; fruit flavor]
Tablet: 200 mg
    Allfen Jr: 400 mg [dye free]
    Humibid® e: 400 mg [DSC]
    Organ-1 NR, Organidin® NR: 200 mg
    XPECT™: 400 mg
Tablet, extended release:
    Humibid® Maximum Strength: 1200 mg
    Mucinex®: 600 mg

♦ **Guaifenesin AC** see Guaifenesin and Codeine on page 815

Guaifenesin and Codeine (gwye FEN e sin & KOE deen)

U.S. Brand Names Brontex®; Cheracol®; Cheratussin AC; Diabetic Tussin C®; Gani-Tuss® NR; Guaifen-C; Guaifenesin AC; Guaituss AC; Iophen-C NR; Kolephrin® #1; Mytussin® AC; Robafen® AC; Romilar® AC; Tussi-Organidin® NR; Tussi-Organidin® S-NR

Index Terms Codeine and Guaifenesin

Pharmacologic Category Antitussive; Cough Preparation; Expectorant

Use Temporary control of cough due to minor throat and bronchial irritation

Restrictions C-V

Pregnancy Risk Factor C

Dosage Oral: **Note:** Also refer to specific product labeling:
Children:
    2-6 years (Diabetic Tussin C® liquid, Tussi-Organidin® NR): Codeine 1 mg/kg/day in 4 divided doses
    6-12 years (Diabetic Tussin C®, Kolephrin® #1, Romilar® AC, Tussi-Organidin® NR liquid): 5 mL every 4 hours; maximum 30 mL/24 hours
Children ≥12 years and Adults:
    Brontex® tablets: 1 tablet every 4 hours; maximum 6 tablets/24 hours
    Diabetic Tussin C®, Kolephrin® #1, Romilar® AC, Tussi-Organidin® NR liquid: 10 mL every 4 hours; maximum 60 mL/24 hours

Additional Information Complete prescribing information for this medication should be consulted for additional detail.

Dosage Forms
Liquid:
    Brontex®: Guaifenesin 75 mg and codeine phosphate 2.5 mg per 5 mL (480 mL) [alcohol free; strawberry mint flavor]
    Diabetic Tussin C®: Guaifenesin 200 mg and codeine phosphate 10 mg per 5 mL (480 mL) [contains phenylalanine 0.03 mcg/5 mL; cherry vanilla flavor]
    Gani-Tuss® NR: Guaifenesin 100 mg and codeine phosphate 10 mg per 5 mL (480 mL) [raspberry flavor]
    Guaifen-C: Guaifenesin 75 mg and codeine phosphate 2.5 mg per 5 mL (480 mL) [cherry flavor]
    Guaifenesin AC: Guaifenesin 100 mg and codeine phosphate 10 mg per 5 mL (120 mL, 480 mL) [alcohol free, sugar free; raspberry flavor]
    Iophen-C NR: Guaifenesin 100 mg and codeine phosphate 10 mg per 5 mL (480 mL) [raspberry flavor]
    Kolephrin® #1: Guaifenesin 100 mg and codeine phosphate 10 mg per 5 mL (120 mL) [contains sodium 1.1 mg/5 mL and sodium benzoate]
    Tussi-Organidin® NR: Guaifenesin 100 mg and codeine phosphate 10 mg per 5 mL (480 mL) [contains sodium benzoate; raspberry flavor]
    Tussi-Organidin® S-NR: Guaifenesin 100 mg and codeine phosphate 10 mg per 5 mL (120 mL) [contains sodium benzoate; raspberry flavor]
Syrup:
    Cheracol®: Guaifenesin 100 mg and codeine phosphate 10 mg per 5 mL (120 mL) [contains alcohol 4.75% and benzoic acid]
    Cheratussin AC: Guaifenesin 100 mg and codeine phosphate 10 mg per 5 mL (120 mL, 240 mL, 480 mL)

(Continued)

Guaifenesin and Codeine *(Continued)*

Guaituss AC: Guaifenesin 100 mg and codeine phosphate 10 mg per 5 mL (120 mL, 480 mL) [contains alcohol; sugar free; fruit-mint flavor]

Mytussin® AC: Guaifenesin 100 mg and codeine phosphate 10 mg per 5 mL (120 mL, 480 mL) [contains alcohol; sugar free; fruit flavor]

Robafen® AC: Guaifenesin 100 mg and codeine phosphate 10 mg per 5 mL (120 mL, 480 mL)

Romilar® AC: Guaifenesin 100 mg and codeine phosphate 10 mg per 5 mL (480 mL) [contains benzoic acid and phenylalanine; alcohol free, sugar free, dye free; grape flavor]

Tablet: Guaifenesin 300 mg and codeine phosphate 10 mg

Brontex®: Guaifenesin 300 mg and codeine phosphate 10 mg

Guaifenesin and Dextromethorphan
(gwye FEN e sin & deks troe meth OR fan)

U.S. Brand Names Allfen-DM; Altarussin DM [OTC]; Amibid DM; Benylin® Expectorant [OTC] [DSC]; Cheracol® D [OTC]; Cheracol® Plus [OTC]; Coricidin HBP® Chest Congestion and Cough [OTC]; Diabetic Tussin® DM [OTC]; Diabetic Tussin® DM Maximum Strength [OTC]; Drituss DM; Duratuss® DM; Gani-Tuss DM NR; Genatuss DM® [OTC]; Guaicon DM [OTC]; Guaicon DMS [OTC]; Guaifenex® DM [OTC]; Guia-D; Guiatuss-DM® [OTC]; Humibid® CS [OTC] [DSC]; Hydro-Tussin™ DM; Iophen DM NR; Kolephrin® GG/DM [OTC]; Mindal DM [DSC]; Mintab DM; Mucinex® DM [OTC]; Phanatuss® DM [OTC]; Q-Bid DM; Q-Tussin DM [OTC]; Respa-DM®; Robafen DM [OTC]; Robitussin® Cough and Congestion [OTC]; Robitussin® DM [OTC]; Robitussin® DM Infant [OTC]; Robitussin® Sugar Free Cough [OTC]; Safe Tussin® [OTC]; Scot-Tussin® Senior [OTC]; Silexin [OTC]; Siltussin DM [OTC]; Siltussin DM DAS [OTC]; Su-Tuss DM; Touro® DM; Vicks® 44E [OTC]; Vicks® Pediatric Formula 44E [OTC]; Z-Cof LA™

Canadian Brand Names Balminil DM E; Benylin® DM-E; Koffex DM-Expectorant; Robitussin® DM

Index Terms Dextromethorphan and Guaifenesin

Pharmacologic Category Antitussive; Cough Preparation; Expectorant

Use Temporary control of cough due to minor throat and bronchial irritation

Pregnancy Risk Factor C

Medication Safety Issues

Sound-alike/look-alike issues:

Benylin® may be confused with Benadryl®, Ventolin®

Dosage Oral:

Children 2-6 years:

General dosing guidelines: Guaifenesin 50-100 mg and dextromethorphan 2.5-5 mg every 4 hours (maximum dose: Guaifenesin 600 mg and dextromethorphan 30 mg per day)

Product-specific labeling:

Benylin®: 5 mL every 4 hour (maximum: 6 doses/24 hours)

Guaifenex® DM, Touro® DM: ½ tablet every 12 hours (maximum: 1 tablet/24 hour)

Robitussin® DM, Robitussin® DM Infant, Robitussin® Sugar Free Cough: 2.5 mL every 4 hours (maximum: 6 doses/24 hours)

Vicks® Pediatric Formula 44E: 7.5 mL every 4 hours (maximum: 6 doses/24 hours)

Children: 6-12 years:

General dosing guidelines: Guaifenesin 100-200 mg and dextromethorphan 5-10 mg every 4 hours (maximum dose: Guaifenesin 1200 mg and dextromethorphan 60 mg per day)

Product-specific labeling:

Benylin®: 10 mL every 4 hours (maximum: 6 doses/24 hours)

Guaifenex® DM, Touro® DM: 1 tablet every 12 hours (maximum: 2 tablets/24 hours)

Humibid® CS: ½ tablet every 4 hours (maximum: 6 doses/24 hours)

Robitussin® DM, Robitussin® Sugar Free Cough: 5 mL every 4 hours (maximum: 6 doses/24 hours)

Vicks® 44E: 7.5 mL every 4 hours (maximum: 6 doses/24 hours)

Vicks® Pediatric Formula 44E: 15 mL every 4 hours (maximum: 6 doses/24 hours)

Z-Cof LA™: ½ tablet very 12 hours

Children ≥12 years and Adults:

General dosing guidelines: Guaifenesin 200-400 mg and dextromethorphan 10-20 mg every 4 hours (maximum dose: Guaifenesin 2400 mg and dextromethorphan 120 mg per day)

Product-specific labeling:

Benylin®: 20 mL every 4 hours (maximum: 6 doses/24 hours)

Guaifenex® DM, Mucinex® DM, Touro® DM: 1-2 tablets every 12 hours (maximum: 4 tablets/24 hours)

Humibid® CD: 1 tablet every 4 hours (maximum: 6 tablets/24 hours)

Robitussin® DM, Robitussin® Sugar Free Cough: 10 mL every 4 hours (maximum: 6 doses/24 hours)

Vicks® 44E: 15 mL every 4 hours (maximum: 6 doses/24 hours)

Vicks® Pediatric Formula 44E: 30 mL every 4 hours (maximum: 6 doses/24 hours)

Z-Cof LA™: 1 tablet every 12 hours

Additional Information Complete prescribing information for this medication should be consulted for additional detail.

Dosage Forms [DSC] = Discontinued product

Caplet, sustained release (Mindal DM [DSC]): Guaifenesin 500 mg and dextromethorphan hydrobromide 30 mg

Capsule, softgel (Coricidin HBP® Chest Congestion and Cough): Guaifenesin 200 mg and dextromethorphan hydrobromide 10 mg

Elixir:

Duratuss DM®: Guaifenesin 225 mg and dextromethorphan hydrobromide 25 mg per 5 mL (480 mL) [contains sodium benzoate; grape flavor]

Drituss DM: Guaifenesin 200 mg and dextromethorphan hydrobromide 20 mg per 5 mL (480 mL) [grape flavor]

Su-Tuss DM: Guaifenesin 200 mg and dextromethorphan hydrobromide 20 mg per 5 mL (480 mL) [fruit flavor]

Liquid: Guaifenesin 100 mg and dextromethorphan hydrobromide 10 mg per 5 mL (480 mL)

Diabetic Tussin® DM: Guaifenesin 100 mg and dextromethorphan hydrobromide 10 mg per 5 mL (120 mL) [alcohol free, sugar free, dye free; contains phenylalanine 8.4 mg/5 mL]

Diabetic Tussin® DM Maximum Strength: Guaifenesin 200 mg and dextromethorphan hydrobromide 10 mg per 5 mL (120 mL) [alcohol free, sugar free, dye free; contains phenylalanine 8.4 mg/5 mL]

Gani-Tuss® DM NR: Guaifenesin 100 mg and dextromethorphan hydrobromide 10 mg per 5 mL (480 mL) [raspberry flavor]

Hydro-Tussin™ DM: Guaifenesin 200 mg and dextromethorphan hydrobromide 20 mg per 5 mL (480 ml) [alcohol free, sugar free; contains sodium benzoate]

Iophen DM NR: Guaifenesin 100 mg and dextromethorphan hydrobromide 10 mg per 5 mL (480 mL) [raspberry flavor]

Kolephrin® GG/DM: Guaifenesin 150 mg and dextromethorphan hydrobromide 10 mg per 5 mL (120 mL) [alcohol free; cherry flavor]

Q-Tussin DM: Guaifenesin 100 mg and dextromethorphan hydrobromide 10 mg per 5 mL (120 mL, 240 mL, 480 mL, 3840 mL) [cherry flavor]

Safe Tussin®: Guaifenesin 100 mg and dextromethorphan hydrobromide 15 mg per 5 mL (120 mL) [alcohol free, sodium free, sugar free, dye free; mint flavor]

Scot-Tussin® Senior: Guaifenesin 200 mg and dextromethorphan hydrobromide 15 mg per 5 mL (120 mL) [alcohol free, sodium free, sugar free]

Vicks® 44E: Guaifenesin 200 mg and dextromethorphan hydrobromide 20 mg per 15 mL (120 mL, 235 mL) [contains sodium 31 mg/15 mL, alcohol, sodium benzoate]

Vicks® Pediatric Formula 44E: Guaifenesin 100 mg and dextromethorphan hydrobromide 10 mg per 15 mL (120 mL) [alcohol free; contains sodium 30 mg/15 mL, sodium benzoate; cherry flavor]

Liquid, oral drops (Robitussin® DM Infant): Guaifenesin 100 mg and dextromethorphan hydrobromide 5 mg per 2.5 mL (30 mL) [alcohol free; contains sodium benzoate; fruit punch flavor]

Syrup: Guaifenesin 100 mg and dextromethorphan hydrobromide 10 mg per 5 mL (120 mL, 480 mL)

Altarussin DM: Guaifenesin 100 mg and dextromethorphan hydrobromide 10 mg per 5 mL (120 mL, 240 mL, 480 mL, 3840 ml)

Benylin® Expectorant: Guaifenesin 100 mg and dextromethorphan hydrobromide 5 mg per 5 mL (120 mL) [alcohol free, sugar free; contains sodium benzoate; raspberry flavor] [DSC]

Cheracol® D: Guaifenesin 100 mg and dextromethorphan hydrobromide 10 mg per 5 mL (120 mL, 180 mL) [contains alcohol 4.75%, benzoic acid]

Cheracol® Plus: Guaifenesin 100 mg and dextromethorphan hydrobromide 10 mg per 5 mL (120 mL) [contains alcohol 4.75%, benzoic acid]

Genatuss DM®: Guaifenesin 100 mg and dextromethorphan hydrobromide 10 mg per 5 mL (120 mL)

Guiatuss® DM: Guaifenesin 100 mg and dextromethorphan hydrobromide 10 mg per 5 mL (120 mL, 480 mL, 3840 mL) [alcohol free; contains sodium benzoate]

Guaicon DM®: Guaifenesin 100 mg and dextromethorphan hydrobromide 10 mg per 5 mL (10 mL) [alcohol free]

Guaicon DMS®: Guaifenesin 100 mg and dextromethorphan hydrobromide 10 mg per 5 mL (10 mL) [alcohol free, sugar free]

Mintab DM: Guaifenesin 200 mg and dextromethorphan hydrobromide 10 mg per 5 mL (480 mL) [alcohol free, dye free; cherry vanilla flavor]

Phanatuss® DM: Guaifenesin 100 mg and dextromethorphan hydrobromide 10 mg per 5 mL (120 mL) [alcohol free, sugar free]

Robafen® DM: Guaifenesin 100 mg and dextromethorphan hydrobromide 10 mg per 5 mL (120 mL, 240 mL, 480 mL) [cherry flavor]

Robitussin® Cough and Congestion: Guaifenesin 100 mg and dextromethorphan hydrobromide 10 mg per 5 mL (120 mL) [alcohol free; contains sodium benzoate]

Robitussin®-DM: Guaifenesin 100 mg and dextromethorphan hydrobromide 10 mg per 5 mL (5 mL, 120 mL, 340 mL, 360 mL) [alcohol free; contains sodium benzoate]

Robitussin® Sugar Free Cough: Guaifenesin 100 mg and dextromethorphan hydrobromide 10 mg per 5 mL (120 mL) [alcohol free, sugar free; contains sodium benzoate]

Silexin: Guaifenesin 100 mg and dextromethorphan hydrobromide 10 mg per 5 mL (45 mL) [alcohol free, sugar free)]

Siltussin DM: Guaifenesin 100 mg and dextromethorphan hydrobromide 10 mg per 5 mL (120 mL, 240 mL, 480 mL) [strawberry flavor]

Siltussin DM DAS: Guaifenesin 100 mg and dextromethorphan hydrobromide 10 mg per 5 mL (120 mL) [alcohol free, dye free, sugar free; strawberry flavor]

Tablet:

Humibid® CS: Guaifenesin 400 mg and dextromethorphan hydrobromide 20 mg [DSC]

Silexin: Guaifenesin 100 mg and dextromethorphan hydrobromide 10 mg

Tablet, extended release: Guaifenesin 500 mg and dextromethorphan hydrobromide 30 mg

Amibid DM, Guaifenex® DM, Mucinex® DM, Q-Bid DM, Respa-DM®: Guaifenesin 600 mg and dextromethorphan hydrobromide 30 mg

Mucophen® DM: Guaifenesin 1000 mg and dextromethorphan hydrobromide 60 mg

Touro® DM: Guaifenesin 575 mg and dextromethorphan hydrobromide 30 mg

Tablet, long-acting: Guaifenesin 500 mg and dextromethorphan hydrobromide 30 mg; guaifenesin 1000 mg and dextromethorphan hydrobromide 50 mg; guaifenesin 1000 mg and dextromethorphan hydrobromide 60 mg

Z-Cof LA [scored]: Guaifenesin 650 mg and dextromethorphan hydrobromide 30 mg

Tablet, sustained release: Guaifenesin 800 mg and dextromethorphan hydrobromide 30 mg; guaifenesin 1000 mg and dextromethorphan hydrobromide 60 mg; guaifenesin 1200 mg and dextromethorphan hydrobromide 60 mg

Allfen-DM: Guaifenesin 1000 mg and dextromethorphan hydrobromide 55 mg

(Continued)

Guaifenesin and Dextromethorphan *(Continued)*

Tussi-Bid®: Guaifenesin 1200 mg and dextromethorphan hydrobromide 60 mg
Tablet, timed release [scored] (Guia-D): Guaifenesin 1000 mg and dextromethorphan hydrobromide 60 mg [dye free]

♦ **Guaifenesin and Hydrocodone** *see* Hydrocodone and Guaifenesin *on page 849*

Guaifenesin and Phenylephrine (gwye FEN e sin & fen il EF rin)

U.S. Brand Names Aldex™; Amidal; Ami-Tex LA; Crantex LA; Deconsal® II; Duratuss®; Duratuss GP®; Entex® [DSC]; Entex® ER [DSC]; Entex® LA [DSC]; ExeFen-PD; ExeTuss; ExeTuss-GP; Gentex LA; Gilphex TR®; Guaifed®; Guaifed-PD®; Guaiphen-D; Guaiphen-D 1200; Guaiphen-PD; Liquibid-D; Liquibid-D® 1200; Liquibid-PD [DSC]; Nasex-G; Nexphen PD; norel® EX; Pendex; PhenaVent™ D; PhenaVent™ LA; PhenaVent™ Ped; Prolex™-D; Prolex®-PD; Rescon GG; Sil-Tex; Simuc; Sina-12X; SINUvent® PE; XPECT-PE™

Index Terms Guaifenesin and Phenylephrine Tannate; Phenylephrine Hydrochloride and Guaifenesin

Pharmacologic Category Decongestant; Expectorant

Use Temporary relief of nasal congestion, sinusitis, rhinitis and hay fever; temporary relief of cough associated with upper respiratory tract conditions, especially when associated with dry, nonproductive cough

Pregnancy Risk Factor C

Medication Safety Issues

Sound-alike/look-alike issues:
Endal® may be confused with Depen®, Intal®
Entex® may be confused with Tenex®
Entex® LA brand name represents a different product in the U.S. than it does in Canada. In the U.S., Entex® LA contains guaifenesin and phenylephrine, while in Canada the product bearing this brand name contains guaifenesin and pseudoephedrine.

Dosage Oral:

Children 2-6 years:
Entex®, Rescon GG, Sil-Tex: 2.5 mL every 4-6 hours; maximum 10 mL/24 hours
Sina-12X suspension: 2.5-5 mL every 12 hours

Children 6-12 years:
Aldex™, Crantex LA, Liquibid-D, PhenaVent™ D, Sina-12X tablet: One-half tablet every 12 hours (maximum: 1 tablet/24 hours)
Deconsal® II: One capsule daily
Entex®, Rescon GG: 5 mL every 4-6 hours (maximum: 20 mL/24 hours)
Guaifed-PD®, PhenaVent™ Ped: One capsule every 12 hours
Liquibid-PD, SINUvent® PE: One tablet every 12 hours (maximum: 2 tablets/24 hours)
Prolex™-D: One-half to 1 tablet every 12 hours
Sina-12X suspension: Refer to Adults dosing.

Children ≥12 years:
Aldex™, Crantex LA, Deconsal® II, Entex®, Entex® LA, Guaifed®, Guaifed-PD®, Liquibid-D, Liquibid-PD, PhenaVent™ D, PhenaVent™ Ped, Prolex™-D, Rescon GG, Sil-Tex, Sina-12X, SINUvent® PE: Refer to Adults dosing
Crantex ER, Entex® ER: One capsule every 12 hours

Adults:
Aldex™, Crantex LA, XPECT-PE™, Liquibid-D, PhenaVent™ D: One tablet every 12 hours
Entex® ER, Guaifed-PD®, PhenaVent™ Ped: 1-2 capsules every 12 hours
Deconsal® II: 1-2 capsules every 12 hours (maximum: 3 capsules/24 hours)
Entex®, Sil-Tex: 5-10 mL every 4-6 hours (maximum: 40 mL/24 hours)
Entex® LA, Guaifed®, PhenaVent™: One capsule every 12 hours (maximum: 2 capsules/24 hours)
Liquibid-PD, Sina-12X tablet: 1-2 tablets every 12 hours (maximum: 4 tablets/24 hours)
Prolex™-D: 1-2 tablets every 12 hours
Rescon GG: 10 mL every 4-6 hours (maximum: 40 mL/24 hours)
Sina-12X suspension: 5-10 mL every 12 hours
SINUvent® PE: Two tablets every 12 hours

Additional Information Complete prescribing information for this medication should be consulted for additional detail.

Dosage Forms [DSC] = Discontinued product

Capsule:
Nexphen PD: Guaifenesin 200 mg and phenylephrine hydrochloride 7 mg

Capsule, variable release:
Deconsal® II: Guaifenesin 375 mg [immediate release] and phenylephrine hydrochloride 20 mg [extended release] [contains tartrazine]
Entex® ER: Guaifenesin 300 mg [immediate release] and phenylephrine hydrochloride 10 mg [extended release] [DSC]
Entex® LA [DSC], PhenaVent™ LA: Guaifenesin 400 mg [immediate release] and phenylephrine hydrochloride 30 mg [extended release]
Guaifed®, PhenaVent™: Guaifenesin 400 mg [immediate release] and phenylephrine hydrochloride 15 mg [extended release]
Guaifed-PD®, PhenaVent™ Ped: Guaifenesin 200 mg [immediate release] and phenylephrine hydrochloride 7.5 mg [extended release]

Liquid: Guaifenesin 100 mg and phenylephrine hydrochloride 7.5 mg per 5 mL (480 mL)
Entex® [DSC], Sil-Tex: Guaifenesin 100 mg and phenylephrine hydrochloride 7.5 mg per 5 mL (480 mL) [alcohol free, dye-free, sugar free; punch flavor]
Rescon GG: Guaifenesin 100 mg and phenylephrine hydrochloride 5 mg per 5 mL (120 mL, 480 mL) [cherry orange-pineapple flavor]

Suspension:
Sina-12X: Guaifenesin 100 mg and phenylephrine tannate 5 mg per 5 mL (120 mL) [contains benzoic acid; grape flavor]

Tablet:
Amidal: Guaifenesin 300 mg and phenylephrine hydrochloride 20 mg
Sina-12X: Guaifenesin 200 mg and phenylephrine tannate 25 mg
Tablet, extended release: Guaifenesin 600 mg and phenylephrine hydrochloride 20 mg; guaifenesin 600 mg and phenylephrine hydrochloride 40 mg; guaifenesin 1200 mg and phenylephrine hydrochloride 40 mg
Aldex™: Guaifenesin 650 mg and phenylephrine hydrochloride 25 mg
Ami-Tex LA: Guaifenesin 600 mg and phenylephrine hydrochloride 30 mg
Duomax: Guaifenesin 1200 mg and phenylephrine hydrochloride 40 mg [Duomatrix release]
ExeFen-PD: Guaifenesin 600 mg and phenylephrine hydrochloride 10 mg
Gentex LA: Guaifenesin 650 mg and phenylephrine hydrochloride 23.75 mg
Liquibid-D: Guaifenesin 600 mg and phenylephrine hydrochloride 40 mg [DSC]
Liquibid-PD: Guaifenesin 275 mg and phenylephrine hydrochloride 25 mg [DSC]
PhenaVent™ D: Guaifenesin 1200 mg and phenylephrine hydrochloride 40 mg
Simuc: Guaifenesin 900 mg and phenylephrine hydrochloride 25 mg
SINUvent® PE: Guaifenesin 600 mg and phenylephrine hydrochloride 15 mg
Tablet, sustained release: Guaifenesin 600 mg and phenylephrine hydrochloride 30 mg
Crantex LA: Guaifenesin 600 mg and phenylephrine hydrochloride 30 mg [dye-free]
Duratuss®, ExeTuss: Guaifenesin 900 mg and phenylephrine hydrochloride 25 mg
Duratuss GP®, ExeTuss-GP: Guaifenesin 1200 mg and phenylephrine hydrochloride 25 mg
Liquibid-D® 1200: Guaifenesin 1200 mg and phenylephrine hydrochloride 40 mg
Nasex-G: Guaifenesin 835 mg and phenylephrine hydrochloride 25 mg
Pendex, Prolex®-PD: Guaifenesin 600 mg and phenylephrine hydrochloride 10 mg
Prolex™-D: Guaifenesin 600 mg and phenylephrine hydrochloride 20 mg [dye-free]
XPECT-PE™: Guaifenesin 1200 mg and phenylephrine hydrochloride 25 mg
Tablet, timed release:
Gilphex TR®: Guaifenesin 600 mg and phenylephrine hydrochloride 25 mg [sugar free, dye free; scored]
Guaiphen-D: Guaifenesin 600 mg and phenylephrine hydrochloride 40 mg
Guaiphen-D 1200: Guaifenesin 1200 mg and phenylephrine hydrochloride 40 mg
Guaiphen-PD: Guaifenesin 275 mg and phenylephrine hydrochloride 25 mg
Tablet, variable release:
Liquibid-D®: Guaifenesin 250 mg [immediate release] and guaifenesin 400 mg and phenylephrine hydrochloride 40 mg [sustained release]
norel® EX: Guaifenesin 400 mg [immediate release] and guaifenesin 400 mg and phenylephrine hydrochloride 40 mg [extended release]

♦ **Guaifenesin and Phenylephrine Tannate** see Guaifenesin and Phenylephrine on page 818

Guaifenesin and Pseudoephedrine (gwye FEN e sin & soo doe e FED rin)

U.S. Brand Names Ambifed-G; Congestac® [OTC]; Dynex; Entex® PSE; Eudal®-SR; Guaifenex® GP; Guaifenex® PSE; Guaimax-D®; Levall G; Maxifed®; Maxifed-G®; Mucinex®-D [OTC]; Nasatab® LA; Pseudo GG TR; Pseudo Max; Pseudovent™; Pseudovent® 400; Pseudovent™-Ped; Refenesen Plus [OTC]; Respaire®-60 SR; Respaire®-120 SR; Robitussin-PE® [OTC] [DSC]; Robitussin® Severe Congestion [OTC] [DSC]; Sinutab® Non-Drying [OTC]; Sudafed® Non-Drying Sinus [OTC] [DSC]; Touro LA®; Zephrex LA® [DSC]
Canadian Brand Names Contac® Cold-Chest Congestion, Non Drowsy, Regular Strength; Entex® LA; Novahistex® Expectorant with Decongestant
Index Terms Pseudoephedrine and Guaifenesin
Pharmacologic Category Alpha/Beta Agonist; Expectorant
Use Temporary relief of nasal congestion and to help loosen phlegm and thin bronchial secretions in the treatment of cough
Pregnancy Risk Factor C
Medication Safety Issues
Sound-alike/look-alike issues:
Entex® may be confused with Tenex®
Entex® LA brand name represents a different product in the U.S. than it does in Canada. In the U.S., Entex® LA contains guaifenesin and phenylephrine, while in Canada the product bearing this brand name contains guaifenesin and pseudoephedrine.
Profen II® may be confused with Profen II DM®, Profen Forte®, Profen Forte™ DM
Profen Forte® may be confused with Profen II®, Profen II DM®, Profen Forte™ DM
Dosage Oral:
Children 2-6 years:
Guaifenex® PSE 60: One-half tablet every 12 hours (maximum: 1 tablet/12 hours)
Maxifed-G®: One-third to ½ tablet every 12 hours (maximum: 1 tablet/12 hours)
Robitussin® PE: 2.5 mL every 4-6 hours (maximum: 4 doses/24 hours)
Children 6-12 years:
Ambifed-G, Dynex, Eudal®-SR, Guaimax-D®, Guaifenex® PSE 80, Guaifenex® PSE 120, Maxifed®, Nasatab® LA, Zephrex® LA: One-half caplet or tablet every 12 hours (maximum: 1 tablet/24 hours)
Congestac®: One-half caplet every 4-6 hours (maximum: 2 caplets/24 hours)
Guaifenex® PSE 60, PanMist®-JR, Pseudovent™-Ped, Respaire®-60 SR: One tablet or capsule every 12 hours (maximum: 2 tablets or capsules every 24 hours)
Levall G: One capsule every 24 hours
Maxifed-G®: One-half to 1 tablet every 12 hours (maximum: 2 tablets/24 hours)
Robitussin® PE: 5 mL every 4-6 hours (maximum: 4 doses/24 hours)
Robitussin® Severe Congestion: One capsule every 4 hours (maximum: 4 doses/24 hours)
Children >12 years and Adults:
Ambifed-G, Dynex, Entex® PSE, Eudal®- SR, G-Phed, Guaifenex® GP, Guaifenex® PSE 120, Guaimax-D®, Levall G, Mucinex®-D 1200/120, Nasatab® LA, Pseudovent™,
(Continued)

Guaifenesin and Pseudoephedrine *(Continued)*

Respaire®-120 SR, Touro LA, Zephrex® LA: One tablet or capsule every 12 hours (maximum: 2 tablets or capsules in 24 hours)

Congestac®: One caplet every 4-6 hours (maximum: 4 caplets in 24 hours)

Guaifenex® PSE 60, Maxifed-G®, Mucinex®-D 600/60, Pseudovent™-Ped, Respaire®-60 SR: 1-2 tablets or capsules every 12 hours (maximum: 4 tablets or capsules/24 hours)

Guaifenex® PSE 80: One tablet every twelve hours (maximum: 3 tablets/24 hours)

Guaifenex™ RX: 1-2 of the AM tablets every morning and 1-2 of the PM tablets 12 hours following morning dose

Maxifed®: One to 1½ tablets every 12 hours (maximum: 3 tablets/24 hours)

Robitussin® PE: 10 mL every 4-6 hours (maximum: 4 doses/24 hours)

Robitussin® Severe Congestion, Sudafed® Non-Drying Sinus: Two capsules every 4 hours (maximum: 4 doses/24 hours)

Additional Information Complete prescribing information for this medication should be consulted for additional detail.

Dosage Forms [DSC] = Discontinued product

Caplet:

Congestac®, Refenesen Plus: Guaifenesin 400 mg and pseudoephedrine hydrochloride 60 mg

Caplet, long acting:

Touro LA®: Guaifenesin 500 mg and pseudoephedrine hydrochloride 120 mg

Caplet, prolonged release:

Ambifed-G: Guaifenesin 1000 mg and pseudoephedrine hydrochloride 60 mg

Capsule, extended release:

Respaire®-60 SR: Guaifenesin 200 mg and pseudoephedrine hydrochloride 60 mg

Respaire®-120 SR: Guaifenesin 250 mg and pseudoephedrine hydrochloride 120 mg

Capsule, liquicap:

Sinutab® Non-Drying: Guaifenesin 200 mg and pseudoephedrine hydrochloride 30 mg

Sudafed® Non-Drying Sinus: Guaifenesin 200 mg and pseudoephedrine hydrochloride 30 mg [DSC]

Capsule, softgel:

Robitussin® Severe Congestion: Guaifenesin 200 mg and pseudoephedrine hydrochloride 30 mg [DSC]

Capsule, variable release:

Entex® PSE: Guaifenesin 400 mg [immediate release] and pseudoephedrine hydrochloride 120 mg [extended release]

Levall G: Guaifenesin 400 mg [immediate release] and pseudoephedrine hydrochloride 90 mg [extended release]

Pseudovent™: Guaifenesin 250 mg [immediate release] and pseudoephedrine hydrochloride 120 mg [prolonged release]

Pseudovent™-Ped: Guaifenesin 300 mg [immediate release] and pseudoephedrine hydrochloride 60 mg [prolonged release]

Pseudovent™ 400: Guaifenesin 400 mg [immediate release] and pseudoephedrine hydrochloride 120 mg [extended release]

Syrup: Guaifenesin 200 mg and pseudoephedrine hydrochloride 40 mg per 5 mL (480 mL)

Robitussin-PE®: Guaifenesin 100 mg and pseudoephedrine hydrochloride 30 mg per 5 mL (120 mL, 240 mL) [alcohol free; contains sodium benzoate] [DSC]

Tablet, extended release:

Guaifenesin 550 mg and pseudoephedrine hydrochloride 60 mg

Guaifenesin 595 mg and pseudoephedrine hydrochloride 48 mg

Guaifenesin 600 mg and pseudoephedrine hydrochloride 120 mg

Guaifenesin 1200 mg and pseudoephedrine hydrochloride 50 mg

Guaifenesin 1200 mg and pseudoephedrine hydrochloride 75 mg

Guaifenesin 1200 mg and pseudoephedrine hydrochloride 120 mg

Guaifenex® GP: Guaifenesin 1200 mg and pseudoephedrine hydrochloride 120 mg [dye free]

Guaifenex® PSE 60: Guaifenesin 600 mg and pseudoephedrine hydrochloride 60 mg

Guaifenex® PSE 80: Guaifenesin 800 mg and pseudoephedrine hydrochloride 80 mg

Guaifenex® PSE 85: Guaifenesin 795 mg and pseudoephedrine hydrochloride 85 mg

Guaifenex® PSE 120: Guaifenesin 600 mg and pseudoephedrine hydrochloride 120 mg [dye free]

Guaimax-D®, Zephrex LA® [DSC]: Guaifenesin 600 mg and pseudoephedrine hydrochloride 120 mg

Maxifed®: Guaifenesin 780 mg and pseudoephedrine hydrochloride 80 mg

Maxifed-G®: Guaifenesin 580 mg and pseudoephedrine hydrochloride 60 mg

Mucinex®-D 600/60: Guaifenesin 600 mg and pseudoephedrine hydrochloride 60 mg

Pseudo Max: Guaifenesin 700 mg and pseudoephedrine hydrochloride 80 mg

Tablet, long acting:

Dynex: Guaifenesin 1200 mg and pseudoephedrine hydrochloride 90 mg

Tablet, sustained release:

Nasatab® LA: Guaifenesin 500 mg and pseudoephedrine hydrochloride 120 mg

♦ **Guaifenesin and Theophylline** see Theophylline and Guaifenesin on page 1663

♦ **Guaifenesin, Dihydrocodeine, and Pseudoephedrine** see Dihydrocodeine, Pseudoephedrine, and Guaifenesin on page 506

♦ **Guaifenesin, Hydrocodone, and Pseudoephedrine** see Hydrocodone, Pseudoephedrine, and Guaifenesin on page 852

Guaifenesin, Pseudoephedrine, and Codeine

(gwye FEN e sin, soo doe e FED rin, & KOE deen)

U.S. Brand Names Guiatuss DAC; Mytussin® DAC; Nucofed® Expectorant [DSC]; Nucofed® Pediatric Expectorant [DSC]

Canadian Brand Names Benylin® 3.3 mg-D-E; Calmylin with Codeine
Index Terms Codeine, Guaifenesin, and Pseudoephedrine; Pseudoephedrine, Guaifenesin, and Codeine
Pharmacologic Category Antitussive/Decongestant/Expectorant
Use Temporarily relieves nasal congestion and controls cough associated with upper respiratory infections and related conditions (common cold, sinusitis, bronchitis, influenza)
Restrictions C-III; C-V
Pregnancy Risk Factor C
Dosage Oral:
Children 2-6 years:
Nucofed® Pediatric: 2.5 mL every 6 hours (maximum 10 mL/24 hours)
Nucofed®: 1.25 mL every 6 hours (maximum 5 mL/24 hours)
Children 6-12 years:
Guaituss DAC: 5 mL every 4 hours (maximum 20 mL/24 hours)
Nucofed® Pediatric: 5 mL every 6 hours (maximum 20 mL/24 hours)
Nucofed®: 2.5 mL every 6 hours (maximum 10 mL/24hours)
Children >12 years and Adults:
Guaituss DAC: 10 mL every 4 hours (maximum 40 mL/24 hours)
Nucofed® Pediatric: 10 mL every 6 hours (maximum 40 mL/24 hours)
Nucofed®: 5 mL every 6 hours (maximum 20 mL/24 hours)
Additional Information Complete prescribing information for this medication should be consulted for additional detail.
Dosage Forms [DSC] = Discontinued product
Syrup:
Guiatuss DAC: Guaifenesin 100 mg, pseudoephedrine hydrochloride 30 mg, and codeine phosphate 10 mg per 5 mL (480 mL)
Mytussin® DAC: Guaifenesin 100 mg, pseudoephedrine hydrochloride 30 mg, and codeine phosphate 10 mg per 5 mL (120 mL, 480 mL) [sugar free; contains alcohol 1.7%; strawberry-raspberry flavor]
Nucofed® Expectorant: Guaifenesin 200 mg, pseudoephedrine hydrochloride 60 mg, and codeine phosphate 20 mg per 5 mL (480 mL) [contains alcohol 12.5%; cherry flavor] [DSC]
Nucofed® Pediatric Expectorant: Guaifenesin 100 mg, pseudoephedrine hydrochloride 30 mg, and codeine phosphate 10 mg per 5 mL (480 mL) [contains alcohol 6%; strawberry flavor] [DSC]

Guaifenesin, Pseudoephedrine, and Dextromethorphan
(gwye FEN e sin, soo doe e FED rin, & deks troe meth OR fan)

U.S. Brand Names Ambifed-G DM; Coldmist DM; Maxifed DM; Maxifed DMX; Medent-DM; Profen Forte™ DM; Profen II DM®; Pseudo Max DMX; Pseudovent™ DM; Relacon-DM NR; Robitussin® Cough and Cold [OTC]; Robitussin® Cough and Cold CF [OTC]; Robitussin® Cough and Cold Infant CF [OTC]; Ru-Tuss DM; Touro® CC; Touro® CC-LD; Tri-Vent™ DM; Tusnel Pediatric®; Z-Cof™ DM
Canadian Brand Names Balminil DM + Decongestant + Expectorant; Benylin® DM-D-E; Koffex DM + Decongestant + Expectorant; Novahistex® DM Decongestant Expectorant; Novahistine® DM Decongestant Expectorant; Robitussin® Cough & Cold®
Index Terms Dextromethorphan, Guaifenesin, and Pseudoephedrine; Pseudoephedrine, Dextromethorphan, and Guaifenesin
Pharmacologic Category Antitussive/Decongestant/Expectorant
Use Temporarily relieves nasal congestion and controls cough due to minor throat and bronchial irritation; helps loosen phlegm and thin bronchial secretions to make coughs more productive
Pregnancy Risk Factor C
Medication Safety Issues
Sound-alike/look-alike issues:
Profen II DM® may be confused with Profen II®, Profen Forte®, Profen Forte™ DM
Profen Forte™ DM may be confused with Profen II®, Profen II DM®, Profen Forte®
Dosage Note: Also refer to specific product labeling.
Children 2-6 years:
Maxifed DM: 1/3 to 1/2 tablet every 12 hours, not to exceed 1 tablet/24 hours
Tri-Vent™ DM: 2.5 mL up to 3-4 times/day, not to exceed pseudoephedrine 4 mg/kg/day
Profen II DM (syrup): 1.25-2.5 mL every 4 hours, not to exceed 15 mL/24 hours
Robitussin® Pediatric Cough and Cold Infant: 2.5 mL every 4-6 hours, not to exceed 4 doses/24 hours
Touro® CC: 1/2 tablet every 12 hour, not to exceed 1 tablet/24 hours
Z-Cof™ DM: 2.5 mL 2-3 times/day, not to exceed 7.5 mL/24 hours

Children 6-12 years:
Ambifed-G DM, Profen Forte™ DM, Profen II DM®: 1/2 tablet every 12 hours not to exceed 1 tablet/24 hours
Maxifed DM: 1/2 to 1 tablet every 12 hours, not to exceed 2 tablets/24 hours
Tri-Vent™ DM: 5 mL up to 3-4 times/day, not to exceed pseudoephedrine 4 mg/kg/day
Touro® CC, Pseudovent™ DM: 1 tablet every 12 hours, not to exceed 2 tablets/24 hours
Profen II DM (syrup): 2.5-5 mL every 4 hours, not to exceed 30 mL/24 hours
Z-Cof™ DM: 5 mL 2-3 times/day, not to exceed 15 mL/24 hours

Children ≥12 years and Adults:
Ambifed-G DM, Aquatab® C, Profen Forte™ DM: 1 tablet every 12 hours not to exceed 2 tablets/24 hours
Maxifed DM, Touro® CC, Pseudovent™ DM: 1-2 tablets every 12 hours not to exceed 4 tablets/24 hours
Tri-Vent™ DM: Up to 10 mL 3-4 times/day, not to exceed pseudoephedrine 240 mg/24 hours
Profen II DM (tablet): 1 to 1 1/2 tablets every 12 hours, not to exceed 3 tablets/24 hours
(Continued)

Guaifenesin, Pseudoephedrine, and Dextromethorphan
(Continued)

Profen II DM (syrup): 5-10 mL every 4 hours, not to exceed 60 mL/24 hours

Z-Cof™ DM: 10 mL 2-3 times/day, not to exceed 30 mL/24 hours

Additional Information Complete prescribing information for this medication should be consulted for additional detail.

Dosage Forms

Caplet, prolonged release:

Ambifed-G DM: Guaifenesin 1000 mg, pseudoephedrine hydrochloride 60 mg, and dextromethorphan hydrobromide 30 mg

Caplet, sustained release [scored]:

Touro® CC: Guaifenesin 575 mg, pseudoephedrine hydrochloride 60 mg, and dextromethorphan hydrobromide 30 mg [dye free]

Touro® CC-LD: Guaifenesin 575 mg, pseudoephedrine hydrochloride 25 mg, and dextromethorphan hydrobromide 30 mg

Capsule, softgel:

Robitussin® Cough and Cold: Guaifenesin 200 mg, pseudoephedrine hydrochloride 30 mg, and dextromethorphan hydrobromide 10 mg

Liquid: Guaifenesin 100 mg, pseudoephedrine hydrochloride 30 mg, and dextromethorphan hydrobromide 10 mg per 5 mL (120 mL)

Profen II DM®: Guaifenesin 200 mg, pseudoephedrine hydrochloride 15 mg, and dextromethorphan hydrobromide 10 mg per 5 mL (480 mL) [alcohol free, dye free, sugar free; cherry flavor]

Relacon-DM NR: Guaifenesin 200 mg, pseudoephedrine hydrochloride 32 mg, and dextromethorphan hydrobromide 15 mg (480 mL) [alcohol free, sugar free; grape flavor]

Tusnel Pediatric®: Guaifenesin 50 mg, pseudoephedrine hydrochloride 15 mg, and dextromethorphan hydrobromide 5 mg per 5 mL (120 mL) [alcohol free]

Z-Cof™ DM: Guaifenesin 200 mg, pseudoephedrine hydrochloride 40 mg, and dextromethorphan hydrobromide 15 mg per 5 mL (480 mL) [alcohol free, sugar free; contains sodium benzoate; grape flavor]

Liquid, oral drops:

Robitussin® Cough and Cold Infant CF: Guaifenesin 100 mg, pseudoephedrine hydrochloride 15 mg, and dextromethorphan hydrobromide 5 mg per 2.5 mL (30 mL) [alcohol free; contains sodium benzoate]

Syrup: Guaifenesin 100 mg, pseudoephedrine hydrochloride 45 mg, and dextromethorphan hydrobromide 15 mg per 5 mL (480 mL)

Robitussin® Cough and Cold CF: Guaifenesin 100 mg, pseudoephedrine hydrochloride 30 mg, and dextromethorphan hydrobromide 10 mg per 5 mL (120 mL, 240 mL, 360 mL) [alcohol free; contains sodium benzoate]

Ru-Tuss DM: Guaifenesin 100 mg, pseudoephedrine hydrochloride 45 mg, and dextromethorphan hydrobromide 15 mg per 5 mL (480 mL) [alcohol free, dye free; strawberry flavor]

Tri-Vent™ DM: Guaifenesin 100 mg, pseudoephedrine hydrochloride 40 mg, and dextromethorphan hydrobromide 15 mg per 5 mL (480 mL) [alcohol free, dye free, sugar free; strawberry flavor]

Tablet, extended release: Guaifenesin 100 mg, pseudoephedrine hydrochloride 30 mg, and dextromethorphan hydrobromide 10 mg; guaifenesin 800 mg, pseudoephedrine hydrochloride 60 mg, and dextromethorphan hydrobromide 30 mg; guaifenesin 1200 mg, pseudoephedrine hydrochloride 60 mg, and dextromethorphan hydrobromide 60 mg; guaifenesin 1200 mg, pseudoephedrine hydrochloride 120 mg, and dextromethorphan hydrobromide 60 mg; guaifenesin 800 mg, pseudoephedrine hydrochloride 90 mg, and dextromethorphan hydrobromide 60 mg; guaifenesin 550 mg, pseudoephedrine hydrochloride 60 mg, and dextromethorphan hydrobromide 30 mg; guaifenesin 595 mg, pseudoephedrine hydrochloride 48 mg, and dextromethorphan hydrobromide 32 mg; guaifenesin 600 mg, pseudoephedrine hydrochloride 60 mg, and dextromethorphan hydrobromide 30 mg

Coldmist DM, Pseudovent™ DM: Guaifenesin 595 mg, pseudoephedrine hydrochloride 48 mg, and dextromethorphan hydrobromide 32 mg

Profen Forte™ DM: Guaifenesin 800 mg, pseudoephedrine hydrochloride 90 mg, and dextromethorphan hydrobromide 60 mg

Profen II DM®: Guaifenesin 800 mg, pseudoephedrine hydrochloride 45 mg, and dextromethorphan hydrobromide 30 mg

Tablet, long acting [scored]:

Medent-DM: Guaifenesin 800 mg, pseudoephedrine hydrochloride 60 mg, and dextromethorphan hydrobromide 30 mg [dye free]

Tablet, sustained release:

Maxifed DM: Guaifenesin 580 mg, pseudoephedrine hydrochloride 60 mg, and dextromethorphan hydrobromide 30 mg [dye free, scored]

Maxifed DM: Guaifenesin 780 mg, pseudoephedrine hydrochloride 80 mg, and dextromethorphan hydrobromide 40 mg [dye free, scored]

Pseudo Max DMX: Guaifenesin 700 mg, pseudoephedrine hydrochloride 80 mg, and dextromethorphan hydrobromide 40 mg

- **Guaifenex® DM** see Guaifenesin and Dextromethorphan on page 816
- **Guaifenex® GP** see Guaifenesin and Pseudoephedrine on page 819
- **Guaifenex® PSE** see Guaifenesin and Pseudoephedrine on page 819
- **Guaimax-D®** see Guaifenesin and Pseudoephedrine on page 819
- **Guaiphen-D** see Guaifenesin and Phenylephrine on page 818
- **Guaiphen-D 1200** see Guaifenesin and Phenylephrine on page 818
- **Guaiphen-PD** see Guaifenesin and Phenylephrine on page 818
- **Guaituss AC** see Guaifenesin and Codeine on page 815

Guanabenz (GWAHN a benz)

Canadian Brand Names Wytensin®
Index Terms Guanabenz Acetate
Pharmacologic Category Alpha₂-Adrenergic Agonist
Use Management of hypertension
Pregnancy Risk Factor C
Medication Safety Issues
Sound-alike/look-alike issues:
Guanabenz may be confused with guanadrel, guanfacine
Dosage Adults: Oral: Initial: 4 mg twice daily; increase in increments of 4-8 mg/day every 1-2 weeks to a maximum of 32 mg twice daily.
Dosing adjustment in hepatic impairment: Probably necessary
Additional Information Complete prescribing information for this medication should be consulted for additional detail.
Dosage Forms Tablet: 4 mg, 8 mg

♦ **Guanabenz Acetate** see Guanabenz on page 823

Guanfacine (GWAHN fa seen)

U.S. Brand Names Tenex® [DSC]
Canadian Brand Names Tenex®
Index Terms Guanfacine Hydrochloride
Pharmacologic Category Alpha₂-Adrenergic Agonist
Use Management of hypertension
Unlabeled/Investigational Use ADHD, tic disorder, aggression
Pregnancy Risk Factor B
Medication Safety Issues
Sound-alike/look-alike issues:
Guanfacine may be confused with guaifenesin, guanabenz, guanidine
Tenex® may be confused with Entex®, Ten-K®, Xanax®

International issues:
Tenex® may be confused with Kinex® which is a brand name for biperiden in Mexico
Dosage Oral: Adults:
Hypertension: 1 mg usually at bedtime, may increase if needed at 3- to 4-week intervals; usual dose range (JNC 7): 0.5-2 mg once daily
ADHD, tic disorder, aggression (unlabeled uses): Initial: 0.5 mg at bedtime; increase as tolerated (every 3-14 days) to usual dose range (1.5-3 mg/day) given in 3 divided doses (maximum: 4 mg/day)
Additional Information Complete prescribing information for this medication should be consulted for additional detail.
Dosage Forms [DSC] = Discontinued product
Tablet: 1 mg, 2 mg
Tenex®: 1 mg, 2 mg [DSC]

♦ **Guanfacine Hydrochloride** see Guanfacine on page 823
♦ **Guia-D** see Guaifenesin and Dextromethorphan on page 816
♦ **Guiatuss™ [OTC]** see Guaifenesin on page 814
♦ **Guiatuss DAC** see Guaifenesin, Pseudoephedrine, and Codeine on page 820
♦ **Guiatuss-DM® [OTC]** see Guaifenesin and Dextromethorphan on page 816
♦ **GW506U78** see Nelarabine on page 1207
♦ **GW433908G** see Fosamprenavir on page 761
♦ **Gynazole-1®** see Butoconazole on page 260
♦ **Gyne-Lotrimin® 3 [OTC]** see Clotrimazole on page 404
♦ **Gynodiol®** see Estradiol on page 620
♦ **Gynol II® [OTC]** see Nonoxynol 9 on page 1239
♦ **Habitrol** see Nicotine on page 1223
♦ **Habitrol® (Can)** see Nicotine on page 1223

Haemophilus b Conjugate and Hepatitis B Vaccine
(he MOF i lus bee KON joo gate & hep a TYE tis bee vak SEEN)

U.S. Brand Names Comvax®
Index Terms Haemophilus b (meningococcal protein conjugate) Conjugate Vaccine; Hepatitis b Vaccine (Recombinant); Hib Conjugate Vaccine
Pharmacologic Category Vaccine
Use
Immunization against invasive disease caused by H. influenzae type b and against infection caused by all known subtypes of hepatitis B virus in infants 6 weeks to 15 months of age born of hepatitis B surface antigen (HBₛAg) negative mothers
Infants born of HBₛAg-positive mothers or mothers of unknown HBₛAg status should receive hepatitis B immune globulin and hepatitis B vaccine (recombinant) at birth and should complete the hepatitis B vaccination series given according to a particular schedule
Pregnancy Risk Factor C
Medication Safety Issues
Sound-alike/look-alike issues:
Comvax® may be confused with Recombivax [Recombivax HB®]
Dosage Infants: I.M.: 0.5 mL at 2, 4, and 12-15 months of age (total of 3 doses)
(Continued)

Haemophilus b Conjugate and Hepatitis B Vaccine *(Continued)*

If the recommended schedule cannot be followed, the interval between the first two doses should be at least 6 weeks and the interval between the second and third dose should be as close as possible to 8-11 months. Minimum age for first dose is 6 weeks.

Modified Schedule: Children who receive one dose of hepatitis B vaccine at or shortly after birth may receive Comvax® on a schedule of 2, 4, and 12-15 months of age

Additional Information Complete prescribing information for this medication should be consulted for additional detail.

Dosage Forms Injection, suspension [preservative free]: *Haemophilus* b PRP 7.5 mcg and HB₅Ag 5 mcg per 0.5 mL (0.5 mL) [vial stopper contains latex]

Haemophilus b Conjugate Vaccine
(he MOF fi lus bee KON joo gate vak SEEN)

U.S. Brand Names ActHIB®; HibTITER®; PedvaxHIB®
Canadian Brand Names ActHIB®; PedvaxHIB®
Index Terms Diphtheria CRM₁₉₇ Protein Conjugate; Diphtheria Toxoid Conjugate; *Haemophilus* b Oligosaccharide Conjugate Vaccine; *Haemophilus* b Polysaccharide Vaccine; HbCV; HbOC; Hib Conjugate Vaccine; Hib Polysaccharide Conjugate; PRP-OMP; PRP-T
Pharmacologic Category Vaccine
Additional Appendix Information
Immunization Recommendations *on page 1929*

Use Routine immunization of children 2 months to 5 years of age against invasive disease caused by *H. influenzae*

Unimmunized children ≥5 years of age with a chronic illness known to be associated with increased risk of *Haemophilus influenzae* type b disease, specifically, persons with anatomic or functional asplenia or sickle cell anemia or those who have undergone splenectomy, should receive *Haemophilus influenzae* type b (Hib) vaccine.

Haemophilus b conjugate vaccines are not indicated for prevention of bronchitis or other infections due to *H. influenzae* in adults; adults with specific dysfunction or certain complement deficiencies who are at especially high risk of *H. influenzae* type b infection (HIV-infected adults); patients with Hodgkin's disease (vaccinated at least 2 weeks before the initiation of chemotherapy or 3 months after the end of chemotherapy)

Pregnancy Risk Factor C
Pregnancy Implications Reproduction studies have not been conducted.
Contraindications Hypersensitivity to *Haemophilus* b polysaccharide vaccine or any component of the formulation
Warnings/Precautions If used in persons with malignancies or those receiving immunosuppressive therapy or who are otherwise immunocompromised, the expected immune response may not be obtained; may be used in patients with HIV infection. Patients who develop symptoms suggestive of hypersensitivity after an injection should not receive further injections of the vaccine. The decision to administer or delay vaccination because of current or recent febrile illness depends on the severity of symptoms and the etiology of the disease. Immunization should be delayed during the course of an acute febrile illness. Use caution in children with coagulation disorders (including thrombocytopenia) where intramuscular injections should not be used. Epinephrine 1:1000 should be readily available.

Children in whom DTP or DT vaccination is deferred: The carrier proteins used in HbOC and PRP-T (but not PRP-OMP) are chemically and immunologically related to toxoids contained in DTP vaccine. Earlier or simultaneous vaccination with diphtheria or tetanus toxoids may be required to elicit an optimal anti-PRP antibody response to HbOC. In contrast, the immunogenicity of PRP-OMP is not affected by vaccination with DTP. In infants in whom DTP or DT vaccination is deferred, PRP-OMP may be advantageous for *Haemophilus influenzae* type b vaccination.

Children with immunologic impairment: Children with chronic illness associated with increased risk of *Haemophilus influenzae* type b disease may have impaired anti-PRP antibody responses to conjugate vaccination. Examples include those with HIV infection, immunoglobulin deficiency, anatomic or functional asplenia, and sickle cell disease, as well as recipients of bone marrow transplants and recipients of chemotherapy for malignancy. Some children with immunologic impairment may benefit from more doses of conjugate vaccine than normally indicated.

Adverse Reactions All serious adverse reactions must be reported to the U.S. Department of Health and Human Services (DHHS) Vaccine Adverse Event Reporting System (VAERS) 1-800-822-7967. Frequency not defined:

Central nervous system: Crying (unusual, high pitched, prolonged); fever, irritability, pain, sleepiness
Dermatologic: Rash
Gastrointestinal: Anorexia, diarrhea, vomiting
Local: Injection site: Erythema, induration, pain, soreness, swelling
Otic: Otitis media
Respiratory: Upper respiratory tract infection
Postmarketing and/or case reports: Anaphylactoid reactions, angioedema, erythema multiforme, facial edema, febrile seizures, Guillain-Barré syndrome, headache, hypersensitivity, hypotonia, inflammation, injection site abscess (sterile), lethargy, lymphadenopathy, malaise, mass, seizure, skin discoloration, urticaria

Drug Interactions
Decreased Effect: The effect of the vaccine may be decreased with immunosuppressive agents; consider deferring vaccination for 3 months after immunosuppressant therapy is discontinued.

Stability Store under refrigeration at 2°C to 8°C (36°F to 46°F); do not freeze.
ActHIB®: Use within 24 hours following reconstitution with saline. Use within 30 minutes following reconstitution with Tripedia®.

Mechanism of Action Stimulates production of anticapsular antibodies and provides active immunity to *Haemophilus influenzae*

Pharmacodynamics/Kinetics Seroconversion following one dose of Hib vaccine for children 18 months or 24 months of age or older is 75% to 90% respectively.

Onset of action: Serum antibody response: 1-2 weeks

Duration: Immunity: 1.5 years

Dosage Children: I.M.: 0.5 mL as a single dose should be administered according to one of the following "brand-specific" schedules; do not inject I.V. (see table)

Vaccination Schedule for Haemophilus b Conjugate Vaccines

Age at 1st Dose (mo)	ActHIBHib®, HibTITER®		PedvaxHIB®	
	Primary Series	Booster	Primary Series	Booster
2-6	3 doses, 2 months apart	15 mo[1]	2 doses, 2 months apart	12-15 mo[1]
7-11	2 doses, 2 months apart	15 mo[1]	2 doses, 2 months apart	12-15 mo[1]
12-14	1 dose	15 mo[1]	1 dose	15 mo[1]
15-71	1 dose	—	1 dose	—

[1]At least 2 months after previous dose.

Note: DTaP/Hib combination vaccines should not be used for infants at ages 2, 4, or 6 months, but can be used as boosters following any Hib vaccine.

Administration For patients at risk of hemorrhage following intramuscular injection, the ACIP recommends "it should be administered intramuscularly if, in the opinion of the physician familiar with the patients bleeding risk, the vaccine can be administered with reasonable safety by this route. If the patient receives antihemophilia or other similar therapy, intramuscular vaccination can be scheduled shortly after such therapy is administered. A fine needle (23 gauge or smaller) can be used for the vaccination and firm pressure applied to the site (without rubbing) for at least 2 minutes. The patient should be instructed concerning the risk of hematoma from the injection."

Test Interactions May interfere with interpretation of antigen detection tests

Additional Information Federal law requires that the date of administration, the vaccine manufacturer, lot number of vaccine, and the administering person's name, title, and address be entered into the patient's permanent medical record.

The three conjugate vaccines currently available consist of *Haemophilus influenzae* type b (Hib) capsular polysaccharide (also referred to as PRP) linked to a carrier protein. The carrier protein for HibTITER® (HbOC) is a nontoxic diphtheria toxoid. PedvaxHIB® (PRP-OMP) is linked to the outer membrane protein complex from *Neisseria meningitidis*. ActHIB® (PRP-T) uses tetanus toxoid conjugate as the carrier protein.

Dosage Forms

Injection, powder for reconstitution (ActHIB®) [preservative free]: *Haemophilus* b capsular polysaccharide 10 mcg and tetanus toxoid 24 mcg per dose [may be reconstituted with provided diluent (forms solution; vial stopper contains latex) or TriHIBit® (forms suspension)]

Injection, solution [preservative free] (HibTITER®): *Haemophilus* b saccharide 10 mcg and diphtheria CRM 197 protein 25 mcg per 0.5 mL (0.5 mL) [vial stopper contains latex]

Injection, suspension (PedvaxHIB®): *Haemophilus* b capsular polysaccharide 7.5 mcg and *Neisseria meningitidis* OMPC 125 mcg per 0.5 mL (0.5 mL) [contains aluminum 225 mcg/0.5 mL]

♦ *Haemophilus* b (meningococcal protein conjugate) Conjugate Vaccine *see Haemophilus b Conjugate and Hepatitis B Vaccine on page 823*

♦ *Haemophilus* b Oligosaccharide Conjugate Vaccine *see Haemophilus b Conjugate Vaccine on page 824*

♦ *Haemophilus* b Polysaccharide Vaccine *see Haemophilus b Conjugate Vaccine on page 824*

♦ *Haemophilus influenzae* b Conjugate Vaccine and Diphtheria, Tetanus Toxoids, and Acellular Pertussis Vaccine *see Diphtheria, Tetanus Toxoids, and Acellular Pertussis Vaccine and Haemophilus influenzae b Conjugate Vaccine on page 524*

Halcinonide (hal SIN oh nide)

U.S. Brand Names Halog®

Canadian Brand Names Halog®

Pharmacologic Category Corticosteroid, Topical

Additional Appendix Information

Corticosteroids *on page 1879*

Use Inflammation of corticosteroid-responsive dermatoses [high potency topical corticosteroid]

Pregnancy Risk Factor C

Medication Safety Issues

Sound-alike/look-alike issues:

Halcinonide may be confused with Halcion®

Halog® may be confused with Haldol®, Mycolog®

Dosage Children and Adults: Topical: Steroid-responsive dermatoses: Apply sparingly 1-3 times/day, occlusive dressing may be used for severe or resistant dermatoses; a thin film is effective; do not overuse. Therapy should be discontinued when control is achieved; if no improvement is seen, reassessment of diagnosis may be necessary.

Additional Information Complete prescribing information for this medication should be consulted for additional detail.

Dosage Forms [DSC] = Discontinued product

Cream (Halog®): 0.1% (15 g, 30 g, 60 g, 240 g) [DSC]

Ointment (Halog®): 0.1% (15 g, 30 g, 60 g, 240 g) [DSC]

Solution, topical (Halog®): 0.1% (20 mL, 60 mL)

♦ **Halcion**® [DSC] see Triazolam on page 1738

♦ **Halcion**® (Can) see Triazolam on page 1738

♦ **Haldol**® see Haloperidol on page 826

♦ **Haldol**® **Decanoate** see Haloperidol on page 826

♦ **Haley's M-O** see Magnesium Hydroxide and Mineral Oil on page 1048

♦ **Halfprin**® [OTC] see Aspirin on page 160

Halobetasol (hal oh BAY ta sol)

U.S. Brand Names Ultravate®
Canadian Brand Names Ultravate®
Index Terms Halobetasol Propionate
Pharmacologic Category Corticosteroid, Topical
Additional Appendix Information
  Corticosteroids on page 1879
Use Relief of inflammatory and pruritic manifestations of corticosteroid-response dermatoses [super high potency topical corticosteroid]
Pregnancy Risk Factor C
Medication Safety Issues
  Sound-alike/look-alike issues:
    Ultravate® may be confused with Cutivate®
Dosage Children ≥12 years and Adults: Topical:
  Inflammatory and pruritic manifestations (dental use): Cream: Apply sparingly to lesion twice daily. Treatment should not exceed 2 consecutive weeks and total dosage should not exceed 50 g/week. Therapy should be discontinued when control is achieved; if no improvement is seen, reassessment of diagnosis may be necessary.
  Steroid-responsive dermatoses: Apply sparingly to skin twice daily, rub in gently and completely; treatment should not exceed 2 consecutive weeks and total dosage should not exceed 50 g/week. Therapy should be discontinued when control is achieved; if no improvement is seen, reassessment of diagnosis may be necessary.
Additional Information Complete prescribing information for this medication should be consulted for additional detail.
Dosage Forms
  Cream, as propionate: 0.05% (15 g, 50 g)
  Ointment, as propionate: 0.05% (15 g, 50 g)

♦ **Halobetasol Propionate** see Halobetasol on page 826

♦ **Halog**® see Halcinonide on page 825

Haloperidol (ha loe PER i dole)

U.S. Brand Names Haldol®; Haldol® Decanoate
Canadian Brand Names Apo-Haloperidol®; Apo-Haloperidol LA®; Haloperidol Injection, USP; Haloperidol-LA; Haloperidol-LA Omega; Haloperidol Long Acting; Novo-Peridol; Peridol; PMS-Haloperidol LA
Index Terms Haloperidol Decanoate; Haloperidol Lactate
Pharmacologic Category Antipsychotic Agent, Typical
Additional Appendix Information
  Antipsychotic Agents on page 1872
Use Management of schizophrenia; control of tics and vocal utterances of Tourette's disorder in children and adults; severe behavioral problems in children
Unlabeled/Investigational Use Treatment of psychosis; may be used for the emergency sedation of severely-agitated or delirious patients; adjunctive treatment of ethanol dependence; antiemetic
Pregnancy Risk Factor C
Lactation Enters breast milk/not recommended (AAP rates "of concern")
Medication Safety Issues
  Sound-alike/look-alike issues:
    Haloperidol may be confused Halotestin®
    Haldol® may be confused with Halcion®, Halenol®, Halog®, Halotestin®, Stadol®
Contraindications Hypersensitivity to haloperidol or any component of the formulation; Parkinson's disease; severe CNS depression; bone marrow suppression; severe cardiac or hepatic disease; coma
Warnings/Precautions Safety and efficacy have not been established in children <3 years of age. Use caution in patients with CNS depression and severe liver or cardiac disease. Hypotension may occur, particularly with parenteral administration. Decanoate form should never be administered I.V. Avoid in thyrotoxicosis. May be sedating, use with caution in disorders where CNS depression is a feature. Caution in patients with hemodynamic instability, predisposition to seizures, subcortical brain damage, renal or respiratory disease. Esophageal dysmotility and aspiration have been associated with antipsychotic use - use with caution in patients at risk of pneumonia (ie, Alzheimer's disease). Caution in breast cancer or other prolactin-dependent tumors (may elevate prolactin levels). May alter temperature regulation or mask toxicity of other drugs due to antiemetic effects. May alter cardiac conduction - life-threatening arrhythmias have occurred with therapeutic doses of antipsychotics. Adverse effects of decanoate may be prolonged. May cause orthostatic hypotension - use with caution in patients at risk of this effect or those who would tolerate transient hypotensive episodes (cerebrovascular disease, cardiovascular disease, or other medications which may predispose). Some tablets contain tartrazine.

May cause anticholinergic effects (confusion, agitation, constipation, xerostomia, blurred vision, urinary retention). Therefore, they should be used with caution in patients with decreased gastrointestinal motility, urinary retention, BPH, xerostomia, or visual problems. Conditions which also may be exacerbated by cholinergic blockade include narrow-angle glaucoma (screening is recommended) and worsening of myasthenia gravis. Relative to other neuroleptics, haloperidol has a low potency of cholinergic blockade.

May cause extrapyramidal reactions, including pseudoparkinsonism, acute dystonic reactions, akathisia, and tardive dyskinesia (risk of these reactions is high relative to other neuroleptics). May be associated with neuroleptic malignant syndrome (NMS) or pigmentary retinopathy.

Adverse Reactions Frequency not defined.

Cardiovascular: Hyper-/hypotension, tachycardia, arrhythmia, abnormal T waves with prolonged ventricular repolarization, torsade de pointes (case-control study ~4%)

Central nervous system: Restlessness, anxiety, extrapyramidal reactions, dystonic reactions, pseudoparkinsonian signs and symptoms, tardive dyskinesia, neuroleptic malignant syndrome (NMS), altered central temperature regulation, akathisia, tardive dystonia, insomnia, euphoria, agitation, drowsiness, depression, lethargy, headache, confusion, vertigo, seizure

Dermatologic: Hyperpigmentation, pruritus, rash, contact dermatitis, alopecia, photosensitivity (rare)

Endocrine & metabolic: Amenorrhea, galactorrhea, gynecomastia, sexual dysfunction, lactation, breast engorgement, mastalgia, menstrual irregularities, hyperglycemia, hypoglycemia, hyponatremia

Gastrointestinal: Nausea, vomiting, anorexia, constipation, diarrhea, hypersalivation, dyspepsia, xerostomia

Genitourinary: Urinary retention, priapism

Hematologic: Cholestatic jaundice, obstructive jaundice

Ocular: Blurred vision

Respiratory: Laryngospasm, bronchospasm

Miscellaneous: Heat stroke, diaphoresis

Overdosage/Toxicology Symptoms include deep sleep, dystonia, agitation, dysrhythmias, and extrapyramidal symptoms. Following initiation of essential overdose management, toxic symptom treatment and supportive treatment should be initiated. Critical cardiac arrhythmias often respond to I.V. lidocaine, while other antiarrhythmics can be used. Neuroleptics often cause extrapyramidal symptoms (eg, dystonic reactions) requiring management with anticholinergic agents such as benztropine mesylate I.V. 1-2 mg (adult). These agents are generally effective within 2-5 minutes.

Drug Interactions

Cytochrome P450 Effect: Substrate of CYP1A2 (minor), 2D6 (major), 3A4 (major); **Inhibits** CYP2D6 (moderate), 3A4 (moderate)

Increased Effect/Toxicity: Haloperidol concentrations/effects may be increased by chloroquine, propranolol, and sulfadoxine-pyridoxine. The levels/effects of haloperidol may be increased by azole antifungals, chlorpromazine, clarithromycin, delavirdine, diclofenac, doxycycline, erythromycin, fluoxetine, imatinib, isoniazid, miconazole, nefazodone, nicardipine, paroxetine, pergolide, propofol, protease inhibitors, quinidine, quinine, ritonavir, ropinirole, telithromycin, verapamil, and other CYP2D6 or 3A4 inhibitors.

Haloperidol may increase the levels/effects of amphetamines, selected beta-blockers, selected benzodiazepines, calcium channel blockers, cisapride, cyclosporine, dextromethorphan, ergot alkaloids, fluoxetine, selected HMG-CoA reductase inhibitors, lidocaine, mesoridazine, mirtazapine, nateglinide, nefazodone, paroxetine, risperidone, ritonavir, sildenafil (and other PDE-5 inhibitors), tacrolimus, thioridazine, tricyclic antidepressants, venlafaxine, and other substrates of CYP2D6 or 3A4.

Haloperidol may increase the effects of antihypertensives, CNS depressants (ethanol, opioid analgesics, sedative-hypnotics), lithium, trazodone, and TCAs. Haloperidol in combination with indomethacin may result in drowsiness, tiredness, and confusion. Metoclopramide may increase risk of extrapyramidal symptoms (EPS). Acetylcholinesterase inhibitors (central) may increase the risk of antipsychotic-related EPS.

Decreased Effect: Haloperidol may inhibit the ability of bromocriptine to lower serum prolactin concentrations. Benztropine (and other anticholinergics) may inhibit the therapeutic response to haloperidol and excess anticholinergic effects may occur. Barbiturates, carbamazepine, and cigarette smoking may enhance the hepatic metabolism of haloperidol. Haloperidol may inhibit the antiparkinsonian effect of levodopa; avoid this combination. The levels/effects of haloperidol may be decreased by aminoglutethimide, carbamazepine, nafcillin, nevirapine, phenobarbital, phenytoin, rifamycins, and other CYP3A4 inducers. Haloperidol may decrease the levels/effects of CYP2D6 prodrug substrates (eg, codeine, hydrocodone, oxycodone, tramadol).

Ethanol/Nutrition/Herb Interactions

Ethanol: Avoid ethanol (may increase CNS depression).

Herb/Nutraceutical: Avoid valerian, St John's wort, kava kava, gotu kola (may increase CNS depression).

Stability

Protect oral dosage forms from light.

Haloperidol lactate injection should be stored at controlled room temperature; do not freeze or expose to temperatures >40°C. Protect from light; exposure to light may cause discoloration and the development of a grayish-red precipitate over several weeks.

Haloperidol lactate may be administered IVPB or I.V. infusion in D_5W solutions. NS solutions should not be used due to reports of decreased stability and incompatibility.

Standardized dose: 0.5-100 mg/50-100 mL D_5W.

Stability of standardized solutions is 38 days at room temperature (24°C).

Mechanism of Action Haloperidol is a butyrophenone antipsychotic which blocks postsynaptic mesolimbic dopaminergic D_1 and D_2 receptors in the brain; depresses the release of hypothalamic and hypophyseal hormones; believed to depress the reticular activating system (Continued)

Haloperidol *(Continued)*

thus affecting basal metabolism, body temperature, wakefulness, vasomotor tone, and emesis

Pharmacodynamics/Kinetics

Onset of action: Sedation: I.V.: ~1 hour

Duration: Decanoate: ~3 weeks

Distribution: Crosses placenta; enters breast milk

Protein binding: 90%

Metabolism: Hepatic to inactive compounds

Bioavailability: Oral: 60%

Half-life elimination: 20 hours

Time to peak, serum: 20 minutes

Excretion: Urine (33% to 40% as metabolites) within 5 days; feces (15%)

Dosage

Children: 3-12 years (15-40 kg): Oral:

Initial: 0.05 mg/kg/day or 0.25-0.5 mg/day given in 2-3 divided doses; increase by 0.25-0.5 mg every 5-7 days; maximum: 0.15 mg/kg/day

Usual maintenance:

Agitation or hyperkinesia: 0.01-0.03 mg/kg/day once daily

Nonpsychotic disorders: 0.05-0.075 mg/kg/day in 2-3 divided doses

Psychotic disorders: 0.05-0.15 mg/kg/day in 2-3 divided doses

Children 6-12 years: Sedation/psychotic disorders: I.M. (as lactate): 1-3 mg/dose every 4-8 hours to a maximum of 0.15 mg/kg/day; change over to oral therapy as soon as able

Adults:

Psychosis:

Oral: 0.5-5 mg 2-3 times/day; usual maximum: 30 mg/day

I.M. (as lactate): 2-5 mg every 4-8 hours as needed

I.M. (as decanoate): Initial: 10-20 times the daily oral dose administered at 4-week intervals

Maintenance dose: 10-15 times initial oral dose; used to stabilize psychiatric symptoms

Delirium in the intensive care unit (unlabeled use, unlabeled route):

I.V.: 2-10 mg; may repeat bolus doses every 20-30 minutes until calm achieved then administer 25% of the maximum dose every 6 hours; monitor ECG and QT_c interval

Intermittent I.V.: 0.03-0.15 mg/kg every 30 minutes to 6 hours

Oral: Agitation: 5-10 mg

Continuous intravenous infusion (100 mg/100 mL D_5W): Rates of 3-25 mg/hour have been used

Rapid tranquilization of severely-agitated patient (unlabeled use): Administer every 30-60 minutes:

Oral: 5-10 mg

I.M.: 5 mg

Average total dose (oral or I.M.) for tranquilization: 10-20 mg

Elderly: Initial: Oral: 0.25-0.5 mg 1-2 times/day; increase dose at 4- to 7-day intervals by 0.25-0.5 mg/day; increase dosing intervals (twice daily, 3 times/day, etc) as necessary to control response or side effects

Hemodialysis/peritoneal dialysis: Supplemental dose is not necessary

Administration The decanoate injectable formulation should be administered I.M. only, **do not administer decanoate I.V.** Dilute the oral concentrate with water or juice before administration. Avoid skin contact with oral suspension or solution; may cause contact dermatitis.

Monitoring Parameters Vital signs; lipid profile, fasting blood glucose/Hgb A_{1c}; BMI; mental status, abnormal involuntary movement scale (AIMS), extrapyramidal symptoms (EPS)

Reference Range

Therapeutic: 5-20 ng/mL (SI: 10-40 nmol/L) (psychotic disorders - less for Tourette's and mania)

Toxic: >42 ng/mL (SI: >84 nmol/L)

Dosage Forms [DSC] = Discontinued product

Note: Strength expressed as base.

Injection, oil, as decanoate: 50 mg/mL (1 mL, 5 mL); 100 mg/mL (1 mL, 5 mL)

Haldol® Decanoate: 50 mg/mL (1 mL; 5 mL [DSC]); 100 mg/mL (1 mL; 5 mL [DSC]) [contains benzyl alcohol, sesame oil]

Injection, solution, as lactate: 5 mg/mL (1 mL, 10 mL)

Haldol®: 5 mg/mL (1 mL)

Solution, oral concentrate, as lactate: 2 mg/mL (15 mL, 120 mL)

Tablet: 0.5 mg, 1 mg, 2 mg, 5 mg, 10 mg, 20 mg

♦ **Haloperidol Decanoate** *see* Haloperidol *on page 826*

♦ **Haloperidol Injection, USP (Can)** *see* Haloperidol *on page 826*

♦ **Haloperidol-LA (Can)** *see* Haloperidol *on page 826*

♦ **Haloperidol Lactate** *see* Haloperidol *on page 826*

♦ **Haloperidol-LA Omega (Can)** *see* Haloperidol *on page 826*

♦ **Haloperidol Long Acting (Can)** *see* Haloperidol *on page 826*

♦ **Halotestin®** *see* Fluoxymesterone *on page 730*

♦ **Havrix®** *see* Hepatitis A Vaccine *on page 833*

♦ **Havrix® and Engerix-B®** *see* Hepatitis A Inactivated and Hepatitis B (Recombinant) Vaccine *on page 832*

♦ **HbCV** *see* Haemophilus b Conjugate Vaccine *on page 824*

♦ **HBIG** *see* Hepatitis B Immune Globulin *on page 834*

♦ **hBNP** *see* Nesiritide *on page 1215*

♦ **HbOC** *see* Haemophilus b Conjugate Vaccine *on page 824*

♦ **hCG** *see* Chorionic Gonadotropin (Human) *on page 363*

♦ **HCTZ (error-prone abbreviation)** *see* Hydrochlorothiazide *on page 845*

♦ **HDA® Toothache [OTC]** *see* Benzocaine *on page 204*

♦ **HDCV** *see* Rabies Virus Vaccine *on page 1479*
♦ **Head & Shoulders® Intensive Treatment [OTC]** *see* Selenium Sulfide *on page 1555*
♦ **Healon®** *see* Hyaluronate and Derivatives *on page 841*
♦ **Healon®5** *see* Hyaluronate and Derivatives *on page 841*
♦ **Healon GV®** *see* Hyaluronate and Derivatives *on page 841*
♦ **Hectorol®** *see* Doxercalciferol *on page 548*
♦ **Helidac®** *see* Bismuth Subsalicylate, Metronidazole, and Tetracycline *on page 225*
♦ **Helistat®** *see* Collagen Hemostat *on page 416*
♦ **Helitene®** *see* Collagen Hemostat *on page 416*
♦ **Helixate® FS** *see* Antihemophilic Factor (Recombinant) *on page 135*
♦ **Hemabate®** *see* Carboprost Tromethamine *on page 293*
♦ **Hemocyte® [OTC]** *see* Ferrous Fumarate *on page 702*
♦ **Hemofil M** *see* Antihemophilic Factor (Human) *on page 133*
♦ **Hemorrhoidal HC** *see* Hydrocortisone *on page 852*
♦ **Hemril®-30** *see* Hydrocortisone *on page 852*
♦ **HepaGam B™** *see* Hepatitis B Immune Globulin *on page 834*
♦ **Hepalean® (Can)** *see* Heparin *on page 829*
♦ **Hepalean® Leo (Can)** *see* Heparin *on page 829*
♦ **Hepalean®-LOK (Can)** *see* Heparin *on page 829*

Heparin (HEP a rin)

U.S. Brand Names HepFlush®-10; Hep-Lock®; Hep-Lock U/P
Canadian Brand Names Hepalean®; Hepalean® Leo; Hepalean®-LOK
Index Terms Heparin Calcium; Heparin Lock Flush; Heparin Sodium
Pharmacologic Category Anticoagulant
Additional Appendix Information
  Anticoagulants, Injectable *on page 1864*
Use Prophylaxis and treatment of thromboembolic disorders
  Note: Heparin lock flush solution is intended only to maintain patency of I.V. devices and is **not** to be used for anticoagulant therapy.
Unlabeled/Investigational Use Acute MI — combination regimen of heparin (unlabeled dose), tenecteplase (half dose), and abciximab (full dose)
Pregnancy Risk Factor C
Lactation Does not enter breast milk/compatible
Medication Safety Issues
  Sound-alike/look-alike issues:
    Heparin may be confused with Hespan®

  High alert medication: The Institute for Safe Medication Practices (ISMP) includes this medication among its list of drugs which have a heightened risk of causing significant patient harm when used in error.

  Heparin lock flush solution is intended only to maintain patency of I.V. devices and is **not** to be used for anticoagulant therapy.

  Note: The 100 unit/mL concentration should not be used in neonates or infants <10 kg, The 10 unit/mL concentration may cause systemic anticoagulation in infants <1 kg who receive frequent flushes.
Contraindications Hypersensitivity to heparin or any component of the formulation; severe thrombocytopenia; uncontrolled active bleeding except when due to DIC; suspected intracranial hemorrhage; not for I.M. use; not for use when appropriate monitoring parameters cannot be obtained
Warnings/Precautions Use cautiously in patients with a documented hypersensitivity reaction and only in life-threatening situations. Hemorrhage is the most common complication. Monitor for signs and symptoms of bleeding. Certain patients are at increased risk of bleeding. Risk factors include bacterial endocarditis; congenital or acquired bleeding disorders; active ulcerative or angiodysplastic GI diseases; severe uncontrolled hypertension; hemorrhagic stroke; or use shortly after brain, spinal, or ophthalmology surgery; patient treated concomitantly with platelet inhibitors; conditions associated with increased bleeding tendencies (hemophilia, vascular purpura); recent GI bleeding; thrombocytopenia or platelet defects; severe liver disease; hypertensive or diabetic retinopathy; or in patients undergoing invasive procedures. A higher incidence of bleeding has been reported in patients >60 years of age, particularly women. They are also more sensitive to the dose. Discontinue heparin if hemorrhage occurs; severe hemorrhage or overdosage may require protamine.

May cause thrombocytopenia; monitor platelet count closely. Patients who develop thrombocytopenia on heparin may be at risk of developing a new thrombus (heparin-induced thrombocytopenia and thrombosis [HITT]). Discontinue therapy and consider alternatives if platelets are <100,000/mm³ and/or thrombosis develops. HIT or HITT can occur up to several weeks after discontinuation of heparin. Hypersensitivity reactions can occur. Osteoporosis can occur following long-term use (>6 months). Monitor for hyperkalemia. Patients >60 years of age may require lower doses of heparin.

Some preparations contain benzyl alcohol as a preservative. In neonates, large amounts of benzyl alcohol (>100 mg/kg/day) have been associated with fatal toxicity (gasping syndrome). The use of preservative-free heparin is, therefore, recommended in neonates. Some preparations contain sulfite which may cause allergic reactions.

Heparin resistance may occur in patients with fever, thrombosis, thrombophlebitis, infections with thrombosing tendencies, MI, cancer, and in postsurgical patients.
Adverse Reactions
  Cardiovascular: Chest pain, hemorrhagic shock, thrombosis, vasospasm (possibly related to thrombosis)
(Continued)

Heparin *(Continued)*

Central nervous system: Fever, headache, chills

Dermatologic: Unexplained bruising, urticaria, alopecia, dysesthesia pedis, purpura, eczema, cutaneous necrosis (following deep SubQ injection), erythematous plaques (case reports)

Endocrine & metabolic: Hyperkalemia (supression of aldosterone), rebound hyperlipidemia on discontinuation

Gastrointestinal: Nausea, vomiting, constipation, hematemesis

Genitourinary: Frequent or persistent erection

Hematologic: Hemorrhage, blood in urine, bleeding from gums, epistaxis, adrenal hemorrhage, ovarian hemorrhage, retroperitoneal hemorrhage, thrombocytopenia (see note)

Hepatic: Elevated liver enzymes (AST/ALT)

Local: Irritation, ulceration, cutaneous necrosis have been rarely reported with deep SubQ injections; I.M. injection (not recommended) is associated with a high incidence of these effects

Neuromuscular & skeletal: Peripheral neuropathy, osteoporosis (chronic therapy effect)

Ocular: Conjunctivitis (allergic reaction)

Respiratory: Hemoptysis, pulmonary hemorrhage, asthma, rhinitis, bronchospasm (case reports)

Miscellaneous: Allergic reactions, anaphylactoid reactions

Note: Thrombocytopenia has been reported to occur at an incidence between 0% and 30%. It is often of no clinical significance. However, immunologically mediated heparin-induced thrombocytopenia has been estimated to occur in 1% to 2% of patients, and is marked by a progressive fall in platelet counts and, in some cases, thromboembolic complications (skin necrosis, pulmonary embolism, gangrene of the extremities, stroke or MI). For recommendations regarding platelet monitoring during heparin therapy, consult "Seventh ACCP Consensus Conference on Antithrombotic and Thrombolytic Therapy."

Overdosage/Toxicology The primary symptom of overdose is bleeding. The antidote is protamine: 1 mg per 100 units of heparin. Discontinue all heparin if evidence of progressive immune thrombocytopenia occurs.

Drug Interactions

Increased Effect/Toxicity: The risk of hemorrhage associated with heparin may be increased by oral anticoagulants (warfarin), thrombolytics, dextran, and drugs which affect platelet function (eg, aspirin, NSAIDs, dipyridamole, ticlopidine, clopidogrel, IIb/IIIa antagonists). However, heparin is often used in conjunction with thrombolytic therapy or during the initiation of warfarin therapy to assure anticoagulation and to protect against possible transient hypercoagulability. Cephalosporins which contain the MTT side chain and parenteral penicillins (may inhibit platelet aggregation) may increase the risk of hemorrhage. Other drugs reported to increase heparin's anticoagulant effect include antihistamines, tetracycline, quinine, nicotine, and cardiac glycosides (digoxin).

Decreased Effect: Nitroglycerin (I.V.) may decrease heparin's anticoagulant effect. This interaction has not been validated in some studies, and may only occur at high nitroglycerin dosages.

Ethanol/Nutrition/Herb Interactions

Food: When taking for >6 months, may interfere with calcium absorption.

Herb/Nutraceutical: Avoid cat's claw, dong quai, evening primrose, feverfew, red clover, horse chestnut, garlic, green tea, ginseng, ginkgo (all have additional antiplatelet activity).

Stability

Heparin solutions are colorless to slightly yellow; minor color variations do not affect therapeutic efficacy.

Heparin should be stored at controlled room temperature. Protect from freezing and temperatures >40°C.

Stability at room temperature and refrigeration:

Prepared bag: 24 hours.

Premixed bag: After seal is broken 4 days.

Out of overwrap stability: 30 days.

Standard diluent: 25,000 units/500 mL D_5W (premixed).

Minimum volume: 250 mL D_5W.

Mechanism of Action Potentiates the action of antithrombin III and thereby inactivates thrombin (as well as activated coagulation factors IX, X, XI, XII, and plasmin) and prevents the conversion of fibrinogen to fibrin; heparin also stimulates release of lipoprotein lipase (lipoprotein lipase hydrolyzes triglycerides to glycerol and free fatty acids)

Pharmacodynamics/Kinetics

Onset of action: Anticoagulation: I.V.: Immediate; SubQ: ~20-30 minutes

Absorption: Oral, rectal, I.M.: Erratic at best from all these routes of administration; SubQ absorption is also erratic, but considered acceptable for prophylactic use

Distribution: Does not cross placenta; does not enter breast milk

Metabolism: Hepatic; may be partially metabolized in the reticuloendothelial system

Half-life elimination: Mean: 1.5 hours; Range: 1-2 hours; affected by obesity, renal function, hepatic function, malignancy, presence of pulmonary embolism, and infections

Excretion: Urine (small amounts as unchanged drug)

Dosage

Children:

Intermittent I.V.: Initial: 50-100 units/kg, then 50-100 units/kg every 4 hours

I.V. infusion: Initial: 50 units/kg, then 15-25 units/kg/hour; increase dose by 2-4 units/kg/hour every 6-8 hours as required

Adults:

Prophylaxis (low-dose heparin): SubQ: 5000 units every 8-12 hours

Intermittent I.V.: Initial: 10,000 units, then 50-70 units/kg (5000-10,000 units) every 4-6 hours

I.V. infusion (weight-based dosing per institutional nomogram recommended):

Acute coronary syndromes: MI: Fibrinolytic therapy:

Full-dose alteplase, reteplase, or tenecteplase with dosing as follows: Concurrent bolus of 60 units/kg (maximum: 4000 units), then 12 units/kg/hour (maximum: 1000 units/hour) as continuous infusion. Check aPTT every 4-6 hours; adjust to target of 1.5-2 times the upper limit of control (50-70 seconds in clinical trials); usual range 10-30 units/kg/hour. Duration of heparin therapy depends on concurrent therapy and the specific patient risks for systemic or venous thromboembolism.

Combination regimen (unlabeled): Half-dose tenecteplase (15-25 mg based on weight) and abciximab 0.25 mg/kg bolus then 0.125 mcg/kg/minute (maximum 10 mcg/minute) for 12 hours with heparin dosing as follows: Concurrent bolus of 40 units/kg (maximum 3000 units), then 7 units/kg/hour (maximum: 800 units/hour) as continuous infusion. Adjust to a aPTT target of 50-70 seconds.

Streptokinase: Heparin use optional depending on concurrent therapy and specific patient risks for systemic or venous thromboembolism (anterior MI, CHF, previous embolus, atrial fibrillation, LV thrombus): If heparin is administered, start when aPTT <2 times the upper limit of control; do not use a bolus, but initiate infusion adjusted to a target aPTT of 1.5-2 times the upper limit of control (50-70 seconds in clinical trials). If heparin is not administered by infusion, 7500-12,500 units SubQ every 12 hours (when aPTT <2 times the upper limit of control) is recommended.

Percutaneous coronary intervention: Heparin bolus and infusion may be administered to an activated clotting time (ACT) of 300-350 seconds if no concurrent GPIIb/IIIa receptor antagonist is administered or 200-250 seconds if a GPIIb/IIIa receptor antagonist is administered.

Treatment of unstable angina (high-risk and some intermediate-risk patients): Initial bolus of 60-70 units/kg (maximum: 5000 units), followed by an initial infusion of 12-15 units/kg/hour (maximum: 1000 units/hour). The American College of Chest Physicians consensus conference has recommended dosage adjustments to correspond to a therapeutic range equivalent to heparin levels of 0.3-0.7 units/mL by antifactor Xa determinations.

Treatment of venous thromboembolism:

DVT/PE: I.V. push: 80 units/kg followed by continuous infusion of 18 units/kg/hour

DVT: SubQ: 17,500 units every 12 hours

Line flushing: When using daily flushes of heparin to maintain patency of single and double lumen central catheters, 10 units/mL is commonly used for younger infants (eg, <10 kg) while 100 units/mL is used for older infants, children, and adults. Capped PVC catheters and peripheral heparin locks require flushing more frequently (eg, every 6-8 hours). Volume of heparin flush is usually similar to volume of catheter (or slightly greater). Additional flushes should be given when stagnant blood is observed in catheter, after catheter is used for drug or blood administration, and after blood withdrawal from catheter.

Addition of heparin (0.5-3 unit/mL) to peripheral and central parenteral nutrition has not been shown to decrease catheter-related thrombosis. The final concentration of heparin used for TPN solutions may need to be decreased to 0.5 units/mL in small infants receiving larger amounts of volume in order to avoid approaching therapeutic amounts. Arterial lines are heparinized with a final concentration of 1 unit/mL.

Dosing adjustments in the elderly: Patients >60 years of age may have higher serum levels and clinical response (longer aPTTs) as compared to younger patients receiving similar dosages; lower dosages may be required

Administration SubQ: Inject in subcutaneous tissue only (not muscle tissue). Injection sites should be rotated (usually left and right portions of the abdomen, above iliac crest).

Do not administer I.M. due to pain, irritation, and hematoma formation; central venous catheters must be flushed with heparin solution when newly inserted, daily (at the time of tubing change), after blood withdrawal or transfusion, and after an intermittent infusion through an injectable cap. A volume of at least 10 mL of blood should be removed and discarded from a heparinized line before blood samples are sent for coagulation testing.

Monitoring Parameters Platelet counts, hemoglobin, hematocrit, signs of bleeding; aPTT or ACT depending upon indication

For intermittent I.V. injections, aPTT is measured 3.5-4 hours after I.V. injection

Note: Continuous I.V. infusion is preferred over I.V. intermittent injections. For full-dose heparin (ie, nonlow-dose), the dose should be titrated according to aPTT results. For anticoagulation, an aPTT 1.5-2.5 times normal is usually desired. Because of variation among hospitals in the control aPTT values, nomograms should be established at each institution, designed to achieve aPTT values in the target range (eg, for a control aPTT of 30 seconds, the target range [1.5-2.5 times control] would be 45-75 seconds). Measurements should be made prior to heparin therapy, 6 hours after initiation, and 6 hours after any dosage change, and should be used to adjust the heparin infusion until the aPTT exhibits a therapeutic level. When two consecutive aPTT values are therapeutic, the measurements may be made every 24 hours, and if necessary, dose adjustment carried out. In addition, a significant change in the patient's clinical condition (eg, recurrent ischemia, bleeding, hypotension) should prompt an immediate aPTT determination, followed by dose adjustment if necessary. Increase or decrease infusion by 2-4 units/kg/hour dependent upon aPTT.

Heparin infusion dose adjustment:

aPTT >3x control: Decrease infusion rate 50%

aPTT 2-3x control: Decrease infusion rate 25%

aPTT 1.5-2x control: No change

aPTT <1.5x control: Increase rate of infusion 25%; max 2500 units/hour

Reference Range Heparin: 0.3-0.5 unit/mL; aPTT: 1.5-2.5 times **the patient's baseline**

Test Interactions Increased thyroxine (S) (competitive protein binding methods); increased PT

Aprotinin significantly increases aPTT and celite Activated Clotting Time (ACT) which may not reflect the actual degree of anticoagulation by heparin. Kaolin-based ACTs are not affected by aprotinin to the same degree as celite ACTs. While institutional protocols may vary, a minimal celite ACT of 750 seconds or kaolin-ACT of 480 seconds is recommended in the presence of aprotinin. Consult the manufacturer's information on specific ACT test interpretation in the presence of aprotinin.

(Continued)

Heparin *(Continued)*

Additional Information Heparin lock flush solution is intended only to maintain patency of I.V. devices and is **not** to be used for anticoagulant therapy.

Dosage Forms

Infusion, as sodium [premixed in NaCl 0.45%; porcine intestinal mucosa source]: 12,500 units (250 mL); 25,000 units (250 mL, 500 mL)

Infusion, as sodium [preservative free; premixed in D$_5$W; porcine intestinal mucosa source]: 10,000 units (100 mL) [contains sodium metabisulfite]; 12,500 units (250 mL) [contains sodium metabisulfite]; 20,000 units (500 mL) [contains sodium metabisulfite]; 25,000 units (250 mL, 500 mL) [contains sodium metabisulfite]

Infusion, as sodium [preservative free; premixed in NaCl 0.9%; porcine intestinal mucosa source]: 1000 units (500 mL); 2000 units (1000 mL)

Injection, solution, as sodium [lock flush preparation; porcine intestinal mucosa source; multidose vial]: 10 units/mL (1 mL, 10 mL, 30 mL) [contains parabens]; 100 units/mL (1 mL, 5 mL) [contains parabens]

Injection, solution, as sodium [lock flush preparation; porcine intestinal mucosa source; multidose vial]: 10 units/mL (10 mL, 30 mL); 100 units/mL (10 mL, 30 mL) [contains benzyl alcohol]

Hep-Lock®: 10 units/mL (1 mL, 2 mL, 10 mL, 30 mL); 100 units/mL (1 mL, 2 mL, 10 mL, 30 mL) [contains benzyl alcohol]

Injection, solution, as sodium [lock flush preparation; porcine intestinal mucosa source; prefilled syringe]: 10 units/mL (1 mL, 2 mL, 3 mL, 5 mL); 100 units/mL (1 mL, 2 mL, 3 mL, 5 mL) [contains benzyl alcohol]

Injection, solution, as sodium [preservative free; lock flush preparation; porcine intestinal mucosa source; prefilled syringe]: 100 units/mL (5 mL)

Injection, solution, as sodium [preservative free; lock flush preparation; porcine intestinal mucosa source; vial]:

HepFlush®-10: 10 units/mL (10 mL)

Hep-Lock U/P: 10 units/mL (1 mL); 100 units/mL (1 mL)

Injection, solution, as sodium [porcine intestinal mucosa source; multidose vial]: 1000 units/mL (1 mL, 10 mL, 30 mL) [contains benzyl alcohol]; 1000 units/mL (1 mL, 10 mL, 30 mL) [contains methylparabens]; 5000 units/mL (1 mL, 10 mL) [contains benzyl alcohol]; 5000 units/mL (1 mL) [contains methylparabens]; 10,000 units/mL (1 mL, 4 mL) [contains benzyl alcohol]; 10,000 units/mL (1 mL, 5 mL) [contains methylparabens]; 20,000 units/mL (1 mL) [contains methylparabens]

Injection, solution, as sodium [porcine intestinal mucosa source; prefilled syringe]: 5000 units/mL (1 mL) [contains benzyl alcohol]

Injection, solution, as sodium [preservative free; porcine intestinal mucosa source; prefilled syringe]: 10,000 units/mL (0.5 mL)

Injection, solution, as sodium [preservative free; porcine intestinal mucosa source; vial]: 1000 units/mL (2 mL); 2000 units/mL (5 mL); 2500 units/mL (10 mL)

♦ **Heparin Calcium** *see* Heparin *on page 829*
♦ **Heparin Cofactor I** *see* Antithrombin III *on page 137*
♦ **Heparin Lock Flush** *see* Heparin *on page 829*
♦ **Heparin Sodium** *see* Heparin *on page 829*

Hepatitis A Inactivated and Hepatitis B (Recombinant) Vaccine
(hep a TYE tis aye in ak ti VAY ted & hep a TYE tis bee ree KOM be nant vak SEEN)

U.S. Brand Names Twinrix®
Canadian Brand Names Twinrix®
Index Terms Engerix-B® and Havrix®; Havrix® and Engerix-B®; Hepatitis B (Recombinant) and Hepatitis A Inactivated Vaccine
Pharmacologic Category Vaccine
Use Active immunization against disease caused by hepatitis A virus and hepatitis B virus (all known subtypes) in populations desiring protection against or at high risk of exposure to these viruses.

Populations include travelers to areas of intermediate/high endemicity for **both** HAV and HBV; those at increased risk of HBV infection due to behavioral or occupational factors; patients with chronic liver disease; laboratory workers who handle live HAV and HBV; healthcare workers, police, and other personnel who render first-aid or medical assistance; workers who come in contact with sewage; employees of day care centers and correctional facilities; patients/staff of hemodialysis units; male homosexuals; patients frequently receiving blood products; military personnel; users of injectable illicit drugs; close household contacts of patients with hepatitis A and hepatitis B infection.

Pregnancy Risk Factor C
Dosage I.M.: Adults: Primary immunization: Three doses (1 mL each) given on a 0-, 1-, and 6-month schedule

Alternative regimen (unlabeled use): Accelerated regimen (1 mL doses at day 0, 7, and 21, followed by a booster at 12 months) has demonstrated similar safety, tolerability, and immunogenicity to the standard regimen. While not formally endorsed in the U.S. for routine vaccination, this administration schedule may be effective for use in individuals with short-notice travel to endemic regions.

Additional Information Complete prescribing information for this medication should be consulted for additional detail.

Dosage Forms

Injection, suspension:

Twinrix®: Inactivated hepatitis A virus 720 ELISA units and hepatitis B surface antigen 20 mcg per mL (1 mL)

Hepatitis A Vaccine (hep a TYE tis aye vak SEEN)

U.S. Brand Names Havrix®; VAQTA®
Canadian Brand Names Avaxim®; Avaxim®-Pediatric; Havrix®; VAQTA®
Pharmacologic Category Vaccine
Additional Appendix Information
Immunization Recommendations *on page 1929*
USPHS / IDSA Guidelines for the Prevention of Opportunistic Infections in Persons Infected With HIV *on page 1966*

Use
Active immunization against disease caused by hepatitis A virus in populations desiring protection against or at high risk of exposure
Populations at high risk of exposure to hepatitis A virus may include children and adolescents in selected states and regions, travelers to developing countries, household and sexual contacts of persons infected with hepatitis A, child day care employees, patients with chronic liver disease, illicit drug users, male homosexuals, institutional workers (eg, institutions for the mentally and physically handicapped persons, prisons), and healthcare workers who may be exposed to hepatitis A virus (eg, laboratory employees)

Pregnancy Risk Factor C
Pregnancy Implications Reproduction studies have not been conducted. The safety of vaccination during pregnancy has not been determined, however, the theoretical risk to the infant is expected to be low.
Lactation Excretion in breast milk unknown/use caution
Contraindications Hypersensitivity to hepatitis A vaccine or any component of the formulation
Warnings/Precautions Use caution in patients on anticoagulants, with thrombocytopenia, or bleeding disorders (bleeding may occur following intramuscular injection). Treatment for anaphylactic reactions should be immediately available. Postpone vaccination with acute infection or febrile illness. May not prevent infection if adequate antibody titers are not achieved (including immunosuppressed patients, patients on immunosuppressant therapy).
Adverse Reactions All serious adverse reactions must be reported to the U.S. Department of Health and Human Services (DHHS) Vaccine Adverse Event Reporting System (VAERS) 1-800-822-7967.
Frequency dependent upon age, product used, and concomitant vaccine administration. In general, injection site reactions were less common in younger children.
>10%:
Central nervous system: Irritability (11% to 36%), drowsiness (15% to 17%), headache (2% to 16%), fever ≥100.4°F (9% to 11%)
Gastrointestinal: Anorexia (1% to 19%)
Local: Injection site: Pain, soreness, tenderness (3% to 56%), erythema (1% to 22%), warmth (<1% to 17%), swelling (1% to 14%)
1% to 10%:
Central nervous system: Fever ≥102°F (3% to 4%)
Dermatologic: Rash (≤1% to 5%)
Endocrine & metabolic: Menstrual disorder (1%)
Gastrointestinal: Diarrhea (<1% to 6%), vomiting (<1% to 4%), nausea (2%), abdominal pain (<1% to 2%), anorexia (1%)
Local: Injection site bruising (1% to 2%)
Neuromuscular & skeletal: Weakness/fatigue (4%), myalgia (<1% to 2%), arm pain (1%), back pain (1%), stiffness (1%)
Ocular: Conjunctivitis (1%)
Otic: Otitis media (8%), otitis (2%)
Respiratory: Upper respiratory tract infection (<1% to 10%), rhinorrhea (6%), cough (1% to 5%), pharyngitis (<1% to 3%), respiratory congestion (2%), nasal congestion (1%), laryngotracheobronchitis (1%)
Miscellaneous: Crying (2%), viral exanthema (1%)
<1% (Limited to important or life threatening): Allergic reaction, anaphylaxis, angioedema, arthralgia, asthma, bronchial constriction, cerebellar ataxia, CK increased, dermatitis, dizziness, dyspnea, encephalitis, erythema multiforme, eosinophilia, Guillain-Barre syndrome, hepatitis, hyperhydrosis, hypertonic episode, injection site hematoma, injection site itching, injection site rash, insomnia, jaundice, liver function tests increased, lymphadenopathy, multiple sclerosis, myelitis, neuropathy, paresthesia, photophobia, pruritus, seizure, somnolence, syncope, taste disturbance, thrombocytopenia, urine protein increased, vertigo, wheezing

Stability Store under refrigeration at 2°C to 8°C (36°F to 46°F); do not freeze.
Mechanism of Action As an inactivated virus vaccine, hepatitis A vaccine offers active immunization against hepatitis A virus infection at an effective immune response rate in up to 99% of subjects
Pharmacodynamics/Kinetics
Onset of action (protection): 4 weeks after a single dose
Duration: Neutralizing antibodies have persisted for up to 8 years; based on kinetic models, antibodies may be present >20 years
Dosage I.M.:
Havrix®:
Children 12 months to 18 years: 720 ELISA units (0.5 mL) with a booster dose of 720 ELISA units 6-12 months following primary immunization
Adults: 1440 ELISA units (1 mL) with a booster dose of 1440 ELISA units 6-12 months following primary immunization
VAQTA®:
Children 12 months to 18 years: 25 units (0.5 mL) with 25 units (0.5 mL) booster dose of 25 units to be given 6-18 months after primary immunization (6-12 months if initial dose was with Havrix®)
(Continued)

Hepatitis A Vaccine *(Continued)*

Adults: 50 units (1 mL) with 50 units (1 mL) booster dose of 50 units to be given 6-18 months after primary immunization (6-12 months if initial dose was with Havrix®)

Administration The deltoid muscle is the preferred site for injection. Shake well prior to use. For optimal protection, travelers should receive 1st dose at least 4 weeks prior to departure. For patients at risk of hemorrhage following intramuscular injection, the ACIP recommends "it should be administered intramuscularly if, in the opinion of the physician familiar with the patients bleeding risk, the vaccine can be administered with reasonable safety by this route. If the patient receives antihemophilia or other similar therapy, intramuscular vaccination can be scheduled shortly after such therapy is administered. A fine needle (23 gauge or smaller) can be used for the vaccination and firm pressure applied to the site (without rubbing) for at least 2 minutes. The patient should be instructed concerning the risk of hematoma from the injection."

Monitoring Parameters Liver function tests

Additional Information Some investigators suggest simultaneous or sequential administration of inactivated hepatitis A vaccine and immune globulin for postexposure protection, especially for travelers requiring rapid immunization, although a slight decrease in vaccine immunogenicity may be observed with this technique. Federal law requires that the date of administration, the vaccine manufacturer, lot number of vaccine, and the administering person's name, title and address be entered into the patient's permanent medical record.

Dosage Forms

Injection, suspension, adult:

Havrix®: Viral antigen 1440 ELISA units/mL (1 mL) [contains trace amounts of neomycin; syringe plunger contains latex rubber; available in prefilled syringe or single-dose vial]

VAQTA®: HAV antigen 50 units/mL (1 mL) [vial stopper and syringe plunger contain latex rubber; available in prefilled syringe or single-dose vial]

Injection, suspension, pediatric (Havrix®): Viral antigen 720 ELISA units/0.5 mL (0.5 mL) [contains trace amounts of neomycin; syringe plunger contains latex rubber; available in prefilled syringe or single-dose vial]

Injection, suspension, pediatric/adolescent (VAQTA®): HAV antigen 25 units/0.5 mL (0.5 mL) [vial stopper and syringe plunger contain latex rubber; available in prefilled syringe or single-dose vial]

Hepatitis B Immune Globulin *(hep a TYE tis bee i MYUN GLOB yoo lin)*

U.S. Brand Names BayHep B® [DSC]; HepaGam B™; HyperHEP B™ S/D; Nabi-HB®

Canadian Brand Names BayHep B®; HyperHEP B®

Index Terms HBIG

Pharmacologic Category Immune Globulin

Additional Appendix Information

Immunization Recommendations *on page 1929*

Use Passive prophylactic immunity to hepatitis B following: Acute exposure to blood containing hepatitis B surface antigen (HBsAg); perinatal exposure of infants born to HBsAg-positive mothers; sexual exposure to HBsAg-positive persons; household exposure to persons with acute HBV infection

Note: Hepatitis B immune globulin is not indicated for treatment of active hepatitis B infection and is ineffective in the treatment of chronic active hepatitis B infection.

Unlabeled/Investigational Use

Prevention of hepatitis B virus recurrence after liver transplantation

Pregnancy Risk Factor C

Pregnancy Implications Reproduction studies have not been conducted.

Lactation Excretion in breast milk unknown/use caution

Contraindications Hypersensitivity to hepatitis B immune globulin or any component of the formulation; severe allergy to gamma globulin or anti-immunoglobulin therapies

Warnings/Precautions Have epinephrine 1:1000 available for anaphylactic reactions. As a product of human plasma, this product may potentially transmit disease; screening of donors, as well as testing and/or inactivation of certain viruses reduces this risk. Use caution in patients with thrombocytopenia or coagulation disorders (I.M. injections may be contraindicated), in patients with isolated IgA deficiency, or in patients with previous systemic hypersensitivity to human immunoglobulins. Not approved for intravenous administration.

Adverse Reactions Frequency not defined.

Central nervous system: Chills, dizziness, fever, headache, lethargy, malaise

Dermatologic: Angioedema, erythema, rash, urticaria

Gastrointestinal: Nausea, vomiting

Genitourinary: Nephrotic syndrome

Local: Muscular stiffness, pain, and tenderness at injection site

Neuromuscular & skeletal: Arthralgia, back pain, myalgia

Miscellaneous: Anaphylaxis, flu-like syndrome

Drug Interactions

Decreased Effect:

Interferes with immune response of live virus vaccines; defer live virus vaccine for about 3 months after immune globulin

Note: HBIG may be administered at the same time (but at a different site) or up to 1 month preceding hepatitis B vaccination without impairing the active immune response

Stability Refrigerate at 2°C to 8°C (36°F to 46°F); do not freeze. Use within 6 hours of entering vial.

Mechanism of Action Hepatitis B immune globulin (HBIG) is a nonpyrogenic sterile solution containing immunoglobulin G (IgG) specific to hepatitis B surface antigen (HBsAg). HBIG differs from immune globulin in the amount of anti-HBs. Immune globulin is prepared from plasma that is not preselected for anti-HBs content. HBIG is prepared from plasma preselected for high titer anti-HBs. In the U.S., HBIG has an anti-HBs high titer >1:100,000 by IRA.

Pharmacodynamics/Kinetics
Absorption: Slow

Half-life: 17-25 days

Distribution: V_d: 7-15 L

Time to peak, serum: 2-10 days

Dosage I.M.:
Newborns: Hepatitis B: 0.5 mL as soon after birth as possible (within 12 hours); may repeat at 3 months in order for a higher rate of prevention of the carrier state to be achieved; at this time an active vaccination program with the vaccine may begin

Infants <12 months: Household exposure prophylaxis: 0.5 mL (to be administered if mother or primary caregiver has acute HBV infection)

Adults: Postexposure prophylaxis: 0.06 mL/kg as soon as possible after exposure (ie, within 24 hours of needlestick, ocular, or mucosal exposure or within 14 days of sexual exposure); usual dose: 3-5 mL; repeat at 28-30 days after exposure in nonresponders or in patients who refuse vaccination

Note: HBIG may be administered at the same time (but at a different site) or up to 1 month preceding hepatitis B vaccination without impairing the active immune response

I.V. (unlabeled route of administration):

Prevention of hepatitis B virus recurrence after liver transplantation (unlabeled use): Consult institutional protocols; specific protocols may vary among transplant centers. Typical HBIG protocols (Nabi-HB®): 10,000-20,000 units intraoperatively during anhepatic phase, followed by 10,000 units daily for 7 days, then as required to maintain adequate quantitative HB_s antibody levels. Used in combination with nucleoside analog (eg, lamivudine) with anti-HBV activity. Subsequent HBIG doses may be administered at fixed intervals or on an "as needed" basis to maintain goal antibody level. Goal antibody titers and HBIG requirements may differ among patients depending upon viral load pretransplant and the presence of other risk factors for recurrence.

Administration I.M. injection only in anterolateral aspect of upper thigh and deltoid muscle of upper arm; to prevent injury from injection, care should be taken when giving to patients with thrombocytopenia or bleeding disorders; has been administered intravenously in hepatitis B-positive liver transplant patients (unlabeled route)

Additional Information Each vial contains anti-HB_s antibody equivalent to or exceeding the potency of anti-HB_s in a U.S. reference standard hepatitis B immune globulin (FDA). The U.S. reference standard has been tested against the WHO standard hepatitis B immune globulin with listed values between 207 int. units/mL and 220 int. units/mL (included in individual product information).

Dosage Forms Note: Potency expressed in international units as compared to the WHO standard

Injection, solution [preservative free]:

BayHepB® [DSC], HyperHEP B™ S/D: 15% to 18% (0.5 mL) [neonatal single-dose syringe]; (1 mL) [single-dose syringe or single-dose vial]; (5 mL) [single-dose vial]

Nabi-HB®: 5% (1 mL, 5 mL) [>312 int. units/mL; single-dose vial]

HepaGam B™: 5% (1 mL, 5 mL) [>312 int. units/mL; contains maltose, single-dose vial]

♦ **Hepatitis B Inactivated Virus Vaccine (recombinant DNA)** *see* Hepatitis B Vaccine *on* page 835

♦ **Hepatitis B (Recombinant) and Hepatitis A Inactivated Vaccine** *see* Hepatitis A Inactivated and Hepatitis B (Recombinant) Vaccine *on* page 832

Hepatitis B Vaccine (hep a TYE tis bee vak SEEN)

U.S. Brand Names Engerix-B®; Recombivax HB®

Canadian Brand Names Engerix-B®; Recombivax HB®

Index Terms Hepatitis B Inactivated Virus Vaccine (recombinant DNA)

Pharmacologic Category Vaccine

Additional Appendix Information

Immunization Recommendations *on page 1929*

Management of Healthcare Worker Exposures to HBV, HCV, and HIV *on page 1941*

USPHS / IDSA Guidelines for the Prevention of Opportunistic Infections in Persons Infected With HIV *on page 1966*

Use Immunization against infection caused by all known subtypes of hepatitis B virus (HBV), in individuals seeking protection from HBV infection and/or in the following individuals considered at high risk of potential exposure to hepatitis B virus or HB_sAg-positive materials:

Workplace Exposure:
- Healthcare workers[1] (including students, custodial staff, lab personnel, etc)
- Police and fire personnel
- Military personnel
- Morticians and embalmers
- Clients/staff of institutions for the developmentally disabled

Lifestyle Factors:
- Homosexual men
- Heterosexually-active persons with multiple partners in a 6-month period or those with recently acquired sexually-transmitted disease
- Intravenous drug users

Specific Patient Groups:
- Those on hemodialysis[2], receiving transfusions[3], or in hematology/oncology units
- Adolescents
- Infants born of HBsAG-positive mothers
- Individuals with chronic liver disease
- Individual with HIV infection

Others:
- Prison inmates and staff of correctional facilities

(Continued)

Hepatitis B Vaccine *(Continued)*

- Household and sexual contacts of HBV carriers
- Residents, immigrants, adoptees, and refugees from areas with endemic HBV infection (eg, Alaskan Eskimos, Pacific Islanders, Indochinese, and Haitian decent)
- International travelers to areas of endemic HBV
- Children born after 11/21/1991

[1]The risk of hepatitis B virus (HBV) infection for healthcare workers varies both between hospitals and within hospitals. Hepatitis B vaccination is recommended for all healthcare workers with blood exposure.

[2]Hemodialysis patients often respond poorly to hepatitis B vaccination; higher vaccine doses or increased number of doses are required. A special formulation of one vaccine is now available for such persons (Recombivax HB®, 40 mcg/mL). The anti-HB$_s$(antibody to hepatitis B surface antigen) response of such persons should be tested after they are vaccinated, and those who have not responded should be revaccinated with 1-3 additional doses. Patients with chronic renal disease should be vaccinated as early as possible, ideally before they require hemodialysis. In addition, their anti-HB$_s$ levels should be monitored at 6- to 12-month intervals to assess the need for revaccination.

[3]Patients with hemophilia should be immunized subcutaneously, not intramuscularly.

Pregnancy Risk Factor C

Pregnancy Implications Reproduction studies have not been conducted. The ACIP suggests vaccination should be considered if otherwise indicated.

Lactation Excretion in breast milk unknown/use caution

Medication Safety Issues
    Sound-alike/look-alike issues:
        Recombivax HB® may be confused with Comvax®

Contraindications Hypersensitivity to yeast, hepatitis B vaccine, or any component of the formulation

Warnings/Precautions Immediate treatment for anaphylactic/anaphylactoid reaction should be available during vaccine use. Consider delaying vaccination during acute, moderate-to-severe febrile illness. Use caution with decreased cardiopulmonary function Unrecognized hepatitis B infection may be present, immunization may not prevent infection in these patients Patients >65 years may have lower response rates. Consider delaying vaccination for ≥3 months after receiving immunosuppressive therapy. Use caution in multiple sclerosis patients; rare exacerbations of symptoms have been observed. Some dosage forms contain dry natural latex rubber.

Adverse Reactions All serious adverse reactions must be reported to the U.S. Department of Health and Human Services (DHHS) Vaccine Adverse Event Reporting System (VAERS) 1-800-822-7967.

Frequency not defined. The most common adverse effects reported with both products included injection site reactions (>10%).

Cardiovascular: Flushing, hypotension

Central nervous system: Agitation, chills, dizziness, fatigue, fever (≥37.5°C / 100°F), headache, insomnia, irritability, lightheadedness, malaise, somnolence, vertigo

Dermatologic: Angioedema, petechiae, pruritus, rash, urticaria

Gastrointestinal: Abdominal pain, appetite decreased, constipation, cramps, diarrhea, dyspepsia, nausea, vomiting

Genitourinary: Dysuria

Local: Injection site reactions: Ecchymosis, erythema, induration, pain, nodule formation, soreness, swelling, tenderness, warmth

Neuromuscular & skeletal: Achiness, arthralgia, back pain, myalgia, neck pain, neck stiffness, paresthesia, shoulder pain, tingling, weakness

Otic: Earache

Respiratory: Cough, pharyngitis, rhinitis, upper respiratory tract infection

Miscellaneous: Diaphoresis, lymphadenopathy, flu-like syndrome

Postmarketing and/or case reports: Alopecia, anaphylaxis, arthritis, Bell's palsy, bronchospasm, conjunctivitis, eczema, encephalitis, erythema nodosum, erythema multiforme, erythrocyte sedimentation rate increased, Guillain-Barré syndrome, herpes zoster, hypoesthesia, keratitis, liver enzymes increased, lupus-like syndrome, migraine, multiple sclerosis, neuropathy, optic neuritis, palpitation, paresis, paresthesia, polyarteritis nodosa, purpura, seizure, serum-sickness like syndrome (may be delayed days to weeks), Stevens-Johnson syndrome, SLE, syncope, tachycardia, thrombocytopenia, tinnitus, transverse myelitis, vasculitis, visual disturbances, vertigo

Drug Interactions
    Decreased Effect: Concomitant immunosuppressive agents may decrease efficacy of vaccine; consider deferring vaccination for at least 3 months after immunosuppressant therapy is discontinued.

Stability Refrigerate at 2°C to 8°C (36°F to 46°F); do not freeze.

Mechanism of Action Recombinant hepatitis B vaccine is a noninfectious subunit viral vaccine, which confers active immunity via formation of antihepatitis B antibodies. The vaccine is derived from hepatitis B surface antigen (HB$_s$Ag) produced through recombinant DNA techniques from yeast cells. The portion of the hepatitis B gene which codes for HB$_s$Ag is cloned into yeast which is then cultured to produce hepatitis B vaccine.

Pharmacodynamics/Kinetics Duration of action: Following a 3-dose series in children, up to 50% of patients will have low or undetectable anti-HB antibody 5-15 years postvaccination. However, anamnestic increases in anti-HB have been shown up to 23 years later suggesting a lifelong immune memory response.

Dosage I.M.:
    Immunization regimen: Regimen consists of 3 doses (0, 1, and 6 months): First dose given on the elected date, second dose given 1 month later, third dose given 6 months after the first dose; see table on next page.
    Note: Infants born to mothers whose HBsAg status is unknown should follow the regimen for HBsAg-positive mothers, omitting the dose of HBIG.

Note: Preterm infants <2000 g and born to HBsAg-negative mothers should have the first dose delayed until 1 month after birth or hospital discharge due to decreased immune response in underweight infants.

Routine Immunization Regimen of Three I.M. Hepatitis B Vaccine Doses

Age	Initial		1 mo		2 mo	6 mo[1]	
	Recombivax HB® (mL)	Engerix-B® (mL)	Recombivax HB® (mL)	Engerix-B® (mL)	Engerix-B® (mL)	Recombivax HB® (mL)	Engerix-B® (mL)
Birth[2] to 19 y	0.5[3]	0.5[4]	0.5[3]	0.5[4]	--	0.5[3]	0.5[4]
≥20 y[5]	1[6]	1[7]	1[6]	1[7]	--	1[6]	1[7]
Dialysis or immuno-compromised patients[8]	1[9]	2[10]	1[9]	2[10]	2[10]	1[9]	2[10]

[1]Final dose in series should not be administered before age of 24 weeks
[2]Infants born of HBsAg **negative** mothers.
[3]5 mcg/0.5 mL pediatric/adolescent formulation
[4]10 mcg/0.5 mL formulation
[5]Alternately, doses may be administered at 0, 1, and 4 months **or** at 0, 2, and 4 months
[6]10 mcg/mL adult formulation
[7]20 mcg/mL formulation
[8]Revaccinate if anti-HBs <10 mIU/mL ≥1-2 months after third dose.
[9]40 mcg/mL dialysis formulation
[10]Two 1 mL doses given at different sites using the 20 mcg/mL formulation

Alternative dosing schedule for **Recombivax HB®**:
  Children 11-15 years (10 mcg/mL adult formulation): First dose of 1 mL given on the elected date, second dose given 4-6 months later
  Adults ≥20 years: Doses may be administered at 0, 1, and 4 months **or** at 0, 2, and 4 months

Alternative dosing schedules for **Engerix-B®**:
  Children ≤10 years (10 mcg/0.5 mL formulation): High-risk children: 0.5 mL at 0, 1, 2, and 12 months; lower-risk children ages 5-10 who are candidates for an extended administration schedule may receive an alternative regimen of 0.5 mL at 0, 12, and 24 months. If booster dose is needed, revaccinate with 0.5 mL.
  Adolescents 11-19 years (20 mcg/mL formulation): 1 mL at 0, 1, and 6 months. High-risk adolescents: 1 mL at 0, 1, 2, and 12 months; lower-risk adolescents 11-16 years who are candidates for an extended administration schedule may receive an alternative regimen of 0.5 mL (using the 10 mcg/0.5 mL) formulation at 0, 12, and 24 months. If booster dose is needed, revaccinate with 20 mcg.
  Adults ≥20 years:
    Doses may be administered at 0, 1, and 4 months **or** at 0, 2, and 4 months
    High-risk adults (20 mcg/mL formulation): 1 mL at 0, 1, 2, and 12 months. If booster dose is needed, revaccinate with 1 mL.

Postexposure prophylaxis: **Note:** High-risk individuals may include children born of hepatitis B-infected mothers, those who have been or might be exposed or those who have traveled to high-risk areas. See table.

Postexposure Prophylaxis Recommended Dosage for Infants Born to HBs Ag-Positive Mothers

Treatment	Birth ≤12 h	1 mo	6 mo
Engerix-B® (pediatric formulation 10 mcg/0.5 mL)[1]	0.5 mL[2]	0.5 mL	0.5 mL
Recombivax HB® (pediatric/adolescent formulation 5 mcg/0.5 mL)	0.5 mL[2]	0.5 mL	0.5 mL
Hepatitis B immune globulin	0.5 mL[2]	—	—

[1]An alternate regimen is administration of the vaccine at birth, and 1, 2, and 12 months later.
[2]The first dose of vaccine may be given at birth at the same time as HBIG, but give in the opposite anterolateral thigh. This may better ensure vaccine absorption. HBIG should be given immediately if mother is determined to be HBsAg-positive within 7 days of birth.

Administration It is possible to interchange the vaccines for completion of a series or for booster doses; the antibody produced in response to each type of vaccine is comparable, however, the quantity of the vaccine will vary

I.M. injection only; in adults, the deltoid muscle is the preferred site; the anterolateral thigh is the recommended site in infants and young children. Not for gluteal administration. Shake well prior to withdrawal and use.

For patients at risk of hemorrhage following intramuscular injection, hepatitis B vaccine may be administered subcutaneously although lower titers and/or increased incidence of local reactions may result. The ACIP recommends "it should be administered intramuscularly if, in the opinion of the physician familiar with the patients bleeding risk, the vaccine can be administered with reasonable safety by this route. If the patient receives antihemophilia or other similar therapy, intramuscular vaccination can be scheduled shortly after such therapy is administered. A fine needle (23 gauge or smaller) can be used for the vaccination and firm pressure applied to the site (without rubbing) for at least 2 minutes. The patient should be instructed concerning the risk of hematoma from the injection."

Federal law requires that the date of administration, the vaccine manufacturer, lot number of vaccine, and the administering person's name, title, and address be entered into the patient's permanent medical record.
(Continued)

Hepatitis B Vaccine *(Continued)*

Additional Information Inactivated virus vaccine. Federal law requires that the date of administration, the vaccine manufacturer, lot number of vaccine, and the administering person's name, title, and address be entered into the patient's permanent medical record.

Dosage Forms Injection, suspension [preservative free] [recombinant DNA]:
Engerix-B®:
Adult: Hepatitis B surface antigen 20 mcg/mL (1 mL) [contains trace amounts of thimerosal; some dosage forms contain dry natural latex rubber]
Pediatric/adolescent: Hepatitis B surface antigen 10 mcg/0.5 mL (0.5 mL) [contains trace amounts of thimerosal; some dosage forms contain dry natural latex rubber]
Recombivax HB®:
Adult: Hepatitis B surface antigen 10 mcg/mL (1 mL, 3 mL)
Dialysis: Hepatitis B surface antigen 40 mcg/mL (1 mL)
Pediatric/adolescent: Hepatitis B surface antigen 5 mcg/0.5 mL (0.5 mL)

- **Hepatitis b Vaccine (Recombinant)** *see* Haemophilus b Conjugate and Hepatitis B Vaccine *on page 823*
- **HepFlush®-10** *see* Heparin *on page 829*
- **Hep-Lock®** *see* Heparin *on page 829*
- **Hep-Lock U/P®** *see* Heparin *on page 829*
- **Hepsera™** *see* Adefovir *on page 49*
- **Heptovir® (Can)** *see* Lamivudine *on page 971*
- **Herceptin®** *see* Trastuzumab *on page 1724*
- **HES** *see* Hetastarch *on page 838*
- **Hespan®** *see* Hetastarch *on page 838*

Hetastarch *(HET a starch)*

U.S. Brand Names Hespan®; Hextend®
Canadian Brand Names Hextend®; Voluven®
Index Terms HES; Hydroxyethyl Starch
Pharmacologic Category Plasma Volume Expander, Colloid
Use Blood volume expander used in treatment of hypovolemia
Hespan®: Adjunct in leukapheresis to improve harvesting and increasing the yield of granulocytes by centrifugal means
Unlabeled/Investigational Use Hextend®: Priming fluid in pump oxygenators during cardiopulmonary bypass, and as a plasma volume expander during cardiopulmonary bypass
Pregnancy Risk Factor C
Medication Safety Issues
Sound-alike/look-alike issues:
Hespan® may be confused with heparin
Dosage I.V. infusion (requires an infusion pump):
Children: Safety and efficacy have not been established
Plasma volume expansion:
Adults: 500-1000 mL (up to 1500 mL/day) or 20 mL/kg/day (up to 1500 mL/day); larger volumes (15,000 mL/24 hours) have been used safely in small numbers of patients
Leukapheresis: 250-700 mL; **Note:** Citrate anticoagulant is added before use.
Dosing adjustment in renal impairment: Cl_{cr} <10 mL/minute: Initial dose is the same but subsequent doses should be reduced by 20% to 50% of normal
Additional Information Complete prescribing information for this medication should be consulted for additional detail.
Dosage Forms
Infusion [premixed in lactated electrolyte injection] (Hextend®): 6% (500 mL)
Infusion, solution [premixed in NaCl 0.9%] (Hespan®): 6% (500 mL)

- **Hexachlorocyclohexane** *see* Lindane *on page 1016*

Hexachlorophene *(heks a KLOR oh feen)*

U.S. Brand Names pHisoHex®
Canadian Brand Names pHisoHex®
Pharmacologic Category Antibiotic, Topical
Use Surgical scrub and as a bacteriostatic skin cleanser; control an outbreak of gram-positive infection when other procedures have been unsuccessful
Pregnancy Risk Factor C
Medication Safety Issues
Sound-alike/look-alike issues:
pHisoHex® may be confused with Fostex®, pHisoDerm®
Dosage Children and Adults: Topical: Apply 5 mL cleanser and water to area to be cleansed; lather and rinse thoroughly under running water
Additional Information Complete prescribing information for this medication should be consulted for additional detail.
Dosage Forms Liquid, topical: 3% (150 mL, 500 mL, 3840 mL)

- **Hexalen®** *see* Altretamine *on page 82*
- **Hexamethylenetetramine** *see* Methenamine *on page 1106*
- **Hexamethylmelamine** *see* Altretamine *on page 82*
- **Hexit™ (Can)** *see* Lindane *on page 1016*
- **HEXM** *see* Altretamine *on page 82*
- **Hextend®** *see* Hetastarch *on page 838*
- **hFSH** *see* Urofollitropin *on page 1759*

- **hGH** *see* Somatropin *on page 1586*
- **Hib Conjugate Vaccine** *see* Haemophilus b Conjugate and Hepatitis B Vaccine *on page 823*
- **Hib Conjugate Vaccine** *see* Haemophilus b Conjugate Vaccine *on page 824*
- **Hibiclens® [OTC]** *see* Chlorhexidine Gluconate *on page 344*
- **Hibidil® 1:2000 (Can)** *see* Chlorhexidine Gluconate *on page 344*
- **Hibistat® [OTC]** *see* Chlorhexidine Gluconate *on page 344*
- **Hib Polysaccharide Conjugate** *see* Haemophilus b Conjugate Vaccine *on page 824*
- **HibTITER®** *see* Haemophilus b Conjugate Vaccine *on page 824*
- **High Gamma Vitamin E Complete™ [OTC]** *see* Vitamin E *on page 1794*
- **Hiprex®** *see* Methenamine *on page 1106*
- **Hirulog** *see* Bivalirudin *on page 227*
- **Histade™** *see* Chlorpheniramine and Pseudoephedrine *on page 350*
- **Hista-Vent® DA** *see* Chlorpheniramine, Phenylephrine, and Methscopolamine *on page 353*
- **Histex™** *see* Chlorpheniramine and Pseudoephedrine *on page 350*
- **Histex™ HC** *see* Hydrocodone, Carbinoxamine, and Pseudoephedrine *on page 851*
- **Histex™ SR** *see* Brompheniramine and Pseudoephedrine *on page 243*

Histrelin (his TREL in)

U.S. Brand Names Vantas™
Canadian Brand Names Vantas™
Index Terms GnRH Agonist; Histrelin Acetate; LH-RH Agonist
Pharmacologic Category Gonadotropin Releasing Hormone Agonist
Use Palliative treatment of advanced prostate cancer
Pregnancy Risk Factor X
Pregnancy Implications Fetal harm and an increase in fetal mortalities have been noted in animal studies. Histrelin is contraindicated for use in females.
Lactation Excretion in breast milk unknown/contraindicated
Contraindications Hypersensitivity to histrelin acetate, GnRH, GnRH-agonist analogs, or any component of the formulation; children; females
Warnings/Precautions Transient increases in testosterone serum levels occur during the first week of use. Worsening symptoms such as bone pain, neuropathy, ureteral or bladder outlet obstruction, and spinal cord compression have been reported. Spinal cord compression and ureteral obstruction may contribute to paralysis; close attention should be given during the first few weeks of therapy to both patients having metastatic vertebral lesions and/or urinary tract obstructions, and to any patients reporting weakness, paresthesias or poor urine output. Safety and efficacy have not been established in patients with hepatic dysfunction.
Adverse Reactions
>10%: Endocrine & metabolic: Expected pharmacological consequence of testosterone suppression: Hot flashes (66%)
2% to 10%:
Central nervous system: Fatigue (10%), headache (3%), insomnia (3%)
Endocrine & metabolic: Expected pharmacological consequences of testosterone suppression: Gynecomastia (4%), sexual dysfunction (4%), libido decreased (2%)
Gastrointestinal: Constipation (4%), weight gain (2%)
Genitourinary: Expected pharmacological consequence of testosterone suppression: Testicular atrophy (5%)
Local: Implant site reaction (6%)
Renal: Renal impairment (5%)
<2% (Limited to important or life-threatening): Abdominal discomfort, alopecia, anemia, appetite increased, arthralgia, AST increased, back pain, bone density decreased, bone pain, breast pain, breast tenderness, contusion, craving food, creatinine increased, depression, diaphoresis, dizziness, dyspnea (exertional), dysuria, feeling cold, fluid retention, genital pruritus, hematuria, hypercalcemia, hypercholesterolemia, hyperglycemia, irritability, LDH increased, lethargy, liver disorder, malaise, muscle twitching, nausea, neck pain, palpitation, peripheral edema, prostatic acid phosphatase increased, renal calculi, renal failure, stent occlusion, testosterone increased, tremor, urinary frequency, urinary retention, ventricular asystoles, weight loss
Drug Interactions
Increased Effect/Toxicity: Not studied
Stability Vantas™: Upon delivery, separate contents of implant carton. Store implant under refrigeration at 2°C to 8°C (36°F to 46°F), wrapped in the amber pouch for protection from light; do not freeze. The implantation kit does not require refrigeration.
Mechanism of Action Potent inhibitor of gonadotropin secretion; continuous administration results in, after an initiation phase, the suppression of luteinizing hormone (LH), follicle-stimulating hormone (FSH), and a subsequent decrease in testosterone.
Pharmacodynamics/Kinetics
Onset: Chemical castration: 14 days
Duration: 1 year
Distribution: V_d: ~58 L
Protein binding: 70% ± 9%
Metabolism: Hepatic via C-terminal dealkylation and hydrolysis
Bioavailability: 92%
Half-life elimination: Terminal: ~4 hours
Time to peak, serum: 12 hours
Dosage SubQ:
Adults: 50 mg implant surgically inserted every 12 months
Elderly: See Adults dosing
Dosage adjustment in renal impairment: Cl_{cr}: 15 60 mL/minute: Adjustment not needed
(Continued)

Histrelin (Continued)

Administration SubQ: Surgical implantation into the inner portion of the upper arm requires the use of the implantation device provided. Use the patient's nondominant arm for placement. Removal must occur after 12 months; a replacement implant may be required.

Monitoring Parameters LH and FSH levels, serum testosterone levels, prostate specific antigen (PSA), bone mineral density; weakness, paresthesias, and urinary tract obstruction (especially during first few weeks of therapy)

Reference Range
Testosterone level: Expected to rise during the first few days and decline to below initiation level by week 2 before reaching ≤50 ng/dL (castrate level)
PSA: Expected to decrease to normal levels after 6 months of therapy
Note: Lack of response (testosterone and PSA decreases) should prompt suspicion that the implant has been expelled.

Test Interactions Results of diagnostic test of pituitary gonadotropic and gonadal functions may be affected during and after therapy

Dosage Forms Implant: 50 mg [released over 12 months; packaged with implantation kit]

- ♦ **Histrelin Acetate** *see Histrelin on page 839*
- ♦ **Histussin D®** **[DSC]** *see Hydrocodone and Pseudoephedrine on page 851*
- ♦ **Hivid®** **[DSC]** *see Zalcitabine on page 1807*
- ♦ **Hivid®** **(Can)** *see Zalcitabine on page 1807*
- ♦ **hMG** *see Menotropins on page 1079*
- ♦ **HMM** *see Altretamine on page 82*
- ♦ **HMR 3647** *see Telithromycin on page 1637*
- ♦ **HMS Liquifilm®** **[DSC]** *see Medrysone on page 1067*
- ♦ **HN₂** *see Mechlorethamine on page 1061*

Homatropine (hoe MA troe peen)

U.S. Brand Names Isopto® Homatropine
Index Terms Homatropine Hydrobromide
Pharmacologic Category Anticholinergic Agent, Ophthalmic; Ophthalmic Agent, Mydriatic
Additional Appendix Information
Cycloplegic Mydriatics *on page 1882*
Use Producing cycloplegia and mydriasis for refraction; treatment of acute inflammatory conditions of the uveal tract
Pregnancy Risk Factor C
Contraindications Hypersensitivity to the drug or any component of the formulation; narrow-angle glaucoma, acute hemorrhage
Warnings/Precautions Use with caution in patients with hypertension, cardiac disease, or increased intraocular pressure; safety and efficacy not established in infants and young children, therefore, use with extreme caution due to susceptibility of systemic effects; use with caution in obstructive uropathy, paralytic ileus, ulcerative colitis, unstable cardiovascular status in acute hemorrhage
Adverse Reactions
>10%: Ocular: Blurred vision, photophobia
1% to 10%:
Local: Irritation
Ocular: Increased intraocular pressure
Respiratory: Congestion
<1% (Limited to important or life-threatening): Eczematoid dermatitis, edema, exudate, follicular conjunctivitis, somnolence, vascular congestion
Overdosage/Toxicology Symptoms include blurred vision, urinary retention, and tachycardia. Anticholinergic toxicity is caused by strong binding of the drug to cholinergic receptors. For anticholinergic overdose with severe life-threatening symptoms, physostigmine 1-2 mg (0.5 mg or 0.02 mg/kg for children) SubQ or slow I.V. may be given to reverse these effects.
Stability Protect from light.
Mechanism of Action Blocks response of iris sphincter muscle and the accommodative muscle of the ciliary body to cholinergic stimulation resulting in dilation and loss of accommodation
Pharmacodynamics/Kinetics
Onset of action: Accommodation and pupil effect: Ophthalmic:
Maximum mydriatic effect: Within 10-30 minutes
Maximum cycloplegic effect: Within 30-90 minutes
Duration:
Mydriasis: 6 hours to 4 days
Cycloplegia: 10-48 hours
Dosage Ophthalmic:
Children:
Mydriasis and cycloplegia for refraction: Instill 1 drop of 2% solution immediately before the procedure; repeat at 10-minute intervals as needed
Uveitis: Instill 1 drop of 2% solution 2-3 times/day
Adults:
Mydriasis and cycloplegia for refraction: Instill 1-2 drops of 2% solution or 1 drop of 5% solution before the procedure; repeat at 5- to 10-minute intervals as needed; maximum of 3 doses for refraction
Uveitis: Instill 1-2 drops of 2% or 5% 2-3 times/day up to every 3-4 hours as needed
Administration Ophthalmic instillation: Finger pressure should be applied to lacrimal sac for 1-2 minutes after instillation to decrease risk of absorption and systemic reactions
Dosage Forms Solution, ophthalmic, as hydrobromide: 2% (5 mL); 5% (5 mL, 15 mL) [contains benzalkonium chloride]

- ◆ **Homatropine and Hydrocodone** *see* Hydrocodone and Homatropine *on page 850*
- ◆ **Homatropine Hydrobromide** *see* Homatropine *on page 840*
- ◆ **Horse Antihuman Thymocyte Gamma Globulin** *see* Antithymocyte Globulin (Equine) *on page 138*
- ◆ **Hp-PAC® (Can)** *see* Lansoprazole, Amoxicillin, and Clarithromycin *on page 979*
- ◆ **HPV Vaccine** *see* Papillomavirus (Types 6, 11, 16, 18) Recombinant Vaccine *on page 1310*
- ◆ **HTF919** *see* Tegaserod *on page 1636*
- ◆ **hu1124** *see* Efalizumab *on page 570*
- ◆ **Humalog®** *see* Insulin Lispro *on page 913*
- ◆ **Humalog® Mix 25 (Can)** *see* Insulin Lispro Protamine and Insulin Lispro *on page 913*
- ◆ **Humalog® Mix 50/50™** *see* Insulin Lispro Protamine and Insulin Lispro *on page 913*
- ◆ **Humalog® Mix 75/25™** *see* Insulin Lispro Protamine and Insulin Lispro *on page 913*
- ◆ **Human Antitumor Necrosis Factor Alpha** *see* Adalimumab *on page 47*
- ◆ **Human Corticotrophin-Releasing Hormone, Analogue** *see* Corticorelin *on page 419*
- ◆ **Human Diploid Cell Cultures Rabies Vaccine** *see* Rabies Virus Vaccine *on page 1479*
- ◆ **Human Growth Hormone** *see* Somatropin *on page 1586*
- ◆ **Humanized IgG1 Anti-CD52 Monoclonal Antibody** *see* Alemtuzumab *on page 63*
- ◆ **Human LFA-3/IgG(1) Fusion Protein** *see* Alefacept *on page 62*
- ◆ **Human Menopausal Gonadotropin** *see* Menotropins *on page 1079*
- ◆ **Human Papillomavirus Vaccine** *see* Papillomavirus (Types 6, 11, 16, 18) Recombinant Vaccine *on page 1310*
- ◆ **Human Thyroid Stimulating Hormone** *see* Thyrotropin Alpha *on page 1677*
- ◆ **Humate-P®** *see* Antihemophilic Factor/von Willebrand Factor Complex (Human) *on page 136*
- ◆ **Humatin®** *see* Paromomycin *on page 1314*
- ◆ **Humatrope®** *see* Somatropin *on page 1586*
- ◆ **Humegon® (Can)** *see* Chorionic Gonadotropin (Human) *on page 363*
- ◆ **Humibid® CS [OTC] [DSC]** *see* Guaifenesin and Dextromethorphan *on page 816*
- ◆ **Humibid® e [OTC] [DSC]** *see* Guaifenesin *on page 814*
- ◆ **Humibid® Maximum Strength** *see* Guaifenesin *on page 814*
- ◆ **Humira®** *see* Adalimumab *on page 47*
- ◆ **Humulin® 20/80 (Can)** *see* Insulin NPH and Insulin Regular *on page 914*
- ◆ **Humulin® 50/50** *see* Insulin NPH and Insulin Regular *on page 914*
- ◆ **Humulin® 70/30** *see* Insulin NPH and Insulin Regular *on page 914*
- ◆ **Humulin® N** *see* Insulin NPH *on page 913*
- ◆ **Humulin® R** *see* Insulin Regular *on page 914*
- ◆ **Humulin® R (Concentrated) U-500** *see* Insulin Regular *on page 914*
- ◆ **Hurricaine® [OTC]** *see* Benzocaine *on page 204*
- ◆ **HXM** *see* Altretamine *on page 82*
- ◆ **Hyalgan®** *see* Hyaluronate and Derivatives *on page 841*
- ◆ **Hyaluronan** *see* Hyaluronate and Derivatives *on page 841*

Hyaluronate and Derivatives (hye al yoor ON ate & dah RIV ah tives)

U.S. Brand Names Biolon™ [DSC]; Euflexxa™; Healon®; Healon®5; Healon GV®; Hyalgan®; Hylaform®; Hylaform® Plus; IPM Wound Gel™ [OTC]; Juvederm™ 24HV; Juvederm™ 30; Juvederm™ 30HV; Orthovisc®; Provisc®; Restylane®; Supartz™; Synvisc®; Vitrax®

Canadian Brand Names Cystistat®; Durolane®; Eyestil; Healon®; Healon GV®; OrthoVisc®; Suplasyn®

Index Terms Hyaluronan; Hyaluronic Acid; Hylan Polymers; Sodium Hyaluronate

Pharmacologic Category Antirheumatic Miscellaneous; Ophthalmic Agent, Viscoelastic; Skin and Mucous Membrane Agent, Miscellaneous

Use
Intra-articular injection: Treatment of pain in osteoarthritis in knee in patients who have failed nonpharmacologic treatment and simple analgesics
Intradermal: Correction of moderate-to-severe facial wrinkles or folds
Ophthalmic: Surgical aid in cataract extraction, intraocular implantation, corneal transplant, glaucoma filtration, and retinal attachment surgery
Topical: Management of skin ulcers and wounds

Pregnancy Risk Factor C

Pregnancy Implications There are no adequate and well-controlled studies in pregnant women.

Lactation Excretion in breast milk unknown/not recommended

Medication Safety Issues
Sound-alike/look-alike issues:
Synvisc® may be confused with Synagis®

Contraindications Hypersensitivity to hyaluronate or any component of the formulation
Intradermal:
Hylaform®, Hylaform® Plus: Additional contraindications include hypersensitivity to avian proteins (egg products, feathers)
Juvederm™, Restylane®: Additional contraindications include history of or presence of multiple severe allergies; sensitivity to gram-positive bacterial proteins
Intra-articular: Knee joint infections, infections or skin diseases at the site of injection
Orthovisc®: Additional contraindications include hypersensitivity to avian proteins (egg products, feathers)

Warnings/Precautions Not for I.V. injection. Do not inject into blood vessels; may cause occlusion, infarction, embolism, or other systemic adverse events.
Intra-articular: Not for use in infected joints; do not use disinfectants containing quaternary salts for skin preparation. Remove effusion, if present, prior to injection. Use with caution if
(Continued)

Hyaluronate and Derivatives *(Continued)*

venous or lymphatic stasis is present in the leg. Avoid strenuous activities for 48 hours after injection. Safety and efficacy have not been established in children.

Intradermal: Do not inject into site of active inflammation or infection. Use in patients susceptible to keloid formation, hypertrophic scarring, or pigmentation disorders has not been studied. Supplemental "touch up" treatments may be required. Use caution with immunosuppressive treatment. Patient must avoid exposure to ultraviolet rays or severe cold until swelling and redness is resolved. Laser treatment or chemical peeling may cause acute inflammatory reaction. Use in lip augmentation has not been established. Strenuous exercise and ethanol consumption should be avoided for 24 hours following use. Safety and efficacy in patients <18 years of age have not been established.

Ophthalmic: Do not overfill the anterior chamber; carefully monitor intraocular pressure

Topical: Cleansing agents other than normal saline are not recommended

Adverse Reactions Frequencies and/or type of local reaction may vary by formulation and site of application/injection.

>10%:
Local: Injection site (intradermal): Bruising (52% to 61%), erythema (85% to 93%), lumps/bumps (79% to 83%), pain (57% to 90%), swelling (86% to 89%); pruritus (28% to 36%), skin discoloration (31% to 34%)
Respiratory: Infection (12%)

1% to 10%:
Cardiovascular: Blood pressure increased (2% to 4%)
Central nervous system: Fatigue (1%)
Gastrointestinal: Nausea (≤2%)
Local: Dry skin (intradermal >1%), peeling (intradermal >1%)
Neuromuscular & skeletal: Back pain (<1% to 6%), tendonitis (2%), parasthesia (1%)
Respiratory: Rhinitis (3%)

Frequency not defined:
Cardiovascular: Edema, flushing, hypotension, tachycardia
Central nervous system: Dizziness, headache
Dermatologic: Rash
Local: Injection site: Arthralgia, nodule
Neuromuscular & skeletal: Hypokinesia (knee)
Ocular (with ophthalmic formulation): Postoperative inflammatory reactions (iritis, hypopyon), corneal edema, corneal decompensation, transient postoperative increase in IOP
Miscellaneous: Abscess formation, allergic reactions, anaphylaxis, respiratory difficulties

Drug Interactions
Increased Effect/Toxicity: Anticoagulants or antiplatelet agents may increase the risk of injection site bleeding or hematoma.

Stability
Euflexxa™: Store under refrigeration at 2°C to 8°C (36°F to 46°F) or at room temperature up to 25°C (77°F); do not freeze. Protect from light. If refrigerated, remove from refrigeration at least 20-30 minutes before use.
Healon® products, Provisc®: Store under refrigeration at 2°C to 8°C (36°F to 46°F); do not freeze. Protect from light.
Hylaform®, Hylaform® Plus: Store at room temperature of 2°C to 30°C; do not freeze. Do not use if gel separates or becomes cloudy.
Hyalgan®, Orthovisc®: Store below 25°C (77°F); do not freeze.
IPM Wound Gel™: Store below 35°C (95°F); do not freeze.
Juvederm™ (all formulations), Restylane®: Store at up to 25°C (77°F); do not freeze. Protect from light. Do not use if gel separates or becomes cloudy.
Synvisc®: Store at room temperature, below 30°C (86°C); do not freeze. Protect from light.

Mechanism of Action Sodium hyaluronate is a polysaccharide which is distributed widely in the extracellular matrix of connective tissue in man (vitreous and aqueous humor of the eye, synovial fluid, skin, and umbilical cord). Sodium hyaluronate and its derivatives form a viscoelastic solution in water (at physiological pH and ionic strength) which makes it suitable for aqueous and vitreous humor in ophthalmic surgery, and functions as a tissue and/or joint lubricant which plays an important role in modulating the interactions between adjacent tissues. Intradermal injection may decrease the depth of facial wrinkles.

Pharmacodynamics/Kinetics
Distribution: Intravitreous injection: Diffusion occurs slowly
Excretion: Ophthalmic: Via Canal of Schlemm

Dosage Adults:
Osteoarthritis of the knee: Intra-articular:
Eulexxa™: Inject 20 mg (2 mL) once weekly for 3 weeks
Hyalgan®: Inject 20 mg (2 mL) once weekly for 5 weeks; some patients may benefit with a total of 3 injections
Orthovisc®: Inject 30 mg (2 mL) once weekly for 3-4 weeks
Supartz™: Inject 25 mg (2.5 mL) once weekly for 5 weeks
Synvisc®: Inject 16 mg (2 mL) once weekly for 3 weeks (total of 3 injections)
Facial wrinkles: Intradermal
Hylaform®, Hylaform® Plus: Inject as required for cosmetic result; typical treatment regimen requires <2 mL; limit injection to ≤1.5 mL per injection site; maximum: 20 mL/60 kg/year
Juvederm™ (all formulations): Inject as required for cosmetic result; typical treatment regimen requires <2 mL; limit injection to 1.6 mL per injection site; maximum: 20 mL/60 kg/year
Restylane®: Inject as required for cosmetic result; typical treatment regimen requires <2 mL; limit injection to ≤1.5 mL per injection site
Ophthalmic (Biolon™, Healon®, Provisc®, Vitrax®): Depends upon procedure (slowly introduce a sufficient quantity into eye)
Topical (IPM Wound Gel™): Apply to clean dry ulcer or wound, and cover with nonstick dressing; repeat daily. Discontinue if wound size increase after 3-4 applications.

Administration

Intra-articular: Inject directly into the knee joint. Do not use disinfectants containing quaternary salts for skin cleansing prior to injection. Remove effusion, if present, prior to injection. If used for bilateral treatment, use a separate syringe for each injection site.

Intradermal: Do not inject into a blood vessel.

Juvederm™: May apply ice pack to injection site for a short period immediately after administration if treatment area swollen.

Ophthalmic: Drug may become cloudy or form a slight precipitate after administration; clinical significance unknown, but cloudy or precipitated material should be removed by irrigation or aspiration

Topical: Clean wound with normal saline; remove excess moisture with dry gauze; apply gel liberally to wound

Monitoring Parameters Intraocular pressure; intradermally administered products, signs and symptoms of excess local inflammation or infection

Additional Information Juvederm™ 24HV provides more versatility in contouring and volumizing of facial wrinkles. Juvederm™ 30 provides subtle correction for facial folds and wrinkles. Juvederm™ 30HV provides greater volumizing for correction of deeper folds and wrinkles.

Dosage Forms [DSC] = Discontinued product

Hylan B: Injection, gel:

Hylaform® [500 micron particle]: 5.5 mg/mL (0.75 mL) [prefilled syringe; derived from avian source]

Hylaform® Plus [700 micron particle]: 5.5 mg/mL (0.75 mL) [prefilled syringe; derived from avian source]

Hylan polymers A and B (Hylan G-F 20): Injection, solution, intra-articular (Synvisc®): 8 mg/mL (2 mL) [prefilled syringe; contains trace amounts of *Streptococcus*]

Sodium Hyaluronate:

Gel, topical (IPM Wound Gel™): 2.5% (10 g)

Injection, gel, intradermal:

Juvederm™ 24HV, Juvederm™ 30, Juvederm™ 30HV: 24 mg/mL [prefilled syringe]

Restylane®: 20 mg/mL [prefilled syringe]

Injection, solution, intra-articular:

Euflexxa™: 10 mg/mL (2 mL) [prefilled syringe; syringe contains latex]

Hyalgan®: 10 mg/mL (2 mL)

Orthovisc®: 15 mg/mL (2 mL) [prefilled syringe; derived from avian source]

Supartz®: 10 mg/mL (2.5 mL) [derived from avian source]

Synvisc®: 8 mg/mL (2 mL) [prefilled syringe; derived from avian source]

Injection, solution, intraocular:

Biolon™: 10 mg/mL (0.5 mL, 1 mL) [DSC]

Healon®: 10 mg/mL (0.4 mL, 0.55 mL, 0.85 mL, 2 mL)

Healon®5: 23 mg/mL

Healon GV®: 14 mg/mL (0.55 mL, 0.85 mL)

Provisc®: 10 mg/mL (0.4 mL, 0.55 mL, 0.8 mL) [prefilled syringe; contains lactose]

Vitrax®: 30 mg/mL (0.65 mL)

♦ **Hyaluronic Acid** see Hyaluronate and Derivatives *on page 841*

♦ **Hycamptamine** see Topotecan *on page 1709*

♦ **Hycamtin®** see Topotecan *on page 1709*

♦ **hycet™** see Hydrocodone and Acetaminophen *on page 848*

♦ **Hycodan®** see Hydrocodone and Homatropine *on page 850*

♦ **Hycomine® Compound** see Hydrocodone, Chlorpheniramine, Phenylephrine, Acetaminophen, and Caffeine *on page 852*

♦ **Hycort™ (Can)** see Hydrocortisone *on page 852*

♦ **Hycotuss®** see Hydrocodone and Guaifenesin *on page 849*

♦ **Hydeltra T.B.A.® (Can)** see PrednisoLONE *on page 1413*

♦ **Hydergine [DSC]** see Ergoloid Mesylates *on page 604*

♦ **Hydergine® (Can)** see Ergoloid Mesylates *on page 604*

♦ **Hyderm (Can)** see Hydrocortisone *on page 852*

HydrALAZINE (hye DRAL a zeen)

Canadian Brand Names Apo-Hydralazine®; Apresoline®; Novo-Hylazin; Nu-Hydral

Index Terms Apresoline [DSC]; Hydralazine Hydrochloride

Pharmacologic Category Vasodilator

Additional Appendix Information

Heart Failure (Systolic) *on page 2051*

Hypertension *on page 2063*

Use Management of moderate to severe hypertension, congestive heart failure, hypertension secondary to pre-eclampsia/eclampsia; treatment of primary pulmonary hypertension

Pregnancy Risk Factor C

Pregnancy Implications Crosses the placenta. One report of fetal arrhythmia; transient neonatal thrombocytopenia and fetal distress reported following late 3rd trimester use. A large amount of clinical experience with the use of this drug for management of hypertension during pregnancy is available. Available evidence suggests safe use during pregnancy.

Lactation Enters breast milk/compatible

Medication Safety Issues

Sound-alike/look-alike issues:

HydrALAZINE may be confused with hydrOXYzine

Contraindications Hypersensitivity to hydralazine or any component of the formulation; mitral valve rheumatic heart disease

Warnings/Precautions May cause a drug-induced lupus-like syndrome (more likely on larger doses, longer duration). Discontinue hydralazine in patients who develop SLE-like syndrome or positive ANA. Use with caution in patients with severe renal disease or cerebral vascular *(Continued)*

HydrALAZINE (Continued)

accidents or with known or suspected coronary artery disease; monitor blood pressure closely with I.V. use. Slow acetylators, patients with decreased renal function, and patients receiving >200 mg/day (chronically) are at higher risk for SLE. Titrate dosage to patient's response. Usually administered with diuretic and a beta-blocker to counteract side effects of sodium and water retention and reflex tachycardia.

Adjust dose in severe renal dysfunction. Use with caution in CAD (increase in tachycardia may increase myocardial oxygen demand). Use with caution in pulmonary hypertension (may cause hypotension). Patients may be poorly compliant because of frequent dosing. Hydralazine-induced fluid and sodium retention may require addition or increased dosage of a diuretics.

Adverse Reactions Frequency not defined.

Cardiovascular: Tachycardia, angina pectoris, orthostatic hypotension (rare), dizziness (rare), paradoxical hypertension, peripheral edema, vascular collapse (rare), flushing

Central nervous system: Increased intracranial pressure (I.V., in patient with pre-existing increased intracranial pressure), fever (rare), chills (rare), anxiety*, disorientation*, depression*, coma*

Dermatologic: Rash (rare), urticaria (rare), pruritus (rare)

Gastrointestinal: Anorexia, nausea, vomiting, diarrhea, constipation, adynamic ileus

Genitourinary: Difficulty in micturition, impotence

Hematologic: Hemolytic anemia (rare), eosinophilia (rare), decreased hemoglobin concentration (rare), reduced erythrocyte count (rare), leukopenia (rare), agranulocytosis (rare), thrombocytopenia (rare)

Neuromuscular & skeletal: Rheumatoid arthritis, muscle cramps, weakness, tremor, peripheral neuritis (rare)

Ocular: Lacrimation, conjunctivitis

Respiratory: Nasal congestion, dyspnea

Miscellaneous: Drug-induced lupus-like syndrome (dose related; fever, arthralgia, splenomegaly, lymphadenopathy, asthenia, myalgia, malaise, pleuritic chest pain, edema, positive ANA, positive LE cells, maculopapular facial rash, positive direct Coombs' test, pericarditis, pericardial tamponade), diaphoresis

*Seen in uremic patients and severe hypertension where rapidly escalating doses may have caused hypotension leading to these effects.

Overdosage/Toxicology Symptoms include hypotension, tachycardia, and shock. Hypotension usually responds to I.V. fluids, Trendelenburg positioning, or vasoconstrictors. Treatment is primarily supportive and symptomatic.

Drug Interactions

Cytochrome P450 Effect: Inhibits CYP3A4 (weak)

Increased Effect/Toxicity: Hydralazine may increase levels of beta-blockers (metoprolol, propranolol). Some beta-blockers (acebutolol, atenolol, and nadolol) are unlikely to be affected due to limited hepatic metabolism. Concurrent use of hydralazine with MAO inhibitors may cause a significant decrease in blood pressure. Propranolol may increase hydralazine serum concentrations.

Decreased Effect: NSAIDs (eg, indomethacin) may decrease the hemodynamic effects of hydralazine.

Ethanol/Nutrition/Herb Interactions

Ethanol: Avoid ethanol (may increase CNS depression).

Food: Food enhances bioavailability of hydralazine.

Herb/Nutraceutical: Avoid dong quai if using for hypertension (has estrogenic activity). Avoid ephedra, yohimbe, ginseng (may worsen hypertension). Avoid garlic (may have increased antihypertensive effect).

Stability Intact ampuls/vials of hydralazine should not be stored under refrigeration because of possible precipitation or crystallization. Hydralazine should be diluted in NS for IVPB administration due to decreased stability in D_5W. Stability of IVPB solution in NS is 4 days at room temperature.

Mechanism of Action Direct vasodilation of arterioles (with little effect on veins) with decreased systemic resistance

Pharmacodynamics/Kinetics

Onset of action: Oral: 20-30 minutes; I.V.: 5-20 minutes

Duration: Oral: Up to 8 hours; I.V.: 1-4 hours; **Note:** May vary depending on acetylator status of patient

Distribution: Crosses placenta; enters breast milk

Protein binding: 85% to 90%

Metabolism: Hepatically acetylated; extensive first-pass effect (oral)

Bioavailability: 30% to 50%; increased with food

Half-life elimination: Normal renal function: 2-8 hours; End-stage renal disease: 7-16 hours

Excretion: Urine (14% as unchanged drug)

Dosage

Children:

Oral: Initial: 0.75-1 mg/kg/day in 2-4 divided doses; increase over 3-4 weeks to maximum of 7.5 mg/kg/day in 2-4 divided doses; maximum daily dose: 200 mg/day

I.M., I.V.: 0.1-0.2 mg/kg/dose (not to exceed 20 mg) every 4-6 hours as needed, up to 1.7-3.5 mg/kg/day in 4-6 divided doses

Adults:

Oral:

Hypertension:

Initial dose: 10 mg 4 times/day for first 2-4 days; increase to 25 mg 4 times/day for the balance of the first week

Increase by 10-25 mg/dose gradually to 50 mg 4 times/day (maximum: 300 mg/day); usual dose range (JNC 7): 25-100 mg/day in 2 divided doses

Congestive heart failure:

Initial dose: 10-25 mg 3-4 times/day

Adjustment: Dosage must be adjusted based on individual response

Target dose: 225-300 mg/day in divided doses; use in combination with isosorbide dinitrate

I.M., I.V.:

Hypertension: Initial: 10-20 mg/dose every 4-6 hours as needed, may increase to 40 mg/dose; change to oral therapy as soon as possible.

Pre-eclampsia/eclampsia: 5 mg/dose then 5-10 mg every 20-30 minutes as needed.

Elderly: Oral: Initial: 10 mg 2-3 times/day; increase by 10-25 mg/day every 2-5 days.

Dosing interval in renal impairment:

Cl$_{cr}$ 10-50 mL/minute: Administer every 8 hours.

Cl$_{cr}$ <10 mL/minute: Administer every 8-16 hours in fast acetylators and every 12-24 hours in slow acetylators.

Hemodialysis: Supplemental dose is not necessary.

Peritoneal dialysis: Supplemental dose is not necessary.

Dietary Considerations Administer with meals.

Administration Inject over 1 minute. Hypotensive effect may be delayed and unpredictable in some patients.

Monitoring Parameters Blood pressure (monitor closely with I.V. use), standing and sitting/supine, heart rate, ANA titer

Dosage Forms

Injection, solution, as hydrochloride: 20 mg/mL (1 mL)

Tablet, as hydrochloride: 10 mg, 25 mg, 50 mg, 100 mg

Extemporaneous Preparations An oral solution (20 mg/5 mL) has been made from 20 mL of the hydralazine injection (20 mg/mL), 8 mL of propylene glycol and purified water USP qs ad 100 mL; expected stability: 30 days if refrigerated

A flavored syrup (1.25 mg/mL) has been made using seventy-five hydralazine hydrochloride 50 mg tablets, dissolved in 250 mL of distilled water with 2250 g of Lycasin® (75% w/w maltitol syrup vehicle); edetate disodium 3 g and sodium saccharin 3 g dissolved in 50 mL distilled water was added; solution was preserved with 30 mL of a solution containing methylparaben 10% (w/v) and propylparaben 2% (w/v) in propylene glycol; flavored with 3 mL orange flavoring; qs ad to 3 L with distilled water and then pH adjusted to pH of 3.7 using glacial acetic acid; measured stability was 5 days at room temperature (25°C); less than 2% loss of hydralazine occurred at 2 weeks when syrup was stored at 5°C

Alexander KS, Pudipeddi M, and Parker GA, "Stability of Hydralazine Hydrochloride Syrup Compounded From Tablets," *Am J Hosp Pharm*, 1993, 50(4):683-6.

Nahata MC and Hipple TF, *Pediatric Drug Formulations*, 2nd ed, Cincinnati, OH: Harvey Whitney Books Co, 1992.

Hydralazine and Hydrochlorothiazide (hye DRAL a zeen & hye droe klor oh THYE a zide)

Index Terms Apresazide [DSC]; Hydrochlorothiazide and Hydralazine

Pharmacologic Category Antihypertensive Agent, Combination

Use Management of moderate to severe hypertension and treatment of congestive heart failure

Pregnancy Risk Factor C

Dosage Adults: Oral: Hydralazine 25-100 mg/day and hydrochlorothiazide 25-50 mg/day in 2 divided doses (maximum: hydrochlorothiazide: 50 mg/day)

Additional Information Complete prescribing information for this medication should be consulted for additional detail.

Dosage Forms Capsule:

25/25: Hydralazine hydrochloride 25 mg and hydrochlorothiazide 25 mg

50/50: Hydralazine hydrochloride 50 mg and hydrochlorothiazide 50 mg

100/50: Hydralazine hydrochloride 100 mg and hydrochlorothiazide 50 mg

♦ **Hydralazine and Isosorbide Dinitrate** *see* Isosorbide Dinitrate and Hydralazine *on page 947*

♦ **Hydralazine Hydrochloride** *see* HydrALAZINE *on page 843*

♦ **Hydramine® [OTC]** *see* DiphenhydrAMINE *on page 515*

♦ **Hydrated Chloral** *see* Chloral Hydrate *on page 339*

♦ **Hydrea®** *see* Hydroxyurea *on page 863*

Hydrochlorothiazide (hye droe klor oh THYE a zide)

U.S. Brand Names Microzide™

Canadian Brand Names Apo-Hydro®; Novo-Hydrazide; PMS-Hydrochlorothiazide

Index Terms HCTZ (error-prone abbreviation)

Pharmacologic Category Diuretic, Thiazide

Additional Appendix Information

Heart Failure (Systolic) *on page 2051*

Sulfonamide Derivatives *on page 1897*

Use Management of mild to moderate hypertension; treatment of edema in congestive heart failure and nephrotic syndrome

Unlabeled/Investigational Use Treatment of lithium-induced diabetes insipidus

Pregnancy Risk Factor B (manufacturer); D (expert analysis)

Pregnancy Implications Although there are no adequate and well-controlled studies using hydrochlorothiazide in pregnancy, thiazide diuretics may cause an increased risk of congenital defects. Hypoglycemia, hypokalemia, hyponatremia, jaundice, and thrombocytopenia are also reported as possible complications to the fetus or newborn.

Lactation Enters breast milk/use caution (AAP rates "compatible")

Medication Safety Issues

Sound-alike/look-alike issues:

Hydrochlorothiazide may be confused with hydrocortisone, hydroflumethiazide

Esidrix may be confused with Lasix®

(Continued)

Hydrochlorothiazide *(Continued)*

HCTZ is an error-prone abbreviation (mistaken as hydrocortisone)

International issues:

Microzide™ may be confused with Nitrobide® which is a brand name for isosorbide dinitrate in Japan

Microzide™ may be confused with Mikrozid® which is a brand name for ethanol/propanol combination in Great Britain

Contraindications Hypersensitivity to hydrochlorothiazide or any component of the formulation, thiazides, or sulfonamide-derived drugs; anuria; renal decompensation; pregnancy

Warnings/Precautions Avoid in severe renal disease (ineffective). Electrolyte disturbances (hypokalemia, hypochloremic alkalosis, hyponatremia) can occur. Use with caution in severe hepatic dysfunction; hepatic encephalopathy can be caused by electrolyte disturbances. Gout can be precipitate in certain patients with a history of gout, a familial predisposition to gout, or chronic renal failure. Cautious use in prediabetics and diabetics; may see a change in glucose control. Can cause SLE exacerbation or activation. Use with caution in patients with moderate or high cholesterol concentrations. Photosensitization may occur. Correct hypokalemia before initiating therapy.

Chemical similarities are present among sulfonamides, sulfonylureas, carbonic anhydrase inhibitors, thiazides, and loop diuretics (except ethacrynic acid). Use in patients with sulfonamide allergy is specifically contraindicated in product labeling, however, a risk of cross-reaction exists in patients with allergy to any of these compounds; avoid use when previous reaction has been severe. Discontinue if signs of hypersensitivity are noted.

Adverse Reactions

1% to 10%:

Cardiovascular: Orthostatic hypotension, hypotension

Dermatologic: Photosensitivity

Endocrine & metabolic: Hypokalemia

Gastrointestinal: Anorexia, epigastric distress

<1% (Limited to important or life-threatening): Agranulocytosis, allergic myocarditis, allergic reactions (possibly with life-threatening anaphylactic shock), alopecia, aplastic anemia, eosinophilic pneumonitis, erythema multiforme, exfoliative dermatitis, hemolytic anemia, hepatic function impairment, hypercalcemia, interstitial nephritis, leukopenia, pancreatitis, renal failure, respiratory distress, Stevens-Johnson syndrome, thrombocytopenia, toxic epidermal necrolysis

Overdosage/Toxicology Symptoms include hypermotility, diuresis, lethargy, confusion, and muscle weakness. Following GI decontamination, therapy is supportive with I.V. fluids, electrolytes, and I.V. pressors if needed.

Drug Interactions

Increased Effect/Toxicity: Increased effect of hydrochlorothiazide with furosemide and other loop diuretics. Increased hypotension and/or renal adverse effects of ACE inhibitors may result in aggressively diuresed patients. Beta-blockers increase hyperglycemic effects of thiazides in type 2 diabetes mellitus. Cyclosporine and thiazides can increase the risk of gout or renal toxicity. Digoxin toxicity can be exacerbated if a thiazide induces hypokalemia or hypomagnesemia. Lithium toxicity can occur with thiazides due to reduced renal excretion of lithium. Thiazides may prolong the duration of action with neuromuscular blocking agents.

Decreased Effect: Effects of oral hypoglycemics may be decreased. Decreased absorption of hydrochlorothiazide with cholestyramine and colestipol. NSAIDs can decrease the efficacy of thiazides, reducing the diuretic and antihypertensive effects.

Ethanol/Nutrition/Herb Interactions

Food: Hydrochlorothiazide peak serum levels may be decreased if taken with food. This product may deplete potassium, sodium, and magnesium.

Herb/Nutraceutical: Avoid dong quai if using for hypertension (has estrogenic activity). Dong quai may also cause photosensitization. Avoid ephedra, ginseng, yohimbe (may worsen hypertension). Avoid garlic (may have increased antihypertensive effect).

Mechanism of Action Inhibits sodium reabsorption in the distal tubules causing increased excretion of sodium and water as well as potassium and hydrogen ions

Pharmacodynamics/Kinetics

Onset of action: Diuresis: ~2 hours

Peak effect: 4-6 hours

Duration: 6-12 hours

Absorption: ~50% to 80%

Distribution: 3.6-7.8 L/kg

Protein binding: 68%

Metabolism: Not metabolized

Bioavailability: 50% to 80%

Half-life elimination: 5.6-14.8 hours

Time to peak: 1-2.5 hours

Excretion: Urine (as unchanged drug)

Dosage Oral (effect of drug may be decreased when used every day):

Children (in pediatric patients, chlorothiazide may be preferred over hydrochlorothiazide as there are more dosage formulations [eg, suspension] available):

<6 months: 2-3 mg/kg/day in 2 divided doses

>6 months: 2 mg/kg/day in 2 divided doses

Adults:

Edema: 25-100 mg/day in 1-2 doses; maximum: 200 mg/day

Hypertension: 12.5-50 mg/day; minimal increase in response and more electrolyte disturbances are seen with doses >50 mg/day

Elderly: 12.5-25 mg once daily

Dosing adjustment/comments in renal impairment: Cl_{cr} <10 mL/minute: Avoid use. Usually ineffective with GFR <30 mL/minute. Effective at lower GFR in combination with a loop diuretic.

Administration May be taken with food or milk. Take early in day to avoid nocturia. Take the last dose of multiple doses no later than 6 PM unless instructed otherwise.

Monitoring Parameters Assess weight, I & O reports daily to determine fluid loss; blood pressure, serum electrolytes, BUN, creatinine

Test Interactions Increased creatine phosphokinase [CPK] (S), ammonia (B), amylase (S), calcium (S), chloride (S), cholesterol (S), glucose, increased acid (S), decreased chloride (S), magnesium, potassium (S), sodium (S); Tyramine and phentolamine tests, histamine tests for pheochromocytoma

Additional Information If given the morning of surgery it may render the patient volume depleted and blood pressure may be labile during general anesthesia. Effect of drug may be decreased when used every day.

Dosage Forms
Capsule: 12.5 mg
   Microzide™: 12.5 mg
Tablet: 25 mg, 50 mg

♦ **Hydrochlorothiazide and Amiloride** see Amiloride and Hydrochlorothiazide on page 93

♦ **Hydrochlorothiazide and Benazepril** see Benazepril and Hydrochlorothiazide on page 203

♦ **Hydrochlorothiazide and Bisoprolol** see Bisoprolol and Hydrochlorothiazide on page 227

♦ **Hydrochlorothiazide and Captopril** see Captopril and Hydrochlorothiazide on page 284

♦ **Hydrochlorothiazide and Enalapril** see Enalapril and Hydrochlorothiazide on page 581

♦ **Hydrochlorothiazide and Eprosartan** see Eprosartan and Hydrochlorothiazide on page 601

♦ **Hydrochlorothiazide and Hydralazine** see Hydralazine and Hydrochlorothiazide on page 845

♦ **Hydrochlorothiazide and Irbesartan** see Irbesartan and Hydrochlorothiazide on page 935

♦ **Hydrochlorothiazide and Lisinopril** see Lisinopril and Hydrochlorothiazide on page 1023

♦ **Hydrochlorothiazide and Losartan** see Losartan and Hydrochlorothiazide on page 1039

♦ **Hydrochlorothiazide and Methyldopa** see Methyldopa and Hydrochlorothiazide on page 1117

♦ **Hydrochlorothiazide and Metoprolol** see Metoprolol and Hydrochlorothiazide on page 1132

♦ **Hydrochlorothiazide and Metoprolol Tartrate** see Metoprolol and Hydrochlorothiazide on page 1132

♦ **Hydrochlorothiazide and Moexipril** see Moexipril and Hydrochlorothiazide on page 1164

♦ **Hydrochlorothiazide and Olmesartan Medoxomil** see Olmesartan and Hydrochlorothiazide on page 1261

♦ **Hydrochlorothiazide and Propranolol** see Propranolol and Hydrochlorothiazide on page 1449

♦ **Hydrochlorothiazide and Quinapril** see Quinapril and Hydrochlorothiazide on page 1471

Hydrochlorothiazide and Spironolactone
(hye droe klor oh THYE a zide & speer on oh LAK tone)

U.S. Brand Names Aldactazide®

Canadian Brand Names Aldactazide 25®; Aldactazide 50®; Novo-Spirozine

Index Terms Spironolactone and Hydrochlorothiazide

Pharmacologic Category Antihypertensive Agent, Combination

Use Management of mild- to-moderate hypertension; treatment of edema in congestive heart failure and nephrotic syndrome, and cirrhosis of the liver accompanied by edema and/or ascites

Pregnancy Risk Factor C

Medication Safety Issues
Sound-alike/look-alike issues:
   Aldactazide® may be confused with Aldactone®

Dosage Oral:
Children: 1.5-3 mg/kg/day in 2-4 divided doses (maximum: 200 mg/day)
Adults: Hydrochlorothiazide 12.5-50 mg/day and spironolactone 12.5-50 mg/day; manufacturer labeling states hydrochlorothiazide maximum 200 mg/day, however, usual dose in JNC-7 is 12.5-50 mg/day

Additional Information Complete prescribing information for this medication should be consulted for additional detail.

Dosage Forms
Tablet: Hydrochlorothiazide 25 mg and spironolactone 25 mg
   Aldactazide®:
      25/25: Hydrochlorothiazide 25 mg and spironolactone 25 mg
      50/50: Hydrochlorothiazide 50 mg and spironolactone 50 mg

♦ **Hydrochlorothiazide and Telmisartan** see Telmisartan and Hydrochlorothiazide on page 1640

Hydrochlorothiazide and Triamterene
(hye droe klor oh THYE a zide & trye AM ter een)

U.S. Brand Names Dyazide®; Maxzide®; Maxzide®-25

Canadian Brand Names Apo-Triazide®; Novo-Triamzide; Nu-Triazide; Penta-Triamterene HCTZ; Riva-Zide

Index Terms Triamterene and Hydrochlorothiazide

Pharmacologic Category Antihypertensive Agent, Combination; Diuretic, Potassium-Sparing; Diuretic, Thiazide

Use Management of mild to moderate hypertension; treatment of edema in congestive heart failure and nephrotic syndrome

Pregnancy Risk Factor C (per manufacturer)
(Continued)

Hydrochlorothiazide and Triamterene *(Continued)*

Medication Safety Issues
Sound-alike/look-alike issues:
Dyazide® may be confused with diazoxide, Dynacin®
Maxzide® may be confused with Maxidex®

Dosage Adults: Oral:
Hydrochlorothiazide 25 mg and triamterene 37.5 mg: 1-2 tablets/capsules once daily
Hydrochlorothiazide 50 mg and triamterene 75 mg: $^1/_2$-1 tablet daily

Additional Information Complete prescribing information for this medication should be consulted for additional detail.

Dosage Forms
Capsule (Dyazide®): Hydrochlorothiazide 25 mg and triamterene 37.5 mg
Tablet:
Maxzide®: Hydrochlorothiazide 50 mg and triamterene 75 mg
Maxzide®-25: Hydrochlorothiazide 25 mg and triamterene 37.5 mg

♦ **Hydrochlorothiazide and Valsartan** *see* Valsartan and Hydrochlorothiazide *on page 1773*
♦ **Hydrocil® Instant [OTC]** *see* Psyllium *on page 1458*

Hydrocodone and Acetaminophen
(hye droe KOE done & a seet a MIN oh fen)

U.S. Brand Names Anexsia®; Ceta-Plus®; Co-Gesic®; hycet™; Lorcet® 10/650; Lorcet® Plus; Lortab®; Margesic® H; Maxidone™; Norco®; Stagesic®; Vicodin®; Vicodin® ES; Vicodin® HP; Xodol®; Xodol® 5/300; Zydone®

Index Terms Acetaminophen and Hydrocodone

Pharmacologic Category Analgesic Combination (Opioid)

Use Relief of moderate to severe pain

Restrictions C-III

Pregnancy Risk Factor C/D (prolonged use or high doses near term)

Medication Safety Issues
Sound-alike/look-alike issues:
Lorcet® may be confused with Fioricet®
Lortab® may be confused with Cortef®, Lorabid®, Luride®
Vicodin® may be confused with Hycodan®, Hycomine®, Indocin®, Uridon®
Zydone® may be confused with Vytone®

Dosage Oral (doses should be titrated to appropriate analgesic effect): Analgesic:
Children 2-13 years or <50 kg: Hydrocodone 0.135 mg/kg/dose every 4-6 hours; do not exceed 6 doses/day or the maximum recommended dose of acetaminophen
Children and Adults ≥50 kg: Average starting dose in opioid naive patients: Hydrocodone 5-10 mg 4 times/day; the dosage of acetaminophen should be limited to ≤4 g/day (and possibly less in patients with hepatic impairment or ethanol use).
Dosage ranges (based on specific product labeling): Hydrocodone 2.5-10 mg every 4-6 hours; maximum: 60 mg hydrocodone/day (maximum dose of hydrocodone may be limited by the acetaminophen content of specific product)
Elderly: Doses should be titrated to appropriate analgesic effect; 2.5-5 mg of the hydrocodone component every 4-6 hours. Do not exceed 4 g/day of acetaminophen.
Dosage adjustment in hepatic impairment: Use with caution. Limited, low-dose therapy usually well tolerated in hepatic disease/cirrhosis; however, cases of hepatotoxicity at daily acetaminophen dosages <4 g/day have been reported. Avoid chronic use in hepatic impairment.

Additional Information Complete prescribing information for this medication should be consulted for additional detail.

Dosage Forms
[DSC] = Discontinued product
Capsule:
Ceta-Plus®, Margesic® H, Stagesic®: Hydrocodone bitartrate 5 mg and acetaminophen 500 mg
Elixir: Hydrocodone bitartrate 7.5 mg and acetaminophen 500 mg per 15 mL (480 mL)
Lortab®: Hydrocodone bitartrate 7.5 mg and acetaminophen 500 mg per 15 mL (480 mL) [contains alcohol 7%; tropical fruit punch flavor]
Solution, oral:
hycet™: Hydrocodone bitartrate 7.5 mg and acetaminophen 325 mg per 15 mL (480 mL) [contains alcohol 7%; tropical fruit punch flavor]
Tablet:
Hydrocodone bitartrate 2.5 mg and acetaminophen 500 mg
Hydrocodone bitartrate 5 mg and acetaminophen 325 mg
Hydrocodone bitartrate 5 mg and acetaminophen 500 mg
Hydrocodone bitartrate 7.5 mg and acetaminophen 325 mg
Hydrocodone bitartrate 7.5 mg and acetaminophen 500 mg
Hydrocodone bitartrate 7.5 mg and acetaminophen 650 mg
Hydrocodone bitartrate 7.5 mg and acetaminophen 750 mg
Hydrocodone bitartrate 10 mg and acetaminophen 325 mg
Hydrocodone bitartrate 10 mg and acetaminophen 500 mg
Hydrocodone bitartrate 10 mg and acetaminophen 650 mg
Hydrocodone bitartrate 10 mg and acetaminophen 660 mg
Hydrocodone bitartrate 10 mg and acetaminophen 750 mg
Anexsia®:
5/325: Hydrocodone bitartrate 5 mg and acetaminophen 325 mg
5/500: Hydrocodone bitartrate 5 mg and acetaminophen 500 mg [DSC]
7.5/325: Hydrocodone bitartrate 7.5 mg and acetaminophen 325 mg
7.5/650: Hydrocodone bitartrate 7.5 mg and acetaminophen 650 mg [DSC]
Co-Gesic® 5/500: Hydrocodone bitartrate 5 mg and acetaminophen 500 mg

Lorcet® 10/650: Hydrocodone bitartrate 10 mg and acetaminophen 650 mg
Lorcet® Plus: Hydrocodone bitartrate 7.5 mg and acetaminophen 650 mg
Lortab®:
  5/500: Hydrocodone bitartrate 5 mg and acetaminophen 500 mg
  7.5/500: Hydrocodone bitartrate 7.5 mg and acetaminophen 500 mg
  10/500: Hydrocodone bitartrate 10 mg and acetaminophen 500 mg
Maxidone™: Hydrocodone bitartrate 10 mg and acetaminophen 750 mg
Norco®:
  Hydrocodone bitartrate 5 mg and acetaminophen 325 mg
  Hydrocodone bitartrate 7.5 mg and acetaminophen 325 mg
  Hydrocodone bitartrate 10 mg and acetaminophen 325 mg
Vicodin®: Hydrocodone bitartrate 5 mg and acetaminophen 500 mg
Vicodin® ES: Hydrocodone bitartrate 7.5 mg and acetaminophen 750 mg
Vicodin® HP: Hydrocodone bitartrate 10 mg and acetaminophen 660 mg
Xodol®: Hydrocodone bitartrate 10 mg and acetaminophen 300 mg
Xodol® 5/300: Hydrocodone bitartrate 5 mg and acetaminophen 300 mg
Zydone®:
  Hydrocodone bitartrate 5 mg and acetaminophen 400 mg
  Hydrocodone bitartrate 7.5 mg and acetaminophen 400 mg
  Hydrocodone bitartrate 10 mg and acetaminophen 400 mg

Hydrocodone and Aspirin (hye droe KOE done & AS pir in)

U.S. Brand Names Damason-P®
Index Terms Aspirin and Hydrocodone
Pharmacologic Category Analgesic Combination (Opioid)
Use Relief of moderate to moderately severe pain
Restrictions C-III
Pregnancy Risk Factor D
Dosage Adults: Oral: 1-2 tablets every 4-6 hours as needed for pain
Additional Information Complete prescribing information for this medication should be consulted for additional detail.
Dosage Forms Tablet: Hydrocodone bitartrate 5 mg and aspirin 500 mg

Hydrocodone and Chlorphenlramine
(hye droe KOE done & klor fen IR a meen)

U.S. Brand Names HyTan™ [DSC]; Tussionex®
Index Terms Chlorpheniramine Maleate and Hydrocodone Bitartrate; Hydrocodone Tannate and Chlorpheniramine Tannate
Pharmacologic Category Antihistamine/Antitussive
Use Symptomatic relief of cough and upper respiratory symptoms associated with cold and allergy
Restrictions C-III
Pregnancy Risk Factor C
Dosage Oral:
Children 6-12 years:
  HyTan™: 5 mL every 12 hours; do not exceed 10 mL/24 hours
  Tussionex®: 2.5 mL every 12 hours; do not exceed 5 mL/24 hours
Children >12 years and Adults:
  HyTan™: 10 mL every 12 hours; do not exceed 20 mL/24 hours
  Tussionex®: 5 mL every 12 hours; do not exceed 10 mL/24 hours
Additional Information Complete prescribing information for this medication should be consulted for additional detail.
Dosage Forms [DSC] = Discontinued product
Suspension:
  HyTan™: Hydrocodone tannate 5 mg and chlorpheniramine tannate 4 mg (120 mL) [contains phenylalanine 12.5 mg/5 mL; tropical fruit flavor] [DSC]
Suspension, extended release:
  Tussionex®: Hydrocodone polistirex [equivalent to hydrocodone bitartrate 10 mg] and chlorpheniramine polistirex [equivalent to chlorpheniramine maleate 8 mg] per 5 mL (480 mL)

Hydrocodone and Guaifenesin (hye droe KOE done & gwye FEN e sin)

U.S. Brand Names Atuss® HX; Codiclear® DH; EndaCof; EndaCof-XP; ExeClear; ExeCof-XP; Extendryl® HC; Hycotuss®; Hydro-Tussin™ HG; Kwelcof®; Maxi-Tuss HCG; Pancof-XP; Phanatuss® HC; Pneumotussin®; Touro® HC; Tusso-DF®; Vitussin; Xpect-HC™; Ztuss™ ZT
Index Terms Guaifenesin and Hydrocodone
Pharmacologic Category Antitussive/Expectorant
Use Symptomatic relief of nonproductive coughs associated with upper and lower respiratory tract congestion
Restrictions C-III
Pregnancy Risk Factor C
Medication Safety Issues
Sound-alike/look-alike issues:
  Vicodin® may be confused with Hycodan®, Hycomine®, Indocin®, Uridon®
Dosage
Children:
  <6 years (unlabeled): Hydrocodone 0.3 mg/kg/day in 4 divided doses
  6-12 years:
    Atuss® Hx: One capsule every 8 hours
(Continued)

Hydrocodone and Guaifenesin *(Continued)*

Codiclear® DH, ExeClear, Hycotuss®, Kwelcof®, Maxi-Tuss HCG: 2.5-5 mL every 4 hours, after meals and at bedtime

Hydro-Tussin™ HG: 2.5 mL after meals and at bedtime

Pneumotussin®: One tablet or 5 mL every 4-6 hours (maximum: 4 doses/24 hours)

>12 years:

Codiclear® DH, ExeClear, Hycotuss®, Kwelcof®, Maxi-Tuss HCG: 5-10 mL every 4 hours, after meals and at bedtime

Hydro-Tussin™ HG: 5 mL after meals and at bedtime; may increase to 10 mL/dose if needed (maximum: 30 mL/day)

Pneumotussin®: 1-2 tablets or 10 mL every 4-6 hours (maximum: 4 doses/24 hours)

Children ≥12 years and Adults (Atuss® HX): 1-2 capsules every 8 hours

Adults:

Codiclear® DH, Kwelcof®, ExeClear, Hycotuss®: 5-15 mL every 4 hours, after meals and at bedtime (maximum: 30 mL/24 hours)

Hydro-Tussin™ HG: 5 mL after meals and at bedtime; may increase to 15 mL/dose if needed (maximum: 30 mL/day)

Maxi-Tuss HCG: 5-10 mL every 4 hours, after meals and at bedtime

Pneumotussin®: 1-2 tablets or 10 mL every 4-6 hours (maximum: 4 doses/24 hours)

Additional Information Complete prescribing information for this medication should be consulted for additional detail.

Dosage Forms [DSC] = Discontinued product

Caplet:

Ztuss™ ZT: Hydrocodone bitartrate 5 mg and guaifenesin 300 mg

Capsule, variable release:

Atuss® HX: Hydrocodone bitartrate 5 mg [immediate release] and guaifenesin 100 mg [sustained release]

Liquid: Hydrocodone bitartrate 5 mg and guaifenesin 100 mg per 5 mL (480 mL, 960 mL)

ExeCof-XP: Hydrocodone bitartrate 3 mg and guaifenesin 90 mg per 5 mL (3840 mL) [contains benzoic acid]

Kwelcof®: Hydrocodone bitartrate 5 mg and guaifenesin 100 mg per 5 mL (480 mL) [alcohol free, dye free, sugar free; contains benzoic acid; apricot-pineapple flavor]

Pancof-XP: Hydrocodone bitartrate 3 mg and guaifenesin 90 mg per 5 mL (3840 mL) [contains benzoic acid]

Phanatuss® HC: Hydrocodone bitartrate 5 mg and guaifenesin 100 mg per 5 mL (480 mL) [alcohol free, sugar free; mint flavor]

Vitussin: Hydrocodone bitartrate 5 mg and guaifenesin 100 mg per 5 mL (480 mL) [alcohol free, sugar free, dye free; cherry flavor]

Tablet:

EndaCof: Hydrocodone bitartrate 2.5 mg and guaifenesin 300 mg

Pneumotussin®: Hydrocodone bitartrate 2.5 mg and guaifenesin 300 mg [dye free] [DSC]

Touro® HC: Hydrocodone bitartrate 5 mg and guaifenesin 575 mg

Tablet, sustained release:

Extendryl® HC: Hydrocodone bitartrate 10 mg and guaifenesin 1000 mg

Xpect-HC™: Hydrocodone bitartrate 5 mg and guaifenesin 600 mg

Syrup: Hydrocodone bitartrate 5 mg and guaifenesin 100 mg per 5 mL (480 mL)

Codiclear® DH: Hydrocodone bitartrate 3.5 mg and guaifenesin 100 mg per 5 mL (120 mL, 480 mL) [alcohol free, dye free, sugar free; contains benzoic acid; grape flavor]

EndaCof-XP: Hydrocodone bitartrate 2.5 mg and guaifenesin 200 mg per 5 mL (480 mL) [alcohol free, dye free, sugar free; contains phenylalanine; cherry punch flavor]

ExeClear: Hydrocodone bitartrate 3.5 mg and guaifenesin 100 mg per 5 mL (480 mL)

Hycotuss®: Hydrocodone bitartrate 5 mg and guaifenesin 100 mg per 5 mL (480 mL) [contains alcohol 10%; butterscotch flavor]

Hydro-Tussin™ HG: Hydrocodone bitartrate 3.5 mg and guaifenesin 100 mg per 5 mL (480 mL) [alcohol free, dye free, sugar free; grape flavor]

Maxi-Tuss HCG: Hydrocodone bitartrate 6 mg and guaifenesin 200 mg per 5 mL (480 mL) [alcohol free, sugar free; contains aspartame; butterscotch flavor]

Pneumotussin®: Hydrocodone bitartrate 2.5 mg and guaifenesin 200 mg per 5 mL (480 mL) [alcohol free, dye free, sugar free; cherry punch flavor]

Tusso-DF®: Hydrocodone bitartrate 2.5 mg and guaifenesin 100 mg per 5 mL (480 mL) [cherry flavor]

Hydrocodone and Homatropine *(hye droe KOE done & hoe MA troe peen)*

U.S. Brand Names Hycodan®; Hydromet®; Tussigon®

Index Terms Homatropine and Hydrocodone

Pharmacologic Category Antitussive

Use Symptomatic relief of cough

Restrictions C-III

Pregnancy Risk Factor C

Medication Safety Issues

Sound-alike/look-alike issues:

Hycodan® may be confused with Hycomine®, Vicodin®

Dosage Oral:

Children 6-12 years: ½ tablet or 2.5 mL every 4-6 hours as needed (maximum: 3 tablets or 15 mL/24 hours)

Children ≥12 years and Adults: 1 tablet or 5 mL every 4-6 hours as needed (maximum: 6 tablets/24 hours or 30 mL/24 hours)

Additional Information Complete prescribing information for this medication should be consulted for additional detail.

Dosage Forms
Syrup:
Hycodan®, Hydromet®: Hydrocodone bitartrate 5 mg and homatropine methylbromide 1.5 mg per 5 mL (480 mL) [cherry flavor]
Tablet: Hydrocodone bitartrate 5 mg and homatropine methylbromide 1.5 mg
Hycodan®, Tussigon®: Hydrocodone bitartrate 5 mg and homatropine methylbromide 1.5 mg

Hydrocodone and Ibuprofen (hye droe KOE done & eye byoo PROE fen)

U.S. Brand Names Reprexain™; Vicoprofen®
Canadian Brand Names Vicoprofen®
Index Terms Ibuprofen and Hydrocodone
Pharmacologic Category Analgesic, Opioid; Nonsteroidal Anti-inflammatory Drug (NSAID), Oral
Use Short-term (generally <10 days) management of moderate to severe acute pain; is not indicated for treatment of such conditions as osteoarthritis or rheumatoid arthritis
Restrictions C-III; An FDA-approved medication guide for NSAIDs must be distributed when dispensing an oral outpatient prescription (new or refill) where this medication is to be used without direct supervision of a healthcare provider. Medication guides are available at http://www.fda.gov/cder/Offices/ODS/medication_guides.htm.
Pregnancy Risk Factor C/D (3rd trimester)
Dosage Adults: Oral: 1 tablet every 4-6 hours as needed for pain; maximum: 5 tablets/day
Additional Information Complete prescribing information for this medication should be consulted for additional detail.
Dosage Forms
Tablet: Hydrocodone bitartrate 5 mg and ibuprofen 200 mg; hydrocodone bitartrate 7.5 mg and ibuprofen 200 mg
Reprexain™: Hydrocodone bitartrate 5 mg and ibuprofen 200 mg
Vicoprofen®: Hydrocodone bitartrate 7.5 mg and ibuprofen 200 mg

Hydrocodone and Pseudoephedrine
(hye droe KOE done & soo doe e FED rin)

U.S. Brand Names Coughcold HCM; Histussin D® [DSC]; Pancof-HC; P-V Tussin Tablet
Index Terms Pseudoephedrine and Hydrocodone
Pharmacologic Category Antitussive/Decongestant
Use Symptomatic relief of cough due to colds, nasal congestion, and cough
Restrictions C-III
Dosage Oral: Adults: 5 mL 4 times/day
Additional Information Complete prescribing information for this medication should be consulted for additional detail.
Dosage Forms
Syrup:
Coldcough HCM: Hydrocodone bitartrate 3 mg and pseudoephedrine hydrochloride 15 mg per 5 mL (480 mL) [alcohol, dye and sugar free; grape flavor]
Histussin D®: Hydrocodone bitartrate 5 mg and pseudoephedrine hydrochloride 60 mg per 5 mL (480 mL) [DSC]
Pancof-HC: Hydrocodone bitartrate 3 mg and pseudoephedrine hydrochloride 15 mg per 5 mL (3700 mL) [contains benzoic acid; grape flavor]
Tablet:
P-V Tussin: Hydrocodone bitartrate 5 mg and pseudoephedrine hydrochloride 60 mg

♦ **Hydrocodone Bitartrate, Carbinoxamine Maleate, and Pseudoephedrine Hydrochloride** see Hydrocodone, Carbinoxamine, and Pseudoephedrine on page 851

Hydrocodone, Carbinoxamine, and Pseudoephedrine
(hye droe KOE done, kar bi NOKS a meen, & soo doe e FED rin)

U.S. Brand Names Histex™ HC; Tri-Vent™ HC
Index Terms Carbinoxamine, Pseudoephedrine, and Hydrocodone; Hydrocodone Bitartrate, Carbinoxamine Maleate, and Pseudoephedrine Hydrochloride; Pseudoephedrine, Hydrocodone, and Carbinoxamine
Pharmacologic Category Antihistamine/Decongestant/Antitussive
Use Symptomatic relief of cough, congestion, and rhinorrhea associated with the common cold, influenza, bronchitis, or sinusitis
Restrictions C-III
Pregnancy Risk Factor C
Dosage Oral: Relief of cough, congestion, and runny nose:
Children:
2-10 years: Dosing based on hydrocodone content: 0.6 mg/kg/day given in 4 divided doses. Alternately, the following dosing may be used based on age:
2-4 years: 1.25 mL every 4-6 hours; maximum dose: 7.5 mL/24 hours
4-10 years: 2.5 mL every 4-6 hours; maximum dose: 15 mL/24 hours
>10 years: Refer to Adults dosing
Adults: 5-10 mL every 4-6 hours; maximum dose: 30 mL/24 hours
Additional Information Complete prescribing information for this medication should be consulted for additional detail.
Dosage Forms [DSC] = Discontinued product
Liquid: Hydrocodone bitartrate 5 mg, carbinoxamine maleate 2 mg, and pseudoephedrine hydrochloride 30 mg per 5 mL (480 mL) [DSC]
(Continued)

Hydrocodone, Carbinoxamine, and Pseudoephedrine
(Continued)

Histex™ HC, Tri-Vent™ HC: Hydrocodone bitartrate 5 mg, carbinoxamine maleate 2 mg, and pseudoephedrine hydrochloride 30 mg per 5 mL (480 mL) [alcohol free, sugar free; peach flavor]

Hydrocodone, Chlorpheniramine, Phenylephrine, Acetaminophen, and Caffeine
(hye droe KOE done, klor fen IR a meen, fen il EF rin, a seet a MIN oh fen, & KAF een)

U.S. Brand Names Hycomine® Compound
Index Terms Acetaminophen, Caffeine, Hydrocodone, Chlorpheniramine, and Phenylephrine; Caffeine, Hydrocodone, Chlorpheniramine, Phenylephrine, and Acetaminophen; Chlorpheniramine, Hydrocodone, Phenylephrine, Acetaminophen, and Caffeine; Phenylephrine, Hydrocodone, Chlorpheniramine, Acetaminophen, and Caffeine
Pharmacologic Category Antitussive/Decongestant
Use Symptomatic relief of cough and symptoms of upper respiratory infection
Restrictions C-III
Pregnancy Risk Factor C
Medication Safety Issues
Sound-alike/look-alike issues:
Hycomine® may be confused with Byclomine®, Hycamtin®, Hycodan®, Vicodin®
Dosage Adults: Oral: 1 tablet every 4 hours, up to 4 times/day
Additional Information Complete prescribing information for this medication should be consulted for additional detail.
Dosage Forms Tablet: Hydrocodone bitartrate 5 mg, chlorpheniramine maleate 2 mg, phenylephrine hydrochloride 10 mg, acetaminophen 250 mg, and caffeine 30 mg [cherry flavor]

Hydrocodone, Pseudoephedrine, and Guaifenesin
(hye droe KOE done, soo doe e FED rin & gwye FEN e sin)

U.S. Brand Names Hydro-Tussin™ HD; Hydro-Tussin™ XP; Su-Tuss®-HD; Tussend® Expectorant [DSC]; Ztuss™ Tablet
Index Terms Guaifenesin, Hydrocodone, and Pseudoephedrine; Pseudoephedrine, Hydrocodone, and Guaifenesin
Pharmacologic Category Antitussive/Decongestant/Expectorant
Use Symptomatic relief of irritating, nonproductive cough associated with upper respiratory conditions and allergies
Restrictions C-III
Pregnancy Risk Factor C
Dosage Oral: Cough/congestion:
Children:
2-6 years: Hydro-Tussin™ XP: 1.25-2.5 mL 4 times/day as needed
6-12 years:
Hydro-Tussin™ XP: 2.5-5 mL 4 times/day as needed
Tussend®, Hydro-Tussin™ HD: 5 mL every 4-6 hours as needed
Ztuss™: One-half to 1 tablet every 4-6 hours (maximum: 6 tablets/24 hours)
Children ≥12 years and Adults:
Hydro-Tussin™ XP: 5-10 mL 4 times/day as needed
Tussend®, Hydro-Tussin™ HD: 10 mL every 4-6 hours as needed
Ztuss™: 1-1¹/₂ tablets every 4-6 hours (maximum: 8 tablets/24 hours)
Additional Information Complete prescribing information for this medication should be consulted for additional detail.
Dosage Forms [DSC] = Discontinued product
Elixir (Su-Tuss®-HD): Hydrocodone bitartrate 2.5 mg, pseudoephedrine hydrochloride 30 mg, and guaifenesin 100 mg per 5 mL (480 mL) [contains alcohol; fruit punch flavor]
Liquid:
Hydro-Tussin™ HD: Hydrocodone bitartrate 2.5 mg, pseudoephedrine hydrochloride 30 mg, and guaifenesin 100 mg per 5 mL (480 mL) [alcohol free; contains sodium benzoate]
Hydro-Tussin® XP: Hydrocodone bitartrate 3 mg, pseudoephedrine hydrochloride 15 mg, and guaifenesin 100 mg per 5 mL (480 mL) [alcohol free, dye free]
Tussend® Expectorant: Hydrocodone bitartrate 2.5 mg, pseudoephedrine hydrochloride 30 mg, and guaifenesin 100 mg per 5 mL (480 mL) [contains alcohol; fruit punch flavor] [DSC]
Tablet (Ztuss™): Hydrocodone bitartrate 5 mg, pseudoephedrine hydrochloride 30 mg, and guaifenesin 300 mg [sugar free]

◆ **Hydrocodone Tannate and Chlorpheniramine Tannate** *see* Hydrocodone and Chlorpheniramine *on page 849*

Hydrocortisone (hye droe KOR ti sone)

U.S. Brand Names Anucort-HC®; Anusol-HC®; Anusol® HC-1 [OTC]; Aquanil™ HC [OTC]; Beta-HC®; Caldecort® [OTC]; Cetacort®; Colocort®; Cortaid® Intensive Therapy [OTC]; Cortaid® Maximum Strength [OTC]; Cortaid® Sensitive Skin [OTC]; Cortef®; Corticool® [OTC]; Cortifoam®; Cortizone®-10 Maximum Strength [OTC]; Cortizone®-10 Plus Maximum Strength [OTC]; Cortizone®-10 Quick Shot [OTC]; Dermarest Dricort® [OTC]; Dermtex® HC [OTC]; EarSol® HC; Encort™; Hemril®-30; HydroZone Plus [OTC]; Hytone®; IvySoothe® [OTC]; Locoid®; Locoid Lipocream®; Nupercainal® Hydrocortisone Cream [OTC]; Nutracort®; Pandel®; Post Peel Healing Balm [OTC]; Preparation H® Hydrocortisone [OTC]; Proctocort®; ProctoCream® HC; Procto-Kit™; Procto-Pak™; Proctosert; Proctosol-HC®; Proctozone-HC™;

Sarnol®-HC [OTC]; Solu-Cortef®; Summer's Eve® SpecialCare™ Medicated Anti-Itch Cream [OTC]; Texacort®; Tucks® Anti-Itch [OTC]; Westcort®

Canadian Brand Names Aquacort®; Cortamed®; Cortef®; Cortenema®; Cortifoam™; Emo-Cort®; Hycort™; Hyderm; HydroVal®; Locoid®; Prevex® HC; Sarna® HC; Solu-Cortef®; Westcort®

Index Terms A-hydroCort; Compound F; Cortisol; Hemorrhoidal HC; Hydrocortisone Acetate; Hydrocortisone Butyrate; Hydrocortisone Probutate; Hydrocortisone Sodium Succinate; Hydrocortisone Valerate

Pharmacologic Category Corticosteroid, Rectal; Corticosteroid, Systemic; Corticosteroid, Topical

Additional Appendix Information
Corticosteroids *on page 1879*

Use Management of adrenocortical insufficiency; relief of inflammation of corticosteroid-responsive dermatoses (low and medium potency topical corticosteroid); adjunctive treatment of ulcerative colitis

Pregnancy Risk Factor C

Pregnancy Implications There are no adequate and well-controlled studies in pregnant women. Corticosteroid use has been associated with cleft palate, neonatal adrenal suppression, low birth weight, and cataracts in the infant; including cases associated with topical administration. Use only if potential benefit to the mother exceeds the potential risk to the fetus. Avoid high doses or prolonged use.

Lactation Excretion in breast milk unknown/use caution

Medication Safety Issues
Sound-alike/look-alike issues:
Hydrocortisone may be confused with hydrocodone, hydroxychloroquine, hydrochlorothiazide

Anusol® may be confused with Anusol-HC®, Aplisol®, Aquasol®

Anusol-HC® may be confused with Anusol®

Cortef® may be confused with Lortab®

Cortizone® may be confused with cortisone

HCT (occasional abbreviation for hydrocortisone) is an error-prone abbreviation (mistaken as hydrochlorothiazide)

Hytone® may be confused with Vytone®

Proctocort® may be confused with ProctoCream®

ProctoCream® may be confused with Proctocort®

International issues:
Hytone® may be confused with Hysone® [Australia]

Nutracort® may be confused with Nitrocor® which is a brand name of nitroglycerin in Chile and Italy

Contraindications Hypersensitivity to hydrocortisone or any component of the formulation; serious infections, except septic shock or tuberculous meningitis; viral, fungal, or tubercular skin lesions

Warnings/Precautions
Use with caution in patients with thyroid disease, hepatic impairment, renal impairment, cardiovascular disease, diabetes, glaucoma, cataracts, myasthenia gravis, patients at risk for osteoporosis, patients at risk for seizures, or GI diseases (diverticulitis, peptic ulcer, ulcerative colitis) due to perforation risk. Use caution following acute MI (corticosteroids have been associated with myocardial rupture). Because of the risk of adverse effects, systemic corticosteroids should be used cautiously in the elderly in the smallest possible effective dose for the shortest duration. May affect growth velocity; growth should be routinely monitored in pediatric patients. Withdraw therapy with gradual tapering of dose.

May cause hypercorticism or suppression of hypothalamic-pituitary-adrenal (HPA) axis, particularly in younger children or in patients receiving high doses for prolonged periods. HPA axis suppression may lead to adrenal crisis. Withdrawal and discontinuation of a corticosteroid should be done slowly and carefully. Particular care is required when patients are transferred from systemic corticosteroids to inhaled products due to possible adrenal insufficiency or withdrawal from steroids, including an increase in allergic symptoms. Patients receiving >20 mg per day of prednisone (or equivalent) may be most susceptible. Fatalities have occurred due to adrenal insufficiency in asthmatic patients during and after transfer from systemic corticosteroids to aerosol steroids; aerosol steroids do not provide the systemic steroid needed to treat patients having trauma, surgery, or infections. Avoid use of topical preparations with occlusive dressings or on weeping or exudative lesions.

Acute myopathy has been reported with high dose corticosteroids, usually in patients with neuromuscular transmission disorders; may involve ocular and/or respiratory muscles; monitor creatine kinase; recovery may be delayed. Corticosteroid use may cause psychiatric disturbances, including depression, euphoria, insomnia, mood swings, and personality changes. Pre-existing psychiatric conditions may be exacerbated by corticosteroid use. Prolonged use of corticosteroids may also increase the incidence of secondary infection, mask acute infection (including fungal infections), prolong or exacerbate viral infections, or limit response to vaccines. Exposure to chickenpox should be avoided; corticosteroids should not be used to treat ocular herpes simplex. Corticosteroids should not be used for cerebral malaria. Close observation is required in patients with latent tuberculosis and/or TB reactivity; restrict use in active TB (only in conjunction with antituberculosis treatment). Prolonged treatment with corticosteroids has been associated with the development of Kaposi's sarcoma (case reports); if noted, discontinuation of therapy should be considered.

Adverse Reactions
Systemic:
>10%:
Central nervous system: Insomnia, nervousness
Gastrointestinal: Increased appetite, indigestion
1% to 10%:
Dermatologic: Hirsutism
Endocrine & metabolic: Diabetes mellitus
(Continued)

Hydrocortisone *(Continued)*

Neuromuscular & skeletal: Arthralgia

Ocular: Cataracts

Respiratory: Epistaxis

<1% (Limited to important or life-threatening): Hypertension, edema, euphoria, headache, delirium, hallucinations, seizure, mood swings, acne, dermatitis, skin atrophy, bruising, hyperpigmentation, hypokalemia, hyperglycemia, Cushing's syndrome, sodium and water retention, bone growth suppression, amenorrhea, peptic ulcer, abdominal distention, ulcerative esophagitis, pancreatitis, muscle wasting, hypersensitivity reactions, immunosuppression

Topical:

>10%: Dermatologic: Eczema (12.5%)

1% to 10%: Dermatologic: Pruritus (6%), stinging (2%), dry skin (2%)

<1% (Limited to important or life-threatening): Allergic contact dermatitis, burning, dermal atrophy, folliculitis, HPA axis suppression, hypopigmentation; metabolic effects (hyperglycemia, hypokalemia); striae

Overdosage/Toxicology Symptoms include cushingoid appearance (systemic), muscle weakness (systemic), and osteoporosis (systemic) - all with long-term use only. When consumed in excessive quantities for prolonged periods, systemic hypercorticism and adrenal suppression may occur. In those cases, discontinuation and withdrawal of the corticosteroid should be done judiciously.

Drug Interactions

Cytochrome P450 Effect: Substrate of CYP3A4 (minor); **Induces** CYP3A4 (weak)

Increased Effect/Toxicity: Hydrocortisone in combination with oral anticoagulants may increase prothrombin time. Potassium-depleting diuretics increase risk of hypokalemia. Cardiac glycosides increase risk of arrhythmias or digitalis toxicity secondary to hypokalemia.

Decreased Effect: Hydrocortisone may decrease the hypoglycemic effect of insulin. Phenytoin, phenobarbital, ephedrine, and rifampin increase metabolism of hydrocortisone resulting in a decreased steroid blood level.

Ethanol/Nutrition/Herb Interactions

Ethanol: Avoid ethanol (may enhance gastric mucosal irritation).

Food: Hydrocortisone interferes with calcium absorption.

Herb/Nutraceutical: St John's wort may decrease hydrocortisone levels. Avoid cat's claw, echinacea (have immunostimulant properties).

Stability Store at controlled room temperature 20°C to 25°C (59°F to 86°F). Hydrocortisone sodium phosphate and hydrocortisone sodium succinate are clear, light yellow solutions which are heat labile.

Sodium succinate: Reconstitute 100 mg vials with bacteriostatic water (not >2 mL). Act-O-Vial (self-contained powder for injection plus diluent) may be reconstituted by pressing the activator to force diluent into the powder compartment. Following gentle agitation, solution may be withdrawn via syringe through a needle inserted into the center of the stopper. May be administered (I.V. or I.M.) without further dilution. After initial reconstitution, hydrocortisone sodium succinate solutions are stable for 3 days at room temperature or under refrigeration when protected from light. Stability of parenteral admixture (Solu-Cortef®) at room temperature (25°C) and at refrigeration temperature (4°C) is concentration-dependent:

Stability of concentration 1 mg/mL: 24 hours.

Stability of concentration 2 mg/mL to 60 mg/mL: At least 4 hours.

Solutions for I.V. infusion: Reconstituted solutions may be added to an appropriate volume of compatible solution for infusion. Concentration should generally not exceed 1 mg/mL. However, in cases where administration of a small volume of fluid is desirable, 100-3000 mg may be added to 50 mL of D_5W or NS (stability limited to 4 hours).

Mechanism of Action Decreases inflammation by suppression of migration of polymorphonuclear leukocytes and reversal of increased capillary permeability

Pharmacodynamics/Kinetics

Onset of action:

Hydrocortisone acetate: Slow

Hydrocortisone sodium succinate (water soluble): Rapid

Duration: Hydrocortisone acetate: Long

Absorption: Rapid by all routes, except rectally

Metabolism: Hepatic

Half-life elimination: Biologic: 8-12 hours

Excretion: Urine (primarily as 17-hydroxysteroids and 17-ketosteroids)

Dosage Dose should be based on severity of disease and patient response

Acute adrenal insufficiency: I.M., I.V.:

Infants and young Children: Succinate: 1-2 mg/kg/dose bolus, then 25-150 mg/day in divided doses every 6-8 hours

Older Children: Succinate: 1-2 mg/kg bolus then 150-250 mg/day in divided doses every 6-8 hours

Adults: Succinate: 100 mg I.V. bolus, then 300 mg/day in divided doses every 8 hours or as a continuous infusion for 48 hours; once patient is stable change to oral, 50 mg every 8 hours for 6 doses, then taper to 30-50 mg/day in divided doses

Chronic adrenal corticoid insufficiency: Adults: Oral: 20-30 mg/day

Anti-inflammatory or immunosuppressive:

Infants and Children:

Oral: 2.5-10 mg/kg/day **or** 75-300 mg/m²/day every 6-8 hours

I.M., I.V.: Succinate: 1-5 mg/kg/day **or** 30-150 mg/m²/day divided every 12-24 hours

Adolescents and Adults: Oral, I.M., I.V.: Succinate: 15-240 mg every 12 hours

Congenital adrenal hyperplasia: Oral: Initial: 10-20 mg/m²/day in 3 divided doses; a variety of dosing schedules have been used. **Note:** Inconsistencies have occurred with liquid formulations; tablets may provide more reliable levels. Doses must be individualized by monitoring growth, bone age, and hormonal levels. Mineralocorticoid and sodium supplementation may be required based upon electrolyte regulation and plasma renin activity.

Physiologic replacement: Children:
    Oral: 0.5-0.75 mg/kg/day **or** 20-25 mg/m^2/day every 8 hours
    I.M.: Succinate: 0.25-0.35 mg/kg/day **or** 12-15 mg/m^2/day once daily

Shock: I.M., I.V.: Succinate:
    Children: Initial: 50 mg/kg, then repeated in 4 hours and/or every 24 hours as needed
    Adolescents and Adults: 500 mg to 2 g every 2-6 hours

Status asthmaticus: Children and Adults: I.V.: Succinate: 1-2 mg/kg/dose every 6 hours for 24 hours, then maintenance of 0.5-1 mg/kg every 6 hours

Adults:
  Rheumatic diseases:
    Intralesional, intra-articular, soft tissue injection: Acetate:
      Large joints: 25 mg (up to 37.5 mg)
      Small joints: 10-25 mg
    Tendon sheaths: 5-12.5 mg
    Soft tissue infiltration: 25-50 mg (up to 75 mg)
    Bursae: 25-37.5 mg
    Ganglia: 12.5-25 mg
  Stress dosing (surgery) in patients known to be adrenally-suppressed or on chronic systemic steroids: I.V.:
    Minor stress (ie, inguinal herniorrhaphy): 25 mg/day for 1 day
    Moderate stress (ie, joint replacement, cholecystectomy): 50-75 mg/day (25 mg every 8-12 hours) for 1-2 days
    Major stress (pancreatoduodenectomy, esophagogastrectomy, cardiac surgery): 100-150 mg/day (50 mg every 8-12 hours) for 2-3 days

Dermatosis: Children >2 years and Adults: Topical: Apply to affected area 2-4 times/day (Buteprate: Apply once or twice daily). Therapy should be discontinued when control is achieved; if no improvement is seen, reassessment of diagnosis may be necessary.

Ulcerative colitis: Adults: Rectal: 10-100 mg 1-2 times/day for 2-3 weeks

Dietary Considerations Systemic use of corticosteroids may require a diet with increased potassium, vitamins A, B$_6$, C, D, folate, calcium, zinc, phosphorus, and decreased sodium. Sodium content of 1 g (sodium succinate injection): 47.5 mg (2.07 mEq)

Administration

Oral: Administer with food or milk to decrease GI upset

Parenteral: Hydrocortisone sodium succinate may be administered by I.M. or I.V. routes
    I.V. bolus: Dilute to 50 mg/mL and administer over 30 seconds to several minutes (depending on the dose)
    I.V. intermittent infusion: Dilute to 1 mg/mL and administer over 20-30 minutes

Topical: Apply a thin film to clean, dry skin and rub in gently

Monitoring Parameters Blood pressure, weight, serum glucose, and electrolytes

Reference Range Therapeutic: AM: 5-25 mcg/dL (SI: 138-690 nmol/L), PM: 2-9 mcg/dL (SI: 55-248 nmol/L) depending on test, assay

Additional Information Hydrocortisone base topical cream, lotion, and ointments in concentrations of 0.25%, 0.5%, and 1% may be OTC or prescription depending on the product labeling.

Dosage Forms [DSC] = Discontinued product

Aerosol, rectal, as acetate (Cortifoam®): 10% (15 g) [90 mg/applicator]

Cream, rectal, as acetate (Nupercainal® Hydrocortisone Cream): 1% (30 g) [strength expressed as base]

Cream, rectal, as base:
    Cortizone®-10: 1% (30 g) [contains aloe]
    Preparation H® Hydrocortisone: 1% (27 g)

Cream, topical, as acetate: 0.5% (9 g, 30 g, 60 g) [available with aloe]; 1% (30 g, 454 g) [available with aloe]

Cream, topical, as base: 0.5% (30 g); 1% (1.5 g, 30 g, 114 g, 454 g); 2.5% (20 g, 30 g, 454 g)
    Anusol-HC®: 2.5% (30 g) [contains benzyl alcohol]
    Caldecort®: 1% (30 g) [contains aloe vera gel]
    Cortaid® Intensive Therapy: 1% (60 g)
    Cortaid® Maximum Strength: 1% (15 g, 30 g, 40 g, 60 g) [contains aloe vera gel and benzyl alcohol]
    Cortaid® Sensitive Skin: 0.5% (15 g) [contains aloe vera gel]
    Cortizone®-10 Maximum Strength: 1% (15 g, 30 g, 60 g) [contains aloe]
    Cortizone®-10 Plus Maximum Strength: 1% (30 g, 60 g) [contains vitamins A, D, E and aloe]
    Dermarest® Dricort®: 1% (15 g, 30 g)
    HydroZone Plus, Proctocort®, Procto-Pak™: 1% (30 g)
    Hytone®: 2.5% (30 g, 60 g)
    IvySoothe®: 1% (30 g) [contains aloe]
    Post Peel Healing Balm: 1% (23 g)
    ProctoCream® HC: 2.5% (30 g) [contains benzyl alcohol]
    Procto-Kit™: 1% (30 g) [packaged with applicator tips and finger cots]; 2.5% (30 g) [packaged with applicator tips and finger cots]
    Proctosol-HC®, Proctozone-HC™: 2.5% (30 g)
    Summer's Eve® SpecialCare™ Medicated Anti-Itch Cream: 1% (30 g)

Cream, topical, as butyrate (Locoid®, Locoid Lipocream®): 0.1% (15 g, 45 g)

Cream, topical, as probutate (Pandel®): 0.1% (15 g, 45 g, 80 g)

Cream, topical, as valerate (Westcort®): 0.2% (15 g, 45 g, 60 g)

Gel, topical, as base (Corticool®): 1% (45 g)

Injection, powder for reconstitution, as sodium succinate (Solu-Cortef®): 100 mg, 250 mg, 500 mg, 1 g [diluent contains benzyl alcohol; strength expressed as base]

Lotion, topical, as base: 1% (120 mL); 2.5% (60 mL)
    Aquanil™ HC: 1% (120 mL)
    Beta-HC®, Cetacort®, Sarnol®-HC: 1% (60 mL)
    HydroZone Plus: 1% (120 mL)

(Continued)

Hydrocortisone *(Continued)*

Hytone®: 2.5% (60 mL)

Nutracort®: 1% (60 mL, 120 mL); 2.5% (60 mL, 120 mL)

Ointment, topical, as acetate: 1% (30 g) [strength expressed as base; available with aloe]

Anusol® HC-1: 1% (21 g) [strength expressed as base]

Cortaid® Maximum Strength: 1% (15 g, 30 g) [strength expressed as base]

Ointment, topical, as base: 0.5% (30 g); 1% (30 g, 454 g); 2.5% (20 g, 30 g, 454 g)

Cortizone®-10 Maximum Strength: 1% (30 g, 60 g)

Hytone®: 2.5% (30 g) [DSC]

Ointment, topical, as butyrate (Locoid®): 0.1% (15 g, 45 g)

Ointment, topical, as valerate (Westcort®): 0.2% (15 g, 45 g, 60 g)

Solution, otic, as base (EarSol® HC): 1% (30 mL) [contains alcohol 44%, benzyl benzoate, yerba santa]

Solution, topical, as base (Texacort®): 2.5% (30 mL) [contains alcohol]

Solution, topical, as butyrate (Locoid®): 0.1% (20 mL, 60 mL) [contains alcohol 50%]

Solution, topical spray, as base:

Cortaid® Intensive Therapy: 1% (60 mL) [contains alcohol]

Cortizone®-10 Quick Shot: 1% (44 mL) [contains benzyl alcohol]

Dermtex® HC: 1% (52 mL) [contains menthol 1%]

Suppository, rectal, as acetate: 25 mg (12s, 24s, 100s)

Anucort-HC®, Tucks® Anti-Itch: 25 mg (12s, 24s, 100s) [strength expressed as base; Anucort-HC® *renamed* Tucks® Anti-Itch]

Anusol-HC®, Proctosol-HC®: 25 mg (12s, 24s)

Encort™: 30 mg (12s)

Hemril®-30, Proctocort®, Proctosert®: 30 mg (12s, 24s)

Suspension, rectal, as base: 100 mg/60 mL (7s)

Colocort®: 100 mg/60 mL (1s, 7s)

Tablet, as base: 20 mg

Cortef®: 5 mg, 10 mg, 20 mg

- ◆ **Hydrocortisone Acetate** *see* Hydrocortisone *on page 852*
- ◆ **Hydrocortisone, Acetic Acid, and Propylene Glycol Diacetate** *see* Acetic Acid, Propylene Glycol Diacetate, and Hydrocortisone *on page 38*
- ◆ **Hydrocortisone and Benzoyl Peroxide** *see* Benzoyl Peroxide and Hydrocortisone *on page 208*
- ◆ **Hydrocortisone and Ciprofloxacin** *see* Ciprofloxacin and Hydrocortisone *on page 377*
- ◆ **Hydrocortisone and Iodoquinol** *see* Iodoquinol and Hydrocortisone *on page 931*
- ◆ **Hydrocortisone and Pramoxine** *see* Pramoxine and Hydrocortisone *on page 1409*
- ◆ **Hydrocortisone and Urea** *see* Urea and Hydrocortisone *on page 1759*
- ◆ **Hydrocortisone, Bacitracin, Neomycin, and Polymyxin B** *see* Bacitracin, Neomycin, Polymyxin B, and Hydrocortisone *on page 192*
- ◆ **Hydrocortisone Butyrate** *see* Hydrocortisone *on page 852*
- ◆ **Hydrocortisone, Neomycin, and Polymyxin B** *see* Neomycin, Polymyxin B, and Hydrocortisone *on page 1212*
- ◆ **Hydrocortisone, Neomycin, Colistin, and Thonzonium** *see* Neomycin, Colistin, Hydrocortisone, and Thonzonium *on page 1211*
- ◆ **Hydrocortisone Probutate** *see* Hydrocortisone *on page 852*
- ◆ **Hydrocortisone Sodium Succinate** *see* Hydrocortisone *on page 852*
- ◆ **Hydrocortisone Valerate** *see* Hydrocortisone *on page 852*
- ◆ **Hydromet®** *see* Hydrocodone and Homatropine *on page 850*
- ◆ **Hydromorph Contin® (Can)** *see* Hydromorphone *on page 856*
- ◆ **Hydromorph-IR® (Can)** *see* Hydromorphone *on page 856*

Hydromorphone *(hye droe MOR fone)*

U.S. Brand Names Dilaudid®; Dilaudid-HP®

Canadian Brand Names Dilaudid®; Dilaudid-HP®; Dilaudid-HP-Plus®; Dilaudid® Sterile Powder; Dilaudid-XP®; Hydromorph Contin®; Hydromorph-IR®; Hydromorphone HP; Hydromorphone HP® 10; Hydromorphone HP® 20; Hydromorphone HP® 50; Hydromorphone HP® Forte; Hydromorphone Hydrochloride Injection, USP; PMS-Hydromorphone

Index Terms Dihydromorphinone; Hydromorphone Hydrochloride

Pharmacologic Category Analgesic, Opioid

Additional Appendix Information

Narcotic Agonists *on page 1888*

Use Management of moderate-to-severe pain

Unlabeled/Investigational Use Antitussive

Restrictions C-II

Pregnancy Risk Factor C/D (prolonged use or high doses at term)

Pregnancy Implications Hydromorphone was teratogenic in some, but not all, animal studies; however, maternal toxicity was also reported. Hydromorphone crosses the placenta. Chronic opioid use during pregnancy may lead to a withdrawal syndrome in the neonate. Symptoms include irritability, hyperactivity, loss of sleep pattern, abnormal crying, tremor, vomiting, diarrhea, weight loss, or failure to gain weight.

Lactation Excretion in breast milk unknown/not recommended

Medication Safety Issues

Sound-alike/look-alike issues:

Dilaudid® may be confused with Demerol®, Dilantin®

Hydromorphone may be confused with morphine; significant overdoses have occurred when hydromorphone products have been inadvertently administered instead of morphine sulfate. Commercially available prefilled syringes of both products looks similar and are often stored in close proximity to each other. **Note:** Hydromorphone 1 mg oral is approximately equal to morphine 4 mg oral; hydromorphone 1 mg I.V. is approximately equal to morphine 5 mg I.V.

Dilaudid®, Dilaudid-HP®: Extreme caution should be taken to avoid confusing the highly-concentrated (Dilaudid-HP®) injection with the less-concentrated (Dilaudid®) injectable product.

Significant differences exist between oral and I.V. dosing. Use caution when converting from one route of administration to another.

Contraindications Hypersensitivity to hydromorphone, any component of the formulation; acute or severe asthma, severe respiratory depression (in absence of resuscitative equipment or ventilatory support); severe CNS depression; pregnancy (prolonged use or high doses at term); obstetrical analgesia

Warnings/Precautions Use with caution in patients with hypersensitivity reactions to other phenanthrene derivative opioid agonists (codeine, hydrocodone, levorphanol, oxycodone, oxymorphone). Hydromorphone shares toxic potential of opiate agonists, including CNS depression and respiratory depression. Precautions associated with opiate agonist therapy should be observed. May cause CNS depression, which may impair physical or mental abilities; patients must be cautioned about performing tasks which require mental alertness (eg, operating machinery or driving). Myoclonus and seizures have been reported with high doses. Critical respiratory depression may occur, even at therapeutic dosages, particularly in elderly or debilitated patients or in patients with pre-existing respiratory compromise (hypoxia and/or hypercapnia). Use caution in COPD or other obstructive pulmonary disease. Use with caution in patients with hypersensitivity to other phenanthrene opiates, kyphoscoliosis, biliary tract disease, acute pancreatitis, morbid obesity, adrenocortical insufficiency, hypothyroidism, acute alcoholism, toxic psychoses, prostatic hyperplasia and/or urinary stricture, or severe liver or renal failure. Use extreme caution in patients with head injury, intracranial lesions, or elevated intracranial pressure; exaggerated elevation of ICP may occur (in addition, hydromorphone may complicate neurologic evaluation due to pupillary dilation and CNS depressant effects). Use with caution in patients with depleted blood volume or drugs which may exaggerate hypotensive effects (including phenothiazines or general anesthetics). May obscure diagnosis or clinical course of patients with acute abdominal conditions.

[U.S. Boxed Warning]: Hydromorphone has a high potential for abuse. Those at risk for opioid abuse include patients with a history of substance abuse or mental illness. Tolerance or drug dependence may result from extended use; however, concerns for abuse should not prevent effective management of pain. In general, abrupt discontinuation of therapy in dependent patients should be avoided.

An opioid-containing analgesic regimen should be tailored to each patient's needs and based upon the type of pain being treated (acute versus chronic), the route of administration, degree of tolerance for opioids (naive versus chronic user), age, weight, and medical condition. The optimal analgesic dose varies widely among patients. Doses should be titrated to pain relief/prevention. I.M. use may result in variable absorption and a lag time to peak effect.

Dosage form specific warnings:
   [U.S. Boxed Warning]: Dilaudid-HP®: Extreme caution should be taken to avoid confusing the highly-concentrated (Dilaudid-HP®) injection with the less-concentrated (Dilaudid®) injectable product. Dilaudid-HP® should only be used in patients who are opioid-tolerant.
   Controlled release: Capsules should only be used when continuous analgesia is required over an extended period of time. Controlled release products are not to be used on an "as needed" (PRN) basis.
   Some dosage forms contain trace amounts of sodium metabisulfite which may cause allergic reactions in susceptible individuals.

Adverse Reactions Frequency not defined.
   Cardiovascular: Bradycardia, flushing of face, hyper-/hypotension, palpitation, peripheral vasodilation, syncope, tachycardia
   Central nervous system: Agitation, chills, CNS depression, dizziness, drowsiness, dysphoria, euphoria, fatigue, hallucinations, headache, increased intracranial pressure, insomnia, lightheadedness, mental depression, nervousness, restlessness, sedation, seizure
   Dermatologic: Pruritus, rash, urticaria
   Endocrine & metabolic: Antidiuretic hormone release
   Gastrointestinal: Anorexia, biliary tract spasm, constipation, diarrhea, nausea, paralytic ileus, stomach cramps, taste perversion, vomiting, xerostomia
   Genitourinary: Ureteral spasm, urinary retention, urinary tract spasm, urination decreased
   Hepatic: AST/ALT increased, LFTs increased
   Local: Pain at injection site (I.M.), wheal/flare over vein (I.V.)
   Neuromuscular & skeletal: Myoclonus, paresthesia, trembling, tremor, weakness
   Ocular: Blurred vision, diplopia, miosis, nystagmus
   Respiratory: Apnea, bronchospasm, dyspnea, laryngospasm, respiratory depression
   Miscellaneous: Diaphoresis, histamine release, physical and psychological dependence

Overdosage/Toxicology Symptoms of overdose include CNS depression, bradycardia, hypotension, respiratory depression, miosis, apnea, pulmonary edema, and convulsions. Along with supportive measures, naloxone, 2 mg I.V. with repeat administration as necessary up to a total of 10 mg, can also be used to reverse toxic effects of the opiate. Longer observation times may be required with overdose of longer duration products. Activated charcoal or gut decontamination may be used with oral overdose.

Drug Interactions
   Increased Effect/Toxicity: Effects may be additive with CNS depressants; hypotensive effects may be increased with phenothiazines or general anesthetics; serotonergic effects may be additive with SSRIs
   Decreased Effect: Hydromorphone may diminish the effects of pegvisomant. Ammonium chloride may decrease the levels/effects of hydromorphone.

Ethanol/Nutrition/Herb Interactions
   Ethanol: Avoid ethanol (may increase CNS depression).
   (Continued)

Hydromorphone (Continued)

Herb/Nutraceutical: Avoid valerian, St John's wort, kava kava, gotu kola (may increase CNS depression).

Stability Store injection and oral dosage forms at 15°C to 30°C (59°F to 86°F). Protect tablets from light. A slightly yellowish discoloration has not been associated with a loss of potency.

Mechanism of Action Binds to opiate receptors in the CNS, causing inhibition of ascending pain pathways, altering the perception of and response to pain; causes cough supression by direct central action in the medulla; produces generalized CNS depression

Pharmacodynamics/Kinetics

Onset of action: Analgesic: Immediate release formulations:

Oral: 15-30 minutes

Peak effect: Oral: 30-60 minutes

Duration: Immediate release formulations: 4-5 hours

Absorption: I.M.: Variable and delayed

Distribution: V_d: 4 L/kg

Protein binding: ~8% to 19%

Metabolism: Hepatic via glucuronidation; to inactive metabolites

Bioavailability: 62%

Half-life elimination: Immediate release formulations: 1-3 hours

Excretion: Urine (primarily as glucuronide conjugates)

Dosage

Acute pain (moderate to severe): **Note:** These are guidelines and do not represent the maximum doses that may be required in all patients. Doses should be titrated to pain relief/prevention.

Children ≥6 months and <50 kg:

Oral: 0.03-0.08 mg/kg/dose every 3-4 hours as needed

I.V.: 0.015 mg/kg/dose every 3-6 hours as needed

Children >50 kg and Adults:

Oral: Initial: Opiate-naive: 2-4 mg every 3-6 hours as needed; elderly/debilitated patients may require lower doses; patients with prior opiate exposure may require higher initial doses; usual dosage range: 2-8 mg every 3-4 hours as needed

I.V.: Initial: Opiate-naive: 0.2-0.6 mg every 2-3 hours as needed; patients with prior opiate exposure may tolerate higher initial doses

Note: More frequent dosing may be needed.

Mechanically-ventilated patients (based on 70 kg patient): 0.7-2 mg every 1-2 hours as needed; infusion (based on 70 kg patient): 0.5-1 mg/hour

Patient-controlled analgesia (PCA): (Opiate-naive: Consider lower end of dosing range)

Usual concentration: 0.2 mg/mL

Demand dose: Usual: 0.1-0.2 mg; range: 0.05-0.5 mg

Lockout interval: 5-15 minutes

4-hour limit: 4-6 mg

Epidural:

Bolus dose: 1-1.5 mg

Infusion concentration: 0.05-0.075 mg/mL

Infusion rate: 0.04-0.4 mg/hour

Demand dose: 0.15 mg

Lockout interval: 30 minutes

I.M., SubQ: **Note:** I.M. use may result in variable absorption and a lag time to peak effect.

Initial: Opiate-naive: 0.8-1 mg every 4-6 hours as needed; patients with prior opiate exposure may require higher initial doses; usual dosage range: 1-2 mg every 3-6 hours as needed

Rectal: 3 mg every 4-8 hours as needed

Chronic pain: Adults: Oral: **Note:** Patients taking opioids chronically may become tolerant and require doses higher than the usual dosage range to maintain the desired effect. Tolerance can be managed by appropriate dose titration. There is no optimal or maximal dose for hydromorphone in chronic pain. The appropriate dose is one that relieves pain throughout its dosing interval without causing unmanageable side effects.

Controlled release formulation (Hydromorph Contin®, not available in U.S.): 3-30 mg every 12 hours. **Note:** A patient's hydromorphone requirement should be established using prompt release formulations; conversion to long acting products may be considered when chronic, continuous treatment is required. Higher dosages should be reserved for use only in opioid-tolerant patients.

Antitussive (unlabeled use): Oral:

Children 6-12 years: 0.5 mg every 3-4 hours as needed

Children >12 years and Adults: 1 mg every 3-4 hours as needed

Dosing adjustment in hepatic impairment: Should be considered

Administration

Parenteral: May be given SubQ or I.M.; vial stopper contains latex

I.V.: For IVP, must be given slowly over 2-3 minutes (rapid IVP has been associated with an increase in side effects, especially respiratory depression and hypotension)

Oral: Hydromorph Contin®: Capsule should be swallowed whole; do not crush or chew; contents may be sprinkled on soft food and swallowed

Monitoring Parameters Pain relief, respiratory and mental status, blood pressure

Test Interactions Some quinolones may produce a false-positive urine screening result for opiates using commercially-available immunoassay kits. This has been demonstrated most consistently for levofloxacin and ofloxacin, but other quinolones have shown cross-reactivity in certain assay kits. Confirmation of positive opiate screens by more specific methods should be considered.

Additional Information Equianalgesic doses: Morphine 10 mg I.M. = hydromorphone 1.5 mg I.M.

Dosage Forms [CAN] = Canadian brand name

Capsule, controlled release (Hydromorph Contin®) [CAN]: 3 mg, 6 mg, 12 mg, 18 mg, 24 mg, 30 mg [not available in U.S.]

Injection, powder for reconstitution, as hydrochloride (Dilaudid-HP®): 250 mg

Injection, solution, as hydrochloride: 1 mg/mL (1 mL); 2 mg/mL (1 mL, 20 mL); 4 mg/mL (1 mL); 10 mg/mL (1 mL, 5 mL, 10 mL)

    Dilaudid®: 1 mg/mL (1 mL); 2 mg/mL (1 mL, 20 mL) [20 mL size contains edetate sodium; vial stopper contains latex]; 4 mg/mL (1 mL)

    Dilaudid-HP®: 10 mg/mL (1 mL, 5 mL, 50 mL)

Liquid, oral, as hydrochloride (Dilaudid®): 1 mg/mL (480 mL) [may contain trace amounts of sodium bisulfite]

Suppository, rectal, as hydrochloride (Dilaudid®): 3 mg (6s)

Tablet, as hydrochloride (Dilaudid®): 2 mg, 4 mg, 8 mg (8 mg tablets may contain trace amounts of sodium bisulfite)

♦ **Hydromorphone HP (Can)** *see* Hydromorphone *on page 856*

♦ **Hydromorphone HP® 10 (Can)** *see* Hydromorphone *on page 856*

♦ **Hydromorphone HP® 20 (Can)** *see* Hydromorphone *on page 856*

♦ **Hydromorphone HP® 50 (Can)** *see* Hydromorphone *on page 856*

♦ **Hydromorphone HP® Forte (Can)** *see* Hydromorphone *on page 856*

♦ **Hydromorphone Hydrochloride** *see* Hydromorphone *on page 856*

♦ **Hydromorphone Hydrochloride Injection, USP (Can)** *see* Hydromorphone *on page 856*

♦ **Hydroquinol** *see* Hydroquinone *on page 859*

Hydroquinone (HYE droe kwin one)

U.S. Brand Names Alphaquin HP®; Claripel™; Dermarest® Skin Correction Cream Plus [OTC]; Eldopaque® [OTC]; Eldopaque Forte®; Eldoquin® [OTC]; Eldoquin Forte®; EpiQuin™ Micro; Esoterica® Regular [OTC]; Glyquin®; Glyquin-XM™; Lustra®; Lustra-AF™; Melanex®; Melpaque HP®; Melquin-3®; Melquin HP®; NeoStrata® AHA [OTC]; Nuquin HP®; Palmer's® Skin Success Eventone® Fade Cream [OTC]; Solaquin® [OTC]; Solaquin Forte®

Canadian Brand Names Eldopaque®; Eldoquin®; Glyquin® XM; Lustra®; NeoStrata® HQ; Solaquin®; Solaquin Forte®; Ultraquin™

Index Terms Hydroquinol; Quinol

Pharmacologic Category Depigmenting Agent

Use Gradual bleaching of hyperpigmented skin conditions

Pregnancy Risk Factor C

Lactation Excretion in breast milk unknown

Medication Safety Issues

Sound-alike/look-alike issues:

    Eldopaque® may be confused with Eldoquin®

    Eldoquin® may be confused with Eldopaque®

    Eldopaque Forte® may be confused with Eldoquin Forte®

    Eldoquin Forte® may be confused with Eldopaque Forte®

Contraindications Hypersensitivity to hydroquinone or any component of the formulation; sunburn, depilatory usage

Warnings/Precautions Limit application to area no larger than face and neck or hands and arms

Adverse Reactions Frequency not defined.

Dermatologic: Dermatitis, dryness, erythema, stinging, inflammatory reaction, sensitization

Local: Irritation

Mechanism of Action Produces reversible depigmentation of the skin by suppression of melanocyte metabolic processes, in particular the inhibition of the enzymatic oxidation of tyrosine to DOPA (3,4-dihydroxyphenylalanine); sun exposure reverses this effect and will cause repigmentation.

Pharmacodynamics/Kinetics Onset and duration of depigmentation produced by hydroquinone varies among individuals

Dosage Children >12 years and Adults: Topical: Apply thin layer and rub in twice daily

Administration For external use only; avoid contact with eyes

Dosage Forms

Cream, topical: 4% (30 g) [may contain sodium metabisulfite]

    Alphaquin HP®: 4% (30 g, 60 g)

    Eldoquin®: 2% (15 g, 30 g)

    Eldoquin Forte®: 4% (30 g) [contains sodium metabisulfite]

    EpiQuin™ Micro: 4% (30 g) [contains benzyl alcohol and sodium metabisulfite]

    Esoterica® Regular: 2% (85 g) [contains sodium bisulfite]

    Lustra®: 4% (30 g) [contains sodium metabisulfite]

    Melquin HP®: 4% (15 g, 30 g) [contains sodium metabisulfite]

Cream, topical [with sunscreen]: 4% (30 g) [may contain sodium metabisulfite]

    Claripel™: 4% (30 g, 45 g) [contains sodium metabisulfite]

    Dermarest® Skin Correcting Cream Plus: 2% (85 g) [contains aloe vera, sodium bisulfite]

    Eldopaque®: 2% (15 g, 30 g)

    Eldopaque Forte®: 4% (30 g) [contains sodium metabisulfite]

    Glyquin®: 4% (30 g)

    Glyquin-XM™: 4% (30 g)

    Lustra-AF™: 4% (30 g, 60 g) [contains sodium metabisulfite]

    Melpaque HP®: 4% (15 g, 30 g) [contains sodium metabisulfite; sunblocking cream base]

    Nuquin HP®: 4% (15 g, 30 g, 60 g) [contains sodium metabisulfite]

    Palmer's® Skin Success Eventone® Fade Cream: 2% (81 g, 132 g) [contains sodium sulfite; available in regular, oily skin, and dry skin formulas]

    Solaquin®: 2% (30 g)

    Solaquin Forte®: 4% (30 g) [contains sodium metabisulfite]

Gel, topical (NeoStrata® AHA): 2% (45 g) [contains glycolic acid 10%, sodium bisulfite, and sodium sulfite]

(Continued)

Hydroquinone *(Continued)*

Gel, topical [with sunscreen]: 4% (30 g)
Nuquin HP: 4% (15 g, 30 g) [contains sodium bisulfite]
Solaquin Forte®: 4% (30 g) [contains sodium metabisulfite]
Solution, topical (Melanex®, Melquin-3®): 3% (30 mL) [contains alcohol]

♦ **Hydroquinone, Fluocinolone Acetonide, and Tretinoin** *see* Fluocinolone, Hydroquinone, and Tretinoin *on page 721*
♦ **Hydro-Tussin™-CBX** *see* Carbinoxamine and Pseudoephedrine *on page 290*
♦ **Hydro-Tussin™ DM** *see* Guaifenesin and Dextromethorphan *on page 816*
♦ **Hydro-Tussin™ EXP** *see* Dihydrocodeine, Pseudoephedrine, and Guaifenesin *on page 506*
♦ **Hydro-Tussin™ HD** *see* Hydrocodone, Pseudoephedrine, and Guaifenesin *on page 852*
♦ **Hydro-Tussin™ HG** *see* Hydrocodone and Guaifenesin *on page 849*
♦ **Hydro-Tussin™ XP** *see* Hydrocodone, Pseudoephedrine, and Guaifenesin *on page 852*
♦ **HydroVal® (Can)** *see* Hydrocortisone *on page 852*

Hydroxocobalamin (hye droks oh koe BAL a min)

Index Terms Vitamin B_{12a}
Pharmacologic Category Antidote; Vitamin, Water Soluble
Use Treatment of pernicious anemia, vitamin B_{12} deficiency due to dietary deficiencies or malabsorption diseases, inadequate secretion of intrinsic factor, and inadequate utilization of B_{12} (eg, during neoplastic treatment); diagnostic agent for Schilling test
Cyanokit®: Treatment of cyanide poisoning (known or suspected)
Unlabeled/Investigational Use Neuropathies
Pregnancy Risk Factor C
Pregnancy Implications Animal studies are insufficient to determine the effect, if any, on pregnancy or fetal development. There are no adequate and well-controlled studies in pregnant women. Use of hydroxocobalamin in pregnancy for the treatment of cyanide poisoning and cobalamin defects is limited.
Lactation Excretion in breast milk unknown/use caution
Contraindications Hypersensitivity to hydroxocobalamin, cyanocobalamin, cobalt, or any component of the formulation
Warnings/Precautions
Solution for I.M. injection: Treatment of severe vitamin B_{12} megaloblastic anemia may result in thrombocytosis and severe hypokalemia, sometimes fatal, due to intracellular potassium shift upon anemia resolution. Use caution in folic acid deficient megaloblastic anemia; administration of vitamin B_{12} alone is not a substitute for folic acid and might mask true diagnosis. Vitamin B_{12} deficiency masks signs of polycythemia vera; vitamin B_{12} administration may unmask this condition. Neurologic manifestations of vitamin B_{12} deficiency will not be prevented with folic acid unless vitamin B_{12} is also given; spinal cord degeneration might also occur when folic acid is used as a substitute for vitamin B_{12} in anemia prevention. Blunted therapeutic response to vitamin B_{12} may occur in certain conditions (eg, infection, uremia, concurrent iron or folic acid deficiency) or in patients on medications with bone marrow suppressant properties (eg, chloramphenicol). Approved for use as I.M. injection only.

Cyanokit®: Use caution or consider alternatives in patients with known allergic reactions, including anaphylaxis, to hydroxocobalamin or cyanocobalamin. Increased blood pressure (≥180 mm Hg systolic or ≥110 mm Hg diastolic) is associated with infusion; elevations usually noted at beginning of infusion, peak toward the end of infusion and return to baseline within 4 hours of infusion. Collection of pretreatment blood cyanide concentrations does not preclude administration and should not delay administration in the emergency management of highly suspected or confirmed cyanide toxicity. Pretreatment levels may be useful as post infusion levels may be inaccurate. Treatment of cyanide poisoning should include decontamination and supportive therapy. Photosensitivity is a potential concern; avoid direct sunlight while skin remains discolored. Safety and efficacy have not been established in children.

Adverse Reactions
I.M. injection: Frequency not defined:
Dermatologic: Exanthema (transient), itching
Gastrointestinal: Diarrhea (mild, transient)
Local: Injection site pain
Miscellaneous: Anaphylaxis

I.V. infusion (Cyanokit®):
>10%:
Cardiovascular: Blood pressure increased (18% to 28%; systolic ≥180 mm Hg or diastolic ≥110 mm Hg)
Central nervous system: Headache (6% to 33%)
Dermatologic: Erythema (94% to 100%; may last up to 2 weeks), rash (predominantly acneiform; 20% to 44%; can appear 7-28 days after administration and usually resolves within a few weeks)
Gastrointestinal: Nausea (6% to 11%)
Genitourinary: Chromaturia (100%; may last up to 5 weeks after administration)
Hematologic: Lymphocytes decreased (8% to 17%)
Local: Infusion site reaction (6% to 39%)
Frequency not defined:
Cardiovascular: Chest discomfort, heart rate increased/decreased, hot flashes, peripheral edema
Central nervous system: Dizziness, memory impairment, restlessness
Dermatologic: Pruritus, urticaria
Gastrointestinal: Abdominal discomfort, diarrhea, dyspepsia, dysphagia, hematochezia, vomiting
Ocular: Irritation, redness, swelling
Respiratory: Dry throat, dyspnea, throat tightness

Miscellaneous: Allergic reaction (including anaphylaxis)

Postmarketing and/or case reports: Angioneurotic edema

Stability

Solution for I.M. injection: Store at 20°C to 25°C (68°F to 77°F). Protect from light.

I.V. infusion (Cyanokit®): Prior to reconstitution, store at 15°C to 30°C (59°F to 86°F).

Temperature variation exposure allowed for transport of lyophilized form:

Usual transport: ≤15 days at 5°C to 40°C (41°F to 104°F)

Desert transport: ≤4 days at 5°C to 60°C (41°F to 140°F)

Freezing/defrosting cycles: ≤15 days at -20°C to 40°C (-4°F to 104°F)

Reconstitute each 2.5 g vial with 100 mL of NS using provided sterile transfer spike. If NS unavailable, may use LR or D_5W. Invert or rock each vial for at least 30 seconds prior to infusion; do not shake. Do not use if solution is **not** dark red. Following reconstitution, store up to 6 hours at ≤40°C (104°F); do not freeze. Discard any remaining solution after 6 hours.

Mechanism of Action Hydroxocobalamin (vitamin B_{12a}) is a precursor to cyanocobalamin (vitamin B_{12}). Cyanocobalamin acts as a coenzyme for various metabolic functions, including fat and carbohydrate metabolism and protein synthesis, used in cell replication and hematopoiesis. In the presence of cyanide, each hydroxocobalamin molecule can bind one cyanide ion by displacing it for the hydroxo ligand linked to the trivalent cobalt ion, forming cyanocobalamin.

Pharmacodynamics/Kinetics Following I.V. administration of Cyanokit®:

Protein binding: Significant; forms various cobalamin-(III) complexes

Half-life elimination: 26-31 hours

Excretion: Urine (50% to 60% within initial 72 hours)

Dosage

Vitamin B_{12} deficiency: I.M.:

Children: 100 mcg once daily for 2 or more weeks (total dose: 1-5 mg); maintenance: 30-50 mcg/month

Adults: 30 mcg/day for 5-10 days, followed by 100-200 mcg/month

Note: Larger doses may be required in critically-ill patients or if patient has neurologic disease, an infectious disease, or hyperthyroidism.

Schilling test: I.M.: Adults: 1000 mcg

Cyanide toxicity (Cyanokit®): I.V.: Adults: Initial: 5 g as single infusion; may repeat a second 5 g dose depending on severity of poisoning and clinical response. Maximum cumulative dose: 10 g. Note: If suspected, antidotal therapy must be given immediately.

Administration

Solution for I.M. injection: Administer 1000 mcg/mL solution I.M. only

Cyanokit®: Administer by I.V. infusion over 15 minutes; if repeat dose needed, administer second dose over 15 minutes to 2 hours

Monitoring Parameters Vitamin B_{12}, hematocrit, hemoglobin, reticulocyte count, red blood cell counts, folate and iron levels should be obtained prior to treatment and periodically during treatment.

Cyanide toxicity: Blood pressure and heart rate during and after infusion, serum lactate levels, venous-arterial PO_2 gradient.

Megaloblastic anemia: In addition to normal hematological parameters, serum potassium and platelet counts should be monitored during therapy, particularly in the first 48 hours of treatment.

Reference Range Blood cyanide levels may be used for diagnosis confirmation; however, reliable levels require prompt testing and proper storage conditions.

Tachycardia/flushing: 0.5-1 mg/L

Obtundation: 1-2.5 mg/L

Coma: 2.5-3 mg/L

Death: >3 mg/L

Test Interactions The following values may be affected, *in vitro*, following hydroxocobalamin 5 g dose. Interference following hydroxocobalamin 10 g dose can be expected to last up to an additional 24 hours. **Note:** Extent and duration of interference dependant on analyzer used and patient variability.

Falsely elevated:

Basophils, hemoglobin, MCH, and MCHC [duration: 12-16 hours]

Albumin, alkaline phosphatase, cholesterol, creatinine, glucose, total protein, and triglycerides [duration: 24 hours]

Bilirubin [duration: up to 4 days]

Urinalysis: Glucose, protein, erythrocytes, leukocytes, ketones, bilirubin, urobilinogen, nitrite [duration: 2-8 days]

Falsely decreased: ALT and amylase [duration: 24 hours]

Unpredictable:

AST, CK, CKMB, LDH, phosphate, and uric acid [duration: 24 hours]

PT (quick or INR) and aPTT [duration: 24-48 hours]

Urine pH [duration: 2-8 days]

May also interfere with colorimetric tests

Additional Information Expert advice from a regional poison control center for appropriate use may be obtained (1-800-222-1222). Cyanide is a clear colorless gas or liquid with a faint bitter almond odor. Cyanide reacts with trivalent ions in cytochrome oxidase in the mitochondria leading to histotoxic hypoxia and lactic acidosis. Signs and symptoms of cyanide toxicity include headache, altered mental status, dyspnea, mydriasis, chest tightness, nausea, vomiting, tachycardia/hypertension (initially), bradycardia/hypotension (later), seizures, cardiovascular collapse, or coma.

Dosage Forms

Injection, solution: 1000 mcg/mL (30 mL)

Injection, powder for reconstitution:

Cyanokit®: 2.5 g (2 vials) [provided in a kit which also contains one I.V. infusion set]

♦ **4-Hydroxybutyrate** see Sodium Oxybate on page 1580

♦ **Hydroxycarbamide** see Hydroxyurea on page 863

Hydroxychloroquine (hye droks ee KLOR oh kwin)

U.S. Brand Names Plaquenil®
Canadian Brand Names Apo-Hydroxyquine®; Gen-Hydroxychloroquine; Plaquenil®
Index Terms Hydroxychloroquine Sulfate
Pharmacologic Category Aminoquinoline (Antimalarial)
Use Suppression and treatment of acute attacks of malaria; treatment of systemic lupus erythematosus and rheumatoid arthritis
Unlabeled/Investigational Use Porphyria cutanea tarda, polymorphous light eruptions
Pregnancy Risk Factor C
Lactation Enters breast milk/compatible
Medication Safety Issues
Sound-alike/look-alike issues:
Hydroxychloroquine may be confused with hydrocortisone
Plaquenil® may be confused with Platinol®
Contraindications Hypersensitivity to hydroxychloroquine, 4-aminoquinoline derivatives, or any component of the formulation; retinal or visual field changes attributable to 4-aminoquinolines
Warnings/Precautions Use with caution in patients with hepatic disease, G6PD deficiency, psoriasis, and porphyria; long-term use in children is not recommended; perform baseline and periodic (6 months) ophthalmologic examinations; test periodically for muscle weakness.
[U.S. Boxed Warning]: Should be prescribed by physicians familiar with its use.
Adverse Reactions Frequency not defined.
Cardiovascular: Cardiomyopathy (rare, relationship to hydroxychloroquine unclear)
Central nervous system: Irritability, nervousness, emotional changes, nightmares, psychosis, headache, dizziness, vertigo, seizure, ataxia, lassitude
Dermatologic: Bleaching of hair, alopecia, pigmentation changes (skin and mucosal; black-blue color), rash (urticarial, morbilliform, lichenoid, maculopapular, purpuric, erythema annulare centrifugum, Stevens-Johnson syndrome, acute generalized exanthematous pustulosis, and exfoliative dermatitis)
Endocrine & metabolic: Weight loss
Gastrointestinal: Anorexia, nausea, vomiting, diarrhea, abdominal cramping
Hematologic: Aplastic anemia, agranulocytosis, leukopenia, thrombocytopenia, hemolysis (in patients with glucose-6-phosphate deficiency)
Hepatic: Abnormal liver function/hepatic failure (isolated cases)
Neuromuscular & skeletal: Myopathy, palsy, or neuromyopathy leading to progressive weakness and atrophy of proximal muscle groups (may be associated with mild sensory changes, loss of deep tendon reflexes, and abnormal nerve conduction)
Ocular: Disturbance in accommodation, keratopathy, corneal changes/deposits (visual disturbances, blurred vision, photophobia - reversible on discontinuation), macular edema, atrophy, abnormal pigmentation, retinopathy (early changes reversible - may progress despite discontinuation if advanced), optic disc pallor/atrophy, attenuation of retinal arterioles, pigmentary retinopathy, scotoma, decreased visual acuity, nystagmus
Otic: Tinnitus, deafness
Miscellaneous: Exacerbation of porphyria and nonlight sensitive psoriasis
Overdosage/Toxicology Symptoms include headache, drowsiness, visual changes, cardiovascular collapse, and seizures, followed by respiratory and cardiac arrest. Treatment is symptomatic. Activated charcoal will bind the drug following GI decontamination. Urinary alkalinization will enhance renal elimination.
Drug Interactions
Increased Effect/Toxicity: Cimetidine increases levels of chloroquine and probably other 4-aminoquinolones.
Decreased Effect: Chloroquine and other 4-aminoquinolones absorption may be decreased due to GI binding with kaolin or magnesium trisilicate.
Ethanol/Nutrition/Herb Interactions Ethanol: Avoid ethanol (due to GI irritation).
Mechanism of Action Interferes with digestive vacuole function within sensitive malarial parasites by increasing the pH and interfering with lysosomal degradation of hemoglobin; inhibits locomotion of neutrophils and chemotaxis of eosinophils; impairs complement-dependent antigen-antibody reactions
Pharmacodynamics/Kinetics
Onset of action: Rheumatic disease: May require 4-6 weeks to respond
Absorption: Complete
Protein binding: 55%
Metabolism: Hepatic
Half-life elimination: 32-50 days
Time to peak: Rheumatic disease: Several months
Excretion: Urine (as metabolites and unchanged drug); may be enhanced by urinary acidification
Dosage Note: Hydroxychloroquine sulfate 200 mg is equivalent to 155 mg hydroxychloroquine base and 250 mg chloroquine phosphate. Oral:
Children:
Chemoprophylaxis of malaria: 5 mg/kg (base) once weekly; should not exceed the recommended adult dose; begin 2 weeks before exposure; continue for 4-6 weeks after leaving endemic area; if suppressive therapy is not begun prior to the exposure, double the initial dose and give in 2 doses, 6 hours apart
Acute attack: 10 mg/kg (base) initial dose; followed by 5 mg/kg at 6, 24, and 48 hours
JRA or SLE: 3-5 mg/kg/day divided 1-2 times/day; avoid exceeding 7 mg/kg/day
Adults:
Chemoprophylaxis of malaria: 310 mg base weekly on same day each week; begin 2 weeks before exposure; continue for 4-6 weeks after leaving endemic area; if suppressive therapy is not begun prior to the exposure, double the initial dose and give in 2 doses, 6 hours apart

Acute attack: 620 mg first dose day 1; 310 mg in 6 hours day 1; 310 mg in 1 dose day 2; and 310 mg in 1 dose on day 3

Rheumatoid arthritis: 310-465 mg/day to start taken with food or milk; increase dose until optimum response level is reached; usually after 4-12 weeks dose should be reduced by $^1/_2$ and a maintenance dose of 155-310 mg/day given

Lupus erythematosus: 310 mg every day or twice daily for several weeks depending on response; 155-310 mg/day for prolonged maintenance therapy

Dietary Considerations May be taken with food or milk.

Administration Administer with food or milk

Monitoring Parameters Ophthalmologic exam, CBC

Dosage Forms Tablet, as sulfate: 200 mg [equivalent to 155 mg base]

Extemporaneous Preparations A 25 mg/mL hydroxychloroquine sulfate suspension is made by removing the coating off of fifteen 200 mg hydroxychloroquine sulfate tablets with a towel moistened with alcohol; tablets are ground to a fine powder and levigated to a paste with 15 mL of Ora-Plus® suspending agent; add an additional 45 mL of suspending agent and levigate until a uniform mixture is obtained; qs ad to 120 mL with sterile water for irrigation; a 30 day expiration date is recommended, although stability testing has not been performed Pesko LJ, "Compounding: Hydroxychloroquine," *Am Druggist*, 1993, 207:57.

♦ **Hydroxychloroquine Sulfate** *see* Hydroxychloroquine *on page 862*
♦ **Hydroxydaunomycin Hydrochloride** *see* DOXOrubicin *on page 549*
♦ **1α-Hydroxyergocalciferol** *see* Doxercalciferol *on page 548*
♦ **Hydroxyethyl Starch** *see* Hetastarch *on page 838*
♦ **Hydroxyldaunorubicin Hydrochloride** *see* DOXOrubicin *on page 549*

Hydroxyurea (hye droks ee yoor EE a)

U.S. Brand Names Droxia®; Hydrea®; Mylocel™

Canadian Brand Names Apo-Hydroxyurea®; Gen-Hydroxyurea; Hydrea®

Index Terms Hydroxycarbamide

Pharmacologic Category Antineoplastic Agent, Antimetabolite

Additional Appendix Information

Antiretroviral Therapy for HIV Infection: Adults and Adolescents *on page 1988*

Use Treatment of melanoma, refractory chronic myelocytic leukemia (CML), relapsed and refractory metastatic ovarian cancer; radiosensitizing agent in the treatment of squamous cell head and neck cancer (excluding lip cancer); adjunct in the management of sickle cell patients who have had at least three painful crises in the previous 12 months (to reduce frequency of these crises and the need for blood transfusions)

Unlabeled/Investigational Use Treatment of HIV; treatment of psoriasis, treatment of hematologic conditions such as essential thrombocythemia, polycythemia vera, hypereosinophilia, and hyperleukocytosis due to acute leukemia; treatment of uterine, cervix and nonsmall cell lung cancers; radiosensitizing agent in the treatment of primary brain tumors; has shown activity against renal cell cancer and prostate cancer

Pregnancy Risk Factor D

Pregnancy Implications Animal studies have demonstrated teratogenicity and embryotoxicity. There are no adequate and well-controlled studies in pregnant women. Women of childbearing potential should be advised to avoid pregnancy.

Lactation Enters breast milk/contraindicated

Medication Safety Issues

Sound-alike/look-alike issues:

Hydroxyurea may be confused with hydrOXYzine

High alert medication: The Institute for Safe Medication Practices (ISMP) includes this medication among its list of drugs which have a heightened risk of causing significant patient harm when used in error.

International issues:

Hydrea® may be confused with Hydra® which is a brand name for isoniazid in Japan

Contraindications Hypersensitivity to hydroxyurea or any component of the formulation; severe anemia; severe bone marrow suppression; WBC <2500/mm^3 or platelet count <100,000/mm^3 (neutrophils <2000/mm^3, platelets <80,000/mm^3, and hemoglobin <4.5 g/dL for sickle cell anemia); pregnancy

Warnings/Precautions Hazardous agent - use appropriate precautions for handling and disposal. Patients with a history of prior cytotoxic chemotherapy and radiation therapy are more likely to experience bone marrow depression. Patients with a history of radiation therapy are also at risk for exacerbation of post irradiation erythema. Megaloblastic erythropoiesis may be seen early in hydroxyurea treatment; plasma iron clearance may be delayed and the rate of utilization of iron by erythrocytes may be delayed. HIV-infected patients treated with hydroxyurea and antiretroviral agents (including didanosine) are at higher risk for potentially fatal pancreatitis, hepatotoxicity, hepatic failure, and severe peripheral neuropathy. **[U.S. Boxed Warning]: Hydroxyurea is mutagenic and clastogenic. Treatment of myeloproliferative disorders (polycythemia vera and thrombocythemia) with long-term hydroxyurea is associated with secondary leukemia**; it is unknown if this is drug-related or disease-related. Cutaneous vasculitic toxicities (vasculitic ulceration and gangrene) have been reported with hydroxyurea treatment, most often in patients with a history of or receiving concurrent interferon therapy; discontinue hydroxyurea and consider alternate cytoreductive therapy if cutaneous vasculitic toxicity develops. Use caution with renal dysfunction; may require dose reductions. **[U.S. Boxed Warning]: Should be administered under the supervision of a physician experienced in cancer chemotherapy or in the treatment of sickle cell anemia.**

Adverse Reactions Frequency not defined.

Cardiovascular: Edema

Central nervous system: Chills, disorientation, dizziness, drowsiness (dose-related), fever, hallucinations, headache, malaise, seizure

(Continued)

Hydroxyurea *(Continued)*

Dermatologic: Alopecia (rare), cutaneous vasculitic toxicities, dermatomyositis-like skin changes, dry skin, facial erythema, gangrene, hyperpigmentation, maculopapular rash, nail atrophy, nail pigmentation, peripheral erythema, scaling, skin atrophy, skin cancer, skin ulcer, vasculitis ulcerations, violet papules

Endocrine & metabolic: Hyperuricemia

Gastrointestinal: Anorexia, constipation, diarrhea, gastrointestinal irritation and mucositis, (potentiated with radiation therapy), nausea, pancreatitis, stomatitis, vomiting

Genitourinary: Dysuria (rare)

Hematologic: Myelosuppression (primarily leukopenia; onset: 24-48 hours; nadir: 10 days; recovery: 7 days after stopping drug; reversal of WBC count occurs rapidly but the platelet count may take 7-10 days to recover); thrombocytopenia and anemia, megaloblastic erythropoiesis, macrocytosis, hemolysis, serum iron decreased, persistent cytopenias, secondary leukemias (long-term use)

Hepatic: Hepatic enzymes increased, hepatotoxicity

Neuromuscular & skeletal: Peripheral neuropathy, weakness

Renal: BUN increased, creatinine increased

Respiratory: Acute diffuse pulmonary infiltrates (rare), dyspnea, pulmonary fibrosis (rare)

Overdosage/Toxicology Symptoms of overdose include myelosuppression, facial swelling, hallucinations, disorientation, soreness, violet erythema, edema on palms and soles, scaling on hands and feet, severe generalized hyperpigmentation of the skin, and stomatitis. Treatment is symptom-directed and supportive.

Drug Interactions

Increased Effect/Toxicity: Hydroxyurea may increase the toxicity of didanosine.

Stability Store at room temperature between 15°C and 30°C (59°F and 86°F).

Mechanism of Action Thought to interfere (unsubstantiated hypothesis) with synthesis of DNA, during the S phase of cell division, without interfering with RNA synthesis; inhibits ribonucleoside diphosphate reductase, preventing conversion of ribonucleotides to deoxyribonucleotides; cell-cycle specific for the S phase and may hold other cells in the G_1 phase of the cell cycle. In sickle cell anemia, hydroxyurea increases red blood cell (RBC) hemoglobin F levels, RBC water content, deformability of sickled cells, and alters adhesion of RBCs to endothelium.

Pharmacodynamics/Kinetics

Absorption: Readily (≥80%)

Distribution: Readily crosses blood-brain barrier; distributes into intestine, brain, lung, kidney tissues, effusions and ascites

Metabolism: 60% via hepatic and GI tract

Half-life elimination: 3-4 hours

Time to peak: 1-4 hours

Excretion: Urine (80%, 50% as unchanged drug, 30% as urea); exhaled gases (as CO_2)

Dosage Oral (refer to individual protocols): All doses should be based on ideal or actual body weight, whichever is less.

Children (unlabeled use):

No FDA-approved dosage regimens have been established; dosages of 1500-3000 mg/m² as a single dose in combination with other agents every 4-6 weeks have been used in the treatment of pediatric astrocytoma, medulloblastoma, and primitive neuroectodermal tumors

CML: Initial: 10-20 mg/kg/day once daily; adjust dosage according to hematologic response

Adults: Dose should always be titrated to patient response and WBC counts; usual oral doses range from 10-30 mg/kg/day or 500-3000 mg/day; if WBC count falls to <2500 cells/mm³, or the platelet count to <100,000/mm³, therapy should be stopped for at least 3 days and resumed when values rise toward normal

Solid tumors:

Intermittent therapy: 80 mg/kg as a single dose every third day

Continuous therapy: 20-30 mg/kg/day given as a single dose/day

Concomitant therapy with irradiation: 80 mg/kg as a single dose every third day starting at least 7 days before initiation of irradiation

Resistant chronic myelocytic leukemia: Continuous therapy: 20-30 mg/kg once daily

HIV (unlabeled use; in combination with antiretroviral agents): 1000-1500 mg daily in a single dose or divided doses

Psoriasis (unlabeled use): 1000-1500 mg/day in a single dose or divided doses

Sickle cell anemia (moderate/severe disease): Initial: 15 mg/kg/day, increased by 5 mg/kg every 12 weeks if blood counts are in an acceptable range until the maximum tolerated dose of 35 mg/kg/day is achieved or the dose that does not produce toxic effects

Acceptable range:

Neutrophils ≥2500 cells/mm³

Platelets ≥95,000/mm³

Hemoglobin >5.3 g/dL, and

Reticulocytes ≥95,000/mm³ if the hemoglobin concentration is <9 g/dL

Toxic range:

Neutrophils <2000 cells/mm³

Platelets <80,000/mm³

Hemoglobin <4.5 g/dL

Reticulocytes <80,000/mm³ if the hemoglobin concentration is <9 g/dL

Monitor for toxicity every 2 weeks; if toxicity occurs, stop treatment until the bone marrow recovers; restart at 2.5 mg/kg/day less than the dose at which toxicity occurs; if no toxicity occurs over the next 12 weeks, then the subsequent dose should be increased by 2.5 mg/kg/day; reduced dosage of hydroxyurea alternating with erythropoietin may decrease myelotoxicity and increase levels of fetal hemoglobin in patients who have not been helped by hydroxyurea alone

Dosing adjustment in renal impairment:

Sickle cell anemia: Cl_{cr} <60 mL/minute or ESRD: Reduce initial dose to 7.5 mg/kg; titrate to response/avoidance of toxicity (refer to usual dosing)

Other indications:
Cl_{cr} 10-50 mL/minute: Administer 50% of normal dose
Cl_{cr} <10 mL/minute: Administer 20% of normal dose
Hemodialysis: Administer dose after dialysis on dialysis days; supplemental dose is not necessary. Hydroxyurea is a low molecular weight compound with high aqueous solubility that may be freely dialyzable, however, clinical studies confirming this hypothesis have not been performed.
CAPD effects: Unknown
CAVH effects: Dose for GFR 10-50 mL/minute

Dietary Considerations In sickle cell patients, supplemental administration of folic acid is recommended; hydroxyurea may mask development of folic acid deficiency.

Administration Capsules may be opened and emptied into water (will not dissolve completely); observe proper handling procedures

Monitoring Parameters CBC with differential and platelets, renal function and liver function tests, serum uric acid

Sickle cell disease: Monitor for toxicity every 2 weeks. If toxicity occurs, stop treatment until the bone marrow recovers; restart at 2.5 mg/kg/day less than the dose at which toxicity occurs. If no toxicity occurs over the next 12 weeks, then the subsequent dose should be increased by 2.5 mg/kg/day. Reduced dosage of hydroxyurea alternating with erythropoietin may decrease myelotoxicity and increase levels of fetal hemoglobin in patients who have not been helped by hydroxyurea alone.

Acceptable range: Neutrophils ≥2500 cells/mm^3, platelets ≥95,000/mm^3, hemoglobin >5.3 g/dL, and reticulocytes ≥95,000/mm^3 if the hemoglobin concentration is <9 g/dL

Toxic range: Neutrophils <2000 cells/mm^3, platelets <80,000/mm^3, hemoglobin <4.5 g/dL, and reticulocytes <80,000/mm^3 if the hemoglobin concentration is <9 g/dL

Additional Information Although I.V. use is reported, no parenteral product is commercially available in the U.S.

If WBC decreases to <2500/mm^3 or platelet count to <100,000/mm^3 (neutrophils <2000/mm^3 and platelets <80,000/mm^3 for patients with sickle cell anemia), interrupt therapy until values rise significantly toward normal. Treat anemia with whole blood replacement; do not interrupt therapy (for sickle cell anemia patients, withhold treatment for hemoglobin <4.5 g/dL until recovery to >5.3 g/dL). Adequate trial period to determine the antineoplastic effectiveness is 6 weeks. Almost all patients receiving hydroxyurea in clinical trials needed to have their medication stopped for a time to allow their low blood count to return to acceptable levels.

Dosage Forms
Capsule: 500 mg
Droxia®: 200 mg, 300 mg, 400 mg
Hydrea®: 500 mg
Tablet:
Mylocel™: 1000 mg

HydrOXYzine (hye DROKS i zeen)

U.S. Brand Names Vistaril®
Canadian Brand Names Apo-Hydroxyzine®; Atarax®; Hydroxyzine Hydrochloride Injection, USP; Novo-Hydroxyzin; PMS-Hydroxyzine; Vistaril®
Index Terms Hydroxyzine Hydrochloride; Hydroxyzine Pamoate
Pharmacologic Category Antiemetic; Antihistamine
Use Treatment of anxiety; preoperative sedative; antipruritic
Unlabeled/Investigational Use Antiemetic; ethanol withdrawal symptoms
Pregnancy Risk Factor C
Pregnancy Implications Hydroxyzine-induced fetal abnormalities at high dosages in animal studies. Neonatal withdrawal symptoms have been reported following long-term maternal use or the use of large doses near term. Use in early pregnancy is contraindicated by the manufacturer.
Lactation Excretion in breast milk unknown/not recommended
Medication Safety Issues
Sound-alike/look-alike issues:
HydrOXYzine may be confused with hydrALAZINE, hydroxyurea
Atarax® may be confused with amoxicillin, Ativan®
Vistaril® may be confused with Restoril®, Versed, Zestril®

International issues:
Vistaril® may be confused with Vastarel® which is a brand name for trimetazidine in multiple international markets

Contraindications Hypersensitivity to hydroxyzine or any component of the formulation; early pregnancy; SubQ, intra-arterial, or I.V. administration of injection
Warnings/Precautions Causes sedation, caution must be used in performing tasks which require alertness (eg, operating machinery or driving). Sedative effects of CNS depressants or ethanol are potentiated. SubQ, I.V., and intra-arterial administration are contraindicated since tissue damage, intravascular hemolysis, thrombosis, and digital gangrene can occur. Use with caution with narrow-angle glaucoma, prostatic hyperplasia, bladder neck obstruction, asthma, or COPD.

Anticholinergic effects are not well tolerated in the elderly. Hydroxyzine may be useful as a short-term antipruritic, but it is not recommended for use as a sedative or anxiolytic in the elderly.

Adverse Reactions Frequency not defined.
Central nervous system: Dizziness, drowsiness, fatigue, hallucination, headache, nervousness, seizure
Dermatologic: Pruritus, rash, urticaria
Gastrointestinal: Xerostomia
Neuromuscular & skeletal: Involuntary movements, paresthesia, tremor
(Continued)

HydrOXYzine *(Continued)*

Ocular: Blurred vision

Respiratory: Thickening of bronchial secretions

Miscellaneous: Allergic reaction

Overdosage/Toxicology Symptoms include seizures, sedation, and hypotension. There is no specific treatment for antihistamine overdose, however, clinical toxicity is mostly due to anticholinergic effects. Anticholinesterase inhibitors may be useful by reducing acetylcholinesterase. For anticholinergic overdose with severe life-threatening symptoms, physostigmine 1-2 mg (0.5 mg or 0.02 mg/kg for children) slow I.V. may be given to reverse these effects.

Drug Interactions

Cytochrome P450 Effect: Inhibits CYP2D6 (weak)

Increased Effect/Toxicity: CNS depressants, anticholinergics, and pramlintide used in combination with hydroxyzine may result in additive effects.

Decreased Effect:

Acetylcholinesterase Inhibitors (Central) may diminish the anticholinergic of hydroxyzine. If the anticholinergic effect is a side effect of the agent, as is the case with hydroxyzine, the result may be beneficial.

Ethanol/Nutrition/Herb Interactions

Ethanol: Avoid ethanol (may increase CNS depression).

Herb/Nutraceutical: Avoid valerian, St John's wort, kava kava, gotu kola (may increase CNS depression).

Stability Injection: Store at 15°C to 30°C. Protect from light.

Mechanism of Action Competes with histamine for H_1-receptor sites on effector cells in the gastrointestinal tract, blood vessels, and respiratory tract. Possesses skeletal muscle relaxing, bronchodilator, antihistamine, antiemetic, and analgesic properties.

Pharmacodynamics/Kinetics

Onset of action: Oral: 15-30 minutes

Duration: 4-6 hours

Absorption: Oral: Rapid

Metabolism: Forms metabolites

Half-life elimination: 3-7 hours

Time to peak: ~2 hours

Excretion: Urine

Dosage

Children:

Preoperative sedation:

Oral: 0.6 mg/kg/dose

I.M.: 0.5-1 mg/kg/dose

Pruritus, anxiety: Oral:

<6 years: 50 mg daily in divided doses

≥6 years: 50-100 mg daily in divided doses

Adults:

Antiemetic (unlabeled use): I.M.: 25-100 mg/dose every 4-6 hours as needed

Anxiety: Oral, I.M.: 50-100 mg 4 times/day

Preoperative sedation:

Oral: 50-100 mg

I.M.: 25-100 mg

Pruritus: Oral, I.M.: 25 mg 3-4 times/day

Dosing interval in hepatic impairment: Change dosing interval to every 24 hours in patients with primary biliary cirrhosis

Administration Do not administer SubQ or intra-arterially. Administer I.M. deep in large muscle. With I.V. administration, extravasation can result in sterile abscess and marked tissue induration.

Monitoring Parameters Relief of symptoms, mental status, blood pressure

Dosage Forms

Capsule, as pamoate: 25 mg, 50 mg, 100 mg

Vistaril®: 25 mg, 50 mg

Injection, solution, as hydrochloride: 25 mg/mL (1 mL); 50 mg/mL (1 mL, 2 mL, 10 mL)

Suspension, oral, as pamoate:

Vistaril®: 25 mg/5 mL (120 mL, 480 mL) [lemon flavor]

Syrup, as hydrochloride: 10 mg/5 mL (120 mL, 480 mL)

Tablet, as hydrochloride: 10 mg, 25 mg, 50 mg

♦ **Hydroxyzine Hydrochloride** *see* HydrOXYzine *on page 865*

♦ **Hydroxyzine Hydrochloride Injection, USP (Can)** *see* HydrOXYzine *on page 865*

♦ **Hydroxyzine Pamoate** *see* HydrOXYzine *on page 865*

♦ **HydroZone Plus [OTC]** *see* Hydrocortisone *on page 852*

♦ **Hyflex-DS®** *see* Acetaminophen and Phenyltoloxamine *on page 32*

♦ **Hygroton** *see* Chlorthalidone *on page 359*

♦ **Hylaform®** *see* Hyaluronate and Derivatives *on page 841*

♦ **Hylaform® Plus** *see* Hyaluronate and Derivatives *on page 841*

♦ **Hylan Polymers** *see* Hyaluronate and Derivatives *on page 841*

♦ **Hyoscine Butylbromide** *see* Scopolamine Derivatives *on page 1550*

♦ **Hyoscine Hydrobromide** *see* Scopolamine Derivatives *on page 1550*

Hyoscyamine *(hye oh SYE a meen)*

U.S. Brand Names Anaspaz®; Cystospaz®; Cystospaz-M® [DSC]; Hyosine; Levbid®; Levsin®; Levsinex®; Levsin/SL®; NuLev™; Spacol [DSC]; Spacol T/S [DSC]; Symax SL; Symax SR

Canadian Brand Names Cystospaz®; Levsin®

Index Terms Hyoscyamine Sulfate; *l*-Hyoscyamine Sulfate

Pharmacologic Category Anticholinergic Agent

Use

Oral: Adjunctive therapy for peptic ulcers, irritable bowel, neurogenic bladder/bowel; treatment of infant colic, GI tract disorders caused by spasm; to reduce rigidity, tremors, sialorrhea, and hyperhidrosis associated with parkinsonism; as a drying agent in acute rhinitis

Injection: Preoperative antimuscarinic to reduce secretions and block cardiac vagal inhibitory reflexes; to improve radiologic visibility of the kidneys; symptomatic relief of biliary and renal colic; reduce GI motility to facilitate diagnostic procedures (ie, endoscopy, hypotonic duodenography); reduce pain and hypersecretion in pancreatitis, certain cases of partial heart block associated with vagal activity; reversal of neuromuscular blockade

Pregnancy Risk Factor C

Pregnancy Implications Crosses the placenta, effects to the fetus not known; use during pregnancy only if clearly needed.

Lactation Enters breast milk/not recommended

Medication Safety Issues

Sound-alike/look-alike issues:

Anaspaz® may be confused with Anaprox®, Antispas®

Levbid® may be confused with Lithobid®, Lopid®, Lorabid®

Levsinex® may be confused with Lanoxin®

Contraindications Hypersensitivity to belladonna alkaloids or any component of the formulation; glaucoma; obstructive uropathy; myasthenia gravis; obstructive GI tract disease, paralytic ileus, intestinal atony of elderly or debilitated patients, severe ulcerative colitis, toxic megacolon complicating ulcerative colitis; unstable cardiovascular status in acute hemorrhage, myocardial ischemia

Warnings/Precautions Heat prostration may occur in hot weather. Diarrhea may be a sign of incomplete intestinal obstruction, treatment should be discontinued if this occurs. May produce side effects as seen with other anticholinergic medications including drowsiness, dizziness, blurred vision, or psychosis. Children and the elderly may be more susceptible to these effects. Use with caution in children with spastic paralysis. Use with caution in patients with autonomic neuropathy, coronary heart disease, CHF, cardiac arrhythmias, prostatic hyperplasia, hyperthyroidism, hypertension, chronic lung disease, renal disease, and hiatal hernia associated with reflux esophagitis. Use with caution in the elderly, may precipitate undiagnosed glaucoma and/or severely impair memory function (especially in those patients with previous memory problems).

NuLev™: Contains phenylalanine

Adverse Reactions Frequency not defined.

Cardiovascular: Palpitations, tachycardia

Central nervous system: Ataxia, dizziness, drowsiness, headache, insomnia, mental confusion/excitement, nervousness, speech disorder

Dermatologic: Urticaria

Endocrine & metabolic: Lactation suppression

Gastrointestinal: Bloating, constipation, dry mouth, loss of taste, nausea, vomiting

Genitourinary: Impotence, urinary hesitancy, urinary retention

Neuromuscular & skeletal: Weakness

Ocular: Blurred vision, cycloplegia, increased ocular tension, mydriasis

Miscellaneous: Allergic reactions, sweating decreased

Overdosage/Toxicology Symptoms include dilated, unreactive pupils; blurred vision; hot, dry, flushed skin; dry mucous membranes; difficulty swallowing, foul breath, diminished or absent bowel sounds, urinary retention, tachycardia, hyperthermia, hypertension, and increased respiratory rate. Anticholinergic toxicity is caused by strong binding of the drug to cholinergic receptors. Anticholinesterase inhibitors reduce acetylcholinesterase, the enzyme that breaks down acetylcholine and thereby allows acetylcholine to accumulate and compete for receptor binding with the offending anticholinergic. For anticholinergic overdose with severe life-threatening symptoms, physostigmine 1-2 mg (0.5 mg or 0.02 mg/kg for children) SubQ or slow I.V. may be given to reverse these effects.

Drug Interactions

Increased Effect/Toxicity: Increased toxicity with amantadine, antihistamines, antimuscarinics, haloperidol, phenothiazines, tricyclic antidepressants, and MAO inhibitors.

Decreased Effect: Decreased effect with antacids.

Stability Store at controlled room temperature. Protect NuLev™ from moisture.

Mechanism of Action Blocks the action of acetylcholine at parasympathetic sites in smooth muscle, secretory glands and the CNS; increases cardiac output, dries secretions, antagonizes histamine and serotonin

Pharmacodynamics/Kinetics

Onset of action: 2-3 minutes

Duration: 4-6 hours

Absorption: Well absorbed

Distribution: Crosses placenta; small amounts enter breast milk

Protein binding: 50%

Metabolism: Hepatic

Half-life elimination: 3-5 hours

Excretion: Urine

Dosage

Oral: Children: Gastrointestinal disorders: Dose as listed, based on age and weight (kg) using 0.125 mg/mL drops; repeat dose every 4 hours as needed:

Children <2 years:

3.4 kg: 4 drops; maximum: 24 drops/24 hours

5 kg: 5 drops; maximum: 30 drops/24 hours

7 kg: 6 drops; maximum: 36 drops/24 hours

10 kg: 8 drops; maximum: 48 drops/24 hours

(Continued)

867

Hyoscyamine *(Continued)*

Oral, S.L.:
Children 2-12 years: Gastrointestinal disorders: Dose as listed, based on age and weight (kg); repeat dose every 4 hours as needed:
10 kg: 0.031-0.033 mg; maximum: 0.75 mg/24 hours
20 kg: 0.0625 mg; maximum: 0.75 mg/24 hours
40 kg: 0.0938 mg; maximum: 0.75 mg/24 hours
50 kg: 0.125 mg; maximum: 0.75 mg/24 hours
Children >12 years and Adults: Gastrointestinal disorders: 0.125-0.25 mg every 4 hours or as needed (before meals or food); maximum: 1.5 mg/24 hours
Cystospaz®: 0.15-0.3 mg up to 4 times/day
Oral (timed release): Children >12 years and Adults: Gastrointestinal disorders: 0.375-0.75 mg every 12 hours; maximum: 1.5 mg/24 hours
I.M., I.V., SubQ: Children >12 years and Adults: Gastrointestinal disorders: 0.25-0.5 mg; may repeat as needed up to 4 times/day, at 4-hour intervals
I.V.: Children >2 year and Adults: I.V.: Preanesthesia: 5 mcg/kg given 30-60 minutes prior to induction of anesthesia or at the time preoperative narcotics or sedatives are administered
I.V.: Adults: Diagnostic procedures: 0.25-0.5 mg given 5-10 minutes prior to procedure
To reduce drug-induced bradycardia during surgery: 0.125 mg; repeat as needed
To reverse neuromuscular blockade: 0.2 mg for every 1 mg neostigmine (or the physostigmine/pyridostigmine equivalent)

Dietary Considerations Should be taken before meals or food; NuLev™ contains phenylalanine

Administration
Oral: Tablets should be administered before meals or food.
Levbid®: Tablets are scored and may be broken in half for dose titration; do not crush or chew.
Levsin/SL®: Tablets may be used sublingually, chewed, or swallowed whole.
NuLev™: Tablet is placed on tongue and allowed to disintegrate before swallowing; may take with or without water.
Symax SL: Tablets may be used sublingually or swallowed whole.
I.M.: May be administered without dilution.
Inject over at least 1 minute. May be administered without dilution.

Dosage Forms [DSC] = Discontinued product
Capsule, timed release, as sulfate (Cystospaz-M® [DSC], Levsinex®): 0.375 mg
Elixir, as sulfate: 0.125 mg/5 mL (480 mL)
Hyosine: 0.125 mg/5 mL (480 mL) [contains alcohol 20% and sodium benzoate; orange flavor]
Levsin®: 0.125 mg/5 mL (480 mL) [contains alcohol 20%; orange flavor]
Injection, solution, as sulfate (Levsin®): 0.5 mg/mL (1 mL)
Liquid, as sulfate (Spacol [DSC]): 0.125 mg/5 mL (120 mL) [sugar free, alcohol free, simethicone based, bubble gum flavor]
Solution, oral drops, as sulfate: 0.125 mg/mL (15 mL)
Hyosine: 0.125 mg/mL (15 mL) [contains alcohol 5% and sodium benzoate; orange flavor]
Levsin®: 0.125 mg/mL (15 mL) [contains alcohol 5%; orange flavor]
Tablet (Cystospaz®): 0.15 mg
Tablet, as sulfate (Anaspaz®, Levsin®, Spacol [DSC]): 0.125 mg
Tablet, extended release, as sulfate (Levbid®, Symax SR, Spacol T/S [DSC]): 0.375 mg
Tablet, orally disintegrating, as sulfate (NuLev™): 0.125 mg [contains phenylalanine 1.7 mg/tablet, mint flavor]
Tablet, sublingual, as sulfate: 0.125 mg
Levsin/SL®: 0.125 mg [peppermint flavor]
Symax SL: 0.125 mg

Hyoscyamine, Atropine, Scopolamine, and Phenobarbital
(hye oh SYE a meen, A troe peen, skoe POL a meen, & fee noe BAR bi tal)

U.S. Brand Names Donnatal®; Donnatal Extentabs®
Index Terms Atropine, Hyoscyamine, Scopolamine, and Phenobarbital; Belladonna Alkaloids With Phenobarbital; Phenobarbital, Hyoscyamine, Atropine, and Scopolamine; Scopolamine, Hyoscyamine, Atropine, and Phenobarbital
Pharmacologic Category Anticholinergic Agent; Antispasmodic Agent, Gastrointestinal
Use Adjunct in treatment of irritable bowel syndrome, acute enterocolitis, duodenal ulcer
Pregnancy Risk Factor C
Medication Safety Issues
Sound-alike/look-alike issues:
Donnatal® may be confused with Donnagel®
Dosage Oral:
Children: Donnatal® elixir: To be given every 4-6 hours; initial dose based on weight:
4.5 kg: 0.5 mL every 4 hours **or** 0.75 mL every 6 hours
10 kg: 1 mL every 4 hours **or** 1.5 mL every 6 hours
14 kg: 1.5 mL every 4 hours **or** 2 mL every 6 hours
23 kg: 2.5 mL every 4 hours **or** 3.8 mL every 6 hours
34 kg: 3.8 mL every 4 hours **or** 5 mL every 6 hours
≥45 kg: 5 mL every 4 hours **or** 7.5 mL every 6 hours
Adults:
Donnatal®: 1-2 tablets or 5-10 mL of elixir 3-4 times/day
Donnatal Extentabs®: 1 tablet every 12 hours; may increase to 1 tablet every 8 hours if needed
Additional Information Complete prescribing information for this medication should be consulted for additional detail.

Dosage Forms

Elixir (Donnatal®): Hyoscyamine sulfate 0.1037 mg, atropine sulfate 0.0194 mg, scopolamine hydrobromide 0.0065 mg, and phenobarbital 16.2 mg per 5 mL (120 mL, 480 mL) [contains alcohol 95%; grape flavor]

Tablet (Donnatal®): Hyoscyamine sulfate 0.1037 mg, atropine sulfate 0.0194 mg, scopolamine hydrobromide 0.0065 mg, and phenobarbital 16.2 mg

Tablet, extended release (Donnatal Extentabs®): Hyoscyamine sulfate 0.3111 mg, atropine sulfate 0.0582 mg, scopolamine hydrobromide 0.0195 mg, and phenobarbital 48.6 mg

♦ **Hyoscyamine, Methenamine, Sodium Biphosphate, Phenyl Salicylate, and Methylene Blue** see Methenamine, Sodium Biphosphate, Phenyl Salicylate, Methylene Blue, and Hyoscyamine on page 1107

♦ **Hyoscyamine Sulfate** see Hyoscyamine on page 866

♦ **Hyosine** see Hyoscyamine on page 866

♦ **Hyperal** see Total Parenteral Nutrition on page 1715

♦ **Hyperalimentation** see Total Parenteral Nutrition on page 1715

♦ **HyperHep B® (Can)** see Hepatitis B Immune Globulin on page 834

♦ **HyperHEP B™ S/D** see Hepatitis B Immune Globulin on page 834

♦ **HyperRAB™ S/D** see Rabies Immune Globulin (Human) on page 1478

♦ **HyperRHO™ S/D Full Dose** see Rh$_o$(D) Immune Globulin on page 1499

♦ **HyperRHO™ S/D Mini Dose** see Rh$_o$(D) Immune Globulin on page 1499

♦ **Hyperstat® [DSC]** see Diazoxide on page 491

♦ **HyperTET® S/D** see Tetanus Immune Globulin (Human) on page 1656

♦ **Hytakerol® [DSC]** see Dihydrotachysterol on page 508

♦ **Hytakerol® (Can)** see Dihydrotachysterol on page 508

♦ **HyTan™ [DSC]** see Hydrocodone and Chlorpheniramine on page 849

♦ **Hytone®** see Hydrocortisone on page 852

♦ **Hytrin®** see Terazosin on page 1647

♦ **Hyzaar®** see Losartan and Hydrochlorothiazide on page 1039

♦ **Hyzaar® DS (Can)** see Losartan and Hydrochlorothiazide on page 1039

Ibandronate (eye BAN droh nate)

U.S. Brand Names Boniva®
Canadian Brand Names Bondronat®
Index Terms Ibandronate Sodium; Ibandronic Acid; NSC-722623
Pharmacologic Category Bisphosphonate Derivative
Use Treatment and prevention of osteoporosis in postmenopausal females
Unlabeled/Investigational Use Hypercalcemia of malignancy; corticosteroid-induced osteoporosis; Paget's disease; reduce bone pain and skeletal complications from metastatic bone disease
Pregnancy Risk Factor C
Pregnancy Implications Safety and efficacy have not been established in pregnant women. Bisphosphonates are incorporated into the bone matrix and are gradually released over time. Theoretically, there may be a risk of fetal harm when pregnancy follows the completion of therapy. Based on limited case reports with pamidronate, serum calcium levels in the newborn may be altered if administered during pregnancy.
Lactation Excretion in breast milk unknown/use caution
Contraindications Hypersensitivity to ibandronate, other bisphosphonates, or any component of the formulation; hypocalcemia; oral tablets are also contraindicated in patients unable to stand or sit upright for at least 60 minutes
Warnings/Precautions Hypocalcemia must be corrected before therapy initiation. Ensure adequate calcium and vitamin D intake. Bisphosphonate therapy has been associated with osteonecrosis, primarily of the jaw; this has been observed mostly in cancer patients, but also in patients with postmenopausal osteoporosis and other diagnoses. Dental exams and preventative dentistry should be performed prior to placing patients with risk factors on chronic bisphosphonate therapy. Invasive dental procedures should be avoided during treatment.

Infrequently, severe (and occasionally debilitating) bone, joint, and/or muscle pain have been reported during bisphosphonate treatment. The onset of pain ranged from a single day to several months. Symptoms usually resolve upon discontinuation. Some patients experienced recurrence when rechallenged with same drug or another bisphosphonate; avoid use in patients with a history of these symptoms in association with bisphosphonate therapy.

Oral bisphosphonates may cause dysphagia, esophagitis, esophageal or gastric ulcer; risk may increase in patients unable to comply with dosing instructions. Intravenous bisphosphonates may cause transient decreases in serum calcium and have also been associated with renal toxicity.

Use not recommended with severe renal impairment (Cl$_{cr}$ <30 mL/minute or serum creatinine >2.3 mg/dL). Safety and efficacy have not been established in patients <18 years of age.
Adverse Reactions Percentages vary based on frequency of administration (daily vs monthly). Unless specified, percentages are reported with oral use.
>10%:
  Gastrointestinal: Dyspepsia (6% to 12%)
  Neuromuscular & skeletal: Back pain (4% to 14%)
1% to 10%:
  Central nervous system: Headache (3% to 7%), dizziness (1% to 4%), insomnia (1% to 2%)
  Dermatologic: Rash (1% to 2%)
  Endocrine & metabolic: Hypercholesterolemia (5%)
(Continued)

Ibandronate *(Continued)*

Gastrointestinal: Abdominal pain (5% to 8%), diarrhea (4% to 7%), nausea (5%), tooth disorder (4%), vomiting (3%), constipation (3% to 4%)

Genitourinary: Urinary tract infection (2% to 6%)

Hepatic: Alkaline phosphatase decreased (frequency not defined)

Local: Injection site reaction (<2%)

Neuromuscular & skeletal: Pain in extremity (8%), myalgia (1% to 6%), joint disorder (4%), weakness (4%), muscle cramp (2%)

Respiratory: Bronchitis (3% to 10%), pneumonia (6%), pharyngitis/nasopharyngitis (3% to 4%), upper respiratory infection (2%)

Miscellaneous: Acute phase reaction (I.V. 10%; oral 4%), allergic reaction (3%), flu-like syndrome (1% to 3%)

Postmarketing and/or case reports: Incapacitating bone, joint or muscle pain, ocular inflammation, scleritis, uveitis

Overdosage/Toxicology Dyspepsia, esophagitis, gastritis, ulcer, hypocalcemia, hypophosphatemia, hypomagnesemia, or upset stomach may be seen with overdose. Milk or antacids may be used to bind ibandronate. Patient should remain fully upright, and vomiting should not be induced to avoid esophageal irritation. Following overdose with I.V. formulation, dialysis may be of benefit if administered within 2 hours of overdose.

Drug Interactions

Increased Effect/Toxicity: Aminoglycosides may lower serum calcium levels with prolonged administration; concomitant use may have an additive hypocalcemic effect. Nonsteroidal anti-inflammatory drugs may enhance the gastrointestinal adverse/toxic effects (increased incidence of GI ulcers) of bisphosphonate derivatives. Bisphosphonate derivatives may enhance the hypocalcemic effect of phosphate supplements.

Decreased Effect: The following agents may decrease the absorption of oral bisphosphonate derivatives: Antacids (aluminum, calcium, magnesium), oral calcium salts, oral iron salts, and oral magnesium salts

Ethanol/Nutrition/Herb Interactions

Ethanol: Avoid ethanol (may increase risk of osteoporosis).

Food: May reduce absorption; mean oral bioavailability is decreased up to 90% when given with food.

Stability Store at controlled room temperature of 15°C to 30°C (59°F to 86°F).

Mechanism of Action A bisphosphonate which inhibits bone resorption via actions on osteoclasts or on osteoclast precursors; decreases the rate of bone resorption, leading to an indirect increase in bone mineral density.

Pharmacodynamics/Kinetics

Distribution: Terminal V_d: 90 L; 40% to 50% of circulating ibandronate binds to bone

Protein binding: 85% to 99%

Bioavailability: Oral: Reduced by 90% following standard breakfast

Half-life elimination:

Oral: 150 mg dose: Terminal: 37-157 hours

I.V.: Terminal: ~5-25 hours

Time to peak, plasma: Oral: 0.5-2 hours

Excretion: Urine (50% to 60% of absorbed dose, excreted as unchanged drug); feces (unabsorbed drug)

Dosage

Oral:

Treatment of postmenopausal osteoporosis: 2.5 mg/day or 150 mg once a month

Prevention of postmenopausal osteoporosis: 2.5 mg/day; 150 mg once a month may be considered

Metastatic bone disease (unlabeled use): 50 mg once daily

I.V.:

Treatment of postmenopausal osteoporosis: 3 mg every 3 months

Hypercalcemia of malignancy (unlabeled use): 2-4 mg over 2 hours

Metastatic bone disease (unlabeled use): 6 mg over 1 hour every 3-4 weeks

Dosage adjustment in renal impairment:

Mild or moderate impairment: Dosing adjustment not needed

Severe impairment (Cl_{cr} <30 mL/minute): Use not recommended

Dose adjustment in renal impairment for oncologic uses (unlabeled): Severe impairment (Cl_{cr} <30 mL/minute):

Oral: 50 mg once weekly

I.V.: 2 mg over 1 hour every 3-4 weeks

Dosage adjustment in hepatic impairment: Dosing adjustment not needed

Dietary Considerations Supplemental calcium or vitamin D may be required if dietary intake is not adequate. Tablet should be taken with a full glass (6-8 oz) of plain water, at least 60 minutes prior to any food, beverages, or medications. Mineral water with a high calcium content should be avoided.

Administration

Oral: Should be administered 60 minutes before the first food or drink of the day (other than water). Ibandronate should be taken in an upright position with a full glass (6-8 oz) of plain water and the patient should avoid lying down for 60 minutes to minimize the possibility of GI side effects. Mineral water with a high calcium content should be avoided. The tablet should be swallowed whole; do not chew or suck.

Once-monthly dosing: The 150 mg tablet should be taken on the same date each month. In case of a missed dose, do not take two 150 mg tablets within the same week. If the next scheduled dose is 1-7 days away, wait until the next scheduled dose to take the tablet. If the next scheduled dose is >7 days away, take the dose the morning it is remembered, and then resume taking the once-monthly dose on the originally scheduled day.

I.V.: Administer as a 15-30 second bolus. Do not mix with calcium-containing solutions or other drugs. For osteoporosis, do not administer more frequently than every 3 months. Infuse over 1 hour for metastatic bone disease and over 2 hours for hypercalcemia of malignancy.

Monitoring Parameters Bone mineral density; serum creatinine prior to each I.V. dose

Test Interactions Bisphosphonates may interfere with diagnostic imaging agents such as technetium-99m-diphosphonate in bone scans.

Dosage Forms

Injection, solution: 1 mg/mL (3 mL) [prefilled syringe]

Tablet: 2.5 mg [once-daily formulation]; 150 mg [once-monthly formulation]

♦ **Ibandronate Sodium** *see* Ibandronate *on page 869*

♦ **Ibandronic Acid** *see* Ibandronate *on page 869*

♦ **Ibidomide Hydrochloride** *see* Labetalol *on page 967*

Ibritumomab (ib ri TYOO mo mab)

U.S. Brand Names Zevalin®

Index Terms Ibritumomab Tiuxetan; In-111 Zevalin; Y-90 Zevalin

Pharmacologic Category Antineoplastic Agent, Monoclonal Antibody; Radiopharmaceutical

Use Treatment of relapsed or refractory low-grade, follicular, or transformed B-cell non-Hodgkin's lymphoma

Pregnancy Risk Factor D

Pregnancy Implications There are no adequate and well-controlled studies in pregnant women. Y-90 ibritumomab may cause fetal harm. Women of childbearing potential should avoid becoming pregnant during treatment with ibritumomab. Both males and females should use effective contraception for 12 months following treatment. The effect on future fertility is unknown.

Lactation Excretion in breast milk unknown/contraindicated

Medication Safety Issues

High alert medication: The Institute for Safe Medication Practices (ISMP) includes this medication among its list of drugs which have a heightened risk of causing significant patient harm when used in error.

Contraindications Known type I hypersensitivity or anaphylactic reactions to ibritumomab, indium chloride, yttrium chloride, or any component of the formulation; murine proteins, rituximab; ≥25% lymphoma marrow involvement; prior myeloablative therapies; platelet count <100,000 cells/mm³; neutrophil count <1500 cells/mm³; hypocellular bone marrow (≤15% cellularity of marked reduction in bone marrow precursors); history of failed stem cell collection; pregnancy; breast-feeding. Y-90 ibritumomab should not be administered to patients with altered In-111 ibritumomab biodistribution.

Warnings/Precautions Hazardous agent - use appropriate precautions for handling and disposal. **[U.S. Boxed Warning: Severe cutaneous and mucocutaneous skin reactions have been reported (with fatalities) in postmarketing experience.** These include erythema multiforme, Stevens-Johnson syndrome, toxic epidermal necrolysis, bullous dermatitis, and exfoliative dermatitis. Onset may occur within days to 3-4 months following infusion. Patients experiencing severe cutaneous or mucocutaneous skin reactions should not receive any further component of the ibritumomab tiuxetan regimen.

To be used as part of the Zevalin® therapeutic regimen (in combination with rituximab). **[U.S. Boxed Warnings]: Do not exceed the Y-90 Ibritumomab maximum allowable dose of 32 mCi; do not administer to patients with altered biodistribution. Use should be reserved to physicians and other professionals qualified and experienced in the safe handling of radiopharmaceuticals, and in monitoring and emergency treatment of infusion reactions.** The contents of the kit are not radioactive until radiolabeling occurs. During and after radiolabeling, adequate shielding should be used with this product, in accordance with institutional radiation safety practices.

[U.S. Boxed Warning]: Severe, potentially-fatal infusion reactions (angioedema, bronchospasm, hypotension, hypoxia) have been reported, typically with the first rituximab infusion (during infusion or within 30-120 minutes of infusion). Patients should be screened for human antimouse antibodies (HAMA); may be at increased risk of allergic or serious hypersensitivity reactions.

[U.S. Boxed Warning]: Prolonged and severe cytopenias are common. Do not administer with ≥25% lymphoma marrow involvement and/or impaired bone marrow reserve. Hemorrhage may occur due to thrombocytopenia; use caution with patients taking anticoagulants or medications interfering with platelet function. Closely monitor patients for up to 3 months after administration.

Safety and efficacy of repeated courses of the therapeutic regimen have not been established. Safety and efficacy have not been established in pediatric patients.

Adverse Reactions Severe, potentially life-threatening allergic reactions have occurred in association with infusions. Also refer to Rituximab monograph.

>10%:

Central nervous system: Chills (24%), fever (17%), pain (13%), headache (12%)

Gastrointestinal: Nausea (31%), abdominal pain (16%), vomiting (12%)

Hematologic: Thrombocytopenia (95%), neutropenia (77%), anemia (61%)

Myelosuppressive:

WBC: Severe

Platelets: Severe

Nadir: 7-9 weeks

Recovery: 22-35 days

Neuromuscular & skeletal: Weakness (43%)

Respiratory: Dyspnea (14%)

Miscellaneous: Infection (29%)

1% to 10%:

Cardiovascular: Peripheral edema (8%), hypotension (6%), flushing (6%), angioedema (5%)

Central nervous system: Dizziness (10%), insomnia (5%), anxiety (4%)

(Continued)

Ibritumomab *(Continued)*

Dermatologic: Pruritus (9%), rash (8%), urticaria (4%), petechia (3%)

Gastrointestinal: Diarrhea (9%), anorexia (8%), abdominal distension (5%), constipation (5%), dyspepsia (4%), melena (2%; life threatening in 1%), gastrointestinal hemorrhage (1%)

Hematologic: Bruising (7%), pancytopenia (2%), secondary malignancies (2%)

Neuromuscular & skeletal: Back pain (8%), arthralgia (7%), myalgia (7%)

Respiratory: Cough (10%), throat irritation (10%), rhinitis (6%), bronchospasm (5%), epistaxis (3%), apnea (1%)

Miscellaneous: Diaphoresis (4%), allergic reaction (2%; life-threatening in 1%)

<1% (Limited to important or life-threatening: Arthritis; cutaneous and mucocutaneous reactions (eg, erythema multiforme, Stevens-Johnson Syndrome, toxic epidermal necrolysis, bullous dermatitis and exfoliative dermatitis); encephalopathy, hematemesis, pulmonary edema, pulmonary embolism, stroke (hemorrhagic), subdural hematoma, tachycardia, vaginal hemorrhage. Myeloid malignancies and dysplasia have also been reported in patients who had received treatment with ibritumomab.

Overdosage/Toxicology Symptoms may include severe hematological toxicity. Treatment is supportive. In early clinical experience with high dosages, some patients required autologous stem cell transplantation.

Drug Interactions

Increased Effect/Toxicity: Due to the high incidence of thrombocytopenia associated with ibritumomab, the use of agents which decrease platelet function may be associated with a higher risk of bleeding (includes aspirin, NSAIDs, glycoprotein IIb/IIIa antagonists, clopidogrel and ticlopidine). In addition, the risk of bleeding may be increased with anticoagulant agents, including heparin, low molecular weight heparins, thrombolytics, and warfarin. The safety of live viral vaccines has not been established.

Decreased Effect: Response to vaccination may be impaired.

Ethanol/Nutrition/Herb Interactions Herb/Nutraceutical: Avoid cat's claw, dong quai, evening primrose, feverfew, garlic, ginger, ginkgo, red clover, horse chestnut, green tea, ginseng (all have antiplatelet activity).

Stability Store at 2°C to 8°C (36°F to 46°F); do not freeze. Kit is not radioactive. To prepare radiolabeled injection, follow preparation guidelines provided by manufacturer.

Mechanism of Action Ibritumomab is a monoclonal antibody directed against the CD20 antigen found on B lymphocytes (normal and malignant). Ibritumomab binding induces apoptosis in B lymphocytes *in vitro*. It is combined with the chelator tiuxetan, which acts as a specific chelation site for either Indium-111 (In-111) or Yttrium-90 (Y-90). The monoclonal antibody acts as a delivery system to direct the radioactive isotope to the targeted cells, however, binding has been observed in lymphoid cells throughout the body and in lymphoid nodules in organs such as the large and small intestines. Indium-111 is a gamma-emitter used to assess biodistribution of ibritumomab, while Y-90 emits beta particles. Beta-emission induces cellular damage through the formation of free radicals (in both target cells and surrounding cells).

Pharmacodynamics/Kinetics

Duration: Beta cell recovery begins in ~12 weeks; generally in normal range within 9 months

Distribution: To lymphoid cells throughout the body and in lymphoid nodules in organs such as the large and small intestines, spleen, testes, and liver

Metabolism: Has not been characterized; the product of yttrium-90 radioactive decay is zirconium-90 (nonradioactive); Indium-111 decays to cadmium-111 (nonradioactive)

Half-life elimination: Y-90 ibritumomab: 30 hours; Indium-111 decays with a physical half-life of 67 hours; Yttrium-90 decays with a physical half-life of 64 hours

Excretion: A median of 7.2% of the radiolabeled activity was excreted in urine over 7 days

Dosage I.V.: Adults: Ibritumomab is administered **only** as part of the Zevalin™ therapeutic regimen (a combined treatment regimen with rituximab). The regimen consists of two steps:

Step 1:

Rituximab infusion: 250 mg/m² at an initial rate of 50 mg/hour. If hypersensitivity or infusion-related events do not occur, increase infusion in increments of 50 mg/hour every 30 minutes, to a maximum of 400 mg/hour. Infusions should be temporarily slowed or interrupted if hypersensitivity or infusion-related events occur. The infusion may be resumed at one-half the previous rate upon improvement of symptoms.

In-111 ibritumomab infusion: Within 4 hours of the completion of rituximab infusion, inject 5 mCi (1.6 mg total antibody dose) over 10 minutes.

Biodistribution of In-111 ibritumomab should be assessed by imaging at 2-24 hours and at 48-72 hours postinjection. An optional third imaging may be performed 90-120 hours following injection. If biodistribution is not acceptable, the patient should not proceed to Step 2.

Step 2 (initiated 7-9 days following Step 1):

Rituximab infusion: 250 mg/m² at an initial rate of 100 mg/hour (50 mg/hour if infusion-related events occurred with the first infusion). If hypersensitivity or infusion-related events do not occur, increase infusion in increments of 100 mg/hour every 30 minutes, to a maximum of 400 mg/hour, as tolerated.

Y-90 ibritumomab infusion: Within 4 hours of the completion of rituximab infusion:

Platelet count >150,000 cells/mm³: Inject 0.4 mCi/kg (14.8 MBq/kg actual body weight) over 10 minutes

Platelet count between 100,000-149,000 cells/mm³: Inject 0.3 mCi/kg (11.1 MBq/kg actual body weight) over 10 minutes

Platelet count <100,000 cells/mm³: Do **not** administer

Maximum dose: The prescribed, measured, and administered dose of Y-90 ibritumomab must not exceed 32 mCi (1184 MBq), regardless of the patient's body weight

Administration

Rituximab: Administer the first infusion of rituximab at an initial rate of 50 mg/hour. If hypersensitivity or infusion-related events do not occur, escalate the infusion rate in 50 mg/hour increments every 30 minutes, to a maximum of 400 mg/hour. If hypersensitivity or an

IBUPROFEN

infusion-related event develops, temporarily slow or interrupt the infusion (discontinue if reaction is severe). The infusion can continue at one-half the previous rate upon improvement of patient symptoms. Subsequent rituximab infusion can be administered at an initial rate of 100 mg/hour and increased in 100 mg/hour increments at 30-minute intervals, to a maximum of 400 mg/hour as tolerated.

In-111 and Y-90 ibritumomab: Inject slowly, over 10 minutes through a 0.22 micron low protein binding in-line filter. After injection, flush line with at least 10 mL normal saline. Y-90 ibritumomab: establish free-flowing I.V. line prior to administration; avoid extravasation.

Monitoring Parameters Human antimurine antibody (HAMA) prior to treatment (if positive, may have an allergic or hypersensitivity reaction when treated with this or other murine or chimeric monoclonal antibodies).

Patients must be monitored for infusion-related allergic reactions (typically within 30-120 minutes of administration). Obtain complete blood counts and platelet counts at regular intervals during rituximab therapy (at least weekly and more frequently in patients who develop cytopenia). Platelet count must be obtained prior to step 2. Monitor for up to 3 months after use.

Biodistribution of In-111 ibritumomab should be assessed by imaging at 2-24 hours and at 48-72 hours post injection. An optional third imaging may be performed 90-120 hours following injection. If biodistribution is not acceptable, the patient should not proceed to Step 2.

Additional Information Ibritumomab tiuxetan is produced in Chinese hamster ovary cell cultures. Kit is not radioactive. Radiolabeling of ibritumomab with Yttrium-90 and Indium-111 (not included in kit) must be performed by appropriate personnel in a specialized facility.

Dosage Forms Each kit contains 4 vials for preparation of either In-111 or Y-90 conjugate (as indicated on container label)

Injection, solution: 1.6 mg/mL (2 mL) [supplied with sodium acetate solution, formulation buffer vial (includes albumin 750 mg), and an empty reaction vial]

♦ **Ibritumomab Tiuxetan** *see* Ibritumomab *on page 871*
♦ **Ibu-200 [OTC]** *see* Ibuprofen *on page 873*

Ibuprofen (eye byoo PROE fen)

U.S. Brand Names Advil® [OTC]; Advil® Children's [OTC]; Advil® Infants' [OTC]; Advil® Junior [OTC]; Advil® Migraine [OTC]; ElixSure™ IB [OTC]; Genpril® [OTC]; Ibu-200 [OTC]; I-Prin [OTC]; Midol® Cramp and Body Aches [OTC]; Motrin®; Motrin® Children's [OTC]; Motrin® IB [OTC]; Motrin® Infants' [OTC]; Motrin® Junior Strength [OTC]; NeoProfen®; Proprinal [OTC]; Ultraprin [OTC]

Canadian Brand Names Advil®; Apo-Ibuprofen®; Motrin® (Children's); Motrin® IB; Novo-Profen; Nu-Ibuprofen

Index Terms Ibuprofen Lysine; *p*-Isobutylhydratropic Acid

Pharmacologic Category Nonsteroidal Anti-inflammatory Drug (NSAID), Oral; Nonsteroidal Anti-inflammatory Drug (NSAID), Parenteral

Additional Appendix Information
Nonsteroidal Anti-inflammatory Agents *on page 1894*
Toxicology Information *on page 2081*

Use
Oral: Inflammatory diseases and rheumatoid disorders including juvenile rheumatoid arthritis, mild-to-moderate pain, fever, dysmenorrhea

Injection: Ibuprofen lysine is for use in premature infants weighing between 500-1500 g and who are ≤32 weeks gestational age (GA) to induce closure of a clinically-significant patent ductus arteriosus (PDA) when usual treatments are ineffective

Unlabeled/Investigational Use Cystic fibrosis, gout, ankylosing spondylitis, acute migraine headache

Restrictions An FDA-approved medication guide must be distributed when dispensing an oral outpatient prescription (new or refill) where this medication is to be used without direct supervision of a healthcare provider. Medication guides are available at http://www.fda.gov/cder/Offices/ODS/medication_guides.htm.

Pregnancy Risk Factor C/D (3rd trimester)

Lactation Enters breast milk/use caution (AAP rates "compatible")

Medication Safety Issues
Sound-alike/look-alike issues:
Haltran® may be confused with Halfprin®

Contraindications Hypersensitivity to ibuprofen, aspirin, other NSAIDs, or any component of the formulation; perioperative pain in the setting of coronary artery bypass surgery (CABG); pregnancy (3rd trimester)

Ibuprofen lysine is contraindicated in preterm infants with untreated proven or suspected infection; congenital heart disease where patency of the PDA is necessary for pulmonary or systemic blood flow; bleeding (especially with active intracranial hemorrhage or GI bleed); thrombocytopenia; coagulation defects; proven or suspected necrotizing enterocolitis (NEC); significant renal dysfunction

Warnings/Precautions [U.S. Boxed Warning]: NSAIDs are associated with an increased risk of adverse cardiovascular events, including MI, stroke, and new onset or worsening of pre-existing hypertension. Risk may be increased with duration of use or pre-existing cardiovascular risk-factors or disease. Carefully evaluate individual cardiovascular risk profiles prior to prescribing. Use caution with fluid retention, CHF or hypertension. Concurrent administration of ibuprofen, and potentially other nonselective NSAIDs, may interfere with aspirin's cardioprotective effect.

Use of NSAIDs can compromise existing renal function. Renal toxicity can occur in patient with impaired renal function, dehydration, heart failure, liver dysfunction, those taking diuretics and ACEI and the elderly. Rehydrate patient before starting therapy. Monitor renal function closely. Ibuprofen is not recommended for patients with advanced renal disease (Continued)

Ibuprofen *(Continued)*

NSAIDs may increase risk of gastrointestinal irritation, ulceration, bleeding, and perforation. These events may occur at any time during therapy and without warning. Use caution with a history of GI disease (bleeding or ulcers), concurrent therapy with aspirin, anticoagulants and/or corticosteroids, smoking, use of alcohol, the elderly or debilitated patients.

Use the lowest effective dose for the shortest duration of time, consistent with individual patient goals, to reduce risk of cardiovascular or GI adverse events. Alternate therapies should be considered for patients at high risk.

NSAIDs may cause serious skin adverse events including exfoliative dermatitis, Stevens-Johnson syndrome (SJS) and toxic epidermal necrolysis (TEN). Anaphylactoid reactions may occur, even without prior exposure; patients with "aspirin triad" (bronchial asthma, aspirin intolerance, rhinitis) may be at increased risk. Do not use in patients who experience bronchospasm, asthma, rhinitis, or urticaria with NSAID or aspirin therapy.

Use with caution in patients with decreased hepatic function. Closely monitor patients with any abnormal LFT. Severe hepatic reactions (eg, fulminant hepatitis, liver failure) have occurred with NSAID use, rarely; discontinue if signs or symptoms of liver disease develop, or if systemic manifestations occur.

The elderly are at increased risk for adverse effects (especially peptic ulceration, CNS effects, renal toxicity) from NSAIDs even at low doses.

Withhold for at least 4-6 half-lives prior to surgical or dental procedures.

Injection: Hold second or third doses if urinary output is <0.6 mL/kg/hour. May alter signs of infection. May inhibit platelet aggregation; monitor for signs of bleeding. May displace bilirubin; use caution when total bilirubin is elevated. Long-term evaluations of neurodevelopment, growth, or diseases associated with prematurity following treatment have not been conducted. A second course of treatment, alternative pharmacologic therapy or surgery may be needed if the ductus arteriosus fails to close or reopens following the initial course of therapy.

OTC labeling: Prior to self-medication, patients should contact healthcare provider if they have had recurring stomach pain or upset, ulcers, bleeding problems, high blood pressure, heart or kidney disease, other serious medical problems, are currently taking a diuretic, or are ≥60 years of age. Recommended dosages should not be exceeded, due to an increased risk of GI bleeding. Consuming ≥3 alcoholic beverages/day or taking longer than recommended may increase the risk of GI bleeding.

Adverse Reactions
Oral:
1% to 10%:
Cardiovascular: Edema (1% to 3%)
Central nervous system: Dizziness (3% to 9%), headache (1% to 3%), nervousness (1% to 3%)
Dermatologic: Itching (1% to 3%), rash (3% to 9%)
Endocrine & metabolic: Fluid retention (1% to 3%)
Gastrointestinal: Dyspepsia (1% to 3%), vomiting (1% to 3%), abdominal pain/cramps/distress (1% to 3%), heartburn (3% to 9%), nausea (3% to 9%), diarrhea (1% to 3%), constipation (1% to 3%), flatulence (1% to 3%), epigastric pain (3% to 9%), appetite decreased (1% to 3%)
Otic: Tinnitus (3% to 9%)
<1% (Limited to important or life-threatening): Acute renal failure, agranulocytosis, anaphylaxis, aplastic anemia, azotemia, blurred vision, bone marrow suppression, confusion, creatinine clearance decreased, duodenal ulcer, edema, eosinophilia, epistaxis, erythema multiforme, gastric ulcer, GI bleed, GI hemorrhage, GI ulceration, hallucinations, hearing decreased, hematuria, hematocrit decreased, hemoglobin decreased, hemolytic anemia, hepatitis, hypertension, inhibition of platelet aggregation, jaundice, liver function tests abnormal, leukopenia, melena, neutropenia, pancreatitis, photosensitivity, Stevens-Johnson syndrome, thrombocytopenia, toxic amblyopia, toxic epidermal necrolysis, urticaria, vesiculobullous eruptions, vision changes

Injection:
>10%:
Cardiovascular: Intraventricular hemorrhage (29%; grade 3/4: 15%)
Dermatologic: Skin irritation (16%)
Endocrine & metabolic: Hypocalcemia (12%), hypoglycemia (12%)
Gastrointestinal: GI disorders, non NEC (22%)
Hematologic: Anemia (32%)
Respiratory: Apnea (28%), respiratory infection (19%)
Miscellaneous: Sepsis (43%)
1% to 10%:
Cardiovascular: Edema (4%)
Endocrine & metabolic: Adrenal insufficiency (7%), hypernatremia (7%)
Genitourinary: Urinary tract infection (9%)
Renal: Urea increased (7%), renal impairment (6%), creatinine increased (3%), urine output decreased (3%; small decrease reported on days 2-6 with compensatory increase in output on day 9)
Respiratory: Respiratory failure (10%), atelectasis (4%)
Frequency not defined: Abdominal distension, cardiac failure, cholestasis, convulsions, feeding problems, gastritis, GI reflux, hyperglycemia, hypotension, ileus, infection, inguinal hernia, injection site reaction, jaundice, neutropenia, tachycardia, thrombocytopenia

Overdosage/Toxicology Symptoms include apnea, metabolic acidosis, coma, and nystagmus; leukocytosis, renal failure. Management of nonsteroidal anti-inflammatory drug (NSAID) intoxication is primarily supportive and symptomatic. Fluid therapy is commonly effective in managing hypotension that may occur following an acute NSAID overdose, except when due to acute blood loss. Seizures tend to be very short-lived and often do not require drug treatment, although recurrent seizures should be treated with I.V. diazepam.

Since many of NSAIDs undergo enterohepatic cycling, multiple doses of charcoal may be needed to reduce the potential for delayed toxicities.

Drug Interactions

Cytochrome P450 Effect: Substrate (minor) of CYP2C9, 2C19; **Inhibits** CYP2C9 (strong)

Increased Effect/Toxicity: Ibuprofen may increase cyclosporine, digoxin, lithium, and methotrexate serum concentrations. The renal adverse effects of ACE inhibitors may be potentiated by NSAIDs. Corticosteroids may increase the risk of GI ulceration. Ibuprofen may increase the levels/effects of bosentan, dapsone, fluoxetine, glimepiride, glipizide, losartan, montelukast, nateglinide, paclitaxel, phenytoin, warfarin, zafirlukast. and other CYP2C9 substrates. Aminoglycosides: NSAIDs may decrease the excretion of aminoglycosides; this is of particular concern in preterm infants. NSAIDs may enhance the adverse/toxic effect of bisphosphonate derivatives. NSAIDs may decrease the excretion of pemetrexed Probenecid may increase the serum concentration of NSAIDs. NSAIDs may decrease the excretion of vancomycin (of particular concern in preterm infants). Concomitant use with fluoroquinolones may rarely increase risk of seizure.

Decreased Effect: Aspirin may decrease ibuprofen serum concentrations. Salicylates antiplatelet effect may be reduced. Ibuprofen may decrease the effect of some antihypertensive agents (including ACE inhibitors, beta blockers, hydralazine, and angiotensin antagonists) and diuretics. Ibuprofen and other COX-1 inhibitors, may reduce the cardioprotective effects of aspirin. Cholestyramine (and other bile acid sequestrants) may decrease the absorption of NSAIDs; separate by at least 2 hours.

Ethanol/Nutrition/Herb Interactions

Ethanol: Avoid ethanol (may enhance gastric mucosal irritation).

Food: Ibuprofen peak serum levels may be decreased if taken with food.

Herb/Nutraceutical: Avoid alfalfa, anise, bilberry, bladderwrack, bromelain, cat's claw, celery, coleus, cordyceps, dong quai, evening primrose, feverfew, fenugreek, garlic, ginger, ginkgo biloba, red clover, horse chestnut, grapeseed, green tea, ginseng, guggul, horse chestnut seed, horseradish, licorice, prickly ash, red clover, reishi, SAMe, sweet clover, turmeric, white willow (all have additional antiplatelet activity).

Stability

Injection: Store at room temperature of 20°C to 25°C (68°F to 77°F). Protect from light. Dilute with dextrose or saline to an appropriate volume. Following dilution, administer within 30 minutes of preparation.

Suspension: Store at room temperature of 15°C to 30°C (59°F to 86°F).

Tablet: Store at room temperature of 20°C to 25°C (68°F to 77°F).

Mechanism of Action Inhibits prostaglandin synthesis by decreasing the activity of the enzyme, cyclooxygenase, which results in decreased formation of prostaglandin precursors

Pharmacodynamics/Kinetics

Onset of action: Analgesic: 30-60 minutes; Anti-inflammatory: ≤7 days
  Peak effect: 1-2 weeks

Duration: 4-6 hours

Absorption: Oral: Rapid (85%)

Distribution: Premature infants with ductal closure (highly variable between studies):
  Day 3: 145-349 mL/kg
  Day 5: 72-222 mL/kg

Protein binding: 90% to 99%

Metabolism: Hepatic via oxidation

Half-life elimination:
  Premature infants (highly variable between studies):
    Day 3: 35-51 hours
    Day 5: 20-33 hours
  Children 3 months to 10 years: 1.6 ± 0.7 hours
  Adults: 2-4 hours; End-stage renal disease: Unchanged

Time to peak: ~1-2 hours

Excretion: Urine (1% as free drug); some feces

Dosage

I.V.: Infants between 500-1500 g and ≤32 weeks GA: Patent ductus arteriosus: Initial dose: Ibuprofen 10 mg/kg, followed by two doses of 5 mg/kg at 24 and 48 hours. Dose should be based on birth weight.

Oral:

Children:

Antipyretic: 6 months to 12 years: Temperature <102.5°F (39°C): 5 mg/kg/dose; temperature >102.5°F: 10 mg/kg/dose given every 6-8 hours (maximum daily dose: 40 mg/kg/day)

Juvenile rheumatoid arthritis: 30-50 mg/kg/24 hours divided every 8 hours; start at lower end of dosing range and titrate upward (maximum: 2.4 g/day)

Analgesic: 4-10 mg/kg/dose every 6-8 hours

Cystic fibrosis (unlabeled use): Chronic (>4 years) twice daily dosing adjusted to maintain serum levels of 50-100 mcg/mL has been associated with slowing of disease progression in younger patients with mild lung disease

Ibuprofen Dosing

Weight (lb)	Age	Dosage (mg)
12-17	6-11 mo	50
18-23	12-23 mo	75
24-35	2-3 y	100
35-47	4-5 y	150
48-59	6-8 y	200
60-71	9-10 y	250
72 06	11 y	300

(Continued)

Ibuprofen *(Continued)*

OTC labeling (analgesic, antipyretic):

Children 6 months to 11 years: See table on previous page; use of weight to select dose is preferred; doses may be repeated every 6-8 hours (maximum: 4 doses/day)

Children ≥12 years: 200 mg every 4-6 hours as needed (maximum: 1200 mg/24 hours)

Adults:

Inflammatory disease: 400-800 mg/dose 3-4 times/day (maximum dose: 3.2 g/day)

Analgesia/pain/fever/dysmenorrhea: 200-400 mg/dose every 4-6 hours (maximum daily dose: 1.2 g, unless directed by physician)

OTC labeling (analgesic, antipyretic): 200 mg every 4-6 hours as needed (maximum: 1200 mg/24 hours)

Dosing adjustment/comments in severe hepatic impairment: Avoid use

Dietary Considerations Should be taken with food. Chewable tablets may contain phenylalanine; amount varies by product, consult manufacturers labeling.

Administration

Oral: Administer with food

I.V.: For I.V. administration only; administration via umbilical line has not been evaluated. Infuse over 15 minutes through port closest to insertion site. Avoid extravasation. Do not administer simultaneously via same line with TPN. If needed, interrupt TPN for 15 minutes prior to and after ibuprofen administration, keeping line open with dextrose or saline.

Monitoring Parameters CBC; occult blood loss and periodic liver function tests; monitor response (pain, range of motion, grip strength, mobility, ADL function), inflammation; observe for weight gain, edema; monitor renal function (urine output, serum BUN and creatinine); observe for bleeding, bruising; evaluate gastrointestinal effects (abdominal pain, bleeding, dyspepsia); mental confusion, disorientation; with long-term therapy, periodic ophthalmic exams

Injection: Renal function, signs of infection or bleeding, ECG

Reference Range Plasma concentrations >200 mcg/mL may be associated with severe toxicity

PDA: Minimum effective level: 10-12 mg/L

Dosage Forms

Caplet: 200 mg [OTC]

Advil®: 200 mg [contains sodium benzoate]

Ibu-200, Motrin® IB: 200 mg

Motrin® Junior Strength: 100 mg

Capsule, liqui-gel:

Advil®: 200 mg

Advil® Migraine: 200 mg [solubilized ibuprofen; contains potassium 20 mg]

Gelcap:

Advil®: 200 mg [contains coconut oil]

Injection, solution, as lysine [preservative free]:

NeoProfen®: 17.1 mg/mL (2 mL) [equivalent to ibuprofen 10 mg/mL]

Suspension, oral: 100 mg/5 mL (5 mL, 120 mL, 480 mL)

Advil® Children's: 100 mg/5 mL (60 mL, 120 mL) [contains sodium benzoate; blue raspberry, fruit, and grape flavors]

ElixSure™ IB: 100 mg/5 mL (120 mL) [berry flavor]

Motrin® Children's: 100 mg/5 mL (60 mL, 120 mL) [contains sodium benzoate; berry, dye free berry, bubble gum, and grape flavors]

Suspension, oral drops: 40 mg/mL (15 mL)

Advil® Infants': 40 mg/mL (15 mL) [contains sodium benzoate; fruit and grape flavors]

Motrin® Infants': 40 mg/mL (15 mL, 30 mL) [contains sodium benzoate; berry and dye-free berry flavors]

Tablet: 200 mg [OTC], 400 mg, 600 mg, 800 mg

Advil®: 200 mg [contains sodium benzoate]

Advil® Junior: 100 mg [contains sodium benzoate; coated tablets]

Genpril®, I-Prin, Midol® Cramp and Body Aches, Motrin® IB, Proprinal, Ultraprin: 200 mg

Motrin®: 400 mg, 600 mg, 800 mg

Tablet, chewable:

Advil® Children's: 50 mg [contains phenylalanine 2.1 mg; grape flavors]

Advil® Junior: 100 mg [contains phenylalanine 4.2 mg; grape flavors]

Motrin® Children's: 50 mg [contains phenylalanine 1.4 mg; grape and orange flavor]

Motrin® Junior Strength: 100 mg [contains phenylalanine 2.1 mg; grape and orange flavors]

♦ **Ibuprofen and Hydrocodone** *see Hydrocodone and Ibuprofen on page 851*

♦ **Ibuprofen and Oxycodone** *see Oxycodone and Ibuprofen on page 1290*

♦ **Ibuprofen and Pseudoephedrine** *see Pseudoephedrine and Ibuprofen on page 1456*

♦ **Ibuprofen Lysine** *see Ibuprofen on page 873*

Ibutilide *(i BYOO ti lide)*

U.S. Brand Names Corvert®

Index Terms Ibutilide Fumarate

Pharmacologic Category Antiarrhythmic Agent, Class III

Use Acute termination of atrial fibrillation or flutter of recent onset; the effectiveness of ibutilide has not been determined in patients with arrhythmias >90 days in duration

Pregnancy Risk Factor C

Pregnancy Implications Teratogenic and embryocidal in rats; avoid use in pregnancy

Lactation Enters breast milk/contraindicated

Contraindications Hypersensitivity to ibutilide or any component of the formulation; QT_c >440 msec

Warnings/Precautions [U.S. Boxed Warning]: Potentially fatal arrhythmias (eg, polymorphic ventricular tachycardia) can occur with ibutilide, usually in association with torsade de pointes (QT prolongation). Studies indicate a 1.7% incidence of arrhythmias in treated patients. The drug should be given in a setting of continuous ECG monitoring and by personnel trained in treating arrhythmias particularly polymorphic ventricular tachycardia. **[U.S. Boxed Warning]: Patients with chronic atrial fibrillation may not be the best candidates for ibutilide since they often revert after conversion and the risks of treatment may not be justified when compared to alternative management.** Dosing adjustments are not required in patients with renal or hepatic dysfunction since a maximum of only two 10-minute infusions are utilized. Drug distribution, rather than administration, is one of the primary mechanisms responsible for termination of the pharmacologic effect. Safety and efficacy in children have not been established. Avoid any drug that can prolong QT interval. Correct hyperkalemia and hypomagnesemia before using. Monitor for heart block.

Adverse Reactions
1% to 10%:
Cardiovascular: Ventricular extrasystoles (5.1%), nonsustained monomorphic ventricular tachycardia (4.9%), nonsustained polymorphic ventricular tachycardia (2.7%), tachycardia/supraventricular tachycardia (2.7%), hypotension (2%), bundle branch block (1.9%), sustained polymorphic ventricular tachycardia (eg, torsade de pointes) (1.7%, often requiring cardioversion), AV block (1.5%), bradycardia (1.2%), QT segment prolongation, hypertension (1.2%), palpitation (1%)
Central nervous system: Headache (4%)
Gastrointestinal: Nausea (>1%)
<1% (Limited to important or life-threatening): CHF, erythematous bullous lesions, idioventricular rhythm, nodal arrhythmia, renal failure, supraventricular extrasystoles, sustained monomorphic ventricular tachycardia, syncope (0.3%, not > placebo)

Overdosage/Toxicology Symptoms include CNS depression, rapid gasping breathing, and convulsions; arrhythmias can occur. Treatment is supportive and should include measures appropriate for the condition. Antiarrhythmics are generally avoided. Pharmacologic therapies may include magnesium sulfate and correction of other electrolyte abnormalities. Overdrive cardiac pacing, electrical cardioversion, or defibrillation may be required.

Drug Interactions
Increased Effect/Toxicity: Class Ia antiarrhythmic drugs (disopyramide, quinidine, and procainamide) and other class III drugs such as amiodarone and sotalol should not be given concomitantly with ibutilide due to their potential to prolong refractoriness. Signs of digoxin toxicity may be masked when coadministered with ibutilide. Toxicity of ibutilide is potentiated by concurrent administration of other drugs which may prolong QT interval: phenothiazines, tricyclic and tetracyclic antidepressants, cisapride, sparfloxacin, gatifloxacin, moxifloxacin, and erythromycin.

Stability Admixtures are chemically and physically stable for 24 hours at room temperature and for 48 hours at refrigerated temperatures. May be administered undiluted or diluted in 50 mL diluent (0.9% NS or D_5W).

Mechanism of Action Exact mechanism of action is unknown; prolongs the action potential in cardiac tissue

Pharmacodynamics/Kinetics
Onset of action: ~90 minutes after start of infusion ($1/2$ of conversions to sinus rhythm occur during infusion)
Distribution: V_d: 11 L/kg
Protein binding: 40%
Metabolism: Extensively hepatic; oxidation
Half-life elimination: 2-12 hours (average: 6 hours)
Excretion: Urine (82%, 7% as unchanged drug and metabolites); feces (19%)

Dosage I.V.: Initial:
Adults:
<60 kg: 0.01 mg/kg over 10 minutes
≥60 kg: 1 mg over 10 minutes
If the arrhythmia does not terminate within 10 minutes after the end of the initial infusion, a second infusion of equal strength may be infused over a 10-minute period
Elderly: Dose selection should be cautious, usually starting at the lower end of the dosing range.

Administration May be administered undiluted or diluted in 50 mL diluent (0.9% NS or D_5W); infuse over 10 minutes

Monitoring Parameters Observe patient with continuous ECG monitoring for at least 4 hours following infusion or until QT_c has returned to baseline; skilled personnel and proper equipment should be available during administration of ibutilide and subsequent monitoring of the patient

Dosage Forms Injection, solution, as fumarate: 0.1 mg/mL (10 mL)

♦ **Ibutilide Fumarate** see Ibutilide on page 876
♦ **ICI-182,780** see Fulvestrant on page 772
♦ **ICI-204,219** see Zafirlukast on page 1805
♦ **ICI-46474** see Tamoxifen on page 1631
♦ **ICI-118630** see Goserelin on page 810
♦ **ICI-176334** see Bicalutamide on page 221
♦ **ICI-D1033** see Anastrozole on page 129
♦ **ICL670** see Deferasirox on page 465

Icodextrin (eye KOE dex trin)

U.S. Brand Names Adept®; Extraneal®
Pharmacologic Category Adhesiolytic; Peritoneal Dialysate, Osmotic
Use
Adept®: Reduction of postsurgical adhesions in gynecologic laparoscopic procedures
Extraneal®: Daily exchange for the long dwell (8- to 16-hour) during continuous ambulatory peritoneal dialysis (CAPD) or automated peritoneal dialysis (APD) for the management of end-stage renal disease (ESRD), improvement of long dwell ultrafiltration and clearance of
(Continued)

Icodextrin *(Continued)*

creatinine and urea nitrogen (compared to 4.25% dextrose) in patients with high/average or greater transport characteristics as measured by peritoneal equilibration test (PET)

Pregnancy Risk Factor C

Dosage Intraperitoneal: Adults:

CAPD or APD (Extraneal®): Given as a single daily exchange in CAPD or APD; dwell time of 8-16 hours is suggested

Laparoscopic gynecologic surgery (Adept®): Irrigate with at least 100 mL every 30 minutes during surgery; aspirate remaining fluid after surgery is completed, then instill 1 L into the cavity

Additional Information Complete prescribing information for this medication should be consulted for additional detail.

Dosage Forms

Solution, intraperitoneal:

Adept®: 4% (1 L, 1.5 L) [for laparoscopic surgery; contains sodium chloride 5.4 g/L, sodium lactate 4.5 g/L, calcium chloride 257 mg/L, magnesium chloride 51 mg/L]

Extraneal®: 7.5% (1.5 L, 2 L, 2.5 L) [for peritoneal dialysis; contains sodium 132 mEq/L, calcium 3.5 mEq/L, magnesium 0.5 mEq/L, chloride 96 mEq/L, and lactate 40 mEq/L]

♦ **ICRF-187** *see Dexrazoxane on page 485*

♦ **Idamycin® (Can)** *see Idarubicin on page 878*

♦ **Idamycin PFS®** *see Idarubicin on page 878*

Idarubicin *(eye da ROO bi sin)*

U.S. Brand Names Idamycin PFS®

Canadian Brand Names Idamycin®

Index Terms 4-Demethoxydaunorubicin; 4-DMDR; Idarubicin Hydrochloride; IDR; IMI 30; NSC-256439; SC 33428

Pharmacologic Category Antineoplastic Agent, Anthracycline; Antineoplastic Agent, Antibiotic

Use Treatment of acute leukemias (AML, ANLL, ALL), accelerated phase or blast crisis of chronic myelogenous leukemia (CML), breast cancer

Unlabeled/Investigational Use Autologous hematopoietic stem cell transplantation

Pregnancy Risk Factor D

Lactation Excretion in breast milk unknown

Medication Safety Issues

Sound-alike/look-alike issues:

Idarubicin may be confused with DOXOrubicin, DAUNOrubicin, epirubicin

Idamycin PFS® may be confused with Adriamycin

High alert medication: The Institute for Safe Medication Practices (ISMP) includes this medication among its list of drugs which have a heightened risk of causing significant patient harm when used in error.

Contraindications Hypersensitivity to idarubicin, other anthracyclines, or any component of the formulation; bilirubin >5 mg/dL; pregnancy

Warnings/Precautions Hazardous agent - use appropriate precautions for handling and disposal. **[U.S. Boxed Warning]: May cause myocardial toxicity (CHF, arrhythmias or cardiomyopathies) and is more common in patients who have previously received anthracyclines or have pre-existing cardiac disease.** The risk of myocardial toxicity is also increased in patients with concomitant or prior mediastinal/pericardial irradiation, patients with anemia, bone marrow depression, infections, leukemic pericarditis or myocarditis. Monitor cardiac function during treatment.

[U.S. Boxed Warnings]: May cause severe myelosuppression; use caution in patients with pre-existing myelosuppression from prior treatment or radiation. Use caution with renal or hepatic impairment; may required dosage reductions. For I.V. use only; may cause severe local tissue necrosis if extravasation occurs. Rapid lysis of leukemic cells may lead to hyperuricemia. Systemic infections should be managed prior to initiation of treatment. **[U.S. Boxed Warning]: Should be administered under the supervision of an experienced cancer chemotherapy physician.** Safety and efficacy in children have not been established.

Adverse Reactions

>10%:

Cardiovascular: Transient ECG abnormalities (supraventricular tachycardia, S-T wave changes, atrial or ventricular extrasystoles); generally asymptomatic and self-limiting. CHF, dose related. The relative cardiotoxicity of idarubicin compared to doxorubicin is unclear. Some investigators report no increase in cardiac toxicity at cumulative oral idarubicin doses up to 540 mg/m²; other reports suggest a maximum cumulative intravenous dose of 150 mg/m².

Central nervous system: Headache

Dermatologic: Alopecia (25% to 30%), radiation recall, skin rash (11%), urticaria

Gastrointestinal: Nausea, vomiting (30% to 60%); diarrhea (9% to 22%); stomatitis (11%); GI hemorrhage (30%)

Emetic potential: Moderate (30% to 60%)

Genitourinary: Discoloration of urine (darker yellow)

Hematologic: Myelosuppression, primarily leukopenia; thrombocytopenia and anemia. Effects are generally less severe with oral dosing.

Nadir: 10-15 days

Recovery: 21-28 days

Hepatic: Bilirubin and transaminases increased (44%)

Local: Tissue necrosis upon extravasation, erythematous streaking

Vesicant chemotherapy

1% to 10%:

Central nervous system: Seizures

878

Neuromuscular & skeletal: Peripheral neuropathy

<1% (Limited to important or life-threatening): Hyperuricemia

Overdosage/Toxicology Symptoms include severe myelosuppression and increased GI toxicity. Treatment is supportive. It is unlikely that therapeutic efficacy or toxicity would be altered by conventional peritoneal or hemodialysis.

Drug Interactions

Decreased Effect: Patients may experience impaired immune response to vaccines; possible infection after administration of live vaccines in patients receiving immunosuppressants.

Stability Store intact vials of solution under refrigeration (2°C to 8°C/36°F to 46°F). Protect from light. Solutions diluted in D_5W or NS for infusion are stable for 4 weeks at room temperature, protected from light. Syringe and IVPB solutions are stable for 72 hours at room temperature and 7 days under refrigeration.

Mechanism of Action Similar to doxorubicin and daunorubicin; inhibition of DNA and RNA synthesis by intercalation between DNA base pairs

Pharmacodynamics/Kinetics

Absorption: Oral: Variable (4% to 77%; mean: ~30%)

Distribution: V_d: 64 L/kg (some reports indicate 2250 L); extensive tissue binding; CSF

Protein binding: 94% to 97%

Metabolism: Hepatic to idarubicinol (pharmacologically active)

Half-life elimination: Oral: 14-35 hours; I.V.: 12-27 hours

Time to peak, serum: 1-5 hours

Excretion:

Oral: Urine (~5% of dose; 0.5% to 0.7% as unchanged drug, 4% as idarubicinol); hepatic (8%)

I.V.: Urine (13% as idarubicinol, 3% as unchanged drug); hepatic (17%)

Dosage Refer to individual protocols. I.V.:

Children:

Leukemia: 10-12 mg/m^2/day for 3 days every 3 weeks.

Solid tumors: 5 mg/m^2/day for 3 days every 3 weeks

Adults:

Leukemia induction: 12 mg/m^2/day for 3 days

Leukemia consolidation: 10-12 mg/m^2/day for 2 days

Stem cell transplantation (unlabeled use): 20 mg/m^2/24 hours continuous I.V. infusion **or** 21 mg/m^2/24 hours continuous infusion for 48 hours (both with high-dose oral busulfan)

Dosing adjustment in renal impairment: S_{cr}: ≥2 mg/dL: Administer 75% of dose

Hemodialysis: Significant drug removal is unlikely based on physiochemical characteristics

Peritoneal dialysis: Significant drug removal is unlikely based on physiochemical characteristics

Dosing adjustment/comments in hepatic impairment:

Bilirubin 1.5-5.0 mg/dL or AST 60-180 int. units/L: Administer 50% of normal dose

Bilirubin >5.0 mg/dL: Do not administer drug

Administration Do not administer I.M. or SubQ; administer as slow push over 3-5 minutes, preferably into the side of a freely-running saline or dextrose infusion **or** as intermittent infusion over 10-15 minutes into a free-flowing I.V. solution of NS or D_5W; also occasionally administered as a bladder lavage.

Extravasation management: Topical cooling may be achieved using ice packs or cooling pad with circulating ice water. Cooling of site for 24 hours as tolerated by the patient. Elevate and rest extremity 24-48 hours, then resume normal activity as tolerated. Application of cold inhibits vesicant's cytotoxicity. **Application of heat can be harmful and is contraindicated.** If pain, erythema, and/or swelling persist beyond 48 hours, refer patient immediately to plastic surgeon for consultation and possible debridement.

Monitoring Parameters CBC with differential, platelet count, cardiac function, serum electrolytes, creatinine, uric acid, ALT, AST, bilirubin, signs of extravasation

Dosage Forms Injection, solution, as hydrochloride [preservative free] (Idamycin PFS®): 1 mg/mL (5 mL, 10 mL, 20 mL)

♦ **Idarubicin Hydrochloride** see Idarubicin on page 878

♦ **IDEC-C2B8** see Rituximab on page 1523

♦ **IDR** see Idarubicin on page 878

Idursulfase (eye dur SUL fase)

U.S. Brand Names Elaprase™

Pharmacologic Category Enzyme

Use Replacement therapy in mucopolysaccharidosis II (MPS II, Hunter syndrome) for improvement of walking capacity

Pregnancy Risk Factor C

Medication Safety Issues

Sound-alike/look-alike issues:

Elaprase™ may be confused with Elspar®

Dosage I.V.: MPS II:

Children ≥5 years and Adults: 0.5 mg/kg once weekly; dose should be rounded up to the nearest whole vial

Elderly: Studies did not include patients ≥65 years

Additional Information Complete prescribing information for this medication should be consulted for additional detail.

Dosage Forms

Injection, solution [preservative free]:

Elaprase™: 2 mg/mL (5 mL) [extractable volume: 3 mL]

♦ **Ifex®** see Ifosfamide on page 880

♦ **IFLrA** see Interferon Alfa-2a on page 918

Ifosfamide (eye FOSS fa mide)

U.S. Brand Names Ifex®
Canadian Brand Names Ifex®
Index Terms Isophosphamide; NSC-109724; Z4942
Pharmacologic Category Antineoplastic Agent, Alkylating Agent; Antineoplastic Agent, Alkylating Agent (Nitrogen Mustard)
Use Treatment of lung cancer, Hodgkin's and non-Hodgkin's lymphoma, breast cancer, acute and chronic lymphocytic leukemias, ovarian cancer, sarcomas, pancreatic and gastric carcinomas
Orphan drug: Treatment of testicular cancer
Pregnancy Risk Factor D
Lactation Enters breast milk/contraindicated
Medication Safety Issues
Sound-alike/look-alike issues:
Ifosfamide may be confused with cyclophosphamide

High alert medication: The Institute for Safe Medication Practices (ISMP) includes this medication among its list of drugs which have a heightened risk of causing significant patient harm when used in error.
Contraindications Hypersensitivity to ifosfamide or any component of the formulation; patients with severely depressed bone marrow function; pregnancy
Warnings/Precautions Hazardous agent - use appropriate precautions for handling and disposal. **[U.S. Boxed Warning]: Urotoxic side effects, primarily hemorrhagic cystitis, may occur.** Hydration and/or mesna administration will protect against hemorrhagic cystitis. **[U.S. Boxed Warning]: Severe bone marrow suppression may occur. May cause CNS toxicity, including confusion and coma**; reversible upon discontinuation of treatment. Use with caution in patients with impaired renal function or those with compromised bone marrow reserve. May interfere with wound healing. **[U.S. Boxed Warning]: Should be administered under the supervision of an experienced cancer chemotherapy physician.** Safety and efficacy in children have not been established.
Adverse Reactions
>10%:
Central nervous system: Somnolence, confusion, hallucinations (12%)
Dermatologic: Alopecia (75% to 100%)
Endocrine & metabolic: Metabolic acidosis (31%)
Gastrointestinal: Nausea and vomiting (58%), may be more common with higher doses or bolus infusions; constipation
Genitourinary: Hemorrhagic cystitis (40% to 50%), patients should be vigorously hydrated (at least 2 L/day) and receive mesna
Hematologic: Myelosuppression, leukopenia (65% to 100%), thrombocytopenia (10%) - dose related
Onset: 7-14 days
Nadir: 21-28 days
Recovery: 21-28 days
Renal: Hematuria (6% to 92%)
1% to 10%:
Central nervous system: Hallucinations, depressive psychoses, polyneuropathy
Dermatologic: Dermatitis, nail banding/ridging, hyperpigmentation
Endocrine & metabolic: SIADH, sterility
Hematologic: Anemia
Hepatic: Transaminases increased (3%)
Local: Phlebitis
Renal: BUN/creatinine increased (6%)
Respiratory: Nasal stuffiness
<1% (Limited to important or life-threatening): Acute tubular necrosis, anorexia, cardiotoxicity, diarrhea, nonconvulsive status epilepticus, pulmonary fibrosis, stomatitis
Overdosage/Toxicology Symptoms include myelosuppression, nausea, vomiting, diarrhea, and alopecia, which is a direct extension of the drug's pharmacologic effect. Treatment is symptom-directed and supportive.
Drug Interactions
Cytochrome P450 Effect: Substrate of CYP2A6 (minor), 2B6 (minor), 2C8 (minor), 2C9 (minor), 2C19 (minor), 3A4 (major); **Inhibits** CYP3A4 (weak); **Induces** CYP2C8 (weak), 2C9 (weak)
Increased Effect/Toxicity: CYP3A4 inducers may increase the levels/effects of acrolein (the active metabolite of ifosfamide); example inducers include aminoglutethimide, carbamazepine, nafcillin, nevirapine, phenobarbital, phenytoin, and rifamycins.
Decreased Effect: CYP3A4 inhibitors may decrease the levels/effects of acrolein (the active metabolite of ifosfamide); example inhibitors include azole antifungals, clarithromycin, diclofenac, doxycycline, erythromycin, imatinib, isoniazid, nefazodone, nicardipine, propofol, protease inhibitors, quinidine, telithromycin, and verapamil.
Ethanol/Nutrition/Herb Interactions Herb/Nutraceutical: St John's wort may decrease ifosfamide levels.
Stability Store intact vials of powder for injection at room temperature; store intact vials of solution under refrigeration at 2°C to 8°C (36°F to 46°F). Dilute powder with SWI or NS to a concentration of 50 mg/mL. Further dilution in 50-1000 mL D_5W or NS is recommended for I.V. infusion. Reconstituted solutions may be stored under refrigeration for up to 21 days. Solutions diluted for administration are stable for 7 days at room temperature and for 6 weeks under refrigeration.
Mechanism of Action Causes cross-linking of strands of DNA by binding with nucleic acids and other intracellular structures; inhibits protein synthesis and DNA synthesis
Pharmacodynamics/Kinetics Pharmacokinetics are dose dependent
Distribution: V_d: 5.7-49 L; does penetrate CNS, but not in therapeutic levels

Protein binding: Negligible

Metabolism: Hepatic to active metabolites phosphoramide mustard, acrolein, and inactive dichloroethylated and carboxy metabolites; acrolein is the agent implicated in development of hemorrhagic cystitis

Bioavailability: Estimated at 100%

Half-life elimination: Beta: High dose: 11-15 hours (3800-5000 mg/m^2); Lower dose: 4-7 hours (1800 mg/m^2)

Time to peak, plasma: Oral: Within 1 hour

Excretion: Urine (15% to 50% as unchanged drug, 41% as metabolites)

Dosage Refer to individual protocols. To prevent bladder toxicity, ifosfamide should be given with the urinary protector mesna and hydration of at least 2 L of oral or I.V. fluid per day. I.V.:

Children:

1200-1800 mg/m^2/day for 3-5 days every 21-28 days **or**

5 g/m^2 once every 21-28 days **or**

3 g/m^2/day for 2 days every 21-28 days

Adults:

50 mg/kg/day or 700-2000 mg/m^2/day for 5 days every 3-4 weeks

Alternatives: 2400 mg/m^2/day for 3 days or 5000 mg/m^2 as a single dose every 3-4 weeks

Dosing adjustment in renal impairment: Limited experience in renal impairment; manufacturer does not provide adjustment. Several published recommendations include dose reductions between 20% and 30% in significant renal impairment. Consult individual protocols.

Dosing adjustment in hepatic impairment: Although no specific guidelines are available from the manufacturer, it is possible that adjusted doses are indicated in hepatic disease. One suggestion in the literature: AST >300 or bilirubin >3.0 mg/dL: Decrease ifosfamide dose by 75%

Administration Administer slow I.V. push, IVPB over 30 minutes to several hours or continuous I.V. over 5 days

Monitoring Parameters CBC with differential, hemoglobin, and platelet count, urine output, urinalysis, liver function, and renal function tests

Dosage Forms

Injection, powder for reconstitution: 1 g

Ifex®: 1 g, 3 g

Injection, solution: 50 mg/mL (20 mL, 60 mL)

♦ **IG** see Immune Globulin (Intramuscular) on page 891

♦ **IgG4-Kappa Monoclonal Antibody** see Natalizumab on page 1203

♦ **IGIM** see Immune Globulin (Intramuscular) on page 891

♦ **IL-1Ra** see Anakinra on page 128

♦ **IL-2** see Aldesleukin on page 59

♦ **IL-11** see Oprelvekin on page 1270

Iloprost (EYE loe prost)

U.S. Brand Names Ventavis™

Index Terms Iloprost Tromethamine; Prostacyclin PGI$_2$

Pharmacologic Category Prostaglandin

Use Treatment of idiopathic pulmonary arterial hypertension in patients with NYHA Class III or IV symptoms

Pregnancy Risk Factor C

Dosage Inhalation: Adults: Initial: 2.5 mcg/dose; if tolerated, increase to 5 mcg/dose; administer 6-9 times daily (dosing at intervals ≥2 hours while awake); maintenance dose: 5 mcg/dose; maximum daily dose: 45 mcg

Dosage adjustment in renal impairment: Adjustments are not necessary. Use caution in dialysis patients; may be more susceptible to hypotension.

Dosage adjustment in hepatic impairment: Use caution

Additional Information Complete prescribing information for this medication should be consulted for additional detail.

Dosage Forms Solution for oral inhalation [preservative-free]: 10 mcg/mL (1 mL, 2 mL) [ampul]

♦ **Iloprost Tromethamine** see Iloprost on page 881

Imatinib (eye MAT eh nib)

U.S. Brand Names Gleevec®

Canadian Brand Names Gleevec®

Index Terms CGP-57148B; Glivec; Imatinib Mesylate; NSC-716051; STI571

Pharmacologic Category Antineoplastic Agent, Tyrosine Kinase Inhibitor

Use Treatment of:

Aggressive systemic mastocytosis (ASM) without D816V c-kit mutation (or c-Kit mutation status unknown)

Dermatofibrosarcoma protuberans (DFSP) (unresectable, recurrent and metastatic)

Gastrointestinal stromal tumors (GIST) kit-positive (CD117) unresectable and/or (metastatic) malignant

Hypereosinophilic syndrome (HES) and/or chronic eosinophilic leukemia (CEL)

Myelodysplastic/myeloproliferative disease (MDS/MPD) associated with platelet-derived growth factor receptor (PDGFR) gene rearrangements

Philadelphia chromosome-positive (Ph+) chronic myeloid leukemia (CML) in chronic phase (newly-diagnosed)

Ph+ acute lymphoblastic leukemia (ALL) (relapsed or refractory)

Ph+ CML in blast crisis, accelerated phase, or chronic phase after failure of interferon therapy

(Continued)

Imatinib *(Continued)*

Ph+ CML in chronic phase in pediatric patients recurring following stem cell transplant or who are resistant to interferon-alpha therapy

Pregnancy Risk Factor D

Pregnancy Implications There are no adequate and well-controlled studies in pregnant women. Animal studies have demonstrated teratogenic effects and fetal loss. Women of childbearing potential are advised not to become pregnant (female patients and female partners of male patients). Adequate contraception is recommended. Case reports of pregnancies while on therapy (both males and females) include reports of spontaneous abortion, minor abnormalities (hypospadias and small intestine rotation) at or shortly after birth. Some women in hematologic or cytogenic response with therapy interruptions for pregnancy failed to respond to imatinib upon treatment reinitiation after pregnancy completion.

Lactation Excretion in breast milk unknown/not recommended

Medication Safety Issues

High alert medication: The Institute for Safe Medication Practices (ISMP) includes this medication among its list of drugs which have a heightened risk of causing significant patient harm when used in error.

Contraindications Hypersensitivity to imatinib or any component of the formulation; pregnancy

Warnings/Precautions Hazardous agent - use appropriate precautions for handling and disposal. Often associated with fluid retention, weight gain, and edema (probability increases with higher doses and age >65 years); occasionally leading to significant complications, including pleural effusion, pericardial effusion, pulmonary edema, and ascites. Use caution in patients where fluid accumulation may be poorly tolerated, such as in cardiovascular disease (CHF or hypertension) and pulmonary disease. CHF and left ventricular dysfunction (LVD) have been reported; carefully monitor patients with cardiac disease or risk factors for heart failure. Cardiogenic shock and/or LVD have been reported in patients with hypereosinophilic syndrome and cardiac involvement (reversible with systemic steroids, circulatory support and temporary cessation of imatinib). Patients with an abnormal echocardiogram or abnormal serum troponin level may benefit from prophylactic systemic steroids with the initiation of imatinib.

Severe dermatologic reactions have been reported; reintroduction has been attempted following resolution. Successful resumption at a lower dose (with corticosteroids and/or antihistamine) has been described; however, some patients may experience recurrent reactions.

Use with caution in renal impairment, hematologic impairment, or hepatic disease. May cause GI irritation, hemorrhage, hepatotoxicity, or hematologic toxicity (anemia, neutropenia, and thrombocytopenia). Median duration of neutropenia is 2-3 weeks; median duration of thrombocytopenia is 3-4 weeks. Hepatotoxic reactions may be severe. Has been associated with development of opportunistic infections. Use with caution in patients receiving concurrent therapy with drugs which alter cytochrome P450 activity or require metabolism by these isoenzymes. Safety and efficacy in patients <2 years of age have not been established. Long-term safety data is limited.

Adverse Reactions

>10%:

Cardiovascular: Chest pain (7% to 11%)

Central nervous system: Fatigue (30% to 53%), pyrexia (15% to 41%), headache (27% to 39%), insomnia (10% to 19%), dizziness (11% to 16%), depression (13%), anxiety (7% to 12%)

Dermatologic: Rash (36% to 53%), pruritus (8% to 14%)

Endocrine & metabolic: Fluid retention (7% to 81% includes aggravated edema, anasarca, ascites, pericardial effusion, pleural effusion, pulmonary edema); hypokalemia (6% to 13%)

Gastrointestinal: Nausea (47% to 74%), diarrhea (39% to 70%), vomiting (21% to 58%), abdominal pain (30% to 40%), flatulence (30% to 34%), weight gain (5% to 32%), dyspepsia (12% to 27%), anorexia (7% to 17%), constipation (9% to 16%), sore throat (10% to 15%), taste disturbance (3% to 15%), loose stools (10% to 12%)

Hematologic: Hemorrhage (24% to 53%; grades 3/4: 1% to 19%), neutropenia (grade 4: 3% to 48%), anemia (grade 4: <1% to 11%), thrombocytopenia (grade 4: <1% to 33%)

Hepatic: Ascites or pleural effusion (GIST: 12% to 15%), hepatotoxicity (6% to 12%)

Neuromuscular & skeletal: Muscle cramps (28% to 62%), musculoskeletal pain (30% to 49%), arthralgia (25% to 40%), joint pain (11% to 30%), myalgia (9% to 27%), back pain (23% to 26%), weakness (15% to 21%), rigors (10% to 12%)

Ocular: Lacrimation increased (16% to 18%)

Respiratory: Cough (14% to 27%), nasopharyngitis (10% to 27%), dyspnea (12% to 21%), upper respiratory tract infection (3% to 19%), pharyngolaryngeal pain (7% to 17%), pneumonia (4% to 13%), sinusitis (4% to 11%)

Miscellaneous: Superficial edema (58% to 81%), night sweats (13% to 17%), influenza (1% to 11%)

1% to 10%:

Central nervous system: CNS hemorrhage (<1% to 9%)

Dermatologic: Alopecia, dry skin

Gastrointestinal: Gastrointestinal hemorrhage (1% to 8%), abdominal distension, gastroesophageal reflux, mouth ulceration

Hepatic: Alkaline phosphatase increased (grade 3: <1% to 6%), ALT increased (grades 3/4: <1% to 7%), bilirubin increased (grades 3/4: <1% to 3%), AST increased (grades 3/4: <1% to 4%)

Neuromuscular & skeletal: Joint swelling, paresthesia

Ocular: Blurred vision, conjunctivitis

Renal: Albumin decreased (grade 3: 3% to 4%), creatinine increased (grades 3/4: <1% to 3%)

Miscellaneous: Flu-like syndrome (<1% to 10%)

<1% (Limited to important or life-threatening): Acute febrile neutropenic dermatosis, acute generalized exanthematous pustulosis, angioedema, aplastic anemia, avascular necrosis, breast enlargement, bullous eruption, cardiac failure, cardiac tamponade, cerebral edema, CHF (severe), colitis, confusion, conjunctival hemorrhage, CPK increased, dehydration, diverticulitis, dry eyes, embolism, erythema multiforme, exfoliative dermatitis, facial edema, flushing, gastric ulcer, gastroenteritis, gastritis, glaucoma, gout, hematuria, hepatic failure, hepatitis, herpes simplex, herpes zoster, hip osteonecrosis, hyperkalemia, hyper-/hypotension, hyponatremia, hypophosphatemia, ileus, intestinal obstruction, intestinal perforation, intracranial pressure increased, interstitial pneumonitis, joint stiffness, LDH increased, leukopenia, LV dysfunction, lymphopenia, macular edema, memory impairment, menorrhagia, migraine, muscle stiffness, pancreatitis, pancytopenia, papilledema, pericarditis, periorbital edema, peripheral neuropathy, photosensitivity, psoriasis, pulmonary fibrosis, purpura, renal failure, respiratory tract (lower) infection, retinal hemorrhage, sciatica, seizure, sepsis, sexual dysfunction, skin pigment changes, somnolence, Stevens-Johnson syndrome, syncope, tachycardia, thrombosis, tinnitus, tumor hemorrhage, tumor necrosis, urinary frequency, vertigo, vesicular rash, vitreous hemorrhage, weight loss

Overdosage/Toxicology Experience with overdose (>800 mg/day) is limited. Patients taking doses of 1200-1600 mg per day experienced ascites, elevated transaminases, elevated bilirubin, and muscle cramps; treatment was interrupted until reversal of abnormalities, then resumed at the normal doses without recurrence of symptoms. Hematologic adverse effects are more common at dosages >750 mg/day. Treatment is symptom-directed and supportive

Drug Interactions

Cytochrome P450 Effect: Substrate of CYP1A2 (minor), 2D6 (minor), 2C9 (minor), 2C19 (minor), 3A4 (major), **Inhibits** CYP2C9 (weak), 2D6 (moderate), 3A4 (strong)

Increased Effect/Toxicity: Imatinib may increase the levels/effects of amphetamines, selected beta blockers, dextromethorphan, fluoxetine, lidocaine, mirtazapine, nefazodone, paroxetine, risperidone, ritonavir, thioridazine, tricyclic antidepressants, venlafaxine and other CYP2D6 substrates. Imatinib may increase the risk of myopathy/rhabdomyolysis with HMG-CoA reductase inhibitors (except pravastatin/fluvastatin). Imatinib may increase the toxicity of pimecrolimus (in patients with widespread and/or erythrodermic disease). Imatinib may increase the levels/effects of benzodiazepines, calcium channel blockers, clarithromycin, cyclosporine, erythromycin, estrogens, mirtazapine, nateglinide, nefazodone, nevirapine, protease inhibitors, tacrolimus, venlafaxine and other CYP3A4 substrates. (Selected benzodiazepines [midazolam and triazolam], cisapride, ergot alkaloids, selected HMG-CoA reductase inhibitors [lovastatin and simvastatin], and pimozide are generally contraindicated with strong CYP3A4 inhibitors.)

The levels/effects of imatinib may be increased by azole antifungals, clarithromycin, diclofenac, doxycycline, erythromycin, isoniazid, nefazodone, nicardipine, propofol, protease inhibitors, quinidine, telithromycin, verapamil, and other CYP3A4 inhibitors. Lansoprazole may enhance the dermatologic adverse effects of Imatinib.

Decreased Effect: The levels/effects of imatinib may be decreased by aminoglutethimide, carbamazepine, nafcillin, nevirapine, phenobarbital, phenytoin, rifamycins, and other CYP3A4 inducers. Dosage of imatinib should be increased by at least 50% (with careful monitoring) when used concurrently with a strong inducer.

Imatinib may decrease the levels/effects of codeine, hydrocodone, oxycodone, tramadol, and other CYP2D6 prodrug substrates. Imatinib may decrease the absorption of digoxin (tablet formulation).

Ethanol/Nutrition/Herb Interactions

Ethanol: Avoid ethanol.

Food: Food may reduce gastrointestinal irritation.

Herb/Nutraceutical: Avoid St John's wort (may increase metabolism and decrease imatinib plasma concentration).

Stability Store at 15°C to 30°C (59°F to 86°F). Protect from moisture.

Mechanism of Action Inhibits Bcr-Abl tyrosine kinase, the constitutive abnormal gene product of the Philadelphia chromosome in chronic myeloid leukemia (CML). Inhibition of this enzyme blocks proliferation and induces apoptosis in Bcr-Abl positive cell lines as well as in fresh leukemic cells in Philadelphia chromosome positive CML. Also inhibits tyrosine kinase for platelet-derived growth factor (PDGF), stem cell factor (SCF), c-kit, and cellular events mediated by PDGF and SCF.

Pharmacodynamics/Kinetics

Protein binding: 95% to albumin and alpha$_1$-acid glycoprotein

Metabolism: Hepatic via CYP3A4 (minor metabolism via CYP1A2, CYP2D6, CYP2C9, CYP2C19); primary metabolite (active): N-demethylated piperazine derivative (CGP74588); severe hepatic impairment (bilirubin >3-10 times ULN) increases AUC by 45% to 55% for imatinib and its active metabolite, respectively

Bioavailability: 98%

Half-life elimination: Parent drug: 18 hours; N-desmethyl metabolite: 40 hours

Time to peak: 2-4 hours

Excretion: Feces (68% primarily as metabolites, 20% as unchanged drug); urine (13% primarily as metabolites, 5% as unchanged drug)

Clearance: Highly variable; Mean: 8-14 L/hour (for 50 kg and 100 kg male, respectively)

Dosage Oral: **Note:** For concurrent use with a strong CYP3A4 enzyme-inducing agent (eg, rifampin, phenytoin), imatinib dosage should be increased by at least 50%.

Children ≥2 years: **Note:** May be administered once daily or in 2 divided doses.

Ph+ CML (chronic phase, recurrent or resistant): 260 mg/m^2/day; maximum: 600 mg /day

Ph+ CML (chronic phase, newly diagnosed): 340 mg/m^2/day; maximum: 600 mg /day

Adults:

Ph+ CML:

Chronic phase: 400 mg once daily; may be increased to 600 mg daily

Accelerated phase or blast crisis: 600 mg once daily; may be increased to 800 mg daily (400 mg twice daily)

Ph+ ALL: 600 mg once daily

GIST: 400-600 mg/day

(Continued)

Imatinib *(Continued)*

ASM with eosinophilia: Initiate at 100 mg once daily; titrate up to a maximum of 400 mg once daily (if tolerated) for insufficient response to lower dose

ASM without D816V c-Kit mutation or c-Kit mutation status unknown: 400 mg once daily

DFSP: 400 mg twice daily

HES/CEL: 400 mg once daily

HES/CEL with FIP1L1-PDGFRα fusion kinase: Initiate at 100 mg once daily; titrate up to a maximum of 400 mg once daily (if tolerated) if insufficient response to lower dose

MDS/MPD: 400 mg once daily

Dosage adjustment for hepatic impairment: Treatment initiation:

Mild-to-moderate impairment: Usual initial dose 400 mg/day (depending on indication)

Severe impairment: Usual initial dose 300 mg/day (depending on indication)

Dosage adjustment for hepatotoxicity or other nonhematologic adverse reactions: If elevations of bilirubin >3 times upper limit of normal (ULN) or transaminases (ALT/AST) >5 times ULN occur, withhold until bilirubin <1.5 times ULN or transaminases <2.5 times ULN. Resume treatment at a reduced dose:

Children ≥2 years:

If initial dose 260 mg/m²/day, reduce dose to 200 mg/m²/day

If initial dose 340 mg/m²/day, reduce dose to 260 mg/m²/day

Adults:

If initial dose 400 mg, reduce dose to 300 mg

If initial dose 600 mg, reduce dose to 400 mg

If initial dose 800 mg, reduce dose to 600 mg

Dosage adjustment for hematologic adverse reactions:

Chronic phase CML (initial dose 400 mg/day in adults or 260-340 mg/m²/day in children), ASM, MDS/MPD, and HES/CEL (initial dose 400 mg/day), or GIST (initial dose 400 mg or 600 mg): If ANC <1 x 10⁹/L and/or platelets <50 x 10⁹/L: Withhold until ANC ≥1.5 x 10⁹/L and platelets ≥75 x 10⁹/L; resume treatment at previous dose. For recurrent neutropenia or thrombocytopenia, withhold until recovery, and reinstitute treatment at a reduced dose:

Children ≥2 years:

If initial dose 260 mg/m²/day, reduce dose to 200 mg/m²/day

If initial dose 340 mg/m²/day, reduce dose to 260 mg/m²/day

Adults:

If initial dose 400 mg, reduce dose to 300 mg

If initial dose 600 mg, reduce dose to 400 mg

CML (accelerated phase or blast crisis) and PH+ ALL: Adults (initial dose 600 mg): If ANC <0.5 x 10⁹/L and/or platelets <10 x 10⁹/L, establish whether cytopenia is related to leukemia (bone marrow aspirate or biopsy). If unrelated to leukemia, reduce dose to 400 mg. If cytopenia persists for an additional 2 weeks, further reduce dose to 300 mg. If cytopenia persists for 4 weeks and is still unrelated to leukemia, withhold treatment until ANC ≥1 x 10⁹/L and platelets ≥20 x 10⁹/L, then resume treatment at 300 mg.

ASM associated with eosinophilia and HES/CEL with FIP1L1-PDGFRα fusion kinase (starting dose 100 mg/day): If ANC <1 x 10⁹/L and/or platelets <50 x 10⁹/L: Withhold until ANC ≥1.5 x 10⁹/L and platelets ≥75 x 10⁹/L; resume treatment at previous dose.

DFSP (initial dose 800 mg/day): If ANC <1 x 10⁹/L and/or platelets <50 x 10⁹/L , withhold until ANC ≥1.5 x 10⁹/L and platelets ≥75 x 10⁹/L; resume treatment at reduced dose of 600 mg/day. If depression in neutrophils or platelets recurs, withhold until recovery, and reinstitute treatment with a further dose reduction to 400 mg/day.

Dietary Considerations Should be taken with food and a large glass of water to decrease gastrointestinal irritation.

Administration Should be administered with food and a large glass of water. Tablets may be dispersed in water or apple juice (using ~50 mL for 100 mg tablet, ~200 mL for 400 mg tablet); stir until dissolved and use immediately. For daily dosing ≥800 mg, the 400 mg tablets should be used in order to reduce iron exposure.

Monitoring Parameters CBC (weekly for first month, biweekly for second month, then periodically thereafter), liver function tests (at baseline and monthly or as clinically indicated), renal function, calcium and phosphorus levels, thyroid function tests; fatigue, weight, and edema/fluid status; consider echocardiogram and serum troponin levels in patients with HES/CEL, and in patients with MDS/MPD or ASM with high eosinophil levels

In Canada, a baseline evaluation of left ventricular ejection fraction is recommended prior to initiation of imatinib therapy in all patients with known underlying heart disease or in elderly patients.

Additional Information Median time to hematologic response was one month; only short-term studies have been completed. Follow-up is insufficient to estimate duration of cytogenic response. Patients with HES/CEL, MDS/MPD or ASM with an abnormal echocardiogram or abnormal serum troponin level may benefit from prophylactic systemic steroids (1-2 mg/kg for 1-2 weeks) with the initiation of imatinib.

Dosage Forms

Tablet:

Gleevec®: 100 mg; 400 mg

♦ **Imatinib Mesylate** *see* Imatinib *on page 881*

♦ **IMC-C225** *see* Cetuximab *on page 336*

♦ **Imdur®** *see* Isosorbide Mononitrate *on page 947*

♦ **IMI 30** *see* Idarubicin *on page 878*

♦ **IMid-3** *see* Lenalidomide *on page 984*

♦ **Imidazole Carboxamide** *see* Dacarbazine *on page 442*

♦ **Imidazole Carboxamide Dimethyltriazene** *see* Dacarbazine *on page 442*

Imiglucerase (i mi GLOO ser ace)

U.S. Brand Names Cerezyme®
Canadian Brand Names Cerezyme®
Pharmacologic Category Enzyme
Use Long-term enzyme replacement therapy for patients with Type 1 Gaucher's disease
Pregnancy Risk Factor C
Medication Safety Issues
Sound-alike/look-alike issues:
Cerezyme® may be confused with Cerebyx®, Ceredase®

Dosage I.V.: Children ≥2 years and Adults: Initial: 30-60 units/kg every 2 weeks; dosing is individualized based on disease severity. Dosing range: 2.5 units/kg 3 times/week up to as much as 60 units/kg administered as frequently as once a week or as infrequently as every 4 weeks. Average dose: 60 units/kg administered every 2 weeks

Additional Information Complete prescribing information for this medication should be consulted for additional detail.

Dosage Forms Injection, powder for reconstitution [preservative free]: 200 units, 400 units

♦ **Imipemide** see Imipenem and Cilastatin on page 885

Imipenem and Cilastatin (i mi PEN em & sye la STAT in)

U.S. Brand Names Primaxin®
Canadian Brand Names Primaxin®; Primaxin® I.V.
Index Terms Imipemide
Pharmacologic Category Antibiotic, Carbapenem
Additional Appendix Information
Antimicrobial Drugs of Choice on page 1981
Use Treatment of lower respiratory tract, urinary tract, intra-abdominal, gynecologic, bone and joint, skin and skin structure, and polymicrobic infections as well as bacterial septicemia and endocarditis. Antibacterial activity includes resistant gram-negative bacilli (*Pseudomonas aeruginosa* and *Enterobacter* sp), gram-positive bacteria (methicillin-sensitive *Staphylococcus aureus* and *Streptococcus* sp) and anaerobes.
Pregnancy Risk Factor C
Pregnancy Implications Teratogenic effects were not observed in animal studies; however, maternal toxicity was noted. There are no well-controlled or adequate studies in pregnant women. Use during pregnancy only if the potential benefits outweigh the potential risks to mother and fetus.
Lactation Enters breast milk/use caution
Medication Safety Issues
Sound-alike/look-alike issues:
Primaxin® may be confused with Premarin®, Primacor®
Contraindications Hypersensitivity to imipenem/cilastatin or any component of the formulation
Warnings/Precautions Dosage adjustment required in patients with impaired renal function; elderly patients often require lower doses (adjust carefully to renal function); Prolonged use may result in superinfection, including pseudomembranous colitis. Has been associated with CNS adverse effects, including confusional states and seizures; use with caution in patients with a history of seizures or hypersensitivity to beta-lactams (including penicillins and cephalosporins); patients with impaired renal function are at increased risk of seizures if not properly dose adjusted. Not recommended in pediatric CNS infections due to seizure potential. Serious hypersensitivity reactions, including anaphylaxis, have been reported (some without a history of previous allergic reactions to beta-lactams). Doses for I.M. administration are mixed with lidocaine, consult information on lidocaine for associated warnings/precautions. Two different imipenem/cilastatin products are available; due to differences in formulation, the I.V. and I.M. preparations **cannot** be interchanged. Safety and efficacy of I.M. administration in children <12 years of age have not been established.
Adverse Reactions Adverse reactions reported with use for both I.V. and I.M. formulations in adults, except where noted.
1% to 10%:
Cardiovascular: Tachycardia (infants 2%; adults <1%)
Central nervous system: Seizure (infants 6%; adults <1%)
Dermatologic: Rash (1%, children 2%)
Gastrointestinal: Nausea (1% to 2%), diarrhea (children 3% to 4%; adults 1% to 2%), vomiting (2%)
Genitourinary: Oliguria/anuria (infants 2%; adults <1%)
Local: Phlebitis/thrombophlebitis (3%), pain at I.M. injection site (1.2%)
<1% (Limited to important or life-threatening): Abdominal pain, abnormal urinalysis, acute renal failure, alkaline phosphatase increased, anaphylaxis, anemia, angioneurotic edema, asthenia, bilirubin increased, bone marrow depression, BUN/creatinine increased, candidiasis, confusion, cyanosis, dizziness, drug fever, dyspnea, encephalopathy, eosinophilia, erythema multiforme, fever, flushing, gastroenteritis, glossitis, hallucinations, headache, hearing loss, hematocrit decreased, hemoglobin decreased, hemolytic anemia, hemorrhagic colitis, hepatitis (including fulminant onset), hepatic failure, hyperchloremia, hyperhidrosis, hyperkalemia, hypersensitivity, hyperventilation, hyponatremia, hypotension, injection site erythema, jaundice, lactate dehydrogenase increased, leukocytosis, leukopenia, myoclonus, neutropenia (including agranulocytosis), palpitation, pancytopenia, paresthesia, pharyngeal pain, polyarthralgia, polyuria, positive Coombs' test, prothrombin time increased, pruritus, pruritus vulvae, pseudomembranous colitis, psychic disturbances, rash, resistant *P. aeruginosa*, salivation increased, somnolence, staining of teeth, Stevens-Johnson syndrome, taste perversion, thoracic spine pain, thrombocythemia, thrombocytopenia, tinnitus, tongue/tooth discoloration, tongue papillar hypertrophy, toxic
(Continued)

Imipenem and Cilastatin *(Continued)*

epidermal necrolysis, transaminases increased, tremor, urine discoloration, urticaria, vertigo

Overdosage/Toxicology Symptoms include neuromuscular hypersensitivity and seizures. Hemodialysis may be helpful to aid in removal of the drug from the blood, otherwise most treatment is supportive or symptom-directed.

Drug Interactions

Increased Effect/Toxicity: Ganciclovir may increase the risk of seizures; concomitant use not recommended. Uricosuric agents (eg, probenecid) may increase the levels/effects of imipenem; monitor. Concurrent cyclosporine may increase the neurotoxic effects of imipenem and cyclosporine levels may also be increased; monitor.

Decreased Effect: Imipenem may decrease valproic acid concentrations to subtherapeutic levels; monitor. Antibiotics may decrease therapeutic effects of Ty21a typhoid vaccine.

Stability Imipenem/cilastatin powder for injection should be stored at <25°C (77°F).

I.M.: Prepare 500 mg vial with 2 mL 1% lidocaine (do not use lidocaine with epinephrine). The I.V. formulation does not form a stable suspension in lidocaine and cannot be used to prepare an I.M dose. The I.M. suspension should be used within 1 hour of reconstitution.

I.V.: Prior to use, dilute dose into 100-250 mL of an appropriate solution. Imipenem is inactivated at acidic or alkaline pH. Final concentration should not exceed 5 mg/mL. The I.M. formulation is not buffered and cannot be used to prepare I.V. solutions. Reconstituted I.V. solutions are stable for 4 hours at room temperature and 24 hours when refrigerated. Do not freeze.

Mechanism of Action Inhibits bacterial cell wall synthesis by binding to one or more of the penicillin binding proteins (PBPs); which in turn inhibits the final transpeptidation step of peptidoglycan synthesis in bacterial cell walls, thus inhibiting cell wall biosynthesis. Bacteria eventually lyse due to ongoing activity of cell wall autolytic enzymes (autolysins and murein hydrolases) while cell wall assembly is arrested. Cilastatin prevents renal metabolism of imipenem by competitive inhibition of dehydropeptidase along the brush border of the renal tubules.

Pharmacodynamics/Kinetics

Absorption: I.M.: Imipenem: 60% to 75%; cilastatin: 95% to 100%

Distribution: Rapidly and widely to most tissues and fluids including sputum, pleural fluid, peritoneal fluid, interstitial fluid, bile, aqueous humor, reproductive organs, and bone; highest concentrations in pleural fluid, interstitial fluid, peritoneal fluid, and reproductive organs; low concentrations in CSF

Protein binding: Imipenem: 20%; cilastatin: 40%

Metabolism: Imipenem is metabolized in the kidney by dehydropeptidase I; cilastatin prevents imipenem metabolism by this enzyme; cilastatin is partially metabolized renally

Half-life elimination: I.V.: Both drugs: 60 minutes; prolonged with renal impairment; I.M.: Imipenem: 2-3 hours

Time to peak: I.M.: 3.5 hours

Excretion: Both drugs: Urine (~70% as unchanged drug)

Dosage

Usual dosage ranges: Note: Dosage based on **imipenem** content:

Neonates ≤3 months and weight ≥1500 g: Non-CNS infections: I.V.:

<1 week: 25 mg/kg every 12 hours

1-4 weeks: 25 mg/kg every 8 hours

4 weeks to 3 months: 25 mg/kg every 6 hours

Children >3 months: Non-CNS infections: I.V.: 15-25 mg/kg every 6 hours; maximum dosage: Susceptible infections: 2 g/day; moderately-susceptible organisms: 4 g/day

Adults: **Note:** For adults weighing <70 kg, refer to Dosing Adjustment in Renal Impairment:

I.M.: Weight ≥70 kg: 500-750 mg every 12 hours

I.V.: Weight ≥70 kg: 250-1000 mg every 6-8 hours; maximum: 4 g/day

Indication-specific dosing: Note: Doses based on imipenem content. I.M. administration is not intended for severe or life-threatening infections (eg, septicemia, endocarditis, shock), UTI, bone/joint or polymicrobic infections:

Children: I.V.:

Burkholderia mallei (melioidosis) (unlabeled use): 20 mg/kg every 8 hours for 10 days

Cystic fibrosis: Doses up to 90 mg/kg/day have been used

Adults:

Burkholderia mallei (melioidosis) (unlabeled use): I.V.: 20 mg/kg (up to 1 g) every 6-8 hours for 10 days

Intra-abdominal infections:

I.V.: Mild infection: 250-500 mg every 6 hours; severe: 500 mg every 6 hours

I.M.: Mild-to-moderate infection: 750 mg every 12 hours

Liver abscess: I.V.: 500 mg every 6 hours for 2-3 weeks, then appropriate oral therapy for a total of 4-6 weeks

Lower respiratory tract, skins/skin structure, gynecologic infections: I.M.: Mild/moderate: 500-750 mg every 12 hours

Mild infection: Note: Rarely a suitable option in mild infections; normally reserved for moderate-severe cases:

I.M.: 500 mg every 12 hours

I.V.:

Fully-susceptible organisms: 250 mg every 6 hours

Moderately-susceptible organisms: 500 mg every 6 hours

Moderate infection:

I.M.: 750 mg every 12 hours

I.V.:

Fully-susceptible organisms: 500 mg every 6-8 hours

Moderately-susceptible organisms: 500 mg every 6 hours or 1 g every 8 hours

Neutropenic fever, otitis externa: I.V.: 500 mg every 6 hours

Pseudomonas **infections:** I.V.: 500 mg every 6 hours; **Note:** Higher doses may be required based on organism sensitivity.

Severe infection: I.V.:
  Fully-susceptible organisms: 500 mg every 6 hours
  Moderately-susceptible organisms: 1 g every 6-8 hours
  Maximum daily dose should not exceed 50 mg/kg or 4 g/day, whichever is lower
Urinary tract infection: I.V.:
  Uncomplicated: 250 mg every 6 hours
  Complicated: 500 mg every 6 hours

Dosage adjustment in renal impairment: I.V.: **Note:** Adjustments have not been established for I.M. dosing:
Patients with a Cl_{cr} ≤5 mL/minute/1.73 m² should not receive imipenem/cilastatin unless hemodialysis is instituted within 48 hours.
Patients weighing <30 kg with impaired renal function should not receive imipenem/cilastatin.
Hemodialysis: Use the dosing recommendation for patients with a Cl_{cr} 6-20 mL/minute; administer dose after dialysis session and every 12 hours thereafter
Peritoneal dialysis: Dose as for Cl_{cr} <10 mL/minute
Continuous arteriovenous or venovenous hemofiltration: Dose as for Cl_{cr} 20-30 mL/minute; monitor for seizure activity; imipenem is well removed by CAVH but cilastatin is not; removes 20 mg of imipenem per liter of filtrate per day

See table.

Imipenem and Cilastatin Dosage in Renal Impairment

Reduced I.V. Dosage Regimen Based on Creatinine Clearance (mL/minute/1.73 m²) and/or Body Weight <70 kg				
Body Weight (kg)				
≥70	60	50	40	30
Total daily dose for normal renal function: 1 g/day				
Cl_{cr} ≥71 — 250 mg q6h	250 mg q8h	125 mg q6h	125 mg q6h	125 mg q8h
Cl_{cr} 41-70 — 250 mg q8h	125 mg q6h	125 mg q6h	125 mg q8h	125 mg q8h
Cl_{cr} 21-40 — 250 mg q12h	250 mg q12h	125 mg q8h	125 mg q12h	125 mg q12h
Cl_{cr} 6-20 — 250 mg q12h	125 mg q12h	125 mg q12h	125 mg q12h	125 mg q12h
Total daily dose for normal renal function: 1.5 g/day				
Cl_{cr} ≥71 — 500 mg q8h	250 mg q6h	250 mg q8h	250 mg q8h	125 mg q6h
Cl_{cr} 41-70 — 250 mg q6h	250 mg q8h	250 mg q8h	125 mg q6h	125 mg q8h
Cl_{cr} 21-40 — 250 mg q8h	250 mg q8h	250 mg q12h	125 mg q8h	125 mg q8h
Cl_{cr} 6-20 — 250 mg q12h	250 mg q12h	250 mg q12h	125 mg q12h	125 mg q12h
Total daily dose for normal renal function: 2 g/day				
Cl_{cr} ≥71 — 500 mg q6h	500 mg q8h	250 mg q6h	250 mg q6h	250 mg q8h
Cl_{cr} 41-70 — 500 mg q8h	250 mg q6h	250 mg q6h	250 mg q8h	125 mg q6h
Cl_{cr} 21-40 — 250 mg q6h	250 mg q8h	250 mg q8h	250 mg q12h	125 mg q8h
Cl_{cr} 6-20 — 250 mg q12h	250 mg q12h	250 mg q12h	250 mg q12h	125 mg q12h
Total daily dose for normal renal function: 3 g/day				
Cl_{cr} ≥71 — 1000 mg q8h	750 mg q8h	500 mg q6h	500 mg q8h	250 mg q6h
Cl_{cr} 41-70 — 500 mg q6h	500 mg q8h	500 mg q8h	250 mg q6h	250 mg q8h
Cl_{cr} 21-40 — 500 mg q8h	500 mg q8h	250 mg q6h	250 mg q8h	250 mg q8h
Cl_{cr} 6-20 — 500 mg q12h	500 mg q12h	250 mg q12h	250 mg q12h	250 mg q12h
Total daily dose for normal renal function: 4 g/day				
Cl_{cr} ≥71 — 1000 mg q6h	1000 mg q8h	750 mg q8h	500 mg q6h	500 mg q8h
Cl_{cr} 41-70 — 750 mg q8h	750 mg q8h	500 mg q6h	500 mg q8h	250 mg q6h
Cl_{cr} 21-40 — 500 mg q6h	500 mg q8h	500 mg q8h	250 mg q6h	250 mg q8h
Cl_{cr} 6-20 — 500 mg q12h	500 mg q12h	500 mg q12h	250 mg q12h	250 mg q12h

Dietary Considerations Sodium content of 500 mg injection:
  I.M.: 32 mg (1.4 mEq)
  I.V.: 37.5 mg (1.6 mEq)
Administration
  I.M.: **Note:** I.M. administration is not intended for severe or life-threatening infections (eg, septicemia, endocarditis, shock). Administer by deep injection into a large muscle (gluteal or lateral thigh). **Only the I.M. formulation can be used for I.M. administration.**
  I.V.: Do not administer I.V. push. Infuse doses ≤500 mg over 20-30 minutes; infuse doses ≥750 mg over 40-60 minutes. **Only the I.V. formulation can be used for I.V. administration.**
Monitoring Parameters Periodic renal, hepatic, and hematologic function tests; monitor for signs of anaphylaxis during first dose
Test Interactions Interferes with urinary glucose determination using Clinitest®
Dosage Forms
  Injection, powder for reconstitution [I.M.]: Imipenem 500 mg and cilastatin 500 mg [contains sodium 32 mg (1.4 mEq)]
  Injection, powder for reconstitution [I.V.]: Imipenem 250 mg and cilastatin 250 mg [contains sodium 18.8 mg (0.8 mEq)]; imipenem 500 mg and cilastatin 500 mg [contains sodium 37.5 mg (1.6 mEq)]

Imipramine (im IP ra meen)

U.S. Brand Names Tofranil®; Tofranil-PM®
Canadian Brand Names Apo-Imipramine®; Novo-Pramine; Tofranil®
Index Terms Imipramine Hydrochloride; Imipramine Pamoate
Pharmacologic Category Antidepressant, Tricyclic (Tertiary Amine)
Additional Appendix Information
Antidepressant Agents *on page 1866*
Use Treatment of depression; treatment of nocturnal enuresis in children
Unlabeled/Investigational Use Analgesic for certain chronic and neuropathic pain; panic disorder; attention-deficit/hyperactivity disorder (ADHD)
Restrictions An FDA-approved medication guide concerning the use of antidepressants in children and teenagers must be distributed when dispensing an outpatient prescription (new or refill) where this medication is to be used without direct supervision of a healthcare provider. Medication guides are available at http://www.fda.gov/cder/Offices/ODS/medication_guides.htm. Dispense to parents or guardians of children and teenagers receiving this medication.
Pregnancy Risk Factor D
Lactation Enters breast milk/not recommended (AAP rates "of concern")
Medication Safety Issues
Sound-alike/look-alike issues:
Imipramine may be confused with amitriptyline, desipramine, Norpramin®
Contraindications Hypersensitivity to imipramine (cross-reactivity with other dibenzodiazepines may occur) or any component of the formulation; concurrent use of MAO inhibitors (within 14 days); in a patient during acute recovery phase of MI; pregnancy
Warnings/Precautions [U.S. Boxed Warning]: Antidepressants increase the risk of suicidal thinking and behavior in children and adolescents with major depressive disorder (MDD) and other depressive disorders; consider risk prior to prescribing. All patients must be closely monitored for clinical worsening, suicidality, or unusual changes in behavior, especially during the initiation of therapy or following an increase or decrease in dosage. When used in children, the child's family or caregiver should be instructed to closely observe the patient and communicate condition with healthcare provider. A medication guide should be dispensed with each prescription. **Imipramine is FDA approved for the treatment of nocturnal enuresis in children ≥6 years of age.**

The possibility of a suicide attempt is inherent in major depression and may persist until remission occurs. Use caution in high-risk patients. Worsening depression and severe abrupt suicidality that are not part of the presenting symptoms may require discontinuation or modification of drug therapy. The patient's family or caregiver should be alerted to monitor patients for the emergence of suicidality and associated behaviors (such as agitation, irritability, hostility, impulsivity, and hypomania) and notify healthcare provider.

May worsen psychosis in some patients or precipitate a shift to mania or hypomania in patients with bipolar disorder. Patients presenting with depressive symptoms should be screened for bipolar disorder. Monotherapy in patients with bipolar disorder should be avoided. **Imipramine is not FDA approved for the treatment of bipolar depression.**

The degree of sedation, anticholinergic effects, orthostasis, and conduction abnormalities are high relative to other antidepressants. Imipramine often causes drowsiness/sedation, resulting in impaired performance of tasks requiring alertness (eg, operating machinery or driving). Sedative effects may be additive with other CNS depressants and/or ethanol. Use with caution in patients with a history of cardiovascular disease (including previous MI, stroke, tachycardia, or conduction abnormalities). Use with caution in patients with urinary retention, benign prostatic hyperplasia, narrow-angle glaucoma, xerostomia, visual problems, constipation, or a history of bowel obstruction.

Consider discontinuing, when possible, prior to elective surgery. Therapy should not be abruptly discontinued in patients receiving high doses for prolonged periods. May lower seizure threshold - use caution in patients with a previous seizure disorder or condition predisposing to seizures such as brain damage, alcoholism, or concurrent therapy with other drugs which lower the seizure threshold. May increase the risks associated with electroconvulsive therapy. Use with caution in hyperthyroid patients or those receiving thyroid supplementation. Use with caution in patients with hepatic or renal dysfunction and in elderly patients. Has been associated with photosensitization.

Adverse Reactions Frequency not defined.
Cardiovascular: Orthostatic hypotension, arrhythmia, tachycardia, hypertension, palpitation, MI, heart block, ECG changes, CHF, stroke
Central nervous system: Dizziness, drowsiness, headache, agitation, insomnia, nightmares, hypomania, psychosis, fatigue, confusion, hallucinations, disorientation, delusions, anxiety, restlessness, seizure
Endocrine & metabolic: Gynecomastia, breast enlargement, galactorrhea, increase or decrease in libido, increase or decrease in blood sugar, SIADH
Gastrointestinal: Nausea, unpleasant taste, weight gain/loss, xerostomia, constipation, ileus, stomatitis, abdominal cramps, vomiting, anorexia, epigastric disorders, diarrhea, black tongue
Genitourinary: Urinary retention, impotence
Neuromuscular & skeletal: Weakness, numbness, tingling, paresthesia, incoordination, ataxia, tremor, peripheral neuropathy, extrapyramidal symptoms
Ocular: Blurred vision, disturbances of accommodation, mydriasis
Otic: Tinnitus
Miscellaneous: Diaphoresis
<1% (Limited to important or life-threatening): Agranulocytosis, alopecia, cholestatic jaundice, eosinophilia, increased liver enzymes, itching, petechiae, photosensitivity, purpura, rash, thrombocytopenia, urticaria

Overdosage/Toxicology Symptoms include confusion, hallucinations, constipation, cyanosis, tachycardia, urinary retention, ventricular tachycardia, and seizures. Following initiation of essential overdose management, toxic symptoms should be treated. Sodium bicarbonate is indicated when the QRS interval is >0.10 seconds or the QT_c interval is >0.42 seconds. Ventricular arrhythmias often respond to concurrent systemic alkalinization (sodium bicarbonate 0.5-2 mEq/kg I.V.). Arrhythmias unresponsive to this therapy may respond to lidocaine 1 mg/kg I.V., followed by a titrated infusion. Physostigmine (1-2 mg slow I.V. for adults or 0.5 mg slow I.V. for children) may be indicated in reversing life-threatening cardiac arrhythmias. Seizures usually respond to diazepam I.V. boluses (5-10 mg for adults up to 30 mg or 0.25-0.4 mg/kg/dose for children up to 10 mg/dose). If seizures are unresponsive or recur, phenytoin or phenobarbital may be required.

Drug Interactions

Cytochrome P450 Effect: Substrate of CYP1A2 (minor), 2B6 (minor), 2C19 (major), 2D6 (major), 3A4 (minor); **Inhibits** CYP1A2 (weak), 2C19 (weak), 2D6 (moderate), 2E1 (weak)

Increased Effect/Toxicity: When used with MAO inhibitors, hyperpyrexia, hypertension, tachycardia, confusion, seizures, and **deaths have been reported** (serotonin syndrome). Serotonin syndrome has also been reported with ritonavir (rare). Use of lithium with a TCA may increase the risk for neurotoxicity.

CYP2C19 inhibitors may increase the levels/effects of imipramine; example inhibitors include delavirdine, fluconazole, fluvoxamine, gemfibrozil, isoniazid, omeprazole, and ticlopidine. Imipramine increases the effects of amphetamines, anticholinergics, other CNS depressants (sedatives, hypnotics, or ethanol), chlorpropamide, tolazamide, and warfarin. CYP2D6 inhibitors may increase the levels/effects of imipramine; example inhibitors include chlorpromazine, delavirdine, fluoxetine, miconazole, paroxetine, pergolide, quinidine, quinine, ritonavir, and ropinirole.

Phenothiazines may increase concentration of some TCAs and TCAs may increase concentration of phenothiazines. Pressor response to I.V. epinephrine, norepinephrine, and phenylephrine may be enhanced in patients receiving TCAs (**Note:** Effect is unlikely with epinephrine or levonordefrin dosages typically administered as infiltration in combination with local anesthetics).

Combined use of beta-agonists or drugs which prolong QT_c (including quinidine, procainamide, disopyramide, cisapride, sparfloxacin, gatifloxacin, moxifloxacin) with TCAs may predispose patients to cardiac arrhythmias.

Decreased Effect: CYP2C19 inducers may decrease the levels/effects of imipramine; example inducers include aminoglutethimide, carbamazepine, phenytoin, and rifampin. Imipramine inhibits the antihypertensive response to bethanidine, clonidine, debrisoquin, guanadrel, guanethidine, guanabenz, and guanfacine. Cholestyramine and colestipol may bind TCAs and reduce their absorption; monitor for altered response.

Ethanol/Nutrition/Herb Interactions

Ethanol: Avoid ethanol (may increase CNS depression).

Food: Grapefruit juice may inhibit the metabolism of some TCAs and clinical toxicity may result.

Herb/Nutraceutical: St John's wort may decrease imipramine levels. Avoid valerian, St John's wort, SAMe, kava kava (may increase risk of serotonin syndrome and/or excessive sedation).

Mechanism of Action Traditionally believed to increase the synaptic concentration of serotonin and/or norepinephrine in the central nervous system by inhibition of their reuptake by the presynaptic neuronal membrane. However, additional receptor effects have been found including desensitization of adenyl cyclase, down regulation of beta-adrenergic receptors, and down regulation of serotonin receptors.

Pharmacodynamics/Kinetics

Onset of action: Peak antidepressant effect: Usually after ≥2 weeks

Absorption: Well absorbed

Distribution: Crosses placenta

Metabolism: Hepatic via CYP to desipramine (active) and other metabolites; significant first-pass effect

Half-life elimination: 6-18 hours

Excretion: Urine (as metabolites)

Dosage Oral:

Children:

Depression (unlabeled use): 1.5 mg/kg/day with dosage increments of 1 mg/kg every 3-4 days to a maximum dose of 5 mg/kg/day in 1-4 divided doses; monitor carefully especially with doses ≥3.5 mg/kg/day

Enuresis: ≥6 years: Initial: 25 mg at bedtime, if inadequate response still seen after 1 week of therapy, increase by 25 mg/day; dose should not exceed 2.5 mg/kg/day or 50 mg at bedtime if 6-12 years of age or 75 mg at bedtime if ≥12 years of age

Adjunct in the treatment of cancer pain (unlabeled use): Initial: 0.2-0.4 mg/kg at bedtime; dose may be increased by 50% every 2-3 days up to 1-3 mg/kg/dose at bedtime

Adolescents: Depression: Initial: 30-40 mg/day; increase gradually; maximum: 100 mg/day in single or divided doses

Adults: Depression: Initial: 25 mg 3-4 times/day, increase dose gradually, total dose may be given at bedtime; maximum: 300 mg/day

Elderly: Initial: 10-25 mg at bedtime; increase by 10-25 mg every 3 days for inpatients and weekly for outpatients if tolerated; average daily dose to achieve a therapeutic concentration: 100 mg/day; range: 50-150 mg/day

Monitoring Parameters Monitor blood pressure and pulse rate prior to and during initial therapy; ECG in older adults; evaluate mental status; blood levels are useful for therapeutic monitoring

Reference Range Therapeutic: Imipramine and desipramine: 150-250 ng/mL (SI: 530-890 nmol/L); desipramine: 150-300 ng/mL (SI: 560-1125 nmol/L); Toxic: >500 ng/mL (SI: 446-893 nmol/L); utility of serum level monitoring controversial

Dosage Forms

Capsule, as pamoate: 75 mg, 100 mg, 125 mg, 150 mg

(Continued)

Imipramine (Continued)

Tofranil-PM®: 75 mg, 100 mg, 125 mg, 150 mg
Tablet, as hydrochloride: 10 mg, 25 mg, 50 mg
Tofranil®): 10 mg, 25 mg, 50 mg

◆ **Imipramine Hydrochloride** *see* Imipramine *on page 888*
◆ **Imipramine Pamoate** *see* Imipramine *on page 888*

Imiquimod (i mi KWI mod)

U.S. Brand Names Aldara™
Canadian Brand Names Aldara™
Pharmacologic Category Skin and Mucous Membrane Agent; Topical Skin Product
Use Treatment of external genital and perianal warts/condyloma acuminata; nonhyperkeratotic, nonhypertrophic actinic keratosis on face or scalp; superficial basal cell carcinoma (sBCC) with a maximum tumor diameter of 2 cm located on the trunk, neck, or extremities (excluding hands or feet)
Unlabeled/Investigational Use Treatment of common warts
Pregnancy Risk Factor C
Pregnancy Implications Safety and efficacy have not been established in pregnant women. A registry has been established for women exposed to imiquimod during pregnancy (800-670-6126).
Lactation Excretion in breast milk unknown/consult prescriber
Medication Safety Issues
Sound-alike/look-alike issues:
Aldara™ may be confused with Alora®
Contraindications Hypersensitivity to imiquimod or any component of the formulation
Warnings/Precautions Imiquimod has not been evaluated for the treatment of urethral, intravaginal, cervical, rectal, or intra-anal human papilloma viral disease and is not recommended for these conditions. Topical imiquimod is not intended for ophthalmic use. Topical imiquimod administration is not recommended until genital/perianal tissue is healed from any previous drug or surgical treatment. Imiquimod has the potential to exacerbate inflammatory conditions of the skin. Intense inflammatory reactions may occur, and may be accompanied by systemic symptoms (fever, malaise, myalgia); interruption of therapy should be considered. May increase sunburn susceptibility; patients should protect themselves from the sun. Use in basal cell carcinoma should be limited to superficial carcinomas with a maximum diameter of 2 cm. Efficacy in treatment of SBCC lesions of the face, head, and anogenital area, or other subtypes of basal cell carcinoma, have not been established. Treatment of actinic keratosis should be limited to areas ≤5 cm². Safety and efficacy of repeated use in the same 25 cm² area has not been established. Safety and efficacy in patients <12 years of age have not been established.
Adverse Reactions
>10%:
Local: Application site reactions are common. Frequency of reactions vary, and are related to the degree of inflammation associated with the treated disease, number of weekly applications, and individual sensitivity. Symptoms of local reaction include burning, edema, erosion, erythema, excoriation/flaking, pain, pruritus, vesicles, and scabbing. In some cases, systemic symptoms (fever, malaise, myalgia, flu-like symptoms) occur, which should prompt consideration of an interruption of therapy.
Respiratory: Upper respiratory infection (15%)
1% to 10%:
Cardiovascular: Hypertension (1% to 3%), atrial fibrillation (1%)
Central nervous system: Pain (2% to 8%), headache (4% to 8%), fatigue (1% to 2%), fever (1% to 2%), dizziness (1%)
Dermatologic: Hyperkeratosis (2% to 9%), eczema (2%), alopecia (1%), hypopigmentation (1%), rash (<1% to 2%)
Endocrine & metabolic: Hypercholesterolemia (2%), gout (1%)
Gastrointestinal: Diarrhea (3%), dyspepsia (2% to 3%), nausea (1%)
Neuromuscular & skeletal: Myalgia (1%), back pain (<1% to 4%)
Respiratory: Sinusitis (7%), rhinitis (3%), pharyngitis (2%), coughing (2%)
Miscellaneous: Influenza-like symptoms (also see Local reactions; 1% to 3%), squamous cell carcinoma (4%)
Postmarketing and/or case reports (limited to important and/or life-threatening): Agitation, angioedema, arrhythmias, capillary leak syndrome, cardiac failure, cardiomyopathy, depression, dyspnea, exfoliative dermatitis, insomnia, ischemia, liver function abnormal, MI, multiple sclerosis aggravated, paresis, proteinuria, pulmonary edema, seizure, stroke, syncope, thyroiditis
Overdosage/Toxicology Overdosage is unlikely because of minimal percutaneous absorption. Persistent topical overdosing of imiquimod could result in severe local skin reactions. The most clinically serious adverse event reported, following multiple oral imiquimod doses ≥200 mg, was hypotension which resolved following oral or I.V. fluid administration. Treat symptomatically.
Drug Interactions
Cytochrome P450 Effect: Substrate (minor) of CYP1A2, 3A4
Stability Store below 25°C (77°F); do not freeze.
Mechanism of Action Mechanism of action is unknown; however, induces cytokines, including interferon-alpha and others
Pharmacodynamics/Kinetics
Absorption: Minimal
Excretion: Urine and feces (<0.9%)
Dosage Topical:
Children ≥12 years and Adults: Perianal warts/condyloma acuminata: Apply a thin layer 3 times/week prior to bedtime and leave on skin for 6-10 hours. Remove with mild soap and

water. Examples of 3 times/week application schedules are: Monday, Wednesday, Friday; or Tuesday, Thursday, Saturday. Continue imiquimod treatment until there is total clearance of the genital/perianal warts for ≤16 weeks. A rest period of several days may be taken if required by the patient's discomfort or severity of the local skin reaction. Treatment may resume once the reaction subsides.

Adults:

Actinic keratosis: Apply twice weekly for 16 weeks to a treatment area on face or scalp; apply prior to bedtime and leave on skin for 8 hours. Remove with mild soap and water.

Common oral warts (dental use): Apply once daily prior to bedtime

Common warts (unlabeled use): Apply once daily prior to bedtime

Superficial basal cell carcinoma: Apply once daily prior to bedtime, 5 days/week for 6 weeks. Treatment area should include a 1 cm margin of skin around the tumor. Leave on skin for 8 hours. Remove with mild soap and water.

Administration

Actinic keratosis: Treatment area should be a single contiguous area (approximately 25 cm^2) on the face or scalp. Both areas should not be treated concurrently. No more than one packet should eb applied at each application. Apply a thin layer to the wart area and rub in until the cream is no longer visible. Avoid contact with the eyes, lips, and nostrils. Do not occlude the application site. Wash hands following application.

External genital warts: Nonocclusive dressings such as cotton gauze or cotton underwear may be used in the management of skin reactions. Handwashing before and after cream application is recommended. Imiquimod is packaged in single-use packets that contain sufficient cream to cover a wart area of up to 20 cm^2; avoid use of excessive amounts of cream. Instruct patients to apply imiquimod to external or perianal warts; not for vaginal use. Apply a thin layer to the wart area and rub in until the cream is no longer visible. Do not occlude the application site. Wash hands following application.

Superficial basal cell carcinoma: Treatment area should have a maximum diameter no more than 2 cm on the trunk, neck, or extremities (excluding the hands and feet). Treatment area should include a 1 cm margin around the tumor. Apply a thin layer to the wart area (and margin) and rub in until the cream is no longer visible. Avoid contact with the eyes, lips, and nostrils. Do not occlude the application site. Wash hands following application.

Monitoring Parameters Reduction in wart size is indicative of a therapeutic response; patients should be monitored for signs and symptoms of hypersensitivity to imiquimod

Dosage Forms Cream: 5% (12s) [contains benzyl alcohol; single-dose packets]

- ◆ **Imitrex**® see Sumatriptan on page 1620
- ◆ **Imitrex**® **DF (Can)** see Sumatriptan on page 1620
- ◆ **Imitrex**® **Nasal Spray (Can)** see Sumatriptan on page 1620
- ◆ **ImmuCyst**® **(Can)** see BCG Vaccine on page 197

Immune Globulin (Intramuscular)
(i MYUN GLOB yoo lin, IN tra MUS kyoo ler)

U.S. Brand Names BayGam® [DSC]; GammaSTAN™ S/D

Canadian Brand Names BayGam®

Index Terms Gamma Globulin; IG; IGIM; Immune Serum Globulin; ISG

Pharmacologic Category Immune Globulin

Additional Appendix Information
Immunization Recommendations on page 1929

Use To provide passive immunity in susceptible individuals under the following circumstances:

Hepatitis A: Within 14 days of exposure and prior to manifestation of disease

Measles: For use within 6 days of exposure in an unvaccinated person, who has not previously had measles

Varicella: When Varicella Zoster Immune Globulin is not available

Rubella: Post exposure prophylaxis (within 72 hours) to reduce the risk of infection in exposed pregnant women who will not consider therapeutic abortion

Immunoglobulin deficiency: To help prevent serious infections

Pregnancy Risk Factor C

Pregnancy Implications Reproduction studies have not been conducted with this product. Immune globulins cross the placenta in increased amounts after 30 weeks gestation.

Contraindications Hypersensitivity to immune globulin or any component of the formulation; IgA deficiency; severe thrombocytopenia or coagulation disorders where I.M. injections are contraindicated

Warnings/Precautions Skin testing should not be performed as local irritation can occur and be misinterpreted as a positive reaction; IG should **not** be used to control outbreaks of measles. As a product of human plasma, this product may potentially transmit disease; screening of donors, as well as testing and/or inactivation of certain viruses reduces this risk. Epidemiologic and laboratory data indicate current IGIM products do not have a discernible risk of transmitting HIV. Use caution in patients with thrombocytopenia or coagulation disorders (I.M. injections may be contraindicated). Not for I.V. administration.

Adverse Reactions Frequency not defined.

Cardiovascular: Flushing, angioedema

Central nervous system: Chills, lethargy, fever

Dermatologic: Urticaria, erythema

Gastrointestinal: Nausea, vomiting

Local: Pain, tenderness, muscle stiffness at I.M. site

Neuromuscular & skeletal: Myalgia

Miscellaneous: Hypersensitivity reactions

Drug Interactions

Decreased Effect:

Do not administer MMR within 3 months after administration of IGIM; do not administer varicella vaccine within 5 months. If IG is given <2 weeks after MMR vaccine or <3 weeks after varicella vaccine, revaccination is required.

Stability Store under refrigeration at 2°C to 8°C (36°F to 46°F).

(Continued)

Immune Globulin (Intramuscular) *(Continued)*

Mechanism of Action Provides passive immunity by increasing the antibody titer and antigen-antibody reaction potential

Pharmacodynamics/Kinetics
Duration: Immune effect: Usually 3-4 weeks
Half-life elimination: 23 days
Time to peak, serum: I.M.: ~48 hours

Dosage I.M.: Children and Adults:

Hepatitis A:
Pre-exposure prophylaxis upon travel into endemic areas (hepatitis A vaccine preferred):
0.02 mL/kg for anticipated risk of exposure <3 months
0.06 mL/kg for anticipated risk of exposure ≥3 months
Repeat approximate dose every 5 months if exposure continues
Postexposure prophylaxis: 0.02 mL/kg given within 14 days of exposure. IG is not needed if at least 1 dose of hepatitis A vaccine was given at ≥1 month before exposure

Measles:
Prophylaxis, immunocompetent: 0.25 mL/kg/dose (maximum dose: 15 mL) given within 6 days of exposure followed by live attenuated measles vaccine in 5-6 months when indicated
Prophylaxis, immunocompromised: 0.5 mL/kg (maximum dose: 15 mL) immediately following exposure

Rubella: Prophylaxis during pregnancy: 0.55 mL/kg/dose within 72 hours of exposure

Varicella: Prophylaxis: 0.6-1.2 mL/kg (varicella zoster immune globulin preferred) within 72 hours of exposure

IgG deficiency: 0.66 mL/kg/dose every 3-4 weeks. A double dose may be given at onset of therapy; some patients may require more frequent injections.

Administration Not for I.V. administration
Administer I.M. in the anterolateral aspects of the upper thigh or deltoid muscle of the upper arm. Avoid gluteal region due to risk of injury to sciatic nerve; use upper outer quadrant only. Divide doses >10 mL.

For patients at risk of hemorrhage following intramuscular injection, the ACIP recommends "it should be administered intramuscularly if, in the opinion of the physician familiar with the patients bleeding risk, the vaccine can be administered with reasonable safety by this route. If the patient receives antihemophilia or other similar therapy, intramuscular vaccination can be scheduled shortly after such therapy is administered. A fine needle (23 gauge or smaller) can be used for the vaccination and firm pressure applied to the site (without rubbing) for at least 2 minutes. The patient should be instructed concerning the risk of hematoma from the injection."

Reference Range Immunoglobulin deficiency: Maintain circulating IgG levels ~200 mg/100 mL plasma to prevent serious infection

Test Interactions Skin tests should **not** be done

Additional Information When administering IG for hepatitis A prophylaxis, use should be considered for the following close contacts of persons with confirmed hepatitis A: unvaccinated household and sexual contacts, persons who have shared illicit drugs, regular babysitters, staff and attendees of child care centers, food handlers within the same establishment.

For travelers, IG is not an alternative to careful selection of foods and water; immune globulin can interfere with the antibody response to parenterally administered live virus vaccines. Frequent travelers should be tested for hepatitis A antibody, immune hemolytic anemia, and neutropenia (with ITP, I.V. route is usually used).

Dosage Forms
Injection, solution [preservative free]:
BayGam® [DSC], GammaSTAN™ S/D: 15% to 18% (2 mL, 10 mL)

Immune Globulin (Intravenous) (i MYUN GLOB yoo lin, IN tra VEE nus)

U.S. Brand Names Carimune™ NF; Gammagard® Liquid; Gammagard® S/D; Gammar®-P I.V.; Gamunex®; Iveegam EN; Octagam®; Panglobulin® NF; Polygam® S/D

Canadian Brand Names Gamimune® N; Gammagard® Liquid; Gammagard® S/D; Gamunex®; Iveegam Immuno®

Index Terms IVIG

Pharmacologic Category Immune Globulin

Additional Appendix Information
Immunization Recommendations *on page 1929*

Use
Treatment of primary immunodeficiency syndromes (congenital agammaglobulinemia, severe combined immunodeficiency syndromes [SCIDS], common variable immunodeficiency, X-linked immunodeficiency, Wiskott-Aldrich syndrome); idiopathic thrombocytopenic purpura (ITP); Kawasaki disease (in combination with aspirin)
Prevention of bacterial infection in B-cell chronic lymphocytic leukemia (CLL); pediatric HIV infection; bone marrow transplant (BMT)

Unlabeled/Investigational Use Autoimmune diseases (myasthenia gravis, SLE, bullous pemphigoid, severe rheumatoid arthritis), Guillain-Barré syndrome; used in conjunction with appropriate anti-infective therapy to prevent or modify acute bacterial or viral infections in patients with iatrogenically-induced or disease-associated immunodepression; autoimmune hemolytic anemia or neutropenia, refractory dermatomyositis/polymyositis

Pregnancy Risk Factor C

Pregnancy Implications Immune globulins cross the placenta in increased amounts after 30 weeks gestation.

Lactation Excretion in breast milk unknown

Medication Safety Issues
Sound-alike/look-alike issues:
Gamimune® N may be confused with CytoGam®

Contraindications Hypersensitivity to immune globulin or any component of the formulation; selective IgA deficiency

Warnings/Precautions [U.S. Boxed Warning]: Acute renal dysfunction (increased serum creatinine, oliguria, acute renal failure) can rarely occur; usually within 7 days of use (more likely with products stabilized with sucrose); use with caution in the elderly, patients with renal disease, diabetes mellitus, volume depletion, sepsis, paraproteinemia, and nephrotoxic medications due to risk of renal dysfunction. Anaphylactic hypersensitivity reactions can occur, especially in IgA-deficient patients; studies indicate that the currently available products have no discernible risk of transmitting HIV or hepatitis B; aseptic meningitis may occur with high doses (≥ 2 g/kg). Patients should be adequately hydrated prior to therapy. Use caution in patients with a history of thrombotic events or cardiovascular disease; there is clinical evidence of a possible association between thrombotic events and administration of intravenous immune globulin. For intravenous administration only.

Adverse Reactions Frequency not defined.

Cardiovascular: Flushing of the face, tachycardia, hyper-/hypotension, chest tightness, angioedema, lightheadedness, chest pain, MI, CHF, pulmonary embolism

Central nervous system: Anxiety, chills, dizziness, drowsiness, fatigue, fever, headache, irritability, lethargy, malaise, aseptic meningitis syndrome

Dermatologic: Pruritus, rash, urticaria

Gastrointestinal: Abdominal cramps, diarrhea, nausea, sore throat, vomiting

Hematologic: Autoimmune hemolytic anemia, hematocrit decreased, leukopenia, mild hemolysis

Hepatic: Liver function test increased

Local: Pain or irritation at the infusion site

Neuromuscular & skeletal: Arthralgia, back or hip pain, myalgia, nuchal rigidity

Ocular: Photophobia, painful eye movements

Renal: Acute renal failure, acute tubular necrosis, anuria, BUN increased, creatinine increased, nephrotic syndrome, oliguria, proximal tubular nephropathy, osmotic nephrosis

Respiratory: Cough, dyspnea, wheezing, nasal congestion, pharyngeal pain, rhinorrhea, sinusitis

Miscellaneous: Diaphoresis, hypersensitivity reactions, anaphylaxis

Postmarketing and/or case reports: Abdominal pain, apnea, ARDS, bronchospasm, bullous dermatitis, cardiac arrest, Coombs' test positive, cyanosis, epidermolysis, erythema multiforme, hepatic dysfunction, hypoxemia, leukopenia, loss of consciousness, pancytopenia, pulmonary edema, rigors, seizure, Stevens-Johnson syndrome, thromboembolism, transfusion-related acute lung injury (TRALI), tremor, vascular collapse

Drug Interactions

Decreased Effect: Decreased effect of live virus vaccines (eg, measles, mumps, rubella); separate administration by at least 3 months

Stability Stability and dilution is dependent upon the manufacturer and brand. Do not freeze or shake. Avoid foaming. Discard unused portion. Do not mix with other drugs.

Carimune™ NF, Panglobulin® NF: Prior to reconstitution, store at or below 30°C (86°F). Reconstitute with NS, D$_5$W, or SWFI. Following reconstitution, store under refrigeration; do not freeze. Use within 24 hours.

Gammagard® Liquid: May be stored for up to 9 months at room temperature of 25°C (77°F) within 24 months of manufacture date. May be stored for up to 36 months under refrigeration at 2°C to 8°C (36°F to 46°F). Do not freeze. May dilute in D$_5$W only.

Gammagard® S/D, Polygam® S/D: Store below 25°C (77°F). Reconstitute with SWFI; may store diluted solution under refrigeration for up to 24 hours.

Gammar®-P I.V.: Store below 25°C (77°F). Reconstitute with SWFI.

Gamunex®: May be stored for up to 5 months at room temperature up to 25°C (up to 77°F) within 18 months of manufacture date. Dilute in D$_5$W only.

Iveegam EN: Store at 2°C to 8°C (36°F to 46°F). Reconstitute with SWFI; use immediately after reconstitution.

Octagam®: Store at 2°C to 8°C (36°F to 46°F) for 24 months or ≤ 25°C (77°F) for 18 months.

Polygam® S/D: Store at room temperature at or below 25°C (77°F); do not freeze.

Mechanism of Action Replacement therapy for primary and secondary immunodeficiencies; interference with F$_c$ receptors on the cells of the reticuloendothelial system for autoimmune cytopenias and ITP; possible role of contained antiviral-type antibodies

Pharmacodynamics/Kinetics

Onset of action: I.V.: Provides immediate antibody levels

Duration: Immune effect: 3-4 weeks (variable)

Distribution: V$_d$: 0.09-0.13 L/kg

Intravascular portion (primarily): Healthy subjects: 41% to 57%; Patients with congenital humoral immunodeficiencies: ~70%

Half-life elimination: IgG (variable among patients): Healthy subjects: 14-24 days; Patients with congenital humoral immunodeficiencies: 26-40 days; hypermetabolism associated with fever and infection have coincided with a shortened half-life

Dosage Approved doses and regimens may vary between brands; check manufacturer guidelines. **Note:** Some clinicians dose IVIG on ideal body weight or an adjusted ideal body weight in morbidly obese patients.

Infants and Children: Prevention of gastroenteritis (unlabeled use): Oral: 50 mg/kg/day divided every 6 hours

Children: I.V.:

Pediatric HIV: 400 mg/kg every 28 days

Severe systemic viral and bacterial infections (unlabeled use): 500-1000 mg/kg/week

Children and Adults: I.V.:

Primary immunodeficiency disorders: 200-400 mg/kg every 4 weeks or as per monitored serum IgG concentrations

Gammagard® Liquid, Gamunex®, Octagam®: 300-600 mg/kg every 3-4 weeks; adjusted based on dosage and interval in conjunction with monitored serum IgG concentrations.

B-cell chronic lymphocytic leukemia (CLL): 400 mg/kg/dose every 3 weeks

(Continued)

Immune Globulin (Intravenous) *(Continued)*

Idiopathic thrombocytopenic purpura (ITP):

Acute: 400 mg/kg/day for 5 days or 1000 mg/kg/day for 1-2 days

Chronic: 400 mg/kg as needed to maintain platelet count >30,000/mm^3; may increase dose to 800 mg/kg (1000 mg/kg if needed)

Kawasaki disease: Initiate therapy within 10 days of disease onset: 2 g/kg as a single dose administered over 10 hours, or 400 mg/kg/day for 4 days. **Note:** Must be used in combination with aspirin: 80-100 mg/kg/day in 4 divided doses for 14 days; when fever subsides, dose aspirin at 3-5 mg/kg once daily for ≥6-8 weeks

Acquired immunodeficiency syndrome (patients must be symptomatic) (unlabeled use): Various regimens have been used, including:

200-250 mg/kg/dose every 2 weeks

or

400-500 mg/kg/dose every month or every 4 weeks

Autoimmune hemolytic anemia and neutropenia (unlabeled use): 1000 mg/kg/dose for 2-3 days

Autoimmune diseases (unlabeled use): 400 mg/kg/day for 4 days

Bone marrow transplant: 500 mg/kg beginning on days 7 and 2 pretransplant, then 500 mg/kg/week for 90 days post-transplant

Adjuvant to severe cytomegalovirus infections (unlabeled use): 500 mg/kg/dose every other day for 7 days

Guillain-Barré syndrome (unlabeled use): Various regimens have been used, including:

400 mg/kg/day for 4 days

or

1000 mg/kg/day for 2 days

or

2000 mg/kg/day for one day

Refractory dermatomyositis (unlabeled use): 2 g/kg/dose every month x 3-4 doses

Refractory polymyositis (unlabeled use): 1 g/kg/day x 2 days every month x 4 doses

Chronic inflammatory demyelinating polyneuropathy (unlabeled use): Various regimens have been used, including:

400 mg/kg/day for 5 doses once each month

or

800 mg/kg/day for 3 doses once each month

or

1000 mg/kg/day for 2 days once each month

Dosing adjustment/comments in renal impairment: Cl$_{cr}$ <10 mL/minute: Avoid use; in patients at risk of renal dysfunction, consider infusion at a rate less than maximum.

Dietary Considerations Octagam® contains sodium 30 mmol/L

Administration I.V. infusion over 2-24 hours; for initial treatment, a lower concentration and/or a slower rate of infusion should be used. Administer in separate infusion line from other medications; if using primary line, flush with saline prior administration. Refrigerated product should be warmed to room temperature prior to infusion. Decrease dose, rate and/or concentration of infusion in patients who may be at risk of renal failure. Decreasing the rate or stopping the infusion may help relieve some adverse effects (flushing, changes in pulse rate, changes in blood pressure). Epinephrine should be available during administration.

Monitoring Parameters Renal function, urine output, hemoglobin and hematocrit, infusion-related adverse reactions, anaphylaxis

Test Interactions Octagam® contains maltose. Falsely-elevated blood glucose levels may occur when glucose monitoring devices and test strips utilizing the glucose dehydrogenase pyrroloquinolinequinone (GDH-PQQ) based methods are used. Glucose monitoring devices and test strips which utilize the glucose-specific method are recommended.

Additional Information

Intravenous Immune Globulin Product Comparison:

Carimune™ NF, Panglobulin® NF:

FDA indication: Primary immunodeficiency, ITP

Contraindication: IgA deficiency

IgA content: 720 mcg/mL

Plasma source: Pooled donors

Half-life: 23 days

IgG subclass (%):

IgG1 (60-70): 60.5

IgG2 (19-31): 30.2

IgG3 (5-8.4): 6.6

IgG4 (0.7-4): 2.8

Storage: Room temperature at or below 30°C (86°F); refrigerate after reconstitution

Recommendations for **initial** infusion rate: 0.5-1 mL/minute

Maximum infusion rate: 2 mg/kg/minute

Gammagard® Liquid:

FDA indication: Primary immunodeficiency

Contraindication: IgA deficiency, history of anaphylaxis with immune globulin

IgA content: 37 mcg/mL

Half-life: 35 days

Storage: Room temperature (stable for 9 months) or refrigeration (stable for 36 months)

Recommendations for **initial** infusion rate: 0.5 mL/kg/hour

Maximum infusion rate: 5 mL/kg/hour; <2 mL/kg/hour in patients at risk for renal impairment or thrombosis

Gammagard® SD:

FDA indication: Primary immunodeficiency, ITP, CLL prophylaxis

Contraindication: None (caution with IgA deficiency)

IgA content: 0.92-1.6 mcg/mL

Adverse reactions (%): 6

Plasma source: 4000-5000 paid donors
Half-life: 24 days
IgG subclass (%):
IgG$_1$ (60-70): 67 (66.8)
IgG$_2$ (19-31): 25 (25.4)
IgG$_3$ (5-8.4): 5 (7.4)
IgG$_4$ (0.7-4): 3 (0.3)
Monomers (%): >95
Gamma globulin (%): >90
Storage: Room temperature
Recommendations for **initial** infusion rate: 0.5 mL/kg/hour
Maximum infusion rate: 4 mL/kg/hour
Maximum concentration for infusion (%): 5

Gammar®-P I.V.:
FDA indication: Primary immunodeficiency
Contraindication: IgA deficiency
IgA content: <20 mcg/mL
Adverse reactions (%): 15
Plasma source: >8000 paid donors
Half-life: 21-24 days
IgG subclass (%):
IgG$_1$ (60-70): 69
IgG$_2$ (19-31): 23
IgG$_3$ (5-8.4): 6
IgG$_4$ (0.7-4): 2
Monomers (%): >98
Gamma globulin (%): >98
Storage: Room temperature
Recommendations for **initial** infusion rate: 0.01-0.02 mL/kg/minute
Maximum infusion rate: 0.06 mL/kg/minute
Maximum concentration for infusion (%): 5

Gamunex®:
FDA indication: Primary immunodeficiency, ITP
Contraindication: Caution in severe, selective IgA deficiency
IgA content: 40 mcg/mL
IgM content: <2 mcg/mL
Plasma source: Pooled donors
Half-life: 36 days
IgG subclass (%):
IgG$_1$ (60-70): 65
IgG$_2$ (19-31): 26
IgG$_3$ (5-8.4): 5.6
IgG$_4$ (0.7-4): 2.6
Monomer + dimer (%): 100
Gamma globulin (%): >98
Storage: 2°C to 8°C; may be stored at room temperature for 5 months (only during first 18 months after manufacture)
Recommendations for **initial** infusion rate: 0.01 mL/kg/minute
Maximum infusion rate: 0.08 mL/kg/minute
Maximum concentration for infusion (%): 10

Octagam®:
FDA indication: Primary immunodeficiency
Contraindications: IgA deficiency
IgA content: 100 mcg/mL
Half-life: Immunodeficiency: 40 days
IgG subclass (%):
IgG$_1$ (60-70): 65
IgG$_2$ (19-31): 30
IgG$_3$ (5-8.4): 3
IgG$_4$ (0.7-4): 2
Monomers (%): ≥90
Gamma globulin (%): 96
Storage: Refrigerated or room temperature
Recommendations for initial infusion rate: 0.6 mL/kg/hour
Maximum infusion rate: 4 mL/kg/hour
Maximum concentration for infusion: 5%

Polygam®:
FDA indication: Primary immunodeficiency, ITP, CLL
Contraindication: None (caution with IgA deficiency)
IgA content: 0.74 ± 0.33 mcg/mL
Adverse reactions (%): 6
Plasma source: 50,000 voluntary donors
Half-life: 21-25 days
IgG subclass (%):
IgG$_1$ (60-70): 67
IgG$_2$ (19-31): 25
IgG$_3$ (5-8.4): 5
IgG$_4$ (0.7-4): 3
Monomers (%): >95
Gamma globulin (%): >90
Storage: Room temperature
Recommendations for **initial** infusion rate: 0.5 mL/kg/hour
Maximum infusion rate: 4 mL/kg/hour
Maximum concentration for infusion (%): 10
(Continued)

Immune Globulin (Intravenous) *(Continued)*

Dosage Forms

Injection, powder for reconstitution [preservative free]:
Gammar®-P I.V.: 5 g, 10 g [stabilized with human albumin and sucrose]
Iveegam EN: 5 g [stabilized with glucose]
Injection, powder for reconstitution [preservative free, nanofiltered]:
Carimune™ NF: 3 g, 6 g, 12 g [contains sucrose]
Panglobulin® NF: 6 g, 12 g [contains sucrose]
Injection, powder for reconstitution [preservative free, solvent detergent-treated]:
Gammagard® S/D: 2.5 g, 5 g, 10 g [stabilized with human albumin, glycine, glucose, and polyethylene glycol]
Polygam® S/D: 5 g, 10 g [stabilized with human albumin, glycine, glucose, and polyethylene glycol]
Injection, solution [preservative free; solvent detergent-treated]:
Gammagard® Liquid: 10% [100 mg/mL] (10 mL, 25 mL, 50 mL, 100 mL, 200 mL) [latex free, sucrose free; stabilized with glycine]
Octagam®: 5% [50 mg/mL] (20 mL, 50 mL, 100 mL, 200 mL) [sucrose free; contains sodium 30 mmol/L and maltose]
Injection, solution [preservative free] (Gamunex®): 10% (10 mL, 25 mL, 50 mL, 100 mL, 200 mL) [caprylate/chromatography purified]

Immune Globulin (Subcutaneous)
(i MYUN GLOB yoo lin sub kyoo TAY nee us)

U.S. Brand Names Vivaglobin®
Index Terms Immune Globulin Subcutaneous (Human); SCIG
Pharmacologic Category Immune Globulin
Use Treatment of primary immune deficiency (PID)
Pregnancy Risk Factor C
Pregnancy Implications Animal studies have not been conducted. There are no adequate and well-controlled studies in pregnant women. Use during pregnancy only if clearly needed.
Lactation Excretion in breast milk unknown/use caution
Contraindications Hypersensitivity to immune globulin or any component of the formulation; history of anaphylactic or severe systemic reaction to immune globulin preparations; selective IgA deficiency with known antibody against IgA
Warnings/Precautions For subcutaneous administration only; not for I.V. use. Hypersensitivity reactions and anaphylactic reactions can occur; use caution with initial treatment, when switching brands of immune globulin, and with treatment interruptions of >8 weeks. Patients should be monitored for adverse events during and after the first infusion. Stop infusion with signs of infusion reaction (fever, chills, nausea, vomiting, and rarely shock); medications for the treatment of hypersensitivity reactions should be available for immediate use. Use caution with IgA deficiency; sensitization to IgA may cause anaphylactic reaction. Product of human plasma; may potentially contain infectious agents which could transmit disease. Screening of donors, as well as testing and/or inactivation or removal of certain viruses, reduces this risk. Infections thought to be transmitted by this product should be reported to ZLB Behring at 1-800-504-5434. Safety and effectiveness for children <2 years of age have not been established.
Adverse Reactions Adverse reactions can be expected to be similar to those experienced with other immune globulin products; percentages are reported as adverse events per patient; injection site reactions decreased with subsequent infusions
>10%:
Central nervous system: Headache (32% to 48%), fever (3% to 25%)
Dermatologic: Rash (6% to 17%)
Gastrointestinal: Gastrointestinal disorder (5% to 37%), nausea (11% to 18%), sore throat (17%)
Local: Injection site reactions (swelling, redness, itching; 92%)
Miscellaneous: Allergic reaction (11%)
1% to 10%:
Cardiovascular: Tachycardia (3%)
Central nervous system: Pain (10%)
Dermatologic: Skin disorder (3%)
Gastrointestinal: Diarrhea (10%)
Genitourinary: Urine abnormality (3%)
Neuromuscular & skeletal: Weakness (5%)
Respiratory: Cough (10%)
<1% (Limited to important or life-threatening): Abdominal pain, dyspnea, nervousness
Overdosage/Toxicology Treatment should be symptom directed and supportive.
Drug Interactions
Decreased Effect: Immune globulin may decrease the efficacy of immune response to live vaccines.
Stability Store at 2°C to 8°C (36°F to 46°F); do not freeze. Do not shake. Store in original box until ready to use. Allow vial(s) to reach room temperature prior to use. The appearance of immune globulin (subcutaneous) may vary from colorless to light brown; do not use if cloudy or contains precipitate.
Mechanism of Action Immune globulin replacement therapy of IgG antibodies against bacteria and viral agents.
Pharmacodynamics/Kinetics
Bioavailability: 73% (compared to I.V.)
Time to peak, plasma: 2.5 days

Dosage Note: Consider premedicating with acetaminophen and diphenhydramine.

SubQ infusion: Children ≥2 years and Adults: 100-200 mg/kg weekly (maximum rate: 20 mL/hour; doses >15 mL should be divided between sites); adjust the dose over time to achieve desired clinical response or target IgG levels

Conversion from I.V. to SubQ: Multiply previous I.V. dose by 1.37, then divide into a weekly regimen by dividing by the previous I.V. dosing interval (eg, if the dosing interval was every 3 weeks, divide by 3); adjust the dose over time to achieve desired clinical response or target IgG levels. SubQ infusion administration should begin 1 week after the last I.V. dose.

Administration Subcutaneous: Initial dose should be administered in a healthcare setting capable of providing monitoring and treatment in the event of hypersensitivity. Using aseptic technique, follow the infusion device manufacturer's instructions for filling the reservoir and preparing the pump. Remove air from administration set and needle by priming. Inject via infusion pump into the abdomen, thigh, upper arm, and/or lateral hip. The maximum rate is 20 mL/hour and maximum volume per injection site is 15 mL (doses >15 mL should be divided and infused into several sites). Select the number of required infusion sites; multiple concurrent injection sites may be achieved with the use of Y-site connection tubing; injection sites must be at least 2 inches apart. After the sites are clean and dry, insert subcutaneous needle and prime administration set. Attach sterile needle to administration set, gently pull back on the syringe to assure a blood vessel has not been inadvertently accessed. Repeat for each injection site; infuse following instructions for the infusion device. Rotate the site(s) weekly. Treatment may be transitioned to the home/home care setting in the absence of adverse reactions.

Monitoring Parameters Infusion-related adverse reactions, anaphylaxis, IgG levels, clinical response

Reference Range Although the trough serum concentration of IgG has not been established, clinical experience has led to the use of 500 mg/dL as a guideline.

Test Interactions Passively-transferred antibodies may yield false-positive serologic testing results; may yield false-positive direct and indirect Coombs' test

Additional Information Serum IgG levels may be drawn at any time. Subcutaneous weekly treatments provide more constant levels rather than the more pronounced peak and trough patterns observed with I.V. monthly immune globulin treatments.

Dosage Forms Injection, solution [preservative free]: IgG 160 mg/mL (3 mL, 10 mL, 20 mL)

♦ **Immune Globulin Subcutaneous (Human)** *see* Immune Globulin (Subcutaneous) *on page 896*

♦ **Immune Serum Globulin** *see* Immune Globulin (Intramuscular) *on page 891*

♦ **Immunine® VH (Can)** *see* Factor IX *on page 679*

♦ **Imodium® (Can)** *see* Loperamide *on page 1027*

♦ **Imodium® A-D [OTC]** *see* Loperamide *on page 1027*

♦ **Imodium® Advanced** *see* Loperamide and Simethicone *on page 1029*

♦ **Imogam® Rabies-HT** *see* Rabies Immune Globulin (Human) *on page 1478*

♦ **Imogam® Rabies Pasteurized (Can)** *see* Rabies Immune Globulin (Human) *on page 1478*

♦ **Imovax® Rabies** *see* Rabies Virus Vaccine *on page 1479*

♦ **Implanon™** *see* Etonogestrel *on page 668*

♦ **Imuran®** *see* Azathioprine *on page 183*

♦ **In-111 Zevalin** *see* Ibritumomab *on page 871*

Inamrinone (eye NAM ri none)

Index Terms Amrinone Lactate

Pharmacologic Category Phosphodiesterase Enzyme Inhibitor

Additional Appendix Information

Hemodynamic Support, Intravenous *on page 1885*

Use Infrequently used as a last resort, short-term therapy in patients with intractable heart failure

Pregnancy Risk Factor C

Medication Safety Issues

Sound-alike/look-alike issues:

Amrinone may be confused with amiloride, amiodarone

Contraindications Hypersensitivity to inamrinone, any component of the formulation, or bisulfites (contains sodium metabisulfite); patients with severe aortic or pulmonic valvular disease

Warnings/Precautions Due to a slight effect on AV conduction, may increase ventricular response rate in atrial fibrillation/atrial flutter; prior treatment with digoxin is recommended. Monitor liver function. Discontinue therapy if alteration in LFTs and clinical symptoms of hepatotoxicity occur. Observe for arrhythmias in this very high-risk patient population. Not recommended in acute MI treatment. Monitor fluid status closely; patients may require adjustment of diuretic and electrolyte replacement therapy. Can cause thrombocytopenia (dose dependent). Correct hypokalemia before initiating therapy. Increase risk of hospitalization and death with long-term therapy.

Adverse Reactions

1% to 10%:

Cardiovascular: Arrhythmias (3%, especially in high-risk patients), hypotension (1% to 2%) (may be infusion rate-related)

Gastrointestinal: Nausea (1% to 2%)

Hematologic: Thrombocytopenia (may be dose related)

<1% (Limited to important or life-threatening): Chest pain, fever, hepatotoxicity, hypersensitivity (especially with prolonged therapy), vomiting; contains sulfites resulting in allergic reactions in susceptible people

(Continued)

Inamrinone *(Continued)*

Drug Interactions

Increased Effect/Toxicity: Diuretics may cause significant hypovolemia and decrease filling pressure. Inotropic effects with digitalis are additive.

Stability May be administered undiluted for I.V. bolus doses. For continuous infusion, dilute with 0.45% or 0.9% sodium chloride to final concentration of 1-3 mg/mL. Use within 24 hours. Do not directly dilute with dextrose-containing solutions, chemical interaction occurs. May be administered I.V. into running dextrose infusions. Furosemide forms a precipitate when injected in I.V. lines containing inamrinone.

Mechanism of Action Inhibits myocardial cyclic adenosine monophosphate (cAMP) phosphodiesterase activity and increases cellular levels of cAMP resulting in a positive inotropic effect and increased cardiac output; also possesses systemic and pulmonary vasodilator effects resulting in pre- and afterload reduction; slightly increases atrioventricular conduction

Pharmacodynamics/Kinetics

Onset of action: I.V.: 2-5 minutes

Peak effect: ~10 minutes

Duration (dose dependent): Low dose: ~30 minutes; Higher doses: ~2 hours

Half-life elimination, serum: Adults: Healthy volunteers: 3.6 hours, Congestive heart failure: 5.8 hours

Dosage Dosage is based on clinical response (**Note:** Dose should not exceed 10 mg/kg/24 hours).

Infants, Children, and Adults: 0.75 mg/kg I.V. bolus over 2-3 minutes followed by maintenance infusion of 5-10 mcg/kg/minute; I.V. bolus may need to be repeated in 30 minutes.

Dosing adjustment in renal failure: Cl_{cr} <10 mL/minute: Administer 50% to 75% of dose.

Administration May be administered undiluted for I.V. bolus doses. For continuous infusion: Dilute with 0.45% or 0.9% sodium chloride to final concentration of 1-3 mg/mL use within 24 hours.

Monitoring Parameters Cardiac index, stroke volume, systemic vascular resistance, and pulmonary vascular resistance (if Swan-Ganz catheter available); CVP, SBP, DBP, heart rate; platelet count, CBC, liver function and renal function tests

Additional Information To avoid confusion with similarly sounding medication names, the name "amrinone" was changed to "inamrinone" in July, 2000.

Dosage Forms Injection, solution, as lactate: 5 mg/mL (20 mL) [contains sodium metabisulfite]

♦ **Inapsine®** see Droperidol on page 559
♦ **Increlex™** see Mecasermin on page 1060

Indapamide *(in DAP a mide)*

U.S. Brand Names Lozol® [DSC]

Canadian Brand Names Apo-Indapamide®; Gen-Indapamide®; Lozide®; Lozol®; Novo-Indapamide; Nu-Indapamide; PMS-Indapamide

Pharmacologic Category Diuretic, Thiazide-Related

Additional Appendix Information

Sulfonamide Derivatives on page 1897

Use Management of mild to moderate hypertension; treatment of edema in congestive heart failure and nephrotic syndrome

Pregnancy Risk Factor B (manufacturer); D (expert analysis)

Lactation Excretion in breast milk unknown

Medication Safety Issues

Sound-alike/look-alike issues:

Indapamide may be confused with Iopidine®

International issues:

Pretanix® [Hungary] may be confused with Protonix® which is a brand name for pantoprazole in the U.S.

Contraindications Hypersensitivity to indapamide or any component of the formulation, thiazides, or sulfonamide-derived drugs; anuria; renal decompensation; pregnancy (based on expert analysis)

Warnings/Precautions Use with caution in severe renal disease. Electrolyte disturbances (hypokalemia, hypochloremic alkalosis, hyponatremia) can occur. Use with caution in severe hepatic dysfunction; hepatic encephalopathy can be caused by electrolyte disturbances. Gout can be precipitate in certain patients with a history of gout, a familial predisposition to gout, or chronic renal failure. Cautious use in prediabetics or diabetics; may see a change in glucose control. I.V. use is generally not recommended (but is available). Can cause SLE exacerbation or activation. Use with caution in patients with moderate or high cholesterol concentrations. Photosensitization may occur. Correct hypokalemia before initiating therapy.

Chemical similarities are present among sulfonamides, sulfonylureas, carbonic anhydrase inhibitors, thiazides, and loop diuretics (except ethacrynic acid). Use in patients with thiazide or sulfonamide allergy is specifically contraindicated in product labeling, however, a risk of cross-reaction exists in patients with allergy to any of these compounds; avoid use when previous reaction has been severe. Discontinue if signs of hypersensitivity are noted.

Adverse Reactions

1% to 10%:

Cardiovascular: Orthostatic hypotension, palpitation, flushing

Central nervous system: Dizziness, lightheadedness, vertigo, headache, weakness, restlessness, drowsiness, fatigue, lethargy, malaise, lassitude, anxiety, agitation, depression, nervousness

Gastrointestinal: Anorexia, gastric irritation, nausea, vomiting, abdominal pain, cramping, bloating, diarrhea, constipation, dry mouth, weight loss

Genitourinary: Nocturia, frequent urination, polyuria

Neuromuscular & skeletal: Muscle cramps, spasm

Ocular: Blurred vision

Respiratory: Rhinorrhea

<1% (Limited to important or life-threatening): Cutaneous vasculitis, glycosuria, hypercalcemia, hyperglycemia, hyperuricemia, impotency, necrotizing angiitis, pancreatitis, purpura, reduced libido, vasculitis

Overdosage/Toxicology Symptoms include lethargy, diuresis, hypermotility, confusion, and muscle weakness. Following GI decontamination, therapy is supportive with I.V. fluids, electrolytes, and I.V. pressors if needed.

Drug Interactions

Increased Effect/Toxicity: The diuretic effect of indapamide is synergistic with furosemide and other loop diuretics. Increased hypotension and/or renal adverse effects of ACE inhibitors may result in aggressively diuresed patients. Cyclosporine and thiazide-type diuretics can increase the risk of gout or renal toxicity. Digoxin toxicity can be exacerbated if a diuretic induces hypokalemia or hypomagnesemia. Lithium toxicity can occur with thiazide-type diuretics due to reduced renal excretion of lithium. Thiazide-type diuretics may prolong the duration of action of neuromuscular blocking agents.

Decreased Effect: Effects of oral hypoglycemics may be decreased. Decreased absorption of indapamide with cholestyramine and colestipol. NSAIDs can decrease the efficacy of thiazide-type diuretics, reducing the diuretic and antihypertensive effects.

Ethanol/Nutrition/Herb Interactions Herb/Nutraceutical: Avoid dong quai if using for hypertension (has estrogenic activity). Avoid ephedra, yohimbe, ginseng (may worsen hypertension). Avoid garlic (may have increased antihypertensive effect).

Mechanism of Action Diuretic effect is localized at the proximal segment of the distal tubule of the nephron; it does not appear to have significant effect on glomerular filtration rate nor renal blood flow; like other diuretics, it enhances sodium, chloride, and water excretion by interfering with the transport of sodium ions across the renal tubular epithelium

Pharmacodynamics/Kinetics

Onset of action: 1-2 hours

Duration: ≤36 hours

Absorption: Complete

Protein binding, plasma: 71% to 79%

Metabolism: Extensively hepatic

Half-life elimination: 14-18 hours

Time to peak: 2-2.5 hours

Excretion: Urine (~60%) within 48 hours; feces (~16% to 23%)

Dosage Adults: Oral.

Edema: 2.5-5 mg/day. **Note:** There is little therapeutic benefit to increasing the dose >5 mg/day; there is, however, an increased risk of electrolyte disturbances

Hypertension: 1.25 mg in the morning, may increase to 5 mg/day by increments of 1.25-2.5 mg; consider adding another antihypertensive and decreasing the dose if response is not adequate

Dietary Considerations May be taken with food or milk to decrease GI adverse effects.

Administration May be taken with food or milk. Administer early in day to avoid nocturia. Administer the last dose of multiple doses no later than 6 PM unless instructed otherwise.

Monitoring Parameters Blood pressure (both standing and sitting/supine), serum electrolytes, renal function, assess weight, I & O reports daily to determine fluid loss

Dosage Forms

Tablet: 1.25 mg, 2.5 mg

Lozol®: 1.25 mg [DSC]

- ♦ **Inderal®** see Propranolol on page 1446
- ♦ **Inderal® LA** see Propranolol on page 1446
- ♦ **Inderal®-LA (Can)** see Propranolol on page 1446
- ♦ **Inderide®** see Propranolol and Hydrochlorothiazide on page 1449

Indinavir (in DIN a veer)

U.S. Brand Names Crixivan®

Canadian Brand Names Crixivan®

Index Terms Indinavir Sulfate

Pharmacologic Category Antiretroviral Agent, Protease Inhibitor

Additional Appendix Information

Antiretroviral Therapy for HIV Infection: Adults and Adolescents on page 1988

Management of Healthcare Worker Exposures to HBV, HCV, and HIV on page 1941

Use Treatment of HIV infection; should always be used as part of a multidrug regimen (at least three antiretroviral agents)

Pregnancy Risk Factor C

Pregnancy Implications Plasma levels of indinavir were 74% lower at weeks 30-32 of gestation when compared to the same women at 14-28 weeks of gestation. Plasma levels were not measurable in some patients 8 hours post dose. It is not known if indinavir will exacerbate hyperbilirubinemia in neonates. Pregnancy and protease inhibitors are both associated with an increased risk of hyperglycemia. Glucose levels should be closely monitored. Until optimal dosing during pregnancy has been established, the manufacturer does not recommend indinavir use in pregnant patients. Healthcare professionals are encouraged to contact the antiretroviral pregnancy registry to monitor outcomes of pregnant women exposed to antiretroviral medications (1-800-258-4263 or www.APRegistry.com).

Lactation Enters breast milk/contraindicated

Medication Safety Issues

Sound-alike/look-alike issues:

Indinavir may be confused with Denavir™

Contraindications Hypersensitivity to indinavir or any component of the formulation; concurrent use of amiodarone, cisapride, triazolam, midazolam, pimozide, or ergot alkaloids

(Continued)

Indinavir *(Continued)*

Warnings/Precautions Because indinavir may cause nephrolithiasis/urolithiasis the drug should be discontinued if signs and symptoms occur; risk is substantially higher in pediatric patients versus adults. Adequate hydration is recommended. May cause tubulointerstitial nephritis (rare); severe asymptomatic leukocyturia may warrant evaluation. Use with caution in patients taking strong CYP3A4 inhibitors, moderate or strong CYP3A4 inducers and major CYP3A4 substrates (see drug interactions); consider alternative agents that avoid or lessen the potential for CYP-mediated interactions. Patients with hepatic insufficiency due to cirrhosis should have dose reduction. Warn patients about fat redistribution that can occur. Indinavir has been associated with hemolytic anemia (discontinue if diagnosed), hepatitis, hyperbilirubinemia, and hyperglycemia (exacerbation or new-onset diabetes). Treatment may result in immune reconstitution syndrome (acute inflammatory response to indolent or residual opportunistic infections). Use caution in patients with hemophilia; spontaneous bleeding has been reported.

Adverse Reactions

>10%:
Gastrointestinal: Abdominal pain (17%), nausea (12%)
Hepatic: Hyperbilirubinemia (14%; dose dependent)
Renal: Nephrolithiasis/urolithiasis, including flank pain with/without hematuria (29%, pediatric patients; 12% adult patients; dose dependent)

1% to 10%:
Central nervous system: Headache (5%), dizziness (3%), somnolence (2%), fever (2%), malaise (2%), fatigue (2%)
Dermatologic: Pruritus (4%), rash (1%)
Gastrointestinal: Vomiting (8%), diarrhea (3%), taste perversion (3%), acid reflux (3%), anorexia (3%), appetite increased (2%), dyspepsia (2%), serum amylase increased (2%)
Hematologic: Neutropenia (2%)
Hepatic: Transaminases increased (4% to 5%), jaundice (2%)
Neuromuscular & skeletal: Back pain (8%), weakness (2%)
Renal: Dysuria (2%)
Respiratory: Cough (2%)

<1% (Limited to important or life-threatening): Abdominal distention, acute renal failure, alopecia, anaphylactoid reactions, anemia, angina, arthralgia, bleeding (spontaneous in patients with hemophilia A or B), cerebrovascular disorder, cholesterol increased, crystalluria, depression, dry skin, erythema multiforme, fat redistribution, hemoglobin decreased, hemolytic anemia, hepatic failure, hepatitis, hydronephrosis, hyperglycemia, hyperpigmentation, immune reconstitution syndrome, interstitial nephritis (with medullary calcification and cortical atrophy), leukocyturia (severe and asymptomatic), MI, new-onset diabetes, pancreatitis, paresthesia (oral), paronychia, pharyngitis, pyelonephritis, renal insufficiency, Stevens-Johnson syndrome, thrombocytopenia, triglycerides increased, upper respiratory infection, urticaria, vasculitis

Overdosage/Toxicology Symptoms of overdose include nausea, vomiting, diarrhea, nephrolithiasis/urolithiasis, flank pain and hematuria. Ensure adequate hydration; treatment is otherwise symptom-directed and supportive.

Drug Interactions

Cytochrome P450 Effect: Substrate of CYP2D6 (minor), 3A4 (major); **Inhibits** CYP2C9 (weak), 2C19 (weak), 2D6 (weak), 3A4 (strong)

Increased Effect/Toxicity: Indinavir may increase the levels/effects of selected benzodiazepines, calcium channel blockers, cyclosporine, fentanyl, mirtazapine, nateglinide, nefazodone, quinidine, sildenafil (and other PDE-5 inhibitors), tacrolimus, trazodone, and other CYP3A4 substrates. Indinavir may also increase the levels of orally inhaled corticosteroids (eg, fluticasone); concomitant use not recommended. Selected benzodiazepines (midazolam, triazolam), cisapride, ergot alkaloids, selected HMG-CoA reductase inhibitors (lovastatin and simvastatin), mesoridazine, pimozide, and thioridazine are generally contraindicated with strong CYP3A4 inhibitors. When used with strong CYP3A4 inhibitors, dosage adjustment/limits are recommended for sildenafil and other PDE-5 inhibitors; refer to individual monographs.

Itraconazole or ketoconazole may increase the serum concentrations of indinavir; dosage adjustment is recommended. The levels/effects of indinavir may be increased by azole antifungals, clarithromycin, diclofenac, doxycycline, erythromycin, imatinib, isoniazid, nefazodone, nicardipine, propofol, protease inhibitors, quinidine, telithromycin, verapamil, and other CYP3A4 inhibitors.

When used with delavirdine, serum levels of indinavir are increased; dosage adjustment of indinavir may be required for this combination. Serum levels of both nelfinavir and indinavir are increased with concurrent use. Serum concentrations of indinavir may be increased by ritonavir; serum levels of ritonavir and saquinavir may be increased; dosage adjustments of indinavir are required during concurrent therapy. Rifabutin serum concentrations has been increased when coadministered with indinavir; dosage adjustments of both agents required. Concurrent use or atazanavir with indinavir may increase the risk of hyperbilirubinemia.

Decreased Effect: The levels/effects of indinavir may be decreased by aminoglutethimide, antacids carbamazepine, nafcillin, nevirapine, phenobarbital, phenytoin, rifamycins, and other CYP3A4 inducers; dosage adjustment may be recommended (see individual agents). Rifampin and/or St John's wort (*Hypericum perforatum*); should not be used with indinavir. Venlafaxine and proton pump inhibitors may decrease indinavir levels/effects.

Ethanol/Nutrition/Herb Interactions

Food: Indinavir bioavailability may be decreased if taken with food. Meals high in calories, fat, and protein result in a significant decrease in drug levels. Indinavir serum concentrations may be decreased by grapefruit juice.

Herb/Nutraceutical: St John's wort (*Hypericum*) appears to induce CYP3A enzymes and has lead to 57% reductions in indinavir AUCs and 81% reductions in trough serum concentrations, which may lead to treatment failures; should not be used concurrently with indinavir.

Stability Medication should be stored at 15°C to 30°C (59°F to 86°F), and used in the original container and the desiccant should remain in the bottle. Capsules are sensitive to moisture.

Mechanism of Action Indinavir is a human immunodeficiency virus protease inhibitor, binding to the protease activity site and inhibiting the activity of this enzyme. HIV protease is an enzyme required for the cleavage of viral polyprotein precursors into individual functional proteins found in infectious HIV. Inhibition prevents cleavage of these polyproteins resulting in the formation of immature noninfectious viral particles.

Pharmacodynamics/Kinetics

Absorption: Administration with a high fat, high calorie diet resulted in a reduction in AUC and in maximum serum concentration (77% and 84% respectively); lighter meal resulted in little or no change in these parameters.

Protein binding, plasma: 60%

Metabolism: Hepatic via CYP3A4; seven metabolites of indinavir identified

Bioavailability: Good

Half-life elimination: 1.8 ± 0.4 hour

Time to peak: 0.8 ± 0.3 hour

Excretion: Feces (83%, 19% as unchanged drug); urine (19%, 9% as unchanged drug)

Dosage

Children 4-15 years (investigational): 500 mg/m^2 every 8 hours

Adults: Oral:

Unboosted regimen: 800 mg every 8 hours

Ritonavir-boosted regimens:

Ritonavir 100-200 mg twice daily plus indinavir 800 mg twice daily **or**

Ritonavir 400 mg twice daily plus indinavir 400 mg twice daily

Dosage adjustments for indinavir when administered in combination therapy:

Delavirdine, itraconazole, or ketoconazole: Reduce indinavir dose to 600 mg every 8 hours

Efavirenz: Increase indinavir dose to 1000 mg every 8 hours

Lopinavir and ritonavir (Kaletra™): Indinavir 600 mg twice daily

Nelfinavir: Increase indinavir dose to 1200 mg twice daily

Nevirapine: Increase indinavir dose to 1000 mg every 8 hours

Rifabutin: Reduce rifabutin to ½ the standard dose plus increase indinavir to 1000 mg every 8 hours

Dosage adjustment in hepatic impairment: Mild-moderate impairment due to cirrhosis: 600 mg every 8 hours

Dietary Considerations Should be taken without food but with water 1 hour before or 2 hours after a meal. Administration with lighter meals (eg, dry toast, skim milk, corn flakes) resulted in little/no change in indinavir concentration. If taking with ritonavir, may take with food. Patient should drink at least 48 oz of water daily. May be taken with food when administered in combination with ritonavir.

Administration Drink at least 48 oz of water daily. Administer with water, 1 hour before or 2 hours after a meal. Administer around-the-clock to avoid significant fluctuation in serum levels. May be taken with food when administered in combination with ritonavir.

Monitoring Parameters Monitor viral load, CD4 count, triglycerides, cholesterol, glucose, liver function tests, CBC, urinalysis (severe leukocyturia should be monitored frequently).

Dosage Forms

Capsule:

Crixivan®: 100 mg, 200 mg, 333 mg, 400 mg

+ **Indinavir Sulfate** see Indinavir on page 899
+ **Indocid® P.D.A. (Can)** see Indomethacin on page 901
+ **Indocin®** see Indomethacin on page 901
+ **Indocin® I.V.** see Indomethacin on page 901
+ **Indocin® SR** see Indomethacin on page 901
+ **Indo-Lemmon (Can)** see Indomethacin on page 901
+ **Indometacin** see Indomethacin on page 901

Indomethacin (in doe METH a sin)

U.S. Brand Names Indocin®; Indocin® I.V.; Indocin® SR

Canadian Brand Names Apo-Indomethacin®; Indocid® P.D.A.; Indocin®; Indo-Lemmon; Indotec; Novo-Methacin; Nu-Indo; Rhodacine®

Index Terms Indometacin; Indomethacin Sodium Trihydrate

Pharmacologic Category Nonsteroidal Anti-inflammatory Drug (NSAID), Oral; Nonsteroidal Anti-inflammatory Drug (NSAID), Parenteral

Additional Appendix Information

Nonsteroidal Anti-inflammatory Agents on page 1894

Use Acute gouty arthritis, acute bursitis/tendonitis, moderate to severe osteoarthritis, rheumatoid arthritis, ankylosing spondylitis; I.V. form used as alternative to surgery for closure of patent ductus arteriosus in neonates

Restrictions An FDA-approved medication guide must be distributed when dispensing an oral outpatient prescription (new or refill) where this medication is to be used without direct supervision of a healthcare provider. Medication guides are available at http://www.fda.gov/cder/Offices/ODS/medication_guides.htm.

Pregnancy Risk Factor C/D (3rd trimester)

Lactation Enters breast milk/use caution (AAP rates "compatible")

Medication Safety Issues

Sound-alike/look-alike issues:

Indocin® may be confused with Imodium®, Lincocin®, Minocin®, Vicodin®

International issues:

Flexin® [Great Britain] may be confused with Floxin® which is a brand name for ofloxacin in the U.S.

(Continued)

Indomethacin *(Continued)*

Flexin® [Great Britain]: Brand name for orphenadrine in Israel

Contraindications Hypersensitivity to indomethacin, aspirin, other NSAIDs, or any component of the formulation; perioperative pain in the setting of coronary artery bypass surgery (CABG); pregnancy (3rd trimester)

Neonates: Necrotizing enterocolitis, impaired renal function, active bleeding, thrombocytopenia, coagulation defects, untreated infection

Warnings/Precautions [U.S. Boxed Warning]: NSAIDs are associated with an increased risk of adverse cardiovascular events, including MI, stroke, and new onset or worsening of pre-existing hypertension. Risk may be increased with duration of use or pre-existing cardiovascular risk-factors or disease. Use caution with fluid retention, CHF or hypertension. Concurrent administration of ibuprofen, and potentially other nonselective NSAIDs, may interfere with aspirin's cardioprotective effect.

Use of NSAIDs can compromise existing renal function. Indomethacin is not recommended for patients with advanced renal disease. Use with caution in patients with decreased hepatic function.

[U.S. Boxed Warning]: NSAIDs may increase risk of gastrointestinal irritation, ulceration, bleeding, and perforation. Use caution with a history of GI disease (bleeding or ulcers), concurrent therapy with aspirin, anticoagulants and/or corticosteroids, smoking, use of alcohol, the elderly or debilitated patients.

Use the lowest effective dose for the shortest duration of time, consistent with individual patient goals, to reduce risk of cardiovascular or GI adverse events.

NSAIDs may cause serious skin adverse events including exfoliative dermatitis, Stevens-Johnson syndrome (SJS) and toxic epidermal necrolysis (TEN). Do not use in patients who experience bronchospasm, asthma, rhinitis, or urticaria with NSAID or aspirin therapy.

The elderly are at increased risk for adverse effects (especially peptic ulceration, CNS effects, renal toxicity) from NSAIDs even at low doses.

Withhold for at least 4-6 half-lives prior to surgical or dental procedures. Safety and efficacy have not been established in children <14 years of age.

Adverse Reactions

>10%: Central nervous system: Headache (12%)

1% to 10%:

Central nervous system: Dizziness (3% to 9%), drowsiness (<1%), fatigue (<3%), vertigo (<3%), depression (<3%), malaise (<3%), somnolence (<3%)

Gastrointestinal: Nausea (3% to 9%), epigastric pain (3% to 9%), abdominal pain/cramps/distress (<3%), heartburn (3% to 9%), indigestion (3% to 9%), constipation (<3%), diarrhea (<3%), dyspepsia (3% to 9%), vomiting

Otic: Tinnitus (<3%)

<1% (Limited to important or life-threatening): Acute respiratory distress, agranulocytosis, allergic rhinitis, anaphylaxis, anemia, angioedema, aplastic anemia, arrhythmia, aseptic meningitis, asthma, bone marrow suppression, bronchospasm, chest pain, cholestatic jaundice, coma, confusion, CHF, cystitis, depersonalization, depression, dilutional hyponatremia (I.V.), diplopia, disseminated intravascular coagulation (DIC), dysarthria, dyspnea, ecchymosis, edema, epistaxis, erythema multiforme, erythema nodosum, exfoliative dermatitis, fluid retention, flushing, hair loss, gastric perforation (rare), gastritis, GI bleeding, GI ulceration, gynecomastia, hearing decreased, hematuria, hemolytic anemia, hepatitis (including fatal cases), hot flashes, hyperkalemia, hypersensitivity reactions, hypertension, hypoglycemia (I.V.), interstitial nephritis, involuntary muscle movements, leukopenia, necrotizing fasciitis, nephrotic syndrome, oliguria, paresthesias, parkinson's exacerbation, peptic ulcer, peripheral neuropathy, proctitis, psychosis, pulmonary edema, purpura, syncope, renal insufficiency, renal failure, retinal/macular disturbances, seizure exacerbation, shock, somnolence, Stevens-Johnson syndrome, stomatitis, thrombocytopenia, thrombocytopenic purpura, thrombophlebitis, toxic amblyopia, toxic epidermal necrolysis

Overdosage/Toxicology Symptoms include drowsiness, lethargy, nausea, vomiting, seizures, paresthesias, headache, dizziness, GI bleeding, cerebral edema, tinnitus, leukocytosis, and renal failure. Management of nonsteroidal anti-inflammatory drug (NSAID) intoxication is primarily supportive and symptomatic. Fluid therapy is commonly effective in managing hypotension that may occur following an acute NSAID overdose, except when due to acute blood loss. Seizures tend to be very short-lived and often do not require drug treatment, although recurrent seizures should be treated with I.V. diazepam.

Drug Interactions

Cytochrome P450 Effect: Substrate (minor) of CYP2C9, 2C19; **Inhibits** CYP2C9 (strong), 2C19 (weak)

Increased Effect/Toxicity: Indomethacin may increase effect/toxicity of anticoagulants (bleeding), antiplatelet agents (bleeding), aminoglycosides, biphosphonates (GI irritation), corticosteroids (GI irritation), cyclosporine (nephrotoxicity), lithium, methotrexate, pemetrexed, treprostinil (bleeding), vancomycin. Tilundronate serum concentrations may be increased. Indomethacin may increase the levels/effects of bosentan, dapsone, fluoxetine, glimepiride, glipizide, losartan, montelukast, nateglinide, paclitaxel, phenytoin, warfarin, zafirlukast, and other CYP2C9 substrates. Concomitant use with fluoroquinolones may rarely increase risk of seizure.

Decreased Effect: May reduce effect of some diuretics and antihypertensive effect of beta-blockers, ACE inhibitors, angiotensin II inhibitors, hydralazine Cholestyramine and colestipol may reduce absorption of indomethacin. Salicylates' antiplatelet effect may be reduced.

Ethanol/Nutrition/Herb Interactions

Ethanol: Avoid ethanol (may enhance gastric mucosal irritation).

Food: Food may decrease the rate but not the extent of absorption. Indomethacin peak serum levels may be delayed if taken with food.

Herb/Nutraceutical: Avoid alfalfa, anise, bilberry, bladderwrack, bromelain, cat's claw, celery, coleus, cordyceps, dong quai, evening primrose, feverfew, fenugreek, garlic, ginger, ginkgo biloba, ginseng, grapeseed, green tea, guggul, horse chestnut seed, horseradish, licorice, prickly ash, red clover, reishi, SAMe, sweet clover, turmeric, white willow (all have additional antiplatelet activity).

Stability I.V.: Store below 30°C (86°F). Protect from light. Not stable in alkaline solution. Reconstitute just prior to administration. Discard any unused portion. Do not use preservative-containing diluents for reconstitution.

Mechanism of Action Inhibits prostaglandin synthesis by decreasing the activity of the enzyme, cyclooxygenase, which results in decreased formation of prostaglandin precursors

Pharmacodynamics/Kinetics

Onset of action: ~30 minutes

Duration: 4-6 hours

Absorption: Prompt and extensive

Distribution: V_d: 0.34-1.57 L/kg; crosses blood brain barrier and placenta; enters breast milk

Protein binding: 99%

Metabolism: Hepatic; significant enterohepatic recirculation

Bioavailability: 100%

Half-life elimination: 4.5 hours; prolonged in neonates

Time to peak, Oral: 2 hours

Excretion: Urine (60%, primarily as glucuronide conjugates); feces (33%, primarily as metabolites)

Dosage

Patent ductus arteriosus:

Neonates: I.V.: Initial: 0.2 mg/kg, followed by 2 doses depending on postnatal age (PNA):

PNA **at time of first dose** <48 hours: 0.1 mg/kg at 12- to 24-hour intervals

PNA **at time of first dose** 2-7 days: 0.2 mg/kg at 12- to 24-hour intervals

PNA **at time of first dose** >7 days: 0.25 mg/kg at 12- to 24-hour intervals

In general, may use 12-hour dosing interval if urine output >1 mL/kg/hour after prior dose; use 24-hour dosing interval if urine output is <1 mL/kg/hour but >0.6 mL/kg/hour; doses should be withheld if patient has oliguria (urine output <0.6 mL/kg/hour) or anuria

Inflammatory/rheumatoid disorders: Oral: Use lowest effective dose.

Children >2 years: 1-2 mg/kg/day in 2-4 divided doses; maximum dose: 4 mg/kg/day; not to exceed 150-200 mg/day

Adults: 25-50 mg/dose 2-3 times/day; maximum dose: 200 mg/day; extended release capsule should be given on a 1-2 times/day schedule; maximum dose for sustained release is 150 mg/day. In patients with arthritis and persistent night pain and/or morning stiffness may give the larger portion (up to 100 mg) of the total daily dose at bedtime.

Bursitis/tendonitis: Oral: Adults: Initial dose: 75-150 mg/day in 3-4 divided doses; usual treatment is 7-14 days

Acute gouty arthritis: Oral: Adults: 50 mg 3 times daily until pain is tolerable then reduce dose; usual treatment <3-5 days

Elderly: Refer to Adults dosing; best to start older adults on 25 mg dose given 2-3 times/day

Dosage adjustment in renal impairment: Not recommended in patients with advanced renal disease

Dietary Considerations May cause GI upset; take with food or milk to minimize

Administration

Oral: Administer with food, milk, or antacids to decrease GI adverse effects; extended release capsules must be swallowed whole, do not crush

I.V.: Administer over 20-30 minutes at a concentration of 0.5-1 mg/mL in preservative-free sterile water for injection or normal saline. Reconstitute I.V. formulation just prior to administration; discard any unused portion; avoid I.V. bolus administration or infusion via an umbilical catheter into vessels near the superior mesenteric artery as these may cause vasoconstriction and can compromise blood flow to the intestines. Do not administer intra-arterially.

Monitoring Parameters Monitor response (pain, range of motion, grip strength, mobility, ADL function), inflammation; observe for weight gain, edema; monitor renal function (serum creatinine, BUN); observe for bleeding, bruising; evaluate gastrointestinal effects (abdominal pain, bleeding, dyspepsia); mental confusion, disorientation, CBC, liver function tests

Test Interactions False-negative dexamethasone suppression test

Dosage Forms

Capsule (Indocin®): 25 mg, 50 mg

Capsule, sustained release (Indocin® SR): 75 mg

Injection, powder for reconstitution, as sodium trihydrate (Indocin® I.V.): 1 mg

Suspension, oral (Indocin®): 25 mg/5 mL (237 mL) [contains alcohol 1%; pineapple-coconut-mint flavor]

♦ **Indomethacin Sodium Trihydrate** see Indomethacin on page 901

♦ **Indotec (Can)** see Indomethacin on page 901

♦ **INF-alpha 2** see Interferon Alfa-2b on page 920

♦ **Infanrix®** see Diphtheria, Tetanus Toxoids, and Acellular Pertussis Vaccine on page 521

♦ **Infantaire [OTC]** see Acetaminophen on page 28

♦ **Infants' Tylenol® Cold Plus Cough Concentrated Drops [OTC] [DSC]** see Acetaminophen, Dextromethorphan, and Pseudoephedrine on page 35

♦ **Infasurf®** see Calfactant on page 275

♦ **INFeD®** see Iron Dextran Complex on page 939

♦ **Infergen®** see Interferon Alfacon-1 on page 924

♦ **Inflamase® Mild (Can)** see PrednisoLONE on page 1413

Infliximab (in FLIKS e mab)

U.S. Brand Names Remicade®

Canadian Brand Names Remicade®

Index Terms Infliximab, Recombinant; NSC-728729

Pharmacologic Category Antirheumatic, Disease Modifying; Gastrointestinal Agent, Miscellaneous; Monoclonal Antibody; Tumor Necrosis Factor (TNF) Blocking Agent

Use Treatment of rheumatoid arthritis (moderate-to-severe, with methotrexate); treatment of Crohn's disease (moderate-to-severe with inadequate response to conventional therapy) for induction and maintenance of remission, and/or to reduce the number of draining enterocutaneous and rectovaginal fistulas, and to maintain fistula closure; treatment of psoriatic arthritis; treatment of plaque psoriasis (chronic severe); treatment of ankylosing spondylitis; treatment of and maintenance of healing of ulcerative colitis (moderately- to severely-active with inadequate response to conventional therapy)

Note: In Canada, infliximab is not approved for use in children.

Unlabeled/Investigational Use Acute graft-versus-host disease (GVHD)

Restrictions An FDA-approved medication guide is available at www.fda.gov/cder/Offices/ODS/labeling.htm; distribute to each patient to whom this medication is dispensed.

Pregnancy Risk Factor B

Pregnancy Implications Reproduction studies have not been conducted. Use during pregnancy only if clearly needed. A Rheumatoid Arthritis and Pregnancy Registry has been established for women exposed to infliximab during pregnancy (Organization of Teratology Information Services, 877-311-8972).

Lactation Excretion in breast milk unknown/not recommended

Medication Safety Issues

Sound-alike/look-alike issues:

Remicade® may be confused with Renacidin®, Rituxan®

Infliximab may be confused with rituximab

Contraindications Hypersensitivity to infliximab, murine proteins or any component of the formulation; doses >5 mg/kg in patients with moderate or severe congestive heart failure (NYHA Class III/IV)

Warnings/Precautions [U.S. Boxed Warning]: Opportunistic infections and/or reactivation of latent infections have been associated with infliximab therapy. Tuberculosis (may be disseminated or extrapulmonary) has been reactivated in patients previously exposed to TB while on infliximab. Most cases have been reported within the first 3-6 months of treatment. Other opportunistic infections (eg, invasive fungal infections, listeriosis, *Pneumocystis*) have occurred during therapy. Patients should be evaluated for latent tuberculosis infection with a tuberculin skin test prior to infliximab therapy. Treatment of latent tuberculosis should be initiated before infliximab is used. The risk/benefit ratio should be weighed in patients who have resided in regions where histoplasmosis is endemic.

Serious infections (including sepsis, pneumonia, and fatal infections) have been reported in patients receiving TNF-blocking agents. Many of the serious infections in patients treated with infliximab have occurred in patients on concomitant immunosuppressive therapy. Caution should be exercised when considering the use of infliximab in patients with a chronic infection or history of recurrent infection. Infliximab should not be given to patients with a clinically important, active infection. Patients who develop a new infection while undergoing treatment with infliximab should be monitored closely. If a patient develops a serious infection or sepsis, infliximab should be discontinued. Patients should be brought up to date with all immunizations before initiating therapy. Live vaccines should not be given concurrently; there is no data available concerning secondary transmission of live vaccines in patients receiving therapy. Rare reactivation of hepatitis B has occurred in chronic virus carriers; evaluate prior to initiation and during treatment.

[U.S. Boxed Warning]: Hepatosplenic T-cell lymphoma has been reported (rarely) in adolescent and young adults with Crohn's disease treated with infliximab and azathioprine or 6-mercaptopurine. The impact of infliximab on the development and course of malignancies is not fully defined, but may be dose dependent. As compared to the general population, an increased risk of lymphoma has been noted in clinical trials; however, rheumatoid arthritis alone has been previously associated with an increased rate of lymphoma. Use caution in patients with a history of COPD; higher rates of malignancy were reported in COPD patients treated with infliximab. Psoriasis patients with a history of phototherapy had a higher incidence of nonmelanoma skin cancers.

Severe hepatic reactions have been reported during treatment; discontinue with jaundice or marked increase in liver enzymes (≥5 times ULN). Use caution with heart failure; if a decision is made to use with heart failure, monitor closely and discontinue if exacerbated or new symptoms occur. Use caution with history of hematologic abnormalities; hematologic toxicities (eg, leukopenia, neutropenia, thrombocytopenia, pancytopenia) have been reported; discontinue if significant abnormalities occur. Autoimmune antibodies and a lupus-like syndrome have been reported. If antibodies to double-stranded DNA are confirmed in a patient with lupus-like symptoms, infliximab should be discontinued. Rare cases of optic neuritis and demyelinating disease have been reported; use with caution in patients with pre-existing or recent onset CNS demyelinating disorders, or seizures; discontinue if significant CNS adverse reactions develop.

Acute infusion reactions may occur. Medication and equipment for management should be available for immediate use. Interruptions and/or reinstitution at a slower rate may be required (consult protocols). Pretreatment may be considered, and may be warranted in all patients with prior infusion reactions. Safety and efficacy for use in juvenile rheumatoid arthritis, pediatric plaque psoriasis, or pediatric ulcerative colitis have not been established.

Adverse Reactions Although profile is similar, frequency of adverse effects may vary with disease state. Except where noted, percentages reported in adults with rheumatoid arthritis:

>10%:
  Central nervous system: Headache (18%)
  Gastrointestinal: Nausea (21%), diarrhea (12%), abdominal pain (12%, Crohn's 26%)
  Hepatic: ALT increased (risk increased with concomitant methotrexate)
  Local: Infusion reactions (20%; severe: <1%)
  Respiratory: Upper respiratory tract infection (32%), sinusitis (14%), cough (12%), pharyngitis (12%)
  Miscellaneous: Development of antinuclear antibodies (~50%), infection (36%), development of antibodies to double-stranded DNA (17%); Crohn's patients with fistulizing disease: Development of new abscess (15%)

5% to 10%:
  Cardiovascular: Hypertension (7%)
  Central nervous system: Fatigue (9%), pain (8%), fever (7%)
  Dermatologic: Rash (1% to 10%), pruritus (7%)
  Gastrointestinal: Dyspepsia (10%)
  Genitourinary: Urinary tract infection (8%)
  Neuromuscular & skeletal: Arthralgia (1% to 8%), back pain (8%)
  Respiratory: Bronchitis (10%), rhinitis (8%), dyspnea (6%)
  Miscellaneous: Moniliasis (5%)

<5%: Abscess, adult respiratory distress syndrome, allergic reaction, anemia, arrhythmia, basal cell carcinoma, biliary pain, bradycardia, brain infarction, breast cancer, cardiac arrest, cellulitis, cholecystitis, cholelithiasis, circulatory failure, confusion, constipation, dehydration, delayed hypersensitivity (plaque psoriasis), diaphoresis increased, dizziness, edema, gastrointestinal hemorrhage, heart failure, hemolytic anemia, hepatitis, hypersensitivity reactions, hypotension, ileus, intervertebral disk herniation, intestinal obstruction, intestinal perforation, intestinal stenosis, leukopenia, lupus-like syndrome, lymphadenopathy, lymphoma, malignancies, meningitis, menstrual irregularity, MI, myalgia, neuritis, pancreatitis, pancytopenia, peripheral neuropathy, peritonitis, pleural effusion, pleurisy, proctalgia, pulmonary edema, pulmonary embolism, renal calculus, renal failure, respiratory insufficiency, seizure, sepsis, serum sickness, suicide attempt, syncope, tachycardia, tendon disorder, thrombocytopenia, thrombophlebitis (deep), ulceration

The following adverse events were reported in children with Crohn's disease and were found more frequently in children than adults:
>10%:
  Hepatic: Liver enzymes increased (18%; ≥5 times ULN: 1%)
  Hematologic: Anemia (11%)
  Miscellaneous: Infections (56%; more common with every 8-week versus every 12-week infusions)

1% to 10%:
  Central nervous system: Flushing (9%)
  Gastrointestinal: Blood in stool (10%)
  Hematologic: Leukopenia (9%), neutropenia (7%)
  Neuromuscular & skeletal: Bone fracture (7%)
  Respiratory: Respiratory tract allergic reaction (6%)
  Miscellaneous: Viral infection (8%), bacterial infection (6%), antibodies to infliximab (3%)

Postmarketing and/or case reports (adults or children): Anaphylactic reactions, angina, angioedema, autoimmune hepatitis, bronchospasm, cholestasis, demyelinating disorders (eg, multiple sclerosis, optic neuritis); drug-induced lupus-like syndrome, erythema multiforme, Guillain-Barré syndrome, heart failure (worsening), hepatitis B reactivation, hepatosplenic T-cell lymphoma (HSTCL), Hodgkin's disease, idiopathic thrombocytopenia purpura, interstitial fibrosis, interstitial pneumonitis, jaundice, laryngeal/pharyngeal edema, latent tuberculosis reactivation, liver failure, liver function tests increased, metallic taste, neuropathy, neutropenia, pericardial effusion, pneumonia, Stevens-Johnson syndrome, thrombotic thrombocytopenia purpura, toxic epidermal necrolysis, transverse myelitis, tuberculosis, urticaria, vasculitis (systemic and cutaneous)

Overdosage/Toxicology Doses up to 20 mg/kg have been given without toxic effects. In case of overdose, treatment is symptom-directed and supportive.

Drug Interactions
  Increased Effect/Toxicity: Specific drug interaction studies have not been conducted. Anti-TNF agents may be associated with increased risk of serious infection when used in combination with anakinra. Abciximab may increase potential for hypersensitivity reaction to infliximab, and may increase risk of thrombocytopenia and/or reduced therapeutic efficacy of infliximab. Infliximab may enhance the adverse/toxic effects of abatacept and live vaccines.

  Decreased Effect: Infliximab may decrease the effect of vaccines (dead organisms).

Ethanol/Nutrition/Herb Interactions Herb/Nutraceutical: Echinacea may diminish the therapeutic effect of infliximab.

Stability Store vials at 2°C to 8°C (36°F to 46°F); do not freeze. Reconstitute vials with 10 mL sterile water for injection. Swirl vial gently to dissolve powder; do not shake. Allow solution to stand for 5 minutes. Total dose of reconstituted product should be further diluted to 250 mL of 0.9% sodium chloride injection to a final concentration of 0.4-4 mg/mL. Infusion of dose should begin within 3 hours of preparation.

Mechanism of Action Infliximab is a chimeric monoclonal antibody that binds to human tumor necrosis factor alpha (TNFα), thereby interfering with endogenous TNFα activity. Biological activities of TNFα include the induction of proinflammatory cytokines (interleukins), enhancement of leukocyte migration, activation of neutrophils and eosinophils, and the induction of acute phase reactants and tissue degrading enzymes. Animal models have shown TNFα expression causes polyarthritis, and infliximab can prevent disease as well as allow diseased joints to heal.

Pharmacodynamics/Kinetics
  Onset of action: Crohn's disease: ~2 weeks
  Half-life elimination: 8-9.5 days
  (Continued)

Infliximab (Continued)

Dosage I.V.: **Note:** Premedication with antihistamines (anti-H_1 and/or anti-H_2), acetaminophen and/or corticosteroids may be considered to prevent and/or manage infusion-related reactions:

Children ≥6 years: Crohn's disease: 5 mg/kg at 0, 2, and 6 weeks, followed by a maintenance dose of 5 mg/kg every 8 weeks

Adults:

Crohn's disease: Induction regimen: 5 mg/kg at 0, 2, and 6 weeks, followed by 5 mg/kg every 8 weeks thereafter; dose may be increased to 10 mg/kg in patients who respond but then lose their response. If no response by week 14, consider discontinuing therapy.

Psoriatic arthritis (with or without methotrexate): 5 mg/kg at 0, 2, and 6 weeks, then every 8 weeks

Rheumatoid arthritis (in combination with methotrexate therapy): 3 mg/kg at 0, 2, and 6 weeks, then every 8 weeks thereafter; doses have ranged from 3-10 mg/kg intravenous infusion repeated at 4- to 8-week intervals

Ankylosing spondylitis: 5 mg/kg at 0, 2, and 6 weeks, followed by 5 mg/kg every 6 weeks thereafter

Plaque psoriasis: 5 mg/kg at 0, 2, and 6 weeks, then every 8 weeks thereafter

Ulcerative colitis: 5 mg/kg at 0, 2, and 6 weeks, followed by 5 mg/kg every 8 weeks thereafter

Acute GVHD (unlabeled use): 10 mg/kg weekly for up to 8 weeks (median 4 weeks of treatment)

Dosage adjustment with CHF: Weigh risk versus benefits for individual patient:
NYHA Class III or IV: ≤5 mg/kg

Dosage adjustment in renal impairment: No specific adjustment is recommended

Dosage adjustment in hepatic impairment: No specific adjustment is recommended

Administration Infuse over at least 2 hours; do not infuse with other agents; use in-line low protein binding filter (≤1.2 micron). Temporarily discontinue or decrease infusion rate with infusion-related reactions. Antihistamines (anti-H_1 and/or anti-H_2), acetaminophen and/or corticosteroids may be used to manage reactions. Infusion may be reinitiated at a lower rate upon resolution of mild-to-moderate symptoms.

Guidelines for the treatment and prophylaxis of infusion reactions: (Note: Limited to dosages used in Crohn's; prospective information on other indications/dosing such as in GVHD are not available).

Treatment of infusion reactions: Medications for the treatment of hypersensitivity reactions should be available for immediate use. A protocol for the treatment of acute infusion reactions, as well a prophylactic therapy for repeat infusions, has been published (Cheifetz, 2003). Decreasing the rate of infusion to 10 mL/hour (mild-to-moderate reactions) or a 20-minute interruption of the infusion (moderate-to-severe reactions) is recommended. Monitor vital signs every 10 minutes until normal. Administration of appropriate symptomatic treatment (acetaminophen and diphenhydramine, as well as hydrocortisone and epinephrine for severe reactions) should be instituted (consult institutional policies, if available). Following initial treatment, the infusion may be reinstituted at 10 mL/hour; then increased at 15-minute intervals, as tolerated (first to 20 mL/hour, then 40 mL/hour, then 80 mL/hour to completion).

Prophylaxis of infusion reactions: Premedication with acetaminophen and diphenhydramine 90 minutes prior to infusion may be considered in all patients with prior infusion reactions, and in patients with severe reactions corticosteroid administration is recommended (Cheifetz, 2003). Steroid dosing may be oral (prednisone 50 mg orally for 3 doses over a 24-hour period prior to infusion) or intravenous (a single dose of hydrocortisone 100 mg or methylprednisolone 20-240 mg administered 20 minutes prior to the infusion) (Cheifetz, 2003). On initiation of the infusion, a test dose (infusion at 10 mL/hour for 15 minutes) may be considered. If tolerated, for patients with mild reactions, the infusion may be completed over 3 hours. For patients with prior moderate-to-severe reactions, the infusion may be increased at 15-minute intervals, as tolerated, to completion (first to 20 mL/hour, then 40 mL/hour, then 100 mL/hour, and finally 125 mL/hour to completion). A maximum rate of 100 mL/hour is recommended in patients who experienced prior severe reactions. In patients with cutaneous flushing, aspirin may be considered (Becker, 2004).

Monitoring Parameters During infusion, if reaction is noted, monitor vital signs every 10 minutes until normal. Follow-up monitoring includes monitoring for improvement of symptoms; signs of infection; LFTs (discontinue if >5 times ULN); place and read PPD before initiation. Psoriasis patients with history of phototherapy should be monitored for nonmelanoma skin cancer.

Dosage Forms
Injection, powder for reconstitution [preservative free]:
Remicade®: 100 mg [contains sucrose and polysorbate 80]

♦ **Infliximab, Recombinant** *see* Infliximab *on page 904*

Influenza Virus Vaccine (in floo EN za VYE rus vak SEEN)

U.S. Brand Names Fluarix®; FluLaval™; fluMist®; Fluvirin®; Fluzone®

Canadian Brand Names Fluviral S/F®; Vaxigrip®

Index Terms Influenza Virus Vaccine (Purified Surface Antigen); Influenza Virus Vaccine (Split-Virus); Influenza Virus Vaccine (Trivalent, Live); Live Attenuated Influenza Vaccine (LAIV); Trivalent Inactivated Influenza Vaccine (TIV)

Pharmacologic Category Vaccine

Additional Appendix Information
Immunization Recommendations *on page 1929*
USPHS / IDSA Guidelines for the Prevention of Opportunistic Infections in Persons Infected With HIV *on page 1966*

Use Provide active immunity to influenza virus strains contained in the vaccine

Groups at Increased Risk for Influenza-Related Complications: Advisory Committee on Immunization Practices (ACIP) recommendations for vaccination:

- Persons ≥50 years of age
- Residents of nursing homes and other chronic-care facilities that house persons of any age with chronic medical conditions
- Adults and children with chronic disorders of the pulmonary or cardiovascular systems, including asthma
- Adults and children who have required regular medical follow-up or hospitalization during the preceding year because of chronic metabolic diseases (including diabetes mellitus), renal dysfunction, hemoglobinopathies, or immunosuppression (including immunosuppression caused by medications or HIV)
- Adults and children with conditions which may compromise respiratory function, the handling of respiratory secretions, or that can increase the risk of aspiration (eg, cognitive dysfunction, spinal; cord injuries, seizure disorders, other neuromuscular disorders)
- Children and adolescents (6 months to 18 years of age) who are receiving long-term aspirin therapy and therefore, may be at risk for developing Reye's syndrome after influenza
- Women who will be pregnant during the influenza season
- Children 6-59 months of age

Vaccination is also recommended for close contacts of children 0-59 months of age, healthy persons who may transmit influenza to those at risk, and all healthcare workers.

Pregnancy Risk Factor C

Pregnancy Implications Reproduction studies have not been conducted. Case reports and limited studies suggest pregnancy may increase the risk of serious medical complications from influenza infection. Vaccination is recommended regardless of stage of pregnancy.

Medication Safety Issues
Sound-alike/look-alike issues:
Fluarix® may be confused with Flarex®
Influenza virus vaccine may be confused with tetanus toxoid and tuberculin products. Medication errors have occurred when tuberculin skin tests (PPD) have been inadvertently administered instead of tetanus toxoid products and influenza virus vaccine. These products are refrigerated and often stored in close proximity to each other.

Contraindications Hypersensitivity to influenza virus vaccine, or any component of the formulation; presence of acute respiratory disease or other active infections or illnesses; active neurological disorder (immunization should be delayed)

In addition, for nasal spray: Patients at increased risk for influenza-related complications (see Use); history of Guillain-Barré syndrome; history of asthma or reactive airway disease; children 5-17 years of age receiving aspirin therapy; underlying medical conditions such as diabetes, renal dysfunction, cardiovascular disease, hemoglobinopathies; immunosuppressed or concomitant immunosuppressant therapy; pregnancy

Warnings/Precautions Antigenic response may not be as great as expected in patients requiring immunosuppressive drug therapy or HIV-infected persons with CD4 cells <100/mm^3 and with viral copies of HIV type 1 >30,000/mL. Some products contain thimerosal, latex, or are manufactured with egg protein, chicken protein, and/or gentamicin; hypersensitivity reactions may occur. Due to potential for febrile reactions, risks and benefits must carefully be considered in patients with history of febrile convulsions. Influenza vaccines from previous seasons must not be used. Inactivated vaccine is preferred over live virus vaccine for household members, healthcare workers and others coming in close contact with severely-immunosuppressed persons requiring care in a protected environment. Treatment for anaphylactic reactions (including epinephrine) should be readily available.

Injection (inactivated, split virus): For I.M. use only; use caution with thrombocytopenia or any coagulation disorder. Safety and efficacy for use in children <6 months of age have not been established. Use caution with history of Guillain-Barré (GBS) (previously reported with older vaccine formulations; relationship to current formulations not known, however, patients with history of GBS have a greater likelihood of developing GBS than those without). Immunization should be delayed during moderate-to-severe febrile illness; minor illnesses with or without fever generally do not preclude use of vaccine.

Nasal spray (live, attenuated virus): For intranasal use only. **Avoid contact with severely immunocompromised individuals for at least 7 days following vaccination.** For use in healthy children and adults 5-49 years of age only; safety and efficacy for use in children <5 years or adults ≥50 years of age have not been established. Defer immunization if nasal congestion is present which may impede delivery of vaccine.

Adverse Reactions All serious adverse reactions must be reported to the U.S. Department of Health and Human Services (DHHS) Vaccine Adverse Event Reporting System (VAERS) 1-800-822-7967.
Injection:
Frequency not defined.
Central nervous system: Chills; fever and malaise (may start within 6-12 hours and last 1-2 days; incidence equal to placebo in adults; occurs more frequently than placebo in children); Guillain-Barré syndrome (GBS)
Dermatologic: Angioedema, rash, urticaria
Local: Tenderness, redness, or induration at the site of injection (10% to 64%; may last up to 2 days); injection site pain
Neuromuscular & skeletal: Myalgia (may start within 6-12 hours and last 1-2 days; incidence equal to placebo in adults; occurs more frequently than placebo in children)
Miscellaneous: Allergic or anaphylactoid reactions (most likely to residual egg protein; includes allergic asthma, angioedema, hives, systemic anaphylaxis)
Postmarketing and/or case reports: Seizures (rare; majority associated with fever)

Nasal spray: Frequency of events reported within 10 days
>10%:
Central nervous system: Headache (children 18% after first dose, < placebo after second dose; adults 40%) irritability (children 10% to 18%)
(Continued)

Influenza Virus Vaccine *(Continued)*

Neuromuscular & skeletal: Tiredness/weakness (adults 26%), muscle aches (children 5% to 6%; adults 17%)

Respiratory: Cough (children 26% to 38%; adults 14%), nasal congestion/ runny nose (children 46% to 48%; adults 9% to 45%), sore throat (children < placebo; adults 28%)

Miscellaneous: Activity decreased (children 14% after first dose, < placebo after second dose)

1% to 10%:

Central nervous system: Chills

Gastrointestinal: Abdominal pain, diarrhea, vomiting

Otic: Otitis media

Respiratory: Rhinitis, sinusitis

Postmarketing and/or case reports: Bell's palsy, epistaxis, hypersensitivity reaction, nausea, rash

Drug Interactions

Increased Effect/Toxicity: Concomitant use of aspirin and the nasal spray formulation may increase the risk of Reye syndrome in patients 5-17 years; concomitant use in this age group is contraindicated.

Decreased Effect: Decreased effect with immunosuppressive agents; some manufacturers and clinicians recommend that the flu vaccine not be administered concomitantly with DTP due to the potential for increased febrile reactions (specifically whole-cell pertussis) and that one should wait at least 3 days. However, ACIP recommends that children at high risk for influenza may get the vaccine concomitantly with DTP. Safety and efficacy of nasal spray with other vaccines have not been established; do not give within 1 month of other live virus vaccines or within 2 weeks of inactivated or subunit vaccines. Live virus vaccines may diminish the diagnostic effect of tuberculin tests. Efficacy of influenza (live) vaccines may be diminished (live virus vaccinations should be withheld for as long as 6 months).

Stability

Injection: Store between 2°C to 8°C (36°F to 46°F). Potency is destroyed by freezing; do not use if product has been frozen.

Fluarix®: Protect from light.

FluLaval™: Discard 28 days after initial entry. Protect from light.

Nasal spray: Store in a freezer at or below -15°C (5°F). May thaw in refrigerator and store at 2°C to 8°C (36°F to 46°F) ≤60 hours. Do not refreeze after thawing.

Mechanism of Action Promotes immunity to influenza virus by inducing specific antibody production. Each year the formulation is standardized according to the U.S. Public Health Service. Preparations from previous seasons must not be used.

Pharmacodynamics/Kinetics

Onset: Protective antibody titers achieved ~2 weeks after vaccination

Duration: Protective antibody titers persist approximately ≥6 months. Elderly: Protective antibody titers may fall ≤4 months after vaccination.

Dosage Optimal time to receive vaccine is October-November, prior to exposure to influenza; however, vaccination can continue into December and throughout the influenza season as long as vaccine is available.

I.M.:

Fluzone®:

Children 6-35 months: 0.25 mL/dose (1 or 2 doses per season; see **Note**)

Children 3-8 years: 0.5 mL/dose (1 or 2 doses per season; see **Note**)

Children ≥9 years and Adults: 0.5 mL/dose (1 dose per season)

Fluvirin®:

Children 4-8 years: 0.5 mL/dose (1 or 2 doses per season; see **Note**)

Children ≥9 years and Adults: 0.5 mL/dose (1 dose per season)

Note: Previously unvaccinated children <9 years should receive 2 doses, given >1 month apart in order to achieve satisfactory antibody response.

Fluarix®, FluLaval™: Adults: 0.5 mL/dose (1 dose per season)

Intranasal (fluMist®):

Children 5-8 years, previously **not vaccinated** with influenza vaccine: Initial season: Two 0.5 mL doses separated by 6-10 weeks

Children 5-8 years, previously **vaccinated** with influenza vaccine: 0.5 mL/dose (1 dose per season)

Children ≥9 years and Adults ≤49 years: 0.5 mL/dose (1 dose per season)

Administration

Injection: For I.M. administration only. Inspect for particulate matter and discoloration prior to administration. Adults and older children should be vaccinated in the deltoid muscle using a ≥1 inch needle length. Infants and young children <12 months of age should be vaccinated in the anterolateral aspect of the thigh using a 7/8 inch to 1 inch needle length. Young children with adequate deltoid muscle mass should be vaccinated using a 7/8 inch to 1.25 inch needle. Suspensions should be shaken well prior to use. **Note:** For patients at risk of hemorrhage following intramuscular injection, the ACIP recommends "it should be administered intramuscularly if, in the opinion of the physician familiar with the patients bleeding risk, the vaccine can be administered with reasonable safety by this route. If the patient receives antihemophilia or other similar therapy, intramuscular vaccination can be scheduled shortly after such therapy is administered. A fine needle (23 gauge or smaller) can be used for the vaccination and firm pressure applied to the site (without rubbing) for at least 2 minutes. The patient should be instructed concerning the risk of hematoma from the injection."

Intranasal: Must be thawed prior to administration. May thaw in refrigerator and store at 2°C to 8°C (36°F to 46°F) ≤60 hours. May also be thawed by holding sprayer in the palm of the hand and supporting the plunger rod with thumb; use immediately. Half the dose (0.25 mL) is administered to each nostril; patient should be in upright position. A dose divider clip is provided. Severely-immunocompromised persons should not administer the live vaccine. If recipient sneezes following administration, the dose should not be repeated.

Additional Information Pharmacies will stock the formulations(s) standardized according to the USPHS requirements for the season. Influenza vaccines from previous seasons must not be used. Federal law requires that the date of administration, the vaccine manufacturer, lot number of vaccine, and the administering person's name, title, and address be entered into the patient's permanent medical record.

The optimal time to receive vaccine is October-November, prior to exposure to influenza; however, vaccination can continue into December and later as long as vaccine is available. To avoid missed opportunities for vaccination, patients at risk for complications can be offered the vaccine during routine healthcare visits as early as September if vaccine is available. Avoid vaccination before October in older persons in nursing homes or similar housing facilities because antibody levels can decline more rapidly following vaccination. When vaccine is available, children aged 6 months to <9 years of age who have not been previously vaccinated, should receive their first dose in September so that both doses can be administered prior to the onset of influenza activity.

During periods of inactivated influenza vaccine shortage, the CDC and ACIP have recommended vaccination be prioritized based on the following three tiers. The grouping is based on influenza associated mortality and hospitalization rates. Those listed in group 1 should be vaccinated first, followed by persons in group 2, and then group 3. If the vaccine supply is extremely limited, group 1 has also been subdivided in three tiers, where those in group 1A should be vaccinated first, followed by 1B, then 1C. When inactivated influenza vaccine is in limited supply, eligible persons should be encouraged to receive live, attenuated vaccine.

Priority groups for vaccination with inactivated influenza vaccine during periods of vaccine shortage:
Tier 1A:
    Persons ≥65 years with comorbid conditions
    Residents of long-term-care facilities
Tier 1B:
    Persons 2-64 years with comorbid conditions
    Persons ≥65 years without comorbid conditions
    Children 6-23 months
    Pregnant women
Tier 1C:
    Healthcare personnel
    Household contacts and out-of-home caregivers of children <6 months
Tier 2:
    Household contacts of children and adults at increased risk of influenza associated complications
    Healthy persons 50-64 years
Tier 3:
    Persons 2-49 years without high-risk conditions
Further information available at http://www.cdc.gov/mmwr/preview/mmwrhtml/mm5430a4.htm

Dosage Forms
Injection, solution, purified split-virus [preservative free]:
    Fluvirin®: (0.5 mL) [TIV; contains thimerosal (trace amounts); manufactured using chicken eggs, neomycin, and polymyxin]
Injection, suspension, purified split-virus:
    FluLaval™: (5 mL) [TIV; latex-free; contains thimerosal; produced in chick embryo cell culture]
    Fluzone®: (5 mL) [TIV; latex free; contains thimerosal; produced in chick embryo cell culture]
Injection, suspension, purified split-virus [preservative free]:
    Fluarix®: (0.5 mL) [TIV; syringe cap and rubber plunger contain natural latex rubber; produced in chick embryo cell culture; may contain residual amounts of thimerosal, hydrocortisone, gentamicin, and ovalbumin]
    Fluzone®: (0.25 mL) [TIV; latex free; produced in chick embryo cell culture]; (0.5 mL) [TIV; latex free; produced in chick embryo cell culture]
Solution, intranasal [preservative free; trivalent; live virus; spray]:
    fluMist®: (0.5 mL) [LAIV; manufactured using eggs and gentamicin]

- ◆ **Influenza Virus Vaccine (Purified Surface Antigen)** see Influenza Virus Vaccine on page 906
- ◆ **Influenza Virus Vaccine (Split-Virus)** see Influenza Virus Vaccine on page 906
- ◆ **Influenza Virus Vaccine (Trivalent, Live)** see Influenza Virus Vaccine on page 906
- ◆ **Infufer® (Can)** see Iron Dextran Complex on page 939
- ◆ **Infumorph®** see Morphine Sulfate on page 1171
- ◆ **INH** see Isoniazid on page 942
- ◆ **Inhaled Insulin** see Insulin Inhalation on page 911
- ◆ **Innohep®** see Tinzaparin on page 1689
- ◆ **InnoPran XL™** see Propranolol on page 1446
- ◆ **Insoluble Prussian Blue** see Ferric Hexacyanoferrate on page 701
- ◆ **Inspra™** see Eplerenone on page 594
- ◆ **Instat™** see Collagen Hemostat on page 416
- ◆ **Instat™ MCH** see Collagen Hemostat on page 416

Insulin Aspart (IN soo lin AS part)

U.S. Brand Names NovoLog®
Canadian Brand Names NovoRapid®
Index Terms Aspart Insulin
Pharmacologic Category Antidiabetic Agent, Insulin
Use Treatment of type 1 diabetes mellitus (insulin dependent, IDDM); type 2 diabetes mellitus (noninsulin dependent, NIDDM) to control hyperglycemia
Pregnancy Risk Factor C
(Continued)

Insulin Aspart *(Continued)*

Medication Safety Issues

Sound-alike/look-alike issues:

NovoLog® may be confused with Novolin®

NovoLog® Mix 70/30 may be confused with NovoLog®

High alert medication: The Institute for Safe Medication Practices (ISMP) includes this medication among its list of drugs which have a heightened risk of causing significant patient harm when used in error. *Due to the number of insulin preparations, it is essential to identify/clarify the type of insulin to be used.*

Dosage Refer to Insulin Regular *on page 914*. Insulin aspart is a rapid-acting insulin analog which is normally administered as a a premeal component of the insulin regimen. It is normally used along with a long-acting (basal) form of insulin.

Dosing adjustment in renal impairment: Insulin requirements are reduced due to changes in insulin clearance or metabolism.

Additional Information Complete prescribing information for this medication should be consulted for additional detail.

Dosage Forms Injection, solution (NovoLog®): 100 units/mL (3 mL) [FlexPen® prefilled syringe or PenFill® prefilled cartridge]; (10 mL) [vial]

♦ **Insulin Aspart and Insulin Aspart Protamine** *see* Insulin Aspart Protamine and Insulin Aspart *on page 910*

Insulin Aspart Protamine and Insulin Aspart
(IN soo lin AS part PROE ta meen & IN soo lin AS part)

U.S. Brand Names NovoLog® Mix 70/30

Index Terms Insulin Aspart and Insulin Aspart Protamine

Pharmacologic Category Antidiabetic Agent, Insulin

Use Treatment of type 1 diabetes mellitus (insulin dependent, IDDM); type 2 diabetes mellitus (noninsulin dependent, NIDDM) to control hyperglycemia

Pregnancy Risk Factor C

Medication Safety Issues

Sound-alike/look-alike issues:

NovoLog® Mix 70/30 may be confused with Novolin® 70/30

High alert medication: The Institute for Safe Medication Practices (ISMP) includes this medication among its list of drugs which have a heightened risk of causing significant patient harm when used in error. *Due to the number of insulin preparations, it is essential to identify/clarify the type of insulin to be used.*

Dosage Refer to Insulin Regular *on page 914*. Fixed ratio insulins (such as insulin aspart protamine and insulin aspart combination) are normally administered in 2 daily doses.

Dosing adjustment in renal impairment: Insulin requirements are reduced due to changes in insulin clearance or metabolism.

Additional Information Complete prescribing information for this medication should be consulted for additional detail.

Dosage Forms Injection, suspension (NovoLog® Mix 70/30): Insulin aspart protamine suspension 70% [intermediate acting] and insulin aspart solution 30% [rapid acting]: 100 units/mL (3 mL) [PenFill® prefilled cartridge or FlexPen® prefilled syringe]; (10 mL) [vial]

Insulin Detemir (IN soo lin DE te mir)

U.S. Brand Names Levemir®

Canadian Brand Names Levemir®

Index Terms Detemir Insulin

Pharmacologic Category Antidiabetic Agent, Insulin

Use Treatment of type 1 diabetes mellitus (insulin dependent, IDDM); type 2 diabetes mellitus (noninsulin dependent, NIDDM) to control hyperglycemia

Pregnancy Risk Factor C

Medication Safety Issues

High alert medication: The Institute for Safe Medication Practices (ISMP) includes this medication among its list of drugs which have a heightened risk of causing significant patient harm when used in error. *Due to the number of insulin preparations, it is essential to identify/clarify the type of insulin to be used.*

Note: Insulin detemir is a clear solution, but it is NOT intended for I.V. or I.M. administration.

Dosage Also refer to Insulin Regular *on page 914*.

SubQ: Children and Adults: Type 1 or type 2 diabetes:

Basal insulin or basal-bolus: May be substituted on a unit-per-unit basis

Insulin-naive patients (type 2 diabetes only): 0.1-0.2 units/kg once daily in the evening or 10 units once or twice daily. Adjust dose to achieve glycemic targets.

Dosage adjustment in renal impairment: Insulin requirements are reduced due to changes in insulin clearance or metabolism.

Additional Information Complete prescribing information for this medication should be consulted for additional detail.

Dosage Forms Injection, solution (Levemir®): 100 units/mL (3 mL) [Innolet® prefilled syringe, Penfill® prefilled cartridge, or FlexPen® prefilled syringe]; (10 mL) [vial]

Insulin Glargine (IN soo lin GLAR jeen)

U.S. Brand Names Lantus®
Canadian Brand Names Lantus®; Lantus® OptiSet®
Index Terms Glargine Insulin
Pharmacologic Category Antidiabetic Agent, Insulin
Use Treatment of type 1 diabetes mellitus (insulin dependent, IDDM); type 2 diabetes mellitus (noninsulin dependent, NIDDM) requiring basal (long-acting) insulin to control hyperglycemia
Pregnancy Risk Factor C
Medication Safety Issues
Sound-alike/look-alike issues:
Lantus® may be confused with Lente®
Lente® may be confused with Lantus®
High alert medication: The Institute for Safe Medication Practices (ISMP) includes this medication among its list of drugs which have a heightened risk of causing significant patient harm when used in error. *Due to the number of insulin preparations, it is essential to identify/clarify the type of insulin to be used.*
Dosage SubQ: Adults:
Type 1 diabetes: Refer to Insulin Regular *on page 914.*
Type 2 diabetes:
Patient not already on insulin: 10 units once daily, adjusted according to patient response (range in clinical study: 2-100 units/day)
Patient already receiving insulin: In clinical studies, when changing to insulin glargine from once-daily NPH or Ultralente® insulin, the initial dose was not changed; when changing from twice-daily NPH to once-daily insulin glargine, the total daily dose was reduced by 20% and adjusted according to patient response
Dosage adjustment in renal impairment: Insulin requirements are reduced due to changes in insulin clearance or metabolism.
Additional Information Complete prescribing information for this medication should be consulted for additional detail.
Dosage Forms Injection, solution (Lantus®): 100 units/mL (3 mL) [cartridge]; (10 mL) [vial]

Insulin Glulisine (IN soo lin gloo LIS een)

U.S. Brand Names Apidra®
Canadian Brand Names Apidra®
Index Terms Glulisine Insulin
Pharmacologic Category Antidiabetic Agent, Insulin
Use Treatment of type 1 diabetes mellitus (insulin dependent, IDDM); type 2 diabetes mellitus (noninsulin dependent, NIDDM) to control hyperglycemia
Pregnancy Risk Factor C
Medication Safety Issues
High alert medication: The Institute for Safe Medication Practices (ISMP) includes this medication among its list of drugs which have a heightened risk of causing significant patient harm when used in error. *Due to the number of insulin preparations, it is essential to identify/clarify the type of insulin to be used.*
Dosage Refer to Insulin Regular *on page 914.*
Dosing adjustment in renal impairment: Insulin requirements are reduced due to changes in insulin clearance or metabolism.
Additional Information Complete prescribing information for this medication should be consulted for additional detail.
Dosage Forms
Injection, solution:
Apidra®: 100 units/mL (3 mL [cartridge], 10 mL [vial])

Insulin Inhalation (IN soo lin in ha LAY shun)

U.S. Brand Names Exubera®
Index Terms Inhaled Insulin
Pharmacologic Category Antidiabetic Agent, Insulin
Use Treatment of type 1 diabetes mellitus (insulin dependent, IDDM); type 2 diabetes mellitus (noninsulin dependent, NIDDM)
Restrictions An FDA-approved medication guide must be distributed when dispensing an outpatient prescription (new or refill) where this medication is to be used without direct supervision of a healthcare provider. Medication guides are available at http://www.fda.gov/cder/Offices/ODS/medication_guides.htm.
Pregnancy Risk Factor C
Pregnancy Implications Animal reproduction studies have not been conducted with this dosage form. Absorption of insulin inhalation (Exubera®) in women with gestational and pregestational type 2 diabetes is similar to nonpregnant women with type 2 diabetes. Does not cross the placenta. Insulin is the drug of choice for control of diabetes mellitus during pregnancy.
Lactation Excretion in breast milk unknown/compatible
Medication Safety Issues
High alert medication: The Institute for Safe Medication Practices (ISMP) includes this medication among its list of drugs which have a heightened risk of causing significant patient harm when used in error. *Due to the number of insulin preparations, it is essential to identify/clarify the type of insulin to be used. The inhalation form of insulin is expressed in milligrams rather than units, potentially leading to confusion. Absolute conversion between doses of inhalation and injection insulin is not possible.*
(Continued)

Insulin Inhalation (Continued)

Contraindications Hypersensitivity to any component of the formulation; smokers or patients who have discontinued smoking for <6 months; poorly-controlled or unstable lung disease

Warnings/Precautions Also refer to Insulin Regular *on page 914*.

Due to increased systemic absorption, the risk of hypoglycemia is greatly increased in patients who smoke or who have stopped smoking for less than 6 months. The effect of passive exposure to smoke has not been fully evaluated but may result in alteration in absorption and/or hypoglycemia. Insulin inhalation should be immediately discontinued in any patient who resumes smoking.

Decreases in pulmonary function have been associated with use. Due the potential impact on pulmonary function, testing should be performed prior to the initiation of inhaled insulin therapy. Not recommended for use in patients with lung disease (asthma, COPD). Monitor closely during periods of intercurrent respiratory illness.

In type 1 diabetes mellitus (insulin dependent, IDDM), rapid-acting insulins including insulin inhalation should be used in combination with a long-acting insulin. However, in type 2 diabetes mellitus (noninsulin dependent, NIDDM), rapid-acting agents may be used without a long-acting insulin when used as monotherapy or combined with an oral antidiabetic agent.

Use caution in renal and/or hepatic impairment.

Adverse Reactions Also refer to Insulin Regular *on page 914*.

Cardiovascular: Chest pain (5%; usually mild-to-moderate)

Dermatologic: Rash (rare)

Endocrine & metabolic: Hypoglycemia

Gastrointestinal: Xerostomia (2%)

Otic: Otitis media (pediatric patients 7%), ear pain (4%), ear disorder (1%)

Respiratory: Respiratory infection (30% to 43%), cough increased (22% to 30%), pharyngitis (10% to 18%), rhinitis (9% to 15%), sinusitis (5% to 10%), dyspnea (4%), sputum increased (3% to 4%), bronchitis (3% to 5%), epistaxis (1%), laryngitis (1%), voice alteration (1%), bronchospasm (rare)

>Note: Decreases in pulmonary function (reduced FEV1, DLco) have been associated with use, usually noted in the initial weeks of therapy; declines from baseline of 20% in, respectively, FEV1 and DLco, were reported in 5.1% and 1.5% of patients as compared to 3.6% and 1.3% in comparator-treated patients.

Miscellaneous: Allergic reactions, anaphylaxis (including tachycardia and hypotension), diaphoresis increased

Overdosage/Toxicology Refer to Insulin Regular *on page 914*.

Drug Interactions

Cytochrome P450 Effect: Refer to Insulin Regular *on page 914*.

Increased Effect/Toxicity: Refer to Insulin Regular *on page 914*.

Decreased Effect: Refer to Insulin Regular *on page 914*.

Ethanol/Nutrition/Herb Interactions Refer to Insulin Regular *on page 914*.

Stability Insulin inhalation (Exubera®): Store unopened blisters, in-use blisters, and inhaler at controlled room temperature (25°C); excursions permitted to 15°C to 30°C (59°F to 86°F); do not freeze or refrigerate. Once foil overwrap is opened, blisters should be used within 3 months. Avoid exposure to excess humidity.

Mechanism of Action Refer to Insulin Regular *on page 914*. Insulin inhalation is a rapid-acting form of human insulin.

Pharmacodynamics/Kinetics

Onset of action: 0.2-0.4 hours

Duration: 6-8 hours

Absorption: Rapid

Bioavailability: Absolute bioavailability not defined (depends on inspiratory flow characteristics); systemic exposure may be up to 2-5 times higher in smokers

Time to peak, plasma: 30-90 minutes

Excretion: Urine

Dosage Inhalation: Children ≥6 years and Adults:

Initial: 0.05 mg/kg (rounded down to nearest whole milligram) 3 times/daily administered within 10 minutes of a meal

Adjustment: Dosage may be increased or decreased based on serum glucose monitoring, meal size, nutrient composition, time of day, and exercise patterns.

>Note: A 1 mg blister is approximately equivalent to 3 units of regular insulin, while a 3 mg blister is approximately equivalent to 8 units of regular insulin administered subcutaneously. Patients should combine 1 mg and 3 mg blisters so that the fewest blisters are required to achieve the prescribed dose. Consecutive inhalation of three 1 mg blisters results in significantly higher insulin levels as compared to inhalation of a single 3 mg blister (do not substitute). In a patient stabilized on a dosage which uses 3 mg blisters, if 3 mg blister is temporarily unavailable, inhalation of two 1 mg blisters may be substituted.

Dosing adjustment in renal impairment: Insulin requirements are reduced due to changes in insulin clearance or metabolism.

Dietary Considerations Dietary modification based on ADA recommendations is a key component of therapy.

Administration Insulin inhalation (Exubera®): Administer no more than 10 minutes before a meal using the Exubera® inhalation device. The Exubera® Release Unit in the inhaler should be changed every 2 weeks; the Exubera® inhaler may be used for 1 year.

Monitoring Parameters Pulmonary function testing at baseline and periodically during therapy; blood glucose, urine sugar and acetone, serum glucose, electrolytes, Hb A_{1c}, lipid profile

Reference Range Refer to Insulin Regular *on page 914*.

Dosage Forms

Combination package:

Exubera® Kit [packaged with inhaler, chamber and release unit]:

Powder for oral inhalation [prefilled blister pack]: 1 mg/blister (180s)

Powder for oral inhalation [prefilled blister pack]: 3 mg/blister (90s)
Exubera® Combination Pack 15 [packaged with 2 release units]:
    Powder for oral inhalation [prefilled blister pack]: 1 mg/blister (180s)
    Powder for oral inhalation [prefilled blister pack]: 3 mg/blister (90s)
Exubera® Combination Pack 12 [packaged with 2 release units]:
    Powder for oral inhalation [prefilled blister pack]: 1 mg/blister (180s)
    Powder for oral inhalation [prefilled blister pack]: 3 mg/blister (90s)

Insulin Lispro (IN soo lin LYE sproe)

U.S. Brand Names Humalog®
Canadian Brand Names Humalog®
Index Terms Lispro Insulin
Pharmacologic Category Antidiabetic Agent, Insulin
Use Treatment of type 1 diabetes mellitus (insulin dependent, IDDM); type 2 diabetes mellitus (noninsulin dependent, NIDDM) to control hyperglycemia
    Note: In type 1 diabetes mellitus (insulin dependent, IDDM), insulin lispro (Humalog®) should be used in combination with a long-acting insulin. However, in type 2 diabetes mellitus (noninsulin dependent, NIDDM), insulin lispro (Humalog®) may be used without a long-acting insulin when used in combination with a sulfonylurea.
Pregnancy Risk Factor B
Medication Safety Issues
    Sound-alike/look-alike issues:
        Humalog® may be confused with Humulin®, Humira®

    High alert medication: The Institute for Safe Medication Practices (ISMP) includes this medication among its list of drugs which have a heightened risk of causing significant patient harm when used in error. *Due to the number of insulin preparations, it is essential to identify/clarify the type of insulin to be used.*
Dosage Refer to Insulin Regular *on page 914.* Insulin lispro is equipotent to insulin regular, but has a more rapid onset.
    Dosing adjustment in renal impairment: Insulin requirements are reduced due to changes in insulin clearance or metabolism.
Additional Information Complete prescribing information for this medication should be consulted for additional detail.
Dosage Forms Injection, solution (Humalog®): 100 units/mL (3 mL) [prefilled cartridge or prefilled disposable pen]; (10 mL) [vial]

♦ **Insulin Lispro and Insulin Lispro Protamine** see Insulin Lispro Protamine and Insulin Lispro *on page 913*

Insulin Lispro Protamine and Insulin Lispro
(IN soo lin LYE sproe PROE ta meen & IN soo lin LYE sproe)

U.S. Brand Names Humalog® Mix 50/50™; Humalog® Mix 75/25™
Canadian Brand Names Humalog® Mix 25
Index Terms Insulin Lispro and Insulin Lispro Protamine
Pharmacologic Category Antidiabetic Agent, Insulin
Use Treatment of type 1 diabetes mellitus (insulin dependent, IDDM); type 2 diabetes mellitus (noninsulin dependent, NIDDM) to control hyperglycemia
Pregnancy Risk Factor B
Medication Safety Issues
    Sound-alike/look-alike issues:
        Humalog® Mix 75/25™ may be confused with Humulin® 70/30.

    High alert medication: The Institute for Safe Medication Practices (ISMP) includes this medication among its list of drugs which have a heightened risk of causing significant patient harm when used in error. *Due to the number of insulin preparations, it is essential to identify/clarify the type of insulin to be used.*
Dosage Refer to Insulin Regular *on page 914.* Fixed ratio insulins (such as insulin lispro protamine and insulin lispro) are normally administered in 2 daily doses.
    Dosage adjustment in renal impairment: Insulin requirements are reduced due to changes in insulin clearance or metabolism.
Additional Information Complete prescribing information for this medication should be consulted for additional detail.
Dosage Forms Injection, suspension:
    Humalog® Mix 50/50™: Insulin lispro protamine suspension 50% [intermediate acting] and insulin lispro solution 50% [rapid acting]: 100 units/mL (3 mL) [disposable pen]
    Humalog® Mix 75/25™: Insulin lispro protamine suspension 75% [intermediate acting] and insulin lispro solution 25% [rapid acting]: 100 units/mL (3 mL) [disposable pen]; (10 mL) [vial]

Insulin NPH (IN soo lin N P H)

U.S. Brand Names Humulin® N; Novolin® N
Canadian Brand Names Humulin® N; Novolin® ge NPH
Index Terms Isophane Insulin; NPH Insulin
Pharmacologic Category Antidiabetic Agent, Insulin
Use Treatment of type 1 diabetes mellitus (insulin dependent, IDDM); type 2 diabetes mellitus (noninsulin dependent, NIDDM) to control hyperglycemia
Pregnancy Risk Factor B
Medication Safety Issues
    Sound-alike/look-alike issues:
        Humulin® may be confused with Humalog®, Humira®
(Continued)

Insulin NPH *(Continued)*

Novolog® may be confused with NovoLog®

High alert medication: The Institute for Safe Medication Practices (ISMP) includes this medication among its list of drugs which have a heightened risk of causing significant patient harm when used in error. *Due to the number of insulin preparations, it is essential to identify/clarify the type of insulin to be used.*

Dosage Refer to Insulin Regular *on page 914*. Insulin NPH is usually administered 1-2 times daily.

Dosing adjustment in renal impairment: Insulin requirements are reduced due to changes in insulin clearance or metabolism.

Additional Information Complete prescribing information for this medication should be consulted for additional detail.

Dosage Forms [CAN] = Canadian brand name

Injection, suspension:

Humulin® N: 100 units/mL (3 mL) [disposable pen]; (10 mL) [vial]

Novolin® ge NPH [CAN]: 100 units/mL (3 mL) [NovolinSet® prefilled syringe or PenFill® prefilled cartridge]; 10 mL [vial]

Novolin® N: 100 units/mL (3 mL) [InnoLet® prefilled syringe or PenFill® prefilled cartridge]; (10 mL) [vial]

Insulin NPH and Insulin Regular (IN soo lin N P H & IN soo lin REG yoo ler)

U.S. Brand Names Humulin® 50/50; Humulin® 70/30; Novolin® 70/30

Canadian Brand Names Humulin® 20/80; Humulin® 70/30; Novolin® ge 10/90; Novolin® ge 20/80; Novolin® ge 30/70; Novolin® ge 40/60; Novolin® ge 50/50

Index Terms Insulin Regular and Insulin NPH; Isophane Insulin and Regular Insulin; NPH Insulin and Regular Insulin

Pharmacologic Category Antidiabetic Agent, Insulin

Use Treatment of type 1 diabetes mellitus (insulin dependent, IDDM); type 2 diabetes mellitus (noninsulin dependent, NIDDM) to control hyperglycemia

Pregnancy Risk Factor C

Medication Safety Issues

Sound-alike/look-alike issues:

Humulin® 70/30 may be confused with Humalog® Mix 75/25

Novolin® 70/30 may be confused with NovoLog® Mix 70/30

High alert medication: The Institute for Safe Medication Practices (ISMP) includes this medication among its list of drugs which have a heightened risk of causing significant patient harm when used in error. *Due to the number of insulin preparations, it is essential to identify/clarify the type of insulin to be used.*

Dosage Refer to Insulin Regular *on page 914*. Fixed ratio insulins are normally administered in 1-2 daily doses.

Additional Information Complete prescribing information for this medication should be consulted for additional detail.

Dosage Forms

Injection, suspension:

Humulin® 50/50: Insulin NPH suspension 50% [intermediate acting] and insulin regular solution 50% [short acting]: 100 units/mL (10 mL) [vial]

Humulin® 70/30: Insulin NPH suspension 70% [intermediate acting] and insulin regular solution 30% [short acting]: 100 units/mL (3 mL) [disposable pen]; (10 mL) [vial]

Novolin® 70/30: Insulin NPH suspension 70% [intermediate acting] and insulin regular solution 30% [short acting]: 100 units/mL (3 mL) [InnoLet® prefilled syringe or PenFill® prefilled cartridge]; (10 mL) [vial]

Additional formulations available in Canada: Injection, suspension:

Humulin® 20/80: Insulin regular solution 20% [short acting] and insulin NPH suspension 80% [intermediate acting]: 100 units/mL (3 mL) [PenFill® prefilled cartridge]

Novolin® ge 10/90: Insulin regular solution 10% [short acting] and insulin NPH suspension 90% [intermediate acting]: 100 units/mL (3 mL) [PenFill® prefilled cartridge]

Novolin® ge 20/80: Insulin regular solution 20% [short acting] and insulin NPH suspension 80% [intermediate acting]: 100 units/mL (3 mL) [PenFill® prefilled cartridge]

Novolin® ge 30/70: Insulin regular solution 30% [short acting] and insulin NPH suspension 70% [intermediate acting]: 100 units/mL (3 mL) [prefilled syringe or PenFill® prefilled cartridge]; (10 mL) [vial]

Novolin® ge 40/60: Insulin regular solution 40% [short acting] and insulin NPH suspension 60% [intermediate acting]: 100 units/mL (3 mL) [PenFill® prefilled cartridge]

Novolin® ge 50/50: Insulin regular solution 50% [short acting] and insulin NPH suspension 50% [intermediate acting]: 100 units/mL (3 mL) [PenFill® prefilled cartridge]

Insulin Regular (IN soo lin REG yoo ler)

U.S. Brand Names Humulin® R; Humulin® R (Concentrated) U-500; Novolin® R

Canadian Brand Names Humulin® R; Novolin® ge Toronto

Index Terms Regular Insulin

Pharmacologic Category Antidiabetic Agent, Insulin; Antidote

Additional Appendix Information

Diabetes Mellitus Management, Adults *on page 2040*

Use Treatment of type 1 diabetes mellitus (insulin dependent, IDDM); type 2 diabetes mellitus (noninsulin dependent, NIDDM) unresponsive to treatment with diet and/or oral hypoglycemics, to control hyperglycemia; adjunct to parenteral nutrition; diabetic ketoacidosis (DKA)

Unlabeled/Investigational Use Hyperkalemia (regular insulin only; use with glucose to shift potassium into cells to lower serum potassium levels)

Pregnancy Risk Factor B

Pregnancy Implications Insulin is the drug of choice for the control of diabetes mellitus during pregnancy.

Lactation Excretion in breast milk unknown/compatible

Medication Safety Issues

Sound-alike/look-alike issues:

Humulin® may be confused with Humalog®, Humira®

Novolin® may be confused with NovoLog®

High alert medication: The Institute for Safe Medication Practices (ISMP) includes this medication among its list of drugs which have a heightened risk of causing significant patient harm when used in error. *Due to the number of insulin preparations, it is essential to identify/clarify the type of insulin to be used.*

Concentrated solutions (eg, U-500) should not be available in patient care areas.

Contraindications Hypersensitivity to any component of the formulation

Warnings/Precautions Hypoglycemia is the most common adverse effect of insulin. The timing of hypoglycemia differs among various insulin formulations. Any change of insulin should be made cautiously; changing manufacturers, type, and/or method of manufacture may result in the need for a change of dosage. Human insulin differs from animal-source insulin. Regular insulin is the only insulin to be used I.V. Hypoglycemia may result from increased work or exercise without eating; use of long-acting insulin preparations (insulin glargine, Ultralente®, insulin U) may delay recovery from hypoglycemia. Use with caution in renal or hepatic impairment.

The general objective of insulin replacement therapy is to approximate the physiologic pattern of insulin secretion. This requires a basal level of insulin throughout the day, supplemented by additional insulin at mealtimes. Since combinations of agents are frequently used, dosage adjustment must address the individual component of the insulin regimen which most directly influences the blood glucose value in question, based on the known onset and duration of the insulin component. The frequency of doses and monitoring must be individualized in consideration of the patient's ability to manage therapy. Diabetic education and nutritional counseling are essential to maximize the effectiveness of therapy.

In type 1 diabetes mellitus (insulin dependent, IDDM), insulin lispro (Humalog®) and insulin glulisine (Apidra™) should be used in combination with a long-acting insulin. However, in type 2 diabetes mellitus (noninsulin dependent, NIDDM), insulin lispro (Humalog®) may be used without a long-acting insulin when used in combination with a sulfonylurea.

Adverse Reactions Frequency not defined.

Cardiovascular: Palpitation, pallor, tachycardia

Central nervous system: Fatigue, headache, hypothermia, loss of consciousness, mental confusion

Dermatologic: Urticaria, redness

Endocrine & metabolic: Hypoglycemia

Gastrointestinal: Hunger, nausea, numbness of mouth

Local: Atrophy or hypertrophy of SubQ fat tissue; edema, itching, pain or warmth at injection site; stinging

Neuromuscular & skeletal: Muscle weakness, paresthesia, tremor

Ocular: Transient presbyopia or blurred vision

Miscellaneous: Anaphylaxis, diaphoresis, local allergy, systemic allergic symptoms

Overdosage/Toxicology Symptoms include tachycardia, anxiety, hunger, tremors, pallor, headache, motor dysfunction, speech disturbances, sweating, palpitations, coma, and death. Antidote includes glucose and glucagon, if necessary.

Drug Interactions

Cytochrome P450 Effect: Induces CYP1A2 (weak)

Increased Effect/Toxicity: Increased hypoglycemic effect of insulin with alcohol, alpha-blockers, anabolic steroids, beta-blockers (nonselective beta-blockers may delay recovery from hypoglycemic episodes and mask signs/symptoms of hypoglycemia; cardioselective beta-blocker agents may be alternatives), clofibrate, guanethidine, MAO inhibitors, pentamidine, phenylbutazone, salicylates, sulfinpyrazone, and tetracyclines.

Insulin increases the risk of hypoglycemia associated with oral hypoglycemic agents (including sulfonylureas, metformin, pioglitazone, rosiglitazone, and troglitazone).

Decreased Effect: Decreased hypoglycemic effect of insulin with corticosteroids, dextrothyroxine, diltiazem, dobutamine, epinephrine, niacin, oral contraceptives, thiazide diuretics, thyroid hormone, and smoking.

Ethanol/Nutrition/Herb Interactions

Ethanol: Caution with ethanol (may increase hypoglycemia).

Food: Insulin shifts potassium from extracellular to intracellular space. Decreases potassium serum concentration.

Herb/Nutraceutical: Use caution with chromium, garlic, gymnema (may increase hypoglycemia).

Stability Insulin, regular (Humulin® R, Novolin® R): Store unopened containers in refrigerator at 2°C to 8°C (36°F to 46°F); do not freeze. Vial in use may be stored under refrigeration or at room temperature; store below 30°C (86°F) away from direct heat or light. Regular insulin should only be used if clear.

Note: Standard diluent for regular insulin: 100 units/100 mL NS; all bags should be prepared fresh; tubing should be flushed 30 minutes prior to administration to allow adsorption as time permits. Can be given as a more diluted solution (eg, 100 units/250 mL 0.45% NS).

Mechanism of Action Insulin acts via specific membrane-bound receptors on target tissues to regulate metabolism of carbohydrate, protein, and fats. Insulin facilitates entry of glucose into muscle, adipose, and other tissues via hexose transporters, including GLUT4. Insulin stimulates the cellular uptake of amino acids and increases cellular permeability to several ions, including potassium, magnesium, and phosphate. By activating sodium-potassium ATPases, insulin promotes the intracellular movement of potassium.

(Continued)

Insulin Regular *(Continued)*

Target organs for insulin include the liver, skeletal muscle, and adipose tissue. Within the liver, insulin stimulates hepatic glycogen synthesis through the activation of the enzymes hexokinase, phosphofructokinase, and glycogen synthase as well as the inhibition of glucose-6 phosphatase. Insulin promotes hepatic synthesis of fatty acids, which are released into the circulation as lipoproteins. Skeletal muscle effects of insulin include increased protein synthesis and increased glycogen synthesis. Within adipose tissue, insulin stimulates the processing of circulating lipoproteins to provide free fatty acids, facilitating triglyceride synthesis and storage by adipocytes. Insulin also directly inhibits the hydrolysis of triglycerides.

Normally secreted by the pancreas, insulin products are manufactured for pharmacologic use through recombinant DNA technology using either *E. coli* or *Saccharomyces cerevisiae*. Insulins are categorized based on promptness and duration of effect, including rapid-, short-, intermediate-, and long-acting insulins.

Pharmacodynamics/Kinetics
Onset of action: 0.5 hours
Duration: 6-8 hours (may increase with dose)
Time to peak: 2-4 hours
Excretion: Urine

Dosage SubQ (regular insulin may also be administered I.V.): The number and size of daily doses, time of administration, and diet and exercise require continuous medical supervision. In addition, specific formulations may require distinct administration procedures.

Type 1 Diabetes Mellitus: Children and Adults: **Note:** Multiple daily doses guided by blood glucose monitoring are the standard of diabetes care. Combinations of insulin are commonly used.

Initial dose: 0.2-0.6 units/kg/day in divided doses. Conservative initial doses of 0.2-0.4 units/kg/day are often recommended to avoid the potential for hypoglycemia.

Division of daily insulin requirement: Generally, 50% to 75% of the daily insulin dose is given as an intermediate- or long-acting form of insulin (in 1-2 daily injections). The remaining portion of the 24-hour insulin requirement is divided and administered as a rapid-acting or short-acting form of insulin. These may be given with meals (before or at the time of meals depending on the form of insulin) or at the same time as injections of intermediate forms (some premixed combinations are intended for this purpose).

Adjustment of dose: Dosage must be titrated to achieve glucose control and avoid hypoglycemia. Adjust dose to maintain premeal and bedtime glucose of 80-140 mg/dL (children <5 years: 100-200 mg/dL). Since combinations of agents are frequently used, dosage adjustment must address the individual component of the insulin regimen which most directly influences the blood glucose value in question, based on the known onset and duration of the insulin component. Also see Additional Information.

Usual maintenance range: 0.5-1.2 units/kg/day in divided doses. An estimate of anticipated needs may be based on body weight and/or activity factors as follows:
Adolescents: May require ≤1.5 units/kg/day during growth spurts
Nonobese: 0.4-0.6 units/kg/day
Obese: 0.8-1.2 units/kg/day
Renal failure: Due to alterations in pharmacokinetics of insulin, may require <0.2 units/kg/day

Type 2 Diabetes Mellitus:
Augmentation therapy: Initial dosage of 0.15 (insulin glargine, corresponding to ~10 units) to 0.2 units/kg/day (insulins other than glargine) have been recommended. Dosage must be carefully adjusted.

Note: Administered when residual beta-cell function is present, as a supplemental agent when oral hypoglycemics have not achieved goal glucose control. Twice daily NPH, or an evening dose of NPH, lente, or glargine insulin may be added to oral therapy with metformin or a sulfonylurea. Augmentation to control postprandial glucose may be accomplished with regular, glulisine, aspart, or lispro insulin.

Monotherapy: Initial dose: Highly variable: See Augmentation therapy dosing.

Note: An empirically-defined scheme for dosage estimation based on fasting plasma glucose and degree of obesity has been published with recommended doses ranging from 6-77 units/day (Holman, 1995). In the setting of glucose toxicity (loss of beta-cell sensitivity to glucose concentrations), insulin therapy may be used for short-term management to restore sensitivity of beta-cells; in these cases, the dose may need to be rapidly reduced/withdrawn when sensitivity is re-established.

Diabetic ketoacidosis:
Children <20 years:
I.V.: Regular insulin infused at 0.1 units/kg/hour; continue until acidosis clears, then decrease to 0.05 units/kg/hour until SubQ replacement dosing can be initiated
SubQ, I.M.: If no I.V. infusion access, regular insulin 0.1 units/kg I.M. bolus followed by 0.1 units/kg/hour SubQ or I.M.; continue until acidosis clears, then decrease to 0.05 units/kg/hour until SubQ replacement dosing can be initiated
Adults:
I.V.: Regular insulin 0.15 units/kg initially followed by an infusion of 0.1 units/kg/hour
SubQ, I.M.: Regular insulin 0.4 units/kg given half as I.V. bolus and half as SubQ or I.M., followed by 0.1 units/kg/hour SubQ or I.M.
If serum glucose does not fall by 50-70 mg/dL in the first hour, double insulin dose hourly until glucose falls at an hourly rate of 50-70 mg/dL. Decrease dose to 0.05-0.1 units/kg/hour once serum glucose reaches 250 mg/dL.
Note: Newly-diagnosed patients with IDDM presenting in DKA and patients with blood sugars <800 mg/dL may be relatively "sensitive" to insulin and should receive loading and initial maintenance doses ~50% of those indicated.
Infusion should continue until reversal of acid-base derangement/ketonemia. Serum glucose is not a direct indicator of these abnormalities, and may decrease more rapidly than correction of the range of metabolic abnormalities.

Hyperkalemia (unlabeled use): Children and Adults: I.V.: Administer dextrose at 0.5-1 mL/kg and regular insulin 1 unit for every 4-5 g dextrose given

Dosing adjustment in renal impairment (regular): Insulin requirements are reduced due to changes in insulin clearance or metabolism

Cl_{cr} 10-50 mL/minute: Administer at 75% of normal dose

Cl_{cr} <10 mL/minute: Administer at 25% to 50% of normal dose and monitor glucose closely

Hemodialysis: Because of a large molecular weight (6000 daltons), insulin is not significantly removed by either peritoneal or hemodialysis

Supplemental dose is not necessary

Peritoneal dialysis: Supplemental dose is not necessary

Continuous arteriovenous or venovenous hemofiltration effects: Supplemental dose is not necessary

Dietary Considerations Dietary modification based on ADA recommendations is a part of therapy.

Administration

SubQ administration: Cold injections should be avoided. SubQ administration is usually made into the thighs, arms, buttocks, or abdomen, with sites rotated. When mixing regular insulin with other preparations of insulin, regular insulin should be drawn into syringe first. Except for rapid-acting, short-acting, or insulin glargine, gently roll vial or pen in the palms of the hands to resuspend before using. When rapid-acting insulin is mixed with an intermediate- or long-acting insulin, it should be administered within 15 minutes before a meal.

Human regular insulin: Should be administered within 30-60 minutes before a meal; may be administered by SubQ, I.M., or I.V. routes.

I.V. administration (requires use of an infusion pump): **Only regular insulin** may be administered I.V.

I.V. infusions: To minimize adsorption problems to I.V. solution bag:

If new tubing is **not** needed: Wait a minimum of 30 minutes between the preparation of the solution and the initiation of the infusion.

If new tubing is needed: After receiving the insulin drip solution, the administration set should be attached to the I.V. container and the line should be flushed with the insulin solution. The nurse should wait 30 minutes, then flush the line again with the insulin solution prior to initiating the infusion.

If insulin is required prior to the availability of the insulin drip, regular insulin should be administered by I.V. push injection.

Because of adsorption, the actual amount of insulin being administered could be substantially less than the apparent amount. Therefore, adjustment of the insulin drip rate should be based on effect and not solely on the apparent insulin dose. Furthermore, the apparent dose should not be used as the basis for determining the subsequent insulin dose upon discontinuing the insulin drip. Dose requires continuous medical supervision.

Monitoring Parameters Urine sugar and acetone, serum glucose, electrolytes, Hb A_{1c}, lipid profile

DKA: Arterial blood gases, CBC with differential, urinalysis, serum glucose (baseline and every hour until reaches 250 mg/dL), BUN, creatinine, electrolytes, anion gap

Hyperkalemia: Serum potassium and glucose must be closely monitored to avoid hypoglycemia and/or hypokalemia.

Reference Range

Therapeutic, serum insulin (fasting): 5-20 µIU/mL (SI: 35-145 pmol/L)

Glucose, fasting:

Newborns: 60-110 mg/dL

Adults: 60-110 mg/dL

Elderly: 100-180 mg/dL

Recommendations for glycemic control, adults with type 1 diabetes:

Hb A_{1c}: <7%

Preprandial capillary plasma glucose: 90-130 mg/dL

Peak postprandial capillary blood glucose: <180 mg/dL

Blood pressure: <130/80 mm Hg

Criteria for diagnosis of DKA:

Serum glucose: >250 mg/dL

Arterial pH: <7.3

Bicarbonate: <15 mEq/L

Moderate ketonuria or ketonemia

Additional Information

Split-mixed or basal-bolus regimens: Combination regimens which exploit differences in the onset and duration of different insulin products are commonly used to approximate physiologic secretion. In split-mixed regimens, an intermediate-acting insulin (such as NPH insulin) is administered once or twice daily and supplemented by short-acting (regular) or rapid-acting (lispro, aspart, or glulisine) insulin. Blood glucose measurements are completed several times daily. Dosages are adjusted emphasizing the individual component of the regimen which most directly influences the blood sugar in question (either the intermediate-acting component or the shorter-acting component). Fixed-ratio formulations (eg, 70/30 mix) may be used as twice daily injections in this scenario; however, the ability to titrate the dosage of an individual component is limited. A example of a "split-mixed" regimen would be 21 units of NPH plus 9 units of regular insulin in the morning and an evening meal dose consisting of 14 units of NPH plus 6 units of regular insulin.

Basal-bolus regimens are designed to more closely mimic physiologic secretion. These employ a long-acting insulin (eg, glargine) to simulate basal insulin secretion. The basal component is frequently administered at bedtime or in the early morning. This is supplemented by multiple daily injections of very rapid-acting products (lispro or aspart) immediately prior to a meal, which provides insulin at the time when nutrients are absorbed. An example of a basal-bolus regimen would be 30 units of glargine at bedtime and 12 units of lispro insulin prior to each meal.

Estimation of the effect per unit: A "Rule of 1500" has been frequently used as a means to estimate the change in blood sugar relative to each unit of insulin administered. In fact, the recommended values used in these calculations may vary from 1500-2200 (a value of 1500 is generally recommended for regular insulin while 1800 is recommended for lispro).

(Continued)

Insulin Regular *(Continued)*

The higher values lead to more conservative estimates of the effect per unit of insulin, and therefore lead to more cautious adjustments. The effect per unit of insulin is approximated by dividing the selected numerical value (eg, 1500-2200) by the number of units/day received by the patient. This may be used as a crude approximation of the patient's insulin sensitivity as adjustments to individual components of the regimen are made. Each additional unit of insulin added to the corresponding insulin dose may be expected to lower the blood glucose by this amount.

To illustrate, in the "basal-bolus" regimen example presented above, the rule of 1800 would indicate an expected change of 27 mg/dL per unit of lispro insulin (the total daily insulin dose is 66 units; using the formula: 1800/66 = 27). A patient may be instructed to add additional insulin if the preprandial glucose is >125 mg/dL. For a prelunch glucose of 195 mg/dL, this would mean the patient would administer the scheduled 12 units of lispro along with an additional "correctional" 3 units for a total of 15 units prior to the meal. If correctional doses are required on a consistent basis, an adjustment of the patients diet and/or scheduled insulin dose may be necessary.

Dosage Forms

Injection, solution:

Humulin® R: 100 units/mL (10 mL) [vial]

Novolin® R: 100 units/mL (3 mL) [InnoLet® prefilled syringe or PenFill® prefilled cartridge]; (10 mL) [vial]

Injection, solution [concentrate] (Humulin® R U-500): 500 units/mL (20 mL vial)

♦ **Insulin Regular and Insulin NPH** *see* Insulin NPH and Insulin Regular *on page 914*

♦ **Intal®** *see* Cromolyn *on page 423*

♦ **Integrilin®** *see* Eptifibatide *on page 601*

♦ **α-2-interferon** *see* Interferon Alfa-2b *on page 920*

♦ **Interferon Alfa-2a (PEG Conjugate)** *see* Peginterferon Alfa-2a *on page 1322*

♦ **Interferon Alfa-2b and Ribavirin Combination Pack** *see* Interferon Alfa-2b and Ribavirin *on page 923*

♦ **Interferon Alfa-2b (PEG Conjugate)** *see* Peginterferon Alfa-2b *on page 1325*

Interferon Alfa-2a (in ter FEER on AL fa too aye)

U.S. Brand Names Roferon-A®

Canadian Brand Names Roferon-A®

Index Terms IFLrA; rIFN-A

Pharmacologic Category Interferon

Use

Patients >18 years of age: Hairy cell leukemia, AIDS-related Kaposi's sarcoma, chronic hepatitis C

Children and Adults: Chronic myelogenous leukemia (CML), Philadelphia chromosome positive, within 1 year of diagnosis (limited experience in children)

Unlabeled/Investigational Use Adjuvant therapy for malignant melanoma, AIDS-related thrombocytopenia, cutaneous ulcerations of Behçet's disease, brain tumors, metastatic ileal carcinoid tumors, cervical and colorectal cancers, genital warts, idiopathic mixed cryoglobulinemia, hemangioma, hepatitis D, hepatocellular carcinoma, idiopathic hypereosinophilic syndrome, mycosis fungoides, Sézary syndrome, low-grade non-Hodgkin's lymphoma, macular degeneration, multiple myeloma, renal cell carcinoma, basal and squamous cell skin cancer, essential thrombocythemia, cutaneous T-cell lymphoma

Restrictions An FDA-approved medication guide must be distributed when dispensing an outpatient prescription (new or refill) where this medication is to be used without direct supervision of a healthcare provider. Medication guides are available at http://www.fda.gov/cder/Offices/ODS/medication_guides.htm.

Pregnancy Risk Factor C

Pregnancy Implications Safety and efficacy for use during pregnancy have not been established. Interferon alpha has been shown to decrease serum estradiol and progesterone levels in humans. Menstrual irregularities and abortion have been reported in animals. Effective contraception is recommended during treatment.

Lactation Enters breast milk/contraindicated (AAP rates "compatible")

Medication Safety Issues

Sound-alike/look-alike issues:

Interferon alfa-2a may be confused with interferon alfa-2b

Roferon-A® may be confused with Rocephin®

Contraindications Hypersensitivity to alfa interferon, benzyl alcohol, or any component of the formulation; autoimmune hepatitis; hepatic decompensation (Child-Pugh class B or C)

Warnings/Precautions Use caution in patients with a history of depression. May cause severe psychiatric adverse events (psychosis, mania, depression, suicidal behavior/ideation) in patients with and without previous psychiatric symptoms; careful neuropsychiatric monitoring is required during therapy. Use with caution in patients with seizure disorders, brain metastases, or compromised CNS function. Higher doses in the elderly or in malignancies other than hairy cell leukemia may result in severe obtundation.

Use caution in patients with autoimmune diseases, pre-existing cardiac disease (ischemic or thromboembolic), arrhythmias, renal impairment (Cl_{cr} <50 mL/minute), mild hepatic impairment, or myelosuppression. Also use caution in patients receiving therapeutic immunosuppression. Use caution in patients with diabetes or pre-existing thyroid disease. Discontinue if persistent unexplained pulmonary infiltrates are noted. Gastrointestinal ischemia, ulcerative colitis and hemorrhage have been associated rarely with alpha interferons; some cases are severe and life-threatening. Ophthalmologic disorders have occurred in patients receiving alpha interferons; close monitoring is warranted.

[U.S. Boxed Warning]: Treatment should be discontinued in patients with worsening or persistently severe signs/symptoms of autoimmune, infectious, ischemic, or neuropsychiatric disorders (including depression and/or suicidal thoughts/behavior). Discontinue treatment if neutrophils <0.5 x 10^9/L or platelets <25 x 10^9/L. **Due to differences in dosage, patients should not change brands of interferons healthcare provider.** Injection solution contains benzyl alcohol; do not use in neonates or infants.

Adverse Reactions Note: A flu-like syndrome (fever, chills, tachycardia, malaise, myalgia, arthralgia, headache) occurs within 1-2 hours of administration; may last up to 24 hours and may be dose-limiting (symptoms in up to 92% of patients).

>10%:
Cardiovascular: Chest pain (4% to 11%), edema (11%), hypertension (11%)
Central nervous system: Psychiatric disturbances (including depression and suicidal behavior/ideation; reported incidence highly variable, generally >15%), fatigue (90%), headache (52%), dizziness (21%), irritability (15%), insomnia (14%), somnolence, lethargy, confusion, mental impairment, and motor weakness (most frequently seen at high doses [>100 million units], usually reverses within a few days); vertigo (19%); mental status changes (12%)
Dermatologic: Rash (usually maculopapular) on the trunk and extremities (7% to 18%), alopecia (19% to 22%), pruritus (13%), dry skin
Endocrine & metabolic: Hypocalcemia (10% to 51%), hyperglycemia (33% to 39%), transaminases increased (25% to 30%), alkaline phosphatase increased (48%)
Gastrointestinal: Loss of taste, anorexia (30% to 70%), nausea (28% to 53%), vomiting (10% to 30%, usually mild), diarrhea (22% to 34%, may be severe), taste change (13%), dry throat, xerostomia, abdominal cramps, abdominal pain
Hematologic: (often due to underlying disease): Myelosuppression; neutropenia (32% to 70%); thrombocytopenia (22% to 70%); anemia (24% to 65%, may be dose-limiting, usually seen only during the first 6 months of therapy)
Onset: 7-10 days
Nadir: 14 days, may be delayed 20-40 days in hairy cell leukemia
Recovery: 21 days
Hepatic: Elevation of AST (SGOT) (77% to 80%), LDH (47%), bilirubin (31%)
Local: Injection site reaction (29%)
Neuromuscular & skeletal: Weakness (may be severe at doses >20,000,000 units/day); arthralgia and myalgia (5% to 73%, usually during the first 72 hours of treatment); rigors
Renal: Proteinuria (15% to 25%)
Respiratory: Cough (27%), irritation of oropharynx (14%)
Miscellaneous: Flu-like syndrome (up to 92% of patients), diaphoresis (15%)

1% to 10%:
Cardiovascular: Hypotension (6%), supraventricular tachyarrhythmia, palpitation (<3%), acute MI (<1% to 1%)
Central nervous system: Confusion (10%), delirium
Dermatologic: Erythema (diffuse), urticaria
Endocrine & metabolic: Hyperphosphatemia (2%)
Gastrointestinal: Stomatitis, pancreatitis (<5%), flatulence, liver pain
Genitourinary: Impotence (6%), menstrual irregularities
Neuromuscular & skeletal: Leg cramps; peripheral neuropathy, paresthesia (7%), and numbness (4%) are more common in patients previously treated with vinca alkaloids or receiving concurrent vinblastine
Ocular: Conjunctivitis (4%)
Respiratory: Dyspnea (7.5%), epistaxis (4%), rhinitis (3%)
Miscellaneous: Antibody production to interferon (10%)

<1% (Limited to important or life-threatening): Angioedema, aplastic anemia, ascites, autoimmune reaction with worsening of liver disease, bronchospasm, bronchiolitis obliterans, cardiomyopathy, coagulopathy, coma, CHF, cutaneous eruptions, diffuse encephalopathy, hallucinations, hemolytic anemia, hyper-/hypothyroidism, hypertriglyceridemia, hyponatremia (SIADH), mania, gastrointestinal hemorrhage, hepatic failure, idiopathic thrombocytopenia purpura, interstitial nephritis, interstitial pneumonitis, ischemic colitis, lupus erythematosus syndrome, myositis, nephrotic syndrome, optic neuritis, pneumonitis, proteinuria, psychotic episodes, Raynaud's phenomenon, renal failure (acute), rhabdomyolysis, sarcoidosis, seizure, stroke, syncope, ulcerative colitis, urticaria, vasculitis, visual acuity decreased

Overdosage/Toxicology Symptoms include CNS depression, obtundation, flu-like symptoms, and myelosuppression. Treatment is supportive.

Drug Interactions
Cytochrome P450 Effect: Inhibits CYP1A2 (weak)
Increased Effect/Toxicity: Note: May exacerbate the toxicity of other agents with respect to CNS, myelotoxicity, or cardiotoxicity. Theophylline clearance has been reported to be decreased in hepatitis patients receiving interferon. Interferons may increase the adverse/toxic effects of ACE inhibitors, specifically the development of granulocytopenia. Agranulocytosis has been reported with concurrent use of clozapine (case report). Interferons may increase the anticoagulant effects of warfarin, and interferons may increase serum levels of zidovudine. Concurrent therapy with ribavirin may increase the risk of hemolytic anemia.
Decreased Effect: Prednisone may decrease the therapeutic effects of interferon alpha. A decreased response to erythropoietin has been reported (case reports) in patients receiving interferons. Interferon alpha may decrease the serum concentrations of melphalan (may or may not decrease toxicity of melphalan).

Stability Refrigerate (2°C to 8°C/36°F to 46°F); do not freeze. Do not shake. Reconstitute vial with the diluent provided, or SWFI, NS, or D$_5$W. Concentrations ≥3 x 10^6 units/mL are hypertonic. After reconstitution, the solution is stable for 24 hours at room temperature and for 1 month when refrigerated.

Mechanism of Action Following activation, multiple effects can be detected including induction of gene transcription. Inhibits cellular growth, alters the state of cellular differentiation, interferes with oncogene expression, alters cell surface antigen expression, increases phagocytic activity of macrophages, and augments cytotoxicity of lymphocytes for target cells
(Continued)

Interferon Alfa-2a (Continued)

Pharmacodynamics/Kinetics

Absorption: Filtered and absorbed at the renal tubule

Distribution: V_d: 0.223-0.748 L/kg

Metabolism: Primarily renal; filtered through glomeruli and undergoes rapid proteolytic degradation during tubular reabsorption

Bioavailability: I.M.: 83%; SubQ: 90%

Half-life elimination: I.V.: 3.7-8.5 hours (mean ~5 hours)

Time to peak, serum: I.M., SubQ: ~6-8 hours

Dosage Refer to individual protocols

Children (limited data):

Chronic myelogenous leukemia (CML): I.M.: 2.5-5 million units/m²/day; **Note:** In juveniles, higher dosages (30 million units/m²/day) have been associated with severe adverse events, including death

Adults:

Hairy cell leukemia: SubQ, I.M.: 3 million units/day for 16-24 weeks, then 3 million units 3 times/week for up to 6-24 months

Chronic myelogenous leukemia (CML): SubQ, I.M.: 9 million units/day, continue treatment until disease progression

AIDS-related Kaposi's sarcoma: SubQ, I.M.: 36 million units/day for 10-12 weeks, then 36 million units 3 times/week; to minimize adverse reactions, can use escalating dose (3-, 9-, then 18 million units each day for 3 days, then 36 million units daily thereafter).

Hepatitis C: SubQ, I.M.: 3 million units 3 times/week for 12 months

Dosage adjustment in renal impairment: Not removed by hemodialysis

Administration SubQ administration is suggested for those who are at risk for bleeding or are thrombocytopenic; rotate SubQ injection site; patient should be well hydrated

Monitoring Parameters Baseline ophthalmologic exam should be performed in all patients, with periodic reassessment in patients with impairment. Patients with thyroid dysfunction should be monitored by TSH levels at baseline and every 3 months during therapy.

Chronic hepatitis C: Monitor ALT (at baseline, after 2 weeks, and monthly thereafter) and HCV-RNA (particularly in first 3 months of therapy)

CML/hairy cell leukemia: Hematologic monitoring should be performed monthly

Dosage Forms Injection, solution [single-dose prefilled syringe; SubQ use only]: 3 million units/0.5 mL (0.5 mL); 6 million units/0.5 mL (0.5 mL); 9 million units/0.5 mL (0.5 mL) [contains benzyl alcohol]

Interferon Alfa-2b (in ter FEER on AL fa too bee)

U.S. Brand Names Intron® A

Canadian Brand Names Intron® A

Index Terms α-2-interferon; INF-alpha 2; rLFN-α2

Pharmacologic Category Interferon

Use

Patients ≥1 year of age: Chronic hepatitis B

Patients ≥18 years of age: Condyloma acuminata, chronic hepatitis C, hairy cell leukemia, malignant melanoma, AIDS-related Kaposi's sarcoma, follicular non-Hodgkin's lymphoma

Unlabeled/Investigational Use AIDS-related thrombocytopenia, cutaneous ulcerations of Behçet's disease, carcinoid syndrome, cervical cancer, lymphomatoid granulomatosis, genital herpes, hepatitis D, chronic myelogenous leukemia (CML), non-Hodgkin's lymphomas (other than follicular lymphoma, see approved use), polycythemia vera, medullary thyroid carcinoma, multiple myeloma, renal cell carcinoma, basal and squamous cell skin cancers, essential thrombocytopenia, thrombocytopenic purpura

Investigational: West Nile virus

Pregnancy Risk Factor C

Pregnancy Implications Safety and efficacy for use during pregnancy have not been established. Interferon alpha has been shown to decrease serum estradiol and progesterone levels in humans. Menstrual irregularities and abortion have been reported in animals. Effective contraception is recommended during treatment.

Lactation Enters breast milk/not recommended (AAP rates "compatible")

Medication Safety Issues

Sound-alike/look-alike issues:

Interferon alfa-2b may be confused with interferon alfa-2a

Contraindications Hypersensitivity to interferon alfa or any component of the formulation; decompensated liver disease; autoimmune hepatitis; history of autoimmune disease; immunosuppressed transplant patients

Warnings/Precautions Suicidal ideation or attempts may occur more frequently in pediatric patients when compared to adults. May cause severe psychiatric adverse events (psychosis, mania, depression, suicidal behavior/ideation) in patients with and without previous psychiatric symptoms, avoid use in severe psychiatric disorders or in patients with a history of depression; careful neuropsychiatric monitoring is required during therapy. Use with caution in patients with a history of seizures, brain metastases, multiple sclerosis, cardiac disease (ischemic or thromboembolic), arrhythmias, myelosuppression, hepatic impairment, or renal dysfunction (use is not recommended if $Cl_{cr}<50$ mL/minute). Use caution in patients with a history of pulmonary disease, coagulopathy, thyroid disease (monitor thyroid function), hypertension, or diabetes mellitus (particularly if prone to DKA). Caution in patients receiving drugs that may cause lactic acidosis (eg, nucleoside analogues).

Avoid use in patients with autoimmune disorders; worsening of psoriasis and/or development of autoimmune disorders has been associated with alpha interferons. Higher doses in elderly patients, or diseases other than hairy cell leukemia, may result in increased CNS toxicity. **[U.S. Boxed Warning]: Treatment should be discontinued in patients who develop severe pulmonary symptoms with chest x-ray changes, autoimmune disorders, worsening of hepatic function, psychiatric symptoms (including depression and/or suicidal**

thoughts/behaviors), ischemic and/or infectious disorders. Ophthalmologic disorders (including retinal hemorrhages, cotton wool spots and retinal artery or vein obstruction) have occurred in patients receiving alpha interferons. Hypertriglyceridemia has been reported (discontinue if severe).

Safety and efficacy in children <1 year of age have not been established. Do not treat patients with visceral AIDS-related Kaposi's sarcoma associated with rapidly-progressing or life-threatening disease. A transient increase in SGOT (>2x baseline) is common in patients treated with interferon alfa-2b for chronic hepatitis. Therapy generally may continue, however, functional indicators (albumin, prothrombin time, bilirubin) should be monitored at 2-week intervals. **Due to differences in dosage, patients should not change brands of interferons without the concurrence of their healthcare provider.**

May cause bone marrow suppression, including very rarely, aplastic anemia. Hemolytic anemia (hemoglobin <10 g/dL) was observed in up to 10% of treated patients in clinical trials when combined with ribavirin; anemia occurred within 1-2 weeks of initiation of therapy.

Adverse Reactions Note: In a majority of patients, a flu-like syndrome (fever, chills, tachycardia, malaise, myalgia, headache), occurs within 1-2 hours of administration; may last up to 24 hours and may be dose-limiting.

>10%:

Cardiovascular: Chest pain (2% to 28%)

Central nervous system: Fatigue (8% to 96%), headache (21% to 62%), fever (34% to 94%), depression (4% to 40%), somnolence (1% to 33%), irritability (1% to 22%), paresthesia (1% to 21%, more common in patients previously treated with vinca alkaloids or receiving concurrent vinblastine), dizziness (7% to 23%), confusion (1% to 12%), malaise (3% to 14%), pain (3% to 15%), insomnia (1% to 12%), impaired concentration (1% to 14%, usually reverses within a few days), amnesia (1% to 14%), chills (45% to 54%)

Dermatologic: Alopecia (8% to 38%), rash (usually maculopapular) on the trunk and extremities (1% to 25%), pruritus (3% to 11%), dry skin (1% to 10%)

Endocrine & metabolic: Hypocalcemia (10% to 51%), hyperglycemia (33% to 39%), amenorrhea (up to 12% in lymphoma), alkaline phosphatase increased (48%)

Gastrointestinal: Anorexia (1% to 69%), nausea (19% to 66%), vomiting (2% to 32%, usually mild), diarrhea (2% to 45%, may be severe), taste change (2% to 24%), xerostomia (1% to 28%), abdominal pain (2% to 23%), gingivitis (2% to 14%), constipation (1% to 14%)

Hematologic: Myelosuppression; neutropenia (30% to 66%); thrombocytopenia (5% to 15%); anemia (15% to 32%, may be dose-limiting, usually seen only during the first 6 months of therapy)

Onset: 7-10 days

Nadir: 14 days, may be delayed 20-40 days in hairy cell leukemia

Recovery: 21 days

Hepatic: Right upper quadrant pain (15% in hepatitis C), transaminases increased (increased SGOT in up to 63%)

Local: Injection site reaction (1% to 20%)

Neuromuscular & skeletal: Weakness (5% to 63%) may be severe at doses >20,000,000 units/day; mild arthralgia and myalgia (5% to 75% - usually during the first 72 hours of treatment), rigors (2% to 42%), back pain (1% to 19%), musculoskeletal pain (1% to 21%), paresthesia (1% to 21%)

Renal: Urinary tract infection (up to 5% in hepatitis C)

Respiratory: Dyspnea (1% to 34%), cough (1% to 31%), pharyngitis (1% to 31%),

Miscellaneous: Loss of smell, flu-like syndrome (5% to 79%), diaphoresis (2% to 21%)

5% to 10%:

Cardiovascular: Hypertension (9% in hepatitis C)

Central nervous system: Anxiety (1% to 9%), nervousness (1% to 3%), vertigo (up to 8% in lymphoma)

Dermatologic: Dermatitis (1% to 8%)

Endocrine & metabolic: Decreased libido (1% to 5%)

Gastrointestinal: Loose stools (1% to 21%), dyspepsia (2% to 8%)

Neuromuscular & skeletal: Hypoesthesia (1% to 10%)

Respiratory: Nasal congestion (1% to 10%)

<5% (Limited to important or life-threatening): Acute hypersensitivity reactions, allergic reactions, angina, aphasia, arrhythmia, ataxia, atrial fibrillation, Bell's palsy, bronchospasm, cardiomyopathy, CHF, coma, depression, epidermal necrolysis, extrapyramidal disorder, gastrointestinal hemorrhage, gingival hyperplasia, granulocytopenia, hallucinations, hemolytic anemia, hemoptysis, hepatic encephalopathy (rare), hepatic failure (rare), hepatotoxic reaction, hypoventilation, jaundice, lupus erythematosus, mania, MI, nephrotic syndrome, pancreatitis, polyarteritis nodosa, psychosis, pulmonary embolism, pulmonary fibrosis, Raynaud's phenomenon, renal failure, seizure, stroke, suicidal ideation, suicide attempt, syncope, tendonitis, thrombocytopenic purpura, thrombosis, vasculitis

Overdosage/Toxicology Symptoms include CNS depression, obtundation, flu-like symptoms, and myelosuppression. Treatment is supportive.

Drug Interactions

Cytochrome P450 Effect: Inhibits CYP1A2 (weak)

Increased Effect/Toxicity: Theophylline clearance has been reported to be decreased in hepatitis patients receiving interferon. Interferons may increase the adverse/toxic effects of ACE inhibitors, specifically the development of granulocytopenia. Agranulocytosis has been reported with concurrent use of clozapine (case report). Interferons may increase the anticoagulant effects of warfarin, and interferons may increase serum levels of zidovudine. Concurrent therapy with ribavirin may increase the risk of hemolytic anemia.

Stability Store powder and solution for injection (vials and pens) under refrigeration (2°C to 8°C). The manufacturer recommends reconstituting vial with the diluent provided (SWFI). To prepare solution for infusion, further dilute appropriate dose in NS 100 mL. Final concentration should not be <10 million units/100 mL.

(Continued)

Interferon Alfa-2b *(Continued)*

Powder for injection: Following reconstitution, should be used immediately, but may be stored under refrigeration for up to 24 hours.

Prefilled pens: After first use, discard unused portion after 1 month.

Mechanism of Action Following activation, multiple effects can be detected including induction of gene transcription. Inhibits cellular growth, alters the state of cellular differentiation, interferes with oncogene expression, alters cell surface antigen expression, increases phagocytic activity of macrophages, and augments cytotoxicity of lymphocytes for target cells

Pharmacodynamics/Kinetics

Distribution: V_d: 31 L; but has been noted to be much greater (370-720 L) in leukemia patients receiving continuous infusion IFN; IFN does not penetrate the CSF

Metabolism: Primarily renal

Bioavailability: I.M.: 83%; SubQ: 90%

Half-life elimination: I.M., I.V.: 2 hours; SubQ: 3 hours

Time to peak, serum: I.M., SubQ: ~3-12 hours

Dosage Refer to individual protocols

Children 1-17 years: Chronic hepatitis B: SubQ: 3 million units/m^2 3 times/week for 1 week; then 6 million units/m^2 3 times/week; maximum: 10 million units 3 times/week; total duration of therapy 16-24 weeks

Adults:

Hairy cell leukemia: I.M., SubQ: 2 million units/m^2 3 times/week for 2-6 months

Lymphoma (follicular): SubQ: 5 million units 3 times/week for up to 18 months

Malignant melanoma: 20 million units/m^2 I.V. for 5 consecutive days per week for 4 weeks, then 10 million units/m^2 SubQ 3 times/week for 48 weeks

AIDS-related Kaposi's sarcoma: I.M., SubQ: 30 million units/m^2 3 times/week

Chronic hepatitis B: I.M., SubQ: 5 million units/day or 10 million units 3 times/week for 16 weeks

Chronic hepatitis C: I.M., SubQ: 3 million units 3 times/week for 16 weeks. In patients with normalization of ALT at 16 weeks, continue treatment for 18-24 months; consider discontinuation if normalization does not occur at 16 weeks. **Note:** May be used in combination therapy with ribavirin in previously untreated patients or in patients who relapse following alpha interferon therapy.

Condyloma acuminata: Intralesionally: 1 million units/lesion (maximum: 5 lesions/treatment) 3 times/week (on alternate days) for 3 weeks; may administer a second course at 12-16 weeks

Dosage adjustment in renal impairment: Combination therapy with ribavirin (hepatitis C) should not be used in patients with reduced renal function (Cl$_{cr}$ <50 mL/minute).

Not removed by peritoneal or hemodialysis

Dosage adjustment for toxicity: Manufacturer-recommended adjustments, listed according to indication:

Lymphoma (follicular):

Severe toxicity (neutrophils <1000 cells/mm^3 or platelets <50,000 cells/mm^3): Reduce dose by 50% or temporarily discontinue

AST/ALT >5 times ULN: Permanently discontinue

Hairy cell leukemia:

Severe toxicity: Reduce dose by 50% or temporarily discontinue; permanently discontinue if persistent or recurrent severe toxicity is noted

Hepatitis B or C:

WBC <1500 cells/mm^3, granulocytes <750 cells/mm^3, or platelet count <50,000 cells/mm^3: Reduce dose by 50%

WBC <1000 cells/mm^3, granulocytes <500 cells/mm^3, or platelet count <25,000 cells/mm^3: Permanently discontinue

Kaposi sarcoma: Severe toxicity: Reduce dose by 50% or temporarily discontinue

Malignant melanoma:

Severe toxicity (neutrophils <500 cells/mm^3 or AST/ALT >5 times ULN): Reduce dose by 50% or temporarily discontinue

Neutrophils <250 cells/mm^3 or AST/ALT >10 times ULN: Permanently discontinue

Administration

I.M.: Administer in evening (if possible)

I.V.: Infuse over ~20 minutes

SubQ: Suggested for those who are at risk for bleeding or are thrombocytopenic. Rotate SubQ injection site. Administer in evening (if possible). Patient should be well hydrated. Reconstitute with recommended amount of SWFI and agitate gently; do not shake. **Note:** Different vial strengths require different amounts of diluent. Not every dosage form is appropriate for every indication; refer to manufacturer's labeling.

Monitoring Parameters Baseline chest x-ray, ECG, CBC with differential, liver function tests, electrolytes, thyroid function tests, platelets, weight; patients with pre-existing cardiac abnormalities, or in advanced stages of cancer should have ECGs taken before and during treatment.

Dosage Forms

Injection, powder for reconstitution: 10 million units; 18 million units; 50 million units [contains human albumin]

Injection, solution [multidose prefilled pen]:

Delivers 3 million units/0.2 mL (1.5 mL) [delivers 6 doses; 18 million units]

Delivers 5 million units/0.2 mL (1.5 mL) [delivers 6 doses; 30 million units]

Delivers 10 million units/0.2 mL (1.5 mL) [delivers 6 doses; 60 million units]

Injection, solution [multidose vial]: 6 million units/mL (3 mL); 10 million units/mL (2.5 mL)

Injection, solution [single-dose vial]: 10 million units/ mL (1 mL)

See also Interferon Alfa-2b and Ribavirin monograph.

Interferon Alfa-2b and Ribavirin
(in ter FEER on AL fa too bee & rye ba VYE rin)

U.S. Brand Names Rebetron®

Index Terms Interferon Alfa-2b and Ribavirin Combination Pack; Ribavirin and Interferon Alfa-2b Combination Pack

Pharmacologic Category Antiviral Agent; Interferon

Use Combination therapy for the treatment of chronic hepatitis C in patients with compensated liver disease previously untreated with alpha interferon or who have relapsed after alpha interferon therapy

Restrictions An FDA-approved medication guide must be distributed when dispensing an outpatient prescription (new or refill) for treatment of hepatitis C where this medication is to be used without direct supervision of a healthcare provider. Medication guides are available at http://www.fda.gov/cder/Offices/ODS/medication_guides.htm.

Pregnancy Risk Factor X

Dosage

Children ≥3 years: Chronic hepatitis C: **Note:** Duration of therapy: genotype 1: 48 weeks; genotype 2 or 3: 24 weeks. Discontinue treatment in any patient if HCV-RNA is not below the limits of detection of the assay after 24 weeks of therapy. Combination therapy:

Intron® A: SubQ:

25-61 kg: 3 million int. units/m² 3 times/week

>61 kg: Refer to Adults dosing

Rebetol®: Oral: **Note:** Oral solution should be used in children 3-5 years of age, children ≤25 kg, or those unable to swallow capsules.

Capsule/solution: 15 mg/kg/day in 2 divided doses (morning and evening)

Capsule dosing recommendations:

25-36 kg: 400 mg/day (200 mg morning and evening)

37-49 kg: 600 mg/day (200 mg in the morning and two 200 mg capsules in the evening)

50-61 kg: 800 mg/day (two 200 mg capsules morning and evening)

>61 kg: Refer to Adults dosing

Adults: Chronic hepatitis C: Recommended dosage of combination therapy:

Intron® A: SubQ: 3 million int. units 3 times/week **and**

Rebetol® capsule: Oral:

≤75 kg (165 lb): 1000 mg/day (two 200 mg capsules in the morning and three 200 mg capsules in the evening)

>75 kg: 1200 mg/day (three 200 mg capsules in the morning and three 200 mg capsules in the evening)

Treatment duration recommendations:

Following relapse after alpha interferon monotherapy: 24 weeks

Previously untreated: 24-48 weeks (individualized based on response, tolerance, and baseline characteristics)

Consider discontinuing therapy in any patient not achieving HCV-RNA below the limit of assay detection by 24 weeks.

Dosing adjustment for toxicity: Note: Recommendations (per manufacturer labeling):

Anemia (RBC depression):

Patient **without** cardiac history:

Hemoglobin <10 g/dL:

Children: Decrease dose by ½

Adults: Decrease dose to 600 mg/day

Hemoglobin <8.5 g/dL: Permanently discontinue treatment

Patient **with** cardiac history:

Hemoglobin has ≥2 g/dL decrease during any 4-week period of treatment:

Children: Decrease ribavirin dose by ½ **and** decrease interferon alfa-2b to 1.5 million int. units 3 times/week

Adults: Decrease dose to ribavirin to 600 mg/day **and** decrease interferon-alfa 2b dose to 1.5 million int. units 3 times/week

Hemoglobin <12 g/dL after 4 weeks of reduced dose: Permanently discontinue treatment

WBC, neutrophil, or platelet depression:

WBC <1500 cells/mm³, neutrophils <750 cells/mm³, or platelet count <50,000 cells/mm³ (<80,000 cells/ mm³ in children): Reduce interferon alfa-2b dose to 1.5 million int. units 3 times/week (50% reduction)

WBC <1000 cells/mm³, neutrophils <500 cells/mm³, or platelet count <25,000 cells/mm³ (<50,000 cells/mm³ in children): Permanently discontinue therapy

Dosage adjustment in renal impairment: Patients with Cl_cr <50 mL/minutes should not receive ribavirin.

Additional Information Complete prescribing information for this medication should be consulted for additional detail.

Dosage Forms Combination package:

For patients ≤75 kg [contains single-dose vials]:

Injection, solution: Interferon alfa-2b (Intron® A): 3 million int. units/0.5 mL (0.5 mL) [6 vials (3 million int. units/vial), 6 syringes, and alcohol swabs]

Capsule: Ribavirin (Rebetol®): 200 mg (70s)

For patients ≤75 kg [contains multidose vials]:

Injection, solution: Interferon alfa-2b (Intron® A): 3 million int. units/0.5 mL (3.8 mL) [1 multidose vial (18 million int. units/vial), 6 syringes, and alcohol swabs]

Capsule: Ribavirin (Rebetol®): 200 mg (70s)

For patients ≤75 kg [contains multidose pen]:

Injection, solution: Interferon alfa-2b (Intron® A): 3 million int. units/0.2 mL (1.5 mL) [1 multidose pen (18 million int. units/pen), 6 needles, and alcohol swabs]

Capsule: Ribavirin (Rebetol®): 200 mg (70s)

(Continued)

Interferon Alfa-2b and Ribavirin *(Continued)*

For patients >75 kg [contains single-dose vials]:
  Injection, solution: Interferon alfa-2b (Intron® A): 3 million int. units/0.5 mL (0.5 mL) [6 vials (3 million int. units/vial), 6 syringes, and alcohol swabs]
  Capsule: Ribavirin (Rebetol®): 200 mg (84s)

For patients >75 kg [contains multidose vials]:
  Injection, solution: Interferon alfa-2b (Intron® A): 3 million int. units/0.5 mL (3.8 mL) [1 multidose vial (18 million int. units/vial), 6 syringes, and alcohol swabs]
  Capsule: Ribavirin (Rebetol®): 200 mg (84s)

For patients >75 kg [contains multidose pen]:
  Injection, solution: Interferon alfa-2b (Intron® A): 3 million int. units/0.2 mL (1.5 mL) [1 multidose pen (18 million int. units/pen), 6 needles, and alcohol swabs]
  Capsule: Ribavirin (Rebetol®): 200 mg (84s)

For Rebetol® dose reduction [contains single-dose vials]:
  Injection, solution: Interferon alfa-2b (Intron® A): 3 million int. units/0.5 mL (0.5 mL) [6 vials (3 million int. units/vial), 6 syringes, and alcohol swabs]
  Capsule: Ribavirin (Rebetol®): 200 mg (42s)

For Rebetol® dose reduction [contains multidose vials]:
  Injection, solution: Interferon alfa-2b (Intron® A): 3 million int. units/0.5 mL (3.8 mL) [1 multidose vial (18 million int. units/vial), 6 syringes, and alcohol swabs]
  Capsule: Ribavirin (Rebetol®): 200 mg (42s)

For Rebetol® dose reduction [contains multidose pen]:
  Injection, solution: Interferon alfa-2b (Intron® A): 3 million int. units/0.2 mL (1.5 mL) [1 multidose pen (18 million int. units/pen), 6 needles, and alcohol swabs]
  Capsule: Ribavirin (Rebetol®): 200 mg (42s)

Interferon Alfacon-1 (in ter FEER on AL fa con one)

U.S. Brand Names Infergen®
Pharmacologic Category Interferon
Use Treatment of chronic hepatitis C virus (HCV) infection in patients ≥18 years of age with compensated liver disease and anti-HCV serum antibodies or HCV RNA.
Restrictions An FDA-approved medication guide must be distributed when dispensing an outpatient prescription (new or refill) where this medication is to be used without direct supervision of a healthcare provider. Medication guides are available at http://www.fda.gov/cder/Offices/ODS/medication_guides.htm.
Pregnancy Risk Factor C
Pregnancy Implications There have been no well-controlled studies in pregnant women. Animal studies have shown embryolethal or abortifacient effects. Males and females who are being treated with interferon alfacon-1 should use effective contraception.
Lactation Excretion in breast milk unknown/use caution (AAP rates "compatible")
Contraindications Hypersensitivity to interferon alfacon-1 or any component of the formulation, other alpha interferons, or *E. coli*-derived products
Warnings/Precautions Severe psychiatric adverse effects, including depression, suicidal ideation, and suicide attempt, may occur. Avoid use in severe psychiatric disorders. Use with caution in patients with a history of depression. Use with caution in patients with prior cardiac disease (ischemic or thromboembolic), arrhythmias, patients who are chronically immunosuppressed, and patients with endocrine disorders. Do not use in patients with hepatic decompensation. Ophthalmologic disorders (including retinal hemorrhages, cotton wool spots and retinal artery or vein obstruction) have occurred in patients using other alpha interferons. Prior to start of therapy, visual exams are recommended for patients with diabetes mellitus or hypertension. **[U.S. Boxed Warning]: Treatment should be discontinued in patients with worsening or persistently severe signs/symptoms of autoimmune, infectious, ischemic (including radiographic changes or worsening hepatic function), or neuropsychiatric disorders (including depression and/or suicidal thoughts/behavior).** Use caution in patients with autoimmune disorders; type-1 interferon therapy has been reported to exacerbate autoimmune diseases. Do not use interferon alfacon-1 in patients with autoimmune hepatitis. Use caution in patients with low peripheral blood counts or myelosuppression, including concurrent use of myelosuppressive therapy. Safety and efficacy have not been determined for patients <18 years of age.
Adverse Reactions Adverse reactions reported using 9 mcg/dose interferon alfacon-1 3 times/week. Reactions listed were reported in ≥5% of patients treated.

>10%:
  Central nervous system: Headache (82%), fatigue (69%), fever (61%), insomnia (39%), nervousness (31%), depression (26%), dizziness (22%), anxiety (19%), noncardiac chest pain (13%), emotional lability (12%), malaise (11%)
  Dermatologic: Alopecia (14%), pruritus (14%), rash (13%)
  Endocrine & metabolic: Hot flashes (13%)
  Gastrointestinal: Abdominal pain (41%), nausea (40%), diarrhea (29%), anorexia (24%), dyspepsia (21%), vomiting (12%)
  Hematologic: Granulocytopenia (23%), thrombocytopenia (19%), leukopenia (15%)
  Local: Injection site erythema (23%)
  Neuromuscular & skeletal: Myalgia (58%), body pain (54%), arthralgia (51%), back pain (42%), limb pain (26%), neck pain (14%), skeletal pain (14%), paresthesia (13%)
  Respiratory: Pharyngitis (34%), upper respiratory tract infection (31%), cough (22%), sinusitis (17%), rhinitis (13%), respiratory tract congestion (12%)
  Miscellaneous: Flu-like syndrome (15%), diaphoresis increased (12%)
1% to 10%:
  Cardiovascular: Peripheral edema (9%), hypertension (5%), tachycardia (4%), palpitation (3%)
  Central nervous system: Amnesia (10%), hypoesthesia (10%), abnormal thinking (8%), agitation (6%), confusion (4%), somnolence (4%)
  Dermatologic: Bruising (6%), erythema (6%), dry skin (6%), wound (4%)

Endocrine & metabolic: Thyroid test abnormalities (9%), dysmenorrhea (9%), increased triglycerides (6%), menstrual disorder (6%), decreased libido (5%), hypothyroidism (4%)

Gastrointestinal: Constipation (9%), flatulence (8%), toothache (7%), decreased salivation (6%), hemorrhoids (6%), weight loss (5%), taste perversion (3%)

Genitourinary: Vaginitis (8%), genital moniliasis (2%)

Hepatic: Hepatomegaly (5%), liver tenderness (5%), increased prothrombin time (3%)

Local: Injection site pain (9%), access pain (8%), injection site bruising (6%)

Neuromuscular & skeletal: Weakness (9%), hypertonia (7%), musculoskeletal disorder (4%)

Ocular: Conjunctivitis (8%), eye pain (5%), vision abnormalities (3%)

Otic: Tinnitus (6%), earache (5%), otitis (2%)

Respiratory: Upper respiratory tract congestion (10%), epistaxis (8%), dyspnea (7%), bronchitis (6%)

Miscellaneous: Allergic reaction (7%), lymphadenopathy (6%), lymphocytosis (5%), infection (3%)

Flu-like symptoms (which included headache, fatigue, fever, myalgia, rigors, arthralgia, and increased diaphoresis) were the most commonly reported adverse reaction. This was reported separately from flu-like syndrome. Most patients were treated symptomatically.

Other adverse reactions associated with interferon therapy include arrhythmia, autoimmune disorders, chest pain, hepatotoxic reactions, lupus erythematosus, MI, neuropsychiatric disorders (including suicidal thoughts/behavior), pneumonia, pneumonitis, severe hypersensitivity reactions (rare), vasculitis

Overdosage/Toxicology One overdose has been reported. A patient received ten times the prescribed dose (150 mcg) for 3 days. In addition to an increase in anorexia, chills, fever, and myalgia, there was also an increase in ALT, AST, and LDH. Laboratory values reportedly returned to baseline within 30 days.

Drug Interactions

Increased Effect/Toxicity: Cimetidine may augment the antitumor effects of interferon in melanoma. Theophylline clearance has been reported to be decreased in hepatitis patients receiving interferon. Vinblastine enhances interferon toxicity in several patients; increased incidence of paresthesia has also been noted. Interferons may increase the adverse/toxic effects of ACE inhibitors, specifically the development of granulocytopenia. Agranulocytosis has been reported with concurrent use of clozapine (case report). Interferons may increase the anticoagulant effects of warfarin, and interferons may increase serum levels of zidovudine.

Decreased Effect: Prednisone may decrease the therapeutic effects of Interferon alpha. A decreased response to erythropoietin has been reported (case reports) in patients receiving interferons. Interferon alpha may decrease the serum concentrations of melphalan (may or may not decrease toxicity of melphalan).

Stability Store in refrigerator 2°C to 8°C (36°F to 46°F); do not freeze. Avoid exposure to direct sunlight. Do not shake vigorously.

Mechanism of Action Alpha interferons are a family of proteins, produced by nucleated cells, that have antiviral, antiproliferative, and immune-regulating activity. There are at least 25 alpha interferons identified. Interferons interact with cells through high affinity cell surface receptors. Following activation, multiple effects can be detected. Interferons induce gene transcription, inhibit cellular growth, alter the state of cellular differentiation, interfere with oncogene expression, alter cell surface antigen expression, increase phagocytic activity of macrophages, and augment cytotoxicity of lymphocytes for target cells. Although all alpha interferons share similar properties, the actual biological effects vary between subtypes.

Pharmacodynamics/Kinetics Pharmacokinetic studies have not been conducted on patients with chronic hepatitis C.

Time to peak: Healthy volunteers: 24-36 hours

Dosage Adults ≥18 years: SubQ:

Chronic HCV infection: 9 mcg 3 times/week for 24 weeks; allow 48 hours between doses

Patients who have previously tolerated interferon therapy but did not respond or relapsed: 15 mcg 3 times/week for 6 months

Dose reduction for toxicity: Dose should be held in patients who experience a severe adverse reaction, and treatment should be stopped or decreased if the reaction does not become tolerable.

Doses were reduced from 9 mcg to 7.5 mcg in the pivotal study.

For patients receiving 15 mcg/dose, doses were reduced in 3 mcg increments. Efficacy is decreased with doses <7.5 mcg

Dosage adjustment in renal impairment: No information available.

Dosage adjustment in hepatic impairment: Avoid use in decompensated hepatic disease.

Elderly: No information available.

Administration Interferon alfacon-1 is administered by SubQ injection, 3 times/week, with at least 48 hours between doses

Monitoring Parameters

Hemoglobin and hematocrit; white blood cell count; platelets; triglycerides; thyroid function. Laboratory tests should be taken 2 weeks prior to therapy, after therapy has begun, and periodically during treatment. HCV RNA, ALT to determine success/response to therapy.

The following guidelines were used during the clinical studies as acceptable baseline values:

Platelet count ≥75 x 10^9/L

Hemoglobin ≥100 g/L

ANC ≥1500 x 10^6/L

S_{cr} <180 µmol/L (<2 mg/dL) or Cl_{cr} >0.83 mL/second (>50 mL/minute)

Serum albumin ≥25 g/L

Bilirubin WNL

TSH and T_4 WNL

Patients should also be monitored for signs of depression. Patients with pre-existing diabetes mellitus or hypertension should have an ophthalmologic exam prior to treatment.

Dosage Forms Injection, solution [preservative free]: 30 mcg/mL (0.3 mL, 0.5 mL)

Interferon Alfa-n3 (in ter FEER on AL fa en three)

U.S. Brand Names Alferon® N
Canadian Brand Names Alferon® N
Pharmacologic Category Interferon
Use Patients ≥18 years of age: Intralesional treatment of refractory or recurring genital or venereal warts (condylomata acuminata)
Pregnancy Risk Factor C
Pregnancy Implications Safety and efficacy for use during pregnancy have not been established. Interferon alpha has been shown to decrease serum estradiol and progesterone levels in humans. Menstrual irregularities and abortion have been reported in animals. Effective contraception is recommended during treatment.
Lactation Excretion in breast milk unknown/not recommended
Medication Safety Issues
Sound-alike/look-alike issues:
Alferon® may be confused with Alkeran®
Contraindications Hypersensitivity to alpha interferon or any component of the formulation; anaphylactic sensitivity to mouse immunoglobulin, egg protein, or neomycin
Warnings/Precautions Use with caution in patients with pre-existing cardiac disease, including unstable angina, uncontrolled CHF, or arrhythmias; severe pulmonary disease; diabetes with ketoacidosis; coagulation disorders (such as thrombophlebitis, pulmonary embolism, hemophilia); severe myelosuppression; or seizure disorder. **Due to differences in dosage, patients should not change brands of interferons.** Safety and efficacy in patients <18 years of age have not been not established.
Adverse Reactions Flu-like reactions, consisting of headache, fever, and/or myalgia, were reported in 30% of patients, and abated with repeated dosing.

>10%:
Central nervous system: Chills, fatigue, fever, headache
Hematologic: Decreased WBC
Neuromuscular & skeletal: Myalgia
Miscellaneous: Flu-like syndrome

1% to 10%:
Central nervous system: Depression, dizziness, insomnia, malaise, thirst
Dermatologic: Pruritus
Gastrointestinal: Diarrhea, dyspepsia, taste disturbance, tongue hyperesthesia, nausea, vomiting
Genitourinary: Groin lymph node swelling
Neuromuscular & skeletal: Arthralgia, back pain, cramps, paresthesia
Ocular: Visual disturbance
Respiratory: Nose bleed, pharyngitis, rhinitis
Miscellaneous: Increased sweating, vasovagal reaction

<1% (Limited to important or life-threatening): Photosensitivity. Rare adverse reactions reported with other alfa-interferons include autoimmune disorders, depression, ophthalmic disorders, suicide.
Overdosage/Toxicology Symptoms include CNS depression, obtundation, flu-like symptoms, and myelosuppression. Treatment is supportive.
Drug Interactions
Increased Effect/Toxicity: Interferons may increase the adverse/toxic effects of ACE inhibitors, specifically the development of granulocytopenia. Risk: Monitor A case report of agranulocytosis has been reported with concurrent use of clozapine. Case reports of decreased hematopoietic effect with erythropoietin. Interferon alpha may decrease the P450 isoenzyme metabolism of theophylline. Interferons may increase the anticoagulant effects of warfarin. Interferons may decrease the metabolism of zidovudine.
Decreased Effect: Interferon alpha may decrease the serum concentrations of melphalan; this may or may not decrease the potential toxicity of melphalan. Prednisone may decrease the therapeutic effects of Interferon alpha.
Stability Store solution at 2°C to 8°C (36°F to 46°F); do not freeze or shake. solution
Mechanism of Action Interferons interact with cells through high affinity cell surface receptors. Following activation, multiple effects can be detected including induction of gene transcription. Inhibits cellular growth, alters the state of cellular differentiation, interferes with oncogene expression, alters cell surface antigen expression, increases phagocytic activity of macrophages, and augments cytotoxicity of lymphocytes for target cells
Dosage Adults: Inject 250,000 units (0.05 mL) in each wart twice weekly for a maximum of 8 weeks; therapy should not be repeated for at least 3 months after the initial 8-week course of therapy
Administration Inject into base of wart with a small 30-gauge needle
Dosage Forms Injection, solution: 5 million int. units (1 mL) [contains albumin]

Interferon Beta-1a (in ter FEER on BAY ta won aye)

U.S. Brand Names Avonex®; Rebif®
Canadian Brand Names Avonex®; Rebif®
Index Terms rIFN beta-1a
Pharmacologic Category Interferon
Use Treatment of relapsing forms of multiple sclerosis (MS)
Restrictions An FDA-approved medication guide must be distributed when dispensing an outpatient prescription (new or refill) where this medication is to be used without direct supervision of a healthcare provider. Medication guides are available at http://www.fda.gov/cder/Offices/ODS/medication_guides.htm.
Pregnancy Risk Factor C

Pregnancy Implications There are no adequate and well-controlled studies in pregnant women. Consideration should be given to discontinue treatment if a woman becomes pregnant, or plans to become pregnant during therapy. A dose-related abortifacient activity was reported in Rhesus monkeys.

Healthcare providers are encouraged to register pregnant women receiving Rebif® during pregnancy online at www.rebifpregnancyregistry.com or by telephone at MS LifeLines 1-877-44-REBIF. A registry has been established for women who become pregnant while receiving Avonex®. Women may be enrolled in the registry by calling 1-800-456-2255.

Lactation Excretion in breast milk unknown/not recommended

Medication Safety Issues
Sound-alike/look-alike issues:
Avonex® may be confused with Avelox®

Contraindications Hypersensitivity to natural or recombinant interferons, human albumin, or any other component of the formulation

Warnings/Precautions Interferons have been associated with severe psychiatric adverse events (psychosis, mania, depression, suicidal behavior/ideation) in patients with and without previous psychiatric symptoms, avoid use in severe psychiatric disorders and use caution in patients with a history of depression; patients exhibiting depressive symptoms should be closely monitored and discontinuation of therapy should be considered.

Allergic reactions, including anaphylaxis, have been reported. Caution should be used in patients with hepatic impairment or in those who abuse alcohol. Rare cases of severe hepatic injury, including hepatic failure, have been reported in patients receiving interferon beta-1a; risk may be increased by ethanol use or concurrent therapy with hepatotoxic drugs. Treatment should be suspended if jaundice or symptoms of hepatic dysfunction occur. Hematologic effects, including pancytopenia (rare) and thrombocytopenia, have been reported. Associated with a high incidence of flu-like adverse effects; use of analgesics and/or antipyretics on treatment days may be helpful. Use caution in patients with pre-existing cardiovascular disease, pulmonary disease, seizure disorders, myelosuppression, or renal impairment. Safety and efficacy in patients <18 years of age have not been established.

Adverse Reactions
>10%:
Central nervous system: Headache (Avonex® 58%; Rebif® 65% to 70%), fatigue (Rebif® 33% to 41%), fever (Avonex® 20%; Rebif® 25% to 28%), pain (Avonex® 23%), chills (Avonex® 19%), depression (Avonex® 18%), dizziness (Avonex® 14%)
Gastrointestinal: Nausea (Avonex® 23%), abdominal pain (Avonex® 8%; Rebif® 20% to 22%)
Genitourinary: Urinary tract infection (Avonex® 17%)
Hematologic: Leukopenia (Rebif® 28% to 36%)
Hepatic: ALT increased (Rebif® 20% to 27%), AST increased (Rebif® 10% to 17%)
Local: Injection site reaction (Avonex® 3%; Rebif® 89% to 92%)
Neuromuscular & skeletal: Myalgia (Avonex® 29%; Rebif® 25%), back pain (Rebif® 23% to 25%), weakness (Avonex® 24%), skeletal pain (Rebif® 10% to 15%), rigors (Rebif® 6% to 13%)
Ocular: Vision abnormal (Rebif® 7% to 13%)
Respiratory: Sinusitis (Avonex® 14%), upper respiratory tract infection (Avonex® 14%)
Miscellaneous: Flu-like syndrome (Avonex® 49%; Rebif® 56% to 59%), neutralizing antibodies (significance not known; Avonex® 5%; Rebif® 24%), lymphadenopathy (Rebif® 11% to 12%)
1% to 10% (reported with one or both products):
Cardiovascular: Chest pain, vasodilation
Central nervous system: Convulsions, malaise, migraine, somnolence
Dermatologic: Alopecia, erythematous rash, maculopapular rash, urticaria
Endocrine & metabolic: Thyroid disorder
Gastrointestinal: Toothache, xerostomia
Genitourinary: Micturition frequency, urinary incontinence
Hematologic: Anemia, thrombocytopenia
Hepatic: Bilirubinemia, hepatic function abnormal
Local: Injection site bruising, injection site inflammation, injection site necrosis, injection site pain
Neuromuscular & skeletal: Arthralgia, coordination abnormal, hypertonia
Ocular: Eye disorder, xerophthalmia
Respiratory: Bronchitis
Miscellaneous: Infection
<1% (Limited to important and life-threatening): Anaphylaxis, autoimmune hepatitis, cardiomyopathy, CHF, hepatic failure, hepatitis, idiopathic thrombocytopenia, menorrhagia, metrorrhagia, pancytopenia, psychiatric disorders (new or worsening), transaminases increased

Overdosage/Toxicology Symptoms include CNS depression, obtundation, flu-like symptoms, and myelosuppression. Treatment is supportive.

Drug Interactions
Increased Effect/Toxicity: Interferons may increase the adverse/toxic effects of ACE inhibitors, specifically the development of granulocytopenia. Agranulocytosis has been reported with concurrent use of clozapine (case report). Interferons may increase the anticoagulant effects of warfarin, and interferons may increase serum levels of zidovudine. Concurrent use of hepatotoxic drugs may increase the risk of hepatic injury in patients receiving interferon beta-1a.

Stability
Avonex®:
Prefilled syringe: Store at 2°C to 8°C (36°F to 46°F); do not freeze. Protect from light. Allow to warm to room temperature prior to use. Use within 12 hours after removing from refrigerator.
Vial: Store unreconstituted vial at 2°C to 8°C (36°F to 46°F). If refrigeration is not available, may be stored at 25°C (77°F) for up to 30 days; do not freeze. Protect from light.
(Continued)

Interferon Beta-1a *(Continued)*

Reconstitute with 1.1 mL of diluent and swirl gently to dissolve. Do not shake. The reconstituted product contains no preservative and is for single-use only; discard unused portion. Following reconstitution, use immediately, but may be stored up to 6 hours at 2°C to 8°C (36°F to 46°F); do not freeze.

Rebif®: Store at 2°C to 8°C (36°F to 46°F); do not freeze. Protect from light. May also be stored ≤25°C (77°F) for up to 30 days if protected from heat and light.

Mechanism of Action Interferon beta differs from naturally occurring human protein by a single amino acid substitution and the lack of carbohydrate side chains; alters the expression and response to surface antigens and can enhance immune cell activities. Properties of interferon beta that modify biologic responses are mediated by cell surface receptor interactions; mechanism in the treatment of MS is unknown.

Pharmacodynamics/Kinetics Limited data due to small doses used

Half-life elimination: Avonex®: 10 hours; Rebif®: 69 hours

Time to peak, serum: Avonex® (I.M.): 3-15 hours; Rebif® (SubQ): 16 hours

Dosage Adults: **Note:** Analgesics and/or antipyretics may help decrease flu-like symptoms on treatment days:

I.M. (Avonex®): 30 mcg once weekly

SubQ (Rebif®): Doses should be separated by at least 48 hours:

Target dose 44 mcg 3 times/week:

Initial: 8.8 mcg (20 % of final dose) 3 times/week for 8 weeks

Titration: 22 mcg (50% of final dose) 3 times/week for 8 weeks

Final dose: 44 mcg 3 times/week

Target dose 22 mcg 3 times/week:

Initial: 4.4 mcg (20 % of final dose) 3 times/week for 8 weeks

Titration: 11 mcg (50% of final dose) 3 times/week for 8 weeks

Final dose: 22 mcg 3 times/week

Dosage adjustment in hepatic impairment: Rebif®: If liver function tests increase or in case of leukopenia: Decrease dose 20% to 50% until toxicity resolves

Administration

Avonex®: Must be administered by I.M. injection

Rebif®: Administer SubQ at the same time of day on the same 3 days each week (ie, late afternoon/evening Mon, Wed, Fri); rotate injection site

Monitoring Parameters Monitor for signs and symptoms of thyroid abnormalities, hematologic suppression, liver functions tests, symptoms of autoimmune disorders

Avonex®: Frequency of monitoring for patients receiving Avonex® has not been specifically defined; in clinical trials, monitoring was at 6-month intervals.

Rebif®: CBC and liver function testing at 1-, 3-, and 6 months, then periodically thereafter. Thyroid function every 6 months (in patients with pre-existing abnormalities and/or clinical indications)

Dosage Forms

Combination package [preservative free] (Rebif® Titration Pack):

Injection, solution: 8.8 mcg/0.2 mL (0.2 mL) [6 prefilled syringes; contains albumin]

Injection, solution: 22 mcg/0.5 mL (0.5 mL) [6 prefilled syringes; contains albumin]

Injection, powder for reconstitution (Avonex®): 33 mcg [6.6 million units; provides 30 mcg/mL following reconstitution] [contains albumin; packaged with SWFI, alcohol wipes, and access pin and needle]

Injection, solution (Avonex®): 30 mcg/0.5 mL (0.5 mL) [albumin free; prefilled syringe; syringe cap contains latex; packaged with alcohol wipes, gauze pad, and adhesive bandages]

Injection, solution [preservative free] (Rebif®): 22 mcg/0.5 mL (0.5 mL) [prefilled syringe; contains albumin]; 44 mcg/0.5 mL (0.5 mL) [prefilled syringe; contains albumin]

Interferon Beta-1b *(in ter FEER on BAY ta won bee)*

U.S. Brand Names Betaseron®

Canadian Brand Names Betaseron®

Index Terms rIFN beta-1b

Pharmacologic Category Interferon

Use Treatment of relapsing forms of multiple sclerosis (MS)

Pregnancy Risk Factor C

Pregnancy Implications A dose-related abortifacient activity was reported in Rhesus monkeys. There are not adequate and well-controlled studies in pregnant women. Treatment should be discontinued if a woman becomes pregnant, or plans to become pregnant during therapy.

Lactation Excretion in breast milk unknown/contraindicated

Contraindications Hypersensitivity to *E. coli*-derived products, natural or recombinant interferon beta, albumin human or any other component of the formulation

Warnings/Precautions Hepatotoxicity has been reported with all beta interferons, including rare reports of hepatitis (autoimmune) and hepatic failure requiring transplant. Interferons have been associated with severe psychiatric adverse events (psychosis, mania, depression, suicidal behavior/ideation) in patients with and without previous psychiatric symptoms, avoid use in severe psychiatric disorders and use caution in patients with a history of depression; patients exhibiting symptoms of depression should be closely monitored and discontinuation of therapy should be considered. Due to high incidence of flu-like adverse effects, use caution in patients with pre-existing cardiovascular disease, pulmonary disease, seizure disorders, myelosuppression, renal impairment or hepatic impairment. Severe injection site reactions (necrosis) may occur, which may or may not heal with continued therapy; patient and/or caregiver competency in injection technique should be confirmed and periodically re-evaluated. Safety and efficacy in patients <18 years of age have not been established.

Adverse Reactions Note: Flu-like syndrome (including at least two of the following - headache, fever, chills, malaise, diaphoresis, and myalgia) are reported in the majority of patients (60%) and decrease over time (average duration ~1 week).

>10%:
  Cardiovascular: Peripheral edema (15%), chest pain (11%)
  Central nervous system: Headache (57%), fever (36%), pain (51%), chills (25%), dizziness (24%), insomnia (24%)
  Dermatologic: Rash (24%), skin disorder (12%)
  Endocrine & metabolic: Metrorrhagia (11%)
  Gastrointestinal: Nausea (27%), diarrhea (19%), abdominal pain (19%), constipation (20%), dyspepsia (14%)
  Genitourinary: Urinary urgency (13%)
  Hematologic: Lymphopenia (88%), neutropenia (14%), leukopenia (14%)
  Local: Injection site reaction (85%), inflammation (53%), pain (18%)
  Neuromuscular & skeletal: Weakness (61%), myalgia (27%), hypertonia (50%), myasthenia (46%), arthralgia (31%), incoordination (21%)
  Miscellaneous: Flu-like syndrome (60%)

1% to 10%:
  Cardiovascular: Palpitation (4%), vasodilation (8%), hypertension (7%), tachycardia (4%), peripheral vascular disorder (6%)
  Central nervous system: Anxiety (10%), malaise (8%), nervousness (7%)
  Dermatologic: Alopecia (4%)
  Endocrine & metabolic: Menorrhagia (8%), dysmenorrhea (7%)
  Gastrointestinal: Weight gain (7%)
  Genitourinary: Impotence (9%), pelvic pain (6%), cystitis (8%), urinary frequency (7%), prostatic disorder (3%)
  Hematologic: Lymphadenopathy (8%)
  Hepatic: SGPT increased >5x baseline (10%), SGOT increased >5x baseline (3%)
  Local: Injection site necrosis (5%), edema (3%), mass (2%)
  Neuromuscular & skeletal: Leg cramps (4%)
  Respiratory: Dyspnea (7%)
  Miscellaneous: Diaphoresis (8%), hypersensitivity (3%)

<1% (Limited to important or life-threatening): Apnea, arrhythmia, ataxia, bronchospasm, capillary leak syndrome (fatal), cardiac arrest, cardiomegaly, cardiomyopathy, cerebral hemorrhage, coma, confusion, convulsion, delirium, depersonalization, depression, DVT, emotional lability, erythema nodosum, ethanol intolerance, exfoliative dermatitis, gamma GT increase, GI hemorrhage, hallucinations, heart failure, hematemesis, hepatic failure, hepatitis, hyperthyroidism, hyperuricemia, hypocalcemia, mania, MI, paresthesia, pericardial effusion, photosensitivity, pneumonia, pruritus, psychosis, pulmonary embolism, rash, sepsis, shock, SIADH, skin discoloration, skin necrosis, suicidal ideation, syncope, thrombocytopenia, thyroid dysfunction, triglyceride increased, urinary tract infection, urosepsis, urticaria, vaginal hemorrhage, vomiting

Overdosage/Toxicology Symptoms include CNS depression, obtundation, flu-like symptoms, and myelosuppression. Treatment is supportive.

Drug Interactions
  Increased Effect/Toxicity: Interferons may increase the adverse/toxic effects of ACE inhibitors, specifically the development of granulocytopenia. Risk: Monitor A case report of agranulocytosis has been reported with concurrent use of clozapine. Case reports of decreased hematopoietic effect with erythropoietin. Interferon alpha may decrease the P450 isoenzyme metabolism of theophylline. Interferons may increase the anticoagulant effects of warfarin. Interferons may decrease the metabolism of zidovudine.

Stability Store at room temperature of 25°C (77°F); excursions permitted to 15°C to 30°C (59°F to 86°F). To reconstitute solution, inject 1.2 mL of diluent (provided); gently swirl to dissolve, do not shake. Reconstituted solution provides 0.25 mg/mL. If not used immediately following reconstitution, refrigerate solution at 2°C to 8°C (36°F to 46°F); do not freeze or shake solution. Use within 3 hours.

Mechanism of Action Interferon beta-1b differs from naturally occurring human protein by a single amino acid substitution and the lack of carbohydrate side chains; mechanism in the treatment of MS is unknown; however, immunomodulatory effects attributed to interferon beta-1b include enhancement of suppressor T cell activity, reduction of proinflammatory cytokines, down-regulation of antigen presentation, and reduced trafficking of lymphocytes into the central nervous system.

Pharmacodynamics/Kinetics Limited data due to small doses used
  Half-life elimination: 8 minutes to 4.3 hours
  Time to peak, serum: 1-8 hours

Dosage SubQ:
  Children <18 years: Not recommended
  Adults: 0.25 mg (8 million units) every other day

Administration Withdraw 1 mL of reconstituted solution from the vial into a sterile syringe fitted with a 27-gauge needle and inject the solution subcutaneously; sites for self-injection include arms, abdomen, hips, and thighs

Monitoring Parameters Complete blood chemistries (including platelet count) and liver function tests are recommended at 1, 3, and 6 months following initiation of therapy and periodically thereafter. Thyroid function should be assessed every 6 months in patients with history of thyroid dysfunction.

Dosage Forms Injection, powder for reconstitution [preservative free]: 0.3 mg [9.6 million units] [contains albumin; packaged with prefilled syringe containing diluent]

Interferon Gamma-1b (in ter FEER on GAM ah won bee)

U.S. Brand Names Actimmune®
Canadian Brand Names Actimmune®
Pharmacologic Category Interferon
Use Reduce frequency and severity of serious infections associated with chronic granulomatous disease; delay time to disease progression in patients with severe, malignant osteopetrosis
Pregnancy Risk Factor C
(Continued)

Interferon Gamma-1b *(Continued)*

Pregnancy Implications Safety and efficacy in pregnant women has not been established. Treatment should be discontinued if a woman becomes pregnant, or plans to become pregnant during therapy. A dose-related abortifacient activity was reported in Rhesus monkeys.

Lactation Excretion in breast milk unknown/contraindicated

Contraindications Hypersensitivity to interferon gamma, *E. coli* derived proteins, or any component of the formulation

Warnings/Precautions Patients with pre-existing cardiac disease, seizure disorders, CNS disturbances, or myelosuppression should be carefully monitored; long-term effects on growth and development are unknown; safety and efficacy in children <1 year of age have not been established.

Adverse Reactions Based on 50 mcg/m^2 dose administered 3 times weekly for chronic granulomatous disease

>10%:
  Central nervous system: Fever (52%), headache (33%), chills (14%), fatigue (14%)
  Dermatologic: Rash (17%)
  Gastrointestinal: Diarrhea (14%), vomiting (13%)
  Local: Injection site erythema or tenderness (14%)
1% to 10%:
  Central nervous system: Depression (3%)
  Gastrointestinal: Nausea (10%), abdominal pain (8%)
  Neuromuscular & skeletal: Myalgia (6%), arthralgia (2%), back pain (2%)

Drug Interactions

Cytochrome P450 Effect: Inhibits CYP1A2 (weak), 2E1 (weak)

Increased Effect/Toxicity: Interferon gamma-1b may increase hepatic enzymes or enhance myelosuppression when taken with other myelosuppressive agents. May decrease cytochrome P450 concentrations leading to increased serum concentrations of drugs metabolized by this pathway.

Ethanol/Nutrition/Herb Interactions Herb/Nutraceutical: Dietary supplements containing aristolochic acid (found most often in Chinese medicines/herbal therapies); cases of nephropathy and ESRD associated with their use.

Stability Store in refrigerator; do not freeze. Do not shake. Discard if left unrefrigerated for >12 hours.

Pharmacodynamics/Kinetics
Absorption: I.M., SubQ: Slowly
Half-life elimination: I.V.: 38 minutes; I.M., SubQ: 3-6 hours
Time to peak, plasma: I.M.: 4 hours (1.5 ng/mL); SubQ: 7 hours (0.6 ng/mL)

Dosage If severe reactions occur, reduce dose by 50% or therapy should be interrupted until adverse reaction abates.

Chronic granulomatous disease: Children >1 year and Adults: SubQ:
  BSA ≤0.5 m^2: 1.5 mcg/kg/dose 3 times/week
  BSA >0.5 m^2: 50 mcg/m^2 (1 million int. units/m^2) 3 times/week

Severe, malignant osteopetrosis: Children >1 year: SubQ:
  BSA ≤0.5 m^2: 1.5 mcg/kg/dose 3 times/week
  BSA >0.5 m^2: 50 mcg/m^2 (1 million int. units/m^2) 3 times/week

Note: Previously expressed as 1.5 million units/m^2; 50 mcg is equivalent to 1 million int. units/m^2.

Monitoring Parameters CBC with differential, platelets, LFTs, electrolytes, BUN, creatinine, and urinalysis prior to therapy and at 3-month intervals

Dosage Forms Injection, solution [preservative free]: 100 mcg [2 million int. units] (0.5 mL)
Previously, 100 mcg was expressed as 3 million units. This is equivalent to 2 million int. units.

♦ **Interleukin-1 Receptor Antagonist** *see* Anakinra *on page 128*
♦ **Interleukin-2** *see* Aldesleukin *on page 59*
♦ **Interleukin-11** *see* Oprelvekin *on page 1270*
♦ **Intralipid**® *see* Fat Emulsion *on page 686*
♦ **Intravenous Fat Emulsion** *see* Fat Emulsion *on page 686*
♦ **Intrifiban** *see* Eptifibatide *on page 601*
♦ **Intron**® **A** *see* Interferon Alfa-2b *on page 920*
♦ **Intropin** *see* DOPamine *on page 539*
♦ **Invanz**® *see* Ertapenem *on page 607*
♦ **Inversine**® *see* Mecamylamine *on page 1059*
♦ **Invirase**® *see* Saquinavir *on page 1546*
♦ **Iodine I 131 Tositumomab and Tositumomab** *see* Tositumomab and Iodine I 131 Tositumomab *on page 1713*

Iodoquinol *(eye oh doe KWIN ole)*

U.S. Brand Names Yodoxin®
Canadian Brand Names Diodoquin®
Index Terms Diiodohydroxyquin
Pharmacologic Category Amebicide
Use Treatment of acute and chronic intestinal amebiasis; asymptomatic cyst passers; *Blastocystis hominis* infections; ineffective for amebic hepatitis or hepatic abscess
Pregnancy Risk Factor C
Lactation Excretion in breast milk unknown
Contraindications Hypersensitivity to iodine or iodoquinol or any component of the formulation; hepatic damage; pre-existing optic neuropathy

Warnings/Precautions Optic neuritis, optic atrophy, and peripheral neuropathy have occurred following prolonged use; avoid long-term therapy
Adverse Reactions Frequency not defined.
Central nervous system: Fever, chills, agitation, retrograde amnesia, headache
Dermatologic: Rash, urticaria, pruritus
Endocrine & metabolic: Thyroid gland enlargement
Gastrointestinal: Diarrhea, nausea, vomiting, stomach pain, abdominal cramps
Neuromuscular & skeletal: Peripheral neuropathy, weakness
Ocular: Optic neuritis, optic atrophy, visual impairment
Miscellaneous: Itching of rectal area
Overdosage/Toxicology Chronic overdose can result in vomiting, diarrhea, abdominal pain, metallic taste, paresthesias, paraplegia, and loss of vision. Can lead to destruction of the long fibers of the spinal cord and optic nerve. Acute overdose symptoms includes delirium, stupor, coma, and amnesia. Following GI decontamination, treatment is symptomatic.
Mechanism of Action Contact amebicide that works in the lumen of the intestine by an unknown mechanism
Pharmacodynamics/Kinetics
Absorption: Poor and erratic
Metabolism: Hepatic
Excretion: Feces (high percentage)
Dosage Oral:
Children: 30-40 mg/kg/day (maximum: 650 mg/dose) in 3 divided doses for 20 days; not to exceed 1.95 g/day
Adults: 650 mg 3 times/day after meals for 20 days; not to exceed 1.95 g/day
Dietary Considerations Should be taken after meals.
Administration Tablets may be crushed and mixed with applesauce or chocolate syrup. May take with food or milk to reduce stomach upset. Complete full course of therapy.
Monitoring Parameters Ophthalmologic exam
Test Interactions May increase protein-bound serum iodine concentrations reflecting a decrease in ^{131}I uptake; false-positive ferric chloride test for phenylketonuria
Dosage Forms Tablet: 210 mg, 650 mg

Iodoquinol and Hydrocortisone
(eye oh doe KWIN ole & hye droe KOR ti sone)

U.S. Brand Names Dermazene®; Vytone®
Index Terms Hydrocortisone and Iodoquinol
Pharmacologic Category Antifungal Agent, Topical; Corticosteroid, Topical
Use Treatment of eczema; infectious dermatitis; chronic eczematoid otitis externa; mycotic dermatoses
Pregnancy Risk Factor C
Medication Safety Issues
Sound-alike/look-alike issues:
Vytone® may be confused with Hytone®, Zydone®
Dosage Apply 3-4 times/day
Additional Information Complete prescribing information for this medication should be consulted for additional detail.
Dosage Forms
Cream: Iodoquinol 1% and hydrocortisone acetate 1% (30 g)
Dermazene®: Iodoquinol 1% and hydrocortisone acetate 1% (30 g, 45 g)
Vytone®: Iodoquinol 1% and hydrocortisone acetate 1% (30 g)

♦ **Ionamin®** see Phentermine on page 1356
♦ **Ionsys™** see Fentanyl on page 693
♦ **Iophen-C NR** see Guaifenesin and Codeine on page 815
♦ **Iophen DM NR** see Guaifenesin and Dextromethorphan on page 816
♦ **Iophen NR** see Guaifenesin on page 814
♦ **Iopidine®** see Apraclonidine on page 144
♦ **Iosat™ [OTC]** see Potassium Iodide on page 1399

Ioxilan (eye OKS ee lan)

U.S. Brand Names Oxilan®
Canadian Brand Names Oxilan® 300; Oxilan® 350
Pharmacologic Category Iodinated Contrast Media; Radiological/Contrast Media, Nonionic
Use
Intra-arterial: Ioxilan 300 mgI/mL is indicated for cerebral arteriography. Ioxilan 350 mgI/mL is indicated for coronary arteriography and left ventriculography, visceral angiography, aortography, and peripheral arteriography
Intravenous: Both products are indicated for excretory urography and contrast-enhanced computed tomographic (CECT) imaging of the head and body
Pregnancy Risk Factor B
Dosage Adults:
Intra-arterial: Coronary arteriography and left ventriculography: For visualization of coronary arteries and left ventricle, ioxilan injection with a concentration of 350 mg iodine/mL is recommended
Usual injection volumes:
Left and right coronary: 2-10 mL (0.7-3.5 g iodine)
Left ventricle: 25-50 mL (8.75-17.5 g iodine)
Total doses should not exceed 250 mL; the injection rate of ioxilan should approximate the flow rate in the vessel injected
(Continued)

Ioxilan *(Continued)*

Cerebral arteriography: For evaluation of arterial lesions of the brain, a concentration of 300 mg iodine/mL is indicated

Recommended doses: 8-12 mL (2.4-3.6 g iodine)

Total dose should not exceed 150 mL

Additional Information Complete prescribing information for this medication should be consulted for additional detail.

Dosage Forms Injection, solution [preservative free]:

Oxilan® 300: 62% (50 mL, 100 mL, 150 mL, 200 mL) [provides organically-bound iodine 300 mg/mL; contains sodium 0.22 mg (0.01 mEq)/mL, edetate calcium disodium]

Oxilan® 350: 73% (50 mL, 100 mL, 150 mL, 200 mL) [provides organically- bound iodine 350 mg/mL; contains sodium 0.22 mg (0.01 mEq)/mL, edetate calcium disodium]

Ipecac Syrup *(IP e kak SIR up)*

Index Terms Syrup of Ipecac

Pharmacologic Category Antidote

Use Treatment of acute oral drug overdosage and in certain poisonings

Pregnancy Risk Factor C

Lactation Excretion in breast milk unknown/use caution

Contraindications Hypersensitivity to ipecac or any component of the formulation; do not use in unconscious patients; patients with no gag reflex; following ingestion of strong bases, acids, or volatile oils; when seizures are likely

Warnings/Precautions Do not confuse ipecac syrup with ipecac fluid extract, which is 14 times more potent; use with caution in patients with cardiovascular disease and bulimics; may not be effective in antiemetic overdose

Adverse Reactions Frequency not defined.

Cardiovascular: Cardiotoxicity

Central nervous system: Lethargy

Gastrointestinal: Protracted vomiting, diarrhea

Neuromuscular & skeletal: Myopathy

Overdosage/Toxicology Ipecac syrup contains cardiotoxin. Symptoms include tachycardia, CHF, atrial fibrillation, depressed myocardial contractility, myocarditis, diarrhea, persistent vomiting, and hypotension. Treatment consists of activated charcoal and gastric lavage.

Drug Interactions

Increased Effect/Toxicity: Phenothiazines (chlorpromazine has been associated with serious dystonic reactions).

Decreased Effect: Activated charcoal, milk, carbonated beverages decrease the effect of ipecac syrup.

Ethanol/Nutrition/Herb Interactions Food: Milk, carbonated beverages may decrease effectiveness.

Mechanism of Action Irritates the gastric mucosa and stimulates the medullary chemore-ceptor trigger zone to induce vomiting

Pharmacodynamics/Kinetics

Onset of action: 15-30 minutes

Duration: 20-25 minutes; 60 minutes in some cases

Absorption: Significant amounts, mainly when it does not produce emesis

Excretion: Urine; emetine (alkaloid component) may be detected in urine 60 days after excess dose or chronic use

Dosage Oral:

Children:

6-12 months: 5-10 mL followed by 10-20 mL/kg of water; repeat dose one time if vomiting does not occur within 20 minutes

1-12 years: 15 mL followed by 10-20 mL/kg of water; repeat dose one time if vomiting does not occur within 20 minutes

If emesis does not occur within 30 minutes after second dose, ipecac must be removed from stomach by gastric lavage

Adults: 15-30 mL followed by 200-300 mL of water; repeat dose one time if vomiting does not occur within 20 minutes

Administration Do **not** administer to unconscious patients. Patients should be kept active and moving following administration of ipecac. If vomiting does not occur after second dose, gastric lavage may be considered to remove ingested substance.

Additional Information The benefit of ipecac syrup to treat poisoning in children has been questioned. In November 2003, the American Academy of Pediatrics recommended that syrup of ipecac no longer be used routinely for the management of poisonings in the home. They advised parents to dispose of existing supplies of ipecac to help prevent inappropriate use.

Dosage Forms Syrup: 70 mg/mL (30 mL) [contains alcohol]

♦ Iplex™ *see* Mecasermin *on page 1060*

♦ IPM Wound Gel™ [OTC] *see* Hyaluronate and Derivatives *on page 841*

♦ IPOL® *see* Poliovirus Vaccine (Inactivated) *on page 1385*

Ipratropium *(i pra TROE pee um)*

U.S. Brand Names Atrovent®; Atrovent® HFA

Canadian Brand Names Alti-Ipratropium; Apo-Ipravent®; Atrovent®; Atrovent® HFA; Gen-Ipratropium; Novo-Ipramide; Nu-Ipratropium; PMS-Ipratropium

Index Terms Ipratropium Bromide

Pharmacologic Category Anticholinergic Agent

Use Anticholinergic bronchodilator used in bronchospasm associated with COPD, bronchitis, and emphysema; symptomatic relief of rhinorrhea associated with the common cold and allergic and nonallergic rhinitis

Pregnancy Risk Factor B

Pregnancy Implications Teratogenic effects were not observed in animal studies.

Lactation Excretion in breast milk unknown/use caution

Medication Safety Issues

Sound-alike/look-alike issues:

Atrovent® may be confused with Alupent®

Contraindications Hypersensitivity to ipratropium, atropine (and its derivatives), or any component of the formulation

Warnings/Precautions Not indicated for the initial treatment of acute episodes of bronchospasm; use with caution in patients with myasthenia gravis, narrow-angle glaucoma, benign prostatic hyperplasia (BPH), or bladder neck obstruction

Adverse Reactions

Inhalation aerosol and inhalation solution:

>10%: Bronchitis (10% to 23%), upper respiratory tract infection (13%)

1% to 10%:

Cardiovascular: Palpitation

Central nervous system: Dizziness (2% to 3%)

Dermatologic: Rash (1%)

Gastrointestinal: Nausea, xerostomia, stomach upset, dry mucous membranes

Renal: Urinary tract infection

Respiratory: Nasal congestion, dyspnea (10%), sputum increased (1%), bronchospasm (2%), pharyngitis (3%), rhinitis (2%), sinusitis (5%)

Miscellaneous: Flu-like syndrome

<1% (Limited to important or life-threatening): Anaphylactic reaction, angioedema, atrial fibrillation, bitter taste, blurred vision, bronchospasm, constipation, eye pain (acute), glaucoma, hypersensitivity reactions, insomnia, laryngospasm, mucosal ulcers, nervousness, palpitations, rash, stomatitis, tachycardia (including supraventricular), tremor, urinary retention, urticaria

Nasal spray: Respiratory: Epistaxis (8%), nasal dryness (5%), nausea (2%)

Overdosage/Toxicology Symptoms include dry mouth, drying of respiratory secretions, cough, nausea, GI distress, blurred vision or impaired visual accommodation, headache, and nervousness. Acute overdose by inhalation is unlikely since it is so poorly absorbed. However, if poisoning occurs, it can be treated like any other anticholinergic toxicity. An anticholinergic overdose with severe life-threatening symptoms may be treated with physostigmine 1-2 mg (0.5 mg or 0.02 mg/kg for children) SubQ or slow I.V.

Drug Interactions

Increased Effect/Toxicity: Increased toxicity with anticholinergics or drugs with anticholinergic properties.

Stability Store at 15°C to 30°C (59°F to 86°F). Do not store near heat or open flame.

Mechanism of Action Blocks the action of acetylcholine at parasympathetic sites in bronchial smooth muscle causing bronchodilation

Pharmacodynamics/Kinetics

Onset of action: Bronchodilation: 1-3 minutes

Peak effect: 1.5-2 hours

Duration: ≤4 hours

Absorption: Negligible

Distribution: Inhalation: 15% of dose reaches lower airways

Dosage

Nebulization:

Infants and Children ≤12 years: 125-250 mcg 3 times/day

Children >12 years and Adults: 500 mcg (one unit-dose vial) 3-4 times/day with doses 6-8 hours apart

Oral inhalation: MDI:

Children 3-12 years: 1-2 inhalations 3 times/day, up to 6 inhalations/24 hours

Children >12 years and Adults: 2 inhalations 4 times/day, up to 12 inhalations/24 hours

Intranasal: Nasal spray:

Symptomatic relief of rhinorrhea associated with the common cold (safety and efficacy of use beyond 4 days in patients with the common cold have not been established):

Children 5-11 years: 0.06%: 2 sprays in each nostril 3 times/day

Children ≥12 years and Adults: 0.06%: 2 sprays in each nostril 3-4 times/day

Symptomatic relief of rhinorrhea associated with allergic/nonallergic rhinitis: Children ≥6 years and Adults: 0.03%: 2 sprays in each nostril 2-3 times/day

Administration Atrovent® HFA: Prime inhaler by releasing 2 test sprays into the air. If the inhaler has not been used for >3 days, reprime.

Dosage Forms

Aerosol for oral inhalation, as bromide:

Atrovent® HFA: 17 mcg/actuation (12.9 g)

Solution for nebulization, as bromide: 0.02% (2.5 mL)

Solution, intranasal, as bromide [spray]:

Atrovent®: 0.03% (30 mL); 0.06% (15 mL)

Ipratropium and Albuterol (i pra TROE pee um & al BYOO ter ole)

U.S. Brand Names Combivent®; DuoNeb™
Canadian Brand Names CO Ipra-Sal; Combivent®; Gen-Combo Sterinebs
Index Terms Albuterol and Ipratropium; Salbutamol and Ipratropium
Pharmacologic Category Bronchodilator
Use Treatment of COPD in those patients that are currently on a regular bronchodilator who continue to have bronchospasms and require a second bronchodilator
Pregnancy Risk Factor C
Medication Safety Issues
Sound-alike/look-alike issues:
Combivent® may be confused with Combivir®
Dosage Adults:
Inhalation: 2 inhalations 4 times/day (maximum: 12 inhalations/24 hours)
Inhalation via nebulization: Initial: 3 mL every 6 hours (maximum: 3 mL every 4 hours)
Additional Information Complete prescribing information for this medication should be consulted for additional detail.
Dosage Forms
Aerosol for oral inhalation (Combivent®): Ipratropium bromide 18 mcg and albuterol sulfate 103 mcg per actuation [200 doses] (14.7 g) [contains soya lecithin]
Solution for nebulization (DuoNeb™): Ipratropium bromide 0.5 mg [0.017%] and albuterol base 2.5 mg [0.083%] per 3 mL vial (30s, 60s)

♦ **Ipratropium Bromide** see Ipratropium on page 932
♦ **I-Prin [OTC]** see Ibuprofen on page 873
♦ **Iproveratril Hydrochloride** see Verapamil on page 1784
♦ **IPV** see Poliovirus Vaccine (Inactivated) on page 1385
♦ **Iquix®** see Levofloxacin on page 1001

Irbesartan (ir be SAR tan)

U.S. Brand Names Avapro®
Canadian Brand Names Avapro®
Pharmacologic Category Angiotensin II Receptor Blocker
Additional Appendix Information
Angiotensin Agents on page 1860
Use Treatment of hypertension alone or in combination with other antihypertensives; treatment of diabetic nephropathy in patients with type 2 diabetes mellitus (noninsulin dependent, NIDDM) and hypertension
Pregnancy Risk Factor C/D (2nd and 3rd trimesters)
Pregnancy Implications The drug should be discontinued as soon as possible after detection of pregnancy. Drugs which act directly on the renin-angiotensin system can cause fetal and neonatal morbidity and death.
Lactation Excretion in breast milk unknown/contraindicated
Medication Safety Issues
Sound-alike/look-alike issues:
Avapro® may be confused with Anaprox®
Contraindications Hypersensitivity to irbesartan or any component of the formulation; hypersensitivity to other A-II receptor antagonists; bilateral renal artery stenosis; pregnancy
Warnings/Precautions [U.S. Boxed Warning]: Based on human data, drugs that act on the angiotensin system can cause injury and death to the developing fetus when used in the second and third trimesters. Angiotensin receptor blockers should be discontinued as soon as possible once pregnancy is detected. May cause hyperkalemia; avoid potassium supplementation unless specifically required by healthcare provider. May be associated with deterioration of renal function and/or increases in serum creatinine, particularly in patients dependent on renin-angiotensin-aldosterone system. Avoid use or use a much smaller dose in patients who are intravascularly volume-depleted; use caution in patients with unilateral or bilateral renal artery stenosis to avoid a decrease in renal function; AUCs of irbesartan (not the active metabolite) are about 50% greater in patients with Cl$_{cr}$ <30 mL/minute and are doubled in hemodialysis patients. Safety and efficacy have not been established in pediatric patients <6 years of age.
Adverse Reactions Unless otherwise indicated, percentage of incidence is reported for patients with hypertension.
>10%: Endocrine & metabolic: Hyperkalemia (19%, diabetic nephropathy; rarely seen in HTN)
1% to 10%:
Cardiovascular: Orthostatic hypotension (5%, diabetic nephropathy)
Central nervous system: Fatigue (4%), dizziness (10%, diabetic nephropathy)
Gastrointestinal: Diarrhea (3%), dyspepsia (2%)
Respiratory: Upper respiratory infection (9%), cough (2.8% versus 2.7% in placebo)
<1% (Limited to important or life-threatening): Angina, angioedema, arrhythmia, cardiopulmonary arrest, conjunctivitis, depression, dyspnea, ecchymosis, edema, epistaxis, gout, heart failure, hepatitis, hypotension, jaundice, libido decreased, MI, orthostatic hypotension, paresthesia, sexual dysfunction, stroke, transaminases increased, urticaria. May be associated with worsening of renal function in patients dependent on renin-angiotensin-aldosterone system.
Overdosage/Toxicology The most likely overdose manifestations would be hypotension and tachycardia. Bradycardia could occur from parasympathetic (vagal) stimulation. If symptomatic hypotension should occur, institute supportive treatment. Not removed by hemodialysis.

Drug Interactions

Cytochrome P450 Effect: Substrate of CYP2C9 (minor); **Inhibits** CYP2C8 (moderate), 2C9 (moderate), 2D6 (weak), 3A4 (weak)

Increased Effect/Toxicity: Potassium salts/supplements, co-trimoxazole (high dose), ACE inhibitors, and potassium-sparing diuretics (amiloride, spironolactone, triamterene) may increase the risk of hyperkalemia. Irbesartan may increase the levels/effects of amiodarone, bosentan, dapsone, fluoxetine, glimepiride, glipizide, losartan, montelukast, nateglinide, paclitaxel, phenytoin, pioglitazone, repaglinide, rosiglitazone, warfarin, zafirlukast, and other CYP2C8 and 2C9 substrates.

Ethanol/Nutrition/Herb Interactions Herb/Nutraceutical: Avoid dong quai if using for hypertension (has estrogenic activity). Avoid ephedra, yohimbe, ginseng (may worsen hypertension). Avoid garlic (may have increased antihypertensive effect).

Stability Store at room temperature of 15°C to 30°C (59°F to 86°F).

Mechanism of Action Irbesartan is an angiotensin receptor antagonist. Angiotensin II acts as a vasoconstrictor. In addition to causing direct vasoconstriction, angiotensin II also stimulates the release of aldosterone. Once aldosterone is released, sodium as well as water are reabsorbed. The end result is an elevation in blood pressure. Irbesartan binds to the AT1 angiotensin II receptor. This binding prevents angiotensin II from binding to the receptor thereby blocking the vasoconstriction and the aldosterone secreting effects of angiotensin II.

Pharmacodynamics/Kinetics

Onset of action: Peak effect: 1-2 hours

Duration: >24 hours

Distribution: V_d: 53-93 L

Protein binding, plasma: 90%

Metabolism: Hepatic, primarily CYP2C9

Bioavailability: 60% to 80%

Half-life elimination: Terminal: 11-15 hours

Time to peak, serum: 1.5-2 hours

Excretion: Feces (80%); urine (20%)

Dosage Oral:

Hypertension:

Children:

<6 years: Safety and efficacy have not been established.

≥6-12 years: Initial: 75 mg once daily; may be titrated to a maximum of 150 mg once daily

Children ≥13 years and Adults: 150 mg once daily; patients may be titrated to 300 mg once daily

Note: Starting dose in volume-depleted patients should be 75 mg

Nephropathy in patients with type 2 diabetes and hypertension: Adults: Target dose: 300 mg once daily

Dosage adjustment in renal impairment: No dosage adjustment necessary with mild to severe impairment unless the patient is also volume depleted.

Dietary Considerations May be taken with or without food.

Dosage Forms Tablet: 75 mg, 150 mg, 300 mg

Irbesartan and Hydrochlorothiazide

(ir be SAR tan & hye droe klor oh THYE a zide)

U.S. Brand Names Avalide®

Canadian Brand Names Avalide®

Index Terms Avapro® HCT; Hydrochlorothiazide and Irbesartan

Pharmacologic Category Angiotensin II Receptor Blocker Combination; Antihypertensive Agent, Combination; Diuretic, Thiazide

Use Combination therapy for the management of hypertension

Pregnancy Risk Factor C/D (2nd and 3rd trimesters)

Medication Safety Issues

Sound-alike/look-alike issues:

Avalide® may be confused with Avandia®

Dosage Dose must be individualized. A patient who is not controlled with either agent alone may be switched to the combination product. Mean effect increases with the dose of each component. The lowest dosage available is irbesartan 150 mg/hydrochlorothiazide 12.5 mg. Dose increases should be made not more frequently than every 2-4 weeks.

Additional Information Complete prescribing information for this medication should be consulted for additional detail.

Dosage Forms Tablet:

Irbesartan 150 mg and hydrochlorothiazide 12.5 mg

Irbesartan 300 mg and hydrochlorothiazide 12.5 mg

Irbesartan 300 mg and hydrochlorothiazide 25 mg

♦ **Ircon® [OTC]** see Ferrous Fumarate on page 702

♦ **IRESSA®** see Gefitinib on page 784

Irinotecan (eye rye no TEE kan)

U.S. Brand Names Camptosar®

Canadian Brand Names Camptosar®; Irinotecan Hydrochloride Trihydrate

Index Terms Camptothecin-11; CPT-11; NSC-616348

Pharmacologic Category Antineoplastic Agent, Natural Source (Plant) Derivative

Use Treatment of metastatic carcinoma of the colon or rectum

Unlabeled/Investigational Use Lung cancer (small cell and nonsmall cell), cervical cancer, gastric cancer, pancreatic cancer, leukemia, lymphoma, breast cancer

Pregnancy Risk Factor D

(Continued)

Irinotecan *(Continued)*

Pregnancy Implications Teratogenic effects were noted in animal studies. There are no adequate and well-controlled studies in pregnant women. Women of childbearing potential should avoid becoming pregnant while receiving treatment.

Lactation Excretion in breast milk unknown/not recommended

Medication Safety Issues

High alert medication: The Institute for Safe Medication Practices (ISMP) includes this medication among its list of drugs which have a heightened risk of causing significant patient harm when used in error.

Contraindications Hypersensitivity to irinotecan or any component of the formulation; concurrent use of atazanavir, ketoconazole, St John's wort; pregnancy

Warnings/Precautions Hazardous agent - use appropriate precautions for handling and disposal. Severe hypersensitivity reactions have occurred.

Patients with diarrhea should be carefully monitored and treated promptly. **[U.S. Boxed Warning]: Severe diarrhea may be dose-limiting and potentially fatal; two severe (life-threatening) forms of diarrhea may occur.** Early diarrhea occurs during or within 24 hours of receiving irinotecan and is characterized by cholinergic symptoms (eg, increased salivation, diaphoresis, abdominal cramping); it is usually responsive to atropine. Late diarrhea occurs more than 24 hours after treatment which may lead to dehydration, electrolyte imbalance, or sepsis; it should be promptly treated with loperamide.

[U.S. Boxed Warning]: May cause severe myelosuppression. Deaths due to sepsis following severe myelosuppression have been reported. Therapy should be temporarily discontinued if neutropenic fever occurs or if the absolute neutrophil count is <1000/mm³. The dose of irinotecan should be reduced if there is a clinically significant decrease in the total WBC (<200/mm³), neutrophil count (<1500/mm³), hemoglobin (<8 g/dL), or platelet count (<100,000/mm³). Routine administration of a colony-stimulating factor is generally not necessary, but may be considered for patients experiencing significant neutropenia.

Patients with even modest elevations in total serum bilirubin levels (1-2 mg/dL) have a significantly greater likelihood of experiencing first-course grade 3 or 4 neutropenia than those with bilirubin levels that were <1 mg/dL. Patients with abnormal glucuronidation of bilirubin, such as those with Gilbert's syndrome, may also be at greater risk of myelosuppression when receiving therapy with irinotecan. Use caution when treating patients with known hepatic dysfunction or hyperbilirubinemia. Dosage adjustments should be considered.

Patients homozygous for the UGT1A1*28 allele are at increased risk of neutropenia; initial one-level dose reduction should be considered for both single-agent and combination regimens. Heterozygous carriers of the UGT1A1*28 allele may also be at increased risk; however, most patients have tolerated normal starting doses.

Renal impairment and acute renal failure have been reported, possible due to dehydration. Patients with bowel obstruction should not be treated with irinotecan until resolution of obstruction. Use caution in patients who previously received pelvic/abdominal radiation, elderly patients with comorbid conditions, or baseline performance status of 2; close monitoring and dosage adjustments are recommended. Contains sorbitol; do not use in patients with hereditary fructose intolerance. **[U.S. Boxed Warning]: Should be administered under the supervision of an experienced cancer chemotherapy physician.**

Adverse Reactions Frequency of adverse reactions reported for single-agent use of irinotecan only.

>10%:

Cardiovascular: Vasodilation (9% to 11%)

Central nervous system: Cholinergic toxicity (47% — includes rhinitis, increased salivation, miosis, lacrimation, diaphoresis, flushing and intestinal hyperperistalsis); fever (44% to 45%), pain (23% to 24%), dizziness (15% to 21%), insomnia (19%), headache (17%), chills (14%)

Dermatologic: Alopecia (46% to 72%), rash (13% to 14%)

Endocrine & metabolic: Dehydration (15%)

Gastrointestinal: Diarrhea, late (83% to 88%; grade 3/4: 5% to 31%), diarrhea, early (43% to 51%; grade 3/4: 6% to 22%), nausea (70% to 86%), abdominal pain (57% to 68%), vomiting (62% to 67%), cramps (57%), anorexia (44% to 55%), constipation (30% to 32%), mucositis (30%), weight loss (30%), flatulence (12%), stomatitis (12%)

Hematologic: Anemia (60% to 97%; grades 3/4: 5% to 22%), leukopenia (63% to 96%, grades 3/4: 14% to 28%), thrombocytopenia (96%, grades 3/4: 1% to 4%), neutropenia (30% to 96%; grades 3/4: 14% to 31%)

Hepatic: Bilirubin increased (84%), alkaline phosphatase increased (13%)

Neuromuscular & skeletal: Weakness (69% to 76%), back pain (14%)

Respiratory: Dyspnea (22%), cough (17% to 20%), rhinitis (16%)

Miscellaneous: Diaphoresis (16%), infection (14%)

1% to 10%:

Cardiovascular: Edema (10%), hypotension (6%), thromboembolic events (5%)

Central nervous system: Somnolence (9%), confusion (3%)

Gastrointestinal: Abdominal fullness (10%), dyspepsia (10%)

Hematologic: Neutropenic fever (grades 3/4: 2% to 6%), hemorrhage (grades 3/4: 1% to 5%), neutropenic infection (grades 3/4: 1% to 2%)

Hepatic: SGOT increased (10%), ascites and/or jaundice (grades 3/4: 9%)

Respiratory: Pneumonia (4%)

<1%, postmarketing, and/or case reports: ALT increased, amylase increased, anaphylactoid reaction, anaphylaxis, angina, arterial thrombosis, bleeding, bradycardia, cardiac arrest, cerebral infarct, cerebrovascular accident, circulatory failure, colitis, deep thrombophlebitis, dysrhythmia, embolus, gastrointestinal bleeding, gastrointestinal obstruction, hepatomegaly, hyperglycemia, hypersensitivity, hyponatremia, ileus, interstitial lung disease, intestinal perforation, ischemic colitis, lipase increased, lymphocytopenia, MI, muscle cramps, myocardial ischemia, pancreatitis, paresthesia, peripheral vascular disorder, pulmonary embolus; pulmonary toxicity (dyspnea, fever, reticulonodular infiltrates on chest

x-ray); renal failure (acute), renal impairment, syncope, thrombophlebitis, thrombosis, ulceration, ulcerative colitis, vertigo

Note: In limited pediatric experience, dehydration (often associated with severe hypokalemia and hyponatremia) was among the most significant grade 3/4 adverse events, with a frequency up to 29%. In addition, grade 3/4 infection was reported in 24%.

Overdosage/Toxicology Symptoms of overdose include bone marrow suppression, including leukopenia, severe neutropenia and thrombocytopenia; nausea, vomiting and severe diarrhea. Treatment is symptom-directed and supportive, including prevention/treatment of dehydration due to diarrhea.

Drug Interactions

Cytochrome P450 Effect: Substrate (major) of CYP2B6, 3A4

Increased Effect/Toxicity: CYP2B6 inhibitors may increase the levels/effects of irinotecan; example inhibitors include desipramine, paroxetine, and sertraline. CYP3A4 inhibitors may increase the levels/effects of irinotecan; example inhibitors include azole antifungals, clarithromycin, diclofenac, doxycycline, erythromycin, imatinib, isoniazid, nefazodone, nicardipine, propofol, protease inhibitors, quinidine, telithromycin, and verapamil. Atazanavir may increase the levels/effects of irinotecan (SN-38) by CYP3A4 and UGT1A1 inhibition. Bevacizumab may increase the adverse effects of irinotecan (eg, diarrhea, neutropenia). Ketoconazole increases the levels/effects of irinotecan and active metabolite; discontinue ketoconazole 1 week prior to irinotecan therapy; **concurrent use is contraindicated.**

Decreased Effect: CYP2B6 inducers may decrease the levels/effects of irinotecan; example inducers include carbamazepine, nevirapine, phenobarbital, phenytoin, and rifampin. CYP3A4 inducers may decrease the levels/effects of irinotecan; example inducers include aminoglutethimide, carbamazepine, nafcillin, nevirapine, phenobarbital, phenytoin, and rifamycins. St John's wort decreases therapeutic effect of irinotecan; discontinue ≥2 weeks prior to irinotecan therapy; **concurrent use is contraindicated.**

Ethanol/Nutrition/Herb Interactions Herb/Nutraceutical: St John's wort decreases the efficacy of irinotecan.

Stability Store intact vials of injection at room temperature of 15°C to 30°C (59°F to 86°F). Protect from light. Doses should be diluted in 250-500 mL D_5W or NS to a final concentration of 0.12-2.8 mg/mL. Due to the relatively acidic pH, irinotecan appears to be more stable in D_5W than NS. Solutions diluted in D_5W are stable for 24 hours at room temperature or 48 hours under refrigeration at 2°C to 8°C. Solutions diluted in NS may precipitate if refrigerated. Do not freeze.

Mechanism of Action Irinotecan and its active metabolite (SN-38) bind reversibly to topoisomerase I-DNA complex preventing religation of the cleaved DNA strand. This results in the accumulation of cleavable complexes and double-strand DNA breaks. As mammalian cells cannot efficiently repair these breaks, cell death consistent with S-phase cell cycle specificity occurs, leading to termination of cellular replication.

Pharmacodynamics/Kinetics

Distribution: V_d: 33-150 L/m^2

Protein binding, plasma: Predominantly albumin; Parent drug: 30% to 68%, SN-38 (active drug): ~95%

Metabolism: Primarily hepatic to SN-38 (active metabolite) by carboxylesterase enzymes; SN-38 undergoes conjugation by UDP- glucuronosyl transferase 1A1 (UGT1A1) to form a glucuronide metabolite. SN-38 is increased by UGT1A1*28 polymorphism (10% of North Americans are homozygous for UGT1A1*28 allele). The lactones of both irinotecan and SN-38 undergo hydrolysis to inactive hydroxy acid forms.

Half-life elimination: SN-38: Mean terminal: 10-20 hours

Time to peak: SN-38: Following 90-minute infusion: ~1 hour

Excretion: Within 24 hours: Urine: Irinotecan (11% to 20%), metabolites (SN-38 <1%, SN-38 glucuronide, 3%)

Dosage I.V. (Refer to individual protocols): **Note:** A reduction in the starting dose by one dose level should be considered for patients ≥65 years of age, prior pelvic/abdominal radiotherapy, performance status of 2, homozygosity for UGT1A1*28 allele, or increased bilirubin (dosing for patients with a bilirubin >2 mg/dL cannot be recommended based on lack of data per manufacturer).

Single-agent therapy:

125 mg/m^2 over 90 minutes on days 1, 8, 15, and 22 of a 6-week treatment cycle

Adjusted dose level -1: 100 mg/m^2

Adjusted dose level -2: 75 mg/m^2

Once-every-3-week regimen: 350 mg/m^2 over 90 minutes, once every 3 weeks

Adjusted dose level -1: 300 mg/m^2

Adjusted dose level -2: 250 mg/m^2

Depending on the patient's ability to tolerate therapy, doses should be adjusted in increments of 25-50 mg/m^2. Irinotecan doses may range from 50-150 mg/m^2 for the weekly regimen. Patients may be dosed as low as 200 mg/m^2 (in 50 mg/m^2 decrements) for the once-every-3-week regimen.

Combination therapy with fluorouracil and leucovorin: Six-week (42-day) cycle:

Regimen 1: 125 mg/m^2 over 90 minutes on days 1, 8, 15, and 22; to be given in combination with bolus leucovorin and fluorouracil (leucovorin administered immediately following irinotecan; fluorouracil immediately following leucovorin)

Adjusted dose level -1: 100 mg/m^2

Adjusted dose level -2: 75 mg/m^2

Regimen 2: 180 mg/m^2 over 90 minutes on days 1, 15, and 29; to be given in combination with infusional leucovorin and bolus/infusion fluorouracil (leucovorin administered immediately following irinotecan; fluorouracil immediately following leucovorin)

Adjusted dose level -1: 150 mg/m^2

Adjusted dose level -2: 120 mg/m^2

Note: For all regimens: It is recommended that new courses begin only after the granulocyte count recovers to ≥1500/mm^3, the platelet count recovers to ≥100,000/mm^3, and treatment-related diarrhea has fully resolved. Treatment should be delayed 1-2 weeks to

(Continued)

Irinotecan *(Continued)*

allow for recovery from treatment-related toxicities. If the patient has not recovered after a 2-week delay, consideration should be given to discontinuing irinotecan.

Dosing adjustment in renal impairment: Effects have not been evaluated

Dosing adjustment in hepatic impairment: The manufacturer recommends that no change in dosage or administration be made for patients with liver metastases and normal hepatic function.

Consideration may be given to starting irinotecan at a lower dose (eg, 100 mg/m^2) if bilirubin is 1-2 mg/dL; for total serum bilirubin elevations >2 mg/dL, specific recommendations are not available.

Dosage adjustment for toxicities: It is recommended that new courses begin only after the granulocyte count recovers to ≥1500/mm^3, the platelet counts recovers to ≥100,000/mm^3, and treatment-related diarrhea has fully resolved. Depending on the patient's ability to tolerate therapy, doses should be adjusted in increments of 25-50 mg/m^2. Treatment should be delayed 1-2 weeks to allow for recovery from treatment-related toxicities. If the patient has not recovered after a 2-week delay, consideration should be given to discontinuing irinotecan. See tables below and on next page.

Dietary Considerations Contains sorbitol; do not use in patients with hereditary fructose intolerance.

Administration Administer by I.V. infusion, usually over 90 minutes.

Monitoring Parameters CBC with differential, platelet count, and hemoglobin with each dose; bilirubin, electrolytes (with severe diarrhea); bowel movements and hydration status; monitor infusion site for signs of inflammation and avoid extravasation

Additional Information Patients who are homozygous for the UGT1A1*28 allele are at increased risk for neutropenia; a decreased dose is recommended. Clinical research of patients who are heterozygous for UGT1A1*28 have been variable for increased neutropenic risk and such patients have tolerated normal starting doses. An FDA-approved test (Invader® Molecular Assay) is available for clinical determination of UGT phenotype.

The recommended regimen to manage late diarrhea is loperamide 4 mg orally at onset of late diarrhea, followed by 2 mg every 2 hours (or 4 mg every 4 hours at night) until 12 hours have passed without a bowel movement. If diarrhea recurs, then repeat administration. Loperamide should not be used for more than 48 consecutive hours.

Dosage Forms

Injection, solution, as hydrochloride:

Camptosar®: 20 mg/mL (2 mL, 5 mL) [contains sorbitol 45 mg/mL]

Combination Schedules: Recommended Dosage Modifications[1]

Toxicity NCI[2] Grade (Value)	During a Cycle of Therapy	At the Start of Subsequent Cycles of Therapy (After Adequate Recovery), Compared to the Starting Dose in the Previous Cycle[1]
No toxicity	Maintain dose level	Maintain dose level
Neutropenia		
1 (1500-1999/mm^3)	Maintain dose level	Maintain dose level
2 (1000-1499/mm^3)	↓ 1 dose level	Maintain dose level
3 (500-999/mm^3)	Omit dose until resolved to ≤ grade 2, then ↓ 1 dose level	↓ 1 dose level
4 (<500/mm^3)	Omit dose until resolved to ≤ grade 2, then ↓ 2 dose levels	↓ 2 dose levels
Neutropenic Fever (grade 4 neutropenia and ≥ grade 2 fever)	Omit dose until resolved, then ↓ 2 dose levels	
Other Hematologic Toxicities	Dose modifications for leukopenia or thrombocytopenia during a course of therapy and at the start of subsequent courses of therapy are also based on NCI toxicity criteria and are the same as recommended for neutropenia above.	
Diarrhea		
1 (2-3 stools/day > pretreatment)	Delay dose until resolved to baseline, then give same dose	Maintain dose level
2 (4-6 stools/day > pretreatment)	Omit dose until resolved to baseline, then ↓ 1 dose level	Maintain dose level
3 (7-9 stools/day > pretreatment)	Omit dose until resolved to baseline, then ↓ by 1 dose level	↓ 1 dose level
4 (≥10 stools/day > pretreatment)	Omit dose until resolved to baseline, then ↓ 2 dose levels	↓ 2 dose levels
Other Nonhematologic Toxicities[3]		
1	Maintain dose level	Maintain dose level
2	Omit dose until resolved to ≤ grade 1, then ↓ 1 dose level	Maintain dose level
3	Omit dose until resolved to ≤ grade 2, then ↓ 1 dose level	↓ 1 dose level
4	Omit dose until resolved to ≤ grade 2, then ↓ 2 dose levels	↓ 2 dose levels
Mucositis and/or stomatitis	Decrease only 5-FU, not irinotecan	Decrease only 5-FU, not irinotecan

[1]All dose modifications should be based on the worst preceding toxicity.

[2]National Cancer Institute Common Toxicity Criteria (version 1.0).

[3]Excludes alopecia, anorexia, asthenia.

Single-Agent Schedule: Recommended Dosage Modifications[1]

Toxicity NCI Grade[2] (Value)	During a Cycle of Therapy	At Start of Subsequent Cycles of Therapy (After Adequate Recovery), Compared to Starting Dose in Previous Cycle[1]	
	Weekly	Weekly	Once Every 3 Weeks
No toxicity	Maintain dose level	↑ 25 mg/m² up to a maximum dose of 150 mg/m²	Maintain dose level
Neutropenia			
1 (1500-1999/mm³)	Maintain dose level	Maintain dose level	Maintain dose level
2 (1000-1499/mm³)	↓ 25 mg/m²	Maintain dose level	Maintain dose level
3 (500-999/mm³)	Omit dose until resolved to ≤ grade 2, then ↓ 25 mg/m²	↓ 25 mg/m²	↓ 50 mg/m²
4 (<500/mm³)	Omit dose until resolved to ≤ grade 2, then ↓ 50 mg/m²	↓ 50 mg/m²	↓ 50 mg/m²
Neutropenic Fever (grade 4 neutropenia and ≥ grade 2 fever)	Omit dose until resolved, then ↓ 50 mg/m²	↓ 50 mg/m²	↓ 50 mg/m²
Other Hematologic Toxicities	Dose modifications for leukopenia, thrombocytopenia, and anemia during a course of therapy and at the start of subsequent courses of therapy are also based on NCI toxicity criteria and are the same as recommended for neutropenia above.		
Diarrhea			
1 (2-3 stools/day > pretreatment)	Maintain dose level	Maintain dose level	Maintain dose level
2 (4-6 stools/day > pretreatment)	↓ 25 mg/m²	Maintain dose level	Maintain dose level
3 (7-9 stools/day > pretreatment)	Omit dose until resolved to ≤ grade 2, then ↓ 25 mg/m²	↓ 25 mg/m²	↓ 50 mg/m²
4 (≥10 stools/day > pretreatment)	Omit dose until resolved to ≤ grade 2, then ↓ 50 mg/m²	↓ 50 mg/m²	↓ 50 mg/m²
Other Nonhematologic Toxicities[3]			
1	Maintain dose level	Maintain dose level	Maintain dose level
2	↓ 25 mg/m²	↓ 25 mg/m²	↓ 50 mg/m²
3	Omit dose until resolved to ≤ grade 2, then ↓ 25 mg/m²	↓ 25 mg/m²	↓ 50 mg/m²
4	Omit dose until resolved to ≤ grade 2, then ↓ 50 mg/m²	↓ 50 mg/m²	↓ 50 mg/m²

[1]All dose modifications should be based on the worst preceding toxicity.
[2]National Cancer Institute Common Toxicity Criteria (version 1.0).
[3]Excludes alopecia, anorexia, asthenia.

♦ **Irinotecan Hydrochloride Trihydrate (Can)** *see* Irinotecan *on page 935*

Iron Dextran Complex (EYE ern DEKS tran KOM pleks)

U.S. Brand Names Dexferrum®; INFeD®
Canadian Brand Names Dexiron™; Infufer®
Pharmacologic Category Iron Salt
Use Treatment of microcytic hypochromic anemia resulting from iron deficiency in patients in whom oral administration is infeasible or ineffective
Pregnancy Risk Factor C
Lactation Enters breast milk/contraindicated
Medication Safety Issues
Sound-alike/look-alike issues:
Dexferrum® may be confused with Desferal®
Contraindications Hypersensitivity to iron dextran or any component of the formulation; all anemias that are not involved with iron deficiency; hemochromatosis; hemolytic anemia
Warnings/Precautions Use with caution in patients with history of asthma, hepatic impairment, rheumatoid arthritis. Not recommended in children <4 months of age. **[U.S. Boxed Warning]: Deaths associated with parenteral administration following anaphylactic-type reactions have been reported.** Use only in patients where the iron deficient state is not amenable to oral iron therapy. A test dose of 0.5 mL I.V. or I.M. should be given to observe for adverse reactions. Anemia in the elderly is often caused by "anemia of chronic disease" or associated with inflammation rather than blood loss. Iron stores are usually normal or increased, with a serum ferritin >50 ng/mL and a decreased total iron binding capacity. I.V. administration of iron dextran is often preferred over I.M. in the elderly secondary to a decreased muscle mass and the need for daily injections.
Adverse Reactions
>10%:
Cardiovascular: Flushing
Central nervous system: Dizziness, fever, headache, pain
Gastrointestinal: Nausea, vomiting, metallic taste
Local: Staining of skin at the site of I.M. injection
Miscellaneous: Diaphoresis
1% to 10%:
Cardiovascular: Hypotension (1% to 2%)
Dermatologic: Urticaria (1% to 2%), phlebitis (1% to 2%)
Gastrointestinal: Diarrhea
Genitourinary: Discoloration of urine
<1% (Limited to important or life-threatening): Anaphylactoid reaction, anaphylaxis, shock (cardiovascular collapse, respiratory difficulty; most frequently within minutes of administration)
Note: Diaphoresis, urticaria, arthralgia, fever, chills, dizziness, headache, and nausea may be delayed 24-48 hours after I.V. administration or 3-4 days after I.M. administration.
Overdosage/Toxicology Symptoms include erosion of GI mucosa, pulmonary edema, hyperthermia, convulsions, tachycardia, hepatic and renal impairment, coma, hematemesis, lethargy, tachycardia, and acidosis. Serum iron >300 mcg/mL requires overdose treatment. (Continued)

Iron Dextran Complex *(Continued)*

due to severe toxicity. Although rare, if a severe iron overdose (when the serum iron concentration exceeds the total iron-binding capacity) occurs, it may be treated with deferoxamine. Deferoxamine may be administered I.V. (80 mg/kg over 24 hours) or I.M. (40-90 mg/kg every 8 hours).

Drug Interactions
Decreased Effect: Decreased effect with chloramphenicol.

Ethanol/Nutrition/Herb Interactions Food: Iron bioavailability may be decreased if taken with dairy products.

Stability Store at room temperature. Stability of parenteral admixture is 3 months refrigerated. Solutions for infusion should be diluted in 250-1000 mL NS.

Mechanism of Action The released iron, from the plasma, eventually replenishes the depleted iron stores in the bone marrow where it is incorporated into hemoglobin

Pharmacodynamics/Kinetics

Absorption:

I.M.: 50% to 90% is promptly absorbed, balance is slowly absorbed over month

I.V.: Uptake of iron by the reticuloendothelial system appears to be constant at about 10-20 mg/hour

Excretion: Urine and feces via reticuloendothelial system

Dosage I.M. (Z-track method should be used for I.M. injection), I.V.:

A 0.5 mL test dose (0.25 mL in infants) should be given prior to starting iron dextran therapy; total dose should be divided into a daily schedule for I.M., total dose may be given as a single continuous infusion

Iron-deficiency anemia:

Children 5-15 kg: Should not normally be given in the first 4 months of life:

Dose (mL) = 0.0442 (desired hemoglobin - observed hemoglobin) x W + (0.26 x W)

Desired hemoglobin: Usually 12 g/dL

W = Total body weight in kg

Children >15 kg and Adults:

Dose (mL) = 0.0442 (desired hemoglobin - observed hemoglobin) x LBW + (0.26 x LBW)

Desired hemoglobin: Usually 14.8 g/dL

LBW = Lean body weight in kg

Iron replacement therapy for blood loss: Replacement iron (mg) = blood loss (mL) x hematocrit

Maximum daily dosage:

Manufacturer's labeling: **Note:** Replacement of larger estimated iron deficits may be achieved by serial administration of smaller incremental dosages. Daily dosages should be limited to:

Children:

5-15 kg: 50 mg iron (1 mL)

15-50 kg: 100 mg iron (2 mL)

Adults >50 kg: 100 mg iron (2 mL)

Total dose infusion (unlabeled): The entire dose (estimated iron deficit) may be diluted and administered as a one-time I.V. infusion.

Administration Note: Test dose: A test dose should be given on the first day of therapy; patient should be observed for 1 hour for hypersensitivity reaction, then the remaining dose (dose minus test dose) should be given. Epinephrine should be available.

I.M.: Use Z-track technique (displacement of the skin laterally prior to injection); injection should be deep into the upper outer quadrant of buttock; subsequent injections should be given into alternate buttock

I.V.: Test dose should be given gradually over at least 5 minutes. Subsequent dose(s) may be administered by I.V. bolus at rate of ≤50 mg/minute or diluted in 250-1000 mL NS and infused over 1-6 hours (initial 25 mL should be given slowly and patient should be observed for allergic reactions); avoid dilutions with dextrose (increased incidence of local pain and phlebitis)

Monitoring Parameters Hemoglobin, hematocrit, reticulocyte count, serum ferritin, serum iron, TIBC

Reference Range

Hemoglobin: Adults:

Males: 13.5-16.5 g/dL

Females: 12.0-15.0 g/dL

Serum iron: 40-160 mcg/dL

Total iron binding capacity: 230-430 mcg/dL

Transferrin: 204-360 mg/dL

Percent transferrin saturation: 20% to 50%

Test Interactions May cause falsely elevated values of serum bilirubin and falsely decreased values of serum calcium

Dosage Forms Note: Strength expressed as elemental iron

Injection, solution:

Dexferrum®: 50 mg/mL (1 mL, 2 mL)

INFeD®: 50 mg/mL (2 mL)

♦ **Iron Fumarate** *see* Ferrous Fumarate *on page 702*

♦ **Iron Gluconate** *see* Ferrous Gluconate *on page 703*

♦ **Iron-Polysaccharide Complex** *see* Polysaccharide-Iron Complex *on page 1390*

Iron Sucrose (EYE ern SOO krose)

U.S. Brand Names Venofer®

Canadian Brand Names Venofer®

Pharmacologic Category Iron Salt

Use Treatment of iron-deficiency anemia in chronic renal failure, including nondialysis-dependent patients (with or without erythropoietin therapy) and dialysis-dependent patients receiving erythropoietin therapy

Pregnancy Risk Factor B

Pregnancy Implications Teratogenic effects were not observed in animal studies. There are no adequate and well-controlled studies in pregnant women. Use in pregnancy only if clearly needed. Based on limited data, may be effective for the treatment of iron-deficiency anemia iin pregnancy.

Lactation Excretion in breast milk unknown/use caution

Contraindications Hypersensitivity to iron sucrose or any component of the formulation; evidence of iron overload; anemia not caused by iron deficiency

Warnings/Precautions Rare anaphylactic and anaphylactoid reactions, including serious or life-threatening reactions, have been reported. Facilities (equipment and personnel) for cardiopulmonary resuscitation should be available during initial administration until response/tolerance has been established. Hypotension has been reported frequently in hemodialysis dependent patients. The incidence of hypotension in nondialysis patients is substantially lower. Hypotension may be related to total dose or rate of administration (avoid rapid I.V. injection), follow recommended guidelines. Withhold iron in the presence of tissue iron overload; periodic monitoring of hemoglobin, hematocrit, serum ferritin, and transferrin saturation is recommended. Safety and efficacy in children have not been established.

Adverse Reactions

>10%:
  Cardiovascular: Hypotension (1% to 7%; 39% in hemodialysis patients; may be related to total dose or rate of administration), peripheral edema (2% to 13%)
  Central nervous system: Headache (3% to 13%)
  Gastrointestinal: Nausea (1% to 15%)
  Neuromuscular & skeletal: Muscle cramps (1% to 3%; 29% in hemodialysis patients)

1% to 10%:
  Cardiovascular: Hypertension (6% to 8%), edema (1% to 7%), chest pain (1% to 6%), murmur (<1% to 3%), CHF
  Central nervous system: Dizziness (1% to 10%), fatigue (2% to 5%), fever (1% to 3%), anxiety
  Dermatologic: Pruritus (1% to 7%), rash (<1% to 2%)
  Endocrine & metabolic: Gout (2% to 7%), hypoglycemia (<1% to 4%), hyperglycemia (3% to 4%), fluid overload (1% to 3%)
  Gastrointestinal: Diarrhea (1% to 10%), vomiting (5% to 9%), taste perversion (1% to 9%), peritoneal infection (8%), constipation (1% to 7%), abdominal pain (1% to 4%), positive fecal occult blood (1% to 3%)
  Genitourinary: Urinary tract infection (≤1%)
  Local: Injection site reaction (2% to 4%), catheter site infection (4%)
  Neuromuscular & skeletal: Muscle pain (1% to 7%), extremity pain (3% to 6%), arthralgia (1% to 4%), weakness (1% to 3%), back pain (1% to 3%)
  Ocular: Conjunctivitis (<1% to 3%)
  Otic: Ear pain (1% to 7%)
  Respiratory: Dyspnea (1% to 10%), pharyngitis (<1% to 7%), cough (1% to 7%), sinusitis (1% to 4%), rhinitis (1% to 3%), upper respiratory infection (1% to 3%), nasal congestion (1%)
  Miscellaneous: Graft complication (1% to 10%), hypersensitivity, sepsis

<1% (Limited to important or life-threatening): Anaphylactoid reactions, anaphylactic shock, bronchospasm (with dyspnea), collapse, facial rash, loss of consciousness, hypoesthesia, necrotizing enterocolitis (reported in premature infants, no causal relationship established), seizure, urticaria

Overdosage/Toxicology Symptoms associated with overdose or rapid infusion include hypotension, headache, vomiting, nausea, dizziness, joint aches, paresthesia, abdominal and muscle pain, edema, and cardiovascular collapse. Reducing rate of infusion can alleviate some symptoms. Most symptoms can be treated with I.V. fluids, hydrocortisone, and/or antihistamines.

For severe iron overdose (serum iron concentration exceeds TIBC), deferoxamine may be administered intravenously.

Drug Interactions

Increased Effect/Toxicity: Iron sucrose injection may reduce the absorption of oral iron preparations.

Stability Store vials at room temperature of 15°C to 30°C (59°F to 86°F); do not freeze. May be administered via the dialysis line as an undiluted solution or by diluting 100 mg (5 mL) in 100 mL normal saline. Doses ≥200mg should be diluted in a maximum of 250 mL normal saline. Following dilution, solutions are stable for 48 hours at room temperature or under refrigeration.

Mechanism of Action Iron sucrose is dissociated by the reticuloendothelial system into iron and sucrose. The released iron increases serum iron concentrations and is incorporated into hemoglobin.

Pharmacodynamics/Kinetics

Distribution: V_{dss}: Healthy adults: 7.9 L
Metabolism: Dissociated into iron and sucrose by the reticuloendothelial system
Half-life elimination: Healthy adults: 6 hours
Excretion: Healthy adults: Urine (5%) within 24 hours

Dosage Doses expressed in mg of **elemental** iron. **Note:** Test dose: Product labeling does not indicate need for a test dose in product-naive patients.
(Continued)

Iron Sucrose *(Continued)*

I.V.: Adults: Iron-deficiency anemia in chronic renal disease:

Hemodialysis-dependent patient: 100 mg (5 mL of iron sucrose injection) administered 1-3 times/week during dialysis; administer no more than 3 times/week to a cumulative total dose of 1000 mg (10 doses); may continue to administer at lowest dose necessary to maintain target hemoglobin, hematocrit, and iron storage parameters

Peritoneal dialysis-dependent patient: Slow intravenous infusion at the following schedule: Two infusions of 300 mg each over $1\frac{1}{2}$ hours 14 days apart followed by a single 400 mg infusion over $2\frac{1}{2}$ hours 14 days later (total cumulative dose of 1000 mg in 3 divided doses)

Nondialysis-dependent patient: 200 mg slow injection (over 2-5 minutes) on 5 different occasions within a 14-day period. Total cumulative dose: 1000 mg in 14-day period. **Note:** Dosage has also been administered as two infusions of 500 mg in a maximum of 250 mL 0.9% NaCl infused over 3.5-4 hours on day 1 and day 14 (limited experience)

Elderly: Insufficient data to identify differences between elderly and other adults; use caution

Administration Not for rapid (bolus) I.V. injection; can be administered through dialysis line. Do not mix with other medications or parenteral nutrient solutions.

Slow I.V. injection: 1 mL (20 mg iron) of undiluted solution per minute (100 mg over 2-5 minutes)

Infusion: Dilute 1 vial (100 mg/5 mL) in maximum of 100 mL 0.9% NaCl; infuse over at least 15 minutes; 300 mg/250 mL should be infused over at least $1\frac{1}{2}$ hours; 400 mg/250 mL should be infused over at least $2\frac{1}{2}$ hours; 500 mg/250 mL should be infused over at least $3\frac{1}{2}$ hours.

Monitoring Parameters Hematocrit, hemoglobin, serum ferritin, transferrin, percent transferrin saturation, TIBC; takes about 4 weeks of treatment to see increased serum iron and ferritin, and decreased TIBC. Serum iron concentrations should be drawn 48 hours after last dose.

Reference Range
Hemoglobin: Adults:
Males: 13.5-16.5 g/dL
Females: 12.0-15.0 g/dL
Serum iron: 40-160 mcg/dL
Total iron binding capacity: 230-430 mcg/dL
Transferrin: 204-360 mg/dL
Percent transferrin saturation: 20% to 50%

Dosage Forms Injection, solution [preservative free]: 20 mg of elemental iron/mL (5 mL)

- **Iron Sulfate** *see* Ferrous Sulfate *on page 704*
- **Iron Sulfate and Vitamin C** *see* Ferrous Sulfate and Ascorbic Acid *on page 705*
- **ISD** *see* Isosorbide Dinitrate *on page 945*
- **ISDN** *see* Isosorbide Dinitrate *on page 945*
- **ISG** *see* Immune Globulin (Intramuscular) *on page 891*
- **ISMN** *see* Isosorbide Mononitrate *on page 947*
- **Ismo® [DSC]** *see* Isosorbide Mononitrate *on page 947*
- **Isoamyl Nitrite** *see* Amyl Nitrite *on page 127*
- **Isobamate** *see* Carisoprodol *on page 294*
- **Isochron™** *see* Isosorbide Dinitrate *on page 945*
- **Isometheptene, Acetaminophen, and Dichloralphenazone** *see* Acetaminophen, Isometheptene, and Dichloralphenazone *on page 36*
- **Isometheptene, Dichloralphenazone, and Acetaminophen** *see* Acetaminophen, Isometheptene, and Dichloralphenazone *on page 36*

Isoniazid *(eye soe NYE a zid)*

U.S. Brand Names Nydrazid® [DSC]
Canadian Brand Names Isotamine®; PMS-Isoniazid
Index Terms INH; Isonicotinic Acid Hydrazide
Pharmacologic Category Antitubercular Agent
Additional Appendix Information
Tuberculosis *on page 2010*
Tyramine Content of Foods *on page 2115*
USPHS / IDSA Guidelines for the Prevention of Opportunistic Infections in Persons Infected With HIV *on page 1966*
Use Treatment of susceptible tuberculosis infections; treatment of latent tuberculosis infection (LTBI)
Pregnancy Risk Factor C
Pregnancy Implications Isoniazid was found to be embryocidal in animal studies; teratogenic effects were not noted. Isoniazid crosses the human placenta. Due to the risk of tuberculosis to the fetus, treatment is recommended when the probability of maternal disease is moderate to high. Pyridoxine supplementation is recommended (25 mg/day).
Lactation Enters breast milk/compatible
Medication Safety Issues
International issues:
Hydra® [Japan] may be confused with Hydrea®
Contraindications Hypersensitivity to isoniazid or any component of the formulation; acute liver disease; previous history of hepatic damage during isoniazid therapy
Warnings/Precautions Use with caution in patients with renal impairment and chronic liver disease. **[U.S. Boxed Warning]: Severe and sometimes fatal hepatitis may occur or develop even after many months of treatment.** Patients must report any prodromal symptoms of hepatitis, such as fatigue, weakness, malaise, anorexia, nausea, or vomiting. Children with low milk and low meat intake should receive concomitant pyridoxine therapy.

Periodic ophthalmic examinations are recommended even when usual symptoms do not occur; pyridoxine (10-50 mg/day) is recommended in individuals likely to develop peripheral neuropathies.

Adverse Reactions Frequency not defined.

Cardiovascular: Hypertension, palpitation, tachycardia, vasculitis

Central nervous system: Dizziness, encephalopathy, memory impairment, slurred speech, lethargy, fever, depression, psychosis, seizure

Dermatologic: Rash (morbilliform, maculopapular, pruritic, or exfoliative), flushing

Endocrine & metabolic: Hyperglycemia, metabolic acidosis, gynecomastia, pellagra, pyridoxine deficiency

Gastrointestinal: Anorexia, nausea, vomiting, stomach pain

Hematologic: Agranulocytosis, anemia (sideroblastic, hemolytic, or aplastic), thrombocytopenia, eosinophilia, lymphadenopathy

Hepatic: LFTs mildly increased (10% to 20%); hyperbilirubinemia, jaundice, hepatitis (may involve progressive liver damage; risk increases with age; 2.3% in patients >50 years)

Neuromuscular & skeletal: Weakness, peripheral neuropathy (dose-related incidence, 10% to 20% incidence with 10 mg/kg/day), hyper-reflexia, arthralgia, lupus-like syndrome

Ocular: Blurred vision, loss of vision, optic neuritis and atrophy

Overdosage/Toxicology Symptoms generally occur within 30 minutes to 3 hours, and may include nausea, vomiting, slurred speech, dizziness, blurred vision, metabolic acidosis, hallucinations, stupor, coma, and intractable seizures. Because of severe morbidity and high mortality rates associated with isoniazid overdose, patients who are asymptomatic after an overdose should be monitored for 4-6 hours. Pyridoxine has been shown to be effective in the treatment of intoxication, especially when seizures occur. Pyridoxine I.V. is administered on a milligram to milligram dose. If the amount of isoniazid ingested is unknown, 5 g of pyridoxine should be given over 3-5 minutes and may be followed by an additional 5 g in 30 minutes. Treatment is supportive. Airway protection and ventilation may be required, with diazepam for seizures, and sodium bicarbonate for acidosis. Forced diuresis and hemodialysis can result in more rapid removal.

Drug Interactions

Cytochrome P450 Effect: Substrate of CYP2E1 (major); **Inhibits** CYP1A2 (weak), 2A6 (moderate), 2C9 (weak), 2C19 (strong), 2D6 (moderate), 2E1 (moderate), 3A4 (strong); **Induces** CYP2E1 (after discontinuation) (weak)

Increased Effect/Toxicity: Concurrent use of disulfiram may result in acute intolerance reactions. Isoniazid may increase the levels/effects of amphetamines, benzodiazepines, beta-blockers, calcium channel blockers, citalopram, dexmedetomidine, dextromethorphan, diazepam, fluoxetine, ifosfamide, inhalational anesthetics, lidocaine, methsuximide, mirtazapine, nateglinide, nefazodone, phenytoin, propranolol, risperidone, ritonavir, sertraline, tacrolimus, theophylline, thioridazine, tricyclic antidepressants, trimethadione, venlafaxine, and other substrates of CYP2A6, 2C19, 2D6, 2E1, or 3A4. Selected benzodiazepines (midazolam and triazolam), cisapride, ergot alkaloids, selected HMG-CoA reductase inhibitors (lovastatin and simvastatin), and pimozide are generally contraindicated with strong CYP3A4 inhibitors. Mesoridazine and thioridazine are generally contraindicated with strong CYP2D6 inhibitors. When used with strong CYP3A4 inhibitors, dosage adjustment/limits are recommended for sildenafil and other PDE-5 inhibitors; consult individual monographs.

Decreased Effect: Decreased effect/levels of isoniazid with aluminum salts or antacids. Isoniazid may decrease the levels/effects of CYP2D6 prodrug substrates (eg, codeine, hydrocodone, oxycodone, tramadol).

Ethanol/Nutrition/Herb Interactions

Ethanol: Avoid ethanol (increases the risk of hepatitis).

Food: Isoniazid serum levels may be decreased if taken with food. Has some ability to inhibit tyramine metabolism; several case reports of mild reactions (flushing, palpitations) after ingestion of cheese with or without wine. Isoniazid decreases folic acid absorption. Isoniazid alters pyridoxine metabolism.

Stability Protect oral dosage forms from light.

Mechanism of Action Unknown, but may include the inhibition of myocolic acid synthesis resulting in disruption of the bacterial cell wall

Pharmacodynamics/Kinetics

Absorption: Rapid and complete; rate can be slowed with food

Distribution: All body tissues and fluids including CSF; crosses placenta; enters breast milk

Protein binding: 10% to 15%

Metabolism: Hepatic with decay rate determined genetically by acetylation phenotype

Half-life elimination: Fast acetylators: 30-100 minutes; Slow acetylators: 2-5 hours; may be prolonged with hepatic or severe renal impairment

Time to peak, serum: 1-2 hours

Excretion: Urine (75% to 95%); feces; saliva

Dosage Recommendations often change due to resistant strains and newly-developed information; consult *MMWR* for current CDC recommendations:

Oral (injectable is available for patients who are unable to either take or absorb oral therapy):

Infants and Children:

Treatment of latent TB infection (LTBI): 10-20 mg/kg/day in 1-2 divided doses (maximum: 300 mg/day) or 20-40 mg/kg (maximum: 900 mg/dose) twice weekly for 9 months

Treatment of active TB infection:

Daily therapy: 10-15 mg/kg/day in 1-2 divided doses (maximum: 300 mg/day)

Twice weekly directly observed therapy (DOT): 20-30 mg/kg (maximum: 900 mg)

Adults:

Treatment of latent tuberculosis infection (LTBI): 300 mg/day or 900 mg twice weekly for 6-9 months in patients who do not have HIV infection (9 months is optimal, 6 months may be considered to reduce costs of therapy) and 9 months in patients who have HIV infection. Extend to 12 months of therapy if interruptions in treatment occur.

Treatment of active TB infection (drug susceptible):

Daily therapy: 5 mg/kg/day given daily (usual dose: 300 mg/day); 10 mg/kg/day in 1-2 divided doses In patients with disseminated disease

(Continued)

Isoniazid *(Continued)*

Twice weekly directly observed therapy (DOT): 15 mg/kg (maximum: 900 mg); 3 times/week therapy: 15 mg/kg (maximum: 900 mg)

Note: Treatment may be defined by the number of doses administered (eg, "six-month" therapy involves 192 doses of INH and rifampin, and 56 doses of pyrazinamide). Six months is the shortest interval of time over which these doses may be administered, assuming no interruption of therapy.

Note: Concomitant administration of 6-50 mg/day pyridoxine is recommended in malnourished patients or those prone to neuropathy (eg, alcoholics, diabetics)

Dosing adjustment in renal impairment:
Cl_{cr} <10 mL/minute: Administer 50% of normal dose
Hemodialysis: Dialyzable (50% to 100%)
    Administer dose postdialysis
Peritoneal dialysis, continuous arteriovenous or venovenous hemofiltration: Dose for Cl_{cr} <10 mL/minute

Dosing adjustment in hepatic impairment: Dose should be reduced in severe hepatic disease

Dietary Considerations Should be taken 1 hour before or 2 hours after meals on an empty stomach; increase dietary intake of folate, niacin, magnesium. No need to restrict tyramine-containing foods.

Administration Should be administered 1 hour before or 2 hours after meals on an empty stomach.

Monitoring Parameters Periodic liver function tests; sputum cultures monthly (until 2 consecutive negative cultures reported); monitoring for prodromal signs of hepatitis

Reference Range Therapeutic: 1-7 mcg/mL (SI: 7-51 µmol/L); Toxic: 20-710 mcg/mL (SI: 146-5176 µmol/L)

Test Interactions False-positive urinary glucose with Clinitest®

Additional Information The AAP recommends that pyridoxine supplementation (1-2 mg/kg/day) should be administered to malnourished patients, children or adolescents on meat or milk-deficient diets, breast-feeding infants, and those predisposed to neuritis to prevent peripheral neuropathy; administration of isoniazid syrup has been associated with diarrhea

Dosage Forms [DSC] = Discontinued product
Injection, solution (Nydrazid®): 100 mg/mL (10 mL) [DSC]
Syrup: 50 mg/5 mL (473 mL) [orange flavor]
Tablet: 100 mg, 300 mg

Extemporaneous Preparations A 10 mg/mL oral suspension was stable for 21 days when refrigerated when compounded as follows:
Triturate ten 100 mg tablets in a mortar, reduce to a fine powder, then add 10 mL of purified water U.S.P. to make a paste; then transfer to a graduate and qs to 100 mL with sorbitol (do not use sugar-based solutions)
Shake well before using and keep in refrigerator
Nahata MC and Hipple TF, *Pediatric Drug Formulations*, 3rd ed, Cincinnati, OH: Harvey Whitney Books Co, 1997.

♦ **Isonicotinic Acid Hydrazide** *see* Isoniazid *on page 942*

♦ **Isonipecaine Hydrochloride** *see* Meperidine *on page 1081*

♦ **Isophane Insulin** *see* Insulin NPH *on page 913*

♦ **Isophane Insulin and Regular Insulin** *see* Insulin NPH and Insulin Regular *on page 914*

♦ **Isophosphamide** *see* Ifosfamide *on page 880*

Isoproterenol *(eye soe proe TER e nole)*

U.S. Brand Names Isuprel®
Index Terms Isoproterenol Hydrochloride
Pharmacologic Category Beta$_1$- & Beta$_2$-Adrenergic Agonist Agent
Additional Appendix Information
Bronchodilators *on page 1877*
Hemodynamic Support, Intravenous *on page 1885*

Use Ventricular arrhythmias due to AV nodal block; hemodynamically compromised bradyarrhythmias or atropine- and dopamine-resistant bradyarrhythmias (when transcutaneous/venous pacing is not available); temporary use in third-degree AV block until pacemaker insertion

Unlabeled/Investigational Use Pharmacologic overdrive pacing for torsade de pointes; diagnostic aid (vasovagal syncope)

Pregnancy Risk Factor C
Lactation Excretion in breast milk unknown
Medication Safety Issues
Sound-alike/look-alike issues:
Isuprel® may be confused with Disophrol®, Ismelin®, Isordil®

Contraindications Hypersensitivity to sulfites or isoproterenol, any component of the formulation, or other sympathomimetic amines; angina, pre-existing cardiac arrhythmias (ventricular); tachycardia or AV block caused by cardiac glycoside intoxication

Warnings/Precautions Use with extreme caution; not currently a treatment of choice; use with caution in elderly patients, diabetics, renal or cardiovascular disease, seizure disorder, or hyperthyroidism; excessive or prolonged use may result in decreased effectiveness.

Adverse Reactions Frequency not defined.
Cardiovascular: Premature ventricular beats, bradycardia, hyper-/hypotension, chest pain, palpitation, tachycardia, ventricular arrhythmia, MI size increased
Central nervous system: Headache, nervousness or restlessness
Endocrine & metabolic: Serum glucose increased, serum potassium decreased, hypokalemia
Gastrointestinal: Nausea, vomiting
Respiratory: Dyspnea

Overdosage/Toxicology Symptoms of overdose include tachycardia, tremor, hypertension or hypotension, angina, and seizures. Hypokalemia also may occur. Cardiac arrest and death may be associated with abuse of beta-agonist bronchodilators. Treatment includes immediate discontinuation and symptomatic and supportive therapies. Cautious use of beta-adrenergic blocking agents may be considered in severe cases.

Drug Interactions
Increased Effect/Toxicity: Sympathomimetic agents may cause headaches and elevate blood pressure. General anesthetics may cause arrhythmias.

Ethanol/Nutrition/Herb Interactions Herb/Nutraceutical: Avoid ephedra, yohimbe (may cause CNS stimulation).

Stability Isoproterenol solution should be stored at room temperature. It should not be used if a color or precipitate is present. Exposure to air, light, or increased temperature may cause a pink to brownish pink color to develop. Stability of parenteral admixture at room temperature (25°C) or at refrigeration (4°C) is 24 hours.
Standard diluent: 2 mg/500 mL D_5W; 4 mg/500 mL D_5W.
Minimum volume: 1 mg/100 mL D_5W.

Mechanism of Action Stimulates beta$_1$- and beta$_2$-receptors resulting in relaxation of bronchial, GI, and uterine smooth muscle, increased heart rate and contractility, vasodilation of peripheral vasculature

Pharmacodynamics/Kinetics
Onset of action: Bronchodilation: I.V.: Immediate
Duration: I.V.: 10-15 minutes
Metabolism: Via conjugation in many tissues including hepatic and pulmonary
Half-life elimination: 2.5-5 minutes
Excretion: Urine (primarily as sulfate conjugates)

Dosage I.V.: Cardiac arrhythmias:
Children: Initial: 0.1 mcg/kg/minute (usual effective dose 0.2-2 mcg/kg/minute)
Adults: Initial: 2 mcg/minute; titrate to patient response (2-10 mcg/minute)

Administration I.V. infusion administration requires the use of an infusion pump. To prepare for infusion: 1 mg isoproterenol to 500 mL D_5W, final concentration 2 mcg/mL

Monitoring Parameters ECG, heart rate, respiratory rate, arterial blood gas, arterial blood pressure, CVP; serum glucose, serum potassium, serum magnesium

Dosage Forms Injection, solution, as hydrochloride: 0.02 mg/mL (10 mL); 0.2 mg/mL (1:5000) (1 mL, 5 mL) [contains sodium metabisulfite]

- ◆ **Isoproterenol Hydrochloride** see Isoproterenol on page 944
- ◆ **Isoptin® SR** see Verapamil on page 1784
- ◆ **Isopto® Atropine** see Atropine on page 176
- ◆ **Isopto® Carbachol** see Carbachol on page 284
- ◆ **Isopto® Carpine** see Pilocarpine on page 1368
- ◆ **Isopto® Eserine (Can)** see Physostigmine on page 1365
- ◆ **Isopto® Homatropine** see Homatropine on page 840
- ◆ **Isopto® Hyoscine** see Scopolamine Derivatives on page 1550
- ◆ **Isordil®** see Isosorbide Dinitrate on page 945

Isosorbide Dinitrate (eye soe SOR bide dye NYE trate)

U.S. Brand Names Dilatrate®-SR; Isochron™; Isordil®
Canadian Brand Names Apo-ISDN®; Cedocard®-SR; Coronex®; Novo-Sorbide; PMS-Isosorbide
Index Terms ISD; ISDN
Pharmacologic Category Vasodilator
Additional Appendix Information
Heart Failure (Systolic) on page 2051
Nitrates on page 1893

Use Prevention and treatment of angina pectoris; for congestive heart failure; to relieve pain, dysphagia, and spasm in esophageal spasm with GE reflux

Unlabeled/Investigational Use Esophageal spastic disorders

Pregnancy Risk Factor C

Lactation Excretion in breast milk unknown

Medication Safety Issues
Sound-alike/look-alike issues:
Isordil® may be confused with Inderal®, Isuprel®

International issues:
Nitrobid® [Japan] may be confused with Microzide™ which is a brand name for hydrochlorothiazide in the U.S.

Contraindications Hypersensitivity to isosorbide dinitrate or any component of the formulation; hypersensitivity to organic nitrates; concurrent use with phosphodiesterase-5 (PDE-5) inhibitors (sildenafil, tadalafil, or vardenafil); angle-closure glaucoma (intraocular pressure may be increased); head trauma or cerebral hemorrhage (increase intracranial pressure); severe anemia

Warnings/Precautions Use with caution in patients with increased intracranial pressure, hypotension, hypovolemia, glaucoma; sustained release products may be absorbed erratically in patients with GI hypermotility or malabsorption syndrome; do not crush or chew sublingual dosage form; abrupt withdrawal may result in angina; tolerance may develop (adjust dose or change agent). Avoid use with sildenafil.

Adverse Reactions Frequency not defined.
Cardiovascular: Hypotension (infrequent), postural hypotension, crescendo angina (uncommon), rebound hypertension (uncommon), pallor, cardiovascular collapse, tachycardia, shock, flushing, peripheral edema, syncope (uncommon)
(Continued)

Isosorbide Dinitrate *(Continued)*

Central nervous system: Headache (most common), lightheadedness (related to blood pressure changes), dizziness, restlessness

Gastrointestinal: Nausea, vomiting, bowel incontinence, xerostomia

Genitourinary: Urinary incontinence

Hematologic: Methemoglobinemia (rare, overdose)

Neuromuscular & skeletal: Weakness

Ocular: Blurred vision

Miscellaneous: Cold sweat

The incidence of hypotension and adverse cardiovascular events may be increased when used in combination with sildenafil (Viagra®).

Overdosage/Toxicology The most common symptoms of overdose include hypotension, throbbing headache, tachycardia, and flushing. Methemoglobinemia may occur with massive doses. Hypotension may aggravate symptoms of cardiac ischemia or cerebrovascular disease, and may even cause seizures (rare). Treatment consists of recumbent positioning and administration of fluids. Alpha-adrenergic vasopressors may be required. Treat methemoglobinemia with oxygen and methylene blue at a dose of 1-2 mg/kg slow I.V.

Drug Interactions

Cytochrome P450 Effect: Substrate of CYP3A4 (major)

Increased Effect/Toxicity: CYP3A4 inhibitors may increase the levels/effects of isosorbide dinitrate; example inhibitors include azole antifungals, clarithromycin, diclofenac, doxycycline, erythromycin, imatinib, isoniazid, nefazodone, nicardipine, propofol, protease inhibitors, quinidine, telithromycin, and verapamil. Significant reduction of systolic and diastolic blood pressure with concurrent use of sildenafil, tadalafil, or vardenafil (contraindicated). Do not administer sildenafil, tadalafil, or vardenafil within 24 hours of a nitrate preparation.

Decreased Effect: CYP3A4 inducers may decrease the levels/effects of isosorbide dinitrate; example inducers include aminoglutethimide, carbamazepine, nafcillin, nevirapine, phenobarbital, phenytoin, and rifamycins.

Ethanol/Nutrition/Herb Interactions Ethanol: Caution with ethanol (may increase risk of hypotension).

Mechanism of Action Stimulation of intracellular cyclic-GMP results in vascular smooth muscle relaxation of both arterial and venous vasculature. Increased venous pooling decreases left ventricular pressure (preload) and arterial dilatation decreases arterial resistance (afterload). Therefore, this reduces cardiac oxygen demand by decreasing left ventricular pressure and systemic vascular resistance by dilating arteries. Additionally, coronary artery dilation improves collateral flow to ischemic regions; esophageal smooth muscle is relaxed via the same mechanism.

Pharmacodynamics/Kinetics

Onset of action: Sublingual tablet: 2-10 minutes; Chewable tablet: 3 minutes; Oral tablet: 45-60 minutes

Duration: Sublingual tablet: 1-2 hours; Chewable tablet: 0.5-2 hours; Oral tablet: 4-6 hours

Metabolism: Extensively hepatic to conjugated metabolites, including isosorbide 5-mononitrate (active) and 2-mononitrate (active)

Half-life elimination: Parent drug: 1-4 hours; Metabolite (5-mononitrate): 4 hours

Excretion: Urine and feces

Dosage Adults (elderly should be given lowest recommended daily doses initially and titrate upward): Oral:

Angina: 5-40 mg 4 times/day or 40 mg every 8-12 hours in sustained-release dosage form

Sublingual: 2.5-5 mg every 5-10 minutes for maximum of 3 doses in 15-30 minutes; may also use prophylactically 15 minutes prior to activities which may provoke an attack

Congestive heart failure:

Initial dose: 20 mg 3-4 times per day

Target dose: 120-160 mg/day in divided doses; use in combination with hydralazine

Esophageal spastic disorders (unlabeled use):

Oral: 5-10 mg before meals

Sublingual: 2.5 mg after meals

Tolerance to nitrate effects develops with chronic exposure: Dose escalation does not overcome this effect. Tolerance can only be overcome by short periods of nitrate absence from the body. Short periods (10-12 hours) of nitrate withdrawal help minimize tolerance. General recommendations are to take the last dose of short-acting agents no later than 7 PM; administer 2-3 times/day rather than 4 times/day. Sustained release preparations could be administered at times to allow a 15- to 17-hour interval between first and last daily dose. Example: Administer sustained release at 8 AM and 2 PM for a twice daily regimen.

Hemodialysis: During hemodialysis, administer dose postdialysis or administer supplemental 10-20 mg dose

Peritoneal dialysis: Supplemental dose is not necessary

Administration Do not administer around-the-clock; the first dose of nitrates should be administered in a physician's office to observe for maximal cardiovascular dynamic effects and adverse effects (orthostatic blood pressure drop, headache); when immediate release products are prescribed twice daily (recommend 7 AM and noon); for 3 times/day dosing (recommend 7 AM, noon, and 5 PM); when sustained-release products are indicated, suggest once a day in morning or via twice daily dosing at 8 AM and 2 PM. Do not crush sublingual tablets.

Monitoring Parameters Monitor for orthostasis

Test Interactions Decreased cholesterol (S)

Dosage Forms [DSC] = Discontinued product

Capsule, sustained release (Dilatrate®-SR): 40 mg

Tablet: 5 mg, 10 mg, 20 mg, 30 mg

Isordil®: 5 mg, 10 mg [DSC], 20 mg [DSC], 30 mg [DSC], 40 mg

Tablet, extended release (Isochron™): 40 mg

Tablet, sublingual: 2.5 mg, 5 mg

Isordil®: 2.5 mg, 5 mg, 10 mg [DSC]

Isosorbide Dinitrate and Hydralazine
(eye soe SOR bide dye NYE trate & hye DRAL a zeen)

U.S. Brand Names BiDil®
Index Terms Hydralazine and Isosorbide Dinitrate
Pharmacologic Category Vasodilator
Use Treatment of heart failure, adjunct to standard therapy, in self-identified African-Americans
Pregnancy Risk Factor C
Dosage Oral: Adults: Initial: 1 tablet 3 times/day; titrate to a maximum dose of 2 tablets 3 times/day
   Dosage adjustment for toxicity: If patient experiences persistent headache, adjust dosing to twice daily.
Additional Information Complete prescribing information for this medication should be consulted for additional detail.
Dosage Forms Tablet: Isosorbide dinitrate 20 mg and hydralazine 37.5 mg

Isosorbide Mononitrate (eye soe SOR bide mon oh NYE trate)

U.S. Brand Names Imdur®; Ismo® [DSC]; Monoket®
Canadian Brand Names Apo-ISMN; Imdur®
Index Terms ISMN
Pharmacologic Category Vasodilator
Additional Appendix Information
   Nitrates *on page 1893*
Use Long-acting metabolite of the vasodilator isosorbide dinitrate used for the prophylactic treatment of angina pectoris
Pregnancy Risk Factor C
Lactation Excretion in breast milk unknown
Medication Safety Issues
   Sound-alike/look-alike issues:
     Imdur® may be confused with Imuran®, Inderal LA®, K-Dur®
     Monoket® may be confused with Monopril®

   International issues:
     Nitrex® [Italy] may be confused with Imitrex® which is a brand name for sumatriptan in the U.S.
Contraindications Hypersensitivity to isosorbide or any component of the formulation; hypersensitivity to organic nitrates; concurrent use with phosphodiesterase-5 (PDE-5) inhibitors (sildenafil, tadalafil, or vardenafil); angle-closure glaucoma (intraocular pressure may be increased); head trauma or cerebral hemorrhage (increase intracranial pressure); severe anemia
Warnings/Precautions Postural hypotension, transient episodes of weakness, dizziness, or syncope may occur even with small doses; ethanol accentuates these effects; tolerance and cross-tolerance to nitrate antianginal and hemodynamic effects may occur during prolonged isosorbide mononitrate therapy; (minimized by using the smallest effective dose, by alternating coronary vasodilators or offering drug-free intervals of as little as 12 hours). Excessive doses may result in severe headache, blurred vision, or xerostomia; increased anginal symptoms may be a result of dosage increases. Avoid use with sildenafil.
Adverse Reactions
   >10%: Central nervous system: Headache (19% to 38%)
   1% to 10%:
     Central nervous system: Dizziness (3% to 5%)
     Gastrointestinal: Nausea/vomiting (2% to 4%)
   <1% (Limited to important or life-threatening): Angina pectoris, arrhythmia, atrial fibrillation, impotence, methemoglobinemia (rare), pruritus, rash, supraventricular tachycardia, syncope, vomiting

The incidence of hypotension and adverse cardiovascular events may be increased when used in combination with sildenafil (Viagra®).
Overdosage/Toxicology The most common symptoms of overdose include hypotension, throbbing headache, tachycardia, and flushing. Methemoglobinemia may occur with massive doses. Hypotension may aggravate symptoms of cardiac ischemia or cerebrovascular disease and may even cause seizures (rare). Treatment consists of placing patient in recumbent position and administering fluids; alpha-adrenergic vasopressors may be required; treat methemoglobinemia with oxygen and methylene blue at a dose of 1-2 mg/kg I.V. slowly.
Drug Interactions
   Cytochrome P450 Effect: Substrate of CYP3A4 (major)
   Increased Effect/Toxicity: CYP3A4 inhibitors may increase the levels/effects of isosorbide dinitrate; example inhibitors include azole antifungals, clarithromycin, diclofenac, doxycycline, erythromycin, imatinib, isoniazid, nefazodone, nicardipine, propofol, protease inhibitors, quinidine, telithromycin, and verapamil. Significant reduction of systolic and diastolic blood pressure with concurrent use of sildenafil, tadalafil, or vardenafil (contraindicated). Do not administer sildenafil, tadalafil, or vardenafil within 24 hours of a nitrate preparation.
Ethanol/Nutrition/Herb Interactions Ethanol: Caution with ethanol (may increase risk of hypotension).
Stability Tablets should be stored in a tight container at room temperature of 15°C to 30°C (59°F to 86°F).
Mechanism of Action Prevailing mechanism of action for nitroglycerin (and other nitrates) is systemic venodilation, decreasing preload as measured by pulmonary capillary wedge pressure and left ventricular end diastolic volume and pressure; the average reduction in left ventricular end diastolic volume is 25% at rest, with a corresponding increase in ejection fractions of 50% to 60%. This effect improves congestive symptoms in heart failure and improves the myocardial perfusion gradient in patients with coronary artery disease.
(Continued)

Isosorbide Mononitrate *(Continued)*

Pharmacodynamics/Kinetics
Onset of action: 30-60 minutes
Absorption: Nearly complete and low intersubject variability in its pharmacokinetic parameters and plasma concentrations
Metabolism: Hepatic
Half-life elimination: Mononitrate: ~4 hours
Excretion: Urine and feces

Dosage Adults and Geriatrics (start with lowest recommended dose): Oral:
Regular tablet: 5-20 mg twice daily with the two doses given 7 hours apart (eg, 8 AM and 3 PM) to decrease tolerance development; then titrate to 10 mg twice daily in first 2-3 days.
Extended release tablet: Initial: 30-60 mg given in morning as a single dose; titrate upward as needed, giving at least 3 days between increases; maximum daily single dose: 240 mg
Dosing adjustment in renal impairment: Not necessary for elderly or patients with altered renal or hepatic function.
Tolerance to nitrate effects develops with chronic exposure. Dose escalation does not overcome this effect. Tolerance can only be overcome by short periods of nitrate absence from the body. Short periods (10-12 hours) of nitrate withdrawal help minimize tolerance. Recommended dosage regimens incorporate this interval. General recommendations are to take the last dose of short-acting agents no later than 7 PM; administer 2 times/day rather than 4 times/day. Administer sustained release tablet once daily in the morning.

Administration Do not administer around-the-clock; Monoket® and Ismo® should be scheduled twice daily with doses 7 hours apart (8 AM and 3 PM); Imdur® may be administered once daily. Extended release tablets should not be chewed or crushed. Should be swallowed with a half-glassful of fluid.

Monitoring Parameters Monitor for orthostasis, increased hypotension

Dosage Forms [DSC] = Discontinued product
Tablet: 10 mg, 20 mg
Ismo®: 20 mg [DSC]
Monoket®: 10 mg, 20 mg
Tablet, extended release: 30 mg, 60 mg, 120 mg
Imdur®: 30 mg, 60 mg, 120 mg

♦ **Isotamine® (Can)** *see* Isoniazid *on page 942*

Isotretinoin *(eye soe TRET i noyn)*

U.S. Brand Names Accutane®; Amnesteem™; Claravis™; Sotret®
Canadian Brand Names Accutane®; Clarus™; Isotrex®
Index Terms 13-*cis*-Retinoic Acid
Pharmacologic Category Acne Products; Retinoic Acid Derivative
Use Treatment of severe recalcitrant nodular acne unresponsive to conventional therapy
Unlabeled/Investigational Use Investigational: Treatment of children with metastatic neuroblastoma or leukemia that does not respond to conventional therapy
Restrictions All patients (male and female), prescribers, wholesalers, and dispensing pharmacists must register and be active in the iPLEDGE™ risk management program, designed to eliminate fetal exposures to isotretinoin. This program covers all isotretinoin products (brand and generic). The iPLEDGE™ program requires that all patients meet qualification criteria and monthly program requirements. Registration, activation, and additional information are provided at www.ipledgeprogram.com or by calling 866-495-0654.

An FDA-approved medication guide must be distributed when dispensing an outpatient prescription (new or refill) where this medication is to be used without direct supervision of a healthcare provider. Medication guides are available at http://www.fda.gov/cder/Offices/ODS/medication_guides.htm.

Pregnancy Risk Factor X
Pregnancy Implications Major fetal abnormalities (both internal and external), spontaneous abortion, premature births and low IQ scores in surviving infants have been reported. This medication is contraindicated in females of childbearing potential unless they are able to comply with the guidelines of the iPLEDGE™ pregnancy prevention program. Females of childbearing potential should not become pregnant during therapy or for 1 month following discontinuation of isotretinoin. Upon discontinuation of treatment, females of childbearing potential should have a pregnancy test after their last dose and again one month after their last dose. Two forms of contraception should be continued during this time. Any pregnancies should be reported to the iPLEDGE™ program (www.ipledgeprogram.com or 866-495-0654).
Lactation Excretion in breast milk unknown/contraindicated
Medication Safety Issues
Sound-alike/look-alike issues:
Accutane® may be confused with Accolate®, Accupril®
Contraindications Hypersensitivity to isotretinoin or any component of the formulation; sensitivity to parabens, vitamin A, or other retinoids; pregnancy
Warnings/Precautions This medication should only be prescribed by prescribers competent in treating severe recalcitrant nodular acne, are experienced in the use of systemic retinoids. **[U.S. Boxed Warning]: Because of the high likelihood of teratogenic effects, all patients (male and female), prescribers, wholesalers, and dispensing pharmacists must register and be active in the iPLEDGE™ risk management program; do not prescribe isotretinoin for women who are or who are likely to become pregnant while using the drug (see Additional Information for details).** Women of childbearing potential must be capable of complying with effective contraceptive measures. Patients must select and commit to two forms of contraception. Therapy is begun after two negative pregnancy tests; effective contraception must be used for at least 1 month before beginning therapy, during therapy, and for 1 month after discontinuation of therapy. Prescriptions should be written for no more than a 1-month supply, and pregnancy testing and counseling should be repeated monthly.

May cause depression, psychosis, aggressive or violent behavior, and changes in mood. Rarely, suicidal thoughts and actions have been reported during isotretinoin usage. All patients should be observed closely for symptoms of depression or suicidal thoughts. Discontinuation of treatment alone may not be sufficient, further evaluation may be necessary. Cases of pseudotumor cerebri (benign intracranial hypertension) have been reported, some with concomitant use of tetracycline (avoid using together). Patients with papilledema, headache, nausea, vomiting, and visual disturbances should be referred to a neurologist and treatment with isotretinoin discontinued. Hearing impairment, which can continue after therapy is discontinued, may occur. Clinical hepatitis, elevated liver enzymes, inflammatory bowel disease, insomnia, lethargy, skeletal hyperostosis, premature epiphyseal closure, vision impairment, corneal opacities, and decreased night vision have also been reported with the use of isotretinoin. Use with caution in patients with diabetes mellitus, hypertriglyceridemia; acute pancreatitis and fatal hemorrhagic pancreatitis (rare) have been reported. Bone mineral density may decrease; use caution in patients with a genetic predisposition to bone disorders (ie osteoporosis, osteomalacia) and with disease states or concomitant medications that can induce bone disorders. Patients may be at risk when participating in activities with repetitive impact (such as sports). Safety of long-term use is not established and is not recommended.

Adverse Reactions Frequency not defined.

Cardiovascular: Palpitation, tachycardia, vascular thrombotic disease, stroke, chest pain, syncope, flushing

Central nervous system: Edema, fatigue, pseudotumor cerebri, dizziness, drowsiness, headache, insomnia, lethargy, malaise, nervousness, paresthesia, seizure, stroke, suicidal ideation, suicide attempts, suicide, depression, psychosis, aggressive or violent behavior, emotional instability

Dermatologic: Cutaneous allergic reactions, purpura, acne fulminans, alopecia, bruising, cheilitis, dry mouth, dry nose, dry skin, epistaxis, eruptive xanthomas, fragility of skin, hair abnormalities, hirsutism, hyperpigmentation, hypopigmentation, peeling of palms, peeling of soles, photoallergic reactions, photosensitizing reactions, pruritus, rash, dystrophy, paronychia, facial erythema, seborrhea, eczema, increased sunburn susceptibility, diaphoresis, urticaria, abnormal wound healing

Endocrine & metabolic: Triglycerides increased (25%), abnormal menses, blood glucose increased, cholesterol increased, HDL decreased

Gastrointestinal: Weight loss, inflammatory bowel disease, regional ileitis, pancreatitis, bleeding and inflammation of the gums, colitis, nausea, nonspecific gastrointestinal symptoms

Genitourinary: Nonspecific urogenital findings

Hematologic: Anemia, thrombocytopenia, neutropenia, agranulocytosis, pyogenic granuloma

Hepatic: Hepatitis

Neuromuscular & skeletal: Skeletal hyperostosis, calcification of tendons and ligaments, premature epiphyseal closure, arthralgia, CPK elevations, arthritis, tendonitis, bone abnormalities, weakness, back pain (29% in pediatric patients), rhabdomyolysis (rare), bone mineral density decreased

Ocular: Corneal opacities, decreased night vision, cataracts, color vision disorder, conjunctivitis, dry eyes, eyelid inflammation, keratitis, optic neuritis, photophobia, visual disturbances

Otic: Hearing impairment, tinnitus

Renal: Vasculitis, glomerulonephritis

Respiratory: Bronchospasms, respiratory infection, voice alteration, Wegener's granulomatosis

Miscellaneous: Allergic reactions, anaphylactic reactions, lymphadenopathy, infection, disseminated herpes simplex, diaphoresis

Overdosage/Toxicology Symptoms include headache, vomiting, flushing, abdominal pain, and ataxia. All signs and symptoms have been transient.

Drug Interactions

Increased Effect/Toxicity: Cases of pseudotumor cerebri have been reported in concurrent use with tetracycline; avoid combination.

Decreased Effect: Isotretinoin may increase clearance of carbamazepine resulting in reduced carbamazepine levels. Retinoic acid derivatives may diminish the therapeutic effect of oral contraceptives (two forms of contraception are recommended in females of childbearing potential during retinoic acid therapy).

Ethanol/Nutrition/Herb Interactions

Ethanol: Avoid or limit ethanol (may increase triglyceride levels if taken in excess).

Food: Isotretinoin bioavailability increased if taken with food or milk.

Herb/Nutraceutical: Avoid dong quai, St John's wort (may also cause photosensitization and may decrease the effectiveness of oral contraceptives). Additional vitamin A supplements may lead to vitamin A toxicity (dry skin, irritation, arthralgias, myalgias, abdominal pain, hepatic changes); avoid use.

Stability Store at room temperature. Protect from light.

Mechanism of Action Reduces sebaceous gland size and reduces sebum production; regulates cell proliferation and differentiation

Pharmacodynamics/Kinetics

Distribution: Crosses placenta

Protein binding: 99% to 100%; primarily albumin

Metabolism: Hepatic via CYP2B6, 2C8, 2C9, 2D6, 3A4; forms metabolites; major metabolite: 4-oxo-isotretinoin (active)

Half-life elimination: Terminal: Parent drug: 21 hours; Metabolite: 21-24 hours

Time to peak, serum: 3-5 hours

Excretion: Urine and feces (equal amounts)

Dosage Oral:

Children: Maintenance therapy for neuroblastoma (investigational): 100-250 mg/m^2/day in 2 divided doses

Children 12-17 years and Adults: Severe recalcitrant nodular acne: 0.5-1 mg/kg/day in 2 divided doses (dosages as low as 0.05 mg/kg/day have been reported to be beneficial) for 15-20 weeks or until the total cyst count decreases by 70%, whichever is sooner. Adults (Continued)

Isotretinoin *(Continued)*

with very severe disease/scarring or primarily involves the trunk may require dosage adjustment up to 2 mg/kg/day. A second course of therapy may be initiated after a period of ≥2 months off therapy.

Dosing adjustment in hepatic impairment: Dose reductions empirically are recommended in hepatitis disease

Dietary Considerations Should be taken with food. Limit intake of vitamin A; avoid use of other vitamin A products. Some formulations may contain soybean oil.

Administration Administer with food. Capsules can be swallowed, or chewed and swallowed. The capsule may be opened with a large needle and the contents placed on applesauce or ice cream for patients unable to swallow the capsule. Whole capsules should be swallowed with a full glass of liquid.

Monitoring Parameters CBC with differential and platelet count, baseline sedimentation rate, glucose, CPK

Pregnancy test (for all female patients of childbearing potential): Two negative tests with a sensitivity of at least 25 mIU/mL prior to beginning therapy (the second performed during the first five days of the menstrual period immediately preceding the start of therapy); monthly tests to rule out pregnancy prior to refilling prescription.

Lipids: Prior to treatment and at weekly or biweekly intervals until response to treatment is established. Test should not be performed <36 hours after consumption of ethanol.

Liver function tests: Prior to treatment and at weekly or biweekly intervals until response to treatment is established.

Additional Information All patients (male and female), must be registered in the iPLEDGE™ risk management program. Females of childbearing potential must receive oral and written information reviewing the hazards of therapy and the effects that isotretinoin can have on a fetus. Therapy should not begin without two negative pregnancy tests. Two forms of contraception (a primary and secondary form as described in the iPLEDGE™ program materials) must be used simultaneously beginning 1 month prior to treatment, during treatment, and for 1 month after therapy is discontinued; limitations to their use must be explained. Prescriptions should be written for no more than a 1-month supply, and pregnancy testing and counseling should be repeated monthly. During therapy, the pregnancy test must be conducted by a CLIA-certified laboratory. Prescriptions must be filled and picked up from the pharmacy within 7 days of prescribing for women of childbearing potential.

Any cases of accidental pregnancy should be reported to the iPLEDGE™ program or FDA MedWatch. All patients (male and female) must read and sign the informed consent material provided in the pregnancy prevention program.

Dosage Forms Capsule:
Accutane®: 10 mg, 20 mg, 40 mg [contains soybean oil and parabens]
Amnesteem™: 10 mg, 20 mg, 40 mg [contains soybean oil]
Claravis™: 10 mg, 20 mg, 40 mg
Sotret®: 10 mg, 20 mg, 30 mg, 40 mg [contains soybean oil]

♦ **Isotrex® (Can)** *see* Isotretinoin *on page 948*

Isoxsuprine (eye SOKS syoo preen)

U.S. Brand Names Vasodilan® [DSC]
Index Terms Isoxsuprine Hydrochloride
Pharmacologic Category Vasodilator
Use Treatment of peripheral vascular diseases, such as arteriosclerosis obliterans and Raynaud's disease
Pregnancy Risk Factor C
Medication Safety Issues
Sound-alike/look-alike issues:
Vasodilan® may be confused with Vasocidin®
Dosage Oral: Adults: 10-20 mg 3-4 times/day; start with lower dose in elderly due to potential hypotension
Additional Information Complete prescribing information for this medication should be consulted for additional detail.
Dosage Forms Tablet, as hydrochloride: 10 mg, 20 mg

♦ **Isoxsuprine Hydrochloride** *see* Isoxsuprine *on page 950*

Isradipine (iz RA di peen)

U.S. Brand Names DynaCirc® [DSC]; DynaCirc® CR
Canadian Brand Names DynaCirc®
Pharmacologic Category Calcium Channel Blocker
Additional Appendix Information
Calcium Channel Blockers *on page 1878*
Use Treatment of hypertension
Pregnancy Risk Factor C
Pregnancy Implications Teratogenic effects were not observed in animal studies. Israpidine crosses the human placenta. There are no adequate and well-controlled studies in pregnant women.
Lactation Excretion in breast milk unknown/not recommended
Medication Safety Issues
Sound-alike/look-alike issues:
DynaCirc® may be confused with Dynabac®, Dynacin®
Contraindications Hypersensitivity to isradipine or any component of the formulation; hypotension (<90 mm Hg systolic)

Warnings/Precautions Increased angina and/or MI has occurred with initiation or dosage titration of calcium channel blockers. The most common side effect is peripheral edema; occurs within 2-3 weeks of starting therapy. Reflex tachycardia may occur with use. Symptomatic hypotension with or without syncope can rarely occur; blood pressure must be lowered at a rate appropriate for the patient's clinical condition. Use cautiously in CHF, hypertrophic cardiomyopathy (IHSS), and in hepatic dysfunction. Use controlled release tablets with caution in patients with severe GI narrowing. Safety and efficacy have not been established in pediatric patients. Adjust doses at 2- to 4-week intervals.

Adverse Reactions Percentages reported with capsule formulation.
>10%: Central nervous system: Headache (dose related 2% to 22%)
1% to 10%:
Cardiovascular: Edema (dose related 1% to 9%), palpitation (dose related 1% to 5%), flushing (dose related 1% to 5%), tachycardia (1% to 3%), chest pain (2% to 3%)
Central nervous system: Dizziness (2% to 8%), fatigue (dose related 1% to 9%)
Dermatologic: Rash (2%)
Gastrointestinal: Nausea (1% to 5%), abdominal discomfort (≤3%), vomiting (≤1%), diarrhea (≤3%)
Neuromuscular & skeletal: Weakness (≤1%)
Renal: Urinary frequency (1% to 3%)
Respiratory: Dyspnea (1% to 3%)
<1% (Limited to important or life-threatening): Angioedema, atrial fibrillation, back pain, constipation, cough, cramps of legs and feet, depression, drowsiness, drug fever, dry mouth, dysuria, epistaxis, gingival hyperplasia (incidence unknown), heart failure, hyperhidrosis, hypotension, impotence, insomnia, joint pain, leg pain, lethargy, leukopenia, libido decreased, liver function tests increased, MI, nasal congestion, nervousness, nocturia, numbness, paresthesia,pruritus, stroke, syncope, throat discomfort,transient ischemic attack, urticaria, ventricular fibrillation, visual disturbance, weight gain

Overdosage/Toxicology
Primary cardiac symptoms of calcium blocker overdose include hypotension and bradycardia. Hypotension is caused by peripheral vasodilation, myocardial depression, and bradycardia. Bradycardia results from sinus bradycardia, second- or third-degree atrioventricular block, or sinus arrest with junctional rhythm. Intraventricular conduction is usually not affected so the QRS duration is normal (verapamil prolongs the PR interval and bepridil prolongs the QT interval and may cause ventricular arrhythmias, including torsade de pointes).

Noncardiac symptoms include confusion, stupor, nausea, vomiting, metabolic acidosis and hyperglycemia. Following initial gastric decontamination, if possible, repeated calcium administration may promptly reverse depressed cardiac contractility (but not sinus node depression or peripheral vasodilation). Glucagon, epinephrine, and inamrinone (amrinone) may treat refractory hypotension. Glucagon and epinephrine also increase the heart rate (outside the U.S., 4-aminopyridine may be available as an antidote). Dialysis and hemoperfusion are not effective in enhancing elimination, although repeat-dose activated charcoal may serve as an adjunct with sustained-release preparations.

In a few reported cases, overdose with calcium channel blockers has been associated with hypotension and bradycardia, initially refractory to atropine, but becoming more responsive to this agent when larger doses (approaching 1 g/hour for more than 24 hours) of calcium chloride were administered.

Treatment should be symptom-directed and supportive. Dialysis is not likely to benefit.

Drug Interactions
Cytochrome P450 Effect: Substrate of CYP3A4 (major); **Inhibits** CYP3A4 (weak)
Increased Effect/Toxicity: Isradipine may increase cardiovascular adverse effects of beta-blockers. Alpha$_1$-blockers may enhance the hypotensive effect of isradipine. Calcium channel blockers may enhance the adverse/toxic effect of magnesium salts. Isradipine may minimally increase cyclosporine levels. CYP3A4 inhibitors may increase the levels/effects of isradipine; example inhibitors include azole antifungals, clarithromycin, diclofenac, doxycycline, erythromycin, imatinib, isoniazid, nefazodone, nicardipine, propofol, protease inhibitors, quinidine, telithromycin, and verapamil. Blood pressure-lowering effects may be additive with sildenafil, tadalafil, and vardenafil (use caution). Cimetidine and cyclosporine may decrease the metabolism, via CYP isoenzymes, of israpidine. Isradipine may enhance the adverse/toxic effect of other QT$_c$-prolonging agents. Isradipine may enhance the QT$_c$-prolonging effect of thioridazine.
Decreased Effect: NSAIDs (diclofenac) may decrease the antihypertensive response of isradipine. Isradipine may cause a decrease in lovastatin effect. CYP3A4 inducers may decrease the levels/effects of isradipine; example inducers include aminoglutethimide, carbamazepine, nafcillin, nevirapine, phenobarbital, phenytoin, and rifamycins.

Ethanol/Nutrition/Herb Interactions
Food: Administration with food delays absorption, but does not affect availability
Herb/Nutraceutical: St John's wort may decrease isradipine levels. Avoid dong quai if using for hypertension. Avoid bayberry, blue cohosh, cayenne, ephedra, ginger, ginseng (American), gotu kola, licorice (may worsen hypertension) Avoid garlic (may have increased antihypertensive effect).

Mechanism of Action Inhibits calcium ion from entering the "slow channels" or select voltage-sensitive areas of vascular smooth muscle and myocardium during depolarization, producing a relaxation of coronary vascular smooth muscle and coronary vasodilation; increases myocardial oxygen delivery in patients with vasospastic angina

Pharmacodynamics/Kinetics
Onset of action: Immediate release: 2-3 hours
Duration: Immediate release: >12 hours
Absorption: 90% to 95%
Distribution: V$_d$: 3 L/kg
Protein binding: 95%
Metabolism: Hepatic; CYP3A4 substrate (major); extensive first-pass effect; forms metabolites (inactive)
Bioavailability: 15% to 24%
(Continued)

Isradipine (Continued)

Half-life elimination: Terminal: 8 hours
Time to peak, serum: 1-1.5 hours
Excretion: Urine (60% to 65% as metabolites); feces (25% to 30%)

Dosage Oral:
Adults:
Capsule: 2.5 mg twice daily; antihypertensive response occurs in 2-3 hours; maximal response in 2-4 weeks; increase dose at 2- to 4-week intervals at 2.5-5 mg increments; usual dose range (JNC 7): 2.5-10 mg/day in 2 divided doses. **Note:** Most patients show no improvement with doses >10 mg/day except adverse reaction rate increases; therefore, maximal dose in older adults should be 10 mg/day.
Controlled release tablet: 5 mg once daily; antihypertensive response occurs in 2 hours. Adjust dose in increments of 5 mg at 2-4 week intervals. Maximum dose 20 mg/day; adverse events are increased at doses >10 mg/day.
Elderly:
Capsule: Refer to adult dosing.
Controlled release tablet: Initial dose: 5 mg once daily

Dosage adjustment in renal impairment: Cl_{cr} 30-80 mL/minute: Bioavailability increased by 45%. Cl_{cr} <10 mL/minute on hemodialysis: Bioavailability decreased by 20% to 50%
Capsule: Refer to adult dosing.
Controlled release tablet: Initial dose: 5 mg once daily
Dosage adjustment in hepatic impairment: Peak serum concentrations are increased by 32% and bioavailability is increased by 52%
Capsule: Refer to adult dosing.
Controlled release tablet: Initial dose: 5 mg once daily

Dietary Considerations May be taken without regard to meals.
Administration Controlled release tablets should be swallowed whole; do not divide or chew
Monitoring Parameters Blood pressure; renal, hepatic dysfunction
Dosage Forms
Capsule: 2.5 mg, 5 mg
DynaCirc®: 2.5 mg [DSC], 5 mg [DSC]
Tablet, controlled release:
DynaCirc® CR: 5 mg, 10 mg
Extemporaneous Preparations A 1 mg/mL oral liquid was stable for 35 days when refrigerated when compounded as follows:
Dissolve the contents of ten 5 mg capsules in simple syrup, qs ad 50 mL
Shake well before using and keep in refrigerator
MacDonald JL, Johnson CE, and Jacobson P, "Stability of Isradipine in Extemporaneously Compounded Oral Liquids," *Am J Hosp Pharm,* 1994, 51(19):2409-11.

♦ **Istalol™** *see* Timolol *on page 1687*
♦ **Isuprel®** *see* Isoproterenol *on page 944*

Itraconazole (i tra KOE na zole)

U.S. Brand Names Sporanox®
Canadian Brand Names Sporanox®
Pharmacologic Category Antifungal Agent, Oral
Additional Appendix Information
Antifungal Agents *on page 1869*
USPHS / IDSA Guidelines for the Prevention of Opportunistic Infections in Persons Infected With HIV *on page 1966*
Use Treatment of susceptible fungal infections in immunocompromised and immunocompetent patients including blastomycosis and histoplasmosis; indicated for aspergillosis, and onychomycosis of the toenail; treatment of onychomycosis of the fingernail without concomitant toenail infection via a pulse-type dosing regimen; has activity against *Aspergillus, Candida, Coccidioides, Cryptococcus, Sporothrix,* tinea unguium

Oral: Useful in superficial mycoses including dermatophytoses (eg, tinea capitis), pityriasis versicolor, sebopsoriasis, vaginal and chronic mucocutaneous candidiases; systemic mycoses including candidiasis, meningeal and disseminated cryptococcal infections, paracoccidioidomycosis, coccidioidomycoses; miscellaneous mycoses such as sporotrichosis, chromomycosis, leishmaniasis, fungal keratitis, alternariosis, zygomycosis
Oral solution: Treatment of oral and esophageal candidiasis
Intravenous solution: Indicated in the treatment of blastomycosis, histoplasmosis (nonmeningeal), and aspergillosis (in patients intolerant or refractory to amphotericin B therapy); empiric therapy of febrile neutropenic fever

Pregnancy Risk Factor C
Pregnancy Implications Should not be used to treat onychomycosis during pregnancy. Effective contraception should be used during treatment and for 2 months following treatment. Congenital abnormalities have been reported during postmarketing surveillance, but a causal relationship has not been established.
Lactation Enters breast milk/not recommended
Medication Safety Issues
Sound-alike/look-alike issues:
Sporanox® may be confused with Suprax®
Contraindications Hypersensitivity to itraconazole, any component of the formulation, or to other azoles; concurrent administration with cisapride, dofetilide, ergot derivatives, levomethadyl, lovastatin, midazolam, pimozide, quinidine, simvastatin, or triazolam; treatment of onychomycosis in patients with evidence of left ventricular dysfunction, CHF, or a history of CHF
Warnings/Precautions Discontinue if signs or symptoms of CHF or neuropathy occur during treatment. **[U.S. Boxed Warning]: Rare cases of serious cardiovascular adverse events**

(including death), ventricular tachycardia, and torsade de pointes have been observed due to increased cisapride, pimozide, quinidine, dofetilide or levomethadyl concentrations induced by itraconazole; concurrent use contraindicated. Use with caution in patients with left ventricular dysfunction or a history of CHF; not recommended for treatment of onychomycosis in these patients. Not recommended for use in patients with active liver disease, elevated liver enzymes, or prior hepatotoxic reactions to other drugs. Itraconazole has been associated with rare cases of serious hepatotoxicity (including fatal cases and cases within the first week of treatment); treatment should be discontinued in patients who develop clinical symptoms of liver dysfunction or abnormal liver function tests during itraconazole therapy except in cases where expected benefit exceeds risk. Large differences in itraconazole pharmacokinetic parameters have been observed in cystic fibrosis patients receiving the solution; if a patient with cystic fibrosis does not respond to therapy, alternate therapies should be considered. Due to differences in bioavailability, oral capsules and oral solution **cannot be used interchangeably.** Intravenous formulation should be used with caution in renal impairment; consider conversion to oral therapy if renal dysfunction/toxicity is noted. Initiation of treatment with oral solution is not recommended in patients at immediate risk for systemic candidiasis (eg, patients with severe neutropenia).

Adverse Reactions Listed incidences are for higher doses appropriate for systemic fungal infection.

>10%: Gastrointestinal: Nausea (11%)

1% to 10%:

Cardiovascular: Edema (4%), hypertension (3%)

Central nervous system: Headache (4%), fatigue (2% to 3%), malaise (1%), fever (3%), dizziness (2%)

Dermatologic: Rash (9%), pruritus (3%)

Endocrine & metabolic: Decreased libido (1%), hypertriglyceridemia, hypokalemia (2%)

Gastrointestinal: Abdominal pain (2%), anorexia (1%), vomiting (5%), diarrhea (3%)

Hepatic: Abnormal LFTs (3%), hepatitis

Renal: Albuminuria (1%)

<1% (Limited to important or life-threatening): Adrenal suppression; allergic reactions (urticaria, angioedema); alopecia, anaphylactoid reactions, anaphylaxis, arrhythmia, CHF, constipation, gastritis, gynecomastia, hepatic failure, impotence, neutropenia, peripheral neuropathy, photosensitivity, pulmonary edema, somnolence, Stevens-Johnson syndrome, tinnitus

Overdosage/Toxicology Overdoses are well tolerated. Following decontamination, if possible, supportive measures only are required. Dialysis is not effective.

Drug Interactions

Cytochrome P450 Effect: Substrate of CYP3A4 (major); **Inhibits** CYP3A4 (strong)

Increased Effect/Toxicity: Itraconazole is a strong inhibitor of CYP3A4, and is contraindicated with cisapride, dofetilide, ergot derivatives, lovastatin, midazolam, pimozide, quinidine, simvastatin, and triazolam. Itraconazole may also increase the levels of alfentanil, benzodiazepines (alprazolam, diazepam, and others), buspirone, busulfan, calcium channel blockers (felodipine, nifedipine, verapamil), carbamazepine, corticosteroids, cyclosporine, digoxin, docetaxel, eletriptan, HMG-CoA reductase inhibitors (except fluvastatin, pravastatin), indinavir, oral hypoglycemics (sulfonylureas), phenytoin, rifabutin, ritonavir, saquinavir, sirolimus, tacrolimus, trimetrexate, vincristine, vinblastine, warfarin, and zolpidem. Other medications metabolized by CYP3A4 should be used with caution. Serum concentrations of itraconazole may be increased by strong CYP3A4 inhibitors. Serum concentrations of PDE-5 inhibitors (sildenafil, tadalafil, and vardenafil) are increased by itraconazole; specific dosage reductions/limitations are recommended.

Decreased Effect: Absorption of itraconazole requires gastric acidity; therefore, antacids, H_2 antagonists (cimetidine, famotidine, nizatidine, and ranitidine), proton pump inhibitors (omeprazole, lansoprazole, rabeprazole), and sucralfate may significantly reduce bioavailability resulting in treatment failures and should not be administered concomitantly. Antacids may decrease serum concentration of itraconazole; administer antacids 1 hour before or 2 hours after itraconazole capsules. Serum levels of itraconazole may be decreased with didanosine, isoniazid, and nevirapine. The levels/effects of itraconazole may be reduced by aminoglutethimide, carbamazepine, nafcillin, phenobarbital, phenytoin, rifamycins, and other CYP3A4 inducers. Oral contraceptive efficacy may be reduced (limited data).

Ethanol/Nutrition/Herb Interactions

Food:

Capsules: Enhanced by food and possibly by gastric acidity. cola drinks have been shown to increase the absorption of the capsules in patients with achlorhydria or those taking H_2-receptor antagonists or other gastric acid suppressors. Avoid grapefruit juice.

Solution: Decreased by food, time to peak concentration prolonged by food.

Herb/Nutraceutical: St John's wort may decrease itraconazole levels.

Stability

Capsule: Store at room temperature, 15°C to 25°C (59°F to 77°F). Protect from light and moisture.

Oral solution: Store at ≤25°C (77°F); do not freeze.

Solution for injection: Store at ≤25°C (77°F); do not freeze. Protect from light. Dilute with 0.9% sodium chloride. Stable for 48 hours at room temperature or under refrigeration. A precise mixing ratio is required to maintain stability (3.33:1) and avoid precipitate formation. Add 25 mL (1 ampul) to 50 mL 0.9% sodium chloride. Mix and withdraw 15 mL of solution before infusing.

Mechanism of Action Interferes with cytochrome P450 activity, decreasing ergosterol synthesis (principal sterol in fungal cell membrane) and inhibiting cell membrane formation

Pharmacodynamics/Kinetics

Absorption: Requires gastric acidity; capsule better absorbed with food, solution better absorbed on empty stomach

Distribution: V_d (average): 796 ± 185 L or 10 L/kg; highly lipophilic and tissue concentrations are higher than plasma concentrations. The highest concentrations: adiposa, omentum, (Continued)

Itraconazole *(Continued)*

endometrium, cervical and vaginal mucus, and skin/nails. Aqueous fluids (eg, CSF and urine) contain negligible amounts.

Protein binding, plasma: 99.9%; metabolite hydroxy-itraconazole: 99.5%

Metabolism: Extensively hepatic via CYP3A4 into >30 metabolites including hydroxy-itraconazole (major metabolite); appears to have *in vitro* antifungal activity. Main metabolic pathway is oxidation; may undergo saturation metabolism with multiple dosing.

Bioavailability: Variable, ~55% (oral solution) in 1 small study; **Note:** Oral solution has a higher degree of bioavailability (149% ± 68%) relative to oral capsules; should not be interchanged

Half-life elimination: Oral: After single 200 mg dose: 21 ± 5 hours; 64 hours at steady-state; I.V.: steady-state: 35 hours; steady-state concentrations are achieved in 13 days with multiple administration of itraconazole 100-400 mg/day.

Excretion: Feces (~3% to 18%); urine (~0.03% as parent drug, 40% as metabolites)

Dosage

Usual dosage ranges:

Children: Efficacy and safety have not been established; a small number of patients 3-16 years of age have been treated with 100 mg/day for systemic fungal infections with no serious adverse effects reported. A dose of 5 mg/kg once daily was used in a pharmacokinetic study using the oral solution in patients 6 months to 12 years; duration of study was 2 weeks.

Adults: Oral, I.V.: 100-400 mg/day; doses >200 mg/day are given in 2 divided doses; length of therapy varies from 1 day to >6 months depending on the condition and mycological response

Indication-specific dosing:

Adults:

Aspergillosis:

Oral: 200-400 mg/day

I.V.: 200 mg twice daily for 4 doses, followed by 200 mg daily

Blastomycosis/histoplasmosis:

Oral: 200 mg once daily, if no obvious improvement or there is evidence of progressive fungal disease, increase the dose in 100 mg increments to a maximum of 400 mg/day; doses >200 mg/day are given in 2 divided doses; length of therapy varies from 1 day to >6 months depending on the condition and mycological response

I.V.: 200 mg twice daily for 4 doses, followed by 200 mg daily

Brain abscess: Cerebral phaeohyphomycosis (dematiaceous): Oral: 200 mg twice daily for at least 6 months with amphotericin

Candidiasis:

Oropharyngeal: Oral solution: 200 mg once daily for 1-2 weeks; in patients unresponsive or refractory to fluconazole: 100 mg twice daily (clinical response expected in 1-2 weeks)

Esophageal: Oral solution: 100-200 mg once daily for a minimum of 3 weeks; continue dosing for 2 weeks after resolution of symptoms

Coccidioides: Oral: 200 mg twice daily

Infections, life-threatening:

Oral: 200 mg 3 times/day (600 mg/day) should be given for the first 3 days of therapy

I.V.: 200 mg twice daily for 4 doses, followed by 200 mg/day

Meningitis:

Coccidioides: Oral: 400-800 mg/day

Cryptococcal: HIV positive (unlabeled use): Induction: Oral: 400 mg/day for 10-12 weeks; maintenance: 200 mg twice daily lifelong

Onychomycosis: Oral: 200 mg once daily for 12 consecutive weeks

Pneumonia:

Coccidioides: Mild to moderate: Oral, I.V.: 200 mg twice daily

Cryptococcal: Mild to moderate (unlabeled use): 200-400 mg/day for 6-12 months (lifelong for HIV positive)

Prototheca infection: 200 mg once daily for 2 months

Sporotrichosis: Oral:

Lymphocutaneous: 100-200 mg/day for 3-6 months

Osteoarticular and pulmonary: 200 mg twice daily for 1-2 years (may use amphotericin B initially for stabilization)

Dosing adjustment in renal impairment: Not necessary; itraconazole injection is not recommended in patients with Cl_{cr} <30 mL/minute; hydroxypropyl-β-cyclodextrin (the excipient) is eliminated primarily by the kidneys.

Hemodialysis: Not dialyzable

Dosing adjustment in hepatic impairment: May be necessary, but specific guidelines are not available. Risk-to-benefit evaluation should be undertaken in patients who develop liver function abnormalities during treatment.

Dietary Considerations

Capsule: Administer with food.

Solution: Take without food, if possible.

Administration

Oral: Doses >200 mg/day are given in 2 divided doses; do not administer with antacids. Capsule absorption is best if taken with food, therefore, it is best to administer itraconazole after meals; solution should be taken on an empty stomach. When treating oropharyngeal and esophageal candidiasis, solution should be swished vigorously in mouth, then swallowed.

I.V.: Infuse 60 mL of the dilute solution (3.33 mg/mL = 200 mg itraconazole, pH ~4.8) over 60 minutes; flush with 15-20 mL of 0.9% sodium chloride over 30 seconds to 15 minutes

Monitoring Parameters Liver function in patients with pre-existing hepatic dysfunction, and in all patients being treated for longer than 1 month

Reference Range Trough serum concentrations may be performed to assure therapeutic levels, especially in the face of oral therapy. Trough concentration of itraconazole plus the metabolite hydroxyitraconazole should be at least 0.5 mcg/mL.

Additional Information Due to potential toxicity, the manufacturer recommends confirmation of diagnosis testing of nail specimens prior to treatment of onychomycosis.

Dosage Forms
Capsule: 100 mg
Injection, solution: 10 mg/mL (25 mL) [packaged in a kit containing sodium chloride 0.9% (50 mL); filtered infusion set (1)]
Solution, oral: 100 mg/10 mL (150 mL) [cherry flavor]

- **Iveegam EN** see Immune Globulin (Intravenous) on page 892
- **Iveegam Immuno® (Can)** see Immune Globulin (Intravenous) on page 892

Ivermectin (eye ver MEK tin)

U.S. Brand Names Stromectol®
Pharmacologic Category Anthelmintic
Use Treatment of the following infections: Strongyloidiasis of the intestinal tract due to the nematode parasite *Strongyloides stercoralis*. Onchocerciasis due to the nematode parasite *Onchocerca volvulus*. Ivermectin is only active against the immature form of *Onchocerca volvulus*, and the intestinal forms of *Strongyloides stercoralis*.
Unlabeled/Investigational Use Has been used for other parasitic infections including *Ascaris lumbricoides*, Bancroftian filariasis, *Brugia malayi*, scabies, *Enterobius vermicularis*, *Mansonella ozzardi*, *Trichuris trichiura*.
Pregnancy Risk Factor C
Pregnancy Implications Safety and efficacy have not been established in pregnant women. The WHO considers use after the first trimester as "probably acceptable."
Lactation Enters breast milk/not recommended
Contraindications Hypersensitivity to ivermectin or any component of the formulation
Warnings/Precautions Data have shown that antihelmintic drugs like ivermectin may cause cutaneous and/or systemic reactions (Mazzoti reaction) of varying severity including ophthalmological reactions in patients with onchocerciasis. These reactions are probably due to allergic and inflammatory responses to the death of microfilariae. Patients with hyper-reactive onchodermatitis may be more likely than others to experience severe adverse reactions, especially edema and aggravation of the onchodermatitis. Repeated treatment may be required in immunocompromised patients (eg, HIV); control of extraintestinal strongyloidiasis may necessitate suppressive (once monthly) therapy. Pretreatment assessment for *Loa loa* infection is recommended in any patient with significant exposure to endemic areas (West and Central Africa); serious and/or fatal encephalopathy has been reported during treatment in patients with loiasis. Safety and efficacy in children <15 kg have not be established.
Adverse Reactions Frequency not defined.
Cardiovascular: Hypotension, mild ECG changes, orthostasis, peripheral and facial edema, transient tachycardia
Central nervous system: Dizziness, encephalopathy (rare; associated with loiasis), headache, hyperthermia, insomnia, seizure, somnolence, vertigo
Dermatologic: Pruritus, rash, Stevens-Johnson syndrome, urticaria, toxic epidermal necrolysis
Gastrointestinal: Abdominal pain, anorexia, constipation, diarrhea, nausea, vomiting
Hematologic: Anemia, eosinophilia, leukopenia
Hepatic: ALT/AST increased, bilirubin increased
Neuromuscular & skeletal: Limbitis, myalgia, tremor, weakness
Ocular: Blurred vision, mild conjunctivitis, punctate opacity
Respiratory: Asthma exacerbation
Miscellaneous: Mazzotti reaction (with onchocerciasis): Arthralgia, edema, fever, lymphadenopathy, ocular damage, pruritus, rash, synovitis
Overdosage/Toxicology Accidental intoxication with, or significant exposure to unknown quantities of veterinary formulations of ivermectin in humans, either by ingestion, inhalation, injection, or exposure to body surfaces, has resulted in the following adverse effects: rash, edema, headache, dizziness, asthenia, nausea, vomiting, and diarrhea. Other adverse effects that have been reported include seizure and ataxia. Treatment is supportive. The usual methods for decontamination are recommended.
Drug Interactions
Cytochrome P450 Effect: Substrate of CYP3A4 (minor)
Ethanol/Nutrition/Herb Interactions
Food: Bioavailability is increased 2.5-fold when administered following a high-fat meal.
Mechanism of Action Ivermectin is a semisynthetic antihelminthic agent; it binds selectively and with strong affinity to glutamate-gated chloride ion channels which occur in invertebrate nerve and muscle cells. This leads to increased permeability of cell membranes to chloride ions then hyperpolarization of the nerve or muscle cell, and death of the parasite.
Pharmacodynamics/Kinetics
Onset of action: Peak effect: 3-6 months
Absorption: Well absorbed
Distribution: Does not cross blood-brain barrier
Half-life elimination: 16-35 hours
Metabolism: Hepatic (>97%)
Excretion: Urine (<1%); feces
Dosage Oral: Children ≥15 kg and Adults:
Strongyloidiasis: 200 mcg/kg as a single dose; follow-up stool examinations
Onchocerciasis: 150 mcg/kg as a single dose; retreatment may be required every 3-12 months until the adult worms die
Dietary Considerations Take on an empty stomach with water.
Administration Administer on an empty stomach with water.
(Continued)

Ivermectin *(Continued)*

Monitoring Parameters Skin and eye microfilarial counts, periodic ophthalmologic exams

Dosage Forms Tablet [scored]: 3 mg

- ◆ **IVIG** *see* Immune Globulin (Intravenous) *on page 892*
- ◆ **IvyBlock® [OTC]** *see* Bentoquatam *on page 204*
- ◆ **Ivy-Rid® [OTC]** *see* Benzocaine *on page 204*
- ◆ **IvySoothe® [OTC]** *see* Hydrocortisone *on page 852*
- ◆ **Jamp® Travel Tablet (Can)** *see* DimenhyDRINATE *on page 511*
- ◆ **Jantoven™** *see* Warfarin *on page 1800*
- ◆ **Januvia™** *see* Sitagliptin *on page 1572*

Japanese Encephalitis Virus Vaccine (Inactivated)
(jap a NEESE en sef a LYE tis VYE rus vak SEEN, in ak ti VAY ted)

U.S. Brand Names JE-VAX®

Canadian Brand Names JE-VAX®

Pharmacologic Category Vaccine

Use Active immunization against Japanese encephalitis for persons 1 year of age and older who plan to spend 1 month or more in endemic areas in Asia, especially persons traveling during the transmission season or visiting rural areas; consider vaccination for shorter trips to epidemic areas or extensive outdoor activities in rural endemic areas; elderly (>55 years of age) individuals should be considered for vaccination, since they have increased risk of developing symptomatic illness after infection; those planning travel to or residence in endemic areas should consult the Travel Advisory Service (Central Campus) for specific advice

Pregnancy Risk Factor C

Contraindications Serious adverse reaction (generalized urticaria or angioedema) to a prior dose of this vaccine; proven or suspected hypersensitivity to proteins or rodent or neural origin; hypersensitivity to thimerosal (used as a preservative). *CDC recommends that the following should not generally receive the vaccine, unless benefit to the individual clearly outweighs the risk:*

- those acutely ill or with active infections
- persons with heart, kidney, or liver disorders
- persons with generalized malignancies such as leukemia or lymphoma
- persons with a history of multiple allergies or hypersensitivity to components of the vaccine
- pregnant women, unless there is a very high risk of Japanese encephalitis during the woman's stay in Asia

Warnings/Precautions Severe adverse reactions manifesting as generalized urticaria or angioedema may occur within minutes following vaccination, or up to 17 days later; most reactions occur within 10 days, with the majority within 48 hours; observe vaccinees for 30 minutes after vaccination; warn them of the possibility of delayed generalized urticaria and to remain where medical care is readily available for 10 days following any dose of the vaccine; because of the potential for severe adverse reactions, Japanese encephalitis vaccine is **not** recommended for all persons traveling to or residing in Asia; safety and efficacy in infants <1 year of age have not been established; therefore, immunization of infants should be deferred whenever possible; it is not known whether the vaccine is excreted in breast milk

Adverse Reactions Report allergic or unusual adverse reactions to the Vaccine Adverse Event Reporting System (VAERS) 1-800-822-7967.

Frequency not defined, common:
Cardiovascular: Hypotension
Central nervous system: Fever, headache, malaise, chills, dizziness
Dermatologic: Rash, urticaria, itching with or without accompanying rash
Gastrointestinal: Nausea, vomiting, abdominal pain
Local: Tenderness, redness, and swelling at injection site
Neuromuscular & skeletal: Myalgia

Frequency not defined, rare:
Cardiovascular: Angioedema
Central nervous system: Seizure, encephalitis, encephalopathy
Dermatologic: Erythema multiforme, erythema nodosum
Neuromuscular & skeletal: Peripheral neuropathy, joint swelling
Respiratory: Dyspnea
Miscellaneous: Anaphylactic reaction

Stability Refrigerate. Discard 8 hours after reconstitution.

Dosage U.S. recommended primary immunization schedule:

Children 1-3 years: SubQ: Three 0.5 mL doses given on days 0, 7, and 30; abbreviated schedules should be used only when necessary due to time constraints

Children >3 years and Adults: SubQ: Three 1 mL doses given on days 0, 7, and 30. Give third dose on day 14 when time does not permit waiting; 2 doses a week apart produce immunity in about 80% of recipients; the longest regimen yields highest titers after 6 months.

Booster dose: Give after 2 years, or according to current recommendation

Note: Travel should not commence for at least 10 days after the last dose of vaccine, to allow adequate antibody formation and recognition of any delayed adverse reaction

Advise concurrent use of other means to reduce the risk of mosquito exposure when possible, including bed nets, insect repellents, protective clothing, avoidance of travel in endemic areas, and avoidance of outdoor activity during twilight and evening periods

Administration The single-dose vial should only be reconstituted with the full 1.3 mL of diluent supplied; administer 1 mL of the resulting liquid as one standard adult dose; discard the unused portion

Additional Information Japanese encephalitis vaccine is currently available only from the Centers for Disease Control. Contact Centers for Disease Control at (404) 639-6370

(Mon-Fri) or (404) 639-2888 (nights, weekends, or holidays). Federal law requires that the date of administration, the vaccine manufacturer, lot number of vaccine, and the administering person's name, title and address be entered into the patient's permanent medical record.

Dosage Forms Injection, powder for reconstitution: 1 mL, 10 mL

♦ **JE-VAX**® *see* Japanese Encephalitis Virus Vaccine (Inactivated) *on page 956*
♦ **Jolessa**™ *see* Ethinyl Estradiol and Levonorgestrel *on page 653*
♦ **Junel**™ *see* Ethinyl Estradiol and Norethindrone *on page 655*
♦ **Junel**™ **Fe** *see* Ethinyl Estradiol and Norethindrone *on page 655*
♦ **Just for Kids**™ **[OTC]** *see* Fluoride *on page 722*
♦ **Juvederm**™ **24HV** *see* Hyaluronate and Derivatives *on page 841*
♦ **Juvederm**™ **30** *see* Hyaluronate and Derivatives *on page 841*
♦ **Juvederm**™ **30HV** *see* Hyaluronate and Derivatives *on page 841*
♦ **K-10**® **(Can)** *see* Potassium Chloride *on page 1396*
♦ **Kadian**® *see* Morphine Sulfate *on page 1171*
♦ **Kala**® **[OTC]** *see* Lactobacillus *on page 969*
♦ **Kaletra**® *see* Lopinavir and Ritonavir *on page 1029*

Kanamycin (kan a MYE sin)

U.S. Brand Names Kantrex®
Canadian Brand Names Kantrex®
Index Terms Kanamycin Sulfate
Pharmacologic Category Antibiotic, Aminoglycoside
Additional Appendix Information
Antimicrobial Drugs of Choice *on page 1981*
Tuberculosis *on page 2010*
Use Treatment of serious infections caused by susceptible strains of *E. coli*, *Proteus* species, *Enterobacter aerogenes*, *Klebsiella pneumoniae*, *Serratia marcescens*, and *Acinetobacter* species; second-line treatment of *Mycobacterium tuberculosis*
Pregnancy Risk Factor D
Medication Safety Issues
Sound-alike/look-alike issues:
Kanamycin may be confused with Garamycin®, gentamicin
Dosage Note: Dosing should be based on ideal body weight
Children: Infections: I.M., I.V.: 15 mg/kg/day in divided doses every 8-12 hours
Adults:
Infections: I.M., I.V.: 5-7.5 mg/kg/dose in divided doses every 8-12 hours (<15 mg/kg/day)
Intraperitoneal: After contamination in surgery: 500 mg
Irrigating solution: 0.25%; maximum 1.5 g/day (via all administration routes)
Aerosol: 250 mg 2-4 times/day
Dosing adjustment/interval in renal impairment:
Cl_{cr} 50-80 mL/minute: Administer 60% to 90% of dose or administer every 8-12 hours
Cl_{cr} 10-50 mL/minute: Administer 30% to 70% of dose or administer every 12 hours
Cl_{cr} <10 mL/minute: Administer 20% to 30% of dose or administer every 24-48 hours
Additional Information Complete prescribing information for this medication should be consulted for additional detail.
Dosage Forms Injection, solution, as sulfate: 1 g/3 mL (3 mL) [contains sodium bisulfate]

♦ **Kanamycin Sulfate** *see* Kanamycin *on page 957*
♦ **Kanka**® **Soft Brush**™ **[OTC]** *see* Benzocaine *on page 204*
♦ **Kantrex**® *see* Kanamycin *on page 957*
♦ **Kaon-Cl-10**® *see* Potassium Chloride *on page 1396*
♦ **Kaon-Cl**® **20** *see* Potassium Chloride *on page 1396*
♦ **Kao-Paverin**® **[OTC]** *see* Loperamide *on page 1027*
♦ **Kaopectate**® **[OTC]** *see* Bismuth *on page 224*
♦ **Kaopectate**® **Extra Strength [OTC]** *see* Bismuth *on page 224*
♦ **Kao-Tin [OTC]** *see* Bismuth *on page 224*
♦ **Kapectolin [OTC]** *see* Bismuth *on page 224*
♦ **Kariva**™ *see* Ethinyl Estradiol and Desogestrel *on page 645*
♦ **Kay Ciel**® *see* Potassium Chloride *on page 1396*
♦ **Kayexalate**® *see* Sodium Polystyrene Sulfonate *on page 1582*
♦ **KCl** *see* Potassium Chloride *on page 1396*
♦ **K-Dur**® **(Can)** *see* Potassium Chloride *on page 1396*
♦ **K-Dur**® **10** *see* Potassium Chloride *on page 1396*
♦ **K-Dur**® **20** *see* Potassium Chloride *on page 1396*
♦ **Keflex**® *see* Cephalexin *on page 331*
♦ **Keftab**® **(Can)** *see* Cephalexin *on page 331*
♦ **Kelnor**™ *see* Ethinyl Estradiol and Ethynodiol Diacetate *on page 648*
♦ **Kemadrin**® *see* Procyclidine *on page 1432*
♦ **Kenalog**® *see* Triamcinolone *on page 1734*
♦ **Kenalog-10**® *see* Triamcinolone *on page 1734*
♦ **Kenalog-40**® *see* Triamcinolone *on page 1734*
♦ **Kenalog**® **in Orabase (Can)** *see* Triamcinolone *on page 1734*
♦ **Keoxifene Hydrochloride** *see* Raloxifene *on page 1480*
♦ **Kepivance**™ *see* Palifermin *on page 1298*
♦ **Keppra**® *see* Levetiracetam *on page 995*
♦ **Keralac**™ *see* Urea *on page 1758*

♦ **Keralac™ Nailstik** *see* Urea *on page 1758*

♦ **Kerlone®** *see* Betaxolol *on page 214*

♦ **Kerr Insta-Char® [OTC]** *see* Charcoal *on page 338*

♦ **Ketalar®** *see* Ketamine *on page 958*

Ketamine (KEET a meen)

U.S. Brand Names Ketalar®
Canadian Brand Names Ketalar®; Ketamine Hydrochloride Injection, USP
Index Terms Ketamine Hydrochloride
Pharmacologic Category General Anesthetic
Use Induction and maintenance of general anesthesia, especially when cardiovascular depression must be avoided (ie, hypotension, hypovolemia, cardiomyopathy, constrictive pericarditis); sedation; analgesia
Restrictions C-III
Pregnancy Risk Factor D
Medication Safety Issues
Sound-alike/look-alike issues:
Ketalar® may be confused with Kenalog®
Contraindications Hypersensitivity to ketamine or any component of the formulation; elevated intracranial pressure; hypertension, aneurysms, thyrotoxicosis, congestive heart failure, angina, psychotic disorders; pregnancy
Warnings/Precautions Use with caution in patients with coronary artery disease, catecholamine depletion, and tachycardia. **[U.S. Boxed Warning]: Postanesthetic emergence reactions which can manifest as vivid dreams, hallucinations, and/or frank delirium occur in 12% of patients; these reactions are less common in patients >65 years of age and when given I.M.** Emergence reactions, confusion, or irrational behavior may occur up to 24 hours postoperatively and may be reduced by pretreatment with a benzodiazepine. May cause dependence (withdrawal symptoms on discontinuation) and tolerance with prolonged use.
Adverse Reactions
>10%:
Cardiovascular: Hypertension, increased cardiac output, paradoxical direct myocardial depression, tachycardia
Central nervous system: Increased intracranial pressure, visual hallucinations, vivid dreams
Neuromuscular & skeletal: Tonic-clonic movements, tremor
Miscellaneous: Emergence reactions, vocalization
1% to 10%:
Cardiovascular: Bradycardia, hypotension
Dermatologic: Pain at injection site, skin rash
Gastrointestinal: Anorexia, nausea, vomiting
Ocular: Diplopia, nystagmus
Respiratory: Respiratory depression
<1% (Limited to important or life-threatening): Anaphylaxis, cardiac arrhythmia, cough reflex may be depressed, decreased bronchospasm, fasciculations, hypersalivation, increased airway resistance, increased intraocular pressure, increased metabolic rate, increased skeletal muscle tone, laryngospasm, myocardial depression, respiratory depression or apnea with large doses or rapid infusions
Overdosage/Toxicology With excessive dosing or too-rapid administration, symptoms include respiratory depression. Supportive care is the treatment of choice. Mechanical respiratory support is preferred.
Drug Interactions
Cytochrome P450 Effect: Substrate (major) of CYP2B6, 2C9, 3A4
Increased Effect/Toxicity: CYP2B6 inhibitors may increase the levels/effects of ketamine; example inhibitors include desipramine, paroxetine, and sertraline. CYP2C9 Inhibitors may increase the levels/effects of ketamine. Example inhibitors include delavirdine, fluconazole, gemfibrozil, ketoconazole, nicardipine, NSAIDs, sulfonamides and tolbutamide. CYP3A4 inhibitors may increase the levels/effects of ketamine; example inhibitors include azole antifungals, clarithromycin, diclofenac, doxycycline, erythromycin, imatinib, isoniazid, nefazodone, nicardipine, propofol, protease inhibitors, quinidine, telithromycin, and verapamil. Barbiturates, narcotics, hydroxyzine increase prolonged recovery; nondepolarizing neuromuscular blockers may increase effects. Muscle relaxants, thyroid hormones may increase blood pressure and heart rate. Halothane may decrease BP.
Stability Do not mix with barbiturates or diazepam (precipitation may occur).
Mechanism of Action Produces a cataleptic-like state in which the patient is dissociated from the surrounding environment by direct action on the cortex and limbic system. Releases endogenous catecholamines (epinephrine, norepinephrine) which maintain blood pressure and heart rate. Reduces polysynaptic spinal reflexes.
Pharmacodynamics/Kinetics
Onset of action:
I.V.: General anesthesia: 1-2 minutes; Sedation: 1-2 minutes
I.M.: General anesthesia: 3-8 minutes
Duration: I.V.: 5-15 minutes; I.M.: 12-25 minutes
Metabolism: Hepatic via hydroxylation and N-demethylation; the metabolite norketamine is 25% as potent as parent compound
Half-life elimination: 11-17 minutes; Elimination: 2.5-3.1 hours
Excretion: Clearance: 18 mL/kg/minute
Dosage Used in combination with anticholinergic agents to decrease hypersalivation

Children:
Oral: 6-10 mg/kg for 1 dose (mixed in 0.2-0.3 mL/kg of cola or other beverage) given 30 minutes before the procedure
I.M.: 3-7 mg/kg
I.V.: Range: 0.5-2 mg/kg, use smaller doses (0.5-1 mg/kg) for sedation for minor procedures; usual induction dosage: 1-2 mg/kg
Continuous I.V. infusion: Sedation: 5-20 mcg/kg/minute

Adults:
I.M.: 3-8 mg/kg
I.V.: Range: 1-4.5 mg/kg; usual induction dosage: 1-2 mg/kg
Children and Adults: Maintenance: Supplemental doses of $^1/_3$ to $^1/_2$ of initial dose

Administration
Oral: Use 100 mg/mL I.V. solution and mix the appropriate dose in 0.2-0.3 mL/kg of cola or other beverage
Parenteral: I.V.: Do not exceed 0.5 mg/kg/minute or administer faster than 60 seconds; do not exceed final concentration of 2 mg/mL; dilute for I.V. administration with normal saline, sterile water, or D_5W

Monitoring Parameters Cardiovascular effects, heart rate, blood pressure, respiratory rate, transcutaneous O_2 saturation

Additional Information Produces emergence psychosis including auditory and visual hallucinations, restlessness, disorientation, vivid dreams, and irrational behavior in 15% to 30% of patients; pretreatment with a benzodiazepine reduces incidence of psychosis by >50%. Spontaneous involuntary movements, nystagmus, hypertonus, and vocalizations are also commonly seen.

The analgesia outlasts the general anesthetic component. Bronchodilation is beneficial in asthmatic or COPD patients. Laryngeal reflexes may remain intact or may be obtunded. The direct myocardial depressant action of ketamine can be seen in stressed, catecholamine-deficient patients. Ketamine increases cerebral metabolism and cerebral blood flow while producing a noncompetitive block of the neuronal postsynaptic NMDA receptor. It lowers seizure threshold and stimulates salivary secretions (atropine/scopolamine treatment is recommended).

Dosage Forms
Injection, solution: 50 mg/mL (10 mL); 100 mg/mL (5 mL)
Ketalar®: 10 mg/mL (20 mL); 50 mg/mL (10 mL); 100 mg/mL (5 mL)

♦ **Ketamine Hydrochloride** see Ketamine on page 958
♦ **Ketamine Hydrochloride Injection, USP (Can)** see Ketamine on page 958
♦ **Ketek®** see Telithromycin on page 1637

Ketoconazole (kee toe KOE na zole)

U.S. Brand Names Kuric™; Nizoral®; Nizoral® A-D [OTC]; Xolegel™
Canadian Brand Names Apo-Ketoconazole®; Ketoderm®; Novo-Ketoconazole
Pharmacologic Category Antifungal Agent, Oral; Antifungal Agent, Topical
Additional Appendix Information
Antifungal Agents on page 1869
USPHS / IDSA Guidelines for the Prevention of Opportunistic Infections in Persons Infected With HIV on page 1966
Use
Systemic: Treatment of susceptible fungal infections, including candidiasis, oral thrush, blastomycosis, histoplasmosis, paracoccidioidomycosis, coccidioidomycosis, chromomycosis, candiduria, chronic mucocutaneous candidiasis, as well as certain recalcitrant cutaneous dermatophytoses
Topical: Treatment of tinea corporis, tinea cruris, tinea versicolor, cutaneous candidiasis, seborrheic dermatitis
Unlabeled/Investigational Use Treatment of prostate cancer (androgen synthesis inhibitor)
Pregnancy Risk Factor C
Pregnancy Implications
Teratogenic effects were noted in animal studies. There are no adequate and well-controlled studies in pregnant women.
Lactation Enters breast milk/not recommended
Medication Safety Issues
Sound-alike/look-alike issues:
Nizoral® may be confused with Nasarel®, Neoral®, Nitrol®
Contraindications Hypersensitivity to ketoconazole or any component of the formulation; CNS fungal infections (due to poor CNS penetration); coadministration with ergot derivatives or cisapride is contraindicated due to risk of potentially fatal cardiac arrhythmias
Warnings/Precautions [U.S. Boxed Warning]: Ketoconazole has been associated with hepatotoxicity, including some fatalities; use with caution in patients with impaired hepatic function and perform periodic liver function tests. **[U.S. Boxed Warning]: Concomitant use with cisapride is contraindicated due to the occurrence of ventricular arrhythmias.**High doses of ketoconazole may depress adrenocortical function.

Topical: Formulations may contain sulfites. Avoid exposure of gel to open flames during or immediately after application.
Adverse Reactions
Oral:
1% to 10%:
Dermatologic: Pruritus (2%)
Gastrointestinal: Nausea/vomiting (3% to 10%), abdominal pain (1%)
<1% (Limited to important or life-threatening): Bulging fontanelles, chills, depression, diarrhea, dizziness, fever, gynecomastia, headache, hemolytic anemia, hepatotoxicity, impotence, leukopenia, photophobia, somnolence, thrombocytopenia

(Continued)

Ketoconazole *(Continued)*

Topical cream/gel: Allergic reaction, contact dermatitis (possibly related to sulfites or propylene glycol), facial swelling, headache, impetigo, local burning, ocular irritation, paresthesia, pruritus, severe irritation, stinging (~5%)

Shampoo: Abnormal hair texture, increases in normal hair loss, irritation (<1%), itching, mild dryness of skin, oiliness/dryness of hair, scalp pustules

Overdosage/Toxicology Symptoms include dizziness, headache, nausea, vomiting, and diarrhea. Overdoses are well tolerated. Treatment includes supportive measures and gastric decontamination.

Drug Interactions

Cytochrome P450 Effect: Substrate of CYP3A4 (major); **Inhibits** CYP1A2 (strong), 2A6 (moderate), 2B6 (weak), 2C8 (weak), 2C9 (strong), 2C19 (moderate), 2D6 (moderate), 3A4 (strong)

Increased Effect/Toxicity: Due to inhibition of hepatic CYP3A4, ketoconazole use is contraindicated with cisapride, lovastatin, midazolam, simvastatin, and triazolam due to large substantial increases in the toxicity of these agents. Ketoconazole may increase the serum levels/effects of amphetamines, benzodiazepines, beta-blockers, bosentan, buspirone, busulfan, calcium channel blockers, citalopram, dapsone, dexmedetomidine, dextromethorphan, diazepam, digoxin, docetaxel, fluoxetine, fluvoxamine, glimepiride, glipizide, ifosfamide, inhalational anesthetics, lidocaine, losartan, mesoridazine, methsuximide, mexiletine, mirtazapine, montelukast, nateglinide, nefazodone, paclitaxel, paroxetine, phenytoin, propranolol, risperidone, ritonavir, ropinirole, sertraline, sirolimus, tacrolimus, theophylline, thioridazine, tricyclic antidepressants, trifluoperazine, trimetrexate, venlafaxine, vincristine, vinblastine, warfarin, zafirlukast, zolpidem, and other substrates of CYP1A2, 2A6, 2C9, 2C19, 2D6, or 3A4. Selected benzodiazepines (midazolam and triazolam), cisapride, ergot alkaloids, selected HMG-CoA reductase inhibitors (lovastatin and simvastatin), and pimozide are generally contraindicated with strong CYP3A4 inhibitors. Mesoridazine and thioridazine are generally contraindicated with strong CYP2D6 inhibitors. When used with strong CYP3A4 inhibitors, dosage adjustment/limits are recommended for sildenafil and other PDE-5 inhibitors; consult individual monographs.

Decreased Effect: Oral: Absorption requires gastric acidity; therefore, antacids, H$_2$ antagonists (cimetidine, famotidine, nizatidine, and ranitidine), proton pump inhibitors (omeprazole, lansoprazole, rabeprazole), and sucralfate may significantly reduce bioavailability resulting in treatment failures and should not be administered concomitantly. Decreased serum levels with didanosine and isoniazid. The levels/effects of ketoconazole may be decreased by aminoglutethimide, carbamazepine, nafcillin, nevirapine, phenobarbital, phenytoin, rifamycins, or other CYP3A4 inducers. **Should not be administered concomitantly with rifampin.** Oral contraceptive efficacy may be reduced (limited data). Ketoconazole may decrease the levels/effects of CYP2D6 prodrug substrates (eg, codeine, hydrocodone, oxycodone, tramadol).

Ethanol/Nutrition/Herb Interactions

Food: Ketoconazole peak serum levels may be prolonged if taken with food.

Herb/Nutraceutical: St John's wort may decrease ketoconazole levels.

Stability Store at 15°C to 30°C (59°F to 86°F).

Mechanism of Action Alters the permeability of the cell wall by blocking fungal cytochrome P450; inhibits biosynthesis of triglycerides and phospholipids by fungi; inhibits several fungal enzymes that results in a build-up of toxic concentrations of hydrogen peroxide; also inhibits androgen synthesis

Pharmacodynamics/Kinetics

Absorption: Oral: Rapid (~75%); Shampoo: None; Gel: Minimal

Distribution: Well into inflamed joint fluid, saliva, bile, urine, breast milk, sebum, cerumen, feces, tendons, skin and soft tissues, and testes; crosses blood-brain barrier poorly; only negligible amounts reach CSF

Protein binding: 93% to 96%

Metabolism: Partially hepatic via CYP3A4 to inactive compounds

Bioavailability: Decreases as gastric pH increases

Half-life elimination: Biphasic: Initial: 2 hours; Terminal: 8 hours

Time to peak, serum: 1-2 hours

Excretion: Feces (57%); urine (13%)

Dosage

Fungal infections:

Oral:

Children ≥2 years: 3.3-6.6 mg/kg/day as a single dose for 1-2 weeks for candidiasis, for at least 4 weeks in recalcitrant dermatophyte infections, and for up to 6 months for other systemic mycoses

Adults: 200-400 mg/day as a single daily dose for durations as stated above

Shampoo: Children >12 years and Adults: Apply twice weekly for 4 weeks with at least 3 days between each shampoo

Topical: Adults:

Tinea infections: Cream: Rub gently into the affected area once daily. Duration of treatment: Tinea corporis, cruris: 2 weeks; tinea pedis: 6 weeks

Seborrheic dermatitis:

Cream: Rub gently into the affected area twice daily for 4 weeks or until clinical response is noted

Gel: Rub gently into the affected area once daily for 2 weeks

Prostate cancer (unlabeled use): Oral: Adults: 400 mg 3 times/day

Dosing adjustment in hepatic impairment: Dose reductions should be considered in patients with severe liver disease

Hemodialysis: Not dialyzable (0% to 5%)

Dietary Considerations May be taken with food or milk to decrease GI adverse effects.

Administration Administer oral tablets 2 hours prior to antacids to prevent decreased absorption due to the high pH of gastric contents. Cream, gel, and shampoo are for external use only.

Monitoring Parameters Liver function tests

Dosage Forms
Cream, topical: 2% (15 g, 30 g, 60 g)
Kuric™: 2%: (25 g, 75 g)
Gel, topical:
Xolegel™: 2% (15 g) [contains dehydrated alcohol 34%]
Shampoo, topical: 1% (120 mL), 2% (120 mL)
Nizoral®: 2% (120 mL)
Nizoral® A-D: 1% (120 mL, 210 mL)
Tablet: 200 mg
Nizoral®: 200 mg

Extemporaneous Preparations A 20 mg/mL suspension may be made by pulverizing twelve 200 mg ketoconazole tablets to a fine powder; add 40 mL Ora-Plus® in small portions with thorough mixing; incorporate Ora-Sweet® to make a final volume of 120 mL and mix thoroughly; refrigerate (no stability information is available)
Allen LV, "Ketoconazole Oral Suspension," *US Pharm*, 1993, 18(2):98-9, 101.

♦ **Ketoderm® (Can)** *see* Ketoconazole *on page 959*

♦ **3-Keto-desogestrel** *see* Etonogestrel *on page 668*

Ketoprofen (kee toe PROE fen)

U.S. Brand Names Orudis® KT [OTC] [DSC]
Canadian Brand Names Apo-Keto®; Apo-Keto-E®; Apo-Keto SR®; Novo-Keto; Novo-Keto-EC; Nu-Ketoprofen; Nu-Ketoprofen-E; Oruvail®; Rhodis™; Rhodis-EC™; Rhodis SR™
Pharmacologic Category Nonsteroidal Anti-inflammatory Drug (NSAID), Oral
Additional Appendix Information
Nonsteroidal Anti-inflammatory Agents *on page 1894*
Use Acute and long-term treatment of rheumatoid arthritis and osteoarthritis; primary dysmenorrhea; mild to moderate pain
Restrictions An FDA-approved medication guide must be distributed when dispensing an oral outpatient prescription (new or refill) where this medication is to be used without direct supervision of a healthcare provider. Medication guides are available at http://www.fda.gov/cder/Offices/ODS/medication_guides.htm.
Pregnancy Risk Factor C/D (3rd trimester)
Pregnancy Implications Teratogenic effects were not observed in animal studies. Embryotoxicity was observed in some, but not all, animal studies. Renal insufficiency and pulmonary hypertension have been noted in premature infants (case reports). Accumulation of the active enantiomer of ketoprofen has also been reported in premature neonates with renal insufficiency. Exposure to NSAIDs late in pregnancy may lead to premature closure of the ductus arteriosus and may inhibit uterine contractions.
Lactation Excretion in breast milk unknown/not recommended
Medication Safety Issues
Sound-alike/look-alike issues:
Oruvail® may be confused with Clinoril®, Elavil®
Contraindications Hypersensitivity to ketoprofen, aspirin, other NSAIDs, or any component of the formulation; perioperative pain in the setting of coronary artery bypass surgery (CABG); pregnancy (3rd trimester)
Warnings/Precautions [U.S. Boxed Warning]: NSAIDs are associated with an increased risk of adverse cardiovascular events, including MI, stroke, and new onset or worsening of pre-existing hypertension. Risk may be increased with duration of use or pre-existing cardiovascular risk-factors or disease. Carefully evaluate individual cardiovascular risk profiles prior to prescribing. Use caution with fluid retention, CHF or hypertension. Concurrent administration of ibuprofen, and potentially other nonselective NSAIDs, may interfere with aspirin's cardioprotective effect.

Use of NSAIDs can compromise existing renal function. Ketoprofen is not recommended for patients with advanced renal disease. **[U.S. Boxed Warning]: NSAIDs may increase risk of gastrointestinal irritation, ulceration, bleeding, and perforation.** Use with caution in patients with decreased hepatic function.

Use the lowest effective dose for the shortest duration of time, consistent with individual patient goals, to reduce risk of cardiovascular or GI adverse events. Alternate therapies should be considered for patients at high risk.

NSAIDs may cause serious skin adverse events including exfoliative dermatitis, Stevens-Johnson syndrome (SJS) and toxic epidermal necrolysis (TEN). Do not use in patients who experience bronchospasm, asthma, rhinitis, or urticaria with NSAID or aspirin therapy.

The elderly are at increased risk for adverse effects (especially peptic ulceration, CNS effects, renal toxicity) from NSAIDs even at low doses.

Withhold for at least 4-6 half-lives prior to surgical or dental procedures. Safety and efficacy have not been established in pediatric patients.

Adverse Reactions
>10%: Gastrointestinal: Dyspepsia (11%)
1% to 10%:
Central nervous system: Headache (3% to 9%), depression, dizziness (>1%), dreams, insomnia, malaise, nervousness, somnolence
Dermatologic: Rash
Gastrointestinal: Abdominal pain (3% to 9%), constipation (3% to 9%), diarrhea (3% to 9%), flatulence (3% to 9%), nausea (3% to 9%), anorexia (>1%), stomatitis (>1%), vomiting (>1%)
Genitourinary: Urinary tract infection (>1%)
Ocular: Visual disturbances
(Continued)

Ketoprofen *(Continued)*

Otic: Tinnitus

Renal: Renal dysfunction (3% to 9%)

<1% (Limited to important or life-threatening): Agranulocytosis, allergic reaction, allergic rhinitis, alopecia, anaphylaxis, anemia, angioedema, arrhythmia, aseptic meningitis, blurred vision, bone marrow suppression, buccal necrosis, bullous rash, cholestatic hepatitis, confusion, CHF, conjunctivitis, cystitis, diabetes mellitus (aggravated), drowsiness, dry eyes, dysphoria, dyspnea, eczema, epistaxis, erythema multiforme, exfoliative dermatitis, gastritis, gastrointestinal perforation, GI ulceration, gynecomastia, hallucinations, hearing decreased, hemolytic anemia, hepatic dysfunction, hepatitis, hot flashes, hypertension, hyponatremia, impotence, interstitial nephritis, intestinal ulceration, jaundice, leukopenia, microvesicular steatosis, migraine, myocardial infarction, nephrotic syndrome, nightmares, onycholysis, pancreatitis, peptic ulcer, peripheral neuropathy, peripheral vascular disease, photosensitivity, polydipsia, polyuria, purpura, renal failure, retinal hemorrhage, Stevens-Johnson syndrome, tachycardia, taste perversion, thrombocytopenia, toxic amblyopia, toxic epidermal necrolysis, tubulopathy, ulcerative colitis, urticaria

Overdosage/Toxicology Common symptoms of acute NSAID overdose include lethargy, drowsiness, nausea, vomiting and epigastric pain. Respiratory depression, coma, convulsions, GI bleeding, or acute renal failure are rare. Management of NSAID intoxication is supportive and symptomatic; multiple dosing of activated charcoal may be effective.

Drug Interactions

Cytochrome P450 Effect: Inhibits CYP2C9 (weak)

Increased Effect/Toxicity: Ketoprofen may increase effect/toxicity of anticoagulants (bleeding), antiplatelet agents (bleeding), aminoglycosides, biphosphonates (GI irritation), corticosteroids (GI irritation), cyclosporine (nephrotoxicity), lithium, methotrexate, pemetrexed, treprostinil (bleeding), vancomycin. Probenecid may increase serum concentrations of ketoprofen. Concomitant use with fluoroquinolones may rarely increase risk of seizure.

Decreased Effect: May reduce effect of some diuretics and antihypertensive effect of beta-blockers, ACE inhibitors, angiotensin II inhibitors, hydralazine. Cholestyramine (and other bile acid sequestrants) may decrease the absorption of NSAIDs; separate by at least 2 hours. Salicylates' antiplatelet effect may be reduced.

Ethanol/Nutrition/Herb Interactions

Ethanol: Avoid ethanol (due to GI irritation).

Food: Food slows rate of absorption resulting in delayed and reduced peak serum concentrations.

Herb/Nutraceutical: Avoid alfalfa, anise, bilberry, bladderwrack, bromelain, cat's claw, celery, coleus, cordyceps, dong quai, evening primrose, feverfew, fenugreek, garlic, ginger, ginkgo biloba, red clover, horse chestnut, grapeseed, green tea, ginseng, guggul, horse chestnut seed, horseradish, licorice, prickly ash, red clover, reishi, SAMe, sweet clover, turmeric, white willow (all have additional antiplatelet activity).

Mechanism of Action Inhibits prostaglandin synthesis by decreasing the activity of the enzyme, cyclooxygenase, which results in decreased formation of prostaglandin precursors

Pharmacodynamics/Kinetics

Absorption: Almost complete

Protein binding: >99%, primarily albumin

Metabolism: Hepatic via glucuronidation; metabolite can be converted back to parent compound; may have enterohepatic recirculation

Half-life elimination:

Capsule: 2-4 hours; moderate-severe renal impairment: 5-9 hours

Capsule, extended release: ~3-7.5 hours

Time to peak, serum:

Capsule: 0.5-2 hours

Capsule, extended release: 6-7 hours

Excretion: Urine (~80%, primarily as glucuronide conjugates)

Dosage Oral:

Children ≥16 years and Adults:

Rheumatoid arthritis or osteoarthritis (lower doses may be used in small patients or in the elderly, or debilitated):

Capsule: 50-75 mg 3-4 times/day up to a maximum of 300 mg/day

Capsule, extended release: 200 mg once daily

Mild-to-moderate pain: Capsule: 25-50 mg every 6-8 hours up to a maximum of 300 mg/day

OTC labeling: 12.5 mg every 4-6 hours, up to a maximum of 6 tablets/24 hours

Elderly: Initial dose should be decreased in patients >75 years; use caution when dosage changes are made

Dosage adjustment in renal impairment: In general, NSAIDs are not recommended for use in patients with advanced renal disease, but the manufacturer of ketoprofen does provide some guidelines for adjustment in renal dysfunction:

Mild impairment: Maximum dose: 150 mg/day

Severe impairment: Cl$_{cr}$ <25 mL/minute: Maximum dose: 100 mg/day

Dosage adjustment in hepatic impairment and serum albumin <3.5 g/dL: Maximum dose: 100 mg/day

Dietary Considerations In order to minimize gastrointestinal effects, ketoprofen can be prescribed to be taken with food or milk.

Administration May take with food to reduce GI upset. Do not crush or break extended release capsules.

Dosage Forms [DSC] = Discontinued product

Capsule: 50 mg, 75 mg

Capsule, extended release: 200 mg

Tablet (Orudis® KT): 12.5 mg [contains tartrazine and sodium benzoate] [DSC]

Ketorolac (KEE toe role ak)

U.S. Brand Names Acular®; Acular LS™; Acular® PF; Toradol®
Canadian Brand Names Acular®; Acular LS™; Apo-Ketorolac®; Apo-Ketorolac Injectable®; Ketorolac Tromethamine Injection, USP; Novo-Ketorolac; ratio-Ketorolac; Toradol®; Toradol® IM
Index Terms Ketorolac Tromethamine
Pharmacologic Category Nonsteroidal Anti-inflammatory Drug (NSAID), Ophthalmic; Nonsteroidal Anti-inflammatory Drug (NSAID), Oral; Nonsteroidal Anti-inflammatory Drug (NSAID), Parenteral
Additional Appendix Information
Nonsteroidal Anti-inflammatory Agents *on page 1894*
Use
Oral, injection: Short-term (≤5 days) management of moderately-severe acute pain requiring analgesia at the opioid level
Ophthalmic: Temporary relief of ocular itching due to seasonal allergic conjunctivitis; postoperative inflammation following cataract extraction; reduction of ocular pain and photophobia following incisional refractive surgery, reduction of ocular pain, burning and stinging following corneal refractive surgery
Restrictions An FDA-approved medication guide must be distributed when dispensing an oral outpatient prescription (new or refill) where this medication is to be used without direct supervision of a healthcare provider. Medication guides are available at http://www.fda.gov/cder/Offices/ODS/medication_guides.htm.
Pregnancy Risk Factor C/D (3rd trimester)
Pregnancy Implications Ketorolac is contraindicated during labor and delivery (may inhibit uterine contractions and adversely affect fetal circulation). Avoid use of ketorolac ophthalmic solution during late pregnancy.
Lactation Enters breast milk/contraindicated (AAP rates "compatible")
Medication Safety Issues
Sound-alike/look-alike issues:
Acular® may be confused with Acthar®, Ocular®
Toradol® may be confused with Foradil®, Inderal®, Tegretol®, Torecan®, tramadol

International issues:
Toradol® may be confused with Theradol which is a brand name for tramadol in the Netherlands
Contraindications Hypersensitivity to ketorolac, aspirin, other NSAIDs, or any component of the formulation; active or history of peptic ulcer disease; recent or history of GI bleeding or perforation; patients with advanced renal disease or risk of renal failure; labor and delivery; nursing mothers; prophylaxis before major surgery; suspected or confirmed cerebrovascular bleeding; hemorrhagic diathesis; concurrent ASA or other NSAIDs; epidural or intrathecal administration; concomitant probenecid; perioperative pain in the setting of coronary artery bypass surgery (CABG); pregnancy (3rd trimester)
Warnings/Precautions
Systemic: Treatment should be started with I.V./I.M. administration then changed to oral only as a continuation of treatment. Total therapy is not to exceed 5 days. Should not be used for minor or chronic pain.

May prolong bleeding time; do not use when hemostasis is critical. Patients should be euvolemic prior to treatment. Low doses of narcotics may be needed for breakthrough pain.

[U.S. Boxed Warning]: NSAIDs are associated with an increased risk of adverse cardiovascular events, including MI, stroke, and new onset or worsening of pre-existing hypertension. Risk may be increased with duration of use or pre-existing cardiovascular risk-factors or disease. Carefully evaluate individual cardiovascular risk profiles prior to prescribing. Use caution with fluid retention, CHF or hypertension. Concurrent administration of ibuprofen, and potentially other nonselective NSAIDs, may interfere with aspirin's cardioprotective effect.

Use of NSAIDs can compromise existing renal function. Renal toxicity can occur in patient with impaired renal function, dehydration, heart failure, liver dysfunction, those taking diuretics and ACEI and the elderly. Rehydrate patient before starting therapy. Monitor renal function closely. Ketorolac is not recommended for patients with advanced renal disease.

[U.S. Boxed Warning]: NSAIDs may increase risk of gastrointestinal irritation, ulceration, bleeding, and perforation. These events may occur at any time during therapy and without warning. Use caution with a history of GI disease (bleeding or ulcers), concurrent therapy with aspirin, anticoagulants and/or corticosteroids, smoking, use of alcohol, the elderly or debilitated patients.

Use the lowest effective dose for the shortest duration of time, consistent with individual patient goals, to reduce risk of cardiovascular or GI adverse events. Alternate therapies should be considered for patients at high risk.

NSAIDs may cause serious skin adverse events including exfoliative dermatitis, Stevens-Johnson syndrome (SJS) and toxic epidermal necrolysis (TEN). Anaphylactoid reactions may occur, even without prior exposure; patients with "aspirin triad" (bronchial asthma, aspirin intolerance, rhinitis) may be at increased risk. Do not use in patients who experience bronchospasm, asthma, rhinitis, or urticaria with NSAID or aspirin therapy.

Use with caution in patients with decreased hepatic function. Closely monitor patients with any abnormal LFT. Severe hepatic reactions (eg, fulminant hepatitis, liver failure) have occurred with NSAID use, rarely; discontinue if signs or symptoms of liver disease develop, or if systemic manifestations occur.

The elderly are at increased risk for adverse effects (especially peptic ulceration, CNS effects, renal toxicity) from NSAIDs even at low doses.
(Continued)

Ketorolac *(Continued)*

Withhold for at least 4-6 half-lives prior to surgical or dental procedures. Safety and efficacy for systemic preparations has not been established in children <2 years of age; a single-dose injection may be used in children 2-16 years of age.

Ophthalmic: May increase bleeding time associated with ocular surgery. Use with caution in patients with known bleeding tendencies or those receiving anticoagulants. Healing time may be slowed or delayed. Corneal thinning, erosion, or ulceration have been reported with topical NSAIDs; discontinue if corneal epithelial breakdown occurs. Use caution with complicated ocular surgery, corneal denervation, corneal epithelial defects, diabetes, rheumatoid arthritis, ocular surface disease, or ocular surgeries repeated within short periods of time; risk of corneal epithelial breakdown may be increased. Use for >24 hours prior to or for >14 days following surgery also increases risk of corneal adverse effects. Do not administer while wearing soft contact lenses. Safety and efficacy in pediatric patients <3 years of age have not been established.

Adverse Reactions

Systemic:

>10%:
 Central nervous system: Headache (17%)
 Gastrointestinal: Gastrointestinal pain (13%), dyspepsia (12%), nausea (12%)

>1% to 10%:
 Cardiovascular: Edema (4%), hypertension
 Central nervous system: Dizziness (7%), drowsiness (6%)
 Dermatologic: Pruritus, purpura, rash
 Gastrointestinal: Diarrhea (7%), constipation, flatulence, gastrointestinal fullness, vomiting, stomatitis
 Local: Injection site pain (2%)
 Miscellaneous: Diaphoresis

≤1% (Limited to important or life-threatening): Abnormal vision, acute renal failure, anaphylactoid reaction, anaphylaxis, asthma, azotemia, bronchospasm, cholestatic jaundice, convulsions, eosinophilia, epistaxis, esophagitis, extrapyramidal symptoms, GI hemorrhage, GI perforation, hallucinations, hearing loss, hematemesis, hematuria, hepatitis, hypersensitivity reactions, liver failure, Lyell's syndrome, maculopapular rash, nephritis, peptic ulceration, Stevens-Johnson syndrome, tinnitus, toxic epidermal necrolysis, urticaria, vertigo, wound hemorrhage (postoperative)

Ophthalmic solution:

>10%: Ocular: Transient burning/stinging (Acular®: 40%; Acular® PF: 20%)

>1% to 10%:
 Central nervous system: Headache
 Ocular: Conjunctival hyperemia, corneal infiltrates, iritis, ocular edema, ocular inflammation, ocular irritation, ocular pain, superficial keratitis, superficial ocular infection
 Miscellaneous: Allergic reactions

≤1% (Limited to important or life-threatening): Blurred vision corneal ulcer, corneal erosion, corneal perforation, corneal thinning, dry eyes, epithelial breakdown

Overdosage/Toxicology Symptoms include abdominal pain, peptic ulcers, and metabolic acidosis. Management of nonsteroidal anti-inflammatory (NSAID) intoxication is supportive and symptomatic. Dialysis is not effective.

Drug Interactions

Increased Effect/Toxicity: Increased toxicity: Lithium, methotrexate, probenecid increased drug level; increased effect/toxicity with salicylates, probenecid, anticoagulants, nondepolarizing muscle relaxants, alprazolam, fluoxetine, thiothixene. Concomitant use with fluoroquinolones may rarely increase risk of seizure.

Decreased Effect: Decreased effect: Decreased antihypertensive effect seen with ACE inhibitors, beta blockers, hydralazine, and angiotensin II antagonists; decreased antiepileptic effect seen with carbamazepine, phenytoin. Cholestyramine (and other bile acid sequestrants) may decrease the absorption of NSAIDs; separate by at least 2 hours. Salicylates' antiplatelet effect may be reduced.

Ethanol/Nutrition/Herb Interactions

Ethanol: Avoid ethanol (may enhance gastric mucosal irritation).

Food: Oral: High-fat meals may delay time to peak (by ~1 hour) and decrease peak concentrations.

Herb/Neutraceuticals: Avoid alfalfa, anise, bilberry, bladderwrack, bromelain, cat's claw, celery, coleus, cordyceps, dong quai, evening primrose, feverfew, fenugreek, garlic, ginger, ginkgo biloba, red clover, horse chestnut, grapeseed, green tea, ginseng, guggul, horse chestnut seed, horseradish, licorice, prickly ash, red clover, reishi, SAMe, sweet clover, turmeric, white willow (all have additional antiplatelet activity).

Stability Ketorolac injection and ophthalmic solution should be stored at controlled room temperature and protected from light. Injection is clear and has a slight yellow color. Precipitation may occur at relatively low pH values. Store tablets at controlled room temperature.

Mechanism of Action Inhibits prostaglandin synthesis by decreasing the activity of the enzyme, cyclooxygenase, which results in decreased formation of prostaglandin precursors

Pharmacodynamics/Kinetics

Onset of action: Analgesic: I.M.: ~10 minutes
 Peak effect: Analgesic: 2-3 hours
Duration: Analgesic: 6-8 hours
Absorption: Oral: Well absorbed
Distribution: Poor penetration into CSF; crosses placenta; enters breast milk
Protein binding: 99%
Metabolism: Hepatic
Half-life elimination: 2-8 hours; prolonged 30% to 50% in elderly
Time to peak, serum: I.M.: 30-60 minutes
Excretion: Urine (61% as unchanged drug)

Dosage

Children 2-16 years: **Do not exceed adult doses**

Single-dose treatment:
    I.M.: 1 mg/kg (maximum: 30 mg)
    I.V.: 0.5 mg/kg (maximum: 15 mg)
    Oral (unlabeled): 1 mg/kg as a single dose reported in one study

Multiple-dose treatment (unlabeled): Limited pediatric studies. The maximum combined duration of treatment (for parenteral and oral) is 5 days.
    I.V.: Initial dose: 0.5 mg/kg, followed by 0.25-1 mg/kg every 6 hours for up to 48 hours (maximum daily dose: 90 mg)
    Oral: 0.25 mg/kg every 6 hours

Children ≥16 years and Adults (pain relief usually begins within 10 minutes with parenteral forms): **Note:** The maximum combined duration of treatment (for parenteral and oral) is 5 days; do not increase dose or frequency; supplement with low-dose opioids if needed for breakthrough pain. For patients <50 kg and/or ≥65 years, see Elderly dosing.
    I.M.: 60 mg as a single dose or 30 mg every 6 hours (maximum daily dose: 120 mg)
    I.V.: 30 mg as a single dose or 30 mg every 6 hours (maximum daily dose: 120 mg)
    Oral: 20 mg, followed by 10 mg every 4-6 hours; do not exceed 40 mg/day; oral dosing is intended to be a continuation of I.M. or I.V. therapy only

Ophthalmic: Children ≥3 years and Adults:
    Allergic conjunctivitis (relief of ocular itching) (Acular®): Instill 1 drop (0.25 mg) 4 times/day for seasonal allergic conjunctivitis
    Inflammation following cataract extraction (Acular®): Instill 1 drop (0.25 mg) to affected eye(s) 4 times/day beginning 24 hours after surgery; continue for 2 weeks
    Pain and photophobia following incisional refractive surgery (Acular® PF): Instill 1 drop (0.25 mg) 4 times/day to affected eye for up to 3 days
    Pain following corneal refractive surgery (Acular LS™): Instill 1 drop 4 times/day as needed to affected eye for up to 4 days

Elderly >65 years: Renal insufficiency or weight <50 kg: **Note:** Ketorolac has decreased clearance and increased half-life in the elderly. In addition, the elderly have reported increased incidence of GI bleeding, ulceration, and perforation. The maximum combined duration of treatment (for parenteral and oral) is 5 days.
    I.M.: 30 mg as a single dose or 15 mg every 6 hours (maximum daily dose: 60 mg)
    I.V.: 15 mg as a single dose or 15 mg every 6 hours (maximum daily dose: 60 mg)
    Oral: 10 mg every 4-6 hours; do not exceed 40 mg/day; oral dosing is intended to be a continuation of I.M. or I.V. therapy only

Dosage adjustment in renal impairment: Do not use in patients with advanced renal impairment. Patients with moderately-elevated serum creatinine should use half the recommended dose, not to exceed 60 mg/day I.M./I.V.

Dosage adjustment in hepatic impairment: Use with caution, may cause elevation of liver enzymes

Dietary Considerations Administer tablet with food or milk to decrease gastrointestinal distress.

Administration
    Oral: May take with food to reduce GI upset
    I.M.: Administer slowly and deeply into the muscle. Analgesia begins in 30 minutes and maximum effect within 2 hours
    I.V.: Administer I.V. bolus over a minimum of 15 seconds; onset within 30 minutes; peak analgesia within 2 hours
    Ophthalmic solution: Contact lenses should be removed before instillation.

Monitoring Parameters Monitor response (pain, range of motion, grip strength, mobility, ADL function), inflammation; observe for weight gain, edema; monitor renal function (serum creatinine, BUN, urine output); observe for bleeding, bruising; evaluate gastrointestinal effects (abdominal pain, bleeding, dyspepsia); mental confusion, disorientation, CBC, liver function tests

Reference Range Serum concentration: Therapeutic: 0.3-5 mcg/mL; Toxic: >5 mcg/mL

Additional Information First parenteral NSAID for analgesia; 30 mg provides the analgesia comparable to 12 mg of morphine or 100 mg of meperidine.

Dosage Forms [DSC] = Discontinued product
    Injection, solution, as tromethamine: 15 mg/mL (1 mL); 30 mg/mL (1 mL, 2 mL, 10 mL) [contains alcohol]
    Solution, ophthalmic, as tromethamine:
        Acular®: 0.5% (3 mL, 5 mL, 10 mL) [contains benzalkonium chloride]
        Acular LS™: 0.4% (5 mL) [contains benzalkonium chloride]
        Acular® P.F. [preservative free]: 0.5% (0.4 mL)
    Tablet, as tromethamine: 10 mg
    Toradol®: 10 mg [DSC]

- **Ketorolac Tromethamine** *see* Ketorolac *on page 963*
- **Ketorolac Tromethamine Injection, USP (Can)** *see* Ketorolac *on page 963*

Ketotifen (kee toe TYE fen)

U.S. Brand Names Zaditor® [OTC]
Canadian Brand Names Apo-Ketotifen®; Novo-Ketotifen; Zaditen®; Zaditor®
Index Terms Ketotifen Fumarate
Pharmacologic Category Antihistamine, H$_1$ Blocker, Ophthalmic
Use Temporary prevention of eye itching due to allergic conjunctivitis
Pregnancy Risk Factor C
Pregnancy Implications Oral treatment administered to pregnant animals have resulted in retarded ossification of the sternebrae, slight increase in postnatal mortality, and a decrease in weight gain in the first 4 days of life. Topical ocular administration has not been studied.
Lactation Use caution
Contraindications Hypersensitivity to ketotifen or any component of the formulation (the preservative is benzalkonium chloride)
(Continued)

Ketotifen *(Continued)*

Warnings/Precautions For topical ophthalmic use only. Not to treat contact lens-related irritation. After ketotifen use, soft contact lens wearers should wait at least 10 minutes before putting their lenses in. Do not wear contact lenses if eyes are red. Do not contaminate dropper tip or solution when placing drops in eyes. Safety and efficacy not established for children <3 years of age.

Adverse Reactions 1% to 10%:
Ocular: Allergic reactions, burning or stinging, conjunctivitis, discharge, dry eyes, eye pain, eyelid disorder, itching, keratitis, lacrimation disorder, mydriasis, photophobia, rash
Respiratory: Pharyngitis
Miscellaneous: Flu syndrome

Overdosage/Toxicology No serious signs or symptoms have been seen after ingestion up to 20 mg.

Stability Stable at room temperature.

Mechanism of Action Relatively selective, noncompetitive H_1-receptor antagonist and mast cell stabilizer, inhibiting the release of mediators from cells involved in hypersensitivity reactions

Pharmacodynamics/Kinetics
Onset of action: Minutes
Duration: 8-12 hours
Absorption: Minimally systemic

Dosage Children ≥3 years and Adults: Ophthalmic: Instill 1 drop into the affected eye(s) twice daily, every 8-12 hours

Dosage Forms
Solution, ophthalmic: 0.025% (5 mL)
Zaditor®: 0.025% (5 mL) [contains benzalkonium chloride]

- **Ketotifen Fumarate** *see* Ketotifen *on page 965*
- **Key-E® [OTC]** *see* Vitamin E *on page 1794*
- **Key-E® Kaps [OTC]** *see* Vitamin E *on page 1794*
- **Keygesic [OTC]** *see* Magnesium Salicylate *on page 1051*
- **KI** *see* Potassium Iodide *on page 1399*
- **Kidkare Cough and Cold [OTC]** *see* Chlorpheniramine, Pseudoephedrine, and Dextromethorphan *on page 355*
- **Kidkare Decongestant [OTC]** *see* Pseudoephedrine *on page 1454*
- **Kidrolase® (Can)** *see* Asparaginase *on page 157*
- **Kineret®** *see* Anakinra *on page 128*
- **Kionex™** *see* Sodium Polystyrene Sulfonate *on page 1582*
- **Kivexa™ (Can)** *see* Abacavir and Lamivudine *on page 19*
- **Klaron®** *see* Sulfacetamide *on page 1609*
- **Klean-Prep® (Can)** *see* Polyethylene Glycol-Electrolyte Solution *on page 1387*
- **Klonopin®** *see* Clonazepam *on page 397*
- **K-Lor®** *see* Potassium Chloride *on page 1396*
- **Klor-Con®** *see* Potassium Chloride *on page 1396*
- **Klor-Con® 8** *see* Potassium Chloride *on page 1396*
- **Klor-Con® 10** *see* Potassium Chloride *on page 1396*
- **Klor-Con®/25** *see* Potassium Chloride *on page 1396*
- **Klor-Con® M** *see* Potassium Chloride *on page 1396*
- **Klor-Con®/EF** *see* Potassium Bicarbonate and Potassium Citrate *on page 1396*
- **K-Lyte®** *see* Potassium Bicarbonate and Potassium Citrate *on page 1396*
- **K-Lyte/Cl®** *see* Potassium Bicarbonate and Potassium Chloride *on page 1396*
- **K-Lyte®/Cl (Can)** *see* Potassium Chloride *on page 1396*
- **K-Lyte/Cl® 50 [DSC]** *see* Potassium Bicarbonate and Potassium Chloride *on page 1396*
- **K-Lyte/Cl® DS** *see* Potassium Bicarbonate and Potassium Citrate *on page 1396*
- **Kodet SE [OTC]** *see* Pseudoephedrine *on page 1454*
- **Koffex DM-D (Can)** *see* Pseudoephedrine and Dextromethorphan *on page 1455*
- **Koffex DM + Decongestant + Expectorant (Can)** *see* Guaifenesin, Pseudoephedrine, and Dextromethorphan *on page 821*
- **Koffex DM-Expectorant (Can)** *see* Guaifenesin and Dextromethorphan *on page 816*
- **Koffex Expectorant (Can)** *see* Guaifenesin *on page 814*
- **Kogenate® (Can)** *see* Antihemophilic Factor (Recombinant) *on page 135*
- **Kogenate® FS** *see* Antihemophilic Factor (Recombinant) *on page 135*
- **Kolephrin® [OTC]** *see* Acetaminophen, Chlorpheniramine, and Pseudoephedrine *on page 35*
- **Kolephrin® #1** *see* Guaifenesin and Codeine *on page 815*
- **Kolephrin® GG/DM [OTC]** *see* Guaifenesin and Dextromethorphan *on page 816*
- **Konakion (Can)** *see* Phytonadione *on page 1366*
- **Konsyl® [OTC]** *see* Psyllium *on page 1458*
- **Konsyl-D® [OTC]** *see* Psyllium *on page 1458*
- **Konsyl® Easy Mix [OTC]** *see* Psyllium *on page 1458*
- **Konsyl® Orange [OTC]** *see* Psyllium *on page 1458*
- **Konyne® 80** *see* Factor IX Complex (Human) *on page 681*
- **Kovia®** *see* Papain and Urea *on page 1309*
- **Koāte®-DVI** *see* Antihemophilic Factor (Human) *on page 133*
- **K-Pek II [OTC]** *see* Loperamide *on page 1027*
- **K-Phos® MF** *see* Potassium Phosphate and Sodium Phosphate *on page 1403*
- **K-Phos® Neutral** *see* Potassium Phosphate and Sodium Phosphate *on page 1403*
- **K-Phos® No. 2** *see* Potassium Phosphate and Sodium Phosphate *on page 1403*

- **K-Phos® Original** *see* Potassium Acid Phosphate *on page 1395*
- **K+ Potassium** *see* Potassium Chloride *on page 1396*
- **Kristalose™** *see* Lactulose *on page 971*
- **Kronofed-A®** *see* Chlorpheniramine and Pseudoephedrine *on page 350*
- **Kronofed-A®-Jr** *see* Chlorpheniramine and Pseudoephedrine *on page 350*
- **K-Tab®** *see* Potassium Chloride *on page 1396*
- **Kuric™** *see* Ketoconazole *on page 959*
- **ku-zyme® HP** *see* Pancrelipase *on page 1302*
- **Kwelcof®** *see* Hydrocodone and Guaifenesin *on page 849*
- **Kwellada-P™ (Can)** *see* Permethrin *on page 1348*
- **Kytril®** *see* Granisetron *on page 811*
- **L-749,345** *see* Ertapenem *on page 607*
- **L-M-X™ 4 [OTC]** *see* Lidocaine *on page 1010*
- **L-M-X™ 5 [OTC]** *see* Lidocaine *on page 1010*
- **L 754030** *see* Aprepitant *on page 144*
- **LA 20304a** *see* Gemifloxacin *on page 788*

Labetalol (la BET a lole)

U.S. Brand Names Trandate®
Canadian Brand Names Apo-Labetalol®; Labetalol Hydrochloride Injection, USP; Normodyne®; Trandate®
Index Terms Ibidomide Hydrochloride; Labetalol Hydrochloride
Pharmacologic Category Beta Blocker With Alpha-Blocking Activity
Additional Appendix Information
  Beta-Blockers *on page 1875*
  Hypertension *on page 2063*
Use Treatment of mild to severe hypertension; I.V. for hypertensive emergencies
Pregnancy Risk Factor C (manufacturer); D (2nd and 3rd trimesters - expert analysis)
Pregnancy Implications Labetalol crosses the placenta. Beta-blockers have been associated with persistent bradycardia, hypotension, and IUGR; IUGR is probably related to maternal hypertension. Available evidence suggests beta-blockers are generally safe during pregnancy (JNC 7). Cases of neonatal hypoglycemia have been reported following maternal use of beta-blockers at parturition or during breast-feeding. Monitor breast-fed infant for symptoms of beta-blockade.
Lactation Enters breast milk/use caution (AAP rates "compatible")
Medication Safety Issues
  Sound-alike/look-alike issues:
    Labetalol may be confused with betaxolol, Hexadrol®, lamotrigine
    Trandate® may be confused with tramadol, Trendar®, Trental®, Tridrate®

  Significant differences exist between oral and I.V. dosing. Use caution when converting from one route of administration to another.
Contraindications Hypersensitivity to labetalol or any component of the formulation; sinus bradycardia; heart block greater than first degree (except in patients with a functioning artificial pacemaker); cardiogenic shock; bronchial asthma; uncompensated cardiac failure; pregnancy (2nd and 3rd trimesters)
Warnings/Precautions Consider pre-existing conditions such as sick sinus syndrome before initiating. Paradoxical increase in blood pressure has been reported with treatment of pheochromocytoma or clonidine withdrawal syndrome; orthostatic hypotension may occur with I.V. administration; patient should remain supine during and for up to 3 hours after I.V. administration; use with caution in impaired hepatic function (discontinue if signs of liver dysfunction occur); may mask the signs and symptoms of hypoglycemia; a lower hemodynamic response rate and higher incidence of toxicity may be observed with administration to elderly patients.

Use only with extreme caution in compensated heart failure and monitor for a worsening of the condition. Beta-blocker therapy should not be withdrawn abruptly (particularly in patients with CAD), but gradually tapered to avoid acute tachycardia, hypertension, and/or ischemia. Use caution with concurrent use of beta-blockers and either verapamil or diltiazem; bradycardia or heart block can occur. Patients with bronchospastic disease should not receive beta-blockers. Labetalol may be used with caution in patients with nonallergic bronchospasm (chronic bronchitis, emphysema). Use cautiously in diabetics because it can mask prominent hypoglycemic symptoms. Use with caution in patients with myasthenia gravis, psychiatric disease (may cause CNS depression), or peripheral vascular disease. Adequate alpha-blockade is required prior to use of any beta-blocker for patients with untreated pheochromocytoma. Use with caution in patients receiving anesthetic agents which decrease myocardial function. Safety and efficacy have not been established in children.
Adverse Reactions
  >10%:
    Central nervous system: Dizziness (1% to 16%)
    Gastrointestinal: Nausea (0% to 19%)
  1% to 10%:
    Cardiovascular: Edema (0% to 2%), hypotension (1% to 5%); with I.V. use, hypotension may occur in up to 58%
    Central nervous system: Fatigue (1% to 10%), headache (2%), vertigo (2%)
    Dermatologic: Rash (1%), scalp tingling (1% to 5%)
    Gastrointestinal: Vomiting (<1% to 3%), dyspepsia (1% to 4%)
    Genitourinary: Ejaculatory failure (0% to 5%), impotence (1% to 4%)
    Hepatic: Transaminases increased (4%)
    Neuromuscular & skeletal: Paresthesia (1% to 5%), weakness (1%)
    Respiratory: Nasal congestion (1% to 6%), dyspnea (2%)
    Miscellaneous: Taste disorder (1%), abnormal vision (1%)
(Continued)

Labetalol *(Continued)*

<1% (Limited to important or life-threatening): Alopecia (reversible), anaphylactoid reaction, angioedema, bradycardia, bronchospasm, cholestatic jaundice, CHF, diabetes insipidus, heart block, hepatic necrosis, hepatitis, hypersensitivity, hypotension, Peyronie's disease, positive ANA, pruritus, Raynaud's syndrome, syncope, systemic lupus erythematosus, toxic myopathy, urinary retention, urticaria, ventricular arrhythmia (I.V.)

Other adverse reactions noted with beta-adrenergic blocking agents include mental depression, catatonia, short-term memory loss, emotional lability, intensification of pre-existing AV block, laryngospasm, respiratory distress, agranulocytosis, thrombocytopenic purpura, nonthrombocytopenic purpura, mesenteric artery thrombosis, and ischemic colitis.

Overdosage/Toxicology Symptoms of intoxication include cardiac disturbances, CNS toxicity, bronchospasm, hypoglycemia and hyperkalemia. The most common cardiac symptoms include hypotension and bradycardia. Atrioventricular block, intraventricular conduction disturbances, cardiogenic shock, and asystole may occur with severe overdose, especially with membrane-depressant drugs (eg, propranolol). CNS effects include convulsions, coma, and respiratory arrest, commonly seen with propranolol and other membrane-depressant and lipid-soluble drugs. Treatment is symptomatic for seizures, hypotension, hyperkalemia and hypoglycemia. Bradycardia and hypotension resistant to atropine, isoproterenol or pacing may respond to glucagon. Wide QRS defects caused by membrane-depressant poisoning may respond to hypertonic sodium bicarbonate. Repeat-dose charcoal, hemoperfusion, or hemodialysis may be helpful in removal of only those beta-blockers with a small V_d, long half-life, or low intrinsic clearance (acebutolol, atenolol, nadolol, sotalol).

Drug Interactions

Cytochrome P450 Effect: Substrate of CYP2D6 (major); **Inhibits** CYP2D6 (weak)

Increased Effect/Toxicity: CYP2D6 inhibitors may increase the levels/effects of labetalol; example inhibitors include chlorpromazine, delavirdine, fluoxetine, miconazole, paroxetine, pergolide, quinidine, quinine, ritonavir, and ropinirole. Cimetidine increases the bioavailability of labetalol. Labetalol has additive hypotensive effects with other antihypertensive agents. Concurrent use with alpha-blockers (prazosin, terazosin) and beta-blockers increases the risk of orthostasis. Concurrent use with diltiazem, verapamil, or digoxin may increase the risk of bradycardia with beta-blocking agents. Halothane, enflurane, isoflurane, and potentially other inhalation anesthetics may cause synergistic hypotension. Beta-blockers may affect the action or levels of ethanol, disopyramide, nondepolarizing muscle relaxants, and theophylline although the effects are difficult to predict.

Decreased Effect: Decreased effect of beta-blockers with aluminum salts, barbiturates, calcium salts, cholestyramine, colestipol, NSAIDs, penicillins (ampicillin), rifampin, salicylates, and sulfinpyrazone due to decreased bioavailability and plasma levels. Beta-blockers may decrease the effect of sulfonylureas.

Ethanol/Nutrition/Herb Interactions

Food: Labetalol serum concentrations may be increased if taken with food.

Herb/Nutraceutical: Avoid dong quai if using for hypertension (has estrogenic activity). Avoid ephedra, yohimbe, ginseng (may worsen hypertension). Avoid natural licorice (causes sodium and water retention and increases potassium loss). Avoid garlic (may have increased antihypertensive effect).

Stability

Labetalol should be stored at room temperature or under refrigeration and should be protected from light and freezing. The solution is clear to slightly yellow.

Stability of parenteral admixture at room temperature (25°C) and refrigeration temperature (4°C): 3 days.

Standard diluent: 500 mg/250 mL D_5W.

Minimum volume: 250 mL D_5W.

Mechanism of Action Blocks alpha-, beta$_1$-, and beta$_2$-adrenergic receptor sites; elevated renins are reduced

Pharmacodynamics/Kinetics

Onset of action: Oral: 20 minutes to 2 hours; I.V.: 2-5 minutes

Peak effect: Oral: 1-4 hours; I.V.: 5-15 minutes

Duration: Oral: 8-24 hours (dose dependent); I.V.: 2-4 hours

Distribution: V_d: Adults: 3-16 L/kg; mean: <9.4 L/kg; moderately lipid soluble, therefore, can enter CNS; crosses placenta; small amounts enter breast milk

Protein binding: 50%

Metabolism: Hepatic, primarily via glucuronide conjugation; extensive first-pass effect

Bioavailability: Oral: 25%; increased with liver disease, elderly, and concurrent cimetidine

Half-life elimination: Normal renal function: 2.5-8 hours

Excretion: Urine (<5% as unchanged drug)

Clearance: Possibly decreased in neonates/infants

Dosage Due to limited documentation of its use, labetalol should be initiated cautiously in pediatric patients with careful dosage adjustment and blood pressure monitoring.

Children:

Oral: Limited information regarding labetalol use in pediatric patients is currently available in literature. Some centers recommend initial oral doses of 4 mg/kg/day in 2 divided doses. Reported oral doses have started at 3 mg/kg/day and 20 mg/kg/day and have increased up to 40 mg/kg/day.

I.V., intermittent bolus doses of 0.3-1 mg/kg/dose have been reported.

For treatment of pediatric hypertensive emergencies, initial continuous infusions of 0.4-1 mg/kg/hour with a maximum of 3 mg/kg/hour have been used. Administration requires the use of an infusion pump.

Adults:

Oral: Initial: 100 mg twice daily, may increase as needed every 2-3 days by 100 mg until desired response is obtained; usual dose: 200-400 mg twice daily; may require up to 2.4 g/day.

Usual dose range (JNC 7): 200-800 mg/day in 2 divided doses

I.V.: 20 mg (0.25 mg/kg for an 80 kg patient) IVP over 2 minutes; may administer 40-80 mg at 10-minute intervals, up to 300 mg total dose.

I.V. infusion (acute loading): Initial: 2 mg/minute; titrate to response up to 300 mg total dose, if needed. Administration requires the use of an infusion pump.

I.V. infusion (500 mg/250 mL D_5W) rates:

1 mg/minute: 30 mL/hour
2 mg/minute: 60 mL/hour
3 mg/minute: 90 mL/hour
4 mg/minute: 120 mL/hour
5 mg/minute: 150 mL/hour
6 mg/minute: 180 mL/hour

Note: Although loading infusions are well described in the product labeling, the labeling is silent in specific clinical situations, such as in the patient who has an initial response to labetalol infusions but cannot be converted to an oral route for subsequent dosing. There is limited documentation of prolonged continuous infusions. In rare clinical situations, higher dosages (up to 6 mg/minute) have been used in the critical care setting (eg, aortic dissection). At the other extreme, continuous infusions at relatively low doses (2-6 mg/hour — note difference in units) have been used in some settings (following loading infusion in patients who are unable to be converted to oral regimens or in some cases as a continuation of outpatient oral regimens). These prolonged infusions should not be confused with loading infusions. Because of wide variation in the use of infusions, an awareness of institutional policies and practices is extremely important. Careful clarification of orders and specific infusion rates/units is required to avoid confusion. Due to the prolonged duration of action, careful monitoring should be extended for the duration of the infusion and for several hours after the infusion. Excessive administration may result in prolonged hypotension and/or bradycardia.

Dialysis: Not removed by hemo- or peritoneal dialysis; supplemental dose is not necessary.

Dosage adjustment in hepatic impairment: Dosage reduction may be necessary.

Administration Bolus administered over 2 minutes. Loading infusions (2 mg/minute) require close monitoring of heart rate and blood pressure and are usually terminated after response or cumulative dose of 300 mg. There is limited documentation of prolonged continuous infusions. In clinical experience, prolonged continuous infusions have been used. In rare clinical situations, higher dosages (up to 6 mg/minute) have been used in the critical care setting (eg, aortic dissection). At the other extreme, continuous infusions at relatively low doses (2-6 mg/hour: note difference in units) have been used in some settings (following loading infusion in patients who are unable to be converted to oral regimens or in some cases as a continuation of outpatient oral regimens). These prolonged infusions should not be confused with loading infusions. Because of wide variation in the use of infusions, an awareness of institutional policies and practices is extremely important. Careful clarification of orders and specific infusion rates/units is required to avoid confusion. Due to the prolonged duration of action, careful monitoring should be extended for the duration of the infusion and for several hours after the infusion. Excessive administration may result in prolonged hypotension and/or bradycardia.

Monitoring Parameters Blood pressure, standing and sitting/supine, pulse, cardiac monitor and blood pressure monitor required for I.V. administration

Test Interactions False-positive urine catecholamines, VMA if measured by fluorometric or photometric methods; use HPLC or specific catecholamine radioenzymatic technique

Dosage Forms

Injection, solution, as hydrochloride: 5 mg/mL (4 mL, 20 mL, 40 mL)
Trandate®: 5 mg/mL (20 mL, 40 mL)
Tablet, as hydrochloride: 100 mg, 200 mg, 300 mg
Trandate®: 100 mg, 200 mg [contains sodium benzoate], 300 mg

Extemporaneous Preparations A 40 mg/mL suspension of labetalol hydrochloride can be made by first crushing sixteen 300 mg labetalol hydrochloride tablets into a fine powder. Using equal amounts of Ora-Sweet® and Ora-Plus® as a vehicle, add a small amount to make a paste; add additional amounts of the vehicle to qs to 120 mL. Suspension is stable for 60 days when stored in the refrigerator. Shake well before using.

Nahata MC and Hipple TF, *Pediatric Drug Formulations*, 4th ed, Cincinnati, OH: Harvey Whitney Books Co, 2000.

♦ **Labetalol Hydrochloride** *see* Labetalol *on page 967*

♦ **Labetalol Hydrochloride Injection, USP (Can)** *see* Labetalol *on page 967*

♦ **Lactinex™ [OTC]** *see* Lactobacillus *on page 969*

Lactobacillus (lak toe ba SIL us)

U.S. Brand Names Bacid® [OTC]; Culturelle™ [OTC]; Dofus [OTC]; Flora-Q™ [OTC]; Kala® [OTC]; Lactinex™ [OTC]; Lacto-Bifidus [OTC]; Lacto-Key [OTC]; Lacto-Pectin [OTC]; Lacto-TriBlend [OTC]; Megadophilus® [OTC]; MoreDophilus® [OTC]; Superdophilus® [OTC]

Canadian Brand Names Bacid®; Fermalac

Index Terms *Lactobacillus acidophilus; Lactobacillus bifidus; Lactobacillus bulgaricus; Lactobacillus casei; Lactobacillus paracasei; Lactobacillus reuteri; Lactobacillus rhamnosus* GG

Pharmacologic Category Dietary Supplement; Probiotic

Use Promote normal bacterial flora of the intestinal tract

Contraindications Hypersensitivity to any component of the formulation

Warnings/Precautions *Lactobacillus* species have been studied for various gastrointestinal disorders including diarrhea, inflammatory bowel disease, gastrointestinal infection. Effectiveness may be dependent upon actual species used; studies are ongoing. Currently, there are no FDA-approved disease-prevention or therapeutic indications for these products.

Adverse Reactions Gastrointestinal: Flatulence

Stability

Bacid®: Store at room temperature.
Flora-Q™: Store at or below room temperature; do not store in bathroom.
Kala®, MoreDophilus®: Refrigeration recommended after opening.
Lactinex™, Dofus: Store in refrigerator.

(Continued)

Lactobacillus (Continued)

Mechanism of Action Helps re-establish normal intestinal flora; suppresses the growth of potentially pathogenic microorganisms by producing lactic acid which favors the establishment of an aciduric flora.

Pharmacodynamics/Kinetics
Absorption: Oral: None
Distribution: Local, primarily colon
Excretion: Feces

Dosage Dietary supplement: Oral: Dosing varies by manufacturer; consult product labeling

Children (Culturelle®): 1 capsule daily
Adults:
Bacid®: 2 caplets/day
Culturelle®: 1 capsule daily; may increase to twice daily
Flora-Q™: 1 capsule/day
Lacto-Key 100 or 600: 1-2 capsules/day
Lactinex™: 1 packet or 4 tablets 3-4 times/day

Dietary Considerations Products may contain whey, evaporated milk, soy peptone casein and/or beef extract; consult individual product labeling. Lactinex™ contains sodium 5.6 mg/4 tablets

Administration
Culturelle®: Capsules may be opened and mixed in a cool beverage or sprinkled onto baby food or applesauce.
Flora-Q™: May be taken with or without food.
Lactinex™: Granules may be added to or administered with cereal, food, or milk.
Megadophilus®, Superdophilus®: Administer on an empty stomach; powder should be mixed in unchilled water.

Dosage Forms
Capsule:
Culturelle®: *L. rhamnosus* GG 10 billion colony-forming units [contains casein and whey]
Dofus: *L. acidophilus* and *L. bifidus* 10:1 ratio [beet root powder base]
Flora-Q™: *L. acidophilus* and *L. paracasei* ≥8 billion colony-forming units [also contains *Bifidobacterium* and *S. thermophilus*]
Lacto-Key:
100: *L. acidophilus* 1 billion colony-forming units [milk, soy, and yeast free; rice derived]
600: *L. acidophilus* 6 billion colony-forming units [milk, soy, and yeast free; rice derived]
Lacto-Bifidus:
100: *L. bifidus* 1 billion colony-forming units [milk, soy, and yeast free; rice derived]
600: *L. bifidus* 6 billion colony-forming units [milk, soy, and yeast free; rice derived]
Lacto-Pectin: *L. acidophilus* and *L. casei* ≥5 billion colony-forming units [also contains *Bifidobacterium lactis* and citrus pectin cellulose complex]
Lacto-TriBlend:
100: *L. acidophilus*, *L. bifidus*, and *L. bulgaricus* 1 billion colony-forming units [milk, soy and yeast free; rice derived]
600: *L. acidophilus*, *L. bifidus*, and *L. bulgaricus* 6 billion colony-forming units [milk, soy and yeast free; rice derived]
Megadophilus®, Superdophilus®: *L. acidophilus* 2 billion units [available in dairy based or dairy free formulations]
Capsule, softgel: *L. acidophilus* 100 active units
Caplet (Bacid®): *L. acidophilus* 80% and *L. bulgaricus* 10% [also contains *Bifidobacterium biffidum* 5% and *S. thermophilus* 5%]
Granules (Lactinex™): *L. acidophilus* and *L. bulgaricus* 100 million live cells per 1 g packet (12s) [contains whey, evaporated milk, soy peptone, lactose, and beef extract]
Powder:
Lacto-TriBlend: *L. acidophilus*, *L. bifidus*, and *L. bulgaricus* 10 billion colony-forming units per ¼ teaspoon (60 g) [milk, soy, and yeast free; rice derived]
Megadophilus®, Superdophilus®: *L. acidophilus* 2 billion units per half-teaspoon (49 g, 70 g, 84 g, 126 g) [available in dairy based or dairy free (garbanzo bean) formulations]
MoreDophilus®: *L. acidophilus* 12.4 billion units per teaspoon (30 g, 120 g) [dairy free, yeast free; soy and carrot derived]
Tablet:
Kala®: *L. acidophilus* 200 million units [dairy free, yeast free; soy based]
Lactinex™: *L. acidophilus* and *L. bulgaricus* 1 million live cells [contains whey, evaporated milk, soy peptone, lactose, and beef extract; contains sodium 5.6 mg/4 tablets]
Tablet, chewable: *L. reuteri* 100 million organisms
Wafer: *L. acidophilus* 90 mg and *L. bifidus* 25 mg (100s) [provides 1 billion organisms/wafer at time of manufacture; milk free]

♦ **Lactobacillus acidophilus** see Lactobacillus on page 969
♦ **Lactobacillus bifidus** see Lactobacillus on page 969
♦ **Lactobacillus bulgaricus** see Lactobacillus on page 969
♦ **Lactobacillus casei** see Lactobacillus on page 969
♦ **Lactobacillus paracasei** see Lactobacillus on page 969
♦ **Lactobacillus reuteri** see Lactobacillus on page 969
♦ **Lactobacillus rhamnosus GG** see Lactobacillus on page 969
♦ **Lacto-Bifidus [OTC]** see Lactobacillus on page 969
♦ **Lactoflavin** see Riboflavin on page 1506
♦ **Lacto-Key [OTC]** see Lactobacillus on page 969
♦ **Lacto-Pectin [OTC]** see Lactobacillus on page 969
♦ **Lacto-TriBlend [OTC]** see Lactobacillus on page 969

Lactulose (LAK tyoo lose)

U.S. Brand Names Constulose; Enulose; Generlac; Kristalose™
Canadian Brand Names Acilac; Apo-Lactulose®; Laxilose; PMS-Lactulose
Pharmacologic Category Ammonium Detoxicant; Laxative, Osmotic
Additional Appendix Information
  Laxatives, Classification and Properties *on page 1886*
Use Adjunct in the prevention and treatment of portal-systemic encephalopathy; treatment of chronic constipation
Pregnancy Risk Factor B
Lactation Excretion in breast milk unknown
Medication Safety Issues
  Sound-alike/look-alike issues:
    Lactulose may be confused with lactose
Contraindications Hypersensitivity to lactulose or any component of the formulation; galactosemia (or patients requiring a low galactose diet)
Warnings/Precautions Use with caution in patients with diabetes mellitus; monitor periodically for electrolyte imbalance when lactulose is used >6 months or in patients predisposed to electrolyte abnormalities (eg, elderly); patients receiving lactulose and an oral anti-infective agent should be monitored for possible inadequate response to lactulose
Adverse Reactions Frequency not defined: Gastrointestinal: Flatulence, diarrhea (excessive dose), abdominal discomfort, nausea, vomiting, cramping
Overdosage/Toxicology Symptoms include diarrhea, abdominal pain, hypochloremic alkalosis, dehydration, hypotension, and hypokalemia. Treatment is supportive.
Drug Interactions
  Decreased Effect: Oral neomycin, laxatives, antacids
Stability Keep solution at room temperature to reduce viscosity. Discard solution if cloudy or very dark.
Mechanism of Action The bacterial degradation of lactulose resulting in an acidic pH inhibits the diffusion of NH_3 into the blood by causing the conversion of NH_3 to NH_4+; also enhances the diffusion of NH_3 from the blood into the gut where conversion to NH_4+ occurs; produces an osmotic effect in the colon with resultant distention promoting peristalsis
Pharmacodynamics/Kinetics
  Absorption: Not appreciable
  Metabolism: Via colonic flora to lactic acid and acetic acid; requires colonic flora for drug activation
  Excretion: Primarily feces and urine (~3%)
Dosage Diarrhea may indicate overdosage and responds to dose reduction
  Prevention of portal systemic encephalopathy (PSE): Oral:
    Infants: 2.5-10 mL/day divided 3-4 times/day; adjust dosage to produce 2-3 stools/day
    Older Children: Daily dose of 40-90 mL divided 3-4 times/day; if initial dose causes diarrhea, then reduce it immediately; adjust dosage to produce 2-3 stools/day
  Constipation: Oral:
    Children: 5 g/day (7.5 mL) after breakfast
    Adults: 15-30 mL/day increased to 60 mL/day in 1-2 divided doses if necessary
  Acute PSE: Adults:
    Oral: 20-30 g (30-45 mL) every 1-2 hours to induce rapid laxation; adjust dosage daily to produce 2-3 soft stools; doses of 30-45 mL may be given hourly to cause rapid laxation, then reduce to recommended dose; usual daily dose: 60-100 g (90-150 mL) daily
    Rectal administration: 200 g (300 mL) diluted with 700 mL of H_2O or NS; administer rectally via rectal balloon catheter and retain 30-60 minutes every 4-6 hours
Dietary Considerations Contraindicated in patients on galactose-restricted diet; may be mixed with fruit juice, milk, water, or citrus-flavored carbonated beverages.
Administration Dilute lactulose in water, usually 60-120 mL, prior to administering through a gastric or feeding tube. Syrup formulation has been used in preparation of rectal solution.
Monitoring Parameters Blood pressure, standing/supine; serum potassium, bowel movement patterns, fluid status, serum ammonia
Dosage Forms
  Crystals for reconstitution:
    Kristalose™: 10 g/packet (30s), 20 g/packet (30s)
  Syrup: 10 g/15 mL (15 mL, 30 mL, 237 mL, 473 mL, 946 mL, 1890 mL)
    Constulose: 10 g/15 mL (240 mL, 960 mL)
    Enulose: 10 g/15 mL (480 mL)
    Generlac: 10 g/15 mL (480 mL, 1920 mL)

♦ **Ladakamycin** *see* Azacitidine *on page 181*
♦ **L-All 12** *see* Carbetapentane and Phenylephrine *on page 289*
♦ **L-AmB** *see* Amphotericin B (Liposomal) *on page 119*
♦ **Lamictal®** *see* Lamotrigine *on page 974*
♦ **Lamisil®** *see* Terbinafine *on page 1648*
♦ **Lamisil® AT™ [OTC]** *see* Terbinafine *on page 1648*

Lamivudine (la MI vyoo deen)

U.S. Brand Names Epivir®; Epivir-HBV®
Canadian Brand Names Heptovir®; 3TC®
Index Terms 3TC
Pharmacologic Category Antiretroviral Agent, Reverse Transcriptase Inhibitor (Nucleoside)
Additional Appendix Information
  Antiretroviral Therapy for HIV Infection: Adults and Adolescents *on page 1988*
  Management of Healthcare Worker Exposure to HBV, HCV, and HIV *on page 1941*
  (Continued)

Lamivudine *(Continued)*

Use

Epivir®: Treatment of HIV infection when antiretroviral therapy is warranted; should always be used as part of a multidrug regimen (at least three antiretroviral agents)

Epivir-HBV®: Treatment of chronic hepatitis B associated with evidence of hepatitis B viral replication and active liver inflammation

Unlabeled/Investigational Use Prevention of HIV following needlesticks (with or without protease inhibitor)

Pregnancy Risk Factor C

Pregnancy Implications Lamivudine crosses the placenta. No increased risk of overall birth defects has been observed following 1st trimester exposure according to data collected by the antiretroviral pregnancy registry. The pharmacokinetics of lamivudine during pregnancy are not significantly altered and dosage adjustment is not required. The Perinatal HIV Guidelines Working Group recommends lamivudine for use during pregnancy; the combination of lamivudine with zidovudine is the recommended dual combination NRTI in pregnancy. It may also be used in combination with zidovudine in HIV-infected women who are in labor, but have had no prior antiretroviral therapy, in order to reduce the maternal-fetal transmission of HIV. Cases of lactic acidosis/hepatic steatosis syndrome have been reported in pregnant women receiving nucleoside analogues. It is not known if pregnancy itself potentiates this known side effect; however, pregnant women may be at increased risk of lactic acidosis and liver damage. Hepatic enzymes and electrolytes should be monitored frequently during the 3rd trimester of pregnancy in women receiving nucleoside analogues. Health professionals are encouraged to contact the antiretroviral pregnancy registry to monitor outcomes of pregnant women exposed to antiretroviral medications (1-800-258-4263 or www.APRegistry.com).

Lactation Enters breast milk/contraindicated

Medication Safety Issues

Sound-alike/look-alike issues:

Lamivudine may be confused with lamotrigine

Epivir® may be confused with Combivir®

Contraindications Hypersensitivity to lamivudine or any component of the formulation

Warnings/Precautions Use caution with renal impairment; dosage reduction recommended. Use with extreme caution in children with history of pancreatitis or risk factors for development of pancreatitis. Do not use as monotherapy in treatment of HIV. Treatment of HBV in patients with unrecognized/untreated HIV may lead to rapid HIV resistance. In addition, treatment of HIV in patients with unrecognized/untreated HBV may lead to rapid HBV resistance. **[U.S. Boxed Warning]: Do not use Epivir-HBV® tablets or Epivir-HBV® oral solution for the treatment of HIV.**

[U.S. Boxed Warning]: Lactic acidosis and severe hepatomegaly with steatosis have been reported, including fatal cases. Use caution in hepatic impairment. Pregnancy, obesity, and/or prolonged therapy may increase the risk of lactic acidosis and liver damage.

Immune reconstitution syndrome may develop resulting in the occurrence of an inflammatory response to an indolent or residual opportunistic infection. May be associated with fat redistribution.

[U.S. Boxed Warning]: Monitor patients closely for several months following discontinuation of therapy for chronic hepatitis B; clinical exacerbations may occur.

Adverse Reactions Reported for treatment of HIV or HBV in adults. Incidence data includes patients on combination therapy with other antiretroviral agents.

>10%:

Central nervous system: Headache (21% to 35%), fatigue (24% to 27%), insomnia (11%)

Gastrointestinal: Nausea (15% to 33%), diarrhea (14% to 18%), pancreatitis (range: 0.3% to 18%; higher percentage in pediatric patients), abdominal pain (9% to 16%), vomiting (13% to 15%)

Hematologic: Neutropenia (7% to 15%)

Hepatic: Transaminases increased (2% to 11%)

Neuromuscular & skeletal: Myalgia (8% to 14%), neuropathy (12%), musculoskeletal pain (12%)

Respiratory: Nasal signs and symptoms (20%), cough (18%), sore throat (13%)

Miscellaneous: Infections (25%; includes ear, nose, and throat)

1% to 10%:

Central nervous system: Dizziness (10%), depression (9%), fever (7% to 10%), chills (7% to 10%)

Dermatologic: Rash (5% to 9%)

Gastrointestinal: Anorexia (10%), lipase increased (10%), abdominal cramps (6%), dyspepsia (5%), amylase increased (<1% to 4%), heartburn

Hematologic: Thrombocytopenia (1% to 4%), hemoglobinemia (2% to 3%)

Neuromuscular & skeletal: Creatine phosphokinase increased (9%), arthralgia (5% to 7%)

<1% (Limited to important or life-threatening): Alopecia, anaphylaxis, anemia, body fat redistribution, hepatitis B exacerbation, hepatomegaly, hyperbilirubinemia, hyperglycemia, immune reconstitution syndrome, lactic acidosis, lymphadenopathy, muscle weakness, paresthesia, peripheral neuropathy, pruritus, red cell aplasia, rhabdomyolysis, splenomegaly, steatosis, stomatitis, urticaria, weakness, wheezing

Overdosage/Toxicology Very limited information is available, although there have been no clinical signs or symptoms noted in overdose, and hematologic tests have remained normal as well. No antidote is available. Limited (negligible) removal following 4-hour hemodialysis. It is not known if continuous 24-hour hemodialysis would be effective.

Drug Interactions

Increased Effect/Toxicity: Sulfamethoxazole/trimethoprim increases lamivudine's blood levels. Concomitant use of ribavirin with or without interferon alfa and nucleoside analogues may increase the risk of developing hepatic decompensation or other signs of mitochondrial toxicity, including pancreatitis or lactic acidosis. Ganciclovir/valganciclovir may increase the adverse effects/toxicity (eg, hematologic) of nucleoside reverse transcriptase inhibitors. Trimethoprim (and other drugs excreted by organic cation transport) may increase serum levels/effects of lamivudine.

Decreased Effect: Zalcitabine and lamivudine may inhibit the intracellular phosphorylation of each other; concomitant use should be avoided.

Ethanol/Nutrition/Herb Interactions Food: Food decreases the rate of absorption and C_{max}; however, there is no change in the systemic AUC. Therefore, may be taken with or without food.

Stability
Oral solution: Store at 2°C to 25°C (68°F to 77°F) tightly closed.
Tablet: Store at 15°C to 30°C (59°F to 86°F).

Mechanism of Action Lamivudine is a cytosine analog. After lamivudine is triphosphorylated, the principle mode of action is inhibition of HIV reverse transcription via viral DNA chain termination; inhibits RNA- and DNA-dependent DNA polymerase activities of reverse transcriptase. The monophosphate form of lamivudine is incorporated into the viral DNA by hepatitis B virus polymerase, resulting in DNA chain termination.

Pharmacodynamics/Kinetics
Absorption: Rapid
Distribution: V_d: 1.3 L/kg
Protein binding, plasma: <36%
Metabolism: 5.2% to trans-sulfoxide metabolite
Bioavailability: Absolute; Cp_{max} decreased with food although AUC not significantly affected
Children: 66%
Adults: 86% to 87%
Half-life elimination: Children: 2 hours; Adults: 5-7 hours
Time to peak, plasma: Fed: 3.2 hours; Fasted: 0.9 hours
Excretion: Primarily urine (as unchanged drug)

Dosage Note: The formulation and dosage of Epivir-HBV® are not appropriate for patients infected with both HBV and HIV. Use with at least two other antiretroviral agents when treating HIV
Oral:
Children 3 months to 16 years: HIV: 4 mg/kg twice daily (maximum: 150 mg twice daily)
Children 2-17 years: Treatment of hepatitis B (Epivir-HBV®): 3 mg/kg once daily (maximum: 100 mg/day)
Adolescents and Adults: Prevention of HIV following needlesticks (unlabeled use): 150 mg twice daily (with zidovudine with or without a protease inhibitor, depending on risk)
Adults:
HIV: 150 mg twice daily **or** 300 mg once daily
<50 kg: 4 mg/kg twice daily (maximum: 150 mg twice daily)
Treatment of hepatitis B (Epivir-HBV®): 100 mg/day

Dosing interval in renal impairment in pediatric patients: Insufficient data; however, dose reduction should be considered.

Dosing interval in renal impairment in patients >16 years for HIV:
Cl_{cr} 30-49 mL/minute: Administer 150 mg once daily
Cl_{cr} 15-29 mL/minute: Administer 150 mg first dose, then 100 mg once daily
Cl_{cr} 5-14 mL/minute: Administer 150 mg first dose, then 50 mg once daily
Cl_{cr} <5 mL/minute: Administer 50 mg first dose, then 25 mg once daily

Dosing interval in renal impairment in adult patients with hepatitis B:
Cl_{cr} 30-49: Administer 100 mg first dose then 50 mg once daily
Cl_{cr} 15-29: Administer 100 mg first dose then 25 mg once daily
Cl_{cr} 5-14: Administer 35 mg first dose then 15 mg once daily
Cl_{cr} <5: Administer 35 mg first dose then 10 mg once daily
Dialysis: Negligible amounts are removed by 4-hour hemodialysis or peritoneal dialysis. Supplemental dosing is not required.

Dietary Considerations May be taken with or without food. Each 5 mL of oral solution contains 1 g of sucrose.

Administration May be taken with or without food. Adjust dosage in renal failure.

Monitoring Parameters Amylase, bilirubin, liver enzymes, hematologic parameters, viral load, and CD4 count; signs and symptoms of pancreatitis

Additional Information Lamivudine has been well studied in the treatment of chronic hepatitis B infection. Potential compliance problems, frequency of administration, and adverse effects should be discussed with patients before initiating therapy to help prevent the emergence of resistance.

A high rate of early virologic nonresponse was observed when abacavir, lamivudine and tenofovir were used as the initial regimen in treatment-naive patients. A high rate of early virologic nonresponse was also observed when didanosine, lamivudine, and tenofovir were used as the initial regimen in treatment-naive patients. Use of either of these combinations is not recommended; patients currently on either of these regimens should be closely monitored for modification of therapy.

Dosage Forms
Solution, oral:
Epivir®: 10 mg/mL (240 mL) [strawberry-banana flavor]
Epivir-HBV®: 5 mg/mL (240 mL) [strawberry-banana flavor]
Tablet:
Epivir®: 150 mg, 300 mg
Epivir-HBV®: 100 mg

◆ **Lamivudine, Abacavir, and Zidovudine** see Abacavir, Lamivudine, and Zidovudine on page 19
◆ **Lamivudine and Abacavir** see Abacavir and Lamivudine on page 19
◆ **Lamivudine and Zidovudine** see Zidovudine and Lamivudine on page 1815

Lamotrigine (la MOE tri jeen)

U.S. Brand Names Lamictal®

Canadian Brand Names Apo-Lamotrigine®; Gen-Lamotrigine; Lamictal®; Novo-Lamotrigine; PMS-Lamotrigine; ratio-Lamotrigine

Index Terms BW-430C; LTG

Pharmacologic Category Anticonvulsant, Miscellaneous

Additional Appendix Information

Anticonvulsants by Seizure Type *on page 1865*

Epilepsy *on page 2048*

Use Adjunctive therapy in the treatment of generalized seizures of Lennox-Gastaut syndrome, primary generalized tonic-clonic seizures, and partial seizures in adults and children ≥2 years of age; conversion to monotherapy in adults with partial seizures who are receiving treatment with valproic acid or a single enzyme-inducing antiepileptic drug (specifically carbamazepine, phenytoin, phenobarbital or primidone); maintenance treatment of bipolar I disorder

Pregnancy Risk Factor C

Pregnancy Implications Lamotrigine has been found to decrease folate concentrations in animal studies. Teratogenic effects in animals were not observed. Lamotrigine crosses the human placenta and can be measured in the plasma of exposed newborns. Preliminary data from the North American Antiepileptic Drug Pregnancy Registry (NAAED) suggest an increased incidence of cleft lip and/or cleft palate following first trimester exposure. Healthcare providers may enroll patients in the Lamotrigine Pregnancy Registry by calling (800) 336-2176. Patients may enroll themselves in the NAAED registry by calling (888) 233-2334. Dose of lamotrigine may need adjustment during pregnancy to maintain clinical response; lamotrigine serum levels may decrease during pregnancy and return to prepartum levels following delivery. Monitor frequently during pregnancy, following delivery, and when adding or discontinuing combination hormonal contraceptives.

Lactation Enters breast milk/not recommended (AAP rates "of concern")

Medication Safety Issues

Sound-alike/look-alike issues:

Lamotrigine may be confused with labetalol, Lamisil®, lamivudine, Lomotil®, ludiomil

Lamictal® may be confused with Lamisil®, Lomotil®, ludiomil

Contraindications Hypersensitivity to lamotrigine or any component of the formulation

Warnings/Precautions [U.S. Boxed Warning]: Severe and potentially life-threatening skin rashes requiring hospitalization have been reported; risk may be increased by coadministration with valproic acid, higher than recommended starting doses, and rapid dose titration. The majority of cases occur in the first 8 weeks; however, isolated cases may occur after prolonged treatment. Discontinue at first sign of rash unless rash is clearly not drug related. Acute multiorgan failure has also been reported. Use caution in patients with impaired renal, hepatic, or cardiac function. Avoid abrupt cessation, taper over at least 2 weeks if possible. May cause CNS depression, which may impair physical or mental abilities. Patients must be cautioned about performing tasks which require mental alertness (eg, operating machinery or driving). Effects with other sedative drugs or ethanol may be potentiated. Binds to melanin and may accumulate in the eye and other melanin-rich tissues; the clinical significance of this is not known. Safety and efficacy has not been established for use as initial monotherapy, conversion to monotherapy from antiepileptic drugs (AED) other than carbamazepine, phenytoin, phenobarbital, primidone or valproic acid or conversion to monotherapy from two or more AEDs. Patients treated for bipolar disorder should be monitored closely for clinical worsening or suicidality; prescriptions should be written for the smallest quantity consistent with good patient care.

Adverse Reactions Percentages reported in adults on monotherapy for epilepsy or bipolar disorder.

>10%: Gastrointestinal: Nausea (7% to 14%)

1% to 10%:

Cardiovascular: Chest pain (5%), peripheral edema (2% to 5%), edema (1% to 5%)

Central nervous system: Somnolence (9%), fatigue (8%), dizziness (7%), anxiety (5%), insomnia (5% to 10%), pain (5%), ataxia (2% to 5%), irritability (2% to 5%), suicidal ideation (2% to 5%), agitation (1% to 5%), amnesia (1% to 5%), depression (1% to 5%), dream abnormality (1% to 5%), emotional lability (1% to 5%), fever (1% to 5%), hypoesthesia (1% to 5%), migraine (1% to 5%), thought abnormality (1% to 5%), confusion (1%)

Dermatologic: Rash (nonserious: 7%), dermatitis (2% to 5%), dry skin (2% to 5%)

Endocrine & metabolic: Dysmenorrhea (5%), libido increased (2% to 5%)

Gastrointestinal: Vomiting (5% to 9%), dyspepsia (7%), abdominal pain (6%), xerostomia (2% to 6%), constipation (5%), weight loss (5%), anorexia (2% to 5%), peptic ulcer (2% to 5%), rectal hemorrhage (2% to 5%), flatulence (1% to 5%), weight gain (1% to 5%)

Genitourinary: Urinary frequency (1% to 5%)

Neuromuscular & skeletal: Back pain (8%), coordination abnormal (7%), weakness (2% to 5%), arthralgia (1% to 5%), myalgia (1% to 5%), neck pain (1% to 5%), paresthesia (1%)

Ocular: Nystagmus (2% to 5%), vision abnormal (2% to 5%), amblyopia (1%)

Respiratory: Rhinitis (7%), cough (5%), pharyngitis (5%), bronchitis (2% to 5%), dyspnea (2% to 5%), epistaxis (2% to 5%), sinusitis (1% to 5%)

Miscellaneous: Infection (5%), diaphoresis (2% to 5%), reflexes increased/decreased (2% to 5%), dyspraxia (1% to 5%)

<1%: Any indication (limited to important or life-threatening): Accommodation abnormality, acne, agranulocytosis, alcohol intolerance, allergic reaction, alopecia, anemia, angina, angioedema, aphasia, aplastic anemia, apnea, appetite increased, arthritis, atrial fibrillation, breast pain, bruising, cerebellar syndrome, cerebral sinus thrombosis, cerebrovascular accident, chills, choreoathetosis, CNS depression/stimulation, conjunctivitis, deafness, deep thrombophlebitis, delirium, delusions, dermatitis (exfoliative, fungal), disseminated intravascular coagulation, dry eyes, dysphagia, dysphoria, dystonia, ear pain, ECG abnormality, ejaculation abnormal, eructation, esophagitis, euphoria, extrapyramidal syndrome, faintness, flushing, gastritis, gingivitis, goiter, halitosis, hallucinations, hematuria, hemiplegia, hemolytic anemia, hemorrhage, hiccup, hirsutism, hot flashes,

hyperalgesia, hyperglycemia, hypersensitivity reactions, hypertension, hyperventilation, hypokinesia, hypothyroidism, hypotonia, impotence, kidney failure (acute), leg cramps, leukopenia, liver function tests abnormal, lupus-like reaction, maculopapular rash, malaise, menorrhagia, MI, mouth ulceration, movement disorder, multiorgan failure, muscle spasm, myasthenia, neuralgia, neurosis, neutropenia, palpitations, pancreatitis, pancytopenia, paralysis, parkinsonian exacerbation, peripheral neuritis, photophobia, polyuria, postural hypotension, progressive immunosuppression, red cell aplasia, rhabdomyolysis, salivation increased, skin discoloration, Stevens-Johnson syndrome, suicide, syncope, tachycardia, taste loss/perversion, thrombocytopenia, tic, tinnitus, tongue edema, toxic epidermal necrolysis, twitching, urinary incontinence, urticaria, vasculitis, vasodilation, yawn

Also observed: Rash requiring hospitalization: Children <16 years 0.8% (epilepsy adjunctive therapy); Adults 0.3% (epilepsy adjunctive therapy), 0.13% (epilepsy monotherapy), 0.8% (bipolar disorder, monotherapy)

Overdosage/Toxicology Most common symptoms reported following lamotrigine overdose include ataxia, drowsiness, lethargy, nausea and vomiting. Coma, respiratory depression, and seizures have also been reported. Symptoms such as hypokalemia, hypertonia, motor weakness, nystagmus, QRS prolongation, tremor, and xerostomia have been noted in case reports. Treatment should be symptom directed and supportive and may include activated charcoal. Effectiveness of hemodialysis is uncertain; ~20% removed during 4-hour dialysis session.

Drug Interactions

Increased Effect/Toxicity: Lamotrigine may increase the epoxide metabolite of carbamazepine resulting in toxicity. Valproic acid increases blood levels of lamotrigine. Valproic acid inhibits the clearance of lamotrigine, dosage adjustment required when adding or withdrawing valproic acid; inhibition appears maximal at valproic acid 250-500 mg/day; the incidence of serious rash may be increased by valproic acid. Lamotrigine may enhance the adverse/toxic effect of other CNS depressants.

Decreased Effect: Carbamazepine, oral contraceptives (estrogens), phenytoin, phenobarbital, primidone may decrease concentrations of lamotrigine; dosage adjustments may be needed when adding or withdrawing agent; monitor. Rifampin may reduce serum concentrations and effects of lamotrigine.

Ethanol/Nutrition/Herb Interactions

Ethanol: Avoid ethanol (may increase CNS depression).

Food: Has no effect on absorption.

Herb/Nutraceutical: Avoid evening primrose (seizure threshold decreased).

Stability Store at 25°C (77°F); excursions are permitted to 15°C to 30°C (59°F to 86°F). Protect from light.

Mechanism of Action A triazine derivative which inhibits release of glutamate (an excitatory amino acid) and inhibits voltage-sensitive sodium channels, which stabilizes neuronal membranes. Lamotrigine has weak inhibitory effect on the 5-HT$_3$ receptor; *in vitro* inhibits dihydrofolate reductase.

Pharmacodynamics/Kinetics

Absorption: Rapid and complete

Distribution: V_d: ~1 L/kg

Protein binding: 55%

Metabolism: Hepatic and renal; metabolized by glucuronic acid conjugation to inactive metabolites

Bioavailability: 98%

Half-life elimination: Adults: 25-33 hours

Concomitant valproic acid therapy: 59-70 hours

Concomitant phenytoin or carbamazepine therapy: 13-14 hours

Chronic renal failure: 43 hours

Hemodialysis: 13 hours during dialysis; 57 hours between dialysis

Hepatic impairment: 26-148 hours

Time to peak, plasma: 1-5 hours

Excretion: Urine (94%, ~90% as glucuronide conjugates and ~10% unchanged); feces (2%)

Dosage Only whole tablets should be used for dosing, round calculated dose down to the nearest whole tablet. Enzyme-inducing regimens specifically refer to those containing carbamazepine, phenytoin, phenobarbital, or primidone. Oral:

Children 2-12 years: Lennox-Gastaut (adjunctive), primary generalized tonic-clonic seizures (adjunctive), or partial seizures (adjunctive): **Note:** Children <30 kg will likely require maintenance doses to be increased as much as 50% based on clinical response regardless of regimen below:

Initial: 0.3 mg/kg/day in 1-2 divided doses for weeks 1 and 2, then increase to 0.6 mg/kg/day in 1-2 divided doses for weeks 3 and 4. Maintenance: Titrate dose to effect; after week 4, increase daily dose every 1-2 weeks by 0.6 mg/kg/day; usual maintenance: 4.5-7.5 mg/kg/day in 2 divided doses; maximum: 300 mg/day in 2 divided doses

Adjustment for AED regimens **containing** valproic acid (see "Note"): Initial: 0.15 mg/kg/day in 1-2 divided doses for weeks 1 and 2, then increase to 0.3 mg/kg/day in 1-2 divided doses for weeks 3 and 4. Maintenance: Titrate dose to effect; after week 4, increase daily dose every 1-2 weeks by 0.3 mg/kg/day; usual maintenance: 1-5 mg/kg/day in 2 divided doses; maximum: 200 mg/day in 1-2 divided doses

Note: For patients >6.7 kg and <14 kg, initial dosing should be 2 mg every other day for first 2 weeks, then increased to 2 mg daily for weeks 3-4. For patients taking lamotrigine with valproic acid alone, the usual maintenance dose is 1-3 mg/kg/day in 2 divided doses

Adjustment for **enzyme-inducing** AED regimens **without** valproic acid: Initial: 0.6 mg/kg/day in 2 divided doses for weeks 1 and 2, then increase to 1.2 mg/kg/day in 2 divided doses for weeks 3 and 4. Maintenance: Titrate dose to effect; after week 4, increase daily dose every 1-2 weeks by 1.2 mg/kg/day; usual maintenance: 5-15 mg/kg/day in 2 divided doses; maximum: 400 mg/day in 2 divided doses

Children >12 years: Lennox-Gastaut (adjunctive), primary generalized tonic-clonic seizures (adjunctive), or partial seizures (adjunctive): Refer to Adults dosing.

(Continued)

Lamotrigine *(Continued)*

Children ≥16 years: Conversion from adjunctive therapy with valproic acid or a single enzyme-inducing AED regimen to monotherapy with lamotrigine: Refer to Adults dosing.

Adults:

Lennox-Gastaut (adjunctive), primary generalized tonic-clonic seizures (adjunctive) or partial seizures (adjunctive): Initial: 25 mg/day for weeks 1 and 2, then increase to 50 mg/day for weeks 3 and 4. Maintenance: Titrate dose to effect; after week 4 increase daily dose every 1-2 weeks by 50 mg/day; usual maintenance: 225-375 mg/day in 2 divided doses

Adjustment for AED regimens **containing** valproic acid (see "Note"): Initial: 25 mg every other day for weeks 1 and 2, then increase to 25 mg every day for weeks 3 and 4. Maintenance: Titrate dose to effect; after week 4 increase daily dose every 1-2 weeks by 25-50 mg/day; usual maintenance: 100-400 mg/day in 1 or 2 divided doses

Note: For patients taking lamotrigine with valproic acid alone, the usual maintenance dose is 100-200 mg/day

Adjustment for **enzyme-inducing** AED regimens **without** valproic acid: Initial: 50 mg/day for weeks 1 and 2, then increase to 100 mg/day in 2 divided doses for weeks 3 and 4. Maintenance: titrate dose to effect; after week 4 increase daily dose every 1-2 weeks by 100 mg/day; usual maintenance: 300-500 mg/day in 2 divided doses. Doses as high as 700 mg/day have been used, though additional benefit has not been established.

Conversion to monotherapy with lamotrigine:

Conversion from adjunctive therapy with valproic acid: Initiate and titrate as per recommendations to a lamotrigine dose of 200 mg/day. Then taper valproic acid dose in decrements of not >500 mg/day at intervals of 1 week (or longer) to a valproic acid dosage of 500 mg/day; this dosage should be maintained for 1 week. The lamotrigine dosage should then be increased to 300 mg/day while valproic acid is decreased to 250 mg/day; this dosage should be maintained for 1 week. Valproic acid may then be discontinued, while the lamotrigine dose is increased by 100 mg/day at weekly intervals to achieve a lamotrigine maintenance dose of 500 mg/day.

Conversion from adjunctive therapy with carbamazepine, phenytoin, phenobarbital, or primidone: Initiate and titrate as per recommendations to a lamotrigine dose of 500 mg/day. Concomitant enzyme-inducing AED should then be withdrawn by 20% decrements each week over a 4-week period. Patients should be monitored for rash.

Conversion from adjunctive therapy with AED other than carbamazepine, phenytoin, phenobarbital, primidone or valproic acid: No specific guidelines available

Bipolar disorder:

Initial: 25 mg/day for weeks 1 and 2, then increase to 50 mg/day for weeks 3 and 4, then increase to 100 mg/day for week 5; maintenance: increase dose to 200 mg/day beginning week 6

Adjustment for regimens **containing** valproic acid: Initial: 25 mg every other day for weeks 1 and 2, then increase to 25 mg every day for weeks 3 and 4, then increase to 50 mg/day for week 5; maintenance: 100 mg/day beginning week 6

Adjustment for **enzyme-inducing** regimens **without** valproic acid: Initial: 50 mg/day for weeks 1 and 2, then increase to 100 mg/day in divided doses for weeks 3 and 4, then increase to 200 mg/day in divided doses for week 5, then increase to 300 mg/day in divided dose for week 6; maintenance: 400 mg/day in divided doses beginning week 7

Adjustment following discontinuation of psychotropic medication:

Discontinuing valproic acid with current dose of lamotrigine 100 mg/day: 150 mg/day for week 1, then increase to 200 mg/day beginning week 2

Discontinuing carbamazepine, phenytoin, phenobarbital, primidone, or rifampin with current dose of lamotrigine 400 mg/day: 400 mg/day for week 1, then decrease to 300 mg/day for week 2, then decrease to 200 mg/day beginning week 3

Discontinuing therapy: Children and Adults: Decrease dose by ~50% per week, over at least 2 weeks unless safety concerns require a more rapid withdrawal. Discontinuing carbamazepine, phenytoin, phenobarbital, or primidone should prolong the half-life of lamotrigine; discontinuing valproic acid should shorten the half-life of lamotrigine

Restarting therapy after discontinuation: If lamotrigine has been withheld for >5 half-lives, consider restarting according to initial dosing recommendations.

Dosage adjustment with combination hormonal contraceptives: Follow initial dosing guidelines, maintenance dose should be adjusted as follows:Patients taking carbamazepine, phenytoin, phenobarbital, primidone or rifampin: No dosing adjustment required

Patients **not** taking carbamazepine, phenytoin, phenobarbital, primidone or rifampin: Maintenance dose may need increased by twofold over target dose. If already taking a stable dose of lamotrigine and starting contraceptive, maintenance dose may need increased by twofold. Dose increases should start when contraceptive is started and titrated to clinical response increasing no more rapidly than 50-100 mg/day every week. Gradual increases of lamotrigine plasma levels may occur during the inactive "pill-free" week and will be greater when dose increases are made the week before. If increased adverse events consistently occur during "pill-free" week, overall dose adjustments may be required. When discontinuing combination hormonal contraceptive, dose of lamotrigine may need decreased by as much as 50%; do not decrease by more than 25% of total daily dose over a 2-week period unless clinical response or plasma levels indicate otherwise. Dose adjustments during "pill-free" week are not recommended.

Dosage adjustment in renal impairment: Decreased dosage may be effective in patients with significant renal impairment; use with caution

Dosage adjustment in hepatic impairment:

Moderate-to-severe impairment without ascites: Decrease initial, escalation, and maintenance doses by ~25%

Moderate-to-severe impairment with ascites: Decrease initial, escalation, and maintenance doses by ~50%

Dietary Considerations Take without regard to meals; drug may cause GI upset.

Administration Doses should be rounded down to the nearest whole tablet. Dispersible tablets may be chewed, dispersed in water or diluted fruit juice, or swallowed whole. To disperse tablets, add to a small amount of liquid (just enough to cover tablet); let sit ~1 minute until dispersed; swirl solution and consume immediately. Do not administer partial amounts of liquid. If tablets are chewed, a small amount of water or diluted fruit juice should be used to aid in swallowing.

Monitoring Parameters Seizure, frequency and duration, serum levels of concurrent anticonvulsants, hypersensitivity reactions, especially rash

Reference Range A therapeutic serum concentration range has not been established for lamotrigine. Dosing should be based on therapeutic response. Lamotrigine plasma concentrations of 0.25-29.1 mcg/mL have been reported in the literature.

Dosage Forms
Tablet:
Lamictal®: 25 mg, 100 mg, 150 mg, 200 mg
Tablet, combination package [each unit-dose starter kit contains]:
Lamictal® (blue kit; for patients taking valproic acid):
Tablet: Lamotrigine 25 mg (35s)
Lamictal® (green kit; for patients taking carbamazepine, phenytoin, phenobarbital, primidone, or rifampin and **not** taking valproic acid):
Tablet: Lamotrigine 25 mg (84s)
Tablet: Lamotrigine 100 mg (14s)
Lamictal® (orange kit; for patients **not** taking carbamazepine, phenytoin, phenobarbital, primidone, rifampin, or valproic acid):
Tablet: Lamotrigine 25 mg (42s)
Tablet: Lamotrigine 100 mg (7s)
Tablet, dispersible/chewable: 5 mg, 25 mg
Lamictal®: 2 mg, 5 mg, 25 mg [black currant flavor]

Extemporaneous Preparations A 1 mg/mL oral suspension may be compounded as follows: Crush one 100 mg tablet and reduce to a fine powder. Add small amount of Ora-Sweet® or Ora-Plus® and mix to uniform paste. Transfer to graduate and qs to 100 mL. Shake well before using and refrigerate. Suspension is stable for 91 days.

Nahata M, Morosco R, Hipple T. "Stability of Lamotrigine in Two Extemporaneously Prepared Oral Suspensions at 4 and 25°C," *Am J Health Syst Pharm*, 1999, 56:240-2.

♦ **Lanacane® [OTC]** *see* Benzocaine *on page 204*
♦ **Lanacane® Maximum Strength [OTC]** *see* Benzocaine *on page 204*
♦ **Lanaphilic® [OTC]** *see* Urea *on page 1758*
♦ **Lanoxicaps®** *see* Digoxin *on page 501*
♦ **Lanoxin®** *see* Digoxin *on page 501*

Lansoprazole (lan SOE pra zole)

U.S. Brand Names Prevacid®; Prevacid® SoluTab™
Canadian Brand Names Prevacid®
Pharmacologic Category Proton Pump Inhibitor; Substituted Benzimidazole
Additional Appendix Information
Helicobacter pylori Treatment *on page 2056*
Use
Oral: Short-term treatment of active duodenal ulcers; maintenance treatment of healed duodenal ulcers; as part of a multidrug regimen for *H. pylori* eradication to reduce the risk of duodenal ulcer recurrence; short-term treatment of active benign gastric ulcer; treatment of NSAID-associated gastric ulcer; to reduce the risk of NSAID-associated gastric ulcer in patients with a history of gastric ulcer who require an NSAID; short-term treatment of symptomatic GERD; short-term treatment for all grades of erosive esophagitis; to maintain healing of erosive esophagitis; long-term treatment of pathological hypersecretory conditions, including Zollinger-Ellison syndrome
I.V.: Short-term treatment (≤7 days) of erosive esophagitis in adults unable to take oral medications
Unlabeled/Investigational Use Active ulcer bleeding (parenteral formulation)
Pregnancy Risk Factor B
Pregnancy Implications Animal studies have not shown teratogenic effects to the fetus. However, there are no adequate and well-controlled studies in pregnant women; use during pregnancy only if clearly needed.
Lactation Excretion in breast milk unknown/not recommended
Medication Safety Issues
Sound-alike/look-alike issues:
Prevacid® may be confused with Pravachol®, Prevpac®, Prilosec®, Prinivil®
Contraindications Hypersensitivity to lansoprazole, substituted benzimidazoles (ie, esomeprazole, omeprazole, pantoprazole, rabeprazole), or any component of the formulation
Warnings/Precautions Relief of symptoms does not preclude the presence of a gastric malignancy. Atrophic gastritis (by biopsy) has been noted with long-term omeprazole therapy; this may also occur with lansoprazole. No reports of enterochromaffin-like (ECL) cell carcinoids, dysplasia, or neoplasia have occurred. Severe liver dysfunction may require dosage reductions. Safety and efficacy have not been established in children <1 year of age.
Adverse Reactions
1% to 10%:
Central nervous system: Headache (children 1-11 years 3%, 12-17 years 7%)
Gastrointestinal: Abdominal pain (children 12-17 years 5%; adults 2%), constipation (children 1-11 years 5%; adults 1%), diarrhea (4%; 4% to 7% at doses of 30-60 mg/day), nausea (children 12-17 years 3%; adults 1%)
<1% (Limited to important or life-threatening): Abnormal vision, agitation, allergic reaction, ALT increased, anaphylactoid reaction, anemia, angina, anxiety, aplastic anemia, (Continued)

Lansoprazole *(Continued)*

arrhythmia, AST increased, chest pain, convulsion, depression, dizziness, dry eyes, dry mouth, erythema multiforme, esophagitis, gastrin levels increased, gastrointestinal disorder, glucocorticoids increased, globulins increased, hemolysis, hemolytic anemia, hepatotoxicity, hyperglycemia, LDH increased, maculopapular rash, pancreatitis, photophobia, rash, RBC abnormal, taste perversion, Stevens-Johnson syndrome, thrombocytopenia, tinnitus, toxic epidermal necrolysis (some fatal), tremor, vertigo, visual field defect, vomiting, WBC abnormal

Overdosage/Toxicology No toxicity has been observed in animal studies. There is limited human overdose experience. Treatment is symptomatic and supportive. Lansoprazole is not removed by hemodialysis.

Drug Interactions

Cytochrome P450 Effect: Substrate of CYP2C9 (minor), 2C19 (major), 3A4 (major); **Inhibits** CYP2C9 (weak), 2C19 (moderate), 2D6 (weak), 3A4 (weak); **Induces** CYP1A2 (weak)

Increased Effect/Toxicity: Lansoprazole may increase the levels/effects of citalopram, diazepam, methsuximide, phenytoin, propranolol, sertraline, and other CYP2C19 substrates.

Decreased Effect: Proton pump inhibitors may decrease the absorption of atazanavir, indinavir, oral iron salts, itraconazole, and ketoconazole. The levels/effects of lansoprazole may be decreased by aminoglutethimide, carbamazepine, nafcillin, nevirapine, phenobarbital, phenytoin, rifamycins, and other CYP2C19 or 3A4 inducers.

Ethanol/Nutrition/Herb Interactions

Ethanol: Avoid ethanol (may cause gastric mucosal irritation).

Food: Lansoprazole serum concentrations may be decreased if taken with food.

Stability Store at 15°C to 30°C (59°F to 86°F). Protect from light and moisture.

Oral suspension: Empty packet into container with 2 tablespoons of water. Do **not** mix with other liquids or food. Stir well and drink immediately.

Powder for injection: Reconstitute with sterile water 5 mL; mix gently until dissolved. Prior to administration, further dilute with 50 mL of NS, LR, or D_5W. After reconstitution, the solution may be stored for up to 1 hour at room temperature prior to final dilution. Following final dilution, solutions mixed with NS or LR are stable at room temperature for 24 hours; solutions mixed with D_5W are stable for 12 hours.

Mechanism of Action A proton pump inhibitor which decreases acid secretion in gastric parietal cells

Pharmacodynamics/Kinetics

Duration: >1 day

Absorption: Rapid

Protein binding: 97%

Metabolism: Hepatic via CYP2C19 and 3A4, and in parietal cells to two inactive metabolites

Bioavailability: 80%; decreased 50% to 70% if given 30 minutes after food

Half-life elimination: 2 hours; Elderly: 2-3 hours; Hepatic impairment: ≤7 hours

Time to peak, plasma: 1.7 hours

Excretion: Feces (67%); urine (33%)

Dosage

Children 1-11 years: GERD, erosive esophagitis: Oral:

≤30 kg: 15 mg once daily

>30 kg: 30 mg once daily

Note: Doses were increased in some pediatric patients if still symptomatic after 2 or more weeks of treatment (maximum dose: 30 mg twice daily)

Children 12-17 years: Oral:

Nonerosive GERD: 15 mg once daily for up to 8 weeks

Erosive esophagitis: 30 mg once daily for up to 8 weeks

Adults:

Duodenal ulcer: Oral: Short-term treatment: 15 mg once daily for 4 weeks; maintenance therapy: 15 mg once daily

Gastric ulcer: Oral: Short-term treatment: 30 mg once daily for up to 8 weeks

NSAID-associated gastric ulcer (healing): Oral: 30 mg once daily for 8 weeks; controlled studies did not extend past 8 weeks of therapy

NSAID-associated gastric ulcer (to reduce risk): Oral: 15 mg once daily for up to 12 weeks; controlled studies did not extend past 12 weeks of therapy

Symptomatic GERD: Oral: Short-term treatment: 15 mg once daily for up to 8 weeks

Erosive esophagitis:

Oral: Short-term treatment: 30 mg once daily for up to 8 weeks; continued treatment for an additional 8 weeks may be considered for recurrence or for patients that do not heal after the first 8 weeks of therapy; maintenance therapy: 15 mg once daily

I.V.: 30 mg once daily for up to 7 days; patients should be switched to an oral formulation as soon as they can take oral medications

Hypersecretory conditions: Oral: Initial: 60 mg once daily; adjust dose based upon patient response and to reduce acid secretion to <10 mEq/hour (5 mEq/hour in patients with prior gastric surgery); doses of 90 mg twice daily have been used; administer doses >120 mg/day in divided doses

Helicobacter pylori eradication: Oral: Currently accepted recommendations (may differ from product labeling): Dose varies with regimen: 30 mg once daily or 60 mg/day in 2 divided doses; requires combination therapy with antibiotics

Prevention of rebleeding in peptic ulcer bleed (unlabeled use): I.V.: 60 mg, followed by 6 mg/hour infusion for 72 hours

Elderly: No dosage adjustment is needed in elderly patients with normal hepatic function

Dosage adjustment in renal impairment: No dosage adjustment is needed

Dosing adjustment in hepatic impairment: Dose reduction is necessary for severe hepatic impairment

Dietary Considerations Should be taken before eating; best if taken before breakfast. Prevacid® SoluTab™ contains phenylalanine 2.5 mg per 15 mg tablet; phenylalanine 5.1 mg per 30 mg tablet.

Administration

Oral: Administer before food; best if taken before breakfast. The intact granules should not be chewed or crushed; however, in addition to oral suspension, several options are available for those patients unable to swallow capsules:

Capsules may be opened and the intact granules sprinkled on 1 tablespoon of applesauce, Ensure® pudding, cottage cheese, yogurt, or strained pears. The granules should then be swallowed immediately.

Capsules may be opened and emptied into ~60 mL orange juice, apple juice, or tomato juice; mix and swallow immediately. Rinse the glass with additional juice and swallow to assure complete delivery of the dose.

Capsule granules may be mixed with apple, cranberry, grape, orange, pineapple, prune, tomato and V-8® juice and stored for up to 30 minutes.

Delayed release oral suspension granules should be mixed with 2 tablespoonfuls (30 mL) of water; no other liquid should be used. Stir well and drink immediately. Should not be administered through enteral administration tubes.

Orally-disintegrating tablets: Should not be swallowed whole or chewed. Place tablet on tongue; allow to dissolve (with or without water) until particles can be swallowed. Orally-disintegrating tablets may also be administered via an oral syringe: Place the 15 mg tablet in an oral syringe and draw up ~4 mL water, or place the 30 mg tablet in an oral syringe and draw up ~10 mL water. After tablet has dispersed, administer within 15 minutes. Refill the syringe with water (2 mL for the 15 mg tablet; 4 mL for the 30 mg tablet), shake gently, then administer any remaining contents.

I.V.: Administer over 30 minutes. Use of an in-line filter is required. Before and after administration, flush I.V. line with NS, LR, or D_5W. Do not administer with other medications.

Nasogastric tube administration:

Capsule: Capsule can be opened, the granules mixed (not crushed) with 40 mL of apple juice and then injected through the NG tube into the stomach, then flush tube with additional apple juice.

Orally-disintegrating tablet: Nasogastric tube ≥8 French: Place a 15 mg tablet in a syringe and draw up ~4 mL water, or place the 30 mg tablet in a syringe and draw up ~10 mL water. After tablet has dispersed, administer within 15 minutes. Refill the syringe with ~5 mL water, shake gently, and then flush the nasogastric tube.

Monitoring Parameters Patients with Zollinger-Ellison syndrome should be monitored for gastric acid output, which should be maintained at ≤10 mEq/hour during the last hour before the next lansoprazole dose; lab monitoring should include CBC, liver function, renal function, and serum gastrin levels

Dosage Forms

Capsule, delayed release (Prevacid®): 15 mg, 30 mg

Granules, for oral suspension, delayed release (Prevacid®): 15 mg/packet (30s), 30 mg/packet (30s) [strawberry flavor]

Injection, powder for reconstitution (Prevacid®): 30 mg

Tablet, orally disintegrating (Prevacid® SoluTab™): 15 mg [contains phenylalanine 2.5 mg; strawberry flavor]; 30 mg [contains phenylalanine 5.1 mg; strawberry flavor]

Extemporaneous Preparations A 3 mg/mL lansoprazole oral solution (Simplified Lansoprazole Solution) can be prepared with ten lansoprazole 30 mg capsules and 100 mL 8.4% sodium bicarbonate. Empty capsules into beaker. Add sodium bicarbonate solution. Gently stir (about 15 minutes) until dissolved. Transfer to amber-colored syringe or bottle. Stable for 8 hours at room temperature or for 14 days under refrigeration.

DiGiancinto JL, Olsen KM, Bergman KL, et al, "Stability of Suspension Formulations of Lansoprazole and Omeprazole Stored in Amber-Colored Plastic Oral Syringes," *Ann Pharmacother*, 2000, 34:600-5

Sharma V, "Comparison of 24-hour Intragastric pH Using Four Liquid Formulations of Lansoprazole and Omeprazole," *Am J Health Syst Pharm*, 1999, 56(Suppl 4):S18-21.

Sharma VK, Vasudeva R, and Howden CW, "Simplified Lansoprazole Suspension - Liquid Formulations of Lansoprazole - Effectively Suppresses Intragastric Acidity When Administered Through a Gastrostomy," *Am J Gastroenterol*, 1999, 94(7):1813-7.

Lansoprazole, Amoxicillin, and Clarithromycin
(lan SOE pra zole, a moks i SIL in, & kla RITH roe mye sin)

U.S. Brand Names Prevpac®

Canadian Brand Names Hp-PAC®; Prevpac®

Index Terms Amoxicillin, Lansoprazole, and Clarithromycin; Clarithromycin, Lansoprazole, and Amoxicillin

Pharmacologic Category Antibiotic, Macrolide Combination; Antibiotic, Penicillin; Gastrointestinal Agent, Miscellaneous

Use Eradication of *H. pylori* to reduce the risk of recurrent duodenal ulcer

Pregnancy Risk Factor C (clarithromycin)

Medication Safety Issues

Sound-alike/look-alike issues:

Prevpac® may be confused with Prevacid®

Dosage Oral: Adults: Lansoprazole 30 mg, amoxicillin 1 g, and clarithromycin 500 mg taken together twice daily for 10 or 14 days

Dosage adjustment in renal impairment: Cl_{cr} <30 mL/minute: Use is not recommended

Additional Information Complete prescribing information for this medication should be consulted for additional detail.

Dosage Forms

Combination package [each administration card contains]:

Prevpac®:

Capsule: Amoxicillin 500 mg (4 capsules/day)

Capsule, delayed release (Prevacid®): Lansoprazole 30 mg (2 capsules/day)

Tablet (Biaxin®): Clarithromycin 500 mg (2 tablets/day)

Lansoprazole and Naproxen (lan SOE pra zole & na PROKS en)

U.S. Brand Names Prevacid® NapraPAC™
Index Terms NapraPAC™; Naproxen and Lansoprazole
Pharmacologic Category Nonsteroidal Anti-inflammatory Drug (NSAID), Oral; Proton Pump Inhibitor
Use Reduction of the risk of NSAID-associated gastric ulcers in patients with history of gastric ulcer who require an NSAID for the treatment of rheumatoid arthritis, osteoarthritis, and ankylosing spondylitis
Pregnancy Risk Factor B (naproxen: D/third trimester)
Medication Safety Issues
Sound-alike/look-alike issues:
Prevacid® may be confused with Pravachol®, Prevpac®, Prilosec®, Prinivil®
Dosage Oral: Adults: Reduce NSAID-associated gastric ulcers during treatment for arthritis: Lansoprazole 15 mg once daily in the morning; naproxen 375 mg or 500 mg twice daily
Elderly: Naproxen: Dosing adjustment should be considered
Dosage adjustment in renal/hepatic impairment: Naproxen: Dosing adjustment should be considered
Additional Information Complete prescribing information for this medication should be consulted for additional detail.
Dosage Forms [DSC] = Discontinued product
Combination package:
Prevacid® NapraPAC™ 375 [each administration card contains] [DSC]:
Capsule, delayed release (Prevacid®): Lansoprazole 15 mg (7 capsules per card)
Tablet (Naprosyn®): Naproxen 375 mg (14 tablets per card)
Prevacid® NapraPAC™ 500 [each administration card contains]:
Capsule, delayed release (Prevacid®): Lansoprazole 15 mg (7 capsules per card)
Tablet (Naprosyn®): Naproxen 500 mg (14 tablets per card)

♦ **Lantus®** see Insulin Glargine on page 911

♦ **Lantus® OptiSet® (Can)** see Insulin Glargine on page 911

♦ **Lanvis® (Can)** see Thioguanine on page 1669

♦ **Largactil® (Can)** see ChlorproMAZINE on page 356

♦ **Lariam®** see Mefloquine on page 1069

Laronidase (lair OH ni days)

U.S. Brand Names Aldurazyme®
Canadian Brand Names Aldurazyme®
Index Terms Recombinant α-L-Iduronidase (Glycosaminoglycan α-L-Iduronohydrolase)
Pharmacologic Category Enzyme
Use Treatment of Hurler and Hurler-Scheie forms of mucopolysaccharidosis I (MPS I); treatment of Scheie form of MPS I in patients with moderate to severe symptoms
Pregnancy Risk Factor B
Pregnancy Implications Teratogenic effects were not observed in animal studies; however, there are no adequate and well-controlled studies in pregnant women. Use during pregnancy only if clearly needed. Patients are encouraged to enroll in the MPS I registry.
Lactation Excretion in breast milk unknown/use caution
Contraindications No known contraindications
Warnings/Precautions Infusion-related hypersensitivity reactions have been reported, may be severe; use caution with pre-existing airway obstruction. Reactions tend to occur within 3 hours of the drug administration. Antipyretics and or antihistamines should be administered prior to infusion to reduce the incidence/severity of headache, fever, and/or flushing. In case of reaction, decrease the rate of infusion, temporarily discontinue the infusion, and/or administer additional antipyretics/antihistamines. Risks and benefits should be carefully considered prior to readministering following a severe hypersensitivity reaction. In the case of anaphylaxis, caution should be used if epinephrine is being considered; many patients with MPS I have pre-existing heart disease. Prepared infusions contain human albumin. Laronidase has not been studied in patients with mild symptoms of the Scheie form of MPS I. Not indicated for the CNS manifestations of the disorder. Safety and efficacy in patients <5 years were not established in clinical trials. A patient registry has been established and all patients are encouraged to participate. Registry information may be obtained at www.MPSIregistry.com or by calling 800-745-4447.
Adverse Reactions
>10%:
Cardiovascular: Vein disorder (14%)
Dermatologic: Rash (36%)
Local: Infusion reactions [31%; may be severe; includes flushing (23%), fever, and headache; frequency decreased over time during open-label extension period], injection site reaction (18%)
Neuromuscular & skeletal: Hyper-reflexia (14%), paresthesia (14%)
Respiratory: Upper respiratory tract infection (32%)
Miscellaneous: Antibody development to laronidase (91%; significance unknown)
1% to 10%:
Cardiovascular: Chest pain (9%), edema (9%), facial edema (9%), hypotension (9%)
Hematologic: Thrombocytopenia (9%)
Hepatic: Bilirubinemia
Local: Abscess (9%), injection site pain (9%)
Ocular: Corneal opacity (9%)

<1% (Limited to important or life-threatening): Airway obstruction, anaphylaxis, angioedema, bronchospasm, cough, dyspnea, pruritus, urticaria

Stability Store vials under refrigeration at 2°C to 8°C (36°F to 46°F). Solution should be prepared based on body weight and should begin by making a solution of NS and albumin 0.1%.

≤20 kg: Using NS 100 mL PVC bag and albumin (human) [2 mL of albumin 5% or 0.4 mL of albumin 25%]:

Remove and discard a volume of NS equal to the amount of albumin to be added to the infusion bag. Add albumin; the total volume of this solution should equal 100 mL. From this bag, remove and discard an equal volume of the laronidase to be added (based on calculated dose). Slowly withdraw and add laronidase to the NS/albumin 0.1% solution; avoid excessive agitation, do not use filtered syringe. Gently rotate infusion bag to mix.

>20 kg: Using NS 250 mL PVC bag and albumin (human) [5 mL of albumin 5% or 1 mL of albumin 25%]:

Remove and discard a volume of NS equal to the amount of albumin to be added to the infusion bag. Add albumin; the total volume of this solution should equal 250 mL. From this bag, remove and discard an equal volume of the laronidase to be added (based on calculated dose). Slowly withdraw and add laronidase to the NS/albumin 0.1% solution; avoid excessive agitation, do not use filtered syringe. Gently rotate infusion bag to mix.

Following dilution, solution for infusion should be used immediately, but may be refrigerated. Infusion of solution should be completed within 36 hours of preparation.

Mechanism of Action Laronidase is a recombinant (replacement) form of α-L-iduronidase derived from Chinese hamster cells. α-L-iduronidase is an enzyme needed to break down endogenous glycosaminoglycans (GAGs) within lysosomes. A deficiency of α-L-iduronidase leads to an accumulation of GAGs, causing cellular, tissue, and organ dysfunction as seen in MPS I. Improved pulmonary function and walking capacity have been demonstrated with the administration of laronidase to patients with Hurler, Hurler-Scheie, or Scheie (with moderate to severe symptoms) forms of MPS.

Pharmacodynamics/Kinetics

Distribution: V_d: 0.24-0.6 L/kg

Half-life elimination: 1.5-3.6 hours

Excretion: Clearance: 1.7 to 2.7 mL/minute/kg; during the first 12 weeks of therapy the clearance of laronidase increases proportionally to the amount of antibodies a given patient develops against the enzyme. However, with long-term use (≥26 weeks) antibody titers have no effect on laronidase clearance.

Dosage I.V.: Children ≥5 years and Adults: 0.58 mg/kg once weekly; dose should be rounded up to the nearest whole vial

Administration Administer using PVC container and PVC infusion set with in-line, low protein-binding 0.2 micrometer filter. Antipyretics and or antihistamines should be administered prior to infusion. Administration schedule is based on body weight. Vital signs should be monitored every 15 minutes, if stable; rate may be increased as follows:

≤20 kg: Total infusion volume: 100 mL

2 mL/hour for 15 minutes

4 mL/hour for 15 minutes

8 mL/hour for 15 minutes

16 mL/hour for 15 minutes

32 mL/hour for remainder of infusion

>20 kg: Total infusion volume: 250 mL

5 mL/hour for 15 minutes

10 mL/hour for 15 minutes

20 mL/hour for 15 minutes

40 mL/hour for 15 minutes

80 mL/hour for remainder of infusion

Note: In case of infusion-related reaction, decrease the rate of infusion, temporarily discontinue the infusion, and/or administer additional antipyretics/antihistamines.

Monitoring Parameters Vital signs; injection site reactions

Dosage Forms Injection, solution [preservative free]: 2.9 mg/5 mL (5 mL)

♦ **Lasix®** see Furosemide on page 773

♦ **Lasix® Special (Can)** see Furosemide on page 773

♦ **L-asparaginase** see Asparaginase on page 157

♦ **Lassar's Zinc Paste** see Zinc Oxide on page 1817

Latanoprost (la TA noe prost)

U.S. Brand Names Xalatan®

Canadian Brand Names Xalatan®

Pharmacologic Category Ophthalmic Agent, Antiglaucoma; Prostaglandin, Ophthalmic

Additional Appendix Information

Glaucoma Drug Therapy on page 2050

Use Reduction of elevated intraocular pressure in patients with open-angle glaucoma or ocular hypertension

Pregnancy Risk Factor C

Medication Safety Issues

Sound-alike/look-alike issues:

Xalatan® may be confused with Travatan®, Zarontin®

Dosage Adults: Ophthalmic: 1 drop (1.5 mcg) in the affected eye(s) once daily in the evening; do not exceed the once daily dosage because it has been shown that more frequent administration may decrease the IOP lowering effect

Note: A medication delivery device (Xal-Ease™) is available for use with Xalatan®.

Additional Information Complete prescribing information for this medication should be consulted for additional detail.

Dosage Forms Solution, ophthalmic: 0.005% (2.5 mL) [contains benzalkonium chloride]

♦ **Laxilose (Can)** *see* Lactulose *on page 971*

♦ **/-Bunolol Hydrochloride** *see* Levobunolol *on page 996*

♦ **L-Carnitine** *see* Levocarnitine *on page 997*

♦ **LCR** *see* VinCRIStine *on page 1789*

♦ **L-Deprenyl** *see* Selegiline *on page 1552*

♦ **LDP-341** *see* Bortezomib *on page 230*

♦ **Leena™** *see* Ethinyl Estradiol and Norethindrone *on page 655*

Leflunomide (le FLOO noh mide)

U.S. Brand Names Arava®
Canadian Brand Names Apo-Leflunomide®; Arava®; Novo-Leflunomide
Pharmacologic Category Antirheumatic, Disease Modifying
Use Treatment of active rheumatoid arthritis; indicated to reduce signs and symptoms, and to retard structural damage and improve physical function
  Orphan drug: Prevention of acute and chronic rejection in recipients of solid organ transplants
Unlabeled/Investigational Use Treatment of cytomegalovirus (CMV) disease
Pregnancy Risk Factor X
Pregnancy Implications Has been associated with teratogenic and embryolethal effects in animal models at low doses. Leflunomide is contraindicated in pregnant women or women of childbearing potential who are not using reliable contraception. Pregnancy must be excluded prior to initiating treatment. Following treatment, pregnancy should be avoided until undetectable plasma levels (< 0.02 mcg/mL) are verified. This may be accomplished by an extended drug elimination procedure: Administer cholestyramine 8 g 3 times/day for 11 days (the 11 days do not need to be consecutive). Plasma levels <0.02 mg/L should be verified by two separate tests performed at least 14 days apart. If plasma levels are >0.02 mg/L, additional cholestyramine treatment should be considered.
Lactation Excretion in breast milk unknown/contraindicated
Contraindications Hypersensitivity to leflunomide or any component of the formulation; pregnancy
Warnings/Precautions Leflunomide has been associated with rare reports of hepatotoxicity, hepatic failure, and death. Multiple risk factors for hepatotoxicity including hepatic disease (including seropositive hepatitis B or C patients) and/or concurrent exposure to other hepatotoxins may increase the risk of hepatotoxicity. Most severe cases occur within 6 months of initiation. Monitoring of hepatic function is required.

Not recommended for patients with severe immune deficiency, bone marrow dysplasia, or uncontrolled infection. Has been associated with rare pancytopenia, agranulocytosis, and thrombocytopenia, particularly when given in combination with methotrexate or other immunosuppressive agents. Monitoring of hematologic function is required. Use with caution in patients with a prior history of significant hematologic abnormalities. Discontinue if evidence of bone marrow suppression or severe dermatologic reaction occurs, and begin procedure to accelerate elimination (cholestyramine or activated charcoal, see Overdosage/Toxicology). Interstitial lung disease has been associated (rarely) with leflunomide use. Discontinue in patients who develop new onset or worsening of pulmonary symptoms; accelerated elimination procedures should be considered if interstitial lung disease occurs; fatal outcomes have been reported. Consider interruption of therapy and accelerated elimination in patients who develop serious infections while receiving leflunomide. The use of live vaccines is not recommended.

[U.S. Boxed Warning]: Women of childbearing potential should not receive leflunomide until pregnancy has been excluded. Patients have been counseled concerning fetal risk and reliable contraceptive measures have been confirmed. Caution in renal impairment. Leflunomide will increase uric acid excretion. Immunosuppression may increase the risk of lymphoproliferative disorders or other malignancies. Safety and efficacy have not been established in children.
Adverse Reactions
>10%:
  Gastrointestinal: Diarrhea (17%)
  Respiratory: Respiratory tract infection (15%)
1% to 10%:
  Cardiovascular: Hypertension (10%), chest pain (2%), vasculitis, edema (peripheral)
  Central nervous system: Headache (7%), dizziness (4%) paresthesia (2%), fever, neuralgia, neuritis, sleep disorder
  Dermatologic: Alopecia (10%), rash (10%), pruritus (4%), dry skin (2%), eczema (2%), dermatitis, hair discoloration, subcutaneous nodule, skin disorder/discoloration
  Endocrine & metabolic: Hypokalemia (1%), diabetes mellitus, hyperlipidemia, hyperthyroidism
  Gastrointestinal: Nausea (9%), weight loss (4%), anorexia (3%), gastroenteritis (3%), stomatitis (3%), vomiting (3%), cholelithiasis, colitis, esophagitis, gingivitis, melena, candidiasis (oral)
  Genitourinary: Urinary tract infection (5%), albuminuria, cystitis, dysuria, hematuria
  Hematologic: Anemia
  Neuromuscular & skeletal: Tenosynovitis (3%), arthralgia (1%), muscle cramps (1%), neck pain, pelvic pain, arthrosis, bursitis, myalgia, bone necrosis, bone pain, tendon rupture
  Ocular: Cataract, conjunctivitis
  Respiratory: Bronchitis (7%), cough (3%), pharyngitis (3%), pneumonia (2%), rhinitis (2%), sinusitis (2%), asthma, dyspnea
  Miscellaneous: Infection (4%), allergic reactions (2%), herpes infection
<1% (Limited to important or life-threatening): Agranulocytosis, anaphylaxis, angioedema, cholestasis, cutaneous necrotizing vasculitis, eosinophilia, erythema multiforme; hepatotoxicity (rare, including hepatic necrosis and hepatic failure, some fatalities reported);

interstitial lung disease, leukopenia, opportunistic infection, pancreatitis, pancytopenia, peripheral neuropathy, pneumonitis (interstitial), pulmonary fibrosis, sepsis, Stevens-Johnson syndrome, thrombocytopenia, toxic epidermal necrolysis, urticaria, vasculitis

Overdosage/Toxicology There is no human experience with overdose. Leflunomide is not dialyzable. Cholestyramine and/or activated charcoal enhance elimination of leflunomide's active metabolite (M1). In cases of significant overdose or toxicity, cholestyramine 8 g every 8 hours for 1-3 days or activated charcoal 50 g every 6 hours for 24 hours may be administered to enhance elimination. Plasma levels are reduced by ~40% in 24 hours and 49% to 65% after 48 hours of cholestyramine dosing. Activated charcoal reduces plasma levels by 37% after 24 hours and 48% after 48 hours of continuous dosing. Activated charcoal without sorbitol should be used.

To reach undetectable levels (recommended in women of childbearing potential who wish to become pregnant), an extended protocol is necessary. Without this procedure, it may take up to 2 years to reach plasma concentrations <0.02 mg/L (a concentration expected to have minimal risk of teratogenicity based on animal models). The procedure consists of the following steps: Administer cholestyramine 8 g 3 times/day for 11 days (the 11 days do not need to be consecutive). Plasma levels <0.02 mg/L should be verified by two separate tests performed at least 14 days apart. If plasma levels are >0.02 mg/L, additional cholestyramine treatment should be considered.

Drug Interactions

Cytochrome P450 Effect: Inhibits CYP2C9 (weak)

Increased Effect/Toxicity: Leflunomide may increase the risk of hepatotoxicity when combined with drugs which may cause hepatic injury. Concomitant treatment of methotrexate with leflunomide may increase the risk of hepatotoxicity or hematologic toxicity. Rifampin may increase the serum concentration of leflunomide's active metabolite. Leflunomide may increase the effects of warfarin.

Decreased Effect: Bile acid sequestrants (cholestyramine) may interfere with enterohepatic recycling of leflunomide; this is used emergently to remove drug from the circulation, but may decrease levels inadvertently if used concomitantly.

Ethanol/Nutrition/Herb Interactions Food: No interactions with food have been noted.

Stability Store at 25°C (77°F). Protect from light.

Mechanism of Action Inhibits pyrimidine synthesis, resulting in antiproliferative and anti-inflammatory effects. For CMV, may interfere with virion assembly.

Pharmacodynamics/Kinetics

Distribution: V_d: 0.13 L/kg

Metabolism: Hepatic to A77 1726 (M1) which accounts for nearly all pharmacologic activity; further metabolism to multiple inactive metabolites; undergoes enterohepatic recirculation

Bioavailability: 80%

Half-life elimination: Mean: 14-15 days; enterohepatic recycling appears to contribute to the long half-life of this agent, since activated charcoal and cholestyramine substantially reduce plasma half-life

Time to peak: 6-12 hours

Excretion: Feces (48%); urine (43%)

Dosage Oral:

Adults:

Rheumatoid arthritis: Initial: 100 mg/day for 3 days, followed by 20 mg/day; dosage may be decreased to 10 mg/day in patients who have difficulty tolerating the 20 mg dose. Due to the long half-life of the active metabolite, plasma levels may require a prolonged period to decline after dosage reduction.

CMV (unlabeled use): Some authors recommend 200 mg/day for 7 days, followed by 40-60 mg/day, targeting blood levels of 100 mcg/mL. Others have utilized the standard arthritis dosing.

Elderly: Although hepatic function may decline with age, no specific dosage adjustment is recommended. Patients should be monitored closely for adverse effects which may require dosage adjustment.

Dosing adjustment in renal impairment: No specific dosage adjustment is recommended. There is no clinical experience in the use of leflunomide in patients with renal impairment. The free fraction of M1 is doubled in dialysis patients. Patients should be monitored closely for adverse effects requiring dosage adjustment.

Dosing adjustment in hepatic impairment: No specific dosage adjustment is recommended. Since the liver is involved in metabolic activation and subsequent metabolism/ elimination of leflunomide, patients with hepatic impairment should be monitored closely for adverse effects requiring dosage adjustment.

Dosing adjustment in hepatic toxicity: Guidelines for dosage adjustment or discontinuation based on the severity and persistence of ALT elevation secondary to leflunomide have been developed. If ALT elevations >2 times but ≤3 times ULN are noted, reduce dose to 10 mg/day, and monitor closely. If elevations persist or if elevations >3 times ULN are observed, discontinue leflunomide and initiate protocol to accelerate elimination. Cholestyramine (8 g 3 times/day for 1-3 days) or activated charcoal (50 g every 6 hours for 24 hours) may be administered to decrease leflunomide concentrations rapidly. If elevations >3 times ULN persist additional cholestyramine and/or activated charcoal may be required.

Dietary Considerations Administer without regard to meals.

Monitoring Parameters A complete blood count (WBC, hemoglobin, hematocrit, and platelet count), serum phosphate, as well as serum transaminase determinations should be monitored at baseline and monthly during the initial 6 months of treatment; if stable, monitoring frequency may be decreased to every 6-8 weeks thereafter (continue monthly when used in combination with other immunosuppressive agents). In addition, monitor for signs/symptoms of severe infection, abnormalities in hepatic function tests, or symptoms of hepatotoxicity. If coadministered with methotrexate, monthly transaminase and serum albumin levels are recommended.

Dosage Forms

Tablet (Arava®): 10 mg, 20 mg

◆ **Legatrin PM®** [OTC] *see* Acetaminophen and Diphenhydramine *on page 31*

Lenalidomide (le na LID oh mide)

U.S. Brand Names Revlimid®

Index Terms CC-5013; IMid-3

Pharmacologic Category Angiogenesis Inhibitor; Antineoplastic Agent; Immunosuppressant Agent; Tumor Necrosis Factor (TNF) Blocking Agent

Use Treatment of myelodysplastic syndrome (MDS) in patients with deletion 5q (del 5q) cytogenetic abnormality; treatment of multiple myeloma

Unlabeled/Investigational Use Treatment of metastatic malignant melanoma; treatment of myelofibrosis

Restrictions Lenalidomide is approved for marketing only under a Food and Drug Administration (FDA) approved, restricted distribution program called RevAssist^SM (www.REVLIMID.com or 1-888-423-5436). Physicians, pharmacies, and patients must be registered; a maximum 28-day supply may be dispensed; a new prescription is required each time it is filled; pregnancy testing is required for females of childbearing potential.

An FDA-approved medication guide must be distributed when dispensing an outpatient prescription (new or refill) where this medication is to be used without direct supervision of a healthcare provider. Medication guides are available at http://www.fda.gov/cder/Offices/ODS/medication_guides.htm.

Pregnancy Risk Factor X

Pregnancy Implications Lenalidomide is an analogue of thalidomide (a human teratogen) and may cause fetal harm when administered to pregnant women. Animal studies with lenalidomide are ongoing; there are no adequate and well-controlled studies in pregnant women. Women of childbearing potential should be treated only if they are able to comply with the conditions of the RevAssist^SM program. Two forms of effective contraception are required beginning 4 weeks prior to, during, and for 4 weeks after therapy and during therapy interruptions. Pregnancy tests (sensitivity of at least 50 mIU/mL) should be performed 10-14 days and 24 hours prior to beginning therapy; weekly for the first 4 weeks and every 4 weeks (every 2 weeks if menstrual cycle irregular) thereafter and during therapy interruptions. Lenalidomide must be immediately discontinued and the patient referred to a reproductive toxicity specialist if pregnancy occurs during treatment. Males (even those vasectomized) should use a latex condom during any sexual contact with women of childbearing age. Risk to the fetus from semen of male patients is unknown. The parent or legal guardian for patients between 12 and 18 years of age must agree to ensure compliance with the required guidelines. Any suspected fetal exposure should be reported to the FDA via the MedWatch program (1-800-FDA-1088) and to Celgene Corporation (1-888-423-5436).

Lactation Excretion in breast milk unknown/not recommended

Medication Safety Issues

High alert medication: The Institute for Safe Medication Practices (ISMP) includes this medication among its list of drugs which have a heightened risk of causing significant patient harm when used in error.

Contraindications Hypersensitivity to lenalidomide or any component of the formulation; pregnancy or women capable of becoming pregnant; patients unable to comply with the RevAssist^SM program

Warnings/Precautions Hazardous agent - use appropriate precautions for handling and disposal. **[U.S. Boxed Warning]: Hematologic toxicity (neutropenia and thrombocytopenia)** occurs in a majority of patients (grade 3/4: 80%) and may require dose reductions and/or delays; the use of blood product support and/or growth factors may be needed. **[U.S. Boxed Warning]: Lenalidomide has been associated with a significant increase in risk for thrombosis and embolism in multiple myeloma patients treated with combination therapy. Deep vein thrombosis (DVT) and pulmonary embolism (PE) have occurred;** monitor for signs and symptoms of thromboembolism (shortness of breath, chest pain, or arm or leg swelling) and seek prompt medical attention with development of these symptoms. Use caution in renal impairment; may experience an increased rate of toxicities.

[U.S. Boxed Warning]: Lenalidomide is an analogue of thalidomide (a human teratogen) and could potentially cause birth defects in humans. Distribution of lenalidomide is restricted and all patients must be enrolled in the RevAssist^SM program. Safety and effectiveness in children <18 years of age have not been established.

Adverse Reactions

>10%:

Cardiovascular: Peripheral edema (8% to 21%)

Central nervous system: Fatigue (31% to 38%), pyrexia (21% to 23%), dizziness (20% to 21%), headache (20%)

Dermatologic: Pruritus (42%), rash (16% to 36%), dry skin (14%)

Endocrine & metabolic: Hyperglycemia (15%), hypokalemia (11%)

Gastrointestinal: Diarrhea (29% to 49%), constipation (24% to 39%), nausea (22% to 24%), weight loss (18%), dyspepsia (14%), anorexia (10% to 14%), taste perversion (6% to 13%), abdominal pain (8% to 12%)

Genitourinary: Urinary tract infection (11%)

Hematologic: Thrombocytopenia (17% to 62%; grades 3/4: 10% to 50%), neutropenia (28% to 59%; grades 3/4: 21% to 53%), anemia (12% to 24%; grades 3/4: 6% to 9%); myelosuppression is dose-dependent and reversible with treatment interruption and/or dose reduction

Neuromuscular & skeletal: Muscle cramp (18% to 30%), arthralgia (10% to 22%), back pain (15% to 21%), tremor (20%), weakness (15%), paresthesia (12%), limb pain (11%)

Ocular: Blurred vision (15%)

Respiratory: Nasopharyngitis (23%), cough (20%), dyspnea (7% to 20%), pharyngitis (16%), epistaxis (15%), upper respiratory infection (14% to 15%), pneumonia (11% to 12%)

1% to 10%:

Cardiovascular: Edema (10%), deep vein thrombosis (≤8%; grades 3/4: 7%), hypertension (6%), chest pain (5%), palpitations (5%), atrial fibrillation (grades 3/4: 3%), syncope (grade 3: 2%)

Central nervous system: Insomnia (10%), hypoesthesia (7%), pain (7%), depression (5%)

Dermatologic: Bruising (5% to 8%), cellulitis (5%), erythema (5%)

Endocrine & metabolic: Hypothyroidism (7%), hypomagnesemia (6%), hypocalcemia (grades 3/4: 4%)

Gastrointestinal: Vomiting (10%), xerostomia (7%), loose stools (6%)

Genitourinary: Dysuria (7%)

Hematologic: Leukopenia (8%; grade 3: 4%), febrile neutropenia (5%), lymphopenia (grade 3: 2%)

Hepatic: ALT increased (8%)

Neuromuscular & skeletal: Myalgia (9%), rigors (6%), neuropathy (peripheral 5%)

Respiratory: Sinusitis (8%), rhinitis (7%), bronchitis (6%), pulmonary embolism (≤3%; grades 3/4: 3%)

Miscellaneous: Night sweats (8%), diaphoresis increased (7%)

<1% or frequency not defined: Acute febrile neutrophilic dermatosis, adrenal insufficiency, angina, aortic disorder, aphasia, azotemia, bacteremia, biliary obstruction, blindness, bone marrow depression, bradycardia, brain edema, cardiac arrest, cardiac failure, cardiogenic shock, cardiomyopathy, cardiopulmonary arrest, cerebellar infarction, cerebral infarction, cerebrovascular accident, CHF, cholecystitis, chondrocalcinosis, chronic obstructive airway disease, circulatory collapse, coagulopathy, dehydration, diabetes mellitus, diabetic ketoacidosis, diverticulitis, dysphagia, encephalitis, gastrointestinal hemorrhage, hematuria, hemoglobin decreased, hemolysis, hemolytic anemia, hemorrhage, hepatitis, herpes virus infection, hyperbilirubinemia, hypernatremia, hypersensitivity, hypoglycemia, hypotension, hypoxia, infection, INR increased, interstitial lung disease, intestinal perforation, intracranial hemorrhage, intracranial venous sinus thrombosis, irritable bowel syndrome, ischemia, ischemic colitis, kidney infection, leukoencephalopathy, liver failure, liver function tests abnormal, lung infiltration, lymphoma, melena, MI, myocardial ischemia, myopathy, neutropenic sepsis, orthostatic hypotension, pancreatitis, pancytopenia, performance status decreased, peripheral ischemia, phlebitis, pseudomembraneous colitis, pulmonary edema, refractory anemia, renal calculus, renal failure, renal tubular necrosis, respiratory failure, septic shock, sepsis, serum creatinine increased, skin desquamation, small bowel obstruction, somnolence, spinal cord compression, splenic infarction, subarachnoid hemorrhage, sudden death, supraventricular arrhythmia, tachyarrhythmia, thrombophlebitis, thrombosis, transient ischemic attack, urinary retention, urosepsis, urticaria, ventricular dysfunction, wheezing

Overdosage/Toxicology Treatment is symptomatic and supportive.

Drug Interactions

Increased Effect/Toxicity: Abatacept and anakinra may increase the risk of serious infection when used in combination with lenalidomide. Lenalidomide may increase the risk of infections associated with vaccines (live organism).

Decreased Effect: Lenalidomide may decrease the effect of vaccines (dead organisms).

Ethanol/Nutrition/Herb Interactions Herb/Nutraceutical: Avoid echinacea (has immunostimulant properties; consider therapy modifications).

Stability Store at controlled room temperature between 15°C and 30°C (59°F and 86°F).

Mechanism of Action Immunomodulatory and antiangiogenic characteristics via multiple mechanisms. Selectively inhibits secretion of proinflammatory cytokines (potent inhibitor of tumor necrosis factor-alpha secretion); enhances cell-mediated immunity by stimulating proliferation of anti-CD3 stimulated T cells (resulting in increased IL-2 and interferon gamma secretion); inhibits trophic signals to angiogenic factors in cells. Inhibits the growth of myeloma cells by inducing cell cycle arrest and cell death.

Pharmacodynamics/Kinetics

Absorption: Rapid

Protein binding: ~30%

Half-life elimination: ~3 hours

Time, to peak, plasma: Healthy volunteers: 0.6-1.5 hours; Myeloma patients: 0.5-4 hours

Excretion: Urine (~67% as unchanged drug)

Dosage Oral:

Adults:

Myelodysplastic syndrome (MDS): 10 mg once daily

Multiple myeloma: 25 mg once daily for 21 days of a 28-day treatment cycle (with dexamethasone 40 mg daily on days 1-4, 9-12, and 17-20 of the 28-day treatment cycle)

Metastatic malignant melanoma (unlabeled/investigational use): 10-25 mg once daily

Myelofibrosis (unlabeled/investigational use): 5-10 mg once daily

Elderly: Refer to adult dosing; due to the potential for decreased renal function in the elderly, select dose carefully and closely monitor renal function

Dosage adjustment in renal impairment: Not studied in renal insufficiency; select dose carefully and closely monitor renal function.

Dosage adjustment for toxicity:

Adjustment for thrombocytopenia in MDS:

Thrombocytopenia developing within 4 weeks of beginning treatment at 10 mg/day:

Baseline platelets ≥100,000/mcL:

If platelets <50,000/mcL: Hold treatment

When platelets return to ≥50,000/mcL: Resume treatment at 5 mg/day

Baseline platelets <100,000/mcL:

If platelets fall to 50% of baseline: Hold treatment

If baseline ≥60,000/mcL and platelet level returns to ≥50,000/mcL: Resume at 5 mg/day

If baseline <60,000/mcL and platelet level returns to ≥30,000/mcL: Resume at 5 mg/day

Thrombocytopenia developing after 4 weeks of beginning treatment at 10 mg/day:

Platelets <30,000/mcL **or** <50,000/mcL with platelet transfusions: Hold treatment

(Continued)

Lenalidomide *(Continued)*

Platelets ≥30,000/mcL (without hemostatic failure): Resume at 5 mg/day
Thrombocytopenia developing with treatment at 5 mg/day:
Platelets <30,000/mcL **or** <50,000/mcL with platelet transfusions: Hold treatment
Platelets ≥30,000/mcL (without hemostatic failure): Resume at 5 mg every other day
day

Adjustment for neutropenia in MDS:
Neutropenia developing within 4 weeks of beginning treatment at 10 mg/day:
For baseline absolute neutrophil count (ANC) ≥1000/mcL:
ANC <750/mcL: Hold treatment
When ANC returns to ≥1000/mcL: Resume at 5 mg/day
For baseline absolute neutrophil count (ANC) <1000/mcL:
ANC <500/mcL: Hold treatment
When ANC returns to ≥500/mcL: Resume at 5 mg/day
Neutropenia developing after 4 weeks of beginning treatment at 10 mg/day:
ANC <500/mcL for ≥7 days or associated with fever: Hold treatment
When ≥500/mcL: Resume at 5 mg/day
Neutropenia developing with treatment at 5 mg/day:
ANC <500/mcL for ≥7 days or associated with fever: Hold treatment
When ≥500/mcL: Resume at 5 mg every other day

Adjustment for thrombocytopenia in multiple myeloma:
Platelets <30,000/mcL: Hold treatment, check CBC weekly
When platelets ≥30,000/mcL: Resume at 15 mg daily
Additional occurrence of platelets <30,000/mcL: Hold treatment
When platelets ≥30,000/mcL: Resume treatment at 5 mg below previous dose; do not dose below 5 mg daily

Adjustment for neutropenia in multiple myeloma:
ANC <1000/mcL: Hold treatment, add G-CSF, check CBC weekly
When ≥1000/mcL (with neutropenia as only toxicity): Resume at 25 mg/day
When ≥1000/mcL (with additional toxicities): Resume at 15 mg/day
Additional occurrence of ANC <1000/mcL: Hold treatment
When ≥1000/mcL: Resume treatment at 5 mg below previous dose; do not dose below 5 mg daily.

Adjustment for other toxicities in multiple myeloma: For additional treatment-related grade 3/4 toxicities, hold treatment and restart at next dose level when toxicity has resolved to ≤ grade 2.

Administration Administer with water. Swallow capsule whole; do not break, open, or chew.

Monitoring Parameters CBC with differential (MDS: weekly for first 8 weeks; MM: every 2 weeks for the first 3 months), then monthly thereafter; serum creatinine, liver function tests, thyroid function tests; monitor for signs and symptoms of thromboembolism
Women of childbearing potential: Pregnancy test 10-14 days **and** 24 hours prior to initiating therapy, then every 2-4 weeks through 4 weeks after therapy discontinued

Additional Information Pregnancy tests are required prior to beginning therapy, throughout treatment and during therapy interruptions for all women of childbearing age. The pregnancy test must be verified by the prescriber and the pharmacist prior to dispensing. Effective contraception with at least two reliable forms of contraception (IUD, hormonal contraception, tubal ligation or partner's vasectomy plus latex condom, diaphragm, or cervical cap) should be used for 4 weeks prior to beginning therapy, during therapy, and for 4 weeks following discontinuance of therapy. Women who have undergone a hysterectomy or have been postmenopausal for at least 24 consecutive months are the only exception. Do not prescribe, administer, or dispense to women of childbearing age or males who may have intercourse with women of childbearing age unless both female and male are capable of complying with contraceptive measures. Even males who have undergone vasectomy must acknowledge these risks in writing, and must use a latex condom during any sexual contact with women of childbearing age. Oral and written warnings concerning contraception and the hazards of thalidomide must be conveyed to females and males and they must acknowledge their understanding in writing. Parents or guardians must consent and sign acknowledgment for patients 12-18 years of age following therapy. A maximum 28-day supply should be dispensed.

Dosage Forms
Capsule:
Revlimid®: 5 mg, 10 mg, 15 mg, 25 mg

Lepirudin *(leh puh ROO din)*

U.S. Brand Names Refludan®
Canadian Brand Names Refludan®
Index Terms Lepirudin (rDNA); Recombinant Hirudin
Pharmacologic Category Anticoagulant, Thrombin Inhibitor
Use Indicated for anticoagulation in patients with heparin-induced thrombocytopenia (HIT) and associated thromboembolic disease in order to prevent further thromboembolic complications
Unlabeled/Investigational Use Investigational: Prevention or reduction of ischemic complications associated with unstable angina
Pregnancy Risk Factor B
Pregnancy Implications Lepirudin crosses the placenta in pregnant rats; however, it is not known if lepirudin crosses the placenta in humans.
Lactation Enters breast milk/consult prescriber
Contraindications Hypersensitivity to hirudins or any component of the formulation
Warnings/Precautions Hemorrhagic events: Intracranial bleeding following concomitant thrombolytic therapy with rt-PA or streptokinase may be life threatening. For patients with an increased risk of bleeding, a careful assessment weighing the risk of lepirudin administration

versus its anticipated benefit has to be made by the treating physician. In particular, this includes the following conditions: Recent puncture of large vessels or organ biopsy; anomaly of vessels or organs; recent cerebrovascular accident, stroke, intracerebral surgery, or other neuroaxial procedures; severe uncontrolled hypertension; bacterial endocarditis; advanced renal impairment; hemorrhagic diathesis; recent major surgery; and recent major bleeding (eg, intracranial, gastrointestinal, intraocular, or pulmonary bleeding). With renal impairment, relative overdose might occur even with standard dosage regimen. The bolus dose and rate of infusion must be reduced in patients with known or suspected renal insufficiency.

Formation of antihirudin antibodies was observed in ~40% of HIT patients treated with lepirudin. This may increase the anticoagulant effect of lepirudin possibly due to delayed renal elimination of active lepirudin-antihirudin complexes. Therefore, strict monitoring of aPTT is necessary also during prolonged therapy. No evidence of neutralization of lepirudin or of allergic reactions associated with positive antibody test results was found. Allergic and hypersensitivity reactions, including anaphylaxis have been reported and may occur frequently in patients treated concomitantly with streptokinase; caution is warranted during re-exposure (anaphylaxis has been reported).

Serious liver injury (eg, liver cirrhosis) may enhance the anticoagulant effect of lepirudin due to coagulation defects secondary to reduced generation of vitamin K-dependent clotting factors.

Clinical trials have provided limited information to support any recommendations for re-exposure to lepirudin (anaphylaxis has been reported). Safety and efficacy have not been established in children.

Adverse Reactions As with all anticoagulants, bleeding is the most common adverse event associated with lepirudin. Hemorrhage may occur at virtually any site. Risk is dependent on multiple variables.

HIT patients:
>10%: Hematologic: Anemia (12%), bleeding from puncture sites (11%), hematoma (11%)
1% to 10%:
  Cardiovascular: Heart failure (3%), pericardial effusion (1%), ventricular fibrillation (1%)
  Central nervous system: Fever (7%)
  Dermatologic: Eczema (3%), maculopapular rash (4%)
  Gastrointestinal: GI bleeding/rectal bleeding (5%)
  Genitourinary: Vaginal bleeding (2%)
  Hepatic: Transaminases increased (6%)
  Renal: Hematuria (4%)
  Respiratory: Epistaxis (4%)
<1% (Limited to important or life-threatening): Allergic reactions, anaphylaxis, hemoperitoneum, hemoptysis, injection site reactions, intracranial bleeding, liver bleeding, mouth bleeding, pruritus, pulmonary bleeding, retroperitoneal bleeding, thrombocytopenia, urticaria

Non-HIT populations (including those receiving thrombolytics and/or contrast media):
1% to 10%: Respiratory: Bronchospasm/stridor/dyspnea/cough
<1% (Limited to important or life-threatening): Allergic reactions (unspecified), anaphylactoid reactions, anaphylaxis, angioedema, intracranial bleeding (0.6%), laryngeal edema, thrombocytopenia, tongue edema

Overdosage/Toxicology In case of overdose (eg, suggested by excessively high aPTT values), the risk of bleeding is increased. No specific antidote for lepirudin is available. If life-threatening bleeding occurs and excessive plasma levels of lepirudin are suspected, the following steps should be followed:
  Immediately STOP LEPIRUDIN administration
  Determine aPTT and other coagulation levels as appropriate
  Determine hemoglobin and prepare for blood transfusion
Follow current guidelines for treating patients with shock
  Individual clinical case reports and *in vitro* data suggest that either hemofiltration or hemodialysis (using high-flux dialysis membranes with a cutoff point of 50,000 daltons, eg, AN/69) may be useful in this situation

Drug Interactions
  Increased Effect/Toxicity: Thrombolytics may enhance anticoagulant properties of lepirudin on aPTT and can increase the risk of bleeding complications. Bleeding risk may also be increased by oral anticoagulants (warfarin) and platelet function inhibitors (NSAIDs, dipyridamole, ticlopidine, clopidogrel, IIb/IIIa antagonists, and aspirin).

Ethanol/Nutrition/Herb Interactions Herb/Nutraceutical: Avoid cat's claw, dong quai, evening primrose, feverfew, garlic, ginger, ginkgo, red clover, horse chestnut, green tea, ginseng (all have additional antiplatelet activity)

Stability
Intact vials should be stored at 2°C to 25°C (36°F to 77°F).
Intravenous bolus: Use a solution with a concentration of 5 mg/mL.
  Preparation of a lepirudin solution with a concentration of 5 mg/mL: Reconstitute one vial (50 mg) of lepirudin with 1 mL of sterile water for injection or 0.9% sodium chloride injection. The final concentration of 5 mg/mL is obtained by transferring the contents of the vial into a sterile, single-use syringe (of at least 10 mL capacity) and diluting the solution to a total volume of 10 mL using sterile water for injection, 0.9% sodium chloride, or 5% dextrose in water.
Intravenous infusion: For continuous intravenous infusion, solutions with concentrations of 0.2 or 0.4 mg/mL may be used.
  Preparation of a lepirudin solution with a concentration of 0.2 mg/mL or 0.4 mg/mL: Reconstitute 2 vials (50 mg each) of lepirudin with 1 mL each using either sterile water for injection or 0.9% sodium chloride injection. The final concentration of 0.2 mg/mL or 0.4 mg/mL is obtained by transferring the contents of both vials into an infusion bag containing 500 mL or 250 mL of 0.9% sodium chloride injection or 5% dextrose injection.
Reconstituted solutions of lepirudin are stable for 24 hours at room temperature. Manufacturer recommends using reconstituted solution immediately after preparation.
(Continued)

Lepirudin *(Continued)*

Mechanism of Action Lepirudin is a highly specific direct inhibitor of thrombin; lepirudin is a recombinant hirudin derived from yeast cells

Pharmacodynamics/Kinetics

Distribution: Two-compartment model; confined to extracellular fluids.

Metabolism: Via release of amino acids via catabolic hydrolysis of parent drug

Half-life elimination: Initial: ~10 minutes: Terminal: Healthy volunteers: 1.3 hours; Marked renal impairment (Cl_{cr} <15 mL/minute and on hemodialysis): ≤2 days

Excretion: Urine (~48%, 35% as unchanged drug and unchanged drug fragments of parent drug); systemic clearance is proportional to glomerular filtration rate or creatinine clearance

Dosage Adults: Maximum dose: Do not exceed 0.21 mg/kg/hour unless an evaluation of coagulation abnormalities limiting response has been completed. **Dosing is weight-based, however, patients weighing >110 kg should not receive doses greater than the recommended dose for a patient weighing 110 kg (44 mg bolus and initial maximal infusion rate of 16.5 mg/hour).**

Heparin-induced thrombocytopenia: Bolus dose: 0.4 mg/kg IVP (over 15-20 seconds), followed by continuous infusion at 0.15 mg/kg/hour; bolus and infusion must be reduced in renal insufficiency

Note: Due to potential renal insufficiency in critical care patients, some clinicians suggest that for isolated HIT (without thromboembolic complications), the initial infusion rate should be 0.1 mg/kg/hour (omit the initial bolus dose unless acute HITTS).

Concomitant use with thrombolytic therapy: Bolus dose: 0.2 mg/kg IVP (over 15-20 seconds), followed by continuous infusion at 0.1 mg/kg/hour

Dosing adjustments during infusions: Monitor first aPTT 4 hours after the start of the infusion. Subsequent determinations of aPTT should be obtained at least once daily during treatment. More frequent monitoring is recommended in renally- or hepatically-impaired patients. Any aPTT ratio measurement out of range (1.5-2.5) should be confirmed prior to adjusting dose, unless a clinical need for immediate reaction exists. If the aPTT is below target range, increase infusion by 20%. If the aPTT is in excess of the target range, stop infusion for 2 hours and when restarted the infusion rate should be decreased by 50%. A repeat aPTT should be obtained 4 hours after any dosing change.

Use in patients scheduled for switch to oral anticoagulants: Once platelets normalize, reduce lepirudin dose gradually to reach aPTT ratio just above 1.5 before starting warfarin therapy. Monitor PT/INR closely until results stabilize in therapeutic range. When lepirudin is discontinued, there may be a small reduction in INR.

Dosing adjustment in renal impairment: All patients with a creatinine clearance of <60 mL/minute or a serum creatinine of >1.5 mg/dL should receive a reduction in lepirudin dosage; there is only limited information on the therapeutic use of lepirudin in HIT patients with significant renal impairment; the following dosage recommendations are mainly based on single-dose studies in a small number of patients with renal impairment.

Initial: Bolus dose: 0.2 mg/kg IVP (over 15-20 seconds), followed by adjusted infusion based on renal function; refer to the following infusion rate adjustments based on creatinine clearance (mL/minute) and serum creatinine (mg/dL):

Lepirudin infusion rates in patients with renal impairment: See table.

Lepirudin Infusion Rates in Patients With Renal Impairment

Creatinine Clearance (mL/min)	Serum Creatinine (mg/dL)	Adjusted Infusion Rate	
		% of Standard Initial Infusion Rate	mg/kg/h
45-60	1.6-2.0	50%	0.075
30-44	2.1-3.0	30%	0.045
15-29	3.1-6.0	15%	0.0225
<15	>6.0	Avoid or STOP infusion	

Note: Acute renal failure or hemodialysis: Infusion is to be avoided or stopped. Following the bolus dose, additional bolus doses of 0.1 mg/kg may be administered every other day (only if aPTT falls below lower therapeutic limit).

Administration Administer **only** intravenously; administer I.V. bolus over 15-20 seconds

Monitoring Parameters aPTT levels; some clinicians recommend obtaining aPTT levels every 4 hours until steady state is reached (2 consecutive aPTTs in the same range) then daily monitoring.

Reference Range aPTT 1.5 to 2.5 times the control value

Dosage Forms Injection, powder for reconstitution: 50 mg

♦ **Lepirudin (rDNA)** *see* Lepirudin *on page 986*

♦ **Lescol®** *see* Fluvastatin *on page 745*

♦ **Lescol® XL** *see* Fluvastatin *on page 745*

♦ **Lessina™** *see* Ethinyl Estradiol and Levonorgestrel *on page 653*

Letrozole *(LET roe zole)*

U.S. Brand Names Femara®

Canadian Brand Names Femara®

Index Terms CGS-20267; NSC-719345

Pharmacologic Category Antineoplastic Agent, Aromatase Inhibitor

Use Adjuvant treatment of postmenopausal hormone receptor positive and treatment of hormone receptor positive or hormone receptor unknown, locally-advanced, or metastatic breast cancer in postmenopausal women

Pregnancy Risk Factor D

Pregnancy Implications Letrozole may cause fetal harm when administered to pregnant women. Animal studies have demonstrated embryotoxicity and fetotoxicity. There are no adequate and well-controlled studies in pregnant women. If used in pregnancy, or if patient becomes pregnant during treatment, the patient should be apprised of potential hazard to the fetus. Letrozole is FDA indicated for postmenopausal women only.

Lactation Excretion in breast milk unknown/use caution

Medication Safety Issues
Sound-alike/look-alike issues:
Femara® may be confused with femhrt®

Contraindications Hypersensitivity to letrozole or any component of the formulation; pregnancy

Warnings/Precautions Hazardous agent - use appropriate precautions for handling and disposal. Use caution with hepatic impairment; dose adjustment may be required. Increases in transaminases ≥5 times the upper limit of normal and in bilirubin ≥1.5 times the upper limit of normal were most often, but not always, associated with metastatic liver disease. May cause dizziness, fatigue, and somnolence; patients should be cautioned before performing tasks which require mental alertness (eg, operating machinery or driving). May increase total serum cholesterol. May cause decreases in bone mineral density. For use in postmenopausal women only.

Adverse Reactions
>10%:
Central nervous system: Headache (8% to 12%), fatigue (6% to 13%)
Endocrine & metabolic: Hot flashes (5% to 19%)
Gastrointestinal: Nausea (13% to 17%)
Neuromuscular & skeletal: Musculoskeletal pain, bone pain (22%), back pain (18%), arthralgia (8% to 16%)
Respiratory: Dyspnea (7% to 18%), cough (5% to 13%)
2% to 10%:
Cardiovascular: Chest pain (3% to 8%), peripheral edema (5%), hypertension (5% to 8%)
Central nervous system: Pain (5%), insomnia (7%), dizziness (3% to 5%), somnolence (2% to 3%), depression (<5%), anxiety (<5%), vertigo (<5%)
Dermatologic: Rash (4% to 5%), alopecia (<5%), pruritus (1% to 2%)
Endocrine & metabolic: Breast pain (7%), hypercholesterolemia (3%), hypercalcemia (<5%)
Gastrointestinal: Vomiting (7%), constipation (6% to 10%), diarrhea (5% to 8%), abdominal pain (5% to 6%), anorexia (3% to 5%), dyspepsia (3% to 4%), weight loss (7%), weight gain (2%)
Neuromuscular & skeletal: Limb pain (10%), arthritis (7%), myalgia (6% to 7%), bone fractures (6%), bone mineral density decreased (3% to 5%), osteoporosis (2%)
Miscellaneous: Flu (6%)
<2% (Limited to important or life-threatening): Angina, bilirubin increased, blurred vision, cardiac ischemia, coronary artery disease, endometrial cancer, endometrial proliferation disorder, hemiparesis, hemorrhagic stroke, hepatic enzymes increased, lymphopenia, MI, portal vein thrombosis, pulmonary embolism, secondary malignancy, thrombocytopenia, thrombophlebitis, thromboembolic event, thrombotic stroke, transaminases increased, transient ischemic attack, venous thrombosis

Overdosage/Toxicology Firm recommendations for treatment are not possible. Emesis could be induced if the patient is alert. In general, supportive care and frequent monitoring of vital signs are appropriate.

Drug Interactions
Cytochrome P450 Effect: Substrate (minor) of CYP2A6, 3A4; **Inhibits** CYP2A6 (strong), 2C19 (weak)
Increased Effect/Toxicity: Letrozole may increase the levels/effects of CYP2A6 substrates; example substrates include dexmedetomidine and ifosfamide.

Stability Store at 15°C to 30°C (59°F to 86°F).

Mechanism of Action Competitive inhibitor of the aromatase enzyme system which binds to the heme group of aromatase, a cytochrome P450 enzyme which catalyzes conversion of androgens to estrogens (specifically, androstenedione to estrone and testosterone to estradiol). This leads to inhibition of the enzyme and a significant reduction in plasma estrogen levels. Does not affect synthesis of adrenal or thyroid hormones, aldosterone, or androgens.

Pharmacodynamics/Kinetics
Absorption: Rapid and well absorbed; not affected by food
Distribution: V_d: ~1.9 L/kg
Protein binding, plasma: Weak
Metabolism: Hepatic via CYP3A4 and 2A6 to an inactive carbinol metabolite
Half-life elimination: Terminal: ~2 days
Time to steady state, plasma: 2-6 weeks
Excretion: Urine (90%; 6% as unchanged drug, 75% as glucuronide carbinol metabolite, 9% as unidentified metabolites)

Dosage Oral (refer to individual protocols): Adults: Breast cancer: 2.5 mg once daily
Elderly: No dosage adjustments required
Dosage adjustment in renal impairment: No dosage adjustment is required in patients with renal impairment if Cl_{cr} ≥10 mL/minute
Dosage adjustment in hepatic impairment:
Mild-to-moderate impairment: No adjustment recommended
Severe impairment: Child-Pugh class C: 2.5 mg every other day

Dietary Considerations May be taken without regard to meals. Calcium and vitamin D supplementation are recommended.

Monitoring Parameters Monitor periodically during therapy: complete blood counts, thyroid function tests; serum electrolytes, cholesterol, transaminases, and creatinine; bone density

Dosage Forms Tablet: 2.5 mg

Leucovorin (loo koe VOR in)

Index Terms Calcium Leucovorin; Citrovorum Factor; Folinic Acid; 5-Formyl Tetrahydrofolate; Leucovorin Calcium

Pharmacologic Category Antidote; Vitamin, Water Soluble

Additional Appendix Information
Management of Overdosages *on page 2075*
USPHS / IDSA Guidelines for the Prevention of Opportunistic Infections in Persons Infected With HIV *on page 1966*

Use Antidote for folic acid antagonists (methotrexate, trimethoprim, pyrimethamine); treatment of megaloblastic anemias when folate is deficient as in infancy, sprue, pregnancy, and nutritional deficiency when oral folate therapy is not possible; in combination with fluorouracil in the treatment of colon cancer

Pregnancy Risk Factor C

Lactation Enters breast milk/compatible

Medication Safety Issues
Sound-alike/look-alike issues:
Leucovorin may be confused with Leukeran®, Leukine®
Folinic acid may be confused with folic acid

Contraindications Hypersensitivity to leucovorin or any component of the formulation; pernicious anemia or vitamin B_{12}-deficient megaloblastic anemias

Adverse Reactions Frequency not defined.
Dermatologic: Rash, pruritus, erythema, urticaria
Hematologic: Thrombocytosis
Respiratory: Wheezing
Miscellaneous: Anaphylactoid reactions

Drug Interactions
Decreased Effect: May decrease efficacy of co-trimoxazole against *Pneumocystis carinii* pneumonitis

Stability Store at room temperature. Protect from light. Leucovorin should be reconstituted with SWFI, bacteriostatic NS, BWFI, NS, or D_5W; dilute in 100-1000 mL NS, D_5W for infusion. Reconstituted solution is chemically stable for 7 days; reconstitutions with bacteriostatic water for injection, U.S.P., must be used within 7 days. Parenteral admixture is stable for 24 hours stored at room temperature (25°C) and for 4 days when stored under refrigeration (4°C).

Mechanism of Action A reduced form of folic acid, leucovorin supplies the necessary cofactor blocked by methotrexate, enters the cells via the same active transport system as methotrexate. Stabilizes the binding of 5-dUMP and thymidylate synthetase, enhancing the activity of fluorouracil.

Pharmacodynamics/Kinetics
Onset of action: Oral: ~30 minutes; I.V.: ~5 minutes
Absorption: Oral, I.M.: Rapid and well absorbed
Metabolism: Intestinal mucosa and hepatically to 5-methyl-tetrahydrofolate (5MTHF; active)
Bioavailability: 31% following 200 mg dose; 98% following doses ≤25 mg
Half-life elimination: Leucovorin: 15 minutes; 5MTHF: 33-35 minutes
Excretion: Urine (80% to 90%); feces (5% to 8%)

Dosage Children and Adults:
Treatment of folic acid antagonist overdosage: Oral: 2-15 mg/day for 3 days or until blood counts are normal, **or** 5 mg every 3 days; doses of 6 mg/day are needed for patients with platelet counts <100,000/mm³

Folate-deficient megaloblastic anemia: I.M.: 1 mg/day

Megaloblastic anemia secondary to congenital deficiency of dihydrofolate reductase: I.M.: 3-6 mg/day

Rescue dose: Initial: I.V.: 10 mg/m², then:
Oral, I.M., I.V., SubQ: 10-15 mg/m² every 6 hours until methotrexate level <0.05 micromole/L; if methotrexate level remains >5 micromole/L at 48-72 hours after the end of the methotrexate infusion, increase to 20-100 mg/m² every 6 hours until methotrexate level <0.05 micromole/L

Investigational: Post I.T. methotrexate: Oral, I.V.: 12 mg/m² as a single dose

Administration Refer to individual protocols. Should be administered I.M., I.V. push, or I.V. infusion (15 minutes to 2 hours). Leucovorin should not be administered concurrently with methotrexate. It is commonly initiated 24 hours after the start of methotrexate. Toxicity to normal tissues may be irreversible if leucovorin is not initiated by ~40 hours after the start of methotrexate.

As a rescue after folate antagonists: Administer by I.V. bolus, I.M., or orally.

In combination with fluorouracil: Fluorouracil activity, the fluorouracil is usually given after, or at the midpoint, of the leucovorin infusion. Leucovorin is usually administered by I.V. bolus injection or short (10-120 minutes) I.V. infusion. Other administration schedules have been used; refer to individual protocols.

Monitoring Parameters Plasma methotrexate concentration as a therapeutic guide to high-dose methotrexate therapy with leucovorin factor rescue. Leucovorin is continued until the plasma methotrexate level <0.05 micromole/L.

With 4- to 6-hour high-dose methotrexate infusions, plasma drug values in excess of 50 and 1 micromole/L at 24 and 48 hours after starting the infusion, respectively, are often predictive of delayed methotrexate clearance

Dosage Forms
Injection, powder for reconstitution, as calcium: 50 mg, 100 mg, 200 mg, 350 mg, 500 mg
Injection, solution, as calcium: 10 mg/mL (50 mL)
Tablet, as calcium: 5 mg, 10 mg, 15 mg, 25 mg

♦ **Leucovorin Calcium** *see* Leucovorin *on page 990*
♦ **Leukeran®** *see* Chlorambucil *on page 340*
♦ **Leukine®** *see* Sargramostim *on page 1548*

Leuprolide (loo PROE lide)

U.S. Brand Names Eligard®; Lupron®; Lupron Depot®; Lupron Depot-Ped®; Viadur®
Canadian Brand Names Eligard®; Lupron®; Lupron® Depot®; Viadur®
Index Terms Abbott-43818; Leuprolide Acetate; Leuprorelin Acetate; NSC-377526; TAP-144
Pharmacologic Category Gonadotropin Releasing Hormone Agonist
Use Palliative treatment of advanced prostate carcinoma; management of endometriosis; treatment of anemia caused by uterine leiomyomata (fibroids); central precocious puberty
Unlabeled/Investigational Use Treatment of breast, ovarian, and endometrial cancer; infertility; prostatic hyperplasia
Pregnancy Risk Factor X
Pregnancy Implications Pregnancy must be excluded prior to the start of treatment. Although leuprolide usually inhibits ovulation and stops menstruation, contraception is not ensured and a nonhormonal contraceptive should be used. Fetal abnormalities and increased fetal mortality have been noted in animal studies.
Lactation Excretion in breast milk unknown/contraindicated
Medication Safety Issues
Sound-alike/look-alike issues:
Lupron® may be confused with Nuprin®
Lupron Depot®-3 Month may be confused with Lupron Depot-Ped®
Contraindications Hypersensitivity to leuprolide, GnRH, GnRH-agonist analogs, or any component of the formulation; spinal cord compression (orchiectomy suggested); undiagnosed abnormal vaginal bleeding; pregnancy; breast-feeding
Warnings/Precautions Hazardous agent - use appropriate precautions for handling and disposal. Transient increases in testosterone serum levels occur at the start of treatment. Tumor flare, bone pain, neuropathy, urinary tract obstruction, and spinal cord compression have been reported when used for prostate cancer; closely observe patients for weakness, paresthesias, hematuria, and urinary tract obstruction in first few weeks of therapy. Observe patients with metastatic vertebral lesions or urinary obstruction closely. Exacerbation of endometriosis or uterine leiomyomata may occur initially. Decreased bone density has been reported when used for ≥6 months. Use caution in patients with a history of psychiatric illness; alteration in mood, memory impairment, and depression have been associated with use. Rare cases of pituitary apoplexy (frequently secondary to pituitary adenoma) have been observed with leuprolide administration (onset from 1 hour to usually <2 weeks); may present as sudden headache, vomiting, visual or mental status changes, and infrequently cardiovascular collapse; immediate medical attention required. Females treated for precocious puberty may experience menses or spotting during the first 2 months of treatment; notify healthcare provider if bleeding continues after the second month.
Adverse Reactions
Children:
2% to 10%:
Central nervous system: Pain (2%)
Dermatologic: Acne (2%), rash (2% including erythema multiforme), seborrhea (2%)
Genitourinary: Vaginitis (2%), vaginal bleeding (2%), vaginal discharge (2%)
Local: Injection site reaction (5%)
<2%: Alopecia, body odor, cervix disorder, dysphagia, emotional lability, epistaxis, fever, gingivitis, gynecomastia, headache, nausea, nervousness, peripheral edema, personality disorder, sexual maturity accelerated, skin striae, somnolence, syncope, urinary incontinence, vasodilation, vomiting, weight gain

Adults (frequency dependent upon formulation and indication):
Cardiovascular: Angina, atrial fibrillation, CHF, deep vein thrombosis, edema, hot flashes, hypertension, MI, peripheral edema, syncope, tachycardia
Central nervous system: Abnormal thinking, agitation, amnesia, anxiety, chills, confusion, convulsion, dementia, depression, dizziness, fatigue, fever, headache, insomnia, malaise, pain, vertigo
Dermatologic: Alopecia, bruising, burning, cellulitis, pruritus
Endocrine & metabolic: Bone density decreased, breast enlargement, breast tenderness, dehydration, hirsutism, hyperglycemia, hyperlipidemia, hyperphosphatemia, libido decreased, menstrual disorders, potassium decreased
Gastrointestinal: Anorexia, appetite increased, constipation, diarrhea, dry mucous membranes, dysphagia, eructation, GI hemorrhage, gingivitis, gum hemorrhage, intestinal obstruction, nausea, peptic ulcer, vomiting, weight gain/loss
Genitourinary: Balanitis, impotence, nocturia, penile shrinkage, testicular atrophy; urinary disorder (eg, urgency, incontinence, retention); UTI, vaginitis
Hematologic: Anemia, platelets decreased, PT prolonged, WBC increased
Hepatic: Hepatomegaly, liver function tests abnormal
Local: Abscess, injection site reaction
Neuromuscular & skeletal: Arthritis, bone pain, leg cramps, myalgia, paresthesia, tremor, weakness
Renal: BUN increased
Respiratory: Allergic reaction, dyspnea, emphysema, hemoptysis, hypoxia, lung edema, pulmonary embolism
Miscellaneous: Body odor, diaphoresis, flu-like syndrome, neoplasm, night sweats, voice alteration

Children and Adults: Postmarketing/case reports: Anaphylactic/anaphylactoid reactions, asthmatic reactions, bone density decreased; fibromyalgia-like symptoms (arthralgia/myalgia, headaches, GI distress); hair growth, hearing disorder, hepatic dysfunction, hypotension, induration at the injection site, peripheral neuropathy, photosensitivity; pituitary apoplexy (cardiovascular collapse, mental status altered, ophthalmoplegia, sudden headache, visual changes, vomiting); prostate pain, pulmonary embolism, rash, spinal fracture/paralysis, tenosynovitis-like symptoms, throat nodule, uric acid increased, urticaria, WBC decreased

(Continued)

Leuprolide *(Continued)*

Overdosage/Toxicology Treatment consists of general supportive care.

Stability

Lupron®: Store unopened vials of injection in refrigerator. Vial in use can be kept at room temperature ≤30°C (86°F) for several months with minimal loss of potency. Protect from light and store vial in carton until use. Do not freeze.

Eligard®: Store at 2°C to 8°C (36°F to 46°F). Allow to reach room temperature prior to using. Once mixed, must be administered within 30 minutes. Eligard® is packaged in two syringes; one contains the Atrigel® polymer system and the second contains leuprolide acetate powder. Follow package instructions for mixing.

Lupron Depot® may be stored at room temperature of 25°C; excursions permitted to 15°C to 30°C (59°F to 86°F). Upon reconstitution, the suspension does not contain a preservative and should be used immediately. Reconstitute only with diluent provided.

Viadur® may be stored at room temperature of 15°C to 30°C (59°F and 86°F).

Mechanism of Action Potent inhibitor of gonadotropin secretion; continuous daily administration results in suppression of ovarian and testicular steroidogenesis due to decreased levels of LH and FSH with subsequent decrease in testosterone (male) and estrogen (female) levels. Leuprolide may also have a direct inhibitory effect on the testes, and act by a different mechanism not directly related to reduction in serum testosterone.

Pharmacodynamics/Kinetics

Onset of action: Following transient increase, testosterone suppression occurs in ~2-4 weeks of continued therapy

Distribution: Males: V_d: 27 L

Protein binding: 43% to 49%

Metabolism: Major metabolite, pentapeptide (M-1)

Bioavailability: Oral: None; SubQ: 94%

Half-life elimination: I.V.: 3 hours

Excretion: Urine (<5% as parent and major metabolite)

Dosage

Children: Precocious puberty (consider discontinuing by age 11 for females and by age 12 for males):

SubQ (Lupron®): Initial: 50 mcg/kg/day (per manufacturer, doses of 20-45 mcg/kg/day have also been reported); titrate dose upward by 10 mcg/kg/day if down-regulation is not achieved

I.M. (Lupron Depot-Ped®): 0.3 mg/kg/dose given every 28 days (minimum dose: 7.5 mg)

≤25 kg: 7.5 mg

>25-37.5 kg: 11.25 mg

>37.5 kg: 15 mg

Titrate dose upward in increments of 3.75 mg every 4 weeks if down-regulation is not achieved.

Adults:

Advanced prostatic carcinoma:

SubQ:

Eligard®: 7.5 mg monthly **or** 22.5 mg every 3 months **or** 30 mg every 4 months **or** 45 mg every 6 months

Lupron®: 1 mg/day

Viadur®: 65 mg implanted subcutaneously every 12 months

I.M.:

Lupron Depot®: 7.5 mg/dose given monthly (every 28-33 days) **or**

Lupron Depot®-3: 22.5 mg every 3 months **or**

Lupron Depot®-4: 30 mg every 4 months

Endometriosis: I.M.: Initial therapy may be with leuprolide alone or in combination with norethindrone; if retreatment for an additional 6 months is necessary, norethindrone should be used. Retreatment is not recommended for longer than one additional 6-month course.

Lupron Depot®: 3.75 mg/month for up to 6 months **or**

Lupron Depot®-3: 11.25 mg every 3 months for up to 2 doses (6 months total duration of treatment)

Uterine leiomyomata (fibroids): I.M. (in combination with iron):

Lupron Depot®: 3.75 mg/month for up to 3 months **or**

Lupron Depot®-3: 11.25 mg as a single injection

Administration

I.M.: Lupron Depot®: Vary injection site periodically

SubQ:

Eligard®: Vary injection site; choose site with adequate subcutaneous tissue (eg, abdomen, upper buttocks)

Lupron®: Vary injection site; if an alternate syringe from the syringe provided is required, insulin syringes should be used

Other: Viadur® implant: Requires surgical implantation (subcutaneous) and removal at 12-month intervals

Monitoring Parameters Bone mineral density

Precocious puberty: GnRH testing (blood LH and FSH levels), measurement of bone age every 6-12 months, testosterone in males and estradiol in females; Tanner staging

Prostatic cancer: LH and FSH levels, serum testosterone (2-4 weeks after initiation of therapy), PSA; weakness, paresthesias, and urinary tract obstruction in first few weeks of therapy

Test Interactions Interferes with pituitary gonadotropic and gonadal function tests during and up to 3 months after therapy. Viadur®: Efficacy and stability of product not affected by MRI or radiographic exposure, although device will be visualized during these diagnostic procedures.

Additional Information

Eligard® Atrigel®: A nongelatin-based, biodegradable, polymer matrix

Viadur®: Leuprolide acetate implant containing 72 mg of leuprolide acetate, equivalent to 65 mg leuprolide free base. One Viadur® implant delivers 120 mcg of leuprolide/day over 12 months.

Dosage Forms
Implant (Viadur®): 65 mg [released over 12 months; packaged with administration kit]
Injection, solution, as acetate (Lupron®): 5 mg/mL (2.8 mL) [contains benzyl alcohol; packaged with syringes and alcohol swabs]
Injection, powder for reconstitution, as acetate [depot formulation; prefilled syringe]:
Eligard®:
7.5 mg [released over 1 month]
22.5 mg [released over 3 months]
30 mg [released over 4 months]
45 mg [released over 6 months]
Lupron Depot®: 3.75 mg, 7.5 mg [released over 1 month; contains polysorbate 80]
Lupron Depot®-3 Month: 11.25 mg, 22.5 mg [released over 3 months; contains polysorbate 80]
Lupron Depot®-4 Month: 30 mg [released over 4 months; contains polysorbate 80]
Lupron Depot-Ped®: 7.5 mg, 11.25 mg, 15 mg [released over 1 month; contains polysorbate 80]

♦ **Leuprolide Acetate** *see Leuprolide on page 991*
♦ **Leuprorelin Acetate** *see Leuprolide on page 991*
♦ **Leurocristine Sulfate** *see VinCRIStine on page 1789*
♦ **Leustatin®** *see Cladribine on page 383*

Levalbuterol (leve al BYOO ter ole)

U.S. Brand Names Xopenex®; Xopenex HFA™
Canadian Brand Names Xopenex®
Index Terms Levalbuterol Hydrochloride; Levalbuterol Tartrate; R-albuterol
Pharmacologic Category Beta$_2$-Adrenergic Agonist
Additional Appendix Information
Bronchodilators *on page 1877*
Use Treatment or prevention of bronchospasm in children and adults with reversible obstructive airway disease
Pregnancy Risk Factor C
Pregnancy Implications Teratogenic effects were not observed in animal studies; however, racemic albuterol was teratogenic in some species. There are no adequate and well-controlled studies in pregnant women. This drug should be used during pregnancy only if benefit exceeds risk. Use caution if needed for bronchospasm during labor and delivery; has potential to interfere with uterine contractions.
Lactation Excretion in breast milk unknown/use caution
Medication Safety Issues
Sound-alike/look-alike issues:
Xopenex® may be confused with Xanax®
Contraindications Hypersensitivity to levalbuterol, albuterol, or any component of the formulation
Warnings/Precautions Optimize anti-inflammatory treatment before initiating maintenance treatment with levalbuterol. Do not use as a component of chronic therapy without an anti-inflammatory agent. Only the mildest form of asthma (Step 1 and/or exercise-induced) would not require concurrent use based upon asthma guidelines. Patient must be instructed to seek medical attention in cases where acute symptoms are not relieved or a previous level of response is diminished. The need to increase frequency of use may indicate deterioration of asthma, and treatment must not be delayed.

Use caution in patients with cardiovascular disease (arrhythmia or hypertension or CHF), convulsive disorders, diabetes, glaucoma, hyperthyroidism, or hypokalemia. Beta agonists may cause elevation in blood pressure, heart rate, and result in CNS stimulation/excitation. Beta$_2$ agonists may increase risk of arrhythmia, increase serum glucose, or decrease serum potassium.

Immediate hypersensitivity reactions (urticaria, angioedema, rash, bronchospasm) have been reported. Do not exceed recommended dose; serious adverse events including fatalities, have been associated with excessive use of inhaled sympathomimetics. Rarely, paradoxical bronchospasm may occur with use of inhaled bronchodilating agents; this should be distinguished from inadequate response. Use with caution during labor and delivery. Safety and efficacy have not been established in patients <4 years of age.

Adverse Reactions Immediate hypersensitivity reactions have occurred, including angioedema, oropharyngeal edema, urticaria, rash, and anaphylaxis.

>10%:
Endocrine & metabolic: Serum glucose increased, serum potassium decreased
Respiratory: Viral infection (7% to 12%), rhinitis (3% to 11%)
>2% to <10%:
Central nervous system: Nervousness (3% to 10%), tremor (≤7%), anxiety (3%), dizziness (1% to 3%), migraine (≤3%), pain (1% to 3%)
Cardiovascular: Tachycardia (~3%)
Gastrointestinal: Dyspepsia (1% to 3%)
Neuromuscular & skeletal: Leg cramps (≤3%)
Respiratory: Asthma (9%), pharyngitis (8%), cough (1% to 4%), nasal edema (1% to 3%), sinusitis (1% to 4%)
Miscellaneous: Flu-like syndrome (1% to 4%), accidental injury (≤3%)
<2% (Limited to important or life-threatening): Angina, arrhythmia, atrial fibrillation, extrasystole, headache, hematuria, hyper-/hypotension, hypokalemia, insomnia, oropharyngeal dryness, paresthesia, supraventricular arrhythmia, syncope, tremor, vertigo; immediate
(Continued)

Levalbuterol (Continued)

hypersensitivity reactions have occurred (including angioedema, oropharyngeal edema, urticaria, rash, and anaphylaxis)

Overdosage/Toxicology Symptoms of overdose include tachycardia, tremor, hypertension, angina, and seizures. Hypokalemia also may occur. Cardiac arrest and death may be associated with abuse of beta-agonist bronchodilators. Treatment includes immediate discontinuation and symptomatic and supportive therapies. Cautious use of beta-adrenergic blocking agents may be considered in severe cases.

Drug Interactions

Increased Effect/Toxicity: May add to effects of medications which deplete potassium (eg, loop or thiazide diuretics). Cardiac effects of levalbuterol may be potentiated in patients receiving MAO inhibitors, tricyclic antidepressants, sympathomimetics (eg, amphetamine, dobutamine), or inhaled anesthetics (eg, enflurane).

Decreased Effect: Beta-blockers (particularly nonselective agents) block the effect of levalbuterol. Digoxin levels may be decreased.

Stability

Aerosol: Store at room temperature of 20°C to 25°C (68°F to 77°F); protect from freezing and direct sunlight. Store with mouthpiece up. Discard after 200 actuations.

Solution for nebulization: Store in protective foil pouch at room temperature of 20°C to 25°C (68°F to 77°F). Protect from light and excessive heat. Vials should be used within 2 weeks after opening protective pouch. Use within 1 week and protect from light if removed from pouch. Vials of concentrated solution should be used immediately after removing from protective pouch. Concentrated solution should be diluted with 2.5 mL NS prior to use.

Mechanism of Action Relaxes bronchial smooth muscle by action on beta-2 receptors with little effect on heart rate

Pharmacodynamics/Kinetics

Onset of action:

Aerosol: 5.5-10.2 minutes

Peak effect: ~77 minutes

Nebulization: 10-17 minutes (measured as a 15% increase in FEV_1)

Peak effect: 1.5 hours

Duration:

Aerosol: 3-4 hours (up to 6 hours in some patients)

Nebulization: 5-6 hours (up to 8 hours in some patients)

Absorption: A portion of inhaled dose is absorbed to systemic circulation

Half-life elimination: 3.3-4 hours

Time to peak, serum:

Aerosol: 0.5 hours

Nebulization: 0.2 hours

Dosage

Metered-dose inhalation: Aerosol: Children ≥4 years and Adults: 1-2 puffs every 4-6 hours

Nebulization:

Children 6-11 years: 0.31 mg 3 times/day (maximum dose: 0.63 mg 3 times/day)

Children >12 years and Adults: 0.63 mg 3 times/day at intervals of 6-8 hours; dosage may be increased to 1.25 mg 3 times/day with close monitoring for adverse effects. Most patients gain optimal benefit from regular use

Elderly: Only a small number of patients have been studied. Although greater sensitivity of some elderly patients cannot be ruled out, no overall differences in safety or effectiveness were observed. An initial dose of 0.63 mg should be used in all patients >65 years of age.

Administration Inhalation:

Aerosol: Shake well before use; prime with 4 test sprays prior to first use or if inhaler has not been use of more than 3 days. Clean actuator (mouthpiece) weekly.

Solution for nebulization: Safety and efficacy were established when administered with the following nebulizers: PARI LC Jet™, PARI LC Plus™, as well as the following compressors: PARI Master®, Dura-Neb® 2000, and Dura-Neb® 3000. Concentrated solution should be diluted prior to use.

Monitoring Parameters Asthma symptoms; FEV_1, peak flow, and/or other pulmonary function tests; heart rate, blood pressure, CNS stimulation; arterial blood gases (if condition warrants); serum potassium, serum glucose (in selected patients)

Dosage Forms Note: Strength expressed as base.

Aerosol, oral, as tartrate:

Xopenex HFA™: 45 mcg/actuation (15 g) [200 doses; chlorofluorocarbon free]

Solution for nebulization, as hydrochloride:

Xopenex®: 0.31 mg/3 mL (24s); 0.63 mg/3 mL (24s); 1.25 mg/3 mL (24s)

Solution for nebulization, concentrate, as hydrochloride:

Xopenex®: 1.25 mg/0.5 mL (30s)

♦ **Levalbuterol Hydrochloride** see Levalbuterol on page 993

♦ **Levalbuterol Tartrate** see Levalbuterol on page 993

♦ **Levall G** see Guaifenesin and Pseudoephedrine on page 819

♦ **Levaquin®** see Levofloxacin on page 1001

♦ **Levarterenol Bitartrate** see Norepinephrine on page 1240

♦ **Levate® (Can)** see Amitriptyline on page 101

♦ **Levbid®** see Hyoscyamine on page 866

♦ **Levemir®** see Insulin Detemir on page 910

Levetiracetam (lee va tye RA se tam)

U.S. Brand Names Keppra®
Canadian Brand Names CO Levetiracetam; Keppra®
Pharmacologic Category Anticonvulsant, Miscellaneous
Additional Appendix Information
Anticonvulsants by Seizure Type *on page 1865*
Use Adjunctive therapy in the treatment of partial onset seizures; adjunctive treatment of myoclonic seizures
Unlabeled/Investigational Use Bipolar disorder
Pregnancy Risk Factor C
Pregnancy Implications Developmental toxicities were observed in animal studies. There are no adequate and well-controlled studies in pregnant women. Two registries are available for women exposed to levetiracetam during pregnancy:
Antiepileptic Drug Pregnancy Registry (888-233-2334 or http://www.mgh.harvard.edu/aed/)
Keppra® pregnancy registry (888-537-7734 or http://www.keppra.com)
Lactation Enters breast milk/not recommended
Medication Safety Issues
Sound-alike/look-alike issues:
Potential for dispensing errors between Keppra® and Kaletra® (lopinavir/ritonavir)
Contraindications Hypersensitivity to levetiracetam or any component of the formulation
Warnings/Precautions Psychotic symptoms (psychosis, hallucinations) and behavioral symptoms (including aggression, anger, anxiety, depersonalization, depression, personality disorder) may occur; incidence may be increased in children. Dose reduction may be required. Levetiracetam should be withdrawn gradually to minimize the potential of increased seizure frequency. Use caution with renal impairment; dosage adjustment may be necessary. Weakness, dizziness, and somnolence occur mostly during the first month of therapy. Safety and efficacy in children <4 years of age (oral formulation) or <16 years or age (I.V. formulation) have not been established.
Adverse Reactions As reported for oral levetiracetam when used for partial onset seizure. Spectrum and frequency of adverse reactions was similar for myoclonic epilepsy.
>10%:
Central nervous system: Behavioral symptoms (agitation, aggression, anger, anxiety, apathy, depersonalization, depression, emotional lability, hostility, hyperkinesias, irritability, nervousness, neurosis and personality disorder: adults 13%; children 38%), somnolence (15% to 23%), headache (14%), hostility (2% to 12%)
Gastrointestinal: Vomiting (15%), anorexia (3% to 13%)
Neuromuscular & skeletal: Weakness (9% to 15%)
Respiratory: Rhinitis (4% to 13%), cough (2% to 11%)
Miscellaneous: Accidental injury (17%), infection (2% to 13%)
1% to 10%:
Cardiovascular: Facial edema (2%)
Central nervous system: Nervousness (4% to 10%), dizziness (7% to 9%), personality disorder (8%), pain (6% to 7%), agitation (6%), emotional lability (2% to 6%), depression (3% to 4%), ataxia (3%), vertigo (3%), amnesia (2%), anxiety (2%), confusion (2%)
Dermatologic: Bruising (2%), pruritus (2%), rash (2%), skin discoloration (2%)
Gastrointestinal: Diarrhea (8%), gastroenteritis (4%), constipation (3%), dehydration (2%)
Hematologic: Decreased leukocytes (2% to 3%)
Neuromuscular & skeletal: Neck pain (2%), paresthesia (2%), reflexes increased (2%)
Ocular: Conjunctivitis (3%), diplopia (2%), amblyopia (2%)
Otic: Ear pain (2%)
Renal: Albuminuria (4%), urine abnormality (2%)
Respiratory: Pharyngitis (6% to 10%), asthma (2%), sinusitis (2%)
Miscellaneous: Flu-like syndrome (3%), viral infection (2%)
<1% (Limited to important or life-threatening): Alopecia, anemia, catatonia, hepatitis, leukopenia, LFTs abnormal, neutropenia, pancreatitis, pancytopenia, suicidal behavior, thrombocytopenia, weight loss
Overdosage/Toxicology Symptoms may include aggression, agitation, ataxia, coma, decreased consciousness, drowsiness, respiratory depression and somnolence. Monitor vital signs. Treatment is symptomatic and supportive. Hemodialysis may be effective (estimated clearance of ~50% in 4 hours).
Drug Interactions
Increased Effect/Toxicity: CNS depressants may enhance the adverse/toxic effect of levetiracetam.
Ethanol/Nutrition/Herb Interactions
Ethanol: Avoid ethanol (may increase CNS depression).
Food: Food may delay, but does not affect the extent of absorption.
Stability
Oral solution, tablet: Store at 15°C to 30°C (59°F to 86°F).
Injection solution: Store at 15°C to 30°C (59°F to 86°F). Must dilute dose in 100 mL of NS, LR, or D_5W. Admixed solution is stable for 24 hours in PVC bags kept at room temperature.
Mechanism of Action The precise mechanism by which levetiracetam exerts its antiepileptic effect is unknown. However, several studies have suggested the mechanism may involve one or more of the following central pharmacologic effects: inhibition of voltage-dependent N-type calcium channels; facilitation of GABA-ergic inhibitory transmission through displacement of negative modulators; reduction of delayed rectifier potassium current; and/or binding to synaptic proteins which modulate neurotransmitter release.
Pharmacodynamics/Kinetics
Onset of action: Oral: Peak effect: 1 hour
Absorption: Oral: Rapid and complete
Distribution: V_d: Similar to total body water
Protein binding: <10%
(Continued)

Levetiracetam (Continued)

Metabolism: Not extensive; primarily by enzymatic hydrolysis; forms metabolites (inactive)

Bioavailability: 100%

Half-life elimination: 6-8 hours

Excretion: Urine (66% as unchanged drug)

Dosage

Oral:

Children 4-15 years: Partial onset seizures: 10 mg/kg/dose given twice daily; may increase every 2 weeks by 10 mg/kg/dose to a maximum of 30 mg/kg/dose twice daily

Children ≥12 years and Adults: Myoclonic seizures: Initial: 500 mg twice daily; may increase every 2 weeks by 500 mg/dose to the recommended dose of 1500 mg twice daily. Efficacy of doses <3000 mg/day has not been established.

Children ≥16 years and Adults:

Partial onset seizure: Initial: 500 mg twice daily; may increase every 2 weeks by 500 mg/dose to a maximum of 1500 mg twice daily. Doses >3000 mg/day have been used in trials; however, there is no evidence of increased benefit.

Bipolar disorder (unlabeled use): Initial: 500 mg twice daily; if tolerated, increase to 500 mg twice daily; dose may be increased every 3 days until target dose of 3000 mg/day is reached; maximum: 4000 mg/day

I.V.: Children ≥16 years and Adults: Partial onset seizure: Initial: 500 mg twice daily; may increase every 2 weeks by 500 mg/dose to a maximum of 1500 mg twice daily. Doses >3000 mg/day have been used in trials; however, there is no evidence of increased benefit.

Note: When switching from oral to I.V. formulations, the total daily dose should be the same.

Dosing adjustment in renal impairment: Adults:

Cl_{cr} >80 mL/minute: 500-1500 mg every 12 hours

Cl_{cr} 50-80 mL/minute: 500-1000 mg every 12 hours

Cl_{cr} 30-50 mL/minute: 250-750 mg every 12 hours

Cl_{cr} <30 mL/minute: 250-500 mg every 12 hours

End-stage renal disease patients using dialysis: 500-1000 mg every 24 hours; a supplemental dose of 250-500 mg following dialysis is recommended

Dosing adjustment in hepatic impairment: No adjustment required

Dietary Considerations May be taken with or without food.

Administration

I.V.: Infuse over 15 minutes

Tablet: Only administer as whole tablet.

Additional Information When switching from oral to I.V. formulations, the total daily dose should be the same.

Dosage Forms

Injection, solution:

Keppra®: 100 mg/mL (5 mL)

Solution, oral:

Keppra®: 100 mg/mL (480 mL) [dye free; grape flavor]

Tablet:

Keppra®: 250 mg, 500 mg, 750 mg, 1000 mg

- ◆ **Levitra®** see Vardenafil on page 1775
- ◆ **Levlen®** see Ethinyl Estradiol and Levonorgestrel on page 653
- ◆ **Levlite™** see Ethinyl Estradiol and Levonorgestrel on page 653

Levobunolol (lee voe BYOO noe lole)

U.S. Brand Names Betagan®

Canadian Brand Names Apo-Levobunolol®; Betagan®; Novo-Levobunolol; Optho-Bunolol®; PMS-Levobunolol; Sandoz-Levobunolol

Index Terms l-Bunolol Hydrochloride; Levobunolol Hydrochloride

Pharmacologic Category Beta-Adrenergic Blocker, Nonselective; Ophthalmic Agent, Antiglaucoma

Additional Appendix Information

Glaucoma Drug Therapy on page 2050

Use To lower intraocular pressure in chronic open-angle glaucoma or ocular hypertension

Pregnancy Risk Factor C

Medication Safety Issues

Sound-alike/look-alike issues:

Levobunolol may be confused with levocabastine

Betagan® may be confused with Betadine®

International issues:

Betagan® may be confused with Betagon® which is a brand name for mepindolol in Italy

Dosage Adults: Ophthalmic: Instill 1 drop in the affected eye(s) 1-2 times/day

Additional Information Complete prescribing information for this medication should be consulted for additional detail.

Dosage Forms

Solution, ophthalmic, as hydrochloride: 0.25% (5 mL, 10 mL); 0.5% (5 mL, 10 mL, 15 mL) [contains benzalkonium chloride and sodium metabisulfite]

Betagan®: 0.25% (5 mL, 10 mL); 0.5% (2 mL, 5 mL, 10 mL, 15 mL) [contains benzalkonium chloride and sodium metabisulfite]

- ◆ **Levobunolol Hydrochloride** see Levobunolol on page 996

Levobupivacaine (LEE voe byoo PIV a kane)

U.S. Brand Names Chirocaine® [DSC]
Canadian Brand Names Chirocaine®
Pharmacologic Category Local Anesthetic
Use Production of local or regional anesthesia for surgery and obstetrics, and for postoperative pain management
Pregnancy Risk Factor B
Dosage Adults: **Note:** Rapid injection of a large volume of local anesthetic solution should be avoided. Fractional (incremental) doses are recommended.
Guidelines (individual response varies): See table.

	Concentration	Volume	Dose	Motor Block
Surgical Anesthesia				
Epidural for surgery	0.5%-0.75%	10-20 mL	50-150 mg	Moderate to complete
Epidural for C-section	0.5%	20-30 mL	100-150 mg	Moderate to complete
Peripheral nerve	0.25%-0.5%	0.4 mL/kg (30 mL)	1-2 mg/kg (75-150 mg)	Moderate to complete
Ophthalmic	0.75%	5-15 mL	37.5-112.5 mg	Moderate to complete
Local infiltration	0.25%	60 mL	150 mg	Not applicable
Pain Management				
Levobupivacaine can be used epidurally with fentanyl or clonidine; dilutions for epidural administration should be made with preservative free 0.9% saline according to standard hospital procedures for sterility				
Labor analgesia (epidural bolus)	0.25%	10-20 mL	25-50 mg	Minimal to moderate
Postoperative pain (epidural infusion)	0.125%[1]-0.25%	4-10 mL/h	5-25 mg/h	Minimal to moderate

[1]0.125%: Adjunct therapy with fentanyl or clonidine.

Maximum dosage: Epidural doses up to 375 mg have been administered incrementally to patients during a surgical procedure.
Intraoperative block and postoperative pain: 695 mg in 24 hours
Postoperative epidural infusion over 24 hours: 570 mg
Single-fractionated injection for brachial plexus block: 300 mg
Additional Information Complete prescribing information for this medication should be consulted for additional detail.
Dosage Forms [DSC] = Discontinued product
Injection, solution [preservative free]: 2.5 mg/mL (10 mL, 30 mL); 5 mg/mL (10 mL, 30 mL); 7.5 mg/mL (10 mL, 30 mL) [DSC]

Levocabastine (LEE voe kab as teen)

U.S. Brand Names Livostin® [DSC]
Canadian Brand Names Livostin®
Index Terms Levocabastine Hydrochloride
Pharmacologic Category Antihistamine, H_1 Blocker, Ophthalmic
Use Treatment of allergic conjunctivitis
Pregnancy Risk Factor C
Medication Safety Issues
Sound-alike/look-alike issues:
Levocabastine may be confused with levobunolol, levocarnitine
Livostin® may be confused with lovastatin

International issues:
Livostin® may be confused with Limoxin® which is a brand name for amoxicillin in Mexico
Livostin® may be confused with Lovastin® which is a brand name for lovastatin in Malaysia and Poland
Dosage Children ≥12 years and Adults: Instill 1 drop in affected eye(s) 4 times/day for up to 2 weeks
Additional Information Complete prescribing information for this medication should be consulted for additional detail.
Dosage Forms [DSC] = Discontinued product
Suspension, ophthalmic: 0.05% (5 mL, 10 mL) [contains benzalkonium chloride] [DSC]

♦ **Levocabastine Hydrochloride** *see* Levocabastine *on page 997*

Levocarnitine (lee voe KAR ni teen)

U.S. Brand Names Carnitor®
Canadian Brand Names Carnitor®
Index Terms L-Carnitine
Pharmacologic Category Dietary Supplement
Use
Oral: Primary systemic carnitine deficiency; acute and chronic treatment of patients with an inborn error of metabolism which results in secondary carnitine deficiency
I.V.: Acute and chronic treatment of patients with an inborn error of metabolism which results in secondary carnitine deficiency; prevention and treatment of carnitine deficiency in patients with end-stage renal disease (ESRD) who are undergoing hemodialysis.
Pregnancy Risk Factor B
Pregnancy Implications Teratogenic effects were not observed in animal studies. There are no adequate and well-controlled studies in pregnant women. However, carnitine is a naturally occurring substance in mammalian metabolism.
(Continued)

Levocarnitine *(Continued)*

Lactation Excretion in breast milk unknown/use caution

Medication Safety Issues

Sound-alike/look-alike issues:

Levocarnitine may be confused with levocabastine

Warnings/Precautions Caution in patients with seizure disorders or in those at risk of seizures (CNS mass or medications which may lower seizure threshold). Both new-onset seizure activity as well as an increased frequency of seizures has been observed. Safety and efficacy of oral carnitine have not been established in ESRD. Chronic administration of high oral doses to patients with severely compromised renal function or ESRD patients on dialysis may result in accumulation of potentially toxic metabolites.

Adverse Reactions Frequencies noted with I.V. therapy (hemodialysis patients).

>10%:

Cardiovascular: Hypertension (18% to 21%), chest pain (6% to 15%)

Central nervous system: Headache (3% to 37%), dizziness (10% to 18%), fever (5% to 12%)

Endocrine & metabolic: Hypercalcemia (6% to 15%)

Gastrointestinal: Diarrhea (9% to 35%), vomiting (9% to 21%), abdominal pain (5% to 21%), nausea (9% to 12%)

Hematologic: Anemia (3% to 12%)

Neuromuscular & skeletal: Weakness (8% to 12%), paresthesia (3% to 12%)

Respiratory: Cough (10% to 18%), rhinitis (6% to 11%)

Miscellaneous: Infection (10% to 24%)

1% to 10%:

Cardiovascular: Tachycardia (5% to 9%), hemorrhage (2% to 9%), palpitation (3% to 8%), peripheral edema (3% to 6%), atrial fibrillation (2% to 6%), ECG abnormality (2% to 6%), vascular disorder (2% to 6%)

Central nervous system: Depression (5% to 6%), vertigo (2% to 6%)

Dermatologic: Rash (3% to 5%)

Endocrine & metabolic: Parathyroid disorder (2% to 6%)

Gastrointestinal: Taste perversion (2% to 9%), weight loss (3% to 8%), anorexia (3% to 6%), gastrointestinal disorder (2% to 6%), melena (2% to 6%), weight gain (2% to 6%)

Ocular: Amblyopia (3% to 6%), eye disorder (3% to 6%)

Respiratory: Bronchitis (3% to 5%)

Miscellaneous: Allergic reaction (2% to 6%)

Frequency not defined: Body odor, gastritis, seizures

Overdosage/Toxicology No reports of overdose. Easily removed by dialysis. Large doses may be associated with diarrhea.

Stability Intravenous solution: Store at 25°C (77°F). Compatible at concentrations between 0.5-8 mg/mL in 0.9% sodium chloride or lactated Ringer's solution. Stable in PVC bags for 24 hours.

Mechanism of Action Carnitine is a naturally occurring metabolic compound which functions as a carrier molecule for long-chain fatty acids within the mitochondria, facilitating energy production. Carnitine deficiency is associated with accumulation of excess acyl CoA esters and disruption of intermediary metabolism. Carnitine supplementation increases carnitine plasma concentrations. The effects on specific metabolic alterations have not been evaluated. ESRD patients on maintenance HD may have low plasma carnitine levels because of reduced intake of meat and dairy products, reduced renal synthesis, and dialytic losses. Certain clinical conditions (malaise, muscle weakness, cardiomyopathy and arrhythmias) in HD patients may be related to carnitine deficiency.

Pharmacodynamics/Kinetics

Metabolism: Hepatic (limited with moderate renal impairment), to trimethylamine (TMA) and trimethylamine N-oxide (TMAO)

Bioavailability: Oral: ~10% to 20%

Half-life elimination: 17.4 hours

Time to peak: Oral: 3.3 hours

Excretion: Urine (76%, 4% to 9% as unchanged drug); feces (<1%)

Dosage

Carnitine deficiency:

Oral:

Infants/Children: Initial: 50 mg/kg/day; titrate to 50-100 mg/kg/day in divided doses with a maximum dose of 3 g/day

Adults: 990 mg (tablet) 2-3 times/day or 1-3 g/day (solution)

I.V.: Children and Adults: 50 mg/kg/day in divided doses; titrate based on patient response. Maximum reported dose: 300 mg/kg. An equivalent loading dose may be used in patients in severe metabolic crisis.

ESRD patients on hemodialysis: I.V.: Adults: 20 mg/kg dry body weight as a slow 2- to 3-minute bolus after each dialysis session

Note: Safety and efficacy of oral carnitine have not been established in ESRD. Chronic administration of high **oral** doses to patients with severely compromised renal function or ESRD patients on dialysis may result in accumulation of **potentially toxic** metabolites.

Administration

Oral: Solution may be dissolved in either drink or liquid food, and should be consumed slowly. Doses should be spaced every 3-4 hours throughout the day, preferably during or following meals.

I.V.:

Hemodialysis patients: Injection should be administered over 2-3 minutes into the venous return line after each dialysis session.

Carnitine deficiency: Administer as a bolus dose over 2-3 minutes or by infusion. Doses should be administered every 3-6 hours

Monitoring Parameters Plasma concentrations should be obtained prior to beginning parenteral therapy, and should be monitored weekly to monthly. In metabolic disorders: monitor blood chemistry, vital signs, and plasma carnitine levels (maintain between 35-60 μmol/L). In

ESRD patients on dialysis: National Kidney Foundation guidelines recommend basing treatment on clinical signs and symptoms; evaluate response at 3-month intervals and discontinue if no clinical improvement noted within 9-12 months. Reimbursement may require documentation of a plasma free carnitine level <40 µmol/L.

Reference Range Normal carnitine levels are 40-50 µmol/L; levels should be maintained on therapy between 35-60 µmol/L

Additional Information Although supplemental carnitine has been shown to increase carnitine concentrations, effects on the signs and symptoms of carnitine deficiency have not been determined.

Dosage Forms
Capsule: 250 mg
Injection, solution: 200 mg/mL (5 mL, 12.5 mL)
　Carnitor®: 200 mg/mL (5 mL)
Solution, oral: 100 mg/mL (118 mL)
　Carnitor®: 100 mg/mL (118 mL) [cherry flavor]
Tablet: 330　mg, 500 mg
　Carnitor®: 330 mg

Levodopa and Carbidopa (lee voe DOE pa & kar bi DOE pa)

U.S. Brand Names Parcopa™; Sinemet®; Sinemet® CR
Canadian Brand Names Apo-Levocarb®; Apo-Levocarb® CR; Endo®-Levodopa/Carbidopa; Novo-Levocarbidopa; Nu-Levocarb®; Sinemet®; Sinemet® CR
Index Terms Carbidopa and Levodopa
Pharmacologic Category Anti-Parkinson's Agent, Dopamine Agonist
Additional Appendix Information
Parkinson's Agents on page 1895
Use Idiopathic Parkinson's disease; postencephalitic parkinsonism; symptomatic parkinsonism
Unlabeled/Investigational Use Restless leg syndrome
Pregnancy Risk Factor C
Pregnancy Implications Teratogenic effects were observed with levodopa and carbidopa in animal studies. There are case reports of levodopa crossing the placenta in humans.
Lactation Excretion in breast milk unknown/use caution
Contraindications Hypersensitivity to levodopa, carbidopa, or any component of the formulation; narrow-angle glaucoma; use of MAO inhibitors within prior 14 days (however, may be administered concomitantly with the manufacturer's recommended dose of an MAO inhibitor with selectivity for MAO type B); history of melanoma or undiagnosed skin lesions
Warnings/Precautions Use with caution in patients with history of cardiovascular disease (including myocardial infarction and arrhythmias); pulmonary diseases such as asthma, psychosis, wide-angle glaucoma, peptic ulcer disease; as well as in renal, hepatic, or endocrine disease. Sudden discontinuation of levodopa may cause a worsening of Parkinson's disease. Elderly may be more sensitive to CNS effects of levodopa. May cause or exacerbate dyskinesias. May cause orthostatic hypotension; Parkinson's disease patients appear to have an impaired capacity to respond to a postural challenge; use with caution in patients at risk of hypotension (such as those receiving antihypertensive drugs) or where transient hypotensive episodes would be poorly tolerated (cardiovascular disease or cerebrovascular disease). Observe patients closely for development of depression with concomitant suicidal tendencies. Has been associated with a syndrome resembling neuroleptic malignant syndrome on withdrawal or significant dosage reduction after long-term use. Protein in the diet should be distributed throughout the day to avoid fluctuations in levodopa absorption.
Adverse Reactions Frequency not defined.
Cardiovascular: Orthostatic hypotension, arrhythmia, chest pain, hypertension, syncope, palpitation, phlebitis
Central nervous system: Dizziness, anxiety, confusion, nightmares, headache, hallucinations, on-off phenomenon, decreased mental acuity, memory impairment, disorientation, delusions, euphoria, agitation, somnolence, insomnia, gait abnormalities, nervousness, ataxia, EPS, falling, psychosis, peripheral neuropathy, seizure (causal relationship not established)
Dermatologic: Rash, alopecia, malignant melanoma, hypersensitivity (angioedema, urticaria, pruritus, bullous lesions, Henoch-Schönlein purpura)
Endocrine & metabolic: Increased libido
Gastrointestinal: Anorexia, nausea, vomiting, constipation, GI bleeding, duodenal ulcer, diarrhea, dyspepsia, taste alterations, sialorrhea, heartburn
Genitourinary: Discoloration of urine, urinary frequency
Hematologic: Hemolytic anemia, agranulocytosis, thrombocytopenia, leukopenia; decreased hemoglobin and hematocrit; abnormalities in AST and ALT, LDH, bilirubin, BUN, Coombs' test
Neuromuscular & skeletal: Choreiform and involuntary movements, paresthesia, bone pain, shoulder pain, muscle cramps, weakness
Ocular: Blepharospasm, oculogyric crises (may be associated with acute dystonic reactions)
Renal: Difficult urination
Respiratory: Dyspnea, cough
Miscellaneous: Hiccups, discoloration of sweat, diaphoresis (increased)
Overdosage/Toxicology Symptoms include palpitations, arrhythmias, spasms, and hypotension. May cause hypertension or hypotension. Treatment is supportive. Initiate gastric lavage, administer I.V. fluids judiciously and monitor ECG. Use fluids judiciously to maintain pressures. May precipitate a variety of arrhythmias.
Drug Interactions
Increased Effect/Toxicity: Concurrent use of levodopa with nonselective MAO inhibitors may result in hypertensive reactions via an increased storage and release of dopamine, norepinephrine, or both. Use with carbidopa to minimize reactions if combination is necessary; otherwise avoid combination.
(Continued)

Levodopa and Carbidopa *(Continued)*

Decreased Effect: Antipsychotics, benzodiazepines, L-methionine, phenytoin, pyridoxine, spiramycin, and tacrine may inhibit the antiparkinsonian effects of levodopa; monitor for reduced effect. Antipsychotics may inhibit the antiparkinsonian effects of levodopa via dopamine receptor blockade. Use antipsychotics with low dopamine blockade (clozapine, olanzapine, quetiapine). High-protein diets may inhibit levodopa's efficacy; avoid high protein foods. Iron binds levodopa and reduces its bioavailability; separate doses of iron and levodopa.

Ethanol/Nutrition/Herb Interactions

Ethanol: Avoid ethanol (due to CNS depression).

Food: Avoid high protein diets and high intakes of vitamin B_6.

Herb/Nutraceutical: Avoid kava kava (may decrease effects). Pyridoxine in doses >10-25 mg (for levodopa alone) or higher doses >200 mg/day (for levodopa/carbidopa) may decrease efficacy.

Stability Store at 20°C to 25°C (68°F to 77°F); excursions permitted between 15°C to 30°C (59°F to 86°F). Protect from light and moisture.

Mechanism of Action Parkinson's symptoms are due to a lack of striatal dopamine; levodopa circulates in the plasma to the blood-brain-barrier (BBB), where it crosses, to be converted by striatal enzymes to dopamine; carbidopa inhibits the peripheral plasma breakdown of levodopa by inhibiting its decarboxylation, and thereby increases available levodopa at the BBB

Pharmacodynamics/Kinetics

Duration: Variable, 6-12 hours; longer with sustained release forms

See individual agents.

Dosage Oral: Adults:

Parkinson's disease:

Immediate release tablet:

Initial: Carbidopa 25 mg/levodopa 100 mg 3 times/day

Dosage adjustment: Alternate tablet strengths may be substituted according to individual carbidopa/levodopa requirements. Increase by 1 tablet every other day as necessary, except when using the carbidopa 25 mg/levodopa 250 mg tablets where increases should be made using 1/2-1 tablet every 1-2 days. Use of more than 1 dosage strength or dosing 4 times/day may be required (maximum: 8 tablets of any strength/day or 200 mg of carbidopa and 2000 mg of levodopa)

Sustained release tablet:

Initial: Carbidopa 50 mg/levodopa 200 mg 2 times/day, at intervals not <6 hours

Dosage adjustment: May adjust every 3 days; intervals should be between 4-8 hours during the waking day (maximum: 8 tablets/day)

Restless leg syndrome (unlabeled use): Carbidopa 25 mg/levodopa 100 mg given 30-60 minutes before bedtime; may repeat dose once

Elderly: Initial: Carbidopa 25 mg/levodopa 100 mg twice daily, increase as necessary

Dietary Considerations Levodopa peak serum concentrations may be decreased if taken with food. High protein diets (>2 g/kg) may decrease the efficacy of levodopa via competition with amino acids in crossing the blood-brain barrier.

Parcopa™: Contains phenylalanine 3.4 mg per 10/100 mg and 25/100 mg strengths; phenylalanine 8.4 mg in 25/250 mg strength

Administration Space doses evenly over the waking hours. Give with meals to decrease GI upset. Sustained release product should not be crushed. Orally-disintegrating tablets do not require water; the tablet should disintegrate on the tongue's surface before swallowing.

Monitoring Parameters Blood pressure, standing and sitting/supine; symptoms of parkinsonism, dyskinesias, mental status

Test Interactions False-positive reaction for urinary glucose with Clinitest®; false-negative reaction using Clinistix®; false-positive urine ketones with Acetest®, Ketostix®, Labstix®

Additional Information 50-100 mg/day of carbidopa is needed to block the peripheral conversion of levodopa to dopamine. "On-off" (a clinical syndrome characterized by sudden periods of drug activity/inactivity), can be managed by giving smaller, more frequent doses of Sinemet® or adding a dopamine agonist or selegiline; when adding a new agent, doses of Sinemet® can usually be decreased. Protein in the diet should be distributed throughout the day to avoid fluctuations in levodopa absorption. Levodopa is the drug of choice when rigidity is the predominant presenting symptom.

Conversion from levodopa to carbidopa/levodopa: **Note:** Levodopa must be discontinued at least 12 hours prior to initiation of levodopa/carbidopa:

Initial dose: Levodopa portion of carbidopa/levodopa should be at least 25% of previous levodopa therapy.

Levodopa <1500 mg/day: Sinemet® or Parcopa™ (levodopa 25 mg/carbidopa 100 mg) 3-4 times/day

Levodopa ≥1500 mg/day: Sinemet® or Parcopa™ (levodopa 25 mg/carbidopa 250 mg) 3-4 times/day

Conversion from immediate release carbidopa/levodopa (Sinemet® or Parcopa™) to Sinemet® CR (50/200):

Sinemet® or Parcopa™ [total daily dose of levodopa]/Sinemet® CR:

Sinemet® or Parcopa™ (levodopa 300-400 mg/day): Sinemet® CR (50/200) 1 tablet twice daily

Sinemet® or Parcopa™ (levodopa 500-600 mg/day): Sinemet® CR (50/200) 1 1/2 tablets twice daily or 1 tablet 3 times/day

Sinemet® or Parcopa™ (levodopa 700-800 mg/day): Sinemet® CR (50/200) 4 tablets in 3 or more divided doses

Sinemet® or Parcopa™ (levodopa 900-1000 mg/day): Sinemet® CR (50/200) 5 tablets in 3 or more divided doses

Intervals between doses of Sinemet® CR should be 4-8 hours while awake; when divided doses are not equal, smaller doses should be given toward the end of the day.

Dosage Forms

Tablet immediate release (Sinemet®):

10/100: Carbidopa 10 mg and levodopa 100 mg

25/100: Carbidopa 25 mg and levodopa 100 mg
25/250: Carbidopa 25 mg and levodopa 250 mg
Tablet, immediate release, orally disintegrating (Parcopa™):
10/100: Carbidopa 10 mg and levodopa 100 mg [contains phenylalanine 3.4 mg/tablet; mint flavor]
25/100: Carbidopa 25 mg and levodopa 100 mg [contains phenylalanine 3.4 mg/tablet; mint flavor]
25/250: Carbidopa 25 mg and levodopa 250 mg [contains phenylalanine 8.4 mg/tablet; mint flavor]
Tablet, sustained release (Sinemet® CR):
Carbidopa 25 mg and levodopa 100 mg
Carbidopa 50 mg and levodopa 200 mg

Levodopa, Carbidopa, and Entacapone
(lee voe DOE pa, kar bi DOE pa, & en TA ka pone)

U.S. Brand Names Stalevo™
Index Terms Carbidopa, Levodopa, and Entacapone; Entacapone, Carbidopa, and Levodopa
Pharmacologic Category Anti-Parkinson's Agent, COMT Inhibitor; Anti-Parkinson's Agent, Dopamine Agonist
Use Treatment of idiopathic Parkinson's disease
Pregnancy Risk Factor C
Dosage Oral: Adults: Parkinson's disease:
Note: All strengths of Stalevo™ contain a carbidopa/levodopa ratio of 1:4 plus entacapone 200 mg.
Dose should be individualized based on therapeutic response; doses may be adjusted by changing strength or adjusting interval. Fractionated doses are not recommended and only 1 tablet should be given at each dosing interval; maximum dose: 8 tablets/day (equivalent to entacapone 1600 mg/day)
Patients previously treated with carbidopa/levodopa immediate release tablets (ratio of 1:4):
With current entacapone therapy: May switch directly to corresponding strength of combination tablet. No data available on transferring patients from controlled release preparations or products with a 1:10 ratio of carbidopa/levodopa.
Without entacapone therapy:
If current levodopa dose is >600 mg/day: Levodopa dose reduction may be required when adding entacapone to therapy; therefore, titrate dose using individual products first (carbidopa/levodopa immediate release with a ratio of 1:4 plus entacapone 200 mg); then transfer to combination product once stabilized.
If current levodopa dose is <600 mg without dyskinesias: May transfer to corresponding dose of combination product; monitor, dose reduction of levodopa may be required.
Dosage adjustment in renal impairment: Use caution with severe renal impairment; specific dosing recommendations not available
Dosage adjustment in hepatic impairment: Use with caution; specific dosing recommendations not available
Additional Information Complete prescribing information for this medication should be consulted for additional detail.
Dosage Forms Tablet:
50: Carbidopa 12.5 mg, levodopa 50 mg, and entacapone 200 mg
100: Carbidopa 25 mg, levodopa 100 mg, and entacapone 200 mg
150: Carbidopa 37.5 mg, levodopa 150 mg, and entacapone 200 mg

♦ **Levo-Dromoran®** see Levorphanol on page 1006

Levofloxacin (lee voe FLOKS a sin)

U.S. Brand Names Iquix®; Levaquin®; Quixin™
Canadian Brand Names Levaquin®; Novo-Levofloxacin
Pharmacologic Category Antibiotic, Quinolone
Additional Appendix Information
Antimicrobial Drugs of Choice on page 1981
Community-Acquired Pneumonia in Adults on page 1999
Prevention of Wound Infection and Sepsis in Surgical Patients on page 1964
Treatment of Sexually Transmitted Infections on page 2007
Tuberculosis on page 2010
Use
Systemic: Treatment of mild, moderate, or severe infections caused by susceptible organisms. Includes the treatment of community-acquired pneumonia, including multidrug resistant strains of *S. pneumoniae* (MDRSP); nosocomial pneumonia; chronic bronchitis (acute bacterial exacerbation); acute bacterial sinusitis; urinary tract infection (uncomplicated or complicated), including acute pyelonephritis caused by *E. coli*; prostatitis (chronic bacterial); skin or skin structure infections (uncomplicated or complicated); reduce incidence or disease progression of inhalational anthrax (postexposure)
Ophthalmic: Treatment of bacterial conjunctivitis caused by susceptible organisms (Quixin™ 0.5% ophthalmic solution); treatment of corneal ulcer caused by susceptible organisms (Iquix® 1.5% ophthalmic solution)
Unlabeled/Investigational Use Diverticulitis, enterocolitis, (*Shigella* sp) gonococcal infections, Legionnaires' disease, peritonitis, PID
Pregnancy Risk Factor C
Pregnancy Implications Reports of arthropathy (observed in immature animals and reported rarely in humans) have limited the use of fluoroquinolones in pregnancy. Teratogenic effects were not observed with levofloxacin in animal studies; however, decreased body weight and increased fetal mortality were reported. Based on limited data, quinolones are not expected to be a major human teratogen. Although quinolone antibiotics should not be used as first-line
(Continued)

Levofloxacin *(Continued)*

agents during pregnancy, when considering treatment for life-threatening infection and/or prolonged duration of therapy, the potential risk to the fetus must be balanced against the severity of the potential illness.

Lactation Excretion in breast milk unknown/not recommended

Contraindications Hypersensitivity to levofloxacin, any component of the formulation, or other quinolones

Warnings/Precautions

Systemic: Not recommended in children <18 years of age; CNS stimulation may occur (tremor, restlessness, confusion, and very rarely hallucinations or seizures). Potential for seizures, although very rare, may be increased with concomitant NSAID therapy. Use with caution in individuals at risk of seizures, with known or suspected CNS disorders or renal dysfunction; use caution to avoid possible photosensitivity reactions during and for several days following fluoroquinolone therapy

Rare cases of torsade de pointes have been reported in patients receiving levofloxacin. Use caution in patients with known prolongation of QT interval, bradycardia, hypokalemia, hypomagnesemia, or in those receiving concurrent therapy with Class Ia or Class III antiarrhythmics.

Severe hypersensitivity reactions, including anaphylaxis, have occurred with quinolone therapy. If an allergic reaction occurs (itching, urticaria, dyspnea or facial edema, loss of consciousness, tingling, cardiovascular collapse), discontinue drug immediately. Prolonged use may result in superinfection; pseudomembranous colitis may occur and should be considered in all patients who present with diarrhea. Tendon inflammation and/or rupture has been reported; risk may be increased with concurrent corticosteroids, particularly in the elderly. Discontinue at first sign of tendon inflammation or pain. Peripheral neuropathies have been linked to levofloxacin use; discontinue if numbness, tingling, or weakness develops. Quinolones may exacerbate myasthenia gravis.

Ophthalmic solution: For topical use only. Do not inject subconjunctivally or introduce into anterior chamber of the eye. Contact lenses should not be worn during treatment for bacterial conjunctivitis. Safety and efficacy in children <1 year of age (Quixin™) or <6 years of age (Iquix®) have not been established. **Note:** Indications for ophthalmic solutions are product concentration-specific and should not be used interchangeably.

Adverse Reactions

1% to 10%:

Cardiovascular: Chest pain (1%)

Central nervous system: Headache (6%), insomnia (5%), dizziness (2%), fatigue (1%), pain (1%), fever

Dermatologic: Pruritus (1%), rash (1%)

Gastrointestinal: Nausea (7%), diarrhea (5%), abdominal pain (3%), constipation (3%), dyspepsia (2%), vomiting (2%), flatulence (1%)

Genitourinary: Vaginitis (1%)

Hematologic: Lymphopenia (2%)

Ocular (with ophthalmic solution use): Decreased vision (transient), foreign body sensation, transient ocular burning, ocular pain or discomfort, photophobia

Respiratory: Pharyngitis (4%), dyspnea (1%), rhinitis (1%), sinusitis (1%)

<1% (Limited to important or life-threatening):

Systemic: Acute renal failure; allergic reaction (including pneumonitis rash, pneumonitis, and anaphylaxis); agranulocytosis, anaphylactoid reaction, anorexia, anxiety, arrhythmia (including atrial/ventricular tachycardia/fibrillation and torsade de pointes), arthralgia, ascites, bradycardia, bronchospasm, carcinoma, cardiac failure, cerebrovascular disorder, cholecystitis, cholelithiasis, confusion, cnjunctivitis, dehydration, depression, ear disorder, edema, EEG abnormalities, electrolyte abnormality, encephalopathy, eosinophilia, erythema multiforme, gangrene, GI hemorrhage, granulocytopenia, hallucination, heart block, hematoma, hemolytic anemia, hemoptysis, hepatic failure, hyper-/hypotension, infection, INR increased, intestinal obstruction, intracranial hypertension, involuntary muscle contractions, jaundice, leukocytosis, leukopenia, leukorrhea, lymphadenopathy, MI, migraine, multiple organ failure, pancreatitis, paralysis, paresthesia, peripheral neuropathy, phlebitis, photosensitivity (<0.1%), pleural effusion, postural hypotension, prothrombin time increased/decreased, pseudomembraneous colitis, pulmonary edema,pulmonary embolism, purpura, QT$_c$ prolongation, respiratory depression, respiratory disorder, rhabdomyolysis, seizure, skin disorder, somnolence,speech disorder, Stevens-Johnson syndrome, stupor, syncope, taste perversion, tendon rupture, tongue edema, transaminases increased, thrombocythemia, thrombocytopenia, tremor, WBC abnormality

Overdosage/Toxicology Symptoms include acute renal failure and seizures. Treatment should include GI decontamination and supportive care. Not removed by peritoneal or hemodialysis.

Drug Interactions

Increased Effect/Toxicity: Levofloxacin may increase the effects/toxicity of glyburide and warfarin. Concomitant use with corticosteroids may increase the risk of tendon rupture. Concomitant use with other QT$_c$-prolonging agents (eg, Class Ia and Class III antiarrhythmics, erythromycin, cisapride, antipsychotics, and cyclic antidepressants) may result in arrhythmias, such as torsade de pointes. Probenecid may increase levofloxacin levels. Concomitant use with NSAIDs may rarely increase risk of seizure.

Decreased Effect: Concurrent administration of metal cations, including most antacids, oral electrolyte supplements, quinapril, sucralfate, some didanosine formulations (pediatric powder for oral suspension), and other highly-buffered oral drugs, may decrease quinolone levels; separate doses.

Stability

Solution for injection:

Vial: Store at room temperature. Protect from light. When diluted to 5 mg/mL in a compatible I.V. fluid, solution is stable for 72 hours when stored at room temperature; stable for 14 days when stored under refrigeration. When frozen, stable for 6 months; do not refreeze. Do not thaw in microwave or by bath immersion.

Premixed: Store at ≤25°C (77°F); do not freeze. Brief exposure to 40°C (104°F) does not affect product. Protect from light.

Tablet, oral solution: Store at 25°C (77°F); excursions permitted to 15°C to 25°C (59°F to 77°F).

Ophthalmic solution: Store at 15°C to 25°C (59°F to 77°F).

Mechanism of Action As the S (-) enantiomer of the fluoroquinolone, ofloxacin, levofloxacin, inhibits DNA-gyrase in susceptible organisms thereby inhibits relaxation of supercoiled DNA and promotes breakage of DNA strands. DNA gyrase (topoisomerase II), is an essential bacterial enzyme that maintains the superhelical structure of DNA and is required for DNA replication and transcription, DNA repair, recombination, and transposition.

Pharmacodynamics/Kinetics
Absorption: Rapid and complete
Distribution: V_d: 1.25 L/kg; CSF concentrations ~15% of serum levels; high concentrations are achieved in prostate, lung, and gynecological tissues, sinus, saliva
Protein binding: 50%
Metabolism: Minimally hepatic
Bioavailability: 99%
Half-life elimination: 6-8 hours
Time to peak, serum: 1-2 hours
Excretion: Primarily urine (as unchanged drug)

Dosage Note: Sequential therapy (intravenous to oral) may be instituted based on prescriber's discretion.
Usual dosage range:
Children ≥1 year: Ophthalmic: 1-2 drops every 2-6 hours
Adults:
Ophthalmic: 1-2 drops every 2-6 hours
Oral, I.V.: 250-500 mg every 24 hours; severe or complicated infections: 750 mg every 24 hours

Indication-specific dosing:
Children ≥1 year and Adults: Ophthalmic:
Conjunctivitis (0.5% ophthalmic solution):
Treatment day 1 and day 2: Instill 1-2 drops into affected eye(s) every 2 hours while awake, up to 8 times/day
Treatment day 3 through day 7: Instill 1-2 drops into affected eye(s) every 4 hours while awake, up to 4 times/day
Children ≥6 years and Adults: Ophthalmic:
Corneal ulceration (1.5% ophthalmic solution): Treatment day 1 through day 3: Instill 1-2 drops into affected eye(s) every 30 minutes to 2 hours while awake and 4-6 hours after retiring.

Adults: Oral, I.V.:
Anthrax (inhalational): 500 mg every 24 hours for 60 days, beginning as soon as possible after exposure
Chronic bronchitis (acute bacterial exacerbation): 500 mg every 24 hours for at least 7 days
Diverticulitis, peritonitis (unlabeled use): 750 mg every 24 hours for 7-10 days; use adjunctive metronidazole therapy
Dysenteric enterocolitis, _Shigella spp._ (unlabeled use): 500 mg every 24 hours for 3-5 days
Gonococcal infection (unlabeled use):
Cervicitis, urethritis: 250 mg for one dose with azithromycin or doxycycline
Disseminated infection: 250 mg I.V. once daily; 24 hours after symptoms improve may change to 500 mg orally every 24 hours to complete total therapy of 7 days
Epididymo-orchitis: 750 mg once daily for 10-14 days
Legionella (unlabeled use): 500 mg every 24 hours for 10-21 days or 750 mg every 24 hours for 5 days
Pelvic inflammatory disease (unlabeled use): 500 mg every 24 hours for 14 days with adjunctive metronidazole
Pneumonia:
Community-acquired: 500 mg every 24 hours for 7-14 days or 750 mg every 24 hours for 5 days (efficacy of 5-day regimen for MDRSP not established)
Nosocomial: 750 mg every 24 hours for 7-14 days
Prostatitis (chronic bacterial): 500 mg every 24 hours for 28 days
Sinusitis (bacterial, acute): 500 mg every 24 hours for 10-14 days or 750 mg every 24 hours for 5 days
Skin and skin structure infections:
Uncomplicated: 500 mg every 24 hours for 7-10 days
Complicated: 750 mg every 24 hours for 7-14 days
Traveler's diarrhea (unlabeled use): 500 mg for one dose
Urinary tract infections:
Uncomplicated: 250 mg once daily for 3 days
Complicated, including pyelonephritis: 250 mg once daily for 10 days

Dosage adjustment in renal impairment:
Chronic bronchitis, acute bacterial sinusitis, uncomplicated skin infection, community-acquired pneumonia, chronic bacterial prostatitis, or inhalational anthrax: Initial: 500 mg, then as follows:
Cl_{cr} 20-49 mL/minute: 250 mg every 24 hours
Cl_{cr} 10-19 mL/minute: 250 mg every 48 hours
Hemodialysis/CAPD: 250 mg every 48 hours
Uncomplicated UTI: No dosage adjustment required
Complicated UTI, acute pyelonephritis: Cl_{cr} 10-19 mL/minute: 250 mg every 48 hours
Complicated skin infection, acute bacterial sinusitis, community-acquired pneumonia, or nosocomial pneumonia: Initial: 750 mg, then as follows:
Cl_{cr} 20-49 mL/minute: 750 mg every 48 hours
Cl_{cr} 10-19 mL/minute: 500 mg every 48 hours
Hemodialysis/CAPD: 500 mg every 48 hours
(Continued)

Levofloxacin *(Continued)*

Dietary Considerations Tablets may be taken without regard to meals. Oral solution should be administered on an empty stomach (1 hour before or 2 hours after a meal).

Administration

Oral: Tablets may be administered without regard to meals. Oral solution should be administered 1 hour before or 2 hours after meals.

I.V.: Infuse 250-500 mg I.V. solution over 60 minutes; infuse 750 mg I.V. solution over 90 minutes. Too rapid of infusion can lead to hypotension. Avoid administration through an intravenous line with a solution containing multivalent cations (eg, magnesium, calcium).

Monitoring Parameters Evaluation of organ system functions (renal, hepatic, ophthalmologic, and hematopoietic) is recommended periodically during therapy; the possibility of crystalluria should be assessed; WBC and signs of infection

Test Interactions Some quinolones may produce a false-positive urine screening result for opiates using commercially-available immunoassay kits. This has been demonstrated most consistently for levofloxacin and ofloxacin, but other quinolones have shown cross-reactivity in certain assay kits. Confirmation of positive opiate screens by more specific methods should be considered.

Dosage Forms

Infusion [premixed in D_5W] (Levaquin®): 250 mg (50 mL); 500 mg (100 mL); 750 mg (150 mL)

Injection, solution [preservative free] (Levaquin®): 25 mg/mL (20 mL, 30 mL)

Solution, ophthalmic:

Iquix®: 1.5% (5 mL)

Quixin™: 0.5% (5 mL) [contains benzalkonium chloride]

Solution, oral (Levaquin®): 25 mg/mL (480 mL) [contains benzyl alcohol]

Tablet (Levaquin®): 250 mg, 500 mg, 750 mg

Levaquin® Leva-Pak: 750 mg (5s)

Levonorgestrel *(LEE voe nor jes trel)*

U.S. Brand Names Mirena®; Plan B® [RX/OTC]

Canadian Brand Names Mirena®; Norplant® Implant; Plan B™

Index Terms LNg 20

Pharmacologic Category Contraceptive; Progestin

Use Prevention of pregnancy

Restrictions Plan B® is approved for OTC use by women ≥18 years of age and available by prescription only for women ≤17 years of age. Sales of Plan B® will be limited to pharmacies or healthcare clinics with a valid license to distribute prescription products. Because there will be one package for both OTC and prescription use, pharmacies are required to keep the product behind the counter.

Pregnancy Risk Factor X

Pregnancy Implications Epidemiologic studies have not shown an increased risk of birth defects when used prior to pregnancy or inadvertently during early pregnancy, although rare reports of congenital anomalies have been reported.

Intrauterine system: Women who become pregnant with an IUD in place risk septic abortion (septic shock and death may occur), removal of IUD may result in pregnancy loss. In addition, miscarriage, premature labor, and premature delivery may occur if pregnancy is continued with IUD in place.

Lactation Enters breast milk/use caution (AAP rates "compatible")

Contraindications Hypersensitivity to levonorgestrel or any component of the formulation; undiagnosed abnormal uterine bleeding, active hepatic disease or malignant tumors, known or suspected carcinoma of the breast; pregnancy

Additional product-specific contraindications: Intrauterine system: Congenital or acquired uterine anomaly, acute pelvic inflammatory disease, history of pelvic inflammatory disease (unless there has been a subsequent intrauterine pregnancy), postpartum endometritis, infected abortion within past 3 months, known or suspected uterine or cervical neoplasia, unresolved/abnormal Pap smear, untreated acute cervicitis or vaginitis, patient or partner with multiple sexual partners, conditions which increase susceptibility to infections (ie, leukemia, AIDS, I.V. drug abuse), unremoved IUD, history of ectopic pregnancy, conditions which predispose to ectopic pregnancy; genital actinomycosis

Note: A previously available levonorgestrel product also had the following contraindications: Active thrombophlebitis, or thromboembolic disorders (current or history of); history of intracranial hypertension

Warnings/Precautions Menstrual bleeding patterns may be altered, missed menstrual periods should not be used to identify early pregnancy. These products do not protect against HIV infection or other sexually-transmitted diseases. Patients presenting with lower abdominal pain should be evaluated for follicular atresia and ectopic pregnancy. Patients receiving enzyme-inducing medications should be evaluated for an alternative method of contraception. Levonorgestrel may affect glucose tolerance, monitor serum glucose in patients with diabetes. Safety and efficacy for use in renal or hepatic impairment have not been established. Use with caution in conditions that may be aggravated by fluid retention, depression, or history of migraine. Only for use in women of reproductive age.

Use of combination hormonal contraceptives increases the risk of cardiovascular side effects in women who smoke cigarettes, especially those who are >35 years of age; although this may be an estrogen-related effect, the risk with progestin-only contraceptives is not known and women should be strongly advised not to smoke. Combination hormonal contraceptives may lead to increased risk of myocardial infarction and should be used with caution in patients with risk factors for coronary artery disease; the actual risk with progestin-only contraceptives is not known, however, there have been postmarketing reports of myocardial infarction in women using levonorgestrel-only contraception. May increase the risk of thromboembolism; discontinue therapy if this occurs. Combination hormonal contraceptives may have a dose-related risk of vascular disease and hypertension; strokes have also been reported with postmarketing use of levonorgestrel-only contraception. Women with hypertension should be encouraged to use a nonhormonal form of contraception. The use of combination hormonal contraceptives has been associated with a slight increase in frequency of breast cancer (studies are not consistent); studies with progestin only contraceptives have been similar. Retinal thrombosis has been reported (rarely) with combination hormonal contraceptives and may be related to the estrogen component, however, progestin-only therapy should also be discontinued with unexplained partial or complete loss of vision.

Additional formulation-specific warnings:

Intrauterine system: Increased incidence of group A streptococcal sepsis and pelvic inflammatory disease (may be asymptomatic). May perforate uterus or cervix; risk of perforation is increased in lactating women. Partial penetration or embedment in the myometrium may decrease effectiveness and lead to difficult removal. Postpartum insertion should be delayed for 6 weeks or until uterine involution is complete. Use caution in patients with coagulopathy or receiving anticoagulants

Oral tablet: Not intended to be used for routine contraception and will not terminate an existing pregnancy

Adverse Reactions

Intrauterine system:
>5%:
  Cardiovascular: Hypertension
  Central nervous system: Headache, depression, nervousness
  Dermatologic: Acne, skin disorder
  Endocrine & metabolic: Breast pain, dysmenorrhea, decreased libido, abnormal Pap smear, amenorrhea (20% at 1 year), enlarged follicles (12%)
  Gastrointestinal: Abdominal pain, nausea, weight gain
  Genitourinary: Leukorrhea, vaginitis
  Neuromuscular & skeletal: Back pain
  Respiratory: Upper respiratory tract infection, sinusitis
<3%: Alopecia, anemia, cervicitis, dyspareunia, eczema, failed insertion, migraine, sepsis, vomiting

Oral tablets:
>10%:
  Central nervous system: Fatigue (17%), headache (17%), dizziness (11%)
  Endocrine & metabolic: Heavier menstrual bleeding (14%), lighter menstrual bleeding (12%), breast tenderness (11%)
  Gastrointestinal: Nausea (23%), abdominal pain (18%)
1% to 10%: Gastrointestinal: Vomiting (6%), diarrhea (5%)

Drug Interactions
  Cytochrome P450 Effect: Substrate of CYP3A4 (major)
  Decreased Effect: CYP3A4 inducers may decrease the levels/effects of levonorgestrel; example inducers include aminoglutethimide, carbamazepine, nafcillin, nevirapine, phenobarbital, phenytoin, and rifamycins.

Ethanol/Nutrition/Herb Interactions Herb/Nutraceutical: St John's wort (an enzyme inducer) may decrease serum levels of levonorgestrel.

Stability Store at room temperature of 25°C (77°F).

Mechanism of Action Pregnancy may be prevented through several mechanisms: Thickening of cervical mucus, which inhibits sperm passage through the uterus and sperm survival; inhibition of ovulation, from a negative feedback mechanism on the hypothalamus, leading to reduced secretion of follicle stimulating hormone (FSH) and luteinizing hormone (LH); inhibition of implantation. Levonorgestrel is not effective once the implantation process has begun.

Pharmacodynamics/Kinetics
  Duration: Intrauterine system: Up to 5 years
  Absorption: Oral: Rapid and complete
  Protein binding: Highly bound to albumin (~50%) and sex hormone-binding globulin (~47%)
  Metabolism: To inactive metabolites
  Half-life elimination: Oral: ~24 hours
  Excretion: Primarily urine

Dosage Adults: Females:
  Long-term prevention of pregnancy: Intrauterine system: To be inserted into uterine cavity; should be inserted within 7 days of onset of menstruation or immediately after 1st trimester abortion; releases 20 mcg levonorgestrel/day over 5 years. May be removed and replaced with a new unit at anytime during menstrual cycle; do not leave any one system in place for >5 years
  Emergency contraception: Oral tablet: One 0.75 mg tablet as soon as possible within 72 hours of unprotected sexual intercourse; a second 0.75 mg tablet should be taken 12 hours after the first dose; may be used at any time during menstrual cycle

  Dosage adjustment in renal impairment: Safety and efficacy have not been established
  Dosage adjustment in hepatic impairment: Safety and efficacy have not been established

  Elderly: Not intended for use in postmenopausal women

Administration Intrauterine system: Inserted in the uterine cavity, to a depth of 6-9 cm, with the provided insertion device; should not be forced into the uterus

Monitoring Parameters Monitor for prolonged menstrual bleeding, amenorrhea, irregularity of menses, Pap smear, blood pressure, serum glucose in patients with diabetes, LDL levels in patients with hyperlipidemias; re-examine following first menses post-insertion of IUD

Reference Range Contraceptive protection usually with plasma levonorgestrel concentrations of 0.29-0.35 ng/mL. Due to variability in individual responses, blood levels alone are not predictive of pregnancy risk.

Test Interactions Decreased concentrations of sex hormone-binding globulin; decreased thyroxine concentrations (slight); increased triiodothyronine uptake
(Continued)

Levonorgestrel *(Continued)*

Additional Information Intrauterine system: The cumulative 5-year pregnancy rate is ~0.7 pregnancies/100 users. Over 70% of women in the trials had previously used IUDs. The reported pregnancy rate after 12 months was ≤0.2 pregnancies/100 users. Approximately 80% of women who wish to conceive have become pregnant within 12 months of device removal. The recommended patient profile for this product: A woman who has at least one child, is in a stable and mutually-monogamous relationship, no history of pelvic inflammatory disease, and no history of ectopic pregnancy or predisposition to ectopic pregnancy.

Oral tablet: When used as directed for emergency contraception, the expected pregnancy rate is decreased from 8% to 1%. Approximately 87% of women have their next menstrual period at approximately the expected time. A rapid return to fertility following use is expected.

Dosage Forms

Intrauterine device:

  Mirena®: 52 mg levonorgestrel/unit [releases levonorgestrel 20 mcg/day]

Tablet:

  Plan B®: 0.75 mg

♦ **Levonorgestrel and Estradiol** *see* Estradiol and Levonorgestrel *on page 624*

♦ **Levonorgestrel and Ethinyl Estradiol** *see* Ethinyl Estradiol and Levonorgestrel *on page 653*

♦ **Levophed®** *see* Norepinephrine *on page 1240*

♦ **Levora®** *see* Ethinyl Estradiol and Levonorgestrel *on page 653*

Levorphanol *(lee VOR fa nole)*

U.S. Brand Names Levo-Dromoran®

Index Terms Levorphanol Tartrate; Levorphan Tartrate

Pharmacologic Category Analgesic, Opioid

Additional Appendix Information

Narcotic Agonists *on page 1888*

Use Relief of moderate to severe pain; also used parenterally for preoperative sedation and an adjunct to nitrous oxide/oxygen anesthesia

Restrictions C-II

Pregnancy Risk Factor B/D (prolonged use or high doses at term)

Lactation Excretion in breast milk unknown/not recommended

Contraindications Hypersensitivity to levorphanol or any component of the formulation; pregnancy (prolonged use or high doses at term)

Warnings/Precautions An opioid-containing analgesic regimen should be tailored to each patient's needs and based upon the type of pain being treated (acute versus chronic), the route of administration, degree of tolerance for opioids (naive versus chronic user), age, weight, and medical condition. The optimal analgesic dose varies widely among patients. Doses should be titrated to pain relief/prevention.

May cause CNS depression, which may impair physical or mental abilities; patients must be cautioned about performing tasks which require mental alertness (eg, operating machinery or driving). Effects may be potentiated when used with other sedative drugs or ethanol. Use with caution in patients with hypersensitivity reactions to other phenanthrene derivative opioid agonists (morphine, hydrocodone, hydromorphone, oxycodone, oxymorphone); respiratory diseases including asthma, emphysema, COPD, hypothiroidism, head trauma, morbid obesity, adrenal insufficiency, prostatic hyperplasia/urinary stricture, or severe liver or renal insufficiency; some preparations contain sulfites which may cause allergic reactions; tolerance or dependence may result from extended use. Use with caution in patients with biliary tract dysfunction; acute pancreatitis may cause constriction of sphincter of Oddi. May cause hypotension; use with caution in patients with depleted blood volume or drugs which may exaggerate hypotensive effects (including phenothiazines or general anesthetics). May obscure diagnosis or clinical course of patients with acute abdominal conditions. Concurrent use of agonist/antagonist analgesics may precipitate withdrawal symptoms and/or reduced analgesic efficacy in patients following prolonged therapy with mu opioid agonists. Abrupt discontinuation following prolonged use may also lead to withdrawal symptoms. Elderly and debilitated patients may be particularly susceptible to the adverse of narcotics. Safety and efficacy have not been established in children.

Adverse Reactions Frequency not defined.

Cardiovascular: Palpitations, hypotension, bradycardia, peripheral vasodilation, cardiac arrest, shock, tachycardia

Central nervous system: CNS depression, fatigue, drowsiness, dizziness, nervousness, headache, restlessness, anorexia, malaise, confusion, coma, convulsion, insomnia, amnesia, mental depression, hallucinations, paradoxical CNS stimulation, intracranial pressure (increased)

Dermatologic: Pruritus, urticaria, rash

Endocrine & metabolic: Antidiuretic hormone release

Gastrointestinal: Nausea, vomiting, dyspepsia, stomach cramps, xerostomia, constipation, abdominal pain, dry mouth, biliary tract spasm, paralytic ileus

Genitourinary: Decreased urination, urinary tract spasm, urinary retention

Local: Pain at injection site

Neuromuscular & skeletal: Weakness

Ocular: Miosis, diplopia

Respiratory: Respiratory depression, apnea, hypoventilation, cyanosis

Miscellaneous: Histamine release, physical and psychological dependence

Overdosage/Toxicology Symptoms include CNS depression, respiratory depression, miosis, apnea, pulmonary edema, and convulsions. Treatment includes naloxone 2 mg I.V. (0.01 mg/kg for children), with repeat administration as necessary, up to a total of 10 mg.

Drug Interactions
Increased Effect/Toxicity: CNS depression is enhanced with coadministration of other CNS depressants.
Ethanol/Nutrition/Herb Interactions
Ethanol: Avoid or limit ethanol (may increase CNS depression). Watch for sedation.
Herb/Nutraceutical: Avoid valerian, St John's wort, kava kava, gotu kola (may increase CNS depression).
Stability Store at room temperature; do not freeze.
Mechanism of Action Levorphanol tartrate is a synthetic opioid agonist that is classified as a morphinan derivative. Opioids interact with stereospecific opioid receptors in various parts of the central nervous system and other tissues. Analgesic potency parallels the affinity for these binding sites. These drugs do not alter the threshold or responsiveness to pain, but the perception of pain.
Pharmacodynamics/Kinetics
Onset of action: Oral: 10-60 minutes
Duration: 4-8 hours
Metabolism: Hepatic
Half-life elimination: 11-16 hours
Excretion: Urine (as inactive metabolite)
Dosage Adults: **Note:** These are guidelines and do not represent the maximum doses that may be required in all patients. Doses should be titrated to pain relief/prevention.
Acute pain (moderate to severe):
Oral: Initial: Opiate-naive: 2 mg every 6-8 hours as needed; patients with prior opiate exposure may require higher initial doses; usual dosage range: 2-4 mg every 6-8 hours as needed
I.M., SubQ: Initial: Opiate-naive: 1 mg every 6-8 hours as needed; patients with prior opiate exposure may require higher initial doses; usual dosage range: 1-2 mg every 6-8 hours as needed
Slow I.V.: Initial: Opiate-naive: Up to 1 mg/dose every 3-6 hours as needed; patients with prior opiate exposure may require higher initial doses
Chronic pain: Patients taking opioids chronically may become tolerant and require doses higher than the usual dosage range to maintain the desired effect. Tolerance can be managed by appropriate dose titration. **There is no optimal or maximal dose for levorphanol in chronic pain. The appropriate dose is one that relieves pain throughout its dosing interval without causing unmanageable side effects.**
Premedication: I.M., SubQ: 1-2 mg/dose 60-90 minutes prior to surgery; older or debilitated patients usually require less drug
Dosing adjustment in hepatic disease: Reduction is necessary in patients with liver disease
Administration I.V.: Inject 3 mg over 4-5 minutes
Monitoring Parameters Pain relief, respiratory and mental status, blood pressure
Dosage Forms
Injection, solution, as tartrate: 2 mg/mL (1 mL, 10 mL)
Tablet, as tartrate: 2 mg

♦ **Levorphanol Tartrate** see Levorphanol on page 1006
♦ **Levorphan Tartrate** see Levorphanol on page 1006
♦ **Levothroid®** see Levothyroxine on page 1007

Levothyroxine (lee voe thye ROKS een)

U.S. Brand Names Levothroid®; Levoxyl®; Synthroid®; Unithroid®
Canadian Brand Names Eltroxin®; Gen-Levothyroxine; Levothyroxine Sodium; Synthroid®
Index Terms Levothyroxine Sodium; L-Thyroxine Sodium; T_4
Pharmacologic Category Thyroid Product
Use Replacement or supplemental therapy in hypothyroidism; pituitary TSH suppression
Pregnancy Risk Factor A
Pregnancy Implications Untreated maternal hypothyroidism may have adverse effects on fetal growth and development and is associated with higher rate of complications (spontaneous abortion, pre-eclampsia, stillbirth, premature delivery). Treatment should not be discontinued during pregnancy. TSH levels should be monitored during each trimester and 6-8 weeks postpartum. Increased doses may be needed during pregnancy.
Lactation Enters breast milk/compatible
Medication Safety Issues
Sound-alike/look-alike issues:
Levothyroxine may be confused with liothyronine
Levoxyl® may be confused with Lanoxin®, Luvox®
Synthroid® may be confused with Symmetrel®

To avoid errors due to misinterpretation of a decimal point, always express dosage in mcg (**not** mg).

Significant differences exist between oral and I.V. dosing. Use caution when converting from one route of administration to another.
Contraindications Hypersensitivity to levothyroxine sodium or any component of the formulation; recent MI or thyrotoxicosis; uncorrected adrenal insufficiency
Warnings/Precautions [U.S. Boxed Warning]: Ineffective and potentially toxic for weight reduction. High doses may produce serious or even life-threatening toxic effects particularly when used with some anorectic drugs. Use with caution and reduce dosage in patients with angina pectoris or other cardiovascular disease; use cautiously in elderly since they may be more likely to have compromised cardiovascular functions. Patients with adrenal insufficiency, myxedema, diabetes mellitus and insipidus may have symptoms exaggerated or aggravated. Chronic hypothyroidism predisposes patients to coronary artery disease. Levoxyl® may rapidly swell and disintegrate causing choking or gagging
(Continued)

Levothyroxine *(Continued)*

(should be administered with a full glass of water); use caution in patients with dysphagia or other swallowing disorders.

Adverse Reactions Frequency not defined.

Cardiovascular: Angina, arrhythmia, blood pressure increased, cardiac arrest, flushing, heart failure, MI, palpitation, pulse increased, tachycardia

Central nervous system: Anxiety, emotional lability, fatigue, fever, headache, hyperactivity, insomnia, irritability, nervousness, pseudotumor cerebri (children), seizure (rare)

Dermatologic: Alopecia

Endocrine & metabolic: Fertility impaired, menstrual irregularities

Gastrointestinal: Abdominal cramps, appetite increased, diarrhea, vomiting, weight loss

Hepatic: Liver function tests increased

Neuromuscular & skeletal: Bone mineral density decreased, muscle weakness, tremor, slipped capital femoral epiphysis (children)

Respiratory: Dyspnea

Miscellaneous: Diaphoresis, heat intolerance, hypersensitivity (to inactive ingredients, symptoms include urticaria, pruritus, rash, flushing, angioedema, GI symptoms, fever, arthralgia, serum sickness, wheezing)

Levoxyl®: Choking, dysphagia, gagging

Overdosage/Toxicology Chronic overdose is treated by withdrawal of the drug. Massive overdose may require beta-blockers for increased sympathomimetic activity. Chronic overdose may cause hyperthyroidism, weight loss, nervousness, sweating, tachycardia, insomnia, heat intolerance, menstrual irregularities, palpitations, psychosis, and fever. Overtreatment of children may result in premature closure of epiphyses or craniosynostosis (infants). Acute overdose may cause fever, hypoglycemia, CHF, and unrecognized adrenal insufficiency. Reduce the dose or temporarily discontinue therapy. The hypothalamic-pituitary-thyroid axis will return to normal in 6-8 weeks. Serum T_4 levels do not correlate well with toxicity. In massive acute ingestion, reduce GI absorption and administer general supportive care. Treat congestive heart failure with digitalis glycosides. Excessive adrenergic activity (tachycardia) requires propranolol 1-3 mg I.V. over 10 minutes or 80-160 mg orally/day. Fever may be treated with acetaminophen.

Drug Interactions

Increased Effect/Toxicity: Also refer to Additional Information. Levothyroxine may potentiate the hypoprothrombinemic effect of warfarin (and other oral anticoagulants). Tricyclic antidepressants (TCAs) coadministered with levothyroxine may increase potential for toxicity of both drugs. Coadministration with ketamine may lead to hypertension and tachycardia.

Decreased Effect: Also refer to Additional Information. Some medications may decrease absorption of levothyroxine: Cholestyramine, colestipol (separate administration by at least 2 hours); aluminum- and magnesium-containing antacids, iron preparations, sucralfate, Kayexalate® (separate administration by at least 4 hours). Enzyme inducers (phenytoin, phenobarbital, carbamazepine, and rifampin/rifabutin) may decrease levothyroxine levels. Levothyroxine may decrease effect of oral sulfonylureas. Serum levels of digoxin and theophylline may be altered by thyroid function. Estrogens may decrease serum free-thyroxine concentrations. Imatinib may decrease the effects of thyroid replacement therapy.

Ethanol/Nutrition/Herb Interactions Food: Taking levothyroxine with enteral nutrition may cause reduced bioavailability and may lower serum thyroxine levels leading to signs or symptoms of hypothyroidism. Limit intake of goitrogenic foods (eg, asparagus, cabbage, peas, turnip greens, broccoli, spinach, Brussels sprouts, lettuce, soybeans). Soybean flour (infant formula), cottonseed meal, walnuts, and dietary fiber may decrease absorption of levothyroxine from the GI tract.

Stability

Tablet: Store at room temperature of 15°C to 30°C (59°F to 86°F). Protect from light and moisture.

Injection: Store at room temperature of 15°C to 30°C (59°F to 86°F). Dilute vials for injection with 5 mL normal saline and shake well. Reconstituted solutions should be used immediately and any unused portions discarded.

Mechanism of Action Exact mechanism of action is unknown; however, it is believed the thyroid hormone exerts its many metabolic effects through control of DNA transcription and protein synthesis; involved in normal metabolism, growth, and development; promotes gluconeogenesis, increases utilization and mobilization of glycogen stores, and stimulates protein synthesis, increases basal metabolic rate

Pharmacodynamics/Kinetics

Onset of action: Therapeutic: Oral: 3-5 days; I.V. 6-8 hours

Peak effect: I.V.: ~24 hours

Absorption: Oral: Erratic (40% to 80%); decreases with age

Protein binding: >99%

Metabolism: Hepatic to triiodothyronine (active)

Time to peak, serum: 2-4 hours

Half-life elimination: Euthyroid: 6-7 days; Hypothyroid: 9-10 days; Hyperthyroid: 3-4 days

Excretion: Urine and feces; decreases with age

Dosage Doses should be adjusted based on clinical response and laboratory parameters.

Oral:

Children: Hypothyroidism:

Newborns: Initial: 10-15 mcg/kg/day. Lower doses of 25 mcg/day should be considered in newborns at risk for cardiac failure. Newborns with T_4 levels <5 mcg/dL should be started at 50 mcg/day. Adjust dose at 4- to 6-week intervals.

Infants and Children: Dose based on body weight and age as listed below. Children with severe or chronic hypothyroidism should be started at 25 mcg/day; adjust dose by 25 mcg every 2-4 weeks. In older children, hyperactivity may be decreased by starting with ¼ of the recommended dose and increasing by ¼ dose each week until the full replacement dose is reached. Refer to adult dosing once growth and puberty are complete.

0-3 months: 10-15 mcg/kg/day
3-6 months: 8-10 mcg/kg/day
6-12 months: 6-8 mcg/kg/day
1-5 years: 5-6 mcg/kg/day
6-12 years: 4-5 mcg/kg/day
>12 years: 2-3 mcg/kg/day

Adults:

Hypothyroidism: 1.7 mcg/kg/day in otherwise healthy adults <50 years old, children in whom growth and puberty are complete, and older adults who have been recently treated for hyperthyroidism or who have been hypothyroid for only a few months. Titrate dose every 6 weeks. Average starting dose ~100 mcg; usual doses are ≤200 mcg/day; doses ≥300 mcg/day are rare (consider poor compliance, malabsorption, and/or drug interactions). **Note:** For patients >50 years or patients with cardiac disease, refer to Elderly dosing.

Severe hypothyroidism: Initial: 12.5-25 mcg/day; adjust dose by 25 mcg/day every 2-4 weeks as appropriate; **Note:** Oral agents are not recommended for myxedema (see I.V. dosing).

Subclinical hypothyroidism (if treated): 1 mcg/kg/day

TSH suppression:

Well-differentiated thyroid cancer: Highly individualized; Doses >2 mcg/kg/day may be needed to suppress TSH to <0.1 mU/L.

Benign nodules and nontoxic multinodular goiter: Goal TSH suppression: 0.1-0.3 mU/L

Elderly: Hypothyroidism:

>50 years without cardiac disease **or** <50 years with cardiac disease: Initial: 25-50 mcg/day; adjust dose at 6- to 8-week intervals as needed

>50 years with cardiac disease: Initial: 12.5-25 mcg/day; adjust dose by 12.5-25 mcg increments at 4- to 6-week intervals. (**Note:** Many clinicians prefer to adjust at 6- to 8-week intervals.)

Note: Elderly patients may require <1 mcg/kg/day

I.M., I.V.: Children, Adults, Elderly: Hypothyroidism: 50% of the oral dose

I.V.:

Adults: Myxedema coma or stupor: 200-500 mcg, then 100-300 mcg the next day if necessary; smaller doses should be considered in patients with cardiovascular disease

Elderly: Myxedema coma: Refer to Adults dosing; lower doses may be needed

Dietary Considerations Should be taken on an empty stomach, at least 30 minutes before food.

Administration

Oral: Administer in the morning on an empty stomach, at least 30 minutes before food. Tablets may be crushed and suspended in 1-2 teaspoonfuls of water; suspension should be used immediately. Levoxyl® should be administered with a full glass of water to prevent gagging (due to tablet swelling).

Parenteral: Dilute vial with 5 mL normal saline; use immediately after reconstitution; should not be admixed with other solutions

Monitoring Parameters Thyroid function test (serum thyroxine, thyrotropin concentrations), resin triiodothyronine uptake (rT$_3$U), free thyroxine index (FTI), T$_4$, TSH, heart rate, blood pressure, clinical signs of hypo- and hyperthyroidism; TSH is the most reliable guide for evaluating adequacy of thyroid replacement dosage. TSH may be elevated during the first few months of thyroid replacement despite patients being clinically euthyroid. In cases where T$_4$ remains low and TSH is within normal limits, an evaluation of "free" (unbound) T$_4$ is needed to evaluate further increase in dosage

Infants: Monitor closely for cardiac overload, arrhythmias, and aspiration from avid suckling

Infants/children: Monitor closely for under/overtreatment. Undertreatment may decrease intellectual development and linear growth, and lead to poor school performance due to impaired concentration and slowed mentation. Overtreatment may adversely affect brain maturation, accelerate bone age (leading to premature closure of the epiphyses and reduced adult height); craniosynostosis has been reported in infants. Treated children may experience a period of catch-up growth. Monitor TSH and total or free T$_4$ at 2 and 4 weeks after starting treatment; every 1-2 months for first year of life; every 2-3 months during years 1-3; every 3-12 months until growth completed.

Adults: Monitor TSH every 6-8 weeks until normalized; 8-12 weeks after dosage changes; every 6-12 months throughout therapy

Reference Range Pediatrics: Cord T$_4$ and values in the first few weeks are much higher, falling over the first months and years. ≥10 years: ~5.8-11 mcg/dL (SI: 75-142 nmol/L). Borderline low: ≤4.5-5.7 mcg/dL (SI: 58-73 nmol/L); low: ≤4.4 mcg/dL (SI: 57 nmol/L); results <2.5 mcg/dL (SI: <32 nmol/L) are strong evidence for hypothyroidism.

Approximate adult normal range: 4-12 mcg/dL (SI: 51-154 nmol/L). Borderline high: 11.1-13 mcg/dL (SI: 143-167 nmol/L); high: ≥13.1 mcg/dL (SI: 169 nmol/L). Normal range is increased in women on birth control pills (5.5-12 mcg/dL); normal range in pregnancy: ~5.5-16 mcg/dL (SI: ~71-206 nmol/L). TSH: 0.4-10 (for those ≥80 years) mIU/L; T$_4$: 4-12 mcg/dL (SI: 51-154 nmol/L); T$_3$ (RIA) (total T$_3$): 80-230 ng/dL (SI: 1.2-3.5 nmol/L); T$_4$ free (free T$_4$): 0.7-1.8 ng/dL (SI: 9-23 pmol/L).

Test Interactions Many drugs may have effects on thyroid function tests (see Additional Information). Pregnancy, infectious hepatitis, and acute intermittent porphyria may increase TBG concentrations; nephrosis, severe hypoproteinemia, severe liver disease, and acromegaly may decrease TBG concentrations.

Additional Information Equivalent doses: The following statement on relative potency of thyroid products is included in a joint statement by American Thyroid Association (ATA), American Association of Clinical Endocrinologists (AACE) and The Endocrine Society (TES): For purposes of conversion, levothyroxine sodium (T$_4$) 100 mcg is usually considered equivalent to desiccated thyroid 60 mg, thyroglobulin 60 mg, or liothyronine sodium (T$_3$) 25 mcg. However, these are rough guidelines only and do not obviate the careful re-evaluation of a patient when switching thyroid hormone preparations, including a change from one brand of

(Continued)

Levothyroxine *(Continued)*

levothyroxine to another. Joint position statement is available at http://www.thyroid.org/professionals/advocacy/04_12_08_thyroxine.html.

Note: Several medications have effects on thyroid production or conversion. The impact in thyroid replacement has not been specifically evaluated, but patient response should be monitored:

Methimazole: Decreases thyroid hormone secretion, while propylthiouracil decrease thyroid hormone secretion and decreases conversion of T_4 to T_3.

Beta-adrenergic antagonists: Decrease conversion of T_4 to T_3 (dose related, propranolol ≥160 mg/day); patients may be clinically euthyroid.

Iodide, iodine-containing radiographic contrast agents may decrease thyroid hormone secretion; may also increase thyroid hormone secretion, especially in patients with Graves' disease.

Other agents reported to impact on thyroid production/conversion include aminoglutethimide, amiodarone, chloral hydrate, diazepam, ethionamide, interferon-alpha, interleukin-2, lithium, lovastatin (case report), glucocorticoids (dose-related), mercaptopurine, sulfonamides, thiazide diuretics, and tolbutamide.

In addition, a number of medications have been noted to cause transient depression in TSH secretion, which may complicate interpretation of monitoring tests for levothyroxine, including corticosteroids, octreotide, and dopamine. Metoclopramide may increase TSH secretion

Dosage Forms

Injection, powder for reconstitution, as sodium: 0.2 mg, 0.5 mg

Tablet, as sodium: 25 mcg, 50 mcg, 75 mcg, 88 mcg, 100 mcg, 112 mcg, 125 mcg, 137 mcg, 150 mcg, 175 mcg, 200 mcg, 300 mcg

Levothroid®: 25 mcg, 50 mcg, 75 mcg, 88 mcg, 100 mcg, 112 mcg, 125 mcg, 150 mcg, 175 mcg, 200 mcg, 300 mcg

Levoxyl®: 25 mcg, 50 mcg, 75 mcg, 88 mcg, 100 mcg, 112 mcg, 125 mcg, 137 mcg, 150 mcg, 175 mcg, 200 mcg; 300 mcg [DSC]

Synthroid®: 25 mcg, 50 mcg, 75 mcg, 88 mcg, 100 mcg, 112 mcg, 125 mcg, 137 mcg, 150 mcg, 175 mcg, 200 mcg, 300 mcg

Unithroid®: 25 mcg, 50 mcg, 75 mcg, 88 mcg, 100 mcg, 112 mcg, 125 mcg, 150 mcg, 175 mcg, 200 mcg, 300 mcg

- **Levothyroxine Sodium** *see Levothyroxine on page 1007*
- **Levoxyl®** *see Levothyroxine on page 1007*
- **Levsin®** *see Hyoscyamine on page 866*
- **Levsinex®** *see Hyoscyamine on page 866*
- **Levsin/SL®** *see Hyoscyamine on page 866*
- **Levulan® (Can)** *see Aminolevulinic Acid on page 95*
- **Levulan® Kerastick®** *see Aminolevulinic Acid on page 95*
- **Lexapro®** *see Escitalopram on page 613*
- **Lexiva®** *see Fosamprenavir on page 761*
- **Lexxel®** *see Enalapril and Felodipine on page 581*
- **LFA-3/IgG(1) Fusion Protein, Human** *see Alefacept on page 62*
- **L-Glutamine** *see Glutamine on page 803*
- **LHRH** *see Gonadorelin on page 809*
- **LH-RH Agonist** *see Histrelin on page 839*
- **l-Hyoscyamine Sulfate** *see Hyoscyamine on page 866*
- **Librax® [reformulation] [DSC]** *see Chlordiazepoxide and Methscopolamine on page 344*
- **Librax® [original formulation]** *see Clidinium and Chlordiazepoxide on page 388*
- **Librax® (Can)** *see Clidinium and Chlordiazepoxide on page 388*
- **Librium®** *see Chlordiazepoxide on page 342*
- **Lice-Aid [OTC]** *see Pyrethrins and Piperonyl Butoxide on page 1461*
- **Licide® [OTC]** *see Pyrethrins and Piperonyl Butoxide on page 1461*
- **LidaMantle®** *see Lidocaine on page 1010*
- **Lidemol® (Can)** *see Fluocinonide on page 721*
- **Lidex®** *see Fluocinonide on page 721*
- **Lidex-E®** *see Fluocinonide on page 721*

Lidocaine *(LYE doe kane)*

U.S. Brand Names Anestacon®; Band-Aid® Hurt-Free™ Antiseptic Wash [OTC]; Burnamycin [OTC]; Burn Jel [OTC]; Burn-O-Jel [OTC]; LidaMantle®; Lidoderm®; L-M-X™ 4 [OTC]; L-M-X™ 5 [OTC]; LTA® 360; Premjact® [OTC]; Solarcaine® Aloe Extra Burn Relief [OTC]; Topicaine® [OTC]; Xylocaine®; Xylocaine® MPF; Xylocaine® Viscous; Zilactin-L® [OTC]

Canadian Brand Names Betacaine®; Lidodan™; Lidoderm®; Xylocaine®; Xylocard®; Zilactin®

Index Terms Lidocaine Hydrochloride; Lignocaine Hydrochloride

Pharmacologic Category Analgesic, Topical; Antiarrhythmic Agent, Class Ib; Local Anesthetic

Use Local anesthetic and acute treatment of ventricular arrhythmias from myocardial infarction, or cardiac manipulation

Rectal: Temporary relief of pain and itching due to anorectal disorders

Topical: Local anesthetic for use in laser, cosmetic, and outpatient surgeries; minor burns, cuts, and abrasions of the skin

Lidoderm® Patch: Relief of allodynia (painful hypersensitivity) and chronic pain in postherpetic neuralgia

Unlabeled/Investigational Use ACLS guidelines (not considered drug of choice): Stable monomorphic VT (preserved ventricular function), polymorphic VT (preserved ventricular function), drug-induced monomorphic VT

Pregnancy Risk Factor B
Pregnancy Implications Animal studies with lidocaine have not shown teratogenic effects.
Lactation Enters breast milk (small amounts)/use caution (AAP rates "compatible")
Medication Safety Issues
    High alert medication: The Institute for Safe Medication Practices (ISMP) includes this medication (I.V. formulation) among its list of drugs which have a heightened risk of causing significant patient harm when used in error.

    Transdermal patch may contain conducting metal (eg, aluminum); remove patch prior to MRI.

    International issues:
      Lidpen® may be confused with Linoten® which is a brand name for pamidronate in Spain
Contraindications Hypersensitivity to lidocaine or any component of the formulation; hypersensitivity to another local anesthetic of the amide type; Adam-Stokes syndrome; severe degrees of SA, AV, or intraventricular heart block (except in patients with a functioning artificial pacemaker); premixed injection may contain corn-derived dextrose and its use is contraindicated in patients with allergy to corn-related products
Warnings/Precautions
    Intravenous: Constant ECG monitoring is necessary during I.V. administration. Use cautiously in hepatic impairment, any degree of heart block, Wolff-Parkinson-White syndrome, CHF, marked hypoxia, severe respiratory depression, hypovolemia, history of malignant hyperthermia, or shock. Increased ventricular rate may be seen when administered to a patient with atrial fibrillation. Correct any underlying causes of ventricular arrhythmias. Monitor closely for signs and symptoms of CNS toxicity. The elderly may be prone to increased CNS and cardiovascular side effects. Reduce dose in hepatic dysfunction and CHF.

    Injectable anesthetic: Follow appropriate administration techniques so as not to administer any intravascularly. Solutions containing antimicrobial preservatives should not be used for epidural or spinal anesthesia. Some solutions contain a bisulfite; avoid in patients who are allergic to bisulfite. Resuscitative equipment, medicine and oxygen should be available in case of emergency. Use products containing epinephrine cautiously in patients with significant vascular disease, compromised blood flow, or during or following general anesthesia (increased risk of arrhythmias). Adjust the dose for the elderly, pediatric, acutely ill, and debilitated patients.

    Topical: L-M-X™ 4 cream: Do not leave on large body areas for >2 hours. Observe young children closely to prevent accidental ingestion. Not for use ophthalmic use or for use on mucous membranes.

    Transdermal patch: May contain conducting metal (eg, aluminum); remove patch prior to MRI.
Adverse Reactions Effects vary with route of administration. Many effects are dose related. Frequency not defined.
    Cardiovascular: Arrhythmia, bradycardia, arterial spasms, cardiovascular collapse, defibrillator threshold increased, edema, flushing, heart block, hypotension, sinus node supression, vascular insufficiency (periarticular injections)
    Central nervous system: Agitation, anxiety, apprehension, coma, confusion, disorientation, dizziness, drowsiness, euphoria, hallucinations, headache, hyperesthesia, hypoesthesia, lethargy, lightheadedness, nervousness, psychosis, seizure, slurred speech, somnolence, unconsciousness
    Dermatologic: Angioedema, bruising (transdermal system), contact dermatitis, depigmentation (transdermal system), edema of the skin, itching, petechia (transdermal system), pruritus, rash, urticaria
    Gastrointestinal: Metallic taste, nausea, vomiting
    Local: Irritation (transdermal system), thrombophlebitis
    Neuromuscular & skeletal: Pain exacerbation (transdermal system), paresthesia, transient radicular pain (subarachnoid administration; up to 1.9%), tremor, twitching, weakness
    Ocular: Diplopia, visual changes
    Otic: Tinnitus
    Respiratory: Bronchospasm, dyspnea, respiratory depression or arrest
    Miscellaneous: Allergic reactions, anaphylactoid reaction, sensitivity to temperature extremes

    Following spinal anesthesia positional headache (3%), shivering (2%) nausea, peripheral nerve symptoms, respiratory inadequacy and double vision (<1%), hypotension, cauda equina syndrome

    Postmarketing and/or case reports: ARDS (inhalation), asystole, disorientation, methemoglobinemia, skin reaction
Overdosage/Toxicology Has a narrow therapeutic index and severe toxicity may occur slightly above the therapeutic range, especially with other antiarrhythmic drugs. Symptoms include sedation, confusion, coma, seizures, respiratory arrest and cardiac toxicity (sinus arrest, AV block, asystole, and hypotension). The QRS and QT intervals are usually normal, although they may be prolonged after massive overdose. Other effects include dizziness, paresthesias, tremor, ataxia, and GI disturbance. Treatment is supportive, using conventional therapies (fluids, positioning, vasopressors, antiarrhythmics, anticonvulsants). Sodium bicarbonate may reverse QRS prolongation, bradyarrhythmias and hypotension. Enhanced elimination with dialysis, hemoperfusion or repeat charcoal is not effective.
Drug Interactions
    Cytochrome P450 Effect: Substrate of CYP1A2 (minor), 2A6 (minor), 2B6 (minor), 2C9 (minor), 2D6 (major), 3A4 (major); **Inhibits** CYP1A2 (strong), 2D6 (moderate), 3A4 (moderate)
    Increased Effect/Toxicity: The levels/effects of lidocaine may be increased by amphetamines, amiodarone, azole antifungals, beta-blockers, chlorpromazine, clarithromycin, delavirdine, diclofenac, doxycycline, erythromycin, fluoxetine, imatinib, isoniazid, miconazole, nefazodone, nicardipine, paroxetine, pergolide, propofol, protease inhibitors, quinidine, quinine, ritonavir, ropinirole, telithromycin, verapamil, and other CYP2D6 or 3A4
(Continued)

Lidocaine *(Continued)*

inhibitors. Concomitant cimetidine or propranolol may result in increased serum concentrations of lidocaine resulting in toxicity.

Lidocaine may increase the levels/effects of aminophylline, amphetamines, selected beta-blockers, selected benzodiazepines, calcium channel blockers, cisapride, cyclosporine, dextromethorphan, ergot alkaloids, fluoxetine, fluvoxamine, selected HMG-CoA reductase inhibitors, lidocaine, mesoridazine, mexiletine, mirtazapine, nateglinide, nefazodone, paroxetine, risperidone, ritonavir, ropinirole, sildenafil (and other PDE-5 inhibitors), tacrolimus, theophylline, thioridazine, tricyclic antidepressants, trifluoperazine, venlafaxine, and other substrates of CYP1A2, 2D6 or 3A4. The effect of succinylcholine may be enhanced by lidocaine.

Decreased Effect: The levels/effects of lidocaine may be decreased by aminoglutethimide, carbamazepine, nafcillin, nevirapine, phenobarbital, phenytoin, rifamycins and other CYP3A4 inducers. Lidocaine may decrease the levels/effects of CYP2D6 prodrug substrates (eg, codeine, hydrocodone, oxycodone, tramadol).

Ethanol/Nutrition/Herb Interactions Herb/Nutraceutical: St John's wort may decrease lidocaine levels; avoid concurrent use.

Stability Lidocaine injection is stable at room temperature. Stability of parenteral admixture at room temperature (25°C) is the expiration date on premixed bag; out of overwrap stability is 30 days.

Standard diluent: 2 g/250 mL D_5W.

Mechanism of Action Class Ib antiarrhythmic; suppresses automaticity of conduction tissue, by increasing electrical stimulation threshold of ventricle, His-Purkinje system, and spontaneous depolarization of the ventricles during diastole by a direct action on the tissues; blocks both the initiation and conduction of nerve impulses by decreasing the neuronal membrane's permeability to sodium ions, which results in inhibition of depolarization with resultant blockade of conduction

Pharmacodynamics/Kinetics

Onset of action: Single bolus dose: 45-90 seconds

Duration: 10-20 minutes

Distribution: V_d: 1.1-2.1 L/kg; alterable by many patient factors; decreased in CHF and liver disease; crosses blood-brain barrier

Protein binding: 60% to 80% to alpha$_1$ acid glycoprotein

Metabolism: 90% hepatic; active metabolites monoethylglycinexylidide (MEGX) and glycinexylidide (GX) can accumulate and may cause CNS toxicity

Half-life elimination: Biphasic: Prolonged with congestive heart failure, liver disease, shock, severe renal disease; Initial: 7-30 minutes; Terminal: Infants, premature: 3.2 hours, Adults: 1.5-2 hours

Dosage

Antiarrhythmic:

Children:

I.V., I.O.: **Note:** For use in pulseless VT or VF, give after defibrillation, CPR, and epinephrine:

Loading dose: 1 mg/kg (maximum 100 mg); follow with continuous infusion; may administer second bolus of 0.5-1 mg/kg if delay between bolus and start of infusion is >15 minutes

Continuous infusion: 20-50 mcg/kg/minute. Use 20 mcg/kg/minute in patients with shock, hepatic disease, cardiac arrest, mild CHF; moderate-to-severe CHF may require 1/2 loading dose and lower infusion rates to avoid toxicity.

E.T. (loading dose only): 2-10 times the I.V. bolus dose; dilute with NS to a volume of 3-5 mL and follow with several positive-pressure ventilations

Adults:

Ventricular fibrillation or pulseless ventricular tachycardia (after defibrillation, CPR, and vasopressor administration): I.V.: Initial: 1-1.5 mg/kg. Refractory ventricular tachycardia or ventricular fibrillation, a repeat 0.5-0.75 mg/kg bolus may be given every 5-10 minutes after initial dose for a maximum of 3 doses. Total dose should not exceed 3 mg/kg. Follow with continuous infusion (1-4 mg/minute) after return of perfusion. Reappearance of arrhythmia during constant infusion: 0.5 mg/kg bolus and reassessment of infusion.

E.T. (loading dose only): 2-2.5 times the recommended I.V. dose; dilute in 10 mL NS or distilled water. **Note:** Absorption is greater with distilled water, but causes more adverse effects on PaO$_2$.

Hemodynamically stable VT: 0.5-0.75 mg/kg followed by synchronized cardioversion

Note: Decrease dose in patients with CHF, shock, or hepatic disease.

Anesthesia, topical:

Cream:

LidaMantle®: Skin irritation: Children and Adults: Apply to affected area 2-3 times/day as needed

L-M-X™ 4: Children ≥2 years and Adults: Apply 1/4 inch thick layer to intact skin. Leave on until adequate anesthetic effect is obtained. Remove cream and cleanse area before beginning procedure.

L-M-X™ 5: Relief of anorectal pain and itching: Children ≥12 years and Adults: Rectal: Apply topically to clean, dry area **or** using applicator, insert rectally, up to 6 times/day

Gel, ointment, solution: Adults: Apply to affected area ≤3 times/day as needed (maximum dose: 4.5 mg/kg, not to exceed 300 mg)

Jelly:

Children ≥10 years: Dose varies with age and weight (maximum dose: 4.5 mg/kg)

Adults (maximum dose: 30 mL [600 mg] in any 12-hour period):

Anesthesia of male urethra: 5-30 mL

Anesthesia of female urethra: 3-5 mL

Lubrication of endotracheal tube: Apply a moderate amount to external surface only

Liquid: Cold sores and fever blisters: Children ≥5 years and Adults: Apply to affected area every 6 hours as needed

Patch: Postherpetic neuralgia: Adults: Apply patch to most painful area. Up to 3 patches may be applied in a single application. Patch may remain in place for up to 12 hours in any 24-hour period.

Anesthetic, local injectable: Children and Adults: Varies with procedure, degree of anesthesia needed, vascularity of tissue, duration of anesthesia required, and physical condition of patient; maximum: 4.5 mg/kg/dose; do not repeat within 2 hours.

Dosage adjustment in renal impairment: Not dialyzable (0% to 5%) by hemo- or peritoneal dialysis; supplemental dose is not necessary.

Dosage adjustment in hepatic impairment: Reduce dose in acute hepatitis and decompensated cirrhosis by 50%.

Dietary Considerations Premixed injection may contain corn-derived dextrose and its use is contraindicated in patients with allergy to corn-related products.

Administration

Intratracheal: Dilute in NS or distilled water. Absorption is greater with distilled water, but causes more adverse effects on PaO₂. Pass catheter beyond tip of tracheal tube, stop compressions, spray drug quickly down tube. Follow immediately with several quick insufflations and continue chest compressions.

I.V.: Use microdrip (60 gtt/mL) or infusion pump to administer an accurate dose

Infusion rates: 2 g/250 mL D₅W (infusion pump should be used):

1 mg/minute: 7.5 mL/hour
2 mg/minute: 15 mL/hour
3 mg/minute: 22.5 mL/hour
4 mg/minute: 30 mL/hour

Buffered lidocaine for injectable local anesthetic: Add 2 mL of sodium bicarbonate 8.4% to 18 mL of lidocaine 1%

Topical:

Gel (Topicaine®): Avoid mucous membranes; remove prior to laser treatment.

Transdermal: Apply to painful area of skin immediately after removal from protective envelope. May be cut to appropriate size. After removal from skin, fold used transdermal systems so the adhesive side sticks to itself. Remove immediately if burning sensation occurs. Wash hands after application.

Reference Range

Therapeutic: 1.5-5.0 mcg/mL (SI: 6-21 μmol/L)
Potentially toxic: >6 mcg/mL (SI: >26 μmol/L)
Toxic: >9 mcg/mL (SI: >38 μmol/L)

Dosage Forms [DSC] = Discontinued product

Cream, rectal (L-M-X™ 5): 5% (15 g) [contains benzyl alcohol; packaged with applicator]; (30 g) [contains benzyl alcohol]

Cream, topical (L-M-X™ 4): 4% (5 g) [contains benzyl alcohol; packaged with Tegaderm™ dressing]; (15 g, 30 g) [contains benzyl alcohol]

Cream, topical, as hydrochloride: 3% (30 g)

LidaMantle®: 3% (30 g, 85 g)

Gel, topical:

Burn-O-Jel: 0.5% (90 g)

Topicaine®: 4% (10 g, 30 g, 113 g) [contains alcohol 35%, benzyl alcohol, aloe vera, and jojoba]

Gel, topical, as hydrochloride:

Burn Jel: 2% (3.5 g, 120 g)

Solarcaine® Aloe Extra Burn Relief: 0.5% (113 g, 226 g) [contains aloe vera gel and tartrazine]

Infusion, as hydrochloride [premixed in D₅W]: 0.4% [4 mg/mL] (250 mL, 500 mL); 0.8% [8 mg/mL] (250 mL, 500 mL)

Injection, solution, as hydrochloride: 0.5% [5 mg/mL] (50 mL); 1% [10 mg/mL] (2 mL, 10 mL, 20 mL, 30 mL, 50 mL); 2% [20 mg/mL] (2 mL, 5 mL, 20 mL, 50 mL)

Xylocaine®: 0.5% [5 mg/mL] (50 mL); 1% [10 mg/mL] (10 mL, 20 mL, 50 mL); 2% [20 mg/mL] (1.8 mL, 10 mL, 20 mL, 50 mL)

Injection, solution, as hydrochloride [preservative free]: 0.5% [5 mg/mL] (50 mL); 1% [10 mg/mL] (2 mL, 5 mL, 30 mL); 1.5% [15 mg/mL] (20 mL); 2% [20 mg/mL] (2 mL, 5 mL, 10 mL); 4% [40 mg/mL] (5 mL)

Xylocaine®: 10% [100 mg/mL] (5 mL) [for ventricular arrhythmias]

Xylocaine® MPF: 0.5% [5 mg/mL] (50 mL); 1% [10 mg/mL] (2 mL, 5 mL, 10 mL, 30 mL); 1.5% [15 mg/mL] (10 mL, 20 mL); 2% [20 mg/mL] (2 mL, 5 mL, 10 mL); 4% [40 mg/mL] (5 mL)

Injection, solution, as hydrochloride [premixed in D₇.₅W, preservative free]: 5% (2 mL)

Xylocaine® MPF: 1.5% (2 mL) [DSC]

Jelly, topical, as hydrochloride: 2% (5 mL, 30 mL)

Anestacon®: 2% (15 mL) [contains benzalkonium chloride]

Xylocaine®: 2% (5 mL, 30 mL)

Liquid, topical (Zilactin®-L): 2.5% (7.5 mL)

Lotion, topical, as hydrochloride (LidaMantle®): 3% (177 mL)

Ointment, topical: 5% (37 g, 50 g)

Solution, topical, as hydrochloride: 4% [40 mg/mL] (50 mL)

Band-Aid® Hurt-Free™ Antiseptic Wash: 2% (180 mL)

LTA® 360: 4% [40 mg/mL] (4 mL) [packaged with cannula for laryngotracheal administration]

Xylocaine®: 4% [40 mg/mL] (50 mL)

Solution, viscous, as hydrochloride: 2% [20 mg/mL] (20 mL, 100 mL)

Xylocaine® Viscous: 2% [20 mg/mL] (100 mL, 450 mL)

Spray, topical:

Burnamycin: 0.5% (60 mL) [contains aloe vera gel and menthol]

Premjact®: 9.6% (13 mL)

Solarcaine® Aloe Extra Burn Relief: 0.5% (127 g) [contains aloe vera]

Transdermal system, topical (Lidoderm®): 5% (30b)

Lidocaine and Bupivacaine (LYE doe kane & byoo PIV a kane)

U.S. Brand Names Duocaine™

Index Terms Bupivacaine and Lidocaine; Lidocaine Hydrochloride and Bupivacaine Hydrochloride

Pharmacologic Category Local Anesthetic

Use Local or regional anesthesia in ophthalmologic surgery by peripheral nerve block techniques such as peribulbar, retrobulbar, and facial blocks; may be used with or without epinephrine

Pregnancy Risk Factor C

Dosage Adults: **Note:** Use lowest effective dose to limit toxic effects. Dosing based on lidocaine 1% and bupivacaine 0.375%

Retrobulbar injection: 2-5 mL; a portion of dose is injected retrobulbarly and remainder may be used to block the facial nerve

Peribulbar block: 6-12 mL

Maximum dose: 0.18 mL/kg or 12 mL; if used with epinephrine, the dose should not exceed 0.28 mL/kg or 20 mL

Dosage adjustment in renal impairment: Lidocaine: Accumulation of metabolites may increase with renal impairment

Dosage adjustment in hepatic impairment:

Lidocaine: Half-life of lidocaine is increased twofold with hepatic impairment

Bupivacaine: Toxicities may be increased with hepatic impairment

Additional Information Complete prescribing information for this medication should be consulted for additional detail.

Dosage Forms Injection, solution [preservative free]: Lidocaine hydrochloride 1% and bupivacaine hydrochloride 0.375% (10 mL)

Lidocaine and Epinephrine (LYE doe kane & ep i NEF rin)

U.S. Brand Names LidoSite™; Xylocaine® MPF With Epinephrine; Xylocaine® With Epinephrine

Canadian Brand Names Xylocaine® With Epinephrine

Index Terms Epinephrine and Lidocaine

Pharmacologic Category Local Anesthetic

Use Local infiltration anesthesia; AVS for nerve block; topical local analgesia for superficial dermatologic procedures

Pregnancy Risk Factor B

Medication Safety Issues

Transdermal patch may contain conducting metal (eg, aluminum); remove patch prior to MRI.

Dosage Dosage varies with the anesthetic procedure, degree of anesthesia needed, vascularity of tissue, duration of anesthesia required, and physical condition of patient.

Dental anesthesia, infiltration, or conduction block:

Children <10 years: 20-30 mg (1-1.5 mL) of lidocaine hydrochloride as a 2% solution with epinephrine 1:100,000; maximum: 4-5 mg of lidocaine hydrochloride/kg of body weight or 100-150 mg as a single dose

Children >10 years and Adults: Do not exceed 6.6 mg/kg body weight or 300 mg of lidocaine hydrochloride and 3 mcg (0.003 mg) of epinephrine/kg of body weight or 0.2 mg epinephrine per dental appointment. The effective anesthetic dose varies with procedure, intensity of anesthesia needed, duration of anesthesia required, and physical condition of the patient. Always use the lowest effective dose along with careful aspiration.

For most routine dental procedures, lidocaine hydrochloride 2% with epinephrine 1:100,000 is preferred. When a more pronounced hemostasis is required, a 1:50,000 epinephrine concentration should be used.

Dermatologic procedure: Children ≥5 and Adults: Topical: Place 1 transdermal patch over area requiring analgesia; attach patch to iontophoretic controller and leave on for 10 minutes. Remove patch and perform procedure within 10-20 minutes of patch removal. Do not use another patch for 30 minutes.

Additional Information Complete prescribing information for this medication should be consulted for additional detail.

Dosage Forms

Injection, solution:

0.5% / 1:200,000: Lidocaine hydrochloride 0.5% and epinephrine 1:200,000 (50 mL)

1% / 1:100,000: Lidocaine hydrochloride 1% and epinephrine 1:100,000 (20 mL, 30 mL, 50 mL)

1% / 1:200,000: Lidocaine hydrochloride 1% and epinephrine 1:200,000 (30 mL)

1.5% / 1:200,000: Lidocaine hydrochloride 1.5% and epinephrine 1:200,000 (30 mL)

2% / 1:50,000: Lidocaine hydrochloride 2% and epinephrine 1:50,000 (1.8 mL)

2% / 1:100,000: Lidocaine hydrochloride 2% and epinephrine 1:100,000 (1.8 mL, 30 mL, 50 mL)

2% / 1:200,000: Lidocaine hydrochloride 2% and epinephrine 1:200,000 (20 mL)

Xylocaine® with Epinephrine:

0.5% / 1:200,000: Lidocaine hydrochloride 0.5% and epinephrine 1:200,000 (50 mL) [contains methylparaben]

1% / 1:100,000: Lidocaine hydrochloride 1% and epinephrine 1:100,000 (10 mL, 20 mL, 50 mL) [contains methylparaben]

2% / 1:50,000: Lidocaine hydrochloride 2% and epinephrine 1:50,000 (1.8 mL) [contains sodium metabisulfite]

2% / 1:100,000: Lidocaine hydrochloride 2% and epinephrine 1:100,000 (1.8 mL) [contains sodium metabisulfite]; (10 mL, 20 mL, 50 mL) [contains methylparaben]

Xylocaine®-MPF with Epinephrine:

1% / 1:200,000: Lidocaine hydrochloride 1% and epinephrine 1:200,000 (5 mL, 10 mL, 30 mL) [contains sodium metabisulfite]

1.5% / 1:200,000: Lidocaine hydrochloride 1.5% and epinephrine 1:200,000 (5 mL, 10 mL, 30 mL) [contains sodium metabisulfite]

2% / 1:200,000: Lidocaine hydrochloride 2% and epinephrine 1:200,000 (5 mL, 10 mL, 20 mL) [contains sodium metabisulfite]

Transdermal system (LidoSite™): Lidocaine hydrochloride 10% and epinephrine 0.1% (25s) [contains sodium metabisulfite; for use only with LidoSite™ controller]

Lidocaine and Prilocaine (LYE doe kane & PRIL oh kane)

U.S. Brand Names EMLA®; Oraquix®
Canadian Brand Names EMLA®
Index Terms Prilocaine and Lidocaine
Pharmacologic Category Local Anesthetic
Use Topical anesthetic for use on normal intact skin to provide local analgesia for minor procedures such as I.V. cannulation or venipuncture; has also been used for painful procedures such as lumbar puncture and skin graft harvesting; for superficial minor surgery of genital mucous membranes and as an adjunct for local infiltration anesthesia in genital mucous membranes.
Pregnancy Risk Factor B
Pregnancy Implications Refer to Lidocaine monograph.
Lactation Enters breast milk/compatible
Contraindications Hypersensitivity to amide-type anesthetic agents (eg, lidocaine, prilocaine, dibucaine, mepivacaine, bupivacaine, etidocaine); hypersensitivity to any component of the formulation selected; application on mucous membranes or broken or inflamed skin; infants <1 month of age if gestational age is <37 weeks; infants <12 months of age receiving therapy with methemoglobin-inducing agents; children with congenital or idiopathic methemoglobinemia, or in children who are receiving medications associated with drug-induced methemoglobinemia (eg, acetaminophen [overdosage], benzocaine, chloroquine, dapsone, nitrofurantoin, nitroglycerin, nitroprusside, phenazopyridine, phenelzine, phenobarbital, phenytoin, quinine, sulfonamides)
Warnings/Precautions Use with caution in patients receiving class I and III antiarrhythmic drugs, since systemic absorption occurs and synergistic toxicity is possible. Although the incidence of systemic adverse reactions with EMLA® is very low, caution should be exercised, particularly when applying over large areas and leaving on for longer than 2 hours. Avoid use on open wounds or near the eyes.
Adverse Reactions Frequency not defined.
Cardiovascular: Hypotension, angioedema
Central nervous system: Shock
Dermatologic: Hyperpigmentation, erythema, itching, rash, burning, urticaria
Genitourinary: Blistering of foreskin (rare)
Local: Burning, stinging, edema
Respiratory: Bronchospasm
Miscellaneous: Alteration in temperature sensation, hypersensitivity reactions
Drug Interactions
Cytochrome P450 Effect: Lidocaine: **Substrate** of CYP1A2 (minor), 2A6 (minor), 2B6 (minor), 2C9 (minor), 2D6 (major), 3A4 (major); **Inhibits** CYP1A2 (strong), 2D6 (strong), 3A4 (moderate)
Increased Effect/Toxicity: The effects of class I antiarrhythmic drugs (eg, mexiletine) are additive and potentially synergistic. The cardiac effects of class III antiarrhythmic drugs (eg, amiodarone, sotalol, dofetilide) may be additive; consider ECG monitoring. Prilocaine may enhance the effect of other drugs known to induce methemoglobinemia.
Stability Store at room temperature.
Mechanism of Action Local anesthetic action occurs by stabilization of neuronal membranes and inhibiting the ionic fluxes required for the initiation and conduction of impulses
Pharmacodynamics/Kinetics
EMLA®:
Onset of action: 1 hour
Peak effect: 2-3 hours
Duration: 1-2 hours after removal
Absorption: Related to duration of application and area where applied
3-hour application: 3.6% lidocaine and 6.1% prilocaine
24-hour application: 16.2% lidocaine and 33.5% prilocaine
See individual agents.
Dosage Although the incidence of systemic adverse effects with EMLA® is very low, caution should be exercised, particularly when applying over large areas and leaving on for >2 hours
Children (intact skin): EMLA® should **not** be used in neonates with a gestation age <37 weeks nor in infants <12 months of age who are receiving treatment with methemoglobin-inducing agents
Dosing is based on child's age and weight:
Age 0-3 months or <5 kg: Apply a maximum of 1 g over no more than 10 cm² of skin; leave on for no longer than 1 hour
Age 3 months to 12 months and >5 kg: Apply no more than a maximum 2 g total over no more than 20 cm² of skin; leave on for no longer than 4 hours
Age 1-6 years and >10 kg: Apply no more than a maximum of 10 g total over no more than 100 cm² of skin; leave on for no longer than 4 hours.
Age 7-12 years and >20 kg: Apply no more than a maximum 20 g total over no more than 200 cm² of skin; leave on for no longer than 4 hours.
Note: If a patient greater than 3 months old does not meet the minimum weight requirement, the maximum total dose should be restricted to the corresponding maximum based on patient weight.
(Continued)

Lidocaine and Prilocaine *(Continued)*

Adults (intact skin):

EMLA® cream and EMLA® anesthetic disc: A thick layer of EMLA® cream is applied to intact skin and covered with an occlusive dressing, or alternatively, an EMLA® anesthetic disc is applied to intact skin

Minor dermal procedures (eg, I.V. cannulation or venipuncture): Apply 2.5 g of cream (1/2 of the 5 g tube) over 20-25 cm of skin surface area, or 1 anesthetic disc (1 g over 10 cm^2) for at least 1 hour. **Note:** In clinical trials, 2 sites were usually prepared in case there was a technical problem with cannulation or venipuncture at the first site.

Major dermal procedures (eg, more painful dermatological procedures involving a larger skin area such as split thickness skin graft harvesting): Apply 2 g of cream per 10 cm^2 of skin and allow to remain in contact with the skin for at least 2 hours.

Adult male genital skin (eg, pretreatment prior to local anesthetic infiltration): Apply a thick layer of cream (1 g/10 cm^2) to the skin surface for 15 minutes. Local anesthetic infiltration should be performed immediately after removal of EMLA® cream.

Note: Dermal analgesia can be expected to increase for up to 3 hours under occlusive dressing and persist for 1-2 hours after removal of the cream

Adult females: Genital mucous membranes: Minor procedures (eg, removal of condylomata acuminata, pretreatment for local anesthetic infiltration): Apply 5-10 g (thick layer) of cream for 5-10 minutes

Periodontal gel (Oraqix®): Adults: Apply on gingival margin around selected teeth using the blunt-tipped applicator included in package. Wait 30 seconds, then fill the periodontal pockets using the blunt-tipped applicator until gel becomes visible at the gingival margin. Wait another 30 seconds before starting treatment. Maximum recommended dose: One treatment session: 5 cartridges (8.5 g)

Administration For external use only. Avoid application to open wounds or near the eyes. In small infants and children, observe patient to prevent accidental ingestion of cream, disc, or dressing. Choose two application sites available for intravenous access. Apply a thick layer (2.5 g/site ~1/2 of a 5 g tube) of cream to each designated site of intact skin. Cover each site with the occlusive dressing (Tegaderm®). Mark the time on the dressing. **Allow at least 1 hour for optimum therapeutic effect.** Remove the dressing and wipe off excess EMLA® cream (gloves should be worn). **Smaller areas of treatment are recommended for debilitated patients.**

Dosage Forms

Cream, topical: Lidocaine 2.5% and prilocaine 2.5% (5 g, 30 g)

EMLA®: Lidocaine 2.5% and prilocaine 2.5% (5 g, 30 g) [each packaged with Tegaderm® dressings]

Disc, topical: Lidocaine 2.5% and prilocaine 2.5% per disc (2s, 10s) [each 1 g disc is 10 cm^2]

Gel, periodontal: Lidocaine 2.5% and prilocaine 2.5% (1.7 g) [cartridge]

Lidocaine and Tetracaine *(LYE doe kane & TET ra kane)*

U.S. Brand Names Synera™

Index Terms Tetracaine and Lidocaine

Pharmacologic Category Analgesic, Topical; Local Anesthetic

Use Topical anesthetic for use on normal intact skin for minor procedures (eg, I.V. cannulation or venipuncture) and superficial dermatologic procedures

Pregnancy Risk Factor B

Dosage Transdermal patch: Children ≥3 years and Adults:

Venipuncture or intravenous cannulation: Prior to procedure, apply to intact skin for 20-30 minutes

Superficial dermatological procedures: Prior to procedure, apply to intact skin for 30 minutes

Note: Adults can use another patch at a new location to facilitate venous access after a failed attempt; remove previous patch.

Dosage adjustment in hepatic impairment: Use caution in patients with severe hepatic dysfunction.

Additional Information Complete prescribing information for this medication should be consulted for additional detail.

Dosage Forms

Transdermal system:

Synera™: Lidocaine 70 mg and tetracaine 70 mg (10s) [contains heating component; each patch is 50 cm^2]

- **Lidocaine Hydrochloride** *see Lidocaine on page 1010*
- **Lidocaine Hydrochloride and Bupivacaine Hydrochloride** *see Lidocaine and Bupivacaine on page 1014*
- **Lidodan™ (Can)** *see Lidocaine on page 1010*
- **Lidoderm®** *see Lidocaine on page 1010*
- **LidoSite™** *see Lidocaine and Epinephrine on page 1014*
- **LID-Pack® (Can)** *see Bacitracin and Polymyxin B on page 192*
- **Lignocaine Hydrochloride** *see Lidocaine on page 1010*
- **Limbitrol** *see Amitriptyline and Chlordiazepoxide on page 103*
- **Limbitrol® DS** *see Amitriptyline and Chlordiazepoxide on page 103*
- **Lin-Amox (Can)** *see Amoxicillin on page 110*
- **Lin-Buspirone (Can)** *see BusPIRone on page 256*

Lindane *(LIN dane)*

Canadian Brand Names Hexit™; PMS-Lindane

Index Terms Benzene Hexachloride; Gamma Benzene Hexachloride; Hexachlorocyclohexane

Pharmacologic Category Antiparasitic Agent, Topical; Pediculocide; Scabicidal Agent

Use Treatment of *Sarcoptes scabiei* (scabies), *Pediculus capitis* (head lice), and *Phthirus pubis* (crab lice); FDA recommends reserving lindane as a second-line agent or with inadequate response to other therapies

Restrictions An FDA-approved medication guide must be distributed when dispensing an outpatient prescription (new or refill) where this medication is to be used without direct supervision of a healthcare provider. Medication guides are available at http://www.fda.gov/cder/Offices/ODS/medication_guides.htm.

Pregnancy Risk Factor C

Pregnancy Implications There are no well-controlled studies in pregnant women.

Lactation Enters breast milk/contraindicated

Contraindications Hypersensitivity to lindane or any component of the formulation; uncontrolled seizure disorders; crusted (Norwegian) scabies, acutely-inflamed skin or raw, weeping surfaces or other skin conditions which may increase systemic absorption

Warnings/Precautions [U.S. Boxed Warning]: Not considered a drug of first choice; use only in patients who have failed first-line treatments, or in patients who cannot tolerate these agents. Because of the potential for systemic absorption and CNS side effects, lindane should be used with caution; consider permethrin or crotamiton agent first. Oil-based hair dressing may increase toxic potential.

[U.S. Boxed Warning]: May be associated with severe neurologic toxicities (contraindicated in premature infants and uncontrolled seizure disorders). Seizures and death have been reported with use; use with caution in infants, small children, patients <50 kg, or patients with a history of seizures; use caution with conditions which may increase risk of seizures or medications which decrease seizure threshold; use caution with hepatic impairment; avoid contact with face, eyes, mucous membranes, and urethral meatus.

[U.S. Boxed Warning]: A lindane medication use guide must be given to all patients along with instructions for proper use. Patients should be informed that itching may occur following successful killing of lice and re-treatment may not be indicated. Should be used as a part of an overall lice management program

Adverse Reactions Frequency not defined (includes postmarketing and/or case reports).
Cardiovascular: Cardiac arrhythmia
Central nervous system: Ataxia, dizziness, headache, restlessness, seizure, pain
Dermatologic: Alopecia, contact dermatitis, skin and adipose tissue may act as repositories, eczematous eruptions, pruritus, urticaria
Gastrointestinal: Nausea, vomiting
Hematologic: Aplastic anemia
Hepatic: Hepatitis
Local: Burning and stinging
Neuromuscular & skeletal: Paresthesias
Renal: Hematuria
Respiratory: Pulmonary edema

Overdosage/Toxicology Symptoms include vomiting, restlessness, ataxia, seizures, arrhythmias, pulmonary edema, hematuria, and hepatitis. The drug is absorbed through skin, mucous membranes, and the GI tract. When used excessively for prolonged periods or when accidental ingestion has occurred, the drug has occasionally caused serious CNS, hepatic, and renal toxicity. If ingested, perform gastric lavage and general supportive measures. Diazepam 0.01 mg/kg can be used to control seizures.

Drug Interactions
Increased Effect/Toxicity: Increased toxicity: Drugs which lower seizure threshold

Mechanism of Action Directly absorbed by parasites and ova through the exoskeleton; stimulates the nervous system resulting in seizures and death of parasitic arthropods

Pharmacodynamics/Kinetics
Absorption: ≤13% systemically
Distribution: Stored in body fat; accumulates in brain; skin and adipose tissue may act as repositories
Metabolism: Hepatic
Half-life elimination: Children: 17-22 hours
Time to peak, serum: Children: 6 hours
Excretion: Urine and feces

Dosage Children and Adults: Topical:
Scabies: Apply a thin layer of lotion and massage it on skin from the neck to the toes; after 8-12 hours, bathe and remove the drug
Head lice, crab lice: Apply shampoo to dry hair and massage into hair for 4 minutes; add small quantities of water to hair until lather forms, then rinse hair thoroughly and comb with a fine tooth comb to remove nits. Amount of shampoo needed is based on length and density of hair; most patients will require 30 mL (maximum: 60 mL).

Administration For topical use only; never administer orally. Caregivers should apply with gloves (avoid natural latex, may be permeable to lindane). Rinse off with warm (not hot) water.
Lotion: Apply to dry, cool skin; do not apply to face or eyes. Wait at least 1 hour after bathing or showering (wet or warm skin increases absorption). Skin should be clean and free of any other lotions, creams, or oil prior to lindane application.
Shampoo: Apply to clean, dry hair. Wait at least 1 hour after washing hair before applying lindane shampoo. Hair should be washed with a shampoo not containing a conditioner; hair and skin of head and neck should be free of any lotions, oils, or creams prior to lindane application.

Dosage Forms
Lotion, topical: 1% (60 mL)
Shampoo, topical: 1% (60 mL) [contains alcohol 0.5%]

♦ **Linessa® (Can)** see Ethinyl Estradiol and Desogestrel *on page 645*

Linezolid (li NE zoh lid)

U.S. Brand Names Zyvox™
Canadian Brand Names Zyvoxam®
Pharmacologic Category Antibiotic, Oxazolidinone
Additional Appendix Information
Antimicrobial Drugs of Choice *on page 1981*
Community-Acquired Pneumonia in Adults *on page 1999*
Use Treatment of vancomycin-resistant *Enterococcus faecium* (VRE) infections, nosocomial pneumonia caused by *Staphylococcus aureus* including MRSA or *Streptococcus pneumoniae* (including multidrug-resistant strains [MDRSP]), complicated and uncomplicated skin and skin structure infections (including diabetic foot infections without concomitant osteomyelitis), and community-acquired pneumonia caused by susceptible gram-positive organisms
Pregnancy Risk Factor C
Pregnancy Implications Teratogenic effects were not observed in animal studies. There are no adequate and well-controlled studies in pregnant women. Should be used in pregnancy only if the potential benefit justifies the risk to the fetus.
Lactation Excretion in breast milk unknown/use caution
Medication Safety Issues
Sound-alike/look-alike issues:
Zyvox™ may be confused with Vioxx®, Ziox™, Zosyn®, Zovirax®
Contraindications Hypersensitivity to linezolid or any other component of the formulation
Warnings/Precautions Myelosuppression has been reported and may be dependent on duration of therapy (generally >2 weeks of treatment); use with caution in patients with pre-existing myelosuppression, in patients receiving other drugs which may cause bone marrow suppression, or in chronic infection (previous or concurrent antibiotic therapy). Weekly CBC monitoring is recommended. Discontinue linezolid in patients developing myelosuppression (or in whom myelosuppression worsens during treatment).

Lactic acidosis has been reported with use. Linezolid exhibits mild MAO inhibitor properties and has the potential to have the same interactions as other MAO inhibitors; use with caution in uncontrolled hypertension, pheochromocytoma, carcinoid syndrome, or untreated hyperthyroidism; avoid use with serotonergic agents such as TCAs, venlafaxine, trazodone, sibutramine, meperidine, dextromethorphan, and SSRIs; concomitant use has been associated with the development of serotonin syndrome. Unnecessary use may lead to the development of resistance to linezolid; consider alternatives before initiating outpatient treatment.

Peripheral and optic neuropathy (with vision loss) has been reported and may occur primarily with extended courses of therapy >28 days; any symptoms of visual change or impairment warrant immediate ophthalmic evaluation and possible discontinuation of therapy. Seizures have been reported; use with caution in patients with a history of seizures. Prolonged use may result in superinfection, including pseudomembranous colitis.

Due to inconsistent therapeutic concentrations in the CSF, empiric use in pediatric patients with CNS infections is not recommended.
Adverse Reactions Percentages as reported in adults; frequency similar in pediatric patients
>10%:
Central nervous system: Headache (<1% to 11%)
Gastrointestinal: Diarrhea (3% to 11%)
1% to 10%:
Central nervous system: Insomnia (3%), dizziness (0.4% to 2%), fever (2%)
Dermatologic: Rash (2%)
Gastrointestinal: Nausea (3% to 10%), vomiting (1% to 4%), pancreatic enzymes increased (<1% to 4%), constipation (2%), taste alteration (1% to 2%), tongue discoloration (0.2% to 1%), oral moniliasis (0.4% to 1%), pancreatitis
Genitourinary: Vaginal moniliasis (1% to 2%)
Hematologic: Thrombocytopenia (0.3% to 10%), hemoglobin decreased (0.9% to 7%), anemia, leukopenia, neutropenia; **Note:** Myelosuppression (including anemia, leukopenia, pancytopenia, and thrombocytopenia; may be more common in patients receiving linezolid for >2 weeks)
Hepatic: Abnormal LFTs (0.4% to 1%)
Renal: BUN increased (<1% to 2%)
Miscellaneous: Fungal infection (0.1% to 2%), lactate dehydrogenase increased (<1% to 2%)
<1% or frequency not defined (limited to important or life-threatening): Blurred vision, *C. difficile*-related complications, creatinine increased, dyspepsia, hypertension, localized abdominal pain, pruritus, lactic acidosis, peripheral neuropathy, optic neuropathy, serotonin syndrome (with concurrent use of other serotonergic agents)
Overdosage/Toxicology Treatment is supportive. Hemodialysis may improve elimination (30% of a dose is removed during a 3-hour hemodialysis session).
Drug Interactions
Increased Effect/Toxicity: Linezolid is a reversible, nonselective inhibitor of MAO. Serotonergic agents (eg, TCAs, venlafaxine, trazodone, sibutramine, meperidine, dextromethorphan, and SSRIs) may cause a serotonin syndrome (eg, hyperpyrexia, cognitive dysfunction) when used concomitantly. Adrenergic agents (eg, phenylpropanolamine, pseudoephedrine, sympathomimetic agents, vasopressor or dopaminergic agents) may cause hypertension. Tramadol may increase the risk of seizures when used concurrently with linezolid. Myelosuppressive medications may increase risk of myelosuppression when used concurrently with linezolid.
Ethanol/Nutrition/Herb Interactions
Ethanol: Avoid ethanol (based on CNS depressant effects and potential tyramine content)
Food: Concurrent ingestion of foods rich in tyramine may cause sudden and severe high blood pressure (hypertensive crisis). Avoid tyramine-containing foods with MAOIs. Food's freshness is also an important concern; improperly stored or spoiled food can create an environment where tyramine concentrations may increase.

Herb/Nutraceuticals. Avoid supplements containing caffeine, tyrosine, tryptophan or phenyl-alanine. Ingestion of large quantities may increase the risk of severe side effects (eg, hypertensive reactions, serotonin syndrome).

Stability
Infusion: Store at 25°C (77°F). Protect from light. Keep infusion bags in overwrap until ready for use. Protect infusion bags from freezing.
Oral suspension: Following reconstitution, store at room temperature. Use reconstituted suspension within 21 days.

Mechanism of Action Inhibits bacterial protein synthesis by binding to bacterial 23S ribosomal RNA of the 50S subunit. This prevents the formation of a functional 70S initiation complex that is essential for the bacterial translation process. Linezolid is bacteriostatic against enterococci and staphylococci and bactericidal against most strains of streptococci.

Pharmacodynamics/Kinetics
Absorption: Rapid and extensive
Distribution: V_{dss}: Adults: 40-50 L
Protein binding: Adults: 31%
Metabolism: Hepatic via oxidation of the morpholine ring, resulting in two inactive metabolites (aminoethoxyacetic acid, hydroxyethyl glycine); does not involve CYP
Bioavailability: 100%
Half-life elimination: Children ≥1 week (full-term) to 11 years: 1.5-3 hours; Adults: 4-5 hours
Time to peak: Adults: Oral: 1-2 hours
Excretion: Urine (30% as parent drug, 50% as metabolites); feces (9% as metabolites)
Nonrenal clearance: 65%; increased in children ≥1 week to 11 years

Dosage
VRE infections: Oral, I.V.:
Preterm neonates (<34 weeks gestational age): 10 mg/kg every 12 hours; neonates with a suboptimal clinical response can be advanced to 10 mg/kg every 8 hours. By day 7 of life, all neonates should receive 10 mg/kg every 8 hours.
Infants (excluding preterm neonates <1 week) and Children ≤11 years: 10 mg/kg every 8 hours for 14-28 days
Children ≥12 years and Adults: 600 mg every 12 hours for 14-28 days
Nosocomial pneumonia, complicated skin and skin structure infections, community acquired pneumonia including concurrent bacteremia: Oral, I.V.:
Infants (excluding preterm neonates <1 week) and Children ≤11 years: 10 mg/kg every 8 hours for 10-14 days
Children ≥12 years and Adults: 600 mg every 12 hours for 10-14 days
Uncomplicated skin and skin structure infections: Oral:
Infants (excluding preterm neonates <1 week) and Children <5 years: 10 mg/kg every 8 hours for 10-14 days
Children 5-11 years: 10 mg/kg every 12 hours for 10-14 days
Children ≥12-18 years: 600 mg every 12 hours for 10-14 days
Adults: 400 mg every 12 hours for 10-14 days
Elderly: No dosage adjustment required

Dosage adjustment in renal impairment: No adjustment is recommended. The two primary metabolites may accumulate in patients with renal impairment but the clinical significance is unknown. Weigh the risk of accumulation of metabolites versus the benefit of therapy. Both linezolid and the two metabolites are eliminated by dialysis. Linezolid should be given after hemodialysis.

Dosage adjustment in hepatic impairment: No dosage adjustment required for mild to moderate hepatic insufficiency (Child-Pugh Class A or B). Use in severe hepatic insufficiency has not been adequately evaluated.

Dietary Considerations Take with or without food. Avoid tyramine-containing foods/beverages. Some examples include aged or matured cheese, air-dried or cured meats (including sausages and salamis), fava or broad bean pods, tap/draft beers, Marmite concentrate, sauerkraut, soy sauce and other soybean condiments.

Suspension contains 20 mg phenylalanine per teaspoonful. Sodium content: 0.1 mEq/tablet; 0.4 mEq/5 mL; 1.7 mEq/100 mL infusion; 3.3 mEq/200 mL infusion; 5 mEq/300 mL infusion

Administration
I.V.: Administer intravenous infusion over 30-120 minutes. Do not mix or infuse with other medications. When the same intravenous line is used for sequential infusion of other medications, flush line with D_5W, NS, or LR before and after infusing linezolid. The yellow color of the injection may intensify over time without affecting potency.
Oral suspension: Invert gently to mix prior to administration, do not shake.

Monitoring Parameters Weekly CBC and platelet counts, particularly in patients at increased risk of bleeding, with pre-existing myelosuppression, on concomitant medications that cause bone marrow suppression, in those who require >2 weeks of therapy, or in those with chronic infection who have received previous or concomitant antibiotic therapy; visual function with extended therapy (≥3 months) or in patients with new onset visual symptoms, regardless of therapy length

Dosage Forms
Infusion [premixed]: 200 mg (100 mL) [contains sodium 1.7 mEq]; 400 mg (200 mL) [contains sodium 3.3 mEq]; 600 mg (300 mL) [contains sodium 5 mEq]
Powder for oral suspension: 20 mg/mL (150 mL) [contains phenylalanine 20 mg/5 mL, sodium benzoate, and sodium 0.4 mEq/5 mL; orange flavor]
Tablet: 600 mg [contains sodium 0.1 mEq/tablet]

♦ **Lin-Sotalol (Can)** *see* Sotalol *on page 1592*
♦ **Lioresal**® *see* Baclofen *on page 193*
♦ **Liotec (Can)** *see* Baclofen *on page 193*

Liothyronine (lye oh THYE roe neen)

U.S. Brand Names Cytomel®; Triostat®
Canadian Brand Names Cytomel®
Index Terms Liothyronine Sodium; Sodium *L*-Triiodothyronine; T$_3$ Sodium (error-prone abbreviation)
Pharmacologic Category Thyroid Product
Use
Oral: Replacement or supplemental therapy in hypothyroidism; management of nontoxic goiter; a diagnostic aid
I.V.: Treatment of myxedema coma/precoma
Pregnancy Risk Factor A
Medication Safety Issues
Sound-alike/look-alike issues:
Liothyronine may be confused with levothyroxine

T3 is an error-prone abbreviation (mistaken as acetaminophen and codeine [ie, Tylenol® #3])
Dosage Doses should be adjusted based on clinical response and laboratory parameters.
Children: Congenital hypothyroidism: Oral: 5 mcg/day increase by 5 mcg every 3-4 days until the desired response is achieved. Usual maintenance dose: 20 mcg/day for infants, 50 mcg/day for children 1-3 years of age, and adult dose for children >3 years.
Adults:
Hypothyroidism: Oral: 25 mcg/day increase by increments of 12.5-25 mcg/day every 1-2 weeks to a maximum of 100 mcg/day; usual maintenance dose: 25-75 mcg/day.
Patients with cardiovascular disease: Refer to Elderly dosing.
T$_3$ suppression test: Oral: 75-100 mcg/day for 7 days; use lowest dose for elderly
Myxedema: Oral: Initial: 5 mcg/day; increase in increments of 5-10 mcg/day every 1-2 weeks. When 25 mcg/day is reached, dosage may be increased at intervals of 5-25 mcg/day every 1-2 weeks. Usual maintenance dose: 50-100 mcg/day.
Myxedema coma: I.V.: 25-50 mcg
Patients with known or suspected cardiovascular disease: 10-20 mcg
Note: Normally, at least 4 hours should be allowed between doses to adequately assess therapeutic response and no more than 12 hours should elapse between doses to avoid fluctuations in hormone levels. Oral therapy should be resumed as soon as the clinical situation has been stabilized and the patient is able to take oral medication. If levothyroxine rather than liothyronine sodium is used in initiating oral therapy, the physician should bear in mind that there is a delay of several days in the onset of levothyroxine activity and that I.V. therapy should be discontinued gradually.
Simple (nontoxic) goiter: Oral: Initial: 5 mcg/day; increase by 5-10 mcg every 1-2 weeks; after 25 mcg/day is reached, may increase dose by 12.5-25 mcg. Usual maintenance dose: 75 mcg/day
Elderly: Oral: 5 mcg/day; increase by 5 mcg/day every 2 weeks
Additional Information Complete prescribing information for this medication should be consulted for additional detail.
Dosage Forms
Injection, solution, as sodium (Triostat®): 10 mcg/mL (1 mL) [contains alcohol 6.8%]
Tablet, as sodium (Cytomel®): 5 mcg, 25 mcg, 50 mcg

♦ **Liothyronine Sodium** see Liothyronine on page 1020

Liotrix (LYE oh triks)

U.S. Brand Names Thyrolar®
Canadian Brand Names Thyrolar®
Index Terms T$_3$/T$_4$ Liotrix
Pharmacologic Category Thyroid Product
Use Replacement or supplemental therapy in hypothyroidism (uniform mixture of T$_4$:T$_3$ in 4:1 ratio by weight); little advantage to this product exists and cost is not justified
Pregnancy Risk Factor A
Medication Safety Issues
Sound-alike/look-alike issues:
Liotrix may be confused with Klotrix®
Thyrolar® may be confused with Theolair™, Thyrogen®, Thytropar®
Dosage Oral:
Congenital hypothyroidism:
Children (dose of T$_4$ or levothyroxine/day):
0-6 months: 8-10 mcg/kg or 25-50 mcg/day
6-12 months: 6-8 mcg/kg or 50-75 mcg/day
1-5 years: 5-6 mcg/kg or 75-100 mcg/day
6-12 years: 4-5 mcg/kg or 100-150 mcg/day
>12 years: 2-3 mcg/kg or >150 mcg/day
Hypothyroidism (dose of thyroid equivalent):
Adults: 30 mg/day (15 mg/day if cardiovascular impairment), increasing by increments of 15 mg/day at 2- to 3-week intervals to a maximum of 180 mg/day (usual maintenance dose: 60-120 mg/day)
Elderly: Initial: 15 mg, adjust dose at 2- to 4-week intervals by increments of 15 mg
Additional Information Complete prescribing information for this medication should be consulted for additional detail.
Dosage Forms Tablet:
¼ [levothyroxine sodium 12.5 mcg and liothyronine sodium 3.1 mcg]
½ [levothyroxine sodium 25 mcg and liothyronine sodium 6.25 mcg]
1 [levothyroxine sodium 50 mcg and liothyronine sodium 12.5 mcg]
2 [levothyroxine sodium 100 mcg and liothyronine sodium 25 mcg]
3 [levothyroxine sodium 150 mcg and liothyronine sodium 37.5 mcg]

♦ **Lipancreatin** *see* Pancrelipase *on page 1302*
♦ **Lipidil EZ® (Can)** *see* Fenofibrate *on page 689*
♦ **Lipidil Micro® (Can)** *see* Fenofibrate *on page 689*
♦ **Lipidil Supra® (Can)** *see* Fenofibrate *on page 689*
♦ **Lipitor®** *see* Atorvastatin *on page 171*
♦ **Lipofen™** *see* Fenofibrate *on page 689*
♦ **Liposyn® II (Can)** *see* Fat Emulsion *on page 686*
♦ **Liposyn® III** *see* Fat Emulsion *on page 686*
♦ **Lipram 4500** *see* Pancrelipase *on page 1302*
♦ **Lipram-CR** *see* Pancrelipase *on page 1302*
♦ **Lipram-PN** *see* Pancrelipase *on page 1302*
♦ **Lipram-UL** *see* Pancrelipase *on page 1302*
♦ **Liqua-Cal [OTC]** *see* Calcium and Vitamin D *on page 268*
♦ **Liquibid-D** *see* Guaifenesin and Phenylephrine *on page 818*
♦ **Liquibid-D® 1200** *see* Guaifenesin and Phenylephrine *on page 818*
♦ **Liquibid-PD [DSC]** *see* Guaifenesin and Phenylephrine *on page 818*
♦ **Liquid Antidote** *see* Charcoal *on page 338*

Lisinopril (lyse IN oh pril)

U.S. Brand Names Prinivil®; Zestril®
Canadian Brand Names Apo-Lisinopril®; Prinivil®; Zestril®
Pharmacologic Category Angiotensin-Converting Enzyme (ACE) Inhibitor
Additional Appendix Information
Angiotensin Agents *on page 1860*
Heart Failure (Systolic) *on page 2051*

Use Treatment of hypertension, either alone or in combination with other antihypertensive agents; adjunctive therapy in treatment of CHF (afterload reduction); treatment of acute myocardial infarction within 24 hours in hemodynamically-stable patients to improve survival; treatment of left ventricular dysfunction after myocardial infarction

Pregnancy Risk Factor C (1st trimester)/D (2nd and 3rd trimesters)

Pregnancy Implications Decreased placental blood flow, low birth weight, fetal hypotension, preterm delivery, and fetal death have been noted with the use of some ACE inhibitors (ACEIs) in animal studies. Neonatal hypotension, skull hypoplasia, anuria, renal failure, oligohydramnios (associated with fetal limb contractures, craniofacial deformities, hypoplastic lung development), prematurity, intrauterine growth retardation, and patent ductus arteriosus have been reported with the use of ACEIs, primarily in the 2nd and 3rd trimesters. The risk of neonatal toxicity has been considered less when ACEIs have been used in the 1st trimester; however, major congenital malformations have been reported. The cardiovascular and/or central nervous systems are most commonly affected. Unless alternative agents are not appropriate, ACEIs should be discontinued as soon as possible once pregnancy is detected.

Lactation Excretion in breast milk unknown/not recommended

Medication Safety Issues
Sound-alike/look-alike issues:
Lisinopril may be confused with fosinopril, Lioresal®, Risperdal®
Prinivil® may be confused with Plendil®, Pravachol®, Prevacid®, Prilosec®, Proventil®
Zestril® may be confused with Desyrel®, Restoril®, Vistaril®, Zetia™, Zostrix®

International issues:
Acepril® [Denmark] may be confused with Accupril® which is a brand name for quinapril in the U.S.
Acepril®: Brand name for enalapril in Hungary and Switzerland; brand name for captopril in Great Britain
Carace® [Ireland; Great Britain] may be confused with Carac™ which is a brand name for fluorouracil in the U.S.
Zetril® may be confused with Nostril® which is a brand name for chlorhexidine/cetrimonium in France

Contraindications Hypersensitivity to lisinopril or any component of the formulation; angioedema related to previous treatment with an ACE inhibitor; bilateral renal artery stenosis; pregnancy (2nd and 3rd trimesters)

Warnings/Precautions Anaphylactic reactions can occur. Angioedema can occur at any time during treatment (especially following first dose). It may involve head and neck (potentially affecting the airway) or the intestine (presenting with abdominal pain). Prolonged monitoring may be required especially if tongue, glottis, or larynx are involved as they are associated with airway obstruction. Those with a history of airway surgery in this situation have a higher risk. Careful blood pressure monitoring with first dose (hypotension can occur especially in volume-depleted patients). **[U.S. Boxed Warning]: Based on human data, ACEIs can cause injury and death to the developing fetus when used in the second and third trimesters. ACEIs should be discontinued as soon as possible once pregnancy is detected.**

Dosage adjustment needed in renal impairment. Use with caution in hypovolemia; collagen vascular diseases; valvular stenosis (particularly aortic stenosis); or before, during, or immediately after anesthesia. Hyperkalemia may occur; risk factors include renal dysfunction, diabetes mellitus, concomitant use of potassium-sparing diuretics, potassium supplements and/or potassium containing salts. Use cautiously, if at all, with these agents and monitor potassium closely. Avoid rapid dosage escalation, which may lead to renal insufficiency. Rare toxicities associated with ACE inhibitors include cholestatic jaundice (which may progress to hepatic necrosis) and neutropenia/agranulocytosis with myeloid hyperplasia. May be associated with deterioration of renal function and/or increases in serum creatinine, particularly in patients dependent on renin-angiotensin-aldosterone system. Use with caution in unilateral renal artery stenosis and pre-existing renal insufficiency; if patient has renal impairment then a baseline WBC with differential and serum creatinine should be evaluated and monitored *(Continued)*

Lisinopril *(Continued)*

closely during the first 3 months of therapy. Hypersensitivity reactions may be seen during hemodialysis with high-flux dialysis membranes (eg, AN69). Safety and efficacy have not been established in children <6 years of age.

Adverse Reactions Note: Frequency ranges include data from hypertension and heart failure trials. Higher rates of adverse reactions have generally been noted in patients with CHF. However, the frequency of adverse effects associated with placebo is also increased in this population.

1% to 10%:
Cardiovascular: Orthostatic effects (1%), hypotension (1% to 4%)
Central nervous system: Headache (4% to 6%), dizziness (5% to 12%), fatigue (3%)
Dermatologic: Rash (1% to 2%)
Endocrine & metabolic: Hyperkalemia (2% to 5%)
Gastrointestinal: Diarrhea (3% to 4%), nausea (2%), vomiting (1%), abdominal pain (2%)
Genitourinary: Impotence (1%)
Hematologic: Decreased hemoglobin (small)
Neuromuscular & skeletal: Chest pain (3%), weakness (1%)
Renal: BUN increased (2%); deterioration in renal function (in patients with bilateral renal artery stenosis or hypovolemia); serum creatinine increased (often transient)
Respiratory: Cough (4% to 9%), upper respiratory infection (2% to 2%)
<1% (Limited to important or life-threatening): Acute renal failure, alopecia, anaphylactoid reactions, angioedema, anuria, arrhythmia, arthralgia, asthma, ataxia, azotemia, bone marrow suppression, bronchospasm, cardiac arrest, decreased libido, gout, hepatic necrosis, hepatitis, hyperkalemia, hyponatremia, increased bilirubin, transaminases increased, infiltrates, jaundice (cholestatic), MI, neutropenia, oliguria, orthostatic hypotension, pancreatitis, paresthesia, pemphigus, peripheral neuropathy, photosensitivity, pleural effusion, pulmonary embolism, Stevens-Johnson syndrome, stroke, systemic lupus erythematosus, thrombocytopenia, TIA, toxic epidermal necrolysis, tremor, urticaria, vasculitis, vertigo, vision loss. In addition, a syndrome which may include fever, myalgia, arthralgia, interstitial nephritis, vasculitis, rash, eosinophilia and positive ANA, and elevated ESR has been reported with ACE inhibitors.

Overdosage/Toxicology Mild hypotension has been the only toxic effect seen with acute overdose; bradycardia may also occur. Hyperkalemia occurs even with therapeutic doses, especially in patients with renal insufficiency and those taking NSAIDs. Following initiation of essential overdose management, toxic symptom and supportive treatment should be initiated. Hypotension usually responds to I.V. fluids or Trendelenburg positioning.

Drug Interactions

Increased Effect/Toxicity: Allopurinol may cause a higher risk of hypersensitivity reaction when taken concurrently. Neutropenia from azathioprine may be enhanced by concurrent use. Adverse events/toxicity of azathioprine (neutropenia), cyclosporine (nephrotoxicity), ferric gluconate, insulin (hypoglycemia), lithium, mercaptopurine (neutropenia), NSAIDs (nephrotoxicity). Concurrent use of eplerenone, potassium-sparing diuretics, or trimethoprim with ACE inhibitor may increase risk of hyperkalemia. Loop and thiazide diuretics may increase risk of hypovolemia, increasing the risk of nephrotoxicity when used with ACE inhibitors. ACE inhibitors may enhance the adverse/toxic effects (nitritoid reaction) of gold sodium thiomalate.

Decreased Effect: Antacids may decrease serum concentrations of ACE inhibitors. Aprotinin may decrease the antihypertensive effect of ACE inhibitors during infusion. NSAIDs and salicylates may attenuate hypertensive efficacy of ACE inhibitors.

Ethanol/Nutrition/Herb Interactions

Food: Potassium-containing salt substitutes may increase risk of hyperkalemia.
Herb/Nutraceutical: Avoid dong quai if using for hypertension (has estrogenic activity). Avoid ephedra, yohimbe, ginseng (may worsen hypertension). Avoid garlic (may have increased antihypertensive effect).

Mechanism of Action Competitive inhibitor of angiotensin-converting enzyme (ACE); prevents conversion of angiotensin I to angiotensin II, a potent vasoconstrictor; results in lower levels of angiotensin II which causes an increase in plasma renin activity and a reduction in aldosterone secretion; a CNS mechanism may also be involved in hypotensive effect as angiotensin II increases adrenergic outflow from CNS; vasoactive kallikreins may be decreased in conversion to active hormones by ACE inhibitors, thus reducing blood pressure

Pharmacodynamics/Kinetics

Onset of action: 1 hour
Peak effect: Hypotensive: Oral: ~6 hours
Duration: 24 hours
Absorption: Well absorbed; unaffected by food
Protein binding: 25%
Half-life elimination: 11-12 hours
Excretion: Primarily urine (as unchanged drug)

Dosage Oral:

Hypertension:
Children ≥6 years: Initial: 0.07 mg/kg once daily (up to 5 mg); increase dose at 1- to 2-week intervals; doses >0.61 mg/kg or >40 mg have not been evaluated.
Adults: Usual dosage range (JNC 7): 10-40 mg/day
Not maintained on diuretic: Initial: 10 mg/day
Maintained on diuretic: Initial: 5 mg/day
Note: Antihypertensive effect may diminish toward the end of the dosing interval especially with doses of 10 mg/day. An increased dose may aid in extending the duration of antihypertensive effect. Doses up to 80 mg/day have been used, but do not appear to give greater effect (Zestril® Product Information, 12/04).
Elderly: Initial: 2.5-5 mg/day; increase doses 2.5-5 mg/day at 1- to 2-week intervals; maximum daily dose: 40 mg
Patients taking diuretics should have them discontinued 2-3 days prior to initiating lisinopril if possible. Restart diuretic after blood pressure is stable if needed. If diuretic cannot be

discontinued prior to therapy, begin with 5 mg with close supervision until stable blood
pressure. In patients with hyponatremia (<130 mEq/L), start dose at 2.5 mg/day
Congestive heart failure: Adults: Initial: 2.5-5 mg once daily; then increase by no more than
10 mg increments at intervals no less than 2 weeks to a maximum daily dose of 40 mg.
Usual maintenance: 5-40 mg/day as a single dose. Target dose: 20-40 mg once daily
(ACC/AHA 2005 Heart Failure Guidelines)

Note: If patient has hyponatremia (serum sodium <130 meq/L) or renal impairment (Cl_{cr}
<30 mL/minute or creatinine >3 mg/dL), then initial dose should be 2.5 mg/day

Acute myocardial infarction (within 24 hours in hemodynamically stable patients): Oral: 5 mg
immediately, then 5 mg at 24 hours, 10 mg at 48 hours, and 10 mg every day thereafter for
6 weeks. Patients should continue to receive standard treatments such as thrombolytics,
aspirin, and beta-blockers.

Dosing adjustment in renal impairment:
Hypertension:
Adults: Initial doses should be modified and upward titration should be cautious, based
on response (maximum: 40 mg/day)
Cl_{cr} >30 mL/minute: Initial: 10 mg/day
Cl_{cr} 10-30 mL/minute: Initial: 5 mg/day
Hemodialysis: Initial: 2.5 mg/day; dialyzable (50%)
Children: Use in not recommended in pediatric patients with GFR <30 mL/minute/1.73
m^2
Congestive heart failure: Adults: Cl_{cr} <30 mL/minute or creatinine >3 mg/dL): Initial: 2.5
mg/day

Dietary Considerations Use potassium-containing salt substitutes cautiously in diabetic
patients, patients with renal dysfunction, or those maintained on potassium supplements or
potassium-sparing diuretics.

Administration Watch for hypotensive effects within 1-3 hours of first dose or new higher
dose.

Monitoring Parameters BUN, serum creatinine, renal function, WBC, and potassium

Test Interactions May cause false-positive results in urine acetone determinations using
sodium nitroprusside reagent; increased potassium (S); increased serum creatinine/BUN

Dosage Forms [DSC] = Discontinued product
Tablet: 2.5 mg, 5 mg, 10 mg, 20 mg, 30 mg, 40 mg
Prinivil®: 5 mg, 10 mg, 20 mg, 30 mg; 40 mg [DSC]
Zestril®: 2.5 mg, 5 mg, 10 mg, 20 mg, 30 mg, 40 mg

Extemporaneous Preparations Preparation of oral suspension (1 mg/mL): Note: Mix in
a polyethylene terephthalate bottle. Add 10 mL of purified water (USP) to a bottle containing
ten lisinopril 20 mg tablets (total 200 mg). Shake for at least 1 minute; then add 30 mL
Bicitra® and 160 mL Ora-Sweet SF™ and shake gently to suspend contents. Store at 25°C
(77°F); stable for up to 4 weeks.

Lisinopril and Hydrochlorothiazide
(lyse IN oh pril & hye droe klor oh THYE a zide)

U.S. Brand Names Prinzide®; Zestoretic®
Canadian Brand Names Prinzide®; Zestoretic®
Index Terms Hydrochlorothiazide and Lisinopril
Pharmacologic Category Antihypertensive Agent, Combination
Use Treatment of hypertension
Pregnancy Risk Factor C/D (2nd and 3rd trimesters)
Dosage Adults: Oral: Dosage is individualized; see each component for appropriate dosing
suggestions; doses >80 mg/day lisinopril or >50 mg/day hydrochlorothiazide are not recom-
mended.
Additional Information Complete prescribing information for this medication should be
consulted for additional detail.
Dosage Forms Tablet:
Lisinopril 10 mg and hydrochlorothiazide 12.5 mg
Lisinopril 20 mg and hydrochlorothiazide 12.5 mg
Lisinopril 20 mg and hydrochlorothiazide 25 mg

♦ **Lispro Insulin** see Insulin Lispro on page 913
♦ **Lithane™ (Can)** see Lithium on page 1023

Lithium (LITH ee um)

U.S. Brand Names Eskalith® [DSC]; Eskalith CR® [DSC]; Lithobid®
Canadian Brand Names Apo-Lithium® Carbonate; Apo-Lithium® Carbonate SR; Carbolith™;
Duralith®; Lithane™; PMS-Lithium Carbonate; PMS-Lithium Citrate
Index Terms Lithium Carbonate; Lithium Citrate
Pharmacologic Category Lithium
Use Management of bipolar disorders; treatment of mania in individuals with bipolar disorder
(maintenance treatment prevents or diminishes intensity of subsequent episodes)
Unlabeled/Investigational Use Potential augmenting agent for antidepressants; aggression,
post-traumatic stress disorder, conduct disorder in children
Pregnancy Risk Factor D
Pregnancy Implications Cardiac malformations in the infant, including Ebstein's anomaly,
are associated with use of lithium during the first trimester of pregnancy. Nontoxic effects to
the newborn include shallow respiration, hypotonia, lethargy, cyanosis, diabetes insipidus,
thyroid depression, and nontoxic goiter when lithium is used near term. Efforts should be
made to avoid lithium use during the first trimester; if an alternative therapy is not appropriate,
the lowest possible dose of lithium should be used throughout the pregnancy. Fetal echocardiography and ultrasound to screen for anomalies should be conducted between 16-20
(Continued)

Lithium (Continued)

weeks of gestation. Lithium levels should be monitored in the mother and may need to be adjusted following delivery.

Lactation Enters breast milk/contraindicated

Medication Safety Issues

Sound-alike/look-alike issues:

Eskalith® may be confused with Estratest®

Lithobid® may be confused with Levbid®, Lithostat®

Do not confuse **mEq** (milliequivalent) with **mg** (milligram). **Note:** 8 mEq lithium carbonate equals 300 mg lithium carbonate. Dosage should be written in **mg** (milligrams) to avoid confusion. Check prescriptions for unusually high volumes of the syrup for dosing errors.

Contraindications Hypersensitivity to lithium or any component of the formulation; avoid use in patients with severe cardiovascular or renal disease, or with severe debilitation, dehydration, or sodium depletion; pregnancy

Warnings/Precautions [U.S. Boxed Warning]: **Lithium toxicity is closely related to serum levels and can occur at therapeutic doses; serum lithium determinations are required to monitor therapy.** Use with caution in patients with thyroid disease, mild-moderate renal impairment, or mild-moderate cardiovascular disease. Use caution in patients receiving medications which alter sodium excretion (eg, diuretics, ACE inhibitors, NSAIDs), or in patients with significant fluid loss (protracted sweating, diarrhea, or prolonged fever); temporary reduction or cessation of therapy may be warranted. Some elderly patients may be extremely sensitive to the effects of lithium, see Dosage and Reference Range. Chronic therapy results in diminished renal concentrating ability (nephrogenic DI); this is usually reversible when lithium is discontinued. Changes in renal function should be monitored, and re-evaluation of treatment may be necessary. Use caution in patients at risk of suicide (suicidal thoughts or behavior).

Use with caution in patients receiving neuroleptic medications - a syndrome resembling NMS has been associated with concurrent therapy. Lithium may impair the patient's alertness, affecting the ability to operate machinery or driving a vehicle. Neuromuscular-blocking agents should be administered with caution; the response may be prolonged.

Higher serum concentrations may be required and tolerated during an acute manic phase; however, the tolerance decreases when symptoms subside. Normal fluid and salt intake must be maintained during therapy.

Safety and efficacy have not been established in children <12 years of age.

Adverse Reactions Frequency not defined.

Cardiovascular: Cardiac arrhythmia, hypotension, sinus node dysfunction, flattened or inverted T waves (reversible), edema, bradycardia, syncope

Central nervous system: Dizziness, vertigo, slurred speech, blackout spells, seizure, sedation, restlessness, confusion, psychomotor retardation, stupor, coma, dystonia, fatigue, lethargy, headache, pseudotumor cerebri, slowed intellectual functioning, tics

Dermatologic: Dry or thinning of hair, folliculitis, alopecia, exacerbation of psoriasis, rash

Endocrine & metabolic: Euthyroid goiter and/or hypothyroidism, hyperthyroidism, hyperglycemia, diabetes insipidus

Gastrointestinal: Polydipsia, anorexia, nausea, vomiting, diarrhea, xerostomia, metallic taste, weight gain, salivary gland swelling, excessive salivation

Genitourinary: Incontinence, polyuria, glycosuria, oliguria, albuminuria

Hematologic: Leukocytosis

Neuromuscular & skeletal: Tremor, muscle hyperirritability, ataxia, choreoathetoid movements, hyperactive deep tendon reflexes, myasthenia gravis (rare)

Ocular: Nystagmus, blurred vision, transient scotoma

Miscellaneous: Coldness and painful discoloration of fingers and toes

Overdosage/Toxicology Symptoms include sedation, confusion, tremors, joint pain, visual changes, seizures, and coma. There is no specific antidote for lithium poisoning. For acute ingestion, following initiation of essential overdose management, discontinue lithium and remove any unabsorbed lithium via gastric lavage (activated charcoal is ineffective as it does not bind lithium). Correct fluid and electrolyte imbalances, provide supportive care. In severe cases, patient should be dialyzed. Hemodialysis is preferred (and more effective) than peritoneal dialysis. The goal is to decrease serum lithium level to <1 mEq/L on a serum sample drawn 6-8 hours after completion of dialysis. Agents that increase the excretion of lithium are of questionable value.

Drug Interactions

Increased Effect/Toxicity: Concurrent use of lithium with carbamazepine, diltiazem, SSRIs (fluoxetine, fluvoxamine), haloperidol, methyldopa, metronidazole (rare), phenothiazines, phenytoin, TCAs, and verapamil may increase the risk for neurotoxicity. A rare encephalopathic syndrome has been reported in association with haloperidol (causal relationship not established). Lithium concentrations/toxicity may be increased by diuretics, NSAIDs (sulindac and aspirin may be exceptions), ACE inhibitors, angiotensin receptor antagonists (losartan), tetracyclines, or COX-2 inhibitors (celecoxib).

Lithium and MAO inhibitors should generally be avoided due to use reports of fatal malignant hyperpyrexia; risk with selective MAO type B inhibitors (selegiline) appears to be lower. Potassium iodide may enhance the hypothyroid effects of lithium. Combined use of lithium with tricyclic antidepressants or sibutramine may increase the risk of serotonin syndrome; this combination is best avoided. Lithium may potentiate effect of neuromuscular blockers.

Decreased Effect: Combined use of lithium and chlorpromazine may lower serum concentrations of both drugs. Lithium may blunt the pressor response to sympathomimetics (epinephrine, norepinephrine). Caffeine (xanthine derivatives) may lower lithium serum concentrations by increasing urinary lithium excretion (monitor).

Ethanol/Nutrition/Herb Interactions Food: Lithium serum concentrations may be increased if taken with food. Limit caffeine.

Mechanism of Action Alters cation transport across cell membrane in nerve and muscle cells and influences reuptake of serotonin and/or norepinephrine; second messenger systems involving the phosphatidylinositol cycle are inhibited; postsynaptic D2 receptor supersensitivity is inhibited

Pharmacodynamics/Kinetics

Absorption: Rapid and complete

Distribution: V_d: Initial: 0.3-0.4 L/kg; V_{dss}: 0.7-1 L/kg; crosses placenta; enters breast milk at 35% to 50% the concentrations in serum; distribution is complete in 6-10 hours

CSF, liver concentrations: $1/3$ to $1/2$ of serum concentration

Erythrocyte concentration: $\sim 1/2$ of serum concentration

Heart, lung, kidney, muscle concentrations: Equivalent to serum concentration

Saliva concentration: 2-3 times serum concentration

Thyroid, bone, brain tissue concentrations: Increase 50% over serum concentrations

Protein binding: Not protein bound

Metabolism: Not metabolized

Bioavailability: Not affected by food; Capsule, immediate release tablet: 95% to 100%; Extended release tablet: 60% to 90%; Syrup: 100%

Half-life elimination: 18-24 hours; can increase to more than 36 hours in elderly or with renal impairment

Time to peak, serum: Nonsustained release: ~0.5-2 hours; slow release: 4-12 hours; syrup: 15-60 minutes

Excretion: Urine (90% to 98% as unchanged drug); sweat (4% to 5%); feces (1%)

Clearance: 80% of filtered lithium is reabsorbed in the proximal convoluted tubules; therefore, clearance approximates 20% of GFR or 20-40 mL/minute

Dosage Oral: Monitor serum concentrations and clinical response (efficacy and toxicity) to determine proper dose

Children 6-12 years:

Bipolar disorder: 15-60 mg/kg/day in 3-4 divided doses; dose not to exceed usual adult dosage

Conduct disorder (unlabeled use): 15-30 mg/kg/day in 3-4 divided doses; dose not to exceed usual adult dosage

Adults: Bipolar disorder: 900-2400 mg/day in 3-4 divided doses or 900-1800 mg/day (sustained release) in 2 divided doses

Elderly: Bipolar disorder: Initial dose: 300 mg once or twice daily; increase weekly in increments of 300 mg/day, monitoring levels; rarely need >900-1200 mg/day

Dosing adjustment in renal impairment:

Cl_{cr} 10-50 mL/minute: Administer 50% to 75% of normal dose

Cl_{cr} <10 mL/minute: Administer 25% to 50% of normal dose

Hemodialysis: Dialyzable (50% to 100%); 4-7 times more efficient than peritoneal dialysis

Dietary Considerations May be taken with meals to avoid GI upset; have patient drink 2-3 L of water daily.

Administration Administer with meals to decrease GI upset. Slow release tablets must be swallowed whole; do not crush or chew.

Monitoring Parameters Serum lithium every 4-5 days during initial therapy; draw lithium serum concentrations 8-12 hours postdose; renal, thyroid, and cardiovascular function; fluid status; serum electrolytes; CBC with differential, urinalysis; monitor for signs of toxicity; beta-hCG pregnancy test for all females not known to be sterile

Reference Range Levels should be obtained twice weekly until both patient's clinical status and levels are stable then levels may be obtained every 1-3 months

Timing of serum samples: Draw trough just before next dose (8-12 hours after previous dose)

Therapeutic levels:

Acute mania: 0.6-1.2 mEq/L (SI: 0.6-1.2 mmol/L)

Protection against future episodes in most patients with bipolar disorder: 0.8-1 mEq/L (SI: 0.8-1.0 mmol/L); a higher rate of relapse is described in subjects who are maintained at <0.4 mEq/L (SI: 0.4 mmol/L)

Elderly patients can usually be maintained at lower end of therapeutic range (0.6-0.8 mEq/L)

Toxic concentration: >1.5 mEq/L (SI: >2 mmol/L)

Adverse effect levels:

GI complaints/tremor: 1.5-2 mEq/L

Confusion/somnolence: 2-2.5 mEq/L

Seizures/death: >2.5 mEq/L

Dosage Forms

[DSC] = Discontinued product

Capsule, as carbonate: 150 mg, 300 mg, 600 mg

Eskalith®: 300 mg [contains benzyl alcohol] [DSC]

Solution, as citrate: 300 mg/5 mL (5 mL, 500 mL) [equivalent to amount of lithium in lithium carbonate]

Syrup, as citrate: 300 mg/5 mL (480 mL) [equivalent to amount of lithium in lithium carbonate]

Tablet, as carbonate: 300 mg

Tablet, controlled release, as carbonate: 450 mg

Eskalith CR®: 450 mg [DSC]

Tablet, slow release, as carbonate: 300 mg

Lithobid®: 300 mg

♦ **Lithium Carbonate** see Lithium on page 1023
♦ **Lithium Citrate** see Lithium on page 1023
♦ **Lithobid®** see Lithium on page 1023
♦ **Live Attenuated Influenza Vaccine (LAIV)** see Influenza Virus Vaccine on page 906
♦ **Livostin® [DSC]** see Levocabastine on page 997
♦ **Livostin® (Can)** see Levocabastine on page 997
♦ **LMD®** see Dextran on page 485
♦ **LNg 20** see Levonorgestrel on page 1004

+ **Locoid**® *see* Hydrocortisone *on page 852*
+ **Locoid Lipocream**® *see* Hydrocortisone *on page 852*
+ **Lodine**® **[DSC]** *see* Etodolac *on page 666*
+ **Lodine**® **(Can)** *see* Etodolac *on page 666*
+ **Lodine**® **XL [DSC]** *see* Etodolac *on page 666*
+ **Lodosyn**® *see* Carbidopa *on page 289*

Lodoxamide (loe DOKS a mide)

U.S. Brand Names Alomide®
Canadian Brand Names Alomide®
Index Terms Lodoxamide Tromethamine
Pharmacologic Category Mast Cell Stabilizer
Use Treatment of vernal keratoconjunctivitis, vernal conjunctivitis, and vernal keratitis
Pregnancy Risk Factor B
Medication Safety Issues
  International issues:
    Thilomide® [Turkey] may be confused with Thalomid® which is a brand name for thalidomide in the U.S.
Dosage Ophthalmic: Instill 1-2 drops in eye(s) 4 times/day for up to 3 months
Additional Information Complete prescribing information for this medication should be consulted for additional detail.
Dosage Forms Solution, ophthalmic: 0.1% (10 mL) [contains benzalkonium chloride]

+ **Lodoxamide Tromethamine** *see* Lodoxamide *on page 1026*
+ **Lodrane**® *see* Brompheniramine and Pseudoephedrine *on page 243*
+ **Lodrane**® **12D** *see* Brompheniramine and Pseudoephedrine *on page 243*
+ **Lodrane**® **12 Hour** *see* Brompheniramine *on page 242*
+ **Lodrane**® **24** *see* Brompheniramine *on page 242*
+ **Lodrane**® **LD** *see* Brompheniramine and Pseudoephedrine *on page 243*
+ **Lodrane**® **XR** *see* Brompheniramine *on page 242*
+ **Loestrin**® *see* Ethinyl Estradiol and Norethindrone *on page 655*
+ **Loestrin**® **1.5/30 (Can)** *see* Ethinyl Estradiol and Norethindrone *on page 655*
+ **Loestrin**® **24 Fe** *see* Ethinyl Estradiol and Norethindrone *on page 655*
+ **Loestrin**® **Fe** *see* Ethinyl Estradiol and Norethindrone *on page 655*
+ **Lofibra**™ *see* Fenofibrate *on page 689*
+ **LoHist-12** *see* Brompheniramine *on page 242*
+ **LoHist-D** *see* Chlorpheniramine and Pseudoephedrine *on page 350*
+ **L-OHP** *see* Oxaliplatin *on page 1277*
+ **LoKara**™ *see* Desonide *on page 478*
+ **Lomine (Can)** *see* Dicyclomine *on page 496*
+ **Lomotil**® *see* Diphenoxylate and Atropine *on page 518*

Lomustine (loe MUS teen)

U.S. Brand Names CeeNU®
Canadian Brand Names CeeNU®
Index Terms CCNU; NSC-79037
Pharmacologic Category Antineoplastic Agent, Alkylating Agent
Use Treatment of brain tumors and Hodgkin's disease
Unlabeled/Investigational Use Non-Hodgkin's lymphoma, melanoma, renal carcinoma, lung cancer, colon cancer
Pregnancy Risk Factor D
Pregnancy Implications Teratogenic effects and embryotoxicity have been observed in animal studies. There are no adequate and well-controlled studies in pregnant women. May cause fetal harm when administered to a pregnant woman. Women of childbearing potential should be advised to avoid pregnancy and should be advised of the potential harm to the fetus.
Lactation Enters breast milk/contraindicated
Medication Safety Issues
  Sound-alike/look-alike issues:
    Lomustine may be confused with carmustine

  High alert medication: The Institute for Safe Medication Practices (ISMP) includes this medication among its list of drugs which have a heightened risk of causing significant patient harm when used in error.

  Lomustine should only be administered as a single dose once every 6 weeks; serious errors have occurred when lomustine was inadvertently administered daily.
Contraindications Hypersensitivity to lomustine, any component of the formulation, or other nitrosoureas; pregnancy
Warnings/Precautions Hazardous agent - use appropriate precautions for handling and disposal. **[U.S. Boxed Warnings]: Bone marrow suppression, notably thrombocytopenia and leukopenia, may lead to bleeding and overwhelming infections in an already compromised patient;** will last for at least 6 weeks after a dose. Do not administer courses more frequently than every 6 weeks because the toxicity is delayed. Use with caution in patients with depressed platelet, leukocyte or erythrocyte counts, renal (may require dosage adjustment) or hepatic impairment. Bone marrow toxicity is cumulative; dose adjustments should be based on nadir counts from prior dose. May cause delayed pulmonary toxicity (infiltrates and/or fibrosis); usually related to cumulative doses >1100 mg/m². Long-term use may be associated with the development of secondary malignancies. **[U.S. Boxed**

Warning]: Should be administered under the supervision of an experienced cancer chemotherapy physician.

Adverse Reactions

>10%:

Gastrointestinal: Nausea and vomiting, usually within 3-6 hours after oral administration. Administration of the dose at bedtime, with an antiemetic, significantly reduces both the incidence and severity of nausea.

Hematologic: Myelosuppression, common, dose-limiting, may be cumulative and irreversible; leukopenia (65%; nadir: 5-6 weeks; recovery 6-8 weeks); thrombocytopenia (nadir: 4 weeks; recovery 5-6 weeks)

Frequency not defined: Acute leukemia, alkaline phosphatase increased, alopecia, anemia, ataxia, azotemia (progressive), bilirubin increased, blindness, bone marrow dysplasia, disorientation, dysarthria, kidney size decreased, lethargy, optic atrophy, pulmonary fibrosis, pulmonary infiltrates, renal failure, stomatitis, transaminases increased, visual disturbances

Overdosage/Toxicology Symptoms include nausea, vomiting, and leukopenia. There are no known antidotes. Treatment is primarily symptom-directed and supportive.

Drug Interactions

Cytochrome P450 Effect: Substrate of CYP2D6 (major); **Inhibits** CYP2D6 (weak), 3A4 (weak)

Increased Effect/Toxicity: CYP2D6 inhibitors may increase the levels/effects of lomustine; example inhibitors include chlorpromazine, delavirdine, fluoxetine, miconazole, paroxetine, pergolide, quinidine, quinine, ritonavir, and ropinirole.

Ethanol/Nutrition/Herb Interactions Ethanol: Avoid ethanol (due to GI irritation).

Stability Store at 15°C to 30°C (59°F to 86°F).

Mechanism of Action Inhibits DNA and RNA synthesis via carbamylation of DNA polymerase, alkylation of DNA, and alteration of RNA, proteins, and enzymes

Pharmacodynamics/Kinetics

Duration: Marrow recovery: ~5-8 weeks

Absorption: Complete

Distribution: Crosses blood-brain barrier to a greater degree than BCNU; CNS concentrations are ≥50% of plasma concentrations

Metabolism: Rapidly hepatic via hydroxylation producing at least two active metabolites; enterohepatically recycled

Half-life elimination: Parent drug: 16-72 hours; Active metabolite: 16-48 hours

Time to peak, serum: Active metabolite: ~3 hours

Excretion: Urine (~50%); feces (<5%); expired air (<10%)

Dosage Oral (refer to individual protocols):

Children: 75-150 mg/m² as a single dose once every 6 weeks; subsequent doses are readjusted after initial treatment according to platelet and leukocyte counts

Adults: 100-130 mg/m² as a single dose once every 6 weeks; readjust after initial treatment according to platelet and leukocyte counts

With compromised marrow function: Initial dose: 100 mg/m² as a single dose once every 6 weeks

Repeat courses should only be administered after adequate recovery: Leukocytes >4000/mm³ and platelet counts >100,000/mm³

Subsequent dosing adjustment based on nadir:

Leukocytes 2000-2999/mm³, platelets 25,000-74,999/mm³: Administer 70% of prior dose

Leukocytes <2000/mm³, platelets <25,000/mm³: Administer 50% of prior dose

Dosage adjustment in renal impairment: There is no FDA-approved renal dosing adjustment guideline; the following guidelines have been used by some clinicians:

Kintzel, 1995:

Cl_{cr} 46-60 mL/minute: Administer 75% of normal dose

Cl_{cr} 31-45 mL/minute: Administer 70% of normal dose

Cl_{cr} ≤30 mL/minute: Consider use of alternative drug

Aronoff, 1999:

Cl_{cr} 10-50 mL/minute: Administer 75% of normal dose

Cl_{cr} <10 mL/minute: Administer 25% to 50% of normal dose

Hemodialysis: Supplemental dose is not necessary

Dietary Considerations Should be taken with fluids on an empty stomach; no food or drink for 2 hours after administration to decrease nausea.

Administration Take with fluids on an empty stomach; no food or drink for 2 hours after administration.

Monitoring Parameters CBC with differential and platelet count (for at least 6 weeks after dose), hepatic and renal function tests (periodic), pulmonary function tests (baseline and periodic)

Test Interactions Liver function tests

Dosage Forms

Capsule:

CeeNU®: 10 mg, 40 mg, 100 mg

Capsule [dose pack]:

CeeNU®: 10 mg (2s); 40 mg (2s); 100 mg (2s)

♦ **Lonox®** see Diphenoxylate and Atropine on page 518

♦ **Lo/Ovral®** see Ethinyl Estradiol and Norgestrel on page 663

♦ **Loperacap (Can)** see Loperamide on page 1027

Loperamide (loe PER a mide)

U.S. Brand Names Diamode [OTC]; Imodium® A-D [OTC]; Kao-Paverin® [OTC]; K-Pek II [OTC]

Canadian Brand Names Apo-Loperamide®; Diarr-Eze; Imodium®; Loperacap; Novo-Loperamide; PMS-Loperamine; Rho®-Loperamine; Riva-Loperamine

(Continued)

Loperamide *(Continued)*

Index Terms Loperamide Hydrochloride

Pharmacologic Category Antidiarrheal

Use Treatment of chronic diarrhea associated with inflammatory bowel disease; acute nonspecific diarrhea; increased volume of ileostomy discharge

OTC labeling: Control of symptoms of diarrhea, including Traveler's diarrhea

Unlabeled/Investigational Use Cancer treatment-induced diarrhea (eg, irinotecan induced); chronic diarrhea caused by bowel resection

Pregnancy Risk Factor C

Pregnancy Implications Teratogenic effects were not observed in animal studies.

Lactation Enters breast milk/not recommended.

Medication Safety Issues

Sound-alike/look-alike issues:

Imodium® A-D may be confused with Indocin®, Ionamin®

International issues:

Diasorb®: Brand name for attapulgite in the U.S.

Contraindications Hypersensitivity to loperamide or any component of the formulation; abdominal pain without diarrhea; children <2 years

Avoid use as primary therapy in acute dysentery, acute ulcerative colitis, bacterial enterocolitis, pseudomembranous colitis

Warnings/Precautions Should not be used if diarrhea is accompanied by high fever or blood in stool. Use caution in young children as response may be variable because of dehydration. Concurrent fluid and electrolyte replacement is often necessary in all age groups depending upon severity of diarrhea. Should not be used when inhibition of peristalsis is undesirable or dangerous. Discontinue if constipation, abdominal pain, or ileus develop. Use caution in patients with hepatic impairment because of reduced first pass metabolism. Use caution in treatment of AIDS patients; stop therapy at the sign of abdominal distention. Cases of toxic megacolon have occurred in this population. Loperamide is a symptom-directed treatment; if an underlying diagnosis is made, other disease-specific treatment may be indicated. Use caution in patients with hepatic impairment because of reduced first-pass metabolism; monitor for signs of CNS toxicity.

OTC labeling: If diarrhea lasts longer than 2 days, patient should stop taking loperamide and consult healthcare provider.

Adverse Reactions 1% to 10%:

Central nervous system: Dizziness (1%)

Gastrointestinal: Constipation (2% to 5%), abdominal cramping (<1% to 3%), nausea (<1% to 3%)

Postmarketing and/or case reports: Abdominal distention, abdominal pain, allergic reactions, anaphylactic shock, anaphylactoid reactions, angioedema, bullous eruption (rare), drowsiness, dry mouth, dyspepsia, erythema multiforme (rare), fatigue, flatulence, paralytic ileus, megacolon, pruritus, rash, Stevens-Johnson syndrome, toxic epidermal necrolysis, toxic megacolon, urinary retention, urticaria, vomiting

Overdosage/Toxicology Symptoms of overdose include CNS depression, urinary retention, and paralytic ileus. Treatment of overdose includes gastric lavage followed by 100 g activated charcoal through a nasogastric tube. Naloxone can be given as an antidote. The prolonged action of loperamide may necessitate naloxone's repeated administration and close patient monitoring for recurrent CNS depression.

Drug Interactions

Cytochrome P450 Effect: Substrate (minor) of CYP2B6

Increased Effect/Toxicity: P-glycoprotein Inhibitors may increase CNS depressant effects.

Decreased Effect: Loperamide may decrease levels/effects of saquinavir.

Stability Store at 15°C to 25°C (59°F to 77°F).

Mechanism of Action Acts directly on circular and longitudinal intestinal muscles, through the opioid receptor, to inhibit peristalsis and prolong transit time; reduces fecal volume, increases viscosity, and diminishes fluid and electrolyte loss; demonstrates antisecretory activity. Loperamide increases tone on the anal sphincter

Pharmacodynamics/Kinetics

Absorption: Poor

Distribution: Poor penetration into brain; low amounts enter breast milk

Metabolism: Hepatic via oxidative N-demethylation

Half-life elimination: 7-14 hours

Time to peak, plasma: Liquid: 2.5 hours; Capsule: 5 hours

Excretion: Urine and feces (1% as metabolites, 30% to 40% as unchanged drug)

Dosage Oral:

Children:

Acute diarrhea: Initial doses (in first 24 hours):

2-5 years (13-20 kg): 1 mg 3 times/day

6-8 years (20-30 kg): 2 mg twice daily

8-12 years (>30 kg): 2 mg 3 times/day

Maintenance: After initial dosing, 0.1 mg/kg doses after each loose stool, but not exceeding initial dosage

Traveler's diarrhea:

6-8 years: 2 mg after first loose stool, followed by 1 mg after each subsequent stool (maximum dose: 4 mg/day)

9-11 years: 2 mg after first loose stool, followed by 1 mg after each subsequent stool (maximum dose: 6 mg/day)

≥12 years: See adult dosing.

Adults:

Acute diarrhea: Initial: 4 mg, followed by 2 mg after each loose stool, up to 16 mg/day

Chronic diarrhea: Initial: Follow acute diarrhea; maintenance dose should be slowly titrated downward to minimum required to control symptoms (typically, 4-8 mg/day in divided doses)

Traveler's diarrhea: Initial: 4 mg after first loose stool, followed by 2 mg after each subsequent stool (maximum dose: 8 mg/day)

Irinotecan-induced diarrhea (unlabeled use): 4 mg after first loose or frequent bowel movement, then 2 mg every 2 hours until 12 hours have passed without a bowel movement. If diarrhea recurs, then repeat administration

Dosage adjustment in hepatic impairment: No specific guidelines available.

Dietary Considerations
Imodium® A-D [new formulation] contains sodium 10 mg/30 mL.

Dosage Forms
Caplet, as hydrochloride: 2 mg
Diamode, Imodium® A-D, Kao-Paverin®: 2 mg
Capsule, as hydrochloride: 2 mg
Liquid, oral, as hydrochloride: 1 mg/5 mL (5 mL, 10 mL, 120 mL)
Imodium® A-D: 1 mg/5 mL (60 mL, 120 mL) [contains alcohol, sodium benzoate, benzoic acid; cherry mint flavor]
Imodium® A-D [new formulation]: 1 mg/7.5 mL (60 mL, 120 mL, 360 mL) [contains sodium 10 mg/30 mL, sodium benzoate; creamy mint flavor]
Tablet, as hydrochloride: 2 mg
K-Pek II: 2 mg

Loperamide and Simethicone (loe PER a mide & sye METH i kone)

U.S. Brand Names Imodium® Advanced
Index Terms Simethicone and Loperamide Hydrochloride
Pharmacologic Category Antidiarrheal; Antiflatulent
Use Control of symptoms of diarrhea and gas (bloating, pressure, and cramps)
Dosage Oral: Acute diarrhea (weight-based dosing is preferred):
Children:
6-8 years (48-59 lbs): 1 caplet or tablet after first loose stool, followed by ½ caplet/tablet with each subsequent loose stool (maximum: 2 caplets or tablets/24 hours)
9-11 years (60-95 lbs): 1 caplet or tablet after first loose stool, followed by ½ caplet or tablet with each subsequent loose stool (maximum: 3 caplets or tablets/24 hours)
Children >12 years and Adults: One caplet or tablet after first loose stool, followed by 1 caplet or tablet with each subsequent loose stool (maximum: 4 caplets or tablets/24 hours)
Additional Information Complete prescribing information for this medication should be consulted for additional detail.

Dosage Forms
Caplet: Loperamide hydrochloride 2 mg and simethicone 125 mg
Tablet, chewable: Loperamide hydrochloride 2 mg and simethicone 125 mg [mint flavor]

♦ **Loperamide Hydrochloride** see Loperamide on page 1027
♦ **Lopid®** see Gemfibrozil on page 787

Lopinavir and Ritonavir (loe PIN a veer & rit ON uh veer)

U.S. Brand Names Kaletra®
Canadian Brand Names Kaletra®
Index Terms Ritonavir and Lopinavir
Pharmacologic Category Antiretroviral Agent, Protease Inhibitor
Additional Appendix Information
Antiretroviral Therapy for HIV Infection: Adults and Adolescents on page 1988
Management of Healthcare Worker Exposures to HBV, HCV, and HIV on page 1941
Use Treatment of HIV infection in combination with other antiretroviral agents
Pregnancy Risk Factor C
Pregnancy Implications Safety and pharmacokinetic studies in pregnant women are not completed. Preliminary information suggests increased dosage may be needed during pregnancy, although specific recommendations with the tablet formulation are not yet available. Once-daily dosing is not recommended during pregnancy. The Perinatal HIV Guidelines Working Group considers this a recommended combination for use during pregnancy. Pregnancy and protease inhibitors are both associated with an increased risk of hyperglycemia. Glucose levels should be closely monitored. Health professionals are encouraged to contact the antiretroviral pregnancy registry to monitor outcomes of pregnant women exposed to antiretroviral medications (1-800-258-4263 or www.APRegistry.com).
Lactation Excretion in breast milk unknown/contraindicated
Medication Safety Issues
Sound-alike/look-alike issues:
Potential for dispensing errors between Kaletra™ and Keppra® (levetiracetam)
Contraindications Hypersensitivity to lopinavir, ritonavir, or any component of the formulation; administration with medications highly dependent upon CYP3A or CYP2D6 for clearance for which increased levels are associated with serious and/or life-threatening events, including cisapride, dihydroergotamine, ergonovine, ergotamine, methylergonovine, midazolam, pimozide, and triazolam.
Warnings/Precautions Use with caution in patients taking strong CYP3A4 inhibitors, moderate or strong CYP3A4 inducers and major CYP3A4 substrates (see drug interactions); consider alternative agents that avoid or lessen the potential for CYP-mediated interactions. Cases of pancreatitis, some fatal, have been associated with lopinavir/ritonavir; use caution in patients with a history of pancreatitis. Patients with signs or symptoms of pancreatitis should be evaluated and therapy suspended as clinically appropriate.

Changes in glucose tolerance, hyperglycemia, exacerbation of diabetes, DKA, and new-onset diabetes mellitus have been reported in patients receiving protease inhibitors. May (Continued)

Lopinavir and Ritonavir *(Continued)*

cause hepatitis or exacerbate pre-existing hepatic dysfunction; use with caution in patients with hepatitis B or C and in hepatic disease; patients with hepatitis or elevations in transaminases prior to the start of therapy may be at increased risk for further increases in transaminases or hepatic dysfunction (rare fatalities reported in postmarketing). Large increases in total cholesterol and triglycerides have been reported; screening should be done prior to therapy and periodically throughout treatment. Increased bleeding may be seen in patients with hemophilia A or B who are taking protease inhibitors. Redistribution or accumulation of body fat has been observed in patients using antiretroviral therapy. An inflammatory response to indolent or residual opportunistic infections (referred to as immune reconstitution syndrome) has occurred with the use of combination retroviral therapy, including Kaletra®; further evaluation and treatment may be required. Safety and efficacy have not been established for children <6 months of age.

Adverse Reactions Protease inhibitors cause dyslipidemia which includes elevated cholesterol and triglycerides and a redistribution of body fat centrally to cause increased abdominal girth, buffalo hump, facial atrophy, and breast enlargement. These agents also cause hyperglycemia.

>10%:
Endocrine & metabolic: Hypercholesterolemia (9% to 39%), triglycerides increased (9% to 36%)
Gastrointestinal: Diarrhea (5% to 27%), nausea (5% to 16%)
Hepatic: GGT increased (6% to 29%)

2% to 10%:
Central nervous system: Headache (2% to 7%), fever (2%), chills (up to 2%), depression (up to 2%), pain (up to 2%), insomnia (up to 2%)
Dermatologic: Rash (up to 4%)
Endocrine & metabolic: Hyperglycemia (1% to 5%), hyperuricemia (up to 3%), sodium decreased (3% children), inorganic phosphorus decreased (up to 2%), amylase increased (3% to 8%), libido decreased (2%)
Gastrointestinal: Abnormal stools (up to 6%), abdominal pain (2% to 10%), vomiting (2% to 6%), dyspepsia (up to 5%), flatulence (1% to 4%), weight loss (up to 3%), dysphagia (up to 2%)
Hematologic: Platelets decreased (4% children), neutrophils decreased (1% to 5%)
Hepatic: AST increased (2% to 9%), ALT increased (4% to 10%), bilirubin increased (children 3%)
Neuromuscular & skeletal: Weakness (up to 9%)
Respiratory: Bronchitis (2%)

<2% (Limited to important or life-threatening): Alopecia, amnesia, apathy, asthma, ataxia, atrial fibrillation, avitaminosis, bacterial infection, bone necrosis, bradyarrhythmia, breast enlargement, cerebral infarction, cholangitis, cholecystitis, Cushing's syndrome, cyst, deep vein thrombosis, diabetes mellitus, dyskinesia, dyspnea, enteritis, erythema multiforme, exfoliative dermatitis, facial paralysis, flu-like syndrome, hemorrhagic colitis, hepatic dysfunction, hypertrophy, jaundice, lactic acidosis, lung edema, maculopapular rash, migraine, nephritis, neuropathy, pancreatitis, paresthesia, periodontitis, peripheral neuritis, pharyngitis, pulmonary edema, renal calculus, rhinitis, seborrhea, seizure, sinusitis, skin ulcer, somnolence, Stevens-Johnson syndrome, tinnitus, varicose veins, vasculitis

Overdosage/Toxicology The solution contains 42.4% alcohol. Overdosage in a child may cause alcohol-related toxicity and may be potentially lethal. Treatment should be symptomatic and supportive. Activated charcoal may aid in the removal of unabsorbed medication. Given extensive protein binding, hemodialysis is unlikely to be effective.

Drug Interactions
Cytochrome P450 Effect:
Lopinavir: **Substrate** of 3A4 (minor)
Ritonavir: **Substrate** of CYP1A2 (minor), 2B6 (minor), 2D6 (major), 3A4 (major); **Inhibits** CYP2C8 (strong), 2C9 (weak), 2C19 (weak), 2D6 (strong), 2E1 (weak), 3A4 (strong); **Induces** CYP1A2 (weak), 2C8 (weak), 2C9 (weak), 3A4 (weak)

Increased Effect/Toxicity: Concurrent use of cisapride, ergot alkaloids, (dihydroergotamine, ergonovine, methylergonovine), lovastatin, midazolam, pimozide, simvastatin, and triazolam is contraindicated. Alfuzosin serum level may be increased by ritonavir; concurrent use is contraindicated (by the manufacturer of ritonavir). Antiarrhythmic agents (including amiodarone, bepridil, flecainide, propafenone, lidocaine (systemic), and quinidine) should be used with caution; life-threatening arrhythmias may result from concurrent use.

Ritonavir may increase the levels/effects of amiodarone, amphetamines, selected beta-blockers, selected benzodiazepines (midazolam and triazolam contraindicated), calcium channel blockers, dextromethorphan, fluoxetine, lidocaine, HMG-CoA reductase inhibitors (lovastatin and simvastatin are not recommended), mesoridazine, mirtazapine, nateglinide, nefazodone, paclitaxel, paroxetine, pioglitazone, repaglinide, risperidone, rosiglitazone, sildenafil (and other PDE-5 inhibitors), thioridazine, tricyclic antidepressants, venlafaxine, and other substrates of CYP2D6 or 3A4. Mesoridazine and thioridazine are generally contraindicated with strong CYP2D6 inhibitors. When used with strong CYP3A4 inhibitors, dosage adjustment/limits are recommended for sildenafil and other PDE-5 inhibitors; refer to individual monographs. Warfarin levels/effects may also be increased. High dosages of itraconazole or ketoconazole (>200 mg/day) are not recommended.

Serum levels of protease inhibitors may be altered during concurrent therapy. Ritonavir may increase serum concentrations of amprenavir, indinavir, or saquinavir. Delavirdine increases levels of lopinavir; dosing recommendations are not yet established. Serum concentrations of corticosteroids (eg, budesonide, dexamethasone, fluticasone, prednisone) may be increased by lopinavir/ritonavir, resulting in decreased serum cortisol, HPA axis suppression; concurrent use is not recommended.

Lopinavir/ritonavir solution contains alcohol, concurrent use with disulfiram or metronidazole should be avoided. May cause disulfiram-like reaction. Serum concentrations of meperidine's neuroexcitatory metabolite (normeperidine) are increased by ritonavir, which may increase the risk of CNS toxicity/seizures. Rifabutin and rifabutin metabolite serum concentrations may be increased by ritonavir; reduce rifabutin dose to 150 mg every other day. Tenofovir serum concentration/effects may be increased by lopinavir/ritonavir. Trazodone serum concentration/effects may be increased by lopinavir/ritonavir; use caution and reduce trazodone dose.

Decreased Effect: The levels/effects of ritonavir may be decreased by aminoglutethimide, carbamazepine, nafcillin, nevirapine, phenobarbital, phenytoin, rifamycins, and other CYP3A4 inducers. Concurrent use of rifampin is not recommended. Ritonavir may decrease the levels/effects of CYP2D6 prodrug substrates (eg, codeine, hydrocodone, oxycodone, tramadol). Non-nucleoside reverse transcriptase inhibitors (efavirenz, nevirapine) may decrease levels of lopinavir. To avoid incompatibility with didanosine, administer didanosine 1 hour before or 2 hours after lopinavir/ritonavir. Decreased levels of ethinyl estradiol may result from concurrent use (alternative contraception is recommended). Lopinavir/ritonavir may decrease levels of abacavir, atovaquone, or zidovudine. Voriconazole serum levels are reduced by ritonavir. Lopinavir/ritonavir may decrease the concentration and effect of amprenavir when administered as fosamprenavir.

Ethanol/Nutrition/Herb Interactions Herb/Nutraceutical: St John's wort may decrease levels of protease inhibitors and lead to possible resistance; concurrent use in not recommended.

Stability

Oral solution: Store at 2°C to 8°C (36°F to 46°F). Avoid exposure to excessive heat. If stored at room temperature (25°C or 77°F), use within 2 months.

Tablet: Store at controlled room temperature of 15°C to 30°C (59°F to 86°F). Exposure to high humidity outside of the original container for >2 weeks is not recommended.

Mechanism of Action A coformulation of lopinavir and ritonavir. The lopinavir component is the active inhibitor of HIV protease. Lopinavir inhibits HIV protease and renders the enzyme incapable of processing polyprotein precursor which leads to production of noninfectious immature HIV particles. The ritonavir component inhibits the CYP3A metabolism of lopinavir, allowing increased plasma levels of lopinavir.

Pharmacodynamics/Kinetics

Ritonavir: See Ritonavir monograph.

Lopinavir:

Protein binding: 98% to 99%; decreased with mild-to-moderate hepatic dysfunction

Metabolism: Hepatic via CYP3A; 13 metabolites identified

Half-life elimination: 5-6 hours

Time to peak, plasma: ~4 hours

Excretion: Feces (83%, 20% as unchanged drug); urine (2%)

Dosage Oral:

Children 6 months to 12 years: Dosage based on weight, presented based on mg of lopinavir (maximum dose: Lopinavir 400 mg/ritonavir 100 mg)

7-<15 kg: 12 mg/kg twice daily

15-40 kg: 10 mg/kg twice daily

>40 kg: Lopinavir 400 mg/ritonavir 100 mg twice daily

Note: For therapy-experienced patients with suspected reduced susceptibility to lopinavir, refer to Adults dosing.

Children >12 years: Therapy-naive: Lopinavir 400 mg/ritonavir 100 mg twice daily (AIDS Info guidelines). **Note:** For therapy-experienced patients with suspected reduced susceptibility to lopinavir, refer to Adults dosing.

Adults:

Therapy-naive: Lopinavir 800 mg/ritonavir 200 mg once daily **or** lopinavir 400 mg/ritonavir 100 mg twice daily

Note: Once-daily dosing regimen should not be used with concurrent indinavir, saquinavir, phenytoin, carbamazepine, or phenobarbital therapy.

Therapy-experienced: Lopinavir 400 mg/ritonavir 100 mg twice daily (per manufacturer labeling)

Note: For therapy-experienced patients with suspected reduced susceptibility to lopinavir, clinicians may consider lopinavir 600 mg/ ritonavir 150 mg twice daily (AIDS Info guidelines)

Elderly: Initial studies did not include enough elderly patients to determine effects based on age. Use with caution due to possible decreased hepatic, renal, and cardiac function.

Dosage adjustment for combination therapy:

When taken with amprenavir, efavirenz, fosamprenavir, nelfinavir, or nevirapine: **Note:** Once-daily dosing regimen should not be used

Children 6 months to 12 years: Solution:

7-<15 kg: 13 mg/kg twice daily

15-45 kg: 11 mg/kg twice daily

>45 kg: Refer to adult dosing

Note: In the USHHS AIDS Info guidelines, the cutoff for adult dosing is 50 kg. (Pediatric Guidelines - October 26, 2006, are available at http://www.aidsinfo.nih.gov)

Children >12 years and Adults:

Therapy-naive: Tablet: Lopinavir 400 mg/ritonavir 100 mg twice daily

Therapy-experienced:

Solution: Lopinavir 533 mg/ritonavir 133 mg twice daily

Tablet: Lopinavir 600 mg/ritonavir 150 mg twice daily

When taken with saquinavir (Invirase®): Lopinavir 400 mg/ritonavir 100 mg twice daily

Dosage adjustment in renal impairment: Has not been studied in patients with renal impairment; however, a decrease in clearance is not expected

Dosage adjustment in hepatic impairment: Plasma levels may be increased in patients with mild-to-moderate hepatic impairment. Lopinavir's AUC may be increased by 30%.

Dietary Considerations Solution should be taken with food. Tablet may be taken with or without food

(Continued)

Lopinavir and Ritonavir *(Continued)*

Administration
Solution: Administer with food; if using didanosine, take didanosine 1 hour before or 2 hours after lopinavir/ritonavir
Tablet: May be taken with or without food. Swallow whole, do not break, crush, or chew. May be taken with didanosine when taken without food.

Monitoring Parameters Triglycerides, cholesterol, LFTs, electrolytes, basic HIV monitoring, viral load and CD4 count, glucose

Dosage Forms
Solution, oral:
Kaletra®: Lopinavir 80 mg and ritonavir 20 mg per mL (160 mL) [contains alcohol 42.4%]
Tablet:
Kaletra®: Lopinavir 200 mg and ritonavir 50 mg

♦ **Lopressor®** *see Metoprolol on page 1129*
♦ **Lopressor HCT®** *see Metoprolol and Hydrochlorothiazide on page 1132*
♦ **Loprox®** *see Ciclopirox on page 366*
♦ **Lorabid® [DSC]** *see Loracarbef on page 1032*
♦ **Lorabid® (Can)** *see Loracarbef on page 1032*

Loracarbef (lor a KAR bef)

U.S. Brand Names Lorabid® [DSC]
Canadian Brand Names Lorabid®
Pharmacologic Category Antibiotic, Carbacephem
Use Treatment of infections caused by susceptible organisms involving the upper and lower respiratory tract, uncomplicated skin and skin structure, and urinary tract (including uncomplicated pyelonephritis)
Pregnancy Risk Factor B
Pregnancy Implications Animal studies have not demonstrated teratogenicity. There are no adequate and well-controlled studies in pregnant women.
Lactation Excretion in breast milk unknown/use caution
Medication Safety Issues
Sound-alike/look-alike issues:
Lorabid® may be confused with Levbid®, Lopid®, Lortab®, Slo-bid™
Contraindications Hypersensitivity to loracarbef, any component of the formulation, or cephalosporins
Warnings/Precautions Modify dosage in patients with severe renal impairment. Prolonged use may result in superinfection. Use with caution in patients with a previous history of hypersensitivity to other beta-lactam antibiotics (eg, penicillins, cephalosporins). Safety and efficacy in children <6 months of age have not been established.
Adverse Reactions
1% to 10%:
Central nervous system: Headache (1% to 3%), somnolence (<1% to 2%)
Dermatologic: Rash (1% to 3%)
Gastrointestinal: Diarrhea (4% to 6%), nausea (2% to 3%), vomiting (1% to 3%), anorexia (<1% to 2%), abdominal pain (1%)
Genitourinary: Vaginitis (1%), vaginal moniliasis (1%)
Respiratory: Rhinitis (2% to 6%)
Miscellaneous: Hypersensitivity reactions (1%; eg, urticaria, pruritus, erythema multiforme)
<1% (Limited to important or life-threatening): Alkaline phosphatase increased, anaphylaxis, cholestasis, eosinophilia, insomnia, jaundice, leukopenia, nephrotoxicity with transient increases of BUN/creatinine, nervousness, prothrombin time increased, serum sickness-like reaction, Stevens-Johnson syndrome, thrombocytopenia (transient), transaminases increased (transient), vasodilatation
Other adverse reactions observed with beta-lactam antibiotics: Agranulocytosis, allergic reactions, aplastic anemia, hemolytic anemia, hemorrhage, interstitial nephritis, LDH increased, neutropenia, pancytopenia, positive direct Coombs' test, pseudomembranous colitis, seizure (with high doses and renal dysfunction), toxic epidermal necrolysis
Overdosage/Toxicology Symptoms include nausea and vomiting, abdominal discomfort and diarrhea. Treatment is symptom-directed and supportive.
Drug Interactions
Increased Effect/Toxicity: Loracarbef serum levels are increased with coadministered probenecid.
Ethanol/Nutrition/Herb Interactions Food: Administration with food decreases and delays the peak plasma concentration.
Stability
Capsule: Store at 15°C to 30°C (59°F to 86°F).
Suspension: Prior to reconstitution, store at 15°C to 30°C (59°F to 86°F). After reconstitution, suspension may be kept at room temperature for 14 days.
Mechanism of Action Inhibits bacterial cell wall synthesis by binding to one or more of the penicillin binding proteins (PBPs); inhibits the final transpeptidation step of peptidoglycan synthesis in bacterial cell walls, thus inhibiting cell wall biosynthesis. It is thought that beta-lactam antibiotics inactivate transpeptidase via acylation of the enzyme with cleavage of the CO-N bond of the beta-lactam ring. Upon exposure to beta-lactam antibiotics, bacteria eventually lyse due to ongoing activity of cell wall autolytic enzymes (autolysins and murein hydrolases) while cell wall assembly is arrested.
Pharmacodynamics/Kinetics
Absorption: Rapid
Protein binding: ~25%
Bioavailability: ~90%; decreased by food
Half-life elimination: ~1 hour

Time to peak, serum: ~1 hour
Excretion: Clearance: Plasma: ~200-300 mL/minute

Dosage

Usual dosage range:
Children 6 months to 12 years: Oral: 7.5-15 mg/kg twice daily
Adults: Oral: 200-400 mg every 12-24 hours

Indication-specific dosing:
Children 6 months to 12 years: Oral:
Acute otitis media: 15 mg/kg twice daily for 10 days
Pharyngitis and impetigo: 7.5-15 mg/kg twice daily for 10 days
Adults: Oral:
Bronchitis: 200-400 mg every 12 hours for 7 days
Pharyngitis/tonsillitis: 200 mg every 12 hours for 10 days
Pneumonia: 400 mg every 12 hours for 14 days
Pyelonephritis (uncomplicated): 400 mg every 12 hours for 14 days
Sinusitis: 400 mg every 12 hours for 10 days
Skin and soft tissue: 200-400 mg every 12-24 hours
Urinary tract infections (uncomplicated): 200 mg once daily for 7 days

Dosing comments in renal impairment:
Cl_{cr} 10-49 mL/minute: 50% of usual dose at usual interval or usual dose given half as often
Cl_{cr} <10 mL/minute: Administer usual dose every 3-5 days
Hemodialysis: Doses should be administered after dialysis sessions

Dietary Considerations Should be taken on an empty stomach at least 1 hour before or 2 hours after meals.

Administration Administer on an empty stomach at least 1 hour before or 2 hours after meals. Finish all medication. Shake suspension well before using.

Dosage Forms [DSC] = Discontinued product
Capsule:
Lorabid®: 200 mg, 400 mg [DSC]
Powder for oral suspension:
Lorabid®: 100 mg/5 mL (100 mL); 200 mg/5 mL (100 mL) [strawberry bubble gum flavor] [DSC]

Loratadine (lor AT a deen)

U.S. Brand Names Alavert® [OTC]; Claritin® 24 Hour Allergy [OTC]; Claritin® Hives Relief [OTC]; Tavist® ND [OTC]; Triaminic® Allerchews™ [OTC]
Canadian Brand Names Apo-Loratadine®; Claritin®; Claritin® Kids
Pharmacologic Category Antihistamine, Nonsedating
Use Relief of nasal and non-nasal symptoms of seasonal allergic rhinitis; treatment of chronic idiopathic urticaria
Pregnancy Risk Factor B
Pregnancy Implications Loratadine was not found to be teratogenic in animal studies. There are no adequate and well-controlled studies in pregnant woman; use during pregnancy only if clearly needed.
Lactation Enters breast milk/not recommended (AAP rates "compatible")
Medication Safety Issues
Sound-alike/look-alike issues:
Dimetapp® may be confused with Dermatop®, Dimetabs®, Dimetane®
Contraindications Hypersensitivity to loratadine or any component of the formulation
Warnings/Precautions Use with caution and modify dose in patients with liver or renal impairment; safety and efficacy in children <2 years of age have not been established
Adverse Reactions
Adults:
Central nervous system: Headache (12%), somnolence (8%), fatigue (4%)
Gastrointestinal: Xerostomia (3%)
Children:
Central nervous system: Nervousness (4% ages 6-12 years), fatigue (3% ages 6-12 years, 2% to 3% ages 2-5 years), malaise (2% ages 6-12 years)
Dermatologic: Rash (2% to 3% ages 2-5 years)
Gastrointestinal: Abdominal pain (2% ages 6-12 years), stomatitis (2% to 3% ages 2-5 years)
Neuromuscular & skeletal: Hyperkinesia (3% ages 6-12 years)
Ocular: Conjunctivitis (2% ages 6-12 years)
Respiratory: Wheezing (4% ages 6-12 years), dysphonia (2% ages 6-12 years), upper respiratory infection (2% ages 6-12 years), epistaxis (2% to 3% ages 2-5 years), pharyngitis (2% to 3% ages 2-5 years)
Miscellaneous: Flu-like syndrome (2% to 3% ages 2-5 years), viral infection (2% to 3% ages 2-5 years)

Adults and Children: <2% (Limited to important or life-threatening): Abnormal hepatic function, agitation, alopecia, altered lacrimation, altered micturition, altered salivation, altered taste, amnesia, anaphylaxis, angioneurotic edema, anorexia, arthralgia, back pain, blepharospasm, blurred vision, breast enlargement, breast pain, bronchospasm, chest pain, confusion, depression, dizziness, dysmenorrhea, dyspnea, erythema multiforme, hemoptysis, hepatic necrosis, hepatitis, hypotension, impaired concentration, impotence, insomnia, irritability, jaundice, menorrhagia, migraine, nausea, palpitation, paresthesia, paroniria, peripheral edema, photosensitivity, pruritus, purpura, rigors, seizure, supraventricular tachyarrhythmia, syncope, tachycardia, tremor, urinary discoloration, urticaria, thrombocytopenia, vaginitis, vertigo, vomiting, weight gain

Overdosage/Toxicology Symptoms include somnolence, tachycardia, and headache. No specific antidote is available. Treatment is symptomatic and supportive. Loratadine is not eliminated by dialysis.
(Continued)

Loratadine (Continued)

Drug Interactions

Cytochrome P450 Effect: Substrate (minor) of CYP2D6, 3A4; **Inhibits** CYP2C8 (weak), 2C19 (moderate), 2D6 (weak)

Increased Effect/Toxicity: Increased toxicity with procarbazine, other antihistamines. Protease inhibitors (amprenavir, ritonavir, nelfinavir) may increase the serum levels of loratadine. Loratadine may increase the levels/effects of citalopram, diazepam, methsuximide, phenytoin, propranolol, sertraline, and other CYP2C19 substrates.

Ethanol/Nutrition/Herb Interactions

Ethanol: Avoid ethanol (although sedation is limited with loratadine, may increase risk of CNS depression).

Food: Increases bioavailability and delays peak.

Herb/Nutraceutical: St John's wort may decrease loratadine levels.

Stability Store at 2°C to 25°C (36°F to 77°F).

Rapidly-disintegrating tablets: Use within 6 months of opening foil pouch, and immediately after opening individual tablet blister. Store in a dry place.

Mechanism of Action Long-acting tricyclic antihistamine with selective peripheral histamine H_1-receptor antagonistic properties

Pharmacodynamics/Kinetics

Onset of action: 1-3 hours

Peak effect: 8-12 hours

Duration: >24 hours

Absorption: Rapid

Distribution: Significant amounts enter breast milk

Metabolism: Extensively hepatic via CYP2D6 and 3A4 to active metabolite

Half-life elimination: 12-15 hours

Excretion: Urine (40%) and feces (40%) as metabolites

Dosage Oral: Seasonal allergic rhinitis, chronic idiopathic urticaria:

Children 2-5 years: 5 mg once daily

Children ≥6 years and Adults: 10 mg once daily

Elderly: Peak plasma levels are increased; elimination half-life is slightly increased; specific dosing adjustments are not available

Dosage adjustment in renal impairment: Cl_{cr} ≤30 mL/minute:

Children 2-5 years: 5 mg every other day

Children ≥6 years and Adults: 10 mg every other day

Dosage adjustment in hepatic impairment: Elimination half-life increases with severity of disease

Children 2-5 years: 5 mg every other day

Children ≥6 years and Adults: 10 mg every other day

Dietary Considerations Take on an empty stomach. Alavert® and Dimetapp® Children's ND contain phenylalanine 8.4 mg per 10 mg tablet.

Administration Take on an empty stomach.

Dosage Forms

Syrup: 1 mg/mL (120 mL)

Claritin®: 1 mg/mL (120 mL) [contains sodium benzoate; fruit flavor]; (60 mL, 120 mL) [alcohol free, dye free, sugar free; contains sodium 6 mg/5 mL and sodium benzoate; grape flavor]

Tablet: 10 mg

Alavert®, Claritin®, Claritin® Hives Relief, Claritin® 24 Hour Allergy, Tavist® ND: 10 mg

Tablet, rapidly disintegrating: 10 mg

Alavert®: 10 mg [contains phenylalanine 8.4 mg/tablet; mint and citrus burst flavors]

Claritin® RediTabs®: 10 mg [mint flavor]

Triaminic® Allerchews™: 10 mg

Loratadine and Pseudoephedrine (lor AT a deen & soo doe e FED rin)

U.S. Brand Names Alavert™ Allergy and Sinus [OTC]; Claritin-D® 12-Hour [OTC]; Claritin-D® 24-Hour [OTC]

Canadian Brand Names Chlor-Tripolon ND®; Claritin® Extra; Claritin® Liberator

Index Terms Pseudoephedrine and Loratadine

Pharmacologic Category Antihistamine/Decongestant Combination

Use Temporary relief of symptoms of seasonal allergic rhinitis, other upper respiratory allergies, or the common cold

Pregnancy Risk Factor B

Dosage Children ≥12 years and Adults: Oral:

Claritin-D® 12-Hour: 1 tablet every 12 hours

Alavert™ Allergy and Sinus, Claritin-D® 24-Hour: 1 tablet daily

Dosage adjustment in renal impairment: Cl_{cr} ≤30 mL/minute:

Claritin-D® 12-Hour: 1 tablet daily

Claritin-D® 24-Hour: 1 tablet every other day

Dosage adjustment in hepatic impairment: Should be avoided

Additional Information Complete prescribing information for this medication should be consulted for additional detail.

Dosage Forms

Tablet, extended release: Loratadine 10 mg and pseudoephedrine sulfate 240 mg

Alavert™ Allergy and Sinus, Claritin-D® 12-hour: Loratadine 5 mg and pseudoephedrine sulfate 120 mg

Claritin-D® 24-hour: Loratadine 10 mg and pseudoephedrine sulfate 240 mg

Lorazepam (lor A ze pam)

U.S. Brand Names Ativan®; Lorazepam Intensol®
Canadian Brand Names Apo-Lorazepam®; Ativan®; Lorazepam Injection, USP; Novo-Lorazepam; Nu-Loraz; PMS-Lorazepam; Riva-Lorazepam
Pharmacologic Category Benzodiazepine
Additional Appendix Information
Benzodiazepines *on page 1874*
Epilepsy *on page 2048*
Use
Oral: Management of anxiety disorders or short-term relief of the symptoms of anxiety or anxiety associated with depressive symptoms
I.V.: Status epilepticus, preanesthesia for desired amnesia, antiemetic adjunct
Unlabeled/Investigational Use Ethanol detoxification; insomnia; psychogenic catatonia; partial complex seizures; agitation (I.V.)
Restrictions C-IV
Pregnancy Risk Factor D
Pregnancy Implications Crosses the placenta. Respiratory depression or hypotonia if administered near time of delivery.
Lactation Enters breast milk/contraindicated (AAP rates "of concern")
Medication Safety Issues
Sound-alike/look-alike issues:
Lorazepam may be confused with alprazolam, clonazepam, diazepam, temazepam
Ativan® may be confused with Atarax®, Atgam®, Avitene®

Injection dosage form contains propylene glycol. Monitor for toxicity when administering continuous lorazepam infusions.
Contraindications Hypersensitivity to lorazepam or any component of the formulation (cross-sensitivity with other benzodiazepines may exist); acute narrow-angle glaucoma; sleep apnea (parenteral); intra-arterial injection of parenteral formulation; severe respiratory insufficiency (except during mechanical ventilation); pregnancy
Warnings/Precautions Use with caution in elderly or debilitated patients, patients with hepatic disease (including alcoholics) or renal impairment. Use with caution in patients with respiratory disease or impaired gag reflex. Initial doses in elderly or debilitated patients should not exceed 2 mg. Prolonged lorazepam use may have a possible relationship to GI disease, including esophageal dilation.

The parenteral formulation of lorazepam contains polyethylene glycol and propylene glycol. Also contains benzyl alcohol - avoid in neonates. Concurrent administration with scopolamine results in an increased risk of hallucinations, sedation, and irrational behavior.

Causes CNS depression (dose-related) resulting in sedation, dizziness, confusion, or ataxia which may impair physical and mental capabilities. Patients must be cautioned about performing tasks which require mental alertness (eg, operating machinery or driving). Use with caution in patients receiving other CNS depressants or psychoactive agents. Effects with other sedative drugs or ethanol may be potentiated. Benzodiazepines have been associated with falls and traumatic injury and should be used with extreme caution in patients who are at risk of these events (especially the elderly).

Lorazepam may cause anterograde amnesia. Paradoxical reactions, including hyperactive or aggressive behavior have been reported with benzodiazepines, particularly in adolescent/pediatric or psychiatric patients. Does not have analgesic, antidepressant, or antipsychotic properties.

Use caution in patients with depression, particularly if suicidal risk may be present. Use with caution in patients with a history of drug dependence. Benzodiazepines have been associated with dependence and acute withdrawal symptoms on discontinuation or reduction in dose. Acute withdrawal, including seizures, may be precipitated after administration of flumazenil to patients receiving long-term benzodiazepine therapy.

As a hypnotic agent, should be used only after evaluation of potential causes of sleep disturbance. Failure of sleep disturbance to resolve after 7-10 days may indicate psychiatric or medical illness. A worsening of insomnia or the emergence of new abnormalities of thought or behavior may represent unrecognized psychiatric or medical illness and requires immediate and careful evaluation.
Adverse Reactions
>10%:
Central nervous system: Sedation
Respiratory: Respiratory depression
1% to 10%:
Cardiovascular: Hypotension
Central nervous system: Confusion, dizziness, akathisia, unsteadiness, headache, depression, disorientation, amnesia
Dermatologic: Dermatitis, rash
Gastrointestinal: Weight gain/loss, nausea, changes in appetite
Neuromuscular & skeletal: Weakness
Respiratory: Nasal congestion, hyperventilation, apnea
<1% (Limited to important or life-threatening): Menstrual irregularities, increased salivation, blood dyscrasias, reflex slowing, physical and psychological dependence with prolonged use, polyethylene glycol or propylene glycol poisoning (prolonged I.V. infusion)
Overdosage/Toxicology Symptoms include confusion, coma, hypoactive reflexes, dyspnea, and labored breathing. **Note:** Prolonged infusions have been associated with toxicity from propylene glycol and/or polyethylene glycol. Treatment for benzodiazepine overdose is supportive. Rarely is mechanical ventilation required. Flumazenil has been shown to selectively block the binding of benzodiazepines to CNS receptors, resulting in a reversal of
(Continued)

Lorazepam *(Continued)*

benzodiazepine-induced CNS depression, but not respiratory depression. Treatment requires blood pressure and respiratory support until drug effects subside.

Drug Interactions

Increased Effect/Toxicity: CNS depressants may increase the CNS effects of lorazepam. There are rare reports of significant respiratory depression, stupor, and/or hypotension with concomitant use of loxapine and lorazepam. Use caution if concomitant administration of loxapine and CNS drugs is required. Benzodiazepines may enhance the toxic effects of clozapine.

Decreased Effect: Theophylline and other CNS stimulants may antagonize the sedative effects of lorazepam.

Ethanol/Nutrition/Herb Interactions

Ethanol: Avoid or limit ethanol (may increase CNS depression).

Herb/Nutraceutical: Avoid valerian, St John's wort, kava kava, gotu kola (may increase CNS depression).

Stability

I.V.: Intact vials should be refrigerated. Protect from light. Do not use discolored or precipitate-containing solutions. May be stored at room temperature for up to 60 days. Parenteral admixture is stable at room temperature (25°C) for 24 hours. Dilute I.V. dose with equal volume of compatible diluent (D$_5$W, NS, SWI).

Infusion: Use 2 mg/mL injectable solution to prepare. Dilute ≤1 mg/mL and mix in glass bottle. Precipitation may develop. Can also be administered undiluted via infusion.

Tablet: Store at room temperature.

Mechanism of Action

Binds to stereospecific benzodiazepine receptors on the postsynaptic GABA neuron at several sites within the central nervous system, including the limbic system, reticular formation. Enhancement of the inhibitory effect of GABA on neuronal excitability results by increased neuronal membrane permeability to chloride ions. This shift in chloride ions results in hyperpolarization (a less excitable state) and stabilization.

Pharmacodynamics/Kinetics

Onset of action:

Hypnosis: I.M.: 20-30 minutes

Sedation: I.V.: 5-20 minutes

Anticonvulsant: I.V.: 5 minutes, oral: 30-60 minutes

Duration: 6-8 hours

Absorption: Oral, I.M.: Prompt

Distribution:

V$_d$: Neonates: 0.76 L/kg, Adults: 1.3 L/kg; crosses placenta; enters breast milk

Protein binding: 85%; free fraction may be significantly higher in elderly

Metabolism: Hepatic to inactive compounds

Half-life elimination: Neonates: 40.2 hours; Older children: 10.5 hours; Adults: 12.9 hours; Elderly: 15.9 hours; End-stage renal disease: 32-70 hours

Excretion: Urine; feces (minimal)

Dosage

Antiemetic:

Children 2-15 years: I.V.: 0.05 mg/kg (up to 2 mg/dose) prior to chemotherapy

Adults: Oral, I.V. (**Note:** May be administered sublingually; not a labeled route): 0.5-2 mg every 4-6 hours as needed

Anxiety and sedation:

Infants and Children: Oral, I.M., I.V.: Usual: 0.05 mg/kg/dose (range: 0.02-0.09 mg/kg) every 4-8 hours

I.V.: May use smaller doses (eg, 0.01-0.03 mg/kg) and repeat every 20 minutes, as needed to titrate to effect

Adults: Oral: 1-10 mg/day in 2-3 divided doses; usual dose: 2-6 mg/day in divided doses

Elderly: 0.5-4 mg/day; initial dose not to exceed 2 mg

Insomnia: Adults: Oral: 2-4 mg at bedtime

Preoperative: Adults:

I.M.: 0.05 mg/kg administered 2 hours before surgery (maximum: 4 mg/dose)

I.V.: 0.044 mg/kg 15-20 minutes before surgery (usual maximum: 2 mg/dose)

Preprocedural anxiety (dental use): Adults: Oral: 1-2 mg 1 hour before procedure

Operative amnesia: Adults: I.V.: Up to 0.05 mg/kg (maximum: 4 mg/dose)

Sedation (preprocedure): Infants and Children:

Oral, I.M., I.V.: Usual: 0.05 mg/kg (range: 0.02-0.09 mg/kg)

I.V.: May use smaller doses (eg, 0.01-0.03 mg/kg) and repeat every 20 minutes, as needed to titrate to effect

Status epilepticus: I.V.:

Infants and Children: 0.1 mg/kg slow I.V. over 2-5 minutes; do not exceed 4 mg/single dose; may repeat second dose of 0.05 mg/kg slow I.V. in 10-15 minutes if needed

Adolescents: 0.07 mg/kg slow I.V. over 2-5 minutes; maximum: 4 mg/dose; may repeat in 10-15 minutes

Adults: 4 mg/dose slow I.V. over 2-5 minutes; may repeat in 10-15 minutes; usual maximum dose: 8 mg

Rapid tranquilization of agitated patient (administer every 30-60 minutes):

Oral: 1-2 mg

I.M.: 0.5-1 mg

Average total dose for tranquilization: Oral, I.M.: 4-8 mg

Agitation in the ICU patient (unlabeled):

I.V.: 0.02-0.06 mg/kg every 2-6 hours

I.V. infusion: 0.01-0.1 mg/kg/hour

Administration

May be administered by I.M., I.V., or orally

I.M.: Should be administered deep into the muscle mass

I.V.: Do not exceed 2 mg/minute or 0.05 mg/kg over 2-5 minutes; dilute I.V. dose with equal volume of compatible diluent (D$_5$W, NS, SWI).

Monitoring Parameters

Respiratory and cardiovascular status, blood pressure, heart rate, symptoms of anxiety

Reference Range Therapeutic: 50-240 ng/mL (SI: 156-746 nmol/L)

Additional Information Oral doses >0.09 mg/kg produced increased ataxia without increased sedative benefit vs lower doses; preferred anxiolytic when I.M. route needed. Abrupt discontinuation after sustained use (generally >10 days) may cause withdrawal symptoms.

Dosage Forms

Injection, solution (Ativan®): 2 mg/mL (1 mL, 10 mL); 4 mg/mL (1 mL, 10 mL) [contains benzyl alcohol]

Solution, oral concentrate (Lorazepam Intensol®): 2 mg/mL (30 mL) [alcohol free, dye free]

Tablet (Ativan®): 0.5 mg, 1 mg, 2 mg

♦ **Lorazepam Injection, USP (Can)** see Lorazepam on page 1035

♦ **Lorazepam Intensol®** see Lorazepam on page 1035

♦ **Lorcet® 10/650** see Hydrocodone and Acetaminophen on page 848

♦ **Lorcet® Plus** see Hydrocodone and Acetaminophen on page 848

♦ **Lortab®** see Hydrocodone and Acetaminophen on page 848

Losartan (loe SAR tan)

U.S. Brand Names Cozaar®

Canadian Brand Names Cozaar®

Index Terms DuP 753; Losartan Potassium; MK594

Pharmacologic Category Angiotensin II Receptor Blocker

Additional Appendix Information

Angiotensin Agents on page 1860

Use Treatment of hypertension (HTN); treatment of diabetic nephropathy in patients with type 2 diabetes mellitus (noninsulin dependent, NIDDM) and a history of hypertension; stroke risk reduction in patients with HTN and left ventricular hypertrophy (LVH)

Pregnancy Risk Factor C/D (2nd and 3rd trimesters)

Pregnancy Implications Discontinue as soon as possible when pregnancy is detected. Drugs which act directly on renin-angiotensin can cause fetal and neonatal morbidity and death.

Lactation Excretion in breast milk unknown/not recommended

Medication Safety Issues

Sound-alike/look-alike issues:

Losartan may be confused with valsartan

Cozaar® may be confused with Hyzaar®, Zocor®

Contraindications Hypersensitivity to losartan or any component of the formulation; hypersensitivity to other A-II receptor antagonists; bilateral renal artery stenosis; pregnancy

Warnings/Precautions [U.S. Boxed Warning]: Based on human data, drugs that act on the angiotensin system can cause injury and death to the developing fetus when used in the second and third trimesters. Angiotensin receptor blockers should be discontinued as soon as possible once pregnancy is detected. Avoid use or use a much smaller dose in patients who are volume-depleted; correct depletion first. Use with caution in patients with pre-existing renal insufficiency or significant aortic/mitral stenosis. May cause hyperkalemia; avoid potassium supplementation unless specifically required by healthcare provider. May be associated with deterioration of renal function and/or increases in serum creatinine, particularly in patients dependent on renin-angiotensin-aldosterone system. Use caution in patients with unilateral or bilateral renal artery stenosis to avoid a decrease in renal function. AUCs of losartan (not the active metabolite) are about 50% greater in patients with Cl$_{cr}$ <30 mL/minute and are doubled in hemodialysis patients. When used to reduce the risk of stroke in patients with HTN and LVH, may not be effective in African-American population. Use caution with hepatic dysfunction, dose adjustment may be needed. Safety and efficacy have not been established in children <6 years of age.

Adverse Reactions

>10%:

Cardiovascular: Chest pain (12% diabetic nephropathy)

Central nervous system: Fatigue (14% diabetic nephropathy)

Endocrine: Hypoglycemia (14% diabetic nephropathy)

Gastrointestinal: Diarrhea (2% hypertension to 15% diabetic nephropathy)

Genitourinary: Urinary tract infection (13% diabetic nephropathy)

Hematologic: Anemia (14% diabetic nephropathy)

Neuromuscular & skeletal: Weakness (14% diabetic nephropathy), back pain (2% hypertension to 12% diabetic nephropathy)

Respiratory: Cough (≤3% to 11%; similar to placebo; incidence higher in patients with previous cough related to ACE inhibitor therapy)

1% to 10%:

Cardiovascular: Hypotension (7% diabetic nephropathy), orthostatic hypotension (4% hypertension to 4% diabetic nephropathy), first-dose hypotension (dose related: <1% with 50 mg, 2% with 100 mg)

Central nervous system: Dizziness (4%), hypoesthesia (5% diabetic nephropathy), fever (4% diabetic nephropathy), insomnia (1%)

Dermatology: Cellulitis (7% diabetic nephropathy)

Endocrine: Hyperkalemia (<1% hypertension to 7% diabetic nephropathy)

Gastrointestinal: Gastritis (5% diabetic nephropathy), weight gain (4% diabetic nephropathy), dyspepsia (1% to 4%), abdominal pain (2%), nausea (2%)

Neuromuscular & skeletal: Muscular weakness (7% diabetic nephropathy), knee pain (5% diabetic nephropathy), leg pain (1% to 5%), muscle cramps (1%), myalgia (1%)

Respiratory: Bronchitis (10% diabetic nephropathy), upper respiratory infection (8%), nasal congestion (2%), sinusitis (1% hypertension to 6% diabetic nephropathy)

Miscellaneous: Infection (5% diabetic nephropathy), flu-like syndrome (10% diabetic nephropathy)

>1% but frequency ≤ placebo: Edema, abdominal pain, nausea, headache, pharyngitis

(Continued)

Losartan (Continued)

<1% (Limited to important or life-threatening): Acute psychosis with paranoid delusions, ageusia, alopecia, anemia, angina, angioedema, arrhythmia, AV block (second degree), depression, dysgeusia, dyspnea, erythroderma, gout, Henoch-Schönlein purpura, hepatitis, hyperkalemia, hyponatremia, impotence, maculopapular rash, MI, panic disorder, pancreatitis, paresthesia, peripheral neuropathy, photosensitivity, renal impairment (patients dependent on renin-angiotensin-aldosterone system), rhabdomyolysis (rare), stroke, syncope, thrombocytopenia (rare), urticaria, vasculitis, vertigo

Overdosage/Toxicology Symptoms including hypotension and tachycardia may occur with very significant overdoses. Treatment should be supportive. Not removed via hemodialysis.

Drug Interactions

Cytochrome P450 Effect: Substrate (major) of CYP2C9, 3A4; **Inhibits** CYP1A2 (weak), 2C8 (moderate), 2C9 (moderate), 2C19 (weak), 3A4 (weak)

Increased Effect/Toxicity: Cimetidine may increase the absorption of losartan by 18% (clinical effect is unknown). Potassium salts/supplements, co-trimoxazole (high dose), ACE inhibitors, and potassium-sparing diuretics (amiloride, spironolactone, triamterene) may increase the risk of hyperkalemia. Risk of lithium toxicity may be increased by losartan. Losartan may increase the levels/effects of amiodarone, bosentan, dapsone, fluoxetine, glimepiride, glipizide, montelukast, nateglinide, paclitaxel, phenytoin, pioglitazone, repaglinide, rosiglitazone, warfarin, zafirlukast, and other CYP2C8 or 2C9 substrates. Fluconazole may increase the levels/effects of losartan.

Decreased Effect: The levels/effects of losartan may be decreased by aminoglutethimide, carbamazepine, nafcillin, nevirapine, phenobarbital, phenytoin, rifampin, rifapentine, secobarbital, and other CYP2C9 or 3A4 inducers. NSAIDs may decrease the efficacy of losartan.

Ethanol/Nutrition/Herb Interactions Herb/Nutraceutical: St John's wort may decrease levels. Avoid dong quai if using for hypertension (has estrogenic activity). Avoid ephedra, yohimbe, ginseng (may worsen hypertension). Avoid garlic (may have increased antihypertensive effect).

Stability Store at 15°C to 30°C (59°F to 86°F). Protect from light.

Mechanism of Action As a selective and competitive, nonpeptide angiotensin II receptor antagonist, losartan blocks the vasoconstrictor and aldosterone-secreting effects of angiotensin II; losartan interacts reversibly at the AT1 and AT2 receptors of many tissues and has slow dissociation kinetics; its affinity for the AT1 receptor is 1000 times greater than the AT2 receptor. Angiotensin II receptor antagonists may induce a more complete inhibition of the renin-angiotensin system than ACE inhibitors, they do not affect the response to bradykinin, and are less likely to be associated with nonrenin-angiotensin effects (eg, cough and angioedema). Losartan increases urinary flow rate and in addition to being natriuretic and kaliuretic, increases excretion of chloride, magnesium, uric acid, calcium, and phosphate.

Pharmacodynamics/Kinetics

Onset of action: 6 hours

Distribution: V_d: Losartan: 34 L; E-3174: 12 L; does not cross blood brain barrier

Protein binding, plasma: High

Metabolism: Hepatic (14%) via CYP2C9 and 3A4 to active metabolite, E-3174 (40 times more potent than losartan); extensive first-pass effect

Bioavailability: 25% to 33%; AUC of E-3174 is four times greater than that of losartan

Half-life elimination: Losartan: 1.5-2 hours; E-3174: 6-9 hours

Time to peak, serum: Losartan: 1 hour; E-3174: 3-4 hours

Excretion: Urine (4% as unchanged drug, 6% as active metabolite)

Clearance: Plasma: Losartan: 600 mL/minute; Active metabolite: 50 mL/minute

Dosage Oral:

Hypertension:

Children 6-16 years: 0.7 mg/kg once daily (maximum: 50 mg/day); adjust dose based on response; doses >1.4 mg/kg (maximum: 100 mg) have not been studied

Adults: Usual starting dose: 50 mg once daily; can be administered once or twice daily with total daily doses ranging from 25-100 mg

Patients receiving diuretics or with intravascular volume depletion: Usual initial dose: 25 mg

Nephropathy in patients with type 2 diabetes and hypertension: Adults: Initial: 50 mg once daily; can be increased to 100 mg once daily based on blood pressure response

Stroke reduction (HTN with LVH): Adults: 50 mg once daily (maximum daily dose: 100 mg); may be used in combination with a thiazide diuretic

Dosing adjustment in renal impairment:

Children: Use is not recommended if Cl_{cr} <30 mL/minute.

Adults: No adjustment necessary.

Dosing adjustment in hepatic impairment: Reduce the initial dose to 25 mg/day; divide dosage intervals into two.

Dietary Considerations May be taken with or without food.

Administration May be administered with or without food.

Monitoring Parameters Supine blood pressure, electrolytes, serum creatinine, BUN, urinalysis, symptomatic hypotension and tachycardia, CBC

Dosage Forms Tablet, as potassium: 25 mg, 50 mg, 100 mg

Extemporaneous Preparations To prepare losartan suspension, combine 10 mL of purified water and ten (10) losartan 50 mg tablets in an 8 ounce bottle. Shake well for ≥2 minutes. Allow concentrate to stand for 1 hour then shake for 1 minute. Separately, prepare 190 mL of a 50/50 mixture of Ora-Plus™ and Ora-Sweet SF™. Add to tablet and water mixture; shake for 1 minute. Resulting 200 mL suspension will contain losartan 2.5 mg/mL. Store under refrigeration for up to 4 weeks; shake well before use.

Product information, October, 2004; Merck & Company, Inc

Losartan and Hydrochlorothiazide
(loe SAR tan & hye droe klor oh THYE a zide)

U.S. Brand Names Hyzaar®
Canadian Brand Names Hyzaar®; Hyzaar® DS
Index Terms Hydrochlorothiazide and Losartan
Pharmacologic Category Angiotensin II Receptor Blocker Combination; Antihypertensive Agent, Combination; Diuretic, Thiazide
Use Treatment of hypertension; stroke risk reduction in patients with HTN and left ventricular hypertrophy (LVH)
Pregnancy Risk Factor C/D (2nd and 3rd trimesters)
Medication Safety Issues
Sound-alike/look-alike issues:
Hyzaar® may be confused with Cozaar®
Dosage
Oral: Adults: Dose is individualized (combination substituted for individual components); dose may be titrated after 2-4 weeks of therapy
Hypertension/stroke reduction in hypertension (with LVH): Usual recommended starting dose of losartan: 50 mg once daily when used as monotherapy in patients who are not volume depleted

Dosage adjustment in renal impairment: Cl_{cr} ≤30 mL/minute: Use of combination formulation not recommended
Dosage adjustment in hepatic impairment: Use is not recommended
Additional Information Complete prescribing information for this medication should be consulted for additional detail.
Dosage Forms
Tablet:
Hyzaar® 50-12.5: Losartan potassium 50 mg and hydrochlorothiazide 12.5 mg
Hyzaar® 100-12.5: Losartan potassium 100 mg and hydrochlorothiazide 12.5 mg
Hyzaar® 100-25: Losartan potassium 100 mg and hydrochlorothiazide 25 mg

♦ **Losartan Potassium** see Losartan on page 1037
♦ **Losec®** (Can) see Omeprazole on page 1264
♦ **Losec MUPS®** (Can) see Omeprazole on page 1264
♦ **Lotemax®** see Loteprednol on page 1039
♦ **Lotensin®** see Benazepril on page 202
♦ **Lotensin® HCT** see Benazepril and Hydrochlorothiazide on page 203

Loteprednol (loe te PRED nol)

U.S. Brand Names Alrex®; Lotemax®
Canadian Brand Names Alrex®; Lotemax®
Index Terms Loteprednol Etabonate
Pharmacologic Category Corticosteroid, Ophthalmic
Use
Suspension, 0.2% (Alrex®): Temporary relief of signs and symptoms of seasonal allergic conjunctivitis
Suspension, 0.5% (Lotemax®): Inflammatory conditions (treatment of steroid-responsive inflammatory conditions of the palpebral and bulbar conjunctiva, cornea, and anterior segment of the globe such as allergic conjunctivitis, acne rosacea, superficial punctate keratitis, herpes zoster keratitis, iritis, cyclitis, selected infective conjunctivitis, when the inherent hazard of steroid use is accepted to obtain an advisable diminution in edema and inflammation) and treatment of postoperative inflammation following ocular surgery
Pregnancy Risk Factor C
Medication Safety Issues
International issues:
Lotemax® may be confused with Lotanax® which is a brand name for terfenadine in the Czech Republic
Dosage Adults: Ophthalmic:
Suspension, 0.2% (Alrex®): Instill 1 drop into affected eye(s) 4 times/day
Suspension, 0.5% (Lotemax®):
Inflammatory conditions: Apply 1-2 drops into the conjunctival sac of the affected eye(s) 4 times/day. During the initial treatment within the first week, the dosing may be increased up to 1 drop every hour. Advise patients not to discontinue therapy prematurely. If signs and symptoms fail to improve after 2 days, re-evaluate the patient.
Postoperative inflammation: Apply 1-2 drops into the conjunctival sac of the operated eye(s) 4 times/day beginning 24 hours after surgery and continuing throughout the first 2 weeks of the postoperative period
Additional Information Complete prescribing information for this medication should be consulted for additional detail.
Dosage Forms Suspension, ophthalmic, as etabonate:
Alrex®: 0.2% (5 mL, 10 mL) [contains benzalkonium chloride]
Lotemax®: 0.5% (2.5 mL, 5 mL, 10 mL, 15 mL) [contains benzalkonium chloride]

Loteprednol and Tobramycin (loe te PRED nol & toe bra MYE sin)

U.S. Brand Names Zylet™
Index Terms Loteprednol Etabonate and Tobramycin; Tobramycin and Loteprednol Etabonate
(Continued)

Loteprednol and Tobramycin (Continued)

Pharmacologic Category Antibiotic/Corticosteroid, Ophthalmic

Use Treatment of steroid-responsive ocular inflammatory conditions where either a superficial bacterial ocular infection or the risk of a superficial bacterial ocular infection exists

Pregnancy Risk Factor C

Dosage Ophthalmic: Adults: Instill 1-2 drops into the affected eye(s) every 4-6 hours; may increase frequency during the first 24-48 hours to every 1-2 hours. Interval should increase as signs and symptoms improve. Further evaluation should occur for use of greater than 20 mL.

Additional Information Complete prescribing information for this medication should be consulted for additional detail.

Dosage Forms Suspension, ophthalmic: Loteprednol 0.5% and tobramycin 0.3% (2.5 mL, 5 mL, 10 mL) [contains benzalkonium chloride]

- ◆ **Loteprednol Etabonate** see Loteprednol on page 1039
- ◆ **Loteprednol Etabonate and Tobramycin** see Loteprednol and Tobramycin on page 1039
- ◆ **Lotrel®** see Amlodipine and Benazepril on page 106
- ◆ **Lotriderm® (Can)** see Betamethasone and Clotrimazole on page 214
- ◆ **Lotrimin® AF Athlete's Foot Cream [OTC]** see Clotrimazole on page 404
- ◆ **Lotrimin® AF Athlete's Foot Solution [OTC]** see Clotrimazole on page 404
- ◆ **Lotrimin® AF Jock Itch Cream [OTC]** see Clotrimazole on page 404
- ◆ **Lotrimin® AF Jock Itch Powder Spray [OTC]** see Miconazole on page 1137
- ◆ **Lotrimin® AF Powder/Spray [OTC]** see Miconazole on page 1137
- ◆ **Lotrimin® Ultra™ [OTC]** see Butenafine on page 260
- ◆ **Lotrisone®** see Betamethasone and Clotrimazole on page 214

Lovastatin (LOE va sta tin)

U.S. Brand Names Altoprev®; Mevacor®

Canadian Brand Names Apo-Lovastatin®; CO Lovastatin; Gen-Lovastatin; Mevacor®; Novo-Lovastatin; Nu-Lovastatin; PMS-Lovastatin; RAN™-Lovastatin; ratio-Lovastatin; Riva-Lovastatin; Sandoz-Lovastatin

Index Terms Mevinolin; Monacolin K

Pharmacologic Category Antilipemic Agent, HMG-CoA Reductase Inhibitor

Additional Appendix Information
Hyperlipidemia Management on page 2058
Lipid-Lowering Agents on page 1887

Use
Adjunct to dietary therapy to decrease elevated serum total and LDL-cholesterol concentrations in primary hypercholesterolemia

Primary prevention of coronary artery disease (patients without symptomatic disease with average to moderately elevated total and LDL-cholesterol and below average HDL-cholesterol); slow progression of coronary atherosclerosis in patients with coronary heart disease

Adjunct to dietary therapy in adolescent patients (10-17 years of age, females >1 year postmenarche) with heterozygous familial hypercholesterolemia having LDL >189 mg/dL, **or** LDL >160 mg/dL with positive family history of premature cardiovascular disease (CVD), or LDL >160 mg/dL with the presence of at least two other CVD risk factors

Pregnancy Risk Factor X

Pregnancy Implications Cholesterol biosynthesis may be important in fetal development. Contraindicated in pregnancy. Administer to women of childbearing potential only when conception is highly unlikely and patients have been informed of potential hazards.

Lactation Excretion unknown/contraindicated

Medication Safety Issues
Sound-alike/look-alike issues:
Lovastatin may be confused with Leustatin®, Livostin®, Lotensin®
Mevacor® may be confused with Mivacron®

International issues:
Lovacol® [Chile and Finland] may be confused with Levatol® which is a brand name for penbutolol in the U.S.
Lovastin® [Poland] may be confused with Livostin® which is a brand name for levocabastine in the U.S.

Contraindications Hypersensitivity to lovastatin or any component of the formulation; active liver disease; unexplained persistent elevations of serum transaminases; pregnancy; breast-feeding

Warnings/Precautions Secondary causes of hyperlipidemia should be ruled out prior to therapy. Liver function must be monitored by periodic laboratory assessment. Rhabdomyolysis with or without acute renal failure has occurred. Risk is dose-related and is increased with concurrent use of lipid-lowering agents which may cause rhabdomyolysis (gemfibrozil, fibric acid derivatives, or niacin at doses ≥1 g/day) or during concurrent use with potent CYP3A4 inhibitors. Avoid concurrent use of azole antifungals, macrolide antibiotics, and protease inhibitors. Use caution/limit dose with amiodarone, cyclosporine, danazol, gemfibrozil (or other fibrates), lipid-lowering doses of niacin, or verapamil. Patients should be instructed to report unexplained muscle pain or weakness; lovastatin should be discontinued if myopathy is suspected/confirmed. Temporarily discontinue in any patient experiencing an acute or serious condition predisposing to renal failure secondary to rhabdomyolysis. Use with caution in patients with advanced age, these patients are predisposed to myopathy. Use with caution in patients who consume large amounts of ethanol or have a history of liver disease. Safety and efficacy of the immediate release tablet have not been evaluated in prepubertal patients, patients <10 years of age, or doses >40 mg/day in appropriately-selected adolescents; extended release tablets have not been studied in patients <20 years of age.

Adverse Reactions Percentages as reported with immediate release tablets; similar adverse reactions seen with extended release tablets.

>10%: Neuromuscular & skeletal: Increased CPK (>2x normal) (11%)

1% to 10%:

Central nervous system: Headache (2% to 3%), dizziness (0.5% to 1%)

Dermatologic: Rash (0.8% to 1%)

Gastrointestinal: Abdominal pain (2% to 3%), constipation (2% to 4%), diarrhea (2% to 3%), dyspepsia (1% to 2%), flatulence (4% to 5%), nausea (2% to 3%)

Neuromuscular & skeletal: Myalgia (2% to 3%), weakness (1% to 2%), muscle cramps (0.6% to 1%)

Ocular: Blurred vision (0.8% to 1%)

<1% (Limited to important or life-threatening): Acid regurgitation, alopecia, arthralgia, chest pain, dermatomyositis, eye irritation, insomnia, leg pain, paresthesia, pruritus, vomiting, xerostomia

Additional class-related events or case reports (not necessarily reported with lovastatin therapy): Alkaline phosphatase increased, alopecia, alteration in taste, anaphylaxis, angioedema, anorexia, anxiety, arthritis, cataracts, chills, cholestatic jaundice, cirrhosis, CPK increased (>10x normal), depression, dryness of skin/mucous membranes, dyspnea, eosinophilia, erectile dysfunction, erythema multiforme, ESR increased, facial paresis, fatty liver, fever, flushing, fulminant hepatic necrosis, GGT increased, gynecomastia, hemolytic anemia, hepatitis, hepatoma, hyperbilirubinemia, hypersensitivity reaction, impaired extraocular muscle movement, impotence, leukopenia, libido decreased, malaise, memory loss, myopathy, nail changes, nodules, ophthalmoplegia, pancreatitis, paresthesia, peripheral nerve palsy, peripheral neuropathy, photosensitivity, polymyalgia rheumatica, positive ANA, pruritus, psychic disturbance, purpura, rash, renal failure (secondary to rhabdomyolysis), rhabdomyolysis, skin discoloration, Stevens-Johnson syndrome, systemic lupus erythematosus-like syndrome, thrombocytopenia, thyroid dysfunction, toxic epidermal necrolysis, transaminases increased, tremor, urticaria, vasculitis, vertigo, vomiting

Overdosage/Toxicology Few adverse events have been reported. Treatment is symptomatic.

Drug Interactions

Cytochrome P450 Effect: Substrate of CYP3A4 (major); **Inhibits** CYP2C9 (weak), 2D6 (weak), 3A4 (weak)

Increased Effect/Toxicity: CYP3A4 inhibitors may increase the levels/effects of lovastatin; example inhibitors include azole antifungals, clarithromycin, diclofenac, doxycycline, erythromycin, imatinib, isoniazid, nefazodone, nicardipine, propofol, protease inhibitors, quinidine, telithromycin, and verapamil. Suspend lovastatin therapy during concurrent clarithromycin, erythromycin, itraconazole, or ketoconazole therapy. Concurrent use of danazol may increase risk of myopathy (limit dose of lovastatin). Cyclosporine, clofibrate, diltiazem, fenofibrate, gemfibrozil, and niacin also may increase the risk of myopathy and rhabdomyolysis. The effect/toxicity of warfarin (elevated PT) and levothyroxine may be increased by lovastatin. Digoxin, norethindrone, and ethinyl estradiol levels may be increased. Effects are additive with other lipid-lowering therapies.

Decreased Effect: Cholestyramine taken with lovastatin reduces lovastatin absorption and effect.

Ethanol/Nutrition/Herb Interactions

Ethanol: Avoid excessive ethanol consumption (due to potential hepatic effects).

Food: Food **decreases** the bioavailability of lovastatin extended release tablets and **increases** the bioavailability of lovastatin immediate release tablets. Lovastatin serum concentrations may be increased if taken with grapefruit juice; avoid concurrent intake of large quantities (>1 quart/day). Red yeast rice contains an estimated 2.4 mg lovastatin per 600 mg rice.

Herb/Nutraceutical: St John's wort may decrease lovastatin levels.

Stability

Tablet, immediate release: Store between 5°C to 30°C (41°F to 86°F). Protect from light

Tablet, extended release: Store between 20°C to 25°C (68°F to 77°F). Avoid excessive heat and humidity.

Mechanism of Action Lovastatin acts by competitively inhibiting 3-hydroxyl-3-methylglutaryl-coenzyme A (HMG-CoA) reductase, the enzyme that catalyzes the rate-limiting step in cholesterol biosynthesis

Pharmacodynamics/Kinetics

Onset of action: LDL-cholesterol reductions: 3 days

Absorption: 30%; increased with extended release tablets when taken in the fasting state

Protein binding: 95%

Metabolism: Hepatic; extensive first-pass effect; hydrolyzed to B-hydroxy acid (active)

Bioavailability: Increased with extended release tablets

Half-life elimination: 1.1-1.7 hours

Time to peak, serum: 2-4 hours

Excretion: Feces (~80% to 85%); urine (10%)

Dosage Oral:

Adolescents 10-17 years: Immediate release tablet:

LDL reduction <20%: Initial: 10 mg/day with evening meal

LDL reduction ≥20%: Initial: 20 mg/day with evening meal

Usual range: 10-40 mg with evening meal, then adjust dose at 4-week intervals

Adults: Initial: 20 mg with evening meal, then adjust at 4-week intervals; maximum dose: 80 mg/day immediate release tablet **or** 60 mg/day extended release tablet

Dosage modification/limits based on concurrent therapy:

Cyclosporine and other immunosuppressant drugs: Initial dose: 10 mg/day with a maximum recommended dose of 20 mg/day

(Continued)

Lovastatin *(Continued)*

Concurrent therapy with fibrates, danazol, and/or lipid-lowering doses of niacin (>1 g/day): Maximum recommended dose: 20 mg/day. Concurrent use with fibrates should be avoided unless risk to benefit favors use.

Concurrent therapy with amiodarone or verapamil: Maximum recommended dose: 40 mg/day of regular release or 20 mg/day with extended release.

Dosage adjustment in renal impairment: Cl_{cr} <30 mL/minute: Use doses >20 mg/day with caution.

Dietary Considerations Before initiation of therapy, patients should be placed on a standard cholesterol-lowering diet for 6 weeks and the diet should be continued during drug therapy. Avoid intake of large quantities of grapefruit juice (≥1 quart/day); may increase toxicity. Red yeast rice contains an estimated 2.4 mg lovastatin per 600 mg rice.

Administration Administer immediate release tablet with meals. Administer extended release tablet at bedtime; do not crush or chew.

Monitoring Parameters

Obtain baseline LFTs and total cholesterol profile. LFTs should also be assessed prior to upwards dosage adjustment to ≥40 mg daily or when otherwise indicated clinically. Enzyme levels should be followed periodically thereafter as clinically warranted.

Reference Range NCEP classification of pediatric patients with familial history of hypercholesterolemia or premature CVD: Acceptable total cholesterol: <170 mg/dL, LDL: <110 mg/dL

Test Interactions Altered thyroid function tests

Dosage Forms

Tablet: 10 mg, 20 mg, 40 mg

Mevacor®: 20 mg, 40 mg

Tablet, extended release:

Altoprev®: 20 mg, 40 mg, 60 mg

♦ **Lovastatin and Niacin** *see* Niacin and Lovastatin *on page 1221*

♦ **Lovenox®** *see* Enoxaparin *on page 583*

♦ **Lovenox® HP (Can)** *see* Enoxaparin *on page 583*

♦ **Low-Ogestrel®** *see* Ethinyl Estradiol and Norgestrel *on page 663*

♦ **Loxapac® IM (Can)** *see* Loxapine *on page 1042*

Loxapine *(LOKS a peen)*

U.S. Brand Names Loxitane®

Canadian Brand Names Apo-Loxapine®; Loxapac® IM; Nu-Loxapine; PMS-Loxapine

Index Terms Loxapine Succinate; Oxilapine Succinate

Pharmacologic Category Antipsychotic Agent, Typical

Additional Appendix Information

Antipsychotic Agents *on page 1872*

Use Management of psychotic disorders

Pregnancy Risk Factor C

Lactation Excretion in breast milk unknown/not recommended

Medication Safety Issues

Sound-alike/look-alike issues:

Loxitane® may be confused with Soriatane®

International issues:

Loxitane® may be confused with Lexotan® which is a brand name for bromazepam in multiple international markets

Contraindications Hypersensitivity to loxapine or any component of the formulation; severe CNS depression; coma

Warnings/Precautions Watch for hypotension when administering I.M.; should not be given I.V. Safety in children <6 months of age has not been established. Moderately sedating, use with caution in disorders where CNS depression is a feature. Use with caution in Parkinson's disease. Caution in patients with hemodynamic instability; bone marrow suppression; predisposition to seizures; subcortical brain damage; severe cardiac, hepatic, renal or respiratory disease. Esophageal dysmotility and aspiration have been associated with antipsychotic use - use with caution in patients at risk of pneumonia (ie, Alzheimer's disease). Caution in breast cancer or other prolactin-dependent tumors (may elevate prolactin levels). May alter temperature regulation or mask toxicity of other drugs due to antiemetic effects. May alter cardiac conduction; life-threatening arrhythmias have occurred with therapeutic doses of phenothiazines. May cause orthostatic hypotension - use with caution in patients at risk of this effect or those who would tolerate transient hypotensive episodes (cerebrovascular disease, cardiovascular disease, or other medications which may predispose). Safety and effectiveness of loxapine in pediatric patients have not been established.

Phenothiazines may cause anticholinergic effects (confusion, agitation, constipation, xerostomia, blurred vision, urinary retention); therefore, they should be used with caution in patients with decreased gastrointestinal motility, urinary retention, BPH, xerostomia, or visual problems. Conditions which also may be exacerbated by cholinergic blockade include narrow-angle glaucoma (screening is recommended) and worsening of myasthenia gravis. Relative to other antipsychotics, loxapine has a low potency of cholinergic blockade.

May cause extrapyramidal reactions, including pseudoparkinsonism, acute dystonic reactions, akathisia, and tardive dyskinesia (risk of these reactions is moderate-high relative to other neuroleptics). May be associated with neuroleptic malignant syndrome (NMS) or pigmentary retinopathy.

Adverse Reactions Frequency not defined.

Cardiovascular: Abnormal T waves with prolonged ventricular repolarization, arrhythmia, hyper-/hypotension, orthostatic hypotension, tachycardia, syncope

Central nervous system: Agitation, altered central temperature regulation, ataxia, confusion, dizziness, drowsiness, extrapyramidal reactions (akathisia, akinesia, dystonia, pseudoparkinsonism, tardive dyskinesia), faintness, headache, insomnia, lightheadedness, neuroleptic malignant syndrome (NMS), seizure, slurred speech, tension

Dermatologic: Alopecia, dermatitis, photosensitivity, pruritus, rash, seborrhea

Endocrine & metabolic: Amenorrhea, enlargement of breasts, galactorrhea, gynecomastia, menstrual irregularity

Gastrointestinal: Adynamic ileus, constipation, nausea, polydipsia, vomiting, weight gain/loss, xerostomia

Genitourinary: Sexual dysfunction, urinary retention

Hematologic: Agranulocytosis, leukopenia, thrombocytopenia

Neuromuscular & skeletal: Weakness

Ocular: Blurred vision

Respiratory: Nasal congestion

Overdosage/Toxicology Symptoms include deep sleep, dystonia, agitation, dysrhythmias, extrapyramidal symptoms, hypotension, and seizures. Following initiation of essential overdose management, toxic symptom and supportive treatment should be initiated. Hypotension usually responds to I.V. fluids or Trendelenburg positioning. If unresponsive to these measures, the use of a parenteral inotrope may be required (eg, norepinephrine 0.1-0.2 mcg/kg/minute titrated to response). Seizures commonly respond to diazepam (I.V. 5-10 mg bolus in adults every 15 minutes, if needed, up to a total of 30 mg; I.V. 0.25-0.4 mg/kg/dose up to a total of 10 mg in children) or to phenytoin or phenobarbital. Critical cardiac arrhythmias often respond to I.V. phenytoin (15 mg/kg up to 1 g), while other antiarrhythmics can be used. Neuroleptics often cause extrapyramidal symptoms (eg, dystonic reactions) requiring management with diphenhydramine 1-2 mg/kg (adults), up to a maximum of 50 mg I.M. or slow I.V. push, followed by a maintenance dose for 48-72 hours. When these reactions are unresponsive to diphenhydramine, anticholinergic agents such as benztropine mesylate I.V. 1-2 mg (adults) may be effective. These agents are generally effective within 2-5 minutes.

Drug Interactions

Increased Effect/Toxicity: Loxapine concentrations may be increased by chloroquine, propranolol, sulfadoxine-pyrimethamine. Loxapine may increased the effect and/or toxicity of antihypertensives, lithium, TCAs, CNS depressants (ethanol, narcotics), and trazodone. There are rare reports of significant respiratory depression, stupor, and/or hypotension with the concomitant use of loxapine and lorazepam. Use caution if the concomitant administration of loxapine and CNS drugs is required. Metoclopramide may increase risk of extrapyramidal symptoms (EPS). Acetylcholinesterase inhibitors (central) may increase the risk of antipsychotic-related EPS. Effects on QT_c interval may be additive with antipsychotics, increasing the risk of malignant arrhythmias; other QT_c-prolonging agents include type Ia antiarrhythmics, TCAs, and some quinolone antibiotics (sparfloxacin, moxifloxacin and gatifloxacin). Concomitant use with thioridazine is contraindicated.

Decreased Effect: Antipsychotics inhibit the activity of bromocriptine and levodopa. Benztropine (and other anticholinergics) may inhibit the therapeutic response to loxapine and excess anticholinergic effects may occur. Loxapine and possibly other low potency antipsychotic may reverse the pressor effects of epinephrine.

Ethanol/Nutrition/Herb Interactions

Ethanol: Avoid ethanol (may increase CNS depression).

Herb/Nutraceutical: Avoid kava kava, gotu kola, valerian, St John's wort (may increase CNS depression).

Stability Protect from light. Dispense in amber or opaque vials.

Mechanism of Action Loxapine is a dibenzoxazepine antipsychotic which blocks postsynaptic mesolimbic D_1 and D_2 receptors in the brain, and also possesses serotonin 5-HT_2 blocking activity

Pharmacodynamics/Kinetics

Onset of action: Neuroleptic: Oral: 20-30 minutes

Peak effect: 1.5-3 hours

Duration: ~12 hours

Metabolism: Hepatic to glucuronide conjugates

Half-life elimination: Biphasic: Initial: 5 hours; Terminal: 12-19 hours

Excretion: Urine; feces (small amounts)

Dosage Oral:

Adults: 10 mg twice daily, increase dose until psychotic symptoms are controlled; usual dose range: 20-100 mg/day in divided doses 2-4 times/day; dosages >250 mg/day are not recommended

Elderly: 20-60 mg/day

Monitoring Parameters Vital signs, orthostatic blood pressures 3-5 days after initiation of therapy or a dose increase; lipid profile, fasting blood glucose/Hgb A_{1c}; BMI; mental status, abnormal involuntary movement scale (AIMS), extrapyramidal symptoms (EPS)

Test Interactions False-positives for phenylketonuria, amylase, uroporphyrins, urobilinogen

Dosage Forms Capsule, as succinate: 5 mg, 10 mg, 25 mg, 50 mg

♦ **Loxapine Succinate** see Loxapine on page 1042

♦ **Loxitane®** see Loxapine on page 1042

♦ **Lozide® (Can)** see Indapamide on page 898

♦ **Lozi-Flur™** see Fluoride on page 722

♦ **Lozol® [DSC]** see Indapamide on page 898

♦ **Lozol® (Can)** see Indapamide on page 898

♦ **L-PAM** see Melphalan on page 1074

♦ **LRH** see Gonadorelin on page 809

♦ **L-Sarcolysin** see Melphalan on page 1074

♦ **LTA® 360** see Lidocaine on page 1010

♦ **LTG** see Lamotrigine on page 974

♦ **Lu-26-054** see Escitalopram on page 613

Lubiprostone (loo bi PROS tone)

U.S. Brand Names Amitiza™
Index Terms RU 0211; SPI 0211
Pharmacologic Category Gastrointestinal Agent, Miscellaneous
Use Treatment of chronic idiopathic constipation
Pregnancy Risk Factor C
Dosage Oral: Adults: 24 mcg twice daily
    Dosage adjustment for toxicity: May decrease dose to 24 mcg once daily in case of severe nausea
    Dosage adjustment for renal/hepatic impairment: Has not been studied
Additional Information Complete prescribing information for this medication should be consulted for additional detail.
Dosage Forms Capsule: 24 mcg

◆ Lucentis™ *see* Ranibizumab *on page 1484*
◆ Ludiomil *see* Maprotiline *on page 1056*
◆ Lugol's Solution *see* Potassium Iodide and Iodine *on page 1401*
◆ Lumigan® *see* Bimatoprost *on page 222*
◆ Luminal® Sodium *see* Phenobarbital *on page 1353*
◆ Lumitene™ *see* Beta-Carotene *on page 211*
◆ Lunesta™ *see* Eszopiclone *on page 639*
◆ Lupron® *see* Leuprolide *on page 991*
◆ Lupron Depot® *see* Leuprolide *on page 991*
◆ Lupron® Depot® (Can) *see* Leuprolide *on page 991*
◆ Lupron Depot-Ped® *see* Leuprolide *on page 991*
◆ Luride® *see* Fluoride *on page 722*
◆ Luride® Lozi-Tab® *see* Fluoride *on page 722*
◆ Lustra® *see* Hydroquinone *on page 859*
◆ Lustra-AF™ *see* Hydroquinone *on page 859*
◆ Luteinizing Hormone Releasing Hormone *see* Gonadorelin *on page 809*
◆ Lutera™ *see* Ethinyl Estradiol and Levonorgestrel *on page 653*
◆ Lutrepulse™ (Can) *see* Gonadorelin *on page 809*

Lutropin Alfa (LOO troe pin AL fa)

U.S. Brand Names Luveris®
Index Terms Recombinant Human Luteinizing Hormone; r-hLH
Pharmacologic Category Gonadotropin; Ovulation Stimulator
Use Stimulation of follicular development in infertile hypogonadotropic hypogonadal (HH) women with profound luteinizing hormone (LH) deficiency; to be used in combination with follitropin alfa
Pregnancy Risk Factor X
Pregnancy Implications An increase in pre- and postimplantation loss was observed in animal studies. Lutropin alfa is contraindicated for use during pregnancy.
Lactation Excretion in breast milk unknown/use caution
Contraindications Hypersensitivity to lutropin alfa or any component of the formulation; primary ovarian failure; uncontrolled thyroid or adrenal dysfunction; uncontrolled organic intracranial lesion; abnormal uterine bleeding of undetermined origin; ovarian cyst or enlargement of undetermined origin; sex hormone-dependent tumors of the reproductive tract and accessory organs; pregnancy
Warnings/Precautions For use by infertility specialists. May cause ovarian hyperstimulation syndrome (OHSS); if severe, treatment should be discontinued and patient should be hospitalized. OHSS results in a rapid (<24 hours to 7 days) accumulation of fluid in the peritoneal cavity, thorax, and possibly the pericardium, which may become more severe if pregnancy occurs; monitor for ovarian enlargement. Patients should be advised of the potential risk for multiple births before beginning therapy. Safety and efficacy have not been established with hepatic or renal dysfunction. Not for use in children or postmenopausal women.
Adverse Reactions
  1% to 10%:
    Central nervous system: Headache (10%), fatigue (2% to 3%)
    Endocrine & metabolic: Ovarian hyperstimulation (6%)
    Gastrointestinal: Nausea (7%), constipation (2% to 3%), diarrhea (2% to 3%)
  Adverse events reported with gonadotropin or menotropin therapy: Adnexal torsion, arterial thromboembolism, congenital abnormalities, ectopic pregnancy, hemoperitoneum, ovarian enlargement (mild-to-moderate), ovarian neoplasms (infrequent), postpartum fever, premature labor, pulmonary complications, spontaneous abortion, vascular complications
Overdosage/Toxicology Multiple gestations and ovarian hyperstimulation may occur following overdose.
Stability Store under refrigeration or at room temperature of 2°C to 25°C (36°F to 77°F). Protect from light. Reconstitute with SWFI. Mix gently, do not shake. Use immediately after reconstitution.
Mechanism of Action Lutropin alfa is a recombinant luteinizing hormone prepared using Chinese hamster cell ovaries. Administration leads to increased follicular estradiol secretion needed for follicle stimulating hormone induced follicular development.
Pharmacodynamics/Kinetics
  Distribution: V_d: 10
  Bioavailability: 56% ± 23%
  Half-life elimination: Terminal: ~18 hours
  Time to peak, serum: 4-16 hours

Excretion: Urine (<5% unchanged)

Dosage SubQ: Adults: Female: Infertility: 75 int. units daily until adequate follicular development is noted; maximum duration of treatment: 14 days; to be used concomitantly with follitropin alfa

Administration SubQ: Administer on the stomach, a few inches above or below the navel.

Monitoring Parameters

Prior to therapy: Baseline LH <1.2 int. units/L, FSH <5 int. units/L, negative progestin challenge test

During therapy: Signs and symptoms of OHSS, ovarian enlargement; follicular maturation (vaginal ultrasound, serum estradiol levels); ovulation (basal body temperature, serum progesterone, menstruation)

Dosage Forms Injection, powder for reconstitution: 75 int. units [contains sucrose; packaged with SWFI]

♦ **Luveris**® *see* Lutropin Alfa *on page 1044*
♦ **Luvox** *see* Fluvoxamine *on page 747*
♦ **Luvox**® **(Can)** *see* Fluvoxamine *on page 747*
♦ **Luxiq**® *see* Betamethasone *on page 211*
♦ **LY139603** *see* Atomoxetine *on page 169*
♦ **LY146032** *see* Daptomycin *on page 452*
♦ **LY170053** *see* Olanzapine *on page 1257*
♦ **LY231514** *see* Pemetrexed *on page 1328*
♦ **LY248686** *see* Duloxetine *on page 562*
♦ **LY303366** *see* Anidulafungin *on page 131*
♦ **LY2148568** *see* Exenatide *on page 676*
♦ **Lyderm**® **(Can)** *see* Fluocinonide *on page 721*
♦ **Lymphocyte Immune Globulin** *see* Antithymocyte Globulin (Equine) *on page 138*
♦ **Lymphocyte Mitogenic Factor** *see* Aldesleukin *on page 59*
♦ **Lyrica**® *see* Pregabalin *on page 1418*
♦ **Lysodren**® *see* Mitotane *on page 1156*
♦ **M-M-R**® **II** *see* Measles, Mumps, and Rubella Vaccines (Combined) *on page 1057*
♦ **Maalox**® **[OTC]** *see* Aluminum Hydroxide, Magnesium Hydroxide, and Simethicone *on page 85*
♦ **Maalox**® **Max [OTC]** *see* Aluminum Hydroxide, Magnesium Hydroxide, and Simethicone *on page 85*
♦ **Maalox**® **Regular Chewable [OTC]** *see* Calcium Carbonate *on page 269*
♦ **Maalox**® **Total Stomach Relief**® **[OTC]** *see* Bismuth *on page 224*
♦ **Macrobid**® *see* Nitrofurantoin *on page 1233*
♦ **Macrodantin**® *see* Nitrofurantoin *on page 1233*
♦ **Macugen**® *see* Pegaptanib *on page 1319*

Mafenide (MA fe nide)

U.S. Brand Names Sulfamylon®
Index Terms Mafenide Acetate
Pharmacologic Category Antibiotic, Topical
Additional Appendix Information
Sulfonamide Derivatives *on page 1897*
Use Adjunct in the treatment of second- and third-degree burns to prevent septicemia caused by susceptible organisms such as *Pseudomonas aeruginosa*
Orphan drug: Prevention of graft loss of meshed autografts on excised burn wounds
Pregnancy Risk Factor C
Dosage Children and Adults: Topical: Apply once or twice daily with a sterile gloved hand; apply to a thickness of approximately 16 mm; the burned area should be covered with cream at all times

Dosage Forms
Cream, topical, as acetate: 85 mg/g (60 g, 120 g, 454 g) [contains sodium metabisulfite]
Powder, for topical solution: 5% (5s) [50 g/packet]

♦ **Mafenide Acetate** *see* Mafenide *on page 1045*
♦ **Mag 64**™ **[OTC]** *see* Magnesium Chloride *on page 1046*

Magaldrate and Simethicone (MAG al drate & sye METH i kone)

U.S. Brand Names Riopan Plus® [OTC] [DSC]; Riopan Plus® Double Strength [OTC] [DSC]
Index Terms Simethicone and Magaldrate
Pharmacologic Category Antacid; Antiflatulent
Use Relief of hyperacidity associated with peptic ulcer, gastritis, peptic esophagitis and hiatal hernia which are accompanied by symptoms of gas
Pregnancy Risk Factor C
Medication Safety Issues
Sound-alike/look-alike issues:
Riopan Plus® may be confused with Repan®
Dosage Adults: Oral: 540-1080 mg magaldrate between meals and at bedtime
Additional Information Complete prescribing information for this medication should be consulted for additional detail.
Dosage Forms [DSC] = Discontinued product
Suspension, oral: Magaldrate 540 mg and simethicone 20 mg per 5 mL (360 mL)
Riopan Plus®: Magaldrate 540 mg and simethicone 20 mg per 5 mL (360 mL) [DSC]
Riopan Plus® Double Strength: Magaldrate 1080 mg and simethicone 40 mg per 5 mL (360 mL) [DSC]

- **Mag-Caps [OTC]** *see* Magnesium Oxide *on page 1050*
- **Mag Delay® [OTC]** *see* Magnesium Chloride *on page 1046*
- **Mag G® [OTC]** *see* Magnesium Gluconate *on page 1047*
- **MagGel™ [OTC]** *see* Magnesium Oxide *on page 1050*
- **Maginex™ [OTC]** *see* Magnesium L-aspartate Hydrochloride *on page 1049*
- **Maginex™ DS [OTC]** *see* Magnesium L-aspartate Hydrochloride *on page 1049*
- **Magnesia Magma** *see* Magnesium Hydroxide *on page 1047*
- **Magnesium L-lactate Dihydrate** *see* Magnesium L-lactate *on page 1050*
- **Magnesium Carbonate and Aluminum Hydroxide** *see* Aluminum Hydroxide and Magnesium Carbonate *on page 84*

Magnesium Chloride (mag NEE zhum KLOR ide)

U.S. Brand Names Chloromag®; Mag 64™ [OTC]; Mag Delay® [OTC]; Slow-Mag® [OTC]
Pharmacologic Category Electrolyte Supplement, Oral; Electrolyte Supplement, Parenteral; Magnesium Salt
Use Correction or prevention of hypomagnesemia; dietary supplement
Pregnancy Risk Factor C
Dosage Note: Serum magnesium is poor reflection of repletional status as the majority of magnesium is intracellular; serum levels may be transiently normal for a few hours after a dose is given, therefore, aim for consistently high normal serum levels in patients with normal renal function for most efficient repletion.
Dietary supplement: Adults: Oral (Mag 64™, Mag Delay®, Slow-Mag®): 2 tablets once daily
Parenteral nutrition supplementation: I.V. (elemental magnesium):
  Children:
    <50 kg: 0.3-0.5 mEq/kg/day
    >50 kg: 10-30 mEq/day
  Adults: 8-20 mEq/day

RDA (elemental magnesium):
  Children:
    1-3 years: 80 mg/day
    4-8 years: 130 mg/day
    9-13 years: 240 mg/day
    14-18 years:
      Female: 360 mg/day
      Pregnant female: 400 mg/day
      Male: 410 mg/day
  Adults:
    19-30 years:
      Female: 310 mg/day
      Pregnant female: 350 mg/day
      Male: 400 mg/day
    ≥31 years:
      Female: 320 mg/day
      Pregnant female: 360 mg/day
      Male: 420 mg/day

Dosage adjustment in renal impairment: Cl_{cr} <30 mL/minute: Use with caution; monitor for hypermagnesemia
Additional Information Complete prescribing information for this medication should be consulted for additional detail.
Dosage Forms
Injection, solution: 200 mg/mL [1.97 mEq/mL] (50 mL)
  Chloromag®: 200 mg/mL [1.97 mEq/mL] (50 mL)
Tablet [enteric coated]:
  Slow-Mag®: Elemental magnesium 64 mg [contains elemental calcium 106 mg]
Tablet, delayed release:
  Mag 64™, Mag Delay®: Magnesium chloride hexahydrate 535 mg [equivalent to elemental magnesium 64 mg; contains elemental calcium 110 mg]

Magnesium Citrate (mag NEE zhum SIT rate)

U.S. Brand Names Citroma® [OTC]
Canadian Brand Names Citro-Mag®
Index Terms Citrate of Magnesia
Pharmacologic Category Laxative, Saline; Magnesium Salt
Additional Appendix Information
Laxatives, Classification and Properties *on page 1886*
Use Evacuation of bowel prior to certain surgical and diagnostic procedures or overdose situations
Pregnancy Risk Factor B
Contraindications Renal failure, appendicitis, abdominal pain, intestinal impaction, obstruction or perforation, diabetes mellitus, complications in gastrointestinal tract, patients with colostomy or ileostomy, ulcerative colitis or diverticulitis
Warnings/Precautions Use with caution in patients with impaired renal function, especially if Cl_{cr} <30 mL/minute (accumulation of magnesium which may lead to magnesium intoxication). Use caution in patients receiving a cardiac glycoside; may increase the AV-blocking effects. Use with caution in patients with lithium administration; use with caution with neuromuscular-blocking agents, and CNS depressants.
Adverse Reactions 1% to 10%:
Cardiovascular: Hypotension
Endocrine & metabolic: Hypermagnesemia

Gastrointestinal: Abdominal cramps, diarrhea, gas formation

Respiratory: Respiratory depression

Overdosage/Toxicology

Due to diarrhea, serious potentially life-threatening electrolyte disturbances may occur with long-term use or overdose; hypermagnesemia may occur, as well as, CNS depression, confusion, hypotension, muscle weakness, and blockage of peripheral neuromuscular transmission.

Serum level >4 mEq/L (4.8 mg/dL): Deep tendon reflexes may be depressed

Serum level ≥10 mEq/L (12 mg/dL): Deep tendon reflexes may disappear, respiratory paralysis may occur, heart block may occur

I.V. calcium (5-10 mEq) will reverse respiratory depression or heart block. In extreme cases, peritoneal dialysis or hemodialysis may be required.

Serum level >12 mEq/L may be fatal, serum level ≥10 mEq/L may cause complete heart block

Mechanism of Action Promotes bowel evacuation by causing osmotic retention of fluid which distends the colon with increased peristaltic activity

Pharmacodynamics/Kinetics

Absorption: Oral: 15% to 30%

Excretion: Urine

Dosage Cathartic: Oral:

Children:

<6 years: 0.5 mL/kg up to a maximum of 200 mL repeated every 4-6 hours until stools are clear

6-12 years: 100-150 mL

Children ≥12 years and Adults: ½ to 1 full bottle (120-300 mL)

Dietary Considerations Magnesium content of 5 mL: 3.85-4.71 mEq

Administration To increase palatability, chill the solution prior to administration.

Reference Range Serum magnesium: 1.5-2.5 mg/dL; slightly different ranges are reported by different laboratories

Test Interactions Increased magnesium; decreased protein, decreased calcium (S), decreased potassium (S)

Dosage Forms

Solution, oral: 290 mg/5 mL (300 mL) [cherry and lemon flavors]

Citroma®: 290 mg/5 mL (300 mL) [contains magnesium 290 mg and potassium 80 mg per 30 mL; cherry and lemon flavors; grape and lemony flavors also contain sodium 45 mg/30 mL]

Tablet: 100 mg [as elemental magnesium]

Magnesium Gluconate (mag NEE zhum GLOO koe nate)

U.S. Brand Names Almora® [OTC]; Mag G® [OTC]; Magonate® [OTC]; Magtrate® [OTC]

Pharmacologic Category Electrolyte Supplement, Oral; Magnesium Salt

Use Dietary supplement

Dosage RDA (elemental magnesium):

Children:

1-3 years: 80 mg/day

4-8 years: 130 mg/day

9-13 years: 240 mg/day

14-18 years:

Female: 360 mg/day

Pregnant female: 400 mg/day

Male: 410 mg/day

Adults:

19-30 years:

Female: 310 mg/day

Pregnant female: 350 mg/day

Male: 400 mg/day

≥31 years:

Female: 320 mg/day

Pregnant female: 360 mg/day

Male: 420 mg/day

Dosing in renal impairment: Cl$_{cr}$ <30 mL/minute: Use with caution; monitor for hypermagnesemia

Additional Information Complete prescribing information for this medication should be consulted for additional detail.

Dosage Forms

Solution:

Magonate®: 1000 mg/5 mL (480 mL) [magnesium 4.8 mEq/5 mL; equivalent to elemental magnesium 54 mg/5 mL; contains sodium benzoate]

Tablet: 500 mg [magnesium 2.4 mEq; equivalent to elemental magnesium 27 mg]

Almora®, Mag G®, Magonate®, Magtrate®): 500 mg [magnesium 2.4 mEq; equivalent to elemental magnesium 27 mg]

Magnesium Hydroxide (mag NEE zhum hye DROKS ide)

U.S. Brand Names Dulcolax® Milk of Magnesia [OTC]; Phillips'® Milk of Magnesia [OTC]

Index Terms Magnesia Magma; Milk of Magnesia; MOM

Pharmacologic Category Antacid; Magnesium Salt

Additional Appendix Information

Laxatives, Classification and Properties *on page 1886*

Use Short-term treatment of occasional constipation and symptoms of hyperacidity, magnesium replacement therapy

(Continued)

Magnesium Hydroxide *(Continued)*

Pregnancy Risk Factor B

Contraindications Hypersensitivity to any component of the formulation; patients with colostomy or an ileostomy, intestinal obstruction, fecal impaction, renal failure, appendicitis

Warnings/Precautions Use with caution in patients with severe renal impairment (especially when doses are >50 mEq magnesium/day); hypermagnesemia and toxicity may occur due to decreased renal clearance of absorbed magnesium. Decreased renal function (Cl_{cr} <30 mL/minute) may result in toxicity; monitor for toxicity.

Adverse Reactions Frequency not defined.

Cardiovascular: Hypotension

Endocrine & metabolic: Hypermagnesemia

Gastrointestinal: Diarrhea, abdominal cramps

Neuromuscular & skeletal: Muscle weakness

Respiratory: Respiratory depression

Overdosage/Toxicology Magnesium antacids are also laxatives and may cause diarrhea and hypokalemia. In patients with renal failure, magnesium may accumulate to toxic levels. I.V. calcium (5-10 mEq) will reverse respiratory depression or heart block. In extreme cases, peritoneal dialysis or hemodialysis may be required.

Drug Interactions

Decreased Effect: Absorption of tetracyclines, digoxin, iron salts, isoniazid, or quinolones may be decreased.

Mechanism of Action Promotes bowel evacuation by causing osmotic retention of fluid which distends the colon with increased peristaltic activity; reacts with hydrochloric acid in stomach to form magnesium chloride

Pharmacodynamics/Kinetics

Onset of action: Laxative: 4-8 hours

Excretion: Urine (up to 30% as absorbed magnesium ions); feces (as unabsorbed drug)

Dosage Oral:

Average daily intakes of dietary magnesium have declined in recent years due to processing of food; the latest estimate of the average American dietary intake was 349 mg/day

Laxative:

Liquid:

Children

<2 years: 0.5 mL/kg/dose

2-5 years: 5-15 mL/day (2.5-7.5 mL/day of liquid concentrate) or in divided doses

6-12 years: 15-30 mL/day (7.5-15 mL/day of liquid concentrate) or in divided doses

Children ≥12 years and Adults: 30-60 mL/day (15-30 mL/day of liquid concentrate) or in divided doses

Tablet:

Children:

2-5 years: 1-2 tablets before bedtime

6-11 years: 3-4 tablets before bedtime

Children ≥12 years and Adults: 6-8 tablets before bedtime

Antacid:

Liquid:

Children: 2.5-5 mL as needed up to 4 times/day

Adults: 5-15 mL (2.5-7.5 mL of liquid concentrate) as needed up to 4 times/day

Tablet:

Children 7-14 years: 1 tablet up to 4 times/day

Adults: 2-4 tablets up to 4 times/day

Dosing in renal impairment: Patients in severe renal failure should not receive magnesium due to toxicity from accumulation. Patients with a Cl_{cr} <25 mL/minute receiving magnesium should be monitored by serum magnesium levels.

Administration Liquid doses may be diluted with a small amount of water prior to administration. All doses should be followed by 8 ounces of water.

Reference Range Serum magnesium: 1.5-2.5 mg/dL; slightly different ranges are reported by different laboratories

Test Interactions Increased magnesium; decreased protein, calcium (S), decreased potassium (S)

Dosage Forms

Liquid, oral: 400 mg/5 mL (360 mL, 480 mL, 960 mL, 3780 mL)

Dulcolax® Milk of Magnesia: 400 mg/5 mL (360 mL, 780 mL) [regular and mint flavors]

Phillips'® Milk of Magnesia: 400 mg/5 mL (120 mL, 360 mL, 780 mL) [original, French vanilla, cherry, and mint flavors]

Liquid, oral concentrate: 800 mg/5 mL (100 mL, 400 mL)

Phillips'® Milk of Magnesia [concentrate]: 800 mg/5 mL (240 mL) [strawberry crème flavor]

Tablet, chewable (Phillips'® Milk of Magnesia): 311 mg [mint flavor]

♦ **Magnesium Hydroxide, Aluminum Hydroxide, and Simethicone** *see* Aluminum Hydroxide, Magnesium Hydroxide, and Simethicone *on page 85*

♦ **Magnesium Hydroxide and Aluminum Hydroxide** *see* Aluminum Hydroxide and Magnesium Hydroxide *on page 85*

♦ **Magnesium Hydroxide and Calcium Carbonate** *see* Calcium Carbonate and Magnesium Hydroxide *on page 271*

Magnesium Hydroxide and Mineral Oil

(mag NEE zhum hye DROKS ide & MIN er al oyl)

U.S. Brand Names Phillips'® M-O [OTC]

Index Terms Haley's M-O; MOM/Mineral Oil Emulsion

Pharmacologic Category Laxative

Use Short-term treatment of occasional constipation

Pregnancy Risk Factor B

Dosage

Children 6-11 years: 5-15 mL at bedtime or upon rising

Children ≥12 years and Adults: 30-60 mL at bedtime or upon rising

Dosage adjustment in renal impairment: Patients in severe renal failure should not receive magnesium due to toxicity from accumulation. Patients with a Cl$_{cr}$ <25 mL/minute should be monitored by serum magnesium levels.

Additional Information Complete prescribing information for this medication should be consulted for additional detail.

Dosage Forms Suspension, oral: Magnesium hydroxide 300 mg and mineral oil 1.25 mL per 5 mL (360 mL, 780 mL) [original and mint flavors]

♦ **Magnesium Hydroxide, Famotidine, and Calcium Carbonate** see Famotidine, Calcium Carbonate, and Magnesium Hydroxide on page 685

Magnesium L-aspartate Hydrochloride
(mag NEE zhum el as PAR tate hye droe KLOR ide)

U.S. Brand Names Maginex™ [OTC]; Maginex™ DS [OTC]

Index Terms MAH

Pharmacologic Category Electrolyte Supplement, Oral; Magnesium Salt

Use Dietary supplement

Pregnancy Implications Magnesium crosses the placenta; serum levels in the fetus correlate with those in the mother.

Lactation Enters breast milk/compatible

Contraindications Hypersensitivity to any component of the formulation

Warnings/Precautions Use magnesium with caution in patients with impaired renal function, hepatitis or Addison's disease (accumulation of magnesium may lead to magnesium intoxication). Use with extreme caution in patients with myasthenia gravis or other neuromuscular disease.

Adverse Reactions Frequency not defined: Gastrointestinal: Diarrhea (excessive oral doses)

Overdosage/Toxicology Serious, potentially life-threatening electrolyte disturbances may occur with long-term use or overdosage due to diarrhea; hypermagnesemia may occur.

Symptoms of overdose usually present with magnesium serum level >4 mEq/L

Serum magnesium >4 mEq/L: Deep tendon reflexes may be depressed; drowsiness, flushing, headache, lethargy, or nausea may be present

Serum magnesium 6-10 mEq/L: Deep tendon reflexes may disappear; respiratory paralysis may occur; bradycardia, ECG changes, hypocalcemia, hypotension, or somnolence may be present

Serum level 10 mEq/L may be fatal; muscle or respiratory paralysis may be present, complete heart block or cardiac arrest may occur

Drug Interactions

Increased Effect/Toxicity: Calcium channel blockers may enhance the adverse/toxic effect of magnesium salts. Magnesium salts may enhance the hypotensive effect of calcium channel blockers. Magnesium salts may enhance the neuromuscular-blocking effect of neuromuscular-blocking agents; only of concern in patients with increased serum magnesium concentrations.

Decreased Effect: Oral magnesium salts may decrease the absorption of bisphosphonate derivatives, mycophenolate, and phosphate supplements. Magnesium salts may decrease the absorption of quinolone and tetracycline antibiotics; of concern only with oral administration of both agents.

Mechanism of Action Magnesium is important as a cofactor in many enzymatic reactions in the body involving protein synthesis and carbohydrate metabolism (at least 300 enzymatic reactions require magnesium). Actions on lipoprotein lipase have been found to be important in reducing serum cholesterol and on sodium/potassium ATPase in promoting polarization (eg, neuromuscular functioning).

Pharmacodynamics/Kinetics

Absorption: Oral: Inversely proportional to amount ingested; 40% to 60% under controlled dietary conditions; 15% to 36% at higher doses. Absorption of the Maginex™ formulation may be increased compared to other magnesium salts.

Distribution: Bone (50% to 60%); extracellular fluid (1% to 2%)

Protein binding: 30%, to albumin

Excretion: Urine (as magnesium)

Dosage

RDA (elemental magnesium):

Children:

1-3 years: 80 mg/day

4-8 years: 130 mg/day

9-13 years: 240 mg/day

14-18 years:

Female: 360 mg/day

Pregnant female: 400 mg/day

Male: 410 mg/day

Adults:

19-30 years:

Female: 310 mg/day

Pregnant female: 350 mg/day

Male: 400 mg/day

≥31 years:

Female: 320 mg/day

Pregnant female: 360 mg/day

Male: 420 mg/day

Dietary supplement: Adults: Oral: Magnesium-L-aspartate 1230 mg (magnesium 122 mg) up to 3 times/day

(Continued)

Magnesium L-aspartate Hydrochloride *(Continued)*

Dosage adjustment in renal impairment: Cl$_{cr}$ <30 mL/minute: Use with caution; monitor for hypermagnesemia

Dietary Considerations Take with food. Whole grains, legumes, and dark-green leafy vegetables are dietary sources of magnesium.

Administration

Granules: Mix each packet in 4 ounces of water or juice prior to administration

Tablet, enteric coated: Do not crush or chew

Reference Range Serum magnesium: 1.5-2.5 mg/dL; slightly different ranges are reported by different laboratories

Dosage Forms

Granules:

Maginex™ DS: 1230 mg [magnesium 10 mEq; equivalent to magnesium 122 mg; lemon flavor]

Tablet [enteric coated]:

Maginex™: 615 mg [magnesium 5 mEq; equivalent to magnesium 61 mg]

Magnesium L-lactate *(mag NEE zhum el LAK tate)*

U.S. Brand Names Mag-Tab® SR

Index Terms Magnesium L-lactate Dihydrate

Pharmacologic Category Electrolyte Supplement; Magnesium Salt

Use Dietary supplement

Dosage

Dietary supplement: Oral: Adults: 1-2 caplets every 12 hours

RDA (elemental magnesium):

Children:

1-3 years: 80 mg/day

4-8 years: 130 mg/day

9-13 years: 240 mg/day

14-18 years:

Female: 360 mg/day

Pregnant female: 400 mg/day

Male: 410 mg/day

Adults:

19-30 years:

Female: 310 mg/day

Pregnant female: 350 mg/day

Male: 400 mg/day

≥31 years:

Female: 320 mg/day

Pregnant female: 360 mg/day

Male: 420 mg/day

Dosage adjustment in renal impairment: Cl$_{cr}$ <30 mL/minute: Use with caution; monitor for hypermagnesemia

Additional Information Complete prescribing information for this medication should be consulted for additional detail.

Dosage Forms

Caplet, sustained-release:

Mag-Tab® SR: Elemental magnesium 84 mg (7 mEq)

Magnesium Oxide *(mag NEE zhum OKS ide)*

U.S. Brand Names Mag-Caps [OTC]; MagGel™ [OTC]; Mag-Ox® 400 [OTC]; Uro-Mag® [OTC]

Pharmacologic Category Electrolyte Supplement, Oral; Magnesium Salt

Use Electrolyte replacement

Pregnancy Implications Magnesium crosses the placenta; serum levels in the fetus correlate with those in the mother.

Lactation Enters breast milk/compatible

Contraindications Hypersensitivity to any component of the formulation

Warnings/Precautions Use magnesium with caution in patients with impaired renal function, hepatitis, or Addison's disease (accumulation of magnesium may lead to magnesium intoxication). Use with extreme caution in patients with myasthenia gravis or other neuromuscular disease.

Adverse Reactions Frequency not defined: Gastrointestinal: Diarrhea (excessive oral doses)

Overdosage/Toxicology Serious, potentially life-threatening electrolyte disturbances may occur with long-term use or overdosage due to diarrhea; hypermagnesemia may occur.

Symptoms of overdose usually present with magnesium serum level >4 mEq/L

Serum magnesium >4 mEq/L: Deep tendon reflexes may be depressed; drowsiness, flushing, headache, lethargy, or nausea may be present

Serum magnesium 6-10 mEq/L: Deep tendon reflexes may disappear; respiratory paralysis may occur; bradycardia, ECG changes, hypocalcemia, hypotension, or somnolence may be present

Serum level 10 mEq/L may be fatal; muscle or respiratory paralysis may be present, complete heart block or cardiac arrest may occur

Drug Interactions

Increased Effect/Toxicity: Calcium channel blockers may enhance the adverse/toxic effect of magnesium salts. Magnesium salts may enhance the hypotensive effect of calcium channel blockers. Magnesium salts may enhance the neuromuscular-blocking effect of neuromuscular-blocking agents; only of concern in patients with increased serum magnesium concentrations.

Decreased Effect: Oral magnesium salts may decrease the absorption of bisphosphonate derivatives, mycophenolate, and phosphate supplements. Magnesium salts may decrease the absorption of quinolone and tetracycline antibiotics; of concern only with oral administration of both agents.

Mechanism of Action Magnesium is important as a cofactor in many enzymatic reactions in the body involving protein synthesis and carbohydrate metabolism (at least 300 enzymatic reactions require magnesium). Actions on lipoprotein lipase have been found to be important in reducing serum cholesterol and on sodium/potassium ATPase in promoting polarization (eg, neuromuscular functioning).

Pharmacodynamics/Kinetics

Absorption: Oral: Inversely proportional to amount ingested; 40% to 60% under controlled dietary conditions; 15% to 36% at higher doses

Distribution: Bone (50% to 60%); extracellular fluid (1% to 2%)

Protein binding: 30%, to albumin

Excretion: Urine (as magnesium)

Dosage

RDA (elemental magnesium):

Children:

1-3 years: 80 mg/day

4-8 years: 130 mg/day

9-13 years: 240 mg/day

14-18 years:

Female: 360 mg/day

Pregnant female: 400 mg/day

Male: 410 mg/day

Adults:

19-30 years:

Female: 310 mg/day

Pregnant female: 350 mg/day

Male: 400 mg/day

≥31 years:

Female: 320 mg/day

Pregnant female: 360 mg/day

Male: 420 mg/day

Dietary supplement: Adults: Oral:

Mag-Ox 400®: 2 tablets daily with food

Mag-Caps, Uro-Mag®: 4-5 capsules daily with food

Dosing in renal impairment: Cl$_{cr}$ <30 mL/minute: Use with caution; monitor for hypermagnesemia

Dietary Considerations Should be taken with food. Whole grains, legumes, and dark-green leafy vegetables are dietary sources of magnesium.

Reference Range Serum magnesium: 1.5-2.5 mg/dL; slightly different ranges are reported by different laboratories

Dosage Forms

Caplet: 250 mg

Capsule:

Mag-Caps: Elemental magnesium 85 mg

Uro-Mag®: 140 mg [magnesium 7 mEq; equivalent to elemental magnesium 84.5 mg]

Capsule, softgel:

MagGel™: 600 mg [magnesium 28.64 mEq; equivalent to elemental magnesium 348 mg]

Tablet: 400 mg [magnesium 20 mEq; equivalent to elemental magnesium 242 mg], 500 mg

Mag-Ox® 400: 400 mg [magnesium 20 mEq; equivalent to elemental magnesium 242 mg]

Magnesium Salicylate (mag NEE zhum sa LIS i late)

U.S. Brand Names Doan's® [OTC]; Doan's® Extra Strength [OTC]; Keygesic [OTC]; Momentum® [OTC]; Novasal™

Pharmacologic Category Salicylate

Use Mild-to-moderate pain, fever, various inflammatory conditions; relief of pain and inflammation of rheumatoid arthritis and osteoarthritis

Pregnancy Risk Factor C

Dosage Oral:

Children ≥12 years and Adults: Relief of mild-to-moderate pain:

Doan's®: Two caplets every 4 hours as needed (maximum: 12 caplets/24 hours)

Doan's® Extra Strength, Momentum®: Two caplets every 6 hours as needed (maximum: 8 caplets/24 hours)

Keygesic: One tablet every 4 hours as needed (maximum 4 tablets/24 hours)

Adults: Treatment of arthritis (Novasal™): Initial: 1 tablet 3-4 times/day. Maximum: 8 tablets/day

Elderly: Treatment of arthritis (Novasal™): Reduce adult dose to lowest effective dose; monitor for signs of toxicity

Additional Information Complete prescribing information for this medication should be consulted for additional detail.

Dosage Forms

Caplet, as anhydrous: 467 mg

Doan's®: 304 mg

Doan's® Extra Strength: 467 mg

Momentum®: 467 mg

Tablet, chelated:

Keygesic: 650 mg

Tablet, as tetrahydrate [scored]:

Novasal™: 600 mg

Magnesium Sulfate (mag NEE zhum SUL fate)

Index Terms Epsom Salts; MgSO$_4$ (error-prone abbreviation)

Pharmacologic Category Anticonvulsant, Miscellaneous; Electrolyte Supplement, Parenteral; Laxative, Saline; Magnesium Salt

Use Treatment and prevention of hypomagnesemia; seizure prevention in severe pre-eclampsia or eclampsia; pediatric acute nephritis; torsade de pointes; treatment of cardiac arrhythmias (VT/VF) caused by hypomagnesemia; short-term treatment of constipation; soaking aid

Pregnancy Risk Factor A/C (manufacturer dependent)

Pregnancy Implications Magnesium crosses the placenta; serum levels in the fetus correlate with those in the mother. Magnesium sulfate is used during pregnancy for the treatment of eclampsia and severe pre-eclampsia.

Lactation Enters breast milk/compatible

Medication Safety Issues
Sound-alike/look-alike issues:
Magnesium sulfate may be confused with manganese sulfate, morphine sulfate
MgSO$_4$ is an error-prone abbreviation (mistaken as morphine sulfate)

High alert medication: The Institute for Safe Medication Practices (ISMP) includes this medication (I.V. formulation) among its list of drugs which have a heightened risk of causing significant patient harm when used in error.

Contraindications Hypersensitivity to any component of the formulation; heart block; myocardial damage

Warnings/Precautions Use with caution in patients with impaired renal function, hepatitis, or Addison's disease (accumulation of magnesium may lead to magnesium intoxication). Monitor serum magnesium level, respiratory rate, deep tendon reflex, renal function when magnesium sulfate is administered parenterally. Use with extreme caution in patients with myasthenia gravis or other neuromuscular disease.

Constipation (self-medication, OTC use): For occasional use only; serious side effects may occur with prolonged use. For use only under the supervision of a healthcare provider in patients with kidney dysfunction, or with a sudden change in bowel habits which persist for >2 weeks. Do not use if abdominal pain, nausea, or vomiting are present.

Adverse Reactions Adverse effects on neuromuscular function may occur at lower levels in patients with neuromuscular disease (eg, myasthenia gravis).
Frequency not defined: Gastrointestinal: Diarrhea (excessive oral doses)

Overdosage/Toxicology Serious, potentially life-threatening electrolyte disturbances may occur with long-term use or overdosage due to diarrhea; hypermagnesemia may occur.
Symptoms of overdose usually present with magnesium serum level >4 mEq/L
Serum magnesium >4 mEq/L: Deep tendon reflexes may be depressed; drowsiness, flushing, headache, lethargy, or nausea may be present
Serum magnesium 6-10 mEq/L: Deep tendon reflexes may disappear; respiratory paralysis may occur; bradycardia, ECG changes, hypocalcemia, hypotension, or somnolence may be present
Serum level 10 mEq/L may be fatal; muscle or respiratory paralysis may be present, complete heart block or cardiac arrest may occur
Calcium chloride 10%: 500-1000 mg can be used to correct arrhythmias; dialysis may be needed for severe hypermagnesemia

Drug Interactions
Increased Effect/Toxicity: Calcium channel blockers may enhance the adverse/toxic effect of magnesium salts. Magnesium salts may enhance the hypotensive effect of calcium channel blockers. Magnesium salts may enhance the neuromuscular-blocking effect of neuromuscular-blocking agents; only of concern in patients with increased serum magnesium concentrations.

Stability Prior to use, store at controlled room temperature. Refrigeration of solution may result in precipitation or crystallization.

Mechanism of Action When taken orally, magnesium promotes bowel evacuation by causing osmotic retention of fluid which distends the colon with increased peristaltic activity; parenterally, magnesium decreases acetylcholine in motor nerve terminals and acts on myocardium by slowing rate of S-A node impulse formation and prolonging conduction time. Magnesium is necessary for the movement of calcium, sodium, and potassium in and out of cells, as well as stabilizing excitable membranes.

Pharmacodynamics/Kinetics
Onset of action: Oral: Cathartic: 1-2 hours; I.M.: 1 hour; I.V.: Immediate
Duration: I.M.: 3-4 hours; I.V.: 30 minutes
Absorption: Oral: Inversely proportional to amount ingested; 40% to 60% under controlled dietary conditions; 15% to 36% at higher doses
Distribution: Bone (50% to 60%); extracellular fluid (1% to 2%)
Protein binding: 30%, to albumin
Excretion: Urine (as magnesium)

Dosage Dose represented as magnesium sulfate unless stated otherwise. **Note:** Serum magnesium is poor reflection of repletional status as the majority of magnesium is intracellular; serum levels may be transiently normal for a few hours after a dose is given, therefore, aim for consistently high normal serum levels in patients with normal renal function for most efficient repletion.

Hypomagnesemia: Note: Treatment depends on severity and clinical status:
Children: I.V., I.O. : 25-50 mg/kg/dose (0.2-0.4 mEq/kg/dose) over 10-20 minutes (faster in torsade); maximum single dose: 2000 mg (16 mEq)
Adults: I.V.:
Severe or smptomatic: 1-2 g over 5-60 minutes
Hypomagnesemia with seizures: 2 g over 10 minutes; calcium administration may also be appropriate
Eclampsia, pre-eclampsia: Adults: I.V.: 4-6 g over 15-20 minutes followed by 2 g/hour

Torsade de pointes: Adults: I.V.:
Pulseless: 1-2 g over 5-20 minutes
With pulse: 1-2 g over 5-60 minutes. **Note:** Slower administration preferable for stable patients.

Cathartic: Oral:
Children:
2-5 years: 2.5-5 g/kg/day in divided doses
6-11 years: 5-10 g/day in divided doses
Children ≥12 years and Adults: 10-30 g/day in divided doses

Parenteral nutrition supplementation (elemental magnesium): I.V.:
Children:
<50 kg: 0.3-0.5 mEq/kg/day
>50 kg: 10-30 mEq/day
Adults: 8-20 mEq/day

Soaking aid: Topical: Adults: Dissolve 2 cupfuls of powder per gallon of warm water

RDA (elemental magnesium):
Children:
1-3 years: 80 mg/day
4-8 years: 130 mg/day
9-13 years: 240 mg/day
14-18 years:
Female: 360 mg/day
Pregnant female: 400 mg/day
Male: 410 mg/day
Adults:
19-30 years:
Female: 310 mg/day
Pregnant female: 350 mg/day
Male: 400 mg/day
≥31 years:
Female: 320 mg/day
Pregnant female: 360 mg/day
Male: 420 mg/day

Dosage adjustment in renal impairment: Cl_{cr} <30 mL/minute: Use with caution; monitor for hypermagnesemia

Dietary Considerations Whole grains, legumes and dark-green leafy vegetables are dietary sources of magnesium.
10% elemental magnesium; 8.1 mEq magnesium/g; 4 mmol magnesium/g
500 mg magnesium sulfate = 4.06 mEq magnesium = 49.3 mg elemental magnesium

Administration
Oral: Dissolve powder in $^1/_2$ glass of water; may add lemon juice to improve taste
Injection: May be administered I.M. or I.V.
I.M.: A 25% or 50% concentration may be used for adults and a 20% solution is recommended for children
I.V.: Magnesium may be administered IVP, IVPB or I.V.; when giving I.V. push, must dilute first and should not be given any faster than 150 mg/minute. Hypotension and asystole may occur with rapid administration.
Maximal rate of infusion: 2 g/hour to avoid hypotension; doses of 4 g/hour have been given in emergencies (eclampsia, seizures); optimally, should add magnesium to I.V. fluids, but bolus doses are also effective
Topical: Dissolve 2 cups of powder per gallon of warm water to use as a soaking aid. To make a compress, dissolve 2 cups of powder per 2 cups of hot water and use a towel to apply as a wet dressing.

Monitoring Parameters Monitor blood pressure when administering magnesium sulfate I.V.; serum magnesium levels should be monitored to avoid overdose; monitor for diarrhea; monitor for arrhythmias, hypotension, respiratory and CNS depression during rapid I.V. administration

Reference Range Serum magnesium: 1.5-2.5 mg/dL; slightly different ranges are reported by different laboratories

Dosage Forms
Infusion [premixed in D_5W]: 10 mg/mL (100 mL); 20 mg/mL (500 mL, 1000 mL)
Infusion [premixed in water for injection]: 40 mg/mL (100 mL, 500 mL, 1000 mL); 80 mg/mL (50 mL)
Injection, solution: 125 mg/mL (8 mL); 500 mg/mL (2 mL, 5 mL, 10 mL, 20 mL, 50 mL)
Powder, oral/topical: Magnesium sulfate USP (227 g, 454 g, 480 g, 1810 g, 1920 g, 2720 g)

♦ **Magnesium Trisilicate and Aluminum Hydroxide** see Aluminum Hydroxide and Magnesium Trisilicate on page 85
♦ **Magonate® [OTC]** see Magnesium Gluconate on page 1047
♦ **Mag-Ox® 400 [OTC]** see Magnesium Oxide on page 1050
♦ **Mag-Tab® SR** see Magnesium L-lactate on page 1050
♦ **Magtrate® [OTC]** see Magnesium Gluconate on page 1047
♦ **MAH** see Magnesium L-aspartate Hydrochloride on page 1049
♦ **Malarone®** see Atovaquone and Proguanil on page 173
♦ **Malarone® Pediatric (Can)** see Atovaquone and Proguanil on page 173

Malathion (mal a THYE on)

U.S. Brand Names Ovide®
Pharmacologic Category Antiparasitic Agent, Topical; Pediculocide; Scabicidal Agent
Use Treatment of head lice and their ova
Pregnancy Risk Factor B
(Continued)

Malathion *(Continued)*

Dosage Sprinkle Ovide® lotion on dry hair and rub gently until the scalp is thoroughly moistened; pay special attention to the back of the head and neck. Allow to dry naturally - use no heat and leave uncovered. After 8-12 hours, the hair should be washed with a nonmedicated shampoo; rinse and use a fine-toothed comb to remove dead lice and eggs. If required, repeat with second application in 7-9 days. Further treatment is generally not necessary. Other family members should be evaluated to determine if infested and if so, receive treatment.

Dosage Forms Lotion: 0.5% (59 mL) [contains isopropyl alcohol 78%]

- ◆ **Maldemar**™ *see* Scopolamine Derivatives *on page 1550*
- ◆ **Mandelamine**® *see* Methenamine *on page 1106*
- ◆ **Mandrake** *see* Podophyllum Resin *on page 1385*

Manganese *(MAN ga nees)*

U.S. Brand Names Mangimin [OTC]
Index Terms Manganese Chloride; Manganese Sulfate
Pharmacologic Category Trace Element, Parenteral
Use Trace element added to total parenteral nutrition (TPN) solution to prevent manganese deficiency; orally as a dietary supplement
Pregnancy Risk Factor C
Lactation Enters breast milk/compatible
Medication Safety Issues
Sound-alike/look-alike issues:
Manganese sulfate may be confused with magnesium sulfate
Contraindications High manganese levels; severe liver dysfunction or cholestasis (conjugated bilirubin >2 mg/dL) due to reduced biliary excretion
Warnings/Precautions Manganese chloride solution for injection contains aluminum; use caution with impaired renal function and in premature infants. Use caution with hepatic impairment.
Overdosage/Toxicology Acute poisoning due to ingestion of manganese or manganese salts is rare (poor oral absorption). Manganese chloride solution for injection contains aluminum; aluminum doses >4-5 mcg/kg/day are associated with toxicity in patients with renal impairment and in premature neonates. In chronic poisoning, either from injection, or usually, from inhalation of manganese dust or fumes, symptoms are mainly extrapyramidal and toxicity can lead to progressive CNS deterioration.
Stability Solution for injection: Store at controlled room temperature of 15°C to 30°C (59°F to 86°F); compatible with electrolytes usually present in amino acid/dextrose solution used for TPN solutions.
Mechanism of Action Cofactor in many enzyme systems, stimulates synthesis of cholesterol and fatty acids in liver, and influences mucopolysaccharide synthesis
Pharmacodynamics/Kinetics
Absorption: Oral: Poor (3% to 4%)
Distribution: Concentrated in mitochondria of pituitary gland, pancreas, liver, kidney, and bone
Excretion: Bile (primarily); urine (negligible)
Dosage
Oral: Adequate intake:
0-6 months: 0.003 mg/day
7-12 months: 0.6 mg/day
1-3 years: 1.2 mg/day
4-8 years: 1.5 mg/day
9 years to Adults, Male: 1.9-2.3 mg/day
9 years to Adults, Female: 1.6-1.8 mg/day
Pregnancy: 2 mg/day
Lactation: 2.6 mg/day
I.V.:
Children: 2-10 mcg/kg/day usually administered in TPN solutions
Note: Use caution in premature neonates; manganese chloride solution for injection contains aluminum
Adults: 150-800 mcg/day usually administered in TPN solutions
Dosage adjustment in renal impairment: Use caution; manganese chloride solution for injection contains aluminum
Dosage adjustment in hepatic impairment: Use caution; dose may need to be decreased or withheld
Administration Solution for injection: Do not administer I.M. or by direct I.V. injection; acidic pH of the solution may cause tissue irritations and it is hypotonic
Monitoring Parameters Periodic manganese plasma level
Reference Range Plasma: 0.6-2 ng/mL
Dosage Forms
Injection, solution, as chloride [preservative free]: 0.1 mg/mL (10 mL) [contains aluminum ≤100 mcg/mL]
Injection, solution, as sulfate: 0.1 mg/mL (10 mL)
Tablet, as aspartate: 93 mg [equivalent to elemental manganese 25 mg]
Tablet, as gluconate: 5.7 mg [as elemental manganese]; 550 mg [equivalent to elemental manganese 30 mg]; 600 mg [equivalent to elemental manganese 50 mg]
Tablet, chelated: 50 mg [as elemental manganese]
Mangimin: 10 mg [as elemental manganese]

- ◆ **Manganese Chloride** *see* Manganese *on page 1054*
- ◆ **Manganese Sulfate** *see* Manganese *on page 1054*
- ◆ **Mangimin [OTC]** *see* Manganese *on page 1054*

Mannitol (MAN i tole)

U.S. Brand Names Osmitrol®; Resectisol®
Canadian Brand Names Osmitrol®
Index Terms *D*-Mannitol
Pharmacologic Category Diuretic, Osmotic; Genitourinary Irrigant
Use Reduction of increased intracranial pressure associated with cerebral edema; promotion of diuresis in the prevention and/or treatment of oliguria or anuria due to acute renal failure; reduction of increased intraocular pressure; promoting urinary excretion of toxic substances; genitourinary irrigant in transurethral prostatic resection or other transurethral surgical procedures
Pregnancy Risk Factor C
Pregnancy Implications
Reproduction studies have not been conducted.
Lactation Excretion in breast milk unknown/use caution
Medication Safety Issues
Sound-alike/look-alike issues:
Osmitrol® may be confused with esmolol
Contraindications Hypersensitivity to mannitol or any component or the formulation; severe renal disease (anuria); severe dehydration; active intracranial bleeding except during craniotomy; progressive heart failure, pulmonary congestion, or renal dysfunction after mannitol administration; severe pulmonary edema or congestion
Warnings/Precautions Should not be administered until adequacy of renal function and urine flow is established;use 1-2 test doses to assess renal response. Excess amounts can lead to profound diuresis with fluid and electrolyte loss; close medical supervision and dose evaluation are required. Watch for and correct electrolyte disturbances; adjust dose to avoid dehydration. May cause renal dysfunction especially with high doses; use caution in patients taking other nephrotoxic agents, with sepsis or pre-existing renal disease. To minimize adverse renal effects, adjust to keep serum osmolality less than 320 mOsm/L. Discontinue if evidence of acute tubular necrosis.

In patients being treated for cerebral edema, mannitol may accumulate in the brain (causing rebound increases in intracranial pressure) if circulating for long periods of time as with continuous infusion; intermittent boluses preferred. Cardiovascular status should also be evaluated; do not administer electrolyte-free mannitol solutions with blood. If hypotension occurs monitor cerebral perfusion pressure to insure adequate.
Adverse Reactions Frequency not defined.
Cardiovascular: Chest pain, CHF, circulatory overload, hyper-/hypotension, tachycardia
Central nervous system: Chills, convulsions, dizziness, headache
Dermatologic: Rash, urticaria
Endocrine & metabolic: Fluid and electrolyte imbalance, dehydration and hypovolemia secondary to rapid diuresis, hyperglycemia, hypernatremia, hyponatremia (dilutional), hyperosmolality-induced hyperkalemia, metabolic acidosis (dilutional), osmolar gap increased, water intoxication
Gastrointestinal: Nausea, vomiting, xerostomia
Genitourinary: Dysuria, polyuria
Local: Pain, thrombophlebitis, tissue necrosis
Ocular: Blurred vision
Renal: Acute renal failure, acute tubular necrosis (>200 g/day; serum osmolality >320 mOsm/L)
Respiratory: Pulmonary edema, rhinitis
Miscellaneous: Allergic reactions
Overdosage/Toxicology Symptoms include acute renal failure, polyuria, hypotension, cardiovascular collapse, pulmonary edema, hyponatremia, hypokalemia, oliguria, and seizures. Increased electrolyte excretion and fluid overload can occur. Hemodialysis will clear mannitol and reduce osmolality.
Drug Interactions
Increased Effect/Toxicity: Lithium toxicity (with diuretic-induced hyponatremia).
Stability Should be stored at room temperature (15°C to 30°C); do not freeze. Crystallization may occur at low temperatures; do not use solutions that contain crystals. Heating in a hot water bath and vigorous shaking may be utilized for resolubilization. Cool solutions to body temperature before using.
Mechanism of Action Increases the osmotic pressure of glomerular filtrate, which inhibits tubular reabsorption of water and electrolytes and increases urinary output
Pharmacodynamics/Kinetics
Onset of action: Diuresis: Injection: 1-3 hours; Reduction in intracranial pressure: ~15-30 minutes
Duration: Reduction in intracranial pressure: 1.5-6 hours
Distribution: Remains confined to extracellular space (except in extreme concentrations); does not penetrate the blood-brain barrier (generally, penetration is low)
Metabolism: Minimally hepatic to glycogen
Half-life elimination: 1.1-1.6 hours
Excretion: Primarily urine (as unchanged drug)
Dosage
Children: I.V.:
Test dose (to assess adequate renal function): 200 mg/kg over 3-5 minutes to produce a urine flow of at least 1 mL/kg for 1-3 hours
Initial: 0.25-1 g/kg
Maintenance: 0.25-0.5 g/kg given every 4-6 hours
Adults:
I.V.:
Test dose (to assess adequate renal function): 12.5 g (200 mg/kg) over 3-5 minutes to produce a urine flow of at least 30-50 mL of urine per hour. If urine flow does not
(Continued)

Mannitol (Continued)

increase, a second test dose may be given. If test dose does not produce an acceptable urine output, then need to reassess management.

Initial: 0.5-1 g/kg

Maintenance: 0.25-0.5 g/kg every 4-6 hours; usual daily dose: 20-200 g/24 hours

Intracranial pressure: Cerebral edema: 0.25-1.5 g/kg/dose I.V. as a 15% to 20% solution over ≥30 minutes; maintain serum osmolality 310 to <320 mOsm/kg

Prevention of acute renal failure (oliguria): 50-100 g dose

Treatment of oliguria: 100 g dose

Preoperative for neurosurgery: 1.5-2 g/kg administered 1-1.5 hours prior to surgery

Reduction of intraocular pressure: 1.5-2 g/kg as a 15% to 20% solution; administer over 30 minutes

Topical: Transurethral irrigation: Use urogenital solution as required for irrigation

Elderly: Consider initiation at lower end of dosing range

Dosage adjustment in renal impairment: Contraindicated in severe renal impairment. If test dose does not produce adequate urine output reassess options. Use caution in patients with underlying renal disease.

Dosage adjustment in hepatic impairment: No adjustment required.

Administration Inspect for crystals prior to administration. If crystals present redissolve by warming solution. Use filter-type administration set; in-line 5-micron filter set should always be used for mannitol infusion with concentrations ≥20%; administer test dose (for oliguria) I.V. push over 3-5 minutes; avoid extravasation; for cerebral edema or elevated ICP, administer over 20-30 minutes; crenation and agglutination of red blood cells may occur if administered with whole blood.

Monitoring Parameters Renal function, daily fluid I & O, serum electrolytes, serum and urine osmolality; for treatment of elevated intracranial pressure, maintain serum osmolality 310 to <320 mOsm/kg

Additional Information May autoclave or heat to redissolve crystals; mannitol 20% has an approximate osmolarity of 1100 mOsm/L and mannitol 25% has an approximate osmolarity of 1375 mOsm/L

Dosage Forms

Injection, solution: 5% [50 mg/mL] (1000 mL); 10% [100 mg/mL] (500 mL, 1000 mL); 15% [150 mg/mL] (500 mL); 20% [200 mg/mL] (150 mL, 250 mL, 500 mL); 25% [250 mg/mL] (50 mL)

Osmitrol®: 5% [50 mg/mL] (1000 mL); 10% [100 mg/mL] (500 mL, 1000 mL); 15% [150 mg/mL] (500 mL); 20% [200 mg/mL] (250 mL, 500 mL)

Solution, urogenital (Resectisol®): 5% [50 mg/mL] (2000 mL, 4000 mL)

- ◆ **D-Mannitol** see Mannitol on page 1055
- ◆ **Mantoux** see Tuberculin Tests on page 1754
- ◆ **Mapap [OTC]** see Acetaminophen on page 28
- ◆ **Mapap Children's [OTC]** see Acetaminophen on page 28
- ◆ **Mapap Extra Strength [OTC]** see Acetaminophen on page 28
- ◆ **Mapap Infants [OTC]** see Acetaminophen on page 28
- ◆ **Mapap Sinus Maximum Strength [OTC]** see Acetaminophen and Pseudoephedrine on page 33
- ◆ **Mapezine® (Can)** see Carbamazepine on page 284

Maprotiline (ma PROE ti leen)

Canadian Brand Names Novo-Maprotiline

Index Terms Ludiomil; Maprotiline Hydrochloride

Pharmacologic Category Antidepressant, Tetracyclic

Additional Appendix Information

Antidepressant Agents on page 1866

Use Treatment of depression and anxiety associated with depression

Unlabeled/Investigational Use Bulimia; duodenal ulcers; enuresis; urinary symptoms of multiple sclerosis; pain; panic attacks; tension headache; cocaine withdrawal

Restrictions An FDA-approved medication guide concerning the use of antidepressants in children and teenagers must be distributed when dispensing an outpatient prescription (new or refill) where this medication is to be used without direct supervision of a healthcare provider. Medication guides are available at http://www.fda.gov/cder/Offices/ODS/medication_guides.htm. Dispense to parents or guardians of children and teenagers receiving this medication.

Pregnancy Risk Factor B

Medication Safety Issues

Sound-alike/look-alike issues:

Ludiomil may be confused with Lamictal®, lamotrigine, Lomotil®

Dosage Oral:

Adults: Depression/anxiety: 75 mg/day to start, increase by 25 mg every 2 weeks up to 150-225 mg/day; given in 3 divided doses or in a single daily dose

Elderly: Depression/anxiety: Initial: 25 mg at bedtime, increase by 25 mg every 3 days for inpatients and weekly for outpatients if tolerated; usual maintenance dose: 50-75 mg/day, higher doses may be necessary in nonresponders

Additional Information Complete prescribing information for this medication should be consulted for additional detail.

Dosage Forms Tablet, as hydrochloride: 25 mg, 50 mg, 75 mg

- ◆ **Maprotiline Hydrochloride** see Maprotiline on page 1056
- ◆ **Marcaine®** see Bupivacaine on page 249
- ◆ **Marcaine® Spinal** see Bupivacaine on page 249
- ◆ **Margesic® H** see Hydrocodone and Acetaminophen on page 848

- **Marinol®** *see* Dronabinol *on page 558*
- **Marvelon® (Can)** *see* Ethinyl Estradiol and Desogestrel *on page 645*
- **Matulane®** *see* Procarbazine *on page 1428*
- **3M™ Avagard™ [OTC]** *see* Chlorhexidine Gluconate *on page 344*
- **Mavik®** *see* Trandolapril *on page 1720*
- **Mavik™ (Can)** *see* Trandolapril *on page 1720*
- **Maxair™ Autohaler™** *see* Pirbuterol *on page 1378*
- **Maxalt®** *see* Rizatriptan *on page 1528*
- **Maxalt™ (Can)** *see* Rizatriptan *on page 1528*
- **Maxalt-MLT®** *see* Rizatriptan *on page 1528*
- **Maxalt RPD™ (Can)** *see* Rizatriptan *on page 1528*
- **Maxidex®** *see* Dexamethasone *on page 479*
- **Maxidone™** *see* Hydrocodone and Acetaminophen *on page 848*
- **Maxifed®** *see* Guaifenesin and Pseudoephedrine *on page 819*
- **Maxifed DM** *see* Guaifenesin, Pseudoephedrine, and Dextromethorphan *on page 821*
- **Maxifed DMX** *see* Guaifenesin, Pseudoephedrine, and Dextromethorphan *on page 821*
- **Maxifed-G®** *see* Guaifenesin and Pseudoephedrine *on page 819*
- **Maxipime®** *see* Cefepime *on page 310*
- **Maxitrol®** *see* Neomycin, Polymyxin B, and Dexamethasone *on page 1211*
- **Maxi-Tuss HCG** *see* Hydrocodone and Guaifenesin *on page 849*
- **Maxivate®** *see* Betamethasone *on page 211*
- **Maxzide®** *see* Hydrochlorothiazide and Triamterene *on page 847*
- **Maxzide®-25** *see* Hydrochlorothiazide and Triamterene *on page 847*
- **May Apple** *see* Podophyllum Resin *on page 1385*
- **MCH** *see* Collagen Hemostat *on page 416*
- **MCV4** *see* Meningococcal Polysaccharide (Groups A / C / Y and W-135) Diphtheria Toxoid Conjugate Vaccine *on page 1077*
- **MDL 73,147EF** *see* Dolasetron *on page 536*

Measles, Mumps, and Rubella Vaccines (Combined)
(MEE zels, mumpz & roo BEL a vak SEENS, kom BINED)

U.S. Brand Names M-M-R® II
Canadian Brand Names M-M-R® II; Priorix™
Index Terms MMR; Mumps, Measles and Rubella Vaccines, Combined; Rubella, Measles and Mumps Vaccines, Combined
Pharmacologic Category Vaccine, Live Virus
Additional Appendix Information
  Immunization Recommendations *on page 1929*
Use Measles, mumps, and rubella prophylaxis
Pregnancy Risk Factor C
Dosage SubQ:
  Infants <12 months: If there is risk of exposure to measles, single-antigen measles vaccine should be administered at 6-11 months of age with a second dose (of MMR) at >12 months of age.
  Children ≥12 months:
    Primary immunization: 0.5 mL at 12-15 months
    Revaccination: 0.5 mL at 4-6 years of age; revaccination is recommended prior to elementary school. If the second dose was not received, the schedule should be completed by the 11- to 12-year old visit. During a mumps outbreak, children ages 1-4 should consider a second dose of a live mumps virus vaccine. (Minimum interval between doses is 28 days.)
  Adults:
    Birth year ≥1957 without evidence of immunity (also see Additional Information): 1 or 2 doses (0.5 mL/dose); minimum interval between doses is 28 days
    Routine vaccination of healthcare workers:
      Birth year ≥1957 without evidence of immunity: 2 doses of a live mumps virus vaccine; minimum interval between doses is 28 days
      Birth year <1957 without evidence of immunity: 1 dose of a live mumps virus vaccine.
    Mumps outbreak:
      Healthcare workers born <1957 without other evidence of immunity: Consider 2 doses of a live mumps virus vaccine; minimum interval between doses is 28 days
      Low-risk adults: A second dose of a live mumps virus vaccine should be considered in adults who previously received 1 dose; minimum interval between doses is 28 days
Additional Information Complete prescribing information for this medication should be consulted for additional detail.
Dosage Forms
  Injection, powder for reconstitution [preservative free]:
    M-M-R® II: Measles virus 1000 $TCID_{50}$, mumps virus 20,000 $TCID_{50}$, and , rubella virus 1000 $TCID_{50}$ [contains neomycin 25 mcg, gelatin, human albumin, and bovine serum; produced in chick embryo cell culture]

Measles, Mumps, Rubella, and Varicella Virus Vaccine
(MEE zels, mumpz, roo BEL a, & var i SEL a VYE rus vak SEEN)

U.S. Brand Names ProQuad®
Index Terms Mumps, Rubella, Varicella, and Measles Vaccine; Rubella, Varicella, Measles, and Mumps Vaccine; Varicella, Measles, Mumps, and Rubella Vaccine
(Continued)

Measles, Mumps, Rubella, and Varicella Virus Vaccine
(Continued)

Pharmacologic Category Vaccine, Live Virus

Use To provide simultaneous active immunization against measles, mumps, rubella, and varicella

Pregnancy Risk Factor C

Dosage SubQ: Children 12 months to 12 years: One dose (0.5 mL)

Allow at least 1 month between administering a dose of a measles containing vaccine (eg, M-M-R® II) and ProQuad®.

Allow at least 3 months between administering a varicella containing vaccine (eg, Varivax®) and ProQuad®.

Additional Information Complete prescribing information for this medication should be consulted for additional detail.

Dosage Forms Injection, powder for reconstitution [preservative free] (ProQuad®): Measles virus ≥3.00 $\log_{10}$ TCID50, mumps virus ≥4.3 $\log_{10}$ TCID50, rubella virus ≥3.0 $\log_{10}$ TCID50, and varicella virus ≥3.99 $\log_{10}$ plaque-forming units [contains neomycin, sucrose, gelatin, human albumin, and bovine serum; produced in chick embryo cell culture]

Measles Virus Vaccine (Live) (MEE zels VYE rus vak SEEN, live)

U.S. Brand Names Attenuvax®

Index Terms More Attenuated Enders Strain; Rubeola Vaccine

Pharmacologic Category Vaccine, Live Virus

Additional Appendix Information

Immunization Recommendations *on page 1929*

Use Adults born before 1957 are generally considered to be immune. All those born in or after 1957 without documentation of live vaccine on or after first birthday, physician-diagnosed measles, or laboratory evidence of immunity should be vaccinated, ideally with two doses of vaccine separated by no less than 1 month. For those previously vaccinated with one dose of measles vaccine, revaccination is recommended for students entering colleges and other institutions of higher education, for healthcare workers at the time of employment, and for international travelers who visit endemic areas.

MMR is the vaccine of choice if recipients are likely to be susceptible to rubella and/or mumps as well as to measles. Persons vaccinated between 1963 and 1967 with a killed measles vaccine, followed by live vaccine within 3 months, or with a vaccine of unknown type should be revaccinated with live measles virus vaccine.

Pregnancy Risk Factor X

Medication Safety Issues

Sound-alike/look-alike issues:

Attenuvax® may be confused with Meruvax®

Contraindications Hypersensitivity to neomycin or any component of the formulation; acute respiratory infections, activated tuberculosis, immunosuppressed patients; pregnancy; known anaphylactoid reaction to eggs

Warnings/Precautions Avoid use in immunocompromised patients; defer administration in presence of acute respiratory or other active infections or inactive, untreated tuberculosis; avoid pregnancy for 3 months following vaccination; history of febrile seizures, hypersensitivity reactions may occur

Adverse Reactions All serious adverse reactions must be reported to the U.S. Department of Health and Human Services (DHHS) Vaccine Adverse Event Reporting System (VAERS) 1-800-822-7967.

>10%:

Cardiovascular: Edema

Central nervous system: Fever (<100°F)

Local: Burning or stinging, induration

1% to 10%:

Central nervous system: Fever between 100°F and 103°F usually between 5th and 12th days postvaccination

Dermatologic: Rash (rarely generalized)

<1% (Limited to important or life-threatening): Allergic reactions, ataxia, confusion, convulsions, coryza, cough, diarrhea, diplopia, dyspnea, encephalitis, erythema multiforme, fatigue, fever (>103°F - prolonged), Guillain-Barré syndrome, headache (severe), itching, lymphadenopathy, palsies, reddening of skin (especially around ears and eyes), rhinitis, sore throat, stiff neck, thrombocytopenic purpura, urticaria, vomiting

Stability Refrigerate at 2°C to 8°C (36°F to 46°F). Protect from light. Discard if left at room temperature for over 8 hours.

Mechanism of Action Promotes active immunity to measles virus by inducing specific measles IgG and IgM antibodies.

Dosage Children ≥15 months and Adults: SubQ: 0.5 mL in outer aspect of the upper arm, no routine boosters

Administration Vaccine should not be administered I.V.; SubQ injection preferred with a 25-gauge ⅝" needle

Test Interactions May temporarily depress tuberculin skin test sensitivity

Additional Information Contains 25 mcg neomycin per dose. Federal law requires that the date of administration, the vaccine manufacturer, lot number of vaccine, and the administering person's name, title, and address be entered into the patient's permanent medical record.

Dosage Forms Injection, powder for reconstitution [preservative free]: 1000 TCID$_{50}$ [contains human albumin, bovine serum, and neomycin; produced in chick embryo cell culture]

♦ **Mebaral®** *see* Mephobarbital *on page 1083*

Mebendazole (me BEN da zole)

U.S. Brand Names Vermox® [DSC]
Canadian Brand Names Vermox®
Pharmacologic Category Anthelmintic
Use Treatment of pinworms (*Enterobius vermicularis*), whipworms (*Trichuris trichiura*), round-worms (*Ascaris lumbricoides*), and hookworms (*Ancylostoma duodenale*)
Pregnancy Risk Factor C
Lactation Excretion in breast milk unknown/use caution
Contraindications Hypersensitivity to mebendazole or any component of the formulation
Warnings/Precautions Pregnancy and children <2 years of age are relative contraindications since safety has not been established; not effective for hydatid disease
Adverse Reactions Frequency not defined.
  Cardiovascular: Angioedema
  Central nervous system: Fever, dizziness, headache, seizure
  Dermatologic: Rash, itching, alopecia (with high doses)
  Gastrointestinal: Abdominal pain, diarrhea, nausea, vomiting
  Hematologic: Neutropenia (sore throat, unusual fatigue)
  Neuromuscular & skeletal: Unusual weakness
Overdosage/Toxicology Symptoms include abdominal pain and altered mental status. Treatment is GI decontamination and supportive care.
Drug Interactions
  Decreased Effect: Anticonvulsants such as carbamazepine and phenytoin may increase metabolism of mebendazole
Ethanol/Nutrition/Herb Interactions Food: Mebendazole serum levels may be increased if taken with food.
Mechanism of Action Selectively and irreversibly blocks glucose uptake and other nutrients in susceptible adult intestine-dwelling helminths
Pharmacodynamics/Kinetics
  Absorption: 2% to 10%
  Distribution: To serum, cyst fluid, liver, omental fat, and pelvic, pulmonary, and hepatic cysts; highest concentrations found in liver; relatively high concentrations found in muscle-encysted *Trichinella spiralis* larvae; crosses placenta
  Protein binding: 95%
  Metabolism: Extensively hepatic
  Half-life elimination: 1-11.5 hours
  Time to peak, serum: 2-4 hours
  Excretion: Primarily feces; urine (5% to 10%)
Dosage Children and Adults: Oral:
  Pinworms: 100 mg as a single dose; may need to repeat after 2 weeks; treatment should include family members in close contact with patient
  Whipworms, roundworms, hookworms: One tablet twice daily, morning and evening on 3 consecutive days; if patient is not cured within 3-4 weeks, a second course of treatment may be administered
  Capillariasis: 200 mg twice daily for 20 days
  Dosing adjustment in hepatic impairment: Dosage reduction may be necessary in patients with liver dysfunction
  Hemodialysis: Not dialyzable (0% to 5%)
Dietary Considerations Tablet can be crushed and mixed with food, swallowed whole, or chewed.
Administration Tablets may be chewed, swallowed whole, or crushed and mixed with food.
Monitoring Parameters Check for helminth ova in feces within 3-4 weeks following the initial therapy
Dosage Forms Tablet, chewable: 100 mg

Mecamylamine (mek a MIL a meen)

U.S. Brand Names Inversine®
Canadian Brand Names Inversine®
Index Terms Mecamylamine Hydrochloride
Pharmacologic Category Ganglionic Blocking Agent
Use Treatment of moderately severe to severe hypertension and in uncomplicated malignant hypertension
Unlabeled/Investigational Use Tourette's syndrome
Pregnancy Risk Factor C
Medication Safety Issues
  Sound-alike/look-alike issues:
  Mecamylamine may be confused with mesalamine
Contraindications Coronary insufficiency, pyloric stenosis, glaucoma, uremia, recent myocardial infarction, unreliable, uncooperative patients
Warnings/Precautions Use with caution in patients receiving sulfonamides or antibiotics that cause neuromuscular blockade; use with caution in patients with impaired renal function, previous CNS abnormalities, prostatic hyperplasia, bladder obstruction, or urethral strictive; do not abruptly discontinue
Adverse Reactions Frequency not defined.
  Cardiovascular: Postural hypotension
  Central nervous system: Drowsiness, convulsions, confusion, mental depression
  Endocrine & metabolic: Sexual ability decreased
  Gastrointestinal: Xerostomia, loss of appetite, nausea, vomiting, bloating; frequent stools followed by severe constipation
  Genitourinary: Dysuria
  Neuromuscular & skeletal: Uncontrolled movements of hands, arms, legs, or face; trembling
(Continued)

Mecamylamine *(Continued)*

Ocular: Blurred vision; enlarged pupils

Respiratory: Dyspnea

Overdosage/Toxicology Symptoms include hypotension, nausea, vomiting, urinary retention, and constipation. Signs and symptoms are a directly result of ganglionic blockade.
Treatment is supportive. Pressor amines may be used to correct hypotension. Use caution as
patients will be unusually sensitive to these agents.

Drug Interactions

Increased Effect/Toxicity: Sulfonamides and antibiotics that cause neuromuscular
blockade may increase effect of mecamylamine. The action of mecamylamine may be
increased by anesthesia, other antihypertensives, and alcohol.

Mechanism of Action Mecamylamine is a ganglionic blocker. This agent inhibits acetylcholine at the autonomic ganglia, causing a decrease in blood pressure. Mecamylamine also
blocks central nicotinic cholinergic receptors, which inhibits the effects of nicotine and may
suppress the desire to smoke.

Dosage Adults: Oral: 2.5 mg twice daily after meals for 2 days; increased by increments of 2.5
mg at intervals ≥2 days until desired blood pressure response is achieved; average daily
dose: 25 mg (usually in 3 divided doses)

Note: Reduce dosage of other antihypertensives when combined with mecamylamine with
exception of thiazide diuretics which may be maintained at usual dose while decreasing
mecamylamine by 50%

Dosing adjustment/comments in renal impairment: Use with caution, if at all, although no
specific guidelines are available

Dietary Considerations Should be taken after meals.

Monitoring Parameters Monitor for orthostatic hypotension; aid with ambulation

Dosage Forms Tablet, as hydrochloride: 2.5 mg

♦ **Mecamylamine Hydrochloride** *see Mecamylamine on page 1059*

Mecasermin *(mek a SER min)*

U.S. Brand Names Increlex™; Iplex™

Index Terms Mecasermin (rDNA Origin); Mecasermin Rinfabate; Recombinant Human
Insulin-Like Growth Factor-1; rhIGF-1; rhIGF-1/rhIGFBP-3

Pharmacologic Category Growth Hormone

Use Treatment of growth failure in children with severe primary insulin-like growth factor-1
deficiency (IGF-1 deficiency; primary IGFD), or with growth hormone (GH) gene deletions
who have developed neutralizing antibodies to GH

Pregnancy Risk Factor C

Pregnancy Implications Teratogenic effects were not observed in animal studies

Lactation Excretion in breast milk unknown/ use caution

Contraindications Hypersensitivity to mecasermin or any component of the formulation;
patients with closed epiphyses; active or suspected neoplasia

Warnings/Precautions Correct thyroid or nutritional deficiencies prior to therapy. May cause
hypoglycemic effects; patients should avoid high risk activities until a tolerated dose is
established. Do not administer on days a patient cannot or will not eat. Increlex™ should be
administered with a meal or a snack; patients using Iplex™ should avoid missing meals and
maintain a balanced diet. Intracranial hypertension has been reported with growth hormone
products and reverses after interruption of dosing; funduscopic examinations are recommended. Lymphoid hypertrophy has been reported and may lead to complications such as
snoring, sleep apnea, and chronic middle-ear effusions. Progression of scoliosis and slipped
capital epiphyses may occur in children experiencing rapid growth. Not intended for use in
patients with secondary forms of IGF-1 deficiency (GH deficiency, malnutrition, hypothyroidism, chronic anti-inflammatory steroid therapy). Safety and efficacy have not been established in adults or in children <2 years of age (Increlex™) or <3 years of age (Iplex™).

Adverse Reactions

≥5%:

Cardiovascular: Cardiac murmur

Central nervous system: Convulsion, dizziness, headache (Iplex™: 22%)

Endocrine & metabolic: Hyper-/hypoglycemia (Increlex™: 42%; Iplex™ 31%),
iron-deficiency anemia, ovarian cysts, thymus hypertrophy, thyromegaly

Gastrointestinal: Vomiting

Hepatic: Liver enzymes increased

Local: Injection site reactions: Erythema, bruising, hair growth, lipohypertrophy

Neuromuscular & skeletal: Arthralgia, bone pain, extremity pain, muscular atrophy

Ocular: Papilledema

Otic: Ear pain, hypoacusis, middle ear fluid, otitis media, serous otitis media, tympa-
nometry abnormal

Renal: Hematuria

Respiratory: Snoring, tonsillar hypertrophy (Increlex™: 15%; Iplex™ 19%)

Miscellanous: Lymphadenopathy

<5% or frequency not defined: Hypoglycemic seizure, intracranial hypertension, loss of
consciousness secondary to hypoglycemia, thickening of soft facial tissue

Overdosage/Toxicology Hypoglycemia would be expected; treatment for hypoglycemia
which may include oral glucose, food, parenteral glucose or glucagon may be required.

Stability

Increlex™: Store under refrigeration at 2°C to 8°C (35°F to 46°F); do not freeze. Protect from
direct light. After initial entry into vial, use within 30 days.

Iplex™: Must be kept frozen. Store at -70°C (-94°F) during distribution and at -20°C (-4°F)
once in the patients home freezer. Transport to home freezer on dry ice. Do not use if
product thaws during transportation or storage. If solution is cloudy, it may indicate that it
has thawed during storage and should not bet used. May be stored up to 2 months at -20°C
(-4°F). Prior to use, remove from freezer and allow to thaw at room temperature of 20°C to

25°C (68° to 77°F) for ~45 minutes. Use within 1 hour of reaching room temperature. Do not use if vial was kept at room temperature for >2 hours.

Mechanism of Action Mecasermin is an insulin-like growth factor (IGF-1) produced using recombinant DNA technology to replace endogenous IGF-1. Endogenous IGF-1 circulates predominately bound to insulin-like growth factor-binding protein-3 (IGFBP-3) and a growth hormone-dependent acid-labile subunit (ALS). Acting at receptors in the liver and other tissues, endogenous growth hormone (GH) stimulates the synthesis and secretion of IGF-1. In patients with primary severe IGF-1 deficiency, growth hormone receptors in the liver are unresponsive to GH, leading to reduced endogenous IGF-I concentrations and decreased growth (skeletal, cell, and organ). Endogenous IGF-1 also suppresses liver glucose production, stimulates peripheral glucose utilization and has an inhibitory effect on insulin secretion. Mecasermin rinfabate is a complex of IGF-1 and IGFBP-3, both produced by recombinant DNA technology.

Pharmacodynamics/Kinetics

Distribution: V_d: Severe primary IGFD: 0.184-0.33 L/kg

Protein binding: >80% bound to IGFBP-3 and an acid-labile subunit (IGFBP-3 reduced with severe primary IGFD)

Metabolism: Hepatic and renal

Half-life elimination: Severe primary IGFD: Mecasermin: 5.8 hours; Mecasermin rinfabate: >12 hours

Dosage

Primary IGFD: SubQ:

Increlex™: Children ≥2 years: Initial: 0.04-0.08 mg/kg twice daily; if tolerated for 7 days, may increase by 0.04 mg/kg/dose (maximum dose: 0.12 mg/kg given twice daily). Must be administered within 20 minutes of a meal or snack; omit dose if patient is unable to eat. Reduce dose if hypoglycemia occurs despite adequate food intake.

Iplex™: Children ≥3 years: Initial: 0.5 mg/kg once daily; dose may be increased to 1-2 mg/kg/ day, given once daily. Withhold dose if hypoglycemia is present.

Dietary Considerations Increlex™ must be administered within 20 minutes of a meal or snack. Patients using Iplex™ should avoid missing meals and maintain a balanced diet.

Administration For SubQ injection only; do not administer I.V. Omit dose and do not make up for omitted dose if patient is unable to eat. Rotate injection site.

Increlex™: Must be administered within 20 minutes of a meal or snack. May cause hypoglycemic effects; patients should avoid high-risk activities within 2-3 hours of dosing until a tolerated dose is established.

Iplex™: Prior to administration, gently swirl vial; do not shake. Do not use if solution is cloudy (may indicate thawing during storage); do not use if stored at room temperature >2 hours. Dose should be administered once daily, at the same time each day. May cause hypoglycemic effects; patients should avoid high risk activities for 3-5 days until a tolerated dose is established. Withhold dose if hypoglycemia is present.

Monitoring Parameters Preprandial glucose during treatment initiation and dose adjustment; facial features; lymphoid tissue; fundoscopic examination; growth; new onset of a limp or complaints of hip or knee pain. Monitor small children closely due to potentially erratic food intake.

Iplex™: Adjust dose based on IGF-1 level obtained 8-18 hours after previous dose.

Target treatment IGF-1 level: 0 to +2 SD score for age

Decrease dose for adverse events and/or IGF-1 levels ≥3 SD above normal

Reference Range Severe primary IGFD is defined as follows:

Height standard deviation score ≤ -3.0 **and**

Basal IGF-1 standard deviation score ≤ -3.0 **and**

Growth hormone: Normal or elevated

Dosage Forms

Injection, solution (Increlex™): 10 mg/mL (4 mL) [contains benzyl alcohol]

Injection, solution, as rinfabate [preservative free] (Iplex™): 36 mg/0.6 mL (0.6 mL)

♦ **Mecasermin (rDNA Origin)** *see* Mecasermin *on page 1060*

♦ **Mecasermin Rinfabate** *see* Mecasermin *on page 1060*

Mechlorethamine (me klor ETH a meen)

U.S. Brand Names Mustargen®

Canadian Brand Names Mustargen®

Index Terms Chlorethazine; Chlorethazine Mustard; HN₂; Mechloramine Hydrochloride; Mustine; Nitrogen Mustard; NSC-762

Pharmacologic Category Antineoplastic Agent, Alkylating Agent (Nitrogen Mustard)

Use Hodgkin's disease; non-Hodgkin's lymphoma; intracavitary injection for treatment of metastatic tumors; pleural and other malignant effusions; topical treatment of mycosis fungoides

Pregnancy Risk Factor D

Lactation Excretion in breast milk unknown/not recommended

Medication Safety Issues

High alert medication: The Institute for Safe Medication Practices (ISMP) includes this medication among its list of drugs which have a heightened risk of causing significant patient harm when used in error.

Contraindications Hypersensitivity to mechlorethamine or any component of the formulation; pre-existing profound myelosuppression or infection; pregnancy

Warnings/Precautions [U.S. Boxed Warnings]: Hazardous agent - use appropriate precautions for handling and disposal. Mechlorethamine is a potent vesicant; if extravasation occurs, severe tissue damage (leading to ulceration and necrosis) and pain may occur. Urate precipitation should be anticipated especially with lymphomas. **[U.S. Boxed Warning]: Should be administered under the supervision of an experienced cancer chemotherapy physician.**

(Continued)

Mechlorethamine *(Continued)*

Adverse Reactions

>10%:

Endocrine & metabolic: Delayed menses, oligomenorrhea, temporary or permanent amenorrhea, impaired spermatogenesis; spermatogenesis may return in patients in remission several years after the discontinuation of chemotherapy, chromosomal abnormalities

Gastrointestinal: Nausea and vomiting usually occur in nearly 100% of patients and onset is within 30 minutes to 2 hours after administration

Emetic potential: Very high (>90%)

Time course of nausea/vomiting: Onset: 1-3 hours; duration 2-8 hours

Genitourinary: Azoospermia

Hematologic: Myelosuppressive: Leukopenia and thrombocytopenia can be severe; caution should be used with patients who are receiving radiotherapy, secondary leukemia

WBC: Severe

Platelets: Severe

Onset (days): 4-7

Nadir (days): 14

Recovery (days): 21

Otic: Ototoxicity

Miscellaneous: Precipitation of herpes zoster

1% to 10%:

Central nervous system: Fever, vertigo

Dermatologic: Alopecia

Endocrine & metabolic: Hyperuricemia

Gastrointestinal: Diarrhea, anorexia, metallic taste

Local: Thrombophlebitis/extravasation: May cause local vein discomfort which may be relieved by warm soaks and pain medication. A brown discoloration of veins may occur. Mechlorethamine is a strong vesicant and can cause tissue necrosis and sloughing.

Vesicant chemotherapy

Secondary malignancies: Have been reported after several years in 1% to 6% of patients treated

Neuromuscular & skeletal: Weakness

Otic: Tinnitus

Miscellaneous: Hypersensitivity, anaphylaxis

<1% (Limited to important or life-threatening): Hemolytic anemia, hepatotoxicity, myelosuppression, peripheral neuropathy

Overdosage/Toxicology Signs and symptoms include suppression of all formed elements of the blood, uric acid crystals, nausea, vomiting, and diarrhea. Sodium thiosulfate is the specific antidote for nitrogen mustard extravasations. Treatment of systemic overdose is supportive.

Drug Interactions

Decreased Effect: Patients may experience impaired immune response to vaccines; possible infection after administration of live vaccines in patients receiving immunosuppressants.

Ethanol/Nutrition/Herb Interactions Ethanol: Avoid ethanol (due to GI irritation).

Stability Store intact vials at room temperature (15°C to 30°C/59°F to 86°F). **Must be prepared immediately before use**; solution is stable for only 15-60 minutes after dilution. Dilute powder with 10 mL SWI to a final concentration of 1 mg/mL. May be diluted in up to 100 mL NS for intracavitary or topical administration. Extemporaneous formulations for topical use have been reported to retain biologic activity for 30 days.

Mechanism of Action Bifunctional alkylating agent that inhibits DNA and RNA synthesis via formation of carbonium ions; cross-links strands of DNA, causing miscoding, breakage, and failure of replication; produces interstrand and intrastrand cross-links in DNA resulting in miscoding, breakage, and failure of replication. Although not cell phase-specific *per se*, mechlorethamine effect is most pronounced in the S phase, and cell proliferation is arrested in the G_2 phase.

Pharmacodynamics/Kinetics

Duration: Unchanged drug is undetectable in blood within a few minutes

Absorption: Intracavitary administration: Incomplete secondary to rapid deactivation by body fluids

Metabolism: Rapid hydrolysis and demethylation, possibly in plasma

Half-life elimination: <1 minute

Excretion: Urine (50% as metabolites, <0.01% as unchanged drug)

Dosage Refer to individual protocols.

Children and Adults: I.V.: 6 mg/m² on days 1 and 8 of a 28-day cycle (MOPP regimen)

Adults:

I.V.: 0.4 mg/kg **or** 12-16 mg/m² for one dose **or** divided into 0.1 mg/kg/day for 4 days, repeated at 4- to 6-week intervals

Intracavitary: 0.2-0.4 mg/kg (10-20 mg) as a single dose; may be repeated if fluid continues to accumulate.

Intrapericardially: 0.2-0.4 mg/kg as a single dose; may be repeated if fluid continues to accumulate.

Topical: 0.01% to 0.02% solution, lotion, or ointment

Hemodialysis: Not removed; supplemental dosing is not required.

Peritoneal dialysis: Not removed; supplemental dosing is not required.

Administration I.V. as a slow push through the side of a freely-flowing saline or dextrose solution. Due to the limited stability of the drug, and the increased risk of phlebitis and venous irritation and blistering with increased contact time, infusions of the drug are not recommended.

Mechlorethamine may cause extravasation. Use within 1 hour of preparation. Avoid extravasation since mechlorethamine is a potent vesicant.

Monitoring Parameters CBC with differential, hemoglobin, and platelet count

Dosage Forms Injection, powder for reconstitution, as hydrochloride: 10 mg

♦ **Mechlorethamine Hydrochloride** *see Mechlorethamine on page 1061*

Meclizine (MEK li zeen)

U.S. Brand Names Antivert®; Bonine® [OTC]; Dramamine® Less Drowsy Formula [OTC]
Canadian Brand Names Bonamine™; Bonine®
Index Terms Meclizine Hydrochloride; Meclozine Hydrochloride
Pharmacologic Category Antiemetic; Antihistamine
Use Prevention and treatment of symptoms of motion sickness; management of vertigo with diseases affecting the vestibular system
Pregnancy Risk Factor B
Pregnancy Implications No data available on crossing the placenta. Probably no effect on the fetus (insufficient data). Available evidence suggests safe use during pregnancy.
Lactation Excretion in breast milk unknown/not recommended
Medication Safety Issues
Sound-alike/look-alike issues:
Antivert® may be confused with Axert™
Contraindications Hypersensitivity to meclizine or any component of the formulation
Warnings/Precautions Use with caution in patients with angle-closure glaucoma, prostatic hyperplasia, pyloric or duodenal obstruction, or bladder neck obstruction; use with caution in hot weather, and during exercise; elderly may be at risk for anticholinergic side effects such as glaucoma, prostatic hyperplasia, constipation, gastrointestinal obstructive disease; if vertigo does not respond in 1-2 weeks, it is advised to discontinue use
Adverse Reactions
>10%:
Central nervous system: Slight to moderate drowsiness
Respiratory: Thickening of bronchial secretions
1% to 10%:
Central nervous system: Headache, fatigue, nervousness, dizziness
Gastrointestinal: Appetite increase, weight gain, nausea, diarrhea, abdominal pain, dry mouth
Neuromuscular & skeletal: Arthralgia
Respiratory: Pharyngitis
<1% (Limited to important or life-threatening): Bronchospasm, hepatitis, hypotension, palpitation
Overdosage/Toxicology Symptoms include CNS depression, confusion, nervousness, hallucinations, dizziness, blurred vision, nausea, vomiting, and hyperthermia. There is no specific treatment for antihistamine overdose, however, clinical toxicity is mostly due to anticholinergic effects. For anticholinergic overdose with severe life-threatening symptoms, physostigmine 1-2 mg (0.5 mg or 0.02 mg/kg for children) slow I.V. may be given to reverse these effects.
Drug Interactions
Increased Effect/Toxicity: Increased toxicity with CNS depressants, neuroleptics, and anticholinergics.
Ethanol/Nutrition/Herb Interactions Ethanol: Avoid ethanol (may increase CNS depression).
Mechanism of Action Has central anticholinergic action by blocking chemoreceptor trigger zone; decreases excitability of the middle ear labyrinth and blocks conduction in the middle ear vestibular-cerebellar pathways
Pharmacodynamics/Kinetics
Onset of action: ~1 hour
Duration: 8-24 hours
Metabolism: Hepatic
Half-life elimination: 6 hours
Excretion: Urine (as metabolites); feces (as unchanged drug)
Dosage Children >12 years and Adults: Oral:
Motion sickness: 12.5-25 mg 1 hour before travel, repeat dose every 12-24 hours if needed; doses up to 50 mg may be needed
Vertigo: 25-100 mg/day in divided doses
Dosage Forms
Tablet, as hydrochloride: 12.5 mg, 25 mg
Antivert®: 12.5 mg, 25 mg, 50 mg
Dramamine® Less Drowsy Formula: 25 mg
Tablet, chewable, as hydrochloride (Bonine®): 25 mg

♦ **Meclizine Hydrochloride** *see Meclizine on page 1063*

Meclofenamate (me kloe fen AM ate)

Canadian Brand Names Meclomen®
Index Terms Meclofenamate Sodium
Pharmacologic Category Nonsteroidal Anti-inflammatory Drug (NSAID), Oral
Additional Appendix Information
Nonsteroidal Anti-inflammatory Agents *on page 1894*
Use Treatment of inflammatory disorders, arthritis, mild to moderate pain, dysmenorrhea
Restrictions An FDA-approved medication guide must be distributed when dispensing an oral outpatient prescription (new or refill) where this medication is to be used without direct supervision of a healthcare provider. Medication guides are available at http://www.fda.gov/cder/Offices/ODS/medication_guides.htm.
Pregnancy Risk Factor C/D (3rd trimester)
(Continued)

Meclofenamate *(Continued)*

Pregnancy Implications May cause premature closure of the ductus arteriosus in the 3rd trimester of pregnancy.

Lactation

Enters breast milk/not recommended

Contraindications Hypersensitivity to meclofenamate, aspirin, other NSAIDs, or any component of the formulation; perioperative pain in the setting of coronary artery bypass surgery (CABG); active GI bleeding, ulcer disease; pregnancy (3rd trimester)

Warnings/Precautions [U.S. Boxed Warning]: NSAIDs are associated with an increased risk of adverse cardiovascular events, including MI, stroke, and new onset or worsening of pre-existing hypertension. Risk may be increased with duration of use or pre-existing cardiovascular risk-factors or disease. Carefully evaluate individual cardiovascular risk profiles prior to prescribing. Use caution with fluid retention, CHF or hypertension. Concurrent administration of ibuprofen, and potentially other nonselective NSAIDs, may interfere with aspirin's cardioprotective effect.

Use of NSAIDs can compromise existing renal function. Renal toxicity can occur in patient with impaired renal function, dehydration, heart failure, liver dysfunction, those taking diuretics and ACEI and the elderly. Rehydrate patient before starting therapy. Monitor renal function closely. Use caution in patients with advanced renal disease.

[U.S. Boxed Warning]: NSAIDs may increase risk of gastrointestinal irritation, ulceration, bleeding, and perforation. These events may occur at any time during therapy and without warning. Use caution with a history of GI disease (bleeding or ulcers), concurrent therapy with aspirin, anticoagulants and/or corticosteroids, smoking, use of alcohol, the elderly or debilitated patients.

Use the lowest effective dose for the shortest duration of time, consistent with individual patient goals, to reduce risk of cardiovascular or GI adverse events. Alternate therapies should be considered for patients at high risk.

NSAIDs may cause serious skin adverse events including exfoliative dermatitis, Stevens-Johnson syndrome (SJS) and toxic epidermal necrolysis (TEN). Anaphylactoid reactions may occur, even without prior exposure; patients with "aspirin triad" (bronchial asthma, aspirin intolerance, rhinitis) may be at increased risk. Do not use in patients who experience bronchospasm, asthma, rhinitis, or urticaria with NSAID or aspirin therapy.

Use with caution in patients with decreased hepatic function. Closely monitor patients with any abnormal LFT. Severe hepatic reactions (eg, fulminant hepatitis, liver failure) have occurred with NSAID use, rarely; discontinue if signs or symptoms of liver disease develop, or if systemic manifestations occur.

The elderly are at increased risk for adverse effects (especially peptic ulceration, CNS effects, renal toxicity) from NSAIDs even at low doses

Withhold for at least 4-6 half-lives prior to surgical or dental procedures. Safety and efficacy have not been established in children <14 years of age.

Adverse Reactions

>10%:

Central nervous system: Dizziness

Dermatologic: Skin rash

Gastrointestinal: Abdominal cramps, heartburn, indigestion, nausea

1% to 10%:

Central nervous system: Headache, nervousness

Dermatologic: Itching

Endocrine & metabolic: Fluid retention

Gastrointestinal: Vomiting

Otic: Tinnitus

<1% (Limited to important or life-threatening): Acute renal failure, agranulocytosis, angioedema, arrhythmia, aseptic meningitis, bone marrow suppression, confusion, CHF, dyspnea, erythema multiforme, GI ulceration, hallucinations, hemolytic anemia, hepatitis, leukopenia, mental depression, peripheral neuropathy, somnolence, Stevens-Johnson syndrome, tachycardia, thrombocytopenia, toxic amblyopia, toxic epidermal necrolysis, urticaria

Overdosage/Toxicology Symptoms include drowsiness, lethargy, nausea, vomiting, seizures, paresthesia, headache, dizziness, GI bleeding, cerebral edema, cardiac arrest, and tinnitus. Management of nonsteroidal anti-inflammatory drug (NSAID) intoxication is primarily supportive and symptomatic. Fluid therapy is commonly effective in managing hypotension that may occur following an acute NSAID overdose, except when due to acute blood loss. Seizures tend to be very short-lived and often do not require drug treatment, although recurrent seizures should be treated with I.V. diazepam. Since many of NSAIDs undergo enterohepatic cycling, multiple doses of charcoal may be needed to reduce the potential for delayed toxicities.

Drug Interactions

Increased Effect/Toxicity: Anticoagulants (warfarin, heparin, LMWHs) in combination with NSAIDs can cause increased risk of bleeding. Other antiplatelet drugs (ticlopidine, clopidogrel, aspirin, abciximab, dipyridamole, eptifibatide, tirofiban) can cause an increased risk of bleeding. NSAIDs may increase serum creatinine, potassium, blood pressure, and cyclosporine levels during concurrent therapy; monitor cyclosporine levels and renal function carefully. Lithium levels can be increased; avoid concurrent use if possible or monitor lithium levels and adjust dose. Sulindac may have the least effect. When NSAID is stopped, lithium will need adjustment again. Corticosteroids may increase the risk of GI ulceration; avoid concurrent use. Serum concentration/toxicity of methotrexate may be increased. Concomitant use with fluoroquinolones may rarely increase risk of seizure.

Decreased Effect: Antihypertensive effects of ACE inhibitors, angiotensin antagonists, beta-blockers, diuretics, and hydralazine may be decreased by concurrent therapy with NSAIDs; monitor blood pressure. Cholestyramine (and other bile acid sequestrants) may decrease the absorption of NSAIDs; separate by at least 2 hours. Salicylates' antiplatelet effect may be reduced.

Ethanol/Nutrition/Herb Interactions
Ethanol: Avoid ethanol (may enhance gastric mucosal irritation).
Herb/Nutraceutical: Avoid alfalfa, anise, bilberry, bladderwrack, bromelain, cat's claw, celery, coleus, cordyceps, dong quai, evening primrose, feverfew, fenugreek, garlic, ginger, ginkgo biloboa, red clover, horse chestnut, grapeseed, green tea, ginseng, guggul, horse chestnut seed, horseradish, licorice, prickly ash, red clover, reishi, SAMe, sweet clover, turmeric, white willow (all have additional antiplatelet activity).

Mechanism of Action Inhibits prostaglandin synthesis by decreasing the activity of the enzyme, cyclooxygenase, which results in decreased formation of prostaglandin precursors

Pharmacodynamics/Kinetics
Duration: 2-4 hours
Distribution: Crosses placenta
Protein binding: 99%
Half-life elimination: 2-3.3 hours
Time to peak, serum: 0.5-1.5 hours
Excretion: Primarily urine and feces (as metabolites)

Dosage Children >14 years and Adults: Oral:
Mild to moderate pain: 50 mg every 4-6 hours; increases to 100 mg may be required; maximum dose: 400 mg
Rheumatoid arthritis and osteoarthritis: 50 mg every 4-6 hours; increase, over weeks, to 200-400 mg/day in 3-4 divided doses; do not exceed 400 mg/day; maximal benefit for any dose may not be seen for 2-3 weeks

Dietary Considerations May be taken with food, milk, or antacids.

Test Interactions Increased chloride (S), increased sodium (S)

Dosage Forms Capsule, as sodium: 50 mg, 100 mg

- ◆ **Meclofenamate Sodium** *see* Meclofenamate *on page 1063*
- ◆ **Meclomen® (Can)** *see* Meclofenamate *on page 1063*
- ◆ **Meclozine Hydrochloride** *see* Meclizine *on page 1063*
- ◆ **Med-Diltiazem (Can)** *see* Diltiazem *on page 509*
- ◆ **Medent-DM** *see* Guaifenesin, Pseudoephedrine, and Dextromethorphan *on page 821*
- ◆ **Medicinal Carbon** *see* Charcoal *on page 338*
- ◆ **Medicinal Charcoal** *see* Charcoal *on page 338*
- ◆ **Medicone® [OTC]** *see* Phenylephrine *on page 1358*
- ◆ **Medigesic®** *see* Butalbital, Acetaminophen, and Caffeine *on page 259*
- ◆ **Medi-Synal [OTC]** *see* Acetaminophen and Pseudoephedrine *on page 33*
- ◆ **Medrol®** *see* MethylPREDNISolone *on page 1122*

MedroxyPROGESTERone (me DROKS ee proe JES te rone)

U.S. Brand Names Depo-Provera®; Depo-Provera® Contraceptive; depo-subQ provera 104™; Provera®

Canadian Brand Names Alti-MPA; Apo-Medroxy®; Depo-Prevera®; Depo-Provera®; Gen-Medroxy; Novo-Medrone; Provera®; Provera-Pak

Index Terms Acetoxymethylprogesterone; Medroxyprogesterone Acetate; Methylacetoxyprogesterone; MPA

Pharmacologic Category Contraceptive; Progestin

Use Endometrial carcinoma or renal carcinoma; secondary amenorrhea or abnormal uterine bleeding due to hormonal imbalance; reduction of endometrial hyperplasia in nonhysterectomized postmenopausal women receiving conjugated estrogens; prevention of pregnancy; management of endometriosis-associated pain

Pregnancy Risk Factor X

Pregnancy Implications There is an increased risk of minor birth defects in children whose mothers take progesterones during the first 4 months of pregnancy. Hypospadias has been reported in male and mild masculinization of the external genitalia has been reported in female babies exposed during the first trimester. High doses are used to impair fertility. Low birth weight has been reported in neonates from unexpected pregnancies which occurred 1-2 months following injection of medroxyprogesterone (MPA) contraceptive. Ectopic pregnancies have been reported with use of the MPA contraceptive injection. When therapy is discontinued, fertility returns sooner in women of lower body weight. Median time to conception/return to ovulation following discontinuation of MPA contraceptive injection is 10 months following the last injection.

Lactation Enters breast milk/compatible

Medication Safety Issues
Sound-alike/look-alike issues:
MedroxyPROGESTERone may be confused with hydroxyprogesterone, methylPREDNISolone, methylTESTOSTERone
Provera® may be confused with Covera®, Parlodel®, Premarin®

The injection dosage form is available in different formulations. Carefully review prescriptions to assure the correct formulation and route of administration.

Contraindications Hypersensitivity to medroxyprogesterone or any component of the formulation; history of or current thrombophlebitis or venous thromboembolic disorders (including DVT, PE); cerebral vascular disease; severe hepatic dysfunction or disease; carcinoma of the breast or genital organs, undiagnosed vaginal bleeding; missed abortion, diagnostic test for pregnancy, pregnancy

Warnings/Precautions [U.S. Boxed Warning]: Prolonged use of medroxyprogesterone contraceptive injection may result in a loss of bone mineral density (BMD). Loss is related to the duration of use, and may not be completely reversible on discontinuation of the drug. The impact on peak bone mass in adolescents should be considered in treatment decisions. **[U.S. Boxed Warning]: Long-term use (ie, >2 years) should be limited to**
(Continued)

MedroxyPROGESTERone *(Continued)*

situations where other birth control methods are inadequate. Consider other methods of birth control in women with (or at risk for) osteoporosis.

Use caution with cardiovascular disease or dysfunction. MPA used in combination with estrogen may increase the risks of hypertension, myocardial infarction (MI), stroke, pulmonary emboli (PE), and deep vein thrombosis; incidence of these effects was shown to be significantly increased in postmenopausal women using conjugated equine estrogens (CEE) in combination with MPA. MPA in combination with estrogens should not be used to prevent coronary heart disease.

The risk of dementia may be increased in postmenopausal women; increased incidence was observed in women ≥65 years of age taking MPA in combination with CEE. An increased risk of invasive breast cancer was observed in postmenopausal women using MPA in combination with CEE. An increase in abnormal mammograms has also been reported with estrogen and progestin therapy.

Discontinue pending examination in cases of sudden partial or complete vision loss, sudden onset of proptosis, diplopia, or migraine; discontinue permanently if papilledema or retinal vascular lesions are observed on examination. Use with caution in patients with diseases that may be exacerbated by fluid retention (including asthma, epilepsy, migraine, diabetes, or renal dysfunction). Use caution with history of depression. Whenever possible, progestins in combination with estrogens should be discontinued at least 4-6 weeks prior to surgeries associated with an increased risk of thromboembolism or during periods of prolonged immobilization. Progestins used in combination with estrogen should be used for shortest duration possible consistent with treatment goals. Conduct periodic risk:benefit assessments.

Adverse Reactions Adverse effects as reported with any dosage form; percent ranges presented are noted with the MPA contraceptive injection:

>5%:
  Central nervous system: Dizziness, headache, nervousness
  Endocrine & metabolic: Libido decreased, menstrual irregularities (includes bleeding, amenorrhea, or both)
  Gastrointestinal: Abdominal pain/discomfort, weight changes (average 3-5 pounds after 1 year, 8 pounds after 2 years)
  Neuromuscular & skeletal: Weakness

1% to 5%:
  Cardiovascular: Edema
  Central nervous system: Depression, fatigue, insomnia, irritability, pain
  Dermatologic: Acne, alopecia, rash
  Endocrine & metabolic: Anorgasmia, breast pain, hot flashes
  Gastrointestinal: Bloating, nausea
  Genitourinary: Cervical smear abnormal, leukorrhea, menometrorrhagia, menorrhagia, pelvic pain, urinary tract infection, vaginitis, vaginal infection, vaginal hemorrhage
  Local: Injection site atrophy, injection site reaction, injection site pain
  Neuromuscular & skeletal: Arthralgia, backache, leg cramp
  Respiratory: Respiratory tract infections

<1% (Limited to important or life-threatening): Allergic reaction, anaphylaxis, anaphylactoid reactions, anemia, angioedema, appetite changes, asthma, axillary swelling, blood dyscrasia, body odor, bone mineral density decreased, breast cancer, breast changes, cervical cancer, chest pain, chills, chloasma, convulsions, deep vein thrombosis, diaphoresis, drowsiness, dry skin, dysmenorrhea, dyspareunia, dyspnea, facial palsy, fever, galactorrhea, genitourinary infections, glucose tolerance decreased, hirsutism, hoarseness, jaundice, lack of return to fertility, lactation decreased, libido increased, melasma, nipple bleeding, osteoporosis, osteoporotic fractures, paralysis, paresthesia, pruritus, pulmonary embolus, rectal bleeding, scleroderma, sensation of pregnancy, somnolence, syncope, tachycardia, thirst, thrombophlebitis, uterine hyperplasia, vaginal cysts, varicose veins; residual lump, sterile abscess, or skin discoloration at the injection site

Overdosage/Toxicology Toxicity is unlikely following single exposures of excessive doses. Supportive treatment is adequate in most cases.

Drug Interactions

Cytochrome P450 Effect: Substrate of CYP3A4 (major); **Induces** CYP3A4 (weak)

Decreased Effect: Acitretin, and griseofulvin may diminish the therapeutic effect of progestin contraceptives (contraceptive failure is possible). CYP3A4 inducers may decrease the levels/effects of medroxyprogesterone; example inducers include aminoglutethimide, carbamazepine, nafcillin, nevirapine, phenobarbital, phenytoin, and rifamycins. Progestins may diminish the anticoagulant effect of coumarin derivatives; and in contrast, enhanced anticoagulant effects have also been noted with some products.

Ethanol/Nutrition/Herb Interactions

Ethanol: Avoid ethanol (may increase risk of osteoporosis).

Food: Bioavailability of the oral tablet is increased when taken with food; half-life is unchanged.

Herb/Nutraceutical: St John's wort may diminish the therapeutic effect of progestin contraceptives (contraceptive failure is possible).

Stability Store at controlled room temperature.

Mechanism of Action Inhibits secretion of pituitary gonadotropins, which prevents follicular maturation and ovulation; causes endometrial thinning

Pharmacodynamics/Kinetics

Absorption: Oral: Well absorbed; I.M.: Slow

Protein binding: 86% to 90% primarily to albumin; does not bind to sex hormone-binding globulin

Metabolism: Extensively hepatic via hydroxylation and conjugation; forms metabolites

Time to peak: Oral: 2-4 hours

Half-life elimination: Oral: 12-17 hours; I.M. (Depo-Provera® Contraceptive): 50 days; SubQ: ~40 days

Excretion: Urine

Dosage

Adolescents and Adults:

Amenorrhea: Oral: 5-10 mg/day for 5-10 days

Abnormal uterine bleeding: Oral: 5-10 mg for 5-10 days starting on day 16 or 21 of cycle

Contraception:

Depo-Provera® Contraceptive: I.M.: 150 mg every 3 months

depo-subQ provera 104™: SubQ: 104 mg every 3 months (every 12-14 weeks)

Endometriosis: depo-subQ provera 104™: SubQ: 104 mg every 3 months (every 12-14 weeks)

Adults:

Endometrial or renal carcinoma (Depo-Provera®): I.M.: 400-1000 mg/week

Accompanying cyclic estrogen therapy, postmenopausal: Oral: 5-10 mg for 12-14 consecutive days each month, starting on day 1 or day 16 of the cycle; lower doses may be used if given with estrogen continuously throughout the cycle

Dosing adjustment in hepatic impairment: Use is contraindicated with severe impairment. Consider lower dose or less frequent administration with mild-to-moderate impairment. Use of the contraceptive injection has not been studied in patients with hepatic impairment; consideration should be given to not readminister if jaundice develops

Dietary Considerations Ensure adequate calcium and vitamin D intake when used for the prevention of pregnancy

Administration

I.M.: Depo-Provera® Contraceptive: Administer first dose during the first 5 days of menstrual period, or within the first 5 days postpartum if not breast-feeding, or at the sixth week postpartum if breast feeding exclusively. Shake vigorously prior to administration. Administer by deep I.M. injection in the gluteal or deltoid muscle.

SubQ: depo-subQ provera 104™: Administer first dose during the first 5 days of menstrual period, or at the sixth week postpartum if breast-feeding. Shake vigorously prior to administration. Administer by SubQ injection in the upper thigh or abdomen; avoid boney areas and the umbilicus. Administer over 5-7 seconds. Do not rub the injection area. When switching from combined hormonal contraceptives (estrogen plus progestin), the first injection should be within 7 days after the last active pill, or removal of patch or ring. If switching from the I.M. to SubQ formulation, the next dose should be given within the prescribed dosing period for the I.M. injection.

Monitoring Parameters Before starting therapy, a physical exam with reference to the breasts and pelvis are recommended, including a Papanicolaou smear. Exam may be deferred if appropriate prior to administration of MPA contraceptive injection; pregnancy should be ruled out prior to use. Monitor patient closely for loss of vision, sudden onset of proptosis, diplopia, migraine; signs and symptoms of thromboembolic disorders; signs or symptoms of depression; glucose in diabetics; blood pressure

Test Interactions

The following tests may be decreased: Steroid levels (plasma and urinary), gonadotropin levels, SHBG concentration, T_3 uptake

The following tests may be increased: Protein-bound iodine, butanol extractable protein-bound iodine, Factors II, VII, VIII, IX, X

Pathologist should be advised of estrogen/progesterone therapy when specimens are submitted.

Dosage Forms

Injection, suspension, as acetate: 150 mg/mL (1 mL)

Depo-Provera®: 400 mg/mL (2.5 mL)

Depo-Provera® Contraceptive: 150 mg/mL (1 mL) [prefilled syringe or vial]

depo-subQ provera 104™: 104 mg/0.65 mL (0.65 mL) [prefilled syringe]

Tablet, as acetate (Provera®): 2.5 mg, 5 mg, 10 mg

- ◆ **Medroxyprogesterone Acetate** see MedroxyPROGESTERone on page 1065
- ◆ **Medroxyprogesterone and Estrogens (Conjugated)** see Estrogens (Conjugated/Equine) and Medroxyprogesterone on page 634

Medrysone (ME dri sone)

U.S. Brand Names HMS Liquifilm® [DSC]

Pharmacologic Category Corticosteroid, Ophthalmic

Use Treatment of allergic conjunctivitis, vernal conjunctivitis, episcleritis, ophthalmic epinephrine sensitivity reaction

Pregnancy Risk Factor C

Lactation Excretion in breast milk unknown/use caution

Contraindications Hypersensitivity to medrysone or any component of the formulation; fungal, viral, or untreated pus-forming bacterial ocular infections; not for use in iritis and uveitis

Warnings/Precautions Prolonged use has been associated with the development of corneal or scleral perforation and posterior subcapsular cataracts; may mask or enhance the establishment of acute purulent untreated infections of the eye; use caution in patients with glaucoma. May mask infection or enhance existing ocular infection. Medrysone is a synthetic corticosteroid; structurally related to progesterone; if no improvement after several days of treatment, discontinue medrysone and institute other therapy; duration of therapy: 3-4 days to several weeks dependent on type and severity of disease; taper dose to avoid disease exacerbation. Safety and efficacy have not been established in children <3 years of age.

Adverse Reactions Frequency not defined: Ocular: Acute anterior uveitis, allergic reactions, blurred vision (mild, temporary), burning, cataracts, conjunctivitis, corneal thinning, corneal ulcers, delayed wound healing, foreign body sensation, glaucoma, IOP increased, keratitis, mydriasis, optic nerve damage, ptosis, secondary ocular infection stinging, visual activity defects

Overdosage/Toxicology Systemic toxicity is unlikely from the ophthalmic preparation.

Stability Store at room temperature of 25°C (77°F); do not freeze.

(Continued)

Medrysone *(Continued)*

Mechanism of Action Decreases inflammation by suppression of migration of polymorpho-nuclear leukocytes and reversal of increased capillary permeability

Pharmacodynamics/Kinetics
Absorption: Through aqueous humor
Metabolism: Hepatic if absorbed
Excretion: Urine and feces

Dosage Children ≥3 years and Adults: Ophthalmic: Instill 1 drop in conjunctival sac 2-4 times/day up to every 4 hours; may use every 1-2 hours during first 1-2 days

Administration Ophthalmic: Shake well before using. Do not touch dropper to the eye.

Monitoring Parameters Intraocular pressure (if duration of therapy is >10 days); periodic examination of lens (with prolonged use)

Dosage Forms [DSC] = Discontinued product
Solution, ophthalmic: 1% (5 mL, 10 mL) [contains benzalkonium chloride] [DSC]

♦ **Mefenamic-250 (Can)** *see* Mefenamic Acid *on page 1068*

Mefenamic Acid (me fe NAM ik AS id)

U.S. Brand Names Ponstel®

Canadian Brand Names Apo-Mefenamic®; Dom-Mefenamic Acid; Mefenamic-250; Nu-Mefenamic; PMS-Mefenamic Acid; Ponstan®

Pharmacologic Category Nonsteroidal Anti-inflammatory Drug (NSAID), Oral

Additional Appendix Information
Nonsteroidal Anti-inflammatory Agents *on page 1894*

Use Short-term relief of mild to moderate pain including primary dysmenorrhea

Restrictions An FDA-approved medication guide must be distributed when dispensing an oral outpatient prescription (new or refill) where this medication is to be used without direct supervision of a healthcare provider. Medication guides are available at http://www.fda.gov/cder/Offices/ODS/medication_guides.htm.

Pregnancy Risk Factor C/D (3rd trimester)

Lactation Enters breast milk (trace amounts)/not recommended (AAP rates "compatible")

Medication Safety Issues
Sound-alike/look-alike issues:
Ponstel® may be confused with Pronestyl®

Contraindications Hypersensitivity to mefenamic acid, aspirin, other NSAIDs, or any component of the formulation; perioperative pain in the setting of coronary artery bypass surgery (CABG); active ulceration or chronic inflammation of the GI tract; renal disease; pregnancy (3rd trimester)

Warnings/Precautions [U.S. Boxed Warning]: NSAIDs are associated with an increased risk of adverse cardiovascular events, including MI, stroke, and new onset or worsening of pre-existing hypertension. Risk may be increased with duration of use or pre-existing cardiovascular risk-factors or disease. Carefully evaluate individual cardiovascular risk profiles prior to prescribing. Use caution with fluid retention, CHF or hypertension. Concurrent administration of ibuprofen, and potentially other nonselective NSAIDs, may interfere with aspirin's cardioprotective effect.

Use of NSAIDs can compromise existing renal function. Renal toxicity can occur in patient with impaired renal function, dehydration, heart failure, liver dysfunction, those taking diuretics and ACEI and the elderly. Rehydrate patient before starting therapy. Monitor renal function closely. Mefenamic acid is not recommended for patients with advanced renal disease.

[U.S. Boxed Warning]: NSAIDs may increase risk of gastrointestinal irritation, ulceration, bleeding, and perforation. These events may occur at any time during therapy and without warning. Use caution with a history of GI disease (bleeding or ulcers), concurrent therapy with aspirin, anticoagulants and/or corticosteroids, smoking, use of alcohol, the elderly or debilitated patients.

Use the lowest effective dose for the shortest duration of time, consistent with individual patient goals, to reduce risk of cardiovascular or GI adverse events. Alternate therapies should be considered for patients at high risk.

NSAIDs may cause serious skin adverse events including exfoliative dermatitis, Stevens-Johnson syndrome (SJS) and toxic epidermal necrolysis (TEN). Anaphylactoid reactions may occur, even without prior exposure; patients with "aspirin triad" (bronchial asthma, aspirin intolerance, rhinitis) may be at increased risk. Do not use in patients who experience bronchospasm, asthma, rhinitis, or urticaria with NSAID or aspirin therapy.

Use with caution in patients with decreased hepatic function. Closely monitor patients with any abnormal LFT. Severe hepatic reactions (eg, fulminant hepatitis, liver failure) have occurred with NSAID use, rarely; discontinue if signs or symptoms of liver disease develop, or if systemic manifestations occur.

The elderly are at increased risk for adverse effects (especially peptic ulceration, CNS effects, renal toxicity) from NSAIDs even at low doses.

Withhold for at least 4-6 half-lives prior to surgical or dental procedures. Safety and efficacy have not been established in children <14 years of age.

Adverse Reactions
1% to 10%:
Central nervous system: Headache, nervousness, dizziness (3% to 9%)
Dermatologic: Itching, rash
Endocrine & metabolic: Fluid retention
Gastrointestinal: Abdominal cramps, heartburn, indigestion, nausea (1% to 10%), vomiting (1% to 10%), diarrhea (1% to 10%), constipation (1% to 10%), abdominal distress/

cramping/pain (1% to 10%), dyspepsia (1% to 10%), flatulence (1% to 10%), gastric or duodenal ulcer with bleeding or perforation (1% to 10%), gastritis (1% to 10%)

Hematologic: Bleeding (1% to 10%)

Hepatic: Elevated LFTs (1% to 10%)

Otic: Tinnitus (1% to 10%)

<1%: CHF, hypertension, arrhythmia, tachycardia, confusion, hallucinations, aseptic meningitis, mental depression, drowsiness, insomnia, urticaria, erythema multiforme, toxic epidermal necrolysis, Stevens-Johnson syndrome, angioedema, polydipsia, hot flashes, gastritis, GI ulceration, cystitis, polyuria, agranulocytosis, anemia, hemolytic anemia, bone marrow suppression, leukopenia, thrombocytopenia, hepatitis, peripheral neuropathy, toxic amblyopia, blurred vision, conjunctivitis, dry eyes, decreased hearing, acute renal failure, dyspnea, allergic rhinitis, epistaxis, stomatitis

Overdosage/Toxicology Symptoms include CNS stimulation, agitation, and seizures. Management of nonsteroidal anti-inflammatory drug (NSAID) intoxication is primarily supportive and symptomatic. Fluid therapy is commonly effective in managing hypotension that may occur following an acute NSAID overdose, except when due to acute blood loss. Seizures tend to be very short-lived and often do not require drug treatment, although recurrent seizures should be treated with I.V. diazepam. Since many of the NSAIDs undergo enterohepatic cycling, multiple doses of charcoal may be needed to reduce the potential for delayed toxicities.

Drug Interactions

Cytochrome P450 Effect: Substrate of CYP2C9 (minor); **Inhibits** CYP2C9 (strong)

Increased Effect/Toxicity: Anticoagulants (warfarin, heparin, LMWHs) in combination with NSAIDs can cause increased risk of bleeding. Other antiplatelet drugs (ticlopidine, clopidogrel, aspirin, abciximab, dipyridamole, eptifibatide, tirofiban) can cause an increased risk of bleeding. Mefenamic acid may increase the levels/effects of CYP2C9 substrates. Example substrates include bosentan, dapsone, fluoxetine, glimepiride, glipizide, losartan, montelukast, nateglinide, paclitaxel, phenytoin, warfarin, and zafirlukast. NSAIDs may increase serum creatinine, potassium, blood pressure, and cyclosporine levels during concurrent therapy; monitor cyclosporine levels and renal function carefully. Lithium levels can be increased; avoid concurrent use if possible or monitor lithium levels and adjust dose. Sulindac may have the least effect. When NSAID is stopped, lithium will need adjustment again. Corticosteroids may increase the risk of GI ulceration; avoid concurrent use. Serum concentration/toxicity of methotrexate may be increased. Concomitant use with fluoroquinolones may rarely increase risk of seizure.

Decreased Effect: Antihypertensive effects of ACE inhibitors, angiotensin antagonists, beta-blockers, diuretics, and hydralazine may be decreased by concurrent therapy with NSAIDs; monitor blood pressure. Salicylates' antiplatelet effect may be reduced. Cholestyramine (and other bile acid sequestrants) may decrease the absorption of NSAIDs; separate by at least 2 hours.

Ethanol/Nutrition/Herb Interactions

Ethanol: Avoid ethanol (may enhance gastric mucosal irritation).

Herb/Nutraceutical: Avoid alfalfa, anise, bilberry, bladderwrack, bromelain, cat's claw, celery, coleus, cordyceps, dong quai, evening primrose, feverfew, fenugreek, garlic, ginger, ginkgo biloba, red clover, horse chestnut, grapeseed, green tea, ginseng, guggul, horse chestnut seed, horseradish, licorice, prickly ash, red clover, reishi, SAMe, sweet clover, turmeric, white willow (all have additional antiplatelet activity).

Mechanism of Action Inhibits prostaglandin synthesis by decreasing the activity of the enzyme, cyclooxygenase, which results in decreased formation of prostaglandin precursors

Pharmacodynamics/Kinetics

Onset of action: Peak effect: 2-4 hours

Duration: ≤6 hours

Protein binding: High

Metabolism: Conjugated hepatically

Half-life elimination: 3.5 hours

Excretion: Urine (50%) and feces as unchanged drug and metabolites

Dosage Children >14 years and Adults: Oral: 500 mg to start then 250 mg every 4 hours as needed; maximum therapy: 1 week

Dosing adjustment/comments in renal impairment: Not recommended for use

Administration May be administered with food, milk, or antacids.

Test Interactions Increased chloride (S), increased sodium (S), positive Coombs' [direct], false-positive urinary bilirubin

Dosage Forms Capsule: 250 mg

Mefloquine (ME floe kwin)

U.S. Brand Names Lariam®

Canadian Brand Names Apo-Mefloquine®; Lariam®

Index Terms Mefloquine Hydrochloride

Pharmacologic Category Antimalarial Agent

Additional Appendix Information

Malaria Treatment *on page 2003*

Use Treatment of acute malarial infections and prevention of malaria

Restrictions An FDA-approved medication guide and wallet card must be distributed when dispensing an outpatient prescription (new or refill) to prevent malaria where this medication is to be used without direct supervision of a healthcare provider. Medication guides are available at http://www.fda.gov/cder/Offices/ODS/medication_guides.htm.

Pregnancy Risk Factor C

Pregnancy Implications Mefloquine crosses the placenta and is teratogenic in animals. There are no adequate and well-controlled studies in pregnant women, however, clinical experience has not shown teratogenic or embryotoxic effects; use with caution during pregnancy if travel to endemic areas cannot be postponed. Nonpregnant women of childbearing potential are advised to use contraception and avoid pregnancy during malaria prophylaxis (Continued)

Mefloquine *(Continued)*

and for 3 months thereafter. In case of an unplanned pregnancy, treatment with mefloquine is not considered a reason for pregnancy termination.

Lactation Enters breast milk/not recommended

Contraindications Hypersensitivity mefloquine, related compounds (such as quinine and quinidine), or any component of the formulation; history of convulsions; cardiac conduction abnormalities; severe psychiatric disorder (including active or recent history of depression, generalized anxiety disorder, psychosis, or schizophrenia)

Warnings/Precautions Use with caution in patients with a previous history of depression (see Contraindications regarding severe psychiatric illness, including active/recent depression). May cause a range of psychiatric symptoms (anxiety, paranoia, depression, hallucinations and psychosis). Occasionally, symptoms have been reported to persist long after mefloquine has been discontinued. Rare cases of suicidal ideation and suicide have been reported (no causal relationship established). The appearance of psychiatric symptoms such as acute anxiety, depression, restlessness or confusion may be considered a prodrome to more serious events. When used as prophylaxis, substitute an alternative medication. Discontinue if unexplained neuropsychiatric disturbances occur. Use caution in patients with significant cardiac disease. If mefloquine is to be used for a prolonged period, periodic evaluations including liver function tests and ophthalmic examinations should be performed. (Retinal abnormalities have not been observed with mefloquine in humans; however, it has with long-term administration to rats.) In cases of life-threatening, serious, or overwhelming malaria infections due to *Plasmodium falciparum*, patients should be treated with intravenous antimalarial drug. Mefloquine may be given orally to complete the course. Dizziness, loss of balance, and other CNS disorders have been reported; due to long half-life, effects may persist after mefloquine is discontinued. Use caution in activities requiring alertness and fine motor coordination (driving, piloting planes, operating machinery, deep sea diving, etc).

Adverse Reactions

Frequency not defined: Neuropsychiatric events

1% to 10%:

Central nervous system: Headache, fever, chills, fatigue

Dermatologic: Rash

Gastrointestinal: Vomiting (3%), diarrhea, stomach pain, nausea, appetite decreased

Neuromuscular & skeletal: Myalgia

Otic: Tinnitus

<1% (Limited to important or life-threatening): Abnormal dreams, alopecia, ataxia, aggressive behavior, agitation, anaphylaxis, anxiety, arthralgia, AV block, bradycardia, chest pain, conduction abnormalities (transient), confusion, convulsions, depression, diaphoresis (increased), dizziness, dyspepsia, dyspnea, edema, emotional lability, encephalopathy, erythema multiforme, exanthema, extrasystoles, hallucinations, hearing impairment, hypotension, insomnia, leukocytosis, malaise, mood changes, muscle cramps/weakness, palpitation, panic attacks, paranoia, paresthesia, psychosis, pruritus, seizure, somnolence, Stevens-Johnson syndrome, suicidal ideation and behavior (causal relationship not established), syncope, tachycardia, thrombocytopenia, tremor, urticaria, vertigo, visual disturbances, weakness

Overdosage/Toxicology Following GI contamination, care is supportive only. Monitor cardiac function and psychiatric status for at least 24 hours.

Drug Interactions

Cytochrome P450 Effect: Substrate of CYP3A4 (major); **Inhibits** CYP2D6 (weak), 3A4 (weak)

Increased Effect/Toxicity: Use caution with drugs that alter cardiac conduction; increased toxicity with chloroquine, quinine, and quinidine (hold treatment until at least 12 hours after these later drugs). CYP3A4 inhibitors may increase the levels/effects of mefloquine; example inhibitors include azole antifungals, clarithromycin, diclofenac, doxycycline, erythromycin, imatinib, isoniazid, nefazodone, nicardipine, propofol, protease inhibitors, quinidine, telithromycin, and verapamil.

Decreased Effect: Mefloquine may decrease the effect of valproic acid, carbamazepine, phenobarbital, and phenytoin. CYP3A4 inducers may decrease the levels/effects of mefloquine; example inducers include aminoglutethimide, carbamazepine, nafcillin, nevirapine, phenobarbital, phenytoin, and rifamycins. Vaccination with oral live attenuated Ty21a vaccine should be delayed for at least 24 hours after the administration of mefloquine.

Ethanol/Nutrition/Herb Interactions Food: Food increases bioavailability by ~40%.

Stability Store at 25°C (77°F); excursions permitted to 15°C to 30°C (59°F to 86°F).

Mechanism of Action Mefloquine is a quinoline-methanol compound structurally similar to quinine; mefloquine's effectiveness in the treatment and prophylaxis of malaria is due to the destruction of the asexual blood forms of the malarial pathogens that affect humans, *Plasmodium falciparum*, *P. vivax*, *P. malariae*, *P. ovale*

Pharmacodynamics/Kinetics

Absorption: Well absorbed

Distribution: V_d: 19 L/kg; blood, urine, CSF, tissues; enters breast milk

Protein binding: 98%

Metabolism: Extensively hepatic; main metabolite is inactive

Bioavailability: Increased by food

Half-life elimination: 21-22 days

Time to peak, plasma: 6-24 hours (median: ~17 hours)

Excretion: Primarily bile and feces; urine (9% as unchanged drug, 4% as primary metabolite)

Dosage Oral (dose expressed as mg of mefloquine hydrochloride):

Children ≥6 months and >5 kg:

Malaria treatment: 20-25 mg/kg in 2 divided doses, taken 6-8 hours apart (maximum: 1250 mg) Take with food and an ample amount of water. If clinical improvement is not seen within 48-72 hours, an alternative therapy should be used for retreatment.

Malaria prophylaxis: 5 mg/kg/once weekly (maximum dose: 250 mg) starting 1 week before, arrival in endemic area, continuing weekly during travel and for 4 weeks after leaving endemic area. Take with food and an ample amount of water.

Adults:

Malaria treatment (mild to moderate infection): 5 tablets (1250 mg) as a single dose. Take with food and at least 8 oz of water. If clinical improvement is not seen within 48-72 hours, an alternative therapy should be used for retreatment.

Malaria prophylaxis: 1 tablet (250 mg) weekly starting 1 week before, arrival in endemic area, continuing weekly during travel and for 4 weeks after leaving endemic area. Take with food and at least 8 oz of water.

Dosage adjustment in renal impairment: No dosage adjustment needed in patients with renal impairment or on dialysis.

Dosage adjustment in hepatic impairment: Half-life may be prolonged and plasma levels may be higher.

Dietary Considerations Take with food and with at least 8 oz of water.

Administration Administer with food and with at least 8 oz of water. When used for malaria prophylaxis, dose should be taken once weekly on the same day each week. If vomiting occurs within 30-60 minutes after dose, an additional half-dose should be given. Tablets may be crushed and suspended in a small amount of water, milk, or another beverage for persons unable to swallow tablets.

Monitoring Parameters LFTS; ocular examination

Dosage Forms Tablet, as hydrochloride: 250 mg [equivalent to 228 mg base]

♦ **Mefloquine Hydrochloride** *see* Mefloquine *on page 1069*

♦ **Mefoxin**® *see* Cefoxitin *on page 316*

♦ **Megace**® *see* Megestrol *on page 1071*

♦ **Megace**® **ES** *see* Megestrol *on page 1071*

♦ **Megace**® **OS (Can)** *see* Megestrol *on page 1071*

♦ **Megadophilus**® **[OTC]** *see* Lactobacillus *on page 969*

Megestrol (me JES trole)

U.S. Brand Names Megace®; Megace® ES

Canadian Brand Names Apo-Megestrol®; Megace®; Megace® OS; Nu-Megestrol

Index Terms 5071-1DL(6); Megestrol Acetate; NSC-10363

Pharmacologic Category Antineoplastic Agent, Hormone; Appetite Stimulant; Progestin

Use Palliative treatment of breast and endometrial carcinoma; treatment of anorexia, cachexia, or unexplained significant weight loss in patients with AIDS

Pregnancy Risk Factor X

Lactation Enters breast milk/contraindicated

Medication Safety Issues

Sound-alike/look-alike issues:

Megace® may be confused with Reglan®

Contraindications Hypersensitivity to megestrol or any component of the formulation; pregnancy

Warnings/Precautions Use during the first few months of pregnancy is not recommended. Use with caution in patients with a history of thrombophlebitis. Elderly females may have vaginal bleeding or discharge.

Adverse Reactions

Cardiovascular: Edema, hypertension (≤8%), cardiomyopathy, palpitation

Central nervous system: Insomnia, fever (2% to 6%), headache (≤10%), pain (≤6%, similar to placebo), confusion (1% to 3%), convulsions (1% to 3%), depression (1% to 3%)

Dermatologic: Allergic rash (2% to 12%) with or without pruritus, alopecia

Endocrine & metabolic: Breakthrough bleeding and amenorrhea, spotting, changes in menstrual flow, changes in cervical erosion and secretions, increased breast tenderness, changes in vaginal bleeding pattern, edema, fluid retention, hyperglycemia (≤6%), diabetes, HPA axis suppression, adrenal insufficiency, Cushing's syndrome

Gastrointestinal: Weight gain (not attributed to edema or fluid retention), nausea, vomiting (7%), diarrhea (8% to 15%, similar to placebo), flatulence (≤10%), constipation (1% to 3%)

Genitourinary: Impotence (4% to 14%), decreased libido (≤5%)

Hepatic: Cholestatic jaundice, hepatotoxicity, hepatomegaly (1% to 3%)

Local: Thrombophlebitis

Neuromuscular & skeletal: Carpal tunnel syndrome, weakness, paresthesia (1% to 3%)

Respiratory: Hyperpnea, dyspnea (1% to 3%), cough (1% to 3%)

Miscellaneous: Diaphoresis

Overdosage/Toxicology Toxicity is unlikely following single exposures of excessive doses.

Ethanol/Nutrition/Herb Interactions Herb/Nutraceutical: Avoid black cohosh, dong quai in estrogen-dependent tumors.

Stability Store at 25°C (77°F); excursions permitted at 15°C to 30°C (59°F to 86°F).

Mechanism of Action A synthetic progestin with antiestrogenic properties which disrupt the estrogen receptor cycle. Megestrol interferes with the normal estrogen cycle and results in a lower LH titer. May also have a direct effect on the endometrium. Megestrol is an antineoplastic progestin thought to act through an antileutenizing effect mediated via the pituitary. May stimulate appetite by antagonizing the metabolic effects of catabolic cytokines.

Pharmacodynamics/Kinetics

Absorption: Well absorbed orally

Metabolism: Completely hepatic to free steroids and glucuronide conjugates

Time to peak, serum: 1-3 hours

Half-life elimination: 15-100 hours

Excretion: Urine (57% to 78% as steroid metabolites and inactive compound); feces (8% to 30%)

Dosage Adults: Oral:

Female (refer to individual protocols):

Breast carcinoma: 40 mg 4 times/day

Endometrial carcinoma: 40-320 mg/day in divided doses; use for 2 months to determine efficacy; maximum doses used have been up to 800 mg/day

(Continued)

Megestrol *(Continued)*

Male/Female: HIV-related cachexia:

Megace®: Initial dose: 800 mg/day; daily doses of 400 and 800 mg/day were found to be clinically effective

Megace ES®: 625 mg/day

Dosing adjustment in renal impairment: No data available; however, the urinary excretion of megestrol acetate administered in doses of 4-90 mg ranged from 56% to 78% within 10 days

Hemodialysis: Megestrol acetate has not been tested for dialyzability; however, due to its low solubility, it is postulated that dialysis would not be an effective means of treating an overdose

Administration Megestrol acetate (Megace®) oral suspension is compatible with water, orange juice, apple juice, or Sustacal H.C. for immediate consumption.

Monitoring Parameters Observe for signs of thromboembolic phenomena

Test Interactions Altered thyroid and liver function tests

Dosage Forms

Suspension, oral, as acetate: 40 mg/mL (240 mL, 480 mL)

Megace®: 40 mg/mL (240 mL) [contains alcohol 0.06% and sodium benzoate; lemon-lime flavor]

Megace® ES: 125 mg/mL (150 mL) [contains alcohol 0.06% and sodium benzoate; lemon-lime flavor]

Tablet, as acetate: 20 mg, 40 mg

♦ **Megestrol Acetate** *see Megestrol on page 1071*

♦ **Melanex®** *see Hydroquinone on page 859*

♦ **Mellaril® (Can)** *see Thioridazine on page 1672*

Meloxicam *(mel OKS i kam)*

U.S. Brand Names Mobic®

Canadian Brand Names Apo-Meloxicam®; CO Meloxicam; Gen-Meloxicam; Mobic®; Mobicox®; Novo-Meloxicam; PMS-Meloxicam

Pharmacologic Category Nonsteroidal Anti-inflammatory Drug (NSAID), Oral

Additional Appendix Information

Nonsteroidal Anti-inflammatory Agents *on page 1894*

Use Relief of signs and symptoms of osteoarthritis, rheumatoid arthritis, and juvenile rheumatoid arthritis (JRA)

Restrictions An FDA-approved medication guide must be distributed when dispensing an oral outpatient prescription (new or refill) where this medication is to be used without direct supervision of a healthcare provider. Medication guides are available at http://www.fda.gov/cder/Offices/ODS/medication_guides.htm.

Pregnancy Risk Factor C/D (3rd trimester)

Pregnancy Implications May cause premature closure of the ductus arteriosus in the 3rd trimester of pregnancy.

Lactation Excretion in breast milk unknown/not recommended

Contraindications Hypersensitivity to meloxicam, aspirin, other NSAIDs, or any component of the formulation; perioperative pain in the setting of coronary artery bypass surgery (CABG); pregnancy (3rd trimester)

Warnings/Precautions [U.S. Boxed Warning]: NSAIDs are associated with an increased risk of adverse cardiovascular events, including MI, stroke, and new onset or worsening of pre-existing hypertension. Risk may be increased with duration of use or pre-existing cardiovascular risk-factors or disease. Carefully evaluate individual cardiovascular risk profiles prior to prescribing. Use caution with fluid retention, CHF or hypertension. Concurrent administration of ibuprofen, and potentially other nonselective NSAIDs, may interfere with aspirin's cardioprotective effect.

Use of NSAIDs can compromise existing renal function. Renal toxicity can occur in patient with impaired renal function, dehydration, heart failure, liver dysfunction, those taking diuretics and ACEI and the elderly. Rehydrate patient before starting therapy. Monitor renal function closely. Meloxicam is not recommended for patients with advanced renal disease

[U.S. Boxed Warning]: NSAIDs may increase risk of gastrointestinal irritation, ulceration, bleeding, and perforation. These events may occur at any time during therapy and without warning. Use caution with a history of GI disease (bleeding or ulcers), concurrent therapy with aspirin, anticoagulants and/or corticosteroids, smoking, use of alcohol, the elderly or debilitated patients.

Use the lowest effective dose for the shortest duration of time, consistent with individual patient goals, to reduce risk of cardiovascular or GI adverse events. Alternate therapies should be considered for patients at high risk.

NSAIDs may cause serious skin adverse events including exfoliative dermatitis, Stevens-Johnson syndrome (SJS) and toxic epidermal necrolysis (TEN). Anaphylactoid reactions may occur, even without prior exposure; patients with "aspirin triad" (bronchial asthma, aspirin intolerance, rhinitis) may be at increased risk. Do not use in patients who experience bronchospasm, asthma, rhinitis, or urticaria with NSAID or aspirin therapy.

Use with caution in patients with decreased hepatic function. Closely monitor patients with any abnormal LFT. Severe hepatic reactions (eg, fulminant hepatitis, liver failure) have occurred with NSAID use, rarely; discontinue if signs or symptoms of liver disease develop, or if systemic manifestations occur.

The elderly are at increased risk for adverse effects (especially peptic ulceration, CNS effects, renal toxicity) from NSAIDs even at low doses.

Withhold for at least 4-6 half-lives prior to surgical or dental procedures. Safety and efficacy have not been established in pediatric patients <2 years of age.

Adverse Reactions Percentages reported in adult patients; abdominal pain, diarrhea, headache, pyrexia, and vomiting were reported more commonly in pediatric patients

2% to 10%:

Cardiovascular: Edema (<1% to 4%)

Central nervous system: Headache (2% to 8%), dizziness (<1% to 4%), insomnia (<1% to 4%)

Dermatologic: Pruritus (<1% to 2%), rash (<1% to 3%)

Gastrointestinal: Diarrhea (3% to 8%), dyspepsia (4% to 9%), nausea (2% to 7%), abdominal pain (2% to 5%), constipation (<1% to 3%), flatulence (<1% to 3%), vomiting (<1% to 3%)

Hematologic: Anemia (<1% to 4%)

Neuromuscular & skeletal: Arthralgia (<1% to 5%), back pain (<1% to 3%)

Respiratory: Upper respiratory infection (2% to 8%), cough (<1% to 2%), pharyngitis (<1% to 3%)

Miscellaneous: Flu-like syndrome (2% to 6%), falls (3%)

<2% (Limited to important or life-threatening): Agranulocytosis, allergic reaction, anaphylactic reaction, anaphylactoid reaction, angina, angioedema, arrhythmia, bronchospasm, bullous eruption, cardiac failure, colitis, depression, duodenal perforation, duodenal ulcer, erythema multiforme, gastric perforation, gastric ulcer, gastroesophageal reflux, gastrointestinal hemorrhage, hepatic failure, hepatitis, hyper-/hypotension, interstitial nephritis, intestinal perforation, jaundice, MI, pancreatitis, paresthesia, photosensitivity reaction, renal failure, seizure, shock, somnolence, Stevens-Johnson syndrome, syncope, thrombocytopenia, tinnitus, toxic epidermal necrolysis, tremor, ulcerative stomatitis, urticaria, vasculitis, vertigo

Overdosage/Toxicology Symptoms include lethargy, drowsiness, nausea, vomiting, and epigastric pain. Rarely, severe symptoms have been associated with NSAID overdose including apnea, metabolic acidosis, coma, nystagmus, seizures, leukocytosis, and renal failure. Management of nonsteroidal anti-inflammatory (NSAID) intoxication is supportive and symptomatic. Since meloxicam undergoes enterohepatic cycling, multiple doses of charcoal may be needed to reduce the potential for delayed toxicities. Cholestyramine has been shown to increase meloxicam clearance. Meloxicam is not dialyzable.

Drug Interactions

Cytochrome P450 Effect: Substrate (minor) of CYP2C9, 3A4; **Inhibits** CYP2C9 (weak)

Increased Effect/Toxicity: Anticoagulants (warfarin, heparin, LMWHs) in combination with NSAIDs can cause increased risk of bleeding. Antiplatelet drugs (ticlopidine, clopidogrel, aspirin, abciximab, dipyridamole, eptifibatide, tirofiban) can cause an increased risk of bleeding. Aspirin increases serum concentrations (AUC) of meloxicam (in addition to potential for additive adverse effects); concurrent use is not recommended. Corticosteroids may increase the risk of GI ulceration; avoid concurrent use. NSAIDs may increase serum creatinine, potassium, blood pressure, and cyclosporine levels; monitor cyclosporine levels and renal function carefully. Lithium levels can be increased; avoid concurrent use if possible or monitor lithium levels and adjust dose. When NSAID is stopped, lithium will need adjustment again. Serum concentration/toxicity of methotrexate may be increased. Warfarin INRs may be increased by meloxicam. Monitor INR closely, particularly during initiation or change in dose. May increase risk of bleeding. Use lowest possible dose for shortest duration possible. Concomitant use with fluoroquinolones may rarely increase risk of seizure.

Decreased Effect: Cholestyramine (and possibly colestipol) increases the clearance of meloxicam. Hydralazine's antihypertensive effect is decreased; avoid concurrent use. Loop diuretic efficacy (diuretic and antihypertensive effect) may be reduced by NSAIDs. Antihypertensive effects of thiazide diuretics are decreased; avoid concurrent use. Salicylates' antiplatelet effect may be reduced. NSAIDs may decrease the antihypertensive effect of beta-blockers, ACE inhibitors, and angiotensin antagonists. Cholestyramine (and other bile acid sequestrants) may decrease the absorption of NSAIDs; separate by at least 2 hours.

Ethanol/Nutrition/Herb Interactions

Ethanol: Avoid ethanol (may enhance gastric mucosal irritation).

Herb/Nutraceutical: Avoid alfalfa, anise, bilberry, bladderwrack, bromelain, cat's claw, celery, coleus, cordyceps, dong quai, evening primrose, feverfew, fenugreek, garlic, ginger, ginkgo biloboa, red clover, horse chestnut, grapeseed, green tea, ginseng, guggul, horse chestnut seed, horseradish, licorice, prickly ash, red clover, reishi, SAMe, sweet clover, turmeric, white willow (all have additional antiplatelet activity).

Stability Store at 25°C (77°F).

Mechanism of Action Inhibits prostaglandin synthesis by decreasing the activity of the enzyme, cyclooxygenase, which results in decreased formation of prostaglandin precursors

Pharmacodynamics/Kinetics

Distribution: 10 L

Protein binding: 99.4%

Metabolism: Hepatic via CYP2C9 and CYP3A4 (minor); forms 4 metabolites (inactive)

Bioavailability: 89%

Half-life elimination: Adults: 15-20 hours

Time to peak: Initial: 5-10 hours; Secondary: 12-14 hours

Excretion: Urine and feces (as inactive metabolites)

Dosage Oral:

Children ≥2 years: JRA: 0.125 mg/kg/day; maximum dose: 7.5 mg/day

Adults: Osteoarthritis, rheumatoid arthritis: Initial: 7.5 mg once daily; some patients may receive additional benefit from an increased dose of 15 mg once daily; maximum dose: 15 mg/day

Elderly: Increased concentrations may occur in elderly patients (particularly in females); however, no specific dosage adjustment is recommended

Dosage adjustment in renal impairment:

Mild-to-moderate impairment: No specific dosage recommendations

Significant impairment (Cl_{cr} ≤15 mL/minute): Avoid use

Hemodialysis: Supplemental dose after dialysis not necessary.

(Continued)

Meloxicam *(Continued)*

Dosage adjustment in hepatic impairment:
Mild (Child-Pugh class A) to moderate (Child-Pugh class B) hepatic dysfunction: No dosage adjustment is necessary

Severe hepatic impairment: Patients with severe hepatic impairment have not been adequately studied

Dietary Considerations Should be taken with food or milk to minimize gastrointestinal irritation.

Monitoring Parameters CBC, periodic liver function, renal function (serum BUN, and creatinine)

Dosage Forms
Suspension: 7.5 mg/5 mL (100 mL)
Mobic®: 7.5 mg/5 mL (100 mL) [contains sodium benzoate; raspberry flavor]
Tablet: 7.5 mg, 15 mg
Mobic®: 7.5 mg, 15 mg

♦ **Melpaque HP®** *see* Hydroquinone *on page 859*

Melphalan (MEL fa lan)

U.S. Brand Names Alkeran®
Canadian Brand Names Alkeran®
Index Terms L-PAM; L-Sarcolysin; NSC-8806; Phenylalanine Mustard
Pharmacologic Category Antineoplastic Agent, Alkylating Agent
Use Palliative treatment of multiple myeloma and nonresectable epithelial ovarian carcinoma
Unlabeled/Investigational Use Treatment of neuroblastoma, rhabdomyosarcoma, breast cancer; part of an induction regimen for marrow and stem cell transplantation
Pregnancy Risk Factor D
Pregnancy Implications Animal studies have demonstrated embryotoxicity and teratogenicity. Therapy may suppress ovarian function leading to amenorrhea. There are no adequate and well-controlled studies in pregnant women. Women of childbearing potential should be advised to avoid pregnancy while on melphalan therapy.
Lactation Excretion in breast milk unknown/not recommended
Medication Safety Issues
Sound-alike/look-alike issues:
Melphalan may be confused with Mephyton®, Myleran®
Alkeran® may be confused with Alferon®, Leukeran®

High alert medication: The Institute for Safe Medication Practices (ISMP) includes this medication among its list of drugs which have a heightened risk of causing significant patient harm when used in error.

Contraindications Hypersensitivity to melphalan or any component of the formulation; severe bone marrow suppression; patients whose disease was resistant to prior melphalan therapy; pregnancy
Warnings/Precautions Hazardous agent - use appropriate precautions for handling and disposal. **[U.S. Boxed Warning]: Is potentially mutagenic, leukemogenic** and carcinogenic. Suppresses ovarian function and produces amenorrhea; may also cause testicular suppression. **[U.S. Boxed Warning]: Bone marrow suppression is common.** Use with caution in patients with prior bone marrow suppression, impaired renal function (consider dose reduction), or who have received prior chemotherapy or irradiation. Toxicity to immunosuppressives is increased in elderly; start with lowest recommended adult doses. Signs of infection, such as fever and WBC rise, may not occur. Lethargy and confusion may be more prominent signs of infection. **[U.S. Boxed Warning]: Hypersensitivity has been reported with I.V. administration** and oral melphalan; may occur after multiple treatment cycles. **[U.S. Boxed Warning]: Should be administered under the supervision of an experienced cancer chemotherapy physician.** Safety and efficacy in children have not been established.
Adverse Reactions
>10%:
Gastrointestinal: Vomiting (oral low-dose: <10%; I.V.: 30% to 90%)
Hematologic: Myelosuppression, leukopenia (onset 7 days; nadir 14-35 days; recovery 28-56 days), thrombocytopenia (onset 7 days; nadir 14-35 days; recovery 28-56 days)
Miscellaneous: Secondary malignancy (<2% to 20%; cumulative dose and duration dependent)
1% to 10%: Miscellaneous: Hypersensitivity (I.V.: 2%)
Infrequent, frequency undefined, postmarketing, and/or case reports: Agranulocytosis, allergic reactions, alopecia, amenorrhea, anaphylaxis, anemia, bladder irritation, bone marrow failure (irreversible), diarrhea, hemolytic anemia, hemorrhagic cystitis, hemorrhagic necrotic enterocolitis, hepatic veno-occlusive disease (I.V. melphalan), hepatitis, interstitial pneumonitis, jaundice, nausea, ovarian suppression, pruritus, pulmonary fibrosis, radiation myelopathy, rash, secondary carcinoma, secondary leukemia, secondary myeloproliferative syndrome, SIADH, skin hypersensitivity, skin necrosis, skin ulceration (injection site), skin vesiculation, sterility, stomatitis, testicular suppression, transaminases increased, vasculitis
Overdosage/Toxicology Symptoms of overdose include hypocalcemia, hyponatremia, pulmonary fibrosis, severe nausea and vomiting, diarrhea, GI hemorrhage, mucositis, stomatitis, and bone marrow suppression (including pancytopenia). Deaths have been reported with I.V. overdoses. Monitor hematologic parameters closely for 3-6 weeks; consider growth factor support, transfusions, and antibiotics. Treatment is otherwise symptom-directed and supportive. Not removed by hemodialysis.
Drug Interactions
Increased Effect/Toxicity: Risk of nephrotoxicity of cyclosporine is increased by melphalan. Concomitant use of I.V. melphalan may cause serious GI toxicity. Cisplatin may increase the levels/effects of melphalan (I.V.). Melphalan may increase risk of vaccinal infection.

Decreased Effect: Melphalan may decrease the levels/effects of digoxin.

Ethanol/Nutrition/Herb Interactions

Ethanol: Avoid ethanol (due to GI irritation).

Food: Food interferes with oral absorption.

Stability

Tablet: Store in refrigerator at 2°C to 8°C (36°F to 46°F). Protect from light.

Injection: Store at room temperature (15°C to 30°C). Protect from light. Must be prepared fresh. **The time between reconstitution/dilution and administration of parenteral melphalan must be kept to a minimum (manufacturer recommends <60 minutes) because reconstituted and diluted solutions are unstable.** Dissolve powder initially with 10 mL of diluent to a concentration of 5 mg/mL. Shake vigorously to dissolve. This solution is chemically and physically stable for at least 90 minutes when stored at 25°C (77°F). **Immediately** dilute dose in 250-500 mL NS to a concentration of 0.1-0.45 mg/mL. This solution is physically and chemically stable for at least 60 minutes at 25°C (77°F). Do not refrigerate solution; precipitation occurs.

Mechanism of Action Alkylating agent which is a derivative of mechlorethamine that inhibits DNA and RNA synthesis via formation of carbonium ions; cross-links strands of DNA; acts on both resting and rapidly dividing tumor cells.

Pharmacodynamics/Kinetics

Absorption: Oral: Variable and incomplete

Distribution: V_d: 0.5-0.6 L/kg throughout total body water

Protein binding: 60% to 90%; primarily to albumin, 20% to α_1-acid glycoprotein

Metabolism: Hepatic; chemical hydrolysis to monohydroxymelphalan and dihydroxymelphalan

Bioavailability: Unpredictable; 61% ± 26%, decreasing with repeated doses

Half-life elimination: Terminal: I.V.: 1.5 hours; oral: 1-1.25 hours

Time to peak, serum: ~1-2 hours

Excretion: Oral: Feces (20% to 50%); urine (10% to 30% as unchanged drug)

Dosage Refer to individual protocols.

Oral: Dose should always be adjusted to patient response and weekly blood counts:

Children (unlabeled use): 4-20 mg/m²/day for 1-21 days

Adults:

Multiple myeloma (multiple regimens have been employed): **Note:** Response is gradual; may require repeated courses to realize benefit:

6 mg daily for 2-3 weeks initially, followed by up to 4 weeks rest, then a maintenance dose of 2 mg daily as hematologic recovery begins **or**

10 mg daily for 7-10 days; institute 2 mg daily maintenance dose after WBC >4000 cells/mcL and platelets >100,000 cells/mcL (~4-8 weeks); titrate maintenance dose to hematologic response **or**

0.15 mg/kg/day for 7 days, with a 2-6 week rest, followed by a maintenance dose of ≤0.05 mg/kg/day as hematologic recovery begins **or**

0.25 mg/kg/day for 4 days (or 0.2 mg/kg/day for 5 days); repeat at 4- to 6-week intervals as ANC and platelet counts return to normal

Ovarian carcinoma: 0.2 mg/kg/day for 5 days, repeat every 4-5 weeks.

I.V.:

Children (unlabeled use):

Pediatric rhabdomyosarcoma: 10-35 mg/m²/dose every 21-28 days

High-dose melphalan with bone marrow transplantation for neuroblastoma: I.V.: 100-220 mg/m² as a single dose or divided into 2-5 daily doses. Infuse over 20-60 minutes.

Adults: Multiple myeloma: 16 mg/m² administered at 2-week intervals for 4 doses, then administer at 4-week intervals after adequate hematologic recovery.

Dosing adjustment in renal impairment: The manufacturer recommends the following adjustments for renal impairment based on route of administration:

Oral: Moderate-to-severe renal impairment: Consider a reduced dose initially

I.V.: BUN >30 mg/dL: Reduce dose by up to 50%

The following guidelines are also used by some clinicians:

Aronoff, 1999 (route of administration not specified):

Cl_{cr} 10-50 mL/minute: Administer at 75% of normal dose

Cl_{cr} <10 mL/minute: Administer at 50% of normal dose

Hemodialysis, CAPD effects: Unknown

CAVH effects: Dose for GFR 10-50 mL/minute

Kintzel, 1995:

Oral: Adjust dose in the presence of hematologic toxicity

I.V.:

Cl_{cr} 46-60 mL/minute: Administer 85% of normal dose

Cl_{cr} 31-45 mL/minute: Administer 75% of normal dose

Cl_{cr} <30 mL/minute: Administer 70% of normal dose

Dietary Considerations Should be taken on an empty stomach (1 hour prior to or 2 hours after meals).

Administration

Oral: Administer on an empty stomach (1 hour prior to or 2 hours after meals)

Parenteral: Due to limited stability, complete administration of I.V. dose should occur within 60 minutes of reconstitution

I.V. infusion: Infuse over 15-20 minutes

I.V. bolus:

Central line: I.V. bolus doses of 17-200 mg/m² (reconstituted and not diluted) have been infused over 2-20 minutes

Peripheral line: I.V. bolus doses of 2-23 mg/m² (reconstituted and not diluted) have been infused over 1-4 minutes

Monitoring Parameters CBC with differential and platelet count, serum electrolytes, serum uric acid

Test Interactions False-positive Coombs' test [direct]

Dosage Forms

Injection, powder for reconstitution: 50 mg [diluent contains ethanol and propylene glycol]

Tablet: 2 mg

♦ **Melquin-3**® see Hydroquinone on page 859

♦ **Melquin HP**® see Hydroquinone on page 859

Memantine (me MAN teen)

U.S. Brand Names Namenda™

Canadian Brand Names Ebixa®

Index Terms Memantine Hydrochloride

Pharmacologic Category N-Methyl-D-Aspartate Receptor Antagonist

Use Treatment of moderate-to-severe dementia of the Alzheimer's type

Unlabeled/Investigational Use Treatment of mild-to-moderate vascular dementia

Pregnancy Risk Factor B

Pregnancy Implications Teratogenic effects were not observed in animal studies. There are no studies in pregnant women.

Lactation Excretion in breast milk unknown/use caution

Contraindications Hypersensitivity to memantine or any component of the formulation

Warnings/Precautions Use caution with seizure disorders or hepatic impairment. Caution with use in severe renal impairment; dose adjustment recommended. Clearance is significantly reduced by alkaline urine; use caution with medications, dietary changes, or patient conditions which may alter urine pH.

Adverse Reactions

1% to 10%:

Cardiovascular: Hypertension (4%), cardiac failure, syncope, cerebrovascular accident, transient ischemic attack

Central nervous system: Dizziness (7%), confusion (6%), headache (6%), hallucinations (3%), pain (3%), somnolence (3%), fatigue (2%), aggressive reaction, ataxia, vertigo

Dermatologic: Rash

Gastrointestinal: Constipation (5%), vomiting (3%), weight loss

Genitourinary: Micturition

Hematologic: Anemia

Hepatic: Alkaline phosphatase increased

Neuromuscular & skeletal: Back pain (3%), hypokinesia

Ocular: Cataract, conjunctivitis

Respiratory: Cough (4%), dyspnea (2%), pneumonia

<1% (Limited to important or life-threatening): Allergic reaction, AV block, cerebral infarction, dyskinesia, dysphagia, hepatic failure, hyperlipidemia, hypoglycemia, ileus, NMS, pancreatitis, renal failure, QT prolongation, seizure, Stevens-Johnson syndrome, sudden death, tardive dyskinesia, thrombocytopenia

Overdosage/Toxicology Loss of consciousness, psychosis, restlessness, somnolence, stupor, and visual hallucinations were reported following ingestion of memantine 400 mg. In case of overdose, treatment should be symptomatic and supportive. Elimination may be increased by acidifying the urine.

Drug Interactions

Increased Effect/Toxicity: Clearance of memantine is decreased 80% at urinary pH 8; use caution with medications (carbonic anhydrase inhibitors, sodium bicarbonate) which may increase urinary pH.

Stability Store at controlled room temperature of 15°C to 30°C (59°F to 86°F).

Mechanism of Action Glutamate, the primary excitatory amino acid in the CNS, may contribute to the pathogenesis of Alzheimer's disease (AD) by overstimulating various glutamate receptors leading to excitotoxicity and neuronal cell death. Memantine is an uncompetitive antagonist of the N-methyl-D-aspartate (NMDA) type of glutamate receptors, located ubiquitously throughout the brain. Under normal physiologic conditions, the (unstimulated) NMDA receptor ion channel is blocked by magnesium ions, which are displaced after agonist-induced depolarization. Pathologic or excessive receptor activation, as postulated to occur during AD, prevents magnesium from reentering and blocking the channel pore resulting in a chronically open state and excessive calcium influx. Memantine binds to the intra-pore magnesium site, but with longer dwell time, and thus functions as an effective receptor blocker only under conditions of excessive stimulation; memantine does not affect normal neurotransmission.

Pharmacodynamics/Kinetics

Distribution: 9-11 L/kg

Protein binding: 45%

Metabolism: Forms 3 metabolites (minimal activity)

Half-life elimination: Terminal: 60-80 hours; severe renal impairment (Cl$_{cr}$ 5-29 mL/minute): 117-156 hours

Time to peak, serum: 3-7 hours

Excretion: Urine (57% to 82% unchanged); excretion reduced by alkaline urine pH

Dosage Oral: Adults:

Alzheimer's disease: Initial: 5 mg/day; increase dose by 5 mg/day to a target dose of 20 mg/day; wait at least 1 week between dosage changes. Doses >5 mg/day should be given in 2 divided doses.

Suggested titration: 5 mg/day for ≥1 week; 5 mg twice daily for ≥1 week; 15 mg/day given in 5 mg and 10 mg separated doses for ≥1 week; then 10 mg twice daily

Mild-to-moderate vascular dementia (unlabeled use): 10 mg twice daily

Dosage adjustment in renal impairment:

Mild-to-moderate impairment: No adjustment required

Severe impairment: Cl$_{cr}$ 5-29 mL/minute): 5 mg twice daily

Dietary Considerations May be taken with or without food.

Dosage Forms
  Solution, oral: 2 mg/mL (360 mL) [alcohol free, dye free, sugar free; peppermint flavor]
  Tablet, as hydrochloride: 5 mg, 10 mg
  Combination package [titration pack contains two separate tablet formulations]: Memantine
    hydrochloride 5 mg (28s) and memantine hydrochloride 10 mg (21s)

♦ **Memantine Hydrochloride** see Memantine on page 1076
♦ **Menactra**® see Meningococcal Polysaccharide (Groups A / C / Y and W-135) Diphtheria Toxoid
  Conjugate Vaccine on page 1077
♦ **Menest**® see Estrogens (Esterified) on page 635

Meningococcal Polysaccharide (Groups A / C / Y and W-135) Diphtheria Toxoid Conjugate Vaccine

(me NIN joe kok al pol i SAK a ride groops aye, see, why & dubl yoo won thur tee fyve dif
THEER ee a TOKS oyds KON joo gate vak SEEN)

U.S. Brand Names Menactra®
Index Terms MCV4
Pharmacologic Category Vaccine
Use Provide active immunization of adolescents and adults (11-55 years of age) against
  invasive meningococcal disease caused by *N. meningitidis* serogroups A, C, Y and W-135

  The ACIP recommends routine vaccination of all adolescents at age 11-12 years. For adoles-
    cents not previously vaccinated, vaccine should be administered prior to high school entry
    (~15 years of age).
  The ACIP also recommends routine vaccination for persons at increased risk for meningo-
    coccal disease. (MCV4 is preferred for persons aged 11-55 years; MPSV4 may be used if
    MCV4 is not available). Persons at increased risk include:
    College freshmen living in dormitories
    Microbiologists routinely exposed to isolates of *N. meningitides*
    Military recruits
    Persons traveling to or who reside in countries where *N. meningitides* is hyperendemic or
      epidemic, particularly if contact with local population will be prolonged
    Persons with terminal complement component deficiencies
    Persons with anatomic or functional asplenia
  Use is also recommended during meningococcal outbreaks caused by vaccine preventable
    serogroups.
Pregnancy Risk Factor C
Pregnancy Implications An isolated teratogenic effect was observed in animal studies; not
  necessarily vaccine related. Carcinogenic or mutagenic studies have not been performed.
  There are no adequate and well-controlled studies in pregnant women. Patients should
  contact the Aventis Pasteur Inc vaccine registry at 1-800-822-2463 if they are pregnant or
  become aware they were pregnant at the time of Menactra® vaccination.
Lactation Excretion in breast milk unknown/use caution
Medication Safety Issues
  Administration issue:
    Menactra® (MCV4) should be administered by intramuscular (I.M.) injection only. Inad-
      vertent subcutaneous (SubQ) administration has been reported; possibly due to confu-
      sion of this product with Menomune® (MPSV4), also a meningococcal polysaccharide
      vaccine, which is administered by the SubQ route.
Contraindications Hypersensitivity to any component of the formulation, including diphtheria
  toxoid; latex hypersensitivity; history of Guillain-Barré syndrome
Warnings/Precautions Due to risk of hemorrhage, avoid using in patients with any bleeding
  disorder, such as thrombocytopenia or hemophilia. Consider risk-to-benefit in patients
  receiving anticoagulant therapy. Defer vaccination until improvement from moderate to
  severe acute illness. Menactra® is not to be used to treat meningococcal infections or to
  provide immunity against *N. meningitidis* serogroup B or diphtheria. Response may not be as
  great as desired in immunosuppressed patients. Vial stopper contains latex. Safety and
  efficacy have not been established in children <11 years of age or adults >55 years.
  Immediate treatment for anaphylactic reactions should be available.
**Adverse Reactions All serious adverse reactions must be reported to the U.S. Depart-
  ment of Health and Human Services Vaccine Adverse Event Reporting System
  (VAERS) 1-800-822-7967 or www.vaers.org.**

  >10%:
    Central nervous system: Pain (54% to 59%), headache (36% to 41%), fatigue (30% to
      35%), malaise (22% to 24%)
    Gastrointestinal: Diarrhea (12% to 16%), anorexia (11% to 12%)
    Local: Redness (11% to 14%), swelling (11% to 13%), induration (16% to 17%)
    Neuromuscular & skeletal: Arthralgia (17% to 20%)
  1% to 10%:
    Central nervous system: Chills (7% to 10%), fever (2% to 5%)
    Gastrointestinal: Vomiting (2%)
    Local: Rash (1% to 2%)
  Postmarketing and/or case reports: Guillain-Barré syndrome, transverse myelitis
Stability Store between 2°C to 8°C (35°F to 46°F); do not freeze. Discard product exposed to
  freezing. Do not mix with other vaccines in the same syringe.
Mechanism of Action Induces immunity against meningococcal disease via the formation of
  bactericidal antibodies directed toward the polysaccharide capsular components of *Neisseria
  meningitidis* serogroups A, C, Y and W-135.
Dosage I.M.:
  Adolescents 11-18 years and Adults ≤55 years: 0.5 mL
    NOTE: Revaccination: May be indicated in patients previously vaccinated with MPSV4 who
      remain at increased risk for infection. The ACIP recommends the use of MCV4 for
  (Continued)

Meningococcal Polysaccharide (Groups A / C / Y and W-135) Diphtheria Toxoid Conjugate Vaccine *(Continued)*

revaccination in patients 11-55 years, however use of MPSV4 is also acceptable. Consider revaccination after 3-5 years. The need for revaccination in patients previously vaccinated with MCV4 is currently under study.

Elderly: Safety and efficacy not established in patients >55 years

Administration Administer by I.M. route, preferably into the upper deltoid region. Do not administer via I.V., SubQ or I.D. route. For patients at risk of hemorrhage, the ACIP recommends "it should be administered intramuscularly if, in the opinion of a physician familiar with the patient's bleeding risk, the vaccine can be administered with reasonable safety by this route. If the patient receives antihemophilia or other similar therapy, intramuscular vaccination can be scheduled shortly after such therapy is administered. A fine needle (≤23 gauge) can be used for the vaccination and firm pressure applied to the site (without rubbing) for at least 2 minutes. The patient or family should be instructed concerning the risk of hematoma from the injection."

Based on limited data, inadvertent SubQ administration provides a lower serologic response, however the response is still considered to be protective. If inadvertently administered by the SubQ route, revaccination is not necessary.

Additional Information Federal law requires that the date of administration, the vaccine manufacturer, lot number of vaccine, and the administering person's name, title and address be entered into the patient's permanent medical record.

Dosage Forms

Injection, solution:

Menactra®: 4 mcg each of polysaccharide antigen groups A, C, Y, and W-135 per 0.5 mL [conjugated to diphtheria toxoid protein 48 mcg; adjuvant and preservative free; vial stopper contains dry, natural latex rubber]

Meningococcal Polysaccharide Vaccine (Groups A / C / Y and W-135)

(me NIN joe kok al pol i SAK a ride vak SEEN groops aye, see, why & dubl yoo won thur tee fyve)

U.S. Brand Names Menomune®-A/C/Y/W-135

Index Terms MPSV4

Pharmacologic Category Vaccine

Additional Appendix Information

Immunization Recommendations *on page 1929*

Use Provide active immunity to meningococcal serogroups contained in the vaccine

The ACIP recommends routine vaccination for persons at increased risk for meningococcal disease. (Use of MPSV4 is recommended in children 2-10 years and adults > 55 years. MCV4 is preferred for persons aged 11-55 years; MPSV4 may be used if MCV4 is not available). Persons at increased risk include:

College freshmen living in dormitories

Microbiologists routinely exposed to isolates of *N. meningitides*

Military recruits

Persons traveling to or who reside in countries where *N. meningitides* is hyperendemic or epidemic, particularly if contact with local population will be prolonged

Persons with terminal complement component deficiencies

Persons with anatomic or functional asplenia

Use is also recommended during meningococcal outbreaks caused by vaccine preventable serogroups.

Pregnancy Risk Factor C

Pregnancy Implications Animal studies have not been conducted. Based on limited data, teratogenic effects have not been reported when used during pregnancy. Pregnancy should not preclude vaccination with MPSV4 if indicated. Patients may contact the Aventis Pasteur Inc vaccine registry at 1-800-822-2463 if they are pregnant or become aware they were pregnant at the time of vaccination.

Lactation Excretion in breast milk unknown/use caution

Medication Safety Issues

Administration issue:

Menomume® (MPSV4) should be administered by subcutaneous (SubQ) injection. Menactra® (MCV4), also a meningococcal polysaccharide vaccine, is to be administered by intramuscular (I.M.) injection only.

Contraindications Hypersensitivity to any component of the formulation; defer immunization during acute illness

Warnings/Precautions Patients who undergo splenectomy secondary to trauma or nonlymphoid tumors respond well; however, those asplenic patients with lymphoid tumors who receive either chemotherapy or irradiation respond poorly. Response may not be as great as desired in immunosuppressed patients. Use in pediatric patients <2 years of age is usually not recommended. Use with caution in patients with latex sensitivity; the stopper to the vial contains dry, natural latex rubber. Some dosage forms contain thimerosal.

Adverse Reactions All serious and serious adverse reactions must be reported to the U.S. Department of Health and Human Services (DHHS) Vaccine Adverse Event Reporting System (VAERS) 1-800-822-7967. Percentages reported in adults; incidence of erythema, swelling, or tenderness may be higher in children

>10%: Local: Tenderness (9% to 36%)

1% to 10%:

Central nervous system: Headache (2% to 5%), malaise (2%), fever (100°F to 106°F: 3%), chills (2%)

Local: Pain at injection site (2% to 3%), erythema (1% to 4%), induration (1% to 4%)

Drug Interactions
  Increased Effect/Toxicity: Should not be administered with whole-cell pertussis or whole-cell typhoid vaccines due to combined endotoxin content.
  Decreased Effect: Decreased effect with administration of immunoglobulin within 1 month.
Stability Prior to and following reconstitution, store at 2°C to 8°C (35°F to 46°F). Reconstitute using provided diluent; shake well. Use single-dose vial within 30 minutes of reconstitution. Use multidose vial within 35 days of reconstitution.
Mechanism of Action Induces the formation of bactericidal antibodies to meningococcal antigens; the presence of these antibodies is strongly correlated with immunity to meningococcal disease caused by *Neisseria meningitidis* groups A, C, Y and W-135.
Pharmacodynamics/Kinetics
  Onset of action: Antibody levels: 7-10 days
  Duration: Antibodies against group A and C polysaccharides decline markedly (to prevaccination levels) over the first 3 years following a single dose of vaccine, especially in children <4 years of age
Dosage SubQ:
  Children <2 years: Not usually recommended. Two doses (0.5 mL/dose), 3 months apart, may be considered in children 3-18 months to elicit short-term protection against serogroup A disease. A single dose may be considered in children 19-23 months.
  Children ≥2 years and Adults: 0.5 mL
  Note: Revaccination: May be indicated in patients previously vaccinated with MPSV4 who remain at increased risk for infection. The ACIP recommends the use of MCV4 for revaccination in patients 11-55 years, however use of MPSV4 is also acceptable.
    Children first vaccinated at <4 years: Revaccinate after 2-3 years.
    Adults: Not determined, consider revaccination after 3-5 years.
Administration Administer by SubQ injection; do not administer intradermally, I.M., or I.V.
Additional Information Federal law requires that the date of administration, the vaccine manufacturer, lot number of vaccine, and the administering person's name, title and address be entered into the patient's permanent medical record.
Dosage Forms Injection, powder for reconstitution: 50 mcg each of polysaccharide antigen groups A, C, Y, and W-135 [contains lactose; packaged with 0.78 mL preservative free diluent or 6 mL diluent containing thimerosal; vial stoppers contain dry, natural latex rubber]

◆ **Menomune®-A/C/Y/W-135** *see* Meningococcal Polysaccharide Vaccine (Groups A / C / Y and W-135) *on page 1078*
◆ **Menopur®** *see* Menotropins *on page 1079*
◆ **Menostar™** *see* Estradiol *on page 620*

Menotropins (men oh TROE pins)

U.S. Brand Names Menopur®; Repronex®
Canadian Brand Names Repronex®
Index Terms hMG; Human Menopausal Gonadotropin
Pharmacologic Category Gonadotropin; Ovulation Stimulator
Use Female:
  In conjunction with hCG to induce ovulation and pregnancy in infertile females experiencing oligoanovulation or anovulation when the cause of anovulation is functional and not caused by primary ovarian failure (Repronex®)
  Stimulation of multiple follicle development in ovulatory patients as part of an assisted reproductive technology (ART) (Menopur®, Repronex®)
Unlabeled/Investigational Use Male: Stimulation of spermatogenesis in primary or secondary hypogonadotropic hypogonadism
Pregnancy Risk Factor X
Pregnancy Implications Ectopic pregnancy and congenital abnormalities have been reported. The incidence of congenital abnormality is similar during natural conception.
Lactation Excretion in breast milk unknown/use caution
Medication Safety Issues
  Sound-alike/look-alike issues:
    Repronex® may be confused with Regranex®
Contraindications Hypersensitivity to menotropins or any component of the formulation; primary ovarian failure as indicated by a high follicle-stimulating hormone (FSH) level; uncontrolled thyroid and adrenal dysfunction; abnormal bleeding of undetermined origin; intracranial lesion (ie, pituitary tumor); ovarian cyst or enlargement not due to polycystic ovary syndrome; infertility due to any cause other than anovulation (except candidates for *in vitro* fertilization); sex hormone-dependent tumors of the reproductive tract and accessory organs; pregnancy
Warnings/Precautions For use by infertility specialists. Advise patient of frequency and potential hazards of multiple pregnancy. May cause ovarian hyperstimulation syndrome (OHSS); if severe, treatment should be discontinued and patient should be hospitalized (may become more severe if pregnancy occurs). Monitor for ovarian enlargement; to minimize the hazard of abnormal ovarian enlargement, use the lowest possible dose. Serious pulmonary conditions (atelectasis, acute respiratory distress syndrome) and arterial thromboembolism have been reported. Safety and efficacy have not been established in renal or hepatic impairment, or in pediatric and geriatric patients.
Adverse Reactions Adverse effects may vary according to specific product, route, and/or dosage.
  >10%:
    Central nervous system: Headache (up to 34%)
    Gastrointestinal: Abdominal pain (up to 18%), nausea (up to 12%)
    Genitourinary: OHSS (up to 13%, dose related)
    Local: Injection site reaction (4% to 12%)
  1% to 10%:
    Cardiovascular: Flushing
  (Continued)

Menotropins *(Continued)*

Central nervous system: Dizziness, malaise, migraine

Endocrine & metabolic: Breast tenderness, hot flashes, menstrual irregularities

Gastrointestinal: Abdominal cramping, abdominal fullness, constipation, diarrhea, enlarged abdomen, vomiting

Genitourinary: Ectopic pregnancy, ovarian disease, vaginal hemorrhage

Local: Injection site edema/pain

Neuromuscular & skeletal: Back pain

Respiratory: Cough increased, respiratory disorder

Miscellaneous: Infection, flu-like syndrome

Frequency not defined:

Cardiovascular: Stroke, tachycardia, thrombosis (venous or arterial)

Central nervous system: Dizziness

Dermatologic: Angioedema, rash, urticaria

Genitourinary: Adnexal torsion, hemoperitoneum, ovarian enlargement

Neuromuscular & skeletal: Limb necrosis

Respiratory: Acute respiratory distress syndrome, atelectasis, dyspnea, embolism, laryngeal edema pulmonary infarction tachypnea

Miscellaneous: Allergic reactions, anaphylaxis

Overdosage/Toxicology Symptoms include ovarian hyperstimulation.

Stability Lyophilized powder may be refrigerated or stored at room temperature. Protect from light. After reconstitution inject immediately; discard any unused portion.

Mechanism of Action Actions occur as a result of both follicle stimulating hormone (FSH) effects and luteinizing hormone (LH) effects; menotropins stimulate the development and maturation of the ovarian follicle (FSH), cause ovulation (LH), and stimulate the development of the corpus luteum (LH); in males it stimulates spermatogenesis (LH)

Pharmacodynamics/Kinetics Excretion: Urine (~10% as unchanged drug)

Dosage Adults:

Repronex®: I.M., SubQ:

Induction of ovulation in patients with oligoanovulation (Female): Initial: 150 int. units daily for the first 5 days of treatment. Adjustments should not be made more frequently than once every 2 days and should not exceed 75-150 int. units per adjustment. Maximum daily dose should not exceed 450 int. units and dosing beyond 12 days is not recommended. If patient's response is appropriate, hCG 5000-10,000 units should be given one day following the last dose of Repronex®. Hold dose if serum estradiol is >2000 pg/mL, if the ovaries are abnormally enlarged, or if abdominal pain occurs; the patient should also be advised to refrain from intercourse. May repeat process if follicular development is inadequate or if pregnancy does not occur.

Assisted reproductive technologies (Female): Initial (in patients who have received GnRH agonist or antagonist pituitary suppression): 225 int. units; adjustments in dose should not be made more frequently than once every 2 days and should not exceed more than 75-150 int. units per adjustment. The maximum daily doses of Repronex® given should not exceed 450 int. units and dosing beyond 12 days is not recommended. Once adequate follicular development is evident, hCG (5000-10,000 units) should be administered to induce final follicular maturation in preparation for oocyte retrieval. Withhold treatment when ovaries are abnormally enlarged on last day of therapy (to reduce chance of developing OHSS).

Menopur®: SubQ: *Assisted reproductive technologies (ART):* Initial (in patients who have received GnRH agonist for pituitary suppression): 225 int. units; adjustments in dose should not be made more frequently than once every 2 days and should not exceed more than 150 int. units per adjustment. The maximum daily dose given should not exceed 450 int. units and dosing beyond 20 days is not recommended. Once adequate follicular development is evident, hCG should be administered to induce final follicular maturation in preparation for oocyte retrieval. Withhold treatment when ovaries are abnormally enlarged on last day of therapy (to reduce chance of developing OHSS).

Spermatogenesis (Male) (unlabeled use): I.M.: Following pretreatment with hCG: 75 int. units 3 times/week and hCG 2000 units twice weekly until sperm is detected in the ejaculate (4-6 months); may then be increased to menotropins 150 int. units 3 times/week

Administration

Menopur®: SubQ: Administer to alternating sites of the abdomen; when administration to the lower abdomen is not possible, the injection may be given into the thigh.

Repronex®:

I.M.: Administer deep in a large muscle.

SubQ: Administer to alternating sites of the lower abdomen.

Monitoring Parameters hCG levels, serum estradiol; vaginal ultrasound; in cases of suspected OHSS, monitor fluid intake and output, weight, hematocrit, serum and urinary electrolytes, urine specific gravity, BUN and creatinine, and abdominal girth

Dosage Forms

Injection, powder for reconstitution:

Menopur®: Follicle stimulating hormone activity 75 int. units and luteinizing hormone activity 75 int. units [packaged with diluent; contains lactose 21 mg]

Repronex®: Follicle stimulating hormone activity 75 int. units and luteinizing hormone activity 75 int. units [packaged with diluent]

♦ **Mentax®** *see Butenafine on page 260*

♦ **292 MEP® (Can)** *see Aspirin and Meprobamate on page 164*

♦ **Mepergan** *see Meperidine and Promethazine on page 1083*

Meperidine (me PER i deen)

U.S. Brand Names Demerol®; Meperitab®
Canadian Brand Names Demerol®
Index Terms Isonipecaine Hydrochloride; Meperidine Hydrochloride; Pethidine Hydrochloride
Pharmacologic Category Analgesic, Opioid
Additional Appendix Information
  Narcotic Agonists *on page 1888*
Use Management of moderate to severe pain; adjunct to anesthesia and preoperative sedation
Unlabeled/Investigational Use
  Reduce postoperative shivering; reduce rigors from amphotericin
Restrictions C-II
Pregnancy Risk Factor C/D (prolonged use or high doses at term)
Pregnancy Implications Meperidine is known to cross the placenta, which may result in respiratory or CNS depression in the newborn.
Lactation Enters breast milk/contraindicated (AAP rates "compatible")
Medication Safety Issues
  Sound-alike/look-alike issues:
    Meperidine may be confused with meprobamate
    Demerol® may be confused with Demulen®, Desyrel®, dicumarol, Dilaudid®, Dymelor®, Pamelor®
Contraindications Hypersensitivity to meperidine or any component of the formulation; use with or within 14 days of MAO inhibitors; pregnancy (prolonged use or high doses near term)
Warnings/Precautions Meperidine is not recommended for the management of chronic pain. When used for acute pain (in patients without renal or CNS disease), treatment should be limited to 48 hours and doses should not exceed 600 mg/24 hours. Oral meperidine is not recommended for acute pain management. Normeperidine (an active metabolite and CNS stimulant) may accumulate and precipitate anxiety, tremors, or seizures; risk increases with renal dysfunction and cumulative dose. Effects may be potentiated when used with other sedative drugs or ethanol.

May cause CNS depression, which may impair physical or mental abilities; patients must be cautioned about performing tasks which require mental alertness (eg, operating machinery or driving). Use only with extreme caution (if at all) in patients with head injury or increased intracranial pressure (ICP). Use caution with pulmonary, hepatic, or renal disorders, supraventricular tachycardias, acute abdominal conditions, hypothyroidism, toxic psychosis, kyphoscoliosis, morbid obesity, Addison's disease, BPH, or urethral stricture. Use with caution in patients with biliary tract dysfunction; acute pancreatitis may cause constriction of sphincter of Oddi. May cause hypotension; use with caution in patients with depleted blood volume or drugs which may exaggerate hypotensive effects (including phenothiazines or general anesthetics).

An opioid-containing analgesic regimen should be tailored to each patient's needs. The optimal analgesic dose varies widely among patients. Some preparations contain sulfites which may cause allergic reaction. Tolerance or drug dependence may result from extended use. Healthcare provider should be alert to problems of abuse, misuse, and diversion. Concurrent use of agonist/antagonist analgesics may precipitate withdrawal symptoms and/or reduced analgesic efficacy in patients following prolonged therapy with mu opioid agonists. Abrupt discontinuation following prolonged use may also lead to withdrawal symptoms. Use with caution in the elderly and debilitated patients; may be more sensitive to adverse effects.

Adverse Reactions Frequency not defined.
  Cardiovascular: Hypotension
  Central nervous system: Fatigue, drowsiness, dizziness, nervousness, headache, restlessness, malaise, confusion, mental depression, hallucinations, paradoxical CNS stimulation, increased intracranial pressure, seizure (associated with metabolite accumulation), serotonin syndrome
  Dermatologic: Rash, urticaria
  Gastrointestinal: Nausea, vomiting, constipation, anorexia, stomach cramps, xerostomia, biliary spasm, paralytic ileus, sphincter of Oddi spasm
  Genitourinary: Ureteral spasms, decreased urination
  Local: Pain at injection site
  Neuromuscular & skeletal: Weakness
  Respiratory: Dyspnea
  Miscellaneous: Histamine release, physical and psychological dependence
Overdosage/Toxicology Symptoms include CNS depression, respiratory depression, mydriasis, bradycardia, pulmonary edema, chronic tremors, CNS excitability, and seizures. Treatment of overdose includes airway support, establishment of an I.V. line, and administration of naloxone 2 mg I.V. (0.01 mg/kg for children), with repeat administration as necessary, up to a total of 10 mg. Naloxone should not be used to treat meperidine-induced seizures. Naloxone does not reverse the adverse effects of normeperidine.

Drug Interactions
  Cytochrome P450 Effect: Substrate (minor) of CYP2B6, 2C19, 3A4
  Increased Effect/Toxicity: MAO inhibitors may enhance the serotonergic effect of meperidine, which may cause serotonin syndrome; concurrent use with or within 14 days of an MAO inhibitor is contraindicated. CNS depressants may potentiate the sedative effects of meperidine or increase respiratory depression. Phenothiazines may potentiate the sedative effects of meperidine and may increase the incidence of hypotension. Serotonin agonists, serotonin reuptake inhibitors, sibutramine, and tricyclic antidepressants may potentiate the effects of meperidine. In addition, concurrent therapy with these drugs potentially may increase the risk of serotonin syndrome. A number of drugs may increase meperidine metabolite concentrations (including acyclovir, cimetidine, and ritonavir).
  (Continued)

Meperidine *(Continued)*

Decreased Effect: Barbiturates may decrease the analgesic efficacy and increase the sedative effects of meperidine. Phenytoin may decrease the analgesic effects of meperidine.

Ethanol/Nutrition/Herb Interactions

Ethanol: Avoid or limit ethanol (may increase CNS depression). Watch for sedation.

Herb/Nutraceutical: Avoid valerian, St John's wort, kava kava, gotu kola (may increase CNS depression).

Stability Meperidine injection should be stored at room temperature; do not freeze. Protect from light. Protect oral dosage forms from light.

Mechanism of Action Binds to opiate receptors in the CNS, causing inhibition of ascending pain pathways, altering the perception of and response to pain; produces generalized CNS depression

Pharmacodynamics/Kinetics

Onset of action: Analgesic: Oral, SubQ: 10-15 minutes; I.V.: ~5 minutes

Peak effect: SubQ.: ~1 hour; Oral: 2 hours

Duration: Oral, SubQ.: 2-4 hours

Absorption: I.M.: Erratic and highly variable

Distribution: Crosses placenta; enters breast milk

Protein binding: 65% to 75%

Metabolism: Hepatic; hydrolyzed to meperidinic acid (inactive) or undergoes N-demethylation to normeperidine (active; has $1/2$ the analgesic effect and 2-3 times the CNS effects of meperidine)

Bioavailability: ~50% to 60%; increased with liver disease

Half-life elimination:

Parent drug: Terminal phase: Adults: 2.5-4 hours, Liver disease: 7-11 hours

Normeperidine (active metabolite): 15-30 hours; can accumulate with high doses or with decreased renal function

Excretion: Urine (as metabolites)

Dosage Note: Doses should be titrated to necessary analgesic effect. When changing route of administration, note that oral doses are about half as effective as parenteral dose. Not recommended for chronic pain. These are guidelines and do not represent the maximum doses that may be required in all patients. In patients with normal renal function, doses of ≤600 mg/24 hours and use for ≤48 hours are recommended (American Pain Society, 1999).

Children: Pain: Oral, I.M., I.V., SubQ: 1-1.5 mg/kg/dose every 3-4 hours as needed; 1-2 mg/kg as a single dose preoperative medication may be used; maximum 100 mg/dose (Note: Oral route is not recommended for acute pain.)

Adults: Pain:

Oral: Initial: Opiate-naive: 50 mg every 3-4 hours as needed; usual dosage range: 50-150 mg every 2-4 hours as needed (manufacturers recommendation; oral route is not recommended for acute pain)

I.M., SubQ: Initial: Opiate-naive: 50-75 mg every 3-4 hours as needed; patients with prior opiate exposure may require higher initial doses

Preoperatively: 50-100 mg given 30-90 minutes before the beginning of anesthesia

Slow I.V.: Initial: 5-10 mg every 5 minutes as needed

Patient-controlled analgesia (PCA): Usual concentration: 10 mg/mL

Initial dose: 10 mg

Demand dose: 1-5 mg (manufacturer recommendations); range 5-25 mg (American Pain Society, 1999).

Lockout interval: 5-10 minutes

Elderly:

Oral: 50 mg every 4 hours

I.M.: 25 mg every 4 hours

Dosing adjustment in renal impairment: Avoid repeated administration of meperidine in renal dysfunction:

Cl_{cr} 10-50 mL/minute: Administer at 75% of normal dose

Cl_{cr} <10 mL/minute: Administer at 50% of normal dose

Dosing adjustment/comments in hepatic disease: Increased narcotic effect in cirrhosis; reduction in dose more important for oral than I.V. route

Administration Meperidine may be administered I.M., SubQ, or I.V.; I.V. push should be administered slowly, use of a 10 mg/mL concentration has been recommended. For continuous I.V. infusions, a more dilute solution (eg, 1 mg/mL) should be used.

Oral: Administer syrup diluted in $1/2$ glass of water; undiluted syrup may exert topical anesthetic effect on mucous membranes

Monitoring Parameters Pain relief, respiratory and mental status, blood pressure; observe patient for excessive sedation, CNS depression, seizures, respiratory depression

Reference Range Therapeutic: 70-500 ng/mL (SI: 283-2020 nmol/L); Toxic: >1000 ng/mL (SI: >4043 nmol/L)

Test Interactions Increased amylase (S), increased BSP retention, increased CPK (I.M. injections)

Dosage Forms

Injection, solution, as hydrochloride [ampul]: 25 mg/0.5 mL (0.5 mL); 25 mg/mL (1 mL); 50 mg/mL (1 mL, 1.5 mL, 2 mL); 75 mg/mL (1 mL); 100 mg/mL (1 mL)

Injection, solution, as hydrochloride [prefilled syringe]: 25 mg/mL (1 mL); 50 mg/mL (1 mL); 75 mg/mL (1 mL); 100 mg/mL (1 mL)

Injection, solution, as hydrochloride [for PCA pump]: 10 mg/mL (30 mL, 50 mL, 60 mL)

Injection, solution, as hydrochloride [vial]: 25 mg/mL (1 mL); 50 mg/mL (1 mL, 30 mL); 75 mg/mL (1 mL); 100 mg/mL (1 mL, 20 mL) [may contain sodium metabisulfite]

Solution, oral, as hydrochloride: 50 mg/5 mL (500 mL)

Syrup, as hydrochloride:

Demerol®: 50 mg/5 mL (480 mL) [contains benzoic acid; banana flavor]

Tablet, as hydrochloride: 50 mg, 100 mg

Demerol®, Meperitab®: 50 mg, 100 mg

Meperidine and Promethazine (me PER i deen & proe METH a zeen)

Index Terms Mepergan; Promethazine and Meperidine
Pharmacologic Category Analgesic Combination (Opioid)
Use Management of moderate pain
Restrictions C-II
Medication Safety Issues
Sound-alike/look-alike issues:
Mepergan may be confused with meprobamate
Dosage Adults: Oral: One (1) capsule every 4-6 hours as needed
Additional Information Complete prescribing information for this medication should be consulted for additional detail.
Dosage Forms Capsule: Meperidine hydrochloride 50 mg and promethazine hydrochloride 25 mg

♦ **Meperidine Hydrochloride** see Meperidine on page 1081
♦ **Meperitab®** see Meperidine on page 1081

Mephobarbital (me foe BAR bi tal)

U.S. Brand Names Mebaral®
Canadian Brand Names Mebaral®
Index Terms Methylphenobarbital
Pharmacologic Category Barbiturate
Use Sedative; treatment of grand mal and petit mal epilepsy
Restrictions C-IV
Pregnancy Risk Factor D
Medication Safety Issues
Sound-alike/look-alike issues:
Mephobarbital may be confused with methocarbamol
Mebaral® may be confused with Medrol®, Mellaril®, Tegretol®
Contraindications Hypersensitivity to mephobarbital, other barbiturates, or any component of the formulation; pre-existing CNS depression; respiratory depression; severe uncontrolled pain; history of porphyria; pregnancy
Adverse Reactions
>10%: Central nervous system: Dizziness, "hangover" effect, lightheadedness, somnolence
1% to 10%:
Central nervous system: Confusion, faint feeling, headache, insomnia, mental depression, nervousness, nightmares, unusual excitement
Gastrointestinal: Constipation, nausea, vomiting
<1% (Limited to important or life-threatening): Agranulocytosis, angioedema, dependence, exfoliative dermatitis, hallucinations, hypotension, megaloblastic anemia, respiratory depression, skin rash, Stevens-Johnson syndrome, thrombocytopenia, thrombophlebitis
Drug Interactions
Cytochrome P450 Effect: Substrate of CYP2B6 (minor), 2C9 (minor), 2C19 (major); **Inhibits** CYP2C19 (weak); **Induces** CYP2A6 (weak)
Increased Effect/Toxicity: When combined with other CNS depressants, ethanol, opioid analgesics, antidepressants, or benzodiazepines, additive respiratory and CNS depression may occur. Barbiturates may enhance the hepatotoxic potential of acetaminophen overdoses. Chloramphenicol, MAO inhibitors, valproic acid, and felbamate may inhibit barbiturate metabolism. Barbiturates may impair the absorption of griseofulvin, and may enhance the nephrotoxic effects of methoxyflurane. Concurrent use of phenobarbital with meperidine may result in increased CNS depression. CYP2C19 inhibitors may increase the levels/effects of mephobarbital; example inhibitors include delavirdine, fluconazole, fluvoxamine, gemfibrozil, isoniazid, omeprazole, and ticlopidine.
Decreased Effect: Barbiturates are hepatic enzyme inducers, and may increase the metabolism of antipsychotics, some beta-blockers (unlikely with atenolol and nadolol), calcium channel blockers, chloramphenicol, cimetidine, corticosteroids, cyclosporine, disopyramide, doxycycline, ethosuximide, felbamate, furosemide, griseofulvin, lamotrigine, phenytoin, propafenone, quinidine, tacrolimus, TCAs, and theophylline. Barbiturates may increase the metabolism of estrogens and reduce the efficacy of oral contraceptives; an alternative method of contraception should be considered. Barbiturates inhibit the hypoprothrombinemic effects of oral anticoagulants via increased metabolism. Barbiturates may enhance the metabolism of methadone resulting in methadone withdrawal. CYP2C19 inducers may decrease the levels/effects of mephobarbital; example inducers include aminoglutethimide, carbamazepine, phenytoin, and rifampin.
Mechanism of Action Increases seizure threshold in the motor cortex; depresses monosynaptic and polysynaptic transmission in the CNS
Pharmacodynamics/Kinetics
Onset of action: 20-60 minutes
Duration: 6-8 hours
Absorption: ~50%
Half-life elimination, serum: 34 hours
Dosage Oral:
Epilepsy:
Children: 6-12 mg/kg/day in 2-4 divided doses
Adults: 200-600 mg/day in 2-4 divided doses
Sedation:
Children:
<5 years: 16-32 mg 3-4 times/day
>5 years: 32-64 mg 3-4 times/day
Adults: 32-100 mg 3-4 times/day
(Continued)

Mephobarbital *(Continued)*

Dosing adjustment in renal or hepatic impairment: Use with caution and reduce dosages
Dietary Considerations High doses of pyridoxine may decrease drug effect; barbiturates may increase the metabolism of vitamin D & K; dietary requirements of vitamin D, K, C, B₁₂, folate and calcium may be increased with long-term use.
Dosage Forms Tablet: 32 mg, 50 mg, 100 mg

♦ **Mephyton**® *see Phytonadione on page 1366*

Mepivacaine *(me PIV a kane)*

U.S. Brand Names Carbocaine®; Polocaine®; Polocaine® Dental; Polocaine® MPF
Canadian Brand Names Carbocaine®; Polocaine®
Index Terms Mepivacaine Hydrochloride
Pharmacologic Category Local Anesthetic
Use Local or regional analgesia; anesthesia by local infiltration, peripheral and central neural techniques including epidural and caudal blocks; **not** for use in spinal anesthesia
Pregnancy Risk Factor C
Pregnancy Implications Animal reproduction studies have not been conducted. Mepivacaine has been used in obstetrical analgesia.
Lactation Excretion in breast milk unknown/use caution
Medication Safety Issues
Sound-alike/look-alike issues:
Mepivacaine may be confused with bupivacaine
Polocaine® may be confused with prilocaine
Contraindications Hypersensitivity to mepivacaine, other amide-type local anesthetics, or any component of the formulation
Warnings/Precautions Use with caution in patients with cardiac disease, hepatic or renal disease, or hyperthyroidism. Local anesthetics have been associated with rare occurrences of sudden respiratory arrest; convulsions due to systemic toxicity leading to cardiac arrest have been reported presumably due to intravascular injection. A test dose is recommended prior to epidural administration and all reinforcing doses with continuous catheter technique. Do not use solutions containing preservatives for caudal or epidural block. Use caution in debilitated, elderly, or acutely-ill patients; dose reduction may be required.
Adverse Reactions Degree of adverse effects in the CNS and cardiovascular system is directly related to the blood levels of mepivacaine, route of administration, and physical status of the patient. The effects below are more likely to occur after systemic administration rather than infiltration.

Cardiovascular: Bradycardia, cardiac arrest, cardiac output decreased, heart block, hyper-/hypotension, myocardial depression, syncope, tachycardia, ventricular arrhythmias
Central nervous system: Anxiety, chills, convulsions, depression, dizziness, excitation, restlessness, tremors
Dermatologic: Angioneurotic edema, diaphoresis, erythema, pruritus, urticaria
Gastrointestinal: Fecal incontinence, nausea, vomiting
Genitourinary: Incontinence, urinary retention
Neuromuscular & skeletal: Paralysis
Ocular: Blurred vision, pupil constriction
Otic: Tinnitus
Respiratory: Apnea, hypoventilation, sneezing
Miscellaneous: Allergic reaction, anaphylactoid reaction

Overdosage/Toxicology Symptoms include dizziness, cyanosis, tremors, and bronchial spasm. Treatment is primarily symptomatic and supportive. Termination of anesthesia by pneumatic tourniquet inflation should be attempted when the agent is administered by infiltration or regional injection. Seizures commonly respond to diazepam, while hypotension responds to I.V. fluids and Trendelenburg positioning. Bradyarrhythmias (when the heart rate is <60) can be treated with I.V., I.M., or SubQ atropine 15 mcg/kg. With the development of metabolic acidosis, I.V. sodium bicarbonate 0.5-2 mEq/kg and ventilatory assistance should be instituted.
Drug Interactions
Increased Effect/Toxicity: Beta-blockers could theoretically decrease clearance.
Stability Store at controlled room temperature of 15°C to 30°C (59°F to 86°F). Brief exposure up to 40°C (104°F) does not adversely affect the product. Solutions may be sterilized. Dental solutions should be protected from light.
Mechanism of Action Mepivacaine is an amide local anesthetic similar to lidocaine; like all local anesthetics, mepivacaine acts by preventing the generation and conduction of nerve impulses
Pharmacodynamics/Kinetics
Onset of action (route and dose dependent): Range: 3-20 minutes
Duration (route and dose dependent): 2-2.5 hours
Protein binding: ~75%
Metabolism: Primarily hepatic via N-demethylation, hydroxylation, and glucuronidation
Half-life elimination: Neonates: 8.7-9 hours; Adults: 1.9-3 hours
Excretion: Urine (95% as metabolites)
Dosage
Injectable local anesthetic: Dose varies with procedure, degree of anesthesia needed, vascularity of tissue, duration of anesthesia required, and physical condition of patient. The smallest dose and concentration required to produce the desired effect should be used.
Children: Maximum dose: 5-6 mg/kg; only concentrations <2% should be used in children <3 years or <14 kg (30 lbs)
Adults: Maximum dose: 400 mg; do not exceed 1000 mg/24 hours
Cervical, brachial, intercostal, pudenal nerve block: 5-40 mL of a 1% solution (maximum: 400 mg) **or** 5-20 mL of a 2% solution (maximum: 400 mg). For pudenal block, inject ½ the total dose each side.

Transvaginal block (paracervical plus pudenal): Up to 30 mL (both sides) of a 1% solution (maximum: 300 mg). Inject ¹/₂ the total dose each side.

Paracervical block: Up to 20 mL (both sides) of a 1% solution (maximum: 200 mg). Inject ¹/₂ the total dose to each side. This is the maximum recommended dose per 90-minute procedure; inject slowly with 5 minutes between sides.

Caudal and epidural block (preservative free solutions only): 15-30 mL of a 1% solution (maximum: 300 mg) **or** 10-25 mL of a 1.5% solution (maximum: 375 mg) **or** 10-20 mL of a 2% solution (maximum: 400 mg)

Infiltration: Up to 40 mL of a 1% solution (maximum: 400 mg)

Therapeutic block (pain management): 1-5 mL of a 1% solution (maximum: 50 mg) **or** 1-5 mL of a 2% solution (maximum: 100 mg)

Dental anesthesia: Adults:

Single site in upper or lower jaw: 54 mg (1.8 mL) as a 3% solution

Infiltration and nerve block of entire oral cavity: 270 mg (9 mL) as a 3% solution. Manufacturer's maximum recommended dose is not more than 400 mg to normal healthy adults.

Administration Before injecting, withdraw syringe plunger to ensure injection is not into vein or artery

Monitoring Parameters Vital signs, state of consciousness; signs of CNS toxicity

Dosage Forms

Injection, solution, as hydrochloride [contains methylparabens]:

Carbocaine®: 1% (50 mL); 2% (50 mL)

Polocaine®: 1% (50 mL); 2% (50 mL)

Injection, solution, as hydrochloride [preservative free]:

Carbocaine®: 1% (30 mL); 1.5% (30 mL); 2% (20 mL); 3% (1.8 mL) [dental cartridge]

Polocaine® Dental: 3% (1.8 mL) [dental cartridge]

Polocaine® MPF: 1% (30 mL); 1.5% (30 mL); 2% (20 mL)

♦ **Mepivacaine Hydrochloride** *see* Mepivacaine *on page 1084*

Meprobamate (me proe BA mate)

U.S. Brand Names Miltown® [DSC]

Canadian Brand Names Novo-Mepro

Index Terms Equanil

Pharmacologic Category Antianxiety Agent, Miscellaneous

Use Management of anxiety disorders

Unlabeled/Investigational Use Demonstrated value for muscle contraction, headache, premenstrual tension, external sphincter spasticity, muscle rigidity, opisthotonos-associated with tetanus

Restrictions C-IV

Pregnancy Risk Factor D

Medication Safety Issues

Sound-alike/look-alike issues:

Meprobamate may be confused with Mepergan, meperidine

Equanil may be confused with Elavil®

Dosage Oral:

Children 6-12 years: Anxiety: 100-200 mg 2-3 times/day

Adults: Anxiety: 400 mg 3-4 times/day, up to 2400 mg/day

Dosing interval in renal impairment:

Cl$_{cr}$ 10-50 mL/minute: Administer every 9-12 hours

Cl$_{cr}$ <10 mL/minute: Administer every 12-18 hours

Hemodialysis: Moderately dialyzable (20% to 50%)

Dosing adjustment in hepatic impairment: Probably necessary in patients with liver disease

Additional Information Complete prescribing information for this medication should be consulted for additional detail.

Dosage Forms

[DSC] = Discontinued product

Tablet: 200 mg, 400 mg

Miltown®: 200 mg, 400 mg [DSC]

♦ **Meprobamate and Aspirin** *see* Aspirin and Meprobamate *on page 164*

♦ **Mepron®** *see* Atovaquone *on page 173*

Mequinol and Tretinoin (ME kwi nole & TRET i noyn)

U.S. Brand Names Solagé™

Canadian Brand Names Solagé™

Index Terms Tretinoin and Mequinol

Pharmacologic Category Retinoic Acid Derivative; Vitamin A Derivative; Vitamin, Topical

Use Treatment of solar lentigines; the efficacy of using Solagé™ daily for >24 weeks has not been established. The local cutaneous safety of Solagé™ in non-Caucasians has not been adequately established.

Pregnancy Risk Factor X

Dosage Solar lentigines: Topical: Apply twice daily to solar lentigines using the applicator tip while avoiding application to the surrounding skin. Separate application by at least 8 hours or as directed by physician.

Dosage Forms Liquid, topical: Mequinol 2% and tretinoin 0.01% (30 mL) [contains alcohol 78%; dispensed in applicator bottle]

Mercaptopurine (mer kap toe PYOOR een)

U.S. Brand Names Purinethol®
Canadian Brand Names Purinethol®
Index Terms 6-Mercaptopurine (error-prone abbreviation); 6-MP (error-prone abbreviation); NSC-755
Pharmacologic Category Antineoplastic Agent, Antimetabolite; Immunosuppressant Agent
Use Treatment (maintenance and induction) of acute lymphoblastic leukemia (ALL)
Unlabeled/Investigational Use Steroid-sparing agent for corticosteroid-dependent Crohn's disease (CD) and ulcerative colitis (UC); maintenance of remission in CD; fistulizing Crohn's disease
Pregnancy Risk Factor D
Lactation Enters breast milk/contraindicated
Medication Safety Issues
Sound-alike/look-alike issues:
Purinethol® may be confused with propylthiouracil

High alert medication: The Institute for Safe Medication Practices (ISMP) includes this medication among its list of drugs which have a heightened risk of causing significant patient harm when used in error.

To avoid potentially serious dosage errors, the terms "6-mercaptopurine" or "6-MP" should be avoided; use of these terms has been associated with sixfold overdosages.
Azathioprine is metabolized to mercaptopurine; concurrent use of these commercially-available products has resulted in profound myelosuppression.
Contraindications Hypersensitivity to mercaptopurine or any component of the formulation; patients whose disease showed prior resistance to mercaptopurine or thioguanine; severe liver disease, severe bone marrow suppression; pregnancy
Warnings/Precautions Hazardous agent - use appropriate precautions for handling and disposal. Adjust dosage in patients with renal impairment or hepatic failure; use with caution in patients with prior bone marrow suppression; patients may be at risk for pancreatitis. Toxicity to immunosuppressives is increased in elderly. Start with lowest recommended adult doses. Signs of infection, such as fever and WBC rise, may not occur. Lethargy and confusion may be more prominent signs of infection. Use caution with other hepatotoxic drugs or in dosages >2.5 mg/kg/day; hepatotoxicity may occur. Patients with genetic deficiency of thiopurine methyltransferase (TPMT) or concurrent therapy with drugs which may inhibit TPMT (eg, olsalazine) or xanthine oxidase (eg, allopurinol) may be sensitive to myelosuppressive effects. Azathioprine is metabolized to mercaptopurine; concomitant use may result in profound myelosuppression and should be avoided. Immune response to vaccines may be diminished.

To avoid potentially serious dosage errors, the terms "6-mercaptopurine" or "6-MP" should be avoided; use of these terms has been associated with sixfold overdosages.
Adverse Reactions
>10%:
Hematologic: Myelosuppression; leukopenia, thrombocytopenia, anemia
Onset: 7-10 days
Nadir: 14-16 days
Recovery: 21-28 days
Hepatic: Intrahepatic cholestasis and focal centralobular necrosis (40%), characterized by hyperbilirubinemia, increased alkaline phosphatase and AST, jaundice, ascites, encephalopathy; more common at doses >2.5 mg/kg/day. Usually occurs within 2 months of therapy but may occur within 1 week, or be delayed up to 8 years.
1% to 10%:
Central nervous system: Drug fever
Dermatologic: Hyperpigmentation, rash
Endocrine & metabolic: Hyperuricemia
Gastrointestinal: Nausea, vomiting, diarrhea, stomatitis, anorexia, stomach pain, mucositis
Renal: Renal toxicity
<1% (Limited to important or life-threatening): Alopecia, dry and scaling rash, glossitis, oligospermia, tarry stools
Overdosage/Toxicology Immediate symptoms are nausea and vomiting. Delayed symptoms include bone marrow suppression, hepatic necrosis, and gastroenteritis. Efforts to minimize absorption (charcoal, gastric lavage) may be ineffective unless instituted within 60 minutes of ingestion.
Drug Interactions
Increased Effect/Toxicity: Allopurinol can cause increased levels of mercaptopurine by inhibition of xanthine oxidase. Decrease dose of mercaptopurine by 75% when both drugs are used concomitantly. May potentiate effect of bone marrow suppression (reduce mercaptopurine to 25% of dose). Synergistic liver toxicity between doxorubicin and mercaptopurine has been reported. Any agent which could potentially alter the metabolic function of the liver could produce higher drug levels and greater toxicities from either mercaptopurine or thioguanine (6-TG). Aminosalicylates (eg, olsalazine, mesalamine, sulfasalazine) may inhibit TPMT, increasing toxicity/myelosuppression of mercaptopurine. Azathioprine is metabolized to mercaptopurine; concomitant use may result in profound myelosuppression and should be avoided
Decreased Effect: Mercaptopurine inhibits the anticoagulation effect of warfarin by an unknown mechanism.
Stability Store at room temperature of 15°C to 25°C (59°F to 77°F). Protect from moisture.
Mechanism of Action Purine antagonist which inhibits DNA and RNA synthesis; acts as false metabolite and is incorporated into DNA and RNA, eventually inhibiting their synthesis; specific for the S phase of the cell cycle
Pharmacodynamics/Kinetics
Absorption: Variable and incomplete (16% to 50%)
Distribution: V_d = total body water; CNS penetration is poor

Protein binding: 19%

Metabolism: Hepatic and in GI mucosa; hepatically via xanthine oxidase and methylation via TPMT to sulfate conjugates, 6-thiouric acid, and other inactive compounds; first-pass effect

Half-life elimination (age dependent): Children: 21 minutes; Adults: 47 minutes

Time to peak, serum: ~2 hours

Excretion: Urine (46% as mercaptopurine and metabolites)

Dosage Oral (refer to individual protocols):

Children: ALL:

Induction: 2.5-5 mg/kg/day **or** 70-100 mg/m^2/day given once daily

Maintenance: 1.5-2.5 mg/kg/day **or** 50-75 mg/m^2/day given once daily

Adults:

ALL:

Induction: 2.5-5 mg/kg/day (100-200 mg)

Maintenance: 1.5-2.5 mg/kg/day **or** 80-100 mg/m^2/day given once daily

Reduction of steroid use in CD or UC, maintenance of remission in CD or fistulizing disease (unlabeled uses): Initial: 50 mg daily; may increase by 25 mg/day every 1-2 weeks as tolerated to target dose of 1-1.5 mg/kg/day

Dosage adjustment with concurrent allopurinol: Reduce mercaptopurine dosage to $\frac{1}{4}$ to $\frac{1}{3}$ the usual dose.

Dosage adjustment in TPMT-deficiency: Not established; substantial reductions are generally required only in homozygous deficiency.

Elderly: Due to renal decline with age, start with lower recommended doses for adults

Note: In ALL, administration in the evening (vs morning administration) may lower the risk of relapse.

Dosing adjustment in renal or hepatic impairment: Dose should be reduced to avoid accumulation, but specific guidelines are not available.

Hemodialysis: Removed; supplemental dosing is usually required

Dietary Considerations Should not be administered with meals.

Administration Preferably on an empty stomach (1 hour before or 2 hours after meals)

Monitoring Parameters CBC with differential and platelet count, liver function tests, uric acid, urinalysis; TPMT genotyping may identify individuals at risk for toxicity

For use as immunomodulatory therapy in CD or UC, monitor CBC with differential weekly for 1 month, then biweekly for 1 month, followed by monitoring every 1-2 months throughout the course of therapy. LFT's should be assessed every 3 months.

Dosage Forms Tablet [scored]: 50 mg

Extemporaneous Preparations A 50 mg/mL oral suspension can be prepared by crushing thirty 50 mg tablets in a mortar, and then mixing in a small amount of vehicle (a 1:1 combination of methylcellulose 1% and syrup) to create a uniform paste. Add a sufficient quantity of vehicle to make 30 mL of suspension. Label "shake well." Room temperature stability is 14 days.

Dressman JB and Poust RI, "Stability of Allopurinol and of Five Antineoplastics in Suspension," *Am J Hosp Pharm*, 1983, 40:616-8.

Nahata MC, Morosco RS, and Hipple TF, 4th ed, *Pediatric Drug Formulations*, Cincinnati, OH: Harvey Whitney Books Co, 2000.

♦ **6-Mercaptopurine (error-prone abbreviation)** *see* Mercaptopurine *on page 1086*

♦ **Mercapturic Acid** *see* Acetylcysteine *on page 39*

♦ **Meridia**® *see* Sibutramine *on page 1562*

Meropenem (mer oh PEN em)

U.S. Brand Names Merrem® I.V.

Canadian Brand Names Merrem®

Pharmacologic Category Antibiotic, Carbapenem

Additional Appendix Information

Antimicrobial Drugs of Choice *on page 1981*

Community-Acquired Pneumonia in Adults *on page 1999*

Use Treatment of intra-abdominal infections (complicated appendicitis and peritonitis); treatment of bacterial meningitis in pediatric patients ≥3 months of age caused by *S. pneumoniae*, *H. influenzae*, and *N. meningitidis*; treatment of complicated skin and skin structure infections caused by susceptible organisms

Unlabeled/Investigational Use Febrile neutropenia, urinary tract infections

Pregnancy Risk Factor B

Pregnancy Implications Teratogenic effects have not been found in animal studies; use during pregnancy only if clearly indicated.

Lactation Excretion in breast milk unknown/use caution

Contraindications Hypersensitivity to meropenem, any component of the formulation, or other carbapenems (eg, imipenem); patients who have experienced anaphylactic reactions to other beta-lactams

Warnings/Precautions

Serious hypersensitivity reactions, including anaphylaxis, have been reported (some without a history of previous allergic reactions to beta-lactams). Has been associated with CNS adverse effects, including confusional states and seizures; use caution with CNS disorders (eg, brain lesions, history of seizures, or renal impairment). Prolonged use may result in superinfection, including pseudomembranous colitis. Use with caution in patients with renal impairment; dosage adjustment required in patients with moderate-to-severe renal dysfunction. Thrombocytopenia has been reported in patients with significant renal dysfunction. Lower doses (based upon renal function) are often required in the elderly. Safety and efficacy have not been established for children <3 months of age.

Adverse Reactions

1% to 10%:

Cardiovascular: Peripheral vascular disorder (<1%)

Central nervous system: Headache (2% to 8%), pain (5%)

Dermatologic: Rash (2% to 3%, includes diaper-area moniliasis in pediatrics), pruritus (1%)

(Continued)

Meropenem *(Continued)*

Gastrointestinal: Diarrhea (4% to 5%), nausea/vomiting (1% to 8%), constipation (1% to 7%), oral moniliasis (up to 2% in pediatric patients), glossitis

Hematologic: Anemia (up to 6%)

Local: Inflammation at the injection site (2%), phlebitis/thrombophlebitis (1%), injection site reaction (1%)

Respiratory: Apnea (1%)

Miscellaneous: Sepsis (2%), septic shock (1%)

<1% (Limited to important or life-threatening): Agitation/delirium, agranulocytosis, angioedema, arrhythmia, bilirubin increased, bradycardia, BUN increased, cholestatic creatinine increased, jaundice/jaundice, decreased prothrombin time, dyspepsia, dyspnea, eosinophilia, epistaxis, erythema multiforme, gastrointestinal hemorrhage, hallucinations, hearing loss, heart failure, hemoperitoneum, hepatic failure, hyper-/hypotension, ileus, leukopenia, melena, MI, neutropenia, paresthesia, pleural effusion, pulmonary edema, pulmonary embolism, renal failure, seizure, Stevens-Johnson syndrome, syncope, thrombocytopenia, toxic epidermal necrolysis, urticaria, vaginal moniliasis

Overdosage/Toxicology No cases of acute overdosage are reported which have resulted in symptoms. Accidental overdose is possible with the use of large doses in patients with renal impairment. Supportive therapy is recommended. Meropenem and its metabolite are removable by dialysis.

Drug Interactions

Increased Effect/Toxicity: Probenecid may increase meropenem serum concentrations.

Decreased Effect: Meropenem may decrease valproic acid serum concentrations to subtherapeutic levels.

Stability Dry powder should be stored at controlled room temperature 20°C to 25°C (68°F to 77°F). Meropenem infusion vials may be reconstituted with SWFI or a compatible diluent (eg, NS). The 500 mg vials should be reconstituted with 10 mL, and 1 g vials with 20 mL. May be further diluted with compatible solutions for infusion. Consult detailed reference/product labeling for compatibility.

Injection reconstitution: Stability in vial when constituted (up to 50 mg/mL) with:

SWFI: Stable for up to 2 hours at room temperature and for up to 12 hours under refrigeration.

Sodium chloride: Stable for up to 2 hours at room temperature or for up to 18 hours under refrigeration.

Dextrose 5% injection: Stable for 1 hour at room temperature or for 8 hours under refrigeration.

Infusion admixture (1-20 mg/mL): Solution stability when diluted in NS is 4 hours at room temperature or 24 hours under refrigeration. Stability in D_5W is 1 hour at room temperature and 4 hours under refrigeration.

Mechanism of Action Inhibits bacterial cell wall synthesis by binding to several of the penicillin-binding proteins, which in turn inhibit the final transpeptidation step of peptidoglycan synthesis in bacterial cell walls, thus inhibiting cell wall biosynthesis; bacteria eventually lyse due to ongoing activity of cell wall autolytic enzymes (autolysins and murein hydrolases) while cell wall assembly is arrested

Pharmacodynamics/Kinetics

Distribution: V_d: Adults: ~0.3 L/kg, Children: 0.4-0.5 L/kg; penetrates well into most body fluids and tissues; CSF concentrations approximate those of the plasma

Protein binding: 2%

Metabolism: Hepatic; metabolized to open beta-lactam form (inactive)

Half-life elimination:

Normal renal function: 1-1.5 hours

Cl_{cr} 30-80 mL/minute: 1.9-3.3 hours

Cl_{cr} 2-30 mL/minute: 3.82-5.7 hours

Time to peak, tissue: 1 hour following infusion

Excretion: Urine (~25% as inactive metabolites)

Dosage

Usual dosage ranges:

Neonates: I.V.:

Postnatal age 0-7 days: 20 mg/kg/dose every 12 hours

Postnatal age >7 days:

Weight 1200-2000 g: 20 mg/kg/dose every 12 hours

Weight >2000 g: 20 mg/kg/dose every 8 hours

Children ≥3 months: I.V.: 60 mg/kg/day divided every 8 hours (maximum dose: 6 g/day)

Adults: I.V.: 1.5-6 g/day divided every 8 hours

Indication-specific dosing:

Children >3 months (<50 kg): I.V.:

Febrile neutropenia (unlabeled use): 20 mg/kg every 8 hours (maximum dose: 1 g every 8 hours)

Intra-abdominal infections: 20 mg/kg every 8 hours (maximum dose: 1 g every 8 hours)

Meningitis: 40 mg/kg every 8 hours (maximum dose: 2 g every 8 hours)

Skin and skin structure infections (complicated): 10 mg/kg every 8 hours (maximum dose: 500 mg every 8 hours)

Children >50 kg and Adults: I.V.:

Burkholderia pseudomallei (melioidosis), *Pseudomonas:* 1 g every 8 hours

Cholangitis, intra-abdominal infections, otitis externa, septic lateral sinus thrombosis: 1 g every 8 hours

Febrile neutropenia, pneumonia, other severe infections (unlabeled use): 1 g every 8 hours

Liver abscess: 1 g every 8 hours for 2-3 weeks, then oral therapy for duration of 4-6 weeks

Meningitis: 2 g every 8 hours

Mild-to-moderate infection: 1.5-3 g/day divided every 8 hours

Skin and skin structure infections (complicated): 500 mg every 8 hours; diabetic foot: 1 g every 8 hours

Urinary tract infections, complicated (unlabeled use): 500 mg to 1 g every 8 hours

Dosing adjustment in renal impairment: Adults:

Cl$_{cr}$ 26-50 mL/minute: Administer recommended dose based on indication every 12 hours

Cl$_{cr}$ 10-25 mL/minute: Administer one-half recommended dose every 12 hours

Cl$_{cr}$ <10 mL/minute: Administer one-half recommended dose every 24 hours

Dialysis: Meropenem and its metabolites are readily dialyzable

Continuous arteriovenous or venovenous hemodiafiltration effects: Dose as Cl$_{cr}$ 10-50 mL/minute

Dietary Considerations 1 g of meropenem contains 90.2 mg of sodium as sodium carbonate (3.92 mEq)

Administration Administer I.V. infusion over 15-30 minutes; I.V. bolus injection over 3-5 minutes

Monitoring Parameters Monitor for signs of anaphylaxis during first dose

Dosage Forms Injection, powder for reconstitution: 500 mg [contains sodium 45.1 mg as sodium carbonate (1.96 mEq)]; 1 g [contains sodium 90.2 mg as sodium carbonate (3.92 mEq)]

♦ **Merrem® (Can)** see Meropenem on page 1087
♦ **Merrem® I.V.** see Meropenem on page 1087
♦ **Meruvax® II** see Rubella Virus Vaccine (Live) on page 1540

Mesalamine (me SAL a meen)

U.S. Brand Names Asacol®; Canasa™; Pentasa®; Rowasa®

Canadian Brand Names Asacol®; Asacol® 800; Mesasal®; Novo-5 ASA; Pendo-5 ASA; Pentasa®; Quintasa®; Rowasa®; Salofalk®

Index Terms 5-Aminosalicylic Acid; 5-ASA; Fisalamine; Mesalazine

Pharmacologic Category 5-Aminosalicylic Acid Derivative

Use

Oral: Treatment and maintenance of remission of mildly to moderately active ulcerative colitis

Rectal: Treatment of active mild to moderate distal ulcerative colitis, proctosigmoiditis, or proctitis

Pregnancy Risk Factor B

Lactation Excretion in breast milk unknown/use caution

Medication Safety Issues

Sound-alike/look-alike issues:

Mesalamine may be confused with mecamylamine

Asacol® may be confused with Ansaid®, Os-Cal®

Contraindications Hypersensitivity to mesalamine, sulfasalazine, salicylates, or any component of the formulation; Canasa™ suppositories contain saturated vegetable fatty acid esters (contraindicated in patients with allergy to these components)

Warnings/Precautions May cause an acute intolerance syndrome (cramping, acute abdominal pain, bloody diarrhea; sometimes fever, headache, rash); discontinue if this occurs. Patients with pyloric stenosis may have prolonged gastric retention of tablets, delaying the release of mesalamine in the colon. Pericarditis should be considered in patients with chest pain; pancreatitis should be considered in patients with new abdominal complaints. Symptomatic worsening of colitis/IBD may occur following initiation of therapy. Oligospermia (rare) has been reported in males. Use caution in patients with impaired renal or hepatic function. Renal impairment (including minimal change nephropathy and acute/chronic interstitial nephritis) has been reported; use caution with other medications converted to mesalamine. Postmarketing reports suggest an increased incidence of blood dyscrasias in patients >65 years of age. In addition, elderly may have difficulty administering and retaining rectal suppositories and decreased renal function; use with caution and monitor. Safety and efficacy in pediatric patients have not been established.

Rowasa® enema: Contains potassium metabisulfite; may cause severe hypersensitivity reactions (ie, anaphylaxis) in patients with sulfite allergies.

Adverse Reactions Adverse effects vary depending upon dosage form. Effects as reported with tablets, unless otherwise noted:

>10%:

Central nervous system: Headache (suppository 14%), pain (14%)

Gastrointestinal: Abdominal pain (18%; enema 8%)

Genitourinary: Eructation (16%)

Respiratory: Pharyngitis (11%)

1% to 10%:

Cardiovascular: Chest pain (3%), peripheral edema (3%)

Central nervous system: Chills (3%), dizziness (suppository 3%), fever (enema 3%; suppository 1%), insomnia (2%), malaise (2%)

Dermatologic: Rash (6%; suppository 1%), pruritus (3%; enema 1%), acne (2%; suppository 1%)

Gastrointestinal: Abdominal pain (enema 8%; suppository 5%), colitis exacerbation (3%; suppository 1%), constipation (5%), diarrhea (suppository 3%), dyspepsia (6%), flatulence (enema 6%; suppository 5%), hemorrhoids (enema 1%), nausea (capsule/suppository 3%), nausea and vomiting (capsule 1%), rectal pain (enema 1%; suppository 2%), vomiting (5%)

Local: Pain on insertion of enema tip (enema 1%)

Neuromuscular & skeletal: Back pain (7%; enema 1%), arthralgia (5%), hypertonia (5%), myalgia (3%), arthritis (2%), leg/joint pain (enema 2%)

Ocular: Conjunctivitis (2%)

Respiratory: Flu-like syndrome (3%; enema 5%), cough increased (2%)

Miscellaneous: Diaphoresis (3%)

(Continued)

Mesalamine *(Continued)*

<1% (Limited to important or life-threatening): Agranulocytosis, alopecia, aplastic anemia, cholestatic jaundice, cholecystitis, edema, erythema nodosum, fibrosing alveolitis, gout, Guillain-Barré syndrome, hepatitis, hepatocellular damage, hepatotoxicity, infertility, interstitial nephritis, Kawasaki-like syndrome, liver enzymes increased, liver failure, liver necrosis, lupus-like syndrome, minimal change nephrotic syndrome, myocarditis, nephropathy, nephrotoxicity, neutropenia, oligospermia (rare), pancreatitis, pancytopenia, pericarditis, thrombocytopenia, vertigo

Overdosage/Toxicology Symptoms include decreased motor activity, diarrhea, vomiting, and renal function impairment. Treatment is supportive following emesis, gastric lavage, and activated charcoal slurry.

Drug Interactions
Increased Effect/Toxicity: Mesalamine may increase the risk of myelosuppression from azathioprine, mercaptopurine, and thioguanine.

Decreased Effect: Decreased digoxin bioavailability.

Ethanol/Nutrition/Herb Interactions Food: Oral: Mesalamine serum levels may be decreased if taken with food.

Stability
Enema: Store at controlled room temperature. Use promptly once foil wrap is removed. Contents may darken with time (do not use if dark brown).

Suppository: Store at controlled room temperature; do not refrigerate. Protect from direct heat, light, and humidity.

Tablet: Store at controlled room temperature.

Mechanism of Action Mesalamine (5-aminosalicylic acid) is the active component of sulfasalazine; the specific mechanism of action of mesalamine is unknown; however, it is thought that it modulates local chemical mediators of the inflammatory response, especially leukotrienes, and is also postulated to be a free radical scavenger or an inhibitor of tumor necrosis factor (TNF); action appears topical rather than systemic

Pharmacodynamics/Kinetics
Absorption: Rectal: Variable and dependent upon retention time, underlying GI disease, and colonic pH; Oral: Tablet: ~28%, Capsule: ~20% to 30%

Metabolism: Hepatic and via GI tract to acetyl-5-aminosalicylic acid

Half-life elimination: 5-ASA: 0.5-1.5 hours; acetyl-5-ASA: 5-10 hours

Time to peak, serum: 4-7 hours

Excretion: Urine (as metabolites); feces (<2%)

Dosage Adults (usual course of therapy is 3-8 weeks):
Oral:
Treatment of ulcerative colitis:
Capsule: 1 g 4 times/day
Tablet: Initial: 800 mg (2 tablets) 3 times/day for 6 weeks
Maintenance of remission of ulcerative colitis:
Capsule: 1 g 4 times/day
Tablet: 1.6 g/day in divided doses
Rectal:
Retention enema: 60 mL (4 g) at bedtime, retained overnight, approximately 8 hours
Rectal suppository (Canasa™):
500 mg: Insert 1 suppository in rectum twice daily; may increase to 3 times/day if inadequate response is seen after 2 weeks
1000 mg: Insert 1 suppository in rectum daily at bedtime
Note: Suppositories should be retained for at least 1-3 hours to achieve maximum benefit.
Note: Some patients may require rectal and oral therapy concurrently.

Elderly: See adult dosing; use with caution

Dietary Considerations Canasa™ rectal suppository contains saturated vegetable fatty acid esters.

Administration
Oral: Swallow capsules or tablets whole, do not chew or crush.

Rectal enema: Shake bottle well. Retain enemas for 8 hours or as long as practical.

Suppository: Remove foil wrapper; avoid excessive handling. Should be retained for at least 1-3 hours to achieve maximum benefit.

Monitoring Parameters CBC and renal function, particularly in elderly patients

Dosage Forms
Capsule, controlled release (Pentasa®): 250 mg, 500 mg

Suppository, rectal (Canasa™): 500 mg [DSC], 1000 mg [contains saturated vegetable fatty acid esters]

Suspension, rectal: 4 g/60 mL (7s, 28s) [contains potassium metabisulfite and sodium benzoate]

Rowasa®: 4 g/60 mL (7s, 28s) [contains potassium metabisulfite and sodium benzoate]

Tablet, delayed release [enteric coated] (Asacol®): 400 mg

- **Mesalazine** *see* Mesalamine *on page 1089*
- **Mesasal® (Can)** *see* Mesalamine *on page 1089*
- **M-Eslon® (Can)** *see* Morphine Sulfate *on page 1171*

Mesna (MES na)

U.S. Brand Names Mesnex®
Canadian Brand Names Mesnex®; Uromitexan
Index Terms Sodium 2-Mercaptoethane Sulfonate
Pharmacologic Category Antidote
Use Orphan drug: Prevention of hemorrhagic cystitis induced by ifosfamide
Unlabeled/Investigational Use Prevention of hemorrhagic cystitis induced by cyclophosphamide
Pregnancy Risk Factor B
Pregnancy Implications Teratogenic effects were not observed in animal studies. There are no adequate and well-controlled studies in pregnant women. Use during pregnancy only if clearly needed.
Lactation Excretion in breast milk unknown/not recommended
Contraindications Hypersensitivity to mesna or other thiol compounds, or any component of the formulation
Warnings/Precautions Examine morning urine specimen for hematuria prior to ifosfamide or cyclophosphamide treatment; if hematuria (>50 RBC/HPF) develops, reduce the ifosfamide/cyclophosphamide dose or discontinue the drug; will not prevent or alleviate other toxicities associated with ifosfamide or cyclophosphamide and will not prevent hemorrhagic cystitis in all patients. Allergic reactions have been reported; patients with autoimmune disorders may be at increased risk. Symptoms ranged from mild hypersensitivity to systemic anaphylactic reactions. I.V. formulation contains benzyl alcohol; do not use in neonates or infants.
Adverse Reactions Reported as part of a chemotherapy regimen.
>10%: Gastrointestinal: Bad taste in mouth with oral administration (100%), vomiting (secondary to the bad taste after oral administration, or with high I.V. doses)
<1% (Limited to important or life-threatening): Anaphylaxis, hypersensitivity, hypertonia, injection site reaction, limb pain, myalgia, platelet count decreased, tachycardia, tachypnea
Drug Interactions
Decreased Effect: Warfarin: Questionable alterations in coagulation control.
Stability Store intact vials and tablets at controlled room temperature of 20°C to 25°C (68°F to 77°F). Opened multidose vials may be stored and used for up to 8 days after opening. Dilute injection in 50-1000 mL D₅W, NS, or lactated Ringer's for infusion. Solutions in D₅W or lactated Ringer's are stable for at least 48 hours at room temperature. Solutions in NS are stable for at least 24 hours at room temperature. Solutions in plastic syringes are stable for 9 days under refrigeration, or at room or body temperature. Solutions of mesna and ifosfamide in lactated Ringer's are stable for 7 days in a PVC ambulatory infusion pump reservoir. Mesna injection is stable for at least 7 days when diluted 1:2 or 1:5 with grape- or orange-flavored syrups or 11:1 to 1:100 in carbonated beverages for oral administration.
Mechanism of Action In blood, mesna is oxidized to dimesna which in turn is reduced in the kidney back to mesna, supplying a free thiol group which binds to and inactivates acrolein, the urotoxic metabolite of ifosfamide and cyclophosphamide
Pharmacodynamics/Kinetics
Distribution: No tissue penetration
Protein binding: 69% to 75%
Metabolism: Rapidly oxidized intravascularly to mesna disulfide; mesna disulfide is reduced in renal tubules back to mesna following glomerular filtration.
Bioavailability: Oral: 45% to 79%
Half-life elimination: Parent drug: 24 minutes; Mesna disulfide: 72 minutes
Time to peak, plasma: 2-3 hours
Excretion: Urine; as unchanged drug (18% to 26%) and metabolites
Dosage Children and Adults (refer to individual protocols):
I.V.: Recommended dose is 60% of the ifosfamide dose given in 3 divided doses (0, 4, and 8 hours after the start of ifosfamide)
Alternative I.V. regimens include 80% of the ifosfamide dose given in 4 divided doses (0, 3, 6, and 9 hours after the start of ifosfamide) and continuous infusions
I.V./Oral: Recommended dose is 100% of the ifosfamide dose, given as 20% of the ifosfamide dose I.V. at hour 0, followed by 40% of the ifosfamide dose given orally 2 and 6 hours after start of ifosfamide
Administration
Oral: Administer orally in tablet formulation or parenteral solution diluted in water, milk, juice, or carbonated beverages; patients who vomit within 2 hours of taking oral mesna should repeat the dose or receive I.V. mesna
I.V.: Administer by short (15-30 minutes) infusion or continuous (24 hour) infusion
Monitoring Parameters Urinalysis
Test Interactions False-positive urinary ketones with Multistix® or Labstix®
Additional Information A parenteral formulation without benzyl alcohol can be requested directly from the manufacturer.
Dosage Forms
Injection, solution: 100 mg/mL (10 mL) [contains benzyl alcohol]
Tablet: 400 mg

♦ **Mesnex®** see Mesna on page 1091

Mesoridazine (mez oh RID a zeen)

U.S. Brand Names Serentil® [DSC]
Canadian Brand Names Serentil®
Index Terms Mesoridazine Besylate
Pharmacologic Category Antipsychotic Agent, Typical, Phenothiazine
Additional Appendix Information
Antipsychotic Agents on page 1872
(Continued)

Mesoridazine *(Continued)*

Use Management of schizophrenic patients who fail to respond adequately to treatment with other antipsychotic drugs, either because of insufficient effectiveness or the inability to achieve an effective dose due to intolerable adverse effects from these drugs

Unlabeled/Investigational Use Psychosis

Pregnancy Risk Factor C

Lactation Enters breast milk/contraindicated (AAP rates "of concern")

Medication Safety Issues
Sound-alike/look-alike issues:
Serentil® may be confused with selegiline, Serevent®, Seroquel®, sertraline, Serzone®, Sinequan®, Surgicel®

Contraindications Hypersensitivity to mesoridazine or any component of the formulation (cross-reactivity between phenothiazines may occur); severe CNS depression and coma; prolonged QT interval (>450 msec), including prolongation due to congenital causes; history of arrhythmias; concurrent use of medications which prolong QT_c (including type Ia and type III antiarrhythmics, cyclic antidepressants, some fluoroquinolones, cisapride)

Warnings/Precautions Safety in children <6 months of age has not been established; use with caution in patients with cardiovascular disease or seizures; benefits of therapy must be weighed against risks of therapy; doses >1 g/day frequently cause pigmentary retinopathy; some products contain sulfites and/or tartrazine; use with caution in patients with narrow-angle glaucoma, bone marrow suppression, severe liver disease.

[U.S. Boxed Warning]: Has been shown to prolong QT_c interval in a dose-dependent manner (associated with an increased risk of torsade de pointes). Patients should have a baseline ECG prior to initiation, and should not receive mesoridazine if baseline QT_c >450 msec. Mesoridazine should be discontinued in patients with a QT_c interval >500 msec. Potassium levels must be evaluated and normalized prior to and throughout treatment.

May cause hypotension, particularly with I.M. administration. Highly sedating, use with caution in disorders where CNS depression is a feature. Use with caution in Parkinson's disease. Caution in patients with hemodynamic instability; bone marrow suppression; predisposition to seizures; subcortical brain damage; severe cardiac, hepatic, renal, or respiratory disease. Esophageal dysmotility and aspiration have been associated with antipsychotic use; use with caution in patients at risk of pneumonia (ie, Alzheimer's disease). Caution in breast cancer or other prolactin-dependent tumors (may elevate prolactin levels). May alter temperature regulation or mask toxicity of other drugs due to antiemetic effects. May cause orthostatic hypotension - use with caution in patients at risk of this effect or those who would tolerate transient hypotensive episodes (cerebrovascular disease, cardiovascular disease, or other medications which may predispose).

Phenothiazines may cause anticholinergic effects (confusion, agitation, constipation, xerostomia, blurred vision, urinary retention). Therefore, they should be used with caution in patients with decreased gastrointestinal motility, urinary retention, BPH, xerostomia, or visual problems. Conditions which also may be exacerbated by cholinergic blockade include narrow-angle glaucoma (screening is recommended) and worsening of myasthenia gravis. Relative to other antipsychotics, mesoridazine has a high potency of cholinergic blockade.

May cause extrapyramidal reactions, including pseudoparkinsonism, acute dystonic reactions, akathisia, and tardive dyskinesia (risk of these reactions is low relative to other neuroleptics). May be associated with neuroleptic malignant syndrome (NMS) or pigmentary retinopathy (particularly at doses >1 g/day).

Adverse Reactions Frequency not defined.
Cardiovascular: Hypotension, orthostatic hypotension, tachycardia, QT prolongation (dose dependent, up to 100% of patients at higher dosages), syncope, edema
Central nervous system: Pseudoparkinsonism, akathisia, dystonias, tardive dyskinesia, dizziness, drowsiness, restlessness, ataxia, slurred speech, neuroleptic malignant syndrome (NMS), impairment of temperature regulation, lowering of seizure threshold
Dermatologic: Increased sensitivity to sun, rash, itching, angioneurotic edema, dermatitis, discoloration of skin (blue-gray)
Endocrine & metabolic: Changes in menstrual cycle, libido (changes in), gynecomastia, lactation, galactorrhea
Gastrointestinal: Constipation, xerostomia, weight gain, nausea, vomiting, stomach pain
Genitourinary: Difficulty in urination, ejaculatory disturbances, impotence, enuresis, incontinence, priapism, urinary retention
Hematologic: Agranulocytosis, leukopenia, eosinophilia, thrombocytopenia, anemia, aplastic anemia
Hepatic: Cholestatic jaundice, hepatotoxicity
Neuromuscular & skeletal: Weakness, tremor, rigidity
Ocular: Pigmentary retinopathy, photophobia, blurred vision, cornea and lens changes
Respiratory: Nasal congestion
Miscellaneous: Diaphoresis (decreased), lupus-like syndrome

Overdosage/Toxicology Symptoms include deep sleep, coma, extrapyramidal symptoms, abnormal involuntary muscle movements, and hypotension. Monitor for cardiac arrhythmias and avoid use of drugs which prolong the QT interval. Following initiation of essential overdose management, toxic symptom supportive treatment should be initiated. Hypotension usually responds to I.V. fluids or Trendelenburg positioning. If unresponsive to these measures, the use of a parenteral inotrope may be required. Seizures commonly respond to diazepam (I.V. 5-10 mg bolus in adults every 15 minutes, if needed, up to a total of 30 mg; I.V. 0.25-0.4 mg/kg/dose up to a total of 10 mg in children) or to phenytoin or phenobarbital. Critical cardiac arrhythmias often respond to I.V. phenytoin (15 mg/kg up to 1 g), while other antiarrhythmics can be used. Extrapyramidal symptoms (eg, dystonic reactions) can be managed with benztropine mesylate I.V. 1-2 mg (adults).

Drug Interactions
Increased Effect/Toxicity: Use of mesoridazine with other agents known to prolong QT_c may increase the risk of malignant arrhythmias; concurrent use is contraindicated -

includes type I and type III antiarrhythmics, TCAs, and some quinolone antibiotics (sparfloxacin, moxifloxacin, gatifloxacin). Mesoridazine may increase the effect and/or toxicity of antihypertensives, anticholinergics, lithium, CNS depressants (ethanol, opioid analgesics), and trazodone. Metoclopramide may increase risk of extrapyramidal symptoms (EPS). Acetylcholinesterase inhibitors (central) may increase the risk of antipsychotic-related EPS.

Decreased Effect: Mesoridazine may inhibit the activity of bromocriptine and levodopa. Benztropine (and other anticholinergics) may inhibit the therapeutic response to mesoridazine and excess anticholinergic effects may occur. Mesoridazine and possibly other low potency antipsychotic may reverse the pressor effects of epinephrine.

Ethanol/Nutrition/Herb Interactions
Ethanol: Avoid ethanol (may increase CNS depression).
Herb/Nutraceutical: Avoid valerian, St John's wort, kava kava, gotu kola (may increase CNS depression).

Stability Protect all dosage forms from light. Clear or slightly yellow solutions may be used. Should be dispensed in amber or opaque vials/bottles. Solutions may be diluted or mixed with fruit juices or other liquids but must be administered immediately after mixing. Do not prepare bulk solutions or store bulk dilutions.

Mechanism of Action Mesoridazine is a piperidine phenothiazine antipsychotic which blocks postsynaptic CNS dopamine$_2$ receptors in the mesolimbic and mesocortical areas

Pharmacodynamics/Kinetics
Duration: 4-6 hours
Absorption: Tablet: Erratic; Liquid: More dependable
Protein binding: 91% to 99%
Half-life elimination: 24-48 hours
Time to peak, serum: 2-4 hours; Steady-state serum: 4-7 days
Excretion: Urine

Dosage Concentrate may be diluted just prior to administration with distilled water, acidified tap water, orange or grape juice; do not prepare and store bulk dilutions

Adults: Schizophrenia/psychoses:
Oral: 25-50 mg 3 times/day; maximum: 100-400 mg/day
I.M.: Initial: 25 mg, repeat in 30-60 minutes as needed; optimal dosage range: 25-200 mg/day

Elderly: Behavioral symptoms associated with dementia:
Oral: Initial: 10 mg 1-2 times/day; if <10 mg/day is desired, consider administering 10 mg every other day (qod). Increase dose at 4- to 7-day intervals by 10-25 mg/day; increase dose intervals (bid, tid, etc) as necessary to control response or side effects. Maximum daily dose: 250 mg. Gradual increases (titration) may prevent some side effects or decrease their severity.
I.M.: Initial: 25 mg; repeat doses in 30-60 minutes if necessary. Dose range: 25-200 mg/day. Elderly usually require less than maximal daily dose.

Hemodialysis: Not dialyzable (0% to 5%)

Administration When administering I.M. or I.V., watch for hypotension. Dilute oral concentrate just prior to administration with distilled water, acidified tap water, orange or grape juice. Do not prepare and store bulk dilutions. Do not mix oral solutions of mesoridazine and lithium, these oral liquids are incompatible when mixed. **Note:** Avoid skin contact with oral medication; may cause contact dermatitis.

Monitoring Parameters Vital signs, orthostatic blood pressures; lipid profile, fasting blood glucose/Hgb A$_{1c}$, baseline (and periodic) serum potassium; BMI; mental status, abnormal involuntary movement scale (AIMS); tremors, gait changes, abnormal movement in trunk, neck, buccal area or extremities; monitor target behaviors for which the agent is given; monitor hepatic function (especially if fever with flu-like symptoms); baseline ECG, do not initiate if QT$_c$ >450 msec (discontinue in any patient with a QT$_c$ >500 msec)

Dosage Forms [DSC] = Discontinued product
Injection, solution, as besylate [DSC]: 25 mg/mL (1 mL)
Liquid, oral, as besylate [DSC]: 25 mg/mL (118 mL) [contains alcohol 0.61%]
Tablet, as besylate [DSC]: 10 mg, 25 mg, 50 mg, 100 mg

- **Mesoridazine Besylate** see Mesoridazine on page 1091
- **Mestinon**® see Pyridostigmine on page 1462
- **Mestinon**®**-SR (Can)** see Pyridostigmine on page 1462
- **Mestinon**® **Timespan**® see Pyridostigmine on page 1462

Mestranol and Norethindrone (MES tra nole & nor eth IN drone)

U.S. Brand Names Necon® 1/50; Norinyl® 1+50; Ortho-Novum® 1/50
Canadian Brand Names Ortho-Novum® 1/50
Index Terms Norethindrone and Mestranol; Ortho Novum 1/50
Pharmacologic Category Contraceptive; Estrogen and Progestin Combination
Use Prevention of pregnancy
Unlabeled/Investigational Use Treatment of hypermenorrhea (menorrhagia); pain associated with endometriosis; dysmenorrhea; dysfunctional uterine bleeding
Pregnancy Risk Factor X
Pregnancy Implications Pregnancy should be ruled out prior to treatment and discontinued if pregnancy occurs. In general, the use of combination hormonal contraceptives when inadvertently taken early in pregnancy have not been associated with teratogenic effects. Due to increased risk of thromboembolism postpartum, combination hormonal contraceptives should not be started earlier than 4-6 weeks following delivery. Hormonal contraceptives may be less effective in obese patients. An increase in oral contraceptive failure was noted in women with a BMI >27.3. Similar findings were noted in patients weighing ≥90 kg (198 lb) using the contraceptive patch.
Lactation Enters breast milk/not recommended (AAP rates "compatible")
(Continued)

Mestranol and Norethindrone *(Continued)*

Medication Safety Issues
Sound-alike/look-alike issues:
Norinyl® may be confused with Nardil®

Contraindications Hypersensitivity to mestranol, norethindrone, or any component of the formulation; history of or current thrombophlebitis or venous thromboembolic disorders (including DVT, PE); active or recent (within 1 year) arterial thromboembolic disease (eg, stroke, MI); cerebral vascular disease, coronary artery disease, valvular heart disease with complications, severe hypertension; diabetes mellitus with vascular involvement; severe headache with focal neurological symptoms; known or suspected breast carcinoma, endometrial cancer, estrogen-dependent neoplasms, undiagnosed abnormal genital bleeding; hepatic dysfunction or tumor, cholestatic jaundice of pregnancy, jaundice with prior combination hormonal contraceptive use; major surgery with prolonged immobilization; heavy smoking (≥15 cigarettes/day) in patients >35 years of age; pregnancy

Warnings/Precautions Combination hormonal contraceptives do not protect against HIV infection or other sexually-transmitted diseases. **[U.S. Boxed Warning]: The risk of cardiovascular side effects increases in women who smoke cigarettes, especially those who are >35 years of age; women who use combination hormonal contraceptives should be strongly advised not to smoke.** Combination hormonal contraceptives may lead to increased risk of myocardial infarction, use with caution in patients with risk factors for coronary artery disease. May increase the risk of thromboembolism. Whenever possible, combination hormonal contraceptives should be discontinued at least 4 weeks prior to and for 2 weeks following elective surgery associated with an increased risk of thromboembolism or during periods of prolonged immobilization. Combination hormonal contraceptives may have a dose-related risk of vascular disease, hypertension, and gallbladder disease. Women with hypertension or renal disease should be encouraged to use a nonhormonal form of contraception. The use of combination hormonal contraceptives has been associated with a slight increase in frequency of breast cancer, however, studies are not consistent. Combination hormonal contraceptives may cause glucose intolerance. Retinal thrombosis has been reported (rarely). Use caution with conditions that may be aggravated by fluid retention, depression, or history of migraine. Not for use prior to menarche.

The minimum dosage combination of estrogen/progestin that will effectively treat the individual patient should be used. New patients should be started on products containing ≤0.035 mg of estrogen per tablet.

Adverse Reactions Frequency not defined.
Cardiovascular: Arterial thromboembolism, cerebral hemorrhage, cerebral thrombosis, edema, hypertension, mesenteric thrombosis, MI
Central nervous system: Depression, dizziness, headache, migraine, nervousness, premenstrual syndrome, stroke
Dermatologic: Acne, erythema multiforme, erythema nodosum, hirsutism, loss of scalp hair, melasma (may persist), rash (allergic)
Endocrine & metabolic: Amenorrhea, breakthrough bleeding, breast enlargement, breast secretion, breast tenderness, carbohydrate intolerance, lactation decreased (postpartum), glucose tolerance decreased, libido changes, menstrual flow changes, sex hormone-binding globulins (SHBG) increased, spotting, temporary infertility (following discontinuation), thyroid-binding globulin increased, triglycerides increased
Gastrointestinal: Abdominal cramps, appetite changes, bloating, cholestasis, colitis, gallbladder disease, jaundice, nausea, vomiting, weight gain/loss
Genitourinary: Cervical erosion changes, cervical secretion changes, cystitis-like syndrome, vaginal candidiasis, vaginitis
Hematologic: Antithrombin III decreased, folate levels decreased, hemolytic uremic syndrome, norepinephrine induced platelet aggregability increased, porphyria, prothrombin increased; factors VII, VIII, IX, and X increased
Hepatic: Benign liver tumors, Budd-Chiari syndrome, cholestatic jaundice, hepatic adenomas
Local: Thrombophlebitis
Ocular: Cataracts, change in corneal curvature (steepening), contact lens intolerance, optic neuritis, retinal thrombosis
Renal: Impaired renal function
Respiratory: Pulmonary thromboembolism
Miscellaneous: Hemorrhagic eruption

Overdosage/Toxicology Toxicity is unlikely following single exposures of excessive doses. Treatment following emesis and charcoal administration should be supportive and symptomatic.

Drug Interactions
Cytochrome P450 Effect:
Mestranol: **Substrate** of CYP2C9 (major); Based on active metabolite ethinyl estradiol: **Substrate** of CYP3A4 (major), 3A5-7 (minor); **Inhibits** CYP1A2 (weak), 2B6 (weak), 2C19 (weak), 3A4 (weak)
Norethindrone: **Substrate** of CYP3A4 (major); **Induces** CYP2C19 (weak)

Increased Effect/Toxicity: Acetaminophen and ascorbic acid may increase plasma levels of estrogen component. Atorvastatin and indinavir increase plasma levels of combination hormonal contraceptives. Combination hormonal contraceptives increase the plasma levels of alprazolam, chlordiazepoxide, cyclosporine, diazepam, prednisolone, selegiline, theophylline, tricyclic antidepressants. Combination hormonal contraceptives may increase (or decrease) the effects of coumarin derivatives.

Decreased Effect: CYP2C9 Inhibitors may increase the levels/effects of (drugname). Example inhibitors include delavirdine, fluconazole, gemfibrozil, ketoconazole, nicardipine, NSAIDs, sulfonamides, and tolbutamide. CYP3A4 inducers may decrease the levels of ethinyl estradiol (active metabolite of mestranol); example inducers include aminoglutethimide, carbamazepine, nafcillin, nevirapine, phenobarbital, phenytoin, and rifamycins. Combination hormonal contraceptives may decrease plasma levels of acetaminophen, clofibric acid, lorazepam, morphine, oxazepam, salicylic acid, temazepam. Contraceptive effect decreased by acitretin, aminoglutethimide, amprenavir, griseofulvin, lopinavir, nelfinavir, nevirapine, penicillins (effect not consistent), ritonavir, tetracyclines (effect not consistent) troglatazone. Combination hormonal contraceptives may decrease (or increase) the effects of coumarin derivatives.

Ethanol/Nutrition/Herb Interactions
Food: CNS effects of caffeine may be enhanced if oral contraceptives are used concurrently with caffeine. Grapefruit juice increases ethinyl estradiol concentrations and would be expected to increase progesterone serum levels as well; clinical implications are unclear.
Herb/Nutraceutical: St John's wort may decrease the effectiveness of combination hormonal contraceptives by inducing hepatic enzymes. Avoid dong quai and black cohosh (have estrogen activity). Avoid saw palmetto, red clover, ginseng.

Stability Store at controlled room temperature of 25°C (77°F).

Mechanism of Action Combination oral contraceptives inhibit ovulation via a negative feed-back mechanism on the hypothalamus, which alters the normal pattern of gonadotropin secretion of a follicle-stimulating hormone (FSH) and luteinizing hormone by the anterior pituitary. The follicular phase FSH and midcycle surge of gonadotropins are inhibited. In addition, combination hormonal contraceptives produce alterations in the genital tract, including changes in the cervical mucus, rendering it unfavorable for sperm penetration even if ovulation occurs. Changes in the endometrium may also occur, producing an unfavorable environment for nidation. Combination hormonal contraceptive drugs may alter the tubal transport of the ova through the fallopian tubes. Progestational agents may also alter sperm fertility.

Pharmacodynamics/Kinetics
Mestranol: Metabolism: Hepatic via demethylation to ethinyl estradiol

Dosage Oral: Adults: Female: Contraception:
Schedule 1 (Sunday starter): Dose begins on first Sunday after onset of menstruation; if the menstrual period starts on Sunday, take first tablet that very same day. **With a Sunday start, an additional method of contraception should be used until after the first 7 days of consecutive administration.**
For 21-tablet package: Dosage is 1 tablet daily for 21 consecutive days, followed by 7 days off of the medication; a new course begins on the 8th day after the last tablet is taken.
For 28-tablet package: Dosage is 1 tablet daily without interruption.
Schedule 2 (Day 1 starter): Dose starts on first day of menstrual cycle taking 1 tablet daily.
For 21-tablet package: Dosage is 1 tablet daily for 21 consecutive days, followed by 7 days off of the medication; a new course begins on the 8th day after the last tablet is taken.
For 28-tablet package: Dosage is 1 tablet daily without interruption.
If all doses have been taken on schedule and one menstrual period is missed, continue dosing cycle. If two consecutive menstrual periods are missed, pregnancy test is required before a new dosing cycle is started.
Missed doses **monophasic formulations** (refer to package insert for complete information):
One dose missed: Take as soon as remembered or take 2 tablets next day
Two consecutive doses missed in the first 2 weeks: Take 2 tablets as soon as remembered or 2 tablets next 2 days. **An additional method of contraception should be used for 7 days after missed dose.**
Two consecutive doses missed in week 3 or three consecutive doses missed at any time: **An additional method of contraception must be used for 7 days after a missed dose:**
Schedule 1 (Sunday starter): Continue dose of 1 tablet daily until Sunday, then discard the rest of the pack, and a new pack should be started that same day.
Schedule 2 (Day 1 starter): Current pack should be discarded, and a new pack should be started that same day.

Dosage adjustment in renal impairment: Specific guidelines not available; use with caution and monitor blood pressure closely. Consider other forms of contraception.

Dosage adjustment in hepatic impairment: Contraindicated in patients with hepatic impairment

Dietary Considerations Should be taken at same time each day.

Administration Administer at the same time each day. Administer at bedtime to minimize occurrence of adverse effects.

Monitoring Parameters Before starting therapy, a physical exam with reference to the breasts and pelvis are recommended, including a Papanicolaou smear. Exam may be deferred if appropriate; pregnancy should be ruled out prior to use. Monitor patient closely for loss of vision, sudden onset of proptosis, diplopia, migraine; blood pressure; signs and symptoms of thromboembolic disorders; signs or symptoms of depression; glycemic control in diabetics; lipid profiles in patients being treated for hyperlipidemias. Adequate diagnostic measures, including endometrial sampling, if indicated, should be performed to rule out malignancy in all cases of undiagnosed abnormal vaginal bleeding.

Additional Information The World Health Organization (WHO) has issued revised management recommendations for missed combined oral contraceptive pills. Refer to the following reference for a complete presentation and discussion of the guidelines:
Faculty of Family Planning and Reproductive Health Care Clinical Effectiveness Unit, "Faculty Statement from the CEU on a New Publication: WHO Selected Practice Recommendations for Contraceptive Use Update. Missed Pills: New Recommendations," *J Fam Plann Reprod Health Care*, 2005, 31(2):153-5.

Dosage Forms Tablet, monophasic formulations:
Necon® 1/50: Norethindrone 1 mg and mestranol 0.05 mg [21 light blue tablets and 7 white inactive tablets] (28s)
Norinyl® 1+50: Norethindrone 1 mg and mestranol 0.05 mg [21 white tablets and 7 orange inactive tablets] (28s)
Ortho-Novum® 1/50: Norethindrone 1 mg and mestranol 0.05 mg [21 yellow tablets and 7 green inactive tablets] (28s)

♦ **Metacortandralone** *see* PrednisoLONE *on page 1413*
♦ **Metadate® CD** *see* Methylphenidate *on page 1119*
♦ **Metadate® ER** *see* Methylphenidate *on page 1119*
♦ **Metadol™ (Can)** *see* Methadone *on page 1100*

♦ **Metaglip™** *see* Glipizide and Metformin *on page 801*

♦ **Metamucil®** **[OTC]** *see* Psyllium *on page 1458*

♦ **Metamucil®** **(Can)** *see* Psyllium *on page 1458*

♦ **Metamucil®** **Plus Calcium [OTC]** *see* Psyllium *on page 1458*

♦ **Metamucil®** **Smooth Texture [OTC]** *see* Psyllium *on page 1458*

Metaproterenol (met a proe TER e nol)

U.S. Brand Names Alupent®
Canadian Brand Names Apo-Orciprenaline®; Ratio-Orciprenaline®; Tanta-Orciprenaline®
Index Terms Metaproterenol Sulfate; Orciprenaline Sulfate
Pharmacologic Category Beta$_2$-Adrenergic Agonist
Additional Appendix Information
Bronchodilators *on page 1877*
Use Bronchodilator in reversible airway obstruction due to asthma or COPD; because of its delayed onset of action (1 hour) and prolonged effect (4 or more hours), this may not be the drug of choice for assessing response to a bronchodilator
Pregnancy Risk Factor C
Pregnancy Implications No data on crossing the placenta. Reported association with poly-dactyly in 1 study; may be secondary to severe maternal disease or chance.
Lactation Excretion in breast milk unknown
Medication Safety Issues
Sound-alike/look-alike issues:
Metaproterenol may be confused with metipranolol, metoprolol
Alupent® may be confused with Atrovent®
Contraindications Hypersensitivity to metaproterenol or any component of the formulation; pre-existing cardiac arrhythmias associated with tachycardia
Warnings/Precautions Optimize anti-inflammatory treatment before initiating maintenance treatment with metaproterenol. Do not use as a component of chronic therapy without an anti-inflammatory agent. Only the mildest form of asthma (Step 1 and/or exercise-induced) would not require concurrent use based upon asthma guidelines. Patient must be instructed to seek medical attention in cases where acute symptoms are not relieved or a previous level of response is diminished. The need to increase frequency of use may indicate deterioration of asthma, and treatment must not be delayed.

Use caution in patients with cardiovascular disease (arrhythmia or hypertension or CHF), convulsive disorders, diabetes, glaucoma, hyperthyroidism, or hypokalemia. Beta agonists may cause elevation in blood pressure, heart rate, and result in CNS stimulation/excitation. Beta$_2$ agonists may increase risk of arrhythmia, increase serum glucose, or decrease serum potassium.

Immediate hypersensitivity reactions (urticaria, angioedema, rash, bronchospasm) have been reported. Do not exceed recommended dose; serious adverse events including fatali-ties, have been associated with excessive use of inhaled sympathomimetics. Rarely, para-doxical bronchospasm may occur with use of inhaled bronchodilating agents; this should be distinguished from inadequate response. All patients should utilize a spacer device when using a metered-dose inhaler; additionally, a face mask should be used in children <4 years of age.

Metaproterenol has more beta$_1$ activity than beta$_2$-selective agents such as albuterol and, therefore, may no longer be the beta agonist of first choice. Oral use should be avoided due to the increased incidence of adverse effects.
Adverse Reactions
>10%:
Cardiovascular: Tachycardia (<17%)
Central nervous system: Nervousness (3% to 14%)
Endocrine & metabolic: Serum glucose increased, serum potassium decreased
Neuromuscular & skeletal: Tremor (1% to 33%)
1% to 10%:
Cardiovascular: Palpitations (<4%)
Central nervous system: Headache (<4%), dizziness (1% to 4%), insomnia (2%)
Gastrointestinal: Nausea, vomiting, bad taste, heartburn (≥4%), xerostomia
Neuromuscular & skeletal: Trembling, muscle cramps, weakness (1%)
Respiratory: Coughing, pharyngitis (≤4%)
Miscellaneous: Diaphoresis (increased) (≤4%)
<1% (Limited to important or life-threatening): Angina, chest pain, diarrhea, drowsiness, hypertension, hypokalemia, paradoxical bronchospasm, taste change
Overdosage/Toxicology Symptoms of overdose include tachycardia, tremor, hypertension, angina, and seizures. Hypokalemia also may occur. Cardiac arrest and death may be associ-ated with abuse of beta-agonist bronchodilators. Treatment includes immediate discontinua-tion and symptomatic and supportive therapies. Cautious use of beta-adrenergic blocking agents may be considered in severe cases.
Drug Interactions
Increased Effect/Toxicity: Sympathomimetics, TCAs, MAO inhibitors taken with metapro-terenol may result in toxicity. Inhaled ipratropium may increase duration of bronchodilation. Halothane may increase risk of malignant arrhythmias; avoid concurrent use.
Decreased Effect: Decreased effect of beta-blockers.
Stability Store in tight, light-resistant container. Do not use if brown solution or contains a precipitate.
Mechanism of Action Relaxes bronchial smooth muscle by action on beta$_2$-receptors with very little effect on heart rate
Pharmacodynamics/Kinetics
Onset of action: Bronchodilation: Oral: ~15 minutes; Inhalation: ~60 seconds
Peak effect: Oral: ~1 hour
Duration: ~1-5 hours

Dosage

Oral:

Children:

<2 years: 0.4 mg/kg/dose given 3-4 times/day; in infants, the dose can be given every 8-12 hours

2-6 years: 1-2.6 mg/kg/day divided every 6 hours

6-9 years: 10 mg/dose 3-4 times/day

Children >9 years and Adults: 20 mg 3-4 times/day

Elderly: Initial: 10 mg 3-4 times/day, increasing as necessary up to 20 mg 3-4 times/day

Inhalation: Children >12 years and Adults: 2-3 inhalations every 3-4 hours, up to 12 inhalations in 24 hours

Nebulizer:

Infants and Children: 0.01-0.02 mL/kg of 5% solution; minimum dose: 0.1 mL; maximum dose: 0.3 mL diluted in 2-3 mL normal saline every 4-6 hours (may be given more frequently according to need)

Adolescents and Adults: 5-20 breaths of full strength 5% metaproterenol **or** 0.2 to 0.3 mL 5% metaproterenol in 2.5-3 mL normal saline until nebulized every 4-6 hours (can be given more frequently according to need)

Administration

Inhalation: Do not use solutions for nebulization if they are brown or contain a precipitate. Shake inhaler well before using.

Oral: Administer around-the-clock to promote less variation in peak and trough serum levels

Monitoring Parameters Assess lung sounds, heart rate, and blood pressure before administration and during peak of medication; observe patient for wheezing after administration, if this occurs, call physician; monitor respiratory rate, arterial or capillary blood gases if applicable; FEV_1, peak flow, and/or other pulmonary function tests; CNS stimulation; serum glucose, serum potassium

Test Interactions Increased potassium (S)

Additional Information Use with caution perioperatively due to $beta_1$ effect of agent. Hypertension and tachycardia are increased with exogenous sympathomimetics. During endotracheal intubation, $beta_2$-specific agent is more appropriate for perioperative use.

Dosage Forms

Aerosol for oral inhalation, as sulfate (Alupent®): 0.65 mg/inhalation (14 g) [200 doses]

Solution for nebulization, as sulfate [preservative free]: 0.4% [4 mg/mL] (2.5 mL); 0.6% [6 mg/mL] (2.5 mL)

Syrup, as sulfate: 10 mg/5 mL (480 mL) [may contain sodium benzoate]

Tablet, as sulfate: 10 mg, 20 mg

♦ **Metaproterenol Sulfate** see Metaproterenol on page 1096

♦ **Metastron®** see Strontium-89 on page 1604

Metaxalone (me TAKS a lone)

U.S. Brand Names Skelaxin®

Canadian Brand Names Skelaxin®

Pharmacologic Category Skeletal Muscle Relaxant

Use Relief of discomfort associated with acute, painful musculoskeletal conditions

Pregnancy Risk Factor C

Medication Safety Issues

Sound-alike/look-alike issues:

Metaxalone may be confused with metolazone

Contraindications Hypersensitivity to metaxalone or any component of the formulation; impaired hepatic or renal function, history of drug-induced hemolytic anemias or other anemias

Warnings/Precautions Use with caution in patients with impaired hepatic function

Adverse Reactions Frequency not defined.

Central nervous system: Paradoxical stimulation, headache, drowsiness, dizziness, irritability

Dermatologic: Allergic dermatitis

Gastrointestinal: Nausea, vomiting, stomach cramps

Hematologic: Leukopenia, hemolytic anemia

Hepatic: Hepatotoxicity

Miscellaneous: Anaphylaxis

Overdosage/Toxicology No major toxicities have been reported.

Drug Interactions

Increased Effect/Toxicity: Additive effects with ethanol or CNS depressants

Ethanol/Nutrition/Herb Interactions Ethanol: Avoid ethanol (may increase CNS depression).

Mechanism of Action Does not have a direct effect on skeletal muscle; most of its therapeutic effect comes from actions on the central nervous system

Pharmacodynamics/Kinetics

Onset of action: ~1 hour

Duration: ~4-6 hours

Metabolism: Hepatic

Bioavailability: Not established; food may increase

Half-life elimination: 9 hours

Time to peak: T_{max}: 3 hours

Excretion: Urine (as metabolites)

Dosage Children >12 years and Adults: Oral: 800 mg 3-4 times/day

Dietary Considerations Administration with food may increase serum concentrations.

Administration May be administered with or without food. However, serum concentrations may be increased when administered with food; clinical significance has not been established. Patients should be monitored.

(Continued)

Metaxalone *(Continued)*

Test Interactions False-positive Benedict's test
Dosage Forms [DSC] = Discontinued product
Tablet: 400 mg [DSC], 800 mg

Metformin *(met FOR min)*

U.S. Brand Names Fortamet®; Glucophage®; Glucophage® XR; Glumetza™; Riomet™
Canadian Brand Names Alti-Metformin; Apo-Metformin®; BCI-Metformin; Gen-Metformin; Glucophage®; Glumetza®; Glycon; Novo-Metformin; Nu-Metformin; PMS-Metformin; RAN™-Metformin; ratio-Metformin; Rho®-Metformin; Sandoz-Metformin FC
Index Terms Metformin Hydrochloride
Pharmacologic Category Antidiabetic Agent, Biguanide
Additional Appendix Information
Diabetes Mellitus Management, Adults *on page 2040*
Hyperglycemia- or Hypoglycemia-Causing Drugs *on page 2057*
Use Management of type 2 diabetes mellitus (noninsulin dependent, NIDDM) as monotherapy when hyperglycemia cannot be managed on diet alone. May be used concomitantly with a sulfonylurea or insulin to improve glycemic control.
Unlabeled/Investigational Use Treatment of HIV lipodystrophy syndrome, gestational diabetes mellitus (GDM), polycystic ovary syndrome (PCOS)
Pregnancy Risk Factor B
Pregnancy Implications Abnormal blood glucose levels are associated with a higher incidence of congenital abnormalities. Insulin is the drug of choice for the control of diabetes mellitus during pregnancy.
Lactation Enters breast milk/not recommended
Medication Safety Issues
Sound-alike/look-alike issues:
Metformin may be confused with metronidazole
Glucophage® may be confused with Glucotrol®, Glutofac®
Contraindications Hypersensitivity to metformin or any component of the formulation; renal disease or renal dysfunction (serum creatinine ≥1.5 mg/dL in males or ≥1.4 mg/dL in females or abnormal creatinine clearance from any cause, including shock, acute myocardial infarction, or septicemia); acute or chronic metabolic acidosis with or without coma (including diabetic ketoacidosis)

Note: Temporarily discontinue in patients undergoing radiologic studies in which intravascular iodinated contrast materials are utilized.
Warnings/Precautions [U.S. Boxed Warning]: Lactic acidosis is a rare, but potentially severe consequence of therapy with metformin. Lactic acidosis should be suspected in any diabetic patient receiving metformin who has evidence of acidosis when evidence of ketoacidosis is lacking. Discontinue metformin in clinical situations predisposing to hypoxemia, including conditions such as cardiovascular collapse, respiratory failure, acute myocardial infarction, acute congestive heart failure, and septicemia. Use caution in patients with congestive heart failure requiring pharmacologic management, particularly in patients with unstable or acute CHF; risk of lactic acidosis may be increased secondary to hypoperfusion.

Metformin is substantially excreted by the kidney. The risk of accumulation and lactic acidosis increases with the degree of impairment of renal function. Patients with renal function below the limit of normal for their age should not receive metformin. In elderly patients, renal function should be monitored regularly; should not be used in any patient ≥80 years of age unless measurement of creatinine clearance verifies normal renal function. Use of concomitant medications that may affect renal function (ie, affect tubular secretion) may also affect metformin disposition. Metformin should be suspended in patients with dehydration and/or prerenal azotemia. Therapy should be suspended for any surgical procedures (resume only after normal intake resumed and normal renal function is verified). Metformin should also be temporarily discontinued for 48 hours in patients undergoing radiologic studies involving the intravascular administration of iodinated contrast materials (potential for acute alteration in renal function). It may be necessary to discontinue metformin and administer insulin if the patient is exposed to stress (fever, trauma, infection, surgery).

Avoid use in patients with impaired liver function. Patient must be instructed to avoid excessive acute or chronic ethanol use. Administration of oral antidiabetic drugs has been reported to be associated with increased cardiovascular mortality; metformin does not appear to share this risk. Safety and efficacy of metformin have been established for use in children ≥10 years of age; the extended release preparation is for use in patients ≥17 years of age.
Adverse Reactions
>10%:
Gastrointestinal: Nausea/vomiting (6% to 25%), diarrhea (10% to 53%), flatulence (12%)
Neuromuscular & skeletal: Weakness (9%)
1% to 10%:
Cardiovascular: Chest discomfort, flushing, palpitation
Central nervous system: Headache (6%), chills, dizziness, lightheadedness
Dermatologic: Rash
Endocrine & metabolic: Hypoglycemia
Gastrointestinal: Indigestion (7%), abdominal discomfort (6%), abdominal distention, abnormal stools, constipation, dyspepsia/ heartburn, taste disorder
Neuromuscular & skeletal: Myalgia
Respiratory: Dyspnea, upper respiratory tract infection
Miscellaneous: Decreased vitamin B_{12} levels (7%), increased diaphoresis, flu-like syndrome, nail disorder
<1% (Limited to important or life-threatening): Lactic acidosis, leukocytoclastic vasculitis, megaloblastic anemia, pneumonitis

Overdosage/Toxicology Hypoglycemia (10% of cases) or lactic acidosis (~32% of cases) may occur. Metformin is dialyzable with a clearance of up to 170 mL/minute. Hemodialysis may be useful for removal of accumulated drug from patients in whom metformin overdose is suspected. Treatment is supportive.

Drug Interactions

Increased Effect/Toxicity: Furosemide and cimetidine may increase metformin blood levels. Cationic drugs (eg, amiloride, digoxin, morphine, procainamide, quinidine, quinine, ranitidine, triamterene, trimethoprim, and vancomycin) which are eliminated by renal tubular secretion have the potential to increase metformin levels by competing for common renal tubular transport systems. Contrast agents may increase the risk of metformin-induced lactic acidosis; discontinue metformin prior to exposure and withhold for 48 hours.

Decreased Effect: Drugs which tend to produce hyperglycemia (eg, diuretics, corticosteroids, phenothiazines, thyroid products, estrogens, oral contraceptives, phenytoin, nicotinic acid, sympathomimetics, calcium channel blocking drugs, isoniazid) may lead to a loss of glucose control.

Ethanol/Nutrition/Herb Interactions

Ethanol: Avoid or limit ethanol (incidence of lactic acidosis may be increased; may cause hypoglycemia).

Food: Food decreases the extent and slightly delays the absorption. May decrease absorption of vitamin B_{12} and/or folic acid.

Herb/Nutraceutical: Caution with chromium, garlic, gymnema (may cause hypoglycemia).

Stability Store tablets and oral solution at 20°C to 25°C (68°F to 77°F).

Mechanism of Action Decreases hepatic glucose production, decreasing intestinal absorption of glucose and improves insulin sensitivity (increases peripheral glucose uptake and utilization)

Pharmacodynamics/Kinetics

Onset of action: Within days; maximum effects up to 2 weeks

Distribution: V_d: 654 ± 358 L; partitions into erythrocytes

Protein binding: Negligible

Metabolism: Not metabolized by the liver

Bioavailability: Absolute: Fasting: 50% to 60%

Half-life elimination:
Plasma: 6.2 hours
Blood: 17.6 hours

Time to peak, serum: Extended release: 7 hours (range: 4-8 hours)

Excretion: Urine (90% as unchanged drug)

Dosage Note: Allow 1-2 weeks between dose titrations: Generally, clinically significant responses are not seen at doses <1500 mg daily; however, a lower recommended starting dose and gradual increased dosage is recommended to minimize gastrointestinal symptoms

Children 10-16 years: Management of type 2 diabetes mellitus: Oral (immediate release tablet or oral solution): Initial: 500 mg twice daily (given with the morning and evening meals); increases in daily dosage should be made in increments of 500 mg at weekly intervals, given in divided doses, up to a maximum of 2000 mg/day

Adults ≥17 years: Management of type 2 diabetes mellitus: Oral:

Immediate release tablet or oral solution: Initial: 500 mg twice daily (give with the morning and evening meals) **or** 850 mg once daily; increase dosage incrementally.

Incremental dosing recommendations based on dosage form:
500 mg tablet: One tablet/day at weekly intervals
850 mg tablet: One tablet/day every other week
Oral solution: 500 mg twice daily every other week

Doses of up to 2000 mg/day may be given twice daily. If a dose >2000 mg/day is required, it may be better tolerated in three divided doses. Maximum recommended dose 2550 mg/day.

Extended release tablet: Initial: 500 mg once daily (with the evening meal); dosage may be increased by 500 mg weekly; maximum dose: 2000 mg once daily. If glycemic control is not achieved at maximum dose, may divide dose to 1000 mg twice daily. If doses >2000 mg/day are needed, switch to regular release tablets and titrate to maximum dose of 2550 mg/day.

Elderly: The initial and maintenance dosing should be conservative, due to the potential for decreased renal function. Generally, elderly patients should not be titrated to the maximum dose of metformin. Do not use in patients ≥80 years of age unless normal renal function has been established.

Transfer from other antidiabetic agents: No transition period is generally necessary except when transferring from chlorpropamide. When transferring from chlorpropamide, care should be exercised during the first 2 weeks because of the prolonged retention of chlorpropamide in the body, leading to overlapping drug effects and possible hypoglycemia.

Concomitant metformin and oral sulfonylurea therapy: If patients have not responded to 4 weeks of the maximum dose of metformin monotherapy, consider a gradual addition of an oral sulfonylurea, even if prior primary or secondary failure to a sulfonylurea has occurred. Continue metformin at the maximum dose.

Failed sulfonylurea therapy: Patients with prior failure on glyburide may be treated by gradual addition of metformin. Initiate with glyburide 20 mg and metformin 500 mg daily. Metformin dosage may be increased by 500 mg/day at weekly intervals, up to a maximum of 2500 mg/day (dosage of glyburide maintained at 20 mg/day).

Concomitant metformin and insulin therapy: Initial: 500 mg metformin once daily, continue current insulin dose; increase by 500 mg metformin weekly until adequate glycemic control is achieved

Maximum dose: 2500 mg metformin; 2000 mg metformin extended release

Decrease insulin dose 10% to 25% when FPG <120 mg/dL; monitor and make further adjustments as needed

Dosing adjustment/comments in renal impairment: The plasma and blood half-life of metformin is prolonged and the renal clearance is decreased in proportion to the decrease in creatinine clearance. Per the manufacturer, metformin is contraindicated in the presence (Continued)

Metformin (Continued)

of renal dysfunction defined as a serum creatinine >1.5 mg/dL in males, or >1.4 mg/dL in females and in patients with abnormal clearance. Clinically, it has been recommended that metformin be avoided in patients with Cl_{cr} <60-70 mL/minute (DeFronzo, 1999).

Dosing adjustment in hepatic impairment: Avoid metformin; liver disease is a risk factor for the development of lactic acidosis during metformin therapy.

Dietary Considerations Drug may cause GI upset; take with food (to decrease GI upset). Take at the same time each day. Dietary modification based on ADA recommendations is a part of therapy. Monitor for signs and symptoms of vitamin B_{12} and/or folic acid deficiency; supplementation may be required.

Administration Extended release dosage form should be swallowed whole; do not crush, break, or chew. Patients who are anorexic or NPO may need to have their dose held to avoid hypoglycemia.

Monitoring Parameters Urine for glucose and ketones, fasting blood glucose, and hemoglobin A_{1c}. Initial and periodic monitoring of hematologic parameters (eg, hemoglobin/hematocrit and red blood cell indices) and renal function should be performed, at least annually. Check vitamin B_{12} and folate if anemia is present.

Reference Range Target range: Adults:
Fasting blood glucose: <120 mg/dL
Glycosylated hemoglobin: <7%

Dosage Forms
Solution, oral, as hydrochloride:
Riomet™: 100 mg/mL (118 mL, 473 mL) [contains saccharin; cherry flavor]
Tablet, as hydrochloride: 500 mg, 850 mg, 1000 mg
Glucophage®: 500 mg, 850 mg, 1000 mg
Tablet, extended release, as hydrochloride: 500 mg, 750 mg
Fortamet®: 500 mg, 1000 mg
Glucophage® XR: 500 mg, 750 mg
Glumetza™: 500 mg

- ♦ **Metformin and Glipizide** *see* Glipizide and Metformin *on page 801*
- ♦ **Metformin and Glyburide** *see* Glyburide and Metformin *on page 805*
- ♦ **Metformin and Rosiglitazone** *see* Rosiglitazone and Metformin *on page 1537*
- ♦ **Metformin Hydrochloride** *see* Metformin *on page 1098*
- ♦ **Metformin Hydrochloride and Pioglitazone Hydrochloride** *see* Pioglitazone and Metformin *on page 1374*
- ♦ **Metformin Hydrochloride and Rosiglitazone Maleate** *see* Rosiglitazone and Metformin *on page 1537*

Methacholine (meth a KOLE leen)

U.S. Brand Names Provocholine®
Canadian Brand Names Methacholine Omega; Provocholine®
Index Terms Methacholine Chloride
Pharmacologic Category Diagnostic Agent
Use Diagnosis of bronchial airway hyperactivity
Pregnancy Risk Factor C
Dosage Before inhalation challenge, perform baseline pulmonary function tests; the patient must have an FEV_1 of at least 70% of the predicted value. The following is a suggested schedule for administration of methacholine challenge. Calculate cumulative units by multiplying number of breaths by concentration given. Total cumulative units is the sum of cumulative units for each concentration given. See table.

Methacholine

Vial	Serial Concentration (mg/mL)	No. of Breaths	Cumulative Units per Concentration	Total Cumulative Units
E	0.025	5	0.125	0.125
D	0.25	5	1.25	1.375
C	2.5	5	12.5	13.88
B	10	5	50	63.88
A	25	5	125	188.88

Determine FEV_1 within 5 minutes of challenge, a positive challenge is a 20% reduction in FEV_1

Additional Information Complete prescribing information for this medication should be consulted for additional detail.

Dosage Forms Powder for oral inhalation, as chloride: 100 mg

- ♦ **Methacholine Chloride** *see* Methacholine *on page 1100*
- ♦ **Methacholine Omega (Can)** *see* Methacholine *on page 1100*

Methadone (METH a done)

U.S. Brand Names Dolophine®; Methadone Diskets®; Methadone Intensol™; Methadose®
Canadian Brand Names Dolophine®; Metadol™; Methadose®
Index Terms Methadone Hydrochloride
Pharmacologic Category Analgesic, Opioid
Additional Appendix Information
Narcotic Agonists *on page 1888*

Use Management of moderate-to-severe pain; detoxification and maintenance treatment of narcotic addiction (if used for detoxification and maintenance treatment of narcotic addiction, it must be part of an FDA-approved program)

Restrictions C-II

When used for treatment of narcotic addiction: May only be dispensed in accordance to guidelines established by the Substance Abuse and Mental Health Services Administration's (SAMHSA) Center for Substance Abuse Treatment (CSAT).

Pregnancy Risk Factor C/D (prolonged use or high doses at term)

Pregnancy Implications Teratogenic effects have been observed in some, but not all, animal studies. Data collected by the Teratogen Information System are complicated by maternal use of illicit drugs, nutrition, infection, and psychosocial circumstances. However, pregnant women in methadone treatment programs are reported to have improved fetal outcomes compared to pregnant women using illicit drugs. Methadone can be detected in the amniotic fluid, cord plasma, and newborn urine. Fetal growth, birth weight, length, and/or head circumference may be decreased in infants born to narcotic-addicted mothers treated with methadone during pregnancy. Growth deficits do not appear to persist; however, decreased performance on psychometric and behavioral tests has been found to continue into childhood. Abnormal fetal nonstress tests have also been reported. Withdrawal symptoms in the neonate may be observed up to 2-4 weeks after delivery. The manufacturer states that methadone should be used during pregnancy only if clearly needed. Because methadone clearance in pregnant women is increased and half-life is decreased during the 2nd and 3rd trimesters of pregnancy, withdrawal symptoms may be observed in the mother; dosage of methadone may need increased or dosing interval decreased during pregnancy.

Lactation Enters breast milk/not recommended (AAP rates "compatible")

Medication Safety Issues

Sound-alike/look-alike issues:

Methadone may be confused with Mephyton®, methylphenidate

Contraindications Hypersensitivity to methadone or any component of the formulation; respiratory depression (in the absence of resuscitative equipment or in an unmonitored setting); acute bronchial asthma or hypercarbia; paralytic ileus; pregnancy (prolonged use or high doses near term)

Warnings/Precautions An opioid-containing analgesic regimen should be tailored to each patient's needs and based upon the type of pain being treated (acute versus chronic), the route of administration, degree of tolerance for opioids (naive versus chronic user), age, weight, and medical condition. The optimal analgesic dose varies widely among patients. Doses should be titrated to pain relief/prevention. Patients maintained on stable doses of methadone may need higher and/or more frequent doses in case of acute pain (eg, postoperative pain, physical trauma). Methadone is ineffective for the relief of anxiety.

[U.S. Boxed Warning]: May prolong the QT interval; use caution in patients at risk for QT prolongation, with medications known to prolong the QT interval, or history of conduction abnormalities. QT interval prolongation and torsade de pointes may be associated with doses >200 mg/day, but have also been observed with lower doses. May cause severe hypotension; use caution with severe volume depletion or other conditions which may compromise maintenance of normal blood pressure. Use caution with cardiovascular disease or patients predisposed to dysrhythmias.

[U.S. Boxed Warning]: May cause respiratory depression. Use caution in patients with respiratory disease or pre-existing respiratory conditions (eg, severe obesity, asthma, COPD, sleep apnea, CNS depression). Because the respiratory effects last longer than the analgesic effects, slow titration is required. Use extreme caution during treatment initiation, dose titration and conversion from other opioid agonists. Incomplete cross tolerance may occur; patients tolerant to other mu opioid agonists may not be tolerant to methadone. Abrupt cessation may precipitate withdrawal symptoms.

May cause CNS depression, which may impair physical or mental abilities. Patients must be cautioned about performing tasks which require mental alertness (eg, operating machinery or driving). Effects with other sedative drugs or ethanol may be potentiated. Use with caution in patients with depression or suicidal tendencies, or in patients with a history of drug abuse. Tolerance or psychological and physical dependence may occur with prolonged use.

Use with caution in patients with head injury or increased intracranial pressure. May obscure diagnosis or clinical course of patients with acute abdominal conditions. Elderly may be more susceptible to adverse effects (eg, CNS, respiratory, gastrointestinal). Decrease initial dose and use caution in the elderly or debilitated; with hyper/hypothyroidism, morbid obesity, adrenal insufficiency, prostatic hyperplasia, or urethral stricture; or with severe renal or hepatic failure. Use with caution in patients with biliary tract dysfunction; acute pancreatitis may cause constriction of sphincter of Oddi. Safety and efficacy have not been established in children. **[U.S. Boxed Warning]: For oral administration only;** excipients to deter use by injection are contained in tablets.

[U.S. Boxed Warning]: When used for treatment of narcotic addiction: May only be dispensed by opioid treatment programs certified by the Substance Abuse and Mental Health Services Administration (SAMHSA) and certified by the designated state authority. Exceptions include inpatient treatment of other conditions and emergency period (not >3 days) while definitive substance abuse treatment is being sought.

Adverse Reactions Frequency not defined. During prolonged administration, adverse effects may decrease over several weeks; however, constipation and sweating may persist.

Cardiovascular: Bradycardia, peripheral vasodilation, cardiac arrest, syncope, faintness, shock, hypotension, edema, arrhythmia, bigeminal rhythms, extrasystoles, tachycardia, torsade de pointes, ventricular fibrillation, ventricular tachycardia, ECG changes, QT interval prolonged, T-wave inversion, cardiomyopathy, flushing, heart failure, palpitation, phlebitis, orthostatic hypotension

Central nervous system: Euphoria, dysphoria, hallucination, headache, insomnia, agitation, disorientation, drowsiness, dizziness, lightheadedness, sedation, confusion, seizure

Dermatologic: Pruritus, urticaria, rash, hemorrhagic urticaria

(Continued)

Methadone *(Continued)*

Endocrine & metabolic: Libido decreased, hypokalemia, hypomagnesemia, antidiuretic effect, amenorrhea

Gastrointestinal: Nausea, vomiting, constipation, anorexia, stomach cramps, xerostomia, biliary tract spasm, abdominal pain, glossitis, weight gain

Genitourinary: Urinary retention or hesitancy, impotence

Hematologic: Thrombocytopenia (reversible, reported in patients with chronic hepatitis)

Neuromuscular & skeletal: Weakness

Local: I.M./SubQ injection: Pain, erythema, swelling; I.V. injection: pruritus, urticaria, rash, hemorrhagic urticaria (rare)

Ocular: Miosis, visual disturbances

Respiratory: Respiratory depression, respiratory arrest, pulmonary edema

Miscellaneous: Physical and psychological dependence, death, diaphoresis

Overdosage/Toxicology Symptoms include respiratory depression, CNS depression, miosis, hypothermia, circulatory collapse, and convulsions. Treatment includes naloxone 2 mg I.V. (0.01 mg/kg for children), with repeat administration as necessary, up to a total of 10 mg, or as a continuous infusion. Nalmefene may also be used to reverse signs of intoxication. Patient should be monitored for depressant effects of methadone for 36-48 hours and other supportive measures should be employed as needed. Forced diuresis, peritoneal dialysis, hemodialysis, or charcoal hemoperfusion have not been established as beneficial for increasing methadone or metabolite elimination.

Drug Interactions

Cytochrome P450 Effect: Substrate of CYP2C9 (minor), 2C19 (minor), 2D6 (minor), 3A4 (major); **Inhibits** CYP2D6 (moderate), 3A4 (weak)

Increased Effect/Toxicity: CYP3A4 inhibitors may increase the levels/effects of methadone (eg, azole antifungals, clarithromycin, diclofenac, doxycycline, erythromycin, imatinib, isoniazid, nefazodone, nicardipine, propofol, protease inhibitors, quinidine, telithromycin, verapamil). Methadone may increase the levels/effects of CYP2D6 substrates (eg, amphetamines, selected beta-blockers, dextromethorphan, fluoxetine, lidocaine, mirtazapine, nefazodone, paroxetine, risperidone, ritonavir, thioridazine, tricyclic antidepressants, venlafaxine). Methadone may increase bioavailability and toxic effects of zidovudine. CNS depressants (including but not limited to opioid analgesics, general anesthetics, sedatives, hypnotics, ethanol) may cause respiratory depression, hypotension, profound sedation, or coma. Levels of desipramine may be increased by methadone. Effects/toxicity of QT_c interval-prolonging agents may be increased; use with caution (including but may not be limited to amitriptyline, astemizole, bepridil, disopyramide, erythromycin, haloperidol, imipramine, quinidine, pimozide, procainamide, sotalol, thioridazine). Ritonavir may increase levels/effects of methadone shortly after initiation.

Decreased Effect: Agonist/antagonist analgesics (buprenorphine, butorphanol, nalbuphine, pentazocine) may decrease analgesic effect of methadone and precipitate withdrawal symptoms; use is not recommended. Efavirenz and nevirapine may decrease levels of methadone (opioid withdrawal syndrome has been reported). Methadone may decrease bioavailability of didanosine and stavudine. Ritonavir (and combinations) may decrease levels of methadone; withdrawal symptoms have inconsistently been observed, monitor. CYP3A4 inducers may decrease the levels/effects of methadone (eg, aminoglutethimide, carbamazepine, nafcillin, nevirapine, phenobarbital, phenytoin, rifamycins). Monitor for methadone withdrawal. Larger doses of methadone may be required. Methadone may decrease the levels/effects of CYP2D6 prodrug substrates (eg, codeine, hydrocodone, oxycodone, tramadol). Ritonavir may decrease levels/effects of methadone with continued dosing.

Ethanol/Nutrition/Herb Interactions

Ethanol: Avoid ethanol (may increase CNS effects). Watch for sedation.

Herb/Nutraceutical: Avoid St John's wort (may decrease methadone levels; may increase CNS depression). Avoid valerian, kava kava, gotu kola (may increase CNS depression). Methadone is metabolized by CYP3A4 in the intestines; avoid concurrent use of grapefruit juice.

Stability

Injection: Store at controlled room temperature of 15°C to 30°C (59°F to 86°F). Protect from light.

Oral concentrate, oral solution, tablet: Store at controlled room temperature of 15°C to 30°C (59°F to 86°F).

Mechanism of Action Binds to opiate receptors in the CNS, causing inhibition of ascending pain pathways, altering the perception of and response to pain; produces generalized CNS depression

Pharmacodynamics/Kinetics

Onset of action: Oral: Analgesic: 0.5-1 hour; Parenteral: 10-20 minutes

Peak effect: Parenteral: 1-2 hours; Oral: continuous dosing: 3-5 days

Duration of analgesia: Oral: 4-8 hours, increases to 22-48 hours with repeated doses

Distribution: V_{dss}: 1-8 L/kg

Protein binding: 85% to 90%

Metabolism: Hepatic; N-demethylation primarily via CYP3A4, CYP2B6, and CYP2C19 to inactive metabolites

Bioavailability: Oral: 36% to 100%

Half-life elimination: 7-59 hours; may be prolonged with alkaline pH, decreased during pregnancy

Excretion: Urine (<10% as unchanged drug); increased with urine pH <6

Dosage Regulations regarding methadone use may vary by state and/or country. Obtain advice from appropriate regulatory agencies and/or consult with pain management/palliative care specialists. **Note:** These are guidelines and do not represent the maximum doses that may be required in all patients. Methadone accumulates with repeated doses and dosage may need reduction after 3-5 days to prevent CNS depressant effects. Some patients may benefit from every 8-12 hour dosing interval for chronic pain management. Doses should be titrated to appropriate effects.

Children:

Pain (analgesia):

Oral (unlabeled use): Initial: 0.1-0.2 mg/kg 4-8 hours initially for 2-3 doses, then every 6-12 hours as needed. Dosing interval may range from 4-12 hours during initial therapy; decrease in dose or frequency may be required (~ days 2-5) due to accumulation with repeated doses (maximum dose: 5-10 mg)

I.V. (unlabeled use): 0.1 mg/kg every 4-8 hours initially for 2-3 doses, then every 6-12 hours as needed. Dosing interval may range from 4-12 hours during initial therapy; decrease in dose or frequency may be required (~ days 2-5) due to accumulation with repeated doses (maximum dose: 5-8 mg)

Iatrogenic narcotic dependency (unlabeled): Oral: General guidelines: Initial: 0.05-0.1 mg/kg/dose every 6 hours; increase by 0.05 mg/kg/dose until withdrawal symptoms are controlled; after 24-48 hours, the dosing interval can be lengthened to every 12-24 hours; to taper dose, wean by 0.05 mg/kg/day; If withdrawal symptoms recur, taper at a slower rate

Adults:

Acute pain (moderate-to-severe):

Oral: Opioid-naive: Initial: 2.5-10 mg every 8-12 hours; more frequent administration may be required during initiation to maintain adequate analgesia. Dosage interval may range from 4-12 hours, since duration of analgesia is relatively short during the first days of therapy, but increases substantially with continued administration.

Chronic pain (opioid-tolerant): **Conversion from oral morphine to oral methadone:**

Daily oral morphine dose <100 mg: Estimated daily oral methadone dose: 20% to 30% of total daily morphine dose

Daily oral morphine dose 100-300 mg: Estimated daily oral methadone dose: 10% to 20% of total daily morphine dose

Daily oral morphine dose 300-600 mg: Estimated daily oral methadone dose: 8% to 12% of total daily morphine dose

Daily oral morphine dose 600-1000 mg: Estimated daily oral methadone dose: 5% to 10% of total daily morphine dose.

Daily oral morphine dose >1000 mg: Estimated daily oral methadone dose: <5% of total daily morphine dose.

Note: The total daily methadone dose should then be divided to reflect the intended dosing schedule.

I.V.: Manufacturers labeling: Initial: 2.5-10 mg every 8-12 hours in opioid-naive patients; titrate slowly to effect; may also be administered by SubQ or I.M. injection

Conversion from oral methadone to parenteral methadone dose: Initial dose: Parenteral:Oral ratio: 1:2 (eg, 5 mg parenteral methadone equals 10 mg oral methadone)

Detoxification: Oral:

Initial: Should not exceed 30 mg; lower doses should be considered in patients with low tolerance at initiation (eg, absence of opioids ≥5 days); an additional 5-10 mg of methadone may be provided if withdrawal symptoms have not been suppressed or if symptoms reappear after 2-4 hours; total daily dose on the first day should not exceed 40 mg, unless the program physician documents in the patient's record that 40 mg did not control opiate abstinence symptoms.

Maintenance: Usual range: 80-120 mg/day (titration should occur cautiously)

Withdrawal: Dose reductions should be <10% of the maintenance dose, every 10-14 days

Detoxification (short-term): Oral:

Initial: Titrate to 40 mg/day in divided doses

Maintenance: Continue 40 mg dose for 2-3 days

Withdrawal: Decrease daily or every other day, keeping withdrawal symptoms tolerable; hospitalized patients may tolerate a 20% reduction/day; ambulatory patients may require a slower reduction

Dosage adjustment during pregnancy: Methadone dose may need to be increased, or the dosing interval decreased; see Pregnancy Implications - use should be reserved for cases where the benefits clearly outweigh the risks

Dosage adjustment in renal impairment: Cl_{cr} <10 mL/minute: Administer 50% to 75% of normal dose

Dosage adjustment in hepatic impairment: Avoid in severe liver disease

Administration Oral dose for detoxification and maintenance may be administered in fruit juice or water.

Monitoring Parameters Pain relief, respiratory and mental status, blood pressure

Reference Range Therapeutic: 100-400 ng/mL (SI: 0.32-1.29 µmol/L); Toxic: >2 mcg/mL (SI: >6.46 µmol/L)

Test Interactions Some quinolones may produce a false-positive urine screening result for opiates using commercially-available immunoassay kits. This has been demonstrated most consistently with levofloxacin and ofloxacin, but other quinolones have shown cross-reactivity in certain assay kits. Confirmation of positive opiate screens by more specific methods should be considered.

Dosage Forms

Injection, solution, as hydrochloride: 10 mg/mL (20 mL)

Solution, oral, as hydrochloride: 5 mg/5 mL (500 mL); 10 mg/5 mL (500 mL) [contains alcohol 8%; citrus flavor]

Solution, oral, as hydrochloride [concentrate]: 10 mg/mL (946 mL)

Methadone Intensol™: 10 mg/mL (30 mL)

Methadose®: 10 mg/mL (1000 mL) [cherry flavor]

Methadose®: 10 mg/mL (1000 mL) [dye free, sugar free, unflavored]

Tablet, as hydrochloride: 5 mg, 10 mg

Dolophine®: 5 mg, 10 mg

Methadose®: 5 mg, 10 mg [DSC]

Tablet, dispersible, as hydrochloride: 40 mg

Methadose®: 40 mg

Methadone Diskets®: 40 mg [orange-pineapple flavor]

♦ **Methadone Diskets®** *see* Methadone *on page 1100*

♦ **Methadone Hydrochloride** *see* Methadone *on page 1100*

♦ **Methadone Intensol™** *see* Methadone *on page 1100*

♦ **Methadose®** *see* Methadone *on page 1100*

♦ **Methaminodiazepoxide Hydrochloride** *see* Chlordiazepoxide *on page 342*

Methamphetamine (meth am FET a meen)

U.S. Brand Names Desoxyn®
Canadian Brand Names Desoxyn®
Index Terms Desoxyephedrine Hydrochloride; Methamphetamine Hydrochloride
Pharmacologic Category Stimulant
Use Treatment of attention-deficit/hyperactivity disorder (ADHD); exogenous obesity (short-term adjunct)
Unlabeled/Investigational Use Narcolepsy
Restrictions C-II
Pregnancy Risk Factor C
Pregnancy Implications Teratogenic and embryocidal effects have been observed in animal studies. Infants may deliver prematurely and suffer withdrawal symptoms. There are no adequate and well-controlled studies in pregnant women.
Lactation Enters breast milk/contraindicated
Medication Safety Issues
Sound-alike/look-alike issues:
Desoxyn® may be confused with digoxin
Contraindications Hypersensitivity to methamphetamine, any component of the formulation, or idiosyncrasy to amphetamines or other sympathomimetic amines; patients with advanced arteriosclerosis, symptomatic cardiovascular disease, moderate-to-severe hypertension, hyperthyroidism, glaucoma, agitated states; patients with a history of drug abuse; use during or within 14 days following MAO inhibitor therapy; stimulant medications are contraindicated for use in children with attention-deficit/hyperactivity disorders and concomitant Tourette's syndrome or tics
Warnings/Precautions [U.S. Boxed Warning]: Dexamphetamine has been associated with serious cardiac cardiovascular events including sudden death in patients with pre-existing structural cardiac abnormalities or other serious heart problems. Using CNS stimulant treatment at usual doses in children and adolescents with serious heart problems and structural cardiac abnormalities has been associated with sudden death. In adults, stimulant use has been associated with sudden deaths, stroke, and myocardial infarction. Stimulant products should be avoided in the patients with known serious structural cardiac abnormalities, cardiomyopathy, serious heart rhythm abnormalities, or other serious cardiac problems that could increase the risk of sudden death that these conditions alone carry. Caution should be used in patients with hypertension and other cardiovascular conditions that might be exacerbated by increases in blood pressure or heart rate. Use of stimulants can cause an increase in blood pressure (average 2-4 mm Hg) and increases in heart rate (average 3-6 bpm), although some patients may have larger than average increases.

Use with caution in patients with bipolar disorder, cardiovascular disease, diabetes, seizure disorders, insomnia, porphyria, mild hypertension, or history of substance abuse. May exacerbate symptoms of behavior and thought disorder in psychotic patients. Stimulants may unmask tics in individuals with coexisting Tourette's syndrome. Potential for drug dependency exists - avoid abrupt discontinuation in patients who have received for prolonged periods. **[U.S. Boxed Warning]: Use in weight reduction programs only when alternative therapy has been ineffective; due to high potential for abuse and/or nontherapeutic use should be prescribed/dispensed sparingly.** Products may contain tartrazine - use with caution in potentially sensitive individuals. Stimulant use in children has been associated with growth suppression.
Adverse Reactions Frequency not defined.
Cardiovascular: Hypertension, tachycardia, palpitation
Central nervous system: Restlessness, headache, exacerbation of motor and phonic tics and Tourette's syndrome, dizziness, psychosis, dysphoria, overstimulation, euphoria, insomnia
Dermatologic: Rash, urticaria
Endocrine & metabolic: Change in libido
Gastrointestinal: Diarrhea, nausea, vomiting, stomach cramps, constipation, anorexia, weight loss, xerostomia, unpleasant taste
Genitourinary: Impotence
Neuromuscular & skeletal: Tremor
Miscellaneous: Suppression of growth in children, tolerance and withdrawal with prolonged use
Overdosage/Toxicology Symptoms include seizures, hyperactivity, coma, and hypertension. There is no specific antidote for amphetamine intoxication and the bulk of treatment is supportive. Hyperactivity and agitation usually respond to reduced sensory input, however, with extreme agitation haloperidol (2-5 mg I.M. for adults) may be required. Hyperthermia is best treated with external cooling measures, or when severe or unresponsive, muscle paralysis with pancuronium may be needed. Hypertension is usually transient and generally does not require treatment unless severe. For diastolic blood pressures >110 mm Hg, a nitroprusside infusion should be initiated. Seizures usually respond to diazepam IVP and/or phenytoin maintenance regimens. Agents which enhance urinary acidification (eg, potassium acid phosphate or ammonium chloride) may increase the renal elimination of amphetamines; very large doses may be required.

Drug Interactions

Cytochrome P450 Effect: Substrate of CYP2D6 (major)

Increased Effect/Toxicity: Amphetamines may precipitate hypertensive crisis or serotonin syndrome in patients receiving MAO inhibitors (selegiline >10 mg/day, isocarboxazid, phenelzine, tranylcypromine, furazolidone). Serotonin syndrome has also been associated with combinations of amphetamines and SSRIs; these combinations should be avoided. TCAs may enhance the effects of amphetamines, potentially leading to hypertensive crisis. CYP2D6 inhibitors may increase the levels/effects of methamphetamine; example inhibitors include chlorpromazine, delavirdine, fluoxetine, miconazole, paroxetine, pergolide, quinidine, quinine, ritonavir, and ropinirole. Large doses of antacids or urinary alkalinizers increase the half-life and duration of action of amphetamines. May precipitate arrhythmias in patients receiving general anesthetics. Inhibitors of CYP2D6 may increase the effects of amphetamines (includes amiodarone, cimetidine, delavirdine, fluoxetine, paroxetine, propafenone, quinidine, and ritonavir).

Decreased Effect: Amphetamines inhibit the antihypertensive response to guanethidine, methyldopa, and guanadrel. Enzyme inducers (barbiturates, carbamazepine, phenytoin, and rifampin) may decrease serum concentrations of amphetamines.

Ethanol/Nutrition/Herb Interactions

Ethanol: Avoid ethanol (may cause CNS depression).

Food: Amphetamine serum levels may be altered if taken with acidic food, juices, or vitamin C. Avoid caffeine.

Herb/Nutraceutical: Avoid ephedra (may cause hypertension or arrhythmias).

Stability Store below 30°C (86°F). Protect from light.

Mechanism of Action A sympathomimetic amine related to ephedrine and amphetamine with CNS stimulant activity; peripheral actions include elevation of systolic and diastolic blood pressure and weak bronchodilator and respiratory stimulant action

Pharmacodynamics/Kinetics

Absorption: Rapid from GI tract

Metabolism: Hepatic; forms metabolite

Half-life elimination: 4-5 hours

Excretion: Urine primarily (dependent on urine pH)

Dosage Oral:

Children ≥6 years and Adults: ADHD: 5 mg 1-2 times/day; may increase by 5 mg increments at weekly intervals until optimum response is achieved, usually 20-25 mg/day

Children ≥12 years and Adults: Exogenous obesity: 5 mg 30 minutes before each meal; treatment duration should not exceed a few weeks

Dietary Considerations Should be taken 30 minutes before meals.

Monitoring Parameters Heart rate, respiratory rate, blood pressure, CNS activity, body weight (BMI); growth rate in children

Additional Information Illicit methamphetamine may contain lead; alkalinizing urine can result in longer methamphetamine half-life and elevated blood level; ephedrine is a precursor in the illicit manufacture of methamphetamine; ephedrine is extracted by dissolving ephedrine tablets in water or alcohol (50,000 tablets can result in 1 kg of ephedrine); conversion to methamphetamine occurs at a rate of 50% to 70% of the weight of ephedrine. 3,4-methylene dioxymethamphetamine (slang: XTC, Ecstasy, Adam) affects the serotonergic, dopaminergic, and noradrenergic pathways. As such, it can cause the serotonin syndrome associated with malignant hyperthermia and rhabdomyolysis.

Dosage Forms Tablet, as hydrochloride: 5 mg

♦ **Methamphetamine Hydrochloride** see Methamphetamine on page 1104

Methazolamide (meth a ZOE la mide)

Canadian Brand Names Apo-Methazolamide®

Pharmacologic Category Carbonic Anhydrase Inhibitor; Diuretic, Carbonic Anhydrase Inhibitor; Ophthalmic Agent, Antiglaucoma

Additional Appendix Information

Glaucoma Drug Therapy on page 2050

Sulfonamide Derivatives on page 1897

Use Adjunctive treatment of open-angle or secondary glaucoma; short-term therapy of narrow-angle glaucoma when delay of surgery is desired

Pregnancy Risk Factor C

Lactation Excretion in breast milk unknown

Medication Safety Issues

Sound-alike/look-alike issues:

Methazolamide may be confused with methenamine, metolazone

Neptazane® may be confused with Nesacaine®

Contraindications Hypersensitivity to methazolamide or any component of the formulation; marked kidney or liver dysfunction; severe pulmonary obstruction

Warnings/Precautions May impair mental alertness and/or physical coordination. Use with caution in patients with prediabetes or diabetes mellitus; may see a change in glucose control. Use with caution in patients with respiratory acidosis. Use with caution in the elderly; may be more sensitive to side effects.

Chemical similarities are present among sulfonamides, sulfonylureas, carbonic anhydrase inhibitors, thiazides, and loop diuretics (except ethacrynic acid). Use in patients with sulfonylurea allergy is specifically contraindicated in product labeling, however, a risk of cross-reaction exists in patients with allergy to any of these compounds; avoid use when previous reaction has been severe. Discontinue if signs of hypersensitivity are noted.

Adverse Reactions Frequency not defined.

Central nervous system: Malaise, fever, mental depression, drowsiness, dizziness, nervousness, headache, confusion, fatigue, trembling, unsteadiness

Dermatologic: Urticaria, pruritus, photosensitivity, rash, Stevens-Johnson syndrome

Endocrine & metabolic: Hyperchloremic metabolic acidosis, hypokalemia, hyperglycemia

(Continued)

Methazolamide *(Continued)*

Gastrointestinal: Metallic taste, anorexia, nausea, vomiting, diarrhea, constipation, weight loss, GI irritation, xerostomia, black tarry stools

Genitourinary: Polyuria, crystalluria, hematuria, renal calculi, impotence

Hematologic: Bone marrow depression, thrombocytopenia, thrombocytopenic purpura, hemolytic anemia, leukopenia, pancytopenia, agranulocytosis

Hepatic: Hepatic insufficiency

Neuromuscular & skeletal: Weakness, ataxia, paresthesia

Miscellaneous: Hypersensitivity

Drug Interactions

Increased Effect/Toxicity: Methazolamide may induce hypokalemia which would sensitize a patient to digitalis toxicity. Hypokalemia may be compounded with concurrent diuretic use or steroids. Methazolamide may increase the potential for salicylate toxicity. Primidone absorption may be delayed.

Decreased Effect: Increased lithium excretion and altered excretion of other drugs by alkalinization of the urine, such as amphetamines, quinidine, procainamide, methenamine, phenobarbital, and salicylates.

Mechanism of Action Noncompetitive inhibition of the enzyme carbonic anhydrase; thought that carbonic anhydrase is located at the luminal border of cells of the proximal tubule. When the enzyme is inhibited, there is an increase in urine volume and a change to an alkaline pH with a subsequent decrease in the excretion of titratable acid and ammonia.

Pharmacodynamics/Kinetics

Onset of action: Slow in comparison with acetazolamide (2-4 hours)

Peak effect: 6-8 hours

Duration: 10-18 hours

Absorption: Slow

Distribution: Well into tissue

Protein binding: ~55%

Metabolism: Slowly from GI tract

Half-life elimination: ~14 hours

Excretion: Urine (~25% as unchanged drug)

Dosage Adults: Oral: 50-100 mg 2-3 times/day

Dosage Forms Tablet: 25 mg, 50 mg

Methenamine *(meth EN a meen)*

U.S. Brand Names Hiprex®; Mandelamine®; Urex®

Canadian Brand Names Dehydral®; Hiprex®; Mandelamine®; Urasal®; Urex®

Index Terms Hexamethylenetetramine; Methenamine Hippurate; Methenamine Mandelate

Pharmacologic Category Antibiotic, Miscellaneous

Use Prophylaxis or suppression of recurrent urinary tract infections; urinary tract discomfort secondary to hypermotility

Pregnancy Risk Factor C

Pregnancy Implications Following a single 1 g dose of methenamine hippurate given prior to delivery, methenamine was found to slowly pass through the placental barrier. There were no signs of accumulation in the fetal circulation. Actual concentrations in the amniotic fluid varied. Methenamine has been considered to be "probably safe" for use during pregnancy. Methenamine has been shown to interfere with urine oestriol concentrations during pregnancy; serum levels are not affected.

Lactation Enters breast milk/compatible

Medication Safety Issues

Sound-alike/look-alike issues:

Methenamine may be confused with methazolamide, methionine

Urex® may be confused with Eurax®, Serax®

International issues:

Urex®: Brand name for furosemide in Australia

Contraindications Hypersensitivity to methenamine or any component of the formulation; severe dehydration, renal insufficiency, hepatic insufficiency in patients receiving hippurate salt; concurrent treatment with sulfonamides

Warnings/Precautions Methenamine should not be used to treat infections outside of the lower urinary tract. Use with caution in patients with hepatic disease, gout, and the elderly; doses of 8 g/day for 3-4 weeks may cause bladder irritation. Use care to maintain an acid pH of the urine, especially when treating infections due to urea splitting organisms (eg, *Proteus* and strains of *Pseudomonas*); reversible increases in LFTs have occurred during therapy especially in patients with hepatic dysfunction. Hiprex® contains tartrazine dye.

Adverse Reactions

1% to 10%:

Dermatologic: Rash (<4%)

Gastrointestinal: Nausea, dyspepsia (<4%)

Genitourinary: Dysuria (<4%)

<1% (Limited to important or life-threatening): Bladder irritation, crystalluria (especially with large doses), increased AST/ALT (reversible, rare)

Overdosage/Toxicology Well tolerated. Treatment includes GI decontamination, if possible, and supportive care.

Drug Interactions

Increased Effect/Toxicity: Sulfonamides may precipitate in the urine; concurrent use is contraindicated.

Decreased Effect: Sodium bicarbonate and acetazolamide will decrease effect secondary to alkalinization of urine.

Ethanol/Nutrition/Herb Interactions Food: Foods/diets which alkalinize urine pH >5.5 decrease therapeutic effect of methenamine.

Stability Protect from excessive heat.

Mechanism of Action Methenamine is hydrolyzed to formaldehyde and ammonia in acidic urine; formaldehyde has nonspecific bactericidal action

Pharmacodynamics/Kinetics
Absorption: Readily
Metabolism: Gastric juices: Hydrolyze 10% to 30% unless protected via enteric coating; Hepatic: ~10% to 25%
Half-life elimination: 3-6 hours
Excretion: Urine (~70% to 90% as unchanged drug) within 24 hours

Dosage Oral:
Children:
>2-6 years: *Mandelate:* 50-75 mg/kg/day in 3-4 doses or 0.25 g/30 lb 4 times/day
6-12 years:
Hippurate: 0.5-1 g twice daily
Mandelate: 50-75 mg/kg/day in 3-4 doses or 0.5 g 4 times/day
>12 years and Adults:
Hippurate: 0.5-1 g twice daily
Mandelate: 1 g 4 times/day after meals and at bedtime

Dosing adjustment/comments in renal impairment: Cl_{cr} <50 mL/minute: Avoid use

Dietary Considerations Foods/diets which alkalinize urine pH >5.5 decrease activity of methenamine; cranberry juice can be used to acidify urine and increase activity of methenamine. Hiprex® contains tartrazine dye.

Administration Administer around-the-clock to promote less variation in effect. Foods/diets which alkalinize urine pH >5.5 decrease activity of methenamine.

Monitoring Parameters Urinalysis, periodic liver function tests

Test Interactions Increased catecholamines and VMA (U); decreased HIAA (U)

Additional Information Should not be used to treat infections outside of the lower urinary tract. Methonamine has little, if any, role in the treatment or prevention of infections in patients with indwelling urinary (Foley) catheters. Furthermore, in noncatheterized patients, more effective antibiotics are available for the prevention or treatment of urinary tract infections. The influence of decreased renal function on the pharmacologic effects of methenamine results are unknown.

Dosage Forms
Tablet, as hippurate (Hiprex®, Urex®): 1 g [Hiprex® contains tartrazine dye]
Tablet, enteric coated, as mandelate (Mandelamine®): 500 mg, 1 g

---

Methenamine and Sodium Acid Phosphate
(meth EN a meen & SOW dee um AS id FOS fate)

U.S. Brand Names Uroqid-Acid® No. 2
Index Terms Methenamine Mandelate and Sodium Acid Phosphate; Sodium Acid Phosphate and Methenamine
Pharmacologic Category Antibiotic, Miscellaneous
Use Prophylaxis or suppression of bacteriuria associated with recurrent urinary tract infections
Pregnancy Risk Factor C
Dosage Oral: Adults: Initial: 2 tablets 4 times daily; maintenance: 2-4 tablets daily in divided doses
Additional Information Complete prescribing information for this medication should be consulted for additional detail.
Dosage Forms Tablet: Methenamine mandelate 500 mg and sodium acid phosphate 500 mg [contains 83 mg sodium]

♦ **Methenamine Hippurate** *see* Methenamine *on page 1106*
♦ **Methenamine Mandelate** *see* Methenamine *on page 1106*
♦ **Methenamine Mandelate and Sodium Acid Phosphate** *see* Methenamine and Sodium Acid Phosphate *on page 1107*

Methenamine, Sodium Biphosphate, Phenyl Salicylate, Methylene Blue, and Hyoscyamine
(meth EN a meen, SOW dee um bye FOS fate, fen nil sa LIS i late, METH i leen bloo, & hye oh SYE a meen)

U.S. Brand Names Urelle®; Urimar-T
Index Terms Hyoscyamine, Methenamine, Sodium Biphosphate, Phenyl Salicylate, and Methylene Blue; Methylene Blue, Methenamine, Sodium Biphosphate, Phenyl Salicylate, and Hyoscyamine; Phenyl Salicylate, Methenamine, Methylene Blue, Sodium Biphosphate, and Hyoscyamine; Sodium Biphosphate, Methenamine, Methylene Blue, Phenyl Salicylate, and Hyoscyamine
Pharmacologic Category Antibiotic, Miscellaneous
Use Treatment of symptoms of irritative voiding; relief of local symptoms associated with urinary tract infections; relief of urinary tract symptoms caused by diagnostic procedures
Pregnancy Risk Factor C
Lactation Enters breast milk/use caution
Contraindications Hypersensitivity to methenamine, hyoscyamine, methylene blue, or any component of the formulation
Warnings/Precautions Use caution in patients with a history of intolerance to belladonna alkaloids or salicylates. Use caution in patients with cardiovascular disease (cardiac arrhythmias, CHF, coronary heart disease, mitral stenosis), gastrointestinal tract obstruction, glaucoma, myasthenia gravis, or obstructive uropathy (bladder neck obstruction or prostatic hyperplasia). Discontinue use immediately if tachycardia, dizziness, or blurred vision occur. Elderly may be more sensitive to anticholinergic effects of hyoscyamine; use caution. May cause urinary discoloration (blue). Safety and efficacy have not been established in children ≤6 years of age.
(Continued)

Methenamine, Sodium Biphosphate, Phenyl Salicylate, Methylene Blue, and Hyoscyamine (Continued)

Adverse Reactions Frequency not defined.
Cardiovascular: Tachycardia, flushing
Central nervous system: Dizziness
Gastrointestinal: Xerostomia, nausea, vomiting
Genitourinary: Urinary retention (acute), micturition difficulty, discoloration of urine (blue)
Ocular: Blurred vision
Respiratory: Dyspnea, shortness of breath

Drug Interactions
Increased Effect/Toxicity: Refer to individual monographs for Hyoscyamine and Methenamine.
Decreased Effect: Refer to individual monographs for Hyoscyamine and Methenamine.

Stability Store at controlled room temperature of 15°C to 30°C (59°F to 86°F).

Dosage Oral:
Children >6 years: Dosage must be individualized
Adults: One tablet 4 times daily (followed by liberal fluid intake)

Dosage Forms
Tablet:
Urelle®: Methenamine 81 mg, sodium biphosphate 40.8 mg, phenyl salicylate 32.4 mg, methylene blue 10.8 mg, hyoscyamine sulfate 0.12 mg
Urimar-T: Methenamine 81.6 mg, sodium biphosphate 40.8 mg, phenyl salicylate 36.2 mg, methylene blue 10.8 mg, hyoscyamine sulfate 0.12 mg

♦ **Methergine**® see Methylergonovine on page 1118

Methimazole (meth IM a zole)

U.S. Brand Names Tapazole®
Canadian Brand Names Dom-Methimazole; PHL-Methimazole; Tapazole®
Index Terms Thiamazole
Pharmacologic Category Antithyroid Agent
Use Palliative treatment of hyperthyroidism, return the hyperthyroid patient to a normal metabolic state prior to thyroidectomy, and to control thyrotoxic crisis that may accompany thyroidectomy. The use of antithyroid thioamides is as effective in elderly as they are in younger adults; however, the expense, potential adverse effects, and inconvenience (compliance, monitoring) make them undesirable. The use of radioiodine due to ease of administration and less concern for long-term side effects and reproduction problems (some older males) makes it a more appropriate therapy.
Pregnancy Risk Factor D
Pregnancy Implications Hypothyroidism and congenital defects (rare) may occur.
Lactation Enters breast milk/contraindicated (AAP rates "compatible")
Medication Safety Issues
Sound-alike/look-alike issues:
Methimazole may be confused with metolazone
Contraindications Hypersensitivity to methimazole or any component of the formulation; nursing mothers (per manufacturer; however, expert analysis and the AAP state this drug may be used with caution in nursing mothers); pregnancy
Warnings/Precautions Use with extreme caution in patients receiving other drugs known to cause myelosuppression particularly agranulocytosis, patients >40 years of age; avoid doses >40 mg/day (increased myelosuppression); may cause acneiform eruptions or worsen the condition of the thyroid
Adverse Reactions Frequency not defined.
Cardiovascular: Edema
Central nervous system: Headache, vertigo, drowsiness, CNS stimulation, depression
Dermatologic: Skin rash, urticaria, pruritus, erythema nodosum, skin pigmentation, exfoliative dermatitis, alopecia
Endocrine & metabolic: Goiter
Gastrointestinal: Nausea, vomiting, stomach pain, abnormal taste, constipation, weight gain, salivary gland swelling
Hematologic: Leukopenia, agranulocytosis, granulocytopenia, thrombocytopenia, aplastic anemia, hypoprothrombinemia
Hepatic: Cholestatic jaundice, jaundice, hepatitis
Neuromuscular & skeletal: Arthralgia, paresthesia
Renal: Nephrotic syndrome
Miscellaneous: SLE-like syndrome
Overdosage/Toxicology Symptoms include nausea, vomiting, epigastric distress, headache, fever, arthralgia, pruritus, edema, pancytopenia, and signs of hypothyroidism. Management of overdose is supportive.
Drug Interactions
Cytochrome P450 Effect: Inhibits CYP1A2 (weak), 2A6 (weak), 2B6 (weak), 2C9 (weak), 2C19 (weak), 2D6 (moderate), 2E1 (weak), 3A4 (weak)
Increased Effect/Toxicity: Dosage of some drugs (including beta-blockers, digoxin, and theophylline) require adjustment during treatment of hyperthyroidism. Methimazole may increase the levels/effects of CYP2D6 substrates (eg, amphetamines, selected beta-blockers, dextromethorphan, fluoxetine, lidocaine, mirtazapine, nefazodone, paroxetine, risperidone, ritonavir, thioridazine, tricyclic antidepressants, venlafaxine).
Decreased Effect: Anticoagulant effect of warfarin may be decreased. Methimazole may decrease the levels/effects of CYP2D6 prodrug substrates (eg, codeine, hydrocodone, oxycodone, tramadol).
Stability Protect from light.

Mechanism of Action Inhibits the synthesis of thyroid hormones by blocking the oxidation of iodine in the thyroid gland, blocking iodine's ability to combine with tyrosine to form thyroxine and triiodothyronine (T_3), does not inactivate circulating T_4 and T_3

Pharmacodynamics/Kinetics
Onset of action: Antithyroid: Oral: 12-18 hours
Duration: 36-72 hours
Distribution: Concentrated in thyroid gland; crosses placenta; enters breast milk (1:1)
Protein binding, plasma: None
Metabolism: Hepatic
Bioavailability: 80% to 95%
Half-life elimination: 4-13 hours
Excretion: Urine (80%)

Dosage Oral: Administer in 3 equally divided doses at approximately 8-hour intervals
Children: Initial: 0.4 mg/kg/day in 3 divided doses; maintenance: 0.2 mg/kg/day in 3 divided doses up to 30 mg/24 hours maximum
Alternatively: Initial: 0.5-0.7 mg/kg/day **or** 15-20 mg/m^2/day in 3 divided doses
Maintenance: $1/3$ to $2/3$ of the initial dose beginning when the patient is euthyroid
Maximum: 30 mg/24 hours
Adults: Initial: 15 mg/day for mild hyperthyroidism; 30-40 mg/day in moderately severe hyperthyroidism; 60 mg/day in severe hyperthyroidism; maintenance: 5-15 mg/day
Adjust dosage as required to achieve and maintain serum T_3, T_4, and TSH levels in the normal range. An elevated T_3 may be the sole indicator of inadequate treatment. An elevated TSH indicates excessive antithyroid treatment.

Dosage adjustment in renal impairment: Adjustment is not necessary

Dietary Considerations Should be taken consistently in relation to meals every day.

Monitoring Parameters Monitor for signs of hypothyroidism, hyperthyroidism, T_4, T_3; CBC with differential, liver function (baseline and as needed), serum thyroxine, free thyroxine index

Dosage Forms
Tablet: 5 mg, 10 mg, 20 mg
Tapazole® 5 mg, 10 mg

♦ **Methitest**™ see MethylTESTOSTERone *on page 1125*

Methocarbamol (meth oh KAR ba mole)

U.S. Brand Names Robaxin®
Canadian Brand Names Robaxin®
Pharmacologic Category Skeletal Muscle Relaxant
Use Treatment of muscle spasm associated with acute painful musculoskeletal conditions; supportive therapy in tetanus
Pregnancy Risk Factor C
Pregnancy Implications Animal reproduction studies have not been conducted. The manufacturer notes that fetal and congenital abnormalities have been rarely reported following *in utero* exposure. Use during pregnancy only if clearly needed.
Lactation Excretion in breast milk unknown/use caution
Medication Safety Issues
Sound-alike/look-alike issues:
Methocarbamol may be confused with mephobarbital
Robaxin® may be confused with Rubex®
Contraindications Hypersensitivity to methocarbamol or any component of the formulation; renal impairment (injection formulation)
Warnings/Precautions
Oral: Use caution with renal or hepatic impairment.
Injection: Rate of injection should not exceed 3 mL/minute; solution is hypertonic; avoid extravasation. Use with caution in patients with a history of seizures. Use caution with hepatic impairment.
Adverse Reactions Frequency not defined.
Cardiovascular: Flushing of face, bradycardia, hypotension, syncope
Central nervous system: Drowsiness, dizziness, lightheadedness, convulsion, vertigo, headache, fever, amnesia, confusion, insomnia, sedation, coordination impaired (mild)
Dermatologic: Allergic dermatitis, urticaria, pruritus, rash, angioneurotic edema
Gastrointestinal: Nausea, vomiting, metallic taste, dyspepsia
Hematologic: Leukopenia
Hepatic: Jaundice
Local: Pain at injection site, thrombophlebitis
Ocular: Nystagmus, blurred vision, diplopia, conjunctivitis
Renal: Renal impairment
Respiratory: Nasal congestion
Miscellaneous: Allergic manifestations, anaphylactic reaction
Overdosage/Toxicology Symptoms include cardiac arrhythmias, nausea, vomiting, drowsiness, and coma. Treatment is supportive following attempts to enhance drug elimination. Hypotension should be treated with I.V. fluids and/or Trendelenburg positioning. Dialysis, hemoperfusion, and osmotic diuresis have all been useful in reducing serum drug concentrations. The patient should be observed for possible relapses due to incomplete gastric emptying.
Drug Interactions
Increased Effect/Toxicity: Increased effect/toxicity with CNS depressants.
Ethanol/Nutrition/Herb Interactions
Ethanol: Avoid ethanol (may increase CNS depression).
Herb/Nutraceutical: Avoid valerian, St John's wort, kava kava, gotu kola (may increase CNS depression).
(Continued)

Methocarbamol *(Continued)*

Stability
Injection: Prior to dilution, store at controlled room temperature of 20°C to 25°C (68°F to 77°F). Injection when diluted to 4 mg/mL in sterile water, 5% dextrose, or 0.9% saline is stable for 6 days at room temperature. Do **not** refrigerate after dilution.

Tablet: Store at controlled room temperature of 20°C to 25°C (68°F to 77°F).

Mechanism of Action Causes skeletal muscle relaxation by general CNS depression

Pharmacodynamics/Kinetics
Onset of action: Muscle relaxation: Oral: ~30 minutes

Protein binding: 46% to 50%

Metabolism: Hepatic via dealkylation and hydroxylation

Half-life elimination: 1-2 hours

Time to peak, serum: ~2 hours

Excretion: Urine (as metabolites)

Dosage
Tetanus: I.V.:

Children: Recommended **only** for use in tetanus: 15 mg/kg/dose or 500 mg/m²/dose, may repeat every 6 hours if needed; maximum dose: 1.8 g/m²/day for 3 days only

Adults: Initial dose: 1-3 g; may repeat dose every 6 hours until oral dosing is possible; injection should not be used for more than 3 consecutive days

Muscle spasm: Children ≥16 years and Adults:

Oral: 1.5 g 4 times/day for 2-3 days (up to 8 g/day may be given in severe conditions), then decrease to 4-4.5 g/day in 3-6 divided doses

I.M., I.V.: 1 g every 8 hours if oral not possible; injection should not be used for more than 3 consecutive days. If condition persists, may repeat course of therapy after a drug-free interval of 48 hours.

Elderly: Muscle spasm: Oral: Initial: 500 mg 4 times/day; titrate to response

Dosing adjustment/comments in renal impairment: Do not administer parenteral formulation to patients with renal dysfunction.

Dosing adjustment in hepatic impairment: Specific dosing guidelines are not available; plasma protein binding and clearance are decreased; half-life is increased

Administration
Injection:

I.M.: A maximum of 5 mL can be administered into each gluteal region.

I.V.: Maximum rate: 3 mL/minute; should not be used for more than 3 consecutive days; may be administered undiluted. Monitor closely for extravasation. Administer I.V. while in recumbent position. Maintain position 15-30 minutes following infusion.

Tablet: May be crushed and mixed with food or liquid if needed. Avoid alcohol.

Test Interactions May cause color interference in certain screening tests for 5-HIAA using nitrosonaphthol reagent and in screening tests for urinary VMA using the Gitlow method.

Dosage Forms
Injection, solution: 100 mg/mL (10 mL) [in polyethylene glycol; vial stopper contains latex]

Tablet: 500 mg, 750 mg

Methohexital *(meth oh HEKS i tal)*

U.S. Brand Names Brevital® Sodium

Canadian Brand Names Brevital®

Index Terms Methohexital Sodium

Pharmacologic Category Barbiturate

Use Induction and maintenance of general anesthesia for short procedures

Can be used in pediatric patients ≥1 month of age as follows: For rectal or intramuscular induction of anesthesia prior to the use of other general anesthetic agents, as an adjunct to subpotent inhalational anesthetic agents for short surgical procedures, or for short surgical, diagnostic, or therapeutic procedures associated with minimal painful stimuli

Unlabeled/Investigational Use Wada test

Restrictions C-IV

Pregnancy Risk Factor C

Medication Safety Issues
Sound-alike/look-alike issues:

Brevital® may be confused with Brevibloc®

Dosage Doses must be titrated to effect

Manufacturer's recommendations:

Infants <1 month: Safety and efficacy not established

Infants ≥1 month and Children:

I.M.: Induction: 6.6-10 mg/kg of a 5% solution

Rectal: Induction: Usual: 25 mg/kg of a 1% solution

Alternative pediatric dosing:

Children 3-12 years:

I.M.: Preoperative: 5-10 mg/kg/dose

I.V.: Induction: 1-2 mg/kg/dose

Rectal: Preoperative/induction: 20-35 mg/kg/dose; usual: 25 mg/kg/dose; maximum dose: 500 mg/dose; give as 10% aqueous solution

Adults: I.V.:

Induction: 50-120 mg to start; 20-40 mg every 4-7 minutes

Wada test (unlabeled): 3-4 mg over 3 second; following signs of recovery, administer a second dose of 2 mg over 2 seconds

Dosing adjustment/comments in hepatic impairment: Lower dosage and monitor closely

Additional Information Complete prescribing information for this medication should be consulted for additional detail.

Dosage Forms Injection, powder for reconstitution, as sodium: 500 mg, 2.5 g, 5 g

♦ **Methohexital Sodium** *see* Methohexital *on page 1110*

Methotrexate (meth oh TREKS ate)

U.S. Brand Names Rheumatrex®; Trexall™

Canadian Brand Names Apo-Methotrexate®; ratio-Methotrexate

Index Terms Amethopterin; Methotrexate Sodium; MTX (error-prone abbreviation); NSC-740

Pharmacologic Category Antineoplastic Agent, Antimetabolite (Antifolate); Antirheumatic, Disease Modifying

Use Treatment of trophoblastic neoplasms; leukemias; psoriasis; rheumatoid arthritis (RA), including polyarticular-course juvenile rheumatoid arthritis (JRA); breast, head and neck, and lung carcinomas; osteosarcoma; soft-tissue sarcomas; carcinoma of gastrointestinal tract, esophagus, testes; lymphomas

Unlabeled/Investigational Use Treatment and maintenance of remission in Crohn's disease; ectopic pregnancy

Pregnancy Risk Factor X (psoriasis, rheumatoid arthritis)

Pregnancy Implications Fetal death or teratogenic effects may occur. Use is contraindicated in pregnant women with psoriasis or rheumatoid arthritis. Use for the treatment of neoplastic diseases only when the potential benefit to the mother outweighs the possible risk to the fetus. Pregnancy should be excluded prior to therapy in women of childbearing potential. Pregnancy should be avoided for ≥3 months following treatment in male patients and ≥1 ovulatory cycle in female patients.

Lactation Enters breast milk/contraindicated

Medication Safety Issues

Sound-alike/look-alike issues:

Methotrexate may be confused with metolazone, mitoxantrone

MTX is an error-prone abbreviation (mistaken as mitoxantrone)

High alert medication: The Institute for Safe Medication Practices (ISMP) includes this medication among its list of drugs which have a heightened risk of causing significant patient harm when used in error.

Errors have occurred (resulting in death) when methotrexate was administered as "daily" dose instead of the recommended "weekly" dose.

International issues:

Trexall™ may be confused with Truxal® which is a brand name for chlorprothixene in Belgium

Trexall™ may be confused with Trexol® which is a brand name for tramadol in Mexico

Contraindications Hypersensitivity to methotrexate or any component of the formulation; severe renal or hepatic impairment; pre-existing profound bone marrow suppression in patients with psoriasis or rheumatoid arthritis, alcoholic liver disease, AIDS, pre-existing blood dyscrasias; pregnancy (in patients with psoriasis or rheumatoid arthritis); breast-feeding

Warnings/Precautions Hazardous agent - use appropriate precautions for handling and disposal.

[U.S. Boxed Warning]: Methotrexate has been associated with acute (elevated transaminases) and potentially fatal chronic (fibrosis, cirrhosis) hepatotoxicity. Risk is related to cumulative dose and prolonged exposure. Monitor closely (with liver function tests, including serum albumin) for liver toxicities. Liver enzyme elevations may be noted, but may not be predictive of hepatic disease in long term treatment for psoriasis (but generally is predictive in rheumatoid arthritis [RA] treatment). With long-term use, liver biopsy may show histologic changes, fibrosis or cirrhosis; periodic liver biopsy is recommended with long-term use for psoriasis and for persistent abnormal liver function tests with RA; discontinue methotrexate with moderate-to-severe change in liver biopsy. Ethanol abuse, obesity, advanced age, and diabetes may increase the risk of hepatotoxic reactions. Use caution with preexisting liver impairment; may require dosage reduction. Use caution when used with other hepatotoxic agents (azathioprine, retinoids, sulfasalazine). **[U.S. Boxed Warning]: Methotrexate elimination is reduced in patients with ascites;** may require dose reduction or discontinuation. Monitor closely for toxicity.

[U.S. Boxed Warning]: May cause renal damage leading to acute renal failure, especially with high-dose methotrexate; monitor renal function and methotrexate levels closely, maintain adequate hydration and urinary alkalinization. Use caution in osteosarcoma patients treated with high-dose methotrexate in combination with nephrotoxic chemotherapy (eg, cisplatin). **[U.S. Boxed Warning]: Methotrexate elimination is reduced in patients with renal impairment;** may require dose reduction or discontinuation; monitor closely for toxicity. **[U.S. Boxed Warning]: Tumor lysis syndrome may occur in patients with high tumor burden;** use appropriate prevention and treatment.

[U.S. Boxed Warning]: May cause potentially life-threatening pneumonitis (may occur at any time during therapy and at any dosage); monitor closely for pulmonary symptoms, particularly dry, nonproductive cough. Other potential symptoms include fever, dyspnea, hypoxemia, or pulmonary infiltrate. **[U.S. Boxed Warning]: Methotrexate elimination is reduced in patients with pleural effusions;** may require dose reduction or discontinuation. Monitor closely for toxicity.

[U.S. Boxed Warning]: Bone marrow suppression may occur, resulting in anemia, aplastic anemia, pancytopenia, leukopenia, neutropenia, and/or thrombocytopenia. Use caution in patients with pre-existing bone marrow suppression. Discontinue therapy in RA or psoriasis if a significant decrease in hematologic components is noted. **[U.S. Boxed Warning]: Use of low dose methotrexate has been associated with the development of malignant lymphomas;** may regress upon discontinuation of therapy; treat lymphoma appropriately if regression is not induced by cessation of methotrexate.

(Continued)

Methotrexate *(Continued)*

[U.S. Boxed Warning]: Diarrhea and ulcerative stomatitis may require interruption of therapy; death from hemorrhagic enteritis or intestinal perforation has been reported. Use with caution in patients with peptic ulcer disease, ulcerative colitis.

May cause neurotoxicity including seizures (usually in pediatric ALL patients), leukoencephalopathy (usually with concurrent cranial irradiation) and stroke-like encephalopathy (usually with high-dose regimens). Chemical arachnoiditis (headache, back pain, nuchal rigidity, fever), myelopathy and chronic leukoencephalopathy may result from intrathecal administration.

[U.S. Boxed Warning]: Any dose level or route of administration may cause severe and potentially fatal dermatologic reactions, including toxic epidermal necrolysis, Stevens-Johnson syndrome, exfoliative dermatitis, skin necrosis, and erythema multiforme. Radiation dermatitis and sunburn may be precipitated by methotrexate administration. Psoriatic lesions may be worsened by concomitant exposure to ultraviolet radiation.

[U.S. Boxed Warning]: Concomitant administration with NSAIDs may cause severe bone marrow suppression, aplastic anemia, and GI toxicity. Do not administer NSAIDs prior to or during high dose methotrexate therapy; may increase and prolong serum methotrexate levels. Doses used for psoriasis may still lead to unexpected toxicities; use caution when administering NSAIDs or salicylates with lower doses of methotrexate for RA. Methotrexate may increase the levels and effects of mercaptopurine; may require dosage adjustments. Vitamins containing folate may decrease response to systemic methotrexate; folate deficiency may increase methotrexate toxicity. **[U.S. Boxed Warning]: Concomitant methotrexate administration with radiotherapy may increase the risk of soft tissue necrosis and osteonecrosis.**

[U.S. Boxed Warnings]: Should be administered under the supervision of a physician experienced in the use of antimetabolite therapy; serious and fatal toxicities have occurred at all dose levels. Immune suppression may lead to potentially fatal opportunistic infections. For rheumatoid arthritis and psoriasis, immunosuppressive therapy should only be used when disease is active and less toxic, traditional therapy is ineffective. Methotrexate formulations and/or diluents containing preservatives should not be used for intrathecal or high-dose therapy. May cause fetal death or congenital abnormalities; do not use for psoriasis or RA treatment in pregnant women. May cause impairment of fertility, oligospermia, and menstrual dysfunction. Toxicity from methotrexate or any immunosuppressive is increased in the elderly. Methotrexate injection may contain benzyl alcohol and should not be used in neonates.

Adverse Reactions Note: Adverse reactions vary by route and dosage. Hematologic and/or gastrointestinal toxicities may be common at dosages used in chemotherapy; these reactions are much less frequent when used at typical dosages for rheumatic diseases.

>10%:
Central nervous system (with I.T. administration or very high-dose therapy):
  Arachnoiditis: Acute reaction manifested as severe headache, nuchal rigidity, vomiting, and fever; may be alleviated by reducing the dose
  Subacute toxicity: 10% of patients treated with 12-15 mg/m² of I.T. methotrexate may develop this in the second or third week of therapy; consists of motor paralysis of extremities, cranial nerve palsy, seizure, or coma. This has also been seen in pediatric cases receiving very high-dose I.V. methotrexate.
  Demyelinating encephalopathy: Seen months or years after receiving methotrexate; usually in association with cranial irradiation or other systemic chemotherapy
Dermatologic: Reddening of skin
Endocrine & metabolic: Hyperuricemia, defective oogenesis or spermatogenesis
Gastrointestinal: Ulcerative stomatitis, glossitis, gingivitis, nausea, vomiting, diarrhea, anorexia, intestinal perforation, mucositis (dose dependent; appears in 3-7 days after therapy, resolving within 2 weeks)
Hematologic: Leukopenia, thrombocytopenia
Renal: Renal failure, azotemia, nephropathy
Respiratory: Pharyngitis

1% to 10%:
Cardiovascular: Vasculitis
Central nervous system: Dizziness, malaise, encephalopathy, seizure, fever, chills
Dermatologic: Alopecia, rash, photosensitivity, depigmentation or hyperpigmentation of skin
Endocrine & metabolic: Diabetes
Genitourinary: Cystitis
Hematologic: Hemorrhage
Myelosuppressive: This is the primary dose-limiting factor (along with mucositis) of methotrexate; occurs about 5-7 days after methotrexate therapy, and should resolve within 2 weeks
  WBC: Mild
  Platelets: Moderate
  Onset: 7 days
  Nadir: 10 days
  Recovery: 21 days
Hepatic: Cirrhosis and portal fibrosis have been associated with chronic methotrexate therapy; acute elevation of liver enzymes are common after high-dose methotrexate, and usually resolve within 10 days.
Neuromuscular & skeletal: Arthralgia
Ocular: Blurred vision
Renal: Renal dysfunction: Manifested by an abrupt rise in serum creatinine and BUN and a fall in urine output; more common with high-dose methotrexate, and may be due to precipitation of the drug.
Respiratory: Pneumonitis: Associated with fever, cough, and interstitial pulmonary infiltrates; treatment is to withhold methotrexate during the acute reaction; interstitial pneumonitis has been reported to occur with an incidence of 1% in patients with RA (dose 7.5-15 mg/week)

<1% (Limited to important or life-threatening): Acute neurologic syndrome (at high dosages - symptoms include confusion, hemiparesis, transient blindness, and coma); anaphylaxis, alveolitis, cognitive dysfunction (has been reported at low dosage), decreased resistance to infection, erythema multiforme, hepatic failure, leukoencephalopathy (especially following craniospinal irradiation or repeated high-dose therapy), lymphoproliferative disorders, osteonecrosis and soft tissue necrosis (with radiotherapy), pericarditis, plaque erosions (psoriasis), seizure (more frequent in pediatric patients with ALL), Stevens-Johnson syndrome, thromboembolism

Overdosage/Toxicology Symptoms include nausea, vomiting, alopecia, melena, and renal failure. Administer leucovorin (see Dosage).

Hydration and alkalinization may be used to prevent precipitation of methotrexate or methotrexate metabolites in the renal tubules. Severe bone marrow toxicity can result from overdose. Generally, neither peritoneal nor hemodialysis have been shown to increase elimination. However, effective clearance of methotrexate has been reported with acute, intermittent hemodialysis using a high-flux dialyzer.

Drug Interactions

Increased Effect/Toxicity: Concurrent therapy with NSAIDs has resulted in severe bone marrow suppression, aplastic anemia, and GI toxicity. NSAIDs should not be used during moderate or high-dose methotrexate due to increased and prolonged methotrexate levels (may increase toxicity); NSAID use during treatment of rheumatoid arthritis has not been fully explored, but continuation of prior regimen has been allowed in some circumstances, with cautious monitoring. Salicylates may increase methotrexate levels, however salicylate doses used for prophylaxis of cardiovascular events are not likely to be of concern.

Penicillins, probenecid, sulfonamides, tetracyclines may increase methotrexate concentrations due to a reduction in renal tubular secretion; primarily a concern with high doses of methotrexate. Hepatotoxic agents (acitretin, azathioprine, retinoids, sulfasalazine) may increase the risk of hepatotoxic reactions with methotrexate.

Concomitant administration of cyclosporine with methotrexate may increase levels and toxicity of each. Methotrexate may increase mercaptopurine or theophylline levels. Methotrexate, when administered prior to cytarabine, may enhance the efficacy and toxicity of cytarabine; some combination treatment regimens (eg, hyper-CVAD) have been designed to take advantage of this interaction.

Concurrent use of live virus vaccines may result in infections.

Decreased Effect: Cholestyramine may decrease levels of methotrexate. Corticosteroids may decrease uptake of methotrexate into leukemia cells. Administration of these drugs should be separated by 12 hours. Dexamethasone has been reported to not affect methotrexate influx into cells.

Ethanol/Nutrition/Herb Interactions

Ethanol: Avoid ethanol (may be associated with increased liver injury).

Food: Methotrexate peak serum levels may be decreased if taken with food. Milk-rich foods may decrease methotrexate absorption. Folate may decrease drug response.

Herb/Nutraceutical: Avoid echinacea (has immunostimulant properties).

Stability Store tablets and intact vials at room temperature (15°C to 25°C). Protect from light. Dilute powder with D_5W or NS to a concentration of ≤25 mg/mL (20 mg and 50 mg vials) and 50 mg/mL (1 g vial). Intrathecal solutions may be reconstituted to 2.5-5 mg/mL with NS, D_5W, lactated Ringer's, or Elliott's B solution. **Use preservative free preparations for intrathecal or high-dose administration.** Further dilution in D_5W or NS is stable for 24 hours at room temperature (21°C to 25°C). Reconstituted solutions with a preservative may be stored under refrigeration for up to 3 months, and up to 4 weeks at room temperature. Intrathecal dilutions are stable at room temperature for 7 days, but it is generally recommended that they be used within 4-8 hours.

Mechanism of Action Methotrexate is a folate antimetabolite that inhibits DNA synthesis. Methotrexate irreversibly binds to dihydrofolate reductase, inhibiting the formation of reduced folates, and thymidylate synthetase, resulting in inhibition of purine and thymidylic acid synthesis. Methotrexate is cell cycle specific for the S phase of the cycle.

The MOA in the treatment of rheumatoid arthritis is unknown, but may affect immune function. In psoriasis, methotrexate is thought to target rapidly proliferating epithelial cells in the skin.

In Crohn's disease, it may have immune modulator and anti-inflammatory activity

Pharmacodynamics/Kinetics

Onset of action: Antirheumatic: 3-6 weeks; additional improvement may continue longer than 12 weeks

Absorption: Oral: Rapid; well absorbed at low doses (<30 mg/m²), incomplete after large doses; I.M.: Complete

Distribution: Penetrates slowly into 3rd space fluids (eg, pleural effusions, ascites), exits slowly from these compartments (slower than from plasma); crosses placenta; small amounts enter breast milk; sustained concentrations retained in kidney and liver

Protein binding: 50%

Metabolism: <10%; degraded by intestinal flora to DAMPA by carboxypeptidase; hepatic aldehyde oxidase converts methotrexate to 7-OH methotrexate; polyglutamates are produced intracellularly and are just as potent as methotrexate; their production is dose- and duration-dependent and they are slowly eliminated by the cell once formed

Half-life elimination: Low dose: 3-10 hours; High dose: 8-12 hours

Time to peak, serum: Oral: 1-2 hours; I.M.: 30-60 minutes

Excretion: Urine (44% to 100%); feces (small amounts)

Dosage Refer to individual protocols.

Note: Doses between 100-500 mg/m² **may require** leucovorin rescue. Doses >500 mg/m² **require** leucovorin rescue: Oral, I.M., I.V.: Leucovorin 10-15 mg/m² every 6 hours for 8 or 10 doses, starting 24 hours after the start of methotrexate infusion. Continue until the methotrexate level is ≤0.1 micromolar (10^{-7}M). Some clinicians continue leucovorin until the methotrexate level is <0.05 micromolar (5×10^{-8}M) or 0.01 micromolar (10^{-8}M).

(Continued)

Methotrexate *(Continued)*

If the 48-hour methotrexate level is >1 micromolar (10^{-7}M) or the 72-hour methotrexate level is >0.2 micromolar (2×10^{-7}M): I.V., I.M, Oral: Leucovorin 100 mg/m^2 every 6 hours until the methotrexate level is ≤0.1 micromolar (10^{-7}M). Some clinicians continue leucovorin until the methotrexate level is <0.05 micromolar (5×10^{-8}M) or 0.01 micromolar (10^{-8}M).

Children:
  Dermatomyositis: Oral: 15-20 mg/m^2/week as a single dose once weekly **or** 0.3-1 mg/kg/dose once weekly
  Juvenile rheumatoid arthritis: Oral, I.M.: 10 mg/m^2 once weekly, then 5-15 mg/m^2/week as a single dose **or** as 3 divided doses given 12 hours apart
  Antineoplastic dosage range:
    Oral, I.M.: 7.5-30 mg/m^2/week **or** every 2 weeks
    I.V.: 10-18,000 mg/m^2 bolus dosing **or** continuous infusion over 6-42 hours
  Pediatric solid tumors (high-dose): I.V.:
    <12 years: 12-25 g/m^2
    ≥12 years: 8 g/m^2
  Acute lymphocytic leukemia (intermediate-dose): I.V.: Loading: 100 mg/m^2 bolus dose, followed by 900 mg/m^2/day infusion over 23-41 hours.
  Meningeal leukemia: I.T.: 10-15 mg/m^2 (maximum dose: 15 mg) **or** an age-based dosing regimen; one possible system is:
    ≤3 months: 3 mg/dose
    4-11 months: 6 mg/dose
    1 year: 8 mg/dose
    2 years: 10 mg/dose
    ≥3 years: 12 mg/dose

Adults: I.V.: Range is wide from 30-40 mg/m^2/week to 100-12,000 mg/m^2 with leucovorin rescue
  Trophoblastic neoplasms:
    Oral, I.M.: 15-30 mg/day for 5 days; repeat in 7 days for 3-5 courses
    I.V.: 11 mg/m^2 days 1 through 5 every 3 weeks
  Head and neck cancer: Oral, I.M., I.V.: 25-50 mg/m^2 once weekly
  Mycosis fungoides (cutaneous T-cell lymphoma): Oral, I.M.: Initial (early stages):
    5-50 mg once weekly **or**
    15-37.5 mg twice weekly
  Bladder cancer: I.V.:
    30 mg/m^2 day 1 and 8 every 3 weeks **or**
    30 mg/m^2 day 1, 15, and 22 every 4 weeks
  Breast cancer: I.V.: 30-60 mg/m^2 days 1 and 8 every 3-4 weeks
  Gastric cancer: I.V.: 1500 mg/m^2 every 4 weeks
  Lymphoma, non-Hodgkin's: I.V.:
    30 mg/m^2 days 3 and 10 every 3 weeks **or**
    120 mg/m^2 day 8 and 15 every 3-4 weeks **or**
    200 mg/m^2 day 8 and 15 every 3 weeks **or**
    400 mg/m^2 every 4 weeks for 3 cycles **or**
    1 g/m^2 every 3 weeks **or**
    1.5 g/m^2 every 4 weeks
  Sarcoma: I.V.: 8-12 g/m^2 weekly for 2-4 weeks
  Rheumatoid arthritis: Oral: 7.5 mg once weekly **or** 2.5 mg every 12 hours for 3 doses/week, not to exceed 20 mg/week
  Psoriasis:
    Oral: 2.5-5 mg/dose every 12 hours for 3 doses given weekly **or**
    Oral, I.M.: 10-25 mg/dose given once weekly
  Ectopic pregnancy (unlabeled use): I.M.: 50 mg/m^2 as a single dose
  Active Crohn's disease (unlabeled use): Induction of remission: I.M., SubQ: 15-25 mg once weekly; remission maintenance: 15 mg once weekly
    Note: Oral dosing has been reported as effective but oral absorption is highly variable. If patient relapses after a switch to oral, may consider returning to injectable.

Elderly: Rheumatoid arthritis/psoriasis: Oral: Initial: 5-7.5 mg/week, not to exceed 20 mg/week

Dosing adjustment in renal impairment:
  Cl$_{cr}$ 61-80 mL/minute: Reduce dose to 75% of usual dose
  Cl$_{cr}$ 51-60 mL/minute: Reduce dose to 70% of usual dose
  Cl$_{cr}$ 10-50 mL/minute: Reduce dose to 30% to 50% of usual dose
  Cl$_{cr}$ <10 mL/minute: Avoid use
Hemodialysis: Not dialyzable (0% to 5%); supplemental dose is not necessary
Peritoneal dialysis: Supplemental dose is not necessary
Dosage adjustment in hepatic impairment:
  Bilirubin 3.1-5 mg/dL **or** AST >180 units: Administer 75% of usual dose
  Bilirubin >5 mg/dL: Do not use

Dietary Considerations
  Sodium content of 100 mg injection: 20 mg (0.86 mEq)
  Sodium content of 100 mg (low sodium) injection: 15 mg (0.65 mEq)

Administration Methotrexate may be administered I.M., I.V., I.T., or SubQ; I.V. administration may be as slow push, short bolus infusion, or 24- to 42-hour continuous infusion

Specific dosing schemes vary, but high dose should be followed by leucovorin calcium to prevent toxicity; refer to Leucovorin monograph *on page 990*

Monitoring Parameters For prolonged use (especially rheumatoid arthritis, psoriasis) a baseline liver biopsy, repeated at each 1-1.5 g cumulative dose interval, should be performed; WBC and platelet counts every 4 weeks; CBC and creatinine, LFTs every 3-4 months; chest x-ray

Reference Range Therapeutic levels: Variable; Toxic concentration: Variable; therapeutic range is dependent upon therapeutic approach.

High-dose regimens produce drug levels that are between 0.1-1 micromole/l 24-72 hours after drug infusion

Toxic: Low-dose therapy: >0.2 micromole/L; high-dose therapy: >1 micromole/L

Additional Information Latex-free products: 50 mg/2 mL, 100 mg/4 mL, and 250 mg/10 mL vials with and without preservatives by Immunex

Dosage Forms

Injection, powder for reconstitution [preservative free]: 20 mg, 1 g

Injection, solution: 25 mg/mL (2 mL, 10 mL) [contains benzyl alcohol]

Injection, solution [preservative free]: 25 mg/mL (2 mL, 4 mL, 8 mL, 10 mL)

Tablet: 2.5 mg

Trexall™: 5 mg, 7.5 mg, 10 mg, 15 mg

Tablet, as sodium [dose pack] (Rheumatrex® Dose Pack): 2.5 mg (4 cards with 2, 3, 4, 5, or 6 tablets each)

♦ **Methotrexate Sodium** see Methotrexate on page 1111

Methoxsalen (meth OKS a len)

U.S. Brand Names 8-MOP®; Oxsoralen®; Oxsoralen-Ultra®; Uvadex®

Canadian Brand Names 8-MOP®; Oxsoralen®; Oxsoralen-Ultra®; Ultramop™; Uvadex®

Index Terms Methoxypsoralen; 8-Methoxypsoralen; 8-MOP

Pharmacologic Category Psoralen

Use

Oral: Symptomatic control of severe, recalcitrant disabling psoriasis; repigmentation of idiopathic vitiligo; palliative treatment of skin manifestations of cutaneous T-cell lymphoma (CTCL)

Topical: Repigmentation of idiopathic vitiligo

Extracorporeal: Palliative treatment of skin manifestations of CTCL

Pregnancy Risk Factor C/D (Uvadex®)

Pregnancy Implications Fetal toxicity has been observed in animal studies, however, there are no adequate and well-controlled studies in pregnant women. Use during pregnancy is not recommended. Women of childbearing potential should be advised to avoid pregnancy.

Lactation Excretion in breast milk unknown/not recommended

Contraindications Hypersensitivity to methoxsalen (psoralens) or any component of the formulation; diseases associated with photosensitivity; cataract; invasive squamous cell cancer; aphakia; melanoma; pregnancy (Uvadex®)

Warnings/Precautions Serious burns may occur from ultraviolet radiation or sunlight even if exposed through glass if dose and/or exposure schedule is not maintained. Therapy may lead to increased risk of melanoma; this risk may be increased with fair skin or prior exposure to prolonged tar and UVB treatment, ionizing radiation, or arsenic. Methoxsalen concentrates in the lens; eyes should be shielded from light for 24 hours to prevent possible formation of cataracts. Use caution with basal cell carcinoma, hepatic, kidney, cardiac disease, or in the elderly. Use caution with other agents that may cause photosensitivity. **[U.S. Boxed Warning]: Soft-gelatin capsule and hard-gelatin capsule are not interchangeable; re-titration is required if the formulation is changed.**

CTCL: For use only if inadequate response to other forms of therapy. Used in conjunction with long wave radiation of white blood cells using the UVAR® photopheresis system. Safety and efficacy in pediatric patients have not been established.

Psoriasis: For use only if inadequate response to other therapies when the diagnosis is biopsy proven. Administer only in conjunction with scheduled controlled doses of long wave ultraviolet (UVA) radiation (combination referred to as PUVA). Safety and efficacy in pediatric patients have not been established.

Vitiligo: Used in conjunction with controlled doses of long wave ultraviolet radiation or sunlight. Lotion should only be applied under direct supervision of prescriber and should not be dispensed to the patient. Safety and efficacy in children <12 years of age have not been established.

[U.S. Boxed Warning]: Should be administered under the supervision of an experienced physician with special competence in the diagnosis and treatment of dermatologic diseases.

Adverse Reactions Frequency not always defined.

Cardiovascular: Severe edema, hypotension

Central nervous system: Nervousness, vertigo, depression, dizziness, headache, malaise

Dermatologic: Painful blistering, burning, and peeling of skin; pruritus (10%), freckling, hypopigmentation, rash, cheilitis, erythema, itching, urticaria

Gastrointestinal: Nausea (10%)

Neuromuscular & skeletal: Loss of muscle coordination, leg cramps

Miscellaneous: Miliaria

Overdosage/Toxicology Symptoms include nausea and severe burns. Follow accepted treatment of severe burns. Keep room darkened until reaction subsides (8-24 hours or more).

Drug Interactions

Cytochrome P450 Effect: Substrate of CYP2A6 (minor); **Inhibits** CYP1A2 (strong), 2A6 (strong), 2C9 (weak), 2C19 (weak), 2D6 (weak), 2E1 (weak), 3A4 (weak)

Increased Effect/Toxicity: Methoxsalen may increase the levels/effects of CYP1A2 substrates (eg, aminophylline, fluvoxamine, mexiletine, mirtazapine, ropinirole, theophylline, trifluoperazine) and CYP2A6 substrates (eg, dexmedetomidine, ifosfamide).

Ethanol/Nutrition/Herb Interactions Food: Methoxsalen serum concentrations may be increased if taken with food. Avoid furocoumarin-containing foods (limes, figs, parsley, celery, cloves, lemon, mustard, carrots).

Mechanism of Action Bonds covalently to pyrimidine bases in DNA, inhibits the synthesis of DNA, and suppresses cell division. The augmented sunburn reaction involves excitation of the methoxsalen molecule by radiation in the long-wave ultraviolet light (UVA), resulting in (Continued)

Methoxsalen *(Continued)*

transference of energy to the methoxsalen molecule producing an excited state ("triplet electronic state"). The molecule, in this "triplet state", then reacts with cutaneous DNA.

Pharmacodynamics/Kinetics

Protein binding: Reversibly bound to albumin

Metabolism: Hepatic; forms metabolites

Bioavailability: Bioavailability increased with soft-gelatin capsules compared to hard-gelatin capsules; exposure using UVAR® system is ~200 times less than with oral administration

Time to peak, serum:

Hard-gelatin capsules: 1.5-6 hours (peak photosensitivity: ~4 hours)

Soft-gelatin capsules: 0.5-4 hours (peak photosensitivity: 1.5-2 hours)

Half-life elimination: ~2 hours

Excretion: Urine (~95% as metabolites)

Dosage Note: Refer to treatment protocols for UVA exposure guidelines.

Children >12 years and Adults: Vitiligo: Topical: Apply lotion 1-2 hours before exposure to UVA light, no more than once weekly

Adults:

Psoriasis: Oral: 10-70 mg 11/2-2 hours before exposure to UVA light; dose may be repeated 2-3 times per week, based on UVA exposure; doses must be given at least 48 hours apart; dosage is based upon patient's body weight and skin type:

<30 kg: 10 mg

30-50 kg: 20 mg

51-65 kg: 30 mg

66-80 kg: 40 mg

81-90 kg: 50 mg

91-115 kg: 60 mg

>115 kg: 70 mg

Vitiligo: (8-MOP®): Oral: 20 mg 2-4 hours before exposure to UVA light; dose may be repeated based on erythema and tenderness of skin; do not give on 2 consecutive days

CTCL: Extracorporeal (Uvadex®): 200 mcg injected into the photoactivation bag during the collection cycle using the UVAR® photopheresis system (consult user's guide). Treatment schedule: Two consecutive days every 4 weeks for a minimum of 7 treatment cycles

Dietary Considerations To reduce nausea, oral drug can be administered with food or milk or in 2 divided doses 30 minutes apart.

Administration Topical: Hands and fingers of person applying the lotion should be protected to prevent possible photosensitization and/or burns.

Dosage Forms

Capsule:

8-MOP®: 10 mg [hard-gelatin capsule]

Oxsoralen-Ultra®: 10 mg [soft-gelatin capsule]

Lotion (Oxsoralen®): 1% (30 mL) [contains alcohol 71%]

Solution, for extracorporeal administration (Uvadex®): 20 mcg/mL (10 mL) **[not for injection]**

♦ **Methoxypsoralen** *see* Methoxsalen *on page 1115*

♦ **8-Methoxypsoralen** *see* Methoxsalen *on page 1115*

♦ **Methscopolamine and Pseudoephedrine** *see* Pseudoephedrine and Methscopolamine *on page 1457*

♦ **Methscopolamine Nitrate and Chlordiazepoxide Hydrochloride** *see* Chlordiazepoxide and Methscopolamine *on page 344*

♦ **Methscopolamine Nitrate, Chlorpheniramine Maleate, and Phenylephrine Hydrochloride** *see* Chlorpheniramine, Phenylephrine, and Methscopolamine *on page 353*

Methsuximide *(meth SUKS i mide)*

U.S. Brand Names Celontin®

Canadian Brand Names Celontin®

Pharmacologic Category Anticonvulsant, Succinimide

Additional Appendix Information

Epilepsy *on page 2048*

Use Control of absence (petit mal) seizures that are refractory to other drugs

Unlabeled/Investigational Use Partial complex (psychomotor) seizures

Pregnancy Risk Factor C

Medication Safety Issues

Sound-alike/look-alike issues:

Methsuximide may be confused with ethosuximide

Dosage Oral:

Children: Anticonvulsant: Initial: 10-15 mg/kg/day in 3-4 divided doses; increase weekly up to maximum of 30 mg/kg/day

Adults: Anticonvulsant: 300 mg/day for the first week; may increase by 300 mg/day at weekly intervals up to 1.2 g/day in 2-4 divided doses/day

Additional Information Complete prescribing information for this medication should be consulted for additional detail.

Dosage Forms Capsule: 150 mg, 300 mg

Methyclothiazide *(meth i kloe THYE a zide)*

U.S. Brand Names Enduron® [DSC]

Canadian Brand Names Aquatensen®; Enduron®

Pharmacologic Category Diuretic, Thiazide

Additional Appendix Information

Sulfonamide Derivatives *on page 1897*

Use Management of mild to moderate hypertension; treatment of edema in congestive heart failure and nephrotic syndrome

Pregnancy Risk Factor B

Medication Safety Issues

Sound-alike/look-alike issues:

Enduron® may be confused with Empirin®, Imuran®, Inderal®

Dosage Adults: Oral:

Edema: 2.5-10 mg/day

Hypertension: 2.5-5 mg/day; may add another antihypertensive if 5 mg is not adequate after a trial of 8-12 weeks of therapy

Additional Information Complete prescribing information for this medication should be consulted for additional detail.

Dosage Forms Tablet: 5 mg

- ♦ **Methylacetoxyprogesterone** *see* MedroxyPROGESTERone *on page 1065*
- ♦ **Methylcellulose, Gelatin, and Pectin** *see* Gelatin, Pectin, and Methylcellulose *on page 785*

Methyldopa (meth il DOE pa)

Canadian Brand Names Apo-Methyldopa®; Nu-Medopa

Index Terms Aldomet; Methyldopate Hydrochloride

Pharmacologic Category Alpha-Adrenergic Inhibitor

Additional Appendix Information

Hypertension *on page 2063*

Use Management of moderate to severe hypertension

Pregnancy Risk Factor B

Medication Safety Issues

Sound-alike/look-alike issues:

Methyldopa may be confused with L-dopa, levodopa

Dosage

Children:

Oral: Initial: 10 mg/kg/day in 2-4 divided doses; increase every 2 days as needed to maximum dose of 65 mg/kg/day; do not exceed 3 g/day.

I.V.: 5-10 mg/kg/dose every 6-8 hours up to a total dose of 65 mg/kg/24 hours or 3 g/24 hours

Adults:

Oral: Initial: 250 mg 2-3 times/day; increase every 2 days as needed (maximum dose: 3 g/day): usual dose range (JNC 7): 250-1000 mg/day in 2 divided doses

I.V.: 250-500 mg every 6-8 hours; maximum dose: 1 g every 6 hours

Dosing interval in renal impairment:

Cl_{cr} >50 mL/minute: Administer every 8 hours.

Cl_{cr} 10-50 mL/minute: Administer every 8-12 hours.

Cl_{cr} <10 mL/minute: Administer every 12-24 hours.

Hemodialysis: Slightly dialyzable (5% to 20%)

Additional Information Complete prescribing information for this medication should be consulted for additional detail.

Dosage Forms

Injection, solution, as methyldopate hydrochloride: 50 mg/mL (5 mL) [contains sodium bisulfite]

Tablet: 250 mg, 500 mg

Methyldopa and Hydrochlorothiazide
(meth il DOE pa & hye droe klor oh THYE a zide)

U.S. Brand Names Aldoril®

Canadian Brand Names Apo-Methazide®

Index Terms Hydrochlorothiazide and Methyldopa

Pharmacologic Category Antihypertensive Agent, Combination

Use Management of moderate to severe hypertension

Pregnancy Risk Factor C

Medication Safety Issues

Sound-alike/look-alike issues:

Aldoril® may be confused with Aldoclor®, Aldomet®, Elavil®

Dosage Oral: Dosage titrated on individual components, then switch to combination product; no more than methyldopa 3 g/day and/or hydrochlorothiazide 50 mg/day; maintain initial dose for first 48 hours, then decrease or increase at intervals of not less than 2 days until an adequate response is achieved

Methyldopa 250 mg and hydrochlorothiazide 15 mg: 2-3 times/day

Methyldopa 250 mg and hydrochlorothiazide 25 mg: Twice daily

Additional Information Complete prescribing information for this medication should be consulted for additional detail.

Dosage Forms

Tablet:

Methyldopa 250 mg and hydrochlorothiazide 15 mg

Methyldopa 250 mg and hydrochlorothiazide 25 mg

Aldoril® 25: Methyldopa 250 mg and hydrochlorothiazide 25 mg

- ♦ **Methyldopate Hydrochloride** *see* Methyldopa *on page 1117*

Methylene Blue (METH i leen bloo)

U.S. Brand Names Urolene Blue®

Pharmacologic Category Antidote

Use Antidote for cyanide poisoning and drug-induced methemoglobinemia, indicator dye

Unlabeled/Investigational Use Has been used topically (0.1% solutions) in conjunction with polychromatic light to photoinactivate viruses such as herpes simplex; has been used alone or in combination with vitamin C for the management of chronic urolithiasis

Pregnancy Risk Factor C/D (injected intra-amniotically)

Medication Safety Issues Due to potential toxicity (hemolytic anemia), do not use methylene blue to color enteral feedings to detect aspiration.

Contraindications Hypersensitivity to methylene blue or any component of the formulation; intraspinal injection; renal insufficiency; pregnancy (injected intra-amniotically)

Warnings/Precautions Do not inject SubQ or intrathecally; use with caution in young patients and in patients with G6PD deficiency; continued use can cause profound anemia

Adverse Reactions Frequency not defined.

Cardiovascular: Hypertension, precordial pain

Central nervous system: Dizziness, mental confusion, headache, fever

Dermatologic: Staining of skin

Gastrointestinal: Fecal discoloration (blue-green), nausea, vomiting, abdominal pain

Genitourinary: Discoloration of urine (blue-green), bladder irritation

Hematologic: Anemia

Miscellaneous: Diaphoresis

Overdosage/Toxicology Symptoms include nausea, vomiting, precordial pain, hypertension, methemoglobinemia, and cyanosis. Overdosage has resulted in methemoglobinemia and cyanosis. Treatment is symptomatic and supportive.

Mechanism of Action Weak germicide in low concentrations, hastens the conversion of methemoglobin to hemoglobin; has opposite effect at high concentrations by converting ferrous ion of reduced hemoglobin to ferric ion to form methemoglobin; in cyanide toxicity, it combines with cyanide to form cyanmethemoglobin preventing the interference of cyanide with the cytochrome system

Pharmacodynamics/Kinetics

Absorption: Oral: 53% to 97%

Excretion: Urine and feces

Dosage

Children: NADPH-methemoglobin reductase deficiency: Oral: 1-1.5 mg/kg/day (maximum: 300 mg/day) given with 5-8 mg/kg/day of ascorbic acid

Children and Adults: Methemoglobinemia: I.V.: 1-2 mg/kg or 25-50 mg/m^2 over several minutes; may be repeated in 1 hour if necessary

Adults: Genitourinary antiseptic: Oral: 65-130 mg 3 times/day with a full glass of water (maximum: 390 mg/day)

Administration Administer I.V. undiluted by direct I.V. injection over several minutes.

Additional Information Skin stains may be removed using a hypochlorite solution.

Dosage Forms

Injection, solution: 10 mg/mL (1 mL, 10 mL)

Tablet (Urolene Blue®): 65 mg

♦ **Methylene Blue, Methenamine, Sodium Biphosphate, Phenyl Salicylate, and Hyoscyamine** see Methenamine, Sodium Biphosphate, Phenyl Salicylate, Methylene Blue, and Hyoscyamine *on page 1107*

♦ **Methylergometrine Maleate** see Methylergonovine *on page 1118*

Methylergonovine (meth il er goe NOE veen)

U.S. Brand Names Methergine®

Canadian Brand Names Methergine®

Index Terms Methylergometrine Maleate; Methylergonovine Maleate

Pharmacologic Category Ergot Derivative

Use Prevention and treatment of postpartum and postabortion hemorrhage caused by uterine atony or subinvolution

Pregnancy Risk Factor C

Pregnancy Implications Prolonged constriction of the uterine vessels and/or increased myometrial tone may lead to reduced placental blood flow. This has contributed to fetal growth retardation in animals. Methylergonovine is intended for use after delivery of the infant.

Lactation Enters breast milk/use caution

Medication Safety Issues

Sound-alike/look-alike issues:

Methylergonovine and terbutaline parenteral dosage forms look similar. Due to their contrasting indications, use care when administering these agents.

Contraindications Hypersensitivity to methylergonovine or any component of the formulation; ergot alkaloids are contraindicated with potent inhibitors of CYP3A4 (includes protease inhibitors, azole antifungals, and some macrolide antibiotics); hypertension; toxemia; pregnancy

Warnings/Precautions Use caution in patients with sepsis, obliterative vascular disease, hepatic, or renal involvement, or second stage of labor; administer with extreme caution if using intravenously. Pleural and peritoneal fibrosis have been reported with prolonged daily use. Cardiac valvular fibrosis has also been associated with ergot alkaloids.

Adverse Reactions Frequency not defined.

Cardiovascular: Acute MI, hypertension, temporary chest pain, palpitation

Central nervous system: Hallucinations, dizziness, seizure, headache

Endocrine & metabolic: Water intoxication

Gastrointestinal: Nausea, vomiting, diarrhea, foul taste
Local: Thrombophlebitis
Neuromuscular & skeletal: Leg cramps
Otic: Tinnitus
Renal: Hematuria
Respiratory: Dyspnea, nasal congestion
Miscellaneous: Diaphoresis

Overdosage/Toxicology Symptoms include vasospastic effects, nausea, vomiting, lassitude, impaired mental function, hypotension, hypertension, unconsciousness, seizures, shock, and death. Treatment includes general supportive therapy, gastric lavage or induction of emesis, activated charcoal, and saline cathartic. Keep extremities warm. Activated charcoal is effective at binding certain chemicals, and this is especially true for ergot alkaloids. Treatment is symptomatic with heparin and vasodilators (nitroprusside). Vasodilators should be used with caution to avoid exaggerating any pre-existing hypotension.

Drug Interactions

Cytochrome P450 Effect: Substrate of CYP3A4 (major)

Increased Effect/Toxicity: CYP3A4 inhibitors may increase the levels/effects of methylergonovine; example inhibitors include azole antifungals, clarithromycin, diclofenac, doxycycline, erythromycin, imatinib, isoniazid, nefazodone, nicardipine, propofol, protease inhibitors, quinidine, telithromycin, and verapamil. Ergot alkaloids are contraindicated with potent CYP3A4 inhibitors. Methylergonovine may increase the effects of 5-HT$_1$ agonists (eg, sumatriptan), MAO inhibitors, sibutramine, and other serotonin agonists (serotonin syndrome). Severe vasoconstriction may occur when peripheral vasoconstrictors or beta-blockers are used in patients receiving ergot alkaloids; concurrent use is contraindicated.

Decreased Effect: Effects of methylergonovine may be diminished by antipsychotics, metoclopramide/

Stability
Ampul: Store under refrigeration at 2°C to 8°C (36°F to 46°F). Protect from light.
Tablet: Store below 25°C (77°F).

Mechanism of Action Similar smooth muscle actions as seen with ergotamine; however, it affects primarily uterine smooth muscles producing sustained contractions and thereby shortens the third stage of labor

Pharmacodynamics/Kinetics
Onset of action: Oxytocic: Oral: 5-10 minutes; I.M.: 2-5 minutes; I.V.: Immediately
Duration: Oral: ~3 hours; I.M.: ~3 hours; I.V.: 45 minutes
Absorption: Rapid
Distribution: V$_d$: 39-73 L
Rapid; primarily to plasma and extracellular fluid following I.V. administration; tissues
Metabolism: Hepatic
Bioavailability: Oral: 60%; I.M.: 78%
Half-life elimination: Biphasic: Initial: 1-5 minutes; Terminal: 0.5-2 hours
Time to peak, serum: Oral: 0.3-2 hours; I.M.: 0.2-0.6 hours
Excretion: Urine and feces

Dosage Adults:
Oral: 0.2 mg 3-4 times/day for 2-7 days
I.M., I.V.: 0.2 mg after delivery of anterior shoulder, after delivery of placenta, or during puerperium; may be repeated as required at intervals of 2-4 hours

Administration Administer over ≥60 seconds. Should not be routinely administered I.V. because of possibility of inducing sudden hypertension and cerebrovascular accident.

Dosage Forms
Injection, solution, as maleate: 0.2 mg/mL (1 mL)
Tablet, as maleate: 0.2 mg

♦ **Methylergonovine Maleate** see Methylergonovine on page 1118
♦ **Methylin**® see Methylphenidate on page 1119
♦ **Methylin**® **ER** see Methylphenidate on page 1119
♦ **Methylmorphine** see Codeine on page 410

Methylphenidate (meth il FEN i date)

U.S. Brand Names Concerta®; Daytrana™; Metadate® CD; Metadate® ER; Methylin®; Methylin® ER; Ritalin®; Ritalin® LA; Ritalin-SR®
Canadian Brand Names Apo-Methylphenidate®; Apo-Methylphenidate® SR; Biphentin®; Concerta®; PMS-Methylphenidate; Riphenidate; Ritalin®; Ritalin® SR
Index Terms Methylphenidate Hydrochloride
Pharmacologic Category Central Nervous System Stimulant
Use Treatment of attention-deficit/hyperactivity disorder (ADHD); symptomatic management of narcolepsy
Unlabeled/Investigational Use Depression (especially elderly or medically ill)
Restrictions C-II
Pregnancy Risk Factor C
Pregnancy Implications Animal studies have shown teratogenic effects to the fetus. There are no adequate and well-controlled studies in pregnant women. Do not use in women of childbearing age unless the potential benefit outweighs the possible risk.
Lactation Enters breast milk/use caution
Medication Safety Issues
Sound-alike/look-alike issues:
Methylphenidate may be confused with methadone
Ritalin® may be confused with Ismelin®, Rifadin®
Contraindications Hypersensitivity to methylphenidate, any component of the formulation, or idiosyncratic reactions to sympathomimetic amines; marked anxiety, tension, and agitation; (Continued)

Methylphenidate *(Continued)*

glaucoma; use during or within 14 days following MAO inhibitor therapy; Tourette's syndrome or tics

Metadate CD™ is contraindicated in patients with severe hypertension, heart failure, arrhythmia, hyperthyroidism, recent MI or angina.

Warnings/Precautions CNS stimulant use has been associated with serious cardiovascular events including sudden death in patients with pre-existing structural cardiac abnormalities or other serious heart problems (sudden death in children and adolescents; sudden death, stroke, and MI in adults). These products should be avoided in patients with known serious structural cardiac abnormalities, cardiomyopathy, serious heart rhythm abnormalities, or other serious cardiac problems that could increase the risk of sudden death that these conditions alone carry. Patients should be carefully evaluated for cardiac disease prior to initiation of therapy. Some products are contraindicated in patients with heart failure, arrhythmias or recent MI. Use of stimulants can cause an increase in blood pressure (average 2-4 mm Hg) and increases in heart rate (average 3-6 bpm), although some patients may have larger than average increases. Use caution with hypertension, hyperthyroidism, or other cardiovascular conditions that might be exacerbated by increases in blood pressure or heart rate. Some products are contraindicated in patients with severe hypertension, hyperthyroidism or angina.

Has demonstrated value as part of a comprehensive treatment program for ADHD. Use with caution in patients with bipolar disorder (may induce mixed/manic episode). May exacerbate symptoms of behavior and thought disorder in psychotic patients; new onset psychosis or mania may occur with stimulant use; observe for symptoms of aggression and/or hostility. Use caution with seizure disorders (may reduce seizure threshold). Use caution in patients with history of ethanol or drug abuse. May exacerbate symptoms of behavior and thought disorder in psychotic patients. **[U.S. Boxed Warning]: Potential for drug dependency exists - avoid abrupt discontinuation in patients who have received for prolonged periods.** Visual disturbances have been reported (rare). Stimulant use has been associated with growth suppression. Growth should be monitored during treatment. Concerta® should not be used in patients with esophageal motility disorders or pre-existing severe gastrointestinal narrowing (small bowel disease, short gut syndrome, history of peritonitis, cystic fibrosis, chronic intestinal pseudo-obstruction, Meckel's diverticulum). Safety and efficacy in children <6 years of age have not been established. Transdermal system may cause allergic contact sensitization, characterized by intense local reactions (edema, papules); sensitization may subsequently manifest systemically with other routes of methylphenidate administration; monitor closely. Avoid exposure of application site to any direct external heat sources (eg, heating pads, electric blankets). Efficacy of transdermal methylphenidate therapy for >7 weeks has not been established.

Adverse Reactions

Transdermal system: Frequency of adverse events as reported in trials of 7-week duration. Incidence of some events reportedly higher with extended use.

>10%:
 Central nervous system: Insomnia (13%)
 Endocrine & metabolic: Appetite decreased (26%)
 Gastrointestinal: Nausea (12%)

1% to 10%:
 Central nervous system: Tic (7%), emotional instability (6%)
 Gastrointestinal: Vomiting (10%), anorexia (5%)
 Respiratory: Nasal congestion (6%), nasopharyngitis (5%)
 Endocrine & metabolic: Weight loss (9%)

All dosage forms: Frequency not defined:

Cardiovascular: Angina, cardiac arrhythmia, cerebral arteritis, cerebral occlusion, hyper-/hypotension, MI, necrotizing vasculitis, palpitation, pulse increase/decrease, tachycardia

Central nervous system: Depression, dizziness, drowsiness, fever, headache, insomnia, nervousness, neuroleptic malignant syndrome (NMS), Tourette's syndrome, toxic psychosis

Dermatologic: Erythema multiforme, exfoliative dermatitis, hair loss, rash, urticaria

Endocrine & metabolic: Growth retardation

Gastrointestinal: Abdominal pain, anorexia, diarrhea, nausea, vomiting, weight loss

Hematologic: Anemia, leukopenia, thrombocytopenic purpura, thrombocytopenia

Hepatic: Liver function tests abnormal, hepatic coma, transaminases increased

Neuromuscular & skeletal: Arthralgia, dyskinesia

Ocular: Blurred vision, visual accommodation disturbance

Renal: Necrotizing vasculitis

Respiratory: Cough increased, pharyngitis, sinusitis, upper respiratory tract infection

Miscellaneous: Accidental injury, hypersensitivity reactions

Overdosage/Toxicology Symptoms include vomiting, agitation, tremors, hyperpyrexia, muscle twitching, hallucinations, tachycardia, mydriasis, sweating, and palpitations. There is no specific antidote for methylphenidate intoxication and the bulk of the treatment is symptom-directed and supportive. Hyperactivity and agitation usually respond to reduced sensory input or benzodiazepines, however, with extreme agitation haloperidol (2-5 mg I.M. for adults) may be required. Hyperthermia is best treated with external cooling measures, or when severe or unresponsive, muscle paralysis with pancuronium may be needed. Hypertension is usually transient and generally does not require treatment unless severe. For diastolic blood pressures >110 mm Hg, a nitroprusside infusion should be initiated. Seizures usually respond to diazepam I.V. and/or phenytoin maintenance regimens. Transdermal system: Remove patch and thoroughly cleanse area; consider that absorption may continue in absence of patch.

Drug Interactions

Cytochrome P450 Effect: Substrate of CYP2D6 (major); **Inhibits** CYP2D6 (weak)

Increased Effect/Toxicity: Methylphenidate may cause hypertensive effects when used in combination with MAO inhibitors or drugs with MAO-inhibiting activity (linezolid). Risk may be less with selegiline (MAO type B selective at low doses); it is best to avoid this combination. CYP2D6 inhibitors may increase the levels/effects of methylphenidate; example inhibitors include chlorpromazine, delavirdine, fluoxetine, miconazole, paroxetine, pergolide, quinidine, quinine, ritonavir, and ropinirole. Methylphenidate may increase levels of phenytoin, phenobarbital, and TCAs. Increased toxicity with clonidine and sibutramine.

Decreased Effect: Effectiveness of antihypertensive agents may be decreased. Carbamazepine may decrease the effect of methylphenidate.

Ethanol/Nutrition/Herb Interactions

Ethanol: Avoid ethanol (may cause CNS depression).

Food: Food may increase oral absorption; Concerta® formulation is not affected. Food delays early peak and high-fat meals increase C_{max} and AUC of Metadate® CD formulation.

Herb/Nutraceutical: Avoid ephedra (may cause hypertension or arrhythmias) and yohimbe (also has CNS stimulatory activity).

Stability

Chewable tablet: Store at room temperature of 20°C to 25°C (68°F to 77°F). Protect from moisture.

Extended release capsule: Store in dose pack provided at 25°C (77°F).

Immediate release tablet: Do not store above 30°C (86°F). Protect from light.

Osmotic controlled release tablet (Concerta®): Store at 25°C (77°F). Protect from humidity.

Solution: Store at room temperature of 20°C to 25°C (68°F to 77°F).

Sustained release tablet: Do not store above 30°C (86°F). Protect from moisture.

Transdermal system: Store at 15°C to 30°C (59°F to 86°F). Keep patches stored in protective pouch. Once tray is opened, use patches within 2 months.

Mechanism of Action Mild CNS stimulant; blocks the reuptake of norepinephrine and dopamine into presynaptic neurons; appears to stimulate the cerebral cortex and subcortical structures similar to amphetamines

Pharmacodynamics/Kinetics

Onset of action: Peak effect:

Immediate release tablet: Cerebral stimulation: ~2 hours

Extended release capsule (Metadate® CD): Biphasic; initial peak similar to immediate release product, followed by second rising portion (corresponding to extended release portion)

Sustained release tablet: 4-7 hours

Osmotic release tablet (Concerta®): Initial: 1-2 hours

Transdermal: ~2 hours

Duration: Immediate release tablet: 3-6 hours; Sustained release tablet: 8 hours; Extended release tablet: Methylin® ER, Metadate® ER, 8 hours, Concerta®: 12 hours

Absorption:

Oral: Readily absorbed

Transdermal: Absorption increased when applied to inflamed skin or exposed to heat. Absorption is continuous for 9 hours after application.

Metabolism: Hepatic via de-esterification to minimally active metabolite

Half-life elimination: *d*-methylphenidate: 3-4 hours; *l*-methylphenidate: 1-3 hours

Time to peak: Concerta®: C_{max}: 6-8 hours; Daytrana™: 7.5-10.5 hours

Excretion: Urine (90% as metabolites and unchanged drug)

Dosage

ADHD:

Oral:

Immediate release products Children ≥6 years and Adults: Initial: 5 mg/dose (~0.3 mg/kg/dose) given twice daily before breakfast and lunch; increase by 5-10 mg/day (0.2 mg/kg/day) at weekly intervals; maximum dose: 60 mg/day (2 mg/kg/day). **Note:** Discontinue periodically to re-evaluate or if no improvement occurs within 1 month.

Extended release products:

Children ≥6 years and Adults:

Metadate® ER, Methylin® ER, Ritalin® SR: May be given in place of immediate release products, once the daily dose is titrated and the titrated 8-hour dosage corresponds to sustained or extended release tablet size; maximum: 60 mg/day

Metadate® CD, Ritalin® LA: Initial: 20 mg once daily; may be adjusted in 10-20 mg increments at weekly intervals; maximum: 60 mg/day

Children 6-12 years and Adolescents 13-17 years: Concerta®:

Patients not currently taking methylphenidate: Initial dose: 18 mg once daily in the morning

Patients currently taking methylphenidate: **Note:** Initial dose: Dosing based on current regimen and clinical judgment; suggested dosing listed below:

— Patients taking methylphenidate 5 mg 2-3 times/day **or** 20 mg/day sustained release formulation: 18 mg once every morning

— Patients taking methylphenidate 10 mg 2-3 times/day **or** 40 mg/day sustained release formulation: 36 mg once every morning

— Patients taking methylphenidate 15 mg 2-3 times/day **or** 60 mg/day sustained release formulation: 54 mg once every morning

Dose adjustment: May increase dose in increments of 18 mg; dose may be adjusted at weekly intervals. A dosage strength of 27 mg is available for situations in which a dosage between 18-36 mg is desired. Maximum dose should not exceed 2 mg/kg/day **or** 54 mg/day in children 6-12 years or 72 mg/day in children 13-17 years.

Transdermal (Daytrana™): Children 6-12 years: Initial: 10 mg patch once daily; remove up to 9 hours after application. Titrate based on response and tolerability; may increase to next transdermal dose no more frequently than every week. **Note:** Application should occur 2 hours prior to desired effect. Drug absorption may continue for a period of time after patch removal.

Narcolepsy: Oral: Adults: 10 mg 2-3 times/day, up to 60 mg/day

Depression (unlabeled use): Oral: Adults: Initial: 2.5 mg every morning before 9 AM; dosage may be increased by 2.5-5 mg every 2-3 days as tolerated to a maximum of 20 mg/day; may be divided (ie, 7 AM and 12 noon), but should not be given after noon; do not use sustained release product

(Continued)

Methylphenidate (Continued)

Dietary Considerations Should be taken 30-45 minutes before meals. Concerta® is not affected by food and should be taken with water, milk, or juice. Metadate® CD should be taken before breakfast. Metadate® ER should be taken before breakfast and lunch. Methylin® chewable tablets contain phenylalanine 0.42 mg/methylphenidate 2.5 mg.

Administration

Oral: Do not crush or allow patient to chew sustained or extended release dosage form. To effectively avoid insomnia, dosing should be completed by noon.

Concerta®: Administer dose once daily in the morning. May be taken with or without food, but must be taken with water, milk, or juice.

Metadate® CD, Ritalin® LA: Capsules may be opened and the contents sprinkled onto a small amount (equal to 1 tablespoon) of applesauce. Swallow applesauce without chewing. Do not crush or chew capsule contents.

Methylin® chewable tablet: Administer with at least 8 ounces of water or other fluid.

Topical: Transdermal (Daytrana™): Apply to clean, dry, non-oily, intact skin to the hip area, avoiding the waistline. Apply at the same time each day to alternating hips. Press firmly for 30 seconds to ensure proper adherence. Avoid exposure of application site to external heat source, which may increase the amount of drug absorbed. If patch should dislodge, may replace with new patch (to different site) but total wear time should not exceed 9 hours. Patch may be removed early if a shorter duration of effect is desired or if late day side effects occur. Wash hands with soap and water after handling. Avoid touching the sticky side of the patch. Dispose of used patch by folding adhesive side onto itself, and discard in toilet or appropriate lidded container.

Monitoring Parameters Blood pressure, heart rate, signs and symptoms of depression, aggression, or hostility; CBC, differential and platelet counts, growth rate in children, signs of central nervous system stimulation

Transdermal: Signs of worsening erythema, blistering or edema which does not improve within 24 hours of patch removal, or spreads beyond patch site.

Additional Information Treatment with methylphenidate may include "drug holidays" or periodic discontinuation in order to assess the patient's requirements and to decrease tolerance and limit suppression of linear growth and weight. Specific patients may require 3 doses/day for treatment of ADHD (ie, additional dose at 4 PM).

Concerta® is an osmotic controlled release formulation (OROS®) of methylphenidate. The tablet has an immediate-release overcoat that provides an initial dose of methylphenidate within 1 hour. The overcoat covers a trilayer core. The trilayer core is composed of two layers containing the drug and excipients, and one layer of osmotic components. As water from the gastrointestinal tract enters the core, the osmotic components expand and methylphenidate is released.

Metadate® CD capsules contain a mixture of immediate release and extended release beads, designed to release 30% of the dose immediately and 70% over an extended period.

Ritalin® LA uses a combination of immediate release and enteric coated, delayed release beads.

Dosage Forms

Capsule, extended release, as hydrochloride:
Metadate® CD: 10 mg, 20 mg, 30 mg, 40 mg, 50 mg, 60 mg
Ritalin® LA: 10 mg, 20 mg, 30 mg, 40 mg

Solution, oral, as hydrochloride:
Methylin®: 5 mg/5 mL (500 mL) [grape flavor]; 10 mg/5 mL (500 mL) [grape flavor]

Tablet, as hydrochloride: 5 mg, 10 mg, 20 mg
Methylin®, Ritalin®: 5 mg, 10 mg, 20 mg

Tablet, chewable, as hydrochloride:
Methylin®: 2.5 mg [contains phenylalanine 0.42 mg; grape flavor]; 5 mg [contains phenylalanine 0.84 mg; grape flavor]; 10 mg [contains phenylalanine 1.68 mg; grape flavor]

Tablet, extended release, as hydrochloride: 20 mg
Concerta®: 18 mg, 27 mg, 36 mg, 54 mg [osmotic controlled release]
Metadate® ER, Methylin® ER: 10 mg, 20 mg

Tablet, sustained release, as hydrochloride:
Ritalin-SR®: 20 mg [dye free]

Transdermal system [once-daily patch]:
Daytrana™: 10 mg/9 hours (10s, 30s) [12.5 cm², total methylphenidate 27.5 mg]; 15 mg/9 hours (10s, 30s) [18.75 cm², total methylphenidate 41.3 mg]; 20 mg/9 hours (10s, 30s) [25 cm², total methylphenidate 55 mg]; 30 mg/9 hours (10s, 30s) [37.5 cm², total methylphenidate 82.5 mg]

- **Methylphenidate Hydrochloride** *see Methylphenidate on page 1119*
- **Methylphenobarbital** *see Mephobarbital on page 1083*
- **Methylphenoxy-Benzene Propanamine** *see Atomoxetine on page 169*
- **Methylphenyl Isoxazolyl Penicillin** *see Oxacillin on page 1276*
- **Methylphytyl Napthoquinone** *see Phytonadione on page 1366*

MethylPREDNISolone (meth il pred NIS oh lone)

U.S. Brand Names Depo-Medrol®; Medrol®; Solu-Medrol®

Canadian Brand Names Depo-Medrol®; Medrol®; Methylprednisolone Acetate; Solu-Medrol®

Index Terms 6-α-Methylprednisolone; A-Methapred; Methylprednisolone Acetate; Methylprednisolone Sodium Succinate

Pharmacologic Category Corticosteroid, Systemic

Additional Appendix Information

Contrast Media Reactions, Premedication for Prophylaxis *on page 2036*

Corticosteroids *on page 1879*

Use Primarily as an anti-inflammatory or immunosuppressant agent in the treatment of a variety of diseases including those of hematologic, allergic, inflammatory, neoplastic, and autoimmune origin. Prevention and treatment of graft-versus-host disease following alloge-neic bone marrow transplantation.

Pregnancy Risk Factor C

Lactation Excretion in breast milk unknown

Medication Safety Issues

Sound-alike/look-alike issues:

MethylPREDNISolone may be confused with medroxyPROGESTERone, predniSONE

Depo-Medrol® may be confused with Solu-Medrol®

Medrol® may be confused with Mebaral®

Solu-Medrol® may be confused with Depo-Medrol®

International issues:

Medor® may be confused with Medral® which is a brand name for omeprazole in Mexico

Contraindications Hypersensitivity to methylprednisolone or any component of the formula-tion; viral, fungal, or tubercular skin lesions; administration of live virus vaccines; serious infections, except septic shock or tuberculous meningitis. Methylprednisolone formulations containing benzyl alcohol preservative are contraindicated in infants.

Warnings/Precautions Use with caution in patients with thyroid disease, hepatic impairment, renal impairment, cardiovascular disease, diabetes, glaucoma, myasthenia gravis, patients at risk for osteoporosis, patients at risk for seizures, or GI diseases (diverticulitis, peptic ulcer, ulcerative colitis) due to perforation risk. Use caution following acute MI (cortico-steroids have been associated with myocardial rupture). Because of the risk of adverse effects, systemic corticosteroids should be used cautiously in the elderly in the smallest possible effective dose for the shortest duration. May affect growth velocity; growth should be routinely monitored in pediatric patients. Withdraw therapy with gradual tapering of dose.

May cause hypercorticism or suppression of hypothalamic-pituitary-adrenal (HPA) axis, particularly in younger children or in patients receiving high doses for prolonged periods. HPA axis suppression may lead to adrenal crisis. Withdrawal and discontinuation of a corticoste-roid should be done slowly and carefully. Particular care is required when patients are transferred from systemic corticosteroids to inhaled products due to possible adrenal insuffi-ciency or withdrawal from steroids, including an increase in allergic symptoms. Patients receiving >20 mg per day of prednisone (or equivalent) may be most susceptible. Fatalities have occurred due to adrenal insufficiency in asthmatic patients during and after transfer from systemic corticosteroids to aerosol steroids; aerosol steroids do not provide the systemic steroid needed to treat patients having trauma, surgery, or infections.

Acute myopathy has been reported with high dose corticosteroids, usually in patients with neuromuscular transmission disorders; may involve ocular and/or respiratory muscles; monitor creatine kinase; recovery may be delayed. Corticosteroid use may cause psychiatric disturbances, including depression, euphoria, insomnia, mood swings, and personality changes. Pre-existing psychiatric conditions may be exacerbated by corticosteroid use. Prolonged use of corticosteroids may also increase the incidence of secondary infection, mask acute infection (including fungal infections), prolong or exacerbate viral infections, or limit response to vaccines. Exposure to chickenpox should be avoided; corticosteroids should not be used to treat ocular herpes simplex. Corticosteroids should not be used for cerebral malaria. Close observation is required in patients with latent tuberculosis and/or TB reactivity; restrict use in active TB (only in conjunction with antituberculosis treatment). Prolonged treatment with corticosteroids has been associated with the development of Kaposi's sarcoma (case reports); if noted, discontinuation of therapy should be considered.

Adverse Reactions Frequency not defined.

Cardiovascular: Edema, hypertension, arrhythmia

Central nervous system: Insomnia, nervousness, vertigo, seizure, psychoses, pseudotumor cerebri, headache, mood swings, delirium, hallucinations, euphoria

Dermatologic: Hirsutism, acne, skin atrophy, bruising, hyperpigmentation

Endocrine & metabolic: Diabetes mellitus, adrenal suppression, hyperlipidemia, Cushing's syndrome, pituitary-adrenal axis suppression, growth suppression, glucose intolerance, hypokalemia, alkalosis, amenorrhea, sodium and water retention, hyperglycemia

Gastrointestinal: Increased appetite, indigestion, peptic ulcer, nausea, vomiting, abdominal distention, ulcerative esophagitis, pancreatitis

Hematologic: Transient leukocytosis

Neuromuscular & skeletal: Arthralgia, muscle weakness, osteoporosis, fractures

Ocular: Cataracts, glaucoma

Miscellaneous: Infections, hypersensitivity reactions, avascular necrosis, secondary malig-nancy, intractable hiccups

Overdosage/Toxicology Arrhythmias and cardiovascular collapse are possible with rapid intravenous infusion of high dose methylprednisolone. Symptoms include cushingoid appear-ance (systemic), muscle weakness (systemic), and osteoporosis (systemic) - all with long-term use only. When consumed in excessive quantities for prolonged periods, systemic hypercorticism and adrenal suppression may occur; in those cases, discontinuation and withdrawal of the corticosteroid should be done judiciously.

Drug Interactions

Cytochrome P450 Effect: Substrate of CYP3A4 (minor); **Inhibits** CYP2C8 (weak), 3A4 (weak)

Increased Effect/Toxicity: Methylprednisolone may increase circulating glucose levels; may need adjustments of insulin or oral hypoglycemics. Methylprednisolone increases cyclosporine and tacrolimus blood levels. Itraconazole increases corticosteroid levels.

Decreased Effect: Phenytoin, phenobarbital, rifampin increase clearance of methylprednis-olone. Potassium-depleting diuretics enhance potassium depletion. Skin test antigens, immunizations decrease antibody response and increase potential infections.

Ethanol/Nutrition/Herb Interactions

Ethanol: Avoid ethanol (may increase gastric mucosal irritation).

Food: Methylprednisolone interferes with calcium absorption. Limit caffeine.

Herb/Nutraceutical: St John's wort may decrease methylprednisolone levels. Avoid cat's claw, echinacea (have immunostimulant properties).

(Continued)

MethylPREDNISolone *(Continued)*

Stability

Intact vials of methylprednisolone sodium succinate should be stored at controlled room temperature.

Reconstituted solutions of methylprednisolone sodium succinate should be stored at room temperature (15°C to 30°C) and used within 48 hours.

Stability of parenteral admixture at room temperature (25°C) and at refrigeration temperature (4°C) is 48 hours.

Standard diluent (Solu-Medrol®): 40 mg/50 mL D_5W; 125 mg/50 mL D_5W.

Minimum volume (Solu-Medrol®): 50 mL D_5W.

Mechanism of Action

In a tissue-specific manner, corticosteroids regulate gene expression subsequent to binding specific intracellular receptors and translocation into the nucleus. Corticosteroids exert a wide array of physiologic effects including modulation of carbohydrate, protein, and lipid metabolism and maintenance of fluid and electrolyte homeostasis. Moreover cardiovascular, immunologic, musculoskeletal, endocrine, and neurologic physiology are influenced by corticosteroids. Decreases inflammation by suppression of migration of polymorphonuclear leukocytes and reversal of increased capillary permeability.

Pharmacodynamics/Kinetics

Onset of action: Peak effect (route dependent): Oral: 1-2 hours; I.M.: 4-8 days; Intra-articular: 1 week; methylprednisolone sodium succinate is highly soluble and has a rapid effect by I.M. and I.V. routes

Duration (route dependent): Oral: 30-36 hours; I.M.: 1-4 weeks; Intra-articular: 1-5 weeks; methylprednisolone acetate has a low solubility and has a sustained I.M. effect

Distribution: V_d: 0.7-1.5 L/kg

Half-life elimination: 3-3.5 hours; reduced in obese

Excretion: Clearance: Reduced in obese

Dosage

Dosing should be based on the lesser of ideal body weight or actual body weight

Only sodium succinate may be given I.V.; methylprednisolone sodium succinate is highly soluble and has a rapid effect by I.M. and I.V. routes. Methylprednisolone acetate has a low solubility and has a sustained I.M. effect.

Children:

Anti-inflammatory or immunosuppressive: Oral, I.M., I.V. (sodium succinate): 0.5-1.7 mg/kg/day or 5-25 mg/m²/day in divided doses every 6-12 hours; "Pulse" therapy: 15-30 mg/kg/dose over ≥30 minutes given once daily for 3 days

Status asthmaticus: I.V. (sodium succinate): Loading dose: 2 mg/kg/dose, then 0.5-1 mg/kg/dose every 6 hours for up to 5 days

Acute spinal cord injury: I.V. (sodium succinate): 30 mg/kg over 15 minutes, followed in 45 minutes by a continuous infusion of 5.4 mg/kg/hour for 23 hours

Lupus nephritis: I.V. (sodium succinate): 30 mg/kg over ≥30 minutes every other day for 6 doses

Adults: **Only sodium succinate may be given I.V.;** methylprednisolone sodium succinate is highly soluble and has a rapid effect by I.M. and I.V. routes. Methylprednisolone acetate has a low solubility and has a sustained I.M. effect.

Acute spinal cord injury: I.V. (sodium succinate): 30 mg/kg over 15 minutes, followed in 45 minutes by a continuous infusion of 5.4 mg/kg/hour for 23 hours

Anti-inflammatory or immunosuppressive:

Oral: 2-60 mg/day in 1-4 divided doses to start, followed by gradual reduction in dosage to the lowest possible level consistent with maintaining an adequate clinical response.

I.M. (sodium succinate): 10-80 mg/day once daily

I.M. (acetate): 10-80 mg every 1-2 weeks

I.V. (sodium succinate): 10-40 mg over a period of several minutes and repeated I.V. or I.M. at intervals depending on clinical response; when high dosages are needed, give 30 mg/kg over a period ≥30 minutes and may be repeated every 4-6 hours for 48 hours.

Status asthmaticus: I.V. (sodium succinate): Loading dose: 2 mg/kg/dose, then 0.5-1 mg/kg/dose every 6 hours for up to 5 days

Lupus nephritis: High-dose "pulse" therapy: I.V. (sodium succinate): 1 g/day for 3 days

Aplastic anemia: I.V. (sodium succinate): 1 mg/kg/day or 40 mg/day (whichever dose is higher), for 4 days. After 4 days, change to oral and continue until day 10 or until symptoms of serum sickness resolve, then rapidly reduce over approximately 2 weeks.

Pneumocystis pneumonia in AIDs patients: I.V.: 40-60 mg every 6 hours for 7-10 days

Intra-articular (acetate): Administer every 1-5 weeks.

Large joints: 20-80 mg

Small joints: 4-10 mg

Intralesional (acetate): 20-60 mg every 1-5 weeks

Dietary Considerations

Should be taken after meals or with food or milk; need diet rich in pyridoxine, vitamin C, vitamin D, folate, calcium, phosphorus, and protein.

Sodium content of 1 g sodium succinate injection: 2.01 mEq; 53 mg of sodium succinate salt is equivalent to 40 mg of methylprednisolone base

Methylprednisolone acetate: Depo-Medrol®

Methylprednisolone sodium succinate: Solu-Medrol®

Administration

Oral: Administer after meals or with food or milk

Parenteral: Methylprednisolone sodium succinate may be administered I.M. or I.V.; I.V. administration may be IVP over one to several minutes or IVPB or continuous I.V. infusion. **Acetate salt should not be given I.V.**

I.V.: Succinate:

Low dose: ≤1.8 mg/kg or ≤125 mg/dose: I.V. push over 3-15 minutes

Moderate dose: ≥2 mg/kg or 250 mg/dose: I.V. over 15-30 minutes

High dose: 15 mg/kg or ≥500 mg/dose: I.V. over ≥30 minutes

Doses >15 mg/kg or ≥1 g: Administer over 1 hour

Do **not** administer high-dose I.V. push; hypotension, cardiac arrhythmia, and sudden death have been reported in patients given high-dose methylprednisolone I.V. push over <20 minutes; intermittent infusion over 15-60 minutes; maximum concentration: I.V. push 125 mg/mL

Monitoring Parameters Blood pressure, blood glucose, electrolytes

Test Interactions Interferes with skin tests

Additional Information Sodium content of 1 g sodium succinate injection: 2.01 mEq; 53 mg of sodium succinate salt is equivalent to 40 mg of methylprednisolone base
  Methylprednisolone acetate: Depo-Medrol®
  Methylprednisolone sodium succinate: Solu-Medrol®

Dosage Forms
  Injection, powder for reconstitution, as sodium succinate: 125 mg [strength expressed as base]
    Solu-Medrol®: 40 mg, 125 mg, 500 mg, 1 g, 2 g [packaged with diluent; diluent contains benzyl alcohol; strength expressed as base]
    Solu-Medrol®: 500 mg, 1 g
  Injection, suspension, as acetate (Depo-Medrol®): 20 mg/mL (5 mL); 40 mg/mL (5 mL); 80 mg/mL (5 mL) [contains benzyl alcohol; strength expressed as base]
  Injection, suspension, as acetate [single-dose vial] (Depo-Medrol®): 40 mg/mL (1 mL, 10 mL); 80 mg/mL (1 mL)
  Tablet: 4 mg
    Medrol®: 2 mg, 4 mg, 8 mg, 16 mg, 32 mg
  Tablet, dose-pack: 4 mg (21s)
    Medrol® Dosepack™: 4 mg (21s)

♦ **6-α-Methylprednisolone** see MethylPREDNISolone on page 1122
♦ **Methylprednisolone Acetate** see MethylPREDNISolone on page 1122
♦ **Methylprednisolone Sodium Succinate** see MethylPREDNISolone on page 1122
♦ **4-Methylpyrazole** see Fomepizole on page 755
♦ **Methylrosaniline Chloride** see Gentian Violet on page 796

MethylTESTOSTERone (meth il tes TOS te rone)

U.S. Brand Names Android®; Methitest™; Testred®; Virilon®

Pharmacologic Category Androgen

Use
  Male: Hypogonadism; delayed puberty; impotence and climacteric symptoms
  Female: Palliative treatment of metastatic breast cancer

Restrictions C-III

Pregnancy Risk Factor X

Lactation Excretion in breast milk unknown/contraindicated

Medication Safety Issues
  Sound-alike/look-alike issues:
    MethylTESTOSTERone may be confused with medroxyPROGESTERone
    Virilon® may be confused with Verelan®

Contraindications Hypersensitivity to methyltestosterone or any component of the formulation; in males, known or suspected carcinoma of the breast or the prostate; pregnancy

Warnings/Precautions Use with extreme caution in patients with liver or kidney disease or serious heart disease; may accelerate bone maturation without producing compensatory gain in linear growth

Adverse Reactions Frequency not defined.
  Male: Virilism, priapism, prostatic hyperplasia, prostatic carcinoma, impotence, testicular atrophy, gynecomastia
  Female: Virilism, menstrual problems (amenorrhea), breast soreness, hirsutism (increase in pubic hair growth), atrophy
  Cardiovascular: Edema
  Central nervous system: Headache, anxiety, depression
  Dermatologic: Acne, "male pattern" baldness, seborrhea
  Endocrine & metabolic: Hypercalcemia, hypercholesterolemia
  Gastrointestinal: GI irritation, nausea, vomiting
  Hematologic: Leukopenia, polycythemia
  Hepatic: Hepatic dysfunction, hepatic necrosis, cholestatic hepatitis
  Miscellaneous: Hypersensitivity reactions

Overdosage/Toxicology Abnormal liver function tests.

Drug Interactions
  Increased Effect/Toxicity: Effects of oral anticoagulants and hypoglycemic agents may be increased. Toxicity may occur with cyclosporine; avoid concurrent use.
  Decreased Effect: Decreased oral anticoagulant effect

Mechanism of Action Stimulates receptors in organs and tissues to promote growth and development of male sex organs and maintains secondary sex characteristics in androgen-deficient males

Pharmacodynamics/Kinetics
  Metabolism: Hepatic
  Excretion: Urine

Dosage Adults (buccal absorption produces twice the androgenic activity of oral tablets):
  Male:
    Hypogonadism, male climacteric and impotence: Oral: 10-40 mg/day
    Androgen deficiency:
      Oral: 10-50 mg/day
      Buccal: 5-25 mg/day
    Postpubertal cryptorchidism: Oral: 30 mg/day
  Female:
    Breast pain/engorgement:
      Oral: 80 mg/day for 3-5 days
      Buccal: 40 mg/day for 3-5 days
(Continued)

MethylTESTOSTERone *(Continued)*

Breast cancer:
 Oral: 50-200 mg/day
 Buccal: 25-100 mg/day

Monitoring Parameters In prepubertal children, perform radiographic examination of the hand and wrist every 6 months to determine the rate of bone maturation and to assess the effect of treatment on the epiphyseal centers.

Dosage Forms

Capsule (Android®, Testred®, Virilon®): 10 mg
Tablet (Methitest™): 10 mg

Metipranolol *(met i PRAN oh lol)*

U.S. Brand Names OptiPranolol®
Canadian Brand Names OptiPranolol®
Index Terms Metipranolol Hydrochloride
Pharmacologic Category Beta-Adrenergic Blocker, Nonselective; Ophthalmic Agent, Antiglaucoma
Additional Appendix Information
Glaucoma Drug Therapy *on page 2050*
Use Agent for lowering intraocular pressure in patients with chronic open-angle glaucoma
Pregnancy Risk Factor C
Medication Safety Issues
Sound-alike/look-alike issues:
 Metipranolol may be confused with metaproterenol

International issues:
 Betanol® [Monaco] may be confused with Beta-Val® which is a brand name for betamethasone in the U.S.
 Betanol® [Monaco] may be confused with Patanol® which is a brand name for olopatadine in the U.S.
 Betanol® [Monaco] may be confused with Betimol® which is a brand name for timolol in the U.S.

Dosage Ophthalmic: Adults: Instill 1 drop in the affected eye(s) twice daily
Additional Information Complete prescribing information for this medication should be consulted for additional detail.
Dosage Forms Solution, ophthalmic: 0.3% (5 mL, 10 mL) [contains benzalkonium chloride]

♦ **Metipranolol Hydrochloride** *see Metipranolol on page 1126*

Metoclopramide *(met oh KLOE pra mide)*

U.S. Brand Names Reglan®
Canadian Brand Names Apo-Metoclop®; Metoclopramide Hydrochloride Injection; Nu-Metoclopramide
Pharmacologic Category Antiemetic; Gastrointestinal Agent, Prokinetic
Use
Oral: Symptomatic treatment of diabetic gastric stasis; gastroesophageal reflux
I.V., I.M.: Symptomatic treatment of diabetic gastric stasis; postpyloric placement of enteral feeding tubes; prevention and/or treatment of nausea and vomiting associated with chemotherapy, or postsurgery; to stimulate gastric emptying and intestinal transit of barium during radiological examination
Pregnancy Risk Factor B
Pregnancy Implications Crosses the placenta; available evidence suggests safe use during pregnancy.
Lactation Enters breast milk/use caution
Medication Safety Issues
Sound-alike/look-alike issues:
 Metoclopramide may be confused with metolazone
 Reglan® may be confused with Megace®, Regonol®, Renagel®
Contraindications Hypersensitivity to metoclopramide or any component of the formulation; GI obstruction, perforation or hemorrhage; pheochromocytoma; history of seizures
Warnings/Precautions Use caution with a history of mental illness; has been associated with extrapyramidal symptoms (EPS) and depression. The frequency of EPS is higher in pediatric patients and adults <30 years of age; risk is increased at higher dosages. Extrapyramidal reactions typically occur within the initial 24-48 hours of treatment. Use caution with concurrent use of other drugs associated with EPS. Use caution in the elderly and with Parkinson's disease; may have increased risk of tardive dyskinesia. Use caution in patients with a history of seizures; risk of metoclopramide-associated seizures is increased. Neuroleptic malignant syndrome (NMS) has been reported (rarely) with metoclopramide. Use lowest recommended doses initially; may cause transient increase in serum aldosterone; use caution in patients who are at risk of fluid overload (CHF, cirrhosis). Use caution in patients with hypertension or following surgical anastomosis/closure. Patients with NADH-cytochrome b5 reductase deficiency are at increased risk of methemoglobinemia and/or sulfhemoglobinemia. Abrupt discontinuation may (rarely) result in withdrawal symptoms (dizziness, headache, nervousness). Use caution and adjust dose in renal impairment.
Adverse Reactions Frequency not always defined.
Cardiovascular: AV block, bradycardia, CHF, fluid retention, flushing (following high I.V. doses), hyper-/hypotension, supraventricular tachycardia
Central nervous system: Drowsiness (~10% to 70%; dose related), fatigue (~10%), restlessness (~10%), acute dystonic reactions (<1% to 25%; dose and age related), akathisia, confusion, depression, dizziness, hallucinations (rare), headache, insomnia, neuroleptic

malignant syndrome (rare), Parkinsonian-like symptoms, suicidal ideation, seizures, tardive dyskinesia

Dermatologic: Angioneurotic edema (rare), rash, urticaria

Endocrine & metabolic: Amenorrhea, galactorrhea, gynecomastia, impotence

Gastrointestinal: Diarrhea, nausea

Genitourinary: Incontinence, urinary frequency

Hematologic: Agranulocytosis, leukopenia, neutropenia, porphyria

Hepatic: Hepatotoxicity (rare)

Ocular: Visual disturbance

Respiratory: Bronchospasm, laryngeal edema (rare)

Miscellaneous: Allergic reactions, methemoglobinemia, sulfhemoglobinemia

Overdosage/Toxicology Symptoms of overdose include drowsiness, ataxia, extrapyramidal symptoms, seizures, methemoglobinemia (in infants). Disorientation, muscle hypertonia, irritability, and agitation are common. Metoclopramide often causes extrapyramidal symptoms (eg, dystonic reactions) requiring management with diphenhydramine 1-2 mg/kg (adults) up to a maximum of 50-100 mg I.M. or I.V. slow push followed by a maintenance dose (25-50 mg orally every 4-6 hours) for 48-72 hours. When these reactions are unresponsive to diphenhydramine, benztropine mesylate I.V. 1-2 mg (adults) may be effective. These agents are generally effective within 2-5 minutes. Methylene blue is not recommended in patients with G6PD deficiency who experience methemoglobinemia due to metoclopramide.

Drug Interactions

Cytochrome P450 Effect: Substrate (minor) of CYP1A2, 2D6; Inhibits CYP2D6 (weak)

Increased Effect/Toxicity: Opiate analgesics may increase CNS depression. Metoclopramide may increase extrapyramidal symptoms (EPS) or risk when used concurrently with antipsychotic agents. Metoclopramide may increase cyclosporine levels.

Decreased Effect: Anticholinergic agents antagonize metoclopramide's actions.

Ethanol/Nutrition/Herb Interactions Ethanol: Avoid ethanol (may increase CNS depression).

Stability

Injection: Store intact vial at controlled room temperature. Injection is photosensitive and should be protected from light during storage. Parenteral admixtures in D_5W or NS are stable for at least 24 hours and do not require light protection if used within 24 hours.

Tablet: Store at controlled room temperature.

Mechanism of Action Blocks dopamine receptors and (when given in higher doses) also blocks serotonin receptors in chemoreceptor trigger zone of the CNS; enhances the response to acetylcholine of tissue in upper GI tract causing enhanced motility and accelerated gastric emptying without stimulating gastric, biliary, or pancreatic secretions; increases lower esophageal sphincter tone

Pharmacodynamics/Kinetics

Onset of action: Oral: 0.5-1 hour; I.V.: 1-3 minutes; I.M.: 10-15 minutes

Duration: Therapeutic: 1-2 hours, regardless of route

Distribution: V_d: 2-4 L/kg

Protein binding: 30%

Bioavailability: Oral: 65% to 95%

Half-life elimination: Normal renal function: 4-6 hours (may be dose dependent)

Time to peak, serum: Oral: 1-2 hours

Excretion: Urine (~85%)

Dosage

Children:

Gastroesophageal reflux (unlabeled use): Oral: 0.1-0.2 mg/kg/dose 4 times/day

Antiemetic (chemotherapy-induced emesis) (unlabeled): I.V.: 1-2 mg/kg 30 minutes before chemotherapy and every 2-4 hours

Postpyloric feeding tube placement: I.V.:

<6 years: 0.1 mg/kg

6-14 years: 2.5-5 mg

>14 years: Refer to Adults dosing.

Adults:

Gastroesophageal reflux: Oral: 10-15 mg/dose up to 4 times/day 30 minutes before meals or food and at bedtime; single doses of 20 mg are occasionally needed for provoking situations. Treatment >12 weeks has not been evaluated.

Diabetic gastric stasis:

Oral: 10 mg 30 minutes before each meal and at bedtime

I.M., I.V. (for severe symptoms): 10 mg over 1-2 minutes; 10 days of I.V. therapy may be necessary for best response

Chemotherapy-induced emesis:

I.V.: 1-2 mg/kg 30 minutes before chemotherapy and repeated every 2 hours for 2 doses, then every 3 hours for 3 doses (manufacturer labeling)

Alternate dosing (with or without diphenhydramine):

Moderate emetic risk chemotherapy: 0.5 mg/kg every 6 hours on days 2-4

Low and minimal risk chemotherapy: 1-2 mg/kg every 3-4 hours

Breakthrough treatment: 1-2 mg/kg every 3-4 hours

Oral (unlabeled use; with or without diphenhydramine):

Moderate emetic risk chemotherapy: 0.5 mg/kg every 6 hours or 20 mg 4 times/day on days 2-4

Low and minimal risk chemotherapy: 20-40 mg every 4-6 hours

Breakthrough treatment: 20-40 mg every 4-6 hours

Postoperative nausea and vomiting: I.M., I.V.: 10-20 mg near end of surgery

Postpyloric feeding tube placement, radiological exam: I.V.: 10 mg

Elderly:

Gastroesophageal reflux: Oral: 5 mg 4 times/day (30 minutes before meals or food and at bedtime); increase dose to 10 mg 4 times/day if no response at lower dose

Gastrointestinal hypomotility:

Oral: Initial: 5 mg 30 minutes before meals and at bedtime; increase if necessary to 10 mg doses

(Continued)

Metoclopramide *(Continued)*

I.V.: Initiate at 5 mg over 1-2 minutes; increase to 10 mg if necessary

Postoperative nausea and vomiting: I.M., I.V.: 5 mg near end of surgery; may repeat dose if necessary

Dosing adjustment in renal impairment: Cl_{cr} <40 mL/minute: Administer at 50% of normal dose

Hemodialysis: Not dialyzable (0% to 5%); supplemental dose is not necessary

Administration Injection solution may be given I.M., direct I.V. push, short infusion (15-30 minutes), or continuous infusion; lower doses (≤10 mg) of metoclopramide can be given I.V. push undiluted over 1-2 minutes; higher doses to be given IVPB over at least 15 minutes; continuous SubQ infusion and rectal administration have been reported. **Note:** Rapid I.V. administration may be associated with a transient (but intense) feeling of anxiety and restlessness, followed by drowsiness.

Monitoring Parameters Dystonic reactions; signs of hypoglycemia in patients using insulin and those being treated for gastroparesis; agitation, and onfusion

Test Interactions Increased aminotransferase [ALT (SGPT)/AST (SGOT)] (S), increased amylase (S)

Dosage Forms
Injection, solution (Reglan®): 5 mg/mL (2 mL, 10 mL, 30 mL)
Syrup: 5 mg/5 mL (10 mL, 480 mL)
Tablet (Reglan®): 5 mg, 10 mg

♦ **Metoclopramide Hydrochloride Injection (Can)** *see* Metoclopramide *on page 1126*

Metolazone *(me TOLE a zone)*

U.S. Brand Names Zaroxolyn®
Canadian Brand Names Zaroxolyn®
Pharmacologic Category Diuretic, Thiazide-Related
Additional Appendix Information
Heart Failure (Systolic) *on page 2051*
Sulfonamide Derivatives *on page 1897*

Use Management of mild to moderate hypertension; treatment of edema in congestive heart failure and nephrotic syndrome, impaired renal function

Pregnancy Risk Factor B (manufacturer); D (expert analysis)

Pregnancy Implications Teratogenic effects were not observed in animal studies. Metolazone crosses the placenta and appears in cord blood. Hypoglycemia, hypokalemia, hyponatremia, jaundice, and thrombocytopenia are reported as complications to the fetus or newborn following maternal use of thiazide diuretics.

Lactation Enters breast milk/not recommended

Medication Safety Issues
Sound-alike/look-alike issues:
Metolazone may be confused with metaxalone, methazolamide, methimazole, methotrexate, metoclopramide, metoprolol, minoxidil
Zaroxolyn® may be confused with Zarontin®

Contraindications Hypersensitivity to metolazone, any component of the formulation, other thiazides, and sulfonamide derivatives; anuria; hepatic coma; pregnancy (expert analysis)

Warnings/Precautions Electrolyte disturbances (hypokalemia, hypochloremic alkalosis, hyponatremia) can occur. Large or prolonged fluid and electrolyte losses may occur with concomitant furosemide administration. Use with caution in severe hepatic dysfunction; hepatic encephalopathy can be caused by electrolyte disturbances. Gout can be precipitate in certain patients with a history of gout, a familial predisposition to gout, or chronic renal failure. Cautious use in patients with prediabetes or diabetes; may see a change in glucose control. Can cause SLE exacerbation or activation. Use caution in severe renal impairment. Use with caution in patients with moderate or high cholesterol concentrations. Photosensitization may occur.

Chemical similarities are present among sulfonamides, sulfonylureas, carbonic anhydrase inhibitors, thiazides, and loop diuretics (except ethacrynic acid). Use in patients with thiazide or sulfonamide allergy is specifically contraindicated in product labeling, however, a risk of cross-reaction exists in patients with allergy to any of these compounds; avoid use when previous reaction has been severe. Discontinue if signs of hypersensitivity are noted.

Adverse Reactions Frequency not defined.
Cardiovascular: Chest pain/discomfort, necrotizing angiitis, orthostatic hypotension, palpitation, syncope, venous thrombosis, vertigo, volume depletion
Central nervous system: chills, depression, dizziness, drowsiness, fatigue, headache, lightheadedness, restlessness
Dermatologic: Petechiae, photosensitivity, pruritus, purpura, rash, skin necrosis, Stevens-Johnson syndrome, toxic epidermal necrolysis, urticaria
Endocrine & metabolic: Gout attacks, hypercalcemia, hyperglycemia, hyperuricemia, hypochloremia, hypochloremic alkalosis, hypokalemia, hypomagnesemia, hyponatremia, hypophosphatemia
Gastrointestinal: Abdominal bloating, abdominal pain, anorexia, constipation, diarrhea, epigastric distress, nausea, pancreatitis, vomiting, xerostomia
Genitourinary: Impotence
Hematologic: Agranulocytosis, aplastic/hypoplastic anemia, hemoconcentration, leukopenia, thrombocytopenia
Hepatic: Cholestatic jaundice, hepatitis
Neuromuscular & skeletal: Joint pain, muscle cramps/spasm, neuropathy, paresthesia, weakness
Ocular: Blurred vision (transient)
Renal: BUN increased, glucosuria

Overdosage/Toxicology Symptoms include hypermotility, diuresis, lethargy, confusion, and muscle weakness. Following GI decontamination, therapy is supportive with I.V. fluids, electrolytes, and I.V. pressors if needed.

Drug Interactions

Increased Effect/Toxicity: Thiazide diuretics may enhance the hypotensive effect and/or nephrotoxic effect of ACE inhibitors. Diazoxide may enhance the hyperglycemic effect of thiazide diuretics. Thiazide diuretics may enhance the serum concentration and QT_c-prolonging effect of dofetilide. Thiazide diuretics may decrease the excretion of lithium; monitor lithium concentration and adjust as needed.

Decreased Effect: Bile acid sequestrants may decrease metolazone absorption.

Ethanol/Nutrition/Herb Interactions

Ethanol: May potentiate hypotensive effect of metazolone.

Herb/Nutraceutical: Avoid dong quai if using for hypertension (has estrogenic activity). Avoid dong quai, St John's wort (may also cause photosensitization). Avoid ephedra, yohimbe, ginseng (may worsen hypertension). Avoid natural licorice. Avoid garlic (may have increased antihypertensive effect).

Mechanism of Action Inhibits sodium reabsorption in the distal tubules causing increased excretion of sodium and water, as well as potassium and hydrogen ions

Pharmacodynamics/Kinetics

Onset of action: Diuresis: ~60 minutes

Duration: ≥24 hours

Absorption: Incomplete

Distribution: Crosses placenta; enters breast milk

Protein binding: 95%

Half-life elimination: 20 hours

Excretion: Urine (80%); bile (10%)

Dosage Oral:

Adults:

Edema: 2.5-20 mg/dose every 24 hours (ACC/AHA 2005 Heart Failure Guidelines)

Hypertension: 2.5-5 mg/dose every 24 hours

Elderly: Initial: 2.5 mg/day or every other day

Dosage adjustment in renal impairment: Dialysis: Not dialyzable (0% to 5%) via hemo- or peritoneal dialysis; supplemental dose is not necessary

Dietary Considerations Should be taken after breakfast; may require potassium supplementation

Administration May be taken with food or milk. Take early in day to avoid nocturia. Take the last dose of multiple doses no later than 6 PM unless instructed otherwise.

Monitoring Parameters Serum electrolytes (potassium, sodium, chloride, bicarbonate), renal function, blood pressure (standing, sitting/supine)

Additional Information Metolazone 5 mg is approximately equivalent to hydrochlorothiazide 50 mg.

Dosage Forms

Tablet: 2.5 mg, 5 mg, 10 mg

Zaroxolyn®: 2.5 mg, 5 mg, 10 mg

Extemporaneous Preparations

A 1 mg/mL suspension may be made by crushing twelve 10 mg Zaroxolyn® tablets; add Ora-Sweet®, Ora-Sweet® SF, Ora-Plus®, or cherry syrup diluted 1:4 with simple syrup to total volume of 120 mL. Label "shake well"; stable 60 days refrigerated.

A 0.25 mg/mL suspension may be made by crushing one 2.5 mg tablet; add 1:1 mixture 1% methylcellulose:simple syrup mixture to a total volume of 10 mL; label "shake well"; refrigerate; stable 91 days refrigerated; 28 days at room temperature in plastic and 14 days at room temperature in glass.

Nahata, MC, Pai VB, and Hipple TF, *Pediatric Drug Formulations*, 5th ed, Cincinnati, OH: Harvey Whitney Books Co, 2004.

Metoprolol (me toe PROE lole)

U.S. Brand Names Lopressor®; Toprol-XL®

Canadian Brand Names Apo-Metoprolol®; Betaloc®; Betaloc® Durules®; Lopressor®; Metoprolol Tartrate Injection, USP; Novo-Metoprolol; Nu-Metop; PMS-Metoprolol; Sandoz-Metoprolol; Toprol-XL®

Index Terms Metoprolol Succinate; Metoprolol Tartrate

Pharmacologic Category Beta Blocker, Beta₁ Selective

Additional Appendix Information

Beta-Blockers *on page 1875*

Heart Failure (Systolic) *on page 2051*

Hypertension *on page 2063*

Use Treatment of hypertension and angina pectoris; prevention of myocardial infarction, atrial fibrillation, flutter, symptomatic treatment of hypertrophic subaortic stenosis

Extended release: To reduce mortality/hospitalization in patients with congestive heart failure (stable NYHA Class II or III) in patients already receiving ACE inhibitors, diuretics, and/or digoxin

Unlabeled/Investigational Use Treatment of ventricular arrhythmias, atrial ectopy, migraine prophylaxis, essential tremor, aggressive behavior

Pregnancy Risk Factor C (manufacturer); D (2nd and 3rd trimesters - expert analysis)

Pregnancy Implications Metoprolol crosses the placenta. Beta-blockers have been associated with bradycardia, hypotension, and IUGR; IUGR is probably related to maternal hypertension. Available evidence suggests beta-blockers are generally safe during pregnancy (JNC 7). Cases of neonatal hypoglycemia have been reported following maternal use of beta-blockers at parturition or during breast-feeding. Monitor breast-fed infant for symptoms of beta-blockade.

Lactation Enters breast milk/use caution (AAP rates "compatible")

(Continued)

Metoprolol *(Continued)*

Medication Safety Issues

Sound-alike/look-alike issues:

Metoprolol may be confused with metaproterenol, metolazone, misoprostol

Toprol-XL® may be confused with Tegretol®, Tegretol®-XR, Topamax®

Significant differences exist between oral and I.V. dosing. Use caution when converting from one route of administration to another.

Contraindications Hypersensitivity to metoprolol or any component of the formulation; sick sinus syndrome; sinus bradycardia; heart block greater than first degree (except in patients with a functioning artificial pacemaker); cardiogenic shock; uncompensated cardiac failure; severe peripheral arterial disease; pheochromocytoma (without alpha blockade); pregnancy (2nd and 3rd trimesters)

Warnings/Precautions [U.S. Boxed Warning]: Beta-blocker therapy should not be withdrawn abruptly (particularly in patients with CAD), but gradually tapered to avoid acute tachycardia, hypertension, and/or ischemia. Consider pre-existing conditions such as sick sinus syndrome before initiating. Use caution in patients with PVD (can aggravate arterial insufficiency). Use caution with concurrent use of beta-blockers and either verapamil or diltiazem; bradycardia or heart block can occur; avoid concurrent I.V. use of both agents. In general, beta-blockers should be avoided in patients with bronchospastic disease. Metoprolol, with B_1 selectivity, should be used cautiously in bronchospastic disease with close monitoring. Use cautiously in diabetics because it can mask prominent hypoglycemic symptoms. Use caution with hepatic dysfunction. Use with caution in patients with myasthenia gravis or psychiatric disease (may cause CNS depression). Use care with anesthetic agents which decrease myocardial function. Use of beta-blockers may unmask cardiac failure in patients without a history of dysfunction. Adequate alpha-blockade is required prior to use of any beta-blocker for patients with untreated pheochromocytoma. Safety and efficacy have not been established in children.

Extended release: Use care in compensated heart failure and monitor closely for a worsening of the condition.

Adverse Reactions Frequency may not be defined.

Cardiovascular: Bradycardia (2% to 16%), hypotension (1% to 2%), arterial insufficiency (usually Raynaud type; 1%), chest pain (1%), CHF (1%), edema (peripheral; 1%), palpitation (1%), syncope (1%), gangrene (rare)

Central nervous system: Dizziness (2% to 10%), fatigue (10%), depression (5%), confusion, headache, insomnia, memory loss (short-term), nightmares, somnolence

Dermatology: Pruritus (5%), rash (5%), psoriasis increased, alopecia (reversible; rare)

Endocrine & metabolic: Libido decreased, Peyronie's disease (<1%)

Gastrointestinal: Diarrhea (5%), constipation (1%), flatulence (1%), gastrointestinal pain (1%), heartburn (1%), nausea (1%), xerostomia (1%)

Hematologic: Agranulocytosis (rare)

Neuromuscular & skeletal: Musculoskeletal pain

Ocular: Blurred vision, dry eyes (rare), oculomucocutaneous syndrome

Otic: Tinnitus

Respiratory: Dyspnea (1% to 3%), bronchospasm (1%), wheezing (1%), rhinitis

Miscellaneous: Cold extremities (1%)

Postmarketing and/or case reports: Arthralgia, arthritis, anxiety, diaphoresis increased, hallucinations, hepatitis, impotence, nervousness, paresthesias, photosensitivity, retroperitoneal fibrosis, second-degree heart block, taste disturbance, third-degree heart block, thrombocytopenia, urticaria, vomiting, weight gain

Other events reported with beta-blockers: Catatonia, emotional lability, fever, hypersensitivity reactions, laryngospasm, nonthrombocytopenic purpura, respiratory distress, thrombocytopenic purpura

Overdosage/Toxicology Symptoms of intoxication include cardiac disturbances, CNS toxicity, bronchospasm, hypoglycemia and hyperkalemia. The most common cardiac symptoms include hypotension and bradycardia. Atrioventricular block, intraventricular conduction disturbances, cardiogenic shock, and asystole may occur with severe overdose, especially with membrane-depressant drugs (eg, propranolol). CNS effects include convulsions, coma, and respiratory arrest. Treatment is symptomatic for seizures, hypotension, hyperkalemia and hypoglycemia. Bradycardia and hypotension resistant to atropine, isoproterenol, or pacing may respond to glucagon. Wide QRS defects caused by membrane-depressant poisoning may respond to hypertonic sodium bicarbonate. Repeat-dose charcoal, hemoperfusion, or hemodialysis may be helpful in removal of only those beta-blockers with a small V_d, long half-life, or low intrinsic clearance (acebutolol, atenolol, nadolol, sotalol).

Drug Interactions

Cytochrome P450 Effect: Substrate of CYP2C19 (minor), 2D6 (major); **Inhibits** CYP2D6 (weak)

Increased Effect/Toxicity: CYP2D6 inhibitors may increase the levels/effects of metoprolol; example inhibitors include chlorpromazine, delavirdine, fluoxetine, miconazole, paroxetine, pergolide, quinidine, quinine, ritonavir, and ropinirole. Aminoquinolones (antimalarial), propafenone, and propoxyphene increase levels of metoprolol. Concomitant therapy with bupropion may result in bradycardia. Metoprolol may increase the effects of other drugs which slow AV conduction (digoxin, verapamil, diltiazem), dipyridamole, disopyramide, acetylcholinesterase inhibitors, amiodarone, alpha₁-blockers (prazosin, terazosin), and alpha₂/beta-agonists (direct acting). Metoprolol may mask the tachycardia from hypoglycemia caused by insulin and sulfonylureas. In patients receiving concurrent therapy, the risk of hypertensive crisis is increased with clonidine (alpha₂-agonist). May increase the levels of antipsychotic agents (phenothiazines) and lidocaine.

Decreased Effect: Decreased effect of beta-blockers with barbiturates, NSAIDs, and rifampin, salicylates; beta-blockers may decrease the effect of theophylline derivatives.

Ethanol/Nutrition/Herb Interactions

Food: Food increases absorption. Metoprolol serum levels may be increased if taken with food.

Herb/Nutraceutical: Avoid dong quai if using for hypertension (has estrogenic activity). Avoid bayberry, blue cohosh, cayenne, ephedra, ginger, ginseng (american), gotu kola, licorice, yohimbe (may worsen hypertension). Avoid black cohosh, california poppy, coleus, garlic, golden seal, hawthorn, mistletoe, periwinkle, quinine, shepherd's purse (have antihypertensive activity, may cause hypotension).

Stability

Injection: Do not store above 30°C (86°F). Protect from light.

Tablet: Store between 15°C to 30°C (59°F to 86°F).

Mechanism of Action Selective inhibitor of beta$_1$-adrenergic receptors; competitively blocks beta$_1$-receptors, with little or no effect on beta$_2$-receptors at doses <100 mg; does not exhibit any membrane stabilizing or intrinsic sympathomimetic activity

Pharmacodynamics/Kinetics

Onset of action: Peak effect: Antihypertensive: Oral: 1.5-4 hours

Duration: 10-20 hours

Absorption: 95%

Protein binding: 12%

Metabolism: Extensively hepatic via CYP2D6; significant first-pass effect

Bioavailability: Oral: 40% to 50%

Half-life elimination: 3-8 hours

Excretion: Urine (3% to 10% as unchanged drug)

Dosage

Children 1-17 years: Hypertension (unlabeled use): Oral: Initial: 1-2 mg/kg/day; maximum 6 mg/kg/day (≤200 mg/day); administer in 2 divided doses

Adults:

Hypertension: Oral: 100-450 mg/day in 2-3 divided doses, begin with 50 mg twice daily and increase doses at weekly intervals to desired effect; usual dosage range (JNC 7): 50-100 mg/day

Extended release: Initial: 25-100 mg/day (maximum: 400 mg/day)

Angina, SVT, MI prophylaxis: Oral: 100-450 mg/day in 2-3 divided doses, begin with 50 mg twice daily and increase doses at weekly intervals to desired effect

Extended release: Initial: 100 mg/day (maximum: 400 mg/day)

Hypertension/ventricular rate control: I.V. (in patients having nonfunctioning GI tract): Initial: 1.25-5 mg every 6-12 hours; titrate initial dose to response. Initially, low doses may be appropriate to establish response; however, up to 15 mg every 3-6 hours has been employed.

Congestive heart failure: Oral (extended release): Initial: 25 mg once daily (reduce to 12.5 mg once daily in NYHA class higher than class II); may double dosage every 2 weeks as tolerated, up to 200 mg/day

Myocardial infarction (acute): I.V.: 5 mg every 2 minutes for 3 doses in early treatment of myocardial infarction; thereafter give 50 mg orally every 6 hours 15 minutes after last I.V. dose and continue for 48 hours; then administer a maintenance dose of 100 mg twice daily.

Note: When switching from immediate release metoprolol to extended release, the same total daily dose of metoprolol should be used.

Elderly: Oral: Initial: 25 mg/day; usual range: 25-300 mg/day

Extended release: 25-50 mg/day initially as a single dose; increase at 1- to 2-week intervals.

Hemodialysis: Administer dose posthemodialysis or administer 50 mg supplemental dose; supplemental dose is not necessary following peritoneal dialysis

Dosing adjustment/comments in hepatic disease: Reduced dose probably necessary

Dietary Considerations Regular tablets should be taken with food. Extended release tablets may be taken without regard to meals.

Administration

Oral: Extended release tablets may be divided in half; do not crush or chew.

I.V.: When administered acutely for cardiac treatment, monitor ECG and blood pressure. May administer by rapid infusion (I.V. push) over 1 minute or by slow infusion (ie, 5-10 mg of metoprolol in 50 mL of fluid) over ~30 minutes. Necessary monitoring for surgical patients who are unable to take oral beta-blockers (prolonged ileus) has not been defined. Some institutions require monitoring of baseline and postinfusion heart rate and blood pressure when a patient's response to beta-blockade has not been characterized (ie, the patient's initial dose or following a change in dose). Consult individual institutional policies and procedures.

Monitoring Parameters Acute cardiac treatment: Monitor ECG and blood pressure with I.V. administration; heart rate and blood pressure with oral administration

Dosage Forms

Injection, solution, as tartrate: 1 mg/mL (5 mL)

Lopressor®: 1 mg/mL (5 mL)

Tablet, as tartrate: 25 mg, 50 mg, 100 mg

Lopressor®: 50 mg, 100 mg

Tablet, extended release, as succinate: 25 mg, 50 mg, 100 mg, 200 mg [expressed as mg equivalent to tartrate]

Toprol-XL®: 25 mg, 50 mg, 100 mg, 200 mg [expressed as mg equivalent to tartrate]

Extemporaneous Preparations A mixture of metoprolol 10 mg/mL plus hydrochlorothiazide 5 mg/mL was found to be stable for 60 days in a refrigerator in a 1:1 preparation of Ora-Sweet® and Ora-Plus®, in Ora-Sweet® SF and Ora-Plus®, and in cherry syrup

Allen LV and Erickson III MA, "Stability of Labetalol Hydrochloride, Metoprolol Tartrate, Verapamil Hydrochloride, and Spironolactone With Hydrochlorothiazide in Extemporaneously Compounded Oral Liquids," *Am J Health Syst Pharm*, 1996, 53:2304-9.

Metoprolol and Hydrochlorothiazide
(me toe PROE lole & hye droe klor oh THYE a zide)

U.S. Brand Names Lopressor HCT®
Index Terms Hydrochlorothiazide and Metoprolol; Hydrochlorothiazide and Metoprolol Tartrate; Metoprolol Tartrate and Hydrochlorothiazide
Pharmacologic Category Beta Blocker, Beta₁ Selective; Diuretic, Thiazide
Use Treatment of hypertension
Pregnancy Risk Factor C/D (expert analysis)
Dosage Oral: Adults: Hypertension: Dosage should be determined by titration of the individual agents and the combination product substituted based upon the daily requirements.
    Usual dose: Metoprolol 50-100 mg and hydrochlorothiazide 25-50 mg administered daily as single or divided doses (twice daily)
    Note: Hydrochlorothiazide >50 mg/day is not recommended.
    Concomitant therapy: It is recommended that if an additional antihypertensive agent is required, gradual titration should occur using ¹/₂ the usual starting dose of the other agent to avoid hypotension.
Additional Information Complete prescribing information for this medication should be consulted for additional detail.
Dosage Forms Tablet:
    50/25: Metoprolol tartrate 50 mg and hydrochlorothiazide 25 mg
    100/25: Metoprolol tartrate 100 mg and hydrochlorothiazide 25 mg
    100/50: Metoprolol tartrate 100 mg and hydrochlorothiazide 50 mg

- **Metoprolol Succinate** see Metoprolol on page 1129
- **Metoprolol Tartrate** see Metoprolol on page 1129
- **Metoprolol Tartrate and Hydrochlorothiazide** see Metoprolol and Hydrochlorothiazide on page 1132
- **Metoprolol Tartrate Injection, USP (Can)** see Metoprolol on page 1129
- **MetroCream®** see Metronidazole on page 1132
- **MetroGel®** see Metronidazole on page 1132
- **Metrogel® (Can)** see Metronidazole on page 1132
- **MetroGel-Vaginal®** see Metronidazole on page 1132
- **MetroLotion®** see Metronidazole on page 1132

Metronidazole (met roe NYE da zole)

U.S. Brand Names Flagyl®; Flagyl ER®; Flagyl I.V. RTU™; MetroCream®; MetroGel®; MetroGel-Vaginal®; MetroLotion®; Noritate®; Vandazole™
Canadian Brand Names Apo-Metronidazole®; Flagyl®; Florazole® ER; MetroCream®; Metrogel®; Nidagel™; Noritate®; Trikacide
Index Terms Metronidazole Hydrochloride
Pharmacologic Category Amebicide; Antibiotic, Miscellaneous; Antibiotic, Topical; Antiprotozoal, Nitroimidazole
Additional Appendix Information
    Antimicrobial Drugs of Choice on page 1981
    Helicobacter pylori Treatment on page 2056
    Prevention of Wound Infection and Sepsis in Surgical Patients on page 1964
    Treatment of Sexually Transmitted Infections on page 2007
Use Treatment of susceptible anaerobic bacterial and protozoal infections in the following conditions: Amebiasis, symptomatic and asymptomatic trichomoniasis; skin and skin structure infections; CNS infections; intra-abdominal infections (as part of combination regimen); systemic anaerobic infections; treatment of antibiotic-associated pseudomembranous colitis (AAPC), bacterial vaginosis; as part of a multidrug regimen for H. pylori eradication to reduce the risk of duodenal ulcer recurrence
    Topical: Treatment of inflammatory lesions and erythema of rosacea
Unlabeled/Investigational Use Crohn's disease
Pregnancy Risk Factor B (may be contraindicated in 1st trimester)
Pregnancy Implications Crosses the placenta (carcinogenic in rats); contraindicated for the treatment of trichomoniasis during the first trimester of pregnancy, unless alternative treatment is inadequate. Until safety and efficacy for other indications have been established, use only during pregnancy when the benefit to the mother outweighs the potential risk to the fetus.
Lactation Enters breast milk/not recommended (AAP rates "of concern")
Medication Safety Issues
    Sound-alike/look-alike issues:
        Metronidazole may be confused with metformin.
Contraindications Hypersensitivity to metronidazole, nitroimidazole derivatives, or any component of the formulation; pregnancy (1st trimester - found to be carcinogenic in rats)
Warnings/Precautions Use with caution in patients with liver impairment due to potential accumulation, blood dyscrasias; history of seizures, CHF, or other sodium retaining states; reduce dosage in patients with severe liver impairment, CNS disease, and severe renal failure; seizures and neuropathies have been reported especially with increased doses and chronic treatment; if this occurs, discontinue therapy. **[U.S. Boxed Warning]: Possibly carcinogenic based on animal data.**
Adverse Reactions
    Systemic: Frequency not defined:
        Cardiovascular: Flattening of the T-wave, flushing
        Central nervous system: Ataxia, confusion, coordination impaired, dizziness, fever, headache, insomnia, irritability, seizure, vertigo
        Dermatologic: Erythematous rash, urticaria
        Endocrine & metabolic: Disulfiram-like reaction, dysmenorrhea, libido decreased

Gastrointestinal: Nausea (~12%), anorexia, abdominal cramping, constipation, diarrhea, furry tongue, glossitis, proctitis, stomatitis, unusual/metallic taste, vomiting, xerostomia

Genitourinary: Cystitis, darkened urine (rare), dysuria, incontinence, polyuria, vaginitis

Hematologic: Neutropenia (reversible), thrombocytopenia (reversible, rare)

Neuromuscular & skeletal: Peripheral neuropathy, weakness

Respiratory: Nasal congestion, rhinitis, sinusitis, pharyngitis

Miscellaneous: Flu-like syndrome, moniliasis

Topical: Frequency not defined:

Central nervous system: Headache

Dermatologic: Burning, contact dermatitis, dryness, erythema, irritation, pruritus, rash

Gastrointestinal: Unusual/metallic taste, nausea, constipation

Local: Local allergic reaction

Neuromuscular & skeletal: Tingling/numbness of extremities

Ocular: Eye irritation

Vaginal:

>10%: Genitourinary: Vaginal discharge (12%)

1% to 10%:

Central nervous system: Headache (5%), dizziness (2%)

Gastrointestinal: Gastrointestinal discomfort (7%), nausea and/or vomiting (4%), unusual/metallic taste (2%), diarrhea (1%)

Genitourinary: Vaginitis (10%), vulva/vaginal irritation (9%), pelvic discomfort (3%)

Hematologic: WBC increased (2%)

<1%: Abdominal bloating, abdominal gas, darkened urine, depression, fatigue, itching, rash, thirst, xerostomia

Overdosage/Toxicology Symptoms include nausea, vomiting, ataxia, seizures, and peripheral neuropathy. Treatment is symptomatic and supportive.

Drug Interactions

Cytochrome P450 Effect: Inhibits CYP2C9 (weak), 3A4 (moderate)

Increased Effect/Toxicity: Ethanol may cause a disulfiram-like reaction. Warfarin and metronidazole may increase bleeding times (PT) which may result in bleeding. Cimetidine may increase metronidazole levels. Metronidazole may inhibit metabolism of cisapride, causing potential arrhythmias; avoid concurrent use. Metronidazole may increase lithium levels/toxicity. Metronidazole may increase the levels/effects of selected benzodiazepines, calcium channel blockers, cyclosporine, ergot derivatives, selected HMG-CoA reductase inhibitors, mirtazapine, nateglinide, nefazodone, sildenafil (and other PDE-5 inhibitors), tacrolimus, venlafaxine, and other CYP3A4 substrates.

Decreased Effect: Phenytoin, phenobarbital (potentially other enzyme inducers) may decrease metronidazole half-life and effects.

Ethanol/Nutrition/Herb Interactions

Ethanol: The manufacturer recommends to avoid all ethanol or any ethanol-containing drugs (may cause disulfiram-like reaction characterized by flushing, headache, nausea, vomiting, sweating or tachycardia).

Food: Peak antibiotic serum concentration lowered and delayed, but total drug absorbed not affected.

Stability Metronidazole injection should be stored at 15°C to 30°C and protected from light. Product may be refrigerated but crystals may form. Crystals redissolve on warming to room temperature. Prolonged exposure to light will cause a darkening of the product. However, short-term exposure to normal room light does not adversely affect metronidazole stability. Direct sunlight should be avoided. Stability of parenteral admixture at room temperature (25°C): Out of overwrap stability: 30 days.

Standard diluent: 500 mg/100 mL NS.

Mechanism of Action After diffusing into the organism, interacts with DNA to cause a loss of helical DNA structure and strand breakage resulting in inhibition of protein synthesis and cell death in susceptible organisms

Pharmacodynamics/Kinetics

Absorption: Oral: Well absorbed; Topical: Concentrations achieved systemically after application of 1 g topically are 10 times less than those obtained after a 250 mg oral dose

Distribution: To saliva, bile, seminal fluid, breast milk, bone, liver, and liver abscesses, lung and vaginal secretions; crosses placenta and blood-brain barrier

CSF:blood level ratio: Normal meninges: 16% to 43%; Inflamed meninges: 100%

Protein binding: <20%

Metabolism: Hepatic (30% to 60%)

Half-life elimination: Neonates: 25-75 hours; Others: 6-8 hours, prolonged with hepatic impairment; End-stage renal disease: 21 hours

Time to peak, serum: Oral: Immediate release: 1-2 hours

Excretion: Urine (20% to 40% as unchanged drug); feces (6% to 15%)

Dosage

Infants and Children:

Amebiasis: Oral: 35-50 mg/kg/day in divided doses every 8 hours for 10 days

Trichomoniasis: Oral: 15-30 mg/kg/day in divided doses every 8 hours for 7 days

Anaerobic infections:

Oral: 15-35 mg/kg/day in divided doses every 8 hours

I.V.: 30 mg/kg/day in divided doses every 6 hours

Clostridium difficile (antibiotic-associated colitis): Oral: 20 mg/kg/day divided every 6 hours

Maximum dose: 2 g/day

Adults:

Anaerobic infections (diverticulitis, intra-abdominal, peritonitis, cholangitis, or abscess): Oral, I.V.: 500 mg every 6-8 hours, not to exceed 4 g/day

Acne rosacea: Topical:

0.75%: Apply and rub a thin film twice daily, morning and evening, to entire affected areas after washing. Significant therapeutic results should be noticed within 3 weeks. Clinical studies have demonstrated continuing improvement through 9 weeks of therapy.

(Continued)

Metronidazole *(Continued)*

1%: Apply thin film to affected area once daily

Amebiasis: Oral: 500-750 mg every 8 hours for 5-10 days

Antibiotic-associated pseudomembranous colitis: Oral: 250-500 mg 3-4 times/day for 10-14 days

Note: Due to the emergence of a new strain of *C. difficile*, some clinicians recommend converting to oral vancomycin therapy if the patient does not show a clear clinical response after 2 days of metronidazole therapy.

Giardiasis: 500 mg twice daily for 5-7 days

Helicobacter pylori eradication: Oral: 250-500 mg with meals and at bedtime for 14 days; requires combination therapy with at least one other antibiotic and an acid-suppressing agent (proton pump inhibitor or H_2 blocker)

Bacterial vaginosis or vaginitis due to *Gardnerella*, *Mobiluncus*:

Oral: 500 mg twice daily (regular release) or 750 mg once daily (extended release tablet) for 7 days

Vaginal: 1 applicatorful (~37.5 mg metronidazole) intravaginally once or twice daily for 5 days; apply once in morning and evening if using twice daily, if daily, use at bedtime

Trichomoniasis: Oral: 250 mg every 8 hours for 7 days **or** 375 mg twice daily for 7 days **or** 2 g as a single dose

Elderly: Use lower end of dosing recommendations for adults, do not administer as a single dose

Dosing adjustment in renal impairment: Cl_{cr} <10 mL/minute: Administer 50% of dose or every 12 hours

Hemodialysis: Extensively removed by hemodialysis and peritoneal dialysis (50% to 100%); administer dose posthemodialysis

Peritoneal dialysis: Dose as for Cl_{cr} <10 mL/minute

Continuous arteriovenous or venovenous hemofiltration: Administer usual dose

Dosing adjustment/comments in hepatic disease: Unchanged in mild liver disease; reduce dosage in severe liver disease

Dietary Considerations Take on an empty stomach. Drug may cause GI upset; if GI upset occurs, take with food. Extended release tablets should be taken on an empty stomach (1 hour before or 2 hours after meals). Sodium content of 500 mg (I.V.): 322 mg (14 mEq). The manufacturer recommends that ethanol be avoided during treatment and for 3 days after therapy is complete.

Administration

Oral: May be taken with food to minimize stomach upset. Extended release tablets should be taken on an empty stomach (1 hour before or 2 hours after meals).

Topical: No disulfiram-like reactions have been reported after **topical** application, although metronidazole can be detected in the blood. Apply to clean, dry skin. Cosmetics may be used after application (wait at least 5 minutes after using lotion).

Test Interactions May interfere with AST, ALT, triglycerides, glucose, and LDH testing

Dosage Forms

Capsule:

Flagyl®: 375 mg

Cream, topical: 0.75% (45 g)

MetroCream®: 0.75% (45 g) [contains benzyl alcohol]

Noritate®: 1% (60 g)

Gel, topical: 0.75% (45 g)

MetroGel®: 1% (60 g)

Gel, vaginal:

MetroGel-Vaginal®, Vandazole™: 0.75% (70 g)

Infusion [premixed iso-osmotic sodium chloride solution]: 500 mg (100 mL)

Flagyl® I.V. RTU™: 500 mg (100 mL) [contains sodium 14 mEq]

Lotion, topical: 0.75% (60 mL)

MetroLotion®: 0.75% (60 mL) [contains benzyl alcohol]

Tablet: 250 mg, 500 mg

Flagyl®: 250 mg, 500 mg

Tablet, extended release:

Flagyl® ER: 750 mg

Extemporaneous Preparations A 20 mg/mL oral suspension can be prepared by crushing ten 250 mg tablets in a mortar, and then adding 10 mL purified water USP to create a uniform paste. Add a small quantity of syrup, then transfer to a graduate and add a sufficient quantity of syrup to make 125 mL. Label "shake well" and "refrigerate." Refrigerated stability is 10 days.

Irwin DB, Dupuis LL, Prober CG, et al, "The Acceptability, Stability, and Relative Bioavailability of an Extemporaneous Metronidazole Suspension," *Can J Hosp Pharm*, 1987, 40:42-6.

Nahata MC, Morosco RS, and Hipple TF, 4th ed, *Pediatric Drug Formulations*, Cincinnati, OH: Harvey Whitney Books Co, 2000.

♦ **Metronidazole, Bismuth Subsalicylate, and Tetracycline** *see* Bismuth Subsalicylate, Metronidazole, and Tetracycline *on page 225*

♦ **Metronidazole Hydrochloride** *see* Metronidazole *on page 1132*

Metyrosine *(me TYE roe seen)*

U.S. Brand Names Demser®

Canadian Brand Names Demser®

Index Terms AMPT; OGMT

Pharmacologic Category Tyrosine Hydroxylase Inhibitor

Use Short-term management of pheochromocytoma before surgery, long-term management when surgery is contraindicated or when chronic malignant pheochromocytoma exists

Pregnancy Risk Factor C

Medication Safety Issues
Sound-alike/look-alike issues:
Metyrosine may be confused with metyrapone

Dosage Children >12 years and Adults: Oral: Initial: 250 mg 4 times/day, increased by 250-500 mg/day up to 4 g/day; maintenance: 2-3 g/day in 4 divided doses; for preoperative preparation, administer optimum effective dosage for 5-7 days

Dosing adjustment in renal impairment: Adjustment should be considered

Additional Information Complete prescribing information for this medication should be consulted for additional detail.

Dosage Forms Capsule: 250 mg

♦ **Mevacor®** see Lovastatin on page 1040
♦ **Mevinolin** see Lovastatin on page 1040
♦ **Mexar™ Wash** see Sulfacetamide on page 1609

Mexiletine (meks IL e teen)

U.S. Brand Names Mexitil® [DSC]
Canadian Brand Names Novo-Mexiletine
Pharmacologic Category Antiarrhythmic Agent, Class Ib
Use Management of serious ventricular arrhythmias; suppression of PVCs
Unlabeled/Investigational Use Diabetic neuropathy
Pregnancy Risk Factor C
Lactation Enters breast milk/compatible
Contraindications Hypersensitivity to mexiletine or any component of the formulation; cardiogenic shock; second- or third-degree AV block (except in patients with a functioning artificial pacemaker)
Warnings/Precautions [U.S. Boxed Warning]: In the Cardiac Arrhythmia Suppression Trial (CAST), recent (>6 days but <2 years ago) myocardial infarction patients with asymptomatic, nonlife-threatening ventricular arrhythmias did not benefit and may have been harmed by attempts to suppress the arrhythmia with flecainide or encainide. An increased mortality or non-fatal cardiac arrest rate (7.7%) was seen in the active treatment group compared with patients in the placebo group (3%). The applicability of the CAST results to other populations is unknown. Antiarrhythmic agents should be reserved for patients with life-threatening ventricular arrhythmias. Can be proarrhythmic. Electrolyte disturbances alter response; should be corrected before initiating therapy. Use cautiously in patients with first-degree block, pre-existing sinus node dysfunction, intraventricular conduction delays, significant hepatic dysfunction, hypotension, or severe CHF. Alterations in urinary pH may change urinary excretion. Rare hepatic toxicity may occur; may cause acute hepatic injury.

Adverse Reactions
>10%:
  Central nervous system: Lightheadedness (11% to 25%), dizziness (20% to 25%), nervousness (5% to 10%), incoordination (10%)
  Gastrointestinal: GI distress (41%), nausea/vomiting (40%)
  Neuromuscular & skeletal: Trembling, unsteady gait, tremor (13%), ataxia (10% to 20%)
1% to 10%:
  Cardiovascular: Chest pain (3% to 8%), premature ventricular contractions (1% to 2%), palpitation (4% to 8%), angina (2%), proarrhythmia (10% to 15% in patients with malignant arrhythmia)
  Central nervous system: Confusion, headache, insomnia (5% to 7%), depression (2%)
  Dermatologic: Rash (4%)
  Gastrointestinal: Constipation or diarrhea (4% to 5%), xerostomia (3%), abdominal pain (1%)
  Neuromuscular & skeletal: Weakness (5%), numbness of fingers or toes (2% to 4%), paresthesia (2%), arthralgia (1%)
  Ocular: Blurred vision (5% to 7%), nystagmus (6%)
  Otic: Tinnitus (2% to 3%)
  Respiratory: Dyspnea (3%)
<1% (Limited to important or life-threatening): Agranulocytosis, alopecia, AV block, cardiogenic shock, CHF, dysphagia, exfoliative dermatitis, hallucinations, hepatic necrosis, hepatitis, hypotension, impotence, leukopenia, myelofibrosis, pancreatitis (rare), psychosis, pulmonary fibrosis, seizure, sinus arrest, SLE syndrome, Stevens-Johnson syndrome, syncope, thrombocytopenia, torsade de pointes, upper GI bleeding, urinary retention, urticaria

Overdosage/Toxicology Has a narrow therapeutic index and severe toxicity may occur slightly above the therapeutic range, especially with other antiarrhythmic drugs. Acute ingestion of twice the daily therapeutic dose is potentially life-threatening. Symptoms include sedation, confusion, coma, seizures, respiratory arrest, and cardiac toxicity (sinus arrest, AV block, asystole, hypotension). The QRS and QT intervals are usually normal, although they may be prolonged after massive overdose. Other effects include dizziness, paresthesias, tremor, ataxia, and GI disturbance. Treatment is supportive, using conventional therapies (fluids, positioning, vasopressors, antiarrhythmics, anticonvulsants). Sodium bicarbonate may reverse QRS prolongation, bradyarrhythmias, and hypotension. Enhanced elimination with dialysis, hemoperfusion, or repeat charcoal is not effective.

Drug Interactions
Cytochrome P450 Effect: Substrate (major) of CYP1A2, 2D6; **Inhibits** CYP1A2 (strong)
Increased Effect/Toxicity: Mexiletine may increase the levels/effects of aminophylline, fluvoxamine, mirtazapine, ropinirole, trifluoperazine, or other CYP1A2 substrates. The levels/effects of mexiletine may be increased by inhibitors of CYP1A2 or 2D6; example inhibitors include chlorpromazine, ciprofloxacin, delavirdine, fluoxetine, fluvoxamine, ketoconazole, miconazole, norfloxacin, ofloxacin, paroxetine, pergolide, quinidine, quinine, ritonavir, rofecoxib, ropinirole, and other CYP1A2 or 2D6 inhibitors. Mexiletine may
(Continued)

Mexiletine (Continued)

increase levels of theophylline and caffeine. Quinidine and urinary alkalinizers (antacids, sodium bicarbonate, acetazolamide) may increase mexiletine blood levels.

Decreased Effect: The levels/effects of mexiletine may be decreased by aminoglutethimide, carbamazepine, phenobarbital, rifampin, and other CYP1A2 inducers. Urinary acidifying agents may decrease mexiletine levels.

Ethanol/Nutrition/Herb Interactions Food: Food may decrease the rate, but not the extent of oral absorption; diets which affect urine pH can increase or decrease excretion of mexiletine. Avoid dietary changes that alter urine pH.

Mechanism of Action Class IB antiarrhythmic, structurally related to lidocaine, which inhibits inward sodium current, decreases rate of rise of phase 0, increases effective refractory period/action potential duration ratio

Pharmacodynamics/Kinetics

Absorption: Elderly have a slightly slower rate, but extent of absorption is the same as young adults

Distribution: V_d: 5-7 L/kg

Protein binding: 50% to 70%

Metabolism: Hepatic; low first-pass effect

Half-life elimination: Adults: 10-14 hours (average: elderly: 14.4 hours, younger adults: 12 hours); prolonged with hepatic impairment or heart failure

Time to peak: 2-3 hours

Excretion: Urine (10% to 15% as unchanged drug); urinary acidification increases excretion, alkalinization decreases excretion

Dosage Adults: Oral: Initial: 200 mg every 8 hours (may load with 400 mg if necessary); adjust dose every 2-3 days; usual dose: 200-300 mg every 8 hours; maximum dose: 1.2 g/day (some patients respond to every 12-hour dosing). When switching from another antiarrhythmic, initiate a 200 mg dose 6-12 hours after stopping former agents, 3-6 hours after stopping procainamide.

Dosage adjustment in hepatic impairment: Reduce dose to 25% to 30% of usual dose

Administration Administer around-the-clock rather than 3 times/day to promote less variation in peak and trough serum levels; administer with food

Reference Range Therapeutic range: 0.5-2 mcg/mL; potentially toxic: >2 mcg/mL

Test Interactions Abnormal liver function test, positive ANA, thrombocytopenia

Dosage Forms [DSC] = Discontinued product

Capsule, as hydrochloride: 150 mg, 200 mg, 250 mg

Mexitil®: 150 mg, 200 mg, 250 mg [DSC]

♦ **Mexitil® [DSC]** see Mexiletine on page 1135

♦ **MgSO₄ (error-prone abbreviation)** see Magnesium Sulfate on page 1052

♦ **Miacalcin®** see Calcitonin on page 264

♦ **Miacalcin® NS (Can)** see Calcitonin on page 264

♦ **Mi-Acid [OTC]** see Aluminum Hydroxide, Magnesium Hydroxide, and Simethicone on page 85

♦ **Mi-Acid™ Double Strength [OTC]** see Calcium Carbonate and Magnesium Hydroxide on page 271

♦ **Mi-Acid Maximum Strength [OTC]** see Aluminum Hydroxide, Magnesium Hydroxide, and Simethicone on page 85

♦ **Micaderm® [OTC]** see Miconazole on page 1137

Micafungin (mi ka FUN gin)

U.S. Brand Names Mycamine®

Index Terms Micafungin Sodium

Pharmacologic Category Antifungal Agent, Parenteral; Echinocandin

Additional Appendix Information

Antifungal Agents on page 1869

Use Esophageal candidiasis; *Candida* prophylaxis in patients undergoing hematopoietic stem cell transplant

Unlabeled/Investigational Use Treatment of infections due to *Aspergillus* spp; prophylaxis of HIV-related esophageal candidiasis

Pregnancy Risk Factor C

Pregnancy Implications Visceral teratogenic and abortifacient effects were noted in animal studies. There are no adequate and well-controlled studies in pregnant women. Use only if benefit outweighs risk.

Lactation Excretion in breast milk unknown/use caution

Contraindications Hypersensitivity to micafungin or any component of the formulation

Warnings/Precautions Anaphylactic reactions, including shock have been reported; new onset or worsening hepatic failure has been reported; use caution in pre-existing mild-moderate hepatic impairment; safety in severe liver failure has not been evaluated; hemolytic anemia and hemoglobinuria have been reported; safety and efficacy in pediatric patients have not been established.

Adverse Reactions

Cardiovascular: Phlebitis (2%), hypertension (1%), flushing (1%)

Central nervous system: Headache (2%), pyrexia (2%), delirium (1%), dizziness (1%), somnolence (1%)

Dermatologic: Rash (2%), pruritus (1%), febrile neutropenia (1%)

Endocrine & metabolic: Hypokalemia (1%), hypocalcemia (1%), hypomagnesemia (1%), hypophosphatemia (1%)

Gastrointestinal: Nausea (3%), diarrhea (2%), vomiting (2%), abdominal pain (1%), appetite decreased (1%), dysgeusia (1%), dyspepsia (1%)

Hematologic: Leukopenia (2%), neutropenia (1%), thrombocytopenia (1%), anemia (1%), lymphopenia (1%), eosinophilia (1%)

Hepatic: Transaminase increased (2% to 3%), serum alkaline phosphatase increased (2%), hyperbilirubinemia (1%)

Local: Infusion site inflammation (1%)

Neuromuscular & skeletal: Rigors (1%), lactate dehydrogenase increased (1%)

Renal: Serum creatinine increased (1%), serum urea increased (1%)

<1% (Limited to important or life-threatening): Acidosis, anorexia, anuria, apnea, arrhythmia, arthralgia, cardiac arrest, coagulopathy, constipation, convulsions, cyanosis, dyspnea, deep vein thrombosis, hypoxia, encephalopathy, erythema multiforme, facial edema, hemoglobinuria, hemolysis, hemolytic anemia, hepatic failure, hepatocellular damage, hepatomegaly, hiccups, hyponatremia, hypotension, infection, injection site necrosis, intracranial hemorrhage, jaundice, MI, mycosal inflammation, oliguria, pancytopenia, pneumonia, pulmonary embolism, renal failure, renal tubular necrosis, sepsis, shock, skin necrosis, tachycardia, thrombotic thrombocytopenia purpura, thrombophlebitis, urticaria, vasodilatation

Overdosage/Toxicology Treatment should be symptom-directed and supportive. Not removed by dialysis.

Drug Interactions
Cytochrome P450 Effect: Substrate of CYP3A4 (minor); **Inhibits** CYP3A4 (weak)
Increased Effect/Toxicity: No clinically-significant interactions have been identified.
Decreased Effect: No clinically-signficant interactions have been identified.

Stability Store at 25°C (77°F). Reconstituted and diluted solutions are stable for 24 hours at room temperature. Protect from light. Aseptically add 5 mL of NS (preservative-free) to each 50 mg vial. Swirl to dissolve; do not shake. Further dilute 50-150 mg in 100 mL NS. Protect from light. Alternatively, D_5W may be used for reconstitution and dilution.

Mechanism of Action Concentration-dependent inhibition of 1,3-beta-D-glucan synthase resulting in reduced formation of 1,3-beta-D-glucan, an essential polysaccharide comprising 30% to 60% of *Candida* cell walls (absent in mammalian cells); decreased glucan content leads to osmotic instability and cellular lysis

Pharmacodynamics/Kinetics
Distribution: 0.28-0.5 L/kg
Protein binding: >99%
Metabolism: Hepatic; forms M-1 (catechol) and M-2 (methoxy) metabolites (activity unknown)
Half-life elimination: 11-21 hours
Excretion: Primarily feces (71%), urine (<15%, unchanged drug)

Dosage I.V.: Adults:
Esophageal candidiasis: 150 mg daily; median duration of therapy (from clinical trials) was 14 days
Prophylaxis of *Candida* infection in hematopoietic stem cell transplantation: 50 mg daily; median duration of therapy (from clinical trials) was 18 days

Administration For intravenous use only; infuse over 1 hour

Monitoring Parameters Liver function tests

Dosage Forms
Injection, powder for reconstitution, as sodium [preservative-free]:
Mycamine®: 50 mg, 100 mg [contains lactose]

♦ **Micafungin Sodium** *see* Micafungin *on page 1136*
♦ **Micanol® (Can)** *see* Anthralin *on page 132*
♦ **Micardis®** *see* Telmisartan *on page 1639*
♦ **Micardis® HCT** *see* Telmisartan and Hydrochlorothiazide *on page 1640*
♦ **Micardis® Plus (Can)** *see* Telmisartan and Hydrochlorothiazide *on page 1640*
♦ **Micatin® (Can)** *see* Miconazole *on page 1137*
♦ **Micatin® Athlete's Foot [OTC]** *see* Miconazole *on page 1137*
♦ **Micatin® Jock Itch [OTC]** *see* Miconazole *on page 1137*

Miconazole (mi KON a zole)

U.S. Brand Names Aloe Vesta® 2-n-1 Antifungal [OTC]; Baza® Antifungal [OTC]; Carrington Antifungal [OTC]; DermaFungal [OTC]; Dermagran® AF [OTC]; DiabetAid™ Antifungal Foot Bath [OTC]; Fungoid® Tincture [OTC]; Lotrimin® AF Jock Itch Powder Spray [OTC]; Lotrimin® AF Powder/Spray [OTC]; Micaderm® [OTC]; Micatin® Athlete's Foot [OTC]; Micatin® Jock Itch [OTC]; Micro-Guard® [OTC]; Mitrazol™ [OTC]; Monistat® 1 Combination Pack [OTC]; Monistat® 3 [OTC]; Monistat® 7 [OTC]; Monistat-Derm®; Neosporin® AF [OTC]; Podactin Cream [OTC]; Secura® Antifungal [OTC]; Zeasorb®-AF [OTC]

Canadian Brand Names Dermazole; Micatin®; Micozole; Monistat®; Monistat® 3

Index Terms Miconazole Nitrate

Pharmacologic Category Antifungal Agent, Topical; Antifungal Agent, Vaginal

Additional Appendix Information
Antifungal Agents *on page 1869*
Treatment of Sexually Transmitted Infections *on page 2007*

Use Treatment of vulvovaginal candidiasis and a variety of skin and mucous membrane fungal infections

Pregnancy Risk Factor C

Lactation Excretion in breast milk unknown/use caution

Medication Safety Issues
Sound-alike/look-alike issues:
Miconazole may be confused with Micronase®, Micronor®
Lotrimin® may be confused with Lotrisone®, Otrivin®
Micatin® may be confused with Miacalcin®

Contraindications Hypersensitivity to miconazole or any component of the formulation

Warnings/Precautions For external use only; discontinue if sensitivity or irritation develop. Petrolatum-based vaginal products may damage rubber or latex condoms or diaphragms. Separate use by 3 days.
(Continued)

Miconazole *(Continued)*

Adverse Reactions Frequency not defined.
Topical: Allergic contact dermatitis, burning, maceration
Vaginal: Abdominal cramps, burning, irritation, itching

Drug Interactions

Cytochrome P450 Effect: Substrate of CYP3A4 (major); **Inhibits** CYP1A2 (moderate), 2A6 (strong), 2B6 (weak), 2C9 (strong), 2C19 (strong), 2D6 (strong), 2E1 (moderate), 3A4 (strong)

Increased Effect/Toxicity: Note: The majority of reported drug interactions were observed following intravenous miconazole administration. Although systemic absorption following topical and/or vaginal administration is low, potential interactions due to CYP isoenzyme inhibition may occur (rarely). This may be particularly true in situations where topical absorption may be increased (ie, inflamed tissue).

Miconazole coadministered with warfarin has increased the anticoagulant effect of warfarin (including reports associated with vaginal miconazole therapy of as little as 3 days). Concurrent administration of cisapride is contraindicated due to an increased risk of cardiotoxicity. Miconazole may increase the serum levels/effects of amiodarone, amphetamines, benzodiazepines, beta-blockers, buspirone, busulfan, calcium channel blockers, citalopram, dexmedetomidine, dextromethorphan, diazepam, digoxin, docetaxel, fluoxetine, fluvoxamine, glimepiride, glipizide, ifosfamide, inhalational anesthetics, lidocaine, mesoridazine, methsuximide, mexiletine, mirtazapine, nateglinide, nefazodone, paroxetine, phenytoin, pioglitazone, propranolol, risperidone, ritonavir, ropinirole, rosiglitazone, sertraline, sirolimus, tacrolimus, theophylline, thioridazine, tricyclic antidepressants, trifluoperazine, trimetrexate, venlafaxine, vincristine, vinblastine, warfarin, zolpidem, and other substrates of CYP1A2, 2A6, 2C9, 2C19, 2D6, or 3A4. Selected benzodiazepines (midazolam and triazolam), cisapride, ergot alkaloids, selected HMG-CoA reductase inhibitors (lovastatin and simvastatin), and pimozide are generally contraindicated with strong CYP3A4 inhibitors. Mesoridazine and thioridazine are generally contraindicated with strong CYP2D6 inhibitors. When used with strong CYP3A4 inhibitors, dosage adjustment/limits are recommended for sildenafil and other PDE-5 inhibitors; consult individual monographs.

Decreased Effect: Amphotericin B may decrease antifungal effect of both agents. The levels/effects of miconazole may be decreased by aminoglutethimide, carbamazepine, nafcillin, nevirapine, phenobarbital, phenytoin, rifamycins or other CYP3A4 inducers. Miconazole may decrease the levels/effects of CYP2D6 prodrug substrates (eg, codeine, hydrocodone, oxycodone, tramadol).

Ethanol/Nutrition/Herb Interactions Herb/Nutraceutical: St John's wort may decrease miconazole levels.

Mechanism of Action Inhibits biosynthesis of ergosterol, damaging the fungal cell wall membrane, which increases permeability causing leaking of nutrients

Pharmacodynamics/Kinetics
Absorption: Topical: Negligible
Distribution: Widely to body tissues; penetrates well into inflamed joints, vitreous humor of eye, and peritoneal cavity, but poorly into saliva and sputum; crosses blood-brain barrier but only to a small extent
Protein binding: 91% to 93%
Metabolism: Hepatic
Half-life elimination: Multiphasic: Initial: 40 minutes; Secondary: 126 minutes; Terminal: 24 hours
Excretion: Feces (~50%); urine (<1% as unchanged drug)

Dosage
Topical: Children and Adults: **Note:** Not for OTC use in children <2 years:
Tinea corporis: Apply twice daily for 4 weeks
Tinea pedis: Apply twice daily for 4 weeks
Effervescent tablet: Dissolve 1 tablet in ~1 gallon of water; soak feet for 15-30 minutes; pat dry
Tinea cruris: Apply twice daily for 2 weeks
Vaginal: Adults: Vulvovaginal candidiasis:
Cream, 2%: Insert 1 applicatorful at bedtime for 7 days
Cream, 4%: Insert 1 applicatorful at bedtime for 3 days
Suppository, 100 mg: Insert 1 suppository at bedtime for 7 days
Suppository, 200 mg: Insert 1 suppository at bedtime for 3 days
Suppository, 1200 mg: Insert 1 suppository (a one-time dose); may be used at bedtime or during the day

Note: Many products are available as a combination pack, with a suppository for vaginal instillation and cream to relieve external symptoms. External cream may be used twice daily, as needed, for up to 7 days.

Dosage Forms [DSC] = Discontinued product
Combination products: Miconazole nitrate vaginal suppository 200 mg (3s) and miconazole nitrate external cream 2%
Monistat® 1 Combination Pack: Miconazole nitrate vaginal insert 1200 mg (1) and miconazole nitrate external cream 2% (5 g) [Note: Do not confuse with 1-Day™ (formerly Monistat® 1) which contains tioconazole]
Monistat® 3 Combination Pack:
Miconazole nitrate vaginal suppository 200 mg (3s) and miconazole nitrate external cream 2%
Miconazole nitrate vaginal cream 4% and miconazole nitrate external cream 2%
Monistat® 7 Combination Pack:
Miconazole nitrate vaginal suppository 100 mg (7s) and miconazole nitrate external cream 2%
Miconazole nitrate vaginal cream 2% (7 prefilled applicators) and miconazole nitrate external cream 2%
Cream, topical, as nitrate: 2% (15 g, 30 g, 45 g)
Baza® Antifungal: 2% (4 g, 57 g, 142 g) [zinc oxide based formula]

Carrington Antifungal: 2% (150 g)
Micaderm®, Neosporin® AF, Podactin: 2% (30 g)
Micatin® Athlete's Foot, Micatin® Jock Itch: 2% (15 g)
Micro-Guard®, Mitrazol™: 2% (60 g)
Monistat-Derm®: 2% (15 g, 30 g, 85 g)
Secura® Antifungal: 2% (60 g, 98 g)
Cream, vaginal, as nitrate [prefilled or refillable applicator]: 2% (45 g)
Monistat® 3: 4% (15 g, 25 g)
Monistat® 7: 2% (45 g)
Liquid, spray, topical, as nitrate:
Micatin® Athlete's Foot: 2% (90 mL) [contains alcohol]
Neosporin AF®: 2% (105 mL)
Lotion, powder, as nitrate (Zeasorb®-AF): 2% (56 g) [contains alcohol 36%]
Ointment, topical, as nitrate:
Aloe Vesta® 2-n-1 Antifungal: 2% (60 g, 150 g)
DermaFungal: 2% (113 g)
Dermagran® AF: (113 g) [contains vitamin A and zinc]
Powder, topical, as nitrate:
Lotrimin® AF: 2% (160 g)
Micro-Guard®: 2% (90 g)
Mitrazol™: 2% (30 g)
Zeasorb®-AF: 2% (70 g)
Powder spray, topical, as nitrate:
Lotrimin® AF, Lotrimin® AF Jock Itch: 2% (140 g)
Micatin® Athlete's Foot, Micatin® Jock Itch: 2% (90 g) [contains alcohol]
Neosporin® AF: 2% (85 g)
Suppository, vaginal, as nitrate: 100 mg (7s); 200 mg (3s)
Monistat® 3: 200 mg (3s)
Monistat® 7: 100 mg (7s)
Tablet, effervescent, topical, as nitrate (DiabetAid™ Antifungal Foot Bath): 2% (10s)
Tincture, topical, as nitrate (Fungoid®): 2% (30 mL, 473 mL) [contains isopropyl alcohol 30%]; 30 mL size also available in a treatment kit which contains nail scrub and nail brush]

Miconazole and Zinc Oxide (mi KON a zole & zink OKS ide)

U.S. Brand Names Vusion™
Index Terms Zinc Oxide and Miconazole Nitrate
Pharmacologic Category Antifungal Agent, Topical
Use Adjunctive treatment of diaper dermatitis complicated by *Candida albicans* infection
Pregnancy Risk Factor C
Dosage Diaper dermatitis: Topical: Children >4 weeks: Apply to affected area with each diaper change for 7 days. Treatment should continue for 7 days, even with initial improvement. Do not use for >7 days.
Additional Information Complete prescribing information for this medication should be consulted for additional detail.
Dosage Forms Ointment, topical (Vusion™): Miconazole nitrate 0.25% and zinc oxide 15% (30 g)

♦ **Miconazole Nitrate** *see* Miconazole *on page 1137*
♦ **Micozole (Can)** *see* Miconazole *on page 1137*
♦ **MICRhoGAM®** *see* Rh₀(D) Immune Globulin *on page 1499*
♦ **Microfibrillar Collagen Hemostat** *see* Collagen Hemostat *on page 416*
♦ **Microgestin™** *see* Ethinyl Estradiol and Norethindrone *on page 655*
♦ **Microgestin™ Fe** *see* Ethinyl Estradiol and Norethindrone *on page 655*
♦ **Micro-Guard® [OTC]** *see* Miconazole *on page 1137*
♦ **microK®** *see* Potassium Chloride *on page 1396*
♦ **microK® 10** *see* Potassium Chloride *on page 1396*
♦ **Micro-K Extencaps® (Can)** *see* Potassium Chloride *on page 1396*
♦ **Micronase®** *see* GlyBURIDE *on page 803*
♦ **Microzide™** *see* Hydrochlorothiazide *on page 845*
♦ **Midamor® [DSC]** *see* Amiloride *on page 92*

Midazolam (MID aye zoe lam)

Canadian Brand Names Apo-Midazolam®; Midazolam Injection
Index Terms Midazolam Hydrochloride; Versed
Pharmacologic Category Benzodiazepine
Additional Appendix Information
Benzodiazepines *on page 1874*
Use Preoperative sedation and provides conscious sedation prior to diagnostic or radiographic procedures; ICU sedation (continuous infusion); intravenous anesthesia (Induction); intravenous anesthesia (maintenance)
Unlabeled/Investigational Use Anxiety, status epilepticus
Restrictions C-IV
Pregnancy Risk Factor D
Pregnancy Implications Midazolam has been found to cross the placenta; not recommended for use during pregnancy.
Lactation Enters breast milk/not recommended (AAP rates "of concern")
Medication Safety Issues
Sound-alike/look-alike issues:
Versed may be confused with VePesid®, Vistaril®
(Continued)

Midazolam *(Continued)*

Contraindications Hypersensitivity to midazolam or any component of the formulation, including benzyl alcohol (cross-sensitivity with other benzodiazepines may exist); parenteral form is not for intrathecal or epidural injection; narrow-angle glaucoma; concurrent use of potent inhibitors of CYP3A4 (amprenavir, atazanavir, or ritonavir); pregnancy

Warnings/Precautions [U.S. Boxed Warning]: May cause severe respiratory depression, respiratory arrest, or apnea. Use with extreme caution, particularly in noncritical care settings. Appropriate resuscitative equipment and qualified personnel must be available for administration and monitoring. Initial dosing must be cautiously titrated and individualized, particularly in elderly or debilitated patients, patients with hepatic impairment (including alcoholics), or in renal impairment, particularly if other CNS depressants (including opiates) are used concurrently. **[U.S. Boxed Warning]: Initial doses in elderly or debilitated patients should be conservative; as little as 1 mg, but not to exceed 2.5 mg.** Use with caution in patients with respiratory disease or impaired gag reflex. Use during upper airway procedures may increase risk of hypoventilation. Prolonged responses have been noted following extended administration by continuous infusion (possibly due to metabolite accumulation) or in the presence of drugs which inhibit midazolam metabolism.

Causes CNS depression (dose-related) resulting in sedation, dizziness, confusion, or ataxia which may impair physical and mental capabilities. Patients must be cautioned about performing tasks which require mental alertness (eg, operating machinery or driving). A minimum of 1 day should elapse after midazolam administration before attempting these tasks. Use with caution in patients receiving other CNS depressants or psychoactive agents. Effects with other sedative drugs or ethanol may be potentiated. Benzodiazepines have been associated with falls and traumatic injury and should be used with extreme caution in patients who are at risk of these events (especially the elderly).

May cause hypotension - hemodynamic events are more common in pediatric patients or patients with hemodynamic instability. Hypotension and/or respiratory depression may occur more frequently in patients who have received opioid analgesics. Use with caution in obese patients, chronic renal failure, and CHF. Does not protect against increases in heart rate or blood pressure during intubation. Should not be used in shock, coma, or acute alcohol intoxication. **[U.S. Boxed Warning]: Parenteral form contains benzyl alcohol; avoid rapid injection in neonates or prolonged infusions.** Avoid intra-arterial administration or extravasation of parenteral formulation.

Midazolam causes anterograde amnesia. Paradoxical reactions, including hyperactive or aggressive behavior have been reported with benzodiazepines, particularly in adolescent/pediatric or psychiatric patients. Does not have analgesic, antidepressant, or antipsychotic properties.

Benzodiazepines have been associated with dependence and acute withdrawal symptoms on discontinuation or reduction in dose. Acute withdrawal, including seizures, may be precipitated after administration of flumazenil to patients receiving long-term benzodiazepine therapy.

Adverse Reactions As reported in adults unless otherwise noted:

>10%: Respiratory: Decreased tidal volume and/or respiratory rate decrease, apnea (3% children)

1% to 10%:
  Cardiovascular: Hypotension (3% children)
  Central nervous system: Drowsiness (1%), oversedation, headache (1%), seizure-like activity (1% children)
  Gastrointestinal: Nausea (3%), vomiting (3%)
  Local: Pain and local reactions at injection site (4% I.M., 5% I.V.; severity less than diazepam)
  Ocular: Nystagmus (1% children)
  Respiratory: Cough (1%)
  Miscellaneous: Physical and psychological dependence with prolonged use, hiccups (4%, 1% children), paradoxical reaction (2% children)

<1% (Limited to important or life-threatening): Agitation, amnesia, bigeminy, bronchospasm, emergence delirium, euphoria, hallucinations, laryngospasm, rash

Overdosage/Toxicology Symptoms include respiratory depression, hypotension, coma, stupor, confusion, and apnea. Treatment for benzodiazepine overdose is supportive. Rarely is mechanical ventilation required. Flumazenil has been shown to selectively block the binding of benzodiazepines to CNS receptors, resulting in a reversal of benzodiazepine-induced CNS depression. Respiratory reaction to hypoxia may not be restored.

Drug Interactions

Cytochrome P450 Effect: Substrate of CYP2B6 (minor), 3A4 (major); **Inhibits** CYP2C8 (weak), 2C9 (weak), 3A4 (weak)

Increased Effect/Toxicity: CYP3A4 inhibitors may increase the levels/effects of midazolam; example inhibitors include azole antifungals, clarithromycin, diclofenac, doxycycline, erythromycin, imatinib, isoniazid, nefazodone, nicardipine, propofol, protease inhibitors, quinidine, telithromycin, and verapamil. Use is contraindicated with amprenavir, atazanavir, and ritonavir. **If narcotics or other CNS depressants are administered concomitantly, the midazolam dose should be reduced by 30% if <65 years of age, or by at least 50% if >65 years of age.**

Decreased Effect: CYP3A4 inducers may decrease the levels/effects of midazolam; example inducers include aminoglutethimide, carbamazepine, nafcillin, nevirapine, phenobarbital, phenytoin, and rifamycins.

Ethanol/Nutrition/Herb Interactions

Ethanol: Avoid ethanol (may increase CNS depression).

Food: Grapefruit juice may increase serum concentrations of midazolam; avoid concurrent use with oral form.

Herb/Nutraceutical: Avoid concurrent use with St John's wort (may decrease midazolam levels, may increase CNS depression). Avoid concurrent use with valerian, kava kava, gotu kola (may increase CNS depression).

Stability Stable for 24 hours at room temperature/refrigeration. At a final concentration of 0.5 mg/mL, stable for up to 24 hours when diluted with D_5W or NS, or for up to 4 hours when diluted with lactated Ringer's. Admixtures do not require protection from light for short-term storage.

Mechanism of Action Binds to stereospecific benzodiazepine receptors on the postsynaptic GABA neuron at several sites within the central nervous system, including the limbic system, reticular formation. Enhancement of the inhibitory effect of GABA on neuronal excitability results in increased neuronal membrane permeability to chloride ions. This shift in chloride ions results in hyperpolarization (a less excitable state) and stabilization.

Pharmacodynamics/Kinetics
Onset of action: I.M.: Sedation: ~15 minutes; I.V.: 1-5 minutes
Peak effect: I.M.: 0.5-1 hour
Duration: I.M.: Up to 6 hours; Mean: 2 hours
Absorption: Oral: Rapid
Distribution: V_d: 0.8-2.5 L/kg; increased with congestive heart failure (CHF) and chronic renal failure
Protein binding: 95%
Metabolism: Extensively hepatic via CYP3A4
Bioavailability: Mean: 45%
Half-life elimination: 1-4 hours; prolonged with cirrhosis, congestive heart failure, obesity, and elderly
Excretion: Urine (as glucuronide conjugated metabolites); feces (~2% to 10%)

Dosage The dose of midazolam needs to be individualized based on the patient's age, underlying diseases, and concurrent medications. Decrease dose (by ~30%) if narcotics or other CNS depressants are administered concomitantly. **Personnel and equipment needed for standard respiratory resuscitation should be immediately available during midazolam administration.**

Children <6 years may require higher doses and closer monitoring than older children; calculate dose on ideal body weight
Conscious sedation for procedures or preoperative sedation:
Oral: 0.25-0.5 mg/kg as a single dose preprocedure, up to a maximum of 20 mg; administer 30-45 minutes prior to procedure. Children <6 years or less cooperative patients may require as much as 1 mg/kg as a single dose; 0.25 mg/kg may suffice for children 6-16 years of age.
Intranasal (not an approved route): 0.2 mg/kg (up to 0.4 mg/kg in some studies), to a maximum of 15 mg; may be administered 30-45 minutes prior to procedure
I.M.: 0.1-0.15 mg/kg 30-60 minutes before surgery or procedure; range 0.05-0.15 mg/kg; doses up to 0.5 mg/kg have been used in more anxious patients; maximum total dose: 10 mg
I.V.:
Infants <6 months: Limited information is available in nonintubated infants; dosing recommendations not clear; infants <6 months are at higher risk for airway obstruction and hypoventilation; titrate dose in small increments to desired effect; monitor carefully
Infants 6 months to Children 5 years: Initial: 0.05-0.1 mg/kg; titrate dose carefully; total dose of 0.6 mg/kg may be required; usual maximum total dose: 6 mg
Children 6-12 years: Initial: 0.025-0.05 mg/kg; titrate dose carefully; total doses of 0.4 mg/kg may be required; usual maximum total dose: 10 mg
Children 12-16 years: Dose as adults; usual maximum total dose: 10 mg
Conscious sedation during mechanical ventilation: Children: Loading dose: 0.05-0.2 mg/kg, followed by initial continuous infusion: 0.06-0.12 mg/kg/hour (1-2 mcg/kg/minute); titrate to the desired effect; usual range: 0.4-6 mcg/kg/minute
Status epilepticus refractory to standard therapy (unlabeled use): Infants >2 months and Children: Loading dose: 0.15 mg/kg followed by a continuous infusion of 1 mcg/kg/minute; titrate dose upward every 5 minutes until clinical seizure activity is controlled; mean infusion rate required in 24 children was 2.3 mcg/kg/minute with a range of 1-18 mcg/kg/minute

Adults:
Preoperative sedation:
I.M.: 0.07-0.08 mg/kg 30-60 minutes prior to surgery/procedure; usual dose: 5 mg; **Note:** Reduce dose in patients with COPD, high-risk patients, patients ≥60 years of age, and patients receiving other narcotics or CNS depressants
I.V.: 0.02-0.04 mg/kg; repeat every 5 minutes as needed to desired effect or up to 0.1-0.2 mg/kg
Intranasal (not an approved route): 0.2 mg/kg (up to 0.4 mg/kg in some studies); administer 30-45 minutes prior to surgery/procedure
Conscious sedation: I.V.: Initial: 0.5-2 mg slow I.V. over at least 2 minutes; slowly titrate to effect by repeating doses every 2-3 minutes if needed; usual total dose: 2.5-5 mg; use decreased doses in elderly
Healthy Adults <60 years: Some patients respond to doses as low as 1 mg; no more than 2.5 mg should be administered over a period of 2 minutes. Additional doses of midazolam may be administered after a 2-minute waiting period and evaluation of sedation after each dose increment. A total dose >5 mg is generally not needed. If narcotics or other CNS depressants are administered concomitantly, the midazolam dose should be reduced by 30%.
Anesthesia: I.V.:
Induction:
Unpremedicated patients: 0.3-0.35 mg/kg (up to 0.6 mg/kg in resistant cases)
Premedicated patients: 0.15-0.35 mg/kg
Maintenance: 0.05-0.3 mg/kg as needed, or continuous infusion 0.25-1.5 mcg/kg/minute
Sedation in mechanically-ventilated patients: I.V. continuous infusion: 100 mg in 250 mL D_5W or NS (if patient is fluid-restricted, may concentrate up to a maximum of 0.5 mg/mL); initial dose: 0.02-0.08 mg/kg (~1 mg to 5 mg in 70 kg adult) initially and either repeated at 5-15 minute intervals until adequate sedation is achieved or continuous infusion rates of 0.04-0.2 mg/kg/hour and titrate to reach desired level of sedation

(Continued)

Midazolam (Continued)

Elderly: I.V.: Conscious sedation: Initial: 0.5 mg slow I.V.; give no more than 1.5 mg in a 2-minute period; if additional titration is needed, give no more than 1 mg over 2 minutes, waiting another 2 or more minutes to evaluate sedative effect; a total dose of >3.5 mg is rarely necessary

Dosage adjustment in renal impairment:
Hemodialysis: Supplemental dose is not necessary
Peritoneal dialysis: Significant drug removal is unlikely based on physiochemical characteristics

Dietary Considerations Injection: Sodium content of 1 mL: 0.14 mEq

Administration
Intranasal: Administer using a 1 mL needleless syringe into the nostrils over 15 seconds; use the 5 mg/mL injection; ½ of the dose may be administered to each nostril
Oral: Do not mix with any liquid (such as grapefruit juice) prior to administration
Parenteral:
I.M.: Administer deep I.M. into large muscle.
I.V.: Administer by slow I.V. injection over at least 2-5 minutes at a concentration of 1-5 mg/mL or by I.V. infusion. Continuous infusions should be administered via an infusion pump.

Monitoring Parameters Respiratory and cardiovascular status, blood pressure, blood pressure monitor required during I.V. administration

Additional Information Abrupt discontinuation after sustained use (generally >10 days) may cause withdrawal symptoms. For neonates, since both concentrations of the injection contain 1% benzyl alcohol, use the 5 mg/mL injection and dilute to 0.5 mg/mL with SWI without preservatives to decrease the amount of benzyl alcohol delivered to the neonate; with continuous infusion, midazolam may accumulate in peripheral tissues; use lowest effective infusion rate to reduce accumulation effects; midazolam is 3-4 times as potent as diazepam; paradoxical reactions associated with midazolam use in children (eg, agitation, restlessness, combativeness) have been successfully treated with flumazenil (see Massanari, 1997).

Dosage Forms
Injection, solution: 1 mg/mL (2 mL, 5 mL, 10 mL); 5 mg/mL (1 mL, 2 mL, 5 mL, 10 mL) [contains benzyl alcohol 1%]
Injection, solution [preservative free]: 1 mg/mL (2 mL, 5 mL); 5 mg/mL (1 mL, 2 mL)
Syrup: 2 mg/mL (118 mL) [contains sodium benzoate; cherry flavor]

♦ **Midazolam Hydrochloride** see Midazolam on page 1139
♦ **Midazolam Injection (Can)** see Midazolam on page 1139

Midodrine (MI doe dreen)

U.S. Brand Names Orvaten™; ProAmatine®
Canadian Brand Names Amatine®; Apo-Midodrine®
Index Terms Midodrine Hydrochloride
Pharmacologic Category Alpha₁ Agonist
Use Orphan drug: Treatment of symptomatic orthostatic hypotension
Unlabeled/Investigational Use Investigational: Management of urinary incontinence
Pregnancy Risk Factor C
Pregnancy Implications Increased rate of embryo resorption and decreased fetal weight were observed in animal studies. Use during pregnancy should be avoided unless the potential benefit outweighs the risk to the fetus.
Lactation Excretion in breast milk is unknown/use caution
Medication Safety Issues
Sound-alike/look-alike issues:
ProAmatine® may be confused with protamine
Contraindications Hypersensitivity to midodrine or any component of the formulation; severe organic heart disease; urinary retention; pheochromocytoma; thyrotoxicosis; persistent and significant supine hypertension
Warnings/Precautions [U.S. Boxed Warning]: Indicated for patients for whom orthostatic hypotension significantly impairs their daily life despite standard clinical care. Use is not recommended with supine hypertension. Caution should be exercised in patients with diabetes, visual problems (especially if receiving fludrocortisone), urinary retention (reduce initial dose), or hepatic dysfunction; monitor renal and hepatic function prior to and periodically during therapy; safety and efficacy has not been established in children; discontinue and re-evaluate therapy if signs of bradycardia occur.
Adverse Reactions
>10%:
Cardiovascular: Supine hypertension (7% to 13%)
Dermatologic: Piloerection (13%), pruritus (12%)
Genitourinary: Urinary urgency, retention, or polyuria, dysuria (up to 13%)
Neuromuscular & skeletal: Paresthesia (18%)
1% to 10%:
Central nervous system: Chills (5%), pain (5%)
Dermatologic: Rash (2%)
Gastrointestinal: Abdominal pain
<1% (Limited to important or life-threatening): Anxiety, canker sore, confusion, dizziness, dry skin, erythema multiforme, facial flushing, flushing, headache, hyperesthesia, insomnia, ICP increased, nausea, somnolence, weakness, xerostomia
Overdosage/Toxicology Symptoms include hypertension, piloerection, and urinary retention. Treatment is symptomatic following gastric decontamination. Alpha-sympatholytics and/or dialysis may be helpful.

Drug Interactions

Increased Effect/Toxicity: Concomitant fludrocortisone results in hypernatremia or an increase in intraocular pressure and glaucoma. Bradycardia may be accentuated with concomitant administration of cardiac glycosides, psychotherapeutics, and beta-blockers. Alpha agonists may increase the pressure effects and alpha antagonists may negate the effects of midodrine.

Mechanism of Action Midodrine forms an active metabolite, desglymidodrine, that is an alpha₁-agonist. This agent increases arteriolar and venous tone resulting in a rise in standing, sitting, and supine systolic and diastolic blood pressure in patients with orthostatic hypotension. See table.

Causes of Orthostatic Hypotension

Primary Autonomic Causes
Pure autonomic failure (Bradbury-Eggleston syndrome, idiopathic orthostatic hypotension)
Autonomic failure with multiple system atrophy (Shy-Drager syndrome)
Familial dysautonomia (Riley-Day syndrome)
Dopamine beta-hydroxylase deficiency
Secondary Autonomic Causes
Chronic alcoholism
Parkinson's disease
Diabetes mellitus
Porphyria
Amyloidosis
Various carcinomas
Vitamin B_1 or B_{12} deficiency
Nonautonomic Causes
Hypovolemia (such as associated with hemorrhage, burns, or hemodialysis) and dehydration
Diminished homeostatic regulation (such as associated with aging, pregnancy, fever, or prolonged bedrest)
Medications (eg, antihypertensives, insulin, tricyclic antidepressants)

Pharmacodynamics/Kinetics

Onset of action: ~1 hour
Duration: 2-3 hours
Absorption: Rapid
Distribution: V_d (desglymidodrine): <1.6 L/kg; poorly across membrane (eg, blood brain barrier)
Protein binding: Minimal
Metabolism: Hepatic; midodrine is a prodrug which undergoes rapid deglycination to desglymidodrine (active metabolite); metabolism occurs in many tissues and plasma
Bioavailability: Desglymidodrine: 93%
Half-life elimination: Desglymidodrine: ~3-4 hours; Midodrine: 25 minutes
Time to peak, serum: Desglymidodrine: 1-2 hours; Midodrine: 30 minutes
Excretion: Urine (2% to 4%)
Clearance: Desglymidodrine: 385 mL/minute (predominantly by renal secretion)

Dosage Adults: Oral: 10 mg 3 times/day during daytime hours (every 3-4 hours) when patient is upright (maximum: 40 mg/day)

Dosing adjustment in renal impairment: 2.5 mg 3 times/day, gradually increasing as tolerated
Hemodialysis: Dialyzable

Administration Doses may be given in approximately 3- to 4-hour intervals (eg, shortly before or upon rising in the morning, at midday, in the late afternoon not later than 6 PM). Avoid dosing after the evening meal or within 4 hours of bedtime. Continue therapy only in patients who appear to attain symptomatic improvement during initial treatment. Standing systolic blood pressure may be elevated 15-30 mm Hg at 1 hour after a 10 mg dose. Some effect may persist for 2-3 hours.

Monitoring Parameters Blood pressure, renal and hepatic parameters

Dosage Forms Tablet, as hydrochloride: 2.5 mg, 5 mg, 10 mg

♦ **Midodrine Hydrochloride** see Midodrine on page 1142
♦ **Midol® Cramp and Body Aches [OTC]** see Ibuprofen on page 873
♦ **Midol® Extended Relief** see Naproxen on page 1199
♦ **Midrin®** see Acetaminophen, Isometheptene, and Dichloralphenazone on page 36
♦ **Mifeprex®** see Mifepristone on page 1143

Mifepristone (mi FE pris tone)

U.S. Brand Names Mifeprex®
Index Terms RU-486; RU-38486
Pharmacologic Category Abortifacient; Antineoplastic Agent, Hormone Antagonist; Antiprogestin
Use Medical termination of intrauterine pregnancy, through day 49 of pregnancy. Patients may need treatment with misoprostol and possibly surgery to complete therapy
Unlabeled/Investigational Use Treatment of unresectable meningioma; has been studied in the treatment of breast cancer, ovarian cancer, and adrenal cortical carcinoma
Restrictions Investigators wishing to obtain the agent for use in oncology patients must apply for a patient-specific IND from the FDA. Mifepristone will be supplied only to licensed physicians who sign and return a "Prescriber's Agreement." Distribution of mifepristone will be subject to specific requirements imposed by the distributor. Mifepristone will not be available
(Continued)

Mifepristone *(Continued)*

to the public through licensed pharmacies. An FDA-approved medication guide must be distributed when dispensing an outpatient prescription (new or refill) where this medication is to be used without direct supervision of a healthcare provider. Medication guides are available at http://www.fda.gov/cder/Offices/ODS/medication_guides.htm.

Not available in Canada

Pregnancy Risk Factor X

Pregnancy Implications This medication is used to terminate pregnancy; there are no approved treatment indications for its use during pregnancy. Prostaglandins (including mifepristone and misoprostol) may have teratogenic effects when used during pregnancy. If treatment fails, there is a risk of fetal malformation. In sexually active women, pregnancy can occur prior to the first menstrual period following treatment. Appropriate contraception can be started as soon as termination of pregnancy is confirmed or before sexual intercourse is resumed.

Lactation Excretion in breast milk unknown/contraindicated

Medication Safety Issues

Sound-alike/look-alike issues:

Mifeprex® may be confused with Mirapex®

Contraindications Hypersensitivity to mifepristone, misoprostol, other prostaglandins, or any component of the formulation; chronic adrenal failure; porphyrias; hemorrhagic disorder or concurrent anticoagulant therapy; pregnancy termination >49 days; intrauterine device (IUD) in place; ectopic pregnancy or undiagnosed adnexal mass; concurrent long-term corticosteroid therapy; inadequate or lack of access to emergency medical services; inability to understand effects and/or comply with treatment

Warnings/Precautions [U.S. Boxed Warning]: Patient must be instructed of the treatment procedure and expected effects. A signed agreement form must be kept in the patient's file. Physicians may obtain patient agreement forms, physician enrollment forms, and medical consultation directly from Danco Laboratories at 1-877-432-7596. Adverse effects (including blood transfusions, hospitalization, ongoing pregnancy, and other major complications) must be reported in writing to the medication distributor. To be administered only by physicians who can date pregnancy, diagnose ectopic pregnancies, provide access to surgical abortion (if needed), and can provide access to emergency care. Medication will be distributed directly to these physicians following signed agreement with the distributor. Must be administered under supervision by the qualified physician. Pregnancy is dated from day 1 of last menstrual period (presuming a 28-day cycle, ovulation occurring midcycle). Pregnancy duration can be determined using menstrual history and clinical examination. Ultrasound should be used if an ectopic pregnancy is suspected or if duration of pregnancy is uncertain. Ultrasonography may not identify all ectopic pregnancies, and healthcare providers should be alert for signs and symptoms which may be related to undiagnosed ectopic pregnancy in any patient who receives mifepristone

[U.S. Boxed Warning]: Patients should be counseled to seek medical attention in cases of excessive bleeding. Bleeding occurs and should be expected (average 9-16 days, may be ≥30 days). In some cases, bleeding may be prolonged and heavy, potentially leading to hypovolemic shock; the manufacturer cites soaking through two thick sanitary pads per hour for two consecutive hours as an example of excessive bleeding. Bleeding may require blood transfusion (rare), curettage, saline infusions, and/or vasoconstrictors. Use caution in patients with severe anemia. Confirmation of pregnancy termination by clinical exam or ultrasound must be made 14 days following treatment. Manufacturer recommends surgical termination of pregnancy when medical termination fails or is not complete. Prescriber should determine in advance whether they will provide such care themselves or through other providers. Preventative measures to prevent rhesus immunization must be taken prior to surgical abortion. Prescriber should also give the patient clear instructions on whom to call and what to do in the event of an emergency following administration of mifepristone.

[U.S. Boxed Warning]: Bacterial infections have been reported following use of this product. In rare cases, these infections may be serious and/or fatal, with septic shock as a potential complication. A causal relationship has not been established. Sustained fever, abdominal pain, or pelvic tenderness should prompt evaluation; however, healthcare professionals are warned that atypical presentations of serious infection without these symptoms have also been noted. Patients presenting with nausea, vomiting, diarrhea, or weakness, with or without abdominal pain or fever, should be evaluated for serious bacterial infection when symptoms occur >24 hours after taking misoprostol. Treatment with antibiotics, including coverage for anaerobic bacteria (eg, *Clostridium sordellii*) should be initiated. **[U.S. Boxed Warning]: Patients undergoing treatment with mifepristone should be instructed to bring their Medication Guide with them when an obtaining treatment from an emergency room or healthcare provider that did not prescribe the medication initially in order to identify that they are undergoing a medical abortion.**

Safety and efficacy have not been established for use in women with chronic cardiovascular, hypertensive, hepatic, respiratory, or renal disease, insulin-dependent diabetes mellitus, severe anemia, or heavy smokers. Women >35 years of age and smokers (>10 cigarettes/day) were excluded from clinical trials. Safety and efficacy in pediatric patients have not been established.

Adverse Reactions Vaginal bleeding and uterine cramping are expected to occur when this medication is used to terminate a pregnancy; 90% of women using this medication for this purpose also report adverse reactions. Bleeding or spotting occurs in most women for a period of 9-16 days. Up to 8% of women will experience some degree of bleeding or spotting for 30 days or more. In some cases, bleeding may be prolonged and heavy, potentially leading to hypovolemic shock.

>10%:

Central nervous system: Headache (2% to 31%), dizziness (1% to 12%)

Gastrointestinal: Abdominal pain (cramping) (96%), nausea (43% to 61%), vomiting (18% to 26%), diarrhea (12% to 20%)

Genitourinary: Uterine cramping (83%)

1% to 10%:
Cardiovascular: Syncope (1%)
Central nervous system: Fatigue (10%), fever (4%), insomnia (3%), anxiety (2%), fainting (2%)
Gastrointestinal: Dyspepsia (3%)
Genitourinary: Uterine hemorrhage (5%), vaginitis (3%), pelvic pain (2%), endometriosis/salpingitis/pelvic inflammatory disease (1%)
Hematologic: Decreased hemoglobin >2 g/dL (6%), anemia (2%), leukorrhea (2%)
Neuromuscular & skeletal: Back pain (9%), rigors (3%), leg pain (2%), weakness (2%)
Respiratory: Sinusitis (2%)
Miscellaneous: Viral infection (4%)
<1% (Limited to important or life-threatening): Adult respiratory distress syndrome (ADRS), allergic reaction including urticaria and hives, bacterial infection (including an ectopic bacteria such as *Clostridium sordellii*), Crohn's disease (exacerbation), disseminated intravascular coagulopathy (DIC), dyspnea, hypotension, lightheadedness, loss of consciousness, MI, pancreatitis (acute), postabortal infection, QT prolongation, ruptured ectopic pregnancy, sepsis, septic shock, sickle cell crisis (exacerbation), tachycardia, toxic shock syndrome

In trials for unresectable meningioma, the most common adverse effects included fatigue, hot flashes, gynecomastia or breast tenderness, hair thinning, and rash. In premenopausal women, vaginal bleeding may be seen shortly after beginning therapy and cessation of menses is common. Thyroiditis and effects related to antiglucocorticoid activity have also been noted.

Overdosage/Toxicology In studies using 3 times the recommended dose for termination of pregnancy, no serious maternal adverse effects were reported. This medication is supplied in single-dose containers to be given under physician supervision, therefore, the risk of overdose should be low. In case of massive ingestion, treat symptomatically and monitor for signs of adrenal failure.

Drug Interactions
Cytochrome P450 Effect: Substrate of CYP3A4 (minor); **Inhibits** CYP2D6 (weak), 3A4 (weak)
Increased Effect/Toxicity: There are no reported interactions. It might be anticipated that the concurrent administration of mifepristone and a progestin would result in an attenuation of the effects of one or both agents.

Ethanol/Nutrition/Herb Interactions
Food: Do not take with grapefruit juice; grapefruit juice may inhibit mifepristone metabolism leading to increased levels.
Herb/Nutraceutical: Avoid St John's wort (may induce mifepristone metabolism, leading to decreased levels).

Stability Store at room temperature of 25°C (77°F).

Mechanism of Action Mifepristone, a synthetic steroid, competitively binds to the intracellular progesterone receptor, blocking the effects of progesterone. When used for the termination of pregnancy, this leads to contraction-inducing activity in the myometrium. In the absence of progesterone, mifepristone acts as a partial progesterone agonist. Mifepristone also has weak antiglucocorticoid and antiandrogenic properties; it blocks the feedback effect of cortisol on corticotropin secretion.

Pharmacodynamics/Kinetics
Absorption: Oral: rapid
Protein binding: 98% to albumin and α_1-acid glycoprotein
Metabolism: Hepatic via CYP3A4 to three metabolites (may possess some antiprogestin and antiglucocorticoid activity)
Bioavailability: Oral: 69%
Half-life elimination: Terminal: 18 hours following a slower phase where 50% eliminated between 12-72 hours
Time to peak: Oral: 90 minutes
Excretion: Feces (83%); urine (9%)

Dosage Oral:
Adults:
Termination of pregnancy: Treatment consists of three office visits by the patient; the patient must read medication guide and sign patient agreement prior to treatment:
Day 1: 600 mg (three 200 mg tablets) taken as a single dose under physician supervision
Day 3: Patient must return to the healthcare provider 2 days following administration of mifepristone; unless abortion has occurred (confirmed using ultrasound or clinical examination): 400 mcg (two 200 mcg tablets) of misoprostol; patient may need treatment for cramps or gastrointestinal symptoms at this time
Day 14: Patient must return to the healthcare provider ~14 days after administration of mifepristone; confirm complete termination of pregnancy by ultrasound or clinical exam. Surgical termination is recommended to manage treatment failures.
Meningioma (unlabeled use): Refer to individual protocols. The dose used in meningioma is usually 200 mg/day, continued based on toxicity and response.
Elderly: Safety and efficacy have not been established

Dosage adjustment in renal impairment: Safety and efficacy have not been established
Dosage adjustment in hepatic impairment: Safety and efficacy have not been established; use with caution due to CYP3A4 metabolism

Monitoring Parameters Clinical exam and/or ultrasound to confirm complete termination of pregnancy; hemoglobin, hematocrit, and red blood cell count in cases of heavy bleeding. Consider CBC in any patient who reports nausea, vomiting, or diarrhea and weakness with or without abdominal pain, and without fever or other signs of infection more than 24 hours after administration of misoprostol.

Test Interactions hCG levels will not be useful to confirm pregnancy termination until at least 10 days following mifepristone treatment

Additional Information Medication will be distributed directly to qualified physicians following signed agreement with the distributor, Danco Laboratories. It will not be available through
(Continued)

Mifepristone *(Continued)*

pharmacies. Major adverse reactions (hospitalization, blood transfusion, ongoing pregnancy, etc) should be reported to Danco Laboratories.

Dosage Forms Tablet: 200 mg

Miglitol *(MIG li tol)*

U.S. Brand Names Glyset®

Canadian Brand Names Glyset®

Pharmacologic Category Antidiabetic Agent, Alpha-Glucosidase Inhibitor

Additional Appendix Information
Diabetes Mellitus Management, Adults *on page 2040*
Hyperglycemia- or Hypoglycemia-Causing Drugs *on page 2057*

Use Type 2 diabetes mellitus (noninsulin-dependent, NIDDM):
Monotherapy adjunct to diet to improve glycemic control in patients with type 2 diabetes mellitus (noninsulin-dependent, NIDDM) whose hyperglycemia cannot be managed with diet alone

Combination therapy with a sulfonylurea when diet plus either miglitol or a sulfonylurea alone do not result in adequate glycemic control. The effect of miglitol to enhance glycemic control is additive to that of sulfonylureas when used in combination.

Pregnancy Risk Factor B

Pregnancy Implications Abnormal blood glucose levels are associated with a higher incidence of congenital abnormalities. Insulin is the drug of choice for the control of diabetes mellitus during pregnancy.

Lactation Enters breast milk (small amounts)/not recommended

Contraindications Hypersensitivity to miglitol or any of component of the formulation; diabetic ketoacidosis; inflammatory bowel disease; colonic ulceration; partial intestinal obstruction or predisposition to intestinal obstruction; chronic intestinal diseases associated with marked disorders of digestion or absorption or with conditions that may deteriorate as a result of increased gas formation in the intestine

Warnings/Precautions GI symptoms are the most common reactions. The incidence of abdominal pain and diarrhea tend to diminish considerably with continued treatment. Long-term clinical trials in diabetic patients with significant renal dysfunction (serum creatinine >2 mg/dL) have not been conducted. Treatment of these patients is not recommended. In combination with a sulfonylurea will cause a further lowering of blood glucose and may increase the hypoglycemic potential of the sulfonylurea. It may be necessary to discontinue miglitol and administer insulin if the patient is exposed to stress (ie, fever, trauma, infection, surgery). Safety and efficacy have not been established in children.

Adverse Reactions
>10%: Gastrointestinal: Flatulence (41.5%), diarrhea (28.7%), abdominal pain (11.7%)
1% to 10%: Dermatologic: Rash (4.3%)

Overdosage/Toxicology An overdose of miglitol will not result in hypoglycemia. An overdose may result in transient increases in flatulence, diarrhea, and abdominal discomfort. No serious systemic reactions are expected in the event of an overdose.

Drug Interactions
Decreased Effect: Miglitol may decrease the absorption and bioavailability of digoxin, propranolol, and ranitidine. Digestive enzymes (amylase, pancreatin, charcoal) may reduce the effect of miglitol and should **not** be taken concomitantly.

Mechanism of Action In contrast to sulfonylureas, miglitol does not enhance insulin secretion; the antihyperglycemic action of miglitol results from a reversible inhibition of membrane-bound intestinal alpha-glucosidases which hydrolyze oligosaccharides and disaccharides to glucose and other monosaccharides in the brush border of the small intestine; in diabetic patients, this enzyme inhibition results in delayed glucose absorption and lowering of postprandial hyperglycemia

Pharmacodynamics/Kinetics
Absorption: Saturable at high doses: 25 mg dose: Completely absorbed; 100 mg dose: 50% to 70% absorbed
Distribution: V_d: 0.18 L/kg
Protein binding: <4%
Metabolism: None
Half-life elimination: ~2 hours
Time to peak: 2-3 hours
Excretion: Urine (as unchanged drug)

Dosage Adults: Oral: 25 mg 3 times/day with the first bite of food at each meal; the dose may be increased to 50 mg 3 times/day after 4-8 weeks; maximum recommended dose: 100 mg 3 times/day

Dosing adjustment in renal impairment: Miglitol is primarily excreted by the kidneys; there is little information of miglitol in patients with a Cl_{cr} <25 mL/minute

Dosing adjustment in hepatic impairment: No adjustment necessary

Administration Should be taken orally at the start (with the first bite) of each main meal

Monitoring Parameters Monitor therapeutic response by periodic blood glucose tests; measurement of glycosylated hemoglobin is recommended for the monitoring of long-term glycemic control

Reference Range Target range: Adults:
Fasting blood glucose: <120 mg/dL
Glycosylated hemoglobin: <7%

Dosage Forms Tablet: 25 mg, 50 mg, 100 mg

Miglustat (MIG loo stat)

U.S. Brand Names Zavesca®
Canadian Brand Names Zavesca®
Index Terms OGT-918
Pharmacologic Category Enzyme Inhibitor
Use Treatment of mild-to-moderate type 1 Gaucher disease when enzyme replacement therapy is not a therapeutic option
Pregnancy Risk Factor X
Pregnancy Implications Decreased fetus weight, fetal loss, and difficult or delayed births were observed in animal studies. Women with reproduction potential should use effective contraception during therapy. In addition, adverse effects on spermatogenesis and reduced fertility were observed in male animal studies. The manufacturer recommends that male patients use reliable contraception during therapy and for 3 months following treatment.
Lactation Excretion in breast milk unknown/not recommended
Contraindications Hypersensitivity to miglustat or any component of the formulation; pregnancy
Warnings/Precautions Peripheral neuropathy has been reported with use and neurologic monitoring is required. Tremor or exacerbations of existing tremor may occur; may resolve over time or respond to dosage reduction. Weigh risk versus benefit of therapy if patient develops numbness and tingling. Use caution in renal impairment. Safety and efficacy in severe type 1 Gaucher disease have not been established. Safety and efficacy in patients <18 or >65 years of age have not been established.
Adverse Reactions Percentages reported from open-label, uncontrolled monotherapy trials.
>10%:
  Central nervous system: Headache (21% to 22%), dizziness (up to 11%)
  Gastrointestinal: Diarrhea (89%; up to 100% in other studies), weight loss (39% to 67%), abdominal pain (18% to 50%), flatulence (29% to 44%), nausea (14% to 22%), vomiting (4% to 11%), cramps (up to 11%)
  Neuromuscular & skeletal: Tremor (11%; up to 30% in other studies), leg cramps (4% to 11%),
  Ocular: Visual disturbances (up to 17%)
1% to 10%:
  Endocrine & metabolic: Menstrual disorder (up to 6%)
  Gastrointestinal: Anorexia (up to 7%), dyspepsia (up to 7%), epigastric pain (up to 6%)
  Hematologic: Thrombocytopenia (6% to 7%)
  Neuromuscular & skeletal: Paresthesia (up to 7%)
Overdosage/Toxicology Doses of up to 3000 mg/day were used in HIV-positive patients during clinical development. Dizziness, granulocytopenia, leukopenia, neutropenia, and paresthesia were observed.
Drug Interactions
  Decreased Effect: Miglustat increases the clearance of imiglucerase; combination therapy is not indicated.
Ethanol/Nutrition/Herb Interactions
  Food: Food decreases the rate, but not the extent, of absorption.
Stability Store at 20°C to 25°C (68°F to 77°F).
Mechanism of Action Miglustat inhibits the enzyme needed to produce glycosphingolipids and decreases the rate of glycosphingolipid glucosylceramide formation. Glucosylceramide accumulates in type 1 Gaucher disease, causing complications specific to this disease.
Pharmacodynamics/Kinetics
  Distribution: V_d: 83-105 L
  Protein binding: No binding to plasma proteins
  Bioavailability: 97%
  Half-life elimination: 6-7 hours
  Time to peak, plasma: 2-2.5 hours
  Excretion: Urine (as unchanged drug)
Dosage Oral: Adults: Type 1 Gaucher disease: 100 mg 3 times/day; dose may be reduced to 100 mg 1-2 times/day in patients with adverse effects (ie, tremor, GI distress)
  Dosage adjustment in renal impairment:
    Cl_{cr} 50-75 mL/minute: 100 mg twice daily
    Cl_{cr} 30-50 mL/minute: 100 mg once daily
    Cl_{cr} <30 mL/minute: Not recommended
Dietary Considerations May be take, with or without food. Patients with diarrhea should avoid foods with high carbohydrate content.
Administration Capsules should be swallowed whole and taken at the same time each day. May be taken with or without food.
Monitoring Parameters Neurologic evaluations baseline and repeated every 6 months; adverse effects; weight
Dosage Forms Capsule: 100 mg

♦ **Migquin** see Acetaminophen, Isometheptene, and Dichloralphenazone on page 36
♦ **Migranal®** see Dihydroergotamine on page 507
♦ **Migratine** see Acetaminophen, Isometheptene, and Dichloralphenazone on page 36
♦ **Migrazone®** see Acetaminophen, Isometheptene, and Dichloralphenazone on page 36
♦ **Migrin-A** see Acetaminophen, Isometheptene, and Dichloralphenazone on page 36
♦ **Milk of Magnesia** see Magnesium Hydroxide on page 1047
♦ **Milophene® (Can)** see ClomiPHENE on page 394

Milrinone (MIL ri none)

U.S. Brand Names Primacor®
Canadian Brand Names Milrinone Lactate Injection; Primacor®
Index Terms Milrinone Lactate
Pharmacologic Category Phosphodiesterase Enzyme Inhibitor
Additional Appendix Information
Hemodynamic Support, Intravenous *on page 1885*
Use Short-term I.V. therapy of congestive heart failure; calcium antagonist intoxication
Pregnancy Risk Factor C
Lactation Excretion in breast milk unknown
Medication Safety Issues
Sound-alike/look-alike issues:
Primacor® may be confused with Primaxin®
Contraindications Hypersensitivity to milrinone, inamrinone, or any component of the formulation; concurrent use of inamrinone
Warnings/Precautions Avoid in severe obstructive aortic or pulmonic valvular disease, history of ventricular arrhythmias; atrial fibrillation, flutter. Life-threatening arrhythmias were infrequent and have been associated with pre-existing arrhythmias, metabolic abnormalities, abnormal digoxin levels, and catheter insertion. It may aggravate outflow tract obstruction in hypertrophic subaortic stenosis. Monitor closely during the infusion. Ensure that ventricular rate controlled in atrial fibrillation/flutter before initiating. Not recommended for use in acute MI patients. Monitor and correct fluid and electrolyte problems. Adjust dose in renal dysfunction.

Adverse Reactions
>10%: Cardiovascular: Ventricular arrhythmia (ectopy 9%, NSVT 3%, sustained ventricular tachycardia 1%, ventricular fibrillation <1%); life-threatening arrhythmia are infrequent, often associated with underlying factors (eg, pre-existing arrhythmia, electrolyte disturbances, catheter insertion)
1% to 10%:
Cardiovascular: Supraventricular arrhythmia (4%), hypotension
Central nervous system: Headache
<1% (Limited to important or life-threatening): Anaphylaxis, atrial fibrillation, bronchospasm, chest pain, hypokalemia, liver function abnormalities, MI, rash, thrombocytopenia, torsade de pointes, tremor, ventricular fibrillation
Overdosage/Toxicology Hypotension should respond to I.V. fluids and Trendelenburg position. Use of vasopressors may be required.
Stability Colorless to pale yellow solution. Store at room temperature. Protect from light. Stable at 0.2 mg/mL in 0.9% sodium chloride or D_5W for 72 hours at room temperature in normal light.

Standard dilution: For a final concentration of 0.2 mg/mL: Dilute Primacor® 1 mg/mL (20 mL) with 80 mL diluent (final volume: 100 mL). May also dilute 1 mg/mL (10 mL) with 40 mL diluent (final volume: 50 mL).
Mechanism of Action Phosphodiesterase inhibitor resulting in vasodilation
Pharmacodynamics/Kinetics
Onset of action: I.V.: 5-15 minutes
Serum level: I.V.: Following a 125 mcg/kg dose, peak plasma concentrations ~1000 ng/mL were observed at 2 minutes postinjection, decreasing to <100 ng/mL in 2 hours
Drug concentration levels:
Therapeutic:
Serum levels of 166 ng/mL, achieved during I.V. infusions of 0.25-1 mcg/kg/minute, were associated with sustained hemodynamic benefit in severe congestive heart failure patients over a 24-hour period
Maximum beneficial effects on cardiac output and pulmonary capillary wedge pressure following I.V. infusion have been associated with plasma milrinone concentrations of 150-250 ng/mL
Toxic: Serum concentrations >250-300 ng/mL have been associated with marked reductions in mean arterial pressure and tachycardia; however, more studies are required to determine the toxic serum levels for milrinone
Distribution: V_{dss}: 0.32 L/kg; Severe congestive heart failure (CHF): V_d: 0.33-0.47 L/kg; not significantly bound to tissues; excretion in breast milk unknown
Protein binding, plasma: ~70%
Metabolism: Hepatic (12%)
Half-life elimination: I.V.: 136 minutes in patients with CHF; patients with severe CHF have a more prolonged half-life, with values ranging from 1.7-2.7 hours. Patients with CHF have a reduction in the systemic clearance of milrinone, resulting in a prolonged elimination half-life. Alternatively, one study reported that 1 month of therapy with milrinone did not change the pharmacokinetic parameters for patients with CHF despite improvement in cardiac function.
Excretion: I.V.: Urine (85% as unchanged drug) within 24 hours; active tubular secretion is a major elimination pathway for milrinone
Clearance: I.V. bolus: 25.9 ± 5.7 L/hour (0.37 L/hour/kg); Severe congestive heart failure: 0.11-0.13 L/hour/kg. The reduction in clearance may be a result of reduced renal function. Creatinine clearance values were ½ those reported for healthy adults in patients with severe congestive heart failure (52 vs 119 mL/minute).
Dosage Adults: I.V.: Loading dose: 50 mcg/kg administered over 10 minutes followed by a maintenance dose titrated according to the hemodynamic and clinical response; see table on next page:

Dosing adjustment in renal impairment:
Cl_{cr} 50 mL/minute/1.73 m²: Administer 0.43 mcg/kg/minute.
Cl_{cr} 40 mL/minute/1.73 m²: Administer 0.38 mcg/kg/minute.
Cl_{cr} 30 mL/minute/1.73 m²: Administer 0.33 mcg/kg/minute.

Cl$_{cr}$ 20 mL/minute/1.73 m²: Administer 0.28 mcg/kg/minute.
Cl$_{cr}$ 10 mL/minute/1.73 m²: Administer 0.23 mcg/kg/minute.
Cl$_{cr}$ 5 mL/minute/1.73 m²: Administer 0.2 mcg/kg/minute.

Maintenance Dosage	Dose Rate (mcg/kg/min)	Total Dose (mg/kg/24 h)
Minimum	0.375	0.59
Standard	0.500	0.77
Maximum	0.750	1.13

Administration Requires an infusion pump; continuous I.V. infusion; 20 mg/100 mL 0.9% sodium chloride or D$_5$W (0.2 mg/mL); see table.

Dose (mcg/kg/min)	Rate (mL/kg/h)
0.375	0.11
0.400	0.12
0.500	0.15
0.600	0.18
0.700	0.21
0.750	0.22

Monitoring Parameters Cardiac monitor and blood pressure monitor required; serum potassium

Therapeutic: Patients should be monitored for improvement in the clinical signs and symptoms of congestive heart failure

Toxic: Patients should be monitored for ventricular arrhythmias and exacerbation of anginal symptoms; during I.V. therapy with milrinone, blood pressure and heart rate should be monitored

Dosage Forms [DSC] = Discontinued product

Infusion [premixed in D$_5$W] (Primacor®): 200 mcg/mL (100 mL, 200 mL)
Injection, solution: 1 mg/mL (10 mL, 20 mL, 50 mL)
Primacor®: 1 mg/mL (10 mL, 20 mL; 50 mL [DSC])

- **Milrinone Lactate** see Milrinone on page 1148
- **Milrinone Lactate Injection (Can)** see Milrinone on page 1148
- **Miltown® [DSC]** see Meprobamate on page 1085
- **Mindal DM [DSC]** see Guaifenesin and Dextromethorphan on page 816
- **Minestrin™ 1/20 (Can)** see Ethinyl Estradiol and Norethindrone on page 655
- **Minidyne® [OTC]** see Povidone-Iodine on page 1404
- **Minipress®** see Prazosin on page 1411
- **Minipress™ (Can)** see Prazosin on page 1411
- **Minirin® (Can)** see Desmopressin on page 476
- **Minitran™** see Nitroglycerin on page 1234
- **Minizide® [DSC]** see Prazosin and Polythiazide on page 1413
- **Minocin®** see Minocycline on page 1149

Minocycline (mi noe SYE kleen)

U.S. Brand Names Dynacin®; Minocin®; myrac™; Solodyn™
Canadian Brand Names Alti-Minocycline; Apo-Minocycline®; Gen-Minocycline; Minocin®; Novo-Minocycline; PMS-Minocycline; Rhoxal-minocycline; Sandoz-Minocycline
Index Terms Minocycline Hydrochloride
Pharmacologic Category Antibiotic, Tetracycline Derivative
Additional Appendix Information
Antimicrobial Drugs of Choice on page 1981
Use Treatment of susceptible bacterial infections of both gram-negative and gram-positive organisms; treatment of anthrax (inhalational, cutaneous, and gastrointestinal); acne; meningococcal (asymptomatic) carrier state; Rickettsial diseases (including Rocky Mountain spotted fever, Q fever); nongonococcal urethritis, gonorrhea; acute intestinal amebiasis
Pregnancy Risk Factor D
Pregnancy Implications May cause permanent discoloration (brown-gray) of teeth. Animal studies indicate possible tumorigenicity, skeletal deformations, and impairment of male fertility. Congenital anomalies have been reported postmarketing. There are no adequate and well-controlled studies in pregnant women. Should be used in pregnancy only if the potential benefit justifies the risk to the fetus.
Lactation Enters breast milk/not recommended
Medication Safety Issues
Sound-alike/look-alike issues:
Dynacin® may be confused with Dyazide®, Dynabac®, DynaCirc®, Dynapen®
Minocin® may be confused with Indocin®, Lincocin®, Minizide®, Mithracin®, niacin
Contraindications Hypersensitivity to minocycline, other tetracyclines, or any component of the formulation; pregnancy
Warnings/Precautions May cause tissue hyperpigmentation or permanent tooth discoloration; avoid use during tooth development (children ≤8 years of age) unless other drugs are not likely to be effective or are contraindicated. May be associated with increases in BUN secondary to antianabolic effects; use caution in patients with renal impairment. Hepatotoxicity has been reported; use caution in patients with hepatic insufficiency. Autoimmune syndromes (eg, lupus-like, hepatitis, and vasculitis) have been reported; discontinue if symptoms. CNS effects (lightheadedness, vertigo) may occur; patients must be cautioned about performing tasks which require mental alertness (eg, operating machinery or driving). Has (Continued)

Minocycline *(Continued)*

been associated (rarely) with pseudotumor cerebri. May cause photosensitivity; discontinue if skin erythema occurs. May cause overgrowth of nonsusceptible organisms, including fungi; discontinue if superinfection occurs. Avoid use in children ≤8 years of age.

Adverse Reactions Frequency not defined.

Cardiovascular: Myocarditis, pericarditis, vasculitis

Central nervous system: Bulging fontanels, dizziness, fatigue, fever, headache, hypoesthesia, malaise, mood changes, paresthesia, pseudotumor cerebri, sedation, seizure, somnolence, vertigo

Dermatologic: Alopecia, angioedema, erythema multiforme, erythema nodosum, erythematous rash, exfoliative dermatitis, hyperpigmentation of nails, maculopapular rash, photosensitivity, pigmentation of the skin and mucous membranes, pruritus, Stevens-Johnson syndrome, toxic epidermal necrolysis, urticaria

Endocrine & metabolic: Thyroid discoloration, thyroid dysfunction

Gastrointestinal: Anorexia, diarrhea, dyspepsia, dysphagia, enamel hypoplasia, enterocolitis, esophageal ulcerations, esophagitis, glossitis, inflammatory lesions (oral/anogenital), moniliasis, nausea, oral cavity discoloration, pancreatitis, pseudomembranous colitis, stomatitis, tooth discoloration, vomiting, xerostomia

Genitourinary: Balanitis, vulvovaginitis

Hematologic: Agranulocytosis, eosinophilia, hemolytic anemia, leukopenia, neutropenia, pancytopenia, thrombocytopenia

Hepatic: Hepatic cholestasis, hepatic failure, hepatitis, hyperbilirubinemia, jaundice, liver enzyme increases

Neuromuscular & skeletal: Arthralgia, arthritis, bone discoloration, joint stiffness, joint swelling, myalgia

Otic: Hearing loss, tinnitus

Renal: Acute renal failure, BUN increased, interstitial nephritis

Respiratory: Asthma, bronchospasm, cough, dyspnea, pneumonitis, pulmonary infiltrate (with eosinophilia)

Miscellaneous: Anaphylaxis, hypersensitivity, lupus erythematosus, lupus-like syndrome, serum sickness

Overdosage/Toxicology Symptoms include diabetes insipidus, nausea, anorexia, dizziness, vomiting, and diarrhea. Following GI decontamination, care is symptom-directed and supportive. Fluid support may be required. Not dialyzable (0% to 5%).

Drug Interactions

Increased Effect/Toxicity: Minocycline may increase the effect of warfarin. Retinoic acid derivatives may increase risk of pseudotumor cerebri.

Decreased Effect: Calcium-, magnesium-, or aluminum-containing antacids, bile acid sequestrants, bismuth, oral contraceptives, iron, zinc, sodium bicarbonate, penicillins, cimetidine, quinapril may decrease absorption of tetracyclines. Methoxyflurane anesthesia (when concurrent with tetracyclines) may cause fatal nephrotoxicity. Tetracyclines may reduce bactericidal efficacy of penicillins and cephalosporins. Tetracycline may reduce the efficacy of the live, attenuated typhoid vaccine (Ty21a).

Ethanol/Nutrition/Herb Interactions

Food: Minocycline serum concentrations are not significantly altered if taken with food or dairy products.

Herb/Nutraceutical: Avoid dong quai, St John's wort (may also cause photosensitization).

Stability

Capsule (including pellet-filled), tablet: Store at 20°C to 25°C (68°F to 77°F). Protect from light and moisture.

Extended release tablet: Store at 15°C to 30°C (59°F to 86°F). Protect from light, moisture, and heat.

Mechanism of Action Inhibits bacterial protein synthesis by binding with the 30S and possibly the 50S ribosomal subunit(s) of susceptible bacteria; cell wall synthesis is not affected

Pharmacodynamics/Kinetics

Absorption: Well absorbed

Distribution: Majority deposits for extended periods in fat; crosses placenta; enters breast milk

Protein binding: 70% to 75%

Half-life elimination: 16 hours (range: 11-23 hours)

Time to peak: Capsule, pellet filled: 1-4 hours; Extended release tablet: 3.5-4 hours

Excretion: Urine

Dosage

Usual dosage range:

Children >8 years: Oral: Initial: 4 mg/kg, followed by 2 mg/kg/dose every 12 hours

Adults: Oral: Initial: 200 mg, followed by 100 mg every 12 hours (maximum: 400 mg/day)

Indication-specific dosing:

Children ≥12 years: **Acne** *(inflammatory, non-nodular, moderate-to-severe)* (Solodyn™): Oral:

45-59 kg: 45 mg once daily

60-90 kg: 90 mg once daily

91-136 kg: 135 mg once daily

Note: Therapy should be continued for 12 weeks. Higher doses do not confer greater efficacy, and safety of use beyond 12 weeks has not been established.

Adults: Oral:

Acne: Capsule or immediate-release tablet: 50-100 mg daily

Inflammatory, non-nodular, moderate-to-severe (Solodyn™):

45-59 kg: 45 mg once daily

60-90 kg: 90 mg once daily

91-136 kg: 135 mg once daily

Note: Therapy should be continued for 12 weeks. Higher doses do not confer greater efficacy, and safety of use beyond 12 weeks has not been established.

Chlamydial or *Ureaplasma urealyticum* infection, uncomplicated: Urethral, endocervical, or rectal: 100 mg every 12 hours for at least 7 days

Gonococcal infection, uncomplicated (males):

Without urethritis or anorectal infection: Initial: 200 mg, followed by 100 mg every 12 hours for at least 4 days (cultures 2-3 days post-therapy)

Urethritis: 100 mg every 12 hours for 5 days

Meningococcal carrier state: 100 mg every 12 hours for 5 days

Mycobacterium marinum: 100 mg every 12 hours for 6-8 weeks

Nocardiosis, cutaneous (non-CNS): 100 mg every 12 hours

Syphilis: Initial: 200 mg, followed by 100 mg every 12 hours for 10-15 days

Dosage adjustment in renal impairment: Consider decreasing dose or increasing dosing interval; total daily dose should not exceed 200 mg

Dietary Considerations May be taken with food or milk.

Administration May be taken with food or milk. Administer with adequate fluid to decrease the risk of esophageal irritation and ulceration.

Monitoring Parameters Culture and sensitivity testing prior to initiating therapy; LFTs, BUN, renal function with long-term treatment; if symptomatic for autoimmune disorder, include ANA, CBC

Test Interactions May cause interference with fluorescence test for urinary catecholamines (false elevations)

Dosage Forms

Capsule: 50 mg, 75 mg, 100 mg

Dynacin®: 75 mg, 100 mg

Capsule, pellet filled: 50 mg, 100 mg

Minocin®: 50 mg, 100 mg

Tablet: 50 mg, 75 mg, 100 mg

Dynacin®, myrac™: 50 mg, 75 mg, 100 mg

Tablet, extended release:

Solodyn™: 45 mg, 90 mg, 135 mg

♦ **Minocycline Hydrochloride** *see* Minocycline *on page 1149*

♦ **Min-Ovral® (Can)** *see* Ethinyl Estradiol and Levonorgestrel *on page 653*

♦ **Minox (Can)** *see* Minoxidil *on page 1151*

Minoxidil (mi NOKS i dil)

U.S. Brand Names Rogaine® Extra Strength for Men [OTC]; Rogaine® for Men [OTC]; Rogaine® for Women [OTC]

Canadian Brand Names Apo-Gain®; Minox; Rogaine®

Pharmacologic Category Topical Skin Product; Vasodilator

Additional Appendix Information

Hypertension *on page 2063*

Use Management of severe hypertension (usually in combination with a diuretic and beta-blocker); treatment (topical formulation) of alopecia androgenetica in males and females

Pregnancy Risk Factor C

Medication Safety Issues

Sound-alike/look-alike issues:

Minoxidil may be confused with metolazone, Monopril®, Noxafil®

International issues:

Noxidil® [Thailand] may be confused with Noxafil® which is a brand name for posaconazole in the U.S.

Contraindications Hypersensitivity to minoxidil or any component of the formulation; pheochromocytoma; acute MI; dissecting aortic aneurysm

Warnings/Precautions [U.S. Boxed Warning]: Minoxidil can cause pericardial effusion, occasionally progressing to tamponade and it can exacerbate angina pectoris; use with caution in patients with pulmonary hypertension, significant renal failure, or CHF; use with caution in patients with coronary artery disease or recent myocardial infarction; renal failure or dialysis patients may require smaller doses; usually used with a beta-blocker (to treat minoxidil-induced tachycardia) and a diuretic (for treatment of water retention/edema); may take 1-6 months for hypertrichosis to totally reverse after minoxidil therapy is discontinued.

Adverse Reactions

>10%:

Cardiovascular: CHF, edema, ECG (transient change in T-wave amplitude and direction), tachycardia

Dermatologic: Hypertrichosis (commonly occurs within 1-2 months of therapy)

1% to 10%: Endocrine & metabolic: Fluid and electrolyte imbalance

<1% (Limited to important or life-threatening): Angina, coarsening facial features, leukopenia, pericardial effusion tamponade, rash, Stevens-Johnson syndrome, thrombocytopenia, weight gain

Overdosage/Toxicology Symptoms include hypotension, tachycardia, headache, nausea, dizziness, weakness syncope, warm flushed skin and palpitations. Lethargy and ataxia may occur in children. Hypotension usually responds to I.V. fluids, Trendelenburg positioning or vasoconstrictor. Treatment is primarily supportive and symptomatic.

Drug Interactions

Increased Effect/Toxicity: Concurrent use of guanethidine can cause severe orthostasis; avoid concurrent use - discontinue 1-3 weeks prior to initiating minoxidil. Effects of other antihypertensives may be additive with minoxidil.

Ethanol/Nutrition/Herb Interactions Herb/Nutraceutical: Avoid natural licorice (causes sodium and water retention and increases potassium loss).

Stability Store at controlled room temperature of 20°C to 25°C (68°F to 77°F).

Mechanism of Action Produces vasodilation by directly relaxing arteriolar smooth muscle, with little effect on veins; effects may be mediated by cyclic AMP; stimulation of hair growth is (Continued)

Minoxidil (Continued)

secondary to vasodilation, increased cutaneous blood flow and stimulation of resting hair follicles

Pharmacodynamics/Kinetics
Onset of action: Hypotensive: Oral: ~30 minutes
  Peak effect: 2-8 hours
Duration: 2-5 days
Protein binding: None
Metabolism: 88%, primarily via glucuronidation
Bioavailability: Oral: 90%
Half-life elimination: Adults: 3.5-4.2 hours
Excretion: Urine (12% as unchanged drug)

Dosage
Children <12 years: Hypertension: Oral: Initial: 0.1-0.2 mg/kg once daily; maximum: 5 mg/day; increase gradually every 3 days; usual dosage: 0.25-1 mg/kg/day in 1-2 divided doses; maximum: 50 mg/day

Children >12 years and Adults: Hypertension: Oral: Initial: 5 mg once daily, increase gradually every 3 days (maximum: 100 mg/day); usual dose range (JNC 7): 2.5-80 mg/day in 1-2 divided doses

Adults: Alopecia: Topical: Apply twice daily; 4 months of therapy may be necessary for hair growth.

Elderly: Initial: 2.5 mg once daily; increase gradually.

Note: Dosage adjustment is needed when added to concomitant therapy.

Dialysis: Supplemental dose is not necessary via hemo- or peritoneal dialysis.

Monitoring Parameters Blood pressure, standing and sitting/supine; fluid and electrolyte balance and body weight should be monitored

Dosage Forms
Aerosol, topical [foam]:
  Men's Rogaine®: 5% (60 g)
Solution, topical: 2% (60 mL); 5% (60 mL)
  Rogaine® for Men, Rogaine® for Women: 2% (60 mL) [supplied with dropper applicator]
  Rogaine® Extra Strength for Men: 5% (60 mL) [supplied with dropper applicator]
Tablet: 2.5 mg, 10 mg

- ◆ **Mintab DM** see Guaifenesin and Dextromethorphan on page 816
- ◆ **Mintezol®** see Thiabendazole on page 1667
- ◆ **Mintox Extra Strength [OTC]** see Aluminum Hydroxide, Magnesium Hydroxide, and Simethicone on page 85
- ◆ **Mintox Plus [OTC]** see Aluminum Hydroxide, Magnesium Hydroxide, and Simethicone on page 85
- ◆ **Miochol®-E** see Acetylcholine on page 38
- ◆ **Miostat®** see Carbachol on page 284
- ◆ **MiraLax™** see Polyethylene Glycol 3350 on page 1387
- ◆ **Mirapex®** see Pramipexole on page 1406
- ◆ **Mircette®** see Ethinyl Estradiol and Desogestrel on page 645
- ◆ **Mirena®** see Levonorgestrel on page 1004

Mirtazapine (mir TAZ a peen)

U.S. Brand Names Remeron®; Remeron SolTab®

Canadian Brand Names CO Mirtazapine; Gen-Mirtazapine; Novo-Mirtazapine; PMS-Mirtazapine; ratio-Mirtazapine; Remeron®; Remeron® RD; Rhoxal-mirtazapine; Rhoxal-mirtazapine FC; Riva-Mirtazapine; Sandoz-Mirtazapine; Sandoz-Mirtazapine FC

Pharmacologic Category Antidepressant, Alpha-2 Antagonist

Additional Appendix Information
Antidepressant Agents on page 1866

Use Treatment of depression

Restrictions An FDA-approved medication guide concerning the use of antidepressants in children and teenagers must be distributed when dispensing an outpatient prescription (new or refill) where this medication is to be used without direct supervision of a healthcare provider. Medication guides are available at http://www.fda.gov/cder/Offices/ODS/medication_guides.htm. Dispense to parents or guardians of children and teenagers receiving this medication.

Pregnancy Risk Factor C

Pregnancy Implications Animal studies did not show teratogenic effects, however, there was an increase in fetal loss and decrease in birth weight; use during pregnancy only if clearly needed.

Lactation Excretion in breast milk unknown/not recommended

Medication Safety Issues
Sound-alike/look-alike issues:
  Remeron® may be confused with Premarin®, Zemuron®

International issues:
  Avanza® [Australia] may be confused with Albenza® which is a brand name for albendazole in the U.S.
  Avanza® [Australia] may be confused with Avandia® which is a brand name for rosiglitazone in the U.S.
  Remeron® my be confused with Reneuron® which is a brand name for fluoxetine in Spain

Contraindications Hypersensitivity to mirtazapine or any component of the formulation; use of MAO inhibitors within 14 days

Warnings/Precautions [U.S. Boxed Warning]: Antidepressants increase the risk of suicidal thinking and behavior in children and adolescents with major depressive disorder (MDD) and other depressive disorders; consider risk prior to prescribing. All patients must be closely monitored for clinical worsening, suicidality, or unusual changes in behavior, especially during the initiation of therapy or following an increase or decrease in dosage. When used in children, the child's family or caregiver should be instructed to closely observe the patient and communicate condition with healthcare provider. A medication guide should be dispensed with each prescription. **Mirtazapine is not FDA approved for use in children.**

The possibility of a suicide attempt is inherent in major depression and may persist until remission occurs. Use caution in high-risk patients. Worsening depression and severe abrupt suicidality that are not part of the presenting symptoms may require discontinuation or modification of drug therapy. The patient's family or caregiver should be alerted to monitor patients for the emergence of suicidality and associated behaviors (such as agitation, irritability, hostility, impulsivity, and hypomania) and call healthcare provider.

May worsen psychosis in some patients or precipitate a shift to mania or hypomania in patients with bipolar disorder. Patients presenting with depressive symptoms should be screened for bipolar disorder. Monotherapy in patients with bipolar disorder should be avoided. **Mirtazapine is not FDA approved for the treatment of bipolar depression.**

Discontinue immediately if signs and symptoms of neutropenia/agranulocytosis occur. May cause sedation, resulting in impaired performance of tasks requiring alertness (eg, operating machinery or driving). Sedative effects may be additive with other CNS depressants and/or ethanol. The degree of sedation is moderate-high relative to other antidepressants. The risks of orthostatic hypotension or anticholinergic effects are low relative to other antidepressants. The incidence of sexual dysfunction with mirtazapine is generally lower than with SSRIs.

May increase appetite and stimulate weight gain. Weight gain of >7% of body weight reported in 7.5% of patients treated with mirtazapine compared to 0% for placebo; 8% of patients receiving mirtazapine discontinued treatment due to the weight gain. In an 8-week pediatric clinical trial, 49% of mirtazapine-treated patients had a weight gain of at least 7% (mean increase 4 kg) as compared to 5.7% of placebo-treated patients (mean increase 1 kg). May increase serum cholesterol and triglyceride levels.

Use caution in patients with a previous seizure disorder or condition predisposing to seizures such as brain damage, alcoholism, or concurrent therapy with other drugs which lower the seizure threshold. Use with caution in patients with hepatic or renal dysfunction and in elderly patients. SolTab® formulation contains phenylalanine.

Adverse Reactions

>10%:
Central nervous system: Somnolence (54%)
Endocrine & metabolic: Cholesterol increased
Gastrointestinal: Constipation (13%), xerostomia (25%), appetite increased (17%), weight gain (12%; weight gain of >7% reported in 8% of adults, ≤49% of pediatric patients)

1% to 10%:
Cardiovascular: Hypertension, vasodilatation, peripheral edema (2%), edema (1%)
Central nervous system: Dizziness (7%), abnormal dreams (4%), abnormal thoughts (3%), confusion (2%), malaise
Endocrine & metabolic: Triglycerides increased
Gastrointestinal: Vomiting, anorexia, abdominal pain
Genitourinary: Urinary frequency (2%)
Neuromuscular & skeletal: Myalgia (2%), back pain (2%), arthralgia, tremor (2%), weakness (8%)
Respiratory: Dyspnea (1%)
Miscellaneous: Flu-like syndrome (5%), thirst (<1%)

<1% (Limited to important or life-threatening): Agranulocytosis, dehydration, liver function test increases, lymphadenopathy, neutropenia, orthostatic hypotension, seizure (1 case reported), torsade de pointes (1 case reported), weight loss

Drug Interactions

Cytochrome P450 Effect: Substrate of CYP1A2 (major), 2C9 (minor), 2D6 (major), 3A4 (major); **Inhibits** CYP1A2 (weak), 3A4 (weak)

Increased Effect/Toxicity: Contraindicated with drugs which inhibit MAO (including linezolid, selegiline, sibutramine, and MAOIs); severe/fatal reactions may occur. CYP1A2 inhibitors may increase the levels/effects of mirtazapine; example inhibitors include ciprofloxacin, fluvoxamine, ketoconazole, norfloxacin, ofloxacin, and rofecoxib. CYP2D6 inhibitors may increase the levels/effects of mirtazapine; example inhibitors include chlorpromazine, delavirdine, fluoxetine, miconazole, paroxetine, pergolide, quinidine, quinine, ritonavir, and ropinirole. CYP3A4 inhibitors may increase the levels/effects of mirtazapine; example inhibitors include azole antifungals, clarithromycin, diclofenac, doxycycline, erythromycin, imatinib, isoniazid, nefazodone, nicardipine, propofol, protease inhibitors, quinidine, telithromycin, and verapamil. Increased sedative effect seen with CNS depressants.

Decreased Effect: CYP1A2 inducers may decrease the levels/effects of mirtazapine; example inducers include aminoglutethimide, carbamazepine, phenobarbital, and rifampin. Decreased effect seen with clonidine. CYP3A4 inducers may decrease the levels/effects of mirtazapine; example inducers include aminoglutethimide, carbamazepine, nafcillin, nevirapine, phenobarbital, phenytoin, and rifamycins.

Ethanol/Nutrition/Herb Interactions

Ethanol: Avoid ethanol (may increase CNS depression).
Herb/Nutraceutical: Avoid St John's wort (may decrease mirtazapine levels). Avoid valerian, St John's wort, SAMe, kava kava (may increase CNS depression).

Stability Store at controlled room temperature.
SolTab®: Protect from light and moisture. Use immediately upon opening tablet blister.

Mechanism of Action Mirtazapine is a tetracyclic antidepressant that works by its central presynaptic alpha₂-adrenergic antagonist effects, which results in increased release of norepinephrine and serotonin. It is also a potent antagonist of 5-HT₂ and 5-HT₃ serotonin receptors and H1 histamine receptors and a moderate peripheral alpha₁-adrenergic and muscarinic antagonist; it does not inhibit the reuptake of norepinephrine or serotonin.
(Continued)

Mirtazapine *(Continued)*

Pharmacodynamics/Kinetics
Protein binding: 85%

Metabolism: Extensively hepatic via CYP1A2, 2C9, 2D6, 3A4 and via demethylation and hydroxylation

Bioavailability: 50%

Half-life elimination: 20-40 hours; hampered with renal or hepatic impairment

Time to peak, serum: 2 hours

Excretion: Urine (75%) and feces (15%) as metabolites

Dosage
Children: Safety and efficacy in children have not been established

Treatment of depression: Adults: Oral: Initial: 15 mg nightly, titrate up to 15-45 mg/day with dose increases made no more frequently than every 1-2 weeks; there is an inverse relationship between dose and sedation

Elderly: Decreased clearance seen (40% males, 10% females); no specific dosage adjustment recommended by manufacturer

Dosage adjustment in renal impairment:
Cl_{cr} 11-39 mL/minute: 30% decreased clearance
Cl_{cr} <10 mL/minute: 50% decreased clearance

Dosage adjustment in hepatic impairment: Clearance decreased by 30%

Dietary Considerations Remeron SolTab® contains phenylalanine: 2.6 mg per 15 mg tablet; 5.2 mg per 30 mg tablet; 7.8 mg per 45 mg tablet

Administration SolTab®: Open blister pack and place tablet on the tongue. Do not split tablet. Tablet is formulated to dissolve on the tongue without water.

Monitoring Parameters Patients should be monitored for signs of agranulocytosis or severe neutropenia such as sore throat, stomatitis or other signs of infection or a low WBC; mental status for depression, suicidal ideation (especially at the beginning of therapy or when doses are increased or decreased), anxiety, social functioning, mania, panic attacks; lipid profile

Additional Information Note: At least 14 days should elapse between discontinuation of an MAO inhibitor and initiation of therapy with mirtazapine; at least 14 days should be allowed after discontinuing mirtazapine before starting an MAO inhibitor.

Dosage Forms
Tablet (Remeron®): 15 mg, 30 mg, 45 mg

Tablet, orally disintegrating: 15 mg, 30 mg

Remeron SolTab®:
15 mg [contains phenylalanine 2.6 mg/tablet; orange flavor]
30 mg [contains phenylalanine 5.2 mg/tablet; orange flavor]
45 mg [contains phenylalanine 7.8 mg/tablet; orange flavor]

Misoprostol *(mye soe PROST ole)*

U.S. Brand Names Cytotec®

Canadian Brand Names Apo-Misoprostol®; Novo-Misoprostol

Pharmacologic Category Prostaglandin

Use Prevention of NSAID-induced gastric ulcers; medical termination of pregnancy of ≤49 days (in conjunction with mifepristone)

Unlabeled/Investigational Use Cervical ripening and labor induction; NSAID-induced nephropathy; fat malabsorption in cystic fibrosis

Pregnancy Risk Factor X

Pregnancy Implications Misoprostol is an abortifacient. During pregnancy, use to prevent NSAID-induced ulcers is contraindicated. Reports of fetal death, congenital anomalies, uterine perforation, and abortion have been received after the use of misoprostol in pregnancy.

Lactation Excretion in breast milk unknown/contraindicated

Medication Safety Issues
Sound-alike/look-alike issues:
Misoprostol may be confused with metoprolol
Cytotec® may be confused with Cytoxan®, Sytobex®

Contraindications Hypersensitivity to misoprostol, prostaglandins, or any component of the formulation; pregnancy (when used to reduce NSAID-induced ulcers)

Warnings/Precautions Safety and efficacy have not been established in children <18 years of age; use with caution in patients with renal impairment and the elderly. **[U.S. Boxed Warning]: Not to be used in pregnant women or women of childbearing potential unless woman is capable of complying with effective contraceptive measures;** therapy is normally begun on the second or third day of next normal menstrual period. Uterine perforation and/or rupture have been reported in association with intravaginal use to induce labor or with combined oral/intravaginal use to induce abortion. Should not be used as a cervical-ripening agent for induction of labor. However, The American College of Obstetricians and Gynecologists (ACOG) continues to support this off-label use.

Adverse Reactions
>10%: Gastrointestinal: Diarrhea, abdominal pain

1% to 10%:
Central nervous system: Headache
Gastrointestinal: Constipation, flatulence, nausea, dyspepsia, vomiting

<1% (Limited to important or life-threatening): Anaphylaxis, anxiety, appetite changes, arrhythmia, arterial thrombosis, bronchospasm, confusion, cramps, depression, drowsiness, edema, fetal or infant death (when used during pregnancy), fever, GI bleeding, GI inflammation, gingivitis, gout, hyper-/hypotension, impotence, loss of libido, MI, neuropathy, neurosis, pulmonary embolism, purpura, rash, reflux, rigors, thrombocytopenia, uterine rupture, weakness, weight changes

Overdosage/Toxicology Symptoms include sedation, tremor, convulsions, dyspnea, abdominal pain, diarrhea, hypotension, and bradycardia.

Drug Interactions
Increased Effect/Toxicity: Misoprostol may increase the effect of oxytocin; wait 6-12 hours after misoprostol administration before initiating oxytocin.
Ethanol/Nutrition/Herb Interactions Food: Misoprostol peak serum concentrations may be decreased if taken with food (not clinically significant).
Stability Store at or below 25°C (77°F).
Mechanism of Action Misoprostol is a synthetic prostaglandin E_1 analog that replaces the protective prostaglandins consumed with prostaglandin-inhibiting therapies (eg, NSAIDs); has been shown to induce uterine contractions
Pharmacodynamics/Kinetics
Absorption: Rapid
Metabolism: Hepatic; rapidly de-esterified to misoprostol acid (active)
Half-life elimination: Metabolite: 20-40 minutes
Time to peak, serum: Active metabolite: Fasting: 15-30 minutes
Excretion: Urine (64% to 73%) and feces (15%) within 24 hours
Dosage
Oral:
Children 8-16 years: Fat absorption in cystic fibrosis (unlabeled use): 100 mcg 4 times/day
Adults:
Prevention of NSAID-induced gastric ulcers: 200 mcg 4 times/day with food; if not tolerated, may decrease dose to 100 mcg 4 times/day with food or 200 mcg twice daily with food; last dose of the day should be taken at bedtime
Medical termination of pregnancy: Refer to Mifepristone monograph.
Intravaginal: Adults: Labor induction or cervical ripening (unlabeled uses): 25 mcg (¼ of 100 mcg tablet); may repeat at intervals no more frequent than every 3-6 hours. Do not use in patients with previous cesarean delivery or prior major uterine surgery.
Dietary Considerations Should be taken with food; incidence of diarrhea may be lessened by having patient take dose right after meals.
Administration Incidence of diarrhea may be lessened by having patient take dose right after meals. Therapy is usually begun on the second or third day of the next normal menstrual period.
Dosage Forms Tablet: 100 mcg, 200 mcg

♦ **Misoprostol and Diclofenac** see Diclofenac and Misoprostol on page 494

Mitomycin (mye toe MYE sin)

U.S. Brand Names Mutamycin®
Canadian Brand Names Mutamycin®
Index Terms Mitomycin-C; Mitomycin-X; MTC; NSC-26980
Pharmacologic Category Antineoplastic Agent, Antibiotic
Use Treatment of adenocarcinoma of stomach or pancreas, bladder cancer, breast cancer, or colorectal cancer
Unlabeled/Investigational Use Prevention of excess scarring in glaucoma filtration procedures in patients at high risk of bleb failure
Pregnancy Risk Factor D
Pregnancy Implications Mitomycin can cause fetal harm in humans. Animal studies show delayed fetal development, fetal external anomalies, and neonatal anomalies.
Lactation Enters breast milk/contraindicated
Medication Safety Issues
Sound-alike/look-alike issues:
Mitomycin may be confused with mithramycin, mitotane, mitoxantrone
High alert medication: The Institute for Safe Medication Practices (ISMP) includes this medication among its list of drugs which have a heightened risk of causing significant patient harm when used in error.
Contraindications Hypersensitivity to mitomycin or any component of the formulation; thrombocytopenia; coagulation disorders, increased bleeding tendency; pregnancy
Warnings/Precautions Hazardous agent - use appropriate precautions for handling and disposal. **[U.S. Boxed Warning]: May cause bone marrow suppression (thrombocytopenia and leukopenia);** monitor for infections. Use with caution in patients who have received radiation therapy or in the presence of hepatobiliary dysfunction; reduce dosage in patients who are receiving radiation therapy simultaneously. Monitor for renal toxicity; do not administer if serum creatinine is >1.7 mg/dL. **[U.S. Boxed Warning]: Hemolytic-uremic syndrome, potentially fatal, has been reported;** is correlated with total dose (single doses ≥60 mg or cumulative doses ≥50 mg/m²) and total duration of therapy (>5-11 months). Bladder fibrosis/contraction has been reported with intravesical administration. **Mitomycin is a potent vesicant, may cause ulceration, necrosis, cellulitis, and tissue sloughing if infiltrated.** Shortness of breath and bronchospasm have been reported in patients receiving vinca alkaloids in combination with or after mitomycin; may be managed with bronchodilators, steroids and/or oxygen. Safety and efficacy in children have not been established. **[U.S. Boxed Warning]: Should be administered under the supervision of an experienced cancer chemotherapy physician.**
Adverse Reactions
>10%:
Cardiovascular: CHF (3% to 15%) (doses >30 mg/m²)
Central nervous system: Fever (14%)
Dermatologic: Alopecia, nail banding/discoloration
Gastrointestinal: Nausea, vomiting and anorexia (14%)
Hematologic: Anemia (19% to 24%); myelosuppression, common, dose-limiting, delayed
Onset: 3 weeks
Nadir: 4-6 weeks
Recovery: 6-8 weeks
(Continued)

Mitomycin *(Continued)*

1% to 10%:
Dermatologic: Rash
Gastrointestinal: Stomatitis
Neuromuscular: Paresthesias
Renal: Creatinine increase (2%)
Respiratory: Interstitial pneumonitis, infiltrates, dyspnea, cough (7%)

<1% (Limited to important or life-threatening): Extravasation reactions, hemolytic uremic syndrome, malaise, pruritus, renal failure, bladder fibrosis/contraction (intravesical administration)

Overdosage/Toxicology Symptoms include bone marrow suppression, nausea, vomiting, and alopecia.

Drug Interactions
Increased Effect/Toxicity: *Vinca* alkaloids or doxorubicin may enhance cardiac toxicity when coadministered with mitomycin.

Ethanol/Nutrition/Herb Interactions Herb/Nutraceutical: Avoid black cohosh, dong quai in estrogen-dependent tumors.

Stability Store intact vials at controlled room temperature. Dilute powder with SWFI or 0.9% sodium chloride to a concentration of 0.5-1 mg/mL. Solution is stable for 7 days at room temperature and 14 days when refrigerated if protected from light. Solution of 0.5 mg/mL in a syringe is stable for 7 days at room temperature and 14 days when refrigerated and protected from light.
Further dilution to 20-40 mcg/mL:
In normal saline: Stable for 12 hours at room temperature.
In sodium lactate: Stable for 24 hours at room temperature.

Mechanism of Action Acts like an alkylating agent and produces DNA cross-linking (primarily with guanine and cytosine pairs); cell-cycle nonspecific; inhibits DNA and RNA synthesis; degrades preformed DNA, causes nuclear lysis and formation of giant cells. While not phase-specific *per se*, mitomycin has its maximum effect against cells in late G and early S phases.

Pharmacodynamics/Kinetics
Distribution: V_d: 22 L/m^2; high drug concentrations found in kidney, tongue, muscle, heart, and lung tissue; probably not distributed into the CNS
Metabolism: Hepatic
Half-life elimination: 23-78 minutes; Terminal: 50 minutes
Excretion: Urine (<10% as unchanged drug), with elevated serum concentrations

Dosage Refer to individual protocols. Children (unlabeled use) and Adults:
Single agent therapy: I.V.: 20 mg/m^2 every 6-8 weeks
Combination therapy: I.V.: 10 mg/m^2 every 6-8 weeks
Bladder carcinoma: Intravesicular instillation (unapproved route): 20-40 mg instilled into the bladder and retained for 3 hours up to 3 times/week for up to 20 procedures per course
Glaucoma surgery (unlabeled use): 0.2-0.5 mg (0.2-0.5 mg/mL solution)

Dosage adjustment in renal impairment: Varying approaches to dosing adjustments have been published; one representative recommendation: Cl_{cr} <10 mL/minute: Administer 75% of normal dose
Note: The manufacturers state that products should not be given to patients with serum creatinine >1.7 mg/dL.
Hemodialysis: Unknown
CAPD effects: Unknown
CAVH effects: Unknown
Dosage adjustment in hepatic impairment: Although some mitomycin may be excreted in the bile, no specific guidelines regarding dosage adjustment in hepatic impairment can be made.

Administration
I.V.: Administer slow I.V. push or by slow (15-30 minute) infusion via a freely-running dextrose or saline infusion. Consider use a central venous catheter.
Intravesicular (unlabeled route): Instill into bladder for up to 3 hours (rotate patient every 15-30 minutes)
Glaucoma surgery (unlabeled route): Apply to pledget and place in contact with surgical wound for 2-5 minutes (doses and techniques may vary)

Monitoring Parameters Platelet count, CBC with differential, hemoglobin, prothrombin time, renal and pulmonary function tests

Dosage Forms Injection, powder for reconstitution: 5 mg, 20 mg, 40 mg

♦ **Mitomycin-X** *see Mitomycin on page 1155*
♦ **Mitomycin-C** *see Mitomycin on page 1155*

Mitotane *(MYE toe tane)*

U.S. Brand Names Lysodren®
Canadian Brand Names Lysodren®
Index Terms NSC-38721; o,p'-DDD
Pharmacologic Category Antineoplastic Agent, Miscellaneous
Use Treatment of adrenocortical carcinoma
Unlabeled/Investigational Use Treatment of Cushing's syndrome
Pregnancy Risk Factor C
Pregnancy Implications Animal studies have not been conducted. There are no adequate and well-controlled studies in pregnant women. Use during pregnancy only if clearly needed.
Lactation Excretion in breast milk unknown/not recommended
Medication Safety Issues
Sound-alike/look-alike issues:
Mitotane may be confused with mitomycin

High alert medication: The Institute for Safe Medication Practices (ISMP) includes this medication among its list of drugs which have a heightened risk of causing significant patient harm when used in error.

Contraindications Hypersensitivity to mitotane or any component of the formulation

Warnings/Precautions Hazardous agent - use appropriate precautions for handling and disposal. Steroid replacement with glucocorticoid, and sometimes mineralocorticoid, is necessary. It has been recommended that replacement therapy be initiated at the start of therapy, rather than waiting for evidence of adrenal insufficiency. Because mitotane can increase the metabolism of hydrocortisone, higher than usual replacement doses of the latter may be required. Surgically remove tumor tissues from metastatic masses prior to initiation of treatment; rapid cytotoxic effect may cause tumor hemorrhage. Observe patients for neuro-toxicity with long term (> 2 years) use. Use caution with hepatic impairment; metabolism may be decreased. **[U.S. Boxed Warnings]: Acute adrenal insufficiency may occur in the face of shock, trauma, or infection. Mitotane should be discontinued temporarily in this setting and appropriate steroid coverage should be administered. Should be administered under the supervision of an experienced cancer chemotherapy physician.** Safety and efficacy in children have not been established.

Adverse Reactions
>10%:
 Central nervous system: CNS depression (32%), somnolence (25%), dizziness/vertigo (15%)
 Dermatologic: Skin rash (15%)
 Gastrointestinal: Anorexia (24%), nausea (39%), vomiting (37%), diarrhea (13%)
 Neuromuscular & skeletal: Weakness (12%)
1% to 10%:
 Central nervous system: Headache (5%), confusion (3%)
 Neuromuscular & skeletal: Muscle tremor (3%)
<1% and/or frequency not defined: Albuminuria, blurred vision, diplopia, flushing, hematuria, hemorrhagic cystitis, hypertension, hyperpyrexia, lens opacity, myalgia, orthostatic hypotension, protein bound iodine decreased, toxic retinopathy

Overdosage/Toxicology Symptoms include diarrhea, vomiting, numbness of limbs, and weakness.

Drug Interactions
 Decreased Effect: Potassium-sparing diuretics (spironolactone) may decrease the effect of mitotane. Mitotane may decrease the effects of warfarin.

Ethanol/Nutrition/Herb Interactions Ethanol: Avoid ethanol (may increase CNS depression).

Stability Store at room temperature.

Mechanism of Action Causes adrenal cortical atrophy; drug affects mitochondria in adrenal cortical cells and decreases production of cortisol; also alters the peripheral metabolism of steroids

Pharmacodynamics/Kinetics
 Absorption: Oral: ~35% to 40%
 Distribution: Stored mainly in fat tissue but is found in all body tissues
 Metabolism: Hepatic and other tissues
 Half-life elimination: 18-159 days
 Time to peak, serum: 3-5 hours
 Excretion: Urine (10% as metabolites) and feces (1% to 17% as metabolites)

Dosage Adrenocortical carcinoma: Oral:
 Children (unlabeled use): 1-2 g/day in divided doses, increasing gradually to a maximum of 5-7 g/day
 Adults: Start at 2-6 g/day in 3-4 divided doses, then increase incrementally to 9-10 g/day in 3-4 divided doses (maximum daily dose: 18 g)
 Dosing adjustment in hepatic impairment: Dose may need to be decreased in patients with liver disease

Monitoring Parameters Adrenal function; neurologic assessments with chronic (>2 years) use

Dosage Forms
 Tablet [scored]:
 Lysodren®: 500 mg

Mitoxantrone (mye toe ZAN trone)

U.S. Brand Names Novantrone®
Canadian Brand Names Mitoxantrone Injection®; Novantrone®
Index Terms DAD; DHAD; DHAQ; Dihydroxyanthracenedione Dihydrochloride; Mitoxantrone Hydrochloride CL-232315; Mitoxantrone; NSC-301739
Pharmacologic Category Antineoplastic Agent, Anthracenedione
Use Treatment of acute leukemias, lymphoma, breast cancer, pediatric sarcoma, secondary progressive or relapsing-remitting multiple sclerosis, prostate cancer
Pregnancy Risk Factor D
Pregnancy Implications Adverse effects were noted in animal studies. May cause fetal harm if administered to a pregnant woman. There are no adequate and well-controlled studies in pregnant women. Pregnancy should be avoided while on treatment. Women with multiple sclerosis and who are biologically capable of becoming pregnant should have a pregnancy test prior to each dose.
Lactation Enters breast milk/contraindicated
Medication Safety Issues
 Sound-alike/look-alike issues:
 Mitoxantrone may be confused with methotrexate, mitomycin

 High alert medication: The Institute for Safe Medication Practices (ISMP) includes this medication among its list of drugs which have a heightened risk of causing significant patient harm when used in error.
 (Continued)

Mitoxantrone *(Continued)*

Contraindications Hypersensitivity to mitoxantrone or any component of the formulation; multiple sclerosis with left ventricular ejection fraction (LVEF) <50% or clinically significant decrease in LVEF; pregnancy

Warnings/Precautions Hazardous agent - use appropriate precautions for handling and disposal.

[U.S. Boxed Warning]: Do not use if baseline neutrophil count <1500 cells/mm³ (except for in the treatment of ANLL). Treatment may lead to severe myelosuppression; use with caution in patients with pre-existing myelosuppression.

[U.S. Boxed Warning]: May cause myocardial toxicity and potentially-fatal CHF; risk increases with cumulative dosing. Predisposing factors for mitoxantrone-induced cardiotoxicity include prior anthracycline therapy, prior cardiovascular disease, concomitant use of cardiotoxic drugs, and mediastinal/pericardial irradiation. Not recommended for use when left ventricular ejection fraction (LVEF) <50%. Use in multiple sclerosis should be limited to a cumulative dose of ≤140 mg/m², and discontinued if a significant decrease in LVEF is observed.

[U.S. Boxed Warnings]: For I.V. use only; may cause severe local tissue damage if extravasation occurs. Do not administer intrathecally; may cause serious and permanent neurologic damage. May cause urine, saliva, tears, and sweat to turn blue-green for 24 hours postinfusion. Whites of eyes may have blue-green tinge. **[U.S. Boxed Warning]: Has been associated with the development of secondary acute myelogenous leukemia and myelodysplasia.**

[U.S. Boxed Warning]: Should be administered under the supervision of an experienced cancer chemotherapy physician. Dosage should be reduced in patients with impaired hepatobiliary function; not for treatment of multiple sclerosis in patients with concurrent hepatic impairment. Not for treatment of primary progressive multiple sclerosis. Safety and efficacy in children have not been established.

Adverse Reactions Includes events reported with any indication; incidence varies based on treatment/dose

>10%:

Cardiovascular: Arrhythmia (3% to 18%), edema (10% to 31%), ECG changes (11%)

Central nervous system: Pain (8% to 41%), fatigue (up to 39%), fever (6% to 78%), headache (6% to 13%)

Dermatologic: Alopecia (20% to 61%), nail bed changes (11%)

Endocrine & metabolic: Amenorrhea (28% to 53%), menstrual disorder (26% to 61%), hyperglycemia (10% to 31%)

Gastrointestinal: Abdominal pain (9% to 15%), anorexia (22% to 25%), nausea (26% to 76%), constipation (10% to 16%), diarrhea (14% to 47%), GI bleeding (2% to 16%), mucositis (10% to 29%), stomatitis (8% to 29%), dyspepsia (5% to 14%), vomiting (6% to 11%), weight gain/loss (13% to 17%)

Genitourinary: Abnormal urine (6% to 11%), urinary tract infection (7% to 32%)

Hematologic: Neutropenia (79% to 100%), leukopenia (9% to 100%), lymphopenia (72% to 95%), anemia (5% to 75%), hemoglobin decreased (43%), thrombocytopenia (33% to 39%), petechiae/bruising (6% to 11%); myelosuppression (WBC: mild; platelets: mild; onset: 7-10 days; nadir: 14 days; recovery: 21 days)

Hepatic: Alkaline phosphatase increased (37%), transaminases increased (5% to 20%), GGT increased (3% to 15%)

Neuromuscular & skeletal: Weakness (24%)

Renal: BUN increased (22%), creatinine increased (13%), hematuria (11%)

Respiratory: Cough (5% to 13%), dyspnea (6% to 18%), upper respiratory tract infection (7% to 53%)

Miscellaneous: Fungal infection (9% to 15%), infection (4% to 18%), sepsis (ANLL 31% to 34%)

1% to 10%:

Cardiovascular: Ischemia (5%), LVEF decreased (≤5%), hypertension (4%), CHF (2% to 5%, risk is much lower with anthracyclines, some reports suggest cumulative doses >160 mg/mL cause CHF in ~10% of patients)

Central nervous system: Chills (5%), anxiety (5%), depression (5%), seizure (2% to 4%)

Dermatologic: Skin infection

Endocrine & metabolic: Hypocalcemia (10%), hypokalemia (7% to 10%), hyponatremia (9%), menorrhagia (7%)

Gastrointestinal: Aphthosis (10%)

Genitourinary: Impotence (7%), sterility (5%)

Hematologic: Granulocytopenia (6%), hemorrhage (6%)

Hepatic: Jaundice (3% to 7%)

Neuromuscular & skeletal: Back pain (8%), myalgia (5%), arthralgia (5%)

Ocular: Conjunctivitis (5%), blurred vision (3%)

Renal: Renal failure (8%), proteinuria (6%)

Respiratory: Rhinitis (10%), pneumonia (9%), sinusitis (6%)

Miscellaneous: Systemic infection, diaphoresis (9%), development of secondary leukemia (~1% to 2%)

<1% or frequency not defined (Limited to important or life-threatening): Acute leukemia, allergic reaction, anaphylactoid reactions, anaphylaxis, extravasation and phlebitis at the infusion site, interstitial pneumonitis (has occurred during combination chemotherapy), irritant chemotherapy with blue skin discoloration, rash, tachycardia

Overdosage/Toxicology Symptoms include leukopenia, tachycardia, and marrow hypoplasia. There is no known antidote.

Drug Interactions

Cytochrome P450 Effect: Inhibits CYP3A4 (weak)

Decreased Effect: Patients may experience impaired immune response to vaccines; possible infection after administration of live vaccines in patients receiving immunosuppressants.

Ethanol/Nutrition/Herb Interactions Herb/Nutraceutical: Avoid black cohosh, dong quai in estrogen-dependent tumors.

Stability Store intact vials at 15°C to 25°C (59°F to 77°F); do not freeze. Opened vials may be stored at room temperature for 7 days or under refrigeration for up to 14 days. Dilute in at least 50 mL of NS or D₅W. Solutions diluted for administration are stable for 7 days at room temperature or under refrigeration.

Mechanism of Action Analogue of the anthracyclines, mitoxantrone intercalates DNA; binds to nucleic acids and inhibits DNA and RNA synthesis by template disordering and steric obstruction; replication is decreased by binding to DNA topoisomerase II and seems to inhibit the incorporation of uridine into RNA and thymidine into DNA; active throughout entire cell cycle

Pharmacodynamics/Kinetics

Absorption: Oral: Poor

Distribution: V_d: 14 L/kg; distributes into pleural fluid, kidney, thyroid, liver, heart, and red blood cells

Protein binding: >95%, 76% to albumin

Metabolism: Hepatic; pathway not determined

Half-life elimination: Terminal: 23-215 hours; may be prolonged with hepatic impairment

Excretion: Urine (6% to 11%; 65% as unchanged drug); feces (25%; 65% as unchanged drug)

Dosage Refer to individual protocols. I.V. (dilute in D₅W or NS):

Acute leukemias:

Children ≤2 years (unlabeled use): 0.4 mg/kg/day once daily for 3-5 days

Children >2 years (unlabeled use): 8-12 mg/m²/day once daily for 4-5 days

Adults:

Induction: 12 mg/m² once daily for 3 days; for incomplete response, may repeat at 12 mg/m² once daily for 2 days

Consolidation: 12 mg/m² once daily for 2 days, repeat in 4 weeks

Solid tumors:

Children (unlabeled use): 18-20 mg/m² every 3-4 weeks **or** 5-8 mg/m² every week

Adults: 12-14 mg/m² every 3-4 weeks **or** 2-4 mg/m²/day for 5 days every 4 weeks

Hormone-refractory prostate cancer: Adults: 12-14 mg/m² every 3 weeks

Multiple sclerosis: Adults: 12 mg/m² every 3 months (maximum lifetime cumulative dose: 140 mg/m²

Dosing adjustment in renal impairment: Safety and efficacy have not been established

Hemodialysis: Supplemental dose is not necessary

Peritoneal dialysis: Supplemental dose is not necessary

Elderly: Clearance is decreased in elderly patients; use with caution

Dosing adjustment in hepatic impairment: Official dosage adjustment recommendations have not been established. Clearance is reduced in hepatic dysfunction; patients with severe hepatic dysfunction (bilirubin >3.4 mg/dL) have an AUC of 3 times greater than patients with normal hepatic function. Consider dose adjustments. **Note:**MS patients with hepatic impairment should not receive mitoxantrone.

Administration Administered as a short (5-30 minutes) I.V. infusion; continuous 24-hour infusions are occasionally used. Although not generally recommended, mitoxantrone has been given as a rapid bolus over 1-3 minutes. High doses for bone marrow transplant are usually given as 1- to 4-hour infusions.

Monitoring Parameters CBC, serum uric acid (for treatment of leukemia), liver function tests, signs and symptoms of CHF; evaluate LVEF prior to start of therapy and regularly during treatment, especially with the development of signs and symptoms of CHF. In addition, for the treatment of multiple sclerosis, obtain pregnancy test and monitor LVEF prior to all doses

Dosage Forms

Injection, solution: 2 mg/mL (10 mL, 12.5 mL, 15 mL)

Novantrone®: 2 mg/mL (10 mL, 12.5 mL, 15 mL)

♦ **Mitoxantrone Hydrochloride CL-232315** *see* Mitoxantrone *on page 1157*

♦ **Mitoxantrone Injection® (Can)** *see* Mitoxantrone *on page 1157*

♦ **Mitozantrone** *see* Mitoxantrone *on page 1157*

♦ **Mitrazol™ [OTC]** *see* Miconazole *on page 1137*

♦ **Mivacron® [DSC]** *see* Mivacurium *on page 1159*

♦ **Mivacron® (Can)** *see* Mivacurium *on page 1159*

Mivacurium (mye va KYOO ree um)

U.S. Brand Names Mivacron® [DSC]

Canadian Brand Names Mivacron®

Index Terms Mivacurium Chloride

Pharmacologic Category Neuromuscular Blocker Agent, Nondepolarizing

Additional Appendix Information

Neuromuscular Blocking Agents *on page 1890*

Use Adjunct to general anesthesia to facilitate endotracheal intubation and to relax skeletal muscles during surgery; to facilitate mechanical ventilation in ICU patients; does not relieve pain or produce sedation

Pregnancy Risk Factor C

Lactation Excretion in breast milk unknown/use caution

Medication Safety Issues

Sound-alike/look-alike issues:

Mivacron® may be confused with Mevacor®

High alert medication: The Institute for Safe Medication Practices (ISMP) includes this medication among its list of drugs which have a heightened risk of causing significant patient harm when used in error.

(Continued)

Mivacurium *(Continued)*

Contraindications Hypersensitivity to mivacurium chloride, any component of the formulation, or other benzylisoquinolinium agents; use of multidose vials in patients with allergy to benzyl alcohol; pre-existing tachycardia

Warnings/Precautions Ventilation must be supported during neuromuscular blockade; does not counteract bradycardia produced by anesthetics/vagal stimulation; prolonged neuromuscular block may be seen in patients with reduced or atypical plasma cholinesterase activity (eg, pregnancy, liver or kidney disease, infections, peptic ulcer, anemia); patients homozygous for the atypical plasma cholinesterase gene are extremely sensitive to the neuromuscular blocking effect of mivacurium (use extreme caution if at all in those patients); duration prolonged in patients with renal and/or hepatic impairment; reduce initial dosage and inject slowly (over 60 seconds) in patients in whom substantial histamine release would be potentially hazardous; certain clinical conditions may result in potentiation or antagonism of neuromuscular blockade:

Potentiation: Electrolyte abnormalities, severe hyponatremia, severe hypocalcemia, severe hypokalemia, hypermagnesemia, neuromuscular diseases, acidosis, acute intermittent porphyria, renal failure, hepatic failure

Antagonism: Alkalosis, hypercalcemia, demyelinating lesions, peripheral neuropathies, diabetes mellitus

Increased sensitivity in patients with myasthenia gravis, Eaton-Lambert syndrome, resistance in burn patients (>30% of body) for period of 5-70 days postinjury; resistance in patients with muscle trauma, denervation, immobilization, infection. Cross-sensitivity with other neuromuscular-blocking agents may occur; use extreme caution in patients with previous anaphylactic reactions.

Adverse Reactions
>10%: Cardiovascular: Flushing of face
1% to 10%: Cardiovascular: Hypotension
<1% (Limited to important or life-threatening): Acute quadriplegic myopathy syndrome (prolonged use), anaphylactoid reaction, anaphylaxis, bradycardia, bronchospasm, cutaneous erythema, dizziness, endogenous histamine release, hypersensitivity reactions, hypoxemia, injection site reaction, muscle spasms, myositis ossificans (prolonged use), rash, tachycardia, wheezing

Drug Interactions
Increased Effect/Toxicity: Increased effects are possible with aminoglycosides, beta-blockers, clindamycin, calcium channel blockers, halogenated anesthetics, imipenem, ketamine, lidocaine, loop diuretics (furosemide), macrolides (case reports), magnesium sulfate, procainamide, quinidine, quinolones, tetracyclines, and vancomycin. May increase risk of myopathy when used with high-dose corticosteroids for extended periods. Drugs which inhibit acetylcholinesterase may prolong effect of mivacurium.

Decreased Effect: Effect of nondepolarizing neuromuscular blockers may be reduced by carbamazepine (chronic use), corticosteroids (also associated with myopathy - see increased effect), phenytoin (chronic use), sympathomimetics, and theophylline.

Stability Store at room temperature of 15°C to 25°C (59°F to 77°F). Protect from direct ultraviolet light.

Mechanism of Action Mivacurium is a short-acting, nondepolarizing, neuromuscular-blocking agent. Like other nondepolarizing drugs, mivacurium antagonizes acetylcholine by competitively binding to cholinergic sites on motor endplates in skeletal muscle. This inhibits contractile activity in skeletal muscle leading to muscle paralysis. This effect is reversible with cholinesterase inhibitors such as edrophonium, neostigmine, and physostigmine.

Pharmacodynamics/Kinetics
Onset of action: Neuromuscular blockade (dose dependent): I.V.: 1.5-3 minutes
Duration: Short due to rapid hydrolysis by plasma cholinesterases; clinically effective block may last for 12-20 minutes; spontaneous recovery may be 95% complete in 25-30 minutes; duration shorter in children and may be slightly longer in elderly
Metabolism: Via plasma cholinesterase, inactive metabolites
Half-life elimination: 2 minutes (more active isomers only)
Excretion: Urine (<10%)

Dosage Continuous infusion requires an infusion pump; dose to effect; doses will vary due to interpatient variability; use ideal body weight for obese patients

Children 2-12 years (duration of action is shorter and dosage requirements are higher): 0.2 mg/kg I.V. followed by average infusion rate of 14 mcg/kg/minute (range: 5-31 mcg/kg/minute) upon evidence of spontaneous recovery from initial dose
Adults: Initial: I.V.: 0.15-0.25 mg/kg bolus followed by maintenance doses of 0.1 mg/kg at approximately 15-minute intervals; for prolonged neuromuscular block, initial infusion of 9-10 mcg/kg/minute is used upon evidence of spontaneous recovery from initial dose, usual infusion rate of 6-7 mcg/kg/minute (1-15 mcg/kg/minute) under balanced anesthesia; initial dose after succinylcholine for intubation (balanced anesthesia): Adults: 0.1 mg/kg
Pretreatment/priming: 10% of intubating dose given 3-5 minutes before initial dose
Dosing adjustment in renal impairment: 0.15 mg/kg I.V. bolus; duration of action of blockade: 1.5 times longer in ESRD, may decrease infusion rates by as much as 50%, dependent on degree of renal impairment
Dosing adjustment in hepatic impairment: 0.15 mg/kg I.V. bolus; duration of blockade: 3 times longer in ESLD, may decrease rate of infusion by as much as 50% in ESLD, dependent on the degree of impairment

Administration Children require higher mivacurium infusion rates than adults; during opioid/nitrous oxide/oxygen anesthesia, the infusion rate required to maintain 89% to 99% neuromuscular block averages 14 mcg/kg/minute (range: 5-31). For adults and children, the amount of infusion solution required per hour depends upon the clinical requirements of the patient, the concentration of mivacurium in the infusion solution, and the patient's weight. The contribution of the infusion solution to the fluid requirements of the patient must be considered.

Additional Information Mivacurium is classified as a short-duration neuromuscular-blocking agent. Do not mix with barbiturates in the same syringe. Mivacurium does not appear to have a cumulative effect on the duration of blockade. It does not relieve pain or produce sedation.

Dosage Forms
Injection, solution [preservative free]:
Mivacron®: 2 mg/mL (5 mL, 10 mL) [DSC]
Injection, solution:
Mivacron®: 2 mg/mL (20 mL, 50 mL) [with benzyl alcohol] [DSC]

- **Mivacurium Chloride** *see* Mivacurium *on page 1159*
- **MK383** *see* Tirofiban *on page 1693*
- **MK-0431** *see* Sitagliptin *on page 1572*
- **MK462** *see* Rizatriptan *on page 1528*
- **MK594** *see* Losartan *on page 1037*
- **MK0826** *see* Ertapenem *on page 607*
- **MK 869** *see* Aprepitant *on page 144*
- **MLN341** *see* Bortezomib *on page 230*
- **MMF** *see* Mycophenolate *on page 1181*
- **MMR** *see* Measles, Mumps, and Rubella Vaccines (Combined) *on page 1057*
- **Moban®** *see* Molindone *on page 1164*
- **Mobic®** *see* Meloxicam *on page 1072*
- **Mobicox® (Can)** *see* Meloxicam *on page 1072*

Modafinil (moe DAF i nil)

U.S. Brand Names Provigil®
Canadian Brand Names Alertec®; Provigil®
Pharmacologic Category Stimulant
Use Improve wakefulness in patients with excessive daytime sleepiness associated with narcolepsy and shift work sleep disorder (SWSD); adjunctive therapy for obstructive sleep apnea/hypopnea syndrome (OSAHS)
Unlabeled/Investigational Use Attention-deficit/hyperactivity disorder (ADHD); treatment of fatigue in MS and other disorders
Restrictions C-IV
Pregnancy Risk Factor C
Pregnancy Implications Embryotoxic effects have been observed in some, but not all animal studies. There are no adequate and well-controlled studies in pregnant women; use only when the potential risk of drug therapy is outweighed by the drug's benefits. Efficacy of steroidal contraceptives may be decreased; alternate means of contraception should be considered during therapy and for 1 month after modafinil is discontinued.
Lactation Excretion in breast milk unknown/use caution
Contraindications Hypersensitivity to modafinil or any component of the formulation
Warnings/Precautions Use is not recommended with a history of angina, cardiac ischemia, recent history of myocardial infarction, left ventricular hypertrophy, or patients with mitral valve prolapse who have developed mitral valve prolapse syndrome with previous CNS stimulant use. Caution should be exercised when modafinil is given to patients with a history of psychosis; caution is warranted when operating machinery or driving, although functional impairment has not been demonstrated with modafinil, all CNS-active agents may alter judgment, thinking and/or motor skills. Stimulants may unmask tics in individuals with coexisting Tourette's syndrome. Use caution with renal or hepatic impairment. Safety and efficacy in children ≤16 years of age have not been established.

Adverse Reactions
>10%:
Central nervous system: Headache (34%, dose related)
Gastrointestinal: Nausea (11%)
1% to 10%:
Cardiovascular: Chest pain (3%), hypertension (3%), palpitation (2%), tachycardia (2%), vasodilation (2%), edema (1%)
Central nervous system: Nervousness (7%), dizziness (5%), depression (2%), anxiety (5%; dose related), insomnia (5%), somnolence (2%), chills (1%), agitation (1%), confusion (1%), emotional lability (1%), vertigo (1%)
Gastrointestinal: Diarrhea (6%), dyspepsia (5%), xerostomia (4%), anorexia (4%), constipation (2%), flatulence (1%), mouth ulceration (1%), taste perversion (1%)
Genitourinary: Abnormal urine (1%), hematuria (1%), pyuria (1%)
Hematologic: Eosinophilia (1%)
Hepatic: LFTs abnormal (2%)
Neuromuscular & skeletal: Back pain (6%), paresthesia (2%), dyskinesia (1%), hyperkinesia (1%), hypertonia (1%), neck rigidity (1%), tremor (1%)
Ocular: Amblyopia (1%), eye pain (1%), vision abnormal (1%)
Respiratory: Pharyngitis (4%), rhinitis (7%), lung disorder (2%), asthma (1%), epistaxis (1%)
Miscellaneous: Diaphoresis
Postmarketing and/or case reports: Agranulocytosis, mania, psychosis

Overdosage/Toxicology Signs and symptoms of overdose include agitation, irritability, aggressiveness, confusion, nervousness, tremor, sleep disturbance, palpitations, decreased prothrombin time, and slight-to-moderate elevations of hemodynamic parameters. Treatment is symptomatic and supportive. There is no data to suggest the utility of dialysis or urinary pH alteration in enhancing elimination. Cardiac monitoring is warranted.

Drug Interactions
Cytochrome P450 Effect: Substrate of CYP3A4 (major); **Inhibits** CYP1A2 (weak), 2A6 (weak), 2C9 (weak), 2C19 (strong), 2E1 (weak), 3A4 (weak); **Induces** CYP1A2 (weak), 2B6 (weak), 3A4 (weak)
(Continued)

Modafinil (Continued)

Increased Effect/Toxicity: Modafinil may increase the levels/effects of citalopram, diazepam, methsuximide, phenytoin, propranolol, sertraline, or other CYP2C19 substrates. Modafinil may increase levels of warfarin. In populations deficient in the CYP2D6 isoenzyme, where CYP2C19 acts as a secondary metabolic pathway, concentrations of tricyclic antidepressants and selective serotonin reuptake inhibitors may be increased during coadministration. The levels/effects of modafinil may be increased by azole antifungals, clarithromycin, diclofenac, doxycycline, erythromycin, imatinib, isoniazid, nefazodone, nicardipine, propofol, protease inhibitors, quinidine, telithromycin, verapamil, or other CYP3A4 inhibitors.

Decreased Effect: Modafinil may decrease serum concentrations of oral contraceptives, cyclosporine, and to a lesser degree, theophylline. The levels/effects of modafinil may be decreased by aminoglutethimide, carbamazepine, nafcillin, nevirapine, phenobarbital, phenytoin, rifamycins, and other CYP3A4 inducers. There is also evidence to suggest that modafinil may induce its own metabolism.

Ethanol/Nutrition/Herb Interactions
Ethanol: Avoid or limit ethanol.
Food: Delays absorption, but does not affect bioavailability.

Mechanism of Action The exact mechanism of action is unclear, it does not appear to alter the release of dopamine or norepinephrine, it may exert its stimulant effects by decreasing GABA-mediated neurotransmission, although this theory has not yet been fully evaluated; several studies also suggest that an intact central alpha-adrenergic system is required for modafinil's activity; the drug increases high-frequency alpha waves while decreasing both delta and theta wave activity, and these effects are consistent with generalized increases in mental alertness

Pharmacodynamics/Kinetics Modafinil is a racemic compound (10% *d*-isomer and 90% *l*-isomer at steady state) whose enantiomers have different pharmacokinetics

Distribution: V_d: 0.9 L/kg
Protein binding: 60%, primarily to albumin
Metabolism: Hepatic; multiple pathways including CYP3A4
Half-life elimination: Effective half-life: 15 hours; Steady-state: 2-4 days
Time to peak, serum: 2-4 hours
Excretion: Urine (as metabolites, <10% as unchanged drug)

Dosage Oral:
Children: ADHD (unlabeled use): 50-100 mg once daily
Adults:
ADHD (unlabeled use): 100-300 mg once daily
Narcolepsy, OSAHS: Initial: 200 mg as a single daily dose in the morning
SWSD: Initial: 200 mg as a single dose taken ~1 hour prior to start of work shift
Note: Doses of 400 mg/day, given as a single dose, have been well tolerated, but there is no consistent evidence that this dose confers additional benefit
Elderly: Elimination of modafinil and its metabolites may be reduced as a consequence of aging and as a result, lower doses should be considered.

Dosing adjustment in renal impairment: Inadequate data to determine safety and efficacy in severe renal impairment

Dosing adjustment in hepatic impairment: Dose should be reduced to one-half of that recommended for patients with normal liver function

Monitoring Parameters Levels of sleepiness; blood pressure in patients with hypertension

Dosage Forms Tablet: 100 mg, 200 mg

- ♦ **Modane® Bulk [OTC]** *see* Psyllium *on page 1458*
- ♦ **Modane Tablets® [OTC]** *see* Bisacodyl *on page 223*
- ♦ **Modecate® (Can)** *see* Fluphenazine *on page 731*
- ♦ **Modecate® Concentrate (Can)** *see* Fluphenazine *on page 731*
- ♦ **Modicon®** *see* Ethinyl Estradiol and Norethindrone *on page 655*
- ♦ **Modified Dakin's Solution** *see* Sodium Hypochlorite Solution *on page 1579*
- ♦ **Modified Shohl's Solution** *see* Sodium Citrate and Citric Acid *on page 1579*
- ♦ **Moduret (Can)** *see* Amiloride and Hydrochlorothiazide *on page 93*

Moexipril (mo EKS i pril)

U.S. Brand Names Univasc®
Index Terms Moexipril Hydrochloride
Pharmacologic Category Angiotensin-Converting Enzyme (ACE) Inhibitor
Additional Appendix Information
Angiotensin Agents *on page 1860*
Use Treatment of hypertension, alone or in combination with thiazide diuretics; treatment of left ventricular dysfunction after myocardial infarction
Pregnancy Risk Factor C (1st trimester)/D (2nd and 3rd trimesters)
Pregnancy Implications Decreased placental blood flow, low birth weight, fetal hypotension, preterm delivery, and fetal death have been noted with the use of some ACE inhibitors (ACEIs) in animal studies. Neonatal hypotension, skull hypoplasia, anuria, renal failure, oligohydramnios (associated with fetal limb contractures, craniofacial deformities, hypoplastic lung development), prematurity, intrauterine growth retardation, and patent ductus arteriosus have been reported with the use of ACEIs, primarily in the 2nd and 3rd trimesters. The risk of neonatal toxicity has been considered less when ACEIs have been used in the 1st trimester; however, major congenital malformations have been reported. The cardiovascular and/or central nervous systems are most commonly affected. Unless alternative agents are not appropriate, ACEIs should be discontinued as soon as possible once pregnancy is detected.
Lactation Excretion in breast milk unknown/use caution

Medication Safety Issues

Sound-alike/look-alike issues:

Moexipril may be confused with Monopril®

Contraindications Hypersensitivity to moexipril, moexiprilat, or any component of the formulation; hypersensitivity or allergic reactions or angioedema related to previous treatment with an ACE inhibitor; pregnancy (2nd or 3rd trimester)

Warnings/Precautions [U.S. Boxed Warning]: Based on human data, ACEIs can cause injury and death to the developing fetus when used in the second and third trimesters. ACEIs should be discontinued as soon as possible once pregnancy is detected. Use with caution and modify dosage in patients with renal impairment especially renal artery stenosis, severe CHF, or with coadministered diuretic therapy. Hyperkalemia may rarely occur. Severe hypotension may occur in patients who are sodium and/or volume depleted; initiate lower doses and monitor closely when starting therapy in these patients; ACE inhibitors may be preferred agents in elderly patients with CHF and diabetes mellitus (diabetic proteinuria is reduced, minimal CNS effects, and enhanced insulin sensitivity), however, due to decreased renal function, tolerance must be carefully monitored; if possible, discontinue the diuretic 2-3 days prior to initiating moexipril in patients receiving them to reduce the risk of symptomatic hypotension.

Anaphylactic reactions can occur. Angioedema can occur at any time during treatment (especially following first dose). It may involve head and neck (potentially affecting the airway) or the intestine (presenting with abdominal pain). Prolonged monitoring may be required especially if tongue, glottis, or larynx are involved as they are associated with airway obstruction. Those with a history of airway surgery in this situation have a higher risk. Use with caution in collagen vascular diseases; valvular stenosis (particularly aortic stenosis); hyperkalemia; or before, during, or immediately after anesthesia. Avoid rapid dosage escalation which may lead to renal insufficiency. Rare toxicities associated with ACE inhibitors include cholestatic jaundice (which may progress to hepatic necrosis) and neutropenia/agranulocytosis with myeloid hyperplasia. May be associated with deterioration of renal function and/or increases in serum creatinine, particularly in patients dependent on renin-angiotensin-aldosterone system. If patient has renal impairment then a baseline WBC with differential and serum creatinine should be evaluated and monitored closely during the first 3 months of therapy. Hypersensitivity reactions may be seen during hemodialysis with high-flux dialysis membranes (eg, AN69). Safety and efficacy have not been established in children.

Adverse Reactions

1% to 10%:

Cardiovascular: Hypotension, peripheral edema

Central nervous system: Headache, dizziness, fatigue

Dermatologic: Alopecia, flushing, rash

Endocrine & metabolic: Hyperkalemia, hyponatremia

Gastrointestinal: Diarrhea, nausea, heartburn

Genitourinary: Polyuria

Neuromuscular & skeletal: Myalgia

Renal: Reversible increases in creatinine or BUN

Respiratory: Cough, pharyngitis, upper respiratory infection, sinusitis

<1% (Limited to important or life-threatening): Alopecia, anemia, angioedema, arrhythmia, bronchospasm, cerebrovascular accident, chest pain, dyspnea, elevated LFTs, eosinophilic pneumonitis, hepatitis, hypercholesterolemia, MI, oliguria, orthostatic hypotension, palpitation, proteinuria, syncope

Overdosage/Toxicology Mild hypotension has been the only toxic effect seen with acute overdose; bradycardia may also occur. Hyperkalemia occurs even with therapeutic doses, especially in patients with renal insufficiency and those taking NSAIDs. Following initiation of essential overdose management, toxic symptom and supportive treatment should be initiated. Hypotension usually responds to I.V. fluids or Trendelenburg positioning.

Drug Interactions

Increased Effect/Toxicity: Potassium supplements, co-trimoxazole (high dose), angiotensin II receptor antagonists (eg, candesartan, losartan, irbesartan), or potassium-sparing diuretics (amiloride, spironolactone, triamterene) may result in elevated serum potassium levels when combined with moexipril. ACE inhibitor effects may be increased by probenecid (increases levels of captopril). ACE inhibitors may increase serum concentrations/effects of lithium. ACE inhibitors may enhance the adverse/toxic effects (nitritoid reaction) of gold sodium thiomalate.

Diuretics have additive hypotensive effects with ACE inhibitors, and hypovolemia increases the potential for adverse renal effects of ACE inhibitors. In patients with compromised renal function, coadministration with NSAIDs may result in further deterioration of renal function. Allopurinol and ACE inhibitors may cause a higher risk of hypersensitivity reaction when taken concurrently.

Decreased Effect: Aspirin (high dose) may reduce the therapeutic effects of ACE inhibitors; at low dosages this does not appear to be significant. Rifampin may decrease the effect of ACE inhibitors. Antacids may decrease the bioavailability of ACE inhibitors (may be more likely to occur with captopril); separate administration times by 1-2 hours. NSAIDs, specifically indomethacin, may reduce the hypotensive effects of ACE inhibitors. More likely to occur in low renin or volume dependent hypertensive patients.

Ethanol/Nutrition/Herb Interactions

Food: Food may delay and reduce peak serum levels.

Herb/Nutraceutical: Avoid dong quai if using for hypertension (has estrogenic activity). Avoid ephedra, yohimbe, ginseng (may worsen hypertension). Avoid garlic (may have increased antihypertensive effect).

Mechanism of Action Competitive inhibitor of angiotensin-converting enzyme (ACE); prevents conversion of angiotensin I to angiotensin II, a potent vasoconstrictor; results in lower levels of angiotensin II which causes an increase in plasma renin activity and a reduction in aldosterone secretion

(Continued)

Moexipril *(Continued)*

Pharmacodynamics/Kinetics
Onset of action: Peak effect: 1-2 hours
Duration: >24 hours
Distribution: V_d (moexiprilat): 180 L
Protein binding, plasma: Moexipril: 90%; Moexiprilat: 50% to 70%
Metabolism: Parent drug: Hepatic and via GI tract to moexiprilat, 1000 times more potent than parent
Bioavailability: Moexiprilat: 13%; reduced with food (AUC decreased by ~40%)
Half-life elimination: Moexipril: 1 hour; Moexiprilat: 2-9 hours
Time to peak: 1.5 hours
Excretion: Feces (50%)

Dosage Adults: Oral: Initial: 7.5 mg once daily (in patients **not** receiving diuretics), 1 hour prior to a meal **or** 3.75 mg once daily (when combined with thiazide diuretics); maintenance dose: 7.5-30 mg/day in 1 or 2 divided doses 1 hour before meals

Dosing adjustment in renal impairment: Cl_{cr} ≤40 mL/minute: Patients may be cautiously placed on 3.75 mg once daily, then upwardly titrated to a maximum of 15 mg/day.

Dietary Considerations Administer on an empty stomach.

Monitoring Parameters Blood pressure, heart rate, electrolytes, CBC, symptoms of hypotension

Test Interactions Increases BUN, creatinine, potassium, positive Coombs' [direct]; decreases cholesterol (S); may cause false-positive results in urine acetone determinations using sodium nitroprusside reagent

Dosage Forms Tablet, as hydrochloride [scored]: 7.5 mg, 15 mg

Moexipril and Hydrochlorothiazide
(mo EKS i pril & hye droe klor oh THYE a zide)

U.S. Brand Names Uniretic®
Canadian Brand Names Uniretic®
Index Terms Hydrochlorothiazide and Moexipril
Pharmacologic Category Antihypertensive Agent, Combination
Use Combination therapy for hypertension, however, not indicated for initial treatment of hypertension; replacement therapy in patients receiving separate dosage forms (for patient convenience); when monotherapy with one component fails to achieve desired antihypertensive effect, or when dose-limiting adverse effects limit upward titration of monotherapy
Pregnancy Risk Factor C/D (2nd and 3rd trimesters)
Dosage Adults: Oral: 7.5-30 mg of moexipril, taken either in a single or divided dose one hour before meals; hydrochlorothiazide dose should be ≤50 mg/day
Additional Information Complete prescribing information for this medication should be consulted for additional detail.
Dosage Forms Tablet [scored]:
7.5/12.5: Moexipril hydrochloride 7.5 mg and hydrochlorothiazide 12.5 mg
15/12.5: Moexipril hydrochloride 15 mg and hydrochlorothiazide 12.5 mg
15/25: Moexipril hydrochloride 15 mg and hydrochlorothiazide 25 mg

♦ **Moexipril Hydrochloride** *see* Moexipril *on page 1162*

Molindone *(moe LIN done)*

U.S. Brand Names Moban®
Canadian Brand Names Moban®
Index Terms Molindone Hydrochloride
Pharmacologic Category Antipsychotic Agent, Typical
Additional Appendix Information
Antipsychotic Agents *on page 1872*
Use Management of schizophrenia
Unlabeled/Investigational Use Management of psychotic disorders
Pregnancy Risk Factor C
Lactation Excretion in breast milk unknown
Medication Safety Issues
Sound-alike/look-alike issues:
Molindone may be confused with Mobidin®
Moban® may be confused with Mobidin®, Modane®
Contraindications Hypersensitivity to molindone or any component of the formulation (cross-reactivity between phenothiazines may occur); severe CNS depression; coma
Warnings/Precautions May be sedating, use with caution in disorders where CNS depression is a feature. Use with caution in Parkinson's disease. Caution in patients with hemodynamic instability; bone marrow suppression; predisposition to seizures; subcortical brain damage; severe cardiac, hepatic, renal, or respiratory disease. Esophageal dysmotility and aspiration have been associated with antipsychotic use - use with caution in patients at risk of pneumonia (ie, Alzheimer's disease). Caution in breast cancer or other prolactin-dependent tumors (may elevate prolactin levels). May alter temperature regulation or mask toxicity of other drugs due to antiemetic effects. May alter cardiac conduction; life-threatening arrhythmias have occurred with therapeutic doses of neuroleptics. May cause orthostatic hypotension - use with caution in patients at risk of this effect or those who would tolerate transient hypotensive episodes (cerebrovascular disease, cardiovascular disease, or other medications which may predispose).

May cause anticholinergic effects (confusion, agitation, constipation, xerostomia, blurred vision, urinary retention); therefore, they should be used with caution in patients with decreased gastrointestinal motility, urinary retention, BPH, xerostomia, or visual problems.

Conditions which also may be exacerbated by cholinergic blockade include narrow-angle glaucoma (screening is recommended) and worsening of myasthenia gravis. Relative to other neuroleptics, molindone has a low potency of cholinergic blockade.

May cause extrapyramidal reactions, including pseudoparkinsonism, acute dystonic reactions, akathisia, and tardive dyskinesia (risk of these reactions is moderate-high relative to other neuroleptics). May be associated with neuroleptic malignant syndrome (NMS) or pigmentary retinopathy.

Adverse Reactions Frequency not defined.

Cardiovascular: Orthostatic hypotension, tachycardia, arrhythmia

Central nervous system: Extrapyramidal reactions (akathisia, pseudoparkinsonism, dystonia, tardive dyskinesia), mental depression, altered central temperature regulation, sedation, drowsiness, restlessness, anxiety, hyperactivity, euphoria, seizure, neuroleptic malignant syndrome (NMS)

Dermatologic: Pruritus, rash, photosensitivity

Endocrine & metabolic: Change in menstrual periods, edema of breasts, amenorrhea, galactorrhea, gynecomastia

Gastrointestinal: Constipation, xerostomia, nausea, salivation, weight gain (minimal compared to other antipsychotics), weight loss

Genitourinary: Urinary retention, priapism

Hematologic: Leukopenia, leukocytosis

Ocular: Blurred vision, retinal pigmentation

Miscellaneous: Diaphoresis (decreased)

Overdosage/Toxicology Symptoms include deep sleep, extrapyramidal symptoms, cardiac arrhythmias, seizures, and hypotension. Following initiation of essential overdose management, toxic symptom and supportive treatment should be initiated. Hypotension usually responds to I.V. fluids or Trendelenburg positioning. If unresponsive to these measures, the use of a parenteral inotrope may be required (eg, norepinephrine 0.1-0.2 mcg/kg/minute titrated to response). Seizures commonly respond to diazepam (I.V. 5-10 mg bolus in adults every 15 minutes, if needed up to a total of 30 mg; I.V. 0.25-0.4 mg/kg/dose up to a total of 10 mg in children) or to phenytoin or phenobarbital. Critical cardiac arrhythmias often respond to I.V. phenytoin (15 mg/kg up to 1 g), while other antiarrhythmics can be used. Neuroleptics often cause extrapyramidal symptoms (eg, dystonic reactions) requiring management with diphenhydramine 1-2 mg/kg (adults), up to a maximum of 50 mg I.M. or slow I.V. push, followed by a maintenance dose for 48-72 hours. When these reactions are unresponsive to diphenhydramine, anticholinergic agents such as benztropine mesylate I.V. 1-2 mg (adults) may be effective. These agents are generally effective within 2-5 minutes.

Drug Interactions

Increased Effect/Toxicity: Molindone concentrations may be increased by chloroquine, propranolol, sulfadoxine-pyrimethamine. Molindone may increase the effect and/or toxicity of antihypertensives, lithium, TCAs, CNS depressants (ethanol, opioid analgesics), and trazodone. Metoclopramide may increase risk of extrapyramidal symptoms (EPS). Acetylcholinesterase inhibitors (central) may increase the risk of antipsychotic-related EPS.

Decreased Effect: Antipsychotics inhibit the activity of bromocriptine and levodopa. Benztropine (and other anticholinergics) may inhibit the therapeutic response to molindone and excess anticholinergic effects may occur. Barbiturates and cigarette smoking may enhance the hepatic metabolism of molindone. Molindone and possibly other low potency antipsychotic may reverse the pressor effects of epinephrine.

Ethanol/Nutrition/Herb Interactions

Ethanol: Avoid ethanol (may increase CNS depression).

Herb/Nutraceutical: Avoid kava kava, gotu kola, valerian, St John's wort (may increase CNS depression).

Stability Protect from light. Dispense in amber or opaque vials.

Mechanism of Action Molindone is a dihydroindoline antipsychotic whose mechanism of action mimics that of chlorpromazine; however, it produces more extrapyramidal symptoms and less sedation than chlorpromazine

Pharmacodynamics/Kinetics

Metabolism: Hepatic

Half-life elimination: 1.5 hours

Time to peak, serum: ~1.5 hours

Excretion: Urine and feces (90%) within 24 hours

Dosage Oral:

Children: Schizophrenia/psychoses:

3-5 years: 1-2.5 mg/day in 4 divided doses

5-12 years: 0.5-1 mg/kg/day in 4 divided doses

Adults: Schizophrenia/psychoses: 50-75 mg/day increase at 3- to 4-day intervals up to 225 mg/day

Elderly: Behavioral symptoms associated with dementia: Initial: 5-10 mg 1-2 times/day; increase at 4- to 7-day intervals by 5-10 mg/day; increase dosing intervals (bid, tid, etc) as necessary to control response or side effects.

Monitoring Parameters Vital signs; lipid profile, fasting blood glucose/Hgb A_{1c}; BMI; mental status, abnormal involuntary movement scale (AIMS), extrapyramidal symptoms (EPS)

Dosage Forms Tablet, as hydrochloride: 5 mg, 10 mg, 25 mg, 50 mg

♦ **Molindone Hydrochloride** see Molindone on page 1164

♦ **MOM** see Magnesium Hydroxide on page 1047

♦ **Momentum® [OTC]** see Magnesium Salicylate on page 1051

Mometasone Furoate (moe MET a sone FYOOR oh ate)

U.S. Brand Names Asmanex® Twisthaler®; Elocon®; Nasonex®

Canadian Brand Names Elocom®; Nasonex®; PMS-Mometasone; ratio-Mometasone; Taro-Mometasone

(Continued)

Mometasone Furoate *(Continued)*

Pharmacologic Category Corticosteroid, Inhalant (Oral); Corticosteroid, Nasal; Corticosteroid, Topical

Additional Appendix Information
Corticosteroids *on page 1879*

Use Relief of the inflammatory and pruritic manifestations of corticosteroid-responsive dermatoses (medium potency topical corticosteroid); treatment of nasal symptoms of seasonal and perennial allergic rhinitis; prevention of nasal symptoms associated with seasonal allergic rhinitis; treatment of nasal polyps in adults; maintenance treatment of asthma as prophylactic therapy or as a supplement in asthma patients requiring oral corticosteroids for the purpose of decreasing or eliminating the oral corticosteroid requirement

Pregnancy Risk Factor C

Pregnancy Implications
There are no adequate and well-controlled studies using topical mometasone during pregnancy. However, teratogenicity and intrauterine growth retardation has been reported in animal studies with some topical steroids. Avoid use of large amounts for long periods of time during pregnancy. Hypoadrenalism may occur in infants born to women receiving corticosteroids during pregnancy. Monitor these infants closely after birth.

Lactation Excretion in breast milk unknown/use caution

Medication Safety Issues
Sound-alike/look-alike issues:
Elocon® lotion may be confused with ophthalmic solutions. Manufacturer's labeling emphasizes the product is **NOT** for use in the eyes.

Contraindications Hypersensitivity to mometasone or any component of the formulation; treatment of acute bronchospasm (oral inhaler)

Warnings/Precautions
May cause hypercorticism or suppression of hypothalamic-pituitary-adrenal (HPA) axis, particularly in younger children or in patients receiving high doses for prolonged periods. HPA axis suppression may lead to adrenal crisis. Withdrawal and discontinuation of a corticosteroid should be done slowly and carefully. Particular care is required when patients are transferred from systemic corticosteroids to inhaled products due to possible adrenal insufficiency or withdrawal from steroids, including an increase in allergic symptoms. Patients receiving >20 mg per day of prednisone (or equivalent) may be most susceptible. Fatalities have occurred due to adrenal insufficiency in asthmatic patients during and after transfer from systemic corticosteroids to aerosol steroids; aerosol steroids do not provide the systemic steroid needed to treat patients having trauma, surgery, or infections. When transferring to oral inhaler, previously-suppressed allergic conditions (rhinitis, conjunctivitis, eczema) may be unmasked.

Bronchospasm may occur with wheezing after inhalation; if this occurs stop steroid and treat with a fast-acting bronchodilator. Supplemental steroids (oral or parenteral) may be needed during stress or severe asthma attacks. Not to be used in status asthmaticus or for the relief of acute bronchospasm. Corticosteroid use may cause psychiatric disturbances, including depression, euphoria, insomnia, mood swings, and personality changes. Pre-existing psychiatric conditions may be exacerbated by corticosteroid use. Prolonged use of corticosteroids may also increase the incidence of secondary infection, mask acute infection (including fungal infections), prolong or exacerbate viral infections, or limit response to vaccines. Exposure to chickenpox should be avoided; corticosteroids should not be used to treat ocular herpes simplex. Corticosteroids should not be used for cerebral malaria. Close observation is required in patients with latent tuberculosis and/or TB reactivity; restrict use in active TB (only in conjunction with antituberculosis treatment). Prolonged treatment with corticosteroids has been associated with the development of Kaposi's sarcoma (case reports); if noted, discontinuation of therapy should be considered.

Use with caution in patients with thyroid disease, hepatic impairment, renal impairment, cardiovascular disease, diabetes, glaucoma, cataracts, myasthenia gravis, patients at risk for osteoporosis, patients at risk for seizures, or GI diseases (diverticulitis, peptic ulcer, ulcerative colitis) due to perforation risk. Use caution following acute MI (corticosteroids have been associated with myocardial rupture). Because of the risk of adverse effects, systemic corticosteroids should be used cautiously in the elderly in the smallest possible effective dose for the shortest duration. Avoid nasal corticosteroid use in patients with recent nasal septal ulcers, nasal surgery or nasal trauma until healing has occurred.

Orally-inhaled and intranasal corticosteroids may cause a reduction in growth velocity in pediatric patients (~1 centimeter per year [range 0.3-1.8 cm per year] and related to dose and duration of exposure). To minimize the systemic effects of orally-inhaled and intranasal corticosteroids, each patient should be titrated to the lowest effective dose. Growth should be routinely monitored in pediatric patients. There have been reports of systemic corticosteroid withdrawal symptoms (eg, joint/muscle pain, lassitude, depression) when withdrawing oral inhalation therapy.

Adverse Reactions
Nasal/oral inhalation:
>10%:
Central nervous system: Headache (17% to 22%), fatigue (oral inhalation 1% to 13%), depression (oral inhalation 11%)
Neuromuscular & skeletal: Musculoskeletal pain (1% to 22%), arthralgia (oral inhalation 13%)
Respiratory: Sinusitis (oral inhalation 22%), rhinitis (2% to 20%), upper respiratory infection (8% to 15%), pharyngitis (8% to 13%), cough (nasal inhalation 7% to 13%), epistaxis (1% to 11%)
Miscellaneous: Viral infection (nasal inhalation 8% to 14%), oral candidiasis (oral inhalation 4% to 22%)
1% to 10%:
Cardiovascular: Chest pain

1166

Gastrointestinal: Abdominal pain, dry throat (oral inhalation), vomiting (1% to 5%), diarrhea, dyspepsia, flatulence, gastroenteritis, nausea, vomiting

Genitourinary: Dysmenorrhea

Neuromuscular & skeletal: Back pain, myalgia

Ocular: Conjunctivitis

Otic: Earache, otitis media

Respiratory: Asthma, dysphonia, epistaxis, nasal irritation, wheezing

Miscellaneous: Accidental injury, flu-like syndrome

<1% (Limited to important or life-threatening): Anaphylaxis, angioedema, growth suppression, nasal candidiasis, nasal burning and irritation, nasal septal perforation, nasal ulcers, oral candidiasis (nasal inhalation), smell disturbance (rare), taste disturbance (rare)

Topical:

1% to 10%: Dermatologic: Bacterial skin infection, burning, furunculosis, pruritus, skin atrophy, tingling/stinging

<1% (Limited to important or life-threatening): Folliculitis, glucocorticoid levels decreased (pediatric patients), moniliasis, paresthesia, rosacea, skin depigmentation, skin atrophy

Cataract formation, reduction in growth velocity, and HPA axis suppression have been reported with other corticosteroids

Drug Interactions

Cytochrome P450 Effect: Substrate of CYP3A4 (minor)

Increased Effect/Toxicity:

Concomittant use with ketoconazole may result in increased mometasone furoate plasma levels.

Stability

Cream: Store between 2°C to 25°C (36°F to 77°F).

Lotion: Store between 2°C to 30°C (36°F to 86°F).

Nasal spray: Store at room temperature of 15°C to 30°C (59°F to 86°F). Protect from light.

Ointment: Store at room temperature of 15°C to 30°C (59°F to 86°F).

Oral Inhaler: Store at room temperature of 15°C to 30°C (59°F to 86°F). Discard when oral dose counter reads "0" (or 45 days after opening the foil pouch).

Mechanism of Action May depress the formation, release, and activity of endogenous chemical mediators of inflammation (kinins, histamine, liposomal enzymes, prostaglandins). Leukocytes and macrophages may have to be present for the initiation of responses mediated by the above substances. Inhibits the margination and subsequent cell migration to the area of injury, and also reverses the dilatation and increased vessel permeability in the area resulting in decreased access of cells to the sites of injury.

Pharmacodynamics/Kinetics

Absorption:

Nasal inhalation: Mometasone furoate monohydrate: Undetectable in plasma

Ointment: 0.7%; increased by occlusive dressings

Oral inhalation: <1%

Protein binding: Mometasone furoate: 98% to 99%

Metabolism: Mometasone furoate: Hepatic via CYP3A4; forms metabolite

Half-life elimination: Oral inhalation: 5 hours

Excretion: Feces, bile, urine

Dosage

Oral inhalation: Children ≥12 years and Adults: Previous therapy:

Bronchodilators or inhaled corticosteroids: Initial: 1 inhalation (220 mcg) daily (maximum 2 inhalations or 440 mcg/day); may be given in the evening or in divided doses twice daily

Oral corticosteroids: Initial: 440 mcg twice daily (maximum 880 mcg/day); prednisone should be reduced no faster than 2.5 mg/day on a weekly basis, beginning after at least 1 week of mometasone furoate use

Note: Maximum effects may not be evident for 1-2 weeks or longer; dose should be titrated to effect, using the lowest possible dose

Nasal spray:

Allergic rhinitis:

Children 2-11 years: 1 spray (50 mcg) in each nostril daily

Children ≥12 years and Adults: 2 sprays (100 mcg) in each nostril daily; when used for the prevention of allergic rhinitis, treatment should begin 2-4 weeks prior to pollen season

Nasal polyps: Adults: 2 sprays (100 mcg) in each nostril twice daily; 2 sprays (100 mcg) once daily may be effective in some patients

Topical: Apply sparingly, do not use occlusive dressings. Therapy should be discontinued when control is achieved; if no improvement is seen in 2 weeks, reassessment of diagnosis may be necessary.

Cream, ointment: Children ≥2 years and Adults: Apply a thin film to affected area once daily; do not use in pediatric patients for longer than 3 weeks

Lotion: Children ≥12 years and Adults: Apply a few drops to affected area once daily

Dietary Considerations

Asmanex® Twisthaler® contains lactose.

Administration

Nasal spray: Prior to first use, prime pump by actuating 10 times or until fine spray appears; may store for a maximum of 1 week without repriming. Spray should be administered once or twice daily, at a regular interval. Shake well prior to use.

Oral inhalation: Exhale fully prior to bringing the Twisthaler® up to the mouth. Place between lips and inhale quickly and deeply. Do not breath out through the inhaler. Remove inhaler and hold breath for 10 seconds if possible.

Topical: Apply sparingly; avoid eyes, face, underarms, and groin. Do not wrap or bandage affected area.

Monitoring Parameters HPA axis suppression

Dosage Forms

Cream, topical:

Elocon®: 0.1% (15 g, 45 g)

(Continued)

Mometasone Furoate *(Continued)*

Lotion, topical:
Elocon®: 0.1% (30 mL, 60 mL) [contains isopropyl alcohol 40%]
Ointment, topical: 0.1% (15 g, 45 g)
Elocon®: 0.1% (15 g, 45 g)
Powder for oral inhalation:
Asmanex® Twisthaler®: 220 mcg (14 units, 30 units, 60 units, 120 units) [contains lactose]
Suspension, intranasal [spray]:
Nasonex®: 50 mcg/spray (17 g) [delivers 120 sprays; contains benzalkonium chloride]

♦ **MOM/Mineral Oil Emulsion** see Magnesium Hydroxide and Mineral Oil on page 1048
♦ **Monacolin K** see Lovastatin on page 1040
♦ **Monarc-M™** see Antihemophilic Factor (Human) on page 133
♦ **Monistat® (Can)** see Miconazole on page 1137
♦ **Monistat® 1 Combination Pack [OTC]** see Miconazole on page 1137
♦ **Monistat® 3 [OTC]** see Miconazole on page 1137
♦ **Monistat® 3 (Can)** see Miconazole on page 1137
♦ **Monistat® 7 [OTC]** see Miconazole on page 1137
♦ **Monistat-Derm®** see Miconazole on page 1137
♦ **Monitan® (Can)** see Acebutolol on page 27
♦ **Monoclate-P®** see Antihemophilic Factor (Human) on page 133
♦ **Monoclonal Antibody** see Muromonab-CD3 on page 1179
♦ **Monocor® (Can)** see Bisoprolol on page 226
♦ **Monodox®** see Doxycycline on page 555
♦ **Monoethanolamine** see Ethanolamine Oleate on page 644
♦ **Monoket®** see Isosorbide Mononitrate on page 947
♦ **MonoNessa™** see Ethinyl Estradiol and Norgestimate on page 660
♦ **Mononine®** see Factor IX on page 679
♦ **Monopril®** see Fosinopril on page 766

Montelukast *(mon te LOO kast)*

U.S. Brand Names Singulair®
Canadian Brand Names Singulair®
Index Terms Montelukast Sodium
Pharmacologic Category Leukotriene-Receptor Antagonist
Use Prophylaxis and chronic treatment of asthma; relief of symptoms of seasonal allergic rhinitis and perennial allergic rhinitis
Unlabeled/Investigational Use Acute asthma
Pregnancy Risk Factor B
Pregnancy Implications Montelukast was not teratogenic in animal studies, however, there are no adequate and well-controlled studies in pregnant women. Use during pregnancy only if clearly needed. Healthcare providers should report any prenatal exposures to the montelukast pregnancy registry at (800) 986-8999.
Lactation Excretion in breast milk unknown/use caution
Medication Safety Issues
Sound-alike/look-alike issues:
Singulair® may be confused with Sinequan®
Contraindications Hypersensitivity to montelukast or any component of the formulation
Warnings/Precautions Montelukast is not FDA approved for use in the reversal of bronchospasm in acute asthma attacks, including status asthmaticus; some clinicians, however, support its use (Cylly, 2003; Camargo, 2003; Ferreira, 2001). Should not be used as monotherapy for the treatment and management of exercise-induced bronchospasm. Advise patients to have appropriate rescue medication available. Appropriate clinical monitoring and caution are recommended when systemic corticosteroid reduction is considered in patients receiving montelukast. Inform phenylketonuric patients that the chewable tablet contains phenylalanine. Safety and efficacy in children <6 months of age have not been established.

In rare cases, patients on therapy with montelukast may present with systemic eosinophilia, sometimes presenting with clinical features of vasculitis consistent with Churg-Strauss syndrome, a condition which is often treated with systemic corticosteroid therapy. Healthcare providers should be alert to eosinophilia, vasculitic rash, worsening pulmonary symptoms, cardiac complications, and/or neuropathy presenting in their patients. A causal association between montelukast and these underlying conditions has not been established.
Adverse Reactions (As reported in adults)
1% to 10%:
Central nervous system: Dizziness (2%), fatigue (2%), fever (2%)
Dermatologic: Rash (2%)
Gastrointestinal: Abdominal pain (3%), dyspepsia (2%), dental pain (2%), gastroenteritis (2%)
Neuromuscular & skeletal: Weakness (2%)
Respiratory: Cough (3%), nasal congestion (2%), upper respiratory infection (2%)
Miscellaneous: Flu-like syndrome (4%), trauma (1%)
<1% (Limited to important or life-threatening): Agitation, anaphylaxis, angioedema, arthralgia, cholestasis (rare), Churg-Strauss syndrome, eosinophilia, hallucinations, hepatic eosinophilic infiltration (rare); hepatitis (mixed pattern, hepatocellular, and cholestatic); hypoesthesia, insomnia, myalgia, palpitation, pancreatitis, paresthesia, pruritus, seizure, vasculitis
Overdosage/Toxicology There is no specific antidote. Remove unabsorbed material from the GI tract, employ clinical monitoring and institute supportive therapy if required. Abdominal pain, hyperkinesia, mydriasis, somnolence, and thirst have been reported with acute overdose of ≥150 mg/day.

Drug Interactions
    Cytochrome P450 Effect: Substrate (major) of CYP2C9, 3A4; **Inhibits** CYP2C8 (weak), 2C9 (weak)
    Decreased Effect: CYP2C9 inducers may decrease the levels/effects of montelukast; example inducers include carbamazepine, phenobarbital, phenytoin, rifampin, rifapentine, and secobarbital. CYP3A4 inducers may decrease the levels/effects of montelukast; example inducers include aminoglutethimide, carbamazepine, nafcillin, nevirapine, phenobarbital, phenytoin, and rifamycins.
Ethanol/Nutrition/Herb Interactions Herb/Nutraceutical: St John's wort may decrease montelukast levels.
Stability Store at room temperature of 15°C to 30°C (59°F to 86°F). Protect from moisture and light.
    Granules: Use within 15 minutes of opening packet.
Mechanism of Action Selective leukotriene receptor antagonist that inhibits the cysteinyl leukotriene receptor. Cysteinyl leukotrienes and leukotriene receptor occupation have been correlated with the pathophysiology of asthma, including airway edema, smooth muscle contraction, and altered cellular activity associated with the inflammatory process, which contribute to the signs and symptoms of asthma.
Pharmacodynamics/Kinetics
    Duration: >24 hours
    Absorption: Rapid
    Distribution: V_d: 8-11 L
    Protein binding, plasma: >99%
    Metabolism: Extensively hepatic via CYP3A4 and 2C8/9
    Bioavailability: Tablet: 10 mg: Mean: 64%; 5 mg: 63% to 73%
    Half-life elimination, plasma: Mean: 2.7-5.5 hours
    Time to peak, serum: Tablet: 10 mg: 3-4 hours; 5 mg: 2-2.5 hours; 4 mg: 2 hours
    Excretion: Feces (86%); urine (<0.2%)
Dosage Oral:
    Children:
        6-11 months: Asthma (unlabeled use): 4 mg (oral granules) once daily, taken in the evening
        6-23 months: Perennial allergic rhinitis: 4 mg (oral granules) once daily
        12-23 months: Asthma: 4 mg (oral granules) once daily, taken in the evening
        2-5 years: Asthma, seasonal or perennial allergic rhinitis: 4 mg (chewable tablet or oral granules) once daily, taken in the evening
        6-14 years: Asthma, seasonal or perennial allergic rhinitis: Chew one 5 mg chewable tablet/day, taken in the evening
    Children ≥15 years and Adults:
        Asthma, seasonal or perennial allergic rhinitis: 10 mg/day, taken in the evening
        Asthma, acute (unlabeled use): 10 mg as a single dose administered with first-line therapy
    Dosing adjustment in renal impairment: No adjustment necessary
    Dosing adjustment in hepatic impairment: Mild-to-moderate: No adjustment necessary. Patients with severe hepatic disease were **not** studied.
Dietary Considerations Tablet, chewable: 4 mg strength contains phenylalanine 0.674 mg; 5 mg strength contains phenylalanine 0.842 mg
Administration When treating asthma, administer dose in the evening. Granules may be administered directly in the mouth or mixed with applesauce, carrots, rice, ice cream, baby formula, or breast milk; do not add to any other liquids. Administer within 15 minutes of opening packet.
Dosage Forms
    Granules: 4 mg/packet
    Tablet: 10 mg
    Tablet, chewable: 4 mg [contains phenylalanine 0.674 mg; cherry flavor]; 5 mg [contains phenylalanine 0.842 mg; cherry flavor]

- **Montelukast Sodium** *see Montelukast on page 1168*
- **Monurol™** *see Fosfomycin on page 765*
- **8-MOP** *see Methoxsalen on page 1115*
- **8-MOP®** *see Methoxsalen on page 1115*
- **More Attenuated Enders Strain** *see Measles Virus Vaccine (Live) on page 1058*
- **MoreDophilus® [OTC]** *see Lactobacillus on page 969*

Moricizine (mor I siz een)

U.S. Brand Names Ethmozine®
Canadian Brand Names Ethmozine®
Index Terms Moricizine Hydrochloride
Pharmacologic Category Antiarrhythmic Agent, Class I
Use Treatment of ventricular tachycardia and life-threatening ventricular arrhythmias
Unlabeled/Investigational Use PVCs, complete and nonsustained ventricular tachycardia, atrial arrhythmias
Pregnancy Risk Factor B
Lactation Enters breast milk/not recommended
Medication Safety Issues
    Sound-alike/look-alike issues:
        Ethmozine® may be confused with Erythrocin®, erythromycin
Contraindications Hypersensitivity to moricizine or any component of the formulation; pre-existing second- or third-degree AV block (except in patients with a functioning artificial pacemaker); right bundle branch block when associated with left hemiblock or bifascicular block (unless functional pacemaker in place); cardiogenic shock
(Continued)

Moricizine *(Continued)*

Warnings/Precautions Considering the known proarrhythmic properties and lack of evidence of improved survival for any antiarrhythmic drug in patients without life-threatening arrhythmias, it is prudent to reserve the use for patients with life-threatening ventricular arrhythmias. **[U.S. Boxed Warning]: The CAST II trial demonstrated a trend towards decreased survival for patients treated with moricizine.** Proarrhythmic effects occur as with other antiarrhythmic agents; hypokalemia, hyperkalemia, hypomagnesemia may effect response to class I agents; use with caution in patients with sick-sinus syndrome, hepatic, and renal impairment; safety and efficacy have not been established in pediatric patients

Adverse Reactions

>10%: Central nervous system: Dizziness

1% to 10%:

Cardiovascular: Proarrhythmia, palpitation, cardiac death, ECG abnormalities, CHF

Central nervous system: Headache, fatigue, insomnia

Endocrine & metabolic: Decreased libido

Gastrointestinal: Nausea, diarrhea, ileus

Ocular: Blurred vision, periorbital edema

Respiratory: Dyspnea

<1% (Limited to important or life-threatening): Apnea, cardiac chest pain, hyper-/hypotension, MI, supraventricular arrhythmia, syncope, ventricular tachycardia

Overdosage/Toxicology Has a narrow therapeutic index and severe toxicity may occur slightly above the therapeutic range, especially if combined with other antiarrhythmic drugs. Acute single ingestion of twice the daily therapeutic dose is life-threatening. Symptoms include increased PR, QRS, and QT intervals, amplitude of the T wave, AV block, bradycardia, hypotension, ventricular arrhythmias (monomorphic or polymorphic ventricular tachycardia), and asystole. Other symptoms include dizziness, blurred vision, headache, and GI upset. Treatment is supportive, using conventional treatment (fluids, positioning, anticonvulsants, antiarrhythmics). **Note:** Type Ia antiarrhythmic agents should not be used to treat cardiotoxicity caused by type Ic antiarrhythmic drugs. Sodium bicarbonate may reverse QRS prolongation, bradycardia and hypotension. Ventricular pacing may be needed.

Drug Interactions

Cytochrome P450 Effect: Substrate of CYP3A4 (major); **Induces** CYP1A2 (weak), 3A4 (weak)

Increased Effect/Toxicity: CYP3A4 inhibitors may increase the levels/effects of moricizine; example inhibitors include azole antifungals, clarithromycin, diclofenac, doxycycline, erythromycin, imatinib, isoniazid, nefazodone, nicardipine, propofol, protease inhibitors, quinidine, telithromycin, and verapamil. Moricizine levels may be increased by cimetidine and diltiazem. Digoxin may result in additive prolongation of the PR interval when combined with moricizine (but not rate of second- and third-degree AV block). Drugs which may prolong QT interval (including cisapride, erythromycin, phenothiazines, cyclic antidepressants, and some quinolones) are contraindicated with type Ia antiarrhythmics. Moricizine has some type Ia activity, and caution should be used.

Decreased Effect: Moricizine may decrease levels of theophylline (50%) and diltiazem. CYP3A4 inducers may decrease the levels/effects of moricizine; example inducers include aminoglutethimide, carbamazepine, nafcillin, nevirapine, phenobarbital, phenytoin, and rifamycins.

Ethanol/Nutrition/Herb Interactions Food: Moricizine peak serum concentrations may be decreased if taken with food.

Mechanism of Action Class I antiarrhythmic agent; reduces the fast inward current carried by sodium ions, shortens Phase I and Phase II repolarization, resulting in decreased action potential duration and effective refractory period

Pharmacodynamics/Kinetics

Protein binding, plasma: 95%

Metabolism: Significant first-pass effect; some enterohepatic recycling

Bioavailability: 38%

Half-life elimination: Healthy volunteers: 3-4 hours; Cardiac disease: 6-13 hours

Excretion: Feces (56%); urine (39%)

Dosage Adults: Oral: 200-300 mg every 8 hours, adjust dosage at 150 mg/day at 3-day intervals.

Recommendations for transferring patients from other antiarrhythmic agents to Ethmozine®: See table.

Moricizine

Transferred From	Start Ethmozine®
Encainide, propafenone, tocainide, or mexiletine	8-12 hours after last dose
Flecainide	12-24 hours after last dose
Procainamide	3-6 hours after last dose
Quinidine, disopyramide	6-12 hours after last dose

Dosing interval in renal or hepatic impairment: Start at 600 mg/day or less.

Dietary Considerations Best if taken on an empty stomach.

Dosage Forms Tablet, as hydrochloride: 200 mg, 250 mg, 300 mg

♦ **Moricizine Hydrochloride** *see* Moricizine *on page 1169*

♦ **Morning After Pill** *see* Ethinyl Estradiol and Norgestrel *on page 663*

♦ **Morphine HP®** **(Can)** *see* Morphine Sulfate *on page 1171*

♦ **Morphine LP® Epidural (Can)** *see* Morphine Sulfate *on page 1171*

Morphine Sulfate (MOR feen SUL fate)

U.S. Brand Names Astramorph/PF™; Avinza®; DepoDur™; Duramorph®; Infumorph®; Kadian®; MS Contin®; Oramorph SR®; RMS®; Roxanol™

Canadian Brand Names Kadian®; M-Eslon®; Morphine HP®; Morphine LP® Epidural; M.O.S.® 10; M.O.S.® 20; M.O.S.® 30; M.O.S.-SR®; M.O.S.-Sulfate®; MS Contin®; MS-IR®; PMS-Morphine Sulfate SR; ratio-Morphine SR; Statex®; Zomorph®

Index Terms MSO₄ (error-prone abbreviation and should not be used)

Pharmacologic Category Analgesic, Opioid

Additional Appendix Information

Narcotic Agonists *on page 1888*

Use Relief of moderate to severe acute and chronic pain; relief of pain of myocardial infarction; relief of dyspnea of acute left ventricular failure and pulmonary edema; preanesthetic medication

DepoDur™: Epidural (lumbar) single-dose management of surgical pain

Infumorph®: Used in microinfusion devices for intraspinal administration in treatment of intractable chronic pain

Restrictions C-II

Pregnancy Risk Factor C/D (prolonged use or high doses at term)

Pregnancy Implications Morphine crosses the placenta. The frequency of congenital malformations has not been reported to be greater than expected in children from mothers treated with morphine during pregnancy. Reduced growth and behavioral abnormalities in offspring have been observed in animal studies. Neonates born to mothers receiving chronic opioids during pregnancy should be monitored for neonatal withdrawal syndrome.

DepoDur™ may be used in women undergoing cesarean section following clamping of the umbilical cord; not for use in vaginal labor and delivery.

Lactation Enters breast milk/use caution (AAP rates "compatible")

Medication Safety Issues

Sound-alike/look-alike issues:

Morphine may be confused with hydromorphone

Morphine sulfate may be confused with magnesium sulfate

MSO₄ is an error-prone abbreviation (mistaken as magnesium sulfate)

Avinza® may be confused with Evista®, Invanz®

Roxanol™ may be confused with OxyFast®, Roxicet™

Use care when prescribing and/or administering morphine solutions. These products are available in different concentrations. Always prescribe dosage in mg; **not** by volume (mL).

Use caution when selecting a morphine formulation for use in neurologic infusion pumps (eg, Medtronic delivery systems). The product should be appropriately labeled as "preservative-free" and suitable for intraspinal use via continuous infusion. In addition, the product should be formulated in a pH range that is compatible with the device operation specifications.

Significant differences exist between oral and I.V. dosing. Use caution when converting from one route of administration to another.

Contraindications Hypersensitivity to morphine sulfate or any component of the formulation; increased intracranial pressure; severe respiratory depression; acute or severe asthma; known or suspected paralytic ileus; sustained release products are not recommended with gastrointestinal obstruction or in acute/postoperative pain; pregnancy (prolonged use or high doses at term)

Warnings/Precautions An opioid-containing analgesic regimen should be tailored to each patient's needs and based upon the type of pain being treated (acute versus chronic), the route of administration, degree of tolerance for opioids (naive versus chronic user), age, weight, and medical condition. The optimal analgesic dose varies widely among patients. Doses should be titrated to pain relief/prevention. When used as an epidural injection, monitor for delayed sedation.

May cause respiratory depression; use with caution in patients (particularly elderly or debilitated) with impaired respiratory function, morbid obesity, adrenal insufficiency, prostatic hyperplasia, urinary stricture, renal impairment, or severe hepatic dysfunction and in patients with hypersensitivity reactions to other phenanthrene derivative opioid agonists (codeine, hydrocodone, hydromorphone, levorphanol, oxycodone, oxymorphone). Use with caution in patients with biliary tract dysfunction; acute pancreatitis may cause constriction of sphincter of Oddi. Some preparations contain sulfites which may cause allergic reactions; infants <3 months of age are more susceptible to respiratory depression, use with caution and generally in reduced doses in this age group. May cause CNS depression, which may impair physical or mental abilities; patients must be cautioned about performing tasks which require mental alertness (eg, operating machinery or driving). Effects may be potentiated when used with other sedative drugs or ethanol. May cause hypotension in patients with acute myocardial infarction, volume depletion, or concurrent drug therapy which may exaggerate vasodilation. Use with extreme caution in patients with head injury, intracranial lesions, or elevated intracranial pressure; exaggerated elevation of ICP may occur. May obscure diagnosis or clinical course of patients with acute abdominal conditions. Tolerance or drug dependence may result from extended use. Concurrent use of agonist/antagonist analgesics may precipitate withdrawal symptoms and/or reduced analgesic efficacy in patients following prolonged therapy with mu opioid agonists. Abrupt discontinuation following prolonged use may also lead to withdrawal symptoms. Elderly may be particularly susceptible to adverse effects of narcotics.

Extended or sustained-release formulations:

[U.S. Boxed Warning]: Extended or sustained release dosage forms should not be crushed or chewed. Controlled-, extended-, or sustained-release products are not

(Continued)

Morphine Sulfate *(Continued)*

intended for "as needed (PRN)" use. MS Contin® 100 or 200 mg tablets are for use only in opioid-tolerant patients requiring >400 mg/day.

[U.S. Boxed Warning]: Avinza®: Do not administer with alcoholic beverages or ethanol-containing products, which may disrupt extended-release characteristic of product.

Injections: Note: Products are designed for administration by specific routes (I.V., intra-thecal, epidural). Use caution when prescribing, dispensing, or administering to use formulations only by intended route(s).

[U.S. Boxed Warning]: Duramorph®: Due to the risk of severe and/or sustained cardiopulmonary depressant effects of Duramorph® must be administered in a fully equipped and staffed environment. Naloxone injection should be immediately available. Patient should remain in this environment for at least 24 hours following the initial dose.

Infumorph® solutions are **for use in microinfusion devices only**; not for I.V., I.M., or SubQ administration.

Depo-Dur™: Freezing may adversely affect modified-release mechanism of drug; check freeze indicator within carton prior to administration.

Adverse Reactions Note: Individual patient differences are unpredictable, and percentage may differ in acute pain (surgical) treatment.

Frequency not defined: Flushing, CNS depression, sedation, antidiuretic hormone release, physical and psychological dependence, diaphoresis

>10%:

Cardiovascular: Palpitations, hypotension, bradycardia

Central nervous system: Drowsiness (48%, tolerance usually develops to drowsiness with regular dosing for 1-2 weeks); dizziness (20%), confusion, headache (following epidural or intrathecal use)

Dermatologic: Pruritus (may be secondary to histamine release)

Note: Pruritus may be dose-related, but not confined to the site of administration.

Gastrointestinal: Nausea (28%, tolerance usually develops to nausea and vomiting with chronic use); constipation (40%, tolerance develops very slowly if at all); xerostomia (78%)

Genitourinary: Urinary retention (16%; may be prolonged, up to 20 hours, following epidural or intrathecal use)

Local: Pain at injection site

Neuromuscular & skeletal: Weakness

Miscellaneous: Histamine release

1% to 10%:

Cardiovascular: Atrial fibrillation (<3%), chest pain (<3%), edema (<3%), syncope (<3%), tachycardia (<3%)

Central nervous system: Amnesia, anxiety, apathy, ataxia, chills, depression, euphoria, false feeling of well being, fever, headache, hypoesthesia, insomnia, lethargy, malaise, restlessness, seizure, vertigo

Endocrine & metabolic: Hyponatremia (<3%), gynecomastia (<3%)

Gastrointestinal: Anorexia, biliary colic, dyspepsia, dysphagia, GERD, GI irritation, paralytic ileus, vomiting (9%)

Genitourinary: Decreased urination

Hematologic: Anemia (<3%), leukopenia (<3%), thrombocytopenia (<3%)

Neuromuscular & skeletal: Arthralgia, back pain, bone pain, paresthesia, trembling

Ocular: Vision problems

Respiratory: Asthma, atelectasis, dyspnea, hiccups, hypoxia, noncardiogenic pulmonary edema, respiratory depression, rhinitis

Miscellaneous: Diaphoresis, flu-like syndrome, withdrawal syndrome

<1% (Limited to important or life-threatening): Amenorrhea, anaphylaxis, biliary tract spasm, hallucinations, intestinal obstruction, intracranial pressure increased, liver function tests increased, menstrual irregularities, mental depression, miosis, muscle rigidity, myoclonus, oliguria, paradoxical CNS stimulation, peripheral vasodilation, urinary tract spasm, transaminases increased

Overdosage/Toxicology Symptoms include respiratory depression, miosis, hypotension, bradycardia, apnea, and pulmonary edema. Treatment includes airway support, establishment of an I.V. line, and administration of naloxone 2 mg I.V. (0.01 mg/kg for children), with repeat administration as necessary, up to a total of 10 mg. Primary attention should be directed to ensuring adequate respiratory exchange.

Drug Interactions

Cytochrome P450 Effect: Substrate of CYP2D6 (minor)

Increased Effect/Toxicity: Antipsychotic agents may increase the hypotensive effects of morphine. Use of selective serotonin reuptake inhibitors (SSRIs) or meperidine may lead to additive serotonergic effects with concomitant morphine, possibly precipitating serotonin syndrome. CNS depressants and tricyclic antidepressants may potentiate the effects of morphine. Concurrent use of MAO inhibitors and meperidine has been associated with significant adverse effects; use caution with morphine. Some manufacturers recommend avoiding use within 14 days of MAO inhibitors.

Decreased Effect: The therapeutic efficacy of pegvisomant may be decreased by concomitant opiates, possibly requiring dosage adjustment of pegvisomant. Rifamycin derivatives may decrease levels or effects of morphine.

Ethanol/Nutrition/Herb Interactions

Ethanol: Avoid ethanol (may increase CNS depression).

Avinza®: Alcoholic beverages or ethanol-containing products may disrupt extended-release formulation resulting in rapid release of entire morphine dose.

Food: Administration of oral morphine solution with food may increase bioavailability (ie, a report of 34% increase in morphine AUC when morphine oral solution followed a high-fat meal). The bioavailability of Oramorph SR® or Kadian® does not appear to be affected by food.

Herb/Nutraceutical: Avoid valerian, St John's wort, kava kava, gotu kola (may increase CNS depression).

Stability

Capsule, sustained release (Kadian®): Store at controlled room temperature 15°C to 30°C (59°F to 86°F). Protect from light and moisture.

Suppositories: Store at controlled room temperature 25°C (77°F). Protect from light.

Injection: Store at controlled room temperature. Protect from light. Degradation depends on pH and presence of oxygen; relatively stable in pH ≤4; darkening of solutions indicate degradation. Usual concentration for continuous I.V. infusion: 0.1-1 mg/mL in D_5W.

DepoDur™: Store under refrigeration, 2°C to 8°C (36°F to 46°F); do not freeze. Check freeze indicator before administration; do not administer if bulb is pink or purple. May store at room temperature for up to 7 days. DepoDur™ may be diluted in preservative-free NS to a volume of 5 mL. Gently invert to suspend particles prior to removal from vial. Once vial is opened, use within 4 hours.

Mechanism of Action Binds to opiate receptors in the CNS, causing inhibition of ascending pain pathways, altering the perception of and response to pain; produces generalized CNS depression

Pharmacodynamics/Kinetics

Onset of action: Oral (immediate release): ~30 minutes; I.V.: 5-10 minutes

Duration: Pain relief:

Immediate release formulations: 4 hours

Extended release epidural injection (DepoDur™): >48 hours

Absorption: Variable

Distribution: V_d: 3-4 L/kg; binds to opioid receptors in the CNS and periphery (eg, GI tract)

Protein binding: 30% to 35%

Metabolism: Hepatic via conjugation with glucuronic acid to morphine-3-glucuronide (inactive), morphine-6-glucuronide (active), and in lesser amounts, morphine-3-6-diglucuronide; other minor metabolites include normorphine (active) and the 3-ethereal sulfate

Bioavailability: Oral: 17% to 33% (first-pass effect limits oral bioavailability; oral:parenteral effectiveness reportedly varies from 1:6 in opioid naive patients to 1:3 with chronic use)

Half-life elimination: Adults: 2-4 hours (immediate release forms)

Time to peak, plasma: Kadian®: ~10 hours

Excretion: Urine (primarily as morphine-3-glucuronide, ~2% to 12% excreted unchanged); feces (~7% to 10%). It has been suggested that accumulation of morphine-6-glucuronide might cause toxicity with renal insufficiency. All of the metabolites (ie, morphine-3-glucuronide, morphine-6-glucuronide, and normorphine) have been suggested as possible causes of neurotoxicity (eg, myoclonus).

Dosage Note: These are guidelines and do not represent the doses that may be required in all patients. Doses should be titrated to pain relief/prevention.

Children >6 months and <50 kg: Acute pain (moderate-to-severe):

Oral (prompt release): 0.15-0.3 mg/kg every 3-4 hours as needed

I.M.: 0.1 mg/kg every 3-4 hours as needed

I.V.: 0.05-0.1 mg/kg every 3-4 hours as needed

I.V. infusion: Range: 10-30 mcg/kg/hour

Adolescents >12 years: Sedation/analgesia for procedures: I.V.: 3-4 mg and repeat in 5 minutes if necessary

Adults:

Acute pain (moderate-to-severe):

Oral: Prompt release formulations: Opiate-naive: Initial: 10 mg every 3-4 hours as needed; patients with prior opiate exposure may require higher initial doses: usual dosage range: 10-30 mg every 3-4 hours as needed

I.M., SubQ: **Note:** Repeated SubQ administration causes local tissue irritation, pain, and induration.

Initial: Opiate-naive: 5-10 mg every 3-4 hours as needed; patients with prior opiate exposure may require higher initial doses; usual dosage range: 5-20 mg every 3-4 hours as needed

Rectal: 10-20 mg every 3-4 hours

I.V.: Initial: Opiate-naive: 2.5-5 mg every 3-4 hours; patients with prior opiate exposure may require higher initial doses. **Note:** Repeated doses (up to every 5 minutes if needed) in small increments (eg, 1-4 mg) may be preferred to larger and less frequent doses.

I.V., SubQ continuous infusion: 0.8-10 mg/hour; usual range: Up to 80 mg/hour

Mechanically-ventilated patients (based on 70 kg patient): 0.7-10 mg every 1-2 hours as needed; infusion: 5-35 mg/hour

Patient-controlled analgesia (PCA): (Opiate-naive: Consider lower end of dosing range):

Usual concentration: 1 mg/mL

Demand dose: Usual: 1 mg; range: 0.5-2.5 mg

Lockout interval: 5-10 minutes

Intrathecal (I.T.): **Note:** Administer with extreme caution and in reduced dosage to geriatric or debilitated patients.

Opioid-naive: 0.2-0.25 mg/dose (may provide adequate relief for 24 hours); repeat doses are **not** recommended.

Epidural: **Note:** Administer with extreme caution and in reduced dosage to geriatric or debilitated patients. Vigilant monitoring is particularly important in these patients.

Pain management:

Single-dose (Duramorph®): Initial: 3-5 mg

Infusion:

Bolus dose: 1-6 mg

Infusion rate: 0.1-0.2 mg/hour

Maximum dose: 10 mg/24 hours

Surgical anesthesia: Epidural: Single-dose (extended release, Depo-Dur™): Lumbar epidural only; not recommended in patients <18 years of age:

Cesarean section: 10 mg

Lower abdominal/pelvic surgery: 10-15 mg

(Continued)

Morphine Sulfate *(Continued)*

Major orthopedic surgery of lower extremity: 15 mg

For Depo-Dur™: To minimize the pharmacokinetic interaction resulting in higher peak serum concentrations of morphine, administer the test dose of the local anesthetic at least 15 minutes prior to Depo-Dur™ administration. Use of Depo-Dur™ with epidural local anesthetics has not been studied. Other medications should not be administered into the epidural space for at least 48 hours after administration of DepoDur™.

Note: Some patients may benefit from a 20 mg dose, however, the incidence of adverse effects may be increased.

Chronic pain: Note: Patients taking opioids chronically may become tolerant and require doses higher than the usual dosage range to maintain the desired effect. Tolerance can be managed by appropriate dose titration. There is no optimal or maximal dose for morphine in chronic pain. The appropriate dose is one that relieves pain throughout its dosing interval without causing unmanageable side effects.

Oral: Controlled-, extended-, or sustained-release formulations: A patient's morphine requirement should be established using prompt-release formulations. Conversion to long-acting products may be considered when chronic, continuous treatment is required. Higher dosages should be reserved for use only in opioid-tolerant patients.

Capsules, extended release (Avinza™): Daily dose administered once daily (for best results, administer at same time each day)

Capsules, sustained release (Kadian®): Daily dose administered once daily or in 2 divided doses daily (every 12 hours)

Tablets, controlled release (MS Contin®), sustained release (Oramorph SR®), or extended release: Daily dose divided and administered every 8 or every 12 hours

Elderly or debilitated patients: Use with caution; may require dose reduction

Dosing adjustment in renal impairment:

Cl_{cr} 10-50 mL/minute: Administer at 75% of normal dose

Cl_{cr} <10 mL/minute: Administer at 50% of normal dose

Dosing adjustment/comments in hepatic disease: Unchanged in mild liver disease; substantial extrahepatic metabolism may occur; excessive sedation may occur in cirrhosis

Dietary Considerations Morphine may cause GI upset; take with food if GI upset occurs. Be consistent when taking morphine with or without meals.

Administration

Oral: Do not crush controlled release drug product, swallow whole. Kadian® and Avinza® can be opened and sprinkled on applesauce; do not crush or chew the beads. Contents of Kadian® capsules may be opened and sprinkled over 10 mL water and flushed through prewetted 16F gastrostomy tube; do not administer Kadian® through nasogastric tube. Administration of oral morphine solution with food may increase bioavailability (not observed with Oramorph SR®).

I.V.: When giving morphine I.V. push, it is best to first dilute in 4-5 mL of sterile water, and then to administer slowly (eg, 15 mg over 3-5 minutes)

Epidural: Use preservative-free solutions

Epidural, extended release liposomal suspension (DepoDur™): May be administered undiluted or diluted up to 5 mL total volume in preservative-free NS. Do not use an in-line filter during administration. Not for I.V. or I.M. administration.

Resedation may occur following epidural administration; this may be delayed ≥48 hours in patients receiving extended-release (DepoDur™) injections.

Administration of an epidural test dose (lidocaine 1.5% and epinephrine 1:200,000) may affect the release of morphine from the liposomal preparation. Delaying the dose for an interval of at least 15 minutes following the test dose minimizes this pharmacokinetic interaction. Except for a test dose, other epidural local anesthetics should not be used before or after this product.

Intrathecal: Use preservative-free solutions

Monitoring Parameters Pain relief, respiratory and mental status, blood pressure

Infumorph®: Patients should be observed in a fully-equipped and staffed environment for at least 24 hours following initiation, and as appropriate for the first several days after catheter implantation.

DepoDur™: Patient should be monitored for at least 48 hours following administration.

Reference Range Therapeutic: Surgical anesthesia: 65-80 ng/mL (SI: 227-280 nmol/L); Toxic: 200-5000 ng/mL (SI: 700-17,500 nmol/L)

Test Interactions Some quinolones may produce a false-positive urine screening result for opiates using commercially-available immunoassay kits. This has been demonstrated most consistently for levofloxacin and ofloxacin, but other quinolones have shown cross-reactivity in certain assay kits. Confirmation of positive opiate screens by more specific methods should be considered.

Dosage Forms

Capsule, extended release:

Avinza®: 30 mg, 60 mg, 90 mg, 120 mg

Capsule, sustained release:

Kadian®: 20 mg, 30 mg, 50 mg, 60 mg, 80 mg, 100 mg

Infusion [premixed in D_5W]: 1 mg/mL (100 mL, 250 mL)

Injection, extended release liposomal suspension [lumbar epidural injection, preservative free]:

DepoDur™: 10 mg/mL (1 mL, 1.5 mL, 2 mL)

Injection, solution: 2 mg/mL (1 mL); 4 mg/mL (1 mL); 5 mg/mL (1 mL); 8 mg/mL (1 mL); 10 mg/mL (1 mL, 10 mL); 15 mg/mL (1 mL, 20 mL); 25 mg/mL (4 mL, 10 mL, 20 mL, 40 mL, 50 mL, 100 mL, 250 mL); 50 mg/mL (20 mL, 40 mL) [some preparations contain sodium metabisulfite]

Injection, solution [epidural, intrathecal, or I.V. infusion; preservative free]:

Astramorph/PF™: 0.5 mg/mL (2 mL, 10 mL); 1 mg/mL (2 mL, 10 mL)

Duramorph®: 0.5 mg/mL (10 mL); 1 mg/mL (10 mL)

Injection, solution [epidural or intrathecal infusion via microinfusion device; preservative free]:

Infumorph®: 10 mg/mL (20 mL); 25 mg/mL (20 mL)

Injection, solution [I.V. infusion via PCA pump]: 0.5 mg/mL (30 mL); 1 mg/mL (30 mL, 50 mL); 2 mg/mL (30 mL); 5 mg/mL (30 mL, 50 mL)

Injection, solution [preservative free]: 0.5 mg/mL (10 mL); 1 mg/mL (10 mL); 25 mg/mL (4 mL, 10 mL, 20 mL)

Solution, oral: 10 mg/5 mL (5 mL, 10 mL, 100 mL, 500 mL); 20 mg/5 mL (100 mL, 500 mL); 20 mg/mL (30 mL, 120 mL, 240 mL)

Roxanol™: 20 mg/mL (30 mL, 120 mL); 100 mg/5 mL (240 mL) [with calibrated spoon]

Suppository, rectal: 5 mg (12s), 10 mg (12s), 20 mg (12s), 30 mg (12s)

RMS®: 5 mg (12s), 10 mg (12s), 20 mg (12s), 30 mg (12s)

Tablet: 10 mg, 15 mg, 30 mg

Tablet, controlled release:
MS Contin®: 15 mg, 30 mg, 60 mg, 100 mg, 200 mg

Tablet, extended release: 15 mg, 30 mg, 60 mg, 100 mg, 200 mg

Tablet, sustained release:
Oramorph SR®: 15 mg, 30 mg, 60 mg, 100 mg

Morrhuate Sodium (MOR yoo ate SOW dee um)

U.S. Brand Names Scleromate®

Pharmacologic Category Sclerosing Agent

Use Treatment of small, uncomplicated varicose veins of the lower extremities

Pregnancy Risk Factor C

Contraindications Hypersensitivity to morrhuate sodium or any component of the formulation; arterial disease, thrombophlebitis

Warnings/Precautions Sloughing and necrosis of tissue may occur following extravasation; anaphylactoid and allergic reactions have occurred; this drug should only be administered by a physician familiar with proper injection techniques; a test dose of 0.25-5 mL of a 5% injection should be given 24 hours before full-dose treatment

Adverse Reactions Frequency not defined.
Cardiovascular: Thrombosis, valvular incompetency, vascular collapse
Central nervous system: Dizziness, drowsiness, headache
Dermatologic: Urticaria
Gastrointestinal: Nausea, vomiting
Local: Burning at the site of injection, severe extravasation effects
Neuromuscular & skeletal: Weakness
Respiratory: Asthma
Miscellaneous: Anaphylaxis, hypersensitivity reactions

Stability Refrigerate

Mechanism of Action Both varicose veins and esophageal varices are treated by the thrombotic action of morrhuate sodium. By causing inflammation of the vein's intima, a thrombus is formed. Occlusion secondary to the fibrous tissue and the thrombus results in the obliteration of the vein.

Pharmacodynamics/Kinetics
Onset of action: ~5 minutes
Absorption: Most stays at site of injection
Distribution: Esophageal varices treatment: ~20% of dose to lungs

Dosage Adults: I.V.: 50-250 mg, repeated at 5- to 7-day intervals (50-100 mg for small veins, 150-250 mg for large veins)

Administration For I.V. use only; avoid extravasation; use only clear solutions, solution should become clear when warmed

Dosage Forms Injection, solution: 50 mg/mL (30 mL)

♦ **M.O.S.® 10 (Can)** *see* Morphine Sulfate *on page 1171*
♦ **M.O.S.® 20 (Can)** *see* Morphine Sulfate *on page 1171*
♦ **M.O.S.® 30 (Can)** *see* Morphine Sulfate *on page 1171*
♦ **M.O.S.-SR® (Can)** *see* Morphine Sulfate *on page 1171*
♦ **M.O.S.-Sulfate® (Can)** *see* Morphine Sulfate *on page 1171*
♦ **Motofen®** *see* Difenoxin and Atropine *on page 499*
♦ **Motrin®** *see* Ibuprofen *on page 873*
♦ **Motrin® Children's [OTC]** *see* Ibuprofen *on page 873*
♦ **Motrin® (Children's) (Can)** *see* Ibuprofen *on page 873*
♦ **Motrin® Cold and Sinus [OTC]** *see* Pseudoephedrine and Ibuprofen *on page 1456*
♦ **Motrin® Cold, Children's [OTC]** *see* Pseudoephedrine and Ibuprofen *on page 1456*
♦ **Motrin® IB [OTC]** *see* Ibuprofen *on page 873*
♦ **Motrin® IB (Can)** *see* Ibuprofen *on page 873*
♦ **Motrin® Infants' [OTC]** *see* Ibuprofen *on page 873*
♦ **Motrin® Junior Strength [OTC]** *see* Ibuprofen *on page 873*
♦ **MoviPrep®** *see* Polyethylene Glycol-Electrolyte Solution *on page 1387*

Moxifloxacin (moxs i FLOKS a sin)

U.S. Brand Names Avelox®; Avelox® I.V.; Vigamox™

Canadian Brand Names Avelox®; Avelox® I.V.; Vigamox™

Index Terms Moxifloxacin Hydrochloride

Pharmacologic Category Antibiotic, Ophthalmic; Antibiotic, Quinolone

Additional Appendix Information
Antimicrobial Drugs of Choice *on page 1981*
Community-Acquired Pneumonia in Adults *on page 1999*
Prevention of Wound Infection and Sepsis in Surgical Patients *on page 1964*
Tuberculosis *on page 2010*
(Continued)

Moxifloxacin *(Continued)*

Use Treatment of mild-to-moderate community-acquired pneumonia, including multi-drug-resistant *Streptococcus pneumoniae* (MDRSP); acute bacterial exacerbation of chronic bronchitis; acute bacterial sinusitis; complicated and uncomplicated skin and skin structure infections; complicated intra-abdominal infections; bacterial conjunctivitis (ophthalmic formulation)

Unlabeled/Investigational Use *Legionella*

Pregnancy Risk Factor C

Pregnancy Implications Reports of arthropathy (observed in immature animals and reported rarely in humans) have limited the use of fluoroquinolones during pregnancy. Teratogenic effects were not observed with moxifloxacin in animal studies; however, delayed skeletal development and smaller fetuses were observed in some species. There are no adequate and well-controlled studies in pregnant women. Based on limited data, quinolones are not expected to be a major human teratogen. Although quinolone antibiotics should not be used as first-line agents during pregnancy, when considering treatment for life-threatening infection and/or prolonged duration of therapy, the potential risk to the fetus must be balanced against the severity of the potential illness.

Lactation Excretion in breast milk unknown/not recommended

Medication Safety Issues
Sound-alike/look-alike issues:
Avelox® may be confused with Avonex®

International issues:
Vigamox™ may be confused with Fisamox® which is a brand name for amoxicillin in Australia

Contraindications Hypersensitivity to moxifloxacin, other quinolone antibiotics, or any component of the formulation

Warnings/Precautions Use with caution in patients with significant bradycardia or acute myocardial ischemia. Moxifloxacin causes a concentration-dependent QT prolongation. Do not exceed recommended dose or infusion rate. Avoid use with uncorrected hypokalemia, with other drugs that prolong the QT interval or induce bradycardia, or with class IA or III antiarrhythmic agents. Use with caution in individuals at risk of seizures (CNS disorders or concurrent therapy with medications which may lower seizure threshold). Potential for seizures, although very rare, may be increased with concomitant NSAID therapy. Discontinue in patients who experience significant CNS adverse effects (dizziness, hallucinations, suicidal ideation or actions). Not recommended in patients with moderate to severe hepatic insufficiency. Use with caution in diabetes; glucose regulation may be altered. Tendon inflammation and/or rupture have been reported with quinolone antibiotics. Risk may be increased with concurrent corticosteroids, particularly in the elderly. Discontinue at first signs or symptoms of tendon pain.

Severe hypersensitivity reactions, including anaphylaxis, have occurred with quinolone therapy. If an allergic reaction occurs (itching, urticaria, dyspnea or facial edema, loss of consciousness, tingling, cardiovascular collapse) discontinue drug immediately. May cause photosensitivity. Prolonged use may result in superinfection; pseudomembranous colitis may occur and should be considered in all patients who present with diarrhea. Quinolones may exacerbate myasthenia gravis. Peripheral neuropathy may rarely occur. Safety and efficacy of systemically administered moxifloxacin (oral, intravenous) in patients <18 years of age have not been established.

Ophthalmic: Eye drops should not be injected subconjunctivally or introduced directly into the anterior chamber of the eye. Contact lenses should not be worn during therapy.

Adverse Reactions
Systemic:
3% to 10%: Gastrointestinal: Nausea (6%), diarrhea (5%)
0.1% to 3%:
Central nervous system: Anxiety, chills, dizziness (2%), headache, insomnia, malaise, nervousness, pain, somnolence, tremor, vertigo
Dermatologic: Dry skin, pruritus, rash (maculopapular, purpuric, pustular)
Endocrine & metabolic: Serum chloride increased (≥2%), serum ionized calcium increased (≥2%), serum glucose decreased (≥2%)
Gastrointestinal: Abdominal pain, amylase increased, amylase decreased (≥2%), anorexia, constipation, dry mouth, dyspepsia, flatulence, glossitis, lactic dehydrogenase increased, stomatitis, taste perversion, vomiting
Genitourinary: Vaginal moniliasis, vaginitis
Hematologic: Eosinophilia, leukopenia, prothrombin time prolonged, increased INR, thrombocytopenia
Increased serum levels of the following (≥2%): MCH, neutrophils, WBC
Decreased serum levels of the following (≥2%): Basophils, eosinophils, hemoglobin, RBC, neutrophils
Hepatic: Bilirubin decreased or increased (≥2%), GGTP increased, liver function test abnormal
Local: Injection site reaction
Neuromuscular & skeletal: Arthralgia, myalgia, weakness
Renal: Serum albumin increased (≥2%)
Respiratory: Pharyngitis, pneumonia, rhinitis, sinusitis, pO_2 increased (≥2%)
Miscellaneous: Allergic reaction, infection, diaphoresis, oral moniliasis

Additional reactions with **ophthalmic** preparation: 1% to 6%: Conjunctivitis, dry eye, ocular discomfort, ocular hyperemia, ocular pain, ocular pruritus, subconjunctival hemorrhage, tearing, visual acuity decreased

Overdosage/Toxicology Potential symptoms of overdose may include CNS excitation, seizures, QT prolongation, and arrhythmias (including torsade de pointes). Patients should be monitored by continuous ECG in the event of an overdose. Management is supportive and symptomatic. Hemodialysis only removes ~9% of dose.

Drug Interactions
   Increased Effect/Toxicity: Moxifloxacin may increase the effects/toxicity of glyburide and warfarin. Concomitant use with corticosteroids may increase the risk of tendon rupture. Concomitant use with other QT_c-prolonging agents (eg, Class Ia and Class III antiarrhythmics, erythromycin, cisapride, antipsychotics, and cyclic antidepressants) may result in arrhythmias, such as torsade de pointes. Concomitant use with NSAIDs may rarely increase risk of seizure.

   Decreased Effect: Concurrent administration of metal cations, including most antacids, oral electrolyte supplements, quinapril, sucralfate, some didanosine formulations (pediatric powder for oral suspension), and other higly-buffered oral drugs, may decrease quinolone levels; separate doses.

Ethanol/Nutrition/Herb Interactions Food: Absorption is not affected by administration with a high-fat meal or yogurt.

Stability Store at 15°C to 30°C (59°F to 86°F). Do not refrigerate infusion solution.

Mechanism of Action Moxifloxacin is a DNA gyrase inhibitor, and also inhibits topoisomerase IV. DNA gyrase (topoisomerase II) is an essential bacterial enzyme that maintains the superhelical structure of DNA. DNA gyrase is required for DNA replication and transcription, DNA repair, recombination, and transposition; inhibition is bactericidal.

Pharmacodynamics/Kinetics
   Absorption: Well absorbed; not affected by high fat meal or yogurt
   Distribution: V_d: 1.7 to 2.7 L/kg; tissue concentrations often exceed plasma concentrations in respiratory tissues, alveolar macrophages, abdominal tissues/fluids, and sinus tissues
   Protein binding: 30% to 50%
   Metabolism: Hepatic (52% of dose) via glucuronide (14%) and sulfate (38%) conjugation
   Bioavailability: 90%
   Half-life elimination: Oral: 12 hours; I.V.: 15 hours
   Excretion: Approximately 45% of a dose is excreted in feces (25%) and urine (20%) as unchanged drug
     Metabolites: Sulfate conjugates in feces, glucuronide conjugates in urine

Dosage
   Usual dosage range:
     Children ≥1 year and Adults: Ophthalmic: Instill 1 drop into affected eye(s) 3 times/day for 7 days
     Adults: Oral, I.V.: 400 mg every 24 hours
   Indication-specific dosing:
     Children ≥1 year and Adults: Ophthalmic:
       Bacterial conjunctivitis: Instill 1 drop into affected eye(s) 3 times/day for 7 days
     Adults: Oral, I.V.:
       Acute bacterial sinusitis: 400 mg every 24 hours for 10 days
       Chronic bronchitis, acute bacterial exacerbation: 400 mg every 24 hours for 5 days
       Intra-abdominal infections (complicated): 400 mg every 24 hours for 5-14 days (initiate with I.V.)
       ***Legionella* (unlabeled use):** 400 mg every 24 hours for 10-21 days
       Pneumonia, community-acquired (including MDRSP): 400 mg every 24 hours for 7-14 days
       Skin and skin structure infections:
        Complicated: 400 mg every 24 hours for 7-21 days
        Uncomplicated: 400 mg every 24 hours for 7 days
     Elderly: No dosage adjustments are required based on age

   Dosage adjustment in renal impairment: No dosage adjustment is required, including patients on hemodialysis or CAPD
   Dosage adjustment in hepatic impairment: No dosage adjustment is required in mild to moderate hepatic insufficiency (Child-Pugh Class A and B). Not recommended in patients with severe hepatic insufficiency.

Dietary Considerations May be taken with or without food. Take 4 hours before or 8 hours after multiple vitamins, antacids, or other products containing magnesium, aluminum, iron, or zinc.

Administration I.V.: Infuse over 60 minutes; do not infuse by rapid or bolus intravenous infusion

Monitoring Parameters WBC, signs of infection

Test Interactions Some quinolones may produce a false-positive urine screening result for opiates using commercially-available immunoassay kits. This has been demonstrated most consistently for levofloxacin and ofloxacin, but other quinolones have shown cross-reactivity in certain assay kits. Confirmation of positive opiate screens by more specific methods should be considered.

Dosage Forms
   Infusion [premixed in sodium chloride 0.8%] (Avelox® I.V.): 400 mg (250 mL)
   Solution, ophthalmic (Vigamox™): 0.5% (3 mL)
   Tablet:
     Avelox®: 400 mg
     Avelox® ABC Pack [unit-dose pack]: 400 mg (5s)

♦ **Moxifloxacin Hydrochloride** *see* Moxifloxacin *on page 1175*
♦ **4-MP** *see* Fomepizole *on page 755*
♦ **MPA** *see* MedroxyPROGESTERone *on page 1065*
♦ **MPA** *see* Mycophenolate *on page 1181*
♦ **MPA and Estrogens (Conjugated)** *see* Estrogens (Conjugated/Equine) and Medroxyprogesterone *on page 634*
♦ **6-MP (error-prone abbreviation)** *see* Mercaptopurine *on page 1086*
♦ **MPSV4** *see* Meningococcal Polysaccharide Vaccine (Groups A / C / Y and W-135) *on page 1078*
♦ **MS Contin®** *see* Morphine Sulfate *on page 1171*
♦ **MS-IR® (Can)** *see* Morphine Sulfate *on page 1171*

- ◆ **MSO₄ (error-prone abbreviation and should not be used)** see Morphine Sulfate on page 1171
- ◆ **MTA** see Pemetrexed on page 1328
- ◆ **MTC** see Mitomycin on page 1155
- ◆ **MTX (error-prone abbreviation)** see Methotrexate on page 1111
- ◆ **Mucinex® [OTC]** see Guaifenesin on page 814
- ◆ **Mucinex®-D [OTC]** see Guaifenesin and Pseudoephedrine on page 819
- ◆ **Mucinex® DM [OTC]** see Guaifenesin and Dextromethorphan on page 816
- ◆ **Mucomyst** see Acetylcysteine on page 39
- ◆ **Mucomyst® (Can)** see Acetylcysteine on page 39
- ◆ **Multitargeted Antifolate** see Pemetrexed on page 1328
- ◆ **Mumps, Measles and Rubella Vaccines, Combined** see Measles, Mumps, and Rubella Vaccines (Combined) on page 1057
- ◆ **Mumps, Rubella, Varicella, and Measles Vaccine** see Measles, Mumps, Rubella, and Varicella Virus Vaccine on page 1057
- ◆ **Mumpsvax®** see Mumps Virus Vaccine (Live/Attenuated) on page 1178

Mumps Virus Vaccine (Live/Attenuated)
(mumpz VYE rus vak SEEN, live, a ten YOO ate ed)

U.S. Brand Names Mumpsvax®
Pharmacologic Category Vaccine
Additional Appendix Information
Immunization Recommendations on page 1929
Use Mumps prophylaxis by promoting active immunity
Note: Trivalent measles-mumps-rubella (MMR) vaccine is the preferred agent for most children and many adults; persons born prior to 1957 are generally considered immune and need not be vaccinated
Pregnancy Risk Factor C
Pregnancy Implications Reproduction studies have not been conducted. Rates of spontaneous abortion may be increased if mumps infection occurs during the first trimester. Although mumps vaccine virus can infect the placenta and fetus, there is not good evidence that it causes congenital malformations. Pregnancy should be avoided for 3 months following vaccination.
Lactation
Excretion in breast milk unknown/use caution
Contraindications
Hypersensitivity to mumps vaccine or any component of the formulation, including gelatin; febrile respiratory illness or active febrile infection; immunosuppressant therapy; primary or acquired immunodeficiency states; blood dyscrasias, leukemia, lymphoma or other malignant neoplasm affecting bone marrow or lymphatic systems; untreated tuberculosis; pregnancy
Warnings/Precautions Use caution with hypersensitivity to eggs or neomycin; patients with history of anaphylactic reaction may be at increased risk of immediate-type hypersensitivity reaction. Patients with minor illnesses (diarrhea, mild upper respiratory tract infection with or without low grade fever or other illnesses with low-grade fever) may receive vaccine. Leukemia patients who are in remission and have not received chemotherapy for at least 3 months may be vaccinated. Patients with a history of congenital or hereditary immunodeficiency should not receive immunization until immune competence is demonstrated. Do not administer to severely immunocompromised persons with the exception of asymptomatic children with HIV. Corticosteroid replacement therapy is not a contraindication for vaccination. Use caution in patients with thrombocytopenia and those who develop thrombocytopenia after first dose; thrombocytopenia may worsen. Immediate treatment for anaphylactic/anaphylactoid reaction should be available during vaccine use. Safety and efficacy in children <12 months of age have not been established.

Adverse Reactions All serious adverse reactions must be reported to the U.S. Department of Health and Human Services (DHHS) Vaccine Adverse Event Reporting System (VAERS) 1-800-822-7967.

Frequency not defined.
   Cardiovascular: Syncope, vasculitis
   Central nervous system: Encephalitis, febrile seizures, fever, Guillain-Barré syndrome, irritability
   Dermatologic: Angioneurotic edema, erythema multiforme, purpura, Stevens-Johnson syndrome, urticaria
   Endocrine & metabolic: Diabetes mellitus, parotitis
   Gastrointestinal: Diarrhea, pancreatitis
   Genitourinary: Orchitis
   Hematologic: Leukocytosis, thrombocytopenia
   Local: Burning/stinging at injection site, wheal and flare at injection site
   Ocular: Conjunctivitis, ocular palsies, optic neuritis, papillitis, retrobulbar neuritis
   Otic: Nerve deafness, otitis media
   Respiratory: Bronchial spasm, cough, rhinitis
   Miscellaneous: Anaphylaxis, anaphylactoid reactions, lymphadenopathy
Drug Interactions
  Decreased Effect:
    In patients receiving high doses of systemic corticosteroids for ≥14 days, wait at least 1 month between discontinuing steroid therapy and administering vaccine. Do not administer this vaccine with Immune globulin, whole blood, plasma; immune response may be compromised (defer vaccine administration for ≥3 months). The effect of the vaccine may be decreased with Immunosuppressant medications. Do not give within 1 month of other live virus vaccine.
Stability Product is shipped at ≤10°C (50°F). Prior to reconstitution, vaccine must be stored at ≤2°C to 8°C (36°F to 46°F). Reconstitute using entire contents of one vial of provided

preservative free diluent. Following reconstitution, use as soon as possible, but may be stored at 2°C to 8°C (36°F to 46°F) for up to 8 hours. Protect from light prior to and after reconstitution.

Mechanism of Action Promotes active immunity to mumps virus by inducing specific antibodies.

Dosage Children ≥12-15 months and Adults: SubQ: 0.5 mL as a single dose

Administration For SubQ administration in outer aspect of the upper arm using a 25G 5/8' needle

Test Interactions Temporary suppression of tuberculosis skin test

Additional Information Federal law requires that the date of administration, the vaccine manufacturer, lot number of vaccine, and the administering person's name, title, and address be entered into the patient's permanent medical record.

Acceptable presumptive evidence of immunity includes one of the following:
1. Documentation of adequate vaccination. Adequate vaccination for mumps is defined as 1 dose of a live mumps virus vaccine for preschool children and adults not at high risk; 2 doses of a live mumps virus vaccine for school-aged children and high-risk adults. Healthcare workers, international travelers, and students in institutions of higher learning are considered high-risk adults.
2. Laboratory evidence of immunity to mumps
3. Birth prior to 1957
4. Documentation of physician-diagnosed mumps

During a mumps outbreak, additional doses of a mumps virus vaccine may need to be considered. MMR vaccine is recommended; refer to Measles Mumps Rubella Vaccine (Combined) monograph. Minimum interval between doses is 28 days.

Dosage Forms
Injection, powder for reconstitution [preservative free]:
Mumpsvax®: $TCID_{50}$ 20,000 [contains human albumin, bovine serum, gelatin, neomycin; packaged with diluent]

Mupirocin (myoo PEER oh sln)

U.S. Brand Names Bactroban®; Bactroban® Nasal; Centany™
Canadian Brand Names Bactroban®
Index Terms Mupirocin Calcium; Pseudomonic Acid A
Pharmacologic Category Antibiotic, Topical
Use
Intranasal: Eradication of nasal colonization with MRSA in adult patients and healthcare workers
Topical: Treatment of impetigo or secondary infected traumatic skin lesions due to *S. aureus* and *S. pyogenes*
Unlabeled/Investigational Use Intranasal: Surgical prophylaxis to prevent wound infections
Pregnancy Risk Factor B
Medication Safety Issues
Sound-alike/look-alike issues:
Bactroban® may be confused with bacitracin, baclofen
Dosage
Intranasal: Children ≥12 years and Adults: Eradication of nasal MRSA: Approximately one-half of the ointment from the single-use tube should be applied into one nostril and the other half into the other nostril twice daily for 5 days
Topical:
Children ≥2 months and Adults: Impetigo: Ointment: Apply to affected area 3 times/day; re-evaluate after 3-5 days if no clinical response
Children ≥3 months and Adults: Secondary skin infections: Cream: Apply to affected area 3 times/day for 10 days; re-evaluate after 3-5 days if no clinical response
Dosage Forms Note: Strength expressed as base
Cream, topical, as calcium:
Bactroban®: 2% (15 g, 30 g) [contains benzyl alcohol]
Ointment, intranasal, as calcium:
Bactroban® Nasal: 2% (1 g) [single-use tube]
Ointment, topical: 2% (0.9 g, 22 g)
Bactroban®: 2% (22 g) [contains polyethylene glycol]
Centany™: 2% (15 g, 30 g)

♦ **Mupirocin Calcium** see Mupirocin on page 1179
♦ **Murine® Ear Wax Removal System [OTC]** see Carbamide Peroxide on page 287
♦ **Muro 128® [OTC]** see Sodium Chloride on page 1576
♦ **Murocoll-2®** see Phenylephrine and Scopolamine on page 1360

Muromonab-CD3 (myoo roe MOE nab see dee three)

U.S. Brand Names Orthoclone OKT® 3
Canadian Brand Names Orthoclone OKT® 3
Index Terms Monoclonal Antibody; OKT3
Pharmacologic Category Immunosuppressant Agent
Use Treatment of acute allograft rejection in renal transplant patients; treatment of acute hepatic, kidney, and pancreas rejection episodes resistant to conventional treatment. Acute graft-versus-host disease following bone marrow transplantation resistant to conventional treatment.

Pregnancy Risk Factor C
Lactation Excretion in breast milk unknown/contraindicated
(Continued)

Muromonab-CD3 *(Continued)*

Contraindications Hypersensitivity to OKT3 or any murine product; patients in fluid overload or those with >3% weight gain within 1 week prior to start of OKT3; mouse antibody titers >1:1000

Warnings/Precautions It is imperative, especially prior to the first few doses, that there be no clinical evidence of volume overload, uncontrolled hypertension, or uncompensated heart failure, including a clear chest x-ray and weight restriction of ≤3% above the patient's minimum weight during the week prior to injection.

May result in an increased susceptibility to infection; dosage of concomitant immunosuppressants should be reduced during OKT3 therapy; cyclosporine should be decreased to 50% usual maintenance dose and maintenance therapy resumed about 4 days before stopping OKT3.

Severe pulmonary edema has occurred in patients with fluid overload.

[U.S. Boxed Warning]: First dose effect (flu-like symptoms, anaphylactic-type reaction) may occur within 30 minutes to 6 hours up to 24 hours after the first dose and may be minimized by using the recommended regimens. See table.

Suggested Prevention/Treatment of Muromonab-CD3 First-Dose Effects

Adverse Reaction	Effective Prevention or Palliation	Supportive Treatment
Severe pulmonary edema	Clear chest x-ray within 24 hours preinjection; weight restriction to ≤3% gain over 7 days preinjection	Prompt intubation and oxygenation; 24 hours close observation
Fever, chills	15 mg/kg methylprednisolone sodium succinate 1 hour preinjection; fever reduction to <37.8°C (100°F) 1 hour preinjection; acetaminophen (1 g orally) and diphenhydramine (50 mg orally) 1 hour preinjection	Cooling blanket Acetaminophen prn
Respiratory effects	100 mg hydrocortisone sodium succinate 30 minutes postinjection	Additional 100 mg hydrocortisone sodium succinate prn for wheezing; if respiratory distress, give epinephrine 1:1000 (0.3 mL SubQ)

Cardiopulmonary resuscitation may be needed. If the patient's temperature is >37.8°C, reduce before administering OKT3. **[U.S. Boxed Warning]: Should be administered under the supervision of a physician experienced in immunosuppressive therapy in a facility appropriate for monitoring and resuscitation.**

Adverse Reactions Note: Signs and symptoms of Cytokine Release Syndrome (characterized by pyrexia, chills, dyspnea, nausea, vomiting, chest pain, diarrhea, tremor, wheezing, headache, tachycardia, rigor, hypertension, pulmonary edema and/or other cardiorespiratory manifestations) occurs in a significant proportion of patients following the first couple of doses of muromonab-CD3. See Warnings/Precautions. Additionally, some patients have experienced immediate hypersensitivity reactions to muromonab-CD3 (characterized by cardiovascular collapse, cardiorespiratory arrest, loss of consciousness, hypotension/shock, tachycardia, tingling, angioedema (including laryngeal, pharyngeal, or facial edema), airway obstruction, bronchospasm, dyspnea, urticaria, and/or pruritus) upon initial exposure and re-exposure.

>10%:

Cardiovascular: Tachycardia (26%), hypotension (25%), hypertension (19%), edema (12%)

Central nervous system: Pyrexia (77%), chills (43%), headache (28%)

Dermatologic: Rash (14%; erythematous 2%)

Gastrointestinal: Diarrhea (37%), nausea (32%), vomiting (25%)

Respiratory: Dyspnea (16%)

1% to 10%:

Cardiovascular: Chest pain (9%), vasodilation (7%), arrhythmia (4%), bradycardia (4%), vascular occlusion (2%)

Central nervous system: Fatigue (9%), confusion (6%), dizziness (6%), lethargy (6%), pain trunk (6%), malaise (5%), nervousness (5%), depression (3%), somnolence (2%), meningitis (1%), seizures (1%)

Dermatologic: Pruritus (7%)

Gastrointestinal: Gastrointestinal pain (7%), abdominal pain (6%), anorexia (4%)

Hematologic: Leukopenia (7%), anemia (2%), thrombocytopenia (2%), leukocytosis (1%)

Neuromuscular & skeletal: Weakness (10%), arthralgia (7%), myalgia (1%), tremor (14%)

Ocular: Photophobia (1%)

Otic: Tinnitus (1%)

Renal: Renal dysfunction (3%)

Respiratory: Abnormal chest sound (10%), hyperventilation (7%), wheezing (6%), respiratory congestion (4%), pulmonary edema (2%), hypoxia (1%), pneumonia (1%)

Miscellaneous: Diaphoresis (7%), infections (various)

<1% (Limited to important or life-threatening): Angina, anuria, apnea, cardiac arrest, coagulation disorder, coma, conjunctivitis, encephalopathy, epilepsy, GI hemorrhage, hallucinations, hearing decreased, heart failure, hepatitis, hypotonia, lymphadenopathy, lymphopenia, MI, mood changes, neoplasms (various), oliguria, paranoia, pneumonitis, psychosis, SGOT/SGPT increased, shock, thrombosis

Drug Interactions

Increased Effect/Toxicity: Recommend decreasing dose of prednisone to 0.5 mg/kg, azathioprine to 0.5 mg/kg (approximate 50% decrease in dose), and discontinuing cyclosporine while patient is receiving OKT3.

Decreased Effect: Decreased effect with immunosuppressive drugs.

Stability Refrigerate; do not freeze. Do not shake. Stable in Becton Dickinson syringe for 16 hours at room temperature or refrigeration.

Mechanism of Action Reverses graft rejection by binding to T cells and interfering with their function by binding T-cell receptor-associated CD3 glycoprotein

Pharmacodynamics/Kinetics
Duration: 7 days after discontinuation
Time to peak: Steady-state: Trough: 3-14 days

Dosage I.V. (refer to individual protocols):
Children <30 kg: 2.5 mg/day once daily for 7-14 days
Children >30 kg: 5 mg/day once daily for 7-14 days
OR
Children <12 years: 0.1 mg/kg/day once daily for 10-14 days
Children ≥12 years and Adults: 5 mg/day once daily for 10-14 days
Hemodialysis: Molecular size of OKT3 is 150,000 daltons; not dialyzed by most standard dialyzers; however, may be dialyzed by high flux dialysis; OKT3 will be removed by plasmapheresis; administer following dialysis treatments
Peritoneal dialysis: Significant drug removal is unlikely based on physiochemical characteristics

Dietary Considerations Injection solution contains sodium 43 mg/5 mL.

Administration Not for I.M. administration. Filter each dose through a low protein-binding 0.22 micron filter (Millex GV) before administration; administer I.V. push over <1 minute at a final concentration of 1 mg/mL

Children and Adults:
Methylprednisolone sodium succinate 15 mg/kg I.V. administered prior to first muromonab-CD3 administration and I.V. hydrocortisone sodium succinate 50-100 mg given 30 minutes after administration are strongly recommended to decrease the incidence of reactions to the first dose
Patient temperature should not exceed 37.8°C (100°F) at time of administration

Monitoring Parameters Chest x-ray, weight gain, CBC with differential, temperature, vital signs (blood pressure, temperature, pulse, respiration); immunologic monitoring of T cells, serum levels of OKT3

Reference Range
OKT3 serum concentrations:
Serum level monitoring should be performed in conjunction with lymphocyte subset determinations; Trough concentration sampling best correlates with clinical outcome. Serial monitoring may provide a better early indicator of inadequate dosing during induction or rejection.
Mean serum trough levels rise during the first 3 days, then average 0.9 mcg/mL on days 3-14
Circulating levels >0.8 mcg/mL block the function of cytotoxic T cells *in vitro* and *in vivo*
Several recent analysis have suggested appropriate dosage adjustments of OKT3 induction course are better determined with OKT3 serum levels versus lymphocyte subset determination; however, no prospective controlled trials have been performed to validate the equivalency of these tests in predicting clinical outcome.

Lymphocyte subset monitoring: CD3+ cells: Trough sample measurement is preferable and reagent utilized defines reference range.
OKT3-FITC: <10-50 cells/mm^3 or <3% to 5%
CD3(IgG1)-FITC: similar to OKT3-FITC
Leu-4a: Higher number of CD3+ cells appears acceptable
Dosage adjustments should be made in conjunction with clinical response and based upon trends over several consecutive days

Dosage Forms Injection, solution: 1 mg/mL (5 mL) [contains sodium 43 mg/5 mL]

- **Muse®** see Alprostadil *on page 77*
- **Muse® Pellet (Can)** see Alprostadil *on page 77*
- **Mustargen®** see Mechlorethamine *on page 1061*
- **Mustine** see Mechlorethamine *on page 1061*
- **Mutamycin®** see Mitomycin *on page 1155*
- **Myambutol®** see Ethambutol *on page 643*
- **Mycamine®** see Micafungin *on page 1136*
- **Mycelex®** see Clotrimazole *on page 404*
- **Mycelex®-3 [OTC]** see Butoconazole *on page 260*
- **Mycelex®-7 [OTC]** see Clotrimazole *on page 404*
- **Mycelex® Twin Pack [OTC]** see Clotrimazole *on page 404*
- **Mycinaire™ [OTC]** see Sodium Chloride *on page 1576*
- **Mycinettes® [OTC]** see Benzocaine *on page 204*
- **Mycobutin®** see Rifabutin *on page 1507*
- **Mycocide® NS [OTC]** see Tolnaftate *on page 1704*
- **Mycolog®-II [DSC]** see Nystatin and Triamcinolone *on page 1251*

Mycophenolate (mye koe FEN oh late)

U.S. Brand Names CellCept®; Myfortic®
Canadian Brand Names CellCept®; Myfortic®
Index Terms MMF; MPA; Mycophenolate Mofetil; Mycophenolate Sodium; Mycophenolic Acid
Pharmacologic Category Immunosuppressant Agent
Use Prophylaxis of organ rejection concomitantly with cyclosporine and corticosteroids in patients receiving allogenic renal (CellCept®, Myfortic®), cardiac (CellCept®), or hepatic (CellCept®) transplants
(Continued)

Mycophenolate *(Continued)*

Unlabeled/Investigational Use Treatment of rejection in liver transplant patients unable to tolerate tacrolimus or cyclosporine due to neurotoxicity; mild rejection in heart transplant patients; treatment of moderate-severe psoriasis; treatment of proliferative lupus nephritis; treatment of myasthenia gravis

Pregnancy Risk Factor C (manufacturer)

Pregnancy Implications There are no adequate and well-controlled studies using mycophenolate in pregnant women, however, based on animal teratogenicity studies, it may cause fetal harm. Women of childbearing potential should have a negative pregnancy test within 1 week prior to beginning therapy. Two reliable forms of contraception should be used prior to, during, and for 6 weeks after therapy.

Lactation Excretion in breast milk unknown/not recommended

Contraindications Hypersensitivity to mycophenolate mofetil, mycophenolic acid, mycophenolate sodium, or any component of the formulation; intravenous formulation is contraindicated in patients who are allergic to polysorbate 80

Warnings/Precautions Hazardous agent - use appropriate precautions for handling and disposal. **[U.S. Boxed Warning]: Risk for infection and development of lymphoproliferative disorders (particularly of the skin) is increased.** Patients should be monitored appropriately, instructed to limit exposure to sunlight/UV light, and given supportive treatment should these conditions occur. Severe neutropenia may occur, requiring interruption of treatment (risk greater from day 31-180 post-transplant). Use caution with active peptic ulcer disease; may be associated with GI bleeding and/or perforation. Use caution in renal impairment as toxicity may be increased; may require dosage adjustment in severe impairment. Patients may be at increased risk of infection.

Because mycophenolate mofetil has demonstrated teratogenic effects in rats and rabbits, tablets should not be crushed, and capsules should not be opened or crushed. Avoid inhalation or direct contact with skin or mucous membranes of the powder contained in the capsules and the powder for oral suspension. Caution should be exercised in the handling and preparation of solutions of intravenous mycophenolate. Avoid skin contact with the intravenous solution and reconstituted suspension. If such contact occurs, wash thoroughly with soap and water, rinse eyes with plain water.

Theoretically, use should be avoided in patients with the rare hereditary deficiency of hypoxanthine-guanine phosphoribosyltransferase (such as Lesch-Nyhan or Kelley-Seegmiller syndrome). Intravenous solutions should be given over at least 2 hours; **never** administer intravenous solution by rapid or bolus injection. **[U.S. Boxed Warning]: Should be administered under the supervision of a physician experienced in immunosuppressive therapy.**

Note: CellCept® and Myfortic® dosage forms should not be used interchangeably due to differences in absorption.

Adverse Reactions As reported in adults following oral dosing of CellCept® alone in renal, cardiac, and hepatic allograft rejection studies. In general, lower doses used in renal rejection patients had less adverse effects than higher doses. Rates of adverse effects were similar for each indication, except for those unique to the specific organ involved. The type of adverse effects observed in pediatric patients was similar to those seen in adults; abdominal pain, anemia, diarrhea, fever, hypertension, infection, pharyngitis, respiratory tract infection, sepsis, and vomiting were seen in higher proportion; lymphoproliferative disorder was the only type of malignancy observed. Percentages of adverse reactions were similar in studies comparing CellCept® to Myfortic® in patients following renal transplant.

>20%:
  Cardiovascular: Hypertension (28% to 77%), hypotension (up to 33%), peripheral edema (27% to 64%), edema (27% to 28%), tachycardia (20% to 22%)

  Central nervous system: Pain (31% to 76%), headache (16% to 54%), insomnia (41% to 52%), fever (21% to 52%), dizziness (up to 29%), anxiety (28%)

  Dermatologic: Rash (up to 22%)

  Endocrine & metabolic: Hyperglycemia (44% to 47%), hypercholesterolemia (41%), hypokalemia (32% to 37%), hypocalcemia (up to 30%), hypomagnesemia (up to 39%), hyperkalemia (up to 22%)

  Gastrointestinal: Abdominal pain (25% to 62%), nausea (20% to 54%), diarrhea (31% to 52%), constipation (18% to 41%), vomiting (33% to 34%), anorexia (up to 25%), dyspepsia (22%)

  Genitourinary: Urinary tract infection (37%)

  Hematologic: Leukopenia (23% to 46%), leukocytosis (22% to 40%), hypochromic anemia (26% to 43%), thrombocytopenia (24% to 36%)

  Hepatic: Liver function tests abnormal (up to 25%), ascites (24%)

  Neuromuscular & skeletal: Back pain (35% to 47%), weakness (35% to 43%), tremor (24% to 34%), paresthesia (21%)

  Renal: BUN increased (up to 35%), creatinine increased (up to 39%)

  Respiratory: Dyspnea (31% to 37%), respiratory tract infection (22% to 37%), cough (31%), lung disorder (22% to 30%)

  Miscellaneous: Infection (18% to 27%), *Candida* (11% to 22%), herpes simplex (10% to 21%)

3% to <20%:
  Cardiovascular: Angina, arrhythmia, arterial thrombosis, atrial fibrillation, atrial flutter, bradycardia, cardiac arrest, cardiac failure, CHF, extrasystole, facial edema, hypervolemia, pallor, palpitation, pericardial effusion, peripheral vascular disorder, postural hypotension, supraventricular extrasystoles, supraventricular tachycardia, syncope, thrombosis, vasodilation, vasospasm, venous pressure increased, ventricular extrasystole, ventricular tachycardia

  Central nervous system: Agitation, chills with fever, confusion, convulsion, delirium, depression, emotional lability, hallucinations, hypoesthesia, malaise, nervousness, psychosis, somnolence, thinking abnormal, vertigo

Dermatologic: Acne, alopecia, bruising, cellulitis, hirsutism, petechia, pruritus, skin carcinoma, skin hypertrophy, skin ulcer, vesiculobullous rash

Endocrine & metabolic: Acidosis, Cushing's syndrome, dehydration, diabetes mellitus, gout, hypercalcemia, hyperlipemia, hyperphosphatemia, hyperuricemia, hypochloremia, hypoglycemia, hyponatremia, hypoproteinemia, hypothyroidism, parathyroid disorder, weight gain/loss

Gastrointestinal: Abdomen enlarged, dry mouth, dysphagia, esophagitis, flatulence, gastritis, gastroenteritis, gastrointestinal hemorrhage, gastrointestinal moniliasis, gingivitis, gum hyperplasia, ileus, melena, mouth ulceration, oral moniliasis, stomach disorder, stomatitis

Genitourinary: Impotence, nocturia, pelvic pain, prostatic disorder, scrotal edema, urinary frequency, urinary incontinence, urinary retention, urinary tract disorder

Hematologic: Coagulation disorder, hemorrhage, neutropenia, pancytopenia, polycythemia, prothrombin time increased, thromboplastin increased

Hepatic: Alkaline phosphatase increased, alkalosis, bilirubinemia, cholangitis, cholestatic jaundice, GGT increased, hepatitis, jaundice, liver damage, transaminases increased

Local: Abscess

Neuromuscular & skeletal: Arthralgia, hypertonia, joint disorder, leg cramps, myalgia, myasthenia, neck pain, neuropathy, osteoporosis

Ocular: Amblyopia, cataract, conjunctivitis, eye hemorrhage, lacrimation disorder, vision abnormal

Otic: Deafness, ear disorder, ear pain, tinnitus

Renal: Albuminuria, creatinine increased, dysuria, hematuria, hydronephrosis, kidney failure, kidney tubular necrosis, oliguria

Respiratory: Apnea, asthma, atelectasis, bronchitis, epistaxis, hemoptysis, hiccup, hyperventilation, hypoxia, respiratory acidosis, lung edema, pharyngitis, pleural effusion, pneumonia, pneumothorax, pulmonary hypertension, respiratory moniliasis, rhinitis, sinusitis, sputum increased, voice alteration

Miscellaneous: *Candida* (mucocutaneous 15% to 18%), CMV viremia/syndrome (12% to 14%), CMV tissue invasive disease (6% to 11%), herpes zoster cutaneous disease (4% to 10%), cyst, diaphoresis, flu-like syndrome, fungal dermatitis, healing abnormal, hernia, ileus infection, lactic dehydrogenase increased, peritonitis, pyelonephritis, thirst

Postmarketing and/or case reports: Atypical mycobacterial infection, colitis, infectious endocarditis, interstitial lung disorder, intestinal villous atrophy, meningitis, pancreatitis, pulmonary fibrosis (fatal), tuberculosis

Overdosage/Toxicology There are no reported overdoses with mycophenolate. At plasma concentrations >100 mcg/mL, small amounts of the inactive metabolite MPAG are removed by hemodialysis. Excretion of the active metabolite, MPA, may be increased by using bile acid sequestrants (cholestyramine).

Drug Interactions

Increased Effect/Toxicity: Acyclovir, valacyclovir, ganciclovir, and valganciclovir levels may increase due to competition for tubular secretion of these drugs. Probenecid may increase mycophenolate levels due to inhibition of tubular secretion. High doses of salicylates may increase free fraction of mycophenolic acid. Azathioprine's bone marrow suppression may be potentiated; do not administer together.

Decreased Effect: Antacids decrease serum levels (C_{max} and AUC); **do not administer together**. Cholestyramine resin decreases serum levels; **do not administer together**. Avoid use of live vaccines; vaccinations may be less effective. Influenza vaccine may be of value. During concurrent use of oral contraceptives, progesterone levels are not significantly affected, however, effect on estrogen component varies; an additional form of contraception should be used.

Ethanol/Nutrition/Herb Interactions

Food: Decreases C_{max} of MPA by 40% following CellCept® administration and 33% following Myfortic® use; the extent of absorption is not changed

Herb/Nutraceutical: Avoid cat's claw, echinacea (have immunostimulant properties)

Stability

Capsules: Store at room temperature of 15°C to 39°C (59°F to 86°F).

Tablets: Store at room temperature of 15°C to 39°C (59°F to 86°F). Protect from light.

Oral suspension: Store powder for oral suspension at room temperature of 15°C to 39°C (59°F to 86°F). Should be constituted prior to dispensing to the patient and **not** mixed with any other medication. Add 47 mL of water to the bottle and shake well for ~1 minute. Add another 47 mL of water to the bottle and shake well for an additional minute. Final concentration is 200 mg/mL of mycophenolate mofetil. Once reconstituted, the oral solution may be stored at room temperature or under refrigeration. Do not freeze. The mixed suspension is stable for 60 days.

I.V.: Store intact vials at room temperature 15°C to 30°C (59°F to 86°F). Reconstitute the contents of each vial with 14 mL of 5% dextrose injection; dilute the contents of a vial with 5% dextrose in water to a final concentration of 6 mg mycophenolate mofetil per mL. **Note:** Vial is vacuum-sealed; if a lack of vacuum is noted during preparation, the vial should not be used. Stability of the infusion solution: 4 hours from reconstitution and dilution of the product. Store solutions at 15°C to 30°C (59°F to 86°F).

Mechanism of Action MPA exhibits a cytostatic effect on T and B lymphocytes. It is an inhibitor of inosine monophosphate dehydrogenase (IMPDH) which inhibits *de novo* guanosine nucleotide synthesis. T and B lymphocytes are dependent on this pathway for proliferation.

Pharmacodynamics/Kinetics

Onset of action: Peak effect: Correlation of toxicity or efficacy is still being developed, however, one study indicated that 12-hour AUCs >40 mcg/mL/hour were correlated with efficacy and decreased episodes of rejection

T_{max}: Oral: MPA:

CellCept®: 1-1.5 hours

Myfortic®: 1.5-2.5 hours

(Continued)

Mycophenolate *(Continued)*

Absorption: AUC values for MPA are lower in the early post-transplant period versus later (>3 months) post-transplant period. The extent of absorption in pediatrics is similar to that seen in adults, although there was wide variability reported.

Oral: Myfortic®: 93%

Distribution:

CellCept®: MPA: Oral: 4 L/kg; I.V.: 3.6 L/kg

Myfortic®: MPA: Oral: 54 L (at steady state); 112 L (elimination phase)

Protein binding: MPA: 97%, MPAG 82%

Metabolism: Hepatic and via GI tract; CellCept® is completely hydrolyzed in the liver to mycophenolic acid (MPA; active metabolite); enterohepatic recirculation of MPA may occur; MPA is glucuronidated to MPAG (inactive metabolite)

Bioavailability: Oral: CellCept®: 94%; Myfortic®: 72%

Half-life elimination:

CellCept®: MPA: Oral: 18 hours; I.V.: 17 hours

Myfortic®: MPA: Oral: 8-16 hours; MPAG: 13-17 hours

Excretion:

CellCept®: MPA: Urine (<1%), feces (6%); MPAG: Urine (87%)

Myfortic®: MPA: Urine (3%), feces; MPAG: Urine (>60%)

Dosage

Children: Renal transplant: Oral:

CellCept® suspension: 600 mg/m²/dose twice daily; maximum dose: 1 g twice daily

Alternatively, may use solid dosage forms according to BSA as follows:

BSA 1.25-1.5 m²: 750 mg capsule twice daily

BSA >1.5 m²: 1 g capsule or tablet twice daily

Myfortic®: 400 mg/m²/dose twice daily; maximum dose: 720 mg twice daily

BSA <1.19 m²: Use of this formulation is not recommended

BSA 1.19-1.58 m²: 540 mg twice daily (maximum: 1080 mg/day)

BSA >1.58 m²: 720 mg twice daily (maximum: 1440 mg/day)

Adults:

Renal transplant:

CellCept®:

Oral: 1 g twice daily. Doses >2 g/day are not recommended.

I.V.: 1 g twice daily

Myfortic®: Oral: 720 mg twice daily (1440 mg/day)

Cardiac transplantation:

Oral (CellCept®): 1.5 g twice daily

I.V. (CellCept®): 1.5 g twice daily

Hepatic transplantation:

Oral (CellCept®): 1.5 g twice daily

I.V. (CellCept®): 1 g twice daily

Myasthenia gravis (unlabeled use): Oral (CellCept®): 1 g twice daily (range 1-3 g/day)

Dosing adjustment in renal impairment:

Renal transplant: GFR <25 mL/minute in patients outside the immediate post-transplant period:

CellCept®: Doses of >1 g administered twice daily should be avoided; patients should also be carefully observed; no dose adjustments are needed in renal transplant patients experiencing delayed graft function postoperatively

Myfortic®: Cl$_{cr}$ <25 mL/minute: Monitor carefully

Cardiac or liver transplant: No data available; mycophenolate may be used in cardiac or hepatic transplant patients with severe chronic renal impairment if the potential benefit outweighs the potential risk

Hemodialysis: Not removed; supplemental dose is not necessary

Peritoneal dialysis: Supplemental dose is not necessary

Dosage adjustment in hepatic impairment: No dosage adjustment is recommended for renal patients with severe hepatic parenchymal disease; however, it is not currently known whether dosage adjustments are necessary for hepatic disease with other etiologies

Elderly: Dosage is the same as younger patients, however, dosing should be cautious due to possibility of increased hepatic, renal or cardiac dysfunction; elderly patients may be at an increased risk of certain infections, gastrointestinal hemorrhage, and pulmonary edema, as compared to younger patients

Dosage adjustment for toxicity (neutropenia): ANC <1.3 x 10³/µL: Dosing should be interrupted or the dose reduced, appropriate diagnostic tests performed and patients managed appropriately

Dietary Considerations Oral dosage formulations should be taken on an empty stomach to avoid variability in MPA absorption. However, in stable renal transplant patients, may be administered with food if necessary. Oral suspension contains 0.56 mg phenylalanine/mL; use caution if administered to patients with phenylketonuria.

Administration

Oral dosage formulations (tablet, capsule, suspension) should be administered on an empty stomach to avoid variability in MPA absorption. The oral solution may be administered via a nasogastric tube (minimum 8 French, 1.7 mm interior diameter); oral suspension should not be mixed with other medications. Delayed release tablets should not be crushed, cut, or chewed.

Intravenous solutions should be administered over at least 2 hours (either peripheral or central vein); do **not** administer intravenous solution by rapid or bolus injection.

Monitoring Parameters Complete blood count; signs and symptoms of infection

Dosage Forms

Capsule, as mofetil (CellCept®): 250 mg

Injection, powder for reconstitution, as mofetil hydrochloride (CellCept®): 500 mg [contains polysorbate 80]

Powder for oral suspension, as mofetil (CellCept®): 200 mg/mL (225 mL) [provides 175 mL suspension following reconstitution; contains phenylalanine 0.56 mg/mL; mixed fruit flavor]

Tablet, as mofetil (CellCept®): 500 mg [may contain ethyl alcohol]
Tablet, delayed release, as mycophenolic acid (Myfortic®): 180 mg, 360 mg [formulated as a sodium salt]

♦ **Mycophenolate Mofetil** see Mycophenolate on page 1181
♦ **Mycophenolate Sodium** see Mycophenolate on page 1181
♦ **Mycophenolic Acid** see Mycophenolate on page 1181
♦ **Mycostatin®** see Nystatin on page 1250
♦ **Mydfrin®** see Phenylephrine on page 1358
♦ **Mydral™** see Tropicamide on page 1752
♦ **Mydriacyl®** see Tropicamide on page 1752
♦ **Myfortic®** see Mycophenolate on page 1181
♦ **Mylanta™ (Can)** see Aluminum Hydroxide and Magnesium Hydroxide on page 85
♦ **Mylanta® Children's [OTC]** see Calcium Carbonate on page 269
♦ **Mylanta® Double Strength (Can)** see Aluminum Hydroxide, Magnesium Hydroxide, and Simethicone on page 85
♦ **Mylanta® Extra Strength (Can)** see Aluminum Hydroxide, Magnesium Hydroxide, and Simethicone on page 85
♦ **Mylanta® Gelcaps® [OTC]** see Calcium Carbonate and Magnesium Hydroxide on page 271
♦ **Mylanta® Liquid [OTC]** see Aluminum Hydroxide, Magnesium Hydroxide, and Simethicone on page 85
♦ **Mylanta® Maximum Strength Liquid [OTC]** see Aluminum Hydroxide, Magnesium Hydroxide, and Simethicone on page 85
♦ **Mylanta® Regular Strength (Can)** see Aluminum Hydroxide, Magnesium Hydroxide, and Simethicone on page 85
♦ **Mylanta® Supreme [OTC]** see Calcium Carbonate and Magnesium Hydroxide on page 271
♦ **Mylanta® Ultra [OTC]** see Calcium Carbonate and Magnesium Hydroxide on page 271
♦ **Myleran®** see Busulfan on page 257
♦ **Mylocel™** see Hydroxyurea on page 863
♦ **Mylotarg®** see Gemtuzumab Ozogamicin on page 790
♦ **Myobloc®** see Botulinum Toxin Type B on page 237
♦ **Myochrysine® (Can)** see Gold Sodium Thiomalate on page 808
♦ **Myotonachol® (Can)** see Bethanechol on page 216
♦ **Myozyme®** see Alglucosidase Alfa on page 70
♦ **myrac™** see Minocycline on page 1149
♦ **Mysoline®** see Primidone on page 1422
♦ **Mytussin® AC** see Guaifenesin and Codeine on page 815
♦ **Mytussin® DAC** see Guaifenesin, Pseudoephedrine, and Codeine on page 820
♦ **N-9** see Nonoxynol 9 on page 1239
♦ **Na2EDTA** see Edetate Disodium on page 568
♦ **Nabi-HB®** see Hepatitis B Immune Globulin on page 834
♦ **NAB-Paclitaxel** see Paclitaxel (Protein Bound) on page 1297

Nabumetone (na BYOO me tone)

U.S. Brand Names Relafen® [DSC]
Canadian Brand Names Apo-Nabumetone®; Gen-Nabumetone; Novo-Nabumetone; Relafen®; Rhoxal-nabumetone; Sandoz-Nabumetone
Pharmacologic Category Nonsteroidal Anti-inflammatory Drug (NSAID), Oral
Additional Appendix Information
Nonsteroidal Anti-inflammatory Agents on page 1894
Use Management of osteoarthritis and rheumatoid arthritis
Unlabeled/Investigational Use Moderate pain
Restrictions An FDA-approved medication guide must be distributed when dispensing an oral outpatient prescription (new or refill) where this medication is to be used without direct supervision of a healthcare provider. Medication guides are available at http://www.fda.gov/cder/Offices/ODS/medication_guides.htm.
Pregnancy Risk Factor C/D (3rd trimester)
Lactation Excretion in breast milk unknown/not recommended
Contraindications Hypersensitivity to nabumetone, aspirin, other NSAIDs, or any component of the formulation; perioperative pain in the setting of coronary artery bypass surgery (CABG); pregnancy (3rd trimester)
Warnings/Precautions [U.S. Boxed Warning]: NSAIDs are associated with an increased risk of adverse cardiovascular events, including MI, stroke, and new onset or worsening of pre-existing hypertension. Risk may be increased with duration of use or pre-existing cardiovascular risk-factors or disease. Carefully evaluate individual cardiovascular risk profiles prior to prescribing. Use caution with fluid retention, CHF or hypertension. Concurrent administration of ibuprofen, and potentially other nonselective NSAIDs, may interfere with aspirin's cardioprotective effect.

Use of NSAIDs can compromise existing renal function. Renal toxicity can occur in patient with impaired renal function, dehydration, heart failure, liver dysfunction, those taking diuretics and ACEI and the elderly. Rehydrate patient before starting therapy. Monitor renal function closely. Not recommended for use in patients with advanced renal disease.

[U.S. Boxed Warning]: NSAIDs may increase risk of gastrointestinal irritation, ulceration, bleeding, and perforation. These events may occur at any time during therapy and without warning. Use caution with a history of GI disease (bleeding or ulcers), concurrent therapy with aspirin, anticoagulants and/or corticosteroids, smoking, use of alcohol, the elderly or debilitated patients.
(Continued)

Nabumetone *(Continued)*

Use the lowest effective dose for the shortest duration of time, consistent with individual patient goals, to reduce risk of cardiovascular or GI adverse events. Alternate therapies should be considered for patients at high risk.

NSAIDs may cause serious skin adverse events including exfoliative dermatitis, Stevens-Johnson syndrome (SJS) and toxic epidermal necrolysis (TEN). Anaphylactoid reactions may occur, even without prior exposure; patients with "aspirin triad" (bronchial asthma, aspirin intolerance, rhinitis) may be at increased risk. Do not use in patients who experience bronchospasm, asthma, rhinitis, or urticaria with NSAID or aspirin therapy.

Use with caution in patients with decreased hepatic function. Closely monitor patients with any abnormal LFT. Severe hepatic reactions (eg, fulminant hepatitis, liver failure) have occurred with NSAID use, rarely; discontinue if signs or symptoms of liver disease develop, or if systemic manifestations occur.

The elderly are at increased risk for adverse effects (especially peptic ulceration, CNS effects, renal toxicity) from NSAIDs even at low doses

Withhold for at least 4-6 half-lives prior to surgical or dental procedures. May cause photosensitivity reactions. Safety and efficacy have not been established in pediatric patients.

Adverse Reactions
>10%: Gastrointestinal: Abdominal pain (12%), diarrhea (14%), dyspepsia (13%)

1% to 10%:
Cardiovascular: Edema (3% to 9%)
Central nervous system: Dizziness (3% to 9%), headache (3% to 9%), fatigue (1% to 3%), insomnia (1% to 3%), nervousness (1% to 3%), somnolence (1% to 3%)
Dermatologic: Pruritus (3% to 9%), rash (3% to 9%)
Gastrointestinal: Constipation (3% to 9%), flatulence (3% to 9%), guaic positive (3% to 9%), nausea (3% to 9%), gastritis (1% to 3%), stomatitis (1% to 3%), vomiting (1% to 3%), xerostomia (1% to 3%)
Otic: Tinnitus
Miscellaneous: Diaphoresis (1% to 3%)

<1% (Limited to important or life-threatening): Abnormal vision, acne, agitation, albuminuria, alopecia, anaphylactoid reaction, anaphylaxis, anemia, angina, angioneurotic edema, anorexia, anxiety, arrhythmia, asthma, azotemia, bilirubinemia duodenitis, bullous eruptions, CHF, chills, confusion, cough, depression, duodenal ulcer, dysphagia, dyspnea, dysuria, eosinophilic pneumonia, eructation, erythema multiforme, fever, gallstones, gastric ulcer, gastroenteritis, gingivitis, GI bleeding, glossitis, granulocytopenia, hematuria, hepatic failure, hyperglycemia, hypersensitivity pneumonitis, hypertension, hyperuricemia, hypokalemia, impotence, interstitial nephritis, interstitial pneumonitis, jaundice, leukopenia, liver function abnormalities, malaise, melena, MI, nephrotic syndrome, nightmares, palpitations, pancreatitis, paresthesia, photosensitivity, pseudoporphyria cutanea tarda, rectal bleeding, renal failure, renal stones, Stevens-Johnson syndrome, syncope, taste disorder, thrombocytopenia, thrombophlebitis, toxic epidermal necrolysis, tremor, urticaria, vasculitis, vertigo, weakness, weight gain/loss

Overdosage/Toxicology Symptoms of overdose include drowsiness, epigastric pain, lethargy, nausea and vomiting. Acute renal failure, coma, hypertension and respiratory depression may also rarely occur. Management of NSAID intoxication is supportive and symptomatic. 6-Methoxy-2-naphthylacetic acid (6MNA) is not dialyzable.

Drug Interactions
Increased Effect/Toxicity: NSAIDs may increase digoxin, methotrexate, and lithium serum concentrations. The renal adverse effects of ACE inhibitors may be potentiated by NSAIDs. Potential for bleeding may be increased with anticoagulants or antiplatelet agents. Concurrent use of corticosteroids may increase the risk of GI ulceration. Concomitant use with fluoroquinolones may rarely increase risk of seizure.

Decreased Effect: NSAIDs may decrease the effect of some antihypertensive agents, including ACE inhibitors, angiotensin receptor antagonists, beta-blockers, and hydralazine. The efficacy of diuretics (loop and/or thiazide) may be decreased. Cholestyramine (and other bile acid sequestrants) may decrease the absorption of NSAIDs; separate by at least 2 hours. Salicylates' antiplatelet effect may be reduced.

Ethanol/Nutrition/Herb Interactions
Ethanol: Avoid ethanol (may enhance gastric mucosal irritation).
Food: Nabumetone peak serum concentrations may be increased if taken with food or dairy products.
Herb/Nutraceutical: Avoid alfalfa, anise, bilberry, bladderwrack, bromelain, cat's claw, celery, coleus, cordyceps, dong quai, evening primrose, feverfew, fenugreek, garlic, ginger, ginkgo biloboa, red clover, horse chestnut, grapeseed, green tea, ginseng, guggul, horse chestnut seed, horseradish, licorice, prickly ash, red clover, reishi, SAMe, sweet clover, turmeric, white willow (all have additional antiplatelet activity).

Mechanism of Action Nabumetone is a nonacidic NSAID that is rapidly metabolized after absorption to a major active metabolite, 6-methoxy-2-naphthylacetic acid. As found with previous NSAIDs, nabumetone's active metabolite inhibits the cyclooxygenase enzyme which is indirectly responsible for the production of inflammation and pain during arthritis by way of enhancing the production of endoperoxides and prostaglandins E_2 and I_2 (prostacyclin). The active metabolite of nabumetone is felt to be the compound primarily responsible for therapeutic effect. Comparatively, the parent drug is a poor inhibitor of prostaglandin synthesis.

Pharmacodynamics/Kinetics
Onset of action: Several days
Distribution: Diffusion occurs readily into synovial fluid
V_d: 6MNA: 29-82 L
Protein binding: 6MNA: >99%
Metabolism: Prodrug, rapidly metabolized in the liver to an active metabolite [6-methoxy-2-naphthylacetic acid (6MNA)] and inactive metabolites; extensive first-pass effect

Half-life elimination: 6MNA: ~24 hours
Time to peak, serum: 6MNA: Oral: 2.5-4 hours; Synovial fluid: 4-12 hours
Excretion: 6MNA: Urine (80%) and feces (9%)

Dosage Adults: Oral: 1000 mg/day; an additional 500-1000 mg may be needed in some patients to obtain more symptomatic relief; may be administered once or twice daily (maximum dose: 2000 mg/day)

Note: Patients <50 kg are less likely to require doses >1000 mg/day.

Dosage adjustment in renal impairment: In general, NSAIDs are not recommended for use in patients with advanced renal disease, but the manufacturer of nabumetone does provide some guidelines for adjustment in renal dysfunction:

Moderate impairment (Cl_{cr} 30-49 mL/minute): Initial dose: 750 mg/day; maximum dose: 1500 mg/day

Severe impairment (Cl_{cr} <30 mL/minute): Initial dose: 500 mg/day; maximum dose: 1000 mg/day

Monitoring Parameters Patients with renal insufficiency: Baseline renal function followed by repeat test within weeks (to determine if renal function has deteriorated)

Dosage Forms [DSC] = Discontinued product
Tablet: 500 mg, 750 mg
Relafen®: 500 mg, 750 mg [DSC]

♦ **NAC** see Acetylcysteine on page 39
♦ **N-Acetyl-L-cysteine** see Acetylcysteine on page 39
♦ **N-Acetylcysteine** see Acetylcysteine on page 39
♦ **N-Acetyl-P-Aminophenol** see Acetaminophen on page 28
♦ **NaCl** see Sodium Chloride on page 1576

Nadolol (NAY doe lol)

U.S. Brand Names Corgard®
Canadian Brand Names Alti-Nadolol; Apo-Nadol®; Corgard®; Novo-Nadolol
Pharmacologic Category Beta-Adrenergic Blocker, Nonselective
Additional Appendix Information
Beta-Blockers on page 1875
Use Treatment of hypertension and angina pectoris; prophylaxis of migraine headaches
Pregnancy Risk Factor C
Pregnancy Implications No data available on crossing the placenta. Beta-blockers have been associated with bradycardia, hypotension, and IUGR; IUGR is probably related to maternal hypertension. Alternative beta-blockers are preferred for use during pregnancy due to limited data and prolonged half-life. Cases of neonatal hypoglycemia have been reported following maternal use of beta-blockers at parturition or during breast-feeding. Monitor breast-fed infant for symptoms of beta-blockade.
Lactation Enters breast milk/use caution (AAP rates "compatible")
Medication Safety Issues
Sound-alike/look-alike issues:
Nadolol may be confused with Mandol®
Corgard® may be confused with Cognex®
Contraindications Hypersensitivity to nadolol or any component of the formulation; bronchial asthma; sinus bradycardia; sinus node dysfunction; heart block greater than first degree (except in patients with a functioning artificial pacemaker); cardiogenic shock; uncompensated cardiac failure
Warnings/Precautions Consider pre-existing conditions such as sick sinus syndrome before initiating. Administer only with extreme caution in patients with compensated heart failure, monitor for a worsening of the condition. Efficacy in heart failure has not been established for nadolol. **[U.S. Boxed Warning]: Beta-blocker therapy should not be withdrawn abruptly (particularly in patients with CAD), but gradually tapered to avoid acute tachycardia, hypertension, and/or ischemia.** Use caution with concurrent use of beta-blockers and either verapamil or diltiazem; bradycardia or heart block can occur. In general, patients with bronchospastic disease should not receive beta-blockers. Nadolol, if used at all, should be used cautiously in bronchospastic disease with close monitoring. Use cautiously in diabetics because it can mask prominent hypoglycemic symptoms. Use cautiously in the renally impaired (dosage adjustments are required). Use with caution in patients with myasthenia gravis, peripheral vascular disease, or psychiatric disease (may cause CNS depression). Use care with anesthetic agents which decrease myocardial function. Adequate alpha-blockade is required prior to use of any beta-blocker for patients with untreated pheochromocytoma. Safety and efficacy have not been established in children.
Adverse Reactions
>10%:
Central nervous system: Drowsiness, insomnia
Endocrine & metabolic: Decreased sexual ability
1% to 10%:
Cardiovascular: Bradycardia, palpitation, edema, CHF, reduced peripheral circulation
Central nervous system: Mental depression
Gastrointestinal: Diarrhea or constipation, nausea, vomiting, stomach discomfort
Respiratory: Bronchospasm
Miscellaneous: Cold extremities
<1% (Limited to important or life-threatening): Arrhythmias, chest pain, confusion (especially in the elderly), depression, dyspnea, hallucinations, leukopenia, orthostatic hypotension, thrombocytopenia
Overdosage/Toxicology Symptoms of intoxication include cardiac disturbances, CNS toxicity, bronchospasm, hypoglycemia, and hyperkalemia. The most common cardiac symptoms include hypotension and bradycardia. Atrioventricular block, intraventricular conduction disturbances, cardiogenic shock, and asystole may occur with severe overdose, especially with membrane-depressant drugs (eg, propranolol). CNS effects include convulsions, coma, (Continued)

Nadolol *(Continued)*

and respiratory arrest (commonly seen with propranolol and other membrane-depressant and lipid-soluble drugs). Treatment is symptomatic for seizures, hypotension, hyperkalemia, and hypoglycemia. Bradycardia and hypotension resistant to atropine, isoproterenol, or pacing may respond to glucagon. Wide QRS defects caused by membrane-depressant poisoning may respond to hypertonic sodium bicarbonate. Repeat-dose charcoal, hemoperfusion, or hemodialysis may be helpful in removal of only those beta-blockers with a small V_d, long half-life, or low intrinsic clearance (acebutolol, atenolol, nadolol, sotalol).

Drug Interactions

Increased Effect/Toxicity: The heart rate lowering effects of nadolol are additive with other drugs which slow AV conduction (digoxin, verapamil, diltiazem). Concurrent use of alpha-blockers (prazosin, terazosin) with beta-blockers may increase risk of orthostasis. Nadolol may mask the tachycardia from hypoglycemia caused by insulin and oral hypoglycemics. In patients receiving concurrent therapy, the risk of hypertensive crisis is increased when either clonidine or the beta-blocker is withdrawn. Reserpine has been shown to enhance the effect of beta-blockers. Avoid using with alpha-adrenergic stimulants (phenylephrine, epinephrine, etc) which may have exaggerated hypertensive responses. Beta-blockers may affect the action or levels of ethanol, disopyramide, nondepolarizing muscle relaxants, and theophylline although the effects are difficult to predict. The vasoconstrictive effects of ergot alkaloids may be enhanced.

Decreased Effect: Decreased effect of beta-blockers with aluminum salts, barbiturates, calcium salts, cholestyramine, colestipol, NSAIDs, penicillins (ampicillin), rifampin, salicylates, and sulfinpyrazone due to decreased bioavailability and plasma levels. Beta-blockers may decrease the effect of sulfonylureas (possibly hyperglycemia). Nonselective beta-blockers blunt the effect of beta-2 adrenergic agonists (albuterol).

Ethanol/Nutrition/Herb Interactions Herb/Nutraceutical: Avoid dong quai if using for hypertension (has estrogenic activity). Avoid ephedra, garlic, yohimbe, ginseng (may worsen hypertension). Avoid natural licorice (causes sodium and water retention and increases potassium loss).

Mechanism of Action Competitively blocks response to beta$_1$- and beta$_2$-adrenergic stimulation; does not exhibit any membrane stabilizing or intrinsic sympathomimetic activity

Pharmacodynamics/Kinetics

Duration: 17-24 hours

Absorption: 30% to 40%

Distribution: Concentration in human breast milk is 4.6 times higher than serum

Protein binding: 28%

Half-life elimination: Adults: 10-24 hours; prolonged with renal impairment; End-stage renal disease: 45 hours

Time to peak, serum: 2-4 hours

Excretion: Urine (as unchanged drug)

Dosage Oral:

Adults: Initial: 40 mg/day, increase dosage gradually by 40-80 mg increments at 3- to 7-day intervals until optimum clinical response is obtained with profound slowing of heart rate; doses up to 160-240 mg/day in angina and 240-320 mg/day in hypertension may be necessary.

Hypertension: Usual dosage range (JNC 7): 40-120 mg once daily

Elderly: Initial: 20 mg/day; increase doses by 20 mg increments at 3- to 7-day intervals; usual dosage range: 20-240 mg/day.

Dosing adjustment in renal impairment:

Cl_{cr} 31-40 mL/minute: Administer every 24-36 hours or administer 50% of normal dose.

Cl_{cr} 10-30 mL/minute: Administer every 24-48 hours or administer 50% of normal dose.

Cl_{cr} <10 mL/minute: Administer every 40-60 hours or administer 25% of normal dose.

Hemodialysis: Moderately dialyzable (20% to 50%); administer dose postdialysis or administer 40 mg supplemental dose.

Peritoneal dialysis: Supplemental dose is not necessary.

Dosing adjustment/comments in hepatic disease: Reduced dose probably necessary.

Dietary Considerations May be taken without regard to meals.

Dosage Forms [DSC] = Discontinued product

Tablet: 20 mg, 40 mg, 80 mg, 120 mg, 160 mg

Corgard®: 20 mg, 40 mg, 80 mg, 120 mg [DSC], 160 mg [DSC]

Nafarelin *(naf a REL in)*

U.S. Brand Names Synarel®

Canadian Brand Names Synarel®

Index Terms Nafarelin Acetate

Pharmacologic Category Gonadotropin Releasing Hormone Agonist

Use Treatment of endometriosis, including pain and reduction of lesions; treatment of central precocious puberty (CPP; gonadotropin-dependent precocious puberty) in children of both sexes

Pregnancy Risk Factor X

Pregnancy Implications Major fetal abnormalities have been reported in some animal studies; a dose-related increase in fetal mortality and decrease in fetal weight was also observed. Ovulation is inhibited and menstruation is stopped when used appropriately for the treatment of endometriosis, however contraception is not assured. Nonhormonal contraception is recommended. Pregnancy should be excluded prior to initiating treatment. There is no evidence that pregnancy rates are enhanced or adversely affected by use.

Lactation Excretion in breast milk unknown/contraindicated

Medication Safety Issues

Sound-alike/look-alike issues:

Nafarelin may be confused with Anafranil®, enalapril

Contraindications Hypersensitivity to gonadotropin-releasing hormone (GnRH), GnRH-agonist analogs, or any component of the formulation; undiagnosed abnormal vaginal bleeding; pregnancy; breast-feeding

Warnings/Precautions Use with caution in patients with risk factors for decreased bone mineral density, nafarelin therapy may pose an additional risk. Ovarian cysts may occur within the first 2 months of therapy and may occur more commonly in women with polycystic ovarian disease. When used for the treatment of CPP, some signs of puberty (eg vaginal bleeding, breast enlargement) may occur but should resolve within the first 2 months of therapy.

Adverse Reactions Note: Adverse events may be more frequent in the first 6 weeks of treatment due to stimulation of the pituitary-gonadal axis. Sensitivity reactions included chest pain, pruritus, shortness of breath, rash.

CPP: 1% to 10%:

Central nervous system: Emotional lability (6%)

Dermatologic: Acne (10%), seborrhea (3%)

Endocrine & metabolic: Breast enlargement (8%; transient), vaginal bleeding (8%), hot flashes (3%; transient), vaginal discharge (3%)

Respiratory: Rhinitis (5%)

Miscellaneous: Pubic hair increased (5%; transient), body odor (4%), sensitivity reactions (3%)

Endometriosis:

>10%:

Central nervous system: Headache, emotional lability

Dermatologic: Acne

Endocrine & metabolic: Hot flashes (90%), hyperphosphatemia, hypertriglyceridemia, hypocalcemia, libido decreased

Genitourinary: Vaginal dryness

Hematologic: Leukopenia

1% to 10%:

Cardiovascular: Edema

Central nervous system: Depression, insomnia

Dermatologic: Hirsutism, seborrhea

Endocrine & metabolic: Breast size reduced, cholesterol increased, hyperlipidemia, libido increased

Gastrointestinal: Weight gain/loss

Neuromuscular & skeletal: Bone mineral density decreased, myalgia

Respiratory: Nasal irritation

<1% (Limited to important or life-threatening): Arthralgia, breast engorgement, chloasma, eye pain, lactation, maculopapular rash, palpitation, paresthesia, sensitivity reactions, weakness

Postmarketing and/or case reports (any indication): ALT/AST increased, pituitary apoplexy, pituitary gland changes

Overdosage/Toxicology Information not available; based on animal studies, nafarelin is not absorbed if used orally

Stability Store at room temperature of 15°C to 30°C (59°F to 86°F). Protect from light.

Mechanism of Action Potent synthetic decapeptide analogue of gonadotropin-releasing hormone (GnRH; LHRH) which is approximately 200 times more potent than GnRH in terms of pituitary release of luteinizing hormone (LH) and follicle-stimulating hormone (FSH). Effects on the pituitary gland and sex hormones are dependent upon its length of administration. After acute administration, an initial stimulation of the release of LH and FSH from the pituitary is observed; an increase in androgens and estrogens subsequently follows. Continued administration of nafarelin, however, suppresses gonadotrope responsiveness to endogenous GnRH resulting in reduced secretion of LH and FSH and, secondarily, decreased ovarian and testicular steroid production.

Pharmacodynamics/Kinetics

Protein binding, plasma: 80%

Metabolism: Degraded by peptidase; forms metabolites

Bioavailability: ~1% to 6%

Half-life elimination: ~3 hours; Metabolites: ~86 hours

Time to peak, serum: 10-45 minutes

Excretion: Urine (44% to 55%, ~3% as unchanged drug); feces (19% to 44%)

Dosage Intranasal:

Endometriosis: Adults: Female: 1 spray (200 mcg) in 1 nostril each morning and the other nostril each evening starting on days 2-4 of menstrual cycle (total: 2 sprays/day). Dose may be increased to 2 sprays (400 mcg; 1 spray in each nostril) in the morning and evening if amenorrhea is not achieved (total: 8 sprays [1600 mcg]/day). Total duration of therapy should not exceed 6 months due to decreases in bone mineral density; retreatment is not recommended by the manufacturer.

Central precocious puberty: Children: Male/Female: 2 sprays (400 mcg) into each nostril in the morning and 2 sprays (400 mcg) into each nostril in the evening (total: 8 sprays [1600 mcg]/day). If inadequate suppression, may increase dose to 3 sprays (600 mcg) into alternating nostrils 3 times/day (total: 9 sprays [1800 mcg]/day).

Administration Nasal spray: Do not use topical nasal decongestant for at least 2 hours after nafarelin use. Allow ~30 seconds to elapse between sprays. Sneezing during or immediately after dosing should be avoided (may decrease drug absorption).

Monitoring Parameters

CPP: Bone mineral density, GnRH testing (blood LH and FSH levels), measurement of bone age, Tanner staging

Endometriosis: Menstruation, vaginal bleeding or spotting which persists after 2 months of treatment

Test Interactions Diagnostic tests of pituitary gonadotropic and gonadal functions during and up to 4-8 weeks after discontinuing treatment may be misleading.

(Continued)

Nafarelin *(Continued)*

Dosage Forms

Solution, intranasal [spray]:

Synarel®: 2 mg/mL (8 mL) [200 mcg/spray: 60 metered sprays; contains benzalkonium chloride]

♦ **Nafarelin Acetate** *see* Nafarelin *on page 1188*

Nafcillin *(naf SIL in)*

Canadian Brand Names Nallpen®; Unipen®

Index Terms Ethoxynaphthamido Penicillin Sodium; Nafcillin Sodium; Nallpen; Sodium Nafcillin

Pharmacologic Category Antibiotic, Penicillin

Additional Appendix Information

Antibiotic Treatment of Adults With Infective Endocarditis *on page 1977*

Use Treatment of infections such as osteomyelitis, septicemia, endocarditis, and CNS infections caused by susceptible strains of staphylococci species

Pregnancy Risk Factor B

Lactation Enters breast milk/use caution

Contraindications Hypersensitivity to nafcillin, or any component of the formulation, or penicillins

Warnings/Precautions Solutions containing dextrose may be contraindicated in patients with allergies to corn or corn products. Extravasation of I.V. infusions should be avoided; modification of dosage is necessary in patients with both severe renal and hepatic impairment; elimination rate will be slow in neonates; use with caution in patients with cephalosporin hypersensitivity

Adverse Reactions Frequency not defined.

Central nervous system: Pain, fever

Dermatologic: Rash

Gastrointestinal: Nausea, diarrhea, pseudomembranous colitis

Hematologic: Agranulocytosis, bone marrow depression, neutropenia

Local: Pain, swelling, inflammation, phlebitis, skin sloughing, and thrombophlebitis at the injection site; oxacillin (less likely to cause phlebitis) is often preferred in pediatric patients

Renal: Interstitial nephritis (acute)

Miscellaneous: Hypersensitivity reactions

Overdosage/Toxicology Symptoms of penicillin overdose include neuromuscular hypersensitivity (agitation, hallucinations, asterixis, encephalopathy, confusion, and seizures) and electrolyte imbalance (with potassium or sodium salts), especially in renal failure. Treatment is supportive or symptom-directed.

Drug Interactions

Cytochrome P450 Effect: Induces CYP3A4 (strong)

Increased Effect/Toxicity: Probenecid may cause an increase in nafcillin levels. Penicillins may increase the exposure to methotrexate during concurrent therapy; monitor.

Decreased Effect: Nafcillin may decrease levels/effects of calcium channel blockers. If taken concomitantly with warfarin, nafcillin may inhibit the anticoagulant response to warfarin. This effect may persist for up to 30 days after nafcillin has been discontinued. Subtherapeutic cyclosporine levels may result when taken concomitantly with nafcillin. Although anecdotal reports suggest oral contraceptive efficacy could be reduced by penicillins, this has been refuted by more rigorous scientific and clinical data. Nafcillin may decrease the levels/effects of benzodiazepines, calcium channel blockers, clarithromycin, cyclosporine, erythromycin, estrogens, mirtazapine, nateglinide, nefazodone, nevirapine, protease inhibitors, tacrolimus, venlafaxine, and other CYP3A4 substrates. Fusidic acid, tetracyclines may decrease the effects of penicillins. The effects of the typhoid vaccine may be decreased by nafcillin.

Stability Reconstituted parenteral solution is stable for 3 days at room temperature and 7 days when refrigerated or 12 weeks when frozen. For I.V. infusion in NS or D_5W, solution is stable for 24 hours at room temperature and 96 hours when refrigerated.

Mechanism of Action Interferes with bacterial cell wall synthesis during active multiplication, causing cell wall death and resultant bactericidal activity against susceptible bacteria

Pharmacodynamics/Kinetics

Distribution: Widely distributed; CSF penetration is poor but enhanced by meningeal inflammation; crosses placenta

Protein binding: 70% to 90%

Metabolism: Primarily hepatic; undergoes enterohepatic recirculation

Half-life elimination:

Neonates: <3 weeks: 2.2-5.5 hours; 4-9 weeks: 1.2-2.3 hours

Children 3 months to 14 years: 0.75-1.9 hours

Adults: 30 minutes to 1.5 hours with normal renal and hepatic function

Time to peak, serum: I.M.: 30-60 minutes

Excretion: Primarily feces; urine (10% to 30% as unchanged drug)

Dosage

Usual dosage range:

Neonates: I.V.:

<2000 g, <7 days: 50 mg/kg/day divided every 12 hours

>2000 g, <7 days: 50 mg/kg/day divided every 8 hours

<2000 g, >7 days: 75 mg/kg/day divided every 8 hours

>2000 g, >7 days: 75 mg/kg/day divided every 6 hours

Children:

I.M.: 25 mg/kg twice daily

I.V.: 50-200 mg/kg/day in divided doses every 4-6 hours (maximum: 12 g/day)

Adults:

I.M.: 500 mg every 4-6 hours

I.V.: 500-2000 mg every 4-6 hours

Indication-specific dosing:
Neonates:
Arthritis, septic: I.V.:
<2000 g, <7 days: 50 mg/kg/day divided every 12 hours
<2000 g, >7 days: 75 mg/kg/day divided every 8 hours
>2000 g, <7 days: 75 mg/kg/day divided every 8 hours
>2000 g, >7 days: 222 mg/kg/day divided every 6 hours
Children:
Epiglottitis: I.V.: 150-200 mg/kg/day divided in 4 doses
Mild to moderate infections: I.M., I.V.: 50-100 mg/kg/day in divided doses every 6 hours
Severe infections: I.M., I.V.: 100-200 mg/kg/day in divided doses every 4-6 hours (maximum dose: 12 g/day)
Toxic epidermal necrolysis: I.V.: 150 mg/kg/day divided every 6 hours for 5-7 days
Adults: I.V.:
Endocarditis: MSSA:
Native valve: 2 g every 4 hours
Prosthetic valve: 1 g every 4 hours with rifampin for 6 weeks with gentamicin for 2 weeks
Tricuspid valve: 2 g every 4 hours with gentamicin for 2 weeks
Joint:
Bursitis, septic: 2 g every 4 hours
Prosthetic: 2 g every 4-6 hours with rifampin for 6 weeks
***Staphylococcus aureus,* methicillin-susceptible infections, including brain abscess, empyema, erysipelas, mastitis, myositis, osteomyelitis, pneumonia, toxic shock, urinary tract (perinephric abscess):** 2 g every 4 hours
Toxic epidermal necrolysis: 2 g every 4 hours

Dosing adjustment in renal impairment: Not necessary
Dosing adjustment in hepatic impairment: In patients with both hepatic and renal impairment, modification of dosage may be necessary; no data available.
Dialysis: Not dialyzable (0% to 5%) via hemodialysis; supplemental dosage not necessary with hemo- or peritoneal dialysis or continuous arteriovenous or venovenous hemofiltration
Dietary Considerations Sodium content of 1 g: 76.6 mg (3.33 mEq)
Administration
I.M.: Rotate injection sites
I.V.: Vesicant. Administer around-the-clock to promote less variation in peak and trough serum levels; infuse over 30-60 minutes

Extravasation management: Use cold packs. Hyaluronidase: Add 1 mL NS to 150 unit vial to make 150 units/mL of concentration; mix 0.1 mL of above with 0.9 mL NS in 1 mL syringe to make final concentration = 15 units/mL.
Monitoring Parameters Periodic CBC, urinalysis, BUN, serum creatinine, AST and ALT; observe for signs and symptoms of anaphylaxis during first dose
Test Interactions Positive Coombs' test (direct), false-positive urinary and serum proteins; may inactivate aminoglycosides *in vitro*
Dosage Forms
Infusion [premixed iso-osmotic dextrose solution]: 1 g (50 mL); 2 g (100 mL)
Injection, powder for reconstitution, as sodium: 1 g, 2 g, 10 g

♦ **Nafcillin Sodium** *see Nafcillin on page 1190*

Naftifine (NAF ti feen)

U.S. Brand Names Naftin®
Index Terms Naftifine Hydrochloride
Pharmacologic Category Antifungal Agent, Topical
Use Topical treatment of tinea cruris (jock itch), tinea corporis (ringworm), and tinea pedis (athlete's foot)
Pregnancy Risk Factor B
Dosage Adults: Topical: Apply cream once daily and gel twice daily (morning and evening) for up to 4 weeks
Additional Information Complete prescribing information for this medication should be consulted for additional detail.
Dosage Forms
Cream, as hydrochloride:
Naftin®: 1% (15 g, 30 g, 60 g, 90 g) [contains benzyl alcohol]
Gel, as hydrochloride:
Naftin®: 1% (20 g, 40 g, 60 g) [contains alcohol 52%]

♦ **Naftifine Hydrochloride** *see Naftifine on page 1191*
♦ **Naftin®** *see Naftifine on page 1191*
♦ **NaHCO₃** *see Sodium Bicarbonate on page 1575*

Nalbuphine (NAL byoo feen)

U.S. Brand Names Nubain®
Index Terms Nalbuphine Hydrochloride
Pharmacologic Category Analgesic, Opioid
Additional Appendix Information
Narcotic Agonists *on page 1888*
Use Relief of moderate to severe pain; preoperative analgesia, postoperative and surgical anesthesia, and obstetrical analgesia during labor and delivery
(Continued)

Nalbuphine *(Continued)*

Unlabeled/Investigational Use Opioid-induced pruritus

Pregnancy Risk Factor B/D (prolonged use or high doses at term)

Pregnancy Implications Severe fetal bradycardia has been reported following use in labor/delivery. Fetal bradycardia may occur when administered earlier in pregnancy (not documented). Use only if clearly needed, with monitoring to detect and manage possible adverse fetal effects. Naloxone has been reported to reverse bradycardia. Newborn should be monitored for respiratory depression or bradycardia following nalbuphine use in labor.

Lactation Enters breast milk/use caution

Medication Safety Issues
Sound-alike/look-alike issues:
Nubain® may be confused with Navane®, Nebcin®

Contraindications Hypersensitivity to nalbuphine or any component of the formulation

Warnings/Precautions Use caution in CNS depression. Sedation and psychomotor impairment are likely, and are additive with other CNS depressants or ethanol. May cause respiratory depression. Ambulatory patients must be cautioned about performing tasks which require mental alertness (eg, operating machinery or driving). Effects may be potentiated when used with other sedative drugs or ethanol. Use with caution in patients with recent myocardial infarction, biliary tract impairment, morbid obesity, thyroid dysfunction, head trauma, or increased intracranial pressure. Use caution in patients with prostatic hyperplasia and/or urinary stricture, adrenal insufficiency, decreased hepatic or renal function. Use with caution in patients with pre-existing respiratory compromise (hypoxia and/or hypercapnia), COPD or other obstructive pulmonary disease; critical respiratory depression may occur, even at therapeutic dosages. May cause hypotension; use with caution in patients with hypovolemia, cardiovascular disease (including acute MI), or drugs which may exaggerate hypotensive effects (including phenothiazines or general anesthetics). May obscure diagnosis or clinical course of patients with acute abdominal conditions. May result in tolerance and/or drug dependence with chronic use; use with caution in patients with a history of drug dependence. Abrupt discontinuation following prolonged use may lead to withdrawal symptoms. May precipitate withdrawal symptoms in patients following prolonged therapy with mu opioid agonists. Use with caution in pregnancy (close neonatal monitoring required when used in labor and delivery). Use with caution in the elderly and debilitated patients; may be more sensitive to adverse effects. Safety and efficacy in children have not been established.

Adverse Reactions
>10%: Central nervous system: Sedation (36%)
1% to 10%:
Central nervous system: Dizziness (5%), headache (3%)
Gastrointestinal: Nausea/vomiting (6%), xerostomia (4%)
Miscellaneous: Clamminess (9%)
<1% (Limited to important or life-threatening): Abdominal pain, agitation, allergic reaction, anaphylaxis, anaphylactoid reaction, anxiety, asthma, bitter taste, blurred vision, bradycardia, cardiac arrest, confusion, crying, delusion, depersonalization, depression, diaphoresis, dreams (abnormal), dyspepsia, dysphoria, dyspnea, euphoria, faintness, fever, floating sensation, flushing, gastrointestinal cramps, hallucinations, hostility, hypertension, hypotension, injection site reactions (pain, swelling, redness, burning); laryngeal edema, loss of consciousness, nervousness, numbness, pruritus, pulmonary edema, rash, respiratory depression, respiratory distress, restlessness, seizure, sensation of warmth/burning, somnolence, speech disorder, stridor, tachycardia, tingling, tremor, unreality, urinary urgency, urticaria

Overdosage/Toxicology Symptoms include CNS depression, respiratory depression, miosis, hypotension, and bradycardia. Treatment of overdose includes airway support, establishment of an I.V. line, and administration of naloxone 2 mg I.V. (0.01 mg/kg for children), with repeat administration as necessary, up to a total of 10 mg.

Drug Interactions
Increased Effect/Toxicity: Barbiturate anesthetics may increase CNS depression.

Ethanol/Nutrition/Herb Interactions
Ethanol: Avoid ethanol (may increase CNS depression).
Herb/Nutraceutical: Avoid valerian, St John's wort, kava kava, gotu kola (may increase CNS depression).

Stability Store at room temperature of 15°C to 30°C (59°F to 86°F). Protect from light.

Mechanism of Action Agonist of kappa opiate receptors and partial antagonist of mu opiate receptors in the CNS, causing inhibition of ascending pain pathways, altering the perception of and response to pain; produces generalized CNS depression

Pharmacodynamics/Kinetics
Onset of action: Peak effect: SubQ, I.M.: <15 minutes; I.V.: 2-3 minutes
Metabolism: Hepatic
Half-life elimination: 5 hours
Excretion: Feces; urine (~7% as metabolites)

Dosage
Children ≥1 year (unlabeled use): Pain management: I.M., I.V., SubQ: 0.1-0.2 mg/kg every 3-4 hours as needed; maximum: 20 mg/dose and/or 160 mg/day
Adults:
Pain management: I.M., I.V., SubQ: 10 mg/70 kg every 3-6 hours; maximum single dose in nonopioid-tolerant patients: 20 mg; maximum daily dose: 160 mg
Surgical anesthesia supplement: I.V.: Induction: 0.3-3 mg/kg over 10-15 minutes; maintenance doses of 0.25-0.5 mg/kg may be given as required
Opioid-induced pruritus (unlabeled use): I.V. 2.5-5 mg; may repeat dose
Dosing adjustment in renal impairment: Use with caution and reduce dose; monitor.
Dosing adjustment in hepatic impairment: Use with caution and reduce dose.

Administration Administer I.M., SubQ, or I.V.

Monitoring Parameters Relief of pain, respiratory and mental status, blood pressure

Dosage Forms [DSC] = Discontinued product
  Injection, solution, as hydrochloride: 10 mg/mL (10 mL); 20 mg/mL (10 mL)
    Nubain®: 10 mg/mL (10 mL) [DSC]; 20 mg/mL (10 mL)
  Injection, solution, as hydrochloride [preservative free]: 10 mg/mL (1 mL); 20 mg/mL (1 mL)
    Nubain®: 10 mg/mL (1 mL); 20 mg/mL (1 mL)

- ◆ **Nalbuphine Hydrochloride** see Nalbuphine on page 1191
- ◆ **Nalcrom® (Can)** see Cromolyn on page 423
- ◆ **Nalex®-A** see Chlorpheniramine, Phenylephrine, and Phenyltoloxamine on page 354
- ◆ **Nalfon®** see Fenoprofen on page 692
- ◆ **Nallpen** see Nafcillin on page 1190
- ◆ **Nallpen® (Can)** see Nafcillin on page 1190
- ◆ **N-allylnoroxymorphine Hydrochloride** see Naloxone on page 1194

Nalmefene (NAL me feen)

U.S. Brand Names Revex®
Index Terms Nalmefene Hydrochloride
Pharmacologic Category Antidote
Use Complete or partial reversal of opioid drug effects, including respiratory depression induced by natural or synthetic opioids; reversal of postoperative opioid depression; management of known or suspected opioid overdose
Pregnancy Risk Factor B
Pregnancy Implications Animal studies have not demonstrated fetal harm or fertility impairment. There are no adequate and well-controlled studies in pregnant women. Use only if clearly needed.
Lactation Excretion in breast milk unknown/use caution
Medication Safety Issues
  Sound-alike/look-alike issues:
    Revex® may be confused with Nimbex®, ReVia®, Rubex®
  Color-coded ampuls denote indication-specific concentrations:
    Blue-labeled ampul (for postoperative use) contains 1 mL (100 mcg/mL)
    Green-labeled ampul (for overdose management) contains 2 mL (1 mg/mL)
  International issues:
    Revex® may be confused with Brivex® which is a brand name for brivudine in Switzerland
    Revex® may be confused with Rubex® which is a brand name for ascorbic acid in Ireland
Contraindications Hypersensitivity to nalmefene, naltrexone, or any component of the formulation
Warnings/Precautions May induce symptoms of acute withdrawal in opioid-dependent patients; recurrence of respiratory depression is possible if the opioid involved is long-acting; observe patients until there is no reasonable risk of recurrent respiratory depression. Safety and efficacy have not been established in children. Avoid abrupt reversal of opioid effects in patients of high cardiovascular risk or who have received potentially cardiotoxic drugs. Pulmonary edema and cardiovascular instability have been reported in association with abrupt reversal with other narcotic antagonists. Use caution with renal impairment.
Adverse Reactions
  >10%: Gastrointestinal: Nausea (18%)
  1% to 10%:
    Cardiovascular: Tachycardia (5%), hypertension (5%), hypotension (1%), vasodilation (1%)
    Central nervous system: Fever (3%), dizziness (3%), headache (1%), chills (1%)
    Gastrointestinal: Vomiting (9%)
    Miscellaneous: Postoperative pain (4%)
  <1% (Limited to important or life-threatening): Agitation, arrhythmia, AST increased, bradycardia, confusion, depression, diarrhea, myoclonus, nervousness, pharyngitis, pruritus, somnolence, tremor, urinary retention, withdrawal syndrome, xerostomia
Overdosage/Toxicology No reported symptoms with significant overdose. Intravenous doses up to 24 mg have been tolerated by healthy volunteers (in the absence of opioid exposure). Large doses of opioids administered to overcome a full blockade of opioid antagonists, however, have resulted in adverse respiratory and circulatory reactions. Treatment is symptom-directed and supportive.
Drug Interactions
  Increased Effect/Toxicity: Potential increased risk of seizures may exist with use of flumazenil and nalmefene coadministration.
Stability Store at controlled room temperature.
Mechanism of Action As a 6-methylene analog of naltrexone, nalmefene acts as a competitive antagonist at opioid receptor sites, preventing or reversing the respiratory depression, sedation, and hypotension induced by opiates; no pharmacologic activity of its own (eg, opioid agonist activity) has been demonstrated
Pharmacodynamics/Kinetics
  Onset of action: I.M., SubQ: 5-15 minutes
  Distribution: V_d: 8.6 L/kg; rapid
  Protein binding: 45%
  Metabolism: Hepatic via glucuronide conjugation to metabolites with little or no activity
  Bioavailability: I.M., SubQ: 100%
  Half-life elimination: 10.8 hours
  Time to peak, serum: Serum: I.M.: 2.3 hours; I.V.: <2 minutes; SubQ: 1.5 hours
  Excretion: Feces (17%); urine (<5% as unchanged drug)
    Clearance: 0.8 L/hour/kg
Dosage I.M., I.V., SubQ:
  Reversal of postoperative opioid depression: Blue-labeled product (100 mcg/mL): Titrate to reverse the undesired effects of opioids; initial dose for nonopioid dependent patients: 0.25 mcg/kg
  (Continued)

Nalmefene *(Continued)*

followed by 0.25 mcg/kg incremental doses at 2- to 5-minute intervals; after a total dose >1 mcg/kg, further therapeutic response is unlikely

Note: In patients with increased cardiovascular risks, dilute 1:1 in NS or SWFI, and initiate/titrate with 0.1 mcg/kg doses.

Management of known/suspected opioid overdose: Green-labeled product (1 mg/mL): Initial dose: 0.5 mg/70 kg; may repeat with 1 mg/70 kg in 2-5 minutes; further increase beyond a total dose of 1.5 mg/70 kg will not likely result in improved response and may result in cardiovascular stress and precipitated withdrawal syndrome. (If opioid dependency is suspected, administer a challenge dose of 0.1 mg/70 kg; if no withdrawal symptoms are observed in 2 minutes, the recommended doses can be administered.)

Note: If recurrence of respiratory depression is noted, dose may again be titrated to clinical effect using incremental doses.

Note: If I.V. access is lost or not readily obtainable, a single SubQ or I.M. dose of 1 mg may be effective in 5-15 minutes.

Dosing adjustment in renal impairment: Not necessary with single use, however, slow administration (over 60 seconds) of incremental doses is recommended to minimize hypertension and dizziness

Dosing adjustment in hepatic impairment: No adjustment necessary with single use.

Administration Check dosage strength carefully before use to avoid error. Slow administration (over 60 seconds) of incremental doses is recommended to minimize hypertension and dizziness in renal patients. Dilute drug (1:1) with diluent and use smaller doses in patients known to be at increased cardiovascular risk. May be administered via I.M. or SubQ routes if I.V. access is not feasible. A single SubQ or I.M. dose of 1 mg may be effective in 5-15 minutes.

Monitoring Parameters Symptoms of withdrawal; signs/symptoms of respiratory depression; pain

Additional Information Proper steps should be used to prevent use of the incorrect dosage strength. The goal of treatment in the postoperative setting is to achieve reversal of excessive opioid effects without inducing a complete reversal and acute pain.

If opioid dependence is suspected, nalmefene should only be used in opioid overdose if the likelihood of overdose is high based on history or the clinical presentation of respiratory depression with concurrent pupillary constriction is present.

Dosage Forms

Injection, solution:

Revex®: 100 mcg/mL (1 mL) [blue label]; 1 mg/mL (2 mL) [green label]

♦ **Nalmefene Hydrochloride** *see* Nalmefene *on page 1193*

Naloxone *(nal OKS one)*

Canadian Brand Names Naloxone Hydrochloride Injection®

Index Terms *N*-allylnoroxymorphine Hydrochloride; Naloxone Hydrochloride; Narcan

Pharmacologic Category Antidote

Additional Appendix Information

Management of Overdosages *on page 2075*

Use

Complete or partial reversal of opioid depression, including respiratory depression, induced by natural and synthetic opioids, including propoxyphene, methadone, and certain mixed agonist-antagonist analgesics: nalbuphine, pentazocine, and butorphanol

Diagnosis of suspected opioid tolerance or acute opioid overdose

Adjunctive agent to increase blood pressure in the management of septic shock

Unlabeled/Investigational Use PCP and ethanol ingestion; opioid-induced pruritus

Pregnancy Risk Factor C

Pregnancy Implications Consider benefit to the mother and the risk to the fetus before administering to a pregnant woman who is known or suspected to be opioid dependent. May precipitate withdrawal in both the mother and fetus.

Lactation Excretion in breast milk unknown/not recommended

Medication Safety Issues

Sound-alike/look-alike issues:

Naloxone may be confused with naltrexone

Narcan® may be confused with Marcaine®, Norcuron®

International issues:

Narcan® may be confused with Marcen® which is a brand name for ketazolam in Spain

Contraindications Hypersensitivity to naloxone or any component of the formulation

Warnings/Precautions Use with caution in patients with cardiovascular disease; excessive dosages should be avoided after use of opiates in surgery, because naloxone may cause an increase in blood pressure and reversal of anesthesia; may precipitate withdrawal symptoms in patients addicted to opiates, including pain, hypertension, sweating, agitation, irritability, shrill cry, failure to feed

Adverse Reactions Frequency not defined.

Cardiovascular: Hyper-/hypotension, tachycardia, ventricular arrhythmia, cardiac arrest

Central nervous system: Irritability, anxiety, narcotic withdrawal, restlessness, seizure

Gastrointestinal: Nausea, vomiting, diarrhea

Neuromuscular & skeletal: Tremulousness

Respiratory: Dyspnea, pulmonary edema, runny nose, sneezing

Miscellaneous: Diaphoresis

Overdosage/Toxicology Naloxone is the drug of choice for respiratory depression that is known or suspected to be caused by an opiate or opioid overdose.

Caution: Naloxone's effects are due to its action on narcotic reversal, not due to direct effect upon opiate receptors. Therefore, adverse events occur secondarily to reversal (withdrawal) of narcotic analgesia and sedation, which can cause severe reactions.

Drug Interactions
Decreased Effect: Decreased effect of opioid analgesics.

Stability Store at 25°C (77°F). Protect from light. Stable in 0.9% sodium chloride and D₅W at 4 mcg/mL for 24 hours.

Mechanism of Action Pure opioid antagonist that competes and displaces narcotics at opioid receptor sites

Pharmacodynamics/Kinetics
Onset of action: Endotracheal, I.M., SubQ: 2-5 minutes; I.V.: ~2 minutes
Duration: 20-60 minutes; since shorter than that of most opioids, repeated doses are usually needed
Distribution: Crosses placenta
Metabolism: Primarily hepatic via glucuronidation
Half-life elimination: Neonates: 1.2-3 hours; Adults: 1-1.5 hours
Excretion: Urine (as metabolites)

Dosage I.M., I.V. (preferred), intratracheal, SubQ:
Postanesthesia narcotic reversal: Infants and Children: 0.01 mg/kg; may repeat every 2-3 minutes, as needed based on response
Opiate intoxication:
Children:
Birth (including premature infants) to 5 years or <20 kg: 0.1 mg/kg; repeat every 2-3 minutes if needed; may need to repeat doses every 20-60 minutes
>5 years or ≥20 kg: 2 mg/dose; if no response, repeat every 2-3 minutes; may need to repeat doses every 20-60 minutes
Children and Adults: Continuous infusion: I.V.: If continuous infusion is required, calculate dosage/hour based on effective intermittent dose used and duration of adequate response seen, titrate dose 0.04-0.16 mg/kg/hour for 2-5 days in children, adult dose typically 0.25-6.25 mg/hour (short-term infusions as high as 2.4 mg/kg/hour have been tolerated in adults during treatment for septic shock); alternatively, continuous infusion utilizes ²/₃ of the initial naloxone bolus on an hourly basis; add 10 times this dose to each liter of D₅W and infuse at a rate of 100 mL/hour; ¹/₂ of the initial bolus dose should be readministered 15 minutes after initiation of the continuous infusion to prevent a drop in naloxone levels; increase infusion rate as needed to assure adequate ventilation
Narcotic overdose: Adults: I.V.: 0.4-2 mg every 2-3 minutes as needed; may need to repeat doses every 20-60 minutes, if no response is observed after 10 mg, question the diagnosis. **Note:** Use 0.1-0.2 mg increments in patients who are opioid dependent and in postoperative patients to avoid large cardiovascular changes.
Opioid induced pruritus (unlabeled use): Adults: I.V. infusion: 0.25 mcg/kg/hour; **Note:** Monitor pain control; verify that the naloxone is not reversing analgesia.

Administration
Intratracheal: Dilute to 1-2 mL with normal saline
I.V. push: Administer over 30 seconds as undiluted preparation
I.V. continuous infusion: Dilute to 4 mcg/mL in D₅W or normal saline

Monitoring Parameters Respiratory rate, heart rate, blood pressure

Additional Information May contain methyl and propylparabens

Dosage Forms Injection, solution, as hydrochloride: 0.4 mg/mL (1 mL, 10 mL); 1 mg/mL (2 mL)

- **Naloxone and Buprenorphine** see Buprenorphine and Naloxone on page 252
- **Naloxone Hydrochloride** see Naloxone on page 1194
- **Naloxone Hydrochloride and Pentazocine Hydrochloride** see Pentazocine on page 1339
- **Naloxone Hydrochloride Dihydrate and Buprenorphine Hydrochloride** see Buprenorphine and Naloxone on page 252
- **Naloxone Hydrochloride Injection® (Can)** see Naloxone on page 1194

Naltrexone (nal TREKS one)

U.S. Brand Names Depade®; ReVia®; Vivitrol™
Canadian Brand Names ReVia®
Index Terms Naltrexone Hydrochloride
Pharmacologic Category Antidote
Use Treatment of ethanol dependence; blockade of the effects of exogenously administered opioids
Pregnancy Risk Factor C
Pregnancy Implications Evidence of early fetal loss has been observed in animal studies with oral naltrexone. There are no adequate and well-controlled studies in pregnant women.
Lactation Enters breast milk/not recommended
Medication Safety Issues
Sound-alike/look-alike issues:
Naltrexone may be confused with naloxone
ReVia® may be confused with Revex®
Contraindications Hypersensitivity to naltrexone or any component of the formulation; narcotic dependence or current use of opioid analgesics; acute opioid withdrawal; failure to pass Narcan® challenge or positive urine screen for opioids; acute hepatitis; liver failure
Warnings/Precautions
[U.S. Boxed Warning]: Dose-related hepatocellular injury is possible; the margin of separation between the apparent safe and hepatotoxic doses appears to be only fivefold or less (contraindicated in acute hepatitis or hepatic failure).

May precipitate withdrawal symptoms in patients addicted to opiates; patients should be opiate-free for a minimum of 7-10 days; use naloxone challenge test to confirm. Use with caution in patients with hepatic or renal impairment. Patients may respond to lower opioid doses than previously used. This could result in potentially life-threatening opioid intoxication. Use of naltrexone does not eliminate or diminish withdrawal symptoms. Warn patients that
(Continued)

Naltrexone *(Continued)*

attempts to overcome opioid blockade could lead to fatal overdose. Suicidal thoughts and depression have been reported; monitor closely. Cases of eosinophilic pneumonia have been reported; monitor for hypoxia and dyspnea. Safety and efficacy in children have not been established.

Adverse Reactions Combined reporting of adverse events from oral and injectable formulations:

>10%:

Cardiovascular: Syncope (13%)

Central nervous system: Headache (25%), insomnia (14%), dizziness (13%), anxiety (12%), somnolence (4%), nervousness, fatigue

Gastrointestinal: Nausea (33%), vomiting (14%), appetite decreased (14%), diarrhea (13%), abdominal pain (11%), abdominal cramping

Local: Injection site reaction (69%)

Neuromuscular & skeletal: Arthralgia (12%), CPK increased (11%)

Respiratory: Upper respiratory tract infection (13%), pharyngitis (11%)

1% to 10%:

Central nervous system: Depression (8%), suicidal thoughts (1%), energy increased, feeling down

Dermatologic: Rash (6%)

Endocrine & metabolic: Polydipsia

Gastrointestinal: Dry mouth (5%)

Genitourinary: Delayed ejaculation, impotency

Hepatic: AST increased (2%)

Neuromuscular & skeletal: Muscle cramps (8%), back pain (6%)

<1% (Limited to important or life-threatening): ALT increased, angina, atrial fibrillation, blood pressure increased, cerebral aneurysm, chest pain, chest tightness, CHF, cholecystitis, cholelithiasis, colitis, COPD, dehydration, delirium, disorientation, DVT, dyspnea, eosinophilic pneumonia, euphoria, GI hemorrhage, hallucinations, hypercholesterolemia, hypersensitivity reaction (includes angioedema and urticaria), hypertension, influenza, ischemic stroke, leukocytosis, lymphadenopathy, MI, narcotic withdrawal, palpitation, paralytic ileus, paranoia, PE, perirectal abscess, pneumonia, pyrexia, rigors, seizures, suicide attempts, tachycardia, thrombocytopenia, tooth abscess, UTI

Overdosage/Toxicology Symptoms include clonic-tonic convulsions and respiratory failure. Patients receiving up to 800 mg/day for 1 week have shown no toxicity. Seizures and respiratory failure have been seen in animals. Treatment should be symptom-directed and supportive.

Drug Interactions

Increased Effect/Toxicity: Lethargy and somnolence have been reported with the combination of naltrexone and thioridazine.

Decreased Effect: Naltrexone decreases effects of opioid-containing products.

Stability

Injection: Store unopened kit at 2°C to 8°C (36°F to 46°F). Kit may be kept at room temperature of ≤25°C (77°F) for ≤7 days prior to use; do not freeze.

Tablet: Store at 20°C to 25°C (68°F to 77°F).

Mechanism of Action Naltrexone (a pure opioid antagonist) is a cyclopropyl derivative of oxymorphone similar in structure to naloxone and nalorphine (a morphine derivative); it acts as a competitive antagonist at opioid receptor sites, showing the highest affinity for mu receptors.

Pharmacodynamics/Kinetics

Duration: Oral: 50 mg: 24 hours; 100 mg: 48 hours; 150 mg: 72 hours; I.M.: 4 weeks

Absorption: Oral: Almost complete

Distribution: V_d: 19 L/kg; widely throughout the body but considerable interindividual variation exists

Protein binding: 21%

Metabolism: Noncytochrome-mediated dehydrogenase conversion to 6-β-naltrexol and related minor metabolites; Oral: Extensive first-pass effect

Half-life elimination: Oral: 4 hours; 6-β-naltrexol: 13 hours; I.M.: naltrexone and 6-β-naltrexol: 5-10 days

Time to peak, serum: Oral: ~60 minutes; I.M.: Biphasic: 2 hours (first peak), 2-3 days (second peak)

Excretion: Primarily urine (as metabolites and unchanged drug)

Dosage Adults: Do not give until patient is opioid-free for 7-10 days as determined by urinalysis

Oral: Alcohol dependence, opioid antidote: 25 mg; if no withdrawal signs within 1 hour give another 25 mg; maintenance regimen is flexible, variable and individualized (50 mg/day to 100-150 mg 3 times/week for 12 weeks); up to 800 mg/day has been tolerated in a small number of healthy adults without an adverse effect

I.M.: Alcohol dependence: 380 mg once every 4 weeks

Dosage adjustment in renal impairment: Use caution. No adjustment needed in mild impairment. Not adequately studied in moderate-to-severe renal impairment.

Dosage adjustment in hepatic impairment: Use caution. An increase in naltrexone AUC of approximately five- and 10-fold in patients with compensated or decompensated liver cirrhosis respectively, compared with normal liver function has been reported No adjustment required with mild-to-moderate hepatic impairment. Not adequately studied in severe hepatic impairment.

Administration If there is any question of occult opioid dependence, perform a naloxone challenge test; do not attempt treatment until naloxone challenge is negative.

Oral: To minimize adverse gastrointestinal effects, administer with food or antacids or after meals; advise patient not to self-administer opiates while receiving naltrexone therapy.

I.M.: Vivitrol™: Administer I.M. into the upper outer quadrant of the gluteal area. Injection should alternate between the two buttocks. Do not substitute any components of the dose-pack; administer with needle provided.

Monitoring Parameters For narcotic withdrawal; liver function tests
Test Interactions May cause cross-reactivity with some opioid immunoassay methods.
Dosage Forms
Injection, powder for suspension [extended-release microspheres]:
Vivitrol™: 380 mg [diluent provided]
Tablet, as hydrochloride: 50 mg
Depade®: 25 mg, 50 mg, 100 mg
ReVia®: 50 mg

♦ **Naltrexone Hydrochloride** *see* Naltrexone *on page 1195*
♦ **Namenda**™ *see* Memantine *on page 1076*

Nandrolone (NAN droe lone)

Canadian Brand Names Deca-Durabolin®; Durabolin®
Index Terms Nandrolone Decanoate; Nandrolone Phenpropionate
Pharmacologic Category Androgen
Use Control of metastatic breast cancer; management of anemia of renal insufficiency
Restrictions C-III
Pregnancy Risk Factor X
Lactation Excretion in breast milk unknown/contraindicated
Contraindications Hypersensitivity to nandrolone or any component of the formulation; carcinoma of breast or prostate; nephrosis; pregnancy; not for use in infants
Warnings/Precautions Monitor diabetic patients carefully. **[U.S. Boxed Warning]: Anabolic steroids may cause peliosis hepatis, liver cell tumors, and blood lipid changes with increased risk of arteriosclerosis.** Use with caution in elderly patients, they may be at greater risk for prostatic hyperplasia; use with caution in patients with cardiac, renal, or hepatic disease or epilepsy
Adverse Reactions
Male: Postpubertal:
>10%:
Dermatologic: Acne
Endocrine & metabolic: Gynecomastia
Genitourinary: Bladder irritability, priapism
1% to 10%:
Central nervous system: Insomnia, chills
Endocrine & metabolic: Decreased libido, hepatic dysfunction
Gastrointestinal: Nausea, diarrhea
Genitourinary: Prostatic hyperplasia (elderly)
Hematologic: Iron-deficiency anemia, suppression of clotting factors
<1% (Limited to important or life-threatening): Hepatic necrosis, hepatocellular carcinoma
Male: Prepubertal:
>10%:
Dermatologic: Acne
Endocrine & metabolic: Virilism
1% to 10%:
Central nervous system: Chills, insomnia, factors
Dermatologic: Hyperpigmentation
Gastrointestinal: Diarrhea, nausea
Hematologic: Iron deficiency anemia, suppression of clotting
<1% (Limited to important or life-threatening): Hepatocellular carcinoma, necrosis
Female:
>10%: Endocrine & metabolic: Virilism
1% to 10%:
Central nervous system: Chills, insomnia
Endocrine & metabolic: Hypercalcemia
Gastrointestinal: Nausea, diarrhea
Hematologic: Iron deficiency anemia, suppression of clotting factors
Hepatic: Hepatic dysfunction
<1% (Limited to important or life-threatening): Hepatic necrosis, hepatocellular carcinoma
Drug Interactions
Increased Effect/Toxicity: Nandrolone may increase the effect of oral anticoagulants, insulin, oral hypoglycemic agents, adrenal steroids, or ACTH when taken together.
Mechanism of Action Promotes tissue-building processes, increases production of erythropoietin, causes protein anabolism; increases hemoglobin and red blood cell volume
Pharmacodynamics/Kinetics
Onset of action: 3-6 months
Duration: Up to 30 days
Absorption: I.M.: 77%
Metabolism: Hepatic
Excretion: Urine
Dosage Deep I.M. (into gluteal muscle):
Children 2-13 years (decanoate): 25-50 mg every 3-4 weeks
Adults:
Male:
Breast cancer (phenpropionate): 50-100 mg/week
Anemia of renal insufficiency (decanoate): 100-200 mg/week
Female: 50-100 mg/week
Breast cancer (phenpropionate): 50-100 mg/week
Anemia of renal insufficiency (decanoate): 50-100 mg/week
Administration Inject deeply I.M., preferably into the gluteal muscle
Test Interactions Altered glucose tolerance tests
Additional Information Both phenpropionate and decanoate are injections in oil.
(Continued)

Nandrolone *(Continued)*

Dosage Forms Injection, solution, as decanoate [in sesame oil]: 100 mg/mL (2 mL); 200 mg/mL (1 mL) [contains benzyl alcohol]

◆ **Nandrolone Decanoate** *see* Nandrolone *on page 1197*
◆ **Nandrolone Phenpropionate** *see* Nandrolone *on page 1197*
◆ **NAPA and NABZ** *see* Sodium Phenylacetate and Sodium Benzoate *on page 1582*

Naphazoline *(naf AZ oh leen)*

U.S. Brand Names AK-Con™; Albalon®; Allersol®; Clear Eyes® ACR [OTC]; Clear Eyes® Extra Relief [OTC]; Naphcon® [OTC]; Privine® [OTC]
Canadian Brand Names Naphcon Forte®; Vasocon®
Index Terms Naphazoline Hydrochloride
Pharmacologic Category Alpha₁ Agonist; Imidazoline Derivative; Ophthalmic Agent, Vasoconstrictor
Use Topical ocular vasoconstrictor; temporary relief of nasal congestion associated with the common cold, upper respiratory allergies or sinusitis; relief of redness of the eye due to minor irritation
Pregnancy Risk Factor C
Pregnancy Implications Animal reproduction studies have not been conducted.
Lactation Excretion in breast milk unknown/use caution
Contraindications Hypersensitivity to naphazoline or any component of the formulation; narrow-angle glaucoma
Warnings/Precautions Rebound congestion may occur with extended use. Use with caution in the presence of hypertension, diabetes, hyperthyroidism, heart disease, coronary artery disease, cerebral arteriosclerosis, local infection or injury, benign prostatic hyperplasia, or long-standing bronchial asthma. Use in children, especially infants, may cause CNS depression, coma and marked reduction in body temperature. Products may contain benzalkonium chloride which may be absorbed by soft contact lenses.

When used for self-medication (OTC): Patients should notify healthcare provider if symptoms last >72 hours or if condition worsens. In addition with ophthalmic products, contact prescriber in case of eye pain or if changes in vision occur.
Adverse Reactions Frequency not defined.
Cardiovascular: Cardiac irregularities, hypertension
Central nervous system: Body temperature decreased, dizziness, drowsiness, headache, nervousness
Endocrine & metabolic: Hyperglycemia
Gastrointestinal: Nausea
Local: Transient stinging, nasal mucosa irritation, dryness, rebound congestion
Neuromuscular & skeletal: Weakness
Ocular: Blurred vision, discomfort, intraocular pressure increased, irritation, lacrimation, mydriasis, punctuate keratitis, redness
Respiratory: Sneezing
Miscellaneous: Diaphoresis
Overdosage/Toxicology Symptoms include CNS depression, hypothermia, bradycardia, cardiovascular collapse, apnea, coma, agitation, tachycardia, hypertension; alternating agitation and hypertension. Overdose may occur following topical administration or inadvertent oral use. Treatment should be symptom-directed and supportive. Following initiation of essential overdose management, toxic symptoms should be treated. The patient should be kept warm and monitored for alterations in vital functions. Seizures commonly respond to diazepam (5-10 mg I.V. bolus in adults every 15 minutes, if needed, up to a total of 30 mg; I.V. 0.25-0.4 mg/kg/dose up to a total of 10 mg for children) or to phenytoin or phenobarbital. Hypotension should be treated with fluids.
Drug Interactions
Increased Effect/Toxicity: Guanadrel and methyldopa may enhance the therapeutic effect of alpha₁-agonists. MAO inhibitors may enhance the hypertensive effects of alpha₁-agonists (avoid use). TCAs may enhance the vasopressor effect of alpha₁-agonists (avoid use).
Stability Store at controlled room temperature.
Mechanism of Action Stimulates alpha-adrenergic receptors in the arterioles of the conjunctiva and the nasal mucosa to produce vasoconstriction
Pharmacodynamics/Kinetics
Onset of action: Decongestant: Topical: ~10 minutes
Duration: 2-6 hours
Dosage
Nasal: Children ≥12 years and Adults: 0.05% instill 1-2 drops or sprays every 6 hours if needed; therapy should not exceed 3 days
Ophthalmic: Adults:
0.1% (prescription): 1-2 drops into conjuctival sac every 3-4 hours as needed
0.012% (OTC): 1-2 drops into affected eye(s) up to 4 times a day; therapy should not exceed 3 days
Administration Ophthalmic: Contact lenses should be removed prior to administering products containing benzalkonium chloride.
Dosage Forms
Solution, intranasal drops, as hydrochloride:
Privine®: 0.05% (25 mL)
Solution, intranasal spray, as hydrochloride:
Privine®: 0.05% (20 mL)
Solution, ophthalmic, as hydrochloride:
AK-Con™, Albalon®, Allersol®: 0.1% (15 mL) [contains benzalkonium chloride]

Clear Eyes® ACR: 0.012% (15 mL, 30 mL) [contains glycerin 0.2%, zinc sulfate 0.25%, and benzalkonium chloride]
Clear Eyes® Extra Relief: 0.012% (6 mL, 15 mL, 30 mL) [contains glycerin 0.2% and benzalkonium chloride]
Naphcon®: 0.012% (15 mL) [contains benzalkonium chloride]

Naphazoline and Pheniramine (naf AZ oh leen & ten NIR a meen)

U.S. Brand Names Naphcon-A® [OTC]; Opcon-A® [OTC]; Visine-A® [OTC]
Canadian Brand Names Naphcon-A®; Visine® Advanced Allergy
Index Terms Pheniramine and Naphazoline
Pharmacologic Category Ophthalmic Agent, Vasoconstrictor
Use Treatment of ocular congestion, irritation, and itching
Pregnancy Risk Factor C
Medication Safety Issues
Sound-alike/look-alike issues:
Visine® may be confused with Visken®
Dosage Ophthalmic: Children ≥6 years and Adults: 1-2 drops up to 4 times/day
Additional Information Complete prescribing information for this medication should be consulted for additional detail.
Dosage Forms
Solution, ophthalmic:
Naphcon-A®: Naphazoline hydrochloride 0.025% and pheniramine maleate 0.3% (5 mL) [contains benzalkonium chloride; 2 bottles/box], (15 mL) [contains benzalkonium chloride]
Opcon-A®: Naphazoline hydrochloride 0.027% and pheniramine maleate 0.3% (15 mL) [contains benzalkonium chloride]
Visine-A®: Naphazoline hydrochloride 0.025% and pheniramine maleate 0.3% (15 mL) [contains benzalkonium chloride]

♦ **Naphazoline Hydrochloride** see Naphazoline on page 1198
♦ **Naphcon®** [OTC] see Naphazoline on page 1198
♦ **Naphcon-A®** [OTC] see Naphazoline and Pheniramine on page 1199
♦ **Naphcon-A®** (Can) see Naphazoline and Pheniramine on page 1199
♦ **Naphcon Forte®** (Can) see Naphazoline on page 1198
♦ **NapraPAC™** see Lansoprazole and Naproxen on page 980
♦ **Naprelan®** see Naproxen on page 1199
♦ **Naprosyn®** see Naproxen on page 1199

Naproxen (na PROKS en)

U.S. Brand Names Aleve® [OTC]; Anaprox®; Anaprox® DS; EC-Naprosyn®; Midol® Extended Relief; Naprelan®; Naprosyn®; Pamprin® Maximum Strength All Day Relief [OTC]
Canadian Brand Names Anaprox®; Anaprox® DS; Apo-Napro-Na®; Apo-Napro-Na DS®; Apo-Naproxen®; Apo-Naproxen EC®; Apo-Naproxen SR®; Gen-Naproxen EC; Naprosyn®; Naxen®; Naxen® EC; Novo-Naproc EC; Novo-Naprox; Novo-Naprox Sodium; Novo-Naprox Sodium DS; Novo-Naprox SR; Nu-Naprox; Riva-Naproxen
Index Terms Naproxen Sodium
Pharmacologic Category Nonsteroidal Anti-inflammatory Drug (NSAID), Oral
Additional Appendix Information
Nonsteroidal Anti-inflammatory Agents on page 1894
Use Management of ankylosing spondylitis, osteoarthritis, and rheumatoid disorders (including juvenile rheumatoid arthritis); acute gout; mild-to-moderate pain; tendonitis, bursitis; dysmenorrhea; fever
Restrictions An FDA-approved medication guide must be distributed when dispensing an oral outpatient prescription (new or refill) where this medication is to be used without direct supervision of a healthcare provider. Medication guides are available at http://www.fda.gov/cder/Offices/ODS/medication_guides.htm.
Pregnancy Risk Factor C/D (3rd trimester)
Lactation Enters breast milk/not recommended (AAP rates "compatible")
Medication Safety Issues
Sound-alike/look-alike issues:
Naproxen may be confused with Natacyn®, Nebcin®
Aleve® may be confused with Alesse®
Anaprox® may be confused with Anaspaz®, Avapro®
Naprelan® may be confused with Naprosyn®
Naprosyn® may be confused with Naprelan®, Natacyn®, Nebcin®

International issues:
Flogen® [Mexico] may be confused with Flovent® which is a brand name for fluticasone in the U.S.
Flogen® [Mexico] may be confused with Floxin® which is a brand name for ofloxacin in the U.S.
Contraindications Hypersensitivity to naproxen, aspirin, other NSAIDs, or any component of the formulation; perioperative pain in the setting of coronary artery bypass surgery (CABG); pregnancy (3rd trimester)
Warnings/Precautions [U.S. Boxed Warning]: NSAIDs are associated with an increased risk of adverse cardiovascular events, including MI, stroke, and new onset or worsening of pre-existing hypertension. Risk may be increased with duration of use or pre-existing cardiovascular risk-factors or disease. Carefully evaluate individual cardiovascular risk profiles prior to prescribing. Use caution with fluid retention, CHF or hypertension. Use the lowest effective dose for the shortest duration of time, consistent with individual patient goals, to reduce risk of cardiovascular or GI adverse events. Alternate therapies (Continued)

Naproxen *(Continued)*

should be considered for patients at high risk. Concurrent administration of ibuprofen, and potentially other nonselective NSAIDs, may interfere with aspirin's cardioprotective effect.

[U.S. Boxed Warning]: NSAIDs may increase risk of gastrointestinal irritation, ulceration, bleeding, and perforation. These events may occur at any time during therapy and without warning. Use caution with a history of GI disease (bleeding or ulcers), concurrent therapy with aspirin, anticoagulants and/or corticosteroids, smoking, use of alcohol, the elderly or debilitated patients.

Use of NSAIDs can compromise existing renal function. Renal toxicity can occur in patient with impaired renal function, dehydration, heart failure, liver dysfunction, those taking diuretics and ACEI and the elderly. Rehydrate patient before starting therapy. Monitor renal function closely. Naproxen is not recommended for patients with advanced renal disease.

NSAIDs may cause serious skin adverse events including exfoliative dermatitis, Stevens-Johnson Syndrome (SJS) and toxic epidermal necrolysis (TEN). Anaphylactoid reactions may occur, even without prior exposure; patients with "aspirin triad" (bronchial asthma, aspirin intolerance, rhinitis) may be at increased risk. Do not use in patients who experience bronchospasm, asthma, rhinitis, or urticaria with NSAID or aspirin therapy.

Use with caution in patients with decreased hepatic function. Closely monitor patients with any abnormal LFT. Severe hepatic reactions (eg, fulminant hepatitis, liver failure) have occurred with NSAID use, rarely; discontinue if signs or symptoms of liver disease develop, or if systemic manifestations occur.

The elderly are at increased risk for adverse effects (especially peptic ulceration, CNS effects, renal toxicity) from NSAIDs even at low doses.

Withhold for at least 4-6 half-lives prior to surgical or dental procedures. Safety and efficacy have not been established in children <2 years of age.

OTC labeling: Prior to self-medication, patients should contact healthcare provider if they have had recurring stomach pain or upset, ulcers, bleeding problems, high blood pressure, heart or kidney disease, other serious medical problems, are currently taking a diuretic, or are ≥60 years of age. Recommended dosages should not be exceeded, due to an increased risk of GI bleeding. Consuming ≥3 alcoholic beverages/day or taking longer than recommended may increase the risk of GI bleeding. Not for self-medication (OTC use) in children <12 years of age.

Adverse Reactions

1% to 10%:

Cardiovascular: Edema (3% to 9%), palpitations (<3%)

Central nervous system: Dizziness (3% to 9%), drowsiness (3% to 9%), headache (3% to 9%), lightheadedness (<3%), vertigo (<3%)

Dermatologic: Pruritus (3% to 9%), skin eruption (3% to 9%), ecchymosis (3% to 9%), purpura (<3%), rash

Endocrine & metabolic: Fluid retention (3% to 9%)

Gastrointestinal: Abdominal pain (3% to 9%), constipation (3% to 9%), nausea (3% to 9%), heartburn (3% to 9%), diarrhea (<3%), dyspepsia (<3%), stomatitis (<3%), flatulence, gross bleeding/perforation, indigestion, ulcers, vomiting

Genitourinary: Abnormal renal function

Hematologic: Hemolysis (3% to 9%), ecchymosis (3% to 9%), anemia, bleeding time increased

Hepatic: LFTs increased

Ocular: Visual disturbances (<3%)

Otic: Tinnitus (3% to 9%), hearing disturbances (<3%)

Respiratory: Dyspnea (3% to 9%)

Miscellaneous: Diaphoresis (<3%), thirst (<3%)

<1% (Limited to important or life-threatening): Agranulocytosis, alopecia, anaphylactic/anaphylactoid reaction, angioneurotic edema, arrhythmia, aseptic meningitis, asthma, blurred vision, cognitive dysfunction, colitis, coma, confusion, CHF, conjunctivitis, cystitis, depression, dream abnormalities, dysuria, eosinophilia, eosinophilic pneumonitis, erythema multiforme, exfoliative dermatitis, glossitis, granulocytopenia, hallucinations, hematemesis, hepatitis, hyper-/hypoglycemia, hyper-/hypotension, infection, interstitial nephritis, melena, jaundice, leukopenia, liver failure, lymphadenopathy, menstrual disorders, malaise, MI, muscle weakness, myalgia, oliguria, pancreatitis, pancytopenia, paresthesia, photosensitivity, pneumonia, polyuria, proteinuria, pyrexia, rectal bleeding, renal failure, renal papillary necrosis, respiratory depression, sepsis, Stevens-Johnson syndrome, tachycardia, seizure, syncope, thrombocytopenia, toxic epidermal necrolysis ulcerative stomatitis, vasculitis

Overdosage/Toxicology Symptoms include drowsiness, heartburn, vomiting, CNS depression, leukocytosis, and renal failure. Management of nonsteroidal anti-inflammatory drug (NSAID) intoxication is primarily supportive and symptomatic. Fluid therapy is commonly effective in managing hypotension that may occur following an acute NSAID overdose, except when due to acute blood loss. Seizures tend to be very short-lived and often do not require drug treatment, although recurrent seizures should be treated with I.V. diazepam. Since many of NSAIDs undergo enterohepatic cycling, multiple doses of charcoal may be needed to reduce the potential for delayed toxicities.

Drug Interactions

Cytochrome P450 Effect: Substrate (minor) of CYP1A2, 2C9

Increased Effect/Toxicity: Naproxen could displace other highly protein-bound drugs, increasing the effect of oral anticoagulants, hydantoins, salicylates, sulfonamides, and first-generation sulfonylureas. Naproxen and warfarin may cause a slight increase in free warfarin. Naproxen and probenecid may cause increased levels of naproxen. Naproxen and methotrexate may significantly increase and prolong blood methotrexate concentration, which may be severe or fatal. May increase lithium or cyclosporine levels. Corticosteroids may increase risk of GI ulceration. Concomitant use with fluoroquinolones may rarely increase risk of seizure.

Decreased Effect: NSAIDs may decrease the effect of some antihypertensive agents, including ACE inhibitors, angiotensin receptor antagonists, beta-blockers, and hydralazine. The efficacy of diuretics (loop and/or thiazide) may be decreased. Cholestyramine (and other bile acid sequestrants) may decrease the absorption of NSAIDs. Separate by at least 2 hours. Salicylates' antiplatelet effect may be reduced.

Ethanol/Nutrition/Herb Interactions

Ethanol: Avoid ethanol (may enhance gastric mucosal irritation).

Food: Naproxen absorption rate/levels may be decreased if taken with food.

Herb/Nutraceutical: Avoid alfalfa, anise, bilberry, bladderwrack, bromelain, cat's claw, celery, coleus, cordyceps, dong quai, evening primrose, feverfew, fenugreek, garlic, ginger, ginkgo biloboa, red clover, horse chestnut, grapeseed, green tea, ginseng, guggul, horse chestnut seed, horseradish, licorice, prickly ash, red clover, reishi, SAMe, sweet clover, turmeric, white willow (all have additional antiplatelet activity).

Stability Store oral suspension and tablet at 15°C to 30°C (59°F to 86°F).

Mechanism of Action Inhibits prostaglandin synthesis by decreasing the activity of the enzyme, cyclooxygenase, which results in decreased formation of prostaglandin precursors

Pharmacodynamics/Kinetics

Onset of action: Analgesic: 1 hour; Anti-inflammatory: ~2 weeks

Peak effect: Anti-inflammatory: 2-4 weeks

Duration: Analgesic: ≤7 hours; Anti-inflammatory: ≤12 hours

Absorption: Almost 100%

Protein binding: >99%; increased free fraction in elderly

Half-life elimination: Normal renal function: 12-17 hours; End-stage renal disease: No change

Time to peak, serum: 1-4 hours

Excretion: Urine (95%)

Dosage Note: Dosage expressed as naproxen base; 200 mg naproxen base is equivalent to 220 mg naproxen sodium.

Oral:

Children >2 years: Juvenile arthritis: 10 mg/kg/day in 2 divided doses

Adults:

Gout, acute: Initial: 750 mg, followed by 250 mg every 8 hours until attack subsides. **Note:** EC-Naprosyn® is not recommended.

Migraine, acute (unlabeled use): Initial: 500-750 mg.; an additional 250-500 mg may be given if needed (maximum: 1250 mg in 24 hours). **Note:** EC-Naprosyn® is not recommended.

Pain (mild-to-moderate), dysmenorrhea, acute tendonitis, bursitis: Initial: 500 mg, then 250 mg every 6-8 hours; maximum: 1250 mg/day naproxen base

Rheumatoid arthritis, osteoarthritis, and ankylosing spondylitis: 500-1000 mg/day in 2 divided doses; may increase to 1.5 g/day of naproxen base for limited time period

OTC labeling: Pain/fever:

Children ≥12 years and Adults ≤65 years: 200 mg naproxen base every 8-12 hours; if needed, may take 400 mg naproxen base for the initial dose; maximum: 600 mg naproxen base/24 hours

Adults >65 years: 200 mg naproxen base every 12 hours

Dosing adjustment in renal impairment: Cl$_{cr}$ <30 mL/minute: use is not recommended

Dietary Considerations Drug may cause GI upset, bleeding, ulceration, perforation; take with food or milk to minimize GI upset.

Administration Administer with food, milk, or antacids to decrease GI adverse effects

Suspension: Shake suspension well before administration.

Tablet, extended release: Swallow tablet whole; do not break, crush, or chew.

Monitoring Parameters Occult blood loss, periodic liver function test, CBC, BUN, serum creatinine; urine output

Test Interactions Naproxen may interfere with 5-HIAA urinary assays; due to an interaction with m-di-nitrobenzene, naproxen should be discontinued 72 hours before adrenal function testing if teh Porter-Silber test is used.

Dosage Forms

Caplet, as sodium (Aleve®, Midol® Extended Relief, Pamprin® Maximum Strength All Day Relief): 220 mg [equivalent to naproxen 200 mg and sodium 20 mg]

Gelcap, as sodium (Aleve®): 220 mg [equivalent to naproxen 200 mg and sodium 20 mg]

Suspension, oral (Naprosyn®): 125 mg/5 mL (480 mL) [contains sodium 0.3 mEq/mL; orange-pineapple flavor]

Tablet (Naprosyn®): 250 mg, 375 mg, 500 mg

Tablet, as sodium: 220 mg [equivalent to naproxen 200 mg and sodium 20 mg]; 275 mg [equivalent to naproxen 250 mg and sodium 25 mg]; 550 mg [equivalent to naproxen 500 mg and sodium 50 mg]

Aleve®: 220 mg [equivalent to naproxen 200 mg and sodium 20 mg]

Anaprox®: 275 mg [equivalent to naproxen 250 mg and sodium 25 mg]

Anaprox® DS: 550 mg [equivalent to naproxen 500 mg and sodium 50 mg]

Tablet, controlled release, as sodium: 550 mg [equivalent to naproxen 500 mg and sodium 50 mg]

Naprelan®: 421.5 mg [equivalent to naproxen 375 mg and sodium 37.5 mg]; 550 mg [equivalent to naproxen 500 mg and sodium 50 mg]

Tablet, delayed release (EC-Naprosyn®): 375 mg, 500 mg

♦ **Naproxen and Lansoprazole** see Lansoprazole and Naproxen on page 980

Naproxen and Pseudoephedrine (na PROKS en & soo doe e FED rin)

U.S. Brand Names Aleve® Cold & Sinus [OTC]; Aleve® Sinus & Headache [OTC]

Index Terms Naproxen Sodium and Pseudoephedrine; Pseudoephedrine and Naproxen

Pharmacologic Category Decongestant/Analgesic

Use Temporary relief of cold, sinus, and flu symptoms (including nasal congestion, sinus congestion/pressure, headache, minor body aches and pains, and fever)

(Continued)

Naproxen and Pseudoephedrine *(Continued)*

Dosage Oral: Children ≥12 years and Adults: Aleve® Cold & Sinus, Aleve® Sinus & Headache: One caplet every 12 hours (maximum dose: 2 caplets/24 hours)

Additional Information Complete prescribing information for this medication should be consulted for additional detail.

Dosage Forms

Caplet, extended release:

Aleve® Cold & Sinus, Aleve ® Sinus & Headache: Naproxen sodium 220 mg [equivalent to naproxen 200 mg and sodium 20 mg] and pseudoephedrine hydrochloride 120 mg

♦ **Naproxen Sodium** *see* Naproxen *on page 1199*

♦ **Naproxen Sodium and Pseudoephedrine** *see* Naproxen and Pseudoephedrine *on page 1201*

Naratriptan *(NAR a trip tan)*

U.S. Brand Names Amerge®

Canadian Brand Names Amerge®

Index Terms Naratriptan Hydrochloride

Pharmacologic Category Antimigraine Agent; Serotonin 5-HT$_{1B, 1D}$ Receptor Agonist

Additional Appendix Information

Antimigraine Drugs: 5-HT$_1$ Receptor Agonists *on page 1871*

Use Treatment of acute migraine headache with or without aura

Pregnancy Risk Factor C

Pregnancy Implications There are no adequate and well-controlled studies using naratriptan in pregnant women. Use only if potential benefit to the mother outweighs the potential risk to the fetus. A pregnancy registry has been established to monitor outcomes of women exposed to naratriptan during pregnancy (800-336-2176). In animal studies, administration was associated with embryolethality, fetal abnormalities, and pup mortality and growth retardation. Tremors were observed in the offspring of female rats when exposed to naratriptan late in gestation.

Lactation Excretion in breast milk unknown/use caution

Medication Safety Issues

Sound-alike/look-alike issues:

Amerge® may be confused with Altace®, Amaryl®

Contraindications Hypersensitivity to naratriptan or any component of the formulation; cerebrovascular, peripheral vascular disease (ischemic bowel disease), ischemic heart disease (angina pectoris, history of myocardial infarction, or proven silent ischemia); or in patients with symptoms consistent with ischemic heart disease, coronary artery vasospasm, or Prinzmetal's angina; uncontrolled hypertension or patients who have received within 24 hours another 5-HT agonist (sumatriptan, zolmitriptan) or ergotamine-containing product; patients with known risk factors associated with coronary artery disease; patients with severe hepatic or renal disease (Cl$_{cr}$ <15 mL/minute); do not administer naratriptan to patients with hemiplegic or basilar migraine

Warnings/Precautions Use only if there is a clear diagnosis of migraine. Do not give to patients with risk factors for CAD until a cardiovascular evaluation has been performed; if evaluation is satisfactory, the healthcare provider should administer the first dose and cardiovascular status should be periodically re-evaluated. Cardiac events (coronary artery vasospasm, transient ischemia, myocardial infarction, ventricular tachycardia/fibrillation, cardiac arrest, and death), cerebral/subarachnoid hemorrhage, stroke, peripheral vascular ischemia, and colonic ischemia have been reported with 5-HT$_1$ agonist administration. Significant elevation in blood pressure, including hypertensive crisis, has also been reported on rare occasions in patients with and without a history of hypertension. If the patient does not respond to the first dose, re-evaluate the diagnosis of migraine before trying a second dose. Safety and efficacy have not been established in children <18 years of age.

Adverse Reactions

1% to 10%:

Central nervous system: Dizziness, drowsiness, malaise/fatigue

Gastrointestinal: Nausea, vomiting

Neuromuscular & skeletal: Paresthesias

Miscellaneous: Pain or pressure in throat or neck

<1% (Limited to important or life-threatening): Allergic reaction, atrial fibrillation, atrial flutter, coronary artery vasospasm, hallucinations, MI, PR prolongation, premature ventricular contractions, QT$_c$ prolongation, seizure, ventricular fibrillation, ventricular tachycardia

Drug Interactions

Increased Effect/Toxicity: Ergot-containing drugs (dihydroergotamine or methysergide) may cause vasospastic reactions when taken with naratriptan. Avoid concomitant use with ergots; separate dose of naratriptan and ergots by at least 24 hours. Oral contraceptives taken with naratriptan reduced the clearance of naratriptan ~30% which may contribute to adverse effects. SSRIs/SNRIs may exhibit additive toxicity with naratriptan or other serotonin agonists (eg, antidepressants, dextromethorphan, tramadol) leading to serotonin syndrome.

Decreased Effect: Smoking increases the clearance of naratriptan.

Mechanism of Action The therapeutic effect for migraine is due to serotonin agonist activity

Pharmacodynamics/Kinetics

Onset of action: 30 minutes

Absorption: Well absorbed

Protein binding, plasma: 28% to 31%

Metabolism: Hepatic via CYP

Bioavailability: 70%

Time to peak: 2-3 hours

Excretion: Urine

Dosage
Adults: Oral: 1-2.5 mg at the onset of headache; it is recommended to use the lowest possible dose to minimize adverse effects. If headache returns or does not fully resolve, the dose may be repeated after 4 hours; do not exceed 5 mg in 24 hours.
Elderly: Not recommended for use in the elderly
Dosing in renal impairment:
Cl$_{cr}$: 18-39 mL/minute: Initial: 1 mg; do not exceed 2.5 mg in 24 hours
Cl$_{cr}$: <15 mL/minute: Do not use
Dosing in hepatic impairment: Contraindicated in patients with severe liver failure; maximum dose: 2.5 mg in 24 hours for patients with mild or moderate liver failure; recommended starting dose: 1 mg
Administration Do **not** crush or chew tablet; swallow whole with water.
Dosage Forms Tablet: 1 mg, 2.5 mg

♦ **Naratriptan Hydrochloride** see Naratriptan on page 1202
♦ **Narcan** see Naloxone on page 1194
♦ **Nardil®** see Phenelzine on page 1351
♦ **Naropin®** see Ropivacaine on page 1533
♦ **Nasacort® AQ** see Triamcinolone on page 1734
♦ **NaSal™ [OTC]** see Sodium Chloride on page 1576
♦ **NasalCrom® [OTC]** see Cromolyn on page 423
♦ **Nasalide® (Can)** see Flunisolide on page 720
♦ **Nasal Moist® [OTC]** see Sodium Chloride on page 1576
♦ **Nasarel®** see Flunisolide on page 720
♦ **Nasatab® LA** see Guaifenesin and Pseudoephedrine on page 819
♦ **Nascobal®** see Cyanocobalamin on page 425
♦ **Nasex-G** see Guaifenesin and Phenylephrine on page 818
♦ **Nasonex®** see Mometasone Furoate on page 1165
♦ **Natacyn®** see Natamycin on page 1203

Natalizumab (na ta LIZ u mab)

U.S. Brand Names Tysabri®
Index Terms AN100226; Anti-4 Alpha Integrin; IgG4-Kappa Monoclonal Antibody
Pharmacologic Category Monoclonal Antibody, Selective Adhesion-Molecule Inhibitor
Use Treatment of relapsing forms of multiple sclerosis
Unlabeled/Investigational Use Crohn's disease
Restrictions Patients must be enrolled in the TOUCH Prescribing Program (800-456-2255) to receive natalizumab. Healthcare providers must also register with the program in order to prescribe, dispense or administer natalizumab. Medication guides are available at http://www.fda.gov/cder/Offices/ODS/MG/natalizumabMG.pdf and should be provided to every patient prior to initiation of therapy.
Pregnancy Risk Factor C
Dosage I.V.: Adults:
Multiple sclerosis: 300 mg infused over 1 hour every 4 weeks
Crohn's disease (unlabeled use): 3-6 mg/kg, followed by a second infusion 4 weeks later
Dosage adjustment in renal impairment: No adjustment recommended
Dosage adjustment in hepatic impairment: Not studied
Additional Information Complete prescribing information for this medication should be consulted for additional detail.
Dosage Forms Injection, solution [preservative free]: 300 mg/15 mL (15 mL) [contains polysorbate-80]

Natamycin (na ta MYE sin)

U.S. Brand Names Natacyn®
Canadian Brand Names Natacyn®
Index Terms Pimaricin
Pharmacologic Category Antifungal Agent, Ophthalmic
Use Treatment of blepharitis, conjunctivitis, and keratitis caused by susceptible fungi (Aspergillus, Candida), Cephalosporium, Curvularia, Fusarium, Penicillium, Microsporum, Epidermophyton, Blastomyces dermatitidis, Coccidioides immitis, Cryptococcus neoformans, Histoplasma capsulatum, Sporothrix schenckii, and Trichomonas vaginalis
Pregnancy Risk Factor C
Lactation Excretion in breast milk unknown
Medication Safety Issues
Sound-alike/look-alike issues:
Natacyn® may be confused with Naprosyn®
Contraindications Hypersensitivity to natamycin or any component of the formulation
Warnings/Precautions Failure to improve (keratitis) after 7-10 days of administration suggests infection caused by a microorganism not susceptible to natamycin; inadequate as a single agent in fungal endophthalmitis
Adverse Reactions Frequency not defined (limited to important or life-threatening): Ocular: Blurred vision, eye irritation not present before therapy, eye pain, photophobia
Drug Interactions
Increased Effect/Toxicity: Topical corticosteroids (concomitant use contraindicated).
Stability Store at room temperature (8°C to 24°C/46°F to 75°F); do not freeze. Protect from excessive heat and light.
Mechanism of Action Increases cell membrane permeability in susceptible fungi
Pharmacodynamics/Kinetics
Absorption: Ophthalmic: Systemic: <2%
(Continued)

Natamycin *(Continued)*

Distribution: Adheres to cornea, retained in conjunctival fornices

Dosage Adults: Ophthalmic: Instill 1 drop in conjunctival sac every 1-2 hours, after 3-4 days reduce to one drop 6-8 times/day; usual course of therapy is 2-3 weeks.

Administration Ophthalmic: Shake well before using, do not touch dropper to eye.

Dosage Forms Suspension, ophthalmic: 5% (15 mL) [contains benzalkonium chloride]

Nateglinide *(na te GLYE nide)*

U.S. Brand Names Starlix®

Canadian Brand Names Starlix®

Pharmacologic Category Antidiabetic Agent, Meglitinide Derivative

Additional Appendix Information

Diabetes Mellitus Management, Adults *on page 2040*

Hyperglycemia- or Hypoglycemia-Causing Drugs *on page 2057*

Use Management of type 2 diabetes mellitus (noninsulin dependent, NIDDM) as monotherapy when hyperglycemia cannot be managed by diet and exercise alone; in combination with metformin or a thiazolidinedione to lower blood glucose in patients whose hyperglycemia cannot be controlled by exercise, diet, or a single agent alone

Pregnancy Risk Factor C

Pregnancy Implications Safety and efficacy in pregnant women have not been established. Do not use during pregnancy. Abnormal blood glucose levels are associated with a higher incidence of congenital abnormalities. Insulin is the drug of choice for the control of diabetes mellitus during pregnancy.

Lactation Excretion in breast milk unknown/not recommended

Contraindications Hypersensitivity to nateglinide or any component of the formulation; diabetic ketoacidosis, with or without coma (treat with insulin); type 1 diabetes mellitus (insulin dependent, IDDM)

Warnings/Precautions Use with caution in patients with moderate-to-severe hepatic impairment. Use caution in severe renal dysfunction, elderly, malnourished, or patients with adrenal/pituitary dysfunction; may be more susceptible to glucose-lowering effects. All oral hypoglycemic agents are capable of producing hypoglycemia. Proper patient selection, dosage, and instructions to the patients are important to avoid hypoglycemic episodes. It may be necessary to discontinue nateglinide and administer insulin if the patient is exposed to stress (ie, fever, trauma, infection, surgery). Indicated for adjunctive therapy with metformin; not to be used as a substitute for metformin monotherapy. Combination treatment with sulfonylureas is not recommended (no additional benefit). Patients not adequately controlled on oral agents which stimulate insulin release (eg, glyburide) should not be switched to nateglinide or have nateglinide added to therapy. Safety and efficacy in pediatric patients have not been established.

Adverse Reactions As reported with nateglinide monotherapy:

1% to 10%:

Central nervous system: Dizziness (4%)

Endocrine & metabolic: Hypoglycemia (2%), increased uric acid

Gastrointestinal: Weight gain

Neuromuscular & skeletal: Arthropathy (3%)

Respiratory: Upper respiratory infection (10%)

Miscellaneous: Flu-like syndrome (4%)

Postmarketing and/or case reports: Cholestatic hepatitis, jaundice, liver enzymes increased, rash, pruritus, urticaria

Overdosage/Toxicology In case of overdose, hypoglycemic symptoms would be expected. Severe hypoglycemic reactions should be treated with intravenous glucose. Dialysis is not effective.

Drug Interactions

Cytochrome P450 Effect: Substrate (major) of CYP2C9, 3A4; **Inhibits** CYP2C9 (weak)

Increased Effect/Toxicity: CYP2C9 inhibitors may increase the levels/effects of nateglinide; example inhibitors include delavirdine, fluconazole, gemfibrozil, ketoconazole, nicardipine, NSAIDs, sulfonamides, and tolbutamide. CYP3A4 inhibitors may increase the levels/effects of nateglinide; example inhibitors include azole antifungals, clarithromycin, diclofenac, doxycycline, erythromycin, imatinib, isoniazid, nefazodone, nicardipine, propofol, protease inhibitors, quinidine, telithromycin, and verapamil. Possible increased hypoglycemic effect may be seen with nonselective beta-adrenergic blocking agents, and pegvisomant; monitor glucose closely when agents are initiated, modified, or discontinued.

Decreased Effect: CYP2C9 inducers may decrease the levels/effects of nateglinide; example inducers include carbamazepine, phenobarbital, phenytoin, rifampin, rifapentine, and secobarbital. CYP3A4 inducers may decrease the levels/effects of nateglinide; example inducers include aminoglutethimide, carbamazepine, nafcillin, nevirapine, phenobarbital, phenytoin, and rifamycins. Possible decreased hypoglycemic effect may be seen with thiazides, corticosteroids; monitor glucose closely when agents are initiated, modified, or discontinued.

Ethanol/Nutrition/Herb Interactions

Ethanol: Avoid ethanol (increased risk of hypoglycemia).

Food: Rate of absorption is decreased and time to T_{max} is delayed when taken with food. Food does not affect AUC. Multiple peak plasma concentrations may be observed if fasting. Not affected by composition of meal.

Herb/Nutraceutical: Avoid alfalfa, aloe, bilberry, bitter melon, burdock, celery, damiana, fenugreek, garcinia, garlic, ginger, ginseng (American), gymnema, marshmallow, and stinging nettle (may enhance the hypoglycemic effects of antidiabetic agents). St. John's wort may decrease the levels/effect of nateglinide.

Stability Store at 25°C (77°F).

Mechanism of Action A phenylalanine derivative, nonsulfonylurea hypoglycemic agent used in the management of type 2 diabetes mellitus (noninsulin dependent, NIDDM); stimulates insulin release from the pancreatic beta cells to reduce postprandial hyperglycemia; amount of insulin release is dependent upon existing glucose levels

Pharmacodynamics/Kinetics
Onset of action: Insulin secretion: ~20 minutes
  Peak effect: 1 hour
Duration: 4 hours
Absorption: Rapid
Distribution: 10 L
Protein binding: 98%, primarily to albumin
Metabolism: Hepatic via hydroxylation followed by glucuronide conjugation via CYP2C9 (70%) and CYP3A4 (30%) to metabolites
Bioavailability: 73%
Half-life elimination: 1.5 hours
Time to peak: ≤1 hour
Excretion: Urine (83%, 16% as unchanged drug); feces (10%)

Dosage
Children: Safety and efficacy have not been established
Adults: Management of type 2 diabetes mellitus: Oral: Initial and maintenance dose: 120 mg 3 times/day, 1-30 minutes before meals; may be given alone or in combination with metformin or a thiazolidinedione; patients close to Hb A_{1c} goal may be started at 60 mg 3 times/day
Elderly: No changes in safety and efficacy were seen in patients ≥65 years; however, some elderly patients may show increased sensitivity to dosing

Dosage adjustment in renal impairment: No specific dosage adjustment is recommended for patients with mild-to-severe renal disease; patients on dialysis showed reduced medication exposure and plasma protein binding. Patients with severe renal dysfunction are more susceptible to glucose-lowering effect; use with caution.

Dosage adjustment in hepatic impairment: Increased serum levels seen with mild hepatic insufficiency; no dosage adjustment is needed. Has not been studied in patients with moderate to severe liver disease; use with caution.

Dietary Considerations Nateglinide should be taken 1-30 minutes prior to meals. Scheduled dose should not be taken if meal is missed. Dietary modification based on ADA recommendations is a part of therapy. Decreases blood glucose concentration. Hypoglycemia may occur. Must be able to recognize symptoms of hypoglycemia (palpitations, sweaty palms, lightheadedness).

Administration Patients who are anorexic or NPO will need to have their dose held to avoid hypoglycemia.

Monitoring Parameters Glucose and Hb A_{1c} levels, weight, lipid profile

Reference Range Target range: Adults:
Fasting blood glucose: <110 mg/dL
Glycosylated hemoglobin: <7%

Additional Information An increase in weight was seen in nateglinide monotherapy, which was not seen when used in combination with metformin.

Dosage Forms
Tablet:
  Starlix®: 60 mg, 120 mg

♦ **Natrecor®** see Nesiritide on page 1215
♦ **Natriuretic Peptide** see Nesiritide on page 1215
♦ **Natulan® (Can)** see Procarbazine on page 1428
♦ **Natural Fiber Therapy [OTC]** see Psyllium on page 1458
♦ **Natural Lung Surfactant** see Beractant on page 210
♦ **Nature-Throid® NT** see Thyroid on page 1676
♦ **Nauseatol (Can)** see DimenhyDRINATE on page 511
♦ **Navane®** see Thiothixene on page 1675
♦ **Navelbine®** see Vinorelbine on page 1791
♦ **Naxen® (Can)** see Naproxen on page 1199
♦ **Naxen® EC (Can)** see Naproxen on page 1199
♦ **Na-Zone® [OTC]** see Sodium Chloride on page 1576
♦ **NC-722665** see Bicalutamide on page 221
♦ **n-Docosanol** see Docosanol on page 533
♦ **NebuPent®** see Pentamidine on page 1338
♦ **Necon® 0.5/35** see Ethinyl Estradiol and Norethindrone on page 655
♦ **Necon® 1/35** see Ethinyl Estradiol and Norethindrone on page 655
♦ **Necon® 1/50** see Mestranol and Norethindrone on page 1093
♦ **Necon® 7/7/7** see Ethinyl Estradiol and Norethindrone on page 655
♦ **Necon® 10/11** see Ethinyl Estradiol and Norethindrone on page 655

Nedocromil (ne doe KROE mil)

U.S. Brand Names Alocril®; Tilade®
Canadian Brand Names Alocril®; Tilade®
Index Terms Nedocromil Sodium
Pharmacologic Category Mast Cell Stabilizer
Additional Appendix Information
Asthma on page 2029
Use
Aerosol: Maintenance therapy in patients with mild to moderate bronchial asthma
Ophthalmic: Treatment of itching associated with allergic conjunctivitis
Pregnancy Risk Factor B
Lactation Excretion in breast milk unknown/use caution
(Continued)

Nedocromil *(Continued)*

Contraindications Hypersensitivity to nedocromil or any component of the formulation

Warnings/Precautions

Aerosol: Safety and efficacy in children <6 years of age have not been established; if systemic or inhaled steroid therapy is at all reduced, monitor patients carefully; nedocromil is **not** a bronchodilator and, therefore, should not be used for reversal of acute bronchospasm

Ophthalmic solution: Users of contact lenses should not wear them during periods of symptomatic allergic conjunctivitis

Adverse Reactions

Inhalation:

>10%: Gastrointestinal: Unpleasant taste after inhalation

1% to 10%:

Cardiovascular: Chest pain

Central nervous system: Dizziness, dysphonia, headache, fatigue

Dermatologic: Rash

Gastrointestinal: Nausea, vomiting, heartburn, diarrhea, abdominal pain, dry mouth

Hepatic: Increased ALT

Neuromuscular & skeletal: Arthritis, tremor

Respiratory: Cough, pharyngitis, rhinitis, bronchitis, upper respiratory infection, bronchospasm, increased sputum production

Ophthalmic solution

>10%:

Central nervous system: Headache

Gastrointestinal: Unpleasant taste

Ocular: Burning, irritation, stinging

Respiratory: Nasal congestion

1% to 10%:

Ocular: Conjunctivitis, eye redness, photophobia

Respiratory: Asthma, rhinitis

Stability Store at 2°C to 30°C/36°F to 86°F; do not freeze.

Mechanism of Action Inhibits the activation of and mediator release from a variety of inflammatory cell types associated with asthma including eosinophils, neutrophils, macrophages, mast cells, monocytes, and platelets; it inhibits the release of histamine, leukotrienes, and slow-reacting substance of anaphylaxis; it inhibits the development of early and late bronchoconstriction responses to inhaled antigen

Pharmacodynamics/Kinetics

Duration: Therapeutic effect: 2 hours

Protein binding, plasma: 89%

Bioavailability: 7% to 9%

Half-life elimination: 1.5-2 hours

Excretion: Urine (as unchanged drug)

Dosage

Inhalation: Children >6 years and Adults: 2 inhalations 4 times/day; may reduce dosage to 2-3 times/day once desired clinical response to initial dose is observed

Ophthalmic: 1-2 drops in each eye twice daily

Additional Information Nedocromil has no known therapeutic systemic activity when delivered by inhalation.

Dosage Forms

Aerosol for oral inhalation, as sodium (Tilade®): 1.75 mg/activation (16.2 g)

Solution, ophthalmic, as sodium (Alocril®): 2% (5 mL) [contains benzalkonium chloride]

♦ **Nedocromil Sodium** *see Nedocromil on page 1205*

Nefazodone *(nef AY zoe done)*

Index Terms Nefazodone Hydrochloride; Serzone

Pharmacologic Category Antidepressant, Serotonin Reuptake Inhibitor/Antagonist

Additional Appendix Information

Antidepressant Agents *on page 1866*

Use Treatment of depression

Unlabeled/Investigational Use Post-traumatic stress disorder

Restrictions An FDA-approved medication guide concerning the use of antidepressants in children and teenagers must be distributed when dispensing an outpatient prescription (new or refill) where this medication is to be used without direct supervision of a healthcare provider. Medication guides are available at http://www.fda.gov/cder/Offices/ODS/medication_guides.htm. Dispense to parents or guardians of children and teenagers receiving this medication.

Pregnancy Risk Factor C

Medication Safety Issues

Sound-alike/look-alike issues:

Serzone® may be confused with selegiline, Serentil®, Seroquel®, sertraline

Dosage Oral:

Children and Adolescents (unlabeled use): Depression: Target dose: 300-400 mg/day (mean: 3.4 mg/kg)

Adults: Depression: 200 mg/day, administered in 2 divided doses initially, with a range of 300-600 mg/day in 2 divided doses thereafter

Additional Information Complete prescribing information for this medication should be consulted for additional detail.

Dosage Forms Tablet, as hydrochloride: 50 mg, 100 mg, 150 mg, 200 mg, 250 mg

♦ **Nefazodone Hydrochloride** *see Nefazodone on page 1206*

Nelarabine (nel AY re been)

U.S. Brand Names Arranon®

Index Terms 2-Amino-6-Methoxypurine Arabinoside; GW506U78; 506U78

Pharmacologic Category Antineoplastic Agent, Antimetabolite

Use Treatment of relapsed or refractory T-cell acute lymphoblastic leukemia (ALL) and T-cell lymphoblastic lymphoma

Unlabeled/Investigational Use CML (Philadelphia chromosome positive) T-Cell blast phase

Pregnancy Risk Factor D

Pregnancy Implications Teratogenic effects were observed in animal studies. There are no adequate and well-controlled studies in pregnant women. Women of childbearing potential should be advised to use effective contraception and avoid becoming pregnant during therapy.

Lactation Excretion in breast milk unknown/not recommended

Medication Safety Issues

High alert medication: The Institute for Safe Medication Practices (ISMP) includes this medication among its list of drugs which have a heightened risk of causing significant patient harm when used in error.

Contraindications Hypersensitivity to nelarabine or any component of the formulation

Warnings/Precautions Hazardous agent - use appropriate precautions for handling and disposal. **[U.S. Boxed Warning]: Neurotoxicity is the dose-limiting toxicity;** observe closely for signs and symptoms of neurotoxicity (somnolence, confusion, convulsions, ataxia, paresthesia, hypoesthesia, coma, status epilepticus, craniospinal demyelination, or ascending neuropathy). Risk of neurotoxicity may increase in patients with concurrent or previous intrathecal chemotherapy or history of craniospinal irradiation. Appropriate measures must be taken to prevent hyperuricemia and tumor lysis syndrome; use extreme caution in patients with increased uric acid, gout, and history of uric acid stones; monitor, consider allopurinol and hydrate accordingly. Bone marrow suppression is common. Avoid administration of live vaccines. Use caution in patients with renal impairment and with severe hepatic impairment; monitor closely. **[U.S. Boxed Warning]: Should be administered under the supervision of an experienced cancer chemotherapy physician.**

Adverse Reactions Note: Pediatric adverse reactions fell within a range similar to adults except where noted.

>10%:

Cardiovascular: Peripheral edema (15%), edema (11%)

Central nervous system: Fatigue (50%), fever (23%), somnolence (7% to 22%; grades 2-4: 3% to 6%), dizziness (21%; grade 2: 8% adults), headache (15% to 17%; grades 2-4: 4% to 8%), hypoesthesia (6% to 17%; grades 2-4: children 5%, adults 12%), pain (11%)

Dermatologic: Petechiae (12%)

Endocrine & metabolic: Hypokalemia (12%)

Gastrointestinal: Nausea (41%), diarrhea (22%), vomiting (10% to 22%), constipation (21%)

Hematologic: Anemia (95% to 99%; grade 4: 10% to 14%), neutropenia (81% to 94%; grade 4: children 62%, adults 49%), thrombocytopenia (86% to 88%; grade 4: 22% to 32%), leukopenia (38%; grade 4: 7%), febrile neutropenia (12%; grade 4: 1%)

Hepatic: Transaminases increased (12%)

Neuromuscular & skeletal: Peripheral neuropathy (12% to 21%; grades 2-4: 11% to 14%), weakness (6% to 17%; grade 4: 1%), paresthesia (4% to 15%; grades 2-4: 3% to 4%), myalgia (13%)

Respiratory: Cough (25%), dyspnea (7% to 20%)

1% to 10%:

Cardiovascular: Hypotension (8%), tachycardia (8%), chest pain (5%)

Central nervous system: Ataxia (2% to 9%; grades 2-4: children 1%, adults 8%), confusion (8%), insomnia (7%), depressed level of consciousness (6%; grades 2-4: 2%), depression (6%), seizure (grade 4: 6% children), motor dysfunction (4%; grades 2-4: 2%), amnesia (3%; grades 2-4: 1%), balance disorder (2%; grades 2-4: 1%), nerve paralysis (2%), sensory loss (1% to 2%), aphasia (1%), cerebral hemorrhage (1%), coma (1%), encephalopathy (1%), hemiparesis (1%), hydrocephalus (1%), lethargy (1%), leukoencephalopathy (1%), loss of consciousness (1%), mental impairment (1%), neuropathic pain (1%), nerve palsy (1%), nystagmus (1%), paralysis (1%), sciatica (1%), sensory disturbance (1%), speech disorder (1%), demyelination, ascending peripheral neuropathy

Endocrine & Metabolic: Hypocalcemia (8%), dehydration (7%), hyper-/hypoglycemia (6%), hypomagnesemia (6%)

Gastrointestinal: Abdominal pain (9%), anorexia (9%), stomatitis (8%), abdominal distension (6%), taste perversion (3%)

Hepatic: Albumin decreased (10%), bilirubin increased (10%), AST increased (6%)

Neuromuscular & skeletal: Arthralgia (9%), back pain (8%), muscle weakness (8%), rigors (8%), limb pain (7%), abnormal gait (6%), noncardiac chest pain (5%), tremor (4% to 5%; grades 2-4: 2% to 3%), dysarthria (1%), hyporeflexia (1%), hypertonia (1%), incoordination (1%)

Ocular: Blurred vision (4%)

Renal: Creatinine increased (6%)

Respiratory: Pleural effusion (10%), epistaxis (8%), pneumonia (8%), sinusitis (7%), wheezing (5%), sinus headache (1%)

Miscellaneous: Infection (5% to 9%)

Overdosage/Toxicology Nelarabine was administered to two adult patients at doses up to 2900 mg/m² on days 1, 3, and 5 in clinical trials. Two patients developed grade 3 neuropathy at a dose of 2200 mg/m² given on days 1, 3, and 5. A single dose of 4800 mg/m² produced neurotoxicity and was fatal in animal studies. If an overdose occurs, it would be expected to cause severe and potentially fatal neurotoxicity and myelosuppression; treatment should be symptom-directed and supportive.

(Continued)

Nelarabine *(Continued)*

Drug Interactions

Increased Effect/Toxicity: Vaccines: Avoid administration of live vaccines in immunosuppressive therapy.

Stability Store unopened vials at 15°C to 30°C (59°F to 86°F). Reconstitution is not required; the appropriate dose should be added to empty plastic bag or glass container. Stable in plastic or glass containers for up to 8 hours at room temperature.

Mechanism of Action Nelarabine is a prodrug of ara-G. It is demethylated by adenosine deaminase to ara-G and then converted to ara-GTP. Ara-GTP is incorporated into the DNA of the leukemic blasts, leading to inhibition of DNA synthesis and inducing apoptosis. Ara-GTP appears to accumulate at higher levels in T-cells, which correlates to clinical response.

Pharmacodynamics/Kinetics

Distribution: Nelarabine: 197-213 L/m^2; ara-G: 33-50 L/m^2

Protein binding: Nelarabine and ara-G: <25%

Metabolism: Hepatic; demethylated by adenosine deaminase to form ara-G (active); also hydrolyzed to form methylguanine. Both ara-G and methylguanine metabolized to guanine. Guanine is deaminated into xanthine, which is further oxidized to form uric acid, which is then oxidized to form allantoin.

Half-life elimination: Nelarabine: 30 minutes; ara-G: 3 hours

Excretion: Urine (nelarabine 7%, ara-G 27%) within 24 hours of infusion on day 1

Dosage I.V.: T-cell ALL, T-cell lymphoblastic lymphoma:

Children: 650 mg/m^2/day on days 1 through 5; repeat every 21 days

Adults: 1500 mg/m^2/day on days 1, 3, and 5; repeat every 21 days

Dosage adjustment for toxicity:

Neurologic toxicity ≥ grade 2: Discontinue treatment.

Hematologic or other (non-neurologic) toxicity: Consider treatment delay.

Dosage adjustment in renal impairment:

Cl$_{cr}$ ≥50 mL/minute: No adjustment recommended

Cl$_{cr}$ <50 mL/minute: Safety has not been established

Cl$_{cr}$ <30 mL/minute: Closely monitor

Dosage adjustment in hepatic impairment: Safety has not been established; closely monitor with severe impairment (bilirubin >3 mg/dL)

Administration Adequate I.V. hydration recommended to prevent tumor lysis syndrome; allopurinol may be used if hyperuricemia is anticipated.

Children: Infuse over 1 hour daily for 5 consecutive days

Adults: Infuse over 2 hours on days 1, 3, and 5

Monitoring Parameters Closely monitor for neurologic toxicity (severe somnolence, seizure, peripheral neuropathy, confusion, ataxia, paresthesia, hypoesthesia, coma, or craniospinal demyelination); signs and symptoms of tumor lysis syndrome; hydration status; CBC with platelet counts, liver and kidney function

Dosage Forms Injection, solution: 5 mg/mL (50 mL)

Nelfinavir *(nel FIN a veer)*

U.S. Brand Names Viracept®

Canadian Brand Names Viracept®

Index Terms NFV

Pharmacologic Category Antiretroviral Agent, Protease Inhibitor

Additional Appendix Information

Antiretroviral Therapy for HIV Infection: Adults and Adolescents *on page 1988*

Desensitization Protocols *on page 1913*

Management of Healthcare Worker Exposures to HBV, HCV, and HIV *on page 1941*

Use In combination with other antiretroviral therapy in the treatment of HIV infection

Pregnancy Risk Factor B

Pregnancy Implications No increased risk of overall birth defects has been observed following 1st trimester exposure according to data collected by the antiretroviral pregnancy registry. The Perinatal HIV Guidelines Working Group recommends nelfinavir as the preferred PI in combination regimens during pregnancy, especially with HAART for perinatal prophylaxis. A dose of 1250 mg twice daily has been shown to provide adequate plasma levels; 750 mg 3 times/day produced low and variable levels. Pregnancy and protease inhibitors are both associated with an increased risk of hyperglycemia. Glucose levels should be closely monitored. Health professionals are encouraged to contact the antiretroviral pregnancy registry to monitor outcomes of pregnant women exposed to antiretroviral medications (1-800-258-4263 or www.APRegistry.com).

Lactation Excretion in breast milk unknown/contraindicated

Medication Safety Issues

Sound-alike/look-alike issues:

Nelfinavir may be confused with nevirapine

Viracept® may be confused with Viramune®

Contraindications Hypersensitivity to nelfinavir or any component of the formulation; concurrent therapy with amiodarone, ergot derivatives, midazolam, pimozide, quinidine, triazolam; additional medications which should not be coadministered (per manufacturer) include lovastatin and simvastatin

Warnings/Precautions Use with caution in patients taking strong CYP3A4 inhibitors, moderate or strong CYP3A4 inducers and major CYP3A4 substrates (see drug interactions); consider alternative agents that avoid or lessen the potential for CYP-mediated interactions. Use caution with hepatic impairment. Warn patients that redistribution of body fat can occur. New onset diabetes mellitus, exacerbation of diabetes, and hyperglycemia have been reported in HIV-infected patients receiving protease inhibitors. Use with caution in patients with hemophilia A or B; increased bleeding during protease inhibitor therapy has been reported. Immune reconstitution syndrome has been reported; may require additional evaluation and treatment. The oral powder contains phenylalanine; use caution in patients with phenylketonuria. Safety and efficacy have not been established in children <2 years.

Adverse Reactions

>10%: Gastrointestinal: Diarrhea

2% to 10%:

Dermatologic: Rash

Gastrointestinal: Nausea, flatulence

Hematologic: Abnormal creatine kinase, hemoglobin, lymphocytes, neutrophils

Hepatic: Abnormal ALT, AST

<2% (Limited to important or life-threatening): Acute iritis, allergic reaction, amylase increased, anemia, anorexia, anxiety, arthralgia, back pain, bilirubinemia, body fat redistribution/accumulation, creatinine phosphokinase increased, dehydration, depression, diaphoresis, dizziness, dyspepsia, dyspnea, epigastric pain, fever, folliculitis, gamma glutarnyl transpeptidase increased, gastrointestinal bleeding, headache, hepatitis, hyperkinesia, hyperglycemia, hyperlipemia; hypersensitivity reaction (bronchospasm, rash, edema); hyperuricemia, hypoglycemia, insomnia, jaundice, kidney calculus, lactic dehydrogenase increased, leukopenia, maculopapular rash, metabolic acidosis, myalgia, myasthenia, myopathy, pain, pancreatitis, paresthesia, pruritus, QT_c prolongation, seizure, sexual dysfunction, sleep disorder, somnolence, suicidal ideation, thrombocytopenia, torsade de pointes, urticaria, vomiting, weakness

Overdosage/Toxicology Limited data are available. However, unabsorbed drug should be removed via gastric lavage and activated charcoal. Significant symptoms beyond gastrointestinal disturbances are likely following acute overdose. Hemodialysis will not be effective due to the high protein binding of nelfinavir.

Drug Interactions

Cytochrome P450 Effect: Substrate of CYP2C9 (minor), 2C19 (major), 2D6 (minor), 3A4 (major); **Inhibits** CYP1A2 (weak), 2B6 (weak), 2C9 (weak), 2C19 (weak), 2D6 (weak), 3A4 (strong)

Increased Effect/Toxicity: Nelfinavir effects may be increased by azithromycin, delavirdine, and protease inhibitors. Nelfinavir may increase the levels/effects of selected benzodiazepines, calcium channel blockers, corticosteroids (eg, fluticasone), cyclosporine, mirtazapine, nateglinide, nefazodone, quinidine, sildenafil (and other PDE-5 inhibitors), tacrolimus, venlafaxine, and other CYP3A4 substrates. Selected benzodiazepines (midazolam, triazolam), cisapride, ergot alkaloids, selected HMG-CoA reductase inhibitors (lovastatin and simvastatin), and pimozide are generally contraindicated with strong CYP3A4 inhibitors. When used with strong CYP3A4 inhibitors, dosage adjustment/limits are recommended for sildenafil and other PDE-5 inhibitors; refer to individual monographs.

Decreased Effect: The levels/effects of nelfinavir may be decreased by aminoglutethimide, carbamazepine, nafcillin, nevirapine, phenobarbital, phenytoin, rifamycins, or other inducers of CYP2C19 or 3A4. Nelfinavir effects may be decreased by St John's wort. Nelfinavir may decrease the effects of delavirdine, methadone, and oral contraceptives

Ethanol/Nutrition/Herb Interactions

Food: Nelfinavir taken with food increases plasma concentration time curve (AUC) by two- to threefold. Do not administer with acidic food or juice (orange juice, apple juice, or applesauce) since the combination may have a bitter taste.

Herb/Nutraceutical: St John's wort may decrease nelfinavir serum concentrations; avoid concurrent use.

Stability Store at room temperature of 15°C to 30°C (59°F to 86°F). Oral powder (or dissolved tablets) diluted in nonacidic liquid is stable for 6 hours under refrigeration.

Mechanism of Action Inhibits the HIV-1 protease; inhibition of the viral protease prevents cleavage of the gag-pol polyprotein resulting in the production of immature, noninfectious virus

Pharmacodynamics/Kinetics

Absorption: Food increases plasma concentration-time curve (AUC) by two- to threefold

Distribution: V_d: 2-7 L/kg

Protein binding: 98%

Metabolism: Hepatic via CYP2C19 and 3A4; major metabolite has activity comparable to parent drug

Half-life elimination: 3.5-5 hours

Time to peak, serum: 2-4 hours

Excretion: Feces (98% to 99%, 78% as metabolites, 22% as unchanged drug); urine (1% to 2%)

Dosage Oral:

Children 2-13 years: 45-55 mg/kg twice daily **or** 25-35 mg/kg 3 times/day (maximum: 2500 mg/day); all doses should be taken with a meal. If tablets are unable to be taken, use oral powder in small amount of water, milk, formula, or dietary supplements; do not use acidic food/juice or store for >6 hours.

Adults: 750 mg 3 times/day with meals or 1250 mg twice daily with meals in combination with other antiretroviral therapies

Dosing adjustment in renal impairment: No adjustment needed

Dosing adjustment in hepatic impairment: Use caution

Dietary Considerations Should be taken as scheduled with food. Oral powder contains phenylalanine 11.2 mg/g.

Administration Mix powder or tablets in a small amount of water, milk, formula, soy milk, soy formula, or dietary supplement. Be sure entire contents is consumed to receive full dose. Do not use acidic food/juice to dilute due to bitter taste. One mixed, solution should be used immediately, but may be stored for up to 6 hours if refrigerated.

Monitoring Parameters Liver function tests, viral load, CD4 count, triglycerides, cholesterol, blood glucose, CBC with differential

Dosage Forms

Powder, oral: 50 mg/g (144 g) [contains phenylalanine 11.2 mg/g]

Tablet: 250 mg, 625 mg

♦ **Nembutal®** *see* Pentobarbital *on page 1340*

♦ **Nembutal® Sodium (Can)** *see* Pentobarbital *on page 1340*

♦ **Neo-Fradin™** *see* Neomycin *on page 1210*

Neomycin (nee oh MYE sin)

U.S. Brand Names Neo-Fradin™; Neo-Rx

Index Terms Neomycin Sulfate

Pharmacologic Category Ammonium Detoxicant; Antibiotic, Aminoglycoside; Antibiotic, Topical

Additional Appendix Information

Prevention of Wound Infection and Sepsis in Surgical Patients *on page 1964*

Use Orally to prepare GI tract for surgery; topically to treat minor skin infections; treatment of diarrhea caused by *E. coli*; adjunct in the treatment of hepatic encephalopathy; bladder irrigation; ocular infections

Pregnancy Risk Factor D

Lactation Excretion in breast milk unknown

Medication Safety Issues

Sound-alike/look-alike issues:

Myciguent may be confused with Mycitracin®

Contraindications Hypersensitivity to neomycin or any component of the formulation, or other aminoglycosides; intestinal obstruction

Warnings/Precautions [U.S. Boxed Warning]: May cause neurotoxicity, nephrotoxicity, and/or neuromuscular blockade and respiratory paralysis; usual risk factors include pre-existing renal impairment, concomitant neuro-/nephrotoxic medications, advanced age and dehydration. The drug's neurotoxicity can result in respiratory paralysis from neuromuscular blockade, especially when the drug is given soon after anesthesia or muscle relaxants. Use with caution in patients with renal impairment, pre-existing hearing impairment, neuromuscular disorders; neomycin is more toxic than other aminoglycosides when given parenterally; **do not administer parenterally;** topical neomycin is a contact sensitizer with sensitivity occurring in 5% to 15% of patients treated with the drug; symptoms include itching, reddening, edema, and failure to heal; **do not use as peritoneal lavage** due to significant systemic adsorption of the drug. Prolonged use may result in superinfection, including pseudomembranous colitis.

Adverse Reactions

Oral:

>10%: Gastrointestinal: Nausea, diarrhea, vomiting, irritation or soreness of the mouth or rectal area

<1% (Limited to important or life-threatening): Dyspnea, eosinophilia, nephrotoxicity, neurotoxicity, ototoxicity (auditory), ototoxicity (vestibular)

Topical: >10%: Dermatologic: Contact dermatitis

Overdosage/Toxicology Symptoms of overdose are rare, due to poor oral bioavailability, but include ototoxicity, nephrotoxicity, and neuromuscular toxicity. The treatment of choice following a single acute overdose appears to be the maintenance of urine output of at least 3 mL/kg/hour. Dialysis is of questionable value in enhancing aminoglycoside elimination. If required, hemodialysis is preferred over peritoneal dialysis in patients with normal renal function. Chelation with penicillin may be of benefit.

Drug Interactions

Increased Effect/Toxicity: Oral neomycin may potentiate the effects of oral anticoagulants. Neomycin may increase the adverse effects with other neurotoxic, ototoxic, or nephrotoxic drugs.

Decreased Effect: May decrease GI absorption of digoxin and methotrexate.

Mechanism of Action Interferes with bacterial protein synthesis by binding to 30S ribosomal subunits

Pharmacodynamics/Kinetics

Absorption: Oral, percutaneous: Poor (3%)

Distribution: 97% of an orally administered dose remains in the GI tract. Absorbed neomycin distributes to tissues and concentrates in the renal cortex. With repeated doses, accumulation also occurs in the inner ear.

V_d: 0.36 L/kg

Protein binding: 0% to 30%

Metabolism: Slightly hepatic

Half-life elimination (age and renal function dependent): 3 hours

Time to peak, serum: Oral: 1-4 hours

Excretion: Feces (97% of oral dose as unchanged drug); urine (30% to 50% of absorbed drug as unchanged drug)

Dosage

Children: Oral:

Preoperative intestinal antisepsis: 90 mg/kg/day divided every 4 hours for 2 days; or 25 mg/kg at 1 PM, 2 PM, and 11 PM on the day preceding surgery as an adjunct to mechanical cleansing of the intestine and in combination with erythromycin base

Hepatic encephalopathy: 50-100 mg/kg/day in divided doses every 6-8 hours or 2.5-7 g/m²/day divided every 4-6 hours for 5-6 days not to exceed 12 g/day

Children and Adults: Topical: Topical solutions containing 0.1% to 1% neomycin have been used for irrigation

Adults: Oral:

Preoperative intestinal antisepsis: 1 g each hour for 4 doses then 1 g every 4 hours for 5 doses; or 1 g at 1 PM, 2 PM, and 11 PM on day preceding surgery as an adjunct to mechanical cleansing of the bowel and oral erythromycin; or 6 g/day divided every 4 hours for 2-3 days

Hepatic encephalopathy: 500-2000 mg every 6-8 hours or 4-12 g/day divided every 4-6 hours for 5-6 days

Chronic hepatic insufficiency: 4 g/day for an indefinite period

Monitoring Parameters Renal function tests, audiometry in symptomatic patients
Dosage Forms
Powder, micronized, as sulfate [for prescription compounding] (Neo-Rx): (10 g, 100 g)
Solution, oral, as sulfate (Neo-Fradin™): 125 mg/5 mL (60 mL, 480 mL) [contains benzoic acid; cherry flavor]
Tablet, as sulfate: 500 mg

Neomycin and Polymyxin B (nee oh MYE sin & pol i MIKS in bee)

U.S. Brand Names Neosporin® G.U. Irrigant
Canadian Brand Names Neosporin® Irrigating Solution
Index Terms Polymyxin B and Neomycin
Pharmacologic Category Antibiotic, Topical; Genitourinary Irrigant
Use Short-term as a continuous irrigant or rinse in the urinary bladder to prevent bacteriuria and gram-negative rod septicemia associated with the use of indwelling catheters; to help prevent infection in minor cuts, scrapes, and burns
Pregnancy Risk Factor C/D (for G.U. irrigant)
Dosage Children and Adults: Bladder irrigation: **Not for injection**; add 1 mL irrigant to 1 liter isotonic saline solution and connect container to the inflow of lumen of 3-way catheter. Continuous irrigant or rinse in the urinary bladder for up to a maximum of 10 days with administration rate adjusted to patient's urine output; usually no more than 1 L of irrigant is used per day.
Additional Information Complete prescribing information for this medication should be consulted for additional detail.
Dosage Forms
Solution, irrigant: Neomycin 40 mg and polymyxin B 200,000 units per mL (1 mL)
Neosporin® G.U. Irrigant: Neomycin 40 mg and polymyxin B 200,000 units per mL (1 mL, 20 mL)

♦ **Neomycin, Bacitracin, and Polymyxin B** see Bacitracin, Neomycin, and Polymyxin B on page 192
♦ **Neomycin, Bacitracin, Polymyxin B, and Hydrocortisone** see Bacitracin, Neomycin, Polymyxin B, and Hydrocortisone on page 192

Neomycin, Colistin, Hydrocortisone, and Thonzonium
(nee oh MYE sin, koe LIS tin, hye droe KOR ti sone, & thon ZOE nee um)

U.S. Brand Names Coly-Mycin® S; Cortisporin®-TC
Index Terms Colistin, Neomycin, Hydrocortisone, and Thonzonium; Hydrocortisone, Neomycin, Colistin, and Thonzonium; Thonzonium, Neomycin, Colistin, and Hydrocortisone
Pharmacologic Category Antibiotic/Corticosteroid, Otic
Use Treatment of superficial and susceptible bacterial infections of the external auditory canal; for treatment of susceptible bacterial infections of mastoidectomy and fenestration cavities
Dosage Otic:
Calibrated dropper:
Children: 4 drops in affected ear 3-4 times/day
Adults: 5 drops in affected ear 3-4 times/day
Dropper bottle:
Children: 3 drops in affected ear 3-4 times/day
Adults: 4 drops in affected ear 3-4 times/day
Note: Alternatively, a cotton wick may be inserted in the ear canal and saturated with suspension every 4 hours; wick should be replaced at least every 24 hours
Additional Information Complete prescribing information for this medication should be consulted for additional detail.
Dosage Forms Suspension, otic [drops]:
Coly-Mycin® S: Neomycin 0.33%, colistin 0.3%, hydrocortisone acetate 1%, and thonzonium bromide 0.05% (5 mL) [contains thimerosal; packaged with dropper]
Cortisporin®-TC: Neomycin 0.33%, colistin 0.3%, hydrocortisone acetate 1%, and thonzonium bromide 0.05% (10 mL) [contains thimerosal; packaged with dropper]

Neomycin, Polymyxin B, and Dexamethasone
(nee oh MYE sin, pol i MIKS in bee, & deks a METH a sone)

U.S. Brand Names AK-Trol® [DSC]; Maxitrol®; Poly-Dex™
Canadian Brand Names Dioptrol®; Maxitrol®
Index Terms Dexamethasone, Neomycin, and Polymyxin B; Polymyxin B, Neomycin, and Dexamethasone
Pharmacologic Category Antibiotic/Corticosteroid, Ophthalmic
Use Steroid-responsive inflammatory ocular conditions in which a corticosteroid is indicated and where bacterial infection or a risk of bacterial infection exists
Pregnancy Risk Factor C
Medication Safety Issues
Sound-alike/look-alike issues:
AK-Trol® may be confused with AKTob®
Dosage Children and Adults: Ophthalmic:
Ointment: Place a small amount (~1/2") in the affected eye 3-4 times/day or apply at bedtime as an adjunct with drops
Suspension: Instill 1-2 drops into affected eye(s) every 3-4 hours; in severe disease, drops may be used hourly and tapered to discontinuation
Additional Information Complete prescribing information for this medication should be consulted for additional detail.
(Continued)

Neomycin, Polymyxin B, and Dexamethasone *(Continued)*

Dosage Forms [DSC] = Discontinued product
Ointment, ophthalmic (Maxitrol®, Poly-Dex™): Neomycin 3.5 mg, polymyxin B sulfate 10,000 units, and dexamethasone 0.1% per g (3.5 g)
Suspension, ophthalmic (AK-Trol® [DSC], Maxitrol®, Poly-Dex®): Neomycin 3.5 mg, polymyxin B sulfate 10,000 units, and dexamethasone 0.1% per mL (5 mL) [contains benzalkonium chloride]

Neomycin, Polymyxin B, and Gramicidin
(nee oh MYE sin, pol i MIKS in bee, & gram i SYE din)

U.S. Brand Names Neosporin® Ophthalmic Solution
Canadian Brand Names Neosporin®; Optimyxin Plus®
Index Terms Gramicidin, Neomycin, and Polymyxin B; Polymyxin B, Neomycin, and Gramicidin
Pharmacologic Category Antibiotic, Ophthalmic
Use Treatment of superficial ocular infection
Pregnancy Risk Factor C
Dosage Children and Adults: Ophthalmic: Instill 1-2 drops 4-6 times/day or more frequently as required for severe infections
Additional Information Complete prescribing information for this medication should be consulted for additional detail.
Dosage Forms Solution, ophthalmic: Neomycin 1.75 mg, polymyxin B 10,000 units, and gramicidin 0.025 mg per mL (10 mL) [contains alcohol 0.5% and thimerosal]

Neomycin, Polymyxin B, and Hydrocortisone
(nee oh MYE sin, pol i MIKS in bee, & hye droe KOR ti sone)

U.S. Brand Names Cortisporin® Cream; Cortisporin® Ophthalmic; Cortisporin® Otic; PediOtic®
Canadian Brand Names Cortimyxin®; Cortisporin® Otic
Index Terms Hydrocortisone, Neomycin, and Polymyxin B; Polymyxin B, Neomycin, and Hydrocortisone
Pharmacologic Category Antibiotic/Corticosteroid, Ophthalmic; Antibiotic/Corticosteroid, Otic; Topical Skin Product
Use Steroid-responsive inflammatory condition for which a corticosteroid is indicated and where bacterial infection or a risk of bacterial infection exists
Pregnancy Risk Factor C
Dosage Duration of use should be limited to 10 days unless otherwise directed by the physician
Otic solution is used **only** for swimmer's ear (infections of external auditory canal)
Otic:
Children: Instill 3 drops into affected ear 3-4 times/day
Adults: Instill 4 drops 3-4 times/day; otic suspension is the preferred otic preparation
Children and Adults:
Ophthalmic: Drops: Instill 1-2 drops 2-4 times/day, or more frequently as required for severe infections; in acute infections, instill 1-2 drops every 15-30 minutes gradually reducing the frequency of administration as the infection is controlled
Topical: Apply a thin layer 1-4 times/day. Therapy should be discontinued when control is achieved; if no improvement is seen, reassessment of diagnosis may be necessary.
Additional Information Complete prescribing information for this medication should be consulted for additional detail.
Dosage Forms
Cream, topical (Cortisporin®): Neomycin 3.5 mg, polymyxin B 10,000 units, and hydrocortisone acetate 5 mg per g (7.5 g)
Solution, otic (Cortisporin®): Neomycin 3.5 mg, polymyxin B 10,000 units, and hydrocortisone 10 mg per mL (10 mL) [contains potassium metabisulfite]
Suspension, ophthalmic (Cortisporin®): Neomycin 3.5 mg, polymyxin B 10,000 units, and hydrocortisone 10 mg per mL (7.5 mL) [contains thimerosal]
Suspension, otic: Neomycin 3.5 mg, polymyxin B 10,000 units, and hydrocortisone 10 mg per mL (10 mL)
Cortisporin®: Neomycin 3.5 mg, polymyxin B 10,000 units, and hydrocortisone 10 mg per mL (10 mL) [contains thimerosal]
PediOtic®: Neomycin 3.5 mg, polymyxin B 10,000 units, and hydrocortisone 10 mg per mL (7.5 mL) [contains thimerosal]

Neomycin, Polymyxin B, and Prednisolone
(nee oh MYE sin, pol i MIKS in bee, & pred NIS oh lone)

U.S. Brand Names Poly-Pred®
Index Terms Polymyxin B, Neomycin, and Prednisolone; Prednisolone, Neomycin, and Polymyxin B
Pharmacologic Category Antibiotic/Corticosteroid, Ophthalmic
Use Steroid-responsive inflammatory ocular condition in which bacterial infection or a risk of bacterial ocular infection exists
Pregnancy Risk Factor C
Dosage Children and Adults: Ophthalmic: Instill 1-2 drops every 3-4 hours; acute infections may require every 30-minute instillation initially with frequency of administration reduced as the infection is brought under control. To treat the lids: Instill 1-2 drops every 3-4 hours, close the eye and rub the excess on the lids and lid margins.
Additional Information Complete prescribing information for this medication should be consulted for additional detail.

Dosage Forms Suspension, ophthalmic: Neomycin 0.35%, polymyxin B 10,000 units per mL, and prednisolone acetate 0.5% (5 mL; 10 mL [DSC]) [contains thimerosal]

◆ **Neomycin Sulfate** *see* Neomycin *on page 1210*
◆ **NeoProfen®** *see* Ibuprofen *on page 873*
◆ **Neoral®** *see* CycloSPORINE *on page 431*
◆ **Neo-Rx** *see* Neomycin *on page 1210*
◆ **Neosar** *see* Cyclophosphamide *on page 428*
◆ **Neosporin® (Can)** *see* Neomycin, Polymyxin B, and Gramicidin *on page 1212*
◆ **Neosporin® AF [OTC]** *see* Miconazole *on page 1137*
◆ **Neosporin® G.U. Irrigant** *see* Neomycin and Polymyxin B *on page 1211*
◆ **Neosporin® Irrigating Solution (Can)** *see* Neomycin and Polymyxin B *on page 1211*
◆ **Neosporin® Neo To Go® [OTC]** *see* Bacitracin, Neomycin, and Polymyxin B *on page 192*
◆ **Neosporin® Ophthalmic Ointment [DSC]** *see* Bacitracin, Neomycin, and Polymyxin B *on page 192*
◆ **Neosporin® Ophthalmic Ointment (Can)** *see* Bacitracin, Neomycin, and Polymyxin B *on page 192*
◆ **Neosporin® Ophthalmic Solution** *see* Neomycin, Polymyxin B, and Gramicidin *on page 1212*
◆ **Neosporin® Topical [OTC]** *see* Bacitracin, Neomycin, and Polymyxin B *on page 192*

Neostigmine (nee oh STIG meen)

U.S. Brand Names Prostigmin®
Canadian Brand Names Prostigmin®
Index Terms Neostigmine Bromide; Neostigmine Methylsulfate
Pharmacologic Category Acetylcholinesterase Inhibitor
Use Diagnosis and treatment of myasthenia gravis; prevention and treatment of postoperative bladder distention and urinary retention; reversal of the effects of nondepolarizing neuromuscular-blocking agents after surgery
Pregnancy Risk Factor C
Lactation Excretion in breast milk unknown/not recommended
Medication Safety Issues
Sound-alike/look-alike issues:
Prostigmin® may be confused with physostigmine
Contraindications Hypersensitivity to neostigmine, bromides, or any component of the formulation; GI or GU obstruction
Warnings/Precautions Does **not** antagonize and may prolong the phase I block of depolarizing muscle relaxants (eg, succinylcholine); use with caution in patients with epilepsy, asthma, bradycardia, hyperthyroidism, cardiac arrhythmias, or peptic ulcer; adequate facilities should be available for cardiopulmonary resuscitation when testing and adjusting dose for myasthenia gravis; have atropine and epinephrine ready to treat hypersensitivity reactions; overdosage may result in cholinergic crisis, this must be distinguished from myasthenic crisis; anticholinesterase insensitivity can develop for brief or prolonged periods
Adverse Reactions Frequency not defined.
Cardiovascular: Arrhythmias (especially bradycardia), hypotension, tachycardia, AV block, nodal rhythm, nonspecific ECG changes, cardiac arrest, syncope, flushing
Central nervous system: Convulsions, dysarthria, dysphonia, dizziness, loss of consciousness, drowsiness, headache
Dermatologic: Skin rash, thrombophlebitis (I.V.), urticaria
Gastrointestinal: Hyperperistalsis, nausea, vomiting, salivation, diarrhea, stomach cramps, dysphagia, flatulence
Genitourinary: Urinary urgency
Neuromuscular & skeletal: Weakness, fasciculations, muscle cramps, spasms, arthralgia
Ocular: Small pupils, lacrimation
Respiratory: Increased bronchial secretions, laryngospasm, bronchiolar constriction, respiratory muscle paralysis, dyspnea, respiratory depression, respiratory arrest, bronchospasm
Miscellaneous: Diaphoresis (increased), anaphylaxis, allergic reactions
Overdosage/Toxicology Symptoms include muscle weakness, blurred vision, excessive sweating, tearing and salivation, nausea, vomiting, diarrhea, hypertension, bradycardia, muscle weakness, and paralysis. Atropine sulfate injection should be readily available as an antagonist for the effects of neostigmine.
Drug Interactions
Increased Effect/Toxicity: Neuromuscular blocking agent effects are increased when combined with neostigmine.
Decreased Effect: Antagonizes effects of nondepolarizing muscle relaxants (eg, pancuronium, tubocurarine). Atropine antagonizes the muscarinic effects of neostigmine.
Mechanism of Action Inhibits destruction of acetylcholine by acetylcholinesterase which facilitates transmission of impulses across myoneural junction
Pharmacodynamics/Kinetics
Onset of action: I.M.: 20-30 minutes; I.V.: 1-20 minutes
Duration: I.M.: 2.5-4 hours; I.V.: 1-2 hours
Absorption: Oral: Poor, <2%
Metabolism: Hepatic
Half-life elimination: Normal renal function: 0.5-2.1 hours; End-stage renal disease: Prolonged
Excretion: Urine (50% as unchanged drug)
Dosage
Myasthenia gravis: Diagnosis: I.M.:
Children: 0.04 mg/kg as a single dose
Adults: 0.02 mg/kg as a single dose
(Continued)

Neostigmine *(Continued)*

Myasthenia gravis: Treatment:
 Children:
  Oral: 2 mg/kg/day divided every 3-4 hours
  I.M., I.V., SubQ: 0.01-0.04 mg/kg every 2-4 hours
 Adults:
  Oral: 15 mg/dose every 3-4 hours up to 375 mg/day maximum; interval between doses
   must be individualized to maximal response
  I.M., I.V., SubQ: 0.5-2.5 mg every 1-3 hours up to 10 mg/24 hours maximum
Reversal of nondepolarizing neuromuscular blockade after surgery in conjunction with atro-
pine (must administer atropine several minutes prior to neostigmine): I.V.:
 Infants: 0.025-0.1 mg/kg/dose
 Children: 0.025-0.08 mg/kg/dose
 Adults: 0.5-2.5 mg; total dose not to exceed 5 mg
Bladder atony: Adults: I.M., SubQ:
 Prevention: 0.25 mg every 4-6 hours for 2-3 days
 Treatment: 0.5-1 mg every 3 hours for 5 doses after bladder has emptied
Dosing adjustment in renal impairment:
 Cl_{cr} 10-50 mL/minute: Administer 50% of normal dose
 Cl_{cr} <10 mL/minute: Administer 25% of normal dose

Administration May be administered undiluted by slow I.V. injection over several minutes

Additional Information In the diagnosis of myasthenia gravis, all anticholinesterase medications should be discontinued for at least 8 hours before administering neostigmine.

Dosage Forms
Injection, solution, as methylsulfate: 0.5 mg/mL (1 mL, 10 mL); 1 mg/mL (10 mL)
Tablet, as bromide: 15 mg

♦ **Neostigmine Bromide** *see Neostigmine on page 1213*
♦ **Neostigmine Methylsulfate** *see Neostigmine on page 1213*
♦ **NeoStrata® AHA [OTC]** *see Hydroquinone on page 859*
♦ **NeoStrata® HQ (Can)** *see Hydroquinone on page 859*
♦ **Neo-Synephrine® (Can)** *see Phenylephrine on page 1358*
♦ **Neo-Synephrine® Extra Strength [OTC]** *see Phenylephrine on page 1358*
♦ **Neo-Synephrine® Mild [OTC]** *see Phenylephrine on page 1358*
♦ **Neo-Synephrine® Ophthalmic [DSC]** *see Phenylephrine on page 1358*
♦ **Neo-Synephrine® Regular Strength [OTC]** *see Phenylephrine on page 1358*

Nepafenac *(ne pa FEN ak)*

U.S. Brand Names Nevanac™
Pharmacologic Category Nonsteroidal Anti-inflammatory Drug (NSAID), Ophthalmic
Use Treatment of pain and inflammation associated with cataract surgery
Pregnancy Risk Factor C/D (3rd trimester)
Pregnancy Implications Teratogenic events were not observed in animal studies. Safety
and efficacy in pregnant women have not been established. Exposure to nonsteroidal
anti-inflammatory drugs late in pregnancy may lead to premature closure of the ductus
arteriosus.
Lactation Excretion in breast milk unknown/use caution
Contraindications Hypersensitivity to nepafenac, other NSAIDs, or any component of the
formulation
Warnings/Precautions Use caution in patients with previous sensitivity to acetylsalicylic acid
and phenylacetic acid derivatives, including patients who experience bronchospasm, asthma,
rhinitis, or urticaria following NSAID or aspirin. May slow/delay healing or prolong bleeding
time following surgery. Use caution in patients with a predisposition to bleeding (bleeding
tendencies or medications which interfere with coagulation).

May cause keratitis; continued use of nepafenac in a patient with keratitis may cause severe
corneal adverse reactions, potentially resulting in loss of vision. Immediately discontinue use
in patients with evidence of corneal epithelial damage.

Use caution in patients with complicated ocular surgeries, corneal denervation, corneal
epithelial defects, diabetes mellitus, ocular surface disease, rheumatoid arthritis, or repeat
ocular surgeries (within a short timeframe); may be at risk of corneal adverse events, potentially resulting in loss of vision. Use more than 1 day prior to surgery or for 14 days beyond
surgery may increase risk and severity of corneal adverse events. Patients using ophthalmic
drops should not wear soft contact lenses.

Safety and efficacy have not been established in children <10 years of age.
Adverse Reactions 1% to 10%:
Cardiovascular: Hypertension (1% to 4%)
Central nervous system: Headache (1% to 4%)
Gastrointestinal: Nausea (1% to 4%), vomiting (1% to 4%)
Ocular: Capsular opacity (5% to 10%), foreign body sensation (5% to 10%), intraocular
 pressure increased (5% to 10%), sticky sensation (5% to 10%), visual acuity decreased
 (5% to 10%), conjunctival edema (1% to 5%), corneal edema (1% to 5%), dry eye (1% to
 5%), lid margin crusting (1% to 5%), ocular discomfort (1% to 5%), ocular hyperemia (1%
 to 5%), ocular pain (1% to 5%), ocular pruritus (1% to 5%), photophobia (1% to 5%),
 tearing (1% to 5%), vitreous detachment (1% to 5%)
Respiratory: Sinusitis (1% to 4%)
Stability Store at 2°C o 25°C (36°F to 77°F).
Mechanism of Action Nepafenac is a prodrug which once converted to amfenac inhibits
prostaglandin synthesis by decreasing the activity of the enzyme, cyclooxygenase, which
results in decreased formation of prostaglandin precursors.

Pharmacodynamics/Kinetics
Absorption: Low levels (0.2-0.5 ng/mL) of nepafenac and amfenac are detected in the plasma following ophthalmic administration

Metabolism: Hydrolyzed in ocular tissue to amfenac (active)

Dosage Ophthalmic: Children ≥10 years and Adults: Instill 1 drop into affected eye(s) 3 times/day, beginning 1 day prior to surgery, the day of surgery, and through the first 2 weeks of the postoperative period

Administration Shake well prior to use.

Dosage Forms Suspension, ophthalmic: 0.1% (3 mL) [contains benzalkonium chloride]

♦ **Nephro-Calci® [OTC]** see Calcium Carbonate on page 269
♦ **Nephro-Fer® [OTC]** see Ferrous Fumarate on page 702
♦ **Nesacaine®** see Chloroprocaine on page 346
♦ **Nesacaine®-CE (Can)** see Chloroprocaine on page 346
♦ **Nesacaine®-MPF** see Chloroprocaine on page 346

Nesiritide (ni SIR i tide)

U.S. Brand Names Natrecor®

Index Terms B-type Natriuretic Peptide (Human); hBNP; Natriuretic Peptide

Pharmacologic Category Natriuretic Peptide, B-Type, Human; Vasodilator

Additional Appendix Information
Hemodynamic Support, Intravenous on page 1885

Use Treatment of acutely decompensated congestive heart failure (CHF) in patients with dyspnea at rest or with minimal activity

Pregnancy Risk Factor C

Lactation Excretion in breast milk unknown/use caution

Medication Safety Issues
High alert medication: The Institute for Safe Medication Practices (ISMP) includes this medication among its list of drugs which have a heightened risk of causing significant patient harm when used in error.

International issues:
Natrecor® may be confused with Nitrocor® which is a brand name for nitroglycerin in Chile and Italy

Contraindications Hypersensitivity to natriuretic peptide or any component of the formulation; cardiogenic shock (when used as primary therapy); hypotension (systolic blood pressure <90 mm Hg)

Warnings/Precautions May cause hypotension; administer in clinical situations when blood pressure may be closely monitored. Use caution in patients with systolic blood pressure <100 mm Hg (contraindicated if <90 mm Hg); more likely to experience hypotension. Effects may be additive with other agents capable of causing hypotension. Hypotensive effects may last for several hours.

Should not be used in patients with low cardiac filling pressures, or in patients with conditions which depend on venous return including significant valvular stenosis, restrictive or obstructive cardiomyopathy, constrictive pericarditis, and pericardial tamponade. May be associated with development of azotemia; use caution in patients with renal impairment or in patients where renal perfusion is dependent on renin-angiotensin-aldosterone system; avoid initiation at doses higher than recommended.

Monitor for allergic or anaphylactic reactions. Use caution with prolonged infusions; limited experience for infusions >48 hours. Safety and efficacy in pediatric patients have not been established.

Adverse Reactions Note: Frequencies cited below were recorded in VMAC trial at dosages similar to approved labeling. Higher frequencies have been observed in trials using higher dosages of nesiritide. The percentages marked with an asterisk (*) indicate frequency less than or equal to placebo or other standard therapy.

>10%:
Cardiovascular: Hypotension (total: 11%; symptomatic: 4% at recommended dose, up to 17% at higher doses)

Renal: Increased serum creatinine (28% with >0.5 mg/dL increase over baseline)

1% to 10%:
Cardiovascular: Ventricular tachycardia (3%)*, ventricular extrasystoles (3%)*, angina (2%)*, bradycardia (1%), tachycardia, atrial fibrillation, AV node conduction abnormalities

Central nervous system: Headache (8%)*, dizziness (3%)*, insomnia (2%)*, anxiety (3%), fever, confusion, paresthesia, somnolence, tremor

Dermatologic: Pruritus, rash

Gastrointestinal: Nausea (4%)*, abdominal pain (1%)*, vomiting (1%)*

Hematologic: Anemia

Local: Injection site reaction

Neuromuscular & skeletal: Back pain (4%), leg cramps

Ocular: Amblyopia

Respiratory: Cough (increased), hemoptysis, apnea

Miscellaneous: Increased diaphoresis

Overdosage/Toxicology Symptoms of overdose would be expected to include excessive and/or prolonged hypotension. Treatment is symptom-directed and supportive.

Drug Interactions
Increased Effect/Toxicity: An increased frequency of symptomatic hypotension was observed with concurrent administration of ACE inhibitors. Other hypotensive agents (eg, diazoxide) are likely to have additive effects on hypotension. In patients receiving diuretic therapy leading to depletion of intravascular volume, the risk of hypotension and/or renal impairment may be increased.

(Continued)

Nesiritide *(Continued)*

Ethanol/Nutrition/Herb Interactions Herb/Nutraceutical: Avoid bayberry, blue cohosh, cayenne, ephedra, ginger, ginseng (American), kola, and licorice (may increase blood pressure). Avoid black cohosh, California poppy, coleus, golden seal, hawthorn, mistletoe, periwinkle, quinine, and shepherd's purse (may enhance decreased blood pressure).

Stability Vials may be stored below 25°C (77°F); do not freeze. Protect from light. Following reconstitution, vials are stable at 2°C to 25°C (36°F to 77°F) for up to 24 hours. Use reconstituted solution within 24 hours.

Reconstitute 1.5 mg vial with 5 mL of diluent removed from a prefilled 250 mL plastic I.V. bag (compatible with 5% dextrose, 0.9% sodium chloride, 5% dextrose and 0.45% sodium chloride, or 5% dextrose and 0.2% sodium chloride). Do not shake vial to dissolve (roll gently). Withdraw entire contents of vial and add to 250 mL I.V. bag. Invert several times to mix. Resultant concentration of solution is ~6 mcg/mL.

Mechanism of Action Binds to guanylate cyclase receptor on vascular smooth muscle and endothelial cells, increasing intracellular cyclic GMP, resulting in smooth muscle cell relaxation. Has been shown to produce dose-dependent reductions in pulmonary capillary wedge pressure (PCWP) and systemic arterial pressure.

Pharmacodynamics/Kinetics

Onset of action: 15 minutes (60% of 3-hour effect achieved)

Duration: >60 minutes (up to several hours) for systolic blood pressure; hemodynamic effects persist longer than serum half-life would predict

Distribution: V_{ss}: 0.19 L/kg

Metabolism: Proteolytic cleavage by vascular endopeptidases and proteolysis following receptor binding and cellular internalization

Half-life elimination: Initial (distribution) 2 minutes; Terminal: 18 minutes

Time to peak: 1 hour

Excretion: Urine

Dosage Adults: I.V.: Initial: 2 mcg/kg (bolus); followed by continuous infusion at 0.01 mcg/kg/minute. **Note:** Should not be initiated at a dosage higher than initial recommended dose. There is limited experience with larger doses; in one trial, a limited number of patients received higher doses that were increased ≥ every 3 hours by 0.005 mcg/kg/minute (preceded by a bolus of 1 mcg/kg), up to a maximum of 0.03 mcg/kg/minute. Increases beyond the initial infusion rate should be limited to selected patients and accompanied by close hemodynamic and renal function monitoring.

Patients experiencing hypotension during the infusion: Infusion should be interrupted. May attempt to restart at a lower dose (reduce initial infusion dose by 30% and omit bolus).

Dosage adjustment in renal impairment: No adjustment required, but use cautiously in patients with renal impairment or those patients who rely on the renin-angiotensin-aldosterone system for renal perfusion. Monitor renal function closely.

Dosage adjustment in hepatic impairment: No dosage adjustment recommended.

Administration Do not administer through a heparin-coated catheter (concurrent administration of heparin via a separate catheter is acceptable, per manufacturer).

Prime I.V. tubing with 5 mL of infusion prior to connection with vascular access port and prior to administering bolus or starting the infusion. Withdraw bolus from the prepared infusion bag and administer over 60 seconds. Begin infusion immediately following administration of the bolus.

Physically incompatible with heparin, insulin, ethacrynate sodium, bumetanide, enalaprilat, hydralazine, and furosemide. Do not administer through the same catheter. Do not administer with any solution containing sodium metabisulfite. Catheter must be flushed between administration of nesiritide and physically incompatible drugs.

Monitoring Parameters Blood pressure, hemodynamic responses (PCWP, RAP, CI), BUN, creatinine; urine output

Additional Information The duration of symptomatic improvement with nesiritide following discontinuation of the infusion has been limited (generally lasting several days). Atrial natriuretic peptide, which is related to nesiritide, has been associated with increased vascular permeability. This has not been observed in clinical trials with nesiritide, but patients should be monitored for this effect.

Dosage Forms

Injection, powder for reconstitution:

Natrecor®: 1.5 mg

♦ **Neulasta**® *see* Pegfilgrastim *on page 1321*

♦ **Neumega**® *see* Oprelvekin *on page 1270*

♦ **Neupogen**® *see* Filgrastim *on page 707*

♦ **Neurontin**® *see* Gabapentin *on page 775*

♦ **Neut**® *see* Sodium Bicarbonate *on page 1575*

♦ **NeutraCare**® *see* Fluoride *on page 722*

♦ **NeutraGard**® **[OTC]** *see* Fluoride *on page 722*

♦ **NeutraGard**® **Advanced** *see* Fluoride *on page 722*

♦ **NeutraGard**® **Plus** *see* Fluoride *on page 722*

♦ **Neutra-Phos**® **[OTC]** *see* Potassium Phosphate and Sodium Phosphate *on page 1403*

♦ **Neutra-Phos**®**-K [OTC]** *see* Potassium Phosphate *on page 1402*

♦ **NeuTrexin**® *see* Trimetrexate *on page 1745*

♦ **Nevanac**™ *see* Nepafenac *on page 1214*

Nevirapine (ne VYE ra peen)

U.S. Brand Names Viramune®

Canadian Brand Names Viramune®

Index Terms NVP

Pharmacologic Category Antiretroviral Agent, Reverse Transcriptase Inhibitor (Non-nucleoside)

Additional Appendix Information

Antiretroviral Therapy for HIV Infection: Adults and Adolescents *on page 1988*

Management of Healthcare Worker Exposures to HBV, HCV, and HIV *on page 1941*

Perinatal HIV-1 *on page 1953*

Use In combination therapy with other antiretroviral agents for the treatment of HIV-1

Restrictions An FDA-approved medication guide must be distributed when dispensing an outpatient prescription (new or refill) where this medication is to be used without direct supervision of a healthcare provider. Medication guides are available at http://www.fda.gov/cder/Offices/ODS/medication_guides.htm.

Pregnancy Risk Factor C

Pregnancy Implications Nevirapine crosses the placenta. No increased risk of overall birth defects has been observed following 1st trimester exposure according to data collected by the antiretroviral pregnancy registry. Pharmacokinetics are not altered during pregnancy and dose adjustment is not needed. The Perinatal HIV Guidelines Working Group recommends nevirapine as the NNRTI for use during pregnancy. When used to prevent perinatal transmission in women who do not need therapy for their own health, use is not recommended if CD4$^+$ lymphocyte counts >250/mm^3 (monitor for liver toxicity during first 18 weeks of therapy). It may also be used in combination with zidovudine in HIV-infected women who are in labor, but have had no prior antiretroviral therapy, in order to reduce the maternal-fetal transmission of HIV; consider adding intrapartum and postpartum zidovudine and lamivudine to reduce nevirapine resistance. Health professionals are encouraged to contact the antiretroviral pregnancy registry to monitor outcomes of pregnant women exposed to antiretroviral medications (1-800-258-4263 or www.APRegistry.com).

Lactation Enters breast milk/contraindicated

Medication Safety Issues

Sound-alike/look-alike issues:

Nevirapine may be confused with nelfinavir

Viramune® may be confused with Viracept®

Contraindications Hypersensitivity to nevirapine or any component of the formulation

Warnings/Precautions [U.S. Boxed Warning]: Severe hepatotoxic reactions may occur (fulminant and cholestatic hepatitis, hepatic necrosis) and, in some cases, have resulted in hepatic failure and death. The greatest risk of these reactions is within the initial 6 weeks of treatment. Patients with a history of chronic hepatitis (B or C) or increased baseline transaminase levels may be at increased risk of hepatotoxic reactions. Female gender and patients with increased CD4$^+$-cell counts may be at substantially greater risk of hepatic events (often associated with rash). Therapy should not be started with elevated CD4$^+$-cell counts unless the benefit of therapy outweighs the risk of serious hepatotoxicity (adult females: CD4$^+$-cell counts >250 cells/mm^3; adult males: CD4$^+$-cell counts >400 cells/mm^3).

[U.S. Boxed Warning]: Severe life-threatening skin reactions (eg, Stevens-Johnson syndrome, toxic epidermal necrolysis, hypersensitivity reactions with rash and organ dysfunction) have occurred; intensive monitoring is required during the initial 18 weeks of therapy to detect potentially life-threatening dermatologic, hypersensitivity, and hepatic reactions. Nevirapine must be initiated with a 14-day lead-in dosing period to decrease the incidence of adverse effects.

If a severe dermatologic or hypersensitivity reaction occurs, or if signs and symptoms of hepatitis occur, nevirapine should be permanently discontinued. These may include a severe rash, or a rash associated with fever, blisters, oral lesions, conjunctivitis, facial edema, muscle or joint aches, general malaise, hepatitis, eosinophilia, granulocytopenia, lymphadenopathy, or renal dysfunction.

Consider alteration of antiretroviral therapies if disease progression occurs while patients are receiving nevirapine. Safety and efficacy have not been established in neonates.

Adverse Reactions Note: Potentially life-threatening nevirapine-associated adverse effects may present with the following symptoms: Abrupt onset of flu-like symptoms, abdominal pain, jaundice, or fever with or without rash; may progress to hepatic failure with encephalopathy. Skin rash is present in ~50% of cases.

Percentages of adverse effects vary by clinical trial:

>10%:

Dermatologic: Rash (grade 1/2: 13%; grade 3/4: 1.5%) is the most common toxicity; occurs most frequently within the first 6 weeks of therapy; women may be at higher risk than men

Hepatic: ALT >250 units/L (5% to 14%); symptomatic hepatic events (4%, range: up to 11%) are more common in women, women with CD4$^+$ cell counts >250 cells/mm^3, and men with CD4$^+$ cell counts >400 cells/mm^3

1% to 10%:

Central nervous system: Headache (1% to 4%), fatigue (up to 5%)

Gastrointestinal: Nausea (<1% to 9%), abdominal pain (<1% to 2%), diarrhea (up to 2%)

Hepatic: AST >250 units/L (4% to 8%); coinfection with hepatitis B or C and/or increased liver function tests at the beginning of therapy are associated with a greater risk of asymptomatic transaminase elevations (ALT or AST >5 times ULN: 6%, range: up to 9%) or symptomatic events occurring ≥6 weeks after beginning treatment

(Continued)

Nevirapine *(Continued)*

Postmarketing and/or case reports: Allergic reactions, anaphylaxis, anemia, angioedema, arthralgia, blisters, bullous eruptions, conjunctivitis, eosinophilia, facial edema, fever, fulminant and cholestatic hepatitis, granulocytopenia, hepatic failure, hepatic necrosis, hypersensitivity syndrome, jaundice, lymphadenopathy, malaise, neutropenia, oral lesions, paresthesia, redistribution/accumulation of body fat, renal dysfunction, Stevens-Johnson syndrome, somnolence, toxic epidermal necrolysis, ulcerative stomatitis, urticaria, vomiting

Overdosage/Toxicology Edema, erythema nodosum, fatigue, fever, headache, insomnia, nausea, pulmonary infiltrates, rash, vertigo, and weight loss have been reported following large doses.

Drug Interactions

Cytochrome P450 Effect: Substrate of CYP2B6 (minor), 2D6 (minor), 3A4 (major); **Inhibits** CYP1A2 (weak), 2D6 (weak), 3A4 (weak); **Induces** CYP2B6 (strong), 3A4 (strong)

Increased Effect/Toxicity: Cimetidine, itraconazole, ketoconazole, and some macrolide antibiotics may increase nevirapine plasma concentrations. Concurrent administration of prednisone for the initial 14 days of nevirapine therapy was associated with an increased incidence and severity of rash. Rifabutin concentrations are increased by nevirapine.

Decreased Effect: The levels/effects of nevirapine may be decreased by aminoglutethimide, carbamazepine, nafcillin, nevirapine, phenobarbital, phenytoin, and rifamycins, and other CYP3A4 inducers; avoid concurrent use. Nevirapine may decrease the levels/effects of benzodiazepines, bupropion, calcium channel blockers, clarithromycin, cyclosporine, efavirenz, erythromycin, estrogens, mirtazapine, nateglinide, nefazodone, promethazine, selegiline, sertraline, tacrolimus, venlafaxine, and other CYP2B6 or 3A4 substrates. Nevirapine may decrease serum concentrations of some protease inhibitors (AUC of indinavir, lopinavir, nelfinavir, and saquinavir may be decreased, however, no effect noted with ritonavir); specific dosage adjustments have not been recommended; no adjustment recommended for ritonavir, unless combined with lopinavir (Kaletra™). Nevirapine may decrease the effectiveness of oral contraceptives; suggest alternate method or additional form of birth control. Nevirapine also decreases the effect of ketoconazole and methadone.

Ethanol/Nutrition/Herb Interactions Herb/Nutraceutical: Nevirapine serum concentration may be decreased by St John's wort; avoid concurrent use.

Stability Store at room temperature.

Mechanism of Action As a non-nucleoside reverse transcriptase inhibitor, nevirapine has activity against HIV-1 by binding to reverse transcriptase. It consequently blocks the RNA-dependent and DNA-dependent DNA polymerase activities including HIV-1 replication. It does not require intracellular phosphorylation for antiviral activity.

Pharmacodynamics/Kinetics

Absorption: >90%

Distribution: Widely; V_d: 1.2-1.4 L/kg; CSF penetration approximates 40% to 50% of plasma

Protein binding, plasma: 60%

Metabolism: Extensively hepatic via CYP3A4 (hydroxylation to inactive compounds); may undergo enterohepatic recycling

Half-life elimination: Decreases over 2- to 4-week time with chronic dosing due to autoinduction (ie, half-life = 45 hours initially and decreases to 25-30 hours)

Time to peak, serum: 2-4 hours

Excretion: Urine (~81%, primarily as metabolites, <3% as unchanged drug); feces (~10%)

Dosage Oral:

Children 2 months to <8 years: Initial: 4 mg/kg/dose once daily for 14 days; increase dose to 7 mg/kg/dose every 12 hours if no rash or other adverse effects occur; maximum dose: 200 mg/dose every 12 hours

Children ≥8 years: Initial: 4 mg/kg/dose once daily for 14 days; increase dose to 4 mg/kg/dose every 12 hours if no rash or other adverse effects occur; maximum dose: 200 mg/dose every 12 hours

Note: Alternative pediatric dosing (AIDSinfo guidelines): 120-200 mg/m² every 12 hours; this dosing has been proposed due to the fact that dosing based on mg/kg may result in an abrupt decrease in dose at the 8th birthday, which may be inappropriate.

Adults: Initial: 200 mg once daily for 14 days; maintenance: 200 mg twice daily (in combination with an additional antiretroviral agent)

Note: If patient experiences a rash during the 14-day lead-in period, dose should not be increased until the rash has resolved. Discontinue if severe rash, or rash with constitutional symptoms, is noted. If therapy is interrupted for >7 days, restart with initial dose for 14 days. Use of prednisone to prevent nevirapine-associated rash is not recommended. Permanently discontinue if symptomatic hepatic events occur.

Prevention of maternal-fetal HIV transmission in women with no prior antiretroviral therapy (AIDS information guidelines):

Mother: 200 mg as a single dose at onset of labor. May be used in combination with zidovudine.

Infant: 2 mg/kg as a single dose at age 48-72 hours. If a maternal dose was given <1 hour prior to delivery, administer a 2 mg/kg dose as soon as possible after birth and repeat at 48-72 hours. May be used in combination with zidovudine.

Dosage adjustment in renal impairment:

Cl_{cr} ≥20 mL/minute: No adjustment required

Hemodialysis: An additional 200 mg dose is recommended following dialysis.

Dosage adjustment in hepatic impairment: Use not recommended with moderate-to-severe hepatic impairment. Permanently discontinue if symptomatic hepatic events occur.

Administration Oral: May be administered with or without food; may be administered with an antacid or didanosine; shake suspension gently prior to administration

Monitoring Parameters Liver function tests should be monitored at baseline, and intensively during the first 18 weeks of therapy (optimal frequency not established, some practitioners recommend more often than once a month, including prior to dose escalation, and at 2 weeks following dose escalation), then periodically throughout therapy; observe for CNS side effects. Assess/evaluate AST/ALT in any patients with a rash. Permanently discontinue if patient experiences severe rash, constitutional symptoms associated with rash, rash with elevated AST/ALT, or clinical hepatitis, Mild-to-moderate rash without AST/ALT elevation may continue treatment per discretion of prescriber. If mild-to-moderate urticarial rash, do not restart if treatment is interrupted.

Additional Information Potential compliance problems, frequency of administration, and adverse effects should be discussed with patients before initiating therapy to help prevent the emergence of resistance. Early virologic failure was observed with tenofovir and didanosine delayed release capsules, plus either efavirenz or nevirapine; use caution in treatment-naive patients with high baseline viral loads.

Dosage Forms
Suspension, oral: 50 mg/5 mL (240 mL)
Tablet: 200 mg

♦ **New-Fill®** *see* Poly-L-Lactic Acid *on page 1388*
♦ **Nexavar®** *see* Sorafenib *on page 1590*
♦ **Nexium®** *see* Esomeprazole *on page 618*
♦ **Nexphen PD** *see* Guaifenesin and Phenylephrine *on page 818*
♦ **NFV** *see* Nelfinavir *on page 1208*

Niacin (NYE a sin)

U.S. Brand Names Niacor®; Niaspan®; Slo-Niacin® [OTC]
Canadian Brand Names Niaspan®
Index Terms Nicotinic Acid; Vitamin B_3
Pharmacologic Category Antilipemic Agent, Miscellaneous; Vitamin, Water Soluble
Additional Appendix Information
Hyperlipidemia Management *on page 2058*
Lipid-Lowering Agents *on page 1887*
Use Adjunctive treatment of dyslipidemias (types IIa and IIb or primary hypercholesterolemia) to lower the risk of recurrent MI and/or slow progression of coronary artery disease, including combination therapy with other antidyslipidemic agents when additional triglyceride-lowering or HDL-increasing effects are desired; treatment of hypertriglyceridemia in patients at risk of pancreatitis; treatment of peripheral vascular disease and circulatory disorders; treatment of pellagra; dietary supplement
Pregnancy Risk Factor A/C (dose exceeding RDA recommendation)
Lactation Enters breast milk/consult prescriber
Medication Safety Issues
Sound-alike/look-alike issues:
Niacin may be confused with Minocin®, Niaspan®, Nispan®
Niaspan® may be confused with niacin
Nicobid® may be confused with Nitro-Bid®

International issues:
Niacor® may be confused with Nacor® which is a brand name for enalapril in Spain
Contraindications Hypersensitivity to niacin, niacinamide, or any component of the formulation; active hepatic disease; active peptic ulcer; arterial hemorrhage
Warnings/Precautions Use caution in heavy ethanol users, unstable angina or MI, diabetes (interferes with glucose control), renal disease, active gallbladder disease (can exacerbate), gout, past history of hepatic disease, or with anticoagulants. Monitor glucose and liver function tests. Rare cases of rhabdomyolysis have occurred during concomitant use with HMG-CoA reductase inhibitors. With concurrent use or if symptoms suggestive of myopathy occur, monitor creatinine phosphokinase (CPK) and potassium. Immediate and extended or sustained release products should not be interchanged. Flushing is common and can be attenuated with a gradual increase in dose, and/or by taking aspirin 30-60 minutes before dosing. Compliance is enhanced with twice daily dosing.

Note: Formulations of niacin (regular release versus extended release) are not interchangeable.

Niaspan®: 500 mg and 750 mg tablets are not interchangeable (eg, three 500 mg tablets are not equivalent to two 750 mg tablets).
Adverse Reactions Frequency not defined.
Cardiovascular: Arrhythmias, atrial fibrillation, edema, flushing, hypotension, orthostasis, palpitation, syncope (rare), tachycardia
Central nervous system: Chills, dizziness, headache, insomnia, migraine
Dermatologic: Acanthosis nigricans, dry skin, hyperpigmentation, maculopapular rash, pruritus, rash, urticaria
Endocrine & metabolic: Glucose tolerance decreased, gout, phosphorous levels decreased, uric acid level increased
Gastrointestinal: Abdominal pain, dyspepsia, eructation, flatulence, nausea, peptic ulcers, vomiting
Hematologic: Platelet counts decreased, prothrombin time increased
Hepatic: Hepatic necrosis (rare), jaundice, liver enzymes increased
Neuromuscular & skeletal: Leg cramps, myalgia, myasthenia, myopathy (with concurrent HMG-CoA reductase inhibitor), pain, rhabdomyolysis (with concurrent HMG-CoA reductase inhibitor; rare), weakness
Ocular: Cystoid macular edema, toxic amblyopia
Respiratory: Dyspnea
Miscellaneous: Diaphoresis, hypersensitivity reactions (rare)
Overdosage/Toxicology Symptoms of acute overdose include flushing, GI distress, and pruritus. Chronic excessive use has been associated with hepatitis. Antihistamines may relieve niacin-induced histamine release, otherwise, treatment is symptomatic.
(Continued)

Niacin *(Continued)*

Drug Interactions

Decreased Effect: Bile acid sequestrants may decrease the absorption of niacin; separate administration by 4-6 hours.

Ethanol/Nutrition/Herb Interactions Ethanol: Avoid heavy use; avoid use around niacin dose.

Mechanism of Action Component of two coenzymes which is necessary for tissue respiration, lipid metabolism, and glycogenolysis; inhibits the synthesis of very low density lipoproteins

Pharmacodynamics/Kinetics

Absorption: Rapid and extensive (60% to 76%)

Distribution: Mainly to hepatic, renal, and adipose tissue

Metabolism: Extensive first-pass effects; converted to nicotinamide adenine dinucleotide, nicotinuric acid, and other metabolites

Half-life elimination: 45 minutes

Time to peak, serum: Immediate release formulation: ~45 minutes; extended release formulation: 4-5 hours

Excretion: Urine 60% to 88% (unchanged drug and metabolites)

Dosage Note: Formulations of niacin (regular release versus extended release) are not interchangeable.

Children: Oral:

Pellagra: 50-100 mg/dose 3 times/day

Recommended daily allowances:

0-0.5 years: 5 mg/day

0.5-1 year: 6 mg/day

1-3 years: 9 mg/day

4-6 years: 12 mg/day

7-10 years: 13 mg/day

Children and Adolescents: Recommended daily allowances:

Male:

11-14 years: 17 mg/day

15-18 years: 20 mg/day

19-24 years: 19 mg/day

Female: 11-24 years: 15 mg/day

Adults: Oral:

Recommended daily allowances:

Male: 25-50 years: 19 mg/day; >51 years: 15 mg/day

Female: 25-50 years: 15 mg/day; >51 years: 13 mg/day

Hyperlipidemia: Usual target dose: 1.5-6 g/day in 3 divided doses with or after meals using a dosage titration schedule; extended release: 375 mg to 2 g once daily at bedtime

Regular release formulation (Niacor®): Initial: 250 mg once daily (with evening meal); increase frequency and/or dose every 4-7 days to desired response or first-level therapeutic dose (1.5-2 g/day in 2-3 divided doses); after 2 months, may increase at 2- to 4-week intervals to 3 g/day in 3 divided doses

Extended release formulation (Niaspan®): 500 mg at bedtime for 4 weeks, then 1 g at bedtime for 4 weeks; adjust dose to response and tolerance; can increase to a maximum of 2 g/day, but only at 500 mg/day at 4-week intervals

With lovastatin: Maximum lovastatin dose: 40 mg/day

Pellagra: 50-100 mg 3-4 times/day, maximum: 500 mg/day

Niacin deficiency: 10-20 mg/day, maximum: 100 mg/day

Dosage adjustment in renal impairment: Use with caution

Dosage adjustment in hepatic impairment: Not recommended for use in patients with significant or unexplained hepatic dysfunction

Dosage adjustment for toxicity: Transaminases rise to 3 times ULN: Discontinue therapy.

Dietary Considerations Should be taken with meal; low-fat meal if treating hyperlipidemia. Avoid hot drinks around the time of niacin dose.

Administration Administer with food. Administer Niaspan® at bedtime. Niaspan® tablet strengths are not interchangeable. When switching from immediate release tablet, initiate Niaspan® at lower dose and titrate. Long-acting forms should not be crushed, broken, or chewed. Do not substitute long-acting forms for immediate release ones.

Monitoring Parameters Blood glucose; liver function tests (dyslipidemia, high dose, prolonged therapy) pretreatment and every 6-12 weeks for first year then periodically; lipid profile

Test Interactions False elevations in some fluorometric determinations of urinary catecholamines; false-positive urine glucose (Benedict's reagent)

Dosage Forms

Capsule, extended release: 125 mg, 250 mg, 400 mg, 500 mg

Capsule, timed release: 250 mg

Tablet: 50 mg, 100 mg, 250 mg, 500 mg

Niacor®: 500 mg

Tablet, controlled release (Slo-Niacin®): 250 mg, 500 mg, 750 mg

Tablet, extended release (Niaspan®): 500 mg, 750 mg, 1000 mg

Note: 500 mg and 750 mg tablets are not interchangeable (eg, three 500 mg tablets are not equivalent to two 750 mg tablets)

Tablet, timed release: 250 mg, 500 mg, 750 mg, 1000 mg

Niacinamide *(nye a SIN a mide)*

U.S. Brand Names Nicomide-T™

Index Terms Nicotinamide; Nicotinic Acid Amide; Vitamin B_3

Pharmacologic Category Vitamin, Water Soluble

Use

Oral: Prophylaxis and treatment of pellagra

Topical: Improve the appearance of acne and decrease visible inflammation and irritation caused by acne medications

Pregnancy Risk Factor A/C (dose exceeding RDA recommendation)

Medication Safety Issues
Sound-alike/look-alike issues:
Niacinamide may be confused with niCARdipine

Contraindications Hypersensitivity to niacin, niacinamide, or any component of the formulation; liver disease; active peptic ulcer

Warnings/Precautions Large doses should be administered with caution to patients with gallbladder disease or diabetes; monitor blood glucose; may elevate uric acid levels; use with caution in patients predisposed to gout; some products may contain tartrazine

Adverse Reactions Frequency not defined.
Cardiovascular: Tachycardia
Dermatologic: Increased sebaceous gland activity, rash
Endocrine & metabolic: Hyperglycemia, hyperuricemia
Gastrointestinal: Bloating, flatulence, nausea
Neuromuscular & skeletal: Paresthesia in extremities
Ocular: Blurred vision
Respiratory: Wheezing

Overdosage/Toxicology Symptoms include GI distress. Treatment is supportive.

Mechanism of Action Used by the body as a source of niacin; is a component of two coenzymes which is necessary for tissue respiration, lipid metabolism, and glycogenolysis; does not have hypolipidemia or vasodilating effects. Niacinamide has anti-inflammatory properties which are believed to help decrease inflammatory acne lesions.

Pharmacodynamics/Kinetics
Absorption: Oral: Rapid; Topical: Absorbed systemically
Metabolism: Hepatic
Half-life elimination: 45 minutes
Time to peak, serum: 20-70 minutes
Excretion: Urine (as metabolites)

Dosage
Pellagra: Oral:
Children: 100-300 mg/day in divided doses
Adults: 300-500 mg/day
Acne: Topical: Adults: Apply to affected area on face twice daily

Administration Topical: Prior to using cream or gel, wash face with mild cleanser. Apply thin layer to affected area. May apply under make-up or other acne medications. Re-evaluate after 8-12 weeks.

Test Interactions False elevations of urinary catecholamines in some fluorometric determinations

Dosage Forms
Cream (Nicomide-T™): 4% (30 g) [contains benzyl alcohol]
Gel (Nicomide-T™): 4% (30 g) [contains alcohol]
Tablet: 100 mg, 250 mg, 500 mg

Niacin and Lovastatin (NYE a sin & LOE va sta tin)

U.S. Brand Names Advicor®
Canadian Brand Names Advicor®
Index Terms Lovastatin and Niacin
Pharmacologic Category Antilipemic Agent, HMG-CoA Reductase Inhibitor; Antilipemic Agent, Miscellaneous
Use Treatment of primary hypercholesterolemia (heterozygous familial and nonfamilial) and mixed dyslipidemia (Fredrickson types IIa and IIb) in patients previously treated with either agent alone (patients who require further lowering of triglycerides (TG) or increase in HDL-cholesterol (HDL-C) from addition of niacin or further lowering of LDL-cholesterol (LDL-C) from addition of lovastatin). Combination product; not intended for initial treatment.

Pregnancy Risk Factor X
Medication Safety Issues
Sound-alike/look-alike issues:
Advicor® may be confused with Advair, Altocor™

Dosage Dosage forms are a fixed combination of niacin and lovastatin.
Oral: Adults: Lowest dose: Niacin 500 mg/lovastatin 20 mg; may increase by not more than 500 mg (niacin) at 4-week intervals (maximum dose: Niacin 2000 mg/lovastatin 40 mg daily); should be taken at bedtime with a low-fat snack
Not for use as initial therapy of dyslipidemias. May be substituted for equivalent dose of Niaspan®, however, manufacturer does not recommend direct substitution with other niacin products.

Additional Information Complete prescribing information for this medication should be consulted for additional detail.

Dosage Forms
Tablet, variable release (Advicor®):
500/20: Niacin 500 mg [extended release] and lovastatin 20 mg [immediate release] [contains polysorbate 80]
750/20: Niacin 750 mg [extended release] and lovastatin 20 mg [immediate release] [contains polysorbate 80]
1000/20: Niacin 1000 mg [extended release] and lovastatin 20 mg [immediate release] [contains polysorbate 80]
1000/40: Niacin 1000 mg [extended release] and lovastatin 40 mg [immediate release] [contains polysorbate 80]

♦ **Niacor®** see Niacin on page 1219
♦ **Niaspan®** see Niacin on page 1219

♦ **Niastase®** **(Can)** *see* Factor VIIa (Recombinant) *on page 678*

NiCARdipine (nye KAR de peen)

U.S. Brand Names Cardene®; Cardene® I.V.; Cardene® SR
Index Terms Nicardipine Hydrochloride
Pharmacologic Category Calcium Channel Blocker
Additional Appendix Information
Calcium Channel Blockers *on page 1878*
Hypertension *on page 2063*
Use Chronic stable angina (immediate-release product only); management of essential hypertension (immediate and sustained release; parenteral only for short time that oral treatment is not feasible)
Unlabeled/Investigational Use Congestive heart failure
Pregnancy Risk Factor C
Pregnancy Implications Crosses the placenta; may exhibit tocolytic effect
Lactation Enters breast milk/not recommended
Medication Safety Issues
Sound-alike/look-alike issues:
NiCARdipine may be confused with niacinamide, NIFEdipine, nimodipine
Cardene® may be confused with Cardizem®, Cardura®, codeine

International issues:
Cardene® may be confused with Cardem® which is a brand name for celiprolol in Spain
Cardene® may be confused with Cardin® which is a brand name for methyldopa in Brazil and a brand name for simvastatin in Poland

Significant differences exist between oral and I.V. dosing. Use caution when converting from one route of administration to another.
Contraindications Hypersensitivity to nicardipine or any component of the formulation; advanced aortic stenosis
Warnings/Precautions Symptomatic hypotension with or without syncope can rarely occur; blood pressure must be lowered at a rate appropriate for the patient's clinical condition. Reflex tachycardia may occur with use. The most common side effect is peripheral edema; occurs within 2-3 weeks of starting therapy. Use with caution in CAD (can cause increase in angina), CHF (can worsen heart failure symptoms), hypertrophic cardiomyopathy, and pheochromocytoma (limited clinical experience). Peripheral infusion sites (for I.V. therapy) should be changed ever 12 hours. Titrate I.V. dose cautiously in patients with CHF, renal, or hepatic dysfunction. Use the I.V. form cautiously in patients with portal hypertension (can cause increase in hepatic pressure gradient). Safety and efficacy have not been demonstrated in pediatric patients. Abrupt withdrawal may cause rebound angina in patients with CAD.
Adverse Reactions
1% to 10%:
Cardiovascular: Flushing (6% to 10%), palpitation (3% to 4%), tachycardia (1% to 3%), peripheral edema (dose related 7% to 8%), increased angina (dose related 5.6%)
Central nervous system: Headache (6% to 8%), dizziness (4% to 7%), somnolence (4% to 6%)
Dermatologic: Rash (1%)
Gastrointestinal: Nausea (2% to 5%), dry mouth (1%)
Neuromuscular & skeletal: Weakness (4% to 6%), myalgia (1%), paresthesia (1%)
<1% (Limited to important or life-threatening): Abnormal ECG, dyspnea, gingival hyperplasia, nervousness, parotitis, sustained tachycardia, syncope
Overdosage/Toxicology Primary cardiac symptoms of calcium blocker overdose include hypotension and bradycardia. Hypotension is caused by peripheral vasodilation, myocardial depression, and bradycardia. Bradycardia results from sinus bradycardia, second- or third-degree atrioventricular block, or sinus arrest with junctional rhythm. Intraventricular conduction is usually not affected so the QRS duration is normal (verapamil prolongs the PR interval and bepridil prolongs the QT interval and may cause ventricular arrhythmias, including torsade de pointes).
Noncardiac symptoms include confusion, stupor, nausea, vomiting, metabolic acidosis, and hyperglycemia. Following initial gastric decontamination, if possible, repeated calcium administration may promptly reverse depressed cardiac contractility (but not sinus node depression or peripheral vasodilation). Glucagon, epinephrine, and amrinone (amrinone) may treat refractory hypotension. Glucagon and epinephrine also increase the heart rate (outside the U.S., 4-aminopyridine may be available as an antidote). Dialysis and hemoperfusion are not effective in enhancing elimination, although repeat-dose activated charcoal may serve as an adjunct with sustained-release preparations.
In a few reported cases, overdose with calcium channel blockers has been associated with hypotension and bradycardia, initially refractory to atropine, but becoming more responsive to this agent when larger doses (approaching 1 g/hour for more than 24 hours) of calcium chloride were administered.
Drug Interactions
Cytochrome P450 Effect: Substrate of CYP1A2 (minor), 2C9 (minor), 2D6 (minor), 2E1 (minor), 3A4 (major); **Inhibits** CYP2C9 (strong), 2C19 (moderate), 2D6 (moderate), 3A4 (strong)
Increased Effect/Toxicity: H$_2$ blockers (cimetidine) may increase the bioavailability of nicardipine. The levels/effects of nicardipine may be increased by azole antifungals, clarithromycin, diclofenac, doxycycline, erythromycin, imatinib, isoniazid, nefazodone, propofol, protease inhibitors, quinidine, telithromycin, verapamil and other CYP3A4 inhibitors.

Nicardipine may increase the effect of vecuronium (reduce dose 25%). Nicardipine increase the levels/effects of amiodarone, amphetamines, selected benzodiazepines, selected beta-blockers, calcium channel blockers, cisapride, citalopram, cyclosporine, dextromethorphan, diazepam, ergot derivatives, fluoxetine, glimepiride, glipizide,

HMG-CoA reductase inhibitors, lidocaine, methsuximide, mirtazapine, nateglinide, nefazodone, paroxetine, phenytoin, pioglitazone, propranolol, risperidone, ritonavir, rosiglitazone, sertraline, sildenafil (and other PDE-5 inhibitors), tacrolimus, thioridazine, tricyclic antidepressants, venlafaxine, warfarin, and other substrates of CYP2C9, 2C19, 2D6, or 3A4.

Decreased Effect: The levels/effects of nicardipine may be decreased by aminoglutethimide, carbamazepine, nafcillin, nevirapine, phenobarbital, phenytoin, rifamycins, and other CYP3A4 inducers. Nicardipine may decrease the levels/effects of CYP2D6 prodrug substrates (eg, codeine, hydrocodone, oxycodone, tramadol). Calcium may reduce the calcium channel blocker's effects, particularly hypotension.

Ethanol/Nutrition/Herb Interactions

Ethanol: Avoid ethanol (may increase CNS depression).

Food: Nicardipine average peak concentrations may be decreased if taken with food. Serum concentrations/toxicity of nicardipine may be increased by grapefruit juice; avoid concurrent use.

Herb/Nutraceutical: St John's wort may decrease levels. Avoid dong quai if using for hypertension (has estrogenic activity). Avoid ephedra, yohimbe, ginseng (may worsen hypertension). Avoid garlic (may have increased antihypertensive effect).

Stability Store at room temperature; stable for 24 hours at room temperature. Protect from light.

Mechanism of Action Inhibits calcium ion from entering the "slow channels" or select voltage-sensitive areas of vascular smooth muscle and myocardium during depolarization, producing a relaxation of coronary vascular smooth muscle and coronary vasodilation; increases myocardial oxygen delivery in patients with vasospastic angina

Pharmacodynamics/Kinetics

Onset of action: Oral: 0.5-2 hours; I.V.: 10 minutes; Hypotension: ~20 minutes

Duration: ≤8 hours

Absorption: Oral: ~100%

Protein binding: >95%

Metabolism: Hepatic; CYP3A4 substrate (major); extensive first-pass effect (saturable)

Bioavailability: 35%

Half-life elimination: 2-4 hours

Time to peak, serum: 30-120 minutes

Excretion: Urine (60% as metabolites); feces (35%)

Dosage Adults:

Oral:

Immediate release: Initial: 20 mg 3 times/day; usual: 20-40 mg 3 times/day (allow 3 days between dose increases)

Sustained release: Initial: 30 mg twice daily, titrate up to 60 mg twice daily

Note: The total daily dose of immediate-release product may not automatically be equivalent to the daily sustained-release dose; use caution in converting.

I.V. (dilute to 0.1 mg/mL):

Acute hypertension: Initial: 5 mg/hour increased by 2.5 mg/hour every 15 minutes to a maximum of 15 mg/hour; consider reduction to 3 mg/hour after response is achieved. Monitor and titrate to lowest dose necessary to maintain stable blood pressure.

Substitution for oral therapy (approximate equivalents):

20 mg every 8 hours oral, equivalent to 0.5 mg/hour I.V. infusion

30 mg every 8 hours oral, equivalent to 1.2 mg/hour I.V. infusion

40 mg every 8 hours oral, equivalent to 2.2 mg/hour I.V. infusion

Dosing adjustment in renal impairment: Titrate dose beginning with 20 mg 3 times/day (immediate release) or 30 mg twice daily (sustained release). Specific guidelines for adjustment of I.V. nicardipine are not available, but careful monitoring/adjustment is warranted.

Dosing adjustment in hepatic impairment: Starting dose: 20 mg twice daily (immediate release) with titration. Specific guidelines for adjustment of I.V. nicardipine are not available, but careful monitoring/adjustment is warranted.

Administration

Oral: The total daily dose of immediate-release product may not automatically be equivalent to the daily sustained-release dose; use caution in converting. Do not chew or crush the sustained release formulation, swallow whole. Do not open or cut capsules.

I.V.: Ampuls must be diluted before use. Administer as a slow continuous infusion.

Dosage Forms

Capsule (Cardene®): 20 mg, 30 mg

Capsule, sustained release (Cardene® SR): 30 mg, 45 mg, 60 mg

Injection, solution (Cardene® IV): 2.5 mg/mL (10 mL)

♦ **Nicardipine Hydrochloride** see NiCARDipine on page 1222

♦ **Nicoderm® (Can)** see Nicotine on page 1223

♦ **NicoDerm® CQ® [OTC]** see Nicotine on page 1223

♦ **Nicomide-T™** see Niacinamide on page 1220

♦ **Nicorette® [OTC]** see Nicotine on page 1223

♦ **Nicorette® (Can)** see Nicotine on page 1223

♦ **Nicorette® Plus (Can)** see Nicotine on page 1223

♦ **Nicotinamide** see Niacinamide on page 1220

Nicotine (nik oh TEEN)

U.S. Brand Names Commit® [OTC]; NicoDerm® CQ® [OTC]; Nicorette® [OTC]; Nicotrol® Inhaler; Nicotrol® NS; Nicotrol® Patch [OTC]

(Continued)

Nicotine (Continued)

Canadian Brand Names Habitrol®; Nicoderm®; Nicorette®; Nicorette® Plus; Nicotrol®

Index Terms Habitrol

Pharmacologic Category Smoking Cessation Aid

Additional Appendix Information
Nicotine Products *on page 1892*

Use Treatment to aid smoking cessation for the relief of nicotine withdrawal symptoms (including nicotine craving)

Unlabeled/Investigational Use Management of ulcerative colitis (transdermal)

Pregnancy Risk Factor D (nasal)

Pregnancy Implications Nicotine is teratogenic in animal studies. Nicotine exposure via cigarette smoke may cause increased ectopic pregnancy, low birth weight, increased risk of spontaneous abortion, increased perinatal mortality; increased aortic blood flow, increased heart rate, decreased uterine blood flow, and decreased breathing have been reported in the fetus. Smoking during pregnancy is associated with sudden infant death syndrome (SIDS), an increased risk of asthma, infantile colic, and childhood obesity. Women who are pregnant should be encouraged not to smoke. The use of nicotine replacement products to aid in smoking cessation has not been adequately studied in pregnant women (amount of nicotine exposure is varied). Nonpharmacologic treatments are recommended. If the benefits of nicotine replacement therapy outweigh the unknown risks, products with intermittent dosing are suggested to be tried first. If a patch is used, it is suggested to remove it overnight while sleeping to decrease fetal exposure.

Lactation Excretion in breast milk unknown/use caution

Medication Safety Issues
Sound-alike/look-alike issues:
NicoDerm® may be confused with Nitroderm
Nicorette® may be confused with Nordette®

Transdermal patch may contain conducting metal (eg, aluminum); remove patch prior to MRI.

Contraindications Hypersensitivity to nicotine or any component of the formulation; patients who are smoking during the postmyocardial infarction period; patients with life-threatening arrhythmias, or severe or worsening angina pectoris; active temporomandibular joint disease (gum); pregnancy; not for use in nonsmokers

Warnings/Precautions Use caution in patients with hyperthyroidism, pheochromocytoma, or insulin-dependent diabetes. Use with caution in oropharyngeal inflammation and in patients with history of esophagitis, peptic ulcer, coronary artery disease, vasospastic disease, angina, hypertension, hyperthyroidism, pheochromocytoma, diabetes, severe renal dysfunction, and hepatic dysfunction. The inhaler should be used with caution in patients with bronchospastic disease. Use of nasal product is not recommended with chronic nasal disorders. Transdermal patch may contain conducting metal (eg, aluminum); remove patch prior to MRI. Dental problems may be worsened by chewing the gum. Urge patients to stop smoking completely when initiating therapy. Safety and efficacy have not been established in pediatric patients.

Adverse Reactions
Nasal spray/inhaler:
>10%:
Central nervous system: Headache (18% to 26%)
Gastrointestinal: Inhaler: Mouth/throat irritation (66%), dyspepsia (18%)
Respiratory: Inhaler: Cough (32%), rhinitis (23%)
1% to 10%:
Dermatologic: Acne (3%)
Endocrine & metabolic: Dysmenorrhea (3%)
Gastrointestinal: Flatulence (4%), gum problems (4%), diarrhea, hiccup, nausea, taste disturbance, tooth disorder
Neuromuscular & skeletal: Back pain (6%), arthralgia (5%), jaw/neck pain
Respiratory: Sinusitis
Miscellaneous: Withdrawal symptoms
<1% (Limited to important or life-threatening): Allergy, amnesia, aphasia, bronchitis, bronchospasm, edema, migraine, numbness, pain, purpura, rash, sputum increased, vision abnormalities, xerostomia

Adverse events previously reported in prescription labeling for chewing gum, lozenge and/or transdermal systems. Frequency not defined; may be product or dose specific:
Central nervous system: Concentration impaired, depression, dizziness, headache, insomnia, nervousness, pain
Gastrointestinal: Aphthous stomatitis, constipation, cough, diarrhea, dyspepsia, flatulence, gingival bleeding, glossitis, hiccups, jaw pain, nausea, salivation increased, stomatitis, taste perversion, tooth disorder, ulcerative stomatitis, xerostomia
Dermatologic: Rash
Local: Application site reaction, local edema, local erythema
Neuromuscular & skeletal: Arthralgia, myalgia, paresthesia
Respiratory: Cough, sinusitis
Miscellaneous: Allergic reaction, diaphoresis

Overdosage/Toxicology Symptoms include nausea, vomiting, abdominal pain, mental confusion, diarrhea, salivation, tachycardia, respiratory and cardiovascular collapse. Treatment after decontamination is symptomatic and supportive. Remove the patch, rinse the area with water and dry; do not use soap as this may increase absorption.

Drug Interactions
Cytochrome P450 Effect: Substrate (minor) of CYP1A2, 2A6, 2B6, 2C9, 2C19, 2D6, 2E1, 3A4; **Inhibits** CYP2A6 (weak), 2E1 (weak)

Increased Effect/Toxicity: Nicotine increases the hemodynamic and AV blocking effects of adenosine; monitor. Cimetidine increases serum nicotine concentrations; therefore, may decrease amount of gum or patches needed. Monitor for treatment-emergent hypertension in patients treated with the combination of nicotine patch and bupropion.

Ethanol/Nutrition/Herb Interactions Food: Lozenge: Acidic foods/beverages decrease absorption of nicotine.

Stability Nicotrol®: Store inhaler cartridge at room temperature not to exceed 30°C (86°F). Protect cartridges from light.

Mechanism of Action Nicotine is one of two naturally-occurring alkaloids which exhibit their primary effects via autonomic ganglia stimulation. The other alkaloid is lobeline which has many actions similar to those of nicotine but is less potent. Nicotine is a potent ganglionic and central nervous system stimulant, the actions of which are mediated via nicotine-specific receptors. Biphasic actions are observed depending upon the dose administered. The main effect of nicotine in small doses is stimulation of all autonomic ganglia; with larger doses, initial stimulation is followed by blockade of transmission. Biphasic effects are also evident in the adrenal medulla; discharge of catecholamines occurs with small doses, whereas prevention of catecholamines release is seen with higher doses as a response to splanchnic nerve stimulation. Stimulation of the central nervous system (CNS) is characterized by tremors and respiratory excitation. However, convulsions may occur with higher doses, along with respiratory failure secondary to both central paralysis and peripheral blockade to respiratory muscles.

Pharmacodynamics/Kinetics
Onset of action: Intranasal: More closely approximate the time course of plasma nicotine levels observed after cigarette smoking than other dosage forms
Duration: Transdermal: 24 hours
Absorption: Transdermal: Slow
Metabolism: Hepatic, primarily to cotinine ($\frac{1}{5}$ as active)
Half-life elimination: 4 hours
Time to peak, serum: Transdermal: 8-9 hours
Excretion: Urine
Clearance: Renal: pH dependent

Dosage
Smoking deterrent: Patients should be advised to completely stop smoking upon initiation of therapy.
Oral:
Gum: Chew 1 piece of gum when urge to smoke, up to 24 pieces/day. Patients who smoke <25 cigarettes/day should start with 2-mg strength; patients smoking ≥25 cigarettes/day should start with the 4-mg strength. Use according to the following 12-week dosing schedule:
Weeks 1-6: Chew 1 piece of gum every 1-2 hours; to increase chances of quitting, chew at least 9 pieces/day during the first 6 weeks
Weeks 7-9: Chew 1 piece of gum every 2-4 hours
Weeks 10-12: Chew 1 piece of gum every 4-8 hours
Inhaler: Usually 6 to 16 cartridges per day; best effect was achieved by frequent continuous puffing (20 minutes); recommended duration of treatment is 3 months, after which patients may be weaned from the inhaler by gradual reduction of the daily dose over 6-12 weeks
Lozenge: Patients who smoke their first cigarette within 30 minutes of waking should use the 4 mg strength; otherwise the 2 mg strength is recommended. Use according to the following 12-week dosing schedule:
Weeks 1-6: One lozenge every 1-2 hours
Weeks 7-9: One lozenge every 2-4 hours
Weeks 10-12: One lozenge every 4-8 hours
Note: Use at least 9 lozenges/day during first 6 weeks to improve chances of quitting; do not use more than one lozenge at a time (maximum: 5 lozenges every 6 hours, 20 lozenges/day)

Topical:
Transdermal patch: Apply new patch every 24 hours to nonhairy, clean, dry skin on the upper body or upper outer arm; each patch should be applied to a different site. **Note:** Adjustment may be required during initial treatment (move to higher dose if experiencing withdrawal symptoms; lower dose if side effects are experienced).
NicoDerm CQ®:
Patients smoking ≥10 cigarettes/day: Begin with **step 1** (21 mg/day) for 4-6 weeks, followed by **step 2** (14 mg/day) for 2 weeks; finish with **step 3** (7 mg/day) for 2 weeks
Patients smoking <10 cigarettes/day: Begin with **step 2** (14 mg/day) for 6 weeks, followed by **step 3** (7 mg/day) for 2 weeks
Note: Initial starting dose for patients <100 pounds, history of cardiovascular disease: 14 mg/day for 4-6 weeks, followed by 7 mg/day for 2-4 weeks
Note: Patients receiving >600 mg/day of cimetidine: Decrease to the next lower patch size
Nicotrol®: One patch daily for 6 weeks
Note: Benefits of use of nicotine transdermal patches beyond 3 months have not been demonstrated.
Ulcerative colitis (unlabeled use): Transdermal: Titrated to 22-25 mg/day

Nasal: Spray: 1-2 sprays/hour; do not exceed more than 5 doses (10 sprays) per hour [maximum: 40 doses/day (80 sprays); each dose (2 sprays) contains 1 mg of nicotine

Dietary Considerations
Commit®: Each lozenge contains phenylalanine 3.4 mg and sodium 18 mg.
Nicorette®: Fruit chill flavor: The 2-mg strength contains calcium 94 mg/gum and sodium 11 mg/gum. The 4-mg strength contains calcium 94 mg/gum and sodium 13 mg/gum.

Administration
Gum: Should be chewed slowly to avoid jaw ache and to maximize benefit. Chew slowly until it tingles, then park gum between cheek and gum until tingle is gone; repeat process until most of tingle is gone (~30 minutes).
Lozenge: Should not be chewed or swallowed; allow to dissolve slowly (~20-30 minutes)
Transdermal patch: Do not cut patch; causes rapid evaporation, rendering the patch useless
(Continued)

Nicotine *(Continued)*

Monitoring Parameters Heart rate and blood pressure periodically during therapy; discontinue therapy if signs of nicotine toxicity occur (eg, severe headache, dizziness, mental confusion, disturbed hearing and vision, abdominal pain; rapid, weak and irregular pulse; salivation, nausea, vomiting, diarrhea, cold sweat, weakness); therapy should be discontinued if rash develops; discontinuation may be considered if other adverse effects of patch occur such as myalgia, arthralgia, abnormal dreams, insomnia, nervousness, dry mouth, sweating

Additional Information A cigarette has 10-25 mg nicotine.

Dosage Forms

Gum, chewing, as polacrilex: 2 mg (48s, 108s); 4 mg (48s, 108s)

Nicorette®:

2 mg (48s, 50s, 110s, 168s, 170s, 192s, 200s, 216s) [fruit chill flavor contains calcium 94 mg/gum and sodium 11 mg/gum; mint, fresh mint, fruit chill, orange, and original flavors]

4 mg (48s, 108s, 168s) [fruit chill flavor contains calcium 94 mg/gum and sodium 13 mg/gum; mint, fresh mint, fruit chill, orange, and original flavors]

Lozenge, as polacrilex:

Commit®: 2 mg (48s, 72s) [contains phenylalanine 3.4 mg/lozenge, sodium 18 mg/lozenge; mint flavor]; 4 mg (48s, 72s) [contains phenylalanine 3.4 mg/lozenge, sodium 18 mg/lozenge; mint flavor]

Oral inhalation system:

Nicotrol® Inhaler: 10 mg cartridge [delivering 4 mg nicotine] (168s) [each unit consists of 5 mouthpieces, 28 storage trays each containing 6 cartridges, and 1 storage case]

Patch, transdermal: 7 mg/24 (30s); 14 mg/24 hours (30s); 21 mg/24 hours (30s)

NicoDerm® CQ®: 7 mg/24 hours (14s); 14 mg/24 hours (14s); 21 mg/24 hours (14s) [available in tan or clear patch]

Nicotrol®: 15 mg/16 hours (7s, 14s) [step 1]; 10 mg/16 hours (14s) [step 2]; 5 mg/16 hours (14s) [step 3]

Solution, intranasal spray (Nicotrol® NS): 10 mg/mL (10 mL) [delivers 0.5 mg/spray; 200 sprays]

♦ **Nicotinic Acid** *see Niacin on page 1219*

♦ **Nicotinic Acid Amide** *see Niacinamide on page 1220*

♦ **Nicotrol® (Can)** *see Nicotine on page 1223*

♦ **Nicotrol® Inhaler** *see Nicotine on page 1223*

♦ **Nicotrol® NS** *see Nicotine on page 1223*

♦ **Nicotrol® Patch [OTC]** *see Nicotine on page 1223*

♦ **Nidagel™ (Can)** *see Metronidazole on page 1132*

♦ **Nifediac™ CC** *see NIFEdipine on page 1226*

♦ **Nifedical™ XL** *see NIFEdipine on page 1226*

NIFEdipine *(nye FED i peen)*

U.S. Brand Names Adalat® CC; Afeditab™ CR; Nifediac™ CC; Nifedical™ XL; Procardia®; Procardia XL®

Canadian Brand Names Adalat® XL®; Apo-Nifed®; Apo-Nifed PA®; Novo-Nifedin; Nu-Nifed; Procardia®

Pharmacologic Category Calcium Channel Blocker

Additional Appendix Information

Calcium Channel Blockers *on page 1878*

Use Angina and hypertension (sustained release only), pulmonary hypertension

Pregnancy Risk Factor C

Pregnancy Implications Use in pregnancy only when clearly needed and when the benefits outweigh the potential hazard to the fetus. No data on crossing the placenta. Hypotension, IUGR reported. IUGR probably related to maternal hypertension. May exhibit tocolytic effects. Available evidence suggests safe use during pregnancy.

Lactation Enters breast milk/compatible

Medication Safety Issues

Sound-alike/look-alike issues:

NIFEdipine may be confused with niCARdipine, nimodipine, nisoldipine

Procardia XL® may be confused with Cartia® XT

International issues:

Nipin® [Italy and Singapore] may be confused with Nipent® which is a brand name for pentostatin in the U.S.

Contraindications Hypersensitivity to nifedipine or any component of the formulation; immediate release preparation for treatment of urgent or emergent hypertension; acute MI

Warnings/Precautions Symptomatic hypotension with or without syncope can rarely occur; blood pressure must be lowered at a rate appropriate for the patient's clinical condition. **The use of sublingual short-acting nifedipine in hypertensive emergencies and urgencies is neither safe nor effective and SHOULD BE ABANDONED!** Serious adverse events (eg, cerebrovascular ischemia, syncope, stroke, acute myocardial infarction, and fetal distress) have been reported in relation to such use.

Severe hypotension may occur in patients taking immediate release concurrently with beta blockers when undergoing CABG with high dose fentanyl anesthesia. When considering surgery with high dose fentanyl, may consider withdrawing nifedipine (>36 hours) before surgery if possible.

Increased angina may be seen upon starting or increasing doses; may increase frequency, duration, and severity of angina during initiation of therapy; use with caution in patients with CHF or aortic stenosis (especially with concomitant beta-adrenergic blocker); severe left ventricular dysfunction, hepatic or renal impairment, hypertrophic cardiomyopathy (especially obstructive), concomitant therapy with beta-blockers or digoxin, edema. The elderly may be more susceptible to adverse effects.

Mild and transient elevations in liver function enzymes may be apparent within 8 weeks of therapy initiation. The most common side effect is peripheral edema; occurs within 2-3 weeks of starting therapy. Reflex tachycardia may occur with use.

Avoid use of extended release tablets (Procardia XL®) in patients with known stricture/narrowing of the GI tract. Therapeutic potential of sustained-release formulation (elementary osmotic pump, gastrointestinal therapeutic system [GITS]) may be decreased in patients with certain GI disorders that accelerate intestinal transit time (eg, short bowel syndrome, inflammatory bowel disease, severe diarrhea).

Adverse Reactions
>10%:
Cardiovascular: Flushing (10% to 25%), peripheral edema (dose related 7% to 10%; up to 50%)

Central nervous system: Dizziness/lightheadedness/giddiness (10% to 27%), headache (10% to 23%)

Gastrointestinal: Nausea/heartburn (10% to 11%)

Neuromuscular & skeletal: Weakness (10% to 12%)

≥1% to 10%:
Cardiovascular: Palpitations (≤2% to 7%), transient hypotension (dose related 5%), CHF (2%)

Central nervous system: Nervousness/mood changes (≤2% to 7%), shakiness (≤2%), jitteriness (≤2%), sleep disturbances (≤2%), difficulties in balance (≤2%), fever (≤2%), chills (≤2%)

Dermatologic: Dermatitis (≤2%), pruritus (≤2%), urticaria (≤2%)

Endocrine & metabolic: Sexual difficulties (≤2%)

Gastrointestinal: Diarrhea (≤2%), constipation (≤2%), cramps (≤2%), flatulence (≤2%), gingival hyperplasia (≤10%)

Neuromuscular & skeletal: Muscle cramps/tremor (≤2% to 8%), inflammation (≤2%), joint stiffness (≤2%)

Ocular: Blurred vision (≤2%)

Respiratory: Cough/wheezing (6%), nasal congestion/sore throat (≤2% to 6%), chest congestion (≤2%), dyspnea (≤2%)

Miscellaneous: Diaphoresis (≤2%)

<1% (Limited to important or life-threatening): Agranulocytosis, allergic hepatitis, angina, angioedema, aplastic anemia, arthritis with positive ANA, bezoars (sustained-release preparations), cerebral ischemia, depression, erythema multiforme, erythromelalgia, exfoliative dermatitis, extrapyramidal symptoms, fever, gingival hyperplasia, gynecomastia, leukopenia, memory dysfunction, paranoid syndrome, photosensitivity, purpura, Stevens-Johnson syndrome, syncope, thrombocytopenia, tinnitus, transient blindness

Reported with use of sublingual short-acting nifedipine: Acute MI, cerebrovascular ischemia, ECG changes, fetal distress, heart block, severe hypotension, sinus arrest, stroke, syncope

Overdosage/Toxicology
Primary cardiac symptoms of calcium blocker overdose include hypotension and bradycardia. Hypotension is caused by peripheral vasodilation, myocardial depression, and bradycardia. Bradycardia results from sinus bradycardia, second- or third-degree atrioventricular block, or sinus arrest with junctional rhythm. Intraventricular conduction is usually not affected so the QRS duration is normal.

Noncardiac symptoms include confusion, stupor, nausea, vomiting, metabolic acidosis and hyperglycemia. Following initial gastric decontamination, if possible, repeated calcium administration may promptly reverse depressed cardiac contractility (but not sinus node depression or peripheral vasodilation). Glucagon, epinephrine, and inamrinone (amrinone) may treat refractory hypotension. Glucagon and epinephrine also increase the heart rate (outside the U.S., 4-aminopyridine may be available as an antidote). Dialysis and hemoperfusion are not effective in enhancing elimination although repeat-dose activated charcoal may serve as an adjunct with sustained-release preparations.

In a few reported cases, overdose with calcium channel blockers has been associated with hypotension and bradycardia, initially refractory to atropine, but becoming more responsive to this agent when larger doses (approaching 1 g/hour for more than 24 hours) of calcium chloride were administered.

Drug Interactions
Cytochrome P450 Effect: Substrate of CYP2D6 (minor), 3A4 (major); Inhibits CYP1A2 (moderate), 2C9 (weak), 2D6 (weak), 3A4 (weak)

Increased Effect/Toxicity: The levels/effects of nifedipine may be increased by alpha-1 blockers, azole antifungals, cisapride, clarithromycin, cyclosporine, diclofenac, doxycycline, erythromycin, grapefruit juice, imatinib, isoniazid, nefazodone, nicardipine, propofol, protease inhibitors, quinidine, quinupristin/dalfopristin, telithromycin, verapamil, and other CYP3A4 inhibitors. Cimetidine may also increase nifedipine levels. Nifedipine may increase the levels/effects of aminophylline, digoxin, fluvoxamine, mexiletine, mirtazapine, ropinirole, trifluoperazine, vincristine, and other CYP1A2 substrates. Digoxin, phenytoin, and vincristine levels may also be increased by nifedipine.

Blood pressure-lowering effects may be additive with sildenafil, tadalafil, and vardenafil (use caution). Concurrent use with magnesium salts may enhance the adverse/toxic effects of magnesium and enhance the hypotensive effects of the calcium channel blocker. Calcium channel blockers may enhance the neuromuscular blocking effect from nondepolarizing neuromuscular blockers. Calcium channel blocker (nondihydropyridine) may enhance the hypotensive effects of calcium channel blocker (dihydropyridine).

Decreased Effect: Nifedipine may decrease quinidine serum levels. Calcium may reduce the hypotension from of calcium channel blockers. The levels/effects of nifedipine may be decreased by aminoglutethimide, barbiturates, carbamazepine, nafcillin, nevirapine, phenobarbital, phenytoin, rifamycins, and other CYP3A4 inducers.

(Continued)

NIFEdipine *(Continued)*

Ethanol/Nutrition/Herb Interactions
Ethanol: Avoid ethanol (may increase CNS depression and may increase the effects of nifedipine). Monitor.

Food: Nifedipine serum levels may be decreased if taken with food. Food may decrease the rate but not the extent of absorption of Procardia XL®. Increased therapeutic and vasodilator side effects, including severe hypotension and myocardial ischemia, may occur if nifedipine is taken by patients ingesting grapefruit.

Herb/Nutraceutical: St John's wort may decrease nifedipine levels. Avoid dong quai if using for hypertension (has estrogenic activity). Avoid ephedra, yohimbe, ginseng (may worsen hypertension). Avoid garlic (may have increased antihypertensive effect).

Mechanism of Action Inhibits calcium ion from entering the "slow channels" or select voltage-sensitive areas of vascular smooth muscle and myocardium during depolarization, producing a relaxation of coronary vascular smooth muscle and coronary vasodilation; increases myocardial oxygen delivery in patients with vasospastic angina

Pharmacodynamics/Kinetics
Onset of action: Immediate release: ~20 minutes

Protein binding (concentration dependent): 92% to 98%

Metabolism: Hepatic to inactive metabolites

Bioavailability: Capsule: 40% to 77%; Sustained release: 65% to 89% relative to immediate release capsules

Half-life elimination: Adults: Healthy: 2-5 hours, Cirrhosis: 7 hours; Elderly: 6.7 hours

Excretion: Urine (as metabolites)

Dosage Oral:
Children: Hypertrophic cardiomyopathy: 0.6-0.9 mg/kg/24 hours in 3-4 divided doses

Adolescents and Adults: (**Note:** When switching from immediate release to sustained release formulations, total daily dose will start the same)

Initial: 30 mg once daily as sustained release formulation, or if indicated, 10 mg 3 times/day as capsules

Usual dose: 10-30 mg 3 times/day as capsules or 30-60 mg once daily as sustained release

Maximum dose: 120-180 mg/day

Increase sustained release at 7- to 14-day intervals

Hemodialysis: Supplemental dose is not necessary.

Peritoneal dialysis effects: Supplemental dose is not necessary.

Dosing adjustment in hepatic impairment: Reduce oral dose by 50% to 60% in patients with cirrhosis.

Dietary Considerations Capsule is rapidly absorbed orally if it is administered without food, but may result in vasodilator side effects; administration with low-fat meals may decrease flushing. Avoid grapefruit juice.

Administration Extended release tablets should be swallowed whole; do not crush or chew.

Monitoring Parameters Heart rate, blood pressure, signs and symptoms of CHF, peripheral edema

Additional Information When measuring smaller doses from the liquid-filled capsules, consider the following concentrations (for Procardia®) 10 mg capsule = 10 mg/0.34 mL; 20 mg capsule = 20 mg/0.45 mL; may be used preoperatively to treat hypertensive urgency.

Considerable attention has been directed to potential increases in mortality and morbidity when short-acting nifedipine is used in treating hypertension. The rapid reduction in blood pressure may precipitate adverse cardiovascular events. At this time, there is no indication for the use of short-acting calcium channel blocker therapy. Nifedipine also has potent negative inotropic effects and can worsen heart failure.

Dosage Forms
Capsule, softgel: 10 mg, 20 mg

Procardia®: 10 mg

Tablet, extended release: 30 mg, 60 mg, 90 mg

Adalat® CC, Procardia XL®: 30 mg, 60 mg, 90 mg

Afeditab™ CR, Nifedical™ XL: 30 mg, 60 mg

Nifediac™ CC: 30 mg, 60 mg, 90 mg [90 mg tablet contains tartrazine]

♦ **Niferex® [OTC]** *see* Polysaccharide-Iron Complex *on page 1390*

♦ **Niftolid** *see* Flutamide *on page 737*

♦ **Nilandron®** *see* Nilutamide *on page 1228*

♦ **Nilstat (Can)** *see* Nystatin *on page 1250*

Nilutamide *(ni LOO ta mide)*

U.S. Brand Names Nilandron®

Canadian Brand Names Anandron®

Index Terms NSC-684588; RU-23908

Pharmacologic Category Antiandrogen; Antineoplastic Agent, Antiandrogen

Use Treatment of metastatic prostate cancer

Pregnancy Risk Factor C

Pregnancy Implications Not indicated for use in women

Lactation Not indicated for use in women

Contraindications Hypersensitivity to nilutamide or any component of the formulation; severe hepatic impairment; severe respiratory insufficiency

Warnings/Precautions Hazardous agent - use appropriate precautions for handling and disposal. **[U.S. Boxed Warning]: Interstitial pneumonitis has been reported in 2% of patients exposed to nilutamide.** Patients typically experienced progressive exertional dyspnea, and possibly cough, chest pain and fever. X-rays showed interstitial or alveolo-interstitial changes. The suggestive signs of pneumonitis most often occurred within the first 3 months of nilutamide treatment.

Hepatitis or marked increases in liver enzymes leading to drug discontinuation occurred in 1% of nilutamide patients. Rare cases of elevated hepatic enzymes followed by death have been reported.

13% to 57% of patients receiving nilutamide reported a delay in adaptation to the dark, ranging from seconds to a few minutes. This effect sometimes does not abate as drug treatment is continued. Caution patients who experience this effect about driving at night or through tunnels. This effect can be alleviated by wearing tinted glasses.

Adverse Reactions
>10%:
Central nervous system: Headache, insomnia
Endocrine & metabolic: Hot flashes (30% to 67%), gynecomastia (10%)
Gastrointestinal: Nausea (mild - 10% to 32%), abdominal pain (10%), constipation, anorexia
Genitourinary: Testicular atrophy (16%), libido decreased
Hepatic: Transaminases increased (8% to 13%; transient)
Ocular: Impaired dark adaptation (13% to 57%), usually reversible with dose reduction, may require discontinuation of the drug in 1% to 2% of patients
Respiratory: Dyspnea (11%)
1% to 10%:
Cardiovascular: Chest pain, edema, heart failure, hypertension, syncope
Central nervous system: Dizziness, drowsiness, malaise, hypoesthesia, depression
Dermatologic: Pruritus, alopecia, dry skin, rash
Endocrine & metabolic: Disulfiram-like reaction (hot flashes, rash) (5%); flu-like syndrome, fever
Gastrointestinal: Vomiting, diarrhea, dyspepsia, GI hemorrhage, melena, weight loss, xerostomia
Genitourinary: Hematuria, nocturia
Hematologic: Anemia
Hepatic: Hepatitis (1%)
Neuromuscular & skeletal: Arthritis, paresthesia
Ocular: Chromatopsia (9%), abnormal vision (6% to 7%), cataracts, photophobia
Respiratory: Interstitial pneumonitis (2% - typically exertional dyspnea, cough, chest pain, and fever; most often occurring within the first 3 months of treatment); rhinitis
Miscellaneous: Diaphoresis
<1% (Limited to important or life-threatening): Aplastic anemia

Overdosage/Toxicology Management is supportive and there is no benefit from dialysis. Induce vomiting if the patient is alert. Administer general supportive care (including frequent monitoring of vital signs and close observation).

Drug Interactions
Cytochrome P450 Effect: Substrate of CYP2C19 (major); **Inhibits** CYP2C19 (weak)
Increased Effect/Toxicity: CYP2C19 inhibitors may increase the levels/effects of nilutamide; example inhibitors include delavirdine, fluconazole, fluvoxamine, gemfibrozil, isoniazid, omeprazole, and ticlopidine.
Decreased Effect: CYP2C19 inducers may decrease the levels/effects of nilutamide; example inducers include aminoglutethimide, carbamazepine, phenytoin, and rifampin.

Ethanol/Nutrition/Herb Interactions
Ethanol: Avoid ethanol. Up to 5% of patients may experience a systemic reaction (flushing, hypotension, malaise) when combined with nilutamide.
Herb/Nutraceutical: St John's wort may decrease nilutamide levels.

Stability Store at room temperature of 15°C to 30°C (59°F to 86°F). Protect from light.
Mechanism of Action Nonsteroidal antiandrogen that inhibits androgen uptake or inhibits binding of androgen in target tissues. It specifically blocks the action of androgens by interacting with cytosolic androgen receptor F sites in target tissue

Pharmacodynamics/Kinetics
Absorption: Rapid and complete
Protein binding: 72% to 85%
Metabolism: Hepatic, forms active metabolites
Half-life elimination: Terminal: 23-87 hours; Metabolites: 35-137 hours
Excretion: Urine (up to 78% at 120 hours; <1% as unchanged drug); feces (1% to 7%)

Dosage Refer to individual protocols.
Adults: Oral: 300 mg daily for 30 days starting the same day or day after surgical castration, then 150 mg/day

Dietary Considerations May be taken without regard to food.
Monitoring Parameters Obtain a chest x-ray if a patient reports dyspnea; if there are findings suggestive of interstitial pneumonitis, discontinue treatment with nilutamide. Measure serum hepatic enzyme levels at baseline and at regular intervals (3 months); if transaminases increase over 2-3 times the upper limit of normal, discontinue treatment. Perform appropriate laboratory testing at the first symptom/sign of liver injury (eg, jaundice, dark urine, fatigue, abdominal pain or unexplained GI symptoms).

Dosage Forms Tablet: 150 mg

◆ **Nimbex**® see Cisatracurium on page 377

Nimodipine (nye MOE di peen)

U.S. Brand Names Nimotop®
Canadian Brand Names Nimotop®
Pharmacologic Category Calcium Channel Blocker
Additional Appendix Information
Calcium Channel Blockers on page 1878
Use Spasm following subarachnoid hemorrhage from ruptured intracranial aneurysms regardless of the patients neurological condition postictus (Hunt and Hess grades I-V)
Pregnancy Risk Factor C
(Continued)

Nimodipine *(Continued)*

Pregnancy Implications Use in pregnancy only when clearly needed and when the benefits outweigh the potential hazard to the fetus. Teratogenic and embryotoxic effects have been demonstrated in small animals. No well-controlled studies have been conducted in pregnant women.

Lactation Enters breast milk/not recommended

Medication Safety Issues
Sound-alike/look-alike issues:
Nimodipine may be confused with niCARdipine, NIFEdipine

Administration issues: **For oral administration only.** For patients unable to swallow a capsule, the drug should be dispensed in an oral syringe labeled **"for oral use only."** Nimodipine has inadvertently been administered I.V. when withdrawn from capsules into a syringe for subsequent nasogastric administration. Severe cardiovascular adverse events, including fatalities, have resulted. Employ precautions against such an event.

Contraindications Hypersensitivity to nimodipine or any component of the formulation

Warnings/Precautions Increased angina and/or MI has occurred with initiation or dosage titration of calcium channel blockers. The most common side effect is peripheral edema; occurs within 2-3 weeks of starting therapy. Reflex tachycardia may occur with use. Symptomatic hypotension with or without syncope can rarely occur; blood pressure must be lowered at a rate appropriate for the patient's clinical condition. Use caution in hepatic impairment. Intestinal pseudo-obstruction and ileus have been reported during the use of nimodipine. Use caution in patients with decreased GI motility of a history of bowel obstruction. Use caution when treating patients with hypertrophic cardiomyopathy. Safety and efficacy have not been established in children.

[U.S. Boxed Warning]: Nimodipine has inadvertently been administered I.V. when withdrawn from capsules into a syringe for subsequent nasogastric administration. Severe cardiovascular adverse events, including fatalities, have resulted; precautions should be employed against such an event.

Adverse Reactions
1% to 10%:
Cardiovascular: Reductions in systemic blood pressure (1% to 8%)
Central nervous system: Headache (1% to 4%)
Dermatologic: Rash (1% to 2%)
Gastrointestinal: Diarrhea (2% to 4%), abdominal discomfort (2%)
<1% (Limited to important or life-threatening): Anemia, CHF, deep vein thrombosis, depression, disseminated intravascular coagulation, dyspnea, ECG abnormalities, GI hemorrhage, hemorrhage, hepatitis, jaundice, neurological deterioration, rebound vasospasm, thrombocytopenia, vomiting

Overdosage/Toxicology Primary cardiac symptoms of calcium blocker overdose include hypotension and bradycardia. Hypotension is caused by peripheral vasodilation, myocardial depression, and bradycardia. Bradycardia results from sinus bradycardia, second- or third-degree atrioventricular block, or sinus arrest with junctional rhythm. Intraventricular conduction is usually not affected so the QRS duration is normal.

Noncardiac symptoms include confusion, stupor, nausea, vomiting, metabolic acidosis and hyperglycemia. Following initial gastric decontamination, if possible, repeated calcium administration may promptly reverse the depressed cardiac contractility (but not sinus node depression or peripheral vasodilation). Glucagon, epinephrine, and inamrinone (amrinone) may treat refractory hypotension. Glucagon and epinephrine also increase the heart rate (outside the U.S., 4-aminopyridine may be available as an antidote). Dialysis and hemoperfusion are not effective in enhancing elimination although repeat-dose activated charcoal may serve as an adjunct with sustained-release preparations.

In a few reported cases, overdose with calcium channel blockers has been associated with hypotension and bradycardia, initially refractory to atropine, but becoming more responsive to this agent when larger doses (approaching 1 g/hour for more than 24 hours) of calcium chloride were administered.

Drug Interactions
Cytochrome P450 Effect: Substrate of CYP3A4 (major)
Increased Effect/Toxicity: Calcium channel blockers and nimodipine may result in enhanced cardiovascular effects of other calcium channel blockers. Cimetidine, omeprazole, and valproic acid may increase serum nimodipine levels. The effects of antihypertensive agents may be increased by nimodipine. Blood pressure-lowering effects may be additive with sildenafil, tadalafil, and vardenafil (use caution). CYP3A4 inhibitors may increase the levels/effects of nimodipine; example inhibitors include azole antifungals, clarithromycin, diclofenac, doxycycline, erythromycin, imatinib, isoniazid, nefazodone, nicardipine, propofol, protease inhibitors, quinidine, telithromycin, and verapamil.
Decreased Effect: CYP3A4 inducers may decrease the levels/effects of nimodipine; example inducers include aminoglutethimide, carbamazepine, nafcillin, nevirapine, phenobarbital, phenytoin, and rifamycins.

Ethanol/Nutrition/Herb Interactions
Food: Nimodipine has shown a 1.5-fold increase in bioavailability when taken with grapefruit juice; avoid concurrent use.
Herb/Nutraceutical: St John's wort may decrease levels. Avoid dong quai if using for hypertension (has estrogenic activity). Avoid ephedra, yohimbe, ginseng (may worsen hypertension). Avoid garlic (may have increased antihypertensive effect).

Mechanism of Action Nimodipine shares the pharmacology of other calcium channel blockers; animal studies indicate that nimodipine has a greater effect on cerebral arterials than other arterials; this increased specificity may be due to the drug's increased lipophilicity and cerebral distribution as compared to nifedipine; inhibits calcium ion from entering the "slow channels" or select voltage sensitive areas of vascular smooth muscle and myocardium during depolarization

Pharmacodynamics/Kinetics
Protein binding: >95%

Metabolism: Extensively hepatic
Bioavailability: 13%
Half-life elimination: 1-2 hours; prolonged with renal impairment
Time to peak, serum: ~1 hour
Excretion: Urine (50%) and feces (32%) within 4 days

Dosage Note: Capsules and contents are for oral administration **ONLY.**
Adults: Oral: 60 mg every 4 hours for 21 days, start therapy within 96 hours after subarachnoid hemorrhage.

Dialysis: Not removed by hemo- or peritoneal dialysis; supplemental dose is not necessary.
Dosing adjustment in hepatic impairment: Reduce dosage to 30 mg every 4 hours in patients with liver failure.

Administration For oral administration **ONLY.** If the capsules cannot be swallowed, the liquid may be removed by making a hole in each end of the capsule with an 18-gauge needle and extracting the contents into a syringe. If administered via NG tube, follow with a flush of 30 mL NS.

Dosage Forms Capsule, liquid filled: 30 mg

♦ **Nimotop®** see Nimodipine on page 1229
♦ **Nipent®** see Pentostatin on page 1342
♦ **Niravam™** see Alprazolam on page 75

Nisoldipine (nye SOL di peen)

U.S. Brand Names Sular®
Pharmacologic Category Calcium Channel Blocker
Additional Appendix Information
Calcium Channel Blockers on page 1878
Use Management of hypertension, alone or in combination with other antihypertensive agents
Pregnancy Risk Factor C
Lactation Excretion in breast milk unknown
Medication Safety Issues
Sound-alike/look-alike issues:
Nisoldipine may be confused with NIFEdipine
Contraindications Hypersensitivity to nisoldipine, any component of the formulation, or other dihydropyridine calcium channel blockers
Warnings/Precautions Increased angina and/or myocardial infarction in patients with coronary artery disease. Use with caution in patients with CHF, hypertrophic cardiomyopathy, and hepatic impairment. The most common side effect is peripheral edema; occurs within 2-3 weeks of starting therapy. Reflex tachycardia may occur with use. Symptomatic hypotension with or without syncope can rarely occur; blood pressure must be lowered at a rate appropriate for the patient's clinical condition. Safety and efficacy have not been established in children.
Adverse Reactions
>10%:
Cardiovascular: Peripheral edema (dose related 7% to 29%)
Central nervous system: Headache (22%)
1% to 10%:
Cardiovascular: Chest pain (2%), palpitation (3%), vasodilation (4%)
Central nervous system: Dizziness (3% to 10%)
Dermatologic: Rash (2%)
Gastrointestinal: Nausea (2%)
Respiratory: Pharyngitis (5%), sinusitis (3%), dyspnea (3%), cough (5%)
<1% (Limited to important or life-threatening): Alopecia, amblyopia, angina, anxiety, ataxia, atrial fibrillation, cerebral ischemia, cholestatic jaundice, confusion, CHF, depression, dyspnea, exfoliative dermatitis, first-degree AV block, GI hemorrhage, gingival hyperplasia, gout, impotence, leukopenia, migraine, myasthenia, MI, paresthesia, pruritus, pulmonary edema, rash, somnolence, stroke, supraventricular tachycardia, syncope, temporary unilateral loss of vision, tinnitus, T-wave abnormalities on ECG (flattening, inversion, nonspecific changes), urticaria, vaginal hemorrhage, ventricular extrasystoles, vertigo
Overdosage/Toxicology Primary cardiac symptoms of calcium blocker overdose include hypotension and bradycardia. Hypotension is caused by peripheral vasodilation, myocardial depression, and bradycardia. Bradycardia results from sinus bradycardia, second- or third-degree atrioventricular block, or sinus arrest with junctional rhythm. Intraventricular conduction is usually not affected so the QRS duration is normal.
Noncardiac symptoms include confusion, stupor, nausea, vomiting, metabolic acidosis and hyperglycemia. Following initial gastric decontamination, if possible, repeated calcium administration may promptly reverse the depressed cardiac contractility (but not sinus node depression or peripheral vasodilation). Glucagon, epinephrine, and inamrinone (amrinone) may treat refractory hypotension. Glucagon and epinephrine also increase the heart rate (outside the U.S., 4-aminopyridine may be available as an antidote). Dialysis and hemoperfusion are not effective in enhancing elimination although repeat-dose activated charcoal may serve as an adjunct with sustained release preparations.
In a few reported cases, overdose with calcium channel blockers has been associated with hypotension and bradycardia, initially refractory to atropine, but becoming more responsive to this agent when larger doses (approaching 1 g/hour for more than 24 hours) of calcium chloride were administered.
Drug Interactions
Cytochrome P450 Effect: **Substrate** of CYP3A4 (major); **Inhibits** CYP1A2 (weak), 3A4 (weak)
Increased Effect/Toxicity: CYP3A4 inhibitors may increase the levels/effects of nisoldipine; example inhibitors include azole antifungals, clarithromycin, diclofenac, doxycycline, erythromycin, imatinib, isoniazid, nefazodone, nicardipine, propofol, protease inhibitors, quinidine, telithromycin, and verapamil. Calcium may reduce the calcium channel blocker's
(Continued)

Nisoldipine *(Continued)*

effects, particularly hypotension. Blood pressure-lowering effects may be additive with sildenafil, tadalafil, and vardenafil (use caution). Digoxin and nisoldipine may increase digoxin effect.

Decreased Effect: CYP3A4 inducers may decrease the levels/effects of nisoldipine; example inducers include aminoglutethimide, carbamazepine, nafcillin, nevirapine, phenobarbital, phenytoin, and rifamycins. Calcium may decrease the hypotension from calcium channel blockers.

Ethanol/Nutrition/Herb Interactions

Food: Nisoldipine bioavailability may be increased if taken with high-lipid foods or with grapefruit juice. Avoid grapefruit products before and after dosing.

Herb/Nutraceutical: St John's wort may decrease nisoldipine levels. Avoid dong quai if using for hypertension (has estrogenic activity). Avoid ephedra, yohimbe, ginseng (may worsen hypertension). Avoid garlic (may have increased antihypertensive effect).

Mechanism of Action As a dihydropyridine calcium channel blocker, structurally similar to nifedipine, nisoldipine impedes the movement of calcium ions into vascular smooth muscle and cardiac muscle. Dihydropyridines are potent vasodilators and are not as likely to suppress cardiac contractility and slow cardiac conduction as other calcium antagonists such as verapamil and diltiazem; nisoldipine is 5-10 times as potent a vasodilator as nifedipine.

Pharmacodynamics/Kinetics

Duration: >24 hours

Absorption: Well absorbed

Protein binding: >99%

Metabolism: Extensively hepatic; 1 active metabolite (10% of parent); first-pass effect

Bioavailability: 5%

Half-life elimination: 7-12 hours

Time to peak: 6-12 hours

Excretion: Urine (as metabolites)

Dosage Adults: Oral: Initial: 20 mg once daily, then increase by 10 mg/week (or longer intervals) to attain adequate control of blood pressure; usual dose range (JNC 7): 10-40 mg once daily; doses >60 mg once daily are not recommended. A starting dose not exceeding 10 mg/day is recommended for the elderly and those with hepatic impairment.

Administration Administer at the same time each day to ensure minimal fluctuation of serum levels. Avoid high-fat diet.

Dosage Forms Tablet, extended release: 10 mg, 20 mg, 30 mg, 40 mg

♦ **Nitalapram** *see* Citalopram *on page 381*

Nitazoxanide *(nye ta ZOX a nide)*

U.S. Brand Names Alinia®

Index Terms NTZ

Pharmacologic Category Antiprotozoal

Use Treatment of diarrhea caused by *Cryptosporidium parvum* or *Giardia lamblia*

Pregnancy Risk Factor B

Pregnancy Implications Teratogenic effects were not observed in animal studies. There are no adequate and well-controlled studies in pregnant women.

Lactation Excretion in breast milk unknown/use caution

Contraindications Hypersensitivity to nitazoxanide or any component of the formulation

Warnings/Precautions Use caution with renal or hepatic impairment. Safety and efficacy have not been established with HIV infection, immunodeficiency, or in children <1 year of age.

Adverse Reactions Rates of adverse effects were similar to those reported with placebo.

1% to 10%:

Central nervous system: Headache (1% to 3%)

Gastrointestinal: Abdominal pain (7% to 8%), diarrhea (2% to 4%), nausea (3%), vomiting (1%)

<1% (Limited to important or life-threatening): Allergic reaction, ALT increased, anemia, anorexia, appetite increased, creatinine increased, diaphoresis, dizziness, eye discoloration (pale yellow), fever, flatulence, hypertension, infection, malaise, nausea, pruritus, rhinitis, salivary glands enlarged, tachycardia, urine discoloration

Overdosage/Toxicology Treatment should be symptomatic and supportive.

Ethanol/Nutrition/Herb Interactions Food: Food increases AUC.

Stability

Suspension: Prior to and following reconstitution, store at room temperature of 15°C to 30°C (59°F to 86°F). For preparation at time of dispensing, add 48 mL incrementally to 60 mL bottle; shake vigorously. Resulting suspension is 20 mg/mL (100 mg per 5 mL). Following reconstitution, discard unused portion of suspension after 7 days.

Tablet: Store at room temperature.

Mechanism of Action Nitazoxanide is rapidly metabolized to the active metabolite tizoxanide *in vivo*. Activity may be due to interference with the pyruvate:ferredoxin oxidoreductase (PFOR) enzyme-dependent electron transfer reaction which is essential to anaerobic metabolism. *In vitro*, nitazoxanide and tizoxanide inhibit the growth of sporozoites and oocysts of *Cryptosporidium parvum* and trophozoites of *Giardia lamblia*.

Pharmacodynamics/Kinetics

Protein binding: Tizoxanide: >99%

Bioavailability: Relative bioavailability of suspension compared to tablet: 70%

Metabolism: Hepatic, to an active metabolite, tizoxanide. Tizoxanide undergoes conjugation to form tizoxanide glucuronide. Nitazoxanide is not detectable in the serum following oral administration.

Time to peak, plasma: Tizoxanide and tizoxanide glucuronide: 1-4 hours

Excretion: Tizoxanide: Urine, bile, and feces; Tizoxanide glucuronide: Urine and bile

Dosage Diarrhea caused by *Cryptosporidium parvum* or *Giardia lamblia*:
Children 1-3 years: 100 mg every 12 hours for 3 days
Children 4-11 years: 200 mg every 12 hours for 3 days
Children ≥12 years and Adults: 500 mg every 12 hours for 3 days
Dosage adjustment in renal/hepatic impairment: Specific recommendations are not available; use with caution
Dietary Considerations Should be taken with food. Suspension contains sucrose 1.48 g/5 mL.
Administration Administer with food. Shake suspension well prior to administration.
Dosage Forms
Powder for oral suspension: 100 mg/5 mL (60 mL) [contains sucrose 1.48 g/5 mL, sodium benzoate; strawberry flavor]
Tablet: 500 mg
Alinia® 3-Day Therapy Packs™ [unit-dose pack]: 500 mg (6s)

Nitisinone (ni TIS i known)

U.S. Brand Names Orfadin®
Pharmacologic Category 4-Hydroxyphenylpyruvate Dioxygenase Inhibitor
Use Treatment of hereditary tyrosinemia type 1 (HT-1); to be used with dietary restriction of tyrosine and phenylalanine
Restrictions Distributed by Rare Disease Therapeutics, Inc (contact 615-399-0700)
Pregnancy Risk Factor C
Dosage Oral: **Note:** Must be used in conjunction with a low protein diet restricted in tyrosine and phenylalanine.
Infants: See dosing for Children and Adults; infants may require maximal dose once liver function has improved
Children and Adults: Initial: 1 mg/kg/day in divided doses, given in the morning and evening, 1 hour before meals; doses do not need to be divided evenly
Dose adjustment: If biochemical parameters are not normalized within in 1-month period, dose may be increased to 1.5 mg/kg/day (maximum dose: 2 mg/kg/day).
Additional Information Complete prescribing information for this medication should be consulted for additional detail.
Dosage Forms Capsule: 2 mg, 5 mg, 10 mg

♦ **Nitrek®** *see* Nitroglycerin *on page 1234*
♦ **Nitro-Bid®** *see* Nitroglycerin *on page 1234*
♦ **Nitro-Dur®** *see* Nitroglycerin *on page 1234*

Nitrofurantoin (nye troe fyoor AN toyn)

U.S. Brand Names Furadantin®; Macrobid®; Macrodantin®
Canadian Brand Names Apo-Nitrofurantoin®; Macrobid®; Macrodantin®; Novo-Furantoin
Pharmacologic Category Antibiotic, Miscellaneous
Additional Appendix Information
Antimicrobial Drugs of Choice *on page 1981*
Use Prevention and treatment of urinary tract infections caused by susceptible strains of *E. coli*, *S. aureus*, *Enterococcus*, *Klebsiella*, and *Enterobacter*
Pregnancy Risk Factor B (contraindicated at term)
Pregnancy Implications Teratogenic effects have not been observed in animal studies, however, may cause hemolytic anemia in infants. Use of nitrofurantoin is contraindicated at term (38-42 weeks gestation), during labor and delivery, or when the onset of labor is imminent.
Lactation Enters breast milk/not recommended (infants <1 month); AAP rates "compatible"
Medication Safety Issues
International issues:
Macrobid® may be confused with Mikrozid® which is a brand name for ethanol/propanol combination in Great Britain
Contraindications Hypersensitivity to nitrofurantoin or any component of the formulation; renal impairment (anuria, oliguria, significantly elevated serum creatinine, or $Cl_{cr} <$ 60 mL/minute); infants <1 month (due to the possibility of hemolytic anemia); pregnancy at term (38-42 weeks gestation), during labor and delivery, or when the onset of labor is imminent
Warnings/Precautions Use with caution in patients with G6PD deficiency or in patients with anemia. Therapeutic concentrations of nitrofurantoin are not attained in urine of patients with $Cl_{cr} <$ 60 mL/minute. Use with caution if prolonged therapy is anticipated due to possible pulmonary toxicity. Acute, subacute, or chronic (usually after 6 months of therapy) pulmonary reactions have been observed in patients treated with nitrofurantoin; if these occur, discontinue therapy immediately; monitor closely for malaise, dyspnea, cough, fever, radiologic evidence of diffuse interstitial pneumonitis or fibrosis. Rare, but severe hepatic reactions have been associated with nitroturantoin (onset may be insidious); discontinue immediately if hepatitis occurs. Has been associated with peripheral neuropathy (rare); risk may be increased by renal impairment, diabetes, vitamin B deficiency, or electrolyte imbalance; use caution. Safety and efficacy have not been established in children <1 month of age.
Adverse Reactions Frequency not defined.
Cardiovascular: Chest pain, cyanosis, ECG changes
Central nervous system: Bulging fontanels (infants), chills, confusion, depression, dizziness, drowsiness, fever, headache, malaise, pseudotumor cerebri, psychotic reaction, vertigo
Dermatologic: Alopecia, angioedema, erythema multiforme, exfoliative dermatitis, pruritus, rash (eczematous, erythematous, maculopapular), Stevens-Johnson syndrome, urticaria
Gastrointestinal: Abdominal pain, *C. difficile* colitis, constipation, diarrhea, dyspepsia, flatulence, nausea, pancreatitis, sialadenitis, vomiting
Hematologic: Agranulocytosis, eosinophilia, granulocytopenia, hemolytic anemia, leukopenia, megaloblastic anemia, thrombocytopenia
(Continued)

Nitrofurantoin *(Continued)*

Hepatic: Cholestasis, hepatitis, hepatic necrosis, transaminases increased, jaundice (cholestatic)

Neuromuscular & skeletal: Arthralgia, myalgia, numbness, paresthesia, peripheral neuropathy, weakness

Ocular: Amblyopia, nystagmus, optic neuritis

Respiratory: Cough, dyspnea, pneumonitis, pulmonary fibrosis (with long-term use), pulmonary infiltration

Miscellaneous: Anaphylaxis, hypersensitivity (including acute pulmonary hypersensitivity), lupus-like syndrome

Overdosage/Toxicology Symptoms include vomiting. Treatment is supportive. Nitrofurantoin is dialyzable.

Drug Interactions

Increased Effect/Toxicity: Probenecid and sulfinpyrazone decreases renal excretion of nitrofurantoin.

Decreased Effect: Antacids containing magnesium trisilicate may decrease absorption of nitrofurantoin.

Ethanol/Nutrition/Herb Interactions

Ethanol: Avoid ethanol (may increase CNS depression).

Food: Nitrofurantoin serum concentrations may be increased if taken with food.

Stability Store at room temperature 15°C to 30°C (59°F to 86°F).

Mechanism of Action Inhibits several bacterial enzyme systems including acetyl coenzyme A interfering with metabolism and possibly cell wall synthesis

Pharmacodynamics/Kinetics

Absorption: Well absorbed; macrocrystalline form absorbed more slowly due to slower dissolution (causes less GI distress)

Distribution: V_d: 0.8 L/kg; crosses placenta; enters breast milk

Protein binding: 60% to 90%

Metabolism: Body tissues (except plasma) metabolize 60% of drug to inactive metabolites

Bioavailability: Increased with food

Half-life elimination: 20-60 minutes; prolonged with renal impairment

Excretion:

Suspension: Urine (40%) and feces (small amounts) as metabolites and unchanged drug

Macrocrystals: Urine (20% to 25% as unchanged drug)

Dosage Oral:

Children >1 month:

UTI treatment (Furadantin®, Macrodantin®): 5-7 mg/kg/day in divided doses every 6 hours; maximum: 400 mg/day. Administer for 7 days or at least 3 days after obtaining sterile urine

UTI prophylaxis (Furadantin®, Macrodantin®): 1-2 mg/kg/day in divided doses every 12-24 hours; maximum: 100 mg/day

Children >12 years: UTI treatment (Macrobid®): 100 mg twice daily for 7 days

Adults:

UTI treatment:

Furadantin®, Macrodantin®: 50-100 mg/dose every 6 hours; administer for 7 days or at least 3 days after obtaining sterile urine

Macrobid®: 100 mg twice daily for 7 days

UTI prophylaxis (Furadantin®, Macrodantin®): 50-100 mg/dose at bedtime

Dosing adjustment in renal impairment: Cl_{cr} <60 mL/minute: Contraindicated

Contraindicated in hemo- and peritoneal dialysis and continuous arteriovenous or venovenous hemofiltration

Administration Administer with meals to improve absorption and decrease adverse effects; suspension may be mixed with water, milk, fruit juice, or infant formula. Shake suspension well before use.

Monitoring Parameters Signs of pulmonary reaction, signs of numbness or tingling of the extremities, periodic liver function tests

Test Interactions False-positive urine glucose (Benedict's and Fehling's methods); no false positives with enzymatic tests

Dosage Forms

Capsule [macrocrystal]: 50 mg, 100 mg

Macrodantin®: 25 mg, 50 mg, 100 mg

Capsule [macrocrystal/monohydrate]: 100 mg [nitrofurantoin macrocrystal 25% and nitrofurantoin monohydrate 75%]

Macrobid®: 100 mg [nitrofurantoin macrocrystal 25% and nitrofurantoin monohydrate 75%]

Suspension, oral:

Furadantin®: 25 mg/5 mL (470 mL)

♦ **Nitrogen Mustard** *see* Mechlorethamine *on page 1061*

Nitroglycerin *(nye troe GLI ser in)*

U.S. Brand Names Minitran™; Nitrek®; Nitro-Bid®; Nitro-Dur®; Nitrolingual®; NitroMist™; Nitro-Quick®; Nitrostat®; NitroTime®

Canadian Brand Names Gen-Nitro; Minitran™; Nitro-Dur®; Nitroglycerin Injection, USP; Nitrol®; Nitrostat™; Rho®-Nitro; Transderm-Nitro®; Trinipatch® 0.2; Trinipatch® 0.4; Trinipatch® 0.6

Index Terms Glyceryl Trinitrate; Nitroglycerol; NTG

Pharmacologic Category Vasodilator

Additional Appendix Information

Hemodynamic Support, Intravenous *on page 1885*

Hypertension *on page 2063*

Nitrates *on page 1893*

Use Treatment of angina pectoris; I.V. for congestive heart failure (especially when associated with acute myocardial infarction); pulmonary hypertension; hypertensive emergencies occurring perioperatively (especially during cardiovascular surgery)

Unlabeled/Investigational Use Esophageal spastic disorders (sublingual)

Pregnancy Risk Factor C

Lactation Excretion in breast milk unknown/use caution

Medication Safety Issues

Sound-alike/look-alike issues:

Nitroglycerin may be confused with nitroprusside

Nitro-Bid® may be confused with Nicobid®

Nitroderm® may be confused with NicoDerm®

Nitrol® may be confused with Nizoral®

Nitrostat® may be confused with Hyperstat®, Nilstat®, nystatin

Nitroglycerin transdermal patches should be removed prior to defibrillation or MRI study.

International issues:

Nitrocor® [Chile and Italy] may be confused with Natrecor® which is a brand name for nesiritide in the U.S.

Nitrocor® [Chile and Italy] may be confused with Nutracort® which is a brand name for hydrocortisone in the U.S.

Nitro-Dur® may be confused with Nitrocor® [Chile and Italy]

Contraindications Hypersensitivity to organic nitrates; hypersensitivity to isosorbide, nitroglycerin, or any component of the formulation; concurrent use with phosphodiesterase-5 (PDE-5) inhibitors (sildenafil, tadalafil, or vardenafil); angle-closure glaucoma (intraocular pressure may be increased); head trauma or cerebral hemorrhage (increase intracranial pressure); severe anemia; allergy to adhesive (transdermal product)

Additional contraindications for I.V. product: Hypotension; uncorrected hypovolemia; inadequate cerebral circulation; constrictive pericarditis; pericardial tamponade

Warnings/Precautions Do not use extended release preparations in patients with GI hypermotility or malabsorptive syndrome; use with caution in patients with hepatic impairment, CHF, or acute myocardial infarction; available preparations of I.V. nitroglycerin differ in concentration or volume; pay attention to dilution and dosage; I.V. preparations contain alcohol and/or propylene glycol; avoid loss of nitroglycerin in standard PVC tubing; dosing instructions must be followed with care when the appropriate infusion sets are used

Hypotension may occur, use with caution in patients who are volume-depleted, are hypotensive, have inadequate circulation; nitrate therapy may aggravate angina caused by hypertrophic cardiomyopathy. Nitroglycerin transdermal patches should be removed prior to defibrillation or MRI study.

Adverse Reactions

Frequency not always defined:

Cardiovascular: Hypotension (4%), postural hypotension, crescendo angina (2%), tachycardia, flushing, peripheral edema

Central nervous system: Headache (most common; 50% to 63%), lightheadedness (6%), syncope (4%), dizziness

Gastrointestinal: Nausea, vomiting, bowel incontinence, xerostomia

Genitourinary: Urinary incontinence

Ocular: Blurred vision

Miscellaneous: Diaphoresis

<1% (Limited to important or life-threatening): Allergic reactions, application site irritation (patch), cardiovascular collapse, exfoliative dermatitis, methemoglobinemia (rare; overdose), pallor, palpitation, rash, rebound hypertension, restlessness, shock, vertigo, weakness

Overdosage/Toxicology Symptoms include hypotension, flushing, syncope, throbbing headache with reflex tachycardia, and methemoglobinemia with extremely large overdoses. I.V. overdose may additionally be associated with increased intracranial pressure, confusion, vertigo, palpitations, nausea, vomiting, dyspnea, diaphoresis, heart block, bradycardia, coma, seizures, and death. After gastric decontamination, treatment is supportive and symptomatic. Hypotension is treated with positioning, fluids, and careful use of low-dose pressors, if needed. Methemoglobinemia may be treated with methylene blue (1-2 mg/kg over 5 minutes). Additional doses may be necessary (0.5-1 mg/kg) based on follow-up methemoglobin levels (obtained after 30 minutes).

Drug Interactions

Increased Effect/Toxicity: Significant reduction of systolic and diastolic blood pressure with concurrent use of sildenafil, tadalafil, or vardenafil (contraindicated); do not administer sildenafil, tadalafil, or vardenafil within 24 hours of a nitrate preparation.

Decreased Effect: I.V. nitroglycerin may antagonize the anticoagulant effect of heparin (possibly only at high nitroglycerin dosages); monitor closely. May need to decrease heparin dosage when nitroglycerin is discontinued. Ergot alkaloids may cause an increase in blood pressure and decrease in antianginal effects; avoid concurrent use.

Ethanol/Nutrition/Herb Interactions

Ethanol: Avoid ethanol (may increase the hypotensive effects of nitroglycerin). Monitor.

Herb/Nutraceutical: Avoid bayberry, blue cohosh, cayenne, ephedra, ginger, ginseng (american), kola, licorice (may worsen hypertension). Avoid black cohosh, California poppy, coleus, golden seal, hawthorn, mistletoe, periwinkle, quinine, shepherd's purse (may cause hypotension).

Stability Doses should be made in glass bottles, Excell® or PAB® containers. Adsorption occurs to soft plastic (ie, PVC).

Nitroglycerin diluted in D_5W or NS in glass containers is physically and chemically stable for 48 hours at room temperature and 7 days under refrigeration. In D_5W or NS in Excell®/PAB® containers it is physically and chemically stable for 24 hours at room temperature and 14 days under refrigeration.

Premixed bottles are stable according to the manufacturer's expiration dating.

Standard diluent: 50 mg/250 mL D_5W; 50 mg/500 mL D_5W.

(Continued)

Nitroglycerin *(Continued)*

Minimum volume: 100 mg/250 mL D_5W; concentration should not exceed 400 mcg/mL. Store sublingual tablets and ointment in tightly closed containers at 15°C to 30°C. Store spray and transdermal patch at 25°C; excursions permitted to 15°C to 30°C (59°F to 86°F).

Mechanism of Action Works by relaxation of smooth muscle, producing a vasodilator effect on the peripheral veins and arteries with more prominent effects on the veins. Primarily reduces cardiac oxygen demand by decreasing preload (left ventricular end-diastolic pressure); may modestly reduce afterload; dilates coronary arteries and improves collateral flow to ischemic regions

Pharmacodynamics/Kinetics

Onset of action: Sublingual tablet: 1-3 minutes; Translingual spray: 2 minutes; Sustained release: 20-45 minutes; Topical: 15-60 minutes; Transdermal: 40-60 minutes; I.V. drip: Immediate

Peak effect: Sublingual tablet: 4-8 minutes; Translingual spray: 4-10 minutes; Sustained release: 45-120 minutes; Topical: 30-120 minutes; Transdermal: 60-180 minutes; I.V. drip: Immediate

Duration: Sublingual tablet: 30-60 minutes; Translingual spray: 30-60 minutes; Sustained release: 4-8 hours; Topical: 2-12 hours; Transdermal: 18-24 hours; I.V. drip: 3-5 minutes

Protein binding: 60%

Metabolism: Extensive first-pass effect

Half-life elimination: 1-4 minutes

Excretion: Urine (as inactive metabolites)

Dosage Note: Hemodynamic and antianginal tolerance often develop within 24-48 hours of continuous nitrate administration. Nitrate-free interval (10-12 hours/day) is recommended to avoid tolerance development; gradually decrease dose in patients receiving NTG for prolonged period to avoid withdrawal reaction.

Children: Pulmonary hypertension: Continuous infusion: Start 0.25-0.5 mcg/kg/minute and titrate by 1 mcg/kg/minute at 20- to 60-minute intervals to desired effect; usual dose: 1-3 mcg/kg/minute; maximum: 5 mcg/kg/minute

Adults:

Oral: 2.5-9 mg 2-4 times/day (up to 26 mg 4 times/day)

I.V.: 5 mcg/minute, increase by 5 mcg/minute every 3-5 minutes to 20 mcg/minute; if no response at 20 mcg/minute increase by 10 mcg/minute every 3-5 minutes, up to 200 mcg/minute

Ointment: 1/2" upon rising and 1/2" 6 hours later; the dose may be doubled and even doubled again as needed

Patch, transdermal: Initial: 0.2-0.4 mg/hour, titrate to doses of 0.4-0.8 mg/hour; tolerance is minimized by using a patch-on period of 12-14 hours and patch-off period of 10-12 hours

Sublingual: 0.2-0.6 mg every 5 minutes for maximum of 3 doses in 15 minutes; may also use prophylactically 5-10 minutes prior to activities which may provoke an attack

Esophageal spastic disorders (unlabeled use): 0.3-0.4 mg 5 minutes before meals

Translingual: 1-2 sprays into mouth under tongue every 5 minutes for maximum of 3 doses in 15 minutes, may also be used 5-10 minutes prior to activities which may provoke an attack prophylactically

Hemodialysis: Supplemental dose is not necessary

Peritoneal dialysis: Supplemental dose is not necessary

Elderly: In general, dose selection should be cautious, usually starting at the low end of the dosing range

Administration

I.V.: I.V. must be prepared in glass bottles; use special sets intended for nitroglycerin. glass I.V. bottles and administration sets provided by manufacturer.

Sublingual: Do not crush sublingual product (tablet). Place under tongue and allow to dissolve.

Translingual spray: Do not shake container. Release spray onto or under tongue. Do not rinse the mouth for at least 5-10 minutes. Priming sprays should be directed away from patient and others. The end of the pump should be covered by the fluid in the bottle.

Nitrolingual®: Prime prior to first use (5 sprays into the air). If unused for 6 weeks, a single priming spray should be completed.

NitroMist™: Prime prior to first use (10 sprays into the air). If unused for 6 weeks, 2 repriming sprays should be completed.

Monitoring Parameters Blood pressure, heart rate

Additional Information I.V. preparations contain alcohol and/or propylene glycol; may need to use nitrate-free interval (10-12 hours/day) to avoid tolerance development. Tolerance may possibly be reversed with acetylcysteine; gradually decrease dose in patients receiving NTG for prolonged period to avoid withdrawal reaction.

Concomitant use of sildenafil (Viagra®) or other phosphodiesterase-5 enzyme inhibitors (PDE-5) may precipitate acute hypotension, myocardial infarction, or death. Nitrates used in right ventricular infarction may induce acute hypotension. Nitrate use in severe pericardial effusion may reduce cardiac filling pressure and precipitate cardiac tamponade. In the management of heart failure, the combination of isosorbide dinitrate and hydralazine confers beneficial effects on disease progression and cardiac outcomes.

Dosage Forms

Capsule, extended release: 2.5 mg, 6.5 mg, 9 mg

Nitro-Time®: 2.5 mg, 6.5 mg, 9 mg

Infusion [premixed in D_5W]: 25 mg (250 mL) [0.1 mg/mL]; 50 mg (250 mL) [0.2 mg/mL]; 50 mg (500 mL) [0.1 mg/mL]; 100 mg (250 mL) [0.4 mg/mL]; 200 mg (500 mL) [0.4 mg/mL]

Injection, solution: 5 mg/mL (5 mL, 10 mL) [contains alcohol and propylene glycol]

Ointment, topical:

Nitro-Bid®: 2% [20 mg/g] (1 g, 30 g, 60 g)

Solution, translingual [spray]:

Nitrolingual®: 0.4 mg/metered spray (4.9 g) [contains alcohol 20%; 60 metered sprays]; (12 g) [contains alcohol 20%; 200 metered sprays]

NitroMist™: 0.4 mg/metered spray (8.5 g) [230 metered sprays]

Tablet, sublingual:
NitroQuick®, Nitrostat®: 0.3 mg, 0.4 mg, 0.6 mg
Transdermal system [once-daily patch]: 0.1 mg/hour (30s); 0.2 mg/hour (30s); 0.4 mg/hour (30s); 0.6 mg/hour (30s)
Minitran™: 0.1 mg/hour (30s); 0.2 mg/hour (30s); 0.4 mg/hour (30s); 0.6 mg/hour (30s)
Nitrek®: 0.2 mg/hour (30s); 0.4 mg/hour (30s); 0.6 mg/hour (30s)
Nitro-Dur®: 0.1 mg/hour (30s); 0.2 mg/hour (30s); 0.3 mg/hour (30s); 0.4 mg/hour (30s); 0.6 mg/hour (30s); 0.8 mg/hour (30s)

♦ **Nitroglycerin Injection, USP (Can)** *see* Nitroglycerin *on page 1234*
♦ **Nitroglycerol** *see* Nitroglycerin *on page 1234*
♦ **Nitrol® (Can)** *see* Nitroglycerin *on page 1234*
♦ **Nitrolingual®** *see* Nitroglycerin *on page 1234*
♦ **NitroMist™** *see* Nitroglycerin *on page 1234*
♦ **Nitropress®** *see* Nitroprusside *on page 1237*

Nitroprusside (nye troe PRUS ide)

U.S. Brand Names Nitropress®
Index Terms Nitroprusside Sodium; Sodium Nitroferricyanide; Sodium Nitroprusside
Pharmacologic Category Vasodilator
Additional Appendix Information
Hemodynamic Support, Intravenous *on page 1885*
Hypertension *on page 2063*
Use Management of hypertensive crises; congestive heart failure; used for controlled hypotension to reduce bleeding during surgery
Pregnancy Risk Factor C
Lactation Excretion in breast milk unknown
Medication Safety Issues
Sound-alike/look-alike issues:
Nitroprusside may be confused with nitroglycerin

High alert medication: The Institute for Safe Medication Practices (ISMP) includes this medication among its list of drugs which have a heightened risk of causing significant patient harm when used in error.
Contraindications Hypersensitivity to nitroprusside or any component of the formulation; treatment of compensatory hypertension (aortic coarctation, arteriovenous shunting); high output failure; congenital optic atrophy or tobacco amblyopia
Warnings/Precautions [U.S. Boxed Warning]: Continuous blood pressure monitoring is needed. Except when used briefly or at low (<2 mcg/kg/minute) infusion rates, nitroprusside gives rise to large cyanide quantities. Do not use the maximum dose for more than 10 minutes; if blood pressure not controlled then discontinue infusion. Monitor for cyanide toxicity via acid-base balance and venous oxygen concentration. Use with caution in patients with increased intracranial pressure (head trauma, cerebral hemorrhage); severe renal impairment; hepatic failure, hypothyroidism. **[U.S. Boxed Warning]: Use only as an infusion with 5% dextrose in water.** Excessive amounts of nitroprusside can cause cyanide toxicity (usually in patients with decreased liver function) or thiocyanate toxicity (usually in patients with decreased renal function, or in patients with normal renal function but prolonged nitroprusside use)
Adverse Reactions 1% to 10%:
Cardiovascular: Excessive hypotensive response, palpitation, substernal distress
Central nervous system: Disorientation, psychosis, headache, restlessness
Endocrine & metabolic: Thyroid suppression
Gastrointestinal: Nausea, vomiting
Neuromuscular & skeletal: Weakness, muscle spasm
Otic: Tinnitus
Respiratory: Hypoxia
Miscellaneous: Diaphoresis, thiocyanate toxicity
Overdosage/Toxicology Symptoms include hypotension, vomiting, hyperventilation, tachycardia, muscular twitching, hypothyroidism, cyanide or thiocyanate toxicity. Thiocyanate toxicity includes psychosis, hyper-reflexia, confusion, weakness, tinnitus, seizures, and coma. Cyanide toxicity includes acidosis (decreased HCO_3, decreased pH, increased lactate), increase in mixed venous blood oxygen tension, tachycardia, altered consciousness, coma, convulsions, and almond smell on breath. Nitroprusside has been shown to release cyanide *in vivo* with hemoglobin. Cyanide toxicity does not usually occur because of the rapid uptake of cyanide by erythrocytes and its eventual incorporation into cyanocobalamin. However, prolonged administration of nitroprusside or its reduced elimination can lead to cyanide intoxication. In these situations, airway support with oxygen therapy is germane, followed closely with antidotal therapy of amyl nitrate perles, sodium nitrate 300 mg I.V. for adults (range based on hemoglobin concentration: 6-12 mg/kg for children), and sodium thiosulfate 12.5 g I.V. for adults (range based on hemoglobin concentration: 0.95-1.95 mL/kg of the 25% solution for children). Nitrates should not be administered to neonates and small children. Thiocyanate is dialyzable. May be mixed with sodium thiosulfate in I.V. to prevent cyanide toxicity.
Stability
Nitroprusside sodium should be reconstituted freshly by diluting 50 mg in 250-1000 mL of D_5W.
Use only clear solutions; solutions of nitroprusside exhibit a color described as brownish, brown, brownish-pink, light orange, and straw. Solutions are highly sensitive to light. Exposure to light causes decomposition, resulting in a highly colored solution of orange, dark brown or blue. **A blue color indicates almost complete degradation and breakdown to cyanide.**
(Continued)

Nitroprusside *(Continued)*

Solutions should be wrapped with aluminum foil or other opaque material to protect from light (do as soon as possible).

Stability of parenteral admixture at room temperature (25°C) and at refrigeration temperature (4°C) is 24 hours.

Mechanism of Action Causes peripheral vasodilation by direct action on venous and arteriolar smooth muscle, thus reducing peripheral resistance; will increase cardiac output by decreasing afterload; reduces aortal and left ventricular impedance

Pharmacodynamics/Kinetics

Onset of action: BP reduction <2 minutes

Duration: 1-10 minutes

Metabolism: Nitroprusside is converted to cyanide ions in the bloodstream; decomposes to prussic acid which in the presence of sulfur donor is converted to thiocyanate (hepatic and renal rhodanase systems)

Half-life elimination: Parent drug: <10 minutes; Thiocyanate: 2.7-7 days

Excretion: Urine (as thiocyanate)

Dosage Administration requires the use of an infusion pump. Average dose: 5 mcg/kg/minute.

Children: Pulmonary hypertension: I.V.: Initial: 1 mcg/kg/minute by continuous I.V. infusion; increase in increments of 1 mcg/kg/minute at intervals of 20-60 minutes; titrating to the desired response; usual dose: 3 mcg/kg/minute, rarely need >4 mcg/kg/minute; maximum: 5 mcg/kg/minute.

Adults: I.V. Initial: 0.3-0.5 mcg/kg/minute; increase in increments of 0.5 mcg/kg/minute, titrating to the desired hemodynamic effect or the appearance of headache or nausea; usual dose: 3 mcg/kg/minute; rarely need >4 mcg/kg/minute; maximum: 10 mcg/kg/minute. When administered by prolonged infusion faster than 2 mcg/kg/minute, cyanide is generated faster than an unaided patient can handle.

Administration I.V. infusion only, not for direct injection

Monitoring Parameters Blood pressure, heart rate; monitor for cyanide and thiocyanate toxicity; monitor acid-base status as acidosis can be the earliest sign of cyanide toxicity; monitor thiocyanate levels if requiring prolonged infusion (>3 days) or dose ≥4 mcg/kg/minute or patient has renal dysfunction; monitor cyanide blood levels in patients with decreased hepatic function; cardiac monitor and blood pressure monitor required

Reference Range Monitor thiocyanate levels if requiring prolonged infusion (>4 days) or ≥4 mcg/kg/minute; not to exceed 100 mcg/mL (or 10 mg/dL) plasma thiocyanate

Thiocyanate:
Therapeutic: 6-29 mcg/mL
Toxic: 35-100 mcg/mL
Fatal: >200 mcg/mL
Cyanide: Normal <0.2 mcg/mL; normal (smoker): <0.4 mcg/mL
Toxic: >2 mcg/mL
Potentially lethal: >3 mcg/mL

Dosage Forms Injection, solution, as sodium: 25 mg/mL (2 mL)

♦ **Nitroprusside Sodium** *see Nitroprusside on page 1237*

♦ **NitroQuick®** *see Nitroglycerin on page 1234*

♦ **Nitrostat®** *see Nitroglycerin on page 1234*

♦ **Nitrostat™ (Can)** *see Nitroglycerin on page 1234*

♦ **NitroTime®** *see Nitroglycerin on page 1234*

♦ **Nix® [OTC]** *see Permethrin on page 1348*

♦ **Nix® (Can)** *see Permethrin on page 1348*

Nizatidine *(ni ZA ti deen)*

U.S. Brand Names Axid®; Axid® AR [OTC]

Canadian Brand Names Apo-Nizatidine®; Axid®; Gen-Nizatidine; Novo-Nizatidine; Nu-Nizatidine; PMS-Nizatidine

Pharmacologic Category Histamine H₂ Antagonist

Use Treatment and maintenance of duodenal ulcer; treatment of benign gastric ulcer; treatment of gastroesophageal reflux disease (GERD); OTC tablet used for the prevention of meal-induced heartburn, acid indigestion, and sour stomach

Unlabeled/Investigational Use Part of a multidrug regimen for *H. pylori* eradication to reduce the risk of duodenal ulcer recurrence

Pregnancy Risk Factor B

Pregnancy Implications Teratogenic effects were not observed in animal studies.

Lactation Enters breast milk/may be compatible

Medication Safety Issues

Sound-alike/look-alike issues:
Axid® may be confused with Ansaid®

International issues:
Tazac® [Australia] may be confused with Tiazac® which is a brand name for diltiazem in the U.S.

Contraindications Hypersensitivity to nizatidine or any component of the formulation; hypersensitivity to other H₂ antagonists (cross-sensitivity has been observed)

Warnings/Precautions Use with caution in children <12 years of age; use with caution in patients with liver and renal impairment; dosage modification required in patients with renal impairment

Adverse Reactions

>10%: Central nervous system: Headache (16%)
1% to 10%:
Central nervous system: Anxiety, dizziness, fever (reported in children), insomnia, irritability (reported in children), somnolence, nervousness

Dermatologic: Pruritus, rash

Gastrointestinal: Abdominal pain, anorexia, constipation, diarrhea, dry mouth, flatulence, heartburn, nausea, vomiting

Respiratory: Reported in children: Cough, nasal congestion, nasopharyngitis

<1% (Limited to important or life-threatening): Alkaline phosphatase increased, anaphylaxis, anemia, AST/ALT increased, bronchospasm, confusion, eosinophilia, exfoliative dermatitis, gynecomastia, hepatitis, jaundice, laryngeal edema, serum-sickness like reactions, thrombocytopenia, thrombocytopenic purpura, vasculitis, ventricular tachycardia

Overdosage/Toxicology Symptoms include muscular tremors, vomiting, rapid respiration. LD_{50}: ~80 mg/kg. Treatment is primarily symptomatic and supportive.

Drug Interactions

Cytochrome P450 Effect: Inhibits 3A4 (weak)

Decreased Effect: May decrease the absorption of itraconazole or ketoconazole.

Ethanol/Nutrition/Herb Interactions

Ethanol: Avoid ethanol (may cause gastric mucosal irritation).

Food: Administration with apple juice may decrease absorption.

Mechanism of Action Competitive inhibition of histamine at H_2-receptors of the gastric parietal cells resulting in reduced gastric acid secretion, gastric volume and hydrogen ion concentration reduced. In healthy volunteers, nizatidine suppresses gastric acid secretion induced by pentagastrin infusion or food.

Pharmacodynamics/Kinetics

Distribution: V_d: 0.8-1.5 L/kg

Protein binding: 35% to α_1-acid glycoprotein

Metabolism: Partially hepatic; forms metabolites

Bioavailability: >70%

Half-life elimination: 1-2 hours; prolonged with renal impairment

Time to peak, plasma: 0.5-3.0 hours

Excretion: Urine (90%; ~60% as unchanged drug); feces (<6%)

Dosage Oral:

Children:

<12 years: GERD (unlabeled use): 10 mg/kg/day in divided doses given twice daily; may not be as effective in children <12 years

≥12 years:

GERD: Refer to Adults dosing

Meal-induced heartburn, acid indigestion and sour stomach: Refer to Adults dosing

Adults:

Duodenal ulcer:

Treatment of active ulcer: 300 mg at bedtime or 150 mg twice daily

Maintenance of healed ulcer: 150 mg/day at bedtime

Gastric ulcer: 150 mg twice daily or 300 mg at bedtime

GERD: 150 mg twice daily

Meal-induced heartburn, acid indigestion, and sour stomach: 75 mg tablet [OTC] twice daily, 30 to 60 minutes prior to consuming food or beverages

Helicobacter pylori eradication (unlabeled use): 150 mg twice daily; requires combination therapy

Dosing adjustment in renal impairment:

Active treatment:

Cl_{cr} 20-50 mL/minute: 150 mg/day

Cl_{cr} <20 mL/minute: 150 mg every other day

Maintenance treatment:

Cl_{cr} 20-50 mL/minute: 150 mg every other day

Cl_{cr} <20 mL/minute: 150 mg every 3 days

Test Interactions False-positive urine protein using Multistix®, gastric acid secretion test, skin tests allergen extracts, serum creatinine and serum transaminase concentrations, urine protein test

Additional Information Giving dose at 6 PM (rather than 10 PM) may better suppress nocturnal acid secretion

Dosage Forms

Capsule (Axid®): 150 mg, 300 mg

Solution, oral (Axid®): 15 mg/mL (120 mL, 480 mL) [bubble gum flavor]

Tablet (Axid® AR): 75 mg

◆ **Nizoral®** *see* Ketoconazole *on page 959*

◆ **Nizoral® A-D [OTC]** *see* Ketoconazole *on page 959*

◆ **N-Methylhydrazine** *see* Procarbazine *on page 1428*

◆ **NoHist** *see* Chlorpheniramine and Phenylephrine *on page 349*

◆ **Nolvadex® [DSC]** *see* Tamoxifen *on page 1631*

◆ **Nolvadex® (Can)** *see* Tamoxifen *on page 1631*

◆ **Nolvadex®-D (Can)** *see* Tamoxifen *on page 1631*

Nonoxynol 9 (non OKS i nole nine)

U.S. Brand Names Advantage-S™ [OTC]; Conceptrol® [OTC]; Delfen® [OTC]; Emko® [OTC] [DSC]; Encare® [OTC]; Gynol II® [OTC]; Shur-Seal® [OTC] [DSC]; Today® Sponge [OTC]; VCF™ [OTC]

Index Terms N-9

Pharmacologic Category Contraceptive; Spermicide

Use Prevention of pregnancy

Medication Safety Issues

Sound-alike/look-alike issues:

Delfen® may be confused with Delsym®

(Continued)

Nonoxynol 9 *(Continued)*

Dosage Note: Prior to use, refer to specific product labeling for complete instructions.

Prevention of pregnancy: Vaginal:

Advantage-S®, Conceptrol®: Insert 1 applicatorful vaginally up to 1 hour prior to intercourse

Encare®: Unwrap and insert 1 suppository vaginally at least 10 minutes prior to intercourse; effective for 1 hour

Today® Sponge: Insert 1 sponge vaginally prior to intercourse; allow to remain in place for 6 hours after intercourse before removing; effective for use up to 24 continuous hours. Do not leave in place for >30 hours.

VCF®:

Film: Insert 1 film vaginally at least 15 minutes, but no more than 3 hours, prior to intercourse. Insert new film for each act of intercourse or if more than 3 hours have elapsed.

Foam: Insert 1 applicatorful at least 15 minutes prior to intercourse; effective for up to 1 hour

Additional Information Complete prescribing information for this medication should be consulted for additional detail.

Dosage Forms [DSC] = Discontinued product

Film, vaginal (VCF™): 28% (3s, 6s,12s)

Foam, vaginal:

Delfen®: 12.5% (18 g)

Emko®: 8% (40 g, 90 g) [DSC]

VCF™: 12.5% (40 g)

Gel, vaginal:

Advantage-S™: 3.5% (1.5 g) [packaged in 3s or with 6 prefilled applicators]; (30g) [packaged with reusable applicator]

Conceptrol®: 4% (2.7 g) [packaged in 6s and 10s with disposable applicators]

Gynol II®: 2% (85 g, 114 g)

Shur-Seal®: 2% (6 g) [packaged in 24s] [DSC]

Sponge, vaginal (Today®): 1 g (3s, 6s, 12s) [contains sodium metabisulfite]

Suppository, vaginal (Encare®): 100 mg (12s, 18s)

♦ **Noradrenaline** *see* Norepinephrine *on page 1240*

♦ **Noradrenaline Acid Tartrate** *see* Norepinephrine *on page 1240*

♦ **Norco®** *see* Hydrocodone and Acetaminophen *on page 848*

♦ **Norcuron® [DSC]** *see* Vecuronium *on page 1780*

♦ **Norcuron® (Can)** *see* Vecuronium *on page 1780*

♦ **Nordeoxyguanosine** *see* Ganciclovir *on page 779*

♦ **Nordette®** *see* Ethinyl Estradiol and Levonorgestrel *on page 653*

♦ **Norditropin®** *see* Somatropin *on page 1586*

♦ **Norditropin® NordiFlex®** *see* Somatropin *on page 1586*

♦ **norel® EX** *see* Guaifenesin and Phenylephrine *on page 818*

♦ **Norelgestromin and Ethinyl Estradiol** *see* Ethinyl Estradiol and Norelgestromin *on page 655*

Norepinephrine *(nor ep i NEF rin)*

U.S. Brand Names Levophed®

Canadian Brand Names Levophed®

Index Terms Levarterenol Bitartrate; Noradrenaline; Noradrenaline Acid Tartrate; Norepinephrine Bitartrate

Pharmacologic Category Alpha/Beta Agonist

Additional Appendix Information

Hemodynamic Support, Intravenous *on page 1885*

Use Treatment of shock which persists after adequate fluid volume replacement

Pregnancy Risk Factor C

Lactation Excretion in breast milk unknown

Contraindications Hypersensitivity to norepinephrine, bisulfites (contains metabisulfite), or any component of the formulation; hypotension from hypovolemia except as an emergency measure to maintain coronary and cerebral perfusion until volume could be replaced; mesenteric or peripheral vascular thrombosis unless it is a lifesaving procedure; during anesthesia with cyclopropane or halothane anesthesia (risk of ventricular arrhythmias)

Warnings/Precautions Assure adequate circulatory volume to minimize need for vasoconstrictors. Avoid hypertension; monitor blood pressure closely and adjust infusion rate. Avoid extravasation; infuse into a large vein if possible. Avoid infusion into leg veins. Watch I.V. site closely. **[U.S. Boxed Warning]: If extravasation occurs, infiltrate the area with diluted phentolamine (5-10 mg in 10-15 mL of saline) with a fine hypodermic needle. Phentolamine should be administered as soon as possible after extravasation is noted.**

Adverse Reactions Frequency not defined.

Cardiovascular: Bradycardia, arrhythmia, peripheral (digital) ischemia

Central nervous system: Headache (transient), anxiety

Local: Skin necrosis (with extravasation)

Respiratory: Dyspnea, respiratory difficulty

Overdosage/Toxicology Symptoms include hypertension, sweating, cerebral hemorrhage, and convulsions. For treatment of extravasation, infiltrate the area of extravasation with phentolamine 5-10 mg in 10-15 mL of saline solution; inject a small amount of this dilution into extravasated area; blanching should reverse immediately. Monitor site; if blanching should recur, additional injections of phentolamine may be needed.

Drug Interactions

Increased Effect/Toxicity: The effects of norepinephrine may be increased by tricyclic antidepressants, MAO inhibitors, antihistamines (diphenhydramine, tripelennamine), beta-blockers (nonselective), guanethidine, ergot alkaloids, reserpine, and methyldopa. Atropine sulfate may block the reflex bradycardia caused by norepinephrine and enhances the vasopressor response.

Decreased Effect: Alpha-blockers may blunt response to norepinephrine.

Stability Readily oxidized. Protect from light. Do not use if brown coloration. Dilute with D_5W or D_5NS, but not recommended to dilute in normal saline. Stability of parenteral admixture at room temperature (25°C) is 24 hours.

Mechanism of Action Stimulates beta$_1$-adrenergic receptors and alpha-adrenergic receptors causing increased contractility and heart rate as well as vasoconstriction, thereby increasing systemic blood pressure and coronary blood flow; clinically alpha effects (vasoconstriction) are greater than beta effects (inotropic and chronotropic effects)

Pharmacodynamics/Kinetics
Onset of action: I.V.: Very rapid-acting
Duration: Limited
Metabolism: Via catechol-o-methyltransferase (COMT) and monoamine oxidase (MAO)
Excretion: Urine (84% to 96% as inactive metabolites)

Dosage Administration requires the use of an infusion pump!
Note: Norepinephrine dosage is stated in terms of norepinephrine base and intravenous formulation is norepinephrine bitartrate
Norepinephrine bitartrate 2 mg = Norepinephrine base 1 mg
Continuous I.V. infusion:
Children: Initial: 0.05-0.1 mcg/kg/minute; titrate to desired effect; maximum dose: 1-2 mcg/kg/minute
Adults: Initial: 0.5-1 mcg/minute and titrate to desired response; 8-30 mcg/minute is usual range; range used in clinical trials: 0.01-3 mcg/kg/minute; ACLS dosage range: 0.5-30 mcg/minute

Administration Administer into large vein to avoid the potential for extravasation; potent drug, must be diluted prior to use; do not administer $NaHCO_3$ through an I.V. line containing norepinephrine.

Dosage Forms Injection, solution, as bitartrate: 1 mg/mL (4 mL) [contains sodium metabisulfite]

♦ **Norepinephrine Bitartrate** see Norepinephrine on page 1240
♦ **Norethindrone Acetate and Ethinyl Estradiol** see Ethinyl Estradiol and Norethindrone on page 655
♦ **Norethindrone and Estradiol** see Estradiol and Norethindrone on page 624
♦ **Norethindrone and Mestranol** see Mestranol and Norethindrone on page 1093
♦ **Norflex™** see Orphenadrine on page 1273

Norfloxacin (nor FLOKS a sin)

U.S. Brand Names Noroxin®
Canadian Brand Names Apo-Norflox®; CO Norfloxacin; Norfloxacine®; Noroxin®; Novo-Norfloxacin; PMS-Norfloxacin; Riva-Norfloxacin
Pharmacologic Category Antibiotic, Quinolone
Use Uncomplicated and complicated urinary tract infections caused by susceptible gram-negative and gram-positive bacteria; sexually-transmitted disease (eg, uncomplicated urethral and cervical gonorrhea) caused by *N. gonorrhoeae*; prostatitis due to *E. coli*
Pregnancy Risk Factor C
Pregnancy Implications Reports of arthropathy (observed in immature animals and reported rarely in humans) have limited the use of fluoroquinolones in pregnancy. Teratogenic effects have not been reported with norfloxacin in animal studies; however, embryonic loss has been reported with one species. Norfloxacin crosses the placenta. The Teratogen Information System concluded that therapeutic doses during pregnancy are unlikely to produce substantial teratogenic risk, but data are insufficient to say that there is no risk. There are no adequate and well-controlled studies in pregnant women. When considering treatment for life-threatening infection and/or prolonged duration of therapy, the potential risk to the fetus must be balanced against the severity of the potential illness.
Lactation Excretion in breast milk unknown/not recommended
Medication Safety Issues
Sound-alike/look-alike issues:
Norfloxacin may be confused with Norflex™, Noroxin®
Noroxin® may be confused with Neurontin®, Norflex™, norfloxacin
Contraindications Hypersensitivity to norfloxacin, quinolones, or any component of the formulation; history of tendonitis or tendon rupture associated with quinolone use
Warnings/Precautions Not recommended in children <18 years of age; other quinolones have caused transient arthropathy in children; use with caution in patients with known or suspected CNS disorders. Tendon inflammation and/or rupture have been reported with norfloxacin and other quinolone antibiotics. Risk may be increased with concurrent corticosteroids, particularly in the elderly. Discontinue at first sign of tendon inflammation or pain. CNS stimulation may occur which may lead to tremor, restlessness, confusion, and very rarely to hallucinations or convulsive seizures. Potential for seizures, although very rare, may be increased with concomitant NSAID therapy. Use with caution in individuals at risk of seizures. Use may be associated (rarely) with prolongation of QT$_c$ interval; avoid concurrent use with class Ia and class III antiarrhythmics; use caution with other drugs may cause QT$_c$ prolongation. Use caution in patients with glucose-6-phosphate dehydrogenase deficiency.

Severe hypersensitivity reactions, including anaphylaxis, have occurred with quinolone therapy. If an allergic reaction occurs (itching, urticaria, dyspnea, facial edema, loss of consciousness, tingling, cardiovascular collapse), discontinue drug immediately. Prolonged use may result in superinfection; pseudomembranous colitis may occur and should be considered in all patients who present with diarrhea. Avoid excessive exposure to sunlight; other quinolones have been associated with phototoxicity. May be associated with the development of peripheral neuropathy and/or paresthesias; discontinue in patients who develop (Continued)

Norfloxacin *(Continued)*

symptoms consistent with neuropathy. Quinolones may exacerbate myasthenia gravis; use with caution (rare, potentially life-threatening weakness of respiratory muscles may occur). Use caution with renal impairment.

Adverse Reactions

1% to 10%:

Central nervous system: Headache (3%), dizziness (3%)

Gastrointestinal: Nausea (4%), abdominal cramping (2%)

Neuromuscular & skeletal: Weakness (1%)

<1% (Limited to important or life-threatening): Acute renal failure, agranulocytosis, albuminuria, alkaline phosphatase increased, anaphylactoid reactions, anaphylaxis, angioedema, candiduria, chest pain, cholestatic jaundice, cholesterol increased, confusion, CPK increased, crystalluria, depression, dyspnea, edema, eosinophilia, erythema, erythema multiforme, exacerbation of myasthenia gravis, exfoliative dermatitis, GI bleeding, glycosuria, Guillain-Barré syndrome, hearing loss, hematocrit decreased, hematuria, hemolytic anemia (sometimes associated with G6PD deficiency), hepatic necrosis, hepatitis, hyperglycemia, hyperkalemia, hypoesthesia, hypoglycemia, interstitial nephritis, jaundice, leukopenia, MI, mouth ulcer, myalgia, myoclonus, neutropenia, palpitation, pancreatitis, paresthesia, peripheral neuropathy, postural hypotension, prothrombin time increased, pseudomembraneous colitis, psychotic reactions, QT_c prolongation, rash, renal colic, seizure, serum creatinine/BUN increased, Stevens-Johnson syndrome, stomatitis, tendon rupture, tendonitis, thrombocytopenia, tingling of fingers, tinnitus, torsade de pointes, toxic epidermal necrolysis, transaminases increased, tremor, triglyceridemia, vasculitis, ventricular arrhythmia

Overdosage/Toxicology Symptoms include acute renal failure and seizures. Following GI decontamination, treatment should be symptom-directed and supportive.

Drug Interactions

Cytochrome P450 Effect: Inhibits CYP1A2 (strong), 3A4 (moderate)

Increased Effect/Toxicity: Norfloxacin may increase the effects/toxicity of caffeine, cyclosporine, CYP1A2 substrates (eg, aminophylline, fluvoxamine, mexiletine, mirtazapine, ropinirole, and trifluoperazine), CYP3A4 substrates (such as benzodiazepines, calcium channel blockers, cisapride, ergot alkaloids, selected HMG-CoA reductase inhibitors, mirtazapine, nateglinide, nefazodone, pimozide, sildenafil (and other PDE-5 inhibitors), tacrolimus, and venlafaxine), glyburide, theophylline, and warfarin. Concomitant use with corticosteroids may increase the risk of tendon rupture. Concomitant use with other QT_c-prolonging agents (eg, Class Ia and Class III antiarrhythmics, erythromycin, cisapride, antipsychotics, and cyclic antidepressants) may result in arrhythmias such as torsade de pointes. Probenecid may increase norfloxacin levels. Concomitant use with NSAIDs may rarely increase risk of seizure.

Decreased Effect: Concurrent administration of metal cations, including most antacids, oral electrolyte supplements, quinapril, sucralfate, some didanosine formulations (pediatric powder for oral suspension), and other highly-buffered oral drugs, may decrease quinolone levels; separate doses.

Ethanol/Nutrition/Herb Interactions

Food: Norfloxacin average peak serum concentrations may be decreased if taken with dairy products. Use caution with caffeine-containing beverages/foods; quinolones may increase blood levels of caffeine.

Herb/Nutraceutical: Avoid dong quai, St John's wort (may also cause photosensitization); avoid administration within 2 hours of multivitamins or other supplements containing iron, zinc, magnesium, or aluminum.

Stability Store at 25°C (77°F). Keep container tightly closed.

Mechanism of Action Norfloxacin is a DNA gyrase inhibitor. DNA gyrase is an essential bacterial enzyme that maintains the superhelical structure of DNA. DNA gyrase is required for DNA replication and transcription, DNA repair, recombination, and transposition; bactericidal

Pharmacodynamics/Kinetics

Absorption: Oral: Rapid, up to 40%

Distribution: Crosses placenta; small amounts enter breast milk

Protein binding: 10% to 15%

Metabolism: Hepatic

Half-life elimination: 3-4 hours; Renal impairment (Cl_{cr} ≤30 mL/minute): 6.5 hours; Elderly: 4 hours

Time to peak, serum: 1-2 hours

Excretion: Urine (26% to 32% as unchanged drug; 5% to 8% as metabolites); feces

Dosage

Usual dosage range:

Adults: Oral: 400 mg every 12 hours (maximum: 800 mg/day)

Indication-specific dosing:

Adults: Oral:

Dysenteric enterocolitis *(Shigella* unlabeled use): 400 mg twice daily for 5 days

Prostatitis: 400 mg every 12 hours for 4 weeks

Traveler's diarrhea (unlabeled use): 400 mg twice daily for 3 days, single dose may also be effective

Uncomplicated gonorrhea: 800 mg as a single dose (CDC recommends as an alternative regimen to ciprofloxacin or ofloxacin)

Urinary tract infections:

Uncomplicated: 400 mg twice daily for 3 days

Uncomplicated due to *E. coli, K. pneumoniae, P. mirabilis*: 400 mg twice daily for 7-10 days

Complicated: 400 mg twice daily for 10-21 days

Dosing interval in renal impairment: Cl_{cr} ≤30 mL/minute/1.73 m²: Administer 400 mg every 24 hours

Dietary Considerations Oral formulations should be administered on an empty stomach with water (1 hour before or 2 hours after meals, milk, or other dairy products). Maintain fluid intake to ensure adequate hydration and urinary output.

Administration Hold antacids, sucralfate, or multivitamins/supplements containing iron, zinc, magnesium, or aluminum for 3-4 hours after giving norfloxacin; do not administer together. Best taken on an empty stomach with water (1 hour before or 2 hours after meals, milk, or other dairy products).

Dosage Forms
Tablet:
Noroxin®: 400 mg

♦ **Norfloxacine® (Can)** *see* Norfloxacin *on page 1241*
♦ **Norgesic™ [DSC]** *see* Orphenadrine, Aspirin, and Caffeine *on page 1273*
♦ **Norgesic™ (Can)** *see* Orphenadrine, Aspirin, and Caffeine *on page 1273*
♦ **Norgesic™ Forte [DSC]** *see* Orphenadrine, Aspirin, and Caffeine *on page 1273*
♦ **Norgesic™ Forte (Can)** *see* Orphenadrine, Aspirin, and Caffeine *on page 1273*
♦ **Norgestimate and Ethinyl Estradiol** *see* Ethinyl Estradiol and Norgestimate *on page 660*
♦ **Norgestrel and Ethinyl Estradiol** *see* Ethinyl Estradiol and Norgestrel *on page 663*
♦ **Norinyl® 1+35** *see* Ethinyl Estradiol and Norethindrone *on page 655*
♦ **Norinyl® 1+50** *see* Mestranol and Norethindrone *on page 1093*
♦ **Noritate®** *see* Metronidazole *on page 1132*
♦ **Normal Human Serum Albumin** *see* Albumin *on page 55*
♦ **Normal Saline** *see* Sodium Chloride *on page 1576*
♦ **Normal Serum Albumin (Human)** *see* Albumin *on page 55*
♦ **Normodyne® (Can)** *see* Labetalol *on page 967*
♦ **Noroxin®** *see* Norfloxacin *on page 1241*
♦ **Norpace®** *see* Disopyramide *on page 526*
♦ **Norpace® CR** *see* Disopyramide *on page 526*
♦ **Norplant® Implant (Can)** *see* Levonorgestrel *on page 1004*
♦ **Norpramin®** *see* Desipramine *on page 473*
♦ **Nortemp Children's [OTC]** *see* Acetaminophen *on page 28*
♦ **Nortrel™** *see* Ethinyl Estradiol and Norethindrone *on page 655*
♦ **Nortrel™ 7/7/7** *see* Ethinyl Estradiol and Norethindrone *on page 655*

Nortriptyline (nor TRIP ti leen)

U.S. Brand Names Pamelor®
Canadian Brand Names Alti-Nortriptyline; Apo-Nortriptyline®; Aventyl®; Gen-Nortriptyline; Norventyl; Novo-Nortriptyline; Nu-Nortriptyline; PMS-Nortriptyline
Index Terms Nortriptyline Hydrochloride
Pharmacologic Category Antidepressant, Tricyclic (Secondary Amine)
Additional Appendix Information
Antidepressant Agents *on page 1866*
Use Treatment of symptoms of depression
Unlabeled/Investigational Use Chronic pain, anxiety disorders, enuresis, attention-deficit/hyperactivity disorder (ADHD); adjunctive therapy for smoking cessation
Restrictions An FDA-approved medication guide concerning the use of antidepressants in children and teenagers must be distributed when dispensing an outpatient prescription (new or refill) where this medication is to be used without direct supervision of a healthcare provider. Medication guides are available at http://www.fda.gov/cder/Offices/ODS/medication_guides.htm. Dispense to parents or guardians of children and teenagers receiving this medication.
Pregnancy Risk Factor D
Lactation Enters breast milk/contraindicated (AAP rates "of concern")
Medication Safety Issues
Sound-alike/look-alike issues:
Nortriptyline may be confused with amitriptyline, desipramine, Norpramin®
Aventyl® HCl may be confused with Bentyl®
Pamelor® may be confused with Demerol®, Dymelor®
Contraindications Hypersensitivity to nortriptyline and similar chemical class, or any component of the formulation; use of MAO inhibitors within 14 days; use in a patient during the acute recovery phase of MI; pregnancy
Warnings/Precautions [U.S. Boxed Warning]: Antidepressants increase the risk of suicidal thinking and behavior in children and adolescents with major depressive disorder (MDD) and other depressive disorders; consider risk prior to prescribing. All patients must be closely monitored for clinical worsening, suicidality, or unusual changes in behavior, especially during the initiation of therapy or following an increase or decrease in dosage. When used in children, the child's family or caregiver should be instructed to closely observe the patient and communicate condition with healthcare provider. A medication guide should be dispensed with each prescription. **Nortriptyline is not FDA approved for use in children.**

The possibility of a suicide attempt is inherent in major depression and may persist until remission occurs. Use caution in high-risk patients. Worsening depression and severe abrupt suicidality that are not part of the presenting symptoms may require discontinuation or modification of drug therapy. The patient's family or caregiver should be alerted to monitor patients for the emergence of suicidality and associated behaviors (such as agitation, irritability, hostility, impulsivity, and hypomania) and call healthcare provider.

May worsen psychosis in some patients or precipitate a shift to mania or hypomania in patients with bipolar disorder. Patients presenting with depressive symptoms should be
(Continued)

Nortriptyline *(Continued)*

screened for bipolar disorder. Monotherapy in patients with bipolar disorder should be avoided. **Nortriptyline is not FDA approved for the treatment of bipolar depression.**

The risk of sedation and orthostatic effects are low relative to other antidepressants. However, nortriptyline may result in impaired performance of tasks requiring alertness (eg, operating machinery or driving). Sedative effects may be additive with other CNS depressants and/or ethanol. The degree of anticholinergic blockade produced by this agent is moderate relative to other cyclic antidepressants, however, caution should still be used in patients with urinary retention, benign prostatic hyperplasia, narrow-angle glaucoma, xerostomia, visual problems, constipation, or history of bowel obstruction. May cause orthostatic hypotension (risk is low relative to other antidepressants) or conduction disturbances. Use with caution in patients with a history of cardiovascular disease (including previous MI, stroke, tachycardia, or conduction abnormalities). The risk conduction abnormalities with this agent is moderate relative to other antidepressants.

Consider discontinuing, when possible, prior to elective surgery. Therapy should not be abruptly discontinued in patients receiving high doses for prolonged periods. May alter glucose regulation - use caution in patients with diabetes. Use caution in patients with a previous seizure disorder or condition predisposing to seizures such as brain damage, alcoholism, or concurrent therapy with other drugs which lower the seizure threshold. May increase the risks associated with electroconvulsive therapy. Use with caution in hyperthyroid patients or those receiving thyroid supplementation. Use with caution in patients with hepatic or renal dysfunction and in elderly patients.

Adverse Reactions Frequency not defined.

Cardiovascular: Postural hypotension, arrhythmia, hypertension, heart block, tachycardia, palpitation, MI

Central nervous system: Confusion, delirium, hallucinations, restlessness, insomnia, disorientation, delusions, anxiety, agitation, panic, nightmares, hypomania, exacerbation of psychosis, incoordination, ataxia, extrapyramidal symptoms, seizure

Dermatologic: Alopecia, photosensitivity, rash, petechiae, urticaria, itching

Endocrine & metabolic: Sexual dysfunction, gynecomastia, breast enlargement, galactorrhea, increase or decrease in libido, increase in blood sugar, SIADH

Gastrointestinal: Xerostomia, constipation, vomiting, anorexia, diarrhea, abdominal cramps, black tongue, nausea, unpleasant taste, weight gain/loss

Genitourinary: Urinary retention, delayed micturition, impotence, testicular edema

Hematologic: Rarely agranulocytosis, eosinophilia, purpura, thrombocytopenia

Hepatic: Increased liver enzymes, cholestatic jaundice

Neuromuscular & skeletal: Tremor, numbness, tingling, paresthesia, peripheral neuropathy

Ocular: Blurred vision, eye pain, disturbances in accommodation, mydriasis

Otic: Tinnitus

Miscellaneous: Diaphoresis (excessive), allergic reactions

Overdosage/Toxicology Signs and symptoms include agitation, confusion, hallucinations, urinary retention, hypothermia, hypotension, seizures, ventricular and tachycardia. Following initiation of essential overdose management, toxic symptoms should be treated. Ventricular arrhythmias often respond to phenytoin 15-20 mg/kg (adults) with concurrent systemic alkalinization (sodium bicarbonate 0.5-2 mEq/kg I.V.). Arrhythmias unresponsive to this therapy may respond to lidocaine 1 mg/kg I.V. followed by a titrated infusion. Physostigmine (1-2 mg slow I.V. for adults or 0.5 mg slow I.V. for children) may be indicated in reversing life-threatening cardiac arrhythmias. Seizures usually respond to diazepam I.V. boluses (5-10 mg for adults up to 30 mg or 0.25-0.4 mg/kg/dose for children up to 10 mg/dose). If seizures are unresponsive or recur, phenytoin or phenobarbital may be required.

Drug Interactions

Cytochrome P450 Effect: Substrate of CYP1A2 (minor), 2C19 (minor), 2D6 (major), 3A4 (minor); **Inhibits** CYP2D6 (weak), 2E1 (weak)

Increased Effect/Toxicity: Nortriptyline increases the effects of amphetamines, anticholinergics, other CNS depressants (sedatives, hypnotics, ethanol), chlorpropamide, tolazamide, and warfarin. When used with MAO inhibitors, hyperpyrexia, hypertension, tachycardia, confusion, seizures, and **deaths have been reported** (serotonin syndrome). Serotonin syndrome has also been reported with ritonavir (rare). CYP2D6 inhibitors may increase the levels/effects of nortriptyline; example inhibitors include chlorpromazine, delavirdine, fluoxetine, miconazole, paroxetine, pergolide, quinidine, quinine, ritonavir, and ropinirole. Cimetidine, grapefruit juice, indinavir, methylphenidate, diltiazem, and verapamil may increase the serum concentrations of TCAs. Use of lithium with a TCA may increase the risk for neurotoxicity. Phenothiazines may increase concentration of some TCAs and TCAs may increase concentration of phenothiazines. Pressor response to I.V. epinephrine, norepinephrine, and phenylephrine may be enhanced in patients receiving TCAs (**Note:** Effect is unlikely with epinephrine or levonordefrin dosages typically administered as infiltration in combination with local anesthetics). Combined use of beta-agonists or drugs which prolong QT_c (including quinidine, procainamide, disopyramide, cisapride, sparfloxacin, gatifloxacin, moxifloxacin) with TCAs may predispose patients to cardiac arrhythmias. Use with altretamine may cause orthostatic hypotension.

Decreased Effect: Carbamazepine, phenobarbital, and rifampin may increase the metabolism of nortriptyline resulting in decreased effect of nortriptyline. Nortriptyline inhibits the antihypertensive response to bethanidine, clonidine, debrisoquin, guanadrel, guanethidine, guanabenz, or guanfacine. Cholestyramine and colestipol may bind TCAs and reduce their absorption; monitor for altered response.

Ethanol/Nutrition/Herb Interactions

Ethanol: Avoid ethanol (may increase CNS depression).

Food: Grapefruit juice may inhibit the metabolism of some TCAs and clinical toxicity may result.

Herb/Nutraceutical: Avoid valerian, St John's wort, SAMe, kava kava (may increase risk of serotonin syndrome and/or excessive sedation).

Stability Protect from light.

Mechanism of Action Traditionally believed to increase the synaptic concentration of sero-tonin and/or norepinephrine in the central nervous system by inhibition of their reuptake by the presynaptic neuronal membrane. However, additional receptor effects have been found including desensitization of adenyl cyclase, down regulation of beta-adrenergic receptors, and down regulation of serotonin receptors.

Pharmacodynamics/Kinetics

Onset of action: Therapeutic: 1-3 weeks

Distribution: V_d: 21 L/kg

Protein binding: 93% to 95%

Metabolism: Primarily hepatic; extensive first-pass effect

Half-life elimination: 28-31 hours

Time to peak, serum: 7-8.5 hours

Excretion: Urine (as metabolites and small amounts of unchanged drug); feces (small amounts)

Dosage Oral:

Nocturnal enuresis: Children (unlabeled use): 10-20 mg/day; titrate to a maximum of 40 mg/day

Depression (unlabeled use): Children: 1-3 mg/kg/day

Depression:

Adults: 25 mg 3-4 times/day up to 150 mg/day

Elderly (**Note:** Nortriptyline is one of the best tolerated TCAs in the elderly)

Initial: 10-25 mg at bedtime

Dosage can be increased by 25 mg every 3 days for inpatients and weekly for outpa-tients if tolerated

Usual maintenance dose: 75 mg as a single bedtime dose or 2 divided doses; however, lower or higher doses may be required to stay within the therapeutic window

Myofascial pain, neuralgia, burning mouth syndrome (dental use): Initial: 10-25 mg at bedtime; dosage may be increased by 25 mg/day weekly, if tolerated; usual maintenance dose: 75 mg as a single bedtime dose or 2 divided doses

Chronic urticaria, angioedema, nocturnal pruritus (unlabeled use): Adults: Oral: 75 mg/day

Smoking cessation (unlabeled use): Adults: 25-75 mg/day beginning 10-14 days before "quit" day; continue therapy for ≥12 weeks after "quit" day

Dosing adjustment in hepatic impairment: Lower doses and slower titration dependent on individualization of dosage is recommended

Monitoring Parameters Blood pressure and pulse rate (ECG, cardiac monitoring) prior to and during initial therapy in older adults; weight; blood levels are useful for therapeutic monitoring

Reference Range

Plasma levels do not always correlate with clinical effectiveness

Therapeutic: 50-150 ng/mL (SI: 190-570 nmol/L)

Toxic: >500 ng/mL (SI: >1900 nmol/L)

Dosage Forms

Capsule, as hydrochloride: 10 mg, 25 mg, 50 mg, 75 mg

Pamelor®: 10 mg, 25 mg, 50 mg, 75 mg [may contain benzyl alcohol; 50 mg may also contain sodium bisulfite]

Solution, as hydrochloride (Pamelor®): 10 mg/5 mL (473 mL) [contains alcohol 4% and benzoic acid]

♦ **Nortriptyline Hydrochloride** see Nortriptyline on page 1243

♦ **Norvasc®** see Amlodipine on page 104

♦ **Norventyl (Can)** see Nortriptyline on page 1243

♦ **Norvir®** see Ritonavir on page 1520

♦ **Norvir® SEC (Can)** see Ritonavir on page 1520

♦ **Novahistex® DM Decongestant (Can)** see Pseudoephedrine and Dextromethorphan on page 1455

♦ **Novahistex® DM Decongestant Expectorant (Can)** see Guaifenesin, Pseudoephedrine, and Dextromethorphan on page 821

♦ **Novahistex® Expectorant with Decongestant (Can)** see Guaifenesin and Pseudoephedrine on page 819

♦ **Novahistine® DM Decongestant (Can)** see Pseudoephedrine and Dextromethorphan on page 1455

♦ **Novahistine® DM Decongestant Expectorant (Can)** see Guaifenesin, Pseudoephedrine, and Dextromethorphan on page 821

♦ **Novamilor (Can)** see Amiloride and Hydrochlorothiazide on page 93

♦ **Novamoxin® (Can)** see Amoxicillin on page 110

♦ **Novantrone®** see Mitoxantrone on page 1157

♦ **Novarel®** see Chorionic Gonadotropin (Human) on page 363

♦ **Novasal™** see Magnesium Salicylate on page 1051

♦ **Novasen (Can)** see Aspirin on page 160

♦ **Novo-5 ASA (Can)** see Mesalamine on page 1089

♦ **Novo-Acebutolol (Can)** see Acebutolol on page 27

♦ **Novo-Alendronate (Can)** see Alendronate on page 65

♦ **Novo-Alprazol (Can)** see Alprazolam on page 75

♦ **Novo-Amiodarone (Can)** see Amiodarone on page 97

♦ **Novo-Ampicillin (Can)** see Ampicillin on page 122

♦ **Novo-Atenol (Can)** see Atenolol on page 167

♦ **Novo-Azathioprine (Can)** see Azathioprine on page 183

♦ **Novo-Azithromycin (Can)** see Azithromycin on page 186

♦ **Novo-Bicalutamide (Can)** see Bicalutamide on page 221

♦ **Novo-Bisoprolol (Can)** see Bisoprolol on page 226

♦ **Novo-Bupropion SR (Can)** see BuPROPion on page 252

♦ **Novo-Buspirone (Can)** see BusPIRone on page 256

- **Novocain®** *see* Procaine *on page 1427*
- **Novo-Captopril (Can)** *see* Captopril *on page 281*
- **Novo-Carbamaz (Can)** *see* Carbamazepine *on page 284*
- **Novo-Carvedilol (Can)** *see* Carvedilol *on page 299*
- **Novo-Cefaclor (Can)** *see* Cefaclor *on page 303*
- **Novo-Cefadroxil (Can)** *see* Cefadroxil *on page 305*
- **Novo-Chloroquine (Can)** *see* Chloroquine *on page 347*
- **Novo-Chlorpromazine (Can)** *see* ChlorproMAZINE *on page 356*
- **Novo-Cholamine (Can)** *see* Cholestyramine Resin *on page 360*
- **Novo-Cholamine Light (Can)** *see* Cholestyramine Resin *on page 360*
- **Novo-Cimetidine (Can)** *see* Cimetidine *on page 369*
- **Novo-Ciprofloxacin (Can)** *see* Ciprofloxacin *on page 372*
- **Novo-Citalopram (Can)** *see* Citalopram *on page 381*
- **Novo-Clavamoxin (Can)** *see* Amoxicillin and Clavulanate Potassium *on page 112*
- **Novo-Clindamycin (Can)** *see* Clindamycin *on page 389*
- **Novo-Clobetasol (Can)** *see* Clobetasol *on page 391*
- **Novo-Clonazepam (Can)** *see* Clonazepam *on page 397*
- **Novo-Clonidine (Can)** *see* Clonidine *on page 399*
- **Novo-Clopate (Can)** *see* Clorazepate *on page 403*
- **Novo-Cycloprine (Can)** *see* Cyclobenzaprine *on page 427*
- **Novo-Difenac (Can)** *see* Diclofenac *on page 492*
- **Novo-Difenac K (Can)** *see* Diclofenac *on page 492*
- **Novo-Difenac-SR (Can)** *see* Diclofenac *on page 492*
- **Novo-Diflunisal (Can)** *see* Diflunisal *on page 500*
- **Novo-Digoxin (Can)** *see* Digoxin *on page 501*
- **Novo-Diltazem (Can)** *see* Diltiazem *on page 509*
- **Novo-Diltazem-CD (Can)** *see* Diltiazem *on page 509*
- **Novo-Diltiazem HCl ER (Can)** *see* Diltiazem *on page 509*
- **Novo-Dimenate (Can)** *see* DimenhyDRINATE *on page 511*
- **Novo-Dipam (Can)** *see* Diazepam *on page 488*
- **Novo-Divalproex (Can)** *see* Valproic Acid and Derivatives *on page 1767*
- **Novo-Docusate Calcium (Can)** *see* Docusate *on page 533*
- **Novo-Docusate Sodium (Can)** *see* Docusate *on page 533*
- **Novo-Doxazosin (Can)** *see* Doxazosin *on page 544*
- **Novo-Doxepin (Can)** *see* Doxepin *on page 545*
- **Novo-Doxylin (Can)** *see* Doxycycline *on page 555*
- **Novo-Famotidine (Can)** *see* Famotidine *on page 683*
- **Novo-Fenofibrate (Can)** *see* Fenofibrate *on page 689*
- **Novo-Ferrogluc (Can)** *see* Ferrous Gluconate *on page 703*
- **Novo-Fluconazole (Can)** *see* Fluconazole *on page 712*
- **Novo-Fluoxetine (Can)** *see* Fluoxetine *on page 727*
- **Novo-Flurprofen (Can)** *see* Flurbiprofen *on page 735*
- **Novo-Flutamide (Can)** *see* Flutamide *on page 737*
- **Novo-Fluvoxamine (Can)** *see* Fluvoxamine *on page 747*
- **Novo-Fosinopril (Can)** *see* Fosinopril *on page 766*
- **Novo-Furantoin (Can)** *see* Nitrofurantoin *on page 1233*
- **Novo-Gabapentin (Can)** *see* Gabapentin *on page 775*
- **Novo-Gemfibrozil (Can)** *see* Gemfibrozil *on page 787*
- **Novo-Gesic (Can)** *see* Acetaminophen *on page 28*
- **Novo-Glimepiride (Can)** *see* Glimepiride *on page 797*
- **Novo-Glyburide (Can)** *see* GlyBURIDE *on page 803*
- **Novo-Hydrazide (Can)** *see* Hydrochlorothiazide *on page 845*
- **Novo-Hydroxyzin (Can)** *see* HydrOXYzine *on page 865*
- **Novo-Hylazin (Can)** *see* HydrALAZINE *on page 843*
- **Novo-Indapamide (Can)** *see* Indapamide *on page 898*
- **Novo-Ipramide (Can)** *see* Ipratropium *on page 932*
- **Novo-Keto (Can)** *see* Ketoprofen *on page 961*
- **Novo-Ketoconazole (Can)** *see* Ketoconazole *on page 959*
- **Novo-Keto-EC (Can)** *see* Ketoprofen *on page 961*
- **Novo-Ketorolac (Can)** *see* Ketorolac *on page 963*
- **Novo-Ketotifen (Can)** *see* Ketotifen *on page 965*
- **Novo-Lamotrigine (Can)** *see* Lamotrigine *on page 974*
- **Novo-Leflunomide (Can)** *see* Leflunomide *on page 982*
- **Novo-Levobunolol (Can)** *see* Levobunolol *on page 996*
- **Novo-Levocarbidopa (Can)** *see* Levodopa and Carbidopa *on page 999*
- **Novo-Levofloxacin (Can)** *see* Levofloxacin *on page 1001*
- **Novo-Lexin (Can)** *see* Cephalexin *on page 331*
- **Novolin® 70/30 (Can)** *see* Insulin NPH and Insulin Regular *on page 914*
- **Novolin® ge 10/90 (Can)** *see* Insulin NPH and Insulin Regular *on page 914*
- **Novolin® ge 20/80 (Can)** *see* Insulin NPH and Insulin Regular *on page 914*
- **Novolin® ge 30/70 (Can)** *see* Insulin NPH and Insulin Regular *on page 914*
- **Novolin® ge 40/60 (Can)** *see* Insulin NPH and Insulin Regular *on page 914*
- **Novolin® ge 50/50 (Can)** *see* Insulin NPH and Insulin Regular *on page 914*
- **Novolin® ge NPH (Can)** *see* Insulin NPH *on page 913*

- **Novolin® ge Toronto (Can)** *see* Insulin Regular *on page 914*
- **Novolin® N** *see* Insulin NPH *on page 913*
- **Novolin® R** *see* Insulin Regular *on page 914*
- **NovoLog®** *see* Insulin Aspart *on page 909*
- **NovoLog® Mix 70/30** *see* Insulin Aspart Protamine and Insulin Aspart *on page 910*
- **Novo-Loperamide (Can)** *see* Loperamide *on page 1027*
- **Novo-Lorazepam (Can)** *see* Lorazepam *on page 1035*
- **Novo-Lovastatin (Can)** *see* Lovastatin *on page 1040*
- **Novo-Maprotiline (Can)** *see* Maprotiline *on page 1056*
- **Novo-Medrone (Can)** *see* MedroxyPROGESTERone *on page 1065*
- **Novo-Meloxicam (Can)** *see* Meloxicam *on page 1072*
- **Novo-Mepro (Can)** *see* Meprobamate *on page 1085*
- **Novo-Metformin (Can)** *see* Metformin *on page 1098*
- **Novo-Methacin (Can)** *see* Indomethacin *on page 901*
- **Novo-Metoprolol (Can)** *see* Metoprolol *on page 1129*
- **Novo-Mexiletine (Can)** *see* Mexiletine *on page 1135*
- **Novo-Minocycline (Can)** *see* Minocycline *on page 1149*
- **Novo-Mirtazapine (Can)** *see* Mirtazapine *on page 1152*
- **Novo-Misoprostol (Can)** *see* Misoprostol *on page 1154*
- **Novo-Nabumetone (Can)** *see* Nabumetone *on page 1185*
- **Novo-Nadolol (Can)** *see* Nadolol *on page 1187*
- **Novo-Naproc EC (Can)** *see* Naproxen *on page 1199*
- **Novo-Naprox (Can)** *see* Naproxen *on page 1199*
- **Novo-Naprox Sodium (Can)** *see* Naproxen *on page 1199*
- **Novo-Naprox Sodium DS (Can)** *see* Naproxen *on page 1199*
- **Novo-Naprox SR (Can)** *see* Naproxen *on page 1199*
- **Novo-Nifedin (Can)** *see* NIFEdipine *on page 1226*
- **Novo-Nizatidine (Can)** *see* Nizatidine *on page 1238*
- **Novo-Norfloxacin (Can)** *see* Norfloxacin *on page 1241*
- **Novo-Nortriptyline (Can)** *see* Nortriptyline *on page 1243*
- **Novo-Ofloxacin (Can)** *see* Ofloxacin *on page 1254*
- **Novo-Oxybutynin (Can)** *see* Oxybutynin *on page 1285*
- **Novo-Paroxetine (Can)** *see* Paroxetine *on page 1314*
- **Novo-Pen-VK (Can)** *see* Penicillin V Potassium *on page 1336*
- **Novo-Peridol (Can)** *see* Haloperidol *on page 826*
- **Novo-Pindol (Can)** *see* Pindolol *on page 1371*
- **Novo-Pirocam (Can)** *see* Piroxicam *on page 1378*
- **Novo-Pramine (Can)** *see* Imipramine *on page 888*
- **Novo-Pranol (Can)** *see* Propranolol *on page 1446*
- **Novo-Pravastatin (Can)** *see* Pravastatin *on page 1409*
- **Novo-Prazin (Can)** *see* Prazosin *on page 1411*
- **Novo-Prednisolone (Can)** *see* PrednisoLONE *on page 1413*
- **Novo-Prednisone (Can)** *see* PredniSONE *on page 1416*
- **Novo-Profen (Can)** *see* Ibuprofen *on page 873*
- **Novo-Propamide (Can)** *see* ChlorproPAMIDE *on page 358*
- **Novo-Purol (Can)** *see* Allopurinol *on page 71*
- **Novo-Quinidin (Can)** *see* Quinidine *on page 1471*
- **Novo-Quinine (Can)** *see* Quinine *on page 1474*
- **Novo-Ranidine (Can)** *see* Ranitidine *on page 1485*
- **NovoRapid® (Can)** *see* Insulin Aspart *on page 909*
- **Novo-Rythro Estolate (Can)** *see* Erythromycin *on page 609*
- **Novo-Rythro Ethylsuccinate (Can)** *see* Erythromycin *on page 609*
- **Novo-Selegiline (Can)** *see* Selegiline *on page 1552*
- **Novo-Semide (Can)** *see* Furosemide *on page 773*
- **Novo-Sertraline (Can)** *see* Sertraline *on page 1557*
- **NovoSeven®** *see* Factor VIIa (Recombinant) *on page 678*
- **Novo-Simvastatin (Can)** *see* Simvastatin *on page 1567*
- **Novo-Sorbide (Can)** *see* Isosorbide Dinitrate *on page 945*
- **Novo-Sotalol (Can)** *see* Sotalol *on page 1592*
- **Novo-Soxazole (Can)** *see* SulfiSOXAZOLE *on page 1617*
- **Novo-Spiroton (Can)** *see* Spironolactone *on page 1596*
- **Novo-Spirozine (Can)** *see* Hydrochlorothiazide and Spironolactone *on page 847*
- **Novo-Sucralate (Can)** *see* Sucralfate *on page 1606*
- **Novo-Sumatriptan (Can)** *see* Sumatriptan *on page 1620*
- **Novo-Sundac (Can)** *see* Sulindac *on page 1618*
- **Novo-Tamoxifen (Can)** *see* Tamoxifen *on page 1631*
- **Novo-Temazepam (Can)** *see* Temazepam *on page 1640*
- **Novo-Terazosin (Can)** *see* Terazosin *on page 1647*
- **Novo-Terbinafine (Can)** *see* Terbinafine *on page 1648*
- **Novo-Ticlopidine (Can)** *see* Ticlopidine *on page 1683*
- **Novo-Topiramate (Can)** *see* Topiramate *on page 1707*
- **Novo-Trazodone (Can)** *see* Trazodone *on page 1727*
- **Novo-Triamzide (Can)** *see* Hydrochlorothiazide and Triamterene *on page 847*
- **Novo-Trifluzine (Can)** *see* Trifluoperazine *on page 1740*

- **Novo-Trimel (Can)** *see* Sulfamethoxazole and Trimethoprim *on page 1613*
- **Novo-Trimel D.S. (Can)** *see* Sulfamethoxazole and Trimethoprim *on page 1613*
- **Novo-Triptyn (Can)** *see* Amitriptyline *on page 101*
- **Novo-Veramil SR (Can)** *see* Verapamil *on page 1784*
- **Novo-Warfarin (Can)** *see* Warfarin *on page 1800*
- **Novoxapram® (Can)** *see* Oxazepam *on page 1281*
- **Noxafil®** *see* Posaconazole *on page 1393*
- **NPH Insulin** *see* Insulin NPH *on page 913*
- **NPH Insulin and Regular Insulin** *see* Insulin NPH and Insulin Regular *on page 914*
- **NSC-740** *see* Methotrexate *on page 1111*
- **NSC-750** *see* Busulfan *on page 257*
- **NSC-752** *see* Thioguanine *on page 1669*
- **NSC-755** *see* Mercaptopurine *on page 1086*
- **NSC-762** *see* Mechlorethamine *on page 1061*
- **NSC-3053** *see* Dactinomycin *on page 444*
- **NSC-3088** *see* Chlorambucil *on page 340*
- **NSC-8806** *see* Melphalan *on page 1074*
- **NSC-10363** *see* Megestrol *on page 1071*
- **NSC-13875** *see* Altretamine *on page 82*
- **NSC-26271** *see* Cyclophosphamide *on page 428*
- **NSC-26980** *see* Mitomycin *on page 1155*
- **NSC-38721** *see* Mitotane *on page 1156*
- **NSC-49842** *see* VinBLAStine *on page 1788*
- **NSC-63878** *see* Cytarabine *on page 437*
- **NSC-66847** *see* Thalidomide *on page 1661*
- **NSC-67574** *see* VinCRIStine *on page 1789*
- **NSC-77213** *see* Procarbazine *on page 1428*
- **NSC-79037** *see* Lomustine *on page 1026*
- **NSC-82151** *see* DAUNOrubicin Hydrochloride *on page 462*
- **NSC-89199** *see* Estramustine *on page 626*
- **NSC-102816** *see* Azacitidine *on page 181*
- **NSC-105014** *see* Cladribine *on page 383*
- **NSC-106977 (*Erwinia*)** *see* Asparaginase *on page 157*
- **NSC-109229 (*E. coli*)** *see* Asparaginase *on page 157*
- **NSC-109724** *see* Ifosfamide *on page 880*
- **NSC-122758** *see* Tretinoin (Oral) *on page 1730*
- **NSC-123127** *see* DOXOrubicin *on page 549*
- **NSC-125066** *see* Bleomycin *on page 229*
- **NSC-125973** *see* Paclitaxel *on page 1295*
- **NSC-127716** *see* Decitabine *on page 463*
- **NSC-147834** *see* Flutamide *on page 737*
- **NSC-180973** *see* Tamoxifen *on page 1631*
- **NSC-218321** *see* Pentostatin *on page 1342*
- **NSC-241240** *see* Carboplatin *on page 291*
- **NSC-256439** *see* Idarubicin *on page 878*
- **NSC-256942** *see* Epirubicin *on page 592*
- **NSC-266046** *see* Oxaliplatin *on page 1277*
- **NSC-301739** *see* Mitoxantrone *on page 1157*
- **NSC-312887** *see* Fludarabine *on page 716*
- **NSC-352122** *see* Trimetrexate *on page 1745*
- **NSC-362856** *see* Temozolomide *on page 1642*
- **NSC-373364** *see* Aldesleukin *on page 59*
- **NSC-377526** *see* Leuprolide *on page 991*
- **NSC-409962** *see* Carmustine *on page 296*
- **NSC-606864** *see* Goserelin *on page 810*
- **NSC606869** *see* Clofarabine *on page 393*
- **NSC-609699** *see* Topotecan *on page 1709*
- **NSC-613327** *see* Gemcitabine *on page 785*
- **NSC-613795** *see* Sargramostim *on page 1548*
- **NSC-614629** *see* Filgrastim *on page 707*
- **NSC-616348** *see* Irinotecan *on page 935*
- **NSC-628503** *see* Docetaxel *on page 530*
- **NSC-644954** *see* Pegaspargase *on page 1320*
- **NSC-671663** *see* Octreotide *on page 1252*
- **NSC-673089** *see* Paclitaxel *on page 1295*
- **NSC-681239** *see* Bortezomib *on page 230*
- **NSC-684588** *see* Nilutamide *on page 1228*
- **NSC-687451** *see* Rituximab *on page 1523*
- **NSC-688097** *see* Trastuzumab *on page 1724*
- **NSC-698037** *see* Pemetrexed *on page 1328*
- **NSC-701852** *see* Vorinostat *on page 1799*
- **NSC-704865** *see* Bevacizumab *on page 217*
- **NSC-706363** *see* Arsenic Trioxide *on page 154*
- **NSC-706725** *see* Raloxifene *on page 1480*

- **NSC-712807** *see* Capecitabine *on page 278*
- **NSC-714692** *see* Cetuximab *on page 336*
- **NSC-714744** *see* Denileukin Diftitox *on page 471*
- **NSC-715055** *see* Gefitinib *on page 784*
- **NSC-716051** *see* Imatinib *on page 881*
- **NSC-718781** *see* Erlotinib *on page 606*
- **NSC-719344** *see* Anastrozole *on page 129*
- **NSC-719345** *see* Letrozole *on page 988*
- **NSC-720568** *see* Gemtuzumab Ozogamicin *on page 790*
- **NSC-721517** *see* Zoledronic Acid *on page 1820*
- **NSC-721631** *see* Rasburicase *on page 1490*
- **NSC-722623** *see* Ibandronate *on page 869*
- **NSC-722848** *see* Oprelvekin *on page 1270*
- **NSC-724223** *see* Epoetin Alfa *on page 595*
- **NSC-725961** *see* Pegfilgrastim *on page 1321*
- **NSC-728729** *see* Infliximab *on page 904*
- **NSC-732517** *see* Dasatinib *on page 458*
- **NSC736511** *see* Sunitinib *on page 1622*
- **NSC-742319** *see* Panitumumab *on page 1305*
- **NTG** *see* Nitroglycerin *on page 1234*
- **N-trifluoroacetyladriamycin-14-valerate** *see* Valrubicin *on page 1770*
- **NTZ** *see* Nitazoxanide *on page 1232*
- **Nu-Acebutolol (Can)** *see* Acebutolol *on page 27*
- **Nu-Acyclovir (Can)** *see* Acyclovir *on page 44*
- **Nu-Alprax (Can)** *see* Alprazolam *on page 75*
- **Nu-Amilzide (Can)** *see* Amiloride and Hydrochlorothiazide *on page 93*
- **Nu-Amoxi (Can)** *see* Amoxicillin *on page 110*
- **Nu-Ampi (Can)** *see* Ampicillin *on page 122*
- **Nu-Atenol (Can)** *see* Atenolol *on page 167*
- **Nu-Baclo (Can)** *see* Baclofen *on page 193*
- **Nubain®** *see* Nalbuphine *on page 1191*
- **Nu-Beclomethasone (Can)** *see* Beclomethasone *on page 198*
- **Nu-Buspirone (Can)** *see* BusPIRone *on page 256*
- **Nu-Capto (Can)** *see* Captopril *on page 281*
- **Nu-Carbamazepine (Can)** *see* Carbamazepine *on page 284*
- **Nu-Cefaclor (Can)** *see* Cefaclor *on page 303*
- **Nu-Cephalex (Can)** *see* Cephalexin *on page 331*
- **Nu-Cimet (Can)** *see* Cimetidine *on page 369*
- **Nu-Clonazepam (Can)** *see* Clonazepam *on page 397*
- **Nu-Clonidine (Can)** *see* Clonidine *on page 399*
- **Nucofed® Expectorant [DSC]** *see* Guaifenesin, Pseudoephedrine, and Codeine *on page 820*
- **Nucofed® Pediatric Expectorant [DSC]** *see* Guaifenesin, Pseudoephedrine, and Codeine *on page 820*
- **Nu-Cotrimox (Can)** *see* Sulfamethoxazole and Trimethoprim *on page 1613*
- **Nu-Cromolyn (Can)** *see* Cromolyn *on page 423*
- **Nu-Cyclobenzaprine (Can)** *see* Cyclobenzaprine *on page 427*
- **Nu-Desipramine (Can)** *see* Desipramine *on page 473*
- **Nu-Diclo (Can)** *see* Diclofenac *on page 492*
- **Nu-Diclo-SR (Can)** *see* Diclofenac *on page 492*
- **Nu-Diflunisal (Can)** *see* Diflunisal *on page 500*
- **Nu-Diltiaz (Can)** *see* Diltiazem *on page 509*
- **Nu-Diltiaz-CD (Can)** *see* Diltiazem *on page 509*
- **Nu-Divalproex (Can)** *see* Valproic Acid and Derivatives *on page 1767*
- **Nu-Doxycycline (Can)** *see* Doxycycline *on page 555*
- **Nu-Erythromycin-S (Can)** *see* Erythromycin *on page 609*
- **Nu-Famotidine (Can)** *see* Famotidine *on page 683*
- **Nu-Fenofibrate (Can)** *see* Fenofibrate *on page 689*
- **Nu-Fluoxetine (Can)** *see* Fluoxetine *on page 727*
- **Nu-Flurprofen (Can)** *see* Flurbiprofen *on page 735*
- **Nu-Fluvoxamine (Can)** *see* Fluvoxamine *on page 747*
- **Nu-Gabapentin (Can)** *see* Gabapentin *on page 775*
- **Nu-Gemfibrozil (Can)** *see* Gemfibrozil *on page 787*
- **Nu-Glyburide (Can)** *see* GlyBURIDE *on page 803*
- **Nu-Hydral (Can)** *see* HydrALAZINE *on page 843*
- **Nu-Ibuprofen (Can)** *see* Ibuprofen *on page 873*
- **Nu-Indapamide (Can)** *see* Indapamide *on page 898*
- **Nu-Indo (Can)** *see* Indomethacin *on page 901*
- **Nu-Ipratropium (Can)** *see* Ipratropium *on page 932*
- **Nu-Iron® 150 [OTC]** *see* Polysaccharide-Iron Complex *on page 1390*
- **Nu-Ketoprofen (Can)** *see* Ketoprofen *on page 961*
- **Nu-Ketoprofen-E (Can)** *see* Ketoprofen *on page 961*
- **NuLev™** *see* Hyoscyamine *on page 866*
- **Nu-Levocarb (Can)** *see* Levodopa and Carbidopa *on page 999*
- **Nu-Loraz (Can)** *see* Lorazepam *on page 1035*

- ◆ **Nu-Lovastatin (Can)** *see* Lovastatin *on page 1040*
- ◆ **Nu-Loxapine (Can)** *see* Loxapine *on page 1042*
- ◆ **NuLYTELY®** *see* Polyethylene Glycol-Electrolyte Solution *on page 1387*
- ◆ **Nu-Medopa (Can)** *see* Methyldopa *on page 1117*
- ◆ **Nu-Mefenamic Acid (Can)** *see* Mefenamic Acid *on page 1068*
- ◆ **Nu-Megestrol (Can)** *see* Megestrol *on page 1071*
- ◆ **Nu-Metformin (Can)** *see* Metformin *on page 1098*
- ◆ **Nu-Metoclopramide (Can)** *see* Metoclopramide *on page 1126*
- ◆ **Nu-Metop (Can)** *see* Metoprolol *on page 1129*
- ◆ **Numorphan®** *see* Oxymorphone *on page 1290*
- ◆ **Nu-Naprox (Can)** *see* Naproxen *on page 1199*
- ◆ **Nu-Nifed (Can)** *see* NIFEdipine *on page 1226*
- ◆ **Nu-Nizatidine (Can)** *see* Nizatidine *on page 1238*
- ◆ **Nu-Nortriptyline (Can)** *see* Nortriptyline *on page 1243*
- ◆ **Nu-Oxybutyn (Can)** *see* Oxybutynin *on page 1285*
- ◆ **Nu-Pentoxifylline SR (Can)** *see* Pentoxifylline *on page 1343*
- ◆ **Nu-Pen-VK (Can)** *see* Penicillin V Potassium *on page 1336*
- ◆ **Nupercainal® Hydrocortisone Cream [OTC]** *see* Hydrocortisone *on page 852*
- ◆ **Nu-Pindol (Can)** *see* Pindolol *on page 1371*
- ◆ **Nu-Pirox (Can)** *see* Piroxicam *on page 1378*
- ◆ **Nu-Prazo (Can)** *see* Prazosin *on page 1411*
- ◆ **Nu-Prochlor (Can)** *see* Prochlorperazine *on page 1429*
- ◆ **Nu-Propranolol (Can)** *see* Propranolol *on page 1446*
- ◆ **Nuquin HP®** *see* Hydroquinone *on page 859*
- ◆ **Nu-Ranit (Can)** *see* Ranitidine *on page 1485*
- ◆ **Nuromax®** *see* Doxacurium *on page 542*
- ◆ **Nu-Selegiline (Can)** *see* Selegiline *on page 1552*
- ◆ **Nu-Sertraline (Can)** *see* Sertraline *on page 1557*
- ◆ **Nu-Sotalol (Can)** *see* Sotalol *on page 1592*
- ◆ **Nu-Sucralate (Can)** *see* Sucralfate *on page 1606*
- ◆ **Nu-Sundac (Can)** *see* Sulindac *on page 1618*
- ◆ **Nu-Temazepam (Can)** *see* Temazepam *on page 1640*
- ◆ **Nu-Terazosin (Can)** *see* Terazosin *on page 1647*
- ◆ **Nu-Tetra (Can)** *see* Tetracycline *on page 1659*
- ◆ **Nu-Ticlopidine (Can)** *see* Ticlopidine *on page 1683*
- ◆ **Nu-Timolol (Can)** *see* Timolol *on page 1687*
- ◆ **Nutracort®** *see* Hydrocortisone *on page 852*
- ◆ **Nutralox® [OTC]** *see* Calcium Carbonate *on page 269*
- ◆ **Nutraplus® [OTC]** *see* Urea *on page 1758*
- ◆ **Nu-Trazodone (Can)** *see* Trazodone *on page 1727*
- ◆ **NutreStore™** *see* Glutamine *on page 803*
- ◆ **Nu-Triazide (Can)** *see* Hydrochlorothiazide and Triamterene *on page 847*
- ◆ **Nu-Trimipramine (Can)** *see* Trimipramine *on page 1747*
- ◆ **Nutropin®** *see* Somatropin *on page 1586*
- ◆ **Nutropin AQ®** *see* Somatropin *on page 1586*
- ◆ **Nutropin® AQ (Can)** *see* Somatropin *on page 1586*
- ◆ **Nutropine® (Can)** *see* Somatropin *on page 1586*
- ◆ **NuvaRing®** *see* Ethinyl Estradiol and Etonogestrel *on page 650*
- ◆ **Nu-Verap (Can)** *see* Verapamil *on page 1784*
- ◆ **NVB** *see* Vinorelbine *on page 1791*
- ◆ **NVP** *see* Nevirapine *on page 1217*
- ◆ **Nyaderm (Can)** *see* Nystatin *on page 1250*
- ◆ **Nyamyc™** *see* Nystatin *on page 1250*
- ◆ **Nydrazid® [DSC]** *see* Isoniazid *on page 942*

Nystatin (nye STAT in)

U.S. Brand Names Bio-Statin®; Mycostatin®; Nyamyc™; Nystat-Rx®; Nystop®; Pedi-Dri®
Canadian Brand Names Candistatin®; Nilstat; Nyaderm; PMS-Nystatin
Pharmacologic Category Antifungal Agent, Oral Nonabsorbed; Antifungal Agent, Topical; Antifungal Agent, Vaginal
Additional Appendix Information
Antifungal Agents *on page 1869*
Treatment of Sexually Transmitted Infections *on page 2007*
Use Treatment of susceptible cutaneous, mucocutaneous, and oral cavity fungal infections normally caused by the *Candida* species
Pregnancy Risk Factor B/C (oral)
Lactation Does not enter breast milk/compatible (not absorbed orally)
Medication Safety Issues
Sound-alike/look-alike issues:
Nystatin may be confused with Nilstat®, Nitrostat®
Nilstat may be confused with Nitrostat®, nystatin
Contraindications Hypersensitivity to nystatin or any component of the formulation
Adverse Reactions
Frequency not defined: Dermatologic: Contact dermatitis, Stevens-Johnson syndrome
1% to 10%: Gastrointestinal: Nausea, vomiting, diarrhea, stomach pain

<1% (Limited to important or life-threatening): Hypersensitivity reactions

Overdosage/Toxicology Symptoms include nausea, vomiting, and diarrhea. Treatment is supportive.

Stability
Vaginal insert: Store in refrigerator. Protect from temperature extremes, moisture, and light.
Oral tablet, ointment, topical powder, and oral suspension: Store at controlled room temperature of 15°C to 25°C (59°F to 77°F).

Mechanism of Action Binds to sterols in fungal cell membrane, changing the cell wall permeability allowing for leakage of cellular contents

Pharmacodynamics/Kinetics
Onset of action: Symptomatic relief from candidiasis: 24-72 hours
Absorption: Topical: None through mucous membranes or intact skin; Oral: Poorly absorbed
Excretion: Feces (as unchanged drug)

Dosage
Oral candidiasis:
Suspension (swish and swallow orally):
Premature infants: 100,000 units 4 times/day
Infants: 200,000 units 4 times/day or 100,000 units to each side of mouth 4 times/day
Children and Adults: 400,000-600,000 units 4 times/day
Powder for compounding: Children and Adults: 1/8 teaspoon (500,000 units) to equal approximately 1/2 cup of water; give 4 times/day
Mucocutaneous infections: Children and Adults: Topical: Apply 2-3 times/day to affected areas; very moist topical lesions are treated best with powder
Intestinal infections: Adults: Oral: 500,000-1,000,000 units every 8 hours
Vaginal infections: Adults: Vaginal tablets: Insert 1 tablet/day at bedtime for 2 weeks

Administration Suspension: Shake well before using. Should be swished about the mouth and retained in the mouth for as long as possible (several minutes) before swallowing.

Dosage Forms
Capsule:
Bio-Statin®: 500,000 units, 1 million units
Cream: 100,000 units/g (15 g, 30 g)
Mycostatin®: 100,000 units/g (30 g)
Ointment, topical: 100,000 units/g (15 g, 30 g)
Powder, for prescription compounding: 50 million units (10 g); 150 million units (30 g); 500 million units (100 g); 2 billion units (400 g)
Nystat-Rx®: 50 million units (10 g); 150 million units (30 g); 500 million units (100 g); 1 billion units (190 g); 2 billion units (350 g)
Powder, topical:
Mycostatin®: 100,000 units/g (15 g) [contains talc]
Nyamyc™: 100,000 units/g (15 g, 30 g) [contains talc]
Nystop®: 100,000 units/g (15 g, 30 g, 60 g) [contains talc]
Pedi-Dri®: 100,000 units/g (56.7 g) [contains talc]
Suspension, oral: 100,000 units/mL (5 mL, 60 mL, 480 mL)
Tablet: 500,000 units
Tablet, vaginal: 100,000 units (15s) [packaged with applicator]

Nystatin and Triamcinolone (nye STAT in & trye am SIN oh lone)

U.S. Brand Names Mycolog®-II [DSC]
Index Terms Triamcinolone and Nystatin
Pharmacologic Category Antifungal Agent, Topical; Corticosteroid, Topical
Use Treatment of cutaneous candidiasis
Pregnancy Risk Factor C
Medication Safety Issues
Sound-alike/look-alike issues:
Mycolog®-II may be confused with Halog®
Dosage Children and Adults: Topical: Apply sparingly 2-4 times/day. Therapy should be discontinued when control is achieved; if no improvement is seen, reassessment of diagnosis may be necessary.
Additional Information Complete prescribing information for this medication should be consulted for additional detail.
Dosage Forms [DSC] = Discontinued product
Cream (Mycolog®-II [DSC]): Nystatin 100,000 units and triamcinolone acetonide 0.1% (15 g, 30 g, 60 g)
Ointment: Nystatin 100,000 units and triamcinolone acetonide 0.1% (15 g, 30 g, 60 g)
Mycolog®-II: Nystatin 100,000 units and triamcinolone acetonide 0.1% (15 g, 30 g, 60 g) [DSC]

♦ **Nystat-Rx®** see Nystatin on page 1250
♦ **Nystop®** see Nystatin on page 1250
♦ **Nytol® (Can)** see DiphenhydrAMINE on page 515
♦ **Nytol® Extra Strength (Can)** see DiphenhydrAMINE on page 515
♦ **Nytol® Quick Caps [OTC]** see DiphenhydrAMINE on page 515
♦ **Nytol® Quick Gels [OTC]** see DiphenhydrAMINE on page 515
♦ **NãSop™** see Phenylephrine on page 1358
♦ **OCBZ** see Oxcarbazepine on page 1282
♦ **Ocean® [OTC]** see Sodium Chloride on page 1576
♦ **Ocean® for Kids [OTC]** see Sodium Chloride on page 1576
♦ **Octagam®** see Immune Globulin (Intravenous) on page 892
♦ **Octostim® (Can)** see Desmopressin on page 476

Octreotide (ok TREE oh tide)

U.S. Brand Names Sandostatin®; Sandostatin LAR®

Canadian Brand Names Octreotide Acetate Injection; Octreotide Acetate Omega; Sandostatin®; Sandostatin LAR®

Index Terms NSC-671663; Octreotide Acetate

Pharmacologic Category Antidiarrheal; Somatostatin Analog

Use Control of symptoms in patients with metastatic carcinoid and vasoactive intestinal peptide-secreting tumors (VIPomas); acromegaly

Unlabeled/Investigational Use AIDS-associated secretory diarrhea (including *Cryptosporidiosis*), control of bleeding of esophageal varices, breast cancer, cryptosporidiosis, Cushing's syndrome (ectopic), insulinomas, small bowel fistulas, pancreatic tumors, gastrinoma, postgastrectomy dumping syndrome, chemotherapy-induced diarrhea, graft-versus-host disease (GVHD) induced diarrhea, Zollinger-Ellison syndrome, congenital hyperinsulinism; hypothalamic obesity

Pregnancy Risk Factor B

Pregnancy Implications Teratogenic effects were not reported in animal studies. Octreotide crosses the human placenta; data concerning use in pregnancy is limited.

Lactation Excretion in breast milk unknown/use caution

Medication Safety Issues
Sound-alike/look-alike issues:
Sandostatin® may be confused with Sandimmune®

Contraindications Hypersensitivity to octreotide or any component of the formulation

Warnings/Precautions May impair gall bladder function; monitor patients for cholelithiasis. Use with caution in patients with renal impairment. Somatostatin analogs may affect glucose regulation; in type I diabetes, severe hypoglycemia may occur; in type II diabetes or nondiabetic patients, hyperglycemia may occur. Insulin and other hypoglycemic medication requirements may change. Bradycardia, conduction abnormalities, and arrhythmia have been observed in acromegalic patients; use caution with CHF or concomitant medications that alter heart rate or rhythm. May alter absorption of dietary fats; monitor for pancreatitis. Chronic treatment has been associated with abnormal Schillings test; monitor vitamin B_{12} levels. Tumors which secrete growth hormone may increase in size; monitor. Suppresses secretion of TSH; monitor for hypothyroidism.

Adverse Reactions Adverse reactions vary by route of administration. Frequency of cardiac, endocrine, and gastrointestinal adverse reactions were generally higher in acromegalics.
>16%:
Cardiovascular: Sinus bradycardia (19% to 25%), chest pain (16% to 20%)
Central nervous system: Fatigue (1% to 20%), malaise (16% to 20%), dizziness (5% to 20%), headache (6% to 20%), fever (16% to 20%)
Endocrine & metabolic: Hyperglycemia (15% to 27%)
Gastrointestinal: Diarrhea (36% to 58%), abdominal discomfort (5% to 61%), flatulence (<10% to 38%), constipation (9% to 21%), nausea (5% to 61%), cholelithiasis (27%; length of therapy dependent), biliary duct dilatation (12%), biliary sludge (24%; length of therapy dependent), loose stools (5% to 61%), vomiting (4% to 21%)
Hematologic: Antibodies to octreotide (up to 25%; no efficacy change)
Local: Injection pain (2% to 50%; dose- and formulation-related)
Neuromuscular & skeletal: Backache (1% to 20%), arthropathy (16% to 20%)
Respiratory: Dyspnea (16% to 20%), upper respiratory infection (16% to 20%)
Miscellaneous: Flu symptoms (1% to 20%)
5% to 15%:
Cardiovascular: Conduction abnormalities (9% to 10%), arrhythmia (3% to 9%), hypertension, palpitations, peripheral edema
Central nervous system: Anxiety, confusion, depression, hypoesthesia, insomnia, vertigo
Dermatologic: Pruritus, rash
Endocrine & metabolic: Hypothyroidism (2% to 12%), goiter (2% to 8%)
Gastrointestinal: Abdominal pain, anorexia, cramping, dehydration, discomfort, hemorrhoids, tenesmus (4% to 6%), dyspepsia (4% to 15%), steatorrhea (4% to 6%), feces discoloration (4% to 6%), weight loss
Genitourinary: UTI
Hematologic: Anemia
Hepatic: Hepatitis
Neuromuscular & skeletal: Arthralgia, leg cramps, myalgia, paresthesia, rigors, weakness
Otic: Ear ache, otitis media
Renal: Renal calculus
Respiratory: Coughing, pharyngitis, rhinitis, sinusitis
Miscellaneous: Allergy, diaphoresis
1% to 4%:
Cardiovascular: Angina, cardiac failure, cerebral vascular disorder, edema, flushing, hematoma, phlebitis, tachycardia
Central nervous system: Abnormal gait, amnesia, dysphonia, hallucinations, nervousness, neuralgia, neuropathy, somnolence, tremor, vertigo
Dermatologic: Acne, alopecia, bruising, cellulitis, urticaria
Endocrine & metabolic: Hypoglycemia (2% to 4%), hypokalemia, hypoproteinemia, gout, cachexia, menstrual irregularities, breast pain, impotence
Gastrointestinal: Colitis, diverticulitis, dysphagia, fat malabsorption, gastritis, gastroenteritis, gingivitis, glossitis, melena, rectal bleeding, stomatitis, taste perversion, xerostomia
Genitourinary: Incontinence
Hematologic: Epistaxis
Hepatic: Ascites, jaundice
Local: Injection hematoma
Neuromuscular & skeletal: Hyperkinesia, hypertonia, joint pain
Ocular: Blurred vision, visual disturbance
Otic: Tinnitus

Renal: Albuminuria, renal abscess

Respiratory: Bronchitis, pleural effusion, pneumonia, pulmonary embolism

Miscellaneous: Bacterial infection, cold symptoms, moniliasis

<1% (Limited to important or life-threatening): Abdomen enlarged, anaphylactic shock, anaphylactoid reaction, aneurysm, aphasia, appendicitis, arthritis, atrial fibrillation, basal cell carcinoma, Bell's palsy, breast carcinoma, burning eyes, cardiac arrest, CHF, CK increased, creatinine increased, deafness, diabetes insipidus, diabetes mellitus, facial edema, fatty liver, galactorrhea, gallbladder polyp, gallstones, GI hemorrhage, glaucoma, gynecomastia, hematuria, hemiparesis, hepatitis, hyperesthesia, hypertensive reaction, hypoadrenalism, intestinal obstruction, intracranial hemorrhage, iron deficiency, ischemia, joint effusion, lactation, leg cramps, LFTs increased, libido decreased, malignant hyperpyrexia, MI, migraine, muscle cramping, nephrolithiasis, orthostatic hypotension, pancreatitis, paranoia, paresis, peptic ulcer, petechiae, pituitary apoplexy, pneumothorax, pulmonary hypertension, pulmonary nodule, Raynaud's syndrome, renal insufficiency, retinal vein thrombosis, rhinorrhea, scotoma, seizure, status asthmaticus, suicide attempt, throat discomfort, thrombocytopenia, thrombophlebitis, thrombosis, vaginitis, visual field defect, wheal/erythema

Overdosage/Toxicology Symptoms of overdose include hypo- or hyperglycemia, blurred vision, dizziness, drowsiness, nausea, flushing, and loss of motor function. Well-tolerated bolus doses up to 1000 mcg have failed to produce adverse effects. Treatment is symptom-directed and supportive.

Drug Interactions

Increased Effect/Toxicity: Bioavailability of bromocriptine may be increased by octreotide. Octreotide may enhance the adverse/toxic effects of other QT_c-prolonging agents.

Decreased Effect: Octreotide may lower cyclosporine serum levels (case reports of transplant rejection due to reduction of serum cyclosporine levels when cyclosporine was given orally in conjunction with a somatostatin analogue).

Ethanol/Nutrition/Herb Interactions

Herb/Nutraceutical: Avoid hypoglycemic herbs, including alfalfa, aloe, bilberry, bitter melon, burdock, celery, damiana, fenugreek, garcinia, garlic, ginger, ginseng, gymnema, marshmallow, and stinging nettle (may enhance the hypoglycemic effect of octreotide).

Stability

Solution: Octreotide is a clear solution and should be stored under refrigeration. May be stored at room temperature for up to 14 days when protected from light. Stability of parenteral admixture is stable in NS for 96 hours at room temperature (25°C) and in D_5W for 24 hours.

Suspension: Prior to dilution, store under refrigeration and protect from light. May be at room temperature for 30-60 minutes prior to use. Use suspension immediately after preparation.

Mechanism of Action Mimics natural somatostatin by inhibiting serotonin release, and the secretion of gastrin, VIP, insulin, glucagon, secretin, motilin, and pancreatic polypeptide. Decreases growth hormone and IGF-1 in acromegaly.

Pharmacodynamics/Kinetics

Duration: SubQ: 6-12 hours

Absorption: SubQ: Rapid

Distribution: V_d: 14 L (13-30 L in acromegaly)

Protein binding: 65%, mainly to lipoprotein (41% in acromegaly)

Metabolism: Extensively hepatic

Bioavailability: SubQ: 100%; I.M.: 60% to 63% of SubQ dose

Half-life elimination: 1.7-1.9 hours; up to 3.7 hours with cirrhosis

Time to peak, plasma: SubQ: 0.4 hours (0.7 hours acromegaly); I.M.: 1 hour

Excretion: Urine (32%)

Dosage

Infants and Children:

Secretory diarrhea (unlabeled use): I.V., SubQ: Doses of 1-10 mcg/kg every 12 hours have been used in children beginning at the low end of the range and increasing by 0.3 mcg/kg/dose at 3-day intervals. Suppression of growth hormone (animal data) is of concern when used as long-term therapy.

Congenital hyperinsulinism (unlabeled use): SubQ: Doses of 3-40 mcg/kg/day have been used

Adults: SubQ, I.V.: Initial: 50 mcg 2-3 times/day and titrate dose based on patient tolerance, response, and indication

Carcinoid: Initial 2 weeks: 100-600 mcg/day in 2-4 divided doses; usual range 50-1500 mcg/day

VIPomas: Initial 2 weeks: 200-300 mcg/day in 2-4 divided doses; usual range 150-750 mcg/day

Diarrhea (unlabeled use): Initial: I.V.: 50-100 mcg every 8 hours; increase by 100 mcg/dose at 48-hour intervals; maximum dose: 500 mcg every 8 hours

Esophageal varices bleeding (unlabeled use): I.V. bolus: 25-50 mcg followed by continuous I.V. infusion of 25-50 mcg/hour

Acromegaly: Initial: SubQ: 50 mcg 3 times/day; titrate to achieve growth hormone levels <5 ng/mL or IGF-I (somatomedin C) levels <1.9 U/mL in males and <2.2 U/mL in females; usual effective dose 100 mcg 3 times/day; range 300-1500 mcg/day

Note: Should be withdrawn yearly for a 4-week interval (8 weeks for depot injection) in patients who have received irradiation. Resume if levels increase and signs/symptoms recur.

Acromegaly, carcinoid tumors, and VIPomas (depot injection): Patients must be stabilized on subcutaneous octreotide for at least 2 weeks before switching to the long-acting depot: Upon switch: 20 mg I.M. intragluteally every 4 weeks for 2-3 months, then the dose may be modified based upon response. Patients receiving depot injection for carcinoid tumor or VIPoma should continue to receive their SubQ injections for the first 2 weeks at the same dose in order to maintain therapeutic levels.

(Continued)

Octreotide *(Continued)*

Dosage adjustment for acromegaly: After 3 months of depot injections the dosage may be continued or modified as follows:

GH ≤2.5 ng/mL, IGF-1 is normal, symptoms controlled: Maintain octreotide LAR® at 20 mg I.M. every 4 weeks

GH >2.5 ng/mL, IGF-1 is elevated, and/or symptoms uncontrolled: Increase octreotide LAR® to 30 mg I.M. every 4 weeks

GH ≤1 ng/mL, IGF-1 is normal, symptoms controlled: Reduce octreotide LAR® to 10 mg I.M. every 4 weeks

Note: Patients not adequately controlled may increase dose to 40 mg every 4 weeks. Dosages >40 mg are not recommended

Dosage adjustment for carcinoid tumors and VIPomas: After 2 months of depot injections the dosage may be continued or modified as follows:

Increase to 30 mg I.M. every 4 weeks if symptoms are inadequately controlled

Decrease to 10 mg I.M. every 4 weeks, for a trial period, if initially responsive to 20 mg dose

Dosage >30 mg is not recommended

Elderly: Elimination half-life is increased by 46% and clearance is decreased by 26%; dose adjustment may be required.

Dosage adjustment in renal impairment: Severe renal failure requiring dialysis: Clearance is reduced by ~50%; specific dosing guidelines not available

Dietary Considerations Schedule injections between meals to decrease GI effects. May alter absorption of dietary fats.

Administration

Regular injection formulation (do not use if solution contains particles or is discolored): Administer SubQ or I.V.; I.V. administration may be IVP, IVPB, or continuous I.V. infusion:

IVP should be administered undiluted over 3 minutes

IVPB should be administered over 15-30 minutes

Continuous I.V. infusion rates have ranged from 25-50 mcg/hour for the treatment of esophageal variceal bleeding

Depot formulation: Administer I.M. intragluteal (avoid deltoid administration); alternate gluteal injection sites to avoid irritation. Do not administer Sandostatin LAR® intravenously or subcutaneously; must be administered immediately after mixing.

Monitoring Parameters

Acromegaly: Growth hormone, somatomedin C (IGF-1)

Carcinoid: 5-HIAA, plasma serotonin and plasma substance P

VIPomas: Vasoactive intestinal peptide

Chronic therapy: Thyroid function (baseline and periodic), vitamin B_{12} level, blood glucose, cardiac function (heart rate, EKG)

Reference Range Vasoactive intestinal peptide: <75 ng/L; levels vary considerably between laboratories

Dosage Forms

Injection, microspheres for suspension, as acetate [depot formulation]:

Sandostatin LAR®: 10 mg, 20 mg, 30 mg [with diluent and syringe]

Injection, solution, as acetate: 0.2 mg/mL (5 mL); 1 mg/mL (5 mL)

Sandostatin®: 0.2 mg/mL (5 mL); 1 mg/mL (5 mL)

Injection, solution, as acetate [preservative free]: 0.05 mg/mL (1 mL); 0.1 mg/mL (1 mL); 0.5 mg/mL (1 mL)

Sandostatin®: 0.05 mg/mL (1 mL); 0.1 mg/mL (1 mL); 0.5 mg/mL (1 mL)

♦ **Octreotide Acetate** *see* Octreotide *on page 1252*

♦ **Octreotide Acetate Injection (Can)** *see* Octreotide *on page 1252*

♦ **Octreotide Acetate Omega (Can)** *see* Octreotide *on page 1252*

♦ **Ocufen®** *see* Flurbiprofen *on page 735*

♦ **Ocuflox®** *see* Ofloxacin *on page 1254*

♦ **Ocupress® [DSC]** *see* Carteolol *on page 298*

♦ **Ocupress® Ophthalmic (Can)** *see* Carteolol *on page 298*

♦ **Oesclim® (Can)** *see* Estradiol *on page 620*

Ofloxacin *(oh FLOKS a sin)*

U.S. Brand Names Floxin®; Ocuflox®

Canadian Brand Names Apo-Oflox®; Apo-Ofloxacin®; Floxin®; Novo-Ofloxacin; Ocuflox®; PMS-Ofloxacin

Index Terms Floxin Otic Singles

Pharmacologic Category Antibiotic, Quinolone

Additional Appendix Information

Antimicrobial Drugs of Choice *on page 1981*

Prevention of Wound Infection and Sepsis in Surgical Patients *on page 1964*

Treatment of Sexually Transmitted Infections *on page 2007*

Tuberculosis *on page 2010*

Use Quinolone antibiotic for the treatment of acute exacerbations of chronic bronchitis, community-acquired pneumonia, skin and skin structure infections (uncomplicated), urethral and cervical gonorrhea (acute, uncomplicated), urethritis and cervicitis (nongonococcal), mixed infections of the urethra and cervix, pelvic inflammatory disease (acute), cystitis (uncomplicated), urinary tract infections (complicated), prostatitis

Ophthalmic: Treatment of superficial ocular infections involving the conjunctiva or cornea due to strains of susceptible organisms

Otic: Otitis externa, chronic suppurative otitis media, acute otitis media

Unlabeled/Investigational Use Epididymitis (gonorrhea), leprosy, Traveler's diarrhea

Pregnancy Risk Factor C

Pregnancy Implications Reports of arthropathy (observed in immature animals and reported rarely in humans) have limited the use of fluoroquinolones in pregnancy. Teratogenic effects were not observed with ofloxacin in animal studies; however, decreased fetal body weight and increased fetal mortality were observed in some species. Ofloxacin crosses the placenta. Although quinolone antibiotics should not be used as first-line agents during pregnancy, when considering treatment for life-threatening infection and/or prolonged duration of therapy, the potential risk to the fetus must be balanced against the severity of the potential illness.

Lactation Enters breast milk/not recommended (AAP rates "compatible")

Medication Safety Issues
Sound-alike/look-alike issues:
Floxin® may be confused with Flexeril®
Ocuflox® may be confused with Ocufen®

International issues:
Floxin® may be confused with Flogen® which is a brand name for naproxen in Mexico
Floxin® may be confused with Fluoxin® which is a brand name for fluoxetine in the Czech Republic and Romania
Floxin® may be confused with Flexin® which is a brand name for orphenadrine in Israel and indomethacin in Great Britain

Contraindications Hypersensitivity to ofloxacin or other members of the quinolone group such as nalidixic acid, oxolinic acid, cinoxacin, norfloxacin, and ciprofloxacin; hypersensitivity to any component of the formulation

Warnings/Precautions Use with caution in patients with epilepsy or other CNS diseases which could predispose seizures; potential for seizures, although very rare, may be increased with concomitant NSAID therapy. Use with caution in patients with renal or hepatic impairment. Tendon inflammation and/or rupture have been reported with quinolone antibiotics, including ofloxacin. Risk may be increased with concurrent corticosteroids, particularly in the elderly. Discontinue at first sign of tendon inflammation or pain. Peripheral neuropathies have been linked to ofloxacin use; discontinue if numbness, tingling, or weakness develops.

Rare cases of torsade de pointes have been reported in patients receiving ofloxacin and other quinolones. Risk may be minimized by avoiding use in patients with known prolongation of the QT interval, bradycardia, hypokalemia, hypomagnesemia, cardiomyopathy, or in those receiving concurrent therapy with Class Ia or Class III antiarrhythmics.

Severe hypersensitivity reactions, including anaphylaxis, have occurred with quinolone therapy. If an allergic reaction occurs (itching, urticaria, dyspnea, facial edema, loss of consciousness, tingling, cardiovascular collapse), discontinue drug immediately. Prolonged use may result in superinfection; pseudomembranous colitis may occur and should be considered in all patients who present with diarrhea. Quinolones may exacerbate myasthenia gravis.

Adverse Reactions
Systemic:
1% to 10%:
Cardiovascular: Chest pain (1% to 3%)
Central nervous system: Headache (1% to 9%), insomnia (3% to 7%), dizziness (1% to 5%), fatigue (1% to 3%), somnolence (1% to 3%), sleep disorders (1% to 3%), nervousness (1% to 3%), pyrexia (1% to 3%)
Dermatologic: Rash/pruritus (1% to 3%)
Gastrointestinal: Diarrhea (1% to 4%), vomiting (1% to 4%), GI distress (1% to 3%), abdominal cramps (1% to 3%), flatulence (1% to 3%), abnormal taste (1% to 3%), xerostomia (1% to 3%), decreased appetite (1% to 3%), nausea (3% to 10%), constipation (1% to 3%)
Genitourinary: Vaginitis (1% to 5%), external genital pruritus in women (1% to 3%)
Ocular: Visual disturbances (1% to 3%)
Respiratory: Pharyngitis (1% to 3%)
Miscellaneous: Trunk pain
<1%, postmarketing, and/or case reports (limited to important or life-threatening): Anaphylaxis reactions, anxiety, blurred vision, chills, cognitive change, cough, depression, dream abnormality, ecchymosis, edema, erythema nodosum, euphoria, extremity pain, hallucinations, hearing acuity decreased, hepatic dysfunction, hepatitis, hyper/hypoglycemia, hypertension, interstitial nephritis, lightheadedness, malaise, myasthenia gravis exacerbation, palpitation, paresthesia, peripheral neuropathy, photophobia, photosensitivity, psychotic reactions, rhabdomyolysis, seizure, Stevens-Johnson syndrome, syncope, tendonitis and tendon rupture, thirst, tinnitus, torsade de pointes, Tourette's syndrome, toxic epidermal necrolysis, vasculitis, vasodilation, vertigo, weakness, weight loss

Ophthalmic: Frequency not defined:
Central nervous system: Dizziness
Gastrointestinal: Nausea
Ocular: Blurred vision, burning, chemical conjunctivitis/keratitis, discomfort, dryness, edema, eye pain, foreign body sensation, itching, photophobia, redness, stinging, tearing

Otic:
>10%: Local: Application site reaction (<1% to 17%)
1% to 10%:
Central nervous system: Dizziness (≤1%), vertigo (≤1%)
Dermatologic: Pruritus (1% to 4%), rash (1%)
Gastrointestinal: Taste perversion (7%)
Neuromuscular & skeletal: Paresthesia (1%)
<1% (Limited to important or life-threatening): Diarrhea, fever, headache, hearing loss (transient), hypertension, nausea, otorrhagia, tinnitus, transient neuropsychiatric disturbances, tremor, vomiting, xerostomia

Overdosage/Toxicology Symptoms include acute renal failure, seizures, nausea, and vomiting. Treatment includes GI decontamination, if possible, and supportive care.
(Continued)

Ofloxacin *(Continued)*

Drug Interactions

Cytochrome P450 Effect: Inhibits CYP1A2 (strong)

Increased Effect/Toxicity: Ofloxacin may increase the effects/toxicity of CYP1A2 substrates (eg, aminophylline, fluvoxamine, mexiletine, mirtazapine, ropinirole, and trifluoperazine). Concomitant use with corticosteroids may increase the risk of tendon rupture. Concomitant use with other QT_c-prolonging agents (eg, Class Ia and Class III antiarrhythmics, erythromycin, cisapride, antipsychotics, and cyclic antidepressants) may result in arrhythmias such as torsade de pointes. Probenecid may increase ofloxacin levels. Concomitant use with NSAIDs may rarely increase risk of seizure.

Decreased Effect: Concurrent administration of metal cations, including most antacids, oral electrolyte supplements, quinapril, sucralfate, some didanosine formulations (pediatric powder for oral suspension), and other highly-buffered oral drugs, may decrease quinolone levels; separate doses.

Ethanol/Nutrition/Herb Interactions

Food: Ofloxacin average peak serum concentrations may be decreased by 20% if taken with food.

Herb/Nutraceutical: Avoid dong quai, St John's wort (may also cause photosensitization).

Stability

Ophthalmic and otic solution: Store at 15°C to 25°C (59°F to 77°F).

Otic Singles™: Store at 15°C to 30°C (59°F to 86°F). Store in pouch to protect from light.

Tablet: Store below 30°C (86°F).

Mechanism of Action

Ofloxacin is a DNA gyrase inhibitor. DNA gyrase is an essential bacterial enzyme that maintains the superhelical structure of DNA. DNA gyrase is required for DNA replication and transcription, DNA repair, recombination, and transposition; bactericidal

Pharmacodynamics/Kinetics

Absorption: Well absorbed; food causes only minor alterations

Distribution: V_d: 2.4-3.5 L/kg

Protein binding: 20%

Bioavailability: Oral: 98%

Half-life elimination: Biphasic: 5-7.5 hours and 20-25 hours (accounts for <5%); prolonged with renal impairment

Excretion: Primarily urine (as unchanged drug)

Dosage

Usual dosage range:

Children ≥6 months: Otic: 5 drops daily

Children >1 year: Ophthalmic: 1-2 drops every 30 minutes to 4 hours initially, decreasing to every 4-6 hours

Children >12 years: Otic: 10 drops once or twice daily

Adults:

Ophthalmic: 1-2 drops every 30 minutes to 4 hours initially, decreasing to every 4-6 hours

Oral: 200-400 mg every 12 hours

Otic: 10 drops once or twice daily

Indication-specific dosing:

Acute otitis media with tympanostomy tubes: Children 1-12 years: Otic: Instill 5 drops (or the contents of 1 single-dose container) into affected ear(s) twice daily for 10 days

Otitis externa: Children 6 months to 13 years: Otic: Instill 5 drops (or the contents of 1 single-dose container) into affected ear(s) once daily for 7 days

Children >1 year and Adults: Ophthalmic:

Conjunctivitis: Instill 1-2 drops in affected eye(s) every 2-4 hours for the first 2 days, then use 4 times/day for an additional 5 days

Corneal ulcer: Instill 1-2 drops every 30 minutes while awake and every 4-6 hours after retiring for the first 2 days; beginning on day 3, instill 1-2 drops every hour while awake for 4-6 additional days; thereafter, 1-2 drops 4 times/day until clinical cure.

Children >12 years and Adults:

Otitis media, chronic suppurative with perforated tympanic membranes: Otic: Instill 10 drops (or the contents of 2 single-dose containers) into affected ear twice daily for 14 days

Children ≥13 years and Adults:

Otitis externa: Otic: Instill 10 drops (or the contents of 2 single-dose containers) into affected ear(s) once daily for 7 days

Adults: Oral:

**Cervicitis/urethritis (nongonococcal) due to *C. trachomatis,* mixed infection of urethra and cervix due to *C. trachomatis* and *N. gonorrhoea:* 300 mg every 12 hours for 7 days

Chronic bronchitis (acute exacerbation), community-acquired pneumonia, skin and skin structure infections (uncomplicated): 400 mg every 12 hours for 10 days

**Cystitis (uncomplicated), *E. coli* or *K. pneumoniae:* 200 mg every 12 hours for 3 days or up to 7 days for other organisms

Epididymitis, gonoccocal (unlabeled use): 300 mg twice daily for 10 days

Leprosy (unlabeled use): 400 mg once daily

Pelvic inflammatory disease (acute): 400 mg every 12 hours for 10-14 days

Prostatitis:

Acute: 400 mg for 1 dose, then 300 mg twice daily for 10 days

Chronic: 200 mg every 12 hours for 6 weeks

Traveler's diarrhea (unlabeled use): 300 mg twice daily for 3 days

Urethral and cervical gonorrhea (acute, uncomplicated): 400 mg as a single dose

UTI (complicated): 200 mg every 12 hours for 10 days

Dosing adjustment/interval in renal impairment: Adults: Oral: After a normal initial dose, adjust as follows:

Cl_{cr} 20-50 mL/minute: Administer usual dose every 24 hours

Cl$_{cr}$ <20 mL/minute: Administer half the usual dose every 24 hours

Continuous arteriovenous or venovenous hemodiafiltration effects: Administer 300 mg every 24 hours

Dosing adjustment in hepatic impairment: Severe impairment: Maximum dose: 400 mg/day

Administration

Ophthalmic: For ophthalmic use only; avoid touching tip of applicator to eye or other surfaces.

Oral: Do not take within 2 hours of food or any antacids which contain zinc, magnesium, or aluminum.

Otic: Prior to use, warm solution by holding container in hands for 1-2 minutes. Patient should lie down with affected ear upward and medication instilled. Pump tragus 4 times to ensure penetration of medication. Patient should remain in this position for 5 minutes.

Test Interactions Some quinolones may produce a false-positive urine screening result for opiates using commercially-available immunoassay kits. This has been demonstrated most consistently for levofloxacin and ofloxacin, but other quinolones have shown cross-reactivity in certain assay kits. Confirmation of positive opiate screens by more specific methods should be considered.

Dosage Forms [DSC] = Discontinued product

Solution, ophthalmic (Ocuflox®): 0.3% (5 mL; 10 mL [DSC]) [contains benzalkonium chloride]

Solution, otic:

Floxin®: 0.3% (5 mL, 10 mL) [contains benzalkonium chloride]

Floxin® Otic Singles™: 0.3% (0.25 mL) [contains benzalkonium chloride; packaged as 2 single-dose containers per pouch, 10 pouches per carton, total net volume 5 mL]

Tablet (Floxin®): 200 mg, 300 mg, 400 mg

♦ **Ogen®** see Estropipate on page 637

♦ **Ogestrel®** see Ethinyl Estradiol and Norgestrel on page 663

♦ **OGMT** see Metyrosine on page 1134

♦ **OGT-918** see Miglustat on page 1147

♦ **OKT3** see Muromonab-CD3 on page 1179

Olanzapine (oh LAN za peen)

U.S. Brand Names Zyprexa®; Zyprexa® Zydis®

Canadian Brand Names Zyprexa®; Zyprexa® Zydis®

Index Terms LY170053; Zyprexa Zydis

Pharmacologic Category Antipsychotic Agent, Atypical

Additional Appendix Information

Antipsychotic Agents on page 1872

Use Treatment of the manifestations of schizophrenia; treatment of acute or mixed mania episodes associated with Bipolar I Disorder (as monotherapy or in combination with lithium or valproate); maintenance treatment of bipolar disorder; acute agitation (patients with schizophrenia or bipolar mania)

Unlabeled/Investigational Use Treatment of psychosis/schizophrenia in children or adolescents; chronic pain

Pregnancy Risk Factor C

Pregnancy Implications No evidence of teratogenicity reported in animal studies. However, fetal toxicity and prolonged gestation have been observed. There are no adequate and well-controlled studies in pregnant women.

Lactation Enters breast milk/not recommended

Medication Safety Issues

Sound-alike/look-alike issues:

Olanzapine may be confused with olsalazine

Zyprexa® may be confused with Celexa™, Zyrtec®

Contraindications Hypersensitivity to olanzapine or any component of the formulation

Warnings/Precautions [U.S. Boxed Warning]: Patients with dementia-related behavioral disorders treated with atypical antipsychotics are at an increased risk of death compared to placebo. An increased incidence of cerebrovascular adverse events (including fatalities) has been reported in elderly patients with dementia-related psychosis. Risk may be increased by dehydration; use caution with concurrent diuretics. Olanzapine is not approved for this indication.

Moderate to highly sedating, use with caution in disorders where CNS depression is a feature; patients must be cautioned about performing tasks which require mental alertness (eg, operating machinery or driving). Use caution in patients with cardiac disease. Use with caution in Parkinson's disease; predisposition to seizures; severe hepatic or renal disease. Life-threatening arrhythmias have occurred with therapeutic doses of some neuroleptics. May induce orthostatic hypotension; use caution with history of cardiovascular disease. Esophageal dysmotility and aspiration have been associated with antipsychotic use; use with caution in patients at risk of aspiration pneumonia. Caution in breast cancer or other prolactin-dependent tumors. Significant weight gain may occur. Impaired core body temperature regulation may occur; caution with strenuous exercise, heat exposure, dehydration, and concomitant medication possessing anticholinergic effects.

May cause anticholinergic effects; use with caution in patients with decreased gastrointestinal motility, urinary retention, BPH, xerostomia, glaucoma, or myasthenia gravis. Relative to other neuroleptics, olanzapine has a moderate potency of cholinergic blockade. May cause extrapyramidal symptoms, although risk of these reactions is lower relative to other neuroleptics). May be associated with neuroleptic malignant syndrome (NMS). May cause extreme and life-threatening hyperglycemia; use with caution in patients with diabetes or other disorders of glucose regulation; monitor. Olanzapine levels may be lower in patients who smoke, requiring dosage adjustment.

The possibility of a suicide attempt is inherent in psychotic illness or bipolar disorder; use caution in high-risk patients during initiation of therapy. Prescriptions should be written for the (Continued)

Olanzapine *(Continued)*

smallest quantity consistent with good patient care. Safety and efficacy in pediatric patients have not been established.

Intramuscular administration: Patients should remain recumbent if drowsy/dizzy until hypotension, bradycardia and/or hypoventilation has been ruled out. Concurrent use of I.M./I.V. benzodiazepines is not recommended (fatalities have been reported, though causality not determined)

Adverse Reactions

>10%:

Central nervous system: Somnolence (6% to 39% dose-dependent), extrapyramidal symptoms (15% to 32% dose-dependent), insomnia (up to 12%), dizziness (4% to 18%)

Gastrointestinal: Dyspepsia (7% to 11%), constipation (9% to 11%), weight gain (5% to 6%, has been reported as high as 40%), xerostomia (9% to 22% dose-dependent)

Neuromuscular & skeletal: Weakness (2% to 20% dose-dependent)

Miscellaneous: Accidental injury (12%)

1% to 10%:

Cardiovascular: Postural hypotension (1% to 5%), tachycardia (up to 3%), peripheral edema (up to 3%), chest pain (up to 3%), hyper-/hypotension (up to 2%)

Central nervous system: Personality changes (8%), speech disorder (7%), fever (up to 6%), abnormal dreams, euphoria, amnesia, delusions, emotional lability, mania, schizophrenia

Dermatologic: Bruising (up to 5%)

Endocrine & metabolic: Cholesterol increased, prolactin increased

Gastrointestinal: Nausea (up to 9% dose-dependent), appetite increased (3% to 6%), vomiting (up to 4%), flatulence, salivation increased, thirst

Genitourinary: Incontinence (up to 2%), UTI (up to 2%), vaginitis

Hepatic: ALT increased (2%)

Local: Injection site pain (I.M. administration)

Neuromuscular & skeletal: Tremor (1% to 7% dose-dependent), abnormal gait (6%), back pain (up to 5%), joint/extremity pain (up to 5%), akathisia (3% to 5% dose-dependent), hypertonia (up to 3%), articulation impairment (up to 2%), falling (particularly in older patients), joint stiffness, paresthesia, twitching

Ocular: Amblyopia (up to 3%), conjunctivitis

Respiratory: Rhinitis (up to 7%), cough (up to 6%), pharyngitis (up to 4%), dyspnea

Miscellaneous: Dental pain, diaphoresis, flu-like syndrome

<1% (Limited to important or life-threatening): Acidosis, akinesia, albuminuria, alkaline phosphatase increased, anaphylactoid reaction, anemia, angioedema, apnea, arteritis, asthma, ataxia, atelectasis, atrial fibrillation, AV block, bilirubinemia, bradycardia, cataract, cerebrovascular accident, CNS stimulation, coma, confusion, congestive heart failure, creatine phosphokinase increased, cyanosis, deafness, dehydration, diabetes mellitus, diabetic acidosis, diabetic coma, diarrhea, dyskinesia, dysphagia, dysuria, encephalopathy, enteritis, esophageal ulcer, facial paralysis, fecal impaction, fecal incontinence, gastritis, gastroenteritis, glaucoma, gout, gynecomastia, heart arrest, heart block, heart failure, hematuria, hemoptysis; hemorrhage (eye, rectal, subarachnoid, vaginal); hepatitis, hyper-/hypoglycemia, hypo-/hyperkalemia, hyperlipemia, hypo-/hypernatremia, hyperuricemia, hyper-/hypoventilation, hypoesthesia, hypokinesia, hypoproteinemia, hypoxia, jaundice, ileus, ketosis, leukocytosis (eosinophilia), leukopenia, liver damage (cholestatic or mixed), liver fatty deposit, lung edema, lymphadenopathy, menstrual irregularities, migraine, myasthenia, myopathy, neuralgia, neuroleptic malignant syndrome, neuropathy, normocytic anemia, osteoporosis, palpitation, pancreatitis, paralysis, priapism, pulmonary embolus, rhabdomyolysis, rheumatoid arthritis, seizure, stridor, sudden death, suicide attempt, syncope, tardive dyskinesia, thrombocythemia, thrombocytopenia, tongue edema, triglycerides increased, urination impaired, uterine fibroids enlarged, ventricular extrasystoles, venous thrombotic events, vomiting, withdrawal syndrome

Overdosage/Toxicology

Signs and symptoms of overdose include CNS depression (ranging from drowsiness to coma), extrapyramidal movements, fasciculations, hypotension (possible, though not described), miosis, respiratory depression, rhinitis (10%), slurred speech, tachycardia, trismus, and possible NMS. Treatment is symptom-directed and supportive. Cardiac monitoring should be initiated, including continuous EEG monitoring. Activated charcoal (1 g) may reduce the C_{max} and AUC of olanzapine by ~60%.

Drug Interactions

Cytochrome P450 Effect: Substrate of CYP1A2 (major), 2D6 (minor); **Inhibits** CYP1A2 (weak), 2C9 (weak), 2C19 (weak), 2D6 (weak), 3A4 (weak)

Increased Effect/Toxicity: Olanzapine levels may be increased by CYP1A2 inhibitors such as cimetidine and fluvoxamine. Sedation from olanzapine is increased with ethanol or other CNS depressants. Concomitant use with pramlintide and other anticholinergic agents may result in increased anticholinergic adverse effects. Concomitant use with ciprofloxacin may increase the levels/effects of olanzapine. Use of acetylcholinesterase inhibitors (central) or lithium may increase the risk of antipsychotic-related EPS. Concurrent use of intramuscular olanzapine and parenteral benzodiazepines may increase the risk of cardiopulmonary toxicity.

Decreased Effect: Olanzapine levels may be decreased by CYP1A2 inducers such as rifampin, omeprazole, and carbamazepine (also cigarette smoking).

Ethanol/Nutrition/Herb Interactions

Ethanol: Avoid ethanol (may increase CNS depression).

Herb/Nutraceutical: Avoid dong quai, St John's wort (may also cause photosensitization). Avoid kava kava, gotu kola, valerian, St John's wort (may increase CNS depression).

Stability

Injection, powder for reconstitution: Store at room temperature 15°C to 30°C (59°F to 86°F); do not freeze. Protect from light. Reconstitute 10 mg vial with 2.1 mL SWFI. Resulting solution is ~5 mg/mL. Use immediately (within 1 hour) following reconstitution. Discard any unused portion.

Tablet and orally-disintegrating tablet: Store at room temperature of 15°C to 30°C (59°F to 86°F). Protect from light and moisture.

Mechanism of Action Olanzapine is a second generation thienobenzodiazepine antipsychotic which displays potent antagonist of serotonin 5-HT$_{2A}$ and 5-HT$_{2C}$, dopamine D$_{1-4}$, muscarinic M$_{1-5}$, histamine H$_1$- and alpha$_1$-adrenergic receptors. Olanzapine shows moderate antagonism of 5-HT$_3$ and muscarinic M$_{1-5}$ receptors, and weak binding to GABA-A, BZD, and beta-adrenergic receptors. Although the precise mechanism of action in schlzophrenia and bipolar disorder is not known, the efficacy of olanzapine is thought to be mediated through combined antagonism of dopamine and serotonin type 2 receptor sites.

Pharmacodynamics/Kinetics

Absorption:

I.M.: Rapidly absorbed

Oral: Well absorbed; not affected by food; tablets and orally-disintegrating tablets are bioequivalent

Distribution: V$_d$: Extensive, 1000 L

Protein binding, plasma: 93% bound to albumin and alpha$_1$-glycoprotein

Metabolism: Highly metabolized via direct glucuronidation and cytochrome P450 mediated oxidation (CYP1A2, CYP2D6); 40% removed via first pass metabolism

Bioavailability: >57%

Half-life elimination: 21-54 hours; ~1.5 times greater in elderly

Time to peak, plasma: Maximum plasma concentrations after I.M. administration are 5 times higher than maximum plasma concentrations produced by an oral dose.

I.M.: 15-45 minutes

Oral: ~6 hours

Excretion: Urine (57%, 7% as unchanged drug); feces (30%)

Clearance: 40% increase in olanzapine clearance in smokers; 30% decrease in females

Dosage

Children: Schizophrenia/bipolar disorder (unlabeled use): Oral: Initial: 2.5 mg/day; titrate as necessary to 20 mg/day (0.12-0.29 mg/kg/day)

Adults:

Schizophrenia: Oral: Initial: 5-10 mg once daily (increase to 10 mg once daily within 5-7 days); thereafter, adjust by 5 mg/day at 1-week intervals, up to a recommended maximum of 20 mg/day. Maintenance: 10-20 mg once daily. **Note:** Doses of 30-50 mg/day have been used; however, doses >10 mg/day have not demonstrated better efficacy, and safety and efficacy of doses >20 mg/day have not been evaluated.

Bipolar I acute mixed or manic episodes: Oral:

Monotherapy: Initial: 10-15 mg once daily; increase by 5 mg/day at intervals of not less than 24 hours. Maintenance: 5-20 mg/day; recommended maximum dose: 20 mg/day

Combination therapy (with lithium or valproate): Initial: 10 mg once daily; dosing range: 5-20 mg/day

Agitation (acute, associated with bipolar I mania or schizophrenia): I.M.: Initial dose: 5-10 mg (a lower dose of 2.5 mg may be considered when clinical factors warrant); additional doses (2.5-10 mg) may be considered; however, 2-4 hours should be allowed between doses to evaluate response (maximum total daily dose: 30 mg, per manufacturer's recommendation)

Elderly: Oral, I.M.: Consider lower starting dose of 2.5-5 mg/day for elderly or debilitated patients; may increase as clinically indicated and tolerated with close monitoring of orthostatic blood pressure

Dosage adjustment in renal impairment: No adjustment required. Not removed by dialysis

Dosage adjustment in hepatic impairment: Dosage adjustment may be necessary, however, there are no specific recommendations. Monitor closely.

Dietary Considerations Tablets may be taken with or without food. Zyprexa® Zydis®: 5 mg tablet contains phenylalanine 0.34 mg; 10 mg tablet contains phenylalanine 0.45 mg; 15 mg tablet contains phenylalanine 0.67 mg; 20 mg tablet contains phenylalanine 0.9 mg

Administration

Injection: For I.M. administration only; do not administer injection intravenously; inject slowly, deep into muscle. If dizziness and/or drowsiness are noted, patient should remain recumbent until examination indicates postural hypotension and/or bradycardia are not a problem.

Tablet: May be administered with or without food.

Orally-disintegrating: Remove from foil blister by peeling back (do not push tablet through the foil); place tablet in mouth immediately upon removal; tablet dissolves rapidly in saliva and may be swallowed with or without liquid. May be administered with or without food/meals.

Monitoring Parameters Vital signs; fasting lipid profile and fasting blood glucose/Hgb A$_{1c}$ (prior to treatment, at 3 months, then annually); periodic assessment of hepatic transaminases (in patients with hepatic disease); BMI, personal/family history of obesity, waist circumference; orthostatic blood pressure; mental status, abnormal involuntary movement scale (AIMS), extrapyramidal symptoms (EPS). Weight should be assessed prior to treatment, at 4 weeks, 8 weeks, 12 weeks, and then at quarterly intervals. Consider titrating to a different antipsychotic agent for a weight gain ≥5% of the initial weight.

Dosage Forms

Injection, powder for reconstitution (Zyprexa® IntraMuscular): 10 mg [contains lactose 50 mg]

Tablet (Zyprexa®): 2.5 mg, 5 mg, 7.5 mg, 10 mg, 15 mg, 20 mg

Tablet, orally disintegrating (Zyprexa® Zydis®): 5 mg [contains phenylalanine 0.34 mg/tablet], 10 mg [contains phenylalanine 0.45 mg/tablet], 15 mg [contains phenylalanine 0.67 mg/tablet], 20 mg [contains phenylalanine 0.9 mg/tablet]

Olanzapine and Fluoxetine (oh LAN za peen & floo OKS e teen)

U.S. Brand Names Symbyax™

Index Terms Fluoxetine and Olanzapine; Olanzapine and Fluoxetine Hydrochloride

Pharmacologic Category Antidepressant, Selective Serotonin Reuptake Inhibitor; Antipsychotic Agent, Atypical

Use Treatment of depressive episodes associated with bipolar disorder

(Continued)

Olanzapine and Fluoxetine *(Continued)*

Restrictions An FDA-approved medication guide concerning the use of antidepressants in children and teenagers must be distributed when dispensing an outpatient prescription (new or refill) where this medication is to be used without direct supervision of a healthcare provider. Medication guides are available at http://www.fda.gov/cder/Offices/ODS/medication_guides.htm. Dispense to parents or guardians of children and teenagers receiving this medication.

Pregnancy Risk Factor C

Dosage Oral:

Adults: Depression associated with bipolar disorder: Initial: Olanzapine 6 mg/fluoxetine 25 mg once daily in the evening. Dosing range: Olanzapine 6-12 mg/fluoxetine 25-50 mg. Use caution adjusting dose in patients predisposed to hypotension, in females, and in nonsmokers (metabolism may be decreased). Safety of daily doses of olanzapine >18 mg/ fluoxetine >75 mg have not been evaluated.

Elderly: Initial: Olanzapine 6 mg/fluoxetine 25 mg once daily in the evening; use caution adjusting dose (metabolism may be decreased). Safety and efficacy have not been established in patients >65 years of age.

Dosage adjustment in hepatic impairment: Initial: Olanzapine 6 mg/fluoxetine 25 mg once daily in the evening; use caution adjusting dose (metabolism may be decreased).

Additional Information Complete prescribing information for this medication should be consulted for additional detail.

Dosage Forms Capsule:

6/25: Olanzapine 6 mg and fluoxetine 25 mg
6/50: Olanzapine 6 mg and fluoxetine 50 mg
12/25: Olanzapine 12 mg and fluoxetine 25 mg
12/50: Olanzapine 12 mg and fluoxetine 50 mg

♦ **Olanzapine and Fluoxetine Hydrochloride** *see* Olanzapine and Fluoxetine *on page 1259*
♦ **Oleovitamin A** *see* Vitamin A *on page 1793*

Olmesartan *(ole me SAR tan)*

U.S. Brand Names Benicar®

Index Terms Olmesartan Medoxomil

Pharmacologic Category Angiotensin II Receptor Blocker

Additional Appendix Information
Angiotensin Agents *on page 1860*

Use Treatment of hypertension with or without concurrent use of other antihypertensive agents

Pregnancy Risk Factor C/D (2nd and 3rd trimesters)

Pregnancy Implications The drug should be discontinued as soon as possible when pregnancy is detected. Drugs which act directly on renin-angiotensin can cause fetal and neonatal morbidity and death.

Lactation Excretion in breast milk unknown/contraindicated

Contraindications Hypersensitivity to olmesartan or any component of the formulation; hypersensitivity to other A-II receptor antagonists; bilateral renal artery stenosis; pregnancy

Warnings/Precautions [U.S. Boxed Warning]: Based on human data, drugs that act on the angiotensin system can cause injury and death to the developing fetus when used in the second and third trimesters. Angiotensin receptor blockers should be discontinued as soon as possible once pregnancy is detected. May cause hyperkalemia; avoid potassium supplementation unless specifically required by healthcare provider. Avoid use or use a smaller dose in patients who are volume depleted; correct depletion first. May be associated with deterioration of renal function and/or increases in serum creatinine, particularly in patients dependent on renin-angiotensin-aldosterone system. Use with caution in unilateral renal artery stenosis and pre-existing renal insufficiency; significant aortic/mitral stenosis. Safety and efficacy in pediatric patients have not been established.

Adverse Reactions

1% to 10%:
Central nervous system: Dizziness (3%), headache
Endocrine & metabolic: Hyperglycemia, hypertriglyceridemia
Gastrointestinal: Diarrhea
Neuromuscular & skeletal: Back pain, CPK increased
Renal: Hematuria
Respiratory: Bronchitis, pharyngitis, rhinitis, sinusitis
Miscellaneous: Flu-like syndrome

<1% (Limited to important or life-threatening): Abdominal pain, acute renal failure, alopecia, angioedema, arthralgia, arthritis, bilirubin increased, chest pain, dyspepsia, facial edema, fatigue, gastroenteritis, hypercholesterolemia, hyperlipidemia, hyperuricemia, insomnia, liver enzymes increased, myalgia, nausea, pain, peripheral edema, pruritus, rash, rhabdomyolysis, serum creatinine increased, skeletal pain, tachycardia, urinary tract infection, urticaria, vertigo, vomiting

Drug Interactions

Increased Effect/Toxicity: The risk of hyperkalemia may be increased during concomitant use with potassium-sparing diuretics, potassium supplements, and trimethoprim; may increase risk of lithium toxicity.

Decreased Effect: NSAIDs may decrease the efficacy of olmesartan.

Ethanol/Nutrition/Herb Interactions

Food: Does not affect olmesartan bioavailability.

Herb/Nutraceutical: Avoid ephedra, yohimbe, ginseng (may worsen hypertension). Avoid garlic (may have increased antihypertensive effect).

Stability Store at 20°C to 25°C (68°F to 77°F).

Mechanism of Action As a selective and competitive, nonpeptide angiotensin II receptor antagonist, olmesartan blocks the vasoconstrictor and aldosterone-secreting effects of angiotensin II; olmesartan interacts reversibly at the AT1 and AT2 receptors of many tissues and has slow dissociation kinetics; its affinity for the AT1 receptor is 12,500 times greater than the AT2 receptor. Angiotensin II receptor antagonists may induce a more complete inhibition of the renin-angiotensin system than ACE inhibitors, they do not affect the response to brady-kinin, and are less likely to be associated with nonrenin-angiotensin effects (eg, cough and angioedema). Olmesartan increases urinary flow rate and, in addition to being natriuretic and kaliuretic, increases excretion of chloride, magnesium, uric acid, calcium, and phosphate.

Pharmacodynamics/Kinetics
Distribution: 17 L; does not cross the blood-brain barrier (animal studies)
Protein binding: 99%
Metabolism: Olmesartan medoxomil is hydrolyzed in the GI tract to active olmesartan. No further metabolism occurs.
Bioavailability: 26%
Half-life elimination: Terminal: 13 hours
Time to peak: 1-2 hours
Excretion: All as unchanged drug: Feces (50% to 65%); urine (35% to 50%)

Dosage Oral:
Adults: Initial: Usual starting dose is 20 mg once daily; if initial response is inadequate, may be increased to 40 mg once daily after 2 weeks. May administer with other antihypertensive agents if blood pressure inadequately controlled with olmesartan. Consider lower starting dose in patients with possible depletion of intravascular volume (eg, patients receiving diuretics).
Elderly: No dosage adjustment necessary
Dosage adjustment in renal impairment: No specific guidelines for dosage adjustment; patients undergoing hemodialysis have not been studied.
Dosage adjustment in hepatic impairment: No adjustment necessary.
Dietary Considerations May be taken with or without food.
Administration May be administered with or without food.
Monitoring Parameters Blood pressure, serum potassium
Dosage Forms Tablet, as medoxomil: 5 mg, 20 mg, 40 mg

Olmesartan and Hydrochlorothiazide
(ole me SAR tan & hye droe klor oh THYE a zide)

U.S. Brand Names Benicar HCT®
Index Terms Hydrochlorothiazide and Olmesartan Medoxomil; Olmesartan Medoxomil and Hydrochlorothiazide
Pharmacologic Category Angiotensin II Receptor Blocker Combination; Antihypertensive Agent, Combination; Diuretic, Thiazide
Use Treatment of hypertension (not recommended for initial treatment)
Pregnancy Risk Factor C/D (2nd and 3rd trimesters)
Dosage Oral: Adults: One tablet daily; dosage must be individualized (see below). May be titrated at 2- to 4-week intervals.
Replacement therapy: May be substituted for previously titrated dosages of the individual components.
Patients not controlled with single-agent therapy: Initiate by adding the lowest available dose of the alternative component (hydrochlorothiazide 12.5 mg or olmesartan 20 mg). Titrate to effect (maximum daily hydrochlorothiazide dose: 25 mg; maximum daily olmesartan dose: 40 mg).
Dosage adjustment in renal impairment: Not recommended in patients with Cl_{cr} <30 mL/minute
Additional Information Complete prescribing information for this medication should be consulted for additional detail.
Dosage Forms Tablet:
20/12.5: Olmesartan medoxomil 20 mg and hydrochlorothiazide 12.5 mg
40/12.5: Olmesartan medoxomil 40 mg and hydrochlorothiazide 12.5 mg
40/25: Olmesartan medoxomil 40 mg and hydrochlorothiazide 25 mg

◆ **Olmesartan Medoxomil** see Olmesartan on page 1260
◆ **Olmesartan Medoxomil and Hydrochlorothiazide** see Olmesartan and Hydrochlorothiazide on page 1261

Olopatadine (oh la PAT a deen)

U.S. Brand Names Patanol®
Canadian Brand Names Patanol®
Pharmacologic Category Antihistamine; Ophthalmic Agent, Miscellaneous
Use Treatment of the signs and symptoms of allergic conjunctivitis
Pregnancy Risk Factor C
Pregnancy Implications Teratogenic effects were not observed in animal studies.
Medication Safety Issues
Sound-alike/look-alike issues:
Patanol® may be confused with Platinol®

International issues:
Patanol® may be confused with Betanol® which is a brand name for metipranolol in Monaco and a brand name for atenolol in Bangladesh
Contraindications Hypersensitivity to olopatadine hydrochloride or any component of the formulation
Warnings/Precautions Contains benzalkonium chloride which may be absorbed by contact lenses; do not wear contact lenses if eyes are red. Safety and efficacy in children <3 years of age have not been established.
Adverse Reactions
>5%: Central nervous system: Headache (7%)
(Continued)

Olopatadine *(Continued)*

<5%:
    Central nervous system: Cold syndrome
    Gastrointestinal: Nausea, taste perversion
    Neuromuscular & skeletal: Weakness
    Ocular: Blurred vision, burning, stinging, dry eyes, foreign body sensation, hyperemia, keratitis, eyelid edema, itching
    Respiratory: Pharyngitis, rhinitis, sinusitis

Pharmacodynamics/Kinetics
Absorption: Low systemic absorption following topical administration
Half-life elimination: ~3 hours
Excretion: Urine (60% to 70%)

Dosage Adults: Ophthalmic: Instill 1 to 2 drops into affected eye(s) twice daily (allowing 6-8 hours between doses); results from an environmental study demonstrated that olopatadine was effective when dosed twice daily for up to 6 weeks

Administration After instilling drops, wait at least 10 minutes before inserting contact lenses. Do not insert contacts if eyes are red.

Dosage Forms Solution, ophthalmic: 0.1% (5 mL) [contains benzalkonium chloride]

Olsalazine (ole SAL a zeen)

U.S. Brand Names Dipentum®
Canadian Brand Names Dipentum®
Index Terms Olsalazine Sodium
Pharmacologic Category 5-Aminosalicylic Acid Derivative
Use Maintenance of remission of ulcerative colitis in patients intolerant to sulfasalazine
Pregnancy Risk Factor C
Lactation Enters breast milk/use caution (monitor for diarrhea)
Medication Safety Issues
Sound-alike/look-alike issues:
    Olsalazine may be confused with olanzapine
    Dipentum® may be confused with Dilantin®
Contraindications Hypersensitivity to olsalazine, salicylates, or any component of the formulation
Warnings/Precautions Diarrhea is a common adverse effect of olsalazine; use with caution in patients with hypersensitivity to salicylates, sulfasalazine, or mesalamine. May exacerbate symptoms of colitis. Use with caution in patients with renal impairment. Safety and efficacy have not been established in children.
Adverse Reactions
>10%: Gastrointestinal: Diarrhea, cramps, abdominal pain
1% to 10%:
    Central nervous system: Headache, fatigue, depression
    Dermatologic: Rash, itching
    Gastrointestinal: Nausea, heartburn, bloating, anorexia
    Neuromuscular & skeletal: Arthralgia
<1% (Limited to important or life-threatening): Blood dyscrasias, cholestatic jaundice, cirrhosis, hepatic necrosis, hepatitis, jaundice, Kawasaki-like syndrome
Overdosage/Toxicology Symptoms include decreased motor activity and diarrhea.
Drug Interactions
Increased Effect/Toxicity: Olsalazine has been reported to increase the prothrombin time in patients taking warfarin. Olsalazine may increase the risk of myelosuppression with azathioprine, mesalamine, or sulfasalazine.
Mechanism of Action The mechanism of action appears to be topical rather than systemic
Pharmacodynamics/Kinetics
Absorption: <3%; very little intact olsalazine is systemically absorbed
Protein binding, plasma: >99%
Metabolism: Primarily via colonic bacteria to active drug, 5-aminosalicylic acid
Half-life elimination: 56 minutes
Time to peak: ~1 hour
Excretion: Primarily feces
Dosage Adults: Oral: 1 g/day in 2 divided doses
Dietary Considerations Administer with food, increases residence of drug in body.
Administration Take with food in evenly divided doses.
Monitoring Parameters Stool frequency
Test Interactions Increased ALT, AST (S)
Dosage Forms Capsule, as sodium: 250 mg

♦ **Olsalazine Sodium** see Olsalazine on page 1262
♦ **Olux®** see Clobetasol on page 391
♦ **Omacor®** see Omega-3-Acid Ethyl Esters on page 1264

Omalizumab (oh mah lye ZOO mab)

U.S. Brand Names Xolair®
Canadian Brand Names Xolair®
Index Terms rhuMAb-E25
Pharmacologic Category Monoclonal Antibody, Anti-Asthmatic
Use Treatment of moderate-to-severe, persistent allergic asthma not adequately controlled with inhaled corticosteroids
Pregnancy Risk Factor B

Pregnancy Implications Teratogenic effects were not observed in animal studies. There are no adequate and well-controlled studies in pregnant women. IgG molecules are known to cross the placenta; use during pregnancy only if clearly needed.

Lactation Excretion in breast milk unknown/use caution

Contraindications Hypersensitivity to omalizumab or any component of the formulation; acute bronchospasm, status asthmaticus

Warnings/Precautions For use in patients with a documented reactivity to a perennial aeroallergen and with symptoms uncontrolled using inhaled corticosteroids; not used to control acute asthma symptoms. Dosing is based on pretreatment IgE serum levels and body weight. IgE levels remain elevated up to 1 year following treatment, therefore, levels taken during treatment can not be used as a dosage guide. Corticosteroid therapy should be tapered gradually, do not discontinue abruptly. Anaphylactic reactions have been reported within 2 hours of initial dose; appropriate medications for the treatment of hypersensitivity reactions should be available. Malignant neoplasms have been reported with use in short-term studies; impact of long-term use is not known. Use caution with and monitor patients at risk for parasitic (helminth) infections. Safety and efficacy in children <12 years of age have not been established.

Adverse Reactions

>10%:
 Central nervous system: Headache (15%)
 Local: Injection site reaction (45%; placebo 43%; severe 12%). Most reactions occurred within 1 hour, lasted <8 days, and decreased in frequency with additional dosing.
 Respiratory: Upper respiratory tract infection (20%), sinusitis (16%), pharyngitis (11%)
 Miscellaneous: Viral infection (23%)

1% to 10%:
 Central nervous system: Pain (7%), fatigue (3%), dizziness (3%)
 Dermatologic: Dermatitis (2%), pruritus (2%)
 Neuromuscular & skeletal: Arthralgia (8%), leg pain (4%), arm pain (2%), fracture (2%)
 Otic: Earache (2%)

<1% (Limited to important or life-threatening): Alopecia, anaphylaxis, antibody formation to omalizumab, dermatitis, malignancy (0.5%; placebo 0.2%), throat edema, thrombocytopenia, tongue edema, urticaria

Overdosage/Toxicology Limited data; single doses up to 4000 mg and cumulative doses up to 44,000 mg (over 20 weeks) have not been associated with toxicity. Treatment is symptom-directed and supportive.

Stability Prior to reconstitution, store under refrigeration at 2°C to 8°C (36°F to 46°F); product may be shipped at room temperature. Prepare using SWFI, USP only; add SWFI 1.4 mL to upright vial and swirl gently for 5-10 seconds every 5 minutes until dissolved, may take >20 minutes to dissolve completely. Resulting solution is 150 mg/1.2 mL. Do not use if powder takes >40 minutes to dissolve. Following reconstitution, protect from direct sunlight. May be stored for up to 8 hours if refrigerated or 4 hours if stored at room temperature.

Mechanism of Action Omalizumab is an IgG monoclonal antibody (recombinant DNA-derived) which inhibits IgE binding to the high-affinity IgE receptor on mast cells and basophils. By decreasing bound IgE, the activation and release of mediators in the allergic response (early and late phase) is limited. Serum free IgE levels and the number of high-affinity IgE receptors are decreased. Long-term treatment in patients with allergic asthma showed a decrease in asthma exacerbations and corticosteroid usage.

Pharmacodynamics/Kinetics

Absorption: Slow following SubQ injection
Distribution: V_d: 78 ± 32 mL/kg
Metabolism: Hepatic; IgG degradation by reticuloendothelial system and endothelial cells
Bioavailability: 62%
Half-life elimination: 26 days
Time to peak: 7-8 days
Excretion: Primarily via hepatic degradation; intact IgG may be secreted in bile

Dosage SubQ: Children ≥12 years and Adults: Asthma: Dose is based on pretreatment IgE serum levels and body weight. Dosing should not be adjusted based on IgE levels taken during treatment or <1 year following discontinuation of therapy; doses should be adjusted during treatment for significant changes in body weight

IgE ≥30-100 int. units/mL:
 30-90 kg: 150 mg every 4 weeks
 >90-150 kg: 300 mg every 4 weeks

IgE >100-200 int. units/mL:
 30-90 kg: 300 mg every 4 weeks
 >90-150 kg: 225 mg every 2 weeks

IgE >200-300 int. units/mL:
 30-60 kg: 300 mg every 4 weeks
 >60-90 kg: 225 mg every 2 weeks
 >90-150 kg: 300 mg every 2 weeks

IgE >300-400 int. units/mL:
 30-70 kg: 225 mg every 2 weeks
 >70-90 kg: 300 mg every 2 weeks
 >90 kg: Do not administer dose

IgE >400-500 int. units/mL:
 30-70 kg: 300 mg every 2 weeks
 >70-90 kg: 375 mg every 2 weeks
 >90 kg: Do not administer dose

IgE >500-600 int. units/mL:
 30-60 kg: 300 mg every 2 weeks
 >60-70 kg: 375 mg every 2 weeks
 >70 kg: Do not administer dose

IgE >600-700 int. units/mL:
 30-60 kg: 375 mg every 2 weeks
 >60 kg: Do not administer dose

(Continued)

Omalizumab (Continued)

Administration For SubQ injection only; doses >150 mg should divided over more than one site. Injections may take 5-10 seconds to administer.

Monitoring Parameters Baseline IgE; FEV$_1$, peak flow, and/or other pulmonary function tests

Test Interactions Total IgE levels are elevated for up to 1 year following treatment. Total serum IgE may be retested after interruption of therapy for 1 year or more.

Dosage Forms
Injection, powder for reconstitution [preservative free]:
Xolair®: 150 mg [contains sucrose 145.5 g]

Omega-3-Acid Ethyl Esters (oh MEG a three AS id ETH il ES ters)

U.S. Brand Names Omacor®

Index Terms Ethyl Esters of Omega-3 Fatty Acids; Fish Oil

Pharmacologic Category Antilipemic Agent, Miscellaneous

Use Omacor®: Treatment of hypertriglyceridemia (≥500 mg/dL)

Note: A number of OTC formulations containing omega-3 fatty acids are marketed as nutritional supplements; these do not have FDA-approved indications.

Unlabeled/Investigational Use Omacor®: Treatment of IgA nephropathy

Pregnancy Risk Factor C

Medication Safety Issues
Sound-alike/look-alike issues:
Omacor® may be confused with Amicar®

Dosage Oral: Adults:
Hypertriglyceridemia: 4 g/day as a single daily dose or in 2 divided doses
Treatment of IgA nephropathy (unlabeled use): 4 g/day

Dosage adjustment in renal impairment: No dosage adjustment required.

Additional Information Complete prescribing information for this medication should be consulted for additional detail.

Dosage Forms Capsule: 1 g [contains EPA ~465 mg and DHA ~375 mg]

Omeprazole (oh MEP ra zole)

U.S. Brand Names Prilosec®; Prilosec OTC™ [OTC]

Canadian Brand Names Apo-Omeprazole®; Losec®; Losec MUPS®

Pharmacologic Category Proton Pump Inhibitor; Substituted Benzimidazole

Additional Appendix Information
Antimicrobial Drugs of Choice on page 1981
Helicobacter pylori Treatment on page 2056

Use Short-term (4-8 weeks) treatment of active duodenal ulcer disease or active benign gastric ulcer; treatment of heartburn and other symptoms associated with gastroesophageal reflux disease (GERD); short-term (4-8 weeks) treatment of endoscopically-diagnosed erosive esophagitis; maintenance healing of erosive esophagitis; long-term treatment of pathological hypersecretory conditions; as part of a multidrug regimen for H. pylori eradication to reduce the risk of duodenal ulcer recurrence

OTC labeling: Short-term treatment of frequent, uncomplicated heartburn occurring ≥2 days/week

Unlabeled/Investigational Use Healing NSAID-induced ulcers; prevention of NSAID-induced ulcers

Pregnancy Risk Factor C

Pregnancy Implications Crosses the placenta; congenital abnormalities have been reported sporadically following omeprazole use during pregnancy. Based on data collected by the Teratogen Information System (TERIS), it was concluded that therapeutic doses used during pregnancy would be unlikely to pose a substantial teratogenic risk (quantity/quality of data: fair). Because the possibility of harm still exists, the manufacturer recommends use during pregnancy only if the potential benefit to the mother outweighs the possible risk to the fetus.

Lactation Enters breast milk/not recommended

Medication Safety Issues
Sound-alike/look-alike issues:
Prilosec® may be confused with Plendil®, Prevacid®, predniSONE, prilocaine, Prinivil®, Proventil®, Prozac®

International issues:
Norpramin®: Brand name for desipramine in the U.S.

Contraindications Hypersensitivity to omeprazole, substituted benzimidazoles (ie, esomeprazole, lansoprazole, pantoprazole, rabeprazole), or any component of the formulation

Warnings/Precautions Relief of symptoms does not preclude the presence of a gastric malignancy. Atrophic gastritis (by biopsy) has been noted with long-term omeprazole therapy. In long-term (2-year) studies in rats, omeprazole produced a dose-related increase in gastric carcinoid tumors. While available endoscopic evaluations and histologic examinations of biopsy specimens from human stomachs have not detected a risk from short-term exposure to omeprazole, further human data on the effect of sustained hypochlorhydria and hypergastrinemia are needed to rule out the possibility of an increased risk for the development of tumors in humans receiving long-term therapy. Bioavailability may be increased in the elderly, Asian population, and with hepatic dysfunction. Safety and efficacy have not been established in children <2 years of age. When used for self-medication (OTC), do not use for >14 days; treatment should not be repeated more often than every 4 months; OTC and oral suspension are not approved for use in children <18 years of age.

Adverse Reactions
1% to 10%:
Central nervous system: Headache (3% to 7%), dizziness (2%)

Dermatologic: Rash (2%)

Gastrointestinal: Diarrhea (3% to 4%), abdominal pain (2% to 5%), nausea (2% to 4%), vomiting (2% to 3%), flatulence (3%), acid regurgitation (2%), constipation (1% to 2%), taste perversion

Neuromuscular & skeletal: Weakness (1%), back pain (1%)

Respiratory: Upper respiratory infection (2%), cough (1%)

<1% (Limited to important or life-threatening; adverse event occurrence may vary based on formulation): Abdominal swelling, abnormal dreams, aggression, agranulocytosis, alkaline phosphatase increased, allergic reactions, alopecia, anaphylaxis, anemia, angina, angioedema, anorexia, anxiety, apathy, atrophic gastritis, benign gastric polyps, blurred vision, confusion, creatinine increased, depression, diaphoresis, double vision, dry mouth, dry skin, epistaxis, erythema multiforme, esophageal candidiasis, fatigue, fecal discoloration, flatulence, glycosuria, gynecomastia, hallucinations, hematuria, hemifacial dysesthesia, hemolytic anemia, hepatic encephalopathy, hepatic failure, hepatic necrosis, hyperhidrosis, hypertension, hypoglycemia, hyponatremia, insomnia, interstitial nephritis, irritable colon, jaundice, joint pain, leg pain, leukocytosis, leukopenia, liver disease (hepatocellular, cholestatic, mixed), malaise, microscopic pyuria, mucosal atrophy (tongue), muscle cramps, muscle weakness, myalgia, nervousness, neutropenia, ocular irritation, optic neuropathy, pain, palpitation, pancreatitis, pancytopenia, paresthesia, peripheral edema, petechiae, pharyngeal pain, photosensitivity, pneumothorax, proteinuria, pruritus, psychic disturbance, purpura, rash, skin inflammation, somnolence, Stevens-Johnson syndrome, stomatitis, tachycardia, taste perversion, testicular pain, thrombocytopenia, tinnitus, toxic epidermal necrolysis, tremor, urinary frequency, urinary tract infection, urticaria, vertigo, weight gain

Overdosage/Toxicology Limited experience with overdose in humans. Doses up to 2400 mg have been reported. Symptoms include confusion, drowsiness, blurred vision, tachycardia, nausea, flushing, diaphoresis, headache, and dry mouth. Treatment is symptom-directed and supportive. Not dialyzable.

Drug Interactions

Cytochrome P450 Effect: Substrate of CYP2A6 (minor), 2C9 (minor), 2C19 (major), 2D6 (minor), 3A4 (minor); **Inhibits** CYP1A2 (weak), 2C9 (moderate), 2C19 (strong), 2D6 (weak), 3A4 (weak); **Induces** CYP1A2 (weak)

Increased Effect/Toxicity: Esomeprazole and omeprazole may increase the levels of benzodiazepines metabolized by oxidation (eg, diazepam, midazolam, triazolam), methotrexate, and carbamazepine. Elimination of phenytoin or warfarin may be prolonged when used concomitantly with omeprazole. Omeprazole may increase the levels/effects of amiodarone, citalopram, diazepam, fluoxetine, glimepiride, glipizide, methsuximide, nateglinide, phenytoin, pioglitazone, propranolol, rosiglitazone, sertraline, warfarin, and other CYP2C9 or 2C19 substrates. Omeprazole may alter the concentrations/effects of clozapine.

Decreased Effect: Proton pump inhibitors may decrease the absorption of atazanavir, indinavir, oral iron salts, itraconazole, and ketoconazole; avoid concurrent use. The levels/effects of omeprazole may be decreased by aminoglutethimide, carbamazepine, phenytoin, rifampin, and other CYP2C19 inducers. Omeprazole may alter the concentrations/effects of clozapine.

Ethanol/Nutrition/Herb Interactions

Ethanol: Avoid ethanol (may cause gastric mucosal irritation).

Food: Food delays absorption.

Herb/Nutraceutical: St John's wort may decrease omeprazole levels.

Stability Store at 15°C to 30°C (59°F to 86°F).

Mechanism of Action Suppresses gastric basal and stimulated acid secretion by inhibiting the parietal cell H+/K+ ATP pump

Pharmacodynamics/Kinetics

Onset of action: Antisecretory: ~1 hour

Peak effect: 2 hours

Duration: 72 hours

Protein binding: 95%

Metabolism: Extensively hepatic to inactive metabolites

Bioavailability: Oral: 30% to 40%; increased in Asian patients and patients with hepatic dysfunction

Half-life elimination: Delayed release capsule: 0.5-1 hour

Excretion: Urine (77% as metabolites, very small amount as unchanged drug); feces

Dosage Oral:

Children ≥2 years: GERD or other acid-related disorders:

<20 kg: 10 mg once daily

≥20 kg: 20 mg once daily

Adults:

Active duodenal ulcer: 20 mg/day for 4-8 weeks

Gastric ulcers: 40 mg/day for 4-8 weeks

Symptomatic GERD: 20 mg/day for up to 4 weeks

Erosive esophagitis: 20 mg/day for 4-8 weeks; maintenance of healing: 20 mg/day for up to 12 months total therapy (including treatment period of 4-8 weeks)

Helicobacter pylori eradication: Dose varies with regimen: 20 mg once daily **or** 40 mg/day as single dose or in 2 divided doses; requires combination therapy with antibiotics

Pathological hypersecretory conditions: Initial: 60 mg once daily; doses up to 120 mg 3 times/day have been administered; administer daily doses >80 mg in divided doses

Frequent heartburn (OTC labeling): 20 mg/day for 14 days; treatment may be repeated after 4 months if needed

Dosage adjustment in hepatic impairment: Specific guidelines are not available; bioavailability is increased with chronic liver disease

Dietary Considerations Should be taken on an empty stomach; best if taken before breakfast.

(Continued)

Omeprazole *(Continued)*

Administration

Capsule: Should be swallowed whole; do not chew or crush. Best if taken before breakfast. Delayed release capsule may be opened and contents added to applesauce. Administration via NG tube should be in an acidic juice.

Tablet: Should be swallowed whole; do not crush or chew.

Dosage Forms

Capsule, delayed release: 10 mg, 20 mg
  Prilosec®: 10 mg, 20 mg, 40 mg
Tablet, delayed release:
  Prilosec OTC™: 20 mg

Extemporaneous Preparations

A 2 mg/mL oral omeprazole solution (Simplified Omeprazole Solution) can be prepared with five omeprazole 20 mg delayed release capsules and 50 mL 8.4% sodium bicarbonate. Empty capsules into beaker. Add sodium bicarbonate solution. Gently stir (about 15 minutes) until a white suspension is formed. Transfer to amber-colored syringe or bottle. Stable for 14 days at room temperature or for 30 days under refrigeration.

DiGiancinto JL, Olsen KM, Bergman KL, et al, "Stability of Suspension Formulations of Lansoprazole and Omeprazole Stored in Amber-Colored Plastic Oral Syringes," *Ann Pharmacother*, 2000, 34:600-5.

Quercia R, Fan C, Liu X, et al, "Stability of Omeprazole in an Extemporaneously Prepared Oral Liquid," *Am J Health Syst Pharm*, 1997, 54:1833-6.

Sharma V, "Comparison of 24-hour Intragastric pH Using Four Liquid Formulations of Lansoprazole and Omeprazole," *Am J Health Syst Pharm*, 1999, 56(Suppl 4):S18-21.

Extemporaneous preparation for NG administration (Prilosec®): The manufacturer recommends the use of an acidic juice for preparation to administer via nasogastric (NG) tube. Alternative methods have been described as follows. NG tube administration for the prevention of stress-related mucosal damage in ventilated, critically-ill patients. The manufacturer makes no judgment regarding the safety or efficacy of these practices.

The contents of one or two 20 mg omeprazole delayed release capsules were poured into a syringe; 10-20 mL of an 8.4% sodium bicarbonate solution was withdrawn in the syringe; 30 minutes were allowed for the enteric-coated omeprazole granules to break down. The resulting milky substance was shaken prior to administration. The NG tube was then flushed with 5-10 mL of water and then clamped for at least 1 hour. Patients received omeprazole 40 mg once, then 40 mg 6-8 hours later, then 20 mg once daily using this technique.

Another study used a different technique. The omeprazole delayed release capsule (20 mg or 40 mg) was opened; then the intact granules were poured into a container holding 30 mL of water. With the plunger removed, $1/3$ to $1/2$ of the granules were then poured into a 30 mL syringe which was attached to a nasogastric tube (NG). The plunger was replaced with 1 cm of air between the granules and the plunger top while the plunger was depressed. This process was repeated until all the granules were flushed, then a final 15 mL of water was flushed through the tube. Patients who received omeprazole 40 mg in this manner had a more predictable increase in intragastric pH than patients who received omeprazole 20 mg.

Omeprazole and Sodium Bicarbonate

(oh MEP ra zole & SOW dee um bye KAR bun ate)

U.S. Brand Names Zegerid®

Pharmacologic Category Proton Pump Inhibitor; Substituted Benzimidazole

Use Short-term (4-8 weeks) treatment of active duodenal ulcer disease or active benign gastric ulcer; treatment of heartburn and other symptoms associated with gastroesophageal reflux disease (GERD); short-term (4-8 weeks) treatment of endoscopically-diagnosed erosive esophagitis; maintenance healing of erosive esophagitis; reduction of risk of upper gastrointestinal bleeding in critically-ill patients

Pregnancy Risk Factor C

Dosage Oral: Adults:

Active duodenal ulcer: 20 mg/day for 4-8 weeks

Gastric ulcers: 40 mg/day for 4-8 weeks

Symptomatic GERD: 20 mg/day for up to 4 weeks

Erosive esophagitis: 20 mg/day for 4-8 weeks; maintenance of healing: 20 mg/day for up to 12 months total therapy (including treatment period of 4-8 weeks)

Risk reduction of upper GI bleeding in critically-ill patients (Zegerid® powder for oral suspension):

Loading dose: Day 1: 40 mg every 6-8 hours for two doses

Maintenance dose: 40 mg/day for up to 14 days; therapy >14 days has not been evaluated

Dosage adjustment in renal impairment: No adjustment necessary

Dosage adjustment in hepatic impairment: Specific guidelines are not available; bioavailability is increased with chronic liver disease

Additional Information Complete prescribing information for this medication should be consulted for additional detail.

Dosage Forms

Capsule, immediate release:
  Zegerid®: 20 mg, 40 mg [both strengths contain sodium bicarbonate 1100 mg, equivalent to sodium 300 mg (13 mEq) per capsule]

Powder for oral suspension [packet]:
  Zegerid®: 20 mg (30s), 40 mg (30s) [both strengths contain sodium bicarbonate 1680 mg, equivalent to sodium 460 mg per packet]

◆ Omnaris™ *see Ciclesonide on page 365*

◆ Omnicef® *see Cefdinir on page 307*

◆ OMNIhist® II L.A. *see Chlorpheniramine, Phenylephrine, and Methscopolamine on page 353*

◆ Omnii Gel™ [OTC] *see Fluoride on page 722*

♦ **Omnitrope**™ see Somatropin on page 1586
♦ **Oncaspar**® see Pegaspargase on page 1320
♦ **Oncotice**™ **(Can)** see BCG Vaccine on page 197

Ondansetron (on DAN se tron)

U.S. Brand Names Zofran®; Zofran® ODT
Canadian Brand Names Zofran®; Zofran® ODT
Index Terms GR38032R; Ondansetron Hydrochloride
Pharmacologic Category Antiemetic; Selective 5-HT$_3$ Receptor Antagonist
Use Prevention of nausea and vomiting associated with moderately- to highly-emetogenic cancer chemotherapy; radiotherapy in patients receiving total body irradiation or fractions to the abdomen; prevention of postoperative nausea and vomiting (PONV); treatment of PONV if no prophylactic dose received
Unlabeled/Investigational Use Treatment of early-onset alcoholism; hyperemesis gravidarum
Pregnancy Risk Factor B
Pregnancy Implications Teratogenic effects were not observed in animal studies; however, there are no adequate and well-controlled studies in pregnant women. Use of ondansetron for the treatment of nausea and vomiting of pregnancy (NVP) has been evaluated. Additional studies are needed to determine safety to the fetus, particularly during the first trimester. Based on preliminary data, use is generally reserved for severe NVP (hyperemesis gravidarum) or when conventional treatments are not effective.
Lactation Excretion in breast milk unknown/use caution
Medication Safety Issues
Sound-alike/look-alike issues:
Ondansetron may be confused with dolasetron, granisetron, palonosetron
Zofran® may be confused with Zantac®, Zosyn®
Contraindications Hypersensitivity to ondansetron, other selective 5-HT$_3$ antagonists, or any component of the formulation
Warnings/Precautions Ondansetron should be used on a scheduled basis, not on an "as needed" (PRN) basis, since data support the use of this drug only in the prevention of nausea and vomiting (due to antineoplastic therapy) and not in the rescue of nausea and vomiting. Ondansetron should only be used in the first 24-48 hours of chemotherapy. Data do not support any increased efficacy of ondansetron in delayed nausea and vomiting. Does not stimulate gastric or intestinal peristalsis; may mask progressive ileus and/or gastric distension. Use with caution in patients allergic to other 5-HT$_3$ receptor antagonists; cross-reactivity has been reported. Transient ECG changes (including QT interval prolongation) have been reported (rarely) with I.V. use. Orally-disintegrating tablets contain phenylalanine. Safety and efficacy for children <1 month of age have not been established.
Adverse Reactions Note: Percentages reported in adult patients.
>10%:
Central nervous system: Headache (9% to 27%), malaise/fatigue (9% to 13%)
Gastrointestinal: Constipation (6% to 11%)
1% to 10%:
Central nervous system: Drowsiness (8%), fever (2% to 8%), dizziness (4% to 7%), anxiety (6%), cold sensation (2%)
Dermatologic: Pruritus (2% to 5%), rash (1%)
Gastrointestinal: Diarrhea (2% to 7%)
Genitourinary: Gynecological disorder (7%), urinary retention (5%)
Hepatic: ALT/AST increased (1% to 5%)
Local: Injection site reaction (4%; pain, redness, burning)
Neuromuscular & skeletal: Paresthesia (2%)
Respiratory: Hypoxia (9%)
<1% (Limited to important or life-threatening): Anaphylactoid reactions, anaphylaxis, angina, angioedema, arrhythmia, blindness (transient/following infusion; lasting ≤48 hours), blurred vision (transient/following infusion), bradycardia, bronchospasm, cardiopulmonary arrest, dyspnea, dystonic reaction, ECG changes, electrocardiographic alterations (second degree heart block and ST-segment depression), extrapyramidal symptoms, flushing, grand mal seizure, hiccups, hypersensitivity reaction, hypokalemia, hypotension, laryngeal edema, laryngospasm, oculogyric crisis, palpitation, premature ventricular contractions (PVC), QT interval increased, shock, stridor, supraventricular tachycardia, syncope, tachycardia, urticaria, vascular occlusive events, ventricular arrhythmia
Overdosage/Toxicology Sudden transient blindness, severe constipation, hypotension, and vasovagal episode with transient secondary heart block have been reported in some cases of overdose. I.V. doses up to 252 mg/day have been inadvertently given without adverse effects. There is no specific antidote. Treatment is symptom-directed and supportive.
Drug Interactions
Cytochrome P450 Effect: Substrate of CYP1A2 (minor), 2C9 (minor), 2D6 (minor), 2E1 (minor), 3A4 (major); Inhibits CYP1A2 (weak), 2C9 (weak), 2D6 (weak)
Increased Effect/Toxicity: Ondansetron may enhance the hypotensive effect of apomorphine; concurrent use is contraindicated.
Decreased Effect: CYP3A4 inducers may decrease the levels/effects of ondansetron; example inducers include aminoglutethimide, carbamazepine, nafcillin, nevirapine, phenobarbital, phenytoin, and rifamycins. The manufacturer does not recommend dosage adjustment in patients receiving CYP3A4 inducers.
Ethanol/Nutrition/Herb Interactions
Food: Food increases the extent of absorption. The C_{max} and T_{max} do not change much.
Herb/Nutraceutical: St John's wort may decrease ondansetron levels.
Stability
Oral solution: Store between 15°C and 30°C (59°F and 86°F). Protect from light.
Premixed bag: Store between 2°C and 30°C (36°F and 86°F). Protect from light.
Tablet: Store between 2°C and 30°C (36°F and 86°F).
(Continued)

Ondansetron *(Continued)*

Vial: Store between 2°C and 30°C (36°F and 86°F). Protect from light. Prior to I.V. infusion, dilute in 50 mL D$_5$W or NS. Solution is stable for 48 hours at room temperature.

Mechanism of Action Selective 5-HT$_3$-receptor antagonist, blocking serotonin, both peripherally on vagal nerve terminals and centrally in the chemoreceptor trigger zone

Pharmacodynamics/Kinetics

Onset of action: ~30 minutes

Distribution: V$_d$: Children: 1.7-3.7 L/kg; Adults: 2.2-2.5 L/kg

Protein binding, plasma: 70% to 76%

Metabolism: Extensively hepatic via hydroxylation, followed by glucuronide or sulfate conjugation; CYP1A2, CYP2D6, and CYP3A4 substrate; some demethylation occurs

Bioavailability: Oral: 56% to 71%; Rectal: 58% to 74%

Half-life elimination: Children <15 years: 2-7 hours; Adults: 3-6 hours

Mild-to-moderate hepatic impairment: Adults: 12 hours

Severe hepatic impairment (Child-Pugh C): Adults: 20 hours

Time to peak: Oral: ~2 hours

Excretion: Urine (44% to 60% as metabolites, 5% to 10% as unchanged drug); feces (~25%)

Dosage Note: Studies in adults have shown a single daily dose of 8-12 mg I.V. or 8-24 mg orally to be as effective as mg/kg dosing, and should be considered for **all** patients whose mg/kg dose exceeds 8-12 mg I.V.; oral solution and ODT formulations are bioequivalent to corresponding doses of tablet formulation

Children:

I.V.:

Prevention of chemotherapy-induced emesis: 6 months to 18 years: 0.15 mg/kg/dose administered 30 minutes prior to chemotherapy, 4 and 8 hours after the first dose **or** 0.45 mg/kg/day as a single dose

Prevention of postoperative nausea and vomiting: 1 month to 12 years:

≤40 kg: 0.1 mg/kg as a single dose

>40 kg: 4 mg as a single dose

Oral: Prevention of chemotherapy-induced emesis:

4-11 years: 4 mg 30 minutes before chemotherapy; repeat 4 and 8 hours after initial dose, then 4 mg every 8 hours for 1-2 days after chemotherapy completed

≥12 years: Refer to adult dosing.

Adults:

I.V.:

Prevention of chemotherapy-induced emesis:

0.15 mg/kg 3 times/day beginning 30 minutes prior to chemotherapy **or**

0.45 mg/kg once daily **or**

8-10 mg 1-2 times/day **or**

24 mg or 32 mg once daily

Treatment of hyperemesis gravidum (unlabeled use): 8 mg administered over 15 minutes every 12 hours **or** 1 mg/hour infused continuously for up to 24 hours

I.M., I.V.: Postoperative nausea and vomiting: 4 mg as a single dose approximately 30 minutes before the end of anesthesia, or as treatment if vomiting occurs after surgery

Note: Repeat doses given in response to inadequate control of nausea/vomiting from preoperative doses are generally ineffective.

Oral:

Chemotherapy-induced emesis:

Highly-emetogenic agents/single-day therapy: 24 mg given 30 minutes prior to the start of therapy

Moderately-emetogenic agents: 8 mg every 12 hours beginning 30 minutes before chemotherapy, continuously for 1-2 days after chemotherapy completed

Total body irradiation: 8 mg 1-2 hours before daily each fraction of radiotherapy

Single high-dose fraction radiotherapy to abdomen: 8 mg 1-2 hours before irradiation, then 8 mg every 8 hours after first dose for 1-2 days after completion of radiotherapy

Daily fractionated radiotherapy to abdomen: 8 mg 1-2 hours before irradiation, then 8 mg 8 hours after first dose for each day of radiotherapy

Postoperative nausea and vomiting: 16 mg given 1 hour prior to induction of anesthesia

Treatment of hyperemesis gravidum (unlabeled use): 8 mg every 12 hours

Elderly: No dosing adjustment required

Dosage adjustment in renal impairment: No dosing adjustment required

Dosage adjustment in hepatic impairment: Severe liver disease (Child-Pugh C): Maximum daily dose: 8 mg

Dietary Considerations Take without regard to meals.

Orally-disintegrating tablet contains <0.03 mg phenylalanine

Administration

Oral: Oral dosage forms should be administered 30 minutes prior to chemotherapy; 1-2 hours before radiotherapy; 1 hour prior to the induction of anesthesia

Orally-disintegrating tablets: Do not remove from blister until needed. Peel backing off the blister, do not push tablet through. Using dry hands, place tablet on tongue and allow to dissolve. Swallow with saliva.

I.M.: Should be administered undiluted

I.V.: Give first dose 30 minutes prior to beginning chemotherapy; the I.V. preparation has been successful when administered orally

I.V. injection: Single doses for prevention of postoperative nausea and vomiting may be administered I.V. over 2-5 minutes as undiluted solution

IVPB: Dilute in 50 mL D$_5$W or NS. Infuse over 15-30 minutes; 24-hour continuous infusions have been reported, but are rarely used

Monitoring Parameters Closely monitor patients <4 months of age

Dosage Forms

Infusion [premixed in D$_5$W, preservative free]: 32 mg (50 mL)

Zofran®: 32 mg (50 mL)

Injection, solution: 2 mg/mL (2 mL, 20 mL)
   Zofran®: 2 mg/mL (2 mL, 20 mL)
Solution, oral: 4 mg/5 mL (50 mL)
   Zofran®: 4 mg/5 mL (50 mL) [contains sodium benzoate; strawberry flavor]
Tablet:
   Zofran®: 4 mg; 8 mg
Tablet, orally disintegrating:
   Zofran® ODT. 4 mg, 8 mg [each strength contains phenylalanine <0.03 mg/tablet; strawberry flavor]

Extemporaneous Preparations A 0.8 mg/mL syrup may be made by crushing ten 8 mg tablets; flaking of the tablet coating occurs. Mix thoroughly with 50 mL of the suspending vehicle, Ora-Plus® (Paddock), in 5 mL increments. Add sufficient volume of any of the following syrups: Cherry syrup USP, Syrpalta® (Humco), Ora-Sweet® (Paddock), or Ora-Sweet® Sugar-Free (Paddock) to make a final volume of 100 mL. Stability is 42 days refrigerated.

   Trissel LA, "Trissel's Stability of Compounded Formulations," American Pharmaceutical Association, 1996.

Rectal suppositories: Calibrate a suppository mold for the base being used. Determine the displacement factor (DF) for ondansetron for the base being used (Fattibase® = 1.1; Polybase® = 0.6). Weigh the ondansetron tablet. Divide the tablet weight by the DF. Subtract the weight of base displaced from the calculated weight of base required for each suppository. Grind the ondansetron tablets to a fine powder in a mortar. Weigh out the appropriate weight of suppository base. Melt the base over a water bath (<55°C). Add the ondansetron powder to the suppository base and mix well. Pour the mixture into the suppository mold and cool. Stable for at least 30 days under refrigeration.

   Allen LV, "Ondansetron Suppositories," US Pharm, 20(7):84-6.

♦ **Ondansetron Hydrochloride** *see* Ondansetron *on page 1267*
♦ **ONTAK®** *see* Denileukin Diftitox *on page 471*
♦ **Onxol™** *see* Paclitaxel *on page 1295*
♦ **Opana®** *see* Oxymorphone *on page 1290*
♦ **Opana® ER** *see* Oxymorphone *on page 1290*
♦ **OPC-13013** *see* Cilostazol *on page 368*
♦ **OPC-14597** *see* Aripiprazole *on page 151*
♦ **Opcon-A® [OTC]** *see* Naphazoline and Pheniramine *on page 1199*
♦ **Operand® [OTC]** *see* Povidone-Iodine *on page 1404*
♦ **Operand® Chlorhexidine Gluconate [OTC]** *see* Chlorhexidine Gluconate *on page 344*
♦ **Ophthetic®** *see* Proparacaine *on page 1440*
♦ **Ophtho-Dipivefrin™ (Can)** *see* Dipivefrin *on page 524*
♦ **Ophtho-Tate® (Can)** *see* PrednisoLONE *on page 1413*
♦ **Opium and Belladonna** *see* Belladonna and Opium *on page 200*

Opium Tincture (OH pee um TING chur)

Index Terms DTO (error-prone abbreviation); Opium Tincture, Deodorized
Pharmacologic Category Analgesic, Opioid; Antidiarrheal
Use Treatment of diarrhea or relief of pain
Restrictions C-II
Pregnancy Risk Factor B/D (prolonged use or high doses at term)
Lactation Enters breast milk/use caution
Medication Safety Issues
   Sound-alike/look-alike issues:
      Opium tincture may be confused with camphorated tincture of opium (paregoric)

   Use care when prescribing opium tincture; each mL contains the equivalent of morphine 10 mg; paregoric contains the equivalent of morphine 0.4 mg/mL

   DTO is an error-prone abbreviation (mistaken as Diluted Tincture of Opium; dose equivalency of paregoric)

Contraindications Hypersensitivity to morphine sulfate or any component of the formulation; increased intracranial pressure; severe respiratory depression; severe hepatic or renal insufficiency; pregnancy (prolonged use or high dosages near term)

Warnings/Precautions May cause CNS depression, which may impair physical or mental abilities; patients must be cautioned about performing tasks which require mental alertness (eg, operating machinery or driving). Effects may be potentiated when used with other sedative drugs or ethanol. Opium shares the toxic potential of opiate agonists, and usual precautions of opiate agonist therapy should be observed; use with caution in patients with CNS depression or coma, hepatic impairment, morbid obesity, adrenal insufficiency, head trauma, thyroid dysfunction, prostatic hyperplasia/urinary stricture, respiratory disease, or a history of drug abuse. Use with caution in patients with biliary tract dysfunction; acute pancreatitis may cause constriction of sphincter of Oddi. May cause hypotension; use with caution in patients with hypovolemia, cardiovascular disease (including acute MI), or drugs which may exaggerate hypotensive effects (including phenothiazines or general anesthetics). May obscure diagnosis or clinical course of patients with acute abdominal conditions. Concurrent use of agonist/antagonist analgesics may precipitate withdrawal symptoms and/or reduced analgesic efficacy in patients following prolonged therapy with mu opioid agonists. Abrupt discontinuation following prolonged use may also lead to withdrawal symptoms. Use with caution in the elderly and debilitated patients; may be more sensitive to adverse effects. Some preparations contain sulfites which may cause allergic reactions; infants <3 months of age are more susceptible to respiratory depression, use with caution and generally in reduced doses in this age group; this is **not** paregoric, dose accordingly.

Adverse Reactions Frequency not defined.
   Cardiovascular: Palpitations, hypotension, bradycardia, peripheral vasodilation
   (Continued)

Opium Tincture *(Continued)*

Central nervous system: Drowsiness, dizziness, restlessness, headache, malaise, CNS depression, increased intracranial pressure, insomnia, mental depression

Gastrointestinal: Nausea, vomiting, constipation, anorexia, stomach cramps, biliary tract spasm

Genitourinary: Decreased urination, urinary tract spasm

Neuromuscular & skeletal: Weakness

Ocular: Miosis

Respiratory: Respiratory depression

Miscellaneous: Histamine release, physical and psychological dependence

Overdosage/Toxicology Primary attention should be directed to ensuring adequate respiratory exchange; opiate agonist-induced respiratory depression may be reversed with parenteral naloxone hydrochloride. Treatment includes naloxone 2 mg I.V. (0.01 mg/kg for children), with repeat administration as necessary, up to a total of 10 mg.

Drug Interactions

Increased Effect/Toxicity: Opium tincture and CNS depressants, MAO inhibitors, tricyclic antidepressants may potentiate the effects of opiate agonists (eg, codeine, morphine). Dextroamphetamine may enhance the analgesic effect of opiate agonists.

Ethanol/Nutrition/Herb Interactions Ethanol: Avoid ethanol (may increase CNS depression).

Stability Protect from light.

Mechanism of Action Contains many narcotic alkaloids including morphine; its mechanism for gastric motility inhibition is primarily due to this morphine content; it results in a decrease in digestive secretions, an increase in GI muscle tone, and therefore a reduction in GI propulsion

Pharmacodynamics/Kinetics

Duration: 4-5 hours

Absorption: Variable

Metabolism: Hepatic

Excretion: Urine

Dosage Oral: **Note:** Opium tincture 10% contains morphine 10 mg/mL. use caution in ordering, dispensing, and/or administering.

Children:

Diarrhea: 0.005-0.01 mL/kg/dose every 3-4 hours for a maximum of 6 doses/24 hours

Analgesia: 0.01-0.02 mL/kg/dose every 3-4 hours

Adults:

Diarrhea: 0.3-1 mL/dose every 2-6 hours to maximum of 6 mL/24 hours

Analgesia: 0.6-1.5 mL/dose every 3-4 hours

Monitoring Parameters Observe patient for excessive sedation, respiratory depression, implement safety measures, assist with ambulation

Test Interactions Increased aminotransferase [ALT (SGPT)/AST (SGOT)] (S)

Dosage Forms Liquid: 10% (120 mL, 480 mL) [0.6 mL equivalent to morphine 6 mg; contains alcohol 19%]

♦ **Opium Tincture, Deodorized** see Opium Tincture on page 1269

Oprelvekin *(oh PREL ve kin)*

U.S. Brand Names Neumega®

Index Terms IL-11; Interleukin-11; NSC-722848; Recombinant Human Interleukin-11; Recombinant Interleukin-11; rhIL-11; rIL-11

Pharmacologic Category Biological Response Modulator; Human Growth Factor

Use Prevention of severe thrombocytopenia and the reduction of the need for platelet transfusions following myelosuppressive chemotherapy

Pregnancy Risk Factor C

Pregnancy Implications Animal studies have demonstrated adverse fetal effects. There are no adequate and well-controlled studies in pregnant women. Use during pregnancy only if the potential benefits outweigh the potential risk to the fetus.

Lactation Excretion in breast milk unknown/not recommended

Medication Safety Issues

Sound-alike/look-alike issues:

Oprelvekin may be confused with aldesleukin, Proleukin®

Neumega® may be confused with Neulasta®, Neupogen®

Contraindications Hypersensitivity to oprelvekin or any component of the formulation

Warnings/Precautions [U.S. Boxed Warning]: Allergic or hypersensitivity reactions, including anaphylaxis have been reported. May occur with the first or with subsequent doses. Permanently discontinue in any patient developing an allergic reaction. May cause serious fluid retention; use cautiously in patients with conditions where expansion of plasma volume should be avoided (eg, left ventricular dysfunction, CHF, hypertension). Closely monitor fluid and electrolytes in patient on chronic diuretic therapy; severe hypokalemia contributing to sudden death have been reported in these patients. Arrhythmia, pulmonary edema, and cardiac arrest have been reported; use in patients with a history of atrial arrhythmia only if the potential benefit exceeds possible risks. Patients experiencing arrhythmia may be at risk for stroke; use caution in patients with a history of transient ischemic attack or stroke. Ventricular arrhythmia has also been reported, occurring within 2-7 days of treatment initiation. Use caution in patients with conduction defects, respiratory disease; history of thromboembolic problems; pre-existing pericardial effusions or ascites. Use with caution in hepatic or renal dysfunction. Not indicated following myeloablative chemotherapy; increased toxicities were reported when used following myeloablative therapy. Efficacy has not been established with chemotherapy regimens of >5 days duration or with regimens associated with delayed myelosuppression (eg, nitrosoureas, mitomycin C). Safety and efficacy have not been established with chronic administration. Papilledema, more frequently associated with use in children, has occurred; use caution in patients with pre-existing papilledema or with tumors involving the central nervous system. Papilledema is dose limiting. Patients experiencing oprelvekin-related papilledema may be at risk for visual acuity changes, including blurred vision or blindness. Although used in children in clinical trials, safety and efficacy have not been established in pediatric patients.

Adverse Reactions
>10%:
Cardiovascular: Tachycardia (children 84%; adults 20%), edema (59%), palpitation (14%), cardiomegaly (children 21%), vasodilation (19%), syncope (13%), atrial arrhythmia (12%)
Central nervous system: Headache (41%), dizziness (38%), fever (36%), insomnia (33%), fatigue (30%)
Dermatologic: Rash (25%)
Endocrine & metabolic: Fluid retention
Gastrointestinal: Nausea/vomiting (77%), diarrhea (43%), oral moniliasis (14%)
Hematologic: Anemia (dilutional); appears within 3 days of initiation of therapy, resolves in about 1 week after cessation of oprelvekin
Neuromuscular & skeletal: Weakness (severe 14%), arthralgia, periostitis (children 11%)
Ocular: Conjunctival injection/redness/swelling (children 57%; adults 19%), papilledema (children 16%; adults 1%)
Respiratory: Dyspnea (48%), rhinitis (42%), cough (29%), pharyngitis (25%)
1% to 10%:
Gastrointestinal: Weight gain (5%)
Respiratory: Pleural effusion (10%)
Postmarketing and/or case reports: Allergic reaction, amblyopia, anaphylaxis/anaphylactoid reactions, blindness, blurred vision, capillary leak syndrome, CHF, dehydration, exfoliative dermatitis, eye hemorrhage, facial edema, fibrinogen increased, fluid overload, hypoalbuminemia, hypocalcemia, hypotension, injection site reactions (dermatitis, pain, discoloration), optic neuropathy, paresthesia, pericardial effusion, pulmonary edema, renal failure, skin discoloration, stroke, ventricular arrhythmia

Overdosage/Toxicology Doses of oprelvekin >50 mcg/kg may be associated with an increased incidence of cardiovascular events. If an overdose is administered, discontinue oprelvekin and closely observe for signs of toxicity. Treatment is symptom-directed and supportive. Base reinstitution of therapy on individual patient factors (evidence of toxicity and continued need for therapy).

Drug Interactions
Increased Effect/Toxicity: Hypokalemia may increase the risk of adverse cardiovascular events with oprelvekin; monitor.

Stability Store vials under refrigeration between 2°C to 8°C (36°F to 46°F); do not freeze. Protect from light. Reconstitute to a final concentration of 5 mg/mL with SWFI; swirl gently, do not shake. Use reconstituted oprelvekin within 3 hours of reconstitution and store in the vial at either 2°C to 8°C (36°F to 46°F) or room temperature of ≤25°C (77°F). Do not freeze or shake reconstituted solution.

Mechanism of Action Oprelvekin is a growth factor which stimulates multiple stages of megakaryocytopoiesis and thrombopoiesis, resulting in proliferation of megakaryocyte progenitors and megakaryocyte maturation, or increased platelet production.

Pharmacodynamics/Kinetics
Bioavailability: >80%
Half-life elimination: Terminal: 5-9 hours
Time to peak, serum: 1-6 hours
Excretion: Urine (primarily as metabolites)

Dosage SubQ: Administer first dose ~6-24 hours after the end of chemotherapy. Discontinue at least 48 hours before beginning the next cycle of chemotherapy.
Children (unlabeled use): 75-100 mcg/kg once daily for 10-21 days (until postnadir platelet count ≥50,000 cells/µL)
Note: A safe and effective dose for use in children has not been established by the manufacturer.
Adults: 50 mcg/kg once daily for ~10-21 days (until postnadir platelet count ≥50,000 cells/µL)

Dosage adjustment in renal impairment: Cl$_{cr}$ <30 mL/minute: 25 mcg/kg once daily

Administration Subcutaneously in the abdomen, thigh, hip, or upper arm.

Monitoring Parameters Monitor electrolytes and fluid balance during therapy; obtain a CBC at regular intervals during therapy; monitor platelet counts until adequate recovery has occurred

Test Interactions Decrease in hemoglobin concentration, serum concentration of albumin and other proteins (result of expansion of plasma volume)

Dosage Forms
Injection, powder for reconstitution:
Neumega®: 5 mg [packaged with diluent]

♦ **Optase**™ *see* Trypsin, Balsam Peru, and Castor Oil *on page 1754*
♦ **Optho-Bunolol® (Can)** *see* Levobunolol *on page 996*
♦ **Opticrom®** *see* Cromolyn *on page 423*
♦ **Optimyxin® (Can)** *see* Bacitracin and Polymyxin B *on page 192*
♦ **Optimyxin Plus® (Can)** *see* Neomycin, Polymyxin B, and Gramicidin *on page 1212*
♦ **OptiPranolol®** *see* Metipranolol *on page 1126*
♦ **Optison**™ *see* Perflutren Protein Type A *on page 1345*
♦ **Optivar®** *see* Azelastine *on page 185*
♦ **o,p′-DDD** *see* Mitotane *on page 1156*
♦ **Orabase® with Benzocaine [OTC]** *see* Benzocaine *on page 204*
♦ **Oracea**™ *see* Doxycycline *on page 555*
♦ **Oracit®** *see* Sodium Citrate and Citric Acid *on page 1579*
♦ **Oracort (Can)** *see* Triamcinolone *on page 1734*
♦ **Orajel® Baby Daytime and Nighttime [OTC]** *see* Benzocaine *on page 204*

- ◆ **Orajel® Baby Teething [OTC]** *see* Benzocaine *on page 204*
- ◆ **Orajel® Baby Teething Nighttime [OTC]** *see* Benzocaine *on page 204*
- ◆ **Orajel® Denture Plus [OTC]** *see* Benzocaine *on page 204*
- ◆ **Orajel® Maximum Strength [OTC]** *see* Benzocaine *on page 204*
- ◆ **Orajel® Medicated Toothache [OTC]** *see* Benzocaine *on page 204*
- ◆ **Orajel® Mouth Sore [OTC]** *see* Benzocaine *on page 204*
- ◆ **Orajel® Multi-Action Cold Sore [OTC]** *see* Benzocaine *on page 204*
- ◆ **Orajel® Perioseptic® Spot Treatment [OTC]** *see* Carbamide Peroxide *on page 287*
- ◆ **Orajel® PM® [OTC]** *see* Benzocaine *on page 204*
- ◆ **Orajel® Ultra Mouth Sore [OTC]** *see* Benzocaine *on page 204*
- ◆ **Oramorph SR®** *see* Morphine Sulfate *on page 1171*
- ◆ **Oranyl [OTC]** *see* Pseudoephedrine *on page 1454*
- ◆ **Oranyl Plus [OTC]** *see* Acetaminophen and Pseudoephedrine *on page 33*
- ◆ **Orap®** *see* Pimozide *on page 1370*
- ◆ **Orapred®** *see* PrednisoLONE *on page 1413*
- ◆ **Orapred ODT™** *see* PrednisoLONE *on page 1413*
- ◆ **Oraquix®** *see* Lidocaine and Prilocaine *on page 1015*
- ◆ **Orazinc® [OTC]** *see* Zinc Sulfate *on page 1817*
- ◆ **Orciprenaline Sulfate** *see* Metaproterenol *on page 1096*
- ◆ **Orencia®** *see* Abatacept *on page 21*
- ◆ **Orfadin®** *see* Nitisinone *on page 1233*
- ◆ **ORG 946** *see* Rocuronium *on page 1529*
- ◆ **Orgalutran® (Can)** *see* Ganirelix *on page 780*
- ◆ **Organ-1 NR** *see* Guaifenesin *on page 814*
- ◆ **Organidin® NR** *see* Guaifenesin *on page 814*
- ◆ **ORG NC 45** *see* Vecuronium *on page 1780*

Orlistat (OR li stat)

U.S. Brand Names Xenical®
Canadian Brand Names Xenical®
Pharmacologic Category Lipase Inhibitor
Additional Appendix Information
Obesity Treatment Guidelines for Adults *on page 2073*
Use Management of obesity, including weight loss and weight management when used in conjunction with a reduced-calorie diet; reduce the risk of weight regain after prior weight loss; indicated for obese patients with an initial body mass index (BMI) ≥30 kg/m² or ≥27 kg/m² in the presence of other risk factors
Pregnancy Risk Factor B
Pregnancy Implications There are no adequate and well-controlled studies of orlistat in pregnant women. Because animal reproductive studies are not always predictive of human response, orlistat is not recommended for use during pregnancy. Teratogenicity studies were conducted in rats and rabbits at doses up to 800 mg/kg/day. Neither study showed embryotoxicity or teratogenicity. This dose is 23 and 47 times the daily human dose calculated on a body surface area basis for rats and rabbits, respectively.
Lactation Excretion in breast milk unknown/not recommended
Medication Safety Issues
Sound-alike/look-alike issues:
Xenical® may be confused with Xeloda®
Contraindications Hypersensitivity to orlistat or any component of the formulation; chronic malabsorption syndrome or cholestasis
Warnings/Precautions Patients should be advised to adhere to dietary guidelines; gastrointestinal adverse events may increase if taken with a diet high in fat (>30% total daily calories from fat). The daily intake of fat should be distributed over three main meals. If taken with any one meal very high in fat, the possibility of gastrointestinal effects increases. Patients should be counseled to take a multivitamin supplement that contains fat-soluble vitamins to ensure adequate nutrition because orlistat has been shown to reduce the absorption of some fat-soluble vitamins and beta-carotene. Some patients may develop increased levels of urinary oxalate following treatment; caution should be exercised when prescribing it to patients with a history of hyperoxaluria or calcium oxalate nephrolithiasis. As with any weight-loss agent, the potential exists for misuse in appropriate patient populations (eg, patients with anorexia nervosa or bulimia). Safety and efficacy have not been established in children <12 years of age. Safety and efficacy with >4 years of use have not been established.
Adverse Reactions
>10%:
Central nervous system: Headache (31%)
Gastrointestinal: Oily spotting (27%), abdominal pain/discomfort (26%), flatus with discharge (24%), fatty/oily stool (20%), fecal urgency (22%), oily evacuation (12%), increased defecation (11%)
Neuromuscular & skeletal: Back pain (14%)
Respiratory: Upper respiratory infection (38%)
1% to 10%:
Central nervous system: Fatigue (7%), anxiety (5%), sleep disorder (4%)
Dermatologic: Dry skin (2%)
Endocrine & metabolic: Menstrual irregularities (10%)
Gastrointestinal: Fecal incontinence (8%), nausea (8%), infectious diarrhea (5%), rectal pain/discomfort (5%), vomiting (4%)
Neuromuscular & skeletal: Arthritis (5%), myalgia (4%)
Otic: Otitis (4%)

<1% (Limited to important or life-threatening): Abdominal distension, allergic reactions, anaphylaxis, angioedema, bronchitis, bronchospasm, bullous eruption, cholelithiasis (may be caused by weight loss), hepatitis (causal relationship not established), hypoglycemia (in diabetic patients), pancreatitis, pruritus, rash, transaminanses increased, urticaria

Overdosage/Toxicology Single doses of 800 mg and multiple doses up to 400 mg 3 times daily for 15 days have been studied in normal weight and obese patients, without significant adverse findings. In significant overdose, observation of the patient is recommended for 24 hours.

Drug Interactions

Decreased Effect: Orlistat may decrease amiodarone absorption (monitor). Coadministration with cyclosporine may decrease plasma levels of cyclosporine (administer cyclosporine 2 hours before or after orlistat and monitor). Orlistat does not alter the pharmacokinetics of warfarin, however, vitamin K absorption may be decreased during orlistat therapy (patients stabilized on warfarin should be monitored for changes in warfarin effects).

Ethanol/Nutrition/Herb Interactions

Fat-soluble vitamins: Absorption of vitamins A, D, E, and K may be decreased by orlistat. A multivitamin containing the fat-soluble vitamins (A, D, E, and K) should be administered once daily at least 2 hours before or after orlistat.

Stability Store at 25°C (77°F); excursions permitted to 15°C to 30°C (59°F to 86°F).

Mechanism of Action A reversible inhibitor of gastric and pancreatic lipases thus inhibiting absorption of dietary fats by 30% (at doses of 120 mg 3 times/day).

Pharmacodynamics/Kinetics

Absorption: Minimal

Metabolism: Metabolized within the gastrointestinal wall; forms inactive metabolites

Excretion: Feces (83% as unchanged drug)

Dosage Oral: Children ≥12 years and Adults: 120 mg 3 times/day with each main meal containing fat (during or up to 1 hour after the meal); omit dose if meal is occasionally missed or contains no fat.

Dietary Considerations Multivitamin supplements that contain fat-soluble vitamins should be taken once daily at least 2 hours before or after the administration of orlistat (ie, bedtime). Distribute the daily intake of fat over 3 main meals. Gastrointestinal effects of orlistat may increase if taken with any 1 meal very high in fat.

Dosage Forms Capsule: 120 mg

♦ **Ornex® [OTC]** *see Acetaminophen and Pseudoephedrine on page 33*
♦ **Ornex® Maximum Strength [OTC]** *see Acetaminophen and Pseudoephedrine on page 33*
♦ **ORO-Clense (Can)** *see Chlorhexidine Gluconate on page 344*
♦ **Orphenace® (Can)** *see Orphenadrine on page 1273*

Orphenadrine (or FEN a dreen)

U.S. Brand Names Norflex™

Canadian Brand Names Norflex™; Orphenace®; Rhoxal-orphendrine

Index Terms Orphenadrine Citrate

Pharmacologic Category Anti-Parkinson's Agent, Anticholinergic; Skeletal Muscle Relaxant

Use Treatment of muscle spasm associated with acute painful musculoskeletal conditions; supportive therapy in tetanus

Pregnancy Risk Factor C

Medication Safety Issues

Sound-alike/look-alike issues:

Norflex™ may be confused with norfloxacin, Noroxin®

International issues:

Flexin® [Israel] may be confused with Floxin® which is a brand name for ofloxacin in the U.S.

Flexin® [Israel]: Brand name for indomethacin in Great Britain

Dosage Adults:

Oral: 100 mg twice daily

I.M., I.V.: 60 mg every 12 hours

Additional Information Complete prescribing information for this medication should be consulted for additional detail.

Dosage Forms

Injection, solution, as citrate: 30 mg/mL (2 mL)

Norflex™: 30 mg/mL (2 mL) [contains sodium bisulfite]

Tablet, extended release, as citrate: 100 mg

Norflex™: 100 mg

Orphenadrine, Aspirin, and Caffeine (or FEN a dreen, AS pir in, & KAF een)

U.S. Brand Names Norgesic™ [DSC]; Norgesic™ Forte [DSC]; Orphengesic [DSC]; Orphengesic Forte [DSC]

Canadian Brand Names Norgesic™; Norgesic™ Forte

Index Terms Aspirin, Orphenadrine, and Caffeine; Caffeine, Orphenadrine, and Aspirin

Pharmacologic Category Skeletal Muscle Relaxant

Use Relief of discomfort associated with skeletal muscular conditions

Pregnancy Risk Factor D

Medication Safety Issues

Sound-alike/look-alike issues:

Norgesic™ Forte may be confused with Norgesic 40®

Dosage Oral: 1-2 tablets 3-4 times/day

(Continued)

Orphenadrine, Aspirin, and Caffeine *(Continued)*

Additional Information Complete prescribing information for this medication should be consulted for additional detail.

Dosage Forms [DSC] = Discontinued product

    Tablet: Orphenadrine citrate 25 mg, aspirin 385 mg, and caffeine 30 mg; orphenadrine citrate 50 mg, aspirin 770 mg, and caffeine 60 mg

        Norgesic™, Orphengesic: Orphenadrine citrate 25 mg, aspirin 385 mg, and caffeine 30 mg [DSC]

        Norgesic™ Forte, Orphengesic Forte: Orphenadrine citrate 50 mg, aspirin 770 mg, and caffeine 60 mg [DSC]

- ♦ **Orphenadrine Citrate** *see* Orphenadrine *on page 1273*
- ♦ **Orphengesic [DSC]** *see* Orphenadrine, Aspirin, and Caffeine *on page 1273*
- ♦ **Orphengesic Forte [DSC]** *see* Orphenadrine, Aspirin, and Caffeine *on page 1273*
- ♦ **Ortho® 0.5/35 (Can)** *see* Ethinyl Estradiol and Norethindrone *on page 655*
- ♦ **Ortho® 1/35 (Can)** *see* Ethinyl Estradiol and Norethindrone *on page 655*
- ♦ **Ortho® 7/7/7 (Can)** *see* Ethinyl Estradiol and Norethindrone *on page 655*
- ♦ **Ortho Cept** *see* Ethinyl Estradiol and Desogestrel *on page 645*
- ♦ **Ortho-Cept®** *see* Ethinyl Estradiol and Desogestrel *on page 645*
- ♦ **Orthoclone OKT® 3** *see* Muromonab-CD3 *on page 1179*
- ♦ **Ortho Cyclen** *see* Ethinyl Estradiol and Norgestimate *on page 660*
- ♦ **Ortho-Cyclen®** *see* Ethinyl Estradiol and Norgestimate *on page 660*
- ♦ **Ortho Est** *see* Estropipate *on page 637*
- ♦ **Ortho-Est®** *see* Estropipate *on page 637*
- ♦ **Ortho-Evra** *see* Ethinyl Estradiol and Norelgestromin *on page 655*
- ♦ **Ortho Evra®** *see* Ethinyl Estradiol and Norelgestromin *on page 655*
- ♦ **Ortho Novum** *see* Ethinyl Estradiol and Norethindrone *on page 655*
- ♦ **Ortho-Novum®** *see* Ethinyl Estradiol and Norethindrone *on page 655*
- ♦ **Ortho Novum 1/50** *see* Mestranol and Norethindrone *on page 1093*
- ♦ **Ortho-Novum® 1/50** *see* Mestranol and Norethindrone *on page 1093*
- ♦ **Ortho Tri Cyclen** *see* Ethinyl Estradiol and Norgestimate *on page 660*
- ♦ **Ortho Tri-Cyclen®** *see* Ethinyl Estradiol and Norgestimate *on page 660*
- ♦ **Ortho Tri-Cyclen® Lo** *see* Ethinyl Estradiol and Norgestimate *on page 660*
- ♦ **Orthovisc®** *see* Hyaluronate and Derivatives *on page 841*
- ♦ **OrthoVisc® (Can)** *see* Hyaluronate and Derivatives *on page 841*
- ♦ **Orudis® KT [OTC] [DSC]** *see* Ketoprofen *on page 961*
- ♦ **Oruvail® (Can)** *see* Ketoprofen *on page 961*
- ♦ **Orvaten™** *see* Midodrine *on page 1142*
- ♦ **Os-Cal® (Can)** *see* Calcium Carbonate *on page 269*
- ♦ **Os-Cal® 500 [OTC] [DSC]** *see* Calcium Carbonate *on page 269*
- ♦ **Os-Cal® 500+D [OTC]** *see* Calcium and Vitamin D *on page 268*

Oseltamivir *(oh sel TAM i vir)*

U.S. Brand Names Tamiflu®
Canadian Brand Names Tamiflu®
Pharmacologic Category Antiviral Agent; Neuraminidase Inhibitor
Additional Appendix Information
    Community-Acquired Pneumonia in Adults *on page 1999*
    USPHS / IDSA Guidelines for the Prevention of Opportunistic Infections in Persons Infected With HIV *on page 1966*
Use Treatment of uncomplicated acute illness due to influenza (A or B) infection in children ≥1 year of age and adults who have been symptomatic for no more than 2 days; prophylaxis against influenza (A or B) infection in children ≥1 year of age and adults
Pregnancy Risk Factor C
Pregnancy Implications There are insufficient human data to determine the risk to a pregnant woman or developing fetus. Studies evaluating the effects on embryo-fetal development in rats and rabbits showed a dose-dependent increase in the rates of minor skeleton abnormalities in exposed offspring. The rate of each abnormality remained within the background rate of occurrence in the species studied.
Lactation Excretion in breast milk unknown/not recommended
Medication Safety Issues
    Sound-alike/look-alike issues:
        Tamiflu® may be confused with Thera-Flu®
Contraindications Hypersensitivity to oseltamivir or any component of the formulation
Warnings/Precautions Oseltamivir is not a substitute for the influenza virus vaccine. Use caution with renal impairment; dosage adjustment is required for creatinine clearance between 10-30 mL/minute. Also consider primary or concomitant bacterial infections. Safety and efficacy for use in hepatic impairment or for treatment or prophylaxis in immunocompromised patients have not been established. Efficacy has not been established if treatment begins >40 hours after the onset of symptoms or in the treatment of patients with chronic cardiac and/or respiratory disease. Rare but severe hypersensitivity reactions (anaphylaxis, severe dermatologic reactions) have been associated with use. Rare occurrences of neuropsychiatric events (including self-injury, confusion, and/or delirium) have been reported in pediatric patients from postmarketing surveillance; monitor closely for signs of any unusual behavior. Safety and efficacy in children (<1 year of age) have not been established.
Adverse Reactions
    >10%: Gastrointestinal: Vomiting (2% to 15%)
    1% to 10%: Gastrointestinal: Nausea (3% to 10%), abdominal pain (2% to 5%)

<1% (Limited to important or life-threatening): Allergy, anaphylactic/anaphylactoid reaction, arrhythmia, confusion, dermatitis, diabetes aggravation, eczema, erythema multiforme, hepatitis, liver function tests abnormal, neuropsychiatric events (self-injury, confusion, delirium), rash, seizure, Stevens-Johnson syndrome, swelling of face or tongue, toxic epidermal necrolysis, urticaria

Overdosage/Toxicology Single doses of 1000 mg resulted in nausea and vomiting.

Drug Interactions

Decreased Effect: Influenza virus vaccine nasal spray (fluMist™): Safety and efficacy for use with influenza virus vaccine nasal spray have not been established. Do not administer nasal spray until 48 hours after stopping antiviral; do not administer antiviral for 2 weeks after receiving influenza virus vaccine nasal spray.

Stability

Capsules: Store at 25°C (77°F).

Oral suspension: Store powder for suspension at 25°C (77°F). Reconstitute with 23 mL of water (to make 25 mL total suspension). Once reconstituted, store suspension under refrigeration at 2°C to 8°C (36°F to 46°F); do not freeze. Use within 10 days of preparation.

Mechanism of Action Oseltamivir, a prodrug, is hydrolyzed to the active form, oseltamivir carboxylate. It is thought to inhibit influenza virus neuraminidase, with the possibility of alteration of virus particle aggregation and release.

Pharmacodynamics/Kinetics

Absorption: Well absorbed

Distribution: V_d: 23-26 L (oseltamivir carboxylate)

Protein binding, plasma: Oseltamivir carboxylate: 3%; Oseltamivir: 42%

Metabolism: Hepatic (90%) to oseltamivir carboxylate; neither the parent drug nor active metabolite has any effect on CYP

Bioavailability: 75% as oseltamivir carboxylate

Half-life elimination: Oseltamivir: 1-3 hours; Oseltamivir carboxylate: 6-10 hours

Excretion: Urine (>90% as oseltamivir carboxylate); feces

Dosage Oral:

Treatment: Initiate treatment within 2 days of onset of symptoms; duration of treatment: 5 days:

Children: 1-12 years:

≤15 kg: 30 mg twice daily

>15 kg to ≤23 kg: 45 mg twice daily

>23 kg to ≤40 kg: 60 mg twice daily

>40 kg: 75 mg twice daily

Adolescents ≥13 years and Adults: 75 mg twice daily

Prophylaxis: Initiate treatment within 2 days of contact with an infected individual; duration of treatment: 10 days

Children: 1-12 years:

≤15 kg: 30 mg once daily

>15 kg to <23 kg: 45 mg once daily

>23 kg to ≤40 kg: 60 mg once daily

>40 kg: 75 mg once daily

Adolescents ≥13 years and Adults: 75 mg once daily. During community outbreaks, dosing is 75 mg once daily. May be used for up to 6 weeks; duration of protection lasts for length of dosing period

Elderly: Refer to Adults dosing.

Dosage adjustment in renal impairment: Adults:

Cl_{cr} 10-30 mL/minute:

Treatment: Reduce dose to 75 mg once daily for 5 days

Prophylaxis: 75 mg every other day or 30 mg once daily

Cl_{cr} <10 mL/minute: Dosing recommendations are not available

Dosage adjustment in hepatic impairment: Dosing recommendations are not available

Dietary Considerations Take with or without food; take with food to improve tolerance.

Monitoring Parameters Signs or symptoms of unusual behavior, including attempts at self-injury, confusion, and/or delirium

Additional Information In clinical studies of the influenza virus, 1.3% of post-treatment isolates in adults and adolescents and 8.6% of isolates in children had decreased neuraminidase susceptibility *in vitro* to oseltamivir carboxylate.

Dosage Forms

Capsule, as phosphate:

Tamiflu®: 75 mg

Powder for oral suspension:

Tamiflu®: 12 mg/mL (25 mL) [contains sodium benzoate; tutti-frutti flavor]

- **OSI-774** see Erlotinib on page 606
- **Osmitrol®** see Mannitol on page 1055
- **Osteocit® (Can)** see Calcium Citrate on page 272
- **Ostoforte® (Can)** see Ergocalciferol on page 603
- **OTFC (Oral Transmucosal Fentanyl Citrate)** see Fentanyl on page 693
- **Oticaine** see Benzocaine on page 204
- **Otocaine™** see Benzocaine on page 204
- **Outgro® [OTC]** see Benzocaine on page 204
- **Ovace®** see Sulfacetamide on page 1609
- **Ovace® Wash** see Sulfacetamide on page 1609
- **Ovcon®** see Ethinyl Estradiol and Norethindrone on page 655
- **Ovide®** see Malathion on page 1053
- **Ovidrel®** see Chorionic Gonadotropin (Recombinant) on page 364
- **Ovine Corticotropin-Releasing Hormone** see Corticorelin on page 419
- **Ovral® (Can)** see Ethinyl Estradiol and Norgestrel on page 663

Oxacillin (oks a SIL in)

Index Terms Methylphenyl Isoxazolyl Penicillin; Oxacillin Sodium
Pharmacologic Category Antibiotic, Penicillin
Additional Appendix Information
Antibiotic Treatment of Adults With Infective Endocarditis *on page 1977*
Use Treatment of infections such as osteomyelitis, septicemia, endocarditis, and CNS infections caused by susceptible strains of *Staphylococcus*
Pregnancy Risk Factor B
Pregnancy Implications Teratogenicity not observed in animal studies.
Lactation Enters breast milk/compatible
Contraindications Hypersensitivity to oxacillin or other penicillins or any component of the formulation
Warnings/Precautions Elimination rate will be slow in neonates; modify dosage in patients with renal impairment and in the elderly; use with caution in patients with cephalosporin hypersensitivity
Adverse Reactions Frequency not defined.
Central nervous system: Fever
Dermatologic: Rash
Gastrointestinal: Nausea, diarrhea, vomiting
Hematologic: Eosinophilia, leukopenia, neutropenia, thrombocytopenia, agranulocytosis
Hepatic: Hepatotoxicity, AST increased
Renal: Acute interstitial nephritis, hematuria
Miscellaneous: Serum sickness-like reactions
Overdosage/Toxicology Symptoms of penicillin overdose include neuromuscular hypersensitivity (agitation, hallucinations, asterixis, encephalopathy, confusion, and seizures) and electrolyte imbalance (with potassium or sodium salts), especially in renal failure. Hemodialysis may be helpful to aid in the removal of the drug from the blood, otherwise most treatment is supportive or symptom-directed.
Drug Interactions
Increased Effect/Toxicity: Probenecid increases penicillin levels. Penicillins and anticoagulants may increase the effect of anticoagulants. Penicillins may increase the exposure to methotrexate during concurrent therapy; monitor.
Decreased Effect: Although anecdotal reports suggest oral contraceptive efficacy could be reduced by penicillins, this has been refuted by more rigorous scientific and clinical data.
Stability Reconstituted parenteral solution is stable for 3 days at room temperature and 7 days when refrigerated. For I.V. infusion in NS or D_5W, solution is stable for 24 hours at room temperature.
Mechanism of Action Inhibits bacterial cell wall synthesis by binding to one or more of the penicillin binding proteins (PBPs); which in turn inhibits the final transpeptidation step of peptidoglycan synthesis in bacterial cell walls, thus inhibiting cell wall biosynthesis. Bacteria eventually lyse due to ongoing activity of cell wall autolytic enzymes (autolysins and murein hydrolases) while cell wall assembly is arrested.
Pharmacodynamics/Kinetics
Distribution: Into bile, synovial and pleural fluids, bronchial secretions, peritoneal, and pericardial fluids; crosses placenta; enters breast milk; penetrates the blood-brain barrier only when meninges are inflamed
Protein binding: ~94%
Metabolism: Hepatic to active metabolites
Half-life elimination: Children 1 week to 2 years: 0.9-1.8 hours; Adults: 23-60 minutes; prolonged in neonates and with renal impairment
Time to peak, serum: I.M.: 30-60 minutes
Excretion: Urine and feces (small amounts as unchanged drug and metabolites)
Dosage
Usual dosage range:
Infants and Children: I.M., I.V.: 100-200 mg/kg/day in divided doses every 6 hours (maximum: 12 g/day)
Adults: I.M., I.V.: 250-2000 mg every 4-6 hours
Indication-specific dosing:
Children:
Arthritis (septic): I.V.: 37 mg/kg every 6 hours
Epiglottitis: I.V.: 150-200 mg/kg/day divided every 6 hours
Mild-to-moderate infections: I.M., I.V.: 100-150 mg/kg/day in divided doses every 6 hours (maximum: 4 g/day)
Severe infections: I.M., I.V.: 150-200 mg/kg/day in divided doses every 6 hours (maximum: 12 g/day)
Staphylococcal scalded-skin syndrome: I.V.: 150 mg/kg/day divided every 6 hours for 5-7 days
Adults:
Endocarditis: I.V.: 2 g every 4 hours with gentamicin
Mild-to-moderate infections: I.M., I.V.: 250-500 mg every 4-6 hours
Prosthetic joint infection: I.V.: 2 g every 4 hours with rifampin
Severe infections: I.M., I.V.: 1-2 g every 4-6 hours
Staphylococcus aureus, **methicillin-susceptible infections, including brain abscess, bursitis, erysipelas, mastitis, mastoiditis, osteomyelitis, perinephric abscess, pneumonia, pyomyositis, scalded skin syndrome, toxic shock syndrome:** I.V.: 2 g every 4 hours
Dosing adjustment in renal impairment: Cl_{cr} <10 mL/minute: Clinical practice varies; some clinicians recommend adjustment to the lower range of the usual dosage as based on severity of infection.
Hemodialysis: Not dialyzable (0% to 5%)
Dietary Considerations Sodium content of 1 g: 92.4 mg (4.02 mEq)

Administration Administer around-the-clock to promote less variation in peak and trough serum levels. Administer IVP over 10 minutes. Administer IVPB over 30 minutes.

Monitoring Parameters Observe for signs and symptoms of anaphylaxis during first dose; monitor periodic CBC, urinalysis, BUN, serum creatinine, AST and ALT

Test Interactions May interfere with urinary glucose tests using cupric sulfate (Benedict's solution, Clinitest®); may inactivate aminoglycosides *in vitro*; false-positive urinary and serum proteins

Dosage Forms
Infusion [premixed iso-osmotic dextrose solution]: 1 g (50 mL); 2 g (50 mL)
Injection, powder for reconstitution, as sodium: 1 g, 2 g, 10 g

♦ **Oxacillin Sodium** *see* Oxacillin *on page 1276*

Oxaliplatin (ox AL i pla tin)

U.S. Brand Names Eloxatin®
Index Terms Diaminocyclohexane Oxalatoplatinum; L-OHP; NSC-266046
Pharmacologic Category Antineoplastic Agent, Alkylating Agent
Use Treatment of advanced colon cancer and advanced rectal carcinoma
Unlabeled/Investigational Use Head and neck cancer, nonsmall cell lung cancer, non-Hodgkin's lymphoma, ovarian cancer
Pregnancy Risk Factor D
Pregnancy Implications Decreased fetal weight, decreased ossification, and increased fetal deaths were observed in animal studies at one-tenth the equivalent human dose. There are no adequate and well-controlled studies in pregnant women. Women of childbearing potential should be advised to avoid pregnancy during treatment.
Lactation Excretion in breast milk unknown/not recommended
Medication Safety Issues
Sound-alike/look-alike issues:
Oxaliplatin may be confused with Aloxi®, carboplatin

High alert medication: The Institute for Safe Medication Practices (ISMP) includes this medication among its list of drugs which have a heightened risk of causing significant patient harm when used in error.

Contraindications Hypersensitivity to oxaliplatin, other platinum-containing compounds, or any component of the formulation; pregnancy

Warnings/Precautions Hazardous agent - use appropriate precautions for handling and disposal. [U.S. Boxed Warning]: **Anaphylactic-like reaction may occur within minutes of oxaliplatin administration; symptoms may be managed with epinephrine, corticosteroids, and antihistamines.** Two different types of neuropathy may occur: First, an acute (within first 2 days), reversible (resolves within 14 days), primarily peripheral symptoms that are often exacerbated by cold (may include pharyngolaryngeal dysesthesia); and secondly, a more persistent (>14 days) presentation that often interferes with daily activities (eg, writing, buttoning, swallowing), these symptoms may improve upon discontinuing treatment. May cause pulmonary fibrosis or hepatotoxicity. The presence of hepatic vascular disorders (including veno-occlusive disease) should be considered, especially in individuals developing portal hypertension or who present with increased liver function tests. Use caution with renal dysfunction; increased toxicity may occur. When administered as sequential infusions, taxane derivatives (docetaxel, paclitaxel) should be administered before platinum derivatives (carboplatin, cisplatin, oxaliplatin) to limit myelosuppression and enhance efficacy. [U.S. Boxed Warning]: **Should be administered under the supervision of an experienced cancer chemotherapy physician.** Safety and efficacy in children have not been established.

Adverse Reactions Percentages reported with monotherapy.
>10%:
Central nervous system: Fatigue (61%), fever (25%), pain (14%), headache (13%), insomnia (11%)
Gastrointestinal: Nausea (64%), diarrhea (46%), vomiting (37%), abdominal pain (31%), constipation (31%), anorexia (20%), stomatitis (14%)
Hematologic: Anemia (64%), thrombocytopenia (30%), leukopenia (13%)
Hepatic: SGOT increased (54%), SGPT increased (36%); total bilirubin increased (13%)
Neuromuscular & skeletal: Peripheral neuropathy (may be dose-limiting; 76%; acute 65%; grades 3/4: 5%; persistent 43%; grades 3/4: 3%), back pain (11%)
Respiratory: Dyspnea (13%), cough (11%)
1% to 10%:
Cardiovascular: Edema (10%), chest pain (5%), peripheral edema (5%), flushing (3%), thromboembolism (2%)
Central nervous system: Dizziness (7%)
Dermatologic: Rash (5%), alopecia (3%), hand-foot syndrome (1%)
Endocrine & metabolic: Dehydration (5%), hypokalemia (3%)
Gastrointestinal: Dyspepsia (7%), taste perversion (5%), flatulence (3%), mucositis (2%), gastroesophageal reflux (1%), dysphagia (acute 1% to 2%)
Genitourinary: Dysuria (1%)
Hematologic: Neutropenia (7%)
Local: Injection site reaction (9%; redness/swelling/pain)
Neuromuscular & skeletal: Rigors (9%), arthralgia (7%)
Ocular: Abnormal lacrimation (1%)
Renal: Serum creatinine increased (5% to 10%)
Respiratory: URI (7%), rhinitis (6%), epistaxis (2%), pharyngitis (2%), pharyngolaryngeal dysesthesia (1% to 2%)
Miscellaneous: Allergic reactions (3%), hiccup (2%)
Postmarketing and/or case reports: Alkaline phosphatase increased, anaphylactic shock, angioedema, colitis, cranial nerve palsies, deep tendon reflex loss, deafness, dysarthria, eosinophilic pneumonia, fasciculations, hemolytic anemia (immuno-allergic), hemolytic uremia syndrome, hepatotoxicity, hypersensitivity (urticaria, pruritus, facial flushing, shortness of breath, bronchospasm, diaphoresis, hypotension, syncope), hypokalemia (due to
(Continued)

Oxaliplatin *(Continued)*

severe diarrhea, vomiting), ileus, interstitial lung diseases, intestinal obstruction, Lhermittes' sign, metabolic acidosis, optic neuritis, pancreatitis, pulmonary fibrosis, thrombocytopenia (immuno-allergic), veno-occlusive liver disease (sinusoidal obstruction syndrome and perisinusoidal fibrosis), visual acuity decreased, visual field disturbance

Overdosage/Toxicology Overdose symptoms are extensions of known side effects (eg, thrombocytopenia, myelosuppression, nausea, vomiting, neurotoxicity, respiratory symptoms). Monitor closely. Treatment should be symptom-directed and supportive.

Drug Interactions

Increased Effect/Toxicity: Taxane derivatives may increase oxaliplatin toxicity if administered before the platin as a sequential infusion. Nephrotoxic agents may increase oxaliplatin toxicity.

Decreased Effect: Oxaliplatin may decrease plasma levels of digoxin.

Stability Store in original outer carton at room temperature of 15°C to 30°C (59°F to 86°F); do not freeze. Protect from light. Diluted solution is stable up to 6 hours at room temperature of 20°C to 25°C (68°F to 77°F) or up to 24 hours under refrigeration at 2°C to 8°C (36°F to 46°F).

Do not prepare using a chloride-containing solution (eg, NaCl). Dilution with D_5W (250 or 500 mL) is required prior to administration. Infusion solutions do not require protection from light.

Mechanism of Action Oxaliplatin, a platinum derivative, is an alkylating agent. Following intracellular hydrolysis, the platinum compound binds to DNA forming cross-links which inhibit DNA replication and transcription, resulting in cell death. Cytotoxicity is cell-cycle nonspecific.

Pharmacodynamics/Kinetics

Distribution: V_d: 440 L

Protein binding: >90% primarily albumin and gamma globulin (irreversible binding to platinum)

Metabolism: Nonenzymatic (rapid and extensive), forms active and inactive derivatives

Half-life elimination: Terminal: 391 hours; Distribution: Alpha phase: 0.4 hours, Beta phase: 16.8 hours

Excretion: Primarily urine (54%); feces (2%)

Dosage Refer to individual protocols.

Adults: Stage III colon cancer and colorectal cancer: I.V.:

85 mg/m² every 2 weeks **or**

Unlabeled doses:

20-25 mg/m² days 1-5 every 3 weeks **or**

100-130 mg/m² every 2-3 weeks

Elderly: No dosing adjustment recommended

Dosage adjustments for toxicity: Longer infusion times may mitigate acute toxicities. In patients experiencing persistent neurosensory events (grade 2) which do not resolve, a dose reduction (65 mg/m² for stage III colon cancer; 75 mg/m² for advanced colorectal cancer) may be considered. Grade 3 neurosensory events may prompt consideration to discontinue oxaliplatin (while fluorouracil/leucovorin are continued or decreased). After recovery from grade 3/4 gastrointestinal toxicity, grade 4 neutropenia, or grade 3/4 thrombocytopenia, a dosage reduction 65 mg/m² for stage III colon cancer; 75 mg/m² for advanced colorectal cancer) is recommended.

Dosage adjustment in renal impairment: Consider omitting dose or changing chemotherapy regimen if Cl_{cr} ≤19 mL/minute. In patients with Cl_{cr} <30 mL/minute, the AUC is increased ~190%.

Administration Administer as I.V. infusion over 2-6 hours. Flush infusion line with D_5W prior to administration of any concomitant medication. Patients should receive an antiemetic premedication regimen.

Monitoring Parameters CBC with differential, serum creatinine, liver function tests; signs of neuropathy, hypersensitivity, and/or respiratory effects; delay dosage until recovery of neutrophils ≥1.5 x 10⁹/L and platelets ≥75 x 10⁹/L

Additional Information Cold temperature may exacerbate acute neuropathy. Do not use ice for mucositis prophylaxis.

Dosage Forms [DSC] = Discontinued product

Injection, powder for reconstitution:

Eloxatin®: 50 mg, 100 mg [contains lactose] [DSC]

Injection, solution [preservative free]:

Eloxatin®: 5 mg/mL (10 mL, 20 mL)

♦ **Oxandrin®** see Oxandrolone on page 1278

Oxandrolone *(oks AN droe lone)*

U.S. Brand Names Oxandrin®

Pharmacologic Category Androgen

Use Adjunctive therapy to promote weight gain after weight loss following extensive surgery, chronic infections, or severe trauma, and in some patients who, without definite pathophysiologic reasons, fail to gain or to maintain normal weight; to offset protein catabolism with prolonged corticosteroid administration; relief of bone pain associated with osteoporosis

Restrictions C-III

Pregnancy Risk Factor X

Pregnancy Implications Masculinization of the fetus has been reported.

Lactation Excretion in breast milk unknown/not recommended

Contraindications Hypersensitivity to oxandrolone or any component of the formulation; nephrosis; carcinoma of breast or prostate; hypercalcemia; pregnancy

Warnings/Precautions [U.S. Boxed Warning]: Anabolic steroids may cause peliosis hepatis or liver cell tumors which may not be apparent until liver failure or intra-abdominal hemorrhage develop. Discontinue in case of cholestatic hepatitis with jaundice or abnormal liver function tests. Use caution with concomitant warfarin therapy; warfarin dose may need significantly decreased. May cause blood lipid changes with increased risk of arteriosclerosis. Use with caution in elderly patients, they may be at greater risk for prostatic hyperplasia, fluid retention, and transaminase elevations. Use with caution in patients with cardiac, renal, or hepatic disease, COPD, diabetes or epilepsy. Discontinue with evidence of mild virilization in women. May stunt bone growth in children.

Adverse Reactions Frequency not defined.

Cardiovascular: Edema

Central nervous system: Depression, excitation, insomnia

Dermatologic: Acne (females and prepubertal males)
Also reported in females: Hirsutism, male-pattern baldness

Endocrine & metabolic: Electrolyte imbalances, glucose intolerance, gonadotropin secretion inhibited, gynecomastia, HDL decreased, LDL increased
Also reported in females: Clitoral enlargement, menstrual irregularities

Genitourinary:
Prepubertal males: Increased or persistent erections, penile enlargement
Postpubertal males: Bladder irritation, epididymitis, impotence, oligospermia, priapism (chronic), testicular atrophy, testicular function

Hepatic: Alkaline phosphatase increased, ALT/AST increased, bilirubin increased, cholestatic jaundice, hepatic necrosis (rare), hepatocellular neoplasms, peliosis hepatitis (with long-term therapy)

Neuromuscular & skeletal: CPK increased, premature closure of epiphyses (in children)

Renal: Creatinine excretion increased

Miscellaneous: Bromsulfophthalein retention, habituation, voice alteration (deepening, in females)

Drug Interactions
Increased Effect/Toxicity: ACTH, adrenal steroids may increase risk of edema and acne. Oxandrolone enhances the hypoprothrombinemic effects of oral anticoagulants, and enhances the hypoglycemic effects of insulin and sulfonylureas (oral hypoglycemics).

Mechanism of Action Synthetic testosterone derivative with similar androgenic and anabolic actions

Pharmacodynamics/Kinetics Half-life elimination: 10-13 hours

Dosage
Children: Total daily dose: ≤0.1 mg/kg **or** ≤0.045 mg/lb
Adults: 2.5-20 mg in divided doses 2-4 times/day based on individual response; a course of therapy of 2-4 weeks is usually adequate. This may be repeated intermittently as needed.
Elderly: 5 mg twice daily
Dosing adjustment in renal impairment: Caution is recommended because of the propensity of oxandrolone to cause edema and water retention
Dosing adjustment in hepatic impairment: Caution is advised but there are not specific guidelines for dosage reduction

Monitoring Parameters Liver function tests, cholesterol profile, hemoglobin/hematocrit; INR/PT in patients on anticoagulant therapy
Children: Radiographs of left wrist every 6 months (to assess bone maturation)
Adult females: Signs of virilization (deepening voice, hirsutism, acne, clitoromegaly); urine and serum calcium in women with breast cancer

Test Interactions May suppress factors II, V, VII, and X; may increase PT; may decrease thyroxine-binding globulin and radioactive iodine uptake

Dosage Forms Tablet: 2.5 mg, 10 mg

Oxaprozin (oks a PROE zin)

U.S. Brand Names Daypro®

Canadian Brand Names Apo-Oxaprozin®; Daypro®

Pharmacologic Category Nonsteroidal Anti-inflammatory Drug (NSAID), Oral

Additional Appendix Information
Nonsteroidal Anti-inflammatory Agents *on page 1894*

Use Acute and long-term use in the management of signs and symptoms of osteoarthritis and rheumatoid arthritis; juvenile rheumatoid arthritis

Restrictions An FDA-approved medication guide must be distributed when dispensing an oral outpatient prescription (new or refill) where this medication is to be used without direct supervision of a healthcare provider. Medication guides are available at http://www.fda.gov/cder/Offices/ODS/medication_guides.htm.

Pregnancy Risk Factor C/D (3rd trimester)

Pregnancy Implications Safety and efficacy in pregnant women have not been established. Exposure late in pregnancy may lead to premature closure of the ductus arteriosus and may inhibit uterine contractions.

Lactation Excretion in breast milk unknown/not recommended

Medication Safety Issues
Sound-alike/look-alike issues:
Daypro® may be confused with Diupres®
Oxaprozin may be confused with oxazepam

Contraindications Hypersensitivity to oxaprozin, aspirin, other NSAIDs, or any component of the formulation; perioperative pain in the setting of coronary artery bypass surgery (CABG); pregnancy (3rd trimester)

Warnings/Precautions [U.S. Boxed Warning]: NSAIDs are associated with an increased risk of adverse cardiovascular events, including MI, stroke, and new onset or worsening of pre-existing hypertension. Risk may be increased with duration of use or pre-existing cardiovascular risk-factors or disease. Carefully evaluate individual cardiovascular risk profiles prior to prescribing. Use caution with fluid retention, CHF or hypertension. Concurrent administration of ibuprofen, and potentially other nonselective NSAIDs, may interfere with aspirin's cardioprotective effect.
(Continued)

Oxaprozin *(Continued)*

Use of NSAIDs can compromise existing renal function. Renal toxicity can occur in patient with impaired renal function, dehydration, heart failure, liver dysfunction, those taking diuretics and ACEI and the elderly. Rehydrate patient before starting therapy. Monitor renal function closely. Oxaprozin is not recommended for patients with advanced renal disease.

[U.S. Boxed Warning]: NSAIDs may increase risk of gastrointestinal irritation, ulceration, bleeding, and perforation. These events may occur at any time during therapy and without warning. Use caution with a history of GI disease (bleeding or ulcers), concurrent therapy with aspirin, anticoagulants and/or corticosteroids, smoking, use of alcohol, the elderly or debilitated patients.

Use the lowest effective dose for the shortest duration of time, consistent with individual patient goals, to reduce risk of cardiovascular or GI adverse events. Alternate therapies should be considered for patients at high risk.

NSAIDs may cause serious skin adverse events including exfoliative dermatitis, Stevens-Johnson syndrome (SJS) and toxic epidermal necrolysis (TEN). Anaphylactoid reactions may occur, even without prior exposure; patients with "aspirin triad" (bronchial asthma, aspirin intolerance, rhinitis) may be at increased risk. Do not use in patients who experience bronchospasm, asthma, rhinitis, or urticaria with NSAID or aspirin therapy.

Use with caution in patients with decreased hepatic function. Closely monitor patients with any abnormal LFT. Severe hepatic reactions (eg, fulminant hepatitis, liver failure) have occurred with NSAID use, rarely; discontinue if signs or symptoms of liver disease develop, or if systemic manifestations occur.

The elderly are at increased risk for adverse effects (especially peptic ulceration, CNS effects, renal toxicity) from NSAIDs even at low doses.

Withhold for at least 4-6 half-lives prior to surgical or dental procedures. May cause mild photosensitivity reactions. Safety and efficacy have not been established in children <6 years of age.

Adverse Reactions

1% to 10%:
Cardiovascular: Edema
Central nervous system: Confusion, depression, dizziness, headache, sedation, sleep disturbance, somnolence
Dermatologic: Pruritus, rash
Gastrointestinal: Abdominal distress, abdominal pain, anorexia, constipation, diarrhea, flatulence, gastrointestinal ulcer, gross bleeding with perforation, heartburn, nausea, vomiting
Hematologic: Anemia, bleeding time increased
Hepatic: Liver enzyme elevation
Otic: Tinnitus
Renal: Dysuria, renal function abnormal, urinary frequency
<1% (Limited to important or life-threatening; effects reported with oxaprozin or other NSAIDs): Acute interstitial nephritis, acute renal failure, agranulocytosis, anaphylaxis, angioedema, asthma, bruising, CHF, erythema multiforme, exfoliative dermatitis, gastritis, gastrointestinal bleeding, hearing decreased, hematemesis, hematuria, hemorrhoidal bleeding, hepatitis, hypersensitivity reaction, hypertension, jaundice, leukopenia, nephrotic syndrome, pancreatitis, peptic ulcer, photosensitivity, rectal bleeding, renal insufficiency, Stevens-Johnson syndrome, toxic epidermal necrolysis, thrombocytopenia

Overdosage/Toxicology

Symptoms include acute renal failure, vomiting, drowsiness, and leukocytosis. Management of nonsteroidal anti-inflammatory drug (NSAID) intoxication is primarily supportive and symptomatic. Fluid therapy is commonly effective in managing hypotension that may occur following an acute NSAID overdose, except when due to acute blood loss. Seizures tend to be very short-lived and often do not require drug treatment, although recurrent seizures should be treated with I.V. diazepam. Since many of NSAIDs undergo enterohepatic cycling, multiple doses of charcoal may be needed to reduce the potential for delayed toxicities.

Drug Interactions

Increased Effect/Toxicity: Oxaprozin may increase cyclosporine, digoxin, lithium, and methotrexate serum concentrations. The renal adverse effects of ACE inhibitors may be potentiated by NSAIDs. Corticosteroids may increase the risk of GI ulceration. The risk of bleeding with anticoagulants (warfarin, antiplatelet agents, low molecular weight heparins) may be increased. Concomitant use with fluoroquinolones may rarely increase risk of seizure.

Decreased Effect: Oxaprozin may decrease the effect of some antihypertensive agents (including ACE inhibitors, beta-blockers, hydralazine, and angiotensin antagonists), diuretics. Cholestyramine (and other bile acid sequestrants) may decrease the absorption of NSAIDs; separate by at least 2 hours. Salicylates' antiplatelet effect may be reduced.

Ethanol/Nutrition/Herb Interactions

Ethanol: Avoid ethanol (may enhance gastric mucosal irritation).
Herb/Nutraceutical: Avoid alfalfa, anise, bilberry, bladderwrack, bromelain, cat's claw, celery, coleus, cordyceps, dong quai, evening primrose, feverfew, fenugreek, garlic, ginger, ginkgo biloboa, red clover, horse chestnut, grapeseed, green tea, ginseng, guggul, horse chestnut seed, horseradish, licorice, prickly ash, red clover, reishi, SAMe, sweet clover, turmeric, white willow (all have additional antiplatelet activity).

Stability Store at 25°C (77°F). Protect from light; keep bottle tightly closed.

Mechanism of Action Inhibits prostaglandin synthesis by decreasing the activity of the enzyme, cyclooxygenase, which results in decreased formation of prostaglandin precursors

Pharmacodynamics/Kinetics

Absorption: Almost complete
Protein binding: >99%
Metabolism: Hepatic via oxidation and glucuronidation; no active metabolites
Half-life elimination: 40-50 hours

Time to peak: 2-4 hours
Excretion: Urine (5% unchanged, 65% as metabolites); feces (35% as metabolites)
Dosage Oral (individualize dosage to lowest effective dose to minimize adverse effects):
Children 6-16 years: Juvenile rheumatoid arthritis:
22-31 kg: 600 mg once daily
32-54 kg: 900 mg once daily
≥55 kg: 1200 mg once daily
Adults:
Osteoarthritis: 600-1200 mg once daily; patients should be titrated to lowest dose possible; patients with low body weight should start with 600 mg daily
Rheumatoid arthritis: 1200 mg once daily; a one-time loading dose of up to 1800 mg/day or 26 mg/kg (whichever is lower) may be given
Maximum doses:
Patient <50 kg: Maximum: 1200 mg/day
Patient >50 kg with normal renal/hepatic function and low risk of peptic ulcer: Maximum: 1800 mg or 26 mg/kg (whichever is lower) in divided doses
Dosing adjustment in renal impairment: In general NSAIDs are not recommended for use in patients with advanced renal disease but the manufacturer of oxaprozin does provide some guidelines for adjustment in renal dysfunction.
Severe renal impairment or on dialysis: 600 mg once daily, may increase cautiously to 1200 mg/day with close monitoring
Dosing adjustment in hepatic impairment: Use caution in patients with severe dysfunction
Monitoring Parameters Monitor CBC; hepatic, renal, and ocular function
Test Interactions False-positive urine immunoassay screening tests for benzodiazepines have been reported and may occur several days after discontinuing oxaprozin.
Dosage Forms Tablet: 600 mg

Oxazepam (oks A ze pam)

U.S. Brand Names Serax®
Canadian Brand Names Apo-Oxazepam®; Novoxapram®; Oxpam®; Oxpram®; PMS-Oxazepam; Riva-Oxazepam
Pharmacologic Category Benzodiazepine
Additional Appendix Information
Benzodiazepines *on page 1874*
Use Treatment of anxiety; management of ethanol withdrawal
Unlabeled/Investigational Use Anticonvulsant in management of simple partial seizures; hypnotic
Restrictions C-IV
Pregnancy Risk Factor D
Lactation Enters breast milk/not recommended
Medication Safety Issues
Sound-alike/look-alike issues:
Oxazepam may be confused with oxaprozin, quazepam
Serax® may be confused with Eurax®, Urex®, Zyrtec®

International issues:
Murelax® [Australia] may be confused with MIralax™ which is a brand name for polyethylene glycol 3350 in the U.S.
Contraindications Hypersensitivity to oxazepam or any component of the formulation (cross-sensitivity with other benzodiazepines may exist); narrow-angle glaucoma (not in product labeling, however, benzodiazepines are contraindicated); not indicated for use in the treatment of psychosis; pregnancy
Warnings/Precautions May cause hypotension (rare) - use with caution in patients with cardiovascular or cerebrovascular disease, or in patients who would not tolerate transient decreases in blood pressure. Serax® 15 contains tartrazine; use is not recommended in pediatric patients <6 years of age; dose has not been established between 6-12 years of age.

Use with caution in elderly or debilitated patients, patients with hepatic disease (including alcoholics), or renal impairment. Use with caution in patients with respiratory disease or impaired gag reflex. Avoid use in patients with sleep apnea.

Causes CNS depression (dose-related) resulting in sedation, dizziness, confusion, or ataxia which may impair physical and mental capabilities. Patients must be cautioned about performing tasks which require mental alertness (eg, operating machinery or driving). Use with caution in patients receiving other CNS depressants or psychoactive agents. Effects with other sedative drugs or ethanol may be potentiated. Benzodiazepines have been associated with falls and traumatic injury and should be used with extreme caution in patients who are at risk of these events (especially the elderly).

Use caution in patients with suicidal risk. Use with caution in patients with a history of drug dependence. Benzodiazepines have been associated with dependence and acute withdrawal symptoms on discontinuation or reduction in dose. Acute withdrawal, including seizures, may be precipitated after administration of flumazenil to patients receiving long-term benzodiazepine therapy.

Benzodiazepines have been associated with anterograde amnesia. Paradoxical reactions, including hyperactive or aggressive behavior have been reported with benzodiazepines, particularly in adolescent/pediatric or psychiatric patients. Does not have analgesic, antidepressant, or antipsychotic properties.
Adverse Reactions Frequency not defined.
Cardiovascular: Syncope (rare), edema
Central nervous system: Drowsiness, ataxia, dizziness, vertigo, memory impairment, headache, paradoxical reactions (excitement, stimulation of effect), lethargy, amnesia, euphoria
Dermatologic: Rash
Endocrine & metabolic: Decreased libido, menstrual irregularities
(Continued)

Oxazepam *(Continued)*

Genitourinary: Incontinence
Hematologic: Leukopenia, blood dyscrasias
Hepatic: Jaundice
Neuromuscular & skeletal: Dysarthria, tremor, reflex slowing
Ocular: Blurred vision, diplopia
Miscellaneous: Drug dependence

Overdosage/Toxicology Symptoms include somnolence, confusion, coma, hypoactive reflexes, dyspnea, hypotension, slurred speech, and impaired coordination. Treatment for benzodiazepine overdose is supportive. Rarely is mechanical ventilation required. Flumazenil has been shown to selectively block the binding of benzodiazepines to CNS receptors, resulting in reversal of benzodiazepine-induced CNS depression, but not respiratory depression due to toxicity.

Drug Interactions

Increased Effect/Toxicity: Ethanol and other CNS depressants may increase the CNS effects of oxazepam. Oxazepam may decrease the antiparkinsonian efficacy of levodopa. Flumazenil may cause seizures if administered following long-term benzodiazepine treatment.

Decreased Effect: Oral contraceptives may increase the clearance of oxazepam. Theophylline and other CNS stimulants may antagonize the sedative effects of oxazepam. Phenytoin may increase the clearance of oxazepam.

Ethanol/Nutrition/Herb Interactions

Ethanol: Avoid ethanol (may increase CNS depression).
Herb/Nutraceutical: Avoid valerian, St John's wort, kava kava, gotu kola (may increase CNS depression).

Mechanism of Action Binds to stereospecific benzodiazepine receptors on the postsynaptic GABA neuron at several sites within the central nervous system, including the limbic system, reticular formation. Enhancement of the inhibitory effect of GABA on neuronal excitability results by increased neuronal membrane permeability to chloride ions. This shift in chloride ions results in hyperpolarization (a less excitable state) and stabilization.

Pharmacodynamics/Kinetics

Absorption: Almost complete
Protein binding: 86% to 99%
Metabolism: Hepatic to inactive compounds (primarily as glucuronides)
Half-life elimination: 2.8-5.7 hours
Time to peak, serum: 2-4 hours
Excretion: Urine (as unchanged drug (50%) and metabolites)

Dosage Oral:

Children: Anxiety: 1 mg/kg/day has been administered
Adults:
Anxiety: 10-30 mg 3-4 times/day
Ethanol withdrawal: 15-30 mg 3-4 times/day
Hypnotic: 15-30 mg
Elderly: Oral: Anxiety: 10 mg 2-3 times/day; increase gradually as needed to a total of 30-45 mg/day. Dose titration should be slow to evaluate sensitivity.
Hemodialysis: Not dialyzable (0% to 5%)

Administration Administer orally in divided doses

Monitoring Parameters Respiratory and cardiovascular status

Reference Range Therapeutic: 0.2-1.4 mcg/mL (SI: 0.7-4.9 μmol/L)

Additional Information Not intended for management of anxieties and minor distresses associated with everyday life. Treatment longer than 4 months should be re-evaluated to determine the patient's need for the drug. Abrupt discontinuation after sustained use (generally >10 days) may cause withdrawal symptoms.

Dosage Forms

Capsule: 10 mg, 15 mg, 30 mg
Tablet: 15 mg [contains tartrazine]

Oxcarbazepine *(ox car BAZ e peen)*

U.S. Brand Names Trileptal®
Canadian Brand Names Trileptal®
Index Terms GP 47680; OCBZ
Pharmacologic Category Anticonvulsant, Miscellaneous
Additional Appendix Information
Anticonvulsants by Seizure Type *on page 1865*
Epilepsy *on page 2048*

Use Monotherapy or adjunctive therapy in the treatment of partial seizures in adults and children ≥4 years of age with epilepsy; adjunctive therapy in the treatment of partial seizures in children ≥2 years of age with epilepsy.

Unlabeled/Investigational Use Bipolar disorder; treatment of neuropathic pain

Pregnancy Risk Factor C

Pregnancy Implications Oxcarbazepine crosses the human placenta. Teratogenic effects have been observed in animal studies. Oxcarbazepine is structurally related to carbamazepine (teratogenic in humans), use during pregnancy only if the benefit to the mother outweighs the potential risk to the fetus. Nonhormonal forms of contraception should be used during therapy.

Lactation Enters breast milk/not recommended

Contraindications Hypersensitivity to oxcarbazepine or any component of the formulation

Warnings/Precautions Clinically-significant hyponatremia (sodium <125 mmol/L) can develop during oxcarbazepine use. Potentially serious, sometimes fatal, dermatologic reactions (eg, Stevens-Johnson, toxic epidermal necrolysis) and multiorgan hypersensitivity reactions have been reported in adults and children; monitor for signs and symptoms of skin reactions and possible disparate manifestations associated with lymphatic, hepatic, renal and/or hematologic organ systems; gradual discontinuation and conversion to alternate therapy may be required. As with all antiepileptic drugs, oxcarbazepine should be withdrawn gradually to minimize the potential of increased seizure frequency. Use of oxcarbazepine has been associated with CNS related adverse events, most significant of these were cognitive symptoms including psychomotor slowing, difficulty with concentration, and speech or language problems, somnolence or fatigue, and coordination abnormalities, including ataxia and gait disturbances. Use caution in patients with previous hypersensitivity to carbamazepine (cross-sensitivity occurs in 25% to 30%). May reduce the efficacy of oral contraceptives (nonhormonal contraceptive measures are recommended).

Adverse Reactions As reported in adults with doses of up to 2400 mg/day (includes patients on monotherapy, adjunctive therapy, and those not previously on AEDs); incidence in children was similar.

>10%:

Central nervous system: Dizziness (22% to 49%), somnolence (20% to 36%), headache (13% to 32%, placebo 23%), ataxia (5% to 31%), fatigue (12% to 15%), vertigo (6% to 15%)

Gastrointestinal: Vomiting (7% to 36%), nausea (15% to 29%), abdominal pain (10% to 13%)

Neuromuscular & skeletal: Abnormal gait (5% to 17%), tremor (3% to 16%)

Ocular: Diplopia (14% to 40%), nystagmus (7% to 26%), abnormal vision (4% to 14%)

1% to 10%:

Cardiovascular: Hypotension (1% to 2%)

Central nervous system: Nervousness (2% to 5%), amnesia (4%), agitation (1% to 2%)

Dermatologic: Rash (4%)

Endocrine & metabolic: Hyponatremia (1% to 3%)

Gastrointestinal: Diarrhea (5% to 7%), gastritis (1% to 2%)

Neuromuscular & skeletal: Weakness (3% to 6%), back pain (4%), falls (4%), abnormal coordination (1% to 4%), muscle weakness (1% to 2%)

Ocular: Abnormal accommodation (2%)

Respiratory: Upper respiratory tract infection (7%)

<1% (Limited to important or life-threatening): Aggressive reaction, alopecia, angioedema, aphasia, asthma, blood in stool, cardiac failure, cataract, cerebral hemorrhage, cholelithiasis, convulsions aggravated, delirium, duodenal ulcer, dysphagia, dysphonia, dyspnea, dystonia, erythema multiforme, eosinophilia, extrapyramidal disorder, gastric ulcer, genital pruritus, gingival hyperplasia, hematemesis, hematuria, hemianopia, hemiplegia, hypersensitivity reaction, intermenstrual bleeding, laryngismus, leukopenia, maculopapular rash, malaise, manic reaction, menorrhagia, migraine, muscle contractions (involuntary), neuralgia, oculogyric crisis, paralysis, photosensitivity reaction, postural hypotension, priapism, purpura, psychosis, scotoma, sialoadenitis, Stevens-Johnson syndrome, stupor, syncope, systemic lupus erythematosus, tetany, thrombocytopenia, toxic epidermal necrolysis, urticaria

Overdosage/Toxicology Symptoms may include CNS depression (somnolence, ataxia). Treatment is symptomatic and supportive.

Drug Interactions

Cytochrome P450 Effect: Inhibits CYP2C19 (weak); **Induces** CYP3A4 (strong)

Increased Effect/Toxicity: Serum concentrations of phenytoin and phenobarbital are increased by oxcarbazepine.

Decreased Effect: Oxcarbazepine serum concentrations may be reduced by carbamazepine, phenytoin, phenobarbital, valproic acid and verapamil (decreases levels of active oxcarbazepine metabolite). Oxcarbazepine reduces the serum concentrations of hormonal contraceptives; use alternative contraceptive measures. Oxcarbazepine may decrease the levels/effects of benzodiazepines, calcium channel blockers, clarithromycin, cyclosporine, erythromycin, estrogens, mirtazapine, nateglinide, nefazodone, nevirapine, protease inhibitors, tacrolimus, venlafaxine, and other CYP3A4 substrates.

Ethanol/Nutrition/Herb Interactions

Ethanol: Avoid ethanol (may increase CNS depression).

Herb/Nutraceutical: St John's wort may decrease oxcarbazepine levels. Avoid evening primrose (seizure threshold decreased). Avoid valerian, St John's wort, kava kava, gotu kola.

Stability Store tablets and suspension at 25°C (77°F). Use suspension within 7 weeks of first opening container.

Mechanism of Action Pharmacological activity results from both oxcarbazepine and its monohydroxy metabolite (MHD). Precise mechanism of anticonvulsant effect has not been defined. Oxcarbazepine and MHD block voltage sensitive sodium channels, stabilizing hyperexcited neuronal membranes, inhibiting repetitive firing, and decreasing the propagation of synaptic impulses. These actions are believed to prevent the spread of seizures. Oxcarbazepine and MHD also increase potassium conductance and modulate the activity of high-voltage activated calcium channels.

Pharmacodynamics/Kinetics

Absorption: Complete; food has no affect on rate or extent

Distribution: MHD: V_d: 49 L

Protein binding, serum: MHD: 40%

Metabolism: Hepatic to 10-monohydroxy metabolite (MHD; active); MHD is further conjugated to DHD (inactive)

Bioavailability: Decreased in children <8 years; increased in elderly >60 years

Half-life elimination: Parent drug: 2 hours; MHD: 9 hours; renal impairment (Cl_{cr} 30 mL/minute): MHD: 19 hours

Clearance of MHD is increased in younger children (~80% in children 2-4 years of age) and approaches that of adults by ~13 years of age

Time to peak, serum: 4.5 hours (3-13 hours)

Excretion: Urine (95%, <1% as unchanged oxcarbazepine, 27% as unchanged MHD, 49% as MHD glucuronides); feces (<4%)

(Continued)

Oxcarbazepine *(Continued)*

Dosage Oral:

Children 2-3 years:

Adjunctive therapy: 8-10 mg/kg/day, not to exceed 600 mg/day, given in 2 divided daily doses. Maintenance dose should be achieved over 2 weeks, and is dependent upon patient weight.

<20 kg: Consider initiating dose at 16-20 mg/kg/day; maximum maintenance dose should be achieved over 2-4 weeks and should not exceed 60 mg/kg/day

Children 4-16 years:

Adjunctive therapy: 8-10 mg/kg/day, not to exceed 600 mg/day, given in 2 divided daily doses. Maintenance dose should be achieved over 2 weeks, and is dependent upon patient weight, according to the following:

20-29 kg: 900 mg/day in 2 divided doses

29.1-39 kg: 1200 mg/day in 2 divided doses

>39 kg: 1800 mg/day in 2 divided doses

Children 4-16 years:

Conversion to monotherapy: Oxcarbazepine 8-10 mg/kg/day in twice daily divided doses, while simultaneously initiating the reduction of the dose of the concomitant antiepileptic drug; the concomitant drug should be withdrawn over 3-6 weeks. Oxcarbazepine dose may be increased by a maximum of 10 mg/kg/day at weekly intervals. See below for recommended total daily dose by weight.

Initiation of monotherapy: Oxcarbazepine should be initiated at 8-10 mg/kg/day in twice daily divided doses; doses may be titrated by 5 mg/kg/day every third day. See below for recommended total daily dose by weight.

Range of maintenance doses by weight during monotherapy:

20 kg: 600-900 mg/day

25-30 kg: 900-1200 mg/day

35-40 kg: 900-1500 mg/day

45 kg: 1200-1500 mg/day

50-55 kg: 1200-1800 mg/day

60-65 kg: 1200-2100 mg/day

70 kg: 1500-2100 mg/day

Adults:

Adjunctive therapy: Initial: 300 mg twice daily; dose may be increased by as much as 600 mg/day at weekly intervals; recommended daily dose: 1200 mg/day in 2 divided doses. Although daily doses >1200 mg/day demonstrated greater efficacy, most patients were unable to tolerate 2400 mg/day (due to CNS effects).

Conversion to monotherapy: Oxcarbazepine 600 mg/day in twice daily divided doses while simultaneously initiating the reduction of the dose of the concomitant antiepileptic drug. The concomitant dosage should be withdrawn over 3-6 weeks, while the maximum dose of oxcarbazepine should be reached in about 2-4 weeks. Recommended daily dose: 2400 mg/day.

Initiation of monotherapy: Oxcarbazepine should be initiated at a dose of 600 mg/day in twice daily divided doses; doses may be titrated upward by 300 mg/day every third day to a final dose of 1200 mg/day given in 2 daily divided doses

Dosing adjustment in renal impairment: Cl_{cr} <30 mL/minute: Therapy should be initiated at one-half the usual starting dose (300 mg/day in adults) and increased slowly to achieve the desired clinical response

Dosing adjustment in hepatic impairment: Adjustment not needed for mild-to-moderate impairment

Dietary Considerations May be taken with or without food.

Administration Suspension: Prior to using for the first time, firmly insert the plastic adapter provided with the bottle. Cover adapter with child-resistant cap when not in use. Shake bottle for at least 10 seconds, remove child-resistant cap and insert the oral dosing syringe provided to withdraw appropriate dose. Dose may be taken directly from oral syringe or may be mixed in a small glass of water immediately prior to swallowing. Rinse syringe with warm water after use and allow to dry thoroughly. Discard any unused portion after 7 weeks of first opening bottle.

Monitoring Parameters Seizure frequency, serum sodium (particularly during first 3 months of therapy), symptoms of CNS depression (dizziness, headache, somnolence). Additional serum sodium monitoring recommended during maintenance treatment in patients receiving other medications known to decrease sodium levels, in patients with signs/symptoms of hyponatremia, and in patients with an increase in seizure frequency or severity.

Dosage Forms

Suspension, oral: 300 mg/5 mL (250 mL) [contains ethanol; packaged with oral syringe]

Tablet: 150 mg, 300 mg, 600 mg

♦ **Oxeze® Turbuhaler® (Can)** *see* Formoterol *on page 759*

Oxiconazole *(oks i KON a zole)*

U.S. Brand Names Oxistat®

Canadian Brand Names Oxistat®

Index Terms Oxiconazole Nitrate

Pharmacologic Category Antifungal Agent, Topical

Use Treatment of tinea pedis (athlete's foot), tinea cruris (jock itch), and tinea corporis (ringworm)

Pregnancy Risk Factor B

Dosage Topical:

Children and Adults:

Tinea corporis/tinea cruris: Cream, lotion: Apply to affected areas 1-2 times daily for 2 weeks

Tinea pedis: Cream, lotion: Apply to affected areas 1-2 times daily for 1 month

Adults: Tinea versicolor: Cream: Apply to affected areas once daily for 2 weeks

Additional Information Complete prescribing information for this medication should be consulted for additional detail.

Dosage Forms

Cream: 1% (15 g, 30 g, 60 g) [contains benzoic acid]
Lotion: 1% (30 mL) [contains benzoic acid]

♦ **Oxiconazole Nitrate** see Oxiconazole on page 1284

♦ **Oxilan®** see Ioxilan on page 931

♦ **Oxilan® 300 (Can)** see Ioxilan on page 931

♦ **Oxilan® 350 (Can)** see Ioxilan on page 931

♦ **Oxilapine Succinate** see Loxapine on page 1042

♦ **Oxistat®** see Oxiconazole on page 1284

♦ **Oxpam® (Can)** see Oxazepam on page 1281

♦ **Oxpentifylline** see Pentoxifylline on page 1343

♦ **Oxpram® (Can)** see Oxazepam on page 1281

♦ **Oxsoralen®** see Methoxsalen on page 1115

♦ **Oxsoralen-Ultra®** see Methoxsalen on page 1115

Oxybutynin (oks i BYOO ti nin)

U.S. Brand Names Ditropan®; Ditropan® XL; Oxytrol®

Canadian Brand Names Apo-Oxybutynin®; Ditropan®; Ditropan® XL; Gen-Oxybutynin; Novo-Oxybutynin; Nu-Oxybutyn; Oxytrol®; PMS-Oxybutynin; Uromax®

Index Terms Oxybutynin Chloride

Pharmacologic Category Antispasmodic Agent, Urinary

Use Antispasmodic for neurogenic bladder (urgency, frequency, urge incontinence) and uninhibited bladder

Pregnancy Risk Factor B

Pregnancy Implications Teratogenic effects were not observed in animal studies. There are no adequate and well-controlled studies in pregnant women; use during pregnancy only if clearly needed.

Lactation Excretion in breast milk unknown/use caution

Medication Safety Issues

Sound-alike/look-alike issues:

Oxybutynin may be confused with OxyContin®
Ditropan® may be confused with Detrol®, diazepam, Diprivan®, dithranol

Transdermal patch may contain conducting metal (eg, aluminum); remove patch prior to MRI.

Contraindications Hypersensitivity to oxybutynin or any component of the formulation; untreated glaucoma; partial or complete GI obstruction; GU obstruction; urinary retention; megacolon; toxic megacolon

Warnings/Precautions Use with caution in patients with urinary tract obstruction, angle-closure glaucoma (treated), hyperthyroidism, reflux esophagitis (including concurrent therapy with oral bisphosphonates or drugs which may increase the risk of esophagitis), heart disease, hepatic or renal disease, prostatic hyperplasia, autonomic neuropathy, ulcerative colitis (may cause ileus and toxic megacolon), hypertension, hiatal hernia, myasthenia gravis, ulcerative colitis, or intestinal atony. Caution should be used in elderly due to anticholinergic activity (eg, confusion, constipation, blurred vision, and tachycardia). May increase the risk of heat prostration.

The extended release formulation consists of drug within a nondeformable matrix; following drug release/absorption, the matrix/shell is expelled in the stool. The use of nondeformable products in patients with known stricture/narrowing of the GI tract has been associated with symptoms of obstruction. Transdermal patch may contain conducting metal (eg, aluminum); remove patch prior to MRI.

Adverse Reactions

Oral:

>10%:

Central nervous system: Dizziness (6% to 16%), somnolence (12% to 13%)
Gastrointestinal: Xerostomia (61% to 71%), constipation (13%)
Genitourinary: Urination impaired (11%)

1% to 10%:

Cardiovascular: Palpitation (2% to <5%), peripheral edema (2% to <5%), hypertension (2% to <5%), vasodilation (2% to <5%)
Central nervous system: Headache (6% to 10%), pain (7%), confusion (2% to <5%), insomnia (2% to <5%), nervousness (2% to <5%)
Dermatologic: Dry skin (2% to <5%), skin rash (2% to <5%)
Gastrointestinal: Nausea (9% to 10%), dyspepsia (7%), abdominal pain (2% to 6%), diarrhea (5% to 9%), flatulence (2% to <5%), gastrointestinal reflux (2% to <5%), taste perversion (2% to <5%)
Genitourinary: Postvoid residuals increased (2% to 9%), urinary tract infection (5%)
Neuromuscular & skeletal: Weakness (2% to 7%)
Ocular: Blurred vision (8% to 9%), dry eyes (2% to 6%)
Respiratory: Rhinitis (6%), dry nasal and sinus membranes (2% to <5%)

Transdermal:

>10%: Local: Application site reaction (17%), pruritus (14%)

1% to 10%:

Gastrointestinal: Xerostomia (4% to 10%), diarrhea (3%), constipation (3%)
Genitourinary: Dysuria (2%)
Local: Erythema (6% to 8%), vesicles (3%), rash (3%)
Ocular: Vision changes (3%)

(Continued)

Oxybutynin *(Continued)*

Postmarketing and/or case reports: Cardiac arrhythmia, cycloplegia, hallucinations, lactation suppressed, myocarditis, impotence, seizure, sweating decreased, tachycardia

Overdosage/Toxicology Symptoms include hypotension, circulatory failure, psychotic behavior, flushing, respiratory failure, paralysis, tremor, irritability, seizures, delirium, hallucinations, and coma. Treatment is symptomatic and supportive. Induce emesis or perform gastric lavage followed by charcoal and a cathartic. Physostigmine may be required. Treat hyperpyrexia with cooling techniques (ice bags, cold applications, alcohol sponges).

Drug Interactions

Cytochrome P450 Effect: Substrate of CYP3A4 (minor); **Inhibits** CYP2C8 (weak), 2D6 (weak), 3A4 (weak)

Increased Effect/Toxicity: Additive sedation with CNS depressants and ethanol. Additive anticholinergic effects with antihistamines and anticholinergic agents.

Ethanol/Nutrition/Herb Interactions Ethanol: Use ethanol with caution (may increase CNS depression and toxicity). Watch for sedation.

Stability Store at controlled room temperature. Protect syrup from light. Keep transdermal patch in sealed pouch.

Mechanism of Action Direct antispasmodic effect on smooth muscle, also inhibits the action of acetylcholine on smooth muscle (exhibits $1/5$ the anticholinergic activity of atropine, but is 4-10 times the antispasmodic activity); does not block effects at skeletal muscle or at autonomic ganglia; increases bladder capacity, decreases uninhibited contractions, and delays desire to void; therefore, decreases urgency and frequency

Pharmacodynamics/Kinetics

Onset of action: Oral: 30-60 minutes

Peak effect: 3-6 hours

Duration: 6-10 hours (up to 24 hours for extended release oral formulation)

Absorption: Oral: Rapid and well absorbed; Transdermal: High

Distribution: V_d: 193 L

Metabolism: Hepatic via CYP3A4; Oral: High first-pass metabolism (not with I.V. or transdermal use). Forms active and inactive metabolites

Half-life elimination: I.V.: ~2 hours (parent drug), 7-8 hours (metabolites)

Time to peak, serum: Oral: ~60 minutes; Transdermal: 24-48 hours

Excretion: Urine, as metabolites (<0.1% as unchanged drug)

Dosage

Oral:

Children:

1-5 years (unlabeled use): 0.2 mg/kg/dose 2-4 times/day

>5 years: 5 mg twice daily, up to 5 mg 3 times/day maximum

>6 years: Extended release: 5 mg once daily; maximum dose: 20 mg/day

Adults: 5 mg 2-3 times/day up to 5 mg 4 times/day maximum

Extended release: Initial: 5-10 mg once daily, may increase in 5-10 mg increments; maximum: 30 mg daily

Elderly: 2.5-5 mg 2-3 times/day

Transdermal: Adults: Apply one 3.9 mg/day patch twice weekly (every 3-4 days)

Note: Should be discontinued periodically to determine whether the patient can manage without the drug and to minimize resistance to the drug

Dietary Considerations Food causes a slight delay in the absorption of the oral solution and bioavailability is deceased by ~25%. Absorption of the extended release tablet is not affected by food.

Administration

Oral: Immediate release tablets and solution should be administered on an empty stomach with water. Extended release tablets may be taken with or without food and must be swallowed whole; do not crush, divide, or chew.

Transdermal: Apply to clean, dry skin on abdomen, hip, or buttock. Select a new site for each new system (avoid reapplication to same site within 7 days).

Monitoring Parameters Incontinence episodes, postvoid residual (PVR)

Test Interactions May suppress the wheal and flare reactions to skin test antigens

Dosage Forms

Syrup, as chloride: 5 mg/5 mL (473 mL)

Ditropan®: 5 mg/5 mL (473 mL)

Tablet, as chloride: 5 mg

Ditropan®: 5 mg

Tablet, extended release, as chloride: 5 mg, 10 mg, 15 mg

Ditropan® XL: 5 mg, 10 mg, 15 mg

Transdermal system:

Oxytrol®: 3.9 mg/day (8s) [39 cm^2; total oxybutynin 36 mg]

♦ **Oxybutynin Chloride** *see Oxybutynin on page 1285*

♦ **Oxycocet® (Can)** *see Oxycodone and Acetaminophen on page 1289*

♦ **Oxycodan® (Can)** *see Oxycodone and Aspirin on page 1289*

Oxycodone *(oks i KOE done)*

U.S. Brand Names ETH-Oxydose™; OxyContin®; OxyFast®; OxyIR®; Roxicodone®

Canadian Brand Names OxyContin®; Oxy.IR®; Supeudol®

Index Terms Dihydrohydroxycodeinone; Oxycodone Hydrochloride

Pharmacologic Category Analgesic, Opioid

Additional Appendix Information

Narcotic Agonists *on page 1888*

Use Management of moderate-to-severe pain, normally used in combination with nonopioid analgesics

OxyContin® is indicated for around-the-clock management of moderate-to-severe pain when an analgesic is needed for an extended period of time.

Restrictions C-II

Pregnancy Risk Factor B/D (prolonged use or high doses at term)

Pregnancy Implications Should be used in pregnancy only if clearly needed. Use of narcotics during pregnancy may produce physical dependence in the neonate; respiratory depression may occur in the newborn if narcotics are used prior to delivery (especially high doses).

Lactation Enters breast milk/use caution

Medication Safety Issues

Sound-alike/look-alike issues:

Oxycodone may be confused with OxyContin®

OxyContin® may be confused with oxybutynin, oxycodone

OxyFast® may be confused with Roxanol™

Contraindications Hypersensitivity to oxycodone or any component of the formulation; significant respiratory depression; hypercarbia; acute or severe bronchial asthma; OxyContin® is also contraindicated in paralytic ileus (known or suspected); pregnancy (prolonged use or high doses at term)

Warnings/Precautions May cause CNS depression, which may impair physical or mental abilities; patients must be cautioned about performing tasks which require mental alertness (eg, operating machinery or driving). Effects may be potentiated when used with other sedative drugs or ethanol. Use with caution in patients with hypersensitivity reactions to other phenanthrene derivative opioid agonists (morphine, hydrocodone, hydromorphone, levorphanol, oxymorphone), respiratory diseases including asthma, emphysema, or COPD. Use with caution in pancreatitis or biliary tract disease, acute alcoholism (including delirium tremens), morbid obesity, adrenocortical insufficiency, history of seizure disorders, CNS depression/coma, kyphoscoliosis (or other skeletal disorder which may alter respiratory function), hypothyroidism (including myxedema), prostatic hyperplasia, urethral stricture, and toxic psychosis. May obscure diagnosis or clinical course of patients with acute abdominal conditions.

Use with caution in the elderly, debilitated, severe hepatic or renal function. Hemodynamic effects (hypotension, orthostasis) may be exaggerated in patients with hypovolemia, concurrent vasodilating drugs, or in patients with head injury. Respiratory depressant effects and capacity to elevate CSF pressure may be exaggerated in presence of head injury, other intracranial lesion, or pre-existing intracranial pressure. Some preparations contain sulfites which may cause allergic reactions.

Concurrent use of agonist/antagonist analgesics may precipitate withdrawal symptoms and/or reduced analgesic efficacy in patients following prolonged therapy with mu opioid agonists. Abrupt discontinuation following prolonged use may also lead to withdrawal symptoms.

[U.S. Boxed Warning]: Healthcare provider should be alert to problems of abuse, misuse, and diversion. Tolerance or drug dependence may result from extended use.

Controlled-release formulations:

[U.S. Boxed Warning]: OxyContin® is not intended for use as an "as needed" analgesic or for immediately-postoperative pain management (should be used postoperatively only if the patient has received it prior to surgery or if severe, persistent pain is anticipated). **[U.S. Boxed Warning]: Do NOT crush, break, or chew controlled-release tablets;** 60 mg, 80 mg, and 160 mg strengths are for use only in opioid-tolerant patients.

Adverse Reactions

>10%:

Central nervous system: Somnolence (23% to 24%), dizziness (13% to 16%)

Dermatologic: Pruritus (12% to 13%)

Gastrointestinal: Nausea (23% to 27%), constipation (23% to 26%), vomiting (12% to 14%)

1% to 10%:

Cardiovascular: Postural hypotension (1% to 5%)

Central nervous system: Headache (7% to 8%), abnormal dreams (1% to 5%), anxiety (1% to 5%), chills (1% to 5%), confusion (1% to 5%), euphoria (1% to 5%), fever (1% to 5%), insomnia (1% to 5%), nervousness (1% to 5%), thought abnormalities (1% to 5%)

Dermatologic: Rash (1% to 5%)

Gastrointestinal: Xerostomia (6% to 7%), abdominal pain (1% to 5%), anorexia (1% to 5%), diarrhea (1% to 5%), dyspepsia (1% to 5%), gastritis (1% to 5%)

Neuromuscular & skeletal: Weakness (6% to 7%), twitching (1% to 5%)

Respiratory: Dyspnea (1% to 5%), hiccups (1% to 5%)

Miscellaneous: Diaphoresis (5% to 6%)

<1% (Limited to important or life-threatening): Agitation, amenorrhea, amnesia, anaphylaxis, anaphylactoid reaction, appetite increased, chest pain, cough, dehydration, depression, dysphagia, dysuria, edema, emotional lability, eructation, exfoliative dermatitis, facial edema, hallucinations, hematuria, histamine release, hyperkinesia, hypesthesia, hyponatremia, hypotonia, ileus,impotence, intracranial pressure increased, libido decreased, malaise, migraine, paradoxical CNS stimulation, paralytic ileus, paresthesias, pharyngitis, physical dependence, polyuria, psychological dependence, seizure, SIADH, speech disorder, ST segment depression, stomatitis, stupor, syncope, tablet in stool (OxyCodone®), taste perversion, thirst, tinnitus, tremor, urinary retention, urticaria, vasodilation, vertigo, vision change, voice alteration, withdrawal syndrome

Overdosage/Toxicology Symptoms of toxicity include CNS depression, respiratory depression, and miosis. Treatment is symptom-directed and supportive. Naloxone can reverse opioid-induced hypotension and respiratory depression. An initial I.V. dose of 0.2-0.4 mg can be administered. Lower initial doses should be considered in opioid-dependent patients or if suspected concurrent stimulant overdose. If no response in 2-3 minutes after initial dose, consider an additional 1-2 mg evey 2-3 minutes up to a total dose of 10 mg. There is no role for dialysis or hemoperfusion.

(Continued)

Oxycodone *(Continued)*

Drug Interactions

Cytochrome P450 Effect: Substrate of CYP2D6 (major)

Increased Effect/Toxicity: Phenothiazine antipsychotic agents may enhance the hypotensive effect of analgesics (opioid). CNS depressants may enhance the adverse/toxic effect of analgesics (opioids).

Decreased Effect: Analgesics (opioid) may diminish the therapeutic effect of pegvisomant. monium chloride may increase the excretion of analgesics (opioid). CYP2D6 inhibitors may decrease the effects of oxycodone; example inhibitors include chlorpromazine, delavirdine, fluoxetine, miconazole, paroxetine, pergolide, quinidine, quinine, ritonavir, and ropinirole. Analgesics (opioid) may enhance the serotonergic effect of SSRIs (may cause serotonin syndrome).

Ethanol/Nutrition/Herb Interactions

Ethanol: Avoid ethanol (may increase CNS depression).

Food: When taken with a high-fat meal, peak concentration is 25% greater following a single OxyContin® 160 mg tablet as compared to two 80 mg tablets.

Herb/Nutraceutical: Avoid valerian, St John's wort, kava kava, gotu kola (may increase CNS depression).

Stability Store at 15°C to 30°C (59°F to 86°F). Protect from light.

Mechanism of Action Binds to opiate receptors in the CNS, causing inhibition of ascending pain pathways, altering the perception of and response to pain; produces generalized CNS depression

Pharmacodynamics/Kinetics

Onset of action: Pain relief: 10-15 minutes

Peak effect: 0.5-1 hour

Duration: Immediate release: 3-6 hours; Controlled release: ≤12 hours

Distribution: V_d: 2.6 L/kg; distributed to skeletal muscle, liver, intestinal tract, lungs, spleen, brain, and breast milk

Protein binding: ~45%

Metabolism: Hepatically via CYP2D6 to various metabolites including noroxycodone (weak analgesic activity), oxymorphone (has analgesic activity; low concentrations in plasma) and their glucuronides

Bioavailability: Controlled release, immediate release: 60% to 87%

Half-life elimination: Immediate release: 2-3 hours; controlled release: ~5 hours

Excretion: Urine (~19% as parent; > 64% as metabolites)

Dosage Oral:

Children: Immediate release:

6-12 years: 1.25 mg every 6 hours as needed

>12 years: 2.5 mg every 6 hours as needed

Adults:

Immediate release: 5 mg every 6 hours as needed

Controlled release:

Opioid naive: 10 mg every 12 hours

Concurrent CNS depressants: Reduce usual dose by 1/3 to 1/2

Conversion from transdermal fentanyl: For each 25 mcg/hour transdermal dose, substitiute 10 mg controlled release oxycodone every 12 hours; should be initiated 18 hours after the removal of the transdermal fentanyl patch

Currently on opioids: Use standard conversion chart to convert daily dose to oxycodone equivalent. Divide daily dose in 2 (for twice-daily dosing, usually every 12-hours) and round down to nearest dosage form.

Note: 60 mg, 80 mg or 160 mg tablets are for use **only** in opioid-tolerant patients. Special safety considerations must be addressed when converting to OxyContin® doses ≥160 mg every 12 hours. Dietary caution must be taken when patients are initially titrated to 160 mg tablets. Using different strengths to obtain the same daily dose is equivalent (eg, four 40 mg tablets, two 80 mg tablets, one 160 mg tablet); all produce similar blood levels.

Multiplication factors for converting the daily dose of current oral opioid to the daily dose of oral oxycodone:

Current opioid mg/day dose x factor = Oxycodone mg/day dose

Codiene mg/day oral dose **x** 0.15 = Oxycodone mg/day dose

Hydrocodone mg/day oral dose **x** 0.9 = Oxycodone mg/day dose

Hydromorphone mg/day oral dose **x** 4 = Oxycodone mg/day dose

Levorphanol mg/day oral dose **x** 7.5 = Oxycodone mg/day dose

Meperidine mg/day oral dose **x** 0.1 = Oxycodone mg/day dose

Methadone mg/day oral dose **x** 1.5 = Oxycodone mg/day dose

Morphine mg/day oral dose **x** 0.5 = Oxycodone mg/day dose

Note: Divide the oxycodone mg/day dose into the appropriate dosing interval for the specific form being used.

Dosing adjustment in hepatic impairment: Reduce dosage in patients with severe liver disease

Dietary Considerations Instruct patient to avoid high-fat meals when taking OxyContin® 160 mg tablets.

Administration Do not crush, break, or chew controlled-release tablets; 60 mg, 80 mg and 160 mg tablets are for use **only** in opioid-tolerant patients. Do not administer OxyContin® 160 mg tablet with a high-fat meal. Controlled release tablets are not indicated for rectal administration; increased risk of adverse events due to better rectal absorption.

Monitoring Parameters Pain relief, respiratory and mental status, blood pressure

Reference Range Blood level of 5 mg/L associated with fatality

Test Interactions Some quinolones may produce a false-positive urine screening result for opiates using commercially-available immunoassay kits. This has been demonstrated most consistently for levofloxacin and ofloxacin, but other quinolones have shown cross-reactivity in certain assay kits. Confirmation of positive opiate screens by more specific methods should be considered.

Additional Information Prophylactic use of a laxative should be considered. OxyContin® 60 mg, 80 mg, and 160 mg tablets are for use in opioid-tolerant patients only.

Dosage Forms

Capsule, as hydrochloride: 5 mg
  OxyIR®: 5 mg
Solution, oral, as hydrochloride: 5 mg/5 mL (500 mL)
  Roxicodone®: 5 mg/5 mL (5 mL, 500 mL) [contains alcohol]
Solution, oral, as hydrochloride [concentrate]: 20 mg/mL (30 mL)
  ETH-Oxydose™: 20 mg/mL (1 mL, 30 mL) [contains sodium benzoate; berry flavor]
  OxyFast®: 20 mg/mL (30 mL) [contains sodium benzoate and dry natural rubber]
  Roxicodone®: 20 mg/mL (30 mL) [contains sodium benzoate]
Tablet, as hydrochloride: 5 mg, 15 mg, 30 mg
  Roxicodone®: 5 mg, 15 mg, 30 mg
Tablet, controlled release, as hydrochloride:
  OxyContin®: 10 mg, 20 mg, 40 mg, 60 mg, 80 mg, 160 mg
Tablet, extended release, as hydrochloride: 10 mg, 20 mg, 40 mg, 80 mg

Oxycodone and Acetaminophen (oks i KOE done & a seet a MIN oh fen)

U.S. Brand Names Endocet®; Percocet®; Roxicet™; Roxicet™ 5/500; Tylox®
Canadian Brand Names Endocet®; Oxycocet®; Percocet®; Percocet®-Demi; PMS-Oxycodone-Acetaminophen
Index Terms Acetaminophen and Oxycodone
Pharmacologic Category Analgesic, Opioid
Use Management of moderate to severe pain
Restrictions C-II
Pregnancy Risk Factor C/D (prolonged periods or high doses at term)
Medication Safety Issues
Sound-alike/look-alike issues:
  Percocet® may be confused with Percodan®
  Roxicet™ may be confused with Roxanol™
  Tylox® may be confused with Trimox®, Tylenol®, Wymox®, Xanax®
Dosage Oral: Doses should be given every 4-6 hours as needed and titrated to appropriate analgesic effects. **Note:** Initial dose is based on the **oxycodone** content; however, the maximum daily dose is based on the **acetaminophen** content.

Children: Maximum acetaminophen dose: Children <45 kg: 90 mg/kg/day; children >45 kg: 4 g/day
  Mild to moderate pain: Initial dose, **based on oxycodone content:** 0.05-0.1 mg/kg/dose
  Severe pain: Initial dose, **based on oxycodone content:** 0.3 mg/kg/dose
Adults:
  Mild to moderate pain: Initial dose, **based on oxycodone content:** 5 mg
  Severe pain: Initial dose, **based on oxycodone content:** 15-30 mg. Do not exceed acetaminophen 4 g/day.
Elderly: Doses should be titrated to appropriate analgesic effects: Initial dose, **based on oxycodone content:** 2.5-5 mg every 6 hours. Do not exceed acetaminophen 4 g/day.
Dosage adjustment in hepatic impairment: Dose should be reduced in patients with severe liver disease.
Additional Information Complete prescribing information for this medication should be consulted for additional detail.

Dosage Forms

Caplet:
  Roxicet™ 5/500: Oxycodone hydrochloride 5 mg and acetaminophen 500 mg
Capsule: 5/500: Oxycodone hydrochloride 5 mg and acetaminophen 500 mg
  Tylox®: 5/500: Oxycodone hydrochloride 5 mg and acetaminophen 500 mg [contains sodium benzoate and sodium metabisulfite]
Solution, oral:
  Roxicet™: Oxycodone hydrochloride 5 mg and acetaminophen 325 mg per 5 mL (5 mL, 500 mL) [contains alcohol <0.5%]
Tablet: 5/325: Oxycodone hydrochloride 5 mg and acetaminophen 325 mg; 7.5/325: Oxycodone hydrochloride 7.5 mg and acetaminophen 325 mg; 7.5/500: Oxycodone hydrochloride 7.5 mg and acetaminophen 500 mg; 10/325: Oxycodone hydrochloride 10 mg and acetaminophen 325 mg; 10/650: Oxycodone hydrochloride 10 mg and acetaminophen 650 mg
  Endocet® 5/325 [scored]: Oxycodone hydrochloride 5 mg and acetaminophen 325 mg
  Endocet® 7.5/325: Oxycodone hydrochloride 7.5 mg and acetaminophen 325 mg
  Endocet® 7.5/500: Oxycodone hydrochloride 7.5 mg and acetaminophen 500 mg
  Endocet® 10/325: Oxycodone hydrochloride 10 mg and acetaminophen 325 mg
  Endocet® 10/650: Oxycodone hydrochloride 10 mg and acetaminophen 650 mg
  Percocet® 2.5/325: Oxycodone hydrochloride 2.5 mg and acetaminophen 325 mg
  Percocet® 5/325 [scored]: Oxycodone hydrochloride 5 mg and acetaminophen 325 mg
  Percocet® 7.5/325: Oxycodone hydrochloride 7.5 mg and acetaminophen 325 mg
  Percocet® 7.5/500: Oxycodone hydrochloride 7.5 mg and acetaminophen 500 mg
  Percocet® 10/325: Oxycodone hydrochloride 10 mg and acetaminophen 325 mg
  Percocet® 10/650: Oxycodone hydrochloride 10 mg and acetaminophen 650 mg
  Roxicet™ [scored]: Oxycodone hydrochloride 5 mg and acetaminophen 325 mg

Oxycodone and Aspirin (oks i KOE done & AS pir in)

U.S. Brand Names Endodan®; Percodan®
Canadian Brand Names Endodan®; Oxycodan®; Percodan®
Index Terms Aspirin and Oxycodone
Pharmacologic Category Analgesic, Opioid
Use Management of moderate to severe pain
(Continued)

Oxycodone and Aspirin *(Continued)*

Restrictions C-II

Pregnancy Risk Factor D

Medication Safety Issues

Sound-alike/look-alike issues:

Percodan® may be confused with Decadron®, Percocet®, Percogesic®, Periactin®

Dosage Oral (based on oxycodone combined salts):

Children: Maximum oxycodone: 5 mg/dose; maximum aspirin dose should not exceed 4 g/day. Doses should be given every 6 hours as needed.

Mild-to-moderate pain: Initial dose, **based on oxycodone content:** 0.05-0.1 mg/kg/dose

Severe pain: Initial dose, **based on oxycodone content:** 0.3 mg/kg/dose

Adults: Percodan®: 1 tablet every 6 hours as needed for pain; maximum aspirin dose should not exceed 4 g/day.

Dosing adjustment in hepatic impairment: Dose should be reduced in patients with severe liver disease.

Additional Information Complete prescribing information for this medication should be consulted for additional detail.

Dosage Forms

Tablet: Oxycodone hydrochloride 4.5 mg, oxycodone terephthalate 0.38 mg, and aspirin 325 mg

Endodan®, Percodan®: Oxycodone hydrochloride 4.8355 mg and aspirin 325 mg

---

Oxycodone and Ibuprofen *(oks i KOE done & eye byoo PROE fen)*

U.S. Brand Names Combunox™

Index Terms Ibuprofen and Oxycodone

Pharmacologic Category Analgesic, Opioid; Nonsteroidal Anti-inflammatory Drug (NSAID), Oral

Use Short-term (≤7 days) management of acute, moderate-to-severe pain

Restrictions C-II

A medication guide should be dispensed with each prescription for oral administration. A template for the required MedGuide can be found on the FDA website at http://www.fda.gov/cder/drug/infopage/COX2/NSAIDmedguide.htm

Pregnancy Risk Factor C/D (3rd trimester)

Dosage Oral: Adults: Pain: Take 1 tablet every 6 hours as needed (maximum: 4 tablets/24 hours); do not take for longer than 7 days

Additional Information Complete prescribing information for this medication should be consulted for additional detail.

Dosage Forms

Tablet:

Combunox™: 5/400: Oxycodone 5 mg and ibuprofen 400 mg

- ◆ **Oxycodone Hydrochloride** *see* Oxycodone *on page 1286*
- ◆ **OxyContin®** *see* Oxycodone *on page 1286*
- ◆ **OxyFast®** *see* Oxycodone *on page 1286*
- ◆ **OxyIR®** *see* Oxycodone *on page 1286*
- ◆ **Oxy.IR® (Can)** *see* Oxycodone *on page 1286*

Oxymetholone *(oks i METH oh lone)*

U.S. Brand Names Anadrol®

Pharmacologic Category Anabolic Steroid

Use Treatment of anemias caused by deficient red cell production

Restrictions C-III

Pregnancy Risk Factor X

Medication Safety Issues

Sound-alike/look-alike issues:

Oxymetholone may be confused with oxymetazoline, oxymorphone

Dosage Children and Adults: Erythropoietic effects: Oral: 1-5 mg/kg/day in one daily dose; usual effective dose: 1-2 mg/kg/day; give for a minimum trial of 3-6 months because response may be delayed

Dosing adjustment in hepatic impairment:

Mild to moderate hepatic impairment: Oxymetholone should be used with caution in patients with liver dysfunction because of its hepatotoxic potential

Severe hepatic impairment: Oxymetholone should **not** be used

Additional Information Complete prescribing information for this medication should be consulted for additional detail.

Dosage Forms Tablet: 50 mg

Oxymorphone *(oks i MOR fone)*

U.S. Brand Names Numorphan®; Opana®; Opana® ER

Index Terms Oxymorphone Hydrochloride

Pharmacologic Category Analgesic, Opioid

Additional Appendix Information

Narcotic Agonists *on page 1888*

Use

Parenteral: Management of moderate-to-severe pain and preoperatively as a sedative and/or supplement to anesthesia

Oral, regular release: Management of moderate-to-severe pain

Oral, extended release: Management of moderate-to-severe pain in patients requiring around-the-clock opioid treatment for an extended period of time

Restrictions C-II

Pregnancy Risk Factor C/D (prolonged use or high doses at term)

Pregnancy Implications Teratogenic effects were not observed in animal studies, however, decreased fetal weight, decreased litter size, increased stillbirths, and increased neonatal death were noted. Chronic opioid use during pregnancy may lead to a withdrawal syndrome in the neonate. Symptoms include irritability, hyperactivity, loss of sleep pattern, abnormal crying, tremor, vomiting, diarrhea, weight loss, or failure to gain weight. Opioid analgesics are considered pregnancy risk factor D if used for prolonged periods or in larger doses near term.

Lactation Excretion in breast milk unknown/use caution

Medication Safety Issues
Sound-alike/look-alike issues:
Oxymorphone may be confused with oxymetholone

Contraindications Hypersensitivity to oxymorphone, other morphine analogs (phenanthrene derivatives) or any component of the formulation; paralytic ileus (known or suspected); increased intracranial pressure; severe respiratory depression (unless in monitored setting with resuscitative equipment); acute/severe bronchial asthma; hypercarbia; pregnancy (prolonged use or high doses at term).

Note: Oral formulations are also contraindicated in moderate-to-severe hepatic impairment

Warnings/Precautions An opioid-containing analgesic regimen should be tailored to each patient's needs and based upon the type of pain being treated (acute versus chronic), the route of administration, degree of tolerance for opioids (naive versus chronic user), age, weight, and medical condition. The optimal analgesic dose varies widely among patients. Doses should be titrated to pain relief/prevention.

May cause CNS depression, which may impair physical or mental abilities; patients must be cautioned about performing tasks which require mental alertness (eg, operating machinery or driving). Effects may be potentiated when used with other sedative drugs or ethanol. Use with caution in patients with hypersensitivity reactions to other phenanthrene derivative opioid agonists (codeine, hydrocodone, hydromorphone, levorphanol, oxycodone). May cause respiratory depression. Use extreme caution in patients with COPD or other chronic respiratory conditions characterized by hypoxia, hypercapnea, or diminished respiratory reserve (myxedema, cor pulmonale, kyphoscoliosis, obstructive sleep apnea, severe obesity). Use with caution in patients (particularly elderly or debilitated) with impaired respiratory function, adrenal disease, morbid obesity, thyroid dysfunction, prostatic hyperplasia, renal impairment, or severe hepatic dysfunction. Use only with extreme caution (if at all) in patients with head injury or increased intracranial pressure (ICP); potential to elevate ICP and/or blunt papillary response may be greatly exaggerated in these patients. Use with caution in biliary tract disease or acute pancreatitis (may cause constriction of sphincter of Oddi). May obscure diagnosis or clinical course of patients with acute abdominal conditions.

Oxymorphone shares the toxic potential of opiate agonists and usual precautions of opiate agonist therapy should be observed; may cause hypotension in patients with acute myocardial infarction, volume depletion, or concurrent drug therapy which may exaggerate vasodilation. The elderly may be particularly susceptible to adverse effects of narcotics. Safety and efficacy have not been established in children <18 years of age.

[U.S. Boxed Warning]: Healthcare provider should be alert to problems of abuse, misuse, and diversion. Tolerance or drug dependence may result from extended use. Use caution in patients with a history of drug dependence or abuse. Abrupt discontinuation may precipitate withdrawal syndrome.

Extended release formulation:

[U.S. Boxed Warnings]: Opana® ER is an extended release oral formulation of oxymorphone and is not suitable for use as an "as needed" analgesic; tablets should not be broken, chewed, dissolved, or crushed; tablets should be swallowed whole. Opana® ER is intended for use in long-term, continuous management of moderate to severe chronic pain. It is not indicated for use in the immediate post-operative period (12-24 hours). **[U.S. Boxed Warning]: The co-ingestion of ethanol or ethanol-containing medications with OPANA ER may result in accelerated release of drug from the dosage form, abruptly increasing plasma levels, which may have fatal consequences.**

Adverse Reactions Frequency not defined.

Cardiovascular: Bradycardia, cardiac shock, flushing, hypotension, palpitation, peripheral vasodilation, shock, tachycardia

Central nervous system: Amnesia, anorexia, anxiety, CNS depression, coma, confusion, convulsion, drowsiness, dizziness, fatigue, fever, hallucinations, headache, insomnia, intracranial pressure (increased), malaise, mental depression, nervousness, restlessness, paradoxical CNS stimulation

Dermatologic: Pruritus, urticaria, rash

Endocrine & metabolic: Antidiuretic hormone release, weight loss

Gastrointestinal: Abdominal pain, appetite depression, biliary tract spasm, constipation, dehydration, dry mouth, dyspepsia, flatulence, nausea, paralytic ileus, stomach cramps, vomiting, xerostomia

Genitourinary: Decreased urination, urinary retention, urinary tract spasm

Local: Pain at injection site

Neuromuscular & skeletal: Weakness

Ocular: Diplopia, miosis

Respiratory: Apnea, cyanosis, dyspnea, hypoventilation, respiratory depression

Miscellaneous: Diaphoresis, histamine release, physical and psychological dependence

Overdosage/Toxicology Symptoms include respiratory depression, miosis, hypotension, bradycardia, apnea, and pulmonary edema. Treatment of overdose includes airway support, establishment of an I.V. line, and administration of naloxone 2 mg I.V. (0.01 mg/kg for children), with repeat administration as necessary, up to a total of 10 mg.

(Continued)

Oxymorphone *(Continued)*

Drug Interactions

Increased Effect/Toxicity: Increased effect/toxicity with CNS depressants (phenothiazines, tricyclic antidepressants, anxiolytics, sedatives, hypnotics, alcohol, and anesthetics). Dextroamphetamine may increase the analgesic effects of opiate agonists. Concurrent use with SSRIs may enhance serotonergic activity and may increase the risk of serotonin syndrome.

Ethanol/Nutrition/Herb Interactions

Ethanol: Avoid ethanol (may increase CNS depression). Ethanol ingestion with extended-release tablets is specifically contraindicated due to possible accelerated release and potentially fatal overdose.

Food: When taken orally with a high-fat meal, peak concentration is 38% to 50% greater. Both immediate-release and extended-release tablets should be taken 1 hour before or 2 hours after eating.

Herb/Nutraceutical: Avoid valerian, St John's wort, kava kava, gotu kola (may increase CNS depression).

Stability Injection solution, tablet: Store at 15°C to 30°C (59°F to 86°F).

Mechanism of Action Oxymorphone hydrochloride (Numorphan®) is a potent narcotic analgesic with uses similar to those of morphine. The drug is a semisynthetic derivative of morphine (phenanthrene derivative) and is closely related to hydromorphone chemically (Dilaudid®).

Pharmacodynamics/Kinetics

Onset of action: Analgesic: I.V., I.M., SubQ: 5-10 minutes

Duration: Analgesic: Parenteral: 3-4 hours

Protein binding: 10% to 12%

Metabolism: Hepatic via glucuronidation to active and inactive metabolites

Bioavailability: Oral: 10%

Half-life elimination: Oral: Immediate release: 7-9 hours; Extended release: 9-11 hours

Excretion: Urine

Dosage Adults: **Note:** Dosage must be individualized. For elderly patients, initiate dosing at the lower end of the dosage range.

I.M., SubQ: Initial: 0.5 mg; may repeat with 1-1.5 mg every 4-6 hours as needed

I.V.: Initial: 0.5 mg every 4-6 hours

Oral:

Immediate release:

Opioid-naive: 10-20 mg every 4-6 hours as needed. Initial dosages as low as 5 mg may be considered in selected patients and/or patients with renal impairment. Dosage adjustment should be based on level of analgesia, side effects, and pain intensity. Initiation of therapy with initial dose >20 mg is **not** recommended.

Currently on stable dose of parenteral oxymorphone: ~10 times the daily parenteral requirement. The calculated amount should be divided and given in 4-6 equal doses.

Currently on other opioids: Use standard conversion chart to convert daily dose to oxymorphone equivalent. Generally start with 1/2 the calculated daily oxymorphone dosage and administered in divided doses every 4-6 hours.

Extended release (Opana® ER):

Opioid-naive: Initial: 5 mg every 12 hours. Supplemental doses of immediate-release oxymorphone may be used as "rescue" medication as dosage is titrated.

Note: Continued requirement for supplemental dosing may be used to titrate the dose of extended-release continuous therapy. Adjust therapy incrementally, by 5-10 mg every 12 hours at intervals of every 3-7 days. Ideally, basal dosage may be titrated to generally mild pain or no pain with the regular use of fewer than 2 supplemental doses per 24 hours.

Currently on stable dose of parenteral oxymorphone: Approximately 10 times the daily parenteral requirement. The calculated amount should be given in 2 divided doses (every 12 hours).

Currently on opioids: Use standard conversion chart to convert daily dose to oxymorphone equivalent. Generally start with 1/2 the calculated daily oxymorphone dosage. Divide daily dose in 2 (for every 12-hour dosing) and round down to nearest dosage form.

Conversion of stable dose of immediate-release oxymorphone to extended-release oxymorphone: Administer 1/2 of the daily dose of immediate-release oxymorphone (Opana®) as the extended-release formulation (Opana® ER) every 12 hours

Dosing adjustment in renal impairment: Cl_{cr} <50 mL/minute: Reduce initial dosage of oral formulations (bioavailability increased 57% to 65%). Begin therapy at lowest dose and titrate carefully.

Dosing adjustment in hepatic impairment: Oral formulations are contraindicated for use in patients with moderate-to-severe liver disease. Initiate with lowest possible dose and titrate slowly in mild impairment.

Dietary Considerations Immediate release and extended release tablets should be taken 1 hour before or 2 hours after eating.

Administration Administer immediate release and extended release tablets 1 hour before or 2 hours after eating. Opana® ER tablet should be swallowed; do not break, crush. or chew.

Monitoring Parameters Respiratory rate, heart rate, blood pressure, CNS activity

Test interactions

Some quinolones may produce a false-positive urine screening result for opiates using commercially-available immunoassay kits. This has been demonstrated most consistently for levofloxacin and ofloxacin, but other quinolones have shown cross-reactivity in certain assay kits. Confirmation of positive opiate screens by more specific methods should be considered. May cause elevation in amylase (due to constriction of the sphincter of Oddi).

Dosage Forms

Injection, solution, as hydrochloride:

Numorphan®: 1 mg (1 mL)

Tablet, as hydrochloride:

Opana®: 5 mg, 10 mg

Tablet, extended release, as hydrochloride:
Opana®: ЕП: 5 mg, 10 mg, 20 mg, 40 mg

♦ **Oxymorphone Hydrochloride** *see Oxymorphone on page 1290*

Oxytetracycline (oks i tet ra SYE kleen)

U.S. Brand Names Terramycin® I.M. [DSC]
Canadian Brand Names Terramycin®
Index Terms Oxytetracycline Hydrochloride
Pharmacologic Category Antibiotic, Tetracycline Derivative
Use Treatment of susceptible bacterial infections; both gram-positive and gram-negative, as well as, *Rickettsia* and *Mycoplasma* organisms
Pregnancy Risk Factor D
Lactation Enters breast milk/not recommended
Medication Safety Issues
Sound-alike/look-alike issues:
Terramycin® may be confused with Garamycin®
Contraindications Hypersensitivity to tetracycline or any component of the formulation
Warnings/Precautions Avoid in children ≤8 years of age, pregnant and nursing women; photosensitivity can occur with oxytetracycline
Adverse Reactions Frequency not defined; also refer to Tetracycline monograph
Cardiovascular: Pericarditis
Central nervous system: Bulging fontanels (infants), intracranial hypertension (adults)
Dermatologic: Angioneurotic edema, erythematous rash, exfoliative dermatitis (uncommon), maculopapular rash, photosensitivity, urticaria
Gastrointestinal: Anogenital inflammatory lesions, diarrhea, dysphagia, enamel hypoplasia, enterocolitis, glossitis, nausea, tooth discoloration, vomiting
Hematologic: Anemia, eosinophilia, neutropenia, thrombocytopenia
Local: Irritation
Renal: BUN increased
Miscellaneous: Anaphylactoid purpura, anaphylaxis, hypersensitivity reaction, SLE exacerbation
Overdosage/Toxicology Symptoms include nausea, anorexia, and diarrhea. Treatment following GI decontamination is supportive care only.
Drug Interactions
Increased Effect/Toxicity: Oral anticoagulant (warfarin) effects may be increased.
Decreased Effect: Barbiturates, phenytoin, and carbamazepine decrease serum levels of tetracyclines. Although anecdotal reports suggest oral contraceptive efficacy could be reduced by tetracyclines, this has been refuted by more rigorous scientific and clinical data.
Mechanism of Action Inhibits bacterial protein synthesis by binding with the 30S and possibly the 50S ribosomal subunit(s) of susceptible bacteria, cell wall synthesis is not affected
Pharmacodynamics/Kinetics
Absorption: Poor
Distribution: Crosses placenta
Metabolism: Hepatic (small amounts)
Half-life elimination: 8.5-9.6 hours; prolonged with renal impairment
Excretion: Urine; feces
Dosage I.M.:
Children >8 years: 15-25 mg/kg/day (maximum: 250 mg/dose) in divided doses every 8-12 hours
Adults: 250 mg every 24 hours or 300 mg/day divided every 8-12 hours
Dosing interval in renal impairment: Cl$_{cr}$ <10 mL/minute: Administer every 24 hours or avoid use if possible
Dosing adjustment/comments in hepatic impairment: Avoid use in patients with severe liver disease
Administration Injection for intramuscular use only.
Dosage Forms
[DSC] = Discontinued product
Injection, solution:
Terramycin® I.M.: 5% [50 mg/mL] (10 mL) [contains lidocaine hydrochloride 2%] [DSC]

♦ **Oxytetracycline Hydrochloride** *see Oxytetracycline on page 1293*

Oxytocin (oks i TOE sin)

U.S. Brand Names Pitocin®
Canadian Brand Names Pitocin®; Syntocinon®
Index Terms Pit
Pharmacologic Category Oxytocic Agent
Use Induction of labor at term; control of postpartum bleeding; adjunctive therapy in management of abortion
Pregnancy Risk Factor X
Pregnancy Implications Reproduction studies have not been conducted. When used as indicated, teratogenic effects would not be expected. Nonteratogenic adverse reactions are reported in the neonate as well as the mother.
Lactation Excretion in breast milk unknown/use caution
Medication Safety Issues
Sound-alike/look-alike issues:
Pitocin® may be confused with Pitressin®
Contraindications Hypersensitivity to oxytocin or any component of the formulation; significant cephalopelvic disproportion; unfavorable fetal positions; fetal distress; hypertonic or
(Continued)

Oxytocin *(Continued)*

hyperactive uterus; contraindicated vaginal delivery (invasive cervical cancer, active genital herpes, prolapse of the cord, cord presentation, total placenta previa, or vasa previa)

Warnings/Precautions [U.S. Boxed Warning]: To be used for medical rather than elective induction of labor. May produce antidiuretic effect (ie, water intoxication and excess uterine contractions); high doses or hypersensitivity to oxytocin may cause uterine hypertonicity, spasm, tetanic contraction, or rupture of the uterus; severe water intoxication with convulsions, coma, and death is associated with a slow oxytocin infusion over 24 hours

Adverse Reactions Frequency not defined.

Fetus or neonate:

Cardiovascular: Arrhythmias (including premature ventricular contractions), bradycardia

Central nervous system: Brain or CNS damage (permanent), neonatal seizure

Hepatic: Neonatal jaundice

Ocular: Neonatal retinal hemorrhage

Miscellaneous: Fetal death, low Apgar score (5 minute)

Mother:

Cardiovascular: Arrhythmias, hypertensive episodes, premature ventricular contractions

Gastrointestinal: Nausea, vomiting

Genitourinary: Pelvic hematoma, postpartum hemorrhage, uterine hypertonicity, tetanic contraction of the uterus, uterine rupture, uterine spasm

Hematologic: Afibrinogenemia (fatal)

Miscellaneous: Anaphylactic reaction, subarachnoid hemorrhage

Overdosage/Toxicology Symptoms include tetanic uterine contractions, impaired uterine blood flow, amniotic fluid embolism, uterine rupture, SIADH, and seizures. Treat SIADH via fluid restriction, diuresis, saline administration, and anticonvulsants, if needed.

Drug Interactions

Increased Effect/Toxicity: Dinoprostone and misoprostol may increase the effect of oxytocin; wait 6-12 hours after dinoprostone or misoprostol administration before initiating oxytocin.

Stability Store oxytocin at 2°C to 8°C (36°F to 46°F); do not freeze. Pitocin® may also be stored at 15°C to 25°C (59°F to 77°F) for up to 30 days. Reconstitution: I.V.:

Induction or stimulation of labor: Add oxytocin 10 units to NS or LR 1000 mL to yield a solution containing oxytocin 10 milliunits/mL. Rotate solution to mix.

Postpartum uterine bleeding: Add oxytocin 10-40 units to running I.V. infusion; maximum: 40 units/1000 mL.

Adjunctive management of abortion: Add oxytocin 10 units to 500 mL of a physiologic saline solution or D₅W.

Mechanism of Action Produces the rhythmic uterine contractions characteristic to delivery

Pharmacodynamics/Kinetics

Onset of action: Uterine contractions: I.M.: 3-5 minutes; I.V.: ~1 minute

Duration: I.M.: 2-3 hour; I.V.: 1 hour

Metabolism: Rapidly hepatic and via plasma (by oxytocinase) and to a smaller degree the mammary gland

Half-life elimination: 1-5 minutes

Excretion: Urine

Dosage I.V. administration requires the use of an infusion pump. Adults:

Induction of labor: I.V.: 0.5-1 milliunits/minute; gradually increase dose in increments of 1-2 milliunits/minute until desired contraction pattern is established; dose may be decreased after desired frequency of contractions is reached and labor has progressed to 5-6 cm dilation. Infusion rates of 6 milliunits/minute provide oxytocin levels similar to those at spontaneous labor; rates of >9-10 milliunits/minute are rarely required.

Postpartum bleeding:

I.M.: Total dose of 10 units after delivery

I.V.: 10-40 units by I.V. infusion in 1000 mL of intravenous fluid at a rate sufficient to control uterine atony

Adjunctive treatment of abortion: I.V.: 10-20 milliunits/minute; maximum total dose: 30 units/ 12 hours

Administration I.V.: Refer to Stability (reconstitution) for dilution information; an infusion pump is required for administration

Monitoring Parameters Fluid intake and output during administration; fetal monitoring

Dosage Forms

Injection, solution: 10 units/mL (1 mL, 10 mL)

Pitocin®: 10 units/mL (1 mL)

♦ **Oxytrol®** *see* Oxybutynin *on page 1285*

♦ **Oysco D [OTC]** *see* Calcium and Vitamin D *on page 268*

♦ **Oysco 500 [OTC]** *see* Calcium Carbonate *on page 269*

♦ **Oysco 500+D [OTC]** *see* Calcium and Vitamin D *on page 268*

♦ **Oyst-Cal-D [OTC]** *see* Calcium and Vitamin D *on page 268*

♦ **Oyst-Cal 500 [OTC]** *see* Calcium Carbonate *on page 269*

♦ **Oyst-Cal-D 500 [OTC]** *see* Calcium and Vitamin D *on page 268*

♦ **P-V Tussin Tablet** *see* Hydrocodone and Pseudoephedrine *on page 851*

♦ **P-071** *see* Cetirizine *on page 334*

♦ **Pacerone®** *see* Amiodarone *on page 97*

♦ **Pacis™ (Can)** *see* BCG Vaccine *on page 197*

Paclitaxel (pac li TAKS el)

U.S. Brand Names Onxol™; Taxol®
Canadian Brand Names Apo-Paclitaxel®; Taxol®
Index Terms NSC-125973; NSC-673089
Pharmacologic Category Antineoplastic Agent, Antimicrotubular; Antineoplastic Agent, Natural Source (Plant) Derivative
Use Treatment of breast, lung (small cell and nonsmall cell), and ovarian cancers; treatment of AIDS-related Kaposi's sarcoma (KS)
Unlabeled/Investigational Use Treatment of bladder, cervical, prostate, and head and neck cancers
Pregnancy Risk Factor D
Pregnancy Implications Animal studies have demonstrated embryotoxicity, fetal toxicity, and maternal toxicity. There are no adequate and well-controlled studies in pregnant women. Women of childbearing potential should be advised to avoid becoming pregnant.
Lactation Excretion in breast milk unknown/contraindicated
Medication Safety Issues
Sound-alike/look-alike issues:
Paclitaxel may be confused with paroxetine, Paxil®
Paclitaxel (conventional) may be confused with paclitaxel (protein-bound)
Taxol® may be confused with Abraxane™, Paxil®, Taxotere®

High alert medication: The Institute for Safe Medication Practices (ISMP) includes this medication among its list of drugs which have a heightened risk of causing significant patient harm when used in error.
Contraindications Hypersensitivity to paclitaxel, Cremophor® EL (polyoxyethylated castor oil), or any component of the formulation; pregnancy
Warnings/Precautions Hazardous agent - use appropriate precautions for handling and disposal. **[U.S. Boxed Warning]: Severe hypersensitivity reactions have been reported;** premedication may minimize this effect. Stop infusion and do not rechallenge for severe hypersensitivity reactions (hypotension requiring treatment, dyspnea requiring bronchodilators, angioedema, urticaria). Minor hypersensitivity reactions (flushing, skin reactions, dyspnea, hypotension, or tachycardia) do not require interruption of treatment. **[U.S. Boxed Warning]: Bone marrow suppression is the dose-limiting toxicity; do not administer if baseline absolute neutrophil count (ANC) is <1500 cells/mm³ (<1000 cells/mm³ for patients with AIDS-related KS);** reduce future doses by 20% for severe neutropenia (<500 cells/mm³ for 7 days or more) and consider the use of supportive therapy, including growth factor treatment.

Use extreme caution with hepatic dysfunction (myelotoxicity may be worsened); dose reductions are recommended. Peripheral neuropathy may occur; patients with pre-existing neuropathies from chemotherapy or coexisting conditions (eg, diabetes mellitus) may be at a higher risk; reduce dose by 20% for severe neuropathy. Paclitaxel formulations contain dehydrated alcohol; may cause adverse CNS effects. Hypotension, bradycardia, and hypertension may occur; frequent monitoring of vital signs is recommended, especially during the first hour of the infusion. Rare but severe conduction abnormalities have been reported; conduct cardiac monitoring during subsequent infusions for these patients. When administered as sequential infusions, taxane derivatives (docetaxel, paclitaxel) should be administered before platinum derivatives (carboplatin, cisplatin) to limit myelosuppression. Elderly patients have an increased risk of toxicity (neutropenia, neuropathy). **[U.S. Boxed Warning]: Should be administered under the supervision of an experienced cancer chemotherapy physician.** Safety and efficacy in children have not been established.
Adverse Reactions Percentages reported with single-agent therapy. **Note:** Myelosuppression is dose related, schedule related, and infusion-rate dependent (increased incidences with higher doses, more frequent doses, and longer infusion times) and, in general, rapidly reversible upon discontinuation.
>10%:
Cardiovascular: Flushing (28%), ECG abnormal (14% to 23%), edema (21%), hypotension (4% to 12%)
Dermatologic: Alopecia (87%), rash (12%)
Gastrointestinal: Nausea/vomiting (52%), diarrhea (38%), mucositis (17% to 35%; grades 3/4: up to 3%), stomatitis (15%; most common at doses >390 mg/m²), abdominal pain (with intraperitoneal paclitaxel)
Hematologic: Neutropenia (78% to 98%; grade 4: 14% to 75%; onset 8-10 days, median nadir 11 days, recovery 15-21 days), leukopenia (90%; grade 4: 17%), anemia (47% to 90%; grades 3/4: 2% to 16%), thrombocytopenia (4% to 20%; grades 3/4: 1% to 7%), bleeding (14%)
Hepatic: Alkaline phosphatase increased (22%), AST increased (19%)
Local: Injection site reaction (erythema, tenderness, skin discoloration, swelling: 13%)
Neuromuscular & skeletal: Peripheral neuropathy (42% to 70%; grades 3/4: up to 7%), arthralgia/myalgia (60%), weakness (17%)
Renal: Creatinine increased (observed in KS patients only: 18% to 34%; severe: 5% to 7%)
Miscellaneous: Hypersensitivity reaction (31% to 45%; grades 3/4: up to 2%), infection (15% to 30%)
1% to 10%:
Cardiovascular: Bradycardia (3%), tachycardia (2%), hypertension (1%), rhythm abnormalities (1%), syncope (1%), venous thrombosis (1%)
Dermatologic: Nail changes (2%)
Hematologic: Febrile neutropenia (2%)
Hepatic: Bilirubin increased (7%)
Respiratory: Dyspnea (2%)
<1% (Limited to important or life-threatening): Ataxia, atrial fibrillation, AV block, back pain, cellulitis, CHF, chills, conjunctivitis, dehydration, enterocolitis, hepatic encephalopathy, (Continued)

Paclitaxel *(Continued)*

hepatic necrosis, induration, intestinal obstruction, intestinal perforation, interstitial pneumonia, ischemic colitis, lacrimation, maculopapular rash, MI, necrotic changes and ulceration following extravasation, neuroencephalopathy, neutropenic enterocolitis, ototoxicity (tinnitus and hearing loss), pancreatitis, paralytic ileus, phlebitis, pruritus, pulmonary embolism, pulmonary fibrosis, radiation recall, radiation pneumonitis, seizure, skin exfoliation, skin fibrosis, skin necrosis, Stevens-Johnson syndrome, supraventricular tachycardia, toxic epidermal necrolysis, ventricular tachycardia (asymptomatic), visual disturbances (scintillating scotomata)

Overdosage/Toxicology Potential symptoms of overdose would include bone marrow suppression, peripheral neurotoxicity, and mucositis. Overdoses in children would be associated with acute ethanol toxicity. There is no known antidote; treatment is symptom-directed and supportive.

Drug Interactions

Cytochrome P450 Effect: Substrate (major) of CYP2C8, 2C9, 3A4; **Induces** CYP3A4 (weak)

Increased Effect/Toxicity: CYP2C8 Inhibitors may increase the levels/effects of paclitaxel; example inhibitors include atazanavir, gemfibrozil, and ritonavir. CYP2C9 Inhibitors may increase the levels/effects of paclitaxel; example inhibitors include delavirdine, fluconazole, gemfibrozil, ketoconazole, nicardipine, NSAIDs, sulfonamides and tolbutamide. CYP3A4 inhibitors may increase the levels/effects of paclitaxel; example inhibitors include azole antifungals, clarithromycin, diclofenac, doxycycline, erythromycin, imatinib, isoniazid, nefazodone, nicardipine, propofol, protease inhibitors, quinidine, telithromycin, and verapamil. In Phase I trials, myelosuppression was more profound when given after cisplatin than with alternative sequence. administered as sequential infusions, studies indicate a potential for increased toxicity when platinum derivatives (carboplatin, cisplatin) are administered before taxane derivatives (docetaxel, paclitaxel). Paclitaxel may increase doxorubicin levels/toxicity.

Decreased Effect: CYP2C8 and 2C9 inducers may decrease the levels/effects of paclitaxel; example inducers include carbamazepine, phenobarbital, phenytoin, rifampin, rifapentine, and secobarbital. CYP3A4 inducers may decrease the levels/effects of paclitaxel; example inducers include aminoglutethimide, carbamazepine, nafcillin, nevirapine, phenobarbital, phenytoin, and rifamycins.

Ethanol/Nutrition/Herb Interactions Herb/Nutraceutical: Avoid black cohosh, dong quai in estrogen-dependent tumors. Avoid valerian, St John's wort, kava kava, gotu kola (may increase CNS depression).

Stability Store intact vials at room temperature of 20°C to 25°C (68°F to 77°F) and protect from light. Dilute in 250-1000 mL D_5W, D_5LR, D_5NS, or NS to a concentration of 0.3-1.2 mg/mL. Solutions in D_5W and NS are stable for up to 3 days at room temperature (25°C). Chemotherapy dispensing devices (eg, Chemo Dispensing Pin™) should not be used to withdraw paclitaxel from the vial.

Paclitaxel should be dispensed in either glass or non-PVC containers (eg, Excel™/PAB™). Use **nonpolyvinyl** (non-PVC) tubing (eg, polyethylene) to minimize leaching. Formulated in a vehicle known as Cremophor® EL (polyoxyethylated castor oil). Cremophor® EL has been found to leach the plasticizer DEHP from polyvinyl chloride infusion bags or administration sets. Contact of the undiluted concentrate with plasticized polyvinyl chloride (PVC) equipment or devices is not recommended.

Mechanism of Action Paclitaxel promotes microtubule assembly by enhancing the action of tubulin dimers, stabilizing existing microtubules, and inhibiting their disassembly, interfering with the late G_2 mitotic phase, and inhibiting cell replication. In addition, the drug can distort mitotic spindles, resulting in the breakage of chromosomes. Paclitaxel may also suppress cell proliferation and modulate immune response.

Pharmacodynamics/Kinetics

Distribution:

V_d: Widely distributed into body fluids and tissues; affected by dose and duration of infusion

V_{dss}:

1- to 6-hour infusion: 67.1 L/m²

24-hour infusion: 227-688 L/m²

Protein binding: 89% to 98%

Metabolism: Hepatic via CYP2C8 and 3A4; forms metabolites (primarily 6α-hydroxypaclitaxel)

Half-life elimination:

1- to 6-hour infusion: Mean (beta): 6.4 hours

3-hour infusion: Mean (terminal): 13.1-20.2 hours

24-hour infusion: Mean (terminal): 15.7-52.7 hours

Excretion: Feces (~70%, 5% as unchanged drug); urine (14%)

Clearance: Mean: Total body: After 1- and 6-hour infusions: 5.8-16.3 L/hour/m²; After 24-hour infusions: 14.2-17.2 L/hour/m²

Dosage Premedication with dexamethasone (20 mg orally or I.V. at 12 and 6 hours **or** 14 and 7 hours before the dose; reduce dexamethasone dose to 10 mg orally with advanced HIV disease), diphenhydramine (50 mg I.V. 30-60 minutes prior to the dose), and cimetidine, famotidine or ranitidine (I.V. 30-60 minutes prior to the dose) is recommended.

Adults: I.V.: Refer to individual protocols

Ovarian carcinoma: 135-175 mg/m² over 3 hours every 3 weeks **or**

135 mg/m² over 24 hours every 3 weeks **or**

50-80 mg/m² over 1-3 hours weekly **or**

1.4-4 mg/m²/day continuous infusion for 14 days every 4 weeks

Metastatic breast cancer: 175-250 mg/m² over 3 hours every 3 weeks **or**

50-80 mg/m² weekly **or**

1.4-4 mg/m²/day continuous infusion for 14 days every 4 weeks

Nonsmall cell lung carcinoma: 135 mg/m² over 24 hours every 3 weeks

AIDS-related Kaposi's sarcoma: 135 mg/m² over 3 hours every 3 weeks **or**

100 mg/m² over 3 hours every 2 weeks

Intraperitoneal (unlabeled route): Ovarian carcinoma: 60 mg/m² on day 8 of a 21-day treatment cycle for 6 cycles, in combination with I.V. paclitaxel and intraperitoneal cisplatin. **Note:** Administration of intraperitoneal paclitaxel should include the standard paclitaxel premedication regimen.

Dosage modification for toxicity (solid tumors, including ovary, breast, and lung carcinoma): Courses of paclitaxel should not be repeated until the neutrophil count is ≥1500 cells/mm³ and the platelet count is ≥100,000 cells/mm³; reduce dosage by 20% for patients experiencing severe peripheral neuropathy or severe neutropenia (neutrophil <500 cells/mm³ for a week or longer)

Dosage modification for immunosuppression in advanced HIV disease: Paclitaxel should not be given to patients with HIV if the baseline or subsequent neutrophil count is <1000 cells/mm³. Additional modifications include: Reduce dosage of dexamethasone in premedication to 10 mg orally; reduce dosage by 20% in patients experiencing severe peripheral neuropathy or severe neutropenia (neutrophil <500 cells/mm³ for a week or longer); initiate concurrent hematopoietic growth factor (G-CSF) as clinically indicated

Dosage adjustment in hepatic impairment: Note: These recommendations are based upon the patient's first course of therapy where the usual dose would be 135 mg/m² dose over 24 hours or the 175 mg/m² dose over 3 hours in patients with normal hepatic function. Dosage in subsequent courses should be based upon individual tolerance. Adjustments for other regimens are not available.

24-hour infusion:
If transaminase levels <2 times upper limit of normal (ULN) and bilirubin level ≤1.5 mg/dL: 135 mg/m²
If transaminase levels 2-<10 times ULN and bilirubin level ≤1.5 mg/dL: 100 mg/m²
If transaminase levels <10 times ULN and bilirubin level 1.6-7.5 mg/dL: 50 mg/m²
If transaminase levels ≥10 times ULN and bilirubin level >7.5 mg/dL: Avoid use

3-hour infusion:
If transaminase levels <10 times ULN and bilirubin level ≤1.25 times ULN: 175 mg/m²
If transaminase levels <10 times ULN and bilirubin level 1.26-2 times ULN: 135 mg/m²
If transaminase levels <10 times ULN and bilirubin level 2.01-5 times ULN: 90 mg/m²
If transaminase levels ≥10 times ULN and bilirubin level >5 times ULN: Avoid use

Administration

I.V.: Infuse over 1-96 hours. When administered as sequential infusions, taxane derivatives should be administered before platinum derivatives (cisplatin, carboplatin) to limit myelosuppression and to enhance efficacy.

Premedication with dexamethasone (20 mg orally or I.V. at 12 and 6 hours **or** 14 and 7 hours before the dose; reduce to 10 mg with advanced HIV disease), diphenhydramine (50 mg I.V. 30-60 minutes prior to the dose), and cimetidine 300 mg, famotidine 20 mg, or ranitidine 50 mg (I.V. 30-60 minutes prior to the dose) is recommended.

Administer I.V. infusion over 1-24 hours; infuse through a 0.22 micron in-line filter and nonsorbing administration set.

Intraperitoneal: 1-2 hour infusion

Monitoring Parameters CBC with differential; monitor for hypersensitivity reactions, vital signs (frequently during the first hour of infusion), continuous cardiac monitoring (patients with conduction abnormalities)

Reference Range Mean maximum serum concentrations: 435-802 ng/mL following 24-hour infusions of 200-275 mg/m² and were approximately 10% to 30% of those following 6-hour infusions of equivalent doses

Additional Information Sensory neuropathy is almost universal at doses >250 mg/m²; motor neuropathy is uncommon at doses <250 mg/m². Myopathic effects are common with doses >200 mg/m², generally occur within 2-3 days of treatment, and resolve over 5-6 days. Intraperitoneal administration of paclitaxel is associated with a higher incidence of chemotherapy related toxicity.

Dosage Forms

Injection, solution: 6 mg/mL (5 mL, 16.7 mL, 25 mL, 50 mL) [contains alcohol and purified Cremophor® EL (polyoxyethylated castor oil)]
Onxol™: 6 mg/mL (5 mL, 25 mL, 50 mL) [contains alcohol and purified Cremophor® EL (polyoxyethylated castor oil)]
Taxol®: 6 mg/mL (5 mL, 16.7 mL, 50 mL) [contains alcohol and purified Cremophor® EL (polyoxyethylated castor oil)]

Paclitaxel (Protein Bound) (pac li TAKS el PROE teen bownd)

U.S. Brand Names Abraxane™
Index Terms BI-007; NAB-Paclitaxel; Protein-Bound Paclitaxel
Pharmacologic Category Antineoplastic Agent, Antimicrotubular; Antineoplastic Agent, Natural Source (Plant) Derivative
Use Treatment of breast cancer (second-line)
Pregnancy Risk Factor D
Medication Safety Issues
Sound-alike/look-alike issues:
Paclitaxel (protein bound) may be confused with paclitaxel (conventional)
Abraxane™ may be confused with Paxil®, Taxol®, Taxotere®

High alert medication: The Institute for Safe Medication Practices (ISMP) includes this medication among its list of drugs which have a heightened risk of causing significant patient harm when used in error.
Dosage I.V.: Adults: Breast cancer: 260 mg/m² every 3 weeks
Dosage adjustment for toxicity:
Severe neutropenia (<500 cells/mm³) ≥1 week: Reduce dose to 220 mg/m² for subsequent courses
Recurrent severe neutropenia: Reduce dose to 180 mg/m²
Severe sensory neuropathy: Reduce dose to 180 mg/m²
(Continued)

Paclitaxel (Protein Bound) *(Continued)*

Sensory neuropathy grade 3 or 4: Hold treatment until resolved to grade 1 or 2, then resume with reduced dose

Dosage adjustment in renal impairment: Safety not established for serum creatinine >2 mg/dL; use with caution

Dosage adjustment in hepatic impairment: Effects of hepatic dysfunction (serum bilirubin >1.5 mg/dL) unknown; dosage adjustment recommendations are not available

Additional Information Complete prescribing information for this medication should be consulted for additional detail.

Dosage Forms Injection, powder for reconstitution: 100 mg [contains human albumin 900 mg]

♦ **Pain Eze [OTC]** *see* Acetaminophen *on page 28*

♦ **Pain-Off [OTC]** *see* Acetaminophen, Aspirin, and Caffeine *on page 34*

♦ **Palafer® (Can)** *see* Ferrous Fumarate *on page 702*

♦ **Palcaps** *see* Pancrelipase *on page 1302*

♦ **Palgic®** *see* Carbinoxamine *on page 289*

♦ **Palgic®-D** *see* Carbinoxamine and Pseudoephedrine *on page 290*

♦ **Palgic®-DS** *see* Carbinoxamine and Pseudoephedrine *on page 290*

Palifermin (pal ee FER min)

U.S. Brand Names Kepivance™

Index Terms AMJ 9701; rHu-KGF

Pharmacologic Category Keratinocyte Growth Factor

Use Decrease the incidence and severity of severe oral mucositis associated with hematologic malignancies in patients receiving myelotoxic therapy requiring hematopoietic stem cell support

Pregnancy Risk Factor C

Pregnancy Implications Palifermin has been shown to be embryotoxic in animal studies at doses also associated with maternal toxicity. There are no adequate and well-controlled studies in pregnant women.

Lactation Excretion in breast milk unknown/use caution

Contraindications Hypersensitivity to palifermin, *E. coli*-derived proteins, or any component of the formulation

Warnings/Precautions Safety and efficacy have not been established with nonhematologic malignancies; effect on the growth of nonhematopoietic human tumors is not known. Palifermin should be administered prior to and following, but not with, chemotherapy. If administered within 24 hours of chemotherapy, palifermin may increase the severity and duration of mucositis due to the increased sensitivity of rapidly-dividing epithelial cells. Safety and efficacy have not been established in children.

Adverse Reactions

>10%:

Cardiovascular: Edema (28%), hypertension (7% to 14%)

Central nervous system: Fever (39%), pain (16%), dysesthesia (12%)

Dermatologic: Rash (62%), pruritus (35%), erythema (32%)

Gastrointestinal: Mouth/tongue discoloration or thickness (17%), taste alteration (16%)

Miscellaneous: Serum amylase increased (grade 3/4, 38%); serum lipase increased (grade 3/4, 11%)

1% to 10%: Neuromuscular & skeletal: Arthralgia (10%)

Overdosage/Toxicology Specific information is not available. Doses higher than those recommended were associated with the reported adverse events, but in general were more severe.

Drug Interactions

Increased Effect/Toxicity: Drug interaction studies have not been conducted.

Stability Store intact vials under refrigeration at 2°C to 8°C (36°F to 46°F). Protect from light. To reconstitute, slowly add SWFI 1.2 mL to vial; final concentration will be 5 mg/mL. Do not shake or vigorously agitate. Following reconstitution, vials are stable for up to 72 hours under refrigeration protected from light; do not freeze. Reconstituted solution should not be used if left at room temperature >2 hours.

Mechanism of Action Palifermin is a recombinant keratinocyte growth factor (KGF) produced in *E. coli*. Endogenous KGF is produced by mesenchymal cells in response to epithelial tissue injury. KGF binds to the KGF receptor resulting in proliferation, differentiation and migration of epithelial cells in multiple tissues, including (but not limited to) the tongue, buccal mucosa, esophagus, and salivary gland.

Pharmacodynamics/Kinetics Half-life elimination: 4.5 hours (range: 3.3-5.7 hours)

Dosage I.V.: Adults: 60 mcg/kg/day for 3 consecutive days before and after myelotoxic therapy; total of 6 doses

Note: Administer first 3 doses prior to myelotoxic therapy, with the 3rd dose given 24-48 hours before therapy begins. The last 3 doses should be administered after myelotoxic therapy, with the first of these doses after but on the same day of hematopoietic stem cell infusion and at least 4 days after the most recent dose of palifermin.

Administration Administer by I.V. bolus. If heparin is used to maintain the patency of the I.V. line, flush line with saline prior to and after palifermin administration. Do not administer palifermin with or within 24 hours of chemotherapy. Allow solution to reach room temperature prior to administration; do not use if at room temperature >1 hour.

Dosage Forms Injection, powder for reconstitution [preservative free]: 6.25 mg [contains mannitol 50 mg, sucrose 25 mg]

Palivizumab (pah li VIZ u mab)

U.S. Brand Names Synagis®
Canadian Brand Names Synagis®
Pharmacologic Category Monoclonal Antibody
Use Prevention of serious lower respiratory tract disease caused by respiratory syncytial virus (RSV) in infants and children <2 years of age at high risk of RSV disease
Pregnancy Risk Factor C
Pregnancy Implications Not for adult use; reproduction studies have not been conducted
Medication Safety Issues
Sound-alike/look-alike issues:
Synagis® may be confused with Synalgos®-DC, Synvisc®
Contraindications History of severe prior reaction to palivizumab or any component of the formulation
Warnings/Precautions Very rare cases of anaphylaxis have been observed following palivizumab. Rare cases of severe acute hypersensitivity reactions have also been reported. Safety and efficacy of palivizumab have not been demonstrated in the treatment of established RSV disease. Use with caution in patients with thrombocytopenia or any coagulation disorder.
Adverse Reactions The incidence of adverse events was similar between the palivizumab and placebo groups.

>1%:
Central nervous system: Nervousness, fever
Dermatologic: Fungal dermatitis, eczema, seborrhea, rash
Gastrointestinal: Diarrhea, vomiting, gastroenteritis
Hematologic: Anemia
Hepatic: ALT increase, abnormal LFTs
Local: Injection site reaction, erythema, induration
Ocular: Conjunctivitis
Otic: Otitis media
Respiratory: Cough, wheezing, bronchiolitis, pneumonia, bronchitis, asthma, croup, dyspnea, sinusitis, apnea, upper respiratory infection, rhinitis
Miscellaneous: Oral moniliasis, failure to thrive, viral infection, flu syndrome
Postmarketing and/or case reports: Hypersensitivity reactions, anaphylaxis (very rare)
Overdosage/Toxicology No data from clinical studies are available.
Stability Store in refrigerator at a temperature between 2°C to 8°C (35.6°F to 46.4°F) in original container; do not freeze.

Powder for injection: Use aseptic technique when reconstituting; add 1 mL of sterile water for injection to a 100 mg vial; swirl vial gently for 30 seconds to avoid foaming. Do not shake vial. Allow to stand at room temperature for 20 minutes until the solution clarifies; solution should be administered within 6 hours of reconstitution.
Mechanism of Action Exhibits neutralizing and fusion-inhibitory activity against RSV; these activities inhibit RSV replication in laboratory and clinical studies
Pharmacodynamics/Kinetics
Half-life elimination: Children <24 months: 20 days; Adults: 18 days
Time to peak, serum: 48 hours
Dosage I.M.: Infants and Children: 15 mg/kg of body weight, monthly throughout RSV season (First dose administered prior to commencement of RSV season)
Administration Injection should (preferably) be in the anterolateral aspect of the thigh; gluteal muscle should not be used routinely; injection volume over 1 mL should be administered as divided doses
Additional Information RSV prophylaxis should be initiated at the onset of the RSV season. In most areas of the United States, onset of RSV outbreaks is October to December, and termination is March to May, but regional differences occur.
Dosage Forms [DSC] = Discontinued product
Injection, powder for reconstitution:
Synagis®: 50 mg, 100 mg [DSC]
Injection, solution [preservative free]:
Synagis®: 50 mg/0.5 mL (0.5 mL); 100 mg/mL (1 mL)

- Palmer's® Skin Success Eventone® Fade Cream [OTC] *see* Hydroquinone *on page 859*
- Palmitate-A® [OTC] *see* Vitamin A *on page 1793*

Palonosetron (pal oh NOE se tron)

U.S. Brand Names Aloxi®
Index Terms Palonosetron Hydrochloride; RS-25259; RS-25259-197
Pharmacologic Category Antiemetic; Selective 5-HT$_3$ Receptor Antagonist
Use Prevention of acute (within 24 hours) and delayed (2-5 days) chemotherapy-induced nausea and vomiting
Pregnancy Risk Factor B
Pregnancy Implications Teratogenic effects were not observed in animal studies. There are no adequate and well-controlled studies in pregnant women; use during pregnancy only if clearly needed.
Lactation Excretion in breast milk unknown/not recommended
Medication Safety Issues
Sound-alike/look-alike issues:
Aloxi® may be confused with oxaliplatin
Palonosetron may be confused with dolasetron, granisetron, ondansetron
Contraindications Hypersensitivity to palonosetron or any component of the formulation
(Continued)

Palonosetron *(Continued)*

Warnings/Precautions Use caution in patients allergic to other 5-HT$_3$ receptor antagonists; cross-reactivity is possible. Caution in patients with congenital QT syndrome or other risk factors for QT prolongation (eg, medications known to prolong QT interval, electrolyte abnormalities, and cumulative high dose anthracycline therapy). Not intended for treatment of nausea and vomiting or for chronic continuous therapy. **For chemotherapy, should be used on a scheduled basis, not on an "as needed" (PRN) basis,** since data support the use of this drug only in the prevention of nausea and vomiting (due to antineoplastic therapy) and not in the rescue of nausea and vomiting. Safety and efficacy in pediatric patients have not been established.

Adverse Reactions
>10%: Dermatologic: Pruritus (8% to 22%)
1% to 10%:
Cardiovascular: Bradycardia (1%), hypotension (1%), tachycardia (nonsustained) (1%)
Central nervous system: Headache (6% to 9%), anxiety (1% to 5%), dizziness (1%)
Endocrine & metabolic: Hyperkalemia (1%)
Gastrointestinal: Constipation (5% to 10%), diarrhea (1%)
Neuromuscular & skeletal: Weakness (1%)
<1% (Limited to important or life-threatening): ALT increased, AST increased, bilirubin increased, electrolyte fluctuations, extrasystoles, fever, glycosuria, hyperglycemia, hypersensitivity, hypertension, injection site reactions (burning/discomfort/induration/pain), metabolic acidosis, myocardial ischemia, QT prolongation, sinus arrhythmia, sinus tachycardia, supraventricular extrasystoles, vein distention

Overdosage/Toxicology Dose-ranging studies in humans using doses up to 25 times the recommended dose of 0.25 mg revealed no increase in the incidence of adverse effects compared to lower dose groups. Due to the large volume of distribution, dialysis would not be effective in the event of an overdose. Treatment is symptom-directed and supportive.

Drug Interactions
Cytochrome P450 Effect: Substrate (minor) of CYP1A2, 2D6, 3A4
Increased Effect/Toxicity: Palonosetron may enhance the hypotensive effect of apomorphine; concurrent use is contraindicated.

Stability Store intact vials at controlled room temperature of 15°C to 30°C (59°F to 86°F); do not freeze. Protect from light. Solutions of 5 mcg/mL and 30 mcg/mL in NS, D$_5$W, D$_5$1/2NS, and D$_5$LR injection are stable for 48 hours at room temperature and 14 days under refrigeration.

Mechanism of Action Selective 5-HT$_3$ receptor antagonist, blocking serotonin, both peripherally on vagal nerve terminals and centrally in the chemoreceptor trigger zone

Pharmacodynamics/Kinetics
Distribution: V$_d$: 8.3 ± 2.5 L/kg
Protein binding: 62%
Metabolism: ~50% metabolized via CYP enzymes (and likely other pathways) to relatively inactive metabolites (N-oxide-palonosetron and 6-S-hydroxy-palonosetron); CYP1A2, 2D6, and 3A4 contribute to its metabolism
Half-life elimination: Terminal: 40 hours
Excretion: Urine (80%, 40% as unchanged drug)

Dosage I.V.: Adults:
Chemotherapy-induced nausea and vomiting: 0.25 mg 30 minutes prior to chemotherapy administration, day 1 of each cycle (doses should not be given more than once weekly)
Breakthrough: Palonosetron has not been shown to be effective in terminating nausea or vomiting once it occurs and should not be used for this purpose.
Elderly: No dosage adjustment necessary
Dosage adjustment in renal/hepatic impairment: No dosage adjustment necessary

Administration I.V.: Infuse over 30 seconds; flush I.V. line with NS prior to and following administration.

Dosage Forms
Injection, solution:
Aloxi®: 0.05 mg/mL (5 mL) [contains disodium edetate]

♦ **Palonosetron Hydrochloride** *see* Palonosetron *on page 1299*
♦ **2-PAM** *see* Pralidoxime *on page 1405*
♦ **Pamelor®** *see* Nortriptyline *on page 1243*

Pamidronate *(pa mi DROE nate)*

U.S. Brand Names Aredia®
Canadian Brand Names Aredia®; Pamidronate Disodium®; Rhoxal-pamidronate
Index Terms Pamidronate Disodium
Pharmacologic Category Antidote; Bisphosphonate Derivative
Use Treatment of hypercalcemia associated with malignancy; treatment of osteolytic bone lesions associated with multiple myeloma or metastatic breast cancer; moderate to severe Paget's disease of bone
Unlabeled/Investigational Use Treatment of pediatric osteoporosis, treatment of osteogenesis imperfecta
Pregnancy Risk Factor D
Pregnancy Implications Pamidronate has been shown to cross the placenta and cause nonteratogenic embryo/fetal effects in animals. There are no adequate and well-controlled studies in pregnant women; manufacturer states pamidronate should not be used in pregnancy. Based on limited case reports, serum calcium levels in the newborn may be altered if pamidronate is administered during pregnancy. Bisphosphonates are incorporated into the bone matrix and gradually released over time. Theoretically, there may be a risk of fetal harm when pregnancy follows the completion of therapy. Women of childbearing potential should be advised to use effective contraception and avoid becoming pregnant during therapy.
Lactation Excretion in breast milk unknown/use caution

Medication Safety Issues
Sound-alike/look-alike issues:
Aredia® may be confused with Adriamycin

International issues:
Linoten® [Spain] may be confused with Lidopen® which is a brand name for lidocaine in the U.S.

Contraindications Hypersensitivity to pamidronate, other bisphosphonates, or any component of the formulation; pregnancy

Warnings/Precautions Bisphosphonate therapy has been associated with osteonecrosis, primarily of the jaw; this has been observed mostly in cancer patients, but also in patients with postmenopausal osteoporosis and other diagnoses. Dental exams and preventative dentistry should be performed prior to placing patients with risk factors on chronic bisphosphonate therapy. Invasive dental procedures should be avoided during treatment.

Infrequently, severe (and occasionally debilitating) bone, joint, and/or muscle pain have been reported during bisphosphonate treatment. The onset of pain ranged from a single day to several months. Symptoms usually resolve upon discontinuation. Some patients experienced recurrence when rechallenged with same drug or another bisphosphonate; avoid use in patients with a history of these symptoms in association with bisphosphonate therapy.

May cause deterioration in renal function. Use caution in patients with renal impairment and avoid in severe renal impairment. Assess serum creatinine prior to each dose; withhold dose in patients with bone metastases who experience deterioration in renal function. Use has been associated with asymptomatic electrolyte abnormalities (including hypophosphatemia, hypokalemia, hypomagnesemia, and hypocalcemia). Rare cases of symptomatic hypocalcemia, including tetany have been reported. Leukopenia has been observed with oral pamidronate and monitoring of white blood cell counts is suggested. Patients with pre-existing anemia, leukopenia, or thrombocytopenia should be closely monitored during the first 2 weeks of treatment.

Vein irritation and thrombophlebitis may occur with infusions. Advise women of childbearing age against becoming pregnant. Safety and efficacy have not been established in children.

Adverse Reactions Percentage of adverse effect varies upon dose and duration of infusion.
>10%:
Central nervous system: Fatigue (12% to 40%), fever (18% to 39%), headache (24% to 27%), anxiety (8% to 18%), insomnia (1% to 25%), pain (13% to 15%)
Endocrine & metabolic: Hypophosphatemia (9% to 18%), hypokalemia (4% to 18%), hypomagnesemia (4% to 12%), hypocalcemia (1% to 12%)
Gastrointestinal: Nausea (4% to 64%), vomiting (4% to 46%), anorexia (1% to 31%), abdominal pain (1% to 24%), dyspepsia (4% to 23%)
Genitourinary: Urinary tract infection (15% to 20%)
Hematologic: Anemia (6% to 48%), leukopenia (4% to 21%)
Local: Infusion site reaction (4% to 18%)
Neuromuscular & skeletal: Weakness (16% to 26%), myalgia (1% to 26%), arthralgia (11% to 15%)
Renal: Serum creatinine increased (19%)
Respiratory: Dyspnea (22% to 35%), cough (25% to 26%), upper respiratory tract infection (3% to 20%), sinusitis (15% to 16%), pleural effusion (3% to 15%)
1% to 10%:
Cardiovascular: Atrial fibrillation (6%), hypertension (6%), syncope (6%), tachycardia (6%), atrial flutter (1%), cardiac failure (1%), edema (1%)
Central nervous system: Somnolence (1% to 6%), psychosis (4%)
Endocrine & metabolic: Hypothyroidism (6%)
Gastrointestinal: Constipation (4% to 6%), gastrointestinal hemorrhage (6%), diarrhea (1%), stomatitis (1%)
Hematologic: Neutropenia (1%), thrombocytopenia (1%)
Neuromuscular & skeletal: Back pain (5%), bone pain (5%)
Renal: Uremia (4%)
Respiratory: Rales (6%), rhinitis (6%)
Miscellaneous: Moniliasis (6%)
<1% (Limited to important or life-threatening): Allergic reaction, anaphylactic shock, angioedema, episcleritis, hypotension, interstitial pneumonitis, iritis, joint and/or muscle pain, malaise, osteonecrosis (primarily jaws), renal deterioration, scleritis, uveitis

Overdosage/Toxicology Symptoms include hypocalcemia, hypotension, ECG changes, seizures, bleeding, paresthesias, carpopedal spasm, and fever. Treat with I.V. calcium gluconate and general supportive care. Fever and hypotension can be treated with corticosteroids.

Drug Interactions
Increased Effect/Toxicity: Aminoglycosides may lower serum calcium levels with prolonged administration; concomitant use may have an additive hypocalcemic effect. NSAIDs may enhance the gastrointestinal adverse/toxic effects (increased incidence of GI ulcers) of bisphosphonate derivatives. Bisphosphonate derivatives may enhance the hypocalcemic effect of phosphate supplements.
Decreased Effect: The following agents may decrease the absorption of oral bisphosphonate derivatives: Antacids (aluminum, calcium, magnesium), oral calcium salts, oral iron salts, and oral magnesium salts.

Stability
Powder for injection: Store below 30°C (86°F). Reconstitute by adding 10 mL of SWFI to each vial of lyophilized pamidronate disodium powder; the resulting solution will be 30 mg/10 mL or 90 mg/10 mL. The reconstituted solution is stable for 24 hours stored under refrigeration at 2°C to 8°C (36°F to 46°F).
Solution for injection: Store below 25°C (77°F).
Pamidronate may be further diluted in 250-1000 mL of 0.45% or 0.9% sodium chloride or 5% dextrose. Pamidronate solution for infusion is stable at room temperature for up to 24 hours.

Mechanism of Action A bisphosphonate which inhibits bone resorption via actions on osteoclasts or on osteoclast precursors. Does not appear to produce any significant effects on
(Continued)

Pamidronate (Continued)

renal tubular calcium handling and is poorly absorbed following oral administration (high oral doses have been reported effective); therefore, I.V. therapy is preferred.

Pharmacodynamics/Kinetics
Onset of action: 24-48 hours
Peak effect: Maximum: 5-7 days
Absorption: Poor; pharmacokinetic studies lacking
Metabolism: Not metabolized
Half-life elimination: 21-35 hours
Excretion: Biphasic; urine (~50% as unchanged drug) within 120 hours

Dosage Drug must be diluted properly before administration and infused intravenously slowly. Due to risk of nephrotoxicity, doses should not exceed 90 mg. I.V.: Adults:
Hypercalcemia of malignancy:
Moderate cancer-related hypercalcemia (corrected serum calcium: 12-13.5 mg/dL): 60-90 mg, as a single dose
Severe cancer-related hypercalcemia (corrected serum calcium: >13.5 mg/dL): 90 mg, as a single dose
A period of 7 days should elapse before the use of second course; repeat infusions every 2-3 weeks have been suggested, however, could be administered every 2-3 months according to the degree of and severity of hypercalcemia and/or the type of malignancy.
Osteolytic bone lesions with multiple myeloma: 90 mg monthly
Osteolytic bone lesions with metastatic breast cancer: 90 mg repeated every 3-4 weeks
Paget's disease: 30 mg daily for 3 consecutive days
Elderly: Begin at lower end of adult dosing range.
Dosing adjustment in renal impairment: Not recommended in severe renal impairment (patients with bone metastases); safety and efficacy have not been established in patients with serum creatinine >5 mg/dL; studies are limited in multiple myeloma patients with serum creatinine ≥3 mg/dL
Dosing adjustment in renal toxicity: In patients with bone metastases, treatment should be withheld in patients who experience deterioration in renal function (increase of serum creatinine ≥0.5 mg/dL in patients with normal baseline or ≥1.0 mg/dL in patients with abnormal baseline). Resumption of therapy may be considered when serum creatinine returns to within 10% of baseline.

Administration I.V. infusion over 2-24 hours.

Monitoring Parameters Serum calcium, electrolytes, phosphate, magnesium, CBC with differential; monitor for hypocalcemia for at least 2 weeks after therapy; monitor serum creatinine prior to each dose; dental exam and preventative dentistry for patients at risk for osteonecrosis; patients with pre-existing anemia, leukopenia or thrombocytopenia should be closely monitored during the first 2 weeks of treatment

Reference Range Calcium (total): Adults: 9.0-11.0 mg/dL (SI: 2.05-2.54 mmol/L), may slightly decrease with aging; Phosphorus: 2.5-4.5 mg/dL (SI: 0.81-1.45 mmol/L)

Test Interactions Bisphosphonates may interfere with diagnostic imaging agents such as technetium-99m-diphosphonate in bone scans.

Dosage Forms
Injection, powder for reconstitution, as disodium: 30 mg, 90 mg
Aredia®: 30 mg, 90 mg
Injection, solution: 3 mg/mL (10 mL); 6 mg/mL (10 mL); 9 mg/mL (10 mL)

♦ **Pamidronate Disodium** see Pamidronate on page 1300
♦ **Pamidronate Disodium® (Can)** see Pamidronate on page 1300
♦ **p-Aminoclonidine** see Apraclonidine on page 144
♦ **Pamix™ [OTC]** see Pyrantel Pamoate on page 1459
♦ **Pamprin® Maximum Strength All Day Relief [OTC]** see Naproxen on page 1199
♦ **Panafil®** see Chlorophyllin, Papain, and Urea on page 345
♦ **Panafil® SE** see Chlorophyllin, Papain, and Urea on page 345
♦ **Pan-B Antibody** see Rituximab on page 1523
♦ **Pancof®-EXP** see Dihydrocodeine, Pseudoephedrine, and Guaifenesin on page 506
♦ **Pancof-HC** see Hydrocodone and Pseudoephedrine on page 851
♦ **Pancof®-PD** see Dihydrocodeine, Chlorpheniramine, and Phenylephrine on page 506
♦ **Pancof-XP** see Hydrocodone and Guaifenesin on page 849
♦ **Pancrease® [DSC]** see Pancrelipase on page 1302
♦ **Pancrease® (Can)** see Pancrelipase on page 1302
♦ **Pancrease® MT** see Pancrelipase on page 1302
♦ **Pancrecarb MS®** see Pancrelipase on page 1302

Pancrelipase (pan kre LYE pase)

U.S. Brand Names Creon®; ku-zyme® HP; Lipram 4500; Lipram-CR; Lipram-PN; Lipram-UL; Palcaps; Pancrease® [DSC]; Pancrease® MT; Pancrecarb MS®; Pangestyme™ CN; Pangestyme™ EC; Pangestyme™ MT; Pangestyme™ UL; Panocaps; Panocaps MT; Panokase®; Panokase® 16; Plaretase® 8000; Ultracaps MT; Ultrase®; Ultrase® MT; Viokase®
Canadian Brand Names Cotazym®; Creon® 5; Creon® 10; Creon® 20; Creon® 25; Pancrease®; Pancrease® MT; Ultrase®; Ultrase® MT; Viokase®
Index Terms Lipancreatin
Pharmacologic Category Enzyme
Use Replacement therapy in symptomatic treatment of malabsorption syndrome caused by pancreatic insufficiency
Unlabeled/Investigational Use Treatment of occluded feeding tubes
Pregnancy Risk Factor B/C (product specific)
Lactation Excretion in breast milk unknown/use caution

Contraindications Hypersensitivity to pork protein or any component of the formulation; acute pancreatitis or acute exacerbations of chronic pancreatic disease

Warnings/Precautions Pancrelipase is inactivated by acids; use microencapsulated products whenever possible, since these products permit better dissolution of enzymes in the duodenum and protect the enzyme preparations from acid degradation in the stomach. Fibrotic strictures in the colon, some requiring surgery, have been reported with high doses; use caution, especially in children with cystic fibrosis. Use caution when adjusting doses or changing brands. Avoid inhalation of powder, may cause nasal and respiratory tract irritation.

Adverse Reactions Frequency not defined; occurrence of events may be dose related.

Central nervous system: Pain

Dermatologic: Rash

Endocrine & metabolic: Hyperuricemia

Gastrointestinal: Nausea, cramps, constipation, diarrhea, perianal irritation/inflammation (large doses), irritation of the mouth, abdominal pain, intestinal obstruction, vomiting, flatulence, melena, weight loss, fibrotic strictures, greasy stools

Ocular: Lacrimation

Renal: Hyperuricosuria

Respiratory: Sneezing, dyspnea, bronchospasm

Miscellaneous: Allergic reactions

Overdosage/Toxicology Symptoms include diarrhea, other transient intestinal upset, hyperuricosuria, and hyperuricemia.

Ethanol/Nutrition/Herb Interactions Food: Avoid placing contents of opened capsules on alkaline food (pH >5.5); pancrelipase may impair absorption of oral iron and folic acid.

Stability Store between 15°C to 25°C (59°F to 77°F); do not refrigerate. Keep in a dry place.

Mechanism of Action Pancrelipase is a natural product harvested from the hog pancreas. It contains a combination of lipase, amylase, and protease. Products are formulated to dissolve in the more basic pH of the duodenum so that they may act locally to break down fats, protein, and starch.

Pharmacodynamics/Kinetics

Absorption: None; acts locally in GI tract

Excretion: Feces

Dosage Oral:

Powder: Actual dose depends on the condition being treated and the digestive requirements of the patient

Children <1 year: Start with $\frac{1}{8}$ teaspoonful with feedings

Adults: 0.7 g ($\frac{1}{4}$ teaspoonful) with meals

Capsules/tablets: The following dosage recommendations are only an approximation for initial dosages. The actual dosage will depend on the condition being treated and the digestive requirements of the individual patient. Adjust dose based on body weight and stool fat content. Total daily dose reflects ~3 meals/day and 2-3 snacks/day, with half the mealtime dose given with a snack. Older patients may need less units/kg due to increased weight, but decreased ingestion of fat/kg. Maximum dose: 2500 units of lipase/kg/meal (10,000 units of lipase/kg/day)

Children:

<1 year: 2000 units of lipase with meals

1-6 years: 4000-8000 units of lipase with meals and 4000 units with snacks

7-12 years: 4000-12,000 units of lipase with meals and snacks

Adults: 4000-48,000 units of lipase with meals and with snacks

Occluded feeding tubes: One tablet of Viokase® crushed with one 325 mg tablet of sodium bicarbonate (to activate the Viokase®) in 5 mL of water can be instilled into the nasogastric tube and clamped for 5 minutes; then, flushed with 50 mL of tap water

Dietary Considerations Should be used as part of a high-calorie diet, appropriate for age and clinical status. Administer with meals or snacks and swallow whole with a generous amount of liquid. Do not crush or chew. Delayed-release capsules containing enteric coated microspheres or microtablets may also be opened and the contents sprinkled on soft food with a low pH such as applesauce, gelatin; apricot, banana, or sweet potato baby food; baby formula. Dairy products such as milk, custard or ice cream may have a high pH and should be avoided.

Administration Oral: Administer with meals or snacks and swallow whole with a generous amount of liquid. Do not crush or chew; retention in the mouth before swallowing may cause mucosal irritation and stomatitis. Delayed-release capsules containing enteric-coated microspheres or microtablets may also be opened and the contents sprinkled on soft food with a low pH that does not require chewing, such as applesauce, gelatin; apricot, banana, or sweet potato baby food; baby formula. Dairy products such as milk, custard, or ice cream may have a high pH and should be avoided. Avoid inhalation of powder, may cause nasal and respiratory tract irritation.

Monitoring Parameters Abdominal symptoms, nutritional intake, growth (in children), stool character, fecal fat

Dosage Forms [DSC] = Discontinued product

Capsule:

ku-zyme® HP: Lipase 8000 units, protease 30,000 units, and amylase 30,000 units

Capsule, delayed release, enteric coated granules:

Pangestyme™ CN-10: Lipase 10,000 units, protease 37,500 units, amylase 33,200 units

Pangestyme™ CN-20: Lipase 20,000 units, protease 75,000 units, amylase 66,400 units

Pangestyme™ EC: Lipase 4500 units, protease 25,000 units, and amylase 20,000 units

Pangestyme™ MT16: Lipase 16,000 units, protease 48,000 units, and amylase 48,000 units

Pangestyme™ UL 12: Lipase 12,000 units, protease 39,000 units, and amylase 39,000 units

Pangestyme™ UL 18: Lipase 18,000 units, protease 58,500 units, and amylase 58,500 units

Pangestyme™ UL 20: Lipase 20,000 units, protease 65,000 units, and amylase 65,000 units

(Continued)

Pancrelipase *(Continued)*

Capsule, delayed release, enteric coated microspheres: Lipase 4500 units, protease 25,000 units, and amylase 20,000 units

Creon® 5: Lipase 5000 units, protease 18,750 units, and amylase 16,600 units

Creon® 10, Palcaps 10: Lipase 10,000 units, protease 37,500 units, and amylase 33,200 units

Creon® 20, Palcaps 20: Lipase 20,000 units, protease 75,000 units, and amylase 66,400 units

Lipram 4500, Panocaps: Lipase 4500 units, protease 25,000 units, and amylase 20,000 units

Lipram-CR5: Lipase 5000 units, protease 18,750 units, and amylase 16,600 units [DSC]

Lipram-CR10: Lipase 10,000 units, protease 37,500 units, and amylase 33,200 units

Lipram-CR20: Lipase 20,000 units, protease 75,000 units, and amylase 66,400 units

Lipram-PN10: Lipase 10,000 units, protease 30,000 units, and amylase 30,000 units

Lipram-PN16, Panocap MT 16: Lipase 16,000 units, protease 48,000 units, and amylase 48,000 units

Lipram-PN20, Panocap MT 20: Lipase 20,000 units, protease 44,000 units, and amylase 56,000 units

Lipram-UL12: Lipase 12,000 units, protease 39,000 units, and amylase 39,000 units [DSC]

Lipram-UL18: Lipase 18,000 units, protease 58,500 units, and amylase 58,500 units [DSC]

Lipram-UL20, Ultracaps MT 20: Lipase 20,000 units, protease 65,000 units, and amylase 65,000 units

Pancrecarb MS-4®: Lipase 4000 units, protease 25,000 units, and amylase 25,000 units [buffered]

Pancrecarb MS-8®: Lipase 8000 units, protease 45,000 units, and amylase 40,000 units [buffered]

Capsule, enteric coated microspheres:

Pancrease® [DSC], Ultrase®: Lipase 4500 units, protease 25,000 units, and amylase 20,000 units

Capsule, enteric coated microtablets:

Pancrease® MT 4: Lipase 4000 units, protease 12,000 units, and amylase 12,000 units

Pancrease® MT 10: Lipase 10,000 units, protease 30,000 units, and amylase 30,000 units

Pancrease® MT 16: Lipase 16,000 units, protease 48,000 units, and amylase 48,000 units

Pancrease® MT 20: Lipase 20,000 units, protease 44,000 units, and amylase 56,000 units

Capsule, enteric coated minitablets:

Ultrase® MT12: Lipase 12,000 units, protease 39,000 units, and amylase 39,000 units

Ultrase® MT18: Lipase 18,000 units, protease 58,500 units, and amylase 58,500 units

Ultrase® MT20: Lipase 20,000 units, protease 65,000 units, and amylase 65,000 units

Powder (Viokase®): Lipase 16,800 units, protease 70,000 units, and amylase 70,000 units per 0.7 g (227 g)

Tablet: Lipase 8000 units, protease 30,000 units, and amylase 30,000 units

Panokase®: Lipase 8000 units, protease 30,000 units, and amylase 30,000 units

Panokase® 16: Lipase 16,000 units, protease 60,000 units, and amylase 60,000 units

Plaretase™ 8000: Lipase 8000 units, protease 30,000 units, and amylase 30,000 units

Viokase® 8: Lipase 8000 units, protease 30,000 units, and amylase 30,000 units

Viokase® 16: Lipase 16,000 units, protease 60,000 units, and amylase 60,000 units

Pancuronium (pan kyoo ROE nee um)

Canadian Brand Names Pancuronium Bromide®

Index Terms Pancuronium Bromide; Pavulon [DSC]

Pharmacologic Category Neuromuscular Blocker Agent, Nondepolarizing

Additional Appendix Information

Neuromuscular Blocking Agents *on page 1890*

Use Adjunct to general anesthesia to facilitate endotracheal intubation and to relax skeletal muscles during surgery; to facilitate mechanical ventilation in ICU patients; does not relieve pain or produce sedation

Drug of choice for neuromuscular blockade except in patients with renal failure, hepatic failure, or cardiovascular instability or in situations not suited for pancuronium's long duration of action

Pregnancy Risk Factor C

Lactation Excretion in breast milk unknown/not recommended

Medication Safety Issues

Sound-alike/look-alike issues:

Pancuronium may be confused with pipecuronium

High alert medication: The Institute for Safe Medication Practices (ISMP) includes this medication among its list of drugs which have a heightened risk of causing significant patient harm when used in error.

Contraindications Hypersensitivity to pancuronium, bromide, or any component of the formulation

Warnings/Precautions Ventilation must be supported during neuromuscular blockade; use with caution in patients with renal and/or hepatic impairment (adjust dose appropriately); certain clinical conditions may result in potentiation or antagonism of neuromuscular blockade:

Potentiation: Electrolyte abnormalities, severe hyponatremia, severe hypocalcemia, severe hypokalemia, hypermagnesemia, neuromuscular diseases, acidosis, acute intermittent porphyria, renal failure, hepatic failure

Antagonism: Alkalosis, hypercalcemia, demyelinating lesions, peripheral neuropathies, diabetes mellitus

Increased sensitivity in patients with myasthenia gravis, Eaton-Lambert syndrome; resistance in burn patients (>30% of body) for period of 5-70 days postinjury; resistance in patients with muscle trauma, denervation, immobilization, infection. Cross-sensitivity with other neuromuscular-blocking agents may occur; use extreme caution in patients with previous anaphylactic reactions. **[U.S. Boxed Warning]: Should be administered by adequately trained individuals familiar with its use.**

Adverse Reactions Frequency not defined.

Cardiovascular: Elevation in pulse rate, elevated blood pressure and cardiac output, tachycardia, edema, skin flushing, circulatory collapse

Dermatologic: Rash, itching, erythema, burning sensation along the vein

Gastrointestinal: Excessive salivation

Neuromuscular & skeletal: Profound muscle weakness

Respiratory: Wheezing, bronchospasm

Miscellaneous: Hypersensitivity reaction

Postmarketing and/or case reports: Acute quadriplegic myopathy syndrome (prolonged use), myositis ossificans (prolonged use)

Overdosage/Toxicology Symptoms include apnea, respiratory depression, and cardiovascular collapse. Pyridostigmine, neostigmine, or edrophonium in conjunction with atropine will usually antagonize the action of pancuronium.

Drug Interactions

Increased Effect/Toxicity: Increased effects are possible with aminoglycosides, beta-blockers, clindamycin, calcium channel blockers, halogenated anesthetics, imipenem, ketamine, lidocaine, loop diuretics (furosemide), macrolides (case reports), magnesium sulfate, procainamide, quinidine, quinolones, tetracyclines, and vancomycin. May increase risk of myopathy when used with high-dose corticosteroids for extended periods.

Decreased Effect: Effect of nondepolarizing neuromuscular blockers may be reduced by carbamazepine (chronic use), corticosteroids (also associated with myopathy - see increased effect), phenytoin (chronic use), sympathomimetics, and theophylline.

Stability Refrigerate; however, stable for up to 6 months at room temperature.

Mechanism of Action Blocks neural transmission at the myoneural junction by binding with cholinergic receptor sites

Pharmacodynamics/Kinetics

Onset of effect: Peak effect: I.V.: 2-3 minutes

Duration (dose dependent): 60-100 minutes

Metabolism: Hepatic (30% to 45%); active metabolite 3-hydroxypancuronium ($1/3$ to $1/2$ the activity of parent drug)

Half-life elimination: 110 minutes

Excretion: Urine (55% to 70% as unchanged drug)

Dosage Administer I.V.; dose to effect; doses will vary due to interpatient variability; use ideal body weight for obese patients

Surgery:

Neonates <1 month:

Test dose: 0.02 mg/kg to measure responsiveness

Initial: 0.03 mg/kg/dose repeated twice at 5- to 10-minute intervals as needed; maintenance: 0.03-0.09 mg/kg/dose every 30 minutes to 4 hours as needed

Infants >1 month, Children, and Adults: Initial: 0.06-0.1 mg/kg or 0.05 mg/kg after initial dose of succinylcholine for intubation; maintenance dose: 0.01 mg/kg 60-100 minutes after initial dose and then 0.01 mg/kg every 25-60 minutes

Pretreatment/priming: 10% of intubating dose given 3-5 minutes before initial dose

ICU: 0.05-0.1 mg/kg bolus followed by 0.8-1.7 mcg/kg/minute once initial recovery from bolus observed or 0.1-0.2 mg/kg every 1-3 hours

Dosing adjustment in renal impairment: Elimination half-life is doubled, plasma clearance is reduced and rate of recovery is sometimes much slower

Cl$_{cr}$ 10-50 mL/minute: Administer 50% of normal dose

Cl$_{cr}$ <10 mL/minute: Do not use

Dosing adjustment/comments in hepatic/biliary tract disease: Elimination half-life is doubled, plasma clearance is reduced, recovery time is prolonged, volume of distribution is increased (50%) and results in a slower onset, higher total initial dosage and prolongation of neuromuscular blockade

Administration May be administered undiluted by rapid I.V. injection

Monitoring Parameters Heart rate, blood pressure, assisted ventilation status; cardiac monitor, blood pressure monitor, and ventilator required

Additional Information Pancuronium is classified as a long-duration neuromuscular-blocking agent. Neuromuscular blockade will be prolonged in patients with decreased renal function. Pancuronium does not relieve pain or produce sedation. It may produce cumulative effect on duration of blockade. It produces tachycardia secondary to vagolytic activity and sympathetic stimulation.

Dosage Forms Injection, solution, as bromide: 1 mg/mL (10 mL); 2 mg/mL (2 mL, 5 mL) [may contain benzyl alcohol]

♦ **Pancuronium Bromide** see Pancuronium on page 1304
♦ **Pancuronium Bromide® (Can)** see Pancuronium on page 1304
♦ **Pandel®** see Hydrocortisone on page 852
♦ **Pangestyme™ CN** see Pancrelipase on page 1302
♦ **Pangestyme™ EC** see Pancrelipase on page 1302
♦ **Pangestyme™ MT** see Pancrelipase on page 1302
♦ **Pangestyme™ UL** see Pancrelipase on page 1302
♦ **Panglobulin® NF** see Immune Globulin (Intravenous) on page 892

Panitumumab (pan i TOOM yoo mab)

U.S. Brand Names Vectibix™

Index Terms ABX-EGF; NSC-742319; rHuMAb-EGFr

Pharmacologic Category Antineoplastic Agent, Monoclonal Antibody; Epidermal Growth Factor Receptor (EGFR) Inhibitor

(Continued)

Panitumumab *(Continued)*

Use Treatment of refractory (EGFR positive) metastatic colorectal cancer

Pregnancy Risk Factor C

Pregnancy Implications Animal reproductive studies have demonstrated adverse fetal effects. Based on animal studies, panitumumab may disrupt normal menstrual cycles. There are no adequate and well-controlled studies in pregnant women. IgG is known to cross the placenta; therefore, it is possible the developing fetus may be exposed to panitumumab. Because panitumumab inhibits epidermal growth factor (EGF), a component of fetal development, adverse effects on pregnancy would be expected. Panitumumab should only be given to a pregnant woman if the potential benefit justifies the potential risk to the fetus. Women of childbearing potential should use effective contraception during and for 6 months after treatment.

Lactation Excretion in breast milk unknown/not recommended

Contraindications Hypersensitivity to panitumumab or any component of the formulation

Warnings/Precautions [U.S. Boxed Warning]: Dermatologic toxicities have been reported in ~90% of patients; may include dermatitis acneiform, pruritus, erythema, rash, skin exfoliation, paronychia, dry skin and skin fissures. Severe skin toxicities may be complicated by infection, sepsis, or abscesses. The median time to development of skin (or ocular) toxicity was 2 weeks, with resolution ~7 weeks after discontinuation. Hold treatment and monitor with severe dermatologic toxicities; may require dose reduction. Patients should minimize sunlight exposure; may exacerbate skin reactions. Gastric mucosal, ocular and nail toxicities have also been reported.

[U.S. Boxed Warning]: Severe infusion reactions (anaphylactic reaction, bronchospasm, fever, chills, and hypotension) have been reported in ~1% of patients. Discontinue infusion for severe reactions; permanently discontinue in patients with persistent severe infusion reactions. Appropriate medical support for the management of infusion reactions should be readily available. Mild to moderate infusion reactions are managed by slowing the infusion rate.

Pulmonary fibrosis has been reported (rarely); permanently discontinue treatment if interstitial lung disease, pneumonitis or lung infiltrates develop. Use caution with lung disease; patients with underlying lung disease were excluded from clinical trials. May cause diarrhea; the incidence and severity of chemotherapy-induced diarrhea is increased with combination chemotherapy. Due to the potential for severe diarrhea, use with the combination regimen containing irinotecan, bolus fluorouracil, and leucovorin regimen (IFL) is not recommended. Electrolyte depletion may occur during treatment and after treatment is discontinued; monitor for hypomagnesemia and hypocalcemia. Safety and efficacy in children have not been established.

Adverse Reactions

>10%:
- Cardiovascular: Peripheral edema (12%)
- Central nervous system: Fatigue (28%)
- Dermatologic: Skin toxicity (90%; grades 3/4: 16%), erythema (65%; grades 3/4: 5%), acneiform rash (57%; grades 3/4: 7%), pruritus (57%; grades 3/4: 2%), exfoliation (25%; grades 3/4: 2%), paronychia (25%), rash (22%; grades 3/4: 1%), fissures (20%; grades 3/4: 1%), acne (13%; grades 3/4: 1%)
- Endocrine & metabolic: Hypomagnesemia (39%; grades 3/4: 4%)
- Gastrointestinal: Abdominal pain (25%), nausea (23%), diarrhea (21%; grades 3/4: 2%), constipation (21%), vomiting (19%)
- Respiratory: Cough (14%)

1% to 10%:
- Dermatologic: Dry skin (10%), nail disorder (other than paronychia: 9%)
- Gastrointestinal: Stomatitis (7%), mucositis (6%)
- Ocular: Eyelash growth (6%), conjunctivitis (4%), ocular hyperemia (3%), lacrimation increased (2%), eye/eye lid irritation (1%)
- Miscellaneous: Infusion reactions (3%; grades 3/4: 1%)

<1% (Limited to important or life-threatening): Allergic reaction, anaphylactoid reaction, chills, dyspnea, fever, hypocalcemia, pulmonary fibrosis

Overdosage/Toxicology Treatment is symptom-directed and supportive.

Stability Store unopened vials under refrigeration at 2°C to 8°C (36°F to 46°F). Do not freeze; do not shake; protect from light. Dilute in 100-150 mL of normal saline to a final concentration of ≤10 mg/mL. Do not shake, invert gently to mix. Preparations in infusion containers are stable for 24 hours under refrigeration at 2°C to 8°C (36°F to 46°F) or for 6 hours at room temperature.

Mechanism of Action Recombinant human IgG2 monoclonal antibody which binds specifically to the epidermal growth factor receptor (EGFR, HER1, c-ErbB-1) and competitively inhibits the binding of epidermal growth factor (EGF) and other ligands. Binding to the EGFR blocks phosphorylation and activation of intracellular tyrosine kinases, resulting in inhibition of cell survival, growth, proliferation and transformation.

Pharmacodynamics/Kinetics Half-life elimination: ~7.5 days (range: 4-11 days)

Dosage I.V.: Adults: Colorectal cancer: 6 mg/kg every 2 weeks

Dosing adjustment for toxicity:
- Infusion reactions, mild-to-moderate (grade 1 or 2): Reduce the infusion rate by 50% for the duration of infusion
- Infusion reactions, severe (grade 3 or 4): Immediately and permanently discontinue treatment
- Skin toxicity (grade 3 or 4): Withhold treatment; if skin toxicity does not improve to ≤ grade 2 within 1 month, permanently discontinue. If skin toxicity improves to ≤ grade 2 within 1 month (with patient missing ≤2 doses), resume treatment at 50% of the original dose. Dose may be increased in increments of 25% of the original dose (up to 6 mg/kg) if skin toxicities do not recur. For recurrent skin toxicity, permanently discontinue.

Dosage adjustment in renal impairment: Has not been studied

Dosage adjustment in hepatic impairment: Has not been studied

Administration Doses ≤1000 mg-infuse over 1 hour; doses >1000 mg-infuse over 90 minutes; reduce infusion rate by 50% for mild-to-moderate infusion reactions; discontinue for severe infusion reactions. Administer through a low protein-binding 0.2 or 0.22 micrometer in-line filter. Flush with NS before and after infusion.

Monitoring Parameters EGF receptor expression testing should be completed prior to treatment. Monitor serum electrolytes, including magnesium and calcium (periodically during and for at least 8 weeks after therapy). Monitor vital signs and temperature before, during, and after infusion. Monitor for skin toxicity.

Dosage Forms
Injection, solution [preservative free]:
Vectibix™: 20 mg/mL (5 mL, 10 mL, 20 mL)

♦ **Panixine DisperDose™ [DSC]** *see* Cephalexin *on page 331*
♦ **Panocaps** *see* Pancrelipase *on page 1302*
♦ **Panocaps MT** *see* Pancrelipase *on page 1302*
♦ **Panokase®** *see* Pancrelipase *on page 1302*
♦ **Panokase® 16** *see* Pancrelipase *on page 1302*
♦ **Panretin®** *see* Alitretinoin *on page 70*
♦ **Panthoderm® [OTC]** *see* Dexpanthenol *on page 485*
♦ **Panto™ IV (Can)** *see* Pantoprazole *on page 1307*
♦ **Pantoloc® (Can)** *see* Pantoprazole *on page 1307*

Pantoprazole (pan TOE pra zole)

U.S. Brand Names Protonix®
Canadian Brand Names Panto™ IV; Pantoloc®; Protonix®
Pharmacologic Category Proton Pump Inhibitor; Substituted Benzimidazole
Use
Oral: Treatment and maintenance of healing of erosive esophagitis associated with GERD; reduction in relapse rates of daytime and nighttime heartburn symptoms in GERD; hypersecretory disorders associated with Zollinger-Ellison syndrome or other neoplastic disorders

I.V.: Short-term treatment (7-10 days) of patients with gastroesophageal reflux disease (GERD) and a history of erosive esophagitis; hypersecretory disorders associated with Zollinger-Ellison syndrome or other neoplastic disorders

Unlabeled/Investigational Use Peptic ulcer disease, active ulcer bleeding (parenteral formulation); adjunct treatment with antibiotics for *Helicobacter pylori* eradication

Pregnancy Risk Factor B

Pregnancy Implications There are no adequate and well-controlled studies in pregnant women. Use in pregnancy only if clearly needed.

Lactation Enters breast milk/not recommended

Medication Safety Issues
Sound-alike/look-alike issues:
Protonix® may be confused with Lotronex®, Lovenox®, protamine

Vials containing Protonix® I.V. for injection are not recommended for use with spiked I.V. system adaptors. Nurses and pharmacists have reported breakage of the glass vials during attempts to connect spiked I.V. system adaptors, which may potentially result in injury to healthcare professionals.

International issues:
Protonix® may be confused with Pretanix® which is a brand name for indapamide in Hungary

Contraindications Hypersensitivity to pantoprazole, substituted benzamidazoles (ie, esomeprazole, lansoprazole, omeprazole, rabeprazole), or any component of the formulation

Warnings/Precautions Relief of symptoms does not preclude the presence of a gastric malignancy. Long-term omeprazole therapy has caused atrophic gastritis (by biopsy); this may also occur with pantoprazole. No reports of enterochromaffin-like (ECL) cell carcinoids, dysplasia, or neoplasia has occurred. Not indicated for maintenance therapy; safety and efficacy for use beyond 16 weeks have not been established. Prolonged treatment (typically >3 years) may lead to vitamin B_{12} malabsorption. Intravenous preparation contains edetate sodium (EDTA); use caution in patients who are risk for zinc deficiency if other EDTA-containing solutions are coadministered. Safety and efficacy in pediatric patients have not been established.

Adverse Reactions
≥1%:
Cardiovascular: Chest pain
Central nervous system: Headache (5% to 9%), insomnia (<1% to 1%), dizziness, migraine, anxiety
Dermatologic: Rash (<1% to 2%)
Endocrine and metabolic: Hyperglycemia (<1% to 1%), hyperlipidemia
Gastrointestinal: Diarrhea (4% to 6%), flatulence (2% to 4%), abdominal pain (1% to 4%), nausea (≤2%), vomiting (≤2%), eructation (≤1%), constipation, dyspepsia, gastroenteritis, rectal disorder
Genitourinary: Urinary frequency, UTI
Hepatic: Liver function abnormal (up to 2%)
Local: Injection site reaction (includes thrombophlebitis and abscess)
Neuromuscular & skeletal: Arthralgia, back pain, hypertonia, neck pain, weakness
Respiratory: Bronchitis, cough, dyspnea, pharyngitis, rhinitis, sinusitis, upper respiratory tract infection
Miscellaneous: Flu syndrome, infection, pain
<1% (Limited to important or life-threatening): Anaphylaxis, angioedema, anterior ischemic optic neuropathy, albuminuria, alkaline phosphatase increased, allergic reaction, anemia, angina pectoris, aphthous stomatitis, arrhythmia, asthma, atrial fibrillation/flutter, atrophic
(Continued)

Pantoprazole *(Continued)*

gastritis, bone pain, breast pain, bursitis, cataract, CHF, cholecystitis, cholelithiasis, CPK increased, colitis, confusion, contact dermatitis, convulsion, creatinine increased, cystitis, deafness, decreased reflexes, dehydration, depression, diabetes mellitus, duodenitis, dysarthria, dysmenorrhea, dysphagia, dysuria, ecchymosis, eczema, ECG abnormality, eosinophilia, epididymitis, erythema multiforme, extraocular palsy, fever, fungal dermatitis, gastrointestinal carcinoma, gastrointestinal hemorrhage, gastrointestinal moniliasis, generalized edema, glaucoma, glycosuria, goiter, gout, hallucinations, hematuria, hemorrhage, hepatic failure, hepatitis, herpes simplex, herpes zoster, hyperkinesia, hyper-/hypotension, hyperuricemia, hypokinesia, impaired urination, impotence, interstitial nephritis, jaundice, kidney calculus, kidney pain, laryngitis, leukocytosis, leukopenia, lichenoid dermatitis, maculopapular rash, mouth ulceration, myalgia, myocardial ischemia, neoplasm, neuralgia, neuritis, optic neuropathy, palpitation, pancreatitis, pancytopenia, paresthesia, pneumonia, pyelonephritis, rhabdomyolysis, rectal hemorrhage, retinal vascular disorder, scrotal edema, skin ulcer, somnolence, Stevens-Johnson syndrome, stomach ulcer, stomatitis, syncope, tachycardia, tenosynovitis, thrombocytopenia, thrombosis, toxic epidermal necrolysis, urethritis, vasodilation, vision abnormal

Overdosage/Toxicology Treatment of an overdose would include appropriate supportive treatment. No adverse events were seen with ingestions of 400 mg and 600 mg. Pantoprazole is not removed by hemodialysis.

Drug Interactions

Cytochrome P450 Effect: Substrate of CYP2C19 (major), 3A4 (minor); **Inhibits** 2C9 (moderate); **Induces** CYP1A2 (weak), 3A4 (weak)

Increased Effect/Toxicity: Pantoprazole may increase the levels/effects of bosentan, dapsone, fluoxetine, glimepiride, glipizide, losartan, montelukast, nateglinide, paclitaxel, phenytoin, warfarin, zafirlukast, and other CYP2C9 substrates.

Decreased Effect: Proton pump inhibitors may decrease the absorption of atazanavir, indinavir, iron salts, itraconazole, and ketoconazole. The levels/effects of pantoprazole may be decreased by aminoglutethimide, carbamazepine, phenytoin, rifampin, and other CYP2C19 inducers.

Ethanol/Nutrition/Herb Interactions

Ethanol: Avoid ethanol (may cause gastric mucosal irritation).

Herb/Nutraceutical: Prolonged treatment (typically >3 years) may lead to vitamin B_{12} malabsorption.

Stability

Oral: Store tablet at 15°C to 30°C (59°F to 77°F).

I.V.:

EDTA-stabilized formulation: Prior to use: Store at 15°C to 30°C (59°F to 86°F). Protect from light. When reconstituted with 10 mL NS (final concentration 4 mg/mL), solution is stable up to 24 hours at room temperature. If further diluting in 100 mL of D_5W, LR, or NS, dilute within 6 hours of reconstitution. Diluted solution is stable at room temperature for up to 24 hours from the time of initial reconstitution; protection from light is not required.

Original formulation (discontinued): Store at 2°C to 8°C (36°F to 46°F). Protect from light. When reconstituted with 10 mL NS (final concentration 4 mg/mL), solution is stable up to 2 hours at room temperature; protection from light is not required. When diluted in 100 mL D_5W, LR, or NS, may be stored at room temperature for up to 12 hours.

Mechanism of Action Suppresses gastric acid secretin by inhibiting the parietal cell H^+/K^+ ATP pump

Pharmacodynamics/Kinetics

Absorption: Well absorbed

Distribution: V_d: 11-24 L

Protein binding: 98%, primarily to albumin

Metabolism: Extensively hepatic; CYP2C19 (demethylation), CYP3A4; no evidence that metabolites have pharmacologic activity

Bioavailability: 77%

Half-life elimination: 1 hour; increased to 3.5-10 hours with CYP2C19 deficiency

Time to peak: Oral: 2.5 hours

Excretion: Urine (71%); feces (18%)

Dosage Adults:

Oral:

Erosive esophagitis associated with GERD:

Treatment: 40 mg once daily for up to 8 weeks; an additional 8 weeks may be used in patients who have not healed after an 8-week course

Maintenance of healing: 40 mg once daily

Note: Lower doses (20 mg once daily) have been used successfully in mild GERD treatment and maintenance of healing

Hypersecretory disorders (including Zollinger-Ellison): Initial: 40 mg twice daily; adjust dose based on patient needs; doses up to 240 mg/day have been administered

Helicobacter pylori eradication (unlabeled use): Doses up to 40 mg twice daily have been used as part of combination therapy

I.V.:

Erosive esophagitis associated with GERD: 40 mg once daily for 7-10 days

Hypersecretory disorders: 80 mg twice daily; adjust dose based on acid output measurements; 160-240 mg/day in divided doses has been used for a limited period (up to 7 days)

Prevention of rebleeding in peptic ulcer bleed (unlabeled use): 80 mg, followed by 8 mg/hour infusion for 72 hours. **Note:** A daily infusion of 40 mg does not raise gastric pH sufficiently to enhance coagulation in active GI bleeds.

Elderly: Dosage adjustment not required

Dosage adjustment in renal impairment: Not required; pantoprazole is not removed by hemodialysis

Dosage adjustment in hepatic impairment: Not required

Dietary Considerations
Oral: May be taken with or without food; best if taken before breakfast.
I.V.: Due to EDTA in preparation, zinc supplementation may be needed in patients prone to zinc deficiency.

Administration
I.V.: Flush I.V. line before and after administration. Solutions prepared from original formulation must be infused through an Inline filter. Solutions prepared from the EDTA-stabilized formulation do not require an in-line filter (per manufacturer).
2-minute infusion: The volume of reconstituted solution (4 mg/mL) to be injected may be administered intravenously over at least 2 minutes.
15-minute infusion: Infuse over 15 minutes at a rate not to exceed 7 mL/minute (3 mg/minute).
Oral: Tablets should be swallowed whole, do not crush or chew. Best if taken before breakfast.

Monitoring Parameters Hypersecretory disorders: Acid output measurements, target level <10 mEq/hour (<5 mEq/hour if prior gastric acid-reducing surgery)

Test Interactions False-positive urine screening tests for tetrahydrocannabinol (THC) have been noted in patients receiving proton pump inhibitors, including pantoprazole.

Dosage Forms Note: Strength expressed as base
Injection, powder for reconstitution, as sodium:
Protonix®: 40 mg [contains edetate sodium 1 mg]
Tablet, delayed release, as sodium:
Protonix®: 20 mg, 40 mg

Extemporaneous Preparations A 2 mg/mL pantoprazole oral liquid can be prepared with twenty pantoprazole 40 mg tablets, 340 mL sterile water, and 33.6 g of sodium bicarbonate powder. Remove the Protonix® imprint from each of the tablets on a paper towel dampened with ethanol (improves the look of product). Let tablets air dry. Grind the tablets into a coarse powder, transfer to a 600 mL beaker and add 340 mL of sterile water for irrigation and place beaker on a magnetic stirrer. Add 16.8 g of sodium bicarbonate powder and stir for about 20 minutes until the tablet remnants have disintegrated. While stirring, add another 16.8 g of sodium bicarbonate powder and stir for about 5 minutes until powder has dissolved. Add enough sterile water for irrigation to bring the final volume to 400 mL. Mix well. Transfer to amber-colored bottle. Stable for 62 days under refrigeration. Shake well before use.
Dentinger PJ, Swenson CF, and Anaizi NH, "Stability of Pantoprazole in an Extemporaneously Compounded Oral Liquid," *Am J Health Syst Pharm*, 2002, 59:953-6.

♦ **Pantothenyl Alcohol** *see* Dexpanthenol *on page 485*

Papain and Urea (pa PAY in & yoor EE a)

U.S. Brand Names Accuzyme®; Allanzyme; Allanzyme 650; Ethezyme™; Ethezyme™ 830; Gladase®; Kovia®

Pharmacologic Category Enzyme, Topical Debridement

Use Debridement of necrotic tissue and liquefaction of slough in acute and chronic lesions such as pressure ulcers, varicose and diabetic ulcers, burns, postoperative wounds, pilonidal cyst wounds, carbuncles, and miscellaneous traumatic or infected wounds

Dosage Topical: Adults: Apply with each dressing change. Daily or twice daily dressing changes are preferred, but may be every 2-3 days. Cover with dressing following application.
Ointment: Apply 1/8-inch thickness over the wound with clean applicator.
Spray: Completely cover the wound site so that the wound is not visible.

Additional Information Complete prescribing information for this medication should be consulted for additional detail.

Dosage Forms
Ointment, topical:
Accuzyme®: Papain 6.5×10^5 units/g and urea 10% (6 g, 30 g)
Allanzyme 650: Papain 6.5×10^5 units/g and urea 10% (30 g)
Ethezyme™: Papain 1.1×10^6 units/g and urea 10% (30 g)
Ethezyme™ 830: Papain 8.3×10^5 units/g and urea 10% (30 g)
Gladase®: Papain 8.3×10^5 units/g and urea 10% (6 g, 30 g)
Kovia®: Papain 8.3×10^5 units/g and urea 10% (3.5 g) [single-dose packet]; 30 g
Spray, topical:
Accuzyme®, Allanzyme: Papain 6.5×10^5 units/g and urea 10% (33 mL)

♦ **Papain, Urea, and Chlorophyllin** *see* Chlorophyllin, Papain, and Urea *on page 345*

Papaverine (pa PAV er een)

U.S. Brand Names Para-Time SR®

Index Terms Papaverine Hydrochloride; Pavabid [DSC]

Pharmacologic Category Vasodilator

Use Oral: Relief of peripheral and cerebral ischemia associated with arterial spasm and myocardial ischemia complicated by arrhythmias

Unlabeled/Investigational Use Investigational: Parenteral: Various vascular spasms associated with muscle spasms as in myocardial infarction, angina, peripheral and pulmonary embolism, peripheral vascular disease, angiospastic states, and visceral spasm (ureteral, biliary, and GI colic); testing for impotence

Pregnancy Risk Factor C

Dosage
I.M., I.V.:
Children: 6 mg/kg/day in 4 divided doses
Adults: 30-65 mg (rarely up to 120 mg); may repeat every 3 hours
Oral, sustained release: Adults: 150-300 mg every 12 hours; in difficult cases: 150 mg every 8 hours
(Continued)

Papaverine *(Continued)*

Additional Information Complete prescribing information for this medication should be consulted for additional detail.

Dosage Forms
Capsule, sustained release, as hydrochloride: 150 mg
Para-Time SR®: 150 mg
Injection, solution, as hydrochloride: 30 mg/mL (2 mL, 10 mL)

♦ **Papaverine Hydrochloride** *see* Papaverine *on page 1309*

Papillomavirus (Types 6, 11, 16, 18) Recombinant Vaccine
(pap ih LO ma VYE rus typs six e LEV en SIX teen aye teen ree KOM be nant vak SEEN)

U.S. Brand Names Gardasil®
Index Terms HPV Vaccine; Human Papillomavirus Vaccine; Papillomavirus Vaccine, Recombinant; Quadrivalent Human Papillomavirus Vaccine
Pharmacologic Category Vaccine
Use Prevention of cervical cancer, genital warts, cervical adenocarcinoma *in situ*, and vulvar, vaginal, or cervical intraepithelial neoplasia caused by human papillomavirus (HPV) types 6, 11, 16, 18
Pregnancy Risk Factor B
Pregnancy Implications Teratogenic effects were not observed in animal studies. Administration of the vaccine in pregnancy is not recommended. In clinical trials, women who were found to be pregnant before the completion of the 3-dose regimen were instructed to defer any remaining dose until pregnancy resolution. Pregnancies detected within 30 days of vaccination had a higher rate of congenital anomalies (pyloric stenosis, congenital megacolon, congenital hydronephrosis, hip dysplasia, club foot) than the placebo group. Pregnancies with onset beyond 30 days of vaccination had a rate of congenital anomalies consistent with the general population. Overall, the type of teratogenic events were the same as those generally observed for this age group. A registry has been established for women exposed to the HPV vaccine during pregnancy (1-800-986-8999).
Lactation Excretion in breast milk unknown/use caution
Contraindications Hypersensitivity to papillomavirus recombinant vaccine or any component of the formulation
Warnings/Precautions Immediate treatment for anaphylactoid reaction should be available during vaccine use. There is no evidence that individuals already infected with HPV will be protected; those already infected with 1 or more HPV types were protected from disease in the remaining HPV types. Not for the treatment of active disease; will not protect against diseases not caused by human papillomavirus (HPV) vaccine types 6, 11, 16, and 18. May administer with mild concurrent febrile illness; consider deferring vaccination with serious illness. Immunocompromised patients may have a reduced response to vaccination. Administered I.M., therefore use caution in patients at risk for bleeding. The entire 3 dose regimen should be completed for maximum efficacy. Not recommended for use during pregnancy. Safety and efficacy in girls <9 years of age or women >26 years have not been established.
Adverse Reactions All serious adverse reactions must be reported to the U.S. Department of Health and Human Services (DHHS) Vaccine Adverse Event Reporting System (VAERS) 1-800-822-7967.
>10%:
Central nervous system: Fever (10% to 13%)
Local: Injection site: Pain (84%), swelling (25%), erythema (25%)
1% to 10%:
Central nervous system: Dizziness (4%), malaise (1%), insomnia (1%)
Gastrointestinal: Nausea (7%), diarrhea (4%), vomiting (2%), toothache (2%)
Local: Injection site pruritus (3%)
Neuromuscular & skeletal: Arthralgia (1%)
Respiratory: Cough (2%), nasal congestion (1%)
<1% (Limited to important or life-threatening): Appendicitis, asthma, bronchospasm, gastroenteritis, headache, pelvic inflammatory disease
Drug Interactions
Decreased Effect: Immunosuppressants may decrease the effect of vaccines.
Stability Store at 2°C to 8°C (36°F to 46°F); do not freeze. Protect from light.
Mechanism of Action Contains inactive human papillomavirus (HPV) proteins HPV 6 L1, HPV 11 L1, HPV 16 L1, and HPV 18 L1 which produce neutralizing antibodies to prevent cervical cancer, cervical adenocarcinoma, cervical, vaginal and vulvar neoplasia and genital warts caused by HPV.
Dosage I.M.: Females: Children ≥9 years and Adults ≤26 years: 0.5 mL followed by 0.5 mL at 2 and 6 months after initial dose
Administration Shake suspension well before use. Inject I.M. into the deltoid region of the upper arm or higher anterolateral thigh area.
Monitoring Parameters Annual gynecologic screening exam, annual papillomavirus test
Additional Information Federal law requires that the date of administration, the vaccine manufacturer, lot number of vaccine, and the administering person's name, title and address be entered into the patient's permanent medical record.
Dosage Forms
Injection, suspension [preservative free]:
Gardasil®: HPV 6 L1 protein 20 mcg, HPV 11 L1 protein 40 mcg, HPV 16 L1 protein 40 mcg, and HPV 18 L1 protein 20 mcg per 0.5 mL (0.5 mL) [contains polysorbate 80; packaged in vials or prefilled syringe]

♦ **Papillomavirus Vaccine, Recombinant** *see* Papillomavirus (Types 6, 11, 16, 18) Recombinant Vaccine *on page 1310*
♦ **Para-Aminosalicylate Sodium** *see* Aminosalicylic Acid *on page 96*

- **Paracetamol** *see* Acetaminophen *on page 28*
- **Parafon Forte® (Can)** *see* Chlorzoxazone *on page 359*
- **Parafon Forte® DSC** *see* Chlorzoxazone *on page 359*
- **Paraplatin® [DSC]** *see* Carboplatin *on page 291*
- **Paraplatin-AQ (Can)** *see* Carboplatin *on page 291*
- **Parathyroid Hormone (1-34)** *see* Teriparatide *on page 1652*
- **Para-Time SR®** *see* Papaverine *on page 1309*
- **Parcopa™** *see* Levodopa and Carbidopa *on page 999*

Paregoric (par e GOR ik)

Index Terms Camphorated Tincture of Opium (error-prone synonym)

Pharmacologic Category Analgesic, Opioid

Use Treatment of diarrhea or relief of pain; neonatal opiate withdrawal

Restrictions C-III

Pregnancy Risk Factor B/D (prolonged use or high doses)

Lactation Enters breast milk/use caution

Medication Safety Issues
Sound-alike/look-alike issues:
Camphorated tincture of opium is an error-prone synonym (mistaken as opium tincture)
Paregoric may be confused with Percogesic®

Use care when prescribing opium tincture; each mL contains the equivalent of morphine 10 mg; paregoric contains the equivalent of morphine 0.4 mg/mL

Contraindications Hypersensitivity to opium or any component of the formulation; diarrhea caused by poisoning until the toxic material has been removed; pregnancy (prolonged use or high doses)

Warnings/Precautions May cause CNS depression, which may impair physical or mental abilities; patients must be cautioned about performing tasks which require mental alertness (eg, operating machinery or driving). Effects may be potentiated when used with other sedative drugs or ethanol. Use with caution in patients with respiratory, hepatic or renal dysfunction, adrenal insufficiency, morbid obesity, severe prostatic hyperplasia, urinary stricture, head trauma, thyroid dysfunction, seizure disorder, CNS depression/coma or history of narcotic abuse. Use with caution in patients with biliary tract dysfunction; acute pancreatitis may cause constriction of sphincter of Oddi. May obscure diagnosis or clinical course of patients with acute abdominal conditions. Opium shares the toxic potential of opiate agonists, and usual precautions of opiate agonist therapy should be observed; some preparations contain sulfites which may cause allergic reactions; infants <3 months of age are more susceptible to respiratory depression, use with caution and generally in reduced doses in this age group; tolerance or drug dependence may result from extended use. Concurrent use of agonist/antagonist analgesics may precipitate withdrawal symptoms and/or reduced analgesic efficacy in patients following prolonged therapy with mu opioid agonists. Abrupt discontinuation following prolonged use may also lead to withdrawal symptoms. Use with caution in the elderly and debilitated patients; may be more sensitive to adverse effects.

Adverse Reactions Frequency not defined.
Cardiovascular: Hypotension, peripheral vasodilation
Central nervous system: Drowsiness, dizziness, insomnia, CNS depression, mental depression, increased intracranial pressure, restlessness, headache, malaise
Gastrointestinal: Constipation, anorexia, stomach cramps, nausea, vomiting, biliary tract spasm
Genitourinary: Ureteral spasms, decreased urination, urinary tract spasm
Hepatic: Increased liver function tests
Neuromuscular & skeletal: Weakness
Ocular: Miosis
Respiratory: Respiratory depression
Miscellaneous: Physical and psychological dependence, histamine release

Overdosage/Toxicology Symptoms include hypotension, drowsiness, seizures, and respiratory depression. Treatment consists of naloxone 2 mg I.V. (0.01 mg/kg for children), with repeat administration as necessary, up to a total of 10 mg.

Drug Interactions
Increased Effect/Toxicity: Increased effect/toxicity with CNS depressants (eg, alcohol, narcotics, benzodiazepines, tricyclic antidepressants, MAO inhibitors, phenothiazine).

Ethanol/Nutrition/Herb Interactions Ethanol: Avoid ethanol (may increase CNS depression).

Stability Store in light-resistant, tightly-closed container.

Mechanism of Action Increases smooth muscle tone in GI tract, decreases motility and peristalsis, diminishes digestive secretions

Pharmacodynamics/Kinetics In terms of opium:
Metabolism: Hepatic
Excretion: Urine (primarily as morphine glucuronide conjugates and unchanged drug - morphine, codeine, papaverine, etc)

Dosage Oral:
Neonatal opiate withdrawal: 3-6 drops every 3-6 hours as needed, or initially 0.2 mL every 3 hours; increase dosage by approximately 0.05 mL every 3 hours until withdrawal symptoms are controlled; it is rare to exceed 0.7 mL/dose. Stabilize withdrawal symptoms for 3-5 days, then gradually decrease dosage over a 2- to 4-week period.
Children: 0.25-0.5 mL/kg 1-4 times/day
Adults: 5-10 mL 1-4 times/day

Additional Information Contains morphine 0.4 mg/mL and alcohol 45%. Do **not** confuse this product with opium tincture which is 25 times **more** potent; each 5 mL of paregoric contains 2 mg morphine equivalent, 0.02 mL anise oil, 20 mg benzoic acid, 20 mg camphor, 0.2 mL glycerin and alcohol; final alcohol content 45%; paregoric also contains papaverine and noscapine; because all of these additives may be harmful to neonates, **a 25-fold dilution of**
(Continued)

Paregoric *(Continued)*

opium tincture is often preferred for treatment of neonatal abstinence syndrome (opiate withdrawal).

Dosage Forms Liquid, oral: Morphine equivalent 2 mg/5 mL (473 mL) [equivalent to opium 20 mg powder; contains alcohol 45% and benzoic acid]

♦ **Parenteral Nutrition** *see Total Parenteral Nutrition* *on page 1715*

Paricalcitol *(pah ri KAL si tole)*

U.S. Brand Names Zemplar®
Canadian Brand Names Zemplar®
Pharmacologic Category Vitamin D Analog
Use
  I.V.: Prevention and treatment of secondary hyperparathyroidism associated with stage 5 chronic kidney disease (CKD)
  Oral: Prevention and treatment of secondary hyperparathyroidism associated with stage 3 and 4 CKD
Pregnancy Risk Factor C
Pregnancy Implications
  Teratogenic effects were not observed in animal studies. There are no adequate and well-controlled studies in pregnant women.
Lactation Excretion in breast milk unknown/not recommended
Contraindications Hypersensitivity to paricalcitol or any component of the formulation; patients with evidence of vitamin D toxicity; hypercalcemia
Warnings/Precautions Excessive administration may lead to over suppression of PTH, hypercalcemia, hypercalciuria, hyperphosphatemia and adynamic bone disease. Acute hypercalcemia may increase risk of cardiac arrhythmias and seizures; use caution with cardiac glycosides as toxicity may be increased. Chronic hypercalcemia may lead to generalized vascular and other soft-tissue calcification. Phosphate and vitamin D (and its derivatives) should be withheld during therapy to avoid hypercalcemia. Safety and efficacy in pediatric patients (oral formulation) and in children <5 years of age (I.V. formulation) have not been established.
Adverse Reactions
  >10%: Gastrointestinal: Nausea (6% to 13%)
  1% to 10%:
    Cardiovascular: Edema (7%), hypertension (7%), hypotension (5%), palpitation (3%), chest pain (3%), syncope (3%), cardiomyopathy (2%), MI (2%), postural hypotension (2%)
    Central nervous system: Pain (8%), chills (5%), dizziness (5%), headache (5%), lightheadedness (5%), vertigo (5%), fever (3% to 5%), depression (3%), insomnia (2%)
    Dermatologic: Rash (2% to 6%), skin ulcer (3%), pruritus (3%), skin hypertrophy (2%)
    Endocrine & metabolic: Dehydration (3%), acidosis (2%), hypokalemia (2%)
    Gastrointestinal: Vomiting (6% to 8%), diarrhea (7%), GI bleeding (5%), abdominal pain (4%), xerostomia (3%), constipation (4%), gastroenteritis (3%), dyspepsia (2%), gastritis (2%), rectal disorder (2%)
    Genitourinary: Urinary tract infection (3%), kidney function abnormal (2%)
    Neuromuscular & skeletal: Arthritis (5%), back pain (4%), leg cramps (3%), weakness (3%), neuropathy (2%)
    Ocular: Amblyopia (2%), retinal disorder (2%)
    Respiratory: Pneumonia (2% to 5%), rhinitis (5%), sinusitis (3%), bronchitis (3%), cough (3%), epistaxis (2%)
    Miscellaneous: Infection (bacterial, fungal, viral: 2% to 8%); allergic reaction (6%), flu-like syndrome (2% to 5%), sepsis (5%), cyst (2%)
  Postmarketing and/or case reports: Facial edema, oral edema, taste perversion (metallic), urticaria
Overdosage/Toxicology Acute overdose may cause hypercalcemia, hypercalciuria, and hyperphosphatemia. Monitor serum calcium and phosphorus closely during titration of paricalcitol. Dosage reduction/interruption and reducing dietary calcium intake may be required if hypercalcemia develops. Signs of hypercalcemia associated with vitamin D intoxication may include:
  Early: Weakness, headache, somnolence, nausea, vomiting, xerostomia, constipation, muscle and bone pain, and metallic taste
  Late: Anorexia, weight loss, conjunctivitis, pancreatitis, photophobia, rhinorrhea, pruritus, hyperthermia, libido decreased, BUN increased, hypercholesterolemia, transaminases increased, ectopic calcification, hypertension, arrhythmias, psychosis (rare)
  Chronic use may predispose to metastatic calcification. Bone lesions may develop if parathyroid hormone is suppressed below normal. Treatment should be supportive and symptom-directed. Institute ECG monitoring for hypercalcemia. For oral overdose, administration of mineral oil may facilitate fecal elimination. Dialysis against a calcium-free dialysate may be beneficial.
Drug Interactions
  Cytochrome P450 Effect:
    Substrate of CYP3A4 (major)
  Increased Effect/Toxicity:
    CYP3A4 inhibitors (strong) may increase the levels/effects of paricalcitol; example CYP3A4 inhibitors include azole antifungals, ciprofloxacin, clarithromycin, diclofenac, doxycycline, erythromycin, imatinib, isoniazid, nefazodone, nicardipine, propofol, protease inhibitors, quinidine, and verapamil. Ketoconazole may increase paricalcitol levels/effects.
Mechanism of Action Decreased renal conversion of vitamin D to its primary active metabolite (1,25-hydroxyvitamin D) in chronic renal failure leads to reduced activation of vitamin D receptor (VDR), which subsequently removes inhibitory suppression of parathyroid hormone (PTH) release; increased serum PTH (secondary hyperparathyroidism) reduces calcium excretion and enhances bone resorption. Paricalcitol is a synthetic vitamin D analog which

binds to and activates the VDR in kidney, parathyroid gland, intestine and bone, thus reducing PTH levels and improving calcium and phosphate homeostasis.

Pharmacodynamics/Kinetics

Distribution: V_d:
Healthy subjects: Oral: 34 L; I.V.: 24 L
Stage 3 and 4 CKD: Oral: 44-46 L;
Stage 5 CKD: I.V.: 31-35 L
Protein binding: >99%
Metabolism: Hydroxylation and glucuronidation via hepatic and nonhepatic enzymes, including CYP24, CYP3A4, UGT1A4; forms metabolites (at least one active)
Bioavailability: Oral: ~72% in healthy subjects
Half-life elimination:
Healthy subjects: Oral: 4-6 hours
Stage 3 and 4 CKD: Oral: 17-20 hours
Stage 5 CKD: I.V.: 14-15 hours
Excretion: Healthy subjects: Feces (oral: 70% to 74%; I.V.: 63%); urine (oral: 16% to 18%, I.V.: 19%); 51% to 59% as metabolites

Dosage Note: If hypercalcemia or Ca x P >75 is observed, reduce or interrupt dosing until parameters are normalized.

Secondary hyperparathyroidism associated with chronic renal failure (stage 5 CKD):
Children ≥5 years and Adults: I.V.: 0.04-0.1 mcg/kg (2.8-7 mcg) given as a bolus dose no more frequently than every other day at any time during dialysis; dose may be increased by 2-4 mcg every 2-4 weeks; doses as high as 0.24 mcg/kg (16.8 mcg) have been administered safely; the dose of paricalcitol should be adjusted based on serum intact PTH (iPTH) levels, as follows:
Same or increasing iPTH level: Increase paricalcitol dose
iPTH level decreased by <30%: Increase paricalcitol dose
iPTH level decreased by >30% and <60%: Maintain paricalcitol dose
iPTH level decrease by >60%: Decrease paricalcitol dose
iPTH level 1.5-3 times upper limit of normal: Maintain paricalcitol dose

Secondary hyperparathyroidism associated with stage 3 and 4 CKD: Adults: Oral: Initial dose based on baseline serum iPTH:
iPTH ≤500 pg/mL: 1 mcg/day or 2 mcg 3 times/week
iPTH >500 pg/mL: 2 mcg/day or 4 mcg 3 times/week
Dosage adjustment based on iPTH level relative to baseline, adjust dose at 2-4 week intervals:
iPTH same or increased: Increase paricalcitol dose by 1 mcg/day or 2 mcg 3 times/week
iPTH decreased by <30%: Increase paricalcitol dose by 1 mcg/day or 2 mcg 3 times// week
iPTH decreased by ≥30% or ≤60%: Maintain paricalcitol dose
iPTH decreased by >60%: Decrease paricalcitol dose by 1 mcg/day* or 2 mcg 3 times/ week
iPTH <60 pg/mL: Decrease paricalcitol dose by 1 mcg/day* or 2 mcg 3 times/week
*If patient is taking the lowest dose on a once-daily regimen, but further dose reduction is needed, decrease dose to 1 mcg 3 times/week. If further dose reduction is required, withhold drug as needed and restart at a lower dose. If applicable, calcium-phosphate binder dosing may also be adjusted or withheld, or switch to noncalcium-based binder

Dosage adjustment in hepatic impairment: Adjustment not needed for mild-to-moderate impairment. Paricalcitol has not been evaluated in severe hepatic impairment.

Dietary Considerations
The capsules may contain coconut or palm kernel oil.

Administration
Oral: May be administered with or without food. With the 3 times/week dosing schedule, doses should not be given more frequently than every other day.
I.V.: Administered as a bolus dose at anytime during dialysis. Doses should not be administered more often than every other day.

Monitoring Parameters
Signs and symptoms of vitamin D intoxication
Serum calcium and phosphorus:
I.V.: Twice weekly during initial phase, then at least monthly once dose established
Oral: At least every 2 weeks for 3 months or following dose adjustment, then monthly for 3 months, then every 3 months
Serum or plasma intact PTH (iPTH):
I.V.: Every 3 months
Oral: At least every 2 weeks for 3 months or following dose adjustment, then monthly for 3 months, then every 3 months
In trials, a mean PTH level reduction of 30% was achieved within 6 weeks with I.V. administration

Reference Range
CKD (definition of stages; chronic disease is kidney damage or GFR <60 mL/minute/1.73 m² for ≥3 months)
Stage 3: GFR 30-59 mL/minute/1.73 m² (moderate decrease GFR)
Stage 4: GFR 15-29 mL/minute/1.73 m² (severe decreased GFR)
Stage 5: GFR <15 mL/minute/1.73 m² or dialysis (kidney failure)
Target range for iPTH:
Stage 3 CKD: 35-70 pg/mL
Stage 4 CKD: 70-110 pg/mL
Stage 5 CKD: 150-300 pg/mL
Serum phosphorous:
Stage 3 and 4 CKD: ≥2.7 to <4.6 mg/dL
Stage 5 CKD: 3.5-5.5 mg/dL

Dosage Forms
Capsule, gelatin: 1 mcg, 2 mcg, 4 mcg [contains alcohol and coconut or palm kernel oil]
Injection, solution: 2 mcg/mL (1 mL); 5 mcg/mL (1 mL, 2 mL) [contains alcohol 20% v/v and propylene glycol 30% v/v]

- **Pariet® (Can)** *see* Rabeprazole *on page 1477*
- **Pariprazole** *see* Rabeprazole *on page 1477*
- **Parlodel®** *see* Bromocriptine *on page 240*
- **Parlodel® SnapTabs®** *see* Bromocriptine *on page 240*
- **Parnate®** *see* Tranylcypromine *on page 1723*

Paromomycin (par oh moe MYE sin)

U.S. Brand Names Humatin®
Canadian Brand Names Humatin®
Index Terms Paromomycin Sulfate
Pharmacologic Category Amebicide
Use Treatment of acute and chronic intestinal amebiasis; hepatic coma
Unlabeled/Investigational Use Treatment of cryptosporidiosis
Pregnancy Risk Factor C
Lactation Does not enter breast milk/compatible
Contraindications Hypersensitivity to paromomycin or any component of the formulation; intestinal obstruction, renal failure
Warnings/Precautions Use with caution in patients with impaired renal function or possible or proven ulcerative bowel lesions
Adverse Reactions
  1% to 10%: Gastrointestinal: Diarrhea, abdominal cramps, nausea, vomiting, heartburn
  <1% (Limited to important or life-threatening): Eosinophilia, exanthema, headache, ototoxicity, pruritus, rash, secondary enterocolitis, steatorrhea, vertigo
Overdosage/Toxicology Symptoms include nausea, vomiting, and diarrhea. Treatment following GI decontamination, if possible, is supportive and symptomatic.
Ethanol/Nutrition/Herb Interactions Food: Paromomycin may cause malabsorption of xylose, sucrose, and fats.
Mechanism of Action Acts directly on ameba; has antibacterial activity against normal and pathogenic organisms in the GI tract; interferes with bacterial protein synthesis by binding to 30S ribosomal subunits
Pharmacodynamics/Kinetics
  Absorption: None
  Excretion: Feces (100% as unchanged drug)
Dosage Oral:
  Intestinal amebiasis: Children and Adults: 25-35 mg/kg/day in 3 divided doses for 5-10 days
  Dientamoeba fragilis: Children and Adults: 25-30 mg/kg/day in 3 divided doses for 7 days
  Cryptosporidium (unlabeled use): Adults with AIDS: 1.5-2.25 g/day in 3-6 divided doses for 10-14 days (occasionally courses of up to 4-8 weeks may be needed)
  Tapeworm (fish, dog, bovine, porcine):
    Children: 11 mg/kg every 15 minutes for 4 doses
    Adults: 1 g every 15 minutes for 4 doses
  Hepatic coma: Adults: 4 g/day in 2-4 divided doses for 5-6 days
  Dwarf tapeworm: Children and Adults: 45 mg/kg/dose every day for 5-7 days
Dosage Forms Capsule: 250 mg

- **Paromomycin Sulfate** *see* Paromomycin *on page 1314*

Paroxetine (pa ROKS e teen)

U.S. Brand Names Paxil®; Paxil CR®; Pexeva®
Canadian Brand Names Apo-Paroxetine®; CO Paroxetine; Gen-Paroxetine; Novo-Paroxetine; Paxil®; Paxil CR®; PMS-Paroxetine; ratio-Paroxetine; Rhoxal-paroxetine; Sandoz-Paroxetine
Index Terms Paroxetine Hydrochloride; Paroxetine Mesylate
Pharmacologic Category Antidepressant, Selective Serotonin Reuptake Inhibitor
Additional Appendix Information
  Antidepressant Agents *on page 1866*
  Selective Serotonin Reuptake Inhibitors (SSRIs) Pharmacokinetics *on page 1896*
Use Treatment of major depressive disorder (MDD); treatment of panic disorder with or without agoraphobia; obsessive-compulsive disorder (OCD); social anxiety disorder (social phobia); generalized anxiety disorder (GAD); post-traumatic stress disorder (PTSD); premenstrual dysphoric disorder (PMDD)
Unlabeled/Investigational Use May be useful in eating disorders, impulse control disorders, self-injurious behavior; vasomotor symptoms of menopause; treatment of depression and obsessive-compulsive disorder (OCD) in children
Restrictions An FDA-approved medication guide concerning the use of antidepressants in children and teenagers must be distributed when dispensing an outpatient prescription (new or refill) where this medication is to be used without direct supervision of a healthcare provider. Medication guides are available at http://www.fda.gov/cder/Offices/ODS/medication_guides.htm. Dispense to parents or guardians of children and teenagers receiving this medication.
Pregnancy Risk Factor D
Pregnancy Implications Teratogenic effects were not observed in animal studies. Preliminary results from a retrospective epidemiologic studies in humans show the risk of congenital malformations, specifically atrial or ventricular septal defects, may be increased with paroxetine relative to other antidepressants. Nonteratogenic effects including respiratory distress, cyanosis, apnea, seizures, temperature instability, feeding difficulty, vomiting, hypoglycemia,

hypo- or hypertonia, hyper-reflexia, jitteriness, irritability, constant crying, and tremor have been reported in the neonate immediately following delivery after exposure late in the third trimester. Exposure to SSRIs late in pregnancy has also been associated with persistent pulmonary hypertension of the newborn (PPHN). Adverse effects may be due to toxic effects of SSRI or drug discontinuation. In some cases, effects may present clinically as serotonin syndrome. There are no adequate and well-controlled studies in pregnant women. Use during pregnancy only if the potential benefit to the mother outweighs the possible risk to the fetus. If treatment during pregnancy is required, consider tapering therapy during the third trimester.

Lactation Enters breast milk/use caution (AAP rates "of concern")

Medication Safety Issues

Sound-alike/look-alike issues:

Paroxetine may be confused with paclitaxel, pyridoxine

Paxil® may be confused with Doxil®, paclitaxel, Plavix®, Taxol®

Contraindications Hypersensitivity to paroxetine or any component of the formulation; use with or within 14 days of MAO inhibitors; concurrent use with thioridazine or pimozide

Warnings/Precautions [U.S. Boxed Warning]: Antidepressants increase the risk of suicidal thinking and behavior in children and adolescents with major depressive disorder (MDD) and other depressive disorders; consider risk prior to prescribing. All patients must be closely monitored for clinical worsening, suicidality, or unusual changes in behavior, especially during the initiation of therapy or following an increase or decrease in dosage. When used in children, the child's family or caregiver should be instructed to closely observe the patient and communicate condition with healthcare provider. A medication guide should be dispensed with each prescription. **Paroxetine is not FDA approved for use in children.**

A higher incidence of suicidal behaviors has been observed in young adults receiving paroxetine for both depressive and nondepressive indications. The possibility of a suicide attempt is inherent in major depression and may persist until remission occurs. Patients treated with antidepressants (for any indication) should be observed for clinical worsening and suicidality, especially during the initial few months of a course of drug therapy, or at times of dose changes, either increases or decreases. Use caution in high-risk patients. Worsening depression and severe abrupt suicidality that are not part of the presenting symptoms may require discontinuation or modification of drug therapy. The patient's family or caregiver should be alerted to monitor patients for the emergence of suicidality and associated behaviors (such as agitation, irritability, hostility, impulsivity, and hypomania) and call healthcare provider.

May worsen psychosis in some patients or precipitate a shift to mania or hypomania in patients with bipolar disorder. Patients presenting with depressive symptoms should be screened for bipolar disorder. Monotherapy in patients with bipolar disorder should be avoided. **Paroxetine is not FDA approved for the treatment of bipolar depression.**

Potential for severe reaction when used with MAO inhibitors, SSRIs/SNRIs or triptans; serotonin syndrome (hyperthermia, muscular rigidity, mental status changes/agitation, autonomic instability) may occur; concurrent use with MAO inhibitors contraindicated. May increase the risks associated with electroconvulsive therapy. Has a low potential to impair cognitive or motor performance - caution operating hazardous machinery or driving. Symptoms of agitation and/or restlessness may occur during initial few weeks of therapy. Low potential for sedation or anticholinergic effects relative to cyclic antidepressants.

Use caution in patients with a previous seizure disorder or condition predisposing to seizures such as brain damage, alcoholism, or concurrent therapy with other drugs which lower the seizure threshold. Use with caution in patients with hepatic dysfunction and in elderly patients. May cause hyponatremia/SIADH. Use with caution in patients at risk of bleeding or receiving anticoagulant therapy - may cause impairment in platelet aggregation. Use with caution in patients with renal insufficiency or other concurrent illness (due to limited experience); dose reduction recommended with severe renal impairment. May cause or exacerbate sexual dysfunction. Use caution in patients with narrow-angle glaucoma. Avoid use in the first trimester of pregnancy.

Upon discontinuation of paroxetine therapy, gradually taper dose and monitor for discontinuation symptoms (eg, dizziness, dysphoric mood, irritability, agitation, confusion, paresthesias). If intolerable symptoms occur following a decrease in dosage or upon discontinuation of therapy, then resuming the previous dose with a more gradual taper should be considered. Safety and efficacy in children have not been established.

Adverse Reactions Frequency varies by dose and indication. Adverse reactions reported as a composite of all indications.

>10%:

Central nervous system: Somnolence (15% to 24%), insomnia (11% to 24%), headache (17% to 18%), dizziness (6% to 14%)

Endocrine & metabolic: Libido decreased (3% to 15%)

Gastrointestinal: Nausea (19% to 26%), xerostomia (9% to 18%), constipation (5% to 16%), diarrhea (9% to 12%)

Genitourinary: Ejaculatory disturbances (10% to 28%)

Neuromuscular & skeletal: Weakness (12% to 22%), tremor (4% to 11%)

Miscellaneous: Diaphoresis (5% to 14%)

1% to 10%:

Cardiovascular: Vasodilation (2% to 4%), chest pain (3%), palpitations (2% to 3%), hypertension (≥1%), tachycardia (≥1%)

Central nervous system: Nervousness (4% to 9%), anxiety (5%), agitation (3% to 5%), abnormal dreams (3% to 4%), concentration impaired (3% to 4%), yawning (2% to 4%), depersonalization (up to 3%), amnesia (2%), emotional lability (≥1%), vertigo (≥1%), confusion (1%), chills (2%)

Dermatologic: Rash (2% to 3%), pruritus (≥1%)

Endocrine & metabolic: Orgasmic disturbance (2% to 9%), dysmenorrhea (5%)

(Continued)

Paroxetine *(Continued)*

Gastrointestinal: Anorexia, appetite decreased (5% to 9%), dyspepsia (2% to 5%), flatulence (4%), abdominal pain (4%), appetite increased (2% to 4%), vomiting (2% to 3%), taste perversion (2%), weight gain (≥1%)

Genitourinary: Impotence (2% to 9%), genital disorder (female 2% to 9%), urinary frequency (2% to 3%), urinary tract infection (2%)

Neuromuscular & skeletal: Paresthesia (4%), myalgia (2% to 4%), back pain (3%), myoclonus (2% to 3%), myopathy (2%), myasthenia (1%), arthralgia (≥1%)

Ocular: Blurred vision (4%), abnormal vision (2% to 4%)

Otic: Tinnitus (≥1%)

Respiratory: Respiratory disorder (up to 7%), pharyngitis (4%), sinusitis (up to 4%), rhinitis (3%)

Miscellaneous: Infection (5% to 6%)

<1%, postmarketing, and/or case reports (limited to important or life-threatening): Acute renal failure, adrenergic syndrome, akinesia, alkaline phosphatase increased, allergic reaction, anaphylaxis, anemias (various), angina pectoris, angioedema, aphasia, aphthous stomatitis, arrhythmias (atrial and ventricular), arthrosis, asthma, behavioral disturbances (various), bilirubinemia, bleeding time increased, blood dyscrasias, bloody diarrhea, bradycardia, bronchitis, bulimia, BUN increased, bundle branch block, cardiospasm, cataract, cellulitis, cerebral ischemia, cerebrovascular accident, cholelithiasis, colitis, congestive heart failure, creatinine phosphokinase increased, deafness, dehydration, delirium, diabetes mellitus, drug dependence, dyskinesia, dysphagia, dyspnea, dystonia, ecchymosis, eclampsia, electrolyte abnormalities, emphysema, erythema, exfoliative dermatitis, extrapyramidal syndrome, fecal impactions, fungal dermatitis, gamma globulins increased, gastroenteritis, glaucoma, goiter, Guillain-Barré syndrome, hallucinations, hematemesis, hematoma, hemorrhage, hemoptysis, hepatic necrosis, hepatitis, hypercholesteremia, hyper-/hypoglycemia, hyper-/hypothyroidism, hypotension, ileus, intestinal obstruction, jaundice, ketosis, lactic dehydrogenase increased, liver function tests abnormal, low cardiac output, lung fibrosis, lymphadenopathy, meningitis, MI, migraine, myelitis, myocardial ischemia, neuroleptic malignant syndrome, neuropathy, osteoporosis, pancreatitis, pancytopenia, peptic ulcer, peritonitis, phlebitis, pneumonia, platelet count abnormalities, pulmonary edema, pulmonary embolus, pulmonary hypertension, seizure, sepsis, serotonin syndrome, status epilepticus, syncope, tetany, thrombophlebitis, thrombosis, tongue edema, torsade de pointes, toxic epidermal necrolysis, vasculitic syndrome

Overdosage/Toxicology Symptoms include somnolence, nausea, vomiting, hepatic dysfunction, drowsiness, sinus tachycardia, urinary retention, renal failure (acute) and dilated pupils. Convulsions, status epilepticus, and ventricular arrhythmias (including torsade de pointes) have been reported, as well as serotonin syndrome and manic reaction. There are no specific antidotes. Following attempts at decontamination, treatment is supportive and symptom-directed. Cardiac monitoring is recommended. Forced diuresis, dialysis, and hemoperfusion are unlikely to be beneficial.

Drug Interactions

Cytochrome P450 Effect: Substrate of CYP2D6 (major); **Inhibits** CYP1A2 (weak), 2B6 (moderate), 2C9 (weak), 2C19 (weak), 2D6 (strong), 3A4 (weak)

Increased Effect/Toxicity: Paroxetine should not be used with nonselective MAO inhibitors (phenelzine, isocarboxazid) or other drugs with MAO inhibition (linezolid); fatal reactions have been reported. Wait 2 weeks after stopping an MAO inhibitor before starting paroxetine. Concurrent selegiline has been associated with mania, hypertension, or serotonin syndrome (risk may be reduced relative to nonselective MAO inhibitors). Serum levels of atomoxetine, carbamazepine, duloxetine, galantamine, mexiletine, propafenone, and risperidone may be increased by paroxetine.

Paroxetine may inhibit the metabolism of thioridazine or mesoridazine, resulting in increased plasma levels and increasing the risk of QT_c interval prolongation. This may lead to serious ventricular arrhythmias, such as torsade de pointes-type arrhythmias and sudden death. Do not use together. Wait at least 5 weeks after discontinuing paroxetine prior to starting thioridazine.

The levels/effects of paroxetine may be increased by chlorpromazine, delavirdine, fluoxetine, miconazole, pergolide, quinidine, quinine, ritonavir, ropinirole, and other CYP2D6 inhibitors. Paroxetine may increase the levels/effects of amphetamines, selected beta-blockers, bupropion, dextromethorphan, fluoxetine, lidocaine, mirtazapine, nefazodone, promethazine, propofol, risperidone, ritonavir, sertraline, tricyclic antidepressants, venlafaxine, and other CYP2B6 or 2D6 substrates.

Concomitant use of paroxetine and NSAIDs, aspirin, or other drugs affecting coagulation has been associated with an increased risk of bleeding. Paroxetine may increase the hypoprothrombinemic response to warfarin. Paroxetine increases levels of procyclidine; this may result in increased anticholinergic effects; procyclidine dose reduction may be necessary. Concomitant use of paroxetine and beta-blockers may increase the risk of bradycardia. Concurrent use of paroxetine with CNS depressants may enhance the adverse effects/toxicity of CNS depressants.

Combined use of SSRIs and amphetamines, buspirone, meperidine, nefazodone, serotonin agonists (such as sumatriptan), sibutramine, other SSRIs/SNRIs, sympathomimetics, ritonavir, tramadol, and venlafaxine may increase the risk of serotonin syndrome. Combined use of sumatriptan (and other serotonin agonists) may result in toxicity; weakness, hyper-reflexia, and incoordination have been observed with sumatriptan and SSRIs. In addition, concurrent use may theoretically increase the risk of serotonin syndrome; includes sumatriptan, naratriptan, rizatriptan, and zolmitriptan. Concurrent lithium may increase risk of nephrotoxicity. Risk of hyponatremia may increase with concurrent use of loop diuretics (bumetanide, furosemide, torsemide).

Decreased Effect: Cyproheptadine, a serotonin antagonist, may inhibit the effects of serotonin reuptake inhibitors (paroxetine). Paroxetine may decrease the levels/effects of CYP2D6 prodrug substrates (eg, codeine, hydrocodone, oxycodone, tramadol).

Ethanol/Nutrition/Herb Interactions

Ethanol: Avoid ethanol (may increase CNS depression).

Food: Peak concentration is increased, but bioavailability is not significantly altered by food.

Herb/Nutraceutical: Avoid valerian, St John's wort, SAMe, kava kava.

Stability

Suspension: Store at ≤25°C (≤77°F).

Tablet: Store at 15°C to 30°C (59°F to 86°F).

Mechanism of Action
Paroxetine is a selective serotonin reuptake inhibitor, chemically unrelated to tricyclic, tetracyclic, or other antidepressants; presumably, the inhibition of serotonin reuptake from brain synapse stimulated serotonin activity in the brain

Pharmacodynamics/Kinetics

Absorption: Completely absorbed following oral administration

Distribution: V_d: 8.7 L/kg (3-28 L/kg)

Protein binding: 93% to 95%

Metabolism: Extensively hepatic via CYP2D6 enzymes; primary metabolites are formed via oxidation and methylation of parent drug, with subsequent glucuronide/sulfate conjugation; nonlinear pharmacokinetics (via 2D6 saturation) may be seen with higher doses and longer duration of therapy. Metabolites exhibit ~2% potency of parent compound. C_{min} concentrations are 70% to 80% greater in the elderly compared to nonelderly patients; clearance is also decreased.

Half-life elimination: 21 hours (3-65 hours)

Time to peak: Immediate release: 5.2 hours; controlled release: 6-10 hours

Excretion: Urine (64%, 2% as unchanged drug); feces (36% primarily via bile, <1% as unchanged drug)

Dosage
Oral:

Children:

Depression (unlabeled use; not recommended by FDA): Initial: 10 mg/day and adjusted upward on an individual basis to 20 mg/day

OCD (unlabeled use): Initial: 10 mg/day and titrate up as necessary to 60 mg/day

Self-Injurious behavior (unlabeled use): 20 mg/day

Social anxiety disorder (unlabeled use): 2.5-15 mg/day

Adults:

MDD:

Paxil®, Pexeva®: Initial: 20 mg once daily, preferably in the morning; increase if needed by 10 mg/day increments at intervals of at least 1 week; maximum dose: 50 mg/day

Paxil CR®: Initial: 25 mg once daily; increase if needed by 12.5 mg/day increments at intervals of at least 1 week; maximum dose: 62.5 mg/day

GAD (Paxil®, Pexeva®): Initial: 20 mg once daily, preferably in the morning (if dose is increased, adjust in increments of 10 mg/day at 1-week intervals); doses of 20-50 mg/day were used in clinical trials, however, no greater benefit was seen with doses >20 mg.

OCD (Paxil®, Pexeva™): Initial: 20 mg once daily, preferably in the morning; increase if needed by 10 mg/day increments at intervals of at least 1 week; recommended dose: 40 mg/day; range: 20-60 mg/day; maximum dose: 60 mg/day

Panic disorder:

Paxil®, Pexeva®: Initial: 10 mg once daily, preferably in the morning; increase if needed by 10 mg/day increments at intervals of at least 1 week; recommended dose: 40 mg/day; range: 10-60 mg/day; maximum dose: 60 mg/day

Paxil CR®: Initial: 12.5 mg once daily; increase if needed by 12.5 mg/day at intervals of at least 1 week; maximum dose: 75 mg/day

PMDD (Paxil CR®): Initial: 12.5 mg once daily in the morning; may be increased to 25 mg/day; dosing changes should occur at intervals of at least 1 week. May be given daily throughout the menstrual cycle or limited to the luteal phase.

PTSD (Paxil®): Initial: 20 mg once daily, preferably in the morning; increase if needed by 10 mg/day increments at intervals of at least 1 week; range: 20-50 mg. Limited data suggest doses of 40 mg/day were not more efficacious than 20 mg/day.

Social anxiety disorder:

Paxil®: Initial: 20 mg once daily, preferably in the morning; recommended dose: 20 mg/day; range: 20-60 mg/day; doses >20 mg may not have additional benefit

Paxil CR®: Initial: 12.5 mg once daily, preferably in the morning; may be increased by 12.5 mg/day at intervals of at least 1 week; maximum dose: 37.5 mg/day

Vasomotor symptoms of menopause (unlabeled use, Paxil CR®): 12.5-25 mg/day

Elderly:

Paxil®, Pexeva®: Initial: 10 mg/day; increase if needed by 10 mg/day increments at intervals of at least 1 week; maximum dose: 40 mg/day

Paxil CR®: Initial: 12.5 mg/day; increase if needed by 12.5 mg/day increments at intervals of at least 1 week; maximum dose: 50 mg/day

Note: Upon discontinuation of paroxetine therapy, gradually taper dose:

Paxil®, Pexeva®: 10 mg/day at weekly intervals; when 20 mg/day dose is reached, continue for 1 week before treatment is discontinued. Some patients may need to be titrated to 10 mg/day for 1 week before discontinuation.

Paxil CR®: Patients receiving 37.5 mg/day in clinical trials had their dose decreased by 12.5 mg/day to a dose of 25 mg/day and remained at a dose of 25 mg/day for 1 week before treatment was discontinued.

Dosage adjustment in severe renal impairment: Adults:

Cl_{cr} <30 mL/minute: Mean plasma concentration is ~4 times that seen in normal function.

Cl_{cr} 30-60 mL/minute: Plasma concentration is 2 times that seen in normal function.

Paxil®, Pexeva®: Initial: 10 mg/day; increase if needed by 10 mg/day increments at intervals of at least 1 week; maximum dose: 40 mg/day

Paxil CR®: Initial: 12.5 mg/day; increase if needed by 12.5 mg/day increments at intervals of at least 1 week; maximum dose: 50 mg/day

Dosage adjustment in severe hepatic impairment: Adults: In hepatic dysfunction, plasma concentration is 2 times that seen in normal function.

Paxil®, Pexeva®: Initial: 10 mg/day; increase if needed by 10 mg/day increments at intervals of at least 1 week; maximum dose: 40 mg/day

(Continued)

Paroxetine *(Continued)*

Paxil CR®: Initial: 12.5 mg/day; increase if needed by 12.5 mg/day increments at intervals of at least 1 week; maximum dose: 50 mg/day

Dietary Considerations May be taken with or without food.

Administration May be administered with or without food. Do not crush, break, or chew controlled release tablets.

Monitoring Parameters Mental status for depression, suicidal ideation (especially at the beginning of therapy or when doses are increased or decreased), anxiety, social functioning, mania, panic attacks; akathisia

Additional Information Paxil CR® incorporates a degradable polymeric matrix (Geomatrix™) to control dissolution rate over a period of 4-5 hours. An enteric coating delays the start of drug release until tablets have left the stomach.

Dosage Forms Note: Strength expressed as base:

Suspension, oral, as hydrochloride:
Paxil®: 10 mg/5 mL (250 mL) [orange flavor]
Tablet, as hydrochloride: 10 mg, 20 mg, 30 mg, 40 mg
Paxil®: 10 mg, 20 mg, 30 mg, 40 mg
Tablet, as mesylate:
Pexeva®: 10 mg, 20 mg, 30 mg, 40 mg
Tablet, controlled release, as hydrochloride:
Paxil CR®: 12.5 mg, 25 mg, 37.5 mg

- ◆ **Paroxetine Hydrochloride** *see* Paroxetine *on page 1314*
- ◆ **Paroxetine Mesylate** *see* Paroxetine *on page 1314*
- ◆ **Parvolex® (Can)** *see* Acetylcysteine *on page 39*
- ◆ **PAS** *see* Aminosalicylic Acid *on page 96*
- ◆ **Paser®** *see* Aminosalicylic Acid *on page 96*
- ◆ **Patanol®** *see* Olopatadine *on page 1261*
- ◆ **Pathocil® (Can)** *see* Dicloxacillin *on page 495*
- ◆ **Pavabid [DSC]** *see* Papaverine *on page 1309*
- ◆ **Pavulon [DSC]** *see* Pancuronium *on page 1304*
- ◆ **Paxil®** *see* Paroxetine *on page 1314*
- ◆ **Paxil CR®** *see* Paroxetine *on page 1314*
- ◆ **PCA (error-prone abbreviation)** *see* Procainamide *on page 1424*
- ◆ **PCE®** *see* Erythromycin *on page 609*
- ◆ **PCEC** *see* Rabies Virus Vaccine *on page 1479*
- ◆ **PCM** *see* Chlorpheniramine, Phenylephrine, and Methscopolamine *on page 353*
- ◆ **PCM Allergy** *see* Chlorpheniramine, Phenylephrine, and Methscopolamine *on page 353*
- ◆ **PCV7** *see* Pneumococcal Conjugate Vaccine (7-Valent) *on page 1382*
- ◆ **PD-Cof** *see* Chlorpheniramine, Phenylephrine, and Dextromethorphan *on page 352*
- ◆ **PD-Hist-D** *see* Chlorpheniramine and Phenylephrine *on page 349*
- ◆ **Pectin, Gelatin, and Methylcellulose** *see* Gelatin, Pectin, and Methylcellulose *on page 785*
- ◆ **PediaCare® Children's Long Acting Cough Plus Cold [OTC] [DSC]** *see* Pseudoephedrine and Dextromethorphan *on page 1455*
- ◆ **PediaCare® Cold and Allergy [OTC] [DSC]** *see* Chlorpheniramine and Pseudoephedrine *on page 350*
- ◆ **PediaCare® Decongestant Infants [OTC]** *see* Pseudoephedrine *on page 1454*
- ◆ **PediaCare® Infants' Decongestant & Cough [OTC]** *see* Pseudoephedrine and Dextromethorphan *on page 1455*
- ◆ **PediaCare® Multi-Symptom Cold [OTC] [DSC]** *see* Chlorpheniramine, Pseudoephedrine, and Dextromethorphan *on page 355*
- ◆ **PediaCare® NightRest Cough and Cold [OTC] [DSC]** *see* Chlorpheniramine, Pseudoephedrine, and Dextromethorphan *on page 355*
- ◆ **Pediacof® [DSC]** *see* Chlorpheniramine, Phenylephrine, Codeine, and Potassium Iodide *on page 354*
- ◆ **Pediaflor® [DSC]** *see* Fluoride *on page 722*
- ◆ **Pediapred®** *see* PrednisoLONE *on page 1413*
- ◆ **Pedia Relief Cough and Cold [OTC]** *see* Pseudoephedrine and Dextromethorphan *on page 1455*
- ◆ **Pedia Relief Infants [OTC]** *see* Pseudoephedrine and Dextromethorphan *on page 1455*
- ◆ **Pediarix™** *see* Diphtheria, Tetanus Toxoids, Acellular Pertussis, Hepatitis B (Recombinant), and Poliovirus (Inactivated) Vaccine *on page 521*
- ◆ **PediaTan™D** *see* Chlorpheniramine and Phenylephrine *on page 349*
- ◆ **Pediatex™-D [DSC]** *see* Carbinoxamine and Pseudoephedrine *on page 290*
- ◆ **Pediatex™ DM [DSC]** *see* Carbinoxamine, Pseudoephedrine, and Dextromethorphan *on page 291*
- ◆ **Pediatric Digoxin CSD (Can)** *see* Digoxin *on page 501*
- ◆ **Pediatrix (Can)** *see* Acetaminophen *on page 28*
- ◆ **Pediazole® [DSC]** *see* Erythromycin and Sulfisoxazole *on page 613*
- ◆ **Pediazole® (Can)** *see* Erythromycin and Sulfisoxazole *on page 613*
- ◆ **Pedi-Boro® [OTC]** *see* Aluminum Sulfate and Calcium Acetate *on page 86*
- ◆ **Pedi-Dri®** *see* Nystatin *on page 1250*
- ◆ **PediOtic®** *see* Neomycin, Polymyxin B, and Hydrocortisone *on page 1212*
- ◆ **PedvaxHIB®** *see* Haemophilus b Conjugate Vaccine *on page 824*
- ◆ **PEG** *see* Polyethylene Glycol 3350 *on page 1387*
- ◆ **PEG-L-asparaginase** *see* Pegaspargase *on page 1320*

Pegademase Bovine (peg A de mase BOE vine)

U.S. Brand Names Adagen®
Canadian Brand Names Adagen®
Pharmacologic Category Enzyme
Use Orphan drug: Enzyme replacement therapy for adenosine deaminase (ADA) deficiency in patients with severe combined immunodeficiency disease (SCID) who can not benefit from bone marrow transplant; not a cure for SCID, unlike bone marrow transplants, injections must be used the rest of the child's life, therefore is not really an alternative
Pregnancy Risk Factor C
Contraindications Hypersensitivity to pegademase bovine or any component of the formulation; not to be used as preparatory or support therapy for bone marrow transplantation
Warnings/Precautions Use with caution in patients with thrombocytopenia.
Adverse Reactions <1% (Limited to important or life-threatening): Headache, pain at injection site
Stability Refrigerate at 2°C to 8°C (36°F to 46°F); do not freeze.
Mechanism of Action Adenosine deaminase is an enzyme that catalyzes the deamination of both adenosine and deoxyadenosine. Hereditary lack of adenosine deaminase activity results in severe combined immunodeficiency disease, a fatal disorder of infancy characterized by profound defects of both cellular and humoral immunity. It is estimated that 25% of patients with the autosomal recessive form of severe combined immunodeficiency lack adenosine deaminase.
Pharmacodynamics/Kinetics
Absorption: Rapid
Half-life elimination: 48-72 hours
Time to peak: Plasma adenosine deaminase activity: 2-3 weeks
Dosage Children: I.M.: Dose given every 7 days, 10 units/kg the first dose, 15 units/kg the second dose, and 20 units/kg the third dose; maintenance dose: 20 units/kg/week is recommended depending on patient's ADA level; maximum single dose: 30 units/kg
Dosage Forms
Injection, solution [preservative free]:
Adagen®: 250 units/mL (1.5 mL)

Pegaptanib (peg AP ta nib)

U.S. Brand Names Macugen®
Canadian Brand Names Macugen®
Index Terms EYE001; Pegaptanib Sodium
Pharmacologic Category Ophthalmic Agent; Vascular Endothelial Growth Factor (VEGF) Inhibitor
Use Treatment of neovascular (wet) age-related macular degeneration (AMD)
Pregnancy Risk Factor B
Pregnancy Implications Teratogenic effects were not reported in animal studies. There are no adequate and well-controlled studies in pregnant women.
Lactation Excretion in breast milk unknown/use caution
Contraindications Hypersensitivity to pegaptanib or any component of the formulation; ocular or periocular infection
Warnings/Precautions Intravitreous injections may be associated with endophthalmitis; patients should be instructed to report any signs of infection immediately. Intraocular pressure may increase following injection. Safety and efficacy for administration into both eyes concurrently have not been studied. Safety and efficacy have not been established with hepatic impairment, or in patients requiring hemodialysis. Rare hypersensitivity reactions (including anaphylaxis) have been associated with pegaptanib, occurring within several hours of use; monitor closely. Equipment and appropriate personnel should be available for monitoring and treatment of anaphylaxis. Safety and efficacy have not been established in children.
Adverse Reactions
10% to 40%:
Cardiovascular: Hypertension
Ocular: Anterior chamber inflammation, blurred vision, cataract, conjunctival hemorrhage, corneal edema, eye discharge, eye irritation, eye pain, intraocular pressure increased, ocular discomfort, punctate keratitis, visual acuity decreased, visual disturbance, vitreous floaters, vitreous opacities
1% to 10%:
Cardiovascular: Carotid artery occlusion (1% to 5%), cerebrovascular accident (1% to 5%), chest pain (1% to 5%), transient ischemic attack (1% to 5%)
Central nervous system: Dizziness (6% to 10%), headache (6% to 10%), vertigo (1% to 5%)
Dermatologic: Contact dermatitis (1% to 5%)
Endocrine & metabolic: Diabetes mellitus (1% to 5%)
Gastrointestinal: Diarrhea (6% to 10%), nausea (6% to 10%), dyspepsia (1% to 5%), vomiting (1% to 5%)
Genitourinary: Urinary retention (1% to 5%)
Neuromuscular & skeletal: Arthritis (1% to 5%), bone spur (1% to 5%)
Ocular: Blepharitis (6% to 10%), conjunctivitis (6% to 10%), photopsia (6% to 10%), vitreous disorder (6% to 10%), allergic conjunctivitis (1% to 5%), conjunctival edema (1% to 5%), corneal abrasion (1% to 5%), corneal deposits (1% to 5%), corneal epithelium disorder (1% to 5%), endophthalmitis (1% to 5%), eye inflammation (1% to 5%), eye swelling (1% to 5%), eyelid irritation (1% to 5%), meibomianitis (1% to 5%), mydriasis (1% to 5%), periorbital hematoma (1% to 5%), retinal edema (1% to 5%), vitreous hemorrhage (1% to 5%)
Otic: Hearing loss (1% to 5%)
(Continued)

Pegaptanib (Continued)

Renal: Urinary tract infection (6% to 10%)
Respiratory: Bronchitis (6% to 10%), pleural effusion (1% to 5%)
Miscellaneous: Contusion (1% to 5%)
<1% (Limited to important or life-threatening): Anaphylaxis, anaphylactoid reaction, angioedema, hypersensitivity, iatrogenic traumatic cataract, endophthalmitis, retinal detachment

Overdosage/Toxicology No additional adverse events were observed with doses up to 3 mg.

Stability Store under refrigeration at 2°C to 8°C (36°F to 46°F); do not freeze. Do not shake vigorously.

Mechanism of Action Pegaptanib is an apatamer, an oligonucleotide covalently bound to polyethylene glycol, which can adopt a three-dimensional shape and bind to vascular endothelial growth factor (VEGF). Pegaptanib binds to extracellular VEGF, inhibiting VEGF from binding to its receptors and thereby suppressing neovascularization and slowing vision loss.

Pharmacodynamics/Kinetics
Absorption: Slow systemic absorption following intravitreous injection
Metabolism: Metabolized by endo- and exonucleases
Half-life elimination: Plasma: 6-14 days

Dosage Intravitreous injection: Adults: AMD: 0.3 mg into affected eye every 6 weeks
Dosage adjustment in renal impairment: Adjustment not required with renal impairment; information not available for patients requiring hemodialysis

Administration For intravitreous injection only; adequate anesthesia and a broad spectrum antibiotic should be administered prior to injection
pH: 6-7

Monitoring Parameters Intraocular pressure (within 30 minutes and 2-7 days after injection); endophthalmitis

Dosage Forms Injection, solution [preservative free]: 0.3 mg/90 µL (90 µL) [prefilled syringe]

♦ **Pegaptanib Sodium** see Pegaptanib on page 1319

Pegaspargase (peg AS par jase)

U.S. Brand Names Oncaspar®
Index Terms NSC-644954; PEG-L-asparaginase
Pharmacologic Category Antineoplastic Agent, Miscellaneous
Use Treatment of acute lymphocytic leukemia (ALL); treatment of ALL with previous hypersensitivity to native L-asparaginase
Pregnancy Risk Factor C
Pregnancy Implications Reproduction studies have not been conducted with pegaspargase.
Lactation Excretion in breast milk unknown/not recommended
Medication Safety Issues
Sound-alike/look-alike issues:
Pegaspargase may be confused with asparaginase

High alert medication: The Institute for Safe Medication Practices (ISMP) includes this medication among its list of drugs which have a heightened risk of causing significant patient harm when used in error.

Contraindications Hypersensitivity to pegaspargase or any component of the formulation; history of serious thrombosis with previous L-asparaginase treatment; pancreatitis or a history of pancreatitis; previous serious allergic reactions (urticaria, bronchospasm, laryngeal edema, hypotension) or other unacceptable adverse reactions to pegaspargase; previous hemorrhagic event with L-asparaginase

Warnings/Precautions Hazardous agent - use appropriate precautions for handling and disposal. Monitor for severe allergic reactions; may be used cautiously in patients who have had hypersensitivity reactions to E. coli asparaginase; however, up to 32% of patients who have an allergic reaction to E. coli asparaginase will also react to pegaspargase; immediate treatment for hypersensitivity reactions should be available during administration. Thrombotic events may occur; discontinue with serious thrombotic event. Discontinue if pancreatitis occurs during treatment. May cause (possibly irreversible) glucose intolerance. Coagulopathy has been reported; monitor coagulation parameters. Use cautiously in patients with an underlying coagulopathy or previous hematologic complications from asparaginase, hepatic dysfunction, concomitant hepatotoxic medications, hyperglycemia, or diabetes.

Adverse Reactions In general, pegaspargase toxicities tend to be less frequent and appear somewhat later than comparable toxicities of asparaginase. Intramuscular rather than intravenous injection may decrease the incidence of coagulopathy; GI, hepatic, and renal toxicity. Except for hypersensitivity reactions, adults tend to have a higher incidence than children.
>5%:
Cardiovascular: Edema
Central nervous system: Fever, malaise
Dermatologic: Rash (1% to >5%)
Gastrointestinal: Nausea, vomiting
Hematologic: Coagulopathy (7%; grades 3/4: 2%)
Hepatic: Transaminases increased (11%; grades 3/4: 3%), SGPT increased
Miscellaneous: Allergic reactions (including bronchospasm, chills, dyspnea, edema, erythema, fever, rash, urticaria: 1% to 10%; 32% in patients with prior hypersensitivity to asparaginase products)
1% to 5%:
Cardiovascular: Hypotension, peripheral edema, tachycardia, thrombosis (4%)
Central nervous system: Chills, CNS thrombosis/hemorrhage (2%), headache, seizure
Dermatologic: Lip edema, urticaria
Endocrine & metabolic: Hyperglycemia (3% to 5%), hyperuricemia, hypoglycemia, hypoproteinemia
Gastrointestinal: Abdominal pain, anorexia, diarrhea, pancreatitis (1% to 2%; grades 3/4: 2%)

Hematologic: Anticoagulant effect decreased, disseminated intravascular coagulation (DIC), fibrinogen decreased, hemolytic anemia, leukopenia, pancytopenia, thrombocytopenia, thromboplastin increased, myelosuppression (mild to moderate; onset: 7 days; nadir: 14 days; recovery: 21 days)

Hepatic: Liver function tests abnormal (5%), hyperbilirubinemia, jaundice, SGOT increased

Local: Injection site hypersensitivity, pain or reaction

Neuromuscular & skeletal: Arthralgia, limb pain, myalgia, paresthesia

Respiratory: Dyspnea

Miscellaneous: Anaphylactic reactions, night sweats

<1% (Limited to important or life-threatening): Abnormal renal function, alopecia, amylase increased, anemia, antithrombin III decreased, appetite increased, ascites, bone pain, bronchospasm, bruising, BUN increased, chest pain, coagulation disorder, coagulation time increased, colitis, coma, confusion, constipation, cough, creatinine increased, dizziness, DVT, emotional lability, endocarditis, epistaxis, erythema, excessive thirst, face edema, fatigue, fatty liver deposits, flatulence, gastrointestinal pain, glucose intolerance, hematuria, hemorrhagic cystitis, hepatomegaly, hyperammonemia, hypertension, hypoalbuminemia, hyponatremia, joint disorder, lesional edema, lipase increased, liver failure, metabolic acidosis, mucositis, petechial rash, polyuria, proteinuria, prothrombin time increased, pruritus, purpura, renal failure, sagittal sinus thrombosis, sepsis, septic shock, somnolence, subacute bacterial endocarditis, superficial venous thrombosis, thirst, upper respiratory infection, uric acid nephropathy, urinary frequency, weight loss

Overdosage/Toxicology Symptoms of overdose include nausea, diarrhea, rash, and increased liver enzymes. Treatment is symptom-directed and supportive.

Stability Refrigerate at 2°C to 8°C (36°F to 46°F); do not freeze. Do not use product if it is known to have been frozen. Do not use if stored at room temperature for >48 hours. Avoid excessive agitation; do **not** shake. Do not use if cloudy or if precipitate is present.

Standard I.M. dilution: Usually not more than 2 mL/injection site.
Standard I.V. dilution: Dilute in 100 mL NS or D₅W; stable for 48 hours at room temperature.

Mechanism of Action Pegaspargase is a modified version of asparaginase. Leukemic cells, especially lymphoblasts, require exogenous asparagine; normal cells can synthesize asparagine. Asparaginase contains L-asparaginase amidohydrolase type EC-2 which inhibits protein synthesis by deaminating asparagine to aspartic acid and ammonia in the plasma and extracellular fluid and therefore deprives tumor cells of the amino acid for protein synthesis. Asparaginase is cycle-specific for the G_1 phase of the cell cycle.

Pharmacodynamics/Kinetics

Duration: Asparaginase was measurable for at least 20 days following initial treatment with pegaspargase

Distribution: V_d: 4-5 L/kg; 70% to 80% of plasma volume; does not penetrate the CSF

Metabolism: Systemically degraded

Half-life elimination: 5.8 days; unaffected by age, renal or hepatic function; half life decreased to 3.2 days in patients with previous hypersensitivity to native L-asparaginase

Excretion: Urine (trace amounts)

Dosage Usually administered as part of a combination chemotherapy regimen.

I.M. administration is **preferred** over I.V. administration due to lower incidence of hepatotoxicity, coagulopathy, gastrointestinal and renal disorders with I.M. administration.

Children: I.M., I.V.:
Body surface area <0.6 m²: 82.5 int. units/kg every 14 days
Body surface area ≥0.6 m²: 2500 int. units/m² every 14 days

Adults: I.M., I.V.: 2500 int. units/m² every 14 days

Hemodialysis: Significant drug removal is unlikely based on physiochemical characteristics

Peritoneal dialysis: Significant drug removal is unlikely based on physiochemical characteristics

Administration

I.M.: Must only be administered as a deep intramuscular injection into a large muscle; if I.M. injection volume is >2 mL, use multiple injection sites.

I.V.: May be administered as a 1 - to 2-hour I.V. infusion; **do not administer I.V. push**.

Monitoring Parameters Vital signs during administration, CBC with differential, platelets, amylase, liver enzymes, fibrinogen, PT, PTT, renal function tests, urine dipstick for glucose, blood glucose; monitor for onset of abdominal pain and mental status changes

Dosage Forms

Injection, solution [preservative free]:
Oncaspar®: 750 units/mL (5 mL)

♦ **Pegasys**® see Peginterferon Alfa-2a on page 1322

Pegfilgrastim (peg fil GRA stim)

U.S. Brand Names Neulasta®

Canadian Brand Names Neulasta®

Index Terms G-CSF (PEG Conjugate); Granulocyte Colony Stimulating Factor (PEG Conjugate); NSC-725961; SD/01

Pharmacologic Category Colony Stimulating Factor

Use Decrease the incidence of infection, by stimulation of granulocyte production, in patients with nonmyeloid malignancies receiving myelosuppressive therapy associated with a significant risk of febrile neutropenia

Pregnancy Risk Factor C

Pregnancy Implications Animal studies have demonstrated adverse effects and fetal loss. There are no adequate and well-controlled studies in pregnant women; use only if potential benefit to mother justifies the potential risk to the fetus.

Lactation Excretion in breast milk unknown/use caution

Medication Safety Issues

Sound-alike/look-alike issues:
Neulasta® may be confused with Neumega® and Lunesta™

(Continued)

Pegfilgrastim *(Continued)*

Contraindications Hypersensitivity to pegfilgrastim, filgrastim, *E. coli*-derived proteins, or any component of the formulation

Warnings/Precautions Do not use pegfilgrastim in the period 14 days before to 24 hours after administration of cytotoxic chemotherapy because of the potential sensitivity of rapidly dividing myeloid cells to cytotoxic chemotherapy. Pegfilgrastim can potentially act as a growth factor for any tumor type, particularly myeloid malignancies. Precaution should be exercised in the usage of pegfilgrastim in any malignancy with myeloid characteristics. Tumors of nonhematopoietic origin may have surface receptors for pegfilgrastim. Pegfilgrastim has not been evaluated with patients receiving radiation therapy, or with chemotherapy associated with delayed myelosuppression (nitrosoureas, mitomycin C). Safety and efficacy have not been evaluated for peripheral blood progenitor cell (PBPC) mobilization.

Allergic-type reactions (anaphylaxis, skin rash, urticaria) have occurred primarily with the initial dose and may recur after discontinuation; close follow up for several days and permanent discontinuation are recommended for severe reactions. Rare cases of splenic rupture have been reported; patients must be instructed to report left upper quadrant pain or shoulder tip pain. Adult respiratory distress syndrome (ARDS) has been associated with the parent compound, filgrastim; withhold pegfilgrastim and evaluate patients with symptoms of ARDS (fever, lung infiltrates, respiratory distress). May precipitate sickle cell crises in patients with sickle cell disease; carefully evaluate potential risks and benefits. The packaging (needle cover) contains latex. Safety and efficacy in pediatric patients have not been established. The 6 mg fixed dose should not be used in adolescents weighing <45 kg.

Adverse Reactions
>10%:
  Cardiovascular: Peripheral edema (12%)
  Central nervous system: Headache (16%)
  Gastrointestinal: Vomiting (13%), constipation (12%)
  Neuromuscular & skeletal: Bone pain (31% to 57%), myalgia (21%), arthralgia (16%), weakness (13%)
<1% (Limited to important or life-threatening): Fever, hyperleukocytosis, leukocytosis, hypoxia. **Note:** Rare adverse reactions reported for filgrastim and pegfilgrastim include adult respiratory distress syndrome, allergic reactions (including urticaria, rash or anaphylaxis), sickle cell crisis, and splenic rupture. Cytopenias resulting from an antibody response to exogenous growth factors have been reported on rare occasions in patients treated with other recombinant growth factors.

Overdosage/Toxicology No clinical adverse effects have been seen with high doses producing ANC >10,000/mm^3. The duration of leukocytosis has ranged from 6-13 days. Leukapheresis may be considered in symptomatic individuals.

Drug Interactions
  Increased Effect/Toxicity: No formal drug interactions studies have been conducted.

Stability Store under refrigeration 2°C to 8°C (36°F to 46°F); do not freeze. If inadvertently frozen, allow to thaw in refrigerator; discard if frozen more than one time. Protect from light. Do not shake. Allow to reach room temperature prior to injection. May be kept at room temperature for 48 hours.

Mechanism of Action Stimulates the production, maturation, and activation of neutrophils, pegfilgrastim activates neutrophils to increase both their migration and cytotoxicity. Pegfilgrastim has a prolonged duration of effect relative to filgrastim and a reduced renal clearance.

Pharmacodynamics/Kinetics Half-life elimination: SubQ: 15-80 hours

Dosage SubQ: Adolescents >45 kg and Adults: 6 mg once per chemotherapy cycle; do not administer in the period between 14 days before and 24 hours after administration of cytotoxic chemotherapy; do not use in infants, children, and smaller adolescents weighing <45 kg
  Dosage adjustment in renal impairment: No adjustment necessary

Administration Do not use 6 mg fixed dose in infants, children, or adolescents <45 kg. Engage/activate needle guard following use to prevent accidental needlesticks.

Monitoring Parameters Complete blood count (with differential) and platelet count should be obtained prior to chemotherapy. Leukocytosis (white blood cell counts 100,000/mm^3) has been observed in <1% of patients receiving pegfilgrastim. Monitor platelets and hematocrit regularly.

Test Interactions May interfere with bone imaging studies; increased hematopoietic activity of the bone marrow may appear as transient positive bone imaging changes

Dosage Forms
Injection, solution [preservative free]:
  Neulasta®: 10 mg/mL (0.6 mL) [prefilled syringe; needle cover contains latex]

Peginterferon Alfa-2a (peg in ter FEER on AL fa too aye)

U.S. Brand Names Pegasys®
Canadian Brand Names Pegasys®
Index Terms Interferon Alfa-2a (PEG Conjugate); Pegylated Interferon Alfa-2a
Pharmacologic Category Interferon
Use Treatment of chronic hepatitis C (CHC), alone or in combination with ribavirin, in patients with compensated liver disease and histological evidence of cirrhosis (Child-Pugh class A) and patients with clinically-stable HIV disease; treatment of patients with HBeAg positive and HBeAg negative chronic hepatitis B with compensated liver disease and evidence of viral replication and liver inflammation
Restrictions An FDA-approved medication guide must be distributed when dispensing an outpatient prescription (new or refill) where this medication is to be used without direct supervision of a healthcare provider. Medication guides are available at http://www.fda.gov/cder/Offices/ODS/medication_guides.htm.
Pregnancy Risk Factor C; X when used with ribavirin

Pregnancy Implications Animal teratogenicity studies have not been conducted; very high doses are abortifacient in Rhesus monkeys. Assumed to have abortifacient potential in humans. There are no adequate and well-controlled studies in pregnant women; use during pregnancy only if the potential benefit to the mother outweighs the possible risk to the fetus. Risk of maternal-infant transmission of hepatitis C is <5%. Reliable contraception should be used in women of childbearing potential.

Lactation Excretion in breast milk unknown/not recommended

Contraindications Hypersensitivity to polyethylene glycol (PEG), interferon alfa, or any component of the formulation; autoimmune hepatitis; decompensated liver disease in cirrhotic patients (Child-Pugh score >6); decompensated liver disease (Child-Pugh score ≥6, class B and C) in CHC coinfected with HIV; neonates and infants

Warnings/Precautions Severe acute hypersensitivity reactions have occurred rarely; prompt discontinuation is advised. Use caution with prior cardiovascular disease, endocrine disorders, autoimmune disorders, and pulmonary dysfunction. **[U.S. Boxed Warning]: Discontinue treatment with worsening or persistently severe signs/symptoms of autoimmune, infectious, ischemic, or neuropsychiatric disorders** Severe psychiatric adverse effects (including depression, suicidal ideation, and suicide attempt) may occur. Avoid use in severe psychiatric disorders; use caution in patients with a history of depression. Patients who experience dizziness, confusion, somnolence or fatigue should use caution when performing tasks which require mental alertness (eg, operating machinery or driving).

Hepatic decompensation and death have been associated with the use of alpha interferons including Pegasys®, in cirrhotic chronic hepatitis C patients; patients coinfected with HIV and receiving highly active antiretroviral therapy have shown an increased risk. Monitor hepatic function; discontinue if decompensation occurs (Child-Pugh score >6) in monoinfected patients and (Child-Pugh score ≥6, class B and C) in patients coinfected with HIV. In hepatitis B patients, flares (transient and potentially severe increases in serum ALT) may occur during or after treatment; more frequent monitoring of LFTs and a dose reduction are recommended. Discontinue if ALT elevation continues despite dose reduction or if increased bilirubin or hepatic decompensation occur.

May cause myelosuppression (including neutropenia, lymphopenia, aplastic anemia); use caution with renal dysfunction (Cl_{cr} <50 mL/minute). Patients with renal dysfunction should be monitored for signs/symptoms of toxicity (dosage adjustment required if toxicity occurs). Discontinue if new or worsening ophthalmologic disorders occur including retinal hemorrhages, cotton wool spots, and retinal artery or vein obstruction; visual exams are recommended in these instances, at the initiation of therapy, and periodically during therapy.

Use caution with baseline neutrophil count <1500/mm^3, platelet count <90,000/mm^3 or hemoglobin <10 g/dL. Discontinue therapy (at least temporarily) if ANC <500/mm^3 or platelet count <25,000/mm^3, colitis develops, or if known or suspected pancreatitis develops. Use caution in patients with an increased risk for severe anemia (eg, spherocytosis, history of GI bleeding).

Use caution in geriatric patients. Safety and efficacy have not been established in patients who have failed other alpha interferon therapy, received organ transplants, been coinfected with HBV and HCV or HIV; or with HCV and HIV with a CD4$^+$ cell count <100 cells/microL, or been treated for >48 weeks. Due to differences in dosage, patients should not change brands of interferon. Safety and efficacy have not been established in children.

Adverse Reactions Note: Percentages are reported for peginterferon alfa-2a in chronic hepatitis C (CHC) patients. Other percentages indicated as "with ribavirin" or "in HIV/CHC" are those which significantly exceed incidence reported for peginterferon monotherapy in CHC patients.

>10%:

Central nervous system: Headache (54%), fatigue (50%), pyrexia (37%; 41% with ribavirin; 54% in hepatitis B), insomnia (19%; 30% with ribavirin), depression (18%), dizziness (16%), irritability/anxiety/nervousness (19%; 33% with ribavirin), pain (11%)

Dermatologic: Alopecia (23%; 28% with ribavirin), pruritus (12%; 19% with ribavirin), dermatitis (16% with ribavirin)

Gastrointestinal: Nausea/vomiting (24%), anorexia (17%; 24% with ribavirin), diarrhea (16%), weight loss (16% in HIV/CHC), abdominal pain (15%)

Hematologic: Neutropenia (21%; 27% with ribavirin; 40% in HIV/CHC), lymphopenia (14% with ribavirin), anemia (11% with ribavirin; 14% in HIV/CHC)

Hepatic: ALT increases 5-10 x ULN during treatment (25% to 27% in hepatitis B); ALT increases >10 x ULN during treatment (12% to 18% in hepatitis B); ALT increases 5-10 x ULN after treatment (13% to 16% in hepatitis B); ALT increases >10 x ULN after treatment (7% to 12% in hepatitis B)

Local: Injection site reaction (22%)

Neuromuscular & skeletal: Weakness (56%; 65% with ribavirin), myalgia (37%), rigors (32%; 25% to 27% in hepatitis B), arthralgia (28%)

Respiratory: Dyspnea (13% with ribavirin)

1% to 10%:

Central nervous system: Concentration impaired (8%), memory impaired (5%), mood alteration (3%; 9% in HIV/CHC)

Dermatologic: Dermatitis (8%), rash (5%), dry skin (4%; 10% with ribavirin), eczema (5% with ribavirin)

Endocrine & metabolic: Hypothyroidism (4%), hyperthyroidism (1%)

Gastrointestinal: Xerostomia (6%), dyspepsia (6% with ribavirin), weight loss (4%; 10% with ribavirin)

Hematologic: Thrombocytopenia (5%), platelets decreased <50,000/mm^3 (5%), lymphopenia (3%), anemia (2%)

Hepatic: Hepatic decompensation (2% CHC/HIV patients)

Neuromuscular & skeletal: Back pain (9%)

Ocular: Blurred vision (4%)

Respiratory: Cough (4%; 10% with ribavirin), dyspnea (4%), exertional dyspnea (4% with ribavirin)

Miscellaneous: Diaphoresis (6%), bacterial infection (3%; 5% in HIV/CHC)

(Continued)

Peginterferon Alfa-2a *(Continued)*

≤1% (Limited to important or life-threatening): Anaphylaxis, angioedema, angina, aggression, arrhythmia, autoimmune disorders, bronchiolitis obliterans, bronchoconstriction, cerebral hemorrhage, chest pain, cholangitis, colitis, coma, corneal ulcer, cotton wool spots, diabetes mellitus, endocarditis, exertional dyspnea, fatty liver, gastrointestinal bleeding, hearing impairment, hearing loss, hemoglobin decreased, hematocrit decreased, hepatic dysfunction, hepatic decompensation, hyper-/hypoglycemia, hypersensitivity reactions, hypertension, influenza, interstitial pneumonitis, MI, myositis, optic neuritis, papilledema, pancreatitis, peptic ulcer, peripheral neuropathy, pneumonia, psychosis, pulmonary embolism, pulmonary infiltrates, retinal hemorrhage, retinopathy, sarcoidosis, substance overdose, suicidal ideation, suicide, supraventricular arrhythmia, thrombotic thrombocytopenic purpura, urticaria, vision decreased/loss

Overdosage/Toxicology Experience with overdosage is limited and no serious reactions have been reported. Dose-limiting toxicities include fatigue, elevated liver enzymes, neutropenia and thrombocytopenia. In case of overdose, treatment should be symptom-directed and supportive. Hemodialysis and peritoneal dialysis are not effective.

Drug Interactions

Cytochrome P450 Effect: Inhibits CYP1A2 (weak)

Increased Effect/Toxicity: Interferons may increase the risk of neutropenia when used with ACE inhibitors; fluorouracil concentrations doubled with interferon alfa-2b; interferon alfa may decrease the metabolism of theophylline and zidovudine; interferons may increase the anticoagulant effects of warfarin. Concurrent therapy with ribavirin may increase the risk of hemolytic anemia.

Decreased Effect: Prednisone may decrease the therapeutic effects of interferon alfa; interferon alfa may decrease the serum concentrations of melphalan

Ethanol/Nutrition/Herb Interactions Ethanol: Avoid use in patients with hepatitis C virus.

Stability Store in refrigerator at 2°C to 8°C (36°F to 46°F); do not freeze or shake. Protect from light. Discard unused solution.

Mechanism of Action Alpha interferons are a family of proteins, produced by nucleated cells, that have antiviral, antiproliferative, and immune-regulating activity. There are 16 known subtypes of alpha interferons. Interferons interact with cells through high affinity cell surface receptors. Following activation, multiple effects can be detected including induction of gene transcription. Inhibits cellular growth, alters the state of cellular differentiation, interferes with oncogene expression, alters cell surface antigen expression, increases phagocytic activity of macrophages, and augments cytotoxicity of lymphocytes for target cells.

Pharmacodynamics/Kinetics

Half-life elimination: Terminal: 50-140 hours; increased with renal dysfunction

Time to peak, serum: 72-96 hours

Dosage SubQ: Adults:

Chronic hepatitis C (monoinfection or coinfection with HIV):

Monotherapy: 180 mcg once weekly for 48 weeks

Combination therapy with ribavirin: Recommended dosage: 180 mcg once/week with ribavirin (Copegus®)

Duration of therapy: Monoinfection (based on genotype):

Genotype 1,4: 48 weeks

Genotype 2,3: 24 weeks

Duration of therapy: Coinfection with HIV: 48 weeks

Chronic hepatitis B: 180 mcg once weekly for 48 weeks

Dose modifications for adverse reactions/toxicity:

For moderate-to-severe adverse reactions: Initial: 135 mcg/week; may need decreased to 90 mcg/week in some cases

Based on hematologic parameters:

ANC <750/mm³: 135 mcg/week

ANC <500/mm³: Suspend therapy until >1000/mm³, then restart at 90 mcg/week and monitor

Platelet count <50,000/mm³: 90 mcg/week

Platelet count <25,000/mm³: Discontinue therapy

Depression (severity based on DSM-IV criteria):

Mild depression: No dosage adjustment required; evaluate once weekly by visit/phone call. If depression remains stable, continue weekly visits. If depression improves, resume normal visit schedule

Moderate depression: Decrease interferon dose to 90-135 mcg once/week; evaluate once weekly with an office visit at least every other week. If depression remains stable, consider psychiatric evaluation and continue with reduced dosing. If symptoms improve and remain stable for 4 weeks, resume normal visit schedule; continue reduced dosing or return to normal dose.

Severe depression: Discontinue interferon permanently. Obtain immediate psychiatric consultation. Discontinue ribavirin if using concurrently.

Dosage adjustment in renal impairment:

Cl$_{cr}$ <50 mL/minute: Use caution; monitor for toxicity

End-stage renal disease requiring hemodialysis: 135 mcg/week; monitor for toxicity

Dosage adjustment in hepatic impairment:

HCV: ALT progressively rising above baseline: Decrease dose to 135 mcg/week. If ALT continues to rise or is accompanied by increased bilirubin or hepatic decompensation, discontinue therapy immediately.

HBV:

ALT >5 x ULN: Monitor LFTs more frequently; consider decreasing dose to 135 mcg/week or temporarily discontinuing (may resume after ALT flare subsides).

ALT >10 x ULN: Consider discontinuing.

Dietary Considerations Avoid ethanol use in patients with hepatitis C virus.

Administration SubQ: Administer in the abdomen or thigh. Rotate injection site. Do not use if solution contains particulate matter or is discolored. Discard unused solution. Administration should be done on the same day and at approximately the same time each week.

Monitoring Parameters Prior to treatment, pregnancy screening should occur for women of childbearing age who are receiving treatment or who have male partners who are receiving treatment. In combination therapy with ribavirin, pregnancy tests should continue monthly up to 6 months after discontinuation of therapy. Standard hematological tests should be performed prior to therapy, at week 2, and periodically. Standard biochemical tests should be performed prior to therapy, at week 4, and periodically. Evaluate for depression and other psychiatric symptoms before and during therapy; baseline eye examination and periodically in patients with baseline disorders; baseline echocardiogram in patients with cardiac disease; serum HCV RNA levels after 12 weeks of treatment. Consider discontinuing treatment if virologic tests indicate no response by week 12.

Clinical studies tested as follows: CBC (including hemoglobin, WBC, and platelets) and chemistries (including liver function tests and uric acid) measured at weeks 1, 2, 4, 6, and 8, and then every 4-6 weeks (more frequently if abnormal) weeks; TSH measured every 12 weeks

In addition, the following baseline values were used as entrance criteria:

Platelet count ≥90,000/mm^3 (as low as 75,000/mm^3 in patients with cirrhosis or transition to cirrhosis)

ANC ≥1500/mm^3

Serum creatinine <1.5 times ULN

TSH and T$_4$ within normal limits or adequately controlled

CD4$^+$ cell count ≥200 cells/microL or CD4$^+$ cell count ≥100 cells/ microL, but <200 cells/ microL and HIV-1 RNA <5000 copies/mL in CHC patients coinfected with HIV

Hemoglobin ≥12 g/dL for women and ≥13 g/dL for men in CHC monoinfected patients

Hemoglobin ≥11 g/dL for women and ≥12 g/dL for men in CHC patients coinfected with HIV

Dosage Forms

Injection solution:

Pegasys®

180 mcg/0.5 mL (0.5 mL) [prefilled syringe; contains benzyl alcohol and polysorbate 80; packaged with needles and alcohol swabs]

180 mcg/mL (1 mL) [vial; contains benzyl alcohol and polysorbate 80]

Peginterferon Alfa-2b (peg in ter FEER on AL fa too bee)

U.S. Brand Names PEG-Intron®

Canadian Brand Names PEG-Intron®

Index Terms Interferon Alfa-2b (PEG Conjugate); Pegylated Interferon Alfa-2b

Pharmacologic Category Interferon

Use Treatment of chronic hepatitis C (as monotherapy or in combination with ribavirin) in adult patients who have never received interferon alpha and have compensated liver disease

Restrictions An FDA-approved medication guide must be distributed when dispensing an outpatient prescription (new or refill) where this medication is to be used without direct supervision of a healthcare provider. Medication guides are available at http://www.fda.gov/cder/Offices/ODS/medication_guides.htm.

Pregnancy Risk Factor C (manufacturer) as monotherapy; X in combination with ribavirin

Pregnancy Implications Very high doses are abortifacient in Rhesus monkeys. Assumed to have abortifacient potential in humans. Case reports of use in pregnant women (usually interferon alfa-2a) did not result in adverse effects in the fetus or newborn. There are no adequate and well-controlled studies in pregnant women. Risk of maternal-infant transmission of hepatitis C is <5%. Reliable contraception should be used in women of childbearing potential. Not recommended for use in pregnancy (per manufacturer).

Lactation Excretion in breast milk unknown/not recommended

Contraindications Hypersensitivity to polyethylene glycol (PEG), interferon alfa, or any component of the formulation; autoimmune hepatitis; decompensated liver disease; previous treatment with interferon; severe psychiatric disorder; pregnancy (in combination with ribavirin)

Warnings/Precautions [U.S. Boxed Warning]: Severe psychiatric adverse effects, including depression, suicidal ideation, and suicide attempt, may occur; use caution with a history of depression. Avoid use in severe psychiatric disorders and discontinue if worsening or persistently severe signs/symptoms of neuropsychiatric disorders (including depression and/or suicidal thoughts/behavior) occur. Use with caution in patients who are chronically immunosuppressed, with low peripheral blood counts or myelosuppression, including concurrent use of myelosuppressive therapy. Discontinue therapy when significant decreases in neutrophil (<0.5 x 10^9/L) or platelet counts (<50,000/mm^3) occur.

[U.S. Boxed Warning]: Use with caution in patients with prior cardiovascular disease, endocrine disorders, autoimmune disorders, and pulmonary dysfunction; may cause or aggravate fatal or life-threatening conditions. Discontinue therapy if colitis develops or known or suspected pancreatitis develops. Patients with renal dysfunction should be monitored for signs/symptoms of toxicity (dosage adjustment required if toxicity occurs); avoid use of combination therapy with ribavirin in renal dysfunction (Cl$_{cr}$ <50 mL/minute). Ophthalmologic disorders (including retinal hemorrhages, cotton wool spots, and retinal artery or vein obstruction) have occurred in patients using other alpha interferons. Prior to start of therapy, visual exams are recommended for patients with diabetes mellitus or hypertension. Transient rashes do not necessitate interruption of therapy.

Due to differences in dosages, patients should not change brands. Safety and efficacy have not been established in patients who have failed other alpha interferon (including peginterferon alfa-2b) therapy, received organ transplants, been infected with HIV or hepatitis B, or received treatment for >48 weeks. Use caution in geriatric patients. Safety and efficacy have not been established in children.

(Continued)

Peginterferon Alfa-2b *(Continued)*

Adverse Reactions

>10%:

Central nervous system: Headache (56%), fatigue (52%), depression (16% to 29%), anxiety/emotional liability/irritability (28%), insomnia (23%), fever (22%), dizziness (12%), impaired concentration (5% to 12%), pain (12%)

Dermatologic: Alopecia (22%), pruritus (12%), dry skin (11%)

Gastrointestinal: Nausea (26%), anorexia (20%), diarrhea (18%), abdominal pain (15%), weight loss (11%)

Local: Injection site inflammation/reaction (47%)

Neuromuscular & skeletal: Musculoskeletal pain (56%), myalgia (38% to 42%), rigors (23% to 45%)

Respiratory: Epistaxis (14%), nasopharyngitis (11%)

Miscellaneous: Flu-like syndrome (46%), viral infection (11%)

>1% to 10%:

Cardiovascular: Flushing (6%)

Central nervous system: Malaise (8%)

Dermatologic: Rash (6%), dermatitis (7%)

Endocrine & metabolic: Hypothyroidism (5%)

Gastrointestinal: Vomiting (7%), dyspepsia (6%), taste perversion

Hematologic: Neutropenia, thrombocytopenia

Hepatic: Hepatomegaly (6%), transaminases increased (10%; transient)

Local: Injection site pain (2%)

Neuromuscular & skeletal: Hypertonia (5%)

Respiratory: Pharyngitis (10%), sinusitis (7%), cough (6%)

Miscellaneous: Diaphoresis (6%)

≤1% (Limited to important or life-threatening): Anaphylaxis, angioedema, aplastic anemia, arrhythmia, autoimmune disorder (eg, thyroiditis, thrombocytopenia, rheumatoid arthritis, interstitial nephritis, systemic lupus erythematosus, psoriasis), diabetes mellitus, dyspnea, facial oculomotor nerve palsy, hallucinations, hemorrhagic colitis, homicidal ideation, hyperthyroidism, hypotension, MI, nerve palsy, neutralizing antibodies, pancreatitis, pneumonia, pneumonitis, psychosis, pulmonary infiltrates, retinal hemorrhage, retinal ischemia, severe depression, severe neutropenia (<0.5 x 10^9/L), severe thrombocytopenia (<50,000/mm^3), suicidal behavior, suicidal ideation, supraventricular arrhythmia, tachycardia, transient ischemic attack, urticaria

Overdosage/Toxicology Limited experience with accidental doses ≥2.5 times the intended dose. No serious side effects have been noted. Treatment is symptom-directed and supportive.

Drug Interactions

Cytochrome P450 Effect: Inhibits CYP1A2 (weak)

Increased Effect/Toxicity: ACE inhibitors, clozapine, erythropoietin may increase risk of bone marrow suppression. Fluorouracil, theophylline, zidovudine concentrations may increase. Warfarin's anticoagulant effect may increase. Concurrent therapy with ribavirin may increase the risk of hemolytic anemia.

Decreased Effect: Melphalan concentrations may decrease. Prednisone may decrease effects of interferon alfa.

Ethanol/Nutrition/Herb Interactions Ethanol: Avoid use in patients with hepatitis C virus.

Stability Prior to reconstitution, store Redipen™ at 2°C to 8°C (36°F to 46°F) and store vials at 15°C to 30°C (59°F to 86°F).

Redipen™: Hold cartridge upright and press the two halves together until there is a "click". Gently invert to mix; do not shake.

Vial: Add 0.7 mL of sterile water for injection, USP (supplied diluent) to the vial. Gently swirl. Do not re-enter vial after dose removed. Discard unused portion.

Once reconstituted each product should be used immediately or may be stored for ≤24 hours at 2°C to 8°C (36°F to 46°F); do not freeze. Products do not contain preservative.

Mechanism of Action Alpha interferons are a family of proteins, produced by nucleated cells, that have antiviral, antiproliferative, and immune-regulating activity. There are 16 known subtypes of alpha interferons. Interferons interact with cells through high affinity cell surface receptors. Following activation, multiple effects can be detected including induction of gene transcription. Inhibits cellular growth, alters the state of cellular differentiation, interferes with oncogene expression, alters cell surface antigen expression, increases phagocytic activity of macrophages, and augments cytotoxicity of lymphocytes for target cells.

Pharmacodynamics/Kinetics

Bioavailability: Increases with chronic dosing

Half-life elimination: 40 hours

Time to peak: 15-44 hours

Excretion: Urine (30%)

Dosage SubQ:

Children: Safety and efficacy have not been established

Adults: Chronic hepatitis C: Administer dose once weekly; **Note:** Usual duration is for 1 year; after 24 weeks of treatment, if serum HCV RNA is not below the limit of detection of the assay, consider discontinuation:

Monotherapy: Initial:

≤45 kg: 40 mcg

46-56 kg: 50 mcg

57-72 kg: 64 mcg

73-88 kg: 80 mcg

89-106 kg: 96 mcg

107-136 kg: 120 mcg

137-160 kg: 150 mcg

Combination therapy with ribavirin (400 mg twice daily): Initial: 1.5 mcg/kg/week

<40 kg: 50 mcg

40-50 kg: 64 mcg

51-60 kg: 80 mcg

61-75 kg: 96 mcg
76-85 kg: 120 mcg
>85 kg: 150 mcg

Elderly: May require dosage reduction based upon renal dysfunction, but no established guidelines are available.

Dosage adjustment if serious adverse event occurs: Depression (severity based upon DSM-IV criteria):

Mild depression: No dosage adjustment required; evaluate once weekly by visit/phone call. If depression remains stable, continue weekly visits. If depression improves, resume normal visit schedule.

Moderate depression: Decrease interferon dose by 50%; evaluate once weekly with an office visit at least every other week. If depression remains stable, consider psychiatric evaluation and continue with reduced dosing. If symptoms improve and remain stable for 4 weeks, resume normal visit schedule; continue reduced dosing or return to normal dose.

Severe depression: Discontinue interferon and ribavirin permanently. Obtain immediate psychiatric consultation.

Dosage adjustment in renal impairment: Monitor for signs and symptoms of toxicity and if toxicity occurs then adjust dose. Do not use patients with Cl_{cr} <50 mL/minute. Patients were excluded from the clinical trials if serum creatinine >1.5 times the upper limits of normal.

Dosage adjustment in hepatic impairment: Contraindicated in decompensated liver disease

Dosage adjustment in hematologic toxicity:

Hemoglobin:

Hemoglobin <10 g/dL: Continue current peginterferon alfa-2b dose; decrease ribavirin dose by 200 mg/day.

Hemoglobin <8.5 g/dL: Permanently discontinue peginterferon alfa-2b and ribavirin.

Hemoglobin decrease >2 g/dL in any 4-week period and stable cardiac disease: Decrease peginterferon alfa-2b dose by half; decrease ribavirin dose by 200 mg per day. Hemoglobin <12 g/dL after ribavirin dose is decreased: Permanently discontinue both peginterferon alfa-2b and ribavirin.

White blood cells:

WBC <1.5 x 10^9/L: Decrease peginterferon alfa-2b dose by half.

WBC <1.0 x 10^9/L: Permanently discontinue peginterferon alfa-2b and ribavirin.

Neutrophils:

Neutrophils <0.75 x 10^9/L: Decrease peginterferon alfa-2b dose by half.

Neutrophils <0.5 x 10^9/L: Permanently discontinue peginterferon alfa-2b and ribavirin.

Platelets:

Platelet count <80 x 10^9/L: Decrease peginterferon alfa-2b dose by half.

Platelet count <50 x 10^9/L: Permanently discontinue peginterferon alfa-2b and ribavirin.

Administration For SubQ administration; rotate injection site

Monitoring Parameters Baseline and periodic TSH, hematology (including CBC with differential, platelets), and chemistry (including LFTs) testing. Evaluate for depression and other psychiatric symptoms before and after initiation of therapy; baseline eye examination in diabetic and hypertensive patients; baseline echocardiogram in patients with cardiac disease; serum HCV RNA levels after 24 weeks of treatment

Dosage Forms

Injection, powder for reconstitution [prefilled syringe]:

PEG-Intron® Redipen®: 50 mcg, 80 mcg, 120 mcg, 150 mcg [contains polysorbate 80 and sucrose; packaged with alcohol swabs and needle for injection]

Injection, powder for reconstitution [vial]:

PEG-Intron®: 50 mcg, 80 mcg, 120 mcg, 150 mcg [contains polysorbate 80 and sucrose; packaged with SWFI, alcohol swabs, and syringes]

♦ **PEG-Intron®** see Peginterferon Alfa-2b on page 1325

♦ **PegLyte® (Can)** see Polyethylene Glycol-Electrolyte Solution on page 1387

Pegvisomant (peg VI soe mant)

U.S. Brand Names Somavert®

Index Terms B2036-PEG

Pharmacologic Category Growth Hormone Receptor Antagonist

Use Treatment of acromegaly in patients resistant to or unable to tolerate other therapies

Pregnancy Risk Factor B

Dosage SubQ: Adults: Initial loading dose: 40 mg; maintenance dose: 10 mg once daily; doses may be adjusted by 5 mg in 4- to 6-week intervals based on IGF-I concentrations (maximum dose: 30 mg/day)

Dosage adjustment in hepatic impairment:

Baseline liver function tests (LFT) >3 times ULN: Do not initiate treatment without comprehensive work-up to determine cause; monitor closely if treatment is started.

LFT ≥3 times but <5 times ULN: Continue treatment, but monitor weekly if no signs or symptoms of hepatitis or liver injury; perform comprehensive hepatic work-up

LFT ≥5 times ULN or transaminase >3 times ULN associated with any increase in total bilirubin: Discontinue immediately and perform comprehensive hepatic work-up. If LFTs return to normal, may cautiously consider restarting therapy with frequent monitoring.

Signs or symptoms of hepatitis or hepatic injury: Evaluate liver function tests; discontinue if liver injury is confirmed

Additional Information Complete prescribing information for this medication should be consulted for additional detail.

Dosage Forms Injection, powder for reconstitution [preservative free]: 10 mg, 15 mg, 20 mg [vial stopper contains latex; packaged with SWFI]

♦ **Pegylated Interferon Alfa-2a** *see* Peginterferon Alfa-2a *on page 1322*
♦ **Pegylated Interferon Alfa-2b** *see* Peginterferon Alfa-2b *on page 1325*

Pemetrexed (pem e TREKS ed)

U.S. Brand Names Alimta®
Canadian Brand Names Alimta®
Index Terms LY231514; MTA; Multitargeted Antifolate; NSC-698037; Pemetrexed Disodium
Pharmacologic Category Antineoplastic Agent, Antimetabolite; Antineoplastic Agent, Antimetabolite (Antifolate)
Use Treatment of malignant pleural mesothelioma; treatment of nonsmall cell lung cancer
Unlabeled/Investigational Use Bladder, breast, cervical, colorectal, esophageal, gastric, head and neck, ovarian, pancreatic, and renal cell cancers
Pregnancy Risk Factor D
Pregnancy Implications In animal studies, was associated with fetotoxicity and teratogenicity (incomplete ossification, cleft palate) when given on gestation days 6-15. Animal studies also demonstrated reduced fertility and embryotoxicity (increased embryo-fetal deaths and decreased litter sizes). There are no adequate and well-controlled studies in pregnant women. Patients should avoid becoming pregnant while using this drug. If used during pregnancy or if patient becomes pregnant during therapy, patient should be educated about the potential hazards to the fetus.
Lactation Excretion in breast milk unknown/not recommended
Medication Safety Issues
  High alert medication: The Institute for Safe Medication Practices (ISMP) includes this medication among its list of drugs which have a heightened risk of causing significant patient harm when used in error.
Contraindications Hypersensitivity to pemetrexed or any component of the formulation
Warnings/Precautions Hazardous agent - use appropriate precautions for handling and disposal. May cause bone marrow suppression (anemia, neutropenia, thrombocytopenia and/or pancytopenia). Prophylactic folic acid and vitamin B$_{12}$ supplements are necessary to reduce hematologic and gastrointestinal toxicity and should be started 1 week before the first dose of pemetrexed. Pretreatment with corticosteroids reduces the incidence and severity of cutaneous reactions. Effects of third space fluid on drug disposition is unknown; consider removal of effusions prior to treatment. Use caution with hepatic dysfunction not due to metastases; may require dose adjustment. Decreased renal function results in increased toxicity. Use caution in patients receiving concurrent nephrotoxins; may result in delayed pemetrexed clearance. The manufacturer does not recommend use for Cl$_{cr}$ <45 mL/minute. Safety and efficacy in children have not been established.
Adverse Reactions Note: Percentages reported with single-agent therapy (in patients who received folate and B$_{12}$ supplementation); dose limiting toxicities include myelosuppression (neutropenia, thrombocytopenia); fatigue and dermatitis.
  >10%:
    Cardiovascular: Chest pain (38%), edema (19%), hypertension (11%; grades 3/4 incidence higher in patients >65 years)
    Central nervous system: Fatigue (87%; grade 3: 14%; grade 4: 2%), fever (26%), depression (11%)
    Dermatologic: Rash/desquamation (17%), alopecia (11%)
    Gastrointestinal: Anorexia (62%), nausea (39%), constipation (30%), vomiting (25%), diarrhea (21%), stomatitis (20%)
    Hematologic: Anemia (33%; grade 4: 2%), leukopenia (13%), neutropenia (11%; grade 4: 2%; nadir: 8-10 days; recovery: 12-17 days)
    Neuromuscular & skeletal: Neuropathy (29%), myalgia (13%)
    Respiratory: Dyspnea (72%), pharyngitis (20%)
    Miscellaneous: Infection (23%)
  1% to 10%:
    Cardiovascular: Thrombosis/embolism (4%), cardiac ischemia (3%)
    Endocrine & metabolic: Dehydration (3%)
    Gastrointestinal: Dysphagia/esophagitis/odynophagia (5%)
    Hematologic: Thrombocytopenia (9%), febrile neutropenia (2% to 6%)
    Hepatic: ALT increased (10%; grade 3: 2%; grade 4: 1%), AST increased (8%; grade 3: <1%; grade 4: 1%)
    Neuromuscular & skeletal: Arthralgia (8%)
    Renal: Creatinine clearance decreased (5%), serum creatinine increased (3%)
    Miscellaneous: Allergic reaction/hypersensitivity (8%)
  <1% (Limited to important or life-threatening): Colitis, renal failure
Overdosage/Toxicology Toxicities include neutropenia, anemia, thrombocytopenia, mucositis, rash, infection, and diarrhea. Treatment is supportive and symptom-directed. Continuing leucovorin may help minimize additional hematologic toxicity. The intravenous leucovorin doses used in clinical trials were 100 mg/m^2 once, followed by 50 mg/m^2 every 6 hours for 8 days. It is unknown if pemetrexed is removed by hemodialysis.
Drug Interactions
  Increased Effect/Toxicity: NSAIDs may increase the toxicity of pemetrexed.
Ethanol/Nutrition/Herb Interactions Lower ANC nadirs occur in patients with elevated baseline cystathionine or homocysteine concentrations. Levels of these substances can be reduced by folic acid and vitamin B$_{12}$ supplementation.
Stability Store unopened vials at 15°C to 30°C (59°F to 86°F). Add 20 mL of 0.9% preservative free sodium chloride injection to make a 25 mg/mL solution. Gently swirl. Solution may be colorless to green-yellow. Reconstituted and infusion solutions are stable for 24 hours when refrigerated at 2°C to 8°C (36°F to 46°F) or stored at room temperature of 15°C to 30°C (59°F to 86°F). Concentrations at 25 mg/mL are stable in polypropylene syringes for 2 days at room temperature (23°C).
Mechanism of Action Inhibits thymidylate synthase (TS), dihydrofolate reductase (DHFR), glycinamide ribonucleotide formyltransferase (GARFT), and aminoimidazole carboxamide

ribonucleotide formyltransferase (AICARFT), the enzymes involved in folate metabolism and DNA synthesis, resulting in inhibition of purine and thymidine nucleotide and protein synthesis.

Pharmacodynamics/Kinetics
Duration: V_{dss}: 16.1 L
Protein binding: ~73% to 81%
Metabolism: Minimal
Half-life elimination: Normal renal function: 3.5 hours; Cl_{cr} 40-59 mL/minute: 5.3-5.8 hours
Excretion: Urine (70% to 90% as unchanged drug)

Dosage I.V.: Adults: Refer to individual protocols:
Nonsmall cell lung cancer: 500 mg/m² on day 1 of each 21-day cycle
Malignant pleural mesothelioma: 500 mg/m² on day 1 of each 21-day cycle (in combination with cisplatin)

Note: Start vitamin supplements 1 week before initial dose of pemetrexed. Folic acid 350-1000 mcg/day orally (continuing for 21 days after last dose of pemetrexed) and vitamin B_{12} 1000 mcg I.M. every 9 weeks. Dexamethasone 4 mg twice daily can be started the day before therapy, and continued the day of and the day after to minimize cutaneous reactions.

Dosage adjustments for toxicities:
Toxicity: Discontinue if patient develops grade 3 or 4 toxicity after two dose reductions (except grade 3 transaminase elevations) or immediately if grade 3 or 4 neurotoxicity develops
Hematologic toxicity: Upon recovery, reinitiate therapy
Nadir ANC <500/mm³ and nadir platelets ≥50,000/mm³: Reduce dose to 75% of previous dose of pemetrexed and cisplatin
Nadir platelets <50,000/mm³ (regardless of nadir ANC): Reduce dose to 50% of previous dose of pemetrexed and cisplatin
Nonhematologic toxicity (excluding neurotoxicity or grade 3 transaminase elevations): Withhold treatment until recovery to baseline, upon recovery, reinitiate therapy
Grade 3 or 4 toxicity (excluding mucositis or grade 3 transaminase elevations): Reduce dose to 75% of previous dose of pemetrexed and cisplatin
Grade 3 or 4 diarrhea or any diarrhea requiring hospitalization: Reduce dose to 75% of previous dose of pemetrexed and cisplatin
Grade 3 or 4 mucositis: Reduce dose to 50% of previous dose of pemetrexed; continue cisplatin at 100% of previous dose
Neurotoxicity:
Common Toxicity Criteria (CTC) Grade 0-1: Continue at 100% of previous dose of pemetrexed and cisplatin.
CTC Grade 2: Continue at previous dose of pemetrexed; Reduce dose to 50% of previous dose of cisplatin.

Dosage adjustment in renal impairment:
Cl_{cr} ≥45 mL/minute: No dosage adjustment required.
Cl_{cr} <45 mL/minute: No dosage adjustment guidelines are available; manufacturer recommends not using the drug.

Dosage adjustment in hepatic impairment: Grade 4 transaminase elevation (>20 times ULN): Reduce dose to 75% of previous dose

Dietary Considerations Initiate folic acid supplementation 1 week before first dose of pemetrexed, continue for full course of therapy, and for 21 days after last dose. Institute vitamin B_{12} 1 week before the first dose; administer every 9 weeks thereafter.

Administration I.V.: Infuse over 10 minutes.

Monitoring Parameters CBC with differential and platelets (before each dose); serum creatinine, total bilirubin, ALT, AST (day 1 of each, or every other, cycle)

Dosage Forms
Injection, powder for reconstitution:
Alimta®: 500 mg

♦ **Pemetrexed Disodium** see Pemetrexed on page 1328

Pemirolast (pe MIR oh last)

U.S. Brand Names Alamast®
Canadian Brand Names Alamast®
Pharmacologic Category Mast Cell Stabilizer; Ophthalmic Agent, Miscellaneous
Use Prevention of itching of the eye due to allergic conjunctivitis
Pregnancy Risk Factor C
Dosage Children >3 years and Adults: 1-2 drops instilled in affected eye(s) 4 times/day
Additional Information Complete prescribing information for this medication should be consulted for additional detail.
Dosage Forms Solution, ophthalmic, as potassium: 0.1% (10 mL) [contains lauralkonium chloride]

Penciclovir (pen SYE kloe veer)

U.S. Brand Names Denavir®
Pharmacologic Category Antiviral Agent
Use Topical treatment of herpes simplex labialis (cold sores)
Pregnancy Risk Factor B
Medication Safety Issues
Sound-alike/look-alike issues:
Denavir® may be confused with indinavir
Dosage Children ≥12 years and Adults: Topical: Apply cream at the first sign or symptom of cold sore (eg, tingling, swelling); apply every 2 hours during waking hours for 4 days
(Continued)

Penciclovir *(Continued)*

Additional Information Complete prescribing information for this medication should be consulted for additional detail.

Dosage Forms Cream: 1% (1.5 g)

♦ **Pendex** *see Guaifenesin and Phenylephrine on page 818*

♦ **Pendo-5 ASA (Can)** *see Mesalamine on page 1089*

Penicillamine *(pen i SIL a meen)*

U.S. Brand Names Cuprimine®; Depen®
Canadian Brand Names Cuprimine®; Depen®
Index Terms β,β-Dimethylcysteine; D-3-Mercaptovaline; D-Penicillamine
Pharmacologic Category Chelating Agent
Additional Appendix Information
Management of Overdosages *on page 2075*
Use Treatment of Wilson's disease, cystinuria; adjunctive treatment of rheumatoid arthritis
Unlabeled/Investigational Use Lead, mercury, copper, arsenic, and possibly gold poisoning **(Note:** Oral succimer [DMSA] is preferable for lead or mercury poisoning)
Pregnancy Risk Factor D
Pregnancy Implications Birth defects, including congenital cutix laxa and associated defects, have been reported in infants following penicillamine exposure during pregnancy. Use for the treatment of rheumatoid arthritis during pregnancy is contraindicated. Use for the treatment of cystinuria only if the possible benefits to the mother outweigh the potential risks to the fetus. Continued treatment of Wilson's disease during pregnancy protects the mother against relapse. Discontinuation has detrimental maternal and fetal effects. Daily dosage should be limited to 750 mg. For planned cesarean section, reduce dose to 250 mg/day for the last 6 weeks of pregnancy, and continue at this dosage until wound healing is complete.
Lactation Excretion in breast milk unknown/contraindicated
Medication Safety Issues
Sound-alike/look-alike issues:
Penicillamine may be confused with penicillin
Depen® may be confused with Endal®

International issues:
Depen® may be confused with Depon® which is a brand name for acetaminophen in Greece
Depen® may be confused with Dipen® which is a brand name for diltiazem in Greece
Pemine® [Italy] may be confused with Pamine® which is a brand name for methscopolamine in the U.S.

Contraindications Hypersensitivity to penicillamine or any component of the formulation; renal insufficiency (in patients with rheumatoid arthritis); patients with previous penicillamine-related aplastic anemia or agranulocytosis; breast-feeding; pregnancy (in patients with rheumatoid arthritis)
Warnings/Precautions Cross-sensitivity with penicillin is possible; therefore, should be used cautiously in patients with a history of penicillin allergy. Once instituted for Wilson's disease or cystinuria, continue treatment on a daily basis; interruptions of even a few days have been followed by hypersensitivity with reinstitution of therapy. Penicillamine has been associated with fatalities due to agranulocytosis, aplastic anemia, thrombocytopenia, Goodpasture's syndrome, and myasthenia gravis. **[U.S. Boxed Warning]: Patients should be warned to report promptly any symptoms suggesting toxicity (fever, sore throat, chills, bruising, or bleeding);** approximately 33% of patients will experience an allergic reaction; toxicity may be dose related, use caution in the elderly. Use caution with other hematopoietic-depressant drugs (eg, gold, immunosuppressants, antimalarials, phenylbutazone); hematologic and renal adverse reactions are similar. Proteinuria or hematuria may develop; monitor for membranous glomerulopathy which can lead to nephrotic syndrome. In rheumatoid arthritis patients, discontinue if gross hematuria or persistent microscopic hematuria develop. Monitor liver function tests periodically due to rare reports of intrahepatic cholestasis or toxic hepatitis. **[U.S. Boxed Warning]: Should be administered under the close supervision of a physician familiar with the toxicity and dosage considerations.**
Adverse Reactions Frequency not defined, may vary by indication. Adverse effects requiring discontinuation of treatment have been reported in 20% to 30% of patients with Wilson's disease.
Cardiovascular: Vasculitis
Central nervous system: Anxiety, agitation, fever, hyperpyrexia, psychiatric disturbances; worsening neurologic symptoms (10% to 50% patients with Wilson's disease)
Dermatologic: Alopecia, cheilosis, dermatomyositis, exfoliative dermatitis, lichen planus, rash (early and late 5%), pemphigus, pruritus, skin friability increased, toxic epidermal necrolysis, urticaria, wrinkling (excessive), yellow nail syndrome
Endocrine & metabolic: Hypoglycemia, thyroiditis
Gastrointestinal: Anorexia, diarrhea (17%), epigastric pain, gingivostomatitis, glossitis, nausea, oral ulcerations, pancreatitis, peptic ulcer reactivation, taste alteration (12%), vomiting
Hematologic: Eosinophilia, hemolytic anemia, leukocytosis, leukopenia (2% to 5%), monocytosis, red cell aplasia, thrombocytopenia (4% to 5%), thrombotic thrombocytopenia purpura, thrombocytosis
Hepatic: Alkaline phosphatase increased, hepatic failure, intrahepatic cholestasis, toxic hepatitis
Local: Thrombophlebitis, white papules at venipuncture and surgical sites
Neuromuscular & skeletal: Arthralgia, dystonia, myasthenia gravis, muscle weakness, neuropathies, polyarthralgia (migratory, often with objective synovitis), polymyositis
Ocular: Diplopia, extraocular muscle weakness, optic neuritis, ptosis, visual disturbances
Otic: Tinnitus

Renal: Goodpasture's syndrome, hematuria, nephrotic syndrome, proteinuria (6%), renal failure, renal vasculitis

Respiratory: Asthma, interstitial pneumonitis, pulmonary fibrosis, obliterative bronchiolitis

Miscellaneous: Allergic alveolitis, anetoderma, elastosis perforans serpiginosa, lupus-like syndrome, lactic dehydrogenase increased, lymphadenopathy, mammary hyperplasia, positive ANA test

Overdosage/Toxicology Symptoms include nausea and vomiting. Following GI decontamination, treatment is supportive.

Drug Interactions

Decreased Effect: Antacids, iron salts may decrease the effects of penicillamine. Penicillamine may decrease the levels of digoxin.

Ethanol/Nutrition/Herb Interactions

Ethanol: Avoid or limit ethanol.

Food: Penicillamine serum levels may be decreased if taken with food. Do not administer with milk.

Stability Store in tight, well-closed containers.

Mechanism of Action Chelates with lead, copper, mercury and other heavy metals to form stable, soluble complexes that are excreted in urine; depresses circulating IgM rheumatoid factor, depresses T-cell but not B-cell activity; combines with cystine to form a compound which is more soluble, thus cystine calculi are prevented

Pharmacodynamics/Kinetics

Onset of action: Rheumatoid arthritis: 2-3 months; Wilson's disease: 1-3 months

Absorption: 40% to 70%

Protein binding: 80% to albumin

Metabolism: Hepatic (small amounts)

Half-life elimination: 1.7-3.2 hours

Time to peak, serum: ~2 hours

Excretion: Urine (30% to 60% as unchanged drug)

Dosage Oral:

Rheumatoid arthritis:

Children (unlabeled use): Initial: 3 mg/kg/day (≤250 mg/day) for 3 months, then 6 mg/kg/day (≤500 mg/day) in divided doses twice daily for 3 months to a maximum of 10 mg/kg/day in 3-4 divided doses; maximum dose: 750 mg/day

Adults: 125-250 mg/day, may increase dose at 1- to 3-month intervals up to 1-1.5 g/day; maximum in older adults: 750 mg/day

Wilson's disease (doses titrated to maintain urinary copper excretion >2 mg/day); decrease dose for surgery and during last trimester of pregnancy

Children <12 years: 20 mg/kg/day in 2-3 divided doses, round off to the nearest 250 mg dose; maximum 1 g/day

Adults: 250 mg 4 times/day (maximum in older adults: 750 mg/day)

Cystinuria: **Note:** Adjust dose to limit cystine excretion to 100-200 mg/day (<100 mg/day with history of stone formation)

Children: 30 mg/kg/day in 4 divided doses

Adults: 1-4 g/day in divided doses every 6 hours; usual dose: 2 g/day

Lead poisoning (unlabeled use): In acute poisoning, continue until blood lead level is <15 mcg/dL; may also be used in other heavy metal poisoning:

Children: 20-30 mg/kg/day, administered in 3-4 divided doses; initiating treatment at 25% of this dose and gradually increasing to the full dose over 2-3 weeks may minimize adverse reactions

Adults: 250-500 mg/dose every 8-12 hours

Arsenic poisoning (unlabeled use): Children: 100 mg/kg/day in divided doses every 6 hours for 5 days; maximum: 1 g/day

Dosing adjustment/comments in renal impairment: Cl_{cr} <50 mL/minute: Avoid use

Hemodialysis: Dialyzable; a dosing decrease from 250 mg/day to 250 mg 3 times/week after dialysis has been suggested in the treatment of rheumatoid arthritis.

Dietary Considerations Should be taken at least 1 hour before a meal on an empty stomach. Iron may decrease drug action. Patients with Wilson's disease or cystinuria should receive pyridoxine supplementation 25 mg/day. For Wilson's disease, decrease copper in diet to <1-2 mg/day and omit chocolate, nuts, shellfish, mushrooms, liver, raisins, broccoli, copper-enriched cereal, multivitamins with copper, and molasses. For lead poisoning, decrease calcium in diet. For cystinuria, increase daily fluid intake including 1 pint of fluid prior to bedtime and 1 additional pint during the night.

Administration For patients who cannot swallow, contents of capsules may be administered in 15-30 mL of chilled puréed fruit or fruit juice. Give on an empty stomach (1 hour before meals and at bedtime).

Cystinuria: If administering 4 equal doses is not feasible, administer the larger dose at bedtime.

Rheumatoid arthritis: Doses ≤500 mg/day may be given as a single dose; >500 mg administer in divided doses

Monitoring Parameters Urinalysis, CBC with differential, platelet count, skin, lymph nodes, and body temperature twice weekly during the first month of therapy, then every 2 weeks for 5 months, then monthly; LFTs every 6 months

Cystinuria: Urinary cystine, annual X-ray for renal stones

Lead poisoning: Serum lead concentration

Wilson's disease: Serum copper, 24-hour urinary copper excretion, LFTs every 3 months during the first year of treatment

CBC: WBC <3500/mm³, neutrophils <2000/mm³, or monocytes >500/mm³ indicate need to stop therapy immediately; platelet counts <100,000/mm³ indicate need to stop therapy until numbers of platelets increase

Urinalysis: Monitor for proteinuria and hematuria. A quantitative 24-hour urine protein at 1- to 2-week intervals initially (first 2-3 months) is recommended if proteinuria develops; in patients with rheumatoid arthritis, discontinue or decrease dose with proteinuria >1 g/24 hours, progressively increasing proteinuria or hematuria.

(Continued)

Penicillamine *(Continued)*

Dosage Forms [DSC] = Discontinued product
Capsule (Cuprimine®): 125 mg [DSC], 250 mg
Tablet (Depen®): 250 mg

Extemporaneous Preparations A 50 mg/mL suspension may be made by mixing twenty 250 mg capsules with 1 g carboxymethylcellulose, 50 g sucrose, 100 mg citric acid, parabens, and purified water to a total volume of 100 mL; cherry flavor may be added. Stability is 30 days refrigerated.

Nahata MC and Hipple TF, *Pediatric Drug Formulations*, 1st ed, Cincinnati, OH: Harvey Whitney Books Co, 1990.

Penicillin G Benzathine *(pen i SIL in jee BENZ a theen)*

U.S. Brand Names Bicillin® L-A
Index Terms Benzathine Benzylpenicillin; Benzathine Penicillin G; Benzylpenicillin Benzathine
Pharmacologic Category Antibiotic, Penicillin
Additional Appendix Information
Treatment of Sexually Transmitted Infections *on page 2007*
Use Active against some gram-positive organisms, few gram-negative organisms such as *Neisseria gonorrhoeae*, and some anaerobes and spirochetes; used in the treatment of syphilis; used only for the treatment of mild to moderately severe infections caused by organisms susceptible to low concentrations of penicillin G or for prophylaxis of infections caused by these organisms
Pregnancy Risk Factor B
Lactation Enters breast milk/compatible
Medication Safety Issues
Sound-alike/look-alike issues:
Penicillin may be confused with penicillamine
Bicillin® may be confused with Wycillin®
Bicillin® C-R (penicillin G benzathine and penicillin G procaine) may be confused with Bicillin® L-A (penicillin G benzathine). Penicillin G benzathine is the only product currently approved for the treatment of syphilis. Administration of penicillin G benzathine and penicillin G procaine combination instead of Bicillin® L-A may result in inadequate treatment response.
Penicillin G benzathine may only be administered by deep intramuscular injection; intravenous administration of penicillin G benzathine has been associated with cardiopulmonary arrest and death.
Contraindications Hypersensitivity to penicillin or any component of the formulation
Warnings/Precautions Use with caution in patients with impaired renal function, seizure disorder, or history of hypersensitivity to other beta-lactams; CDC and AAP do not currently recommend the use of penicillin G benzathine to treat congenital syphilis or neurosyphilis due to reported treatment failures and lack of published clinical data on its efficacy
Adverse Reactions Frequency not defined.
Central nervous system: Convulsions, confusion, drowsiness, myoclonus, fever
Dermatologic: Rash
Endocrine & metabolic: Electrolyte imbalance
Hematologic: Positive Coombs' reaction, hemolytic anemia
Local: Pain, thrombophlebitis
Renal: Acute interstitial nephritis
Miscellaneous: Anaphylaxis, hypersensitivity reactions, Jarisch-Herxheimer reaction
Overdosage/Toxicology Symptoms of penicillin overdose include neuromuscular hypersensitivity (agitation, hallucinations, asterixis, encephalopathy, confusion, seizures) and electrolyte imbalance with potassium or sodium salts, especially in renal failure. Hemodialysis may be helpful to aid in removal of the drug from the blood, otherwise, most treatment is supportive or symptom-directed.
Drug Interactions
Increased Effect/Toxicity: Probenecid increases penicillin levels. Aminoglycosides may lead to synergistic efficacy. Penicillins may increase the exposure to methotrexate during concurrent therapy; monitor.
Decreased Effect: Tetracyclines may decrease penicillin effectiveness. Although anecdotal reports suggest oral contraceptive efficacy could be reduced by penicillins, this has been refuted by more rigorous scientific and clinical data.
Stability Refrigerate
Mechanism of Action Interferes with bacterial cell wall synthesis during active multiplication, causing cell wall death and resultant bactericidal activity against susceptible bacteria
Pharmacodynamics/Kinetics
Duration: 1-4 weeks (dose dependent); larger doses result in more sustained levels
Absorption: I.M.: Slow
Time to peak, serum: 12-24 hours
Dosage Note: Administer undiluted injection; higher doses result in more sustained rather than higher levels. Use a penicillin G benzathine-penicillin G procaine combination to achieve early peak levels in acute infections.
Usual dosage range:
Children: I.M.: 25,000-50,000 units/kg as a single dose (maximum: 2.4 million units)
Adults: I.M.: 1.2-2.4 million units as a single dose
Indication-specific dosing:
Neonates >1200 g: I.M.:
Congenital syphilis (asymptomatic): 50,000 units/kg as a single dose
Infants and Children: I.M.:
Group A streptococcal upper respiratory infection: 25,000-50,000 units/kg as a single dose (maximum: 1.2 million units)
Prophylaxis of recurrent rheumatic fever: 25,000-50,000 units/kg every 3-4 weeks (maximum: 1.2 million units/dose)

Syphilis:
> *Early:* 50,000 units/kg as a single injection (maximum: 2.4 million units)
> *More than 1-year duration:* 50,000 units/kg every week for 3 doses (maximum: 2.4 million units/dose)

Adults: I.M.:

Group A streptococcal upper respiratory infection: 1.2 million units as a single dose

Prophylaxis of recurrent rheumatic fever: 1.2 million units every 3-4 weeks or 600,000 units twice monthly

Syphilis:
> *Early:* 2.4 million units as a single dose in 2 injection sites
> *More than 1-year duration:* 2.4 million units in 2 injection sites once weekly for 3 doses
> *Neurosyphilis:* Not indicated as single-drug therapy, but may be given once weekly for 3 weeks following I.V. treatment; refer to Penicillin G Parenteral/Aqueous monograph for dosing

Administration Administer by deep I.M. injection in the upper outer quadrant of the buttock do **not** administer I.V., intra-arterially, or SubQ; in children <2 years of age, I.M. injections should be made into the midlateral muscle of the thigh, not the gluteal region; when doses are repeated, rotate the injection site

Monitoring Parameters Observe for signs and symptoms of anaphylaxis during first dose

Test Interactions Positive Coombs' [direct], false-positive urinary and/or serum proteins; false-positive or negative urinary glucose using Clinitest®

Dosage Forms Injection, suspension [prefilled syringe]: 600,000 units/mL (1 mL, 2 mL, 4 mL)

Penicillin G Benzathine and Penicillin G Procaine
(pen i SIL in jee BENZ a theen & pen i SIL in jee PROE kane)

U.S. Brand Names Bicillin® C-R; Bicillin® C-R 900/300

Index Terms Penicillin G Procaine and Benzathine Combined

Pharmacologic Category Antibiotic, Penicillin

Use May be used in specific situations in the treatment of streptococcal infections

Pregnancy Risk Factor B

Medication Safety Issues

Bicillin® C-R (penicillin G benzathine and penicillin G procaine) may be confused with Bicillin® L-A (penicillin G benzathine). Penicillin G benzathine is the only product currently approved for the treatment of syphilis. Administration of penicillin G benzathine and penicillin G procaine combination instead of Bicillin® L-A may result in inadequate treatment response.

Penicillin G benzathine may only be administered by deep intramuscular injection; intravenous administration of penicillin G benzathine has been associated with cardiopulmonary arrest and death.

Sound-alike/look-alike issues:

Penicillin may be confused with penicillamine

Bicillin® may be confused with Wycillin®

Dosage

Usual dosage range and indication-specific dosing:

Streptococcal infections:

Children: I.M.:
<14 kg: 600,000 units in a single dose
14-27 kg: 900,000 units to 1.2 million units in a single dose
Children >27 kg and Adults: 2.4 million units in a single dose

Additional Information Complete prescribing information for this medication should be consulted for additional detail.

Dosage Forms Injection, suspension [prefilled syringe]:

Bicillin® C-R:

600,000 units: Penicillin G benzathine 300,000 units and penicillin G procaine 300,000 units per 1 mL (1 mL)

1,200,000 units: Penicillin G benzathine 600,000 units and penicillin G procaine 600,000 units per 2 mL (2 mL)

2,400,000 units: Penicillin G benzathine 1,200,000 units and penicillin G procaine 1,200,000 units per 4 mL (4 mL)

Bicillin® C-R 900/300: 1,200,000 units: Penicillin G benzathine 900,000 units and penicillin G procaine 300,000 units per 2 mL (2 mL)

Penicillin G (Parenteral/Aqueous)
(pen i SIL in jee, pa REN ter al, AYE kwee us)

U.S. Brand Names Pfizerpen®

Canadian Brand Names Pfizerpen®

Index Terms Benzylpenicillin Potassium; Benzylpenicillin Sodium; Crystalline Penicillin; Penicillin G Potassium; Penicillin G Sodium

Pharmacologic Category Antibiotic, Penicillin

Additional Appendix Information
Antibiotic Treatment of Adults With Infective Endocarditis *on page 1977*
Antimicrobial Drugs of Choice *on page 1981*
Desensitization Protocols *on page 1913*
Treatment of Sexually Transmitted Infections *on page 2007*

Use Active against some gram-positive organisms, generally not *Staphylococcus aureus*; some gram-negative organisms such as *Neisseria gonorrhoeae*, and some anaerobes and spirochetes

Pregnancy Risk Factor B

Lactation Enters breast milk/compatible
(Continued)

Penicillin G (Parenteral/Aqueous) *(Continued)*

Medication Safety Issues
Sound-alike/look-alike issues:
Penicillin may be confused with penicillamine

Contraindications Hypersensitivity to penicillin or any component of the formulation

Warnings/Precautions Avoid intra-arterial administration or injection into or near major peripheral nerves or blood vessels since such injections may cause severe and/or permanent neurovascular damage; use with caution in patients with renal impairment (dosage reduction required), pre-existing seizure disorders, or with a history of hypersensitivity to cephalosporins

Adverse Reactions Frequency not defined.
Central nervous system: Convulsions, confusion, drowsiness, myoclonus, fever
Dermatologic: Rash
Endocrine & metabolic: Electrolyte imbalance
Hematologic: Positive Coombs' reaction, hemolytic anemia
Local: Injection site reaction, thrombophlebitis
Renal: Acute interstitial nephritis
Miscellaneous: Anaphylaxis, hypersensitivity reactions, Jarisch-Herxheimer reaction

Overdosage/Toxicology Symptoms of penicillin overdose include neuromuscular hypersensitivity (agitation, hallucinations, asterixis, encephalopathy, confusion, seizures) and electrolyte imbalance with potassium or sodium salts, especially in renal failure. Hemodialysis may be helpful to aid in removal of the drug from the blood, otherwise, most treatment is supportive or symptom-directed.

Drug Interactions
Increased Effect/Toxicity: Probenecid increases penicillin levels. Aminoglycosides may lead to synergistic efficacy. Penicillins may increase the exposure to methotrexate during concurrent therapy; monitor.

Decreased Effect: Tetracyclines may decrease penicillin effectiveness. Although anecdotal reports suggest oral contraceptive efficacy could be reduced by penicillins, this has been refuted by more rigorous scientific and clinical data.

Stability
Penicillin G potassium powder for injection should be stored below 86°F (30°C). Following reconstitution, solution may be stored for up to 7 days under refrigeration. Premixed bags for infusion should be stored in the freezer (-20°C to -4°F); frozen bags may be thawed at room temperature or in refrigerator. Once thawed, solution is stable for 14 days if stored in refrigerator or for 24 hours when stored at room temperature. Do not refreeze once thawed.

Penicillin G sodium powder for injection should be stored at controlled room temperature. Reconstituted solution may be stored under refrigeration for up to 3 days.

Mechanism of Action Interferes with bacterial cell wall synthesis during active multiplication, causing cell wall death and resultant bactericidal activity against susceptible bacteria

Pharmacodynamics/Kinetics
Distribution: Poor penetration across blood-brain barrier, despite inflamed meninges; crosses placenta; enters breast milk
Relative diffusion from blood into CSF: Good only with inflammation (exceeds usual MICs)
CSF:blood level ratio: Normal meninges: <1%; Inflamed meninges: 3% to 5%
Protein binding: 65%
Metabolism: Hepatic (30%) to penicilloic acid
Half-life elimination:
Neonates: <6 days old: 3.2-3.4 hours; 7-13 days old: 1.2-2.2 hours; >14 days old: 0.9-1.9 hours
Children and Adults: Normal renal function: 20-50 minutes
End-stage renal disease: 3.3-5.1 hours
Time to peak, serum: I.M.: ~30 minutes; I.V. ~1 hour
Excretion: Urine

Dosage
Usual dosage range:
Neonates: I.M., I.V.:
<7 days, <2000 g: 25,000-50,000 units/kg every 12 hours
<7 days, >2000 g: 25,000-50,000 units/kg every 8 hours
>7 days, <2000 g: 25,000-50,000 units/kg every 8 hours
>7 days, >2000 g: 25,000-50,000 units/kg every 6 hours
Infants and Children: I.M., I.V.: 25,000-400,000 units/kg/day in divided doses every 4-6 hours (maximum dose: 24 million units/day)
Adults: I.M., I.V.: 2-24 million units/day in divided doses every 4 hours depending on sensitivity of the organism and severity of the infection
Indication-specific dosing:
Infants and Children:
Gonococcal:
Disseminated or ophthalmia: I.V.: 100,000 units/kg/day in 2 divided doses (>1 week of age: 4 divided doses)
Meningitis: I.V.: 150,000 units/kg in 2 divided doses (>1 week of age: 4 divided doses)
Mild infections: I.M., I.V.: 25,000-50,000 units/kg/day in 4 divided doses
Moderate infections: I.M., I.V.: 100,000-200,000 units/kg/day in 4 divided doses
Severe infections: I.M., I.V.: 250,000-400,000 units/kg/day in divided doses every 4-6 hours (maximum dose: 24 million units/day)
Syphilis (congenital):
Neonates:
≤7 days: 50,000 units/kg I.V. every 12 hours for a total of 10 days
>7 days: 50,000 units/kg I.V. every 8 hours for a total of 10 days
Infants: I.V.: 50,000 units/kg every 4-6 hours for 10 days

Adults:
Actinomyces species: I.V.: 10-20 million units/day divided every 4-6 hours for 4-6 weeks

Anthrax (cutaneous): I.V.: 2 million units every 3 hours for 5-7 days

Clostridium perfringens: I.V.: 24 million units/day divided every 4-6 hours with clindamycin

Corynebacterium diphtheriae: I.V.: 25,000-50,000 units/kg to maximum 1.2 million units every 12 hours, until oral therapy tolerated

Erysipelas: I.V.: 1-2 million units every 4-6 hours

Erysipelothrix: I.V.: 2-4 million units every 4 hours

Fascial space infections: I.V.: 2-4 million units every 4-6 hours with metronidazole

Leptospirosis: I.V.: 1.5 million units every 6 hours for 7 days

Listeria: I.V.: 300,000 units/kg/day every 4 hours

Lyme disease (meningitis): I.V.: 20 million units/day in divided doses

Neurosyphilis: I.M., I.V.: 18-24 million units/day in divided doses every 4 hours (or by continuous infusion) for 10-14 days

Streptococcus:
Brain abscess: I.V.: 20-24 million units/day in divided doses with metronidazole
Endocarditis or osteomyelitis: I.V.: 3-4 million units every 4 hours for at least 4 weeks
Meningitis: I.V.: 3-4 million units every 4 hours for 2-3 weeks
Pregnancy (prophylaxis GBS): I.V.: 5-6 million units x 1 dose, then 2.5-3 million units every 4 hours until delivery
Skin and soft tissue: I.V.: 3-4 million units every 4 hours for 10 days
Toxic shock: I.V.: 24 million units/day in divided doses with clindamycin

Streptococcal pneumonia:
Meningitis: I.V.: 2-4 million units every 2-4 hours
Nonmeningitis: I.V.: 2-3 million units every 4 hours

Whipple's disease: I.V.: 2 million units every 4 hours (with streptomycin) for 10-14 days, followed by oral trimethoprim/sulfamethoxazole or doxycycline for 1 year

Dosing interval in renal impairment:
Cl$_{cr}$ >10 mL/minute: Administer full loading dose followed by ½ loading dose given every 4-5 hours
Cl$_{cr}$ <10 mL/minute: Administer full loading dose followed by ½ loading dose given every 8-10 hours

Dietary Considerations Injection powder for reconstitution as potassium contains sodium 6.8 mg (0.3 mEq) and potassium 65.6 mg (1.68 mEq) per 1 million units

Administration Administer I.M. by deep injection in the upper outer quadrant of the buttock

Monitoring Parameters Observe for signs and symptoms of anaphylaxis during first dose

Test Interactions False-positive or negative urinary glucose determination using Clinitest®; positive Coombs' [direct]; false-positive urinary and/or serum proteins

Additional Information 1 million units is approximately equal to 625 mg.

Dosage Forms
Infusion, as potassium [premixed iso-osmotic dextrose solution, frozen]: 1 million units (50 mL), 2 million units (50 mL), 3 million units (50 mL) [contains sodium 1.02 mEq and potassium 1.7 mEq per 1 million units]
Injection, powder for reconstitution, as potassium (Pfizerpen®): 5 million units, 20 million units [contains sodium 6.8 mg (0.3 mEq) and potassium 65.6 mg (1.68 mEq) per 1 million units]
Injection, powder for reconstitution, as sodium: 5 million units [contains sodium 1.68 mEq per 1 million units]

♦ **Penicillin G Potassium** *see* Penicillin G (Parenteral/Aqueous) *on page 1333*

Penicillin G Procaine (pen i SIL in jee PROE kane)

Canadian Brand Names Pfizerpen-AS®; Wycillin®
Index Terms APPG; Aqueous Procaine Penicillin G; Procaine Benzylpenicillin; Procaine Penicillin G; Wycillin [DSC]
Pharmacologic Category Antibiotic, Penicillin
Additional Appendix Information
Treatment of Sexually Transmitted Infections *on page 2007*
Use Moderately severe infections due to *Treponema pallidum* and other penicillin G-sensitive microorganisms that are susceptible to low, but prolonged serum penicillin concentrations; anthrax due to *Bacillus anthracis* (postexposure) to reduce the incidence or progression of disease following exposure to aerolized *Bacillus anthracis*
Pregnancy Risk Factor B
Lactation Enters breast milk/compatible
Medication Safety Issues
Sound-alike/look-alike issues:
Penicillin G procaine may be confused with penicillin V potassium
Wycillin® may be confused with Bicillin®
Contraindications Hypersensitivity to penicillin, procaine, or any component of the formulation
Warnings/Precautions May need to modify dosage in patients with severe renal impairment, seizure disorders, or history of hypersensitivity to cephalosporins; avoid I.V., intravascular, or intra-arterial administration of penicillin G procaine since severe and/or permanent neurovascular damage may occur; use of penicillin for longer than 2 weeks may be associated with an increased risk for some adverse reactions (neutropenia, serum sickness)
Adverse Reactions Frequency not defined.
Cardiovascular: Myocardial depression, vasodilation, conduction disturbances
Central nervous system: Confusion, drowsiness, myoclonus, CNS stimulation, seizure
Hematologic: Positive Coombs' reaction, hemolytic anemia, neutropenia
Local: Pain at injection site, thrombophlebitis, sterile abscess at injection site
Renal: Interstitial nephritis
(Continued)

Penicillin G Procaine *(Continued)*

Miscellaneous: Pseudoanaphylactic reactions, hypersensitivity reactions, Jarisch-Herxheimer reaction, serum sickness

Overdosage/Toxicology Symptoms of penicillin overdose include neuromuscular hypersensitivity (agitation, hallucinations, asterixis, encephalopathy, confusion, seizures) and electrolyte imbalance with potassium or sodium salts, especially in renal failure. Hemodialysis may be helpful to aid in removal of the drug from the blood, otherwise, most treatment is supportive or symptom-directed.

Drug Interactions

Increased Effect/Toxicity: Probenecid increases penicillin levels. Aminoglycosides may lead to synergistic efficacy. Penicillins may increase the exposure to methotrexate during concurrent therapy; monitor.

Decreased Effect: Tetracyclines may decrease penicillin effectiveness. Although anecdotal reports suggest oral contraceptive efficacy could be reduced by penicillins, this has been refuted by more rigorous scientific and clinical data.

Stability Refrigerate

Mechanism of Action Inhibits bacterial cell wall synthesis by binding to one or more of the penicillin binding proteins (PBPs); which in turn inhibits the final transpeptidation step of peptidoglycan synthesis in bacterial cell walls, thus inhibiting cell wall biosynthesis. Bacteria eventually lyse due to ongoing activity of cell wall autolytic enzymes (autolysins and murein hydrolases) while cell wall assembly is arrested.

Pharmacodynamics/Kinetics

Duration: Therapeutic: 15-24 hours

Absorption: I.M.: Slow

Distribution: Penetration across the blood-brain barrier is poor, despite inflamed meninges; enters breast milk

Protein binding: 65%

Metabolism: ~30% hepatically inactivated

Time to peak, serum: 1-4 hours

Excretion: Urine (60% to 90% as unchanged drug)

Clearance: Renal: Delayed in neonates, young infants, and with impaired renal function

Dosage

Usual dosage range:

Infants and Children: I.M.: 25,000-50,000 units/kg/day in divided doses 1-2 times/day; (maximum: 4.8 million units/day)

Adults: I.M.: 0.6-4.8 million units/day in divided doses every 12-24 hours

Indication-specific dosing:

Children: I.M.:

Anthrax, inhalational (postexposure prophylaxis): 25,000 units/kg every 12 hours (maximum: 1,200,000 units every 12 hours); see "Note" in Adults dosing

Syphilis (congenital): 50,000 units/kg/day for 10 days; if more than 1 day of therapy is missed, the entire course should be restarted

Adults: I.M.:

Anthrax:

Inhalational (postexposure prophylaxis): 1,200,000 units every 12 hours

Note: Overall treatment duration should be 60 days. Available safety data suggest continued administration of penicillin G procaine for longer than 2 weeks may incur additional risk for adverse reactions. Clinicians may consider switching to effective alternative treatment for completion of therapy beyond 2 weeks.

Cutaneous (treatment): 600,000-1,200,000 units/day; alternative therapy is recommended in severe cutaneous or other forms of anthrax infection

Endocarditis caused by susceptible viridans *Streptococcus* (when used in conjunction with an aminoglycoside): 1.2 million units every 6 hours for 2-4 weeks

Gonorrhea (uncomplicated): 4.8 million units as a single dose divided in 2 sites given 30 minutes after probenecid 1 g orally

Neurosyphilis: 2.4 million units/day with 500 mg probenecid by mouth 4 times/day for 10-14 days; **Note: Penicillin G aqueous I.V. is the preferred agent**

Whipple's disease: 1.2 million units/day (with streptomycin) for 10-14 days, followed by oral trimethoprim/sulfamethoxazole or doxycycline for 1 year

Hemodialysis: Moderately dialyzable (20% to 50%)

Administration Procaine suspension for deep I.M. injection only; do not inject in gluteal muscle in children <2 years of age; rotate the injection site; avoid I.V., intravascular, or intra-arterial administration of penicillin G procaine since severe and/or permanent neurovascular damage may occur

Monitoring Parameters Periodic renal and hematologic function tests with prolonged therapy; fever, mental status, WBC count

Test Interactions Positive Coombs' [direct], false-positive urinary and/or serum proteins

Dosage Forms Injection, suspension: 600,000 units/mL (1 mL, 2 mL)

♦ **Penicillin G Procaine and Benzathine Combined** *see* Penicillin G Benzathine and Penicillin G Procaine *on page 1333*

♦ **Penicillin G Sodium** *see* Penicillin G (Parenteral/Aqueous) *on page 1333*

Penicillin V Potassium *(pen i SIL in vee poe TASS ee um)*

Canadian Brand Names Apo-Pen VK®; Novo-Pen-VK; Nu-Pen-VK

Index Terms Pen VK; Phenoxymethyl Penicillin

Pharmacologic Category Antibiotic, Penicillin

Additional Appendix Information

Antimicrobial Drugs of Choice *on page 1981*

Desensitization Protocols *on page 1913*

Use Treatment of infections caused by susceptible organisms involving the respiratory tract, otitis media, sinusitis, skin, and urinary tract; prophylaxis in rheumatic fever

Pregnancy Risk Factor B

Lactation Enters breast milk (other penicillins are compatible with breast-feeding)

Medication Safety Issues
Sound-alike/look-alike issues:
Penicillin V procaine may be confused with penicillin G potassium

Contraindications Hypersensitivity to penicillin or any component of the formulation

Warnings/Precautions Use with caution in patients with severe renal impairment (modify dosage), history of seizures, or hypersensitivity to cephalosporins

Adverse Reactions
>10%: Gastrointestinal: Mild diarrhea, vomiting, nausea, oral candidiasis
<1% (Limited to important or life-threatening): Acute interstitial nephritis, convulsions, hemolytic anemia, positive Coombs' reaction

Overdosage/Toxicology Symptoms of penicillin overdose include neuromuscular hypersensitivity (agitation, hallucinations, asterixis, encephalopathy, confusion, seizures) and electrolyte imbalance with potassium or sodium salts, especially in renal failure. Hemodialysis may be helpful to aid in removal of the drug from the blood, otherwise, most treatment is supportive or symptom-directed.

Drug Interactions
Increased Effect/Toxicity: Probenecid increases penicillin levels. Aminoglycosides may cause synergistic efficacy. Penicillins may increase the exposure to methotrexate during concurrent therapy; monitor.
Decreased Effect: Tetracyclines may decrease penicillin effectiveness. Although anecdotal reports suggest oral contraceptive efficacy could be reduced by penicillins, this has been refuted by more rigorous scientific and clinical data.

Ethanol/Nutrition/Herb Interactions Food: Decreases drug absorption rate; decreases drug serum concentration.

Stability Refrigerate suspension after reconstitution; discard after 14 days

Mechanism of Action Inhibits bacterial cell wall synthesis by binding to one or more of the penicillin binding proteins (PBPs); which in turn inhibits the final transpeptidation step of peptidoglycan synthesis in bacterial cell walls, thus inhibiting cell wall biosynthesis. Bacteria eventually lyse due to ongoing activity of cell wall autolytic enzymes (autolysins and murein hydrolases) while cell wall assembly is arrested.

Pharmacodynamics/Kinetics
Absorption: 60% to 73%
Distribution: Enters breast milk
Protein binding, plasma: 80%
Half-life elimination: 30 minutes; prolonged with renal impairment
Time to peak, serum: 0.5-1 hour
Excretion: Urine (as unchanged drug and metabolites)

Dosage
Usual dosage range:
Children <12 years: Oral: 25-50 mg/kg/day in divided doses every 6-8 hours (maximum dose: 3 g/day)
Children ≥12 years and Adults: Oral: 125-500 mg every 6-8 hours
Indication-specific dosing:
Children: Oral:
Pharyngitis (streptococcal): 250 mg 2-3 times/day for 10 days
Prophylaxis of pneumococcal infections:
Children <5 years: 125 mg twice daily
Children ≥5 years: 250 mg twice daily
Prophylaxis of recurrent rheumatic fever:
Children <5 years: 125 mg twice daily
Children ≥5 years: 250 mg twice daily
Adults: Oral:
Acintomycosis:
Mild: 2-4 g/day in 4 divided doses for 8 weeks
Surgical: 2-4 g/day in 4 divided doses for 6-12 months (after I.V. penicillin G therapy of 4-6 weeks)
Erysipelas: 500 mg 4 times/day
Periodontal infections: 250-500 mg every 6 hours for 5-7 days
Note: Efficacy of antimicrobial therapy in periapical abscess is questionable; the American Academy of Periodontology recommends use of antibiotic therapy only when systemic symptoms (eg, fever, lymphadenopathy) are present or in immunocompromised patients.
Pharyngitis (streptococcal): 500 mg 3-4 times/day for 10 days
Prophylaxis of pneumococcal or recurrent rheumatic fever infections: 250 mg twice daily

Dosing interval in renal impairment: Cl_{cr} <10 mL/minute: Administer 250 mg every 6 hours

Dietary Considerations Take on an empty stomach 1 hour before or 2 hours after meals.

Administration Administer on an empty stomach to increase oral absorption

Monitoring Parameters Periodic renal and hematologic function tests during prolonged therapy; monitor for signs of anaphylaxis during first dose

Test Interactions False-positive or negative urinary glucose determination using Clinitest®; positive Coombs' [direct]; false-positive urinary and/or serum proteins

Additional Information 0.7 mEq of potassium per 250 mg penicillin V; 250 mg equals 400,000 units of penicillin

Dosage Forms Note: 250 mg = 400,000 units
Powder for oral solution: 125 mg/5 mL (100 mL, 200 mL); 250 mg/5 mL (100 mL, 200 mL)
Tablet: 250 mg, 500 mg

- ♦ **Penicilloyl-polylysine** *see* Benzylpenicilloyl-polylysine *on page 209*
- ♦ **Penlac®** *see* Ciclopirox *on page 366*
- ♦ **Pennsaid® (Can)** *see* Diclofenac *on page 492*

♦ **Pentahydrate** *see Sodium Thiosulfate on page 1584*
♦ **Pentam-300®** *see Pentamidine on page 1338*

Pentamidine (pen TAM i deen)

U.S. Brand Names NebuPent®; Pentam-300®
Index Terms Pentamidine Isethionate
Pharmacologic Category Antibiotic, Miscellaneous
Additional Appendix Information
USPHS / IDSA Guidelines for the Prevention of Opportunistic Infections in Persons Infected With HIV *on page 1966*
Use Treatment and prevention of pneumonia caused by *Pneumocystis carinii* (PCP)
Unlabeled/Investigational Use Treatment of trypanosomiasis and visceral leishmaniasis
Pregnancy Risk Factor C
Lactation Excretion in breast milk unknown/contraindicated
Contraindications Hypersensitivity to pentamidine isethionate or any component of the formulation (inhalation and injection)
Warnings/Precautions Use with caution in patients with diabetes mellitus, renal or hepatic dysfunction; hypertension or hypotension; leukopenia, thrombocytopenia, asthma, hypo/hyperglycemia
Adverse Reactions
Inhalation:
>10%:
Cardiovascular: Chest pain
Dermatologic: Rash
Respiratory: Wheezing, dyspnea, cough, pharyngitis
1% to 10%: Gastrointestinal: Bitter or metallic taste
<1% (Limited to important or life-threatening): Hypoglycemia, renal insufficiency
Systemic:
>10%:
Cardiovascular: Hypotension
Dermatologic: Rash
Endocrine & metabolic: Hyperglycemia or hypoglycemia
Gastrointestinal: Nausea, vomiting, anorexia, diarrhea
Hematologic: Leukopenia or neutropenia, thrombocytopenia
Hepatic: Elevated LFTs
Renal: Nephrotoxicity
1% to 10%:
Cardiovascular: Cardiac arrhythmia
Gastrointestinal: Pancreatitis, metallic taste
Hematologic: Anemia
Local: Local reactions at injection site
<1% (Limited to important or life-threatening): Arrhythmia
Overdosage/Toxicology Symptoms include hypotension, hypoglycemia, and cardiac arrhythmias. Treatment is supportive.
Drug Interactions
Cytochrome P450 Effect: Substrate of CYP2C19 (major); **Inhibits** CYP2C8/9 (weak), 2C19 (weak), 2D6 (weak), 3A4 (weak)
Increased Effect/Toxicity: CYP2C19 inhibitors may increase the levels/effects of pentamidine; example inhibitors include delavirdine, fluconazole, fluvoxamine, gemfibrozil, isoniazid, omeprazole, and ticlopidine. Pentamidine may potentiate the effect of other drugs which prolong QT interval (cisapride, sparfloxacin, gatifloxacin, moxifloxacin, pimozide, and type Ia and type III antiarrhythmics).
Decreased Effect: CYP2C19 inducers may decrease the levels/effects of pentamidine; example inducers include aminoglutethimide, carbamazepine, phenytoin, and rifampin.
Ethanol/Nutrition/Herb Interactions Ethanol: Avoid ethanol (may increase CNS depression or aggravate hypoglycemia).
Stability Store intact vials at controlled room temperature. Protect from light. Reconstituted vials with SWFI (60-100 mg/mL) are stable for 48 hours at room temperature protected from light. Diluted solutions in 50-250 mL D$_5$W for infusion (1-2.5 mg/mL) are stable for at least 24 hours at room temperature.
Powder for inhalation should be reconstituted with SWFI (6 mL per 300 mg vial).
Powder for injection may be reconstituted with SWFI or D$_5$W (SWFI should be used for I.M. injections). **Do not use NS as a diluent.**
Mechanism of Action Interferes with RNA/DNA, phospholipids and protein synthesis, through inhibition of oxidative phosphorylation and/or interference with incorporation of nucleotides and nucleic acids into RNA and DNA, in protozoa
Pharmacodynamics/Kinetics
Absorption: I.M.: Well absorbed; Inhalation: Limited systemic absorption
Half-life elimination: Terminal: 6.4-9.4 hours; may be prolonged with severe renal impairment
Excretion: Urine (33% to 66% as unchanged drug)
Dosage
Children:
Treatment of PCP pneumonia: I.M., I.V. (I.V. preferred): 4 mg/kg/day once daily for 10-14 days
Prevention of PCP pneumonia:
I.M., I.V.: 4 mg/kg monthly or every 2 weeks
Inhalation (aerosolized pentamidine in children ≥5 years): 300 mg/dose given every 3-4 weeks via Respirgard® II inhaler (8 mg/kg dose has also been used in children <5 years)
Treatment of trypanosomiasis (unlabeled use): I.V.: 4 mg/kg/day once daily for 10 days
Adults:
Treatment: I.M., I.V. (I.V. preferred): 4 mg/kg/day once daily for 14-21 days

Prevention: Inhalation: 300 mg every 4 weeks via Respirgard® II nebulizer

Dialysis: Not removed by hemo or peritoneal dialysis or continuous arteriovenous or venovenous hemofiltration; supplemental dosage is not necessary

Dosing adjustment in renal impairment: Adults: I.V.:

Cl_{cr} 10-50 mL/minute: Administer 4 mg/kg every 24-36 hours

Cl_{cr} <10 mL/minute: Administer 4 mg/kg every 48 hours

Administration

Inhalation: Deliver until nebulizer is gone (30-45 minutes)

I.V.: Infuse slowly over a period of at least 60 minutes or administer deep I.M.

Monitoring Parameters Liver function tests, renal function tests, blood glucose, serum potassium and calcium, ECG, blood pressure

Additional Information Virtually undetectable amounts are transferred to healthcare personnel during aerosol administration.

Dosage Forms

Injection, powder for reconstitution, as isethionate [preservative free]:

Pentam-300®: 300 mg

Powder for nebulization, as isethionate [preservative free]:

NebuPent®: 300 mg

♦ **Pentamidine Isethionate** see Pentamidine on page 1338

♦ **Pentamycetin® (Can)** see Chloramphenicol on page 341

♦ **Pentasa®** see Mesalamine on page 1089

♦ **Penta-Triamterene HCTZ (Can)** see Hydrochlorothiazide and Triamterene on page 847

♦ **Pentavalent Human-Bovine Reassortant Rotavirus Vaccine** see Rotavirus Vaccine on page 1539

Pentazocine (pen TAZ oh seen)

U.S. Brand Names Talwin®; Talwin® NX

Canadian Brand Names Talwin®

Index Terms Naloxone Hydrochloride and Pentazocine Hydrochloride; Pentazocine Hydrochloride; Pentazocine Hydrochloride and Naloxone Hydrochloride; Pentazocine Lactate

Pharmacologic Category Analgesic, Opioid

Additional Appendix Information

Narcotic Agonists on page 1888

Use Relief of moderate to severe pain; has also been used as a sedative prior to surgery and as a supplement to surgical anesthesia

Restrictions C-IV

Pregnancy Risk Factor C/D (prolonged use or high doses at term)

Pregnancy Implications Pentazocine was not found to be teratogenic in animal studies. Pentazocine and naloxone have been shown to cross the human placenta. Use should be avoided during labor and delivery of premature infants. Abstinence syndromes in the newborn have been reported after long-term use of pentazocine during pregnancy. Other adverse effects in the newborn have been reported following abuse of pentazocine during pregnancy; these effects may be due to pentazocine, other drugs abused, the mother's lifestyle, or a combination of all factors.

Lactation Excretion in breast milk unknown/use caution

Contraindications Hypersensitivity to pentazocine, naloxone, or any component of the formulation; increased intracranial pressure (unless the patient is mechanically ventilated); pregnancy (prolonged use or high doses at term)

Warnings/Precautions May cause CNS depression, which may impair physical or mental abilities; patients must be cautioned about performing tasks which require mental alertness (eg, operating machinery or driving). Effects may be potentiated when used with other sedative drugs or ethanol. Use with caution in seizure-prone patients, acute myocardial infarction, patients undergoing biliary tract impairment, thyroid dysfunction, prostatic hyperplasia/urinary stricture, patients with respiratory, adrenal insufficiency, morbid obesity, renal and hepatic dysfunction, head trauma, increased intracranial pressure, and patients with a history of prior opioid dependence or abuse; pentazocine may precipitate opiate withdrawal symptoms in patients who have been receiving opiates regularly; injection contains sulfites which may cause allergic reaction; tolerance or drug dependence may result from extended use. May cause hypotension; use with caution in patients with hypovolemia, cardiovascular disease (including acute MI), or drugs which may exaggerate hypotensive effects (including phenothiazines or general anesthetics). May obscure diagnosis or clinical course of patients with acute abdominal conditions. **[U.S. Boxed Warning]: Talwin® NX is intended for oral administration only - severe vascular reactions have resulted from misuse by injection.** Severe sclerosis has occurred at the injection-site following multiple injections; rotate sites of injection. Use with caution in the elderly and debilitated patients; may be more sensitive adverse effects. Safety and efficacy have not been established in children <1 year of age.

Adverse Reactions Frequency not defined.

Cardiovascular: Circulatory depression, facial edema, flushing, hypotension, shock, syncope, tachycardia

Central nervous system: Chills, CNS depression, confusion, disorientation, dizziness, drowsiness, euphoria, excitement, hallucinations, headache, insomnia, irritability, lightheadedness, malaise, nightmares, sedation

Dermatologic: dermatitis, erythema multiforme, pruritus, rash, Stevens-Johnson syndrome, toxic epidermal necrolysis, urticaria

Gastrointestinal: Abdominal distress, anorexia, constipation, diarrhea, nausea, vomiting, xerostomia

Genitourinary: Urinary retention

Hematologic: Decreased WBCs, eosinophilia

Local: Tissue damage and irritation with I.M./SubQ use

Neuromuscular & skeletal: Paresthesia, tremor, weakness

(Continued)

Pentazocine *(Continued)*

Ocular: Blurred vision, miosis

Otic: Tinnitus

Respiratory: Dyspnea, respiratory depression (rare)

Miscellaneous: Anaphylaxis, diaphoresis, physical and psychological dependence

Overdosage/Toxicology Symptoms include drowsiness, sedation, respiratory depression, and coma. Treatment consists of naloxone 2 mg I.V. (0.01 mg/kg for children), with repeat administration as necessary, up to a total of 10 mg.

Drug Interactions

Increased Effect/Toxicity: Increased effect/toxicity with tripelennamine (can be lethal), CNS depressants (eg, phenothiazines, tranquilizers, anxiolytics, sedatives, hypnotics, alcohol).

Decreased Effect: May potentiate or reduce analgesic effect of opiate agonist (eg, morphine) depending on patients tolerance to opiates; can precipitate withdrawal in narcotic addicts.

Ethanol/Nutrition/Herb Interactions Ethanol: Avoid ethanol (may increase CNS depression).

Stability Store at room temperature; do not freeze. Protect from heat.

Mechanism of Action Binds to opiate receptors in the CNS, causing inhibition of ascending pain pathways, altering the perception of and response to pain; produces generalized CNS depression; partial agonist-antagonist

Pharmacodynamics/Kinetics

Onset of action: Oral, I.M., SubQ: 15-30 minutes; I.V.: 2-3 minutes

Duration: Oral: 4-5 hours; Parenteral: 2-3 hours

Protein binding: 60%

Metabolism: Hepatic via oxidative and glucuronide conjugation pathways; extensive first-pass effect

Bioavailability: Oral: ~20%; increased to 60% to 70% with cirrhosis

Half-life elimination: 2-3 hours; prolonged with hepatic impairment

Excretion: Urine (small amounts as unchanged drug)

Dosage

Preoperative/preanesthetic: Children 1-16 years: I.M.: 0.5 mg/kg

Analgesia:

Children: I.M.:

5-8 years: 15 mg

8-14 years: 30 mg

Children >12 years and Adults: Oral: 50 mg every 3-4 hours; may increase to 100 mg/dose if needed, but should not exceed 600 mg/day

Adults:

I.M., SubQ: 30-60 mg every 3-4 hours; do not exceed 60 mg/dose (maximum: 360 mg/day)

I.V.: 30 mg every 3-4 hours; do not exceed 30 mg/dose (maximum: 360 mg/day)

Elderly: Elderly patients may be more sensitive to the analgesic and sedating effects. The elderly may also have impaired renal function. If needed, dosing should be started at the lower end of dosing range and adjust dose for renal function.

Dosing adjustment in renal impairment:

Cl_{cr} 10-50 mL/minute: Administer 75% of normal dose

Cl_{cr} <10 mL/minute: Administer 50% of normal dose

Dosing adjustment in hepatic impairment: Reduce dose or avoid use in patients with liver disease

Administration Rotate injection site for I.M., SubQ use; avoid intra-arterial injection; avoid SubQ use unless absolutely necessary (may cause tissue damage)

Monitoring Parameters Relief of pain, respiratory and mental status, blood pressure

Additional Information Pentazocine hydrochloride: Talwin® NX tablet (with naloxone); naloxone is used to prevent abuse by dissolving tablets in water and using as injection.

Dosage Forms

Injection, solution:

Talwin®: 30 mg/mL (1 mL, 10 mL) [10 mL size contains sodium bisulfite]

Tablet: Pentazocine 50 mg and naloxone 0.5 mg

Talwin® NX: Pentazocine 50 mg and naloxone 0.5 mg

♦ **Pentazocine Hydrochloride** *see* Pentazocine *on page 1339*

♦ **Pentazocine Hydrochloride and Naloxone Hydrochloride** *see* Pentazocine *on page 1339*

♦ **Pentazocine Lactate** *see* Pentazocine *on page 1339*

Pentobarbital *(pen toe BAR bi tal)*

U.S. Brand Names Nembutal®

Canadian Brand Names Nembutal® Sodium

Index Terms Pentobarbital Sodium

Pharmacologic Category Anticonvulsant, Barbiturate; Barbiturate

Use Sedative/hypnotic; preanesthetic; high-dose barbiturate coma for treatment of increased intracranial pressure or status epilepticus unresponsive to other therapy

Restrictions C-II

Pregnancy Risk Factor D

Lactation Enters breast milk/contraindicated

Medication Safety Issues

Sound-alike/look-alike issues:

Pentobarbital may be confused with phenobarbital

Nembutal® may be confused with Myambutol®

Contraindications Hypersensitivity to barbiturates or any component of the formulation; marked hepatic impairment; dyspnea or airway obstruction; porphyria; pregnancy

Warnings/Precautions Tolerance to hypnotic effect can occur; do not use for >2 weeks to treat insomnia. Potential for drug dependency exists; abrupt cessation may precipitate withdrawal, including status epilepticus in epileptic patients. Do not administer to patients in acute pain. Use caution in elderly, debilitated, renally impaired, hepatic dysfunction, or pediatric patients. May cause paradoxical responses, including agitation and hyperactivity, particularly in acute pain and pediatric patients. Use with caution in patients with depression or suicidal tendencies, or in patients with a history of drug abuse. Tolerance, psychological and physical dependence may occur with prolonged use.

May cause CNS depression, which may impair physical or mental abilities. Patients must be cautioned about performing tasks which require mental alertness (eg, operating machinery or driving). Effects with other sedative drugs or ethanol may be potentiated. Use of this agent as a hypnotic in the elderly is not recommended due to its long half-life and potential for physical and psychological dependence.

May cause respiratory depression or hypotension, particularly when administered intravenously. Use with caution in hemodynamically unstable patients or patients with respiratory disease. High doses (loading doses of 15-35 mg/kg given over 1-2 hours) have been utilized to induce pentobarbital coma, but these higher doses often cause hypotension requiring vasopressor therapy.

Adverse Reactions Frequency not defined.
Cardiovascular: Bradycardia, hypotension, syncope
Central nervous system: Drowsiness, lethargy, CNS excitation or depression, impaired judgment, "hangover" effect, confusion, somnolence, agitation, hyperkinesia, ataxia, nervousness, headache, insomnia, nightmares, hallucinations, anxiety, dizziness
Dermatologic: Rash, exfoliative dermatitis, Stevens-Johnson syndrome
Gastrointestinal: Nausea, vomiting, constipation
Hematologic: Agranulocytosis, thrombocytopenia, megaloblastic anemia
Local: Pain at injection site, thrombophlebitis with I.V. use
Renal: Oliguria
Respiratory: Laryngospasm, respiratory depression, apnea (especially with rapid I.V. use), hypoventilation
Miscellaneous: Gangrene with inadvertent intra-arterial injection

Overdosage/Toxicology Symptoms include unsteady gait, slurred speech, confusion, jaundice, hypothermia, hypotension, respiratory depression, and coma. If hypotension occurs, administer I.V. fluids and place in the Trendelenburg position. If unresponsive, an I.V. vasopressor (eg, dopamine, epinephrine) may be required. Forced alkaline diuresis is of no value in the treatment of intoxications with short-acting barbiturates. Charcoal hemoperfusion or hemodialysis may be useful in harder-to-treat intoxications, especially in the presence of very high serum barbiturate levels when the patient is in a coma, shock, or renal failure.

Drug Interactions
Cytochrome P450 Effect: Induces CYP2A6 (strong), 3A4 (strong)
Increased Effect/Toxicity: When combined with other CNS depressants, ethanol, opioid analgesics, antidepressants, or benzodiazepines, additive respiratory and CNS depression may occur. Barbiturates may enhance the hepatotoxic potential of acetaminophen overdoses. Chloramphenicol, MAO inhibitors, valproic acid, and felbamate may inhibit barbiturate metabolism. Barbiturates may impair the absorption of griseofulvin, and may enhance the nephrotoxic effects of methoxyflurane.
Decreased Effect: Pentobarbital may decrease the levels/effects of benzodiazepines, calcium channel blockers, clarithromycin, cyclosporine, erythromycin, ifosfamide, mirtazapine, nateglinide, nefazodone, nevirapine, protease inhibitors, rifampin, tacrolimus, venlafaxine, and other CYP2A6 or 3A4 substrates. Barbiturates may increase the metabolism of estrogens and reduce the efficacy of oral contraceptives; an alternative method of contraception should be considered. Barbiturates inhibit the hypoprothrombinemic effects of oral anticoagulants via increased metabolism. Barbiturates may enhance the metabolism of methadone resulting in methadone withdrawal.

Ethanol/Nutrition/Herb Interactions Ethanol: Avoid ethanol (may increase CNS depression).

Stability Protect from freezing. Aqueous solutions are not stable; a commercially available vehicle (containing propylene glycol) is more stable. When mixed with an acidic solution, precipitate may form. Use only clear solution.

Mechanism of Action Short-acting barbiturate with sedative, hypnotic, and anticonvulsant properties. Barbiturates depress the sensory cortex, decrease motor activity, alter cerebellar function, and produce drowsiness, sedation, and hypnosis. In high doses, barbiturates exhibit anticonvulsant activity; barbiturates produce dose-dependent respiratory depression.

Pharmacodynamics/Kinetics
Onset of action: I.M.: 10-15 minutes; I.V.: ~1 minute
Duration: I.V.: 15 minutes
Distribution: V_d: Children: 0.8 L/kg; Adults: 1 L/kg
Protein binding: 35% to 55%
Metabolism: Extensively hepatic via hydroxylation and oxidation pathways
Half-life elimination: Terminal: Children: 25 hours; Adults: Healthy: 22 hours (range: 15-50 hours)
Excretion: Urine (<1% as unchanged drug)

Dosage
Children:
Hypnotic: I.M.: 2-6 mg/kg; maximum: 100 mg/dose
Preoperative/preprocedure sedation: ≥6 months:
Note: Limited information is available for infants <6 months of age.
I.M.: 2-6 mg/kg; maximum: 100 mg/dose
I.V.: 1-3 mg/kg to a maximum of 100 mg until asleep
Conscious sedation prior to a procedure: Children 5-12 years: I.V.: 2 mg/kg 5-10 minutes before procedures, may repeat one time
Adolescents: Conscious sedation: I.V.: 100 mg prior to a procedure
(Continued)

Pentobarbital *(Continued)*

Children and Adults: Barbiturate coma in head injury patients: I.V.: Loading dose: 5-10 mg/kg given slowly over 1-2 hours; monitor blood pressure and respiratory rate; Maintenance infusion: Initial: 1 mg/kg/hour; may increase to 2-3 mg/kg/hour; maintain burst suppression on EEG

Status epilepticus: I.V.: **Note**: Intubation required; monitor hemodynamics

Children: Loading dose: 5-15 mg/kg given slowly over 1-2 hours; maintenance infusion: 0.5-5 mg/kg/hour

Adults: Loading dose: 2-15 mg/kg given slowly over 1-2 hours; maintenance infusion: 0.5-3 mg/kg/hour

Adults:

Hypnotic:

I.M.: 150-200 mg

I.V.: Initial: 100 mg, may repeat every 1-3 minutes up to 200-500 mg total dose

Preoperative sedation: I.M.: 150-200 mg

Dosing adjustment in hepatic impairment: Reduce dosage in patients with severe liver dysfunction

Administration Pentobarbital may be administered by deep I.M. or slow I.V. injection.

I.M.: No more than 5 mL (250 mg) should be injected at any one site because of possible tissue irritation.

I.V.: I.V. push doses can be given undiluted, but should be administered no faster than 50 mg/minute; parenteral solutions are highly alkaline; avoid extravasation; avoid rapid I.V. administration >50 mg/minute; avoid intra-arterial injection

Monitoring Parameters Respiratory status (for conscious sedation, includes pulse oximetry), cardiovascular status, CNS status; cardiac monitor and blood pressure monitor required

Reference Range

Therapeutic:

Hypnotic: 1-5 mcg/mL (SI: 4-22 µmol/L)

Coma: 10-50 mcg/mL (SI: 88-221 µmol/L)

Toxic: >10 mcg/mL (SI: >44 µmol/L)

Dosage Forms Injection, solution, as sodium: 50 mg/mL (20 mL, 50 mL) [contains alcohol 10% and propylene glycol 40%]

♦ **Pentobarbital Sodium** *see Pentobarbital on page 1340*

Pentosan Polysulfate Sodium *(PEN toe san pol i SUL fate SOW dee um)*

U.S. Brand Names Elmiron®
Canadian Brand Names Elmiron®
Index Terms PPS
Pharmacologic Category Analgesic, Urinary
Use Orphan drug: Relief of bladder pain or discomfort due to interstitial cystitis
Pregnancy Risk Factor B
Medication Safety Issues

Sound-alike/look-alike issues:

Pentosan may be confused with pentostatin

Elmiron® may be confused with Imuran®

Dosage Adults: Oral: 100 mg 3 times/day taken with water 1 hour before or 2 hours after meals

Patients should be evaluated at 3 months and may be continued an additional 3 months if there has been no improvement and if there are no therapy-limiting side effects. **The risks and benefits of continued use beyond 6 months in patients who have not responded is not yet known.**

Additional Information Complete prescribing information for this medication should be consulted for additional detail.

Dosage Forms Capsule: 100 mg

Pentostatin *(pen toe STAT in)*

U.S. Brand Names Nipent®
Canadian Brand Names Nipent®
Index Terms CL-825; Co-Vidarabine; dCF; Deoxycoformycin; NSC-218321; 2'-Deoxycoformycin
Pharmacologic Category Antineoplastic Agent, Antibiotic; Antineoplastic Agent, Antimetabolite (Purine Antagonist)
Use Treatment of hairy cell leukemia; non-Hodgkin's lymphoma, cutaneous T-cell lymphoma
Pregnancy Risk Factor D
Pregnancy Implications Pentostatin has been found to be teratogenic in animals. There are no adequate and well-controlled studies in humans. Women of childbearing potential should be advised to avoid becoming pregnant. If used during pregnancy, the patient should be apprised of the potential risk to the fetus.
Lactation Excretion in breast milk unknown/contraindicated
Medication Safety Issues

Sound-alike/look-alike issues:

Pentostatin may be confused with pentosan

High alert medication: The Institute for Safe Medication Practices (ISMP) includes this medication among its list of drugs which have a heightened risk of causing significant patient harm when used in error.

International issues:

Nipent® may be confused with Nipin® which is a brand name for nifedipine in Italy and Singapore

Contraindications Hypersensitivity to pentostatin or any component; pregnancy

Warnings/Precautions Hazardous agent - use appropriate precautions for handling and disposal. **[U.S. Boxed Warnings]: Severe renal, liver, pulmonary and CNS toxicities have occurred with doses higher than recommended; do not exceed the recommended dose. Do not administer concurrently with fludarabine; concomitant use has resulted in serious and fatal pulmonary toxicity.** Bone marrow suppression may occur, primarily early in treatment; if neutropenia persists beyond early cycles, evaluate for disease status. In patients who present with infections prior to treatment , infections should be resolved, if possible, prior to initiation of treatment. Use cautiously in patients with renal dysfunction; appropriate dosing guidelines in renal insufficiency have not been determined. May cause elevations (reversible) in liver function tests. Withhold treatment for CNS toxicity or severe rash. Pulmonary edema and hypotension have been reported in patients treated with pentostatin in combination with carmustine, etoposide, or high-dose cyclophosphamide as part of a myeloablative regimen for bone marrow transplant. **[U.S. Boxed Warning]: Should be administered under the supervision of an experienced cancer chemotherapy physician.** Safety and efficacy in children have not been established.

Adverse Reactions
>10%:
Central nervous system: Fever, chills, headache
Dermatologic: Skin rash (25% to 30%), alopecia (10%)
Gastrointestinal: Mild to moderate nausea, vomiting (60%), stomatitis, diarrhea (13%), anorexia
Genitourinary: Acute renal failure (35%)
Hematologic: Thrombocytopenia (50%), dose-limiting in 25% of patients; anemia (40% to 45%), neutropenia, mild to moderate, not dose-limiting (11%)
Nadir: 7 days
Recovery: 10-14 days
Hepatic: Transaminases increased, mild-moderate, usually transient (30%); hepatitis (19%), usually reversible
Respiratory: Pulmonary edema (15%), may be exacerbated by fludarabine
Miscellaneous: Infection (57%; 35% severe, life-threatening)
1% to 10%:
Cardiovascular: Chest pain, arrhythmia, peripheral edema
Central nervous system: Opportunistic infection (8%); anxiety, confusion, depression, dizziness, insomnia, nervousness, somnolence, myalgia, malaise
Dermatologic: Dry skin, eczema, pruritus
Gastrointestinal: Constipation, flatulence, weight loss
Neuromuscular & skeletal: Paresthesia, weakness
Ocular: Moderate to severe keratoconjunctivitis, abnormal vision, eye pain
Otic: Ear pain
Respiratory: Dyspnea, pneumonia, bronchitis, pharyngitis, rhinitis, epistaxis, sinusitis (3% to 7%)
<1%: Dysuria, hematuria, hypersensitivity reactions, BUN increased, thrombophlebitis; lethargy, seizure, coma (uncommon at doses <4 mg/m^2)

Overdosage/Toxicology Symptoms include severe renal, hepatic, pulmonary, and CNS toxicity. Treatment is supportive.

Drug Interactions
Increased Effect/Toxicity: Increased toxicity with vidarabine and allopurinol; combined use with fludarabine may lead to severe, even fatal, pulmonary toxicity

Stability Vials are stable under refrigeration at 2°C to 8°C; reconstituted vials, or further dilutions, are stable at room temperature for 24 hours in D$_5$W or 48 hours in NS or lactated Ringer's. Reconstitute with SWFI to a concentration of 2 mg/mL. The injection may be further diluted with 25-50 mL NS or D$_5$W for infusion.

Mechanism of Action Pentostatin is a purine antimetabolite that inhibits adenosine deaminase, preventing the deamination of adenosine to inosine. Accumulation of deoxyadenosine (dAdo) and deoxyadenosine 5'-triphosphate (dATP) results in a reduction of purine metabolism and DNA synthesis and cell death.

Pharmacodynamics/Kinetics
Distribution: I.V.: V$_d$: 36.1 L (20.1 L/m^2); rapidly to body tissues
Half-life elimination: Distribution half-life: 30-85 minutes; Terminal: 5-15 hours
Excretion: Urine (~50% to 96%) within 24 hours (30% to 90% as unchanged drug)

Dosage Refractory hairy cell leukemia: Adults (refer to individual protocols):
4 mg/m^2 every other week **or**
4 mg/m^2 weekly for 3 weeks, then every 2 weeks **or**
5 mg/m^2 daily for 3 days every 3 weeks

Dosing interval in renal impairment:
Cl$_{cr}$ <60 mL/minute: Use extreme caution
Cl$_{cr}$ 50-60 mL/minute: 2 mg/m^2/dose

Administration Administer I.V. as a 15- to 30-minute infusion; continuous infusion regimens have been reported, but are not commonly used
I.V. bolus over ≥3-5 minutes

Dosage Forms
Injection, powder for reconstitution [preservative free]:
Nipent®: 10 mg

♦ **Pentothal**® see Thiopental on page 1670

Pentoxifylline (pen toks IF i lin)

U.S. Brand Names Pentoxil®; Trental®
Canadian Brand Names Albert® Pentoxifylline; Apo-Pentoxifylline SR®; Nu-Pentoxifylline SR; ratio-Pentoxifylline; Trental®
(Continued)

Pentoxifylline *(Continued)*

Index Terms Oxpentifylline

Pharmacologic Category Blood Viscosity Reducer Agent

Use Treatment of intermittent claudication on the basis of chronic occlusive arterial disease of the limbs; may improve function and symptoms, but not intended to replace more definitive therapy

Unlabeled/Investigational Use AIDS patients with increased TNF, CVA, cerebrovascular diseases, diabetic atherosclerosis, diabetic neuropathy, gangrene, hemodialysis shunt thrombosis, vascular impotence, cerebral malaria, septic shock, sickle cell syndromes, and vasculitis

Pregnancy Risk Factor C

Pregnancy Implications Teratogenic effects were not observed in animal studies. There are no adequate and well-controlled studies in pregnant women.

Lactation Enters breast milk/not recommended

Medication Safety Issues
Sound-alike/look-alike issues:
Pentoxifylline may be confused with tamoxifen
Trental® may be confused with Bentyl®, Tegretol®, Trandate®

Contraindications Hypersensitivity to pentoxifylline, xanthines (eg, caffeine, theophylline), or any component of the formulation; recent cerebral and/or retinal hemorrhage

Warnings/Precautions Use with caution in patients with renal and hepatic impairment; start with lower doses in elderly patients and monitor renal function. Use caution in patients receiving anticoagulant therapy or at risk for bleeding complications; monitor PT/INR, hematocrit and/or hemoglobin as necessary. May lower blood pressure; monitor with concomitant antihypertensive agent use. Safety and efficacy in pediatric patients have not been established.

Adverse Reactions
1% to 10%: Gastrointestinal: Nausea (2%), vomiting (1%)
<1% (Limited to important or life-threatening): Anaphylactoid reaction, angioedema, angina, anorexia, anxiety, aplastic anemia, arrhythmia, aseptic meningitis, bloating, blurred vision, brittle fingernails, chest pain, cholecystitis, confusion, conjunctivitis, constipation, depression, dyspnea, ear ache, edema, epistaxis, eructation, fibrinogen decreased (serum), flatus, flu-like syndrome, hallucinations, hepatitis, hypotension, jaundice, laryngitis, leukemia, leukopenia, liver enzymes increased, malaise, nasal congestion, pancytopenia, pruritus, purpura, rash, scotoma, seizure, sialism, sore throat, taste perversion, tachycardia, thrombocytopenia, tremor, urticaria, weight change, xerostomia

Overdosage/Toxicology Symptoms of overdose have been reported to occur 4-5 hours postingestion and last approximately 12 hours. Symptoms may include hypotension, flushing, convulsions, deep sleep, agitation, bradycardia, and AV block. Treatment should be symptom-directed and supportive. Seizures can be treated with diazepam 5-10 mg (0.25-0.4 mg/kg in children). Arrhythmias respond to lidocaine.

Drug Interactions
Cytochrome P450 Effect: Inhibits CYP1A2 (weak)
Increased Effect/Toxicity:
Pentoxifylline may increase the serum levels of theophylline.

Ethanol/Nutrition/Herb Interactions Food: Food may decrease rate but not extent of absorption. Pentoxifylline peak serum levels may be decreased if taken with food.

Stability Store between 15°C to 30°C (59°F to 86°F).

Mechanism of Action Reduces blood viscosity via increased leukocyte and erythrocyte deformability and decreased neutrophil adhesion/activation; improves peripheral tissue oxygenation presumably through enhanced blood flow.

Pharmacodynamics/Kinetics
Absorption: Well absorbed
Metabolism: Hepatic and via erythrocytes; extensive first-pass effect
Half-life elimination: Parent drug: 24-48 minutes; Metabolites: 60-96 minutes
Time to peak, serum: 2-4 hours
Excretion: Primarily urine (active metabolites); feces (4%)

Dosage Adults: Oral: 400 mg 3 times/day with meals; maximal therapeutic benefit may take 2-4 weeks to develop; recommended to maintain therapy for at least 8 weeks. May reduce to 400 mg twice daily if GI or CNS side effects occur.

Dietary Considerations May be taken with meals or food.

Administration Tablets should be swallowed whole; do not chew, break, or crush.

Test Interactions Decreased calcium (S), magnesium (S); false-positive theophylline levels

Dosage Forms
Tablet, controlled release:
Trental®: 400 mg
Tablet, extended release: 400 mg
Pentoxil®: 400 mg

♦ **Pentoxil®** *see* Pentoxifylline *on page 1343*
♦ **Pen VK** *see* Penicillin V Potassium *on page 1336*
♦ **Pepcid®** *see* Famotidine *on page 683*
♦ **Pepcid® AC [OTC]** *see* Famotidine *on page 683*
♦ **Pepcid® AC (Can)** *see* Famotidine *on page 683*
♦ **Pepcid® Complete [OTC]** *see* Famotidine, Calcium Carbonate, and Magnesium Hydroxide *on page 685*
♦ **Pepcid® I.V. (Can)** *see* Famotidine *on page 683*
♦ **Pepto-Bismol® [OTC]** *see* Bismuth *on page 224*
♦ **Pepto-Bismol® Maximum Strength [OTC]** *see* Bismuth *on page 224*
♦ **Percocet®** *see* Oxycodone and Acetaminophen *on page 1289*
♦ **Percocet®-Demi (Can)** *see* Oxycodone and Acetaminophen *on page 1289*
♦ **Percodan®** *see* Oxycodone and Aspirin *on page 1289*

◆ **Percogesic**® **[OTC]** *see* Acetaminophen and Phenyltoloxamine *on page 32*

◆ **Percogesic**® **Extra Strength [OTC]** *see* Acetaminophen and Diphenhydramine *on page 31*

Perflutren Protein Type A (per FLOO tren PRO teen typ aye)

U.S. Brand Names Optison™

Pharmacologic Category Diagnostic Agent

Use Opacification of left ventricular chamber and improvement of delineation of the left ventricular endocardial border in patients with suboptimal echocardiograms

Pregnancy Risk Factor C

Dosage I.V.: Adults: 0.5 mL via peripheral vein; flush with D_5W or NS following dose; may repeat in increments of 0.5 mL up to 5 mL cumulatively in 10 minutes (maximum total dose: 8.7 mL in any one patient study)

Additional Information Complete prescribing information for this medication should be consulted for additional detail.

Dosage Forms

Injection, suspension [preservative free]:

Optison™: Perflutren 0.11-0.33 mg and protein-type A microspheres 5-8 x 10^8 per mL (3 mL) [contains human albumin 10 mg/mL]

Pergolide (PER go lide)

U.S. Brand Names Permax®

Canadian Brand Names Permax®

Index Terms Pergolide Mesylate

Pharmacologic Category Anti-Parkinson's Agent, Dopamine Agonist; Ergot Derivative

Additional Appendix Information

Parkinson's Agents *on page 1895*

Use Adjunctive treatment to levodopa/carbidopa in the management of Parkinson's disease

Unlabeled/Investigational Use Tourette's disorder, chronic motor or vocal tic disorder

Pregnancy Risk Factor B

Lactation Excretion in breast milk unknown/not recommended

Medication Safety Issues

Sound-alike/look-alike issues:

Permax® may be confused with Bumex®, Pentrax®, Pernox®

Contraindications Hypersensitivity to pergolide mesylate, other ergot derivatives, or any component of the formulation; ergot alkaloids are contraindicated with potent inhibitors of CYP3A4 (includes protease inhibitors, azole antifungals, and some macrolide antibiotics)

Warnings/Precautions Symptomatic hypotension occurs in 10% of patients; use with caution in patients with a history of cardiac arrhythmias, hallucinations, or mental illness. Cardiac valvular, pleural, and peritoneal fibrosis have been reported with prolonged daily use. Avoid rapid dose reduction or abrupt discontinuation.

Pergolide has been associated with somnolence. Some patients have been reported to fall asleep during activities of daily living, including driving, while taking this medication. Not all patients exhibited somnolence prior to these events.

Adverse Reactions

>10%:

Central nervous system: Dizziness (19%), hallucinations (14%), dystonia (12%), somnolence (10%), confusion (10%)

Gastrointestinal: Nausea (24%), constipation (11%)

Neuromuscular & skeletal: Dyskinesia (62%)

Respiratory: Rhinitis (12%)

1% to 10%:

Cardiovascular: Hypotension or postural hypotension (10%), peripheral edema (7%), chest pain (4%), vasodilation (3%), palpitation (2%), syncope (2%), arrhythmia (1%), hypertension (2%), MI (1%)

Central nervous system: Insomnia (8%), pain (7%), anxiety (6%), psychosis (2%), EPS (2%), incoordination (2%), chills (1%)

Dermatologic: Rash (3%)

Gastrointestinal: Diarrhea (6%), dyspepsia (6%), abdominal pain (6%), anorexia (5%), xerostomia (4%), vomiting (3%), dysphagia (1%)

Hematologic: Anemia (1%)

Neuromuscular & skeletal: Myalgia (1%), neuralgia (1%)

Ocular: Abnormal vision (6%), diplopia (2%)

Respiratory: Dyspnea (5%), epistaxis (2%)

Miscellaneous: Flu syndrome (3%), hiccups (1%)

<1% (Limited to important or life-threatening): AV block, facial paralysis, intestinal obstruction, intracranial hypertension, laryngeal edema, neuritis, neuroleptic malignant syndrome (NMS; associated with rapid discontinuation), pancreatitis, pericarditis, pericardial effusion, pleural effusion, pleural fibrosis, pleuritis, pneumothorax, retroperitoneal fibrosis, somnolence/falling asleep during daily activities, vasculitis, valvular fibrosis

Overdosage/Toxicology Symptoms include vomiting, hypotension, agitation, hallucinations, ventricular extrasystoles, and possible seizures. Data on overdose are limited. Treatment is supportive and may require antiarrhythmics and/or neuroleptics for agitation. Hypotension, when unresponsive to I.V. fluids or Trendelenburg positioning, often responds to norepinephrine infusions started at 0.1-0.2 mcg/kg/minute, followed by a titrated infusion. If signs of CNS stimulation are present, a neuroleptic may be indicated. Monitor ECG. Activated charcoal is useful in preventing further absorption and hastening elimination.

Drug Interactions

Cytochrome P450 Effect: Substrate of CYP3A4 (major); **Inhibits** CYP2D6 (strong), 3A4 (weak)

(Continued)

Pergolide (Continued)

Increased Effect/Toxicity: Effects of pergolide may be increased by levodopa (hallucinations) and MAO inhibitors. Pergolide may increase the levels/effects of amphetamines, selected beta-blockers, dextromethorphan, fluoxetine, lidocaine, mirtazapine, nefazodone, paroxetine, risperidone, ritonavir, thioridazine, tricyclic antidepressants, venlafaxine, and other CYP2D6 substrates. Pergolide may increase the levels/effects of sibutramine and other serotonin agonists (serotonin syndrome). Macrolide antibiotics may increase the effects of pergolide. The levels/effects of pergolide may be increased by azole antifungals, clarithromycin, diclofenac, doxycycline, erythromycin, imatinib, isoniazid, nefazodone, nicardipine, propofol, protease inhibitors, quinidine, telithromycin, verapamil, and other CYP3A4 inhibitors.

Decreased Effect: Effects of pergolide may be diminished by antipsychotics, metoclopramide. Pergolide may decrease the levels/effects of CYP2D6 prodrug substrates (eg, codeine, hydrocodone, oxycodone, tramadol).

Ethanol/Nutrition/Herb Interactions Ethanol: Avoid ethanol (may cause CNS depression).

Mechanism of Action Pergolide is a semisynthetic ergot alkaloid similar to bromocriptine but stated to be more potent (10-1000 times) and longer-acting; it is a centrally-active dopamine agonist stimulating both D_1 and D_2 receptors. Pergolide is believed to exert its therapeutic effect by directly stimulating postsynaptic dopamine receptors in the nigrostriatal system.

Pharmacodynamics/Kinetics
Absorption: Well absorbed
Protein binding, plasma: 90%
Metabolism: Extensively hepatic
Half-life elimination: 27 hours
Excretion: Urine (~50%); feces (50%)

Dosage When adding pergolide to levodopa/carbidopa, the dose of the latter can usually and should be decreased. Patients no longer responsive to bromocriptine may benefit by being switched to pergolide. Oral:
Children and Adolescents: Tourette's disorder, chronic motor or vocal disorder (unlabeled uses): Up to 300 mcg/day
Adults: Parkinson's disease: Start with 0.05 mg/day for 2 days, then increase dosage by 0.1 or 0.15 mg/day every 3 days over next 12 days, increase dose by 0.25 mg/day every 3 days until optimal therapeutic dose is achieved, up to 5 mg/day maximum; usual dosage range: 2-3 mg/day in 3 divided doses

Monitoring Parameters Blood pressure (both sitting/supine and standing), symptoms of parkinsonism, dyskinesias, mental status

Dosage Forms
Tablet [scored]: 0.05 mg, 0.25 mg, 1 mg
Permax®: 0.05 mg, 0.25 mg, 1 mg

♦ **Pergolide Mesylate** see Pergolide on page 1345
♦ **Periactin** see Cyproheptadine on page 436
♦ **Peri-Colace®** [OTC] see Docusate and Senna on page 534
♦ **Peridex®** see Chlorhexidine Gluconate on page 344
♦ **Peridol (Can)** see Haloperidol on page 826

Perindopril Erbumine (per IN doe pril er BYOO meen)

U.S. Brand Names Aceon®
Canadian Brand Names Coversyl®
Pharmacologic Category Angiotensin-Converting Enzyme (ACE) Inhibitor
Additional Appendix Information
Angiotensin Agents on page 1860

Use Treatment of essential hypertension; reduction of cardiovascular mortality or nonfatal myocardial infarction in patients with stable coronary artery disease

Unlabeled/Investigational Use As a class, ACE inhibitors are recommended in the treatment of congestive heart failure with left ventricular dysfunction

Pregnancy Risk Factor C (1st trimester) / D (2nd and 3rd trimesters)

Pregnancy Implications Decreased placental blood flow, low birth weight, fetal hypotension, preterm delivery, and fetal death have been noted with the use of some ACE inhibitors (ACEIs) in animal studies. Neonatal hypotension, skull hypoplasia, anuria, renal failure, oligohydramnios (associated with fetal limb contractures, craniofacial deformities, hypoplastic lung development), prematurity, intrauterine growth retardation, and patent ductus arteriosus have been reported with the use of ACEIs, primarily in the 2nd and 3rd trimesters. The risk of neonatal toxicity has been considered less when ACEIs have been used in the 1st trimester; however, major congenital malformations have been reported. The cardiovascular and/or central nervous systems are most commonly affected. Unless alternative agents are not appropriate, ACEIs should be discontinued as soon as possible once pregnancy is detected.

Lactation Excretion in breast milk unknown/use caution

Contraindications Hypersensitivity to perindopril or any component of the formulation; angioedema related to previous treatment with an ACE inhibitor; bilateral renal artery stenosis; pregnancy (2nd and 3rd trimesters)

Warnings/Precautions Anaphylactic reactions can occur. Angioedema can occur at any time during treatment (especially following first dose). It may involve head and neck (potentially affecting the airway) or the intestine (presenting with abdominal pain). Prolonged monitoring may be required especially if tongue, glottis, or larynx are involved as they are associated with airway obstruction. Those with a history of airway surgery in this situation have a higher risk. Careful blood pressure monitoring with first dose (hypotension can occur especially in volume- and/or salt-depleted patients); caution in patients receiving hypotensive-inducing anesthesia. **[U.S. Boxed Warning]: Based on human data, ACEIs can cause injury and death to the developing fetus when used in the second and third trimesters. ACEIs should be discontinued as soon as possible once pregnancy is detected.** Dosage adjustment needed in renal impairment. Avoid rapid dosage escalation, which may lead to renal insufficiency.

Use with caution in hypovolemia; collagen vascular diseases; valvular stenosis (particularly aortic stenosis); concomitant use with potassium-sparing agents, potassium supplements or salt substitutes not recommended; risk of hyperkalemia may be increased with renal insufficiency. Rare toxicities associated with ACE inhibitors include cholestatic jaundice (which may progress to hepatic necrosis) and neutropenia/agranulocytosis with myeloid hyperplasia. May be associated with deterioration of renal function and/or increases in serum creatinine, particularly in patients dependent on renin-angiotensin-aldosterone system. Use with caution in unilateral renal artery stenosis and pre-existing renal insufficiency; if patient has renal impairment then a baseline WBC with differential and serum creatinine should be evaluated and monitored closely during the first 3 months of therapy. Hypersensitivity reactions may be seen during hemodialysis with high-flux dialysis membranes (eg, AN69). Safety and efficacy have not been established in children.

Adverse Reactions

>10%:
Central nervous system: Headache (24%)
Respiratory: Cough (incidence is higher in women, 3:1) (12%)

1% to 10%:
Cardiovascular: Edema (4%), chest pain (2%), ECG abnormal (2%), palpitation (1%)
Central nervous system: Dizziness (8%, less than placebo), sleep disorders (3%), depression (2%), fever (2%), nervousness (1%), somnolence (1%)
Dermatologic: Rash (2%)
Endocrine & metabolic: Hyperkalemia (1%, less than placebo), triglycerides increased (1%), menstrual disorder (1%)
Gastrointestinal: Nausea (2%), diarrhea (4%), vomiting (2%), dyspepsia (2%), abdominal pain (3%), flatulence (1%)
Genitourinary: Urinary tract infection (3%), sexual dysfunction (male 1%)
Hepatic: Increased ALT (2%)
Neuromuscular & skeletal: Weakness (8%), back pain (6%), lower extremity pain (5%), upper extremity pain (3%), hypertonia (3%), paresthesia (2%), joint pain (1%), myalgia (1%), arthritis (1%), neck pain (1%)
Renal: Proteinuria (2%)
Respiratory: Upper respiratory tract infection (9%), sinusitis (5%), rhinitis (5%), pharyngitis (3%)
Otic: Tinnitus (2%), ear infection (1%)
Miscellaneous: Viral infection (3%), allergy (2%)
Note: Some reactions occurred at an incidence >1% but ≤ placebo.

<1% (Limited to important or life-threatening): Amnesia, anaphylaxis, angioedema, anxiety, dyspnea, erythema, gout, migraine, MI, nephrolithiasis, orthostatic hypotension, pruritus, psychosocial disorder, pulmonary fibrosis, purpura, stroke, syncope, urinary retention, vertigo

Additional adverse effects that have been reported with **ACE inhibitors** include agranulocytosis (especially in patients with renal impairment or collagen vascular disease), neutropenia, anemia, bullous pemphigus, cardiac arrest, eosinophilic pneumonitis, exfoliative dermatitis, hepatic failure, hyponatremia, jaundice, pancreatitis (acute), pancytopenia, thrombocytopenia; decreases in creatinine clearance in some elderly hypertensive patients or those with chronic renal failure, and worsening of renal function in patients with bilateral renal artery stenosis or hypovolemic patients (diuretic therapy). In addition, a syndrome which may include fever, myalgia, arthralgia, interstitial nephritis, vasculitis, rash, eosinophilia and positive ANA, and elevated ESR has been reported with ACE inhibitors.

Overdosage/Toxicology Mild hypotension has been the primary toxic effect seen with acute overdose. Bradycardia may also occur. Hyperkalemia occurs even with therapeutic doses, especially in patients with renal insufficiency and those taking NSAIDs. Treatment is symptom-directed and supportive. Hemodialysis may be beneficial.

Drug Interactions

Increased Effect/Toxicity: Potassium supplements, co-trimoxazole (high dose), angiotensin II receptor antagonists (eg, candesartan, losartan, irbesartan), or potassium-sparing diuretics (amiloride, eplerenone, spironolactone, triamterene) may result in elevated serum potassium levels when combined with perindopril. ACE inhibitor effects may be increased by phenothiazines or probenecid (increases levels of captopril). ACE inhibitors may increase serum concentrations/effects of lithium. ACE inhibitors may enhance the adverse/toxic effects (nitritoid reaction) of gold sodium thiomalate.

Diuretics have additive hypotensive effects with ACE inhibitors, and hypovolemia increases the potential for adverse renal effects of ACE inhibitors. ACE inhibitors may increase nephrotoxicity of cyclosporine. In patients with compromised renal function, coadministration with NSAIDs may result in further deterioration of renal function. Allopurinol and ACE inhibitors may cause a higher risk of hypersensitivity reaction when taken concurrently.

Decreased Effect: Aspirin (high dose) may reduce the therapeutic effects of ACE inhibitors; at low dosages this does not appear to be significant. Rifampin may decrease the effect of ACE inhibitors. Antacids may decrease the bioavailability of ACE inhibitors (may be more likely to occur with captopril); separate administration times by 1-2 hours. NSAIDs, specifically indomethacin, may reduce the hypotensive effects of ACE inhibitors. More likely to occur in low renin or volume dependent hypertensive patients.

Ethanol/Nutrition/Herb Interactions

Food: Perindopril active metabolite concentrations may be lowered if taken with food.
Herb/Nutraceutical: Avoid dong quai if using for hypertension (has estrogenic activity). Avoid ephedra, yohimbe, ginseng (may worsen hypertension). Avoid garlic (may have increased antihypertensive effect).

Stability Store at room temperature of 20°C to 25°C (68°F to 77°F). Protect from moisture.

Mechanism of Action Perindopril is a prodrug for perindoprilat, which acts as a competitive inhibitor of angiotensin-converting enzyme (ACE); prevents conversion of angiotensin I to (Continued)

Perindopril Erbumine *(Continued)*

angiotensin II, a potent vasoconstrictor; results in lower levels of angiotensin II which, in turn, causes an increase in plasma renin activity and a reduction in aldosterone secretion

Pharmacodynamics/Kinetics

Onset of action: Peak effect: 1-2 hours

Distribution: Small amounts enter breast milk

Protein binding: Perindopril: 60%; Perindoprilat: 10% to 20%

Metabolism: Hepatically hydrolyzed to active metabolite, perindoprilat (~17% to 20% of a dose) and other inactive metabolites

Bioavailability: Perindopril: 75%; Perindoprilat ~25% (~16% with food)

Half-life elimination: Parent drug: 1.5-3 hours; Metabolite: Effective: 3-10 hours, Terminal: 30-120 hours

Time to peak: Chronic therapy: Perindopril: 1 hour; Perindoprilat: 3-7 hours (maximum perindoprilat serum levels are 2-3 times higher and T_{max} is shorter following chronic therapy); CHF: Perindoprilat: 6 hours

Excretion: Urine (75%, 4% to 12% as unchanged drug)

Dosage Oral:

Adults:

Essential hypertension: Initial: 4 mg/day but may be titrated to response; usual range: 4-8 mg/day (may be given in 2 divided doses); increase at 1- to 2-week intervals (maximum: 16 mg/day)

Concomitant therapy with diuretics: To reduce the risk of hypotension, discontinue diuretic, if possible, 2-3 days prior to initiating perindopril. If unable to stop diuretic, initiate perindopril at 2-4 mg/day and monitor blood pressure closely for the first 2 weeks of therapy, and after any dose adjustment of perindopril or diuretic.

Stable coronary artery disease: Initial: 4 mg once daily for 2 weeks; increase as tolerated to 8 mg once daily.

Congestive heart failure (unlabeled use): Initial: 2 mg once daily; increase at 1- to 2-week intervals; target dose: 8-16 mg once daily (ACC/AHA 2005 Heart Failure Guidelines)

Elderly:

Essential hypertension: >65 years of age: Initial: 4 mg/day; maintenance: 8 mg/day

Stable coronary artery disease: >70 years of age: Initial: 2 mg/day for 1 week; increase as tolerated to 4 mg/day for 1 week; then increase as tolerated to 8 mg/day

Dosing adjustment in renal impairment:

Cl_{cr} >30 mL/minute: Initial: 2 mg/day; maintenance dosing not to exceed 8 mg/day

Cl_{cr} <30 mL/minute: Safety and efficacy not established.

Hemodialysis: Perindopril and its metabolites are dialyzable

Dosing adjustment in hepatic impairment: None needed

Monitoring Parameters Serum creatinine, electrolytes, and WBC with differential initially and repeated at 2-week intervals for at least 90 days; urinalysis for protein

Dosage Forms Tablet: 2 mg, 4 mg, 8 mg

♦ **PerioChip®** *see* Chlorhexidine Gluconate *on page 344*
♦ **PerioGard®** *see* Chlorhexidine Gluconate *on page 344*
♦ **PerioMed™** *see* Fluoride *on page 722*
♦ **Periostat®** *see* Doxycycline *on page 555*
♦ **Permax®** *see* Pergolide *on page 1345*

Permethrin *(per METH rin)*

U.S. Brand Names A200® Lice [OTC]; Acticin®; Elimite®; Nix® [OTC]; Rid® Spray [OTC]

Canadian Brand Names Kwellada-P™; Nix®

Pharmacologic Category Antiparasitic Agent, Topical; Scabicidal Agent

Use Single-application treatment of infestation with *Pediculus humanus capitis* (head louse) and its nits or *Sarcoptes scabiei* (scabies); indicated for prophylactic use during epidemics of lice

Pregnancy Risk Factor B

Dosage Topical:

Head lice: Children >2 months and Adults: After hair has been washed with shampoo, rinsed with water, and towel dried, apply a sufficient volume of topical liquid (lotion or cream rinse) to saturate the hair and scalp. Leave on hair for 10 minutes before rinsing off with water; remove remaining nits; may repeat in 1 week if lice or nits still present.

Scabies: Apply cream from head to toe; leave on for 8-14 hours before washing off with water; for infants, also apply on the hairline, neck, scalp, temple, and forehead; may reapply in 1 week if live mites appear

Permethrin 5% cream was shown to be safe and effective when applied to an infant <1 month of age with neonatal scabies; time of application was limited to 6 hours before rinsing with soap and water

Dosage Forms

Cream, topical (Acticin®, Elimite®): 5% (60 g) [contains coconut oil]

Lotion, topical: 1% (59 mL)

Liquid, topical [creme rinse formulation] (Nix®): 1% (60 mL) [contains isopropyl alcohol 20%]

Solution, spray [for bedding and furniture]:

A200® Lice: 0.5% (180 mL)

Nix®: 0.25% (148 mL)

Rid®: 0.5% (150 mL)

Perphenazine (per FEN a zeen)

Canadian Brand Names Apo-Perphenazine®
Pharmacologic Category Antipsychotic Agent, Typical, Phenothiazine
Additional Appendix Information
  Antipsychotic Agents *on page 1872*
Use Treatment of schizophrenia; nausea and vomiting
Unlabeled/Investigational Use Ethanol withdrawal; dementia in elderly; Tourette's syndrome; Huntington's chorea; spasmodic torticollis; Reye's syndrome; psychosis
Pregnancy Risk Factor C
Lactation Enters breast milk/not recommended (AAP rates "of concern")
Medication Safety Issues
  Sound-alike/look-alike issues:
    Trilafon® may be confused with Tri-Levlen®
Contraindications Hypersensitivity to perphenazine or any component of the formulation (cross-reactivity between phenothiazines may occur); severe CNS depression; subcortical brain damage; bone marrow suppression; blood dyscrasias; coma
Warnings/Precautions Safety in children <6 months of age has not been established. May cause hypotension. May be sedating, use with caution in disorders where CNS depression is a feature. Use with caution in Parkinson's disease. Caution in patients with hemodynamic instability; predisposition to seizures; severe cardiac, hepatic, renal, or respiratory disease. Esophageal dysmotility and aspiration have been associated with antipsychotic use - use with caution in patients at risk of pneumonia (ie, Alzheimer's disease). Caution in breast cancer or other prolactin-dependent tumors (may elevate prolactin levels). May alter temperature regulation or mask toxicity of other drugs due to antiemetic effects. May alter cardiac conduction - life-threatening arrhythmias have occurred with therapeutic doses of phenothiazines. May cause orthostatic hypotension - use with caution in patients at risk of this effect or those who would tolerate transient hypotensive episodes (cerebrovascular disease, cardiovascular disease, or other medications which may predispose).

Phenothiazines may cause anticholinergic effects (confusion, agitation, constipation, xerostomia, blurred vision, urinary retention); therefore, they should be used with caution in patients with decreased gastrointestinal motility, urinary retention, BPH, xerostomia, or visual problems. Conditions which also may be exacerbated by cholinergic blockade include narrow-angle glaucoma (screening is recommended) and worsening of myasthenia gravis. Relative to other neuroleptics, perphenazine has a low potency of cholinergic blockade.

May cause extrapyramidal reactions, including pseudoparkinsonism, acute dystonic reactions, akathisia, and tardive dyskinesia (risk of these reactions is moderate-high relative to other neuroleptics). May be associated with neuroleptic malignant syndrome (NMS) or pigmentary retinopathy.

Adverse Reactions Frequency not defined.
  Cardiovascular: Hyper-/hypotension, orthostatic hypotension, tachycardia, bradycardia, dizziness, cardiac arrest
  Central nervous system: Extrapyramidal symptoms (pseudoparkinsonism, akathisia, dystonias, tardive dyskinesia), dizziness, cerebral edema, seizure, headache, drowsiness, paradoxical excitement, restlessness, hyperactivity, insomnia, neuroleptic malignant syndrome (NMS), impairment of temperature regulation
  Dermatologic: Rash, discoloration of skin (blue-gray), photosensitivity
  Endocrine & metabolic: Hypoglycemia, hyperglycemia, galactorrhea, lactation, breast enlargement, gynecomastia, menstrual irregularity, amenorrhea, SIADH, libido (changes in)
  Gastrointestinal: Constipation, weight gain, vomiting, stomach pain, nausea, xerostomia, salivation, diarrhea, anorexia, ileus
  Genitourinary: Difficulty in urination, ejaculatory disturbances, incontinence, polyuria, ejaculating dysfunction, priapism
  Hematologic: Agranulocytosis, leukopenia, eosinophilia, hemolytic anemia, thrombocytopenic purpura, pancytopenia
  Hepatic: Cholestatic jaundice, hepatotoxicity
  Neuromuscular & skeletal: Tremor
  Ocular: Pigmentary retinopathy, blurred vision, cornea and lens changes
  Respiratory: Nasal congestion
  Miscellaneous: Diaphoresis
Overdosage/Toxicology Symptoms include deep sleep, dystonia, agitation, coma, abnormal involuntary muscle movements, hypotension, and arrhythmias. Following initiation of essential overdose management, toxic symptom and supportive treatment should be initiated. Hypotension usually responds to I.V. fluids or Trendelenburg positioning. If unresponsive to these measures, the use of a parenteral inotrope may be required (eg, norepinephrine 0.1-0.2 mcg/kg/minute titrated to response). Seizures commonly respond to diazepam (I.V. 5-10 mg bolus in adults every 15 minutes, if needed, up to a total of 30 mg; I.V. 0.25-0.4 mg/kg/dose up to a total of 10 mg in children) or to phenytoin or phenobarbital. Extrapyramidal symptoms (eg, dystonic reactions) may be managed with diphenhydramine. When these reactions are unresponsive to diphenhydramine, benztropine mesylate may be effective.

Drug Interactions
  Cytochrome P450 Effect: Substrate of CYP1A2 (minor), 2C9 (minor), 2C19 (minor), 2D6 (major), 3A4 (minor); **Inhibits** CYP1A2 (weak), 2D6 (weak)
  Increased Effect/Toxicity: CYP2D6 inhibitors may increase the levels/effects of perphenazine; example inhibitors include chlorpromazine, delavirdine, fluoxetine, miconazole, paroxetine, pergolide, quinidine, quinine, ritonavir, and ropinirole. Effects on CNS depression may be additive when perphenazine is combined with CNS depressants (opioid analgesics, ethanol, barbiturates, cyclic antidepressants, antihistamines, or sedative-hypnotics). Perphenazine may increase the effects/toxicity of anticholinergics, antihypertensives, lithium (rare neurotoxicity), trazodone, or valproic acid. Concurrent use with TCA may produce increased toxicity or altered therapeutic response. Chloroquine and
(Continued)

Perphenazine *(Continued)*

propranolol may increase perphenazine concentrations. Hypotension may occur when perphenazine is combined with epinephrine. May increase the risk of arrhythmia when combined with antiarrhythmics, cisapride, pimozide, sparfloxacin, or other drugs which prolong QT interval. Metoclopramide may increase risk of extrapyramidal symptoms (EPS). Acetylcholinesterase inhibitors (central) may increase the risk of antipsychotic-related EPS.

Decreased Effect: Phenothiazines inhibit the ability of bromocriptine to lower serum prolactin concentrations. Benztropine (and other anticholinergics) may inhibit the therapeutic response to perphenazine and excess anticholinergic effects may occur. Cigarette smoking and barbiturates may enhance the hepatic metabolism of chlorpromazine. Antihypertensive effects of guanethidine and guanadrel may be inhibited by perphenazine. Perphenazine may inhibit the antiparkinsonian effect of levodopa. Perphenazine and possibly other low potency antipsychotics may reverse the pressor effects of epinephrine.

Ethanol/Nutrition/Herb Interactions

Ethanol: Avoid ethanol (may increase CNS depression).

Herb/Nutraceutical: Avoid kava kava, gotu kola, valerian, St John's wort (may increase CNS depression).

Stability Store at 2°C to 25°C (36°F to 77°F). Protect from light.

Mechanism of Action Perphenazine is a piperazine phenothiazine antpsychotic which blocks postsynaptic mesolimbic dopaminergic receptors in the brain; exhibits alpha-adrenergic blocking effect and depresses the release of hypothalamic and hypophyseal hormones

Pharmacodynamics/Kinetics

Absorption: Oral: Well absorbed

Distribution: Crosses placenta

Metabolism: Extensively hepatic to metabolites via sulfoxidation, hydroxylation, dealkylation, and glucuronidation

Half-life elimination: Perphenazine: 9-12 hours; 7-hydroxyperphenazine: 11.3 hours

Time to peak, serum: Perphenazine: 1-3 hours; 7-hydroxyperphenazine: 2-4 hours

Excretion: Urine and feces

Dosage Oral:

Children:

Schizophrenia/psychoses:

1-6 years: 4-6 mg/day in divided doses

6-12 years: 6 mg/day in divided doses

>12 years: 4-16 mg 2-4 times/day

Adults:

Schizophrenia/psychoses: 4-16 mg 2-4 times/day not to exceed 64 mg/day

Nausea/vomiting: 8-16 mg/day in divided doses up to 24 mg/day

Elderly: Behavioral symptoms associated with dementia: Initial: 2-4 mg 1-2 times/day; increase at 4- to 7-day intervals by 2-4 mg/day. Increase dose intervals (bid, tid, etc) as necessary to control behavior response or side effects. Maximum daily dose: 32 mg; gradual increase (titration) and bedtime administration may prevent some side effects or decrease their severity.

Hemodialysis: Not dialyzable (0% to 5%)

Dosing adjustment in hepatic impairment: Dosage reductions should be considered in patients with liver disease although no specific guidelines are available

Monitoring Parameters Vital signs; lipid profile, fasting blood glucose/Hgb A_{1c}; BMI; mental status, abnormal involuntary movement scale (AIMS), extrapyramidal symptoms (EPS)

Reference Range 2-6 nmol/L

Dosage Forms Tablet: 2 mg, 4 mg, 8 mg, 16 mg

◆ **Perphenazine and Amitriptyline Hydrochloride** *see* Amitriptyline and Perphenazine *on page 103*

◆ **Persantine®** *see* Dipyridamole *on page 525*

◆ **Pethidine Hydrochloride** *see* Meperidine *on page 1081*

◆ **Pexeva®** *see* Paroxetine *on page 1314*

◆ **Pexicam® (Can)** *see* Piroxicam *on page 1378*

◆ **PFA** *see* Foscarnet *on page 762*

◆ **Pfizerpen®** *see* Penicillin G (Parenteral/Aqueous) *on page 1333*

◆ **Pfizerpen-AS® (Can)** *see* Penicillin G Procaine *on page 1335*

◆ **PGE₁** *see* Alprostadil *on page 77*

◆ **PGE₂** *see* Dinoprostone *on page 513*

◆ **PGI₂** *see* Epoprostenol *on page 598*

◆ **PGX** *see* Epoprostenol *on page 598*

◆ **Phanasin® [OTC]** *see* Guaifenesin *on page 814*

◆ **Phanasin® Diabetic Choice [OTC]** *see* Guaifenesin *on page 814*

◆ **Phanatuss® DM [OTC]** *see* Guaifenesin and Dextromethorphan *on page 816*

◆ **Phanatuss® HC** *see* Hydrocodone and Guaifenesin *on page 849*

◆ **Pharmaflur®** *see* Fluoride *on page 722*

◆ **Pharmaflur® 1.1** *see* Fluoride *on page 722*

◆ **Pharmorubicin® (Can)** *see* Epirubicin *on page 592*

◆ **Phenabid®** *see* Chlorpheniramine and Phenylephrine *on page 349*

◆ **Phenabid DM®** *see* Chlorpheniramine, Phenylephrine, and Dextromethorphan *on page 352*

◆ **Phenadoz™** *see* Promethazine *on page 1435*

◆ **Phenagesic [OTC]** *see* Acetaminophen and Phenyltoloxamine *on page 32*

◆ **PhenaVent™** *see* Guaifenesin and Phenylephrine *on page 818*

◆ **PhenaVent™ D** *see* Guaifenesin and Phenylephrine *on page 818*

◆ **PhenaVent™ LA** *see* Guaifenesin and Phenylephrine *on page 818*

◆ **PhenaVent™ Ped** *see* Guaifenesin and Phenylephrine *on page 818*

♦ Phenazo™ **(Can)** see Phenazopyridine on page 1351

Phenazopyridine (fen az oh PEER i deen)

U.S. Brand Names AZO-Gesic® [OTC]; AZO-Standard® [OTC]; Baridium® [OTC]; Pyridium®; ReAzo [OTC]; Uristat® [OTC]; UTI Relief® [OTC]
Canadian Brand Names Phenazo™
Index Terms Phenazopyridine Hydrochloride; Phenylazo Diamino Pyridine Hydrochloride
Pharmacologic Category Analgesic, Urinary
Use Symptomatic relief of urinary burning, itching, frequency and urgency in association with urinary tract infection or following urologic procedures
Pregnancy Risk Factor B
Lactation Excretion in breast milk unknown
Medication Safety Issues
Sound-alike/look-alike issues:
Pyridium® may be confused with Dyrenium®, Perdiem®, pyridoxine, pyrithione
Contraindications Hypersensitivity to phenazopyridine or any component of the formulation; kidney or liver disease; patients with a Cl_{cr} <50 mL/minute
Warnings/Precautions Does not treat infection, acts only as an analgesic; drug should be discontinued if skin or sclera develop a yellow color; use with caution in patients with renal impairment. Use of this agent in the elderly is limited since accumulation of phenazopyridine can occur in patients with renal insufficiency. Use is contraindicated in patients with a Cl_{cr} <50 mL/minute.
Adverse Reactions
1% to 10%:
Central nervous system: Headache, dizziness
Gastrointestinal: Stomach cramps
<1% (Limited to important or life-threatening): Acute renal failure, hemolytic anemia, hepatitis, methemoglobinemia
Overdosage/Toxicology Symptoms include methemoglobinemia, hemolytic anemia, skin pigmentation, and renal and hepatic impairment. The antidote for methemoglobinemia is methylene blue 1-2 mg/kg I.V.
Mechanism of Action An azo dye which exerts local anesthetic or analgesic action on urinary tract mucosa through an unknown mechanism
Pharmacodynamics/Kinetics
Metabolism: Hepatic and via other tissues
Excretion: Urine (65% as unchanged drug)
Dosage Oral:
Children: 12 mg/kg/day in 3 divided doses administered after meals for 2 days
Adults: 100-200 mg 3 times/day after meals for 2 days when used concomitantly with an antibacterial agent
Dosing interval in renal impairment:
Cl_{cr} 50-80 mL/minute: Administer every 8-16 hours
Cl_{cr} <50 mL/minute: Avoid use
Dietary Considerations Should be taken after meals.
Test Interactions Phenazopyridine may cause delayed reactions with glucose oxidase reagents (Clinistix®, Tes-Tape®); occasional false-positive tests occur with Tes-Tape®; cupric sulfate tests (Clinitest®) are not affected; interference may also occur with urine ketone tests (Acetest®, Ketostix®) and urinary protein tests; tests for urinary steroids and porphyrins may also occur
Dosage Forms
Tablet, as hydrochloride: 100 mg, 200 mg
AZO-Gesic®, AZO-Standard®, Uristat®: 95 mg
Baridium®: 97.2 mg
ReAzo: 95 mg
Pyridium®: 100 mg, 200 mg
UTI Relief®: 97.2 mg

♦ **Phenazopyridine Hydrochloride** see Phenazopyridine on page 1351

Phenelzine (FEN el zeen)

U.S. Brand Names Nardil®
Canadian Brand Names Nardil®
Index Terms Phenelzine Sulfate
Pharmacologic Category Antidepressant, Monoamine Oxidase Inhibitor
Additional Appendix Information
Antidepressant Agents on page 1866
Tyramine Content of Foods on page 2115
Use Symptomatic treatment of atypical, nonendogenous, or neurotic depression
Unlabeled/Investigational Use Selective mutism
Restrictions An FDA-approved medication guide concerning the use of antidepressants in children and teenagers must be distributed when dispensing an outpatient prescription (new or refill) where this medication is to be used without direct supervision of a healthcare provider. Medication guides are available at http://www.fda.gov/cder/Offices/ODS/medication_guides.htm. Dispense to parents or guardians of children and teenagers receiving this medication.
Pregnancy Risk Factor C
Lactation Excretion in breast milk unknown/not recommended
Medication Safety Issues
Sound-alike/look-alike issues:
Phenelzine may be confused with phenytoin
Nardil® may be confused with Norinyl®
(Continued)

Phenelzine *(Continued)*

Contraindications Hypersensitivity to phenelzine or any component of the formulation; uncontrolled hypertension; pheochromocytoma; hepatic disease; congestive heart failure; CNS depressants, ethanol, meperidine, bupropion, buspirone, guanethidine, serotonergic drugs (including SSRIs) - do not use within 5 weeks of fluoxetine discontinuation or 2 weeks of other antidepressant discontinuation; general anesthesia, local vasoconstrictors; spinal anesthesia (hypotension may be exaggerated); sympathomimetics (and related compounds); foods high in tyramine content; supplements containing tyrosine, phenylalanine, tryptophan, or caffeine

Warnings/Precautions [U.S. Boxed Warning]: Antidepressants increase the risk of suicidal thinking and behavior in children and adolescents with major depressive disorder (MDD) and other depressive disorders; consider risk prior to prescribing. All patients must be closely monitored for clinical worsening, suicidality, or unusual changes in behavior, especially during the initiation of therapy or following an increase or decrease in dosage. When used in children, the child's family or caregiver should be instructed to closely observe the patient and communicate condition with healthcare provider. A medication guide should be dispensed with each prescription. **Phenelzine is FDA approved for the treatment of depression in children ≥16 years of age.**

The possibility of a suicide attempt is inherent in major depression and may persist until remission occurs. Use caution in high-risk patients. Worsening depression and severe abrupt suicidality that are not part of the presenting symptoms may require discontinuation or modification of drug therapy. The patient's family or caregiver should be alerted to monitor patients for the emergence of suicidality and associated behaviors (such as agitation, irritability, hostility, impulsivity, and hypomania) and call healthcare provider.

May worsen psychosis in some patients or precipitate a shift to mania or hypomania in patients with bipolar disorder. Patients presenting with depressive symptoms should be screened for bipolar disorder. Monotherapy in patients with bipolar disorder should be avoided. **Phenelzine is not FDA approved for the treatment of bipolar depression.**

Use with caution in patients who are hyperactive, hyperexcitable, or who have glaucoma, hyperthyroidism, suicidal tendencies, or diabetes. Hypertensive crisis may occur with tyramine, tryptophan, or dopamine-containing foods. Should not be used in combination with other antidepressants. Hypotensive effects of antihypertensives (beta-blockers, thiazides) may be exaggerated. May cause orthostatic hypotension - use with caution in patients with hypotension or patients who would not tolerate transient hypotensive episodes (cardiovascular or cerebrovascular disease) - effects may be additive with other agents which cause orthostasis. Use with caution in patients at risk of seizures, or in patients receiving other drugs which may lower seizure threshold. Toxic reactions have occurred with dextromethorphan. Discontinue at least 48 hours prior to myelography. May increase the risks associated with electroconvulsive therapy. Consider discontinuing, when possible, prior to elective surgery.

Adverse Reactions Frequency not defined.

Cardiovascular: Orthostatic hypotension, edema

Central nervous system: Dizziness, headache, drowsiness, sleep disturbances, fatigue, hyper-reflexia, twitching, ataxia, mania

Dermatologic: Rash, pruritus

Endocrine & metabolic: Decreased sexual ability (anorgasmia, ejaculatory disturbances, impotence), hypernatremia, hypermetabolic syndrome

Gastrointestinal: Xerostomia, constipation, weight gain

Genitourinary: Urinary retention

Hematologic: Leukopenia

Hepatic: Hepatitis

Neuromuscular & skeletal: Weakness, tremor, myoclonus

Ocular: Blurred vision, glaucoma

Miscellaneous: Diaphoresis

Overdosage/Toxicology Symptoms include tachycardia, palpitations, muscle twitching, seizures, insomnia, restlessness, transient hypertension, hypotension, drowsiness, hyperpyrexia, and coma. Competent supportive care is the most important treatment for overdose with a monoamine oxidase (MAO) inhibitor. Both hypertension or hypotension can occur with intoxication. Hypotension may respond to I.V. fluids or vasopressors and hypertension usually responds to an alpha-adrenergic blocker. While treating the hypertension, care is warranted to avoid sudden drops in blood pressure, since this may worsen MAO inhibitor toxicity. Muscle irritability and seizures often respond to diazepam, while hyperthermia is best treated with antipyretics and cooling blankets.

Drug Interactions

Increased Effect/Toxicity: In general, the combined use of phenelzine with TCAs, venlafaxine, trazodone, dexfenfluramine, sibutramine, lithium, meperidine, fenfluramine, dextromethorphan, and SSRIs should be avoided due to the potential for severe adverse reactions (serotonin syndrome, death); avoid meperidine within 2 weeks of phenelzine use, allow 5 weeks between discontinuing fluoxetine and starting MAO inhibitors, allow at least 10 days after discontinuing MAO inhibitors and starting fluoxetine; concurrent use with dextromethorphan is contraindicated. MAO inhibitors (including phenelzine) may inhibit the metabolism of barbiturates and prolong their effect. Phenelzine in combination with amphetamines, other stimulants (methylphenidate), levodopa, metaraminol, reserpine, and decongestants (pseudoephedrine) may result in severe hypertensive reactions. Concurrent use with amphetamines, methylphenidate, metaraminol, and pseudoephedrine is contraindicated.

Phenelzine may increase the pressor response of norepinephrine and may prolong neuromuscular blockade produced by succinylcholine. Tramadol may increase the risk of seizures and serotonin syndrome in patients receiving an MAO inhibitor. Phenelzine may produce additive hypoglycemic effect in patients receiving hypoglycemic agents and may produce delirium in patients receiving disulfiram. Concurrent use with bupropion is contraindicated; allow at least 14 days between discontinuing MAO inhibitors and starting bupropion. Concurrent use with buspirone may cause hypertension; wait at least 14 days between discontinuing one agent and starting the other.

Decreased Effect: Phenelzine (and other MAO inhibitors) inhibits the antihypertensive response to guanadrel or guanethidine; concurrent use is contraindicated.

Ethanol/Nutrition/Herb Interactions

Ethanol: Avoid ethanol (based on CNS depressant effects and potential tyramine content)

Food: Concurrent ingestion of foods rich in tyramine may cause sudden and severe high blood pressure (hypertensive crisis). Avoid tyramine-containing foods with MAOIs. Food's freshness is also an important concern; improperly stored or spoiled food can create an environment where tyramine concentrations may increase.

Herb/Nutraceuticals: Avoid supplements containing caffeine, tyrosine, tryptophan or phenylalanine. Ingestion of large quantities may increase the risk of severe side effects (eg, hypertensive reactions, serotonin syndrome).

Stability Protect from light.

Mechanism of Action Thought to act by increasing endogenous concentrations of norepinephrine, dopamine, and serotonin through inhibition of the enzyme (monoamine oxidase) responsible for the breakdown of these neurotransmitters

Pharmacodynamics/Kinetics

Onset of action: Therapeutic: 2-4 weeks; geriatric patients receiving an average of 55 mg/day developed a mean platelet MAO activity inhibition of about 85%.

Duration: May continue to have a therapeutic effect and interactions 2 weeks after discontinuing therapy

Absorption: Well absorbed

Metabolism: Oxidized via monoamine oxidase (primary pathway) and acetylation (minor pathway)

Half-life elimination: 11 hours

Excretion: Urine (primarily as metabolites and unchanged drug)

Dosage Oral:

Children: Selective mutism (unlabeled use): 30-60 mg/day

Adults: Depression: 15 mg 3 times/day; may increase to 60-90 mg/day during early phase of treatment, then reduce dose for maintenance therapy slowly after maximum benefit is obtained; takes 2-4 weeks for a significant response to occur

Elderly: Depression: Initial: 7.5 mg/day; increase by 7.5-15 mg/day every 3-4 days as tolerated; usual therapeutic dose: 15-60 mg/day in 3-4 divided doses

Monitoring Parameters Blood pressure, heart rate, diet, weight, mood (if depressive symptoms)

Additional Information Pyridoxine deficiency has occurred; symptoms include numbness and edema of hands; may respond to supplementation.

The MAO inhibitors are usually reserved for patients who do not tolerate or respond to other antidepressants. The brain activity of monoamine oxidase increases with age and even more so in patients with Alzheimer's disease. Therefore, the MAO inhibitors may have an increased role in patients with Alzheimer's disease who are depressed. Phenelzine is less stimulating than tranylcypromine.

Dosage Forms Tablet: 15 mg

♦ **Phenelzine Sulfate** *see* Phenelzine *on page 1351*
♦ **Phenergan®** *see* Promethazine *on page 1435*
♦ **Pheniramine and Naphazoline** *see* Naphazoline and Pheniramine *on page 1199*

Phenobarbital (fee noe BAR bi tal)

U.S. Brand Names Luminal® Sodium

Canadian Brand Names PMS-Phenobarbital

Index Terms Phenobarbital Sodium; Phenobarbitone; Phenylethylmalonylurea

Pharmacologic Category Anticonvulsant, Barbiturate; Barbiturate

Additional Appendix Information

Anticonvulsants by Seizure Type *on page 1865*

Epilepsy *on page 2048*

Use Management of generalized tonic-clonic (grand mal) and partial seizures; sedative

Unlabeled/Investigational Use Febrile seizures in children; may also be used for prevention and treatment of neonatal hyperbilirubinemia and lowering of bilirubin in chronic cholestasis; neonatal seizures; management of sedative/hypnotic withdrawal

Restrictions C-IV

Pregnancy Risk Factor D

Pregnancy Implications Crosses the placenta. Cardiac defect reported; hemorrhagic disease of newborn due to fetal vitamin K depletion may occur; may induce maternal folic acid deficiency; withdrawal symptoms observed in infant following delivery. Epilepsy itself, number of medications, genetic factors, or a combination of these probably influence the teratogenicity of anticonvulsant therapy. Benefit:risk ratio usually favors continued use during pregnancy and breast-feeding.

Lactation Enters breast milk/not recommended (AAP recommends use "with caution")

Medication Safety Issues

Sound-alike/look-alike issues:

Phenobarbital may be confused with pentobarbital

Luminal® may be confused with Tuinal®

Contraindications Hypersensitivity to barbiturates or any component of the formulation; marked hepatic impairment; dyspnea or airway obstruction; porphyria; pregnancy

Warnings/Precautions Use with caution in patients with hypovolemic shock, CHF, hepatic impairment, respiratory dysfunction or depression, previous addiction to the sedative/hypnotic group, chronic or acute pain, renal dysfunction, and the elderly, due to its long half-life and risk of dependence, phenobarbital is not recommended as a sedative in the

(Continued)

Phenobarbital *(Continued)*

elderly; tolerance or psychological and physical dependence may occur with prolonged use. Use with caution in patients with depression or suicidal tendencies, or in patients with a history of drug abuse. **Abrupt withdrawal in patients with epilepsy may precipitate status epilepticus.**

Adverse Reactions Frequency not defined.

Cardiovascular: Bradycardia, hypotension, syncope

Central nervous system: Drowsiness, lethargy, CNS excitation or depression, impaired judgment, "hangover" effect, confusion, somnolence, agitation, hyperkinesia, ataxia, nervousness, headache, insomnia, nightmares, hallucinations, anxiety, dizziness

Dermatologic: Rash, exfoliative dermatitis, Stevens-Johnson syndrome

Gastrointestinal: Nausea, vomiting, constipation

Hematologic: Agranulocytosis, thrombocytopenia, megaloblastic anemia

Local: Pain at injection site, thrombophlebitis with I.V. use

Renal: Oliguria

Respiratory: Laryngospasm, respiratory depression, apnea (especially with rapid I.V. use), hypoventilation

Miscellaneous: Gangrene with inadvertent intra-arterial injection

Overdosage/Toxicology Symptoms include unsteady gait, slurred speech, confusion, jaundice, hypothermia, hypotension, respiratory depression, and coma. If hypotension occurs, administer I.V. fluids and place in Trendelenburg position. If unresponsive, an I.V. vasopressor (eg, dopamine, epinephrine) may be required. Repeat oral doses of activated charcoal significantly reduce the half-life of phenobarbital resulting from enhancement of nonrenal elimination. The usual dose is 0.1-1 g/kg every 4-6 hours for 3-4 days, unless the patient has no bowel movement, causing charcoal to remain in the GI tract. Assure adequate hydration and renal function. Urinary alkalinization with I.V. sodium bicarbonate also helps enhance elimination. Hemodialysis or hemoperfusion is of uncertain status. Patients in stage IV coma, due to high serum barbiturate levels, may require charcoal hemoperfusion.

Drug Interactions

Cytochrome P450 Effect: Substrate of CYP2C9 (minor), 2C19 (major), 2E1 (minor); **Induces** CYP1A2 (strong), 2A6 (strong), 2B6 (strong), 2C8 (strong), 2C9 (strong), 3A4 (strong)

Increased Effect/Toxicity: When combined with other CNS depressants, ethanol, opioid analgesics, antidepressants, or benzodiazepines, additive respiratory and CNS depression may occur. Barbiturates may enhance the hepatotoxic potential of acetaminophen overdoses. Chloramphenicol, MAO inhibitors, valproic acid, and felbamate may inhibit barbiturate metabolism. Barbiturates may impair the absorption of griseofulvin, and may enhance the nephrotoxic effects of methoxyflurane. Concurrent use of phenobarbital with meperidine may result in increased CNS depression. Concurrent use of phenobarbital with primidone may result in elevated phenobarbital serum concentrations. The levels/effects of phenobarbital may be increased by delavirdine, fluconazole, fluvoxamine, gemfibrozil, isoniazid, omeprazole, ticlopidine, and other CYP2C19 inhibitors.

Decreased Effect: Barbiturates may increase the metabolism of estrogens and reduce the efficacy of oral contraceptives; an alternative method of contraception should be considered. Barbiturates inhibit the hypoprothrombinemic effects of oral anticoagulants via increased metabolism. Barbiturates may enhance the metabolism of methadone resulting in methadone withdrawal. The levels/effects of phenobarbital may be decreased by aminoglutethimide, carbamazepine, phenytoin, rifampin, and other CYP2C19 inducers.

Phenobarbital may decrease the levels/effects of aminophylline, amiodarone, benzodiazepines, bupropion, calcium channel blockers, carbamazepine, citalopram, clarithromycin, cyclosporine, diazepam, efavirenz, erythromycin, estrogens, fluoxetine, fluvoxamine, glimepiride, glipizide, ifosfamide, losartan, methsuximide, mirtazapine, nateglinide, nefazodone, nevirapine, phenytoin, pioglitazone, promethazine, propranolol, protease inhibitors, proton pump inhibitors, rifampin, ropinirole, rosiglitazone, selegiline, sertraline, sulfonamides, tacrolimus, theophylline, venlafaxine, voriconazole, warfarin, zafirlukast, and other CYP1A2, 2A6, 2B6, 2C8, 2C9, or 3A4 substrates.

Ethanol/Nutrition/Herb Interactions

Ethanol: Avoid ethanol (may increase CNS depression).

Food: May cause decrease in vitamin D and calcium.

Herb/Nutraceutical: Avoid evening primrose (seizure threshold decreased). Avoid valerian, St John's wort, kava kava, gotu kola (may increase CNS depression).

Stability Protect elixir from light. Not stable in aqueous solutions; use only clear solutions. Do not add to acidic tendencies; precipitation may occur.

Mechanism of Action Short-acting barbiturate with sedative, hypnotic, and anticonvulsant properties. Barbiturates depress the sensory cortex, decrease motor activity, alter cerebellar function, and produce drowsiness, sedation, and hypnosis. In high doses, barbiturates exhibit anticonvulsant activity; barbiturates produce dose-dependent respiratory depression.

Pharmacodynamics/Kinetics

Onset of action: Oral: Hypnosis: 20-60 minutes; I.V.: ~5 minutes

Peak effect: I.V.: ~30 minutes

Duration: Oral: 6-10 hours; I.V.: 4-10 hours

Absorption: Oral: 70% to 90%

Protein binding: 20% to 45%; decreased in neonates

Metabolism: Hepatic via hydroxylation and glucuronide conjugation

Half-life elimination: Neonates: 45-500 hours; Infants: 20-133 hours; Children: 37-73 hours; Adults: 53-140 hours

Time to peak, serum: Oral: 1-6 hours

Excretion: Urine (20% to 50% as unchanged drug)

Dosage

Children:

Sedation: Oral: 2 mg/kg 3 times/day

Hypnotic: I.M., I.V., SubQ: 3-5 mg/kg at bedtime

Preoperative sedation: Oral, I.M., I.V.: 1-3 mg/kg 1-1.5 hours before procedure

Adults:
Sedation: Oral, I.M.: 30-120 mg/day in 2-3 divided doses
Hypnotic: Oral, I.M., I.V., SubQ: 100-320 mg at bedtime
Preoperative sedation: I.M.: 100-200 mg 1-1.5 hours before procedure

Anticonvulsant: Status epilepticus: **Loading dose:** I.V.:
Infants and Children: 10-20 mg/kg in a single or divided dose; in select patients may administer additional 5 mg/kg/dose every 15-30 minutes until seizure is controlled or a total dose of 40 mg/kg is reached
Adults: 300-800 mg initially followed by 120-240 mg/dose at 20-minute intervals until seizures are controlled or a total dose of 1-2 g

Anticonvulsant maintenance dose: Oral, I.V.:
Infants: 5-8 mg/kg/day in 1-2 divided doses
Children:
1-5 years: 6-8 mg/kg/day in 1-2 divided doses
5-12 years: 4-6 mg/kg/day in 1-2 divided doses
Children >12 years and Adults: 1-3 mg/kg/day in divided doses or 50-100 mg 2-3 times/day
Sedative/hypnotic withdrawal (unlabeled use): Initial daily requirement is determined by substituting phenobarbital 30 mg for every 100 mg pentobarbital used during tolerance testing; then daily requirement is decreased by 10% of initial dose

Dosing interval in renal impairment: Cl$_{cr}$ <10 mL/minute: Administer every 12-16 hours
Hemodialysis: Moderately dialyzable (20% to 50%)
Dosing adjustment/comments in hepatic disease: Increased side effects may occur in severe liver disease; monitor plasma levels and adjust dose accordingly

Dietary Considerations Vitamin D: Loss in vitamin D due to malabsorption; increase intake of foods rich in vitamin D. Supplementation of vitamin D and/or calcium may be necessary. Sodium content of injection (65 mg, 1 mL): 6 mg (0.3 mEq).

Administration Avoid rapid I.V. administration >50 mg/minute; avoid intra-arterial injection; parenteral solutions are highly alkaline; avoid extravasation

Monitoring Parameters Phenobarbital serum concentrations, mental status, CBC, LFTs, seizure activity

Reference Range
Therapeutic:
Infants and children: 15-30 mcg/mL (SI: 65-129 µmol/L)
Adults: 20-40 mcg/mL (SI: 86-172 µmol/L)
Toxic: >40 mcg/mL (SI: >172 µmol/L)
Toxic concentration: Slowness, ataxia, nystagmus: 35-80 mcg/mL (SI: 150-344 µmol/L)
Coma with reflexes: 65-117 mcg/mL (SI: 279-502 µmol/L)
Coma without reflexes: >100 mcg/mL (SI: >430 µmol/L)

Test Interactions Assay interference of LDH
Additional Information Injectable solutions contain propylene glycol.

Dosage Forms
Elixir: 20 mg/5 mL (473 mL) [contains alcohol]
Injection, solution, as sodium: 65 mg/mL (1 mL); 130 mg/mL (1 mL) [contains alcohol and propylene glycol]
Luminal® Sodium: 60 mg/mL (1 mL); 130 mg/mL (1 mL) [contains alcohol 10% and propylene glycol]
Tablet: 15 mg, 30 mg, 32 mg, 60 mg, 65 mg, 100 mg

♦ **Phenobarbital, Belladonna, and Ergotamine Tartrate** *see* Belladonna, Phenobarbital, and Ergotamine *on page 201*
♦ **Phenobarbital, Hyoscyamine, Atropine, and Scopolamine** *see* Hyoscyamine, Atropine, Scopolamine, and Phenobarbital *on page 868*
♦ **Phenobarbital Sodium** *see* Phenobarbital *on page 1353*
♦ **Phenobarbitone** *see* Phenobarbital *on page 1353*

Phenoxybenzamine (fen oks ee BEN za meen)

U.S. Brand Names Dibenzyline®
Canadian Brand Names Dibenzyline®
Index Terms Phenoxybenzamine Hydrochloride
Pharmacologic Category Alpha$_1$ Blocker
Use Symptomatic management of pheochromocytoma; treatment of hypertensive crisis caused by sympathomimetic amines
Unlabeled/Investigational Use Micturition problems associated with neurogenic bladder, functional outlet obstruction, and partial prostate obstruction
Pregnancy Risk Factor C
Dosage Oral:
Children: Initial: 0.2 mg/kg (maximum: 10 mg) once daily, increase by 0.2 mg/kg increments; usual maintenance dose: 0.4-1.2 mg/kg/day every 6-8 hours, higher doses may be necessary
Adults: Initial: 10 mg twice daily, increase by 10 mg every other day until optimum dose is achieved; usual range: 20-40 mg 2-3 times/day
Additional Information Complete prescribing information for this medication should be consulted for additional detail.
Dosage Forms Capsule, as hydrochloride: 10 mg [contains benzyl alcohol]

♦ **Phenoxybenzamine Hydrochloride** *see* Phenoxybenzamine *on page 1355*
♦ **Phenoxymethyl Penicillin** *see* Penicillin V Potassium *on page 1336*

Phentermine (FEN ter meen)

U.S. Brand Names Adipex-P®; Ionamin®
Canadian Brand Names Ionamin®
Index Terms Phentermine Hydrochloride
Pharmacologic Category Anorexiant
Use Short-term adjunct in a regimen of weight reduction based on exercise, behavioral modification, and caloric reduction in the management of exogenous obesity for patients with an initial body mass index ≥30 kg/m^2 or ≥27 kg/m^2 in the presence of other risk factors (diabetes, hypertension)
Restrictions C-IV
Pregnancy Risk Factor C
Medication Safety Issues
Sound-alike/look-alike issues:
Phentermine may be confused with phentolamine, phenytoin
Ionamin® may be confused with Imodium®
Contraindications Hypersensitivity or idiosyncrasy to sympathomimetic amines or any component of the formulation; patients with advanced arteriosclerosis, symptomatic cardiovascular disease, moderate to severe hypertension (stage II or III), hyperthyroidism, glaucoma, agitated states; patients with a history of drug abuse; use during or within 14 days following MAO inhibitor therapy; children <16 years of age (per manufacturer)
Warnings/Precautions Use with caution in patients with bipolar disorder, diabetes mellitus, cardiovascular disease, seizure disorders, insomnia, porphyria, or mild hypertension (stage I). May exacerbate symptoms of behavior and thought disorder in psychotic patients. Stimulants may unmask tics in individuals with coexisting Tourette's syndrome. Potential for drug dependency exists; avoid abrupt discontinuation in patients who have received for prolonged periods. Stimulant use has been associated with growth suppression, and careful monitoring is recommended.

Primary pulmonary hypertension (PPH), a rare and frequently fatal pulmonary disease, has been reported to occur in patients receiving a combination of phentermine and fenfluramine or dexfenfluramine. The possibility of an association between PPH and the use of phentermine alone cannot be ruled out.

Use in weight reduction programs only when alternative therapy has been ineffective. Serious, potentially life-threatening toxicities may occur when thyroid hormones (at dosages above usual daily hormonal requirements) are used in combination with sympathomimetic amines to induce weight loss. Treatment of obesity is not an approved use for thyroid hormone.
Adverse Reactions Frequency not defined.
Cardiovascular: Hypertension, palpitation, tachycardia, primary pulmonary hypertension and/or regurgitant cardiac valvular disease
Central nervous system: Euphoria, insomnia, overstimulation, dizziness, dysphoria, headache, restlessness, psychosis
Dermatologic: Urticaria
Endocrine & metabolic: Changes in libido, impotence
Gastrointestinal: Nausea, constipation, xerostomia, unpleasant taste, diarrhea
Hematologic: Blood dyscrasias
Neuromuscular & skeletal: Tremor
Ocular: Blurred vision
Overdosage/Toxicology Symptoms include hyperactivity, agitation, hyperthermia, hypertension, and seizures. There is no specific antidote for phentermine intoxication and the bulk of the treatment is supportive. Hyperactivity and agitation usually respond to reduced sensory input; however, with extreme agitation haloperidol (2-5 mg I.M. for adults) may be required. Hyperthermia is best treated with external cooling measures, or when severe or unresponsive, muscle paralysis with pancuronium may be needed. Hypertension is usually transient and generally does not require treatment unless severe. For diastolic blood pressures >110 mm Hg, a nitroprusside infusion should be initiated. Seizures usually respond to diazepam IVP and/or phenytoin maintenance regimens.
Drug Interactions
Increased Effect/Toxicity: Dosage of hypoglycemic agents may need to be adjusted when phentermine is used in a diabetic receiving a special diet. Concurrent use of MAO inhibitors and drugs with MAO activity (furazolidone, linezolid) may be associated with hypertensive episodes. Concurrent use of SSRIs may be associated with a risk of serotonin syndrome.
Decreased Effect: Phentermine may decrease the effect of antihypertensive medications The efficacy of anorexiants may be decreased by antipsychotics; in addition, amphetamines or related compounds may induce an increase in psychotic symptoms in some patients. Amphetamines (and related compounds) inhibit the antihypertensive response to guanethidine; probably also may occur with guanadrel.
Mechanism of Action Phentermine is structurally similar to dextroamphetamine and is comparable to dextroamphetamine as an appetite suppressant, but is generally associated with a lower incidence and severity of CNS side effects. Phentermine, like other anorexiants, stimulates the hypothalamus to result in decreased appetite; anorexiant effects are most likely mediated via norepinephrine and dopamine metabolism. However, other CNS effects or metabolic effects may be involved.
Pharmacodynamics/Kinetics
Duration: Resin produces more prolonged clinical effects
Absorption: Well absorbed; resin absorbed slower
Half-life elimination: 20 hours
Excretion: Primarily urine (as unchanged drug)
Dosage Oral: Adults: Obesity: 8 mg 3 times/day 30 minutes before meals or food or 15-37.5 mg/day before breakfast or 10-14 hours before retiring
Monitoring Parameters CNS

Dosage Forms
Capsule, as hydrochloride: 15 mg, 30 mg
  Adipex-P®: 37.5 mg
Capsule, resin complex:
  Ionamin®: 15 mg; 30 mg [DSC]
Tablet, as hydrochloride: 37.5 mg
  Adipex-P®: 37.5 mg

♦ **Phentermine Hydrochloride** *see Phentermine on page 1356*

Phentolamine (fen TOLE a meen)

Canadian Brand Names Regitine®; Rogitine®
Index Terms Phentolamine Mesylate; Regitine [DSC]
Pharmacologic Category Alpha₁ Blocker
Additional Appendix Information
  Hypertension *on page 2063*
Use Diagnosis of pheochromocytoma and treatment of hypertension associated with pheochromocytoma or other forms of hypertension caused by excess sympathomimetic amines; as treatment of dermal necrosis after extravasation of drugs with alpha-adrenergic effects (norepinephrine, dopamine, epinephrine)
Unlabeled/Investigational Use Treatment of pralidoxime-induced hypertension
Pregnancy Risk Factor C
Lactation Excretion in breast milk unknown
Medication Safety Issues
  Sound-alike/look-alike issues:
    Phentolamine may be confused with phentermine, Ventolin®
Contraindications Hypersensitivity to phentolamine or any component of the formulation; renal impairment; coronary or cerebral arteriosclerosis; concurrent use with phosphodiesterase-5 (PDE-5) inhibitors including sildenafil (>25 mg), tadalafil, or vardenafil
Warnings/Precautions Myocardial infarction, cerebrovascular spasm, and cerebrovascular occlusion have occurred following administration; use with caution in patients with gastritis or peptic ulcer, tachycardia, or a history of cardiac arrhythmias. Discontinue if symptoms of angina occur or worsen.
Adverse Reactions Frequency not defined.
  Cardiovascular: Hypotension, tachycardia, arrhythmia, flushing, orthostatic hypotension
  Central nervous system: Dizziness
  Gastrointestinal: Nausea, vomiting, diarrhea
  Neuromuscular & skeletal: Weakness
  Respiratory: Nasal congestion
  Postmarketing and/or case reports: Pulmonary hypertension
Overdosage/Toxicology Symptoms include tachycardia, shock, vomiting, and dizziness. Hypotension and shock should be treated with fluids and Trendelenburg positioning. Only alpha-adrenergic pressors, such as norepinephrine should be used. Mixed agents such as epinephrine, may cause more hypotension. Take care not to cause so much swelling of the extremity or digit that a compartment syndrome would occur.
Drug Interactions
  Increased Effect/Toxicity: Phentolamine's toxicity is increased with ethanol (disulfiram reaction). Blood pressure-lowering effects are additive with sildenafil (use with extreme caution at a dose ≤25 mg), tadalafil (use is contraindicated by the manufacturer), and vardenafil (use is contraindicated by the manufacturer).
  Decreased Effect: Decreased effect of phentolamine with epinephrine and ephedrine.
Stability Reconstituted solution is stable for 48 hours at room temperature and 1 week when refrigerated.
Mechanism of Action Competitively blocks alpha-adrenergic receptors to produce brief antagonism of circulating epinephrine and norepinephrine to reduce hypertension caused by alpha effects of these catecholamines; also has a positive inotropic and chronotropic effect on the heart
Pharmacodynamics/Kinetics
  Onset of action: I.M.: 15-20 minutes; I.V.: Immediate
  Duration: I.M.: 30-45 minutes; I.V.: 15-30 minutes
  Metabolism: Hepatic
  Half-life elimination: 19 minutes
  Excretion: Urine (10% as unchanged drug)
Dosage
  Treatment of alpha-adrenergic drug extravasation: SubQ:
    Children: 0.1-0.2 mg/kg diluted in 10 mL 0.9% sodium chloride infiltrated into area of extravasation within 12 hours
    Adults: Infiltrate area with small amount of solution made by diluting 5-10 mg in 10 mL 0.9% sodium chloride within 12 hours of extravasation; do not exceed 0.1-0.2 mg/kg or 5 mg total
    If dose is effective, normal skin color should return to the blanched area within 1 hour
  Diagnosis of pheochromocytoma: I.M., I.V.:
    Children: 0.05-0.1 mg/kg/dose, maximum single dose: 5 mg
    Adults: 5 mg
  Surgery for pheochromocytoma: Hypertension: I.M., I.V.:
    Children: 0.05-0.1 mg/kg/dose given 1-2 hours before procedure; repeat as needed every 2-4 hours until hypertension is controlled; maximum single dose: 5 mg
    Adults: 5 mg given 1-2 hours before procedure and repeated as needed every 2-4 hours
  Hypertensive crisis: Adults: 5-20 mg
  Treatment of pralidoxime-induced hypertension (unlabeled use): I.V.:
    Children: 1 mg
    Adults and Elderly: 5 mg
(Continued)

Phentolamine *(Continued)*

Administration Infiltrate the area of dopamine extravasation with multiple small injections using only 27- or 30-gauge needles and changing the needle between each skin entry; take care not to cause so much swelling of the extremity or digit that a compartment syndrome occurs. If infiltration is severe, may also need to consult vascular surgeon

Monitoring Parameters Blood pressure, heart rate; area of infiltration; monitor patient for orthostasis; assist with ambulation

Test Interactions Increased LFTs rarely

Dosage Forms Injection, powder for reconstitution, as mesylate: 5 mg

♦ **Phentolamine Mesylate** *see* Phentolamine *on page 1357*

♦ **Phenylalanine Mustard** *see* Melphalan *on page 1074*

♦ **Phenylazo Diamino Pyridine Hydrochloride** *see* Phenazopyridine *on page 1351*

Phenylephrine *(fen il EF rin)*

U.S. Brand Names AH-chew® D [OTC] [DSC]; AK-Dilate®; Altafrin; Anu-Med [OTC]; Formulation R™ [OTC]; Medicone® [OTC]; Mydfrin®; NāSop™; Neo-Synephrine® Extra Strength [OTC]; Neo-Synephrine® Mild [OTC]; Neo-Synephrine® Ophthalmic [DSC]; Neo-Synephrine® Regular Strength [OTC]; Rectacaine [OTC]; Relief® [OTC]; Rhinall [OTC]; Sudafed PE™ [OTC]; Tronolane® Suppository [OTC]; Vicks® Sinex® Nasal Spray [OTC]; Vicks® Sinex® UltraFine Mist [OTC]

Canadian Brand Names Dionephrine®; Mydfrin®; Neo-Synephrine®

Index Terms Phenylephrine Hydrochloride; Phenylephrine Tannate

Pharmacologic Category Alpha/Beta Agonist; Ophthalmic Agent, Antiglaucoma; Ophthalmic Agent, Mydriatic

Additional Appendix Information
Hemodynamic Support, Intravenous *on page 1885*

Use Treatment of hypotension, vascular failure in shock; as a vasoconstrictor in regional analgesia; as a mydriatic in ophthalmic procedures and treatment of wide-angle glaucoma; supraventricular tachycardia

For OTC use as symptomatic relief of nasal and nasopharyngeal mucosal congestion, treatment of hemorrhoids, relief of redness of the eye due to irritation

Pregnancy Risk Factor C

Lactation Excretion in breast milk unknown/not recommended

Medication Safety Issues
Sound-alike/look-alike issues:
Mydfrin® may be confused with Midrin®

Contraindications Hypersensitivity to phenylephrine or any component of the formulation; hypertension; ventricular tachycardia
Oral: Use with or within 14 days of MAO inhibitor therapy
Ophthalmic: Narrow-angle glaucoma

Warnings/Precautions Some products contain sulfites which may cause allergic reactions in susceptible individuals.

Intravenous: Use with caution in the elderly, patients with hyperthyroidism, bradycardia, partial heart block, myocardial disease, or severe CAD. Not a substitute for volume replacement. Avoid hypertension; monitor blood pressure closely and adjust infusion rate. Infuse into a large vein if possible. Watch I.V. site closely. Avoid extravasation. **[U.S. Boxed Warning]: Should be administered by adequately trained individuals familiar with its use.**

Nasal, oral, rectal: Use caution with hyperthyroidism, diabetes mellitus, cardiovascular disease, ischemic heart disease, increased intraocular pressure, prostatic hyperplasia or in the elderly. Rebound congestion may occur when nasal products are discontinued after chronic use. When used for self-medication (OTC), notify healthcare provider if symptoms do not improve within 7 days (oral, rectal) or 3 days (nasal), are accompanied by fever (oral), or if bleeding occurs (rectal).

Ophthalmic: Use caution with or within 21 days of MAO inhibitor therapy. When used for self-medication (OTC), notify healthcare provider in case of vision changes, continued redness, or if symptoms worsen or do not improve within 3 days.

Adverse Reactions Frequency not defined.
Cardiovascular: Reflex bradycardia, excitability, restlessness, arrhythmia (rare), precordial pain or discomfort, pallor, hypertension, severe peripheral and visceral vasoconstriction, decreased cardiac output
Central nervous system: Headache, anxiety, dizziness, tremor, paresthesia, restlessness
Endocrine & metabolic: Metabolic acidosis
Local: I.V.: Extravasation which may lead to necrosis and sloughing of surrounding tissue, blanching of skin
Neuromuscular & skeletal: Pilomotor response, weakness
Renal: Decreased renal perfusion, reduced urine output
Respiratory: Respiratory distress

Overdosage/Toxicology Symptoms include vomiting, hypertension, palpitations, paresthesia, and ventricular extrasystoles. Treatment is supportive. In extreme cases, I.V. phentolamine may be used.

Drug Interactions
Increased Effect/Toxicity: Phenylephrine, taken with sympathomimetics, may induce tachycardia or arrhythmias. If taken with MAO inhibitors or oxytocic agents, actions may be potentiated. Nonselective beta-blockers may increase hypertensive effects; MAO inhibitors may potentiate hypertension and hypertensive crisis; TCAs may enhance vasopressor effect; avoid concurrent use with these agents. Methyldopa may increase pressor response.

Ethanol/Nutrition/Herb Interactions Herb/Nutraceutical: Avoid ephedra, yohimbe (may cause CNS stimulation).

Stability

Solution for injection: Store vials at controlled room temperature of 15°C to 30°C (59°F to 86°F). Protect from light. Do not use solution if brown or contains a precipitate.

I.V. infusion: May dilute 10 mg in 500 mL NS or D₅W.

I.V. injection: Dilute with SWFI to a concentration of 1 mg/mL.

Ophthalmic solution:

0.12%: Store at controlled room temperature. Protect from light and excessive heat.

2.5% and 10%: Refer to product labeling. Some products are labeled to store at room temperature, others should be stored under refrigeration at 2°C to 8°C (36°F to 46°F). Do not use solution if brown or contains a precipitate.

Mechanism of Action Potent, direct-acting alpha-adrenergic stimulator with weak beta-adrenergic activity; causes vasoconstriction of the arterioles of the nasal mucosa and conjunctiva; activates the dilator muscle of the pupil to cause contraction; produces vasoconstriction of arterioles in the body; produces systemic arterial vasoconstriction

Pharmacodynamics/Kinetics

Onset of action: I.M., SubQ: 10-15 minutes; I.V.: Immediate; Ophthalmic: 10-15 minutes

Duration: I.M.: 0.5-2 hours; I.V.: 15-30 minutes; SubQ: 1 hour; Ophthalmic: Maximal mydriasis: 1 hour, recover time: 3-6 hours

Metabolism: Hepatic, via intestinal monoamine oxidase to phenolic conjugates

Excretion: Urine (90%)

Dosage

Hemorrhoids: Children ≥12 years and Adults: Rectal:

Cream/ointment: Apply to clean dry area, up to 4 times/day; may be used externally or inserted rectally using applicator.

Suppository: Insert 1 suppository rectally, up to 4 times/day

Hypotension/shock:

Children:

I.V. bolus: 5-20 mcg/kg/dose every 10-15 minutes as needed

I.V. infusion: 0.1-0.5 mcg/kg/minute

Adults:

I.V. bolus: 0.1-0.5 mg/dose every 10-15 minutes as needed (initial dose should not exceed 0.5 mg)

I.V. infusion: Initial dose: 100-180 mcg/minute; when blood pressure is stabilized, maintenance rate: 40-60 mcg/minute; rates up to 360 mcg/minute have been reported; dosing range: 0.4-9.1 mcg/kg/minute

Nasal decongestant:

Children:

2-6 years:

Intranasal: Instill 1 drop every 2-4 hours of 0.125% solution as needed. (**Note:** Therapy should not exceed 3 continuous days.)

Oral: Tannate salt (NāSop™ suspension): 1.87-3.75 mg every 12 hours

6-12 years:

Intranasal: Instill 1-2 sprays or instill 1-2 drops every 4 hours of 0.25% solution as needed. (**Note:** Therapy should not exceed 3 continuous days.)

Oral:

Hydrochloride salt: 10 mg every 4 hours

Tannate salt (NāSop™ suspension): 3.75-7.5 mg every 12 hours

Children >12 years and Adults:

Intranasal: Instill 1-2 sprays or instill 1-2 drops every 4 hours of 0.25% to 0.5% solution as needed; 1% solution may be used in adult in cases of extreme nasal congestion; do not use nasal solutions more than 3 days

Oral:

Hydrochloride salt: 10-20 mg every 4 hours

Tannate salt (NāSop™ suspension): 7.5-15 mg every 12 hours

Ocular procedures:

Infants <1 year: Instill 1 drop of 2.5% 15-30 minutes before procedures

Children and Adults: Instill 1 drop of 2.5% or 10% solution, may repeat in 10-60 minutes as needed

Ophthalmic irritation (OTC formulation for relief of eye redness): Adults: Instill 1-2 drops 0.12% solution into affected eye, up to 4 times/day; do not use for >72 hours

Paroxysmal supraventricular tachycardia: I.V.:

Children: 5-10 mcg/kg/dose over 20-30 seconds

Adults: 0.25-0.5 mg/dose over 20-30 seconds

Dietary Considerations NāSop™ contains phenylalanine 4 mg/tablet.

Administration

I.V.: May cause necrosis or sloughing tissue if extravasation occurs during I.V. administration or SubQ administration.

Extravasation management: Use phentolamine as antidote; mix 5 mg with 9 mL of NS. Inject a small amount of this dilution into extravasated area. Blanching should reverse immediately. Monitor site. If blanching should recur, additional injections of phentolamine may be needed.

Oral: NāSop™: Place tablet on tongue and allow to dissolve

Monitoring Parameters Blood pressure, pulse; excitability, irritability, anxiety

Additional Information Phenylephrine allows for close titration of blood pressure and should be used in patients with hypotension or shock due to peripheral vasodilation. Phenylephrine should not constitute sole therapy in patients with hypotension due to aortic dysfunction or hypovolemia. An important benefit of this drug is the short half-life, allowing rapid changes in dosage with prompt appropriate blood pressure responses. When administered intravenously, it should be used in intensive care settings or under very close monitoring.

Dosage Forms [DSC] = Discontinued product

Cream, rectal, as hydrochloride (Formulation R™): 0.25% (54 g) [contains sodium benzoate]

Injection, solution, as hydrochloride: 1% [10 mg/mL] (1 mL, 5 mL) [may contain sodium metabisulfite]

Neo-Synephrine®: 1% (1 mL) [contains sodium metabisulfite]

(Continued)

Phenylephrine *(Continued)*

Ointment, rectal, as hydrochloride:
  Formulation R™: 0.25% (30 g, 60 g) [contains benzoic acid]
  Rectacaine: 0.25% (30 g) [contains shark liver oil]
Solution, intranasal drops, as hydrochloride:
  Neo-Synephrine® Extra Strength: 1% (15 mL) [contains benzalkonium chloride]
  Neo-Synephrine® Regular Strength: 0.5% (15 mL) [contains benzalkonium chloride]
  Rhinall: 0.25% (30 mL) [contains benzalkonium chloride and sodium bisulfite]
Solution, intranasal spray, as hydrochloride:
  Neo-Synephrine® Extra Strength: 1% (15 mL) [contains benzalkonium chloride]
  Neo-Synephrine® Mild: 0.25% (15 mL) [contains benzalkonium chloride]
  Neo-Synephrine® Regular Strength: 0.5% (15 mL) [contains benzalkonium chloride]
  Rhinall: 0.25% (40 mL) [contains benzalkonium chloride and sodium bisulfite]
  Vicks® Sinex®, Vicks® Sinex® UltraFine Mist: 0.5% (15 mL) [contains benzalkonium chloride]
Solution, ophthalmic, as hydrochloride: 2.5% (1 mL, 2 mL, 3 mL, 5 mL, 15 mL) [may contain sodium bisulfite]
  AK-Dilate®: 2.5% (2 mL, 15 mL); 10% (5 mL)
  Altrafrin: 0.12% (15 mL) [OTC]; 2.5% (5 mL, 15 mL) [RX; contains benzalkonium chloride]; 10% (5 mL) [RX; contains benzalkonium chloride]
  Mydfrin®: 2.5% (3 mL, 5 mL) [contains sodium bisulfite]
  Neo-Synephrine®: 2.5% (15 mL); 10% (5 mL) [contains benzalkonium chloride] [DSC]
  Neo-Synephrine® Viscous: 10% (5 mL) [contains benzalkonium chloride] [DSC]
Suppository, rectal, as hydrochloride: 0.25% (12s)
  Anu-Med, Tronolane®: 0.25% (12s)
  Medicone®: 0.25% (18s, 24s)
  Rectacaine: 0.25% (12s) [contains shark liver oil]
Suspension, oral, as tannate (NāSop™): 7.5 mg/5 mL (120 mL) [orange flavor]
Tablet, as hydrochloride (Sudafed PE™): 10 mg
Tablet, chewable, as hydrochloride:
  AH-chew® D: 10 mg [DSC]
Tablet, orally dissolving, as hydrochloride (NāSop™): 10 mg [contains phenylalanine 4 mg/tablet; bubble gum flavor]

- ◆ **Phenylephrine and Chlorpheniramine** *see* Chlorpheniramine and Phenylephrine *on page 349*
- ◆ **Phenylephrine and Cyclopentolate** *see* Cyclopentolate and Phenylephrine *on page 428*
- ◆ **Phenylephrine and Promethazine** *see* Promethazine and Phenylephrine *on page 1438*

Phenylephrine and Scopolamine *(fen il EF rin & skoe POL a meen)*

U.S. Brand Names Murocoll-2®
Index Terms Scopolamine and Phenylephrine
Pharmacologic Category Anticholinergic/Adrenergic Agonist
Use Mydriasis, cycloplegia, and to break posterior synechiae in iritis
Pregnancy Risk Factor C
Medication Safety Issues
  Sound-alike/look-alike issues:
    Murocoll-2® may be confused with Murocel®
Dosage Ophthalmic: Instill 1-2 drops into eye(s); repeat in 5 minutes
Additional Information Complete prescribing information for this medication should be consulted for additional detail.
Dosage Forms Solution, ophthalmic: Phenylephrine hydrochloride 10% and scopolamine hydrobromide 0.3% (5 mL) [contains benzalkonium chloride and sodium metabisulfite]

- ◆ **Phenylephrine, Chlorpheniramine, and Dextromethorphan** *see* Chlorpheniramine, Phenylephrine, and Dextromethorphan *on page 352*
- ◆ **Phenylephrine, Chlorpheniramine, and Dihydrocodeine** *see* Dihydrocodeine, Chlorpheniramine, and Phenylephrine *on page 506*
- ◆ **Phenylephrine, Chlorpheniramine, and Phenyltoloxamine** *see* Chlorpheniramine, Phenylephrine, and Phenyltoloxamine *on page 354*
- ◆ **Phenylephrine, Chlorpheniramine, Codeine, and Potassium Iodide** *see* Chlorpheniramine, Phenylephrine, Codeine, and Potassium Iodide *on page 354*
- ◆ **Phenylephrine, Ephedrine, Chlorpheniramine, and Carbetapentane** *see* Chlorpheniramine, Ephedrine, Phenylephrine, and Carbetapentane *on page 351*
- ◆ **Phenylephrine Hydrochloride** *see* Phenylephrine *on page 1358*
- ◆ **Phenylephrine Hydrochloride and Guaifenesin** *see* Guaifenesin and Phenylephrine *on page 818*
- ◆ **Phenylephrine, Hydrocodone, Chlorpheniramine, Acetaminophen, and Caffeine** *see* Hydrocodone, Chlorpheniramine, Phenylephrine, Acetaminophen, and Caffeine *on page 852*
- ◆ **Phenylephrine, Promethazine, and Codeine** *see* Promethazine, Phenylephrine, and Codeine *on page 1438*
- ◆ **Phenylephrine Tannate** *see* Phenylephrine *on page 1358*
- ◆ **Phenylephrine Tannate and Carbetapentane Tannate** *see* Carbetapentane and Phenylephrine *on page 289*
- ◆ **Phenylephrine Tannate, Chlorpheniramine Tannate, and Methscopolamine Nitrate** *see* Chlorpheniramine, Phenylephrine, and Methscopolamine *on page 353*
- ◆ **Phenylethylmalonylurea** *see* Phenobarbital *on page 1353*
- ◆ **Phenylgesic [OTC]** *see* Acetaminophen and Phenyltoloxamine *on page 32*
- ◆ **Phenyl Salicylate, Methenamine, Methylene Blue, Sodium Biphosphate, and Hyoscyamine** *see* Methenamine, Sodium Biphosphate, Phenyl Salicylate, Methylene Blue, and Hyoscyamine *on page 1107*

♦ **Phenyltoloxamine, Chlorpheniramine, and Phenylephrine** *see* Chlorpheniramine, Phenylephrine, and Phenyltoloxamine *on page 354*

♦ **Phenyltoloxamine Citrate and Acetaminophen** *see* Acetaminophen and Phenyltoloxamine *on page 32*

♦ **Phenytek™** *see* Phenytoin *on page 1361*

Phenytoin (FEN i toyn)

U.S. Brand Names Dilantin®; Phenytek™
Canadian Brand Names Dilantin®
Index Terms Diphenylhydantoin; DPH; Phenytoin Sodium; Phenytoin Sodium, Extended; Phenytoin Sodium, Prompt
Pharmacologic Category Antiarrhythmic Agent, Class Ib; Anticonvulsant, Hydantoin
Additional Appendix Information
Anticonvulsants by Seizure Type *on page 1865*
Epilepsy *on page 2048*
Fosphenytoin and Phenytoin *on page 1883*
Use Management of generalized tonic-clonic (grand mal), complex partial seizures; prevention of seizures following head trauma/neurosurgery
Unlabeled/Investigational Use Ventricular arrhythmias, including those associated with digitalis intoxication, prolonged QT interval and surgical repair of congenital heart diseases in children; epidermolysis bullosa
Pregnancy Risk Factor D
Pregnancy Implications Phenytoin crosses the placenta. Congenital malformations (including a pattern of malformations termed the "fetal hydantoin syndrome" or "fetal anticonvulsant syndrome") have been reported in infants. Isolated cases of malignancies (including neuroblastoma) and coagulation defects in the neonate following delivery have also been reported. Epilepsy itself, the number of medications, genetic factors, or a combination of these probably influence the teratogenicity of anticonvulsant therapy.

Total plasma concentrations of phenytoin are decreased by 56% in the mother during pregnancy; unbound plasma (free) concentrations are decreased by 31%. Because protein binding is decreased, monitoring of unbound plasma concentrations is recommended. Concentrations should be monitored through the 8th week postpartum. The use of folic acid throughout pregnancy and vitamin K during the last month of pregnancy is recommended.

A pregnancy registry is available for women exposed to antiepileptic drug (including phenytoin) at the Genetics and Teratology Unit Massachusetts General Hospital, 1-888-233-2334.
Lactation Enters breast milk/not recommended (AAP rates "compatible")
Medication Safety Issues
Sound-alike/look-alike issues:
Phenytoin may be confused with phenelzine, phentermine
Dilantin® may be confused with Dilaudid®, diltiazem, Dipentum®
Contraindications Hypersensitivity to phenytoin, other hydantoins, or any component of the formulation; pregnancy
Warnings/Precautions May increase frequency of petit mal seizures; I.V. form may cause hypotension, skin necrosis at I.V. site; avoid I.V. administration in small veins; use with caution in patients with porphyria; discontinue if rash or lymphadenopathy occurs; use with caution in patients with hepatic dysfunction, sinus bradycardia, S-A block, or AV block; use with caution in elderly or debilitated patients, or in any condition associated with low serum albumin levels, which will increase the free fraction of phenytoin in the serum and, therefore, the pharmacologic response. Sedation, confusional states, or cerebellar dysfunction (loss of motor coordination) may occur at higher total serum concentrations, or at lower total serum concentrations when the free fraction of phenytoin is increased. Abrupt withdrawal may precipitate status epilepticus.
Adverse Reactions I.V. effects: Hypotension, bradycardia, cardiac arrhythmia, cardiovascular collapse (especially with rapid I.V. use), venous irritation and pain, thrombophlebitis

Effects not related to plasma phenytoin concentrations: Hypertrichosis, gingival hypertrophy, thickening of facial features, carbohydrate intolerance, folic acid deficiency, peripheral neuropathy, vitamin D deficiency, osteomalacia, systemic lupus erythematosus
Concentration-related effects: Nystagmus, blurred vision, diplopia, ataxia, slurred speech, dizziness, drowsiness, lethargy, coma, rash, fever, nausea, vomiting, gum tenderness, confusion, mood changes, folic acid depletion, osteomalacia, hyperglycemia
Related to elevated concentrations:
>20 mcg/mL: Far lateral nystagmus
>30 mcg/mL: 45° lateral gaze nystagmus and ataxia
>40 mcg/mL: Decreased mentation
>100 mcg/mL: Death
Cardiovascular: Hypotension, bradycardia, cardiac arrhythmia, cardiovascular collapse
Central nervous system: Psychiatric changes, slurred speech, dizziness, drowsiness, headache, insomnia
Dermatologic: Rash
Gastrointestinal: Constipation, nausea, vomiting, gingival hyperplasia, enlargement of lips
Hematologic: Leukopenia, thrombocytopenia, agranulocytosis
Hepatic: Hepatitis
Local: Thrombophlebitis
Neuromuscular & skeletal: Tremor, peripheral neuropathy, paresthesia
Ocular: Diplopia, nystagmus, blurred vision
Rarely seen effects: Blood dyscrasias, coarsening of facial features, dyskinesias, hepatitis, hypertrichosis, lymphadenopathy, lymphoma, pseudolymphoma, SLE-like syndrome, Stevens-Johnson syndrome, venous irritation and pain
Overdosage/Toxicology Symptoms include unsteady gait, slurred speech, confusion, nausea, hypothermia, fever, hypotension, respiratory depression, and coma. Treatment is (Continued)

Phenytoin *(Continued)*

supportive for hypotension. Treat with I.V. fluids and place in Trendelenburg position. Seizures may be controlled with diazepam 5-10 mg (0.25-0.4 mg/kg in children).

Drug Interactions

Cytochrome P450 Effect: Substrate of CYP2C9 (major), 2C19 (major), 3A4 (minor); **Induces** CYP2B6 (strong), 2C8 (strong), 2C9 (strong), 2C19 (strong), 3A4 (strong)

Increased Effect/Toxicity: The sedative effects of phenytoin may be additive with other CNS depressants including ethanol, barbiturates, sedatives, antidepressants, opioid analgesics, and benzodiazepines. Selected anticonvulsants (felbamate, gabapentin, and topiramate) have been reported to increase phenytoin levels/effects. In addition, serum phenytoin concentrations may be increased by allopurinol, amiodarone, calcium channel blockers (including diltiazem and nifedipine), cimetidine, disulfiram, methylphenidate, metronidazole, omeprazole, selective serotonin reuptake inhibitors (SSRIs), ticlopidine, tricyclic antidepressants, trazodone, and trimethoprim.

The levels/effects of phenytoin may be increased by delavirdine, fluconazole, fluvoxamine, gemfibrozil, isoniazid, ketoconazole, nicardipine, NSAIDs, omeprazole, sulfonamides, ticlopidine, tolbutamide, and other CYP2C9 or 2C19 inhibitors.

Phenytoin enhances the conversion of primidone to phenobarbital resulting in elevated phenobarbital serum concentrations. Concurrent use of acetazolamide with phenytoin may result in an increased risk of osteomalacia. Concurrent use of phenytoin and lithium has resulted in lithium intoxication. Valproic acid (and sulfisoxazole) may displace phenytoin from binding sites; valproic acid may increase, decrease, or have no effect on phenytoin serum concentrations. Phenytoin transiently increased the response to warfarin initially; this is followed by an inhibition of the hypoprothrombinemic response. Phenytoin may enhance the hepatotoxic potential of acetaminophen overdoses. Concurrent use of dopamine and intravenous phenytoin may lead to an increased risk of hypotension.

Decreased Effect: Phenytoin may enhance the metabolism of estrogen and/or oral contraceptives, decreasing their clinical effect; an alternative method of contraception should be considered. Phenytoin may increase the metabolism of anticonvulsants including barbiturates, carbamazepine, ethosuximide, felbamate, lamotrigine, tiagabine, topiramate, and zonisamide. Valproic acid may increase, decrease, or have no effect on phenytoin serum concentrations. Phenytoin may also decrease the serum concentrations/effects of some antiarrhythmics (disopyramide, propafenone, quinidine, quetiapine) and tricyclic antidepressants may be reduced by phenytoin. Phenytoin may enhance the metabolism of doxycycline, decreasing its clinical effect; higher dosages may be required. Phenytoin may increase the metabolism of chloramphenicol or itraconazole.

Phenytoin may decrease the levels/effects of amiodarone, benzodiazepines, bupropion, calcium channel blockers, carbamazepine, citalopram, clarithromycin, clozapine, cyclosporine, efavirenz, erythromycin, estrogens, fluoxetine, glimepiride, glipizide, losartan, methsuximide, mirtazapine, nateglinide, nefazodone, nevirapine, phenytoin, pioglitazone, promethazine, propranolol, protease inhibitors, proton pump inhibitors, rosiglitazone, selegiline, sertraline, sulfonamides, tacrolimus, venlafaxine, voriconazole, warfarin, zafirlukast, and other CYP2B6, 2C8, 2C9, 2C19, or 3A4 substrates.

The levels/effects of phenytoin may be decreased by aminoglutethimide, carbamazepine, phenobarbital, rifampin, rifapentine, secobarbital, and other CYP2C9 or 2C19 inducers. Clozapine and vigabatrin may reduce phenytoin serum concentrations. Ciprofloxacin may decrease serum phenytoin concentrations. Dexamethasone may decrease serum phenytoin concentrations. Replacement of folic acid has been reported to increase the metabolism of phenytoin, decreasing its serum concentrations and/or increasing seizures.

Initially, phenytoin increases the response to warfarin; this is followed by a decrease in response to warfarin. Phenytoin may inhibit the anti-Parkinson effect of levodopa. The duration of neuromuscular blockade from neuromuscular-blocking agents may be decreased by phenytoin. Phenytoin may enhance the metabolism of methadone resulting in methadone withdrawal. Phenytoin may decrease serum levels/effects of digitalis glycosides, theophylline, and thyroid hormones.

Several chemotherapeutic agents have been associated with a decrease in serum phenytoin levels; includes cisplatin, bleomycin, carmustine, methotrexate, and vinblastine. Enzyme-inducing anticonvulsant therapy may reduce the effectiveness of some chemotherapy regimens (specifically in ALL). Teniposide and methotrexate may be cleared more rapidly in these patients.

Ethanol/Nutrition/Herb Interactions

Ethanol:

Acute use: Avoid or limit ethanol (inhibits metabolism of phenytoin). Watch for sedation.

Chronic use: Avoid or limit ethanol (stimulates metabolism of phenytoin).

Food: Phenytoin serum concentrations may be altered if taken with food. If taken with enteral nutrition, phenytoin serum concentrations may be decreased. Tube feedings decrease bioavailability; hold tube feedings 2 hours before and 2 hours after phenytoin administration. May decrease calcium, folic acid, and vitamin D levels.

Herb/Nutraceutical: Avoid evening primrose (seizure threshold decreased). Avoid valerian, St John's wort, kava kava, gotu kola (may increase CNS depression).

Stability

Capsule, tablet: Store below 30°C (86°F). Protect from light and moisture.

Oral suspension: Store at room temperature of 20°C to 25°C (68°F to 77°F); do not freeze. Protect from light.

Solution for injection: Store at room temperature of 15°C to 30°C (59°F to 86°F). Use only clear solutions free of precipitate and haziness; slightly yellow solutions may be used. Precipitation may occur if solution is refrigerated and may dissolve at room temperature. Further dilution of the solution for I.V. infusion is controversial and no consensus exists as to the optimal concentration and length of stability. Stability is concentration and pH dependent. Based on limited clinical consensus, NS or LR are recommended diluents. Dilutions of 1-10 mg/mL have been used and should be administered as soon as possible after preparation (some recommend to discard if not used within 4 hours). Do not refrigerate.

Mechanism of Action Stabilizes neuronal membranes and decreases seizure activity by increasing efflux or decreasing influx of sodium ions across cell membranes in the motor cortex during generation of nerve impulses; prolongs effective refractory period and suppresses ventricular pacemaker automaticity, shortens action potential in the heart

Pharmacodynamics/Kinetics

Onset of action: I.V.: ~ 0.5-1 hour

Absorption: Oral: Slow

Distribution: V_d:

Neonates: Premature: 1-1.2 L/kg; Full-term: 0.8-0.9 L/kg

Infants: 0.7-0.8 L/kg

Children: 0.7 L/kg

Adults: 0.6-0.7 L/kg

Protein binding:

Neonates: ≥80% (≤20% free)

Infants: ≥85% (≤15% free)

Adults: 90% to 95%

Others: Decreased protein binding

Disease states resulting in a decrease in serum albumin concentration: Burns, hepatic cirrhosis, nephrotic syndrome, pregnancy, cystic fibrosis

Disease states resulting in an apparent decrease in affinity of phenytoin for serum albumin: Renal failure, jaundice (severe), other drugs (displacers), hyperbilirubinemia (total bilirubin >15 mg/dL), Cl_{cr} <25 mL/minute (unbound fraction is increased two- to threefold in uremia)

Metabolism: Follows dose-dependent capacity-limited (Michaelis-Menten) pharmacokinetics with increased V_{max} in infants >6 months of age and children versus adults; major metabolite (via oxidation), HPPA, undergoes enterohepatic recirculation

Bioavailability: Form dependent

Half-life elimination: Oral: 22 hours (range: 7-42 hours)

Time to peak, serum (form dependent): Oral: Extended-release capsule: 4-12 hours; Immediate release preparation: 2-3 hours

Excretion: Urine (<5% as unchanged drug); as glucuronides

Clearance: Highly variable, dependent upon intrinsic hepatic function and dose administered; increased clearance and decreased serum concentrations with febrile illness

Dosage

Status epilepticus: I.V.:

Infants and Children: Loading dose: 15-20 mg/kg in a single or divided dose; maintenance dose: Initial: 5 mg/kg/day in 2 divided doses; usual doses:

6 months to 3 years: 8-10 mg/kg/day

4-6 years: 7.5-9 mg/kg/day

7-9 years: 7-8 mg/kg/day

10-16 years: 6-7 mg/kg/day, some patients may require every 8 hours dosing

Adults: Loading dose: Manufacturer recommends 10-15 mg/kg, however, 15-25 mg/kg has been used clinically; maintenance dose: 300 mg/day or 5-6 mg/kg/day in 3 divided doses or 1-2 divided doses using extended release

Anticonvulsant: Children and Adults: Oral:

Loading dose: 15-20 mg/kg; based on phenytoin serum concentrations and recent dosing history; administer oral loading dose in 3 divided doses given every 2-4 hours to decrease GI adverse effects and to ensure complete oral absorption; maintenance dose: same as I.V.

Neurosurgery (prophylactic): 100-200 mg at approximately 4-hour intervals during surgery and during the immediate postoperative period

Dosing adjustment/comments in renal impairment or hepatic disease: Safe in usual doses in mild liver disease; clearance may be substantially reduced in cirrhosis and plasma level monitoring with dose adjustment advisable. Free phenytoin levels should be monitored closely.

Dietary Considerations

Folic acid: Phenytoin may decrease mucosal uptake of folic acid; to avoid folic acid deficiency and megaloblastic anemia, some clinicians recommend giving patients on anticonvulsants prophylactic doses of folic acid and cyanocobalamin. However, folate supplementation may increase seizures in some patients (dose dependent). Discuss with healthcare provider prior to using any supplements.

Calcium: Hypocalcemia has been reported in patients taking prolonged high-dose therapy with an anticonvulsant. Some clinicians have given an additional 4000 units/week of vitamin D (especially in those receiving poor nutrition and getting no sun exposure) to prevent hypocalcemia.

Vitamin D: Phenytoin interferes with vitamin D metabolism and osteomalacia may result; may need to supplement with vitamin D

Tube feedings: Tube feedings decrease phenytoin absorption. To avoid decreased serum levels with continuous NG feeds, hold feedings for 2 hours prior to and 2 hours after phenytoin administration, if possible. There is a variety of opinions on how to administer phenytoin with enteral feedings. Be **consistent** throughout therapy.

Sodium content of 1 g injection: 88 mg (3.8 mEq)

Administration

Oral: Suspension: Shake well prior to use. Absorption is impaired when phenytoin suspension is given concurrently to patients who are receiving continuous nasogastric feedings. A method to resolve this interaction is to divide the daily dose of phenytoin and withhold the administration of nutritional supplements for 1-2 hours before and after each phenytoin dose.

I.M.: Although approved for I.M. use, I.M. administration is not recommended due to erratic absorption and pain on injection. Fosphenytoin may be considered.

I.V.: Vesicant. Fosphenytoin may be considered for loading in patients who are in status epilepticus, hemodynamically unstable, or develop hypotension/bradycardia with I.V. (Continued)

Phenytoin *(Continued)*

administration of phenytoin. Phenytoin may be administered by IVP or IVPB administration. The maximum rate of I.V. administration is 50 mg/minute. Highly sensitive patients (eg, elderly, patients with pre-existing cardiovascular conditions) should receive phenytoin more slowly (eg, 20 mg/minute). An in-line 0.22-5 micron filter is recommended for IVPB solutions due to the high potential for precipitation of the solution. Avoid extravasation. Following I.V. administration, NS should be injected through the same needle or I.V. catheter to prevent irritation.

pH: 10.0-12.3

SubQ: SubQ administration is not recommended because of the possibility of local tissue damage.

Monitoring Parameters Blood pressure, vital signs (with I.V. use), plasma phenytoin level, CBC, liver function tests

Reference Range Timing of serum samples: Because it is slowly absorbed, peak blood levels may occur 4-8 hours after ingestion of an oral dose. The serum half-life varies with the dosage and the drug follows Michaelis-Menten kinetics. The average adult half-life is about 24 hours. Steady-state concentrations are reached in 5-10 days.

Children and Adults: Toxicity is measured clinically, and some patients require levels outside the suggested therapeutic range

Therapeutic range:

Total phenytoin: 10-20 mcg/mL (children and adults), 8-15 mcg/mL (neonates)

Concentrations of 5-10 mcg/mL may be therapeutic for some patients but concentrations <5 mcg/mL are not likely to be effective

50% of patients show decreased frequency of seizures at concentrations >10 mcg/mL

86% of patients show decreased frequency of seizures at concentrations >15 mcg/mL

Add another anticonvulsant if satisfactory therapeutic response is not achieved with a phenytoin concentration of 20 mcg/mL

Free phenytoin: 1-2.5 mcg/mL

Toxic: >30 mcg/mL (SI: <120-200 μmol/L)

Lethal: >100 mcg/mL (SI: >400 μmol/L)

When to draw levels: This is dependent on the disease state being treated and the clinical condition of the patient

Key points:

Slow absorption of extended capsules and prolonged half-life minimize fluctuations between peak and trough concentrations, timing of sampling not crucial

Trough concentrations are generally recommended for routine monitoring. Daily levels are not necessary and may result in incorrect dosage adjustments. If it is determined essential to monitor free phenytoin concentrations, concomitant monitoring of total phenytoin concentrations is not necessary and expensive.

After a loading dose: Draw level within 48-96 hours

Rapid achievement: Draw within 2-3 days of therapy initiation to ensure that the patient's metabolism is not remarkably different from that which would be predicted by average literature-derived pharmacokinetic parameters; early levels should be used cautiously in design of new dosing regimens

Second concentration: Draw within 6-7 days with subsequent doses of phenytoin adjusted accordingly

If plasma concentrations have not changed over a 3- to 5-day period, monitoring interval may be increased to once weekly in the acute clinical setting

In stable patients requiring long-term therapy, generally monitor levels at 3- to 12-month intervals

Adjustment of serum concentration: See tables.

Adjustment of Serum Concentration in Patients With Low Serum Albumin

Measured Total Phenytoin Concentration (mcg/mL)	Patient's Serum Albumin (g/dL)			
	3.5	3	2.5	2
	Adjusted Total Phenytoin Concentration (mcg/mL)[1]			
5	6	7	8	10
10	13	14	17	20
15	19	21	25	30

[1]Adjusted concentration = measured total concentration divided by [(0.2 x albumin) + 0.1].

Adjustment of Serum Concentration in Patients With Renal Failure (Cl_cr ≤10 mL/min)

Measured Total Phenytoin Concentration (mcg/mL)	Patient's Serum Albumin (g/dL)				
	4	3.5	3	2.5	2
	Adjusted Total Phenytoin Concentration (mcg/mL)[1]				
5	10	11	13	14	17
10	20	22	25	29	33
15	30	33	38	43	50

[1]Adjusted concentration = measured total concentration divided by [(0.1 x albumin) + 0.1].

Dosage Forms

Capsule, extended release, as sodium: 100 mg

Dilantin®: 30 mg [contains sodium benzoate], 100 mg

Phenytek™: 200 mg, 300 mg

Capsule, prompt release, as sodium: 100 mg

Injection, solution, as sodium: 50 mg/mL (2 mL, 5 mL) [contains alcohol and propylene glycol]

Suspension, oral: 125 mg/5 mL (240 mL)
Dilantin®: 125 mg/5 mL (240 mL) [contains alcohol <0.6%, sodium benzoate; orange vanilla flavor]
Tablet, chewable:
Dilantin®: 50 mg

◆ **Phenytoin Sodium** *see* Phenytoin *on page 1361*
◆ **Phenytoin Sodium, Extended** *see* Phenytoin *on page 1361*
◆ **Phenytoin Sodium, Prompt** *see* Phenytoin *on page 1361*
◆ **Phillips'® M-O [OTC]** *see* Magnesium Hydroxide and Mineral Oil *on page 1048*
◆ **Phillips'® Milk of Magnesia [OTC]** *see* Magnesium Hydroxide *on page 1047*
◆ **Phillips'® Stool Softener Laxative [OTC]** *see* Docusate *on page 533*
◆ **pHisoHex®** *see* Hexachlorophene *on page 838*
◆ **PHL-Amoxicillin (Can)** *see* Amoxicillin *on page 110*
◆ **PHL-Citalopram (Can)** *see* Citalopram *on page 381*
◆ **PHL-Fenofibrate Supra (Can)** *see* Fenofibrate *on page 689*
◆ **PHL-Methimazole (Can)** *see* Methimazole *on page 1108*
◆ **PHL-Sumatriptan (Can)** *see* Sumatriptan *on page 1620*
◆ **PHL-Topiramate (Can)** *see* Topiramate *on page 1707*
◆ **Phos-Flur®** *see* Fluoride *on page 722*
◆ **Phos-Flur® Rinse [OTC]** *see* Fluoride *on page 722*
◆ **PhosLo®** *see* Calcium Acetate *on page 267*
◆ **Phos-NaK** *see* Potassium Phosphate and Sodium Phosphate *on page 1403*
◆ **Phospha 250™ Neutral** *see* Potassium Phosphate and Sodium Phosphate *on page 1403*
◆ **Phosphate, Potassium** *see* Potassium Phosphate *on page 1402*
◆ **Phospholine Iodide®** *see* Echothiophate Iodide *on page 566*
◆ **Phosphonoformate** *see* Foscarnet *on page 762*
◆ **Phosphonoformic Acid** *see* Foscarnet *on page 762*
◆ **Photofrin®** *see* Porfimer *on page 1391*
◆ **Phoxal-timolol (Can)** *see* Timolol *on page 1687*
◆ **Phrenilin®** *see* Butalbital and Acetaminophen *on page 259*
◆ **Phrenilin® Forte** *see* Butalbital and Acetaminophen *on page 259*
◆ **p-Hydroxyampicillin** *see* Amoxicillin *on page 110*
◆ **Phylloquinone** *see* Phytonadione *on page 1366*

Physostigmine (fye zoe STIG meen)

Canadian Brand Names Eserine®; Isopto® Eserine
Index Terms Eserine Salicylate; Physostigmine Salicylate; Physostigmine Sulfate
Pharmacologic Category Acetylcholinesterase Inhibitor
Additional Appendix Information
Glaucoma Drug Therapy *on page 2050*
Management of Overdosages *on page 2075*
Use Reverse toxic CNS effects caused by anticholinergic drugs
Pregnancy Risk Factor C
Lactation Excretion in breast milk unknown
Medication Safety Issues
Sound-alike/look-alike issues:
Physostigmine may be confused with Prostigmin®, pyridostigmine
Contraindications Hypersensitivity to physostigmine or any component of the formulation; GI or GU obstruction; physostigmine therapy of drug intoxications should be used with extreme caution in patients with asthma, gangrene, severe cardiovascular disease, or mechanical obstruction of the GI tract or urogenital tract. In these patients, physostigmine should be used only to treat life-threatening conditions.
Warnings/Precautions Use with caution in patients with epilepsy, asthma, diabetes, gangrene, cardiovascular disease, bradycardia. Discontinue if excessive salivation or emesis, frequent urination or diarrhea occur. Reduce dosage if excessive sweating or nausea occurs. Administer I.V. slowly or at a controlled rate not faster than 1 mg/minute. Due to the possibility of hypersensitivity or overdose/cholinergic crisis, atropine should be readily available; not intended as a first-line agent for anticholinergic toxicity or Parkinson's disease.
Adverse Reactions Frequency not defined.
Cardiovascular: Palpitations, bradycardia
Central nervous system: Restlessness, nervousness, hallucinations, seizure
Gastrointestinal: Nausea, salivation, diarrhea, stomach pain
Genitourinary: Frequent urge to urinate
Neuromuscular & skeletal: Muscle twitching
Ocular: Lacrimation, miosis
Respiratory: Dyspnea, bronchospasm, respiratory paralysis, pulmonary edema
Miscellaneous: Diaphoresis
Overdosage/Toxicology Symptoms include muscle weakness, blurred vision, excessive sweating, tearing and salivation, nausea, vomiting, bronchospasm, and seizures. If physostigmine is used in excess or in the absence of an anticholinergic overdose, patients may manifest signs of cholinergic toxicity. At this point, an anticholinergic agent (eg, atropine 0.015-0.05 mg/kg) may be necessary.
Drug Interactions
Increased Effect/Toxicity: Increased toxicity with bethanechol, methacholine. Succinylcholine may increase neuromuscular blockade with systemic administration.
Stability Do not use solution if cloudy or dark brown.
(Continued)

Physostigmine *(Continued)*

Mechanism of Action Inhibits destruction of acetylcholine by acetylcholinesterase which facilitates transmission of impulses across myoneural junction and prolongs the central and peripheral effects of acetylcholine

Pharmacodynamics/Kinetics
Onset of action: ~5 minutes
Duration: 0.5-5 hours
Absorption: I.M., SubQ: Readily absorbed
Distribution: Crosses blood-brain barrier readily and reverses both central and peripheral anticholinergic effects
Metabolism: Hepatic and via hydrolysis by cholinesterases
Half-life elimination: 15-40 minutes

Dosage
Children: Anticholinergic drug overdose: Reserve for life-threatening situations only: I.V.: 0.01-0.03 mg/kg/dose (maximum: 0.5 mg/minute); may repeat after 5-10 minutes to a maximum total dose of 2 mg or until response occurs or adverse cholinergic effects occur
Adults: Anticholinergic drug overdose:
I.M., I.V., SubQ: 0.5-2 mg to start, repeat every 20 minutes until response occurs or adverse effect occurs
Repeat 1-4 mg every 30-60 minutes as life-threatening signs (arrhythmias, seizures, deep coma) recur; maximum I.V. rate: 1 mg/minute

Administration Injection: Infuse slowly I.V. at a maximum rate of 0.5 mg/minute in children or 1 mg/minute in adults. Too rapid administration (I.V. rate not to exceed 1 mg/minute) can cause bradycardia, hypersalivation leading to respiratory difficulties and seizures.

Monitoring Parameters Heart rate, respiratory rate

Test Interactions Increased aminotransferase [ALT (SGPT)/AST (SGOT)] (S), increased amylase (S)

Dosage Forms Injection, solution, as salicylate: 1 mg/mL (2 mL) [contains benzyl alcohol and sodium metabisulfite]

- ◆ **Physostigmine Salicylate** *see* Physostigmine *on page 1365*
- ◆ **Physostigmine Sulfate** *see* Physostigmine *on page 1365*
- ◆ **Phytomenadione** *see* Phytonadione *on page 1366*

Phytonadione *(fye toe na DYE one)*

U.S. Brand Names Mephyton®
Canadian Brand Names AquaMEPHYTON®; Konakion; Mephyton®
Index Terms Methylphytyl Napthoquinone; Phylloquinone; Phytomenadione; Vitamin K$_1$
Pharmacologic Category Vitamin, Fat Soluble
Additional Appendix Information
Management of Overdosages *on page 2075*
Use Prevention and treatment of hypoprothrombinemia caused by coumarin derivative-induced or other drug-induced vitamin K deficiency, hypoprothrombinemia caused by malabsorption or inability to synthesize vitamin K; hemorrhagic disease of the newborn
Pregnancy Risk Factor C
Lactation Enters breast milk/use caution (APP rates "compatible")
Medication Safety Issues
Sound-alike/look-alike issues:
Mephyton® may be confused with melphalan, methadone
Contraindications Hypersensitivity to phytonadione or any component of the formulation
Warnings/Precautions [U.S. Boxed Warning]: Severe reactions resembling hypersensitivity (eg, anaphylaxis) reactions have occurred rarely during or immediately after I.V. administration. Allergic reactions have also occurred with I.M. and SubQ injections; oral administration is the safest. In obstructive jaundice or with biliary fistulas concurrent administration of bile salts is necessary. Manufacturers recommend the SubQ route over other parenteral routes. SubQ is less predictable when compared to the oral route. The American College of Chest Physicians recommends the I.V. route in patients with serious or life-threatening bleeding secondary to warfarin. The I.V. route should be restricted to emergency situations where oral phytonadione cannot be used. Efficacy is delayed regardless of route of administration; patient management may require other treatments in the interim. Administer a dose that will quickly lower the INR into a safe range without causing resistance to warfarin. Use caution in newborns especially premature infants; hemolysis, jaundice and hyperbilirubinemia have been reported with larger than recommended doses. Some dosage forms contain benzyl alcohol. In liver disease, if initial doses do not reverse coagulopathy then higher doses are unlikely to have any effect. Ineffective in hereditary hypoprothrombinemia. Use caution with renal dysfunction (including premature infants). Injectable products may contain aluminum.

Adverse Reactions Parenteral administration: Frequency not defined.
Cardiovascular: Cyanosis, flushing, hypotension
Central nervous system: Dizziness
Dermatologic: Scleroderma-like lesions
Endocrine & metabolic: Hyperbilirubinemia (newborn; greater than recommended doses)
Gastrointestinal: Abnormal taste
Local: Injection site reactions
Respiratory: Dyspnea
Miscellaneous: Anaphylactoid reactions, diaphoresis, hypersensitivity reactions

Drug Interactions
Decreased Effect: Phytonadione may diminish the anticoagulant effect of coumarin derivatives (monitor INR). Phytonadione (oral) may not be properly absorbed when administered concurrently with orlistat (separate doses by at least 2 hours).

Stability
Injection: Store at 15°C to 30°C (59°F to 86°F). Dilute in preservative-free NS, D$_5$W, or D$_5$NS.

Note: Store Hospira product at 20°C to 25°C (68°F to 77°F).

Oral: Store tablets at 15°C to 30°C (59°F to 86°F). Protect from light.

Mechanism of Action Promotes liver synthesis of clotting factors (II, VII, IX, X); however, the exact mechanism as to this stimulation is unknown. Menadiol is a water soluble form of vitamin K; phytonadione has a more rapid and prolonged effect than menadione; menadiol sodium diphosphate (K_4) is half as potent as menadione (K_3).

Pharmacodynamics/Kinetics

Onset of action: Increased coagulation factors: Oral: 6-10 hours; I.V.: 1-2 hours

Peak effect: INR values return to normal: Oral: 24-48 hours; I.V.: 12-14 hours

Absorption: Oral: From intestines in presence of bile; SubQ: Variable

Metabolism: Rapidly hepatic

Excretion: Urine and feces

Dosage

Adequate intake:

Children:

1-3 years: 30 mcg/day

4-8 years: 55 mcg/day

9-13 years: 60 mcg/day

14-18 years: 75 mcg/day

Adults: Males: 120 mcg/day; Females: 90 mcg/day

Hemorrhagic disease of the newborn:

Prophylaxis: I.M.: 0.5-1 mg within 1 hour of birth

Treatment: I.M., SubQ: 1 mg/dose/day; higher doses may be necessary if mother has been receiving oral anticoagulants

Hypoprothrombinemia due to drugs (other than coumarin derivatives) or factors limiting absorption or synthesis: Adults: Oral, SubQ, I.M., I.V.: Initial: 2.5-25 mg (rarely up to 50 mg)

Vitamin K deficiency secondary to coumarin derivative: Adults: See table:

Management of Elevated INR

INR	Symptom	Action
Above therapeutic range to <5	No significant bleeding	Lower or hold the next dose and monitor frequently; when INR approaches desired range, may resume dosing with a lower dose if INR was significantly above therapeutic range.
≥5 and <9	No significant bleeding	Omit the next 1or 2 doses; monitor INR and resume with a lower dose when the INR approaches the desired range. Alternatively, if there are other risk factors for bleeding, omit the next dose and give vitamin K_1 orally ≤5 mg; resume with a lower dose when the INR approaches the desired range. If rapid reversal is required for surgery, then given vitamin K_1 orally 2-4 mg and hold warfarin. Expect a response within 24 hours; another 1-2 mg may be given orally if needed.
≥9	No significant bleeding	Hold warfarin, give vitamin K_1 orally 5-10 mg, expect the INR to be reduced within 24-48 hours; monitor INR and administer additional vitamin K if necessary. Resume warfarin at lower doses when INR is in the desired range.
Any INR elevation	Serious bleeding	Hold warfarin, give vitamin K_1 (10 mg by slow I.V. infusion), and supplement with fresh plasma transfusion or prothrombin complex concentrate (Factor X complex); recombinant factor VIIa is an alternative to prothrombin complex concentrate. Vitamin K_1 injection can be repeated every 12 hours.
Any INR elevation	Life-threatening bleeding	Hold warfarin, give prothrombin complex concentrate, supplemented with vitamin K_1 (10 mg by slow I.V. infusion); repeat if necessary. Recombinant factor VIIa is an alternative to prothrombin complex concentrate.

Note: Use of high doses of vitamin K_1 (10.0-15.0) may cause resistance to warfarin for up to a week. Heparin or low molecular weight heparin can be given until the patient becomes responsive to warfarin.

Reference: Ansell J, Hirsh J, Poller L et al. "The Pharmacology and Management of the Vitamin K Antagonists," *Chest*, 2004, 126 (3 Suppl):204-33.

Administration I.V. administration: Infuse slowly; rate of infusion should not exceed 1 mg/minute. The injectable route should be used only if the oral route is not feasible or there is a greater urgency to reverse anticoagulation.

Oral: The parenteral preparation has been administered orally to neonates.

Monitoring Parameters PT, INR

Dosage Forms

Injection, aqueous colloidal: 2 mg/mL (0.5 mL); 10 mg/mL (1 mL)

Tablet: 100 mcg [OTC]

Mephyton®: 5 mg

Extemporaneous Preparations A 1 mg/mL oral suspension was stable for only 3 days when refrigerated when compounded as follows:

Triturate six 5 mg tablets in a mortar, reduce to a fine powder, then add 5 mL each of water and methylcellulose 1% while mixing; then transfer to a graduate and qs to 30 mL with sorbitol

Shake well before using and keep in refrigerator

Nahata MC and Hipple TF, *Pediatric Drug Formulations*, 3rd ed, Cincinnati, OH: Harvey Whitney Books Co, 1997.

♦ **Pidorubicin** *see* Epirubicin *on page 592*
♦ **Pidorubicin Hydrochloride** *see* Epirubicin *on page 592*

Pilocarpine (pye loe KAR peen)

U.S. Brand Names Isopto® Carpine; Pilopine HS®; Salagen®
Canadian Brand Names Diocarpine; Isopto® Carpine; Pilopine HS®; Salagen®
Index Terms Pilocarpine Hydrochloride
Pharmacologic Category Cholinergic Agonist; Ophthalmic Agent, Antiglaucoma; Ophthalmic Agent, Miotic
Additional Appendix Information
Glaucoma Drug Therapy *on page 2050*
Use
Ophthalmic: Management of chronic simple glaucoma, chronic and acute angle-closure glaucoma
Oral: Symptomatic treatment of xerostomia caused by salivary gland hypofunction resulting from radiotherapy for cancer of the head and neck or Sjögren's syndrome
Unlabeled/Investigational Use Counter effects of cycloplegics
Pregnancy Risk Factor C
Lactation Excretion in breast milk unknown/not recommended
Medication Safety Issues
Sound-alike/look-alike issues:
Isopto® Carpine may be confused with Isopto® Carbachol
Salagen® may be confused with Salacid®, selegiline

International issues:
Salagen® may be confused with Poagen® which is a brand name for grass pollen extract in Portugal
Contraindications Hypersensitivity to pilocarpine or any component of the formulation; acute inflammatory disease of the anterior chamber of the eye; in addition, tablets are also contraindicated in patients with uncontrolled asthma, angle-closure glaucoma, severe hepatic impairment
Warnings/Precautions Use with caution in patients with corneal abrasion, CHF, asthma, peptic ulcer, urinary tract obstruction, Parkinson's disease, or narrow-angle glaucoma
Adverse Reactions
Ophthalmic: Frequency not defined:
Cardiovascular: Hypertension, tachycardia
Gastrointestinal: Diarrhea, nausea, salivation, vomiting
Ocular: Burning, ciliary spasm, conjunctival vascular congestion, corneal granularity (gel 10%), lacrimation, lens opacity, myopia, retinal detachment, supraorbital or temporal headache, visual acuity decreased
Respiratory: Bronchial spasm, pulmonary edema
Miscellaneous: Diaphoresis

Oral (frequency varies by indication and dose):
>10%:
Cardiovascular: Flushing (8% to 13%)
Central nervous system: Chills (3% to 15%), dizziness (5% to 12%), headache (11%)
Gastrointestinal: Nausea (6% to 15%)
Genitourinary: Urinary frequency (9% to 12%)
Neuromuscular & skeletal: Weakness (2% to 12%)
Respiratory: Rhinitis (5% to 14%)
Miscellaneous: Diaphoresis (29% to 68%)
1% to 10%:
Cardiovascular: Edema (<1% to 5%), facial edema, hypertension (3%), palpitation, tachycardia
Central nervous system: Pain (4%), fever, somnolence
Dermatologic: Pruritus, rash
Gastrointestinal: Diarrhea (4% to 7%), dyspepsia (7%), vomiting (3% to 4%), constipation, flatulence, glossitis, salivation increased, stomatitis, taste perversion
Genitourinary: Vaginitis, urinary incontinence
Neuromuscular & skeletal: Myalgias, tremor
Ocular: Lacrimation (6%), amblyopia (4%), abnormal vision, blurred vision, conjunctivitis
Otic: Tinnitus
Respiratory: Cough increased, dysphagia, epistaxis, sinusitis
Miscellaneous: Allergic reaction, voice alteration
<1% (Limited to important or life-threatening): Abnormal dreams, alopecia, angina pectoris, anorexia, anxiety, arrhythmia, body odor, bone disorder, cholelithiasis, colitis, confusion, dry eyes, dry mouth, ECG abnormality, myasthenia, photosensitivity reaction, nervousness, pancreatitis, paresthesia, salivary gland enlargement, sputum increased, taste loss, tongue disorder, urinary impairment, urinary urgency, yawning
Overdosage/Toxicology Symptoms include bronchospasm, bradycardia, involuntary urination, vomiting, hypotension, and tremors. Atropine is the treatment of choice for intoxications manifesting with significant muscarinic symptoms. Atropine I.V. 2-4 mg every 3-60 minutes (or 0.04-0.08 mg I.V. every 5-60 minutes, if needed, for children) should be repeated to control symptoms and then continued as needed for 1-2 days following acute ingestion. Epinephrine 0.1-1 mg SubQ may be useful in reversing severe cardiovascular or pulmonary sequelae.
Drug Interactions
Cytochrome P450 Effect: Inhibits CYP2A6 (weak), 2E1 (weak), 3A4 (weak)
Increased Effect/Toxicity: Concurrent use with beta-blockers may cause conduction disturbances.

Decreased Effect: May decrease effects of anticholinergic drugs (atropine, ipratropium).

Ethanol/Nutrition/Herb Interactions Food: Avoid administering oral formulation with high-fat meal; fat decreases the rate of absorption, maximum concentration and increases the time it takes to reach maximum concentration.

Stability

Gel: Store at room temperature of 2°C to 27°C (36°F to 80°F); do not freeze. Avoid excessive heat.

Tablets: Store at controlled room temperature of 15°C to 30°C (59°F to 86°F).

Mechanism of Action Directly stimulates cholinergic receptors in the eye causing miosis (by contraction of the iris sphincter), loss of accommodation (by constriction of ciliary muscle), and lowering of intraocular pressure (with decreased resistance to aqueous humor outflow)

Pharmacodynamics/Kinetics

Onset of action:

Ophthalmic: Miosis: 10-30 minutes; Intraocular pressure reduction: 1 hour

Oral: 20 minutes

Duration:

Ophthalmic: Miosis: 4-8 hours; Intraocular pressure reduction: 4-12 hours

Oral: 3-5 hours

Half-life elimination: Oral: 0.76-1.35 hours; increased with hepatic impairment

Excretion: Urine

Dosage Adults:

Ophthalmic:

Glaucoma:

Solution: Instill 1-2 drops up to 6 times/day; adjust the concentration and frequency as required to control elevated intraocular pressure

Gel: Instill 0.5" ribbon into lower conjunctival sac once daily at bedtime

To counteract the mydriatic effects of sympathomimetic agents (unlabeled use): Solution: Instill 1 drop of a 1% solution in the affected eye

Oral: Xerostomia:

Following head and neck cancer: 5 mg 3 times/day, titration up to 10 mg 3 times/day may be considered for patients who have not responded adequately; do not exceed 2 tablets/dose

Sjögren's syndrome: 5 mg 4 times/day

Dosage adjustment in hepatic impairment: Oral: Patients with moderate impairment: 5 mg 2 times/day regardless of indication; adjust dose based on response and tolerability. Do not use with severe impairment (Child-Pugh score 10-15).

Administration

Oral: Avoid administering with high-fat meal. Fat decreases the rate of absorption, maximum concentration, and increases the time it takes to reach maximum concentration.

Ophthalmic: If both solution and gel are used, the solution should be applied first, then the gel at least 5 minutes later. Following administration of the solution, finger pressure should be applied on the lacrimal sac for 1-2 minutes.

Monitoring Parameters Intraocular pressure, funduscopic exam, visual field testing

Dosage Forms

Gel, ophthalmic, as hydrochloride (Pilopine HS®): 4% (4 g) [contains benzalkonium chloride]

Solution, ophthalmic, as hydrochloride: 0.5% (15 mL); 1% (2 mL, 15 mL); 2% (2 mL, 15 mL); 3% (15 mL); 4% (2 mL, 15 mL); 6% (15 mL) [may contain benzalkonium chloride]

Isopto® Carpine: 1% (15 mL); 2% (15 mL); 4% (15 mL) [contains benzalkonium chloride]

Tablet, as hydrochloride: 5 mg

Salagen®: 5 mg, 7.5 mg

- ♦ **Pilocarpine Hydrochloride** see Pilocarpine on page 1368
- ♦ **Pilopine HS** see Pilocarpine on page 1368
- ♦ **Pima®** see Potassium Iodide on page 1399
- ♦ **Pimaricin** see Natamycin on page 1203

Pimecrolimus (pim e KROE li mus)

U.S. Brand Names Elidel®

Canadian Brand Names Elidel®

Pharmacologic Category Immunosuppressant Agent; Topical Skin Product

Use Short-term and intermittent long-term treatment of mild to moderate atopic dermatitis in patients not responsive to conventional therapy or when conventional therapy is not appropriate

Restrictions An FDA-approved medication guide must be distributed when dispensing an outpatient prescription (new or refill) where this medication is to be used without direct supervision of a healthcare provider. Medication guides are available at http://www.fda.gov/cder/Offices/ODS/medication_guides.htm.

Pregnancy Risk Factor C

Pregnancy Implications There are no adequate and well-controlled studies in pregnant women; use only if clearly needed.

Lactation Excretion in breast milk unknown/not recommended

Contraindications Hypersensitivity to pimecrolimus or any component of the formulation; Netherton's syndrome

Warnings/Precautions [U.S. Boxed Warning]: Topical calcineurin inhibitors have been associated with rare cases of malignancy. Avoid use on malignant or premalignant skin conditions (eg, cutaneous T-cell lymphoma). Topical calcineurin agents are considered second-line therapies in the treatment of atopic dermatitis/eczema, and should be limited to use in patients who have failed treatment with other therapies. **[U.S. Boxed Warning]: They should be used for short-term and intermittent treatment using the minimum amount necessary for the control of symptoms should be used.** Application should be limited to involved areas. Safety of intermittent use for >1 year has not been established.

(Continued)

Pimecrolimus *(Continued)*

Should not be used in immunocompromised patients. Do not apply to areas of active viral infection; infections at the treatment site should be cleared prior to therapy. Patients with atopic dermatitis are predisposed to skin infections, and tacrolimus therapy has been associated with risk of developing eczema herpeticum, varicella zoster, and herpes simplex. May be associated with development of lymphadenopathy; possible infectious causes should be investigated. Discontinue use in patients with unknown cause of lymphadenopathy or acute infectious mononucleosis. Not recommended for use in patients with skin disease which may increase systemic absorption (eg, Netherton's syndrome). Avoid artificial or natural sunlight exposure, even when Elidel® is not on the skin. Safety not established in patients with generalized erythroderma. **[U.S. Boxed Warning]: The use of Elidel® in children <2 years of age is not recommended,** particularly since the effect on immune system development is unknown.

Adverse Reactions
>10%:
Central nervous system: Headache (7% to 25%), pyrexia (1% to 13%)
Local: Burning at application site (2% to 26%; tends to resolve/improve as lesions resolve)
Respiratory: Nasopharyngitis (8% to 27%), cough (2% to 16%), upper respiratory tract infection (4% to 19%), bronchitis (0.4% to 11%)
Miscellaneous: Influenza (3% to 13%)
1% to 10%:
Dermatologic: Skin papilloma (warts) (up to 3%), molluscum contagiosum (0.7% to 2%), herpes simplex dermatitis (up to 2%)
Gastrointestinal: Diarrhea (0.6% to 8%), constipation (up to 4%)
Local: Irritation at application site (0.4% to 6%), erythema at application site (0.4% to 2%), pruritus at application site (0.6% to 6%)
Ocular: Eye infection (up to 1%)
Otic: Ear infection (0.6% to 6%)
Respiratory: Pharyngitis (0.7% to 8%), sinusitis (0.6% to 3%), nasal congestion (0.6% to 3%)
Miscellaneous: Viral infection (up to 7%), herpes simplex infection (0.4% to 4%), tonsillitis (0.4% to 6%)
<1% (Limited to important or life-threatening): Anaphylaxis, angioneurotic edema, eczema herpeticum, facial edema, flushing (ethanol-associated), lymphadenopathy, ocular irritation (following application near eyes), malignancy (basal cell carcinoma, squamous cell carcinoma, malignant melanoma, lymphoma)

Overdosage/Toxicology No experience with overdose reported.

Drug Interactions
Cytochrome P450 Effect: Substrate of CYP3A4 (minor)
Increased Effect/Toxicity: CYP3A inhibitors may increase pimecrolimus levels in patients where increased absorption expected.

Stability Store at 25°C (77°F); excursions permitted to 15°C to 30°C (59°F to 86°F). Do not freeze.

Mechanism of Action Penetrates inflamed epidermis to inhibit T cell activation by blocking transcription of proinflammatory cytokine genes such as interleukin-2, interferon gamma (Th1-type), interleukin-4, and interleukin-10 (Th2-type). Blocks catalytic function of calcineurin. Prevents release of inflammatory cytokines and mediators from mast cells *in vitro* after stimulation by antigen/IgE.

Pharmacodynamics/Kinetics Absorption: Poor when applied to 13% to 62% body surface area for up to a year

Dosage Children ≥2 years and Adults: Topical: Apply thin layer to affected area twice daily; rub in gently and completely. **Note:** Limit application to involved areas. Continue as long as signs and symptoms persist; discontinue if resolution occurs; re-evaluate if symptoms persist >6 weeks.

Administration Do not use with occlusive dressings. Burning at the application site is most common in first few days; improves as atopic dermatitis improves. Limit application to areas of involvement. Continue as long as signs and symptoms persist; discontinue if resolution occurs; re-evaluate if symptoms persist >6 weeks.

Dosage Forms Cream, topical: 1% (30 g, 60 g, 100 g)

Pimozide *(PI moe zide)*

U.S. Brand Names Orap®
Canadian Brand Names Apo-Pimozide®; Orap®
Pharmacologic Category Antipsychotic Agent, Typical
Additional Appendix Information
Antipsychotic Agents *on page 1872*
Use Suppression of severe motor and phonic tics in patients with Tourette's disorder who have failed to respond satisfactorily to standard treatment
Unlabeled/Investigational Use Psychosis; reported use in individuals with delusions focused on physical symptoms (ie, preoccupation with parasitic infestation); Huntington's chorea
Pregnancy Risk Factor C
Dosage Oral: **Note:** An ECG should be performed baseline and periodically thereafter, especially during dosage adjustment:
Children ≤12 years: Tourette's disorder: Initial: 0.05 mg/kg preferably once at bedtime; may be increased every third day; usual range: 2-4 mg/day; do not exceed 10 mg/day (0.2 mg/kg/day)
Children >12 years and Adults: Tourette's disorder: Initial: 1-2 mg/day in divided doses, then increase dosage as needed every other day; range is usually 7-16 mg/day, maximum dose: 10 mg/day or 0.2 mg/kg/day are not generally recommended
Note: Sudden unexpected deaths have occurred in patients taking doses >10 mg. Therefore, dosages exceeding 10 mg/day are generally not recommended.

Dosing adjustment in hepatic impairment: Reduction of dose is necessary in patients with liver disease

Additional Information Complete prescribing information for this medication should be consulted for additional detail.

Dosage Forms Tablet: 1 mg, 2 mg

♦ **Pin-X® [OTC]** *see* Pyrantel Pamoate *on page 1459*

Pindolol (PIN doe lole)

Canadian Brand Names Apo-Pindol®; Gen-Pindolol; Novo-Pindol; Nu-Pindol; PMS-Pindolol; Visken®

Pharmacologic Category Beta Blocker With Intrinsic Sympathomimetic Activity

Additional Appendix Information
Beta-Blockers *on page 1875*

Use Management of hypertension

Unlabeled/Investigational Use Potential augmenting agent for antidepressants; ventricular arrhythmias/tachycardia, antipsychotic-induced akathisia, situational anxiety; aggressive behavior associated with dementia

Pregnancy Risk Factor B

Pregnancy Implications Pindolol crosses the placenta. Beta-blockers have been associated with bradycardia, hypotension, and IUGR; IUGR is probably related to maternal hypertension. Available evidence suggests beta-blockers are generally safe during pregnancy (JNC 7). Cases of neonatal hypoglycemia have been reported following maternal use of beta-blockers at parturition or during breast-feeding. Monitor breast-fed infant for symptoms of beta-blockade.

Lactation Enters breast milk/use caution

Medication Safety Issues
Sound-alike/look-alike issues:
Pindolol may be confused with Parlodel®, Plendil®
Visken® may be confused with Visine®

Contraindications Hypersensitivity to pindolol, beta-blockers, or any component of the formulation; uncompensated congestive heart failure; cardiogenic shock; bradycardia, sinus node dysfunction, or heart block (2nd or 3rd degree) except in patients with a functioning artificial pacemaker; pulmonary edema; severe hyperactive airway disease (asthma or COPD); Raynaud's disease

Warnings/Precautions Consider pre-existing conditions such as sick sinus syndrome before initiating. Use with caution in patients with inadequate myocardial function, undergoing anesthesia, bronchospastic disease, myasthenia gravis, peripheral vascular disease, renal impairment, psychiatric disease (may cause CNS depression) or impaired hepatic function. Use with caution in patients with diabetes mellitus; may potentiate hypoglycemia and/or mask signs and symptoms. Beta-blockers with intrinsic sympathomimetic activity (including pindolol) do not appear to be of benefit in CHF. Beta-blocker therapy should not be withdrawn abruptly (particularly in patients with CAD), but gradually tapered to avoid acute tachycardia, hypertension, and/or ischemia. Adequate alpha-blockade is required prior to use of any beta-blocker for patients with untreated pheochromocytoma. Safety and efficacy have not been established in children.

Adverse Reactions
1% to 10%:
Cardiovascular: Chest pain (3%), edema (6%)
Central nervous system: Nightmares/vivid dreams (5%), dizziness (9%), insomnia (10%), fatigue (8%), nervousness (7%), anxiety (<2%)
Dermatologic: Rash, itching (4%)
Gastrointestinal: Nausea (5%), abdominal discomfort (4%)
Neuromuscular & skeletal: Weakness (4%), paresthesia (3%), arthralgia (7%), muscle pain (10%)
Respiratory: Dyspnea (5%)
<1% (Limited to important or life-threatening): Bradycardia, CHF, confusion, hallucinations, hypotension, mental depression, thrombocytopenia

Overdosage/Toxicology Symptoms of intoxication include cardiac disturbances, CNS toxicity, bronchospasm, hypoglycemia, and hyperkalemia. The most common cardiac symptoms include hypotension and bradycardia. Atrioventricular block, intraventricular conduction disturbances, cardiogenic shock, and asystole may occur with severe overdose, especially with membrane-depressant drugs (eg, propranolol). CNS effects include convulsions, coma, and respiratory arrest and are commonly seen with propranolol and other membrane-depressant and lipid-soluble drugs. Treatment is symptomatic for seizures, hypotension, hyperkalemia and hypoglycemia; bradycardia and hypotension resistant to atropine, isoproterenol or pacing may respond to glucagon. Wide QRS defects caused by membrane-depressant poisoning may respond to hypertonic sodium bicarbonate. Repeat-dose charcoal, hemoperfusion, or hemodialysis may be helpful in removal of only those beta-blockers with a small V_d, long half-life, or low intrinsic clearance (acebutolol, atenolol, nadolol, sotalol).

Drug Interactions
Cytochrome P450 Effect: Substrate of CYP2D6 (major); **Inhibits** CYP2D6 (weak)
Increased Effect/Toxicity: CYP2D6 inhibitors may increase the levels/effects of pindolol; example inhibitors include chlorpromazine, delavirdine, fluoxetine, miconazole, paroxetine, pergolide, quinidine, quinine, ritonavir, and ropinirole. Pindolol may increase the effects of other drugs which slow AV conduction (digoxin, verapamil, diltiazem), alpha-blockers (prazosin, terazosin), and alpha-adrenergic stimulants (epinephrine, phenylephrine). Pindolol may mask the tachycardia from hypoglycemia caused by insulin and oral hypoglycemics. In patients receiving concurrent therapy, the risk of hypertensive crisis is increased when either clonidine or the beta-blocker is withdrawn. Reserpine has been shown to enhance the effect of beta-blockers. Beta-blockers may increase the action of
(Continued)

Pindolol *(Continued)*

levels of ethanol, disopyramide, nondepolarizing muscle relaxants, and theophylline although the effects are difficult to predict.

Decreased Effect: Decreased levels/effect of pindolol with aluminum salts, barbiturates, calcium salts, cholestyramine, colestipol, NSAIDs, penicillins (ampicillin), rifampin, salicylates, and sulfinpyrazone due to decreased bioavailability and plasma levels. Beta-blockers may decrease the effect of sulfonylureas (possibly hyperglycemia). Nonselective beta-blockers blunt the effect of beta-2 adrenergic agonists (albuterol).

Ethanol/Nutrition/Herb Interactions Herb/Nutraceutical: Avoid dong quai if using for hypertension (has estrogenic activity). Avoid ephedra, yohimbe, ginseng (may worsen hypertension).

Stability Protect from light.

Mechanism of Action Blocks both beta$_1$- and beta$_2$-receptors and has mild intrinsic sympathomimetic activity; pindolol has negative inotropic and chronotropic effects and can significantly slow AV nodal conduction. Augmentive action of antidepressants thought to be mediated via a serotonin 1A autoreceptor antagonism.

Pharmacodynamics/Kinetics
Absorption: Rapid, 50% to 95%
Protein binding: 50%
Metabolism: Hepatic (60% to 65%) to conjugates
Half-life elimination: 2.5-4 hours; prolonged with renal impairment, age, and cirrhosis
Time to peak, serum: 1-2 hours
Excretion: Urine (35% to 50% as unchanged drug)

Dosage Oral:
Adults:
Hypertension: Initial: 5 mg twice daily, increase as necessary by 10 mg/day every 3-4 weeks (maximum daily dose: 60 mg); usual dose range (JNC 7): 10-40 mg twice daily
Antidepressant augmentation: 2.5 mg 3 times/day
Elderly: Initial: 5 mg once daily, increase as necessary by 5 mg/day every 3-4 weeks

Dosing adjustment in renal and hepatic impairment: Reduction is necessary in severely impaired

Dietary Considerations May be taken without regard to meals.

Monitoring Parameters Blood pressure, standing and sitting/supine, pulse, respiratory function

Dosage Forms Tablet: 5 mg, 10 mg

♦ **Pink Bismuth** *see* Bismuth *on page 224*

Pioglitazone *(pye oh GLI ta zone)*

U.S. Brand Names Actos®
Canadian Brand Names Actos®
Pharmacologic Category Antidiabetic Agent, Thiazolidinedione
Additional Appendix Information
Hyperglycemia- or Hypoglycemia-Causing Drugs *on page 2057*
Use
Type 2 diabetes mellitus (noninsulin dependent, NIDDM), monotherapy: Adjunct to diet and exercise, to improve glycemic control
Type 2 diabetes mellitus (noninsulin dependent, NIDDM), combination therapy with sulfonylurea, metformin, or insulin: When diet, exercise, and a single agent alone does not result in adequate glycemic control
Unlabeled/Investigational Use
Polycystic ovary syndrome (PCOS)
Pregnancy Risk Factor C
Pregnancy Implications Treatment during mid-late gestation was associated with delayed parturition, embryotoxicity and postnatal growth retardation in animal models. Abnormal blood glucose levels are associated with a higher incidence of congenital abnormalities. Insulin is the drug of choice for the control of diabetes mellitus during pregnancy. In anovulatory, premenopausal women, ovulation may occur, increasing the risk of pregnancy; adequate contraception is recommended.
Lactation Excretion in breast milk unknown/not recommended
Medication Safety Issues
Sound-alike/look-alike issues:
Actos® may be confused with Actidose®, Actonel®
Contraindications Hypersensitivity to pioglitazone or any component of the formulation; active liver disease (transaminases >2.5 times the upper limit of normal at baseline); patients who have experienced jaundice during troglitazone therapy
Warnings/Precautions Should not be used in diabetic ketoacidosis. Mechanism requires the presence of insulin, therefore use in type 1 diabetes is not recommended. May potentiate hypoglycemia when used in combination with sulfonylureas or insulin. Use with caution in premenopausal, anovulatory women - may result in a resumption of ovulation, increasing the risk of pregnancy. Use with caution in patients with anemia (may reduce hemoglobin and hematocrit). Use with caution in patients with edema; may increase plasma volume and/or increase cardiac hypertrophy. Monitor closely for signs and symptoms of heart failure (including weight gain, edema, or dyspnea). Not recommended for use in patients with NYHA Class III or IV heart failure, unless serum glucose control outweighs the risk of excessive fluid retention. Discontinue if heart failure develops. Use with caution in patients with minor elevations in transaminases (AST or ALT). Idiosyncratic hepatotoxicity has been reported with another thiazolidinedione agent (troglitazone) and postmarketing case reports of hepatitis (with rare hepatic failure) have been received for pioglitazone. Monitoring should include periodic determinations of liver function. Use caution with pre-existing macular edema or diabetic retinopathy. Postmarketing reports of new-onset or worsening diabetic macular

edema with decreased visual acuity has been reported. Safety and efficacy have not been established in children.

Adverse Reactions

>10%:
- Cardiovascular: Edema (5%; in combination trials with sulfonlyureas or insulin, the incidence of edema was as high as 15%)
- Respiratory: Upper respiratory tract infection (13%)

1% to 10%:
- Central nervous system: Headache (9%), fatigue (4%)
- Gastrointestinal: Tooth disorder (5%)
- Hematologic: Anemia (≤2%)
- Neuromuscular & skeletal: Myalgia (5%)
- Respiratory: Sinusitis (6%), pharyngitis (5%)

<1% (Limited to important or life-threatening): CHF, CPK increased, dyspnea (associated with weight gain and/or edema), hepatic failure (very rare), hepatitis, macular edema (new onset or worsening), transaminases increased, visual acuity decreased

Frequency not defined: HDL-cholesterol increased, hypoglycemia (in combination trials with sulfonylureas or insulin), serum triglycerides decreased, weight gain/loss

Overdosage/Toxicology
Experience in overdose is limited. Symptoms may include hypoglycemia. Treatment is symptom-directed and supportive.

Drug Interactions

Cytochrome P450 Effect: Substrate of CYP2C8 (major), 3A4 (minor); **Inhibits** CYP2C8 (moderate), 2C9 (weak), 2C19 (weak), 2D6 (moderate); **Induces** CYP3A4 (weak)

Increased Effect/Toxicity: Concomitant use with thioridazine is contraindicated, due to a risk of arrhythmias. The levels/effects of pioglitazone may be increased by atazanavir, gemfibrozil, ritonavir, and other CYP2C8 inhibitors. Pioglitazone level/effect may be increased if trimethoprim, and pioglitazone effect on fluid retention may be enhanced with pregabalin.

Pioglitazone may increase the levels/effects of amiodarone, amphetamines, selected beta-blockers, dextromethorphan, fluoxetine, lidocaine, mirtazapine, nefazodone, paclitaxel, paroxetine, risperidone, repaglinide, ritonavir, rosiglitazone, thioridazine, and other CYP2D6 or 2C8 substrates.

Decreased Effect: The levels/effects of pioglitazone may be decreased by carbamazepine, phenobarbital, phenytoin, rifampin, rifapentine, secobarbital, and other CYP2C8 inducers. Pioglitazone may decrease the levels/effects of CYP2D6 prodrug substrates (eg, codeine, hydrocodone, oxycodone, tramadol). Bile acid sequestrants may decrease pioglitazone levels.

Ethanol/Nutrition/Herb Interactions

Ethanol: Caution with ethanol (may cause hypoglycemia).

Food: Peak concentrations are delayed when administered with food, but the extent of absorption is not affected. Pioglitazone may be taken without regard to meals.

Herb/Nutraceutical: Caution with alfalfa, aloe, bilberry, bitter melon, burdock, celery, damiana, fenugreek, garcinia, garlic, ginger, ginseng (American), gymnema, marshmallow, and stinging nettle (may cause hypoglycemia).

Mechanism of Action
Thiazolidinedione antidiabetic agent that lowers blood glucose by improving target cell response to insulin, without increasing pancreatic insulin secretion. It has a mechanism of action that is dependent on the presence of insulin for activity. Pioglitazone is a potent and selective agonist for peroxisome proliferator-activated receptor-gamma (PPARgamma). Activation of nuclear PPARgamma receptors influences the production of a number of gene products involved in glucose and lipid metabolism.

Pharmacodynamics/Kinetics

Onset of action: Delayed

Peak effect: Glucose control: Several weeks

Distribution: V_{ss} (apparent): 0.63 L/kg

Protein binding: 99.8%; primarily to albumin

Metabolism: Hepatic (99%) via CYP2C8 and 3A4 to both active and inactive metabolites

Half-life elimination: Parent drug: 3-7 hours; Total: 16-24 hours

Time to peak: ~2 hours; delayed with food

Excretion: Urine (15% to 30%) and feces as metabolites

Dosage
Oral:

Adults:
- Monotherapy: Initial: 15-30 mg once daily; if response is inadequate, the dosage may be increased in increments up to 45 mg once daily; maximum recommended dose: 45 mg once daily
- Combination therapy: Maximum recommended dose: 45 mg/day
  - With sulfonylureas: Initial: 15-30 mg once daily; dose of sulfonylurea should be reduced if the patient reports hypoglycemia
  - With metformin: Initial: 15-30 mg once daily; it is unlikely that the dose of metformin will need to be reduced due to hypoglycemia
  - With insulin: Initial: 15-30 mg once daily; dose of insulin should be reduced by 10% to 25% if the patient reports hypoglycemia or if the plasma glucose falls to <100 mg/dL.

Dosage adjustment in patients with CHF (NYHA Class II) in mono- or combination therapy: Initial: 15 mg once daily; may be increased after several months of treatment, with close attention to heart failure symptoms

Elderly: No dosage adjustment is recommended in elderly patients.

Dosage adjustment in renal impairment: No dosage adjustment is required.

Dosage adjustment in hepatic impairment: Clearance is significantly lower in hepatic impairment (Child-Pugh Grade B/C). Therapy should not be initiated if the patient exhibits active liver disease or increased transaminases (>2.5 times ULN) at baseline. During treatment if ALT levels elevate >3 times ULN, the test should be repeated as soon as possible. If ALT levels remain >3 times ULN or if the patient is jaundiced, therapy should be discontinued.

Dietary Considerations
Management of type 2 diabetes mellitus (noninsulin dependent, NIDDM) should include diet control. May be taken without regard to meals.

(Continued)

Pioglitazone *(Continued)*

Administration May be administered without regard to meals

Monitoring Parameters Hemoglobin A$_{1c}$, serum glucose; signs and symptoms of heart failure; liver enzymes prior to initiation and periodically during treatment (per clinician judgment). If the ALT is increased to >2.5 times the upper limit of normal, liver function testing should be performed more frequently until the levels return to normal or pretreatment values. Patients with an elevation in ALT >3 times the upper limit of normal should be rechecked as soon as possible. If the ALT levels remain >3 times the upper limit of normal, therapy with pioglitazone should be discontinued. Routine ophthalmic exams are recommended; patients reporting visual deterioration should have a prompt referral to an ophthalmologist and consideration should be given to discontinuing pioglitazone.

Dosage Forms

Tablet:
Actos®: 15 mg, 30 mg, 45 mg

Pioglitazone and Glimepiride (pye oh GLI ta zone & GLYE me pye ride)

U.S. Brand Names Duetact™

Index Terms Glimepiride and Pioglitazone; Glimepiride and Pioglitazone Hydrochloride

Pharmacologic Category Antidiabetic Agent, Sulfonylurea; Antidiabetic Agent, Thiazolidinedione; Hypoglycemic Agent, Oral

Use Management of type 2 diabetes mellitus (noninsulin dependent, NIDDM) as an adjunct to diet and exercise

Pregnancy Risk Factor C

Dosage Oral: Type 2 diabetes mellitus:

Adults: Initial dose should be based on current dose of pioglitazone and/or sulfonylurea.

Patients inadequately controlled on **glimepiride** alone: Initial dose: 30 mg/2 mg or 30 mg/4 mg once daily

Patients inadequately controlled on **pioglitazone** alone: Initial dose: 30 mg/2 mg once daily

Patients with systolic dysfunction (eg, NYHA Class I and II): Initiate only after patient has been safely titrated to 30 mg of pioglitazone. Initial dose: 30 mg/2 mg or 30 mg/4 mg once daily.

Note: No exact dosing relationship exists between glimepiride and other sulfonlyureas. Dosing should be limited to less than or equal to the maximum initial dose of glimepiride (2 mg). When converting patients from other sulfonylureas with longer half lives (eg, chlorpropamide) to glimepiride, observe patient carefully for 1-2 weeks due to overlapping hypoglycemic effects.

Dosing adjustment: Dosage may be increased up to max dose and formulation strengths available; tablet should not be given more than once daily; see individual agents for frequency of adjustments. Dosage adjustments in patients with systolic dysfunction should be done carefully and patient monitored for symptoms of worsening heart failure. Maximum dose: Pioglitazone 45 mg/glimepiride 8 mg daily

Elderly: Initial: Glimepiride 1 mg/day prior to initiating Duetact™; dose titration and maintenance dosing should be conservative to avoid hypoglycemia

Dosage adjustment in renal impairment: Cl$_{cr}$ <22 mL/minute: Initial dose should be 1 mg of glimepiride and dosage increments should be based on fasting blood glucose levels

Dosage adjustment in hepatic impairment: Do not initiate treatment with active liver disease or ALT >2.5 times ULN. During treatment, if ALT levels elevate >3 times ULN, the test should be repeated as soon as possible. If ALT levels remain >3 times ULN or if the patient is jaundiced, Duetact™ should be discontinued.

Additional Information Complete prescribing information for this medication should be consulted for additional detail.

Dosage Forms

Tablet:
Duetact™:
30 mg/2 mg: Pioglitazone 30 mg and glimepiride 2 mg
30 mg/4 mg: Pioglitazone 30 mg and glimepiride 4 mg

Pioglitazone and Metformin (pye oh GLI ta zone & met FOR min)

U.S. Brand Names Actoplus Met™

Index Terms Metformin Hydrochloride and Pioglitazone Hydrochloride

Pharmacologic Category Antidiabetic Agent, Biguanide; Antidiabetic Agent, Thiazolidinedione

Use Management of type 2 diabetes mellitus (noninsulin dependent, NIDDM)

Pregnancy Risk Factor C

Dosage Oral: Type 2 diabetes mellitus:

Adults: Initial dose should be based on current dose of pioglitazone and/or metformin; daily dose should be divided and given with meals

Patients inadequately controlled on **metformin alone**: Initial dose: Pioglitazone 15-30 mg/day plus current dose of metformin

Patients inadequately controlled on **pioglitazone alone**: Initial dose: Metformin 1000-1700 mg/day plus current dose of pioglitazone

Note: When switching from combination pioglitazone and metformin as separate tablets: Use current dose.

Dosing adjustment: Doses may be increased as increments of pioglitazone 15 mg and/or metformin 500-850 mg, up to the maximum dose; doses should be titrated gradually. Guidelines for frequency of adjustment (adapted from rosiglitazone/metformin combination labeling):

After a change in the **metformin** dosage, titration can be done after 1-2 weeks
After a change in the **pioglitazone** dosage, titration can be done after 8-12 weeks

Maximum dose: Pioglitazone 45 mg/metformin 2550 mg daily

Elderly: The initial and maintenance dosing should be conservative, due to the potential for decreased renal function (monitor). Generally, elderly patients should not be titrated to the maximum; do not use in patients ≥80 years of age unless normal renal function has been established.

Dosage adjustment in renal impairment: Do not use with renal disease or renal dysfunction (serum creatinine ≥1.5 mg/dL in males or ≥1.4 mg/dL in females or abnormal clearance).

Dosage adjustment in hepatic impairment: Do not initiate treatment with active liver disease or ALT >2.5 times ULN. During treatment if ALT levels elevate >3 times ULN, the test should be repeated as soon as possible. If ALT levels remain >3 times ULN or if the patient is jaundiced, therapy should be discontinued.

Additional Information Complete prescribing information for this medication should be consulted for additional detail.

Dosage Forms
Tablet:
Actoplus Met™:
15/500: Pioglitazone 15 mg and metformin hydrochloride 500 mg
15/850: Pioglitazone 15 mg and metformin hydrochloride 850 mg

---

Piperacillin (pi PER a sil in)

Canadian Brand Names Piperacillin for Injection, USP
Index Terms Piperacillin Sodium
Pharmacologic Category Antibiotic, Penicillin
Additional Appendix Information
Antimicrobial Drugs of Choice *on page 1981*
Community-Acquired Pneumonia in Adults *on page 1999*

Use Treatment of susceptible infections such as septicemia, acute and chronic respiratory tract infections, skin and soft tissue infections, and urinary tract infections due to susceptible strains of *Pseudomonas*, *Proteus*, and *Escherichia coli* and *Enterobacter*; active against some streptococci and some anaerobic bacteria; febrile neutropenia (as part of combination regimen)

Pregnancy Risk Factor B

Dosage
Usual dosage range:
Neonates: I.M., I.V.: 100 mg/kg every 12 hours
Infants and Children: I.M., I.V.: 200-300 mg/kg/day in divided doses every 4-6 hours
Adults: I.M., I.V.: 2-4 g/dose every 4-6 hours (maximum: 24 g/day)
Indication-specific dosing:
Children: I.M., I.V.:
Cystic fibrosis: 350-500 mg/kg/day in divided doses every 4-6 hours
Adults:
Burn wound sepsis: I.V.: 4 g every 4 hours with vancomycin and amikacin
Cholangitis, acute: I.V.: 4 g every 6 hours
Keratitis *(Pseudomonas):* Ophthalmic: 6-12 mg/mL every 15-60 minutes around the clock for 24-72 hours, then slow reduction
Malignant otitis externa: I.V.: 4-6 g every 4-6 hours with tobramycin
Moderate infections: I.M., I.V.: 2-3 g/dose every 6-12 hours (maximum: 2 g I.M./site)
Prosthetic joint *(Pseudomonas):* I.V.: 3 g every 6 hours with aminoglycoside
Pseudomonas infections: I.V.: 4 g every 4 hours
Severe infections: I.M., I.V.: 3-4 g/dose every 4-6 hours (maximum: 24 g/24 hours)
Urinary tract infections: I.V.: 2-3 g/dose every 6-12 hours
Uncomplicated gonorrhea: I.M.: 2 g in a single dose accompanied by 1 g probenecid 30 minutes prior to injection

Dosing adjustment in renal impairment: Adults: I.V.:
Cl$_{cr}$ 20-40 mL/minute: Administer 3-4 g every 8 hours
Cl$_{cr}$ <20 mL/minute: Administer 3-4 g every 12 hours
Moderately dialyzable (20% to 50%)
Continuous arteriovenous or venovenous hemodiafiltration effects: Dose as for Cl$_{cr}$ 10-50 mL/minute

Additional Information Complete prescribing information for this medication should be consulted for additional detail.

Dosage Forms Injection, powder for reconstitution: 2 g, 3 g, 4 g, 40 g

---

Piperacillin and Tazobactam Sodium
(pi PER a sil in & ta zoe BAK tam SOW dee um)

U.S. Brand Names Zosyn®
Canadian Brand Names Tazocin®
Index Terms Piperacillin Sodium and Tazobactam Sodium; Tazobactam and Piperacillin
Pharmacologic Category Antibiotic, Penicillin
Additional Appendix Information
Antimicrobial Drugs of Choice *on page 1981*
Community-Acquired Pneumonia in Adults *on page 1999*

Use Treatment of moderate-to-severe infections caused by susceptible organisms, including infections of the lower respiratory tract (community-acquired pneumonia, nosocomial pneumonia); urinary tract; uncomplicated and complicated skin and skin structures; gynecologic (endometritis, pelvic inflammatory disease); bone and joint infections; intra-abdominal infections (appendicitis with rupture/abscess, peritonitis); and septicemia. Tazobactam expands activity of piperacillin to include beta-lactamase producing strains of *S. aureus*, *H. influenzae*, *Bacteroides*, and other gram-negative bacteria.

(Continued)

Piperacillin and Tazobactam Sodium *(Continued)*

Pregnancy Risk Factor B

Pregnancy Implications Piperacillin and tazobactam were not teratogenic in animal studies. Both piperacillin and tazobactam cross the human placenta.

Lactation Enters breast milk/use caution

Medication Safety Issues

Sound-alike/look-alike issues:

Zosyn® may be confused with Zofran®, Zyvox™

Contraindications Hypersensitivity to penicillins, beta-lactamase inhibitors, or any component of the formulation

Warnings/Precautions Bleeding disorders have been observed, particularly in patients with renal impairment; discontinue if thrombocytopenia or bleeding occurs. Due to sodium load and to the adverse effects of high serum concentrations of penicillins, dosage modification is required in patients with impaired or underdeveloped renal function; use with caution in patients with seizures or in patients with history of beta-lactam allergy; associated with an increased incidence of rash and fever in cystic fibrosis patients. Prolonged use may result in superinfection, including pseudomembranous colitis. Safety and efficacy have not been established in children <2 months of age.

Adverse Reactions

>10%: Gastrointestinal: Diarrhea (7% to 11%)

>1% to 10%:

Cardiovascular: Hypertension (2%)

Central nervous system: Insomnia (7%), headache (8%), fever (2% to 5%), agitation (2%), pain (2%)

Dermatologic: Rash (4%), pruritus (3%)

Gastrointestinal: Constipation (1% to 8%), nausea (7%), vomiting (3% to 4%), dyspepsia (3%), stool changes (2%), abdominal pain (1% to 2%)

Hepatic: Transaminases increased

Local: Local reaction (3%), abscess (2%)

Respiratory: Pharyngitis (2%)

Miscellaneous: Moniliasis (2%), sepsis (2%), infection (2%)

≤1% (Limited to important and life-threatening): Agranulocytosis, anaphylaxis/anaphylactoid reaction, anemia, anxiety, arrhythmia, arthralgia, atrial fibrillation, back pain, bradycardia, bronchospasm, candidiasis, cardiac arrest, cardiac failure, circulatory failure, chest pain, cholestatic jaundice, confusion, convulsions, coughing, depression, diaphoresis, dizziness, dyspnea, dysuria, edema, epistaxis, erythema multiforme, flatulence, flushing, gastritis, genital pruritus, hallucination, hematuria, hemolytic anemia, hemorrhage, hepatitis, hiccough, hypoglycemia, hypotension, ileus, incontinence, inflammation, injection site reaction, interstitial nephritis, leukorrhea, malaise, mesenteric embolism, myalgia, myocardial infarction, oliguria, pancytopenia, phlebitis, photophobia, pseudomembranous colitis, pulmonary edema, pulmonary embolism, purpura, renal failure, rhinitis, rigors, Stevens-Johnson syndrome, syncope, tachycardia (supraventricular and ventricular), taste perversion, thirst, thrombocytosis, thrombophlebitis, tinnitus, toxic epidermal necrolysis, tremor, ulcerative stomatitis, urinary retention, vaginitis, ventricular fibrillation, vertigo

Overdosage/Toxicology Symptoms of penicillin overdose include neuromuscular hypersensitivity (agitation, hallucinations, asterixis, encephalopathy, confusion, and seizures) and electrolyte imbalance (with potassium or sodium salts), especially in renal dysfunction. Hemodialysis may be helpful to aid in the removal of the drug from the blood, otherwise, most treatment is supportive or symptom-directed.

Drug Interactions

Increased Effect/Toxicity: Probenecid may increase penicillin levels. Neuromuscular blockers may increase duration of blockade. Penicillins may increase methotrexate exposure; clinical significance has not been established.

Decreased Effect: Tetracyclines may decrease penicillin effectiveness. Aminoglycosides may cause physical inactivation of aminoglycosides in the presence of high concentrations of piperacillin and potential toxicity in patients with mild-moderate renal dysfunction. Although anecdotal reports suggest oral contraceptive efficacy could be reduced by penicillins, this has been refuted by more rigorous scientific and clinical data.

Stability

Vials: Store at controlled room temperature of 20°C to 25°C (68°F to 77°F). Use single-dose vials immediately after reconstitution (discard unused portions after 24 hours at room temperature and 48 hours if refrigerated). Reconstitute with 5 mL of diluent per 1 g of piperacillin and then further dilute. After reconstitution, vials or solution are stable in NS or D_5W for 24 hours at room temperature and 48 hours (vials) or 7 days (solution) when refrigerated.

Premixed solution: Store frozen at -20°C (-4°F). Thawed solution is stable for 24 hours at room temperature or 14 days under refrigeration; do not refreeze.

Mechanism of Action Inhibits bacterial cell wall synthesis by binding to one or more of the penicillin binding proteins (PBPs); which in turn inhibits the final transpeptidation step of peptidoglycan synthesis in bacterial cell walls, thus inhibiting cell wall biosynthesis. Bacteria eventually lyse due to ongoing activity of cell wall autolytic enzymes (autolysins and murein hydrolases) while cell wall assembly is arrested. Tazobactam inhibits many beta-lactamases, including staphylococcal penicillinase and Richmond and Sykes types II, III, IV, and V, including extended spectrum enzymes; it has only limited activity against class I beta-lactamases other than class Ic types.

Pharmacodynamics/Kinetics Both AUC and peak concentrations are dose proportional; hepatic impairment does not affect kinetics

Distribution: Well into lungs, intestinal mucosa, skin, muscle, uterus, ovary, prostate, gallbladder, and bile; penetration into CSF is low in subject with noninflamed meninges

Protein binding: Piperacillin and tazobactam: ~30%

Metabolism:

Piperacillin: 6% to 9% to desethyl metabolite (weak activity)

Tazobactam: ~26% to inactive metabolite

Half-life elimination: Piperacillin and tazobactam: 0.7-1.2 hours

Time to peak, plasma: Immediately following infusion of 30 minutes

Excretion: Clearance of both piperacillin and tazobactam are directly proportional to renal function

Piperacillin: Urine (68% as unchanged drug); feces (10% to 20%)

Tazobactam: Urine (80% as inactive metabolite)

Dosage

Usual dosage range:

Children ≥6 months (unlabeled use): I.V.: 240 mg of piperacillin component/kg/day in 3 divided doses for severe infections; maximum: Piperacillin 18 g/day

Adults: I.V.: 2.25-4.5 g every 6-8 hours; maximum: Piperacillin 18 g/day

Indication-specific dosing: I.V.:

Children: **Note:** Dosing based on piperacillin component:

Appendicitis, peritonitis:

2-9 months: 80 mg/kg every 8 hours

≥9 months and ≤40 kg: 100 mg/kg every 8 hours

>40 kg: refer to Adult dosing

Cystic fibrosis, pseudomonal infections (unlabeled use): 350-450 mg/kg/day in divided doses

Adults:

Diverticulitis, intra-abdominal abscess, peritonitis: I.V.: 4.5 g every 8 hours or 3.375 g every 6 hours

Moderate infections: I.M.: 2.25 g every 6-8 hours; treatment should be continued for ≥7-10 days depending on severity of disease (**Note:** I.M. route not FDA-approved)

Pneumonia (nosocomial): I.V.: 4.5 g every 6 hours for 7-14 days (when used empirically, combination with an aminoglycoside is recommended; consider discontinuation of aminoglycoside if *P. aeruginosa* is not isolated)

Severe infections: I.V.: 4.5 g every 8 hours or 3.375 g every 6 hours for 7-10 days

Dosing interval in renal impairment:

Cl_{cr} 20-40 mL/minute: Administer 2.25 g every 6 hours (3.375 g every 6 hours for nosocomial pneumonia)

Cl_{cr} <20 mL/minute: Administer 2.25 g every 8 hours (2.25 g every 6 hours for nosocomial pneumonia)

Hemodialysis/CAPD: Administer 2.25 g every 12 hours (2.25 g every 8 hours for nosocomial pneumonia) with an additional dose of 0.75 g after each dialysis

Dietary Considerations

Infusion, premixed: 2.25 g contains sodium 5.58 mEq (128 mg); 3.375 g contains sodium 8.38 mEq (192 mg); 4.5 g contains sodium 11.17 mEq (256 mg)

Injection, powder for reconstitution: 2.25 g contains sodium 5.58 mEq (128 mg); 3.375 g contains sodium 8.38 mEq (192 mg); 4.5 g contains sodium 11.17 mEq (256 mg); 40.5 g contains sodium 100.4 mEq (2304 mg, bulk pharmacy vial)

Administration Administer by I.V. infusion over 30 minutes

Some penicillins (eg, carbenicillin, ticarcillin and piperacillin) have been shown to inactivate aminoglycosides *in vitro*. This has been observed to a greater extent with tobramycin and gentamicin, while amikacin has shown greater stability against inactivation. Concurrent use of these agents may pose a risk of reduced antibacterial efficacy *in vivo*, particularly in the setting of profound renal impairment. However, definitive clinical evidence is lacking. If combination penicillin/aminoglycoside therapy is desired in a patient with renal dysfunction, separation of doses (if feasible), and routine monitoring of aminoglycoside levels, CBC, and clinical response should be considered. **Note:** Reformulated Zosyn® containing EDTA has been shown to be compatible *in vitro* for Y-site infusion with amikacin and gentamicin, but not compatible with tobramycin.

Monitoring Parameters Creatinine, BUN, CBC with differential, PT, PTT; signs of bleeding; monitor for signs of anaphylaxis during first dose

Test Interactions Positive Coombs' [direct] test; false positive reaction for urine glucose using copper-reduction method (Clinitest®); may result in false positive results with the Platelia® *Aspergillus* enzyme immunoassay (EIA)

Some penicillin derivatives may accelerate the degradation of aminoglycosides *in vitro*, leading to a potential underestimation of aminoglycoside serum concentration. **Note:** Reformulated Zosyn® containing EDTA has been shown to be compatible *in vitro* for Y-site infusion with amikacin and gentamicin, but not compatible with tobramycin.

Dosage Forms Note: 8:1 ratio of piperacillin sodium/tazobactam sodium

Infusion [premixed iso-osmotic solution, frozen]:

2.25 g: Piperacillin 2 g and tazobactam 0.25 g (50 mL) [contains sodium 5.58 mEq (128 mg) and EDTA]

3.375 g: Piperacillin 3 g and tazobactam 0.375 g (50 mL) [contains sodium 8.38 mEq (192 mg) and EDTA]

4.5 g: Piperacillin 4 g and tazobactam 0.5 g (50 mL) [contains sodium 11.17 mEq (256 mg) and EDTA]

Injection, powder for reconstitution:

2.25 g: Piperacillin 2 g and tazobactam 0.25 g [contains sodium 5.58 mEq (128 mg) and EDTA]

3.375 g: Piperacillin 3 g and tazobactam 0.375 g [contains sodium 8.38 mEq (192 mg) and EDTA]

4.5 g: Piperacillin 4 g and tazobactam 0.5 g [contains sodium 11.17 mEq (256 mg) and EDTA]

40.5 g: Piperacillin 36 g and tazobactam 4.5 g [contains sodium 100.4 mEq (2304 mg) and EDTA; bulk pharmacy vial]

♦ **Piperacillin for Injection, USP (Can)** see Piperacillin on page 1375

♦ **Piperacillin Sodium** see Piperacillin on page 1375

♦ **Piperacillin Sodium and Tazobactam Sodium** see Piperacillin and Tazobactam Sodium on page 1375

♦ **Piperazine Estrone Sulfate** see Estropipate on page 637

♦ **Piperonyl Butoxide and Pyrethrins** *see* Pyrethrins and Piperonyl Butoxide *on page 1461*

Pirbuterol (peer BYOO ter ole)

U.S. Brand Names Maxair™ Autohaler™
Index Terms Pirbuterol Acetate
Pharmacologic Category Beta$_2$-Adrenergic Agonist
Additional Appendix Information
Bronchodilators *on page 1877*
Use Prevention and treatment of reversible bronchospasm including asthma
Pregnancy Risk Factor C
Lactation Excretion in breast milk unknown
Contraindications Hypersensitivity to pirbuterol, albuterol, or any component of the formulation
Warnings/Precautions Optimize anti-inflammatory treatment before initiating maintenance treatment with pirbuterol. Do not use as a component of chronic therapy without an anti-inflammatory agent. Only the mildest form of asthma (Step 1 and/or exercise-induced) would not require concurrent use based upon asthma guidelines. Patient must be instructed to seek medical attention in cases where acute symptoms are not relieved or a previous level of response is diminished. The need to increase frequency of use may indicate deterioration of asthma, and treatment must not be delayed.

Use caution in patients with cardiovascular disease (arrhythmia or hypertension or CHF), convulsive disorders, diabetes, glaucoma, hyperthyroidism, or hypokalemia. Beta agonists may cause elevation in blood pressure, heart rate, and result in CNS stimulation/excitation. Beta$_2$ agonists may increase risk of arrhythmia, increase serum glucose, or decrease serum potassium.

Do not exceed recommended dose; serious adverse events including fatalities, have been associated with excessive use of inhaled sympathomimetics. Rarely, paradoxical bronchospasm may occur with use of inhaled bronchodilating agents; this should be distinguished from inadequate response. All patients should utilize a spacer device when using a metered-dose inhaler. Safety and efficacy have not been established in children <12 years of age.

Adverse Reactions
>10%:
 Central nervous system: Nervousness, restlessness
 Endocrine & metabolic: Serum glucose increased, serum potassium decreased
 Neuromuscular & skeletal: Trembling
1% to 10%:
 Cardiovascular: Tachycardia, pounding heartbeat
 Central nervous system: Headache, dizziness, lightheadedness
 Gastrointestinal: Taste changes, vomiting, nausea
<1% (Limited to important or life-threatening): Arrhythmias, chest pain, hypertension, hypokalemia, insomnia, paradoxical bronchospasm

Overdosage/Toxicology Symptoms of overdose include tachycardia, tremor, hypertension, angina, and seizures. Hypokalemia also may occur. Cardiac arrest and death may be associated with abuse of beta-agonist bronchodilators. Treatment includes immediate discontinuation and symptomatic and supportive therapies. Cautious use of beta-adrenergic blocking agents may be considered in severe cases.

Drug Interactions
 Increased Effect/Toxicity: Increased toxicity with other beta agonists, MAO inhibitors, tricyclic antidepressants.
 Decreased Effect: Decreased effect with beta-blockers.
Stability Store between 15°C and 30°C (59°F and 86°F).
Mechanism of Action Pirbuterol is a beta$_2$-adrenergic agonist with a similar structure to albuterol, specifically a pyridine ring has been substituted for the benzene ring in albuterol. The increased beta$_2$ selectivity of pirbuterol results from the substitution of a tertiary butyl group on the nitrogen of the side chain, which additionally imparts resistance of pirbuterol to degradation by monoamine oxidase and provides a lengthened duration of action in comparison to the less selective previous beta-agonist agents.

Pharmacodynamics/Kinetics
 Onset of action: Peak effect: Therapeutic: Oral: 2-3 hours with peak serum concentration of 6.2-9.8 mcg/L; Inhalation: 0.5-1 hour
 Half-life elimination: 2-3 hours
 Metabolism: Hepatic
 Excretion: Urine (10% as unchanged drug)
Dosage Children ≥12 years and Adults: 2 inhalations every 4-6 hours for prevention; two inhalations at an interval of at least 1-3 minutes, followed by a third inhalation in treatment of bronchospasm, not to exceed 12 inhalations/day
Administration Inhalation: Shake inhaler well before use.
Monitoring Parameters Respiratory rate; FEV$_1$, peak flow, and/or other pulmonary function tests; blood pressure, heart rate; CNS stimulation; serum glucose, serum potassium
Dosage Forms Aerosol for oral inhalation, as acetate:
 Maxair™ Autohaler™: 14 g [400 inhalations; contains chlorofluorocarbons]

♦ **Pirbuterol Acetate** *see* Pirbuterol *on page 1378*

Piroxicam (peer OKS i kam)

U.S. Brand Names Feldene®
Canadian Brand Names Apo-Piroxicam®; Gen-Piroxicam; Novo-Pirocam; Nu-Pirox; Pexicam®

Pharmacologic Category Nonsteroidal Anti-inflammatory Drug (NSAID), Oral
Additional Appendix Information
Nonsteroidal Anti-inflammatory Agents *on page 1894*

Use Symptomatic treatment of acute and chronic rheumatoid arthritis and osteoarthritis

Unlabeled/Investigational Use Ankylosing spondylitis

Restrictions An FDA-approved medication guide must be distributed when dispensing an oral outpatient prescription (new or refill) where this medication is to be used without direct supervision of a healthcare provider. Medication guides are available at http://www.fda.gov/cder/Offices/ODS/medication_guides.htm.

Pregnancy Risk Factor C/D (3rd trimester)

Lactation Enters breast milk (small amounts)/not recommended (AAP rates "compatible")

Medication Safety Issues
International issues:
Flogene® [Brazil] may be confused with Florone® which is a brand name for diflorasone in the U.S.

Contraindications Hypersensitivity to piroxicam, aspirin, other NSAIDs or any component of the formulation; perioperative pain in the setting of coronary artery bypass surgery (CABG); pregnancy (3rd trimester or near term)

Warnings/Precautions [U.S. Boxed Warning]: NSAIDs are associated with an increased risk of adverse cardiovascular events, including MI, stroke, and new onset or worsening of pre-existing hypertension. Risk may be increased with duration of use or pre-existing cardiovascular risk-factors or disease. Carefully evaluate individual cardiovascular risk profiles prior to prescribing. Use caution with fluid retention, CHF or hypertension. Concurrent administration of ibuprofen, and potentially other nonselective NSAIDs, may interfere with aspirin's cardioprotective effect.

Use of NSAIDs can compromise existing renal function. Renal toxicity can occur in patient with impaired renal function, dehydration, heart failure, liver dysfunction, those taking diuretics and ACEI and the elderly. Rehydrate patient before starting therapy. Monitor renal function closely. Not recommended for use in patients with advanced renal disease.

[U.S. Boxed Warning]: NSAIDs may increase risk of gastrointestinal irritation, ulceration, bleeding, and perforation. These events may occur at any time during therapy and without warning. Use caution with a history of GI disease (bleeding or ulcers), concurrent therapy with aspirin, anticoagulants and/or corticosteroids, smoking, use of alcohol, the elderly or debilitated patients.

Use the lowest effective dose for the shortest duration of time, consistent with individual patient goals, to reduce risk of cardiovascular or GI adverse events. Alternate therapies should be considered for patients at high risk.

NSAIDs may cause serious skin adverse events including exfoliative dermatitis, Stevens-Johnson syndrome (SJS) and toxic epidermal necrolysis (TEN). Anaphylactoid reactions may occur, even without prior exposure; patients with "aspirin triad" (bronchial asthma, aspirin intolerance, rhinitis) may be at increased risk. Do not use in patients who experience bronchospasm, asthma, rhinitis, or urticaria with NSAID or aspirin therapy. A serum sickness-like reaction can rarely occur; watch for arthralgias, pruritus, fever, fatigue, and rash.

Use with caution in patients with decreased hepatic function. Closely monitor patients with any abnormal LFT. Severe hepatic reactions (eg, fulminant hepatitis, liver failure) have occurred with NSAID use, rarely; discontinue if signs or symptoms of liver disease develop, or if systemic manifestations occur.

The elderly are at increased risk for adverse effects (especially peptic ulceration, CNS effects, renal toxicity) from NSAIDs even at low doses

Withhold for at least 4-6 half-lives prior to surgical or dental procedures. Safety and efficacy have not been established in children.

Adverse Reactions
>10%:
Central nervous system: Dizziness
Dermatologic: Rash
Gastrointestinal: Abdominal cramps, heartburn, indigestion, nausea
1% to 10%:
Central nervous system: Headache, nervousness
Dermatologic: Itching
Endocrine & metabolic: Fluid retention
Gastrointestinal: Vomiting
Otic: Tinnitus
<1%: Acute renal failure, agranulocytosis, allergic rhinitis, anemia, angioedema, arrhythmia, aseptic meningitis, blurred vision, bone marrow suppression, confusion, CHF, conjunctivitis, cystitis, decreased hearing, drowsiness, dry eyes, dyspnea, epistaxis, erythema multiforme, gastritis, GI ulceration, hallucinations, hemolytic anemia, hepatitis, hot flashes, hypertension, insomnia, leukopenia, mental depression, peripheral neuropathy, photosensitivity, polydipsia, polyuria, Stevens-Johnson syndrome, tachycardia, thrombocytopenia, toxic amblyopia, toxic epidermal necrolysis, urticaria

Overdosage/Toxicology Symptoms include nausea, epigastric distress, CNS depression, leukocytosis, and renal failure. Management of nonsteroidal anti-inflammatory drug (NSAID) intoxication is primarily supportive and symptomatic. Fluid therapy is commonly effective in managing hypotension that may occur following an acute NSAID overdose, except when due to acute blood loss. Seizures tend to be very short-lived and often do not require drug treatment; although, recurrent seizures should be treated with I.V. diazepam. Since many of the NSAIDs undergo enterohepatic cycling, multiple doses of charcoal may be needed to reduce the potential for delayed toxicities.

Drug Interactions
Cytochrome P450 Effect: Substrate of CYP2C9 (minor); **Inhibits** CYP2C9 (strong)
Increased Effect/Toxicity: Increased effect/toxicity of lithium and methotrexate (controversial). Piroxicam may increase the levels/effects of CYP2C9 substrates; example substrates
(Continued)

Piroxicam *(Continued)*

include bosentan, dapsone, fluoxetine, glimepiride, glipizide, losartan, montelukast, nateglinide, paclitaxel, phenytoin, warfarin, and zafirlukast. Concomitant use with fluoroquinolones may rarely increase risk of seizure.

Decreased Effect: Decreased effect of diuretics, ACE inhibitors, angiotensin antagonists, beta-blockers, and hydralazine. Decreased effect with aspirin, antacids. Cholestyramine (and other bile acid sequestrants) may decrease the absorption of NSAIDs; separate by at least 2 hours. Salicylates' antiplatelet effect may be reduced.

Ethanol/Nutrition/Herb Interactions

Ethanol: Avoid ethanol (may enhance gastric mucosal irritation).

Food: Onset of effect may be delayed if piroxicam is taken with food.

Herb/Nutraceutical: Avoid alfalfa, anise, bilberry, bladderwrack, bromelain, cat's claw, celery, coleus, cordyceps, dong quai, evening primrose, feverfew, fenugreek, garlic, ginger, ginkgo biloboa, red clover, horse chestnut, grapeseed, green tea, ginseng, guggul, horse chestnut seed, horseradish, licorice, prickly ash, red clover, reishi, SAMe, sweet clover, turmeric, white willow (all have additional antiplatelet activity).

Mechanism of Action Inhibits prostaglandin synthesis, acts on the hypothalamus heat-regulating center to reduce fever, blocks prostaglandin synthetase action which prevents formation of the platelet-aggregating substance thromboxane A_2; decreases pain receptor sensitivity. Other proposed mechanisms of action for salicylate anti-inflammatory action are lysosomal stabilization, kinin and leukotriene production, alteration of chemotactic factors, and inhibition of neutrophil activation. This latter mechanism may be the most significant pharmacologic action to reduce inflammation.

Pharmacodynamics/Kinetics

Onset of action: Analgesic: ~1 hour

Peak effect: 3-5 hours

Protein binding: 99%

Metabolism: Hepatic

Half-life elimination: 45-50 hours

Excretion: Primarily urine and feces (small amounts) as unchanged drug (5%) and metabolites

Dosage Oral:

Children (unlabeled use): 0.2-0.3 mg/kg/day once daily; maximum dose: 15 mg/day

Adults: 10-20 mg/day once daily; although associated with increase in GI adverse effects, doses >20 mg/day have been used (ie, 30-40 mg/day)

Dosing adjustment in renal impairment: Not recommended in patients with advanced renal disease

Dosing adjustment in hepatic impairment: Reduction of dosage is necessary

Dietary Considerations May be taken with food to decrease GI adverse effect.

Monitoring Parameters Occult blood loss, hemoglobin, hematocrit, and periodic renal and hepatic function tests; periodic ophthalmologic exams with chronic use

Test Interactions Increased chloride (S), increased sodium (S), increased bleeding time

Dosage Forms Capsule: 10 mg, 20 mg

- ◆ *p*-Isobutylhydratropic Acid *see* Ibuprofen *on page 873*
- ◆ Pit *see* Oxytocin *on page 1293*
- ◆ Pitocin® *see* Oxytocin *on page 1293*
- ◆ Pitressin® *see* Vasopressin *on page 1779*
- ◆ Pitrex (Can) *see* Tolnaftate *on page 1704*
- ◆ PLA *see* Poly-L-Lactic Acid *on page 1388*
- ◆ Plan B® [RX/OTC] *see* Levonorgestrel *on page 1004*
- ◆ Plan B™ (Can) *see* Levonorgestrel *on page 1004*
- ◆ Plantago Seed *see* Psyllium *on page 1458*
- ◆ Plantain Seed *see* Psyllium *on page 1458*
- ◆ Plaquenil® *see* Hydroxychloroquine *on page 862*
- ◆ Plaretase® 8000 *see* Pancrelipase *on page 1302*
- ◆ Plasbumin® *see* Albumin *on page 55*
- ◆ Plasbumin®-5 (Can) *see* Albumin *on page 55*
- ◆ Plasbumin®-25 (Can) *see* Albumin *on page 55*
- ◆ Platinol®-AQ [DSC] *see* Cisplatin *on page 379*
- ◆ Plavix® *see* Clopidogrel *on page 401*
- ◆ Plenaxis™ [DSC] *see* Abarelix *on page 20*
- ◆ Plendil® *see* Felodipine *on page 687*
- ◆ Pletal® *see* Cilostazol *on page 368*
- ◆ Plexion® *see* Sulfur and Sulfacetamide *on page 1618*
- ◆ Plexion SCT® *see* Sulfur and Sulfacetamide *on page 1618*
- ◆ Plexion TS® *see* Sulfur and Sulfacetamide *on page 1618*
- ◆ PMPA *see* Tenofovir *on page 1645*
- ◆ PMS-Alendronate (Can) *see* Alendronate *on page 65*
- ◆ PMS-Amantadine (Can) *see* Amantadine *on page 86*
- ◆ PMS-Amitriptyline (Can) *see* Amitriptyline *on page 101*
- ◆ PMS-Amoxicillin (Can) *see* Amoxicillin *on page 110*
- ◆ PMS-Anagrelide (Can) *see* Anagrelide *on page 128*
- ◆ PMS-Atenolol (Can) *see* Atenolol *on page 167*
- ◆ PMS-Azithromycin (Can) *see* Azithromycin *on page 186*
- ◆ PMS-Baclofen (Can) *see* Baclofen *on page 193*
- ◆ PMS-Bethanechol (Can) *see* Bethanechol *on page 216*
- ◆ PMS-Bicalutamide (Can) *see* Bicalutamide *on page 221*
- ◆ PMS-Brimonidine Tartrate (Can) *see* Brimonidine *on page 239*

♦ **PMS-Bromocriptine (Can)** *see* Bromocriptine *on page 240*
♦ **PMS-Buspirone (Can)** *see* BusPIRone *on page 256*
♦ **PMS-Butorphanol (Can)** *see* Butorphanol *on page 261*
♦ **PMS-Captopril (Can)** *see* Captopril *on page 281*
♦ **PMS-Carbamazepine (Can)** *see* Carbamazepine *on page 284*
♦ **PMS-Carvedilol (Can)** *see* Carvedilol *on page 299*
♦ **PMS-Cefaclor (Can)** *see* Cefaclor *on page 303*
♦ **PMS-Chloral Hydrate (Can)** *see* Chloral Hydrate *on page 339*
♦ **PMS-Cholestyramine (Can)** *see* Cholestyramine Resin *on page 360*
♦ **PMS-Cimetidine (Can)** *see* Cimetidine *on page 369*
♦ **PMS-Ciprofloxacin (Can)** *see* Ciprofloxacin *on page 372*
♦ **PMS-Citalopram (Can)** *see* Citalopram *on page 381*
♦ **PMS-Clonazepam (Can)** *see* Clonazepam *on page 397*
♦ **PMS-Deferoxamine (Can)** *see* Deferoxamine *on page 466*
♦ **PMS-Desipramine (Can)** *see* Desipramine *on page 473*
♦ **PMS-Desonide (Can)** *see* Desonide *on page 478*
♦ **PMS-Dexamethasone (Can)** *see* Dexamethasone *on page 479*
♦ **PMS-Dicitrate (Can)** *see* Sodium Citrate and Citric Acid *on page 1579*
♦ **PMS-Diclofenac (Can)** *see* Diclofenac *on page 492*
♦ **PMS-Diclofenac SR (Can)** *see* Diclofenac *on page 492*
♦ **PMS-Diphenhydramine (Can)** *see* DiphenhydrAMINE *on page 515*
♦ **PMS-Dipivefrin (Can)** *see* Dipivefrin *on page 524*
♦ **PMS-Docusate Calcium (Can)** *see* Docusate *on page 533*
♦ **PMS-Docusate Sodium (Can)** *see* Docusate *on page 533*
♦ **PMS-Erythromycin (Can)** *see* Erythromycin *on page 609*
♦ **PMS-Fenofibrate Micro (Can)** *see* Fenofibrate *on page 689*
♦ **PMS-Fenofibrate Supra (Can)** *see* Fenofibrate *on page 689*
♦ **PMS-Flunisolide (Can)** *see* Flunisolide *on page 720*
♦ **PMS-Fluorometholone (Can)** *see* Fluorometholone *on page 724*
♦ **PMS-Fluoxetine (Can)** *see* Fluoxetine *on page 727*
♦ **PMS-Fluphenazine Decanoate (Can)** *see* Fluphenazine *on page 731*
♦ **PMS-Fluvoxamine (Can)** *see* Fluvoxamine *on page 747*
♦ **PMS-Gabapentin (Can)** *see* Gabapentin *on page 775*
♦ **PMS-Gemfibrozil (Can)** *see* Gemfibrozil *on page 787*
♦ **PMS-Glyburide (Can)** *see* GlyBURIDE *on page 803*
♦ **PMS-Haloperidol LA (Can)** *see* Haloperidol *on page 826*
♦ **PMS-Hydrochlorothiazide (Can)** *see* Hydrochlorothiazide *on page 845*
♦ **PMS-Hydromorphone (Can)** *see* Hydromorphone *on page 856*
♦ **PMS-Hydroxyzine (Can)** *see* HydrOXYzine *on page 865*
♦ **PMS-Indapamide (Can)** *see* Indapamide *on page 898*
♦ **PMS-Ipratropium (Can)** *see* Ipratropium *on page 932*
♦ **PMS-Isoniazid (Can)** *see* Isoniazid *on page 942*
♦ **PMS-Isosorbide (Can)** *see* Isosorbide Dinitrate *on page 945*
♦ **PMS-Lactulose (Can)** *see* Lactulose *on page 971*
♦ **PMS-Lamotrigine (Can)** *see* Lamotrigine *on page 974*
♦ **PMS-Levobunolol (Can)** *see* Levobunolol *on page 996*
♦ **PMS-Lindane (Can)** *see* Lindane *on page 1016*
♦ **PMS-Lithium Carbonate (Can)** *see* Lithium *on page 1023*
♦ **PMS-Lithium Citrate (Can)** *see* Lithium *on page 1023*
♦ **PMS-Loperamine (Can)** *see* Loperamide *on page 1027*
♦ **PMS-Lorazepam (Can)** *see* Lorazepam *on page 1035*
♦ **PMS-Lovastatin (Can)** *see* Lovastatin *on page 1040*
♦ **PMS-Loxapine (Can)** *see* Loxapine *on page 1042*
♦ **PMS-Mefenamic Acid (Can)** *see* Mefenamic Acid *on page 1068*
♦ **PMS-Meloxicam (Can)** *see* Meloxicam *on page 1072*
♦ **PMS-Metformin (Can)** *see* Metformin *on page 1098*
♦ **PMS-Methylphenidate (Can)** *see* Methylphenidate *on page 1119*
♦ **PMS-Metoprolol (Can)** *see* Metoprolol *on page 1129*
♦ **PMS-Minocycline (Can)** *see* Minocycline *on page 1149*
♦ **PMS-Mirtazapine (Can)** *see* Mirtazapine *on page 1152*
♦ **PMS-Mometasone (Can)** *see* Mometasone Furoate *on page 1165*
♦ **PMS-Morphine Sulfate SR (Can)** *see* Morphine Sulfate *on page 1171*
♦ **PMS-Nizatidine (Can)** *see* Nizatidine *on page 1238*
♦ **PMS-Norfloxacin (Can)** *see* Norfloxacin *on page 1241*
♦ **PMS-Nortriptyline (Can)** *see* Nortriptyline *on page 1243*
♦ **PMS-Nystatin (Can)** *see* Nystatin *on page 1250*
♦ **PMS-Ofloxacin (Can)** *see* Ofloxacin *on page 1254*
♦ **PMS-Oxazepam (Can)** *see* Oxazepam *on page 1281*
♦ **PMS-Oxybutynin (Can)** *see* Oxybutynin *on page 1285*
♦ **PMS-Oxycodone-Acetaminophen (Can)** *see* Oxycodone and Acetaminophen *on page 1289*
♦ **PMS-Paroxetine (Can)** *see* Paroxetine *on page 1314*
♦ **PMS-Phenobarbital (Can)** *see* Phenobarbital *on page 1353*
♦ **PMS-Pindolol (Can)** *see* Pindolol *on page 1371*
♦ **PMS-Polytrimethoprim (Can)** *see* Trimethoprim and Polymyxin B *on page 1745*

+ **PMS-Pravastatin (Can)** *see* Pravastatin *on page 1409*
+ **PMS-Procyclidine (Can)** *see* Procyclidine *on page 1432*
+ **PMS-Pseudoephedrine (Can)** *see* Pseudoephedrine *on page 1454*
+ **PMS-Ranitidine (Can)** *see* Ranitidine *on page 1485*
+ **PMS-Salbutamol (Can)** *see* Albuterol *on page 57*
+ **PMS-Sertraline (Can)** *see* Sertraline *on page 1557*
+ **PMS-Simvastatin (Can)** *see* Simvastatin *on page 1567*
+ **PMS-Sodium Polystyrene Sulfonate (Can)** *see* Sodium Polystyrene Sulfonate *on page 1582*
+ **PMS-Sotalol (Can)** *see* Sotalol *on page 1592*
+ **PMS-Sucralate (Can)** *see* Sucralfate *on page 1606*
+ **PMS-Sumatriptan (Can)** *see* Sumatriptan *on page 1620*
+ **PMS-Temazepam (Can)** *see* Temazepam *on page 1640*
+ **PMS-Terazosin (Can)** *see* Terazosin *on page 1647*
+ **PMS-Terbinafine (Can)** *see* Terbinafine *on page 1648*
+ **PMS-Timolol (Can)** *see* Timolol *on page 1687*
+ **PMS-Tobramycin (Can)** *see* Tobramycin *on page 1696*
+ **PMS-Topiramate (Can)** *see* Topiramate *on page 1707*
+ **PMS-Trazodone (Can)** *see* Trazodone *on page 1727*
+ **PMS-Trifluoperazine (Can)** *see* Trifluoperazine *on page 1740*
+ **PMS-Valproic Acid (Can)** *see* Valproic Acid and Derivatives *on page 1767*
+ **PMS-Valproic Acid E.C. (Can)** *see* Valproic Acid and Derivatives *on page 1767*
+ **PN** *see* Total Parenteral Nutrition *on page 1715*
+ **Pneumo 23™ (Can)** *see* Pneumococcal Polysaccharide Vaccine (Polyvalent) *on page 1384*
+ **Pneumococcal 7-Valent Conjugate Vaccine** *see* Pneumococcal Conjugate Vaccine (7-Valent) *on page 1382*

Pneumococcal Conjugate Vaccine (7-Valent)
(noo moe KOK al KON ju gate vak SEEN, seven vay lent)

U.S. Brand Names Prevnar®
Canadian Brand Names Prevnar®
Index Terms Diphtheria CRM$_{197}$ Protein; PCV7; Pneumococcal 7-Valent Conjugate Vaccine
Pharmacologic Category Vaccine
Additional Appendix Information
Immunization Recommendations *on page 1929*
Use Immunization of infants and toddlers against *Streptococcus pneumoniae* infection caused by serotypes included in the vaccine

Advisory Committee on Immunization Practices (ACIP) guidelines also recommend PCV7 for use in:
All children 2-23 months
Children ≥2-59 months with cochlear implants
Children ages 24-59 months with: Sickle cell disease (including other sickle cell hemoglobinopathies, asplenia, splenic dysfunction), HIV infection, immunocompromising conditions (congenital immunodeficiencies, renal failure, nephrotic syndrome, diseases associated with immunosuppressive or radiation therapy, solid organ transplant), chronic illnesses (cardiac disease, cerebrospinal fluid leaks, diabetes mellitus, pulmonary disease excluding asthma unless on high dose corticosteroids)
Consider use in all children 24-59 months with priority given to:
Children 24-35 months
Children 24-59 months who are of Alaska native, American Indian, or African-American descent
Children 24-59 months who attend group day care centers
Pregnancy Risk Factor C
Pregnancy Implications
Reproduction studies have not been conducted. This product is indicated for use in infants and toddlers.
Lactation
Excretion in breast milk unknown/not recommended
Medication Safety Issues
Sound-alike/look-alike issues:
Prevnar® may be confused with PREVEN®
Contraindications Hypersensitivity to pneumococcal vaccine or any component of the formulation, including diphtheria toxoid; current or recent severe or moderate febrile illness
Warnings/Precautions Use caution in latex sensitivity. Children with impaired immune responsiveness may have a reduced response to active immunization. The decision to administer or delay vaccination because of current or recent febrile illness depends on the severity of symptoms and the etiology of the disease. Immunization should be delayed during the course of an acute febrile illness. Use caution in children with coagulation disorders (including thrombocytopenia) where intramuscular injections should not be used. Epinephrine 1:1000 should be readily available. Use of pneumococcal conjugate vaccine does not replace use of the 23-valent pneumococcal polysaccharide vaccine in children ≥24 months of age with sickle cell disease, asplenia, HIV infection, chronic illness or if immunocompromised. Safety and efficacy have not been established in children <6 weeks or ≥10 years of age. Not for I.V. use.
Adverse Reactions All serious adverse reactions must be reported to the U.S. Department of Health and Human Services (DHHS) Vaccine Adverse Event Reporting System (VAERS) 1-800-822-7967.
>10%:
Central nervous system: Fever, irritability, drowsiness, restlessness

Dermatologic: Erythema

Gastrointestinal: Decreased appetite, vomiting, diarrhea

Local: Induration, tenderness, nodule

1% to 10%: Dermatologic: Rash

Postmarketing and/or case reports: Anaphylactic reaction, anaphylactoid reaction, angioneurotic edema, apnea, bronchospasm, dyspnea, erythema multiforme, facial edema, febrile seizure, hypersensitivity reaction, injection site reaction (eg, dermatitis, lymphadenopathy, pruritus, urticaria, shock)

Overdosage/Toxicology

Higher than recommended doses, and doses administered closer than the recommended interval, have been reported. Adverse events were similar to those reported with single doses; most patients were asymptomatic.

Drug Interactions

Decreased Effect: Immunosuppressants may decrease response to active immunizations.

Stability Store refrigerated at 2°C to 8°C (36°F to 46°F).

Mechanism of Action Promotes active immunization against invasive disease caused by *S. pneumoniae* capsular serotypes 4, 6B, 9V, 18C, 19F, and 23F, all which are individually conjugated to CRM197 protein

Dosage I.M.:

Infants: 2-6 months: 0.5 mL at approximately 2-month intervals for 3 consecutive doses, followed by a fourth dose of 0.5 mL at 12-15 months of age; first dose may be given as young as 6 weeks of age, but is typically given at 2 months of age. In case of a moderate shortage of vaccine, defer the fourth dose until shortage is resolved; in case of a severe shortage of vaccine, defer third and fourth doses until shortage is resolved.

Previously Unvaccinated Older Infants and Children:

7-11 months: 0.5 mL for a total of 3 doses; 2 doses at least 4 weeks apart, followed by a third dose after the 1-year birthday (12-15 months), separated from the second dose by at least 2 months. In case of a severe shortage of vaccine, defer the third dose until shortage is resolved.

12-23 months: 0.5 mL for a total of 2 doses, separated by at least 2 months. In case of a severe shortage of vaccine, defer the second dose until shortage is resolved.

24-59 months:

Healthy Children: 0.5 mL as a single dose. In case of a severe shortage of vaccine, defer dosing until shortage is resolved.

Children with sickle cell disease, asplenia, HIV infection, chronic illness or immunocompromising conditions (not including bone marrow transplants - results pending; use PPV23 [pneumococcal polysaccharide vaccine, polyvalent] at 12- and 24-months until studies are complete): 0.5 mL for a total of 2 doses, separated by 2 months

Previously Vaccinated Children with a lapse in vaccine administration:

7-11 months: Previously received 1 or 2 doses PCV7: 0.5 mL dose at 7-11 months of age, followed by a second dose ≥2 months later at 12-15 months of age

12-23 months:

Previously received 1 dose before 12 months of age: 0.5 mL dose, followed by a second dose ≥2 months later

Previously received 2 doses before age 12 months: 0.5 mL dose ≥2 months after the most recent dose

24-59 months: Any incomplete schedule: 0.5 mL as a single dose; **Note:** Patients with chronic diseases or immunosuppressing conditions should receive 2 doses ≥2 months apart

Administration Shake well prior to use. Do not inject I.V.; avoid intradermal route; administer I.M. (deltoid muscle for toddlers and young children or lateral midthigh in infants)

For patients at risk of hemorrhage following intramuscular injection, the ACIP recommends "it should be administered intramuscularly if, in the opinion of the physician familiar with the patients bleeding risk, the vaccine can be administered with reasonable safety by this route. If the patient receives antihemophilia or other similar therapy, intramuscular vaccination can be scheduled shortly after such therapy is administered. A fine needle (23 gauge or smaller) can be used for the vaccination and firm pressure applied to the site (without rubbing) for at least 2 minutes. The patient should be instructed concerning the risk of hematoma from the injection."

Additional Information Children 24-59 months of age at high risk for pneumococcal disease but that have already received pneumococcal polysaccharide vaccine (PPV23) may benefit from the immunologic response induced by PCV7. Suggested dosing: Starting ≥2 months after last PPV23 dose: 0.5 mL dose of PCV7, followed by a second dose ≥2 months later. (**Note:** Although it is believed that this will provide additional protection, safety data is limited.)

Federal law requires that the date of administration, the vaccine manufacturer, lot number of vaccine, and the administering person's name, title and address be entered into the patient's permanent medical record.

Dosage Forms

Injection, suspension:

Prevnar®: 2 mcg of each saccharide for serotypes 4, 9V, 14, 18C, 19F, and 23F, and 4 mcg of serotype 6B per 0.5 mL (0.5 mL) [contains 16 mcg total saccharide; also contains diphtheria CRM197 carrier protein ~20 mcg/0.5 mL and aluminum 0.125 mg/0.5 mL (as aluminum phosphate adjuvant); serotypes grown in soy peptone broth; packaging contains latex]

Pneumococcal Polysaccharide Vaccine (Polyvalent)
(noo moe KOK al pol i SAK a ride vak SEEN, pol i VAY lent)

U.S. Brand Names Pneumovax® 23
Canadian Brand Names Pneumo 23™; Pneumovax® 23
Index Terms PPV23; 23PS; 23-Valent Pneumococcal Polysaccharide Vaccine
Pharmacologic Category Vaccine
Additional Appendix Information
    Immunization Recommendations *on page 1929*
    USPHS / IDSA Guidelines for the Prevention of Opportunistic Infections in Persons Infected
    With HIV *on page 1966*
Use Children ≥2 years of age and adults who are at increased risk of pneumococcal disease
    and its complications because of underlying health conditions (including patients with
    cochlear implants); routine use in older adults >50 years of age, including all those ≥65 years
    Current Advisory Committee on Immunization Practices (ACIP) guidelines recommend **pneu-**
    mococcal 7-valent conjugate vaccine (PCV7) be used for children 2-23 months of age
    and, in certain situations, children up to 59 months of age
Pregnancy Risk Factor C
Pregnancy Implications The safety of vaccine in pregnant women has not been evaluated; it
    should not be given during pregnancy unless the risk of infection is high
Lactation Excretion in breast milk unknown/use caution
Contraindications Hypersensitivity to pneumococcal vaccine or any component of the formu-
    lation
Warnings/Precautions Use caution in patients with severe cardiovascular or pulmonary
    disease where a systemic reaction may pose a significant risk. Use caution and consider
    delay of vaccination in any active infection. Use caution in individuals who have had
    episodes of pneumococcal infection within the preceding 3 years (pre-existing pneumococcal
    antibodies may result in increased reactions to vaccine); may cause relapse in patients with
    stable idiopathic thrombocytopenia purpura. Epinephrine injection (1:1000) must be immedi-
    ately available in the case of anaphylaxis.

Patients who will be receiving immunosuppressive therapy (including Hodgkin's disease,
cancer chemotherapy, or transplantation) should be vaccinated at least 2 weeks prior to the
initiation of therapy. Immune responses may be impaired for several months following intensive immunosuppressive therapy (up to 2 years in Hodgkin's disease patients). Patients who
will undergo splenectomy should also be vaccinated 2 weeks prior to surgery, if possible.
Patients with HIV should be vaccinated as soon as possible (following confirmation of the
diagnosis). Not recommended in children <2 years of age.

**Adverse Reactions All serious adverse reactions must be reported to the U.S. Depart-
ment of Health and Human Services (DHHS) Vaccine Adverse Event Reporting System
(VAERS) 1-800-822-7967.**

Frequency not defined.
Cardiovascular: Malaise
Central nervous system: Guillain-Barré syndrome, fever ≤102°F*, fever >102°F, headache,
    radiculoneuropathy
Dermatologic: Angioneurotic edema, cellulitis, rash, urticaria
Gastrointestinal: Nausea, vomiting
Hematologic: Hemolytic anemia (in patients with other hematologic disorders), thrombocyto-
    penia (in patients with stabilized ITP)
Local: Injection site reaction* (erythema, induration, swelling, soreness, warmth)
Neuromuscular & skeletal: Arthralgia, arthritis, myalgia, paresthesia, weakness
Miscellaneous: Anaphylactoid reaction, lymphadenitis, serum sickness
*Reactions most commonly reported in clinical trials.

Drug Interactions
    Decreased Effect: The effect of the vaccine may be decreased with immunosuppressant
    medications.
Stability Store under refrigeration at 2°C to 8°C (36°F to 46°F).
Mechanism of Action Although there are more than 80 known pneumococcal capsular types,
    pneumococcal disease is mainly caused by only a few types of pneumococci. Pneumococcal
    vaccine contains capsular polysaccharides of 23 pneumococcal types of *Streptococcal pneu-*
    moniae which represent at least 85% to 90% of pneumococcal disease isolates in the United
    States. The pneumococcal vaccine with 23 pneumococcal capsular polysaccharide types
    became available in 1983. The 23 capsular pneumococcal vaccine contains purified capsular
    polysaccharides of pneumococcal types 1, 2, 3, 4, 5, 6B, 7F, 8, 9N, 9V, 10A, 11A, 12F, 14,
    15B, 17F, 18C, 19F, 19A, 20, 22F, 23F, and 33F. These are the main pneumococcal types
    associated with serious infections in the United States.
Dosage I.M., SubQ:
    Children >2 years and Adults: 0.5 mL
    Previously vaccinated with PCV7 vaccine: Children ≥2 years and Adults:
        With sickle cell disease, asplenia, immunocompromised or HIV infection: 0.5 mL at ≥2
        years of age and ≥2 months after last dose of PCV7; revaccination with PPV23 should
        be given ≥5 years for children >10 years of age and every 3-5 years for children ≤10
        years of age; revaccination should not be administered <3 years after the previous
        PPV23 dose
        With chronic illness: 0.5 mL at ≥2 years of age and ≥2 months after last dose of PCV7;
        revaccination with PPV23 is not recommended
    Following bone marrow transplant (use of PCV7 under study): Administer one dose PPV23
        at 12- and 24-months following BMT

    Revaccination should be considered:
        1. If ≥6 years since initial vaccination has elapsed, or
        2. In patients who received 14-valent pneumococcal vaccine and are at highest risk
           (asplenic) for fatal infection or
        3. At ≥6 years in patients with nephrotic syndrome, renal failure, or transplant recipients, or

4. 3-5 years in children with nephrotic syndrome, asplenia, or sickle cell disease

Administration Do not inject I.V., avoid intradermal, administer SubQ or I.M. (deltoid muscle or lateral midthigh)

For patients at risk of hemorrhage following intramuscular injection, the ACIP recommends "it should be administered intramuscularly if, in the opinion of the physician familiar with the patients bleeding risk, the vaccine can be administered with reasonable safety by this route. If the patient receives antihemophilia or other similar therapy, intramuscular vaccination can be scheduled shortly after such therapy is administered. A fine needle (23 gauge or smaller) can be used for the vaccination and firm pressure applied to the site (without rubbing) for at least 2 minutes. The patient should be instructed concerning the risk of hematoma from the injection."

Additional Information Inactivated bacteria vaccine. Federal law requires that the date of administration, the vaccine manufacturer, lot number of vaccine, and the administering person's name, title, and address be entered into the patient's permanent medical record.

Dosage Forms Injection, solution: 25 mcg each of 23 polysaccharide isolates/0.5 mL (0.5 mL, 2.5 mL)

- ◆ **Pneumotussin**® see Hydrocodone and Guaifenesin on page 849
- ◆ **Pneumovax**® **23** see Pneumococcal Polysaccharide Vaccine (Polyvalent) on page 1384
- ◆ **PNU-140690E** see Tipranavir on page 1692
- ◆ **Podactin Cream [OTC]** see Miconazole on page 1137
- ◆ **Podactin Powder [OTC]** see Tolnaftate on page 1704
- ◆ **Podocon-25**® see Podophyllum Resin on page 1385
- ◆ **Podofilm**® **(Can)** see Podophyllum Resin on page 1385
- ◆ **Podophyllin** see Podophyllum Resin on page 1385

Podophyllum Resin (po DOF fil um REZ in)

U.S. Brand Names Podocon-25®
Canadian Brand Names Podofilm®
Index Terms Mandrake; May Apple; Podophyllin
Pharmacologic Category Keratolytic Agent
Use Topical treatment of benign growths including external genital and perianal warts, papillomas, fibroids; compound benzoin tincture generally is used as the medium for topical application
Pregnancy Risk Factor X
Dosage Topical:
Children and Adults: 10% to 25% solution in compound benzoin tincture; apply drug to dry surface, use 1 drop at a time allowing drying between drops until area is covered; total volume should be limited to <0.5 mL per treatment session
Condylomata acuminatum: 25% solution is applied daily; use a 10% solution when applied to or near mucous membranes
Verrucae: 25% solution is applied 3-5 times/day directly to the wart
Additional Information Complete prescribing information for this medication should be consulted for additional detail.
Dosage Forms Liquid, topical: 25% (15 mL) [in benzoin tincture]

Poliovirus Vaccine (Inactivated) (POE lee oh VYE rus vak SEEN, in ak ti VAY ted)

U.S. Brand Names IPOL®
Canadian Brand Names IPOL®
Index Terms Enhanced-potency Inactivated Poliovirus Vaccine; IPV; Salk Vaccine
Pharmacologic Category Vaccine
Additional Appendix Information
Immunization Recommendations on page 1929
Use Active immunization against poliomyelitis caused by poliovirus types 1, 2 and 3. Routine immunization of adults in the United States is generally not recommended. Adults with previous wild poliovirus disease, who have never been immunized, or those who are incompletely immunized may receive inactivated poliovirus vaccine if they fall into one of the following categories:
- Travelers to regions or countries where poliomyelitis is endemic or epidemic
- Healthcare workers in close contact with patients who may be excreting poliovirus
- Laboratory workers handling specimens that may contain poliovirus
- Members of communities or specific population groups with diseases caused by wild poliovirus
- Incompletely vaccinated or unvaccinated adults in a household or with other close contact with children receiving oral poliovirus (may be at increased risk of vaccine associated paralytic poliomyelitis)

Pregnancy Risk Factor C
Pregnancy Implications Animal reproduction studies have not been conducted. Although adverse effects of IPV have not been documented in pregnant women or their fetuses, vaccination of pregnant women should be avoided on theoretical grounds. Pregnant women at increased risk for infection and requiring immediate protection against polio may be administered the vaccine.
Lactation Excretion into breast milk unknown/use caution
Contraindications Hypersensitivity to any component of the vaccine
Warnings/Precautions Patients with prior clinical poliomyelitis, incomplete immunization with oral poliovirus vaccine (OPV), HIV infection, severe combined immunodeficiency, hypogammaglobulinemia, agammaglobulinemia, or altered immunity (due to corticosteroids, alkylating agents, antimetabolites or radiation) may receive inactivated poliovirus vaccine (IPV). Immune response may be decreased in patients receiving immune globulin. Vaccination may (Continued)

Poliovirus Vaccine (Inactivated) *(Continued)*

be deferred with an acute febrile illness; minor illnesses with or without a low-grade fever are not reasons to postpone vaccination. Immediate treatment for anaphylactic/anaphylactoid reaction should be available during vaccine use.

The injection contains 2-phenoxyethanol, calf serum protein, formaldehyde, neomycin, streptomycin, and polymyxin B; the packaging contains natural latex rubber. Safety and efficacy have not been established in children <6 weeks of age.

Adverse Reactions All serious adverse reactions must be reported to the U.S. Department of Health and Human Services (DHHS) Vaccine Adverse Event Reporting System (VAERS) 1-800-822-7967.

Percentages noted with concomitant administration of DTP or DTaP vaccine and observed within 48 hours of injection.

>10%:

Central nervous system: Irritability (7% to 65%), tiredness (4% to 61%), fever ≥39°C (≤38%)

Gastrointestinal: Anorexia (1% to 17%)

Local: Injection Site: Tenderness (≤29%), pain (13%), swelling (≤11%)

1% to 10%:

Gastrointestinal: Vomiting (1% to 3%)

Local: Injection site: Erythema (≤3%), induration (1%)

Miscellaneous: Persistent crying (up to 1% reported within 72 hours)

Postmarketing and/or case reports: Guillain-Barré syndrome has been temporally related to another inactivated poliovirus vaccine

Drug Interactions

Decreased Effect:

The effect of the vaccine may be decreased when administered with immunosuppressant medications.

Stability Store under refrigeration 2°C to 8°C (35°F to 46°F); do not freeze.

Dosage I.M., SubQ:

Children:

Primary immunization: Administer three 0.5 mL doses, preferably 8 or more weeks apart, at 2,4, and 6-18 months of age. First dose may be given as early as 6 weeks of age. Do not administer more frequently than 4 weeks apart.

Booster dose: 0.5 mL at 4-6 years of age

Adults:

Previously unvaccinated: Two 0.5 mL doses administered at 1- to 2-month intervals, followed by a third dose 6-12 months later. If <3 months, but at least 2 months are available before protection is needed, 3 doses may be administered at least 1 month apart. If administration must be completed within 1-2 months, give 2 doses at least 1 month apart. If <1 month is available, give 1 dose.

Incompletely vaccinated: Adults with at least 1 previous dose of OPV, <3 doses of IPV, or a combination of OPV and IPV equaling <3 doses, administer at least one 0.5 mL dose of IPV. Additional doses to complete the series may be given if time permits.

Completely vaccinated: One 0.5 mL dose

Administration Do not administer I.V.; for I.M. or SubQ administration. Administer to midlateral aspect of the thigh in infants and small children. Administer in the deltoid area to adults or older children.

Additional Information Federal law requires that the date of administration, the vaccine manufacturer, lot number of vaccine, and the administering person's name, title, and address be entered into the patient's permanent medical record.

As the global eradication of poliomyelitis continues, the risk for importation of wild-type poliovirus into the United States decreases dramatically. To eliminate the risk for vaccine-associated paralytic poliomyelitis (VAPP), an all-IPV schedule is recommended for routine childhood vaccination in the United States. Oral poliovirus vaccine (OPV), is not commercially available in the United States, but has been stockpiled for use in the following special circumstances:

Mass vaccination campaigns to control outbreaks of paralytic polio

Unvaccinated children who will be traveling within 4 weeks to areas where polio is endemic or epidemic

Children of parents who do not accept the recommended number of vaccine injections; these children may receive OPV only for the third or fourth dose or both. In this situation, healthcare providers should administer OPV only after discussing the risk for VAPP with parents or caregivers

Currently, the primary risk for paralytic polio in U.S. residents is through travel to countries where polio remains endemic or where polio outbreaks are occurring. Unvaccinated persons traveling to countries that use OPV should be aware of the risk caused by OPV and should consider polio vaccination prior to travel.

Dosage Forms

Injection, suspension:

IPOL®: Type 1 poliovirus 40 D antigen units, type 2 poliovirus 8 D antigen units, and type 3 poliovirus 32 D antigen units per 0.5 mL (5 mL) [contains 2-phenoxyethanol, formaldehyde, calf serum protein, neomycin, streptomycin, and polymyxin B; packaging contains natural latex rubber]

♦ **Polocaine**® *see* Mepivacaine *on page 1084*

♦ **Polocaine® Dental** *see* Mepivacaine *on page 1084*

♦ **Polocaine® MPF** *see* Mepivacaine *on page 1084*

♦ **Polycitra**® *see* Citric Acid, Sodium Citrate, and Potassium Citrate *on page 383*

♦ **Polycitra®-K** *see* Potassium Citrate and Citric Acid *on page 1398*

♦ **Polycitra®-LC** *see* Citric Acid, Sodium Citrate, and Potassium Citrate *on page 383*

♦ **Poly-Dex**™ *see* Neomycin, Polymyxin B, and Dexamethasone *on page 1211*

Polyethylene Glycol 3350 (pol i ETH i leen GLY kol 3350)

U.S. Brand Names GlycoLax™; MiraLax™
Index Terms PEG
Pharmacologic Category Laxative, Osmotic
Use Treatment of occasional constipation in adults
Unlabeled/Investigational Use Treatment of constipation in children
Pregnancy Risk Factor C
Medication Safety Issues
Sound-alike/look-alike issues:
MiraLax™ may be confused with Mirapex®

International issues:
MiraLax™ may be confused with Murelax® which is a brand name for oxazepam in Australia
Dosage Oral: Adults: Occasional constipation: 17 g of powder (~1 heaping tablespoon) dissolved in 8 oz of water, once daily; do not use for >2 weeks.
Additional Information Complete prescribing information for this medication should be consulted for additional detail.
Dosage Forms [DSC] = Discontinued product
Powder, for oral solution: PEG 3350 17 g/packet (12s); PEG 3350 255 g (14 oz); PEG 3350 527 g (26 oz)
GlycoLax™: PEG 3350 17 g/packet (14s); PEG 3350 255 g (16 oz); PEG 3350 527 g (24 oz)
MiraLax™: PEG 3350 17 g/packet (12s) [DSC]; PEG 3350 255 g (14 oz); PEG 3350 527 g (26 oz) [DSC]

Polyethylene Glycol-Electrolyte Solution
(pol i ETH i leen GLY kol ee LEK troe lite soe LOO shun)

U.S. Brand Names Colyte®; GoLYTELY®; MoviPrep®; NuLYTELY®; TriLyte™
Canadian Brand Names Colyte™; Klean-Prep®; PegLyte®
Index Terms Electrolyte Lavage Solution
Pharmacologic Category Laxative, Osmotic
Additional Appendix Information
Laxatives, Classification and Properties *on page 1886*
Use Bowel cleansing prior to GI examination or following toxic ingestion
Pregnancy Risk Factor C
Pregnancy Implications Reproduction studies have not been conducted in animals or in humans.
Lactation Excretion in breast milk unknown/use caution
Medication Safety Issues
Sound-alike/look-alike issues:
GoLYTELY® may be confused with NuLYTELY®
NuLYTELY® may be confused with GoLYTELY®
Contraindications Hypersensitivity to polyethylene glycol or any component of the formulation; ileus, gastrointestinal obstruction, gastric retention, bowel perforation, toxic colitis, megacolon
Warnings/Precautions Seizures associated with electrolyte abnormalities (eg, hyponatremia, hypokalemia) have occurred. Use caution with other medications that alter electrolyte balance or in patients with underlying hyponatremia. Do not add flavorings as additional ingredients before use; observe unconscious or semiconscious patients with impaired gag reflex or those who are otherwise prone to regurgitation or aspiration during administration; use with caution in patients with severe ulcerative colitis. Evaluate patients with symptoms of bowel obstruction (nausea, vomiting, abdominal pain or distension) prior to use.

MoviPrep®: May be safer to use in patients who cannot tolerate fluid load (eg, heart failure, renal insufficiency, ascites). Use cautiously in patients with G6PD deficiency. Use caution in phenylketonuria. Safety and efficacy in children have not been established.
Adverse Reactions
>10%:
Central nervous system: Malaise (18% to 27%)
Gastrointestinal: Abdominal distension (<60%), anal irritation (<52%), nausea (14% to 47%), abdominal pain (13% to 39%), vomiting (7% to 12%)
Neuromuscular & skeletal: Rigors (34%)
Miscellaneous: Thirst (<47%)
1% to 10%:
Central nervous system: Dizziness (7%), headache (2%)
Gastrointestinal: Dyspepsia (1% to 3%)
Frequency not defined, postmarketing, and/or case reports: Abdominal cramps, abdominal fullness, allergic reactions, anaphylaxis, asystole, bloating, dehydration (children), dermatitis, dyspnea (acute), esophageal perforation, flatulence, hypokalemia (children), pulmonary edema, Mallory-Weiss tear, rash, rhinorrhea, seizure, upper GI bleeding, urticaria
Overdosage/Toxicology May cause severe electrolyte disturbances (eg, hyponatremia, hypokalemia), dehydration, hypovolemia. Treatment is symptom-directed and supportive.
Stability
Colyte®, GoLYTELY®, NuLYTELY®, TriLyte®: Store at 15°C to 30°C (59°F to 86°F) before reconstitution. Use within 48 hours of preparation; refrigerate reconstituted solution; tap water may be used for preparation of the solution; shake container vigorously several times to ensure dissolution of powder.
(Continued)

Polyethylene Glycol-Electrolyte Solution *(Continued)*

MoviPrep®: Store at 15°C to 30°C (59°F to 86°F) before reconstitution. Mix pouch A and pouch B in container provided. Add 1 L of lukewarm water; mix the solution. Use within 24 hours. May refrigerate solution prior to drinking.

Mechanism of Action Induces catharsis by strong electrolyte and osmotic effects

Pharmacodynamics/Kinetics Onset of effect: Oral: ~1-2 hours

Dosage

Oral:

Children ≥6 months: Bowel cleansing prior to GI exam (CoLyte®, GoLYTELY®, NuLYTELY®, TriLyte®): 25-40 mL/kg/hour for 4-10 hours (until rectal effluent is clear). Ideally, patients should fast for ~3-4 hours prior to administration; absolutely no solid food for at least 2 hours before the solution is given. The solution may be given via nasogastric tube to patients who are unwilling or unable to drink the solution. Patients <2 years should be monitored closely.

Adults: Bowel cleansing prior to GI exam:

CoLyte®, GoLYTELY®, NuLYTELY®, TriLyte®: 240 mL (8 oz) every 10 minutes, until 4 L are consumed or the rectal effluent is clear; rapid drinking of each portion is preferred to drinking small amounts continuously. Ideally, patients should fast for ~3-4 hours prior to administration; absolutely no solid food for at least 2 hours before the solution is given. The solution may be given via nasogastric tube to patients who are unwilling or unable to drink the solution.

MoviPrep®: Administer 2 L total with an additional L of clear fluid prior to colonoscopy.

Split dose: Evening before and morning of the colonoscopy: 240 mL (8 oz) every 15 minutes until 1L is consumed. Then drink 16 oz of clear liquid. On the morning of the colonoscopy, repeat process at least 1 hour before the procedure.

Full dose: Evening before colonoscopy (6 PM): 240 mL (8 oz every 15 minutes) until 1 L is consumed; 90 minutes later (~7:30 PM), repeat dose. Then drink 32 oz of clear liquid.

Note: Patient should not eat solid food from start of solution administration until after colonoscopy. Clear liquid/plain yogurt for dinner; finishing 1 hour before start of colon prep.

Nasogastric tube (CoLyte®, GoLYTELY®, NuLYTELY®, TriLyte®):

Children ≥6 months: Bowel cleansing prior to GI exam: 25 mL/kg/hour until rectal effluent is clear. Ideally, patients should fast for ~3-4 hours prior to administration; absolutely no solid food for at least 2 hours before the solution is given.

Adults: Bowel cleansing prior to GI exam: 20-30 mL/minute (1.2-1.8 L/hour); the first bowel movement should occur ~1 hour after the start of administration. Ideally, patients should fast for ~3-4 hours prior to administration; absolutely no solid food for at least 2 hours before the solution is given.

Dietary Considerations Ideally, the patient should fast for ~3-4 hours prior to administration, but in no case should solid food be given for at least 2 hours before the solution is given. Some products contain aspartame which is metabolized to phenylalanine.

Administration Oral: Rapid drinking of each portion is preferred to drinking small amounts continuously. Do not add flavorings as additional ingredients before use. Chilled solution often more palatable. Oral medications should not be administered within 1 hour of start of therapy.

Monitoring Parameters Electrolytes, serum glucose, BUN, urine osmolality; children <2 years of age should be monitored for hypoglycemia, dehydration, hypokalemia

Dosage Forms

Powder, for oral solution: PEG 3350 240 g, sodium sulfate 22.72 g, sodium bicarbonate 6.72 g, sodium chloride 5.84 g, and potassium chloride 2.98 g (4000 mL)

Colyte®:

PEG 3350 240 g, sodium sulfate 22.72 g, sodium bicarbonate 6.72 g, sodium chloride 5.84 g, and potassium chloride 2.98 g (4000 mL) [available with citrus berry, lemon lime, cherry, and pineapple flavor packets]

PEG 3350 227.1 g, sodium sulfate 21.5 g, sodium bicarbonate 6.36 g, sodium chloride 5.53 g, and potassium chloride 2.82 g (4000 mL) [regular and pineapple flavor]

GoLYTELY®:

Disposable jug: PEG 3350 236 g, sodium sulfate 22.74 g, sodium bicarbonate 6.74 g, sodium chloride 5.86 g, and potassium chloride 2.97 g (4000 mL) [regular and pineapple flavor]

Packets: PEG 3350 227.1 g, sodium sulfate 21.5 g, sodium bicarbonate 6.36 g, sodium chloride 5.53 g, and potassium chloride 2.82 g (4000 mL) [regular flavor]

MoviPrep®: Disposable jug: Pouch A: PEG 3350 100g, sodium sulfate 7.5 g, sodium chloride 2.69 g, potassium chloride 1.015 g; Pouch B: Ascorbic acid 4.7 g, sodium ascorbate 5.9 g (1000 mL) [contains phenylalanine 2.33 mg/treatment; lemon flavor; packaged with 2 of Pouch A and 2 of Pouch B in carton]

NuLYTELY®: PEG 3350 420 g, sodium bicarbonate 5.72 g, sodium chloride 11.2 g, and potassium chloride 1.48 (4000 mL) [cherry, lemon-lime, and orange flavors]

TriLyte™: PEG 3350 420 g, sodium bicarbonate 5.72 g, sodium chloride 11.2 g, and potassium chloride 1.48 (4000 mL) [supplied with flavor packets]

♦ **Polygam® S/D** see Immune Globulin (Intravenous) on page 892

Poly-L-Lactic Acid *(POL i el LAK tik AS id)*

U.S. Brand Names Sculptra™

Index Terms New-Fill®; PLA

Pharmacologic Category Cosmetic Agent, Implant

Use Restoration and/or correction of facial lipoatrophy in patients with HIV

Pregnancy Implications Safety for use during pregnancy has not been established.

Contraindications Hypersensitivity to poly-L-lactic acid or any component of the formulation

Warnings/Precautions Not for use if skin inflammation or infection exists in or near the treatment area; control inflammation or infection before use. Avoid use with implants. Avoid overcorrection of contour deficit; improvement occurs over weeks of treatment. Avoid IV injection; may lead to occlusion, infarction, or embolism. Use caution in patients on anticoagulants or antiplatelet medications. Patients should be instructed to limit exposure to excessive sunlight or UV lamps until any swelling or redness is resolved. Safety and efficacy in non-Caucasians and in women are limited. Safety and efficacy for use in the periorbital area or in pediatric patients have not been established.

Adverse Reactions
>10%:
Dermatologic: Bruising (1% to 38%)
Hematologic: Hematoma (up to 28%)
Local: Injection site: Papules (6% to 52%), edema (3% to 17%)
Miscellaneous: Discomfort (up to 19%)
1% to 10%:
Central nervous system: Fever (<5%)
Local: Erythema (up to 10%), injection site reactions (<5%)
Postmarketing/case reports: Allergic reaction, angioedema, brittle nails, colitis, ectropion, fatigue, hair breakage, hypersensitivity reaction, hypertrophy, joint aches, malaise, photosensitivity, Quicke's edema, rash, skin roughness, telangiectasia, visible nodules
Injection site reactions: Abscess, atrophy, discharge, fat atrophy, granuloma

Stability Prior to and following reconstitution, store at room temperature. Slowly add 3-5 mL SWFI to vial and allow to stand for 2 hours to hydrate. **Do not shake.** After 2 hours, agitate vial until a uniform suspension is formed. Use within 72 hours.

Mechanism of Action Poly-L-lactic acid is an immunologically inert synthetic polymer. It increases dermal thickness by causing a local reaction leading to an increase in collagen deposits. It is eventually degraded and undergoes resorption.

Pharmacodynamics/Kinetics
Onset: Weeks to months for full effect of treatment

Dosage Intradermal or SubQ: Adults: Lipoatrophy: ~0.05-0.2 mL per individual injection depending on technique used; ~20 injections may be needed per cheek. Treatment should be individualized. Separate treatments by ≥2 weeks. Typical course involves 3-6 treatments. Supplemental injections may be needed. Do not overfill contour deficiency. For patients with severe facial fat loss, the average treatment requires ~1 vial per cheek area per treatment.

Administration For injection into deep dermis or subcutaneous layer. Avoid intravenous injection. Administer using 26 gauge needle; do not bend needle. Massage treatment area periodically during session to evenly distribute.

Dosage Forms Injection, powder for suspension: Poly-L-lactic acid USP

Polymyxin B (pol i MIKS in bee)

U.S. Brand Names Poly-Rx
Index Terms Polymyxin B Sulfate
Pharmacologic Category Antibiotic, Irrigation; Antibiotic, Miscellaneous
Additional Appendix Information
Prevention of Wound Infection and Sepsis in Surgical Patients *on page 1964*

Use Treatment of acute infections caused by susceptible strains of *Pseudomonas aeruginosa*; used occasionally for gut decontamination; parenteral use of polymyxin B has mainly been replaced by less toxic antibiotics, reserved for life-threatening infections caused by organisms resistant to the preferred drugs (eg, pseudomonal meningitis - intrathecal administration)

Pregnancy Risk Factor B (per expert opinion)
Pregnancy Implications Safety and efficacy for use in pregnant women have not been established.

Lactation Excretion in breast milk unknown/use caution

Contraindications Hypersensitivity to polymyxin B or any component of the formulation; concurrent use of neuromuscular blockers

Warnings/Precautions [U.S. Boxed Warning]: May cause neurotoxicity, nephrotoxicity, and/or neuromuscular blockade and respiratory paralysis; usual risk factors include pre-existing renal impairment, concomitant neuro-/nephrotoxic medications, advanced age and dehydration. Use with caution in patients with impaired renal function (modify dosage); polymyxin B-induced nephrotoxicity may be manifested by albuminuria, cellular casts, and azotemia. Discontinue therapy with decreasing urinary output and increasing BUN; neurotoxic reactions are usually associated with high serum levels, often in patients with renal dysfunction. Avoid concurrent or sequential use of other nephrotoxic and neurotoxic drugs (eg, aminoglycosides). The drug's neurotoxicity can result in respiratory paralysis from neuromuscular blockade, especially when the drug is given soon after anesthesia or muscle relaxants. Polymyxin B sulfate is most toxic when given parenterally; avoid parenteral use whenever possible. **[U.S. Boxed Warnings]: Safety in pregnant women not established; intramuscular/intrathecal administration only to hospitalized patients.**

Adverse Reactions Frequency not defined (limited to important or life-threatening):
Central nervous system: Neurotoxicity (irritability, drowsiness, ataxia, perioral paresthesia, numbness of the extremities, and blurred vision); dizziness
Neuromuscular & skeletal: Neuromuscular blockade
Renal: Nephrotoxicity
Respiratory: Respiratory arrest

Overdosage/Toxicology Symptoms include respiratory paralysis, ototoxicity, and nephrotoxicity. Supportive care is indicated. Ventilatory support may be necessary.

Drug Interactions
Increased Effect/Toxicity: Increased/prolonged effect of neuromuscular blocking agents.

Stability Prior to reconstitution, store at room temperature of 15°C to 30°C (59°F to 86°F). Protect from light. After reconstitution, store under refrigeration at 2°C to 8°C (36°F to 46°F). Discard any unused solution after 72 hours.
(Continued)

Polymyxin B *(Continued)*

Mechanism of Action Binds to phospholipids, alters permeability, and damages the bacterial cytoplasmic membrane permitting leakage of intracellular constituents

Pharmacodynamics/Kinetics

Absorption: Well absorbed from peritoneum; minimal from GI tract (except in neonates) from mucous membranes or intact skin

Distribution: Minimal into CSF; does not cross placenta

Half-life elimination: 4.5-6 hours; prolonged with renal impairment

Time to peak, serum: I.M.: ~2 hours

Excretion: Urine (>60% primarily as unchanged drug)

Dosage

Otic (in combination with other drugs): 1-2 drops, 3-4 times/day; should be used sparingly to avoid accumulation of excess debris

Infants <2 years:

I.M.: Up to 40,000 units/kg/day divided every 6 hours (not routinely recommended due to pain at injection sites)

I.V.: Up to 40,000 units/kg/day divided every 12 hours

Intrathecal: 20,000 units/day for 3-4 days, then 25,000 units every other day for at least 2 weeks after CSF cultures are negative and CSF (glucose) has returned to within normal limits

Children ≥2 years and Adults:

I.M.: 25,000-30,000 units/kg/day divided every 4-6 hours (not routinely recommended due to pain at injection sites)

I.V.: 15,000-25,000 units/kg/day divided every 12 hours

Intrathecal: 50,000 units/day for 3-4 days, then every other day for at least 2 weeks after CSF cultures are negative and CSF (glucose) has returned to within normal limits

Total daily dose should not exceed 2,000,000 units/day

Bladder irrigation: Continuous irrigant or rinse in the urinary bladder for up to 10 days using 20 mg (equal to 200,000 units) added to 1 L of normal saline; usually no more than 1 L of irrigant is used per day unless urine flow rate is high; administration rate is adjusted to patient's urine output

Topical irrigation or topical solution: 500,000 units/L of normal saline; topical irrigation should not exceed 2 million units/day in adults

Gut sterilization: Oral: 15,000-25,000 units/kg/day in divided doses every 6 hours

Clostridium difficile enteritis: Oral: 25,000 units every 6 hours for 10 days

Ophthalmic: A concentration of 0.1% to 0.25% is administered as 1-3 drops every hour, then increasing the interval as response indicates to 1-2 drops 4-6 times/day

Dosing adjustment/interval in renal impairment:

Cl_{cr} 20-50 mL/minute: Administer 75% to 100% of the normal daily dose given in divided doses every 12 hours

Cl_{cr} 5-20 mL/minute: Administer 50% of normal daily dose given in divided doses every 12 hours

Cl_{cr} <5 mL/minute: Administer 15% of normal daily dose given in divided doses every 12 hours

Administration Dissolve 500,000 units in 300-500 mL D_5W for continuous I.V. drip; dissolve 500,000 units in 2 mL water for injection, saline, or 1% procaine solution for I.M. injection; dissolve 500,000 units in 10 mL physiologic solution for intrathecal administration

Extravasation management: Monitor I.V. site closely; extravasation may cause serious injury with possible necrosis and tissue sloughing. Rotate infusion site frequently.

Monitoring Parameters Neurologic symptoms and signs of superinfection; renal function (decreasing urine output and increasing BUN may require discontinuation of therapy)

Reference Range Serum concentrations >5 mcg/mL are toxic in adults

Additional Information 1 mg = 10,000 units

Dosage Forms

Injection, powder for reconstitution: 500,000 units

Powder [for prescription compounding] (Poly-Rx): 100 million units (13 g)

♦ **Polymyxin B and Bacitracin** *see* Bacitracin and Polymyxin B *on page 192*

♦ **Polymyxin B and Neomycin** *see* Neomycin and Polymyxin B *on page 1211*

♦ **Polymyxin B and Trimethoprim** *see* Trimethoprim and Polymyxin B *on page 1745*

♦ **Polymyxin B, Bacitracin, and Neomycin** *see* Bacitracin, Neomycin, and Polymyxin B *on page 192*

♦ **Polymyxin B, Bacitracin, Neomycin, and Hydrocortisone** *see* Bacitracin, Neomycin, Polymyxin B, and Hydrocortisone *on page 192*

♦ **Polymyxin B, Neomycin, and Dexamethasone** *see* Neomycin, Polymyxin B, and Dexamethasone *on page 1211*

♦ **Polymyxin B, Neomycin, and Gramicidin** *see* Neomycin, Polymyxin B, and Gramicidin *on page 1212*

♦ **Polymyxin B, Neomycin, and Hydrocortisone** *see* Neomycin, Polymyxin B, and Hydrocortisone *on page 1212*

♦ **Polymyxin B, Neomycin, and Prednisolone** *see* Neomycin, Polymyxin B, and Prednisolone *on page 1212*

♦ **Polymyxin B Sulfate** *see* Polymyxin B *on page 1389*

♦ **Poly-Pred®** *see* Neomycin, Polymyxin B, and Prednisolone *on page 1212*

♦ **Poly-Rx** *see* Polymyxin B *on page 1389*

Polysaccharide-Iron Complex *(pol i SAK a ride-EYE ern KOM pleks)*

U.S. Brand Names Ferrex 150 [OTC]; Niferex® [OTC]; Nu-Iron® 150 [OTC]

Index Terms Iron-Polysaccharide Complex

Pharmacologic Category Iron Salt

Use Prevention and treatment of iron-deficiency anemias

Pregnancy Risk Factor A
Medication Safety Issues
Sound-alike/look-alike issues:
Niferex® may be confused with Nephrox®
Adverse Reactions
>10%: Gastrointestinal: Stomach cramping, constipation, nausea, vomiting, dark stools, GI irritation, epigastric pain
1% to 10%:
Gastrointestinal: Heartburn, diarrhea
Genitourinary: Discolored urine
Miscellaneous: Staining of teeth
<1% (Limited to important or life-threatening): Contact irritation
Dosage
Children ≥6 years: Tablets/elixir: 50-100 mg/day; may be given in divided doses
Adults:
Elixir: 50-100 mg twice daily
Capsules: 150-300 mg/day
Additional Information 100% elemental iron
Dosage Forms
Capsule: Elemental iron 150 mg
Ferrex 150, Nu-Iron® 150: Elemental iron 150 mg
Niferex®: Elemental iron 60 mg
Elixir:
Niferex®: Elemental iron 100 mg/5 mL (240 mL) [contains alcohol 10%; dye free, sugar free]

♦ **Polysporin® [OTC]** see Bacitracin and Polymyxin B on page 192

Polythiazide (pol i THYE a zide)

U.S. Brand Names Renese®
Pharmacologic Category Diuretic, Thiazide
Additional Appendix Information
Sulfonamide Derivatives on page 1897
Use Adjunctive therapy in treatment of edema and hypertension
Pregnancy Risk Factor D
Dosage Adults: Oral:
Edema: 1-4 mg/day
Hypertension: 2-4 mg/day
Additional Information Complete prescribing information for this medication should be consulted for additional detail.
Dosage Forms Tablet: 2 mg

♦ **Polythiazide and Prazosin** see Prazosin and Polythiazide on page 1413
♦ **Polytrim®** see Trimethoprim and Polymyxin B on page 1745
♦ **Polytrim™ (Can)** see Trimethoprim and Polymyxin B on page 1745
♦ **Polyvinylpyrrolidone with Iodine** see Povidone-Iodine on page 1404
♦ **Ponstan® (Can)** see Mefenamic Acid on page 1068
♦ **Ponstel®** see Mefenamic Acid on page 1068
♦ **Pontocaine®** see Tetracaine on page 1659
♦ **Pontocaine® Niphanoid®** see Tetracaine on page 1659

Porfimer (POR fi mer)

U.S. Brand Names Photofrin®
Canadian Brand Names Photofrin®
Index Terms CL-184116; Dihematoporphyrin Ether; Porfimer Sodium
Pharmacologic Category Antineoplastic Agent, Miscellaneous
Use Adjunct to laser light therapy for obstructing esophageal cancer, obstructing endobronchial nonsmall cell lung cancer (NSCLC), ablation of high-grade dysplasia in Barrett's esophagus
Unlabeled/Investigational Use Transitional cell carcinoma in situ of the urinary bladder; gastric and rectal cancers
Pregnancy Risk Factor C
Pregnancy Implications Animal studies have shown maternal and fetal toxicity, but no major malformations. Effective contraception is recommended for women of childbearing potential.
Lactation Excretion in breast milk unknown/contraindicated
Contraindications Hypersensitivity to porfimer, porphyrins, or any component of the formulation; porphyria; photodynamic therapy is contraindicated in tracheoesophageal or bronchoesophageal fistula; tumors eroding into a major blood vessel; severe acute respiratory distress when caused by endobronchial lesion; esophageal ulcers >1 cm
Warnings/Precautions Hazardous agent - use appropriate precautions for handling and disposal. When treating endobronchial tumors, use caution if treatment-induced inflammation may obstruct airway. Assess patient for possibility of tumor erosion into a pulmonary blood vessel; fatal massive pulmonary hemoptysis (FMH) may occur. Risk factors for FMH include large, centrally located tumors, cavitating tumors, or extensive tumor extrinsic to the bronchus. Generally not suited for treatment of patients with esophageal or gastric varices; if used in esophageal varices, extreme caution is warranted and light exposure to the varices should be avoided. In patients with Barrett's esophagus, rigorous surveillance (endoscopic biopsy every 3 months until 4 consecutive negative results for high-grade dysplasia followed by further follow-up per physician judgement). Esophageal strictures are common adverse events associated with photodynamic therapy of Barrett's esophagus; esophageal dilation may be required
(Continued)

Porfimer *(Continued)*

Photosensitivity reactions are common is patients are exposed to direct sunlight or bright indoor light (eg fluorescent lights, unshaded light bulbs, examination/operating lights). Photosensitivity may last 30-90 days. Ocular discomfort has been reported; for at least 30 days, when outdoors, patients should wear dark sunglasses which have an average white light transmittance of <4%. Patients should be educated to test for residual photosensitivity before resuming exposure to sunlight. Conventional sunscreens are NOT protective. Allow 2-4 weeks to elapse after phototherapy prior to initiating radiation therapy; 4 weeks should elapse after radiation therapy prior to initiating phototherapy. Safety and efficacy in children have not been established.

Adverse Reactions

>10%:

Cardiovascular: Chest pain (7% to 35%), edema (3% to 18%)

Central nervous system: Fever (5% to 31%), pain (1% to 22%), insomnia (4% to 14%)

Dermatologic: Photosensitivity reaction (4% to 37%, minor reactions may occur in up to 100%; severe: 10%)

Endocrine & metabolic: Dehydration (7% to 11%)

Gastrointestinal: Esophageal stricture (6% in esophageal cancer patients; up to 39% in Barrett's esophagus patients), nausea (24% to 39%), vomiting (17% to 34%), constipation (5% to 24%), dysphagia (10% to 24%), abdominal pain (12% to 20%)

Genitourinary: Urinary tract irritation including frequency, urgency, nocturia, painful urination, or bladder spasm (~100% of bladder cancer patients)

Hematologic: Anemia (32% in esophageal cancer patients)

Neuromuscular & skeletal: Back pain (3% to 11%)

Respiratory: Pleural effusion (32% in esophageal cancer patients; 11% in Barrett's esophagus patients), dyspnea (6% to 20%), pneumonia (6% to 18%), hemoptysis (7% to 16%), cough (6% to 15%), pharyngitis (11%)

Miscellaneous: Mild-moderate allergic-type reactions (34% of lung cancer patients)

5% to 10%:

Cardiovascular: Atrial fibrillation (10%), hyper-/hypotension (3% to 7%), cardiac failure (7% in esophageal cancer), tachycardia (6%), chest pain (substernal; 5%)

Central nervous system: Confusion (7% to 8%), headache (6%), anxiety (3% to 7%), depression (3% to 5%)

Dermatologic: Rash (7%), pruritus (4%)

Gastrointestinal: Diarrhea (5% to 10%), weight loss (6% to 9%), esophageal edema (8%), esophageal tumor bleeding (8%), anorexia (4% to 8%), dyspepsia (1% to 6%), eructation (5%), esophagitis (5%), hematemesis (5%), melena (5%), odynophagia (5%)

Genitourinary: Urinary tract infection (7%)

Neuromuscular & skeletal: Weakness (6%), arthralgia (3% to 5%)

Respiratory: Respiratory insufficiency (6% to 10%), bronchitis (4% to 10%), tracheoesophageal fistula (6%), sinusitis (4%)

Miscellaneous: Moniliasis (9%), surgical complication (5% in esophageal cancer patients)

<5% (Limited to important or life-threatening): Abnormal vision, bronchospasm, bradycardia, cataracts, diplopia, esophageal perforation, eye pain, fluid imbalance, gastric ulcer, hair growth increased, ileus, jaundice, lung abscess, myocardial infarction, peritonitis, photophobia, pulmonary edema, pulmonary embolism, pulmonary hemorrhage, pulmonary thrombosis, respiratory failure, sepsis, sick sinus syndrome, skin discoloration, skin fragility, skin nodules, skin wrinkles, stridor, supraventricular tachycardia

Overdosage/Toxicology Laser treatment should not be given if an overdose of porfimer is administered. In the event of an overdose, patients should protect their eyes and skin from direct sunlight or bright indoor lights for 30 days. Patients should test for residual photosensitivity. Porfimer is not dialyzable.

Drug Interactions

Increased Effect/Toxicity: Concomitant administration of other photosensitizing agents (eg, tetracyclines, sulfonamides, phenothiazines, sulfonylureas, thiazide diuretics, griseofulvin) could increase the photosensitivity reaction.

Decreased Effect: Compounds that quench active oxygen species or scavenge radicals (eg, dimethyl sulfoxide, beta-carotene, ethanol, mannitol) would be expected to decrease photodynamic therapy (PDT) activity. Allopurinol, calcium channel blockers, and some prostaglandin synthesis inhibitors could interfere with porfimer. Drugs that decrease clotting, vasoconstriction, or platelet aggregation could decrease the efficacy of PDT. Glucocorticoid hormones may decrease the efficacy of the treatment.

Stability Store intact vials at controlled room temperature of 20°C to 25°C (68°F to 77°F). Reconstitute each vial of porfimer with 31.8 mL of either D_5W or NS injection resulting in a final concentration of 2.5 mg/mL. Shake well until dissolved. Protect the reconstituted product from bright light and use immediately. Reconstituted solutions are stable for 24 hours under refrigeration and protected from light.

Mechanism of Action Porfimer's cytotoxic activity is dependent on light and oxygen. Following administration, the drug is selectively retained in neoplastic tissues. Exposure of the drug to laser light at wavelengths >630 nm results in the production of oxygen free-radicals. Release of thromboxane A_2, leading to vascular occlusion and ischemic necrosis, may also occur.

Pharmacodynamics/Kinetics

Distribution: V_{dss}: 0.49 L/kg

Protein binding, plasma: 90%

Half-life elimination: Mean: 21.5 days (range: 11-28 days)

Time to peak, serum: ~2 hours

Excretion: Feces; Clearance: Plasma: Total: 0.051 mL/minute/kg

Dosage I.V. (refer to individual protocols):

Children: Safety and efficacy have not been established

Adults: 2 mg/kg, followed by exposure to the appropriate laser light; repeat courses must be separated by at least 30 days (esophageal or endobronchial cancer) or 90 days (Barrett's esophagus) for a maximum of 3 courses

Administration Administer slow I.V. injection over 3-5 minutes.

Dosage Forms

Injection, powder for reconstitution, as sodium:
Photofrin®: 75 mg

♦ **Porfimer Sodium** see Porfimer on page 1391
♦ **Portia™** see Ethinyl Estradiol and Levonorgestrel on page 653

Posaconazole (poe sa KON a zole)

U.S. Brand Names Noxafil®
Index Terms SCH 56592
Pharmacologic Category Antifungal Agent, Oral
Additional Appendix Information
Antifungal Agents on page 1869
Use Prophylaxis of invasive *Aspergillus* and *Candida* infections in severely-immunocompromised patients [eg, hematopoietic stem cell transplant (HSCT) recipients with graft-versus-host disease (GVHD) or those with prolonged neutropenia secondary to chemotherapy for hematologic malignancies]; treatment of oropharyngeal candidiasis (including patients refractory to itraconazole and/or fluconazole)
Unlabeled/Investigational Use Salvage therapy of refractory invasive fungal infections
Pregnancy Risk Factor C
Pregnancy Implications Posaconazole has been shown to be teratogenic in animal studies. There are no adequate and well-controlled studies in pregnant women. Use only if the benefit to the mother justifies potential risk to the fetus.
Lactation Excretion in breast milk unknown/use caution
Medication Safety Issues
Sound-alike/look-alike issues:
Noxafil® may be confused with minoxidil

International issues:
Noxafil® may be confused with Noxidil® which is a brand name for minoxidil in Thailand
Contraindications Hypersensitivity to posaconazole or any component of the formulation; coadministration of cisapride, pimozide, quinidine, or ergot alkaloids
Warnings/Precautions Use caution in hepatic impairment; hepatic dysfunction has occurred, ranging from mild/moderate increases of ALT/AST, alkaline phosphatase, and/or clinical hepatitis to severe reactions (cholestasis, hepatic failure including death). Use caution in patients with an increased risk of arrhythmia (concurrent QT_c-prolonging drugs, hypokalemia). Correct electrolyte abnormalities (eg, potassium, magnesium, and calcium) before initiating therapy.

Use caution in hypersensitivity with other azole antifungal agents; cross-reaction may occur, but has not been established. Alternative antifungal therapy should be considered in any patient unable to eat or tolerate an oral liquid nutritional supplement. Use caution in severe renal impairment; monitor for breakthrough fungal infections. Safety and efficacy have not been established in children <13 years of age.
Adverse Reactions Note: A higher frequency of adverse reactions was observed in studies with refractory oropharyngeal candidiasis patients and percentages are included below.
>10%: Gastrointestinal: Diarrhea (3% to 11%)
1% to 10%:
Cardiovascular: QT_c prolongation (up to 4%), hypertension (1%)
Central nervous system: Headache (1% to 8%), dizziness (1% to 3%), fatigue (1% to 3%), insomnia (1% to 3%), fever (up to 3%), somnolence (1%)
Dermatologic: Rash (1% to 4%), pruritus (1% to 2%)
Endocrine & metabolic: Hypokalemia (3%)
Gastrointestinal: Nausea (5% to 8%), vomiting (4% to 7%), abdominal pain (1% to 5%), flatulence (1% to 5%), anorexia (1% to 3%), mucositis (2%), dyspepsia (1% to 2%), xerostoma (1% to 2%), taste perversion (1%), constipation (up to 1%)
Hematologic: Neutropenia (2% to 8%), anemia (up to 3%), thrombocytopenia (up to 2%)
Hepatic: Bilirubin increased (2% to 3%), ALT increased (2% to 3%), AST increased (2% to 3%), GGT increased (2% to 3%), alkaline phosphatase increased (2%), hepatocellular damage (1%)
Neuromuscular & skeletal: Weakness (1% to 3%), myalgia (up to 2%), tremor (1%)
Ocular: Blurred vision (1%)
Renal: Serum creatinine increased (2%)
<1% (Limited to important or life-threatening): Adrenal insufficiency, allergic/hypersensitivity reactions, cholestasis, hemolytic uremic syndrome, hepatic failure, hepatitis, pulmonary embolus, thrombotic thrombocytopenic purpura, torsade de pointes
Overdosage/Toxicology Experience with overdosage is limited; treatment is symptom-directed and supportive. Posaconazole is not removed by hemodialysis.
Drug Interactions
Cytochrome P450 Effect: Inhibits CYP3A4 (moderate)
Increased Effect/Toxicity: Posaconazole may increase the levels/effects of calcium channel blockers (eg, felodipine, nifedipine, verapamil), cyclosporine, CYP3A4 substrates, ergot alkaloids, HMG-CoA reductase inhibitors, midazolam, phenytoin, rifabutin, sirolimus, tacrolimus and vinca alkaloids. Use with QT_c-prolonging agents may increase risk of malignant arrhythmias
Decreased Effect: Cimetidine, phenytoin, and rifabutin may decrease the effects/levels of posaconazole.
Ethanol/Nutrition/Herb Interactions Food: Bioavailability increased ~3-4 times when posaconazole administered with a meal or an oral liquid nutritional supplement.
Stability Store at 15°C to 30°C (59°F to 86°F); do not freeze.
Mechanism of Action Interferes with fungal cytochrome P450 activity, decreasing ergosterol synthesis (principal sterol in fungal cell membrane) and inhibiting fungal cell membrane formation.
(Continued)

Posaconazole *(Continued)*

Pharmacodynamics/Kinetics

Absorption: Food and/or liquid nutritional supplements increase absorption; fasting states do not provide sufficient absorption to ensure adequate plasma concentrations

Distribution: V_d: 465-1774 L

Protein binding: ≥97%; predominantly bound to albumin

Metabolism: Not significantly metabolized; ~15% to 17% undergoes non-CYP-mediated metabolism, primarily via hepatic glucuronidation into metabolites

Half-life elimination: 35 hours (range: 20-66 hours)

Time to peak, plasma: 3-5 hours

Excretion: Feces 71% to 77% (~66% as unchanged drug); urine 13% to 14% (<0.2% as unchanged drug)

Dosage Oral: Children ≥13 years and Adults:

Prophylaxis of invasive *Aspergillus* and *Candida* species: 200 mg 3 times/day

Treatment of oropharyngeal candidiasis: Initial: 100 mg twice daily for 1 day; maintenance: 100 mg once daily for 13 days

Treatment of refractory oropharyngeal candidiasis: 400 mg twice daily

Treatment of refractory invasive fungal infections (unlabeled use): 800 mg/day in divided doses

Dosage adjustment in renal impairment: No adjustment necessary; use caution in severe renal impairment and monitor for breakthrough fungal infections. Variability in posaconazole exposure observed with Cl_{cr}<20 mL/minute.

Dosage adjustment in hepatic impairment: No adjustment necessary; use with caution

Dietary Considerations Give with meals. If alternative antifungal therapy can not be given to patients without food intake or severe diarrhea/vomiting, close monitoring for breakthrough fungal infections must be performed. Adequate posaconazole absorption from GI tract and subsequent plasma concentrations are dependent on food for efficacy. Lower average plasma concentrations have been associated with an increased risk of treatment failure.

Administration Must be administered with a full meal or an oral liquid nutritional supplement.

Monitoring Parameters Hepatic function (eg, SGOT, SGPT, alkaline phosphatase and bilirubin) prior to initiation and during treatment; renal function; electrolyte disturbances (eg, calcium, magnesium, potassium)

Dosage Forms

Suspension, oral:

Noxafil®: 40 mg/mL (123 mL) [contains sodium benzoate; delivers 105 mL of suspension; cherry flavor; packaged with calibrated dosing spoon]

♦ Post Peel Healing Balm [OTC] *see* Hydrocortisone *on page 852*

Potassium Acetate *(poe TASS ee um AS e tate)*

Pharmacologic Category Electrolyte Supplement, Parenteral

Use Potassium deficiency; to avoid chloride when high concentration of potassium is needed, source of bicarbonate

Pregnancy Risk Factor C

Medication Safety Issues

Consider special storage requirements for intravenous potassium salts; I.V. potassium salts have been administered IVP in error, leading to fatal outcomes.

Contraindications Severe renal impairment; hyperkalemia

Warnings/Precautions Use with caution in patients with renal disease, hyperkalemia, cardiac disease, metabolic alkalosis; must be administered in patients with adequate urine flow. Potassium acetate solution for injection contains aluminum; use caution with impaired renal function and in premature infants.

Adverse Reactions

1% to 10%:

Cardiovascular: Bradycardia

Endocrine & metabolic: Hyperkalemia

Neuromuscular & skeletal: Weakness

Respiratory: Dyspnea

Local: Local tissue necrosis with extravasation

<1% (Limited to important or life-threatening): Abdominal pain, alkalosis, chest pain, mental confusion, paralysis, paresthesia, phlebitis, throat pain

Overdosage/Toxicology Symptoms include muscle weakness, paralysis, peaked T waves, flattened P waves, prolongation of chloride, QRS complex, and ventricular arrhythmias. Removal of potassium can be accomplished by various means such as removal through the GI tract with Kayexalate® administration, by way of the kidney through diuresis, mineralocorticoid administration or increased sodium intake, by hemodialysis or peritoneal dialysis, or by shifting potassium back into the cells by insulin and glucose infusion or administration of sodium bicarbonate. Calcium chloride will reverse cardiac effects.

Drug Interactions

Increased Effect/Toxicity: Potassium-sparing diuretics, salt substitutes, and ACE inhibitors

Mechanism of Action Potassium is the major cation of intracellular fluid and is essential for the conduction of nerve impulses in heart, brain, and skeletal muscle; contraction of cardiac, skeletal and smooth muscles; maintenance of normal renal function, acid-base balance, carbohydrate metabolism, and gastric secretion

Pharmacodynamics/Kinetics

Distribution: Enters cells via active transport from extracellular fluid

Excretion: Primarily urine; skin and feces (small amounts); most intestinal potassium reabsorbed

Dosage I.V. doses should be incorporated into the patient's maintenance I.V. fluids, intermittent I.V. potassium administration should be reserved for severe depletion situations and requires ECG monitoring; doses listed as mEq of potassium

Children:
   Treatment of hypokalemia: I.V.: 2-5 mEq/kg/day
   I.V. intermittent infusion (must be diluted prior to administration): 0.5-1 mEq/kg/dose
      (maximum: 30 mEq/dose) to infuse at 0.3-0.5 mEq/kg/hour (maximum: 1 mEq/kg/hour)
   Note: Use caution in premature neonates; potassium acetate for injection contains
      aluminum.
Adults:
   Treatment of hypokalemia: I.V.: 40-100 mEq/day
   I.V. intermittent infusion (must be diluted prior to administration): 5-10 mEq/dose
      (maximum: 40 mEq/dose) to infuse over 2-3 hours (maximum: 40 mEq over 1 hour)

Note: Continuous cardiac monitor recommended for rates >0.5 mEq/hour
Potassium dosage/rate of infusion guidelines:
   Serum potassium >2.5 mEq/L: Maximum infusion rate: 10 mEq/hour; maximum concentra-
      tion: 40 mEq/L; maximum 24-hour dose: 200 mEq
   Serum potassium <2.5 mEq/L: Maximum infusion rate: 40 mEq/hour; maximum concentra-
      tion: 80 mEq/L; maximum 24-hour dose: 400 mEq

Dosage adjustment in renal impairment: Use caution; potassium acetate injection contains
aluminum

Administration Potassium must be diluted prior to parenteral administration; maximum
recommended concentration (peripheral line): 80 mEq/L; maximum recommended concentration (central line): 150 mEq/L or 15 mEq/100 mL; in severely fluid-restricted patients (with
central lines): 200 mEq/L or 20 mEq/100 mL has been used; maximum rate of infusion, see
Dosage, I.V. intermittent infusion

Additional Information 1 mEq of acetate is equivalent to the alkalinizing effect of 1 mEq of
bicarbonate.

Dosage Forms Injection, solution: 2 mEq/mL (20 mL, 50 mL, 100 mL); 4 mEq/mL (50 mL)
[contains aluminum ≤200 mcg/mL]

Potassium Acid Phosphate (poe TASS ee um AS id FOS fate)

U.S. Brand Names K-Phos® Original

Pharmacologic Category Urinary Acidifying Agent

Use Acidifies urine and lowers urinary calcium concentration; reduces odor and rash caused by
ammoniacal urine; increases the antibacterial activity of methenamine

Pregnancy Risk Factor C

Contraindications Severe renal impairment; hyperkalemia, hyperphosphatemia; infected
magnesium ammonium phosphate stones

Warnings/Precautions Use with caution in patients receiving other potassium supplementation and in patients with renal insufficiency, or severe tissue breakdown (eg, chemotherapy or
hemodialysis)

Adverse Reactions
   >10%: Gastrointestinal: Diarrhea, nausea, stomach pain, flatulence, vomiting
   1% to 10%:
      Cardiovascular: Bradycardia
      Endocrine & metabolic: Hyperkalemia
      Local: Local tissue necrosis with extravasation
      Neuromuscular & skeletal: Weakness
      Respiratory: Dyspnea
   <1% (Limited to important or life-threatening): Arrhythmia, dyspnea, edema, hyperphospha-
      temia, hypocalcemia, mental confusion, paralysis, paresthesia, tetany

Overdosage/Toxicology Symptoms include muscle weakness, paralysis, peaked T waves,
flattened P waves, prolongation of QRS complex, and ventricular arrhythmias. Removal of
potassium can be accomplished by various means such as through the GI tract with Kayexa-
late® administration, by way of the kidney through diuresis, mineralocorticoid administration
or increased sodium intake, by hemodialysis or peritoneal dialysis, or by shifting potassium
back into the cells by insulin and glucose infusion or sodium bicarbonate. Calcium chloride
will reverse cardiac effects.

Drug Interactions
   Increased Effect/Toxicity: Potassium-sparing diuretics, salt substitutes, salicylates, and
      ACE inhibitors
   Decreased Effect: Antacids containing magnesium, calcium or aluminum (bind phosphate
      and decreased its absorption)

Mechanism of Action The principal intracellular cation; involved in transmission of nerve
impulses, muscle contractions, enzyme activity, and glucose utilization

Pharmacodynamics/Kinetics
   Absorption: Well absorbed from upper GI tract
   Distribution: Enters cells via active transport from extracellular fluid
   Excretion: Primarily urine; skin and feces (small amounts); most intestinal potassium reab-
      sorbed

Dosage Adults: Oral: 1000 mg dissolved in 6-8 oz of water 4 times/day with meals and at
bedtime; for best results, soak tablets in water for 2-5 minutes, then stir and swallow

Dietary Considerations May be taken with meals.

Monitoring Parameters Serum potassium, sodium, phosphate, calcium; serum salicylates (if
taking salicylates)

Test Interactions Decreased ammonia (B)

Dosage Forms Tablet [scored]: 500 mg [phosphorus 114 mg and potassium 144 mg (3.7
mEq) per tablet; sodium free]

Potassium Bicarbonate and Potassium Chloride
(poe TASS ee um bye KAR bun ate & poe TASS ee um KLOR ide)

U.S. Brand Names K-Lyte/Cl®; K-Lyte/Cl® 50 [DSC]
Index Terms Potassium Bicarbonate and Potassium Chloride (Effervescent)
Pharmacologic Category Electrolyte Supplement, Oral
Use Treatment or prevention of hypokalemia
Pregnancy Risk Factor C
Dosage Oral:
  Children: 1-4 mEq/kg/24 hours in divided doses as required to maintain normal serum potassium
  Adults:
    Prevention: 16-24 mEq/day in 2-4 divided doses
    Treatment: 40-100 mEq/day in 2-4 divided doses
Additional Information Complete prescribing information for this medication should be consulted for additional detail.
Dosage Forms [DSC] = Discontinued product
  Tablet for oral solution, effervescent:
    K-Lyte/Cl®: Potassium chloride 25 mEq [potassium chloride 1.5 g and potassium bicarbonate 0.5 g; citrus or fruit punch flavor]
    K-Lyte/Cl® 50: Potassium chloride 50 mEq [potassium chloride 2.24 g and potassium bicarbonate 2 g; citrus flavor] [DSC]

♦ Potassium Bicarbonate and Potassium Chloride (Effervescent) *see* Potassium Bicarbonate and Potassium Chloride *on page 1396*

Potassium Bicarbonate and Potassium Citrate
(poe TASS ee um bye KAR bun ate & poe TASS ee um SIT rate)

U.S. Brand Names Effer-K™; Klor-Con®/EF; K-Lyte®; K-Lyte® DS
Index Terms Potassium Bicarbonate and Potassium Citrate (Effervescent)
Pharmacologic Category Electrolyte Supplement, Oral
Use Treatment or prevention of hypokalemia
Pregnancy Risk Factor C
Medication Safety Issues
  Sound-alike/look-alike issues:
    Klor-Con® may be confused with Klaron®, K-Lor®
Dosage Oral:
  Children: 1-4 mEq/kg/24 hours in divided doses as required to maintain normal serum potassium
  Adults:
    Prevention: 16-24 mEq/day in 2-4 divided doses
    Treatment: 40-100 mEq/day in 2-4 divided doses
Additional Information Complete prescribing information for this medication should be consulted for additional detail.
Dosage Forms
  Tablet, effervescent: Potassium 25 mEq
    Effer-K™: Potassium 25 mEq
    Klor-Con®/EF: Potassium 25 mEq [orange flavor]
    K-Lyte®: Potassium 25 mEq [orange flavor]
    K-Lyte® DS: Potassium 50 mEq [lime or orange flavor]

♦ Potassium Bicarbonate and Potassium Citrate (Effervescent) *see* Potassium Bicarbonate and Potassium Citrate *on page 1396*

Potassium Chloride (poe TASS ee um KLOR ide)

U.S. Brand Names Kaon-Cl-10®; Kaon-Cl® 20; Kay Ciel®; K-Dur® 10; K-Dur® 20; K-Lor®; Klor-Con®; Klor-Con® 8; Klor-Con® 10; Klor-Con®/25; Klor-Con® M; K+ Potassium; K-Tab®; microK®; microK® 10; Rum-K®
Canadian Brand Names Apo-K®; K-10®; K-Dur®; K-Lor®; K-Lyte®/Cl; Micro-K Extencaps®; Roychlor®; Slo-Pot; Slow-K®
Index Terms KCl
Pharmacologic Category Electrolyte Supplement, Oral; Electrolyte Supplement, Parenteral
Use Treatment or prevention of hypokalemia
Pregnancy Risk Factor A
Medication Safety Issues
  Sound-alike/look-alike issues:
    Kaon-Cl-10® may be confused with kaolin
    KCl may be confused with HCl
    K-Dur® may be confused with Cardura®, Imdur®
    K-Lor® may be confused with Kaochlor®, Klor-Con®
    Klor-Con® may be confused with Klaron®, K-Lor®
    Klotrix® may be confused with liotrix
    microK® may be confused with Micronase®

  High alert medication: The Institute for Safe Medication Practices (ISMP) includes this medication (I.V. formulation) among its list of drugs which have a heightened risk of causing significant patient harm when used in error.

Per JCAHO recommendations, concentrated electrolyte solutions should not be available in patient care areas.

Consider special storage requirements for intravenous potassium salts; I.V. potassium salts have been administered IVP in error, leading to fatal outcomes.

Contraindications Severe renal impairment, untreated Addison's disease, heat cramps, hyperkalemia, severe tissue trauma; solid oral dosage forms are contraindicated in patients in whom there is a structural, pathological, and/or pharmacologic cause for delay or arrest in passage through the GI tract; an oral liquid potassium preparation should be used in patients with esophageal compression or delayed gastric emptying time

Warnings/Precautions Use with caution in patients with cardiac disease, severe renal impairment, hyperkalemia

Adverse Reactions

>10%: Gastrointestinal: Diarrhea, nausea, stomach pain, flatulence, vomiting (oral)

1% to 10%:
Cardiovascular: Bradycardia
Endocrine & metabolic: Hyperkalemia
Local: Local tissue necrosis with extravasation, pain at the site of injection
Neuromuscular & skeletal: Weakness
Respiratory: Dyspnea

<1% (Limited to important or life-threatening): Abdominal pain, alkalosis, arrhythmia, chest pain, heart block, hypotension, mental confusion, paralysis, paresthesia, phlebitis, rash, throat pain

Overdosage/Toxicology Symptoms include muscle weakness, paralysis, peaked T waves, flattened P waves, prolongation of QRS complex, and ventricular arrhythmias. Removal of potassium can be accomplished by various means such as through the GI tract with Kayexalate® administration, by way of the kidney through diuresis, mineralocorticoid administration or increased sodium intake, by hemodialysis or peritoneal dialysis, or by shifting potassium back into the cells by insulin and glucose infusion or sodium bicarbonate. Calcium chloride reverses cardiac effects.

Drug Interactions

Increased Effect/Toxicity: Potassium-sparing diuretics, salt substitutes, ACE inhibitors

Stability Store at room temperature; do not freeze. Use only clear solutions. Use admixtures within 24 hours.

Mechanism of Action Potassium is the major cation of intracellular fluid and is essential for the conduction of nerve impulses in heart, brain, and skeletal muscle; contraction of cardiac, skeletal and smooth muscles; maintenance of normal renal function, acid-base balance, carbohydrate metabolism, and gastric secretion

Pharmacodynamics/Kinetics

Absorption: Well absorbed from upper GI tract

Distribution: Enters cells via active transport from extracellular fluid

Excretion: Primarily urine; skin and feces (small amounts); most intestinal potassium reabsorbed

Dosage I.V. doses should be incorporated into the patient's maintenance I.V. fluids; intermittent I.V. potassium administration should be reserved for severe depletion situations in patients undergoing ECG monitoring.

Normal daily requirements: Oral, I.V.:
Premature infants: 2-6 mEq/kg/24 hours
Term infants 0-24 hours: 0-2 mEq/kg/24 hours
Infants >24 hours: 1-2 mEq/kg/24 hours
Children: 2-3 mEq/kg/day
Adults: 40-80 mEq/day

Prevention during diuretic therapy: Oral:
Children: 1-2 mEq/kg/day in 1-2 divided doses
Adults: 20-40 mEq/day in 1-2 divided doses

Treatment of hypokalemia: Children:
Oral: 1-2 mEq/kg initially, then as needed based on frequently obtained lab values. If deficits are severe or ongoing losses are great, I.V. route should be considered.
I.V.: 1 mEq/kg over 1-2 hours initially, then repeated as needed based on frequently obtained lab values; severe depletion or ongoing losses may require >200% of normal limit needs
I.V. intermittent infusion: Dose should not exceed 1 mEq/kg/hour, or 40 mEq/hour; if it exceeds 0.5 mEq/kg/hour, physician should be at bedside and patient should have continuous ECG monitoring; usual pediatric maximum: 3 mEq/kg/day or 40 mEq/m²/day

Treatment of hypokalemia: Adults:
I.V. intermittent infusion: 5-10 mEq/hour (continuous cardiac monitor recommended for rates >5 mEq/hour), not to exceed 40 mEq/hour; usual adult maximum per 24 hours: 400 mEq/day.

Potassium dosage/rate of infusion guidelines:
Serum potassium >2.5 mEq/L: Maximum infusion rate: 10 mEq/hour; maximum concentration: 40 mEq/L; maximum 24-hour dose: 200 mEq
Serum potassium <2.5 mEq/L: Maximum infusion rate: 40 mEq/hour; maximum concentration: 80 mEq/L; maximum 24-hour dose: 400 mEq

Potassium >2.5 mEq/L:
Oral: 60-80 mEq/day plus additional amounts if needed
I.V.: 10 mEq over 1 hour with additional doses if needed

Potassium <2.5 mEq/L:
Oral: Up to 40-60 mEq initial dose, followed by further doses based on lab values
I.V.: Up to 40 mEq over 1 hour, with doses based on frequent lab monitoring; deficits at a plasma level of 2 mEq/L may be as high as 400-800 mEq of potassium

Dietary Considerations Administer with plenty of fluid and/or food because of stomach irritation and discomfort.

Administration

Parenteral: Potassium must be diluted prior to parenteral administration; maximum recommended concentration (peripheral line): 80 mEq/L; maximum recommended concentration

(Continued)

Potassium Chloride *(Continued)*

(central line): 150 mEq/L or 15 mEq/100 mL; in severely fluid-restricted patients (with central lines): 200 mEq/L or 20 mEq/100 mL has been used; maximum rate of infusion, see Dosage, I.V. intermittent infusion

Oral: Wax matrix tablets must be swallowed and not allowed to dissolve in mouth.

Monitoring Parameters Serum potassium, glucose, chloride, pH, urine output (if indicated), cardiac monitor (if intermittent infusion or potassium infusion rates >0.25 mEq/kg/hour)

Dosage Forms [DSC] = Discontinued product

Capsule, extended release: 10 mEq [750 mg]

micro-K® [microencapsulated]: 8 mEq [600 mg]

micro-K® 10 [microencapsulated]: 10 mEq [750 mg]

Infusion [premixed in D_5W]: 20 mEq (1000 mL); 30 mEq (1000 mL); 40 mEq (1000 mL)

Infusion [premixed in D_5W and LR]: 20 mEq (1000 mL); 30 mEq (1000 mL); 40 mEq (1000 mL)

Infusion [premixed in D_5W and $^1/_4NS$]: 10 mEq (500 mL, 1000 mL); 20 mEq (250 mL, 500 mL, 1000 mL); 30 mEq (1000 mL); 40 mEq (1000 mL)

Infusion [premixed in D_5W and $^1/_2NS$]: 10 mEq (500 mL, 1000 mL); 20 mEq (500 mL, 1000 mL); 30 mEq (1000 mL); 40 mEq (1000 mL)

Infusion [premixed in D_5 and NS]: 20 mEq (1000 mL); 40 mEq (1000 mL)

Infusion [premixed in D_5W and sodium chloride 0.3%]: 10 mEq (500 mL); 20 mEq (1000 mL); 30 mEq (1000 mL); 40 mEq (1000 mL)

Infusion [premixed in $D_{10}W$ and sodium chloride 0.2%]: 20 mEq (250 mL)

Infusion [premixed in NS]: 20 mEq (1000 mL); 40 mEq (1000 mL)

Infusion [premixed in SWFI; concentrate]: 10 mEq (50 mL, 100 mL); 20 mEq (50 mL, 100 mL); 30 mEq (100 mL); 40 mEq (100 mL)

Injection, solution [concentrate]: 2 mEq/mL (5 mL, 10 mL, 15 mL, 20 mL, 30 mL, 250 mL, 500 mL)

Powder, for oral solution: 20 mEq/packet (30s, 100s, 1000s)

K-Lor™: 20 mEq/packet (30s, 100s) [fruit flavor]

K+ Potassium: 20 mEq/packet (30s) [orange flavor]

Kay Ciel® 10%: 20 mEq/packet (30s, 100s) [sugar free]

Klor-Con®: 20 mEq/packet (30s, 100s) [sugar free; fruit flavor]

Klor-Con®/25: 25 mEq/packet (30s, 100s) [sugar free; fruit flavor]

Solution, oral: 20 mEq/15 mL (480 mL, 3840 mL); 40 mEq/15 mL (480 mL)

Kaon-Cl® 20: 40 mEq/15 mL (480 mL) [sugar free; contains alcohol; cherry flavor]

Kay Ciel®: 10%: 20 mEq/15 mL (480 mL) [sugar free; contains alcohol] [DSC]

Rum-K®: 20 mEq/10 mL (480 mL) [alcohol free, sugar free; butter/rum flavor]

Tablet, extended release: 8 mEq [600 mg]; 10 mEq [750 mg]; 20 mEq [1500 mg]

K-Dur® 10 [microencapsulated]: 10 mEq [750 mg]

K-Dur® 20 [microencapsulated]: 20 mEq [1500 mg; scored]

K-Tab®: 10 mEq [750 mg]

Kaon-Cl® 10: 10 mEq [750 mg]

Klor-Con® 8: 8 mEq [600 mg; wax matrix]

Klor-Con® 10: 10 mEq [750 mg; wax matrix]

Klor-Con® M10 [microencapsulated]: 10 mEq [750 mg]

Klor-Con® M15 [microencapsulated]: 15 mEq [1125 mg; scored]

Klor-Con® M20 [microencapsulated]: 20 mEq [1500 mg; scored]

Potassium Citrate and Citric Acid *(poe TASS ee um SIT rate & SI trik AS id)*

U.S. Brand Names Cytra-K; Polycitra®-K

Index Terms Citric Acid and Potassium Citrate

Pharmacologic Category Alkalinizing Agent, Oral

Use Treatment of metabolic acidosis; alkalinizing agent in conditions where long-term maintenance of an alkaline urine is desirable

Pregnancy Risk Factor A

Dosage Urine alkalizing agent:

Children: Solution: 5-15 mL after meals and at bedtime; adjust dose based on urinary pH

Adults:

Powder: One packet dissolved in water after meals and at bedtime; adjust dose to urinary pH

Solution: 15-30 mL after meals and at bedtime; adjust dose based on urinary pH

Additional Information Complete prescribing information for this medication should be consulted for additional detail.

Dosage Forms Note: Equivalent to potassium 2 mEq/mL and bicarbonate 2 mEq/mL

Powder:

Cytra-K: Potassium citrate 3300 mg and citric acid 1002 mg per packet (100s) [sugar free; fruit flavor]

Polycitra®-K: Potassium citrate 3300 mg and citric acid 1002 mg per packet (100s) [sugar free]

Solution:

Cytra-K: Potassium citrate 1100 mg and citric acid monohydrate 334 mg per 5 mL (480 mL) [alcohol free, sugar free; contains sodium benzoate; cherry flavor]

Polycitra®-K: Potassium citrate 1100 mg and citric acid monohydrate 334 mg per 5 mL (480 mL) [alcohol free, sugar free]

♦ **Potassium Citrate, Citric Acid, and Sodium Citrate** *see* Citric Acid, Sodium Citrate, and Potassium Citrate *on page 383*

Potassium Gluconate (poe TASS ee um GLOO coe nate)

U.S. Brand Names Glu-K® [OTC]
Pharmacologic Category Electrolyte Supplement, Oral
Use Treatment or prevention of hypokalemia
Pregnancy Risk Factor A
Contraindications Severe renal impairment, untreated Addison's disease, heat cramps, hyperkalemia, severe tissue trauma; solid oral dosage forms are contraindicated in patients in whom there is a structural, pathological, and/or pharmacologic cause for delay or arrest in passage through the GI tract
Warnings/Precautions Use with caution in patients with cardiac disease, severe renal impairment, hyperkalemia; patients must be on a cardiac monitor during intermittent infusions
Adverse Reactions
>10%: Gastrointestinal: Diarrhea, nausea, stomach pain, flatulence, vomiting (oral)
1% to 10%:
Cardiovascular: Bradycardia
Endocrine & metabolic: Hyperkalemia
Neuromuscular & skeletal: Weakness
Respiratory: Dyspnea
<1% (Limited to important or life-threatening): Mental confusion, paralysis, paresthesia, phlebitis
Overdosage/Toxicology Symptoms of hyperkalemia include muscle weakness, paralysis, peaked T waves, flattened P waves, prolongation of QRS complex, and ventricular arrhythmias. Removal of potassium can be accomplished by various means such as through the GI tract with Kayexalate® administration, by way of the kidney through diuresis, mineralocorticoid administration or increased sodium intake, by hemodialysis or peritoneal dialysis, or by shifting potassium back into the cells by insulin, glucose infusion, or sodium bicarbonate. Calcium chloride reverses cardiac effects.
Drug Interactions
Increased Effect/Toxicity: Potassium-sparing diuretics, salt substitutes, ACE inhibitors; increased effect of digitalis
Stability Store at room temperature.
Mechanism of Action Potassium is the major cation of intracellular fluid and is essential for the conduction of nerve impulses in heart, brain, and skeletal muscle; contraction of cardiac, skeletal and smooth muscles; maintenance of normal renal function, acid-base balance, carbohydrate metabolism, and gastric secretion
Pharmacodynamics/Kinetics
Absorption: Well absorbed from upper GI tract
Distribution: Enters cells via active transport from extracellular fluid
Excretion: Primarily urine; skin and feces (small amounts); most intestinal potassium reabsorbed
Dosage Oral (doses listed as mEq of potassium):
Normal daily requirement:
Children: 2-3 mEq/kg/day
Adults: 40-80 mEq/day
Prevention of hypokalemia during diuretic therapy:
Children: 1-2 mEq/kg/day in 1-2 divided doses
Adults: 16-24 mEq/day in 1-2 divided doses
Treatment of hypokalemia:
Children: 2-5 mEq/kg/day in 2-4 divided doses
Adults: 40-100 mEq/day in 2-4 divided doses
Monitoring Parameters Serum potassium, chloride, glucose, pH, urine output (if indicated)
Test Interactions Decreased ammonia (B)
Additional Information 9.4 g potassium gluconate is approximately equal to 40 mEq potassium (4.3 mEq potassium/g potassium gluconate).
Dosage Forms
Tablet: 500 mg, 610 mg
Glu-K®: 486 mg
Tablet, timed release: 595 mg

Potassium Iodide (poe TASS ee um EYE oh dide)

U.S. Brand Names Iosat™ [OTC]; Pima®; SSKI®; ThyroSafe™ [OTC]; ThyroShield™ [OTC]
Index Terms KI
Pharmacologic Category Antithyroid Agent; Expectorant
Use Expectorant for the symptomatic treatment of chronic pulmonary diseases complicated by mucous; reduce thyroid vascularity prior to thyroidectomy and management of thyrotoxic crisis; block thyroidal uptake of radioactive isotopes of iodine in a radiation emergency or other exposure to radioactive iodine
Unlabeled/Investigational Use Lymphocutaneous and cutaneous sporotrichosis
Pregnancy Risk Factor D
Pregnancy Implications Iodide crosses the placenta (may cause hypothyroidism and goiter in fetus/newborn). Use as an expectorant during pregnancy is contraindicated by the AAP. Use for protection against thyroid cancer secondary to radioactive iodine exposure is considered acceptable based upon risk/benefit, keeping in mind the dose and duration. Repeat dosing should be avoided if possible.
Lactation Enters breast milk/use caution (AAP rates "compatible")
Medication Safety Issues
Sound-alike/look-alike issues:
Potassium iodide products, including saturated solution of potassium iodide (SSKI®) may be confused with potassium iodide and iodine (Strong Iodide Solution or Lugol's solution)
(Continued)

Potassium Iodide *(Continued)*

Contraindications Hypersensitivity to iodine or any component of the formulation; hyperkalemia; pulmonary edema; impaired renal function; hyperthyroidism; iodine-induced goiter; dermatitis herpetiformis; hypocomplementemic vasculitis

Warnings/Precautions Prolonged use can lead to hypothyroidism; cystic fibrosis patients have an exaggerated response; can cause acne flare-ups, can cause dermatitis; use with caution in patients with a history of thyroid disease, Addison's disease, cardiac disease, myotonia congenita, tuberculosis, acute bronchitis

Adverse Reactions Frequency not defined.
Cardiovascular: Irregular heart beat
Central nervous system: Confusion, tiredness, fever
Dermatologic: Skin rash
Endocrine & metabolic: Goiter, salivary gland swelling/tenderness, thyroid adenoma, swelling of neck/throat, myxedema, lymph node swelling, hyper-/hypothyroidism
Gastrointestinal: Diarrhea, gastrointestinal bleeding, metallic taste, nausea, stomach pain, stomach upset, vomiting
Neuromuscular & skeletal: Numbness, tingling, weakness, joint pain
Miscellaneous: Chronic iodine poisoning (with prolonged treatment/high doses); iodism; hypersensitivity reactions (angioedema, cutaneous and mucosal hemorrhage, serum sickness-like symptoms)

Overdosage/Toxicology Symptoms include angioedema, laryngeal edema in patients with hypersensitivity; muscle weakness, paralysis, peaked T waves, flattened P waves, prolongation of QRS complex, ventricular arrhythmias. Removal of potassium can be accomplished by various means such as through the GI tract with Kayexalate® administration, by way of the kidney through diuresis, mineralocorticoid administration or increased sodium intake, by hemodialysis or peritoneal dialysis, or by shifting potassium back into the cells by insulin and glucose infusion.

Drug Interactions
Increased Effect/Toxicity: Lithium may cause additive hypothyroid effects; ACE inhibitors, potassium-sparing diuretics, and potassium/potassium-containing products may lead to hyperkalemia, cardiac arrhythmias, or cardiac arrest

Stability Store at controlled room temperature of 25°C (77°F); excursions permitted to 15°C to 30°C (59°F to 86°F). Protect from light; keep tightly closed.
SSKI®: If exposed to cold, crystallization may occur. Warm and shake to redissolve. If solution becomes brown/yellow, it should be discarded. May be mixed in water, fruit juice, or milk.
Preparation of oral solution:
Concentration of 16.25 mg/5 mL oral solution: Crush one 130 mg tablet into a fine powder. Add 20 mL of water and mix until powder is dissolved. Add an additional 20 mL of low-fat milk (white or chocolate), orange juice, flat soda, raspberry syrup or infant formula. Final concentration will be 16.25 mg/5 mL. Stable for 7 days under refrigeration.
Concentration of 8.125 mg/5 mL oral solution: Crush one 65 mg tablet into a fine powder. Add 20 mL of water and mix until powder is dissolved. Add an additional 20 mL of low-fat milk (white or chocolate), orange juice, flat soda, raspberry syrup, or infant formula. Final concentration will be 8.125 mg/5 mL. Stable for 7 days under refrigeration.

Mechanism of Action Reduces viscosity of mucus by increasing respiratory tract secretions; inhibits secretion of thyroid hormone, fosters colloid accumulation in thyroid follicles. Following radioactive iodine exposure, potassium iodide blocks uptake of radioiodine by the thyroid, reducing the risk of thyroid cancer.

Pharmacodynamics/Kinetics
Onset of action: Hyperthyroidism: 24-48 hours
Peak effect: 10-15 days after continuous therapy
Duration: Radioactive iodine exposure: ~ 24 hours

Dosage Oral:
Adults: RDA: 150 mcg (iodine)
Expectorant:
Children (Pima®):
<3 years: 162 mg 3 times day
>3 years: 325 mg 3 times/day
Adults:
Pima®: 325-650 mg 3 times/day
SSKI®: 300-600 mg 3-4 times/day
Preoperative thyroidectomy: Children and Adults: 50-250 mg (1-5 drops SSKI®) 3 times/day; administer for 10 days before surgery
Radiation protectant to radioactive isotopes of iodine (Pima®):
Children:
Infants up to 1 year: 65 mg once daily for 10 days; start 24 hours prior to exposure
>1 year: 130 mg once daily for 10 days; start 24 hours prior to exposure
Adults: 195 mg once daily for 10 days; start 24 hours prior to exposure 7
To reduce risk of thyroid cancer following nuclear accident (Iosat™, ThyroSafe™, ThyroShield™): Dosing should continue until risk of exposure has passed or other measures are implemented:
Children (see adult dose for children >68 kg):
Infants <1 month: 16.25 mg once daily
1 month to 3 years: 32.5 mg once daily
3-18 years: 65 mg once daily
Children >68 kg and Adults (including pregnant/lactating women): 130 mg once daily
Thyrotoxic crisis:
Infants <1 year: 150-250 mg (3-5 drops SSKI®) 3 times/day
Children and Adults: 300-500 mg (6-10 drops SSKI®) 3 times/day
Sporotrichosis (cutaneous, lymphocutaneous; unlabeled use): Adults: Oral: Initial: 5 drops (SSKI®) 3 times/day; increase to 40-50 drops (SSKI®) 3 times/day as tolerated for 3-6 months

Dietary Considerations SSKI®: Take with food to decrease gastric irritation.

Administration
Pima®: When used as an expectorant, take each dose with at least 4-6 ounces of water

SSKI®: Dilute in a glassful of water, fruit juice or milk. Take with food to decrease gastric irritation

Monitoring Parameters Thyroid function tests, signs/symptoms of hyperthyroidism; thyroid function should be monitored in pregnant women, neonates, and young infants if repeat doses are required following radioactive iodine exposure

Test Interactions May alter thyroid function tests

Additional Information 10 drops of SSKI® = potassium iodide 500 mg

Dosage Forms
Solution, oral:

SSKI®: 1 g/mL (30 mL, 240 mL) [contains sodium thiosulfate]

ThyroShield™: 65 mg/mL (30 mL) [black raspberry flavor]

Syrup (Pima®): 325 mg/5 mL (473 mL) [equivalent to iodide 249 mg/5 mL; black raspberry flavor]

Tablet:

Iosat™: 130 mg

ThyroSafe™: 65 mg [equivalent to iodine 50 mg]

Extemporaneous Preparations Preparation of oral solution:

Concentration of 16.25 mg/5 mL oral solution: Crush one 130 mg tablet into a fine powder. Add 20 mL of water and mix until powder is dissolved. Add an additional 20 mL of low-fat milk (white or chocolate), orange juice, flat soda, raspberry syrup or infant formula. Final concentration will be 16.25 mg/5 mL.

Concentration of 8.125 mg/5 mL oral solution: Crush one 65 mg tablet into a fine powder. Add 20 mL of water and mix until powder is dissolved. Add an additional 20 mL of low-fat milk (white or chocolate), orange juice, flat soda, raspberry syrup, or infant formula. Final concentration will be 8.125 mg/5 mL.

Potassium Iodide and Iodine (poe TASS ee um EYE oh dide & EYE oh dine)

Index Terms Lugol's Solution; Strong Iodine Solution

Pharmacologic Category Antithyroid Agent

Use Reduce thyroid vascularity prior to thyroidectomy and management of thyrotoxic crisis; block thyroidal uptake of radioactive isotopes of iodine in a radiation emergency or other exposure to radioactive iodine

Pregnancy Risk Factor D (potassium iodide)

Pregnancy Implications Iodide crosses the placenta (may cause hypothyroidism and goiter in fetus/newborn). Use for protection against thyroid cancer secondary to radioactive iodine exposure is considered acceptable based upon risk/benefit, keeping in mind the dose and duration. Repeat dosing should be avoided if possible.

Lactation Enters breast milk/use caution (AAP rates "compatible")

Medication Safety Issues
Sound-alike/look-alike issues:

Potassium iodide and iodine (Strong Iodine Solution or Lugol's solution) may be confused with potassium iodide products, including saturated solution of potassium iodide (SSKI®)

Contraindications Hypersensitivity to iodine or any component of the formulation; hyperkalemia; pulmonary edema; impaired renal function; hyperthyroidism; iodine-induced goiter; dermatitis herpetiformis; hypocomplementemic vasculitis

Warnings/Precautions Prolonged use can lead to hypothyroidism; cystic fibrosis patients have an exaggerated response; can cause acne flare-ups, can cause dermatitis; use with caution in patients with a history of thyroid disease, Addison's disease, cardiac disease, myotonia congenita, tuberculosis, acute bronchitis

Adverse Reactions Frequency not defined.

Cardiovascular: Irregular heart beat

Central nervous system: Confusion, tiredness, fever

Dermatologic: Skin rash

Endocrine & metabolic: Goiter, salivary gland swelling/tenderness, thyroid adenoma, swelling of neck/throat, myxedema, lymph node swelling, hyper-/hypothyroidism

Gastrointestinal: Diarrhea, gastrointestinal bleeding, metallic taste, nausea, stomach pain, stomach upset, vomiting

Neuromuscular & skeletal: Numbness, tingling, weakness, joint pain

Miscellaneous: Chronic iodine poisoning (with prolonged treatment/high doses); iodism; hypersensitivity reactions (angioedema, cutaneous and mucosal hemorrhage, serum sickness-like symptoms)

Overdosage/Toxicology Symptoms of overdose include angioedema, laryngeal edema or cutaneous hemorrhages, muscle weakness, paralysis, peaked T waves, flattened P waves, prolongation of QRS complex, and ventricular arrhythmias.

Symptoms of iodism or chronic iodine poisoning may manifest as burning of mouth or throat, severe headache, metallic taste, sore teeth and gums, head cold symptoms, eye irritation including eyelid swelling, unusual increase in salivation, acneform skin lesions in seborrheic areas, or severe skin eruption (rare).

Removal of potassium can be accomplished by various means: Removal through the GI tract with Kayexalate® administration; by way of the kidney through diuresis, mineralocorticoid administration, or increased sodium intake; by hemodialysis or peritoneal dialysis; or by shifting potassium back into the cells by insulin and glucose infusion or by administration of sodium bicarbonate. Calcium chloride reverses cardiac effects.

Drug Interactions
Increased Effect/Toxicity: Concurrent use of ACE inhibitors, potassium-sparing diuretics, or potassium (and potassium-containing products) may lead to hyperkalemia, cardiac arrhythmias or cardiac arrest. Lithium may cause additive hypothyroid effects.

Stability Store at controlled room temperature of 25°C (77°F); excursions permitted to 15°C to 30°C (59°F to 86°F). Protect from light and keep container tightly closed.

(Continued)

Potassium Iodide and Iodine *(Continued)*

Mechanism of Action Inhibits secretion of thyroid hormone, fosters colloid accumulation in thyroid follicles. Following radioactive iodine exposure, potassium iodide blocks uptake of radioiodine by the thyroid, reducing the risk of thyroid cancer.

Pharmacodynamics/Kinetics
Onset of action: Hyperthyroidism: 24-48 hours
Peak effect: 10-15 days after continuous therapy

Dosage RDA, Adults: 150 mcg (iodine)
Children and Adults: Oral:
Preoperative thyroidectomy: 0.1-0.3 mL (3-5 drops) of strong iodine (Lugol's solution) 3 times/day; administer for 10 days before surgery
Thyrotoxic crisis: 1 mL strong iodine (Lugol's solution) 3 times/day

Monitoring Parameters
Thyroid function tests, signs/symptoms of hyperthyroidism; thyroid function should be monitored in pregnant women, neonates, and young infants if repeat doses are required following radioactive iodine exposure

Test Interactions May alter thyroid function tests.

Dosage Forms Solution, oral (Lugol's solution, strong iodine): Potassium iodide 100 mg/mL and iodine 50 mg/mL (15 mL, 480 mL)

♦ **Potassium Iodide, Chlorpheniramine, Phenylephrine, and Codeine** *see* Chlorpheniramine, Phenylephrine, Codeine, and Potassium Iodide *on page 354*

Potassium Phosphate *(poe TASS ee um FOS fate)*

U.S. Brand Names Neutra-Phos®-K [OTC]
Index Terms Phosphate, Potassium
Pharmacologic Category Electrolyte Supplement, Oral; Electrolyte Supplement, Parenteral
Use Treatment and prevention of hypophosphatemia or hypokalemia
Pregnancy Risk Factor C
Medication Safety Issues
Sound-alike/look-alike issues:
Neutra-Phos®-K may be confused with K-Phos Neutral®

High alert medication: The Institute for Safe Medication Practices (ISMP) includes this medication (I.V. formulation) among its list of drugs which have a heightened risk of causing significant patient harm when used in error.
Per JCAHO recommendations, concentrated electrolyte solutions should not be available in patient care areas.
Consider special storage requirements for intravenous potassium salts; I.V. potassium salts have been administered IVP in error, leading to fatal outcomes.

Contraindications Hyperphosphatemia, hyperkalemia, hypocalcemia, hypomagnesemia, renal failure

Warnings/Precautions Use with caution in patients with renal insufficiency, cardiac disease, metabolic alkalosis; admixture of phosphate and calcium in I.V. fluids can result in calcium phosphate precipitation

Adverse Reactions
>10%: Gastrointestinal: Diarrhea, nausea, stomach pain, flatulence, vomiting
1% to 10%:
Cardiovascular: Bradycardia
Endocrine & metabolic: Hyperkalemia
Neuromuscular & skeletal: Weakness
Respiratory: Dyspnea
<1% (Limited to important or life-threatening): Acute renal failure, arrhythmia, chest pain, decreased urine output, dyspnea, edema, mental confusion, paralysis, paresthesia, phlebitis, tetany (with large doses of phosphate)

Overdosage/Toxicology Symptoms include muscle weakness, paralysis, peaked T waves, flattened P waves, prolongation of QRS complex, ventricular arrhythmias, tetany, and calcium-phosphate precipitation. Removal of potassium can be accomplished by various means such as through the GI tract with Kayexalate® administration, by way of the kidney through diuresis, mineralocorticoid administration or increased sodium intake, by hemodialysis or peritoneal dialysis, or by shifting potassium back into the cells by insulin, glucose infusion, or sodium bicarbonate. Calcium chloride reverses cardiac effects.

Drug Interactions
Increased Effect/Toxicity: Potassium-sparing diuretics, salt substitutes, or ACE inhibitors; increased effect of digitalis
Decreased Effect: Aluminum and magnesium-containing antacids or sucralfate can act as phosphate binders

Ethanol/Nutrition/Herb Interactions Food: Avoid administering with oxalate (berries, nuts, chocolate, beans, celery, tomato) or phytate-containing foods (bran, whole wheat).

Stability Store at room temperature; do not freeze. Use only clear solutions. Up to 10-15 mEq of calcium may be added per liter before precipitate may occur.

Stability of parenteral admixture at room temperature (25°C) is 24 hours.

Phosphate salts may precipitate when mixed with calcium salts. Solubility is improved in amino acid parenteral nutrition solutions. Check with a pharmacist to determine compatibility.

Dosage I.V. doses should be incorporated into the patient's maintenance I.V. fluids; intermittent I.V. infusion should be reserved for severe depletion situations in patients undergoing continuous ECG monitoring. It is difficult to determine total body phosphorus deficit; the following dosages are empiric guidelines:

Normal requirements elemental phosphorus: Oral:
0-6 months: 240 mg
6-12 months: 360 mg

1-10 years: 800 mg
>10 years: 1200 mg
Pregnancy lactation: Additional 400 mg/day
Adults: 800 mg

Treatment: It is difficult to provide concrete guidelines for the treatment of severe hypophosphatemia because the extent of total body deficits and response to therapy are difficult to predict. Aggressive doses of phosphate may result in a transient serum elevation followed by redistribution into intracellular compartments or bone tissue. It is recommended that repletion of severe hypophosphatemia (<1 mg/dL in adults) be done I.V. because large doses of oral phosphate may cause diarrhea and intestinal absorption may be unreliable

Pediatric I.V. phosphate repletion:
Children: 0.25-0.5 mmol/kg **administer over 4-6 hours and repeat if symptomatic hypophosphatemia persists**; to assess the need for further phosphate administration, obtain serum inorganic phosphate after administration of the first dose and base further doses on serum levels and clinical status

Adult I.V. phosphate repletion:
Initial dose: 0.08 mmol/kg if recent uncomplicated hypophosphatemia
Initial dose: 0.16 mmol/kg if prolonged hypophosphatemia with presumed total body deficits; increase dose by 25% to 50% if patient symptomatic with severe hypophosphatemia

Do not exceed 0.24 mmol/kg/dose; administer over 6-12 hours by I.V. infusion. Some investigators have used more rapid infusions.

With orders for I.V. phosphate, there is considerable confusion associated with the use of millimoles (mmol) versus milliequivalents (mEq) to express the phosphate requirement. Because inorganic phosphate exists as monobasic and dibasic anions, with the mixture of valences dependent on pH, ordering by mEq amounts is unreliable and may lead to large dosing errors. In addition, I.V. phosphate is available in the sodium and potassium salt; therefore, the content of these cations must be considered when ordering phosphate. The most reliable method of ordering I.V. phosphate is by millimoles, then specifying the potassium or sodium salt. For example, an order for 15 mmol of phosphate as potassium phosphate in one liter of normal saline. The dosing of phosphate should be 0.2-0.3 mmol/kg with a usual daily requirement of 30-60 mmol/day or 15 mmol of phosphate per liter of TPN or 15 mmol phosphate per 1000 calories of dextrose. Would also provide 22 mEq of potassium.

Maintenance:
I.V. solutions:
Children: 0.5-1.5 mmol/kg/24 hours I.V. or 2-3 mmol/kg/24 hours orally in divided doses
Adults: 15-30 mmol/24 hours I.V. or 50-150 mmol/24 hours orally in divided doses
Oral:
Children <4 years: 1 capsule (250 mg phosphorus/8 mmol) 4 times/day; dilute as instructed
Children >4 years and Adults: 1-2 capsules (250-500 mg phosphorus/8-16 mmol) 4 times/day; dilute as instructed

Administration Injection must be diluted in appropriate I.V. solution and volume prior to administration and administered over a minimum of 4 hours

Monitoring Parameters Serum potassium, calcium, phosphate, sodium, cardiac monitor (when intermittent infusion or high-dose I.V. replacement needed)

Test Interactions Decreased ammonia (B)

Dosage Forms
Injection, solution: Potassium 4.4 mEq and phosphorus 3 mmol per mL (5 mL, 15 mL, 50 mL) [equivalent to potassium 170 mg and phosphate 285 mg per mL]
Powder for oral solution [packet] (Neutra-Phos®-K): Monobasic potassium phosphate and dibasic potassium phosphate/packet (100s) [equivalent to elemental potassium 556 mg (14.2 mEq) and phosphorus 250 mg per packet; sodium and sugar free; fruit flavor]

Potassium Phosphate and Sodium Phosphate
(poe TASS ee um FOS fate & SOW dee um FOS fate)

U.S. Brand Names K-Phos® MF; K-Phos® Neutral; K-Phos® No. 2; Neutra-Phos® [OTC]; Phos-NaK; Phospha 250™ Neutral; Uro-KP-Neutral®

Index Terms Sodium Phosphate and Potassium Phosphate

Pharmacologic Category Electrolyte Supplement, Oral

Use Treatment of conditions associated with excessive renal phosphate loss or inadequate GI absorption of phosphate; to acidify the urine to lower calcium concentrations; to increase the antibacterial activity of methenamine; reduce odor and rash caused by ammonia in urine

Pregnancy Risk Factor C

Medication Safety Issues
Sound-alike/look-alike issues:
K-Phos® Neutral may be confused with Neutra-Phos-K®

Dosage All dosage forms to be mixed in 6-8 oz of water prior to administration
Children ≥4 years: Elemental phosphorus 250 mg 4 times/day after meals and at bedtime
Adults: Elemental phosphorus 250-500 mg 4 times/day after meals and at bedtime

Additional Information Complete prescribing information for this medication should be consulted for additional detail.

Dosage Forms
Caplet:
Uro-KP-Neutral®: Sodium phosphate monobasic, dipotassium phosphate, and disodium phosphate [equivalent to elemental phosphorus 258 mg, sodium 262.4 mg (10.8 mEq), and potassium 49.4 mg (1.3 mEq)]
Powder, for oral solution:
Neutra-Phos®, Phos-NaK): Monobasic sodium, dibasic sodium, and potassium phosphate/packet (100s) [equivalent to elemental phosphorus 250 mg, sodium 164 mg (7.1 mEq), and potassium 278 mg (7.1 mEq) per packet]

(Continued)

Potassium Phosphate and Sodium Phosphate *(Continued)*

Tablet:
K-Phos® MF: Potassium acid phosphate 155 mg and sodium acid phosphate 350 mg [equivalent to elemental phosphorus 125.6 mg, sodium 67 mg (2.9 mEq), and potassium 44.5 mg (1.1 mEq)]

K-Phos® Neutral: Dibasic sodium phosphate 852 mg, monobasic potassium phosphate 155 mg, and monobasic sodium phosphate 130 mg [equivalent to elemental phosphorus 250 mg, sodium 298 mg (13 mEq), and potassium 45 mg (1.1 mEq)]

K-Phos® No. 2: Potassium acid phosphate 305 mg and sodium acid phosphate 700 mg [equivalent to elemental phosphorus 250 mg, sodium 134 mg (5.8 mEq), and potassium 88 mg (2.3 mEq)]

Phospha 250™ Neutral: Dibasic sodium phosphate 852 mg, monobasic potassium phosphate 155 mg, and monobasic sodium phosphate 130 mg [equivalent to elemental phosphorus 250 mg, sodium 298 mg (13 mEq), and potassium 45 mg (1.1 mEq)]

♦ **Povidine™ [OTC]** *see* Povidone-Iodine *on page 1404*

Povidone-Iodine *(POE vi done EYE oh dyne)*

U.S. Brand Names Betadine® [OTC]; Betadine® Ophthalmic; Minidyne® [OTC]; Operand® [OTC]; Povidine™ [OTC]; Summer's Eve® Medicated Douche [OTC]; Vagi-Gard® [OTC]

Canadian Brand Names Betadine®; Proviodine

Index Terms Polyvinylpyrrolidone with Iodine; PVP-I

Pharmacologic Category Antiseptic, Ophthalmic; Antiseptic, Topical; Antiseptic, Vaginal; Topical Skin Product

Use External antiseptic with broad microbicidal spectrum for the prevention or treatment of topical infections associated with surgery, burns, minor cuts/scrapes; relief of minor vaginal irritation

Pregnancy Risk Factor C (ophthalmic)

Medication Safety Issues

Sound-alike/look-alike issues:
Betadine® may be confused with Betagan®, betaine

International issues:
Alphadine®: Brand name for ranitidine in Greece
Oralon® [Japan] may be confused with Oralone® which is a brand name for triamcinolone in the U.S.

Dosage

Antiseptic: Apply topically to affected area as needed. Ophthalmic solution may be used to irrigate the eye or applied to area around the eye such as skin, eyelashes, or lid margins.

Surgical scrub: Topical: Apply solution to wet skin or hands, scrub for ~5 minutes, rinse; refer to product labeling for specific procedure-related instructions.

Vaginal irritation: Douche: Insert 0.3% solution vaginally once daily for 5-7 days

Dosage Forms [DSC] = Discontinued product

Gel, topical (Operand®): 10% (120 g)

Liquid, topical: 10% (30 mL)

Ointment, topical: 10% (1 g, 30 g)
Betadine®: 10% (0.9 g, 3.7 g, 30 g) [DSC]
Povidine™: 10% (30 g)

Pad [prep pads]: 10% (200s)
Betadine® SwabAids: 10% (100s)

Scrub brush [solution impregnated]: 7.5% (30s)

Solution, ophthalmic (Betadine®): 5% (50 mL)

Solution, perineal (Operand®): 10% (240 mL) [concentrate]

Solution, topical: 10% (240 mL, 480 mL, 3840 mL)
Betadine®: 10% (15 mL, 120 mL, 240 mL, 480 mL, 960 mL, 3840 mL)
Minidyne®: 10% (15 mL)
Operand®: 10% (60 mL, 120 mL, 240 mL, 480 mL, 960 mL, 3840 mL)

Solution, topical scrub:
Betadine® Surgical Scrub: 7.5% (120 mL, 480 mL, 960 mL, 3840 mL)
Betadine® Skin Cleanser: 7.5% (120 mL)
Operand®: 7.5% (60 mL, 120 mL, 240 mL, 480 mL, 960 mL, 3840 mL)

Solution, topical spray:
Betadine®: 5% (90 mL) [CFC free; contains dry natural rubber]
Operand®: 10% (59 mL)

Solution, vaginal douche:
Operand®: 10% (240 mL) [concentrate]
Summer's Eve® Medicated Douche: 0.3% (135 mL)
Vagi-Gard®: 10% (180 mL, 240 mL) [concentrate]

Solution, whirlpool (Operand®): 10% (3840 mL) [concentrate]

Swab [prep-swab ampul]: 10% (0.65 mL)

Swabsticks: 10% (25s, 50s)
Betadine®: 10% (50s, 150s, 200s)

Swabsticks [gel saturated]: 10% (50s)

Swabsticks, topical scrub: 7.5% (25s, 50s)

♦ **PPD** *see* Tuberculin Tests *on page 1754*

♦ **PPI-149** *see* Abarelix *on page 20*

♦ **PPL** *see* Benzylpenicilloyl-polylysine *on page 209*

♦ **PPS** *see* Pentosan Polysulfate Sodium *on page 1342*

♦ **PPV23** *see* Pneumococcal Polysaccharide Vaccine (Polyvalent) *on page 1384*

Pralidoxime (pra li DOKS eem)

U.S. Brand Names Protopam®
Canadian Brand Names Protopam®
Index Terms 2-PAM; Pralidoxime Chloride; 2-Pyridine Aldoxime Methochloride
Pharmacologic Category Antidote
Additional Appendix Information
Management of Overdosages *on page 2075*
Use Reverse muscle paralysis caused by toxic exposure to organophosphate anticholinesterase pesticides and chemicals; control of overdose of anticholinesterase medications used to treat myasthenia gravis (ambenonium, neostigmine, pyridostigmine)
Unlabeled/Investigational Use Treatment of nerve agent toxicity (chemical warfare) in combination with atropine
Pregnancy Risk Factor C
Lactation Excretion in breast milk unknown/not recommended
Medication Safety Issues
Sound-alike/look-alike issues:
Pralidoxime may be confused with pramoxine, pyridoxine
Protopam® may be confused with Proloprim®, protamine, Protropin®
Contraindications Hypersensitivity to pralidoxime or any component of the formulation; poisonings due to phosphorus, inorganic phosphates, or organic phosphates without anticholinesterase activity; poisonings due to pesticides or carbamate class (may increase toxicity of carbaryl)
Warnings/Precautions Use with caution in patients with myasthenia gravis; dosage modification required in patients with impaired renal function; use with caution in patients receiving theophylline, succinylcholine, phenothiazines, respiratory depressants (eg, narcotics, barbiturates)
Adverse Reactions Frequency not defined.
Cardiovascular: Tachycardia, hypertension
Central nervous system: Dizziness, headache, drowsiness
Dermatologic: Rash
Gastrointestinal: Nausea
Hepatic: Transient increases in ALT, AST
Local: Pain at injection site after I.M. administration
Neuromuscular & skeletal: Muscle rigidity, weakness
Ocular: Accommodation impaired, blurred vision, diplopia
Renal: Renal function decreased
Respiratory: Hyperventilation, laryngospasm
Overdosage/Toxicology Symptoms include blurred vision, nausea, tachycardia, and dizziness. Therapy is supportive. Mechanical ventilation may be required.
Drug Interactions
Increased Effect/Toxicity: Increased effect with barbiturates (potentiated). Use with aminophylline, morphine, theophylline, and succinylcholine is contraindicated. Use with reserpine and phenothiazines should be avoided in patients with organophosphate poisoning.
Decreased Effect: Atropine is often used concurrently with pralidoxime to blunt excessive cholinergic stimulation. However, the onset of atropine's effect may be unpredictable, and may occur earlier than anticipated, diminishing the therapeutic response to pralidoxime
Stability Store at controlled room temperature of 20°C to 25°C (68°F to 77°F). For I.V. administration, dilute 1 g with 20 mL SWI. Solution should be further diluted and administered as 1-2 g in 100 mL NS. If not practical or in cases of fluid overload, may prepare as a 5% solution.
Mechanism of Action Reactivates cholinesterase that had been inactivated by phosphorylation due to exposure to organophosphate pesticides by displacing the enzyme from its receptor sites; removes the phosphoryl group from the active site of the inactivated enzyme
Pharmacodynamics/Kinetics
Protein binding: None
Metabolism: Hepatic
Half-life elimination: 74-77 minutes
Time to peak, serum: I.V.: 5-15 minutes
Excretion: Urine (80% to 90% as metabolites and unchanged drug)
Dosage
Organic phosphorus poisoning (use in conjunction with atropine; atropine effects should be established before pralidoxime is administered): I.V. (may be given I.M. or SubQ if I.V. is not feasible):
Children: 20-50 mg/kg/dose; repeat in 1-2 hours if muscle weakness has not been relieved, then at 8- to 12-hour intervals if cholinergic signs recur
Adults: 1-2 g; repeat in 1 hour if muscle weakness has not been relieved, then at 8- to 12-hour intervals if cholinergic signs recur. When the poison has been ingested, continued absorption from the lower bowel may require additional doses; patients should be titrated as long as signs of poisoning recur; dosing may need repeated every 3-8 hours.
Treatment of acetylcholinesterase inhibitor toxicity: Adults: I.V.: Initial: 1-2 g followed by increments of 250 mg every 5 minutes until response is observed
Nerve agent toxicity management (unlabeled use): **Note:** Atropine is a component of the management of nerve agent toxicity; consult atropine monograph for specific route and dose. To be effective, pralidoxime must be administered within minutes to a few hours following exposure (depending on the nerve agent).
Infants and Children:
Prehospital ("in the field"): Mild-to-moderate symptoms: I.M.: 15 mg/kg; severe symptoms: 25 mg/kg
Hospital/emergency department: Mild-to-severe symptoms: I.V.: 15 mg/kg (up to 1 g)
(Continued)

Pralidoxime *(Continued)*

Adults:
Prehospital ("in the field"): Mild-to-moderate symptoms: I.M.: 600 mg; severe symptoms: 1800 mg
Hospital/emergency department: Mild-to-severe symptoms: I.V.: 15 mg/kg (up to 1 g)
Frail patients, elderly:
Prehospital ("in the field"): Mild-to-moderate symptoms: I.M.: 10 mg/kg; severe symptoms: 25 mg/kg
Hospital/emergency department: Mild-to-severe symptoms: I.V.: 5-10 mg/kg
Elderly: Refer to Adults dosing; dosing should be cautious, considering possibility of decreased hepatic, renal, or cardiac function
Dosing adjustment in renal impairment: Dose should be reduced
Administration I.V.: Infuse over 15-30 minutes at a rate not to exceed 200 mg/minute; may administer I.M. or SubQ if I.V. is not accessible. If a more concentrated 5% solution is used, infuse over at least 5 minutes.
Monitoring Parameters Heart rate, respiratory rate, blood pressure, continuous ECG; cardiac monitor and blood pressure monitor required for I.V. administration
Reference Range Minimum therapeutic concentration: 4 mcg/mL
Additional Information Pralidoxime is most effective when given immediately after poisoning. If the poison has been ingested, exposure may continue due to slow absorption from the lower bowel; relapses may occur after initial improvement and treatment may need continued for several days in these patients. In cases of dermal exposure to organophosphate poisoning, clothing should be removed and hair and skin washed with sodium bicarbonate or alcohol as soon as possible.
Dosage Forms Injection, powder for reconstitution, as chloride: 1 g

◆ **Pralidoxime Chloride** see Pralidoxime on page 1405

Pramipexole *(pra mi PEKS ole)*

U.S. Brand Names Mirapex®
Canadian Brand Names Mirapex®
Pharmacologic Category Anti-Parkinson's Agent, Dopamine Agonist
Additional Appendix Information
Parkinson's Agents *on page 1895*
Use Treatment of the signs and symptoms of idiopathic Parkinson's disease; treatment of moderate-to-severe primary Restless Legs Syndrome (RLS)
Unlabeled/Investigational Use Treatment of depression
Pregnancy Risk Factor C
Pregnancy Implications Early embryonic loss and postnatal growth inhibition were observed in animal studies. There are no adequate and well-controlled studies in pregnant women.
Lactation Excretion in breast milk unknown/not recommended
Medication Safety Issues
Sound-alike/look-alike issues:
Mirapex® may be confused with Mifeprex®, MiraLax™
Contraindications Hypersensitivity to pramipexole or any component of the formulation
Warnings/Precautions Caution should be taken in patients with renal insufficiency; dose adjustment necessary. Caution in patients with pre-existing dyskinesias; may be exacerbated. May cause orthostatic hypotension; Parkinson's disease patients appear to have an impaired capacity to respond to a postural challenge. Use with caution in patients at risk of hypotension or where transient hypotensive episodes would be poorly tolerated. Parkinson's patients being treated with dopaminergic agonists ordinarily require careful monitoring for signs and symptoms of postural hypotension, especially during dose escalation. May cause hallucinations.

Other dopaminergic agents have been associated with a syndrome resembling neuroleptic malignant syndrome on withdrawal or significant dosage reduction after long-term use. Ergot-derived dopamine agonists have also been associated with fibrotic complications (eg, retroperitoneal fibrosis, pleural thickening, and pulmonary infiltrates). There have been postmarketing reports of possible fibrotic complications with pramipexole.

Pramipexole has been associated with somnolence, particularly at higher dosages (>1.5 mg/day). In addition, patients have been reported to fall asleep during activities of daily living, including driving, while taking this medication. Whether these patients exhibited somnolence prior to these events is not clear. Patients should be advised of this issue and factors which may increase risk (sleep disorders, other sedating medications, or concomitant medications which increase pramipexole concentrations) and instructed to report daytime somnolence or sleepiness to the prescriber. Patients should use caution in performing activities which require alertness (driving or operating machinery), and to avoid other medications which may cause CNS depression, including ethanol.

Augmentation (earlier onset of symptoms in the evening/afternoon, increase and/or spread of symptoms to other extremities) or rebound (shifting of symptoms to early morning hours) may occur in some RLS patients.
Adverse Reactions Parkinson's disease (PD) unless identified as RLS:
>10%:
Cardiovascular: Postural hypotension (dose related; PD 53%)
Central nervous system: Dizziness (PD 25%), headache (RLS 16%), somnolence (dose related; RLS 6%; PD 9% to 22%), insomnia (RLS 13%; PD 17% to 27%), hallucinations (PD 9% to 17%), abnormal dreams (RLS up to 8%)
Gastrointestinal: Nausea (dose related; RLS: 5% to 27%; PD 28%), constipation (dose related; RLS: 4%; PD 10% to 14%)
Neuromuscular & skeletal: Weakness (PD 10% to 14%), dyskinesia (PD 47%), EPS
1% to 10%:
Cardiovascular: Edema, syncope, tachycardia, chest pain

Central nervous system: Malaise, confusion (PD 4% to 10%), amnesia (dose related), dystonias, akathisia, thinking abnormalities, myoclonus, hyperesthesia, paranoia, fever

Endocrine & metabolic: Decreased libido

Gastrointestinal: Anorexia, diarrhea (RLS 3% to7%), dysphagia, weight loss, xerostomia (up to 7%)

Genitourinary: Urinary frequency (PD 6%), impotence, urinary incontinence

Neuromuscular & skeletal: Muscle twitching, leg cramps, arthritis, bursitis, myasthenia, gait abnormalities, hypertonia

Ocular: Vision abnormalities

Respiratory: Dyspnea, nasal congestion (RLS up to 6%), rhinitis

Miscellaneous: Influenza (RLS 3%)

<1% (Limited to important or life-threatening): Augmentation (RLS ~20% but similar to placebo), compulsive gambling, liver transaminases increased, rebound (RLS), rhabdomyolysis, tolerance (RLS)

Frequency not defined, dose related: Falling asleep during activities of daily living

Drug Interactions

Increased Effect/Toxicity: Cimetidine may increase level/effects of pramipexole. CNS depressants may enhance the adverse/toxic effect of pramipexole.

Decreased Effect: Dopamine antagonists (antipsychotics, metoclopramide) may decrease the efficiency of pramipexole.

Ethanol/Nutrition/Herb Interactions

Ethanol: Avoid ethanol (may increase CNS depression).

Food: Food intake does not affect the extent of drug absorption, although the time to maximal plasma concentration is delayed by 60 minutes when taken with a meal.

Herb/Nutraceutical: Avoid valerian, St John's wort, SAMe, kava kava (may increase risk of serotonin syndrome and/or excessive sedation).

Stability Store at 15°C to 30°C (59°F to 86°F). Protect from light.

Mechanism of Action Pramipexole is a nonergot dopamine agonist with specificity for the D_2 subfamily dopamine receptor, and has also been shown to bind to D_3 and D_4 receptors. By binding to these receptors, it is thought that pramipexole can stimulate dopamine activity on the nerves of the striatum and substantia nigra.

Pharmacodynamics/Kinetics

Absorption: Rapid

Distribution: V_d: 500 L

Protein binding: 15%

Bioavailability: >90%

Half-life elimination: ~8 hours; Elderly: 12-14 hours

Time to peak, serum: ~2 hours

Excretion: Urine (90% as unchanged drug)

Dosage Oral: Adults:

Parkinson's disease: Initial: 0.375 mg/day given in 3 divided doses, increase gradually by 0.125 mg/dose every 5-7 days; range: 1.5-4.5 mg/day

Restless legs syndrome: Initial: 0.125 mg once daily 2-3 hours before bedtime. Dose may be doubled every 4-7 days up to 0.5 mg/day. Maximum dose: 0.5 mg/day (manufacturer's recommendation).

Note: Most patients require <0.5 mg/day, but higher doses have been used (2 mg/day). If augmentation occurs, dose earlier in the day.

Dosage adjustment in renal impairment: Parkinson's disease:

Cl_{cr} 35-59 mL/minute: Initial: 0.125 mg twice daily (maximum dose: 1.5 mg twice daily)

Cl_{cr} 15-34 mL/minute: Initial: 0.125 mg once daily (maximum dose: 1.5 mg once daily)

Cl_{cr} <15 mL/minute (or hemodialysis patients): Not adequately studied

Dietary Considerations May be taken with food to decrease nausea.

Administration Doses should be titrated gradually in all patients to avoid the onset of intolerable side effects. The dosage should be increased to achieve a maximum therapeutic effect, balanced against the side effects of dyskinesia, hallucinations, somnolence, and dry mouth.

Monitoring Parameters Monitor for improvement in symptoms of Parkinson's disease (eg, mentation, behavior, daily living activities, motor examinations), blood pressure, body weight changes, and heart rate

Dosage Forms

Tablet, as dihydrochloride monohydrate:

Mirapex®: 0.125 mg, 0.25 mg, 0.5 mg, 1 mg, 1.5 mg

Pramlintide (PRAM lin tide)

U.S. Brand Names Symlin®

Index Terms Pramlintide Acetate

Pharmacologic Category Amylinomimetic; Antidiabetic Agent

Use

Adjunctive treatment with mealtime insulin in type 1 diabetes mellitus (insulin dependent, IDDM) patients who have failed to achieve desired glucose control despite optimal insulin therapy

Adjunctive treatment with mealtime insulin in type 2 diabetes mellitus (noninsulin dependent, NIDDM) patients who have failed to achieve desired glucose control despite optimal insulin therapy, with or without concurrent sulfonylurea and/or metformin

Restrictions An FDA-approved medication guide must be distributed when dispensing an outpatient prescription (new or refill) where this medication is to be used without direct supervision of a healthcare provider. Medication guides are available at http://www.fda.gov/cder/Offices/ODS/medication_guides.htm.

Pregnancy Risk Factor C

Pregnancy Implications Congenital abnormalities have been observed in animal studies. There are no adequate and well-controlled studies in pregnant women. Use only if potential benefit outweighs potential risk.

Lactation Excretion in breast milk unknown/use caution

(Continued)

Pramlintide (Continued)

Medication Safety Issues

Dosing: The concentration of this product is 600 micrograms (mcg)/mL. Manufacturer recommended dosing ranges from 15 mcg to 120 mcg, which corresponds to injectable volumes of 0.025 mL to 0.2 mL. Patients and healthcare providers should exercise caution when administering this product to avoid inadvertent calculation of the dose based on "units," which could result in a sixfold overdose.

Contraindications Hypersensitivity to pramlintide or any component of the formulation; confirmed diagnosis of gastroparesis; hypoglycemia unawareness

Warnings/Precautions [U.S. Boxed Warning]: Coadministration with insulin may induce severe hypoglycemia (usually within 3 hours following administration); coadministration with insulin therapy is an approved indication but does require an initial dosage reduction of insulin and frequent pre and post blood glucose monitoring to reduce risk of severe hypoglycemia. Concurrent use of other glucose-lowering agents may increase risk of hypoglycemia. Avoid use in patients with poor compliance with their insulin regimen and/or blood glucose monitoring. Do not use in patients with Hb A$_{1c}$ levels >9% or recent, recurrent episodes of hypoglycemia; obtain detailed history of glucose control (eg, Hb A$_{1c}$, incidence of hypoglycemia, glucose monitoring, and medication compliance) and body weight before initiating therapy. Use caution when driving or operating heavy machinery until effects on blood sugar are known. Use caution with certain antihypertensive agents (eg, beta adrenergic blockers) or neuropathic conditions which may mask signs/symptoms of hypoglycemia. Use caution in patients with history of nausea; avoid use in patients with conditions or concurrent medications likely to impair gastric motility (eg, anticholinergics); do not use in patients requiring medication(s) to stimulate gastric emptying. Safety and efficacy in pediatric patients have not been established.

Adverse Reactions

>10%:
  Central nervous system: Headache (5% to 13%)
  Gastrointestinal: Nausea (28% to 48%), vomiting (7% to 11%), anorexia (<1% to 17%)
  Endocrine & metabolic: Severe hypoglycemia (type 1 diabetes: <1% to 17%)
  Miscellaneous: Inflicted injury (8% to 14%)
1% to 10%:
  Central nervous system: Fatigue (3% to 7%), dizziness (2% to 6%)
  Endocrine & metabolic: Severe hypoglycemia (type 2 diabetes: <1% to 8%)
  Gastrointestinal: Abdominal pain (2% to 8%)
  Respiratory: Pharyngitis (3% to 5%), cough (2% to 6%)
  Neuromuscular & skeletal: Arthralgia (2% to 7%)
  Miscellaneous: Allergic reaction (<1% to 6%)

Overdosage/Toxicology Severe nausea and vomiting likely to occur, possibly accompanied by diarrhea, vasodilatation and dizziness. Treatment should be symptom-directed and supportive.

Drug Interactions

Increased Effect/Toxicity: Medications which may induce or exacerbate hypoglycemia include ACE inhibitors, alcohol, alpha-blockers, anabolic steroids, beta-blockers, clofibrate, clonidine, disopyramide, fenfluramine, fibrates, fluoxetine, guanethidine, MAO inhibitors, pentamidine, pentoxifylline, phenylbutazone, propoxyphene, reserpine, salicylates, sulfinpyrazone, sulfonamides, and tetracyclines. Nonselective beta-blockers may delay recovery from hypoglycemic episodes and mask signs/symptoms of hypoglycemia. Anticholinergic agents may cause synergistic impairment of gastric motility.

Decreased Effect: Pramlintide may delay absorption of concomitantly administered medication due to increased gastric emptying time; coadministration with agents in which a rapid onset of action is desired (eg, analgesics) may delay drug response.

Ethanol/Nutrition/Herb Interactions

Ethanol: Use caution with ethanol (may increase hypoglycemia).

Herb/Nutraceutical: Use caution with garlic, chromium, gymnema (may increase hypoglycemia).

Stability Store unopened vials at 2°C to 8°C (36°F to 46°F); do not freeze. Opened vials may be kept refrigerated or at room temperature ≤25°C (≤77°F). Discard opened vial after 28 days. Protect from light.

Mechanism of Action Synthetic analog of human amylin cosecreted with insulin by pancreatic beta cells; reduces postprandial glucose increases via the following mechanisms: 1) prolongation of gastric emptying time, 2) reduction of postprandial glucagon secretion, and 3) reduction of caloric intake through centrally-mediated appetite suppression

Pharmacodynamics/Kinetics

Duration: 3 hours
Protein binding: 60%
Metabolism: Primarily renal to des-lys^1 pramlintide (active metabolite)
Bioavailability: 30% to 40%
Half-life elimination: 48 minutes
Time to peak, plasma: 20 minutes
Excretion: Primarily urine

Dosage SubQ: Adults: **Note:** When initiating pramlintide, reduce current insulin dose (including rapidly- and mixed-acting preparations) by 50% to avoid hypoglycemia.

Type 1 diabetes mellitus (insulin dependent, IDDM): Initial: 15 mcg immediately prior to meals; titrate in 15 mcg increments every 3 days (if no significant nausea occurs) to target dose of 30-60 mcg (consider discontinuation if intolerant of 30 mcg dose)

Type 2 diabetes mellitus (noninsulin dependent, NIDDM): Initial: 60 mcg immediately prior to meals; after 3-7 days, increase to 120 mcg prior to meals if no significant nausea occurs (if nausea occurs at 120 mcg dose, reduce to 60 mcg)

If pramlintide is discontinued for any reason, restart therapy with same initial titration protocol.

Dosage adjustment in renal impairment: No dosage adjustment required; not evaluated in dialysis patients

Dietary Considerations Dietary modification based on ADA recommendations is a part of therapy; pramlintide to be administered prior to major meals consisting of ≥250 Kcal or ≥30 g carbohydrates

Administration Do not mix with other insulins; administer subcutaneously into abdominal or thigh areas at sites distinct from concomitant insulin injections (do not administer into arm due to variable absorption); rotate injection sites frequently. For oral medications in which a rapid onset of action is desired, administer 1 hour before, or 2 hours after pramlintide, if possible.

Monitoring Parameters Prior to initiating therapy: Hb A_{1c}, hypoglycemic history, body weight. During therapy: urine sugar and acetone, pre- and postprandial and bedtime serum glucose, electrolytes, Hb A_{1c}, lipid profile

Dosage Forms Injection, solution: Pramlintide acetate 0.6 mg/mL (5 mL) [contains phenol-derivative metacresol]

♦ **Pramlintide Acetate** see Pramlintide on page 1407

♦ **Pramosone**® see Pramoxine and Hydrocortisone on page 1409

♦ **Pramox**® **HC (Can)** see Pramoxine and Hydrocortisone on page 1409

Pramoxine and Hydrocortisone (pra MOKS een & hye droe KOH ti sone)

U.S. Brand Names Analpram-HC®; Enzone®; Epifoam®; Pramosone®; ProctoFoam®-HC; Zone-A®; Zone-A Forte®

Canadian Brand Names Pramox® HC; Proctofoam™-HC

Index Terms Hydrocortisone and Pramoxine

Pharmacologic Category Anesthetic/Corticosteroid

Use Relief of inflammatory and pruritic manifestations of corticosteroid-responsive dermatoses

Pregnancy Risk Factor C

Medication Safety Issues

Sound-alike/look-alike issues:

Pramosone® may be confused with predniSONE

Zone-A Forte® may be confused with Zonalon®

Dosage Topical/rectal: Apply to affected areas 3-4 times/day

Additional Information Complete prescribing information for this medication should be consulted for additional detail.

Dosage Forms

Cream, topical:

Analpram-HC®: Pramoxine hydrochloride 1% and hydrocortisone acetate 1% (30 g); pramoxine hydrochloride 1% and hydrocortisone acetate 2.5% (30 g)

Enzone®: Pramoxine hydrochloride 1% and hydrocortisone acetate 1% (30 g)

Pramosone®: Pramoxine hydrochloride 1% and hydrocortisone acetate 1% (30 g, 60 g); pramoxine hydrochloride 1% and hydrocortisone acetate 2.5% (30 g, 60 g)

Foam, rectal (ProctoFoam®-HC): Pramoxine hydrochloride 1% and hydrocortisone acetate 1% (10 g)

Foam, topical (Epifoam®): Pramoxine hydrochloride 1% and hydrocortisone acetate 1% (10 g)

Lotion, topical:

Analpram-HC®: Pramoxine hydrochloride 1% and hydrocortisone 2.5% (60 mL)

Pramosone®: Pramoxine hydrochloride 1% and hydrocortisone 1% (60 mL, 120 mL, 240 mL); pramoxine hydrochloride 1% and hydrocortisone 2.5% (60 mL, 120 mL)

Zone-A®: Pramoxine hydrochloride 1% and hydrocortisone 1% (60 mL)

Zone-A Forte®: Pramoxine hydrochloride 1% and hydrocortisone 2.5% (60 mL)

Ointment, topical (Pramosone®): Pramoxine hydrochloride 1% and hydrocortisone 1% (30 g); pramoxine hydrochloride 1% and hydrocortisone 2.5% (30 g)

♦ **Prandase**® **(Can)** see Acarbose on page 25

♦ **Prandin**® see Repaglinide on page 1494

♦ **Pravachol**® see Pravastatin on page 1409

♦ **PravASA (Can)** see Aspirin and Pravastatin on page 164

Pravastatin (prav a STAT in)

U.S. Brand Names Pravachol®

Canadian Brand Names Apo-Pravastatin®; CO Pravastatin; Novo-Pravastatin; PMS-Pravastatin; Pravachol®; ratio-Pravastatin; Riva-Pravastatin; Sandoz-Pravastatin

Index Terms Pravastatin Sodium

Pharmacologic Category Antilipemic Agent, HMG-CoA Reductase Inhibitor

Additional Appendix Information

Hyperlipidemia Management on page 2058

Lipid-Lowering Agents on page 1887

Use Use with dietary therapy for the following:

Primary prevention of coronary events: In hypercholesterolemic patients without established coronary heart disease to reduce cardiovascular morbidity (myocardial infarction, coronary revascularization procedures) and mortality.

Secondary prevention of cardiovascular events in patients with established coronary heart disease: To slow the progression of coronary atherosclerosis; to reduce cardiovascular morbidity (myocardial infarction, coronary vascular procedures) and to reduce mortality; to reduce the risk of stroke and transient ischemic attacks

Hyperlipidemias: Reduce elevations in total cholesterol, LDL-C, apolipoprotein B, and triglycerides (elevations of 1 or more components are present in Fredrickson type IIa, IIb, III, and IV hyperlipidemias)

Heterozygous familial hypercholesterolemia (HeFH): In pediatric patients, 8-18 years of age, with HeFH having LDL-C ≥190 mg/dL or LDL ≥160 mg/dL with positive family

(Continued)

Pravastatin *(Continued)*

history of premature cardiovascular disease (CVD) or 2 or more CVD risk factors in the pediatric patient

Pregnancy Risk Factor X

Pregnancy Implications Cholesterol biosynthesis may be important in fetal development. Contraindicated in pregnancy. Administer to women of childbearing potential only when conception is highly unlikely and patients have been informed of potential hazards.

Lactation Enters breast milk/contraindicated

Medication Safety Issues

Sound-alike/look-alike issues:

Pravachol® may be confused with Prevacid®, Prinivil®, propranolol

Contraindications Hypersensitivity to pravastatin or any component of the formulation; active liver disease; unexplained persistent elevations of serum transaminases; pregnancy; breast-feeding

Warnings/Precautions Secondary causes of hyperlipidemia should be ruled out prior to therapy. Liver function must be monitored by periodic laboratory assessment. Rhabdomyolysis with acute renal failure has occurred. Risk may be increased with concurrent use of other drugs which may cause rhabdomyolysis (including gemfibrozil, fibric acid derivatives, or niacin at doses ≥1 g/day). Temporarily discontinue in any patient experiencing an acute or serious condition predisposing to renal failure secondary to rhabdomyolysis. Use with caution in patients with advanced age, these patients are predisposed to myopathy. Use caution in patients with previous liver disease or heavy ethanol use. Treatment in patients <8 years of age is not recommended.

Adverse Reactions As reported in short-term trials; safety and tolerability with long-term use were similar to placebo

1% to 10%:

Cardiovascular: Chest pain (4%)

Central nervous system: Headache (2% to 6%), fatigue (4%), dizziness (1% to 3%)

Dermatologic: Rash (4%)

Gastrointestinal: Nausea/vomiting (7%), diarrhea (6%), heartburn (3%)

Hepatic: Transaminases increased (>3x normal on two occasions - 1%)

Neuromuscular & skeletal: Myalgia (2%)

Respiratory: Cough (3%)

Miscellaneous: Influenza (2%)

<1% (Limited to important or life-threatening): Allergy, lens opacity, libido change, memory impairment, muscle weakness, neuropathy, paresthesia, taste disturbance, tremor, vertigo

Postmarketing and/or case reports: Anaphylaxis, angioedema, cholestatic jaundice, cirrhosis, cranial nerve dysfunction, dermatomyositis, erythema multiforme, ESR increase, fulminant hepatic necrosis, gynecomastia, hemolytic anemia, hepatitis, hepatoma, lupus erythematosus-like syndrome, myopathy, pancreatitis, peripheral nerve palsy, polymyalgia rheumatica, positive ANA, purpura, rhabdomyolysis, Stevens-Johnson syndrome, vasculitis

Additional class-related events or case reports (not necessarily reported with pravastatin therapy): Angioedema, cataracts, depression, dyspnea, eosinophilia, erectile dysfunction, facial paresis, hypersensitivity reaction, impaired extraocular muscle movement, impotence, leukopenia, malaise, memory loss, ophthalmoplegia, paresthesia, peripheral neuropathy, photosensitivity, psychic disturbance, skin discoloration, thrombocytopenia, thyroid dysfunction, toxic epidermal necrolysis, transaminases increased, vomiting

Overdosage/Toxicology Treatment is symptomatic.

Drug Interactions

Cytochrome P450 Effect: Substrate of CYP3A4 (minor); **Inhibits** CYP2C9 (weak), 2D6 (weak), 3A4 (weak)

Increased Effect/Toxicity: Clofibrate, cyclosporine, fenofibrate, gemfibrozil, and niacin may increase the risk of myopathy and rhabdomyolysis. Imidazole antifungals (itraconazole, ketoconazole), P-glycoprotein inhibitors may increase pravastatin concentrations.

Decreased Effect: Concurrent administration of cholestyramine or colestipol can decrease pravastatin absorption.

Ethanol/Nutrition/Herb Interactions

Ethanol: Consumption of large amounts of ethanol may increase the risk of liver damage with HMG-CoA reductase inhibitors.

Food: Red yeast rice contains an estimated 2.4 mg lovastatin per 600 mg rice.

Herb/Nutraceutical: St John's wort may decrease pravastatin levels.

Stability Store at 25°C (77°F); excursions permitted to 15°C to 30°C (59°F to 86°F). Protect from moisture and light.

Mechanism of Action Pravastatin is a competitive inhibitor of 3-hydroxy-3-methylglutaryl coenzyme A (HMG-CoA) reductase, which is the rate-limiting enzyme involved in *de novo* cholesterol synthesis.

Pharmacodynamics/Kinetics

Onset of action: Several days

Peak effect: 4 weeks

Absorption: Rapidly absorbed; average absorption 34%

Protein binding: 50%

Metabolism: Hepatic to at least two metabolites

Bioavailability: 17%

Half-life elimination: ~2-3 hours

Time to peak, serum: 1-1.5 hours

Excretion: Feces (70%); urine (≤20%, 8% as unchanged drug)

Dosage Oral: **Note:** Doses should be individualized according to the baseline LDL-cholesterol levels, the recommended goal of therapy, and patient response; adjustments should be made at intervals of 4 weeks or more; doses may need adjusted based on concomitant medications

Children: HeFH:

8-13 years: 20 mg/day

14-18 years: 40 mg/day

Dosage adjustment for pravastatin based on concomitant immunosuppressants (ie, cyclosporine): Refer to Adults dosing section

Adults: Hyperlipidemias, primary prevention of coronary events, secondary prevention of cardiovascular events: Initial: 40 mg once daily; titrate dosage to response; usual range: 10-80 mg; (maximum dose: 80 mg once daily)

Dosage adjustment for pravastatin based on concomitant immunosuppressants (ie, cyclosporine): Initial: 10 mg/day, titrate with caution (maximum dose: 20 mg/day)

Elderly: No specific dosage recommendations. Clearance is reduced in the elderly, resulting in an increase in AUC between 25% to 50%. However, substantial accumulation is not expected.

Dosing adjustment in renal impairment: Initial: 10 mg/day

Dosing adjustment in hepatic impairment: Initial: 10 mg/day

Dietary Considerations May be taken without regard to meals. Before initiation of therapy, patients should be placed on a standard cholesterol-lowering diet for 6 weeks and the diet should be continued during drug therapy. Red yeast rice contains an estimated 2.4 mg lovastatin per 600 mg rice.

Administration May be taken without regard to meals.

Monitoring Parameters Obtain baseline LFTs and total cholesterol profile; creatine phosphokinase due to possibility of myopathy. Repeat LFTs prior to elevation of dose. May be measured when clinically indicated and/or periodically thereafter.

Dosage Forms

Tablet, as sodium: 10 mg, 20 mg, 40 mg
  Pravachol®: 10 mg, 20 mg, 40 mg, 80 mg

♦ **Pravastatin and Aspirin** see Aspirin and Pravastatin on page 164
♦ **Pravastatin Sodium** see Pravastatin on page 1409
♦ **Pravigard™ PAC [DSC]** see Aspirin and Pravastatin on page 164

Praziquantel (pray zi KWON tel)

U.S. Brand Names Biltricide®
Canadian Brand Names Biltricide®
Pharmacologic Category Anthelmintic
Use All stages of schistosomiasis caused by all *Schistosoma* species pathogenic to humans; clonorchiasis and opisthorchiasis
Unlabeled/Investigational Use Cysticercosis and many intestinal tapeworms
Pregnancy Risk Factor B
Lactation Enters breast milk
Contraindications Hypersensitivity to praziquantel or any component of the formulation; ocular cysticercosis
Warnings/Precautions Use caution in patients with severe hepatic disease; patients with cerebral cysticercosis require hospitalization
Adverse Reactions
1% to 10%:
  Central nervous system: Dizziness, drowsiness, headache, malaise, CSF reaction syndrome in patients being treated for neurocysticercosis
  Gastrointestinal: Abdominal pain, loss of appetite, nausea, vomiting
  Miscellaneous: Diaphoresis
<1% (Limited to important or life-threatening): Diarrhea, fever, itching, rash, urticaria
Overdosage/Toxicology Symptoms include dizziness, drowsiness, headache, and liver function impairment. Treatment is supportive following GI decontamination. Administer fast-acting laxative.
Drug Interactions
Cytochrome P450 Effect: Inhibits CYP2D6 (weak)
Mechanism of Action Increases the cell permeability to calcium in schistosomes, causing strong contractions and paralysis of worm musculature leading to detachment of suckers from the blood vessel walls and to dislodgment
Pharmacodynamics/Kinetics
Absorption: Oral: ~80%
Distribution: CSF concentration is 14% to 20% of plasma concentration; enters breast milk
Protein binding: ~80%
Metabolism: Extensive first-pass effect
Half-life elimination: Parent drug: 0.8-1.5 hours; Metabolites. 4.5 hours
Time to peak, serum: 1-3 hours
Excretion: Urine (99% as metabolites)
Dosage Children >4 years and Adults: Oral:
Schistosomiasis: 20 mg/kg/dose 2-3 times/day for 1 day at 4- to 6-hour intervals
Flukes (unlabeled use): 25 mg/kg/dose every 8 hours for 1-2 days
Cysticercosis (unlabeled use): 50 mg/kg/day divided every 8 hours for 14 days
Tapeworms (unlabeled use): 10-20 mg/kg as a single dose (25 mg/kg for *Hymenolepis nana*)
Clonorchiasis/opisthorchiasis: 3 doses of 25 mg/kg as a 1-day treatment
Dosage Forms Tablet [tri-scored]: 600 mg

Prazosin (PRAZ oh sin)

U.S. Brand Names Minipress®
Canadian Brand Names Apo-Prazo®; Minipress™; Novo-Prazin; Nu-Prazo
Index Terms Furazosin; Prazosin Hydrochloride
Pharmacologic Category Alpha₁ Blocker
Use Treatment of hypertension
Unlabeled/Investigational Use Benign prostatic hyperplasia; Raynaud's syndrome
Pregnancy Risk Factor C
(Continued)

Prazosin *(Continued)*

Lactation Excretion in breast milk unknown/use caution

Medication Safety Issues

Sound-alike/look-alike issues:

Prazosin may be confused with predniSONE

International issues:

Prazac® [Denmark] may be confused with Prozac® which is a brand name for fluoxetine in the U.S.

Prazepam [multiple international markets] may be confused with prazosin.

Contraindications Hypersensitivity to quinazolines (doxazosin, prazosin, terazosin) or any component of the formulation; concurrent use with phosphodiesterase-5 (PDE-5) inhibitors including sildenafil (>25 mg), tadalafil, or vardenafil

Warnings/Precautions May cause significant orthostatic hypotension and syncope, especially with first dose; anticipate a similar effect if therapy is interrupted for a few days, if dosage is rapidly increased, or if another antihypertensive drug (particularly vasodilators) or a PDE5 inhibitor is introduced. Patients should be cautioned about performing hazardous tasks when starting new therapy or adjusting dosage upward. Discontinue if symptoms of angina occur or worsen. Should rule out prostatic carcinoma before beginning therapy. Safety and efficacy have not been established in children.

Adverse Reactions

>10%: Central nervous system: Dizziness (10%)

1% to 10%:

Cardiovascular: Palpitations (5%), edema, orthostatic hypotension, syncope (1%)

Central nervous system: Headache (8%), drowsiness (8%), vertigo, depression, nervousness

Dermatologic: Rash (1% to 4%)

Endocrine & metabolic: Decreased energy (7%)

Gastrointestinal: Nausea (5%), vomiting, diarrhea, constipation

Genitourinary: Urinary frequency (1% to 5%)

Neuromuscular & skeletal: Weakness (7%)

Ocular: Blurred vision, reddened sclera, xerostomia

Respiratory: Dyspnea, epistaxis, nasal congestion

<1% (Limited to important or life-threatening): Allergic reaction, alopecia, angina, cataplexy, cataracts (both development and disappearance have been reported), hallucinations, impotence, leukopenia, lichen planus, MI, narcolepsy (worsened), pancreatitis, paresthesia, pigmentary mottling and serous retinopathy, priapism, pruritus, systemic lupus erythematosus, tinnitus, urticaria, vasculitis

Overdosage/Toxicology Symptoms include hypotension and drowsiness. Hypotension usually responds to I.V. fluids, Trendelenburg positioning, or vasoconstrictors. Treatment is otherwise supportive and symptomatic.

Drug Interactions

Increased Effect/Toxicity: Prazosin's hypotensive effect may be increased with beta-blockers, diuretics, ACE inhibitors, calcium channel blockers, other antihypertensive medications, sildenafil (use with extreme caution at a dose ≤25 mg), tadalafil (use is contraindicated by the manufacturer), and vardenafil (use is contraindicated by the manufacturer). Concurrent use with tricyclic antidepressants (TCAs) and low-potency antipsychotics may increase risk of orthostasis.

Decreased Effect: Decreased antihypertensive effect if taken with NSAIDs.

Ethanol/Nutrition/Herb Interactions

Ethanol: Avoid ethanol (may increase vasodilation).

Food: Food has variable effects on absorption.

Herb/Nutraceutical: Avoid dong quai if using for hypertension (has estrogenic activity). Avoid ephedra, yohimbe, ginseng (may worsen hypertension). Avoid saw palmetto (due to limited experience with this combination). Avoid garlic (may have increased antihypertensive effect).

Stability Store in airtight container. Protect from light.

Mechanism of Action Competitively inhibits postsynaptic alpha-adrenergic receptors which results in vasodilation of veins and arterioles and a decrease in total peripheral resistance and blood pressure

Pharmacodynamics/Kinetics

Onset of action: BP reduction: ~2 hours

Maximum decrease: 2-4 hours

Duration: 10-24 hours

Distribution: Hypertensive adults: V_d: 0.5 L/kg

Protein binding: 92% to 97%

Metabolism: Extensively hepatic

Bioavailability: 43% to 82%

Half-life elimination: 2-4 hours; prolonged with congestive heart failure

Excretion: Urine (6% to 10% as unchanged drug)

Dosage Oral:

Children: Initial: 5 mcg/kg/dose (to assess hypotensive effects); usual dosing interval: every 6 hours; increase dosage gradually up to maximum of 25 mcg/kg/dose every 6 hours

Adults:

Hypertension: Initial: 1 mg/dose 2-3 times/day; usual maintenance dose: 3-15 mg/day in divided doses 2-4 times/day; maximum daily dose: 20 mg

Hypertensive urgency: 10-20 mg once, may repeat in 30 minutes

Raynaud's (unlabeled use): 0.5-3 mg twice daily

Benign prostatic hyperplasia (unlabeled use): 2 mg twice daily

Monitoring Parameters Blood pressure, standing and sitting/supine

Test Interactions Increased urinary VMA 17%, norepinephrine metabolite 42%

Dosage Forms Capsule, as hydrochloride: 1 mg, 2 mg, 5 mg

Prazosin and Polythiazide (PRAZ oh sin & pol i THYE a zide)

U.S. Brand Names Minizide® [DSC]
Index Terms Polythiazide and Prazosin
Pharmacologic Category Antihypertensive Agent, Combination
Use Management of mild-to-moderate hypertension
Pregnancy Risk Factor C
Medication Safety Issues
Sound-alike/look-alike issues:
Minizide® may be confused with Minocin®
Dosage Hypertension: Adults: Oral: Initial: One capsule 2-3 times/day. Maintenance: May be slowly increased to a total daily prazosin dose of 20 mg; polythiazide dose is 1-4 mg/day.
Additional Information Complete prescribing information for this medication should be consulted for additional detail.
Dosage Forms [DSC] = Discontinued product
Capsule:
Minizide® 1: Prazosin 1 mg and polythiazide 0.5 mg [DSC]
Minizide® 2: Prazosin 2 mg and polythiazide 0.5 mg [DSC]
Minizide® 5: Prazosin 5 mg and polythiazide 0.5 mg [DSC]

♦ **Prazosin Hydrochloride** see Prazosin on page 1411
♦ **Precedex™** see Dexmedetomidine on page 483
♦ **Precose®** see Acarbose on page 25
♦ **Pred Forte®** see PrednisoLONE on page 1413
♦ **Pred-G®** see Prednisolone and Gentamicin on page 1416
♦ **Pred Mild®** see PrednisoLONE on page 1413

Prednicarbate (pred ni KAR bate)

U.S. Brand Names Dermatop®
Canadian Brand Names Dermatop®
Pharmacologic Category Corticosteroid, Topical
Additional Appendix Information
Corticosteroids on page 1879
Use Relief of the inflammatory and pruritic manifestations of corticosteroid-responsive dermatoses (medium potency topical corticosteroid)
Pregnancy Risk Factor C
Medication Safety Issues
Sound-alike/look-alike issues:
Dermatop® may be confused with Dimetapp®
Dosage Adults: Topical: Apply a thin film to affected area twice daily. Therapy should be discontinued when control is achieved; if no improvement is seen, reassessment of diagnosis may be necessary.
Additional Information Has been shown that the atrophic activity of prednicarbate is many times less than agents with similar clinical potency, nevertheless, avoid use on the face.
Dosage Forms
Cream: 0.1% (15 g, 60 g)
Dermatop®: 0.1% (15 g, 60 g)
Ointment:
Dermatop®: 0.1% (15 g, 60 g)

PrednisoLONE (pred NISS oh lone)

U.S. Brand Names Econopred® Plus; Orapred®; Orapred ODT™; Pediapred®; Pred Forte®; Pred Mild®; Prelone®
Canadian Brand Names Diopred®; Hydeltra T.B.A.®; Inflamase® Mild; Novo-Prednisolone; Ophtho-Tate®; Pediapred®; Pred Forte®; Pred Mild®; Sab-Prenase
Index Terms Deltahydrocortisone; Metacortandralone; Prednisolone Acetate; Prednisolone Acetate, Ophthalmic; Prednisolone Sodium Phosphate; Prednisolone Sodium Phosphate, Ophthalmic
Pharmacologic Category Corticosteroid, Ophthalmic; Corticosteroid, Systemic
Additional Appendix Information
Corticosteroids on page 1879
Use Treatment of palpebral and bulbar conjunctivitis; corneal injury from chemical, radiation, thermal burns, or foreign body penetration; endocrine disorders, rheumatic disorders, collagen diseases, dermatologic diseases, allergic states, ophthalmic diseases, respiratory diseases, hematologic disorders, neoplastic diseases, edematous states, and gastrointestinal diseases; resolution of acute exacerbations of multiple sclerosis; management of fulminating or disseminated tuberculosis and trichinosis; acute or chronic solid organ rejection
Pregnancy Risk Factor C
Pregnancy Implications Animal studies have demonstrated teratogenic effects. There are no adequate and well-controlled studies in pregnant women.
Lactation Enters breast milk/use caution (AAP rates "compatible")
Medication Safety Issues
Sound-alike/look-alike issues:
PrednisoLONE may be confused with predniSONE
Pediapred® may be confused with Pediazole®
Contraindications Hypersensitivity to prednisolone or any component of the formulation; acute superficial herpes simplex keratitis; live or attenuated virus vaccines (with immunosuppressive doses of corticosteroids); systemic fungal infections; varicella
(Continued)

PrednisoLONE *(Continued)*

Warnings/Precautions May cause hypercorticism or suppression of hypothalamic-pituitary-adrenal (HPA) axis, particularly in younger children or in patients receiving high doses for prolonged periods. HPA axis suppression may lead to adrenal crisis. Withdrawal and discontinuation of a corticosteroid should be done slowly and carefully. Particular care is required when patients are transferred from systemic corticosteroids to inhaled products due to possible adrenal insufficiency or withdrawal from steroids, including an increase in allergic symptoms. Patients receiving >20 mg per day of prednisone (or equivalent) may be most susceptible. Fatalities have occurred due to adrenal insufficiency in asthmatic patients during and after transfer from systemic corticosteroids to aerosol steroids; aerosol steroids do **not** provide the systemic steroid needed to treat patients having trauma, surgery, or infections.

Acute myopathy has been reported with high dose corticosteroids, usually in patients with neuromuscular transmission disorders; may involve ocular and/or respiratory muscles; monitor creatine kinase; recovery may be delayed. Corticosteroid use may cause psychiatric disturbances, including depression, euphoria, insomnia, mood swings, and personality changes. Pre-existing psychiatric conditions may be exacerbated by corticosteroid use. Prolonged use of corticosteroids may also increase the incidence of secondary infection, mask acute infection (including fungal infections), prolong or exacerbate viral infections, or limit response to vaccines. Exposure to chickenpox should be avoided; corticosteroids should not be used to treat ocular herpes simplex. Corticosteroids should not be used for cerebral malaria. Close observation is required in patients with latent tuberculosis and/or TB reactivity; restrict use in active TB (only in conjunction with antituberculosis treatment). Prolonged use of corticosteroids may result in glaucoma; damage to the optic nerve (not indicated for treatment of optic neuritis), defects in visual acuity and fields of vision, and posterior subcapsular cataract formation may occur. Use following cataract surgery may delay healing or increase the incidence of bleb formation. Prolonged treatment with corticosteroids has been associated with the development of Kaposi's sarcoma (case reports); if noted, discontinuation of therapy should be considered.

Use with caution in patients with thyroid disease, hepatic impairment, renal impairment, cardiovascular disease, diabetes, glaucoma, cataracts, myasthenia gravis, patients at risk for osteoporosis, patients at risk for seizures, or GI diseases (diverticulitis, peptic ulcer, ulcerative colitis) due to perforation risk. Use caution following acute MI (corticosteroids have been associated with myocardial rupture). Because of the risk of adverse effects, systemic corticosteroids should be used cautiously in the elderly in the smallest possible effective dose for the shortest duration. Do not use occlusive dressings on weeping or exudative lesions and general caution with occlusive dressings should be observed; adverse effects may be increased. Discontinue if skin irritation or contact dermatitis should occur; do not use in patients with decreased skin circulation. Withdraw therapy with gradual tapering of dose. May affect growth velocity; growth should be routinely monitored in pediatric patients.

Adverse Reactions Frequency not defined.

Ophthalmic formulation:

Endocrine & metabolic: Hypercorticoidism (rare)

Ocular: Conjunctival hyperemia, conjunctivitis, corneal ulcers, delayed wound healing, glaucoma, intraocular pressure increased, keratitis, loss of accommodation, optic nerve damage, mydriasis, posterior subcapsular cataract formation, ptosis, secondary ocular infection

Oral formulation:

Cardiovascular: Cardiomyopathy, CHF, edema, facial edema, hypertension

Central nervous system: Convulsions, headache, insomnia, malaise, nervousness, pseudotumor cerebri, psychic disorders, vertigo

Dermatologic: Bruising, facial erythema, hirsutism, petechiae, skin test reaction suppression, thin fragile skin, urticaria

Endocrine & metabolic: Carbohydrate tolerance decreased, Cushing's syndrome, diabetes mellitus, growth suppression, hyperglycemia, hypernatremia, hypokalemia, hypokalemic alkalosis, menstrual irregularities, negative nitrogen balance, pituitary adrenal axis suppression

Gastrointestinal: Abdominal distention, increased appetite, indigestion, nausea, pancreatitis, peptic ulcer, ulcerative esophagitis, weight gain

Hepatic: LFTs increased (usually reversible)

Neuromuscular & skeletal: Arthralgia, aseptic necrosis (humeral/femoral heads), fractures, muscle mass decreased, muscle weakness, osteoporosis, steroid myopathy, tendon rupture, weakness

Ocular: Cataracts, exophthalmus, eyelid edema, glaucoma, intraocular pressure increased, irritation

Respiratory: Epistaxis

Miscellaneous: Diaphoresis increased, impaired wound healing

Overdosage/Toxicology When consumed in excessive quantities for prolonged periods, systemic hypercorticism and adrenal suppression may occur; in those cases, discontinuation and withdrawal of the corticosteroid should be done judiciously. Treatment should be symptom-directed and supportive.

Drug Interactions

Cytochrome P450 Effect: Substrate of CYP3A4 (minor); **Inhibits** CYP3A4 (weak)

Increased Effect/Toxicity: Aprepitant, azole antifungals (eg, ketoconazole), calcium channel blockers (nondihydropyridine), cyclosporine, estrogens, and macrolide antibiotics may increase effects of corticosteroids. Corticosteroids may increase the serum levels of cyclosporine; concurrent use of fluoroquinolones may increase the risk of tendon rupture; concurrent use of neuromuscular-blocking agents may increase the risk of myopathy; concurrent use of NSAIDs (ophthalmic) with corticosteroids (ophthalmic) may lead to delayed healing; use of potassium-depleting agents increase the risk of hypokalemia; salicylates may increase the risk of gastrointestinal adverse events; immunosuppressants may enhance the adverse/toxic effects of vaccines (live organisms).

Decreased Effect: Aminoglutethimide, barbiturates, isoniazid, and rifampin may reduce the serum levels/effects of prednisolone. Antacids and bile acid sequestrants may reduce the absorption of corticosteroids; corticosteroids may suppress reactions to skin tests and vaccines (dead organisms).

Ethanol/Nutrition/Herb Interactions

Ethanol: Avoid ethanol (may increase gastric mucosal irritation).

Food: Prednisolone interferes with calcium absorption. Limit caffeine.

Herb/Nutraceutical: St John's wort may decrease prednisolone levels. Avoid cat's claw, echinacea (have immunostimulant properties).

Stability Store Orapred ODT™ at 20°C to 25°C (68°F to 77°F) in blister pack. Protect from moisture.

Mechanism of Action Decreases inflammation by suppression of migration of polymorphonuclear leukocytes and reversal of increased capillary permeability; suppresses the immune system by reducing activity and volume of the lymphatic system

Pharmacodynamics/Kinetics

Duration: 18-36 hours

Protein binding (concentration dependent): 65% to 91%; decreased in elderly

Metabolism: Primarily hepatic, but also metabolized in most tissues, to inactive compounds

Half-life elimination: 3.6 hours; End-stage renal disease: 3-5 hours

Excretion: Primarily urine (as glucuronides, sulfates, and unconjugated metabolites)

Dosage Dose depends upon condition being treated and response of patient; dosage for infants and children should be based on severity of the disease and response of the patient rather than on strict adherence to dosage indicated by age, weight, or body surface area. Consider alternate day therapy for long-term therapy. Discontinuation of long-term therapy requires gradual withdrawal by tapering the dose. Patients undergoing unusual stress while receiving corticosteroids, should receive increased doses prior to, during, and after the stressful situation.

Children: Oral:

Acute asthma: 1-2 mg/kg/day in divided doses 1-2 times/day for 3-5 days

Anti-inflammatory or immunosuppressive dose: 0.1-2 mg/kg/day in divided doses 1-4 times/day

Nephrotic syndrome:

Initial (first 3 episodes): 2 mg/kg/day **or** 60 mg/m²/day (maximum: 80 mg/day) in divided doses 3-4 times/day until urine is protein free for 3 consecutive days (maximum: 28 days); followed by 1-1.5 mg/kg/dose **or** 40 mg/m²/dose given every other day for 4 weeks

Maintenance (long-term maintenance dose for frequent relapses): 0.5-1 mg/kg/dose given every other day for 3-6 months

Adults: Oral:

Usual range: 5-60 mg/day

Multiple sclerosis: 200 mg/day for 1 week followed by 80 mg every other day for 1 month

Rheumatoid arthritis: Initial: 5-7.5 mg/day; adjust dose as necessary

Ophthalmic suspension/solution: Conjunctivitis, corneal injury: Children and Adults: Instill 1-2 drops into conjunctival sac every hour during day, every 2 hours at night until favorable response is obtained, then use 1 drop every 4 hours.

Elderly: Use lowest effective dose

Dosing adjustment in hyperthyroidism: Prednisolone dose may need to be increased to achieve adequate therapeutic effects

Hemodialysis: Slightly dialyzable (5% to 20%); administer dose posthemodialysis

Peritoneal dialysis: Supplemental dose is not necessary

Dietary Considerations Should be taken after meals or with food or milk to decrease GI effects; increase dietary intake of pyridoxine, vitamin C, vitamin D, folate, calcium, and phosphorus.

Administration Administer oral formulation with food or milk to decrease GI effects.

Orapred ODT™: Do not break or use partial tablet. Remove tablet from blister pack just prior to use. May swallow whole or allow to dissolve on tongue.

Monitoring Parameters Blood pressure; blood glucose, electrolytes; intraocular pressure (use >6 weeks); bone mineral density

Test Interactions Response to skin tests

Dosage Forms

Solution, ophthalmic, as sodium phosphate: 1% (5 mL, 10 mL, 15 mL) [contains benzalkonium chloride]

Solution, oral, as sodium phosphate: Prednisolone base 5 mg/5 mL (120 mL)

Orapred®: 20 mg/5 mL (20 mL, 240 mL) [equivalent to prednisolone base 15 mg/5 mL; dye free; contains alcohol 2%, sodium benzoate; grape flavor]

Pediapred®: 6.7 mg/5 mL (120 mL) [equivalent to prednisolone base 5 mg/5 mL; dye free; raspberry flavor]

Suspension, ophthalmic, as acetate: 1% (5 mL, 10 mL, 15 mL)

Econopred® Plus: 1% (5 mL, 10 mL) [contains benzalkonium chloride]

Pred Forte®: 1% (1 mL, 5 mL, 10 mL, 15 mL) [contains benzalkonium chloride and sodium bisulfite]

Pred Mild®: 0.12% (5 mL, 10 mL) [contains benzalkonium chloride and sodium bisulfite]

Syrup, as base: 5 mg/5 mL (120 mL); 15 mg/5 mL (240 mL, 480 mL)

Prelone®: 15 mg/5 mL (240 mL, 480 mL) [contains alcohol 5%, benzoic acid; cherry flavor]

Tablet, as base: 5 mg

Tablet, orally disintegrating, as base:

Orapred ODT™: 10 mg, 15 mg, 30 mg [grape flavor]

♦ **Prednisolone Acetate** see PrednisoLONE on page 1413

♦ **Prednisolone Acetate, Ophthalmic** see PrednisoLONE on page 1413

Prednisolone and Gentamicin (pred NIS oh lone & jen ta MYE sin)

U.S. Brand Names Pred-G®
Index Terms Gentamicin and Prednisolone
Pharmacologic Category Antibiotic/Corticosteroid, Ophthalmic
Use Treatment of steroid responsive inflammatory conditions and superficial ocular infections due to microorganisms susceptible to gentamicin
Pregnancy Risk Factor C
Dosage Ophthalmic: Children and Adults:
Ointment: Apply ½ inch ribbon in the conjunctival sac 1-3 times/day
Suspension: 1 drop 2-4 times/day; during the initial 24-48 hours, the dosing frequency may be increased if necessary up to 1 drop every hour
Additional Information Complete prescribing information for this medication should be consulted for additional detail.
Dosage Forms
Ointment, ophthalmic: Prednisolone acetate 0.6% and gentamicin sulfate 0.3% (3.5 g)
Suspension, ophthalmic: Prednisolone acetate 1% and gentamicin sulfate 0.3% (2 mL, 5 mL, 10 mL) [contains benzalkonium chloride]

♦ **Prednisolone and Sulfacetamide** see Sulfacetamide and Prednisolone on page 1610
♦ **Prednisolone, Neomycin, and Polymyxin B** see Neomycin, Polymyxin B, and Prednisolone on page 1212
♦ **Prednisolone Sodium Phosphate** see PrednisoLONE on page 1413
♦ **Prednisolone Sodium Phosphate, Ophthalmic** see PrednisoLONE on page 1413

PredniSONE (PRED ni sone)

U.S. Brand Names Prednisone Intensol™; Sterapred®; Sterapred® DS
Canadian Brand Names Apo-Prednisone®; Novo-Prednisone; Winpred™
Index Terms Deltacortisone; Deltadehydrocortisone
Pharmacologic Category Corticosteroid, Systemic
Additional Appendix Information
Contrast Media Reactions, Premedication for Prophylaxis on page 2036
Corticosteroids on page 1879
Use Treatment of a variety of diseases including adrenocortical insufficiency, hypercalcemia, rheumatic, and collagen disorders; dermatologic, ocular, respiratory, gastrointestinal, and neoplastic diseases; organ transplantation and a variety of diseases including those of hematologic, allergic, inflammatory, and autoimmune in origin; not available in injectable form, prednisolone must be used
Unlabeled/Investigational Use Investigational: Prevention of postherpetic neuralgia and relief of acute pain in the early stages
Pregnancy Risk Factor B
Pregnancy Implications Crosses the placenta. Immunosuppression reported in 1 infant exposed to high-dose prednisone plus azathioprine throughout gestation. One report of congenital cataracts. Available evidence suggests safe use during pregnancy.
Lactation Enters breast milk/compatible
Medication Safety Issues
Sound-alike/look-alike issues:
PredniSONE may be confused with methylPREDNISolone, Pramosone®, prazosin, prednisoLONE, Prilosec®, primidone, promethazine
Contraindications Hypersensitivity to prednisone or any component of the formulation; serious infections, except tuberculous meningitis; systemic fungal infections; varicella
Warnings/Precautions May cause hypercorticism or suppression of hypothalamic-pituitary-adrenal (HPA) axis, particularly in younger children or in patients receiving high doses for prolonged periods. HPA axis suppression may lead to adrenal crisis. Withdrawal and discontinuation of a corticosteroid should be done slowly and carefully. Particular care is required when patients are transferred from systemic corticosteroids to inhaled products due to possible adrenal insufficiency or withdrawal from steroids, including an increase in allergic symptoms. Patients receiving >20 mg per day of prednisone (or equivalent) may be most susceptible. Fatalities have occurred due to adrenal insufficiency in asthmatic patients during and after transfer from systemic corticosteroids to aerosol steroids; aerosol steroids do **not** provide the systemic steroid needed to treat patients having trauma, surgery, or infections.

Acute myopathy has been reported with high dose corticosteroids, usually in patients with neuromuscular transmission disorders; may involve ocular and/or respiratory muscles; monitor creatine kinase; recovery may be delayed. Corticosteroid use may cause psychiatric disturbances, including depression, euphoria, insomnia, mood swings, and personality changes. Pre-existing psychiatric conditions may be exacerbated by corticosteroid use. Prolonged use of corticosteroids may also increase the incidence of secondary infection, mask acute infection (including fungal infections), prolong or exacerbate viral infections, or limit response to vaccines. Exposure to chickenpox should be avoided; corticosteroids should not be used to treat ocular herpes simplex. Corticosteroids should not be used for cerebral malaria. Close observation is required in patients with latent tuberculosis and/or TB reactivity; restrict use in active TB (only in conjunction with antituberculosis treatment). Prolonged treatment with corticosteroids has been associated with the development of Kaposi's sarcoma (case reports); if noted, discontinuation of therapy should be considered.

Use with caution in patients with thyroid disease, hepatic impairment, renal impairment, cardiovascular disease, diabetes, glaucoma, cataracts, myasthenia gravis, patients at risk for osteoporosis, patients at risk for seizures, or GI diseases (diverticulitis, peptic ulcer, ulcerative colitis) due to perforation risk. Use caution following acute MI (corticosteroids have been associated with myocardial rupture). Because of the risk of adverse effects, systemic corticosteroids should be used cautiously in the elderly in the smallest possible effective dose for the shortest duration. Withdraw therapy with gradual tapering of dose. May affect growth velocity; growth should be routinely monitored in pediatric patients.

Adverse Reactions

>10%:
  Central nervous system: Insomnia, nervousness
  Gastrointestinal: Increased appetite, indigestion
1% to 10%:
  Central nervous system: Dizziness or lightheadedness, headache
  Dermatologic: Hirsutism, hypopigmentation
  Endocrine & metabolic: Diabetes mellitus, glucose intolerance, hyperglycemia
  Neuromuscular & skeletal: Arthralgia
  Ocular: Cataracts, glaucoma
  Respiratory: Epistaxis
  Miscellaneous: Diaphoresis
<1% (Limited to important or life-threatening): Cushing's syndrome, edema, fractures, hallucinations, hypertension, muscle-wasting, osteoporosis, pancreatitis, pituitary-adrenal axis suppression, seizure

Overdosage/Toxicology When consumed in excessive quantities for prolonged periods, systemic hypercorticism and adrenal suppression may occur; in those cases, discontinuation and withdrawal of the corticosteroid should be done judiciously.

Drug Interactions

Cytochrome P450 Effect: Substrate of CYP3A4 (minor); **Induces** CYP2C19 (weak), 3A4 (weak)

Increased Effect/Toxicity: Concurrent use with NSAIDs may increase the risk of GI ulceration.

Decreased Effect: Decreased effect with barbiturates, phenytoin, rifampin; decreased effect of salicylates, vaccines, and toxoids.

Ethanol/Nutrition/Herb Interactions

Ethanol: Avoid ethanol (may increase gastric mucosal irritation)
Food: Prednisone interferes with calcium absorption. Limit caffeine.
Herb/Nutraceutical: St John's wort may decrease prednisone levels. Avoid cat's claw, echinacea (have immunostimulant properties).

Mechanism of Action Decreases inflammation by suppression of migration of polymorphonuclear leukocytes and reversal of increased capillary permeability; suppresses the immune system by reducing activity and volume of the lymphatic system; suppresses adrenal function at high doses. Antitumor effects may be related to inhibition of glucose transport, phosphorylation, or induction of cell death in immature lymphocytes. Antiemetic effects are thought to occur due to blockade of cerebral innervation of the emetic center via inhibition of prostaglandin synthesis.

Pharmacodynamics/Kinetics

Protein binding (concentration dependent): 65% to 91%
Metabolism: Hepatically converted from prednisone (inactive) to prednisolone (active); may be impaired with hepatic dysfunction
Half-life elimination: Normal renal function: 2.5-3.5 hours
See Prednisolone monograph for complete information.

Dosage Oral: Dose depends upon condition being treated and response of patient; dosage for infants and children should be based on severity of the disease and response of the patient rather than on strict adherence to dosage indicated by age, weight, or body surface area. Consider alternate day therapy for long-term therapy. Discontinuation of long-term therapy requires gradual withdrawal by tapering the dose.

Children:
  Anti-inflammatory or immunosuppressive dose: 0.05-2 mg/kg/day divided 1-4 times/day
  Acute asthma: 1-2 mg/kg/day in divided doses 1-2 times/day for 3-5 days
    Alternatively (for 3- to 5-day "burst"):
    <1 year: 10 mg every 12 hours
    1-4 years: 20 mg every 12 hours
    5-13 years: 30 mg every 12 hours
    >13 years: 40 mg every 12 hours
  Asthma long-term therapy (alternative dosing by age):
    <1 year: 10 mg every other day
    1-4 years: 20 mg every other day
    5-13 years: 30 mg every other day
    >13 years: 40 mg every other day
  Nephrotic syndrome:
    Initial (first 3 episodes): 2 mg/kg/day **or** 60 mg/m^2/day (maximum: 80 mg/day) in divided doses 3-4 times/day until urine is protein free for 3 consecutive days (maximum: 28 days); followed by 1-1.5 mg/kg/dose **or** 40 mg/m^2/dose given every other day for 4 weeks
    Maintenance dose (long-term maintenance dose for frequent relapses): 0.5-1 mg/kg/dose given every other day for 3-6 months
Children and Adults: Physiologic replacement: 4-5 mg/m^2/day
Children ≥5 years and Adults: Asthma:
  Moderate persistent: Inhaled corticosteroid (medium dose) or inhaled corticosteroid (low-medium dose) with a long-acting bronchodilator
  Severe persistent: Inhaled corticosteroid (high dose) and corticosteroid tablets or syrup long term: 2 mg/kg/day, generally not to exceed 60 mg/day
Adults:
  Immunosuppression/chemotherapy adjunct: Range: 5-60 mg/day in divided doses 1-4 times/day
  Allergic reaction (contact dermatitis):
    Day 1: 30 mg divided as 10 mg before breakfast, 5 mg at lunch, 5 mg at dinner, 10 mg at bedtime
    Day 2: 5 mg at breakfast, 5 mg at lunch, 5 mg at dinner, 10 mg at bedtime
    Day 3: 5 mg 4 times/day (with meals and at bedtime)
(Continued)

PredniSONE (Continued)

Day 4: 5 mg 3 times/day (breakfast, lunch, bedtime)
Day 5: 5 mg 2 times/day (breakfast, bedtime)
Day 6: 5 mg before breakfast
Pneumocystis carinii pneumonia (PCP):
40 mg twice daily for 5 days **followed by**
40 mg once daily for 5 days **followed by**
20 mg once daily for 11 days or until antimicrobial regimen is completed
Thyrotoxicosis: Oral: 60 mg/day
Chemotherapy (refer to individual protocols): Oral: Range: 20 mg/day to 100 mg/m^2/day
Rheumatoid arthritis: Oral: Use lowest possible daily dose (often ≤7.5 mg/day)
Idiopathic thrombocytopenia purpura (ITP): Oral: 60 mg daily for 4-6 weeks, gradually tapered over several weeks
Systemic lupus erythematosus (SLE): Oral:
Acute: 1-2 mg/kg/day in 2-3 divided doses
Maintenance: Reduce to lowest possible dose, usually <1 mg/kg/day as single dose (morning)
Elderly: Use the lowest effective dose
Dosing adjustment in hepatic impairment: Prednisone is inactive and must be metabolized by the liver to prednisolone. This conversion may be impaired in patients with liver disease, however, prednisolone levels are observed to be higher in patients with severe liver failure than in normal patients. Therefore, compensation for the inadequate conversion of prednisone to prednisolone occurs.
Dosing adjustment in hyperthyroidism: Prednisone dose may need to be increased to achieve adequate therapeutic effects
Hemodialysis: Supplemental dose is not necessary
Peritoneal dialysis: Supplemental dose is not necessary
Dietary Considerations Should be taken after meals or with food or milk; increase dietary intake of pyridoxine, vitamin C, vitamin D, folate, calcium, and phosphorus.
Administration Administer with meals to decrease gastrointestinal upset
Monitoring Parameters Blood pressure, blood glucose, electrolytes
Test Interactions Response to skin tests
Additional Information Tapering of corticosteroids after a short course of therapy (<7-10 days) is generally not required unless the disease/inflammatory process is slow to respond. Tapering after prolonged exposure is dependent upon the individual patient, duration of corticosteroid treatments, and size of steroid dose. Recovery of the HPA axis may require several months. Subtle but important HPA axis suppression may be present for as long as several months after a course of as few as 10-14 days duration. Testing of HPA axis (cosyntropin) may be required, and signs/symptoms of adrenal insufficiency should be monitored in patients with a history of use.
Dosage Forms
Solution, oral: 1 mg/mL (5 mL, 120 mL, 500 mL) [contains alcohol 5%, sodium benzoate; vanilla flavor]
Solution, oral concentrate (Prednisone Intensol™): 5 mg/mL (30 mL) [contains alcohol 30%]
Tablet: 1 mg, 2.5 mg, 5 mg, 10 mg, 20 mg, 50 mg
Sterapred®: 5 mg [supplied as 21 tablet 6-day unit-dose package or 48 tablet 12-day unit-dose package]
Sterapred® DS: 10 mg [supplied as 21 tablet 6-day unit-dose package or 48 tablet 12-day unit-dose package]

♦ **Prednisone Intensol**™ *see* PredniSONE *on page 1416*

Pregabalin (pre GAB a lin)

U.S. Brand Names Lyrica®
Canadian Brand Names Lyrica®
Index Terms CI-1008; S-(+)-3-isobutylgaba
Pharmacologic Category Analgesic, Miscellaneous; Anticonvulsant, Miscellaneous
Use Management of pain associated with diabetic peripheral neuropathy; management of postherpetic neuralgia; adjunctive therapy for partial-onset seizure disorder in adults
Restrictions C-V
Pregnancy Risk Factor C
Pregnancy Implications Increased incidence of fetal abnormalities, particularly skeletal malformations, were observed in animal studies. Male-mediated teratogenicity has been observed in animal studies; implications in humans are not defined. Impaired male and female fertility has been noted in animal studies. There are no adequate and well-controlled studies in pregnant women. Use only when potential benefit to the mother outweighs possible risk to the fetus.
Lactation Excretion in breast milk unknown/not recommended
Contraindications Hypersensitivity to pregabalin or any component of the formulation
Warnings/Precautions May cause CNS depression and/or dizziness, which may impair physical or mental abilities. Patients must be cautioned about performing tasks which require mental alertness (eg, operating machinery or driving). Effects with other sedative drugs or ethanol may be potentiated. Visual disturbances (blurred vision, decreased acuity and visual field changes) have been associated with pregabalin therapy; patients should be instructed to notify their physician if these effects are noted.

Pregabalin has been associated with increases in CPK and rare cases of rhabdomyolysis. Patients should be instructed to notify their prescriber if unexplained muscle pain, tenderness, or weakness, particularly if fever and/or malaise are associated with these symptoms. Use may be associated with weight gain and peripheral edema; use caution in patients with congestive heart failure, hypertension, or diabetes. Effect on weight gain/edema may be additive to thiazolidinedione antidiabetic agent; particularly in patients with prior cardiovascular disease. May decrease platelet count or prolong PR interval.

Has been noted to be tumorigenic (increased incidence of hemangiosarcoma) in animal studies; significance of these findings in humans is unknown. Pregabalin has been associated with discontinuation symptoms following abrupt cessation, and increases in seizure frequency (when used as an antiepileptic) may occur. Should not be discontinued abruptly; dosage tapering over at least 1 week is recommended. Use caution in renal impairment; dosage adjustment required. Safety and efficacy have not been established in pediatric patients.

Adverse Reactions Note: Frequency of adverse effects may be influenced by dose or concurrent therapy. In add-on trials in epilepsy, frequency of CNS and adverse effects were higher than those reported in pain management trials. Range noted below is inclusive of all trials.

>10%:
Cardiovascular: Peripheral edema (up to 16%)
Central nervous system: Dizziness (8% to 38%), somnolence (4% to 28%), ataxia (1% to 20%)
Gastrointestinal: Weight gain (up to 16%), xerostomia (1% to 15%)
Neuromuscular & skeletal: Tremor (1% to 11%)
Ocular: Blurred vision (1% to 12%), diplopia (up to 12%)
Miscellaneous: Infection (up to 14%), accidental injury (2% to 11%)

1% to 10%:
Cardiovascular: Chest pain (up to 4%), edema (up to 6%)
Central nervous system: Neuropathy (up to 9%), headache (up to 9%), thinking abnormal (up to 9%), confusion (up to 7%), speech disorder (up to 7%), incoordination (up to 6%), amnesia (up to 6%), pain (up to 5%), vertigo (up to 4%), nervousness (>2%), euphoria (up to 3%), fever (≥1%), anxiety (≥1%), depersonalization (≥1%), hypertonia (≥1%), hypoesthesia (≥1%), stupor (≥1%)
Dermatologic: Facial edema (up to 3%), ecchymosis (≥1%), pruritus (≥1%)
Endocrine & metabolic: Appetite increased (up to 6%), hypoglycemia (up to 3%), libido decreased (≥1%)
Gastrointestinal: Constipation (up to 7%), flatulence (up to 3%), vomiting (up to 3%), abdominal pain (≥1%), gastroenteritis (≥1%)
Genitourinary: Anorgasmia (≥1%), impotence (≥1%), urinary frequency (≥1%), incontinence (≥1%)
Hematologic: Thrombocytopenia (3%)
Neuromuscular & skeletal: Abnormal gait (up to 8%), weakness (up to 7%), twitching (up to 5%), myoclonus (up to 4%), back pain (up to 3%), paresthesia (>2%), CPK increased (2%), arthralgia (≥1%), leg cramps (≥1%), myalgia (≥1%), myasthenia (≥1%)
Ocular: Visual abnormalities (up to 5%), visual field defect (≥2%), eye disorder (up to 2%), nystagmus (>2%), conjunctivitis (≥1%)
Otic: Otitis media (≥1%), tinnitus (≥1%)
Respiratory: Dyspnea (up to 3%), bronchitis (up to 3%)
Miscellaneous: Flu-like syndrome (up to 2%), allergic reaction (≥1%)

<1% (Limited to important or life-threatening): Abscess, acute renal failure, addiction (rare), agitation, albuminuria, anaphylactoid reaction, anemia, angioedema, aphasia, aphthous stomatitis, apnea, ascites, atelectasis, blepharitis, blindness, bronchiolitis, cellulitis, cerebellar syndrome, cervicitis, chills, cholecystitis, cholelithiasis, circumoral paresthesia, cogwheel rigidity, colitis, coma, corneal ulcer, crystalluria (urate), delirium, delusions, dysarthria, dysautonomia, dyskinesia, dysphagia, dystonia, dysuria, encephalopathy, eosinophilia, esophageal ulcer, exfoliative dermatitis, extraocular palsy, extrapyramidal syndrome, gastritis, GI hemorrhage, glomerulitis, granuloma, Guillain-Barré syndrome, hallucinations, heart failure, hematuria, hostility, hyper-/hypokinesia, hypotension, hypotonia, intracranial hypertension, laryngismus, leukopenia, leukorrhea, leukocytosis, lymphadenopathy, manic reaction, melena, myelofibrosis, nephritis, neuralgia, ocular hemorrhage, oliguria, optic atrophy, pancreatitis, papilledema, paranoid reaction, pelvic pain, peripheral neuritis, polycythemia, postural hypotension, prothrombin decreased, psychotic depression, ptosis, pulmonary edema, pulmonary fibrosis, rectal hemorrhage, renal calculus, retinal edema, retinal vascular disorder, retroperitoneal fibrosis, rhabdomyolysis, schizophrenic reaction, shock, skin necrosis, skin ulcer, spasm (generalized), ST depression, Stevens-Johnson syndrome, subcutaneous nodule, suicide attempt, suicide, syncope, thrombocythemia, thrombophlebitis, tongue edema, torticollis, trismus, uveitis, ventricular fibrillation

Overdosage/Toxicology Symptoms are similar to those experienced at therapeutic doses (somnolence). Treatment is symptom-directed and supportive. A 4-hour hemodialysis procedure reduces plasma concentrations by ~50%.

Drug Interactions
Increased Effect/Toxicity: Sedative effects may be additive with CNS depressants (includes ethanol, barbiturates, opioid analgesics, and other sedative agents). Pregabalin's effect on weight gain/edema may be additive with thiazolidinedione antidiabetic agents (includes pioglitazone, rosiglitazone).

Ethanol/Nutrition/Herb Interactions
Ethanol: Avoid ethanol (may increase CNS depression).
Herb/Nutraceutical: Avoid valerian, St John's wort, kava kava, gotu kola (may increase CNS depression).

Stability Store at 25°C (77°F); excursions permitted to 15°C to 30°C (59°F to 86°F).

Mechanism of Action Binds to alpha$_2$-delta subunit of voltage-gated calcium channels within the CNS, inhibiting excitatory neurotransmitter release. Although structurally related to GABA, it does not bind to GABA or benzodiazepine receptors. Exerts antinociceptive and anticonvulsant activity. Decreases symptoms of painful peripheral neuropathies and, as adjunctive therapy in partial seizures, decreases the frequency of seizures.

Pharmacodynamics/Kinetics
Onset: Pain management: Effects may be noted as early as the first week of therapy.
Distribution: V_d: 0.5 L/kg
Protein binding: 0%
Metabolism: Negligible
(Continued)

Pregabalin *(Continued)*

Bioavailability: >90%

Half-life elimination: 6.3 hours

Time to peak, plasma: 1.5 hours (3 hours with food)

Excretion: Urine (90% as unchanged drug; minor metabolites)

Dosage Oral: Adults:

Neuropathic pain (diabetes-associated): Initial: 150 mg/day in divided doses (50 mg 3 times/day); may be increased within 1 week based on tolerability and effect; maximum dose: 300 mg/day (dosages up to 600 mg/day were evaluated with no significant additional benefit and an increase in adverse effects)

Postherpetic neuralgia: Initial: 150 mg/day in divided doses (75 mg 2 times/day or 50 mg 3 times/day); may be increased to 300 mg/day within 1 week based on tolerability and effect; further titration (to 600 mg/day) after 2-4 weeks may be considered in patients who do not experience sufficient relief of pain provided they are able to tolerate pregabalin. Maximum dose: 600 mg/day

Partial-onset seizures (adjunctive therapy): Initial: 150 mg per day in divided doses (75 mg 2 times/day or 50 mg 3 times/day); may be increased based on tolerability and effect (optimal titration schedule has not been defined). Maximum dose: 600 mg/day

Discontinuing therapy: Pregabalin should not be abruptly discontinued; taper dosage over at least 1 week

Dosage adjustment in renal impairment: Cl$_{cr}$ ≥60 mL/minute: No dosage adjustment required. In renally-impaired patients, dosage adjustment depends on renal function and daily dosage:

Cl$_{cr}$ 30-60 mL/minute: Total daily dose:
75 mg in 2-3 divided doses **or**
150 mg in 2-3 divided doses **or**
300 mg in 2-3 divided doses

Cl$_{cr}$ 15-30 mL/minute: Total daily dose:
25-50 mg in once daily or in 2 divided doses **or**
75 mg once daily or in 2 divided doses **or**
150 mg once daily or in 2 divided doses

Cl$_{cr}$ <15 mL/minute: Total daily dose:
25 mg once daily **or**
25-50 mg once daily **or**
75 mg once daily

Hemodialysis: Total daily dose:
25 mg: Single supplementary dose of 25 mg **or** 50 mg
25-50 mg: Single supplementary dose of 50 mg **or** 75 mg
75 mg: Single supplementary dose of 100 mg **or** 150 mg

Dietary Considerations May be taken with or without food.

Administration May be administered with or without food.

Monitoring Parameters Measures of efficacy (pain intensity/seizure frequency); degree of sedation; symptoms of myopathy or ocular disturbance; weight gain/edema; CPK; skin integrity (in diabetic patients).

Dosage Forms Capsule: 25 mg, 50 mg, 75 mg, 100 mg, 150 mg, 200 mg, 225 mg, 300 mg

♦ **Pregnenedione** *see* Progesterone *on page 1433*
♦ **Pregnyl®** *see* Chorionic Gonadotropin (Human) *on page 363*
♦ **Prelone®** *see* PrednisoLONE *on page 1413*
♦ **Premarin®** *see* Estrogens (Conjugated/Equine) *on page 631*
♦ **Premjact® [OTC]** *see* Lidocaine *on page 1010*
♦ **Premphase®** *see* Estrogens (Conjugated/Equine) and Medroxyprogesterone *on page 634*
♦ **Premplus® (Can)** *see* Estrogens (Conjugated/Equine) and Medroxyprogesterone *on page 634*
♦ **Prempro™** *see* Estrogens (Conjugated/Equine) and Medroxyprogesterone *on page 634*
♦ **Preparation H® Hydrocortisone [OTC]** *see* Hydrocortisone *on page 852*
♦ **Pre-Pen® [DSC]** *see* Benzylpenicilloyl-polylysine *on page 209*
♦ **Prepidil®** *see* Dinoprostone *on page 513*
♦ **Preservative-Free Cosopt® (Can)** *see* Dorzolamide and Timolol *on page 542*
♦ **Pressyn® (Can)** *see* Vasopressin *on page 1779*
♦ **Pressyn® AR (Can)** *see* Vasopressin *on page 1779*
♦ **Pretz® [OTC]** *see* Sodium Chloride *on page 1576*
♦ **Pretz-D® [OTC]** *see* Ephedrine *on page 587*
♦ **Prevacid®** *see* Lansoprazole *on page 977*
♦ **Prevacid® NapraPAC™** *see* Lansoprazole and Naproxen *on page 980*
♦ **Prevacid® SoluTab™** *see* Lansoprazole *on page 977*
♦ **Prevalite®** *see* Cholestyramine Resin *on page 360*
♦ **Prevex® B (Can)** *see* Betamethasone *on page 211*
♦ **Prevex® HC (Can)** *see* Hydrocortisone *on page 852*
♦ **PreviDent®** *see* Fluoride *on page 722*
♦ **PreviDent® 5000 Plus™** *see* Fluoride *on page 722*
♦ **Previfem™** *see* Ethinyl Estradiol and Norgestimate *on page 660*
♦ **Prevnar®** *see* Pneumococcal Conjugate Vaccine (7-Valent) *on page 1382*
♦ **Prevpac®** *see* Lansoprazole, Amoxicillin, and Clarithromycin *on page 979*
♦ **Prezista™** *see* Darunavir *on page 457*
♦ **Prialt®** *see* Ziconotide *on page 1811*
♦ **Priftin®** *see* Rifapentine *on page 1510*
♦ **Prilocaine and Lidocaine** *see* Lidocaine and Prilocaine *on page 1015*
♦ **Prilosec®** *see* Omeprazole *on page 1264*

- **Prilosec OTC™ [OTC]** *see* Omeprazole *on page 1264*
- **Primaclone** *see* Primidone *on page 1422*
- **Primacor®** *see* Milrinone *on page 1148*

Primaquine (PRIM a kween)

Index Terms Primaquine Phosphate; Prymaccone
Pharmacologic Category Aminoquinoline (Antimalarial)
Additional Appendix Information
Malaria Treatment *on page 2003*
Use Treatment of malaria
Unlabeled/Investigational Use Prevention of malaria; treatment *Pneumocystis carinii* pneumonia
Pregnancy Risk Factor C
Lactation Excretion in breast milk unknown
Contraindications Hypersensitivity to primaquine, similar alkaloids, or any component of the formulation; acutely ill patients who have a tendency to develop granulocytopenia (rheumatoid arthritis, SLE); patients receiving other drugs capable of depressing the bone marrow (eg, quinacrine and primaquine)
Warnings/Precautions Use with caution in patients with G6PD deficiency, NADH methemoglobin reductase deficiency; do not exceed recommended dosage. Promptly discontinue with signs of hemolytic anemia (darkening of urine, marked fall in hemoglobin or erythrocyte count). **[U.S. Boxed Warning]: Should be prescribed only by physicians familiar with its use.**
Adverse Reactions Frequency not defined.
Cardiovascular: Arrhythmias
Central nervous system: Headache
Dermatologic: Pruritus
Gastrointestinal: Abdominal pain, nausea, vomiting
Hematologic: Agranulocytosis, hemolytic anemia in G6PD deficiency, leukopenia, leukocytosis, methemoglobinemia in NADH-methemoglobin reductase-deficient individuals
Ocular: Interference with visual accommodation
Overdosage/Toxicology Symptoms of acute overdose include abdominal cramps, vomiting, cyanosis, methemoglobinemia (possibly severe), leukopenia, acute hemolytic anemia (often significant), and granulocytopenia. With chronic overdose, symptoms include ototoxicity and retinopathy. Following GI decontamination, treatment is supportive (fluids, anticonvulsants, blood transfusions, methylene blue if methemoglobinemia is severe - 1-2 mg/kg over several minutes).
Drug Interactions
Cytochrome P450 Effect: Substrate of CYP3A4 (major); **Inhibits** CYP1A2 (strong), 2D6 (weak), 3A4 (weak); **Induces** CYP1A2 (weak)
Increased Effect/Toxicity: Increased toxicity/levels with quinacrine. Primaquine may increase the levels/effects of aminophylline, fluvoxamine, mexiletine, mirtazapine, ropinirole, theophylline, trifluoperazine, and other CYP1A2 substrates.
Decreased Effect: The levels/effects of primaquine may be decreased by aminoglutethimide, carbamazepine, nafcillin, nevirapine, phenobarbital, phenytoin, rifamycins, and other CYP3A4 inducers.
Ethanol/Nutrition/Herb Interactions Ethanol: Avoid ethanol (due to GI irritation).
Mechanism of Action Eliminates the primary tissue exoerythrocytic forms of *P. falciparum*; disrupts mitochondria and binds to DNA
Pharmacodynamics/Kinetics
Absorption: Well absorbed
Metabolism: Hepatic to carboxyprimaquine (active)
Half-life elimination: 3.7-9.6 hours
Time to peak, serum: 1-2 hours
Excretion: Urine (small amounts as unchanged drug)
Dosage Oral: Dosage expressed as mg of base (15 mg base = 26.3 mg primaquine phosphate)
Treatment of malaria (decrease risk of delayed primary attacks and prevent relapse):
Children: 0.3 mg base/kg/day once daily for 14 days (not to exceed 15 mg/day) or 0.9 mg base/kg once weekly for 8 weeks not to exceed 45 mg base/week
Adults: 15 mg/day (base) once daily for 14 days or 45 mg base once weekly for 8 weeks CDC treatment recommendations. Begin therapy during last 2 weeks of, or following a course of, suppression with chloroquine or a comparable drug
Note: A second course (30 mg/day) for 14 days may be required in patients with relapse. Higher initial doses (30 mg/day) have also been used following exposure in S.E. Asia or Somalia.
Prevention of malaria (unlabeled use): Initiate prior to travel and continue for 7 days after departure from malaria-endemic area:
Children: 0.5 mg/kg once daily
Adults: 30 mg once daily
Pneumocystis carinii pneumonia (unlabeled use): Adults: 30 mg once daily for 21 days (in conjunction with clindamycin)
Administration Take with meals to decrease adverse GI effects. Drug has a bitter taste.
Monitoring Parameters Periodic CBC, visual color check of urine, glucose, electrolytes; if hemolysis suspected, monitor CBC, haptoglobin, peripheral smear, urinalysis dipstick for occult blood
Dosage Forms Tablet, as phosphate: 26.3 mg [15 mg base]

- **Primaquine Phosphate** *see* Primaquine *on page 1421*
- **Primatene® Mist [OTC]** *see* Epinephrine *on page 589*
- **Primaxin®** *see* Imipenem and Cilastatin *on page 885*
- **Primaxin® I.V. (Can)** *see* Imipenem and Cilastatin *on page 885*

Primidone (PRI mi done)

U.S. Brand Names Mysoline®
Canadian Brand Names Apo-Primidone®
Index Terms Desoxyphenobarbital; Primaclone
Pharmacologic Category Anticonvulsant, Miscellaneous; Barbiturate
Additional Appendix Information
 Anticonvulsants by Seizure Type *on page 1865*
 Epilepsy *on page 2048*
Use Management of grand mal, psychomotor, and focal seizures
Unlabeled/Investigational Use Benign familial tremor (essential tremor)
Pregnancy Risk Factor D
Pregnancy Implications Crosses the placenta. Dysmorphic facial features; hemorrhagic disease of newborn due to fetal vitamin K depletion, maternal folic acid deficiency may occur. Epilepsy itself, number of medications, genetic factors, or a combination of these probably influence the teratogenicity of anticonvulsant therapy. Benefit:risk ratio usually favors continued use during pregnancy.
Lactation Enters breast milk/not recommended (AAP recommends use "with caution")
Medication Safety Issues
 Sound-alike/look-alike issues:
 Primidone may be confused with predniSONE
Contraindications Hypersensitivity to primidone, phenobarbital, or any component of the formulation; porphyria; pregnancy
Warnings/Precautions Use with caution in patients with renal or hepatic impairment, pulmonary insufficiency; abrupt withdrawal may precipitate status epilepticus. Potential for drug dependency exists. Do not administer to patients in acute pain. Use caution in elderly, debilitated, or pediatric patients - may cause paradoxical responses. May cause CNS depression, which may impair physical or mental abilities. Patients must cautioned about performing tasks which require mental alertness (eg, operating machinery or driving). Effects with other sedative drugs or ethanol may be potentiated. Use with caution in patients with depression or suicidal tendencies, or in patients with a history of drug abuse. Tolerance or psychological and physical dependence may occur with prolonged use. Primidone's metabolite, phenobarbital, has been associated with cognitive deficits in children. Use with caution in patients with hypoadrenalism.
Adverse Reactions Frequency not defined.
 Central nervous system: Drowsiness, vertigo, ataxia, lethargy, behavior change, fatigue, hyperirritability
 Dermatologic: Rash
 Gastrointestinal: Nausea, vomiting, anorexia
 Genitourinary: Impotence
 Hematologic: Agranulocytopenia, agranulocytosis, anemia
 Ocular: Diplopia, nystagmus
Overdosage/Toxicology Symptoms include unsteady gait, slurred speech, confusion, jaundice, hypothermia, fever, hypotension, coma, and respiratory arrest. Assure adequate hydration and renal function. Urinary alkalinization with I.V. sodium bicarbonate also helps enhance elimination. Repeat oral doses of activated charcoal significantly reduce the half-life of primidone resulting from enhancement of nonrenal elimination. The usual dose is 0.1-1 g/kg every 4-6 hours for 3-4 days, unless the patient has no bowel movement, causing charcoal to remain in the GI tract. Hemodialysis or hemoperfusion is of uncertain value. Patients in stage IV coma, due to high serum drug levels, may require charcoal hemoperfusion.
Drug Interactions
 Cytochrome P450 Effect: Metabolized to phenobarbital; **Induces** CYP1A2 (strong), 2B6 (strong), 2C8 (strong), 2C9 (strong), 3A4 (strong)
 Increased Effect/Toxicity: When combined with other CNS depressants, ethanol, opioid analgesics, antidepressants, or benzodiazepines, additive respiratory and CNS depression may occur. Barbiturates may enhance the hepatotoxic potential of acetaminophen overdoses. Chloramphenicol, MAO inhibitors, valproic acid, and felbamate may inhibit barbiturate metabolism. Barbiturates may impair the absorption of griseofulvin, and may enhance the nephrotoxic effects of methoxyflurane. Concurrent use of phenobarbital with meperidine may result in increased CNS depression. Concurrent use of phenobarbital with primidone may result in elevated phenobarbital serum concentrations. CYP2C19 inhibitors may increase the levels/effects of primidone; example inhibitors include delavirdine, fluconazole, fluvoxamine, gemfibrozil, isoniazid, omeprazole, and ticlopidine.
 Decreased Effect: Barbiturates may increase the metabolism of estrogens and reduce the efficacy of oral contraceptives; an alternative method of contraception should be considered. Barbiturates inhibit the hypoprothrombinemic effects of oral anticoagulants via increased metabolism. Barbiturates may enhance the metabolism of methadone resulting in methadone withdrawal. The levels/effects of primidone may be decreased by aminoglutethimide, carbamazepine, phenytoin, rifampin, and other CYP2C19 inducers.

 Primidone may decrease the levels/effects of aminophylline, amiodarone, benzodiazepines, bupropion, calcium channel blockers, carbamazepine, citalopram, clarithromycin, cyclosporine, diazepam, efavirenz, erythromycin, estrogens, fluoxetine, fluvoxamine, glimepiride, glipizide, ifosfamide, losartan, methsuximide, mirtazapine, nateglinide, nefazodone, nevirapine, phenytoin, pioglitazone, promethazine, propranolol, protease inhibitors, proton pump inhibitors, rifampin, ropinirole, rosiglitazone, selegiline, sertraline, sulfonamides, tacrolimus, theophylline, venlafaxine, voriconazole, warfarin, zafirlukast, and other CYP1A2, 2A6, 2B6, 2C8, 2C9, or 3A4 substrates.
Ethanol/Nutrition/Herb Interactions
 Ethanol: Avoid ethanol (may increase CNS depression).
 Food: Protein-deficient diets increase duration of action of primidone.
 Herb/Nutraceutical: Avoid valerian, St John's wort, kava kava, gotu kola (may increase CNS depression).

Stability Protect from light.

Mechanism of Action Decreases neuron excitability, raises seizure threshold similar to phenobarbital; primidone has two active metabolites, phenobarbital and phenylethylmalonamide (PEMA); PEMA may enhance the activity of phenobarbital

Pharmacodynamics/Kinetics

Distribution: Adults: V_d: 2-3 L/kg

Protein binding: 99%

Metabolism: Hepatic to phenobarbital (active) and phenylethylmalonamide (PEMA)

Bioavailability: 60% to 80%

Half-life elimination (age dependent): Primidone: 10-12 hours; PEMA: 16 hours; Phenobarbital: 52-118 hours

Time to peak, serum: ~4 hours

Excretion: Urine (15% to 25% as unchanged drug and active metabolites)

Dosage Oral:

Children <8 years: Initial: 50-125 mg/day given at bedtime; increase by 50-125 mg/day increments every 3-7 days; usual dose: 10-25 mg/kg/day in divided doses 3-4 times/day

Children ≥8 years and Adults: Initial: 125-250 mg/day at bedtime; increase by 125-250 mg/day every 3-7 days; usual dose: 750-1500 mg/day in divided doses 3-4 times/day with maximum dosage of 2 g/day

Adults: Essential tremor (unlabeled use): 750 mg early in divided doses

Dosing interval in renal impairment:

Cl_{cr} 50-80 mL/minute: Administer every 8 hours

Cl_{cr} 10-50 mL/minute: Administer every 8-12 hours

Cl_{cr} <10 mL/minute: Administer every 12-24 hours

Hemodialysis: Moderately dialyzable (20% to 50%); administer dose postdialysis or administer supplemental 30% dose

Dietary Considerations Folic acid: Low erythrocyte and CSF folate concentrations. Megaloblastic anemia has been reported. To avoid folic acid deficiency and megaloblastic anemia, some clinicians recommend giving patients on anticonvulsants prophylactic doses of folic acid and cyanocobalamin.

Monitoring Parameters Serum primidone and phenobarbital concentration, CBC, neurological status. Due to CNS effects, monitor closely when initiating drug in elderly. Monitor CBC at 6-month intervals to compare with baseline obtained at start of therapy. Since elderly metabolize phenobarbital at a slower rate than younger adults, it is suggested to measure both primidone and phenobarbital levels together.

Reference Range Therapeutic: Children <5 years: 7-10 mcg/mL (SI: 32-46 μmol/L); Adults: 5-12 mcg/mL (SI: 23-55 μmol/L); toxic effects rarely present with levels <10 mcg/mL (SI: 46 μmol/L) if phenobarbital concentrations are low. Dosage of primidone is adjusted with reference mostly to the phenobarbital level; Toxic: >15 mcg/mL (SI: >69 μmol/L)

Dosage Forms Tablet: 50 mg, 250 mg [generic tablet may contain sodium benzoate]

Dosage forms available in Canada: Tablet: 125 mg, 250 mg. **Note:** 50 mg tablet is **not** available in Canada.

♦ **Primsol**® see Trimethoprim on page 1744

♦ **Prinivil**® see Lisinopril on page 1021

♦ **Prinzide**® see Lisinopril and Hydrochlorothiazide on page 1023

♦ **Priorix**™ **(Can)** see Measles, Mumps, and Rubella Vaccines (Combined) on page 1057

♦ **Priscoline**® **[DSC]** see Tolazoline on page 1701

♦ **Pristinamycin** see Quinupristin and Dalfopristin on page 1476

♦ **Privine**® **[OTC]** see Naphazoline on page 1198

♦ **ProAir**™ **HFA** see Albuterol on page 57

♦ **ProAmatine**® see Midodrine on page 1142

Probenecid (proe BEN e sid)

Canadian Brand Names Benuryl™

Index Terms Benemid [DSC]

Pharmacologic Category Uricosuric Agent

Additional Appendix Information

Treatment of Sexually Transmitted Infections on page 2007

Use Prevention of hyperuricemia associated with gout or gouty arthritis; prolongation and elevation of beta-lactam plasma levels

Lactation Excretion in breast milk unknown

Medication Safety Issues

Sound-alike/look-alike issues:

Probenecid may be confused with Procanbid®

Contraindications Hypersensitivity to probenecid or any component of the formulation; high-dose aspirin therapy; blood dyscrasias; uric acid kidney stones; children <2 years of age

Warnings/Precautions Use with caution in patients with peptic ulcer. Salicylates may diminish the therapeutic effect of probenecid. This effect may be more pronounced with high, chronic doses, however, the manufacturer recommends the use of an alternative analgesic even in place of small doses of aspirin. Use of probenecid with penicillin in patients with renal insufficiency is not recommended. Probenecid monotherapy may not be effective in patients with a creatinine clearance <30 mL/minute. May cause exacerbation of acute gouty attack

Adverse Reactions Frequency not defined.

Cardiovascular: Flushing

Central nervous system: Dizziness, fever, headache

Dermatologic: Alopecia, dermatitis, pruritus, rash

Gastrointestinal: Anorexia, nausea, sore gums, vomiting

Genitourinary: Hematuria, polyuria

Hematologic: Anemia, aplastic anemia, hemolytic anemia, leukopenia

Hepatic: Hepatic necrosis

(Continued)

Probenecid *(Continued)*

Neuromuscular & skeletal: Costovertebral pain, gouty arthritis (acute)

Renal: Nephrotic syndrome, renal colic

Miscellaneous: Anaphylaxis, hypersensitivity

Drug Interactions

Cytochrome P450 Effect: Inhibits CYP2C19 (weak)

Increased Effect/Toxicity: Probenecid may decrease the excretion of carbapenems, cephalosporins, dapsone, methotrexate, and penicillins. Concomitant use with methotrexate should be avoided. Probenecid may increase the serum concentration of NSAIDs; the manufacturer of ketorolac contraindicates concomitant use. Probenecid may enhance the therapeutic effect of thiopental. Probenecid may decrease the metabolism of zidovudine.

Decreased Effect: Salicylates may diminish the therapeutic effect of probenecid.

Mechanism of Action Competitively inhibits the reabsorption of uric acid at the proximal convoluted tubule, thereby promoting its excretion and reducing serum uric acid levels; increases plasma levels of weak organic acids (penicillins, cephalosporins, or other beta-lactam antibiotics) by competitively inhibiting their renal tubular secretion

Pharmacodynamics/Kinetics

Onset of action: Effect on penicillin levels: 2 hours

Absorption: Rapid and complete

Metabolism: Hepatic

Half-life elimination (dose dependent): Normal renal function: 6-12 hours

Time to peak, serum: 2-4 hours

Excretion: Urine

Dosage Oral:

Children:

<2 years: Contraindicated

2-14 years: Prolong penicillin serum levels: Initial: 25 mg/kg, then 40 mg/kg/day given 4 times/day (maximum: 500 mg/dose)

Gonorrhea: >45 kg: Refer to adult guidelines

Adults:

Hyperuricemia with gout: 250 mg twice daily for one week; increase to 250-500 mg/day; may increase by 500 mg/month, if needed, to maximum of 2-3 g/day (dosages may be increased by 500 mg every 6 months if serum urate concentrations are controlled)

Prolong penicillin serum levels: 500 mg 4 times/day

Gonorrhea: CDC guidelines (alternative regimen): Probenecid 1 g orally with cefoxitin 2 g I.M.

Pelvic inflammatory disease: CDC guidelines: Cefoxitin 2 g I.M. plus probenecid 1 g orally as a single dose

Neurosyphilis: CDC guidelines (alternative regimen): Procaine penicillin 2.4 million units/day I.M. plus probenecid 500 mg 4 times/day; both administered for 10-14 days

Dosing adjustment in renal impairment: Cl$_{cr}$ <30 mL/minute: Avoid use

Dietary Considerations Drug may cause GI upset; take with food if GI upset. Drink plenty of fluids.

Administration Administer with food or antacids to minimize GI effects

Monitoring Parameters Uric acid, renal function, CBC

Test Interactions False-positive glucosuria with Clinitest®, a falsely high determination of theophylline has occurred and the renal excretion of phenolsulfonphthalein 17-ketosteroids and bromsulfophthalein (BSP) may be inhibited

Additional Information Avoid fluctuation in uric acid (increase or decrease); may precipitate gout attack. Use of sodium bicarbonate or potassium citrate is suggested until serum uric acid normalizes and tophaceous deposits disappear.

Dosage Forms Tablet: 500 mg

♦ **Probenecid and Colchicine** *see Colchicine and Probenecid on page 414*

Procainamide *(pro KANE a mide)*

U.S. Brand Names Procanbid®

Canadian Brand Names Apo-Procainamide®; Procainamide Hydrochloride Injection, USP; Procan® SR; Pronestyl®-SR

Index Terms PCA (error-prone abbreviation); Procainamide Hydrochloride; Procaine Amide Hydrochloride

Pharmacologic Category Antiarrhythmic Agent, Class Ia

Use Treatment of ventricular tachycardia (VT), premature ventricular contractions, paroxysmal atrial tachycardia (PSVT), and atrial fibrillation (AF); prevent recurrence of ventricular tachycardia, paroxysmal supraventricular tachycardia, atrial fibrillation or flutter

Unlabeled/Investigational Use ACLS guidelines:

Stable monomorphic VT (EF >40%, no CHF)

Stable wide complex tachycardia, likely VT (EF >40%, no CHF, patient stable)

Atrial fibrillation or flutter, including pre-excitation syndrome (EF >40%, no CHF)

AV reentrant, narrow complex tachycardia (eg, reentrant SVT) [preserved ventricular function]

PALS guidelines: Tachycardia with pulses and poor perfusion (possible VT)

Pregnancy Risk Factor C

Lactation Enters breast milk/use caution (AAP rates "compatible")

Medication Safety Issues

Sound-alike/look-alike issues:

Procanbid® may be confused with probenecid

Pronestyl® may be confused with Ponstel®

PCA is an error-prone abbreviation (mistaken as patient controlled analgesia)

Contraindications Hypersensitivity to procaine, other ester-type local anesthetics, or any component of the formulation; complete heart block (except in patients with a functioning artificial pacemaker); second-degree AV block (without a functional pacemaker); various types of hemiblock (without a functional pacemaker); SLE; torsade de pointes; concurrent cisapride use; QT prolongation

Warnings/Precautions Use with caution in patients with marked AV conduction distur-bances, myasthenia gravis, bundle-branch block, or severe cardiac glycoside intoxication, ventricular arrhythmias with organic heart disease or coronary occlusion, CHF supraventric-ular tachyarrhythmias unless adequate measures are taken to prevent marked increases in ventricular rates; concurrent therapy with other class Ia drugs may accumulate in patients with renal or hepatic dysfunction; some tablets contain tartrazine; injection may contain bisulfite (allergens). **[U.S. Boxed Warning]: Long-term administration leads to the devel-opment of a positive antinuclear antibody (ANA) test in 50% of patients which may result in a lupus erythematosus-like syndrome (in 20% to 30% of patients);** discontinue procainamide with SLE symptoms and choose an alternative agent; elderly have reduced clearance and frequent drug interactions. Potentially fatal blood dyscrasias have occurred with therapeutic doses; close monitoring is recommended during the first 3 months of therapy.

Adverse Reactions

>1%:

Cardiovascular: Hypotension (I.V., up to 5%)

Dermatologic: Rash

Gastrointestinal: Diarrhea (3% to 4%), nausea, vomiting, taste disorder, GI complaints (3% to 4%)

<1% (Limited to important or life-threatening): Agranulocytosis, angioneurotic edema, aplastic anemia, arrhythmia (proarrhythmic effect, new or worsened), bone marrow suppression, cerebellar ataxia, cholestasis, demyelinating polyradiculoneuropathy, depressed myocardial contractility, depression, disorientation, drug fever, granulomatous hepatitis, hallucinations, hemolytic anemia, hepatic failure, hypoplastic anemia, leuko-penia, mania, myasthenia gravis (worsened), myocarditis, myopathy, neuromuscular blockade, neutropenia, pancreatitis, pancytopenia, paradoxical increase in ventricular rate in atrial fibrillation/flutter, pericarditis, peripheral neuropathy, pleural effusion, positive ANA, positive Coombs' test, pruritus, pseudo-obstruction, psychosis, pulmonary embolism, QT prolongation (excessive), rash, respiratory failure due to myopathy, second-degree heart block, SLE-like syndrome, thrombocytopenia (0.5%), torsade de pointes, tremor, urticaria, vasculitis, ventricular arrhythmia

Overdosage/Toxicology Has a low toxic:therapeutic ratio and may easily produce fatal intoxication (acute toxic dose: 5 g in adults). Symptoms of include sinus bradycardia, sinus node arrest or asystole; PR, QRS or QT interval prolongation; torsade de pointes (polymor-phous ventricular tachycardia); and depressed myocardial contractility, which along with alpha-adrenergic or ganglionic blockade, may result in hypotension and pulmonary edema. Other effects are seizures, coma, and respiratory arrest.

Treatment is primarily symptomatic and effects usually respond to conventional therapies (fluids, positioning, vasopressors, anticonvulsants, antiarrhythmics). **Note:** Do not use other type 1a or 1c antiarrhythmic agents to treat ventricular tachycardia. Sodium bicar-bonate may treat wide QRS intervals or hypotension. Markedly impaired conduction or high degree AV block, unresponsive to bicarbonate, indicates consideration of a pacemaker is needed.

Drug Interactions

Cytochrome P450 Effect: Substrate of CYP2D6 (major)

Increased Effect/Toxicity: Amiodarone, cimetidine, ofloxacin (and potentially other renally eliminated quinolones), ranitidine, and trimethoprim increase procainamide and NAPA blood levels; consider reducing procainamide dosage by 25% with concurrent use. Cisapride and procainamide may increase the risk of malignant arrhythmia; concurrent use is contraindicated. Procainamide may potentiate neuromuscular blockade of neuromus-cular-blocking agents. CYP2D6 inhibitors may increase the levels/effects of procainamide; example inhibitors include chlorpromazine, delavirdine, fluoxetine, miconazole, paroxetine, pergolide, quinidine, quinine, ritonavir, and ropinirole.

Drugs which may prolong the QT interval include amiodarone, amitriptyline, bepridil, cisapride, disopyramide, erythromycin, haloperidol, imipramine, pimozide, quinidine, sotalol, mesoridazine, thioridazine, and some quinolone antibiotics (sparfloxacin, gatiflox-acin, moxifloxacin); concurrent use may result in additional prolongation of the QT interval.

Ethanol/Nutrition/Herb Interactions

Ethanol: Avoid ethanol (acute ethanol administration reduces procainamide serum concen-trations).

Herb/Nutraceutical: Avoid ephedra (may worsen arrhythmia).

Stability Procainamide may be stored at room temperature up to 27°C; however, refrigeration retards oxidation, which causes color formation. The solution is initially colorless but may turn slightly yellow on standing. Injection of air into the vial causes the solution to darken. Solutions darker than a light amber should be discarded.

Minimum volume: 1 g/250 mL NS/D$_5$W.

Stability of admixture at room temperature in D$_5$W or NS: 24 hours.

Some information that procainamide may be subject to greater decomposition in D$_5$W unless the admixture is refrigerated or the pH is adjusted. Procainamide is believed to form an association complex with dextrose - the bioavailability of procainamide in this complex is not known and the complex formation is reversible.

Mechanism of Action Decreases myocardial excitability and conduction velocity and may depress myocardial contractility, by increasing the electrical stimulation threshold of ventricle, His-Purkinje system and through direct cardiac effects

Pharmacodynamics/Kinetics

Onset of action: I.M. 10-30 minutes

Distribution: V$_d$: Children: 2.2 L/kg; Adults: 2 L/kg; Congestive heart failure or shock: Decreased V$_d$

(Continued)

Procainamide *(Continued)*

Protein binding: 15% to 20%

Metabolism: Hepatic via acetylation to produce N-acetyl procainamide (NAPA) (active metabolite)

Bioavailability: Oral: 75% to 95%

Half-life elimination:

Procainamide (hepatic acetylator, phenotype, cardiac and renal function dependent):
Children: 1.7 hours; Adults: 2.5-4.7 hours; Anephric: 11 hours

NAPA (dependent upon renal function):
Children: 6 hours; Adults: 6-8 hours; Anephric: 42 hours

Time to peak, serum: Capsule: 45 minutes to 2.5 hours; I.M.: 15-60 minutes

Excretion: Urine (25% as NAPA)

Dosage Must be titrated to patient's response

Children:

Oral: 15-50 mg/kg/24 hours divided every 3-6 hours

I.M.: 50 mg/kg/24 hours divided into doses of $1/8$ to $1/4$ every 3-6 hours in divided doses until oral therapy is possible

I.V. (infusion requires use of an infusion pump):

Load: 3-6 mg/kg/dose over 5 minutes not to exceed 100 mg/dose; may repeat every 5-10 minutes to maximum of 15 mg/kg/load

Maintenance as continuous I.V. infusion: 20-80 mcg/kg/minute; maximum: 2 g/24 hours

Possible VT (pulses and poor perfusion) [PALS 2005 Guidelines]: I.V.; I.O.: 15 mg/kg over 30-60 minutes

Adults:

Oral: Usual dose: 50 mg/kg/24 hours: maximum: 5 g/24 hours (**Note:** Twice-daily dosing approved for Procanbid®.)

Immediate release formulation: 250-500 mg/dose every 3-6 hours

Extended release formulation: 500 mg to 1 g every 6 hours; Procanbid®: 1000-2500 mg every 12 hours

I.M.: 0.5-1 g every 4-8 hours until oral therapy is possible

I.V. (infusion requires use of an infusion pump):

Loading dose: 15-18 mg/kg administered as slow infusion over 25-30 minutes **or** 100-200 mg/dose repeated every 5 minutes as needed to a total dose of 1 g. Reduce loading dose to 12 mg/kg in severe renal or cardiac impairment.

Maintenance dose: 1-4 mg/minute by continuous infusion. Maintenance infusions should be reduced by one-third in patients with moderate renal or cardiac impairment and by two-thirds in patients with severe renal or cardiac impairment.

ACLS guidelines: Infuse 20 mg/minute until arrhythmia is controlled, hypotension occurs, QRS complex widens by 50% of its original width, or total of 17 mg/kg is given.

Dosing interval in renal impairment:

Oral:

Cl_{cr} 10-50 mL/minute: Administer every 6-12 hours.

Cl_{cr} <10 mL/minute: Administer every 8-24 hours.

I.V.:

Loading dose: Reduce dose to 12 mg/kg in severe renal impairment.

Maintenance infusion: Reduce dose by one-third in patients with mild renal impairment. Reduce dose by two-thirds in patients with severe renal impairment.

Dialysis:

Procainamide: Moderately hemodialyzable (20% to 50%): 200 mg supplemental dose posthemodialysis is recommended.

N-acetylprocainamide: Not dialyzable (0% to 5%)

Procainamide/N-acetylprocainamide: Not peritoneal dialyzable (0% to 5%)

Procainamide/N-acetylprocainamide: Replace by blood level during continuous arteriovenous or venovenous hemofiltration

Dosing adjustment in hepatic impairment: Reduce dose by 50%.

Dietary Considerations Should be taken with water on an empty stomach.

Administration

Oral: Do **not** crush or chew extended release drug products.

Must dilute prior to I.V. administration; maximum rate: 50 mg/minute; administer around-the-clock rather than 4 times/day to promote less variation in peak and trough serum levels.

Infusion rate: **2 g/250 mL** (I.V. infusion requires use of an infusion pump):

1 mg/minute: 7.5 mL/hour

2 mg/minute: 15 mL/hour

3 mg/minute: 22.5 mL/hour

4 mg/minute: 30 mL/hour

5 mg/minute: 37.5 mL/hour

6 mg/minute: 45 mL/hour

Monitoring Parameters ECG, blood pressure, CBC with differential, platelet count; cardiac monitor and blood pressure monitor required during I.V. administration; blood levels in patients with renal failure or receiving constant infusion >3 mg/minute for longer than 24 hours

Reference Range

Timing of serum samples: Draw trough just before next oral dose; draw 6-12 hours after I.V. infusion has started; half-life is 2.5-5 hours

Therapeutic levels: Procainamide: 4-10 mcg/mL; NAPA 15-25 mcg/mL; Combined: 10-30 mcg/mL

Toxic concentration: Procainamide: >10-12 mcg/mL

Dosage Forms

Capsule, as hydrochloride: 250 mg, 500 mg

Injection, solution, as hydrochloride: 100 mg/mL (10 mL); 500 mg/mL (2 mL) [contains sodium metabisulfite]

Tablet, extended release, as hydrochloride: 500 mg, 750 mg, 1000 mg

Procanbid®: 500 mg, 1000 mg

Extemporaneous Preparations Note: Several formulations have been described, some being more complex; for all formulations, the pH must be 4-6 to prevent degradation; some preparations require adjustment of pH; shake well before use

A suspension of 50 mg/mL can be made with the capsules, distilled water, and a 2:1 simple syrup/cherry syrup mixture; stability 2 weeks under refrigeration (ASHP, 1987)

Concentrations of 5, 50, and 100 mg/mL oral liquid preparations (made with the capsules, sterile water for irrigation and cherry syrup) stored at 4°C to 6°C (pH 6) were stable for at least 6 months (Metras, 1992).

A sucrose-based syrup (procainamide 50 mg/mL) made with capsules, distilled water, simple syrup, parabens, and cherry flavoring had a calculated stability of 456 days at 25°C and measured stability of 42 days at 40°C (pH ~5) while a maltitol-based syrup (procainamide 50 mg/mL) made with capsules, distilled water, Lycasin® (a syrup vehicle with 75% w/w maltitol), parabens, sodium bisulfate, saccharin, sodium acetate, pineapple and apricot flavoring, FD & C yellow number 6 (pH adjusted to 5 with glacial acetic acid) had a calculated stability of 97 days at 25°C and a measured stability of 94 days at 40°C. The maltitol-based syrup was more stable than the sucrose-based syrup when temperature was >37°C, but the sucrose-based syrup was more stable at temperatures <37°C (Alexander, 1993).

Alexander KS, Pudipeddi M, and Parker GA, "Stability of Procainamide Hydrochloride Syrups Compounded From Capsules," *Am J Hosp Pharm*, 1993, 50(4):693-8.

Handbook in Extemporaneous Formulations, Bethesda, MD: American Society of Hospital Pharmacists, 1987.

Metras JI, Swenson CF, and MacDermott MP, "Stability of Procainamide Hydrochloride in an Extemporaneously Compounded Oral Liquid," *Am J Hosp Pharm*, 1992, 49(7):1720-4.

Swenson CF, "Importance of Following Instructions When Compounding," *Am J Hosp Pharm*, 1993, 50(2):261.

♦ **Procainamide Hydrochloride** *see* Procainamide *on page 1424*
♦ **Procainamide Hydrochloride Injection, USP (Can)** *see* Procainamide *on page 1424*

Procaine (PROE kane)

U.S. Brand Names Novocain®
Index Terms Procaine Hydrochloride
Pharmacologic Category Local Anesthetic
Use Produces spinal anesthesia and epidural and peripheral nerve block by injection and infiltration methods
Pregnancy Risk Factor C
Lactation Excretion in breast milk unknown
Contraindications Hypersensitivity to procaine, PABA, parabens, other ester local anesthetics, or any component of the formulation
Warnings/Precautions Patients with cardiac diseases, hyperthyroidism, or other endocrine diseases may be more susceptible to toxic effects of local anesthetics; some preparations contain metabisulfite
Adverse Reactions
1% to 10%: Local: Burning sensation at site of injection, tissue irritation, pain at injection site
<1% (Limited to important or life-threatening): Aseptic meningitis resulting in paralysis, chills, CNS stimulation followed by CNS depression
Overdosage/Toxicology Treatment is primarily symptomatic and supportive. Termination of anesthesia by pneumatic tourniquet inflation should be attempted when the agent is administered by infiltration or regional injection. Seizures commonly respond to diazepam, while hypotension responds to I.V. fluids and Trendelenburg positioning. Bradyarrhythmias (heart rate <60) can be treated with I.V., I.M., or SubQ atropine 15 mcg/kg. With the development of metabolic acidosis, I.V. sodium bicarbonate 0.5-2 mEq/kg and ventilatory assistance should be instituted.
Drug Interactions
Decreased Effect: Decreased effect of sulfonamides with the PABA metabolite of procaine, chloroprocaine, and tetracaine. Decreased/increased effect of vasopressors, ergot alkaloids, and MAO inhibitors on blood pressure when using anesthetic solutions with a vasoconstrictor.
Mechanism of Action Blocks both the initiation and conduction of nerve impulses by decreasing the neuronal membrane's permeability to sodium ions, which results in inhibition of depolarization with resultant blockade of conduction
Pharmacodynamics/Kinetics
Onset of action: 2-5 minutes
Duration (patient, type of block, concentration, and method of anesthesia dependent): 0.5-1.5 hours
Metabolism: Rapidly hydrolyzed by plasma enzymes to para-aminobenzoic acid and diethylaminoethanol (80% conjugated before elimination)
Half-life elimination: 7.7 minutes
Excretion: Urine (as metabolites and some unchanged drug)
Dosage Dose varies with procedure, desired depth, and duration of anesthesia, desired muscle relaxation, vascularity of tissues, physical condition, and age of patient
Administration Prior to instillation of anesthetic agent, withdraw plunger to ensure needle is not in artery or vein; resuscitative equipment should be available when local anesthetics are administered
Dosage Forms Injection, solution, as hydrochloride: 1% [10 mg/mL] (2 mL) [contains sodium bisulfite]; 10% (2 mL) [contains sodium bisulfite]

♦ **Procaine Amide Hydrochloride** *see* Procainamide *on page 1424*
♦ **Procaine Benzylpenicillin** *see* Penicillin G Procaine *on page 1335*
♦ **Procaine Hydrochloride** *see* Procaine *on page 1427*

♦ **Procaine Penicillin G** *see* Penicillin G Procaine *on page 1335*
♦ **Procanbid®** *see* Procainamide *on page 1424*
♦ **Procan® SR (Can)** *see* Procainamide *on page 1424*

Procarbazine (proe KAR ba zeen)

U.S. Brand Names Matulane®
Canadian Brand Names Matulane®; Natulan®
Index Terms Benzmethyzin; N-Methylhydrazine; NSC-77213; Procarbazine Hydrochloride
Pharmacologic Category Antineoplastic Agent, Alkylating Agent
Additional Appendix Information
   Tyramine Content of Foods *on page 2115*
Use Treatment of Hodgkin's disease
Unlabeled/Investigational Use Treatment of non-Hodgkin's lymphoma, brain tumors, melanoma, lung cancer, multiple myeloma
Pregnancy Risk Factor D
Pregnancy Implications Animal studies have demonstrated teratogenic effects. There are no adequate and well-controlled studies in pregnant women. There are, however, case reports of fetal malformations in the offspring of pregnant women exposed to procarbazine as part of a combination chemotherapy regimen. Women of childbearing potential should avoid becoming pregnant during treatment.
Lactation Excretion in breast milk unknown/not recommended
Medication Safety Issues
   Sound-alike/look-alike issues:
      Procarbazine may be confused with dacarbazine
      Matulane® may be confused with Modane®

   High alert medication: The Institute for Safe Medication Practices (ISMP) includes this medication among its list of drugs which have a heightened risk of causing significant patient harm when used in error.
Contraindications Hypersensitivity to procarbazine or any component of the formulation; pre-existing bone marrow aplasia; ethanol ingestion; pregnancy
Warnings/Precautions Hazardous agent - use appropriate precautions for handling and disposal. Use with caution in patients with pre-existing renal or hepatic impairment. Procarbazine possesses MAO inhibitor activity and has potential for severe drug and food interactions; follow MAOI diet. Avoid ethanol consumption, could cause disulfiram-like reaction. May cause hemolysis and/or presence of Heinz inclusion bodies in erythrocytes. Bone marrow depression may occur 2-8 weeks after treatment initiation. Allow ≥1 month interval between radiation therapy or myelosuppressive chemotherapy and initiation of treatment. Withhold treatment for CNS toxicity, leukopenia (WBC <4000/mm^3), thrombocytopenia (platelets <100,000/mm^3), hypersensitivity, stomatitis, diarrhea or hemorrhage. Procarbazine is a carcinogen which may cause acute leukemia. May cause infertility. **[U.S. Boxed Warning]: Should be administered under the supervision of an experienced cancer chemotherapy physician.**
Adverse Reactions Most frequencies not defined.
   Cardiovascular: Edema, flushing, hypotension, syncope, tachycardia
   Central nervous system: Apprehension, ataxia, chills, coma, confusion, depression, dizziness, drowsiness, fatigue, fever, hallucination, headache, insomnia, lethargy, nervousness, nightmares, pain, seizure, slurred speech
   Dermatologic: Alopecia, dermatitis, hyperpigmentation, petechiae, pruritus, purpura, rash, urticaria
   Endocrine & metabolic: Gynecomastia (in prepubertal and early pubertal males)
   Hematologic: Eosinophilia; hemolysis (in patients with G6PD deficiency); hemolytic anemia; myelosuppression (leukopenia, anemia, thrombocytopenia); pancytopenia
   Gastrointestinal: Abdominal pain, anorexia, constipation, diarrhea, dysphagia, hematemesis, melena; nausea and vomiting ([60% to 90%], increasing the dose in a stepwise fashion over several days may minimize); stomatitis, xerostomia
   Genitourinary: Azoospermia (reported with combination chemotherapy), hematuria, nocturia, polyuria, reproductive dysfunction (>10%)
   Hepatic: Hepatic dysfunction, jaundice
   Neuromuscular & skeletal: Arthralgia, falling, foot drop, myalgia, neuropathy, paresthesia, reflex diminished, tremor, unsteadiness, weakness
   Ocular: Diplopia, inability to focus, nystagmus, papilledema, photophobia, retinal hemorrhage
   Otic: Hearing loss
   Respiratory: Cough, epistaxis, hemoptysis, hoarseness, pleural effusion, pneumonitis, pulmonary toxicity (<1%)
   Miscellaneous: Allergic reaction, diaphoresis, herpes, infection, secondary malignancies (2% to 15%; reported with combination therapy)
Overdosage/Toxicology Symptoms of overdose include hypotension, paresthesia, bone marrow suppression, hallucinations, nausea, vomiting, diarrhea, enteritis, tremors, seizures, and coma. In addition to I.V. hydration, treatment is symptom-directed and supportive. Emesis and/or gastric lavage may be useful. Adverse effects such as marrow toxicity may begin as late as 2 weeks after exposure. Monitor CBC and liver function tests for at least 2 weeks.
Drug Interactions
   Increased Effect/Toxicity: Procarbazine may enhance the vasopressor effect of direct-acting alpha-/beta-agonists. Procarbazine may enhance the hypertensive effect of indirect-acting alpha-/beta-agonists, alpha$_1$-agonists, alpha$_2$-agonists (ophthalmic), amphetamines, dexmethylphenidate, and methylphenidate. Procarbazine may enhance the serotonergic effect of serotonin/norepinephrine reuptake inhibitors, cyclobenzaprine, dextromethorphan, meperidine, selective serotonin reuptake inhibitors, serotonin modulators, and tricyclic antidepressants. Procarbazine may enhance the neurotoxic (central) effect of atomoxetine, bupropion, lithium and mirtazapine. Procarbazine may enhance the adverse/toxic effect of disulfiram and rauwolfia alkaloids. Procarbazine may increase the

levels/effects of serotonin 5-HT$_{1D}$ receptor agonists. Altretamine may enhance the orthostatic effect of procarbazine. Buspirone may enhance the adverse/toxic effect of procarbazine. COMT Inhibitors may enhance the cardiovascular adverse/toxic effects of procarbazine. Levodopa may enhance the hypertensive effect of procarbazine. Sibutramine may enhance the serotonergic effect of procarbazine. Tramadol may enhance the neurotoxic effects of procarbazine.

Decreased Effect: Procarbazine may decrease the absorption of digoxin tablets. Procarbazine may diminish the antihypertensive effect of false neurotransmitters.

Ethanol/Nutrition/Herb Interactions
Ethanol: May enhance the adverse/toxic effects of procarbazine; concurrent use not recommended.
Food: Concurrent ingestion of foods rich in tyramine may cause sudden and severe high blood pressure (hypertensive crisis). Avoid tyramine-containing foods with MAOIs. Food's freshness is also an important concern; improperly stored or spoiled food can create an environment where tyramine concentrations may increase.
Herb/Nutraceuticals: Avoid supplements containing caffeine, tyrosine, tryptophan or phenylalanine. Ingestion of large quantities may increase the risk of severe side effects (eg, hypertensive reactions, serotonin syndrome).

Stability Protect from light.

Mechanism of Action Mechanism of action is not clear, methylating of nucleic acids; inhibits DNA, RNA, and protein synthesis; may damage DNA directly and suppresses mitosis; metabolic activation required by host

Pharmacodynamics/Kinetics
Absorption: Rapid and complete
Distribution: Crosses blood-brain barrier; equilibrates between plasma and CSF
Metabolism: Hepatic and renal
Half-life elimination: 1 hour
Time to peak, plasma: 1 hour
Excretion: Urine and respiratory tract (<5% as unchanged drug, 70% as metabolites)

Dosage Refer to Individual protocols. Manufacturer states that the dose is based on patient's ideal weight if the patient is obese or has abnormal fluid retention. Other studies suggest that ideal body weight may not be necessary. Oral (may be given as a single daily dose or in 2-3 divided doses):

Children:
BMT aplastic anemia conditioning regimen: 12.5 mg/kg/day every other day for 4 doses
Hodgkin's disease: MOPP/IC-MOPP regimens: 100 mg/m^2/day for 14 days and repeated every 4 weeks
Neuroblastoma and medulloblastoma: Doses as high as 100-200 mg/m^2/day once daily have been used
Adults: Initial: 2-4 mg/kg/day in single or divided doses for 7 days then increase dose to 4-6 mg/kg/day until response is obtained or leukocyte count decreased <4000/mm^3 or the platelet count decreased <100,000/mm^3; maintenance: 1-2 mg/kg/day
Dosing in renal/hepatic impairment: Use with caution, may result in increased toxicity; decrease dose if serum creatinine >2 mg/dL or total bilirubin >3 mg/dL

Dietary Considerations Avoid tyramine-containing foods/beverages. Some examples include aged or matured cheese, air-dried or cured meats (including sausages and salamis), fava or broad bean pods, tap/draft beers, Marmite concentrate, sauerkraut, soy sauce and other soybean condiments.

Administration May be given as a single daily dose or in 2-3 divided doses.

Monitoring Parameters CBC with differential, platelet and reticulocyte count, urinalysis, liver function test, renal function test.

Dosage Forms
Capsule, as hydrochloride:
Matulane®: 50 mg

♦ **Procarbazine Hydrochloride** *see Procarbazine on page 1428*
♦ **Procardia**® *see NIFEdipine on page 1226*
♦ **Procardia XL**® *see NIFEdipine on page 1226*
♦ **Procetofene** *see Fenofibrate on page 689*
♦ **Prochieve**™ *see Progesterone on page 1433*

Prochlorperazine (proe klor PER a zeen)

U.S. Brand Names Compro™
Canadian Brand Names Apo-Prochlorperazine®; Compazine®; Nu-Prochlor; Stemetil®
Index Terms Chlormeprazine; Compazine; Prochlorperazine Edisylate; Prochlorperazine Maleate
Pharmacologic Category Antiemetic; Antipsychotic Agent, Typical, Phenothiazine
Use Management of nausea and vomiting; psychotic disorders including schizophrenia; anxiety
Unlabeled/Investigational Use Behavioral syndromes in dementia
Pregnancy Implications Crosses the placenta. Isolated reports of congenital anomalies, however, some included exposures to other drugs. Jaundice, extrapyramidal signs, hyper-/hyporeflexes have been noted in newborns. Available evidence with use of occasional low doses suggests safe use during pregnancy.
Lactation Excretion in breast milk unknown/use caution
Medication Safety Issues
Sound-alike/look-alike issues:
Prochlorperazine may be confused with chlorproMAZINE
Compazine® may be confused with Copaxone®, Coumadin®

CPZ (occasional abbreviation for Compazine®) is an error-prone abbreviation (mistaken as chlorpromazine)
(Continued)

Prochlorperazine *(Continued)*

Contraindications Hypersensitivity to prochlorperazine or any component of the formulation (cross-reactivity between phenothiazines may occur); severe CNS depression; coma; pediatric surgery; Reye's syndrome; should not be used in children <2 years of age or <9 kg

Warnings/Precautions May be sedating; use with caution in disorders where CNS depression is a feature. May obscure intestinal obstruction or brain tumor. May impair physical or mental abilities. Effects with other sedative drugs or ethanol may be potentiated. Use with caution in Parkinson's disease; hemodynamic instability; bone marrow suppression; predisposition to seizures; subcortical brain damage; and in severe cardiac, hepatic, renal or respiratory disease. Caution in breast cancer or other prolactin-dependent tumors. May alter temperature regulation or mask toxicity of other drugs. Use caution with exposure to heat. May alter cardiac conduction. May cause orthostatic hypotension. Hypotension may occur following administration, particularly when parenteral form is used or in high dosages.

Phenothiazines may cause anticholinergic effects; therefore, they should be used with caution in patients with decreased gastrointestinal motility, urinary retention, BPH, xerostomia, or visual problems. Conditions which also may be exacerbated by cholinergic blockade include narrow-angle glaucoma (screening is recommended) and worsening of myasthenia gravis. May cause extrapyramidal symptoms. Use caution in the elderly. Children with acute illness or dehydration are more susceptible to neuromuscular reactions; use cautiously. May be associated with neuroleptic malignant syndrome (NMS).

Adverse Reactions Reported with prochlorperazine or other phenothiazines. Frequency not defined

Cardiovascular: Cardiac arrest, hypotension, peripheral edema, Q-wave distortions, T-wave distortions

Central nervous system: Agitation, catatonia, cerebral edema, cough reflex suppressed, dizziness, drowsiness, fever (mild — I.M.), headache, hyperactivity, hyperpyrexia, impairment of temperature regulation, insomnia, neuroleptic malignant syndrome (NMS), paradoxical excitement, restlessness, seizure

Dermatologic: Angioedema, contact dermatitis, discoloration of skin (blue-gray), epithelial keratopathy, erythema, eczema, exfoliative dermatitis (injectable), itching, photosensitivity, rash, skin pigmentation, urticaria

Endocrine & metabolic: Amenorrhea, breast enlargement, galactorrhea, gynecomastia, glucosuria, hyperglycemia, hypoglycemia, lactation, libido (changes in), menstrual irregularity, SIADH

Gastrointestinal: Appetite increased, atonic colon, constipation, ileus, nausea, weight gain, xerostomia

Genitourinary: Ejaculating dysfunction, ejaculatory disturbances, impotence, incontinence, polyuria, priapism, urinary retention, urination difficulty

Hematologic: Agranulocytosis, aplastic anemia, eosinophilia, hemolytic anemia, leukopenia, pancytopenia, thrombocytopenic purpura

Hepatic: Biliary stasis, cholestatic jaundice, hepatotoxicity

Neuromuscular & skeletal: Dystonias (torticollis, opisthotonos, carpopedal spasm, trismus, oculogyric crisis, protusion of tongue); extrapyramidal symptoms (pseudoparkinsonism, akathisia, dystonias, tardive dyskinesia); SLE-like syndrome, tremor

Ocular: blurred vision, cornea and lens changes, lenticular/corneal deposits, miosis, mydriasis, pigmentary retinopathy

Respiratory: Asthma, laryngeal edema, nasal congestion

Miscellaneous: Allergic reactions, diaphoresis

Overdosage/Toxicology Symptoms include deep sleep, coma, extrapyramidal symptoms, abnormal involuntary muscle movements, and hypotension. Following initiation of essential overdose management, toxic symptom and supportive treatment should be initiated. Hypotension usually responds to I.V. fluids or Trendelenburg positioning. If unresponsive to these measures, the use of a parenteral medication may be required (eg, norepinephrine 0.1-0.2 mcg/kg/minute titrated to response). Seizures commonly respond to diazepam (I.V. 5-10 mg bolus in adults every 15 minutes, if needed, up to a total of 30 mg; I.V. 0.25-0.4 mg/kg/dose up to a total of 10 mg in children) or to phenytoin or phenobarbital. Critical cardiac arrhythmias often respond to I.V. phenytoin (15 mg/kg up to 1 g), while other antiarrhythmics can be used. Extrapyramidal symptoms (eg, dystonic reactions) may require management with diphenhydramine 1-2 mg/kg (adults) up to a maximum of 50 mg I.M. or slow I.V. push followed by a maintenance dose for 48-72 hours. When these reactions are unresponsive to diphenhydramine, anticholinergic agents such as benztropine mesylate I.V. 1-2 mg (adults) may be effective. These agents are generally effective within 2-5 minutes.

Drug Interactions

Increased Effect/Toxicity: Prochlorperazine plus lithium may rarely produce neurotoxicity. Prochlorperazing may produce additive CNS depressant effects with other CNS depressants. Acetylcholinesterase inhibitors may increase the risk of EPS. Alpha-/beta-agonists, antihistamines, QT_c-prolonging agents may enhance the arrhythmogenic effects of phenothiazines. Concurrent use may enhance the hypotensive effects of narcotics and beta blockers. SSRIs may increase risk of hypotension. Antimalarials and beta blockers may increase serum levels of prochlorperazine.Pramlintide may increase anticholinergic effects of prochlorperazine.

Decreased Effect: The antihypertensive effects of methyldopa and guanadrel may be inhibited by prochlorperazine. Prochlorperazine may inhibit the antiparkinsonian effect of levodopa. Prochlorperazine may reverse the pressor effects of epinephrine. Antacids and attapulgite may decreased absorption of phenothiazines. Anticholinertics may decrease the therapeutic response to phenothiazines.

Ethanol/Nutrition/Herb Interactions

Ethanol: Avoid ethanol (may increase CNS depression).

Food: Limit caffeine.

Herb/Nutraceutical: Avoid dong quai, St John's wort (may also cause photosensitization). Avoid kava kava, gotu kola, valerian, St John's wort (may increase CNS depression).

Stability

Injection: Store at <30°C (<86°F); do not freeze. Protect from light. Clear or slightly yellow solutions may be used.

I.V. infusion: Injection may be diluted in 50-100 mL NS or D$_5$W.

Suppository, tablet: Store at 15°C to 30°C (59°F to 86°F). Protect from light.

Mechanism of Action

Prochlorperazine is a piperazine phenothiazine antipsychotic which blocks postsynaptic mesolimbic dopaminergic D$_1$ and D$_2$ receptors in the brain, including the chemoreceptor trigger zone; exhibits a strong alpha-adrenergic and anticholinergic blocking effect and depresses the release of hypothalamic and hypophyseal hormones; believed to depress the reticular activating system, thus affecting basal metabolism, body temperature, wakefulness, vasomotor tone and emesis

Pharmacodynamics/Kinetics

Onset of action: Oral: 30-40 minutes; I.M.: 10-20 minutes; Rectal: ~60 minutes

Peak antiemetic effect: I.V.: 30-60 minutes

Duration: Rectal: 12 hours; Oral: 3-4 hours; I.M., I.V.: Adults: 4-6 hours; I.M.: Children: 12 hours

Distribution: V$_d$: 1400-1548 L; crosses placenta; enters breast milk

Metabolism: Primarily hepatic; N-desmethyl prochlorperazine (major active metabolite)

Bioavailability: Oral: 12.5%

Half-life elimination: Oral: 3-5 hours; I.V.: ~7 hours

Dosage

Antiemetic: Children (therapy >1 day usually not required): **Note:** Not recommended for use in children <9 kg or <2 years:

Oral, rectal: >9 kg: 0.4 mg/kg/24 hours in 3-4 divided doses; **or**

9-13 kg: 2.5 mg every 12-24 hours as needed; maximum: 7.5 mg/day

13.1-17 kg: 2.5 mg every 8-12 hours as needed; maximum: 10 mg/day

17.1-37 kg: 2.5 mg every 8 hours or 5 mg every 12 hours as needed; maximum: 15 mg/day

I.M.: 0.13 mg/kg/dose; change to oral as soon as possible

Antiemetic: Adults:

Oral (tablet): 5-10 mg 3-4 times/day; usual maximum: 40 mg/day; larger doses may rarely be required

I.M. (deep): 5-10 mg every 3-4 hours; usual maximum: 40 mg/day

I.V.: 2.5-10 mg; maximum 10 mg/dose or 40 mg/day; may repeat dose every 3-4 hours as needed

Rectal: 25 mg twice daily

Surgical nausea/vomiting: Adults: **Note:** Should not exceed 40 mg/day

I.M.: 5-10 mg 1-2 hours before induction or to control symptoms during or after surgery; may repeat once if necessary

I.V. (administer slow IVP <5 mg/minute): 5-10 mg 15-30 minutes before induction or to control symptoms during or after surgery; may repeat once if necessary

Rectal (unlabeled use): 25 mg

Antipsychotic:

Children 2-12 years (not recommended in children <9 kg or <2 years):

Oral, rectal: 2.5 mg 2-3 times/day; do not give more than 10 mg the first day; increase dosage as needed to maximum daily dose of 20 mg for 2-5 years and 25 mg for 6-12 years

I.M.: 0.13 mg/kg/dose; change to oral as soon as possible

Adults:

Oral: 5-10 mg 3-4 times/day; titrate dose slowly every 2-3 days; doses up to 150 mg/day may be required in some patients for treatment of severe disturbances

I.M.: Initial: 10-20 mg; if necessary repeat initial dose every 1-4 hours to gain control; more than 3-4 doses are rarely needed. If parenteral administration is still required; give 10-20 mg every 4-6 hours; change to oral as soon as possible.

Nonpsychotic anxiety: Oral (tablet): Adults: Usual dose: 15-20 mg/day in divided doses; do not give doses >20 mg/day or for longer than 12 weeks

Elderly: Behavioral symptoms associated with dementia (unlabeled use): Initial: 2.5-5 mg 1-2 times/day; increase dose at 4- to 7-day intervals by 2.5-5 mg/day; increase dosing intervals (twice daily, 3 times/day, etc) as necessary to control response or side effects; maximum daily dose should probably not exceed 75 mg in elderly; gradual increases (titration) may prevent some side effects or decrease their severity

Dietary Considerations

Increase dietary intake of riboflavin; should be administered with food or water. Rectal suppositories may contain coconut and palm oil.

Administration

May be administered orally, I.M., or I.V.

I.M.: Inject by deep IM into outer quadrant of buttocks.

I.V.: Doses should be given as a short (~30 minute) infusion to avoid orthostatic hypotension; administer at ≤5 mg/minute

Monitoring Parameters

Vital signs; lipid profile, fasting blood glucose/Hgb A$_{1c}$; BMI; mental status, abnormal involuntary movement scale (AIMS); periodic ophthalmic exams (if chronically used); extrapyramidal symptoms (EPS)

Test Interactions

False-positives for phenylketonuria, pregnancy, urinary amylase, uroporphyrins, urobilinogen

Additional Information

Not recommended as an antipsychotic due to inferior efficacy compared to other phenothiazines.

Dosage Forms

Injection, solution, as edisylate: 5 mg/mL (2 mL, 10 mL) [contains benzyl alcohol]

Suppository, rectal: 2.5 mg (12s), 5 mg (12s), 25 mg (12s) [may contain coconut and palm oil]

Compro™: 25 mg (12s) [contains coconut and palm oils]

Tablet, as maleate: 5 mg, 10 mg

- ◆ **Prochlorperazine Edisylate** see Prochlorperazine on page 1429
- ◆ **Prochlorperazine Maleate** see Prochlorperazine on page 1429
- ◆ **Procrit**® see Epoetin Alfa on page 595
- ◆ **Proctocort**® see Hydrocortisone on page 852

- **ProctoCream® HC** *see* Hydrocortisone *on page 852*
- **Proctofene** *see* Fenofibrate *on page 689*
- **ProctoFoam®-HC** *see* Pramoxine and Hydrocortisone *on page 1409*
- **Proctofoam™-HC (Can)** *see* Pramoxine and Hydrocortisone *on page 1409*
- **Procto-Kit™** *see* Hydrocortisone *on page 852*
- **Procto-Pak™** *see* Hydrocortisone *on page 852*
- **Proctosert** *see* Hydrocortisone *on page 852*
- **Proctosol-HC®** *see* Hydrocortisone *on page 852*
- **Proctozone-HC™** *see* Hydrocortisone *on page 852*

Procyclidine (proe SYE kli deen)

U.S. Brand Names Kemadrin®
Canadian Brand Names PMS-Procyclidine
Index Terms Procyclidine Hydrochloride
Pharmacologic Category Anti-Parkinson's Agent, Anticholinergic; Anticholinergic Agent
Use Relieves symptoms of parkinsonian syndrome and drug-induced extrapyramidal symptoms
Pregnancy Risk Factor C
Lactation Excretion in breast milk unknown/not recommended
Medication Safety Issues
Sound-alike/look-alike issues:
Kemadrin® may be confused with Coumadin®
Contraindications Hypersensitivity to procyclidine or any component of the formulation; angle-closure glaucoma; myasthenia gravis; safe use in children not established
Warnings/Precautions Use with caution in hot weather or during exercise. Elderly patients frequently develop increased sensitivity and require strict dosage regulation - side effects may be more severe in elderly patients with atherosclerotic changes. Use with caution in patients with tachycardia, cardiac arrhythmias, hypertension, hypotension, prostatic hyperplasia (especially in the elderly) or any tendency toward urinary retention, liver or kidney disorders and obstructive disease of the GI or GU tract. When given in large doses or to susceptible patients, may cause weakness and inability to move particular muscle groups.
Adverse Reactions Frequency not defined.
Cardiovascular: Palpitation, tachycardia
Central nervous system: Ataxia, confusion, drowsiness, fatigue, giddiness, headache, light-headedness, loss of memory
Dermatologic: Dry skin, photosensitivity, rash
Gastrointestinal: Constipation, dry throat, epigastric distress, nausea, vomiting, xerostomia
Genitourinary: Difficult urination
Neuromuscular & skeletal: Weakness
Ocular: Blurred vision, increased intraocular pain, mydriasis
Respiratory: Dry nose
Miscellaneous: Diaphoresis decreased
Overdosage/Toxicology Symptoms include disorientation, hallucinations, delusions, blurred vision, dysphagia, absent bowel sounds, hyperthermia, hypertension, and urinary retention. Anticholinergic toxicity is caused by strong binding of the drug to cholinergic receptors. Anticholinesterase inhibitors reduce acetylcholinesterase, the enzyme that breaks down acetylcholine and thereby allows acetylcholine to accumulate and compete for receptor binding with the offending anticholinergic. For anticholinergic overdose with severe life-threatening symptoms, physostigmine 1-2 mg (0.5 mg or 0.02 mg/kg for children) SubQ or slow I.V. may be given to reverse these effects.
Drug Interactions
Increased Effect/Toxicity: Central and/or peripheral anticholinergic syndrome can occur when administered with amantadine, rimantadine, opioid analgesics, phenothiazines and other antipsychotics (especially with high anticholinergic activity), tricyclic antidepressants, quinidine and some other antiarrhythmics, and antihistamines.
Decreased Effect: May increase gastric degradation of levodopa and decrease the amount of levodopa absorbed by delaying gastric emptying; the opposite may be true for digoxin. Therapeutic effects of cholinergic agents (tacrine, donepezil) and neuroleptics may be antagonized.
Ethanol/Nutrition/Herb Interactions Ethanol: Avoid ethanol.
Mechanism of Action Thought to act by blocking excess acetylcholine at cerebral synapses; many of its effects are due to its pharmacologic similarities with atropine; it exerts an antispasmodic effect on smooth muscle, is a potent mydriatic; inhibits salivation
Pharmacodynamics/Kinetics
Onset of action: 30-40 minutes
Duration: 4-6 hours
Dosage Adults: Oral: 2.5 mg 3 times/day after meals; if tolerated, gradually increase dose, maximum of 20 mg/day if necessary
Dosing adjustment in hepatic impairment: Decrease dose to a twice daily dosing regimen
Dietary Considerations Should be taken after meals to minimize stomach upset.
Administration Should be administered after meals to minimize stomach upset.
Monitoring Parameters Symptoms of EPS or Parkinson's disease, pulse, anticholinergic effects (ie, CNS, bowel and bladder function)
Dosage Forms Tablet, as hydrochloride [scored]: 5 mg

- **Procyclidine Hydrochloride** *see* Procyclidine *on page 1432*
- **Procytox® (Can)** *see* Cyclophosphamide *on page 428*
- **Profasi® HP (Can)** *see* Chorionic Gonadotropin (Human) *on page 363*
- **Profen II DM®** *see* Guaifenesin, Pseudoephedrine, and Dextromethorphan *on page 821*
- **Profen Forte™ DM** *see* Guaifenesin, Pseudoephedrine, and Dextromethorphan *on page 821*
- **Profilnine® SD** *see* Factor IX Complex (Human) *on page 681*

♦ **Proflavanol C™ (Can)** *see* Ascorbic Acid *on page 156*

Progesterone (proe JES ter one)

U.S. Brand Names Crinone®; Prochieve™; Prometrium®
Canadian Brand Names Crinone®; Prometrium®
Index Terms Pregnenedione; Progestin
Pharmacologic Category Progestin
Use
Oral: Prevention of endometrial hyperplasia in nonhysterectomized, postmenopausal women who are receiving conjugated estrogen tablets; secondary amenorrhea
I.M.: Amenorrhea; abnormal uterine bleeding due to hormonal imbalance
Intravaginal gel: Part of assisted reproductive technology (ART) for infertile women with progesterone deficiency; secondary amenorrhea
Pregnancy Risk Factor B (Prometrium®, per manufacturer); none established for vaginal gel or injection (contraindicated)
Pregnancy Implications There is an increased risk of minor birth defects in children whose mothers take progesterones during the first 4 months of pregnancy. Hypospadias has been reported in male and mild masculinization of the external genitalia has been reported in female babies exposed during the first trimester. Cleft lip, cleft palate, congenital heart disease, patent ductus arteriosus, ventricular septal defect, intrauterine death, and spontaneous abortion have been noted in case reports following use of oral progesterone during pregnancy. High doses of progesterone would be expected to impair fertility. According to the American College of Obstetricians and Gynecologists, additional studies are needed to evaluate the use of progesterone to reduce the risk of preterm birth. If needed, use should be restricted to women with history of previous spontaneous abortion at <37 weeks. The vaginal gel is indicated for use in ART.
Lactation Enters breast milk/use caution (AAP rates "compatible")
Contraindications Hypersensitivity to progesterone or any component of the formulation; undiagnosed abnormal vaginal bleeding; history of or current thrombophlebitis or venous thromboembolic disorders (including DVT, PE); active or recent (within 1 year) arterial thromboembolic disease (eg, stroke, MI); carcinoma of the breast or genital organs; hepatic dysfunction or disease; missed abortion; diagnostic test for pregnancy; pregnancy (see Pregnancy Implications)
The following are also contraindicated in patients with allergies to their inactive ingredient:
Crinone® and Prochieve™ vaginal gels contain palm oil
Prometrium® capsules contain peanut oil
Oil for injection contains sesame oil
Warnings/Precautions Use caution with cardiovascular disease or dysfunction. Progestins used in combination with estrogen may increase the risks of hypertension, myocardial infarction (MI), stroke, pulmonary emboli (PE), and deep vein thrombosis; incidence of these effects was shown to be significantly increased in postmenopausal women using conjugated equine estrogens (CEE) in combination with medroxyprogesterone acetate (MPA). Similar risk should be assumed with other progestins. Progestins in combination with estrogens should not be used to prevent coronary heart disease.

The risk of dementia may be increased in postmenopausal women; increased incidence was observed in women ≥65 years of age taking CEE in combination with MPA. An increased risk of invasive breast cancer was observed in postmenopausal women using CEE in combination with MPA. An increase in abnormal mammograms has also been reported with estrogen and progestin therapy.

Discontinue pending examination in cases of sudden partial or complete vision loss, sudden onset of proptosis, diplopia, or migraine; discontinue permanently if papilledema or retinal vascular lesions are observed on examination. Use with caution in patients with diseases that may be exacerbated by fluid retention, including asthma, epilepsy, migraine, diabetes or renal dysfunction. Use caution with history of depression. Patients should be warned that progesterone might cause transient dizziness or drowsiness during initial therapy. Whenever possible, progestins in combination with estrogens should be discontinued at least 4-6 weeks prior to surgeries associated with an increased risk of thromboembolism or during periods of prolonged immobilization. Progestins used in combination with estrogen should be used for shortest duration possible consistent with treatment goals. Conduct periodic risk:benefit assessments.
Adverse Reactions
Injection (I.M.):
Cardiovascular: Edema
Central nervous system: Depression, fever, insomnia, somnolence
Dermatologic: Acne, allergic rash (rare), alopecia, hirsutism, pruritus, rash, urticaria
Endocrine & metabolic: Amenorrhea, breakthrough bleeding, breast tenderness, galactorrhea, menstrual flow changes, spotting
Gastrointestinal: Nausea, weight gain, weight loss
Genitourinary: Cervical erosion changes, cervical secretion changes
Hepatic: Cholestatic jaundice
Local: Pain at the injection site
Miscellaneous: Anaphylactoid reactions

Oral capsule (percentages reported when used in combination with or cycled with conjugated estrogens):
>10%:
Central nervous system: Headache (10% to 31%), dizziness (15% to 24%), depression (19%)
Endocrine & metabolic: Breast tenderness (27%), breast pain (6% to 16%)
Gastrointestinal: Abdominal pain (6% to 12%), abdominal bloating (10% to 20%)
Genitourinary: Urinary problems (11%)
Neuromuscular & skeletal: Joint pain (20%), musculoskeletal pain (6% to 12%)
Miscellaneous: Viral infection (7% to 12%)
(Continued)

Progesterone *(Continued)*

5% to 10%:

Cardiovascular: Chest pain (7%)

Central nervous system: Fatigue (8% to 9%), emotional lability (6%), irritability (5% to 8%), worry (8%)

Gastrointestinal: Nausea/vomiting (8%), diarrhea (8%)

Respiratory: Upper respiratory tract infection (5%), cough (8%)

Miscellaneous: Night sweats (7%)

<5% (Limited to important or life-threatening): Acne, aggression, alopecia, ALT/AST increased, anaphylactic reaction, angina pectoris, anxiety, arthralgia, arthritis, blurred vision, breast cancer, cholecystectomy, cholestasis, cholestatic hepatitis, circulatory collapse, confusion, consciousness depressed/loss, constipation, convulsion, depersonalization, diplopia, disorientation, dyspepsia, dysphagia, edema, endometrial carcinoma, facial edema, fungal vaginitis, gastroenteritis, GGT increased, hemorrhagic rectum, hepatic enzymes increased, hepatic failure, hepatic necrosis, hepatitis, hernia, hiatus, hyperglycemia, hypersensitivity, hypertension, hypertonia, hypotension, insomnia, jaundice, leg cramps, leukorrhea, lymphadenopathy, muscle cramps, ovarian cyst, palpitation, pancreatitis (acute), paresthesia, personality disorder, pruritus, sedation, somnolence, speech disorder, stupor, suicidal ideation, syncope, tachycardia, TIA, tinnitus, tongue swelling, urticaria, uterine fibroid, vaginal dryness, vaginitis, verruca, vertigo, vision abnormal, visual disturbance, xerostomia

Vaginal gel (percentages reported with ART); also refer to oral capsule reactions listing for additional effects noted with progesterone:

>10%:

Central nervous system: Somnolence (27%), headache (13% to 17%), nervousness (16%), depression (11%)

Endocrine & metabolic: Breast enlargement (40%), breast pain (13%), libido decreased (11%)

Gastrointestinal: Constipation (27%), nausea (7% to 22%), cramps (15%), abdominal pain (12%)

Genitourinary: Perineal pain (17%), nocturia (13%)

5% to 10%:

Central nervous system: Pain (8%), dizziness (5%)

Gastrointestinal: Diarrhea (8%), bloating (7%), vomiting (5%)

Genitourinary: Vaginal discharge (7%), dyspareunia (6%), genital moniliasis (5%), genital pruritus (5%)

Neuromuscular & skeletal: Arthralgia (8%)

Overdosage/Toxicology Toxicity is unlikely following single exposures of excessive doses. Supportive treatment is adequate in most cases.

Drug Interactions

Cytochrome P450 Effect: Substrate of CYP1A2 (minor), 2A6 (minor), 2C9 (minor), 2C19 (major), 2D6 (minor), 3A4 (major); **Inhibits** CYP2C9 (weak), 2C19 (weak), 3A4 (weak)

Increased Effect/Toxicity: Ketoconazole may increase the bioavailability of progesterone. Progesterone may increase concentrations of estrogenic compounds during concurrent therapy with conjugated estrogens.

Decreased Effect: CYP2C19 inducers may decrease the levels/effects of progesterone; example inducers include aminoglutethimide, carbamazepine, phenytoin, and rifampin. CYP3A4 inducers may decrease the levels/effects of progesterone; example inducers include aminoglutethimide, carbamazepine, nafcillin, nevirapine, phenobarbital, phenytoin, and rifamycins.

Ethanol/Nutrition/Herb Interactions

Food: Food increases oral bioavailability.

Herb/Nutraceutical: St John's wort may decrease progesterone levels.

Stability Store at controlled room temperature.

Mechanism of Action Natural steroid hormone that induces secretory changes in the endometrium, promotes mammary gland development, relaxes uterine smooth muscle, blocks follicular maturation and ovulation, and maintains pregnancy

Pharmacodynamics/Kinetics

Absorption: Vaginal gel: Prolonged

Absorption half-life: 25-50 hours

Protein binding: 96% to 99%

Metabolism: Hepatic to metabolites

Half-life elimination: Vaginal gel: 5-20 minutes

Time to peak: Oral: Within 3 hours

Excretion: Urine, bile, feces

Dosage Adults:

I.M.: Female:

Amenorrhea: 5-10 mg/day for 6-8 consecutive days

Functional uterine bleeding: 5-10 mg/day for 6 doses

Oral: Female:

Prevention of endometrial hyperplasia (in postmenopausal women with a uterus who are receiving daily conjugated estrogen tablets): 200 mg as a single daily dose every evening for 12 days sequentially per 28-day cycle

Amenorrhea: 400 mg every evening for 10 days

Intravaginal gel: Female:

ART in women who require progesterone supplementation: 90 mg (8% gel) once daily; if pregnancy occurs, may continue treatment for up to 10-12 weeks

ART in women with partial or complete ovarian failure: 90 mg (8% gel) intravaginally twice daily; if pregnancy occurs, may continue up to 10-12 weeks

Secondary amenorrhea: 45 mg (4% gel) intravaginally every other day for up to 6 doses; women who fail to respond may be increased to 90 mg (8% gel) every other day for up to 6 doses

Administration

I.M.: Administer deep I.M. only

Intravaginal: Vaginal gel: (A small amount of gel will remain in the applicator following insertion): Administer into the vagina directly from sealed applicator. Remove applicator from wrapper; holding applicator by thickest end, shake down to move contents to thin end; while holding applicator by flat section of thick end, twist off tab; gently insert into vagina and squeeze thick end of applicator.

For use at altitudes above 2500 feet: Remove applicator from wrapper; hold applicator on both sides of bubble in the thick end; using a lancet, make a single puncture in the bubble to relieve air pressure; holding applicator by thickest end, shake down to move contents to thin end; while holding applicator by flat section of thick end, twist off tab; gently insert into vagina and squeeze thick end of applicator.

Monitoring Parameters Before starting therapy, a physical exam including the breasts and pelvis are recommended, also a Pap smear; signs or symptoms of depression, glucose in diabetics

Test Interactions Thyroid function, metyrapone, liver function, coagulation tests, endocrine function tests

Dosage Forms

Capsule (Prometrium®): 100 mg, 200 mg [contains peanut oil]

Gel, vaginal (Crinone®, Prochieve™): 4% (45 mg); 8% (90 mg) [contains palm oil; prefilled applicators]

Injection, oil: 50 mg/mL (10 mL) [contains benzyl alcohol 10%, sesame oil]

♦ **Progestin** see Progesterone on page 1433

♦ **Proglycem®** see Diazoxide on page 491

♦ **Prograf®** see Tacrolimus on page 1626

♦ **Proguanil and Atovaquone** see Atovaquone and Proguanil on page 173

♦ **Proleukin®** see Aldesleukin on page 59

♦ **Prolex™-D** see Guaifenesin and Phenylephrine on page 818

♦ **Prolex®-PD** see Guaifenesin and Phenylephrine on page 818

♦ **Prolixin® [DSC]** see Fluphenazine on page 731

♦ **Prolixin Decanoate®** see Fluphenazine on page 731

♦ **Proloprim®** see Trimethoprim on page 1744

♦ **Promacet** see Butalbital and Acetaminophen on page 259

Promethazine (proe METH a zeen)

U.S. Brand Names Phenadoz™; Phenergan®; Promethegan™

Canadian Brand Names Phenergan®

Index Terms Promethazine Hydrochloride

Pharmacologic Category Antiemetic; Antihistamine; Phenothiazine Derivative; Sedative

Use Symptomatic treatment of various allergic conditions; antiemetic; motion sickness; sedative; postoperative pain (adjunctive therapy); anesthetic (adjunctive therapy); anaphylactic reactions (adjunctive therapy)

Pregnancy Risk Factor C

Pregnancy Implications Teratogenic effects were not observed in animal studies. Crosses the placenta. Possible respiratory depression if drug is administered near time of delivery; behavioral changes, EEG alterations, impaired platelet aggregation reported with use during labor.

Lactation Excretion in breast milk unknown/use caution

Medication Safety Issues

Sound-alike/look-alike issues:

Promethazine may be confused with chlorproMAZINE, predniSONE, promazine

Phenergan® may be confused with Phenaphen®, Phrenilin®, Theragran®

Administration issues:

To prevent or minimize tissue damage during I.V. administration, the Institute for Safe Medication Practices (ISMP) has the following recommendations:

Limit concentration available to the 25 mg/mL product

Consider limiting initial doses to 6.25-12.5 mg

Further dilute the 25 mg/mL strength into 10-20 mL NS

Administer through a large bore vein (not hand or wrist)

Administer via running I.V. line at port furthest from patient's vein

Consider administering over 10-15 minutes

Instruct patients to report immediately signs of pain or burning

Contraindications Hypersensitivity to promethazine or any component of the formulation (cross-reactivity between phenothiazines may occur); coma; treatment of lower respiratory tract symptoms, including asthma; children <2 years of age

Warnings/Precautions [U.S. Boxed Warning]: Respiratory fatalities have been reported in children <2 years of age. In children ≥2 years, use the lowest possible dose; other drugs with respiratory depressant effects should be avoided. Not for SubQ or intra-arterial administration. Injection may contain sodium metabisulfite. I.M. is the preferred route of parenteral administration. I.V. use has been associated with severe tissue damage; discontinue immediately if burning or pain occurs with administration. May be sedating; use with caution in disorders where CNS depression is a feature. May impair physical or mental abilities; patients must be cautioned about performing tasks which require mental alertness. Use with caution in Parkinson's disease; hemodynamic instability; bone marrow suppression; subcortical brain damage; and in severe cardiac, hepatic, renal, or respiratory disease. Avoid use in Reye's syndrome. May lower seizure threshold; use caution in persons with seizure disorders or in persons using narcotics or local anesthetics which may also affect seizure threshold. May alter temperature regulation or mask toxicity of other drugs due to antiemetic effects. May alter cardiac conduction (life-threatening arrhythmias have occurred with therapeutic doses of phenothiazines). May cause orthostatic hypotension; use with caution in (Continued)

Promethazine *(Continued)*

patients at risk of hypotension or where transient hypotensive episodes would be poorly tolerated (cardiovascular disease or cerebrovascular disease).

Phenothiazines may cause anticholinergic effects; therefore, they should be used with caution in patients with decreased gastrointestinal motility, urinary retention, BPH, xerostomia, or visual problems. Conditions which also may be exacerbated by cholinergic blockade include narrow-angle glaucoma (screening is recommended) and worsening of myasthenia gravis. May cause extrapyramidal symptoms, including pseudoparkinsonism, acute dystonic reactions, akathisia, and tardive dyskinesia. May be associated with neuroleptic malignant syndrome (NMS).

Adverse Reactions

Cardiovascular: Bradycardia, hypertension, nonspecific QT changes, postural hypotension, tachycardia

Central nervous system: Akathisia, catatonic states, confusion, delirium, disorientation, dizziness, drowsiness, dystonias, euphoria, excitation, extrapyramidal symptoms, fatigue, hallucinations, hysteria, insomnia, lassitude, nervousness, neuroleptic malignant syndrome, nightmares, pseudoparkinsonism, sedation, seizure, somnolence, tardive dyskinesia

Dermatologic: Angioneurotic edema, dermatitis, photosensitivity, skin pigmentation (slate gray), urticaria

Endocrine & metabolic: Amenorrhea, breast engorgement, gynecomastia, hyper-/hypoglycemia, lactation

Gastrointestinal: Constipation, nausea, vomiting, xerostomia

Genitourinary: Ejaculatory disorder, impotence, urinary retention

Hematologic: Agranulocytosis, aplastic anemia, eosinophilia, hemolytic anemia, leukopenia, thrombocytopenia, thrombocytopenic purpura

Hepatic: Jaundice

Local: Venous thrombosis; injection site reactions (burning, erythema, pain, edema)

Neuromuscular & skeletal: Incoordination, tremor

Ocular: Blurred vision, corneal and lenticular changes, diplopia, epithelial keratopathy, pigmentary retinopathy

Otic: Tinnitus

Respiratory: Apnea, asthma, nasal congestion, respiratory depression

Overdosage/Toxicology

Symptoms include CNS depression, respiratory depression, possible CNS stimulation, dry mouth, fixed and dilated pupils, and hypotension. Following initiation of essential overdose management, toxic symptom and supportive treatment should be initiated. Hypotension usually responds to I.V. fluids or Trendelenburg positioning. If unresponsive to these measures, norepinephrine 0.1-0.2 mcg/kg/minute titrated to response may be tried. Seizures commonly respond to diazepam (I.V. 5-10 mg bolus in adults every 15 minutes if needed up to a total of 30 mg; I.V. 0.25-0.4 mg/kg/dose up to a total of 10 mg in children) or to phenytoin or phenobarbital. Critical cardiac arrhythmias often respond to I.V. phenytoin (15 mg/kg up to 1 g), while other antiarrhythmics can be used. Neuroleptics often cause extrapyramidal symptoms (eg, dystonic reactions) requiring management with diphenhydramine 1-2 mg/kg (adults) up to a maximum of 50 mg I.M. or slow I.V. push followed by a maintenance dose for 48-72 hours. When these reactions are unresponsive to diphenhydramine, anticholinergic agents such as benztropine mesylate I.V. 1-2 mg (adults) may be effective. These agents are generally effective within 2-5 minutes. Epinephrine should not be used. Hemodialysis: Not dialyzable (0% to 5%)

Drug Interactions

Cytochrome P450 Effect: Substrate (major) of CYP2B6, 2D6; **Inhibits** CYP2D6 (weak)

Increased Effect/Toxicity: CYP2B6 inhibitors may increase the levels/effects of promethazine; example inhibitors include desipramine, paroxetine, and sertraline. CYP2D6 inhibitors may increase the levels/effects of promethazine; example inhibitors include chlorpromazine, delavirdine, fluoxetine, miconazole, paroxetine, pergolide, quinidine, quinine, ritonavir, and ropinirole. Pramlintide may enhance the gastrointestinal anticholinergic effects of promethazine.

Decreased Effect: Acetylcholinesterase inhibitors (centrally-acting) may diminish the effects of promethazine. CYP2B6 inducers may decrease the levels/effects of promethazine; example inducers include carbamazepine, nevirapine, phenobarbital, phenytoin, and rifampin. Benztropine (and other anticholinergics) may inhibit the therapeutic response to promethazine. Promethazine may diminish the effect of centrally-acting acetylcholinesterase inhibitors.

Ethanol/Nutrition/Herb Interactions

Ethanol: Avoid ethanol (may increase CNS depression).

Herb/Nutraceutical: Avoid valerian, St John's wort, kava kava, gotu kola (may increase CNS depression).

Stability

Injection: Prior to dilution, store at room temperature. Protect from light. Solutions in NS or D_5W are stable for 24 hours at room temperature.

Suppositories: Store refrigerated at 2°C to 8°C (36°F to 46°F).

Tablets: Store at room temperature. Protect from light.

Mechanism of Action

Blocks postsynaptic mesolimbic dopaminergic receptors in the brain; exhibits a strong alpha-adrenergic blocking effect and depresses the release of hypothalamic and hypophyseal hormones; competes with histamine for the H_1-receptor; reduces stimuli to the brainstem reticular system

Pharmacodynamics/Kinetics

Onset of action: I.M.: ~20 minutes; I.V.: 3-5 minutes

Peak effect: C_{max}: 9.04 ng/mL (suppository); 19.3 ng/mL (syrup)

Duration: 2-6 hours

Absorption:

I.M.: Bioavailability may be greater than with oral or rectal administration

Oral: Rapid and complete; large first pass effect limits systemic bioavailability

Distribution: V_d: 171 L

Protein binding: 93%

Metabolism: Hepatic; primarily oxidation; forms metabolites
Half-life elimination: 9-16 hours
Time to maximum serum concentration: 4.4 hours (syrup); 6.7-8.6 hours (suppositories)
Excretion: Primarily urine and feces (as inactive metabolites)

Dosage
Children ≥2 years:
Allergic conditions: Oral, rectal: 0.1 mg/kg/dose (maximum: 12.5 mg) every 6 hours during the day and 0.5 mg/kg/dose (maximum: 25 mg) at bedtime as needed
Antiemetic: Oral, I.M., I.V., rectal: 0.25-1 mg/kg 4-6 times/day as needed (maximum: 25 mg/dose)
Motion sickness: Oral, rectal: 0.5 mg/kg/dose 30 minutes to 1 hour before departure, then every 12 hours as needed (maximum dose: 25 mg twice daily)
Sedation: Oral, I.M., I.V., rectal: 0.5-1 mg/kg/dose every 6 hours as needed (maximum: 50 mg/dose)
Adults:
Allergic conditions (including allergic reactions to blood or plasma):
Oral, rectal: 25 mg at bedtime **or** 12.5 mg before meals and at bedtime (range: 6.25-12.5 mg 3 times/day)
I.M., I.V.: 25 mg, may repeat in 2 hours when necessary; switch to oral route as soon as feasible
Antiemetic: Oral, I.M., I.V., rectal: 12.5-25 mg every 4-6 hours as needed
Motion sickness: Oral, rectal: 25 mg 30-60 minutes before departure, then every 12 hours as needed
Sedation: Oral, I.M., I.V., rectal: 12.5-50 mg/dose

Dietary Considerations Increase dietary intake of riboflavin.

Administration Formulations available for oral, rectal, I.M./I.V.; not for SubQ or intra-arterial administration. Administer I.M. into deep muscle (preferred route of administration). I.V. administration is **not** the preferred route; severe tissue damage may occur. Solution for injection should be administered in a maximum concentration of 25 mg/mL (more dilute solutions are recommended). Administer via running I.V. line at port furthest from patient's vein, or through a large bore vein (not hand or wrist). Consider administering over 10-15 minutes (maximum: 25 mg/minute). Discontinue immediately if burning or pain occurs with administration.

Monitoring Parameters Relief of symptoms, mental status

Test Interactions Alters the flare response in intradermal allergen tests; hCG-based pregnancy tests may result in false-negatives or false-positives; increased serum glucose may be seen with glucose tolerance tests

Dosage Forms [DSC] = Discontinued product
Injection, solution, as hydrochloride: 25 mg/mL (1 mL); 50 mg/mL (1 mL)
Phenergan®: 25 mg/mL (1 mL); 50 mg/mL (1 mL) [contains sodium metabisulfite]
Suppository, rectal, as hydrochloride: 12.5 mg, 25 mg, 50 mg
Phenadoz™: 12.5 mg, 25 mg
Phenergan®: 25 mg, 50 mg [DSC]
Promethegan™: 12.5 mg, 25 mg, 50 mg
Syrup, as hydrochloride: 6.25 mg/5 mL (120 mL, 480 mL) [contains alcohol]
Tablet, as hydrochloride: 12.5 mg, 25 mg, 50 mg
Phenergan®: 25 mg [DSC]

Promethazine and Codeine (proe METH a zeen & KOE deen)

Index Terms Codeine and Promethazine
Pharmacologic Category Antihistamine/Antitussive
Use Temporary relief of coughs and upper respiratory symptoms associated with allergy or the common cold
Restrictions C-V
Pregnancy Risk Factor C
Medication Safety Issues
Sound-alike/look-alike issues:
Phenergan® may be confused with Phenaphen®, Phrenilin®, Theragran®
Dosage Oral:
Children:
<2 years: Use of promethazine is contraindicated
2 to <6 years:
12 kg: 1.25-2.5 mL every 4-6 hours (maximum: 6 mL/24 hours)
14 kg: 1.25-2.5 mL every 4-6 hours (maximum: 7 mL/24 hours)
16 kg: 1.25-2.5 mL every 4-6 hours (maximum: 8 mL/24 hours)
18 kg: 1.25-2.5 mL every 4-6 hours (maximum: 9 mL/24 hours)
6-12 years: 2.5-5 mL every 4-6 hours (maximum: 30 mL/24 hours)
Adults: 5 mL every 4-6 hours (maximum 30 mL/24 hours)
Additional Information Complete prescribing information for this medication should be consulted for additional detail.
Dosage Forms Syrup: Promethazine hydrochloride 6.25 mg and codeine phosphate 10 mg per 5 mL (120 mL, 473 mL) [contains alcohol]

Promethazine and Dextromethorphan
(proe METH a zeen & deks troe meth OR fan)

Index Terms Dextromethorphan and Promethazine
Pharmacologic Category Antihistamine/Antitussive
Use Temporary relief of coughs and upper respiratory symptoms associated with allergy or the common cold
Pregnancy Risk Factor C
(Continued)

Promethazine and Dextromethorphan *(Continued)*

Dosage Oral:

Children:

<2 years: Use of promethazine is contraindicated

2-6 years: 1.25-2.5 mL every 4-6 hours up to 10 mL in 24 hours

6-12 years: 2.5-5 mL every 4-6 hours up to 20 mL in 24 hours

Adults: 5 mL every 4-6 hours up to 30 mL in 24 hours

Additional Information Complete prescribing information for this medication should be consulted for additional detail.

Dosage Forms Syrup: Promethazine hydrochloride 6.25 mg and dextromethorphan hydrobromide 15 mg per 5 mL (120 mL, 480 mL) [contains alcohol 7%]

♦ **Promethazine and Meperidine** *see* Meperidine and Promethazine *on page 1083*

Promethazine and Phenylephrine (proe METH a zeen & fen il EF rin)

Index Terms Phenylephrine and Promethazine

Pharmacologic Category Antihistamine/Decongestant Combination

Use Temporary relief of upper respiratory symptoms associated with allergy or the common cold

Pregnancy Risk Factor C

Dosage Oral:

Children:

<2 years: Use of promethazine is contraindicated

2-6 years: 1.25-2.5 mL every 4-6 hours, not to exceed 7.5 mL in 24 hours

6-12 years: 2.5-5 mL every 4-6 hours, not to exceed 30 mL in 24 hours

Children >12 years and Adults: 5 mL every 4-6 hours, not to exceed 30 mL in 24 hours

Additional Information Complete prescribing information for this medication should be consulted for additional detail.

Dosage Forms Syrup: Promethazine hydrochloride 6.25 mg and phenylephrine hydrochloride 5 mg per 5 mL (473 mL) [contains alcohol]

♦ **Promethazine Hydrochloride** *see* Promethazine *on page 1435*

Promethazine, Phenylephrine, and Codeine
(proe METH a zeen, fen il EF rin, & KOE deen)

Index Terms Codeine, Promethazine, and Phenylephrine; Phenylephrine, Promethazine, and Codeine

Pharmacologic Category Antihistamine/Decongestant/Antitussive

Use Temporary relief of coughs and upper respiratory symptoms including nasal congestion associated with allergy or the common cold

Restrictions C-V

Pregnancy Risk Factor C

Dosage Oral:

Children:

<2 years: Use of promethazine is contraindicated

2 to <6 years:

12 kg: 1.25-2.5 mL every 4-6 hours, not to exceed 6 mL/24 hours

14 kg: 1.25-2.5 mL every 4-6 hours, not to exceed 7 mL/24 hours

16 kg: 1.25-2.5 mL every 4-6 hours, not to exceed 8 mL/24 hours

18 kg: 1.25-2.5 mL every 4-6 hours, not to exceed 9 mL/24 hours

6 to <12 years: 2.5-5 mL every 4-6 hours, not to exceed 30 mL/24 hours

Adults: 5 mL every 4-6 hours, not to exceed 30 mL/24 hours

Additional Information Complete prescribing information for this medication should be consulted for additional detail.

Dosage Forms Syrup: Promethazine hydrochloride 6.25 mg, phenylephrine hydrochloride 5 mg, and codeine phosphate 10 mg per 5 mL (480 mL) [contains alcohol and sodium benzoate]

♦ **Promethegan™** *see* Promethazine *on page 1435*

♦ **Prometrium®** *see* Progesterone *on page 1433*

♦ **Promit® [DSC]** *see* Dextran 1 *on page 486*

♦ **Pronap-100®** *see* Propoxyphene and Acetaminophen *on page 1445*

♦ **Pronestyl®-SR (Can)** *see* Procainamide *on page 1424*

♦ **Pronto® Complete Lice Killing Kit [OTC]** *see* Pyrethrins and Piperonyl Butoxide *on page 1461*

♦ **Pronto® Lice Control (Can)** *see* Pyrethrins and Piperonyl Butoxide *on page 1461*

♦ **Pronto® Plus Hair and Scalp Masque [OTC]** *see* Pyrethrins and Piperonyl Butoxide *on page 1461*

♦ **Pronto® Plus Mousse [OTC]** *see* Pyrethrins and Piperonyl Butoxide *on page 1461*

♦ **Pronto® Plus Warm Oil Treatment and Conditioner [OTC]** *see* Pyrethrins and Piperonyl Butoxide *on page 1461*

♦ **Pronto® Plus with Natural Extracts and Oils [OTC]** *see* Pyrethrins and Piperonyl Butoxide *on page 1461*

♦ **Propaderm® (Can)** *see* Beclomethasone *on page 198*

Propafenone (pro PAF en one)

U.S. Brand Names Rythmol®; Rythmol® SR
Canadian Brand Names Apo-Propafenone®; Rythmol® Gen-Propafenone
Index Terms Propafenone Hydrochloride
Pharmacologic Category Antiarrhythmic Agent, Class Ic
Use Treatment of life-threatening ventricular arrhythmias
Rythmol® SR: Maintenance of normal sinus rhythm in patients with symptomatic atrial fibrillation
Unlabeled/Investigational Use Supraventricular tachycardias, including those patients with Wolff-Parkinson-White syndrome
Pregnancy Risk Factor C
Pregnancy Implications There are no adequate and well-controlled studies in pregnant women; use only if potential benefit to the mother justifies potential risk to the fetus.
Lactation Enters breast milk/use caution
Contraindications Hypersensitivity to propafenone or any component of the formulation; sinoatrial, AV, and intraventricular disorders of impulse generation and/or conduction (except in patients with a functioning artificial pacemaker); sinus bradycardia; cardiogenic shock; uncompensated cardiac failure; hypotension; bronchospastic disorders; uncorrected electrolyte abnormalities; concurrent use of ritonavir (see Drug Interactions)
Warnings/Precautions Monitor for proarrhythmic events. May prolong QT_c interval; use caution with other QT_c-prolonging drugs. **[U.S. Boxed Warning]: In the Cardiac Arrhythmia Suppression Trial (CAST), recent (>6 days but <2 years ago) myocardial infarction patients with asymptomatic, nonlife-threatening ventricular arrhythmias did not benefit and may have been harmed by attempts to suppress the arrhythmia with flecainide or encainide. An increased mortality or nonfatal cardiac arrest rate (7.7%) was seen in the active treatment group compared with patients in the placebo group (3%). The applicability of the CAST results to other populations is unknown. Antiarrhythmic agents should be reserved for patients with life-threatening ventricular arrhythmias.** Can cause or unmask a variety of conduction disturbances. May alter pacing and sensing thresholds of artificial pacemakers. Patients with bronchospastic disease should generally not receive this drug. Monitor for worsening CHF if patient has underlying condition. Administer cautiously in significant hepatic dysfunction.

Adverse Reactions
1% to 10%:
Cardiovascular: New or worsened arrhythmia (proarrhythmic effect) (2% to 10%), angina (2% to 5%), CHF (1% to 4%), ventricular tachycardia (1% to 3%), palpitation (1% to 3%), AV block (first-degree) (1% to 3%), syncope (1% to 2%), increased QRS interval (1% to 2%), chest pain (1% to 2%), PVCs (1% to 2%), bradycardia (1% to 2%), edema (0% to 1%), bundle branch block (0% to 1%), atrial fibrillation (1%), hypotension (0% to 1%), intraventricular conduction delay (0% to 1%)
Central nervous system: Dizziness (4% to 15%), fatigue (2% to 6%), headache (2% to 5%), ataxia (0% to 2%), insomnia (0% to 2%), anxiety (1% to 2%), drowsiness (1%)
Dermatologic: Rash (1% to 3%)
Gastrointestinal: Nausea/vomiting (2% to 11%), unusual taste (3% to 23%), constipation (2% to 7%), dyspepsia (1% to 3%), diarrhea (1% to 3%), xerostomia (1% to 2%), anorexia (1% to 2%), abdominal pain (1% to 2%), flatulence (0% to 1%)
Neuromuscular & skeletal: Tremor (0% to 1%), arthralgia (0% to 1%), weakness (1% to 2%)
Ocular: Blurred vision (1% to 6%)
Respiratory: Dyspnea (2% to 5%)
Miscellaneous: Diaphoresis (1%)
<1% (Limited to important or life-threatening): Agranulocytosis, alopecia, amnesia, anemia, apnea, AV block (second or third degree), AV dissociation, cardiac arrest, cholestasis (0.1%), coma, confusion, CHF, depression, granulocytopenia, hepatitis (0.03%), hyperglycemia, impotence, increased bleeding time, leukopenia, lupus erythematosus, mania, memory loss, nephrotic syndrome, paresthesia, peripheral neuropathy, pruritus, psychosis, purpura, renal failure, seizure (0.3%), SIADH, sinus node dysfunction, thrombocytopenia, tinnitus, vertigo

Overdosage/Toxicology Has a narrow therapeutic index and severe toxicity may occur slightly above the therapeutic range, especially if combined with other antiarrhythmic drugs. Acute single ingestion of twice the daily therapeutic dose is life-threatening. Symptoms include increases in PR, QRS, QT intervals and amplitude of the T wave, as well as AV block, bradycardia, hypotension, ventricular arrhythmias (monomorphic or polymorphic ventricular tachycardia), and asystole. Other symptoms include dizziness, blurred vision, headache, and GI upset. Treatment is supportive, using conventional treatment (fluids, positioning, anticonvulsants, antiarrhythmics). **Note:** Type Ia antiarrhythmic agents should not be used to treat cardiotoxicity caused by type Ic antiarrhythmic drugs. Sodium bicarbonate may reverse QRS prolongation, bradycardia and hypotension; ventricular pacing may be needed. Hemodialysis is only of possible benefit for tocainide or flecainide overdose in patients with renal failure.

Drug Interactions
Cytochrome P450 Effect: Substrate of CYP1A2 (minor), 2D6 (major), 3A4 (minor); **Inhibits** CYP1A2 (weak), 2D6 (weak)
Increased Effect/Toxicity: Cimetidine and quinidine may increase propafenone levels. Ritonavir may increase propafenone levels; concurrent use is contraindicated. CYP2D6 inhibitors may increase the levels/effects of propafenone; example inhibitors include chlorpromazine, delavirdine, fluoxetine, miconazole, paroxetine, pergolide, quinine, and ropinirole. Digoxin (reduce dose by 25%), metoprolol, propranolol, theophylline, and warfarin blood levels are increased by propafenone. Use caution with Class Ia and Class III antiarrhythmics, erythromycin, cisapride, antipsychotics, and cyclic antidepressants; QT_c-prolonging effects may be additive with propafenone.
Decreased Effect: Enzyme inducers (phenobarbital, phenytoin, rifabutin, rifampin) may decrease propafenone blood levels
(Continued)

Propafenone *(Continued)*

Ethanol/Nutrition/Herb Interactions

Food: Propafenone serum concentrations may be increased if taken with food.

Herb/Nutraceutical: St John's wort may decrease propafenone levels. Avoid ephedra (may worsen arrhythmia).

Stability Store at 25°C (77°F); excursions permitted to 15°C to 30°C (59°F to 86°F).

Mechanism of Action Propafenone is a class 1c antiarrhythmic agent which possesses local anesthetic properties, blocks the fast inward sodium current, and slows the rate of increase of the action potential. Prolongs conduction and refractoriness in all areas of the myocardium, with a slightly more pronounced effect on intraventricular conduction; it prolongs effective refractory period, reduces spontaneous automaticity and exhibits some beta-blockade activity.

Pharmacodynamics/Kinetics

Absorption: Well absorbed

Metabolism: Hepatic; two genetically determined metabolism groups exist: fast or slow metabolizers; 10% of Caucasians are slow metabolizers; exhibits nonlinear pharmacokinetics; when dose is increased from 300-900 mg/day, serum concentrations increase tenfold; this nonlinearity is thought to be due to saturable first-pass effect

Bioavailability: 150 mg: 3.4%; 300 mg: 10.6%

Half-life elimination: Single dose (100-300 mg): 2-8 hours; Chronic dosing: 10-32 hours

Time to peak: 150 mg dose: 2 hours, 300 mg dose: 3 hours

Dosage Oral: Adults: **Note:** Patients who exhibit significant widening of QRS complex or second- or third-degree AV block may need dose reduction.

Immediate release tablet: Initial: 150 mg every 8 hours, increase at 3- to 4-day intervals up to 300 mg every 8 hours.

Extended release capsule: Initial: 225 mg every 12 hours; dosage increase may be made at a minimum of 5-day intervals; may increase to 325 mg every 12 hours; if further increase is necessary, may increase to 425 mg every 12 hours

Dosing adjustment in hepatic impairment: Reduction is necessary; however, specific guidelines are not available.

Dietary Considerations

Capsule: May be taken without regard to food.

Rythmol® SR capsules contain soy lecithin.

Tablet: Should be taken at the same time in relation to meals each day, either always with meals or always between meals.

Administration Capsules should be swallowed whole; do not crush or chew.

Monitoring Parameters ECG, blood pressure, pulse (particularly at initiation of therapy)

Dosage Forms

Capsule, extended release, as hydrochloride (Rythmol® SR): 225 mg, 325 mg, 425 mg [contains soy lecithin]

Tablet, as hydrochloride (Rythmol®): 150 mg, 225 mg, 300 mg

♦ **Propafenone Hydrochloride** *see Propafenone on page 1439*

Propantheline *(proe PAN the leen)*

Index Terms Propantheline Bromide

Pharmacologic Category Anticholinergic Agent

Use Adjunctive treatment of peptic ulcer, irritable bowel syndrome, pancreatitis, ureteral and urinary bladder spasm; reduce duodenal motility during diagnostic radiologic procedures

Pregnancy Risk Factor C

Dosage Oral:

Antisecretory:

Children: 1-2 mg/kg/day in 3-4 divided doses

Adults: 15 mg 3 times/day before meals or food and 30 mg at bedtime

Elderly: 7.5 mg 3 times/day before meals and at bedtime

Antispasmodic:

Children: 2-3 mg/kg/day in divided doses every 4-6 hours and at bedtime

Adults: 15 mg 3 times/day before meals or food and 30 mg at bedtime

Additional Information Complete prescribing information for this medication should be consulted for additional detail.

Dosage Forms Tablet, as bromide: 15 mg [contains lactose 23.2 mg]

♦ **Propantheline Bromide** *see Propantheline on page 1440*

Proparacaine *(proe PAR a kane)*

U.S. Brand Names Alcaine®; Ophthetic®

Canadian Brand Names Alcaine®; Diocaine®

Index Terms Proparacaine Hydrochloride; Proxymetacaine

Pharmacologic Category Local Anesthetic, Ophthalmic

Use Anesthesia for tonometry, gonioscopy; suture removal from cornea; removal of corneal foreign body; cataract extraction, glaucoma surgery; short operative procedure involving the cornea and conjunctiva

Pregnancy Risk Factor C

Medication Safety Issues

Sound-alike/look-alike issues:

Proparacaine may be confused with propoxyphene

Contraindications Hypersensitivity to proparacaine or any component of the formulation

Warnings/Precautions Use with caution in patients with cardiac disease, hyperthyroidism; for topical ophthalmic use only; prolonged use not recommended

Adverse Reactions
1% to 10%: Local: Burning, stinging, redness
<1% (Limited to important or life-threatening): Allergic contact dermatitis, arrhythmia, blurred vision, CNS depression, conjunctival congestion and hemorrhage, corneal opacification, diaphoresis (increased), epithelium, erosion of the corneal iritis, irritation, keratitis, lacrimation, sensitization

Drug Interactions
Increased Effect/Toxicity: Effects of phenylephrine and tropicamide (ophthalmics) are increased

Stability Store under refrigeration at 2°C to 8°C (36°F to 46°F). Protect from light.

Mechanism of Action Prevents initiation and transmission of impulse at the nerve cell membrane by decreasing ion permeability through stabilizing

Pharmacodynamics/Kinetics
Onset of action: ~20 seconds
Duration: 15-20 minutes

Dosage Children and Adults:
Ophthalmic surgery: Instill 1 drop of 0.5% solution in eye every 5-10 minutes for 5-7 doses
Tonometry, gonioscopy, suture removal: Instill 1-2 drops of 0.5% solution in eye just prior to procedure

Administration Do not use if discolored; protect eye from irritating chemicals, foreign bodies, and blink reflex; use eye patch if necessary

Dosage Forms Solution, ophthalmic, as hydrochloride: 0.5% (15 mL) [contains benzalkonium chloride]

Proparacaine and Fluorescein (proe PAR a kane & FLURE e seen)

U.S. Brand Names Flucaine®; Fluoracaine®
Index Terms Fluorescein and Proparacaine
Pharmacologic Category Diagnostic Agent; Local Anesthetic
Use Anesthesia for tonometry, gonioscopy; suture removal from cornea; removal of corneal foreign body; cataract extraction, glaucoma surgery
Pregnancy Risk Factor C
Dosage
Ophthalmic surgery: Children and Adults: Instill 1 drop in each eye every 5-10 minutes for 5-7 doses
Tonometry, gonioscopy, suture removal: Adults: Instill 1-2 drops in each eye just prior to procedure

Additional Information Complete prescribing information for this medication should be consulted for additional detail.
Dosage Forms Solution, ophthalmic: Proparacaine hydrochloride 0.5% and fluorescein sodium 0.25% (5 mL)

♦ **Proparacaine Hydrochloride** see Proparacaine on page 1440
♦ **Propecia®** see Finasteride on page 708
♦ **Propine®** see Dipivefrin on page 524
♦ **Proplex® T** see Factor IX Complex (Human) on page 681

Propofol (PROE po fole)

U.S. Brand Names Diprivan®
Canadian Brand Names Diprivan®
Pharmacologic Category General Anesthetic
Use Induction of anesthesia for inpatient or outpatient surgery in patients ≥3 years of age; maintenance of anesthesia for inpatient or outpatient surgery in patients >2 months of age; in adults, for the induction and maintenance of monitored anesthesia care sedation during diagnostic procedures; treatment of agitation in intubated, mechanically-ventilated ICU patients

Unlabeled/Investigational Use Postoperative antiemetic; refractory delirium tremens (case reports); conscious sedation
Pregnancy Risk Factor B
Pregnancy Implications Propofol is not recommended for obstetrics, including cesarean section deliveries. Propofol crosses the placenta and may be associated with neonatal depression.
Lactation Enters breast milk/not recommended
Medication Safety Issues
Sound-alike/look-alike issues:
Diprivan® may be confused with Diflucan®, Ditropan®

Contraindications Hypersensitivity to propofol or any component of the formulation; propofol is also contraindicated when general anesthesia or sedation is contraindicated
Warnings/Precautions Use requires careful patient monitoring, should only be used by experienced personnel who are not actively engaged in the procedure or surgery. If used in a nonintubated and/or nonmechanically-ventilated patient, qualified personnel and appropriate equipment for rapid institution of respiratory and/or cardiovascular support must be immediately available.

Use a slower rate of induction and avoid rapid bolus administration in the elderly, debilitated, or ASA III/IV patients. Use with caution in patients who are hypotensive, hypovolemic, hemodynamically unstable, or have abnormally low vascular tone (eg, sepsis). Use caution in patients with severe cardiac disease (ejection fraction <50%) or respiratory disease. Use caution in patients with a history of epilepsy or seizures. Use caution in patients with increased intracranial pressure or impaired cerebral circulation.

Use caution in patients with hyperlipidemia. Transient local pain may occur during I.V. injection; perioperative myoclonia has occurred. Not recommended for use in obstetrics. (Continued)

Propofol *(Continued)*

including cesarean section deliveries. Safety and efficacy in pediatric intensive care unit patients have not been established. Several deaths associated with severe metabolic acidosis have been reported in pediatric ICU patients on long-term propofol infusion. Concurrent use of fentanyl and propofol in pediatric patients may result in bradycardia.

Abrupt discontinuation prior to weaning or daily wake up assessments should be avoided. Abrupt discontinuation can result in rapid awakening, anxiety, agitation, and resistance to mechanical ventilation; titrate the infusion rate so the patient awakens slowly. Propofol does not have analgesic properties; pain should be treated with analgesic agents, propofol must be titrated separately from the analgesic agent. Propofol emulsion contains soybean oil, egg phosphatide, and glycerol; some formulations also contain sulfites. Some products may contain benzyl alcohol; benzyl alcohol has been associated with the "gasping syndrome" in neonates and low-birth-weight infants.

Adverse Reactions

>10%:

Cardiovascular: Hypotension (children 17%, adults 3% to 26%)

Central nervous system: Dystonic or choreiform movement (children 17%)

Local: Injection site burning, stinging, or pain (children 10%, adults 18%)

Respiratory: Apnea, lasting 30-60 seconds (children 10%, adults 24%); apnea, lasting >60 seconds (children 5%, adults 12%)

1% to 10%:

Cardiovascular: Hypertension (children 8%), arrhythmia, bradycardia, cardiac output decreased, tachycardia

Central nervous system: Movement (adults)

Dermatologic: Pruritus (children 2%), rash (children 5%)

Endocrine & metabolic: Hyperlipidemia, hypertriglyceridemia

Respiratory: Respiratory acidosis during weaning

<1% (Limited to important or life-threatening): Agitation, amblyopia, anaphylaxis, anaphylactoid reaction, anticholinergic syndrome, asystole, atrial arrhythmia, bigeminy, cardiac arrest, chills, cough, dizziness, delirium; discoloration (green - urine, hair, or nailbeds); dystonia; extremity pain, fever, flushing, hemorrhage, hypersalivation, hypertonia, hypomagnesemia, hypoxia, laryngospasm, leukocytosis, lung function decreased, metabolic acidosis (not associated with "propofol infusion syndrome"), myalgia, nausea, paresthesia, perioperative myoclonia (rarely including convulsions and opisthotonos), phlebitis, postoperative pancreatitis, postoperative unconsciousness with or without increase in muscle tone, premature atrial contractions, premature ventricular contractions, pulmonary edema, rhabdomyolysis, serum triglycerides increased, somnolence, syncope, thrombosis, urine cloudy, vision abnormality, wheezing.

Infusion site reactions include pain, swelling, blisters and/or tissue necrosis following accidental extravasation. **Note:** A "propofol infusion syndrome" has been described in patients receiving high-dose, prolonged infusion; symptoms include severe, sporadic metabolic acidosis and/or lactic acidosis which may be associated with tachycardia, myocardial dysfunction, and/or rhabdomyolysis.

Overdosage/Toxicology Symptoms include hypotension, bradycardia, and cardiovascular collapse. Treatment is symptomatic and supportive. Hypotension usually responds to I.V. fluids and/or Trendelenburg positioning. Parenteral inotropes may be needed.

Drug Interactions

Cytochrome P450 Effect: Substrate of CYP1A2 (minor), 2A6 (minor), 2B6 (major), 2C9 (major), 2C19 (minor), 2D6 (minor), 2E1 (minor), 3A4 (minor); **Inhibits** CYP1A2 (moderate), 2C9 (weak), 2C19 (moderate), 2D6 (weak), 2E1 (weak), 3A4 (strong)

Increased Effect/Toxicity: Additive CNS depression and respiratory depression may necessitate dosage reduction when used with anesthetics, benzodiazepines, opiates, ethanol, narcotics, phenothiazines. The levels/effects of propofol may be increased by delavirdine, desipramine, fluconazole, gemfibrozil, ketoconazole, nicardipine, NSAIDs, paroxetine, sertraline, sulfonamides, tolbutamide, and other inhibitors of CYP2B6 or 2C9.

Propofol may potentiate the neuromuscular blockade of vecuronium (and possibly other neuromuscular-blocking agents). Propofol may increase the levels/effects of aminophylline, benzodiazepines, calcium channel blockers, cyclosporine, fluvoxamine, selected HMG-CoA reductase inhibitors, mexiletine, mirtazapine, nateglinide, nefazodone, ropinirole, sildenafil (and other PDE-5 inhibitors) tacrolimus, theophylline, trifluoperazine, venlafaxine, and other CYP1A2 or 3A4 substrates. Selected benzodiazepines (midazolam and triazolam), cisapride, ergot alkaloids, selected HMG-CoA reductase inhibitors (lovastatin and simvastatin), and pimozide are generally contraindicated with strong CYP3A4 inhibitors.

Ethanol/Nutrition/Herb Interactions Food: EDTA, an ingredient of propofol emulsion, may lead to decreased zinc levels in patients on prolonged therapy (>5 days) or those predisposed to deficiency (burns, diarrhea, and/or major sepsis).

Stability Store at room temperature 4°C to 22°C (40°F to 72°F); refrigeration is not recommended. Protect from light. If transferred to a syringe or other container prior to administration, use within 6 hours. If used directly from vial/prefilled syringe, use within 12 hours. Shake well before use. Do not use if there is evidence of separation of phases of emulsion.

Does not need to be diluted; however, propofol may be further diluted in 5% dextrose in water to a concentration of 2 mg/mL and is stable for 8 hours at room temperature.

Mechanism of Action Propofol is a hindered phenolic compound with intravenous general anesthetic properties. The drug is unrelated to any of the currently used barbiturate, opioid, benzodiazepine, arylcyclohexylamine, or imidazole intravenous anesthetic agents.

Pharmacodynamics/Kinetics

Onset of action: Anesthetic: Bolus infusion (dose dependent): 9-51 seconds (average 30 seconds)

Duration (dose and rate dependent): 3-10 minutes

Distribution: V_d: 2-10 L/kg; highly lipophilic

Protein binding: 97% to 99%

Metabolism: Hepatic to water-soluble sulfate and glucuronide conjugates

Half-life elimination: Biphasic: Initial: 40 minutes; Terminal: 4-7 hours (up to 1-3 days)

Excretion: Urine (~88% as metabolites, 40% as glucuronide metabolite); feces (<2%)

Clearance: 20-30 mL/kg/minute; total body clearance exceeds liver blood flow

Dosage Dosage must be individualized based on total body weight and titrated to the desired clinical effect; wait at least 3-5 minutes between dosage adjustments to clinically assess drug effects; smaller doses are required when used with narcotics; the following are general dosing guidelines:

General anesthesia:

Induction: I.V.:

Children 3-16 years, ASA I or II: 2.5-3.5 mg/kg over 20-30 seconds; use a lower dose for children ASA III or IV

Adults, ASA I or II, <55 years: 2-2.5 mg/kg (~40 mg every 10 seconds until onset of induction)

Elderly, debilitated, hypovolemic, or ASA III or IV: 1-1.5 mg/kg (~20 mg every 10 seconds until onset of induction)

Cardiac anesthesia: 0.5-1.5 mg/kg (~20 mg every 10 seconds until onset of induction)

Neurosurgical patients: 1-2 mg/kg (~20 mg every 10 seconds until onset of induction)

Maintenance: I.V. infusion:

Children 2 months to 16 years, ASA I or II: Initial: 200-300 mcg/kg/minute; decrease dose after 30 minutes if clinical signs of light anesthesia are absent; usual infusion rate: 125-150 mcg/kg/minute (range: 125-300 mcg/kg/minute; 7.5-18 mg/kg/hour); children ≤5 years may require larger infusion rates compared to older children

Adults, ASA I or II, <55 years: Initial: 150-200 mcg/kg/minute for 10-15 minutes; decrease by 30% to 50% during first 30 minutes of maintenance; usual infusion rate: 100-200 mcg/kg/minute (6-12 mg/kg/hour)

Elderly, debilitated, hypovolemic, ASA III or IV: 50-100 mcg/kg/minute (3-6 mg/kg/ hour)

Cardiac anesthesia:

Low-dose propofol with primary opioid: 50-100 mcg/kg/minute (see manufacturer's labeling)

Primary propofol with secondary opioid: 100-150 mcg/kg/minute

Neurosurgical patients: 100-200 mcg/kg/minute (6-12 mg/kg/hour)

Maintenance: I.V. intermittent bolus: Adults, ASA I or II, <55 years: 20-50 mg increments as needed

Monitored anesthesia care sedation:

Initiation:

Adults, ASA I or II, <55 years: Slow I.V. infusion: 100-150 mcg/kg/minute for 3-5 minutes **or** slow injection: 0.5 mg/kg over 3-5 minutes

Elderly, debilitated, neurosurgical, or ASA III or IV patients: Use similar doses to healthy adults; avoid rapid I.V. boluses

Maintenance:

Adults, ASA I or II, <55 years: I.V. infusion using variable rates (preferred over intermittent boluses): 25-75 mcg/kg/minute **or** incremental bolus doses: 10 mg or 20 mg

Elderly, debilitated, neurosurgical, or ASA III or IV patients: Use 80% of healthy adult dose; **do not** use rapid bolus doses (single or repeated)

ICU sedation in intubated mechanically-ventilated patients: Avoid rapid bolus injection; individualize dose and titrate to response Continuous infusion: Initial: 0.3 mg/kg/hour (5 mcg/kg/min); increase by 0.3-0.6 mg/kg/hour (5-10 mcg/kg/min) every 5-10 minutes until desired sedation level is achieved; usual maintenance: 0.3-4.8 mg/kg/hour (5-80 mcg/kg/min) or higher; reduce dose by 80% in elderly, debilitated, and ASA III or IV patients; reduce dose after adequate sedation established and adjust to response (ie, evaluate frequently to use minimum dose for sedation). Some clinicians recommend daily interruption of infusion to perform clinical evaluation.

Dietary Considerations Propofol is formulated in an oil-in-water emulsion. If on parenteral nutrition, may need to adjust the amount of lipid infused. Propofol emulsion contains 1.1 kcal/mL. Soybean fat emulsion is used as a vehicle for propofol. Formulations also contain egg phosphatide and glycerol.

Administration To reduce pain associated with injection, use larger veins of forearm or antecubital fossa; lidocaine I.V. (1 mL of a 1% solution) may also be used prior to administration. Do not use filter with <5 micron for administration. Tubing and any unused portions of propofol vials should be discarded after 12 hours. Strict aseptic technique must be maintained in handling although a preservative has been added. Do not administer through the same I.V. catheter with blood or plasma. The American College of Critical Care Medicine recommends the use of a central vein for administration in an ICU setting.

Monitoring Parameters Cardiac monitor, blood pressure monitor required; serum triglyceride levels should be obtained prior to initiation of therapy (ICU setting) and every 3-7 days thereafter; daily sedation levels using standardized scale. Monitor vital signs (blood pressure, heart rate) during infusion. Unexplained tachycardia should prompt evaluation of metabolic status (including consideration of acid-base status). In patients at risk for renal impairment, urinalysis and urine sediment should be monitored prior to treatment and every other day of sedation.

Diprivan®: Monitor zinc levels in patients predisposed to deficiency (burns, diarrhea, major sepsis) or after 5 days of treatment.

Test Interactions Decreased cholesterol (S); increased porphyrin (U); decreased cortisol (S), but does not appear to inhibit adrenal responsiveness to ACTH

Additional Information On March 26, 2001, a specific warning was issued concerning the use of propofol in pediatric ICU patients. In the opinion of the FDA, a clinical trial evaluating the use of propofol as a sedative agent in this population was associated with a higher number of deaths as compared to standard sedative agents. The warning reminded healthcare professionals that propofol is not approved in the U.S. for sedation in pediatric ICU patients. A new clinical trial is planned to evaluate differences in safety within this population. (Continued)

Propofol (Continued)

Dosage Forms

Injection, emulsion: 10 mg/mL (20 mL, 50 mL, 100 mL) [products may contain egg lecithin, and soybean oil; may contain benzyl alcohol, sodium benzoate, or sodium metabisulfite]

Diprivan®: 10 mg/mL (20 mL, 50 mL, 100 mL) [contains egg lecithin, soybean oil, and disodium edetate]

Propoxyphene (proe POKS i feen)

U.S. Brand Names Darvon®; Darvon-N®

Canadian Brand Names Darvon-N®; 642® Tablet

Index Terms Dextropropoxyphene; Propoxyphene Hydrochloride; Propoxyphene Napsylate

Pharmacologic Category Analgesic, Opioid

Additional Appendix Information

Narcotic Agonists *on page 1888*

Use Management of mild to moderate pain

Restrictions C-IV

Pregnancy Risk Factor C/D (prolonged use)

Pregnancy Implications Withdrawal symptoms have been reported in the neonate following propoxyphene use during pregnancy. Teratogenic effects have also been noted in case reports. Opioid analgesics are considered pregnancy risk factor D if used for prolonged periods or in large doses near term.

Lactation Enters breast milk/use caution (AAP rates "compatible")

Medication Safety Issues

Sound-alike/look-alike issues:

Propoxyphene may be confused with proparacaine

Darvon® may be confused with Devrom®, Diovan®

Darvon-N® may be confused with Darvocet-N®

Contraindications Hypersensitivity to propoxyphene or any component of the formulation

Warnings/Precautions [U.S. Boxed Warning]: When given in excessive doses, either alone or in combination with other CNS depressants (including alcohol), propoxyphene is a major cause of drug-related deaths; recommended dosage must not be exceeded and alcohol intake should be limited. Avoid use in severely depressed or suicidal patients. Should not be prescribed in patients who are addiction prone or suicidal. Use caution in patients taking CNS depressant medications or antidepressants, and in patients who use alcohol in excess. Use with caution in patients with CNS depression coma, head trauma, thyroid dysfunction, adrenal insufficiency, morbid obesity, and prostatic hyperplasia/urinary stricture. Use with caution in patients with biliary tract dysfunction; acute pancreatitis may cause constriction of sphincter of Oddi. May cause hypotension; use with caution in patients with hypovolemia, cardiovascular disease (including acute MI), or drugs which may exaggerate hypotensive effects (including phenothiazines or general anesthetics). May obscure diagnosis or clinical course of patients with acute abdominal conditions.

May cause CNS depression, which may impair physical or mental abilities; patients must be cautioned about performing tasks which require mental alertness (eg, operating machinery or driving). Effects may be potentiated when used with other sedative drugs or ethanol. Use caution in patients dependent on opiates, substitution may result in acute opiate withdrawal symptoms. Tolerance or drug dependence may result from extended use. Propoxyphene should be used with caution in patients with renal or hepatic dysfunction, debilitated patients or in the elderly; consider dosing adjustment.

An opioid-containing analgesic regimen should be tailored to each patient's needs and based upon the type of pain being treated (acute versus chronic), the route of administration, degree of tolerance for opioids (naive versus chronic user), age, weight, and medical condition. The optimal analgesic dose varies widely among patients; doses should be titrated to pain relief/prevention. Safety and efficacy have not been established in children.

Adverse Reactions Frequency not defined.

Cardiovascular: Bundle branch block, hypotension

Central nervous system: Confusion, dizziness, dysphoria, drowsiness, fatigue, hallucinations, headache, increased intracranial pressure, lightheadedness, malaise, mental depression, nervousness, paradoxical CNS stimulation, paradoxical excitement and insomnia, restlessness, sedation, vertigo

Dermatologic: Rash, urticaria

Endocrine & metabolic: Decreased urinary 17-OHCS, hypoglycemia

Gastrointestinal: Abdominal pain, anorexia, biliary spasm, constipation, nausea, paralytic ileus, stomach cramps, vomiting, xerostomia

Genitourinary: Decreased urination, ureteral spasms

Hepatic: LFTs increased, jaundice

Neuromuscular & skeletal: Weakness

Ocular: Visual disturbances

Respiratory: Dyspnea

Miscellaneous: Histamine release, hypersensitivity reaction psychologic and physical dependence with prolonged use

Overdosage/Toxicology Symptoms include CNS and respiratory depression, hypotension, pulmonary edema, and seizures. Treatment includes airway support, establishment of an I.V. line, and administration of naloxone 2 mg I.V. (0.01 mg/kg for children), with repeat administration as necessary, up to a total of 10 mg. Emesis is not indicated as overdose may cause seizures. Charcoal is very effective (>95%) at binding propoxyphene.

Drug Interactions

Cytochrome P450 Effect: Inhibits CYP2C9 (weak), 2D6 (weak), 3A4 (weak)

Increased Effect/Toxicity: CNS depressants (phenothiazines, tranquilizers, anxiolytics, sedatives, hypnotics, or alcohol) may potentiate pharmacologic effects. Propoxyphene may inhibit the metabolism and increase the serum concentrations of carbamazepine, phenobarbital, MAO inhibitors, tricyclic antidepressants, and warfarin.

Decreased Effect: Decreased effect with cigarette smoking.

Ethanol/Nutrition/Herb Interactions

Ethanol: Avoid or limit ethanol (may increase CNS depression). Watch for sedation.

Food: May decrease rate of absorption, but may slightly increase bioavailability.

Stability Store at controlled room temperature of 15°C to 30°C (59°F to 86°F).

Mechanism of Action Propoxyphene is a weak narcotic analgesic which acts through binding to opiate receptors to inhibit ascending pain pathways. Propoxyphene, as with other narcotic (opiate) analgesics, blocks pain perception in the cerebral cortex by binding to specific receptor molecules (opiate receptors) within the neuronal membranes of synapses. This binding results in a decreased synaptic chemical transmission throughout the CNS thus inhibiting the flow of pain sensations into the higher centers. Mu and kappa are the two subtypes of the opiate receptor which propoxyphene binds to cause analgesia.

Pharmacodynamics/Kinetics

Onset of action: 0.5-1 hour

Duration: 4-6 hours

Metabolism: Hepatic to active metabolite (norpropoxyphene) and inactive metabolites; first-pass effect

Half-life elimination: Adults: Parent drug: 6-12 hours; Norpropoxyphene: 30-36 hours

Excretion: Urine (primarily as metabolites)

Dosage Oral:

Children: Doses for children are not well established; doses of the hydrochloride of 2-3 mg/kg/d divided every 6 hours have been used

Adults:

Hydrochloride: 65 mg every 3-4 hours as needed for pain; maximum: 390 mg/day

Napsylate: 100 mg every 4 hours as needed for pain; maximum: 600 mg/day

Elderly:

Hydrochloride: 65 mg every 4-6 hours as needed for pain

Napsylate: 100 mg every 4-6 hours as needed for pain

Dosing adjustment in renal impairment: Serum concentrations of propoxyphene may be increased or elimination may be delayed. Avoid use in Cl_{cr} <10 mL/minute. Specific dosing recommendations not available for less severe impairment.

Not dialyzable (0% to 5%)

Dosing adjustment in hepatic impairment: Serum concentrations of propoxyphene may be increased or elimination may be delayed; specific dosing recommendations not available.

Dietary Considerations May administer with food if gastrointestinal distress occurs.

Administration Should be administered with glass of water on an empty stomach. Food may decrease rate of absorption, but may slightly increase bioavailability.

Monitoring Parameters Pain relief, respiratory and mental status, blood pressure

Reference Range

Therapeutic: Ranges published vary between laboratories and may not correlate with clinical effect

Therapeutic concentration: 0.1-0.4 mcg/mL (SI: 0.3-1.2 µmol/L)

Toxic: >0.5 mcg/mL (SI: >1.5 µmol/L)

Test Interactions False-positive methadone test

Additional Information 100 mg of napsylate = 65 mg of hydrochloride

Propoxyphene hydrochloride: Darvon®

Propoxyphene napsylate: Darvon-N®

Dosage Forms

Capsule, as hydrochloride (Darvon®): 65 mg

Tablet, as napsylate (Darvon-N®): 100 mg

Propoxyphene and Acetaminophen

(proe POKS i feen & a seet a MIN oh fen)

U.S. Brand Names Balacet 325™; Darvocet A500™; Darvocet-N® 50; Darvocet-N® 100; Pronap-100®

Canadian Brand Names Darvocet-N® 50; Darvocet-N® 100

Index Terms Acetaminophen and Propoxyphene; Propoxyphene Hydrochloride and Acetaminophen; Propoxyphene Napsylate and Acetaminophen

Pharmacologic Category Analgesic Combination (Opioid)

Use Management of mild to moderate pain

Restrictions C-IV

Pregnancy Risk Factor C

Medication Safety Issues

Sound-alike/look-alike issues:

Darvocet-N® may be confused with Darvon-N®

Dosage Oral: Adults:

Darvocet A500™, Darvocet-N® 100: 1 tablet every 4 hours as needed; maximum: 600 mg propoxyphene napsylate/day

Darvocet-N® 50: 1-2 tablets every 4 hours as needed; maximum: 600 mg propoxyphene napsylate/day

Propoxyphene hydrochloride 65 mg and acetaminophen 650 mg: 1 tablet every 4 hours as needed; maximum: 390 mg/day propoxyphene hydrochloride, 4 g/day acetaminophen)

Note: Dosage of acetaminophen should not exceed 4 g/day (6 tablets of Darvocet-N® 100); possibly less in patients with ethanol

Elderly: Refer to Adults dosing

Dosing adjustment in renal/hepatic impairment: Serum concentrations of propoxyphene may be increased or elimination may be delayed; specific dosing recommendations not available.

Additional Information Complete prescribing information for this medication should be consulted for additional detail.

(Continued)

Propoxyphene and Acetaminophen *(Continued)*

Dosage Forms

Tablet: Propoxyphene hydrochloride 65 mg and acetaminophen 650 mg, propoxyphene napsylate 100 mg, and acetaminophen 650 mg

Balacet 325™: Propoxyphene napsylate 100 mg and acetaminophen 325 mg

Darvocet A500™: Propoxyphene napsylate 100 mg and acetaminophen 500 mg [contains lactose]

Darvocet-N® 50: Propoxyphene napsylate 50 mg and acetaminophen 325 mg

Darvocet-N® 100, Pronap-100®: Propoxyphene napsylate 100 mg and acetaminophen 650 mg

Propoxyphene, Aspirin, and Caffeine
(proe POKS i feen, AS pir in, & KAF een)

U.S. Brand Names Darvon® Compound [DSC]

Index Terms Aspirin, Caffeine, and Propoxyphene; Caffeine, Propoxyphene, and Aspirin; Propoxyphene Hydrochloride, Aspirin, and Caffeine

Pharmacologic Category Analgesic Combination (Opioid)

Use Treatment of mild-to-moderate pain

Restrictions C-IV

Pregnancy Risk Factor C

Medication Safety Issues

Sound-alike/look-alike issues:

Darvon® may be confused with Devrom®, Diovan®

Dosage Oral: Adults: Pain: One capsule (providing propoxyphene 65 mg) every 4 hours as needed; maximum propoxyphene 390 mg/day. This will also provide aspirin 389 mg and caffeine 32.4 mg per capsule.

Elderly: Refer to Adults dosing; consider increasing dosing interval

Dosage adjustment in renal impairment: Serum concentrations of propoxyphene may be increased or elimination may be delayed; specific dosing recommendations not available. Avoid use with Cl$_{cr}$ <10 mL/minute.

Dosage adjustment in hepatic impairment: Serum concentrations or propoxyphene may be increased or elimination may be delayed; specific dosing recommendations not available.

Additional Information Complete prescribing information for this medication should be consulted for additional detail.

Dosage Forms [DSC] = Discontinued product

Capsule (Darvon® Compound 65): Propoxyphene hydrochloride 65 mg, aspirin 389 mg, and caffeine 32.4 mg [DSC]

♦ **Propoxyphene Hydrochloride** *see* Propoxyphene *on page 1444*

♦ **Propoxyphene Hydrochloride and Acetaminophen** *see* Propoxyphene and Acetaminophen *on page 1445*

♦ **Propoxyphene Hydrochloride, Aspirin, and Caffeine** *see* Propoxyphene, Aspirin, and Caffeine *on page 1446*

♦ **Propoxyphene Napsylate** *see* Propoxyphene *on page 1444*

♦ **Propoxyphene Napsylate and Acetaminophen** *see* Propoxyphene and Acetaminophen *on page 1445*

Propranolol (proe PRAN oh lole)

U.S. Brand Names Inderal®; Inderal® LA; InnoPran XL™

Canadian Brand Names Apo-Propranolol®; Inderal®; Inderal®-LA; Novo-Pranol; Nu-Propranolol; Propranolol Hydrochloride Injection, USP

Index Terms Propranolol Hydrochloride

Pharmacologic Category Antiarrhythmic Agent, Class II; Beta-Adrenergic Blocker, Nonselective

Additional Appendix Information

Beta-Blockers *on page 1875*

Use Management of hypertension; angina pectoris; pheochromocytoma; essential tremor; supraventricular arrhythmias (such as atrial fibrillation and flutter, AV nodal re-entrant tachycardias), ventricular tachycardias (catecholamine-induced arrhythmias, digoxin toxicity); prevention of myocardial infarction; migraine headache prophylaxis; symptomatic treatment of hypertrophic subaortic stenosis

Unlabeled/Investigational Use Tremor due to Parkinson's disease; ethanol withdrawal; aggressive behavior; antipsychotic-induced akathisia; prevention of bleeding esophageal varices; anxiety; schizophrenia; acute panic; gastric bleeding in portal hypertension; thyrotoxicosis; tetralogy of Fallot (TOF) hypercyanotic spells

Pregnancy Risk Factor C (manufacturer); D (2nd and 3rd trimesters - expert analysis)

Pregnancy Implications Propranolol crosses the placenta. Beta-blockers have been associated with bradycardia, hypotension, and IUGR. IUGR is probably related to maternal hypertension. Available evidence suggests beta-blockers are generally safe during pregnancy (JNC 7). Cases of neonatal hypoglycemia have been reported following maternal use of beta-blockers at parturition or during breast-feeding. Monitor breast-fed infant for symptoms of beta-blockade.

Lactation Enters breast milk/use caution (AAP rates "compatible")

Medication Safety Issues

Sound-alike/look-alike issues:

Propranolol may be confused with Pravachol®, Propulsid®

Inderal® may be confused with Adderall®, Enduron®, Enduronyl®, Imdur®, Imuran®, Inderide®, Isordil®, Toradol®

Inderal® 40 may be confused with Enduronyl® Forte

Significant differences exist between oral and I.V. dosing. Use caution when converting from one route of administration to another.

International issues:
Inderal® may be confused with Indiaral® which is a brand name for loperamide in France

Contraindications Hypersensitivity to propranolol, beta-blockers, or any component of the formulation; uncompensated congestive heart failure (unless the failure is due to tachyarrhythmias being treated with propranolol), cardiogenic shock, bradycardia or heart block (2nd or 3rd degree), pulmonary edema, severe hyperactive airway disease (asthma or COPD), Raynaud's disease; pregnancy (2nd and 3rd trimesters)

Warnings/Precautions Consider pre-existing conditions such as sick sinus syndrome before initiating. Administer cautiously in compensated heart failure and monitor for a worsening of the condition (efficacy of propranolol in CHF has not been demonstrated). Beta-blocker therapy should not be withdrawn abruptly (particularly in patients with CAD), but gradually tapered to avoid acute tachycardia, hypertension, and/or ischemia. Use caution in patient with peripheral vascular disease (PVD). Use caution with concurrent use of beta-blockers and either verapamil or diltiazem; bradycardia or heart block can occur. Avoid concurrent I.V. use of both agents. Use cautiously in diabetics because it can mask prominent hypoglycemic symptoms. Use with caution in myasthenia gravis or psychiatric disease (may cause CNS depression). Use cautiously in renal and hepatic dysfunction; dosage adjustment required in hepatic impairment. Use care with anesthetic agents which decrease myocardial function. In general, patients with bronchospastic disease should not receive beta-blockers; if used at all, should be used cautiously with close monitoring. Not indicated for hypertensive emergencies. Adequate alpha-blockade is required prior to use of any beta-blocker for patients with untreated pheochromocytoma. Safety and efficacy in children have not been established.

Adverse Reactions Frequency not defined.
Cardiovascular: Arterial insufficiency, AV conduction disturbance increased, bradycardia, cardiogenic shock, CHF, chest pain, hypotension, impaired myocardial contractility, mesenteric thrombosis (rare), Raynaud's syndrome, syncope

Central nervous system: Amnesia, cognitive dysfunction, cold extremities, confusion, depression, dizziness, emotional lability, fatigue, hallucinations, hypersomnolence, insomnia, lethargy, lightheadedness, memory loss (short-term), psychosis, vertigo, vivid dreams

Dermatologic: Alopecia, contact dermatitis, eczematous eruptions, erythema multiforme, exfoliative dermatitis, hyperkeratosis, nail changes, oculomucocutaneous reactions, pruritus, psoriasiform eruptions, rash, Stevens-Johnson syndrome, toxic epidermal necrolysis, ulcers, ulcerative lichenoid, urticaria

Endocrine & metabolic: Hyper-/hypoglycemia, hyperkalemia, hyperlipidemia

Gastrointestinal: Anorexia, cramping, constipation, diarrhea, ischemic colitis, mesenteric arterial thrombosis, nausea, stomach discomfort, vomiting

Genitourinary: Impotence, interstitial nephritis (rare), oliguria (rare), Peyronie's disease, proteinuria (rare)

Hematologic: Agranulocytosis, nonthrombocytopenic purpura, thrombocytopenia, thrombocytopenic purpura

Neuromuscular & skeletal: Arthropathy, carpal tunnel syndrome (rare), myotonus, paresthesia, polyarthritis, weakness

Ocular: Hyperemia of the conjunctiva, mydriasis, tear production decreased, visual acuity decreased

Respiratory: Bronchospasm, laryngospasm, pharyngitis, pulmonary edema, respiratory distress, wheezing

Miscellaneous: Anaphylactic/anaphylactoid allergic reaction, lupus-like syndrome (rare)

Overdosage/Toxicology Symptoms of intoxication include cardiac disturbances, CNS toxicity, bronchospasm, hypoglycemia, and hyperkalemia. The most common cardiac symptoms include hypotension and bradycardia. Atrioventricular block, intraventricular conduction disturbances, cardiogenic shock, and asystole may occur with severe overdose, especially with membrane-depressant drugs (eg, propranolol). CNS effects include convulsions, coma, and respiratory arrest and are commonly seen with propranolol and other membrane-depressant and lipid-soluble drugs. Treatment is symptomatic for seizures, hypotension, hyperkalemia, and hypoglycemia. Bradycardia and hypotension resistant to atropine, isoproterenol, or pacing may respond to glucagon. Wide QRS defects caused by membrane-depressant poisoning may respond to hypertonic sodium bicarbonate. Repeat-dose charcoal, hemoperfusion, or hemodialysis may be helpful in removal of only those beta-blockers with a small V_d, long half-life, or low intrinsic clearance (acebutolol, atenolol, nadolol, sotalol). Atropine can be administered for symptomatic bradycardia; glucagon can reverse the negative inotropy/chronotropy. Norepinephrine is the preferred vasopressor. Propranolol is not dialyzable. Avoid epinephrine because it may cause uncontrolled hypertension.

Drug Interactions
Cytochrome P450 Effect: Substrate of CYP1A2 (major), 2C19 (minor), 2D6 (major), 3A4 (minor); **Inhibits** CYP1A2 (weak), 2D6 (weak)

Increased Effect/Toxicity: Beta-blockers may enhance the vasopressor effect of alpha-/beta-agonists (direct-acting). Concurrent use of alpha$_1$-blockers may increase risk of orthostasis. Beta-blockers may increase the rebound hypertensive effect when alpha$_2$-agonists are abruptly withdrawn.

CYP1A2 inhibitors (eg, rifamycin derivatives) may increase the levels/effects of propranolol. CYP2D6 inhibitors may increase the levels/effects of propranolol. Aminoquinolines (antimalarial), propoxyphene, propafenone, quinidine, and zileuton may increase levels/effects of beta-blockers. Propafenone possesses some beta-blocking activity and can contribute to bradycardia. The negative chronotropic effects of propranolol are enhanced with other drugs including: acetylcholinesterase inhibitors, amiodarone, digoxin, diltiazem, dipyridamole, disopyramide, SSRIs, and verapamil. Beta-blockers may mask the tachycardia from hypoglycemia caused by insulin and sulfonylureas; the hypoglycemic effect may be enhanced. Beta-blockers may increase the levels/effects of antipsychotics (phenothiazines), lidocaine, rizatriptan, and warfarin.

(Continued)

Propranolol *(Continued)*

Decreased Effect: CYP1A2 inducers may decrease the levels/effects of propranolol. Nonselective beta-blockers blunt the response to beta$_2$-agonists and theophylline. NSAIDs may blunt the antihypertensive effect of beta-blockers.

Ethanol/Nutrition/Herb Interactions

Ethanol: Ethanol may decrease plasma levels of propranolol by increasing metabolism.

Food: Propranolol serum levels may be increased if taken with food. Protein-rich foods may increase bioavailability; a change in diet from high carbohydrate/low protein to low carbohydrate/high protein may result in increased oral clearance.

Cigarette: Smoking may decrease plasma levels of propranolol by increasing metabolism.

Herb/Nutraceutical: Avoid dong quai if using for hypertension (has estrogenic activity). Avoid bayberry, blue cohosh, cayenne, ephedra, ginger, ginseng (american), gotu kola, licorice, yohimbe (may worsen hypertension). Avoid black cohosh, california poppy, coleus, garlic, golden seal, hawthorn, mistletoe, periwinkle, quinine, shepherd's purse (have antihypertensive activity, may cause hypotension).

Stability Propranolol is stable for 24 hours at room temperature in D$_5$W or NS. Protect injection from light. Solutions have a maximum stability at pH of 3 and decompose rapidly in alkaline pH.

Mechanism of Action Nonselective beta-adrenergic blocker (class II antiarrhythmic); competitively blocks response to beta$_1$- and beta$_2$-adrenergic stimulation which results in decreases in heart rate, myocardial contractility, blood pressure, and myocardial oxygen demand

Pharmacodynamics/Kinetics

Onset of action: Beta-blockade: Oral: 1-2 hours

Duration: ~6 hours

Distribution: V$_d$: 3.9 L/kg in adults; crosses placenta; small amounts enter breast milk

Protein binding: Newborns: 68%; Adults: 93%

Metabolism: Hepatic to active and inactive compounds; extensive first-pass effect

Bioavailability: 30% to 40%; may be increased in Down syndrome

Half-life elimination: Neonates and Infants: Possible increased half-life; Children: 3.9-6.4 hours; Adults: 4-6 hours

Excretion: Urine (96% to 99%)

Dosage

Akathisia: Oral: Adults: 30-120 mg/day in 2-3 divided doses

Essential tremor: Oral: Adults: 20-40 mg twice daily initially; maintenance doses: usually 120-320 mg/day

Hypertension:

Oral:

Children (unlabeled use): Initial: 0.5-1 mg/kg/day in divided doses every 6-12 hours; increase gradually every 5-7 days; maximum: 16 mg/kg/24 hours

Adults: Initial: 40 mg twice daily; increase dosage every 3-7 days; usual dose: ≤320 mg divided in 2-3 doses/day; maximum daily dose: 640 mg; usual dosage range (JNC 7): 40-160 mg/day in 2 divided doses

Long-acting formulation: Initial: 80 mg once daily; usual maintenance: 120-160 mg once daily; maximum daily dose: 640 mg; usual dosage range (JNC 7): 60-180 mg/day once daily

I.V.: Children (unlabeled use): 0.01-0.05 mg/kg over 1 hour; maximum dose: 10 mg

Hypertrophic subaortic stenosis: Oral: Adults: 20-40 mg 3-4 times/day

Long-acting formulation: 80-160 mg once daily

Migraine headache prophylaxis: Oral:

Children (unlabeled use): Initial: 2-4 mg/kg/day **or**

≤35 kg: 10-20 mg 3 times/day

>35 kg: 20-40 mg 3 times/day

Adults: Initial: 80 mg/day divided every 6-8 hours; increase by 20-40 mg/dose every 3-4 weeks to a maximum of 160-240 mg/day given in divided doses every 6-8 hours; if satisfactory response not achieved within 6 weeks of starting therapy, drug should be withdrawn gradually over several weeks

Long-acting formulation: Initial: 80 mg once daily; effective dose range: 160-240 mg once daily

Postmyocardial infarction prophylaxis: Oral: Adults: 180-240 mg/day in 3-4 divided doses

Pheochromocytoma: Oral: Adults: 30-60 mg/day in divided doses

Stable angina: Oral: Adults: 80-320 mg/day in doses divided 2-4 times/day

Long-acting formulation: Initial: 80 mg once daily; maximum dose: 320 mg once daily

Tachyarrhythmias:

Oral:

Children (unlabeled use): Initial: 0.5-1 mg/kg/day in divided doses every 6-8 hours; titrate dosage upward every 3-7 days; usual dose: 2-6 mg/kg/day; higher doses may be needed; do not exceed 16 mg/kg/day or 60 mg/day

Adults: 10-30 mg/dose every 6-8 hours

Elderly: Initial: 10 mg twice daily; increase dosage every 3-7 days; usual dosage range: 10-320 mg given in 2 divided doses

I.V.:

Children (unlabeled use): 0.01-0.1 mg/kg/dose slow IVP over 10 minutes; maximum dose: 1 mg for infants; 3 mg for children

Adults (in patients having nonfunctional GI tract): 1 mg/dose slow IVP; repeat every 5 minutes up to a total of 5 mg; titrate initial dose to desired response

Elderly: Use caution; initiate at lower end of the dosing range.

Hypercyanotic spells (TOF) (unlabeled use): Children:

Oral: Palliation: Initial: 1 mg/kg/day every 6 hours; if ineffective, may increase dose after 1 week by 1 mg/kg/day to a maximum of 5 mg/kg/day; if patient becomes refractory, may increase slowly to a maximum of 10-15 mg/kg/day. Allow 24 hours between dosing changes.

I.V.: 0.01-0.2 mg/kg/dose infused over 10 minutes; maximum initial dose: 1 mg

Thyrotoxicosis:
Oral:
Children (unlabeled use): 2 mg/kg/day, divided every 6-8 hours, titrate to effective dose
Adolescents and Adults: Oral: 10-40 mg/dose every 6 hours
I.V.: Adults: 1-3 mg/dose slow IVP as a single dose

Dosing adjustment in renal impairment:
Not dialyzable (0% to 5%); supplemental dose is not necessary.
Peritoneal dialysis effects: Supplemental dose is not necessary.

Dosing adjustment in hepatic disease: Marked slowing of heart rate may occur in chronic liver disease with conventional doses; low initial dose and regular heart rate monitoring

Dietary Considerations Tablets should be taken on an empty stomach; capsules may be taken with or without food, but should always be taken consistently (with food or on an empty stomach)

Administration I.V. dose is much smaller than oral dose. When administered acutely for cardiac treatment, monitor ECG and blood pressure. May administer by rapid infusion (I.V. push) at a rate of 1 mg/minute or by slow infusion over ~30 minutes. Necessary monitoring for surgical patients who are unable to take oral beta-blockers (prolonged ileus) has not been defined. Some institutions require monitoring of baseline and postinfusion heart rate and blood pressure when a patient's response to beta-blockade has not been characterized (ie, the patient's initial dose or following a change in dose). Consult individual institutional policies and procedures. Do not crush long-acting oral forms.

Monitoring Parameters
Acute cardiac treatment: Monitor ECG and blood pressure with I.V. administration; heart rate and blood pressure with oral administration

Reference Range Therapeutic: 50-100 ng/mL (SI: 190-390 nmol/L) at end of dose interval

Dosage Forms [DSC] = Discontinued product
Capsule, extended release, as hydrochloride:
InnoPran XL™: 80 mg, 120 mg
Capsule, sustained release, as hydrochloride:
Inderal® LA: 60 mg, 80 mg, 120 mg, 160 mg
Injection, solution, as hydrochloride: 1 mg/mL (1 mL)
Inderal®: 1 mg/mL (1 mL)
Solution, oral, as hydrochloride: 4 mg/mL (500 mL); 8 mg/mL (500 mL) [strawberry-mint flavor; contains alcohol 0.6%]
Tablet, as hydrochloride: 10 mg, 20 mg, 40 mg, 60 mg, 80 mg
Inderal®: 10 mg [DSC], 20 mg, 40 mg, 60 mg, 80 mg

Propranolol and Hydrochlorothiazide
(proe PRAN oh lole & hye droe klor oh THYE a zide)

U.S. Brand Names Inderide®
Index Terms Hydrochlorothiazide and Propranolol
Pharmacologic Category Antihypertensive Agent, Combination
Use Management of hypertension
Pregnancy Risk Factor C
Medication Safety Issues
Sound-alike/look-alike issues:
Inderide® may be confused with Inderal®
Dosage Oral: Adults: Hypertension: Dose is individualized; typical dosages of **hydrochlorothiazide**: 12.5-50 mg/day; initial dose of **propranolol**: 80 mg/day
Daily dose of tablet form should be divided into 2 daily doses; may be used to maximum dosage of up to 160 mg of propranolol; higher dosages would result in higher than optimal thiazide dosages.
Additional Information Complete prescribing information for this medication should be consulted for additional detail.
Dosage Forms [DSC] = Discontinued product
Tablet: Propranolol hydrochloride 40 mg and hydrochlorothiazide 25 mg; propranolol hydrochloride 80 mg and hydrochlorothiazide 25 mg
Inderide®:
40/25: Propranolol hydrochloride 40 mg and hydrochlorothiazide 25 mg
80/25: Propranolol hydrochloride 80 mg and hydrochlorothiazide 25 mg [DSC]

♦ **Propranolol Hydrochloride** see Propranolol on page 1446
♦ **Propranolol Hydrochloride Injection, USP (Can)** see Propranolol on page 1446
♦ **Proprinal [OTC]** see Ibuprofen on page 873
♦ **Proprinal® Cold and Sinus [OTC]** see Pseudoephedrine and Ibuprofen on page 1456
♦ **Propulsid®** see Cisapride on page 377
♦ **Propylene Glycol Diacetate, Acetic Acid, and Hydrocortisone** see Acetic Acid, Propylene Glycol Diacetate, and Hydrocortisone on page 38
♦ **2-Propylpentanoic Acid** see Valproic Acid and Derivatives on page 1767

Propylthiouracil (proe pil thye oh YOOR a sil)

Canadian Brand Names Propyl-Thyracil®
Index Terms PTU (error-prone abbreviation)
Pharmacologic Category Antithyroid Agent
Use Palliative treatment of hyperthyroidism as an adjunct to ameliorate hyperthyroidism in preparation for surgical treatment or radioactive iodine therapy; management of thyrotoxic crisis
Pregnancy Risk Factor D
Pregnancy Implications Crosses the placenta and may induce goiter and hypothyroidism in the developing fetus (cretinism). May need to monitor infant's thyroid function periodically.
(Continued)

Propylthiouracil *(Continued)*

Lactation Enters breast milk/use caution (AAP rates "compatible")

Medication Safety Issues
Sound-alike/look-alike issues:
Propylthiouracil may be confused with Purinethol®
PTU is an error-prone abbreviation (mistaken as mercaptopurine [Purinethol®; 6-MP])

Contraindications Hypersensitivity to propylthiouracil or any component of the formulation; pregnancy

Warnings/Precautions Use with caution in patients >40 years of age because PTU may cause hypoprothrombinemia and bleeding; use with extreme caution in patients receiving other drugs known to cause agranulocytosis; may cause agranulocytosis, thyroid hyperplasia, thyroid carcinoma (usage >1 year). Discontinue in the presence of agranulocytosis, aplastic anemia, ANCA-positive vasculitis, hepatitis, unexplained fever, or exfoliative dermatitis. Safety and efficacy have not been established in children <6 years of age.

Adverse Reactions Frequency not defined.
Cardiovascular: ANCA-positive vasculitis, cutaneous vasculitis, edema, leukocytoclastic vasculitis
Central nervous system: Dizziness, drowsiness, drug fever, fever, headache, neuritis, vertigo
Dermatologic: Alopecia, erythema nodosum, exfoliative dermatitis, pruritus, skin rash, urticaria
Endocrine & metabolic: Goiter, swollen salivary glands, weight gain
Gastrointestinal: Constipation, loss of taste perception, nausea, stomach pain, vomiting
Hematologic: Agranulocytosis, aplastic anemia, bleeding, leukopenia, thrombocytopenia
Hepatic: Cholestatic jaundice, hepatitis
Neuromuscular & skeletal: Arthralgia, paresthesia
Renal: Acute renal failure, glomerulonephritis, nephritis
Respiratory: Alveolar hemorrhage, interstitial pneumonitis
Miscellaneous: SLE-like syndrome

Overdosage/Toxicology Symptoms include nausea, vomiting, epigastric pain, headache, fever, arthralgia, pruritus, edema, pancytopenia, epigastric distress, headache, fever, CNS stimulation or depression. Treatment is supportive and includes monitoring bone marrow response, forced diuresis, peritoneal and hemodialysis, as well as charcoal hemoperfusion.

Drug Interactions
Increased Effect/Toxicity: Propylthiouracil may increase the anticoagulant activity of warfarin.
Decreased Effect: Oral anticoagulant activity is increased only until metabolic effect stabilizes. Anticoagulants may be potentiated by antivitamin K effect of propylthiouracil. Correction of hyperthyroidism may alter disposition of beta-blockers, digoxin, and theophylline, necessitating a dose reduction of these agents.

Ethanol/Nutrition/Herb Interactions Food: Propylthiouracil serum levels may be altered if taken with food.

Mechanism of Action Inhibits the synthesis of thyroid hormones by blocking the oxidation of iodine in the thyroid gland; blocks synthesis of thyroxine and triiodothyronine

Pharmacodynamics/Kinetics
Onset of action: Therapeutic: 24-36 hours
Peak effect: Remission: 4 months of continued therapy
Duration: 2-3 hours
Distribution: Concentrated in the thyroid gland
Protein binding: 75% to 80%
Metabolism: Hepatic
Bioavailability: 80% to 95%
Half-life elimination: 1.5-5 hours; End-stage renal disease: 8.5 hours
Time to peak, serum: ~1 hour
Excretion: Urine (35%)

Dosage Oral: Administer in 3 equally divided doses at approximately 8-hour intervals. Adjust dosage to maintain T_3, T_4, and TSH levels in normal range; elevated T_3 may be sole indicator of inadequate treatment. Elevated TSH indicates excessive antithyroid treatment.

Children: Initial: 5-7 mg/kg/day **or** 150-200 mg/m^2/day in divided doses every 8 hours
or
6-10 years: 50-150 mg/day
>10 years: 150-300 mg/day
Maintenance: Determined by patient response **or** $1/3$ to $2/3$ of the initial dose in divided doses every 8-12 hours. This usually begins after 2 months on an effective initial dose.
Adults: Initial: 300 mg/day in divided doses every 8 hours. In patients with severe hyperthyroidism, very large goiters, or both, the initial dosage is usually 450 mg/day; an occasional patient will require 600-900 mg/day; maintenance: 100-150 mg/day in divided doses every 8-12 hours
Elderly: Use lower dose recommendations; Initial: 150-300 mg/day
Withdrawal of therapy: Therapy should be withdrawn gradually with evaluation of the patient every 4-6 weeks for the first 3 months then every 3 months for the first year after discontinuation of therapy to detect any reoccurrence of a hyperthyroid state.
Dosing adjustment in renal impairment: Adjustment is not necessary

Dietary Considerations Administer at the same time in relation to meals each day, either always with meals or always between meals.

Monitoring Parameters CBC with differential, prothrombin time, liver function tests, thyroid function tests (TSH, T_3, T_4); periodic blood counts are recommended chronic therapy

Reference Range Normal laboratory values:
Total T_4: 5-12 mcg/dL
Serum T_3: 90-185 ng/dL
Free thyroxine index (FT_4 I): 6-10.5
TSH: 0.5-4.0 microunits/mL

Additional Information Preferred over methimazole in thyroid storm due to inhibition of peripheral conversion as well as synthesis of thyroid hormone.

Dosage Forms Tablet: 50 mg

Extemporaneous Preparations A 5 mg/mL oral suspension was stable for 10 days when refrigerated when compounded as follows:

Triturate six 50 mg tablets in a mortar, reduce to a fine powder, add 30 mL of carboxymethyl-cellulose 1.5%, transfer to a graduate and qs to 60 mL

Shake well before using and keep in refrigerator; protect from light

Nahata MC and Hipple TF, *Pediatric Drug Formulations*, 3rd ed, Cincinnati, OH: Harvey Whitney Books Co, 1997.

♦ **Propyl-Thyracil® (Can)** see Propylthiouracil *on page 1449*

♦ **2-Propylvaleric Acid** see Valproic Acid and Derivatives *on page 1767*

♦ **ProQuad®** see Measles, Mumps, Rubella, and Varicella Virus Vaccine *on page 1057*

♦ **Proquin® XR** see Ciprofloxacin *on page 372*

♦ **Proscar®** see Finasteride *on page 708*

♦ **ProSom®** see Estazolam *on page 619*

♦ **Prostacyclin** see Epoprostenol *on page 598*

♦ **Prostacyclin PGI₂** see Iloprost *on page 881*

♦ **Prostaglandin E₁** see Alprostadil *on page 77*

♦ **Prostaglandin E₂** see Dinoprostone *on page 513*

♦ **Prostaglandin F₂** see Carboprost Tromethamine *on page 293*

♦ **Prostigmin®** see Neostigmine *on page 1213*

♦ **Prostin E₂®** see Dinoprostone *on page 513*

♦ **Prostin® VR (Can)** see Alprostadil *on page 77*

♦ **Prostin VR Pediatric®** see Alprostadil *on page 77*

Protamine Sulfate (PROE ta meen SUL fate)

Pharmacologic Category Antidote

Additional Appendix Information

Management of Overdosages *on page 2075*

Use Treatment of heparin overdosage; neutralize heparin during surgery or dialysis procedures

Unlabeled/Investigational Use Treatment of low molecular weight heparin (LMWH) overdose

Pregnancy Risk Factor C

Lactation Excretion in breast milk unknown

Medication Safety Issues

Sound-alike/look-alike issues:

Protamine may be confused with ProAmatine®, protamine, Protopam®, Protropin®

Contraindications Hypersensitivity to protamine or any component of the formulation

Warnings/Precautions May not be totally effective in some patients following cardiac surgery despite adequate doses; may cause hypersensitivity reaction in patients with a history of allergy to fish (have epinephrine 1:1000 available) and in patients sensitized to protamine (via protamine zinc insulin); too rapid administration can cause severe hypotensive and anaphylactoid-like reactions. Heparin rebound associated with anticoagulation and bleeding has been reported to occur occasionally; symptoms typically occur 8-9 hours after protamine administration, but may occur as long as 18 hours later.

Adverse Reactions Frequency not defined.

Cardiovascular: Sudden fall in blood pressure, bradycardia, flushing, hypotension

Central nervous system: Lassitude

Gastrointestinal: Nausea, vomiting

Hematologic: Hemorrhage

Respiratory: Dyspnea, pulmonary hypertension

Miscellaneous: Hypersensitivity reactions

Overdosage/Toxicology Symptoms include hypertension; may cause hemorrhage. Doses exceeding 100 mg may cause paradox anticoagulation.

Stability Refrigerate; do not freeze. Stable for at least 2 weeks at room temperature. Preservative-free formulation does not require refrigeration. Reconstitute vial with 5 mL sterile water. If using protamine in neonates, reconstitute with preservative-free sterile water for injection; resulting solution equals 10 mg/mL.

Mechanism of Action Combines with strongly acidic heparin to form a stable complex (salt) neutralizing the anticoagulant activity of both drugs

Pharmacodynamics/Kinetics Onset of action: I.V.: Heparin neutralization: ~5 minutes

Dosage

Heparin neutralization: I.V.: Protamine dosage is determined by the dosage of heparin; 1 mg of protamine neutralizes 90 USP units of heparin (lung) and 115 USP units of heparin (intestinal); maximum dose: 50 mg

Heparin overdosage, following intravenous administration: I.V.: Since blood heparin concentrations decrease rapidly **after** administration, adjust the protamine dosage depending upon the duration of time since heparin administration as follows: See table.

Time Elapsed	Dose of Protamine (mg) to Neutralize 100 units of Heparin
Immediate	1-1.5
30-60 min	0.5-0.75
>2 h	0.25-0.375

Heparin overdosage, following SubQ injection: I.V.: 1-1.5 mg protamine per 100 units heparin; this may be done by a portion of the dose (eg, 25-50 mg) given slowly I.V. followed by the remaining portion as a continuous infusion over 8-16 hours (the expected absorption time of the SubQ heparin dose)

(Continued)

Protamine Sulfate *(Continued)*

LMWH overdose (unlabeled use): **Note:** Antifactor Xa activity never completely neutralized (maximum: ~60% to 75%)

Enoxaparin: 1 mg protamine for each mg of enoxaparin; if PTT prolonged 2-4 hours after first dose, consider additional dose of 0.5 mg for each mg of enoxaparin.

Dalteparin or tinzaparin: 1 mg protamine for each 100 anti-Xa int. units of dalteparin or tinzaparin; if PTT prolonged 2-4 hours after first dose, consider additional dose of 0.5 mg for each 100 anti-Xa int. units of dalteparin or tinzaparin.

Note: Excessive protamine doses may worsen bleeding potential.

Administration For I.V. use only; **incompatible** with cephalosporins and penicillins; administer slow IVP (50 mg over 10 minutes); rapid I.V. infusion causes hypotension; resulting solution equals 10 mg/mL; inject without further dilution over 1-3 minutes; maximum of 50 mg in any 10-minute period

Monitoring Parameters Coagulation test, aPTT or ACT, cardiac monitor and blood pressure monitor required during administration

Dosage Forms Injection, solution, as sulfate [preservative free]: 10 mg/mL (5 mL, 25 mL)

- ♦ **Protein C (Activated), Human, Recombinant** *see Drotrecogin Alfa on page 561*
- ♦ **Protein-Bound Paclitaxel** *see Paclitaxel (Protein Bound) on page 1297*
- ♦ **Prothrombin Complex Concentrate** *see Factor IX Complex (Human) on page 681*
- ♦ **Protonix®** *see Pantoprazole on page 1307*
- ♦ **Protopam®** *see Pralidoxime on page 1405*
- ♦ **Protopic®** *see Tacrolimus on page 1626*

Protriptyline *(proe TRIP ti leen)*

U.S. Brand Names Vivactil®

Index Terms Protriptyline Hydrochloride

Pharmacologic Category Antidepressant, Tricyclic (Secondary Amine)

Additional Appendix Information

Antidepressant Agents *on page 1866*

Use Treatment of depression

Restrictions An FDA-approved medication guide concerning the use of antidepressants in children and teenagers must be distributed when dispensing an outpatient prescription (new or refill) where this medication is to be used without direct supervision of a healthcare provider. Medication guides are available at http://www.fda.gov/cder/Offices/ODS/medication_guides.htm. Dispense to parents or guardians of children and teenagers receiving this medication.

Pregnancy Risk Factor C

Lactation Excretion in breast milk unknown/not recommended

Contraindications Hypersensitivity to protriptyline (cross-reactivity to other cyclic antidepressants may occur) or any component of the formulation; use of MAO inhibitors within 14 days; use of cisapride; use in a patient during the acute recovery phase of MI

Warnings/Precautions [U.S. Boxed Warning]: Antidepressants increase the risk of suicidal thinking and behavior in children and adolescents with major depressive disorder (MDD) and other depressive disorders; consider risk prior to prescribing. All patients must be closely monitored for clinical worsening, suicidality, or unusual changes in behavior, especially during the initiation of therapy or following an increase or decrease in dosage. When used in children, the child's family or caregiver should be instructed to closely observe the patient and communicate condition with healthcare provider. A medication guide should be dispensed with each prescription. **Protriptyline is FDA approved for the treatment of depression in adolescents.**

The possibility of a suicide attempt is inherent in major depression and may persist until remission occurs. Use caution in high-risk patients. Worsening depression and severe abrupt suicidality that are not part of the presenting symptoms may require discontinuation or modification of drug therapy. The patient's family or caregiver should be alerted to monitor patients for the emergence of suicidality and associated behaviors (such as agitation, irritability, hostility, impulsivity, and hypomania) and call healthcare provider.

May worsen psychosis in some patients or precipitate a shift to mania or hypomania in patients with bipolar disorder. Patients presenting with depressive symptoms should be screened for bipolar disorder. Monotherapy in patients with bipolar disorder should be avoided. **Protriptyline is not FDA approved for the treatment of bipolar depression.**

Although the degree of sedation is low relative to other antidepressant agents, protriptyline may cause sedation, resulting in impaired performance of tasks requiring alertness (eg, operating machinery or driving). Sedative effects may be additive with other CNS depressants and/or ethanol. Protriptyline may aggravate aggressive behavior. Consider discontinuing, when possible, prior to elective surgery. Therapy should not be abruptly discontinued in patients receiving high doses for prolonged periods. May alter glucose regulation - use with caution in patients with diabetes.

May cause orthostatic hypotension or conduction abnormalities (risks are moderate relative to other antidepressants). Use with caution in patients with a history of cardiovascular disease (including previous MI, stroke, tachycardia, or conduction abnormalities). The degree of anticholinergic blockade produced by this agent is moderate relative to other cyclic antidepressants, however, caution should still be used in patients with urinary retention, benign prostatic hyperplasia, narrow-angle glaucoma, xerostomia, visual problems, constipation, or history of bowel obstruction.

Use caution in patients with a previous seizure disorder or condition predisposing to seizures such as brain damage, alcoholism, or concurrent therapy with other drugs which lower the seizure threshold. May increase the risks associated with electroconvulsive therapy. Use with caution in hyperthyroid patients or those receiving thyroid supplementation. Use with caution in patients with hepatic or renal dysfunction and in elderly patients.

Adverse Reactions Frequency not defined.

Cardiovascular: Arrhythmias, heart block, hyper-/hypotension, MI, palpitation, stroke, tachycardia

Central nervous system: agitation, anxiety, ataxia, confusion, delirium, delusions, dizziness, drowsiness, EPS, exacerbation of psychosis, fatigue, hallucinations, headache, hypomania, incoordination, insomnia, nightmares, panic, restlessness, seizure

Dermatologic: Alopecia, itching, petechiae, photosensitivity, rash, urticaria

Endocrine & metabolic: Breast enlargement, galactorrhea, gynecomastia, increased or decreased libido, syndrome of inappropriate ADH secretion (SIADH)

Gastrointestinal: Anorexia, constipation, decreased lower esophageal sphincter tone may cause GE reflux, diarrhea, heartburn, increased appetite, nausea, trouble with gums, unpleasant taste, vomiting, weight gain/loss, xerostomia

Genitourinary: Difficult urination, impotence, testicular edema

Hematologic: Agranulocytosis, eosinophilia, leukopenia, purpura, thrombocytopenia

Hepatic: Cholestatic jaundice, increased liver enzymes

Neuromuscular & skeletal: Fine muscle tremor, numbness, tingling, tremor, weakness

Ocular: Blurred vision, eye pain, increased intraocular pressure

Otic: Tinnitus

Miscellaneous: Allergic reactions, excessive diaphoresis

Overdosage/Toxicology Symptoms include confusion, hallucinations, urinary retention, hypotension, tachycardia, seizures, and hyperthermia. Following initiation of essential overdose management, toxic symptoms should be treated. Sodium bicarbonate is indicated when the QRS interval is >0.10 seconds or the QT_c >0.42 seconds. Ventricular arrhythmias often respond to systemic alkalinization (sodium bicarbonate 0.5-2 mEq/kg I.V.). Arrhythmias unresponsive to this therapy may respond to lidocaine 1 mg/kg I.V. followed by a titrated infusion. Physostigmine (1-2 mg I.V. slowly for adults or 0.5 mg slow I.V. for children) may be indicated in reversing life-threatening cardiac arrhythmias. Seizures usually respond to diazepam I.V. boluses (5-10 mg for adults up to 30 mg or 0.25-0.4 mg/kg/dose for children up to 10 mg/dose). If seizures are unresponsive or recur, phenytoin or phenobarbital may be required.

Drug Interactions

Cytochrome P450 Effect: Substrate of CYP2D6 (major)

Increased Effect/Toxicity: Protriptyline increases the effects of amphetamines, anticholinergics, other CNS depressants (sedatives, hypnotics, or ethanol), chlorpropamide, tolazamide, and warfarin. When used with MAO inhibitors, hyperpyrexia, hypertension, tachycardia, confusion, seizures, and **deaths have been reported** (serotonin syndrome). The SSRIs (to varying degrees), cimetidine, grapefruit juice, indinavir, methylphenidate, ritonavir, quinidine, diltiazem, and verapamil inhibit the metabolism of TCAs. Levels/effects of protriptyline may be increased by chlorpromazine, delavirdine, fluoxetine, miconazole, paroxetine, pergolide, quinidine, quinine, ritonavir, ropinirole, and other CYP2D6 inhibitors. Use of lithium with a TCA may increase the risk for neurotoxicity. Phenothiazines may increase concentration of some TCAs and TCAs may increase concentration of phenothiazines. Pressor response to I.V. epinephrine, norepinephrine, and phenylephrine may be enhanced in patients receiving TCAs (**Note:** Effect is unlikely with epinephrine or levonordefrin dosages typically administered as infiltration in combination with local anesthetics). Combined use of beta-agonists or drugs which prolong QT_c (including quinidine, procainamide, disopyramide, cisapride, sparfloxacin, gatifloxacin, moxifloxacin) with TCAs may predispose patients to cardiac arrhythmias.

Decreased Effect: Carbamazepine, phenobarbital, and rifampin may increase the metabolism of protriptyline, decreasing its effects. Protriptyline inhibits the antihypertensive response to bethanidine, clonidine, debrisoquin, guanadrel, guanethidine, guanabenz, guanfacine. Cimetidine and methylphenidate may decrease the metabolism of protriptyline. Cholestyramine and colestipol may bind TCAs and reduce their absorption.

Ethanol/Nutrition/Herb Interactions

Ethanol: Avoid ethanol (may increase CNS depression).

Food: Grapefruit juice may inhibit the metabolism of some TCAs and clinical toxicity may result.

Herb/Nutraceutical: Avoid valerian, St John's wort, SAMe, kava kava (may increase risk of serotonin syndrome and/or excessive sedation).

Mechanism of Action Increases the synaptic concentration of serotonin and/or norepinephrine in the central nervous system by inhibition of their reuptake by the presynaptic neuronal membrane

Pharmacodynamics/Kinetics

Distribution: Crosses placenta

Protein binding: 92%

Metabolism: Extensively hepatic via N-oxidation, hydroxylation, and glucuronidation; first-pass effect (10% to 25%)

Half-life elimination: 54-92 hours (average: 74 hours)

Time to peak, serum: 24-30 hours

Excretion: Urine

Dosage Oral:

Adolescents: 15-20 mg/day

Adults: 15-60 mg/day in 3-4 divided doses

Elderly: Initial: 5-10 mg/day; increase every 3-7 days by 5-10 mg; usual dose: 15-20 mg/day

Dietary Considerations May be taken with food to decrease GI distress.

Administration Make any dosage increase in the morning dose

Monitoring Parameters Monitor for cardiac abnormalities in elderly patients receiving doses >20 mg

Reference Range Therapeutic: 70-250 ng/mL (SI: 266-950 nmol/L); Toxic: >500 ng/mL (SI: >1900 nmol/L)

Dosage Forms Tablet, as hydrochloride: 5 mg, 10 mg

- ♦ **Protriptyline Hydrochloride** see Protriptyline on page 1452
- ♦ **Proventil®** see Albuterol on page 57
- ♦ **Proventil® HFA** see Albuterol on page 57

- **Provera**® *see* MedroxyPROGESTERone *on page 1065*
- **Provera-Pak (Can)** *see* MedroxyPROGESTERone *on page 1065*
- **Provigil**® *see* Modafinil *on page 1161*
- **Proviodine (Can)** *see* Povidone-Iodine *on page 1404*
- **Provisc**® *see* Hyaluronate and Derivatives *on page 841*
- **Provocholine**® *see* Methacholine *on page 1100*
- **Proxymetacaine** *see* Proparacaine *on page 1440*
- **Prozac**® *see* Fluoxetine *on page 727*
- **Prozac**® **Weekly**™ *see* Fluoxetine *on page 727*
- **PRP-OMP** *see* Haemophilus b Conjugate Vaccine *on page 824*
- **PRP-T** *see* Haemophilus b Conjugate Vaccine *on page 824*
- **Prudoxin**™ *see* Doxepin *on page 545*
- **Prussian Blue** *see* Ferric Hexacyanoferrate *on page 701*
- **Prymaccone** *see* Primaquine *on page 1421*
- **23PS** *see* Pneumococcal Polysaccharide Vaccine (Polyvalent) *on page 1384*
- **PS-341** *see* Bortezomib *on page 230*

Pseudoephedrine (soo doe e FED rin)

U.S. Brand Names Contac® Cold [OTC] [DSC]; Dimetapp® 12-Hour Non-Drowsy Extentabs® [OTC] [DSC]; Dimetapp® Decongestant Infant [OTC] [DSC]; Genaphed® [OTC]; Kidkare Decongestant [OTC]; Kodet SE [OTC]; Oranyl [OTC]; PediaCare® Decongestant Infants [OTC]; Silfedrine Children's [OTC]; Simply Stuffy™ [OTC] [DSC]; Sudafed® 12 Hour [OTC]; Sudafed® 24 Hour [OTC]; Sudafed® Children's [OTC]; Sudafed® Maximum Strength Nasal Decongestant [OTC]; Sudodrin [OTC]; SudoGest [OTC]; Sudo-Tab® [OTC]

Canadian Brand Names Balminil Decongestant; Benylin® D for Infants; Contac® Cold 12 Hour Relief Non Drowsy; Drixoral® ND; Eltor®; PMS-Pseudoephedrine; Pseudofrin; Robidrine®; Sudafed® Decongestant

Index Terms d-Isoephedrine Hydrochloride; Pseudoephedrine Hydrochloride; Pseudoephedrine Sulfate

Pharmacologic Category Alpha/Beta Agonist

Use Temporary symptomatic relief of nasal congestion due to common cold, upper respiratory allergies, and sinusitis; also promotes nasal or sinus drainage

Pregnancy Risk Factor C

Lactation Enters breast milk/use caution (AAP rates "compatible")

Medication Safety Issues
Sound-alike/look-alike issues:
Dimetapp® may be confused with Dermatop®, Dimetabs®, Dimetane®
Sudafed® may be confused with Sufenta®

Contraindications Hypersensitivity to pseudoephedrine or any component of the formulation; with or within 14 days of MAO inhibitor therapy

Warnings/Precautions Use with caution in patients >60 years of age; administer with caution, to patients with hypertension, hyperthyroidism, diabetes mellitus, cardiovascular disease, ischemic heart disease, increased intraocular pressure, or prostatic hyperplasia. Elderly patients are more likely to experience adverse reactions to sympathomimetics. Overdosage may cause hallucinations, seizures, CNS depression, and death. When used for self-medication (OTC), notify healthcare provider if symptoms do not improve within 7 days or are accompanied by fever.

Adverse Reactions Frequency not defined.
Cardiovascular: Arrhythmia, palpitaion, tachycardia
Central nervous system: Convulsion, dizziness, drowsiness, excitability, hallucination, headache, insomnia, nervousness, transient stimulation
Gastrointestinal: Nausea, vomiting
Genitourinary: Dysuria
Neuromuscular & skeletal: Tremor, weakness
Respiratory: Dyspnea
Miscellaneous: Diaphoresis

Overdosage/Toxicology Symptoms include seizures, nausea, vomiting, cardiac arrhythmias, hypertension, and agitation. There is no specific antidote. The bulk of treatment is supportive. Hyperactivity and agitation usually respond to reduced sensory input; however, with extreme agitation, haloperidol (2-5 mg I.M. for adults) may be required. Hyperthermia is best treated with external cooling measures; or when severe or unresponsive, muscle paralysis with pancuronium may be needed. Hypertension is usually transient and generally does not require treatment unless severe. For diastolic blood pressures >110 mm Hg, a nitroprusside infusion should be initiated. Seizures usually respond to diazepam I.V. and/or phenytoin maintenance regimens.

Drug Interactions
Increased Effect/Toxicity: MAO inhibitors may increase blood pressure effects of pseudoephedrine. Sympathomimetic agents may increase toxicity.
Decreased Effect: Decreased effect of methyldopa, reserpine.

Ethanol/Nutrition/Herb Interactions
Food: Onset of effect may be delayed if pseudoephedrine is taken with food.
Herb/Nutraceutical: Avoid ephedra, yohimbe (may cause hypertension).

Mechanism of Action Directly stimulates alpha-adrenergic receptors of respiratory mucosa causing vasoconstriction; directly stimulates beta-adrenergic receptors causing bronchial relaxation, increased heart rate and contractility

Pharmacodynamics/Kinetics
Onset of action: Decongestant: Oral: 15-30 minutes
Duration: Immediate release tablet: 4-6 hours; Extended release: ≤12 hours
Absorption: Rapid
Metabolism: Partially hepatic

Half-life elimination: 9-16 hours

Excretion: Urine (70% to 90% as unchanged drug, 1% to 6% as active norpseudoephedrine); dependent on urine pH and flow rate; alkaline urine decreases renal elimination of pseudoephedrine

Dosage Oral: General dosing guidelines:

Children:

<2 years: 4 mg/kg/day in divided doses every 6 hours

2-5 years: 15 mg every 4-6 hours; maximum: 60 mg/24 hours

6-12 years: 30 mg every 4-6 hours; maximum: 120 mg/24 hours

Adults: 30-60 mg every 4-6 hours, sustained release: 120 mg every 12 hours; maximum: 240 mg/24 hours

Dosing adjustment in renal impairment: Reduce dose

Dietary Considerations Should be taken with water or milk to decrease GI distress.

Administration Do not crush extended release drug product, swallow whole.

Test Interactions Interferes with urine detection of amphetamine (false-positive)

Dosage Forms [DSC] = Discontinued product

Caplet, extended release, as hydrochloride:

Contac® Cold [DSC], Sudafed® 12 Hour: 120 mg

Liquid, as hydrochloride: 30 mg/5 mL (120 mL, 480 mL)

Silfedrine Children's: 15 mg/5 mL (120 mL, 480 mL) [alcohol and sugar free; grape flavor]

Simply Stuffy™: 15 mg/5 mL (120 mL) [alcohol free; contains sodium benzoate; cherry berry flavor] [DSC]

Sudafed® Children's: 15 mg/5 mL (120 mL) [alcohol and sugar free; contains sodium benzoate; grape flavor]

Liquid, oral, as hydrochloride [drops]:

Dimetapp® Decongestant Infant Drops: 7.5 mg/0.8 mL (15 mL) [alcohol free; contains sodium benzoate; grape flavor] [DSC]

Kidkare Decongestant: 7.5 mg/0.8 mL (30 mL) [alcohol free; contains benzoic acid and sodium benzoate; cherry flavor]

PediaCare® Decongestant: 7.5 mg/0.8 mL (15 mL) [alcohol free, dye free; contains benzoic acid, sodium benzoate; fruit flavor]

Tablet, as hydrochloride: 30 mg, 60 mg

Genaphed®, Kodet SE, Oranyl, Sudafed®, Sudodrin, Sudo-Tab®: 30 mg

SudoGest: 30 mg, 60 mg

Tablet, chewable, as hydrochloride:

Sudafed® Children's: 15 mg [sugar free; contains phenylalanine 0.78 mg/tablet; orange flavor]

Tablet, extended release, as hydrochloride:

Dimetapp® 12-Hour Non-Drowsy Extentabs®: 120 mg [DSC]

Sudafed® 24 Hour: 240 mg

♦ **Pseudoephedrine, Acetaminophen, and Chlorpheniramine** see Acetaminophen, Chlorpheniramine, and Pseudoephedrine on page 35

♦ **Pseudoephedrine, Acetaminophen, and Dextromethorphan** see Acetaminophen, Dextromethorphan, and Pseudoephedrine on page 35

♦ **Pseudoephedrine and Acetaminophen** see Acetaminophen and Pseudoephedrine on page 33

♦ **Pseudoephedrine and Brompheniramine** see Brompheniramine and Pseudoephedrine on page 243

♦ **Pseudoephedrine and Carbetapentane** see Carbetapentane and Pseudoephedrine on page 289

♦ **Pseudoephedrine and Carbinoxamine** see Carbinoxamine and Pseudoephedrine on page 290

♦ **Pseudoephedrine and Chlorpheniramine** see Chlorpheniramine and Pseudoephedrine on page 350

♦ **Pseudoephedrine and Desloratadine** see Desloratadine and Pseudoephedrine on page 476

♦ **Pseudoephedrine and Dexbrompheniramine** see Dexbrompheniramine and Pseudoephedrine on page 482

Pseudoephedrine and Dextromethorphan

(soo doe e FED rin & deks troe meth OR fan)

U.S. Brand Names Dimetapp® Infant Decongestant Plus Cough [OTC] [DSC]; PediaCare® Children's Long Acting Cough Plus Cold [OTC] [DSC]; PediaCare® Infants' Decongestant & Cough [OTC]; Pedia Relief Cough and Cold [OTC]; Pedia Relief Infants [OTC]; Robitussin® Maximum Strength Cough & Cold [OTC] [DSC]; Robitussin® Pediatric Cough & Cold [OTC] [DSC]; Sudafed® Children's Cold & Cough [OTC]; SudoGest Children's [OTC]; Triaminic® Cough [OTC] [DSC]; Triaminic® Cough & Nasal Congestion [OTC] [DSC]; Vicks® 44D Cough & Head Congestion [OTC] [DSC]

Canadian Brand Names Balminil DM D; Benylin® DM-D; Koffex DM-D; Novahistex® DM Decongestant; Novahistine® DM Decongestant; Robitussin® Childrens Cough & Cold

Index Terms Dextromethorphan and Pseudoephedrine

Pharmacologic Category Antitussive/Decongestant

Use Temporary symptomatic relief of nasal congestion and cough due to common cold, hay fever, upper respiratory allergies

Dosage Relief of nasal congestion and cough: Oral:

General dosing guidelines base on pseudoephedrine component:

Children 2-6 years: 15 mg every 4-6 hours (maximum: 60 mg/24 hours)

Children 6-12 years: 30 mg every 4-6 hours (maximum: 120 mg/24 hours)

Children ≥12 years and Adults: 60 mg every 4-6 hours (maximum: 240 mg/24 hours)

Product-specific dosing:

Children 2-3 years (PediaCare® Infants Decongestant & Cough): 1.6 mL every 4-6 hours (maximum: 6.4 mL/24 hours)

(Continued)

Pseudoephedrine and Dextromethorphan *(Continued)*

Children 2-6 years:

PediaCare® Children's Long Acting Cough Plus Cold: One chewable tablet or 5 mL every 6-8 hours (maximum: 4 doses/24 hours)

Robitussin® Pediatric Cough & Cold, Triaminic® Cough and Nasal Congestion: 5 mL every 6 hours (maximum: 20 mL/24 hours)

Sudafed® Children's Cold & Cough: 5 mL every 4 hours (maximum: 20 mL/24 hours)

Triaminic® Cough: 5 mL every 4-6 hours (maximum: 20 mL/24 hours)

Children 6-12 years:

PediaCare® Children's Long Acting Cough Plus Cold: Two chewable tablets or 10 mL every 6-8 hours (maximum: 4 doses/24 hours)

Robitussin® Pediatric Cough & Cold, Triaminic® Cough and Nasal Congestion: 10 mL every 6 hours (maximum: 40 mL/24 hours)

Sudafed® Children's Cold & Cough: 10 mL every 4 hours (maximum: 40 mL/24 hours)

Triaminic Cough: 10 mL every 4-6 hours (maximum: 40 mL/24 hours)

Vicks® 44D Cough & Head Congestion: 7.5 mL every 6 hours (maximum: 30 mL/24 hours)

Children ≥12 years and Adults:

Robitussin® Maximum Strength Cough & Cold: 10 mL every 6 hours as needed (maximum: 40 mL/24 hours)

Sudafed® Children's Cold & Cough: 20 mL every 4 hours (maximum: 80 mL/24 hours)

Vicks® 44D Cough & Head Congestion: 15 mL every 6 hours (maximum: 60 mL/24 hours)

Additional Information Complete prescribing information for this medication should be consulted for additional detail.

Dosage Forms [DSC] = Discontinued product

Liquid:

PediaCare® Children's Long Acting Cough Plus Cold: Pseudoephedrine hydrochloride 15 mg and dextromethorphan hydrobromide 7.5 mg per 5 mL (120 mL) [alcohol free; contains sodium benzoate; grape flavor] [DSC]

Sudafed® Children's Cold & Cough: Pseudoephedrine hydrochloride 15 mg and dextro-methorphan hydrobromide 5 mg per 5 mL (120 mL) [alcohol free, sugar free; contains sodium benzoate; cherry berry flavor]

Triaminic® Cough: Pseudoephedrine hydrochloride 15 mg and dextromethorphan hydro-bromide 5 mg per 5 mL (120 mL, 150 mL) [alcohol free; contains benzoic acid, sodium 20 mg/5 mL; berry flavor] [DSC]

Triaminic® Cough & Nasal Congestion: Pseudoephedrine hydrochloride 15 mg and dextro-methorphan hydrobromide 7.5 mg per 5 mL (120 mL) [alcohol free; contains benzoic acid, sodium 7 mg/5 mL; orange strawberry flavor] [DSC]

Vicks® 44D Cough & Head Congestion: Pseudoephedrine hydrochloride 20 mg and dextro-methorphan hydrobromide 10 mg per 5 mL (120 mL, 240 mL) [contains alcohol 5%, sodium 10.3 mg/5 mL and sodium benzoate; cherry flavor] [DSC]

Liquid, oral [drops]:

Dimetapp® Infant Decongestant Plus Cough: Pseudoephedrine hydrochloride 7.5 mg and dextromethorphan hydrobromide 2.5 mg per 0.8 mL (15 mL) [alcohol free, sugar free; grape flavor] [DSC]

PediaCare® Infants' Decongestant & Cough: Pseudoephedrine hydrochloride 7.5 mg and dextromethorphan hydrobromide 2.5 mg per 0.8 mL (15 mL) [alcohol free; contains sodium benzoate; cherry flavor]

Pedia Relief Infants: Pseudoephedrine hydrochloride 7.5 mg and dextromethorphan hydro-bromide 2.5 mg per 0.8 mL (15 mL) [cherry flavor]

Syrup:

Pedia Relief Cough and Cold: Pseudoephedrine hydrochloride 15 mg and dextromethor-phan hydrobromide 7.5 mg per 5 mL (120 mL) [cherry flavor]

Robitussin® Maximum Strength Cough & Cold: Pseudoephedrine hydrochloride 30 mg and dextromethorphan hydrobromide 15 mg per 5 mL (120 mL, 240 mL) [contains alcohol 1.4% and sodium benzoate] [DSC]

Robitussin® Pediatric Cough & Cold: Pseudoephedrine hydrochloride 15 mg and dextro-methorphan hydrobromide 7.5 mg per 5 mL (120 mL, 240 mL) [alcohol free; contains sodium benzoate; fruit punch flavor] [DSC]

SudoGest Children's: Pseudoephedrine hydrochloride 15 mg and dextromethorphan hydrobromide 5 mg per 5 mL (120 mL)

Tablet, chewable:

PediaCare® Children's Long Acting Cough Plus Cold: Pseudoephedrine hydrochloride 15 mg and dextromethorphan hydrobromide 7.5 mg [contains phenylalanine 5 mg per tablet; grape flavor] [DSC]

♦ **Pseudoephedrine and Diphenhydramine** *see* Diphenhydramine and Pseudoephedrine *on page 517*

♦ **Pseudoephedrine and Fexofenadine** *see* Fexofenadine and Pseudoephedrine *on page 706*

♦ **Pseudoephedrine and Guaifenesin** *see* Guaifenesin and Pseudoephedrine *on page 819*

♦ **Pseudoephedrine and Hydrocodone** *see* Hydrocodone and Pseudoephedrine *on page 851*

Pseudoephedrine and Ibuprofen *(soo doe e FED rin & eye byoo PROE fen)*

U.S. Brand Names Advil® Cold & Sinus [OTC]; Advil® Cold, Children's [OTC]; Motrin® Cold and Sinus [OTC]; Motrin® Cold, Children's [OTC]; Proprinal® Cold and Sinus [OTC]

Canadian Brand Names Advil® Cold & Sinus; Children's Advil® Cold; Sudafed® Sinus Advance

Index Terms Ibuprofen and Pseudoephedrine

Pharmacologic Category Decongestant/Analgesic

Use For temporary relief of cold, sinus and flu symptoms (including nasal congestion, headache, sore throat, minor body aches and pains, and fever)

Pregnancy Risk Factor Ibuprofen: B/D (3rd trimester)

Dosage OTC labeling: Oral:

Children: Ibuprofen 100 mg and pseudoephedrine 15 mg per 5 mL: May repeat dose every 6 hours (maximum: 4 doses/24 hours); dose should be based on weight when possible. Contact healthcare provider if symptoms have not improved within 3 days (2 days if treating sore throat accompanied by fever).

2-5 years or 11 to <22 kg (24-47 pounds): 5 mL

6-11 years or 22-43 kg (48-95 pounds): 10 mL

Children ≥12 years and Adults: Ibuprofen 200 mg and pseudoephedrine 30 mg per dose: One dose every 4-6 hours as needed; may increase to 2 doses if necessary (maximum: 6 doses/24 hours). Contact healthcare provider if symptoms have not improved within 7 days when treating cold symptoms or within 3 days when treating fever.

Additional Information Complete prescribing information for this medication should be consulted for additional detail.

Dosage Forms [DSC] = Discontinued product

Caplet:

Advil® Cold and Sinus [DSC], Motrin® Cold and Sinus, Proprinal® Cold and Sinus: Pseudoephedrine hydrochloride 30 mg and ibuprofen 200 mg

Capsule, liquid filled:

Advil® Cold and Sinus: Pseudoephedrine hydrochloride 30 mg and ibuprofen 200 mg [solubilized ibuprofen as free acid and potassium salt; contains coconut oil]

Suspension:

Advil® Cold, Children's: Pseudoephedrine hydrochloride 15 mg and ibuprofen 100 mg per 5 mL (120 mL) [alcohol free; contains sodium benzoate; grape flavor]

Motrin® Cold, Children's: Pseudoephedrine hydrochloride 15 mg and ibuprofen 100 mg per 5 mL (120 mL) [contains sodium benzoate; berry, dye free berry, and grape flavors]

Tablet:

Advil® Cold and Sinus: Pseudoephedrine hydrochloride 30 mg and ibuprofen 200 mg [DSC]

♦ **Pseudoephedrine and Loratadine** see Loratadine and Pseudoephedrine on page 1034

Pseudoephedrine and Methscopolamine
(soo doe e FED rin & meth skoe POL a meen)

U.S. Brand Names Allerx™-D; Amdry-D

Index Terms Methscopolamine and Pseudoephedrine; Pseudoephedrine hydrochloride and Methscopolamine Nitrate

Pharmacologic Category Decongestant/Anticholinergic Combination

Use Relief of symptoms of allergic rhinitis, vasomotor rhinitis, sinusitis, and the common cold

Pregnancy Risk Factor C

Dosage Oral: Children ≥12 years and Adults (Allerx™-D, Amdry-D): One tablet every 12 hours (maximum: 2 tablets/24 hours)

Additional Information Complete prescribing information for this medication should be consulted for additional detail.

Dosage Forms

Tablet: Pseudoephedrine hydrochloride 120 mg and methscopolamine nitrate 2.5 mg

Allerx™-D, Amdry-D: Pseudoephedrine hydrochloride 120 mg and methscopolamine nitrate 2.5 mg

♦ **Pseudoephedrine and Naproxen** see Naproxen and Pseudoephedrine on page 1201

♦ **Pseudoephedrine and Triprolidine** see Triprolidine and Pseudoephedrine on page 1749

♦ **Pseudoephedrine, Carbinoxamine, and Dextromethorphan** see Carbinoxamine, Pseudoephedrine, and Dextromethorphan on page 291

♦ **Pseudoephedrine, Chlorpheniramine, and Acetaminophen** see Acetaminophen, Chlorpheniramine, and Pseudoephedrine on page 35

♦ **Pseudoephedrine, Chlorpheniramine, and Codeine** see Chlorpheniramine, Pseudoephedrine, and Codeine on page 355

♦ **Pseudoephedrine, Chlorpheniramine, and Dextromethorphan** see Chlorpheniramine, Pseudoephedrine, and Dextromethorphan on page 355

♦ **Pseudoephedrine, Codeine, and Triprolidine** see Triprolidine, Pseudoephedrine, and Codeine on page 1750

♦ **Pseudoephedrine, Dextromethorphan, and Acetaminophen** see Acetaminophen, Dextromethorphan, and Pseudoephedrine on page 35

♦ **Pseudoephedrine, Dextromethorphan, and Carbinoxamine** see Carbinoxamine, Pseudoephedrine, and Dextromethorphan on page 291

♦ **Pseudoephedrine, Dextromethorphan, and Guaifenesin** see Guaifenesin, Pseudoephedrine, and Dextromethorphan on page 821

♦ **Pseudoephedrine, Guaifenesin, and Codeine** see Guaifenesin, Pseudoephedrine, and Codeine on page 820

♦ **Pseudoephedrine Hydrochloride** see Pseudoephedrine on page 1454

♦ **Pseudoephedrine Hydrochloride and Acrivastine** see Acrivastine and Pseudoephedrine on page 43

♦ **Pseudoephedrine hydrochloride and Methscopolamine Nitrate** see Pseudoephedrine and Methscopolamine on page 1457

♦ **Pseudoephedrine Hydrochloride, Guaifenesin, and Dihydrocodeine Bitartrate** see Dihydrocodeine, Pseudoephedrine, and Guaifenesin on page 506

♦ **Pseudoephedrine, Hydrocodone, and Carbinoxamine** see Hydrocodone, Carbinoxamine, and Pseudoephedrine on page 851

♦ **Pseudoephedrine, Hydrocodone, and Guaifenesin** *see* Hydrocodone, Pseudoephedrine, and Guaifenesin *on page 852*
♦ **Pseudoephedrine Sulfate** *see* Pseudoephedrine *on page 1454*
♦ **Pseudoephedrine Tannate and Dexchlorpheniramine Tannate** *see* Dexchlorpheniramine and Pseudoephedrine *on page 483*
♦ **Pseudoephedrine, Triprolidine, and Codeine** *see* Triprolidine, Pseudoephedrine, and Codeine *on page 1750*
♦ **Pseudofrin (Can)** *see* Pseudoephedrine *on page 1454*
♦ **Pseudo GG TR** *see* Guaifenesin and Pseudoephedrine *on page 819*
♦ **Pseudo Max** *see* Guaifenesin and Pseudoephedrine *on page 819*
♦ **Pseudo Max DMX** *see* Guaifenesin, Pseudoephedrine, and Dextromethorphan *on page 821*
♦ **Pseudomonic Acid A** *see* Mupirocin *on page 1179*
♦ **Pseudovent™** *see* Guaifenesin and Pseudoephedrine *on page 819*
♦ **Pseudovent™ 400** *see* Guaifenesin and Pseudoephedrine *on page 819*
♦ **Pseudovent™ DM** *see* Guaifenesin, Pseudoephedrine, and Dextromethorphan *on page 821*
♦ **Pseudovent™-Ped** *see* Guaifenesin and Pseudoephedrine *on page 819*
♦ **Psorcon® (Can)** *see* Diflorasone *on page 499*
♦ **Psorcon® e™ [DSC]** *see* Diflorasone *on page 499*
♦ **Psoriatec™** *see* Anthralin *on page 132*

Psyllium (SIL i yum)

U.S. Brand Names Fiberall®; Fibro-Lax [OTC]; Fibro-XL [OTC]; Genfiber® [OTC]; Hydrocil® Instant [OTC]; Konsyl® [OTC]; Konsyl-D® [OTC]; Konsyl® Easy Mix [OTC]; Konsyl® Orange [OTC]; Metamucil® [OTC]; Metamucil® Plus Calcium [OTC]; Metamucil® Smooth Texture [OTC]; Modane® Bulk [OTC]; Natural Fiber Therapy [OTC]; Reguloid® [OTC]; Serutan® [OTC]
Canadian Brand Names Metamucil®
Index Terms Plantago Seed; Plantain Seed; Psyllium Hydrophilic Mucilloid
Pharmacologic Category Antidiarrheal; Laxative, Bulk-Producing
Additional Appendix Information
Laxatives, Classification and Properties *on page 1886*
Use Treatment of chronic atonic or spastic constipation and in constipation associated with rectal disorders; management of irritable bowel syndrome; labeled for OTC use as fiber supplement, treatment of constipation
Pregnancy Risk Factor B
Lactation Excretion in breast milk unknown/compatible
Medication Safety Issues
Sound-alike/look-alike issues:
Fiberall® may be confused with Feverall®
Hydrocil® may be confused with Hydrocet®
Modane® may be confused with Matulane®, Moban®
Perdiem® may be confused with Pyridium®
Contraindications Hypersensitivity to psyllium or any component of the formulation; fecal impaction; GI obstruction
Warnings/Precautions Products must be taken with adequate fluid. Use with caution in patients with esophageal strictures, ulcers, stenosis, or intestinal adhesions; elderly may have insufficient fluid intake which may predispose them to fecal impaction and bowel obstruction.
Adverse Reactions Frequency not defined.
Gastrointestinal: Abdominal cramps, constipation, diarrhea, esophageal or bowel obstruction
Respiratory: Bronchospasm
Miscellaneous: Anaphylaxis upon inhalation in susceptible individuals, rhinoconjunctivitis
Overdosage/Toxicology Symptoms include abdominal pain, diarrhea, and constipation.
Drug Interactions
Decreased Effect: Decreased effect of warfarin, digitalis, potassium-sparing diuretics, salicylates, tetracyclines, nitrofurantoin when taken together. Separate administration times to reduce potential for drug-drug interaction.
Mechanism of Action Adsorbs water in the intestine to form a viscous liquid which promotes peristalsis and reduces transit time
Pharmacodynamics/Kinetics
Onset of action: 12-24 hours
Peak effect: 2-3 days
Absorption: None; small amounts of grain extracts present in the preparation have been reportedly absorbed following colonic hydrolysis
Dosage Oral (administer at least 2 hours before or after other drugs):
Children 6-11 years: Approximately ½ adult dosage
Children ≥12 years and Adults: Take 1 dose up to 3 times/day; all doses should be followed with 8 oz of water or liquid
Capsule: 4 capsules/dose (range: 2-6); swallow capsules one at a time
Powder: 1 rounded tablespoonful/dose (1 teaspoonful/dose for many sugar free or select concentrated products) mixed in 8 oz liquid
Tablet: 1 tablet/dose
Wafer: 2 wafers/dose
Dietary Considerations Products should be taken with large amount of fluids. Some products contain aspartame, dextrose, or sucrose, as well as additional ingredients. Check individual product information for caloric and nutritional value.
Fiberall® (sugar free formulation) contains phenylalanine.
Metamucil®. Smooth Texture (sugar free formulation) contains phenylalanine 25 mg per teaspoonful.

Administration Inhalation of psyllium dust may cause sensitivity to psyllium (eg, runny nose, watery eyes, wheezing). Drink a full glass of liquid with each dose. Powder must be mixed in a glass of water or juice. Separate dose from other drug therapies.

Dosage Forms

Capsule:

Fibro XL: 675 mg

Metamucil®: 0.52 g [contains potassium 5 mg/capsule; provides 3 g dietary fiber 2.4 g per 6 capsules]

Metamucil® Plus Calcium: 0.42 g [contains potassium 6 mg/capsule; provides dietary fiber 2.1 g and calcium 300 mg per 5 capsules]

Granules (Serutan®): 2.5 g/teaspoon (510 g) [contains sodium benzoate]

Powder: 3.4 g/dose (390 g, 570 g)

Bulk-K: 4.725 g/dose (392 g)

Fiberall®: 3.5 g/dose (454 g) [sugar free; contains phenylalanine; orange flavor]

Fibro-Lax: 4.725 g /dose (140 g, 392g)

Genfiber®: 3.4 g/dose (397 g, 595 g) [regular flavor]

Genfiber®: 3.5 g/dose (283 g) [sugar free; orange flavor]

Hydrocil® Instant: 3.5 g/dose (3.7 g unit-dose packets, 300 g) [sugar free]

Konsyl®: 6 g/dose (6 g unit-dose packets, 300 g, 450 g) [sugar free; contains sodium 4.1 mg/dose; regular flavor]

Konsyl-D®: 3.4 g/dose (6.5 g unit-dose packets, 325 g, 397 g, 500 g) [contains sodium 2.3 mg/dose and dextrose]

Konsyl® Easy Mix: 6 g/dose (6 g unit-dose packets, 250 g) [sugar free; contains sodium 4.4 mg/dose]

Konsyl® Orange: 3.4 g/dose (12 g unit-dose packets, 538 g) [contains sodium 2.3 mg/dose and sucrose; orange flavor]

Konsyl® Orange: 3.4 g/dose (425 g) [sugar free; contains sodium 2.3 mg/dose; orange flavor]

Metamucil®: 3.4 g/dose:

(390 g, 570 g, 870 g) [contains sodium 3 mg and potassium 30 mg per dose; regular flavor]

(570 g, 870 g, 1254 g) [contains sodium 5 mg and potassium 30 mg per dose; orange flavor]

Metamucil® Smooth Texture: 3.4 g/dose:

(unit-dose packets, 609 g, 912 g, 1446 g) [contains sodium 5 mg and potassium 30 mg per dose; orange flavor]

(300 g, 450 g, 690 g) [contains sodium 4 mg and potassium 30 mg per dose; regular flavor]

(unit-dose packets, 183 g, 300 g, 450 g, 699 g, 1104 g) [sugar free; contains phenylalanine 25 mg, sodium 5 mg, and potassium 30 mg per dose; orange flavor]

Modane® Bulk: 3.4 g/dose (390 g) [contains dextrose; flavor free]

Natural Fiber Therapy: 3.4 g/dose (369 g, 539 g) [natural and orange flavors]

Reguloid®: 3.4 g/dose (300 g, 450 g) [sugar free; regular or orange flavors]; (390 g, 570g) [regular or orange flavors]

Wafers (Metamucil®): 3.4 g/dose (24s) [one dose = 2 wafers; contains sodium 20 mg and potassium 60 mg per dose; apple crisp and cinnamon spice flavors]

- **Psyllium Hydrophilic Mucilloid** see Psyllium on page 1458
- **Pteroylglutamic Acid** see Folic Acid on page 749
- **PTU (error-prone abbreviation)** see Propylthiouracil on page 1449
- **Pulmicort® (Can)** see Budesonide on page 244
- **Pulmicort Respules®** see Budesonide on page 244
- **Pulmicort Turbuhaler®** see Budesonide on page 244
- **Pulmozyme®** see Dornase Alfa on page 541
- **Pulmozyme™ (Can)** see Dornase Alfa on page 541
- **Puregon® (Can)** see Follitropin Beta on page 753
- **Purified Chick Embryo Cell** see Rabies Virus Vaccine on page 1479
- **Purinethol®** see Mercaptopurine on page 1086
- **PVP-I** see Povidone-Iodine on page 1404

Pyrantel Pamoate (pi RAN tel PAM oh ate)

U.S. Brand Names Pamix™ [OTC]; Pin-X® [OTC]; Reese's® Pinworm Medicine [OTC]

Canadian Brand Names Combantrin™

Pharmacologic Category Anthelmintic

Use Treatment of pinworms (*Enterobius vermicularis*) and roundworms (*Ascaris lumbricoides*)

Unlabeled/Investigational Use Treatment of whipworms (*Trichuris trichiura*) and hookworms (*Ancylostoma duodenale*)

Pregnancy Risk Factor C

Contraindications Hypersensitivity to pyrantel pamoate or any component of the formulation

Warnings/Precautions Use with caution in patients with liver impairment, anemia, malnutrition, or pregnancy. Since pinworm infections are easily spread to others, treat all family members in close contact with the patient.

Adverse Reactions Frequency not defined.

Central nervous system: Dizziness, drowsiness, insomnia, headache

Dermatologic: Rash

Gastrointestinal: Abdominal cramps, anorexia, diarrhea, nausea, vomiting, tenesmus

Hepatic: Liver enzymes increased

Neuromuscular & skeletal: Weakness

Overdose/Toxicology Symptoms include anorexia, nausea, vomiting, cramps, diarrhea, and ataxia. Treatment is supportive following GI decontamination.

(Continued)

Pyrantel Pamoate *(Continued)*

Drug Interactions
Decreased Effect: Decreased effect with piperazine
Stability Protect from light.
Mechanism of Action Causes the release of acetylcholine and inhibits cholinesterase; acts as a depolarizing neuromuscular blocker, paralyzing the helminths
Pharmacodynamics/Kinetics
Absorption: Oral: Poor
Metabolism: Partially hepatic
Time to peak, serum: 1-3 hours
Excretion: Feces (50% as unchanged drug); urine (7% as unchanged drug)
Dosage Children and Adults (purgation is not required prior to use): Oral:
Roundworm, pinworm, or trichostrongyliasis: 11 mg/kg administered as a single dose; maximum dose: 1 g. (**Note:** For pinworm infection, dosage should be repeated in 2 weeks and all family members should be treated).
Hookworm (unlabeled use): 11 mg/kg administered once daily for 3 days
Administration May be mixed with milk or fruit juice
Monitoring Parameters Stool for presence of eggs, worms, and occult blood, serum AST and ALT
Dosage Forms
Suspension, oral as pamoate:
Pamix™: 144 mg/mL (30 mL, 60 mL, 240 mL) [equivalent to pyrantel base 50 mg/mL; contains sodium benzoate]
Pin-X®: 144 mg/mL (30 mL, 60 mL) [equivalent to pyrantel base 50 mg/mL; contains sodium benzoate; caramel flavor]
Reese's® Pinworm Medicine: 144 mg/mL (30 mL) [equivalent to pyrantel base 50 mg/mL]
Tablet, as pamoate (Reese's® Pinworm Medicine): 180 mg [equivalent to pyrantel base 62.5 mg/tablet]

Pyrazinamide *(peer a ZIN a mide)*

Canadian Brand Names Tebrazid™
Index Terms Pyrazinoic Acid Amide
Pharmacologic Category Antitubercular Agent
Additional Appendix Information
Antimicrobial Drugs of Choice *on page 1981*
Tuberculosis *on page 2010*
Use Adjunctive treatment of tuberculosis in combination with other antituberculosis agents
Pregnancy Risk Factor C
Lactation Enters breast milk/use caution
Contraindications Hypersensitivity to pyrazinamide or any component of the formulation; acute gout; severe hepatic damage
Warnings/Precautions Use with caution in patients with renal failure, chronic gout, diabetes mellitus, or porphyria
Adverse Reactions
1% to 10%:
Central nervous system: Malaise
Gastrointestinal: Anorexia, nausea, vomiting
Neuromuscular & skeletal: Arthralgia, myalgia
<1% (Limited to important or life-threatening): Acne, angioedema (rare), anticoagulant effect, dysuria, fever, gout, hepatotoxicity, interstitial nephritis, itching, photosensitivity, porphyria, rash, sideroblastic anemia, thrombocytopenia, urticaria
Overdosage/Toxicology Symptoms include gout, gastric upset, and hepatic damage (mild). Treatment following GI decontamination is supportive.
Drug Interactions
Increased Effect/Toxicity: Combination therapy with rifampin and pyrazinamide has been associated with severe and fatal hepatotoxic reactions.
Mechanism of Action Converted to pyrazinoic acid in susceptible strains of *Mycobacterium* which lowers the pH of the environment; exact mechanism of action has not been elucidated
Pharmacodynamics/Kinetics Bacteriostatic or bactericidal depending on drug's concentration at infection site

Absorption: Well absorbed
Distribution: Widely into body tissues and fluids including liver, lung, and CSF
Relative diffusion from blood into CSF: Adequate with or without inflammation (exceeds usual MICs)
CSF:blood level ratio: Inflamed meninges: 100%
Protein binding: 50%
Metabolism: Hepatic
Half-life elimination: 9-10 hours
Time to peak, serum: Within 2 hours
Excretion: Urine (4% as unchanged drug)
Dosage Oral: Treatment of tuberculosis:
Note: Used as part of a multidrug regimen. Treatment regimens consist of an initial 2-month phase, followed by a continuation phase of 4 or 7 additional months; frequency of dosing may differ depending on phase of therapy.

Children:
Daily therapy: 15-30 mg/kg/day (maximum: 2 g/day)
Twice weekly directly observed therapy (DOT): 50 mg/kg/dose (maximum: 4 g/dose)
Adults (dosing is based on lean body weight):
Daily therapy: 15-30 mg/kg/day
40-55 kg: 1000 mg

        56-75 kg: 1500 mg
        76-90 kg: 2000 mg (maximum dose regardless of weight)
    Twice weekly directly observed therapy (DOT): 50 mg/kg
        40-55 kg: 2000 mg
        56-75 kg: 3000 mg
        76-90 kg: 4000 mg (maximum dose regardless of weight)
    Three times/week DOT: 25-30 mg/kg (maximum: 2.5 g)
        40-55 kg: 1500 mg
        56-75 kg: 2500 mg
        76-90 kg: 3000 mg (maximum dose regardless of weight)
    Elderly: Start with a lower daily dose (15 mg/kg) and increase as tolerated.

Dosing adjustment in renal impairment: Cl_{cr} <50 mL/minute: Avoid use or reduce dose to 12-20 mg/kg/day
    Avoid use in hemo- and peritoneal dialysis as well as continuous arteriovenous or venovenous hemofiltration.

Dosing adjustment in hepatic impairment: Reduce dose

Monitoring Parameters Periodic liver function tests, serum uric acid, sputum culture, chest x-ray 2-3 months into treatment and at completion

Test Interactions Reacts with Acetest® and Ketostix® to produce pinkish-brown color

Dosage Forms Tablet: 500 mg

Extemporaneous Preparations Pyrazinamide suspension can be compounded with simple syrup or 0.5% methylcellulose with simple syrup at a concentration of 100 mg/mL; the suspension is stable for 2 months at 4°C or 25°C when stored in glass or plastic bottles

To prepare pyrazinamide suspension in 0.5% methylcellulose with simple syrup: Crush 200 pyrazinamide 500 mg tablets and mix with a suspension containing 500 mL of 1% methylcellulose and 500 mL simple syrup. Add to this a suspension containing 140 crushed pyrazinamide tablets in 350 mL of 1% methylcellulose and 350 mL of simple syrup to make 1.7 L of suspension containing pyrazinamide 100 mg/mL in 0.5% methylcellulose with simple syrup.
    Nahata MC, Morosco RS, and Peritre SP, "Stability of Pyrazinamide in Two Suspensions," *Am J Health Syst Pharm*, 1995, 52:1558-60.

♦ **Pyrazinoic Acid Amide** *see* Pyrazinamide *on page 1460*

Pyrethrins and Piperonyl Butoxide
(pye RE thrins & pi PER oh nil byo TOKS ide)

U.S. Brand Names A-200® Maximum Strength [OTC]; Lice-Aid [OTC]; Licide® [OTC]; Pronto® Complete Lice Killing Kit [OTC]; Pronto® Plus Hair and Scalp Masque [OTC]; Pronto® Plus Mousse [OTC]; Pronto® Plus Warm Oil Treatment and Conditioner [OTC]; Pronto® Plus with Natural Extracts and Oils [OTC]; Pyrinyl Plus® [OTC]; RID® Maximum Strength [OTC]; Tisit® [OTC]; Tisit® Blue Gel [OTC]

Canadian Brand Names Pronto® Lice Control; R & C™ II; R & C™ Shampoo/Conditioner; RID® Mousse

Index Terms Piperonyl Butoxide and Pyrethrins

Pharmacologic Category Antiparasitic Agent, Topical; Pediculocide; Shampoo, Pediculocide

Use Treatment of *Pediculus humanus* infestations (head lice, body lice, pubic lice and their eggs)

Pregnancy Risk Factor C

Dosage Application of pyrethrins:
    Topical products:
        Apply enough solution to completely wet infested area, including hair
        Allow to remain on area for 10 minutes
        Wash and rinse with large amounts of warm water.
        Use fine-toothed comb to remove lice and eggs from hair
        Shampoo hair to restore body and luster
        Treatment may be repeated if necessary once in a 24-hour period
        Repeat treatment in 7-10 days to kill newly hatched lice
        Note: Keep out of eyes when rinsing hair; protect eyes with a wash cloth or towel
    Solution for furniture, bedding: Spray on entire area to be treated; allow to dry before use. Intended for use on items which cannot be laundered or dry cleaned. **Not for use on humans or animals.**

Dosage Forms
    Cream, topical (Pronto® Plus Hair and Scalp Masque): Pyrethrins 0.33% and piperonyl butoxide 4% (60 g) [green cream shampoo; contains coconut and sesame oil; apple herb scent; packaged with nit removal comb]
    Foam, topical [mousse] (RID® Maximum Strength): Pyrethrins 0.33% and piperonyl butoxide 4% (156 g) [packaged with nit removal comb]
    Gel (Tisit® Blue Gel): Pyrethrins 0.33% and piperonyl butoxide 3% (30 g)
    Liquid, topical (Tisit®): Pyrethrins 0.33% and piperonyl butoxide 2% (60 mL, 120 mL) [packaged with nit removal comb]
    Oil, topical (Pronto® Plus Warm Oil Treatment and Conditioner): Pyrethrins 0.33% and piperonyl butoxide 4% (36 mL) [fruity herbal scent; packaged with nit removal comb]
    Shampoo: Pyrethrins 0.33% and piperonyl butoxide 4% (60 mL, 120 mL)
        A-200® Maximum Strength: Pyrethrins 0.33% and piperonyl butoxide 4% (60 mL, 120 mL) [contains benzyl alcohol; packaged with nit removal comb]
        Lice-Aid: Pyrethrins 0.33% and piperonyl butoxide 4% (120 mL)
        Licide®: Pyrethrins 0.33% and piperonyl butoxide 4% (120 mL) [packaged with nit removal comb; also available in a kit containing shampoo, household spray and nit removal comb]
        Pronto® Complete Lice Killing Kit: Pyrethrins 0.33% and piperonyl butoxide 4% (120 mL) [contains benzyl alcohol; packaged in a kit containing shampoo, creme rinse, hair separators, nit removal comb, magnifying glass, and furniture spray]
(Continued)

Pyrethrins and Piperonyl Butoxide *(Continued)*

Pronto® Plus Mousse: Pyrethrins 0.33% and piperonyl butoxide 4% (120 mL) [blue mousse shampoo; contains vitamin E; packaged with nit removal comb]

Pronto® Plus with Natural Extracts and Oils: Pyrethrins 0.33% and piperonyl butoxide 4% (60 mL) [orange scent; packaged with metal nit removal comb; also available in a kit packaged with lice/egg remover and household spray]

Pyrinyl Plus®: Pyrethrins 0.33% and piperonyl butoxide 4% (60 mL) [contains benzyl alcohol; packaged with nit removal comb]

RID® Maximum Strength: Pyrethrins 0.33% and piperonyl butoxide 4% (60 mL, 120 mL, 180 mL, 240 mL) [packaged with nit removal comb; also available in a kit containing shampoo, gel, and furniture spray]

Tisit®: Pyrethrins 0.33% and piperonyl butoxide 3% (60 mL, 120 mL) [also available in a kit containing shampoo, nit removal comb, and furniture spray]

Solution, spray [for furniture, garments, bedding; not for human or animal use] (Tisit®): Pyrethrins 0.4% and piperonyl butoxide 2% (150 mL)

- ♦ **2-Pyridine Aldoxime Methochloride** *see Pralidoxime on page 1405*
- ♦ **Pyridium®** *see Phenazopyridine on page 1351*

Pyridostigmine *(peer id oh STIG meen)*

U.S. Brand Names Mestinon®; Mestinon® Timespan®; Regonol®

Canadian Brand Names Mestinon®; Mestinon®-SR

Index Terms Pyridostigmine Bromide

Pharmacologic Category Acetylcholinesterase Inhibitor

Use Symptomatic treatment of myasthenia gravis; antidote for nondepolarizing neuromuscular blockers

Military use: Pretreatment for Soman nerve gas exposure

Pregnancy Risk Factor B

Pregnancy Implications Safety has not been established for use during pregnancy. The potential benefit to the mother should outweigh the potential risk to the fetus. When pyridostigmine is needed in myasthenic mothers, giving dose parenterally 1 hour before completion of the second stage of labor may facilitate delivery and protect the neonate during the immediate postnatal state.

Lactation Enters breast milk/compatible

Medication Safety Issues

Sound-alike/look-alike issues:

Pyridostigmine may be confused with physostigmine

Mestinon® may be confused with Metatensin®

Regonol® may be confused with Reglan®, Renagel®

Contraindications Hypersensitivity to pyridostigmine, bromides, or any component of the formulation; GI or GU obstruction

Warnings/Precautions Use with caution in patients with epilepsy, asthma, bradycardia, hyperthyroidism, cardiac arrhythmias, or peptic ulcer; adequate facilities should be available for cardiopulmonary resuscitation when testing and adjusting dose for myasthenia gravis; have atropine and epinephrine ready to treat hypersensitivity reactions; overdosage may result in cholinergic crisis, this must be distinguished from myasthenic crisis; anticholinesterase insensitivity can develop for brief or prolonged periods. Safety and efficacy in pediatric patients have not been established. Regonol® injection contains 1% benzyl alcohol as the preservative (not intended for use in newborns).

Adverse Reactions Frequency not defined.

Cardiovascular: Arrhythmias (especially bradycardia), AV block, cardiac arrest, decreased carbon monoxide, flushing, hypotension, nodal rhythm, nonspecific ECG changes, syncope, tachycardia

Central nervous system: Convulsions, dizziness, drowsiness, dysphonia, headache, loss of consciousness

Dermatologic: Skin rash, thrombophlebitis (I.V.), urticaria

Gastrointestinal: Abdominal pain, diarrhea, dysphagia, flatulence, hyperperistalsis, nausea, salivation, stomach cramps, vomiting

Genitourinary: Urinary urgency

Neuromuscular & skeletal: Arthralgia, dysarthria, fasciculations, muscle cramps, myalgia, spasms, weakness

Ocular: Amblyopia, lacrimation, small pupils

Respiratory: Bronchial secretions increased, bronchiolar constriction, bronchospasm, dyspnea, laryngospasm, respiratory arrest, respiratory depression, respiratory muscle paralysis

Miscellaneous: Allergic reactions, anaphylaxis, diaphoresis increased

Overdosage/Toxicology Symptoms include muscle weakness, blurred vision, excessive sweating, tearing and salivation, nausea, vomiting, diarrhea, hypertension, bradycardia, and paralysis. Atropine is the treatment of choice for intoxications manifesting with significant muscarinic symptoms. Atropine I.V. 2-4 mg every 3-60 minutes (or 0.04-0.08 mg I.V. every 5-60 minutes if needed for children) should be repeated to control symptoms and then continued as needed for 1-2 days following the acute ingestion.

Drug Interactions

Increased Effect/Toxicity: Increased effect of depolarizing neuromuscular blockers (succinylcholine). Increased toxicity with edrophonium. Increased bradycardia/hypotension with beta-blockers.

Decreased Effect: Neuromuscular blockade reversal effect of pyridostigmine may be decreased by aminoglycosides, quinolones, tetracyclines, bacitracin, colistin, polymyxin B, sodium colistimethate, quinidine, elevated serum magnesium concentrations.

Stability

Injection: Protect from light.

Tablet:
    30 mg: Store under refrigeration at 2°C to 8°C (36°F to 46°F). Protect from light. Stable at room temperature for up to 3 months.
    Mestinon®: Store at 25°C (77°F). Protect from moisture.

Mechanism of Action Inhibits destruction of acetylcholine by acetylcholinesterase which facilitates transmission of impulses across myoneural junction

Pharmacodynamics/Kinetics
    Onset of action: Oral, I.M.: 15-30 minutes; I.V. injection: 2-5 minutes
    Duration: Oral: Up to 6-8 hours (due to slow absorption); I.V.: 2-3 hours
    Absorption: Oral: Very poor
    Distribution: 19 ± 12 L
    Metabolism: Hepatic
    Bioavailability: 10% to 20%
    Half-life elimination: 1-2 hours; Renal failure: ≤6 hours
    Excretion: Urine (80% to 90% as unchanged drug)

Dosage
    Myasthenia gravis:
      Oral:
        Children: 7 mg/kg/24 hours divided into 5-6 doses
        Adults: Highly individualized dosing ranges: 60-1500 mg/day, usually 600 mg/day divided into 5-6 doses, spaced to provide maximum relief
          Sustained release formulation: Highly individualized dosing ranges: 180-540 mg once or twice daily (doses separated by at least 6 hours); **Note:** Most clinicians reserve sustained release dosage form for bedtime dose only.
      I.M., slow I.V. push:
        Children: 0.05-0.15 mg/kg/dose
        Adults: To supplement oral dosage pre- and postoperatively during labor and post-partum, during myasthenic crisis, or when oral therapy is impractical: ~1/30th of oral dose; observe patient closely for cholinergic reactions
        or
        I.V. infusion: Initial: 2 mg/hour with gradual titration in increments of 0.5-1 mg/hour, up to a maximum rate of 4 mg/hour

    Pretreatment for Soman nerve gas exposure (military use): Oral: Adults: 30 mg every 8 hours beginning several hours prior to exposure; discontinue at first sign of nerve agent exposure, then begin atropine and pralidoxime

    Reversal of nondepolarizing muscle relaxants: **Note:** Atropine sulfate (0.6-1.2 mg) I.V. immediately prior to pyridostigmine to minimize side effects: I.V.:
      Children: Dosing range: 0.1-0.25 mg/kg/dose*
      Adults: 0.1-0.25 mg/kg/dose; 10-20 mg is usually sufficient*
      *Full recovery usually occurs ≤15 minutes, but ≥30 minutes may be required

    Dosage adjustment in renal dysfunction: Lower dosages may be required due to prolonged elimination; no specific recommendations have been published

Administration Do **not** crush sustained release tablet.

Monitoring Parameters Observe for cholinergic reactions, particularly when administered I.V.

Test Interactions Increased aminotransferase [ALT (SGPT)/AST (SGOT)] (S), increased amylase (S)

Dosage Forms
    Injection, solution, as bromide:
      Mestinon®: 5 mg/mL (2 mL)
      Regonol®: 5 mg/mL (2 mL) [contains benzyl alcohol]
    Syrup, as bromide (Mestinon®): 60 mg/5 mL (480 mL) [raspberry flavor; contains alcohol 5%, sodium benzoate]
    Tablet, as bromide (Mestinon®): 60 mg
    Tablet, sustained release, as bromide (Mestinon® Timespan®): 180 mg

♦ **Pyridostigmine Bromide** see Pyridostigmine on page 1462

Pyridoxine (peer i DOKS een)

U.S. Brand Names Aminoxin® [OTC]
Index Terms Pyridoxine Hydrochloride; Vitamin B₆
Pharmacologic Category Vitamin, Water Soluble
Additional Appendix Information
    Anticonvulsants by Seizure Type on page 1865
    Epilepsy on page 2048
    Management of Overdosages on page 2075
    USPHS / IDSA Guidelines for the Prevention of Opportunistic Infections in Persons Infected With HIV on page 1966
Use Prevention and treatment of vitamin B₆ deficiency, pyridoxine-dependent seizures in infants; adjunct to treatment of acute toxicity from isoniazid, cycloserine, or hydrazine overdose
Pregnancy Risk Factor A/C (dose exceeding RDA recommendation)
Pregnancy Implications Crosses the placenta; available evidence suggests safe use during pregnancy
Lactation Enters breast milk/compatible
Medication Safety Issues
    Sound-alike/look-alike issues:
      Pyridoxine may be confused with paroxetine, pralidoxime, Pyridium®
Contraindications Hypersensitivity to pyridoxine or any component of the formulation
Warnings/Precautions Dependence and withdrawal may occur with doses >200 mg/day
Adverse Reactions Frequency not defined.
    (Continued)

Pyridoxine *(Continued)*

Central nervous system: Headache, seizure (following very large I.V. doses), sensory neuropathy

Endocrine & metabolic: Decreased serum folic acid secretions

Gastrointestinal: Nausea

Hepatic: Increased AST

Neuromuscular & skeletal: Paresthesia

Miscellaneous: Allergic reactions

Overdosage/Toxicology Symptoms include ataxia and sensory neuropathy with doses of 50 mg to 2 g daily over prolonged periods. Acute doses of 70-357 mg/kg have been well tolerated.

Drug Interactions

Decreased Effect: Pyridoxine may decrease serum levels of levodopa, phenobarbital, and phenytoin (patients taking levodopa without carbidopa should avoid supplemental vitamin B_6 >5 mg per day, which includes multivitamin preparations).

Stability Protect from light.

Mechanism of Action Precursor to pyridoxal, which functions in the metabolism of proteins, carbohydrates, and fats; pyridoxal also aids in the release of liver and muscle-stored glycogen and in the synthesis of GABA (within the central nervous system) and heme

Pharmacodynamics/Kinetics

Absorption: Enteral, parenteral: Well absorbed

Metabolism: Via 4-pyridoxic acid (active form) and other metabolites

Half-life elimination: 15-20 days

Excretion: Urine

Dosage

Recommended daily allowance (RDA):

Children:

1-3 years: 0.9 mg

4-6 years: 1.3 mg

7-10 years: 1.6 mg

Adults:

Male: 1.7-2.0 mg

Female: 1.4-1.6 mg

Pyridoxine-dependent Infants:

Oral: 2-100 mg/day

I.M., I.V., SubQ: 10-100 mg

Dietary deficiency: Oral:

Children: 5-25 mg/24 hours for 3 weeks, then 1.5-2.5 mg/day in multiple vitamin product

Adults: 10-20 mg/day for 3 weeks

Drug-induced neuritis (eg, isoniazid, hydralazine, penicillamine, cycloserine): Oral:

Children:

Treatment: 10-50 mg/24 hours

Prophylaxis: 1-2 mg/kg/24 hours

Adults:

Treatment: 100-200 mg/24 hours

Prophylaxis: 25-100 mg/24 hours

Treatment of seizures and/or coma from acute isoniazid toxicity, a dose of pyridoxine hydrochloride equal to the amount of INH ingested can be given I.M./I.V. in divided doses together with other anticonvulsants; if the amount INH ingested is not known, administer 5 g I.V. pyridoxine

Treatment of acute hydrazine toxicity, a pyridoxine dose of 25 mg/kg in divided doses I.M./I.V. has been used

Administration Burning may occur at the injection site after I.M. or SubQ administration; seizures have occurred following I.V. administration of very large doses

Reference Range Over 50 ng/mL (SI: 243 nmol/L) (varies considerably with method). A broad range is ~25-80 ng/mL (SI: 122-389 nmol/L). HPLC method for pyridoxal phosphate has normal range of 3.5-18 ng/mL (SI: 17-88 nmol/L).

Test Interactions Urobilinogen

Dosage Forms

Capsule, as hydrochloride: 250 mg

Injection, solution, as hydrochloride: 100 mg/mL (1 mL)

Tablet, as hydrochloride: 25 mg, 50 mg, 100 mg, 200 mg, 250 mg, 500 mg

Tablet, enteric coated, as hydrochloride (Aminoxin®): 20 mg

Extemporaneous Preparations A 1 mg/mL oral solution was stable for 30 days when refrigerated when compounded as follows:

Withdraw 100 mg (1 mL of a 100 mg/mL injection) from a vial with a needle and syringe, add to 99 mL of simple syrup in an amber bottle

Keep in refrigerator

Nahata MC and Hipple TF, *Pediatric Drug Formulations*, 3rd ed, Cincinnati, OH: Harvey Whitney Books Co, 1997.

♦ **Pyridoxine, Folic Acid, and Cyanocobalamin** *see* Folic Acid, Cyanocobalamin, and Pyridoxine *on page 750*

♦ **Pyridoxine Hydrochloride** *see* Pyridoxine *on page 1463*

Pyrimethamine *(peer i METH a meen)*

U.S. Brand Names Daraprim®

Canadian Brand Names Daraprim®

Pharmacologic Category Antimalarial Agent

Additional Appendix Information

Malaria Treatment *on page 2003*

USPHS / IDSA Guidelines for the Prevention of Opportunistic Infections in Persons Infected With HIV *on page 1966*

Use Prophylaxis of malaria due to susceptible strains of plasmodia; used in conjunction with quinine and sulfadiazine for the treatment of uncomplicated attacks of chloroquine-resistant *P. falciparum* malaria; used in conjunction with fast-acting schizonticide to initiate transmission control and suppression cure; synergistic combination with sulfonamide in treatment of toxoplasmosis

Pregnancy Risk Factor C

Pregnancy Implications There are no adequate or well-controlled studies in pregnant women. Teratogenicity has been reported in animal studies. If administered during pregnancy (ie, for toxoplasmosis), supplementation of folate is strongly recommended. Pregnancy should be avoided during therapy.

Lactation Enters breast milk/not recommended (AAP rates "compatible")

Medication Safety Issues
Sound-alike/look-alike issues:
Daraprim® may be confused with Dantrium®, Daranide®

Contraindications Hypersensitivity to pyrimethamine or any component of the formulation; chloroguanide; resistant malaria; megaloblastic anemia secondary to folate deficiency

Warnings/Precautions When used for more than 3-4 days, it may be advisable to administer leucovorin to prevent hematologic complications; monitor CBC and platelet counts every 2 weeks; use with caution in patients with impaired renal or hepatic function or with possible G6PD. Use caution in patients with seizure disorders or possible folate deficiency (eg, malabsorption syndrome, pregnancy, alcoholism).

Adverse Reactions Frequency not defined.
Cardiovascular: Arrhythmias (large doses)
Central nervous system: Depression, fever, insomnia, lightheadedness, malaise, seizure
Dermatologic: Abnormal skin pigmentation, dermatitis, erythema multiforme, rash, Stevens-Johnson syndrome, toxic epidermal necrolysis
Gastrointestinal: Anorexia, abdominal cramps, vomiting, diarrhea, xerostomia, atrophic glossitis
Hematologic: Megaloblastic anemia, leukopenia, pancytopenia, thrombocytopenia, pulmonary eosinophilia
Genitourinary: Hematuria
Miscellaneous: Anaphylaxis

Overdosage/Toxicology Symptoms include megaloblastic anemia, leukopenia, thrombocytopenia, anorexia, CNS stimulation, seizures, nausea, vomiting, and hematemesis. Following GI decontamination, leucovorin should be administered in a dosage of 5-15 mg/day I.M., I.V., or oral for 5-7 days, or as required to reverse symptoms of folic acid deficiency. Diazepam 0.1-0.25 mg/kg can be used to treat seizures.

Drug Interactions
Cytochrome P450 Effect: Inhibits CYP2C9 (moderate), 2D6 (moderate)
Increased Effect/Toxicity: Serum levels of antipsychotic agents may be increased by pyrimethamine. Sulfonamides (synergy), methotrexate, TMP/SMZ, and zidovudine may increase the risk of bone marrow suppression. Pyrimethamine may increase the levels/effects of amphetamines, selected beta-blockers, bosentan, dapsone, dextromethorphan, fluoxetine, glimepiride, glipizide, lidocaine, losartan, mirtazapine, montelukast, nateglinide, nefazodone, paclitaxel, paroxetine, phenytoin, risperidone, ritonavir, thioridazine, tricyclic antidepressants, venlafaxine, warfarin, zafirlukast, and other CYP2C9 and 2D6 substrates.
Decreased Effect: Pyrimethamine may decrease the levels/effects of CYP2D6 prodrug substrates (eg, codeine, hydrocodone, oxycodone, tramadol).

Stability Store at 15°C to 25°C (59°F to 77°F). Protect from light.

Mechanism of Action Inhibits parasitic dihydrofolate reductase, resulting in inhibition of vital tetrahydrofolic acid synthesis

Pharmacodynamics/Kinetics
Onset of action: ~1 hour
Absorption: Well absorbed
Distribution: Widely, mainly in blood cells, kidneys, lungs, liver, and spleen; crosses into CSF; crosses placenta; enters breast milk
Protein binding: 80% to 87%
Metabolism: Hepatic
Half-life elimination: 80-95 hours
Time to peak, serum: 1.5-8 hours
Excretion: Urine (20% to 30% as unchanged drug)

Dosage
Malaria chemoprophylaxis (for areas where chloroquine-resistant *P. falciparum* exists): Begin prophylaxis 2 weeks before entering endemic area:
Children: 0.5 mg/kg once weekly; not to exceed 25 mg/dose
or
Children:
<4 years: 6.25 mg once weekly
4-10 years: 12.5 mg once weekly
Children >10 years and Adults: 25 mg once weekly
Dosage should be continued for all age groups for at least 6-10 weeks after leaving endemic areas
Chloroquine-resistant *P. falciparum* malaria (when used in conjunction with quinine and sulfadiazine):
Children:
<10 kg: 6.25 mg/day once daily for 3 days
10-20 kg: 12.5 mg/day once daily for 3 days
20-40 kg: 25 mg/day once daily for 3 days
Adults: 25 mg twice daily for 3 days
Toxoplasmosis:
Infants (congenital toxoplasmosis): Oral: 1 mg/kg once daily for 6 months with sulfadiazine then every other month with sulfa, alternating with spiramycin.
(Continued)

Pyrimethamine *(Continued)*

Children: Loading dose: 2 mg/kg/day divided into 2 equal daily doses for 1-3 days (maximum: 100 mg/day) followed by 1 mg/kg/day divided into 2 doses for 4 weeks; maximum: 25 mg/day

With sulfadiazine or trisulfapyrimidines: 2 mg/kg/day divided every 12 hours for 3 days, followed by 1 mg/kg/day once daily or divided twice daily for 4 weeks given with trisulfapyrimidines or sulfadiazine

Adults: 50-75 mg/day together with 1-4 g of a sulfonamide for 1-3 weeks depending on patient's tolerance and response, then reduce dose by 50% and continue for 4-5 weeks **or** 25-50 mg/day for 3-4 weeks

Prophylaxis for first episode of *Toxoplasma gondii*:

Children ≥1 month of age: 1 mg/kg/day once daily with dapsone, plus oral folinic acid 5 mg every 3 days

Adolescents and Adults: 50 mg once weekly with dapsone, plus oral folinic acid 25 mg once weekly

Prophylaxis to prevent recurrence of *Toxoplasma gondii*:

Children ≥1 month of age: 1 mg/kg/day once daily given with sulfadiazine or clindamycin, plus oral folinic acid 5 mg every 3 days

Adolescents and Adults: 25-50 mg once daily in combination with sulfadiazine or clindamycin, plus oral folinic acid 10-25 mg daily; atovaquone plus oral folinic acid has also been used in combination with pyrimethamine.

Administration Administer with meals to minimize GI distress.

Monitoring Parameters CBC, including platelet counts

Additional Information Leucovorin may be administered in a dosage of 3-9 mg/day for 3 days or 5 mg every 3 days or as required to reverse symptoms of or to prevent hematologic problems due to folic acid deficiency

Dosage Forms Tablet: 25 mg

Extemporaneous Preparations Pyrimethamine tablets may be crushed to prepare oral suspensions of the drug in water, cherry syrup or sucrose-containing solutions at a concentration of 1 mg/mL; stable at room temperature for 5-7 days

AHFS Drug Information, McEvoy G, ed, Bethesda, MD: American Society of Health-System Pharmacists, 1996.

- ◆ **Pyrimethamine and Sulfadoxine** *see* Sulfadoxine and Pyrimethamine *on page 1611*
- ◆ **Pyrinyl Plus® [OTC]** *see* Pyrethrins and Piperonyl Butoxide *on page 1461*
- ◆ **Q-Bid DM** *see* Guaifenesin and Dextromethorphan *on page 816*
- ◆ **QDALL®** *see* Chlorpheniramine and Pseudoephedrine *on page 350*
- ◆ **Q-Dryl [OTC]** *see* DiphenhydrAMINE *on page 515*
- ◆ **Q-Naftate [OTC]** *see* Tolnaftate *on page 1704*
- ◆ **Q-Tussin [OTC]** *see* Guaifenesin *on page 814*
- ◆ **Q-Tussin DM [OTC]** *see* Guaifenesin and Dextromethorphan *on page 816*
- ◆ **Quadrivalent Human Papillomavirus Vaccine** *see* Papillomavirus (Types 6, 11, 16, 18) Recombinant Vaccine *on page 1310*
- ◆ **Qualaquin™** *see* Quinine *on page 1474*
- ◆ **Quasense™** *see* Ethinyl Estradiol and Levonorgestrel *on page 653*
- ◆ **Quaternium-18 Bentonite** *see* Bentoquatam *on page 204*

Quazepam *(KWAZ e pam)*

U.S. Brand Names Doral®

Canadian Brand Names Doral®

Pharmacologic Category Benzodiazepine

Additional Appendix Information
Benzodiazepines *on page 1874*

Use Treatment of insomnia

Restrictions C-IV

Pregnancy Risk Factor X

Medication Safety Issues

Sound-alike/look-alike issues:

Quazepam may be confused with oxazepam

Dosage Adults: Oral: Initial: 15 mg at bedtime, in some patients the dose may be reduced to 7.5 mg after a few nights

Elderly: Dosing should be cautious; begin at lower end of dosing range (ie, 7.5 mg)

Dosing adjustment in hepatic impairment: Dose reduction may be necessary

Additional Information Complete prescribing information for this medication should be consulted for additional detail.

Dosage Forms Tablet: 7.5 mg, 15 mg

- ◆ **Quelicin®** *see* Succinylcholine *on page 1605*
- ◆ **Quenalin [OTC]** *see* DiphenhydrAMINE *on page 515*
- ◆ **Questran®** *see* Cholestyramine Resin *on page 360*
- ◆ **Questran® Light** *see* Cholestyramine Resin *on page 360*
- ◆ **Questran® Light Sugar Free (Can)** *see* Cholestyramine Resin *on page 360*

Quetiapine (kwe TYE a peen)

U.S. Brand Names Seroquel®
Canadian Brand Names Seroquel®
Index Terms Quetiapine Fumarate
Pharmacologic Category Antipsychotic Agent, Atypical
Additional Appendix Information
Antipsychotic Agents on page 1872
Use Treatment of schizophrenia; treatment of acute manic episodes associated with bipolar disorder (as monotherapy or in combination with lithium or valproate); treatment of depressive episodes associated with bipolar disorder
Unlabeled/Investigational Use Autism, psychosis (children)
Restrictions An FDA-approved medication guide concerning the use of antidepressants in children and teenagers must be distributed when dispensing an outpatient prescription (new or refill) where this medication is to be used without direct supervision of a healthcare provider. Medication guides are available at http://www.fda.gov/cder/drug/antidepressants/MG_template.pdf. Dispense to parents or guardians of children and teenagers receiving this medication.
Pregnancy Risk Factor C
Lactation Excretion in breast milk unknown/not recommended
Medication Safety Issues
Sound-alike/look-alike issues:
Seroquel® may be confused with Serentil®, Serzone®, Sinequan®
Contraindications Hypersensitivity to quetiapine or any component of the formulation; severe CNS depression; bone marrow suppression; blood dyscrasias; severe hepatic disease, coma
Warnings/Precautions [U.S. Boxed Warning]: Patients with dementia-related behavioral disorders treated with atypical antipsychotics are at an increased risk of death compared to placebo. An increased incidence of cerebrovascular adverse events (including fatalities) has been reported in elderly patients with dementia-related psychosis. Risk may be increased by dehydration; use caution with concurrent diuretics. Quetiapine is not approved for this indication.

[U.S. Boxed Warning]: Antidepressants increase the risk of suicidal thinking and behavior in children and adolescents with major depressive disorder (MDD) and other depressive disorders; consider risk prior to prescribing. The possibility of a suicide attempt is inherent in psychotic illness, bipolar disorder, or major depression; use caution in high-risk patients during initiation of therapy. Prescriptions should be written for the smallest quantity consistent with good patient care. Safety and efficacy have not been established in children.

May be sedating, use with caution in disorders where CNS depression is a feature. Use with caution in Parkinson's disease. May induce orthostatic hypotension associated with dizziness, tachycardia, and, in some cases, syncope, especially during the initial dose titration period. Should be used with particular caution in patients with known cardiovascular disease (history of MI or ischemic heart disease, heart failure, or conduction abnormalities), cerebrovascular disease, or conditions that predispose to hypotension. Esophageal dysmotility and aspiration have been associated with antipsychotic use; use with caution in patients at risk of aspiration pneumonia (ie, Alzheimer's disease). Development of cataracts has been observed in animal studies, therefore, lens examinations should be made upon initiation of therapy and every 6 months thereafter.

Due to anticholinergic effects, use with caution in patients with decreased gastrointestinal motility, urinary retention, BPH, xerostomia, visual problems, narrow-angle glaucoma (screening is recommended), and myasthenia gravis. Relative to other antipsychotics, quetiapine has a moderate potency of cholinergic blockade. May cause extrapyramidal symptoms, pseudoparkinsonism, and/or tardive dyskinesia. Impaired core body temperature regulation may occur; caution with strenuous exercise, heat exposure, dehydration, and concomitant medication possessing anticholinergic effects. Neuroleptic malignant syndrome (NMS) is a potentially fatal symptom complex that has been reported in association with administration of antipsychotic drugs. Clinical manifestations of NMS are hyperpyrexia, muscle rigidity, altered mental status, and evidence of autonomic instability (irregular pulse or blood pressure, tachycardia, diaphoresis, and cardiac dysrhythmia). Management of NMS should include immediate discontinuation of antipsychotic drugs and other drugs not essential to concurrent therapy, intensive symptomatic treatment and medication monitoring, and treatment of any concomitant medical problems for which specific treatment are available.

Use caution in patients with a history of seizures. May cause decreases in total free thyroxine, elevations of liver enzymes, cholesterol levels and/or triglyceride increases.

May cause hyperglycemia; in some cases may be extreme and associated with ketoacidosis, hyperosmolar coma, or death. Use with caution in patients with diabetes or other disorders of glucose regulation; monitor for worsening of glucose control. Significant weight gain has been observed with antipsychotic therapy; incidence varies with product.

Adverse Reactions
>10%:
Central nervous system: Agitation, dizziness, headache, somnolence
Endocrine & metabolic: Cholesterol increased (11%), triglycerides increased (17%)
Gastrointestinal: Weight gain (≥7% body weight, dose related), xerostomia
1% to 10%:
Cardiovascular: Palpitation, peripheral edema, postural hypotension, tachycardia
Central nervous system: Anxiety, fever, pain
Dermatologic: Rash
Gastrointestinal: Abdominal pain (dose related), anorexia, constipation, dyspepsia (dose related), gastroenteritis, vomiting
Hematologic: Leukopenia
Hepatic: AST increased, ALT increased, GGT increased
Neuromuscular & skeletal: Back pain, dysarthria, hypertonia, tremor, weakness
(Continued)

Quetiapine *(Continued)*

Ocular: Amblyopia

Respiratory: Cough, dyspnea, pharyngitis, rhinitis

Miscellaneous: Diaphoresis, flu-like syndrome

<1% (Limited to important or life-threatening): Agranulocytosis, anaphylaxis, diabetes mellitus, hyperglycemia, hyperlipidemia, hyponatremia, hypothyroidism, increased appetite, increased salivation, involuntary movements, leukocytosis, neutropenia, photosensitivity, priapism, QT prolongation, rash, rhabdomyolysis, SIADH, Stevens-Johnson syndrome, tardive dyskinesia, vertigo

Drug Interactions

Cytochrome P450 Effect: Substrate of CYP2D6 (minor), 3A4 (major)

Increased Effect/Toxicity: Quetiapine increases levels of lorazepam. The effects of other centrally-acting drugs, sedatives, or ethanol may be potentiated by quetiapine. Quetiapine may enhance the effects of antihypertensive agents. CYP3A4 inhibitors may increase the levels/effects of quetiapine; example inhibitors include azole antifungals, clarithromycin, diclofenac, doxycycline, erythromycin, imatinib, isoniazid, nefazodone, nicardipine, propofol, protease inhibitors, quinidine, telithromycin, and verapamil; ketoconazole increased serum concentrations of quetiapine by 335%. Cimetidine increases blood levels of quetiapine. Acetylcholinesterase inhibitors (central) may increase the risk of antipsychotic-related EPS. Concurrent use with other QT_c-prolonging agents may increase risk of serious arrhythmias.

Decreased Effect: Thioridazine increases quetiapine's clearance (by 65%), decreasing serum levels. CYP3A4 inducers may decrease the levels/effects of quetiapine. Example inducers include aminoglutethimide, carbamazepine, nafcillin, nevirapine, phenobarbital, phenytoin, and rifamycins.

Ethanol/Nutrition/Herb Interactions

Ethanol: Avoid ethanol (may cause excessive impairment in cognition/motor function).

Food: In healthy volunteers, administration of quetiapine with food resulted in an increase in the peak serum concentration and AUC (each by ~15%) compared to the fasting state.

Herb/Nutraceutical: St John's wort may decrease quetiapine levels. Avoid valerian, St John's wort, kava kava, gotu kola (may increase CNS depression).

Mechanism of Action Quetiapine is a dibenzothiazepine atypical antipsychotic. It has been proposed that this drug's antipsychotic activity is mediated through a combination of dopamine type 2 (D_2) and serotonin type 2 (5-HT_2) antagonism. It is an antagonist at multiple neurotransmitter receptors in the brain: serotonin 5-HT_{1A} and 5-HT_2, dopamine D_1 and D_2, histamine H_1, and adrenergic alpha$_1$- and alpha$_2$- receptors; but appears to have no appreciable affinity at cholinergic muscarinic and benzodiazepine receptors.

Antagonism at receptors other than dopamine and 5-HT_2 with similar receptor affinities may explain some of the other effects of quetiapine. The drug's antagonism of histamine H_1-receptors may explain the somnolence observed with it. The drug's antagonism of adrenergic alpha$_1$-receptors may explain the orthostatic hypotension observed with it.

Pharmacodynamics/Kinetics

Absorption: Rapidly absorbed following oral administration

Distribution: V_d: 10 ± 4 L/kg; V_{dss}: ~2 days

Protein binding, plasma: 83%

Metabolism: Primarily hepatic; via CYP3A4; forms two inactive metabolites

Bioavailability: 9% ± 4%; tablet is 100% bioavailable relative to solution

Half-life elimination: Mean: Terminal: ~6 hours

Time to peak, plasma: 1.5 hours

Excretion: Urine (73% as metabolites, <1% as unchanged drug); feces (20%)

Dosage Oral:

Children and Adolescents:

Autism (unlabeled use): 100-350 mg/day (1.6-5.2 mg/kg/day)

Psychosis and mania (unlabeled use): Initial: 25 mg twice daily; titrate as necessary to 450 mg/day

Adults:

Bipolar depression: Initial: 50 mg/day the first day; increase to 100 mg/day on day 2, further increasing by 100 mg/day each day to a target of 300 mg/day by day 4. Further increases up to 600 mg/day by day 8 have been evaluated in clinical trials, but no additional antidepressant efficacy was noted.

Bipolar mania: Initial: 50 mg twice daily on day 1, increase dose in increments of 100 mg/day to 200 mg twice daily on day 4; may increase to a target dose of 800 mg/day by day 6 at increments of ≤200 mg/day. Usual dosage range: 400-800 mg/day.

Schizophrenia/psychoses: Initial: 25 mg twice daily; increase in increments of 25-50 mg 2-3 times/day on the second and third day, if tolerated, to a target dose of 300-400 mg in 2-3 divided doses by day 4. Make further adjustments as needed at intervals of at least 2 days in adjustments of 25-50 mg twice daily. Usual maintenance range: 300-800 mg/day.

Note: Dose reductions should be attempted periodically to establish lowest effective dose in patients with psychosis. Patients being restarted after 1 week of no drug need to be titrated as above.

Elderly: 40% lower mean oral clearance of quetiapine in adults >65 years of age; higher plasma levels expected and, therefore, dosage adjustment may be needed; elderly patients usually require 50-200 mg/day with a slower titration schedule. See "Note" in Adults dosing.

Dosing comments in renal insufficiency: 25% lower mean oral clearance of quetiapine than normal subjects; however, plasma concentrations similar to normal subjects receiving the same dose; no dosage adjustment required

Dosing comments in hepatic insufficiency: 30% lower mean oral clearance of quetiapine than normal subjects; higher plasma levels expected in hepatically impaired subjects; dosage adjustment may be needed

Initial: 25 mg/day, increase dose by 25-50 mg/day to effective dose, based on clinical response and tolerability to patient

Dietary Considerations May be taken with or without food.

Monitoring Parameters Vital signs; fasting lipid profile and fasting blood glucose/Hgb A₁c (prior to treatment, at 3 months, then annually); BMI, personal/family history of obesity, waist circumference; blood pressure; mental status, abnormal involuntary movement scale (AIMS); Weight should be assessed prior to treatment, at 4 weeks, 8 weeks, 12 weeks, and then at quarterly intervals. Consider titrating to a different antipsychotic agent for a weight gain ≥5% of the initial weight. Patients should have eyes checked for cataracts every 6 months while on this medication. Observe for new or worsening depression, anxiety, irritability, aggression, or other symptoms of unusual behavior or mood.

Dosage Forms
Tablet, as fumarate:
Seroquel®: 25 mg, 50 mg, 100 mg, 200 mg, 300 mg, 400 mg

♦ **Quetiapine Fumarate** see Quetiapine on page 1467

♦ **Quibron® [DSC]** see Theophylline and Guaifenesin on page 1663

♦ **Quibron®-T** see Theophylline Salts on page 1664

♦ **Quibron®-T/SR** see Theophylline Salts on page 1664

♦ **Quinalbarbitone Sodium** see Secobarbital on page 1552

Quinapril (KWIN a pril)

U.S. Brand Names Accupril®
Canadian Brand Names Accupril®
Index Terms Quinapril Hydrochloride
Pharmacologic Category Angiotensin-Converting Enzyme (ACE) Inhibitor
Additional Appendix Information
Angiotensin Agents on page 1860
Heart Failure (Systolic) on page 2051
Use Management of hypertension; treatment of congestive heart failure
Unlabeled/Investigational Use Treatment of left ventricular dysfunction after myocardial infarction
Pregnancy Risk Factor C (1st trimester)/D (2nd and 3rd trimesters)
Pregnancy Implications Decreased placental blood flow, low birth weight, fetal hypotension, preterm delivery, and fetal death have been noted with the use of some ACE inhibitors (ACEIs) in animal studies. Neonatal hypotension, skull hypoplasia, anuria, renal failure, oligohydramnios (associated with fetal limb contractures, craniofacial deformities, hypoplastic lung development), prematurity, intrauterine growth retardation, and patent ductus arteriosus have been reported with the use of ACEIs, primarily in the 2nd and 3rd trimesters. The risk of neonatal toxicity has been considered less when ACEIs have been used in the 1st trimester; however, major congenital malformations have been reported. The cardiovascular and/or central nervous systems are most commonly affected. Unless alternative agents are not appropriate, ACEIs should be discontinued as soon as possible once pregnancy is detected.
Lactation Enters breast milk/use caution
Medication Safety Issues
Sound-alike/look-alike issues:
Accupril® may be confused with Accolate®, Accutane®, AcipHex®, Monopril®

International issues:
Accupril® may be confused with Acepril® which is a brand name for lisinopril in Denmark, a brand name for enalapril in Hungary and Switzerland, and a brand name for captopril in Great Britain
Contraindications Hypersensitivity to quinapril or any component of the formulation; angioedema related to previous treatment with an ACE inhibitor; bilateral renal artery stenosis; patients with idiopathic or hereditary angioedema; pregnancy (2nd and 3rd trimesters)
Warnings/Precautions Anaphylactic reactions can occur. Use with caution in patients with renal insufficiency, autoimmune disease, renal artery stenosis; excessive hypotension may be more likely in volume-depleted patients, the elderly, and following the first dose (first dose phenomenon); quinapril should be discontinued if laryngeal stridor or angioedema is observed. Angioedema can occur at any time during treatment (especially following first dose). It may involve head and neck (potentially affecting the airway) or the intestine (presenting with abdominal pain). Prolonged monitoring may be required especially if tongue, glottis, or larynx are involved as they are associated with airway obstruction. Those with a history of airway surgery in this situation have a higher risk. **[U.S. Boxed Warning]: Based on human data, ACEIs can cause injury and death to the developing fetus when used in the second and third trimesters. ACEIs should be discontinued as soon as possible once pregnancy is detected.** Rare toxicities associated with ACE inhibitors include cholestatic jaundice (which may progress to hepatic necrosis) and neutropenia/agranulocytosis with myeloid hyperplasia. Hyperkalemia may rarely occur. May be associated with deterioration of renal function and/or increases in serum creatinine, particularly in patients dependent on renin-angiotensin-aldosterone system. Use with caution in unilateral renal artery stenosis and pre-existing renal insufficiency; if patient has renal impairment then a baseline WBC with differential and serum creatinine should be evaluated and monitored closely during the first 3 months of therapy. Hypersensitivity reactions may be seen during hemodialysis with high-flux dialysis membranes (eg, AN69). Safety and efficacy have not been established in children.
Adverse Reactions Note: Frequency ranges include data from hypertension and heart failure trials. Higher rates of adverse reactions have generally been noted in patients with CHF. However, the frequency of adverse effects associated with placebo is also increased in this population.

1% to 10%:
Cardiovascular: Hypotension (3%), chest pain (2%), first-dose hypotension (up to 3%)
Central nervous system: Dizziness (4% to 8%), headache (2% to 6%), fatigue (3%)
Dermatologic: Rash (1%)
Endocrine & metabolic: Hyperkalemia (2%)
Gastrointestinal: Vomiting/nausea (1% to 2%), diarrhea (1.7%)
(Continued)

Quinapril *(Continued)*

Neuromuscular & skeletal: Myalgias (2% to 5%), back pain (1%)

Renal: Increased BUN/serum creatinine (2%, transient elevations may occur with a higher frequency), worsening of renal function (in patients with bilateral renal artery stenosis or hypovolemia)

Respiratory: Upper respiratory symptoms, cough (2% to 4%; up to 13% in some studies), dyspnea (2%)

<1% (Limited to important or life-threatening): Acute renal failure, agranulocytosis, alopecia, amblyopia, anaphylactoid reaction, angina, angioedema, arrhythmia, arthralgia, depression, dermatopolymyositis, edema, eosinophilic pneumonitis, exfoliative dermatitis, hemolytic anemia, hepatitis, hyperkalemia, hypertensive crisis, impotence, insomnia, MI, orthostatic hypotension, pancreatitis, paresthesia, pemphigus, photosensitivity, pruritus, shock, somnolence, stroke, syncope, thrombocytopenia, vertigo

A syndrome which may include fever, myalgia, arthralgia, interstitial nephritis, vasculitis, rash, eosinophilia and positive ANA, and elevated ESR has been reported with ACE inhibitors. In addition, pancreatitis, hepatic necrosis, neutropenia, and/or agranulocytosis (particularly in patients with collagen-vascular disease or renal impairment) have been associated with many ACE inhibitors.

Overdosage/Toxicology Mild hypotension has been the only toxic effect seen with acute overdose; bradycardia may also occur. Hyperkalemia occurs even with therapeutic doses, especially in patients with renal insufficiency and those taking NSAIDs. Following initiation of essential overdose management, toxic symptom and supportive treatment should be initiated. Hypotension usually responds to I.V. fluids or Trendelenburg positioning.

Drug Interactions

Increased Effect/Toxicity: Potassium supplements, co-trimoxazole (high dose), angiotensin II receptor antagonists (eg, candesartan, losartan, irbesartan), or potassium-sparing diuretics (amiloride, spironolactone, triamterene) may result in elevated serum potassium levels when combined with quinapril. ACE inhibitor effects may be increased by phenothiazines or probenecid (increases levels of captopril). ACE inhibitors may increase serum concentrations/effects of lithium. ACE inhibitors may enhance the adverse/toxic effects (nitritoid reaction) of gold sodium thiomalate.

Diuretics have additive hypotensive effects with ACE inhibitors, and hypovolemia increases the potential for adverse renal effects of ACE inhibitors. In patients with compromised renal function, coadministration with NSAIDs may result in further deterioration of renal function. Allopurinol and ACE inhibitors may cause a higher risk of hypersensitivity reaction when taken concurrently.

Decreased Effect: Quinapril may reduce the absorption of quinolones and tetracycline antibiotics. Aspirin (high dose) may reduce the therapeutic effects of ACE inhibitors; at low dosages this does not appear to be significant. Rifampin may decrease the effect of ACE inhibitors. Antacids may decrease the bioavailability of ACE inhibitors (may be more likely to occur with captopril); separate administration times by 1-2 hours. NSAIDs, specifically indomethacin, may reduce the hypotensive effects of ACE inhibitors.

Ethanol/Nutrition/Herb Interactions Herb/Nutraceutical: Avoid dong quai if using for hypertension (has estrogenic activity). Avoid ephedra, yohimbe, ginseng (may worsen hypertension). Avoid garlic (may have increased antihypertensive effect).

Stability Store at room temperature. To prepare solution for oral administration, mix prior to administration and use within 10 minutes.

Mechanism of Action Competitive inhibitor of angiotensin-converting enzyme (ACE); prevents conversion of angiotensin I to angiotensin II, a potent vasoconstrictor; results in lower levels of angiotensin II which causes an increase in plasma renin activity and a reduction in aldosterone secretion; a CNS mechanism may also be involved in hypotensive effect as angiotensin II increases adrenergic outflow from CNS; vasoactive kallikreins may be decreased in conversion to active hormones by ACE inhibitors, thus reducing blood pressure

Pharmacodynamics/Kinetics

Onset of action: 1 hour

Duration: 24 hours

Absorption: Quinapril: ≥60%

Protein binding: Quinapril: 97%; Quinaprilat: 97%

Metabolism: Rapidly hydrolyzed to quinaprilat, the active metabolite

Half-life elimination: Quinapril: 0.8 hours; Quinaprilat: 3 hours; increases as Cl_{cr} decreases

Time to peak, serum: Quinapril: 1 hour; Quinaprilat: ~2 hours

Excretion: Urine (50% to 60% primarily as quinaprilat)

Dosage

Adults: Oral:

Hypertension: Initial: 10-20 mg once daily, adjust according to blood pressure response at peak and trough blood levels; initial dose may be reduced to 5 mg in patients receiving diuretic therapy if the diuretic is continued; usual dose range (JNC 7): 10-40 mg once daily

Congestive heart failure or post-MI: Initial: 5 mg once or twice daily, titrated at weekly intervals to 20-40 mg daily in 2 divided doses; target dose (heart failure): 20 mg twice daily (ACC/AHA 2005 Heart Failure Guidelines)

Elderly: Initial: 2.5-5 mg/day; increase dosage at increments of 2.5-5 mg at 1- to 2-week intervals.

Dosing adjustment in renal impairment: Lower initial doses should be used; after initial dose (if tolerated), administer initial dose twice daily; may be increased at weekly intervals to optimal response:

Hypertension: Initial:

Cl_{cr} >60 mL/minute: Administer 10 mg/day

Cl_{cr} 30-60 mL/minute: Administer 5 mg/day

Cl_{cr} 10-30 mL/minute: Administer 2.5 mg/day

Congestive heart failure: Initial:

Cl_{cr} >30 mL/minute: Administer 5 mg/day

Cl_{cr} 10-30 mL/minute: Administer 2.5 mg/day

Dosing comments in hepatic impairment: In patients with alcoholic cirrhosis, hydrolysis of quinapril to quinaprilat is impaired; however, the subsequent elimination of quinaprilat is unaltered.

Dosage Forms
Tablet: 5 mg, 10 mg, 20 mg, 40 mg
Accupril®: 5 mg, 10 mg, 20 mg, 40 mg

Quinapril and Hydrochlorothiazide
(KWIN a pril & hye droe klor oh THYE a zide)

U.S. Brand Names Accuretic®; Quinaretic
Canadian Brand Names Accuretic®
Index Terms Hydrochlorothiazide and Quinapril
Pharmacologic Category Angiotensin-Converting Enzyme (ACE) Inhibitor; Antihypertensive; Diuretic, Thiazide
Use Treatment of hypertension (not for initial therapy)
Pregnancy Risk Factor C (1st trimester); D (2nd and 3rd trimesters)
Dosage Oral:
Children: Safety and efficacy have not been established.
Adults: Initial:
Patients who have failed quinapril monotherapy:
Quinapril 10 mg/hydrochlorothiazide 12.5 mg **or**
Quinapril 20 mg/hydrochlorothiazide 12.5 mg once daily
Patients with adequate blood pressure control on hydrochlorothiazide 25 mg/day, but significant potassium loss:
Quinapril 10 mg/hydrochlorothiazide 12.5 mg **or**
Quinapril 20 mg/hydrochlorothiazide 12.5 mg once daily
Note: Clinical trials of quinapril/hydrochlorothiazide combinations used quinapril doses of 2.5-40 mg/day and hydrochlorothiazide doses of 6.25-25 mg/day.
Elderly: If previous response to individual components is unknown, initial dose selection should be cautious, at the low end of adult dosage range; titration should occur at 1- to 2-week intervals.
Dosage adjustment in renal impairment: Cl_{cr} <30 mL/minute/1.73 m^2 or serum creatinine ≤3 mg/dL: Use is not recommended.
Additional Information Complete prescribing information for this medication should be consulted for additional detail.
Dosage Forms Tablet:
10/12.5: Quinapril 10 mg and hydrochlorothiazide 12.5 mg
20/12.5: Quinapril 20 mg and hydrochlorothiazide 12.5 mg
20/25: Quinapril 20 mg and hydrochlorothiazide 25 mg

♦ **Quinapril Hydrochloride** *see* Quinapril *on page 1469*
♦ **Quinaretic** *see* Quinapril and Hydrochlorothiazide *on page 1471*
♦ **Quinate® (Can)** *see* Quinidine *on page 1471*

Quinidine (KWIN i deen)

Canadian Brand Names Apo-Quinidine®; BioQuin® Durules™; Novo-Quinidin; Quinate®
Index Terms Quinidine Gluconate; Quinidine Polygalacturonate; Quinidine Sulfate
Pharmacologic Category Antiarrhythmic Agent, Class Ia
Additional Appendix Information
Malaria Treatment *on page 2003*
Use Prophylaxis after cardioversion of atrial fibrillation and/or flutter to maintain normal sinus rhythm; prevent recurrence of paroxysmal supraventricular tachycardia, paroxysmal AV junctional rhythm, paroxysmal ventricular tachycardia, paroxysmal atrial fibrillation, and atrial or ventricular premature contractions; has activity against *Plasmodium falciparum* malaria
Pregnancy Risk Factor C
Lactation Enters breast milk/compatible
Medication Safety Issues
Sound-alike/look-alike issues:
Quinidine may be confused with clonidine, quinine, Quinora®
Contraindications Hypersensitivity to quinidine or any component of the formulation; thrombocytopenia; thrombocytopenic purpura; myasthenia gravis; heart block greater than first degree; idioventricular conduction delays (except in patients with a functioning artificial pacemaker); those adversely affected by anticholinergic activity; concurrent use of quinolone antibiotics which prolong QT interval, cisapride, amprenavir, or ritonavir
Warnings/Precautions Monitor and adjust dose to prevent QT_c prolongation. Watch for proarrhythmic effects. Correct hypokalemia before initiating therapy. Hypokalemia may worsen toxicity. **[U.S. Boxed Warning]: Antiarrhythmic drugs have not been shown to enhance survival in nonlife-threatening ventricular arrhythmias and may increase mortality; the risk is greatest with structural heart disease. Quinidine may increase mortality in treatment of atrial fibrillation/flutter.** May precipitate or exacerbate CHF. Reduce dosage in hepatic impairment. Use may cause digoxin-induced toxicity (adjust digoxin's dose). Use caution with concurrent use of other antiarrhythmics. Hypersensitivity reactions can occur. Can unmask sick sinus syndrome (causes bradycardia). Has been associated with severe hepatotoxic reactions, including granulomatous hepatitis. Hemolysis may occur in patients with G6PD (glucose-6-phosphate dehydrogenase) deficiency. Different salt products are not interchangeable.
Adverse Reactions
Frequency not defined: Hypotension, syncope
(Continued)

Quinidine *(Continued)*

>10%:

Cardiovascular: QT$_c$ prolongation (modest prolongation is common, however, excessive prolongation is rare and indicates toxicity)

Central nervous system: Lightheadedness (15%)

Gastrointestinal: Diarrhea (35%), upper GI distress, bitter taste, diarrhea, anorexia, nausea, vomiting, stomach cramping (22%)

1% to 10%:

Cardiovascular: Angina (6%), palpitation (7%), new or worsened arrhythmia (proarrhythmic effect)

Central nervous system: Syncope (1% to 8%), headache (7%), fatigue (7%), sleep disturbance (3%), tremor (2%), nervousness (2%), incoordination (1%)

Dermatologic: Rash (5%)

Neuromuscular & skeletal: Weakness (5%)

Ocular: Blurred vision

Otic: Tinnitus

Respiratory: Wheezing

<1% (Limited to important or life-threatening): Abnormal pigmentation, acute psychotic reactions, agranulocytosis, angioedema, arthralgia, bronchospasm, cerebral hypoperfusion (possibly resulting in ataxia, apprehension, and seizure), cholestasis, confusion, delirium, depression, drug-induced lupus-like syndrome, eczematous dermatitis, esophagitis, exacerbated bradycardia (in sick sinus syndrome), exfoliative rash, fever, flushing, granulomatous hepatitis, hallucinations, heart block, hemolytic anemia, hepatotoxic reaction (rare), impaired hearing, increased CPK, lichen planus, livedo reticularis, lymphadenopathy, melanin pigmentation of the hard palate, myalgia, mydriasis, nephropathy, optic neuritis, pancytopenia, paradoxical increase in ventricular rate during atrial fibrillation/flutter, photosensitivity, pneumonitis, pruritus, psoriaform rash, QT$_c$ prolongation (excessive), respiratory depression, sicca syndrome, tachycardia, thrombocytopenia, thrombocytopenic purpura, torsade de pointes, urticaria, uveitis, vascular collapse, vasculitis, ventricular fibrillation, ventricular tachycardia, vertigo, visual field loss

Note: Cinchonism, a syndrome which may include tinnitus, high-frequency hearing loss, deafness, vertigo, blurred vision, diplopia, photophobia, headache, confusion, and delirium has been associated with quinidine use. Usually associated with chronic toxicity, this syndrome has also been described after brief exposure to a moderate dose in sensitive patients. Vomiting and diarrhea may also occur as isolated reactions to therapeutic quinidine levels.

Overdosage/Toxicology Has a low toxic:therapeutic ratio and may easily produce fatal intoxication (acute toxic dose: 1 g in adults); symptoms include sinus bradycardia, sinus node arrest or asystole, PR, QRS, or QT interval prolongation, torsade de pointes (polymorphous ventricular tachycardia) and depressed myocardial contractility, which along with alpha-adrenergic or ganglionic blockade, may result in hypotension and pulmonary edema. Other effects are anticholinergic (dry mouth, dilated pupils, and delirium) as well as seizures, coma and respiratory arrest.

Treatment is primarily symptomatic and effects usually respond to conventional therapies (fluids, positioning, vasopressors, anticonvulsants, antiarrhythmics). **Note:** Do not use other type 1a or 1c antiarrhythmic agents to treat ventricular tachycardia. Sodium bicarbonate may treat wide QRS intervals or hypotension. Markedly impaired conduction or high degree AV block, unresponsive to bicarbonate, indicates consideration of a pacemaker is needed.

Drug Interactions

Cytochrome P450 Effect: Substrate of CYP2C9 (minor), 2E1 (minor), 3A4 (major); **Inhibits** CYP2C9 (weak), 2D6 (strong), 3A4 (strong)

Increased Effect/Toxicity: Effects may be additive with drugs which prolong the QT interval, including amiodarone, amitriptyline, bepridil, cisapride (use is contraindicated), disopyramide, erythromycin, haloperidol, imipramine, pimozide, procainamide, sotalol, thioridazine, and some quinolones (sparfloxacin, gatifloxacin, moxifloxacin - concurrent use is contraindicated). Concurrent use of amprenavir, or ritonavir is contraindicated. Quinidine increases digoxin serum concentrations; digoxin dosage may need to be reduced (by 50%) when quinidine is initiated; new steady-state digoxin plasma concentrations occur in 5-7 days.

Quinidine may increase the levels/effects of amphetamines, selected beta-blockers, selected benzodiazepines, calcium channel blockers, cisapride, cyclosporine, dextromethorphan, ergot alkaloids, fluoxetine, selected HMG-CoA reductase inhibitors, lidocaine, mesoridazine, mirtazapine, nateglinide, nefazodone, paroxetine, risperidone, ritonavir, sildenafil (and other PDE-5 inhibitors), tacrolimus, thioridazine, tricyclic antidepressants, venlafaxine, and other substrates of CYP2D6 or 3A4. Selected benzodiazepines (midazolam and triazolam), cisapride, ergot alkaloids, selected HMG-CoA reductase inhibitors (lovastatin and simvastatin), mesoridazine, pimozide, and thioridazine are generally contraindicated with strong CYP3A4 inhibitors. When used with strong CYP3A4 inhibitors, dosage adjustment/limits are recommended for sildenafil and other PDE-5 inhibitors; refer to individual monographs.

The levels/effects of quinidine may be increased by azole antifungals, clarithromycin, diclofenac, doxycycline, erythromycin, imatinib, isoniazid, nefazodone, nicardipine, propofol, protease inhibitors (amprenavir and ritonavir are contraindicated), telithromycin, verapamil, and other CYP3A4 inhibitors. Quinidine potentiates nondepolarizing and depolarizing muscle relaxants. When combined with quinidine, amiloride may cause prolonged ventricular conduction leading to arrhythmias. Urinary alkalinizers (antacids, sodium bicarbonate, acetazolamide) increase quinidine blood levels. Warfarin effects may be increased by quinidine.

Decreased Effect: The levels/effects of quinidine may be decreased by aminoglutethimide, carbamazepine, nafcillin, nevirapine, phenobarbital, phenytoin, rifamycins, and other CYP3A4 inducers. Quinidine may decrease the levels/effects of CYP2D6 prodrug substrates (eg, codeine, hydrocodone, oxycodone, tramadol).

Ethanol/Nutrition/Herb Interactions

Food: Dietary salt intake may alter the rate and extent of quinidine absorption. A decrease in dietary salt may lead to an increase in quinidine serum concentrations. Avoid changes in dietary salt intake. Quinidine serum levels may be increased if taken with food. Food has a variable effect on absorption of sustained release formulation. The rate of absorption of quinidine may be decreased following the ingestion of grapefruit juice. In addition, CYP3A4 metabolism of quinidine may be reduced by grapefruit juice. Grapefruit juice should be avoided. Excessive intake of fruit juices or vitamin C may decrease urine pH and result in increased clearance of quinidine with decreased serum concentration. Alkaline foods may result in increased quinidine serum concentrations.

Herb/Nutraceutical: St John's wort may decrease quinidine levels. Avoid ephedra (may worsen arrhythmia).

Stability Do not use discolored parenteral solution.

Mechanism of Action Class 1a antiarrhythmic agent; depresses phase O of the action potential; decreases myocardial excitability and conduction velocity, and myocardial contractility by decreasing sodium influx during depolarization and potassium efflux in repolarization; also reduces calcium transport across cell membrane

Pharmacodynamics/Kinetics

Distribution: V_d: Adults: 2-3.5 l/kg, decreased with congestive heart failure, malaria; increased with cirrhosis; crosses placenta; enters breast milk

Protein binding:
Newborns: 60% to 70%; decreased protein binding with cyanotic congenital heart disease, cirrhosis, or acute myocardial infarction
Adults: 80% to 90%

Metabolism: Extensively hepatic (50% to 90%) to inactive compounds

Bioavailability: Sulfate: 80%; Gluconate: 70%

Half-life elimination, plasma: Children: 2.5-6.7 hours; Adults: 6-8 hours; prolonged with elderly, cirrhosis, and congestive heart failure

Excretion: Urine (15% to 25% as unchanged drug)

Dosage Dosage expressed in terms of the salt; 267 mg of quinidine gluconate = 200 mg of quinidine sulfate.

Children: Test dose for idiosyncratic reaction (sulfate, oral or gluconate, I.M.): 2 mg/kg or 60 mg/m^2
Oral (quinidine sulfate): 15-60 mg/kg/day in 4-5 divided doses or 6 mg/kg every 4-6 hours; usual 30 mg/kg/day or 900 mg/m^2/day given in 5 daily doses
I.V. **not** recommended (quinidine gluconate): 2-10 mg/kg/dose given at a rate ≤10 mg/minute every 3-6 hours as needed

Adults: Test dose: Oral, I.M.: 200 mg administered several hours before full dosage (to determine possibility of idiosyncratic reaction)
Oral (for malaria):
Sulfate: 100-600 mg/dose every 4-6 hours; begin at 200 mg/dose and titrate to desired effect (maximum daily dose: 3-4 g)
Gluconate: 324-972 mg every 8-12 hours
I.M.: 400 mg/dose every 2-6 hours; initial dose: 600 mg (gluconate)
I.V.: 200-400 mg/dose diluted and given at a rate ≤10 mg/minute; may require as much as 500-750 mg

Dosing adjustment in renal impairment: Cl_{cr} <10 mL/minute: Administer 75% of normal dose.

Hemodialysis: Slightly hemodialyzable (5% to 20%); 200 mg supplemental dose posthemodialysis is recommended.

Peritoneal dialysis: Not dialyzable (0% to 5%)

Dosing adjustment/comments in hepatic impairment: Larger loading dose may be indicated, reduce maintenance doses by 50% and monitor serum levels closely.

Dietary Considerations Administer with food or milk to decrease gastrointestinal irritation. Avoid changes in dietary salt intake.

Administration Administer around-the-clock to promote less variation in peak and trough serum levels

Oral: Do not crush, chew, or break sustained release dosage forms.
Parenteral: When injecting I.M., aspirate carefully to avoid injection into a vessel; maximum I.V. infusion rate: 10 mg/minute

Monitoring Parameters Cardiac monitor required during I.V. administration; CBC, liver and renal function tests, should be routinely performed during long-term administration

Reference Range Therapeutic: 2-5 mcg/mL (SI: 6.2-15.4 µmol/L). Patient dependent therapeutic response occurs at levels of 3-6 mcg/mL (SI: 9.2-18.5 µmol/L). Optimal therapeutic level is method dependent; >6 mcg/mL (SI: >18 µmol/L).

Dosage Forms

Injection, solution, as gluconate: 80 mg/mL (10 mL) [equivalent to quinidine base 50 mg/mL]
Tablet, as sulfate: 200 mg, 300 mg
Tablet, extended release, as gluconate: 324 mg [equivalent to quinidine base 202 mg]
Tablet, extended release, as sulfate: 300 mg [equivalent to quinidine base 249 mg]

Extemporaneous Preparations A 10 mg/mL oral liquid preparation made from tablets and 3 different vehicles (cherry syrup, a 1:1 mixture of Ora-Sweet® and Ora-Plus®, or a 1:1 mixture of Ora-Sweet® SF and Ora-Plus®) was stable for 60 days when stored in amber plastic prescription bottles in the dark at room temperature (25°C) or under refrigeration (5°C); Grind six 200 mg tablets in a mortar into a fine powder; add 15 mL of the vehicle and mix well to form a uniform paste; mix while adding the vehicle in geometric proportions to **almost** 120 mL; transfer to a calibrated bottle and qsad to 120 mL; label "shake well" and "protect from light" (Allen 1998).

Allen LV and Erickson MA, "Stability of Bethanechol Chloride, Pyrazinamide, Quinidine Sulfate, Rifampin, and Tetracycline in Extemporaneously Compounded Oral Liquids," *Am J Health Syst Pharm*, 1998, 55(17):1804-9.

♦ **Quinidine Gluconate** *see* Quinidine *on page 1471*
♦ **Quinidine Polygalacturonate** *see* Quinidine *on page 1471*

♦ **Quinidine Sulfate** *see* Quinidine *on page 1471*

Quinine (KWYE nine)

U.S. Brand Names Qualaquin™
Canadian Brand Names Apo-Quinine®; Novo-Quinine; Quinine-Odan™
Index Terms Quinine Sulfate
Pharmacologic Category Antimalarial Agent
Additional Appendix Information
  Malaria Treatment *on page 2003*
Use In conjunction with other antimalarial agents, treatment of uncomplicated chloroquine-resistant *P. falciparum* malaria
Unlabeled/Investigational Use Treatment of *Babesia microti* infection in conjunction with clindamycin

Note: Prevention/treatment of nocturnal leg cramps (unapproved) removed following FDA issued warning regarding severe adverse events (eg, cardiac arrhythmias, thrombocytopenia and severe hypersensitivity reactions) and potentially serious drug interactions associated with quinine does not justify use in this condition.

Pregnancy Risk Factor C
Pregnancy Implications Teratogenic effects have been reported in some animal studies. Quinine crosses the human placenta. Cord plasma to maternal plasma quinine ratios have been reported as 0.18-0.46 and should not be considered therapeutic to the infant. Teratogenic effects, optic nerve hypoplasia, and deafness have been reported in the infant following maternal use of very high doses; however, therapeutic doses used for malaria are generally considered safe. Quinine may also cause significant hypoglycemia when used during pregnancy. Malaria infection in pregnant women may be more severe than in nonpregnant women. The CDC recommends the use of quinine sulfate for the treatment of chloroquine-resistant *P. falciparum* malaria during pregnancy. Pregnant women should be advised not to travel to areas of *P. falciparum* resistance to chloroquine.
Lactation Enters breast milk/use caution (AAP rate "compatible")
Medication Safety Issues
  Sound-alike/look-alike issues:
    Quinine may be confused with quinidine
Contraindications Hypersensitivity to quinine or any component of the formulation; hypersensitivity to mefloquine or quinidine (cross sensitivity reported); prolonged QT interval; myasthenia gravis; optic neuritis; G6PD deficiency; history of black water fever; thrombotic thrombocytopenia purpura, hemolytic uremic syndrome, thrombocytopenia
Warnings/Precautions Use caution with medications or clinical conditions which may prolong the QT interval or cause cardiac arrhythmias. Use may cause significant hypoglycemia. Use caution with atrial fibrillation or flutter, renal or hepatic impairment. Quinine interacts with many medications due to its hepatic metabolism; use caution with other medications metabolized via the CYP3A4 isoenzyme system. Severe hypersensitivity reactions (eg, Stevens-Johnson syndrome, anaphylactic shock) have occurred; discontinue following any signs of sensitivity. Other events including, thrombocytopenia and hemolytic uremic syndrome may also be attributed to hypersensitivity reactions. Because of the potential for severe and/or life-threatening side effects, as well as the absence of clinical effectiveness, quinine is no longer recommended for the treatment of nocturnal leg cramps.
Adverse Reactions
Frequency not defined.
Cardiovascular: Atrial fibrillation, atrioventricular block, bradycardia, cardiac arrest, chest pain, hypotension, irregular rhythm, nodal escape beats, palpitations, postural hypotension, QT prolongation, syncope, tachycardia, torsade de pointes, unifocal premature ventricular contractions, U waves, vasodilation, ventricular fibrillation, ventricular tachycardia
Central nervous system: Aphasia, ataxia, chills, coma, confusion, disorientation, dizziness, dystonic reaction, fever, flushing, headache, mental status altered, restlessness, seizures, suicide, vertigo
Dermatologic: Acral necrosis, allergic contact dermatitis, bullous dermatitis, bruising, cutaneous rash (urticaria, papular, scarlatinal), cutaneous vasculitis, diaphoresis, exfoliative dermatitis, erythema multiforme, petechiae, photosensitivity, pruritus, Stevens-Johnson syndrome, toxic epidermal necrolysis
Endocrine & metabolic: Hypoglycemia
Gastrointestinal: Abdominal pain, anorexia, diarrhea, esophagitis, gastric irritation, nausea, vomiting
Hematologic: Agranulocytosis, aplastic anemia, coagulopathy, disseminated intravascular coagulation, hemolytic anemia, hemolytic uremic syndrome, hemorrhage, hypoprothrombinemia, leukopenia, neutropenia, pancytopenia, thrombocytopenia, thrombotic thrombocytopenic purpura
Hepatic: Granulomatous hepatitis, hepatitis, jaundice, liver function test abnormalities
Neuromuscular & skeletal: Myalgia, tremor, weakness
Ocular: Blindness, blurred vision (with or without scotomata), color vision disturbance, diminished visual fields, diplopia, night blindness, optic neuritis, photophobia, pupillary dilation, vision loss (sudden)
Otic: Deafness, hearing impairment, tinnitus
Respiratory: Asthma, dyspnea, pulmonary edema
Renal: Acute interstitial nephritis, hemoglobinuria, renal failure, renal impairment
Miscellaneous: Black water fever, hypersensitivity syndrome, lupus anticoagulant, lupus-like syndrome
Overdosage/Toxicology Symptoms of mild toxicity include nausea, vomiting, and cinchonism. Severe intoxication may cause ataxia, obtundation, convulsions, coma, and respiratory arrest. With massive intoxication quinidine-like cardiotoxicity (hypotension, QRS and QT interval prolongation, AV block, and ventricular arrhythmias) may be fatal. Retinal toxicity occurs 9-10 hours after ingestion (blurred vision, impaired color perception, constriction of

visual fields, blindness). Other toxic effects include hypokalemia, hypoglycemia, and hemolysis. Treatment includes symptomatic therapy with conventional agents (anticonvulsants, fluids, positioning, vasoconstrictors, antiarrhythmias). **Note:** Avoid type 1a and 1c antiarrhythmic drugs. Treat cardiotoxicity with sodium bicarbonate. Dialysis and hemoperfusion procedures are ineffective in enhancing elimination. Activated charcoal may enhance elimination if administered repeatedly (every 4 hours) and within a reasonable period of time after quinine ingestion (≤4 hours).

Drug Interactions

Cytochrome P450 Effect: Substrate of CYP1A2 (minor), 2C19 (minor), 3A4 (major); **Inhibits** CYP2C8 (moderate), 2C9 (moderate), 2D6 (strong), 3A4 (weak)

Increased Effect/Toxicity: Antacids products containing aluminum or magnesium may decrease absorption of quinine; avoid concurrent administration. Quinine may increase the serum concentration of cardiac glycosides. Quinine may increase the levels/effects of CYP2C8 substrates (example substrates include amiodarone, paclitaxel, pioglitazone, repaglinide, and rosiglitazone). Quinine may increase the levels/effects of CYP2C9 substrates (example substrates include bosentan, dapsone, fluoxetine, glimepiride, glipizide, losartan, montelukast, nateglinide, paclitaxel, phenytoin, warfarin, and zafirlukast). Quinine may increase the levels/effects of CYP2D6 substrates (example substrates include amphetamines, selected beta-blockers, dextromethorphan, fluoxetine, lidocaine, mirtazapine, nefazodone, paroxetine, risperidone, ritonavir, thioridazine, tricyclic antidepressants, and venlafaxine).

Quinine may increase the serum concentration of phenothiazine antipsychotic agents. QT$_c$-prolonging agents (eg, amiodarone, amitriptyline, bepridil, disopyramide, erythromycin, haloperidol, imipramine, pimozide, procainamide, sotalol, thioridazine) may have additive additive; use with caution. Urinary alkalinizers (sodium bicarbonate, acetazolamide) may increase quinine blood levels.

Decreased Effect: Phenobarbital, phenytoin, and rifampin may decrease quinine serum concentrations. Quinine may decrease the levels/effects of CYP2D6 prodrug substrates (eg, codeine, hydrocodone, oxycodone, tramadol). CYP3A4 inducers may decrease the levels/effects of quinine (example inducers include aminoglutethimide, carbamazepine, nafcillin, nevirapine, phenobarbital, phenytoin, and rifamycins).

Ethanol/Nutrition/Herb Interactions Herb/Nutraceutical: St John's wort may decrease quinine levels. Black cohosh, California poppy, coleus, golden seal, hawthorn, mistletoe, periwinkle, and shepherd's purse may cause excessive decreases in blood pressure.

Stability Store at 25°C to 30°C (77°F to 86°F); do not refrigerate or freeze.

Mechanism of Action Depresses oxygen uptake and carbohydrate metabolism; intercalates into DNA, disrupting the parasite's replication and transcription; cardiovascular effects similar to quinidine

Pharmacodynamics/Kinetics

Absorption: Readily, mainly from upper small intestine

Distribution: 2.5-7.1 L/kg; varies with severity of infection
Intraerythrocytic levels are ~30% to 50% of the plasma concentration; distributes poorly to the CSF (~2% to 7% of plasma concentration)

Protein binding: 69% to 92% in healthy subjects; 78% to 95% with malaria

Metabolism: Primarily hepatic via CYP450 enzymes, including CYP3A4 and 2C19; forms metabolites

Bioavailability: 76% to 88% in healthy subjects; increased with malaria

Half-life elimination:
Children: ~3 hours in healthy subjects; ~12 hours with malaria
Healthy adults: 10-13 hours

Time to peak, serum:
Children: 2 hours in healthy subjects; 4 hours with malaria
Adults: 1-3 hours in healthy subjects; 1.2-11 hours with malaria

Excretion: Urine (<20% as unchanged drug)

Dosage Note: Actual duration of treatment for malaria may be dependent upon the geographic region or pathogen.

Children: Oral:
Treatment of chloroquine-resistant malaria (CDC guidelines): 30 mg/kg/day in divided doses every 8 hours for 3-7 days with tetracycline, doxycycline, or clindamycin (consider risk versus benefit of using tetracycline or doxycycline in children <8 years of age)
Babesiosis (unlabeled use): 25 mg/kg/day divided every 8 hours for 7 days with clindamycin

Adults: Oral:
Treatment of chloroquine-resistant malaria: 648 mg every 8 hours for 7 days with tetracycline, doxycycline, or clindamycin
Babesiosis (unlabeled use): 650 mg every 8 hours for 7 days with clindamycin

Dosing interval/adjustment in renal impairment:
Cl$_{cr}$ 10-50 mL/minute: Administer every 8-12 hours
Cl$_{cr}$ <10 mL/minute: Administer every 24 hours
Severe chronic renal failure not on dialysis: Initial dose: 648 mg followed by 324 mg every 12 hours
Dialysis: Administer dose after dialysis
Peritoneal dialysis: Dose as for Cl$_{cr}$ <10 mL/minute
Continuous arteriovenous or hemodialysis: Dose for Cl$_{cr}$ 10-50 mL/minute

Dosing adjustment in hepatic impairment:
Child-Pugh Class B: No dosing adjustment required; monitor closely
Child-Pugh Class C: Data not available

Dietary Considerations Take with food to decrease incidence of gastric upset.

Administration Avoid use of aluminum- or magnesium-containing antacids because of drug absorption problems. Swallow dose whole to avoid bitter taste. May be administered with food.

Monitoring Parameters Monitor CBC with platelet count, liver function tests, blood glucose, ophthalmologic examination
(Continued)

Quinine *(Continued)*

Reference Range Toxic: >10 mcg/mL

Test Interactions Positive Coombs' [direct]; false elevation of urinary steroids (when assayed by Zimmerman method) and catecholamines

Dosage Forms [DSC] = Discontinued product
Capsule, as sulfate: 325 mg [DSC]
  Qualaquin™: 324 mg
Tablet, as sulfate: 260 mg [DSC]

♦ **Quinine-Odan™ (Can)** *see* Quinine *on page 1474*

♦ **Quinine Sulfate** *see* Quinine *on page 1474*

♦ **Quinol** *see* Hydroquinone *on page 859*

♦ **Quintasa® (Can)** *see* Mesalamine *on page 1089*

Quinupristin and Dalfopristin (kwi NYOO pris tin & dal FOE pris tin)

U.S. Brand Names Synercid®
Canadian Brand Names Synercid®
Index Terms Pristinamycin; RP-59500
Pharmacologic Category Antibiotic, Streptogramin
Additional Appendix Information
  Antimicrobial Drugs of Choice *on page 1981*

Use Treatment of serious or life-threatening infections associated with vancomycin-resistant *Enterococcus faecium* bacteremia; treatment of complicated skin and skin structure infections caused by methcillin-susceptible *Staphylococcus aureus* or *Streptococcus pyogenes*

Has been studied in the treatment of a variety of infections caused by *Enterococcus faecium* (not *E. fecalis*) including vancomycin-resistant strains. May also be effective in the treatment of serious infections caused by *Staphylococcus* species including those resistant to methicillin.

Pregnancy Risk Factor B

Pregnancy Implications No evidence of impaired fertility or harm to the fetus in animal reproductive studies.

Lactation Excretion in breast milk unknown/use caution

Contraindications Hypersensitivity to quinupristin, dalfopristin, pristinamycin, or virginiamycin, or any component of the formulation

Warnings/Precautions Use with caution in patients with hepatic or renal dysfunction. May cause pain and phlebitis when infused through a peripheral line (not relieved by hydrocortisone or diphenhydramine). Prolonged use may result in superinfection, including pseudomembranous colitis. May cause arthralgias, myalgias, and hyperbilirubinemia. May inhibit the metabolism of many drugs metabolized by CYP3A4. Concurrent therapy with cisapride (which may prolong QT_c interval and lead to arrhythmias) should be avoided. Safety and efficacy have not been established in children <16 years of age.

Adverse Reactions
>10%:
  Hepatic: Hyperbilirubinemia (3% to 35%)
  Local: Inflammation at infusion site (38% to 42%), local pain (40% to 44%), local edema (17% to 18%), infusion site reaction (12% to 13%)
  Neuromuscular & skeletal: Arthralgia (up to 47%), myalgia (up to 47%)
1% to 10%:
  Central nervous system: Pain (2% to 3%), headache (2%)
  Dermatologic: Pruritus (2%), rash (3%)
  Endocrine & metabolic: Hyperglycemia (1%)
  Gastrointestinal: Nausea (3% to 5%), diarrhea (3%), vomiting (3% to 4%)
  Hematologic: Anemia (3%)
  Hepatic: GGT increased (2%), LDH increased (3%)
  Local: Thrombophlebitis (2%)
  Neuromuscular & skeletal: CPK increased (2%)
<1% (Limited to important or life-threatening): Allergic reaction, anaphylactoid reaction, angina, apnea, arrhythmia, cardiac arrest, coagulation disorder, dysautonomia, dyspnea, encephalopathy, gout, hematuria, hemolytic anemia, hepatitis, hyperkalemia, hypotension, maculopapular rash, mesenteric artery occlusion, myasthenia, neuropathy, pancreatitis, pancytopenia, paraplegia, paresthesia, pericarditis, pleural effusion, pseudomembranous colitis, respiratory distress, seizure, shock, stomatitis, syncope, thrombocytopenia, urticaria

Overdosage/Toxicology Symptoms may include dyspnea, emesis, tremors, and ataxia. Treatment is supportive. Not removed by hemodialysis or peritoneal dialysis.

Drug Interactions
Cytochrome P450 Effect: Quinupristin: **Inhibits** CYP3A4 (weak)
  Increased Effect/Toxicity: The manufacturer states that quinupristin/dalfopristin may increase cisapride concentrations and cause QT_c prolongation, and recommends to avoid concurrent use with cisapride. Quinupristin/dalfopristin may increase cyclosporine concentrations; monitor.

Stability Store unopened vials under refrigeration (2°C to 8°C/36°F to 46°F). Reconstitute single dose vial with 5 mL of 5% dextrose in water or sterile water for injection. Swirl gently to dissolve; do not shake (to limit foam formation). The reconstituted solution should be diluted within 30 minutes. Stability of the diluted solution prior to the infusion is established as 5 hours at room temperature or 54 hours if refrigerated at 2°C to 8°C. Reconstituted solution should be added to at least 250 mL of 5% dextrose in water for peripheral administration (increase to 500 mL or 750 mL if necessary to limit venous irritation). An infusion volume of 100 mL may be used for central line infusions. Do not freeze solution.

Mechanism of Action Quinupristin/dalfopristin inhibits bacterial protein synthesis by binding to different sites on the 50S bacterial ribosomal subunit thereby inhibiting protein synthesis

Pharmacodynamics/Kinetics
Distribution: Quinupristin: 0.45 L/kg; Dalfopristin: 0.24 L/kg
Protein binding: Moderate
Metabolism: To active metabolites via nonenzymatic reactions
Half-life elimination: Quinupristin: 0.85 hour; Dalfopristin: 0.7 hour (mean elimination half-lives, including metabolites: 3 and 1 hours, respectively)
Excretion: Feces (75% to 77% as unchanged drug and metabolites); urine (15% to 19%)

Dosage I.V.:
Children (limited information): Dosages similar to adult dosing have been used in the treatment of complicated skin/soft tissue infections and infections caused by vancomycin-resistant *Enterococcus faecium*
CNS shunt infection due to vancomycin-resistant *Enterococcus faecium*: 7.5 mg/kg/dose every 8 hours; concurrent intrathecal doses of 1-2 mg/day have been administered for up to 68 days
Adults:
Vancomycin-resistant *Enterococcus faecium*: 7.5 mg/kg every 8 hours
Complicated skin and skin structure infection: 7.5 mg/kg every 12 hours
Dosage adjustment in renal impairment: No adjustment required in renal failure, hemodialysis, or peritoneal dialysis
Dosage adjustment in hepatic impairment: Pharmacokinetic data suggest dosage adjustment may be necessary; however, specific recommendations have not been proposed
Elderly: No dosage adjustment is required

Administration Line should be flushed with 5% dextrose in water prior to and following administration. Incompatible with saline. Infusion should be completed over 60 minutes (toxicity may be increased with shorter infusion). Compatible (Y-site injection) with aztreonam, ciprofloxacin, haloperidol, metoclopramide or potassium chloride when admixed in 5% dextrose in water. Also compatible (Y-site injection) with fluconazole (used as undiluted solution). If severe venous irritation occurs following peripheral administration of quinupristin/dalfopristin diluted in 250 mL 5% dextrose in water, consideration should be given to increasing the infusion volume to 500 mL or 750 mL, changing the infusion site, or infusing by a peripherally inserted central catheter (PICC) or a central venous catheter.

Dosage Forms Injection, powder for reconstitution:
500 mg: Quinupristin 150 mg and dalfopristin 350 mg
600 mg: Quinupristin 180 mg and dalfopristin 420 mg

♦ **Quixin**™ *see* Levofloxacin *on page 1001*
♦ **QVAR**® *see* Beclomethasone *on page 198*
♦ **R 14-15** *see* Erlotinib *on page 606*
♦ **R & C**™ **II (Can)** *see* Pyrethrins and Piperonyl Butoxide *on page 1461*
♦ **R & C**™ **Shampoo/Conditioner (Can)** *see* Pyrethrins and Piperonyl Butoxide *on page 1461*
♦ **R-3827** *see* Abarelix *on page 20*
♦ **RabAvert**® *see* Rabies Virus Vaccine *on page 1479*

Rabeprazole (ra BEP ra zole)

U.S. Brand Names AcipHex®
Canadian Brand Names AcipHex®; Pariet®
Index Terms Pariprazole
Pharmacologic Category Proton Pump Inhibitor; Substituted Benzimidazole
Use Short-term (4-8 weeks) treatment and maintenance of erosive or ulcerative gastroesophageal reflux disease (GERD); symptomatic GERD; short-term (up to 4 weeks) treatment of duodenal ulcers; long-term treatment of pathological hypersecretory conditions, including Zollinger-Ellison syndrome; *H. pylori* eradication (in combination with amoxicillin and clarithromycin)
Unlabeled/Investigational Use Maintenance of duodenal ulcer
Pregnancy Risk Factor B
Pregnancy Implications Not shown to be teratogenic in animal studies, however, adequate and well-controlled studies have not been done in humans; use during pregnancy only if clearly needed
Lactation Excretion in breast milk unknown/not recommended
Medication Safety Issues
Sound-alike/look-alike issues:
AcipHex® may be confused with Acephen®, Accupril®, Aricept®
Rabeprazole may be confused with aripiprazole
Contraindications Hypersensitivity to rabeprazole, substituted benzimidazoles (ie, esomeprazole, lansoprazole, omeprazole, pantoprazole), or any component of the formulation
Warnings/Precautions Use caution in severe hepatic impairment; relief of symptoms with rabeprazole does not preclude the presence of a gastric malignancy
Adverse Reactions
1% to 10%: Central nervous system: Headache (2.4%)
<1% (Limited to important or life-threatening): Anaphylaxis, agranulocytosis, allergic reactions, alopecia, amnesia, angina, angioedema, apnea, asthma, bradycardia, bundle branch block, cholecystitis, coma, delirium, depression, dysphagia, dyspnea, erythema multiforme, extrapyramidal reaction, gout, hemolytic anemia, interstitial pneumonia, jaundice, leukopenia, MI, neuralgia, neuropathy, pancreatitis, pancytopenia, paresthesia, photosensitivity, pulmonary embolus, QT prolongation, rash, renal calculus, retinal degeneration, rhabdomyolysis, seizure, strabismus, syncope, tachycardia, thrombocytopenia, toxic epidermal necrolysis, Stevens-Johnson syndrome, ventricular tachycardia, vertigo
Overdosage/Toxicology There has been no experience with large overdoses. Seven reports of accidental overdosage have been reported. The maximum reported overdose was 80 mg. There were no clinical signs or symptoms associated with any reported overdose. Patients
(Continued)

Rabeprazole *(Continued)*

with Zollinger-Ellison syndrome have been treated with up to 120 mg/day. No specific antidote is known. A single oral dose of 2000 mg/kg was not lethal to dogs.

Drug Interactions

Cytochrome P450 Effect: Substrate (major) of CYP2C19, 3A4; **Inhibits** CYP2C8 (moderate), 2C19 (moderate), 2DC (weak), 3A4 (weak)

Increased Effect/Toxicity: Rabeprazole may increase the levels/effects of citalopram, diazepam, methsuximide, phenytoin, propranolol, sertraline, and other CYP2C19 substrates. Rabeprazole may increase the levels/effects of amiodarone, paclitaxel, pioglitazone, repaglinide, rosiglitazone, and other CYP2C8 substrates.

Decreased Effect: Proton pump inhibitors may decrease the absorption of atazanavir, indinavir, oral iron salts, itraconazole, and ketoconazole. The levels/effects of rabeprazole may be decreased by aminoglutethimide, carbamazepine, nafcillin, nevirapine, phenobarbital, phenytoin, rifampin, and other CYP2C19 or 3A4 inducers.

Ethanol/Nutrition/Herb Interactions

Ethanol: Avoid ethanol (may cause gastric mucosal irritation).

Food: High-fat meals may delay absorption, but C_{max} and AUC are not altered.

Stability Rapidly degraded in acid conditions.

Mechanism of Action Potent proton pump inhibitor; suppresses gastric acid secretion by inhibiting the parietal cell H+/K+ ATP pump

Pharmacodynamics/Kinetics

Onset of action: 1 hour

Duration: 24 hours

Absorption: Oral: Well absorbed within 1 hour

Distribution: 96.3%

Protein binding, serum: 94.8% to 97.5%

Metabolism: Hepatic via CYP3A and 2C19 to inactive metabolites

Bioavailability: Oral: 52%

Half-life elimination (dose dependent): 0.85-2 hours

Time to peak, plasma: 2-5 hours

Excretion: Urine (90% primarily as thioether carboxylic acid); remainder in feces

Dosage Oral: Adults >18 years and Elderly:

GERD: 20 mg once daily for 4-8 weeks; maintenance: 20 mg once daily

Duodenal ulcer: 20 mg/day before breakfast for 4 weeks

H. pylori eradication: 20 mg twice daily for 7 days; to be administered with amoxicillin 1000 mg and clarithromycin 500 mg, also given twice daily for 7 days.

Hypersecretory conditions: 60 mg once daily; dose may need to be adjusted as necessary. Doses as high as 100 mg once daily and 60 mg twice daily have been used.

Dosage adjustment in renal impairment: No dosage adjustment required

Dosage adjustment in hepatic impairment:

Mild to moderate: Elimination decreased; no dosage adjustment required

Severe: Use caution

Dietary Considerations May be taken with or without food; best if taken before breakfast.

Administration May be administered with or without food; best if taken before breakfast. Do not crush, split, or chew tablet. May be administered with an antacid.

Dosage Forms Tablet, delayed release, enteric coated, as sodium: 20 mg

---

Rabies Immune Globulin (Human)
(RAY beez i MYUN GLOB yoo lin, HYU man)

U.S. Brand Names BayRab® [DSC]; HyperRAB™ S/D; Imogam® Rabies-HT

Canadian Brand Names BayRab™; Imogam® Rabies Pasteurized

Index Terms RIG

Pharmacologic Category Immune Globulin

Additional Appendix Information

Immunization Recommendations *on page 1929*

Use Part of postexposure prophylaxis of persons with rabies exposure who lack a history of pre-exposure or postexposure prophylaxis with rabies vaccine or a recently documented neutralizing antibody response to previous rabies vaccination; although it is preferable to administer RIG with the first dose of vaccine, it can be given up to 8 days after vaccination

Pregnancy Risk Factor C

Contraindications Hypersensitivity to thimerosal or any component of the formulation

Warnings/Precautions Have epinephrine 1:1000 available for anaphylactic reactions. As a product of human plasma, this product may potentially transmit disease; screening of donors, as well as testing and/or inactivation of certain viruses reduces this risk. Use caution in patients with thrombocytopenia or coagulation disorders (I.M. injections may be contraindicated), in patients with isolated IgA deficiency, or in patients with previous systemic hypersensitivity to human immunoglobulins. Not for intravenous administration.

Adverse Reactions

1% to 10%:

Central nervous system: Fever (mild)

Local: Soreness at injection site

<1% (Limited to important or life-threatening): Anaphylactic shock, angioedema, soreness of muscles, stiffness, urticaria

Stability Refrigerate

Mechanism of Action Rabies immune globulin is a solution of globulins dried from the plasma or serum of selected adult human donors who have been immunized with rabies vaccine and have developed high titers of rabies antibody. It generally contains 10% to 18% of protein of which not less than 80% is monomeric immunoglobulin G.

Dosage Children and Adults: Postexposure prophylaxis: Local wound infiltration: 20 units/kg in a single dose, RIG should always be administered as part of rabies vaccine (HDCV) regimen as soon as possible (after the first dose of vaccine, up to 8 days). If anatomically feasible, the full rabies immune globulin dose should be infiltrated around and into the wound(s); remaining volume should be administered I.M. at a site distant from the vaccine administration site. If rabies vaccine was initiated without rabies immune globulin, rabies immune globulin may be administered through the seventh day after the first vaccine dose.

Note: Persons known to have an adequate titer or who have been completely immunized with rabies vaccine should not receive RIG, only booster doses of HDCV

Administration Do not administer I.V. Do not administer vaccine with or at same site as RIG administration.

Postexposure wound infiltration: If anatomically feasible, the full rabies immune globulin dose should be infiltrated around and into the wound(s); remaining volume should be administered I.M. at a site distant from the vaccine administration site.

Dosage Forms Injection, solution:

BayRab® [DSC], HyperRAB™ S/D: 150 int. units/mL (2 mL, 10 mL) [solvent/detergent treated]

Imogam® Rabies-HT: 150 int. units/mL (2 mL, 10 mL) [heat treated]

Rabies Virus Vaccine (RAY beez VYE rus vak SEEN)

U.S. Brand Names Imovax® Rabies; RabAvert®

Canadian Brand Names Imovax® Rabies; RabAvert®

Index Terms HDCV; Human Diploid Cell Cultures Rabies Vaccine; PCEC; Purified Chick Embryo Cell

Pharmacologic Category Vaccine

Use Pre-exposure immunization: Vaccinate persons with greater than usual risk due to occupation or avocation including veterinarians, rangers, animal handlers, certain laboratory workers, and persons living in or visiting countries for longer than 1 month where rabies is a constant threat.

Postexposure prophylaxis: If a bite from a carrier animal is unprovoked, if it is not captured and rabies is present in that species and area, administer rabies immune globulin (RIG) and the vaccine as indicated

Pregnancy Risk Factor C

Pregnancy Implications Pregnancy is not a contraindication to postexposure prophylaxis. Pre-exposure prophylaxis during pregnancy may also be considered if risk of rabies is great.

Contraindications Hypersensitivity to any component of the formulation; developing febrile illness (during pre-exposure therapy only); life-threatening allergic reactions to rabies vaccine or any components of the formulation (however, carefully consider a patient's risk of rabies before continuing therapy)

Warnings/Precautions Report serious reactions to the State Health Department or the manufacturer/distributor, an immune complex reaction is possible 2-21 days following booster doses of HDCV; hypersensitivity reactions may be treated with antihistamines or epinephrine, if severe. Immune response may be decreased in immunosuppressed patients. Imovax® Rabies contains albumin and neomycin. RabAvert® contains amphotericin B, bovine gelatin, chicken protein, chlortetracycline, and neomycin. For I. M. administration only.

Adverse Reactions All serious adverse reactions must be reported to the U.S. Department of Health and Human Services (DHHS) Vaccine Adverse Event Reporting System (VAERS) 1-800-822-7967.

Frequency not defined.

Cardiovascular: Edema

Central nervous system: Dizziness, malaise, encephalomyelitis, transverse myelitis, fever, pain, headache, neuroparalytic reactions

Gastrointestinal: Nausea, abdominal pain

Local: Local discomfort, pain at injection site, itching, erythema, swelling or pain

Neuromuscular & skeletal: Myalgia

Postmarketing and/or case reports: Anaphylaxis, encephalitis, Guillain-Barré syndrome, meningitis, transient paralysis, urticaria pigmentosa

Stability Store under refrigeration at 2°C to 8°C (36°F to 46°F); do not freeze. Protect from light.

Mechanism of Action Rabies vaccine is an inactivated virus vaccine which promotes immunity by inducing an active immune response. The production of specific antibodies requires about 7-10 days to develop. Rabies immune globulin or antirabies serum, equine (ARS) is given in conjunction with rabies vaccine to provide immune protection until an antibody response can occur.

Pharmacodynamics/Kinetics

Onset of action: I.M.: Rabies antibody: ~7-10 days

Peak effect: ~30-60 days

Duration: ≥1 year

Dosage

Pre-exposure prophylaxis: 1 mL I.M. on days 0, 7, and 21 to 28. **Note:** Prolonging the interval between doses does not interfere with immunity achieved after the concluding dose of the basic series.

Postexposure prophylaxis: All postexposure treatment should begin with immediate cleansing of the wound with soap and water

Persons not previously immunized as above: I.M.: 5 doses (1 mL each) on days 0, 3, 7, 14, 28. In addition, patients should receive rabies immune globulin 20 units/kg body weight, half infiltrated at bite site if possible, remainder I.M.)

Persons who have previously received postexposure prophylaxis with rabies vaccine, received a recommended I.M. pre-exposure series of rabies vaccine or have a previously documented rabies antibody titer considered adequate: 1 mL of either vaccine I.M. only on days 0 and 3; do not administer RIG

Booster (for occupational or other continuing risk): 1 mL I.M. every 2-5 years or based on antibody titers

(Continued)

Rabies Virus Vaccine *(Continued)*

Administration For I.M. administration only; this rabies vaccine product must not be administered intradermally; in adults and children, administer I.M. injections in the deltoid muscle, not the gluteal; for younger children, use the outer aspect of the thigh.

For patients at risk of hemorrhage following intramuscular injection, the ACIP recommends "it should be administered intramuscularly if, in the opinion of the physician familiar with the patients bleeding risk, the vaccine can be administered with reasonable safety by this route. If the patient receives antihemophilia or other similar therapy, intramuscular vaccination can be scheduled shortly after such therapy is administered. A fine needle (23 gauge or smaller) can be used for the vaccination and firm pressure applied to the site (without rubbing) for at least 2 minutes. The patient should be instructed concerning the risk of hematoma from the injection."

Monitoring Parameters Serum rabies antibody every 6 months to 2 years in patients at high risk for exposure

Reference Range Antibody titers ≥115 as determined by rapid fluorescent-focus inhibition test are indicative of adequate response; collect titers on day 28 postexposure

Additional Information Federal law requires that the date of administration, the vaccine manufacturer, lot number of vaccine, and the administering person's name, title, and address be entered into the patient's permanent medical record.

Dosage Forms Injection, powder for reconstitution:
Imovax® Rabies: 2.5 int. units [HDCV; grown in human diploid cell culture; contains albumin <100 mg, neomycin <150 mcg]
RabAvert®: 2.5 int. units [PCEC; grown in chicken fibroblasts; contains amphotericin <2 ng, chlortetracycline <20 ng, and neomycin <1 mcg]

- ◆ **Racepinephrine** *see* Epinephrine *on page 589*
- ◆ **Radiogardase™** *see* Ferric Hexacyanoferrate *on page 701*
- ◆ **rAHF** *see* Antihemophilic Factor (Recombinant) *on page 135*
- ◆ **R-albuterol** *see* Levalbuterol *on page 993*
- ◆ **Ralix** *see* Chlorpheniramine, Phenylephrine, and Methscopolamine *on page 353*

Raloxifene *(ral OKS i feen)*

U.S. Brand Names Evista®
Canadian Brand Names Evista®
Index Terms Keoxifene Hydrochloride; NSC-706725; Raloxifene Hydrochloride
Pharmacologic Category Selective Estrogen Receptor Modulator (SERM)
Use Prevention and treatment of osteoporosis in postmenopausal women
Unlabeled/Investigational Use Risk reduction for invasive breast cancer in postmenopausal women at increased risk for breast cancer

Pregnancy Risk Factor X

Pregnancy Implications Animal studies have demonstrated teratogenicity and fetal loss. There are no adequate and well-controlled studies in pregnant women. Raloxifene should not be used by pregnant women or by women planning to become pregnant in the immediate future.

Lactation Excretion in breast milk unknown/contraindicated

Medication Safety Issues
Sound-alike/look-alike issues:
Evista® may be confused with Avinza™

Contraindications Hypersensitivity to raloxifene or any component of the formulation; active or history of venous thromboembolic events; pregnancy; breast-feeding

Warnings/Precautions Use caution in patients at high risk for venous thromboembolism (deep vein thrombosis, pulmonary embolism); patients with cardiovascular disease; history of cervical/uterine carcinoma; renal/hepatic insufficiency (however, pharmacokinetic data are lacking); concurrent use of estrogens; women with a history of elevated triglycerides in response to treatment with oral estrogens (or estrogen/progestin). Safety and efficacy in premenopausal women or men have not been established.

Adverse Reactions Note: Raloxifene has been associated with increased risk of thromboembolism (DVT, PE) and superficial thrombophlebitis; risk is similar to reported risk of HRT
>10%:
Endocrine & metabolic: Hot flashes (10% to 29%)
Neuromuscular & skeletal: Arthralgia (11% to 16%)
Miscellaneous: Flu syndrome (14% to 15%), infection (11% to 15%)
1% to 10%:
Cardiovascular: Peripheral edema (3% to 5%), chest pain (3% to 4%), syncope (2%), varicose vein (2%)
Central nervous system: Headache (9%), depression (6%), insomnia (6%), vertigo (4%), fever (3% to 4%), migraine (3%)
Dermatologic: Rash (6%)
Endocrine & metabolic: Breast pain (4%)
Gastrointestinal: Nausea (8% to 9%), weight gain (9%), abdominal pain (7%), diarrhea (7%), dyspepsia (6%), vomiting (3% to 5%), flatulence (2% to 3%), gastroenteritis (≤3%)
Genitourinary: Vaginal bleeding (6%), cystitis (3% to 5%), urinary tract infection (4%), vaginitis (4%), leukorrhea (3%), urinary tract disorder (3%), uterine disorder (3%), vaginal hemorrhage (3%), endometrial disorder (≤3%)
Neuromuscular & skeletal: Myalgia (7%), leg cramps (6% to 7%), arthritis (4%), tendon disorder (4%), hypoesthesia (≤2%), neuralgia (≤2%)
Ocular: Conjunctivitis (2%)
Respiratory: Bronchitis (10%), rhinitis (10%), sinusitis (8% to 10%), cough (6% to 9%), pharyngitis (5% to 8%), pneumonia (3%), laryngitis (≤2%)
Miscellaneous: Diaphoresis (3%)

<1% (Limited to important or life-threatening): Apolipoprotein A1 increased, apolipoprotein B decreased, fibrinogen decreased, hypertriglyceridemia (in women with a history of increased triglycerides in response to oral estrogens), LDL cholesterol decreased, lipoprotein decreased, retinal vein occlusion, total serum cholesterol decreased

Overdosage/Toxicology Incidence of overdose in humans has not been reported. In an 8-week study of postmenopausal women, a dose of raloxifene 600 mg/day was safely tolerated. No mortality was seen after a single oral dose in rats or mice (at 810 times the human dose for rats and 405 times the human dose for mice). There is no specific antidote for raloxifene. Treatment is symptom-directed and supportive.

Drug Interactions

Decreased Effect: Cholestyramine decreases raloxifene absorption; raloxifene decreases levothyroxine absorption

Ethanol/Nutrition/Herb Interactions Ethanol: Avoid ethanol (may increase risk of osteoporosis).

Stability Store between 15°C to 30°C (59°F to 86°F).

Mechanism of Action A selective estrogen receptor modulator, meaning that it affects some of the same receptors that estrogen does, but not all, and in some instances, it antagonizes or blocks estrogen; it acts like estrogen to prevent bone loss and improve lipid profiles (decreases total and LDL-cholesterol but does not raise triglycerides), but it has the potential to block some estrogen effects such as those that lead to breast cancer and uterine cancer

Pharmacodynamics/Kinetics
Onset of action: 8 weeks
Absorption: ~60%
Distribution: 2348 L/kg
Protein binding: >95% to albumin and α-glycoprotein
Metabolism: Hepatic, extensive first-pass effect; metabolized to glucuronide conjugates
Bioavailability: ~2%
Half-life elimination: 27.7-32.5 hours
Excretion: Primarily feces; urine (0.2%)

Dosage Adults: Female: Oral:
Osteoporosis: 60 mg/day
Invasive breast cancer risk reduction (investigational use): 60 mg/day for 5 years

Dosage adjustment in hepatic impairment: Child-Pugh class A: Plasma concentrations were higher and correlated with total bilirubin. Safety and efficacy in hepatic insufficiency have not been established.

Dietary Considerations Supplemental calcium or vitamin D may be required if dietary intake is not adequate.

Administration May be administered any time of the day without regard to meals.

Monitoring Parameters Bone mineral density (BMD), CBC, lipid profile

Additional Information The decrease in estrogen-related adverse effects with the selective estrogen-receptor modulators in general and raloxifene in particular should improve compliance and decrease the incidence of cardiovascular events and fractures while not increasing breast cancer.

Dosage Forms
Tablet, as hydrochloride:
Evista®: 60 mg

♦ **Raloxifene Hydrochloride** see Raloxifene on page 1480

Ramelteon (ra MEL tee on)

U.S. Brand Names Rozerem™
Index Terms TAK-375
Pharmacologic Category Hypnotic, Nonbenzodiazepine
Use Treatment of insomnia characterized by difficulty with sleep onset
Pregnancy Risk Factor C
Pregnancy Implications Animal studies have demonstrated teratogenic effects. May cause disturbances of reproductive hormonal regulation (eg, disruption of menses or decreased libido). There are no adequate and well-controlled studies in pregnant women.
Lactation Excretion in breast milk unknown/not recommended
Medication Safety Issues
Sound-alike/look-alike issues:
Rozerem™ may be confused with Razadyne™
Contraindications Hypersensitivity to ramelteon or any component of the formulation; severe hepatic impairment; concurrent use with fluvoxamine
Warnings/Precautions
Symptomatic treatment of insomnia should be initiated only after careful evaluation of potential causes of sleep disturbance. Failure of sleep disturbance to resolve after a reasonable period of treatment may indicate psychiatric and/or medical illness. Because of the rapid onset of action, administer immediately prior to bedtime or after the patient has gone to bed and is having difficulty falling asleep. Hypnotics/sedatives have been associated with abnormal thinking and behavior changes including decreased inhibition, aggression, bizarre behavior, agitation, hallucinations, and depersonalization. These changes may occur unpredictably and may indicate previously unrecognized psychiatric disorders; evaluate appropriately. Use caution with pre-existing depression or other psychiatric conditions. Caution when using with other CNS depressants; avoid engaging in hazardous activities or activities requiring mental alertness. Not recommended for use in patients with severe sleep apnea or COPD. Use caution with moderate hepatic impairment. May cause disturbances of hormonal regulation. Use caution when administered concomitantly with strong CYP1A2 inhibitors. Safety and efficacy in pediatric patients have not been established.
Adverse Reactions 1% to 10%:
Central nervous system: Headache (7%, same as placebo), somnolence (5%), dizziness (5%), fatigue (4%), insomnia worsened (3%), depression (2%)
(Continued)

Ramelteon *(Continued)*

Endocrine & metabolic: Serum cortisol decreased (1%)
Gastrointestinal: Nausea (3%), diarrhea (2%, same as placebo), taste perversion (2%)
Neuromuscular & skeletal: Myalgia (2%), arthralgia (2%)
Respiratory: Upper respiratory infection (3%; 2% with placebo)
Miscellaneous: Influenza (1%)

Postmarketing and/or case reports: Prolactin levels increased, testosterone levels decreased

Overdosage/Toxicology Single doses of up to 160 mg have been administered, with no safety or tolerability concerns noted. Treatment should be symptom-directed and supportive. Hemodialysis is not effective in removing ramelteon.

Drug Interactions

Cytochrome P450 Effect: Substrate of CYP1A2 (major), CYP3A4 (minor), CYP2C family (minor)

Increased Effect/Toxicity: The following agents may increase the levels/effects of ramelteon: CNS depressants, CYP1A2 inhibitors (example inhibitors include ciprofloxacin, fluvoxamine (concomitant use not recommended), ketoconazole, norfloxacin, ofloxacin, and rofecoxib), fluvoxamine, fluconazole, and ketoconazole.

Decreased Effect: Rifampin may decrease the levels/effects of ramelteon.

Ethanol/Nutrition/Herb Interactions

Ethanol: Avoid ethanol (may increase CNS depression).
Food: Taking with high-fat meal delays T_{max} and increases AUC (~31%); do not take with high-fat meal.

Stability Store at 15°C to 30°C (59°F to 86°F).

Mechanism of Action Potent, selective agonist of melatonin receptors MT_1 and MT_2 (with little affinity for MT_3) within the suprachiasmic nucleus of the hypothalamus, an area responsible for determination of circadian rhythms and synchronization of the sleep-wake cycle. Agonism of MT_1 is thought to preferentially induce sleepiness, while MT_2 receptor activation preferentially influences regulation of circadian rhythms. Ramelteon is eightfold more selective for MT_1 than MT_2 and exhibits nearly sixfold higher affinity for MT_1 than melatonin, presumably allowing for enhanced effects on sleep induction.

Pharmacodynamics/Kinetics

Onset of action: 30 minutes
Absorption: Rapid; high-fat meal delays T_{max} and increases AUC (~31%)
Distribution: 74 L
Protein binding: 82%
Metabolism: Extensive first-pass effect; oxidative metabolism primarily through CYP1A2 and to a lesser extent through CYP2C and CYP3A4; forms active metabolite (M-II)
Bioavailability: Absolute: 1.8%
Half-life elimination: Ramelteon: 1-2.6 hours; M-II: 2-5 hours
Time to peak, plasma: Median: 0.5-1.5 hours
Excretion: Primarily as metabolites: Urine (84%); feces (4%)

Dosage

Oral: Adults: One 8 mg tablet within 30 minutes of bedtime
Dosage adjustment in renal impairment: No dosage adjustment required
Dosage adjustment in hepatic impairment: No adjustment required for mild-to-moderate impairment. Avoid use with severe impairment.

Dietary Considerations Taking with high-fat meal delays T_{max} and increases AUC (~31%); do not take with high-fat meal.

Administration Do not administer with a high-fat meal.

Dosage Forms Tablet: 8 mg

Ramipril *(RA mi pril)*

U.S. Brand Names Altace®
Canadian Brand Names Altace®
Pharmacologic Category Angiotensin-Converting Enzyme (ACE) Inhibitor
Additional Appendix Information
Angiotensin Agents *on page 1860*
Heart Failure (Systolic) *on page 2051*

Use Treatment of hypertension, alone or in combination with thiazide diuretics; treatment of left ventricular dysfunction after myocardial infarction; to reduce risk of heart attack, stroke, and death in patients at increased risk for these problems

Unlabeled/Investigational Use Treatment of heart failure

Pregnancy Risk Factor C (1st trimester)/D (2nd and 3rd trimesters)

Pregnancy Implications Decreased placental blood flow, low birth weight, fetal hypotension, preterm delivery, and fetal death have been noted with the use of some ACE inhibitors (ACEIs) in animal studies. Neonatal hypotension, skull hypoplasia, anuria, renal failure, oligohydramnios (associated with fetal limb contractures, craniofacial deformities, hypoplastic lung development), prematurity, intrauterine growth retardation, and patent ductus arteriosus have been reported with the use of ACEIs, primarily in the 2nd and 3rd trimesters. The risk of neonatal toxicity has been considered less when ACEIs have been used in the 1st trimester; however, major congenital malformations have been reported. The cardiovascular and/or central nervous systems are most commonly affected. Unless alternative agents are not appropriate, ACEIs should be discontinued as soon as possible once pregnancy is detected.

Lactation Excretion in breast milk unknown/not recommended

Medication Safety Issues
Sound-alike/look-alike issues:
Ramipril may be confused with enalapril, Monopril®
Altace® may be confused with alteplase, Amaryl®, Amerge®, Artane®

Contraindications Hypersensitivity to ramipril or any component of the formulation; prior hypersensitivity (including angioedema) to ACE inhibitors; bilateral renal artery stenosis; pregnancy (2nd and 3rd trimesters)

Warnings/Precautions Anaphylactic or anaphylactoid reactions can occur. Use with caution and modify dosage in patients with renal impairment (especially renal artery stenosis), severe CHF. Severe hypotension may occur in the elderly and patients who are sodium and/or volume depleted, initiate lower doses and monitor closely when starting therapy in these patients. Angioedema can occur at any time during treatment (especially following first dose). It may involve head and neck (potentially affecting the airway) or the intestine (presenting with abdominal pain). Prolonged monitoring may be required especially if tongue, glottis, or larynx are involved as they are associated with airway obstruction. Those with a history of airway surgery in this situation have a higher risk. **[U.S. Boxed Warning]: Based on human data, ACEIs can cause injury and death to the developing fetus when used in the second and third trimesters. ACEIs should be discontinued as soon as possible once pregnancy is detected.** Careful blood pressure monitoring with first dose (hypotension can occur especially in volume-depleted patients). Use with caution in hypovolemia; collagen vascular diseases; valvular stenosis (particularly aortic stenosis); hyperkalemia; or before, during, or immediately after anesthesia. Avoid rapid dosage escalation, which may lead to renal insufficiency. Hyperkalemia may rarely occur. Rare toxicities associated with ACE inhibitors include cholestatic jaundice (which may progress to hepatic necrosis) and neutropenia/agranulocytosis with myeloid hyperplasia. May be associated with deterioration of renal function and/or increases in serum creatinine, particularly in patients dependent on renin-angiotensin-aldosterone system. Use with caution in unilateral renal artery stenosis and pre-existing renal insufficiency; if patient has renal impairment then a baseline WBC with differential and serum creatinine should be evaluated and monitored closely during the first 3 months of therapy. Hypersensitivity reactions may be seen during hemodialysis with high-flux dialysis membranes (eg, AN69). Safety and efficacy have not been established in children.

Adverse Reactions Note: Frequency ranges include data from hypertension and heart failure trials. Higher rates of adverse reactions have generally been noted in patients with CHF. However, the frequency of adverse effects associated with placebo is also increased in this population.

>10%: Respiratory: Cough (increased) (7% to 12%)

1% to 10%:

Cardiovascular: Hypotension (11%), angina (3%), postural hypotension (2%), syncope (2%)

Central nervous system: Headache (1% to 5%), dizziness (2% to 4%), fatigue (2%), vertigo (2%)

Endocrine & metabolic: Hyperkalemia (1% to 10%)

Gastrointestinal: Nausea/vomiting (1% to 2%)

Neuromuscular & skeletal: Chest pain (noncardiac) (1%)

Renal: Renal dysfunction (1%), elevation in serum creatinine (1% to 2%), increased BUN (<1% to 3%); transient elevations of creatinine and/or BUN may occur more frequently

Respiratory: Cough (estimated 1% to 10%)

<1% (Limited to important or life-threatening): Agitation, agranulocytosis, amnesia, anaphylactoid reaction, angina, angioedema, arrhythmia, bone marrow depression, convulsions, depression, dysphagia, dyspnea, edema, eosinophilia, erythema multiforme, hearing loss, hemolytic anemia, hepatitis, hypersensitivity reactions (urticaria, rash, fever), impotence, insomnia, myalgia, MI, neuropathy, onycholysis, pancreatitis, pancytopenia, paresthesia, pemphigoid, pemphigus, photosensitivity, proteinuria, somnolence, Stevens-Johnson syndrome, symptomatic hypotension, syncope, thrombocytopenia, toxic epidermal necrolysis, vertigo

Worsening of renal function may occur in patients with bilateral renal artery stenosis or in hypovolemia. In addition, a syndrome which may include fever, myalgia, arthralgia, interstitial nephritis, vasculitis, rash, eosinophilia and positive ANA, and elevated ESR has been reported with ACE inhibitors. Risk of pancreatitis and/or agranulocytosis may be increased in patients with collagen vascular disease or renal impairment.

Overdosage/Toxicology Mild hypotension has been the only toxic effect seen with acute overdose; bradycardia may also occur. Mild hyperkalemia may occur even with therapeutic doses, especially in patients with renal insufficiency and those taking NSAIDs. Following initiation of essential overdose management, toxic symptom and supportive treatment should be initiated. Hypotension usually responds to I.V. fluids or Trendelenburg positioning.

Drug Interactions

Increased Effect/Toxicity: Potassium supplements, co-trimoxazole (high dose), angiotensin II receptor antagonists (eg, candesartan, losartan, irbesartan), or potassium-sparing diuretics (amiloride, spironolactone, triamterene) may result in elevated serum potassium levels when combined with ramipril. ACE inhibitor effects may be increased by phenothiazines or probenecid (increases levels of captopril). ACE inhibitors may increase serum concentrations/effects of lithium. ACE inhibitors may enhance the adverse/toxic effects (nitritoid reaction) of gold sodium thiomalate.

Diuretics have additive hypotensive effects with ACE inhibitors, and hypovolemia increases the potential for adverse renal effects of ACE inhibitors. In patients with compromised renal function, coadministration with NSAIDs may result in further deterioration of renal function. Allopurinol and ACE inhibitors may cause a higher risk of hypersensitivity reaction when taken concurrently.

Decreased Effect: Aspirin (high dose) may reduce the therapeutic effects of ACE inhibitors; at low dosages this does not appear to be significant. Rifampin may decrease the effect of ACE inhibitors. Antacids may decrease the bioavailability of ACE inhibitors (may be more likely to occur with captopril); separate administration times by 1-2 hours. NSAIDs, specifically indomethacin, may reduce the hypotensive effects of ACE inhibitors. More likely to occur in low renin or volume dependent hypertensive patients.

Ethanol/Nutrition/Herb Interactions Herb/Nutraceutical: Avoid dong quai if using for hypertension (has estrogenic activity). Avoid ephedra, yohimbe, ginseng (may worsen hypertension). Avoid garlic (may have increased antihypertensive effect).

Stability Store at controlled room temperature.

Mechanism of Action Ramipril is an ACE inhibitor which prevents the formation of angiotensin II from angiotensin I and exhibits pharmacologic effects that are similar to captopril. Ramipril must undergo enzymatic saponification by esterases in the liver to its biologically (Continued)

Ramipril (Continued)

active metabolite, ramiprilat. The pharmacodynamic effects of ramipril result from the high-affinity, competitive, reversible binding of ramiprilat to angiotensin-converting enzyme thus preventing the formation of the potent vasoconstrictor angiotensin II. This isomerized enzyme-inhibitor complex has a slow rate of dissociation, which results in high potency and a long duration of action; a CNS mechanism may also be involved in the hypotensive effect as angiotensin II increases adrenergic outflow from CNS; vasoactive kallikreins may be decreased in conversion to active hormones by ACE inhibitors, thus reducing blood pressure

Pharmacodynamics/Kinetics

Onset of action: 1-2 hours

Duration: 24 hours

Absorption: Well absorbed (50% to 60%)

Distribution: Plasma levels decline in a triphasic fashion; rapid decline is a distribution phase to peripheral compartment, plasma protein and tissue ACE (half-life 2-4 hours); 2nd phase is an apparent elimination phase representing the clearance of free ramiprilat (half-life: 9-18 hours); and final phase is the terminal elimination phase representing the equilibrium phase between tissue binding and dissociation

Metabolism: Hepatic to the active form, ramiprilat

Half-life elimination: Ramiprilat: Effective: 13-17 hours; Terminal: >50 hours

Time to peak, serum: ~1 hour

Excretion: Urine (60%) and feces (40%) as parent drug and metabolites

Dosage Adults: Oral:

Hypertension: 2.5-5 mg once daily, maximum: 20 mg/day

Reduction in risk of MI, stroke, and death from cardiovascular causes: Initial: 2.5 mg once daily for 1 week, then 5 mg once daily for the next 3 weeks, then increase as tolerated to 10 mg once daily (may be given as divided dose)

Heart failure postmyocardial infarction: Initial: 2.5 mg twice daily titrated upward, if possible, to 5 mg twice daily.

Heart failure (unlabeled use): Initial: 1.25-2.5 mg once daily; target dose: 10 mg once daily (ACC/AHA 2005 Heart Failure Guidelines)

Note: The dose of any concomitant diuretic should be reduced. If the diuretic cannot be discontinued, initiate therapy with 1.25 mg. After the initial dose, the patient should be monitored carefully until blood pressure has stabilized.

Dosing adjustment in renal impairment:

Cl_{cr} <40 mL/minute: Administer 25% of normal dose.

Renal failure and hypertension: Administer 1.25 mg once daily, titrated upward as possible.

Renal failure and heart failure: Administer 1.25 mg once daily, increasing to 1.25 mg twice daily up to 2.5 mg twice daily as tolerated.

Administration Capsule is usually swallowed whole, but may be may be mixed in water, apple juice, or applesauce.

Test Interactions Increases BUN, creatinine, potassium, positive Coombs' [direct]; decreases cholesterol (S); may cause false-positive results in urine acetone determinations using sodium nitroprusside reagent

Dosage Forms Capsule: 1.25 mg, 2.5 mg, 5 mg, 10 mg

♦ **RAN™-Atenolol (Can)** see Atenolol on page 167
♦ **RAN™-Carvedilol (Can)** see Carvedilol on page 299
♦ **RAN™-Ciprofloxacin (Can)** see Ciprofloxacin on page 372
♦ **RAN™-Citalopram (Can)** see Citalopram on page 381
♦ **Ranexa™** see Ranolazine on page 1487

Ranibizumab (ra ni BIZ oo mab)

U.S. Brand Names Lucentis™

Index Terms rhuFabV2

Pharmacologic Category Monoclonal Antibody; Ophthalmic Agent; Vascular Endothelial Growth Factor (VEGF) Inhibitor

Use Treatment of neovascular (wet) age-related macular degeneration (AMD)

Pregnancy Risk Factor C

Pregnancy Implications Reproduction studies have not been conducted. Use during pregnancy only if clearly needed.

Lactation Excretion in breast milk unknown/use caution

Contraindications Hypersensitivity to ranibizumab or any component of the formulation; ocular or periocular infection

Warnings/Precautions Intravitreous injections may be associated with endophthalmitis and retinal detachments. Proper aseptic injection techniques should be used and patients should be instructed to report any signs of infection immediately. Intraocular pressure may increase following injection. Use for >24 months has not been evaluated.

Risk of thromboembolic events may be increased following intravitreal administration of VEGF inhibitors. Rare hypersensitivity reactions (including anaphylaxis) have been associated with another VEGF inhibitor, pegaptanib, occurring within several hours of use; monitor closely. Equipment and appropriate personnel should be available for monitoring and treatment of anaphylaxis. Safety and efficacy have not been established in children.

Adverse Reactions Note: Rates of ocular adverse reactions reported for control group when percentages overlapped with treatment group.

>10%:

Central nervous system: Headache (2% to 15%)

Neuromuscular & skeletal: Arthralgia (3% to 11%)

Ocular: Conjunctival hemorrhage (43% to 77%; control: 29% to 66%), eye pain (17% to 37%; control 11% to 33%), vitreous floaters (3% to 32%), retinal hemorrhage (15% to 26%; control 37% to 56%), intraocular pressure increased (8% to 24%), vitreous detachment (7% to 22%; control 13% to 18%), intraocular inflammation (5% to 18%; control 3%

to 11%), eye irritation (4% to 19%; control 6% to 20%), visual disturbance (up to 14%), blepharitis (3% to 13%)

Note: Cataract, foreign body sensation, lacrimation increased, pruritus, and subretinal fibrosis occurred in >10% of patients, but also occurred in similar percentages to the control; visual acuity blurred/decreased occurred more often in the control.

Respiratory: Nasopharyngitis (5% to 16%), upper respiratory tract infection (2% to 15%)

1% to 10%:

Cardiovascular: Arterial thromboembolic events (<4%)

Gastrointestinal: Nausea (2% to 9%)

Ocular: Conjunctival hyperemia (up to 9%), posterior capsule opacification (up to 8%)

Note: Ocular hyperemia, maculopathy, dry eye, and ocular discomfort occurred in 1% to 10% of patients, but also occurred in similar percentages to the control; retinal exudates occurred more often in the control.

Respiratory: Bronchitis (3% to 10%), cough (3% to 10%), sinusitis (2% to 8%)

Miscellaneous: Influenza (2% to 10%), ranibizumab antibodies (1% to 6%)

<1% (Limited to important or life-threatening): Endophthalmitis, iatrogenic traumatic cataracts, rhegmatogenous retinal detachments

Overdosage/Toxicology Significant intraocular inflammation was noted with initial doses of 1 mg; when using escalating regimens, doses up to 2 mg have been tolerated

Stability Store in original carton under refrigeration at 2°C to 8°C (36°F to 46°F); protect from light. Do not freeze.

Mechanism of Action Ranibizumab is a recombinant humanized monoclonal antibody fragment which binds to and inhibits human vascular endothelial growth factor A (VEGF-A). Ranibizumab inhibits VEGF from binding to its receptors and thereby suppressing neovascularization and slowing vision loss.

Pharmacodynamics/Kinetics

Absorption: Low levels are detected in the serum following intravitreal injection

Half-life elimination: Vitreous: 9 days

Dosage Ophthalmic:

Adults: AMD: Intravitreal injection: 0.5 mg once a month. Although not as effective, frequency may be reduced after the first 4 injections to once every 3 months if monthly injections are not feasible. Dosing every 3 months will lead to an ~5 letter (1 line) loss of visual acuity over 9 months, as compared to monthly dosing.

Elderly: Initial studies were conducted in patients ≥50 years of age; 94% of patients were ≥65 years and 68% were ≥75 years

Dosage adjustment in renal impairment: Dose adjustment not expected

Dosage adjustment in hepatic impairment: Dose adjustment not expected

Administration For ophthalmic intravitreal injection only. Remove contents from vial using a 5 micron 19-gauge filter needle attached to a tuberculin syringe. Discard filter needle and replace with a sterile 30 gauge 1/2 inch needle for injection. Adequate anesthesia and a broad-spectrum antimicrobial agent should be administered prior to the procedure.

Monitoring Parameters Intraocular pressure (within 30 minutes and between 2-7 days following administration); endophthalmitis

Dosage Forms

Injection, solution [preservative free]:

Lucentis™: 10 mg/mL (0.05 mL)

♦ **Raniclor**™ *see Cefaclor on page 303*

Ranitidine (ra NI ti deen)

U.S. Brand Names Zantac®; Zantac 75® [OTC]; Zantac 150™ [OTC]; Zantac® EFFERdose®

Canadian Brand Names Alti-Ranitidine; Apo-Ranitidine®; BCI-Ranitidine; CO Ranitidine; Gen-Ranidine; Novo-Ranidine; Nu-Ranit; PMS-Ranitidine; Ranitidine Injection, USP; Rhoxal-ranitidine; Sandoz-Ranitidine; Zantac®; Zantac 75®

Index Terms Ranitidine Hydrochloride

Pharmacologic Category Histamine H_2 Antagonist

Use

Zantac®: Short-term and maintenance therapy of duodenal ulcer, gastric ulcer, gastroesophageal reflux, active benign ulcer, erosive esophagitis, and pathological hypersecretory conditions; as part of a multidrug regimen for *H. pylori* eradication to reduce the risk of duodenal ulcer recurrence

Zantac® 75 [OTC]: Relief of heartburn, acid indigestion, and sour stomach

Unlabeled/Investigational Use Recurrent postoperative ulcer, upper GI bleeding, prevention of acid-aspiration pneumonitis during surgery, and prevention of stress-induced ulcers

Pregnancy Risk Factor B

Pregnancy Implications Ranitidine crosses the placenta, teratogenic effects to the fetus have not been reported in animal studies. Use with caution during pregnancy.

Lactation Enters breast milk/use caution

Medication Safety Issues

Sound-alike/look-alike issues:

Ranitidine may be confused with amantadine, rimantadine

Zantac® may be confused with Xanax®, Zarontin®, Zofran®, Zyrtec®

International issues:

Antagon®: Brand name for astemizole in Mexico; brand name for ganirelix in the U.S.

Contraindications Hypersensitivity to ranitidine or any component of the formulation

Warnings/Precautions Ranitidine has been associated with confusional states (rare). Use with caution in patients with hepatic impairment; use with caution in renal impairment, dosage modification required. Avoid use in patients with history of acute porphyria (may precipitate attacks); long-term therapy may be associated with vitamin B_{12} deficiency. Symptoms of GI distress may be associated with a variety of conditions; symptomatic response to H_2 antagonists does not rule out the potential for significant pathology (eg, malignancy). EFFERdose® (Continued)

Ranitidine *(Continued)*

formulations contain phenylalanine. Safety and efficacy of ranitidine have not been established for pediatric patients <1 month of age

Adverse Reactions Frequency not defined (limited to important or life-threatening):

Cardiovascular: Arrhythmias, vasculitis

Central nervous system: Dizziness, hallucinations, headache, mental confusion, somnolence, vertigo

Dermatologic: Erythema multiforme, rash

Gastrointestinal: Pancreatitis

Hematologic: Acquired hemolytic anemia, agranulocytosis, aplastic anemia, granulocytopenia, leukopenia, pancytopenia, thrombocytopenia

Hepatic: Hepatic failure

Respiratory: Pneumonia (causal relationship not established)

Miscellaneous: Anaphylaxis, hypersensitivity reactions

Overdosage/Toxicology Symptoms include abnormal gait, hypotension, and adverse effects seen with normal use. Treatment is primarily symptomatic and supportive.

Drug Interactions

Cytochrome P450 Effect: Substrate (minor) of CYP1A2, 2C19, 2D6; **Inhibits** CYP1A2 (weak), 2D6 (weak)

Increased Effect/Toxicity: Increased the effect/toxicity of cyclosporine (increased serum creatinine).

Decreased Effect: Ranitidine may have variable effects on warfarin (monitor INR closely). The absorption/efficacy of ketoconazole and itraconazole are decreased by ranitidine; avoid concurrent therapy. The absorption of some cephalosporins (cefuroxime, cefpodoxime) may be reduced by ranitidine (separate administrations times by at least 2 hours). The absorption of atazanavir and cyanocobalamin may be decreased by ranitidine.

Ethanol/Nutrition/Herb Interactions

Ethanol: Avoid ethanol (may cause gastric mucosal irritation).

Food: Does not interfere with absorption of ranitidine.

Stability

Injection: Vials: Store between 4°C to 30°C (39°F to 86°F). Protect from light. Solution is a clear, colorless to yellow solution; slight darkening does not affect potency.

Premixed bag: Store between 2°C to 25°C (36°F to 77°F). Protect from light.

EFFERdose® formulations: Store between 2°C to 30°C (36°F to 86°F).

Syrup: Store between 4°C to 25°C (39°F to 77°F). Protect from light.

Tablet: Store in dry place, between 15°C to 30°C (59°F to 86°F). Protect from light.

Vials can be mixed with NS or D_5W; solutions are stable for 48 hours at room temperature. Intermittent bolus injection: Dilute to maximum of 2.5 mg/mL. Intermittent infusion: Dilute to maximum of 0.5 mg/mL.

Mechanism of Action Competitive inhibition of histamine at H_2-receptors of the gastric parietal cells, which inhibits gastric acid secretion, gastric volume, and hydrogen ion concentration are reduced. Does not affect pepsin secretion, pentagastrin-stimulated intrinsic factor secretion, or serum gastrin.

Pharmacodynamics/Kinetics

Absorption: Oral: 50%

Distribution: Normal renal function: V_d: 1.7 L/kg; Cl_{cr} 25-35 mL/minute: 1.76 L/kg minimally penetrates the blood-brain barrier; enters breast milk

Protein binding: 15%

Metabolism: Hepatic to N-oxide, S-oxide, and N-desmethyl metabolites

Bioavailability: Oral: 48%

Half-life elimination:

Oral: Normal renal function: 2.5-3 hours; Cl_{cr} 25-35 mL/minute: 4.8 hours

I.V.: Normal renal function: 2-2.5 hours

Time to peak, serum: Oral: 2-3 hours; I.M.: ≤15 minutes

Excretion: Urine: Oral: 30%, I.V.: 70% (as unchanged drug); feces (as metabolites)

Dosage

Children 1 month to 16 years:

Duodenal and gastric ulcer:

Oral:

Treatment: 2-4 mg/kg/day divided twice daily; maximum treatment dose: 300 mg/day

Maintenance: 2-4 mg/kg once daily; maximum maintenance dose: 150 mg/day

I.V.: 2-4 mg/kg/day divided every 6-8 hours; maximum: 200 mg/day

GERD and erosive esophagitis:

Oral: 5-10 mg/kg/day divided twice daily; maximum: GERD: 300 mg/day, erosive esophagitis: 600 mg/day

I.V. (unlabeled): 2-4 mg/kg/day divided every 6-8 hours; maximum: 200 mg/day **or as an alternative**

Continuous infusion: Initial: 1 mg/kg/dose for one dose followed by infusion of 0.08-0.17 mg/kg/hour or 2-4 mg/kg/day

Children ≥12 years: Prevention of heartburn: Oral: Zantac® 75 [OTC]: 75 mg 30-60 minutes before eating food or drinking beverages which cause heartburn; maximum: 150 mg/24 hours; do not use for more than 14 days

Adults:

Duodenal ulcer: Oral: Treatment: 150 mg twice daily, or 300 mg once daily after the evening meal or at bedtime; maintenance: 150 mg once daily at bedtime

Helicobacter pylori eradication: 150 mg twice daily; requires combination therapy

Pathological hypersecretory conditions:

Oral: 150 mg twice daily; adjust dose or frequency as clinically indicated; doses of up to 6 g/day have been used

I.V.: Continuous infusion for Zollinger-Ellison: 1 mg/kg/hour; measure gastric acid output at 4 hours, if >10 mEq or if patient is symptomatic, increase dose in increments of 0.5 mg/kg/hour; doses of up to 2.5 mg/kg/hour have been used

Gastric ulcer, benign: Oral: 150 mg twice daily; maintenance: 150 mg once daily at bedtime

Erosive esophagitis: Oral: Treatment: 150 mg 4 times/day; maintenance: 150 mg twice daily

Prevention of heartburn: Oral: Zantac® 75 [OTC]: 75 mg 30-60 minutes before eating food or drinking beverages which cause heartburn; maximum: 150 mg in 24 hours; do not use for more than 14 days

Patients not able to take oral medication:

I.M.: 50 mg every 6-8 hours

I.V.: Intermittent bolus or infusion: 50 mg every 6-8 hours

Continuous I.V. infusion: 6.25 mg/hour

Elderly: Ulcer healing rates and incidence of adverse effects are similar in the elderly, when compared to younger patients; dosing adjustments not necessary based on age alone

Dosing adjustment in renal impairment: Adults: Cl_{cr} <50 mL/minute:

Oral: 150 mg every 24 hours; adjust dose cautiously if needed

I.V.: 50 mg every 18-24 hours; adjust dose cautiously if needed

Hemodialysis: Adjust dosing schedule so that dose coincides with the end of hemodialysis

Dosing adjustment/comments in hepatic disease: Patients with hepatic impairment may have minor changes in ranitidine half-life, distribution, clearance, and bioavailability; dosing adjustments not necessary, monitor

Dietary Considerations Oral dosage forms may be taken with or without food.

Zantac® EFFERdose®:

Effervescent tablet 25 mg contains sodium 1.33 mEq/tablet and phenylalanine 2.81 mg/tablet

Effervescent tablet 150 mg contains sodium 7.96 mEq/tablet and phenylalanine 16.84 mg/tablet

Administration

Ranitidine injection may be administered I.M. or I.V.:

I.M.: Injection is administered undiluted

I.V.: Must be diluted; may be administered IVP or IVPB or continuous I.V. infusion

IVP: Ranitidine (usually 50 mg) should be diluted to a total of 20 mL with NS or D_5W and administered over at least 5 minutes

IVPB: Administer over 15-20 minutes

Continuous I.V. infusion: Administer at 6.25 mg/hour and titrate dosage based on gastric pH by continuous infusion over 24 hours

EFFERdose®: Should not be chewed, swallowed whole, or dissolved on tongue:

25 mg tablet: Dissolve in at least 5 mL (1 teaspoonful) of water; wait until completely dissolved before administering

150 mg tablet: Dissolve each dose in 6-8 ounces of water before drinking

Monitoring Parameters AST, ALT, serum creatinine; when used to prevent stress-related GI bleeding, measure the intragastric pH and try to maintain pH >4; signs and symptoms of peptic ulcer disease, occult blood with GI bleeding, monitor renal function to correct dose; monitor for side effects

Test Interactions False-positive urine protein using Multistix®, gastric acid secretion test, skin test allergen extracts, serum creatinine, urine protein test

Dosage Forms

Capsule 150 mg, 300 mg

Infusion [premixed in NaCl 0.45%; preservative free]:

Zantac®: 50 mg (50 mL)

Injection, solution: 25 mg/mL (2 mL, 6 mL)

Zantac®: 25 mg/mL (2 mL, 6 mL, 40 mL) [contains phenol 0.5% as preservative]

Syrup: 15 mg/mL (10 mL) [contains alcohol 7.5%; peppermint flavor]

Zantac®: 15 mg/mL (473 mL) [contains alcohol 7.5%; peppermint flavor]

Tablet: 75 mg [OTC], 150 mg, 300 mg

Zantac®: 150 mg, 300 mg

Zantac 75®: 75 mg

Zantac 150™: 150 mg

Tablet, effervescent:

Zantac® EFFERdose®: 25 mg [contains sodium 1.33 mEq/tablet, phenylalanine 2.81 mg/tablet, and sodium benzoate]; 150 mg [contains sodium 7.96 mEq/tablet, phenylalanine 16.84 mg/tablet, and sodium benzoate]

- ♦ **Ranitidine Hydrochloride** see Ranitidine on page 1485
- ♦ **Ranitidine Injection, USP (Can)** see Ranitidine on page 1485
- ♦ **RAN™-Lovastatin (Can)** see Lovastatin on page 1040
- ♦ **RAN™-Metformin (Can)** see Metformin on page 1098

Ranolazine (ra NOE la zeen)

U.S. Brand Names Ranexa™

Pharmacologic Category Cardiovascular Agent, Miscellaneous

Use Treatment of chronic angina in combination with amlodipine, beta-blockers, or nitrates

Pregnancy Implications There are no adequate and well-controlled studies in pregnant women.

Lactation Excretion in breast milk unknown/not recommended

Contraindications Hypersensitivity to ranolazine or any component of the formulation; pre-existing QT prolongation (including congenital long-QT syndrome, uncorrected hypokalemia); known history of ventricular tachycardia; hepatic dysfunction (of any degree); concurrent QT_c-prolonging drugs; concurrent strong or moderate CYP3A4 inhibitors (including diltiazem and grapefruit juice)

Warnings/Precautions Ranolazine will not relieve acute angina attacks. Has been shown to prolong QT_c interval in a dose/plasma concentration-related manner. Hepatically-impaired patients may have a more significant increase in QT_c. Use caution in patients ≥75 years of (Continued)

Ranolazine *(Continued)*

age; they may experience more adverse events. Use caution in patients with renal dysfunction. In general, avoid use in severe renal dysfunction. Monitor blood pressure in patients with renal dysfunction. Safety and efficacy in children have not been established.

Adverse Reactions
>10%: Gastrointestinal: Constipation (5% to 8%; 19% in the elderly)
>0.5% to 10%:
Cardiovascular: Syncope (0.7%), palpitation, peripheral edema
Central nervous system: Dizziness (5% to 6%), headache (3% to 6%), vertigo
Gastrointestinal: Nausea (4% to 6%), abdominal pain, vomiting, xerostomia
Hematologic: Hematocrit decreased
Neuromuscular & skeletal: Weakness
Respiratory: Dyspnea
<0.5% (Limited to important or life-threatening): Blood pressure increased, blurred vision, bradycardia, eosinophilia, hematuria, hypoesthesia, hypotension, orthostatic hypotension, paresthesia, tremor, QT_c prolongation, serum creatinine increased, T-wave amplitude decreased, T-wave changes (notched)

Overdosage/Toxicology Symptoms may include dizziness, nausea, vomiting, diplopia, paresthesias, confusion, syncope, and prolonged loss of consciousness. QT prolongation may occur and continuous ECG monitoring may be warranted. Treatment is symptom-directed and supportive. Complete clearance of ranolazine by hemodialysis is unlikely.

Drug Interactions
Cytochrome P450 Effect: Substrate of CYP3A4 (major), 2D6 (minor); **Inhibits** CYP3A4 (weak), 2D6 (weak)
Increased Effect/Toxicity: CYP3A4 inhibitors (eg, diltiazem, ketoconazole, verapamil) may increase the effects of ranolazine. Ranolazine may increase the effects of simvastatin and digoxin. Concurrent use of QT_c-prolonging agents may further increase QT interval.
Decreased Effect: CYP3A4 inducers may decrease the effect of ranolazine.

Stability Store at 15°C to 30°C (59°F to 86°F).

Mechanism of Action A proposed mechanism suggests ranolazine is a partial fatty acid oxidation inhibitor; may change myocardial energy metabolism from fatty acids to glucose, increasing the efficiency of ATP production under hypoxic conditions. Exerts antianginal and anti-ischemic effects without changing hemodynamic parameters. In addition, it is a late sodium channel inhibitor.

Pharmacodynamics/Kinetics
Absorption: Highly variable; ranolazine is a substrate of P-glycoprotein; concurrent use of P-glycoprotein inhibitors may increase absorption
Protein binding: 62%
Metabolism: Hepatic via CYP3A (major) and 2D6 (minor)
Half-life elimination: Terminal: 7 hours
Time to peak, plasma: 2-5 hours
Excretion: Primarily urine (75% mostly as metabolites, <5% to 7% excreted unchanged); feces (25% mostly as metabolites)

Dosage Oral: Chronic angina:
Adults: Initial: 500 mg twice daily; maximum recommended dose: 1000 mg twice daily
Elderly: Select dose cautiously, starting at the lower end of the dosing range
Dosage adjustment in renal impairment: Dosage adjustment recommendations have not been established. However, plasma ranolazine levels increased ~50% in patients with varying degrees of renal dysfunction. Patients with severe renal dysfunction had an increase in mean diastolic blood pressure of 10-15 mm Hg. Monitor blood pressure closely in these patients. Patients on dialysis have not been studied. Avoid use in severe renal dysfunction.
Dosage adjustment in hepatic impairment: Use is contraindicated

Dietary Considerations May be taken with or without food. Concurrent consumption of grapefruit or grapefruit juice is contraindicated.

Administration May be taken with or without meals. Swallow tablet whole; do not crush, break, or chew.

Monitoring Parameters Baseline and follow up ECG to evaluate QT interval; blood pressure in patients with renal dysfunction; correct and maintain serum potassium in normal limits

Dosage Forms Tablet, extended release: 500 mg

♦ **Rapamune®** *see* Sirolimus *on page 1569*
♦ **Raphon [OTC]** *see* Epinephrine *on page 589*
♦ **Raptiva®** *see* Efalizumab *on page 570*

Rasagiline *(ra SA ji leen)*

U.S. Brand Names Azilect®
Index Terms AGN 1135; Rasagiline Mesylate; TVP-1012
Pharmacologic Category Anti-Parkinson's Agent, MAO Type B Inhibitor
Use Initial monotherapy or as adjunct to levodopa in the treatment of idiopathic Parkinson's disease
Pregnancy Risk Factor C
Pregnancy Implications Animal studies have documented decreased offspring survival and birth weight. An increased incidence of teratogenic effects, embryo-fetal deaths, and cardiovascular abnormalities were also noted with rasagiline in combination with levodopa/carbidopa. There are no adequate and well-controlled studies in pregnant women.
Lactation Excretion in breast milk unknown/use caution
Medication Safety Issues
Sound-alike/look-alike issues:
Azilect® may be confused with Aricept®

Contraindications Hypersensitivity to rasagiline or any component of the formulation; concomitant use of amphetamine, tramadol, propoxyphene, methadone, dextromethorphan, St John's wort, mirtazapine, cyclobenzaprine, or sympathomimetic amines (eg, pseudoephedrine, ephedrine); use of meperidine or other MAO inhibitor within 14 days of rasagiline; elective surgery requiring general anesthesia, local anesthesia containing sympathomimetic vasoconstrictors; patients with pheochromocytoma

Warnings/Precautions

Cardiovascular system: Hypertensive crisis may occur with tyramine, tryptophan, or dopamine-containing foods; avoid for at least 2 weeks following discontinuation of rasagiline. May cause orthostatic hypotension, particularly in combination with levodopa; use with caution in patients with hypotension or patients who would not tolerate transient hypotensive episodes (cardiovascular or cerebrovascular disease); orthostasis is usually most problematic during first 2 months of therapy and tends to abate thereafter. Due to the potential for hemodynamic instability, patients should not undergo elective surgery requiring general anesthesia and should avoid local anesthesia containing sympathomimetic vasoconstrictors within 14 days of discontinuing rasagiline. If surgery is required, benzodiazepines, mivacurium, fentanyl, morphine or codeine may be used cautiously.

Central nervous system: May cause hallucinations; signs of severe CNS toxicity (some fatal), including hyporpyrexia, hyperthermia, rigidity, altered mental status, seizure and coma have been reported with selective and nonselective MAO inhibitor use in combination with antidepressants; Do not use within 5 weeks of fluoxetine discontinuation; do not initiate tricyclic, SSRI or SNRI therapy within 2 weeks of discontinuing rasagiline. Addition to levodopa therapy may result in exacerbation of dyskinesias, requiring a reduction in levodopa dosage.

Dermatologic: Risk of melanoma may be increased with rasagiline, although increased risk has been associated with Parkinson's disease itself; patients should have regular and frequent skin examinations.

Organ dysfunction: Use caution in mild hepatic impairment; dose reduction recommended. Do not use with moderate to severe hepatic impairment.

Safety and efficacy in pediatric patients have not been established.

Adverse Reactions Unless otherwise noted, the following adverse reactions are as reported for monotherapy. Spectrum of adverse events was generally similar with adjunctive (levodopa) therapy, though the incidence tended to be higher.

>10%:
  Central nervous system: Dyskinesia (18% adjunct therapy), headache (14%)
  Gastrointestinal: Nausea (10% to 12% adjunct therapy)

1% to 10%:
  Cardiovascular: Postural hypotension (6% to 9% adjunct therapy; dose dependent), bundle branch block angina, chest pain, syncope
  Central nervous system: Depression (5%), hallucinations (4% to 5% adjunct therapy), fever (3%), malaise (2%), vertigo (2%), anxiety, dizziness
  Dermatologic: Bruising (2%), alopecia, skin carcinoma, vesiculobullous rash
  Endocrine & metabolic: Impotence, libido decreased
  Gastrointestinal: Constipation (4% to 9% adjunct therapy), weight loss (2% to 9% adjunct therapy; dose dependent), dyspepsia (7%), xerostomia (2% to 6% adjunct therapy; dose dependent), gastroenteritis (3%), anorexia, diarrhea, gastrointestinal hemorrhage, vomiting
  Genitourinary: Hematuria, urinary incontinence
  Hematologic: Leukopenia
  Hepatic: Liver function tests increased
  Neuromuscular & skeletal: Arthralgia (7%), neck pain (2%), arthritis (2%), paresthesia (2%), abnormal gait, hyperkinesias, hypertonia, neuropathy, tremor, weakness
  Ocular: Conjunctivitis (3%)
  Renal: Albuminuria
  Respiratory: Rhinitis (3%), asthma, cough increased
  Miscellaneous: Fall (5%), flu-like syndrome (5%), allergic reaction

<1% (Limited to important or life-threatening): Acute kidney failure, aphasia, apnea, atrial arrhythmia, bigeminy, blepharitis, blindness, bone necrosis, cerebral hemorrhage, cerebral ischemia, circumoral paresthesia, deafness, deep thrombophlebitis, delirium, diplopia, dysautonomia, dysesthesia, emphysema, esophageal ulcer, exfoliative dermatitis, facial paralysis, glaucoma, gynecomastia, heart failure, hematemesis, hemiplegia, hemorrhage (various locations), hostility, hypocalcemia, incoordination, interstitial pneumonia, intestinal obstruction, intestinal perforation, intestinal stenosis, jaundice, keratitis, kidney calculus, large intestine perforation, laryngismus, larynx edema, leukoderma, leukorrhea, lung fibrosis, macrocytic anemia, manic depressive reaction, mania, megacolon, menstrual abnormalities, MI, muscle atrophy, myelitis, neuralgia, neuritis, neurosis, nocturia, paranoid reaction, parosmia, personality disorder, pleural effusion, pneumothorax, polyuria, psychosis, psychotic depression, ptosis, purpura, retinal degeneration, retinal detachment, seizure, stomach ulcer, strabismus, stupor, thrombocythemia, thrombosis, tongue edema, urinary disorders, vaginal moniliasis, ventricular fibrillation, ventricular tachycardia, vestibular disorder, visual field defect

Overdosage/Toxicology No reports of overdose have been documented. Symptoms of overdose would be expected to present similar to other MAO inhibitors, including cardiovascular events (eg, arrhythmia, rapid blood pressure changes), altered mental status, muscle twitching or seizure and respiratory failure. Treatment should be symptom-directed and supportive.

Drug Interactions

Cytochrome P450 Effect: Substrate of CYP1A2 (major)

Increased Effect/Toxicity: CYP1A2 inhibitors may increase the levels/effects of rasagiline (example inhibitors include amiodarone, ciprofloxacin, fluvoxamine, ketoconazole, norfloxacin, and ofloxacin). Concurrent use of rasagiline in combination with amphetamines, methylphenidate, dextromethorphan, meperidine, methadone, mirtazapine, propoxyphene, tramadol, tricyclic or tetracyclic antidepressants may result in serotonin syndrome; these (Continued)

Rasagiline *(Continued)*

combinations are contraindicated. Concurrent use of rasagiline with an SSRI or SNRI may result in mania or hypertension; it is generally best to avoid these combinations.

Decreased Effect: CYP1A2 Inducers may decrease the levels/effects of rasagiline (example inducers include aminoglutethimide, carbamazepine, phenobarbital, and rifampin).

Ethanol/Nutrition/Herb Interactions

Ethanol: Avoid ethanol. Avoid beverages containing tyramine (hearty red wine and beer).

Food: Concurrent ingestion of foods rich in tyramine may cause sudden and severe high blood pressure (hypertensive crisis). Avoid tyramine-containing foods with MAOIs. Food's freshness is also an important concern; improperly stored or spoiled food can create an environment where tyramine concentrations may increase.

Herb/Nutraceutical: Avoid valerian, St John's wort, SAMe, kava kava (may increase risk of serotonin syndrome and/or excessive sedation); Avoid supplements containing caffeine, tyrosine, tryptophan or phenylalanine. Ingestion of large quantities may increase the risk of severe side effects (eg, hypertensive reactions, serotonin syndrome).

Stability Store at 15°C to 30°C (59°F to 86°F).

Mechanism of Action Potent, irreversible and selective inhibitor of brain monoamine oxidase (MAO) type B, which plays a major role in the catabolism of dopamine. Inhibition of dopamine depletion in the striatal region of the brain reduces the symptomatic motor deficits of Parkinson's disease. There is also experimental evidence of rasagiline conferring neuroprotective effects (antioxidant, antiapoptotic), which may delay onset of symptoms and progression of neuronal deterioration.

Pharmacodynamics/Kinetics

Onset of action: Therapeutic: Within 1 hour

Duration: ~1 week (irreversible inhibition); may require ~14-40 days for complete restoration of (brain) MAO-B activity

Absorption: Rapid

Protein binding: 88% to 94%

Metabolism: Hepatic N-dealkylation and/or hydroxylation via CYP1A2 to multiple inactive metabolites (nonamphetamine derivatives)

Distribution: V_{dss}: 87 L

Bioavailability: 36%

Half-life elimination: ~1.3-3 hours (no correlation with biologic effect due to irreversible inhibition)

Time to peak, plasma: 30 minutes to 1 hour

Excretion: Urine (62%, >99% as metabolites); feces (7%)

Dosage Oral: Adults: Parkinson's disease:

Monotherapy: 1 mg once daily

Adjunctive therapy with levodopa: Initial: 0.5 mg once daily; may increase to 1 mg once daily based on response and tolerability

Note: When added to existing levodopa therapy, a dose reduction of levodopa may be required to avoid exacerbation of dyskinesias; typical dose reductions of ~9% to 13% were employed in clinical trials

Dose reduction with concomitant ciprofloxacin or other CYP1A2 inhibitors: 0.5 mg once daily

Dosage adjustment in renal impairment:

Mild impairment: No adjustment necessary

Moderate-to-severe impairment: No data available

Dosage adjustment in hepatic impairment:

Mild impairment (Child-Pugh ≤6): 0.5 mg once daily

Moderate-to-severe impairment: Not recommended

Dietary Considerations Avoid tyramine-containing foods/beverages. Some examples include aged or matured cheese, air-dried or cured meats (including sausages and salamis), fava or broad bean pods, tap/draft beers, Marmite concentrate, sauerkraut, soy sauce and other soybean condiments.

Monitoring Parameters Blood pressure; symptoms of parkinsonism; general mood and behavior (increased anxiety, or presence of mania or agitation); skin examination for presence of melanoma (higher incidence in Parkinson's patients- drug causation not established)

Additional Information When adding rasagiline to levodopa/carbidopa, the dose of the latter can usually be decreased. Studies are investigating the use of rasagiline in early Parkinson's disease to slow the progression of the disease.

Dosage Forms

Tablet, as mesylate:

Azilect®: 0.5 mg, 1 mg

♦ **Rasagiline Mesylate** *see Rasagiline on page 1488*

Rasburicase *(ras BYOOR i kayse)*

U.S. Brand Names Elitek™

Canadian Brand Names Fasturtec®

Index Terms NSC-721631; Recombinant Urate Oxidase

Pharmacologic Category Enzyme; Enzyme, Urate-Oxidase (Recombinant)

Use Initial management of uric acid levels in pediatric patients with leukemia, lymphoma, and solid tumor malignancies receiving anticancer therapy expected to result in tumor lysis and elevation of plasma uric acid

Unlabeled/Investigational Use Prevention and treatment of malignancy-associated hyperuricemia in adults

Pregnancy Risk Factor C

Pregnancy Implications Reproduction studies have not been conducted.

Lactation Excretion in breast milk unknown/not recommended

Contraindications Hypersensitivity, hemolytic or methemoglobinemia reactions to rasburicase or any component of the formulation; glucose-6-phosphatase dehydrogenase (G6PD) deficiency

Warnings/Precautions [U.S. Boxed Warning]: Hypersensitivity reactions (including anaphylaxis), methemoglobinemia, and severe hemolysis have been reported; reactions may occur at any time during treatment (including the initial dose); discontinue **immediately and permanently** in patients developing any of these reactions. Hemolysis may be associated with G6PD deficiency; patients at higher risk for G6PD deficiency should be screened prior to therapy. **[U.S. Boxed Warning]: Enzymatic degradation of uric acid in blood samples will occur if left at room temperature;** specific guidelines for the collection of plasma uric acid samples must be followed. Rasburicase is immunogenic and can elicit an antibody response; administration of more than one course is not recommended.

Adverse Reactions As reported in patients receiving rasburicase with antitumor therapy versus active-control:
>10%:
Central nervous system: Fever (5% to 46%), headache (26%)
Dermatologic: Rash (13%)
Gastrointestinal: Vomiting (50%), nausea (27%), abdominal pain (20%), constipation (20%), mucositis (2% to 15%), diarrhea (≤1% to 20%)
1% to 10%:
Hematologic: Neutropenia with fever (4%), neutropenia (2%)
Respiratory: Respiratory distress (3%)
Miscellaneous: Sepsis (3%)
<1% (Limited to important or life-threatening): Anaphylaxis, convulsions, hemolysis, methemoglobinemia, pulmonary edema

Overdosage/Toxicology No cases of overdose have been reported; low or undetectable serum levels of uric acid would be expected. Treatment should be symptom-directed and supportive.

Stability Prior to reconstitution, store with diluent at 2°C to 8°C (36°F to 46°F); do not freeze. Protect from light. Reconstitute each vial with 1 mL of the provided diluent. Mix by gently swirling; do **not** shake or vortex. Discard it discolored or containing particulate matter. Total dose should be further diluted in NS to a final volume of 50 mL. Reconstituted and final solution may be stored up to 24 hours at 2°C to 8°C (36°F to 46°F). Discard unused product.

Mechanism of Action Rasburicase is a recombinant urate-oxidase enzyme, which converts uric acid to allantoin (an inactive and soluble metabolite of uric acid); it does not inhibit the formation of uric acid.

Pharmacodynamics/Kinetics
Distribution: Pediatric patients: 110-127 mL/kg
Half-life elimination: Pediatric patients: 18 hours

Dosage I.V.:
Children: Management of uric acid levels: 0.15 mg/kg or 0.2 mg/kg once daily for 5 days (manufacturer-recommended duration); begin chemotherapy 4-24 hours after the first dose Limited data suggest that a single prechemotherapy dose (versus multiple-day administration) may be sufficiently efficacious. Monitoring electrolytes, hydration status, and uric acid concentrations are necessary to identify the need for additional doses. Other clinical manifestations of tumor lysis syndrome (eg, hyperphosphatemia, hypocalcemia, and hyperkalemia) may occur.
Adults (unlabeled use): Management of malignancy-associated hyperuricemia: 0.2 mg/kg/day for 3-7 days, beginning the day before or day of chemotherapy **or** 0.15-0.2 mg/kg as a single dose, repeated if needed based on uric acid levels **or** 3-6 mg as a single dose, repeated (1.5-6 mg) if needed based on uric acid levels

Administration I.V. infusion over 30 minutes; do **not** administer as a bolus infusion. Do **not** filter during infusion. If not possible to administer through a separate line, I.V. line should be flushed with at least 15 mL saline prior to and following rasburicase infusion.

Monitoring Parameters Plasma uric acid levels, CBC

Test Interactions Specific handling procedures must be followed to prevent the degradation of uric acid in plasma samples. Blood must be collected in prechilled tubes containing heparin anticoagulant. Samples must then be **immediately** immersed in an ice water bath. Prepare samples by centrifugation in a precooled centrifuge (4°C). Samples must be kept in ice water bath and analyzed within 4 hours of collection.

Dosage Forms
Injection, powder for reconstitution:
Elitek™: 1.5 mg [packaged with three 1 mL ampuls of diluent]

♦ **ratio-Aclavulanate (Can)** *see* Amoxicillin and Clavulanate Potassium *on page 112*
♦ **ratio-Acyclovir (Can)** *see* Acyclovir *on page 44*
♦ **ratio-Alendronate (Can)** *see* Alendronate *on page 65*
♦ **ratio-Amcinonide (Can)** *see* Amcinonide *on page 88*
♦ **ratio-Azithromycin (Can)** *see* Azithromycin *on page 186*
♦ **ratio-Bicalutamide (Can)** *see* Bicalutamide *on page 221*
♦ **ratio-Brimonidine (Can)** *see* Brimonidine *on page 239*
♦ **ratio-Carvedilol (Can)** *see* Carvedilol *on page 299*
♦ **ratio-Cefuroxime (Can)** *see* Cefuroxime *on page 326*
♦ **ratio-Ciprofloxacin (Can)** *see* Ciprofloxacin *on page 372*
♦ **ratio-Citalopram (Can)** *see* Citalopram *on page 381*
♦ **ratio-Clarithromycin (Can)** *see* Clarithromycin *on page 385*
♦ **ratio-Cotridin (Can)** *see* Triprolidine, Pseudoephedrine, and Codeine *on page 1750*
♦ **ratio-Diltiazem CD (Can)** *see* Diltiazem *on page 509*
♦ **ratio-Emtec (Can)** *see* Acetaminophen and Codeine *on page 31*
♦ **ratio-Famotidine (Can)** *see* Famotidine *on page 683*
♦ **ratio-Fenofibrate MC (Can)** *see* Fenofibrate *on page 689*
♦ **ratio-Fosinopril (Can)** *see* Fosinopril *on page 766*

♦ **ratio-Glimepiride (Can)** *see Glimepiride on page 797*
♦ **ratio-Glyburide (Can)** *see GlyBURIDE on page 803*
♦ **ratio-Inspra-Sal (Can)** *see Albuterol on page 57*
♦ **ratio-Ketorolac (Can)** *see Ketorolac on page 963*
♦ **ratio-Lamotrigine (Can)** *see Lamotrigine on page 974*
♦ **ratio-Lenoltec (Can)** *see Acetaminophen and Codeine on page 31*
♦ **ratio-Lovastatin (Can)** *see Lovastatin on page 1040*
♦ **ratio-Metformin (Can)** *see Metformin on page 1098*
♦ **ratio-Methotrexate (Can)** *see Methotrexate on page 1111*
♦ **ratio-Mirtazapine (Can)** *see Mirtazapine on page 1152*
♦ **ratio-Mometasone (Can)** *see Mometasone Furoate on page 1165*
♦ **ratio-Morphine SR (Can)** *see Morphine Sulfate on page 1171*
♦ **Ratio-Orciprenaline® (Can)** *see Metaproterenol on page 1096*
♦ **ratio-Paroxetine (Can)** *see Paroxetine on page 1314*
♦ **ratio-Pentoxifylline (Can)** *see Pentoxifylline on page 1343*
♦ **ratio-Pravastatin (Can)** *see Pravastatin on page 1409*
♦ **ratio-Salbutamol (Can)** *see Albuterol on page 57*
♦ **ratio-Sertraline (Can)** *see Sertraline on page 1557*
♦ **ratio-Simvastatin (Can)** *see Simvastatin on page 1567*
♦ **ratio-Sumatriptan (Can)** *see Sumatriptan on page 1620*
♦ **ratio-Temazepam (Can)** *see Temazepam on page 1640*
♦ **ratio-Topiramate (Can)** *see Topiramate on page 1707*
♦ **ratio-Trazodone (Can)** *see Trazodone on page 1727*
♦ **Razadyne™** *see Galantamine on page 777*
♦ **Razadyne™ ER** *see Galantamine on page 777*
♦ **Reactine™ (Can)** *see Cetirizine on page 334*
♦ **Rea-Lo® [OTC]** *see Urea on page 1758*
♦ **ReAzo [OTC]** *see Phenazopyridine on page 1351*
♦ **Rebetol®** *see Ribavirin on page 1503*
♦ **Rebetron®** *see Interferon Alfa-2b and Ribavirin on page 923*
♦ **Rebif®** *see Interferon Beta-1a on page 926*
♦ **Reclipsen™** *see Ethinyl Estradiol and Desogestrel on page 645*
♦ **Recombinant α-L-Iduronidase (Glycosaminoglycan α-L-Iduronohydrolase)** *see Laronidase on page 980*
♦ **Recombinant Hirudin** *see Lepirudin on page 986*
♦ **Recombinant Human Deoxyribonuclease** *see Dornase Alfa on page 541*
♦ **Recombinant Human Insulin-Like Growth Factor-1** *see Mecasermin on page 1060*
♦ **Recombinant Human Interleukin-11** *see Oprelvekin on page 1270*
♦ **Recombinant Human Luteinizing Hormone** *see Lutropin Alfa on page 1044*
♦ **Recombinant Human Parathyroid Hormone (1-34)** *see Teriparatide on page 1652*
♦ **Recombinant Human Platelet-Derived Growth Factor B** *see Becaplermin on page 198*
♦ **Recombinant Interleukin-11** *see Oprelvekin on page 1270*
♦ **Recombinant Plasminogen Activator** *see Reteplase on page 1498*
♦ **Recombinant Urate Oxidase** *see Rasburicase on page 1490*
♦ **Recombinate** *see Antihemophilic Factor (Recombinant) on page 135*
♦ **Recombivax HB®** *see Hepatitis B Vaccine on page 835*
♦ **Rectacaine [OTC]** *see Phenylephrine on page 1358*
♦ **Red Cross™ Canker Sore [OTC]** *see Benzocaine on page 204*
♦ **Reese's® Pinworm Medicine [OTC]** *see Pyrantel Pamoate on page 1459*
♦ **ReFacto®** *see Antihemophilic Factor (Recombinant) on page 135*
♦ **Refenesen Plus [OTC]** *see Guaifenesin and Pseudoephedrine on page 819*
♦ **Refludan®** *see Lepirudin on page 986*
♦ **Regitine [DSC]** *see Phentolamine on page 1357*
♦ **Regitine® (Can)** *see Phentolamine on page 1357*
♦ **Reglan®** *see Metoclopramide on page 1126*
♦ **Regonol®** *see Pyridostigmine on page 1462*
♦ **Regranex®** *see Becaplermin on page 198*
♦ **Regular Insulin** *see Insulin Regular on page 914*
♦ **Regulex® (Can)** *see Docusate on page 533*
♦ **Reguloid® [OTC]** *see Psyllium on page 1458*
♦ **Rejuva-A® (Can)** *see Tretinoin (Topical) on page 1732*
♦ **Relacon-DM NR** *see Guaifenesin, Pseudoephedrine, and Dextromethorphan on page 821*
♦ **Relafen® [DSC]** *see Nabumetone on page 1185*
♦ **Relafen® (Can)** *see Nabumetone on page 1185*
♦ **Relenza®** *see Zanamivir on page 1809*
♦ **Relera** *see Chlorpheniramine and Phenylephrine on page 349*
♦ **Relief® [OTC]** *see Phenylephrine on page 1358*
♦ **Relpax®** *see Eletriptan on page 575*
♦ **Remeron®** *see Mirtazapine on page 1152*
♦ **Remeron® RD (Can)** *see Mirtazapine on page 1152*
♦ **Remeron SolTab®** *see Mirtazapine on page 1152*
♦ **Remicade®** *see Infliximab on page 904*

Remifentanil (rem i FEN ta nil)

U.S. Brand Names Ultiva®
Canadian Brand Names Ultiva®
Index Terms GI87084B
Pharmacologic Category Analgesic, Opioid
Additional Appendix Information
Narcotic Agonists *on page 1888*
Use Analgesic for use during the induction and maintenance of general anesthesia; for continued analgesia into the immediate postoperative period; analgesic component of monitored anesthesia
Unlabeled/Investigational Use Management of pain in mechanically-ventilated patients
Restrictions C-II
Pregnancy Risk Factor C
Pregnancy Implications Remifentanil has been shown to cross the placenta. Neonatal respiratory depression and sedation may occur.
Lactation Excretion in breast milk unknown/use caution
Medication Safety Issues
Sound-alike/look-alike issues:
Remifentanil may be confused with alfentanil
Contraindications Not for intrathecal or epidural administration, due to the presence of glycine in the formulation; hypersensitivity to remifentanil, fentanyl, or fentanyl analogs, or any component of the formulation
Warnings/Precautions Remifentanil is not recommended as the sole agent in general anesthesia, because the loss of consciousness cannot be assured and due to the high incidence of apnea, hypotension, tachycardia and muscle rigidity; it should be administered by individuals specifically trained in the use of anesthetic agents and should not be used in diagnostic or therapeutic procedures outside the monitored anesthesia setting; resuscitative and intubation equipment should be readily available. May cause hypotension; use with caution in patients with hypovolemia, cardiovascular disease (including acute MI), or drugs which may exaggerate hypotensive effects (including phenothiazines or general anesthetics). Shares the toxic potentials of opiate agonists, and precautions of opiate agonist therapy should be observed. In patients <55 years of age, intraoperative awareness has been reported when used with propofol rates of ≤75 mcg/kg/minute.

Use with caution when administering to patients with bradycardia. Inject slowly over 3-5 minutes; rapid I.V. infusion may result in skeletal muscle and chest wall rigidity, impaired ventilation, or respiratory distress/arrest; nondepolarizing skeletal muscle relaxant may be required. Interruption of an infusion will result in offset of effects within 5-10 minutes; the discontinuation of remifentanil infusion should be preceded by the establishment of adequate postoperative analgesia orders, especially for patients in whom postoperative pain is anticipated. Use caution in the morbidly obese. Safety and efficacy for postoperative analgesic or monitored anesthesia care have not been established in children.

Adverse Reactions
>10%: Gastrointestinal: Nausea, vomiting
1% to 10%:
Cardiovascular: Hypotension (dose dependent), bradycardia (dose dependent), tachycardia, hypertension
Central nervous system: Dizziness, headache, agitation, fever
Dermatologic: Pruritus
Neuromuscular & skeletal: Muscle rigidity (dose dependent)
Ocular: Visual disturbances
Respiratory: Respiratory depression, apnea, hypoxia
Miscellaneous: Shivering, postoperative pain
<1% (Limited to important or life-threatening): Anaphylactic/anaphylactoid reactions, anemia, anxiety, arrhythmia, asystole, bronchospasm, confusion, constipation, CPK-MB increased, diarrhea, dysphagia, electrolyte disorders, hallucinations, heart block, pleural effusion, prolonged emergence from anesthesia, pulmonary edema, syncope, thrombocytopenia, xerostomia

Overdosage/Toxicology Symptoms include apnea, chest wall rigidity, seizures, hypoxemia, hypotension, and bradycardia. Treatment includes airway support, establishment of an I.V. line, administration of I.V. fluids and naloxone 2 mg I.V. (0.01 mg/kg for children) with repeat administration as needed up to a total of 10 mg. Glycopyrrolate or atropine may be useful for the treatment of bradycardia or hypotension.

Drug Interactions
Increased Effect/Toxicity: Additive effects with other CNS depressants. Synergistic with other anesthetics, may need to decrease thiopental, propofol, isoflurane, and midazolam by up to 75%.
Stability Prior to reconstitution, store at 2°C to 25°C (36°F to 77°F). Prepare solution by adding 1 mL of diluent per 1 mg of remifentanil. Shake well. Further dilute to a final concentration of 20, 25, 50, or 250 mcg/mL. Stable for 24 hours at room temperature after reconstitution and further dilution to concentrations of 20-250 mcg/mL (4 hours if diluted with LR).
Mechanism of Action Binds with stereospecific mu-opioid receptors at many sites within the CNS, increases pain threshold, alters pain reception, inhibits ascending pain pathways
Pharmacodynamics/Kinetics
Onset of action: I.V.: 1-3 minutes
Distribution: V_d: 100 mL/kg; increased in children
Protein binding: ~70% (primarily alpha$_1$ acid glycoprotein)
Metabolism: Rapid via blood and tissue esterases
Half-life elimination (dose dependent): Terminal: 10-20 minutes; effective: 3-10 minutes
Excretion: Urine
Dosage I.V. continuous infusion: Dose should be based on ideal body weight (IBW) in obese patients (>30% over IBW).
(Continued)

Remifentanil *(Continued)*

Children birth to 2 months: Maintenance of anesthesia with nitrous oxide (70%): 0.4 mcg/kg/minute (range: 0.4-1 mcg/kg/minute); supplemental bolus dose of 1 mcg/kg may be administered, smaller bolus dose may be required with potent inhalation agents, potent neuraxial anesthesia, significant comorbidities, significant fluid shifts, or without atropine pretreatment. Clearance in neonates is highly variable; dose should be carefully titrated.

Children 1-12 years: Maintenance of anesthesia with halothane, sevoflurane or isoflurane: 0.25 mcg/kg/minute (range 0.05-1.3 mcg/kg/minute); supplemental bolus dose of 1 mcg/kg may be administered every 2-5 minutes. Consider increasing concomitant anesthetics with infusion rate >1 mcg/kg/minute. Infusion rate can be titrated upward in increments up to 50% or titrated downward in decrements of 25% to 50%. May titrate every 2-5 minutes.

Adults:

Induction of anesthesia: 0.5-1 mcg/kg/minute; if endotracheal intubation is to occur in <8 minutes, an initial dose of 1 mcg/kg may be given over 30-60 seconds
Coronary bypass surgery: 1 mcg/kg/minute

Maintenance of anesthesia: **Note:** Supplemental bolus dose of 1 mcg/kg may be administered every 2-5 minutes. Consider increasing concomitant anesthetics with infusion rate >1 mcg/kg/minute. Infusion rate can be titrated upward in increments of 25% to 100% or downward in decrements of 25% to 50%. May titrate every 2-5 minutes.
With nitrous oxide (66%): 0.4 mcg/kg/minute (range: 0.1-2 mcg/kg/minute)
With isoflurane: 0.25 mcg/kg/minute (range: 0.05-2 mcg/kg/minute)
With propofol: 0.25 mcg/kg/minute (range: 0.05-2 mcg/kg/minute)
Coronary bypass surgery: 1 mcg/kg/minute (range: 0.125-4 mcg/kg/minute); supplemental dose: 0.5-1 mcg/kg

Continuation as an analgesic in immediate postoperative period: 0.1 mcg/kg/minute (range: 0.025-0.2 mcg/kg/minute). Infusion rate may be adjusted every 5 minutes in increments of 0.025 mcg/kg/minute. Bolus doses are not recommended. Infusion rates >0.2 mcg/kg/minute are associated with respiratory depression.

Coronary bypass surgery, continuation as an analgesic into the ICU: 1 mcg/kg/minute (range: 0.05-1 mcg/kg/minute)

Analgesic component of monitored anesthesia care: **Note:** Supplemental oxygen is recommended:
Single I.V. dose given 90 seconds prior to local anesthetic:
Remifentanil alone: 1 mcg/kg over 30-60 seconds
With midazolam: 0.5 mcg/kg over 30-60 seconds
Continuous infusion beginning 5 minutes prior to local anesthetic:
Remifentanil alone: 0.1 mcg/kg minute
With midazolam: 0.05 mcg/kg minute
Continuous infusion given after local anesthetic:
Remifentanil alone: 0.05 mcg/kg/minute (range: 0.025-0.2 mcg/kg/minute)
With midazolam: 0.025 mcg/kg/minute (range: 0.025-0.2 mcg/kg/minute)
Note: Following local or anesthetic block, infusion rate should be decreased to 0.05 mcg/kg/minute; rate adjustments of 0.025 mcg/kg/minute may be done at 5-minute intervals

Mechanically-ventilated patients: Acute pain (moderate-to-severe) (unlabeled use): 0.6-15 mcg/kg/hour

Elderly: Elderly patients have an increased sensitivity to effect of remifentanil, doses should be decreased by ½ and titrated

Administration An infusion device should be used to administer continuous infusions. During the maintenance of general anesthesia, I.V. boluses may be administered over 30-60 seconds. Injections should be given into I.V. tubing close to the venous cannula; tubing should be cleared after treatment to prevent residual effects when other fluids are administered through the same I.V. line.

Monitoring Parameters Respiratory and cardiovascular status, blood pressure, heart rate

Additional Information Ultra short-acting narcotic that is unique compared to other short-acting narcotics. This agent is not considered suitable as the sole agent for induction; remifentanil should be used in combination with other induction agents. Bolus doses are not recommended for sedation cases and in treatment of postoperative pain due to risk of respiratory depression and muscle rigidity. Due to remifentanil's short duration of action, when postoperative pain is anticipated, discontinuation of an infusion of remifentanil should be preceded by an adequate postoperative analgesic (ie, fentanyl, morphine).

Dosage Forms Injection, powder for reconstitution: 1 mg, 2 mg, 5 mg [contains glycine 15 mg]

♦ **Reminyl® [DSC]** *see* Galantamine *on page 777*
♦ **Reminyl® (Can)** *see* Galantamine *on page 777*
♦ **Reminyl® ER (Can)** *see* Galantamine *on page 777*
♦ **Remodulin®** *see* Treprostinil *on page 1729*
♦ **Renagel®** *see* Sevelamer *on page 1560*
♦ **Renedil® (Can)** *see* Felodipine *on page 687*
♦ **Renese®** *see* Polythiazide *on page 1391*
♦ **Renova®** *see* Tretinoin (Topical) *on page 1732*
♦ **ReoPro®** *see* Abciximab *on page 22*
♦ **Reopro® (Can)** *see* Abciximab *on page 22*

Repaglinide *(re PAG li nide)*

U.S. Brand Names Prandin®
Canadian Brand Names GlucoNorm®; Prandin®
Pharmacologic Category Antidiabetic Agent, Meglitinide Derivative
Additional Appendix Information
Diabetes Mellitus Management, Adults *on page 2040*
Hyperglycemia- or Hypoglycemia-Causing Drugs *on page 2057*
Use Management of type 2 diabetes mellitus (noninsulin dependent, NIDDM); may be used in combination with metformin or thiazolidinediones

Pregnancy Risk Factor C

Pregnancy Implications Safety in pregnant women has not been established. Use during pregnancy only if clearly needed. Abnormal blood glucose levels are associated with a higher incidence of congenital abnormalities. Insulin is the drug of choice for the control of diabetes mellitus during pregnancy.

Lactation Excretion in breast milk unknown/not recommended

Medication Safety Issues
Sound-alike/look-alike issues:
Prandin® may be confused with Avandia®

Contraindications Hypersensitivity to repaglinide or any component of the formulation; diabetic ketoacidosis, with or without coma (treat with insulin); type 1 diabetes (insulin dependent, IDDM)

Warnings/Precautions Use with caution in patients with moderate-to-severe hepatic impairment. Use caution in severe renal dysfunction, elderly, malnourished, or patients with adrenal/pituitary dysfunction; may be more susceptible to glucose-lowering effects. May cause hypoglycemia; appropriate patient selection, dosage, and patient education are important to avoid hypoglycemic episodes. It may be necessary to discontinue repaglinide and administer insulin if the patient is exposed to stress (fever, trauma, infection, surgery). Not indicated for use in combination with NPH insulin due to potential cardiovascular events. Safety and efficacy have not been established in pediatric patients.

Adverse Reactions
>10%:
Central nervous system: Headache (9% to 11%)
Endocrine & metabolic: Hypoglycemia (16% to 31%)
Respiratory: Upper respiratory tract infection (10% to 16%)
1% to 10%:
Cardiovascular: Ischemia (4%), chest pain (2% to 3%)
Gastrointestinal: Diarrhea (4% to 5%), constipation (2% to 3%), tooth disorder (<1% to 2%)
Genitourinary: Urinary tract infection (2% to 3%)
Neuromuscular & skeletal: Arthralgia (3% to 6%), back pain (5% to 6%)
Respiratory: Sinusitis (3% to 6%), bronchitis (2% to 6%)
Miscellaneous: Allergy (1% to 2%)
<1% (Limited to important or life-threatening): Alopecia, anaphylactoid reaction, arrhythmias, hemolytic anemia, hepatic dysfunction (severe), hepatitis, hypertension, jaundice, leukopenia, liver function tests increased, MI, palpitation, pancreatitis, Stevens-Johnson syndrome, thrombocytopenia

Overdosage/Toxicology Symptoms include severe hypoglycemia, seizures, cerebral damage, tingling of lips and tongue, nausea, yawning, confusion, agitation, tachycardia, sweating, convulsions, stupor, and coma. Intoxications are best managed with glucose administration (oral for milder hypoglycemia or by injection in more severe forms) and symptomatic management.

Drug Interactions
Cytochrome P450 Effect: Substrate of CYP2C8 (major), 3A4 (major)
Increased Effect/Toxicity: Concurrent use of other hypoglycemic agents may increase risk of hypoglycemia. Gemfibrozil may increase the serum concentration of repaglinide (resulting in severe, prolonged hypoglycemia), and the addition of itraconazole may augment the effects of gemfibrozil on repaglinide. Macrolide antibiotics or trimethoprim may increase the effects of repaglinide. CYP2C8 Inhibitors may increase the levels/effects of repaglinide; example inhibitors include atazanavir, gemfibrozil, and ritonavir. CYP3A4 inhibitors may increase the levels/effects of repaglinide; example inhibitors include azole antifungals, clarithromycin, diclofenac, doxycycline, erythromycin, imatinib, isoniazid, nefazodone, nicardipine, propofol, protease inhibitors, quinidine, telithromycin, and verapamil.
Decreased Effect: CYP2C8 inducers may decrease the levels/effects of repaglinide; example inducers include carbamazepine, phenobarbital, phenytoin, rifampin, rifapentine, and secobarbital. CYP3A4 inducers may decrease the levels/effects of repaglinide; example inducers include aminoglutethimide, carbamazepine, nafcillin, nevirapine, phenobarbital, phenytoin, and rifamycins.

Ethanol/Nutrition/Herb Interactions
Ethanol: Avoid ethanol (may cause hypoglycemia).
Food: When given with food, the AUC of repaglinide is decreased.
Herb/Nutraceutical: St John's wort may decrease repaglinide levels. Avoid gymnema, garlic (may cause hypoglycemia).

Stability Do not store above 25°C (77°F). Protect from moisture.

Mechanism of Action Nonsulfonylurea hypoglycemic agent of the meglitinide class (the nonsulfonylurea moiety of glyburide) used in the management of type 2 diabetes mellitus; stimulates insulin release from the pancreatic beta cells

Pharmacodynamics/Kinetics
Onset of action: Single dose: Increased insulin levels: ~15-60 minutes
Duration: 4-6 hours
Absorption: Rapid and complete
Distribution: V_d: 31 L
Protein binding, plasma: >98%
Metabolism: Hepatic via CYP3A4 isoenzyme and glucuronidation to inactive metabolites
Bioavailability: Mean absolute: ~56%
Half-life elimination: 1 hour
Time to peak, plasma: ~1 hour
Excretion: Within 96 hours: Feces (~90%, <2% as parent drug); Urine (~8%)

Dosage Adults: Oral: Should be taken within 15 minutes of the meal, but time may vary from immediately preceding the meal to as long as 30 minutes before the meal

Initial: For patients not previously treated or whose Hb A_{1c} is <8%, the starting dose is 0.5 mg. For patients previously treated with blood glucose-lowering agents whose Hb A_{1c} is ≥8%, the initial dose is 1 or 2 mg before each meal.

(Continued)

Repaglinide *(Continued)*

Dose adjustment: Determine dosing adjustments by blood glucose response, usually fasting blood glucose. Double the preprandial dose up to 4 mg until satisfactory blood glucose response is achieved. At least 1 week should elapse to assess response after each dose adjustment.

Dose range: 0.5-4 mg taken with meals. Repaglinide may be dosed preprandial 2, 3 or 4 times/day in response to changes in the patient's meal pattern. Maximum recommended daily dose: 16 mg.

Patients receiving other oral hypoglycemic agents: When repaglinide is used to replace therapy with other oral hypoglycemic agents, it may be started the day after the final dose is given. Observe patients carefully for hypoglycemia because of potential overlapping of drug effects. When transferred from longer half-life sulfonylureas (eg, chlorpropamide), close monitoring may be indicated for up to ≥1 week.

Combination therapy: If repaglinide monotherapy does not result in adequate glycemic control, metformin or a thiazolidinedione may be added. Or, if metformin or thiazolidinedione therapy does not provide adequate control, repaglinide may be added. The starting dose and dose adjustments for combination therapy are the same as repaglinide monotherapy. Carefully adjust the dose of each drug to determine the minimal dose required to achieve the desired pharmacologic effect. Failure to do so could result in an increase in the incidence of hypoglycemic episodes. Use appropriate monitoring of FPG and Hb A_{1c} measurements to ensure that the patient is not subjected to excessive drug exposure or increased probability of secondary drug failure. If glucose is not achieved after a suitable trial of combination therapy, consider discontinuing these drugs and using insulin.

Dosing adjustment in renal impairment:

Cl_{cr} 40-80 mL/minute (mild to moderate renal dysfunction): Initial dosage adjustment does not appear to be necessary.

Cl_{cr} 20-40 mL/minute: Initiate 0.5 mg with meals; titrate carefully.

Dosing adjustment in hepatic impairment: Use conservative initial and maintenance doses. Use longer intervals between dosage adjustments.

Dietary Considerations Administer repaglinide 15-30 minutes before meals. Dietary modification based on ADA recommendations is a part of therapy. May cause hypoglycemia. Must be able to recognize symptoms of hypoglycemia (palpitations, tachycardia, sweaty palms, diaphoresis, lightheadedness).

Administration Administer repaglinide 15-30 minutes before meals. Patients who are anorexic or NPO, may need to have their dose held to avoid hypoglycemia.

Monitoring Parameters Periodically monitor fasting blood glucose and glycosylated hemoglobin (Hb A_{1c}) levels with a goal of decreasing these levels towards the normal range. During dose adjustment, fasting glucose can be used to determine response.

Reference Range Target range: Adults:

Fasting blood glucose: <120 mg/dL

Glycosylated hemoglobin: <7%

Dosage Forms

Tablet:

Prandin®: 0.5 mg, 1 mg, 2 mg

- ◆ **Repan®** *see* Butalbital, Acetaminophen, and Caffeine *on page 259*
- ◆ **Reprexain™** *see* Hydrocodone and Ibuprofen *on page 851*
- ◆ **Repronex®** *see* Menotropins *on page 1079*
- ◆ **Requip®** *see* Ropinirole *on page 1531*
- ◆ **Rescon® MX** *see* Chlorpheniramine, Phenylephrine, and Methscopolamine *on page 353*
- ◆ **Rescon DM [OTC]** *see* Chlorpheniramine, Pseudoephedrine, and Dextromethorphan *on page 355*
- ◆ **Rescon GG** *see* Guaifenesin and Phenylephrine *on page 818*
- ◆ **Rescon-Jr** *see* Chlorpheniramine and Phenylephrine *on page 349*
- ◆ **Rescriptor®** *see* Delavirdine *on page 468*
- ◆ **Resectisol®** *see* Mannitol *on page 1055*

Reserpine *(re SER peen)*

Pharmacologic Category Central Monoamine-Depleting Agent; Rauwolfia Alkaloid

Additional Appendix Information

Hypertension *on page 2063*

Use Management of mild-to-moderate hypertension; treatment of agitated psychotic states (schizophrenia)

Unlabeled/Investigational Use Management of tardive dyskinesia

Pregnancy Risk Factor C

Medication Safety Issues

Sound-alike/look-alike issues:

Reserpine may be confused with Risperdal®, risperidone

Dosage Note: When used for management of hypertension, full antihypertensive effects may take as long as 3 weeks.

Oral:

Children: Hypertension: 0.01-0.02 mg/kg/24 hours divided every 12 hours; maximum dose: 0.25 mg/day (not recommended in children)

Adults:

Hypertension:

Manufacturer's labeling: Initial: 0.5 mg/day for 1-2 weeks; maintenance: 0.1-0.25 mg/day

Note: Clinically, the need for a "loading" period (as recommended by the manufacturer) is not well supported, and alternative dosing is preferred.

Alternative dosing (unlabeled): Initial: 0.1 mg once daily; adjust as necessary based on response.

Usual dose range (JNC 7): 0.05-0.25 mg once daily; 0.1 mg every other day may be given to achieve 0.05 mg once daily

Schizophrenia (labeled use) or tardive dyskinesia (unlabeled use): Dosing recommendations vary; initial dose recommendations generally range from 0.05-0.25 mg (although manufacturer recommends 0.5 mg once daily initially in schizophrenia). May be increased in increments of 0.1-0.25 mg; maximum dose in tardive dyskinesia: 5 mg/day.

Elderly: Initial: 0.05 mg once daily, increasing by 0.05 mg every week as necessary

Dosing adjustment in renal impairment: Cl_{cr} <10 mL/minute: Avoid use

Dialysis: Not removed by hemo or peritoneal dialysis; supplemental dose is not necessary

Additional Information Complete prescribing information for this medication should be consulted for additional detail.

Dosage Forms Tablet: 0.1 mg, 0.25 mg

- ◆ **Resource® GlutaSolve® [OTC]** *see* Glutamine *on page 803*
- ◆ **Respa-DM®** *see* Guaifenesin and Dextromethorphan *on page 816*
- ◆ **Respaire®-60 SR** *see* Guaifenesin and Pseudoephedrine *on page 819*
- ◆ **Respaire®-120 SR** *see* Guaifenesin and Pseudoephedrine *on page 819*
- ◆ **RespiGam® [DSC]** *see* Respiratory Syncytial Virus Immune Globulin (Intravenous) *on page 1497*

Respiratory Syncytial Virus Immune Globulin (Intravenous)
(RES peer rah tor ee sin SISH al VYE rus i MYUN GLOB yoo lin in tra VEE nus)

U.S. Brand Names RespiGam® [DSC]
Index Terms RSV-IGIV
Pharmacologic Category Immune Globulin
Use Orphan drug: Prevention of serious lower respiratory infection caused by respiratory syncytial virus (RSV) in children <24 months of age with bronchopulmonary dysplasia (BPD) or a history of premature birth (≤35 weeks gestation)
Pregnancy Risk Factor C
Contraindications Hypersensitivity to any component of the formulation; selective IgA deficiency; history of severe prior reaction to any immunoglobulin preparation
Warnings/Precautions Use caution to avoid fluid overload in patients, particularly infants with bronchopulmonary dysplasia (BPD), when administering RSV-IGIV; hypersensitivity including anaphylaxis or angioneurotic edema may occur; keep epinephrine 1:1000 readily available during infusion; rare occurrences of aseptic meningitis syndrome have been associated with IGIV treatment, particularly with high doses; observe carefully for signs and symptoms and treat promptly.

RespiGam® contains sucrose. Renal dysfunction and /or acute renal failure has been reported with the administration of IVIG; the majority of cases were associated with sucrose-containing IVIG products. Use caution in patients at increased risk of renal failure (including pre-existing renal insufficiency, volume depletion, or concurrent treatment with nephrotoxic drugs). Ensure adequate hydration prior to infusion.

Adverse Reactions
1% to 10%:
Cardiovascular: Tachycardia (1%), hypertension (1%), hypotension
Central nervous system: Fever (6%)
Dermatologic: Rash (1%)
Endocrine & metabolic: Fluid overload (1%)
Gastrointestinal: Vomiting (2%), diarrhea (1%), gastroenteritis (1%)
Local: Injection site inflammation (1%)
Respiratory: Respiratory distress (2%), wheezing (2%), rales, hypoxia (1%), tachypnea (1%)
<1% (Limited to important or life-threatening): Abdominal cramps, anxiety, arthralgia, chest tightness, cough, cyanosis, dizziness, dyspnea, eczema, edema, flushing, heart murmur, myalgia, pallor, palpitation, pruritus, rhinorrhea

Overdosage/Toxicology Likely symptoms of overdose include those associated with fluid overload. Treatment is supportive (eg, diuretics).

Stability Store between 2°C and 8°C; do not freeze. Do not shake vial; avoid foaming. Discard after single use since it is preservative free.

Mechanism of Action RSV-IGIV is a sterile liquid immunoglobulin G containing neutralizing antibody to respiratory syncytial virus. It is effective in reducing the incidence and duration of RSV hospitalization and the severity of RSV illness in high risk infants.

Dosage I.V.: Children <24 months of age: Prevention of respiratory syncytial virus (RSV) infection: 750 mg/kg/month according to the following infusion schedule:
Initial infusion rate for the first 15 minutes: 1.5 mL/kg/hour; after 15 minutes increase to 3.6 mL/kg/hour (maximum infusion rate: 3.6 mL/kg/hour); rate should be decreased in patients at risk of renal dysfunction

Dietary Considerations Contains sodium 1-1.5 mEq per 50 mL, sucrose 50 mg, human albumin 10 mg

Administration Begin infusion within 6 hours and complete within 12 hours after entering vial. Observe for signs of intolerance during and after infusion; administer through an I.V. line using a constant infusion pump and through a separate I.V. line, if possible; if needed, RSV-IGIV may be "piggybacked" into dextrose with or without saline solutions, avoiding dilutions >2:1 with such line configurations. An in-line filter with a pore size >15 micrometers may be used.

Monitoring Parameters Monitor for symptoms of allergic reaction; check vital signs, cardiopulmonary status after each rate increase and thereafter at 30-minute intervals until 30 minutes following completion of the infusion
(Continued)

Respiratory Syncytial Virus Immune Globulin (Intravenous)
(Continued)

Dosage Forms [DSC] = Discontinued product

Injection, solution [preservative free]: 50 mg/mL (50 mL) [contains sodium 1-1.5 mEq per 50 mL, sucrose 50 mg, human albumin 10 mg] [DSC]

♦ **Respi-Tann™** *see* Carbetapentane and Pseudoephedrine *on page 289*
♦ **Restasis®** *see* CycloSPORINE *on page 431*
♦ **Restoril®** *see* Temazepam *on page 1640*
♦ **Restylane®** *see* Hyaluronate and Derivatives *on page 841*
♦ **Retavase®** *see* Reteplase *on page 1498*

Reteplase (RE ta plase)

U.S. Brand Names Retavase®
Canadian Brand Names Retavase®
Index Terms Recombinant Plasminogen Activator; r-PA
Pharmacologic Category Thrombolytic Agent
Use Management of acute myocardial infarction (AMI); improvement of ventricular function; reduction of the incidence of CHF and the reduction of mortality following AMI
Pregnancy Risk Factor C
Lactation Excretion in breast milk unknown/use caution
Medication Safety Issues
 High alert medication: The Institute for Safe Medication Practices (ISMP) includes this medication (I.V.) among its list of drugs which have a heightened risk of causing significant patient harm when used in error.
Contraindications Hypersensitivity to reteplase or any component of the formulation; active internal bleeding; history of cerebrovascular accident; recent intracranial or intraspinal surgery or trauma; intracranial neoplasm, arteriovenous malformations, or aneurysm; known bleeding diathesis; severe uncontrolled hypertension
Warnings/Precautions Concurrent heparin anticoagulation can contribute to bleeding; careful attention to all potential bleeding sites. I.M. injections and nonessential handling of the patient should be avoided. Venipunctures should be performed carefully and only when necessary. If arterial puncture is necessary, use an upper extremity vessel that can be manually compressed. If serious bleeding occurs then the infusion of anistreplase and heparin should be stopped.

For the following conditions the risk of bleeding is higher with use of reteplase and should be weighed against the benefits of therapy: recent major surgery (eg, CABG, obstetrical delivery, organ biopsy, previous puncture of noncompressible vessels), cerebrovascular disease, recent gastrointestinal or genitourinary bleeding, recent trauma including CPR, hypertension (systolic BP >180 mm Hg and/or diastolic BP >110 mm Hg), high likelihood of left heart thrombus (eg, mitral stenosis with atrial fibrillation), acute pericarditis, subacute bacterial endocarditis, hemostatic defects including ones caused by severe renal or hepatic dysfunction, significant hepatic dysfunction, pregnancy, diabetic hemorrhagic retinopathy or other hemorrhagic ophthalmic conditions, septic thrombophlebitis or occluded AV cannula at seriously infected site, advanced age (eg, >75 years), patients receiving oral anticoagulants, any other condition in which bleeding constitutes a significant hazard or would be particularly difficult to manage because of location.

Coronary thrombolysis may result in reperfusion arrhythmias. Follow standard MI management. Rare anaphylactic reactions can occur. Safety and efficacy in pediatric patients have not been established.
Adverse Reactions Bleeding is the most frequent adverse effect associated with reteplase. Heparin and aspirin have been administered concurrently with reteplase in clinical trials. The incidence of adverse events is a reflection of these combined therapies, and are comparable with comparison thrombolytics.

>10%: Local: Injection site bleeding (4.6% to 48.6%)
1% to 10%:
 Gastrointestinal: Bleeding (1.8% to 9.0%)
 Genitourinary: Bleeding (0.9% to 9.5%)
 Hematologic: Anemia (0.9% to 2.6%)
<1% (Limited to important or life-threatening): Allergic/anaphylactoid reactions, cholesterol embolization, intracranial hemorrhage (0.8%)
Other adverse effects noted are frequently associated with MI (and therefore may or may not be attributable to Retavase®) and include arrhythmia, arrest, cardiac reinfarction, cardiogenic shock, embolism, hypotension, pericarditis, pulmonary edema, tamponade, thrombosis
Overdosage/Toxicology Symptoms include increased incidence of intracranial bleeding.
Drug Interactions
 Increased Effect/Toxicity: The risk of bleeding associated with reteplase may be increased by oral anticoagulants (warfarin), heparin, low molecular weight heparins, and drugs which affect platelet function (eg, NSAIDs, dipyridamole, ticlopidine, clopidogrel, IIb/IIIa antagonists). Concurrent use with aspirin and heparin may increase the risk of bleeding; however, aspirin and heparin were used concomitantly with reteplase in the majority of patients in clinical studies.
 Decreased Effect: Aminocaproic acid (antifibrinolytic agent) may decrease effectiveness of thrombolytic agents.
Stability Dosage kits should be stored at 2°C to 25°C (36°F to 77°F) and remain sealed until use in order to protect from light. Reteplase should be reconstituted using the diluent, syringe, needle, and dispensing pin provided with each kit.
Mechanism of Action Reteplase is a nonglycosylated form of tPA produced by recombinant DNA technology using *E. coli*; it initiates local fibrinolysis by binding to fibrin in a thrombus (clot) and converts entrapped plasminogen to plasmin

Pharmacodynamics/Kinetics
Onset of action: Thrombolysis: 30-90 minutes
Half-life elimination: 13-16 minutes
Excretion: Feces and urine
Clearance: Plasma: 250-450 mL/minute

Dosage
Children: Not recommended
Adults: 10 units I.V. over 2 minutes, followed by a second dose 30 minutes later of 10 units I.V. over 2 minutes
Withhold second dose if serious bleeding or anaphylaxis occurs

Administration Reteplase should be reconstituted using the diluent, syringe, needle and dispensing pin provided with each kit and the each reconstituted dose should be administered I.V. over 2 minutes; no other medication should be added to the injection solution

Monitoring Parameters Monitor for signs of bleeding (hematuria, GI bleeding, gingival bleeding)

Dosage Forms Injection, powder for reconstitution [preservative free]: 10.4 units [equivalent to reteplase 18.1 mg; contains sucrose and polysorbate 80; packaged with sterile water for injection]

♦ **Retin-A**® *see* Tretinoin (Topical) *on page 1732*
♦ **Retin-A**® **Micro** *see* Tretinoin (Topical) *on page 1732*
♦ **Retinoic Acid** *see* Tretinoin (Topical) *on page 1732*
♦ **Retinova**® **(Can)** *see* Tretinoin (Topical) *on page 1732*
♦ **Retisert**™ *see* Fluocinolone *on page 721*
♦ **Retrovir**® *see* Zidovudine *on page 1812*
♦ **Revatio**™ *see* Sildenafil *on page 1564*
♦ **Reversol**® *see* Edrophonium *on page 569*
♦ **Revex**® *see* Nalmefene *on page 1193*
♦ **ReVia**® *see* Naltrexone *on page 1195*
♦ **Revitalose C-1000**® **(Can)** *see* Ascorbic Acid *on page 156*
♦ **Revlimid**® *see* Lenalidomide *on page 984*
♦ **Reyataz**® *see* Atazanavir *on page 165*
♦ **rFSH-alpha** *see* Follitropin Alfa *on page 751*
♦ **rFSH-beta** *see* Follitropin Beta *on page 753*
♦ **rFVIIa** *see* Factor VIIa (Recombinant) *on page 678*
♦ **R-Gene**® *see* Arginine *on page 151*
♦ **rGM-CSF** *see* Sargramostim *on page 1548*
♦ **r-hCG** *see* Chorionic Gonadotropin (Recombinant) *on page 364*
♦ **Rheumatrex**® *see* Methotrexate *on page 1111*
♦ **rhFSH-alpha** *see* Follitropin Alfa *on page 751*
♦ **rhFSH-beta** *see* Follitropin Beta *on page 753*
♦ **rhGAA** *see* Alglucosidase Alfa *on page 70*
♦ **r-h** α-**GAL** *see* Agalsidase Beta *on page 53*
♦ **RhIG** *see* Rho(D) Immune Globulin *on page 1499*
♦ **rhIGF-1** *see* Mecasermin *on page 1060*
♦ **rhIGF-1/rhIGFBP-3** *see* Mecasermin *on page 1060*
♦ **rhIL-11** *see* Oprelvekin *on page 1270*
♦ **Rhinalar**® **(Can)** *see* Flunisolide *on page 720*
♦ **Rhinall [OTC]** *see* Phenylephrine *on page 1358*
♦ **Rhinocort**® **Aqua**® *see* Budesonide *on page 244*
♦ **Rhinocort**® **Turbuhaler**® **(Can)** *see* Budesonide *on page 244*
♦ **RhinoFlex**™ *see* Acetaminophen and Phenyltoloxamine *on page 32*
♦ **RhinoFlex 650** *see* Acetaminophen and Phenyltoloxamine *on page 32*
♦ **r-hLH** *see* Lutropin Alfa *on page 1044*
♦ **Rho(D) Immune Globulin (Human)** *see* Rho(D) Immune Globulin *on page 1499*
♦ **Rho**®-**Clonazepam (Can)** *see* Clonazepam *on page 397*
♦ **Rhodacine**® **(Can)** *see* Indomethacin *on page 901*

Rho(D) Immune Globulin (ar aych oh (dee) i MYUN GLOB yoo lin)

U.S. Brand Names BayRho-D® Full-Dose [DSC]; BayRho-D® Mini-Dose [DSC]; HyperRHO™ S/D Full Dose; HyperRHO™ S/D Mini Dose; MICRhoGAM®; RhoGAM®; Rhophylac®; WinRho® SDF

Canadian Brand Names BayRho-D® Full-Dose

Index Terms RhIG; Rho(D) Immune Globulin (Human); RhoIGIV; RhoIVIM

Pharmacologic Category Immune Globulin

Use

Suppression of Rh isoimmunization: Use in the following situations when an Rho(D)-negative individual is exposed to Rho(D)-positive blood: During delivery of an Rho(D)-positive infant; abortion; amniocentesis; chorionic villus sampling; ruptured tubal pregnancy; abdominal trauma; transplacental hemorrhage. Used when the mother is Rho(D) negative, the father of the child is either Rho(D) positive or Rho(D) unknown, the baby is either Rho(D) positive or Rho(D) unknown.

Transfusion: Suppression of Rh isoimmunization in Rho(D)-negative female children and female adults in their childbearing years transfused with Rho(D) antigen-positive RBCs or blood components containing Rho(D) antigen-positive RBCs

Treatment of idiopathic thrombocytopenic purpura (ITP): Used in the following nonsplenectomized Rho(D) positive individuals: Children with acute or chronic ITP, adults with chronic ITP, children and adults with ITP secondary to HIV infection

(Continued)

Rhₒ(D) Immune Globulin *(Continued)*

Pregnancy Risk Factor C

Pregnancy Implications Animal studies have not been conducted. Available evidence suggests that Rhₒ(D) immune globulin administration during pregnancy does not harm the fetus or affect future pregnancies.

Lactation Does not enter breast milk

Contraindications Hypersensitivity to immune globulins or any component of the formulation; prior sensitization to Rhₒ(D)

Warnings/Precautions Rare but serious signs and symptoms (eg, back pain, shaking, chills, fever, discolored urine; onset within 4 hours of infusion) of intravascular hemolysis (IVH) have been reported in postmarketing experience in patients treated for ITP. Clinically-compromising anemia, acute renal insufficiency and disseminated intravascular coagulation (DIC) have also been reported. ITP patients should be advised of the signs and symptoms of IVH and instructed to report them immediately.

As a product of human plasma, may potentially transmit disease; screening of donors, as well as testing and/or inactivation of certain viruses reduces this risk. Not for replacement therapy in immune globulin deficiency syndromes. Use caution with IgA deficiency, may contain trace amounts of IgA; patients who are IgA deficient may have the potential for developing IgA antibodies, anaphylactic reactions may occur. Administer I.M. injections with caution in patients with thrombocytopenia or coagulation disorders. Some products may contain maltose, which may result in falsely-elevated blood glucose readings. Use caution with renal dysfunction; may require an infusion rate reduction or discontinuation.

Do not administer I.M. or SubQ for the treatment of ITP; administer dose I.V. only. Safety and efficacy not established in Rhₒ(D) negative, non-ITP thrombocytopenia, or splenectomized patients. Decrease dose with hemoglobin <10 g/dL; use with extreme caution if hemoglobin <8 g/dL

Rhₒ(D) suppression: For use in the mother; do not administer to the neonate.

Adverse Reactions Frequency not defined.

Cardiovascular: Hyper-/hypotension, pallor, tachycardia, vasodilation

Central nervous system: Chills, dizziness, fever, headache, malaise, somnolence

Dermatologic: Pruritus, rash

Gastrointestinal: Abdominal pain, diarrhea, nausea, vomiting

Hematologic: Hemoglobin decreased (patients with ITP), intravascular hemolysis (patients with ITP)

Hepatic: LDH increased

Local: Injection site reaction: Discomfort, induration, mild pain, redness, swelling

Neuromuscular & skeletal: Arthralgia, back pain, hyperkinesia, myalgia, weakness

Renal: Acute renal insufficiency

Miscellaneous: Anaphylaxis, diaphoresis, infusion-related reactions

Postmarketing and/or case reports: Signs and symptoms of IVH are associated with treatment for ITP with WinRho® SDF: Anemia (clinically-compromising), DIC

Overdosage/Toxicology No symptoms are likely, however, high doses have been associated with a mild, transient hemolytic anemia. Treatment should be symptom-directed and supportive.

Drug Interactions

Decreased Effect: Rhₒ(D) immune globulin may interfere with the response of live vaccines; vaccines should not be administered within 3 months after Rhₒ(D)

Stability Store at 2°C to 8°C (35°F to 46°F); do not freeze.

Rhophylac®: Stored at this temperature, Rhophylac® has a shelf life of 36 months. Protect from light.

WinRho® SDF lyophilized powder: Dilute with provided NS only with volumes specified below. Inject diluent slowly into vial and gently swirl until dissolved; do not shake. Following reconstitution, may store at room temperature for up to 12 hours.

I.V. administration:

600 units (120 mcg) vial: 2.5 mL diluent

1500 units (300 mcg) vial: 2.5 mL diluent

5000 units (1000 mcg) vial: 8.5 mL diluent

I.M. administration:

600 units (120 mcg) vial: 1.25 mL diluent

1500 units (300 mcg) vial: 1.25 mL diluent

5000 units (1000 mcg) vial: 8.5 mL diluent (administer into several sites)

Mechanism of Action

Rh suppression: Prevents isoimmunization by suppressing the immune response and antibody formation by Rhₒ(D) negative individuals to Rhₒ(D) positive red blood cells.

ITP: Not completely characterized; Rhₒ(D) immune globulin is thought to form anti-D-coated red blood cell complexes which bind to macrophage Fc receptors within the spleen; blocking or saturating the spleens ability to clear antibody-coated cells, including platelets. In this manner, platelets are spared from destruction.

Pharmacodynamics/Kinetics

Onset of platelet increase: ITP: Platelets should rise within 1-2 days

Peak effect: In 7-14 days

Duration: Suppression of Rh isoimmunization: ~12 weeks; Treatment of ITP: 30 days (variable)

Distribution: V_d: I.M.: 8.59 L

Half-life elimination: 21-30 days

Time to peak, plasma: I.M.: 5-10 days; I.V. (WinRho® SDF): ≤2 hours

Dosage

ITP: Children and Adults: WinRho® SDF: I.V.:

Initial: 50 mcg/kg as a single injection, or can be given as a divided dose on separate days. If hemoglobin is <10 g/dL: Dose should be reduced to 25-40 mcg/kg.

Subsequent dosing: 25-60 mcg/kg can be used if required to elevate platelet count

Maintenance dosing if patient **did respond** to initial dosing: 25-60 mcg/kg based on platelet and hemoglobin levels:

Maintenance dosing if patient **did not respond** to initial dosing:

Hemoglobin 8-10 g/dL: Redose between 25-40 mcg/kg

Hemoglobin >10 g/dL: Redose between 50-60 mcg/kg

Hemoglobin <8 g/dL: Use with caution

Rh₀(D) suppression: Adults: **Note:** One "full dose" (300 mcg) provides enough antibody to prevent Rh sensitization if the volume of RBC entering the circulation is ≤15 mL. When >15 mL is suspected, a fetal red cell count should be performed to determine the appropriate dose.

Pregnancy:

Antepartum prophylaxis: In general, dose is given at 28 weeks. If given early in pregnancy, administer every 12 weeks to ensure adequate levels of passively acquired anti-Rh

BayRho-D® Full Dose, HyperRHO™ S/D Full Dose, RhoGAM®: I.M.: 300 mcg

Rhophylac®, WinRho® SDF: I.M., I.V.: 300 mcg

Postpartum prophylaxis: In general, dose is administered as soon as possible after delivery, preferably within 72 hours. Can be given up to 28 days following delivery

BayRho-D® Full Dose, HyperRHO™ S/D Full Dose, RhoGAM®: I.M.: 300 mcg

Rhophylac®: I.M., I.V.: 300 mcg

WinRho® SDF: I.M., I.V.: 120 mcg

Threatened abortion, any time during pregnancy (with continuation of pregnancy):

BayRho-D® Full Dose, HyperRHO™ S/D Full Dose, RhoGAM®: I.M.: 300 mcg; administer as soon as possible

Rhophylac®, WinRho® SDF: I.M., I.V.: 300 mcg; administer as soon as possible

Abortion, miscarriage, termination of ectopic pregnancy:

BayRho-D®, RhoGAM®: I.M.: ≥13 weeks gestation: 300 mcg.

BayRho-D® Mini Dose, HyperRHO™ S/D Mini Dose, MICRhoGAM®: <13 weeks gestation: I.M.: 50 mcg

Rhophylac®: I.M., I.V.: 300 mcg

WinRho® SDF: I.M., I.V.: After 34 weeks gestation: 120 mcg; administer immediately or within 72 hours

Amniocentesis, chorionic villus sampling:

BayRho-D®, HyperRHO™ S/D Full Dose, RhoGAM®: I.M.: At 15-18 weeks gestation or during the 3rd trimester: 300 mcg. If dose is given between 13-18 weeks, repeat at 26-28 weeks and within 72 hours of delivery.

Rhophylac®: I.M., I.V.: 300 mcg

WinRho® SDF: I.M., I.V.: Before 34 weeks gestation: 300 mcg; administer immediately, repeat dose every 12 weeks during pregnancy; After 34 weeks gestation: 120 mcg, administered immediately or within 72 hours

Abdominal trauma, manipulation:

BayRho-D®, HyperRHO™ S/D Full Dose, RhoGAM®: I.M.: 2nd or 3rd trimester: 300 mcg. If dose is given between 13-18 weeks, repeat at 26-28 weeks and within 72 hours of delivery

WinRho® SDF: I.M./I.V.: After 34 weeks gestation: 120 mcg; administer immediately or within 72 hours

Transfusion:

Children and Adults: WinRho® SDF: Administer within 72 hours after exposure of incompatible blood transfusions or massive fetal hemorrhage.

I.V.: Calculate dose as follows; administer 600 mcg every 8 hours until the total dose is administered:

Exposure to Rh₀(D) positive whole blood: 9 mcg/mL blood

Exposure to Rh₀(D) positive red blood cells: 18 mcg/mL cells

I.M.: Calculate dose as follows; administer 1200 mcg every 12 hours until the total dose is administered:

Exposure to Rh₀(D) positive whole blood: 12 mcg/mL blood

Exposure to Rh₀(D) positive red blood cells: 24 mcg/mL cells

Adults:

BayRho-D®, HyperRHO™ S/D Full Dose, RhoGAM®: I.M.: Multiply the volume of Rh positive whole blood administered by the hematocrit of the donor unit to equal the volume of RBCs transfused. The volume of RBCs is then divided by 15 mL, providing the number of 300 mcg doses (vials/syringes) to administer. If the dose calculated results in a fraction, round up to the next higher whole 300 mcg dose (vial/syringe).

Rhophylac®: I.M., I.V.: 20 mcg/2 mL transfused blood or 20 mcg/mL erythrocyte concentrate

Dosage adjustment in renal impairment: I.V. infusion: Use caution; may require infusion rate reduction or discontinuation.

Administration The total volume can be administered in divided doses at different sites at one time or may be divided and given at intervals, provided the total dosage is given within 72 hours of the fetomaternal hemorrhage or transfusion.

I.M.: Administer into the deltoid muscle of the upper arm or anterolateral aspect of the upper thigh; avoid gluteal region due to risk of sciatic nerve injury. If large doses (>5 mL) are needed, administration in divided doses at different sites is recommended. **Note:** Do not administer I.M. Rho(D) immune globulin for ITP.

I.V.: WinRho® SDF: Infuse over at least 3-5 minutes; do not administer with other medications **Note:** If preparing dose using liquid formulation, withdraw the entire contents of the vial to ensure accurate calculation of the dosage requirement.

Monitoring Parameters Signs and symptoms of intravascular hemolysis (IVH), anemia, and renal insufficiency; observe patient for side effects for at least 20 minutes following administration; patients with suspected IVH should have CBC, haptoglobulin, plasma hemoglobin, urine dipstick, BUN, serum creatinine, liver function tests, DIC-specific tests (D-dimer, fibrin degradation products [FDP] or fibrin split products [FSP]) for differential diagnosis. Clinical response may be determined by monitoring platelets, red blood cell (RBC) counts, hemoglobulin, and reticulocyte levels.

(Continued)

Rh_o(D) Immune Globulin *(Continued)*

Test Interactions Some infants born to women given Rh_o(D) antepartum have a weakly positive Coombs' test at birth. Fetal-maternal hemorrhage may cause false blood-typing result in the mother; when there is any doubt to the patients' Rh type, Rh_o(D) immune globulin should be administered. WinRho® SDF liquid contains maltose; may result in falsely elevated blood glucose levels with dehydrogenase pyrroloquinolinequinone or glucose-dye-oxidoreductase testing methods. WinRho® SDF contains trace amounts of anti-A, B, C and E; may alter Coombs' tests following administration.

Additional Information A "full dose" of Rh_o(D) immune globulin has previously been referred to as a 300 mcg dose. It is not the actual anti-D content. Although dosing has traditionally been expressed in mcg, potency is listed in int. units (1 mcg = 5 int. units). ITP patients requiring transfusions should be transfused with Rho-negative blood cells to avoid exacerbating hemolysis; platelet products may contain red blood cells; caution should be exercised if platelets are from Rh_o-positive donors.

Dosage Forms [DSC] = Discontinued product

Injection, solution [preservative free]:

BayRho-D® Full-Dose [DSC], HyperRHO™ S/D Full Dose, RhoGAM®: 300 mcg [for I.M. use only]

BayRho-D® Mini-Dose [DSC], HyperRHO™ S/D Mini Dose, MICRhoGAM®: 50 mcg [for I.M. use only]

Rhophylac®: 300 mcg/2 mL (2 mL) [1500 int. units; for I.M. or I.V. use]

WinRho® SDF:

120 mcg/~0.5 mL (~0.5 mL) [600 int. units; contains maltose and polysorbate 80; for I.M. or I.V. use]

300 mcg/~1.3 mL (~1.3 mL) [1500 int. units; contains maltose and polysorbate 80; for I.M. or I.V. use]

500 mcg/~2.2 mL (~2.2 mL) [2500 int. units; contains maltose and polysorbate 80; for I.M. or I.V. use]

1000 mcg/~4.4 mL (~4.4 mL) [5000 int. units; contains maltose and polysorbate 80; for I.M. or I.V. use]

3000 mcg/~13 mL (~13 mL) [15,000 int. units; contains maltose and polysorbate 80; for I.M. or I.V. use]

Injection, powder for reconstitution [preservative free] (WinRho® SDF):

120 mcg [600 int. units; for I.M. or I.V. use] [DSC]

300 mcg [1500 int. units; for I.M. or I.V. use] [DSC]

1000 mcg [5000 int. units; for I.M. or I.V. use] [DSC]

◆ **Rhodis™ (Can)** *see* Ketoprofen *on page 961*
◆ **Rhodis-EC™ (Can)** *see* Ketoprofen *on page 961*
◆ **Rhodis SR™ (Can)** *see* Ketoprofen *on page 961*
◆ **RhoGAM®** *see* Rh_o(D) Immune Globulin *on page 1499*
◆ **RholGIV** *see* Rh_o(D) Immune Globulin *on page 1499*
◆ **RholVIM** *see* Rh_o(D) Immune Globulin *on page 1499*
◆ **Rho®-Loperamide (Can)** *see* Loperamide *on page 1027*
◆ **Rho®-Metformin (Can)** *see* Metformin *on page 1098*
◆ **Rho®-Nitro (Can)** *see* Nitroglycerin *on page 1234*
◆ **Rhophylac®** *see* Rh_o(D) Immune Globulin *on page 1499*
◆ **Rho®-Sotalol (Can)** *see* Sotalol *on page 1592*
◆ **Rhotral (Can)** *see* Acebutolol *on page 27*
◆ **Rhotrimine® (Can)** *see* Trimipramine *on page 1747*
◆ **Rhoxal-acebutolol (Can)** *see* Acebutolol *on page 27*
◆ **Rhoxal-amiodarone (Can)** *see* Amiodarone *on page 97*
◆ **Rhoxal-anagrelide (Can)** *see* Anagrelide *on page 128*
◆ **Rhoxal-atenolol (Can)** *see* Atenolol *on page 167*
◆ **Rhoxal-ciprofloxacin (Can)** *see* Ciprofloxacin *on page 372*
◆ **Rhoxal-citalopram (Can)** *see* Citalopram *on page 381*
◆ **Rhoxal-cyclosporine (Can)** *see* CycloSPORINE *on page 431*
◆ **Rhoxal-diltiazem CD (Can)** *see* Diltiazem *on page 509*
◆ **Rhoxal-diltiazem SR (Can)** *see* Diltiazem *on page 509*
◆ **Rhoxal-diltiazem T (Can)** *see* Diltiazem *on page 509*
◆ **Rhoxal-fluoxetine (Can)** *see* Fluoxetine *on page 727*
◆ **Rhoxal-fluvoxamine (Can)** *see* Fluvoxamine *on page 747*
◆ **Rhoxal-glimepiride (Can)** *see* Glimepiride *on page 797*
◆ **Rhoxal-minocycline (Can)** *see* Minocycline *on page 1149*
◆ **Rhoxal-mirtazapine (Can)** *see* Mirtazapine *on page 1152*
◆ **Rhoxal-mirtazapine FC (Can)** *see* Mirtazapine *on page 1152*
◆ **Rhoxal-nabumetone (Can)** *see* Nabumetone *on page 1185*
◆ **Rhoxal-orphendrine (Can)** *see* Orphenadrine *on page 1273*
◆ **Rhoxal-pamidronate (Can)** *see* Pamidronate *on page 1300*
◆ **Rhoxal-paroxetine (Can)** *see* Paroxetine *on page 1314*
◆ **Rhoxal-ranitidine (Can)** *see* Ranitidine *on page 1485*
◆ **Rhoxal-salbutamol (Can)** *see* Albuterol *on page 57*
◆ **Rhoxal-sertraline (Can)** *see* Sertraline *on page 1557*
◆ **Rhoxal-sumatriptan (Can)** *see* Sumatriptan *on page 1620*
◆ **Rhoxal-ticlopidine (Can)** *see* Ticlopidine *on page 1683*
◆ **Rhoxal-topiramate (Can)** *see* Topiramate *on page 1707*
◆ **Rhoxal-valproic (Can)** *see* Valproic Acid and Derivatives *on page 1767*
◆ **rhPTH(1-34)** *see* Teriparatide *on page 1652*
◆ **rHuEPO-α** *see* Epoetin Alfa *on page 595*

- **rhuFabV2** *see* Ranibizumab *on page 1484*
- **rHu-KGF** *see* Palifermin *on page 1298*
- **rhuMAb-E25** *see* Omalizumab *on page 1262*
- **rHuMAb-EGFr** *see* Panitumumab *on page 1305*
- **rhuMAb-VEGF** *see* Bevacizumab *on page 217*
- **RibaPak™** *see* Ribavirin *on page 1503*
- **Ribasphere™** *see* Ribavirin *on page 1503*

Ribavirin (rye ba VYE rin)

U.S. Brand Names Copegus®; Rebetol®; RibaPak™; Ribasphere™; Virazole®
Canadian Brand Names Virazole®
Index Terms RTCA; Tribavirin
Pharmacologic Category Antiviral Agent
Use

Inhalation: Treatment of patients with respiratory syncytial virus (RSV) infections; specially indicated for treatment of severe lower respiratory tract RSV infections in patients with an underlying compromising condition (prematurity, bronchopulmonary dysplasia and other chronic lung conditions, congenital heart disease, immunodeficiency, immunosuppression), and recent transplant recipients

Oral capsule:

In combination with interferon alfa-2b (Intron® A) injection for the treatment of chronic hepatitis C in patients with compensated liver disease who have relapsed after alpha interferon therapy or were previously untreated with alpha interferons

In combination with peginterferon alfa-2b (PEG-Intron®) injection for the treatment of chronic hepatitis C in patients with compensated liver disease who were previously untreated with alpha interferons

Oral solution: In combination with interferon alfa 2b (Intron® A) injection for the treatment of chronic hepatitis C in patients >3 years of age with compensated liver disease who were previously untreated with alpha interferons or patients ≥18 years of age who have relapsed after alpha interferon therapy

Oral tablet: In combination with peginterferon alfa-2a (Pegasys®) injection for the treatment of chronic hepatitis C in patients with compensated liver disease who were previously untreated with alpha interferons (includes patients with histological evidence of cirrhosis [Child-Pugh class A] and patients with clinically-stable HIV disease)

Unlabeled/Investigational Use Used in other viral infections including influenza A and B and adenovirus

Restrictions An FDA-approved medication guide must be distributed when dispensing an outpatient prescription (new or refill) for treatment of hepatitis C where this medication is to be used without direct supervision of a healthcare provider. Medication guides are available at http://www.fda.gov/cder/Offices/ODS/medication_guides.htm.

Pregnancy Risk Factor X

Pregnancy Implications Produced significant embryocidal and/or teratogenic effects in all animal studies at ~0.01 times the maximum recommended daily human dose. Use is contraindicated in pregnancy. Negative pregnancy test is required before initiation and monthly thereafter. Avoid pregnancy in female patients and female partners of male patients during therapy by using two effective forms of contraception; continue contraceptive measures for at least 6 months after completion of therapy. If patient or female partner becomes pregnant during treatment, she should be counseled about potential risks of exposure. If pregnancy occurs during use or within 6 months after treatment, report to company (800-593-2214).

Lactation Excretion in breast milk unknown/not recommended

Medication Safety Issues

Sound-alike/look-alike issues:

Ribavirin may be confused with riboflavin

Contraindications Hypersensitivity to ribavirin or any component of the formulation; women of childbearing age who will not use contraception reliably; pregnancy

Additional contraindications for oral formulation: Male partners of pregnant women; $Cl_{cr} < 50$ mL/minute; hemoglobinopathies (eg, thalassemia major, sickle cell anemia); as monotherapy for treatment of chronic hepatitis C; patients with autoimmune hepatitis, anemia, severe heart disease

Refer to individual monographs for Interferon Alfa-2b (Intron® A) and Peginterferon Alfa-2a (Pegasys®) for additional contraindication information.

Warnings/Precautions [U.S. Boxed Warning]: Negative pregnancy test is required before initiation and monthly thereafter. Avoid pregnancy in female patients and female partners of male patients, during therapy, and for at least 6 months after treatment; two forms of contraception should be used. Elderly patients are more susceptible to adverse effects; use caution. Safety and efficacy have not been established in patients who have failed other alpha interferon therapy, received organ transplants, or been coinfected with hepatitis B or HIV (Copegus® may be used in HIV coinfected patients unless CD4+ cell count is <100 cells/microL). **[U.S. Boxed Warning]: Monotherapy not effective for chronic hepatitis C infection.** Safety and efficacy have not been established in patients <3 years of age.

Inhalation: **[U.S. Boxed Warning]: Use with caution in patients requiring assisted ventilation because precipitation of the drug in the respiratory equipment may interfere with safe and effective patient ventilation; sudden deterioration of respiratory function has been observed;** monitor carefully in patients with COPD and asthma for deterioration of respiratory function. Ribavirin is potentially mutagenic, tumor-promoting, and gonadotoxic. Although anemia has not been reported with inhalation therapy, consider monitoring for anemia 1-2 weeks post-treatment. Pregnant healthcare workers may consider unnecessary occupational exposure; ribavirin has been detected in healthcare workers' urine. Healthcare professionals or family members who are pregnant (or may become pregnant) should be counseled about potential risks of exposure and counseled about risk reduction strategies. (Continued)

Ribavirin (Continued)

Oral: Severe psychiatric events have occurred including depression and suicidal behavior during combination therapy. Avoid use in patients with a psychiatric history; discontinue if severe psychiatric symptoms occur. **[U.S. Boxed Warning]: Hemolytic anemia is a significant toxicity; usually occurring within 1-2 weeks.** Assess cardiac disease before initiation. Anemia may worsen underlying cardiac disease; use caution. If any deterioration in cardiovascular status occurs, discontinue therapy. Use caution in pulmonary disease; pulmonary symptoms have been associated with administration. Discontinue therapy in suspected/confirmed pancreatitis or if hepatic decompensation occurs. Use caution in patients with sarcoidosis (exacerbation reported).

Hemolytic anemia (hemoglobin <10 g/dL) was observed in up to 10% of treated patients in clinical trials when alfa interferons were combined with ribavirin; anemia occurred within 1-2 weeks of initiation of therapy.

Dental and periodontal disorders have been reported with ribavirin and interferon therapy.

Adverse Reactions

Inhalation:

1% to 10%:

Central nervous system: Fatigue, headache, insomnia

Gastrointestinal: Nausea, anorexia

Hematologic: Anemia

<1%: Hypotension, cardiac arrest, digitalis toxicity, conjunctivitis, mild bronchospasm, worsening of respiratory function, apnea

Note: Incidence of adverse effects (approximate) in healthcare workers: Headache (51%); conjunctivitis (32%); rhinitis, nausea, rash, dizziness, pharyngitis, and lacrimation (10% to 20%)

Oral (all adverse reactions are documented while receiving combination therapy with interferon alpha-2b or interferon alpha-2a; percentages as reported in adults):

>10%:

Central nervous system: Fatigue (60% to 70%)*, headache (43% to 66%)*, fever (32% to 46%)*, insomnia (26% to 41%), depression (20% to 36%)*, irritability (23% to 32%), dizziness (14% to 26%), impaired concentration (10% to 14%)*, emotional lability (7% to 12%)*

Dermatologic: Alopecia (27% to 36%), pruritus (13% to 29%), dry skin (13% to 24%), rash (5% to 28%), dermatitis (up to 16%)

Gastrointestinal: Nausea (33% to 47%), anorexia (21% to 32%), weight decrease (10% to 29%), diarrhea (10% to 22%), dyspepsia (8% to 16%), vomiting (9% to 14%)*, abdominal pain (8% to 13%), xerostomia (up to 12%), RUQ pain (up to 12%)

Hematologic: Neutropenia (8% to 27%; 40% with HIV coinfection), hemoglobin decreased (25% to 36%), hyperbilirubinemia (24% to 34%), anemia (11% to 17%), lymphopenia (12% to 14%), absolute neutrophil count <0.5 x 10^9/L (5% to 11%), thrombocytopenia (<1% to 14%), hemolytic anemia (10% to 13%), WBC decreased

Neuromuscular & skeletal: Myalgia (40% to 64%)*, rigors (40% to 48%), arthralgia (22% to 34%)*, musculoskeletal pain (19% to 28%)

Respiratory: Dyspnea (13% to 26%), cough (7% to 23%), pharyngitis (up to 13%), sinusitis (up to 12%)*, nasal congestion

Miscellaneous: Flu-like syndrome (13% to 18%)*, viral infection (up to 12%), diaphoresis increased (up to 11%)

*Similar to interferon alone

1% to 10%:

Cardiovascular: Chest pain (5% to 9%)*, flushing (up to 4%)

Central nervous system: Mood alteration (up to 6%; 9% with HIV coinfection), memory impairment (up to 6%), malaise (up to 6%), nervousness (~5%)*

Dermatologic: Eczema (4% to 5%)

Endocrine & metabolic: Hypothyroidism (up to 5%)

Gastrointestinal: Taste perversion (4% to 9%), constipation (up to 5%)

Genitourinary: Menstrual disorder (up to 7%)

Hepatic: Hepatomegaly (up to 4%)

Neuromuscular & skeletal: Weakness (9% to 10%), back pain (5%)

Ocular: Conjunctivitis (up to 6%), blurred vision (up to 5%)

Respiratory: Rhinitis (up to 8%), exertional dyspnea (up to 7%)

Miscellaneous: Fungal infection (up to 6%)

*Similar to interferon alone

<1% (Limited to important or life-threatening): Aggression, angina, anxiety, aplastic anemia, arrhythmia; autoimmune disorders (systemic lupus erythematosus, rheumatoid arthritis, sarcoidosis); cerebral hemorrhage, cholangitis, colitis, coma, diabetes mellitus, fatty liver, gastrointestinal bleeding, gout, hepatic dysfunction, hyper-/hypothyroidism, myositis, pancreatitis, peptic ulcer, peripheral neuropathy, psychosis, pulmonary dysfunction, pulmonary embolism, suicidal ideation, suicide, thrombotic thrombocytopenic purpura, thyroid function test abnormalities

Note: Incidence of anorexia, headache, fever, suicidal ideation, and vomiting are higher in children.

Drug Interactions

Increased Effect/Toxicity: Concomitant use of ribavirin and nucleoside analogues may increase the risk of developing lactic acidosis (includes adefovir, didanosine, lamivudine, stavudine, zalcitabine, zidovudine). Concurrent therapy of zidovudine with ribavirin/interferon alfa-2a may cause increased risk of severe anemia and/or severe neutropenia. Concurrent use with didanosine has been noted to increase the risk of pancreatitis and/or peripheral neuropathy in addition to lactic acidosis. Suspend therapy if signs/symptoms of toxicity are present. Concurrent therapy with Interferons (alfa) may increase the risk of hemolytic anemia.

Decreased Effect: Decreased effect of lamivudine, stavudine, and zidovudine (in vitro).

Ethanol/Nutrition/Herb Interactions Food: Oral: High-fat meal increases the AUC and C_{max}.

Stability

Inhalation: Store vials in a dry place at 15°C to 25°C (59°F to 78°F). Do not use any water containing an antimicrobial agent to reconstitute drug. Reconstituted solution is stable for 24 hours at room temperature. Should not be mixed with other aerosolized medication.

Oral: Store at 15°C to 30°C (59°F to 86°F). Solution may also be refrigerated at 2°C to 8°C (36°F to 46°F).

Mechanism of Action Inhibits replication of RNA and DNA viruses; inhibits influenza virus RNA polymerase activity and inhibits the initiation and elongation of RNA fragments resulting in inhibition of viral protein synthesis

Pharmacodynamics/Kinetics

Absorption: Inhalation: Systemic; dependent upon respiratory factors and method of drug delivery; maximal absorption occurs with the use of aerosol generator via endotracheal tube; highest concentrations in respiratory tract and erythrocytes

Distribution: Oral capsule: Single dose: V_d 2825 L; distribution significantly prolonged in the erythrocyte (16-40 days), which can be used as a marker for intracellular metabolism

Protein binding: Oral: None

Metabolism: Hepatically and intracellularly (forms active metabolites); may be necessary for drug action

Bioavailability: Oral: 64%

Half-life elimination, plasma:

Children: Inhalation: 6.5-11 hours

Adults: Oral:

Capsule, single dose (Rebetol®, Ribasphere™): 24 hours in healthy adults, 44 hours with chronic hepatitis C infection (increases to ~298 hours at steady state)

Tablet, single dose (Copegus®): 120-170 hours

Time to peak, serum: Inhalation: At end of inhalation period; Oral capsule: Multiple doses: 3 hours; Tablet: 2 hours

Excretion: Inhalation: Urine (40% as unchanged drug and metabolites); Oral capsule: Urine (61%), feces (12%)

Dosage

Aerosol inhalation: Infants and children: Use with Viratek® small particle aerosol generator (SPAG-2) at a concentration of 20 mg/mL (6 g reconstituted with 300 mL of sterile water without preservatives). Continuous aerosol administration: 12-18 hours/day for 3 days, up to 7 days in length

Oral capsule or solution: Children ≥3 years: Chronic hepatitis C (in combination with interferon alfa-2b):

Rebetol®: Oral: **Note:** Oral solution should be used in children 3-5 years of age, children ≤25 kg, or those unable to swallow capsules.

Capsule/solution: 15 mg/kg/day in 2 divided doses (morning and evening)

Capsule dosing recommendations:

25-36 kg: 400 mg/day (200 mg morning and evening)

37-49 kg: 600 mg/day (200 mg in the morning and two 200 mg capsules in the evening)

50-61 kg: 800 mg/day (two 200 mg capsules morning and evening)

>61 kg: Refer to Adults dosing

Note: Duration of therapy is 48 weeks in pediatric patients with genotype 1 and 24 weeks in patients with genotype 2,3. Discontinue treatment in any patient if HCV-RNA is not below the limit of detection of the assay after 24 weeks of therapy.

Note: Also refer to Interferon Alfa-2b/Ribavirin combination pack monograph.

Oral capsule (Rebetol®, Ribasphere™): Adults:

Chronic hepatitis C (in combination with interferon alfa-2b):

≤75 kg: 400 mg in the morning, then 600 mg in the evening

>75 kg: 600 mg in the morning, then 600 mg in the evening

Note: If HCV-RNA is undetectable at 24 weeks, duration of therapy is 48 weeks. In patients who relapse following interferon therapy, duration of dual therapy is 24 weeks.

Note: Also refer to Interferon Alfa-2b/Ribavirin combination pack monograph.

Chronic hepatitis C (in combination with peginterferon alfa-2b): 400 mg twice daily; duration of therapy is 1 year; after 24 weeks of treatment, if serum HCV-RNA is not below the limit of detection of the assay, consider discontinuation.

Oral tablet (Copegus®, in combination with peginterferon alfa-2b): Adults: Chronic hepatitis C:

Monoinfection, genotype 1,4:

<75kg: 1000 mg/day in 2 divided doses for 48 weeks

≥75kg: 1200 mg/day in 2 divided doses for 48 weeks

Monoinfection, genotype 2,3: 800 mg/day in 2 divided doses for 24 weeks

Coinfection with HIV: 800 mg/day in 2 divided doses for 48 weeks

Note: Also refer to Peginterferon Alfa-2a monograph.

Dosage adjustment in renal impairment: Cl_{cr} <50 mL/minute: Oral route is contraindicated

Dosage adjustment for toxicity: Oral: Capsule, solution, tablet:

Patient **without** cardiac history:

Hemoglobin <10 g/dL:

Children: 7.5 mg/kg/day

Adults: Decrease dose to 600 mg/day

Hemoglobin <8.5 g/dL: Children and Adults: Permanently discontinue treatment

Patient **with** cardiac history:

Hemoglobin has decreased ≥2 g/dL during any 4-week period of treatment:

Children: 7.5 mg/kg/day

Adults: Decrease dose to 600 mg/day

Hemoglobin <12 g/dL after 4 weeks of reduced dose: Children and Adults: Permanently discontinue treatment

Dietary Considerations When used in combination with interferon alfa-2b, capsules and solution may be taken with or without food, but always in a consistent manner in regard to food intake (ie, always take with food or always take on an empty stomach). When used in combination with peginterferon alfa-2b, capsules should be taken with food. Tablets should be taken with food.

(Continued)

Ribavirin *(Continued)*

Administration

Inhalation: Ribavirin should be administered in well-ventilated rooms (at least 6 air changes/hour). In mechanically-ventilated patients, ribavirin can potentially be deposited in the ventilator delivery system depending on temperature, humidity, and electrostatic forces; this deposition can lead to malfunction or obstruction of the expiratory valve, resulting in inadvertently high positive end-expiratory pressures. The use of one-way valves in the inspiratory lines, a breathing circuit filter in the expiratory line, and frequent monitoring and filter replacement have been effective in preventing these problems. Solutions in SPAG-2 unit should be discarded at least every 24 hours and when the liquid level is low before adding newly reconstituted solution. Should not be mixed with other aerosolized medication.

Oral: Administer concurrently with interferon alfa injection. Capsule should not be opened, crushed, chewed, or broken. Capsules are not for use in children <5 years of age. Use oral solution for children 3-5 years, those ≤25 kg, or those who cannot swallow capsules.

Capsule, in combination with interferon alfa-2b: May be administered with or without food, but always in a consistent manner in regard to food intake.

Capsule, in combination with peginterferon alfa 2b: Administer with food.

Solution, in combination with interferon alfa-2b: May be administered with or without food, but always in a consistent manner in regard to food intake.

Tablet: Should be administered with food.

Monitoring Parameters

Inhalation: Respiratory function, hemoglobin, reticulocyte count, CBC, I & O

Oral: CBC with differential (pretreatment, 2- and 4 weeks after initiation); pretreatment and monthly pregnancy test for women of childbearing age; LFTs, TSH, HCV-RNA after 24 weeks of therapy; ECG in patients with pre-existing cardiac disease; dental exams

Dosage Forms

Capsule: 200 mg

Rebetol®, Ribasphere™: 200 mg

Powder for solution, inhalation [for aerosol administration]:

Virazole®: 6 g [reconstituted product provides 20 mg/mL]

Solution, oral:

Rebetol®: 40 mg/mL (100 mL) [contains sodium benzoate; bubble-gum flavor]

Tablet: 200 mg

Copegus®: 200 mg

Tablet [dose pack]:

RibaPak™: 400 mg (14s), 600 mg (14s)

♦ **Ribavirin and Interferon Alfa-2b Combination Pack** *see* Interferon Alfa-2b and Ribavirin *on page 923*

♦ **Ribo-100** *see* Riboflavin *on page 1506*

Riboflavin *(RYE boe flay vin)*

U.S. Brand Names Ribo-100

Index Terms Lactoflavin; Vitamin B₂; Vitamin G

Pharmacologic Category Vitamin, Water Soluble

Use Prevention of riboflavin deficiency and treatment of ariboflavinosis

Pregnancy Risk Factor A/C (dose exceeding RDA recommendation)

Lactation Enters breast milk/compatible

Medication Safety Issues

Sound-alike/look-alike issues:

Riboflavin may be confused with ribavirin

Warnings/Precautions Riboflavin deficiency often occurs in the presence of other B vitamin deficiencies

Adverse Reactions Frequency not defined: Genitourinary: Discoloration of urine (yellow-orange)

Drug Interactions

Decreased Effect: Decreased absorption with probenecid.

Mechanism of Action Component of flavoprotein enzymes that work together, which are necessary for normal tissue respiration; also needed for activation of pyridoxine and conversion of tryptophan to niacin

Pharmacodynamics/Kinetics

Absorption: Readily via GI tract, however, food increases extent; decreased with hepatitis, cirrhosis, or biliary obstruction

Metabolism: None

Half-life elimination: Biologic: 66-84 minutes

Excretion: Urine (9%) as unchanged drug

Dosage Oral:

Riboflavin deficiency:

Children: 2.5-10 mg/day in divided doses

Adults: 5-30 mg/day in divided doses

Recommended daily allowance:

Children: 0.4-1.8 mg

Adults: 1.2-1.7 mg

Monitoring Parameters CBC and reticulocyte counts (if anemic when treating deficiency)

Test Interactions Large doses may interfere with urinalysis based on spectrometry; may cause false elevations in fluorometric determinations of catecholamines and urobilinogen

Additional Information Dietary sources of riboflavin include liver, kidney, dairy products, green vegetables, eggs, whole grain cereals, yeast, and mushroom.

Dosage Forms

Tablet: 25 mg, 50 mg, 100 mg

Ribo-100: 100 mg

♦ **Rid-A-Pain Dental Drops [OTC]** *see* Benzocaine *on page 204*
♦ **Ridaura®** *see* Auranofin *on page 179*
♦ **RID® Maximum Strength [OTC]** *see* Pyrethrins and Piperonyl Butoxide *on page 1461*
♦ **RID® Mousse (Can)** *see* Pyrethrins and Piperonyl Butoxide *on page 1461*
♦ **Rid® Spray [OTC]** *see* Permethrin *on page 1348*

Rifabutin (rif a BYOO tin)

U.S. Brand Names Mycobutin®
Canadian Brand Names Mycobutin®
Index Terms Ansamycin
Pharmacologic Category Antibiotic, Miscellaneous; Antitubercular Agent
Additional Appendix Information
Antimicrobial Drugs of Choice *on page 1981*
Tuberculosis *on page 2010*
USPHS / IDSA Guidelines for the Prevention of Opportunistic Infections in Persons Infected With HIV *on page 1966*
Use Prevention of disseminated *Mycobacterium avium* complex (MAC) in patients with advanced HIV infection
Unlabeled/Investigational Use Utilized in multidrug regimens for treatment of MAC
Pregnancy Risk Factor B
Lactation Excretion in breast milk unknown
Medication Safety Issues
Sound-alike/look-alike issues:
Rifabutin may be confused with rifampin
Contraindications Hypersensitivity to rifabutin, any other rifamycins, or any component of the formulation; rifabutin is contraindicated in patients with a WBC <1000/mm^3 or a platelet count <50,000/mm^3
Warnings/Precautions Rifabutin as a single agent must not be administered to patients with active tuberculosis since its use may lead to the development of tuberculosis that is resistant to both rifabutin and rifampin; rifabutin should be discontinued in patients with AST >500 units/L or if total bilirubin is >3 mg/dL. Use with caution in patients with liver impairment; modification of dosage should be considered in patients with renal impairment.
Adverse Reactions
>10%:
Dermatologic: Rash
Gastrointestinal: Vomiting, nausea; discoloration of feces, saliva (reddish orange)
Genitourinary: Discoloration of urine (reddish orange)
Miscellaneous: Discoloration of sputum, sweat, and/or tears (reddish orange)
1% to 10%:
Central nervous system: Headache
Gastrointestinal: Abdominal pain, diarrhea, anorexia, flatulence, eructation
Hematologic: Anemia, thrombocytopenia
<1% (Limited to important or life-threatening): Chest pain, dyspnea, leukopenia, neutropenia, uveitis
Overdosage/Toxicology Symptoms include nausea, vomiting, hepatotoxicity, lethargy, and CNS depression. Treatment is supportive. Hemodialysis will remove rifabutin, its effect on outcome is unknown.
Drug Interactions
Cytochrome P450 Effect: Substrate of CYP3A4 (major); **Induces** CYP3A4 (strong)
Increased Effect/Toxicity: Rifabutin may increase the therapeutic effect of clopidogrel; concurrent use with isoniazid may increase risk of hepatotoxicity; the levels/toxicity of rifabutin may be increased by imidazole antifungals, macrolide antibiotics, and protease inhibitors
Decreased Effect: Rifabutin may decrease the levels/effects of alfentanil, amiodarone, angiotensin II receptor blockers (irbesartan, losartan), CYP3A4 substrates (eg, clarithromycin, erythromycin, mirtazapine, nefazodone, venlafaxine), 5-HT$_3$ antagonists, imidazole antifungals, aprepitant, barbiturates, benzodiazepines (metabolized by oxidation), beta blockers, buspirone, calcium channel blockers, chloramphenicol, corticosteroids, cyclosporine, dapsone, disopyramide, estrogen and progestin contraceptives, fluconazole, gefitinib, HMG-CoA reductase inhibitors, methadone, morphine, phenytoin, propafenone, protease inhibitors, quinidine, repaglinide, reverse transcriptase inhibitors (non-nucleoside), tacrolimus, tamoxifen, terbinafine, tocainide, tricyclic antidepressants, warfarin, zaleplon, zolpidem. The effects of rifabutin may be decreased by CYP3A4 inducers (eg, aminoglutethimide, carbamazepine, nafcillin, nevirapine, phenobarbital, phenytoin).
Ethanol/Nutrition/Herb Interactions Food: High-fat meal may decrease the rate but not the extent of absorption.
Mechanism of Action Inhibits DNA-dependent RNA polymerase at the beta subunit which prevents chain initiation
Pharmacodynamics/Kinetics
Absorption: Readily, 53%
Distribution: V$_d$: 9.32 L/kg; distributes to body tissues including the lungs, liver, spleen, eyes, and kidneys
Protein binding: 85%
Metabolism: To active and inactive metabolites
Bioavailability: Absolute: HIV: 20%
Half-life elimination: Terminal: 45 hours (range: 16-69 hours)
Time to peak, serum: 2-4 hours
Excretion: Urine (10% as unchanged drug, 53% as metabolites); feces (10% as unchanged drug, 30% as metabolites)
(Continued)

Rifabutin (Continued)

Dosage Oral:
Children >1 year:
Prophylaxis: 5 mg/kg daily; higher dosages have been used in limited trials
Treatment (unlabeled use): Patients not receiving NNRTIs or protease inhibitors:
Initial phase (2 weeks to 2 months): 10-20 mg/kg daily (maximum: 300 mg).
Second phase: 10-20 mg/kg daily (maximum: 300 mg) or twice weekly
Adults:
Prophylaxis: 300 mg once daily (alone or in combination with azithromycin)
Treatment (unlabeled use):
Patients not receiving NNRTIs or protease inhibitors:
Initial phase: 5 mg/kg daily (maximum: 300 mg)
Second phase: 5 mg/kg daily or twice weekly
Patients receiving nelfinavir, amprenavir, indinavir: Reduce dose to 150 mg/day; no
change in dose if administered twice weekly
Dosage adjustment in renal impairment: Cl_{cr} <30 mL/minute: Reduce dose by 50%

Dietary Considerations May be taken with meals or without food or mix with applesauce.

Administration Should be administered on an empty stomach, but may be taken with meals
to minimize nausea or vomiting.

Monitoring Parameters Periodic liver function tests, CBC with differential, platelet count

Dosage Forms Capsule: 150 mg

♦ **Rifadin®** see Rifampin on page 1508
♦ **Rifampicin** see Rifampin on page 1508

Rifampin (rif AM pin)

U.S. Brand Names Rifadin®

Canadian Brand Names Rifadin®; Rofact™

Index Terms Rifampicin

Pharmacologic Category Antibiotic, Miscellaneous; Antitubercular Agent

Additional Appendix Information
Antibiotic Treatment of Adults With Infective Endocarditis on page 1977
Antimicrobial Drugs of Choice on page 1981
Desensitization Protocols on page 1913
Tuberculosis on page 2010
USPHS / IDSA Guidelines for the Prevention of Opportunistic Infections in Persons Infected
With HIV on page 1966

Use Management of active tuberculosis in combination with other agents; elimination of meningococci from the nasopharynx in asymptomatic carriers

Unlabeled/Investigational Use Prophylaxis of *Haemophilus influenzae* type b infection;
Legionella pneumonia; used in combination with other anti-infectives in the treatment of
staphylococcal infections; treatment of *M. leprae* infections

Pregnancy Risk Factor C

Pregnancy Implications Teratogenic effects have bee reported in animal studies. Rifampin
crosses the human placenta. Due to the risk of tuberculosis to the fetus, treatment is
recommended when the probability of maternal disease is moderate to high. Postnatal
hemorrhages have been reported in the infant and mother with isoniazid administration
during the last few weeks of pregnancy.

Lactation Enters breast milk/not recommended (AAP rates "compatible")

Medication Safety Issues
Sound-alike/look-alike issues:
Rifampin may be confused with rifabutin, Rifamate®, rifapentine, rifaximin
Rifadin® may be confused with Ritalin®

Contraindications Hypersensitivity to rifampin, any rifamycins, or any component of the
formulation; concurrent use of amprenavir, saquinavir/ritonavir (possibly other protease inhibitors)

Warnings/Precautions Use with caution and modify dosage in patients with liver impairment;
observe for hyperbilirubinemia; discontinue therapy if this in conjunction with clinical symptoms or any signs of significant hepatocellular damage develop; since rifampin has
enzyme-inducing properties, porphyria exacerbation is possible; use with caution in patients
with porphyria; do not use for meningococcal disease, only for short-term treatment of
asymptomatic carrier states

Monitor for compliance and effects including hypersensitivity, thrombocytopenia in patients
on intermittent therapy; urine, feces, saliva, sweat, tears, and CSF may be discolored to red/
orange; do not administer I.V. form via I.M. or SubQ routes; restart infusion at another site if
extravasation occurs; remove soft contact lenses during therapy since permanent staining
may occur; regimens of 600 mg once or twice weekly have been associated with a high
incidence of adverse reactions including a flu-like syndrome.

Adverse Reactions
Frequency not defined:
Cardiovascular: Edema, flushing
Central nervous system: Ataxia, behavioral changes, concentration impaired, confusion,
dizziness, drowsiness, fatigue, fever, headache, numbness, psychosis
Dermatologic: Pemphigoid reaction, pruritus, urticaria
Endocrine & metabolic: Adrenal insufficiency, menstrual disorders
Hematologic: Agranulocytosis (rare), DIC, eosinophilia, hemoglobin decreased, hemolysis,
hemolytic anemia, leukopenia, thrombocytopenia (especially with high-dose therapy)
Hepatic: Hepatitis (rare), jaundice
Neuromuscular & skeletal: Myalgia, osteomalacia, weakness
Ocular: Exudative conjunctivitis, visual changes
Renal: Acute renal failure, BUN increased, hemoglobinuria, hematuria, interstitial nephritis,
uric acid increased

Miscellaneous: Flu-like syndrome

1% to 10%:

Dermatologic: Rash (1% to 5%)

Gastrointestinal (1% to 2%): Anorexia, cramps, diarrhea, epigastric distress, flatulence, heartburn, nausea, pseudomembranous colitis, pancreatitis vomiting

Hepatic: LFTs increased (up to 14%)

Overdosage/Toxicology Symptoms include nausea, vomiting, discoloration of bodily fluids, skin, and/or feces, and hepatotoxicity. Treatment is supportive. Lavage with activated charcoal is preferred to ipecac, as emesis is frequently present with overdose. Hemodialysis will remove rifampin, but its effect on outcome is unknown.

Drug Interactions

Cytochrome P450 Effect: Induces CYP1A2 (strong), 2A6 (strong), 2B6 (strong), 2C8 (strong), 2C9 (strong), 2C19 (strong), 3A4 (strong)

Increased Effect/Toxicity: Rifampin may increase the therapeutic effect of clopidogrel; concurrent use with isoniazid, pyrazinamide, or protease inhibitors (amprenavir, saquinavir/ ritonavir) may increase risk of hepatotoxicity; macrolide antibiotics may increase levels/ toxicity of rifampin

Decreased Effect: Rifampin may decrease the levels/effects of the following drugs: Acetaminophen, alfentanil, amiodarone, angiotensin II receptor blockers (irbesartan and losartan), 5-HT₃ antagonists, imidazole antifungals, aprepitant, barbiturates, benzodiazepines (metabolized by oxidation), beta blockers, buspirone, calcium channel blockers, chloramphenicol, corticosteroids, cyclosporine; CYP1A2, 2A6, 2B6, 2C8, 2C9, 2C19, and 3A4 substrates (eg, aminophylline, amiodarone, bupropion, fluoxetine, fluvoxamine, ifosfamide, methsuximide, mirtazapine, nateglinide, pioglitazone, promethazine, proton pump inhibitors, ropinirole, rosiglitazone, selegiline, sertraline, theophylline, venlafaxine, and zafirlukast); dapsone, disopyramide, estrogen and progestin contraceptives, fexofenadine, fluconazole, fusidic acid, gefitinib, HMG-CoA reductase inhibitors, methadone, morphine, phenytoin, propafenone, protease inhibitors, quinidine, repaglinide, reverse transcriptase inhibitors (non-nucleoside), sulfonylureas, tacrolimus, tamoxifen, terbinafine, tocainide, tricyclic antidepressants, warfarin, zaleplon, zidovudine, zolpidem.

Ethanol/Nutrition/Herb Interactions

Ethanol: Avoid ethanol (may increase risk of hepatotoxicity).

Food: Food decreases the extent of absorption; rifampin concentrations may be decreased if taken with food.

Herb/Nutraceutical: St John's wort may decrease rifampin levels.

Stability Rifampin powder is reddish brown. Intact vials should be stored at room temperature and protected from excessive heat and light. Reconstitute powder for injection with SWFI. Prior to injection, dilute in appropriate volume of compatible diluent (eg, 100 mL D₅W). Reconstituted vials are stable for 24 hours at room temperature.

Stability of parenteral admixture at room temperature (25°C) is 4 hours for D₅W and 24 hours for NS.

Mechanism of Action Inhibits bacterial RNA synthesis by binding to the beta subunit of DNA-dependent RNA polymerase, blocking RNA transcription

Pharmacodynamics/Kinetics

Duration: ≤24 hours

Absorption: Oral: Well absorbed; food may delay or slightly reduce peak

Distribution: Highly lipophilic; crosses blood-brain barrier well

Relative diffusion from blood into CSF: Adequate with or without inflammation (exceeds usual MICs)

CSF:blood level ratio: Inflamed meninges: 25%

Protein binding: 80%

Metabolism: Hepatic; undergoes enterohepatic recirculation

Half-life elimination: 3-4 hours; prolonged with hepatic impairment; End-stage renal disease: 1.8-11 hours

Time to peak, serum: Oral: 2-4 hours

Excretion: Feces (60% to 65%) and urine (~30%) as unchanged drug

Dosage Oral (I.V. infusion dose is the same as for the oral route):

Tuberculosis therapy (drug susceptible): Note: A four-drug regimen (isoniazid, rifampin, pyrazinamide, and ethambutol) is preferred for the initial, empiric treatment of TB. When the drug susceptibility results are available, the regimen should be altered as appropriate.

Infants and Children <12 years:

Daily therapy: 10-20 mg/kg/day usually as a single dose (maximum: 600 mg/day)

Twice weekly directly observed therapy (DOT): 10-20 mg/kg (maximum: 600 mg)

Adults:

Daily therapy: 10 mg/kg/day (maximum: 600 mg/day)

Twice weekly directly observed therapy (DOT): 10 mg/kg (maximum: 600 mg); 3 times/ week: 10 mg/kg (maximum: 600 mg)

Latent tuberculosis infection (LTBI): As an alternative to isoniazid:

Children: 10-20 mg/kg/day (maximum: 600 mg/day) for 6 months

Adults: 10 mg/kg/day (maximum: 600 mg/day) for 4 months. **Note:** Combination with pyrazinamide should not generally be offered (*MMWR*, Aug 8, 2003).

***H. influenzae* prophylaxis (unlabeled use):**

Infants and Children: 20 mg/kg every 24 hours for 4 days, not to exceed 600 mg/dose

Adults: 600 mg every 24 hours for 4 days

Leprosy (unlabeled use): Adults:

Multibacillary: 600 mg once monthly for 24 months in combination with ofloxacin and minocycline

Paucibacillary: 600 mg once monthly for 6 months in combination with dapsone

Single lesion: 600 mg as a single dose in combination with ofloxacin 400 mg and minocycline 100 mg

Meningococcal meningitis prophylaxis:

Infants <1 month: 10 mg/kg/day in divided doses every 12 hours for 2 days

Infants ≥1 month and Children: 20 mg/kg/day in divided doses every 12 hours for 2 days (maximum: 600 mg/dose)

(Continued)

Rifampin *(Continued)*

Meningitis *(Pneumococcus* or *Staphylococcus)*: I.V.: Adults: 600 mg once daily
Adults: 600 mg every 12 hours for 2 days

Nasal carriers of *Staphylococcus aureus* (unlabeled use):
Children: 15 mg/kg/day divided every 12 hours for 5-10 days in combination with other antibiotics
Adults: 600 mg/day for 5-10 days in combination with other antibiotics

Synergy for *Staphylococcus aureus* infections (unlabeled use): Adults: 300-600 mg twice daily with other antibiotics

Dosing adjustment in hepatic impairment: Dose reductions may be necessary to reduce hepatotoxicity
Hemodialysis or peritoneal dialysis: Plasma rifampin concentrations are not significantly affected by hemodialysis or peritoneal dialysis.

Dietary Considerations Rifampin should be taken on an empty stomach.

Administration
I.V.: Administer I.V. preparation once daily by slow I.V. infusion over 30 minutes to 3 hours at a final concentration not to exceed 6 mg/mL.
Oral: Administer on an empty stomach (ie, 1 hour prior to, or 2 hours after meals or antacids) to increase total absorption. The compounded oral suspension must be shaken well before using. May mix contents of capsule with applesauce or jelly.

Monitoring Parameters Periodic (baseline and every 2-4 weeks during therapy) monitoring of liver function (AST, ALT, bilirubin), CBC; hepatic status and mental status, sputum culture, chest x-ray 2-3 months into treatment

Test Interactions Positive Coombs' reaction [direct], rifampin inhibits standard assay's ability to measure serum folate and B_{12}; transient increase in LFTs and decreased biliary excretion of contrast media

Dosage Forms
Capsule: 150 mg, 300 mg
Injection, powder for reconstitution: 600 mg

Extemporaneous Preparations For pediatric and adult patients with difficulty swallowing or where lower doses are needed, the package insert lists an extemporaneous liquid suspension as follows:

Rifampin 1% w/v suspension (10 mg/mL) can be compounded using one of four syrups (Syrup NF, simple syrup, Syrpalta® syrup, or raspberry syrup)
Empty contents of four 300 mg capsules or eight 150 mg capsules onto a piece of weighing paper
If necessary, crush contents to produce a fine powder
Transfer powder blend to a 4 oz amber glass or plastic prescription bottle
Rinse paper and spatula with 20 mL of syrup and add the rinse to bottle; shake vigorously
Add 100 mL of syrup to the bottle and shake vigorously

This compounding procedure results in a 1% w/v suspension containing 10 mg rifampin/mL; stability studies indicate suspension is stable at room temperature (25°C ± 3°C) or in refrigerator (2°C to 8°C) for 4 weeks; shake well prior to administration

Rifapentine *(rif a PEN teen)*

U.S. Brand Names Priftin®
Canadian Brand Names Priftin®
Pharmacologic Category Antitubercular Agent
Additional Appendix Information
Tuberculosis *on page 2010*

Use Treatment of pulmonary tuberculosis; rifapentine must always be used in conjunction with at least one other antituberculosis drug to which the isolate is susceptible; it may also be necessary to add a third agent (either streptomycin or ethambutol) until susceptibility is known.

Pregnancy Risk Factor C

Pregnancy Implications Has been shown to be teratogenic in rats and rabbits. Rat offspring showed cleft palates, right aortic arch, and delayed ossification and increased number of ribs. Rabbits displayed ovarian agenesis, pes varus, arhinia, microphthalmia, and irregularities of the ossified facial tissues. Rat studies also show decreased fetal weight, increased number of stillborns, and decreased gestational survival. There are no adequate and well-controlled studies in pregnant women. Rifapentine should be used during pregnancy only if the potential benefits justifies the potential risk to the fetus.

Lactation Excretion in breast milk unknown/contraindicated

Medication Safety Issues
Sound-alike/look-alike issues:
Rifapentine may be confused with rifampin

Contraindications Hypersensitivity to rifapentine, rifampin, rifabutin, any rifamycin analog, or any component of the formulation

Warnings/Precautions Patients with abnormal liver tests and/or liver disease should only be given rifapentine when absolutely necessary and under strict medical supervision. If signs of liver disease occur or worsen, rifapentine should be discontinued. Experience in treating TB in HIV-infected patients is limited.

Rifapentine may produce a red-orange discoloration of body tissues/fluids including skin, teeth, tongue, urine, feces, saliva, sputum, tears, sweat, and cerebral spinal fluid. Contact lenses may become permanently stained. All patients treated with rifapentine should have baseline measurements of liver function tests and enzymes, bilirubin, and a complete blood count. Patients should be seen and monitored monthly and specifically questioned regarding symptoms associated with adverse reactions. Routine laboratory monitoring in people with normal baseline measurements is generally not necessary.

Adverse Reactions
>10%: Endocrine & metabolic: Hyperuricemia (most likely due to pyrazinamide from initiation phase combination therapy)
1% to 10%:
  Cardiovascular: Hypertension
  Central nervous system: Headache, dizziness
  Dermatologic: Rash, pruritus, acne
  Gastrointestinal: Anorexia, nausea, vomiting, dyspepsia, diarrhea
  Genitourinary: Pyuria, proteinuria, hematuria, urinary casts
  Hematologic: Neutropenia, lymphopenia, anemia, leukopenia, thrombocytosis
  Hepatic: Increased ALT, AST
  Neuromuscular & skeletal: Arthralgia, pain
  Respiratory: Hemoptysis
<1% (Limited to important or life-threatening): Aggressive reaction, arthrosis, gout, hepatitis, hyperkalemia, pancreatitis, purpura, thrombocytopenia

Overdosage/Toxicology There is no experience with treatment of acute overdose. Experience with other rifamycins suggests that gastric lavage, followed by activated charcoal, may help adsorb any remaining drug from the GI tract. Hemodialysis or forced diuresis is not expected to enhance elimination of unchanged rifapentine in an overdose.

Drug Interactions
  Cytochrome P450 Effect: Induces CYP2C8 (strong), 2C9 (strong), 3A4 (strong)
  Increased Effect/Toxicity: Rifapentine may increase the therapeutic effect of clopidogrel; concurrent use with isoniazid may increase risk of hepatotoxicity
  Decreased Effect: Rifapentine may decrease the levels/effects of the following drugs: alfentanil, amiodarone, angiotensin II receptor blockers (irbesartan, losartan), 5-HT$_3$ antagonists, imidazole antifungals, aprepitant, barbiturates, benzodiazepines (metabolized by oxidation), beta blockers, buspirone, calcium channel blockers, corticosteroids, cyclosporine; CYP2C8, 2C9 and 3A4 substrates (eg, amiodarone, clarithromycin, erythromycin, fluoxetine, mirtazapine, nateglinide, nefazodone, nevirapine, pioglitazone, rosiglitazone, sertraline, venlafaxine, and zafirlukast); dapsone, disopyramide, estrogen and progestin contraceptives, fluconazole, gefitinib, HMG-CoA reductase inhibitors, methadone, morphine, phenytoin, propafenone, protease inhibitors, quinidine, repaglinide, reverse transcriptase inhibitors (non-nucleoside), tacrolimus, tamoxifen, terbinafine, tocainide, tricyclic antidepressants, warfarin, zaleplon, zidovudine, and zolpidem.

Ethanol/Nutrition/Herb Interactions Food: Food increases AUC and maximum serum concentration by 43% and 44% respectively as compared to fasting conditions.

Stability Store at room temperature (15°C to 30°C; 59°F to 86°F). Protect from excessive heat and humidity.

Mechanism of Action Inhibits DNA-dependent RNA polymerase in susceptible strains of *Mycobacterium tuberculosis* (but not in mammalian cells). Rifapentine is bactericidal against both intracellular and extracellular MTB organisms. MTB resistant to other rifamycins including rifampin are likely to be resistant to rifapentine. Cross-resistance does not appear between rifapentine and other nonrifamycin antimycobacterial agents.

Pharmacodynamics/Kinetics
  Absorption: Food increases AUC and C$_{max}$ by 43% and 44% respectively.
  Distribution: V$_d$: ~70.2 L; rifapentine and metabolite accumulate in human monocyte-derived macrophages with intracellular/extracellular ratios of 24:1 and 7:1 respectively
  Protein binding: Rifapentine and 25-desacetyl metabolite: 97.7% and 93.2%, primarily to albumin
  Metabolism: Hepatic; hydrolyzed by an esterase and esterase enzyme to form the active metabolite 25-desacetyl rifapentine
  Bioavailability: ~70%
  Half-life elimination: Rifapentine: 14-17 hours; 25-desacetyl rifapentine: 13 hours
  Time to peak, serum: 5-6 hours
  Excretion: Urine (17% primarily as metabolites)

Dosage
  Children: No dosing information available
  Adults: **Rifapentine should not be used alone**; initial phase should include a 3- to 4-drug regimen
    Intensive phase (initial 2 months) of short-term therapy: 600 mg (four 150 mg tablets) given twice weekly (with an interval of not less than 72 hours between doses); following the intensive phase, treatment should continue with rifapentine 600 mg once weekly for 4 months in combination with INH or appropriate agent for susceptible organisms
  Dosing adjustment in renal or hepatic impairment: Unknown

Monitoring Parameters Patients with pre-existing hepatic problems should have liver function tests monitored every 2-4 weeks during therapy

Test Interactions Rifampin has been shown to inhibit standard microbiological assays for serum folate and vitamin B$_{12}$; this should be considered for rifapentine; therefore, alternative assay methods should be considered.

Additional Information Rifapentine has only been studied in patients with tuberculosis receiving a 6-month short-course intensive regimen approval. Outcomes have been based on 6-month follow-up treatment observed in clinical trial 008 as a surrogate for the 2-year follow-up generally accepted as evidence for efficacy in the treatment of pulmonary tuberculosis.

Dosage Forms Tablet: 150 mg

Rifaximin (rif AX i min)

U.S. Brand Names Xifaxan™
Pharmacologic Category Antibiotic, Miscellaneous
Use Treatment of travelers' diarrhea caused by noninvasive strains of *E. coli*
Pregnancy Risk Factor C
  (Continued)

Rifaximin *(Continued)*

Pregnancy Implications Teratogenic effects were observed in animal studies. There are no adequate and well-controlled studies in pregnant women.

Lactation Excretion in breast milk unknown/not recommended

Medication Safety Issues
Sound-alike/look-alike issues:
Rifaximin may be confused with rifampin

Contraindications Hypersensitivity to rifaximin, other rifamycin antibiotics, or any component of the formulation; diarrhea with fever or blood in the stool

Warnings/Precautions Efficacy has not been established for the treatment of diarrhea due to pathogens other than *E. coli*, including *C. jejuni*, *Shigella* and *Salmonella*. Consider alternative therapy if symptoms persist or worsen after 24-48 hours of treatment. Not for treatment of systemic infections; <1% is absorbed orally. Safety and efficacy have not been established in children <12 years of age.

Adverse Reactions Incidence of adverse effects reported as ≥2% occurred more in the placebo group than the rifaximin group except for headache.
2% to 10%: Central nervous system: Headache (10%; placebo 9%)
<2%, postmarketing, and/or case reports (limited to important or life-threatening): Abnormal dreams, allergic dermatitis, angioneurotic edema, fatigue, hypersensitivity reactions, insomnia, motion sickness, pruritus, rash, sunburn, tinnitus, urticaria

Overdosage/Toxicology Specific information not available. Treatment should be symptom-directed and supportive.

Drug Interactions
Cytochrome P450 Effect: Induces CYP3A4 (minor)

Stability Store at controlled room temperature of 20°C to 25°C (68°F to 77°F).

Mechanism of Action Rifaximin inhibits bacterial RNA synthesis by binding to bacterial DNA-dependent RNA polymerase.

Pharmacodynamics/Kinetics
Absorption: Oral: <0.4%
Distribution: 80% to 90% in the gut
Half-life elimination: ~6 hours
Excretion: Feces (~97% as unchanged drug); urine (<1%)

Dosage Oral: Children ≥12 years and Adults: Travelers' diarrhea: 200 mg 3 times/day for 3 days

Dietary Considerations May be taken with or without food.

Administration May be administered with or without food.

Monitoring Parameters Temperature, blood in stool, change in symptoms

Dosage Forms Tablet: 200 mg

♦ **rIFN-A** *see* Interferon Alfa-2a *on page 918*
♦ **rIFN beta-1a** *see* Interferon Beta-1a *on page 926*
♦ **rIFN beta-1b** *see* Interferon Beta-1b *on page 928*
♦ **RIG** *see* Rabies Immune Globulin (Human) *on page 1478*
♦ **rIL-11** *see* Oprelvekin *on page 1270*
♦ **Rilutek**® *see* Riluzole *on page 1512*

Riluzole *(RIL yoo zole)*

U.S. Brand Names Rilutek®
Canadian Brand Names Rilutek®
Index Terms 2-Amino-6-Trifluoromethoxy-benzothiazole; RP-54274
Pharmacologic Category Glutamate Inhibitor
Use Treatment of amyotrophic lateral sclerosis (ALS); riluzole can extend survival or time to tracheostomy
Pregnancy Risk Factor C
Pregnancy Implications Impaired fertility, decreased implantation, increased intrauterine death, and adverse effects on offspring growth and viability were observed in animal studies. There are no adequate or well-controlled studies in pregnant women.
Lactation Excretion in breast milk unknown/not recommended
Contraindications Severe hypersensitivity reactions to riluzole or any component of the formulation
Warnings/Precautions Among 4000 patients given riluzole for ALS, there were 3 cases of marked neutropenia (ANC <500/mm³), all seen within the first 2 months of treatment. Use with caution in patients with concomitant renal insufficiency. Use with caution in patients with current evidence or history of abnormal liver function; do not administer if baseline liver function tests are elevated. The elderly, female, or Japanese patients may have decreased clearance of riluzole; use with caution. May cause dizziness or somnolence; caution should be used performing tasks which require alertness (operating machinery or driving).
Adverse Reactions
>10%:
Gastrointestinal: Nausea (12% to 21%)
Neuromuscular & skeletal: Weakness (15% to 20%)
Respiratory: Lung function decreased (10% to 16%)
1% to 10%:
Cardiovascular: Edema, hypertension, tachycardia
Central nervous system: Agitation, circumoral paresthesia, depression, dizziness, headache, insomnia, malaise, somnolence, tremor, vertigo
Dermatologic: Alopecia, eczema, pruritus
Gastrointestinal: Abdominal pain, anorexia, diarrhea, dyspepsia, flatulence, oral moniliasis, stomatitis, vomiting
Hepatic: Liver function tests increased
Neuromuscular & skeletal: Arthralgia, back pain

Respiratory: Cough increased, rhinitis, sinusitis

Miscellaneous: Aggravation reaction

<1% (Limited to important or life-threatening): Exfoliative dermatitis, neutropenia, postural hypertension, seizure

Overdosage/Toxicology Methemoglobinemia has been reported with overdose. No specific antidote or treatment information is available. Treatment should be supportive and directed toward alleviating symptoms.

Drug Interactions

Cytochrome P450 Effect: Substrate of CYP1A2 (major)

Increased Effect/Toxicity: CYP1A2 inhibitors may increase the levels/effects of riluzole; example inhibitors include amiodarone, ciprofloxacin, fluvoxamine, ketoconazole, norfloxacin, ofloxacin, and rofecoxib.

Decreased Effect: CYP1A2 inducers may decrease the levels/effects of riluzole; example inducers include aminoglutethimide, carbamazepine, phenobarbital, and rifampin.

Ethanol/Nutrition/Herb Interactions

Ethanol: Avoid ethanol (due to CNS depression and possible risk of liver toxicity).

Food: A high-fat meal decreases absorption of riluzole (decreasing AUC by 20% and peak blood levels by 45%). Charbroiled food may increase riluzole elimination.

Stability Store at 20°C to 25°C (68°F to 77°F). Protect from bright light.

Mechanism of Action Mechanism of action is not known. Pharmacologic properties include inhibitory effect on glutamate release, inactivation of voltage-dependent sodium channels; and ability to interfere with intracellular events that follow transmitter binding at excitatory amino acid receptors

Pharmacodynamics/Kinetics

Absorption: 90%; high-fat meal decreases AUC by 20% and peak blood levels by 45%

Protein binding, plasma: 96%, primarily to albumin and lipoproteins

Metabolism: Extensively hepatic to six major and a number of minor metabolites via CYP1A2 dependent hydroxylation and glucuronidation

Bioavailability: Oral: Absolute: 60%

Half-life elimination: 12 hours

Excretion: Urine (90%; 85% as metabolites, 2% as unchanged drug) and feces (5%) within 7 days

Dosage Adults: Oral: 50 mg every 12 hours; no increased benefit can be expected from higher daily doses, but adverse events are increased

Dosage adjustment in smoking: Cigarette smoking is known to induce CYP1A2; patients who smoke cigarettes would be expected to eliminate riluzole faster. There is no information, however, on the effect of, or need for, dosage adjustment in these patients.

Dosage adjustment in special populations: Females and Japanese patients may possess a lower metabolic capacity to eliminate riluzole compared with male and Caucasian subjects, respectively

Dosage adjustment in renal impairment: Use with caution in patients with concomitant renal insufficiency

Dosage adjustment in hepatic impairment: Use with caution in patients with current evidence or history of abnormal liver function indicated by significant abnormalities in serum transaminase, bilirubin or GGT levels. Baseline elevations of several LFTs (especially elevated bilirubin) should preclude use of riluzole.

Dietary Considerations Take at least 1 hour before, or 2 hours after, a meal.

Administration Administer at the same time each day, 1 hour before or 2 hours after a meal.

Monitoring Parameters Monitor serum aminotransferases including ALT levels before and during therapy. Evaluate serum ALT levels every month during the first 3 months of therapy, every 3 months during the remainder of the first year and periodically thereafter. Evaluate ALT levels more frequently in patients who develop elevations. Maximum increases in serum ALT usually occurred within 3 months after the start of therapy and were usually transient when <5 times ULN (upper limits of normal).

In trials, if ALT levels were <5 times ULN, treatment continued and ALT levels usually returned to below 2 times ULN within 2-6 months. There is no experience with continued treatment of ALS patients once ALT values exceed 5 times ULN.

If a decision is made to continue treatment in patients when the ALT exceeds 5 times ULN, frequent monitoring (at least weekly) of complete liver function is recommended. Discontinue treatment if ALT exceeds 10 times ULN or if clinical jaundice develops. Monitor temperature, especially during first 2 months of therapy.

Dosage Forms Tablet: 50 mg

Rimantadine (ri MAN ta deen)

U.S. Brand Names Flumadine®

Canadian Brand Names Flumadine®

Index Terms Rimantadine Hydrochloride

Pharmacologic Category Antiviral Agent, Adamantane

Additional Appendix Information

Community-Acquired Pneumonia in Adults *on page 1999*

USPHS / IDSA Guidelines for the Prevention of Opportunistic Infections in Persons Infected With HIV *on page 1966*

Use Prophylaxis (adults and children >1 year of age) and treatment (adults) of influenza A viral infection (per manufacturer labeling; also refer to current CDC guidelines for recommendations during current flu season)

Pregnancy Risk Factor C

Pregnancy Implications Embryotoxic in high dose rat studies.

Lactation Excretion in breast milk unknown/ not recommended

Medication Safety Issues

Sound-alike/look-alike issues:

Rimantadine may be confused with amantadine, ranitidine, Rimactane®

(Continued)

Rimantadine *(Continued)*

Flumadine® may be confused with fludarabine, flunisolide, flutamide

Contraindications Hypersensitivity to drugs of the adamantine class, including rimantadine and amantadine, or any component of the formulation

Warnings/Precautions Use with caution in patients with renal and hepatic dysfunction; avoid use, if possible, in patients with recurrent and eczematoid dermatitis, uncontrolled psychosis, or severe psychoneurosis. An increase in seizure incidence may occur in patients with seizure disorders; discontinue drug if seizures occur; resistance may develop during treatment; viruses exhibit cross-resistance between amantadine and rimantadine. Due to increased resistance, in June 2006, the CDC recommended that rimantadine no longer be used for the treatment or prophylaxis of influenza A in the United States until susceptibility has been re-established.

Adverse Reactions

1% to 10%:

Central nervous system: Dizziness (2%), insomnia (2%), anxiety (1%), fatigue (1%), headache (1%), nervousness (1%)

Gastrointestinal: Nausea (3%), anorexia (2%), vomiting (2%), xerostomia (2%), abdominal pain (1%)

Neuromuscular and skeletal: Weakness (1%)

<1% (Limited to important or life-threatening): Agitation, ataxia, bronchospasm, cardiac failure, concentration impaired, confusion, convulsions, cough, depression, diarrhea, dyspepsia, dyspnea, euphoria, gait abnormality, hallucinations, heart block, hyperkinesias, hypertension, lactation, palpitation, pallor, parosmia, pedal edema, rash, somnolence, syncope, tachycardia, taste alteration, tinnitus, tremor

Overdosage/Toxicology Agitation, hallucinations, ventricular cardiac arrhythmias (torsade de pointes and PVCs), slurred speech, anticholinergic effects (dry mouth, urinary retention and mydriasis), ataxia, tremor, myoclonus, seizures, and death have been reported with amantadine (a related drug). Treatment is symptomatic (do not use physostigmine). Tachyarrhythmias may be treated with beta-blockers such as propranolol. Dialysis is not recommended except possibly in renal failure.

Drug Interactions

Increased Effect/Toxicity: Cimetidine increases blood levels/toxicity of rimantadine.

Decreased Effect: Acetaminophen may cause a small reduction in AUC and peak concentration of rimantadine. Peak plasma and AUC concentrations of rimantadine are slightly reduced by aspirin.

Ethanol/Nutrition/Herb Interactions Food: Food does not affect rate or extent of absorption

Mechanism of Action Exerts its inhibitory effect on three antigenic subtypes of influenza A virus (H1N1, H2N2, H3N2) early in the viral replicative cycle, possibly inhibiting the uncoating process; it has no activity against influenza B virus and is two- to eightfold more active than amantadine

Pharmacodynamics/Kinetics

Onset of action: Antiviral activity: No data exist establishing a correlation between plasma concentration and antiviral effect

Absorption: Tablet and syrup formulations are equally absorbed

Metabolism: Extensively hepatic

Half-life elimination: 25.4 hours; prolonged in elderly

Time to peak: 6 hours

Excretion: Urine (<25% as unchanged drug)

Clearance: Hemodialysis does not contribute to clearance

Dosage Oral:

Prophylaxis:

Children 1-10 years: 5 mg/kg/day; maximum: 150 mg/day

Children >10 years and Adults: 100 mg twice daily

Elderly: 100 mg/day in nursing home patients or all elderly patients who may experience adverse effects using the adult dose

Treatment:

Adults: 100 mg twice daily

Elderly: 100 mg once daily in patients ≥65 years

Dosage adjustment in renal impairment:

Cl$_{cr}$ >10 mL/minute: Dose adjustment not required

Cl$_{cr}$ ≤10 mL/minute: 100 mg/day

Dosage adjustment in hepatic impairment: Severe dysfunction: 100 mg/day

Administration Initiation of rimantadine within 48 hours of the onset of influenza A illness halves the duration of illness and significantly reduces the duration of viral shedding and increased peripheral airways resistance; continue therapy for 5-7 days after symptoms begin

Monitoring Parameters Monitor for CNS or GI effects in elderly or patients with renal or hepatic impairment

Dosage Forms

Syrup, as hydrochloride:

Flumadine®: 50 mg/5 mL (240 mL) [raspberry flavor]

Tablet, as hydrochloride: 100 mg

Flumadine®: 100 mg

♦ **Rimantadine Hydrochloride** *see* Rimantadine *on page 1513*

Rimexolone *(ri MEKS oh lone)*

U.S. Brand Names Vexol®

Canadian Brand Names Vexol®

Pharmacologic Category Corticosteroid, Ophthalmic

Use Treatment of inflammation after ocular surgery and the treatment of anterior uveitis

Pregnancy Risk Factor C

Medication Safety Issues

Sound-alike/look-alike issues:

Vexol® may be confused with VoSol®

Contraindications Hypersensitivity to rimexolone or any component of the formulation; fungal, viral, or untreated pus-forming bacterial ocular infections

Warnings/Precautions Prolonged use has been associated with the development of corneal or scleral perforation and posterior subcapsular cataracts; may mask or enhance the establishment of acute purulent untreated infections of the eye; may delay healing after cataract surgery; intraocular pressure should be monitored if this product is used >10 days; effectiveness and safety have not been established in children.

Adverse Reactions

1% to 10%: Ocular: Temporary mild blurred vision

<1% (Limited to important or life-threatening): Burning or stinging eyes, cataracts, corneal thinning, glaucoma, increased intraocular pressure, optic nerve damage, secondary ocular infection, visual acuity defects

Mechanism of Action Decreases inflammation by suppression of migration of polymorphonuclear leukocytes and reversal of increased capillary permeability

Pharmacodynamics/Kinetics

Absorption: Through aqueous humor

Metabolism: Hepatic for any amount of drug absorbed

Excretion: Urine and feces

Dosage Adults: Ophthalmic: Instill 1 drop in conjunctival sac 2-4 times/day up to every 4 hours; may use every 1-2 hours during first 1-2 days

Monitoring Parameters Intraocular pressure and periodic examination of lens (with prolonged use)

Dosage Forms Suspension, ophthalmic: 1% (5 mL, 10 mL) [contains benzalkonium chloride]

♦ **Riomet**™ *see* Metformin *on page 1098*

♦ **Riopan Plus**® **[OTC] [DSC]** *see* Magaldrate and Simethicone *on page 1045*

♦ **Riopan Plus**® **Double Strength [OTC] [DSC]** *see* Magaldrate and Simethicone *on page 1045*

♦ **Riphenidate (Can)** *see* Methylphenidate *on page 1119*

Risedronate (ris ED roe nate)

U.S. Brand Names Actonel®

Canadian Brand Names Actonel®

Index Terms Risedronate Sodium

Pharmacologic Category Bisphosphonate Derivative

Use Paget's disease of the bone; treatment and prevention of glucocorticoid-induced osteoporosis; treatment and prevention of osteoporosis in postmenopausal women; treatment of osteoporosis in men

Pregnancy Risk Factor C

Pregnancy Implications Teratogenic and nonteratogenic embryo/fetal effects have been reported in animal studies. There are no adequate and well-controlled studies in pregnant women. Bisphosphonates are incorporated into the bone matrix and gradually released over time. Theoretically, there may be a risk of fetal harm when pregnancy follows the completion of therapy. Based on limited case reports with pamidronate, serum calcium levels in the newborn may be altered if administered during pregnancy.

Lactation Excretion in breast milk unknown/not recommended

Contraindications Hypersensitivity to risedronate, bisphosphonates, or any component of the formulation; hypocalcemia; abnormalities of the esophagus which delay esophageal emptying such as stricture or achalasia; inability to stand or sit upright for at least 30 minutes; severe renal impairment (Cl_{cr} <30 mL/minute)

Warnings/Precautions Bisphosphonates may cause upper gastrointestinal disorders such as dysphagia, esophagitis, esophageal ulcer, and gastric ulcer. Use caution in patients with renal impairment (not recommended in patients with a Cl_{cr} <30 mL/minute). Hypocalcemia must be corrected before therapy initiation with risedronate. Ensure adequate calcium and vitamin D intake, especially for patients with Paget's disease in whom the pretreatment rate of bone turnover may be greatly elevated.

Bisphosphonate therapy has been associated with osteonecrosis, primarily of the jaw; this has been observed mostly in cancer patients, but also in patients with postmenopausal osteoporosis and other diagnoses. Dental exams and preventative dentistry should be performed prior to placing patients with risk factors on chronic bisphosphonate therapy. Invasive dental procedures should be avoided during treatment.

Infrequently, severe (and occasionally debilitating) bone, joint, and/or muscle pain have been reported during bisphosphonate treatment. The onset of pain ranged from a single day to several months. Symptoms usually resolve upon discontinuation. Some patients experienced recurrence when rechallenged with same drug or another bisphosphonate; avoid use in patients with a history of these symptoms in association with bisphosphonate therapy.

Safety and efficacy in pediatric patients have not been established.

Adverse Reactions Frequency may vary with dose and indication.

>10%:

Central nervous system: Headache (18%), pain (14%)

Dermatologic: Rash (8% to 12%)

Gastrointestinal: Diarrhea (11% to 20%), abdominal pain (12%)

Genitourinary: Urinary tract infection (11%)

Neuromuscular & skeletal: Arthralgia (14% to 33%), back pain (26%)

1% to 10%:

Cardiovascular: Hypertension (10%), peripheral edema (8%), chest pain (5% to 7%), cardiovascular disorder (3%), angina (3%), arrhythmia (2%)

(Continued)

Risedronate *(Continued)*

Central nervous system: Depression (7%), dizziness (6% to 7%), insomnia (5%), anxiety (4%)

Dermatologic: Pruritus (3%)

Gastrointestinal: Constipation (7%), nausea (7%), flatulence (5%), belching (3%), colitis (3%), gastritis (3%)

Genitourinary: Prostatic hyperplasia (5%), cystitis (4%), nephrolithiasis (3%)

Hematologic: Anemia (2%)

Neuromuscular & skeletal: Joint disorder (7%), myalgia (7%), neck pain (5%), bone pain (5%), weakness (5%), neuralgia (4%), leg cramps (4%), myasthenia (3%), tendon disorder (3%)

Ocular: Cataract (6%), dry eyes (3%)

Respiratory: Pharyngitis (6%), rhinitis (6%), sinusitis (5%), dyspnea (4%), bronchitis (3%)

Miscellaneous: Flu symptoms (10%), neoplasm (3%), hernia (3%)

<1% (Limited to important or life-threatening): Angioedema, bullous skin reaction, duodenitis, glossitis, hypersensitivity reaction, iritis, liver function test abnormality, musculoskeletal pain (rarely severe or incapacitating), osteonecrosis, uveitis

Overdosage/Toxicology Symptoms include hypophosphatemia and upper GI adverse events (upset stomach, heartburn, esophagitis, gastritis, or ulcer). Signs and symptoms of hypocalcemia may also occur in some patients. Milk or antacids containing calcium should be given to bind Actonel® and reduce absorption of the drug. Decreases in serum calcium and phosphorus following substantial overdose may be expected in some patients. In cases of substantial overdose, use of gastric lavage to remove unabsorbed drug and I.V. calcium may be required. Standard procedures that are effective for treating hypocalcemia, including the administration of calcium intravenously, would be expected to restore physiologic amounts of ionized calcium and to relieve signs and symptoms of hypocalcemia.

Drug Interactions

Increased Effect/Toxicity:

Aminoglycosides may lower serum calcium levels with prolonged administration; concomitant use may have an additive hypocalcemic effect. NSAIDs may enhance the gastrointestinal adverse/toxic effects (increased incidence of GI ulcers) of bisphosphonate derivatives. Bisphosphonate derivatives may enhance the hypocalcemic effect of phosphate supplements.

Decreased Effect: The following agents may decrease the absorption of oral bisphosphonate derivatives: Antacids (aluminum, calcium, magnesium), oral calcium salts, oral iron salts, and oral magnesium salts

Ethanol/Nutrition/Herb Interactions

Ethanol: Avoid ethanol (may increase risk of osteoporosis).

Food: Food may reduce absorption (similar to other bisphosphonates); mean oral bioavailability is decreased when given with food.

Stability Store at room temperature of 20°C to 25°C (68°F to 77°F).

Mechanism of Action A bisphosphonate which inhibits bone resorption via actions on osteoclasts or on osteoclast precursors; decreases the rate of bone resorption, leading to an indirect increase in bone mineral density. In Paget's disease, characterized by disordered resorption and formation of bone, inhibition of resorption leads to an indirect decrease in bone formation; but the newly-formed bone has a more normal architecture.

Pharmacodynamics/Kinetics

Onset of action: May require weeks

Absorption: Rapid

Distribution: V_d: 6.3 L/kg

Protein binding: ~24%

Metabolism: None

Bioavailability: Poor, ~0.54% to 0.75%

Half-life elimination: Initial: 1.5 hours; Terminal: 480 hours

Excretion: Urine (up to 85%); feces (as unabsorbed drug)

Dosage Oral: Adults:

Paget's disease of bone: 30 mg once daily for 2 months

Retreatment may be considered (following post-treatment observation of at least 2 months) if relapse occurs, or if treatment fails to normalize serum alkaline phosphatase. For retreatment, the dose and duration of therapy are the same as for initial treatment. No data are available on more than one course of retreatment.

Osteoporosis (postmenopausal) prevention and treatment: 5 mg once daily or 35 mg once weekly

Osteoporosis (male) treatment: 35 mg once weekly

Osteoporosis (glucocorticoid-induced) prevention and treatment: 5 mg once daily

Dosage adjustment in renal impairment: Cl_{cr} <30 mL/minute: **Not** recommended for use

Dietary Considerations Take ≥30 minutes before the first food or drink of the day other than water. Supplemental calcium or vitamin D may be required if dietary intake is not adequate.

Administration It is imperative to administer risedronate 30-60 minutes before the patient takes any food, drink, or other medications orally to avoid interference with absorption. The patient should take risedronate on an empty stomach with a full glass (8 oz) of **plain water** (not mineral water) and avoid lying down for 30 minutes after swallowing tablet to help delivery to stomach. Tablet should be swallowed whole; do not crush or chew.

Monitoring Parameters Alkaline phosphatase should be periodically measured; serum calcium, phosphorus; monitor pain and fracture rate; bone mineral density

Reference Range Calcium (total): Adults: 9.0-11.0 mg/dL (2.05-2.54 mmol/L), may slightly decrease with aging; phosphorus: 2.5-4.5 mg/dL (0.81-1.45 mmol/L)

Test Interactions Bisphosphonates may interfere with diagnostic imaging agents such as technetium-99m-diphosphonate in bone scans.

Dosage Forms

Tablet, as sodium:

Actonel®: 5 mg, 30 mg, 35 mg

Risedronate and Calcium (ris ED roc nate & KAL see um)

U.S. Brand Names Actonel® and Calcium
Index Terms Calcium and Risedronate; Risedronate Sodium and Calcium Carbonate
Pharmacologic Category Bisphosphonate Derivative; Calcium Salt
Use Treatment and prevention of osteoporosis in postmenopausal women
Pregnancy Risk Factor C
Dosage
   Oral: Adults: Osteoporosis in postmenopausal females:
      Risedronate: 35 mg once weekly on day 1 of 7-day treatment cycle
      Calcium carbonate: 1250 mg (elemental calcium 500 mg) once daily on days 2 through 7 of
      7-day treatment cycle
   Dosage adjustment in renal impairment: Cl$_{cr}$ <30 mL/minute: Not recommended for use
Additional Information Complete prescribing information for this medication should be
   consulted for additional detail.
Dosage Forms Combination package [each package contains]:
   Tablet (Actonel®): Risedronate 35 mg (4s)
   Tablet: Calcium carbonate 1250 mg (24s) [equivalent to elemental calcium 500 mg]

♦ **Risedronate Sodium** see Risedronate on page 1515
♦ **Risedronate Sodium and Calcium Carbonate** see Risedronate and Calcium on page 1517
♦ **Risperdal®** see Risperidone on page 1517
♦ **Risperdal M-Tab** see Risperidone on page 1517
♦ **Risperdal® M-Tab®** see Risperidone on page 1517
♦ **Risperdal® Consta®** see Risperidone on page 1517

Risperidone (ris PER i done)

U.S. Brand Names Risperdal®; Risperdal® Consta®; Risperdal® M-Tab®
Canadian Brand Names Apo-Risperidone®; Risperdal®; Risperdal® Consta®; Risperdal®
   M-Tab®
Index Terms Risperdal M-Tab
Pharmacologic Category Antipsychotic Agent, Atypical
Additional Appendix Information
   Antipsychotic Agents on page 1872
Use Treatment of schizophrenia; treatment of acute mania or mixed episodes associated with
   bipolar I disorder (as monotherapy or in combination with lithium or valproate); treatment of
   irritability/aggression associated with autistic disorder
Unlabeled/Investigational Use Behavioral symptoms associated with dementia in elderly;
   treatment of Tourette's disorder; treatment of pervasive developmental disorder
Pregnancy Risk Factor C
Pregnancy Implications Animal studies indicate an increase in fetal mortality. Reversible
   EPS symptoms were noted in neonates following use of risperidone during the last trimester.
   There are no adequate and well-controlled studies in pregnant women.
Lactation Enters breast milk/not recommended
Medication Safety Issues
   Sound-alike/look-alike issues:
      Risperidone may be confused with reserpine
      Risperdal® may be confused with lisinopril, reserpine
Contraindications Hypersensitivity to risperidone or any component of the formulation
**Warnings/Precautions [U.S. Boxed Warning]: Patients with dementia-related behavioral
   disorders treated with atypical antipsychotics are at an increased risk of death
   compared to placebo.** An increased incidence of cerebrovascular adverse events (including
   fatalities) has been reported in elderly patients with dementia-related psychosis. Risk may be
   increased by dehydration; use caution with concurrent diuretics. Risperidone is not approved
   for the treatment of dementia-related psychosis.

   Low to moderately sedating, use with caution in disorders where CNS depression is a
   feature. Use with caution in Parkinson's disease. Caution in patients with predisposition to
   seizures; or severe cardiac disease. Use with caution in renal or hepatic dysfunction; dose
   reduction recommended. Esophageal dysmotility and aspiration have been associated with
   antipsychotic use; use with caution in patients at risk of aspiration pneumonia (eg,
   Alzheimer's disease). May elevate prolactin levels; effects seen in adults and children. Use
   with caution in breast cancer or other prolactin-dependent tumors. May alter temperature
   regulation. May mask toxicity of other drugs or conditions (eg intestinal obstruction, Reyes
   syndrome, brain tumor) due to antiemetic effects.

   May cause orthostasis. Use with caution in patients with cardiovascular diseases (eg, heart
   failure, history of myocardial infarction or ischemia, cerebrovascular disease, conduction
   abnormalities). Use caution in patients receiving medications for hypertension (orthostatic
   effects may be exacerbated) or in patients with hypovolemia or dehydration. May alter
   cardiac conduction (low risk relative to other neuroleptics); life-threatening arrhythmias have
   occurred with therapeutic doses of neuroleptics.

   May cause anticholinergic effects (confusion, agitation, constipation, xerostomia, blurred
   vision, urinary retention); therefore, they should be used with caution in patients with
   decreased gastrointestinal motility, urinary retention, BPH, xerostomia, or visual problems.
   Conditions which also may be exacerbated by cholinergic blockade include narrow-angle
   glaucoma (screening is recommended) and worsening of myasthenia gravis. Relative to
   other neuroleptics, risperidone has a low potency of cholinergic blockade.

   May cause extrapyramidal symptoms, including pseudoparkinsonism, acute dystonic reactions, akathisia, and tardive dyskinesia (risk of these reactions is low relative to other neuroleptics, and is dose dependent). Risk of neuroleptic malignant syndrome (NMS) may be
   (Continued)

Risperidone *(Continued)*

increased in patients with Parkinson's disease or Lewy Body Dementia; monitor for symptoms of confusion, obtundation, postural instability and extrapyramidal symptoms. May cause hyperglycemia; in some cases may be extreme and associated with ketoacidosis, hyperosmolar coma, or death. Use with caution in patients with diabetes or other disorders of glucose regulation; monitor for worsening of glucose control. Significant weight gain has been observed with antipsychotic therapy; incidence varies with product.

The possibility of a suicide attempt is inherent in psychotic illness or bipolar disorder; use caution in high-risk patients during initiation of therapy. Prescriptions should be written for the smallest quantity consistent with good patient care. Safety and efficacy have not been established in children for schizophrenia or bipolar disorder. Long-term effects on growth or sexual maturation have not been evaluated.

Adverse Reactions

The frequency of adverse effects is reported as absolute percentages and is not based upon net frequencies as compared to placebo. Unless otherwise noted, frequency of adverse effects is reported for the oral formulation in adults.

>10%:

Central nervous system: Fatigue (adults 4%; children 42%), extrapyramidal symptoms (adults 17% to 34%; children 28%), somnolence (adults 3% to 28%; children 67%), insomnia (23% to 26%), agitation (8% to 26%), anxiety (4% to 20%), dystonia (adults 18%; children 12%), akathisia (16%), headache (12% to 14%), dizziness (4% to 11%)

Gastrointestinal: Appetite increased (children 49%), salivation increased (adults up to 5%; children 22%), weight gain (adults 2% to 18%; children 5%), constipation (adults 7% to 13%; children 21%), xerostomia (adults 3% to ≥5%; children 13%), dyspepsia (5% to 11%), nausea (4% to 11%)

Neuromuscular & skeletal: Tremor (children 12%)

Respiratory: Upper respiratory infection (adults 3%; children 34%)

1% to 10%:

Cardiovascular: Tachycardia (adults 3% to 5%; children 7%), hypertension (3%), chest pain (2% to 3%), hypotension (2%; especially orthostatic)

Central nervous system: Mania (8%), automatism (children 7%), pseudoparkinsonism (adults 6%; children 7%), dreaming increased (≥5%), sleep prolonged (≥5%), confusion (children 5%), pain (5%), fever (2% to 3%), aggressiveness (1% to 3%), concentration impaired (2%), hypoesthesia (2%), tardive dyskinesia, neuroleptic malignant syndrome, altered central temperature regulation, nervousness, sleep duration increased

Dermatologic: Rash (2% to 5%), dry skin (2% to 4%), acne (2%), pruritus (2%), seborrhea (up to 1%), pigmentation increased, photosensitivity

Endocrine & metabolic: Sexual dysfunction (3%), menorrhagia (≥5%), galactorrhea (children 1%), gynecomastia (children 2%)

Gastrointestinal: Vomiting (5% to 7%), diarrhea (≥5%), abdominal pain (1% to 4%), toothache (up to 2%), anorexia

Genitourinary: Micturition disturbances (≥5%)

Hematologic: Anemia (≥1% I.M. injection)

Hepatic: Transaminases increased (≥1% I.M. injection)

Neuromuscular & skeletal: Dyskinesia (children 7%), myalgia (5%), arthralgia (2% to 3%), skeletal pain (2%), back pain (up to 2%)

Ocular: Abnormal vision (1% to 6%), accommodation disturbances (≥5%)

Renal: Polydipsia, polyuria

Respiratory: Rhinitis (3% to 10%), sinusitis (1% to 4%), cough (2% to 3%), pharyngitis (2% to 3%), dyspnea (up to 1%)

Miscellaneous: Injury (2%)

≤1% (Limited to important or life-threatening): Allergic reaction, amenorrhea, amnesia, anaphylactic reaction, anemias (oral formulations), angina pectoris, angioedema, antidiuretic hormone disorder, aphasia, apnea, ascites, aspiration, asthma, atrial fibrillation, AV block, bronchospasm, cachexia, catatonic reaction, cerebrovascular accident, cerebrovascular disorder, cholecystitis, cholelithiasis, cholestatic hepatitis, cholinergic syndrome, coma, creatine phosphokinase increase, dehydration, delirium, depression, diabetes mellitus, diabetic ketoacidosis, diverticulitis, dysphagia, esophagitis, esophageal dysmotility, fecal incontinence, flu-like symptoms, flushing, gastroenteritis, hematemesis, hematuria, hemorrhage, hepatic failure, hepatocellular damage, hyper-/hypoglycemia, hyperphosphatemia, hypertriglyceridemia, hyperuricemia, hypokalemia, hyponatremia, hypoproteinemia, flu-like symptoms, intestinal obstruction, jaundice, leukocytosis, leukopenia, leukorrhea, liver enzymes increased (oral formulations), lymphadenopathy, mastitis, menstrual irregularities, migraine, myocardial infarction, myocarditis, palpitation, pancreatitis, Pelger-Huët anomaly, pituitary adenomas, pneumonia, precocious puberty, premature atrial contractions, priapism, pulmonary embolism, purpura, QT$_c$ prolongation, RBC disorders, renal insufficiency, rigors, sarcoidosis, skin exfoliation, skin ulceration, ST depression, stomatitis, stridor, stroke, superficial phlebitis, synostosis, T wave inversions, thirst, thrombocytopenia, thrombophlebitis, thrombotic thrombocytopenic purpura, tinnitus, tongue discoloration, tongue edema, tongue paralysis, torticollis, transient ischemic attack, urinary incontinence, urinary retention, urticaria, ventricular extrasystoles, ventricular tachycardia, withdrawal syndrome, xerophthalmia

Overdosage/Toxicology Ingestion of doses as high as 360 mg have been reported. Symptoms of overdose are commonly drowsiness, sedation, tachycardia, hypotension, and extrapyramidal symptoms (EPS). Other reactions reported include torsade de pointes, prolonged QT interval, seizures, and cardiopulmonary arrest. Treatment should be symptom-directed and supportive. Gastric lavage and activated charcoal should be initiated. Risk of aspiration should be considered; cardiac monitoring should be initiated. Avoid antiarrhythmic therapy with agents known to prolong the QT interval (eg, disopyramide or procainamide) Avoid use of epinephrine and dopamine as vasopressors which may worsen hypotensive effects of risperidone. Anticholinergics may be used for severe EPS.

Drug Interactions

Cytochrome P450 Effect: Substrate of CYP2D6 (major), 3A4 (minor); Inhibits CYP2D6 (weak), 3A4 (weak)

Increased Effect/Toxicity: CNS depressants and valproic acid may increase adverse effects/toxicity of risperidone. CYP2D6 inhibitors may increase the levels/effects of risperidone; example inhibitors include chlorpromazine, delavirdine, fluoxetine, miconazole, paroxetine, pergolide, quinidine, quinine, ritonavir, and ropinirole. Clozapine decreases clearance of risperidone. Acetylcholinesterase inhibitors (central) may increase the risk of antipsychotic-related EPS. Pramlintide may increase anticholinergic effects of risperidone on the GI tract. Verapamil, SSRIs, and lithium may increase the levels and effects of risperidone. May enhance the effects of other anticholinergics.

Decreased Effect: Carbamazepine decreases risperidone serum concentrations.

Ethanol/Nutrition/Herb Interactions

Ethanol: Avoid ethanol (may increase CNS depression).

Herb/Nutraceutical: Avoid kava kava, gotu kola, valerian, St John's wort (may increase CNS depression).

Stability

Injection: Risperdal® Consta®: Store in refrigerator at 2°C to 8°C (36°F to 46°F) and protect from light. May be stored at room temperature of 25°C (77°F) for up to 7 days prior to administration. Bring to room temperature prior to reconstitution. Reconstitute with provided diluent only. Shake vigorously to mix; will form thick, milky suspension. Following reconstitution, store at room temperature and use within 6 hours. If suspension settles prior to use, shake vigorously to resuspend.

Oral solution, tablet: Store at 15°C to 25°C (59°F to 77°F). Protect from light and moisture. Keep orally-disintegrating tablets sealed in foil pouch until ready to use. Do not freeze solution.

Mechanism of Action

Risperidone is a benzisoxazole atypical antipsychotic with mixed serotonin-dopamine antagonist activity that binds to $5-HT_2$-receptors in the CNS and in the periphery with a very high affinity; binds to dopamine-D_2 receptors with less affinity. The binding affinity to the dopamine-D_2 receptor is 20 times lower than the $5-HT_2$ affinity. The addition of serotonin antagonism to dopamine antagonism (classic neuroleptic mechanism) is thought to improve negative symptoms of psychoses and reduce the incidence of extrapyramidal side effects. Alpha$_1$, alpha$_2$ adrenergic, and histaminergic receptors are also antagonized with high affinity. Risperidone has low to moderate affinity for $5-HT_{1C}$, $5-HT_{1D}$, and $5-HT_{1A}$ receptors, weak affinity for D_1 and no affinity for muscarinics or beta$_1$ and beta$_2$ receptors

Pharmacodynamics/Kinetics

Absorption:

Oral: Rapid and well absorbed; food does not affect rate or extent

Injection: <1% absorbed initially; main release occurs at ~3 weeks and is maintained from 4-6 weeks

Distribution: V_d: 1-2 L/kg

Protein binding, plasma: Risperidone 90%; 9-hydroxyrisperidone: 77%

Metabolism: Extensively hepatic via CYP2D6 to 9-hydroxyrisperidone (similar pharmacological activity as risperidone); N-dealkylation is a second minor pathway

Bioavailability: Solution: 70%; Tablet: 66%; orally-disintegrating tablets and oral solution are bioequivalent to tablets

Half-life elimination: Active moiety (risperidone and its active metabolite 9-hydroxyrisperidone)

Oral: 20 hours (mean)

Extensive metabolizers: Risperidone: 3 hours; 9-hydroxyrisperidone: 21 hours

Poor metabolizers: Risperidone: 20 hours; 9-hydroxyrisperidone: 30 hours

Injection: 3-6 days; related to microsphere erosion and subsequent absorption of risperidone

Time to peak, plasma: Oral: Risperidone: Within 1 hour; 9-hydroxyrisperidone: Extensive metabolizers: 3 hours; Poor metabolizers: 17 hours

Excretion: Urine (70%); feces (15%)

Dosage

Oral:

Children ≥5 years and Adolescents: Autism:

<15 kg: Use with caution; specific dosing recommendations not available

<20 kg: Initial: 0.25 mg/day; may increase dose to 0.5 mg/day after ≥4 days, maintain dose for ≥14 days. In patients not achieving sufficient clinical response, may increase dose by 0.25 mg/day in ≥2-week intervals. Therapeutic effect reached plateau at 1 mg/day in clinical trials. Following clinical response, consider gradually lowering dose. May be administered once daily or in divided doses twice daily.

≥20 kg: Initial: 0.5 mg/day; may increase dose to 1 mg/day after ≥4 days, maintain dose for ≥14 days. In patients not achieving sufficient clinical response, may increase dose by 0.5 mg/day in ≥2-week intervals. Therapeutic effect reached plateau at 2.5 mg/day (3 mg/day in children >45 kg) in clinical trials. Following clinical response, consider gradually lowering dose. May be administered once daily or in divided doses twice daily.

Children and Adolescents:

Pervasive developmental disorder (unlabeled use). Initial: 0.25 mg twice daily; titrate up 0.25 mg/day every 5-7 days; optimal dose range: 0.75-3 mg/day

Schizophrenia (unlabeled use): Initial: 0.5 mg once or twice daily; titrate as necessary up to 2-6 mg/day

Bipolar disorder (unlabeled use): Initial: 0.5 mg; titrate to 0.5-3 mg/day

Tourette's disorder (unlabeled use): Initial: 0.5 mg; titrate to 2-4 mg/day

Adults:

Schizophrenia:

Initial: 1 mg twice daily; may be increased by 2 mg/day to a target dose of 6 mg/day; usual range: 4-8 mg/day; may be given as a single daily dose once maintenance dose is achieved; daily dosages >6 mg do not appear to confer any additional benefit, and the incidence of extrapyramidal symptoms is higher than with lower doses. Further dose adjustments should be made in increments/decrements of 1-2 mg/day on a weekly basis. Dose range studied in clinical trials: 4-16 mg/day.

Maintenance: Target dose: 4 mg once daily (range 2-8 mg/day)

(Continued)

Risperidone *(Continued)*

Bipolar mania:

Initial: 2-3 mg once daily; if needed, adjust dose by 1 mg/day in intervals ≥24 hours; dosing range: 1-6 mg/day

Maintenance: No dosing recommendation available for treatment >3 weeks duration.

Elderly: A starting dose of 0.5 mg twice daily, and titration should progress slowly in increments of no more than 0.5 mg twice daily; increases to dosages >1.5 mg twice daily should occur at intervals of ≥1 week.

Additional monitoring of renal function and orthostatic blood pressure may be warranted. If once-a-day dosing in the elderly or debilitated patient is considered, a twice daily regimen should be used to titrate to the target dose, and this dose should be maintained for 2-3 days prior to attempts to switch to a once-daily regimen.

I.M.: Adults: Schizophrenia (Risperdal® Consta®): 25 mg every 2 weeks; some patients may benefit from larger doses; maximum dose not to exceed 50 mg every 2 weeks. Dosage adjustments should not be made more frequently than every 4 weeks.

Note: Oral risperidone (or other antipsychotic) should be administered with the initial injection of Risperdal® Consta® and continued for 3 weeks (then discontinued) to maintain adequate therapeutic plasma concentrations prior to main release phase of risperidone from injection site. When switching from depot administration to a short-acting formulation, administer short-acting agent in place of the next regularly-scheduled depot injection.

Dosing adjustment in renal impairment: Oral: Starting dose of 0.5 mg twice daily; clearance of the active moiety is decreased by 60% in patients with moderate to severe renal disease compared to healthy subjects.

Dosing adjustment in hepatic impairment: Oral: Starting dose of 0.5 mg twice daily; the mean free fraction of risperidone in plasma was increased by 35% compared to healthy subjects.

Dietary Considerations May be taken with or without food. Risperdal® M-Tabs® contain phenylalanine.

Administration

Oral: Oral solution can be mixed with water, coffee, orange juice, or low-fat milk, but is **not compatible** with cola or tea. May be administered with or without food.

Risperdal® M-Tabs® should not be removed from blister pack until administered. Using dry hands, place immediately on tongue. Tablet will dissolve within seconds, and may be swallowed with or without liquid. Do not split or chew.

I.M.: Risperdal® Consta® should be administered into the upper outer quadrant of the gluteal area. Injection should alternate between the two buttocks. Do not combine two different dosage strengths into one single administration. Do not substitute any components of the dose-pack; administer with needle provided.

Monitoring Parameters Vital signs; fasting lipid profile and fasting blood glucose/Hgb A_{1c} (prior to treatment, at 3 months, then annually); BMI, personal/family history of obesity, waist circumference; blood pressure; mental status; abnormal involuntary movement scale (AIMS), extrapyramidal symptoms; orthostatic blood pressure changes for 3-5 days after starting or increasing dose. Weight should be assessed prior to treatment, at 4 weeks, 8 weeks, 12 weeks, and then at quarterly intervals. Consider titrating to a different antipsychotic agent for a weight gain ≥5% of the initial weight.

Additional Information Risperdal® Consta® is an injectable formulation of risperidone using the extended release Medisorb® drug-delivery system; small polymeric microspheres degrade slowly, releasing the medication at a controlled rate.

Dosage Forms

Injection, microspheres for reconstitution, extended release:

Risperdal® Consta®: 25 mg, 37.5 mg, 50 mg [supplied in a dose-pack containing vial with active ingredient in microsphere formulation, prefilled syringe with diluent, needle-free vial access device, and safety needle]

Solution, oral:

Risperdal®: 1 mg/mL (30 mL) [contains benzoic acid]

Tablet:

Risperdal®: 0.25 mg, 0.5 mg, 1 mg, 2 mg, 3 mg, 4 mg

Tablet, orally disintegrating:

Risperdal® M-Tabs®: 0.5 mg [contains phenylalanine 0.42 mg]; 1 mg [contains phenylalanine 0.28 mg]; 2 mg [contains phenylalanine 0.56 mg]; 3 mg [contains phenylalanine 0.63 mg]; 4 mg [contains phenylalanine 0.84 mg]

♦ **Ritalin®** *see* Methylphenidate *on page 1119*

♦ **Ritalin® LA** *see* Methylphenidate *on page 1119*

♦ **Ritalin-SR®** *see* Methylphenidate *on page 1119*

♦ **Ritalin® SR (Can)** *see* Methylphenidate *on page 1119*

Ritonavir (ri TOE na veer)

U.S. Brand Names Norvir®

Canadian Brand Names Norvir®; Norvir® SEC

Pharmacologic Category Antiretroviral Agent, Protease Inhibitor

Additional Appendix Information

Antiretroviral Therapy for HIV Infection: Adults and Adolescents *on page 1988*

Management of Healthcare Worker Exposures to HBV, HCV, and HIV *on page 1941*

Use Treatment of HIV infection; should always be used as part of a multidrug regimen (at least three antiretroviral agents); may be used as a pharmacokinetic "booster" for other protease inhibitors

Pregnancy Risk Factor B

Pregnancy Implications No increased risk of overall birth defects has been observed following 1st trimester exposure according to data collected by the antiretroviral pregnancy registry. Early studies have shown lower plasma levels during pregnancy compared to postpartum. If needed during pregnancy, use in combination with another PI to boost levels of second PI. Pregnancy and protease inhibitors are both associated with an increased risk of hyperglycemia. Glucose levels should be closely monitored. The Perinatal HIV Guidelines Working Group considers ritonavir to be an alternative PI for use during pregnancy. Health-care professionals are encouraged to contact the antiretroviral pregnancy registry to monitor outcomes of pregnant women exposed to antiretroviral medications (1-800-258-4263 or www.APRegistry.com).

Lactation Excretion in breast milk unknown/contraindicated

Medication Safety Issues
Sound-alike/look-alike issues:
Ritonavir may be confused with Retrovir®
Norvir® may be confused with Norvasc®

Contraindications Hypersensitivity to ritonavir or any component of the formulation; concurrent alfuzosin, amiodarone, cisapride, dihydroergotamine, ergonovine, ergotamine, flecainide, methylergonovine, midazolam, pimozide, propafenone, quinidine, triazolam, and voriconazole (when ritonavir ≥800 mg/day)

Warnings/Precautions [U.S. Boxed Warning]: Ritonavir may interact with many medications, resulting in potentially serious and/or life-threatening adverse events. Use with caution in patients taking strong CYP3A4 inhibitors, moderate or strong CYP3A4 inducers and major CYP3A4 substrates (see drug interactions); consider alternative agents that avoid or lessen the potential for CYP-mediated interactions. Pancreatitis has been observed; use with caution in patients with increased triglycerides; monitor serum lipase and amylase. Increases in total cholesterol and triglycerides have been reported; screening should be done prior to therapy and periodically throughout treatment.

Protease inhibitors have been associated with a variety of dermatologic adverse events (some severe), including rash, erythema multiforme, and/or Stevens-Johnson syndrome. It is generally recommended to discontinue treatment if severe rash or moderate symptoms accompanied by other systemic symptoms occur. Use with caution in patients with hemophilia A or B; increased bleeding during protease inhibitor therapy has been reported. Changes in glucose tolerance, hyperglycemia, exacerbation of diabetes, DKA, and new-onset diabetes mellitus have been reported in patients receiving protease inhibitors. May be associated with fat redistribution (buffalo hump, increased abdominal girth, breast engorgement, facial atrophy, and dyslipidemia). Immune reconstitution syndrome may develop resulting in the occurrence of an inflammatory response to an indolent or residual opportunistic infection; further evaluation and treatment may be required. May cause hepatitis or exacerbate pre-existing hepatic dysfunction; use with caution in patients with hepatitis B or C and in hepatic disease. Safety and efficacy have not been established in children <1 month of age.

Adverse Reactions Protease inhibitors cause dyslipidemia which includes elevated cholesterol and triglycerides and a redistribution of body fat centrally to cause increased abdominal girth, buffalo hump, facial atrophy, and breast enlargement. These agents also cause hyperglycemia. Percentages as reported in adults:

>10%:
Endocrine & metabolic: Hypercholesterolemia (>240 mg/dL: 37% to 45%), triglycerides increased (>800 mg/dL: 17% to 34%; >1500 mg/dL: 1% to 13%)
Gastrointestinal: Nausea (26% to 30%), diarrhea (15% to 23%), vomiting (14% to 17%), taste perversion (7% to 11%)
Hematologic: WBCs decreased
Hepatic: GGT increased (5% to 20%)
Neuromuscular & skeletal: Weakness (10% to 15%), creatine phosphokinase increased (9% to 12%)

2% to 10%:
Cardiovascular: Syncope (<1% to 2%), vasodilation (2%)
Central nervous system: Fever (4% to 5%), dizziness (3% to 4%), insomnia (2% to 3%), somnolence (2% to 3%), anxiety (2%),
Dermatologic: Rash
Endocrine & metabolic: Uric acid increased (up to 4%)
Gastrointestinal: Abdominal pain (6% to 8%), anorexia (2% to 8%), dyspepsia (up to 6%), local throat irritation (2% to 3%)
Hematologic: Eosinophilia, neutropenia, neutrophilia
Hepatic: LFTs increased (6% to 10%)
Neuromuscular & skeletal: Paresthesia (3% to 7%), arthralgia (up to 2%), myalgia (2%)
Respiratory: Pharyngitis
Miscellaneous: Circumoral paresthesia, diaphoresis (2% to 3%)

<2% (Limited to important or life-threatening): Acute myeloblastic leukemia, adrenal cortex insufficiency, allergic reaction, amnesia, anemia, aphasia, asthma, bleeding increased (in patients with hemophilia A or B), cachexia, cardiovascular disorder, cerebral ischemia, cerebral venous thrombosis, chest pain, cholestatic jaundice, coma, convulsion, Cushing's syndrome, dehydration, dementia, depersonalization, diabetes mellitus, dyspnea, esophageal ulcer, gastroenteritis, gastrointestinal hemorrhage, hallucinations, hepatic coma, hepatitis, hepatomegaly, hypercholesteremia, hyper-/hypotension, hypothermia, hypoventilation, ileus, interstitial pneumonia, kidney failure, larynx edema, leukopenia, lymphadenopathy, lymphocytosis, manic reaction, MI, myeloproliferative disorder, neuropathy, palpitation, pancreatitis, paralysis, postural hypotension, pseudomembranous colitis, rectal hemorrhage, redistribution of body fat, skin melanoma, subdural hematoma, tachycardia, thrombocytopenia, tongue edema, ulcerative colitis

Overdosage/Toxicology Human experience is limited. There is no specific antidote for overdose with ritonavir. The oral solution contains 43% ethanol by volume, potentially causing significant ethanol-related toxicity in younger patients. Dialysis is unlikely to be beneficial in significant removal of the drug. Charcoal or gastric lavage may be useful to remove unabsorbed drug.
(Continued)

Ritonavir *(Continued)*

Drug Interactions

Cytochrome P450 Effect: Substrate of CYP1A2 (minor), 2B6 (minor), 2D6 (major), 3A4 (major); **Inhibits** CYP2C8 (strong), 2C9 (weak), 2C19 (weak), 2D6 (strong), 2E1 (weak), 3A4 (strong); **Induces** CYP1A2 (weak), 2C8 (weak), 2C9 (weak), 3A4 (weak)

Increased Effect/Toxicity: Concurrent use of alfuzosin, amiodarone, cisapride, ergot alkaloids (including dihydroergotamine, ergonovine, methylergonovine), flecainide, midazolam, pimozide, propafenone, quinidine, and triazolam is contraindicated.

Saquinavir's serum concentrations are increased by ritonavir; the dosage of both agents should be reduced to 400 mg twice daily. Concurrent therapy with amprenavir may result in increased serum concentrations: dosage adjustment is recommended. Metronidazole or disulfiram may cause disulfiram reaction (oral solution contains 43% ethanol). Serum levels/effects of corticosteroids (eg, budesonide, fluticasone) and immunosuppressants (cyclosporine, sirolimus, tacrolimus; monitor) may be increased by ritonavir. Serum concentrations of the parent drug and/or metabolite(s) of several analgesics (eg, tramadol, meperidine, propoxyphene) may be increased by ritonavir; increased levels of normeperidine may increase the risk of CNS toxicity/seizures. Rifabutin and rifabutin metabolite serum concentrations may be increased by ritonavir; reduce rifabutin dose to 150 mg every other day.

Ritonavir may increase the levels/effects of amiodarone, amphetamines, selected beta-blockers, selected benzodiazepines (midazolam and triazolam contraindicated), calcium channel blockers, bupropion, carbamazepine, cisapride (contraindicated), delavirdine, dextromethorphan, digoxin, eplerenone, ergot alkaloids (contraindicated), ethosuximide, fentanyl, fluoxetine, lidocaine, HMG-CoA reductase inhibitors, mirtazapine, nateglinide, nefazodone, paclitaxel, paroxetine, perphenazine, pimozide (contraindicated), propafenone (contraindicated), repaglinide, risperidone, rosiglitazone, sildenafil (and other PDE-5 inhibitors), thioridazine, trazodone, tricyclic antidepressants, venlafaxine, zolpidem, and other substrates of CYP2D6 or 3A4. Thioridazine is generally contraindicated with strong CYP2D6 inhibitors. When used with strong CYP3A4 inhibitors, dosage adjustment/limits are recommended for sildenafil and other PDE-5 inhibitors; refer to individual monographs.

Decreased Effect: The administration of didanosine (buffered formulation) should be separated from ritonavir by 2.5 hours to limit interaction with ritonavir. Concurrent use of rifampin, rifabutin, dexamethasone, and many anticonvulsants may lower serum concentration of ritonavir. Ritonavir may reduce the concentration of ethinyl estradiol which may result in loss of contraception (including combination products). Theophylline concentrations may be reduced in concurrent therapy. Levels of didanosine and zidovudine may be decreased by ritonavir, however, no dosage adjustment is necessary. Voriconazole serum levels are reduced by ritonavir. In addition, ritonavir may decrease the serum concentrations of the following drugs: Atovaquone, divalproex, lamotrigine, methadone, phenytoin. The levels/effects of ritonavir may be decreased by aminoglutethimide, carbamazepine, nafcillin, nevirapine, phenobarbital, phenytoin, rifamycins, and other CYP3A4 inducers. Ritonavir may decrease the levels/effects of CYP2D6 prodrug substrates (eg, codeine, hydrocodone, oxycodone, tramadol).

Ethanol/Nutrition/Herb Interactions

Food: Food enhances absorption.

Herb/Nutraceutical: St John's wort may decrease ritonavir serum levels. Avoid use.

Stability

Capsule: Store under refrigeration at 2°C to 8°C (36°F to 46°F); may be left out at room temperature of <25°C (<77°F) if used within 30 days. Protect from light. Avoid exposure to excessive heat.

Solution: Store at room temperature at 20°C to 25°C (68°F to 77°F); do not refrigerate.

Mechanism of Action

Ritonavir inhibits HIV protease and renders the enzyme incapable of processing of polyprotein precursor which leads to production of noninfectious immature HIV particles

Pharmacodynamics/Kinetics

Absorption: Variable; increased with food

Distribution: High concentrations in serum and lymph nodes

Protein binding: 98% to 99%

Metabolism: Hepatic via CYP3A4 and 2D6; five metabolites, low concentration of an active metabolite achieved in plasma (oxidative)

Half-life elimination: 3-5 hours

Time to peak, plasma: 2 hours (fasted); 4 hours (nonfasted)

Excretion: Urine (~11%); feces (~86%)

Dosage Treatment of HIV infection: Oral:

Children >1 month: 350-400 mg/m² twice daily (maximum dose: 600 mg twice daily). Initiate dose at 250 mg/m² twice daily; titrate dose upward every 2-3 days by 50 mg/m² twice daily.

Adults: 600 mg twice daily; dose escalation tends to avoid nausea that many patients experience upon initiation of full dosing. Escalate the dose as follows: 300 mg twice daily for 1 day, 400 mg twice daily for 2 days, 500 mg twice daily for 1 day, then 600 mg twice daily. Ritonavir may be better tolerated when used in combination with other antiretrovirals by initiating the drug alone and subsequently adding the second agent within 2 weeks.

Pharmacokinetic "booster" in combination with other protease inhibitors: 100-400 mg/day

Refer to individual monographs; specific dosage recommendations often require adjustment of both agents.

Note: Dosage adjustments for ritonavir when administered in combination therapy:

Amprenavir: Adjustments necessary for each agent:

Amprenavir 1200 mg with ritonavir 200 mg once daily **or**

Amprenavir 600 mg with ritonavir 100 mg twice daily

Amprenavir plus efavirenz (3-drug regimen): Amprenavir 1200 mg twice daily plus ritonavir 200 mg twice daily plus efavirenz at standard dose

Indinavir: Adjustments necessary for both agents:

Indinavir 800 mg twice daily plus ritonavir 100-200 mg twice daily **or**

Indinavir 400 mg twice daily plus ritonavir 400 mg twice daily

Nelfinavir: Ritonavir 400 mg twice daily

Rifabutin: Decrease rifabutin dose to 150 mg every other day

Saquinavir: Ritonavir 400 mg twice daily

Dosing adjustment in renal impairment: None necessary

Dosing adjustment in hepatic impairment: No adjustment required in mild or moderate impairment; however, careful monitoring is required in moderate hepatic impairment (levels may be decreased); caution advised with severe impairment (no data available)

Dietary Considerations Should be taken with food. Oral solution contains 43% ethanol by volume.

Administration Administer with food. Liquid formulations usually have an unpleasant taste. Consider mixing it with chocolate milk or a liquid nutritional supplement. Whenever possible, administer oral solution with calibrated dosing syringe.

Monitoring Parameters Triglycerides, cholesterol, CBC, LFTs, CPK, uric acid, basic HIV monitoring, viral load, CD4 count, glucose, serum amylase and lipase

Additional Information Potential compliance problems, frequency of administration and adverse effects should be discussed with patients before initiating therapy to help prevent the emergence of resistance.

Dosage Forms

Capsule: 100 mg [contains ethanol and polyoxyl 35 castor oil]

Solution: 80 mg/mL (240 mL) [contains ethanol and polyoxyl 35 castor oil; peppermint and caramel flavor]

♦ **Ritonavir and Lopinavir** see Lopinavir and Ritonavir on page 1029

♦ **Rituxan®** see Rituximab on page 1523

Rituximab (ri TUK si mab)

U.S. Brand Names Rituxan®

Canadian Brand Names Rituxan®

Index Terms Anti-CD20 Monoclonal Antibody; C2B8; C2B8 Monoclonal Antibody; IDEC-C2B8; NSC-687451; Pan-B Antibody

Pharmacologic Category Antineoplastic Agent, Monoclonal Antibody; Monoclonal Antibody

Use Treatment of low-grade or follicular CD20-positive, B-cell non-Hodgkin's lymphoma (NHL); treatment of diffuse large B-cell CD20-positive NHL; treatment of rheumatoid arthritis (RA) in combination with methotrexate

Unlabeled/Investigational Use Treatment of autoimmune hemolytic anemia (AIHA) in children; chronic immune thrombocytopenic purpura (ITP); chronic lymphocytic leukemia (CLL); small lymphocytic lymphoma (SLL); pemphigus vulgaris, Waldenström's macroglobulinemia (WM); treatment of systemic autoimmune diseases (other than rheumatoid arthritis)

Pregnancy Risk Factor C

Pregnancy Implications Animal studies have demonstrated adverse effects including decreased (reversible) B-cells and immunosuppression. There are no adequate and well-controlled studies in pregnant women. Rituximab administration during pregnancy could potentially cause fetal B-cell depletion. Use during pregnancy only if clearly needed. Effective contraception is recommended during treatment and for up to 12 months following treatment.

Lactation Excretion in breast milk unknown/not recommended

Medication Safety Issues

Sound-alike/look-alike issues:

Rituxan® may be confused with Remicade®

Rituximab may be confused with infliximab

High alert medication: The Institute for Safe Medication Practices (ISMP) includes this medication among its list of drugs which have a heightened risk of causing significant patient harm when used in error.

The rituximab dose for rheumatoid arthritis is a flat dose (1000 mg) and is not based on body surface area (BSA).

Contraindications Type I hypersensitivity or anaphylactic reactions to rituximab, murine proteins, or any component of the formulation

Warnings/Precautions [U.S. Boxed Warning]: Severe and occasionally fatal infusion-related reactions have been reported during the first 30-120 minutes of the first infusion. Reactions include hypotension, angioedema, bronchospasm, hypoxia, and in more severe cases pulmonary infiltrates, acute respiratory distress syndrome, myocardial infarction, ventricular fibrillation, and/or cardiogenic shock. Risk factors associated with fatal outcomes include chronic lymphocytic leukemia, female gender, mantle cell lymphoma, or pulmonary infiltrates. Discontinue infusion for severe reactions; treatment is symptomatic. Medications for the treatment of hypersensitivity reactions (eg, epinephrine, antihistamines, corticosteroids) should be available for immediate use. Discontinue infusion for serious or life-threatening cardiac arrhythmias; subsequent doses should include cardiac monitoring during and after the infusion. Mild-to-moderate infusion-related reactions (eg, chills, fever, rigors) occur frequently and are typically managed through slowing or interrupting the infusion. Infusion may be resumed at a 50% infusion rate reduction upon resolution of symptoms. Due to the potential for hypotension, consider withholding antihypertensives 12 hours prior to treatment.

[U.S. Boxed Warning]: Tumor lysis syndrome leading to acute renal failure requiring dialysis may occur 12-24 hours following the first dose. Consider prophylaxis (allopurinol, hydration) in patients at high risk (high numbers of circulating malignant cells ≥25,000/mm³ or high tumor burden). May cause renal toxicity; consider discontinuation with increasing (Continued)

Rituximab *(Continued)*

serum creatinine or oliguria. **[U.S. Boxed Warning]: Severe and sometimes fatal mucocutaneous reactions (lichenoid dermatitis, paraneoplastic pemphigus, Stevens-Johnson syndrome, toxic epidermal necrolysis and vesiculobullous dermatitis) have been reported,** occurring from 1-13 weeks following exposure. Patients experiencing severe mucocutaneous skin reactions should not receive further rituximab infusions and should seek prompt medical evaluation. Use caution with pre-existing cardiac or pulmonary disease, or prior cardiopulmonary events. Rheumatoid arthritis patients are at increased risk for cardiovascular events; monitor closely during and after each infusion. Elderly patients are at higher risk for cardiac (supraventricular arrhythmia) and pulmonary adverse events (pneumonia, pneumonitis). Reactivation of hepatitis B has been reported in association with rituximab (rare); consider screening in high-risk patients. Other serious and potentially fatal viral infections, either new or reactivated, associated with rituximab use include JC virus (progressive multifocal leukoencephalopathy [PML]), cytomegalovirus, herpes simplex virus, parvovirus B19, varicella zoster virus, West Nile virus, and hepatitis C. Viral infections may be delayed; occurring up to 1 year after discontinuation of rituximab. Bowel obstruction and perforation have been reported; complaints of abdominal pain should be evaluated. Safety and efficacy of rituximab in combination with biologic agents or disease-modifying antirheumatic drugs (DMARD) other than methotrexate have not been established. Safety and efficacy of retreatment for RA have not been established. Safety and efficacy in children have not been established.

Adverse Reactions Note: Patients treated with rituximab for rheumatoid arthritis (RA) may experience fewer adverse reactions.

>10%:

Central nervous system: Fever (5% to 53%), chills (3% to 33%), headache (19%), pain (12%)

Dermatologic: Rash (15%), pruritus (5% to 14%), angioedema (11%)

Gastrointestinal: Nausea (8% to 23%), abdominal pain (2% to 14%)

Hematologic: Lymphopenia (48%; grade 3/4: 40%; median duration 14 days), leukopenia (14%; grade 3/4: 4%), neutropenia (14%; grade 3/4: 6%; median duration 13 days), thrombocytopenia (12%; grade 3/4: 2%)

Neuromuscular & skeletal: Weakness (2% to 26%)

Respiratory: Cough (13%), rhinitis (3% to 12%)

Miscellaneous: Infection (31%; grade 3/4: 2%), night sweats (15%)

Mild-to-moderate infusion-related reactions: Chills, fever, rigors, dizziness, hypertension, myalgia, nausea, pruritus, rash, and vomiting (lymphoma: first dose 77%; fourth dose 30%; eighth dose 14%); infusion-related reactions reported are lower in RA

1% to 10%:

Cardiovascular: Hypotension (10%), peripheral edema (8%), hypertension (6% to 8%), flushing (5%), edema (<5%)

Central nervous system: Dizziness (10%), anxiety (2% to 5%), agitation (<5%), depression (<5%), hypoesthesia (<5%), insomnia (<5%), malaise (<5%), nervousness (<5%), neuritis (<5%), somnolence (<5%), vertigo (<5%), migraine (RA: 2%)

Dermatologic: Urticaria (2% to 8%)

Endocrine & metabolic: Hyperglycemia (9%), hypoglycemia (<5%), hypercholesterolemia (2%)

Gastrointestinal: Diarrhea (10%), vomiting (10%), dyspepsia (3% to 5%), anorexia (<5%), weight loss (<5%)

Hematologic: Anemia (8%; grade 3/4: 3%)

Local: Pain at the injection site (<5%)

Neuromuscular & skeletal: Back pain (10%), myalgia (10%), arthralgia (6% to 10%), paresthesia (2% to 5%), arthritis (<5%), hyperkinesia (<5%), hypertonia (<5%), neuropathy (<5%)

Ocular: Conjunctivitis (<5%), lacrimation disorder (<5%)

Respiratory: Throat irritation (2% to 9%), bronchospasm (8%), dyspnea (7%), upper respiratory tract infection (RA: 7%), sinusitis (6%)

Miscellaneous: LDH increased (7%)

Postmarketing and/or case reports: Acute renal failure (associated with tumor lysis syndrome), anaphylactoid reaction/anaphylaxis, angina, aplastic anemia, ARDS, arrhythmia, bowel obstruction, bronchiolitis obliterans, cardiac failure, cardiogenic shock, fatal infusion-related reactions, gastrointestinal perforation, hemolytic anemia, hepatic failure, hepatitis, hepatitis B reactivation, hyperviscosity syndrome (in Waldenström's macroglobulinemia), hypoxia, interstitial pneumonitis, lichenoid dermatitis, lupus-like syndrome, marrow hypoplasia, MI, neutropenia (late-onset occurring >40 days after last dose), optic neuritis, pancytopenia, paraneoplastic pemphigus (uncommon), pleuritis, pneumonia, pneumonitis, pure red cell aplasia, renal toxicity, serum sickness, Stevens-Johnson syndrome, supraventricular arrhythmia, toxic epidermal necrolysis, urticaria, uveitis, vasculitis with rash, ventricular fibrillation, ventricular tachycardia, vesiculobullous dermatitis, viral reactivation (includes JC virus [PML], cytomegalovirus, herpes simplex virus, parvovirus B19, varicella zoster virus, West Nile virus, and hepatitis C)

Overdosage/Toxicology There has been no experience with overdosage in human clinical trials. Treatment is symptom-directed and supportive.

Drug Interactions

Increased Effect/Toxicity: Monoclonal antibodies may increase the risk for allergic reactions to rituximab due to the presence of HACA antibody. Antihypertensive medications may exacerbate hypotension.

Decreased Effect: Currently recommended not to administer live vaccines during rituximab treatment.

Ethanol/Nutrition/Herb Interactions Herb/Nutraceutical: Avoid hypoglycemic herbs, including alfalfa, bilberry, bitter melon, burdock, celery, damiana, fenugreek, garcinia, garlic, ginger, ginseng, gymnema, marshmallow, and stinging nettle (may enhance the hypoglycemic effect of rituximab). Monitor.

Stability

Store vials at refrigeration at 2°C to 8°C (36°F to 46°F); do not freeze. Do not shake. Protect vials from direct sunlight.

Withdraw the necessary amount of rituximab and dilute to a final concentration of 1-4 mg/mL with 0.9% sodium chloride or 5% dextrose in water. Gently invert the bag to mix the solution; do not shake. Solutions for infusion are stable at 2°C to 8°C (36°F to 46°F) for 24 hours and at room temperature for an additional 24hours.

Mechanism of Action Rituximab is a monoclonal antibody directed against the CD20 antigen on B-lymphocytes. CD20 regulates cell cycle initiation; and, possibly, functions as a calcium channel. Rituximab binds to the antigen on the cell surface, activating complement-dependent cytotoxicity; and to human Fc receptors, mediating cell killing through an antibody-dependent cellular toxicity. B-cells are believed to play a role in the development and progression of rheumatoid arthritis. Signs and symptoms of RA are reduced by targeting B-cells.

Pharmacodynamics/Kinetics

Duration: Detectable in serum 3-6 months after completion of treatment; B-cell recovery begins ~6 months following completion of treatment; median B-cell levels return to normal by 12 months following completion of treatment

Absorption: I.V.: Immediate and results in a rapid and sustained depletion of circulating and tissue-based B cells

Distribution: 4.3 L (following two 1000 mg doses for rheumatoid arthritis)

Half-life elimination:

Cancer: Proportional to dose; wide ranges reflect variable tumor burden and changes in CD20 positive B-cell populations with repeated doses:

>100 mg/m^2: 4.4 days (range 1.6-10.5 days)

375 mg/m^2:

Following first dose: Mean half-life: 3.2 days (range 1.3-6.4 days)

Following fourth dose: Mean half-life: 8.6 days (range 3.5-17 days)

RA: Mean terminal half-life: 19 days

Excretion: Uncertain; may undergo phagocytosis and catabolism in the reticuloendothelial system (RES)

Dosage Note: Pretreatment with acetaminophen and diphenhydramine is recommended.

Children: AIHA, chronic ITP (unlabeled uses): I.V.: 375 mg/m^2 once weekly for 2-4 doses

Adults: I.V. infusion (refer to individual protocols):

NHL (relapsed/refractory, low-grade or follicular CD20-positive, B-cell): 375 mg/m^2 once weekly for 4 or 8 doses

Retreatment following disease progression: 375 mg/m^2 once weekly for 4 doses

NHL (diffuse large B-cell): 375 mg/m^2 given on day 1 of each chemotherapy cycle for up to 8 doses

NHL (follicular, CD20-positive, B-cell, previously untreated): 375 mg/m^2 given on day 1 of each chemotherapy cycle for up to 8 doses

NHL (low-grade, CD20-positive, B-cell, previously untreated): 375 mg/m^2 once weekly for 4 doses every 6 months for up to 4 cycles (initiate after 6-8 cycles of chemotherapy are completed)

Rheumatoid arthritis: 1000 mg on days 1 and 15 in combination with methotrexate

Note: Premedication with a corticosteroid (eg, methylprednisolone 100 mg I.V.) prior to each rituximab dose is recommended. In clinical trials, patients received oral corticosteroids on a tapering schedule from baseline through day 16.

CLL/SLL (unlabeled use): 100 mg day 1, then 375 mg/m^2 3 times/week for 11 doses

Refractory pemphigus vulgaris (unlabeled use): 375 mg/m^2 once weekly of weeks 1, 2, and 3 of a 4-week cycle, repeat for 1 additional cycle, then 1 dose per month for 4 months (total of 10 doses in 6 months)

Waldenström's macroglobulinemia (unlabeled use): 375 mg/m^2 once weekly for 4 weeks

Combination therapy with ibritumomab: 250 mg/m^2 I.V. day 1; repeat in 7-9 days with ibritumomab (also see Ibritumomab monograph):

Administration Do **not** administer I.V. push or bolus.

Initial infusion: Start rate of 50 mg/hour; if there is no reaction, increase the rate 50 mg/hour every 30 minutes, to a maximum of 400 mg/hour.

Subsequent infusions: If patient did not tolerate initial infusion follow initial infusion guidelines. If patient tolerated initial infusion, start at 100 mg/hour; if there is no reaction, increase the rate 100 mg/hour every 30 minutes, to a maximum of 400 mg/hour.

Note: If a reaction occurs, slow or stop the infusion. If the reaction abates, restart infusion at 50% of the previous rate.

Monitoring Parameters CBC with differential and platelets, peripheral CD20$^+$ cells; HAMA/HACA titers (high levels may increase the risk of allergic reactions); renal function, fluid balance; vital signs; cardiac monitoring during and after infusion in rheumatoid arthritis patients and in patients with pre-existing cardiac disease or if arrhythmias develop during or after subsequent infusions

Screening for hepatitis B in high-risk persons may be considered prior to initiation of rituximab therapy. In addition, carriers and patients with evidence of recovery from prior hepatitis B infection should be monitored closely for clinical and laboratory signs of HBV infection during therapy and for up to a year following completion of treatment.

Complaints of abdominal pain, especially early in the course of treatment, should prompt a thorough diagnostic evaluation and appropriate treatment. Signs or symptoms of progressive multifocal leukoencephalopathy (focal neurologic deficits, which may present as hemiparesis, visual field deficits, cognitive impairment, aphasia, ataxia, and/or cranial nerve deficits).

Reference Range Peripheral CD20+ cells: High level pretreatment (500-1600 cells/μL, malignant or normal) may indicate risk of more severe infusion reactions

Dosage Forms

Injection, solution [preservative free]:

Rituxan®: 10 mg/mL (10 mL, 50 mL) [contains polysorbate 80]

♦ **Riva-Alendronate (Can)** see Alendronate on page 65

♦ **Riva-Atenolol (Can)** see Atenolol on page 167

♦ **Riva-Diclofenac (Can)** *see Diclofenac on page 492*
♦ **Riva-Diclofenac-K (Can)** *see Diclofenac on page 492*
♦ **Riva-Dicyclomine (Can)** *see Dicyclomine on page 496*
♦ **Riva-Famotidine (Can)** *see Famotidine on page 683*
♦ **Riva-Fluconazole (Can)** *see Fluconazole on page 712*
♦ **Riva-Fosinopril (Can)** *see Fosinopril on page 766*
♦ **Riva-Loperamine (Can)** *see Loperamide on page 1027*
♦ **Riva-Lorazepam (Can)** *see Lorazepam on page 1035*
♦ **Riva-Lovastatin (Can)** *see Lovastatin on page 1040*
♦ **Riva-Mirtazapine (Can)** *see Mirtazapine on page 1152*
♦ **Riva-Naproxen (Can)** *see Naproxen on page 1199*
♦ **Rivanase AQ (Can)** *see Beclomethasone on page 198*
♦ **Riva-Norfloxacin (Can)** *see Norfloxacin on page 1241*
♦ **Riva-Oxazepam (Can)** *see Oxazepam on page 1281*
♦ **Riva-Pravastatin (Can)** *see Pravastatin on page 1409*
♦ **Riva-Simvastatin (Can)** *see Simvastatin on page 1567*
♦ **Rivasol (Can)** *see Zinc Sulfate on page 1817*
♦ **Riva-Sotalol (Can)** *see Sotalol on page 1592*

Rivastigmine (ri va STIG meen)

U.S. Brand Names Exelon®
Canadian Brand Names Exelon®
Index Terms ENA 713; Rivastigmine Tartrate; SDZ ENA 713
Pharmacologic Category Acetylcholinesterase Inhibitor (Central)
Use Treatment of mild-to-moderate dementia associated with Alzheimer's disease and Parkinson's disease
Pregnancy Risk Factor B
Pregnancy Implications Teratogenic effects were not observed in animal studies. There are no adequate and well-controlled studies in pregnant women. Should be used only if the benefit outweighs the potential risk to the fetus.
Lactation Excretion in breast milk unknown/use caution
Contraindications Hypersensitivity to rivastigmine, other carbamate derivatives (eg, neostigmine, pyridostigmine, physostigmine), or any component of the formulation
Warnings/Precautions Significant nausea, vomiting, anorexia, and weight loss are associated with use; occurs more frequently in women and during the titration phase. If treatment is interrupted for more than several days, reinstate at the lowest daily dose. Use caution in patients with a history of peptic ulcer disease or concurrent NSAID use. Use caution in patients undergoing anesthesia who will receive succinylcholine-type muscle relaxation, patients with sick sinus syndrome, bradycardia or supraventricular conduction conditions, urinary obstruction, seizure disorders, or pulmonary conditions such as asthma or COPD. Safety and efficacy in children have not been established.
Adverse Reactions
>10%:
    Central nervous system: Dizziness (6% to 21%), headache (4% to 17%)
    Gastrointestinal: Nausea (29% to 47%), vomiting (17% to 31%), diarrhea (7% to 19%), anorexia (6% to 17%), abdominal pain (4% to 13%)
2% to 10%:
    Cardiovascular: Syncope (3%), hypertension (3%)
    Central nervous system: Fatigue (4% to 9%), insomnia (9%), confusion (8%), depression (6%), anxiety (5%), malaise (5%), somnolence (4% to 5%), hallucinations (4%), aggressiveness (3%), parkinsonism symptoms worsening (2% to 3%)
    Gastrointestinal: Dyspepsia (9%), constipation (5%), flatulence (4%), weight loss (3%), eructation (2%), dehydration (2%)
    Genitourinary: Urinary tract infection (7%)
    Neuromuscular & skeletal: Weakness (2% to 6%), tremor (4%; up to 10% in Parkinson's patients)
    Respiratory: Rhinitis (4%)
    Miscellaneous: Diaphoresis (4%), flu-like syndrome (3%)
≥1% (Drug causality indeterminate; frequency most often similar to placebo): Accidental trauma, agitation, allergy, anemia, angina, arthralgia, arthritis, ataxia, atrial fibrillation, back pain, bone fracture, bradycardia, bronchitis, cardiac failure, cataract, chest pain, confusion, cough, delusion, depression, dyspnea, dyskinesia, edema, epistaxis, fecal incontinence, fever, gait abnormal, gastritis, hematuria, hot flushes, hypokalemia, hypotension (including postural), infection, leg cramps, MI, myalgia, nervousness, pain, palpitation, paranoid reaction, paresthesia, peripheral edema, pharyngitis, rash, restlessness, rigors, salivation increased, seizure, tinnitus, transient ischemic attack, upper respiratory tract infection, urinary incontinence, vertigo
<1% (Limited to important or life-threatening symptoms; reactions may be at a similar frequency to placebo): Abnormal hepatic function, acute renal failure, albuminuria, alkaline phosphatase increased, aneurysm, apathy, aphasia, apnea, apraxia, AV block, bronchospasm, bundle branch block, cachexia, cardiac arrest, cellulitis, cholecystitis, colitis, conjunctival hemorrhage, diabetes mellitus, diplopia, diverticulitis, dysphagia, dysphonia, endometrial hypertrophy, esophagitis, extrasystoles, gastroesophageal reflux, GGT increased, GI hemorrhage, glaucoma, hematoma, hyper-/hypoglycemia, hypercholesterolemia, hyper-/hypokinesia, hypertonia, hypochromic anemia, hyponatremia, hypothermia, hypothyroidism, intestinal obstruction, intracranial hemorrhage, leukocytosis, lymphadenopathy, mastitis, migraine, neuralgia, otitis media, pancreatitis, peptic ulcer, periorbital or facial edema, peripheral ischemia, peripheral neuropathy, peritonitis, prostatic adenoma, psychiatric disorders (eg, delirium, depersonalization, psychosis, emotional lability, suicidal ideation or tendencies), pulmonary embolism, purpura, rectal hemorrhage, retinopathy,

sick sinus syndrome, sudden cardiac death, supraventricular tachycardia, tachycardia, thrombocytopenia, thrombophlebitis, thrombosis, ulcerative stomatitis, urticaria, vasovagal syncope

Postmarketing and/or case reports: Stevens-Johnson syndrome, severe vomiting with esophageal rupture (following inappropriate reinitiation of dose)

Overdosage/Toxicology In cases of asymptomatic overdoses, rivastigmine should be held for 24 hours. Cholinergic crisis, caused by significant acetylcholinesterase inhibition, is characterized by severe nausea, vomiting, salivation, sweating, bradycardia, hypotension, respiratory depression, cardiovascular collapse, and convulsions. Treatment is supportive and symptomatic. Dialysis would not be helpful.

Drug Interactions

Increased Effect/Toxicity: Acetylcholinesterase inhibitors (central) may increase the risk of antipsychotic-related extrapyramidal symptoms. Beta-blockers without ISA activity may increase risk of bradycardia. Calcium channel blockers (diltiazem or verapamil) may increase risk of bradycardia. Cholinergic agonists effects may be increased with rivastigmine. Depolarizing neuromuscular blocking agents effects may be increased with rivastigmine. Digoxin may increase risk of bradycardia.

Decreased Effect: Anticholinergic agents effects may be reduced with rivastigmine.

Ethanol/Nutrition/Herb Interactions

Smoking: Nicotine increases the clearance of rivastigmine by 23%.

Ethanol: Avoid ethanol (due to risk of sedation; may increase GI irritation).

Food: Food delays absorption by 90 minutes, lowers C_{max} by 30% and increases AUC by 30%.

Stability Store below 25°C (77°F); do not freeze. Store solution in an upright position.

Mechanism of Action A deficiency of cortical acetylcholine is thought to account for some of the symptoms of Alzheimer's disease and the dementia of Parkinson's disease; rivastigmine increases acetylcholine in the central nervous system through reversible inhibition of its hydrolysis by cholinesterase

Pharmacodynamics/Kinetics

Duration: Anticholinesterase activity (CSF): ~10 hours (6 mg dose)

Absorption: Fasting: Rapid and complete within 1 hour

Distribution: V_d: 1.8-2.7 L/kg

Protein binding: 40%

Metabolism: Extensively via cholinesterase-mediated hydrolysis in the brain; metabolite undergoes N-demethylation and/or sulfate conjugation hepatically; CYP minimally involved; linear kinetics at 3 mg twice daily, but nonlinear at higher doses

Bioavailability: 36% to 40%

Half-life elimination: 1.5 hours

Time to peak: 1 hour

Excretion: Urine (97% as metabolites); feces (0.4%)

Dosage Note: Exelon® oral solution and capsules are bioequivalent.

Adults: Oral:

Mild-to-moderate Alzheimer's dementia: Initial: 1.5 mg twice daily; may increase by 3 mg/day (1.5 mg/dose) every 2 weeks based on tolerability (maximum recommended dose: 6 mg twice daily)

Note: If GI adverse events occur, discontinue treatment for several doses then restart at the same or next lower dosage level; antiemetics have been used to control GI symptoms. If treatment is interrupted for longer than several days, restart the treatment at the lowest dose and titrate as previously described.

Mild-to-moderate Parkinson's-related dementia: Initial: 1.5 mg twice daily; may increase by 3 mg/day (1.5 mg/dose) every 4 weeks based on tolerability (maximum recommended dose: 6 mg twice daily)

Elderly: Clearance is significantly lower in patients >60 years of age, but dosage adjustments are not recommended. Titrate dose to individual's tolerance.

Dosage adjustment in renal impairment: Dosage adjustments are not recommended, however, titrate the dose to the individual's tolerance.

Dosage adjustment in hepatic impairment: Clearance is significantly reduced in mild to moderately impaired patients. Although dosage adjustments are not recommended, use lowest possible dose and titrate according to individual's tolerance. Consider intervals of >2 weeks between dosage adjustments.

Dietary Considerations Should be taken with meals.

Administration Should be administered with meals (breakfast or dinner). Capsule should be swallowed whole. Liquid form is available for patients who cannot swallow capsules (can be swallowed directly from syringe or mixed with water, soda, or cold fruit juice). Stir well and drink within 4 hours of mixing.

Monitoring Parameters Cognitive function at periodic intervals, symptoms of GI intolerance

Dosage Forms

Capsule:

Exelon®: 1.5 mg, 3 mg, 4.5 mg, 6 mg

Solution, oral:

Exelon®: 2 mg/mL (120 mL) [contains sodium benzoate]

♦ **Rivastigmine Tartrate** *see* Rivastigmine *on page 1526*

♦ **Riva-Sumatriptan (Can)** *see* Sumatriptan *on page 1620*

♦ **Riva-Verapamil SR (Can)** *see* Verapamil *on page 1784*

♦ **Riva-Zide (Can)** *see* Hydrochlorothiazide and Triamterene *on page 847*

♦ **Rivotril® (Can)** *see* Clonazepam *on page 397*

Rizatriptan (rye za TRIP tan)

U.S. Brand Names Maxalt®; Maxalt-MLT®
Canadian Brand Names Maxalt™; Maxalt RPD™
Index Terms MK462
Pharmacologic Category Antimigraine Agent; Serotonin 5-HT$_{1B, 1D}$ Receptor Agonist
Additional Appendix Information
Antimigraine Drugs: 5-HT$_1$ Receptor Agonists *on page 1871*
Use Acute treatment of migraine with or without aura
Pregnancy Risk Factor C
Pregnancy Implications There are no adequate and well-controlled studies using rizatriptan in pregnant women. Use only if potential benefit to the mother outweighs the potential risk to the fetus. A pregnancy registry has been established to monitor outcomes of women exposed to rizatriptan during pregnancy (800-986-8999). In some animal studies, administration was associated with decreased weight gain, developmental toxicity and increased mortality in the offspring. Teratogenic effects were not observed.
Lactation Excretion in breast milk unknown/use caution
Contraindications Hypersensitivity to rizatriptan or any component of the formulation; documented ischemic heart disease or Prinzmetal's angina; uncontrolled hypertension; basilar or hemiplegic migraine; during or within 2 weeks of MAO inhibitors; during or within 24 hours of treatment with another 5-HT$_1$ agonist, or an ergot-containing or ergot-type medication (eg, methysergide, dihydroergotamine)
Warnings/Precautions Use only in patients with a clear diagnosis of migraine. May cause vasospastic reactions resulting in colonic, peripheral, or coronary ischemia. Use with caution in elderly or patients with hepatic or renal impairment (including dialysis patients); history of hypersensitivity to sumatriptan or adverse effects from sumatriptan, and in patients at risk of coronary artery disease (as predicted by presence of risk factors) unless cardiovascular evaluation provides evidence that the patient is free of cardiovascular disease. In patients with risk factors for coronary artery disease, following adequate evaluation to establish the absence of coronary artery disease, the initial dose should be administered in a setting where response may be evaluated (physician's office or similarly staffed setting). ECG monitoring may be considered. May increase blood pressure transiently; may cause coronary vasospasm (less than sumatriptan); avoid in patients with signs/symptoms suggestive of reduced arterial flow (ischemic bowel, Raynaud's) which could be exacerbated by vasospasm. Cerebral/subarachnoid hemorrhage and stroke have been reported with 5-HT$_1$ agonist administration.

Patients who experience sensations of chest pain/pressure/tightness or symptoms suggestive of angina following dosing should be evaluated for coronary artery disease or Prinzmetal's angina before receiving additional doses. Symptoms of agitation, confusion, hallucinations, hyperreflexia, myoclonus, shivering, and tachycardia (serotonin syndrome) may occur with concomitant proserotonergic drugs (ie, SSRIs/SNRIs or triptans) or agents which reduce rizatriptan's metabolism. Concurrent use of serotonin precursors (eg, tryptophan) is not recommended.

Reconsider diagnosis of migraine if no response to initial dose. Long-term effects on vision have not been evaluated. Safety and efficacy have not been established in children <18 years of age. Maxalt-MLT® tablets contain phenylalanine.
Adverse Reactions
1% to 10%:
Cardiovascular: Systolic/diastolic blood pressure increases (5-10 mm Hg), chest pain (5%), palpitation
Central nervous system: Dizziness, drowsiness, fatigue (13% to 30%, dose related)
Dermatologic: Skin flushing
Endocrine & metabolic: Mild increase in growth hormone, hot flashes
Gastrointestinal: Abdominal pain, dry mouth (<5%), nausea
Respiratory: Dyspnea
<1% (Limited to important or life-threatening): Akinesia, angina, angioedema, arrhythmia, bradycardia, bradykinesia, decreased mental activity, myalgia, myocardial ischemia, MI, neck pain/stiffness, neurological/psychiatric abnormalities, pruritus, stroke, syncope, tachycardia, tinnitus, toxic epidermal necrolysis, wheezing
Drug Interactions
Increased Effect/Toxicity: Use within 24 hours of another selective 5-HT$_1$ antagonist or ergot-containing drug should be avoided due to possible additive vasoconstriction. Use with propranolol increased plasma concentration of rizatriptan by 70%. SSRIs/SNRIs may exhibit additive toxicity with rizatriptan or other serotonin agonists (eg, antidepressants, dextromethorphan, tramadol) leading to serotonin syndrome. MAO inhibitors and nonselective MAO inhibitors increase concentration of rizatriptan.
Ethanol/Nutrition/Herb Interactions Food: Food delays absorption.
Stability Store in blister pack until administration.
Mechanism of Action Selective agonist for serotonin (5-HT$_{1D}$ receptor) in cranial arteries to cause vasoconstriction and reduce sterile inflammation associated with antidromic neuronal transmission correlating with relief of migraine
Pharmacodynamics/Kinetics
Onset of action: ~30 minutes
Duration: 14-16 hours
Protein binding: 14%
Metabolism: Via monoamine oxidase-A; first-pass effect
Bioavailability: 40% to 50%
Half-life elimination: 2-3 hours
Time to peak: 1-1.5 hours
Excretion: Urine (82%, 8% to 16% as unchanged drug); feces (12%)
Dosage Note: In patients with risk factors for coronary artery disease, following adequate evaluation to establish the absence of coronary artery disease, the initial dose should be

administered in a setting where response may be evaluated (physician's office or similarly staffed setting). ECG monitoring may be considered.

Oral: 5-10 mg, repeat after 2 hours if significant relief is not attained; maximum: 30 mg in a 24-hour period (use 5 mg dose in patients receiving propranolol with a maximum of 15 mg in 24 hours)

Note: For orally-disintegrating tablets (Maxalt-MLT®): Patient should be instructed to place tablet on tongue and allow to dissolve. Dissolved tablet will be swallowed with saliva.

Dietary Considerations Orally-disintegrating tablet contains phenylalanine (1.05 mg per 5 mg tablet, 2.10 mg per 10 mg tablet).

Monitoring Parameters Headache severity, signs/symptoms suggestive of angina; consider monitoring blood pressure, heart rate, and/or ECG with first dose in patients with likelihood of unrecognized coronary disease, such as patients with significant hypertension, hypercholesterolemia, obese patients, diabetics, smokers with other risk factors or strong family history of coronary artery disease

Dosage Forms

Tablet, as benzoate:
Maxalt®: 5 mg, 10 mg
Tablet, orally disintegrating, as benzoate:
Maxalt-MLT®: 5 mg [contains phenylalanine 1.05 mg/tablet; peppermint flavor]; 10 mg [contains phenylalanine 2.1 mg/tablet; peppermint flavor]

♦ **rLFN-α2** see Interferon Alfa-2b on page 920

♦ **RMS®** see Morphine Sulfate on page 1171

♦ **Ro 5488** see Tretinoin (Oral) on page 1730

♦ **Robafen® AC** see Guaifenesin and Codeine on page 815

♦ **Robafen DM [OTC]** see Guaifenesin and Dextromethorphan on page 816

♦ **Robaxin®** see Methocarbamol on page 1109

♦ **Robidrine® (Can)** see Pseudoephedrine on page 1454

♦ **Robinul®** see Glycopyrrolate on page 807

♦ **Robinul® Forte** see Glycopyrrolate on page 807

♦ **Robitussin® [OTC]** see Guaifenesin on page 814

♦ **Robitussin® (Can)** see Guaifenesin on page 814

♦ **Robitussin® Childrens Cough & Cold (Can)** see Pseudoephedrine and Dextromethorphan on page 1455

♦ **Robitussin® Cough and Cold [OTC]** see Guaifenesin, Pseudoephedrine, and Dextromethorphan on page 821

♦ **Robitussin® Cough and Cold CF [OTC]** see Guaifenesin, Pseudoephedrine, and Dextromethorphan on page 821

♦ **Robitussin® Cough and Cold Infant CF [OTC]** see Guaifenesin, Pseudoephedrine, and Dextromethorphan on page 821

♦ **Robitussin® Cough and Congestion [OTC]** see Guaifenesin and Dextromethorphan on page 816

♦ **Robitussin® Cough & Cold® (Can)** see Guaifenesin, Pseudoephedrine, and Dextromethorphan on page 821

♦ **Robitussin® DM [OTC]** see Guaifenesin and Dextromethorphan on page 816

♦ **Robitussin® DM (Can)** see Guaifenesin and Dextromethorphan on page 816

♦ **Robitussin® DM Infant [OTC]** see Guaifenesin and Dextromethorphan on page 816

♦ **Robitussin® Maximum Strength Cough & Cold [OTC] [DSC]** see Pseudoephedrine and Dextromethorphan on page 1455

♦ **Robitussin®-PE [OTC] [DSC]** see Guaifenesin and Pseudoephedrine on page 819

♦ **Robitussin® Pediatric Cough & Cold [OTC] [DSC]** see Pseudoephedrine and Dextromethorphan on page 1455

♦ **Robitussin® Pediatric Night Relief [OTC] [DSC]** see Chlorpheniramine, Pseudoephedrine, and Dextromethorphan on page 355

♦ **Robitussin® Severe Congestion [OTC] [DSC]** see Guaifenesin and Pseudoephedrine on page 819

♦ **Robitussin® Sugar Free Cough [OTC]** see Guaifenesin and Dextromethorphan on page 816

♦ **Rocaltrol®** see Calcitriol on page 266

♦ **Rocephin®** see Ceftriaxone on page 324

Rocuronium (roe kyoor OH nee um)

U.S. Brand Names Zemuron®
Canadian Brand Names Zemuron®
Index Terms ORG 946; Rocuronium Bromide
Pharmacologic Category Neuromuscular Blocker Agent, Nondepolarizing
Additional Appendix Information
Neuromuscular Blocking Agents on page 1890
Use Adjunct to general anesthesia to facilitate both rapid sequence and routine endotracheal intubation and to relax skeletal muscles during surgery; to facilitate mechanical ventilation in ICU patients; does not relieve pain or produce sedation
Pregnancy Risk Factor C
Pregnancy Implications There are no adequate and well-controlled studies in pregnant women; use only when potential benefit justifies potential risk to the fetus.
Lactation Excretion in breast milk unknown/use caution
Medication Safety Issues
Sound-alike/look-alike issues:
Zemuron® may be confused with Remeron®
(Continued)

Rocuronium *(Continued)*

High alert medication: The Institute for Safe Medication Practices (ISMP) includes this medication among its list of drugs which have a heightened risk of causing significant patient harm when used in error.

Contraindications Hypersensitivity to rocuronium or any component of the formulation

Warnings/Precautions Use with caution in patients with valvular heart disease, pulmonary disease, hepatic impairment; ventilation must be supported during neuromuscular blockade; certain clinical conditions may result in potentiation or antagonism of neuromuscular blockade:

Potentiation: Electrolyte abnormalities, severe hyponatremia, severe hypocalcemia, severe hypokalemia, hypermagnesemia, neuromuscular diseases, acidosis, acute intermittent porphyria, renal failure, hepatic failure

Antagonism: Alkalosis, hypercalcemia, demyelinating lesions, peripheral neuropathies, diabetes mellitus

Increased sensitivity in patients with myasthenia gravis, Eaton-Lambert syndrome; resistance in burn patients (>30% of body) for period of 5-70 days postinjury; resistance in patients with muscle trauma, denervation, immobilization, infection. Cross-sensitivity with other neuromuscular-blocking agents may occur; use extreme caution in patients with previous anaphylactic reactions.

Adverse Reactions

>1%: Cardiovascular: Transient hypotension and hypertension

<1% (Limited to important or life-threatening): Abnormal ECG, acute quadriplegic myopathy syndrome (prolonged use), anaphylaxis, arrhythmia, bronchospasm, edema, hiccups, injection site pruritus, myositis ossificans (prolonged use), nausea, rash, rhonchi, shock, tachycardia, vomiting, wheezing

Overdosage/Toxicology Symptoms include prolonged skeletal muscle block, muscle weakness and apnea. Treatment consists of airway support and controlled ventilation until recovery of normal neuromuscular block is observed. Further recovery may be facilitated by administering an anticholinesterase agent (eg, neostigmine, edrophonium, or pyridostigmine) with atropine, to antagonize skeletal muscle relaxation. Support of the cardiovascular system with fluids and pressors may be necessary.

Drug Interactions

Increased Effect/Toxicity: Increased effects are possible with aminoglycosides, beta-blockers, clindamycin, calcium channel blockers, halogenated anesthetics, imipenem, ketamine, lidocaine, loop diuretics (furosemide), macrolides (case reports), magnesium sulfate, procainamide, quinidine, quinolones, tetracyclines, and vancomycin. May increase risk of myopathy when used with high- dose corticosteroids for extended periods.

Decreased Effect: Effect of nondepolarizing neuromuscular blockers may be reduced by carbamazepine (chronic use), corticosteroids (also associated with myopathy - see increased effect), phenytoin (chronic use), sympathomimetics, and theophylline.

Stability Store under refrigeration (2°C to 8°C), do not freeze. When stored at room temperature, it is stable for 30 days. Unlike vecuronium, it is stable in 0.9% sodium chloride and 5% dextrose in water. This mixture should be used within 24 hours of preparation.

Mechanism of Action Blocks acetylcholine from binding to receptors on motor endplate inhibiting depolarization

Pharmacodynamics/Kinetics

Onset of action: Good intubation conditions in 1-2 minutes; maximum neuromuscular blockade within 4 minutes

Duration: ~30 minutes (with standard doses, increases with higher doses)

Metabolism: Minimally hepatic; 17-desacetylrocuronium (5% to 10% activity of parent drug)

Half-life elimination: 60-70 minutes

Excretion: Feces (50%); urine (30%)

Dosage Administer I.V.; dose to effect; doses will vary due to interpatient variability; use ideal body weight for obese patients

Children:

Initial: 0.6 mg/kg under halothane anesthesia produce excellent to good intubating conditions within 1 minute and will provide a median time of 41 minutes of clinical relaxation in children 3 months to 1 year of age, and 27 minutes in children 1-12 years

Maintenance: 0.075-0.125 mg/kg administered upon return of T_1 to 25% of control provides clinical relaxation for 7-10 minutes

Adults:

Tracheal intubation: I.V.:

Initial: 0.6 mg/kg is expected to provide approximately 31 minutes of clinical relaxation under opioid/nitrous oxide/oxygen anesthesia with neuromuscular block sufficient for intubation attained in 1-2 minutes; lower doses (0.45 mg/kg) may be used to provide 22 minutes of clinical relaxation with median time to neuromuscular block of 1-3 minutes; maximum blockade is achieved in <4 minutes

Maximum: 0.9-1.2 mg/kg may be given during surgery under opioid/nitrous oxide/oxygen anesthesia without adverse cardiovascular effects and is expected to provide 58-67 minutes of clinical relaxation; neuromuscular blockade sufficient for intubation is achieved in <2 minutes with maximum blockade in <3 minutes

Maintenance: 0.1, 0.15, and 0.2 mg/kg administered at 25% recovery of control T_1 (defined as 3 twitches of train-of-four) provides a median of 12, 17, and 24 minutes of clinical duration under anesthesia

Rapid sequence intubation: 0.6-1.2 mg/kg in appropriately premedicated and anesthetized patients with excellent or good intubating conditions within 2 minutes

Continuous infusion: Initial: 0.01-0.012 mg/kg/minute only after early evidence of spontaneous recovery of neuromuscular function is evident; infusion rates have ranged from 4-16 mcg/kg/minute

ICU: 10 mcg/kg/minute; adjust dose to maintain appropriate degree of neuromuscular blockade (eg, 1 or 2 twitches on train-of-four)

Dosing adjustment in hepatic impairment: Reductions are necessary in patients with liver disease

Administration Administer I.V. only; may be administered undiluted as a bolus injection or via a continuous infusion using an infusion pump

Monitoring Parameters Peripheral nerve stimulator measuring twitch response, heart rate, blood pressure, assisted ventilation status

Additional Information Rocuronium is classified as an intermediate-duration neuromuscular-blocking agent. Do not mix in the same syringe with barbiturates. Rocuronium does not relieve pain or produce sedation.

Dosage Forms Injection, solution, as bromide: 10 mg/mL (5 mL, 10 mL)

- **Rocuronium Bromide** *see* Rocuronium *on page 1529*
- **Rofact™ (Can)** *see* Rifampin *on page 1508*
- **Roferon-A®** *see* Interferon Alfa-2a *on page 918*
- **Rogaine® (Can)** *see* Minoxidil *on page 1151*
- **Rogaine® Extra Strength for Men [OTC]** *see* Minoxidil *on page 1151*
- **Rogaine® for Men [OTC]** *see* Minoxidil *on page 1151*
- **Rogaine® for Women [OTC]** *see* Minoxidil *on page 1151*
- **Rogitine® (Can)** *see* Phentolamine *on page 1357*
- **Rolaids® [OTC]** *see* Calcium Carbonate and Magnesium Hydroxide *on page 271*
- **Rolaids® Extra Strength [OTC]** *see* Calcium Carbonate and Magnesium Hydroxide *on page 271*
- **Rolaids® Softchews [OTC]** *see* Calcium Carbonate *on page 269*
- **Romazicon®** *see* Flumazenil *on page 718*
- **Romilar® AC** *see* Guaifenesin and Codeine *on page 815*
- **Romycin®** *see* Erythromycin *on page 609*
- **Rondec®** *see* Chlorpheniramine and Phenylephrine *on page 349*
- **Rondec®-DM** *see* Chlorpheniramine, Phenylephrine, and Dextromethorphan *on page 352*
- **Rondec® Tablets** *see* Carbinoxamine and Pseudoephedrine *on page 290*
- **Rondec-TR®** *see* Carbinoxamine and Pseudoephedrine *on page 290*

Ropinirole (roe PIN i role)

U.S. Brand Names Requip®
Canadian Brand Names Requip®
Index Terms Ropinirole Hydrochloride
Pharmacologic Category Anti-Parkinson's Agent, Dopamine Agonist
Additional Appendix Information
Parkinson's Agents *on page 1895*
Use Treatment of idiopathic Parkinson's disease; in patients with early Parkinson's disease who were not receiving concomitant levodopa therapy as well as in patients with advanced disease on concomitant levodopa; treatment of moderate-to-severe primary Restless Legs Syndrome (RLS)
Pregnancy Risk Factor C
Lactation Excretion in breast milk unknown/not recommended
Medication Safety Issues
Sound-alike/look-alike issues:
Ropinirole may be confused with ropivacaine
Contraindications Hypersensitivity to ropinirole or any component of the formulation
Warnings/Precautions Syncope, sometimes associated with bradycardia, was observed in association with ropinirole in both early Parkinson's disease (without levodopa) patients and advanced Parkinson's disease (with levodopa) patients. Dopamine agonists appear to impair the systemic regulation of blood pressure resulting in postural hypotension, especially during dose escalation. Parkinson's disease patients appear to have an impaired capacity to respond to a postural challenge; use with caution in patients at risk of hypotension (ie, those receiving antihypertensive drugs) or where transient hypotensive episodes would be poorly tolerated (cardiovascular disease or cerebrovascular disease). Parkinson's patients being treated with dopaminergic agonists ordinarily require careful monitoring for signs and symptoms of postural hypotension, especially during dose escalation, and should be informed of this risk. May cause hallucinations. Use with caution in patients with pre-existing dyskinesia, severe hepatic or renal dysfunction.

Patients treated with ropinirole have reported falling asleep while engaging in activities of daily living; this has been reported to occur without significant warning signs. Monitor for daytime somnolence or pre-existing sleep disorder; caution with concomitant sedating medication; discontinue if significant daytime sleepiness or episodes of falling asleep occur. Patients must be cautioned about performing tasks which require mental alertness (eg, operating machinery or driving). Use with caution in patients receiving other CNS depressants or psychoactive agents. Effects with other sedative drugs or ethanol may be potentiated.

Some patients treated for RLS may experience worsening of symptoms in the early morning hours (rebound) or an increase and/or spread of daytime symptoms (augmentation); clinical management of these phenomena has not been evaluated in controlled clinical trials. Pathologic degenerative changes were observed in the retinas of albino rats during studies with this agent, but were not observed in the retinas of albino mice or in other species. The significance of these data for humans remains uncertain.

Other dopaminergic agents have been associated with a syndrome resembling neuroleptic malignant syndrome on withdrawal or significant dosage reduction after long-term use. Risk of fibrotic complications (eg, pleural effusion/fibrosis, interstitial lung disease) and melanoma has been reported in patients receiving ropinirole; drug causation has not been established. (Continued)

Ropinirole (Continued)

Adverse Reactions

Data inclusive of trials in both early and late Parkinson's disease (may include levo-dopa) and restless legs syndrome; frequencies of some adverse effects may be influenced by disease state, particularly in advanced Parkinson's disease:

>10%:

Cardiovascular: Syncope (12%)

Central nervous system: Somnolence (12% to 40%), dizziness (11% to 40%), fatigue (8% to 11%)

Gastrointestinal: Nausea (40% to 60%), vomiting (12%)

Miscellaneous: Viral infection (11%)

1% to 10%:

Cardiovascular: Dependent/leg edema (2% to 7%), orthostasis (1% to 6%), hypertension (2% to 5%), chest pain (4%), flushing (3%), palpitation (3%), peripheral ischemia (3%), hypotension (2%), tachycardia (2%)

Central nervous system: Pain (3% to 8%), confusion (5% to 9%), hallucinations (5% to 10%, dose related), anxiety (6%), pain (5%), hypoesthesia (4%), amnesia (3% to 5%), malaise (3%), paresis (3%), vertigo (2%), yawning (3%), abnormal dreams (3%), insomnia, neuralgia (>1%)

Gastrointestinal: Constipation (5% to 6%), dyspepsia (4% to 10%), abdominal pain (3% to 9%), vomiting (7%), xerostomia (3% to 5%), diarrhea (4%), flatulence (2% to 3%), dysphagia (2%), salivation increased (2%), weight loss (2%)

Genitourinary: Urinary tract infection (1% to 5%), impotence (3%)

Hematologic: Anemia (2%)

Hepatic: Alkaline phosphatase increased (3%)

Neuromuscular & skeletal: Falls (10%), arthralgia (4% to 7%), weakness (6%), tremor (6%), hypokinesia (5%), paresthesia (5%), arthritis (3%), muscle cramps (3%)

Ocular: Abnormal vision (6%), xerophthalmia (2%)

Renal: BUN increased (>1%)

Respiratory: Upper respiratory tract infection (9%), pharyngitis (6% to 9%), rhinitis (4%), sinusitis (4%), dyspnea (3%), influenza (3%), cough (3%), nasal congestion (2%)

Miscellaneous: Injury, diaphoresis increased (3% to 7%), viral infection, increased drug level (7%)

<1% (Limited to important or life-threatening): Abnormal coordination, acidosis, agitation, aneurysm, angina, aphasia, asthma, behavioral disorders, bradycardia, bundle branch block, cardiac arrest, cardiac failure, cardiomegaly, cellulitis, cholecystitis, cholelithiasis, choreoathetosis, colitis, coma, conjunctival hemorrhage, dehydration, diabetes mellitus, diverticulitis, Dupuytren's contracture, dysphonia, electrolyte disturbances, eosinophilia, extrapyramidal symptoms, gangrene, gastrointestinal hemorrhage, gastrointestinal ulceration, glaucoma, goiter, gynecomastia, hematuria, hemiparesis, hemiplegia, hepatitis (ischemic), hyperbilirubinemia, hypercholesterolemia, hyperphosphatemia, hyperuricemia, hyper-/hypothyroidism, hyper-/hypotonia, hypoglycemia, hyponatremia; infections (bacterial, viral or fungal); intestinal obstruction, leukocytosis, leukopenia, limb embolism, liver enzymes increased, lymphadenopathy, lymphedema, lymphocytosis, lymphopenia, menstrual abnormalities, mitral insufficiency, MI, neoplasms (various), neuralgia, pancreatitis, paralysis, psychiatric disorders, peripheral neuropathy, photosensitivity, pleural effusion, proteinuria, pulmonary edema, pulmonary embolism, rash, renal calculus, renal failure (acute), seizure, sepsis, SIADH, skin disorders, stomatitis, stupor, subarachnoid hemorrhage, suicide attempt, SVT, tachycardia, thrombocytopenia, thrombosis, tinnitus, tongue edema, torticollis, urticaria, vagina/uterine hemorrhage, ventricular tachycardia, visual disturbances

Overdosage/Toxicology

There have been no reports of intentional overdose. Symptoms reported with accidental overdosage included agitation, increased dyskinesia, sedation, orthostatic hypotension, chest pain, confusion, nausea, and vomiting. It is anticipated that the symptoms of overdose will be related to its dopaminergic activity. General supportive measures are recommended. Vital signs should be maintained, if necessary. Removal of any unabsorbed material (eg, by gastric lavage) should be considered.

Drug Interactions

Cytochrome P450 Effect: Substrate of CYP1A2 (major), 3A4 (minor); Inhibits CYP1A2 (weak), 2D6 (strong)

Increased Effect/Toxicity: The levels/effects of ropinirole may be increased by ciprofloxacin, fluvoxamine, ketoconazole, norfloxacin, ofloxacin, rofecoxib, and other CYP1A2 inhibitors. Estrogens may also reduce the metabolism of ropinirole; dosage adjustments may be needed. Ropinirole may increase the levels/effects of amphetamines, selected beta-blockers, dextromethorphan, fluoxetine, lidocaine, mirtazapine, nefazodone, paroxetine, risperidone, ritonavir, thioridazine, tricyclic antidepressants, venlafaxine, and other CYP2D6 substrates.

Decreased Effect: The levels/effects of ropinirole may be decreased by aminoglutethimide, carbamazepine, phenobarbital, rifampin, and other CYP1A2 inducers. Antipsychotics, cigarette smoking, and metoclopramide may reduce the effect or serum concentrations of ropinirole. Ropinirole may decrease the levels/effects of CYP2D6 prodrug substrates (eg, codeine, hydrocodone, oxycodone, tramadol).

Ethanol/Nutrition/Herb Interactions

Ethanol: Avoid ethanol (may increase CNS depression).

Herb/Nutraceutical: Avoid kava kava, gotu kola, valerian, St John's wort (may increase CNS depression).

Mechanism of Action

Ropinirole has a high relative in vitro specificity and full intrinsic activity at the D_2 and D_3 dopamine receptor subtypes, binding with higher affinity to D_3 than to D_2 or D_4 receptor subtypes; relevance of D_3 receptor binding in Parkinson's disease is unknown. Ropinirole has moderate in vitro affinity for opioid receptors. Ropinirole and its metabolites have negligible in vitro affinity for dopamine D_1, $5-HT_1$, $5-HT_2$, benzodiazepine, GABA, muscarinic, alpha$_1$-, alpha$_2$-, and beta-adrenoreceptors. Although precise mechanism of action of ropinirole is unknown, it is believed to be due to stimulation of postsynaptic dopamine D_2-type receptors within the caudate putamen in the brain. Ropinirole caused decreases in systolic and diastolic blood pressure at doses >0.25 mg. The mechanism of ropinirole-induced postural hypotension is believed to be due to D_2-mediated blunting of the noradrenergic response to standing and subsequent decrease in peripheral vascular resistance.

Pharmacodynamics/Kinetics

Absorption: Not affected by food

Distribution: V_d: 525 L

Metabolism: Extensively hepatic via CYP1A2 to inactive metabolites; first-pass effect

Bioavailability: Absolute: 55%

Half-life elimination: ~6 hours

Time to peak: ~1-2 hours; T_{max} increased by 2.5 hours when drug taken with food

Excretion: Clearance: Reduced by 30% in patients >65 years of age

Dosage Oral: Adults:

Parkinson's disease: The dosage should be increased to achieve a maximum therapeutic effect, balanced against the principal side effects of nausea, dizziness, somnolence and dyskinesia. Recommended starting dose is 0.25 mg 3 times/day; based on individual patient response, the dosage should be titrated with weekly increments as described below:

- Week 1: 0.25 mg 3 times/day; total daily dose: 0.75 mg
- Week 2: 0.5 mg 3 times/day; total daily dose: 1.5 mg
- Week 3: 0.75 mg 3 times/day; total daily dose: 2.25 mg
- Week 4: 1 mg 3 times/day; total daily dose: 3 mg

  Note: After week 4, if necessary, daily dosage may be increased by 1.5 mg per day on a weekly basis up to a dose of 9 mg/day, and then by up to 3 mg/day weekly to a total of 24 mg/day

Parkinson's disease discontinuation taper: Ropinirole should be gradually tapered over 7 days as follows: reduce frequency of administration from 3 times daily to twice daily for 4 days, then reduce to once daily for remaining 3 days.

Restless Legs Syndrome: Initial: 0.25 mg once daily 1-3 hours before bedtime. Dose may be increased after 2 days to 0.5 mg daily, and after 7 days to 1 mg daily. Dose may be further titrated upward in 0.5 mg increments every week until reaching a daily dose of 3 mg during week 6. If symptoms persist or reappear, the daily dose may be increased to a maximum of 4 mg beginning week 7.

Note: Doses up to 4 mg per day may be discontinued without tapering.

Dietary Considerations May be taken with or without food.

Monitoring Parameters

Blood pressure (orthostatic); daytime alertness

Additional Information If therapy with a drug known to be a potent inhibitor of CYP1A2 is stopped or started during treatment with ropinirole, adjustment of ropinirole dose may be required. Ropinirole binds to melanin-containing tissues (ie, eyes, skin) in pigmented rats. After a single dose, long-term retention of drug was demonstrated, with a half-life in the eye of 20 days; not known if ropinirole accumulates in these tissues over time.

Dosage Forms

Combination package:

Requip® [starter kit; contents per each administration card]: Tablet: 0.25 mg (2s), 0.5 mg (5s), 1 mg (7s)

Tablet:

Requip®: 0.25 mg, 0.5 mg, 1 mg, 2 mg, 3 mg, 4 mg, 5 mg

♦ **Ropinirole Hydrochloride** *see* Ropinirole *on page 1531*

Ropivacaine (roe PIV a kane)

U.S. Brand Names Naropin®

Canadian Brand Names Naropin®

Index Terms Ropivacaine Hydrochloride

Pharmacologic Category Local Anesthetic

Use Local anesthetic for use in surgery, postoperative pain management, and obstetrical procedures when local or regional anesthesia is needed

Pregnancy Risk Factor B

Pregnancy Implications Teratogenic events were not observed in animal studies. When used for epidural block during labor and delivery, systemically absorbed ropivacaine may cross the placenta, resulting in varying degrees of fetal or neonatal effects (eg, CNS or cardiovascular depression). Fetal or neonatal adverse events include fetal bradycardia (12%), neonatal jaundice (8%), low Apgar scores (3%), fetal distress (2%), neonatal respiratory disorder (3%). Maternal hypotension may also result from systemic absorption. In cases of hypotension, position pregnant woman in left lateral decubitus position to prevent aortocaval compression by the gravid uterus. Epidural anesthesia may prolong the second stage of labor.

Lactation Excretion in breast milk unknown/use caution

Medication Safety Issues

Sound-alike/look-alike issues:

Ropivacaine may be confused with bupivacaine, ropinirole

Contraindications Hypersensitivity to ropivacaine, amide-type local anesthetics (eg, bupivacaine, mepivacaine, lidocaine), or any component of the formulation

Warnings/Precautions When administering this agent, have ready access to drugs and equipment for resuscitation. Use with caution in patients with liver disease, cardiovascular disease, neurological or psychiatric disorders, and in the elderly or debilitated; these patients may be at greater risk for toxicity. Bradycardia and hypotension may be age-related (more common in patients >61 years of age). Use caution in patients on antiarrhythmics, such as amiodarone; consider ECG monitoring since cardiac effects may be additive. Use cautiously in hypotension, hypovolemia, or heart block. Ropivacaine is not recommended for use in emergency situations where rapid administration is necessary. Safety and efficacy have not been established in pediatric patients.

(Continued)

Ropivacaine (Continued)

Adverse Reactions

>10%:

Cardiovascular: Hypotension (dose-related and age-related: 32% to 69%), bradycardia (6% to 20%)

Gastrointestinal: Nausea (11% to 29%), vomiting (7% to 14%)

Neuromuscular & skeletal: Back pain (7% to 16%)

1% to 10%:

Cardiovascular: Hypertension, tachycardia, chest pain (1% to 5%)

Central nervous system: Fever (3% to 9%), headache (5% to 8%), dizziness (3%), chills (2% to 3%), anxiety (1%), lightheadedness

Dermatologic: Pruritus (1% to 5%)

Endocrine & metabolic: Hypokalemia

Genitourinary: Urinary retention (1% to 5%), urinary tract infection (1% to 5%)

Hematologic: Anemia (6%)

Neuromuscular & skeletal: Paresthesia (2% to 6%), hypoesthesia, rigors, circumoral paresthesia

Renal: Oliguria

Respiratory: Dyspnea

Miscellaneous: Shivering

<1% (Limited to important or life-threatening): Accidental I.V. injection (0.2%), angioedema, allergic reaction, apnea (usually associated with epidural block in head/neck region), bronchospasm, cardiac arrest, cardiovascular collapse, dyskinesia, hallucination, hyperthermia, laryngeal edema, myocardial depression, MI, rash, seizure, syncope, tinnitus, urticaria, ventricular arrhythmia

Overdosage/Toxicology Incidence of cardiovascular and CNS toxicity appears to be low with inadvertent intravascular injection but this can occur. Treatment is primarily symptomatic and supportive. Termination of anesthesia by pneumatic tourniquet inflation should be attempted when the agent is administered by infiltration or regional injection. Seizures commonly respond to diazepam, while hypotension responds to I.V. fluids and Trendelenburg positioning. Bradyarrhythmias (when the heart rate is <60) can be treated with I.V. or SubQ atropine 15 mcg/kg. With the development of metabolic acidosis, I.V. sodium bicarbonate 0.5-2 mEq/kg and ventilatory assistance should be instituted. Methemoglobinemia should be treated with methylene blue 1-2 mg/kg in a 1% sterile aqueous solution I.V. push over 4-6 minutes repeated up to a total dose of 7 mg/kg.

Lipid infusion has been used in animals studies and one human ropivacaine case (Litz RJ, 2006) where asystole, unresponsive to conventional resuscitation, resulted. Additional information is available at http://www.lipidrescue.org.

Drug Interactions

Cytochrome P450 Effect: Substrate of CYP1A2 (major), 2B6 (minor), 2D6 (minor), 3A4 (minor); may be major in cases of 1A2 inhibition/deficiency)

Increased Effect/Toxicity: Cardiac effects may be additive with amiodarone and other class III antiarrhythmics. Amiodarone, ciprofloxacin, fluvoxamine, and propofol may increase ropivacaine levels/effects (monitor). Other CYP1A2 inhibitors may increase the levels/effects of ropivacaine; example inhibitors include ketoconazole, norfloxacin, ofloxacin, and rofecoxib.

Stability Store at 20°C to 25°C (68°F to 77°F). Infusions should be discarded after 24 hours.

Mechanism of Action Blocks both the initiation and conduction of nerve impulses by decreasing the neuronal membrane's permeability to sodium ions, which results in inhibition of depolarization with resultant blockade of conduction

Pharmacodynamics/Kinetics

Onset of action: Anesthesia (route dependent): 3-15 minutes

Duration (dose and route dependent): 3-15 hours

Metabolism: Hepatic, via CYP1A2 to metabolites

Half-life elimination: Epidural: 5-7 hours

Excretion: Urine (86% as metabolites)

Dosage Dose varies with procedure, onset and depth of anesthesia desired, vascularity of tissues, duration of anesthesia, and condition of patient: Adults:

Surgical anesthesia:

Lumbar epidural: 15-30 mL of 0.5% to 1% solution

Lumbar epidural block for cesarean section:

20-30 mL dose of 0.5% solution

15-20 mL dose of 0.75% solution

Thoracic epidural block: 5-15 mL dose of 0.5% to 0.75% solution

Major nerve block:

35-50 mL dose of 0.5% solution (175-250 mg)

10-40 mL dose of 0.75% solution (75-300 mg)

Field block: 1-40 mL dose of 0.5% solution (5-200 mg)

Labor pain management: Lumbar epidural: Initial: 10-20 mL 0.2% solution; continuous infusion dose: 6-14 mL/hour of 0.2% solution with incremental injections of 10-15 mL/hour of 0.2% solution

Postoperative pain management:

Lumbar or thoracic epidural: Continuous infusion dose: 6-14 mL/hour of 0.2% solution

Infiltration/minor nerve block:

1-100 mL dose of 0.2% solution

1-40 mL dose of 0.5% solution

Administration Administered via local infiltration, epidural block and epidural infusion, or intermittent bolus

Monitoring Parameters Heart rate, blood pressure, ECG monitoring (if used with antiarrhythmics)

Dosage Forms

Infusion, as hydrochloride:

Naropin®: 2 mg/mL (100 mL, 200 mL)

Injection, solution, as hydrochloride [preservative free]:
Naropin®: 2 mg/mL (10 mL, 20 mL); 5 mg/mL (20 mL, 30 mL); 7.5 mg/mL (20 mL); 10 mg/mL (10 mL, 20 mL)

♦ **Ropivacaine Hydrochloride** *see* Ropivacaine *on page 1533*
♦ **Rosac®** *see* Sulfur and Sulfacetamide *on page 1618*
♦ **Rosanil®** *see* Sulfur and Sulfacetamide *on page 1618*

Rosiglitazone (roh si GLI ta zone)

U.S. Brand Names Avandia®
Canadian Brand Names Avandia®
Pharmacologic Category Antidiabetic Agent, Thiazolidinedione
Additional Appendix Information
Hyperglycemia- or Hypoglycemia-Causing Drugs *on page 2057*
Use Type 2 diabetes mellitus (noninsulin dependent, NIDDM):
Monotherapy: Improve glycemic control as an adjunct to diet and exercise
Combination therapy: In combination with a sulfonylurea, metformin, or insulin, or sulfonylurea plus metformin when diet, exercise, and a single agent do not result in adequate glycemic control
Unlabeled/Investigational Use
Polycystic ovary syndrome (PCOS)
Pregnancy Risk Factor C
Pregnancy Implications Treatment during mid to late gestation was associated with fetal death and growth retardation in animal models. Abnormal blood glucose levels are associated with a higher incidence of congenital abnormalities. Insulin is the drug of choice for the control of diabetes mellitus during pregnancy. In anovulatory, premenopausal women, ovulation may occur, increasing the risk of pregnancy; adequate contraception is recommended.
Lactation Excretion in breast milk unknown/not recommended
Medication Safety Issues
Sound-alike/look-alike issues:
Avandia® may be confused with Avalide®, Coumadin®, Prandin®

International issues:
Avandia® may be confused with Avanza® which is a brand name for mirtazapine in Australia
Contraindications Hypersensitivity to rosiglitazone or any component of the formulation; active liver disease (transaminases >2.5 times the upper limit of normal at baseline); contraindicated in patients who previously experienced jaundice during troglitazone therapy
Warnings/Precautions Should not be used in diabetic ketoacidosis. Mechanism requires the presence of insulin, therefore use in type 1 diabetes (insulin dependent, IDDM) is not recommended.

May increase plasma volume and/or increase cardiac hypertrophy. Use with caution in patients with edema. Assess for fluid accumulation in patients with unusually rapid weight gain. Monitor closely for signs and symptoms of heart failure. Drug discontinuation is recommended if cardiovascular status worsens. A higher frequency of cardiovascular events has been noted in patients with NYHA Class I or II heart failure; up to 33% require adjustment of medications. Not recommended for use in patients with NYHA Class III or IV heart failure, unless serum glucose control outweighs the risk of excessive fluid retention. Use with caution in patients with anemia or depressed leukocyte counts (may reduce hemoglobin, hematocrit, and/or WBC).

Use with caution in patients with elevated transaminases (AST or ALT). Idiosyncratic hepatotoxicity has been reported with another thiazolidinedione agent (troglitazone) and (rarely) with rosiglitazone; discontinue if jaundice occurs. Monitoring should include periodic determinations of liver function. Rosiglitazone has been associated with new onset and/or worsening of macular edema in diabetic patients. Rosiglitazone should be used with caution in patients with a pre-existing macular edema or diabetic retinopathy. Discontinuation of rosiglitazone should be considered in any patient who reports visual deterioration. In addition, ophthalmological consultation should be initiated in these patients. May result in hormonal imbalance; development of menstrual irregularities should prompt reconsideration of therapy. Use with caution in premenopausal, anovulatory women; may result in resumption of ovulation, increasing the risk of pregnancy. Safety and efficacy in pediatric patients have not been established.
Adverse Reactions
>10%: Endocrine & metabolic: Weight gain, increase in total cholesterol, increased LDL-cholesterol, increased HDL-cholesterol
1% to 10%:
Cardiovascular: Edema (5%)
Central nervous system: Headache (6%), fatigue (4%)
Endocrine & metabolic: Hyperglycemia (4%), hypoglycemia (1%; increased with insulin to 12% to 14%)
Gastrointestinal: Diarrhea (2%)
Hematologic: Anemia (2%)
Neuromuscular & skeletal: Back pain (4%)
Respiratory: Upper respiratory tract infection (10%), sinusitis (3%)
Miscellaneous: Injury (8%)
<1%, postmarketing, and/or case reports: Angina, angioedema, CHF or exacerbation of CHF (increased with insulin to 2% to 3%), hepatic failure, hepatitis, bilirubin increased, macular edema, MI, pleural effusion, pulmonary edema, transaminases increased, urticaria, weight gain (rapid, excessive; usually due to fluid accumulation)
Isolated case reports of hepatotoxic reactions have been reported in patients receiving rosiglitazone; causality not established
Overdosage/Toxicology Experience in overdose is limited. Symptoms may include hypoglycemia. Treatment is supportive.
(Continued)

Rosiglitazone *(Continued)*

Drug Interactions

Cytochrome P450 Effect: Substrate of CYP2C8 (major), 2C9 (minor); **Inhibits** CYP2C8 (moderate), 2C9 (weak), 2C19 (weak), 2D6 (weak)

Increased Effect/Toxicity: The levels/effects of rosiglitazone may be increased by atazanavir, ritonavir, and other CYP2C8 inhibitors. Gemfibrozil may increase rosiglitazone levels; severe hypoglycemic episodes have been reported. Rosiglitazone may increase the levels/effects of amiodarone, paclitaxel, pioglitazone, repaglinide, rosiglitazone, and other CYP2C8 substrates.

Decreased Effect: The levels/effects of rosiglitazone may be decreased by carbamazepine, phenobarbital, phenytoin, rifampin, rifapentine, and secobarbital, and other CYP2C8 inducers. Bile acid sequestrants may decrease rosiglitazone levels.

Ethanol/Nutrition/Herb Interactions

Ethanol: Avoid ethanol (may cause hypoglycemia).

Food: Peak concentrations are lower by 28% and delayed when administered with food, but these effects are not believed to be clinically significant.

Herb/Nutraceutical: Avoid garlic, gymnema (may cause hypoglycemia).

Stability Store at 25°C (77°F); excursions permitted to 15°C to 30°C (59°F to 86°F). Protect from light.

Mechanism of Action Thiazolidinedione antidiabetic agent that lowers blood glucose by improving target cell response to insulin, without increasing pancreatic insulin secretion. It has a mechanism of action that is dependent on the presence of insulin for activity.

Pharmacodynamics/Kinetics

Onset of action: Delayed; Maximum effect: Up to 12 weeks

Distribution: V_{dss} (apparent): 17.6 L

Protein binding: 99.8%; primarily albumin

Metabolism: Hepatic (99%) via CYP2C8; minor metabolism via CYP2C9

Bioavailability: 99%

Half-life elimination: 3-4 hours

Time to peak, plasma: 1 hour; delayed with food

Excretion: Urine (64%) and feces (23%) as metabolites

Dosage Oral:

Adults: **Note:** All patients should be initiated at the lowest recommended dose.

Monotherapy: Initial: 4 mg daily as a single daily dose or in divided doses twice daily. If response is inadequate after 8-12 weeks of treatment, the dosage may be increased to 8 mg daily as a single daily dose or in divided doses twice daily. In clinical trials, the 4 mg twice-daily regimen resulted in the greatest reduction in fasting plasma glucose and Hb A_{1c}.

Combination therapy: When adding rosiglitazone to existing therapy, continue current dose(s) of previous agents:

With sulfonylureas or metformin (or sulfonylurea plus metformin): Initial: 4 mg daily as a single daily dose or in divided doses twice daily. If response is inadequate after 8-12 weeks of treatment, the dosage may be increased to 8 mg daily as a single daily dose or in divided doses twice daily. Reduce dose of sulfonylurea if hypoglycemia occurs. It is unlikely that the dose of metformin will need to be reduced to hypoglycemia.

With insulin: Initial: 4 mg daily as a single daily dose or in divided doses twice daily. Dose of insulin should be reduced by 10% to 25% if the patient reports hypoglycemia or if the plasma glucose falls to <100 mg/dL. Doses of rosiglitazone >4 mg/day are not indicated in combination with insulin.

Elderly: No dosage adjustment is recommended

Dosage adjustment in renal impairment: No dosage adjustment is required

Dosage comment in hepatic impairment: Clearance is significantly lower in hepatic impairment. Therapy should not be initiated if the patient exhibits active liver disease of increased transaminases (>2.5 times the upper limit of normal) at baseline.

Dietary Considerations Management of type 2 diabetes mellitus (noninsulin dependent, NIDDM) should include diet control. May be taken without regard to meals.

Monitoring Parameters Hemoglobin A_{1c}, serum glucose; signs and symptoms of fluid retention or heart failure; liver enzymes (prior to initiation of therapy, then periodically thereafter). Patients with an elevation in ALT >3 times the upper limit of normal should be rechecked as soon as possible. If the ALT levels remain >3 times the upper limit of normal, therapy with rosiglitazone should be discontinued.

Dosage Forms Tablet: 2 mg, 4 mg, 8 mg

Rosiglitazone and Glimepiride *(roh si GLI ta zone & GLYE me pye ride)*

U.S. Brand Names Avandaryl™

Index Terms Glimepiride and Rosiglitazone Maleate

Pharmacologic Category Antidiabetic Agent, Sulfonylurea; Antidiabetic Agent, Thiazolidinedione

Use Management of type 2 diabetes mellitus (noninsulin dependent, NIDDM) as an adjunct to diet and exercise

Pregnancy Risk Factor C

Dosage Oral: Adults: Type 2 diabetes mellitus:

Initial: Rosiglitazone 4 mg and glimepiride 1 mg once daily **or** rosiglitazone 4 mg and glimepiride 2 mg once daily (for patients previously treated with sulfonylurea or thiazolidinedione monotherapy)

Patients switching from combination rosiglitazone and glimepiride as separate tablets: Use current dose. Maximum: Rosiglitazone 8 mg and glimepiride 4 mg once daily

Titration:

Dose adjustment in patients previously on sulfonylurea monotherapy: May take 2 weeks to observe decreased blood glucose and 2-3 months to see full effects of rosiglitazone component. If not adequately controlled after 8-12 weeks, increase daily dose of rosiglitazone component. Maximum: Rosiglitazone 8 mg and glimepiride 4 mg once daily

Dose adjustment in patients previously on thiazolidinedione monotherapy: If not adequately controlled after 1-2 weeks, increase daily dose of glimepiride component in ≤2 mg increments in 1-2 week intervals. Maximum: Rosiglitazone 8 mg and glimepiride 4 mg once daily

Elderly: Rosiglitazone 4 mg and glimepiride 1 mg once daily; carefully titrate dose.

Dosage adjustment in renal impairment: Rosiglitazone 4 mg and glimepiride 1 mg once daily; carefully titrate dose.

Dosage adjustment in hepatic impairment: Rosiglitazone 4 mg and glimepiride 1 mg once daily; carefully titrate dose.
ALT ≤2.5 times ULN: Use with caution
ALT >2.5 times ULN: Do not initiate therapy
ALT >3 times ULN or jaundice: Discontinue

Additional Information Complete prescribing information for this medication should be consulted for additional detail.

Dosage Forms
Tablet:
Avandaryl™ 4 mg/1 mg: Rosiglitazone 4 mg and glimepiride 1 mg
Avandaryl™ 4 mg/2 mg: Rosiglitazone 4 mg and glimepiride 2 mg
Avandaryl™ 4 mg/4 mg: Rosiglitazone 4 mg and glimepiride 4 mg

Rosiglitazone and Metformin (roh si GLI ta zone & met FOR min)

U.S. Brand Names Avandamet®
Canadian Brand Names Avandamet®
Index Terms Metformin and Rosiglitazone; Metformin Hydrochloride and Rosiglitazone Maleate; Rosiglitazone Maleate and Metformin Hydrochloride
Pharmacologic Category Antidiabetic Agent, Biguanide; Antidiabetic Agent, Thiazolidinedione
Use Management of type 2 diabetes mellitus (noninsulin dependent, NIDDM) as an adjunct to diet and exercise in patients where dual rosiglitazone and metformin therapy is appropriate
Pregnancy Risk Factor C
Dosage Oral:
Adults: Type 2 diabetes mellitus: Daily dose should be divided and given with meals:
First-line therapy (drug-naive patients): Initial: Rosiglitazone 2 mg and metformin 500 mg once or twice daily; may increase by 2 mg/500 mg per day after 4 weeks to a maximum of 8 mg/2000 mg per day.
Second-line therapy:
Patients inadequately controlled on **metformin alone**: Initial dose: Rosiglitazone 4 mg/day plus current dose of metformin
Patients inadequately controlled on **rosiglitazone alone**: Initial dose: Metformin 1000 mg/day plus current dose of rosiglitazone
Note: When switching from combination rosiglitazone and metformin as separate tablets: Use current dose
Dose adjustment: Doses may be increased as increments of rosiglitazone 4 mg and/or metformin 500 mg, up to the maximum dose; doses should be titrated gradually.
After a change in the metformin dosage, titration can be done after 1-2 weeks
After a change in the rosiglitazone dosage, titration can be done after 8-12 weeks
Maximum dose: Rosiglitazone 8 mg/metformin 2000 mg daily
Elderly: The initial and maintenance dosing should be conservative, due to the potential for decreased renal function (monitor). Generally, elderly patients should not be titrated to the maximum; do not use in patients ≥80 years unless normal renal function has been established.
Dosage adjustment in renal impairment: Do not use with renal disease or renal dysfunction (serum creatinine ≥1.5 mg/dL in males or ≥1.4 mg/dL in females or abnormal clearance)
Dosage adjustment in hepatic impairment: Do not use with active liver disease or ALT >2.5 times the upper limit of normal
Additional Information Complete prescribing information for this medication should be consulted for additional detail.
Dosage Forms [DSC] = Discontinued product
Tablet:
Avandamet®: 1/500: Rosiglitazone 1 mg and metformin hydrochloride 500 mg [DSC]
Avandamet®: 2/500: Rosiglitazone 2 mg and metformin hydrochloride 500 mg
Avandamet®: 4/500: Rosiglitazone 4 mg and metformin hydrochloride 500 mg
Avandamet®: 2/1000: Rosiglitazone 2 mg and metformin hydrochloride 1000 mg
Avandamet®: 4/1000: Rosiglitazone 4 mg and metformin hydrochloride 1000 mg

♦ **Rosiglitazone Maleate and Metformin Hydrochloride** *see* Rosiglitazone and Metformin *on page 1537*
♦ **Rosula®** *see* Sulfur and Sulfacetamide *on page 1618*
♦ **Rosula® NS** *see* Sulfacetamide *on page 1609*

Rosuvastatin (roe soo va STAT in)

U.S. Brand Names Crestor®
Canadian Brand Names Crestor®
Index Terms Rosuvastatin Calcium
Pharmacologic Category Antilipemic Agent, HMG-CoA Reductase Inhibitor
Additional Appendix Information
Lipid-Lowering Agents *on page 1887*
Use Used with dietary therapy for hyperlipidemias to reduce elevations in total cholesterol (TC), LDL-C, apolipoprotein B, and triglycerides (TG) in patients with primary hypercholesterolemia
(Continued)

Rosuvastatin *(Continued)*

(elevations of 1 or more components are present in Fredrickson type IIa, IIb, and IV hyperlipidemias); treatment of homozygous familial hypercholesterolemia (FH)

Pregnancy Risk Factor X

Pregnancy Implications Cholesterol biosynthesis may be important in fetal development. Contraindicated in pregnancy. Administer to women of childbearing potential only when conception is highly unlikely and patients have been informed of potential hazards.

Lactation Excretion in breast milk unknown/contraindicated

Contraindications Hypersensitivity to rosuvastatin or any component of the formulation; active liver disease; unexplained persistent elevations of serum transaminases (>3 times ULN); pregnancy; breast-feeding

Warnings/Precautions Secondary causes of hyperlipidemia should be ruled out prior to therapy. Liver function must be monitored by periodic laboratory assessment. Use with caution in patients who consume large amounts of ethanol or have a history of liver disease. Rhabdomyolysis with acute renal failure has occurred. Discontinue in any patient in which CPK levels are markedly elevated (>10 times ULN) or if myopathy is suspected/diagnosed. An increased incidence of rosuvastatin-associated myopathy has been reported during concomitant therapy with fibric acid derivatives, niacin, cyclosporine, and in certain subgroups of the Asian population. Risk is also elevated at higher dosages of rosuvastatin. Patients should be instructed to report unexplained muscle pain, tenderness, or weakness, particularly if associated with fever and/or malaise. Use caution in patients predisposed to myopathy (eg, renal failure, advanced age, inadequately treated hypothyroidism). Temporarily withhold in patients experiencing an acute or serious condition predisposing to renal failure secondary to rhabdomyolysis (sepsis, hypotension, major surgery, trauma, severe metabolic or endocrine or electrolyte disorders, uncontrolled seizures). Use with caution in patients with advanced age, these patients are predisposed to myopathy. Safety and efficacy have not been established in children (limited experience with homozygous FH in patients >8 years of age).

Adverse Reactions

1% to 10%:

Cardiovascular: Chest pain, hypertension, palpitation, peripheral edema

Central nervous system: Headache (6%), anxiety, depression, dizziness, insomnia, neuralgia, pain, vertigo

Dermatologic: Rash

Gastrointestinal: Pharyngitis (9%), abdominal pain, constipation, diarrhea, dyspepsia, gastroenteritis, nausea, vomiting

Hematologic: Anemia, bruising

Neuromuscular & skeletal: Myalgia (3%), arthralgia, arthritis, back pain, hypertonia, paresthesia, weakness

Respiratory: Bronchitis, cough, rhinitis, sinusitis

Miscellaneous: Flu-like syndrome

<1% (Limited to important or life-threatening): Arrhythmia, angioedema, hematuria (microscopic), hepatitis, hypersensitivity reactions, jaundice, kidney failure, myasthenia, myositis, myopathy, pancreatitis, photosensitivity, proteinuria (dose related), rhabdomyolysis, syncope

Adverse reactions reported with other HMG-CoA reductase inhibitors include a hypersensitivity syndrome (symptoms may include anaphylaxis, angioedema, arthralgia, erythema multiforme, eosinophilia, hemolytic anemia, lupus syndrome, photosensitivity, polymyalgia rheumatica, positive ANA, purpura, Stevens-Johnson syndrome, toxic epidermal necrolysis, urticaria, vasculitis)

Overdosage/Toxicology No specific experience in overdose. Treatment is supportive. Rosuvastatin is not removed by hemodialysis. CNS vascular lesions and corneal opacities have been reported following high-dose, long-term exposure to HMG-CoA reductase inhibitors in animal studies. The relationship to human exposures has not been established.

Drug Interactions

Cytochrome P450 Effect: Substrate (minor) of CYP2C9, 3A4

Increased Effect/Toxicity: Cyclosporine may increase serum concentrations of rosuvastatin (up to 10-fold); limit dose to 5 mg/day. Serum concentrations of rosuvastatin may be increased (doubled) during concurrent administration of gemfibrozil; combination should be avoided; limit dose to 10 mg/day. Clofibrate, fenofibrate, or niacin may increase the risk of myopathy and rhabdomyolysis with HMG-CoA reductase inhibitors; the effects on lipids may be additive. The anticoagulant effects of warfarin may be increased by rosuvastatin (monitor). Rosuvastatin increases serum concentrations of hormonal contraceptives (ethinyl estradiol and norgestrel).

Decreased Effect: Plasma concentrations of rosuvastatin may be decreased when given with magnesium/aluminum hydroxide-containing antacids; antacids should be administered at least 2 hours after rosuvastatin. Cholestyramine and colestipol (bile acid sequestrants) may reduce absorption of several HMG-CoA reductase inhibitors; separate administration times by at least 4 hours; cholesterol-lowering effects are additive.

Ethanol/Nutrition/Herb Interactions Ethanol: Avoid excessive ethanol consumption (due to potential hepatic effects).

Food: Red yeast rice contains an estimated 2.4 mg lovastatin per 600 mg rice.

Stability Store between 20°C and 25°C (68°F to 77°F). Protect from moisture.

Mechanism of Action Inhibitor of 3-hydroxy-3-methylglutaryl coenzyme A (HMG-CoA) reductase, the rate-limiting enzyme in cholesterol synthesis (reduces the production of mevalonic acid from HMG-CoA); this then results in a compensatory increase in the expression of LDL receptors on hepatocyte membranes and a stimulation of LDL catabolism

Pharmacodynamics/Kinetics

Onset: Within 1 week; maximal at 4 weeks

Distribution: V_d: 134 L

Protein binding: 90%

Metabolism: Hepatic (10%), via CYP2C9 (1 active metabolite identified)

Bioavailability: 20% (high first-pass extraction by liver)

Asian patients have been noted to have increased bioavailability.

Half-life elimination: 19 hours

Time to peak, plasma: 3-5 hours

Excretion: Feces (90%), primarily as unchanged drug

Dosage Adults: Oral:

Heterozygous familial and nonfamilial hypercholesterolemia; mixed dyslipidemia:

Initial dose:

General dosing: 10 mg once daily (20 mg in patients with severe hypercholesterolemia)

Conservative dosing: Patients requiring less aggressive treatment or predisposed to myopathy (including patients of Asian descent): 5 mg once daily

Titration: After 2 weeks, may be increased by 5-10 mg once daily; dosing range: 5-40 mg/day (maximum dose: 40 mg once daily)

Note: The 40 mg dose should be reserved for patients who have not achieved goal cholesterol levels on a dose of 20 mg/day, including patients switched from another HMG-CoA reductase inhibitor.

Homozygous FH: Initial: 20 mg once daily (maximum dose: 40 mg/day)

Dosage adjustment with concomitant medications:

Cyclosporine: Rosuvastatin dose should not exceed 5 mg/day

Gemfibrozil: Rosuvastatin dose should not exceed 10 mg/day

Dosage adjustment for persistent, unexplained proteinuria while on 40 mg/day:

Reduce dose and evaluate causes

Dosage adjustment in renal impairment:

Mild-to-moderate impairment: No dosage adjustment required.

Cl_{cr} <30 mL/minute/1.73 m²: Initial: 5 mg/day; do not exceed 10 mg once daily

Dietary Considerations May be taken with or without food. Red yeast rice contains an estimated 2.4 mg lovastatin per 600 mg rice.

Administration May be administered with or without food.

Monitoring Parameters Total cholesterol, LDL, and HDL cholesterol; liver function tests should be determined at baseline (prior to initiation), 3 months following initiation, and 3 months after any increase in dose; baseline CPK (recheck CPK in any patient with symptoms suggestive of myopathy)

Dosage Forms Tablet, as calcium: 5 mg, 10 mg, 20 mg, 40 mg

♦ **Rosuvastatin Calcium** *see* Rosuvastatin *on page 1537*

♦ **RotaTeq**® *see* Rotavirus Vaccine *on page 1539*

Rotavirus Vaccine (ROE ta vye rus vak SEEN)

U.S. Brand Names RotaTeq®

Index Terms Pentavalent Human-Bovine Reassortant Rotavirus Vaccine; Rotavirus Vaccine, Pentavalent

Pharmacologic Category Vaccine

Use Prevention of rotavirus gastroenteritis in infants and children

Pregnancy Implications

Infants living in households with pregnant women may be vaccinated.

Contraindications Hypersensitivity to rotavirus vaccine or any component of the formulation

Warnings/Precautions Information is not available for use in postexposure prophylaxis. Immunization may be delayed during febrile illness; low grade fever (<38.1°C/<100.5°F) and mild upper respiratory tract infections generally do not preclude use of vaccine. Use caution with history of GI disorders, acute GI illness, chronic diarrhea, failure to thrive, congenital abdominal disorders, abdominal surgery, and intussusception. Vaccine may be used with controlled gastroesophageal reflux disease. Live virus vaccines may be transmitted to nonvaccinated contacts; use caution in presence immunocompromised family members. Safety and efficacy have not been established for use in immunocompromised infants (including blood dyscrasias, leukemia, lymphoma, malignant neoplasms affecting bone marrow or lymphatic system), infants on immunosuppressants (including high-dose corticosteroids; may be administered with topical corticosteroids or inhaled steroids), primary and acquired immunodeficiencies (including HIV), or infants receiving blood products or immunoglobulins within 42 days. Intussusception was observed with a previous licensed rotavirus vaccine; an increased risk in intussusception was not observed in clinical trials with RotaTeq®, however, a postlicensure study will be conducted to monitor all serious side effects. Use caution with a history of intussusception. Safety and efficacy have not been established in children <6 weeks or >32 weeks of age. Not intended for use in adults.

Adverse Reactions All serious adverse reactions must be reported to the U.S. Department of Health and Human Services (DHHS) Vaccine Adverse Event Reporting System (VAERS) 1-800-822-7967.

Note: An increased risk of intussusception was not noted in clinical trials

>10%:

Central nervous system: Fever (43%, equal to placebo)

Gastrointestinal: Diarrhea (4% to 24%), vomiting (3% to 15%)

Otic: Otitis media (15%)

1% to 10%:

Central nervous system: Irritability (3% to 8%)

Respiratory: Nasopharyngitis (7%), bronchospasm (1%)

<1% (Limited to important or life-threatening): Seizure

Drug Interactions

Increased Effect/Toxicity: In clinical trials, rotavirus vaccine was administered with DTaP, IPV, HiB, hepatitis B vaccine, and pneumococcal conjugate vaccine. Antibody response was not decreased, with the exception of pertussis (insufficient data). Infants needing oral polio vaccine were excluded from clinical studies.

Decreased Effect: In clinical trials, rotavirus vaccine was administered with DTaP, IPV, HiB, hepatitis B vaccine and pneumococcal conjugate vaccine. Antibody response was not decreased, with the exception of pertussis (insufficient data). Infants needing oral polio

(Continued)

Rotavirus Vaccine *(Continued)*

vaccine were excluded from clinical studies. When used concurrently with immunosuppressant medications, the effect of the vaccine may be decreased.

Stability Store and transport under refrigeration at 2°C to 8°C (36°F to 46°F). Use as soon as possible once removed from refrigerator. Protect from light.

Mechanism of Action A live vaccine obtained from human and bovine sources; replicates in the small intestine and promotes active immunity to rotavirus gastroenteritis caused by serotypes G1, G2, G3, and G4.

Pharmacodynamics/Kinetics
Onset of action: A threefold increase in antirotavirus IgA was noted following completion of the 3-dose regimen in 93% to 100% of infants.
Duration: At least 2 years

Dosage Oral: Children 6-32 weeks: Three 2 mL doses at 2-, 4-, and 6 months of age, the first given at 6-12 weeks of age, followed by subsequent doses at 4- to 10-week intervals. Routine administration of the first dose at >12 weeks of age is not recommended (insufficient data). Administer all doses by 32 weeks of age. Infants who have had rotavirus gastroenteritis before getting the full course of vaccine should still initiate or complete the 3-dose schedule; initial infection provides only partial immunity.

Dietary Considerations Do not mix or dilute vaccine. May be administered before or after food, milk, or breast milk.

Administration Gently squeeze dose from ready-to-use dosing tube. If infant spits or regurgitates vaccine, a replacement dose is not recommended. In general, vaccine administration should be deferred for 42 days following an antibody-containing product. However, if deferral causes first dose of vaccine to be scheduled at ≥13 weeks of age, a shorter deferral interval should be used.

Dosage Forms
Suspension, oral [preservative free]:
RotaTeq®: G1 ≥2.2 10^6 infectious units, G2 ≥2.8 10^6 infectious units, G3 ≥2.2 10^6 infectious units, G4 ≥2.0 10^6 infectious units, and P1 [8] ≥2.3 10^6 infectious units (2 mL) [bovine and human derived; available in a prefilled, ready-to-use dosing tube]

- **Rotavirus Vaccine, Pentavalent** *see* Rotavirus Vaccine *on page 1539*
- **Rowasa®** *see* Mesalamine *on page 1089*
- **Roxanol™** *see* Morphine Sulfate *on page 1171*
- **Roxicet™** *see* Oxycodone and Acetaminophen *on page 1289*
- **Roxicet™ 5/500** *see* Oxycodone and Acetaminophen *on page 1289*
- **Roxicodone®** *see* Oxycodone *on page 1286*
- **Roychlor® (Can)** *see* Potassium Chloride *on page 1396*
- **Rozerem™** *see* Ramelteon *on page 1481*
- **RP-6976** *see* Docetaxel *on page 530*
- **RP-54274** *see* Riluzole *on page 1512*
- **RP-59500** *see* Quinupristin and Dalfopristin *on page 1476*
- **r-PA** *see* Reteplase *on page 1498*
- **rPDGF-BB** *see* Becaplermin *on page 198*
- **(R,R)-Formoterol L-Tartrate** *see* Arformoterol *on page 148*
- **RS-25259** *see* Palonosetron *on page 1299*
- **RS-25259-197** *see* Palonosetron *on page 1299*
- **RSV-IGIV** *see* Respiratory Syncytial Virus Immune Globulin (Intravenous) *on page 1497*
- **R-Tanna** *see* Chlorpheniramine and Phenylephrine *on page 349*
- **RTCA** *see* Ribavirin *on page 1503*
- **RU 0211** *see* Lubiprostone *on page 1044*
- **RU-486** *see* Mifepristone *on page 1143*
- **RU-23908** *see* Nilutamide *on page 1228*
- **RU-38486** *see* Mifepristone *on page 1143*
- **Rubella, Measles and Mumps Vaccines, Combined** *see* Measles, Mumps, and Rubella Vaccines (Combined) *on page 1057*
- **Rubella, Varicella, Measles, and Mumps Vaccine** *see* Measles, Mumps, Rubella, and Varicella Virus Vaccine *on page 1057*

Rubella Virus Vaccine (Live) (rue BEL a VYE rus vak SEEN, live)

U.S. Brand Names Meruvax® II
Index Terms German Measles Vaccine
Pharmacologic Category Vaccine
Additional Appendix Information
Immunization Recommendations *on page 1929*
Use Selective active immunization against rubella; vaccination is routinely recommended for persons from 12 months of age to puberty. All adults, both male and female, lacking documentation of live vaccine on or after first birthday, or laboratory evidence of immunity (particularly women of childbearing age and young adults who work in or congregate in hospitals, colleges, and on military bases) should be vaccinated. Susceptible travelers should be vaccinated.
Note: Trivalent measles - mumps - rubella (MMR) vaccine is the preferred immunizing agent for most children and many adults.

Pregnancy Risk Factor C
Pregnancy Implications Women who are pregnant when vaccinated or who become pregnant within 28 days of vaccination should be counseled on the theoretical risks to the fetus. The risk of rubella-associated malformations in these women is so small as to be negligible. MMR is the vaccine of choice if recipients are likely to be susceptible to measles or mumps as well as to rubella.

Lactation Enters breast milk/use caution

Medication Safety Issues
Sound-alike/look-alike issues:
Meruvax® II may be confused with Attenuvax®

Contraindications Hypersensitivity to gelatin or any other component of the vaccine; history of anaphylactic reactions to neomycin; individuals with blood dyscrasias, leukemia, lymphomas, or other malignant neoplasms affecting the bone marrow or lymphatic systems; concurrent immunosuppressive therapy; primary and acquired immunodeficiency states; family history of congenital or hereditary immunodeficiency; active/untreated tuberculosis; current febrile illness or active febrile infection; pregnancy

Warnings/Precautions Immediate treatment for anaphylactic/anaphylactoid reaction should be available during vaccine use. Use with caution in patients with thrombocytopenia and those who develop thrombocytopenia after first dose; thrombocytopenia may worsen. Defer vaccine following blood, plasma, or immune globulin (human) administration; children with HIV infection, who are asymptomatic and not immunosuppressed may be vaccinated.

Adverse Reactions All serious adverse reactions must be reported to the U.S. Department of Health and Human Services (DHHS) Vaccine Adverse Event Reporting System (VAERS) 1-800-822-7967.
Frequency not defined.
Cardiovascular: Syncope, vasculitis
Central nervous system: Dizziness, encephalitis, fever, Guillain-Barré syndrome, headache, irritability, malaise, polyneuritis, polyneuropathy
Dermatologic: Angioneurotic edema, erythema multiforme, purpura, rash, Stevens-Johnson syndrome, urticaria
Gastrointestinal: Diarrhea, nausea, sore throat, vomiting
Hematologic: Leukocytosis, thrombocytopenia
Local: Injection site reactions which include burning, induration, pain, redness, stinging, wheal and flare
Neuromuscular & skeletal: Arthralgia/arthritis (variable; highest rates in women, 12% to 26% versus children, up to 3%), myalgia, paresthesia
Ocular: Conjunctivitis, optic neuritis, papillitis, retrobulbar neuritis
Otic: Nerve deafness, otitis media
Respiratory: Bronchial spasm, cough, rhinitis
Miscellaneous: Anaphylactoid reactions, anaphylaxis, regional lymphadenopathy

Drug Interactions
Decreased Effect: The effect of the vaccine may be decreased in individuals who are receiving immunosuppressant drugs (including high-dose systemic corticosteroids). Effect of vaccine may be decreased in given with immune globulin, whole blood or plasma; do not administer with vaccine. Effectiveness may be decreased if given within 30 days of varicella vaccine (effectiveness not decreased when administered simultaneously).

Stability Vaccine is to be shipped at 10°C (50°F). May use dry ice. Protect from light at all times. Prior to reconstitution, store at 2°C to 8°C (36°F to 46°F) or colder. Discard reconstituted vaccine after 8 hours.

Mechanism of Action Rubella vaccine is a live attenuated vaccine that contains the Wistar Institute RA 27/3 strain, which is adapted to and propagated in human diploid cell culture. Promotes active immunity by inducing rubella hemagglutination-inhibiting antibodies.

Pharmacodynamics/Kinetics Onset of action: Antibodies to vaccine: 2-4 weeks

Dosage Children ≥12 months and Adults: SubQ: 0.5 mL in outer aspect of upper arm; children vaccinated before 12 months of age should be revaccinated. Recommended age for primary immunization is 12-15 months; revaccination with MMR-II is recommended prior to elementary school.

Administration SubQ injection only in outer aspect of upper arm; avoid injection into blood vessel. **Not for I.V. administration.** Federal law requires that the date of administration, the vaccine manufacturer, lot number of vaccine, and the administering person's name, title and address be entered into the patient's permanent medical record.

Test Interactions May depress tuberculin skin test sensitivity

Additional Information Live virus vaccine. Federal law requires that the date of administration, the vaccine manufacturer, lot number of vaccine, and the administering person's name, title, and address be entered into the patient's permanent record.

Using separate sites and syringes, rubella virus vaccine may be administered concurrently with DTaP, *Haemophilus* b conjugate vaccine (PedvaxHIB®), or hepatitis B vaccine. Unless otherwise specified, rubella virus vaccine should be given 1 month before or 1 month after other live viral vaccines. OPV and rubella virus vaccines may be administered together. Rubella virus vaccine and varicella virus vaccine may be administered together (using separate sites and syringes); however, if vaccines are not administered simultaneously, doses should be separated by at least 30 days.

Dosage Forms Injection, powder for reconstitution [single dose]: 1000 $TCID_{50}$ (Wistar RA 27/3 Strain) [contains gelatin, human albumin, and neomycin]

♦ **Rubeola Vaccine** *see* Measles Virus Vaccine (Live) *on page 1058*
♦ **Rubex®** *see* DOXOrubicin *on page 549*
♦ **Rubidomycin Hydrochloride** *see* DAUNOrubicin Hydrochloride *on page 462*
♦ **Rulox [OTC]** *see* Aluminum Hydroxide and Magnesium Hydroxide *on page 85*
♦ **Rulox No. 1 [DSC]** *see* Aluminum Hydroxide and Magnesium Hydroxide *on page 85*
♦ **Rum-K®** *see* Potassium Chloride *on page 1396*
♦ **Ru-Tuss DM** *see* Guaifenesin, Pseudoephedrine, and Dextromethorphan *on page 821*
♦ **Rylosol (Can)** *see* Sotalol *on page 1592*
♦ **Rynatan®** *see* Chlorpheniramine and Phenylephrine *on page 349*
♦ **Rynatan® Pediatric Suspension** *see* Chlorpheniramine and Phenylephrine *on page 349*
♦ **Rynatuss®** *see* Chlorpheniramine, Ephedrine, Phenylephrine, and Carbetapentane *on page 351*
♦ **Rynatuss® Pediatric [DSC]** *see* Chlorpheniramine, Ephedrine, Phenylephrine, and Carbetapentane *on page 351*

♦ **Rythmodan® (Can)** *see* Disopyramide *on page 526*

♦ **Rythmodan®-LA (Can)** *see* Disopyramide *on page 526*

♦ **Rythmol®** *see* Propafenone *on page 1439*

♦ **Rythmol® Gen-Propafenone (Can)** *see* Propafenone *on page 1439*

♦ **Rythmol® SR** *see* Propafenone *on page 1439*

♦ **Rēv-Eyes™** *see* Dapiprazole *on page 450*

♦ **S2® [OTC]** *see* Epinephrine *on page 589*

♦ **S-(+)-3-isobutylgaba** *see* Pregabalin *on page 1418*

♦ **SAB-Dimenhydrinate (Can)** *see* DimenhyDRINATE *on page 511*

♦ **SAB-Gentamicin (Can)** *see* Gentamicin *on page 793*

♦ **Sab-Prenase (Can)** *see* PrednisoLONE *on page 1413*

♦ **SAB-Trifluridine (Can)** *see* Trifluridine *on page 1741*

Sacrosidase (sak ROE si dase)

U.S. Brand Names Sucraid®
Canadian Brand Names Sucraid®
Pharmacologic Category Enzyme, Gastrointestinal
Use Orphan drug: Oral replacement therapy in sucrase deficiency, as seen in congenital sucrase-isomaltase deficiency (CSID)
Pregnancy Risk Factor C
Pregnancy Implications Animal studies have not been conducted. Should be administered to a pregnant woman only when indicated.
Lactation Enters breast milk/compatible
Contraindications Hypersensitivity to yeast, yeast products, or glycerin
Warnings/Precautions Hypersensitivity reactions to sacrosidase, including bronchospasm, have been reported. Administer initial doses in a setting where acute hypersensitivity reactions may be treated within a few minutes. Skin testing for hypersensitivity may be performed prior to administration to identify patients at risk.
Adverse Reactions
1% to 10%: Gastrointestinal: Abdominal pain, constipation, diarrhea, nausea, vomiting
<1% (Limited to important or life-threatening symptoms): Bronchospasm, dehydration, headache, hypersensitivity reaction, insomnia, nervousness
Overdosage/Toxicology Symptoms may include epigastric pain, drowsiness, lethargy, nausea, and vomiting. Gastrointestinal bleeding may occur. Rare manifestations include hypertension, respiratory depression, coma, and acute renal failure. Treatment is symptomatic and supportive. Forced diuresis, hemodialysis, and/or urinary alkalinization are not likely to be useful.
Drug Interactions
Increased Effect/Toxicity: Drug-drug interactions have not been evaluated.
Ethanol/Nutrition/Herb Interactions Food: May be inactivated or denatured if administered with fruit juice, warm or hot food or liquids. Since isomaltase deficiency is not addressed by supplementation of sacrosidase, adherence to a low-starch diet may be required.
Stability Store under refrigeration at 4°C to 8°C (36°F to 46°F). Protect from heat or light.
Mechanism of Action Sacrosidase is a naturally-occurring gastrointestinal enzyme which breaks down the disaccharide sucrose to its monosaccharide components. Hydrolysis is necessary to allow absorption of these nutrients.
Pharmacodynamics/Kinetics
Absorption: Amino acids
Metabolism: GI tract to individual amino acids
Dosage Oral:
Infants ≥5 months and Children <15 kg: 8500 int. units (1 mL) per meal or snack
Children >15 kg and Adults: 17,000 int. units (2 mL) per meal or snack
Doses should be diluted with 2-4 oz of water, milk, or formula with each meal or snack. Approximately one-half of the dose may be taken before, and the remainder of a dose taken at the completion of each meal or snack.
Administration Do not administer with fruit juices, warm or hot liquids; the solution is fully soluble with water, milk, or formula
Additional Information Oral solution contains 50% glycerol.
Dosage Forms Solution, oral: 8500 int. units per mL (118 mL)

♦ **Safe Tussin® [OTC]** *see* Guaifenesin and Dextromethorphan *on page 816*

♦ **SAHA** *see* Vorinostat *on page 1799*

♦ **Saizen®** *see* Somatropin *on page 1586*

♦ **Salagen®** *see* Pilocarpine *on page 1368*

♦ **Salazopyrin® (Can)** *see* Sulfasalazine *on page 1615*

♦ **Salazopyrin En-Tabs® (Can)** *see* Sulfasalazine *on page 1615*

♦ **Salbu-2 (Can)** *see* Albuterol *on page 57*

♦ **Salbu-4 (Can)** *see* Albuterol *on page 57*

♦ **Salbutamol** *see* Albuterol *on page 57*

♦ **Salbutamol and Ipratropium** *see* Ipratropium and Albuterol *on page 934*

♦ **Salflex® (Can)** *see* Salsalate *on page 1544*

♦ **Salicylazosulfapyridine** *see* Sulfasalazine *on page 1615*

♦ **Salicylsalicylic Acid** *see* Salsalate *on page 1544*

♦ **SalineX® [OTC]** *see* Sodium Chloride *on page 1576*

♦ **Salk Vaccine** *see* Poliovirus Vaccine (Inactivated) *on page 1385*

Salmeterol (sal ME te role)

U.S. Brand Names Serevent® Diskus®
Canadian Brand Names Serevent®
Index Terms Salmeterol Xinafoate
Pharmacologic Category Beta₂-Adrenergic Agonist

Additional Appendix Information
Bronchodilators *on page 1877*

Use Maintenance treatment of asthma and in prevention of bronchospasm with reversible obstructive airway disease, including patients with symptoms of nocturnal asthma; prevention of exercise-induced bronchospasm; maintenance treatment of bronchospasm associated with COPD

Restrictions An FDA-approved medication guide must be distributed when dispensing an outpatient prescription (new or refill) where this medication is to be used without direct supervision of a healthcare provider. Medication guides are available at http://www.fda.gov/cder/Offices/ODS/medication_guides.htm.

Pregnancy Risk Factor C

Pregnancy Implications Animal studies have demonstrated (? dose-dependent) teratogenicity. There are no adequate and well-controlled studies in pregnant women. Beta-agonists may interfere with uterine contractility if administered during labor. Use only if clearly needed.

Lactation Enters breast milk/use caution

Medication Safety Issues
Sound-alike/look-alike issues:
Salmeterol may be confused with Salbutamol
Serevent® may be confused with Serentil®

Contraindications Hypersensitivity to salmeterol, adrenergic amines, or any component of the formulation; need for acute bronchodilation

Warnings/Precautions

Asthma treatment: [U.S. Boxed Warning]: Long-acting beta₂ agonists may increase the risk of asthma-related deaths. In a large, randomized clinical trial (SMART, 2006), salmeterol was associated with an increase in asthma-related deaths (when added to usual asthma therapy); risk may be greater in African-American patients versus Caucasians. Should only be used as adjuvant therapy in patients not adequately controlled on inhaled corticosteroids or whose disease requires two maintenance therapies. Salmeterol is not meant to relieve acute asthmatic symptoms, should not be initiated in patients with significantly worsening or acutely deteriorating asthma, and is not a substitute for inhaled or oral corticosteroids. Short-acting beta₂ agonist should be used for acute symptoms and symptoms occurring between treatments. Corticosteroids should not be stopped or reduced when salmeterol is initiated. During the initiation of salmeterol watch for signs of worsening asthma.

Concurrent diseases: Use caution in patients with cardiovascular disease (eg, arrhythmia, hypertension, or CHF); seizure disorders, diabetes, glaucoma, hyperthyroidism, hepatic impairment, or hypokalemia. Beta agonists may cause elevation in blood pressure, heart rate, CNS stimulation/excitation, increased risk of arrhythmia, increase serum glucose, or decrease serum potassium.

Adverse events: Immediate hypersensitivity reactions (urticaria, angioedema, rash, bronchospasm) have been reported. There have been reports of laryngeal spasm, irritation, swelling (stridor, choking) with use. Salmeterol should not be used more than twice daily; do not exceed recommended dose; do not use with other long-acting beta₂ agonists; serious adverse events including fatalities, have been associated with excessive use of inhaled sympathomimetics. Rarely, paradoxical bronchospasm may occur; distinguished from inadequate response. Powder for oral inhalation contains lactose; very rare anaphylactic reactions have been reported in patients with severe milk protein allergy.

Safety and efficacy have not been established in children <4 years of age.

Adverse Reactions
>10%:
Central nervous system: Headache (13% to 17%)
Neuromuscular & skeletal: Pain (1% to 12%)
1% to 10%:
Cardiovascular: Hypertension (4%), edema (1% to <3%)
Central nervous system: Dizziness (4%), sleep disturbance (1% to 3%), fever (1% to 3%), anxiety (1% to <3%), migraine (1% to <3%)
Dermatologic: Rash (1% to 4%), contact dermatitis (1% to 3%), eczema (1% to 3%), urticaria (3%), photodermatitis (1% to 2%)
Endocrine & metabolic: Hyperglycemia (1% to <3%)
Gastrointestinal: Nausea (1% to 3%), dyspepsia (1% to <3%), dental pain (1% to <3%), infections (1% to <3%), oropharyngeal candidiasis (1% to <3%), xerostomia (1% to <3%)
Neuromuscular & skeletal: Muscular cramps/spasm (3%), paresthesia (1% to 3%), arthralgia (1% to <3%), muscular stiffness, rigidity (1% to <3%)
Ocular: Keratitis/conjunctivitis (1% to <3%)
Respiratory: Tracheitis/bronchitis (7%), pharyngitis (up to 6%), cough (5%), influenza (5%), infection (5%), sinusitis (4% to 5%), rhinitis (4% to 5%), nasal congestion (4%), asthma (3% to 4%)
<1% (Limited to important or life-threatening): Anaphylaxis, anaphylactic reaction (severe milk protein allergy), angioedema, arrhythmia (atrial fibrillation, supraventricular tachycardia, extrasystoles), bronchospasm, choking, hypersensitivity reaction, laryngeal spasm, paradoxical bronchospasm, stridor, tachycardia, tremor

Overdosage/Toxicology Symptoms of overdose include tachycardia, tremor, hypertension, angina, and seizures. Hypokalemia also may occur. Cardiac arrest and death may be associated with abuse of beta-agonist bronchodilators. Treatment includes immediate discontinuation and symptomatic and supportive therapies. Cautious use of beta-adrenergic blocking agents may be considered in severe cases.
(Continued)

Salmeterol (Continued)

Drug Interactions

Cytochrome P450 Effect: Substrate of CYP3A4 (major)

Increased Effect/Toxicity: CYP3A4 inhibitors may increase the levels/effects of fluticasone and salmeterol; example inhibitors include amprenavir, atazanavir, clarithromycin, delavirdine, diclofenac, fosamprenavir, imatinib, indinavir, isoniazid, itraconazole, ketoconazole, miconazole, nefazodone, nelfinavir, nicardipine, propofol, quinidine, ritonavir, and telithromycin. Atomoxetine may enhance the tachycardia effect of beta$_2$-agonists. Sympathomimetics may enhance the adverse/toxic effect of salmeterol.

Decreased Effect: Beta$_2$-agonists may diminish the bradycardia effect of beta-blockers (beta$_1$ selective). Beta-blockers (nonselective) may diminish the bronchodilator effect of beta$_2$-agonists.

Stability Inhalation powder: Store at controlled room temperature 20°C to 25°C (68°F to 77°F) in a dry place away from direct heat or sunlight. Stable for 6 weeks after removal from foil pouch.

Mechanism of Action Relaxes bronchial smooth muscle by selective action on beta$_2$-receptors with little effect on heart rate; because salmeterol acts locally in the lung, therapeutic effect is not predicted by plasma levels

Pharmacodynamics/Kinetics

Onset of action: Asthma: 30-48 minutes, COPD: 2 hours

Peak effect: 2-4 hours, COPD: 3.27-4.75 hours

Duration: 12 hours

Protein binding: 96%

Metabolism: Hepatically hydroxylated

Half-life elimination: 5.5 hours

Excretion: Feces (60%), urine (25%)

Dosage Inhalation, powder (Serevent® Diskus®):

Asthma, maintenance and prevention: Children ≥4 years and Adults: One inhalation (50 mcg) twice daily (~12 hours apart); maximum: 1 inhalation twice daily

Exercise-induced asthma, prevention: Children ≥4 years and Adults: One inhalation (50 mcg) at least 30 minutes prior to exercise; additional doses should not be used for 12 hours; should not be used in individuals already receiving salmeterol twice daily

COPD (maintenance treatment of associated bronchospasm): Adults: One inhalation (50 mcg) twice daily (~12 hours apart); maximum: 1 inhalation twice daily

Dietary Considerations Powder for oral inhalation contains lactose; very rare anaphylactic reactions have been reported in patients with severe milk protein allergy.

Administration Inhalation: **Not** to be used for the relief of acute attacks. Not for use with a spacer device. Administer with Diskus® in a level, horizontal position. Do not wash mouthpiece; Diskus® should be kept dry.

Monitoring Parameters FEV$_1$, peak flow, and/or other pulmonary function tests; blood pressure, heart rate; CNS stimulation; serum glucose, serum potassium. Monitor for increased use of short-acting beta$_2$-agonist inhalers; may be marker of a deteriorating asthma condition.

Dosage Forms Powder for oral inhalation: 50 mcg (28s, 60s) [delivers 50 mcg/inhalation; contains lactose]

- **Salmeterol and Fluticasone** see Fluticasone and Salmeterol on page 742
- **Salmeterol Xinafoate** see Salmeterol on page 1543
- **Salofalk® (Can)** see Mesalamine on page 1089

Salsalate (SAL sa late)

U.S. Brand Names Amigesic®

Canadian Brand Names Amigesic®; Salflex®

Index Terms Disalicylic Acid; Salicylsalicylic Acid

Pharmacologic Category Salicylate

Additional Appendix Information

Antiretroviral Therapy for HIV Infection: Adults and Adolescents on page 1988

Use Treatment of minor pain or fever; arthritis

Pregnancy Risk Factor C/D (3rd trimester)

Lactation Enters breast milk/contraindicated

Medication Safety Issues

Sound-alike/look-alike issues:

Salsalate may be confused with sucralfate, sulfasalazine

Contraindications Hypersensitivity to salsalate or any component of the formulation; GI ulcer or bleeding; pregnancy (3rd trimester)

Warnings/Precautions Use with caution in patients with platelet and bleeding disorders, dehydration, renal dysfunction, erosive gastritis, or peptic ulcer disease, previous nonreaction does not guarantee future safe taking of medication; do not use aspirin in children <16 years of age for chickenpox or flu symptoms due to the association with Reye's syndrome

Adverse Reactions

>10%: Gastrointestinal: Nausea, heartburn, stomach pain, dyspepsia

1% to 10%:

Central nervous system: Drowsiness

Dermatologic: Rash

Gastrointestinal: Gastrointestinal ulceration

Hematologic: Hemolytic anemia

Neuromuscular & skeletal: Weakness

Respiratory: Dyspnea

Miscellaneous: Anaphylactic shock

<1% (Limited to important or life-threatening): Bronchospasm, does not appear to inhibit platelet aggregation, hepatotoxicity, impaired renal function, iron-deficiency anemia, leukopenia, occult bleeding, thrombocytopenia

Overdosage/Toxicology Symptoms include respiratory alkalosis, hyperpnea, tachypnea, tinnitus, headache, hyperpyrexia, metabolic acidosis, hypoglycemia, and coma. The "Done" nomogram is very helpful for estimating the severity of aspirin poisoning and directing treatment using serum salicylate levels. Treatment can also be based upon symptomatology.

Drug Interactions

Increased Effect/Toxicity: Increased effect/toxicity of oral anticoagulants, hypoglycemics, and methotrexate.

Decreased Effect: Decreased effect with urinary alkalinizers, antacids, and corticosteroids. Decreased effect of uricosurics and spironolactone.

Ethanol/Nutrition/Herb Interactions

Ethanol: Avoid ethanol (may enhance gastric mucosal irritation).

Food: Salsalate peak serum levels may be delayed if taken with food.

Herb/Nutraceutical: Avoid cat's claw, dong quai, evening primrose, feverfew, garlic, ginger, ginkgo, red clover, horse chestnut, green tea, ginseng (all have additional antiplatelet activity).

Mechanism of Action Inhibits prostaglandin synthesis, acts on the hypothalamus heat-regulating center to reduce fever, blocks prostaglandin synthetase action which prevents formation of the platelet-aggregating substance thromboxane A_2

Pharmacodynamics/Kinetics

Onset of action: Therapeutic: 3-4 days of continuous dosing

Absorption: Complete from small intestine

Metabolism: Hepatically hydrolyzed to two moles of salicylic acid (active)

Half-life elimination: 7-8 hours

Excretion: Primarily urine

Dosage Adults: Oral: 3 g/day in 2-3 divided doses

Dosing comments in renal impairment: In patients with end-stage renal disease undergoing hemodialysis: 750 mg twice daily with an additional 500 mg after dialysis

Dietary Considerations May be taken with food to decrease GI distress.

Test Interactions False-negative results for glucose oxidase urinary glucose tests (Clinistix®); false-positives using the cupric sulfate method (Clinitest®); also, interferes with Gerhardt test, VMA determination; 5-HIAA, xylose tolerance test and T_3 and T_4

Additional Information Does not appear to inhibit platelet aggregation

Dosage Forms

Tablet: 500 mg, 750 mg

Amigesic®: 500 mg, 750 mg

♦ **Salt** see Sodium Chloride on page 1576

♦ **Salt Poor Albumin** see Albumin on page 55

♦ **Sal-Tropine™** see Atropine on page 176

♦ **Sanctura™** see Trospium on page 1753

♦ **Sandimmune®** see CycloSPORINE on page 431

♦ **Sandimmune® I.V. (Can)** see CycloSPORINE on page 431

♦ **Sandostatin®** see Octreotide on page 1252

♦ **Sandostatin LAR®** see Octreotide on page 1252

♦ **Sandoz-Acebutolol (Can)** see Acebutolol on page 27

♦ **Sandoz-Amiodarone (Can)** see Amiodarone on page 97

♦ **Sandoz-Anagrelide (Can)** see Anagrelide on page 128

♦ **Sandoz-Atenolol (Can)** see Atenolol on page 167

♦ **Sandoz-Azithromycin (Can)** see Azithromycin on page 186

♦ **Sandoz-Betaxolol (Can)** see Betaxolol on page 214

♦ **Sandoz-Bicalutamide (Can)** see Bicalutamide on page 221

♦ **Sandoz-Bisoprolol (Can)** see Bisoprolol on page 226

♦ **Sandoz-Ciprofloxacin (Can)** see Ciprofloxacin on page 372

♦ **Sandoz-Citalopram (Can)** see Citalopram on page 381

♦ **Sandoz-Clonazepam (Can)** see Clonazepam on page 397

♦ **Sandoz-Cyclosporine (Can)** see CycloSPORINE on page 431

♦ **Sandoz-Diltiazem CD (Can)** see Diltiazem on page 509

♦ **Sandoz-Diltiazem T (Can)** see Diltiazem on page 509

♦ **Sandoz-Estradiol Derm 50 (Can)** see Estradiol on page 620

♦ **Sandoz-Estradiol Derm 75 (Can)** see Estradiol on page 620

♦ **Sandoz-Estradiol Derm 100 (Can)** see Estradiol on page 620

♦ **Sandoz-Fluoxetine (Can)** see Fluoxetine on page 727

♦ **Sandoz-Fluvoxamine (Can)** see Fluvoxamine on page 747

♦ **Sandoz-Glimepiride (Can)** see Glimepiride on page 797

♦ **Sandoz-Glyburide (Can)** see GlyBURIDE on page 803

♦ **Sandoz-Levobunolol (Can)** see Levobunolol on page 996

♦ **Sandoz-Lovastatin (Can)** see Lovastatin on page 1040

♦ **Sandoz-Metformin FC (Can)** see Metformin on page 1098

♦ **Sandoz-Metoprolol (Can)** see Metoprolol on page 1129

♦ **Sandoz-Minocycline (Can)** see Minocycline on page 1149

♦ **Sandoz-Mirtazapine (Can)** see Mirtazapine on page 1152

♦ **Sandoz-Mirtazapine FC (Can)** see Mirtazapine on page 1152

♦ **Sandoz-Nabumetone (Can)** see Nabumetone on page 1185

♦ **Sandoz-Paroxetine (Can)** see Paroxetine on page 1314

♦ **Sandoz-Pravastatin (Can)** see Pravastatin on page 1409

♦ **Sandoz-Ranitidine (Can)** see Ranitidine on page 1485

♦ **Sandoz-Sertraline (Can)** see Sertraline on page 1557

♦ **Sandoz-Simvastatin (Can)** see Simvastatin on page 1567

♦ **Sandoz-Sumatriptan (Can)** see Sumatriptan on page 1620

♦ **Sandoz-Ticlopidine (Can)** *see* Ticlopidine *on page 1683*
♦ **Sandoz-Timolol (Can)** *see* Timolol *on page 1687*
♦ **Sandoz-Tobramycin (Can)** *see* Tobramycin *on page 1696*
♦ **Sandoz-Topiramate (Can)** *see* Topiramate *on page 1707*
♦ **Sandoz-Trifluridine (Can)** *see* Trifluridine *on page 1741*
♦ **Sandoz-Valproic (Can)** *see* Valproic Acid and Derivatives *on page 1767*
♦ **Sans Acne® (Can)** *see* Erythromycin *on page 609*
♦ **Santyl®** *see* Collagenase *on page 416*

Saquinavir (sa KWIN a veer)

U.S. Brand Names Fortovase® [DSC]; Invirase®
Canadian Brand Names Fortovase®; Invirase®
Index Terms Saquinavir Mesylate
Pharmacologic Category Antiretroviral Agent, Protease Inhibitor
Additional Appendix Information
  Antiretroviral Therapy for HIV Infection: Adults and Adolescents *on page 1988*
  Management of Healthcare Worker Exposures to HBV, HCV, and HIV *on page 1941*
Use Treatment of HIV infection; used in combination with at least two other antiretroviral agents
Pregnancy Risk Factor B
Pregnancy Implications Saquinavir soft gelatin capsules (Fortovase®) provide adequate levels when used in normal doses during pregnancy, however, this product is no longer available. Based on limited data, Invirase® 1000 mg (capsules) administered twice daily with ritonavir 100 mg twice daily provide adequate levels in pregnant women. The Perinatal HIV Guidelines Working Group considers Invirase® capsules and ritonavir to be an alternative combination for use during pregnancy. Pregnancy and protease inhibitors are both associated with an increased risk of hyperglycemia. Glucose levels should be closely monitored. Health professionals are encouraged to contact the antiretroviral pregnancy registry to monitor outcomes of pregnant women exposed to antiretroviral medications (1-800-258-4263 or www.APRegistry.com).
Lactation Excretion in breast milk unknown/contraindicated
Medication Safety Issues
  Sound-alike/look-alike issues:
    Saquinavir may be confused with Sinequan®
    Fortovase® may be confused with Invirase®
    Invirase® may be confused with Fortovase®
Contraindications Hypersensitivity to saquinavir or any component of the formulation; exposure to direct sunlight without sunscreen or protective clothing; severe hepatic impairment; coadministration with amiodarone, bepridil, cisapride, flecainide, midazolam, pimozide, propafenone, quinidine, rifampin, triazolam, or ergot derivatives
Warnings/Precautions Use caution in patients with hepatic insufficiency. May exacerbate pre-existing hepatic dysfunction; use with caution in patients with hepatitis B or C and in cirrhosis. May be associated with fat redistribution (buffalo hump, increased abdominal girth, breast engorgement, facial atrophy). Use caution in hemophilia. May increase cholesterol and/or triglycerides. Changes in glucose tolerance, hyperglycemia, exacerbation of diabetes, DKA, and new-onset diabetes mellitus have been reported in patients receiving protease inhibitors.

Use with caution in patients taking strong CYP3A4 inhibitors, moderate or strong CYP3A4 inducers and major CYP3A4 substrates (see drug interactions); consider alternative agents that avoid or lessen the potential for CYP-mediated interactions. Patients may develop immune reconstitution syndrome resulting in the occurrence of an inflammatory response to an indolent or residual opportunistic infection; further evaluation and treatment may be required.**[U.S. Boxed Warning]: Fortovase® and Invirase® are not bioequivalent and should not be used interchangeably; only Fortovase® should be used to initiate therapy.** Fortovase® is recommended when saquinavir will be given as the sole protease inhibitor; Invirase® may be used only if combined with ritonavir. Safety and efficacy have not been established in children ≤16 years of age.

Adverse Reactions Protease inhibitors cause dyslipidemia which includes elevated cholesterol and triglycerides and a redistribution of body fat centrally to cause increased abdominal girth, buffalo hump, facial atrophy, and breast enlargement. These agents also cause hyperglycemia.

10%: Gastrointestinal: Diarrhea, nausea
1% to 10%:
  Cardiovascular: Chest pain
  Central nervous system: Anxiety, depression, fatigue, headache, insomnia, pain
  Dermatologic: Rash, verruca
  Endocrine & metabolic: Hyper-/hypoglycemia, hyperkalemia, libido disorder, serum amylase increased
  Gastrointestinal: Abdominal discomfort, abdominal pain, appetite decreased, buccal mucosa ulceration, constipation, dyspepsia, flatulence, taste alteration, vomiting
  Hepatic: AST increased, ALT increased, bilirubin increased
  Neuromuscular & skeletal: CPK increased, paresthesia, weakness
  Renal: Creatinine kinase increased
  <1% (Limited to important or life-threatening): Acute myeloblastic leukemia, alkaline phosphatase increased, allergic reaction, ascites, ataxia, bullous skin eruption, calcium increased, cholangitis, chronic liver disease exacerbation, confusion, hemoglobin decreased, hemolytic anemia, hepatitis, hypokalemia, jaundice, LFTs increased, neuropathy, pain, pancreatitis, polyarthritis, portal hypertension, seizure, serum phosphate decreased, Stevens-Johnson syndrome, syncope, thrombocytopenia, thrombophlebitis, triglycerides increased, upper quadrant abdominal pain

Drug Interactions

Cytochrome P450 Effect: Substrate of CYP2D6 (minor), 3A4 (major); **Inhibits** CYP2C9 (weak), 2C19 (weak), 2D6 (weak), 3A4 (moderate)

Increased Effect/Toxicity: Concurrent use of amiodarone, bepridil, cisapride, flecainide, midazolam, pimozide, propafenone, quinidine, rifampin, triazolam, or ergot derivatives is contraindicated.

Saquinavir may increase the levels/effects of selected benzodiazepines, calcium channel blockers, cisapride, cyclosporine, ergot alkaloids, selected HMG-CoA reductase inhibitors, mirtazapine, nateglinide, nefazodone, pimozide, quinidine, sildenafil (and other PDE-5 inhibitors), tacrolimus, venlafaxine, and other CYP3A4 substrates. The effects of warfarin may also be increased.

Serum concentrations of saquinavir may be increased by azole antifungals (itraconazole, ketoconazole); dose adjustment was not needed at the study dose when used for a limited time (ketoconazole 400 mg once daily and Fortovase® 1200 mg 3 times/day). Saquinavir serum concentrations may be increased by delavirdine. Atazanavir, indinavir, and ritonavir may increase serum levels of saquinavir. Serum levels of saquinavir and nelfinavir may be increased with concurrent use. Lopinavir/ritonavir (combination product) may increase serum levels of saquinavir. Refer to Dosage (dosage adjustment recommendations with atazanavir have not been established).

Serum concentrations of saquinavir and clarithromycin may both be increased. Dose adjustment not was not needed at the study dose when used for 7 days (clarithromycin 500 mg twice daily and Fortovase® 1200 mg 3 times/day); dosage adjustment of clarithromycin is recommended in patients with renal impairment.

Serum concentrations of saquinavir are decreased and levels of rifabutin are increased when used together. Saquinavir should not be used as the sole protease inhibitor when given with rifabutin.

Decreased Effect: The levels/effects of saquinavir may be reduced by aminoglutethimide, carbamazepine, nafcillin, nevirapine, phenobarbital, phenytoin, rifamycins, and other CYP3A4 inducers. Loss of efficacy and potential resistance may occur. Concurrent use with rifampin is contraindicated.

Serum concentrations of methadone may be decreased; an increased dose may be needed when administered with saquinavir. Serum levels of the hormones in oral contraceptives may decrease significantly with administration of saquinavir. Patients should use alternative methods of contraceptives during saquinavir therapy.

Serum levels of saquinavir and efavirenz may be decreased with concurrent use; saquinavir should not be used as the sole protease inhibitor with efavirenz or nevirapine.

Dexamethasone may decrease serum concentrations of saquinavir; use with caution. Serum concentrations of saquinavir are decreased and levels of rifabutin are increased when used together. Saquinavir should not be used as the sole protease inhibitor when given with rifabutin.

Ethanol/Nutrition/Herb Interactions

Food: A high-fat meal maximizes bioavailability. Saquinavir levels may increase if taken with grapefruit juice.

Herb/Nutraceutical: Saquinavir serum concentrations may be decreased by St John's wort; avoid concurrent use. Garlic capsules may decrease saquinavir serum concentrations; avoid use if saquinavir is the only protease inhibitor.

Stability

Fortovase®: Store in refrigerator. Stable for 3 months when stored at room temperature.

Invirase®: Store at room temperature.

Mechanism of Action

As an inhibitor of HIV protease, saquinavir prevents the cleavage of viral polyprotein precursors which are needed to generate functional proteins in and maturation of HIV-infected cells

Pharmacodynamics/Kinetics

Absorption: Poor; increased with high fat meal; Fortovase® has improved absorption over Invirase®

Distribution: V_d: 700 L; does not distribute into CSF

Protein binding, plasma: ~98%

Metabolism: Extensively hepatic via CYP3A4; extensive first-pass effect

Bioavailability: Invirase®: ~4%; Fortovase®: 12% to 15%

Excretion: Feces (81% to 88%), urine (1% to 3%) within 5 days

Dosage

Oral: Children >16 years and Adults: **Note:** Fortovase® and Invirase® are not bioequivalent and should not be used interchangeably; only Fortovase® should be used to initiate therapy:

Unboosted regimen: Fortovase®: 1200 mg (six 200 mg capsules) 3 times/day or 1600 mg twice daily within 2 hours after a meal in combination with a nucleoside analog

Note: Saquinavir hard-gel capsules (Invirase®) should not be used in "unboosted regimens."

Ritonavir-boosted regimens:

Fortovase®: 1000 mg (five 200 mg capsules) twice daily in combination with ritonavir 100 mg twice daily

Invirase®: 1000 mg (five 200 mg capsules or two 500 mg tablets) twice daily given in combination with ritonavir 100 mg twice daily. This combination should be given together and within 2 hours after a full meal in combination with a nucleoside analog.

Dosage adjustments of Fortovase® when administered in combination therapy:

Delavirdine: Fortovase® 800 mg 3 times/day

Lopinavir and ritonavir (Kaletra™): Fortovase® or Invirase® 1000 mg twice daily

Nelfinavir: Fortovase® 1200 mg twice daily

Elderly: Clinical studies did not include sufficient numbers of patients ≥65 years of age; use caution due to increased frequency of organ dysfunction

Dietary Considerations

Administer within 2 hours of a meal. Invirase® capsules contain lactose 63.3 mg/capsule (not expected to induce symptoms of intolerance).

(Continued)

Saquinavir (Continued)

Administration Take saquinavir within 2 hours after a full meal. Avoid direct sunlight when taking saquinavir. When used with ritonavir, saquinavir and ritonavir should be administered at the same time.

Monitoring Parameters Monitor viral load, CD4 count, triglycerides, cholesterol, glucose

Dosage Forms Note: Strength expressed as base; [DSC] = Discontinued product

Capsule, as mesylate:
Invirase®: 200 mg [contains lactose 63.3 mg/capsule]
Capsule, soft gelatin, as base:
Fortovase®: 200 mg [DSC]
Tablet, as mesylate:
Invirase®: 500 mg

◆ **Saquinavir Mesylate** see Saquinavir on page 1546

◆ **Sarafem®** see Fluoxetine on page 727

Sargramostim (sar GRAM oh stim)

U.S. Brand Names Leukine®
Canadian Brand Names Leukine®
Index Terms GM-CSF; Granulocyte-Macrophage Colony Stimulating Factor; NSC-613795; rGM-CSF
Pharmacologic Category Colony Stimulating Factor
Use

Acute myelogenous leukemia (AML) following induction chemotherapy in older adults (≥55 years of age) to shorten time to neutrophil recovery and to reduce the incidence of severe and life-threatening infections and infections resulting in death

Bone marrow transplant (allogeneic or autologous) failure or engraftment delay

Myeloid reconstitution after allogeneic bone marrow transplantation

Myeloid reconstitution after autologous bone marrow transplantation: Non-Hodgkin's lymphoma (NHL), acute lymphoblastic leukemia (ALL), Hodgkin's lymphoma

Peripheral stem cell transplantation: Mobilization and myeloid reconstitution following peripheral stem cell transplantation

Pregnancy Risk Factor C

Pregnancy Implications Clinical effects to the fetus: Animal reproduction studies have not been conducted. It is not known whether sargramostim can cause fetal harm when administered to a pregnant woman or can affect reproductive capability. Sargramostim should be given to a pregnant woman only if clearly needed.

Lactation Excretion in breast milk unknown/use caution

Medication Safety Issues

Sound-alike/look-alike issues:
Leukine® may be confused with Leukeran®

Contraindications Hypersensitivity to sargramostim, yeast-derived products, or any component of the formulation; concurrent (24 hours preceding/following) myelosuppressive chemotherapy or radiation therapy; patients with excessive (≥10%) leukemic myeloid blasts in bone marrow or peripheral blood

Warnings/Precautions Simultaneous administration, or administration 24 hours preceding/following cytotoxic chemotherapy or radiotherapy is not recommended. Use with caution in patients with pre-existing cardiac problems or CHF; supraventricular arrhythmias have been reported in patients with history of arrhythmias. Edema, capillary leak syndrome, pleural and/or pericardial effusion have been reported; use with caution in patients with pre-existing fluid retention; may worsen. Use with caution in patients with hepatic or renal impairment; monitor hepatic and/or renal function in patients with history of hepatic or renal dysfunction. Dyspnea may occur; monitor respiratory symptoms during and following infusion; use with caution in patients with hypoxia or pulmonary infiltrates.

With rapid increase in blood counts (ANC >20,000/mm³ or platelets >500,000/mm³); decrease dose by 50% or discontinue drug (counts will fall to normal within 3-7 days after discontinuing drug). May potentially act as a growth factor for any tumor type, particularly myeloid malignancies; caution should be exercised when using in any malignancy with myeloid characteristics; tumors of nonhematopoietic origin may have surface receptors for sargramostim.

There is a "first-dose effect" (refer to Adverse Reactions for details)which is seen (rarely) with the first dose of a cycle and does not usually occur with subsequent doses within that cycle. Anaphylaxis or other serious allergic reactions have been reported; discontinue immediately if occur. Solution contains benzyl alcohol; do not use in premature infants or neonates.

Adverse Reactions

>10%:
Cardiovascular: Hypertension (34%), pericardial effusion (4% to 25%), edema (13% to 25%), chest pain (15%), peripheral edema (11%), tachycardia (11%)
Central nervous system: Fever (81%), malaise (57%), headache (26%), chills (25%), anxiety (11%), insomnia (11%)
Dermatologic: Rash (44%), pruritus (23%)
Endocrine & metabolic: Hyperglycemia (25%), hypercholesterolemia (17%)
Gastrointestinal: Diarrhea (52% to 89%), nausea (58% to 70%), vomiting (46% to 70%), abdominal pain (38%), weight loss (37%), hematemesis (13%), dysphagia (11%), gastrointestinal hemorrhage (11%)
Genitourinary: Urinary tract disorder (14%)
Hepatic: Hyperbilirubinemia (30%)
Neuromuscular & skeletal: Weakness (66%), bone pain (21%), arthralgia (11% to 21%), myalgia (18%)
Ocular: Eye hemorrhage (11%)
Renal: BUN increased (23%), serum creatinine increased (15%)

Respiratory: Pharyngitis (23%), epistaxis (17%), dyspnea (15%)

1% to 10%: Respiratory: Pleural effusion (1%)

<1% (Limited to important or life-threatening): Allergic reaction, anaphylaxis, anorexia, arrhythmia, capillary leak syndrome, constipation, eosinophilia, fever, first-dose effect (syndrome with respiratory distress, hypoxia, flushing, hypotension, syncope, and/or tachycardia occurring with the first dose of a treatment cycle); injection site reaction, lethargy, leukocytosis, malaise, pain, pericarditis, rigors, sore throat, supraventricular arrhythmia (transient), thrombocytosis, thrombophlebitis, thrombosis

Overdosage/Toxicology Symptoms of overdose include dyspnea, malaise, nausea, fever, sinus tachycardia, headache, and chills. Discontinue drug and wait for levels to fall. Treatment is symptom-directed and supportive. Monitor CBC, respiratory symptoms, fluid status, and for pulmonary edema. Toxicity of GM-CSF is dose dependent. Severe reactions such as capillary leak syndrome are seen at higher doses (>15 mcg/kg/day).

Stability Store at 2°C to 8°C (36°F to 46°F); do not freeze. Do not shake.

Solution for injection: May be stored for up to 20 days at 2°C to 8°C (36°F to 46°F) once the vial has been entered. Discard remaining solution after 20 days.

Powder for injection: May be reconstituted with preservative free SWFI or bacteriostatic water for injection (with benzyl alcohol 0.9%). Preparations made with SWFI should be administered as soon as possible, and discarded within 6 hours of reconstitution. Preparations made with bacteriostatic water may be stored for up to 20 days at 2°C to 8°C (36°F to 46°F). Gently swirl to reconstitute; do not shake.

Sargramostim may also be further diluted in 25-50 mL NS to a concentration ≥10 mcg/mL for I.V. infusion administration; preparations diluted with NS are stable for 48 hours at room temperature and refrigeration.

If the final concentration of sargramostim is <10 mcg/mL, 1 mg of human albumin/1 mL of NS (eg, 1 mL of 5% human albumin/50 mL of NS) should be added.

Mechanism of Action Stimulates proliferation, differentiation and functional activity of neutrophils, eosinophils, monocytes, and macrophages, as indicated.

Pharmacodynamics/Kinetics

Onset of action: Increase in WBC: 7-14 days

Duration: WBCs return to baseline within 1 week of discontinuing drug

Half-life elimination: I.V.: 60 minutes; SubQ: 2.7 hours

Time to peak, serum: SubQ: 1-2 hours

Dosage

Children (unlabeled use) and Adults: I.V. infusion over ≥2 hours or SubQ: **Rounding the dose to the nearest vial size enhances patient convenience and reduces costs without clinical detriment**

Myeloid reconstitution after peripheral stem cell, allogeneic or autologous bone marrow transplant: I.V.: 250 mcg/m^2/day (over 2 hours), begin 2-4 hours after the marrow infusion and ≥24 hours after chemotherapy or radiotherapy, when the post marrow infusion ANC is <500 cells/mm^3, and continue until ANC >1500 cells/mm^3 for 3 consecutive days

If a severe adverse reaction occurs, reduce or temporarily discontinue the dose until the reaction abates

If blast cells appear or progression of the underlying disease occurs, disrupt treatment

Interrupt or reduce the dose by half if ANC is >20,000 cells/mm^3

Neutrophil recovery following chemotherapy in AML: I.V.: 250 mcg/m^2/day (over 4 hours) starting approximately day 11 or 4 days following the completion of induction chemotherapy, if day 10 bone marrow is hypoblastic with <5% blasts

If a second cycle of chemotherapy is necessary, administer ~4 days after the completion of chemotherapy if the bone marrow is hypoblastic with <5% blasts

Continue sargramostim until ANC is >1500 cells/mm^3 for 3 consecutive days or a maximum of 42 days

Discontinue sargramostim immediately if leukemic regrowth occurs

If a severe adverse reaction occurs, reduce the dose by 50% or temporarily discontinue the dose until the reaction abates

Mobilization of peripheral blood progenitor cells: I.V., SubQ: 250 mcg/m^2/day I.V. over 24 hours or SubQ once daily

Continue the same dose through the period of PBPC collection

The optimal schedule for PBPC collection has not been established (usually begun by day 5 and performed daily until protocol specified targets are achieved)

If WBC >50,000 cells/mm^3, reduce the dose by 50%

If adequate numbers of progenitor cells are not collected, consider other mobilization therapy

Postperipheral blood progenitor cell transplantation: I.V., SubQ: 250 mcg/m^2/day I.V. over 24 hours or SubQ once daily beginning immediately following infusion of progenitor cells and continuing until ANC is >1500 cells/mm^3 for 3 consecutive days is attained

BMT failure or engraftment delay: I.V.: 250 mcg/m^2/day over 2 hours for 14 days

May be repeated after 7 days off therapy if engraftment has not occurred

If engraftment still has not occurred, a third course of 500 mcg/m^2/day for 14 days may be tried after another 7 days off therapy; if there is still no improvement, it is unlikely that further dose escalation will be beneficial

If a severe adverse reaction occurs, reduce or temporarily discontinue the dose until the reaction abates

If blast cells appear or disease progression occurs, discontinue treatment

Administration Can premedicate with analgesics and antipyretics; control bone pain with non-narcotic analgesics. Sargramostim is administered as a subcutaneous injection or intravenous infusion; intravenous infusion should be over 2-24 hours; continuous infusions may be more effective than short infusion or bolus injection. An in-line membrane filter should not be used for intravenous administration. When administering GM-CSF subcutaneously, rotate injection sites.

Monitoring Parameters Vital signs, weight, CBC with differential, platelets, renal/liver function tests, especially with previous dysfunction, pulmonary function

Reference Range Excessive leukocytosis: ANC >20,000/mm^3 or WBC >50,000 cells/mm^3

(Continued)

Sargramostim *(Continued)*

Test Interactions May interfere with bone imaging studies; increased hematopoietic activity of the bone marrow may appear as transient positive bone imaging changes

Additional Information Reimbursement Hotline (Leukine®): 1-800-321-4669

Dosage Forms

Injection, powder for reconstitution:

Leukine®: 250 mcg [contains mannitol 40 mg/mL and sucrose 10 mg/mL]

Injection, solution:

Leukine®: 500 mcg/mL (1 mL) [contains benzyl alcohol, disodium edetate, mannitol 40 mg/mL, and sucrose 10 mg/mL]

- ♦ **Sarna® HC (Can)** *see* Hydrocortisone *on page 852*
- ♦ **Sarnol®-HC [OTC]** *see* Hydrocortisone *on page 852*
- ♦ **SB-265805** *see* Gemifloxacin *on page 788*
- ♦ **SC 33428** *see* Idarubicin *on page 878*
- ♦ **SCH 13521** *see* Flutamide *on page 737*
- ♦ **SCH 56592** *see* Posaconazole *on page 1393*
- ♦ **SCIG** *see* Immune Globulin (Subcutaneous) *on page 896*
- ♦ **S-Citalopram** *see* Escitalopram *on page 613*
- ♦ **Scleromate®** *see* Morrhuate Sodium *on page 1175*
- ♦ **Scopace™** *see* Scopolamine Derivatives *on page 1550*
- ♦ **Scopolamine and Phenylephrine** *see* Phenylephrine and Scopolamine *on page 1360*
- ♦ **Scopolamine Butylbromide** *see* Scopolamine Derivatives *on page 1550*

Scopolamine Derivatives *(skoe POL a meen dah RIV ah tives)*

U.S. Brand Names Isopto® Hyoscine; Maldemar™; Scopace™; Transderm Scōp®

Canadian Brand Names Buscopan®; Transderm-V®

Index Terms Hyoscine Butylbromide; Hyoscine Hydrobromide; Scopolamine Butylbromide; Scopolamine Hydrobromide

Pharmacologic Category Anticholinergic Agent

Additional Appendix Information

Cycloplegic Mydriatics *on page 1882*

Use

Scopolamine hydrobromide:

Injection: Preoperative medication to produce amnesia, sedation, and decrease salivary and respiratory secretions

Ophthalmic: Produce cycloplegia and mydriasis; treatment of iridocyclitis

Oral: Symptomatic treatment of postencephalitic parkinsonism and paralysis agitans; inhibits excessive motility and hypertonus of the genitourinary or gastrointestinal tract in such conditions as the irritable colon syndrome, mild dysentery, diverticulitis, pylorospasm, and cardiospasm

Transdermal: Prevention of nausea/vomiting associated with anesthesia or opiate analgesia; prevention of motion sickness

Scopolamine butylbromide:

Oral/injection: Treatment of smooth muscle spasm of the genitourinary or gastrointestinal tract; injection may also be used to prior to radiological/diagnostic procedures to prevent spasm

Pregnancy Risk Factor C

Pregnancy Implications Crosses the placenta; except when used prior to cesarean section, use during pregnancy only if the benefit to the mother outweighs the potential risk to the fetus.

Lactation Enters breast milk/use caution (AAP rates "compatible")

Medication Safety Issues

Transdermal patch may contain conducting metal (eg, aluminum); remove patch prior to MRI.

Contraindications Hypersensitivity to scopolamine or any component of the formulation; narrow-angle glaucoma; acute hemorrhage; paralytic ileus, GI or GU obstruction; thyrotoxicosis; tachycardia secondary to cardiac insufficiency; myasthenia gravis

Warnings/Precautions Use with caution with hepatic or renal impairment since adverse CNS effects occur more often in these patients; use with caution in infants and children since they may be more susceptible to adverse effects of scopolamine; use with caution in patients with GI obstruction, prostatic hyperplasia (nonobstructive), or urinary retention. Discontinue if patient reports unusual visual disturbances or pain within the eye. Use caution in hiatal hernia, reflux esophagitis, and ulcerative colitis. Scopolamine (hyoscine) hydrobromide should not be interchanged with scopolamine butylbromide formulations; dosages are not equivalent. Transdermal patch may contain conducting metal (eg, aluminum); remove patch prior to MRI.

Adverse Reactions Frequency not defined.

Ophthalmic: Note: Systemic adverse effects have been reported following ophthalmic administration.

Cardiovascular: Vascular congestion, edema

Central nervous system: Drowsiness

Dermatologic: Eczematoid dermatitis

Ocular: Blurred vision, photophobia, local irritation, increased intraocular pressure, follicular conjunctivitis, exudate

Respiratory: Congestion

Systemic:

Cardiovascular: Orthostatic hypotension, ventricular fibrillation, tachycardia, palpitation

Central nervous system: Confusion, drowsiness, headache, loss of memory, ataxia, fatigue

Dermatologic: Dry skin, increased sensitivity to light, rash

Endocrine & metabolic: Decreased flow of breast milk

Gastrointestinal: Constipation, xerostomia, dry throat, dysphagia, bloated feeling, nausea, vomiting

Genitourinary: Dysuria

Local: Irritation at injection site

Neuromuscular & skeletal: Weakness

Ocular: Increased intraocular pain, blurred vision

Respiratory: Dry nose

Miscellaneous: Diaphoresis (decreased)

<1% (Limited to important or life-threatening): Anaphylactoid reaction, anaphylaxis, hallucinations, restlessness, retinal pigmentation

Overdosage/Toxicology Symptoms include dilated pupils, flushed skin, tachycardia, hypertension, ECG abnormalities, and CNS manifestations resembling acute psychosis. CNS depression, circulatory collapse, respiratory failure, and death can occur. Pure scopolamine intoxication is extremely rare. However, for a scopolamine overdose with severe life-threatening symptoms, physostigmine 1-2 mg (0.5 mg or 0.02 mg/kg for children) SubQ or slow I.V. should be given to reverse the toxic effects.

Drug Interactions

Increased Effect/Toxicity: Adverse anticholinergic effects may be additive with other anticholinergic agents (includes tricyclic antidepressants, antihistamines, and phenothiazines). Sedative effects of other CNS depressants may be additive with scopolamine.

Decreased Effect: Decreased effect of acetaminophen, levodopa, ketoconazole, digoxin, riboflavin, and potassium chloride in wax matrix preparations.

Ethanol/Nutrition/Herb Interactions Ethanol: Avoid ethanol (may increase CNS depression).

Stability Store tablets and/or injection at room temperature of 15°C to 30°C. Protect injection from light.

Hydrobromide injection: Avoid acid solutions, hydrolysis occurs at pH <3.

Butylbromide injection: Stable in D_5W, NS, $D_{10}W$, and LR for up to 8 hours.

Mechanism of Action Blocks the action of acetylcholine at parasympathetic sites in smooth muscle, secretory glands and the CNS, increases cardiac output, dries secretions, antagonizes histamine and serotonin

Pharmacodynamics/Kinetics

Onset of action: Oral, I.M.: 0.5-1 hour; I.V.: 10 minutes

Peak effect: 20-60 minutes; may take 3-7 days for full recovery; transdermal: 24 hours

Duration: Oral, I.M.: 4-6 hours; I.V.: 2 hours

Absorption: Tertiary salts (hydrobromide) are well absorbed; quaternary salts (butylbromide) are poorly absorbed (local concentrations in the GI tract following oral dosing may be high)

Metabolism: Hepatic

Half-life elimination: 4.8 hours

Excretion: Urine (as metabolites)

Dosage Note: Scopolamine (hyoscine) hydrobromide should not be interchanged with scopolamine butylbromide formulations. Dosages are not equivalent.

Scopolamine hydrobromide:

Preoperative:

Children: I.M., SubQ: 6 mcg/kg/dose (maximum: 0.3 mg/dose) every 6-8 hours

Adults:

I.M., I.V., SubQ: 0.3-0.65 mg; may be repeated every 4-6 hours

Transdermal patch: Apply 2.5 cm² patch to hairless area behind ear the night before surgery or 1 hour prior to cesarean section (the patch should be applied no sooner than 1 hour before surgery for best results and removed 24 hours after surgery)

Motion sickness: Transdermal: Adults: Apply 1 disc behind the ear at least 4 hours prior to exposure and every 3 days as needed; effective if applied as soon as 2-3 hours before anticipated need, best if 12 hours before

Refraction: Ophthalmic:

Children: Instill 1 drop of 0.25% to eye(s) twice daily for 2 days before procedure

Adults: Instill 1-2 drops of 0.25% to eye(s) 1 hour before procedure

Iridocyclitis: Ophthalmic:

Children: Instill 1 drop of 0.25% to eye(s) up to 3 times/day

Adults: Instill 1-2 drops of 0.25% to eye(s) up to 4 times/day

Parkinsonism, spasticity, motion sickness: Oral: 0.4-0.8 mg. May repeat every 8-12 hours as needed; the dosage may be cautiously increased in parkinsonism and spastic states. For motion sickness, administration at least 1 hour before exposure is recommended.

Scopolamine butylbromide:

Gastrointestinal/genitourinary spasm (Buscopan® [CAN]; not available in the U.S.): Adults:

Oral: 10-20 mg daily (1-2 tablets); maximum: 6 tablets/day

I.M., I.V., SubQ: 10-20 mg; maximum: 100 mg/day. Intramuscular injections should be administered 10-15 minutes prior to radiological/diagnostic procedures

Administration

I.V.:

Hydrobromide: Dilute with an equal volume of sterile water and administer by direct I.V.; inject over 2-3 minutes

Butylbromide: No dilution is necessary prior to injection; inject at a rate of 1 mL/minute

Transdermal: Topical disc is programmed to deliver *in vivo* 1 mg over 3 days. Once applied, do not remove the patch for 3 full days. Apply to hairless area of skin behind the ear. Wash hands before and after applying the disc to avoid drug contact with eyes.

Dosage Forms [CAN] = Canadian brand name

Injection, solution, as hydrobromide: 0.4 mg/mL (1 mL)

Injection, solution, as hyoscine-N-butylbromide:

Buscopan® [CAN]: 20 mg/mL [not available in U.S.]

Solution, ophthalmic, as hydrobromide:

Isopto® Hyoscine: 0.25% (5 mL, 15 mL) [contains benzalkonium chloride]

Tablet, as hyoscine-N-butylbromide:

Buscopan® [CAN]: 10 mg [not available in U.S.]

(Continued)

Scopolamine Derivatives *(Continued)*

Tablet, soluble, as hydrobromide:
  Maldemar™, Scopace™: 0.4 mg
Transdermal system:
  Transderm Scōp®: 1.5 mg (4s, 10s, 24s) [releases ~1 mg over 72 hours]

♦ **Scopolamine Hydrobromide** *see* Scopolamine Derivatives *on page 1550*
♦ **Scopolamine, Hyoscyamine, Atropine, and Phenobarbital** *see* Hyoscyamine, Atropine, Scopolamine, and Phenobarbital *on page 868*
♦ **Scot-Tussin® Expectorant [OTC]** *see* Guaifenesin *on page 814*
♦ **Scot-Tussin® Senior [OTC]** *see* Guaifenesin and Dextromethorphan *on page 816*
♦ **Sculptra™** *see* Poly-L-Lactic Acid *on page 1388*
♦ **SD/01** *see* Pegfilgrastim *on page 1321*
♦ **SDZ ENA 713** *see* Rivastigmine *on page 1526*
♦ **Seasonale®** *see* Ethinyl Estradiol and Levonorgestrel *on page 653*
♦ **Seasonique™** *see* Ethinyl Estradiol and Levonorgestrel *on page 653*

Secobarbital *(see koe BAR bi tal)*

U.S. Brand Names Seconal®
Index Terms Quinalbarbitone Sodium; Secobarbital Sodium
Pharmacologic Category Barbiturate
Use Preanesthetic agent; short-term treatment of insomnia
Restrictions C-II
Pregnancy Risk Factor D
Medication Safety Issues
  Sound-alike/look-alike issues:
    Seconal® may be confused with Sectral®
Dosage Oral:
  Children:
    Preoperative sedation: 2-6 mg/kg (maximum dose: 100 mg/dose) 1-2 hours before procedure
    Sedation: 6 mg/kg/day divided every 8 hours
  Adults:
    Hypnotic: Usual: 100 mg/dose at bedtime; range 100-200 mg/dose
    Preoperative sedation: 100-300 mg 1-2 hours before procedure
Additional Information Complete prescribing information for this medication should be consulted for additional detail.
Dosage Forms Capsule, as sodium: 100 mg

♦ **Secobarbital and Amobarbital** *see* Amobarbital and Secobarbital *on page 108*
♦ **Secobarbital Sodium** *see* Secobarbital *on page 1552*
♦ **Seconal®** *see* Secobarbital *on page 1552*
♦ **Sectral® [DSC]** *see* Acebutolol *on page 27*
♦ **Sectral® (Can)** *see* Acebutolol *on page 27*
♦ **Secura® Antifungal [OTC]** *see* Miconazole *on page 1137*
♦ **Sedapap®** *see* Butalbital and Acetaminophen *on page 259*
♦ **Selax® (Can)** *see* Docusate *on page 533*
♦ **Select™ 1/35 (Can)** *see* Ethinyl Estradiol and Norethindrone *on page 655*

Selegiline *(se LE ji leen)*

U.S. Brand Names Eldepryl®; Emsam®; Zelapar™
Canadian Brand Names Apo-Selegiline®; Gen-Selegiline; Novo-Selegiline; Nu-Selegiline
Index Terms Deprenyl; L-Deprenyl; Selegiline Hydrochloride
Pharmacologic Category Anti-Parkinson's Agent, MAO Type B Inhibitor; Antidepressant, Monoamine Oxidase Inhibitor
Additional Appendix Information
  Parkinson's Agents *on page 1895*
  Tyramine Content of Foods *on page 2115*
Use Adjunct in the management of parkinsonian patients in which levodopa/carbidopa therapy is deteriorating (oral products); treatment of major depressive disorder (transdermal product)
Unlabeled/Investigational Use Early Parkinson's disease; attention-deficit/hyperactivity disorder (ADHD); negative symptoms of schizophrenia; extrapyramidal symptoms; Alzheimer's disease (studies have shown some improvement in behavioral and cognitive performance)
Restrictions An FDA-approved medication guide concerning the use of antidepressants in children and teenagers must be distributed when dispensing a transdermal selegiline outpatient prescription (new or refill) where this medication is to be used without direct supervision of a healthcare provider. Medication guides are available at http://www.fda.gov/cder/Offices/ODS/medication_guides.htm. Dispense to parents or guardians of children and teenagers receiving this medication.
Pregnancy Risk Factor C
Pregnancy Implications Teratogenic and adverse behavioral events were noted in animal studies. There are no adequate and well-controlled studies in pregnant women.
Lactation Excretion in breast milk unknown/use caution
Medication Safety Issues
  Sound-alike/look-alike issues:
    Selegiline may be confused with Salagen®, Serentil®, sertraline, Serzone®, Stelazine®
    Eldepryl® may be confused with Elavil®, enalapril
    Zelapar™ may be confused with zaleplon, Zemplar®

Contraindications Hypersensitivity to selegiline or any component of the formulation; concomitant use of meperidine

Orally disintegrating tablet: Additional contraindications: Concomitant use of dextromethorphan, methadone, propoxyphene, tramadol, oral selegiline, other MAO inhibitors

Transdermal: Additional contraindications: Pheochromocytoma; concomitant use of bupropion, selective or dual serotonin reuptake inhibitors (including SSRIs and SNRIs), tricyclic antidepressants, buspirone, tramadol, propoxyphene, methadone, dextromethorphan, St. John's wort, mirtazapine, cyclobenzaprine, oral selegiline and other MAO inhibitors; carbamazepine, and oxcarbazepine; elective surgery requiring general anesthesia, local anesthesia containing sympathomimetic vasoconstrictors; sympathomimetics (and related compounds); foods high in tyramine content; supplements containing tyrosine, phenylalanine, tryptophan, or caffeine

Warnings/Precautions

Oral: MAO-B selective inhibition should not pose a problem with tyramine-containing products as long as the typical oral doses are employed, however, rare reactions have been reported. Increased risk of nonselective MAO inhibition occurs with oral capsule/tablet doses >10 mg/day or orally disintegrating tablet doses >2.5 mg/day. Use of oral selegiline with tricyclic antidepressants and SSRIs has also been associated with rare reactions and should generally be avoided. Addition to levodopa therapy may result in exacerbation of levodopa adverse effects, requiring a reduction in levodopa dosage.

Transdermal: Nonselective MAO inhibition occurs with transdermal delivery and is necessary for antidepressant efficacy. Hypertensive crisis as a result of ingesting tyramine-rich foods is always a concern with nonselective MAO inhibition. Although transdermal delivery minimizes inhibition of MAO-A in the gut, there is limited data with higher transdermal doses; dietary restrictions are recommended with doses >6 mg/24hours. Monitor for worsening of depression, suicidality and/or associated behaviors such as anxiety, agitation, panic attacks, insomnia, irritability, hostility, impulsivity, hypomania, and mania; worsening depression and severe abrupt suicidality that are not part of the presenting symptoms may require discontinuation or modification of drug therapy. Use caution in high-risk patients during initiation of therapy; prescriptions should be written for the smallest quantity. The patient's family or caregiver should be alerted to monitor patients for the emergence of suicidality and associated behaviors such as anxiety, agitation, panic attacks, insomnia, irritability, hostility, impulsivity, akathisia, hypomania, and mania; patients should be instructed to notify their healthcare provider if any of these symptoms or worsening depression occur.

Transdermal selegiline may worsen psychosis in some patients or precipitate a shift to mania or hypomania in patients with bipolar disorder. Monotherapy in patients with bipolar disorder should be avoided. Patients presenting with depressive symptoms should be screened for bipolar disorder. Selegiline is not FDA approved for the treatment of bipolar depression. **[U.S. Boxed Warning]: Antidepressants increase the risk of suicidal thinking and behavior in children and adolescents with major depressive disorder (MDD) and other depressive disorders. Selegiline is not FDA approved for use in children.**

Adverse Reactions Unless otherwise noted, the percentage of adverse events is reported for the transdermal patch (**Note:** ODT = orally disintegrating tablet, Oral = capsule/tablet)

> 10%:

Central nervous system: Headache (18%; ODT 7%; oral 2%), insomnia (12%; ODT 7%), dizziness (ODT 11%; oral 7%)

Gastrointestinal: Nausea (ODT 11%; oral 10%)

Local: Application site reaction (24%)

1% to 10%:

Cardiovascular: Hypotension (including postural 3% to 10%), chest pain (≥1%; ODT 2%), hypertension (≥1%), peripheral edema (≥1%)

Central nervous system: Pain (ODT 8%), hallucinations (ODT 4%; oral 3%), confusion (ODT 4%; oral 3%), headache (ODT 7%; oral 2%), ataxia (ODT 3%), somnolence (ODT 3%), agitation (≥1%), amnesia (≥1%), paresthesia (≥1%), thinking abnormal (≥1%), depression (<1%; ODT 2%)

Dermatologic: Rash (4%), ecchymosis (ODT 2%), bruising (≥1%), pruritus (≥1%), acne (≥1%)

Endocrine and metabolic: Weight loss (5%), hypokalemia (ODT 2%), sexual side effects (≤1%)

Gastrointestinal: Diarrhea (9%; ODT 2%), xerostomia (8%; ODT 4%), stomatitis (ODT 5%), abdominal pain (oral 4%), dyspepsia (4%; ODT 5%), constipation (≥1%; ODT 4%), flatulence (≥1%; ODT 2%), anorexia (≥1%), gastroenteritis (≥1%), taste perversion (≥1%; ODT 2%), vomiting (≥1%; ODT 3%), tooth disorder (ODT 2%), dysphagia (ODT 2%)

Genitourinary: Dysmenorrhea (≥1%), metrorrhagia (≥1%), UTI (≥1%), urinary frequency (≥1%)

Neuromuscular & skeletal: Dyskinesia (ODT 6%), back pain (ODT 5%), ataxia (<1%; ODT 3%), leg cramps (ODT 3%), myalgia (≥1%; ODT 3%), neck pain (≥1%), tremor (<1%; ODT 3%)

Otic: Tinnitus (≥1%)

Respiratory: Rhinitis (ODT 7%), pharyngitis (3%; ODT 4%), sinusitis (3%; ODT 4%), cough (≥1%), bronchitis (≥1%), dyspnea (<1%; ODT 3%)

Miscellaneous: Diaphoresis (≥1%)

Oral and/or transdermal patch: <1% or frequency not defined (limited to important or life-threatening): Abnormal liver function tests, alkaline phosphatase increased, appetite increased, arrhythmia, asthma, ataxia, atrial fibrillation, bacterial infection, behavior/mood changes, bilirubinemia, bradycardia, bradykinesia, breast neoplasm (female), breast pain, chorea, circumoral paresthesia, colitis, dehydration, delusions, dental caries, depersonalization, depression, emotional lability, epistaxis, eructation, euphoria, face edema, fever, fungal infection, gastritis, generalized spasm, glossitis, heat stroke, hematuria (female), hernia, hostility, hypercholesterolemia, hyperesthesia, hyperglycemia, hyperkinesias, hypertonia, hypoglycemic reaction, hyponatremia, kidney calculus (female), lactate dehydrogenase increased, laryngismus, leukocytosis, leukopenia, libido increased, loss of balance, lymphadenopathy, maculopapular rash, manic reaction, melena, migraine, moniliasis, myasthenia, myocardial infarct, myoclonus, neoplasia, neurosis, osteoporosis, otitis

(Continued)

Selegiline *(Continued)*

external, palpitation, paranoid reaction, parasitic infection, parosmia, pelvic pain, periodontal abscess, peripheral vascular disorder, pneumonia, polyuria (female), prostatic hyperplasia, rectal hemorrhage, salivation increased, skin hypertrophy, skin benign neoplasm, suicide attempt, syncope, tachycardia, tenosynovitis, tongue edema, twitching, urinary retention, urinary urgency (male and female), urination impaired (male), urticaria, vaginal hemorrhage, vaginal moniliasis, vaginitis, vasodilatation, vertigo, vesiculobullous rash, viral infection, visual field defect

Overdosage/Toxicology Symptoms include tachycardia, palpitations, muscle twitching, and seizures. Competent supportive care is the most important treatment. Both hypertension or hypotension can occur with intoxication. Hypotension may respond to I.V. fluids or vasopressors, and hypertension usually responds to an alpha-adrenergic blocker. While treating the hypertension, care is warranted to avoid sudden drops in blood pressure, since this may worsen MAO inhibitor toxicity. Muscle irritability and seizures often respond to diazepam, while hyperthermia is best treated with antipyretics and cooling blankets. Cardiac arrhythmias are best treated with phenytoin or procainamide. Restrict dietary tyramine for several weeks after overdose.

Drug Interactions

Cytochrome P450 Effect: Substrate of CYP1A2 (minor), 2A6 (minor), 2B6 (major), 2C8 (minor), 2C19 (minor), 2D6 (minor), 3A4 (minor); **Inhibits** CYP1A2 (weak), 2A6 (weak), 2C9 (weak), 2C19 (weak), 2D6 (weak), 2E1 (weak), 3A4 (weak)

Increased Effect/Toxicity: CYP2B6 inhibitors may increase the levels/effects of selegiline; example inhibitors include desipramine, paroxetine, and sertraline. Concurrent use of oral selegiline (high dose) in combination with amphetamines, methylphenidate, dextromethorphan, fenfluramine, meperidine, nefazodone, sibutramine, tramadol, trazodone, tricyclic antidepressants, and venlafaxine may result in serotonin syndrome; these combinations are best avoided. Concurrent use of selegiline with an SSRI or SNRI may result in mania or hypertension; it is generally best to avoid these combinations. Transdermal selegiline is contraindicated with amphetamines, sympathomimetics or other CNS stimulants, dextromethorphan, meperidine, methadone, mirtazapine, propoxyphene, SSRIs/SNRIs, tramadol, tricyclic antidepressants. The toxicity of levodopa (hypertension), lithium (hyperpyrexia), and reserpine may be increased by MAO inhibitors.

Decreased Effect: CYP2B6 inducers may decrease the levels/effects of selegiline; example inducers include carbamazepine, nevirapine, phenobarbital, phenytoin, and rifampin.

Ethanol/Nutrition/Herb Interactions

Ethanol: Avoid ethanol (based on CNS depressant effects and potential tyramine content)

Food: Concurrent ingestion of foods rich in tyramine may cause sudden and severe high blood pressure (hypertensive crisis). Avoid tyramine-containing foods with MAOIs. Food's freshness is also an important concern; improperly stored or spoiled food can create an environment where tyramine concentrations may increase.

Herb/Nutraceuticals: Avoid valerian, St John's wort, SAMe, kava kava. Avoid supplements containing caffeine, tryptophan, or phenylalanine. Ingestion of large quantities may increase the risk of severe side effects (eg, hypertensive reactions, serotonin syndrome).

Stability

Capsule, tablet: Store at controlled room temperature 15°C to 30°C (59°F to 86°F).

Orally-disintegrating tablet: Store at controlled room temperature 15°C to 30°C (59°F to 86°F). Use within 3 months of opening pouch and immediately after opening individual blister.

Transdermal: Store at 20°C to 25°C (68°F to 77°F).

Mechanism of Action Potent, irreversible inhibitor of monoamine oxidase (MAO). Plasma concentrations achieved via administration of oral dosage forms in recommended doses confer selective inhibition of MAO type B, which plays a major role in the metabolism of dopamine; selegiline may also increase dopaminergic activity by interfering with dopamine reuptake at the synapse. When administered transdermally in recommended doses, selegiline achieves higher blood levels and effectively inhibits both MAO-A and MAO-B, which blocks catabolism of other centrally-active biogenic amine neurotransmitters.

Pharmacodynamics/Kinetics

Onset of action: Therapeutic: Oral: Within 1 hour

Duration: Oral: 24-72 hours

Absorption:

Orally disintegrating tablet: Rapid; greater bioavailability than capsule/tablet

Transdermal: 25% to 30% (of total selegiline content) over 24 hours

Protein binding: ~90%

Metabolism: Hepatic, primarily via CYP2B6 to active (N-desmethylselegiline, amphetamine, methamphetamine) and inactive metabolites

Half-life elimination: Oral: 10 hours; Transdermal: 18-25 hours

Excretion: Urine (primarily metabolites); feces

Dosage

Capsule/tablet:

Children and Adolescents: ADHD (unlabeled use): 5-15 mg/day

Adults: Parkinson's disease: 5 mg twice daily with breakfast and lunch or 10 mg in the morning

Elderly: Parkinson's disease: Initial: 5 mg in the morning, may increase to a total of 10 mg/day

Orally disintegrating tablet (Zelapar™): Adults: Parkinson's disease: Initial 1.25 mg daily for at least 6 weeks; may increase to 2.5 mg daily based on clinical response (maximum: 2.5 mg daily)

Transdermal (Emsam®): Depression:

Adults: Initial: 6 mg/24 hours once daily; may titrate based on clinical response in increments of 3 mg/day every 2 weeks up to a maximum of 12 mg/24 hours

Elderly: 6 mg/24 hours

Dosage adjustment in renal impairment: No adjustment necessary.

Dosage adjustment in hepatic impairment: No adjustment necessary in mild-moderate hepatic impairment.

Dietary Considerations Avoid tyramine-containing foods/beverages. Some examples include aged or matured cheese, air-dried or cured meats (including sausages and salamis), fava or broad bean pods, tap/draft beers, Marmite concentrate, sauerkraut, soy sauce and other soybean condiments.

Emsam® 9 mg/24 hours or 12 mg/24 hours: Avoid tyramine-rich foods or beverages beginning the first day of treatment or for 2 weeks after discontinuation or dose reduction to 6 mg/24 hours.

Zelapar™: Phenylalanine 1.25 mg per 1.25 mg tablet; do not take with food or liquid

Administration

Oral: Orally disintegrating tablet (Zelapar™): Take in morning before breakfast; place on top of tongue and allow to dissolve. Avoid food or liquid 5 minutes before and after administration.

Topical: Transdermal (Emsam®): Apply to clean, dry, intact skin to the upper torso (below the neck and above the waist), upper thigh, or outer surface of the upper arm. Avoid exposure of application site to external heat source, which may increase the amount of drug absorbed. Apply at the same time each day and rotate application sites. Wash hands with soap and water after handling. Avoid touching the sticky side of the patch.

Monitoring Parameters Blood pressure; symptoms of parkinsonism; general mood and behavior (increased anxiety, presence of mania or agitation, or suicidal ideation/tendencies)

Additional Information When adding selegiline to levodopa/carbidopa, the dose of the latter can usually be decreased.

Dosage Forms

Capsule, as hydrochloride: 5 mg
Eldepryl®: 5 mg
Tablet, as hydrochloride: 5 mg
Tablet, orally-disintegrating:
Zelapar™: 1.25 mg [contains phenylalanine 1.25 mg/tablet]
Transdermal system [once-daily patch]:
Emsam®: 6 mg/24 hours (30s); 9 mg/24 hours (30s); 12 mg/24 hours (30s)

♦ **Selegiline Hydrochloride** see Selegiline on page 1552
♦ **Selenicaps [OTC]** see Selenium on page 1555
♦ **Selenimin [OTC]** see Selenium on page 1555

Selenium (se LEE nee um)

U.S. Brand Names Selenicaps [OTC]; Selenimin [OTC]; Selepen®
Pharmacologic Category Trace Element, Parenteral
Use Trace metal supplement
Pregnancy Risk Factor C
Contraindications Hypersensitivity to selenium or any component of the formulation
Adverse Reactions Frequency not defined.
Central nervous system: Lethargy
Dermatologic: Alopecia or hair discoloration
Gastrointestinal: Vomiting following long-term use on damaged skin; abdominal pain, garlic breath
Local: Irritation
Neuromuscular & skeletal: Tremor
Miscellaneous: Diaphoresis
Overdosage/Toxicology Symptoms include nausea, vomiting, and diarrhea.
Mechanism of Action Part of glutathione peroxidase which protects cell components from oxidative damage due to peroxidases produced in cellular metabolism
Pharmacodynamics/Kinetics Excretion: Urine, feces, lungs, skin
Dosage I.V. in TPN solutions:
Children: 3 mcg/kg/day
Adults:
Metabolically stable: 20-40 mcg/day
Deficiency from prolonged TPN support: 100 mcg/day for 24 and 31 days
Dosage Forms
Capsule (Selenicaps): 200 mcg [sugar, starch, wheat, yeast, gluten free]
Injection, solution: 40 mcg/mL (10 mL)
Selepen®: 40 mcg/mL (10 mL, 30 mL) [30 mL size contains benzyl alcohol]
Tablet: 50 mcg, 100 mcg, 200 mcg
Selenimin: 50 mcg, 125 mcg, 200 mcg
Tablet, timed release: 200 mcg

Selenium Sulfide (se LEE nee um SUL fide)

U.S. Brand Names Exsel® [DSC]; Head & Shoulders® Intensive Treatment [OTC]; Selsun®; Selsun Blue® 2-in-1 Treatment [OTC]; Selsun Blue® Balanced Treatment [OTC]; Selsun Blue® Medicated Treatment [OTC]; Selsun Blue® Moisturizing Treatment [OTC]
Canadian Brand Names Versel®
Pharmacologic Category Topical Skin Product
Use Treatment of itching and flaking of the scalp associated with dandruff, to control scalp seborrheic dermatitis; treatment of tinea versicolor
Pregnancy Risk Factor C
Dosage Topical:
Dandruff, seborrhea: Massage 5-10 mL into wet scalp, leave on scalp 2-3 minutes, rinse thoroughly
Tinea versicolor: Apply the 2.5% lotion to affected area and lather with small amounts of water; leave on skin for 10 minutes, then rinse thoroughly; apply every day for 7 days
(Continued)

Selenium Sulfide *(Continued)*

Additional Information Complete prescribing information for this medication should be consulted for additional detail.

Dosage Forms [DSC] = Discontinued product

Lotion, topical: 2.5% (120 mL)

Shampoo, topical: 1% (210 mL)

Exsel® [DSC], Selsun®: 2.5% (120 mL)

Head & Shoulders® Intensive Treatment: 1% (400 mL)

Selsun Blue® Balanced Treatment, Selsun Blue® Medicated Treatment, Selsun Blue® Moisturizing Treatment, Selsun Blue® 2-in-1 Treatment: 1% (120 mL, 210 mL, 330 mL)

- ◆ **Selepen**® *see* Selenium *on page 1555*
- ◆ **Selsun**® *see* Selenium Sulfide *on page 1555*
- ◆ **Selsun Blue**® **2-in-1 Treatment [OTC]** *see* Selenium Sulfide *on page 1555*
- ◆ **Selsun Blue**® **Balanced Treatment [OTC]** *see* Selenium Sulfide *on page 1555*
- ◆ **Selsun Blue**® **Medicated Treatment [OTC]** *see* Selenium Sulfide *on page 1555*
- ◆ **Selsun Blue**® **Moisturizing Treatment [OTC]** *see* Selenium Sulfide *on page 1555*
- ◆ **Semprex**®**-D** *see* Acrivastine and Pseudoephedrine *on page 43*
- ◆ **Senna and Docusate** *see* Docusate and Senna *on page 534*
- ◆ **Senna-S** *see* Docusate and Senna *on page 534*
- ◆ **Senokot-S**® **[OTC]** *see* Docusate and Senna *on page 534*
- ◆ **SenoSol**™**-SS [OTC]** *see* Docusate and Senna *on page 534*
- ◆ **Sensipar**™ *see* Cinacalcet *on page 371*
- ◆ **Sensorcaine**® *see* Bupivacaine *on page 249*
- ◆ **Sensorcaine**®**-MPF** *see* Bupivacaine *on page 249*
- ◆ **Sensorcaine**®**-MPF Spinal** *see* Bupivacaine *on page 249*
- ◆ **Septra**® *see* Sulfamethoxazole and Trimethoprim *on page 1613*
- ◆ **Septra**® **DS** *see* Sulfamethoxazole and Trimethoprim *on page 1613*
- ◆ **Septra**® **Injection (Can)** *see* Sulfamethoxazole and Trimethoprim *on page 1613*
- ◆ **Serax**® *see* Oxazepam *on page 1281*
- ◆ **Serentil**® **[DSC]** *see* Mesoridazine *on page 1091*
- ◆ **Serentil**® **(Can)** *see* Mesoridazine *on page 1091*
- ◆ **Serevent**® **(Can)** *see* Salmeterol *on page 1543*
- ◆ **Serevent**® **Diskus**® *see* Salmeterol *on page 1543*

Sermorelin Acetate *(ser moe REL in AS e tate)*

U.S. Brand Names Geref® Diagnostic

Pharmacologic Category Diagnostic Agent; Growth Hormone

Use

Geref® Diagnostic: For evaluation of the ability of the pituitary gland to secrete growth hormone (GH)

Pregnancy Risk Factor C

Pregnancy Implications Sermorelin has been shown to produce minor variations in fetuses of rats and rabbits. There are no adequate and well-controlled studies in pregnant women.

Lactation Excretion in breast milk unknown/use caution

Contraindications Hypersensitivity to sermorelin acetate, mannitol, or any component of the formulation

Warnings/Precautions Not used for the diagnosis of acromegaly. Thyroid status should be evaluated prior to treatment.

Adverse Reactions Frequency not defined.

Cardiovascular: Tightness in the chest

Central nervous system: Headache, dizziness, hyperactivity, somnolence

Dermatologic: Transient flushing of the face, urticaria

Gastrointestinal: Dysphagia, nausea, vomiting

Local: Pain, redness, and/or swelling at the injection site

Overdosage/Toxicology Changes of heart rate and blood pressure have been reported with sermorelin in I.V. doses exceeding 10 mcg/kg. Cardiovascular collapse is a conceivable, but as of yet, unreported, complication of overdosage with sermorelin.

Drug Interactions

Decreased Effect: The test should not be conducted in the presence of drugs that directly affect the pituitary secretion of somatotropin. These include preparations that contain or release somatostatin, insulin, glucocorticoids, or cyclooxygenase inhibitors such as ASA or indomethacin. Somatotropin levels may be transiently elevated by clonidine, levodopa, and insulin-induced hypoglycemia. Response to sermorelin may be blunted in patients who are receiving muscarinic antagonists (atropine) or who are hypothyroid or being treated with antithyroid medications such as propylthiouracil. Obesity, hyperglycemia, and elevated plasma fatty acids generally are associated with subnormal GH responses to sermorelin. Exogenous growth hormone therapy should be discontinued at least 1 week before administering the test.

Stability Lyophilized preparation must be stored in the refrigerator. Use immediately after reconstitution. Each ampul should be reconstituted with a minimum of 0.5 mL of the accompanying sterile diluent.

Pharmacodynamics/Kinetics Onset of action: Peak response: Diagnostic: Children 30 ± 27 minutes; Adults: 35 ± 29 minutes

Dosage

Children and Adults: Diagnostic: I.V.: 1 mcg/kg as a single dose in the morning following an overnight fast

Note: Response to diagnostic test may be decreased in patients >40 years

Administration Diagnostic: Venous blood samples for growth hormone determinations should be drawn 15 minutes before and immediately prior to sermorelin administration. Administer a bolus of 1 mcg/kg/body weight sermorelin I.V. over 1-3 minutes at a final concentration not to exceed 100 mcg/mL followed by a 3 mL normal saline flush. Draw venous blood samples for growth hormone determinations at 15, 30, 45, and 60 minutes after sermorelin administration.

Reference Range Peak growth hormone levels of >7-10 mcg/L are rarely achieved upon provocation in patients with classic growth hormone deficiency; a marked growth hormone response in these patients (>10-12 mcg/L) is strongly suggestive of hypothalamic dysfunction, as opposed to pituitary dysfunction

Test Interactions See Drug Interactions

Dosage Forms Injection, powder for reconstitution, as acetate: 50 mcg [packaged with diluent]

♦ **Seromycin**® *see* CycloSERINE *on page 430*

♦ **Serophene**® *see* ClomiPHENE *on page 394*

♦ **Seroquel**® *see* Quetiapine *on page 1467*

♦ **Serostim**® *see* Somatropin *on page 1586*

Sertaconazole (ser ta KOE na zole)

U.S. Brand Names Ertaczo™

Index Terms Sertaconazole Nitrate

Pharmacologic Category Antifungal Agent, Topical

Use Topical treatment of tinea pedis (athlete's foot)

Pregnancy Risk Factor C

Dosage Topical: Children ≥12 years and Adults: Apply between toes and to surrounding healthy skin twice daily for 4 weeks

Additional Information Complete prescribing information for this medication should be consulted for additional detail.

Dosage Forms Cream, topical, as nitrate: 2% (30 g)

♦ **Sertaconazole Nitrate** *see* Sertaconazole *on page 1557*

Sertraline (SER tra leen)

U.S. Brand Names Zoloft®

Canadian Brand Names Apo-Sertraline®; Gen-Sertraline; GMD-Sertraline; Novo-Sertraline; Nu-Sertraline; PMS-Sertraline; ratio-Sertraline; Rhoxal-sertraline; Sandoz-Sertraline; Zoloft®

Index Terms Sertraline Hydrochloride

Pharmacologic Category Antidepressant, Selective Serotonin Reuptake Inhibitor

Additional Appendix Information
Antidepressant Agents *on page 1866*
Selective Serotonin Reuptake Inhibitors (SSRIs) Pharmacokinetics *on page 1896*

Use Treatment of major depression; obsessive-compulsive disorder (OCD); panic disorder; post-traumatic stress disorder (PTSD); premenstrual dysphoric disorder (PMDD); social anxiety disorder

Unlabeled/Investigational Use Eating disorders; generalized anxiety disorder (GAD); impulse control disorders

Restrictions An FDA-approved medication guide concerning the use of antidepressants in children and teenagers must be distributed when dispensing an outpatient prescription (new or refill) where this medication is to be used without direct supervision of a healthcare provider. Medication guides are available at http://www.fda.gov/cder/Offices/ODS/medication_guides.htm. Dispense to parents or guardians of children and teenagers receiving this medication.

Pregnancy Risk Factor C

Pregnancy Implications Nonteratogenic effects including respiratory distress, cyanosis, apnea, seizures, temperature instability, feeding difficulty, vomiting, hypoglycemia, hypo- or hypertonia, hyper-reflexia, jitteriness, irritability, constant crying, and tremor have been reported in the neonate immediately following delivery after exposure of SSRIs late in the third trimester. Exposure to SSRIs late in pregnancy has also been associated with persistent pulmonary hypertension of the newborn (PPHN). Adverse effects may be due to toxic effects of SSRI or drug discontinuation. In some cases, effects may present clinically as serotonin syndrome. There are no adequate and well-controlled studies in pregnant women. Use during pregnancy only if the potential benefit to the mother outweighs the possible risk to the fetus. If treatment during pregnancy is required, consider tapering therapy during the third trimester.

Lactation Enters breast milk/not recommended (AAP rates "of concern")

Medication Safety Issues
Sound-alike/look-alike issues:
Sertraline may be confused with selegiline, Serentil®
Zoloft® may be confused with Zocor®

Contraindications Hypersensitivity to sertraline or any component of the formulation; use of MAO inhibitors within 14 days; concurrent use of pimozide; concurrent use of sertraline oral concentrate with disulfiram

Warnings/Precautions [U.S. Boxed Warning]: Antidepressants increase the risk of suicidal thinking and behavior in children and adolescents with major depressive disorder (MDD) and other depressive disorders; consider risk prior to prescribing. All patients must be closely monitored for clinical worsening, suicidality, or unusual changes in behavior, especially during the initiation of therapy or following an increase or decrease in dosage. When used in children, the child's family or caregiver should be instructed to closely observe the patient and communicate condition with healthcare provider. A medication guide should be dispensed with each prescription. **Sertraline is not FDA approved for use in** (Continued)

Sertraline *(Continued)*

children with major depressive disorder (MDD). However, it is approved for the treatment of obsessive-compulsive disorder (OCD) in children ≥6 years of age.

The possibility of a suicide attempt is inherent in major depression and may persist until remission occurs. Use caution in high-risk patients. Worsening depression and severe abrupt suicidality that are not part of the presenting symptoms may require discontinuation or modification of drug therapy. The patient's family or caregiver should be alerted to monitor patients for the emergence of suicidality and associated behaviors (such as agitation, irritability, hostility, impulsivity, and hypomania) and call healthcare provider.

May worsen psychosis in some patients or precipitate a shift to mania or hypomania in patients with bipolar disorder. Patients presenting with depressive symptoms should be screened for bipolar disorder. Monotherapy in patients with bipolar disorder should be avoided. **Sertraline is not FDA approved for the treatment of bipolar depression.**

The potential for severe reaction exists when used with MAO inhibitors, SSRIs/SNRIs or triptans; serotonin syndrome (hyperthermia, muscular rigidity, mental status changes/agitation, autonomic instability) may occur; concomitant use with MAO inhibitors is contraindicated. Has a very low potential to impair cognitive or motor performance. However, caution patients regarding activities requiring alertness until response to sertraline is known. Does not appear to potentiate the effects of alcohol, however, ethanol use is not advised.

Use caution in patients with a previous seizure disorder or condition predisposing to seizures such as brain damage, alcoholism, or concurrent therapy with other drugs which lower the seizure threshold. May increase the risks associated with electroconvulsive therapy. Use with caution in patients with hepatic or renal dysfunction and in elderly patients. May cause hyponatremia/SIADH. Use with caution in patients with renal insufficiency or other concurrent illness (due to limited experience). Sertraline acts as a mild uricosuric; use with caution in patients at risk of uric acid nephropathy. Use with caution in patients at risk of bleeding or receiving anticoagulant therapy; may cause impairment in platelet aggregation. Use with caution in patients where weight loss is undesirable. May cause or exacerbate sexual dysfunction.

Use oral concentrate formulation with caution in patients with latex sensitivity; dropper dispenser contains dry natural rubber. Monitor growth in pediatric patients. Discontinuation symptoms (eg, dysphoric mood, irritability, agitation, confusion, anxiety, insomnia, hypomania) may occur upon abrupt discontinuation. Taper dose when discontinuing therapy.

Adverse Reactions

>10%:
    Central nervous system: Dizziness, fatigue, headache, insomnia, somnolence
    Endocrine & metabolic: Libido decreased
    Gastrointestinal: Anorexia, diarrhea, nausea, xerostomia
    Genitourinary: Ejaculatory disturbances
    Neuromuscular & skeletal: Tremors
    Miscellaneous: Diaphoresis

1% to 10%:
    Cardiovascular: Chest pain, palpitation
    Central nervous system: Agitation, anxiety, hypoesthesia, malaise, nervousness, pain
    Dermatologic: Rash
    Endocrine & metabolic: Impotence
    Gastrointestinal: Appetite increased, constipation, dyspepsia, flatulence, vomiting, weight gain
    Neuromuscular & skeletal: Back pain, hypertonia, myalgia, paresthesia, weakness
    Ocular: Visual difficulty, abnormal vision
    Otic: Tinnitus
    Respiratory: Rhinitis
    Miscellaneous: Yawning

<1% (Limited to important or life-threatening): Abdominal pain, acute renal failure, agranulocytosis, allergic reaction, anaphylactoid reaction, angioedema, aplastic anemia, atrial arrhythmia, AV block, bilirubin increased, blindness, bradycardia, cataract, dystonia, extrapyramidal symptoms, galactorrhea, gum hyperplasia, gynecomastia, hallucinations, hepatic failure, hepatitis, hepatomegaly, hyperglycemia, hyperprolactinemia, hypothyroidism, jaundice, leukopenia, lupus-like syndrome, micturition disorders, neuroleptic malignant syndrome, oculogyric crisis, serotonin syndrome, SIADH, Stevens-Johnson syndrome (and other severe dermatologic reactions), optic neuritis, pancreatitis (rare), photosensitivity, priapism, psychosis, PT/INR increased, pulmonary hypertension, QT_c prolongation, serum sickness, thrombocytopenia, torsade de pointes, transaminases increased, vasculitis, ventricular tachycardia

Additional adverse reactions reported in pediatric patients (frequency >2%): Aggressiveness, epistaxis, hyperkinesia, purpura, sinusitis, urinary incontinence

Overdosage/Toxicology Among 634 patients who overdosed on sertraline alone, 8 resulted in a fatal outcome. Symptoms include somnolence, vomiting, tachycardia, nausea, dizziness, agitation, and tremor. Treatment is symptomatic and supportive.

Drug Interactions

Cytochrome P450 Effect: Substrate of CYP2B6 (minor), 2C9 (minor), 2C19 (major), 2D6 (major), 3A4 (minor); **Inhibits** CYP1A2 (weak), 2B6 (moderate), 2C8 (weak), 2C9 (weak), 2C19 (moderate), 2D6 (moderate), 3A4 (moderate)

Increased Effect/Toxicity: Sertraline should not be used with nonselective MAO inhibitors (phenelzine, isocarboxazid) or other drugs with MAO inhibition (linezolid); fatal reactions have been reported. Wait 2 weeks after stopping an MAO inhibitor before starting sertraline. Concurrent selegiline has been associated with mania, hypertension, or serotonin syndrome (risk may be reduced relative to nonselective MAO inhibitors). Sertraline may increase serum concentrations of pimozide; concurrent use is contraindicated. Avoid use of oral concentrate with disulfiram.

Sertraline may inhibit the metabolism of thioridazine or mesoridazine, resulting in increased plasma levels and increasing the risk of QT$_c$ interval prolongation. This may lead to serious ventricular arrhythmias, such as torsade de pointes-type arrhythmias and sudden death. Do not use together. Wait at least 5 weeks after discontinuing sertraline prior to starting thioridazine.

Sertraline may increase the levels/effects of levels/effects of amphetamines, selected beta-blockers, bupropion, selected benzodiazepines, calcium channel blockers, cisapride, cyclosporine, dextromethorphan, ergot alkaloids, fluoxetine, selected HMG-CoA reductase inhibitors, lidocaine, mesoridazine, mirtazapine, nateglinide, nefazodone, paroxetine, phenytoin, promethazine, propofol, risperidone, ritonavir, selegiline, sildenafil (and other PDE-5 inhibitors), tacrolimus, thioridazine, tricyclic antidepressants, venlafaxine, and other substrates of CYP2B6, 2D6 or 3A4. Sertraline may increase the hypoprothrombinemic response to warfarin.

The levels/effects of sertraline may be increased by chlorpromazine, delavirdine, fluconazole, fluoxetine, fluvoxamine, gemfibrozil, isoniazid, miconazole, omeprazole, paroxetine, pergolide, quinidine, quinine, ritonavir, ropinirole, ticlopidine, and other CYP2C19 or 2D6 inhibitors.

Combined use of SSRIs and amphetamines, buspirone, meperidine, nefazodone, serotonin agonists (such as sumatriptan), sibutramine, other SSRIs/SNRIs, sympathomimetics, ritonavir, tramadol, and venlafaxine may increase the risk of serotonin syndrome. Combined use of sumatriptan (and other serotonin agonists) may result in toxicity; weakness, hyper-reflexia, and incoordination have been observed with sumatriptan and SSRIs. In addition, concurrent use may theoretically increase the risk of serotonin syndrome; includes sumatriptan, naratriptan, rizatriptan, and zolmitriptan.

Concurrent lithium may increase risk of nephrotoxicity. Risk of hyponatremia may increase with concurrent use of loop diuretics (bumetanide, furosemide, torsemide). Concomitant use of sertraline and NSAIDs, aspirin, or other drugs affecting coagulation has been associated with an increased risk of bleeding; monitor.

Decreased Effect: The levels/effects of sertraline may be decreased by aminoglutethimide, carbamazepine, phenytoin, rifampin, and other CYP2C19 inducers. Sertraline may decrease the metabolism of tolbutamide; monitor for changes in glucose control. Sertraline may decrease the levels/effects of CYP2D6 prodrug substrates (eg, codeine, hydrocodone, oxycodone, tramadol).

Ethanol/Nutrition/Herb Interactions
Ethanol: Avoid ethanol (may increase CNS depression).
Food: Sertraline average peak serum levels may be increased if taken with food.
Herb/Nutraceutical: Avoid valerian, St John's wort, kava kava, gotu kola (may increase CNS depression).

Stability Tablets and oral solution should be stored at controlled room temperature of 15°C to 30°C (59°F to 86°F).

Mechanism of Action Antidepressant with selective inhibitory effects on presynaptic serotonin (5-HT) reuptake and only very weak effects on norepinephrine and dopamine neuronal uptake. *In vitro* studies demonstrate no significant affinity for adrenergic, cholinergic, GABA, dopaminergic, histaminergic, serotonergic, or benzodiazepine receptors.

Pharmacodynamics/Kinetics
Absorption: Slow
Protein binding: 98%
Metabolism: Hepatic; may involve CYP2C19 and CYP2D6; extensive first pass metabolism; forms metabolite N-desmethylsertraline
Bioavailability: Bioavailability of tablets and solution are equivalent
Half-life elimination: Sertraline: 26 hours; N-desmethylsertraline: 66 hours (range: 62-104 hours)
Time to peak, plasma: Sertraline: 4.5-8.4 hours
Excretion: Urine and feces

Dosage Oral:
Children and Adolescents: OCD:
6-12 years: Initial: 25 mg once daily
13-17 years: Initial: 50 mg once daily
Note: May increase daily dose, at intervals of not less than 1 week, to a maximum of 200 mg/day. If somnolence is noted, give at bedtime.

Adults:
Depression/OCD: Oral: Initial: 50 mg/day (see "Note" above)
Panic disorder, PTSD, social anxiety disorder: Initial: 25 mg once daily; increase to 50 mg once daily after 1 week (see "Note" above)
PMDD: 50 mg/day either daily throughout menstrual cycle **or** limited to the luteal phase of menstrual cycle, depending on physician assessment. Patients not responding to 50 mg/day may benefit from dose increases (50 mg increments per menstrual cycle) up to 150 mg/day when dosing throughout menstrual cycle **or** up to 100 mg day when dosing during luteal phase only. If a 100 mg/day dose has been established with luteal phase dosing, a 50 mg/day titration step for 3 days should be utilized at the beginning of each luteal phase dosing period.
Elderly: Depression/OCD: Start treatment with 25 mg/day in the morning and increase by 25 mg/day increments every 2-3 days if tolerated to 50-100 mg/day; additional increases may be necessary; maximum dose: 200 mg/day

Dosage adjustment/comment in renal impairment: Multiple-dose pharmacokinetics are unaffected by renal impairment.
Hemodialysis: Not removed by hemodialysis
Dosage adjustment/comment in hepatic impairment: Sertraline is extensively metabolized by the liver; caution should be used in patients with hepatic impairment; a lower dose or less frequent dosing should be used.

Administration Oral concentrate: Must be diluted before use. Immediately before administration, use the dropper provided to measure the required amount of concentrate; mix with 4 (Continued)

Sertraline *(Continued)*

ounces (¹/₂ cup) of water, ginger ale, lemon/lime soda, lemonade, or orange juice **only**. Do not mix with any other liquids than these. The dose should be taken immediately after mixing; do not mix in advance. A slight haze may appear after mixing; this is normal. **Note:** Use with caution in patients with latex sensitivity; dropper dispenser contains dry natural rubber.

Monitoring Parameters Monitor nutritional intake and weight; mental status for depression, suicidal ideation, anxiety, social functioning, mania, panic attacks; akathisia; growth in pediatric patients

Additional Information Buspirone (15-60 mg/day) may be useful in treatment of sexual dysfunction during treatment with a selective serotonin reuptake inhibitor. May exacerbate tics in Tourette's syndrome.

Dosage Forms Note: Available as sertraline hydrochloride; mg strength refers to sertraline
Solution, oral [concentrate]: 20 mg/mL (60 mL)
  Zoloft®: 20 mg/mL (60 mL) [contains alcohol 12%; dropper contains dry natural rubber]
Tablet: 25 mg, 50 mg, 100 mg
  Zoloft®: 25 mg, 50 mg, 100 mg

- ♦ **Sertraline Hydrochloride** *see* Sertraline *on page 1557*
- ♦ **Serutan® [OTC]** *see* Psyllium *on page 1458*
- ♦ **Serzone** *see* Nefazodone *on page 1206*

Sevelamer *(se VEL a mer)*

U.S. Brand Names Renagel®
Canadian Brand Names Renagel®
Index Terms Sevelamer Hydrochloride
Pharmacologic Category Phosphate Binder
Use Reduction of serum phosphorous in patients with chronic kidney disease on hemodialysis
Pregnancy Risk Factor C
Pregnancy Implications Because sevelamer may cause a reduction in the absorption of some vitamins, it should be used with caution in pregnant women.
Lactation Excretion in breast milk unknown/use caution (not absorbed systemically but may alter maternal nutrition)
Medication Safety Issues
Sound-alike/look-alike issues:
  Renagel® may be confused with Reglan®, Regonol®
International issues:
  Renagel® may be confused with Remegel® which is a brand name for calcium carbonate in Ireland, Italy, and Great Britain
Contraindications Hypersensitivity to sevelamer or any component of the formulation; hypophosphatemia; bowel obstruction
Warnings/Precautions Use with caution in patients with gastrointestinal disorders including dysphagia, swallowing disorders, severe gastrointestinal motility disorders, or major gastrointestinal surgery. May cause reductions in vitamin D, E, K, and folic acid absorption. Long-term studies of carcinogenic potential have not been completed. Tablets should not be taken apart or chewed; broken or crushed tablets will rapidly expand in water/saliva and may be a choking hazard..
Adverse Reactions
>10%:
  Dermatologic: Rash (13%)
  Gastrointestinal: Vomiting (22%), nausea (7% to 20%), diarrhea (4% to 19%), dyspepsia (5% to 16%)
  Neuromuscular & skeletal: Limb pain (13%), arthralgia (12%)
  Respiratory: Nasopharyngitis (14%), bronchitis (11%)
1% to 10%:
  Cardiovascular: Hypertension (10%)
  Central nervous system: Headache (9%), pyrexia (5%)
  Gastrointestinal: Constipation (2% to 8%), flatulence (4%)
  Neuromuscular & skeletal: Back pain (4%)
  Respiratory: Dyspnea (10%), cough (7%), upper respiratory tract infection (5%)
Postmarketing and/or case reports: Abdominal pain
Overdosage/Toxicology Sevelamer is not absorbed systemically. Doses up to 14 g/day for 8 days have been administered without adverse effects. There are no reports of overdosage in patients.
Drug Interactions
Decreased Effect: Sevelamer may bind to some drugs in the gastrointestinal tract and decrease their absorption. When changes in absorption of oral medications may have significant clinical consequences (such as antiarrhythmic and antiseizure medications), these medications should be taken at least 1 hour before or 3 hours after a dose of sevelamer. Sevelamer may decrease the bioavailability of ciprofloxacin by 50%.
Stability Store at controlled room temperature of 15°C to 30°C (59°F to 86°F).
Mechanism of Action Sevelamer (a polymeric compound) binds phosphate within the intestinal lumen, limiting absorption and decreasing serum phosphate concentrations without altering calcium, aluminum, or bicarbonate concentrations
Pharmacodynamics/Kinetics
Absorption: None
Excretion: Feces
Dosage
Adults: Oral: Patients not taking a phosphate binder: 800-1600 mg 3 times/day with meals; the initial dose may be based on serum phosphorous levels:
  >5.5 mg/dL to <7.5 mg/dL: 800 mg 3 times/day
  ≥7.5 mg/dL to <9.0 mg/dL: 1200-1600 mg 3 times/day
  ≥9.0 mg/dL: 1600 mg 3 times/day

Maintenance dose adjustment based on serum phosphorous concentration (goal of lowering to <5.5 mg/dL; maximum daily dose studied was equivalent to 13 g/day):
>5.5 mg/dL: Increase by 1 tablet per meal every 2 weeks
3.5-5.5 mg/dL: Maintain current dose
<3.5 mg/dL: Decrease by 1 tablet per meal
Dosage adjustment when switching between phosphate binder products: 667 mg of calcium acetate is equivalent to 800 mg sevelamer

Dietary Considerations Take with meals.

Administration Must be administered with meals

Monitoring Parameters Serum phosphorus, calcium, bicarbonate, chloride

Dosage Forms Tablet, as hydrochloride: 400 mg, 800 mg

♦ **Sevelamer Hydrochloride** *see* Sevelamer *on page 1560*

Sevoflurane (see voe FLOO rane)

U.S. Brand Names Ultane®

Canadian Brand Names Sevorane™

Pharmacologic Category General Anesthetic, Inhalation

Use Induction and maintenance of general anesthesia

Pregnancy Risk Factor B

Medication Safety Issues
Sound-alike/look-alike issues:
Ultane® may be confused with Ultram®

Contraindications Previous hypersensitivity to sevoflurane, other halogenated anesthetics, or any component of the formulation; known or suspected susceptibility to malignant hyperthermia

Warnings/Precautions Reaction of sevoflurane with CO_2 absorbents that become desiccated within circle breathing equipment can lead to formation of formaldehyde (causing respiratory irritation) and carbon monoxide; maintain fresh absorbent as per manufacturer guidelines regardless of state of colorimetric indicator. Exothermic reaction of sevoflurane with desiccated CO_2 absorbents has been reported to generate extreme heat, smoke and/or fire within breathing circuit. This reaction also leads to formation of a fluorinated byproduct, compound A, which has been reported to cause nephrotoxicity (eg, proteinuria, glycosuria) in animal studies. Compound A-induced renal toxicity is dose- and exposure time-dependent; minimize exposure risk by not exceeding 2 MAC hours and fresh flow rates <2 L/minute (low fresh gas flow rates maximize rebreathing of the anesthetic).

Causes dose-dependent respiratory depression and blunted ventilatory response to hypoxia and hypercapnia. Hypoxic pulmonary vasoconstriction is blunted which may lead to increased pulmonary shunt. May dilate the cerebral vasculature and increase intracranial pressure. Use cautiously in patients with risk of elevation in intracranial pressure. May cause malignant hyperthermia. Perioperative hyperkalemia may occur in pediatric patients with underlying neuromuscular disease (eg, Duchenne muscular dystrophy). Concomitant use of succinylcholine was associated with many of the cases. Other abnormalities may include elevation in CPK and myoglobinuria. Monitor closely for arrhythmias. Aggressively identify and treat hyperkalemia. Use cautiously in patients with renal dysfunction. Use with caution in patients at risk for seizures; seizures have been reported in children and young adults. Monitor for emergence agitation or delirium. Postoperative hepatitis or hepatic dysfunction with or without jaundice has rarely been reported. Safety in patients with severe renal dysfunction or severe hepatic dysfunction has not been determined.

Adverse Reactions
>10%:
Cardiovascular: Hypotension (4% to 11% dose dependent)
Central nervous system: Agitation (7% to 15%)
Gastrointestinal: Nausea (25%), vomiting (18%)
Respiratory: Cough increased (5% to 11%)
1% to 10%:
Cardiovascular: Bradycardia (5%), tachycardia (2% to 6%), hypertension (2%)
Central nervous system: Somnolence (8%), dizziness (4%), hypothermia (1%), headache (1%), fever (1%), emergence delirium
Gastrointestinal: Salivation (2% to 4%)
Respiratory: Laryngospasm (2% to 8%), airway obstruction (8%), breath-holding (2% to 5%), apnea (2%)
Miscellaneous: Shivering (6%)
<1% (Limited to important or life-threatening): Acidosis, albuminuria, alkaline phosphatase increased, allergic reactions, ALT/AST increased, amblyopia, anaphylactic/anaphylactoid reaction, arrhythmia, asthenia, atrial arrhythmia, atrial fibrillation, bigeminy, bilirubinemia, bronchospasm, BUN increased, complete AV block, confusion, conjunctivitis, creatinine increased, creatinine phosphokinase increased, crying, dry mouth, dyspnea, fluorosis, glycosuria, hemorrhage, hepatic dysfunction, hepatic failure, hepatic necrosis, hepatitis, hiccup, hyperglycemia, hyperkalemia (pediatric patients, postoperative), hypertonia, hyper-/hypoventilation, hypophosphatemia, hypoxia, insomnia, inverted T wave, jaundice, leukocytosis, LDH increased, liver enzymes increased, malignant hyperthermia, myoglobinuria, nervousness, oliguria, pain, pharyngitis, pruritus, rash, second degree AV block, seizure, sputum, ST depression, stridor, supraventricular extrasystoles, syncope, taste perversion, thrombocytopenia, urinary retention, ventricular extrasystoles, wheezing

Drug Interactions
Cytochrome P450 Effect: Substrate of CYP2A6 (minor), 2B6 (minor), 2E1 (major), 3A4 (minor)
Increased Effect/Toxicity: CYP2E1 inhibitors may increase the levels/effects of sevoflurane; example inhibitors include disulfiram, isoniazid, and miconazole. Administration of 60% to 65% N_2O reduces the minimum alveolar concentration (MAC) equivalent dose of sevoflurane in adults and in children; benzodiazepines and opioids also reduce the MAC
(Continued)

Sevoflurane *(Continued)*

of sevoflurane. Sevoflurane may increase the nephrotoxicity of aminoglycosides. Excessive hypotension may occur when combined with antihypertensive drugs. Sevoflurane potentiates the actions of nondepolarizing, neuromuscular-blocking agents.

Decreased Effect: Concurrent use of opioids and/or benzodiazepines decreases the MAC of sevoflurane. Concurrent use of nitrous oxide may reduce the anesthetic requirement of sevoflurane.

Stability Store at 15°C to 30°C (59°F to 86°F).

Mechanism of Action Inhaled anesthetics alter activity of neuronal ion channels particularly the fast synaptic neurotransmitter receptors (nicotinic acetylcholine, GABA, and glutamate receptors). Limited effects on sympathetic stimulation including cardiovascular system. Seroflurane does not cause respiratory irritation or circulatory stimulation. May depress myocardial contractility, decrease blood pressure through a decrease in systemic vascular resistance and decrease sympathetic nervous activity.

Pharmacodynamics/Kinetics Sevoflurane has a low blood/gas partition coefficient and therefore is associated with a rapid onset of anesthesia and recovery

Onset of action: Time to induction: Within 2 minutes

Duration: Emergence time: Depends on blood concentration when sevoflurane is discontinued. The rate of change of anesthetic concentration in the lung is rapid with sevoflurane because of its low blood gas solubility (0.63). The 90% decrement time (time required for anesthetic concentration in vessel-rich tissues to decrease by 90%) for sevoflurane is short when the duration of anesthesia is <2 hours but increases dramatically as the duration of administration is lengthened.

Metabolism: 3% to 5% hepatic via CYP2E1

Excretion: Exhaled gases

Dosage Minimum alveolar concentration (MAC), the concentration that abolishes movement in response to a noxious stimulus (surgical incision) in 50% of patients, is 2.6% (25 years of age) for sevoflurane. Surgical levels of anesthesia are generally achieved with concentrations from 0.5% to 3%; the concentration at which amnesia and loss of awareness occur is 0.6%.

Minimum alveolar concentrations (MAC) values for surgical levels of anesthesia:

0 to 1 month old full-term neonates: Sevoflurane in oxygen: 3.3%

1 to <6 months: Sevoflurane in oxygen: 3%

6 months to <3 years:

Sevoflurane in oxygen: 2.8%

Sevoflurane in 60% N_2O/40% oxygen: 2%

3-12 years: Sevoflurane in oxygen: 2.5%

25 years:

Sevoflurane in oxygen: 2.6%

Sevoflurane in 65% N_2O/35% oxygen: 1.4%

40 years:

Sevoflurane in oxygen: 2.1%

Sevoflurane in 65% N_2O/35% oxygen: 1.1%

60 years:

Sevoflurane in oxygen: 1.7%

Sevoflurane in 65% N_2O/35% oxygen: 0.9%

80 years:

Sevoflurane in oxygen: 1.4%

Sevoflurane in 65% N_2O/35% oxygen: 0.7%

Dosage adjustment in renal impairment: Use with caution in renal insufficiency.

Dosage adjustment in hepatic impairment: Use with caution in patients with underlying hepatic conditions.

Administration Via sevoflurane-specific calibrated vaporizers; use cautiously in low-flow or closed-circuit systems since sevoflurane is unstable and potentially toxic breakdown products have been liberated.

Monitoring Parameters Blood pressure, temperature, heart rate and rhythm, oxygen saturation, end-tidal CO_2 and end-tidal sevoflurane concentrations should be monitored prior to and throughout anesthesia; temperature of CO_2 absorbent canister

Dosage Forms Liquid for inhalation: 100% (250 mL)

♦ **Sevorane™ (Can)** *see* Sevoflurane *on page 1561*

♦ **Shingles Vaccine** *see* Zoster Vaccine *on page 1827*

♦ **Shur-Seal® [OTC] [DSC]** *see* Nonoxynol 9 *on page 1239*

Sibutramine *(si BYOO tra meen)*

U.S. Brand Names Meridia®

Canadian Brand Names Meridia®

Index Terms Sibutramine Hydrochloride Monohydrate

Pharmacologic Category Anorexiant

Additional Appendix Information

Obesity Treatment Guidelines for Adults *on page 2073*

Use Management of obesity, including weight loss and maintenance of weight loss; should be used in conjunction with a reduced-calorie diet

Restrictions C-IV; recommended only for obese patients with a body mass index ≥30 kg/m² or ≥27 kg/m² in the presence of other risk factors such as hypertension, diabetes, and/or dyslipidemia; rule out obesity due to untreated hypothyroidism

Pregnancy Risk Factor C

Pregnancy Implications Teratogenic effects were not observed in animal studies at doses exceeding the therapeutic range. There are no adequate and well-controlled studies in pregnant women. Use in pregnancy is not recommended.

Lactation Excretion in breast milk unknown/not recommended

Contraindications Hypersensitivity to sibutramine or any component of the formulation; during or within 2 weeks of MAO inhibitors (eg, phenelzine, selegiline) or concomitant centrally-acting appetite suppressants; anorexia nervosa; bulimia nervosa

Warnings/Precautions Use with caution in mild-moderate renal impairment or hepatic dysfunction, seizure disorder, hypertension, gallstones, narrow-angle glaucoma, nursing mothers, and elderly patients; not for use in patients with severe renal or hepatic impairment or history of cardiovascular disorders (eg, CHF, stroke, arrhythmia). Primary pulmonary hypertension (PPH), a rare and frequently fatal pulmonary disease, has been reported to occur in patients receiving other agents with serotonergic activity which have been used as anorexiants. Although not reported in clinical trials, it is possible that sibutramine may share this potential, and patients should be monitored closely. Avoid concurrent use with other serotonergic agents, due to the risk of developing serotonin syndrome. Rare cases of bleeding have been reported; use caution in patients with bleeding disorders. Stimulants may unmask tics in individuals with coexisting Tourette's syndrome. Rare reports of depression, suicide and suicidal ideation have been documented; use caution and monitor closely in patients with history of psychiatric symptoms. Safety and efficacy have not been established in children <16 years of age.

Adverse Reactions

>10%:
  Central nervous system: Headache (30%), insomnia (11%)
  Gastrointestinal: Xerostomia (17%), anorexia (13%), constipation (12%)

1% to 10%:
  Cardiovascular: Tachycardia (3%), vasodilation (2%), hypertension (2%), palpitation (2%), chest pain (2%), edema (1%)
  Central nervous system: Dizziness (7%), nervousness (5%), anxiety (5%), depression (4%), migraine (2%), somnolence (2%), CNS stimulation (2%), emotional lability (1%)
  Dermatologic: Rash (4%), acne (1%)
  Endocrine & metabolic: Dysmenorrhea (4%), metrorrhagia (1%)
  Gastrointestinal: Appetite increased (9%), nausea (6%), abdominal pain (5%), dyspepsia (5%), gastritis (2%), vomiting (2%), taste perversion (2%), rectal disorder (1%)
  Genitourinary: Urinary tract infection (2%), vaginal *Monilia* (1%)
  Hepatic: Abnormal LFTs (2%)
  Neuromuscular & skeletal: Back pain (8%), weakness (6%), arthralgia (6%), neck pain (2%), myalgia (2%), paresthesia (2%), tenosynovitis (1%), joint disorder (1%)
  Otic: Ear disorder (2%), ear pain (1%)
  Respiratory: Pharyngitis (10%), rhinitis (10%), sinusitis (5%), cough (4%), laryngitis (1%)
  Miscellaneous: Flu-like syndrome (8%), diaphoresis (3%), allergic reactions (2), thirst (2%), herpes simplex (1%)

<1% (Limited to important or life-threatening): Bruising, interstitial nephritis, seizure

Frequency not defined:
  Cardiovascular: Peripheral edema
  Central nervous system: Thinking abnormal, agitation, fever
  Dermatologic: Pruritus
  Endocrine & metabolic: Menstrual disorders/irregularities
  Gastrointestinal: Diarrhea, flatulence, gastroenteritis, tooth disorder
  Neuromuscular & skeletal: Arthritis, hypertonia, leg cramps
  Ocular: Amblyopia
  Respiratory: Bronchitis, dyspnea

Postmarketing and/or case reports (frequency not defined; limited to important or life-threatening): Amnesia, anaphylactic shock, anaphylactoid reaction, anemia, angina, angioedema, arrhythmia, arthrosis, atrial fibrillation, cardiac arrest, cerebrovascular accident, CHF, cholecystitis, cholelithiasis, depression aggravated, GI hemorrhage, goiter, hematuria, hyper-/hypoglycemia, hyper-/hypothyroidism, impotence, intestinal obstruction, intraocular pressure increased, leukopenia, lymphadenopathy, mania, mouth/stomach ulcer, serotonin syndrome, stroke, suicidal ideation, syncope, thrombocytopenia, tongue edema, torsade de pointes, Tourette's syndrome, urinary retention, urticaria, transient ischemic attack, vascular headache, ventricular dysrhythmias

Overdosage/Toxicology There is no specific antidote. Treatment should consist of general supportive measures employed in the management of overdosage. Treatment is supportive. Monitor vitals; beta-blockers may be beneficial to control elevated pressure and heart rate; dialysis not likely to be effective.

Drug Interactions

Cytochrome P450 Effect: Substrate of CYP3A4 (major)

Increased Effect/Toxicity: Serotonergic agents such as buspirone, selective serotonin reuptake inhibitors (eg, citalopram, fluoxetine, fluvoxamine, paroxetine, sertraline), sumatriptan (and similar serotonin agonists), dihydroergotamine, lithium, tryptophan, some opioid/analgesics (eg, meperidine, tramadol), and venlafaxine, when combined with sibutramine may result in serotonin syndrome. Dextromethorphan, MAO inhibitors and other drugs that can raise the blood pressure (eg decongestants, centrally-acting weight loss products, amphetamines, and amphetamine-like compounds) can increase the possibility of sibutramine-associated cardiovascular complications. Sibutramine may increase serum levels of tricyclic antidepressants. CYP3A4 inhibitors may increase the levels/effects of sibutramine; example inhibitors include azole antifungals, clarithromycin, diclofenac, doxycycline, erythromycin, imatinib, isoniazid, nefazodone, nicardipine, propofol, protease inhibitors, quinidine, telithromycin, and verapamil.

Decreased Effect: Inducers of CYP3A4 (including phenytoin, phenobarbital, carbamazepine, and rifampin) theoretically may reduce sibutramine serum concentrations.

Ethanol/Nutrition/Herb Interactions

Ethanol: Avoid excess ethanol ingestion.
Herb/Nutraceutical: St John's wort may decrease sibutramine levels.

Stability Store at room temperature of 15°C to 30°C (59°F to 86°F).
(Continued)

Sibutramine *(Continued)*

Mechanism of Action Sibutramine and its two primary metabolites block the neuronal uptake of norepinephrine, serotonin, and (to a lesser extent) dopamine. There is no mono-amine-releasing (or depleting) activity.

Pharmacodynamics/Kinetics

Absorption: 77%; rapid

Protein binding, plasma: Parent drug and metabolites: >94%

Metabolism: Hepatic; undergoes first-pass metabolism via CYP3A4; forms two primary metabolites (active)

Half-life elimination: Sibutramine: 1 hour; Metabolites: M_1: 14 hours; M_2: 16 hours

Time to peak: Sibutramine: 1.2 hours; Metabolites (M_1 and M_2): 3-4 hours

Excretion: Primarily urine (77%); feces

Dosage Adults ≥16 years: Initial: 10 mg once daily; after 4 weeks may titrate up to 15 mg once daily as needed and tolerated (may be used for up to 2 years, per manufacturer labeling)

Dosage adjustment in renal/hepatic impairment: Should not be used in patients with severe renal or hepatic impairment

Dietary Considerations Sibutramine, as an appetite suppressant, is the most effective when combined with a low calorie diet and behavior modification counseling.

Administration May take with or without food.

Monitoring Parameters Do initial blood pressure and heart rate evaluation and then monitor regularly during therapy. If patient has sustained increases in either blood pressure or pulse rate, consider discontinuing or reducing the dose of the drug.

Additional Information Physicians should carefully evaluate patients for history of drug abuse and follow such patients closely, observing them for signs of misuse or abuse (eg, development of tolerance, excessive increases of doses, drug seeking behavior).

Unlike dexfenfluramine and fenfluramine, the medication does not cause the release of serotonin from neurons. Tests done on humans show no evidence of valvular heart disease and experiments done on animals show no evidence of the neurotoxicity which was found in similar testing using animals treated with fenfluramine and dexfenfluramine; has minimal potential for abuse.

Dosage Forms Capsule, as hydrochloride: 5 mg, 10 mg, 15 mg

- ◆ **Sibutramine Hydrochloride Monohydrate** *see* Sibutramine *on page 1562*
- ◆ **Silace [OTC]** *see* Docusate *on page 533*
- ◆ **Siladryl® Allergy [OTC]** *see* DiphenhydrAMINE *on page 515*
- ◆ **Siladryl® DAS [OTC]** *see* DiphenhydrAMINE *on page 515*
- ◆ **Silafed® [OTC]** *see* Triprolidine and Pseudoephedrine *on page 1749*
- ◆ **Silapap® Children's [OTC]** *see* Acetaminophen *on page 28*
- ◆ **Silapap® Infants [OTC]** *see* Acetaminophen *on page 28*
- ◆ **Sildec [DSC]** *see* Carbinoxamine and Pseudoephedrine *on page 290*
- ◆ **Sildec-DM [DSC]** *see* Carbinoxamine, Pseudoephedrine, and Dextromethorphan *on page 291*
- ◆ **Sildec PE** *see* Chlorpheniramine and Phenylephrine *on page 349*
- ◆ **Sildec PE-DM** *see* Chlorpheniramine, Phenylephrine, and Dextromethorphan *on page 352*

Sildenafil *(sil DEN a fil)*

U.S. Brand Names Revatio™; Viagra®

Canadian Brand Names Viagra®

Index Terms UK92480

Pharmacologic Category Phosphodiesterase-5 Enzyme Inhibitor

Use Treatment of erectile dysfunction; treatment of pulmonary arterial hypertension

Unlabeled/Investigational Use Psychotropic-induced sexual dysfunction; pulmonary arterial hypertension in children

Pregnancy Risk Factor B

Pregnancy Implications There are no adequate and well-controlled studies in pregnant women.

Lactation Excretion in breast milk unknown/use caution

Medication Safety Issues

Sound-alike/look-alike issues:

Viagra® may be confused with Allegra®, Vaniqa™

Contraindications Hypersensitivity to sildenafil or any component of the formulation; concurrent use of organic nitrates (nitroglycerin) in any form (potentiates the hypotensive effects)

Warnings/Precautions Decreases in blood pressure may occur due to vasodilator effects; use caution in patients with resting hypotension (BP <90/50), hypertension (BP >170/110), fluid depletion, severe left ventricular outflow obstruction, or autonomic dysfunction, and patients receiving alpha-blockers or other antihypertensive medication. Not recommended for use with pulmonary veno-occlusive disease.

Use caution in patients with cardiovascular disease, including cardiac failure, unstable angina, or a recent history (within the last 6 months) of myocardial infarction, stroke, or life-threatening arrhythmia. Use caution in patients receiving concurrent bosentan. Use caution in patients with bleeding disorders or with active peptic ulcer disease; safety and efficacy have not been established.

There is a degree of cardiac risk associated with sexual activity; therefore, physicians may wish to consider the cardiovascular status of their patients prior to initiating any treatment for erectile dysfunction. Sildenafil should be used with caution in patients with anatomical deformation of the penis (angulation, cavernosal fibrosis, or Peyronie's disease), or in patients who have conditions which may predispose them to priapism (sickle cell anemia, multiple myeloma, leukemia).

Rare cases of nonarteritic ischemic optic neuropathy (NAION) have been reported; risk may be increased with history of vision loss. Other risk factors for NAION include low cup-to-disc ratio ("crowded disc"), coronary artery disease, diabetes, hypertension, hyperlipidemia, smoking, and age >50 years.

The safety and efficacy of sildenafil with other treatments for erectile dysfunction have not been established; use is not recommended. May cause dose-related impairment of color discrimination. Use caution in patients with retinitis pigmentosa; a minority have generic disorders of retinal phosphodiesterases (no safety information available). Safety and efficacy in pediatric patients have not been established.

Adverse Reactions Based upon normal doses. (Adverse effects such as flushing, diarrhea, myalgia, and visual disturbances may be increased with doses >100 mg/24 hours.)

>10%:
Central nervous system: Headache (16% to 46%)
Gastrointestinal: Dyspepsia (7% to 17%)

1% to 10%:
Cardiovascular: Flushing (10%)
Central nervous system: Dizziness, insomnia, pyrexia
Dermatologic: Erythema, rash
Gastrointestinal: Diarrhea (3% to 9%), gastritis
Genitourinary: Urinary tract infection
Hematologic: Anemia, leukopenia
Hepatic: LFTs increased
Neuromuscular & skeletal: Myalgia, paresthesia
Ocular: Abnormal vision (color changes, blurred or increased sensitivity to light 3%; up to 11% with doses >100 mg)
Respiratory: Dyspnea exacerbated, epistaxis, nasal congestion, rhinitis, sinusitis

<2% (Limited to important or life-threatening): Abnormal dreams, allergic reaction, anemia, angina pectoris, anorgasmia, asthma, AV block, cardiac arrest, cardiomyopathy, cataract, cerebrovascular hemorrhage, cystitis, depression, dysphagia, hearing decreased, hemorrhage, cerebral thrombosis, colitis, dyspnea, edema, epistaxis, exfoliative dermatitis, eye hemorrhage, gout, heart failure, hematuria, hyper-/hypoglycemia, hypernatremia, hyper-/hypotension, hyperuricemia, intracerebral hemorrhage, intraocular pressure increased, leukopenia, migraine, myocardial ischemia, MI, myasthenia, mydriasis, neuralgia, nonarteritic ischemic optic neuropathy (NAION), palpitation, photosensitivity, postural hypotension, priapism, pulmonary hemorrhage, rectal hemorrhage, retinal vascular disease or bleeding, seizure, shock, stomatitis, subarachnoid hemorrhage, syncope, tachycardia, tendon rupture, TIA, urinary incontinence, ventricular arrhythmia, vertigo, visual field loss, vitreous detachment/traction, vomiting

Overdosage/Toxicology In studies of healthy volunteers with single doses up to 800 mg, adverse events were similar to those seen at lower doses, but incidence rates were increased. Dialysis not likely to be beneficial due to protein binding.

Drug Interactions

Cytochrome P450 Effect: Substrate of CYP2C9 (minor), 3A4 (major); **Inhibits** CYP1A2 (weak), 2C9 (weak), 2C19 (weak), 2D6 (weak), 2E1 (weak), 3A4 (weak)

Increased Effect/Toxicity: Sildenafil potentiates the hypotensive effects of nitrates (amyl nitrate, isosorbide dinitrate, isosorbide mononitrate, nitroglycerin); severe reactions have occurred and concurrent use is contraindicated. Concomitant use of alpha-blockers (doxazosin) may lead to symptomatic hypotension. Macrolide antibiotics may increase the effects of sildenafil.

CYP3A4 inhibitors may increase the levels/effects of sildenafil; example inhibitors include azole antifungals, clarithromycin, diclofenac, doxycycline, erythromycin, imatinib, isoniazid, nefazodone, nicardipine, propofol, protease inhibitors, quinidine, telithromycin, and verapamil. Sildenafil may potentiate the effect of other antihypertensives. Reduce sildenafil dose to 25 mg/24 hours in patients receiving azole antifungals or protease inhibitors (use of Revatio™ with concurrent protease inhibitors is not recommended).

Decreased Effect: Enzyme inducers (including phenytoin, carbamazepine, phenobarbital, rifampin) may decrease the serum concentration and efficacy of sildenafil. Bosentan may decrease serum concentration and effect of sildenafil.

Ethanol/Nutrition/Herb Interactions

Food: Amount and rate of absorption of sildenafil is reduced when taken with a high-fat meal. Serum concentrations/toxicity may be increased with grapefruit juice; avoid concurrent use.

Herb/Nutraceutical: St John's wort may decrease sildenafil levels.

Stability Store tablets at controlled room temperature of 15°C to 30°C (59°F to 86°F).

Mechanism of Action

Erectile dysfunction: Does not directly cause penile erections, but affects the response to sexual stimulation. The physiologic mechanism of erection of the penis involves release of nitric oxide (NO) in the corpus cavernosum during sexual stimulation. NO then activates the enzyme guanylate cyclase, which results in increased levels of cyclic guanosine monophosphate (cGMP), producing smooth muscle relaxation and inflow of blood to the corpus cavernosum. Sildenafil enhances the effect of NO by inhibiting phosphodiesterase type 5 (PDE-5), which is responsible for degradation of cGMP in the corpus cavernosum; when sexual stimulation causes local release of NO, inhibition of PDE-5 by sildenafil causes increased levels of cGMP in the corpus cavernosum, resulting in smooth muscle relaxation and inflow of blood to the corpus cavernosum; at recommended doses, it has no effect in the absence of sexual stimulation.

Pulmonary arterial hypertension (PAH): Inhibits phosphodiesterase type 5 (PDE-5) in smooth muscle of pulmonary vasculature where PDE-5 is responsible for the degradation of cyclic guanosine monophosphate (cGMP). Increased cGMP concentration results in pulmonary vasculature relaxation; vasodilation in the pulmonary bed and the systemic circulation (to a lesser degree) may occur.

Pharmacodynamics/Kinetics

Onset of action: ~60 minutes
Duration: 2-4 hours
(Continued)

Sildenafil *(Continued)*

Absorption: Rapid; slower with a high-fat meal

Distribution: V_{dss}: 105 L

Protein binding, plasma: ~96%

Metabolism: Hepatic via CYP3A4 (major) and CYP2C9 (minor route)

Bioavailability: 40%

Half-life elimination: 4 hours

Time to peak: 30-120 minutes; delayed by 60 minutes with a high-fat meal

Excretion: Feces (80%); urine (13%)

Dosage Adults: Oral:

Erectile dysfunction (Viagra®): For most patients, the recommended dose is 25-50 mg taken as needed, approximately 1 hour before sexual activity. However, sildenafil may be taken anywhere from 30 minutes to 4 hours before sexual activity. Based on effectiveness and tolerance, the dose may be increased to a maximum recommended dose of 100 mg or decreased to 25 mg. The maximum recommended dosing frequency is once daily.

Pulmonary arterial hypertension (Revatio™): 20 mg 3 times/day, taken 4-6 hours apart

Dosage adjustment for patients >65 years of age: Hepatic impairment (cirrhosis), severe renal impairment (creatinine clearance <30 mL/minute): Higher plasma levels have been associated which may result in increase in efficacy and adverse effects; Viagra®: Starting dose of 25 mg should be considered

Dosage considerations for patients stable on alpha blockers: Viagra®: Initial 25 mg

Dosage adjustment for concomitant use of potent CYP34A inhibitors:

Revatio™:

Erythromycin, saquinavir: No dosage adjustment

Itraconazole, ketoconazole, ritonavir: Not recommended

Viagra®:

Erythromycin, itraconazole, ketoconazole, saquinavir: Starting dose of 25 mg should be considered

Ritonavir: Maximum: 25 mg every 48 hours

Administration

Revatio™: Administer tablets at least 4-6 hours apart

Viagra®: Administer orally ~1 hour before sexual activity (may be used anytime from 4 hours to 30 minutes before).

Additional Information Sildenafil is ~10 times more selective for PDE-5 as compared to PDE6. This enzyme is found in the retina and is involved in phototransduction. At higher plasma levels, interference with PDE6 is believed to be the basis for changes in color vision noted in some patients.

Dosage Forms Tablet:

Revatio™: 20 mg

Viagra®: 25 mg, 50 mg, 100 mg

Extemporaneous Preparations A stable suspension of sildenafil citrate (2.5 mg/mL) may be prepared as follows: Triturate thirty (30) sildenafil 25 mg tablets (Viagra®) to a fine powder in a mortar and pestle. Create a uniform paste by stirring in a small volume of suspending agent (1:1 mixture of methylcellulose 1% and simple syrup NF or a 1:1 mixture of Ora-Sweet® and Ora-Plus®). Continue adding vehicle to the paste in a geometric manner, with mixing, until near the desired volume. Transfer suspension to a graduated cylinder and QS to 300 mL with vehicle. Final suspension should be transferred to amber plastic bottles, labeled with "shake well" and dated for 90-day expiration at room temperature (25°C) or under refrigeration (4°C).

Nahata MC, Morosco RS, and Brady MT, "Extemporaneous Sildenafil Citrate Oral Suspensions for the Treatment of Pulmonary Hypertension in Children," *Am J Health-Syst Pharm*, 2006, 63:254-7.

♦ **Silexin [OTC]** *see* Guaifenesin and Dextromethorphan *on page 816*

♦ **Silfedrine Children's [OTC]** *see* Pseudoephedrine *on page 1454*

♦ **Silphen® [OTC]** *see* DiphenhydrAMINE *on page 515*

♦ **Sil-Tex** *see* Guaifenesin and Phenylephrine *on page 818*

♦ **Siltussin DAS [OTC]** *see* Guaifenesin *on page 814*

♦ **Siltussin DM [OTC]** *see* Guaifenesin and Dextromethorphan *on page 816*

♦ **Siltussin DM DAS [OTC]** *see* Guaifenesin and Dextromethorphan *on page 816*

♦ **Siltussin SA [OTC]** *see* Guaifenesin *on page 814*

♦ **Silvadene®** *see* Silver Sulfadiazine *on page 1567*

Silver Nitrate *(SIL ver NYE trate)*

Index Terms $AgNO_3$

Pharmacologic Category Antibiotic, Topical; Cauterizing Agent, Topical; Topical Skin Product, Antibacterial

Use Cauterization of wounds and sluggish ulcers, removal of granulation tissue and warts; aseptic prophylaxis of burns

Pregnancy Risk Factor C

Dosage Children and Adults:

Sticks: Apply to mucous membranes and other moist skin surfaces only on area to be treated 2-3 times/week for 2-3 weeks

Topical solution: Apply a cotton applicator dipped in solution on the affected area 2-3 times/week for 2-3 weeks

Additional Information Silver nitrate solutions stain skin and utensils.

Dosage Forms

Applicator sticks, topical: Silver nitrate 75% and potassium nitrate 25% (6", 12", 18")

Solution, topical: 10% (30 mL); 25% (30 mL); 50% (30 mL)

Silver Sulfadiazine (SIL ver sul fa DYE a zeen)

U.S. Brand Names Silvadene®; SSD®; SSD® AF; Thermazene®
Canadian Brand Names Flamazine®
Pharmacologic Category Antibiotic, Topical
Additional Appendix Information
Sulfonamide Derivatives *on page 1897*
Use Prevention and treatment of infection in second and third degree burns
Pregnancy Risk Factor B
Dosage Children and Adults: Topical: Apply once or twice daily with a sterile-gloved hand; apply to a thickness of $^1/_{16}$"; burned area should be covered with cream at all times
Additional Information Contains methylparaben and propylene glycol
Dosage Forms
Cream, topical: 1% (25 g, 50 mg, 85 g, 400 g)
Silvadene®, Thermazene®: 1% (20 g, 50 g, 85 g, 400 g, 1000 g)
SSD®: 1% (25 g, 50 g, 85 g, 400 g)
SSD® AF: 1% (50 g, 400 g)

♦ **Simethicone, Aluminum Hydroxide, and Magnesium Hydroxide** *see* Aluminum Hydroxide, Magnesium Hydroxide, and Simethicone *on page 85*

♦ **Simethicone and Loperamide Hydrochloride** *see* Loperamide and Simethicone *on page 1029*

♦ **Simethicone and Magaldrate** *see* Magaldrate and Simethicone *on page 1045*

♦ **Simply Saline® [OTC]** *see* Sodium Chloride *on page 1576*

♦ **Simply Saline® Baby [OTC]** *see* Sodium Chloride *on page 1576*

♦ **Simply Saline® Nasal Moist® [OTC]** *see* Sodium Chloride *on page 1576*

♦ **Simply Sleep® [OTC]** *see* DiphenhydrAMINE *on page 515*

♦ **Simply Sleep® (Can)** *see* DiphenhydrAMINE *on page 515*

♦ **Simply Stuffy™ [OTC] [DSC]** *see* Pseudoephedrine *on page 1454*

♦ **Simuc** *see* Guaifenesin and Phenylephrine *on page 818*

♦ **Simulect®** *see* Basiliximab *on page 195*

Simvastatin (sim va STAT in)

U.S. Brand Names Zocor®
Canadian Brand Names Apo-Simvastatin®; BCI-Simvastatin; CO Simvastatin; Gen-Simvastatin; Novo-Simvastatin; PMS-Simvastatin; ratio-Simvastatin; Riva-Simvastatin; Sandoz-Simvastatin; Taro-Simvastatin; Zocor®
Pharmacologic Category Antilipemic Agent, HMG-CoA Reductase Inhibitor
Additional Appendix Information
Hyperlipidemia Management *on page 2058*
Lipid-Lowering Agents *on page 1887*
Use Used with dietary therapy for the following:
Secondary prevention of cardiovascular events in hypercholesterolemic patients with established coronary heart disease (CHD) or at high risk for CHD: To reduce cardiovascular morbidity (myocardial infarction, coronary revascularization procedures) and mortality; to reduce the risk of stroke and transient ischemic attacks
Hyperlipidemias: To reduce elevations in total cholesterol, LDL-C, apolipoprotein B, and triglycerides in patients with primary hypercholesterolemia (elevations of 1 or more components are present in Fredrickson type IIa, IIb, III, and IV hyperlipidemias); treatment of homozygous familial hypercholesterolemia
Heterozygous familial hypercholesterolemia (HeFH): In adolescent patients (10-17 years of age, females >1 year postmenarche) with HeFH having LDL-C ≥190 mg/dL or LDL ≥160 mg/dL with positive family history of premature cardiovascular disease (CVD), or 2 or more CVD risk factors in the adolescent patient
Pregnancy Risk Factor X
Pregnancy Implications Cholesterol biosynthesis may be important in fetal development. Contraindicated in pregnancy. Administer to women of childbearing potential only when conception is highly unlikely and patients have been informed of potential hazards.
Lactation Excretion in breast milk unknown/contraindicated
Medication Safety Issues
Sound-alike/look-alike issues:
Zocor® may be confused with Cozaar®, Yocon®, Zoloft®

International issues:
Cardin® [Poland] may be confused with Cardene® which is a brand name for nicardipine in the U.S.
Cardin® [Poland] may be confused with Cardem® which is a brand name for celiprolol in Spain
Contraindications Hypersensitivity to simvastatin or any component of the formulation; acute liver disease; unexplained persistent elevations of serum transaminases; pregnancy; breast-feeding
Warnings/Precautions Secondary causes of hyperlipidemia should be ruled out prior to therapy. Liver function must be monitored by laboratory assessment. Rhabdomyolysis with acute renal failure has occurred. Risk is dose-related and is increased with concurrent use of lipid-lowering agents which may cause rhabdomyolysis (gemfibrozil, fibric acid derivatives, or niacin at doses ≥1 g/day), during concurrent use with danazol or strong CYP3A4 inhibitors (including amiodarone, clarithromycin, cyclosporine, erythromycin, telithromycin, itraconazole, ketoconazole, nefazodone, grapefruit juice in large quantities, verapamil, or protease inhibitors such as indinavir, nelfinavir, or ritonavir). Weigh the risk versus benefit when combining any of these drugs with simvastatin. Do not initiate simvastatin-containing treatment in a patient with pre-existing therapy of cyclosporine or danazol, unless the patient
(Continued)

Simvastatin *(Continued)*

has previously demonstrated tolerance to ≥5 mg/day simvastatin. Temporarily discontinue in any patient experiencing an acute or serious major medical or surgical condition which may increase the risk of rhabdomyolysis. Discontinue temporarily for elective surgical procedures. Use caution in patients with renal insufficiency. Use with caution in patients with advanced age, these patients are predisposed to myopathy. Use with caution in patients who consume large amounts of ethanol or have a history of liver disease. Safety and efficacy have not been established in patients <10 years of age or in premenarcheal girls.

Adverse Reactions

1% to 10%:
Gastrointestinal: Constipation (2%), dyspepsia (1%), flatulence (2%)
Neuromuscular & skeletal: CPK elevation (>3x normal on one or more occasions - 5%)
Respiratory: Upper respiratory infection (2%)

<1% (Limited to important or life-threatening): Depression, lichen planus, photosensitivity, thrombocytopenia, vertigo

Additional class-related events: Alopecia, anaphylaxis, angioedema, anxiety, cataracts, cholestatic jaundice, depression, dermatomyositis, dyspnea, eosinophilia, erythema multiforme, facial paresis, fulminant hepatic necrosis, gynecomastia, hemolytic anemia, hepatitis, hypersensitivity reaction, impotence, leukopenia, myopathy, ophthalmoplegia, pancreatitis, paresthesia, peripheral nerve palsy, peripheral neuropathy, photosensitivity, polymyalgia rheumatica, psychic disturbance, rash, renal failure (secondary to rhabdomyolysis), rhabdomyolysis, Stevens-Johnson syndrome, systemic lupus erythematosus-like syndrome, thrombocytopenia, thyroid dysfunction, toxic epidermal necrolysis, urticaria, vasculitis, vertigo

Overdosage/Toxicology Very few adverse events. Treatment is symptomatic.

Drug Interactions

Cytochrome P450 Effect: Substrate of CYP3A4 (major); **Inhibits** CYP2C8 (weak), 2C9 (weak), 2D6 (weak)

Increased Effect/Toxicity: Risk of myopathy/rhabdomyolysis may be increased by concurrent use of lipid-lowering agents which may cause rhabdomyolysis (gemfibrozil, fibric acid derivatives, or niacin at doses ≥1 g/day), or during concurrent use of strong CYP3A4 inhibitors.

CYP3A4 inhibitors may increase the levels/effects of simvastatin; example inhibitors include azole antifungals, clarithromycin, diclofenac, diltiazem, doxycycline, erythromycin, imatinib, isoniazid, nefazodone, nicardipine, propofol, protease inhibitors, quinidine, telithromycin, and verapamil. In large quantities (ie, >1 quart/day), grapefruit juice may also increase simvastatin serum concentrations, increasing the risk of rhabdomyolysis. In general, concurrent use with CYP3A4 inhibitors is not recommended; manufacturer recommends limiting simvastatin dose to 20 mg/day when used with amiodarone or verapamil, and 10 mg/day when used with cyclosporine, gemfibrozil, or fibric acid derivatives.

The anticoagulant effect of warfarin may be increased by simvastatin. Cholesterol-lowering effects are additive with bile-acid sequestrants (colestipol and cholestyramine).

Decreased Effect: When taken within 1 before or up to 2 hours after cholestyramine, a decrease in absorption of simvastatin can occur.

Ethanol/Nutrition/Herb Interactions

Ethanol: Avoid excessive ethanol consumption (due to potential hepatic effects).
Food: Simvastatin serum concentration may be increased when taken with grapefruit juice; avoid concurrent intake of large quantities (>1 quart/day). Red yeast rice contains an estimated 2.4 mg lovastatin per 600 mg rice.
Herb/Nutraceutical: St John's wort may decrease simvastatin levels.

Stability Tablets should be stored in tightly-closed containers at temperatures between 5°C to 30°C (41°F to 86°F).

Mechanism of Action Simvastatin is a methylated derivative of lovastatin that acts by competitively inhibiting 3-hydroxy-3-methylglutaryl-coenzyme A (HMG-CoA) reductase, the enzyme that catalyzes the rate-limiting step in cholesterol biosynthesis

Pharmacodynamics/Kinetics

Onset of action: >3 days
Peak effect: 2 weeks
Absorption: 85%
Protein binding: ~95%
Metabolism: Hepatic via CYP3A4; extensive first-pass effect
Bioavailability: <5%
Half-life elimination: Unknown
Time to peak: 1.3-2.4 hours
Excretion: Feces (60%); urine (13%)

Dosage Oral: **Note:** Doses should be individualized according to the baseline LDL-cholesterol levels, the recommended goal of therapy, and the patient's response; adjustments should be made at intervals of 4 weeks or more; doses may need adjusted based on concomitant medications

Children 10-17 years (females >1 year postmenarche): HeFH: 10 mg once daily in the evening; range: 10-40 mg/day (maximum: 40 mg/day)
Dosage adjustment for simvastatin with concomitant cyclosporine, danazol, fibrates, niacin, amiodarone, or verapamil: Refer to drug-specific dosing in Adults dosing section

Adults:
Homozygous familial hypercholesterolemia: 40 mg once daily in the evening **or** 80 mg/day (given as 20 mg, 20 mg, and 40 mg evening dose)
Prevention of cardiovascular events, hyperlipidemias: 20-40 mg once daily in the evening; range: 5-80 mg/day
Patients requiring only moderate reduction of LDL-cholesterol may be started at 10 mg once daily
Patients requiring reduction of >45% in low-density lipoprotein (LDL) cholesterol may be started at 40 mg once daily in the evening

Patients with CHD or at high risk for CHD: Dosing should be started at 40 mg once daily in the evening; simvastatin may be started simultaneously with diet

Dosage adjustment with concomitant medications:

Cyclosporine or danazol (patient must first demonstrate tolerance to simvastatin ≥5 mg once daily): Initial: 5 mg simvastatin, should **not** exceed 10 mg/day

Fibrates or niacin: Simvastatin dose should **not** exceed 10 mg/day

Amiodarone or verapamil: Simvastatin dose should **not** exceed 20 mg/day

Dosing adjustment/comments in renal impairment: Because simvastatin does not undergo significant renal excretion, modification of dose should not be necessary in patients with mild to moderate renal insufficiency.

Severe renal impairment: Cl_{cr} <10 mL/minute: Initial: 5 mg/day with close monitoring.

Dietary Considerations Red yeast rice contains an estimated 2.4 mg lovastatin per 600 mg rice.

Administration May be taken without regard to meals.

Monitoring Parameters Creatine phosphokinase levels due to possibility of myopathy; serum cholesterol (total and fractionated)

Obtain liver function tests prior to initiation, dose, and thereafter when clinically indicated. Patients titrated to the 80 mg dose should be tested prior to initiation and 3 months after initiating the 80 mg dose. Thereafter, periodic monitoring (ie, semiannually) is recommended for the first year of treatment. Patients with elevated transaminase levels should have a second (confirmatory) test and frequent monitoring until values normalize. Discontinue if increase in ALT/AST is persistently >3 times ULN.

Dosage Forms

Tablet: 5 mg, 10 mg, 20 mg, 40 mg

Zocor®: 5 mg, 10 mg, 20 mg, 40 mg, 80 mg

♦ **Sina-12X** see Guaifenesin and Phenylephrine on page 818

♦ **Sinemet®** see Levodopa and Carbidopa on page 999

♦ **Sinemet® CR** see Levodopa and Carbidopa on page 999

♦ **Sinequan® [DSC]** see Doxepin on page 545

♦ **Sinequan® (Can)** see Doxepin on page 545

♦ **Singulair®** see Montelukast on page 1168

♦ **Sinus-Relief [OTC] [DSC]** see Acetaminophen and Pseudoephedrine on page 33

♦ **Sinutab® Non Drowsy (Can)** see Acetaminophen and Pseudoephedrine on page 33

♦ **Sinutab® Non-Drying [OTC]** see Guaifenesin and Pseudoephedrine on page 819

♦ **Sinutab® Sinus & Allergy (Can)** see Acetaminophen, Chlorpheniramine, and Pseudoephedrine on page 35

♦ **Sinutab® Sinus Allergy Maximum Strength [OTC]** see Acetaminophen, Chlorpheniramine, and Pseudoephedrine on page 35

♦ **SINUvent® PE** see Guaifenesin and Phenylephrine on page 818

♦ **Sirdalud®** see Tizanidine on page 1695

Sirolimus (sir OH li mus)

U.S. Brand Names Rapamune®

Canadian Brand Names Rapamune®

Pharmacologic Category Immunosuppressant Agent

Use Prophylaxis of organ rejection in patients receiving renal transplants, in combination with corticosteroids and cyclosporine (cyclosporine may be withdrawn in low-to-moderate immunological risk patients after 2-4 months, in conjunction with an increase in sirolimus dosage)

Unlabeled/Investigational Use Investigational: Immunosuppression in other forms of solid organ transplantation and peripheral stem cell/bone marrow transplantation

Pregnancy Risk Factor C

Pregnancy Implications Embryotoxicity and fetotoxicity may occur, as evidenced by increased mortality, reduced fetal weights and delayed ossification in animal studies. There are no adequate and well-controlled studies in pregnant women. Effective contraception must be initiated before therapy with sirolimus and continued for 12 weeks after discontinuation.

Lactation Excretion in breast milk unknown/not recommended

Contraindications Hypersensitivity to sirolimus or any component of the formulation

Warnings/Precautions [U.S. Boxed Warning]: Immunosuppressive agents, including sirolimus, increase the risk of infection and may be associated with the development of lymphoma. Immune suppression may also increase the risk of opportunistic infections and sepsis. May increase serum lipids (cholesterol and triglycerides). Use with caution in patients with hyperlipidemia. May increase serum creatinine and decrease GFR. Use caution in patients with renal impairment, or when used concurrently with medications which may alter renal function. Monitor renal function closely when combined with cyclosporine; consider dosage adjustment or discontinue in patients with increasing serum creatinine. Use caution with hepatic impairment; reduced dosage is recommended. Has been associated with an increased risk of lymphocele. Cases of interstitial lung disease (eg, pneumonitis, bronchiolitis obliterans organizing pneumonia, pulmonary fibrosis) have been observed; risk may be increased with higher trough levels. Avoid concurrent use of strong CYP3A4 inhibitors or strong inducers of either CYP3A4 or P-glycoprotein. Concurrent use with a calcineurin inhibitor (cyclosporine, tacrolimus) may increase the risk of calcineurin inhibitor-induced hemolytic uremic syndrome/thrombotic thrombocytopenic purpura/thrombotic microangiopathy (HUS/TTP/TMA). Anaphylactic reactions, angioedema and hypersensitivity vasculitis have been reported. May increase sensitivity to UV light; use appropriate sun protection.

Sirolimus is not recommended for use in liver transplant patients; studies indicate an association with an increase risk of hepatic artery thrombosis and graft failure in these patients. Cases of bronchial anastomotic dehiscence have been reported in lung transplant patients when sirolimus was used as part of an immunosuppressive regimen; most of these reactions were fatal. Use in patients with lung transplants is not recommended. Safety and efficacy of (Continued)

Sirolimus *(Continued)*

cyclosporine withdrawal in high-risk patients is not currently recommended. Safety and efficacy in children <13 years of age, or in adolescent patients <18 years of age considered at high immunological risk, have not been established.

Adverse Reactions Incidence of many adverse effects is dose related

>20%:

Cardiovascular: Peripheral edema (54% to 64%), hypertension (39% to 49%), edema (16% to 24%), chest pain (16% to 24%)

Central nervous system: Fever (23% to 34%), headache (23% to 34%), pain (24% to 33%), insomnia (13% to 22%)

Dermatologic: Acne (20% to 31%), rash (10% to 20%)

Endocrine & metabolic: Hyperlipidemia (38% to 57%), hypercholesterolemia (38% to 46%), hypophosphatemia (15% to 23%), hypokalemia (11% to 21%)

Gastrointestinal: Diarrhea (25% to 42%), constipation (28% to 38%), abdominal pain (28% to 36%), nausea (25% to 36%), vomiting (19% to 25%), dyspepsia (17% to 25%), weight gain (8% to 21%)

Genitourinary: Urinary tract infection (20% to 33%)

Hematologic: Anemia (23% to 37%), thrombocytopenia (13% to 40%)

Neuromuscular & skeletal: Weakness (22% to 40%), arthralgia (25% to 31%), tremor (21% to 31%), back pain (16% to 26%)

Renal: Serum creatinine increased (35% to 40%)

Respiratory: Dyspnea (22% to 30%), upper respiratory infection (20% to 26%), pharyngitis (16% to 21%)

3% to 20%:

Cardiovascular: Atrial fibrillation, CHF, facial edema, hypervolemia, hypotension, palpitation, peripheral vascular disorder, postural hypotension, syncope, tachycardia, thrombosis, vasodilation, venous thromboembolism

Central nervous system: Chills, malaise, anxiety, confusion, depression, dizziness, emotional lability, hypoesthesia, hypotonia, neuropathy, somnolence

Dermatologic: Dermatitis (fungal), hirsutism, pruritus, skin hypertrophy, dermal ulcer, ecchymosis, cellulitis, skin carcinoma

Endocrine & metabolic: Cushing's syndrome, diabetes mellitus, glycosuria, acidosis, dehydration, hypercalcemia, hyperglycemia, hyperphosphatemia, hypocalcemia, hypoglycemia, hypomagnesemia, hyponatremia, hyperkalemia (12% to 17%)

Gastrointestinal: Enlarged abdomen, anorexia, dysphagia, eructation, esophagitis, flatulence, gastritis, gastroenteritis, gingivitis, gingival hyperplasia, ileus, mouth ulceration, oral moniliasis, stomatitis, weight loss

Genitourinary: Pelvic pain, scrotal edema, testis disorder, impotence

Hematologic: Leukocytosis, polycythemia, TTP, hemolytic-uremic syndrome, hemorrhage, leukopenia (9% to 15%)

Hepatic: Abnormal liver function tests, alkaline phosphatase increased, ascites, LDH increased, transaminases increased

Local: Thrombophlebitis

Neuromuscular & skeletal: Arthrosis, bone necrosis, CPK increased, leg cramps, myalgia, osteoporosis, tetany, hypertonia, paresthesia

Ocular: Abnormal vision, cataract, conjunctivitis

Otic: Ear pain, deafness, otitis media, tinnitus

Renal: Albuminuria, bladder pain, BUN increased, dysuria, hematuria, hydronephrosis, kidney pain, tubular necrosis, nocturia, oliguria, pyelonephritis, pyuria, nephropathy (toxic), urinary frequency, urinary incontinence, urinary retention

Respiratory: Asthma, atelectasis, bronchitis, cough, epistaxis, hypoxia, lung edema, pleural effusion, pneumonia, rhinitis, sinusitis

Miscellaneous: Abscess, diaphoresis, facial edema, flu-like syndrome, herpes simplex, hernia, infection, lymphadenopathy, lymphocele, lymphoproliferative disease, peritonitis, sepsis

Postmarketing and/or case reports: Abnormal wound healing, anaphylactoid reaction, anaphylaxis, anastomotic disruption, angioedema, fascial dehiscence, hepatic necrosis, hepatotoxicity, hypersensitivity vasculitis; interstitial lung disease (pneumonitis, pulmonary fibrosis, and bronchiolitis obliterans organizing pneumonia) with no identified infectious etiology, lymphedema, neutropenia, pancreatitis, pancytopenia, proteinuria, pulmonary hemorrhage. In liver transplant patients (not an approved use), an increase in hepatic artery thrombosis and graft failure were noted in clinical trials. In lung transplant patients (not an approved use), bronchial anastomotic dehiscence has been reported. Calcineurin inhibitor-induced hemolytic uremic syndrome/thrombotic thrombocytopenic purpura/thrombotic microangiopathy (HUS/TTP/TMA) have been reported (with concurrent cyclosporine or tacrolimus).

Overdosage/Toxicology Experience with overdosage has been limited. Dose-limiting toxicities include immune suppression. Reported symptoms of overdose include atrial fibrillation. Treatment is symptom-directed and supportive; dialysis is not likely to facilitate removal.

Drug Interactions

Cytochrome P450 Effect: Substrate of CYP3A4 (major); **Inhibits** CYP3A4 (weak)

Increased Effect/Toxicity: Cyclosporine increases sirolimus concentrations during concurrent therapy, and cyclosporine levels may be increased; sirolimus should be taken 4 hours after cyclosporine oral solution (modified) and/or cyclosporine capsules (modified). CYP3A4 inhibitors may increase the levels/effects of sirolimus; example inhibitors include azole antifungals, clarithromycin, diclofenac, diltiazem, doxycycline, erythromycin, imatinib, isoniazid, nefazodone, nicardipine, propofol, protease inhibitors, quinidine, telithromycin, and verapamil; avoid concurrent use. Concurrent live organism vaccines may increase the adverse/toxic effect of the vaccine; vaccinial infections are possible (avoid concurrent use). Concurrent therapy with calcineurin inhibitors (cyclosporine, tacrolimus) may increase the risk of HUS/TTP/TMA.

Decreased Effect: CYP3A4 inducers may decrease the levels/effects of sirolimus; example inducers include aminoglutethimide, carbamazepine, nafcillin, nevirapine, phenobarbital, phenytoin, and rifamycins. Vaccination (dead organisms) may be less effective with concurrent sirolimus (monitor).

Ethanol/Nutrition/Herb Interactions

Food: Do not administer with grapefruit juice; may decrease clearance of sirolimus. Ingestion with high-fat meals decreases peak concentrations but increases AUC by 35%. Sirolimus should be taken consistently either with or without food to minimize variability.

Herb/Nutraceutical: St John's wort may decrease sirolimus levels; avoid concurrent use. Avoid cat's claw, echinacea (have immunostimulant properties; consider therapy modifications).

Stability

Oral solution: Store under refrigeration, 2°C to 8°C (36°F to 46°F). Protect from light. A slight haze may develop in refrigerated solutions, but the quality of the product is not affected. After opening, solution should be used in 1 month. If necessary, may be stored at temperatures up to 25°C (77°F) for ≤15 days after opening. Product may be stored in amber syringe for a maximum of 24 hours (at room temperature or refrigerated). Solution should be used immediately following dilution.

Tablet: Store at room temperature of 20°C to 25°C (68°F to 77°F). Protect from light.

Mechanism of Action Sirolimus inhibits T-lymphocyte activation and proliferation in response to antigenic and cytokine stimulation and inhibits antibody production. Its mechanism differs from other immunosuppressants. It inhibits acute rejection of allografts and prolongs graft survival.

Pharmacodynamics/Kinetics

Absorption: Rapid

Distribution: 12 L/kg (range: 4-20 L/kg)

Protein binding: 92%, primarily to albumin

Metabolism: Extensively hepatic via CYP3A4; P-glycoprotein-mediated efflux into gut lumen

Bioavailability: Oral solution: 14%; Oral tablet: 18%

Half-life elimination: Mean: 62 hours

Time to peak: 1-2hours

Excretion: Feces (91%); urine (2%)

Dosage Oral:

Combination therapy with cyclosporine: Doses should be taken 4 hours after cyclosporine, and should be taken consistently either with or without food.

Children ≥13 years and Adults: Dosing by body weight:

<40 kg: Loading dose: Loading dose: 3 mg/m^2 on day 1, followed by maintenance dosing of 1 mg/m^2 once daily

≥40 kg: Loading dose: 6 mg on day 1; maintenance: 2 mg once daily

Maintenance therapy after withdrawal of cyclosporine: Following 2-4 months of combined therapy, withdrawal of cyclosporine may be considered in low-to-moderate risk patients. Cyclosporine withdrawal in not recommended in high immunological risk patients. Cyclosporine should be discontinued over 4-8 weeks, and a necessary increase in the dosage of sirolimus (up to fourfold) should be anticipated due to removal of metabolic inhibition by cyclosporine and to maintain adequate immunosuppressive effects.

Sirolimus dosages should be adjusted to maintain trough concentrations of 16-24 ng/mL for 1 year after transplant. Dosage should be adjusted at intervals of 7-14 days to account for the long half-life of sirolimus.

Dosage adjustments: New sirolimus dose **equals** current dose **multiplied by** (target concentration/current concentration). **Note:** If large dose increase is required, consider loading dose calculated as:

Loading dose **equals** (new maintenance dose **minus** current maintenance dose) **multiplied by** 3

Loading doses >40 mg may be administered over 2 days. Serum concentrations should not be used as the sole basis for dosage adjustment (monitor clinical signs/symptoms, tissue biopsy, and laboratory parameters).

Dosage adjustment in renal impairment: No dosage adjustment is necessary in renal impairment. However, adjustment of regimen (including discontinuation of therapy) should be considered when used concurrently with cyclosporine and elevated or increasing serum creatinine is noted.

Dosage adjustment in hepatic impairment: Reduce maintenance dose by approximately 33% in hepatic impairment. Loading dose is unchanged.

Dietary Considerations Take consistently, with or without food, to minimize variability of absorption.

Administration The solution should be mixed with at least 2 ounces of water or orange juice. No other liquids should be used for dilution. Patient should drink diluted solution immediately. The cup should then be refilled with an additional 4 ounces of water or orange juice, stirred vigorously, and the patient should drink the contents at once. Sirolimus should be taken 4 hours after cyclosporine oral solution (modified) or cyclosporine capsules (modified)

Monitoring Parameters Monitor sirolimus levels in pediatric patients, patients ≥13 years of age weighing <40 kg, patients with hepatic impairment, or on concurrent potent inhibitors or inducers of CYP3A4, and/or if cyclosporine dosing is markedly reduced or discontinued. Also monitor serum cholesterol and triglycerides, blood pressure, and serum creatinine. Serum drug concentrations should be determined 3-4 days after loading doses; however, these concentrations should not be used as the sole basis for dosage adjustment, especially during withdrawal of cyclosporine (monitor clinical signs/symptoms, tissue biopsy, and laboratory parameters).

Reference Range Serum trough concentrations (based on HPLC methods):

Concomitant cyclosporine: 4-12 ng/mL (5-15 ng/mL if measured via immunoassay)

After cyclosporine withdrawal: 16-24 ng/mL for 1 year after transplant; after 1 year: 12-20 ng/mL

Note: Differences in sensitivity and specificity exist between methods of detection (eg, immunoassay vs. HPLC); on average, chromatographic methods yield values ~20% lower than (whole blood) immunoassay determinations. Target range may vary based on assay conditions.

(Continued)

Sirolimus (Continued)

Additional Information Sirolimus tablets and oral solution are not bioequivalent, due to differences in absorption. Clinical equivalence was seen using 2 mg tablet and 2 mg solution. It is not known if higher doses are also clinically equivalent.

Dosage Forms

Solution, oral [bottle]: 1 mg/mL (60 mL) [contains ethanol 1.5% to 2.5%; packaged with oral syringes and a carrying case]

Tablet: 1 mg, 2 mg

Sitagliptin (sit a GLIP tin)

U.S. Brand Names Januvia™

Index Terms MK-0431; Sitagliptin Phosphate

Pharmacologic Category Antidiabetic Agent, Dipeptidyl Peptidase IV (DPP-IV) Inhibitor

Use Management of type 2 diabetes mellitus (noninsulin dependent, NIDDM) as an adjunct to diet and exercise as monotherapy or in combination therapy with metformin or a peroxisome proliferator-actived receptor (PPAR) gamma agonist (eg, a thiazolidinedione)

Pregnancy Risk Factor B

Pregnancy Implications Teratogenic events were reported in some, but not all animal studies. There are no adequate and well-controlled studies in pregnant women. Insulin is the drug of choice for the control of diabetes mellitus during pregnancy. Health professionals are encouraged to report any prenatal exposure to sitagliptin by contacting Merck's pregnancy registry (1-800-986-8999).

Lactation Excretion in breast milk unknown/use caution

Medication Safety Issues

Sound-alike/look-alike issues:

Januvia™ may be confused with Jantoven™

Contraindications Hypersensitivity to sitagliptin or any component of the formulation

Warnings/Precautions Mechanism of sitagliptin requires the presence of insulin; therefore, use in type 1 diabetes (insulin dependent, IDDM) or diabetic ketoacidosis is not recommended. Use with caution in patients with moderate-to-severe renal dysfunction and end-stage renal disease (ESRD) requiring hemodialysis or peritoneal dialysis; dosing adjustment required. Safety and efficacy have not been established in children <18 years of age.

Adverse Reactions

1% to 10%:

Central nervous system: Headache (5%)

Gastrointestinal: Diarrhea (3%)

Respiratory: Upper respiratory tract infection (6%), nasopharyngitis (5%)

Incidence less than or equal to placebo: Abdominal pain (2%), hypoglycemia (1%), nausea (1%), neutrophils increased, serum creatinine increased

Overdosage/Toxicology Experience in overdose is limited. Treatment should be symptom-directed and supportive. QT_c prolongation, reported as not clinically significant, occurred in one study using doses of 800 mg. Sitagliptin is modestly dialyzable by hemodialysis (~14% of dose removed after a 3-4 hour hemodialysis session); unknown if dialyzable by peritoneal dialysis.

Drug Interactions

Cytochrome P450 Effect: Substrate (minor) of CYP2C8, 3A4

Stability Store at 20°C to 25°C (68°F to 77°F).

Mechanism of Action Sitagliptin inhibits dipeptidyl peptidase IV (DPP-IV) enzyme resulting in prolonged active incretin levels. Incretin hormones [eg, glucagon-like peptide-1 (GLP-1) and glucose-dependent insulinotropic polypeptide (GIP)] regulate glucose homeostasis by increasing insulin synthesis and release from pancreatic beta cells and decreasing glucagon secretion from pancreatic alpha cells. Decreased glucagon secretion results in decreased hepatic glucose production. Under normal physiologic circumstances, incretin hormones are released by the intestine throughout the day and levels are increased in response to a meal; incretin hormones are rapidly inactivated by the DPP-IV enzyme.

Pharmacodynamics/Kinetics

Absorption: Rapid

Distribution: 198 L

Protein binding: 38%

Metabolism: Not extensively metabolized; minor metabolism via CYP3A4 and 2C8 to metabolites (inactive) suggested by *in vitro* studies

Bioavailability: 87%

Half-life elimination: 12 hours

Time to peak, plasma: 1-4 hours

Excretion: Urine 87% (79% as unchanged drug, 16% as metabolites); feces 13%

Dosage Oral: Adults: Type 2 diabetes: 100 mg once daily

Dosage adjustment in renal impairment:

Cl_{cr} ≥30 to <50 mL/minute: 50 mg once daily

S_{cr}: Males: >1.7 to ≤3.0 mg/dL; Females: >1.5 to ≤2.5 mg/dL: 50 mg once daily

Cl_{cr}<30 mL/minute: 25 mg once daily

S_{cr}: Males: >3.0 mg/dL; Females: >2.5 mg/dL: 25 mg once daily

ESRD requiring hemodialysis or peritoneal dialysis: 25 mg once daily; administered without regard to timing of hemodialysis

Dosage adjustment in hepatic impairment:

Mild-to-moderate impairment (Child-Pugh score 7-9): No dosage adjustment required

Severe impairment (Child-Pugh score >9): Not studied

Administration May be administered with or without food.

Monitoring Parameters Hgb A_{1C} and serum glucose; renal function prior to initiation and periodically during treatment.

Reference Range Target range: Adults:

Fasting blood glucose: 90-130 mg/dL

Glycosylated hemoglobin: <7%

Dosage Forms
Tablet:
Januvia™: 25 mg, 50 mg, 100 mg

- **Sitagliptin Phosphate** *see* Sitagliptin *on page 1572*
- **SK** *see* Streptokinase *on page 1600*
- **SK and F 104864** *see* Topotecan *on page 1709*
- **Skeeter Stik [OTC]** *see* Benzocaine *on page 204*
- **Skelaxin**® *see* Metaxalone *on page 1097*
- **Skelid**® *see* Tiludronate *on page 1686*
- **SKF 104864** *see* Topotecan *on page 1709*
- **SKF 104864-A** *see* Topotecan *on page 1709*
- **Sleep-ettes D [OTC]** *see* DiphenhydrAMINE *on page 515*
- **Sleepinal**® **[OTC]** *see* DiphenhydrAMINE *on page 515*
- **Slo-Niacin**® **[OTC]** *see* Niacin *on page 1219*
- **Slo-Pot (Can)** *see* Potassium Chloride *on page 1396*
- **Slow FE**® **[OTC]** *see* Ferrous Sulfate *on page 704*
- **Slow-K**® **(Can)** *see* Potassium Chloride *on page 1396*
- **Slow-Mag**® **[OTC]** *see* Magnesium Chloride *on page 1046*

Smallpox Vaccine (SMAL poks vak SEEN)

U.S. Brand Names Dryvax®
Index Terms Dried Smallpox Vaccine; Vaccinia Vaccine
Pharmacologic Category Vaccine
Use Active immunization against vaccinia virus, the causative agent of smallpox in persons determined to be at risk for smallpox infection. The ACIP recommends vaccination of laboratory workers at risk of exposure from cultures or contaminated animals which may be a source of vaccinia or related Orthopoxviruses capable of causing infections in humans (monkeypox, cowpox, or variola). The ACIP also recommends that consideration be given for vaccination in healthcare workers having contact with clinical specimens, contaminated material, or patients receiving vaccinia or recombinant vaccinia viruses. Revaccination is recommended every 10 years. The Armed Forces recommend vaccination of certain personnel categories. Recommendations for use in response to bioterrorism are regularly updated by the CDC, and may be found at www.cdc.gov.
Restrictions In October 2002, the FDA approved the licensing of the current stockpile of smallpox vaccine. This approval allows the vaccine to be distributed and administered in the event of a smallpox attack. The bulk of current supplies have been designated for use by the U.S. military. Additionally, laboratory workers who may be at risk of exposure may require vaccination. Bioterrorism experts have proposed immunization of first responders (including police, fire, and emergency workers), but these plans may not be implemented until additional stocks of vaccine are licensed.
Pregnancy Risk Factor C
Pregnancy Implications Animal reproduction studies have not been conducted. Vaccinia vaccine has not been associated with the development of congenital malformations. On rare occasions, vaccination has been reported to cause fetal infection. Fetal vaccinia infection is associated with stillbirth or neonatal mortality. Pregnancy should be avoided for at least 28 days following vaccination. Healthcare providers may enroll pregnant women who were inadvertently vaccinated during pregnancy (or within 42 days prior to conception) in the CDC pregnancy registry by calling 404-639-8253 or 877-554-4625. Military cases should be reported to the Department of Defense.
Lactation Excretion in breast milk unknown/not recommended
Contraindications Hypersensitivity to the vaccine or any component, including polymyxin B, dihydrostreptomycin, chlortetracycline, and neomycin; patients with a history of eczema or patients whose household contacts have acute or chronic exfoliative skin conditions (atopic dermatitis, eczema, burns, impetigo, Varicella zoster, or wounds); history of Darier disease (or if household contact has active disease); immunosuppressed patients and their household contacts, including patients with congenital or acquired immune deficiencies (including HIV, agammaglobulinemia, leukemia, lymphoma, neoplastic disease of the bone marrow or lymphatic system), patients receiving radiation, Immunosuppressive drugs, or systemic corticosteroids ≥20 mg/day or ≥2 mg/kg body weight of prednisone for >2 weeks; patients using ocular steroid medications; moderate to severe intercurrent illness; cardiac disease, including previous MI, angina, CHF, cardiomyopathy, chest pain, or shortness of breath requiring medical therapy; pregnancy or suspected pregnancy (including household contacts of pregnant women); breast-feeding

Note: There are no absolute contraindications regarding vaccination of individuals with a high-risk exposure to smallpox. The decision to vaccinate in an emergency situation must be based on a careful analysis of potential benefits and possible risks.
Warnings/Precautions Acute myopericarditis and encephalitis have been observed following vaccination. Progressive vaccinia may occur in the immunocompromised. Severe skin infections may occur in patients with eczema. Immunocompromised patients or those with eczema or cardiovascular disease should not be vaccinated in nonemergency situations. For vaccination by scarification (multiple punctures into superficial layers of the skin) only. Not for I.M., I.V., or SubQ injection. Packaging contains latex, which may cause hypersensitivity reactions in allergic individuals. Materials used to prepare and vaccinate should be disposed of per manufacturer's recommendations. Virus may be cultured from vaccination sites until scab separates from lesion. Individuals should be instructed to avoid contact with patients at high risk of transmission/adverse effects, including patients with eczema or immunodeficiency during this time. Patients should be advised not to donate blood for 21 days or until the scab has separated; contacts who have inadvertently contracted vaccinia should avoid
(Continued)

Smallpox Vaccine (Continued)

donating blood for 14 days. Not for use in infants <12 months of age (in emergency conditions) or for use in pediatric patients <18 years of age (nonemergency conditions).

Adverse Reactions All serious adverse reactions must be reported to the U.S. Department of Health and Human Services (DHHS) Vaccine Adverse Event Reporting System (VAERS) 1-800-822-7967. In addition, clinicians may enroll patients with adverse reactions in the CDC Registry at 877-554-4625.

Cardiovascular: Cardiomyopathy (nonischemic, dilated); myopericarditis (asymptomatic or symptomatic)

Central nervous system: Encephalitis, encephalomyelitis, encephalopathy, fever (up to 70%; may be ≥102°F in up to 20% of children; frequency in adults may be lower), headache

Dermatologic: Eczema vaccinatum, rash (erythematous, urticarial, nonspecific), Stevens-Johnson syndrome (rare)

Local: Injection site: Secondary pyogenic infection

Ocular: Photophobia

Miscellaneous: Inadvertent inoculation at other sites (including autoinoculation to face, genitalia, eyelid, mouth, nose, rectum); progressive vaccinia

Overdosage/Toxicology No specific experience in overdose. Symptoms may include headache, nausea, vomiting, and hypotension. Treatment is supportive.

Drug Interactions

Decreased Effect: Smallpox vaccine may suppress tuberculin (PPD) skin test; avoid skin test for ≥1 month after vaccine to prevent false-negative reactions.

Stability Store at 2°C to 8°C (36°F to 46°F); do not freeze. Following reconstitution, stable for up to 90 days when refrigerated at 2°C to 8°C (36°F to 46°F).

Release vacuum in vial prior to reconstitution by inserting a sterile 21-gauge needle (or smaller) through the stopper. Do not use this needle to reconstitute vaccine. Use the vented needle (provided with kit) to reconstitute solution. Solution should be reconstituted with the diluent provided (to reduce viscosity, this solution may require warming in hands prior to drawing into the syringe). Reconstitute with entire volume of diluent. Following reconstitution, allow to stand for 3-5 minutes, then swirl gently (if necessary) to effect complete reconstitution.

Mechanism of Action Live vaccinia virus at a concentration of ~100 million infectious particles per mL. Vaccination results in viral replication, production of neutralizing antibodies, immunity, and cellular hypersensitivity.

Pharmacodynamics/Kinetics Onset: Neutralizing antibodies appear 10-13 days after vaccination.

Dosage Not for I.M., I.V., or SubQ injection: Vaccination by scarification (multiple-puncture technique) only: **Note:** A trace of blood should appear at vaccination site after 15-20 seconds; if no trace of blood is visible, an additional 3 insertions should be made using the same needle, without reinserting the needle into the vaccine bottle.

Adults (children ≥12 months in emergency conditions only):

Primary vaccination: Use a single drop of vaccine suspension and 2 or 3 needle punctures (using the same needle) into the superficial skin

Revaccination: Use a single drop of vaccine suspension and 15 needle punctures (using the same needle) into the superficial skin

Dosage adjustment in renal impairment: No dosage adjustment required

Administration Using a bifurcated needle, 1 drop of vaccine is introduced into the superficial layers of the skin using a multiple-puncture technique. The skin over the insertion of the deltoid muscle or the posterior aspect of the arm over the triceps are the preferred sites for vaccination.

A single-use bifurcated needle should be dipped carefully into the reconstituted vaccine (following removal of rubber stopper). Visually confirm that the needle picks up a drop of vaccine solution. Deposit the drop of vaccine onto clean, dry skin at the vaccination site. Holding the bifurcated needle perpendicular to the skin, punctures are to be made rapidly into the superficial skin of the vaccination site. The puncture strokes should be vigorous enough to allow a trace of blood to appear after approximately 15-20 seconds. Wipe off any remaining vaccine with dry sterile gauze. Dispose of all materials in a biohazard waste container. All materials must be burned, boiled, or autoclaved. If no evidence of vaccine take is apparent after 7 days, the individual may be vaccinated again.

To prevent transmission of the virus, cover vaccination site with gauze and cover gauze with a semipermeable barrier or clothing. Good handwashing prevents inadvertent inoculation. Vaccinees should change bandages away from others and launder their own linens to prevent transmission.

Monitoring Parameters Monitor vaccination site; inspect after 6-8 days. Evidence of a major reaction (vesicular or pustular lesion or an area of palpable induration surrounding a central lesion) confirms success of vaccination. An equivocal reaction (all responses other than a major reaction) requires revaccination (preferably with another vial or vaccine lot, if available). Consult CDC or state or local health department if response to a second vaccination is equivocal.

Additional Information Initial reaction of the vaccine includes formation of a papule (2-5 days following vaccination). The papule forms a vesicle on day 5 or day 6, which becomes pustular, with surrounding erythema and induration. The maximal area of erythema usually occurs around day 10, and crusting of the lesion normally occurs between day 12 and day 21. At the peak of the reaction, systemic symptoms (fever, malaise) and lymphadenopathy may occur. All materials used in vaccination must be burned, boiled, or autoclaved. Vaccination can decrease the rate of severe or fatal smallpox if administered during the first 4 days of exposure.

Dosage Forms Injection, powder for reconstitution [calf liver source]: ~100 million vaccinia virions per mL following reconstitution [contains polymyxin B, neomycin, dihydrostreptomycin sulfate, and chlortetracycline (trace amounts); packed with diluent, venting needle, and 100 bifurcated needles; vial stopper contains latex]

♦ **SMZ-TMP** see Sulfamethoxazole and Trimethoprim on page 1613

- **(+)-(S)-N-Methyl-γ-(1-naphthyloxy)-2-thiophenepropylamine Hydrochloride** see Duloxetine on page 562
- **Sodium 2-Mercaptoethane Sulfonate** see Mesna on page 1091
- **Sodium 4-Hydroxybutyrate** see Sodium Oxybate on page 1580
- **Sodium L-Triiodothyronine** see Liothyronine on page 1020

Sodium Acetate (SOW dee um AS e tate)

Pharmacologic Category Electrolyte Supplement, Parenteral
Use Sodium source in large volume I.V. fluids to prevent or correct hyponatremia in patients with restricted intake; used to counter acidosis through conversion to bicarbonate
Pregnancy Risk Factor C
Contraindications Alkalosis, hypocalcemia, low sodium diets, edema, cirrhosis
Warnings/Precautions Avoid extravasation, use with caution in patients with hepatic failure
Adverse Reactions 1% to 10%:
  Cardiovascular: Thrombosis, hypervolemia
  Dermatologic: Chemical cellulitis at injection site (extravasation)
  Endocrine & metabolic: Hypernatremia, dilution of serum electrolytes, overhydration, hypokalemia, metabolic alkalosis, hypocalcemia
  Gastrointestinal: Gastric distension, flatulence
  Local: Phlebitis
  Respiratory: Pulmonary edema
  Miscellaneous: Congestive conditions
Stability Protect from light, heat, and freezing.
Dosage Sodium acetate is metabolized to bicarbonate on an equimolar basis outside the liver; administer in large volume I.V. fluids as a sodium source. Refer to Sodium Bicarbonate monograph.
  Maintenance electrolyte requirements of sodium in parenteral nutrition solutions:
  Daily requirements: 3-4 mEq/kg/24 hours or 25-40 mEq/1000 kcal/24 hours
  Maximum: 100-150 mEq/24 hours
Dietary Considerations Sodium and acetate content of 1 g: 7.3 mEq
Administration Must be diluted prior to I.V. administration; infusion hypertonic solutions (>154 mEq/L) via a central line; maximum rate of administration: 1 mEq/kg/hour
Dosage Forms Injection, solution: 2 mEq/mL (20 mL, 50 mL, 100 mL); 4 mEq/mL (50 mL, 100 mL)

- **Sodium Acid Carbonate** see Sodium Bicarbonate on page 1575
- **Sodium Acid Phosphate and Methenamine** see Methenamine and Sodium Acid Phosphate on page 1107
- **Sodium Benzoate and Sodium Phenylacetate** see Sodium Phenylacetate and Sodium Benzoate on page 1582

Sodium Bicarbonate (SOW dee um bye KAR bun ate)

U.S. Brand Names Brioschi® [OTC]; Neut®
Index Terms Baking Soda; NaHCO₃; Sodium Acid Carbonate; Sodium Hydrogen Carbonate
Pharmacologic Category Alkalinizing Agent; Antacid; Electrolyte Supplement, Oral; Electrolyte Supplement, Parenteral
Use Management of metabolic acidosis; gastric hyperacidity; as an alkalinization agent for the urine; treatment of hyperkalemia; management of overdose of certain drugs, including tricyclic antidepressants and aspirin
Pregnancy Risk Factor C
Lactation Enters breast milk/compatible
Contraindications Alkalosis, hypernatremia, severe pulmonary edema, hypocalcemia, unknown abdominal pain
Warnings/Precautions Rapid administration in neonates and children <2 years of age has led to hypernatremia, decreased CSF pressure and intracranial hemorrhage. **Use of I.V. NaHCO₃ should be reserved for documented metabolic acidosis and for hyperkalemia-induced cardiac arrest.** Routine use in cardiac arrest is not recommended. Avoid extravasation, tissue necrosis can occur due to the hypertonicity of NaHCO₃. May cause sodium retention especially if renal function is impaired; not to be used in treatment of peptic ulcer; use with caution in patients with CHF, edema, cirrhosis, or renal failure. Not the antacid of choice for the elderly because of sodium content and potential for systemic alkalosis.
Adverse Reactions Frequency not defined.
  Cardiovascular: Cerebral hemorrhage, CHF (aggravated), edema
  Central nervous system: Tetany
  Gastrointestinal: Belching, flatulence (with oral), gastric distension
  Endocrine & metabolic: Hypernatremia, hyperosmolality, hypocalcemia, hypokalemia, increased affinity of hemoglobin for oxygen-reduced pH in myocardial tissue necrosis when extravasated, intracranial acidosis, metabolic alkalosis, milk-alkali syndrome (especially with renal dysfunction)
  Respiratory: Pulmonary edema
Overdosage/Toxicology Symptoms include hypocalcemia, hypokalemia, hypernatremia, and seizures. Seizures can be treated with diazepam 0.1-0.25 mg/kg. Hypernatremia is resolved through the use of diuretics and free water replacement.
Drug Interactions
  Increased Effect/Toxicity: Increased toxicity/levels of amphetamines, ephedrine, pseudoephedrine, flecainide, quinidine, and quinine due to urinary alkalinization.
  Decreased Effect: Decreased effect/levels of lithium, chlorpropamide, and salicylates due to urinary alkalinization.
  (Continued)

Sodium Bicarbonate *(Continued)*

Ethanol/Nutrition/Herb Interactions Herb/Nutraceutical: Concurrent doses with iron may decrease iron absorption.

Stability Store injection at room temperature; do not freeze. Protect from heat. Use only clear solutions.

Mechanism of Action Dissociates to provide bicarbonate ion which neutralizes hydrogen ion concentration and raises blood and urinary pH

Pharmacodynamics/Kinetics

Onset of action: Oral: Rapid; I.V.: 15 minutes

Duration: Oral: 8-10 minutes; I.V.: 1-2 hours

Absorption: Oral: Well absorbed

Excretion: Urine (<1%)

Dosage

Cardiac arrest: **Routine use of NaHCO₃ is not recommended and should be given only after adequate alveolar ventilation has been established and effective cardiac compressions are provided**

Infants and Children: I.V.: 0.5-1 mEq/kg/dose repeated every 10 minutes or as indicated by arterial blood gases; rate of infusion should not exceed 10 mEq/minute; neonates and children <2 years of age should receive 4.2% (0.5 mEq/mL) solution

Adults: I.V.: Initial: 1 mEq/kg/dose one time; maintenance: 0.5 mEq/kg/dose every 10 minutes or as indicated by arterial blood gases

Metabolic acidosis: Infants, Children, and Adults: Dosage should be based on the following formula if blood gases and pH measurements are available:

HCO_3^- (mEq) = 0.3 x weight (kg) x base deficit (mEq/L)

Administer ½ dose initially, then remaining ½ dose over the next 24 hours; monitor pH, serum HCO_3^-, and clinical status

Note: If acid-base status is not available: Dose for older Children and Adults: 2-5 mEq/kg I.V. infusion over 4-8 hours; subsequent doses should be based on patient's acid-base status

Chronic renal failure: Oral: Initiate when plasma HCO_3^- <15 mEq/L

Children: 1-3 mEq/kg/day

Adults: Start with 20-36 mEq/day in divided doses, titrate to bicarbonate level of 18-20 mEq/L

Hyperkalemia: Adults: I.V.: 1 mEq/kg over 5 minutes

Renal tubular acidosis: Oral:

Distal:

Children: 2-3 mEq/kg/day

Adults: 0.5-2 mEq/kg/day in 4-5 divided doses

Proximal: Children and Adults: Initial: 5-10 mEq/kg/day; maintenance: Increase as required to maintain serum bicarbonate in the normal range

Urine alkalinization: Oral:

Children: 1-10 mEq (84-840 mg)/kg/day in divided doses every 4-6 hours; dose should be titrated to desired urinary pH

Adults: Initial: 48 mEq (4 g), then 12-24 mEq (1-2 g) every 4 hours; dose should be titrated to desired urinary pH; doses up to 16 g/day (200 mEq) in patients <60 years and 8 g (100 mEq) in patients >60 years

Antacid: Adults: Oral: 325 mg to 2 g 1-4 times/day

Dietary Considerations Oral product should be administered 1-3 hours after meals.

Sodium content:

Injection: 50 mL, 8.4% = 1150 mg = 50 mEq; each mL of 8.4% NaHCO₃ contains 23 mg sodium; 1 mEq NaHCO₃ = 84 mg

Granules: 2.69 g packet or capful = 770 mg sodium

Powder: 30 mEq sodium per ½ teaspoon

Administration For I.V. administration to infants, use the 0.5 mEq/mL solution or dilute the 1 mEq/mL solution 1:1 with **sterile water**; for direct I.V. infusion in emergencies, administer slowly (maximum rate in infants: 10 mEq/minute); for infusion, dilute to a maximum concentration of 0.5 mEq/mL in dextrose solution and infuse over 2 hours (maximum rate of administration: 1 mEq/kg/hour)

Dosage Forms

Granules, effervescent (Brioschi®): 2.69 g/packet (6 g) [unit-dose packets; contains sodium 770 mg/packet; lemon flavor]; 2.69 g/capful (120 g, 240 g) [contains sodium 770 mg/capful; lemon flavor]

Infusion [premixed in sterile water]: 5% (500 mL)

Injection, solution:

4.2% [42 mg/mL = 5 mEq/10 mL] (10 mL)

7.5% [75 mg/mL = 8.92 mEq/10 mL] (50 mL)

8.4% [84 mg/mL = 10 mEq/10 mL] (10 mL, 50 mL)

Neut®: 4% [40 mg/mL = 2.4 mEq/5 mL] (5 mL)

Powder: Sodium bicarbonate USP (120 g, 480 g) [contains sodium 30 mEq per ½ teaspoon]

Tablet: 325 mg [3.8 mEq]; 650 mg [7.6 mEq]

♦ **Sodium Biphosphate, Methenamine, Methylene Blue, Phenyl Salicylate, and Hyoscyamine** *see* Methenamine, Sodium Biphosphate, Phenyl Salicylate, Methylene Blue, and Hyoscyamine *on page 1107*

Sodium Chloride *(SOW dee um KLOR ide)*

U.S. Brand Names Altachlore [OTC]; Altamist [OTC]; Ayr® Baby Saline [OTC]; Ayr® Saline [OTC]; Ayr® Saline No-Drip [OTC]; Breathe Right® Saline [OTC]; Broncho Saline® [OTC]; Deep Sea [OTC]; Entsol® [OTC]; Muro 128® [OTC]; Mycinaire™ [OTC]; NaSal™ [OTC]; Nasal Moist® [OTC]; Na-Zone® [OTC]; Ocean® [OTC]; Oceant® for Kids [OTC]; Pretz® [OTC]; SalineX® [OTC]; Simply Saline® [OTC]; Simply Saline® Baby [OTC]; Simply Saline® Nasal Moist® [OTC]; Syrex® [OTC]; 4-Way® Saline Moisturizing Mist [OTC]; Wound Wash Saline™ [OTC]

Index Terms NaCl; Normal Saline; Salt

Pharmacologic Category Electrolyte Supplement, Parenteral; Genitourinary Irrigant; Irrigant; Lubricant, Ocular; Sodium Salt

Use

Parenteral: Restores sodium ion in patients with restricted oral intake (especially hyponatremia states or low salt syndrome). In general, parenteral saline uses:

Bacteriostatic sodium chloride: Dilution or dissolving drugs for I.M., I.V., or SubQ injections

Concentrated sodium chloride: Additive for parenteral fluid therapy

Hypertonic sodium chloride: For severe hyponatremia and hypochloremia

Hypotonic sodium chloride: Hydrating solution

Normal saline: Restores water/sodium losses

Pharmaceutical aid/diluent for infusion of compatible drug additives

Ophthalmic: Reduces corneal edema

Inhalation: Restores moisture to pulmonary system; loosens and thins congestion caused by colds or allergies; diluent for bronchodilator solutions that require dilution before inhalation

Intranasal: Restores moisture to nasal membranes

Irrigation: Wound cleansing, irrigation, and flushing

Unlabeled/Investigational Use Traumatic brain injury (hypertonic sodium chloride)

Pregnancy Risk Factor C

Medication Safety Issues

Per JCAHO recommendations, concentrated electrolyte solutions (eg, NaCl >0.9%) should not be available in patient care areas.

High alert medication: The Institute for Safe Medication Practices (ISMP) includes this medication (I.V. formulation) among its list of drugs which have a heightened risk of causing significant patient harm when used in error.

Contraindications Hypersensitivity to sodium chloride or any component of the formulation; hypertonic uterus, hypernatremia, fluid retention

Warnings/Precautions Use with caution in patients with CHF, renal insufficiency, liver cirrhosis, hypertension, edema; sodium toxicity is almost exclusively related to how fast a sodium deficit is corrected; both rate and magnitude are extremely important; do not use bacteriostatic sodium chloride in newborns since benzyl alcohol preservatives have been associated with toxicity

Irrigants: For external use only; not for parenteral use. Do not use during electrosurgical procedures. Irrigating fluids may be absorbed into systemic circulation; monitor for fluid or solute overload.

Adverse Reactions Frequency not defined.

Cardiovascular: Congestive conditions

Endocrine & metabolic: Extravasation, hypervolemia, hypernatremia, dilution of serum electrolytes, overhydration, hypokalemia

Local: Thrombosis, phlebitis, extravasation

Respiratory: Pulmonary edema

Overdosage/Toxicology Symptoms include nausea, vomiting, diarrhea, abdominal cramps, hypocalcemia, hypokalemia, and hypernatremia. Hypernatremia is resolved through the use of diuretics and free water replacement.

Drug Interactions

Decreased Effect: Lithium levels/effects may be decreased.

Stability Store injection at room temperature; do not freeze. Protect from heat. Use only clear solutions.

Mechanism of Action Principal extracellular cation; functions in fluid and electrolyte balance, osmotic pressure control, and water distribution

Pharmacodynamics/Kinetics

Absorption: Oral, I.V.: Rapid

Distribution: Widely distributed

Excretion: Primarily urine; also sweat, tears, saliva

Dosage

Children: I.V.: Hypertonic solutions (>0.9%) should only be used for the initial treatment of acute serious symptomatic hyponatremia; maintenance: 3-4 mEq/kg/day; maximum: 100-150 mEq/day; dosage varies widely depending on clinical condition

Replacement: Determined by laboratory determinations mEq

Sodium deficiency (mEq/kg) = [% dehydration (L/kg)/100 x 70 (mEq/L)] + [0.6 (L/kg) x (140 - serum sodium) (mEq/L)]

Children ≥2 years and Adults:

Intranasal: 2-3 sprays in each nostril as needed

Irrigation: Spray affected area

Children and Adults: Inhalation: Bronchodilator diluent: 1-3 sprays (1-3 mL) to dilute bronchodilator solution in nebulizer prior to administration

Adults:

GU irrigant: 1-3 L/day by intermittent irrigation

Replacement I.V.: Determined by laboratory determinations mEq

Sodium deficiency (mEq/kg) = [% dehydration (L/kg)/100 x 70 (mEq/L)] + [0.6 (L/kg) x (140 - serum sodium) (mEq/L)]

To correct acute, serious hyponatremia: mEq sodium = [desired sodium (mEq/L) - actual sodium (mEq/L)] x [0.6 x wt (kg)]; for acute correction use 125 mEq/L as the desired serum sodium; acutely correct serum sodium in 5 mEq/L/dose increments; more gradual correction in increments of 10 mEq/L/day is indicated in the asymptomatic patient

Chloride maintenance electrolyte requirement in parenteral nutrition: 2-4 mEq/kg/24 hours or 25-40 mEq/1000 kcals/24 hours; maximum: 100-150 mEq/24 hours

Sodium maintenance electrolyte requirement in parenteral nutrition: 3-4 mEq/kg/24 hours or 25-40 mEq/1000 kcals/24 hours; maximum: 100-150 mEq/24 hours.

Ophthalmic:

Ointment: Apply once daily or more often

Solution: Instill 1-2 drops into affected eye(s) every 3-4 hours

(Continued)

Sodium Chloride *(Continued)*

Approximate Deficits of Water and Electrolytes in Moderately Severe Dehydration[1]

Condition	Water (mL/kg)	Sodium (mEq/kg)
Fasting and thirsting	100-120	5-7
Diarrhea		
isonatremic	100-120	8-10
hypernatremic	100-120	2-4
hyponatremic	100-120	10-12
Pyloric stenosis	100-120	8-10
Diabetic acidosis	100-120	9-10

[1]A **negative** deficit indicates total body **excess** prior to treatment.

Adapted from Behrman RE, Kleigman RM, Nelson WE, et al, eds, *Nelson Textbook of Pediatrics*, 14th ed, WB Saunders Co, 1992.

Administration Irrigation solution: Do not warm >66°C (150°F); not for I.V. use. Wound Wash Saline™: Before use, expel a short stream into air to clear nozzle.

Monitoring Parameters Serum sodium, potassium, chloride, and bicarbonate levels; I & O, weight

Reference Range Serum/plasma sodium levels:
Neonates:
  Full-term: 133-142 mEq/L
  Premature: 132-140 mEq/L
Children ≥2 months to Adults: 135-145 mEq/L

Dosage Forms
Gel, intranasal:
  Ayr® Saline No-Drip: 0.5% (22 mL) [spray gel; contains benzalkonium chloride, benzyl alcohol and soybean oil]
  Ayr® Saline: 0.5% (14 g) [contains soybean oil]
  Entsol®: 3% (20 g) [contains aloe, benzalkonium chloride, and vitamin E]
  Simply Saline® Nasal Moist®: 0.65% (30 g)
Injection, solution [preservative free]: 0.9% (2 mL, 5 mL, 10 mL, 20 mL, 100 mL)
Injection, solution [preservative free, prefilled I.V. flush syringe]: 0.9% (2 mL, 2.5 mL, 3 mL, 5 mL, 10 mL)
Injection, solution: 0.45% (25 mL, 50 mL, 100 mL, 250 mL, 500 mL, 1000 mL); 0.9% (3 mL, 5 mL, 10 mL, 20 mL, 25 mL, 30 mL, 50 mL, 100 mL, 150 mL, 250 mL, 500 mL, 1000 mL); 3% (500 mL); 5% (500 mL)
  Syrex: 0.9% (2.5 mL, 5 mL, 10 mL) [prefilled syringe]
Injection, solution [bacteriostatic]: 0.9% (10 mL, 20 mL, 30 mL) [contains benzyl alcohol]
Injection, solution [concentrate]: 14.6% (2.5 mEq/mL) (20 mL, 40 mL); 23.4% (4 mEq/mL) (30 mL, 100 mL, 200 mL, 250 mL)
Ointment, ophthalmic: 5% (3.5 g)
  Altachlore, Muro 128®: 5% (3.5 g)
Powder for nasal solution (Entsol®): 3% (10.5 g)
Solution for inhalation: 0.45% (3 mL, 5 mL); 0.9% (3 mL, 5 mL, 15 mL); 3% (15 mL); 10% (15 mL)
  Broncho® Saline: 0.9% (90 mL, 240 mL) [for dilution of bronchodilator solutions]
Solution, intranasal: 0.65% (45 mL)
  Altamist: 0.65% (60 mL) [spray; contains benzalkonium chloride]
  Ayr® Baby Saline: 0.65% (30 mL) [spray/drops; contains benzalkonium chloride]
  Ayr® Saline: 0.65% (50 mL) [drops; contains benzalkonium chloride]
  Ayr® Saline: 0.65% (50 mL) [mist, contains benzalkonium chloride]
  Breathe Right® Saline: 0.65% (44 mL) [spray; contains benzalkonium chloride]
  Deep Sea: 0.65% (45 mL) [spray; contains benzalkonium chloride]
  Entsol® Mist: 3% (30 mL) [spray; contains benzalkonium chloride]
  Entsol® [preservative free]: 3% (100 mL) [spray]
  Entsol® [preservative free]: 3% (240 mL) [nasal wash]
  Mycinaire™: 0.65% (30 mL) [mist; contains benzalkonium chloride]
  Na-Zone®: 0.65% (60 mL) [spray; contains benzalkonium chloride]
  NaSal™: 0.65% (15 mL) [drops; contains benzalkonium chloride], (30 mL) [spray; contains benzalkonium chloride]
  Nasal Moist®: 0.65% (45 mL) [spray]
  Ocean®: 0.65% (45 mL) [mist/spray/drops; contains benzalkonium chloride]; (473 mL) [refill bottle; contains benzalkonium chloride]
  Ocean® for Kids: 0.65% (37.5 mL) [drops/spray/stream; contains benzalkonium chloride]
  Pretz®: 0.75% (50 mL) [spray; contains benzalkonium chloride and yerba santa]; (240 mL) [irrigation; contains benzalkonium chloride and yerba santa]; (960 mL) [refill bottle; contains benzalkonium chloride and yerba santa]
  SalineX®: 0.4% (15 mL) [drops]; (50 mL) [spray]
  Simply Saline®: 0.9% (44 mL, 90 mL) [mist]
  Simply Saline® Baby: 0.9% (45 mL) [mist]
  4-Way® Saline Moisturizing Mist: 0.74% (30 mL) [alcohol free; contains benzalkonium chloride, eucalyptol, and menthol]
Solution for irrigation: 0.45% (1500 mL, 2000 mL); 0.9% (250 mL, 500 mL, 1000 mL, 1500 mL, 2000 mL, 3000 mL, 4000 mL, 5000 mL)
  Wound Wash Saline™: 0.9% (90 mL, 210 mL)
Solution, ophthalmic: 5% (15 mL)
  Altachlore: 5% (15 mL, 30 mL)
  Muro 128®: 2% (15 mL); 5% (15 mL, 30 mL)

Sodium Citrate and Citric Acid (SOW dee um SIT rate & SI trik AS id)

U.S. Brand Names Bicitra®; Cytra-2; Oracit®
Canadian Brand Names PMS-Dicitrate
Index Terms Modified Shohl's Solution
Pharmacologic Category Alkalinizing Agent, Oral
Use Treatment of metabolic acidosis; alkalinizing agent in conditions where long-term maintenance of an alkaline urine is desirable
Pregnancy Risk Factor Not established
Pregnancy Implications Use caution with toxemia of pregnancy.
Lactation Excretion in breast milk unknown/compatible
Contraindications Hypersensitivity to sodium citrate, citric acid, or any component of the formulation; severe renal insufficiency; sodium-restricted diet
Warnings/Precautions Conversion to bicarbonate may be impaired in patients with hepatic failure, in shock, or who are severely ill. Use caution with cardiac failure, hypertension, impaired renal function, and peripheral or pulmonary edema.
Adverse Reactions Frequency not defined. Generally well tolerated with normal renal function.
Central nervous system: Tetany
Endocrine & metabolic: Metabolic alkalosis, hyperkalemia
Gastrointestinal: Diarrhea, nausea, vomiting
Overdosage/Toxicology Symptoms include hypokalemia, hypernatremia, tetany, and seizures. Hypernatremia is resolved through the use of diuretics and free water replacement.
Drug Interactions
  Increased Effect/Toxicity: Increased toxicity/levels of amphetamines, ephedrine, pseudoephedrine, flecainide, quinidine, and quinine due to urinary alkalinization.
  Decreased Effect: Decreased effect/levels of lithium, chlorpropamide, and salicylates due to urinary alkalinization.
Stability Store at controlled room temperature of 15°C to 30°C (59°F to 86°F); do not freeze. Protect from excessive heat.
Pharmacodynamics/Kinetics
Metabolism: Oxidized to sodium bicarbonate
Excretion: Urine (<5% as sodium citrate)
Dosage Oral: Systemic alkalization:
Infants and Children: 2-3 mEq/kg/day in divided doses 3-4 times/day **or** 5-15 mL with water after meals and at bedtime
Adults: 10-30 mL with water after meals and at bedtime
Dietary Considerations Should be taken after meals to avoid laxative effect.
Administration Administer after meals. Dilute with 30-90 mL of water to enhance taste. Chilling solution prior to dosing helps to enhance palatability.
Dosage Forms Note: Contains sodium 1 mEq/mL and the equivalent to bicarbonate 1 mEq/mL
Solution, oral: Sodium citrate 500 mg and citric acid 334 mg per 5 mL (480 mL)
  Bicitra®: Sodium citrate 500 mg and citric acid 334 mg per 5 mL (480 mL) [sugar free; grape flavor]
  Cytra-2: Sodium citrate 500 mg and citric acid 334 mg per 5 mL (480 mL) [alcohol free, dye free, sugar free; grape flavor]
  Oracit®: Sodium citrate 490 mg and citric acid 640 mg per 5 mL (15 mL, 30 mL, 500 mL, 3840 mL)

♦ **Sodium Citrate, Citric Acid, and Potassium Citrate** *see* Citric Acid, Sodium Citrate, and Potassium Citrate *on page 383*
♦ **Sodium Edetate** *see* Edetate Disodium *on page 568*
♦ **Sodium Etidronate** *see* Etidronate Disodium *on page 665*
♦ **Sodium Ferric Gluconate** *see* Ferric Gluconate *on page 699*
♦ **Sodium Fluoride** *see* Fluoride *on page 722*
♦ **Sodium Hyaluronate** *see* Hyaluronate and Derivatives *on page 841*
♦ **Sodium Hyaluronate and Chondroitin Sulfate** *see* Chondroitin Sulfate and Sodium Hyaluronate *on page 362*
♦ **Sodium Hydrogen Carbonate** *see* Sodium Bicarbonate *on page 1575*

Sodium Hypochlorite Solution (SOW dee um hye poe KLOR ite soe LOO shun)

U.S. Brand Names Dakin's Solution; Di-Dak-Sol
Index Terms Modified Dakin's Solution
Pharmacologic Category Disinfectant, Antibacterial (Topical)
Use Treatment of athlete's foot (0.5%); wound irrigation (0.5%); disinfection of utensils and equipment (5%)
Pregnancy Risk Factor C
Dosage Topical irrigation
Additional Information Dakin's solution may hinder wound healing.
Dosage Forms Solution, topical:
Dakin's: 0.25% (480 mL); 0.5% (480 mL, 3840 mL)
Di-Dak-Sol: 0.0125% (480 mL)

♦ **Sodium Hyposulfate** *see* Sodium Thiosulfate *on page 1584*
♦ **Sodium Nafcillin** *see* Nafcillin *on page 1190*
♦ **Sodium Nitroferricyanide** *see* Nitroprusside *on page 1237*
♦ **Sodium Nitroprusside** *see* Nitroprusside *on page 1237*

Sodium Oxybate (SOW dee um ox i BATE)

U.S. Brand Names Xyrem®
Canadian Brand Names Xyrem®
Index Terms Gamma Hydroxybutyric Acid; GHB; 4-Hydroxybutyrate; Sodium 4-Hydroxybutyrate
Pharmacologic Category Central Nervous System Depressant
Use Treatment of cataplexy and daytime sleepiness in patients with narcolepsy
Restrictions C-I (illicit use); C-III (medical use)

Sodium oxybate oral solution will be available only to prescribers enrolled in the Xyrem® Patient Success Program® and dispensed to the patient through the designated centralized pharmacy (1-866-997-3688). Prior to dispensing the first prescription, prescribers will be sent educational materials to be reviewed with the patient and enrollment forms for the postmarketing surveillance program. Patients must be seen at least every 3 months; prescriptions can be written for a maximum of 3 months (the first prescription may only be written for a 1-month supply).

An FDA-approved medication guide must be distributed when dispensing an outpatient prescription (new or refill) where this medication is to be used without direct supervision of a healthcare provider. Medication guides are available at http://www.fda.gov/cder/Offices/ODS/medication_guides.htm.

Pregnancy Risk Factor B
Pregnancy Implications Reproduction studies in animals have not shown teratogenic effects. However, there are no well-controlled studies in pregnant women. Use during pregnancy only if clearly needed. Past use during labor and delivery as an anesthetic has shown a slight decrease in Apgar scores due to sleepiness in the neonate.
Lactation Excretion in breast milk unknown/use caution
Contraindications Hypersensitivity to sodium oxybate or any component of the formulation; ethanol and other CNS depressants; semialdehyde dehydrogenase deficiency
Warnings/Precautions [U.S. Boxed Warning]: Sodium oxybate is a CNS depressant with abuse potential; it should not be used with ethanol or other CNS depressants. Seizures, respiratory depression, decreases in level of consciousness, coma, and death have been reported when used for nonprescription purposes. Due to the rapid onset of CNS depressant effects, doses should be administered only at bedtime and while the patient is sitting up in bed. May impair respiratory drive; use caution with compromised respiratory function. Most patients (~80%) in clinical trials were also treated with stimulants; therefore, an independent assessment of the effects of sodium oxybate is lacking. May cause confusion, psychosis, paranoia, hallucinations, agitation, and depression; use caution with history of depression or suicide attempt. May cause sleepwalking, urinary, and/or fecal incontinence. Use caution with hepatic dysfunction. Contains significant amounts of sodium; use caution with heart failure, hypertension, or compromised renal function.

Patients should be instructed not to engage in hazardous activities requiring mental alertness for at least 6 hours after taking this medication and that CNS effects may carryover to the next day. Tolerance to sodium oxybate, or withdrawal following its discontinuation, have not been clearly defined in controlled clinical trials, but have been reported at larger doses used for illicit purposes. Safety and efficacy have not been established in patients <16 years of age.

[U.S. Boxed Warning]: Sodium oxybate oral solution will be available only to prescribers enrolled in the Xyrem® Patient Success Program® and dispensed to the patient through the designated centralized pharmacy (1-866-997-3688).

Adverse Reactions
>10%:
Central nervous system: Dizziness (8% to 37%), headache (9% to 37%), pain (9% to 20%), somnolence (1% to 14%), confusion (3% to 17%), sleep disorder (6% to 14%)
Gastrointestinal: Nausea (8% to 40%), vomiting (2% to 23%), abdominal pain (3% to 11%)
Genitourinary: Urinary incontinence (<1% to 14%, usually nocturnal), enuresis (3% to 17%), cystitis, metrorrhagia, urinary frequency
Miscellaneous: Diaphoresis (3% to 11%)
1% to 10%:
Cardiovascular: Hypertension (6%), chest pain, edema
Central nervous system: Disorientation (up to 9%), inebriation (up to 9%), concentration decreased (3% to 9%), dream abnormality (3% to 9%), sleepwalking (4% to 7%), depression (3% to 6%), amnesia (3% to 6%), anxiety (3% to 6%), thinking abnormality (3% to 6%), lethargy (up to 6%), insomnia (5%), agitation, ataxia, chills, fatigue, malaise, memory impairment, nervousness, pyrexia, seizure, stupor, tremor, vertigo
Dermatologic: Hyperhidrosis (3% to 6%), pruritus, rash
Endocrine & metabolic: Dysmenorrhea (3% to 6%)
Gastrointestinal: Dyspepsia (6% to 9%), diarrhea (6% to 8%), abdominal pain (6%), nausea and vomiting (6%), anorexia, constipation, tooth ache, weight gain
Hepatic: Alkaline phosphatase increased, hypercholesteremia, hypocalcemia
Neuromuscular & skeletal: Hypoesthesia (6%), weakness (6% to 8%), myasthenia (3% to 6%), pain (3% to 6%), arthritis, leg cramps, myalgia
Ocular: Amblyopia (6%), blurred vision (6%)
Otic: Tinnitus (6%), ear pain
Renal: Albuminuria, hematuria
Respiratory: Pharyngitis (6% to 8%), rhinitis (8%), nasopharyngitis (3% to 8%), infection (3% to 6%), bronchitis, cough, dyspnea
Miscellaneous: Infection (3% to 6%), viral infection (3% to 9%), allergic reaction, flu-like syndrome
<1% (Limited to important or life-threatening): Abdominal distension, accident, acne, affect lability, akathisia, ALT/AST increased, allergic reaction, alopecia, anemia, apathy, apnea, arthritis, asthma, bilirubinemia, bronchitis, bruising, coma, conjunctivitis, contusion, contact dermatitis, creatinine increased, dehydration, depersonalization, dysgeusia, dysphagia,

edema, epistaxis, eructation, euphoria, eye irritation, eye pain, eye redness, eye swelling, fall, fecal incontinence, flatulence, fracture, gastroinesophageal reflux disease, gait abnormal, hangover, hematuria, hiccups, hypersensitivity, hyperuricemia, hyperglycemia, hypernatremia, hypertonia, hypotension, infection, injury, keratoconjunctivitis sicca, laceration, leukocytosis, leukopenia, libido decreased, lymphadenopathy, mental impairment, migraine, miosis, mouth ulceration, myoclonus, neck rigidity, neuralgia, night sweats, paralysis, paranoia, polyarthritis, polycythemia, positive ANA test, proteinuria, psychomotor activity, restless leg syndrome, rosacea, salivary hypersecretion, sinusitis, snoring, stomatitis, suicidal behavior/thoughts, suicidal attempts, syncope, tachycardia, taste loss, tendonitis, thirst, urinary urgency, urticaria

Overdosage/Toxicology Signs and symptoms of overdose may be dependent upon dose ingested, time since ingestion, coingestion of CNS depressants, and the fed or fasted state. Signs and symptoms may include depressed consciousness (may fluctuate rapidly between confusion, agitation, combativeness, ataxia, coma); emesis; diaphoresis; headache; impaired psychomotor skills; blurred vision; myoclonus; tonic-clonic seizures; apnea; Cheyne-Stokes respiration; bradycardia; hypothermia; and muscular hypotonia (with tendon reflexes intact). Pupillary reactivity to light is maintained and no typical pupillary changes have been described. Treatment should be symptom-directed and supportive. Atropine may be given for bradycardia.

Drug Interactions

Increased Effect/Toxicity: CNS depressants: CNS depressant effects are potentiated; concomitant use with sodium oxybate is contraindicated.

Ethanol/Nutrition/Herb Interactions

Ethanol: Avoid ethanol (increases CNS depression).

Food: High-fat meal decreases bioavailability, delays absorption, and decreases peak serum level.

Herb/Nutraceutical: Avoid any products that may cause CNS depression (eg, kava kava or valerian).

Stability Store at controlled room temperature of 15°C to 30°C (59°F to 86°F) in the original bottle and in a safe and secure place (may need to be locked up). Prepare both doses prior to bedtime and place safely near bed, out of reach of pets and children. Each dose should be diluted with 2 ounces of water in the child-resistant dosing cups. Once diluted, solutions should be used within 24 hours.

Mechanism of Action Sodium oxybate is derived from gamma aminobutyric acid (GABA) and acts as an inhibitory chemical transmitter in the brain. May function through specific receptors for gamma hydroxybutyrate (GHB) and GABA (B).

Pharmacodynamics/Kinetics

Absorption: Rapid

Distribution: 190-384 mL/kg

Protein binding: <1%

Metabolism: Primarily via the Krebs cycle to form water and carbon dioxide; secondarily via beta oxidation; significant first-pass effect; no active metabolites; metabolic pathways are saturable

Bioavailability: 25%

Half-life elimination: 30-60 minutes

Time to peak: 30-75 minutes

Excretion: Primarily pulmonary (as carbon dioxide); urine (<5% unchanged drug)

Dosage Oral:

Children ≥16 years and Adults: Narcolepsy: Initial: 4.5 g/day, in 2 equal doses; first dose to be given at bedtime after the patient is in bed, and second dose to be given 2.5-4 hours later. Dose may be increased or adjusted in 2-week intervals; average dose: 6-9 g/day (maximum: 9 g/day)

Elderly: Safety and efficacy have not been studied in patients >65 years.

Dosage adjustment in renal impairment: Adjustment not necessary; consider sodium content

Dosage adjustment in hepatic impairment: Decrease starting dose to half and titrate doses carefully in patients with liver dysfunction. Elimination half-life significantly longer in patients with Child's class C liver dysfunction.

Dietary Considerations Take on an empty stomach; separate last meal (or food) and first dose by several hours; try to take at similar time each day.

Contains sodium 0.5 g per 3 g dose or 1.6 g per 9 g dose.

Administration Take on an empty stomach; separate last meal (or food) and first dose by several hours; try to take at similar time each day. Doses should be administered while patient is sitting up in bed. Both doses should be prepared prior to bedtime. The first dose is taken at bedtime and the second dose is taken 2.5-4 hours later; an alarm clock may need to be set for the second dose. After taking the dose, patient is to lie down and remain in bed.

Monitoring Parameters

Signs and symptoms of depression, drug abuse

Additional Information Sodium oxybate is a known substance of abuse. When used illegally, it has been referred to as a "date-rape drug". Street names include Liquid Ecstasy, Liquid X, Liquid E, Georgia Home Boy, Grievous Bodily Harm, G-Riffick, Soap, Scoop, Salty Water, Somatomax, and Organic Quaalude. As part of the FDA approval for prescription use, all patients and prescribers must be enrolled in a program designed to restrict its distribution and to provide postmarketing evaluations. Detailed instructions for the use of sodium oxybate will be provided to the patient and healthcare provider prior dispensing the first dose.

Dosage Forms Solution, oral: 500 mg/mL (180 mL) [supplied in a kit containing two dosing cups and measuring device]

♦ **Sodium PAS** *see* Aminosalicylic Acid *on page 96*

Sodium Phenylacetate and Sodium Benzoate
(SOW dee um fen il AS e tate & SOW dee um BENZ oh ate)

U.S. Brand Names Ammonul®
Index Terms NAPA and NABZ; Sodium Benzoate and Sodium Phenylacetate
Pharmacologic Category Antidote; Urea Cycle Disorder (UCD) Treatment Agent
Use Adjunct to treatment of acute hyperammonemia and encephalopathy in patients with urea cycle disorders involving partial or complete deficiencies of carbamyl-phosphate synthetase (CPS), ornithine transcarbamoylase (OTC), argininosuccinate lyase (ASL), or argininosuccinate synthetase (ASS); for use with hemodialysis in acute neonatal hyperammonemic coma, moderate-to-severe hyperammonemic encephalopathy and hyperammonemia which fails to respond to initial therapy
Pregnancy Risk Factor C
Dosage Administer as a loading dose over 90-120 minutes, followed by an equivalent maintenance infusion given over 24 hours. Dosage based on weight and specific enzyme deficiency; therapy should continue until ammonia levels are in normal range.
  ≤20 kg:
    CPS and OTC deficiency: Ammonul® 2.5 mL/kg and arginine 10% 2 mL/kg (provides sodium phenylacetate 250 mg/kg, sodium benzoate 250 mg/kg, and arginine hydrochloride 200 mg/kg).
    ASS and ASL deficiency: Ammonul® 2.5 mL/kg and arginine 10% 6 mL/kg (provides sodium phenylacetate 250 mg/kg, sodium benzoate 250 mg/kg, and arginine hydrochloride 600 mg/kg)
    Note: Pending a specific diagnosis in infants, the bolus and maintenance dose of arginine should be 6 mL/kg. If ASS or ASL are excluded as diagnostic possibilities, reduce dose of arginine to 2 mL/kg/day.
  >20 kg:
    CPS and OTC deficiency: Ammonul® 55 mL/m^2 and arginine 10% 2 mL/kg (provides sodium phenylacetate 5.5 g/m^2, sodium benzoate 5.5 g/m^2, and arginine hydrochloride 200 mg/kg)
    ASS and ASL deficiency: Ammonul® 55 mL/m^2 and arginine 10% 6 mL/kg (provides sodium phenylacetate 5.5 g/m^2, sodium benzoate 5.5 g/m^2, and arginine hydrochloride 600 mg/kg)
Dosage adjustment in renal impairment: Use with caution; monitor closely
  Dialysis: Ammonia clearance is ~10 times greater with hemodialysis than by peritoneal dialysis or hemofiltration. Exchange transfusion is ineffective.
Dosage adjustment in hepatic impairment: Use with caution
Additional Information Complete prescribing information for this medication should be consulted for additional detail.
Dosage Forms Injection, solution: Sodium phenylacetate 100 mg and sodium benzoate 100 mg per mL (50 mL)

Sodium Phenylbutyrate (SOW dee um fen il BYOO ti rate)

U.S. Brand Names Buphenyl®
Index Terms Ammonapse
Pharmacologic Category Urea Cycle Disorder (UCD) Treatment Agent
Use Orphan drug: Adjunctive therapy in the chronic management of patients with urea cycle disorder involving deficiencies of carbamoylphosphate synthetase, ornithine transcarbamylase, or argininosuccinic acid synthetase
Pregnancy Risk Factor C
Dosage Oral:
  Powder: Patients weighing <20 kg: 450-600 mg/kg/day or 9.9-13 g/m^2/day, administered in equally divided amounts with each meal or feeding, four to six times daily; safety and efficacy of doses >20 g/day has not been established
  Tablet: Children >20 kg and Adults: 450-600 mg/kg/day or 9.9-13 g/m^2/day, administered in equally divided amounts with each meal; safety and efficacy of doses >20 g/day have not been established
Additional Information Complete prescribing information for this medication should be consulted for additional detail.
Dosage Forms
  Powder, for oral solution: 3 g/level teaspoon (250 g) [contains sodium 125 mg/g; packaged with measuring device]
  Tablet: 500 mg [contains sodium 124 mg/g]

♦ **Sodium Phosphate and Potassium Phosphate** *see* Potassium Phosphate and Sodium Phosphate *on page 1403*

Sodium Polystyrene Sulfonate (SOW dee um pol ee STYE reen SUL fon ate)

U.S. Brand Names Kayexalate®; Kionex™; SPS®
Canadian Brand Names Kayexalate®; PMS-Sodium Polystyrene Sulfonate
Pharmacologic Category Antidote
Use Treatment of hyperkalemia
Pregnancy Risk Factor C
Lactation Excretion in breast milk unknown/use caution
Medication Safety Issues
  Sound-alike/look-alike issues:
    Kayexalate® may be confused with Kaopectate®

  Always prescribe either one-time doses or as a specific number of doses (eg, 15 g q6h x 2 doses). Scheduled doses with no dosage limit could be given for days leading to dangerous hypokalemia.

International issues:

Kionex™ may be confused with Kinex® which is a brand name for biperiden in Mexico

Contraindications Hypersensitivity to sodium polystyrene sulfonate or any component of the formulation; hypernatremia, hypokalemia, obstructive bowel disease

Warnings/Precautions Use with caution in patients with severe CHF, hypertension, edema, or renal failure; avoid using the commercially available liquid product in neonates due to the preservative content; large oral doses may cause fecal impaction (especially in elderly); enema will reduce the serum potassium faster than oral administration, but the oral route will result in a greater reduction over several hours.

Adverse Reactions Frequency not defined.

Endocrine & metabolic: Hypernatremia, hypokalemia, hypocalcemia, hypomagnesemia

Gastrointestinal: Anorexia, colonic necrosis (rare), constipation, fecal impaction, intestinal obstruction (due to concretions in association with aluminum hydroxide), nausea, vomiting

Overdosage/Toxicology Symptoms include hypokalemia including cardiac dysrhythmias, confusion, irritability, ECG changes, muscle weakness, and gastrointestinal effects. Treatment is supportive and is limited to management of fluid and electrolytes.

Drug Interactions

Increased Effect/Toxicity: Systemic alkalosis and seizure has occurred after cation-exchange resins were administered with nonabsorbable cation-donating antacids and laxatives (eg, magnesium hydroxide, aluminum carbonate). Digitalis toxicity may occur with hypokalemia.

Stability Store prepared suspensions at 15°C to 30°C (59°F to 86°F). Store repackaged product in refrigerator and use within 14 days. Freshly prepared suspensions should be used within 24 hours. Do not heat resin suspension.

Mechanism of Action Removes potassium by exchanging sodium ions for potassium ions in the intestine before the resin is passed from the body

Pharmacodynamics/Kinetics

Onset of action: 2-24 hours

Absorption: None

Excretion: Completely feces (primarily as potassium polystyrene sulfonate)

Dosage

Children:

Oral: 1 g/kg/dose every 6 hours

Rectal: 1 g/kg/dose every 2-6 hours (In small children and infants, employ lower doses by using the practical exchange ratio of 1 mEq K⁺/g of resin as the basis for calculation)

Adults: Hyperkalemia:

Oral: 15 g (60 mL) 1-4 times/day

Rectal: 30-50 g every 6 hours

Dietary Considerations Do **not** mix in orange juice. Sodium content of 1 g: 31 mg (1.3 mEq).

Administration

Oral: Administer oral (or NG) as ~25% sorbitol solution; never mix in orange juice. Chilling the oral mixture will increase palatability.

Rectal: Enema route is less effective than oral administration. Administer cleansing enema first. Retain enema in colon for at least 30-60 minutes and for several hours, if possible. Enema should be followed by irrigation with normal saline to prevent necrosis.

Monitoring Parameters Exchange capacity is 1 mEq/g *in vivo*, and *in vitro* capacity is 3.1 mEq/g, therefore, a wide range of exchange capacity exists such that close monitoring of serum electrolytes (potassium, sodium, calcium, magnesium) is necessary; ECG

Reference Range Serum potassium: Adults: 3.5-5.2 mEq/L

Additional Information 1 g of resin binds approximately 1 mEq of potassium

Dosage Forms

Powder for suspension, oral/rectal:

Kayexalate®: 15 g/4 level teaspoons (480 g) [contains sodium 100 mg (4.1 mEq)/g]

Kionex™: 15 g/4 level teaspoons (454 g) [contains sodium 100 mg (4.1 mEq)/g]

Suspension, oral/rectal: 15 g/60 mL (60 mL, 120 mL, 200 mL, 500 mL) [contains sodium 1500 mg (65 mEq)/60 mL, sorbitol, and alcohol 0.1%; cherry/caramel flavor]

SPS®: 15 g/60 mL (60 mL, 120 mL, 480 mL) [contains alcohol 0.3%, sodium 1500 mg (65 mEq)/60 mL, and sorbitol; cherry flavor]

♦ **Sodium Sulfacetamide** *see* Sulfacetamide *on page 1609*

♦ **Sodium Sulfacetamide and Sulfur** *see* Sulfur and Sulfacetamide *on page 1618*

Sodium Tetradecyl (SOW dee um tetra DEK il)

U.S. Brand Names Sotradecol®

Canadian Brand Names Trombovar®

Index Terms Sodium Tetradecyl Sulfate

Pharmacologic Category Sclerosing Agent

Use Treatment of small, uncomplicated varicose veins of the lower extremities

Pregnancy Risk Factor C

Dosage I.V.: Test dose: 0.5 mL given several hours prior to administration of larger dose; 0.5-2 mL (preferred maximum: 1 mL) in each vein, maximum: 10 mL per treatment session; 3% solution reserved for large varices

Additional Information Complete prescribing information for this medication should be consulted for additional detail.

Dosage Forms Injection, as sulfate: 1% [10 mg/mL] (2 mL) [contains benzyl alcohol]; 3% [30 mg/mL] (2 mL) [contains benzyl alcohol]

♦ **Sodium Tetradecyl Sulfate** *see* Sodium Tetradecyl *on page 1583*

Sodium Thiosulfate (SOW dee um thye oh SUL fate)

U.S. Brand Names Versiclear™
Index Terms Disodium Thiosulfate Pentahydrate; Pentahydrate; Sodium Hyposulfate; Sodium Thiosulphate; Thiosulfuric Acid Disodium Salt
Pharmacologic Category Antidote
Use
Parenteral: Used alone or with sodium nitrite or amyl nitrite in cyanide poisoning; reduce the risk of nephrotoxicity associated with cisplatin therapy
Topical: Treatment of tinea versicolor
Unlabeled/Investigational Use Management of I.V. extravasation
Pregnancy Risk Factor C
Pregnancy Implications Safety has not been established in pregnant women. Use only when potential benefit to the mother outweighs the possible risk to the fetus.
Contraindications Hypersensitivity to sodium thiosulfate or any component of the formulation
Warnings/Precautions Safety in pregnancy has not been established; discontinue topical use if irritation or sensitivity occurs; rapid I.V. infusion has caused transient hypotension and ECG changes in dogs; can increase risk of thiocyanate intoxication
Adverse Reactions
1% to 10%:
Cardiovascular: Hypotension
Central nervous system: Coma, CNS depression secondary to thiocyanate intoxication, psychosis, confusion
Dermatologic: Contact dermatitis, local irritation
Neuromuscular & skeletal: Weakness
Otic: Tinnitus
<1% (Limited to important or life-threatening): Gastrointestinal: Diarrhea (following large oral doses)
Mechanism of Action
Cyanide toxicity: Increases the rate of detoxification of cyanide by the enzyme rhodanese by providing an extra sulfur
Cisplatin toxicity: Complexes with cisplatin to form a compound that is nontoxic to either normal or cancerous cells
Pharmacodynamics/Kinetics
Absorption: Oral: Poor
Distribution: Extracellular fluid
Half-life elimination: 0.65 hour
Excretion: Urine (28.5% as unchanged drug)
Dosage
Cyanide and nitroprusside antidote: I.V.:
Children <25 kg: 50 mg/kg after receiving 4.5-10 mg/kg sodium nitrite; a half dose of each may be repeated if necessary
Children >25 kg and Adults: 12.5 g after 300 mg of sodium nitrite; a half dose of each may be repeated if necessary
Cyanide poisoning: I.V.: Dose should be based on determination as with nitrite, at rate of 2.5-5 mL/minute to maximum of 50 mL.

Variation of sodium nitrite and sodium thiosulfate dose, based on hemoglobin concentration: See table.

Variation of Sodium Nitrite and Sodium Thiosulfate Dose With Hemoglobin Concentration[1]

Hemoglobin (g/dL)	Initial Dose Sodium Nitrite (mg/kg)	Initial Dose Sodium Nitrite 3% (mL/kg)	Initial Dose Sodium Thiosulfate 25% (mL/kg)
7	5.8	0.19	0.95
8	6.6	0.22	1.10
9	7.5	0.25	1.25
10	8.3	0.27	1.35
11	9.1	0.30	1.50
12	10.0	0.33	1.65
13	10.8	0.36	1.80
14	11.6	0.39	1.95

[1]Adapted from Berlin DM Jr, "The Treatment of Cyanide Poisoning in Children," *Pediatrics*, 1970, 46:793.

Cisplatin rescue should be given before or during cisplatin administration: I.V. infusion (in sterile water): 12 g/m^2 over 6 hours or 9 g/m^2 I.V. push followed by 1.2 g/m^2 continuous infusion for 6 hours
Tinea versicolor: Children and Adults: Topical: 20% to 25% solution: Apply a thin layer to affected areas twice daily
Drug extravasation (unlabeled use): Children and Adults: SubQ:
2% solution: Infiltrate SubQ into the affected area
1/6 M (~4%) solution: 5-10 mL infused through I.V. line and SubQ into the affected area
Administration
I.V.: Inject slowly, over at least 10 minutes; rapid administration may cause hypotension.
Topical: Do not apply to or near eyes.
Monitoring Parameters Monitor for signs of thiocyanate toxicity
Dosage Forms
Injection, solution [preservative free]: 100 mg/mL (10 mL); 250 mg/mL (50 mL)
Lotion: Sodium thiosulfate 25% and salicylic acid 1% (120 mL) [contains isopropyl alcohol 10%]

- **Sodium Thiosulphate** *see* Sodium Thiosulfate *on page 1584*
- **Soflax™ (Can)** *see* Docusate *on page 533*
- **Solagé™** *see* Mequinol and Tretinoin *on page 1085*
- **Solaquin® [OTC]** *see* Hydroquinone *on page 859*
- **Solaquin® (Can)** *see* Hydroquinone *on page 859*
- **Solaquin Forte®** *see* Hydroquinone *on page 859*
- **Solaraze®** *see* Diclofenac *on page 492*
- **Solarcaine® Aloe Extra Burn Relief [OTC]** *see* Lidocaine *on page 1010*
- **Solia™** *see* Ethinyl Estradiol and Desogestrel *on page 645*

Solifenacin (sol i FEN a sin)

U.S. Brand Names VESIcare®
Index Terms Solifenacin Succinate
Pharmacologic Category Anticholinergic Agent
Use Treatment of overactive bladder with symptoms of urinary frequency, urgency, or urge incontinence
Pregnancy Risk Factor C
Pregnancy Implications Decreased fetal weight, increased incidence of cleft palate, and delayed physical development were observed in some animal studies. There are no adequate or well-controlled studies in pregnant women. Use during pregnancy only if the benefit to the mother outweighs the potential risk to the fetus.
Lactation Excretion in breast milk unknown/not recommended
Medication Safety Issues
 Sound-alike/look-alike issues:
  VESIcare® may be confused with Visicol®
Contraindications Hypersensitivity to solifenacin or any component of the formulation; urinary retention; gastric retention; uncontrolled narrow-angle glaucoma.
Warnings/Precautions Use with caution in patients with bladder outflow obstruction, gastrointestinal obstructive disorders, and decreased gastrointestinal motility. Use with caution in patients with controlled (treated) narrow-angle glaucoma. Dosage adjustment is required for patients with renal and hepatic impairment. Patients on potent CYP3A4 inhibitors require lower dose. Safety and efficacy in pediatric patients have not been established.
Adverse Reactions Adverse reactions are dose related.
 >10%: Gastrointestinal: Xerostomia (11% to 28%), constipation (5% to 13%)
 1% to 10%:
  Cardiovascular: Edema (up to 1%), hypertension (up to 1%)
  Central nervous system: Dizziness (2%), fatigue (1% to 2%), depression (up to 1%)
  Gastrointestinal: Nausea (2% to 3%), dyspepsia (1% to 4%), upper abdominal pain (1% to 2%), vomiting (up to 1%)
  Genitourinary: Urinary tract infection (3% to 5%), urinary retention (up to 1%)
  Ocular: Blurred vision (4% to 5%), dry eyes (up to 2%)
  Respiratory: Cough (up to 1%), pharyngitis (up to 1%)
  Miscellaneous: Influenza (1% to 2%)
 <1% (Limited to important or life-threatening): Angioneurotic edema, gastrointestinal obstruction
Overdosage/Toxicology Overdosage can potentially result in severe central anticholinergic effects. Treatment should include gastric lavage and supportive measures.
Drug Interactions
 Cytochrome P450 Effect: Substrate of CYP3A4 (major)
 Increased Effect/Toxicity: CYP3A4 inhibitors may increase the levels/effects of solifenacin; example inhibitors include azole antifungals, clarithromycin, diclofenac, doxycycline, erythromycin, ketoconazole, imatinib, isoniazid, nefazodone, nicardipine, propofol, protease inhibitors, quinidine, telithromycin, and verapamil; solifenacin dose should not exceed 5 mg/day.
 Decreased Effect: CYP3A4 inducers may decrease the levels/effects of solifenacin; example inducers include aminoglutethimide, carbamazepine, nafcillin, nevirapine, phenobarbital, and phenytoin.
Ethanol/Nutrition/Herb Interactions
 Food: Grapefruit juice may increase the serum level effects of solifenacin.
 Herb/Nutraceutical: St John's wort (*Hypericum*) may decrease the levels/effects of solifenacin.
Stability Store at room temperature between 15°C to 30°C (59°F to 86°F).
Mechanism of Action Inhibits muscarinic receptors resulting in decreased urinary bladder contraction, increased residual urine volume, and decreased detrusor muscle pressure.
Pharmacodynamics/Kinetics
 Distribution: V_d: 600 L
 Protein binding: 98% bound to alpha$_1$-acid glycoprotein
 Metabolism: Extensively hepatic; via N-oxidation and 4 R-hydroxylation, forms one active and three inactive metabolites; primary pathway for elimination is via CYP3A4 route
 Bioavailability: 90%
 Half-life elimination: 45-68 hours following chronic dosing
 Time to peak, plasma: 3-8 hours
 Excretion: Urine 69% (<15% as unchanged drug); feces 23%
Dosage Oral:
 Children: Use is not recommended.
 Adults: 5 mg/day; if tolerated, may increase to 10 mg/day
 Dosage adjustment in renal impairment: Use with caution in reduced renal function
  Cl_{cr} <30 mL/minute: 5 mg/day
 Dosage adjustment in hepatic impairment: Use with caution in reduced hepatic function
  Moderate: 5 mg/day
  Severe: Not recommended
(Continued)

Solifenacin *(Continued)*

Administration Swallow tablet whole; may take with liquids, without regard to food.

Monitoring Parameters Anticholinergic effects (eg, fixed and dilated pupils, blurred vision, tremors or dry skin)

Dosage Forms Tablet: 5 mg, 10 mg

♦ **Solifenacin Succinate** *see* Solifenacin *on page 1585*
♦ **Solodyn**™ *see* Minocycline *on page 1149*
♦ **Soltamox**™ *see* Tamoxifen *on page 1631*
♦ **Soluble Fluorescein** *see* Fluorescein Sodium *on page 722*
♦ **Solu-Cortef**® *see* Hydrocortisone *on page 852*
♦ **Solu-Medrol**® *see* MethylPREDNISolone *on page 1122*
♦ **Soma**® *see* Carisoprodol *on page 294*
♦ **Soma**® **Compound** *see* Carisoprodol and Aspirin *on page 295*
♦ **Soma**® **Compound w/Codeine** *see* Carisoprodol, Aspirin, and Codeine *on page 295*
♦ **Somatrem** *see* Somatropin *on page 1586*

Somatropin *(soe ma TROE pin)*

U.S. Brand Names Genotropin®; Genotropin Miniquick®; Humatrope®; Norditropin®; Norditropin® NordiFlex®; Nutropin®; Nutropin AQ®; Omnitrope™; Saizen®; Serostim®; Tev-Tropin®; Zorbtive®

Canadian Brand Names Humatrope®; Nutropin® AQ; Nutropine®; Saizen®; Serostim®

Index Terms hGH; Human Growth Hormone; Somatrem

Pharmacologic Category Growth Hormone

Use

Children:

Long-term treatment of growth failure due to inadequate endogenous growth hormone secretion (Genotropin®, Humatrope®, Norditropin®, Nutropin®, Nutropin AQ®, Omnitrope™, Saizen®, Tev-Tropin®)

Long-term treatment of short stature associated with Turner syndrome (Genotropin®, Humatrope®, Nutropin®, Nutropin AQ®)

Treatment of Prader-Willi syndrome (Genotropin®)

Treatment of growth failure associated with chronic renal insufficiency (CRI) up until the time of renal transplantation (Nutropin®, Nutropin AQ®)

Long-term treatment of growth failure in children born small for gestational age who fail to manifest catch-up growth by 2 years of age (Genotropin®)

Long-term treatment of idiopathic short stature (nongrowth hormone-deficient short stature) defined by height standard deviation score (SDS) less than or equal to -2.25 and growth rate not likely to attain normal adult height (Humatrope®, Nutropin®, Nutropin AQ®)

Treatment of short stature or growth failure associated with short stature homeobox gene (SHOX) deficiency (Humatrope®)

Adults:

HIV patients with wasting or cachexia with concomitant antiviral therapy (Serostim®)

Replacement of endogenous growth hormone in patients with adult growth hormone deficiency who meet both of the following criteria (Genotropin®, Humatrope®, Norditropin®, Nutropin®, Nutropin AQ®, Omnitrope™, Saizen®):

Biochemical diagnosis of adult growth hormone deficiency by means of a subnormal response to a standard growth hormone stimulation test (peak growth hormone ≤5 mcg/L). Confirmatory testing may not be required in patients with congenital/genetic growth hormone deficiency or multiple pituitary hormone deficiencies due to organic diseases.

and

Adult-onset: Patients who have adult growth hormone deficiency whether alone or with multiple hormone deficiencies (hypopituitarism) as a result of pituitary disease, hypothalamic disease, surgery, radiation therapy, or trauma

or

Childhood-onset: Patients who were growth hormone deficient during childhood, confirmed as an adult before replacement therapy is initiated

Treatment of short-bowel syndrome (Zorbtive®)

Unlabeled/Investigational Use Investigational: Congestive heart failure; pediatric HIV patients with wasting/cachexia (Serostim®)

Pregnancy Risk Factor B/C (depending upon manufacturer)

Pregnancy Implications Reproduction studies have not been conducted with all agents. Teratogenic effects were not observed in animal studies. During normal pregnancy, maternal production of endogenous growth hormone decreases as placental growth hormone production increases. Data with somatropin use during pregnancy is limited.

Lactation Excretion in breast milk unknown/not recommended

Medication Safety Issues

Sound-alike/look-alike issues:

Somatrem may be confused with somatropin

Somatropin may be confused with somatrem, sumatriptan

International issues:

Genotropin® may be confused with Genatropine® which is a brand name for atropine in France

Contraindications Hypersensitivity to growth hormone or any component of the formulation; growth promotion in pediatric patients with closed epiphyses; progression of any underlying intracranial lesion or actively growing intracranial tumor; acute critical illness due to complications following open heart or abdominal surgery; multiple accidental trauma or acute respiratory failure; evidence of active malignancy; use in patients with Prader-Willi syndrome **without** growth hormone deficiency (except Genotropin®) or in patients with Prader-Willi syndrome **with** growth hormone deficiency who are severely obese or have severe respiratory impairment. Humatrope®, Saizen®, and Norditropin® are contraindicated with proliferative or preproliferative retinopathy.

Warnings/Precautions Somatropin may decrease insulin sensitivity; use with caution in patients with diabetes or with risk factors for glucose intolerance. Untreated/undiagnosed hypothyroidism may decrease response to therapy. Intracranial hypertension with headache, nausea, papilledema, visual changes, and/or vomiting has been reported with growth hormone product, funduscopic examinations are recommended. Progression of scoliosis may occur in children experiencing rapid growth. Patients with growth hormone deficiency may develop slipped capital epiphyses more frequently, evaluate any child with new onset of a limp or with complaints of hip or knee pain. Patients with Turner syndrome are at increased risk for otitis media and other ear/hearing disorders, cardiovascular disorders (including stroke, aortic aneurysm, hypertension), and thyroid disease, monitor carefully. Concurrent glucocorticoid therapy may inhibit growth promotion effects; may require dosage adjustment or replacement glucocorticoid therapy in patients with ACTH deficiency. Products may contain benzyl alcohol. When administering to newborns, reconstitute with sterile water or saline for injection. Not for I.V. injection.

Fatalities have been reported in pediatric patients with Prader-Willi syndrome following the use of growth hormone. The reported fatalities occurred in patients with one or more risk factors, including severe obesity, sleep apnea, respiratory impairment, or unidentified respiratory infection; male patients with one or more of these factors may be at greater risk. Treatment interruption is recommended in patients who show signs of upper airway obstruction, including the onset of, or increased, snoring. In addition, evaluation of and/or monitoring for sleep apnea and respiratory infections are recommended.

Patients with HIV infection should be maintained on antiretroviral therapy to prevent the potential increase in viral replication.

Adverse Reactions

Growth hormone deficiency: Adverse reactions reported with growth hormone deficiency vary greatly by age. Generally, percentages are less in pediatric patients than adults, and many of the reactions reported in adults are dose related. Percentages reported also vary by product. Below is a listing by age group; events reported more commonly overall are noted with an asterisk (*).

Children: Antibodies development, arthralgia, edema, eosinophilia, glycosuria, Hb A$_{1c}$ increased, headache, hematoma, hematuria, hyperglycemia (mild), hypertriglyceridemia, hypoglycemia, hypothyroidism, injection site reaction, leg pain, lipoatrophy, muscle pain, rash, weakness

Adults: Arthralgia*, bronchitis, carpal tunnel syndrome, chest pain, depression, diaphoresis, dizziness, edema*, fatigue, flu-like syndrome*, glucose intolerance, glucosuria, headache*, hyperglycemia (mild), hypertension, hypoesthesia, hypothyroidism, infection, insomnia, leg edema, muscle pain, myalgia*, nausea, pain in extremities, paresthesia*, peripheral edema*, rhinitis, skeletal pain*, stiffness in extremities, upper respiratory tract, weakness

Additional/postmarketing reactions observed with growth hormone deficiency: Gynecomastia, increased growth of pre-existing nevi, pancreatitis

Idiopathic short stature: Percentages reported using Humatrope® versus placebo: Myalgia (24%), scoliosis (19%), otitis media (16%), arthralgia (11%), arthrosis (11 %), hyperlipidemia (8%), gynecomastia (5%), hip pain (3%), hypertension (3%). Additional adverse reactions listed as reported using other products from ISS NCGS Cohort (frequencies <1%): Aggressiveness, benign intracranial hypertension, diabetes, edema, hair loss, headache, injection site reaction

Prader-Willi syndrome: Genotropin® (frequency not defined): Aggressiveness, arthralgia, edema, hair loss, headache, benign intracranial hypertension, myalgia; fatalities associated with use in this population have been reported

Turner syndrome: Percentages reported using Humatrope® compared to untreated patients. Additional adverse reactions reported from other products, frequency not specified: Surgical procedures (45%), otitis media (43%), ear disorders (18%), hypothyroidism (14%), nevi increased (11%), peripheral edema (7%), joint pain, respiratory illness, urinary tract infection

HIV patients with wasting or cachexia: Serostim® (limited to ≥5%): Musculoskeletal disorders (arthralgia, arthrosis, myalgia: 78%), peripheral edema (26%), headache (13%), nausea (9%), paresthesia (8%), edema (6%), gynecomastia (6%), hypoesthesia (5%)

Short-bowel syndrome: Zorbtive® (limited to >10%): Peripheral edema (69% to 81%), facial edema (44% to 50%), arthralgia (31% to 44%), nausea (13% to 31%), injection site pain (up to 31%), flatulence (25%), injection site reaction (19% to 25%), abdominal pain (13% to 25%), vomiting (19%), pain (6% to 19%), chest pain (up to 19%), dehydration (up to 19%), infection (up to 19%), rhinitis (up to 19%), hearing symptoms (13%), dizziness (6% to 13%), rash (6% to 13%), diaphoresis (up to 13%), generalized edema (up to 13%), malaise (up to 13%), moniliasis (up to 13%), myalgia (up to 13%)

SHOX deficiency: Humatrope®: Arthralgia (11%), gynecomastia (8%), excessive cutaneous nevi (7%), scoliosis (4%)

Small for gestational age: Genotropin® (frequency not defined): Mild, transient hyperglycemia; benign intracranial hypertension (rare); central precocious puberty; jaw prominence (rare); aggravation of pre-existing scoliosis (rare); injection site reactions; progression of pigmented nevi

Overdosage/Toxicology Symptoms of acute overdose may include initial hypoglycemia (with subsequent hyperglycemia), fluid retention, headache, nausea, and vomiting. Long-term overdose may result in signs and symptoms of acromegaly.

Drug Interactions

Increased Effect/Toxicity: Larger doses of somatropin may be needed for women taking oral estrogen replacement products; dosing not affected by topical products.

Decreased Effect: Glucocorticoid therapy may inhibit growth-promoting effects. Growth hormone may induce insulin resistance in patients with diabetes mellitus; monitor glucose and adjust insulin dose as necessary.

(Continued)

Somatropin *(Continued)*

Stability

Genotropin®: Store at 2°C to 8°C (36°F to 46°F); do not freeze. Protect from light. Reconstitute with diluent provided. Following reconstitution of 5.8 mg and 13.8 mg cartridge, store under refrigeration and use within 21 days.

Genotropin® Miniquick®: Store in refrigerator prior to dispensing, but may be stored ≤25°C (77°F) for up to 3 months after dispensing. Reconstitute with diluent provided. Consult the instructions provided with the reconstitution device. Once reconstituted, solution must be refrigerated and used within 24 hours. Discard unused portion.

Omnitrope™: Prior to reconstitution, store under refrigeration at 2°C to 8°C (36°F to 46°F); do not freeze. Protect from light. Reconstitute with provided diluent. Swirl gently; do not shake. Following reconstitution with the provided diluents, the 1.5 mg vial may be stored under refrigeration for up to 24 hours and the 5.8 mg vial may be stored under refrigeration for up to 3 weeks. Store vial in carton to protect from light.

Humatrope®:

Vial: Before and after reconstitution, store at 2°C to 8°C (36°F to 46°F); do not freeze. When reconstituted with provided diluent or bacteriostatic water for injection, use within 14 days. When reconstituted with sterile water for injection, use within 24 hours and discard unused portion. Reconstitute 5.5 mg vial with 1.5-5 mL diluent provided; swirl gently, do not shake.

Cartridge: Before and after reconstitution, store at 2°C to 8°C (36°F to 46°F); do not freeze. Consult HumatroPen™ User Guide for complete instructions for reconstitution. **Do not use diluent provided with vials.** Following reconstitution with provided diluent, stable for 28 days under refrigeration. Dilute with solution provided with cartridges **ONLY**; do not use diluent provided with vials.

Norditropin®: Store at 2°C to 8°C (36°F to 46°F); do not freeze. Avoid direct light.

Cartridge: When refrigerated, must be used within 4 weeks once inserted into pen. Orange and blue cartridges may also be stored up to 3 weeks at ≤25°C (77°F).

Prefilled pen: When refrigerated, must be used within 4 weeks once inserted into pen. Orange and blue cartridges may also be stored up to 3 weeks at ≤25°C (77°F).

Nutropin®: Before and after reconstitution, store at 2°C to 8°C (36°F to 46°F); do not freeze.

Vial: Reconstitute with bacteriostatic water for injection. Use reconstituted vials within 14 days. When reconstituted with sterile water for injection, use immediately and discard unused portion.

AQ formulation: Use within 28 days following initial use.

Saizen®: Prior to reconstitution, store at room temperature 15°C to 30°C (59°F to 86°F). Following reconstitution with bacteriostatic water for injection, reconstituted solution should be refrigerated and used within 14 days. When reconstituted with sterile water for injection, use immediately and discard unused portion. The Saizen® 8.8 mg easy click cartridge, when reconstituted with the provided bacteriostatic water, should be stored under refrigeration and used within 21 days.

5 mg vial: Reconstitute with 1-3 mL bacteriostatic water for injection or sterile water for injection; Gently swirl; do not shake.

8.8 mg vial: Reconstitute with 2-3 mL bacteriostatic water for injection or sterile water for injection. Gently swirl; do not shake.

Serostim®: Prior to reconstitution, store at room temperature 15°C to 30°C (59°F to 86°F). Reconstitute with sterile water for injection. When reconstituted with sterile water for injection, use immediately and discard unused portion.

Tev-Tropin®: Prior to reconstitution, store at 2°C to 8°C (36°F to 46°F). Reconstitute with 1-5 mL of diluent provided. Gently swirl; do not shake. May use preservative free NS for use in newborns. Following reconstitution with bacteriostatic NS, solution should be refrigerated and used within 14 days. Some cloudiness may occur; do not use if cloudiness persists after warming to room temperature.

Zorbtive®: Store unopened vials and diluent at room temperature of 15°C to 30°C (59°F to 86°F). Store reconstituted vial under refrigeration at 2°C to 8°C (36°F to 46°F) for up to 14 days; do not freeze.

8.8 mg vial: Reconstitute with 1-2 mL bacteriostatic water for injection. Swirl gently.

Mechanism of Action Somatropin is a purified polypeptide hormones of recombinant DNA origin; somatropin contains the identical sequence of amino acids found in human growth hormone; human growth hormone stimulates growth of linear bone, skeletal muscle, and organs; stimulates erythropoietin which increases red blood cell mass; exerts both insulin-like and diabetogenic effects; enhances the transmucosal transport of water, electrolytes, and nutrients across the gut

Pharmacodynamics/Kinetics

Duration: Maintains supraphysiologic levels for 18-20 hours

Absorption: I.M., SubQ: Well absorbed

Distribution: ~1 L/kg

Metabolism: Hepatic and renal (~90%)

Bioavailability: SubQ: ~70% to 90%

Half-life elimination: Preparation and route of administration dependent; SubQ: ~2-4 hours

Excretion: Urine

Dosage

Children (individualize dose):

Growth hormone deficiency:

Genotropin®, Omnitrope™: SubQ: Weekly dosage: 0.16-0.24 mg/kg divided into 6-7 doses

Humatrope®: I.M., SubQ: Weekly dosage: 0.18 mg/kg; maximum replacement dose: 0.3 mg/kg/week; dosing should be divided into equal doses given 3 times/week on alternating days, 6 times/week, or daily

Norditropin®: SubQ: 0.024-0.034 mg/kg/day, 6-7 times/week

Nutropin®, Nutropin® AQ: SubQ: Weekly dosage: 0.3 mg/kg divided into daily doses; pubertal patients: ≤0.7 mg/kg/week divided daily

Tev-Tropin®: SubQ: Up to 0.1 mg/kg administered 3 times/week

Saizen®: I.M., SubQ: 0.06 mg/kg/dose administered 3 times/week

Note: Therapy should be discontinued when patient has reached satisfactory adult height, when epiphyses have fused, or when the patient ceases to respond. Growth of 5 cm/year or more is expected, if growth rate does not exceed 2.5 cm in a 6-month period, double the dose for the next 6 months; if there is still no satisfactory response, discontinue therapy

Chronic renal insufficiency (CRI): Nutropin®, Nutropin® AQ: SubQ: Weekly dosage: 0.35 mg/kg divided into daily injections; continue until the time of renal transplantation

Dosage recommendations in patients treated for CRI who require dialysis:

Hemodialysis: Administer dose at night prior to bedtime or at least 3-4 hours after hemodialysis to prevent hematoma formation from heparin

CCPD: Administer dose in the morning following dialysis

CAPD: Administer dose in the evening at the time of overnight exchange

Turner syndrome:

Genotropin®: SubQ: Weekly dosage: 0.33 mg/kg divided into 6-7 doses

Humatrope®, Nutropin®, Nutropin® AQ: SubQ: Weekly dosage: ≤0.375 mg/kg divided into equal doses 3-7 times per week

Prader-Willi syndrome: Genotropin®: SubQ: Weekly dosage: 0.24 mg/kg divided into 6-7 doses

Small for gestational age: Genotropin®: SubQ: Weekly dosage: 0.48 mg/kg divided into 6-7 doses

Idiopathic short stature:

Humatrope®: SubQ: Weekly dosage: 0.37 mg/kg divided into equal doses 6-7 times per week

Nutropin®, Nutropin AQ®: SubQ: Weekly dosage: Up to 0.3 mg/kg divided into daily doses

SHOX deficiency: Humatrope®: SubQ: 0.35 mg/kg/week divided into equal daily doses

HIV patients with wasting or cachexia (unlabeled use): Serostim®: SubQ: Limited data; doses of 0.04 mg/kg/day were reported in five children, 6-17 years of age; doses of 0.07 mg/kg/day were reported in six children, 8-14 years of age

Adults:

Growth hormone deficiency: Adjust dose based on individual requirements: To minimize adverse events in older or overweight patients, reduced dosages may be necessary. During therapy, dosage should be decreased if required by the occurrence of side effects or excessive IGF-I levels.

Norditropin®: SubQ: Initial dose ≤0.004 mg/kg/day; after 6 weeks of therapy, may increase dose up to 0.016 mg/kg/day

Nutropin®, Nutropin® AQ: SubQ: ≤0.006 mg/kg/day; dose may be increased up to a maximum of 0.025 mg/kg/day in patients <35 years of age, or up to a maximum of 0.0125 mg/kg/day in patients ≥35 years of age

Humatrope®: SubQ: ≤0.006 mg/kg/day; dose may be increased up to a maximum of 0.0125 mg/kg/day

Genotropin®, Omnitrope™: SubQ: Weekly dosage: ≤0.04 mg/kg divided into 6-7 doses; dose may be increased at 4- to 8-week intervals to a maximum of 0.08 mg/kg/week

Saizen®: SubQ: ≤0.005 mg/kg/day; dose may be increased to not more than 0.01 mg/kg/day after 4 weeks

Alternate dosing (growth hormone deficiency): SubQ: Initial: 0.2 mg/day (range: 0.15-0.3 mg/day); may increase every 1-2 months by 0.1-0.2 mg/day

Dosage adjustment with estrogen supplementation (growth hormone deficiency): Larger doses of somatropin may be needed for women taking oral estrogen replacement products; dosing not affected by topical products

HIV patients with wasting or cachexia: Serostim®: SubQ: 0.1 mg/kg once daily at bedtime (maximum 6 mg/day). Alternately, patients at risk for side effects may be started at 0.1 mg/kg every other day. Patients who continue to lose weight after 12 weeks should be re-evaluated for opportunistic infections or other clinical events; rotate injection sites to avoid lipodystrophy Adjust dose if needed to manage side effects.

Daily dose based on body weight:

<35 kg: 0.1 mg/kg

35-45 kg: 4 mg

45-55 kg: 5 mg

>55 kg: 6 mg

Short-bowel syndrome (Zorbtive®): SubQ: 0.1 mg/kg once daily for 4 weeks (maximum: 8 mg/day)

Fluid retention (moderate) or arthralgias: Treat symptomatically or reduce dose by 50%

Severe toxicity: Discontinue therapy for up to 5 days; when symptoms resolve, restart at 50% of dose. If severe toxicity recurs or does not disappear within 5 days after discontinuation, permanently discontinue treatment.

Elderly: Patients ≥65 years of age may be more sensitive to the action of growth hormone and more prone to adverse effects; in general, dosing should be cautious, beginning at low end of dosing range

Dosage adjustment in renal impairment Reports indicate patients with chronic renal failure tend to have decreased clearance; specific dosing suggestions not available

Dosage adjustment in hepatic impairment: Clearance may be reduced in patients with severe hepatic dysfunction; specific dosing suggestions not available

Dietary Considerations

Prader-Willi syndrome: All patients should have effective weight control (use is contraindicated in severely-obese patients).

Short-bowel syndrome: Intravenous parenteral nutrition requirements may need reassessment as gastrointestinal absorption improves.

Administration Do not shake; administer SubQ or I.M. (not all products are approved for I.M. administration). Rotate administration sites to avoid tissue atrophy). When administering to newborns, reconstitute with sterile water for injection. Norditropin® cartridge must be administered using the corresponding color-coded NordiPen® injection pen.

Norditropin® cartridge must be administered using the corresponding color-coded NordiPen® injection pen.

(Continued)

Somatropin *(Continued)*

Humatrope®: When administering for growth hormone deficiency, SubQ route is preferred

Monitoring Parameters Growth curve, periodic thyroid function tests, bone age (annually), periodical urine testing for glucose, somatomedin C (IGF-I) levels; funduscopic examinations at initiation of therapy and periodically during treatment; serum phosphorus, alkaline phosphatase and parathyroid hormone. If growth deceleration is observed in children treated for growth hormone deficiency, and not due to other causes, evaluate for presence of antibody formation. Strict blood glucose monitoring in diabetic patients.

CRI: Progression of renal osteodystrophy

Prader-Willi syndrome: Monitor for sleep apnea, respiratory infections, snoring (onset of or increased)

Turner Syndrome: Ear disorders including otitis media; cardiovascular disorders

Dosage Forms

Injection, powder for reconstitution [rDNA origin]:

Genotropin®: 5.8 mg [15 units/mL; delivers 5 mg/mL]; 13.8 mg [36 int units/mL; delivers 12 mg/mL]

Genotropin Miniquick® [preservative free]: 0.2 mg, 0.4 mg, 0.6 mg, 0.8 mg, 1 mg, 1.2 mg, 1.4 mg, 1.6 mg, 1.8 mg, 2 mg [each strength delivers 0.25 mL]

Humatrope®: 5 mg [~15 int. units], 6 mg [18 int. units], 12 mg [36 int. units], 24 mg [72 int. units]

Nutropin®: 5 mg [~15 int. units; packaged with diluent containing benzyl alcohol]; 10 mg [~30 int. units; packaged with diluent containing benzyl alcohol]

Omnitrope™: 1.5 mg [~4.5 int. units; packaged with preservative free diluent]; 5.8 mg [~17.4 int. units; packaged with diluent containing benzyl alcohol]

Tev-Tropin®: 5 mg [15 int. units/mL; packaged with diluent containing benzyl alcohol]

Saizen®: 5 mg [~15 int. units; contains sucrose 34.2 mg; packaged with diluent containing benzyl alcohol]; 8.8 mg [~26.4 int. units; contains sucrose 60.2 mg; packaged with diluent containing benzyl alcohol]

Serostim®: 4 mg [12 int. units; contains sucrose 27.3 mg]; 5 mg [15 int. units; contains sucrose 34.2 mg]; 6 mg [18 int. units; contains sucrose 41 mg]

Zorbtive®: 8.8 mg [~26.4 int. units; contains sucrose 60.19 mg; packaged with diluent containing benzyl alcohol]

Injection, solution [rDNA origin]:

Norditropin®: 5 mg/1.5 mL (1.5 mL); 15 mg/1.5 mL (1.5 mL) [prefilled pen]

Norditropin® NordiFlex®: 5 mg/1.5 mL (1.5 mL); 10 mg/1.5 mL (1.5 mL); 15 mg/1.5 mL (1.5 mL) [prefilled pen]

Nutropin AQ®: 5 mg/mL (2 mL) [~15 int. units/mL; vial or cartridge]

♦ **Somavert**® *see* Pegvisomant *on page 1327*

♦ **Sominex**® **[OTC]** *see* DiphenhydrAMINE *on page 515*

♦ **Sominex**® **Maximum Strength [OTC]** *see* DiphenhydrAMINE *on page 515*

♦ **Somnote**™ *see* Chloral Hydrate *on page 339*

♦ **Som Pam (Can)** *see* Flurazepam *on page 733*

♦ **Sonata**® *see* Zaleplon *on page 1808*

Sorafenib *(sor AF e nib)*

U.S. Brand Names Nexavar®

Index Terms BAY 43-9006; Sorafenib Tosylate

Pharmacologic Category Antineoplastic Agent, Tyrosine Kinase Inhibitor; Vascular Endothelial Growth Factor (VEGF) Inhibitor

Use Treatment of advanced renal cell cancer

Unlabeled/Investigational Use Treatment of hepatocellular, breast, colon, colorectal, nonsmall cell lung, ovarian, pancreatic and thyroid cancers; melanoma, sarcoma

Pregnancy Risk Factor D

Pregnancy Implications Animal studies have demonstrated teratogenicity and fetal loss. There are no adequate and well-controlled studies in pregnant women. Because sorafenib inhibits angiogenesis, a critical component of fetal development, adverse effects on pregnancy would be expected. Women of childbearing potential should be advised to avoid pregnancy. Men and women should use effective birth control during treatment and for at least 2 weeks after treatment is discontinued.

Lactation Excretion in breast milk unknown/not recommended

Medication Safety Issues

High alert medication: The Institute for Safe Medication Practices (ISMP) includes this medication among its list of drugs which have a heightened risk of causing significant patient harm when used in error.

Contraindications Hypersensitivity to sorafenib or any component of the formulation; pregnancy

Warnings/Precautions May cause hypertension, especially in the first 6 weeks of treatment; use caution in patients with underlying or poorly-controlled hypertension. May cause cardiac ischemia or infarction; avoid use in patients with unstable coronary artery disease or recent myocardial infarction. Serious bleeding events may occur; monitor PT/INR in patients on warfarin therapy. May complicate wound healing; temporarily withhold treatment for patients undergoing major surgical procedures. Use caution when administering sorafenib with compounds that are metabolized predominantly via UGT1A1 (eg, irinotecan). Hand-foot skin reaction and rash are the most common adverse events. Has not been studied in patients with severe hepatic or renal impairment. Safety and efficacy have not been established in children.

Adverse Reactions Note: Dose-limiting toxicities (diarrhea, fatigue, and hand-foot syndrome) were reversible upon discontinuation; rash and hand-foot syndrome are dose-related; percentages not always reported.

>10%:

Cardiovascular: Hypertension (17%)

Central nervous system: Fatigue (32% to 33%; grade 3/4: 5% to <6%), sensory neuropathy (13%)

Dermatologic: Rash (38% to 40%), hand-foot syndrome (30% to 35%; grade 3/4: 6%), alopecia (27%), pruritus (19%), dry skin (11%), erythema

Endocrine & metabolic: Hypophosphatemia (45%; grade 3: 13%)

Gastrointestinal: Diarrhea (37% to 43%; grade 3/4: 2%), lipase increased (41%), amylase increased (30%), nausea (23%), anorexia (16%), vomiting (16%), constipation (15%), abdominal pain (11%), mouth pain

Hematologic: Lymphopenia (23%), neutropenia (<10% to 18%), hemorrhage (15%), thrombocytopenia (<10% to 12%), leukopenia

Neuromuscular & skeletal: Bone pain, muscle pain, weakness

Respiratory: Dyspnea (14%), cough (13%)

1% to 10%:

Cardiovascular: Flushing

Central nervous system: Headache (10%), depression, fever

Dermatologic: Acne, exfoliative dermatitis

Gastrointestinal: Weight loss (10%), appetite decreased, dyspepsia, dysphagia, glossodynia, mucositis, stomatitis, xerostomia

Genitourinary: Erectile dysfunction

Hematologic: Anemia

Hepatic: Transaminases increased

Neuromuscular & skeletal: Joint pain (10%), arthralgia, myalgia

Respiratory: Hoarseness

Miscellaneous: Influenza-like symptoms

<1% (Limited to important or life-threatening): Acute renal failure, alkaline phosphatase increased, arrhythmia, bilirubin increased, cardiac failure, cerebral hemorrhage, dehydration, erythema multiform, hypersensitivity (skin reaction, urticaria), hypertensive crisis, hyponatremia, hypothyroidism, infection, INR abnormal, jaundice, MI, myocardial ischemia, pancreatitis, thromboembolism, transient ischemic attack

Overdosage/Toxicology In clinical trials, doses of 800 mg twice daily produced diarrhea and dermatologic reactions. In the event of an overdose, treatment is symptomatic and supportive.

Drug Interactions

Cytochrome P450 Effect: Substrate of CYP3A4 (minor); **Inhibits** CYP2B6 (weak) and 2C8 (weak)

Increased Effect/Toxicity: Sorafenib may increase the levels/effects of doxorubicin.

Ethanol/Nutrition/Herb Interactions Herb/Nutraceutical: Avoid St John's wort (may decrease the levels/effects of sorafenib).

Stability Store at room temperature between 15°C and 30°C (59°F and 86°F). Protect from moisture.

Mechanism of Action Multikinase inhibitor; inhibits tumor growth and angiogenesis by inhibiting intracellular Raf kinases (CRAF, BRAF, and mutant BRAF), and cell surface kinase receptors (VEGFR-2, VEGFR-3, PDGFR-β, cKIT, and FLT-3)

Pharmacodynamics/Kinetics

Absorption: Bioavailability decreased 29% with a high-fat meal (bioavailability similar to fasting state when administered with a moderate-fat meal).

Protein binding: 99.5%

Metabolism: Hepatic, via CYP3A4 (primarily oxidated to the pyridine N-oxide; active, minor) and UGT1A9 (glucuronidation)

Bioavailability: 38% to 49%

Half-life elimination: 25-48 hours

Time to peak, plasma: 3 hours

Excretion: Feces (77%, 51% as unchanged drug); urine (19%, as metabolites)

Dosage Oral: Adults:

Advanced renal cell carcinoma: 400 mg twice daily

Nonsmall cell lung cancer (unlabeled use): 400 mg twice daily

Pancreatic cancer (unlabeled use): 400 mg twice daily in combination with gemcitabine

Dosage adjustment in renal impairment: Not studied in severe renal impairment (Cl$_{cr}$ <30 mL/minute)

Dosage adjustment in hepatic impairment: No adjustment required for mild (Child-Pugh class A) to moderate (Child-Pugh class B) hepatic impairment; not studied in severe hepatic impairment (Child-Pugh class C)

Dosage adjustment for toxicity: Temporary interruption and/or dosage reduction may be necessary for management of adverse drug reactions. The dose may be reduced to 400 mg once daily and then further reduced to 400 mg every other day.

Dose modification for skin toxicity:

Grade 1 (numbness, dysesthesia, paresthesia, tingling, painless swelling, erythema or discomfort of the hands or feet which do not disrupt normal activities): Continue sorafenib and consider symptomatic treatment with topical therapy.

Grade 2 (painful erythema and swelling of the hands or feet and/or discomfort affecting normal activities):

1st occurrence: Continue sorafenib and consider symptomatic treatment with topical therapy. **Note:** If no improvement, see dosing for 2nd or 3rd occurrence.

2nd or 3rd occurrence: Hold treatment until resolves to grade 0-1; resume treatment with dose reduced by one dose level (400 mg daily or 400 mg every other day)

4th occurrence: Discontinue treatment

Grade 3 (moist desquamation, ulceration, blistering, or severe pain of the hands or feet or severe discomfort that prevents working or performing daily activities):

1st or 2nd occurrence: Hold treatment until resolves to grade 0-1; resume treatment with dose reduced by one dose level (400 mg daily or 400 mg every other day)

3rd occurrence: Discontinue treatment

Dietary Considerations Take without food (1 hour before or 2 hours after eating).

Administration Administer on an empty stomach (1 hour before or 2 hours after eating).

Monitoring Parameters CBC with differential, electrolytes, phosphorus; blood pressure

Dosage Forms Tablet, as tosylate: 200 mg

♦ **Sorafenib Tosylate** *see* Sorafenib *on page 1590*

Sorbitol (SOR bi tole)

Pharmacologic Category Genitourinary Irrigant; Laxative, Osmotic
Additional Appendix Information
 Laxatives, Classification and Properties *on page 1886*
Use Genitourinary irrigant in transurethral prostatic resection or other transurethral resection or other transurethral surgical procedures; diuretic; humectant; sweetening agent; hyperosmotic laxative; facilitate the passage of sodium polystyrene sulfonate through the intestinal tract
Pregnancy Risk Factor C
Lactation Excretion in breast milk unknown
Contraindications Anuria
Warnings/Precautions Use with caution in patients with severe cardiopulmonary or renal impairment and in patients unable to metabolize sorbitol; large volumes may result in fluid overload and/or electrolyte changes
Adverse Reactions Frequency not defined.
 Cardiovascular: Edema
 Endocrine & metabolic: Fluid and electrolyte losses, hyperglycemia, lactic acidosis
 Gastrointestinal: Diarrhea, nausea, vomiting, abdominal discomfort, dry mouth
Overdosage/Toxicology Symptoms include nausea, diarrhea, fluid and electrolyte loss. Treatment is supportive to ensure fluid and electrolyte balance.
Stability Avoid storage in temperatures >150°F; do not freeze.
Mechanism of Action A polyalcoholic sugar with osmotic cathartic actions
Pharmacodynamics/Kinetics
 Onset of action: 0.25-1 hour
 Absorption: Oral, rectal: Poor
 Metabolism: Primarily hepatic to fructose
Dosage Hyperosmotic laxative (as single dose, at infrequent intervals):
 Children 2-11 years:
  Oral: 2 mL/kg (as 70% solution)
  Rectal enema: 30-60 mL as 25% to 30% solution
 Children >12 years and Adults:
  Oral: 30-150 mL (as 70% solution)
  Rectal enema: 120 mL as 25% to 30% solution
  Adjunct to sodium polystyrene sulfonate: 15 mL as 70% solution orally until diarrhea occurs (10-20 mL/2 hours) or 20-100 mL as an oral vehicle for the sodium polystyrene sulfonate resin
 When administered with charcoal:
  Oral:
   Children: 4.3 mL/kg of 35% sorbitol with 1 g/kg of activated charcoal
   Adults: 4.3 mL/kg of 70% sorbitol with 1 g/kg of activated charcoal every 4 hours until first stool containing charcoal is passed
  Topical: 3% to 3.3% as transurethral surgical procedure irrigation
Monitoring Parameters Monitor for fluid overload and/or electrolyte disturbances following large volumes; changes may be delayed due to slow absorption
Dosage Forms
 Solution, genitourinary irrigation: 3% (3000 mL, 5000 mL); 3.3% (2000 mL, 4000 mL)
 Solution, oral: 70% (30 mL, 480 mL, 3840 mL)

♦ **Soriatane®** *see* Acitretin *on page 41*

♦ **Sorine®** *see* Sotalol *on page 1592*

♦ **Sotacor® (Can)** *see* Sotalol *on page 1592*

Sotalol (SOE ta lole)

U.S. Brand Names Betapace®; Betapace AF®; Sorine®
Canadian Brand Names Alti-Sotalol; Apo-Sotalol®; Betapace AF®; CO Sotalol; Gen-Sotalol; Lin-Sotalol; Novo-Sotalol; Nu-Sotalol; PMS-Sotalol; Rho®-Sotalol; Riva-Sotalol; Rylosol; Sotacor®
Index Terms Sotalol Hydrochloride
Pharmacologic Category Antiarrhythmic Agent, Class II; Antiarrhythmic Agent, Class III; Beta-Adrenergic Blocker, Nonselective
Additional Appendix Information
 Beta-Blockers *on page 1875*
Use Treatment of documented ventricular arrhythmias (ie, sustained ventricular tachycardia), that in the judgment of the physician are life-threatening; maintenance of normal sinus rhythm in patients with symptomatic atrial fibrillation and atrial flutter who are currently in sinus rhythm. Manufacturer states substitutions should not be made for Betapace AF® since Betapace AF® is distributed with a patient package insert specific for atrial fibrillation/flutter.
Pregnancy Risk Factor B
Pregnancy Implications There are no adequate and well-controlled studies in pregnant women. Beta-blockers have been associated with bradycardia, hypotension, and IUGR; IUGR is probably related to maternal hypertension. Sotalol has been shown to cross the placenta, and is found in amniotic fluid; therefore, sotalol should be used during pregnancy only if the potential benefit outweighs the potential risk. Cases of neonatal hypoglycemia have been reported following maternal use of beta-blockers at parturition or during breast-feeding. Monitor breast-fed infant for symptoms of beta-blockade.
Lactation Enters breast milk/use caution (AAP rates "compatible")

Medication Safety Issues

Sound-alike/look-alike issues:

Sotalol may be confused with Stadol®

Betapace® may be confused with Betapace AF®

Betapace AF® may be confused with Betapace®

Contraindications Hypersensitivity to sotalol or any component of the formulation; bronchial asthma; sinus bradycardia; second- and third-degree AV block (unless a functioning pacemaker is present); congenital or acquired long QT syndromes; cardiogenic shock; uncontrolled congestive heart failure. Betapace AF® is contraindicated in patients with significantly reduced renal filtration (Cl_{cr} <40 mL/minute).

Warnings/Precautions [U.S. Boxed Warning] Manufacturer recommends initiation (or reinitiation) and doses increased in a hospital setting with continuous monitoring and staff familiar with the recognition and treatment of life-threatening arrhythmias. Dosage of sotalol should be adjusted gradually with 3 days between dosing increments to achieve steady-state concentrations, and to allow time to monitor QT intervals. Some experts will initiate therapy on an outpatient basis in a patient without heart disease or bradycardia, who has a baseline uncorrected QT interval <450 msec, and normal serum potassium and magnesium levels; close EKG monitoring during this time is necessary. ACC/AHA guidelines for management of atrial fibrillation also recommend that for outpatient initiation the patient not have risk factors predisposing to drug-induced ventricular proarrhythmia (Fuster, 2001). Creatinine clearance must be calculated prior to dosing. Use cautiously in the renally-impaired (dosage adjustment required).

Monitor and adjust dose to prevent QT_c prolongation. Concurrent use with other QT_c-prolonging drugs (including Class I and Class III antiarrhythmics) is generally not recommended; withhold for 3 half-lives. Watch for proarrhythmic effects. Correct electrolyte imbalances before initiating (especially hypokalemia and hypomagnesemia). Consider pre-existing conditions such as sick sinus syndrome before initiating. Conduction abnormalities can occur particularly sinus bradycardia. Use cautiously within the first 2 weeks post-MI (experience limited). Administer cautiously in compensated heart failure and monitor for a worsening of the condition. Use caution in patients with PVD (can aggravate arterial insufficiency). Beta-blocker therapy should not be withdrawn abruptly (particularly in patients with CAD), but gradually tapered to avoid acute tachycardia, hypertension, and/or ischemia. Use caution with concurrent use of beta-blockers and either verapamil or diltiazem; bradycardia or heart block can occur. Use cautiously in diabetics because it can mask prominent hypoglycemic symptoms. Use with caution in patients with bronchospastic disease, myasthenia gravis, peripheral vascular disease, or psychiatric disease. Use care with anesthetic agents which decrease myocardial function. Adequate alpha-blockade is required prior to use of any beta-blocker for patients with untreated pheochromocytoma. Safety and efficacy have not been established in children.

[U.S. Boxed Warning]: Betapace® should not be substituted for Betapace® AF; Betapace® AF is distributed with an educational insert specifically for patients with atrial fibrillation/flutter.

Adverse Reactions

>10%:

Cardiovascular: Bradycardia (16%), chest pain (16%), palpitation (14%)

Central nervous system: Fatigue (20%), dizziness (20%), lightheadedness (12%)

Neuromuscular & skeletal: Weakness (13%)

Respiratory: Dyspnea (21%)

1% to 10%:

Cardiovascular: CHF (5%), peripheral vascular disorders (3%), edema (8%), abnormal ECG (7%), hypotension (6%), proarrhythmia (5% in ventricular arrhythmia patients; less than 1% in atrial fibrillation/flutter), syncope (5%)

Central nervous system: Mental confusion (6%), anxiety (4%), headache (8%), sleep problems (8%), depression (4%)

Dermatologic: Itching/rash (5%)

Endocrine & metabolic: Sexual ability decreased (3%)

Gastrointestinal: Diarrhea (7%), nausea/vomiting (10%), stomach discomfort (3% to 6%), flatulence (2%)

Genitourinary: Impotence (2%)

Hematologic: Bleeding (2%)

Neuromuscular & skeletal: Paresthesia (4%), extremity pain (7%), back pain (3%)

Ocular: Visual problems (5%)

Respiratory: Upper respiratory problems (5% to 8%), asthma (2%)

<1% (Limited to Important or life-threatening): Alopecia, bronchiolitis obliterans with organized pneumonia (BOOP), cold extremities, diaphoresis, eosinophilia, leukocytoclastic vasculitis, leukopenia, paralysis, phlebitis, photosensitivity reaction, pruritus, pulmonary edema, Raynaud's phenomenon, red crusted skin, retroperitoneal fibrosis, serum transaminases increased, skin necrosis after extravasation, thrombocytopenia, vertigo

Overdosage/Toxicology Symptoms of intoxication include cardiac disturbances, CNS toxicity, bronchospasm, hypoglycemia and hyperkalemia. The most common cardiac symptoms include hypotension and bradycardia. Atrioventricular block, intraventricular conduction disturbances, cardiogenic shock, and asystole may occur with severe overdose, especially with membrane-depressant drugs (eg, propranolol). CNS effects include convulsions, coma, and respiratory arrest and are commonly seen with propranolol and other membrane-depressant and lipid-soluble drugs. Treatment is symptomatic for seizures, hypotension, hyperkalemia and hypoglycemia. Bradycardia and hypotension resistant to atropine, isoproterenol or pacing may respond to glucagon. Wide QRS defects caused by membrane-depressant poisoning may respond to hypertonic sodium bicarbonate. Repeat-dose charcoal, hemoperfusion, or hemodialysis may be helpful in removal of only those beta-blockers with a small V_d, long half-life, or low intrinsic clearance (acebutolol, atenolol, nadolol, sotalol).

Drug Interactions

Increased Effect/Toxicity: Increased effect/toxicity of beta-blockers with calcium blockers since there may be additive effects on AV conduction or ventricular function. Other agents (Continued)

Sotalol (Continued)

which prolong QT interval, including Class I antiarrhythmic agents, bepridil, cisapride, erythromycin, haloperidol, pimozide, phenothiazines, tricyclic antidepressants, and specific quinolones (including sparfloxacin, gatifloxacin, moxifloxacin) may increase the effect of sotalol on the prolongation of QT interval. Amiodarone may cause additive effects on QT_c prolongation as well as decreased heart rate, and has been associated with cardiac arrest in patients receiving some beta-blockers. When used concurrently with clonidine, sotalol may increase the risk of rebound hypertension after or during withdrawal of either agent. Beta-blocker and catecholamine depleting agents (reserpine or guanethidine) may result in additive hypotension or bradycardia. Beta-blockers may increase the action or levels of ethanol, nondepolarizing muscle relaxants, and theophylline although the effects are difficult to predict.

Decreased Effect: Decreased effect of sotalol may occur with aluminum-magnesium antacids (if taken within 2 hours), aluminum salts, barbiturates, calcium salts, cholestyramine, colestipol, NSAIDs, penicillins (ampicillin), rifampin, salicylates, and sulfinpyrazone due to decreased bioavailability and plasma levels. Beta-blockers may decrease the effect of sulfonylureas. Beta-agonists such as albuterol, terbutaline may have less of a therapeutic effect when administered concomitantly.

Ethanol/Nutrition/Herb Interactions

Food: Sotalol peak serum concentrations may be decreased if taken with food.

Herb/Nutraceutical: Avoid ephedra (may worsen arrhythmia).

Stability Store at 25°C (77°F); excursions permitted to 15°C to 30°C (59°F to 86°F).

Mechanism of Action

Beta-blocker which contains both beta-adrenoreceptor-blocking (Vaughan Williams Class II) and cardiac action potential duration prolongation (Vaughan Williams Class III) properties

Class II effects: Increased sinus cycle length, slowed heart rate, decreased AV nodal conduction, and increased AV nodal refractoriness

Class III effects: Prolongation of the atrial and ventricular monophasic action potentials, and effective refractory prolongation of atrial muscle, ventricular muscle, and atrioventricular accessory pathways in both the antegrade and retrograde directions

Sotalol is a racemic mixture of *d*- and *l*-sotalol; both isomers have similar Class III antiarrhythmic effects while the *l*-isomer is responsible for virtually all of the beta-blocking activity

Sotalol has both beta$_1$- and beta$_2$-receptor blocking activity

The beta-blocking effect of sotalol is a noncardioselective [half maximal at about 80 mg/day and maximal at doses of 320-640 mg/day]. Significant beta-blockade occurs at oral doses as low as 25 mg/day.

The Class III effects are seen only at oral doses ≥160 mg/day

Pharmacodynamics/Kinetics

Onset of action: Rapid, 1-2 hours

Peak effect: 2.5-4 hours

Duration: 8-16 hours

Absorption: Decreased 20% to 30% by meals compared to fasting

Distribution: Low lipid solubility; enters milk of laboratory animals and is reported to be present in human milk

Protein binding: None

Metabolism: None

Bioavailability: 90% to 100%

Half-life elimination: 12 hours; Children: 9.5 hours; terminal half-life decreases with age <2 years (may by ≥1 week in neonates)

Excretion: Urine (as unchanged drug)

Dosage Sotalol should be initiated and doses increased in a hospital with facilities for cardiac rhythm monitoring and assessment. Proarrhythmic events can occur after initiation of therapy and with each upward dosage adjustment.

Children: Oral: The safety and efficacy of sotalol in children have not been established

Note: Dosing per manufacturer, based on pediatric pharmacokinetic data; wait at least 36 hours between dosage adjustments to allow monitoring of QT intervals

≤2 years: Dosage should be adjusted (decreased) by plotting of the child's age on a logarithmic scale; see graph on next page or refer to manufacturer's package labeling.

>2 years: Initial: 90 mg/m^2/day in 3 divided doses; may be incrementally increased to a maximum of 180 mg/m^2/day

Adults: Oral:

Ventricular arrhythmias (Betapace®, Sorine®):

Initial: 80 mg twice daily

Dose may be increased gradually to 240-320 mg/day; allow 3 days between dosing increments in order to attain steady-state plasma concentrations and to allow monitoring of QT intervals

Most patients respond to a total daily dose of 160-320 mg/day in 2-3 divided doses.

Some patients, with life-threatening refractory ventricular arrhythmias, may require doses as high as 480-640 mg/day; however, these doses should only be prescribed when the potential benefit outweighs the increased of adverse events.

Atrial fibrillation or atrial flutter (Betapace AF®): Initial: 80 mg twice daily

If the initial dose does not reduce the frequency of relapses of atrial fibrillation/flutter and is tolerated without excessive QT prolongation (not >520 msec) after 3 days, the dose may be increased to 120 mg twice daily. This may be further increased to 160 mg twice daily if response is inadequate and QT prolongation is not excessive.

Elderly: Age does not significantly alter the pharmacokinetics of sotalol, but impaired renal function in elderly patients can increase the terminal half-life, resulting in increased drug accumulation

Dosage adjustment in renal impairment: Adults: Impaired renal function can increase the terminal half-life, resulting in increased drug accumulation. Sotalol (Betapace AF®) is contraindicated per the manufacturer for treatment of atrial fibrillation/flutter in patients with a Cl_{cr} <40 mL/minute.

Ventricular arrhythmias (Betapace®, Sorine®):
  Cl_{cr} >60 mL/minute: Administer every 12 hours
  Cl_{cr} 30-60 mL/minute: Administer every 24 hours
  Cl_{cr} 10-30 mL/minute: Administer every 36-48 hours
  Cl_{cr} <10 mL/minute: Individualize dose
Atrial fibrillation/flutter (Betapace AF®):
  Cl_{cr} >60 mL/minute: Administer every 12 hours
  Cl_{cr} 40-60 mL/minute: Administer every 24 hours
  Cl_{cr} <40 mL/minute: Use is contraindicated
Dialysis: Hemodialysis would be expected to reduce sotalol plasma concentrations because sotalol is not bound to plasma proteins and does not undergo extensive metabolism; administer dose postdialysis or administer supplemental 80 mg dose; peritoneal dialysis does not remove sotalol; supplemental dose is not necessary

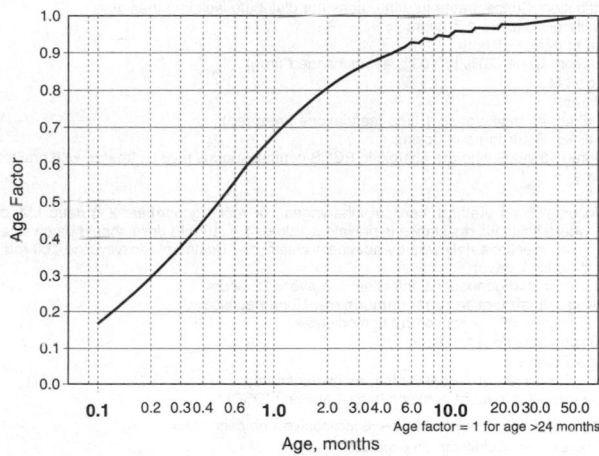

Sotalol Age Factor Nomogram for Patients ≤2 Years of Age

Age factor = 1 for age >24 months

Age, months

Adapted from U.S. Food and Drug Administration.
http://www.fda.gov/cder/foi/label/2001/2115s3lbl.PDF

Dietary Considerations Administer on an empty stomach.
Administration Food may decrease adsorption
Monitoring Parameters Serum magnesium, potassium, ECG
Additional Information Pharmacokinetics in children are more relevant for BSA than age.
Dosage Forms
Tablet, as hydrochloride: 80 mg, 80 mg [AF], 120 mg, 120 mg [AF], 160 mg, 160 mg [AF], 240 mg
  Betapace® [light blue]: 80 mg, 120 mg, 160 mg, 240 mg
  Betapace AF® [white]: 80 mg, 120 mg, 160 mg
  Sorine® [white]: 80 mg, 120 mg, 160 mg, 240 mg
Extemporaneous Preparations To make a 5 mg/mL oral solution, using a 6-ounce amber plastic prescription bottle, add five sotalol 120 mg tablets to 120 mL of simple syrup containing 0.1% sodium benzoate (tablets do not need to be crushed). Shake well. Allow tablets to hydrate for ~2 hours; shake intermittently until tablets completely disintegrate. Store at room temperature; shake well before use. Stable for 3 months. (Refer to manufacturer's current labeling.)

♦ **Sotalol Hydrochloride** see Sotalol on page 1592
♦ **Sotradecol®** see Sodium Tetradecyl on page 1583
♦ **Sotret®** see Isotretinoin on page 948
♦ **SPA** see Albumin on page 55
♦ **Spacol [DSC]** see Hyoscyamine on page 866
♦ **Spacol T/S [DSC]** see Hyoscyamine on page 866
♦ **Spastrin®** see Belladonna, Phenobarbital, and Ergotamine on page 201
♦ **SPD417** see Carbamazepine on page 284
♦ **Spectazole®** see Econazole on page 566
♦ **Spectazole™ (Can)** see Econazole on page 566

Spectinomycin (spek ti noe MYE sin)

U.S. Brand Names Trobicin® [DSC]
Index Terms Spectinomycin Hydrochloride
Pharmacologic Category Antibiotic, Miscellaneous
Additional Appendix Information
  Treatment of Sexually Transmitted Infections on page 2007
Use Treatment of uncomplicated gonorrhea
  (Continued)

Spectinomycin *(Continued)*

Pregnancy Risk Factor B

Lactation Enters breast milk/effect on infant unknown

Medication Safety Issues
Sound-alike/look-alike issues:
Trobicin® may be confused with tobramycin

Contraindications Hypersensitivity to spectinomycin or any component of the formulation

Adverse Reactions <1% (Limited to important or life-threatening): Abdominal cramps, chills, dizziness, headache, nausea, vomiting

Overdosage/Toxicology Symptoms include paresthesias, dizziness, blurred vision, ototoxicity, renal damage, nausea, sleeplessness, and decreased hemoglobin.

Stability Reconstitute with supplied diluent only. Use reconstituted solutions within 24 hours.

Mechanism of Action A bacteriostatic antibiotic that selectively binds to the 30s subunits of ribosomes, and thereby inhibiting bacterial protein synthesis

Pharmacodynamics/Kinetics
Duration: Up to 8 hours
Absorption: I.M.: Rapid and almost complete
Distribution: Concentrates in urine; does not distribute well into the saliva
Half-life elimination: 1.7 hours
Time to peak: ~1 hour
Excretion: Urine (70% to 100% as unchanged drug)

Dosage I.M.:
Children:
<45 kg: 40 mg/kg/dose 1 time (ceftriaxone preferred)
≥45 kg: Refer to adult dosing.
Children >8 years who are allergic to PCNS/cephalosporins may be treated with oral tetracycline

Adults:
Uncomplicated urethral, cervical, pharyngeal, or rectal gonorrhea: 2 g deep I.M. or 4 g where antibiotic resistance is prevalent 1 time; 4 g (10 mL) dose should be given as two 5 mL injections, followed by adequate chlamydial treatment (doxycycline 100 mg twice daily for 7 days)
Disseminated gonococcal infection: 2 g every 12 hours

Dosing adjustment in renal impairment: None necessary
Hemodialysis: 50% removed by hemodialysis

Administration For I.M. use only

Dosage Forms
Injection, powder for reconstitution, as hydrochloride:
Trobicin®: 2 g [diluent contains benzyl alcohol] [DSC]

♦ **Spectinomycin Hydrochloride** *see* Spectinomycin *on page 1595*
♦ **Spectracef**™ *see* Cefditoren *on page 309*
♦ **SPI 0211** *see* Lubiprostone *on page 1044*

Spironolactone *(speer on oh LAK tone)*

U.S. Brand Names Aldactone®

Canadian Brand Names Aldactone®; Novo-Spiroton

Pharmacologic Category Diuretic, Potassium-Sparing; Selective Aldosterone Blocker

Additional Appendix Information
Heart Failure (Systolic) *on page 2051*

Use Management of edema associated with excessive aldosterone excretion; hypertension; congestive heart failure; primary hyperaldosteronism; hypokalemia; cirrhosis of liver accompanied by edema or ascites

Unlabeled/Investigational Use Female acne (adjunctive therapy); hirsutism; hypertension (pediatric); diuretic (pediatric)

Pregnancy Risk Factor C/D in pregnancy-induced hypertension (per expert analysis)

Pregnancy Implications Teratogenic effects were not observed in animal studies; however, doses used were less than or equal to equivalent doses in humans. The antiandrogen effects of spironolactone have been shown to cause feminization of the male fetus in animal studies. Two case reports did not demonstrate this effect in humans however, the authors caution that adequate data is lacking. Diuretics are generally avoided in pregnancy due to the theoretical risk that decreased plasma volume may cause placental insufficiency. Diuretics should not be used during pregnancy in the presence of reduced placental perfusion (eg, pre-eclampsia, intrauterine growth restriction).

Lactation Enters breast milk/not recommended (AAP rates "compatible")

Medication Safety Issues
Sound-alike/look-alike issues:
Aldactone® may be confused with Aldactazide®

International issues:
Aldactone®: Brand name for potassium canrenoate in Austria, Czech Republic, Germany, and Hungary

Contraindications Hypersensitivity to spironolactone or any component of the formulation; anuria; acute renal insufficiency; significant impairment of renal excretory function; hyperkalemia; pregnancy (pregnancy-induced hypertension - per expert analysis)

Warnings/Precautions Avoid potassium supplements, potassium-containing salt substitutes, a diet rich in potassium, or other drugs that can cause hyperkalemia. Excess amounts can lead to profound diuresis with fluid and electrolyte loss; close medical supervision and dose evaluation are required. Watch for and correct electrolyte disturbances; adjust dose to avoid dehydration. In cirrhosis, avoid electrolyte and acid/base imbalances that might lead to hepatic encephalopathy. Gynecomastia is related to dose and duration of therapy. Discontinue use prior to adrenal vein catheterization. When evaluating a heart failure patient for spironolactone treatment, creatinine should be ≤2.5 mg/dL in men or ≤2 mg/dL in women and potassium <5 mEq/L. **[U.S. Boxed Warning]: Shown to be a tumorigen in chronic toxicity animal studies. Avoid unnecessary use.**

Adverse Reactions Incidence of adverse events is not always reported (mean daily dose 26 mg).

Cardiovascular: Edema (2%, placebo 2%)

Central nervous system: Disorders (23%, placebo 21%) which may include drowsiness, lethargy, headache, mental confusion, drug fever, ataxia, fatigue

Dermatologic: Maculopapular, erythematous cutaneous eruptions, urticaria, hirsutism, eosinophilia

Endocrine & metabolic: Gynecomastia (men 9%; placebo 1%), breast pain (men 2%; placebo 0.1%), serious hyperkalemia (2%, placebo 1%), hyponatremia, dehydration, hyperchloremic metabolic acidosis (in decompensated hepatic cirrhosis), impotence, menstrual irregularities, amenorrhea, postmenopausal bleeding

Gastrointestinal: Disorders (29%, placebo 29%) which may include anorexia, nausea, cramping, diarrhea, gastric bleeding, ulceration, gastritis, vomiting

Hematologic: Agranulocytosis

Hepatic: Cholestatic/hepatocellular toxicity

Renal: Increased BUN concentration

Miscellaneous: Deepening of the voice, anaphylactic reaction, breast cancer

Overdosage/Toxicology Symptoms include drowsiness, confusion, clinical signs of dehydration and electrolyte imbalance, and hyperkalemia. Ingestion of large amounts of potassium-sparing diuretics, may result in life-threatening hyperkalemia. This can be treated with I.V. glucose, with concurrent regular insulin. Sodium bicarbonate may also be used as a temporary measure. If needed, Kayexalate® oral or rectal solutions in sorbitol may also be used.

Drug Interactions

Increased Effect/Toxicity: Concurrent use of spironolactone with other potassium-sparing diuretics, potassium supplements, angiotensin receptor antagonists, co-trimoxazole (high dose), and ACE inhibitors can increase the risk of hyperkalemia, especially in patients with renal impairment. Cholestyramine can cause hyperchloremic acidosis in cirrhotic patients; avoid concurrent use.

Decreased Effect: The effects of digoxin (loss of positive inotropic effect) and mitotane may be reduced by spironolactone. Salicylates and NSAIDs (indomethacin) may decrease the natriuretic effect of spironolactone.

Ethanol/Nutrition/Herb Interactions

Food: Food increases absorption.

Herb/Nutraceutical: Avoid natural licorice (due to mineralocorticoid activity)

Stability Protect from light.

Mechanism of Action Competes with aldosterone for receptor sites in the distal renal tubules, increasing sodium chloride and water excretion while conserving potassium and hydrogen ions; may block the effect of aldosterone on arteriolar smooth muscle as well

Pharmacodynamics/Kinetics

Duration of action: 2-3 days

Protein binding: 91% to 98%

Metabolism: Hepatic to multiple metabolites, including canrenone (active)

Half-life elimination: 78-84 minutes

Time to peak, serum: 1-3 hours (primarily as the active metabolite)

Excretion: Urine and feces

Dosage To reduce delay in onset of effect, a loading dose of 2 or 3 times the daily dose may be administered on the first day of therapy. Oral:

Children:

Diuretic, hypertension (unlabeled use): Children 1-17 years: Initial: 1 mg/kg/day divided every 12-24 hours (maximum dose: 3.3 mg/kg/day, up to 100 mg/day)

Diagnosis of primary aldosteronism (unlabeled use): 125-375 mg/m²/day in divided doses

Adults:

Edema, hypokalemia: 25-200 mg/day in 1-2 divided doses

Hypertension (JNC 7): 25-50 mg/day in 1-2 divided doses

Diagnosis of primary aldosteronism: 100-400 mg/day in 1-2 divided doses

Acne in women (unlabeled use): 25-200 mg once daily

Hirsutism in women (unlabeled use): 50-200 mg/day in 1-2 divided doses

CHF, severe (with ACE inhibitor and a loop diuretic ± digoxin): 12.5-25 mg/day; maximum daily dose: 50 mg (higher doses may occasionally be used). In the RALES trial, 25 mg every other day was the lowest maintenance dose possible.

Note: If potassium >5.4 mEq/L, consider dosage reduction.

Elderly: Initial: 25-50 mg/day in 1-2 divided doses, increasing by 25-50 mg every 5 days as needed.

Dosing interval in renal impairment:

Cl_{cr} 10-50 mL/minute: Administer every 12-24 hours.

Cl_{cr} <10 mL/minute: Avoid use.

Dietary Considerations Should be taken with food to decrease gastrointestinal irritation and to increase absorption. Excessive potassium intake (eg, salt substitutes, low-salt foods, bananas, nuts) should be avoided.

Monitoring Parameters Blood pressure, serum electrolytes (potassium, sodium), renal function, I & O ratios and daily weight throughout therapy

CHF: Potassium levels and renal function should be checked in 3 days and 1 week after initiation, then every 2-4 weeks for 3-12 months, then every 3-6 months.

Test Interactions May cause false elevation in serum digoxin concentrations measured by RIA

Additional Information Maximum diuretic effect may be delayed 2-3 days and maximum hypertensive effects may be delayed 2-3 weeks.

Dosage Forms Tablet: 25 mg, 50 mg, 100 mg

(Continued)

Spironolactone (Continued)

Extemporaneous Preparations A 25 mg/mL oral suspension can be prepared by crushing one hundred twenty (120) 25 mg tablets in a mortar (reducing to a fine powder), and then mixing in 20 mL of vehicle (a 1:1 combination of Ora-Sweet® or Ora-Sweet® SF and Ora-Plus®) to create a uniform paste. Continue to add vehicle in geometric amounts (while mixing) until near-final volume is achieved. Transfer to a graduate and add sufficient quantity to make 120 mL. Label "shake well" and "refrigerate." Refrigerated stability is 60 days.

> Allen LV Jr and Erickson MA III, "Stability of Ketoconazole, Metolazone, Metronidazole, Procainamide Hydrochloride, and Spironolactone in Extemporaneously Compounded Oral Liquids," *Am J Health Syst Pharm*, 1996, 53:2073-8.

> Nahata MC, Morosco RS, and Hipple TF, 4th ed, *Pediatric Drug Formulations*, Cincinnati, OH: Harvey Whitney Books Co, 2000.

♦ **Spironolactone and Hydrochlorothiazide** see Hydrochlorothiazide and Spironolactone on page 847

♦ **Sporanox®** see Itraconazole on page 952

♦ **Sprintec™** see Ethinyl Estradiol and Norgestimate on page 660

♦ **Sprycel™** see Dasatinib on page 458

♦ **SPS®** see Sodium Polystyrene Sulfonate on page 1582

♦ **Sronyx™** see Ethinyl Estradiol and Levonorgestrel on page 653

♦ **SSD®** see Silver Sulfadiazine on page 1567

♦ **SSD® AF** see Silver Sulfadiazine on page 1567

♦ **SSKI®** see Potassium Iodide on page 1399

♦ **Stadol®** see Butorphanol on page 261

♦ **Staflex** see Acetaminophen and Phenyltoloxamine on page 32

♦ **Stagesic®** see Hydrocodone and Acetaminophen on page 848

♦ **Stalevo™** see Levodopa, Carbidopa, and Entacapone on page 1001

♦ **StanGard®** see Fluoride on page 722

♦ **StanGard® Perio** see Fluoride on page 722

♦ **Stannous Fluoride** see Fluoride on page 722

Stanozolol (stan OH zoe lole)

U.S. Brand Names Winstrol®

Pharmacologic Category Anabolic Steroid

Use Prophylactic use against hereditary angioedema

Restrictions C-III

Pregnancy Risk Factor X

Lactation Enters breast milk/contraindicated

Contraindications Hypersensitivity to stanozolol or any component of the formulation; nephrosis; carcinoma of breast or prostate; pregnancy

Warnings/Precautions May stunt bone growth in children; anabolic steroids may cause peliosis hepatis, liver cell tumors, and blood lipid changes with increased risk of arteriosclerosis; monitor diabetic patients carefully; use with caution in elderly patients, they may be at greater risk for prostatic hyperplasia; use with caution in patients with cardiac, renal, or hepatic disease or epilepsy

Adverse Reactions

Male: Postpubertal:

>10%:
  Dermatologic: Acne
  Endocrine & metabolic: Gynecomastia
  Genitourinary: Bladder irritability, priapism

1% to 10%:
  Central nervous system: Insomnia, chills
  Endocrine & metabolic: Decreased libido, hepatic dysfunction
  Gastrointestinal: Nausea, diarrhea
  Genitourinary: Prostatic hyperplasia (elderly)
  Hematologic: Iron-deficiency anemia, suppression of clotting factors

<1% (Limited to important or life-threatening): Hepatic necrosis, hepatocellular carcinoma

Female:

>10%: Endocrine & metabolic: Virilism

1% to 10%:
  Central nervous system: Chills, insomnia
  Endocrine & metabolic: Hypercalcemia
  Gastrointestinal: Nausea, diarrhea
  Hematologic: Iron deficiency anemia, suppression of clotting factors
  Hepatic: Hepatic dysfunction

<1% (Limited to important or life-threatening): Hepatic necrosis, hepatocellular carcinoma

Drug Interactions

Increased Effect/Toxicity: ACTH, adrenal steroids may increase risk of edema and acne. Stanozolol enhances the hypoprothrombinemic effects of oral anticoagulants and enhances the hypoglycemic effects of insulin and sulfonylureas (oral hypoglycemics).

Mechanism of Action Synthetic testosterone derivative with similar androgenic and anabolic actions

Pharmacodynamics/Kinetics

Metabolism: Hepatic

Excretion: Urine (90%); feces (6%)

Dosage

Children: Acute attacks:
  <6 years: 1 mg/day
  6-12 years: 2 mg/day

Adults: Oral: Initial: 2 mg 3 times/day, may then reduce to a maintenance dose of 2 mg/day or 2 mg every other day after 1-3 months

Dosing adjustment in hepatic impairment: Stanozolol is **not** recommended for patients with severe liver dysfunction

Dosage Forms Tablet: 2 mg

♦ **Starlix**® *see* Nateglinide *on page 1204*

♦ **Starnoc**® **(Can)** *see* Zaleplon *on page 1808*

♦ **Statex**® **(Can)** *see* Morphine Sulfate *on page 1171*

♦ **Staticin**® **[DSC]** *see* Erythromycin *on page 609*

♦ **Statuss**™ **DM** *see* Chlorpheniramine, Phenylephrine, and Dextromethorphan *on page 352*

Stavudine (STAV yoo deen)

U.S. Brand Names Zerit®
Canadian Brand Names Zerit®
Index Terms d4T
Pharmacologic Category Antiretroviral Agent, Reverse Transcriptase Inhibitor (Nucleoside)
Additional Appendix Information
   Antiretroviral Therapy for HIV Infection: Adults and Adolescents *on page 1988*
   Management of Healthcare Worker Exposures to HBV, HCV, and HIV *on page 1941*
Use Treatment of HIV infection in combination with other antiretroviral agents
Pregnancy Risk Factor C
Pregnancy Implications No increased risk of overall birth defects has been observed following 1st trimester exposure according to data collected by the antiretroviral pregnancy registry. Cases of fatal and nonfatal lactic acidosis, with or without pancreatitis, have been reported in pregnant women. It is not known if pregnancy itself potentiates this known side effect; however, pregnant women may be at increased risk of lactic acidosis and liver damage. Hepatic enzymes and electrolytes should be monitored frequently during the 3rd trimester of pregnancy. Pharmacokinetics of stavudine are not significantly altered during pregnancy; dose adjustments are not needed. The Perinatal HIV Guidelines Working Group considers stavudine to be an alternative NRTI in dual nucleoside combination regimens; use with didanosine only if no alternatives are available, do not use with zidovudine. Health professionals are encouraged to contact the antiretroviral pregnancy registry to monitor outcomes of pregnant women exposed to antiretroviral medications (1 800-258-4263 or www.APRegistry.com).
Lactation Excretion in breast milk unknown/contraindicated
Medication Safety Issues
   Sound-alike/look-alike issues:
      Zerit® may be confused with Ziac®
Contraindications Hypersensitivity to stavudine or any component of the formulation
Warnings/Precautions Use with caution in patients who demonstrate previous hypersensitivity to zidovudine, didanosine, zalcitabine, pre-existing bone marrow suppression, renal insufficiency, or peripheral neuropathy. Peripheral neuropathy may be the dose-limiting side effect. Zidovudine should not be used in combination with stavudine. **[U.S. Boxed Warning]: Lactic acidosis and severe hepatomegaly with steatosis have been reported with stavudine use, including fatal cases.** Risk may be increased in obesity, prolonged nucleoside exposure, or in female patients. Suspend therapy in patients with suspected lactic acidosis; consider discontinuation of stavudine if lactic acidosis is confirmed. Pregnant women may be at increased risk of lactic acidosis and liver damage. Severe motor weakness (resembling Guillain-Barré syndrome) has also been reported (including fatal cases, usually in association with lactic acidosis); manufacturer recommends discontinuation if motor weakness develops (with or without lactic acidosis). **[U.S. Boxed Warning]: Pancreatitis (including some fatal cases) has occurred during combination therapy (didanosine with or without hydroxyurea).** Risk increased when used in combination regimen with didanosine and hydroxyurea. Suspend therapy with agents toxic to the pancreas (including stavudine, didanosine, or hydroxyurea) in patients with suspected pancreatitis.
Adverse Reactions All adverse reactions reported below were similar to comparative agent, zidovudine, except for peripheral neuropathy, which was greater for stavudine. Selected adverse events reported as monotherapy or in combination therapy include:

>10%:
   Central nervous system: Headache
   Dermatologic: Rash
   Gastrointestinal: Nausea, vomiting, diarrhea
   Hepatic: Transaminases increased
   Neuromuscular & skeletal: Peripheral neuropathy
   Miscellaneous: Amylase increased
1% to 10%: Hepatic: Bilirubin increased
Postmarketing and/or case reports: Abdominal pain, allergic reaction, anemia, anorexia, chills, fever, hepatitis, hepatomegaly, hepatic failure, hepatic steatosis, insomnia, lactic acidosis, leukopenia, motor weakness (severe), myalgia, pancreatitis, redistribution/accumulation of body fat, thrombocytopenia
Overdosage/Toxicology Acute toxicity was not reported following administration of 12-24 times the recommended dose in adults. Peripheral neuropathy and hepatic toxicity have been reported following chronic overdose. Stavudine may be removed by hemodialysis.
Drug Interactions
   Increased Effect/Toxicity: Risk of pancreatitis may be increased with concurrent didanosine use; cases of fatal lactic acidosis have been reported with this combination when used during pregnancy (use only if clearly needed). Risk of hepatotoxicity or pancreatitis may be increased with concurrent hydroxyurea use. Zalcitabine may increase risk of peripheral neuropathy; concurrent use not recommended. Concomitant use of ribavirin with or without interferon alfa and nucleoside analogues may increase the risk of developing
(Continued)

Stavudine *(Continued)*

hepatic decompensation or other signs of mitochondrial toxicity, including pancreatitis or lactic acidosis.

Decreased Effect: Zidovudine inhibits intracellular phosphorylation of stavudine; concurrent use not recommended. Doxorubicin may inhibit intracellular phosphorylation of stavudine; use with caution. Ribavirin may inhibit intracellular phosphorylation of stavudine; use with caution.

Stability Capsules and powder for reconstitution may be stored at room temperature. Reconstituted oral solution should be refrigerated and is stable for 30 days.

Mechanism of Action Stavudine is a thymidine analog which interferes with HIV viral DNA dependent DNA polymerase resulting in inhibition of viral replication; nucleoside reverse transcriptase inhibitor

Pharmacodynamics/Kinetics

Distribution: V_d: 0.5 L/kg

Bioavailability: 86.4%

Metabolism: Undergoes intracellular phosphorylation to an active metabolite

Half-life elimination: 1-1.6 hours

Time to peak, serum: 1 hour

Excretion: Urine (40% as unchanged drug)

Dosage Oral:

Newborns (Birth to 13 days): 0.5 mg/kg every 12 hours

Children:

>14 days and <30 kg: 1 mg/kg every 12 hours

≥30 kg: Refer to Adults dosing

Adults:

≥60 kg: 40 mg every 12 hours

<60 kg: 30 mg every 12 hours

Dosing adjustment for toxicity: If symptoms of peripheral neuropathy occur, discontinue until symptoms resolve. Treatment may then be resumed at 50% the recommended dose. If symptoms recur at lower dose, permanent discontinuation should be considered.

Dosing adjustment in renal impairment:

Children: Specific recommendations not available. Reduction in dose or increase in dosing interval should be considered.

Adults:

Cl_{cr} >50 mL/minute:

≥60 kg: 40 mg every 12 hours

<60 kg: 30 mg every 12 hours

Cl_{cr} 26-50 mL/minute:

≥60 kg: 20 mg every 12 hours

<60 kg: 15 mg every 12 hours

Cl_{cr} 10-25 mL/minute, hemodialysis (administer dose after hemodialysis on day of dialysis):

≥60 kg: 20 mg every 24 hours

<60 kg: 15 mg every 24 hours

Elderly: Older patients should be closely monitored for signs and symptoms of peripheral neuropathy; dosage should be carefully adjusted to renal function

Dietary Considerations May be taken without regard to meals.

Administration May be administered without regard to meals. Oral solution should be shaken vigorously prior to use.

Monitoring Parameters Monitor liver function tests and signs and symptoms of peripheral neuropathy; monitor viral load and CD4 count

Additional Information Potential compliance problems, frequency of administration and adverse effects should be discussed with patients before initiating therapy to help prevent the emergence of resistance.

Dosage Forms

Capsule: 15 mg, 20 mg, 30 mg, 40 mg

Powder, for oral solution: 1 mg/mL (200 mL) [dye free; fruit flavor]

♦ Stemetil® **(Can)** *see* Prochlorperazine *on page 1429*

♦ Sterapred® *see* PredniSONE *on page 1416*

♦ Sterapred® **DS** *see* PredniSONE *on page 1416*

♦ STI571 *see* Imatinib *on page 881*

♦ Stieprox® **(Can)** *see* Ciclopirox *on page 366*

♦ Stimate™ *see* Desmopressin *on page 476*

♦ Sting-Kill **[OTC]** *see* Benzocaine *on page 204*

♦ St. Joseph® **Adult Aspirin [OTC]** *see* Aspirin *on page 160*

♦ Stop® *see* Fluoride *on page 722*

♦ Strattera® *see* Atomoxetine *on page 169*

♦ Streptase® *see* Streptokinase *on page 1600*

Streptokinase *(strep toe KYE nase)*

U.S. Brand Names Streptase®

Canadian Brand Names Streptase®

Index Terms SK

Pharmacologic Category Thrombolytic Agent

Use Thrombolytic agent used in treatment of recent severe or massive deep vein thrombosis, pulmonary emboli, myocardial infarction, and occluded arteriovenous cannulas

Pregnancy Risk Factor C

Lactation Excretion in breast milk unknown

Medication Safety Issues

High alert medication: The Institute for Safe Medication Practices (ISMP) includes this medication (I.V.) among its list of drugs which have a heightened risk of causing significant patient harm when used in error.

Contraindications Hypersensitivity to anistreplase, streptokinase, or any component of the formulation; active internal bleeding; history of CVA; recent (within 2 months) intracranial or intraspinal surgery or trauma; intracranial neoplasm, arteriovenous malformation, or aneurysm; known bleeding diathesis; severe uncontrolled hypertension

Warnings/Precautions Concurrent heparin anticoagulation can contribute to bleeding; careful attention to all potential bleeding sites. I.M. injections and nonessential handling of the patient should be avoided. Venipunctures should be performed carefully and only when necessary. If arterial puncture is necessary, use an upper extremity vessel that can be manually compressed. If serious bleeding occurs then the infusion of streptokinase and heparin should be stopped. Use with caution in patients >75 years of age, patients with a history of cardiac arrhythmias, septic thrombophlebitis or occluded AV cannula at seriously infected site, patients with a high likelihood of left heart thrombus (eg, mitral stenosis with atrial fibrillation), major surgery within last 10 days, GI bleeding, diabetic hemorrhagic retinopathy, subacute bacterial endocarditis, cerebrovascular disease, recent trauma including cardiopulmonary resuscitation, or severe hypertension (systolic BP >180 mm Hg and/or diastolic BP >110 mm Hg); antibodies to streptokinase remain for 3-6 months after initial dose, use another thrombolytic enzyme (ie, alteplase) if thrombolytic therapy is indicated in patients with prior streptokinase therapy

Coronary thrombolysis may result in reperfusion arrhythmias. Hypotension, occasionally severe, can occur (not from bleeding or anaphylaxis). Follow standard MI management. Rare anaphylactic reactions can occur. Cautious repeat administration in patients who have received anistreplase or streptokinase within 1 year (streptokinase antibody may decrease effectiveness or risk of allergic reactions). Safety and efficacy in pediatric patients have not been established.

Streptokinase is not indicated for restoration of patency of intravenous catheters. Serious adverse events relating to the use of streptokinase in the restoration of patency of occluded intravenous catheters have involved the use of high doses of streptokinase in small volumes (250,000 international units in 2 mL). Uses of lower doses of streptokinase in infusions over several hours, generally into partially occluded catheters, or local instillation into the catheter lumen and subsequent aspiration, have been described in the medical literature. Healthcare providers should consider the risk for potentially life-threatening reactions (eg, hypotension, hypersensitivity reactions, apnea, bleeding) associated with the use of streptokinase in the management of occluded intravenous catheters.

Adverse Reactions As with all drugs which may affect hemostasis, bleeding is the major adverse effect associated with streptokinase. Hemorrhage may occur at virtually any site. Risk is dependent on multiple variables, including the dosage administered, concurrent use of multiple agents which alter hemostasis, and patient predisposition (including hypertension). Rapid lysis of coronary artery thrombi by thrombolytic agents may be associated with reperfusion-related atrial and/or ventricular arrhythmia.

>10%:
Cardiovascular: Hypotension
Local: Injection site bleeding
1% to 10%:
Central nervous system: Fever (1% to 4%)
Dermatologic: Bruising, rash, pruritus
Gastrointestinal: Gastrointestinal hemorrhage, nausea, vomiting
Genitourinary: Genitourinary hemorrhage
Hematologic: Anemia
Neuromuscular & skeletal: Muscle pain
Ocular: Eye hemorrhage, periorbital edema
Respiratory: Bronchospasm, epistaxis
Miscellaneous: Diaphoresis
<1% (Limited to important or life-threatening): Acute tubular necrosis, allergic reactions, anaphylactic shock, anaphylactoid reactions, anaphylaxis, angioneurotic edema, ARDS, back pain (during infusion), cholesterol embolization, erysipelas-like rash, Guillain-Barré syndrome, hemarthrosis, intracranial hemorrhage, laryngeal edema, morbilliform, Parsonage-Turner syndrome, pericardial hemorrhage, respiratory depression, retroperitoneal hemorrhage, splenic rupture, transaminases increased, urticaria

Additional cardiovascular events associated with use in MI: Asystole, AV block, cardiac arrest, cardiac tamponade, cardiogenic shock, electromechanical dissociation, heart failure, mitral regurgitation, myocardial rupture, pericardial effusion, pericarditis, pulmonary edema, recurrent ischemia/infarction, thromboembolism, ventricular tachycardia

Overdosage/Toxicology Symptoms include epistaxis, bleeding gums, hematoma, spontaneous ecchymoses, and oozing at catheter site. If uncontrollable bleeding occurs, discontinue infusion; whole blood or blood products may be used to reverse bleeding.

Drug Interactions

Increased Effect/Toxicity: The risk of bleeding with streptokinase is increased by oral anticoagulants (warfarin), heparin, low molecular weight heparins, and drugs which affect platelet function (eg, NSAIDs, dipyridamole, ticlopidine, clopidogrel, IIb/IIIa antagonists). Although concurrent use with aspirin and heparin may increase the risk of bleeding. Aspirin and heparin were used concomitantly with streptokinase in the majority of patients in clinical studies of MI.

Decreased Effect: Antifibrinolytic agents (aminocaproic acid) may decrease effectiveness to thrombolytic agents.

Ethanol/Nutrition/Herb Interactions Herb/Nutraceutical: Avoid cat's claw, dong quai, evening primrose, feverfew, red clover, horse chestnut, garlic, green tea, ginseng, ginkgo (all have additional antiplatelet activity). (Continued)

Streptokinase (Continued)

Stability Streptokinase, a white lyophilized powder, may have a slight yellow color in solution due to the presence of albumin. Intact vials should be stored at room temperature. Reconstituted solutions should be refrigerated and are stable for 24 hours.

Stability of parenteral admixture at room temperature (25°C) is 8 hours; 24 hours when refrigerated (4°C).

Mechanism of Action Activates the conversion of plasminogen to plasmin by forming a complex, exposing plasminogen-activating site, and cleaving a peptide bond that converts plasminogen to plasmin; plasmin degrades fibrin, fibrinogen and other procoagulant proteins into soluble fragments; effective both outside and within the formed thrombus/embolus

Pharmacodynamics/Kinetics

Onset of action: Activation of plasminogen occurs almost immediately

Duration: Fibrinolytic effect: Several hours; Anticoagulant effect: 12-24 hours

Half-life elimination: 83 minutes

Excretion: By circulating antibodies and the reticuloendothelial system

Dosage I.V.:

Children: Safety and efficacy have not been not established. Limited studies have used 3500-4000 units/kg over 30 minutes followed by 1000-1500 units/kg/hour.

Clotted catheter: **Note:** Not recommended due to possibility of allergic reactions with repeated doses: 10,000-25,000 units diluted in NS to a final volume equivalent to catheter volume; instill into catheter and leave in place for 1 hour, then aspirate contents out of catheter and flush catheter with normal saline.

Adults: Antibodies to streptokinase remain for at least 3-6 months after initial dose: Administration requires the use of an infusion pump.

An intradermal skin test of 100 units has been suggested to predict allergic response to streptokinase. If a positive reaction is not seen after 15-20 minutes, a therapeutic dose may be administered.

Guidelines for acute myocardial infarction (AMI): 1.5 million units over 60 minutes

Administration:

Dilute two 750,000 unit vials of streptokinase with 5 mL dextrose 5% in water (D_5W) each, gently swirl to dissolve.

Add this dose of the 1.5 million units to 150 mL D_5W.

This should be infused over 60 minutes; an in-line filter ≥0.45 micron should be used.

Monitor for the first few hours for signs of anaphylaxis or allergic reaction. **Infusion should be slowed if blood pressure falls by 25 mm Hg or terminated if asthmatic symptoms appear**.

Following completion of streptokinase, initiate heparin, if directed, when aPTT returns to less than 2 times the upper limit of control; do not use a bolus, but initiate infusion adjusted to a target aPTT of 1.5-2 times the upper limit of control. If prolonged (>48 hours) heparin is required, infusion may be switched to subcutaneous therapy.

Guidelines for acute pulmonary embolism (APE): 3 million unit dose over 24 hours

Administration:

Dilute four 750,000 unit vials of streptokinase with 5 mL dextrose 5% in water (D_5W) each, gently swirl to dissolve.

Add this dose of 3 million units to 250 mL D_5W, an in-line filter ≥0.45 micron should be used.

Administer 250,000 units (23 mL) over 30 minutes followed by 100,000 units/hour (9 mL/hour) for 24 hours.

Monitor for the first few hours for signs of anaphylaxis or allergic reaction. **Infusion should be slowed if blood pressure is lowered by 25 mm Hg or if asthmatic symptoms appear**.

Begin heparin 1000 units/hour about 3-4 hours after completion of streptokinase infusion or when PTT is <100 seconds.

Monitor PT, PTT, and fibrinogen levels during therapy.

Thromboses: 250,000 units to start, then 100,000 units/hour for 24-72 hours depending on location.

Cannula occlusion: 250,000 units into cannula, clamp for 2 hours, then aspirate contents and flush with normal saline; **Not recommended; see Warnings/Precautions**

Administration Avoid I.M. injections

Monitoring Parameters Blood pressure, PT, aPTT, platelet count, hematocrit, fibrinogen concentration, signs of bleeding

Reference Range

Partial thromboplastin time (aPTT) activated: 20.4-33.2 seconds

Prothrombin time (PT): 10.9-13.7 seconds (same as control)

Fibrinogen: 200-400 mg/dL

Dosage Forms [DSC] = Discontinued product

Injection, powder for reconstitution: 250,000 int. units; 750,000 int. units; 1,500,000 int. units [DSC]

Streptomycin (strep toe MYE sin)

Index Terms Streptomycin Sulfate

Pharmacologic Category Antibiotic, Aminoglycoside; Antitubercular Agent

Additional Appendix Information

Antimicrobial Drugs of Choice on page 1981

Tuberculosis on page 2010

Use Part of combination therapy of active tuberculosis; used in combination with other agents for treatment of streptococcal or enterococcal endocarditis, mycobacterial infections, plague, tularemia, and brucellosis

Pregnancy Risk Factor D

Lactation Enters breast milk/compatible

Medication Safety Issues
Sound-alike/look-alike issues:
Streptomycin may be confused with streptozocin

Contraindications Hypersensitivity to streptomycin or any component of the formulation; pregnancy

Warnings/Precautions [U.S. Boxed Warning]: May cause neurotoxicity, nephrotoxicity, and/or neuromuscular blockade and respiratory paralysis; usual risk factors include pre-existing renal impairment, concomitant neuro-/nephrotoxic medications, advanced age and dehydration. The drug's neurotoxicity can result in respiratory paralysis from neuromuscular blockade, especially when the drug is given soon after anesthesia or muscle relaxants. Use with caution in patients with pre-existing vertigo, tinnitus, hearing loss, neuromuscular disorders, or renal impairment; modify dosage in patients with renal impairment; ototoxicity is directly proportional to the amount of drug given and the duration of treatment; tinnitus or vertigo are indications of vestibular injury and impending bilateral irreversible damage; renal damage is usually reversible. **[U.S. Boxed Warning]: Parenteral form should be used only where appropriate audiometric and laboratory testing facilities are available.** Prolonged use may result in superinfection, including pseudomembranous colitis.

Adverse Reactions Frequency not defined.
Cardiovascular: Hypotension
Central nervous system: Neurotoxicity, drowsiness, headache, drug fever, paresthesia
Dermatologic: Skin rash
Gastrointestinal: Nausea, vomiting
Hematologic: Eosinophilia, anemia
Neuromuscular & skeletal: Arthralgia, weakness, tremor
Otic: Ototoxicity (auditory), ototoxicity (vestibular)
Renal: Nephrotoxicity
Respiratory: Difficulty in breathing

Overdosage/Toxicology Symptoms include ototoxicity, nephrotoxicity, and neuromuscular toxicity. The treatment of choice following a single acute overdose appears to be the maintenance of urine output of at least 3 mL/kg/hour. Dialysis is of questionable value in the enhancement of aminoglycoside elimination. If required, hemodialysis is preferred over peritoneal dialysis in patients with normal renal function. Careful hydration may be all that is required to promote diuresis and therefore enhance elimination.

Drug Interactions
Increased Effect/Toxicity: Increased/prolonged effect with depolarizing and nondepolarizing neuromuscular blocking agents. Concurrent use with amphotericin or loop diuretics may increase nephrotoxicity.

Stability Depending upon manufacturer, reconstituted solution remains stable for 2-4 weeks when refrigerated. Exposure to light causes darkening of solution without apparent loss of potency.

Mechanism of Action Inhibits bacterial protein synthesis by binding directly to the 30S ribosomal subunits causing faulty peptide sequence to form in the protein chain

Pharmacodynamics/Kinetics
Absorption:
Oral: Poorly absorbed
I.M.: Well absorbed
Distribution: To extracellular fluid including serum, abscesses, ascitic, pericardial, pleural, synovial, lymphatic, and peritoneal fluids; poorly distributed into CSF; crosses placenta; small amounts enter breast milk
Protein binding: 34%
Half-life elimination: Newborns: 4-10 hours; Adults: 2-4.7 hours, prolonged with renal impairment
Time to peak: I.M.: Within 1 hour
Excretion: Urine (90% as unchanged drug); feces, saliva, sweat, and tears (<1%)

Dosage Note: For I.M. administration; I.V. use is not recommended
Usual dosage range:
Children: 20-40 mg/kg/day (maximum: 1 g)
Adults: 15-30 mg/kg/day or 1-2 g/day

Indication-specific dosing:
Children: **Tuberculosis:** I.M.:
Daily therapy: 20-40 mg/kg/day (maximum: 1 g/day)
Directly observed therapy (DOT): Twice weekly: 25-30 mg/kg (maximum: 1.5 g)
Directly observed therapy DOT: 3 times/week: 25-30 mg/kg (maximum: 1.5 g)
Adults: I.M.:
Brucellosis: 1 g/day for 14-21 days (with doxycycline, 100 mg twice daily for 6 weeks)
Endocarditis:
Enterococcal: 1 g every 12 hours for 2 weeks, 500 mg every 12 hours for 4 weeks in combination with penicillin
Streptococcal: 1 g every 12 hours for 1 week, 500 mg every 12 hours for 1 week
***Mycobacterium avium* complex:** Adjunct therapy (with macrolide, rifamycin, and ethambutol): 15 mg/kg 3 times/week for first 2-3 months for severe disease
Plague: 15 mg/kg (or 1 g) every 12 hours until the patient is afebrile for at least 3 days
Tuberculosis:
Daily therapy: 15 mg/kg/day (maximum: 1 g)
Directly observed therapy (DOT): Twice weekly: 25-30 mg/kg (maximum: 1.5 g)
Directly observed therapy DOT: 3 times/week: 25-30 mg/kg (maximum: 1.5 g)
Tularemia: 10-15 mg/kg every 12 hours (maximum: 2 g/day) for 7-10 days or until patient is afebrile for 5-7 days

Elderly: I.M.: 10 mg/kg/day, not to exceed 750 mg/day; dosing interval should be adjusted for renal function; some authors suggest not to give more than 5 days/week or give as 20-25 mg/kg/dose twice weekly

Dosing interval in renal impairment:
Cl$_{cr}$ 10-50 mL/minute: Administer every 24-72 hours
(Continued)

Streptomycin *(Continued)*

Cl$_{cr}$ <10 mL/minute: Administer every 72-96 hours

Removed by hemo- and peritoneal dialysis: Administer dose postdialysis

Administration Inject deep I.M. into large muscle mass; I.V. administration is not recommended; has been administered intravenously over 30-60 minutes.

Monitoring Parameters Hearing (audiogram), BUN, creatinine; serum concentration of the drug should be monitored in all patients; eighth cranial nerve damage is usually preceded by high-pitched tinnitus, roaring noises, sense of fullness in ears, or impaired hearing and may persist for weeks after drug is discontinued

Reference Range Therapeutic: Peak: 20-30 mcg/mL; Trough: <5 mcg/mL; Toxic: Peak: >50 mcg/mL; Trough: >10 mcg/mL

Test Interactions False-positive urine glucose with Benedict's solution or Clinitest®; penicillin may decrease aminoglycoside serum concentrations *in vitro*

Dosage Forms Injection, powder for reconstitution: 1 g

♦ **Streptomycin Sulfate** *see* Streptomycin *on page 1602*
♦ **Striant®** *see* Testosterone *on page 1653*
♦ **Strifon Forte® (Can)** *see* Chlorzoxazone *on page 359*
♦ **Stromectol®** *see* Ivermectin *on page 955*
♦ **Strong Iodine Solution** *see* Potassium Iodide and Iodine *on page 1401*
♦ **Strontium-89 Chloride** *see* Strontium-89 *on page 1604*

Strontium-89 *(STRON shee um atey nine)*

U.S. Brand Names Metastron®
Canadian Brand Names Metastron®
Index Terms Strontium-89 Chloride
Pharmacologic Category Radiopharmaceutical
Use Relief of bone pain in patients with skeletal metastases
Pregnancy Risk Factor D
Contraindications Hypersensitivity to any strontium-containing compounds or any other component of the formulation; pregnancy; breast-feeding
Warnings/Precautions Use caution in patients with bone marrow compromise; incontinent patients may require urinary catheterization. Body fluids may remain radioactive up to one week after injection. Not indicated for use in patients with cancer not involving bone and should be used with caution in patients whose platelet counts fall <60,000 or whose white blood cell counts fall <2400. A small number of patients have experienced a transient increase in bone pain at 36-72 hours postdose; this reaction is generally mild and self-limiting. It should be handled cautiously, in a similar manner to other radioactive drugs. Appropriate safety measures to minimize radiation to personnel should be instituted.
Adverse Reactions Most severe reactions of marrow toxicity can be managed by conventional means

Frequency not defined:
  Cardiovascular: Flushing (most common after rapid injection)
  Central nervous system: Fever and chills (rare)
  Hematologic: Thrombocytopenia, leukopenia
  Neuromuscular & skeletal: Increase in bone pain may occur (10% to 20% of patients)

Stability Store vial and its contents inside its transportation container at room temperature.
Dosage Adults: I.V.: 148 megabecquerel (4 millicurie) administered by slow I.V. injection over 1-2 minutes or 1.5-2.2 megabecquerel (40-60 microcurie)/kg; repeated doses are generally not recommended at intervals <90 days; measure the patient dose by a suitable radioactivity calibration system immediately prior to administration
Monitoring Parameters Routine blood tests
Additional Information During the first week after injection, strontium-89 will be present in the blood and urine, therefore, the following common sense precautions should be instituted:
1. Where a normal toilet is available, use in preference to a urinal, flush the toilet twice
2. Wipe away any spilled urine with a tissue and flush it away
3. Have patient wash hands after using the toilet
4. Immediately wash any linen or clothes that become stained with blood or urine
5. Wash away any spilled blood if a cut occurs

Dosage Forms Injection, solution, as chloride [preservative free]: 10.9-22.6 mg/mL [148 megabecquerel, 4 millicurie] (10 mL)

♦ **SU11248** *see* Sunitinib *on page 1622*
♦ **Suberoylanilide Hydroxamic Acid** *see* Vorinostat *on page 1799*
♦ **Sublimaze®** *see* Fentanyl *on page 693*
♦ **Suboxone®** *see* Buprenorphine and Naloxone *on page 252*
♦ **Subutex®** *see* Buprenorphine *on page 250*

Succimer *(SUKS si mer)*

U.S. Brand Names Chemet®
Canadian Brand Names Chemet®
Index Terms DMSA
Pharmacologic Category Antidote
Additional Appendix Information
Management of Overdosages *on page 2075*
Use Orphan drug: Treatment of lead poisoning in children with blood levels >45 mcg/dL. It is not indicated for prophylaxis of lead poisoning in a lead-containing environment. Following oral administration, succimer is generally well tolerated and produces a linear dose-dependent reduction in serum lead concentrations. This agent appears to offer advantages over existing lead chelating agents.

Pregnancy Risk Factor C

Contraindications Hypersensitivity to succimer or any component of the formulation

Warnings/Precautions Caution in patients with renal or hepatic impairment; adequate hydration should be maintained during therapy

Adverse Reactions

>10%:

Central nervous system: Fever

Gastrointestinal: Nausea, vomiting, diarrhea, appetite loss, hemorrhoidal symptoms, metallic taste

Neuromuscular & skeletal: Back pain

1% to 10%:

Central nervous system: Drowsiness, dizziness

Dermatologic: Rash

Endocrine & metabolic: Serum cholesterol increased

Gastrointestinal: Sore throat

Hepatic: Elevated AST/ALT, alkaline phosphatase

Respiratory: Nasal congestion, cough

Miscellaneous: Flu-like syndrome

<1% (Limited to important or life-threatening): Arrhythmias

Overdosage/Toxicology Symptoms include anorexia, vomiting, nephritis, hepatotoxicity, renal tubular necrosis, and GI bleeding.

Drug Interactions

Decreased Effect: Not recommended for concomitant administration with edetate calcium disodium or penicillamine.

Mechanism of Action Succimer is an analog of dimercaprol. It forms water soluble chelates with heavy metals which are subsequently excreted renally. Initial data have shown encouraging results in the treatment of mercury and arsenic poisoning. Succimer binds heavy metals; however, the chemical form of these chelates is not known.

Pharmacodynamics/Kinetics

Absorption: Rapid but incomplete

Metabolism: Rapidly and extensively to mixed succimer cysteine disulfides

Half-life elimination: 2 days

Time to peak, serum: ~1-2 hours

Excretion: Urine (~25%) with peak urinary excretion between 2-4 hours (90% as mixed succimer-cysteine disulfide conjugates, 10% as unchanged drug); feces (as unabsorbed drug)

Dosage Children and Adults: Oral: 10 mg/kg/dose every 8 hours for 5 days followed by 10 mg/kg/dose every 12 hours for 14 days

Dosing adjustment in renal/hepatic impairment: Administer with caution and monitor closely

Concomitant iron therapy has been reported in a small number of children without the formation of a toxic complex with iron (as seen with dimercaprol); courses of therapy may be repeated if indicated by weekly monitoring of blood lead levels; lead levels should be stabilized <15 mcg/dL; 2 weeks between courses is recommended unless more timely treatment is indicated by lead levels

Monitoring Parameters Blood lead levels, serum aminotransferases

Test Interactions False-positive ketones (U) using nitroprusside methods, falsely elevated serum CPK; falsely decreased uric acid measurement

Dosage Forms Capsule: 100 mg

Succinylcholine (suks in il KOE leen)

U.S. Brand Names Quelicin®

Canadian Brand Names Quelicin®

Index Terms Succinylcholine Chloride; Suxamethonium Chloride

Pharmacologic Category Neuromuscular Blocker Agent, Depolarizing

Additional Appendix Information

Neuromuscular Blocking Agents on page 1890

Use Adjunct to general anesthesia to facilitate both rapid sequence and routine endotracheal intubation and to relax skeletal muscles during surgery; to reduce the intensity of muscle contractions of pharmacologically- or electrically-induced convulsions; does not relieve pain or produce sedation

Pregnancy Risk Factor C

Lactation Excretion in breast milk unknown/use caution

Medication Safety Issues

High alert medication: The Institute for Safe Medication Practices (ISMP) includes this medication among its list of drugs which have a heightened risk of causing significant patient harm when used in error.

Contraindications Hypersensitivity to succinylcholine or any component of the formulation; personal or familial history of malignant hyperthermia; myopathies associated with elevated serum creatine phosphokinase (CPK) values; narrow-angle glaucoma, penetrating eye injuries; disorders of plasma pseudocholinesterase

Warnings/Precautions [U.S. Boxed Warning]: Use with caution in pediatrics and adolescents secondary to undiagnosed skeletal muscle myopathy and potential for ventricular dysrhythmias and cardiac arrest resulting from hyperkalemia; use with caution in patients with pre-existing hyperkalemia, paraplegia, extensive or severe burns, extensive denervation of skeletal muscle because of disease or injury to the CNS or with degenerative or dystrophic neuromuscular disease; may increase vagal tone

Adverse Reactions

>10%:

Ocular: Increased intraocular pressure

Miscellaneous: Postoperative stiffness

(Continued)

Succinylcholine *(Continued)*

1% to 10%:
Cardiovascular: Bradycardia, hypotension, cardiac arrhythmia, tachycardia
Gastrointestinal: Intragastric pressure, salivation

<1% (Limited to important or life-threatening): Acute quadriplegic myopathy syndrome (prolonged use), apnea, bronchospasm, circulatory collapse, erythema, hyperkalemia, hypertension, itching, malignant hyperthermia, myalgia, myoglobinuria, myositis ossificans (prolonged use), rash

Overdosage/Toxicology Symptoms include respiratory paralysis and cardiac arrest. Brady-arrhythmias can often be treated with atropine 0.1 mg (infants). Do not treat with anticholinesterase drugs (eg, neostigmine, physostigmine), since they may worsen toxicity by interfering with succinylcholine metabolism.

Drug Interactions
Increased Effect/Toxicity:

Increased toxicity: Anticholinesterase drugs (neostigmine, physostigmine, or pyridostigmine) in combination with succinylcholine can cause cardiorespiratory collapse; cyclophosphamide, oral contraceptives, lidocaine, thiotepa, pancuronium, lithium, magnesium salts, aprotinin, chloroquine, metoclopramide, terbutaline, and procaine enhance and prolong the effects of succinylcholine

Prolonged neuromuscular blockade: Inhaled anesthetics, local anesthetics, calcium channel blockers, antiarrhythmics (eg, quinidine or procainamide), antibiotics (eg, aminoglycosides, tetracyclines, vancomycin, clindamycin), immunosuppressants (eg, cyclosporine)

Stability
Refrigerate at 2°C to 8°C (36°F to 46°F); however, stable for ≤3 months unrefrigerated. Powder form does not require refrigeration.
Stability of parenteral admixture at refrigeration temperature (4°C) is 24 hours in D_5W or NS.

Mechanism of Action Acts similar to acetylcholine, produces depolarization of the motor endplate at the myoneural junction which causes sustained flaccid skeletal muscle paralysis produced by state of accommodation that developes in adjacent excitable muscle membranes

Pharmacodynamics/Kinetics
Onset of action: I.M.: 2-3 minutes; I.V.: Complete muscular relaxation: 30-60 seconds
Duration: I.M.: 10-30 minutes; I.V.: 4-6 minutes with single administration
Metabolism: Rapidly hydrolyzed by plasma pseudocholinesterase

Dosage I.M., I.V.: Dose to effect; doses will vary due to interpatient variability; use ideal body weight for obese patients
I.M.: 2.5-4 mg/kg, total dose should not exceed 150 mg
I.V.:
Children: Initial: 1-2 mg/kg; maintenance: 0.3-0.6 mg/kg every 5-10 minutes as needed; because of the risk of malignant hyperthermia, use of continuous infusions is not recommended in infants and children
Adults: 1-1.5 mg/kg, up to 150 mg total dose
Maintenance: 0.04-0.07 mg/kg every 5-10 minutes as needed
Continuous infusion: 10-100 mcg/kg/minute (or 0.5-10 mg/minute); dilute to concentration of 1-2 mg/mL in D_5W or NS

Note: Initial dose of succinylcholine must be increased when nondepolarizing agent pretreatment used because of the antagonism between succinylcholine and nondepolarizing neuromuscular blocking agents

Dosing adjustment in hepatic impairment: Dose should be decreased in patients with severe liver disease

Administration May be administered by rapid I.V. injection without further dilution; I.M. injections should be made deeply, preferably high into deltoid muscle

Monitoring Parameters Cardiac monitor, blood pressure monitor, and ventilator required during administration; temperature, serum potassium and calcium, assisted ventilator status

Test Interactions Increased potassium (S)

Dosage Forms Injection, solution, as chloride: 20 mg/mL (5 mL, 10 mL); 50 mg/mL (10 mL); 100 mg/mL (10 mL)

♦ **Succinylcholine Chloride** *see* Succinylcholine *on page 1605*
♦ **Sucraid®** *see* Sacrosidase *on page 1542*

Sucralfate *(soo KRAL fate)*

U.S. Brand Names Carafate®
Canadian Brand Names Novo-Sucralate; Nu-Sucralate; PMS-Sucralate; Sulcrate®; Sulcrate® Suspension Plus
Index Terms Aluminum Sucrose Sulfate, Basic
Pharmacologic Category Gastrointestinal Agent, Miscellaneous
Use Short-term management of duodenal ulcers; maintenance of duodenal ulcers
Unlabeled/Investigational Use Gastric ulcers; suspension may be used topically for treatment of stomatitis due to cancer chemotherapy and other causes of esophageal and gastric erosions; GERD, esophagitis; treatment of NSAID mucosal damage; prevention of stress ulcers; postsclerotherapy for esophageal variceal bleeding
Pregnancy Risk Factor B
Pregnancy Implications No data available; available evidence suggests safe use during pregnancy.
Lactation Enters breast milk/compatible
Medication Safety Issues
Sound-alike/look-alike issues:
Sucralfate may be confused with salsalate

Carafate® may be confused with Cafergot®

Contraindications Hypersensitivity to sucralfate or any component of the formulation

Warnings/Precautions Successful therapy with sucralfate should not be expected to alter the posthealing frequency of recurrence or the severity of duodenal ulceration; use with caution in patients with chronic renal failure who have an impaired excretion of absorbed aluminum. Because of the potential for sucralfate to alter the absorption of some drugs, separate administration (take other medication 2 hours before sucralfate) should be considered when alterations in bioavailability are believed to be critical

Adverse Reactions

1% to 10%: Gastrointestinal: Constipation

<1% (Limited to important or life-threatening): Bezoar formation, hypersensitivity (pruritus, urticaria, angioedema), rash

Overdosage/Toxicology Toxicity is minimal. May cause constipation.

Drug Interactions

Decreased Effect: Sucralfate may alter the absorption of digoxin, phenytoin (hydantoins), warfarin, ketoconazole, quinidine, quinolones, tetracycline, theophylline. Because of the potential for sucralfate to alter the absorption of some drugs; separate administration (take other medications at least 2 hours before sucralfate). The potential for decreased absorption should be considered when alterations in bioavailability are believed to be critical.

Ethanol/Nutrition/Herb Interactions Food: Sucralfate may interfere with absorption of vitamin A, vitamin D, vitamin E, and vitamin K.

Stability Suspension: Shake well. Refrigeration is **not** necessary; do **not** freeze.

Mechanism of Action Forms a complex by binding with positively charged proteins in exudates, forming a viscous paste-like, adhesive substance. This selectively forms a protective coating that protects the lining against peptic acid, pepsin, and bile salts.

Pharmacodynamics/Kinetics

Onset of action: Paste formation and ulcer adhesion: 1-2 hours

Duration: Up to 6 hours

Absorption: Oral: <5%

Distribution: Acts locally at ulcer sites; unbound in GI tract to aluminum and sucrose octasulfate

Metabolism: None

Excretion: Urine (small amounts as unchanged compounds)

Dosage Oral:

Children: Dose not established, doses of 40-80 mg/kg/day divided every 6 hours have been used

Stomatitis (unlabeled use): 2.5-5 mL (1 g/10 mL suspension), swish and spit or swish and swallow 4 times/day

Adults:

Stress ulcer prophylaxis: 1 g 4 times/day

Stress ulcer treatment: 1 g every 4 hours

Duodenal ulcer:

Treatment: 1 g 4 times/day on an empty stomach and at bedtime for 4-8 weeks, or alternatively 2 g twice daily; treatment is recommended for 4-8 weeks in adults, the elderly may require 12 weeks

Maintenance: Prophylaxis: 1 g twice daily

Stomatitis (unlabeled use): 1 g/10 mL suspension, swish and spit or swish and swallow 4 times/day

Dosage comment in renal impairment: Aluminum salt is minimally absorbed (<5%), however, may accumulate in renal failure

Dietary Considerations Administer with water on an empty stomach.

Administration Tablet may be broken or dissolved in water before ingestion. Administer with water on an empty stomach.

Dosage Forms

Suspension, oral: 1 g/10 mL (10 mL)

Carafate®: 1 g/10 mL (420 mL)

Tablet: 1 g

Carafate®: 1 g

♦ **Sucrets®** [OTC] *see* Dyclonine *on page 565*

♦ **Sudafed® 12 Hour** [OTC] *see* Pseudoephedrine *on page 1454*

♦ **Sudafed® 24 Hour** [OTC] *see* Pseudoephedrine *on page 1454*

♦ **Sudafed® Children's** [OTC] *see* Pseudoephedrine *on page 1454*

♦ **Sudafed® Children's Cold & Cough** [OTC] *see* Pseudoephedrine and Dextromethorphan *on page 1455*

♦ **Sudafed® Cold & Cough Extra Strength (Can)** *see* Acetaminophen, Dextromethorphan, and Pseudoephedrine *on page 35*

♦ **Sudafed® Decongestant (Can)** *see* Pseudoephedrine *on page 1454*

♦ **Sudafed® Head Cold and Sinus Extra Strength (Can)** *see* Acetaminophen and Pseudoephedrine *on page 33*

♦ **Sudafed® Maximum Strength Nasal Decongestant** [OTC] *see* Pseudoephedrine *on page 1454*

♦ **Sudafed® Maximum Strength Sinus Nighttime** [OTC] [DSC] *see* Triprolidine and Pseudoephedrine *on page 1749*

♦ **Sudafed® Multi-Symptom Sinus and Cold** [OTC] *see* Acetaminophen and Pseudoephedrine *on page 33*

♦ **Sudafed® Non-Drying Sinus** [OTC] [DSC] *see* Guaifenesin and Pseudoephedrine *on page 819*

♦ **Sudafed PE™** [OTC] *see* Phenylephrine *on page 1358*

♦ **Sudafed® Severe Cold** [OTC] *see* Acetaminophen, Dextromethorphan, and Pseudoephedrine *on page 35*

♦ **Sudafed® Sinus Advance (Can)** *see* Pseudoephedrine and Ibuprofen *on page 1456*

♦ **Sudafed® Sinus & Allergy [OTC]** *see* Chlorpheniramine and Pseudoephedrine *on page 350*

♦ **Sudal® 12** *see* Chlorpheniramine and Pseudoephedrine *on page 350*

♦ **Sudodrin [OTC]** *see* Pseudoephedrine *on page 1454*

♦ **SudoGest [OTC]** *see* Pseudoephedrine *on page 1454*

♦ **SudoGest Children's [OTC]** *see* Pseudoephedrine and Dextromethorphan *on page 1455*

♦ **Sudo-Tab® [OTC]** *see* Pseudoephedrine *on page 1454*

♦ **Sufenta®** *see* Sufentanil *on page 1608*

Sufentanil (soo FEN ta nil)

U.S. Brand Names Sufenta®
Canadian Brand Names Sufenta®; Sufentanil Citrate Injection, USP
Index Terms Sufentanil Citrate
Pharmacologic Category Analgesic, Opioid; General Anesthetic
Additional Appendix Information
Narcotic Agonists *on page 1888*
Use Analgesic supplement in maintenance of balanced general anesthesia
Restrictions C-II
Pregnancy Risk Factor C
Medication Safety Issues
Sound-alike/look-alike issues:
Sufentanil may be confused with alfentanil, fentanyl
Sufenta® may be confused with Alfenta®, Sudafed®, Survanta®
Contraindications Hypersensitivity to sufentanil or any component of the formulation
Warnings/Precautions Sufentanil can cause severely compromised respiratory depression; use with caution in patients with head injuries, morbid obesity, hepatic or renal impairment or with pulmonary disease; sufentanil shares the toxic potential of opiate agonists, precaution of opiate agonist therapy should be observed; rapid I.V. infusion may result in skeletal muscle and chest wall rigidity, impaired ventilation, respiratory distress/arrest; inject slowly over 3-5 minutes; nondepolarizing skeletal muscle relaxant may be required. Should be administered by trained individuals.
Adverse Reactions
>10%:
Cardiovascular: Bradycardia, hypotension
Central nervous system: Somnolence
Gastrointestinal: Nausea, vomiting
Respiratory: Respiratory depression
1% to 10%:
Cardiovascular: Cardiac arrhythmia, orthostatic hypotension
Central nervous system: CNS depression, confusion
Gastrointestinal: Biliary spasm
Ocular: Blurred vision
<1% (Limited to important or life-threatening): Bronchospasm, circulatory depression, convulsions, laryngospasm, mental depression, paradoxical CNS excitation or delirium, physical and psychological dependence with prolonged use, rash, urticaria
Overdosage/Toxicology Treatment consists of naloxone 2 mg I.V. (0.01 mg/kg for children), with repeat administration as necessary, up to a total of 10 mg. Supportive care includes establishment of respiratory change. Naloxone may be used to treat respiratory depression. Muscular rigidity may also respond to opiate antagonist therapy or to neuromuscular blocking agents.
Drug Interactions
Cytochrome P450 Effect: Substrate of CYP3A4 (major)
Increased Effect/Toxicity: Additive effect/toxicity with CNS depressants or beta-blockers. May increase response to neuromuscular-blocking agents. CYP3A4 inhibitors may increase the levels/effects of sufentanil; example inhibitors include azole antifungals, clarithromycin, diclofenac, doxycycline, erythromycin, imatinib, isoniazid, nefazodone, nicardipine, propofol, protease inhibitors, quinidine, telithromycin, and verapamil.
Mechanism of Action Binds to opioid receptors throughout the CNS. Once receptor binding occurs, effects are exerted by opening K+ channels and inhibiting Ca++ channels. These mechanisms increase pain threshold, alter pain perception, inhibit ascending pain pathways; short-acting narcotic
Pharmacodynamics/Kinetics
Onset of action: 1-3 minutes
Duration: Dose dependent
Metabolism: Primarily hepatic
Dosage
Children 2-12 years: 10-25 mcg/kg (10-15 mcg/kg most common dose) with 100% O_2, maintenance: up to 1-2 mcg/kg total dose
Adults: Dose should be based on body weight. **Note:** In obese patients (ie, >20% above ideal body weight), use lean body weight to determine dosage.
1-2 mcg/kg with N_2O/O_2 for endotracheal intubation; maintenance: 10-25 mcg as needed
2-8 mcg/kg with N_2O/O_2 more complicated major surgical procedures; maintenance: 10-50 mcg as needed
8-30 mcg/kg with 100% O_2 and muscle relaxant produces sleep; at doses ≥8 mcg/kg maintains a deep level of anesthesia; maintenance: 10-50 mcg as needed
Administration Parenteral: I.V.: Slow I.V. injection or by infusion
Additional Information Short-acting narcotic; sufentanil is 5-10 times more potent than fentanyl. Sufentanil is packaged in the same concentration as fentanyl, 50 mcg/mL. Keep in mind the differences in potency to prevent overdose with sufentanil. May choose to dilute sufentanil to decrease concentration; this will decrease the potential for administering excessive doses.
Dosage Forms Injection, solution [preservative free]: 50 mcg/mL (1 mL, 2 mL, 5 mL)

♦ **Sufentanil Citrate** *see* Sufentanil *on page 1608*
♦ **Sufentanil Citrate Injection, USP (Can)** *see* Sufentanil *on page 1608*
♦ **Sular®** *see* Nisoldipine *on page 1231*
♦ **Sulbactam and Ampicillin** *see* Ampicillin and Sulbactam *on page 124*

Sulconazole (sul KON a zole)

U.S. Brand Names Exelderm®
Canadian Brand Names Exelderm®
Index Terms Sulconazole Nitrate
Pharmacologic Category Antifungal Agent, Topical
Use Treatment of superficial fungal infections of the skin, including tinea cruris (jock itch), tinea corporis (ringworm), tinea versicolor, and possibly tinea pedis (athlete's foot, cream only)
Pregnancy Risk Factor C
Dosage Adults: Topical: Apply a small amount to the affected area and gently massage once or twice daily for 3 weeks (tinea cruris, tinea corporis, tinea versicolor) to 4 weeks (tinea pedis).
Dosage Forms
Cream, as nitrate: 1% (15 g, 30 g, 60 g)
Solution, topical, as nitrate: 1% (30 mL)

♦ **Sulconazole Nitrate** *see* Sulconazole *on page 1609*
♦ **Sulcrate® (Can)** *see* Sucralfate *on page 1606*
♦ **Sulcrate® Suspension Plus (Can)** *see* Sucralfate *on page 1606*

Sulfacetamide (sul fa SEE ta mide)

U.S. Brand Names Bleph®-10; Carmol® Scalp; Klaron®; Mexar™ Wash; Ovace®; Ovace® Wash; Rosula® NS
Canadian Brand Names Cetamide™; Diosulf™
Index Terms Sodium Sulfacetamide; Sulfacetamide Sodium
Pharmacologic Category Acne Products; Antibiotic, Ophthalmic; Antibiotic, Sulfonamide Derivative; Topical Skin Product, Acne
Additional Appendix Information
Sulfonamide Derivatives *on page 1897*
Use
Ophthalmic: Treatment and prophylaxis of conjunctivitis due to susceptible organisms; corneal ulcers; adjunctive treatment with systemic sulfonamides for therapy of trachoma
Dermatologic: Scaling dermatosis (seborrheic); bacterial infections of the skin; acne vulgaris
Pregnancy Risk Factor C
Medication Safety Issues
Sound-alike/look-alike issues:
Bleph®-10 may be confused with Blephamide®
Klaron® may be confused with Klor-Con®
Dosage
Children >2 months and Adults: Ophthalmic:
Ointment: Apply to lower conjunctival sac 1-4 times/day and at bedtime
Solution: Instill 1-2 drops several times daily up to every 2-3 hours in lower conjunctival sac during waking hours and less frequently at night; increase dosing interval as condition responds. Usual duration of treatment: 7-10 days
Trachoma: Instill 2 drops into the conjunctival sac every 2 hours; must be used in conjunction with systemic therapy
Children >12 years and Adults: Topical:
Acne: Apply thin film to affected area twice daily
Seborrheic dermatitis: Apply at bedtime and allow to remain overnight; in severe cases, may apply twice daily. Duration of therapy is usually 8-10 applications; dosing interval may be increased as eruption subsides. Applications once or twice weekly, or every other week may be used to prevent eruptions.
Secondary cutaneous bacterial infections: Apply 2-4 times/day until infection clears
Dosage Forms
Cream, topical, as sodium:
Ovace®: 10% (30 g, 60 g)
Foam, topical, as sodium:
Ovace®: 10% (50 g, 100 g)
Gel, topical, as sodium:
Ovace®: 10% (30 g, 60 g)
Lotion, as sodium:
Carmol® Scalp: 10% (85 g) [contains urea 10%]
Klaron®: 10% (120 mL) [contains sodium metabisulfite]
Mexar™ Wash: 10% (170 mL)
Ovace® Wash: 10% (180 mL, 360 mL)
Ointment, ophthalmic, as sodium: 10% (3.5 g)
Pad: topical:
Rosula® NS: 10% (30s) [contains urea 10%]
Solution, ophthalmic, as sodium: 10% (15 mL)
Bleph®-10: 10% (5 mL) [contains benzalkonium chloride]
Suspension, topical: 10% (118 mL)

Sulfacetamide and Prednisolone (sul fa SEE ta mide & pred NIS oh lone)

U.S. Brand Names Blephamide®
Canadian Brand Names Blephamide®; Dioptimyd®
Index Terms Prednisolone and Sulfacetamide
Pharmacologic Category Antibiotic/Corticosteroid, Ophthalmic
Use Steroid-responsive inflammatory ocular conditions where infection is present or there is a risk of infection; ophthalmic suspension may be used as an otic preparation
Pregnancy Risk Factor C
Medication Safety Issues
Sound-alike/look-alike issues:
Blephamide® may be confused with Bleph®-10
Vasocidin® may be confused with Vasodilan®
Dosage Children >2 months and Adults: Ophthalmic:
Ointment: Apply to lower conjunctival sac 1-4 times/day
Solution, suspension: Instill 1-3 drops every 2-3 hours while awake
Additional Information Complete prescribing information for this medication should be consulted for additional detail.
Dosage Forms
Ointment, ophthalmic (Blephamide®): Sulfacetamide sodium 10% and prednisolone acetate 0.2% (3.5 g)
Solution, ophthalmic: Sulfacetamide sodium 10% and prednisolone sodium phosphate 0.25% (5 mL, 10 mL)
Suspension, ophthalmic (Blephamide®): Sulfacetamide sodium 10% and prednisolone acetate 0.2% (5 mL, 10 mL) [contains benzalkonium chloride]

♦ **Sulfacetamide and Sulfur** see Sulfur and Sulfacetamide on page 1618
♦ **Sulfacetamide Sodium** see Sulfacetamide on page 1609

Sulfacetamide Sodium and Fluorometholone
(sul fa SEE ta mide SOW dee um & flure oh METH oh lone)

U.S. Brand Names FML-S®
Index Terms Fluorometholone and Sulfacetamide
Pharmacologic Category Antibiotic/Corticosteroid, Ophthalmic
Use Steroid-responsive inflammatory ocular conditions where infection is present or there is a risk of infection
Pregnancy Risk Factor C
Dosage Ophthalmic: Children >2 years and Adults: Instill 1 drop into affected eye(s) 4 times/day
Note: Dose may be decreased but should not be discontinued prematurely; re-evaluation should occur if improvement is not seen within 2 days; in chronic conditions, dosing frequency should be gradually decreased prior to discontinuing treatment
Additional Information Complete prescribing information for this medication should be consulted for additional detail.
Dosage Forms Suspension, ophthalmic: Sulfacetamide sodium 10% and fluorometholone 0.1% (5 mL, 10 mL) [contains benzalkonium chloride]

♦ **Sulfacet-R® [DSC]** see Sulfur and Sulfacetamide on page 1618
♦ **Sulfacet-R® (Can)** see Sulfur and Sulfacetamide on page 1618

SulfaDIAZINE (sul fa DYE a zeen)

Pharmacologic Category Antibiotic, Sulfonamide Derivative
Additional Appendix Information
Sulfonamide Derivatives on page 1897
USPHS / IDSA Guidelines for the Prevention of Opportunistic Infections in Persons Infected With HIV on page 1966
Use Treatment of urinary tract infections and nocardiosis; adjunctive treatment in toxoplasmosis; uncomplicated attack of malaria
Unlabeled/Investigational Use Rheumatic fever prophylaxis
Pregnancy Risk Factor B/D (at term)
Lactation Enters breast milk/contraindicated
Medication Safety Issues
Sound-alike/look-alike issues:
SulfaDIAZINE may be confused with sulfasalazine, sulfiSOXAZOLE
Contraindications Hypersensitivity to any sulfa drug or any component of the formulation; porphyria; children <2 months of age unless indicated for the treatment of congenital toxoplasmosis; sunscreens containing PABA; pregnancy (at term)
Warnings/Precautions Use with caution in patients with impaired hepatic function or impaired renal function, G6PD deficiency; dosage modification required in patients with renal impairment; fluid intake should be maintained ≥1500 mL/day, or administer sodium bicarbonate to keep urine alkaline; more likely to cause crystalluria because it is less soluble than other sulfonamides. Chemical similarities are present among sulfonamides, sulfonylureas, carbonic anhydrase inhibitors, thiazides, and loop diuretics (except ethacrynic acid). Use in patients with sulfonamide allergy is specifically contraindicated in product labeling, however, a risk of cross-reaction exists in patients with allergy to any of these compounds; avoid use when previous reaction has been severe.
Adverse Reactions Frequency not defined.
Central nervous system: Fever, dizziness, headache
Dermatologic: Lyell's syndrome, Stevens-Johnson syndrome, itching, rash, photosensitivity
Endocrine & metabolic: Thyroid function disturbance

Gastrointestinal: Anorexia, nausea, vomiting, diarrhea

Genitourinary: Crystalluria

Hematologic: Granulocytopenia, leukopenia, thrombocytopenia, aplastic anemia, hemolytic anemia

Hepatic: Hepatitis, jaundice

Renal: Hematuria, acute nephropathy, interstitial nephritis

Miscellaneous: Serum sickness-like reactions

Overdosage/Toxicology Symptoms include drowsiness, dizziness, anorexia, abdominal pain, nausea, vomiting, hemolytic anemia, acidosis, jaundice, fever, and agranulocytosis. Doses of as little as 2-6 g/day in divided doses every 6 hours may produce toxicity. The aniline radical is responsible for hematologic toxicity. High volume diuresis may aid in elimination and prevention of renal failure.

Drug Interactions

Cytochrome P450 Effect: Substrate of CYP2C9 (major), 2E1 (minor), 3A4 (minor); **Inhibits** CYP2C9 (strong)

Increased Effect/Toxicity: Increased effect of oral anticoagulants and oral hypoglycemic agents. Sulfadiazine may increase the levels/effects of CYP2C9 substrates; example substrates include bosentan, dapsone, fluoxetine, glimepiride, glipizide, losartan, montelukast, nateglinide, paclitaxel, phenytoin, warfarin, and zafirlukast

Decreased Effect: The levels/effects of sulfadiazine may be decreased by carbamazepine, phenobarbital, phenytoin, rifampin, rifapentine, secobarbital, and other CYP2C9 inducers. Decreased effect with PABA or PABA metabolites of drugs (eg, procaine, proparacaine, tetracaine, sunblock).

Ethanol/Nutrition/Herb Interactions

Food: Avoid large quantities of vitamin C or acidifying agents (cranberry juice) to prevent crystalluria.

Herb/Nutraceutical: Avoid dong quai, St John's wort (may also cause photosensitization).

Stability Tablets may be crushed to prepare oral suspension of the drug in water or with a sucrose-containing solution. Aqueous suspension with concentrations of 100 mg/mL should be stored in the refrigerator and used within 7 days.

Mechanism of Action Interferes with bacterial growth by inhibiting bacterial folic acid synthesis through competitive antagonism of PABA

Pharmacodynamics/Kinetics

Absorption: Well absorbed

Distribution: Throughout body tissues and fluids including pleural, peritoneal, synovial, and ocular fluids; throughout total body water; readily diffused into CSF; enters breast milk

Metabolism: Via N-acetylation

Half-life elimination: 10 hours

Time to peak: Within 3-6 hours

Excretion: Urine (43% to 60% as unchanged drug, 15% to 40% as metabolites)

Dosage Oral:

Asymptomatic meningococcal carriers:

Infants 1-12 months: 500 mg once daily for 2 days

Children 1-12 years: 500 mg twice daily for 2 days

Adults: 1 g twice daily for 2 days

Congenital toxoplasmosis:

Newborns and Children <2 months: 100 mg/kg/day divided every 6 hours in conjunction with pyrimethamine 1 mg/kg/day once daily and supplemental folinic acid 5 mg every 3 days for 6 months

Children >2 months: 25-50 mg/kg/dose 4 times/day

Nocardiosis: 4-8 g/day for a minimum of 6 weeks

Toxoplasmosis:

Children >2 months: Loading dose: 75 mg/kg; maintenance dose: 120-150 mg/kg/day, maximum dose: 6 g/day; divided every 4-6 hours in conjunction with pyrimethamine 2 mg/kg/day divided every 12 hours for 3 days followed by 1 mg/kg/day once daily with supplemental folinic acid

Adults: 2-6 g/day in divided doses every 6 hours in conjunction with pyrimethamine 50-75 mg/day and with supplemental folinic acid

Prevention of recurrent attacks of rheumatic fever (unlabeled use):

>30 kg: 1 g/day

<30 kg: 0.5 g/day

Dietary Considerations Supplemental folinic acid should be administered to reverse symptoms or prevent problems due to folic acid deficiency.

Administration Tablets may be crushed to prepare oral suspension of the drug in water or with a sucrose-containing solution. Aqueous suspension with concentrations of 100 mg/mL should be stored in the refrigerator and used within 7 days. Administer around-the-clock to promote less variation in peak and trough serum levels.

Dosage Forms Tablet: 500 mg

Sulfadoxine and Pyrimethamine (sul fa DOKS een & peer i METH a meen)

U.S. Brand Names Fansidar®

Index Terms Pyrimethamine and Sulfadoxine

Pharmacologic Category Antimalarial Agent

Use Treatment of *Plasmodium falciparum* malaria in patients in whom chloroquine resistance is suspected; malaria prophylaxis for travelers to areas where chloroquine-resistant malaria is endemic

Pregnancy Risk Factor C/D (at term)

Contraindications Hypersensitivity to any sulfa drug, pyrimethamine, or any component of the formulation; porphyria, megaloblastic anemia; repeated prophylactic use is contraindicated in patients with renal failure, hepatic failure, or blood dyscrasias; children <2 months of age due to competition with bilirubin for protein binding sites; pregnancy (at term)

(Continued)

Sulfadoxine and Pyrimethamine *(Continued)*

Warnings/Precautions [U.S. Boxed Warning]: Fatalities have occurred due to severe reactions including Stevens-Johnson syndrome and toxic epidermal necrolysis. Discontinue use at first sign of rash, myelosuppression or active bacterial/fungal infection; fatalities associated with sulfonamides, although rare, have occurred due to hepatic necrosis, agranulocytosis, aplastic anemia and other blood dyscrasias; hemolysis occurs in patients with G6PD deficiency; leucovorin should be administered to reverse signs and symptoms of folic acid deficiency. Use with caution in patients with renal or hepatic impairment, patients with possible folate deficiency, and patients with seizure disorders, increased adverse reactions are seen in patients also receiving chloroquine. May cause photosensitivity.

Chemical similarities are present among sulfonamides, sulfonylureas, carbonic anhydrase inhibitors, thiazides, and loop diuretics (except ethacrynic acid). Use in patients with sulfonamide allergy is specifically contraindicated in product labeling, however, a risk of cross-reaction exists in patients with allergy to any of these compounds; avoid use when previous reaction has been severe.

Adverse Reactions Frequency not defined.
Cardiovascular: Myocarditis (allergic), pericarditis (allergic), periorbital edema
Central nervous system: Ataxia, hallucinations, headache, polyneuritis, seizure
Dermatologic: Photosensitivity, Stevens-Johnson syndrome, erythema multiforme, toxic epidermal necrolysis, rash
Endocrine & metabolic: Thyroid function dysfunction
Gastrointestinal: Anorexia, atrophic glossitis, gastritis, pancreatitis, vomiting
Genitourinary: Crystalluria
Hematologic: Megaloblastic anemia, leukopenia, thrombocytopenia, pancytopenia
Hepatic: Hepatic necrosis, hepatitis
Neuromuscular & skeletal: Tremors
Renal: BUN increased, interstitial nephritis, renal failure, serum creatinine increased
Respiratory: Respiratory failure, alveolitis (resembling eosinophilic or allergic)
Miscellaneous: Anaphylactoid reaction, drug fever, hypersensitivity, Lupus-like syndrome, periarteritis nodosum

Overdosage/Toxicology Symptoms include anorexia, vomiting, CNS stimulation including seizures, megaloblastic anemia, leukopenia, thrombocytopenia, and crystalluria. Leucovorin should be administered in a dosage of 3-9 mg/day for 3 days or as required to reverse symptoms of folic acid deficiency. Doses of as little as 2-5 g/day may produce toxicity. The aniline radical is responsible for hematologic toxicity. High volume diuresis may aid in elimination and prevention of renal failure. Diazepam can be used to control seizures.

Drug Interactions
Cytochrome P450 Effect: Pyrimethamine: **Inhibits** CYP2C8/9 (moderate), 2D6 (moderate)
Increased Effect/Toxicity: Effect of oral hypoglycemics (rare, but severe) may occur. Combination with methenamine may result in crystalluria; avoid use. May increase methotrexate-induced bone marrow suppression. NSAIDs and salicylates may increase sulfonamide concentrations. Pyrimethamine may increase the levels/effects of amiodarone, amphetamines, selected beta-blockers, dextromethorphan, fluoxetine, glimepiride, glipizide, lidocaine, mirtazapine, nateglinide, nefazodone, paroxetine, phenytoin, pioglitazone, risperidone, ritonavir, rosiglitazone, sertraline, thioridazine, tricyclic antidepressants, venlafaxine, warfarin, and other CYP2C8/9 and 2D6 substrates.
Decreased Effect: Cyclosporine concentrations may be decreased; monitor levels and renal function. PABA (para-aminobenzoic acid - may be found in some vitamin supplements): interferes with the antibacterial activity of sulfonamides; avoid concurrent use. Pyrimethamine may decrease the levels/effects of CYP2D6 prodrug substrates (eg, codeine, hydrocodone, oxycodone, tramadol).

Stability Protect from light.

Mechanism of Action Sulfadoxine interferes with bacterial folic acid synthesis and growth via competitive inhibition of para-aminiobenzoic acid; pyrimethamine inhibits microbial dihydrofolate reductase, resulting in inhibition of tetrahydrofolic acid synthesis

Pharmacodynamics/Kinetics
Absorption: Well absorbed
Distribution: Sulfadoxine: Well distributed like other sulfonamides; Pyrimethamine: Widely distributed, mainly in blood cells, kidneys, lungs, liver, and spleen
Metabolism: Pyrimethamine: Hepatic; Sulfadoxine: None
Half-life elimination: Pyrimethamine: 80-95 hours; Sulfadoxine: 5-8 days
Time to peak, serum: 2-8 hours
Excretion: Urine (as unchanged drug and several unidentified metabolites)

Dosage Children and Adults: Oral:
Treatment of acute attack of malaria: A single dose of the following number of Fansidar® tablets is used in sequence with quinine or alone:
2-11 months: 1/4 tablet
1-3 years: 1/2 tablet
4-8 years: 1 tablet
9-14 years: 2 tablets
>14 years: 3 tablets
Malaria prophylaxis: A single dose should be carried for self-treatment in the event of febrile illness when medical attention is not immediately available:
2-11 months: 1/4 tablet
1-3 years: 1/2 tablet
4-8 years: 1 tablet
9-14 years: 2 tablets
>14 years and Adults: 3 tablets

Monitoring Parameters CBC, including platelet counts, and urinalysis should be performed periodically

Dosage Forms Tablet: Sulfadoxine 500 mg and pyrimethamine 25 mg

Sulfamethoxazole and Trimethoprim
(sul fa meth OKS a zole & trye METH oh prim)

U.S. Brand Names Bactrim™; Bactrim™ DS; Septra®; Septra® DS

Canadian Brand Names Apo-Sulfatrim®; Apo-Sulfatrim® DS; Apo-Sulfatrim® Pediatric; Novo-Trimel; Novo-Trimel D.S.; Nu-Cotrimox; Septra® Injection

Index Terms Co-Trimoxazole; SMZ-TMP; Sulfatrim; TMP-SMZ; Trimethoprim and Sulfamethoxazole

Pharmacologic Category Antibiotic, Miscellaneous; Antibiotic, Sulfonamide Derivative

Additional Appendix Information
Animal and Human Bites *on page 1976*
Antimicrobial Drugs of Choice *on page 1981*
Desensitization Protocols *on page 1913*
USPHS / IDSA Guidelines for the Prevention of Opportunistic Infections in Persons Infected With HIV *on page 1966*

Use
Oral treatment of urinary tract infections due to *E. coli, Klebsiella* and *Enterobacter* sp, *M. morganii, P. mirabilis* and *P. vulgaris*; acute otitis media in children; acute exacerbations of chronic bronchitis in adults due to susceptible strains of *H. influenzae* or *S. pneumoniae*; treatment and prophylaxis of *Pneumocystis jiroveci* pneumonitis (PCP); traveler's diarrhea due to enterotoxigenic *E. coli*; treatment of enteritis caused by *Shigella flexneri* or *Shigella sonnei*

I.V. treatment or severe or complicated infections when oral therapy is not feasible, for documented PCP, empiric treatment of PCP in immune compromised patients; treatment of documented or suspected shigellosis, typhoid fever, *Nocardia asteroides* infection, or other infections caused by susceptible bacteria

Unlabeled/Investigational Use Cholera and *Salmonella*-type infections and nocardiosis; chronic prostatitis; as prophylaxis in neutropenic patients with *P. jiroveci* infections, in leukemics, and in patients following renal transplantation, to decrease incidence of PCP; treatment of *Cyclospora* infection, typhoid fever, *Nocardia asteroides* infection

Pregnancy Risk Factor C/D (at term - expert analysis)

Pregnancy Implications Do not use at term to avoid kernicterus in the newborn; use during pregnancy only if risks outweigh the benefits since folic acid metabolism may be affected.

Lactation Enters breast milk/contraindicated (AAP rates "compatible with restrictions")

Medication Safety Issues
Sound-alike/look-alike issues:
Bactrim™ may be confused with bacitracin, Bactine®
Co-trimoxazole may be confused with clotrimazole
Septra® may be confused with Ceptaz®, Sectral®, Septa®

Contraindications Hypersensitivity to any sulfa drug, trimethoprim, or any component of the formulation; porphyria; megaloblastic anemia due to folate deficiency; infants <2 months of age; marked hepatic damage; severe renal disease; pregnancy (at term)

Warnings/Precautions Use with caution in patients with G6PD deficiency, impaired renal or hepatic function or potential folate deficiency (malnourished, chronic anticonvulsant therapy, or elderly); maintain adequate hydration to prevent crystalluria; adjust dosage in patients with renal impairment. Injection vehicle contains benzyl alcohol and sodium metabisulfite.

Chemical similarities are present among sulfonamides, sulfonylureas, carbonic anhydrase inhibitors, thiazides, and loop diuretics (except ethacrynic acid). Use in patients with sulfonamide allergy is specifically contraindicated in product labeling, however, a risk of cross-reaction exists in patients with allergy to any of these compounds; avoid use when previous reaction has been severe.

Fatalities associated with severe reactions including Stevens-Johnson syndrome, toxic epidermal necrolysis, hepatic necrosis, agranulocytosis, aplastic anemia and other blood dyscrasias; discontinue use at first sign of rash. Elderly patients appear at greater risk for more severe adverse reactions. May cause hypoglycemia, particularly in malnourished, or patients with renal or hepatic impairment. Use with caution in patients with porphyria or thyroid dysfunction. Slow acetylators may be more prone to adverse reactions. Caution in patients with allergies or asthma. May cause hyperkalemia (associated with high doses of trimethoprim). Incidence of adverse effects appears to be increased in patients with AIDS.

Adverse Reactions The most common adverse reactions include gastrointestinal upset (nausea, vomiting, anorexia) and dermatologic reactions (rash or urticaria). Rare, life-threatening reactions have been associated with co-trimoxazole, including severe dermatologic reactions and hepatotoxic reactions. Most other reactions listed are rare, however, frequency cannot be accurately estimated.

Cardiovascular: Allergic myocarditis
Central nervous system: Confusion, depression, hallucinations, seizure, aseptic meningitis, peripheral neuritis, fever, ataxia, kernicterus in neonates
Dermatologic: Rashes, pruritus, urticaria, photosensitivity; rare reactions include erythema multiforme, Stevens-Johnson syndrome, toxic epidermal necrolysis, exfoliative dermatitis, and Henoch-Schönlein purpura
Endocrine & metabolic: Hyperkalemia (generally at high dosages), hypoglycemia
Gastrointestinal: Nausea, vomiting, anorexia, stomatitis, diarrhea, pseudomembranous colitis, pancreatitis
Hematologic: Thrombocytopenia, megaloblastic anemia, granulocytopenia, eosinophilia, pancytopenia, aplastic anemia, methemoglobinemia, hemolysis (with G6PD deficiency), agranulocytosis
Hepatic: Hepatotoxicity (including hepatitis, cholestasis, and hepatic necrosis), hyperbilirubinemia, transaminases increased
Neuromuscular & skeletal: Arthralgia, myalgia, rhabdomyolysis
Renal: Interstitial nephritis, crystalluria, renal failure, nephrotoxicity (in association with cyclosporine), diuresis
Respiratory: Cough, dyspnea, pulmonary infiltrates
(Continued)

Sulfamethoxazole and Trimethoprim *(Continued)*

Miscellaneous: Serum sickness, angioedema, periarteritis nodosa (rare), systemic lupus erythematosus (rare)

Overdosage/Toxicology Symptoms of acute overdose include nausea, vomiting, GI distress, hematuria, and crystalluria. Following GI decontamination, treatment is supportive. Adequate fluid intake is essential. Peritoneal dialysis is not effective and hemodialysis is only moderately effective in removing sulfamethoxazole and trimethoprim.

Drug Interactions

Cytochrome P450 Effect:

Sulfamethoxazole: **Substrate** of CYP2C9 (major), 3A4 (minor); **Inhibits** CYP2C9 (moderate)

Trimethoprim: **Substrate** (major) of CYP2C9, 3A4; **Inhibits** CYP2C8 (moderate), 2C9 (moderate)

Increased Effect/Toxicity: Sulfamethoxazole/trimethoprim may increase toxicity of methotrexate. Sulfamethoxazole/trimethoprim may increase the serum levels of procainamide. Concurrent therapy with pyrimethamine (in doses >25 mg/week) may increase the risk of megaloblastic anemia. Sulfamethoxazole/trimethoprim may increase the levels/effects of amiodarone, fluoxetine, glimepiride, glipizide, nateglinide, phenytoin, pioglitazone, rosiglitazone, sertraline, warfarin, and other CYP2C8 and 2C9 substrates.

ACE Inhibitors, angiotensin receptor antagonists, or potassium-sparing diuretics may increase the risk of hyperkalemia. Concurrent use with cyclosporine may result in an increased risk of nephrotoxicity when used with sulfamethoxazole/trimethoprim. Trimethoprim may increase the serum concentration of dapsone.

Decreased Effect: The levels/effects of sulfamethoxazole may be decreased by carbamazepine, phenobarbital, phenytoin, rifampin, rifapentine, secobarbital, and other CYP2C9 inducers. Although occasionally recommended to limit or reverse hematologic toxicity of high-dose sulfamethoxazole/trimethoprim, concurrent use has been associated with a decreased effectiveness in treating *Pneumocystis carinii*.

Ethanol/Nutrition/Herb Interactions Herb/Nutraceutical: Avoid dong quai, St John's wort (may also cause photosensitization).

Stability

Injection: Store at room temperature; do not refrigerate. Less soluble in more alkaline pH. Protect from light. Solution must be diluted prior to administration. Following dilution, store at room temperature; do not refrigerate. Manufacturer recommended dilutions and stability of parenteral admixture at room temperature (25°C):

5 mL/125 mL D_5W; stable for 6 hours.

5 mL/100 mL D_5W; stable for 4 hours.

5 mL/75 mL D_5W; stable for 2 hours.

Studies have also confirmed limited stability in NS; detailed references should be consulted.

Suspension, tablet: Store at room temperature. Protect from light.

Mechanism of Action Sulfamethoxazole interferes with bacterial folic acid synthesis and growth via inhibition of dihydrofolic acid formation from para-aminobenzoic acid; trimethoprim inhibits dihydrofolic acid reduction to tetrahydrofolate resulting in sequential inhibition of enzymes of the folic acid pathway

Pharmacodynamics/Kinetics

Absorption: Oral: Almost completely, 90% to 100%

Protein binding: SMX: 68%, TMP: 45%

Metabolism: SMX: N-acetylated and glucuronidated; TMP: Metabolized to oxide and hydroxylated metabolites

Half-life elimination: SMX: 9 hours, TMP: 6-17 hours; both are prolonged in renal failure

Time to peak, serum: Within 1-4 hours

Excretion: Both are excreted in urine as metabolites and unchanged drug

Effects of aging on the pharmacokinetics of both agents has been variable; increase in half-life and decreases in clearance have been associated with reduced creatinine clearance

Dosage Dosage recommendations are based on the trimethoprim component. Double-strength tablets are equivalent to sulfamethoxazole 800 mg and trimethoprim 160 mg.

Children >2 months:

General dosing guidelines:

Mild-to-moderate infections: Oral: 8-12 mg TMP/kg/day in divided doses every 12 hours

Serious infection:

Oral: 20 mg TMP/kg/day in divided doses every 6 hours

I.V.: 8-12 mg TMP/kg/day in divided doses every 6 hours

Acute otitis media: Oral: 8 mg TMP/kg/day in divided doses every 12 hours for 10 days

Urinary tract infection:

Treatment:

Oral: 6-12 mg TMP/kg/day in divided doses every 12 hours

I.V.: 8-10 mg TMP/kg/day in divided doses every 6, 8, or 12 hours for up to 4 days with serious infections

Prophylaxis: Oral: 2 mg TMP/kg/dose daily or 5 mg TMP/kg/dose twice weekly

Pneumocystis:

Treatment: Oral, I.V.: 15-20 mg TMP/kg/day in divided doses every 6-8 hours

Prophylaxis: Oral, 150 mg TMP/m²/day in divided doses every 12 hours for 3 days/week; dose should not exceed trimethoprim 320 mg and sulfamethoxazole 1600 mg daily

Alternative prophylaxis dosing schedules include:

150 mg TMP/m²/day as a single daily dose 3 times/week on consecutive days

or

150 mg TMP/m²/day in divided doses every 12 hours administered 7 days/week

or

150 mg TMP/m²/day in divided doses every 12 hours administered 3 times/week on alternate days

Shigellosis:
  Oral: 8 mg TMP/kg/day in divided doses every 12 hours for 5 days
  I.V.: 8-10 mg TMP/kg/day in divided doses every 6, 8, or 12 hours for up to 5 days
Cyclospora (unlabeled use): Oral, I.V.: 5 mg TMP/kg twice daily for 7-10 days
Adults:
Urinary tract infection:
  Oral: One double-strength tablet every 12 hours
    Duration of therapy: Uncomplicated: 3-5 days; Complicated: 7-10 days
      Pyelonephritis: 14 days
      Prostatitis: Acute: 2 weeks; Chronic: 2-3 months
  I.V.: 8-10 mg TMP/kg/day in divided doses every 6, 8, or 12 hours for up to 14 days with
    severe infections
Chronic bronchitis: Oral: One double-strength tablet every 12 hours for 10-14 days
Meningitis (bacterial): I.V.: 10-20 mg TMP/kg/day in divided doses every 6-12 hours
Shigellosis:
  Oral: One double strength tablet every 12 hours for 5 days
  I.V.: 8-10 mg TMP/kg/day in divided doses every 6, 8, or 12 hours for up to 5 days
Travelers' diarrhea: Oral: One double strength tablet every 12 hours for 5 days
Sepsis: I.V.: 20 TMP/kg/day divided every 6 hours
Pneumocystis jiroveci:
  Prophylaxis: Oral: 1 double strength tablet daily or 3 times/week
  Treatment: Oral, I.V.: 15-20 mg TMP/kg/day in 3-4 divided doses
Cyclospora (unlabeled use): Oral, I.V.: 160 mg TMP twice daily for 7-10 days
Nocardia (unlabeled use): Oral, I.V.:
  Cutaneous infections: 5 mg TMP/kg/day in 2 divided doses
  Severe infections (pulmonary/cerebral): 10-15 mg TMP/kg/day in 2-3 divided doses.
    Treatment duration is controversial; an average of 7 months has been reported.
  Note: Therapy for severe infection may be initiated I.V. and converted to oral therapy
    (frequently converted to approximate dosages of oral solid dosage forms: 2 DS tablets
    every 8-12 hours). Although not widely available, sulfonamide levels should be consid-
    ered in patients with questionable absorption, at risk for dose-related toxicity, or those
    with poor therapeutic response.

Dosing adjustment in renal impairment: Oral, I.V.:
  Cl$_{cr}$ 15-30 mL/minute: Administer 50% of recommended dose
  Cl$_{cr}$ <15 mL/minute: Use is not recommended
Dietary Considerations Should be taken with 8 oz of water on empty stomach.
Administration I.V.: Infuse over 60-90 minutes, must dilute well before giving; may be given
less diluted in a central line; not for I.M. injection
  Oral: May be taken with food and water.
Test Interactions Increased creatinine (Jaffé alkaline picrate reaction); increased serum
methotrexate by dihydrofolate reductase method
Dosage Forms Note: The 5:1 ratio (SMX:TMP) remains constant in all dosage forms.
  Injection, solution: Sulfamethoxazole 80 mg and trimethoprim 16 mg per mL (5 mL, 10 mL, 30
    mL) [contains propylene glycol ~400 mg/mL, alcohol, benzyl alcohol, and sodium metabi-
    sulfite]
  Suspension, oral: Sulfamethoxazole 200 mg and trimethoprim 40 mg per 5 mL (480 mL)
    [contains alcohol]
    Septra®: Sulfamethoxazole 200 mg and trimethoprim 40 mg per 5 mL (480 mL) [contains
      alcohol 0.26% and sodium benzoate; cherry and grape flavors] [DSC]
  Tablet: Sulfamethoxazole 400 mg and trimethoprim 80 mg
    Bactrim™: Sulfamethoxazole 400 mg and trimethoprim 80 mg [contains sodium benzoate]
    Septra®: Sulfamethoxazole 400 mg and trimethoprim 80 mg
  Tablet, double strength: Sulfamethoxazole 800 mg and trimethoprim 160 mg
    Bactrim™ DS: Sulfamethoxazole 800 mg and trimethoprim 160 mg [contains sodium
      benzoate]
    Septra® DS: Sulfamethoxazole 800 mg and trimethoprim 160 mg

♦ **Sulfamylon®** *see* Mafenide *on page 1045*

Sulfasalazine (sul fa SAL a zeen)

U.S. Brand Names Azulfidine®; Azulfidine® EN-tabs®; Sulfazine; Sulfazine EC
Canadian Brand Names Alti-Sulfasalazine; Salazopyrin®; Salazopyrin En-Tabs®
Index Terms Salicylazosulfapyridine
Pharmacologic Category 5-Aminosalicylic Acid Derivative
Additional Appendix Information
  Sulfonamide Derivatives *on page 1897*
Use Management of ulcerative colitis; enteric coated tablets are also used for rheumatoid
  arthritis (including juvenile rheumatoid arthritis) in patients who inadequately respond to
  analgesics and NSAIDs
Unlabeled/Investigational Use Ankylosing spondylitis, collagenous colitis, Crohn's disease,
  psoriasis, psoriatic arthritis, juvenile chronic arthritis
Pregnancy Risk Factor B/D (at term)
Lactation Enters breast milk/use caution (AAP recommends use "with caution")
Medication Safety Issues
  Sound-alike/look-alike issues:
    Sulfasalazine may be confused with salsalate, sulfaDIAZINE, sulfiSOXAZOLE
    Azulfidine® may be confused with Augmentin®, azathioprine
Contraindications Hypersensitivity to sulfasalazine, sulfa drugs, salicylates, or any compo-
  nent of the formulation; porphyria; GI or GU obstruction; pregnancy (at term)
Warnings/Precautions Use with caution in patients with renal impairment; impaired hepatic
  function or urinary obstruction, blood dyscrasias severe allergies or asthma, or G6PD deficiency; may cause folate deficiency (consider providing 1 mg/day folate supplement). Deaths
  from irreversible neuromuscular, central nervous system, fibrosing alveolitis, agranulocytosis,
  (Continued)

Sulfasalazine *(Continued)*

aplastic anemia, and other blood dyscrasias have been reported. In males, oligospermia (rare) has been reported. Chemical similarities are present among sulfonamides, sulfonylureas, carbonic anhydrase inhibitors, thiazides, and loop diuretics (except ethacrynic acid). Use in patients with sulfonamide allergy is specifically contraindicated in product labeling, however, a risk of cross-reaction exists in patients with allergy to any of these compounds; avoid use when previous reaction has been severe. Safety and efficacy have not been established in children <2 years of age.

Adverse Reactions

>10%:

Central nervous system: Headache (33%)

Dermatologic: Photosensitivity

Gastrointestinal: Anorexia, nausea, vomiting, diarrhea (33%), gastric distress

Genitourinary: Reversible oligospermia (33%)

<3% (Limited to important or life-threatening): Alopecia, anaphylaxis, aplastic anemia, ataxia, crystalluria, depression, epidermal necrolysis, exfoliative dermatitis, granulocytopenia, hallucinations, Heinz body anemia, hemolytic anemia, hepatitis, interstitial nephritis, jaundice, leukopenia, Lyell's syndrome, myelodysplastic syndrome, nephropathy (acute), neutropenic enterocolitis, pancreatitis, peripheral neuropathy, photosensitization, pruritus, rhabdomyolysis, seizure, serum sickness-like reactions, skin discoloration, Stevens-Johnson syndrome, thrombocytopenia, thyroid function disturbance, urine discoloration, urticaria, vasculitis, vertigo

Additional events reported with sulfonamides and/or 5-ASA derivatives: Cholestatic jaundice, eosinophilia pneumonitis, erythema multiforme, fibrosing alveolitis, hepatic necrosis, Kawasaki-like syndrome, SLE-like syndrome, pericarditis, seizure, transverse myelitis

Overdosage/Toxicology Symptoms include drowsiness, dizziness, anorexia, abdominal pain, nausea, vomiting, hemolytic anemia, acidosis, jaundice, fever, and agranulocytosis. The aniline radical is responsible for hematologic toxicity. High volume diuresis may aid in elimination and prevention of renal failure, gastric lavage or emesis plus catharsis, alkalinize urine. Dialysis may be helpful.

Drug Interactions

Increased Effect/Toxicity: Sulfasalazine may increase hydantoin levels. Effects of thiopental, oral hypoglycemics, and oral anticoagulants may be increased. Sulfasalazine may increase the risk of myelosuppression with azathioprine, mercaptopurine, or thioguanine (due to TPMT inhibition); may also increase the toxicity of methotrexate. Risk of thrombocytopenia may be increased with thiazide diuretics. Concurrent methenamine may increase risk of crystalluria.

Decreased Effect: Decreased effect with iron, digoxin and PABA or PABA metabolites of drugs (eg, procaine, proparacaine, tetracaine). Sulfasalazine may decrease serum cyclosporine concentrations.

Ethanol/Nutrition/Herb Interactions

Food: May impair folate absorption.

Herb/Nutraceutical: Avoid dong quai, St John's wort (may also cause photosensitization)

Stability Protect from light.

Mechanism of Action Acts locally in the colon to decrease the inflammatory response and systemically interferes with secretion by inhibiting prostaglandin synthesis

Pharmacodynamics/Kinetics

Absorption: 10% to 15% as unchanged drug from small intestine

Distribution: Small amounts enter feces and breast milk

Metabolism: Via colonic intestinal flora to sulfapyridine and 5-aminosalicylic acid (5-ASA); following absorption, sulfapyridine undergoes N-acetylation and ring hydroxylation while 5-ASA undergoes N-acetylation

Half-life elimination: 5.7-10 hours

Excretion: Primarily urine (as unchanged drug, components, and acetylated metabolites)

Dosage Oral:

Children ≥2 years: Ulcerative colitis: Initial: 40-60 mg/kg/day in 3-6 divided doses; maintenance dose: 20-30 mg/kg/day in 4 divided doses

Children ≥6 years: Juvenile rheumatoid arthritis: Enteric coated tablet: 30-50 mg/kg/day in 2 divided doses; Initial: Begin with ¼ to ⅓ of expected maintenance dose; increase weekly; maximum: 2 g/day typically

Adults:

Ulcerative colitis: Initial: 1 g 3-4 times/day, 2 g/day maintenance in divided doses; may initiate therapy with 0.5-1 g/day

Rheumatoid arthritis: Enteric coated tablet: Initial: 0.5-1 g/day; increase weekly to maintenance dose of 2 g/day in 2 divided doses; maximum: 3 g/day (if response to 2 g/day is inadequate after 12 weeks of treatment)

Dosing interval in renal impairment:

Cl_cr 10-30 mL/minute: Administer twice daily

Cl_cr <10 mL/minute: Administer once daily

Dosing adjustment in hepatic impairment: Avoid use

Dietary Considerations Since sulfasalazine impairs folate absorption, consider providing 1 mg/day folate supplement.

Administration GI intolerance is common during the first few days of therapy (administer with meals).

Dosage Forms

Tablet (Azulfidine®, Sulfazine): 500 mg

Tablet, delayed release, enteric coated (Azulfidine® EN-tabs®, Sulfazine EC): 500 mg

♦ **Sulfatrim** *see* Sulfamethoxazole and Trimethoprim *on page 1613*

♦ **Sulfazine** *see* Sulfasalazine *on page 1615*

♦ **Sulfazine EC** *see* Sulfasalazine *on page 1615*

SulfiSOXAZOLE (sul fi SOKS a zole)

U.S. Brand Names Gantrisin®
Canadian Brand Names Novo-Soxazole; Sulfizole®
Index Terms Sulfisoxazole Acetyl; Sulphafurazole
Pharmacologic Category Antibiotic, Sulfonamide Derivative
Additional Appendix Information
Antimicrobial Drugs of Choice *on page 1981*
Sulfonamide Derivatives *on page 1897*
Use Treatment of urinary tract infections, otitis media, *Chlamydia*; nocardiosis
Pregnancy Risk Factor B/D (near term)
Lactation Enters breast milk/compatible
Medication Safety Issues
Sound-alike/look-alike issues:
SulfiSOXAZOLE may be confused with sulfaDIAZINE, sulfamethoxazole, sulfasalazine
Gantrisin® may be confused with Gastrosed™
Contraindications Hypersensitivity to sulfisoxazole, any sulfa drug, or any component of the formulation; porphyria; infants <2 months of age (sulfas compete with bilirubin for protein binding sites); patients with urinary obstruction; sunscreens containing PABA; pregnancy (at term)
Warnings/Precautions Use with caution in patients with G6PD deficiency (hemolysis may occur), hepatic or renal impairment; dosage modification required in patients with renal impairment; risk of crystalluria should be considered in patients with impaired renal function. Chemical similarities are present among sulfonamides, sulfonylureas, carbonic anhydrase inhibitors, thiazides, and loop diuretics (except ethacrynic acid). Use in patients with sulfonamide allergy is specifically contraindicated in product labeling, however, a risk of cross-reaction exists in patients with allergy to any of these compounds; avoid use when previous reaction has been severe.
Adverse Reactions Frequency not defined.
Cardiovascular: Vasculitis
Central nervous system: Dizziness, fever, headache
Dermatologic: Itching, Lyell's syndrome, rash, photosensitivity, Stevens-Johnson syndrome
Endocrine & metabolic: Thyroid function disturbance
Gastrointestinal: Anorexia, diarrhea, nausea, vomiting
Genitourinary: Crystalluria, hematuria
Hematologic: Aplastic anemia, granulocytopenia, hemolytic anemia, leukopenia, thrombocytopenia
Hepatic: Hepatitis, jaundice
Renal: Interstitial nephritis
Miscellaneous: Serum sickness-like reactions
Overdosage/Toxicology Symptoms include drowsiness, dizziness, anorexia, abdominal pain, nausea, vomiting, hemolytic anemia, acidosis, jaundice, fever, and agranulocytosis. Doses of as little as 2-5 g/day may produce toxicity. The aniline radical is responsible for hematologic toxicity. High volume diuresis may aid in elimination and prevention of renal failure.
Drug Interactions
Cytochrome P450 Effect: Substrate of CYP2C9 (major); **Inhibits** CYP2C9 (strong)
Increased Effect/Toxicity: Sulfisoxazole may increase the levels/effects of CYP2C9 substrates; example substrates include bosentan, dapsone, fluoxetine, glimepiride, glipizide, losartan, montelukast, nateglinide, paclitaxel, phenytoin, warfarin, and zafirlukast. Sulfisoxazole may increase the effect of methotrexate. Risk of adverse reactions (thrombocytopenia purpura) may be increased by thiazide diuretics.
Decreased Effect: Decreased effect with PABA or PABA metabolites of drugs (eg, procaine, proparacaine, tetracaine), thiopental. May decrease cyclosporine levels. CYP2C9 Inducers may decrease the levels/effects of Sulfisoxazole; example inducers include carbamazepine, phenobarbital, phenytoin, rifampin, rifapentine, and secobarbital.
Ethanol/Nutrition/Herb Interactions
Food: Interferes with folate absorption.
Herb/Nutraceutical: Avoid dong quai, St John's wort (may also cause photosensitization).
Stability Protect from light.
Mechanism of Action Interferes with bacterial growth by inhibiting bacterial folic acid synthesis through competitive antagonism of PABA
Pharmacodynamics/Kinetics
Absorption: Sulfisoxazole acetyl is hydrolyzed in GI tract to sulfisoxazole which is readily absorbed
Distribution: Crosses placenta; enters breast milk
CSF:blood level ratio: Normal meninges: 50% to 80%; Inflamed meninges: 80+%
Protein binding: 85% to 88%
Metabolism: Hepatic via acetylation and glucuronide conjugation to inactive compounds
Half-life elimination: 4-7 hours; prolonged with renal impairment
Time to peak, serum: 2-3 hours
Excretion: Urine (95%, 40% to 60% as unchanged drug) within 24 hours
Dosage Oral: Not for use in patients <2 months of age:
Children >2 months: Initial: 75 mg/kg, followed by 120-150 mg/kg/day in divided doses every 4-6 hours; not to exceed 6 g/day
Adults: Initial: 2-4 g, then 4-8 g/day in divided doses every 4-6 hours
Dosing interval in renal impairment:
Cl_{cr} 10-50 mL/minute: Administer every 8-12 hours
Cl_{cr} <10 mL/minute: Administer every 12-24 hours
Hemodialysis: >50% removed by hemodialysis
Dietary Considerations Should be taken with a glass of water on an empty stomach.
(Continued)

SulfiSOXAZOLE *(Continued)*

Administration Administer around-the-clock to promote less variation in peak and trough serum levels.

Monitoring Parameters CBC, urinalysis, renal function tests, temperature

Test Interactions False-positive protein in urine; false-positive urine glucose with Clinitest®

Dosage Forms

Suspension, oral, pediatric, as acetyl (Gantrisin®): 500 mg/5 mL (480 mL) [contains alcohol 0.3%; raspberry flavor]

Tablet: 500 mg

- ♦ **Sulfisoxazole Acetyl** *see* SulfiSOXAZOLE *on page 1617*
- ♦ **Sulfisoxazole and Erythromycin** *see* Erythromycin and Sulfisoxazole *on page 613*
- ♦ **Sulfizole® (Can)** *see* SulfiSOXAZOLE *on page 1617*

Sulfur and Sulfacetamide *(SUL fur & sul fa SEE ta mide)*

U.S. Brand Names AVAR™; AVAR™-e; AVAR™-e Green; AVAR™ Green; Clenia™; Plexion®; Plexion SCT®; Plexion TS®; Rosac®; Rosanil®; Rosula®; Sulfacet-R® [DSC]; Suphera™; Zetacet®

Canadian Brand Names Sulfacet-R®

Index Terms Sodium Sulfacetamide and Sulfur; Sulfacetamide and Sulfur; Sulfur and Sulfacetamide Sodium

Pharmacologic Category Acne Products; Antibiotic, Sulfonamide Derivative; Antiseborrheic Agent, Topical; Topical Skin Product, Acne

Use Aid in the treatment of acne vulgaris, acne rosacea, and seborrheic dermatitis

Pregnancy Risk Factor C

Dosage Topical: Children ≥12 years and Adults: Apply in a thin film 1-3 times/day. Cleansing products should be used 1-2 times/day.

Dosage adjustment in renal impairment: Use is contraindicated.

Additional Information Complete prescribing information for this medication should be consulted for additional detail.

Dosage Forms [DSC] = Discontinued product

Cleanser, topical:

AVAR™ : Sulfur 5% and sulfacetamide sodium 10% (228 g)

Plexion®: Sulfur 5% and sulfacetamide sodium 10% (170 g, 340 g)

Rosanil®: Sulfur 5% and sulfacetamide sodium 10% (170 g)

Rosula®: Sulfur 5% and sulfacetamide sodium 10% (355 mL) [contains urea 10%]

Cream, topical:

AVAR™-e: Sulfur 5% and sulfacetamide sodium 10% (45 g) [contains benzyl alcohol]

AVAR™-e Green: Sulfur 5% and sulfacetamide sodium 10% (45 g) [contains benzyl alcohol; color corrective cream]

Clenia™: Sulfur 5% and sulfacetamide sodium 10% (28 g)

Plexion SCT®: Sulfur 5% and sulfacetamide sodium 10% (120 g) [contains benzyl alcohol]

Rosac®: Sulfur 5% and sulfacetamide sodium 10% (45 g) [contains benzyl alcohol and sunscreen]

Suphera™: Sulfur 5% and sulfacetamide sodium 10% (113 g)

Gel, topical:

AVAR™: Sulfur 5% and sulfacetamide sodium 10% (45 g) [contains benzyl alcohol]

AVAR™ Green: Sulfur 5% and sulfacetamide sodium 10% (45 g) [contains benzyl alcohol; color corrective gel]

Rosula®: Sulfur 5% and sulfacetamide sodium 10% (45 mL) [contains urea 10% and benzyl alcohol]

Lotion, topical: Sulfur 5% and sulfacetamide sodium 10% (25 g, 30 g, 45 g, 60 g)

Sulfacet-R®: Sulfur 5% and sulfacetamide sodium 10% (25 g) [contains sodium metabisulfate; available with tint or tint-free formulations] [DSC]

Zetacet®: Sulfur 5% and sulfacetamide sodium 10% (25 g) [contains sodium metabisulfite]

Pad [cleansing cloth]:

Plexion®: Sulfur 5% and sulfacetamide sodium 10% (30s) [contains aloe vera]

Suspension, topical:

Plexion® TS: Sulfur 5% and sulfacetamide sodium 10% (30 g) [contains benzyl alcohol]

Zetacet®: Sulfur 5% and sulfacetamide sodium 10% (30 g) [contains benzyl alcohol]

Wash, topical: Sulfur 5% and sulfacetamide sodium 10% (170 g, 340 g)

Clenia™: Sulfur 5% and sulfacetamide sodium 10% (170 g, 340 g)

Zetacet®: Sulfur 5% and sulfacetamide sodium 10% (170 g, 340 g)

- ♦ **Sulfur and Sulfacetamide Sodium** *see* Sulfur and Sulfacetamide *on page 1618*

Sulindac *(SUL in dak)*

U.S. Brand Names Clinoril®

Canadian Brand Names Apo-Sulin®; Novo-Sundac; Nu-Sundac

Pharmacologic Category Nonsteroidal Anti-inflammatory Drug (NSAID), Oral

Additional Appendix Information

Nonsteroidal Anti-inflammatory Agents *on page 1894*

Use Management of inflammatory disease, osteoarthritis, rheumatoid disorders, acute gouty arthritis, ankylosing spondylitis, bursitis/tendonitis of shoulder

Restrictions An FDA-approved medication guide must be distributed when dispensing an oral outpatient prescription (new or refill) where this medication is to be used without direct supervision of a healthcare provider. Medication guides are available at http://www.fda.gov/cder/Offices/ODS/medication_guides.htm.

Pregnancy Risk Factor C/D (3rd trimester)

Pregnancy Implications Animal studies have not documented teratogenic effects. However, known effects of NSAIDs suggest the potential for premature ductus arteriosus closeure, particularly in late pregnancy.

Lactation Excretion in breast milk unknown/not recommended

Medication Safety Issues
Sound-alike/look-alike issues:
Clinoril® may be confused with Cleocin®, Clozaril®, Oruvail®

Contraindications Hypersensitivity to sulindac, aspirin, other NSAIDs, or any component of the formulation; perioperative pain in the setting of coronary artery bypass surgery (CABG); pregnancy (3rd trimester)

Warnings/Precautions [U.S. Boxed Warning]: NSAIDs are associated with an increased risk of adverse cardiovascular events, including MI, stroke, and new onset or worsening of pre-existing hypertension. Use caution with fluid retention, CHF or hypertension. Concurrent administration of ibuprofen, and potentially other nonselective NSAIDs, may interfere with aspirin's cardioprotective effect. Use of NSAIDs can compromise existing renal function. Sulindac is not recommended for patients with advanced renal disease. Use caution in patients with renal lithiasis; sulindac metabolites have been reported as components of renal stones. Use hydration in patients with a history of renal stones. Use with caution in patients with decreased hepatic function. May require dosage adjustment in hepatic dysfunction; sulfide and sulfone metabolites may accumulate.

[U.S. Boxed Warning]: NSAIDs may increase risk of gastrointestinal irritation, ulceration, bleeding, and perforation. Use the lowest effective dose for the shortest duration of time, consistent with individual patient goals, to reduce risk of cardiovascular or GI adverse events.

NSAIDs may cause serious skin adverse events including exfoliative dermatitis, Stevens-Johnson syndrome (SJS) and toxic epidermal necrolysis (TEN). Anaphylactoid reactions may occur. Do not use in patients who experience bronchospasm, asthma, rhinitis, or urticaria with NSAID or aspirin therapy.

Withhold for at least 4-6 half-lives prior to surgical or dental procedures.

Adverse Reactions
1% to 10%:
Cardiovascular: Edema (1% to 3%)
Central nervous system: Dizziness (3% to 9%), headache (3% to 9%), nervousness (1% to 3%)
Dermatologic: Rash (3% to 9%), pruritus (1% to 3%)
Gastrointestinal: GI pain (10%), constipation (3% to 9%), diarrhea (3% to 9%), dyspepsia (3% to 9%), nausea (3% to 9%), abdominal cramps (1% to 3%), anorexia (1% to 3%), flatulence (1% to 3%), vomiting (1% to 3%)
Otic: Tinnitus (1% to 3%)
<1% (Limited to important or life-threatening): Agranulocytosis, ageusia, alopecia, anaphylaxis, angioneurotic edema, aplastic anemia, arrhythmia, aseptic meningitis, bitter taste, blurred vision, bone marrow depression, bronchial spasm, cholestasis, colitis, CHF, crystalluria, depression, dry mucous membranes, dyspnea, dysuria, ecchymosis, epistaxis, erythema multiforme, exfoliative dermatitis, fever, gastritis, GI bleeding, GI perforation, glossitis, gynecomastia, hearing decreased, hematuria, hemolytic anemia, hepatitis, hepatic failure, hyperglycemia, hyperkalemia, hypersensitivity reaction, hypersensitivity vasculitis, hypertension, insomnia, intestinal stricture, interstitial nephritis, jaundice, leukopenia, metallic taste, necrotizing fascitis, nephrotic syndrome, neuritis, neutropenia, palpitation, pancreatitis, paresthesia, peptic ulcer, photosensitivity, proteinuria, psychosis, purpura, renal calculi, renal impairment, renal failure, retinal disturbances, seizures, somnolence, Stevens-Johnson syndrome, stomatitis, syncope, thrombocytopenia, toxic epidermal necrolysis, urine discoloration, vaginal bleeding, vertigo, weakness

Overdosage/Toxicology Symptoms include dizziness, vomiting, nausea, abdominal pain, hypotension, coma, stupor, metabolic acidosis, leukocytosis, and renal failure. Management of nonsteroidal anti-inflammatory drug (NSAID) intoxication is primarily supportive and symptomatic. Fluid therapy is commonly effective managing hypotension that may occur following an acute NSAID overdose, except when due to acute blood loss. Seizures tend to be very short-lived and often do not require drug treatment; although, recurrent seizures should be treated with I.V. diazepam.

Drug Interactions
Increased Effect/Toxicity: Sulindac may increase effect/toxicity of anticoagulants (bleeding), antiplatelet agents (bleeding), aminoglycosides, bisphosphonates (GI irritation), corticosteroids (GI irritation), cyclosporine (nephrotoxicity), lithium, methotrexate, pemetrexed, treprostinil (bleeding), vancomycin. Concomitant use with fluoroquinolones may rarely increase risk of seizure.
Decreased Effect: May reduce effect of some diuretics and antihypertensive effect of beta-blockers, ACE inhibitors, angiotensin II inhibitors, and hydralazine. Dimethyl sulfoxide may decrease active metabolite of sulindac; combination may cause peripheral neuropathy. Cholestyramine (and other bile acid sequestrants) may decrease the absorption of NSAIDs; separate by at least 2 hours. Salicylates' antiplatelet effect may be reduced.

Ethanol/Nutrition/Herb Interactions
Ethanol: Avoid ethanol (may enhance gastric mucosal irritation).
Food: Food may decrease the rate but not the extent of oral absorption. The therapeutic effect of sulindac may be decreased if taken with food.
Herb/Nutraceutical: Avoid alfalfa, anise, bilberry, bladderwrack, bromelain, cat's claw, celery, coleus, cordyceps, dong quai, evening primrose, feverfew, fenugreek, garlic, ginger, ginkgo biloba, red clover, horse chestnut, grapeseed, green tea, ginseng, guggul, horse chestnut seed, horseradish, licorice, prickly ash, red clover, reishi, SAMe, sweet clover, turmeric, white willow (all have additional antiplatelet activity).

Mechanism of Action Inhibits prostaglandin synthesis by decreasing the activity of the enzyme, cyclooxygenase, which results in decreased formation of prostaglandin precursors

Pharmacodynamics/Kinetics
Onset of action: Analgesic: ~1 hour
(Continued)

Sulindac *(Continued)*

Duration: 12-24 hours

Absorption: 90%

Protein binding: Parent, sulfide metabolite (active): 93% to 98% primarily to albumin

Distribution: Crosses blood-brain barrier and placental barriers

Metabolism: Hepatic; prodrug metabolized to sulfide metabolite (active) for therapeutic effects and to sulfone metabolites (inactive); parent and inactive sulfone metabolite undergo extensive enterohepatic recirculation

Half-life elimination: Parent drug: ~8 hours; Active metabolite: ~16 hours

Excretion: Urine (50%, primarily as inactive metabolites); feces (25%, primarily as metabolites)

Dosage Oral:

Children: Dose not established

Adults: **Note:** Maximum daily dose: 400 mg

Osteoarthritis, rheumatoid arthritis, ankylosing spondylitis: 150 mg twice/daily

Bursitis/tendonitis: 200 mg twice daily; usual treatment: 7-14 days

Acute gouty arthritis: 200 mg twice daily; usual treatment: 7 days

Dosing adjustment in renal impairment: Not recommended with advanced renal impairment; if required, decrease dose and monitor closely

Dosing adjustment in hepatic impairment: Dose reduction is necessary; discontinue if abnormal liver function tests occur

Dietary Considerations Drug may cause GI upset, bleeding, ulceration, perforation; take with food or milk to minimize GI upset.

Administration Should be administered with food or milk.

Monitoring Parameters Liver enzymes, BUN, serum creatinine, CBC, blood pressure; signs and symptoms of GI bleeding

Test Interactions Increased chloride (S), increased sodium (S), increased bleeding time

Dosage Forms

Tablet: 150 mg, 200 mg

Clinoril®: 200 mg

Extemporaneous Preparations A suspension of sulindac can be prepared by triturating 1000 mg sulindac (5 x 200 mg tablets) with 50 mg of kelco and 400 mg of Veegum® until a powder mixture is formed; then add 30 mL of sorbitol 35% (prepared from 70% sorbitol) to form a slurry; finally add a sufficient quantity of 35% sorbitol to make a final volume of 100 mL; the final suspension is 10 mg/mL and is stable for 7 days

♦ **Sulphafurazole** *see* SulfISOXAZOLE *on page 1617*

Sumatriptan *(soo ma TRIP tan)*

U.S. Brand Names Imitrex®

Canadian Brand Names Apo-Sumatriptan®; CO Sumatriptan; Dom-Sumatriptan; Gen-Sumatriptan; Imitrex®; Imitrex® DF; Imitrex® Nasal Spray; Novo-Sumatriptan; PHL-Sumatriptan; PMS-Sumatriptan; ratio-Sumatriptan; Rhoxal-sumatriptan; Riva-Sumatriptan; Sandoz-Sumatriptan; Sumatryx

Index Terms Sumatriptan Succinate

Pharmacologic Category Antimigraine Agent; Serotonin 5-HT$_{1B, 1D}$ Receptor Agonist

Additional Appendix Information

Antimigraine Drugs: 5-HT$_1$ Receptor Agonists *on page 1871*

Sulfonamide Derivatives *on page 1897*

Use

Oral, SubQ: Acute treatment of migraine with or without aura

SubQ: Acute treatment of cluster headache episodes

Pregnancy Risk Factor C

Pregnancy Implications There are no adequate and well-controlled studies using sumatriptan in pregnant women. Use only if potential benefit to the mother outweighs the potential risk to the fetus. A pregnancy registry has been established to monitor outcomes of women exposed to sumatriptan during pregnancy (800-336-2176). Preliminary data from the registry do not suggest a greater risk of birth defects than the general population and so far a specific pattern of malformations has not been identified. However, sample sizes are small and studies are ongoing. In some (but not all) animal studies, administration was associated with embryolethality, fetal malformations and pup mortality.

Lactation Enters breast milk/use caution (AAP rates "compatible")

Medication Safety Issues

Sound-alike/look-alike issues:

Sumatriptan may be confused with somatropin, zolmitriptan

International issues:

Imitrex® may be confused with Nitrex® which is a brand name for isosorbide mononitrate in Italy

Contraindications Hypersensitivity to sumatriptan or any component of the formulation; patients with ischemic heart disease or signs or symptoms of ischemic heart disease (including Prinzmetal's angina, angina pectoris, myocardial infarction, silent myocardial ischemia); cerebrovascular syndromes (including strokes, transient ischemic attacks); peripheral vascular syndromes (including ischemic bowel disease); uncontrolled hypertension; use within 24 hours of ergotamine derivatives; use within 24 hours of another 5-HT$_1$ agonist; concurrent administration or within 2 weeks of discontinuing an MAO inhibitor, specifically MAO type A inhibitors; management of hemiplegic or basilar migraine; prophylactic treatment of migraine; severe hepatic impairment; not for I.V. administration

Warnings/Precautions Sumatriptan is indicated only in patients ≥18 years of age with a clear diagnosis of migraine or cluster headache. Cardiac events (coronary artery vasospasm, transient ischemia, myocardial infarction, ventricular tachycardia/fibrillation, cardiac arrest and death), cerebral/subarachnoid hemorrhage, and stroke have been reported with 5-HT$_1$ agonist administration. Do not give to patients with risk factors for CAD until a cardiovascular evaluation has been performed; if evaluation is satisfactory, the healthcare provider should administer the first dose and cardiovascular status should be periodically evaluated.

Significant elevation in blood pressure, including hypertensive crisis, has also been reported on rare occasions in patients with and without a history of hypertension. Vasospasm-related reactions have been reported other than coronary artery vasospasm. Peripheral vascular ischemia and colonic ischemia with abdominal pain and bloody diarrhea have occurred. Use with caution in patients with a history of seizure disorder or in patients with a lowered seizure threshold. Use with caution in patients with hepatic impairment. Symptoms of agitation, confusion, hallucinations, hyperreflexia, myoclonus, shivering, and tachycardia (serotonin syndrome) may occur with concomitant proserotonergic drugs (ie, SSRIs/SNRIs or triptans) or agents which reduce sumatriptan's metabolism. Concurrent use of serotonin precursors (eg, tryptophan) is not recommended. Safety and efficacy in pediatric patients have not been established.

Adverse Reactions

Injection:

>10%:
Central nervous system: Dizziness (12%), warm/hot sensation (11%)
Local: Pain at injection site (59%)
Neuromuscular & skeletal: Paresthesia (14%)

1% to 10%:
Cardiovascular: Chest pain/tightness/heaviness/pressure (2% to 3%), hyper-/hypotension (1%)
Central nervous system: Burning (7%), feeling of heaviness (7%), flushing (7%), pressure sensation (7%), feeling of tightness (5%), drowsiness (3%), malaise/fatigue (1%), feeling strange (2%), headache (2%), tight feeling in head (2%), cold sensation (1%), anxiety (1%)
Gastrointestinal: Abdominal discomfort (1%), dysphagia (1%)
Neuromuscular & skeletal: Neck, throat, and jaw pain/tightness/pressure (2% to 5%), mouth/tongue discomfort (5%), weakness (5%), myalgia (2%); muscle cramps (1%), numbness (5%)
Ocular: Vision alterations (1%)
Respiratory: Throat discomfort (3%), nasal disorder/discomfort (2%)
Miscellaneous: Diaphoresis (2%)

Nasal spray:

>10%: Gastrointestinal: Bad taste (13% to 24%), nausea (11% to 13%), vomiting (11% to 13%)

1% to 10%:
Central nervous system: Dizziness (1% to 2%)
Respiratory: Nasal disorder/discomfort (2% to 4%), throat discomfort (1% to 2%)

Tablet:

1% to 10%:
Cardiovascular: Chest pain/tightness/heaviness/pressure (1% to 2%), hyper-/hypotension (1%), palpitation (1%), syncope (1%)
Central nervous system: Burning (1%), dizziness (>1%), drowsiness (>1%), malaise/fatigue (2% to 3%), headache (>1%), nonspecified pain (1% to 2%, placebo 1%), vertigo (<1% to 2%), migraine (>1%), sleepiness (>1%)
Gastrointestinal: Diarrhea (1%), nausea (>1%), vomiting (>1%), hyposalivation (>1%)
Genitourinary: Hematuria (1%)
Hematologic: Hemolytic anemia (1%)
Neuromuscular & skeletal: Neck, throat, and jaw pain/tightness/pressure (2% to 3%), paresthesia (3% to 5%), myalgia (1%), numbness (1%)
Otic: Ear hemorrhage (1%), hearing loss (1%), sensitivity to noise (1%), tinnitus (1%)
Respiratory: Allergic rhinitis (1%), dyspnea (1%), nasal inflammation (1%), nose/throat hemorrhage (1%), sinusitis (1%), upper respiratory inflammation (1%)
Miscellaneous: Hypersensitivity reactions (1%), nonspecified pressure/tightness/heaviness (1% to 3%, placebo 2%); warm/cold sensation (2% to 3%, placebo 2%)

Route unspecified: <1%: Postmarketing and uncontrolled studies (limited to important or life-threatening): Abdominal aortic aneurysm, abdominal discomfort, abnormal menstrual cycle, abnormal/elevated liver function tests, accommodation disorders, acute renal failure, agitation, anaphylactoid reaction, anaphylaxis, anemia, angioneurotic edema, arrhythmia, atrial fibrillation, bronchospasm, cerebral ischemia, cerebrovascular accident, convulsions, deafness, death, decreased appetite, dental pain, diarrhea, dyspeptic symptoms, dysphagia, dystonic reaction, ECG changes, fluid disturbances (including retention), flushing, gastrointestinal pain, hallucinations, heart block, hematuria, hemolytic anemia, hiccups, hypersensitivity reactions, intestinal obstruction, intracranial pressure increased, ischemic colitis, joint ache, muscle stiffness, nose/throat hemorrhage, numbness of tongue, optic neuropathy (ischemic), pancytopenia, paresthesia, phlebitis, photosensitivity, Prinzmetal's angina, pruritus, psychomotor disorders, pulmonary embolism, rash, Raynaud syndrome, sensation changes, shock, subarachnoid hemorrhage, swallowing disorders, syncope, thrombocytopenia, thrombophlebitis, thrombosis, transient myocardial ischemia, TSH increased, vasculitis, vision loss, xerostomia

Overdosage/Toxicology Single oral doses up to 400 mg, injectable doses up to 16 mg, and nasal doses of 40 mg have been reported without adverse effects. Treatment should be supportive and symptomatic. Monitor for at least 12 hours or until signs and symptoms subside. It is not known if hemodialysis or peritoneal dialysis is effective.

Drug Interactions

Increased Effect/Toxicity: Increased toxicity with ergot-containing drugs, avoid use, wait 24 hours from last ergot containing drug (dihydroergotamine, or methysergide) before administering sumatriptan. MAO inhibitors decrease clearance of sumatriptan increasing the risk of systemic sumatriptan toxic effects. SSRIs/SNRIs or other serotonin agonists may increase symptoms of hyper-reflexia, weakness, and incoordination. **Note:** Use cautiously in patients receiving concomitant medications that can lower the seizure threshold.
(Continued)

Sumatriptan *(Continued)*

Stability Store at 2°C to 20°C (36°F to 86°F). Protect from light.

Mechanism of Action Selective agonist for serotonin (5-HT$_{1D}$ receptor) in cranial arteries to cause vasoconstriction and reduces sterile inflammation associated with antidromic neuronal transmission correlating with relief of migraine

Pharmacodynamics/Kinetics

Onset of action: ~30 minutes

Distribution: V$_d$: 2.4 L/kg

Protein binding: 14% to 21%

Metabolism: Hepatic, primarily via MAO-A isoenzyme

Bioavailability: SubQ: 97% ± 16% of that following I.V. injection; Oral: 15%

Half-life elimination: Injection, tablet: 2.5 hours; Nasal spray: 2 hours

Time to peak, serum: 5-20 minutes

Excretion:

Injection: Urine (38% as indole acetic acid metabolite, 22% as unchanged drug)

Nasal spray: Urine (42% as indole acetic acid metabolite, 3% as unchanged drug)

Tablet: Urine (60% as indole acetic acid metabolite, 3% as unchanged drug); feces (40%)

Dosage Adults:

Oral: A single dose of 25 mg, 50 mg, or 100 mg (taken with fluids). If a satisfactory response has not been obtained at 2 hours, a second dose may be administered. Results from clinical trials show that initial doses of 50 mg and 100 mg are more effective than doses of 25 mg, and that 100 mg doses do not provide a greater effect than 50 mg and may have increased incidence of side effects. Although doses of up to 300 mg/day have been studied, the total daily dose should not exceed 200 mg. The safety of treating an average of >4 headaches in a 30-day period have not been established.

Intranasal: A single dose of 5 mg, 10 mg, or 20 mg administered in one nostril. A 10 mg dose may be achieved by administering a single 5 mg dose in each nostril. If headache returns, the dose may be repeated once after 2 hours, not to exceed a total daily dose of 40 mg. The safety of treating an average of >4 headaches in a 30-day period has not been established.

SubQ: Up to 6 mg; if side effects are dose-limiting, lower doses may be used. A second injection may be administered at least 1 hour after the initial dose, but not more than 2 injections in a 24-hour period.

Dosage adjustment in renal impairment: Dosage adjustment not necessary

Dosage adjustment in hepatic impairment: Bioavailability of oral sumatriptan is increased with liver disease. If treatment is needed, do not exceed single doses of 50 mg. The nasal spray has not been studied in patients with hepatic impairment, however, because the spray does not undergo first-pass metabolism, levels would not be expected to alter. Use of all dosage forms is contraindicated with severe hepatic impairment.

Administration

Oral: Should be taken with fluids as soon as symptoms appear

Injection solution: For SubQ administration; do not administer I.V.; may cause coronary vasospasm. An autoinjection device (STATdose System®) is available for use with the 4 mg and 6 mg cartridges.

Dosage Forms Note: Strength expressed as sumatriptan base

Injection, solution, as succinate: 8 mg/mL (0.5 mL) [disposable cartridge for use with STAT-dose System®]; 12 mg/mL (0.5 mL) [disposable cartridge for use with STATdose System® or vial]

Solution, intranasal spray: 5 mg (100 µL unit dose spray device); 20 mg (100 µL unit dose spray device)

Tablet, as succinate: 25 mg, 50 mg, 100 mg

- ◆ **Sumatriptan Succinate** *see* Sumatriptan *on page 1620*
- ◆ **Sumatryx (Can)** *see* Sumatriptan *on page 1620*
- ◆ **Summer's Eve® Medicated Douche [OTC]** *see* Povidone-Iodine *on page 1404*
- ◆ **Summer's Eve® SpecialCare™ Medicated Anti-Itch Cream [OTC]** *see* Hydrocortisone *on page 852*
- ◆ **Sumycin® [DSC]** *see* Tetracycline *on page 1659*

Sunitinib *(su NIT e nib)*

U.S. Brand Names Sutent®

Index Terms NSC736511; SU11248; Sunitinib Maleate

Pharmacologic Category Antineoplastic Agent, Tyrosine Kinase Inhibitor; Vascular Endothelial Growth Factor (VEGF) Inhibitor

Use Treatment of gastrointestinal stromal tumor (GIST) following failure of or intolerance to imatinib; treatment of advanced renal cell cancer (RCC)

Unlabeled/Investigational Use Treatment of acute myeloid leukemia (AML)

Restrictions Pharmacies must obtain an Order Authorization Number (OAN) from McKesson Specialty at 1-800-496-6540 prior to ordering sunitinib.

Pregnancy Risk Factor D

Pregnancy Implications Animal studies have demonstrated teratogenicity and fetal loss. There are no adequate and well-controlled studies in pregnant women. Because sunitinib inhibits angiogenesis, a critical component of fetal development, adverse effects on pregnancy would be expected. Women of childbearing potential should be advised to avoid pregnancy.

Lactation Excretion in breast milk unknown/not recommended

Medication Safety Issues

High alert medication: The Institute for Safe Medication Practices (ISMP) includes this medication among its list of drugs which have a heightened risk of causing significant patient harm when used in error.

Contraindications Hypersensitivity to sunitinib or any other component of the formulation; pregnancy

Warnings/Precautions May cause a decrease in left ventricular ejection fraction (LVEF), including grade 3 reductions; monitor with baseline and periodic LVEF evaluations. Interrupt therapy or decrease dose with LVEF <50% or >20% reduction from baseline. Discontinue with clinical signs and symptoms of congestive heart failure (CHF). Use caution with cardiac dysfunction; patients with MI, bypass grafts, CHF, CVA, TIA, and PE were excluded from clinical trials. May cause hypertension; monitor and control with antihypertensives if needed; interrupt therapy until hypertension is controlled for severe hypertension. Use caution and closely monitor in patients with underlying or poorly-controlled hypertension. Use with caution in patients concurrently taking strong CYP3A4 inhibitors or inducers; dosage adjustments of sunitinib may be required.

Hemorrhagic events have been reported including epistaxis, rectal, gingival, upper GI, genital, wound bleeding, and tumor-related and pulmonary hemorrhage. Serious and fatal gastrointestinal complications have occurred. Adrenal function abnormalities have been reported; monitor for adrenal insufficiency for patients with trauma, severe infection, or undergoing surgery. May cause skin and/or hair depigmentation or discoloration. Safety and effectiveness in children have not been established.

Adverse Reactions
>10%:
  Cardiovascular: Hypertension (15% to 28%), edema (peripheral 17%)
  Central nervous system: Fatigue (42% to 74%), headache (13% to 25%), fever (15% to 18%), dizziness (16%)
  Dermatologic: Rash (14% to 38%), hyperpigmentation (30% to 33%), dry skin (17%), hair color changes (7% to 17%), hand-foot syndrome (12% to 14%), alopecia (5% to 12%)
  Endocrine & metabolic: Hyperuricemia (10% to 15%), hypokalemia (12%), dehydration (11%)
  Gastrointestinal: Diarrhea (40% to 55%), nausea (31% to 54%), mucositis/stomatitis (29% to 53%), dyspepsia (46%), taste perversion (21% to 43%), vomiting (24% to 37%), constipation (20% to 34%), anorexia (31% to 33%), abdominal pain (20% to 33%), hyperlipasemia (16% to 25%), amylase increased (5% to 17%), glossodynia (15%), flatulence (14%)
  Hematologic: Neutropenia (53%; grades 3/4: 10% to 13%), lymphopenia (38%; grades 3/4: 21%), thrombocytopenia (38%; grades 3/4: 3% to 5%), anemia (26%; grades 3/4: 3% to 7%), bleeding (18% to 26%)
  Hepatic: AST/ALT increased (39%), alkaline phosphatase increased (24%), hyperbilirubinemia (10% to 16%)
  Neuromuscular & skeletal: Arthralgia (12% to 28%), weakness (22%), limb pain (18%), myalgia (14% to 17%), back pain (11% to 17%)
  Renal: Creatinine increased (12%)
  Respiratory: Dyspnea (10% to 28%), cough (8% to 17%)
1% to 10%:
  Cardiovascular: LVEF decreased (10%; grade 3/4: 1%), DVT (1% to 3%), myocardial ischemia (1%)
  Central nervous system: Neuropathy (peripheral 10%)
  Dermatologic: Skin blistering (7%)
  Endocrine & metabolic: Hypernatremia (10%), hypophosphatemia (9% to 10%), hypothyroidism (4% to 7%), hyperkalemia (6%), hyponatremia (6%)
  Gastrointestinal: Appetite disturbance (9%), oral pain (6%)
  Ocular: Periorbital edema (7%), lacrimation increased (6%)
  Respiratory: Pulmonary embolism (1%)
<1% (Limited to important or life-threatening): Febrile neutropenia, MI, pancreatitis, reversible posterior leukoencephalopathy syndrome (RPLS), seizure

Overdosage/Toxicology There is no antidote for sunitinib overdose; emesis or gastric lavage may eliminate unabsorbed drug. Treatment is symptom-directed and supportive.

Drug Interactions
  Cytochrome P450 Effect: Substrate of CYP3A4 (major)
  Increased Effect/Toxicity: CYP3A4 inhibitors may increase the levels/effects of sunitinib (example inhibitors include azole antifungals, clarithromycin, diclofenac, doxycycline, erythromycin, imatinib, isoniazid, nefazodone, nicardipine, propofol, protease inhibitors, quinidine, telithromycin, and verapamil). Ketoconazole may increase the effects of sunitinib.
  Decreased Effect: CYP3A4 inducers may decrease the levels/effects of sunitinib (example inducers include aminoglutethimide, carbamazepine, dexamethasone, nafcillin, nevirapine, phenobarbital, and phenytoin. Rifamycins may decrease the effects of sunitinib.

Ethanol/Nutrition/Herb Interactions
  Food: Grapefruit juice may increase the levels/effects of sunitinib. Food has no effect on the bioavailability of sunitinib.
  Herb/Nutraceutical: Avoid St John's wort (may increase metabolism and decrease sunitinib concentrations).

Stability Store at room temperature between 15°C and 30°C (59°F and 86°F).

Mechanism of Action Exhibits antitumor and antiangiogenic properties by inhibiting multiple receptor tyrosine kinases, including platelet-derived growth factors (PDGFRα and PDGFRβ), vascular endothelial growth factors (VEGFR1, VEGFR2, and VEGFR3), FMS-like tyrosine kinase-3 (FLT3), colony-stimulating factor type 1 (CSF-1R), and glial cell-line-derived neurotrophic factor receptor (RET).

Pharmacodynamics/Kinetics
  Distribution: V_d/F: 2230 L
  Protein binding: Sunitinib: 95%; SU12662: 90%
  Metabolism: Hepatic; primarily metabolized by CYP3A4 to the N-desethyl metabolite SU12662 (active)
  Half-life elimination: Sunitinib: 40-60 hours; SU12662: 80-110 hours
  Time to peak, plasma: 6-12 hours
  Excretion: Feces (61%); urine (16%)
(Continued)

Sunitinib *(Continued)*

Dosage Oral: Adults: Gastrointestinal stromal tumor, renal cell cancer: 50 mg once daily for 4 weeks of a 6-week treatment cycle (4 weeks on, 2 weeks off). **Note:** Dose increase or reduction should be done in increments of 12.5 mg; individualize based on safety and tolerability.

Dosage adjustment with concurrent CYP3A4 inhibitor: Dose reductions are more likely to be needed when sunitinib is administered concomitantly with strong CYP3A4 inhibitors; dose reductions to a minimum of 37.5 mg/day should be considered with ketoconazole. (See Drug Interactions for examples of CYP3A4 inhibitors.)

Dosage adjustment with concurrent CYP3A4 inducer: May require increased doses; dosage increases to a maximum of 87.5 mg/day should be considered with rifampin. (See Drug Interactions for examples of CYP3A4 inducers.)

Dosage adjustment in renal/hepatic impairment: Not studied.

Dietary Considerations May be taken with or without food. Avoid grapefruit juice.

Administration May be taken with or without food.

Monitoring Parameters LVEF, baseline (and periodic with cardiac risk factors), blood pressure, adrenal function, CBC with differential and platelets (prior to each treatment cycle), serum chemistries including phosphate (prior to each treatment cycle), thyroid function (if symptomatic)

Dosage Forms Capsule: 12.5 mg, 25 mg, 50 mg

- **Sunitinib Maleate** *see* Sunitinib *on page 1622*
- **Supartz™** *see* Hyaluronate and Derivatives *on page 841*
- **Superdophilus® [OTC]** *see* Lactobacillus *on page 969*
- **Supeudol® (Can)** *see* Oxycodone *on page 1286*
- **Suphera™** *see* Sulfur and Sulfacetamide *on page 1618*
- **Suplasyn® (Can)** *see* Hyaluronate and Derivatives *on page 841*
- **Suprax®** *see* Cefixime *on page 312*
- **Sureprin 81™ [OTC]** *see* Aspirin *on page 160*
- **Surfak® [OTC]** *see* Docusate *on page 533*
- **Surmontil®** *see* Trimipramine *on page 1747*
- **Survanta®** *see* Beractant *on page 210*
- **Sustiva®** *see* Efavirenz *on page 571*
- **Sutent®** *see* Sunitinib *on page 1622*
- **Su-Tuss DM** *see* Guaifenesin and Dextromethorphan *on page 816*
- **Su-Tuss®-HD** *see* Hydrocodone, Pseudoephedrine, and Guaifenesin *on page 852*
- **Suxamethonium Chloride** *see* Succinylcholine *on page 1605*
- **Sween Cream® [OTC]** *see* Vitamin A and Vitamin D *on page 1794*
- **Symax SL** *see* Hyoscyamine *on page 866*
- **Symax SR** *see* Hyoscyamine *on page 866*
- **Symbicort®** *see* Budesonide and Formoterol *on page 247*
- **Symbyax™** *see* Olanzapine and Fluoxetine *on page 1259*
- **Symlin®** *see* Pramlintide *on page 1407*
- **Symmetrel®** *see* Amantadine *on page 86*
- **Sympt-X [OTC]** *see* Glutamine *on page 803*
- **Sympt-X G.I. [OTC]** *see* Glutamine *on page 803*
- **Synacthen** *see* Cosyntropin *on page 422*
- **Synagis®** *see* Palivizumab *on page 1299*
- **Synalar®** *see* Fluocinolone *on page 721*
- **Synalgos®-DC** *see* Dihydrocodeine, Aspirin, and Caffeine *on page 506*
- **Synarel®** *see* Nafarelin *on page 1188*
- **Syn-Diltiazem® (Can)** *see* Diltiazem *on page 509*
- **Synera™** *see* Lidocaine and Tetracaine *on page 1016*
- **Synercid®** *see* Quinupristin and Dalfopristin *on page 1476*
- **Synphasic® (Can)** *see* Ethinyl Estradiol and Norethindrone *on page 655*
- **Syntest D.S.** *see* Estrogens (Esterified) and Methyltestosterone *on page 637*
- **Syntest H.S.** *see* Estrogens (Esterified) and Methyltestosterone *on page 637*
- **Synthroid®** *see* Levothyroxine *on page 1007*
- **Syntocinon® (Can)** *see* Oxytocin *on page 1293*
- **Synvisc®** *see* Hyaluronate and Derivatives *on page 841*
- **Syprine®** *see* Trientine *on page 1739*
- **Syrex** *see* Sodium Chloride *on page 1576*
- **SyringeAvitene™** *see* Collagen Hemostat *on page 416*
- **Syrup of Ipecac** *see* Ipecac Syrup *on page 932*
- **T_3 Sodium (error-prone abbreviation)** *see* Liothyronine *on page 1020*
- **T_3/T_4 Liotrix** *see* Liotrix *on page 1020*
- **T_4** *see* Levothyroxine *on page 1007*
- **T-20** *see* Enfuvirtide *on page 581*
- **642® Tablet (Can)** *see* Propoxyphene *on page 1444*
- **Tabloid®** *see* Thioguanine *on page 1669*
- **Taclonex®** *see* Calcipotriene and Betamethasone *on page 264*

Tacrine (TAK reen)

U.S. Brand Names Cognex®
Index Terms Tacrine Hydrochloride; Tetrahydroaminoacrine; THA
Pharmacologic Category Acetylcholinesterase Inhibitor (Central)
Use Treatment of mild to moderate dementia of the Alzheimer's type
Pregnancy Risk Factor C
Lactation Excretion in breast milk unknown/not recommended
Medication Safety Issues
Sound-alike/look-alike issues:
Cognex® may be confused with Corgard®

International issues:
Cognex® may be confused with Codex® which is a brand name for saccharomyces boulardii in Italy

Contraindications Hypersensitivity to tacrine, acridine derivatives, or any component of the formulation; patients previously treated with tacrine who developed jaundice

Warnings/Precautions The use of tacrine has been associated with elevations in serum transaminases; serum transaminases (specifically ALT) must be monitored throughout therapy; use extreme caution in patients with current evidence of a history of abnormal liver function tests; use caution in patients with urinary tract obstruction (bladder outlet obstruction or prostatic hyperplasia), asthma, and sick-sinus syndrome, bradycardia, or conduction abnormalities (tacrine may cause bradycardia and/or heart block). Also, patients with cardiovascular disease, asthma, or peptic ulcer should use cautiously. Adverse cardiovascular events may also occur in patients without known cardiac disease. Use with caution in patients with a history of seizures. May cause nausea, vomiting, or loose stools. Abrupt discontinuation or dosage decrease may worsen cognitive function. May be associated with neutropenia.

Adverse Reactions
>10%:
Central nervous system: Dizziness, headache
Gastrointestinal: Diarrhea, nausea, vomiting
Miscellaneous: Transaminases increased
1% to 10%:
Cardiovascular: Flushing
Central nervous system: Ataxia, confusion, depression, fatigue, insomnia, somnolence
Dermatologic: Rash
Gastrointestinal: Abdominal pain, anorexia, constipation, dyspepsia, flatulence, weight loss
Neuromuscular & skeletal: Myalgia, tremor
Respiratory: Rhinitis

Overdosage/Toxicology Symptoms included cholinergic crisis characterized by severe nausea, vomiting, salivation, sweating, bradycardia, hypotension, cardiovascular collapse, and convulsions. Increased muscle weakness is a possibility and may result in death if respiratory muscles are involved. Treatments includes general supportive measures. Tertiary anticholinergics, such as atropine, may be used as an antidote. I.V. atropine sulfate titrated to effect is recommended. Atypical increases in blood pressure and heart rate have been reported with other cholinomimetics when coadministered with quaternary anticholinergics such as glycopyrrolate.

Drug Interactions
Cytochrome P450 Effect: Substrate of CYP1A2 (major); **Inhibits** CYP1A2 (weak)
Increased Effect/Toxicity: CYP1A2 inhibitors may increase the levels/effects of tacrine; example inhibitors include ciprofloxacin, fluvoxamine, ketoconazole, norfloxacin, ofloxacin, and rofecoxib. Tacrine in combination with other cholinergic agents (eg, ambenonium, edrophonium, neostigmine, pyridostigmine, bethanechol), will likely produce additive cholinergic effects. Tacrine in combination with beta-blockers may produce additive bradycardia. Tacrine may increase the levels/effect of succinylcholine and theophylline. in elevated plasma levels. Fluvoxamine, enoxacin, and cimetidine increase tacrine concentrations via enzyme inhibition (CYP1A2). Acetylcholinesterase inhibitors (central) may increase the risk of antipsychotic-related extrapyramidal symptoms.
Decreased Effect: CYP1A2 inducers may decrease the levels/effects of tacrine; example inducers include aminoglutethimide, carbamazepine, phenobarbital, rifampin, and cigarette smoking. Tacrine may worsen Parkinson's disease and inhibit the effects of levodopa. Tacrine may antagonize the therapeutic effect of anticholinergic agents (benztropine, trihexyphenidyl).

Ethanol/Nutrition/Herb Interactions Food: Food decreases bioavailability.
Mechanism of Action Centrally-acting cholinesterase inhibitor. It elevates acetylcholine in cerebral cortex by slowing the degradation of acetylcholine.
Pharmacodynamics/Kinetics
Absorption: Oral: Rapid
Distribution: V_d: Mean: 349 L; reduced by food
Protein binding, plasma: 55%
Metabolism: Extensively by CYP450 to multiple metabolites; first pass effect
Bioavailability: Absolute: 17%
Half-life elimination, serum: 2-4 hours; Steady-state: 24-36 hours
Time to peak, plasma: 1-2 hours
Dosage Adults: Initial: 10 mg 4 times/day; may increase by 40 mg/day adjusted every 6 weeks; maximum: 160 mg/day; best administered separate from meal times.
Dose adjustment based upon transaminase elevations:
ALT ≤3 times ULN*: Continue titration
ALT >3 to ≤5 times ULN*: Decrease dose by 40 mg/day, resume when ALT returns to normal
ALT >5 times ULN*: Stop treatment, may rechallenge upon return of ALT to normal
*ULN = upper limit of normal
(Continued)

Tacrine (Continued)

Patients with clinical jaundice confirmed by elevated total bilirubin (>3 mg/dL) should not be rechallenged with tacrine

Dietary Considerations Give with food if GI side effects are intolerable.

Monitoring Parameters ALT (SGPT) levels and other liver enzymes weekly for at least the first 18 weeks, then monitor once every 3 months

Reference Range In clinical trials, serum concentrations >20 ng/mL were associated with a much higher risk of development of symptomatic adverse effects

Dosage Forms Capsule, as hydrochloride: 10 mg, 20 mg, 30 mg, 40 mg

♦ **Tacrine Hydrochloride** see Tacrine on page 1625

Tacrolimus (ta KROE li mus)

U.S. Brand Names Prograf®; Protopic®

Canadian Brand Names Prograf®; Protopic®

Index Terms FK506

Pharmacologic Category Immunosuppressant Agent; Topical Skin Product

Use

Oral/injection: Potent immunosuppressive drug used in heart, kidney, or liver transplant recipients

Topical: Moderate-to-severe atopic dermatitis in patients not responsive to conventional therapy or when conventional therapy is not appropriate

Unlabeled/Investigational Use Potent immunosuppressive drug used in lung, small bowel transplant recipients; immunosuppressive drug for peripheral stem cell/bone marrow transplantation

Restrictions An FDA-approved medication guide must be distributed when dispensing the outpatient prescription (new or refill) for tacrolimus ointment where this medication is to be used without direct supervision of a healthcare provider. Medication guides are available at http://www.fda.gov/cder/Offices/ODS/medication_guides.htm.

Pregnancy Risk Factor C

Pregnancy Implications Tacrolimus crosses the placenta and reaches concentrations four times greater than maternal plasma concentrations. Neonatal hyperkalemia and renal dysfunction have been reported.

Lactation Enters breast milk/contraindicated

Medication Safety Issues

Sound-alike/look-alike issues:

Prograf® may be confused with Gengraf®

Contraindications Hypersensitivity to tacrolimus or any component of the formulation

Warnings/Precautions

Oral/injection: Insulin-dependent post-transplant diabetes mellitus (PTDM) has been reported (1% to 20%); risk increases in African-American and Hispanic kidney transplant patients. **[U.S. Boxed Warning]: Increased susceptibility to infection and the possible development of lymphoma may occur after administration of tacrolimus.** Nephrotoxicity and neurotoxicity have been reported, especially with higher doses; to avoid excess nephrotoxicity do not administer simultaneously with cyclosporine; monitoring of serum concentrations (trough for oral therapy) is essential to prevent organ rejection and reduce drug-related toxicity; tonic clonic seizures may have been triggered by tacrolimus. A period of 24 hours should elapse between discontinuation of cyclosporine and the initiation of tacrolimus. Use caution in renal or hepatic dysfunction, dosing adjustments may be required. Delay initiation if postoperative oliguria occurs. Use may be associated with the development of hypertension (common). Myocardial hypertrophy has been reported (rare). Each mL of injection contains polyoxyl 60 hydrogenated castor oil (HCO-60) (200 mg) and dehydrated alcohol USP 80% v/v. Anaphylaxis has been reported with the injection, use should be reserved for those patients not able to take oral medications.

Topical: [U.S. Boxed Warning]: Topical calcineurin inhibitors have been associated with rare cases of malignancy. Avoid use on malignant or premalignant skin conditions (eg cutaneous T-cell lymphoma). Topical calcineurin agents are considered second-line therapies in the treatment of atopic dermatitis/eczema, and should be limited to use in patients who have failed treatment with other therapies. **[U.S. Boxed Warning]: They should be used for short-term and intermittent treatment using the minimum amount necessary for the control of symptoms should be used.** Application should be limited to involved areas. Safety of intermittent use for >1 year has not been established.

Should not be used in immunocompromised patients. Do not apply to areas of active viral infection; infections at the treatment site should be cleared prior to therapy. Patients with atopic dermatitis are predisposed to skin infections, and tacrolimus therapy has been associated with risk of developing eczema herpeticum, varicella zoster, and herpes simplex. May be associated with development of lymphadenopathy; possible infectious causes should be investigated. Discontinue use in patients with unknown cause of lymphadenopathy or acute infectious mononucleosis. Not recommended for use in patients with skin disease which may increase systemic absorption (eg, Netherton's syndrome). Avoid artificial or natural sunlight exposure, even when Protopic® is not on the skin. Safety not established in patients with generalized erythroderma. **[U.S. Boxed Warning]: The use of Protopic® in children <2 years of age is not recommended,** particularly since the effect on immune system development is unknown.

Adverse Reactions

Oral, I.V.:

≥15%:

Cardiovascular: Chest pain, hypertension, pericardial effusion (heart transplant)

Central nervous system: Dizziness, headache, insomnia, tremor (headache and tremor are associated with high whole blood concentrations and may respond to decreased dosage)

Dermatologic: Pruritus, rash

Endocrine & metabolic: Diabetes mellitus, hyperglycemia, hyper-/hypokalemia, hyperlipemia, hypomagnesemia, hypophosphatemia

Gastrointestinal: Abdominal pain, constipation, diarrhea, dyspepsia, nausea, vomiting

Genitourinary: Urinary tract infection

Hematologic: Anemia, leukocytosis, leukopenia, thrombocytopenia

Hepatic: Ascites

Neuromuscular & skeletal: Arthralgia, back pain, paresthesia, tremor, weakness

Renal: Abnormal kidney function, BUN increased, creatinine increased, oliguria, urinary tract infection

Respiratory: Atelectasis, bronchitis, dyspnea, increased cough, pleural effusion

Miscellaneous: CMV infection, infection

<15%:

Cardiovascular: Abnormal ECG (QRS or ST segment abnormal), angina pectoris, cardiopulmonary failure, deep thrombophlebitis, heart rate decreased, hemorrhage, hemorrhagic stroke, hypervolemia, hypotension, generalized edema, peripheral vascular disorder, phlebitis, postural hypotension, tachycardia, thrombosis, vasodilation

Central nervous system: Abnormal dreams, abnormal thinking, agitation, amnesia, anxiety, chills, confusion, depression, dizziness, elevated mood, emotional lability, encephalopathy, hallucinations, nervousness, paralysis, psychosis, quadriparesis, seizure, somnolence

Dermatologic: Acne, alopecia, cellulitis, exfoliative dermatitis, fungal dermatitis, hirsutism, increased diaphoresis, photosensitivity reaction, skin discoloration, skin disorder, skin ulcer

Endocrine & metabolic: Acidosis, alkalosis, Cushing's syndrome, decreased bicarbonate, decreased serum iron, diabetes mellitus, hypercalcemia, hypercholesterolemia, hyperphosphatemia, hypoproteinemia, increased alkaline phosphatase

Gastrointestinal: Anorexia, appetite increased, cramps, duodenitis, dysphagia, enlarged abdomen, esophagitis (including ulcerative), flatulence, gastritis, gastroesophagitis, GI perforation/hemorrhage, ileus, oral moniliasis, pancreatic pseudocyst, rectal disorder, stomatitis, weight gain

Genitourinary: Bladder spasm, cystitis, dysuria, nocturia, oliguria, urge incontinence, urinary frequency, urinary incontinence, urinary retention, vaginitis

Hematologic: Bruising, coagulation disorder, decreased prothrombin, hypochromic anemia, polycythemia

Hepatic: Abnormal liver function tests, ALT/AST increased, bilirubinemia, cholangitis, cholestatic jaundice, GGT increased, hepatitis (including granulomatous), jaundice, liver damage, increase LDH

Neuromuscular & skeletal: Hypertonia, incoordination, joint disorder, leg cramps, myalgia, myasthenia, myoclonus, nerve compression, neuropathy, osteoporosis

Ocular: Abnormal vision, amblyopia

Otic: Ear pain, otitis media, tinnitus

Renal: Albuminuria, renal tubular necrosis, toxic nephropathy

Respiratory: Asthma, lung disorder, pharyngitis, pneumonia, pneumothorax, pulmonary edema, respiratory disorder, rhinitis, sinusitis, voice alteration

Miscellaneous: Abscess, abnormal healing, allergic reaction, crying, flu-like syndrome, generalized spasm, hernia, herpes simplex, peritonitis, sepsis, writing impaired

Topical:

>10%:

Central nervous system: Headache (5% to 20%), fever (1% to 21%)

Dermatologic: Skin burning (43% to 58%; tends to improve as lesions resolve), pruritus (41% to 46%), erythema (12% to 28%)

Respiratory: Increased cough (18% children)

Miscellaneous: Flu-like syndrome (23% to 28%), allergic reaction (4% to 12%)

Oral, I.V., topical: Postmarketing and/or case reports (limited to important or life-threatening): Acute renal failure, alopecia, anaphylaxis, anaphylactoid reaction, angioedema, ARDS, arrhythmia, atrial fibrillation, atrial flutter, bile duct stenosis, blindness, cardiac arrest, cerebral infarction, cerebrovascular accident, deafness, delirium, depression, DIC, hemiparesis, hemolytic-uremic syndrome, hemorrhagic cystitis, hepatic necrosis, hepatotoxicity, hyperglycemia, leukoencephalopathy, lymphoproliferative disorder (related to EBV), myocardial hypertrophy (associated with ventricular dysfunction; reversible upon discontinuation), MI, neutropenia, pancreatitis (hemorrhagic and necrotizing), pancytopenia, paresthesia, photosensitivity reaction (topical), quadriplegia, QT$_c$ prolongation, respiratory failure, seizure, skin discoloration (topical), Stevens-Johnson syndrome, syncope, toxic epidermal necrolysis, thrombocytopenic purpura, torsade de pointes, TTP, veno-occlusive hepatic disease, venous thrombosis, ventricular fibrillation

Note: Calcineurin inhibitor-induced hemolytic uremic syndrome/thrombotic thrombocytopenic purpura/thrombotic microangiopathy (HUS/TTP/TMA) have been reported (with concurrent sirolimus).

Overdosage/Toxicology Symptoms are extensions of pharmacologic activity and listed adverse effects. Symptomatic and supportive treatment is required. Hemodialysis is not effective.

Drug Interactions

Cytochrome P450 Effect: Substrate of CYP3A4 (major); **Inhibits** CYP3A4 (weak)

Increased Effect/Toxicity: Amphotericin B and other nephrotoxic antibiotics have the potential to increase tacrolimus-associated nephrotoxicity. Cisapride and metoclopramide may increase tacrolimus levels. Synergistic immunosuppression results from concurrent use of cyclosporine. Voriconazole may increase tacrolimus serum concentrations; decrease tacrolimus dosage by 66% when initiating voriconazole. CYP3A4 inhibitors may increase the levels/effects of tacrolimus; example inhibitors include azole antifungals, clarithromycin, diclofenac, doxycycline, erythromycin, imatinib, isoniazid, nefazodone, nicardipine, propofol, protease inhibitors, quinidine, telithromycin, and verapamil. Macrolides may increase tacrolimus concentration (limited documentation). Calcium channel (Continued)

Tacrolimus *(Continued)*

blockers (dihydropyridine) may increase tacrolimus serum concentrations (monitor). Concurrent therapy with sirolimus may increase the risk of HUS/TTP/TMA.

Decreased Effect: Antacids impair tacrolimus absorption (separate administration by at least 2 hours). St John's wort may reduce tacrolimus serum concentrations (avoid concurrent use). CYP3A4 inducers may decrease the levels/effects of tacrolimus; example inducers include aminoglutethimide, carbamazepine, nafcillin, nevirapine, phenobarbital, phenytoin, and rifamycins. Caspofungin and sirolimus may decrease the serum concentrations of tacrolimus.

Ethanol/Nutrition/Herb Interactions

Ethanol: Localized flushing (redness, warm sensation) may occur at application site of topical tacrolimus following ethanol consumption.

Food: Decreases rate and extent of absorption. High-fat meals have most pronounced effect (35% decrease in AUC, 77% decrease in C_{max}). Grapefruit juice, CYP3A4 inhibitor, may increase serum level and/or toxicity of tacrolimus; avoid concurrent use.

Herb/Nutraceutical: St John's wort: May reduce tacrolimus serum concentrations (avoid concurrent use).

Stability

Injection: Prior to dilution, store at 5°C to 25°C (41°F to 77°F). Following dilution, stable for 24 hours in D_5W or NS in glass or polyolefin containers. Dilute with 5% dextrose injection or 0.9% sodium chloride injection to a final concentration between 0.004 mg/mL and 0.02 mg/mL.

Capsules and ointment: Store at room temperature of 15°C to 30°C (59°F to 86°F).

Mechanism of Action Suppresses cellular immunity (inhibits T-lymphocyte activation), possibly by binding to an intracellular protein, FKBP-12

Pharmacodynamics/Kinetics

Absorption: Better in resected patients with a closed stoma; unlike cyclosporine, clamping of the T-tube in liver transplant patients does not alter trough concentrations or AUC

Oral: Incomplete and variable; food within 15 minutes of administration decreases absorption (27%)

Topical: Serum concentrations range from undetectable to 20 ng/mL (<5 ng/mL in majority of adult patients studied)

Protein binding: 99%

Metabolism: Extensively hepatic via CYP3A4 to eight possible metabolites (major metabolite, 31-demethyl tacrolimus, shows same activity as tacrolimus *in vitro*)

Bioavailability: Oral: Adults: 7% to 28%, Children: 10% to 52%; Topical: <0.5%; Absolute: Unknown

Half-life elimination: Variable, 21-61 hours in healthy volunteers

Time to peak: 0.5-4 hours

Excretion: Feces (~92%); feces/urine (<1% as unchanged drug)

Dosage

Oral:

Children: **Notes:** Patients without pre-existing renal or hepatic dysfunction have required (and tolerated) higher doses than adults to achieve similar blood concentrations. It is recommended that therapy be initiated at high end of the recommended adult I.V. and oral dosing ranges; dosage adjustments may be required. If switching from I.V. to oral, the oral dose should be started 8-12 hours after stopping the infusion. Adjunctive therapy with corticosteroids is recommended early post-transplant.

Liver transplant: Initial dose: 0.15-0.20 mg/kg/day in 2 divided doses, given every 12 hours; begin oral dose no sooner than 6 hours post-transplant

Adults: **Notes:** If switching from I.V. to oral, the oral dose should be started 8-12 hours after stopping the infusion. Adjunctive therapy with corticosteroids is recommended early post-transplant.

Heart transplant: Initial dose: 0.075 mg/kg/day in 2 divided doses, given every 12 hours; begin oral dose no sooner than 6 hours post-transplant

Kidney transplant: Initial dose: 0.2 mg/kg/day in 2 divided doses, given every 12 hours; initial dose may be given within 24 hours of transplant, but should be delayed until renal function has recovered; African-American patients may require larger doses to maintain trough concentration

Liver transplant: Initial dose: 0.1-0.15 mg/kg/day in 2 divided doses, given every 12 hours; begin oral dose no sooner than 6 hours post-transplant

I.V.: Children and Adults: **Note:** I.V. route should only be used in patients not able to take oral medications and continued until oral medication can be tolerated; anaphylaxis has been reported. Begin no sooner than 6 hours post-transplant; adjunctive therapy with corticosteroids is recommended.

Heart transplant: Initial dose: 0.01 mg/kg/day as a continuous infusion

Kidney, liver transplant: Initial dose: 0.03-0.05 mg/kg/day as a continuous infusion

Prevention of graft-vs-host disease: 0.03 mg/kg/day as continuous infusion

Topical: Children ≥2 years and Adults: Atopic dermatitis (moderate to severe): Apply minimum amount of 0.03% or 0.1% ointment to affected area twice daily; rub in gently and completely. Discontinue use when symptoms have cleared. If no improvement within 6 weeks, patients should be re-examined to confirm diagnosis.

Dosing adjustment in renal impairment: Evidence suggests that lower doses should be used; patients should receive doses at the lowest value of the recommended I.V. and oral dosing ranges; further reductions in dose below these ranges may be required.

Tacrolimus therapy should usually be delayed up to 48 hours or longer in patients with postoperative oliguria.

Hemodialysis: Not removed by hemodialysis; supplemental dose is not necessary.

Peritoneal dialysis: Significant drug removal is unlikely based on physiochemical characteristics.

Dosing adjustment in hepatic impairment: Use of tacrolimus in liver transplant recipients experiencing post-transplant hepatic impairment may be associated with increased risk of developing renal insufficiency related to high whole blood levels of tacrolimus. The presence of moderate-to-severe hepatic dysfunction (serum bilirubin >2 mg/dL; Child-Pugh score ≥10) appears to affect the metabolism of tacrolimus. The half-life of the drug was prolonged and the clearance reduced after I.V. administration. The bioavailability of tacrolimus was also increased after oral administration. The higher plasma concentrations as determined by ELISA, in patients with severe hepatic dysfunction are probably due to the accumulation of metabolites of lower activity. These patients should be monitored closely and dosage adjustments should be considered. Some evidence indicates that lower doses could be used in these patients.

Dietary Considerations Capsule: Take on an empty stomach; be consistent with timing and composition of meals if GI intolerance occurs (per manufacturer).

Administration
I.V.: Administer by I.V. continuous infusion only. Do not use PVC tubing when administering dilute solutions. Usually intended to be administered as a continuous infusion over 24 hours.

Oral: If dosed once daily (not common), administer in the morning. If dosed twice daily, doses should be 12 hours apart. If the morning and evening doses differ, the larger dose (differences are never >0.5-1 mg) should be given in the morning. If dosed 3 times/day, separate doses by 8 hours.

Topical: Do not use with occlusive dressings. Burning at the application site is most common in first few days; improves as atopic dermatitis improves. Limit application to involved areas. Continue as long as signs and symptoms persist; discontinue if resolution occurs; re-evaluate if symptoms persist >6 weeks.

Monitoring Parameters Renal function, hepatic function, serum electrolytes (especially potassium), glucose and blood pressure, measure 3 times/week for first few weeks, then gradually decrease frequency as patient stabilizes. Whole blood concentrations should be used for monitoring (trough for oral therapy). Signs/symptoms of anaphylactic reactions during infusion should also be monitored. Patients should be monitored during the first 30 minutes of the infusion, and frequently thereafter.

Reference Range
Heart: Typical whole blood trough concentrations:
One week to 3 months: 8-20 ng/mL
Months 3-18: 6-18 ng/mL
Kidney transplant: whole blood trough concentrations:
Months 1-3: 7-20 ng/mL
Months 4-12: 5-15 ng/mL
Liver transplant: whole blood trough concentrations: Months 1-12: 5-20 ng/mL

Additional Information Additional dosing considerations:
Switch from I.V. to oral therapy: Threefold increase in dose
Pediatric patients: About 2 times higher dose compared to adults
Liver dysfunction: Decrease I.V. dose; decrease oral dose
Renal dysfunction: Does not affect kinetics; decrease dose to decrease levels if renal dysfunction is related to the drug

Dosage Forms
Capsule (Prograf®): 0.5 mg, 1 mg, 5 mg
Injection, solution (Prograf®): 5 mg/mL (1 mL) [contains dehydrated alcohol 80% and polyoxyl 60 hydrogenated castor oil]
Ointment, topical (Protopic®): 0.03% (30 g, 60 g, 100 g); 0.1% (30 g, 60 g, 100 g)

Extemporaneous Preparations Tacrolimus 0.5 mg/mL oral suspension: Mix the contents of six 5-mg tacrolimus capsules with equal amounts of Ora-Plus® and Simple Syrup, N.F., to make a final volume of 60 mL. The suspension is stable for 56 days at room temperature in glass or plastic amber prescription bottles.

Esquivel C, So S, McDiarmid S, Andrews W, and Colombani PM, "Suggested Guidelines for the Use of Tacrolimus in Pediatric Liver Transplant Patients," *Transplantation*, 1996, 61(5):847-8.

Foster JA, Jacobson PA, Johnson CE, et al, "Stability of Tacrolimus in an Extemporaneously Compounded Oral Liquid (Abstract of Meeting Presentation)," *American Society of Health-System Pharmacists Annual Meeting*, 1996, 53:P-52(E).

Tacrolimus 1 mg/mL oral suspension: Mix the contents of six 5-mg capsules in approximately 5 mL of sterile water; add capsule contents to an empty amber bottle first, then add sterile water and agitate bottle until drug disperses and a slurry is formed. Add equal parts of Ora-Plus® (suspending agent) and Ora-Sweet® (sweetening agent) to a total volume of 30 mL. The suspension is stable for 4 months at room temperature in plastic amber prescription bottles.

Elefante A, Muindi J, West K, et al, "Long-Term Stability of a Patient-Convenient 1 mg/mL Suspension of Tacrolimus for Accurate Maintenance of Stable Therapeutic Levels," *Bone Marrow Transplant*, 2006, 37(8):781-4.

Tadalafil (tah DA la fil)

U.S. Brand Names Cialis®
Canadian Brand Names Cialis®
Index Terms GF196960
Pharmacologic Category Phosphodiesterase-5 Enzyme Inhibitor
Use Treatment of erectile dysfunction
Pregnancy Risk Factor B
Pregnancy Implications Tadalafil is not indicated for use in women.
Contraindications Hypersensitivity to tadalafil or any component of the formulation; concurrent use of organic nitrates (nitroglycerin) in any form
Warnings/Precautions There is a degree of cardiac risk associated with sexual activity; therefore, physicians may wish to consider the cardiovascular status of their patients prior to initiating any treatment for erectile dysfunction. Use caution in patients with left ventricular outflow obstruction (aortic stenosis or IHSS); may be more sensitive to hypotensive actions. (Continued)

Tadalafil (Continued)

Concurrent use with alpha-adrenergic antagonist therapy may cause symptomatic hypotension; patients should be hemodynamically stable prior to initiating tadalafil therapy at the lowest possible dose. Use caution in patients receiving strong CYP3A4 inhibitors, the elderly, or those with hepatic impairment or renal impairment; dosage adjustment/limitation is needed. Use caution in patients with peptic ulcer disease.

Agents for the treatment of erectile dysfunction should be used with caution in patients with anatomical deformation of the penis (angulation, cavernosal fibrosis, or Peyronie's disease), or in patients who have conditions which may predispose them to priapism (sickle cell anemia, multiple myeloma, leukemia). All patients should be instructed to seek medical attention if erection persists >4 hours. The safety and efficacy of tadalafil with other treatments for erectile dysfunction have not been studied and are, therefore, not recommended as combination therapy.

Rare cases of nonarteritic ischemic optic neuropathy (NAION) have been reported; risk may be increased with history of vision loss. Other risk factors for NAION include heart disease, diabetes, hypertension, smoking, age >50 years, or history of certain eye problems.

Safety and efficacy have not been studied in patients with the following conditions, therefore, use in these patients is not recommended: Arrhythmias, hypotension, uncontrolled hypertension, unstable angina or angina during intercourse, cardiac failure (NYHA Class II or greater), myocardial infarction within the last 3 months, or stroke within the last 6 months. A minority of patients with retinitis pigmentosa have genetic disorders of retinal phosphodiesterases; use is not recommended. Safety and efficacy in children have not been established.

Adverse Reactions

>10%: Central nervous system: Headache (11% to 15%)

2% to 10%:

Cardiovascular: Flushing (2% to 3%)

Gastrointestinal: Dyspepsia (4% to 10%)

Neuromuscular & skeletal: CPK increased (2%), back pain (3% to 6%), myalgia (1% to 4%), limb pain (1% to 3%)

Respiratory: Nasal congestion (2% to 3%)

<2%, postmarketing, and/or case reports: Abdominal pain (upper), abnormal liver function tests, angina pectoris, arthralgia, blurred vision, chest pain, color perception change, color vision decreased, conjunctival hyperemia, conjunctivitis, diaphoresis, diarrhea, dizziness, dysphagia, dyspnea, epistaxis, esophagitis, exfoliative dermatitis, eye pain, eyelid swelling, facial edema, fatigue, gastritis, gastroesophageal reflux, hepatic enzymes increased, hyper-/hypotension, hypoesthesia, GGTP increased, insomnia, migraine, MI, nausea, nonarteritic ischemic optic neuropathy, pain, palpitation, paresthesia, pharyngitis, photophobia, postural hypotension, priapism (reported with drugs in this class), pruritus, rash, retinal artery occlusion, retinal vein occlusion, somnolence, Stevens-Johnson syndrome, stroke, sudden cardiac death, syncope, tachycardia, urticaria, vertigo, visual changes (color vision), visual field loss, vomiting, weakness, xerostomia

Overdosage/Toxicology Symptoms similar to those seen at lower doses (headache, back pain, myalgias). Treatment is symptomatic and supportive.

Drug Interactions

Cytochrome P450 Effect: Substrate of CYP3A4 (major)

Increased Effect/Toxicity:

Tadalafil increases the hypotensive effects of alpha1-blockers. Concurrent use with organic nitrates may cause severe hypotension. Antifungals agents (imidazole), macrolide antibiotics (clarithromycin, erythromycin, telithromycin, troleandomycin), protease inhibitors (amprenavir, atazanavir, fosamprenavir, indinavir, lopinavir, nelfinavir, ritonavir, saquinavir), and other CYP3A4 inhibitors may increase tadalafil levels.

Ethanol/Nutrition/Herb Interactions

Ethanol: Substantial consumption of ethanol may increase the risk of hypotension and orthostasis. Lower ethanol consumption has not been associated with significant changes in blood pressure or increase in orthostatic symptoms.

Food: Rate and extent of absorption are not affected by food. Grapefruit juice may increase serum levels/toxicity of tadalafil. Do not give more than a single 10 mg dose of tadalafil more frequently than every 72 hours in patients who regularly consume grapefruit juice.

Stability Store at controlled room temperature of 15°C to 30°C (59°F to 86°F).

Mechanism of Action Does not directly cause penile erections, but affects the response to sexual stimulation. The physiologic mechanism of erection of the penis involves release of nitric oxide (NO) in the corpus cavernosum during sexual stimulation. NO then activates the enzyme guanylate cyclase, which results in increased levels of cyclic guanosine monophosphate (cGMP), producing smooth muscle relaxation and inflow of blood to the corpus cavernosum. Tadalafil enhances the effect of NO by inhibiting phosphodiesterase type 5 (PDE-5), which is responsible for degradation of cGMP in the corpus cavernosum; when sexual stimulation causes local release of NO, inhibition of PDE-5 by tadalafil causes increased levels of cGMP in the corpus cavernosum, resulting in smooth muscle relaxation and inflow of blood to the corpus cavernosum. At recommended doses, it has no effect in the absence of sexual stimulation.

Pharmacodynamics/Kinetics

Onset: Within 1 hour

Duration: Up to 36 hours

Distribution: V_d: 63 L

Protein binding: 94%

Metabolism: Hepatic, via CYP3A4 to metabolites (inactive)

Half-life elimination: 17.5 hours

Time to peak, plasma: 2 hours

Excretion: Feces (61%, as metabolites); urine (36%, as metabolites)

Dosage Oral: Adults: Erectile dysfunction: 10 mg prior to anticipated sexual activity (dosing range: 5-20 mg); to be given as one single dose and not given more than once daily. **Note:** Erectile function may be improved for up to 36 hours following a single dose; adjust dose.

Elderly: Dosage is based on renal function; refer to "Dosage adjustment in renal impairment"

Dosing adjustment with concomitant medications:

Alpha$_1$-blockers: If stabilized on either alpha blockers or tadalafil therapy, initiate new therapy with the other agent at the lowest possible dose.

CYP3A4 inhibitors: Dose reduction of tadalafil is recommended with strong CYP3A4 inhibitors. The dose of tadalafil should not exceed 10 mg, and tadalafil should not be taken more frequently than once every 72 hours. Examples of such inhibitors include amprenavir, atazanavir, clarithromycin, conivaptan, delavirdine, diclofenac, fosamprenavir, imatinib, indinavir, isoniazid, itraconazole, ketoconazole, miconazole, nefazodone, nelfinavir, nicardipine, propofol, quinidine, ritonavir, and telithromycin.

Dosage adjustment in renal impairment:

Cl_{cr} 31-50 mL/minute: Initial dose 5 mg once daily; maximum dose 10 mg not to be given more frequently than every 48 hours.

Cl_{cr} <30 mL/minute or hemodialysis: Maximum dose 5 mg.

Dosage adjustment in hepatic impairment:

Mild-to-moderate hepatic impairment (Child-Pugh class A or B): Dose should not exceed 10 mg once daily

Severe hepatic impairment: Use is not recommended

Dietary Considerations May be taken with or without food.

Administration May be administered with or without food, prior to anticipated sexual activity.

Monitoring Parameters Monitor for response and adverse effects.

Dosage Forms Tablet: 5 mg, 10 mg, 20 mg

♦ **Tagamet®** [DSC] see Cimetidine on page 369

♦ **Tagamet® HB (Can)** see Cimetidine on page 369

♦ **Tagamet® HB 200 [OTC]** see Cimetidine on page 369

♦ **TAK-375** see Ramelteon on page 1481

♦ **Talwin®** see Pentazocine on page 1339

♦ **Talwin® NX** see Pentazocine on page 1339

♦ **TAM** see Tamoxifen on page 1631

♦ **Tambocor™** see Flecainide on page 710

♦ **Tamiflu®** see Oseltamivir on page 1274

♦ **Tamofen® (Can)** see Tamoxifen on page 1631

Tamoxifen (ta MOKS i fen)

U.S. Brand Names Nolvadex® [DSC]; Soltamox™

Canadian Brand Names Apo-Tamox®; Gen-Tamoxifen; Nolvadex®; Nolvadex®-D; Novo-Tamoxifen; Tamofen®

Index Terms ICI-46474; NSC-180973; TAM; Tamoxifen Citrate

Pharmacologic Category Antineoplastic Agent, Estrogen Receptor Antagonist

Use Palliative or adjunctive treatment of advanced breast cancer; reduce the incidence of breast cancer in women at high risk; reduce risk of invasive breast cancer in women with ductal carcinoma in situ (DCIS); metastatic female and male breast cancer

Unlabeled/Investigational Use Treatment of mastalgia, gynecomastia, pancreatic carcinoma, melanoma and desmoid tumors; induction of ovulation; treatment of precocious puberty in females, secondary to McCune-Albright syndrome

Restrictions An FDA-approved medication guide must be distributed when dispensing the outpatient prescription (new or refill) to females for breast cancer prevention or treatment of ductal carcinoma in situ where this medication is to be used without direct supervision of a healthcare provider. Medication guides are available at http://www.fda.gov/cder/Offices/ODS/medication_guides.htm.

Pregnancy Risk Factor D

Pregnancy Implications Animal studies have demonstrated fetal adverse effects and fetal loss. There are no adequate and well-controlled studies in pregnant women. There have been reports of vaginal bleeding, birth defects and fetal loss in pregnant women. Tamoxifen use during pregnancy may have a potential long term risk to the fetus of a DES-like syndrome. For sexually-active women of childbearing age, initiate during menstruation (negative β-hCG immediately prior to initiation in women with irregular cycles). Tamoxifen may induce ovulation. Barrier or nonhormonal contraceptives are recommended. Pregnancy should be avoided during treatment and for 2 months after treatment has been discontinued.

Lactation Excretion in breast milk unknown/contraindicated

Medication Safety Issues

Sound-alike/look-alike issues:

Tamoxifen may be confused with pentoxifylline, Tambocor™

Contraindications Hypersensitivity to tamoxifen or any component of the formulation; concurrent warfarin therapy or history of deep vein thrombosis or pulmonary embolism (when tamoxifen is used for cancer risk reduction); pregnancy

Warnings/Precautions Hazardous agent - use appropriate precautions for handling and disposal. **[U.S. Boxed Warning]: Serious and life-threatening events (including stroke, pulmonary emboli, and uterine malignancy) have occurred at an incidence greater than placebo during use for breast cancer risk reduction.** These events are rare, but require consideration in risk:benefit evaluation. An increased incidence of thromboembolic events has been associated with use for breast cancer; risk may increase with chemotherapy addition; use caution in individuals with a history of thromboembolic events. Use with caution in patients with leukopenia, thrombocytopenia, or hyperlipidemias. Decreased visual acuity, retinopathy, corneal changes, and increased incidence of cataracts have been reported. Hypercalcemia has occurred in patients with bone metastasis. Significant bone loss of the lumbar spine and hip was associated with use in premenopausal women. Liver abnormalities such as cholestasis, fatty liver, hepatitis, and hepatic necrosis have occurred. Hepatocellular (Continued)

Tamoxifen *(Continued)*

carcinomas have been reported in some studies; relationship to treatment is unclear. Endometrial hyperplasia, polyps, endometriosis, uterine fibroids, and ovarian cysts have occurred. Increased risk of uterine or endometrial cancer; monitor. Safety and efficacy in children <2 years of age, or for treatment durations >1 year in children 2-10 years, have not been established.

Adverse Reactions

>10%:

Cardiovascular: Flushing (33% to 41%), hypertension (11%), peripheral edema (11%)

Central nervous system: Pain (3% to 16%), mood changes (12% to 18%), depression (2% to 12%)

Dermatologic: Skin changes (6% to 19%), rash (13%)

Endocrine & metabolic: Hot flashes (3% to 80%), fluid retention (32%), altered menses (13% to 25%), amenorrhea (16%)

Gastrointestinal: Nausea (5% to 26%), weight loss (23%)

Genitourinary: Vaginal bleeding (2% to 23%), vaginal discharge (13% to 55%)

Neuromuscular & skeletal: Weakness (19%), arthritis (14%), arthralgia (11%)

Respiratory: Pharyngitis (14%)

1% to 10%:

Cardiovascular: Chest pain (5%), venous thrombotic events (5%), edema (4%), cardiovascular ischemia (3%), cerebrovascular ischemia (3%), angina (2%), deep venous thrombus (2%), MI (1%)

Central nervous system: Insomnia (9%), dizziness (8%), headache (8%), anxiety (6%), fatigue (4%)

Dermatologic: Alopecia (<1% to 5%)

Endocrine & metabolic: Oligomenorrhea (9%), breast pain (6%), menstrual disorder (6%), breast neoplasm (5%), hypercholesterolemia (4%)

Gastrointestinal: Abdominal pain (9%), weight gain (9%), throat irritation (oral solution 5%), constipation (4% to 8%), diarrhea (7%), dyspepsia (6%), abdominal cramps (1%), anorexia (1%)

Genitourinary: Urinary tract infection (10%), leukorrhea (9%), vaginal hemorrhage (6%), vaginitis (5%), ovarian cyst (3%)

Hematologic: Thrombocytopenia (<1% to 10%), anemia (5%)

Hepatic: SGOT increased (5%), serum bilirubin increased (2%)

Neuromuscular & skeletal: Bone pain (6% to 10%), osteoporosis (7%), fracture (7%), arthrosis (5%), myalgia (5%), paresthesia (5%), musculoskeletal pain (3%)

Ocular: Cataract (7%)

Renal: Serum creatinine increased (up to 2%)

Respiratory: Cough (4% to 9%), dyspnea (8%), bronchitis (5%), sinusitis (5%)

Miscellaneous: Infection/sepsis (up to 9%), diaphoresis (6%), flu-like syndrome (6%), allergic reaction (3%)

<1%, infrequent, or frequency not defined: Angioedema, bullous pemphigoid, cholestasis, corneal changes, endometriosis, endometrial cancer, endometrial hyperplasia, endometrial polyps, erythema multiforme, fatty liver, hepatic necrosis, hepatitis, hypercalcemia, hyperlipidemia, hypersensitivity reactions, hypertriglyceridemia, impotence (males), interstitial pneumonitis, lightheadedness, loss of libido (males), pancreatitis, phlebitis, pruritus vulvae, pulmonary embolism, retinal vein thrombosis, retinopathy, second primary tumors, Stevens-Johnson syndrome, stroke, taste disturbances, tumor pain and local disease flare (including increase in lesion size and erythema) during treatment of metastatic breast cancer (generally resolves with continuation), uterine fibroids, vaginal dryness

Overdosage/Toxicology Overdose produced respiratory difficulties and seizure in animal studies. In humans, loading doses of 400 mg/m^2 followed by 150 mg/m^2 twice daily produced reversible neurotoxicity (tremor, hyperreflexia, unsteady gait, and dizziness). Loading doses of >250 mg/m^2 followed by 80 mg/m^2 twice daily produced QT prolongation in some patients. In the case of an overdose, treatment is symptom-directed and supportive.

Drug Interactions

Cytochrome P450 Effect: Substrate of CYP2A6 (minor), 2B6 (minor), 2C9 (major), 2D6 (major), 2E1 (minor), 3A4 (major); **Inhibits** CYP2B6 (weak), 2C8 (moderate), 2C9 (weak), 3A4 (weak)

Increased Effect/Toxicity: Concomitant use of warfarin is contraindicated when used for risk reduction; results in significant enhancement of the anticoagulant effects of warfarin. Tamoxifen may increase the levels/effects of CYP2C8 substrates; example substrates include amiodarone, paclitaxel, pioglitazone, repaglinide, and rosiglitazone. CYP2C9 inhibitors may increase the levels/effects of tamoxifen; example inhibitors include delavirdine, fluconazole, gemfibrozil, ketoconazole, nicardipine, NSAIDs, sulfonamides, and tolbutamide. CYP2D6 inhibitors may increase the levels/effects of tamoxifen; example inhibitors include chlorpromazine, delavirdine, fluoxetine, miconazole, paroxetine, pergolide, quinidine, quinine, ritonavir, and ropinirole. CYP3A4 inhibitors may increase the levels/effects of tamoxifen; example inhibitors include azole antifungals, clarithromycin, diclofenac, doxycycline, erythromycin, imatinib, isoniazid, nefazodone, nicardipine, propofol, protease inhibitors, quinidine, telithromycin, and verapamil. Rifamycin derivatives may increase the metabolism (via CYP isoenzymes) of tamoxifen.

Decreased Effect: CYP2C9 inducers may decrease the levels/effects of tamoxifen; example inducers include carbamazepine, phenobarbital, phenytoin, rifampin, rifapentine, and secobarbital. CYP3A4 inducers may decrease the levels/effects of tamoxifen; example inducers include aminoglutethimide, carbamazepine, nafcillin, nevirapine, phenobarbital, phenytoin, and rifamycins. Tamoxifen may reduce the levels/effects of anastrozole (concurrent therapy is not recommended per manufacturer).

Ethanol/Nutrition/Herb Interactions Herb/Nutraceutical: Avoid black cohosh, dong quai in estrogen-dependent tumors. Avoid St John's wort (may decrease levels/effects of tamoxifen).

Stability

Solution: Store at room temperature at or below 25°C (77°F); do not refrigerate or freeze. Protect from light. Use within 3 months of opening.

Tablet: Store at room temperature of 20°C to 25°C (68°F to 77°F).

Mechanism of Action Competitively binds to estrogen receptors on tumors and other tissue targets, producing a nuclear complex that decreases DNA synthesis and inhibits estrogen effects; nonsteroidal agent with potent antiestrogenic properties which compete with estrogen for binding sites in breast and other tissues; cells accumulate in the G_0 and G_1 phases; therefore, tamoxifen is cytostatic rather than cytocidal.

Pharmacodynamics/Kinetics

Absorption: Well absorbed; tablet and oral solution are bioequivalent

Distribution: High concentrations found in uterus, endometrial and breast tissue

Protein binding: 99%

Metabolism: Hepatic (via CYP3A4) to major metabolites, N-desmethyl tamoxifen (major) and 4-hydroxytamoxifen (minor), and a tamoxifen derivative (minor); undergoes enterohepatic recirculation

Half-life elimination: Distribution: 7-14 hours; Elimination: 5-7 days; Metabolites: 14 days

Time to peak, serum: 5 hours

Excretion: Feces (26% to 51%); urine (9% to 13%)

Dosage Oral (refer to individual protocols):

Children: Female: Precocious puberty and McCune-Albright syndrome (unlabeled use): A dose of 20 mg/day has been reported in patients 2-10 years of age; safety and efficacy have not been established for treatment of longer than 1 year duration

Adults:

Breast cancer:

Metastatic (males and females) or adjuvant therapy (females): 20-40 mg/day; daily doses >20 mg should be given in 2 divided doses (morning and evening)

Prevention (high-risk females): 20 mg/day for 5 years

DCIS (females): 20 mg once daily for 5 years

Note: Higher dosages (up to 700 mg/day) have been investigated for use in modulation of multidrug resistance (MDR), but are not routinely used in clinical practice

Induction of ovulation (unlabeled use): 5-40 mg twice daily for 4 days

Administration Administer once or twice daily. Doses >20 mg/day should be given in divided doses.

Monitoring Parameters CBC with platelets, serum calcium, LFTs; abnormal vaginal bleeding; annual gynecologic exams, mammogram

Test Interactions T_4 elevations (which may be explained by increases in thyroid-binding globulin) have been reported; not accompanied by clinical hyperthyroidism

Additional Information Oral clonidine is being studied for the treatment of tamoxifen-induced "hot flashes." The tumor flare reaction may indicate a good therapeutic response, and is often considered a good prognostic factor.

Dosage Forms

Solution, oral:

Soltamox™: 10 mg/5 mL (150 mL) [licorice flavor]

Tablet: 10 mg, 20 mg

Nolvadex®: 10 mg, 20 mg [DSC]

♦ **Tamoxifen Citrate** see Tamoxifen on page 1631

Tamsulosin (tam SOO loe sin)

U.S. Brand Names Flomax®

Canadian Brand Names Flomax®; Flomax® CR

Index Terms Tamsulosin Hydrochloride

Pharmacologic Category Alpha₁ Blocker

Use Treatment of signs and symptoms of benign prostatic hyperplasia (BPH)

Pregnancy Risk Factor B

Pregnancy Implications Teratogenic effects were not observed in animal studies, however, tamsulosin is not indicated for use in women.

Lactation Not indicated for use in women

Medication Safety Issues

Sound-alike/look-alike issues:

Flomax® may be confused with Fosamax®, Volmax®

International issues:

Flomax®: Brand name for morniflumate in Italy

Flomax® may be confused with Flomox® which is a brand name for cefcapene in Japan

Contraindications Hypersensitivity to tamsulosin or any component of the formulation; concurrent use with phosphodiesterase-5 (PDE-5) inhibitors including sildenafil (>25 mg), tadalafil (if tamsulosin dose >0.4 mg/day), or vardenafil

Warnings/Precautions Not intended for use as an antihypertensive drug. May cause significant orthostatic hypotension and syncope, especially with first dose; anticipate a similar effect if therapy is interrupted for a few days, if dosage is rapidly increased, or if another antihypertensive drug (particularly vasodilators) or a PDE5 inhibitor is introduced. Patients should be cautioned about performing hazardous tasks when starting new therapy or adjusting dosage upward. Discontinue if symptoms of angina occur or worsen. Rule out prostatic carcinoma before beginning therapy with tamsulosin. Intraoperative floppy iris syndrome has been observed in cataract surgery patients who were on or were previously treated with alpha₁ blockers; causality has not been established and there appears to be no benefit in discontinuing alpha blocker therapy prior to surgery. Rarely, patients with a sulfa allergy have also developed an allergic reaction to tamsulosin; avoid use when previous reaction has been severe. Safety and efficacy have not been established in children.

Adverse Reactions

>10%:

Cardiovascular: Studies specific for orthostatic hypotension: Overall, at least one positive test was observed in 16% of patients receiving 0.4 mg and 19% of patients receiving the 0.8 mg dose. "First-dose" orthostatic hypotension following a 0.4 mg dose was reported as 7% at 4 hours postdose and 6% at 8 hours postdose.

(Continued)

Tamsulosin *(Continued)*

Central nervous system: Headache (19% to 21%), dizziness (15% to 17%)
Genitourinary: Abnormal ejaculation (8% to 18%)
Respiratory: Rhinitis (13% to 18%)
1% to 10%:
Cardiovascular: Chest pain (~4%)
Central nervous system: Somnolence (3% to 4%), insomnia (1% to 2%), vertigo (0.6% to 1%)
Endocrine & metabolic: Libido decreased (1% to 2%)
Gastrointestinal: Diarrhea (4% to 6%), nausea (3% to 4%), stomach discomfort (2% to 3%), bitter taste (2% to 3%)
Neuromuscular & skeletal: Weakness (8% to 9%), back pain (7% to 8%)
Ocular: Amblyopia (0.2% to 2%)
Respiratory: Pharyngitis (5% to 6%), cough (3% to 5%), sinusitis (2% to 4%)
Miscellaneous: Infection (9% to 11%), tooth disorder (1% to 2%)
<1% (Limited to important or life-threatening): Allergic reactions (rash, angioedema, pruritus, urticaria) priapism; constipation, intraoperative floppy iris syndrome, orthostasis (symptomatic) (0.2% to 0.4%), palpitation, syncope (0.2% to 0.4%), transaminases increased, vomiting

Drug Interactions
Cytochrome P450 Effect: Substrate (major) of CYP2D6, 3A4
Increased Effect/Toxicity: Alpha-adrenergic blockers and calcium channel blockers may increase risk of hypotension. Risk of first-dose orthostatic hypotension may increase with beta-blockers. Cimetidine may decrease tamsulosin clearance. Blood pressure-lowering effects are additive with sildenafil (use with extreme caution), tadalafil (may be used when tamsulosin dose is ≤0.4 mg/day), and vardenafil (use is contraindicated by the manufacturer).

CYP2D6 inhibitors may increase the levels/effects of tamsulosin; example inhibitors include chlorpromazine, delavirdine, fluoxetine, miconazole, paroxetine, pergolide, quinidine, quinine, ritonavir, and ropinirole. CYP3A4 inhibitors may increase the levels/effects of tamsulosin; example inhibitors include azole antifungals, clarithromycin, diclofenac, doxycycline, erythromycin, imatinib, isoniazid, nefazodone, nicardipine, propofol, protease inhibitors, quinidine, telithromycin, and verapamil.

Decreased Effect: CYP3A4 inducers may decrease the levels/effects of tamsulosin; example inducers include aminoglutethimide, carbamazepine, nafcillin, nevirapine, phenobarbital, phenytoin, and rifamycins.

Ethanol/Nutrition/Herb Interactions
Food: Fasting increases bioavailability by 30% and peak concentration 40% to 70%.
Herb/Nutraceutical: Avoid saw palmetto (due to limited experience with this combination).
Mechanism of Action Tamsulosin is an antagonist of alpha$_{1A}$ adrenoreceptors in the prostate. Smooth muscle tone in the prostate is mediated by alpha$_{1A}$ adrenoreceptors; blocking them leads to relaxation of smooth muscle in the bladder neck and prostate causing an improvement of urine flow and decreased symptoms of BPH. Approximately 75% of the alpha$_1$ receptors in the prostate are of the alpha$_{1A}$ subtype.
Pharmacodynamics/Kinetics
Absorption: >90%
Protein binding: 94% to 99%, primarily to alpha$_1$ acid glycoprotein (AAG)
Metabolism: Hepatic via CYP; metabolites undergo extensive conjugation to glucuronide or sulfate
Bioavailability: Fasting: 30% increase
Distribution: V$_d$: 16 L
Steady-state: By the fifth day of once-daily dosing
Half-life elimination: Healthy volunteers: 9-13 hours; Target population: 14-15 hours
Time to peak: Fasting: 4-5 hours; With food: 6-7 hours
Excretion: Urine (76%, <10% as unchanged drug); feces (21%)
Dosage Oral: Adults: 0.4 mg once daily ~30 minutes after the same meal each day; dose may be increased after 2-4 weeks to 0.8 mg once daily in patients who fail to respond. If therapy is interrupted for several days, restart with 0.4 mg once daily.
Dosage adjustment in renal impairment:
Cl$_{cr}$ ≥10 mL/minute: No adjustment needed
Cl$_{cr}$ <10 mL/minute: Not studied
Dietary Considerations Take once daily, 30 minutes after the same meal each day.
Administration Capsules should be swallowed whole; do not crush, chew, or open.
Dosage Forms Capsule, as hydrochloride: 0.4 mg

♦ **Tamsulosin Hydrochloride** *see* Tamsulosin *on page 1633*
♦ **Tanac®** [OTC] *see* Benzocaine *on page 204*
♦ **TanaCof-XR** *see* Brompheniramine *on page 242*
♦ **Tanafed DMX™** *see* Chlorpheniramine, Pseudoephedrine, and Dextromethorphan *on page 355*
♦ **Tanafed DP™** *see* Dexchlorpheniramine and Pseudoephedrine *on page 483*
♦ **Tanta-Orciprenaline®** (Can) *see* Metaproterenol *on page 1096*
♦ **TAP-144** *see* Leuprolide *on page 991*
♦ **Tapazole®** *see* Methimazole *on page 1108*
♦ **Tarceva®** *see* Erlotinib *on page 606*
♦ **Targretin®** *see* Bexarotene *on page 219*
♦ **Tarka®** *see* Trandolapril and Verapamil *on page 1722*
♦ **Taro-Amcinonide (Can)** *see* Amcinonide *on page 88*
♦ **Taro-Carbamazepine Chewable (Can)** *see* Carbamazepine *on page 284*
♦ **Taro-Ciprofloxacin (Can)** *see* Ciprofloxacin *on page 372*
♦ **Taro-Clindamycin (Can)** *see* Clindamycin *on page 389*

- **Taro-Clobetasol (Can)** *see* Clobetasol *on page 391*
- **Taro-Desoximetasone (Can)** *see* Desoximetasone *on page 479*
- **Taro-Mometasone (Can)** *see* Mometasone Furoate *on page 1165*
- **Taro-Simvastatin (Can)** *see* Simvastatin *on page 1567*
- **Taro-Sone® (Can)** *see* Betamethasone *on page 211*
- **Taro-Warfarin (Can)** *see* Warfarin *on page 1800*
- **Tasmar®** *see* Tolcapone *on page 1701*
- **Tavist® Allergy [OTC]** *see* Clemastine *on page 387*
- **Tavist® ND [OTC]** *see* Loratadine *on page 1033*
- **Taxol®** *see* Paclitaxel *on page 1295*
- **Taxotere®** *see* Docetaxel *on page 530*

Tazarotene (taz AR oh teen)

U.S. Brand Names Avage™; Tazorac®
Canadian Brand Names Tazorac®
Pharmacologic Category Acne Products; Keratolytic Agent; Topical Skin Product, Acne
Use Topical treatment of facial acne vulgaris; topical treatment of stable plaque psoriasis of up to 20% body surface area involvement; mitigation (palliation) of facial skin wrinkling, facial mottled hyper-/hypopigmentation, and benign facial lentigines
Pregnancy Risk Factor X
Pregnancy Implications May cause fetal harm if administered to a pregnant woman. A negative pregnancy test should be obtained 2 weeks prior to treatment; treatment should begin during a normal menstrual period.
Lactation Excretion in breast milk unknown/use caution
Contraindications Hypersensitivity to tazarotene, other retinoids or vitamin A derivatives (isotretinoin, tretinoin, etretinate); or any component of the formulation; use in women of childbearing potential who are unable to comply with birth control requirements; pregnancy (negative pregnancy test required)
Warnings/Precautions Women of childbearing potential must use adequate contraceptive measures because of potential teratogenicity. May cause photosensitivity; exposure to sunlight should be avoided unless deemed medically necessary, and in such cases, exposure should be minimized (including use of sunscreens/protective clothing) during use of tazarotene. Risk may be increased by concurrent therapy with known photosensitizers (thiazides, tetracyclines, fluoroquinolones, phenothiazines, sulfonamides). For external use only; avoid contact with eyes, eyelids, and mouth. Not for use on eczematous, broken, or sunburned skin; not for treatment of lentigo maligna. Avoid application over extensive areas; specifically, safety and efficacy of gel applied over >20% of BSA have not been established. Safety and efficacy in children <12 years of age have not been established.
Adverse Reactions Percentage of incidence varies with formulation and/or strength:

>10%: Dermatologic: Burning/stinging, desquamation, dry skin, erythema, pruritus, skin pain, worsening of psoriasis

1% to 10%: Dermatologic: Contact dermatitis, discoloration, fissuring, hypertriglyceridemia, inflammation, irritation, localized bleeding, rash

Frequency not defined:
Dermatologic: Photosensitization
Neuromuscular & skeletal: Peripheral neuropathy

Overdosage/Toxicology Excessive topical use may lead to marked redness, peeling, or discomfort. Oral ingestion may lead to the same adverse effects as those associated with excessive oral intake of Vitamin A (hypervitaminosis A) or other retinoids. If oral ingestion occurs, monitor the patient and administer appropriate supportive measures as necessary.

Drug Interactions
Increased Effect/Toxicity: Increased toxicity may occur with sulfur, benzoyl peroxide, salicylic acid, resorcinol, or any product with strong drying effects (including alcohol-containing compounds) due to increased drying actions. May augment phototoxicity of sensitizing medications (thiazides, tetracyclines, fluoroquinolones, phenothiazines, sulfonamides).

Stability Store at room temperature of 25°C (77°F), away from heat and direct light; do not freeze.

Mechanism of Action Synthetic, acetylenic retinoid which modulates differentiation and proliferation of epithelial tissue and exerts some degree of anti-inflammatory and immunological activity

Pharmacodynamics/Kinetics
Duration: Therapeutic: Psoriasis: Effects have been observed for up to 3 months after a 3-month course of topical treatment
Absorption: Minimal following cutaneous application (≤6% of dose)
Distribution: Retained in skin for prolonged periods after topical application.
Protein binding: >99%
Metabolism: Prodrug, rapidly metabolized via esterases to an active metabolite (tazarotenic acid) following topical application and systemic absorption; tazarotenic acid undergoes further hepatic metabolism
Half-life elimination: 18 hours
Excretion: Urine and feces (as metabolites)

Dosage Topical: **Note:** In patients experiencing excessive pruritus, burning, skin redness, or peeling, discontinue until integrity of the skin is restored, or reduce dosing to an interval the patient is able to tolerate.
Children ≥12 years and Adults:
Acne: Tazorac® cream/gel 0.1%: Cleanse the face gently. After the skin is dry, apply a thin film of tazarotene (2 mg/cm²) once daily, in the evening, to the skin where the acne lesions appear; use enough to cover the entire affected area
(Continued)

Tazarotene *(Continued)*

Psoriasis: Tazorac® gel 0.05% or 0.1%: Apply once daily, in the evening, to psoriatic lesions using enough (2 mg/cm^2) to cover only the lesion with a thin film to no more than 20% of body surface area. If a bath or shower is taken prior to application, dry the skin before applying. Unaffected skin may be more susceptible to irritation, avoid application to these areas.

Children ≥17 years and Adults: Palliation of fine facial wrinkles, facial mottled hyper/hypopigmentation, benign facial lentigines: Avage™: Apply a pea-sized amount once daily to clean dry face at bedtime; lightly cover entire face including eyelids if desired. Emollients or moisturizers may be applied before or after; if applied before tazarotene, ensure cream or lotion has absorbed into the skin and has dried completely.

Adults: Psoriasis: Tazorac® cream 0.05% or 0.1%: Apply once daily, in the evening, to psoriatic lesions using enough (2 mg/cm^2) to cover only the lesion with a thin film to no more than 20% of body surface area. If a bath or shower is taken prior to application, dry the skin before applying. Unaffected skin may be more susceptible to irritation, avoid application to these areas.

Administration Do not apply to eczematous or sunburned skin; apply thin film to affected areas; avoid eyes and mouth

Monitoring Parameters Disease severity in plaque psoriasis during therapy (reduction in erythema, scaling, induration); routine blood chemistries (including transaminases) are suggested during long-term topical therapy; pregnancy test prior to treatment of female patients

Dosage Forms

Cream:

Avage™: 0.1% (30 g) [contains benzyl alcohol]

Tazorac®: 0.05% (30 g, 60 g); 0.1% (30 g, 60 g) [contains benzyl alcohol]

Gel (Tazorac®): 0.05% (30 g, 100 g); 0.1% (30 g, 100 g) [contains benzyl alcohol]

- ◆ **Tazicef®** *see* Ceftazidime *on page 320*
- ◆ **Tazobactam and Piperacillin** *see* Piperacillin and Tazobactam Sodium *on page 1375*
- ◆ **Tazocin® (Can)** *see* Piperacillin and Tazobactam Sodium *on page 1375*
- ◆ **Tazorac®** *see* Tazarotene *on page 1635*
- ◆ **Taztia XT™** *see* Diltiazem *on page 509*
- ◆ **TB Skin Test** *see* Tuberculin Tests *on page 1754*
- ◆ **3TC** *see* Lamivudine *on page 971*
- ◆ **3TC® (Can)** *see* Lamivudine *on page 971*
- ◆ **3TC, Abacavir, and Zidovudine** *see* Abacavir, Lamivudine, and Zidovudine *on page 19*
- ◆ **T-Cell Growth Factor** *see* Aldesleukin *on page 59*
- ◆ **TCGF** *see* Aldesleukin *on page 59*
- ◆ **TCN** *see* Tetracycline *on page 1659*
- ◆ **Td** *see* Diphtheria and Tetanus Toxoid *on page 519*
- ◆ **Td Adsorbed (Can)** *see* Diphtheria and Tetanus Toxoid *on page 519*
- ◆ **Tdap** *see* Diphtheria, Tetanus Toxoids, and Acellular Pertussis Vaccine *on page 521*
- ◆ **TDF** *see* Tenofovir *on page 1645*
- ◆ **Tebamide™** *see* Trimethobenzamide *on page 1743*
- ◆ **Tebrazid™ (Can)** *see* Pyrazinamide *on page 1460*

Tegaserod *(teg a SER od)*

U.S. Brand Names Zelnorm®

Canadian Brand Names Zelnorm®

Index Terms HTF919; Tegaserod Maleate

Pharmacologic Category Serotonin 5-HT$_4$ Receptor Agonist

Use Short-term treatment of constipation-predominate irritable bowel syndrome (IBS) in women; treatment of chronic idiopathic constipation

Pregnancy Risk Factor B

Pregnancy Implications Safety and efficacy have not been established in pregnant women. Use during pregnancy only if clearly needed.

Lactation Excretion in breast milk unknown/not recommended

Contraindications Hypersensitivity to tegaserod or any component of the formulation; severe renal impairment; moderate or severe hepatic impairment; history of bowel obstruction, symptomatic gallbladder disease, suspected sphincter of Oddi dysfunction, or abdominal adhesions. Treatment should **not** be started in patients with diarrhea or in those who experience diarrhea frequently.

Warnings/Precautions Has been associated with rare intestinal ischemic events. Discontinue immediately with new or sudden worsening abdominal pain or rectal bleeding. Diarrhea may occur after the start of treatment, most cases reported as a single episode within the first week of therapy, and may resolve with continued dosing. However, serious consequences of diarrhea (hypovolemia, syncope) have been reported. Patients should be warned to contact healthcare provider immediately if they develop severe diarrhea, or diarrhea with severe cramping, abdominal pain, or dizziness. Use caution with mild hepatic impairment; not recommended with moderate or severe impairment. Safety and efficacy have not been established in males with IBS or patients <18 years of age.

Adverse Reactions

>10%:

Central nervous system: Headache (15%)

Gastrointestinal: Abdominal pain (12%)

1% to 10%:

Central nervous system: Dizziness (4%), migraine (2%)

Gastrointestinal: Diarrhea (9%; severe <1%), nausea (8%), flatulence (6%)

Neuromuscular & skeletal: Back pain (5%), arthropathy (2%), leg pain (1%)

<1% (Limited to important or life-threatening): Albuminuria, angina pectoris, arrhythmia, bile duct stone, cramps, cholecystitis (with increased transaminases), gangrenous bowel, hypokalemia (secondary to diarrhea), hypotension, ischemic colitis, mesenteric ischemia, pruritus, rectal bleeding, renal pain; severe diarrhea (complicated by hypovolemia, hypotension, syncope); SGOT increased, SGPT increased, sphincter of Oddi spasm (suspected), syncope, tenesmus, vertigo

Overdosage/Toxicology Treatment should be symptom-directed and supportive. Diarrhea, headache, abdominal pain, orthostatic hypotension, flatulence, nausea, and vomiting were reported in healthy volunteers with doses of 90-180 mg. Unlikely to be removed by dialysis.

Ethanol/Nutrition/Herb Interactions Food: Bioavailability is decreased by 40% to 65% and C_{max} is decreased by 20% to 40% when taken with food. T_{max} is prolonged from 1 hour up to 2 hours when taken following a meal, but decreased to 0.7 hours when taken 30 minutes before a meal.

Stability Store at controlled room temperature of 15°C to 30°C (59°F to 86°F). Protect from moisture.

Mechanism of Action Tegaserod is a partial neuronal 5-HT$_4$ receptor agonist. Its action at the receptor site leads to stimulation of the peristaltic reflex and intestinal secretion, and moderation of visceral sensitivity.

Pharmacodynamics/Kinetics
Distribution: V_d: 368 ± 223 L
Protein binding: 98% primarily to α_1-acid glycoprotein
Metabolism: GI: Hydrolysis in the stomach; Hepatic: Oxidation, conjugation, and glucuronidation; metabolite (negligible activity); significant first-pass effect
Bioavailability: Fasting: 10%
Half-life elimination: I.V.: 11 ± 5 hours
Time to peak: 1 hour
Excretion: Feces (~66% as unchanged drug); urine (~33% as metabolites)

Dosage Oral:
Adults:
IBS with constipation (females): 6 mg twice daily, before meals, for 4-6 weeks, may consider continuing treatment for an additional 4-6 weeks in patients who respond initially
Chronic idiopathic constipation: 6 mg twice daily, before meals; the need for continued therapy should be reassessed periodically
Elderly: Dosing adjustment not recommended
Dosage adjustment in renal impairment: C_{max} and AUC of the inactive metabolite are increased with renal impairment.
Mild to moderate impairment: No dosage adjustment recommended
Severe impairment: Use is contraindicated
Dosage adjustment in hepatic impairment: C_{max} and AUC of tegaserod are increased with hepatic impairment.
Mild impairment: No dosage adjustment recommended; however, use caution
Moderate to severe impairment: Use is contraindicated

Dietary Considerations Take on an empty stomach, 30 minutes before meals.

Administration Administer 30 minutes before meals.

Additional Information In clinical trials, constipation was defined as <3 bowel movements per week, hard or lumpy stools, or straining with a bowel movement.

Dosage Forms Tablet: 2 mg, 6 mg

♦ **Tegaserod Maleate** see Tegaserod on page 1636
♦ **Tegretol®** see Carbamazepine on page 284
♦ **Tegretol®-XR** see Carbamazepine on page 284

Telithromycin (tel ith roe MYE sin)

U.S. Brand Names Ketek®
Canadian Brand Names Ketek®
Index Terms HMR 3647
Pharmacologic Category Antibiotic, Ketolide
Use Treatment of community-acquired pneumonia (mild-to-moderate) caused by susceptible strains of *Streptococcus pneumoniae* (including multidrug-resistant isolates), *Haemophilus influenzae*, *Chlamydia pneumoniae*, *Moraxella catarrhalis*, and *Mycoplasma pneumoniae*; treatment of bacterial exacerbation of chronic bronchitis caused by susceptible strains of *S. pneumoniae*, *H. influenzae* and *Moraxella catarrhalis*; treatment of acute bacterial sinusitis caused by *Streptococcus pneumoniae*, *Haemophilus influenzae*, *Moraxella catarrhalis*, and *Staphylococcus aureus*

Unlabeled/Investigational Use Approved in Canada for use in the treatment of tonsillitis/pharyngitis due to *S. pyogenes* (as an alternative to beta-lactam antibiotics when necessary/appropriate)

Pregnancy Risk Factor C

Pregnancy Implications Teratogenic effects were not observed in animal studies. There are no adequate or well-controlled studies in pregnant women.

Lactation Excretion in breast milk unknown/use caution

Contraindications Hypersensitivity to telithromycin, macrolide antibiotics, or any component of the formulation; history of hepatitis and/or jaundice associated with telithromycin or other macrolide antibiotic use; concurrent use of cisapride or pimozide

Warnings/Precautions Acute hepatic failure and severe liver injury, including hepatitis and hepatic necrosis (leading to some fatalities) have been reported; use caution with hepatic impairment or previous history of jaundice, and discontinue with signs/symptoms of hepatitis or liver damage. May prolong QT_c interval, leading to a risk of ventricular arrhythmias; closely-related antibiotics have been associated with malignant ventricular arrhythmias and torsade de pointes. Avoid in patients with prolongation of QT_c interval due to congenital causes, history of long QT syndrome, uncorrected electrolyte disturbances (hypokalemia or (Continued)

Telithromycin *(Continued)*

hypomagnesemia), significant bradycardia (<50 bpm), or concurrent therapy with QT_c-prolonging drugs (eg, class Ia and class III antiarrhythmics). Avoid use in patients with a prior history of confirmed cardiogenic syncope or ventricular arrhythmias while receiving macrolide antibiotics or other QT_c-prolonging drugs. Use caution in renal impairment; severe impairment (Cl_{cr} <30 mL/minute) requires dosage adjustment. Use caution in patients with myasthenia gravis; exacerbations have occurred (use only if suitable alternatives are not available). Inform patients of potential for blurred vision, which may interfere with ability to operate machinery or drive; use caution until effects are known. Safety and efficacy not established in pediatric patients <13 years of age per Canadian approved labeling and <18 years of age per U.S. approved labeling. Pseudomembranous colitis has been reported.

Adverse Reactions
>10%: Gastrointestinal: Diarrhea (10% to 11%)

2% to 10%:
Central nervous system: Headache (2% to 6%), dizziness (3% to 4%)
Gastrointestinal: Nausea (7% to 8%), vomiting (2% to 3%), loose stools (2%), dysgeusia (2%)

≥0.2% to <2%:
Central nervous system: Vertigo, fatigue, somnolence, insomnia
Dermatologic: Rash
Gastrointestinal: Abdominal distension, abdominal pain, anorexia, constipation, dyspepsia, flatulence, gastritis, gastroenteritis, GI upset, glossitis, stomatitis, watery stools, xerostomia
Genitourinary: Vaginal candidiasis, vaginitis
Hematologic: Platelets increased
Hepatic: Transaminases increased
Ocular: Blurred vision, accommodation delayed, diplopia
Miscellaneous: Candidiasis, diaphoresis increased

<0.2% (Limited to important or life-threatening): Alkaline phosphatase increased, anaphylaxis, angioedema, anxiety, arrhythmia, bilirubin increased, bradycardia, eczema, edema (facial), eosinophilia, erythema multiforme, flushing, hepatitis, hepatocellular injury (including necrosis), hypotension, jaundice, liver failure, muscle cramps, myasthenia gravis exacerbation (rare), palpitation, pancreatitis, paresthesia, pruritus, QT_c prolongation, syncope, urticaria

Overdosage/Toxicology Treatment should be symptomatic and supportive. Gastric lavage recommended. ECG and electrolytes should be monitored. Effectiveness of dialysis unknown.

Drug Interactions
Cytochrome P450 Effect: Substrate of CYP1A2 (minor), 3A4 (major); **Inhibits** CYP2D6 (weak), 3A4 (strong)

Increased Effect/Toxicity: Concurrent use of cisapride or pimozide is contraindicated. Concurrent use with antiarrhythmics (eg, class Ia and class III) or other drugs which prolong QT_c (eg, disopyramide, gatifloxacin, moxifloxacin, pimozide, thioridazine) may be additive; serious arrhythmias may occur. Neuromuscular-blocking agents may be potentiated by telithromycin.

Telithromycin may increase the levels/effects of alfentanil, selected benzodiazepines, buspirone, calcium channel blockers, cilostazol, clozapine, corticosteroids, cyclosporine, eletriptan, eplerenone, ergot alkaloids, selected HMG-CoA reductase inhibitors, mirtazapine, nateglinide, nefazodone, pimozide, repaglinide, quinidine, sildenafil (and other PDE-5 inhibitors), SSRIs, tacrolimus, venlafaxine, warfarin (monitor), and other CYP3A4 substrates. Selected benzodiazepines (midazolam, triazolam), and selected HMG-CoA reductase inhibitors (atorvastatin, lovastatin and simvastatin) are generally contraindicated with strong CYP3A4 inhibitors. When used with strong CYP3A4 inhibitors, dosage adjustment/limits are recommended for sildenafil and other PDE-5 inhibitors; refer to individual monographs.

The levels/effects of telithromycin may be increased by azole antifungals, clarithromycin, diclofenac, doxycycline, erythromycin, imatinib, isoniazid, nefazodone, nicardipine, propofol, protease inhibitors, quinidine, verapamil, and other CYP3A4 inhibitors.

Decreased Effect: The levels/effects of telithromycin may be decreased by aminoglutethimide, carbamazepine, nafcillin, nevirapine, phenobarbital, phenytoin, rifamycins, and other CYP3A4 inducers; avoid concurrent use. Telithromycin may decrease the levels/effects of clopidogrel.

Ethanol/Nutrition/Herb Interactions Herb/nutraceutical: St John's wort: May decrease the levels/effects of telithromycin.

Stability Store at room temperature between 15°C and 30°C.

Mechanism of Action Inhibits bacterial protein synthesis by binding to two sites on the 50S ribosomal subunit. Telithromycin has also been demonstrated to alter secretion of IL-1alpha and TNF-alpha; the clinical significance of this immunomodulatory effect has not been evaluated.

Pharmacodynamics/Kinetics
Absorption: Rapid
Distribution: 2.9 L/kg
Protein binding: 60% to 70%
Metabolism: Hepatic, via CYP3A4 (50%) and non-CYP-mediated pathways
Bioavailability: 57% (significant first-pass metabolism)
Half-life elimination: 10 hours
Time to peak, plasma: 1 hour
Excretion: Urine (13% unchanged drug, remainder as metabolites); feces (7%)

Dosage Oral:
Children ≥13 years and Adults: Tonsillitis/pharyngitis (unlabeled U.S. indication): 800 mg once daily for 5 days

Adults:
Acute exacerbation of chronic bronchitis, acute bacterial sinusitis: 800 mg once daily for 5 days

Community-acquired pneumonia: 800 mg once daily for 7-10 days

Dosage adjustment in renal impairment:
U.S. product labeling: Cl_{cr} <30 mL/minute: 600 mg once daily; when renal impairment is accompanied by hepatic impairment, reduce dosage to 400 mg once daily

Canadian product labeling: Cl_{cr} <30 mL/minute: Reduce dose to 400 mg once daily

Hemodialysis: Administer following dialysis

Dosage adjustment in hepatic impairment: No adjustment recommended, unless concurrent severe renal impairment is present

Dietary Considerations May be taken with or without food.

Administration May be administered with or without food.

Monitoring Parameters Liver function tests; signs/symptoms of liver failure (eg, jaundice, fatigue, malaise, anorexia, nausea, bilirubinemia, acholic stools, liver tenderness, hepatomegaly); visual acuity

Dosage Forms
Tablet:
Ketek® : 300 mg [not available in Canada], 400 mg
Ketek Pak™ [blister pack]: 400 mg (10s) [packaged as 10 tablets/card; 2 tablets/blister]

Telmisartan (tel mi SAR tan)

U.S. Brand Names Micardis®
Canadian Brand Names Micardis®
Pharmacologic Category Angiotensin II Receptor Blocker
Additional Appendix Information
Angiotensin Agents *on page 1860*

Use Treatment of hypertension; may be used alone or in combination with other antihypertensive agents

Pregnancy Risk Factor C (1st trimester); D (2nd and 3rd trimesters)

Pregnancy Implications The drug should be discontinued as soon as possible when pregnancy is detected. Drugs which act directly on renin-angiotensin can cause fetal and neonatal morbidity and death.

Lactation Enters breast milk/not recommended

Contraindications Hypersensitivity to telmisartan or any component of the formulation; hypersensitivity to other A-II receptor antagonists; bilateral renal artery stenosis; pregnancy

Warnings/Precautions [U.S. Boxed Warning]: Based on human data, drugs that act on the angiotensin system can cause injury and death to the developing fetus when used in the second and third trimesters. Angiotensin receptor blockers should be discontinued as soon as possible once pregnancy is detected. May cause hyperkalemia; avoid potassium supplementation unless specifically required by healthcare provider. Avoid use or use a smaller dose in patients who are volume depleted; correct depletion first. May be associated with deterioration of renal function and/or increases in serum creatinine, particularly in patients dependent on renin-angiotensin-aldosterone system. Use with caution in unilateral renal artery stenosis and pre-existing renal insufficiency; significant aortic/mitral stenosis. Use with caution in patients who have biliary obstructive disorders or hepatic dysfunction. Safety and efficacy have not been established in children.

Adverse Reactions May be associated with worsening of renal function in patients dependent on renin-angiotensin-aldosterone system.

1% to 10%:
Cardiovascular: Hypertension (1%), chest pain (1%), peripheral edema (1%)
Central nervous system: Headache (1%), dizziness (1%), pain (1%), fatigue (1%)
Gastrointestinal: Diarrhea (3%), dyspepsia (1%), nausea (1%), abdominal pain (1%)
Genitourinary: Urinary tract infection (1%)
Neuromuscular & skeletal: Back pain (3%), myalgia (1%)
Respiratory: Upper respiratory infection (7%), sinusitis (3%), pharyngitis (1%), cough (2%)
Miscellaneous: Flu-like syndrome (1%)
<1% (Limited to important or life-threatening): Abnormal vision, allergic reaction, angina, angioedema, angioneurotic edema, atrial fibrillation, CHF, cramps, depression, dyspnea, edema, epistaxis, erectile dysfunction, erythema, facial edema, gout, hyperkalemia, hypersensitivity, hypotension, impotence, increased serum creatinine and BUN, insomnia, MI, migraine, muscle cramps, paresthesia, pruritus, rash, somnolence, syncope, tinnitus, urticaria, vertigo, weakness

Overdosage/Toxicology Signs and symptoms of overdose include hypotension, dizziness, and tachycardia. Treatment is supportive. Vagal stimulation may result in bradycardia.

Drug Interactions
Cytochrome P450 Effect: Inhibits CYP2C19 (weak)
Increased Effect/Toxicity: Telmisartan may increase serum digoxin concentrations. Potassium salts/supplements, co-trimoxazole (high dose), ACE inhibitors, and potassium-sparing diuretics (amiloride, spironolactone, triamterene) may increase the risk of hyperkalemia with telmisartan.
Decreased Effect: Telmisartan decreased the trough concentrations of warfarin during concurrent therapy, however, INR was not changed.

Ethanol/Nutrition/Herb Interactions Herb/Nutraceutical: Avoid dong quai if using for hypertension (has estrogenic activity). Avoid ephedra, yohimbe, ginseng (may worsen hypertension). Avoid garlic (may have increased antihypertensive effect).

Mechanism of Action Angiotensin II acts as a vasoconstrictor. In addition to causing direct vasoconstriction, angiotensin II also stimulates the release of aldosterone. Once aldosterone is released, sodium as well as water are reabsorbed. The end result is an elevation in blood pressure. Telmisartan is a nonpeptide AT1 angiotensin II receptor antagonist. This binding prevents angiotensin II from binding to the receptor thereby blocking the vasoconstriction and the aldosterone secreting effects of angiotensin II.

(Continued)

Telmisartan *(Continued)*

Pharmacodynamics/Kinetics Orally active, not a prodrug
Onset of action: 1-2 hours
Peak effect: 0.5-1 hours
Duration: Up to 24 hours
Protein binding: >99.5%
Metabolism: Hepatic via conjugation to inactive metabolites; not metabolized via CYP
Bioavailability (dose dependent): 42% to 58%
Half-life elimination: Terminal: 24 hours
Excretion: Feces (97%)
Clearance: Total body: 800 mL/minute

Dosage Adults: Oral: Initial: 40 mg once daily; usual maintenance dose range: 20-80 mg/day. Patients with volume depletion should be initiated on the lower dosage with close supervision.

Dosage adjustment in hepatic impairment: Supervise patients closely.

Dietary Considerations May be taken without regard to food.

Monitoring Parameters Supine blood pressure, electrolytes, serum creatinine, BUN, urinalysis, symptomatic hypotension, and tachycardia

Dosage Forms Tablet: 20 mg, 40 mg, 80 mg

Telmisartan and Hydrochlorothiazide
(tel mi SAR tan & hye droe klor oh THYE a zide)

U.S. Brand Names Micardis® HCT
Canadian Brand Names Micardis® Plus
Index Terms Hydrochlorothiazide and Telmisartan
Pharmacologic Category Angiotensin II Receptor Blocker Combination; Antihypertensive Agent, Combination; Diuretic, Thiazide
Use Treatment of hypertension; combination product should not be used for initial therapy
Pregnancy Risk Factor C (1st trimester); D (2nd and 3rd trimesters)
Dosage Adults: Oral: Replacement therapy: Combination product can be substituted for individual titrated agents. Initiation of combination therapy when monotherapy has failed to achieve desired effects:

Patients currently on telmisartan: Initial dose if blood pressure is not currently controlled on monotherapy of 80 mg telmisartan: Telmisartan 80 mg/hydrochlorothiazide 12.5 mg once daily; may titrate up to telmisartan 160 mg/hydrochlorothiazide 25 mg if needed

Patients currently on HCTZ: Initial dose if blood pressure is not currently controlled on monotherapy of 25 mg once daily: Telmisartan 80 mg/hydrochlorothiazide 12.5 mg once daily or telmisartan 80 mg/hydrochlorothiazide 25 mg once daily; may titrate up to telmisartan 160 mg/hydrochlorothiazide 25 mg if blood pressure remains uncontrolled after 2-4 weeks of therapy. Patients who develop hypokalemia may be switched to telmisartan 80 mg/hydrochlorothiazide 12.5 mg.

Dosage adjustment in renal impairment:
Cl_{cr} >30 mL/minute: Usual recommended dose
Cl_{cr} ≤30 mL/minute: Not recommended

Dosage adjustment in hepatic impairment: Dosing should be started at telmisartan 40 mg/hydrochlorothiazide 12.5 mg; do **not** use in patients with severe hepatic impairment
Elderly: No dosing adjustment needed based on age; monitor renal and hepatic function

Additional Information Complete prescribing information for this medication should be consulted for additional detail.

Dosage Forms [CAN]: Canadian brand name
Tablet:
Micardis® HCT [available in U.S.]:
40/12.5: Telmisartan 40 mg and hydrochlorothiazide 12.5 mg
80/12.5: Telmisartan 80 mg and hydrochlorothiazide 12.5 mg
80/25: Telmisartan 80 mg and hydrochlorothiazide 25 mg
Micardis® Plus [CAN]: 80/25: Telmisartan 80 mg and hydrochlorothiazide 25 mg [Not available in U.S.]

♦ **Telzir® (Can)** *see* Fosamprenavir *on page 761*

Temazepam (te MAZ e pam)

U.S. Brand Names Restoril®
Canadian Brand Names Apo-Temazepam®; CO Temazepam; Gen-Temazepam; Novo-Temazepam; Nu-Temazepam; PMS-Temazepam; ratio-Temazepam; Restoril®
Pharmacologic Category Hypnotic, Benzodiazepine
Additional Appendix Information
Benzodiazepines *on page 1874*
Use Short-term treatment of insomnia
Unlabeled/Investigational Use Treatment of anxiety; adjunct in the treatment of depression; management of panic attacks
Restrictions C-IV
Pregnancy Risk Factor X
Lactation Enters breast milk/not recommended (AAP rates "of concern")
Medication Safety Issues
Sound-alike/look-alike issues:
Temazepam may be confused with flurazepam, lorazepam
Restoril® may be confused with Vistaril®, Zestril®
Contraindications Hypersensitivity to temazepam or any component of the formulation (cross-sensitivity with other benzodiazepines may exist); narrow-angle glaucoma (not in product labeling, however, benzodiazepines are contraindicated); pregnancy

Warnings/Precautions Should be used only after evaluation of potential causes of sleep disturbance. Failure of sleep disturbance to resolve after 7-10 days may indicate psychiatric or medical illness. A worsening of insomnia or the emergence of new abnormalities of thought or behavior may represent unrecognized psychiatric or medical illness and requires immediate and careful evaluation.

Use with caution in elderly or debilitated patients, patients with hepatic disease (including alcoholics), or renal impairment. Use with caution in patients with respiratory disease, or impaired gag reflex. Avoid use inpatients with sleep apnea.

Causes CNS depression (dose-related) resulting in sedation, dizziness, confusion, or ataxia which may impair physical and mental capabilities. Patients must be cautioned about performing tasks which require mental alertness (eg, operating machinery or driving). Use with caution in patients receiving other CNS depressants or psychoactive agents. Effects with other sedative drugs or ethanol may be potentiated. Benzodiazepines have been associated with falls and traumatic injury and should be used with extreme caution in patients who are at risk of these events (especially the elderly).

Use caution in patients with suicidal risk. Use with caution in patients with a history of drug dependence. Benzodiazepines have been associated with dependence and acute withdrawal symptoms on discontinuation or reduction in dose (may occur after as little as 10 days). Acute withdrawal, including seizures, may be precipitated after administration of flumazenil to patients receiving long-term benzodiazepine therapy.

Benzodiazepines have been associated with anterograde amnesia. Paradoxical reactions, including hyperactive or aggressive behavior, have been reported with benzodiazepines, particularly in adolescent/pediatric or psychiatric patients. Does not have analgesic, antidepressant, or antipsychotic properties.

Adverse Reactions
1% to 10%:
Central nervous system: Confusion, dizziness, drowsiness, fatigue, anxiety, headache, lethargy, hangover, euphoria, vertigo
Dermatologic: Rash
Endocrine & metabolic: Decreased libido
Gastrointestinal: Diarrhea
Neuromuscular & skeletal: Dysarthria, weakness
Ocular: Blurred vision
Miscellaneous: Diaphoresis
<1% (Limited to important or life-threatening): Amnesia, ataxia, blood dyscrasias, drug dependence, paradoxical reactions, vomiting

Overdosage/Toxicology Symptoms include somnolence, confusion, coma, hypoactive reflexes, dyspnea, hypotension, slurred speech, and impaired coordination. Treatment for benzodiazepine overdose is supportive. Rarely is mechanical ventilation required. Flumazenil has been shown to selectively block the binding of benzodiazepines to CNS receptors, resulting in reversal of benzodiazepine-induced CNS depression.

Drug Interactions
Cytochrome P450 Effect: Substrate (minor) of CYP2B6, 2C9, 2C19, 3A4
Increased Effect/Toxicity: Temazepam potentiates the CNS depressant effects of opioid analgesics, barbiturates, phenothiazines, ethanol, antihistamines, MAO inhibitors, sedative-hypnotics, and cyclic antidepressants. Serum levels of temazepam may be increased by inhibitors of CYP3A4, including cimetidine, ciprofloxacin, clarithromycin, clozapine, diltiazem, disulfiram, digoxin, erythromycin, ethanol, fluconazole, fluoxetine, fluvoxamine, grapefruit juice, isoniazid, itraconazole, ketoconazole, labetalol, levodopa, loxapine, metoprolol, metronidazole, miconazole, nefazodone, omeprazole, phenytoin, rifabutin, rifampin, troleandomycin, valproic acid, and verapamil.
Decreased Effect: Oral contraceptives may increase the clearance of temazepam. Temazepam may decrease the antiparkinsonian efficacy of levodopa. Theophylline and other CNS stimulants may antagonize the sedative effects of temazepam. Carbamazepine, rifampin, rifabutin may enhance the metabolism of temazepam and decrease its therapeutic effect.

Ethanol/Nutrition/Herb Interactions
Ethanol: Avoid ethanol (may increase CNS depression).
Food: Serum levels may be increased by grapefruit juice.
Herb/Nutraceutical: St John's wort may decrease temazepam levels. Avoid valerian, St John's wort, kava kava, gotu kola (may increase CNS depression).

Mechanism of Action Binds to stereospecific benzodiazepine receptors on the postsynaptic GABA neuron at several sites within the central nervous system, including the limbic system, reticular formation. Enhancement of the inhibitory effect of GABA on neuronal excitability results by increased neuronal membrane permeability to chloride ions. This shift in chloride ions results in hyperpolarization (a less excitable state) and stabilization.

Pharmacodynamics/Kinetics
Distribution: V_d: 1.4 L/kg
Protein binding: 96%
Metabolism: Hepatic
Half-life elimination: 9.5-12.4 hours
Time to peak, serum: 2-3 hours
Excretion: Urine (80% to 90% as inactive metabolites)

Dosage Oral:
Adults: 15-30 mg at bedtime
Elderly or debilitated patients: 15 mg

Monitoring Parameters Respiratory and cardiovascular status

Reference Range Therapeutic: 26 ng/mL after 24 hours

Additional Information Abrupt discontinuation after sustained use (generally >10 days) may cause withdrawal symptoms.

Dosage Forms
Capsule: 15 mg, 30 mg
Restoril®: 7.5 mg, 15 mg, 30 mg

♦ **Temodal**™ **(Can)** *see* Temozolomide *on page 1642*

♦ **Temodar**® *see* Temozolomide *on page 1642*

♦ **Temovate**® *see* Clobetasol *on page 391*

♦ **Temovate E**® *see* Clobetasol *on page 391*

Temozolomide (te moe ZOE loe mide)

U.S. Brand Names Temodar®
Canadian Brand Names Temodal™; Temodar®
Index Terms NSC-362856; TMZ
Pharmacologic Category Antineoplastic Agent, Alkylating Agent
Use Treatment of adult patients with refractory (first relapse) anaplastic astrocytoma who have experienced disease progression on nitrosourea and procarbazine; newly-diagnosed glioblastoma multiforme
Unlabeled/Investigational Use Glioma, melanoma
Pregnancy Risk Factor D
Pregnancy Implications May cause fetal harm when administered to pregnant women. Animal studies, at doses less than used in humans, resulted in numerous birth defects. Testicular toxicity was demonstrated in animal studies using smaller doses than recommended for cancer treatment. Male and female patients should avoid pregnancy while receiving drug.
Lactation Excretion in breast milk unknown/not recommended
Medication Safety Issues
  High alert medication: The Institute for Safe Medication Practices (ISMP) includes this medication among its list of drugs which have a heightened risk of causing significant patient harm when used in error.
Contraindications Hypersensitivity to temozolomide or any component of the formulation; hypersensitivity to dacarbazine (since both drugs are metabolized to MTIC); pregnancy
Warnings/Precautions Hazardous agent - use appropriate precautions for handling and disposal. *Pneumocystis carinii* pneumonia (PCP) may occur; risk is increased in those receiving steroids or longer dosing regimens; PCP prophylaxis is required with radiotherapy for the 42-day regimen. Myelosuppression may occur; an increased incidence has been reported in geriatric and female patients. Rare cases of myelodysplastic syndrome and secondary malignancies, including acute myeloid leukemia have been reported. Use caution in patients with severe hepatic or renal impairment. Safety and efficacy in pediatric patients have not been established.
Adverse Reactions Adverse reactions are listed as the combined incidence in studies for treatment of newly-diagnosed glioblastoma multiforme during the maintenance phase (after radiotherapy) and refractory anaplastic astrocytoma in adults.
  >10%:
    Cardiovascular: Peripheral edema (up to 11%)
    Central nervous system: Fatigue (34% to 61%), headache (23% to 41%), fatigue (34% to 61%), convulsions (6% to 23%), hemiparesis (18%), dizziness (5% to 12%), fever (up to 13%), coordination abnormality (up to 11%). In the case of CNS malignancies, it is difficult to distinguish the relative contributions of temozolomide and progressive disease to CNS symptoms.
    Dermatologic: Alopecia (55% - maintenance phase after radiotherapy), rash (8% to 13%)
    Gastrointestinal: Nausea (49% to 53%), vomiting (29% to 42%), constipation (22% to 33%), anorexia (9% to 27%), diarrhea (10% to 16%)
    Hematologic: Lymphopenia (grade 3/4 in 55%), thrombocytopenia (grade 3/4 in 4% to 19%), neutropenia (grade 3/4 in 8% to 14%), leukopenia (grade 3/4 in 11%)
    Neuromuscular & skeletal: Weakness (7% to 13%)
    Miscellaneous: Viral infection (up to 11%)
  1% to 10%:
    Central nervous system: Ataxia (8%), memory impairment (up to 7%), confusion (5%), anxiety (7%), depression (up to 6%), amnesia (up to 10%), paresis (up to 8%), somnolence (up to 9%), insomnia (4% to 10%)
    Dermatologic: Rash (8% to 13%), pruritus (5% to 8%), dry skin (up to 5%), radiation injury (2% - maintenance phase after radiotherapy), erythema (1%)
    Endocrine & metabolic: Hypercorticism (8%), breast pain (up to 6%)
    Gastrointestinal: Dysphagia (up to 7%), abdominal pain (5% to 9%), stomatitis (up to 9%), weight gain (up to 5%)
    Genitourinary: Micturition frequency increased (up to 6%), incontinence (up to 8%), urinary tract infection (up to 8%)
    Hematologic: Anemia (8%; grade 3/4 in up to 4%)
    Neuromuscular & skeletal: Paresthesia (up to 9%), back pain (up to 8%), arthralgia (up to 6%), abnormal gait (up to 6%), myalgia (up to 5%),
    Ocular: Diplopia (5%); vision abnormality (blurred vision, visual deficit, vision changes) (5% to 8%)
    Respiratory: Pharyngitis (up to 8%), sinusitis (up to 6%), cough (5% to 8%), upper respiratory tract infection (up to 8%), dyspnea (5%)
    Miscellaneous: Taste perversion (up to 5%), allergic reaction (up to 3%)
  Postmarketing and/or case reports: Anaphylaxis, erythema multiforme, myelodysplastic syndrome, opportunistic infection (eg, PCP), secondary malignancies (including myeloid leukemia)
Overdosage/Toxicology Dose-limiting toxicity is hematological. In the event of an overdose, hematological evaluation is necessary. Treatment is supportive.
Ethanol/Nutrition/Herb Interactions Food: Food reduces rate and extent of absorption.
Stability Store at controlled room temperature (15°C to 10°C/59°F to 86°F)

Mechanism of Action Like dacarbazine, temozolomide is converted to the active alkylating metabolite MTIC [(methyl-triazene-1-yl)-imidazole-4-carboxamide]. Unlike dacarbazine, however, this conversion is spontaneous, nonenzymatic, and occurs under physiologic conditions in all tissues to which the drug distributes.

Pharmacodynamics/Kinetics

Distribution: V_d: Parent drug: 0.4 L/kg

Protein binding: 15%

Metabolism: Prodrug, hydrolyzed to the active form, MTIC; MTIC is eventually eliminated as CO_2 and 5-aminoimidazole-4-carboxamide (AIC), a natural constituent in urine

Bioavailability: 100%

Half-life elimination: Mean: Parent drug: 1.8 hours

Time to peak: Empty stomach: 1 hour

Excretion: Urine (~38%; parent drug 6%); feces 0.8%

Dosage Oral (refer to individual protocols): Adults:

Anaplastic astrocytoma (refractory): Initial dose: 150 mg/m²/day for 5 days; repeat every 28 days. Subsequent doses of 100-200 mg/m²/day for 5 days per treatment cycle; based upon hematologic tolerance. This monthly-cycle regimen may be preceded by a 6- to 7-week regimen of 75 mg/m²/day.

ANC <1000/mm³ or platelets <50,000/mm³ on day 22 or day 29 (day 1 of next cycle): Postpone therapy until ANC >1500/mm³ and platelets >100,000/mm³; reduce dose by 50 mg/m²/day for subsequent cycle

ANC 1000-1500/mm³ or platelets 50,000-100,000/mm³ on day 22 or day 29 (day 1 of next cycle): Postpone therapy until ANC >1500/mm³ and platelets >100,000/mm³; maintain initial dose

ANC >1500/mm³ and platelets >100,000/mm³ on day 22 or day 29 (day 1 of next cycle): Increase dose to or maintain dose at 200 mg/m²/day for 5 days for subsequent cycle

Glioblastoma multiforme (high-grade glioma):

Concomitant phase: 75 mg/m²/day for 42 days with radiotherapy (60Gy administered in 30 fractions). **Note:** PCP prophylaxis is required during concomitant phase and should continue in patients who develop lymphocytopenia until recovery (common toxicity criteria [CTC] ≤1). Obtain weekly CBC.

ANC ≥1500/mm³, platelet count ≥100,000/mm³, and nonhematologic CTC ≤grade 1 (excludes alopecia, nausea/vomiting): Temodar® 75 mg/m²/day may be continued throughout the 42-day concomitant period up to 49 days

Dosage modification:

ANC ≥500/mm³ but <1500/mm³ **or** platelet count ≥10,000/mm³ but <100,000/mm³ **or** nonhematologic CTC grade 2 (excludes alopecia, nausea/vomiting): Interrupt therapy

ANC <500/mm³ **or** platelet count <10,000/mm³ **or** nonhematologic CTC grade 3/4 (excludes alopecia, nausea/vomiting): Discontinue therapy

Maintenance phase (consists of 6 treatment cycles): Begin 4 weeks after concomitant phase completion. **Note:** Each subsequent cycle is 28 days (consisting of 5 days of drug treatment followed by 23 days without treatment). Draw CBC within 48 hours of day 22; hold next cycle and do weekly CBC until ANC >1500/mm³ and platelet count >100,000/mm³; dosing modification should be based on lowest blood counts and worst nonhematologic toxicity during the previous cycle.

Cycle 1: 150 mg/m²/day for 5 days

Dosage modification for next cycle:

ANC <1000/mm³, platelet count <50,000/mm³, or nonhematologic CTC grade 3 (excludes for alopecia, nausea/vomiting) during previous cycle: Decrease dose by 50 mg/m²/day for 5 days, unless dose has already been lowered to 100 mg/m²/day, then discontinue therapy.

If dose reduction <100 mg/m²/day is required or nonhematologic CTC grade 4 (excludes for alopecia, nausea/vomiting), or if the same grade 3 nonhematologic toxicity occurs after dose reduction: Discontinue therapy

Cycle 2: 200 mg/m²/day for 5 days unless prior toxicity, then refer to Dosage Modifications under "Cycle 1" and give adjusted dose for 5 days

Cycles 3-6: Continue with previous cycle's dose for 5 days unless toxicity has occurred then, refer to Dosage Modifications under "Cycle 1" and give adjusted dose for 5 days

Elderly: Patients ≥70 years of age had a higher incidence of grade 4 neutropenia and thrombocytopenia in the first cycle of therapy than patients <70 years of age.

Dosage adjustment in renal impairment: No guidelines exist. Caution should be used when administered to patients with severe renal impairment (Cl_{cr} <39 mL/minute).

Dosage adjustment in hepatic impairment: Caution should be used when administering to patients with severe hepatic impairment.

Dietary Considerations The incidence of nausea/vomiting is decreased when the drug is taken on an empty stomach.

Administration Capsules should not be opened or chewed but swallowed whole with a glass of water. May be administered on an empty stomach to reduce nausea and vomiting. Bedtime administration may be advised.

Monitoring Parameters CBC; platelet count >100,000/mm³ and WBC >1500/mm³ before initiating therapy

Dosage Forms Capsule: 5 mg, 20 mg, 100 mg, 250 mg

♦ **Tempra®** **(Can)** see Acetaminophen on page 28

Tenecteplase (ten EK te plase)

U.S. Brand Names TNKase™

Canadian Brand Names TNKase™

Pharmacologic Category Thrombolytic Agent

Use Thrombolytic agent used in the management of acute myocardial infarction for the lysis of thrombi in the coronary vasculature to restore perfusion and reduce mortality.

(Continued)

Tenecteplase *(Continued)*

Unlabeled/Investigational Use Acute MI — combination regimen of tenecteplase (unlabeled dose), abciximab, and heparin (unlabeled dose)

Pregnancy Risk Factor C

Pregnancy Implications Administer to pregnant women only if the potential benefits justify the risk to the fetus.

Lactation Use caution

Medication Safety Issues

Sound-alike/look-alike issues:

TNKase™ may be confused with t-PA

TNK (occasional abbreviation for TNKase™) is an error-prone abbreviation (mistaken as TPA)

High alert medication: The Institute for Safe Medication Practices (ISMP) includes this medication (I.V.) among its list of drugs which have a heightened risk of causing significant patient harm when used in error.

Contraindications Hypersensitivity to tenecteplase or any component of the formulation; active internal bleeding; history of stroke; intracranial/intraspinal surgery or trauma within 2 months; intracranial neoplasm; arteriovenous malformation or aneurysm; bleeding diathesis; severe uncontrolled hypertension

Warnings/Precautions Stop antiplatelet agents and heparin if serious bleeding occurs. Avoid I.M. injections and nonessential handling of the patient for a few hours after administration. Monitor for bleeding complications. Venipunctures should be performed carefully and only when necessary. If arterial puncture is necessary, then use an upper extremity that can be easily compressed manually. For the following conditions, the risk of bleeding is higher with use of tenecteplase and should be weighed against the benefits: Recent major surgery, cerebrovascular disease, recent GI or GU bleed, recent trauma, uncontrolled hypertension (systolic BP ≥180 mm Hg and/or diastolic BP ≥110 mm Hg), suspected left heart thrombus, acute pericarditis, subacute bacterial endocarditis, hemostatic defects, severe hepatic dysfunction, pregnancy, hemorrhagic diabetic retinopathy or other hemorrhagic ophthalmic conditions, septic thrombophlebitis or occluded arteriovenous cannula at seriously infected site, advanced age (see Usual Dosing, Elderly), anticoagulants, recent administration of GP IIb/IIIa inhibitors. Coronary thrombolysis may result in reperfusion arrhythmias. Caution with readministration of tenecteplase. Safety and efficacy have not been established in pediatric patients. Cholesterol embolism has rarely been reported.

Adverse Reactions As with all drugs which may affect hemostasis, bleeding is the major adverse effect associated with tenecteplase. Hemorrhage may occur at virtually any site. Risk is dependent on multiple variables, including the dosage administered, concurrent use of multiple agents which alter hemostasis, and patient predisposition. Rapid lysis of coronary artery thrombi by thrombolytic agents may be associated with reperfusion-related arterial and/or ventricular arrhythmia.

>10%:

Local: Hematoma (12% minor)

Hematologic: Bleeding (22% minor: ASSENT-2 trial)

1% to 10%:

Central nervous system: Stroke (2%)

Gastrointestinal: GI hemorrhage (1% major, 2% minor), epistaxis (2% minor)

Genitourinary: GU bleeding (4% minor)

Hematologic: Bleeding (5% major; ASSENT-2 trial)

Local: Bleeding at catheter puncture site (4% minor), hematoma (2% major)

Respiratory: Pharyngeal (3% minor)

The incidence of stroke and bleeding increase with age above 65 years.

<1% (Limited to important or life-threatening): Anaphylaxis, angioedema, bleeding at catheter puncture site (<1% major), cholesterol embolism (clinical features may include livedo reticularis, "purple toe" syndrome, acute renal failure, gangrenous digits, hypertension, pancreatitis, MI, cerebral infarction, spinal cord infarction, retinal artery occlusion, bowel infarction, rhabdomyolysis), GU bleeding (<1% major), intracranial hemorrhage (0.9%), laryngeal edema, rash, respiratory tract bleeding, retroperitoneal bleeding, urticaria

Additional cardiovascular events associated with use in MI: Arrhythmias, AV block, cardiac arrest, cardiac tamponade, cardiogenic shock, electromechanical dissociation, embolism, fever, heart failure, hypotension, mitral regurgitation, myocardial reinfarction, myocardial rupture, nausea, pericardial effusion, pericarditis, pulmonary edema, recurrent myocardial ischemia, thrombosis, vomiting

Overdosage/Toxicology Symptom include increased incidence of bleeding.

Drug Interactions

Increased Effect/Toxicity: Drugs which affect platelet function (eg, NSAIDs, dipyridamole, ticlopidine, clopidogrel, IIb/IIIa antagonists) may potentiate the risk of hemorrhage; use with caution.

Heparin and aspirin: Use with aspirin and heparin may increase bleeding. However, aspirin and heparin were used concomitantly with tenecteplase in the majority of patients in clinical studies.

Warfarin or oral anticoagulants: Risk of bleeding may be increased during concurrent therapy.

Decreased Effect: Aminocaproic acid (antifibrinolytic agent) may decrease effectiveness.

Stability Store at room temperature not to exceed 30°C (86°F) or under refrigeration 2°C to 8°C (36°F to 46°F). Tenecteplase should be reconstituted using the supplied 10 mL syringe with TwinPak™ Dual Cannula Device and 10 mL sterile water for injection. If reconstituted and not used immediately, store in refrigerator and use within 8 hours.

Mechanism of Action Initiates fibrinolysis by binding to fibrin and converting plasminogen to plasmin.

Pharmacodynamics/Kinetics

Distribution: V_d is weight related and approximates plasma volume

Metabolism: Primarily hepatic

Half-life elimination: 90-130 minutes

Excretion: Clearance: Plasma: 99-119 mL/minute

Dosage I.V.:

Adult: Recommended total dose should not exceed 50 mg and is based on patient's weight; administer as a bolus over 5 seconds

If patient's weight:

<60 kg, dose: 30 mg

≥60 to <70 kg, dose: 35 mg

≥70 to <80 kg, dose: 40 mg

≥80 to <90 kg, dose: 45 mg

≥90 kg, dose: 50 mg

All patients received 150-325 mg of aspirin as soon as possible and then daily. Intravenous heparin was initiated as soon as possible and aPTT was maintained between 50-70 seconds.

Elderly: Although dosage adjustments are not recommended, the elderly have a higher incidence of morbidity and mortality with the use of tenecteplase. The 30-day mortality in the ASSENT-2 trial was 2.5% for patients <65 years, 8.5% for patients 65-74 years, and 16.2% for patients ≥75 years. The intracranial hemorrhage rate was 0.4% for patients <65, 1.6 % for patients 65-74 years, and 1.7 % for patients ≥75 years. The risks and benefits of use should be weighted carefully in the elderly.

Combination regimen (unlabeled): Half-dose tenecteplase (15-25 mg based on weight) and abciximab 0.25 mg/kg bolus then 0.125 mcg/kg/minute (maximum 10 mcg/minute) for 12 hours with heparin dosing as follows: Concurrent bolus of 40 units/kg (maximum 3000 units), then 7 units/kg/hour (maximum 800 units/hour) as continuous infusion. Adjust to aPTT target of 50-70 seconds.

Dosage adjustment in renal impairment: No formal recommendations for renal impairment

Dosage adjustment in hepatic impairment: Severe hepatic failure is a relative contraindication. Recommendations were not made for mild to moderate hepatic impairment.

Administration Tenecteplase should be reconstituted using the supplied 10 mL syringe with TwinPak™ dual cannula device and 10 mL sterile water for injection. Do not shake when reconstituting. Slight foaming is normal and will dissipate if left standing for several minutes. The reconstituted solution is 5 mg/mL. Any unused solution should be discarded. Tenecteplase is **incompatible** with dextrose solutions. Dextrose-containing lines must be flushed with a saline solution before and after administration. Administer as a single I.V. bolus over 5 seconds. Avoid I.M. injections and nonessential handling of patient.

Monitoring Parameters CBC, aPTT, signs and symptoms of bleeding, ECG monitoring

Dosage Forms Injection, powder for reconstitution, recombinant: 50 mg [packaged with diluent and syringe]

♦ **Tenex® [DSC]** *see* Guanfacine *on page 823*

♦ **Tenex® (Can)** *see* Guanfacine *on page 823*

Teniposide (ten i POE side)

U.S. Brand Names Vumon®

Canadian Brand Names Vumon®

Index Terms EPT; VM-26

Pharmacologic Category Antineoplastic Agent, Miscellaneous

Use Treatment of acute lymphocytic leukemia, small cell lung cancer

Pregnancy Risk Factor D

Medication Safety Issues

Sound-alike/look-alike issues:

Teniposide may be confused with etoposide

High alert medication: The Institute for Safe Medication Practices (ISMP) includes this medication among its list of drugs which have a heightened risk of causing significant patient harm when used in error.

Dosage I.V.:

Children: 130 mg/m^2/week, increasing to 150 mg/m^2 after 3 weeks and up to 180 mg/m^2 after 6 weeks

Acute lymphoblastic leukemia (ALL): 165 mg/m^2 twice weekly for 8-9 doses **or** 250 mg/m^2 weekly for 4-8 weeks

Adults: 50-180 mg/m^2 once or twice weekly for 4-6 weeks or 20-60 mg/m^2/day for 5 days

Small cell lung cancer: 80-90 mg/m^2/day for 5 days every 4-6 weeks

Dosage adjustment in renal/hepatic impairment: Data is insufficient, but dose adjustments may be necessary in patient with significant renal or hepatic impairment

Dosage adjustment in Down syndrome patients: Reduce initial dosing; administer the first course at half the usual dose. Patients with both Down syndrome and leukemia may be especially sensitive to myelosuppressive chemotherapy.

Additional Information Complete prescribing information for this medication should be consulted for additional detail.

Dosage Forms Injection, solution: 10 mg/mL (5 mL) [contains benzyl alcohol, dehydrated alcohol, and polyoxyethylated castor oil]

Tenofovir (te NOE fo veer)

U.S. Brand Names Viread®

Canadian Brand Names Viread®

Index Terms PMPA; TDF; Tenofovir Disoproxil Fumarate

Pharmacologic Category Antiretroviral Agent, Reverse Transcriptase Inhibitor (Nucleotide)

Additional Appendix Information

Antiretroviral Therapy for HIV Infection: Adults and Adolescents *on page 1988*

Management of Healthcare Worker Exposures to HBV, HCV, and HIV *on page 1941*

(Continued)

Tenofovir *(Continued)*

Use Management of HIV infections in combination with at least two other antiretroviral agents

Pregnancy Risk Factor B

Pregnancy Implications There are no adequate and well-controlled studies in pregnant women. Animal studies have shown decreased fetal growth and reduced fetal bone porosity. Clinical studies in children have shown bone demineralization with chronic use. Use in pregnancy only if clearly needed. Cases of lactic acidosis/hepatic steatosis syndrome have been reported in pregnant women receiving nucleoside analogues. It is not known if pregnancy itself potentiates this known side effect; however, pregnant women may be at increased risk of lactic acidosis and liver damage. Hepatic enzymes and electrolytes should be monitored frequently during the 3rd trimester of pregnancy in women receiving nucleoside analogues. Health professionals are encouraged to contact the Antiretroviral Pregnancy Registry to monitor outcomes of pregnant women exposed to antiretroviral medications (1-800-258-4263 or www.APRegistry.com).

Lactation Excretion in breast milk unknown/contraindicated

Contraindications Hypersensitivity to tenofovir or any component of the formulation

Warnings/Precautions [U.S Boxed Warning]: Lactic acidosis and severe hepatomegaly with steatosis have been reported with nucleoside analogues, including fatal cases; use with caution in patients with risk factors for liver disease (risk may be increased in obese patients or prolonged exposure) and suspend treatment in any patient who develops clinical or laboratory findings suggestive of lactic acidosis (transaminase elevation may/may not accompany hepatomegaly and steatosis). Immune reconstitution syndrome may develop resulting in the occurrence of an inflammatory response to an indolent or residual opportunistic infection; further evaluation and treatment may be required.

May cause osteomalacia; increased biochemical markers of bone metabolism, serum parathyroid hormone levels, and 1,25 vitamin D levels have been noted with tenofovir use. A 5% to 7% loss of bone mineral density (BMD) has been reported in some patients. BMD monitoring should be considered in patients with a history of bone fracture or risk factors for osteopenia.

Use caution in renal impairment (Cl_{cr} <50 mL/minute); dosage adjustment required. May cause acute renal failure or Fanconi syndrome; use caution with other nephrotoxic agents (especially those which compete for active tubular secretion), patients with low body weight, or concurent medications which increase tenofovir levels. Use caution in hepatic impairment. All patients with HIV should be tested for HBV prior to initiation of treatment. **[U.S Boxed Warning]: Safety and efficacy of tenofovir during coinfection of HIV and HBV have not been established; acute, severe exacerbations of HBV have been reported following tenofovir discontinuation.** In HBV coinfected patients, monitor hepatic function closely for several months following discontinuation. Safety and efficacy have not been established in pediatric patients.

Adverse Reactions

>10%:

Central nervous system: Pain (7% to 12%)

Gastrointestinal: Diarrhea (11% to 16%), nausea (8% to 11%)

Neuromuscular & skeletal: Weakness (7% to 11%)

1% to 10%:

Central nervous system: Headache (5% to 8%), depression (4% to 8%; treatment naïve 11%), insomnia (3% to 4%), fever (2% to 4%; treatment naïve 8%), dizziness (1% to 3%)

Dermatologic: Rash event (maculopapular, pustular, or vesiculobullous rash, pruritus or urticaria 5% to 7%; treatment naïve 18%)

Endocrine & metabolic: Amylase increased (treatment naïve 9%)

Gastrointestinal: Vomiting (4% to 7%), abdominal pain (4% to 7%), dyspepsia (3% to 4%), flatulence (3% to 4%), anorexia (3% to 4%), weight loss (2% to 4%)

Hematologic: Neutropenia (1% to 2%)

Hepatic: Transaminases increased (2% to 4%)

Neuromuscular & skeletal: Back pain (3% to 4%; treatment naïve 9%), myalgia (3% to 4%), neuropathy (peripheral 1% to 3%)

Respiratory: Pneumonia (2% to 3%)

Miscellaneous: Diaphoresis (3%)

Postmarketing and/or case reports: Acute tubular necrosis, allergic reaction, bone mineral density decreased, serum creatinine increased, dyspnea, Fanconi syndrome, hepatitis, hypophosphatemia, immune reconstitution syndrome, lactic acidosis, nephrogenic diabetes insipidus, nephrotoxicity, pancreatitis, proteinuria, proximal tubulopathy, renal failure

Note: Uncommon, but significant adverse reactions reported with other reverse transcriptase inhibitors include pancreatitis, peripheral neuropathy, and myopathy.

Overdosage/Toxicology Limited experience with overdose. Treatment is supportive. Hemodialysis may be beneficial; reportedly 10% of an administered single dose of 300 mg was removed during a 4-hour session.

Drug Interactions

Cytochrome P450 Effect: Inhibits CYP1A2 (weak)

Increased Effect/Toxicity: Concurrent use has been noted to increase serum concentrations/exposure to didanosine and its metabolites, potentially increasing the risk of didanosine toxicity (hyperglycemia, pancreatitis, peripheral neuropathy, or lactic acidosis); decreased CD4 cell counts and decreased virologic response have been reported. Use caution and monitor closely; suspend therapy if signs/symptoms of toxicity are present. Drugs which may compete for renal tubule secretion (including acyclovir, cidofovir, ganciclovir, valacyclovir, valganciclovir) may increase the serum concentrations of tenofovir. Drugs causing nephrotoxicity may reduce elimination of tenofovir. Protease inhibitors (especially ritonavir and combinations with ritonavir) may increase serum concentrations of tenofovir.

Decreased Effect: Tenofovir may decrease serum concentrations of atazanavir and other protease inhibitors, resulting in a loss of virologic response (specific atazanavir dosing recommendations provided by manufacturer).

Ethanol/Nutrition/Herb Interactions Food: Fatty meals may increase the bioavailability of tenofovir. Tenofovir may be taken with or without food.

Stability Store at 25°C (77°F); excursions permitted to 15°C to 30°C (59°F to 86°F).

Mechanism of Action Tenofovir disoproxil fumarate (TDF) is an analog of adenosine 5'-monophosphate; it interferes with the HIV viral RNA dependent DNA polymerase resulting in inhibition of viral replication. TDF is first converted intracellularly by hydrolysis to tenofovir and subsequently phosphorylated to the active tenofovir diphosphate; nucleotide reverse transcriptase inhibitor.

Pharmacodynamics/Kinetics
Distribution: 1.2-1.3 L/kg
Protein binding: 7% to serum proteins
Metabolism: Tenofovir disoproxil fumarate (TDF) is converted intracellularly by hydrolysis (by non-CYP enzymes) to tenofovir, then phosphorylated to the active tenofovir diphosphate
Bioavailability: 25% (fasting); increases ~40% with high-fat meal
Half-life elimination: 17 hours
Time to peak, serum: Fasting: 36-84 minutes; With food: 96-144 minutes
Excretion: Urine (70% to 80%) via filtration and active secretion, primarily as unchanged tenofovir

Dosage Oral: Adults: HIV infection: 300 mg once daily
Dosage adjustment in renal impairment:
Cl_{cr} 30-49 mL/minute: 300 mg every 48 hours
Cl_{cr} 10-29 mL/minute: 300 mg twice weekly
Cl_{cr} <10 mL/minute without hemodialysis: No recommendation available.
Hemodialysis: 300 mg every 7 days or after a total of 12 hours of dialysis (usually once weekly assuming 3 dialysis sessions lasting about 4 hours each)
Dosage adjustment in hepatic impairment: No dosage adjustment required.

Dietary Considerations May be taken with or without food. Consider calcium and vitamin D supplementation in patients with history of bone fracture or osteopenia.

Administration May be administered with or without food.

Monitoring Parameters CBC with differential, reticulocyte count, serum creatine kinase, CD4 count, HIV RNA plasma levels, renal and hepatic function tests, bone density (long-term), serum phosphorus; testing for HBV is recommended prior to the initiation of antiretroviral therapy
Patients with HIV and HVB coinfection should be monitored for several months following tenofovir discontinuation.

Additional Information Approval was based on two clinical trials involving patients who were previously treated with antiretrovirals with continued evidence of HIV replication despite therapy. The risk:benefit ratio for untreated patients has not been established (studies currently ongoing); however, patients who received tenofovir showed significant decreases in HIV replication as compared to continuation of standard therapy.

A high rate of early virologic nonresponse was observed when abacavir, lamivudine, and tenofovir were used as the initial regimen in treatment-naïve patients. A high rate of early virologic nonresponse was also observed when didanosine, lamivudine, and tenofovir were used as the initial regimen in treatment-naïve patients. Use of either of these combinations is not recommended; patients currently on either of these regimens should be closely monitored for modification of therapy. Early virologic failure was also observed with tenofovir and didanosine delayed release capsules, plus either efavirenz or nevirapine; use caution in treatment-naïve patients with high baseline viral loads.

Dosage Forms Tablet, as disoproxil fumarate: 300 mg [equivalent to 245 mg tenofovir disoproxil]

◆ **Tenofovir and Emtricitabine** *see* Emtricitabine and Tenofovir *on page 578*
◆ **Tenofovir Disoproxil Fumarate** *see* Tenofovir *on page 1645*
◆ **Tenofovir Disoproxil Fumarate, Efavirenz, and Emtricitabine** *see* Efavirenz, Emtricitabine, and Tenofovir *on page 573*
◆ **Tenolin (Can)** *see* Atenolol *on page 167*
◆ **Tenoretic®** *see* Atenolol and Chlorthalidone *on page 169*
◆ **Tenormin®** *see* Atenolol *on page 167*
◆ **Tensilon® (Can)** *see* Edrophonium *on page 569*
◆ **Tenuate® [DSC]** *see* Diethylpropion *on page 499*
◆ **Tenuate® (Can)** *see* Diethylpropion *on page 499*
◆ **Tenuate® Dospan® [DSC]** *see* Diethylpropion *on page 499*
◆ **Tenuate® Dospan® (Can)** *see* Diethylpropion *on page 499*
◆ **Tequin® [DSC]** *see* Gatifloxacin *on page 781*
◆ **Tequin® (Can)** *see* Gatifloxacin *on page 781*
◆ **Terazol® (Can)** *see* Terconazole *on page 1652*
◆ **Terazol® 3** *see* Terconazole *on page 1652*
◆ **Terazol® 7** *see* Terconazole *on page 1652*

Terazosin (ter AY zoe sin)

U.S. Brand Names Hytrin®
Canadian Brand Names Alti-Terazosin; Apo-Terazosin®; Hytrin®; Novo-Terazosin; Nu-Terazosin; PMS-Terazosin
Pharmacologic Category Alpha₁ Blocker
Use Management of mild to moderate hypertension; alone or in combination with other agents such as diuretics or beta-blockers; benign prostate hyperplasia (BPH)
Pregnancy Risk Factor C
(Continued)

Terazosin *(Continued)*

Lactation Excretion in breast milk unknown

Contraindications Hypersensitivity to quinazolines (doxazosin, prazosin, terazosin) or any component of the formulation; concurrent use with phosphodiesterase-5 (PDE-5) inhibitors including sildenafil (>25 mg), tadalafil, or vardenafil

Warnings/Precautions Can cause significant orthostatic hypotension and syncope, especially with first dose; anticipate a similar effect if therapy is interrupted for a few days, if dosage is rapidly increased, or if another antihypertensive drug (particularly vasodilators) or a PDE5 inhibitor is introduced. Discontinue if symptoms of angina occur or worsen. Patients should be cautioned about performing hazardous tasks when starting new therapy or adjusting dosage upward. Prostate cancer should be ruled out before starting for BPH. Use with caution in hepatic impairment. Intraoperative floppy iris syndrome has been observed in cataract surgery patients who were on or were previously treated with alpha$_1$ blockers. Causality has not been established and there appears to be no benefit in discontinuing alpha blocker therapy prior to surgery. Safety and efficacy in children have not been established.

Adverse Reactions Asthenia, postural hypotension, dizziness, somnolence, nasal congestion/rhinitis, and impotence were the only events noted in clinical trials to occur at a frequency significantly greater than placebo (p <0.05).

>10%:
Central nervous system: Dizziness, headache
Neuromuscular & skeletal: Muscle weakness

1% to 10%:
Cardiovascular: Edema, palpitation, chest pain, peripheral edema (3%), orthostatic hypotension (3% to 4%), tachycardia
Central nervous system: Fatigue, nervousness, drowsiness
Gastrointestinal: Dry mouth
Genitourinary: Urinary incontinence
Ocular: Blurred vision
Respiratory: Dyspnea, nasal congestion

<1% (Limited to important or life-threatening): Allergic reactions, anaphylaxis, atrial fibrillation, priapism, sexual dysfunction, syncope (0.8%), thrombocytopenia

Overdosage/Toxicology Symptoms include hypotension, drowsiness, and shock (but very unusual). Hypotension usually responds to I.V. fluids or Trendelenburg positioning. If unresponsive to these measures, the use of a parenteral vasoconstrictor may be required. Treatment is primarily supportive and symptomatic.

Drug Interactions
Increased Effect/Toxicity: Terazosin's hypotensive effect is increased with beta-blockers, diuretics, ACE inhibitors, calcium channel blockers, other antihypertensive medications, sildenafil (use with extreme caution at a dose ≤25 mg), tadalafil (use is contraindicated by the manufacturer), and vardenafil (use is contraindicated by the manufacturer).
Decreased Effect: Decreased antihypertensive response with NSAIDs. Alpha-blockers reduce the response to pressor agents (norepinephrine).

Ethanol/Nutrition/Herb Interactions Herb/Nutraceutical: Avoid dong quai if using for hypertension (has estrogenic activity). Avoid ephedra, yohimbe, ginseng (may worsen hypertension). Avoid saw palmetto. Avoid garlic (may have increased antihypertensive effect).

Mechanism of Action Alpha$_1$-specific blocking agent with minimal alpha$_2$ effects; this allows peripheral postsynaptic blockade, with the resultant decrease in arterial tone, while preserving the negative feedback loop which is mediated by the peripheral presynaptic alpha$_2$-receptors; terazosin relaxes the smooth muscle of the bladder neck, thus reducing bladder outlet obstruction

Pharmacodynamics/Kinetics
Onset of action: 1-2 hours
Absorption: Rapid
Protein binding: 90% to 95%
Metabolism: Extensively hepatic
Half-life elimination: 9.2-12 hours
Time to peak, serum: ~1 hour
Excretion: Feces (60%); urine (40%)

Dosage Oral: Adults:
Hypertension: Initial: 1 mg at bedtime; slowly increase dose to achieve desired blood pressure, up to 20 mg/day; usual dose range (JNC 7): 1-20 mg once daily
Dosage reduction may be needed when adding a diuretic or other antihypertensive agent; if drug is discontinued for greater than several days, consider beginning with initial dose and retitrate as needed; dosage may be given on a twice daily regimen if response is diminished at 24 hours and hypotensive is observed at 2-4 hours following a dose
Benign prostatic hyperplasia: Initial: 1 mg at bedtime, increasing as needed; most patients require 10 mg day; if no response after 4-6 weeks of 10 mg/day, may increase to 20 mg/day

Dietary Considerations May be taken without regard to meals at the same time each day.

Monitoring Parameters Standing and sitting/supine blood pressure, especially following the initial dose at 2-4 hours following the dose and thereafter at the trough point to ensure adequate control throughout the dosing interval; urinary symptoms

Dosage Forms Capsule: 1 mg, 2 mg, 5 mg, 10 mg

Terbinafine *(TER bin a feen)*

U.S. Brand Names Lamisil®; Lamisil® AT™ [OTC]
Canadian Brand Names Apo-Terbinafine®; CO Terbinafine; Gen-Terbinafine; Lamisil®; Novo-Terbinafine; PMS-Terbinafine

Index Terms Terbinafine Hydrochloride
Pharmacologic Category Antifungal Agent, Oral; Antifungal Agent, Topical
Additional Appendix Information
  Antifungal Agents *on page 1869*
Use Active against most strains of *Trichophyton mentagrophytes*, *Trichophyton rubrum*; may be effective for infections of *Microsporum gypseum* and *M. nanum*, *Trichophyton verrucosum*, *Epidermophyton floccosum*, *Candida albicans*, and *Scopulariopsis brevicaulis*
  Oral: Onychomycosis of the toenail or fingernail due to susceptible dermatophytes
  Topical: Antifungal for the treatment of tinea pedis (athlete's foot), tinea cruris (jock itch), and tinea corporis (ringworm) [OTC/prescription formulations]; tinea versicolor [prescription formulations]
Pregnancy Risk Factor B
Pregnancy Implications Avoid use in pregnancy since treatment of onychomycosis is postponable.
Lactation Enters breast milk/not recommended
Medication Safety Issues
  Sound-alike/look-alike issues:
    Terbinafine may be confused with terbutaline
    Lamisil® may be confused with Lamictal®, Lomotil®

  International issues:
    Lamisil® may be confused with Lemesil® which is a brand name for nimesulide in Greece and Romania
Contraindications Hypersensitivity to terbinafine, naftifine, or any component of the formulation
Warnings/Precautions While rare, the following complications have been reported and may require discontinuation of therapy: Changes in the ocular lens and retina, pancytopenia, neutropenia, Stevens-Johnson syndrome, toxic epidermal necrolysis. Rare cases of hepatic failure (including fatal cases) have been reported following oral treatment of onychomycosis. Not recommended for use in patients with active or chronic liver disease. Discontinue if symptoms or signs of hepatobiliary dysfunction or cholestatic hepatitis develop. If irritation/sensitivity develop with topical use, discontinue therapy. Oral products are not recommended for use with pre-existing liver or renal disease (≤50 mL/minute GFR). **Use caution in writing and/or filling prescription/orders. Confusion between Lamictal® (lamotrigine) and Lamisil® (terbinafine) has occurred.**
Adverse Reactions
  Oral:
  1% to 10%:
    Central nervous system: Headache, dizziness, vertigo
    Dermatologic: Rash, pruritus, urticaria
    Gastrointestinal: Diarrhea, dyspepsia, abdominal pain, appetite decrease, taste disturbance
    Hematologic: Lymphocytopenia
    Hepatic: Liver enzymes increased
    Ocular: Visual disturbance
  <1% (Limited to important or life-threatening): Angioedema, agranulocytosis, allergic reactions, alopecia, anaphylaxis, arthralgia, changes in ocular lens and retina, fatigue, generalized exanthematous pustulosis (acute), hepatic failure, malaise, myalgia, neutropenia, precipitation/exacerbation of cutaneous and systemic lupus erythematosus, psoriaform eruption, psoriasis exacerbation, Stevens-Johnson syndrome, thrombocytopenia, toxic epidermal necrolysis, vomiting

  Topical: 1% to 10%:
    Dermatologic: Pruritus, contact dermatitis, irritation, burning, dryness
    Local: Irritation, stinging
Drug Interactions
  Cytochrome P450 Effect: Substrate (minor) of 1A2, 2C9, 2C19, 3A4; **Inhibits** CYP2D6 (strong); **Induces** CYP3A4 (weak)
  Increased Effect/Toxicity: Terbinafine may increase the levels/effects of amphetamines, beta-blockers, dextromethorphan, fluoxetine, lidocaine, mirtazapine, nefazodone, paroxetine, risperidone, ritonavir, thioridazine, tricyclic antidepressants, venlafaxine, and other CYP2D6 substrates. The effects of warfarin may be increased.
  Decreased Effect: Terbinafine may decrease the levels/effects of CYP2D6 prodrug substrates (eg, codeine, hydrocodone, oxycodone, tramadol).
Stability
  Cream: Store at 5°C to 30°C (41°F to 86°F).
  Solution: Store at 5°C to 25°C (41°F to 77°F); do not refrigerate.
  Tablet: Store below 25°C (77°F). Protect from light.
Mechanism of Action Synthetic allylamine derivative which inhibits squalene epoxidase, a key enzyme in sterol biosynthesis in fungi. This results in a deficiency in ergosterol within the fungal cell wall and results in fungal cell death.
Pharmacodynamics/Kinetics
  Absorption: Topical: Limited (<5%); Oral: >70%
  Distribution: V_d: 2000 L; distributed to sebum and skin predominantly
  Protein binding, plasma: >99%
  Metabolism: Hepatic; no active metabolites; first-pass effect; little effect on CYP
  Bioavailability: Oral: 40%
  Half-life elimination:
    Topical: 22-26 hours
    Oral: Terminal half-life: 200-400 hours; very slow release of drug from skin and adipose tissues occurs; effective half-life: ~36 hours
  Time to peak, plasma: 1-2 hours
  Excretion: Urine (70% to 75%)
  (Continued)

Terbinafine *(Continued)*

Dosage

Children ≥12 years and Adults:

Topical cream, solution:

Athlete's foot (tinea pedis): Apply to affected area twice daily for at least 1 week, not to exceed 4 weeks [OTC/prescription formulations]

Ringworm (tinea corporis) and jock itch (tinea cruris): Apply cream to affected area once or twice daily for at least 1 week, not to exceed 4 weeks; apply solution once daily for 7 days [OTC formulations]

Adults:

Oral:

Superficial mycoses: Fingernail: 250 mg/day for up to 6 weeks; toenail: 250 mg/day for 12 weeks; doses may be given in two divided doses

Systemic mycosis: 250-500 mg/day for up to 16 months

Topical solution: Tinea versicolor: Apply to affected area twice daily for 1 week [prescription formulation]

Children: Oral (unlabeled use in children):

10-20 kg: 62.5 mg/day

20-40 kg: 125 mg/day

>40 kg: 250 mg/day

Treatment duration:

Tinea pedis: 2 weeks

Tinea capitis: 2-4 weeks

Onychomycosis: Fingernails: 6 weeks; Toenails: 12 weeks

Dosing adjustment in renal impairment: GFR <50 mL/minute: Oral administration is not recommended.

Dosing adjustment in hepatic impairment: Clearance is decreased by ~50% with hepatic cirrhosis; use is not recommended.

Monitoring Parameters CBC and LFTs at baseline and repeated if use is for >6 weeks

Additional Information Due to potential toxicity, the manufacturer recommends confirmation of diagnosis testing of nail specimens prior to treatment of onychomycosis. Patients should not be considered therapeutic failures until they have been symptom-free for 2-4 weeks off following a course of treatment; GI complaints usually subside with continued administration.

A meta-analysis of efficacy studies for toenail infections revealed that weighted average mycological cure rates for continuous therapy were 36.7% (griseofulvin), 54.7% (itraconazole), and 77% (terbinafine). Cure rate for 4-month pulse therapy for itraconazole and terbinafine were 73.3% and 80%. Additionally, the final outcome measure of final costs per cured infections for continuous therapy was significantly lower for terbinafine.

Dosage Forms

Cream, as hydrochloride:

Lamisil® AT™: 1% (12 g) [contains benzyl alcohol]

Solution, as hydrochloride [topical spray]:

Lamisil® [DSC], Lamisil® AT™: 1% (30 mL)

Tablet:

Lamisil®: 250 mg

♦ **Terbinafine Hydrochloride** *see* Terbinafine *on page 1648*

Terbutaline *(ter BYOO ta leen)*

Canadian Brand Names Bricanyl®

Index Terms Brethaire [DSC]; Bricanyl [DSC]

Pharmacologic Category Beta₂-Adrenergic Agonist

Additional Appendix Information

Bronchodilators *on page 1877*

Use Bronchodilator in reversible airway obstruction and bronchial asthma

Unlabeled/Investigational Use Tocolytic agent (management of preterm labor)

Pregnancy Risk Factor B

Lactation Enters breast milk/compatible

Medication Safety Issues

Sound-alike/look-alike issues:

Terbutaline may be confused with terbinafine, TOLBUTamide

Contraindications Hypersensitivity to terbutaline or any component of the formulation; cardiac arrhythmias associated with tachycardia; tachycardia caused by digitalis intoxication

Warnings/Precautions When used for tocolysis, there is some risk of maternal pulmonary edema, which has been associated with the following risk factors, excessive hydration, multiple gestation, occult sepsis and underlying cardiac disease. To reduce risk, limit fluid intake to 2.5-3 L/day, limit sodium intake, maintain maternal pulse to <130 beats/minute.

Use caution in patients with cardiovascular disease (arrhythmia or hypertension or CHF), convulsive disorders, diabetes, glaucoma, hyperthyroidism, or hypokalemia. Beta agonists may cause elevation in blood pressure, heart rate, and result in CNS stimulation/excitation. Beta₂ agonists may increase risk of arrhythmia, increase serum glucose, or decrease serum potassium.

When used as a bronchodilator, optimize anti-inflammatory treatment before initiating maintenance treatment with terbutaline. Do not use as a component of chronic therapy without an anti-inflammatory agent. Only the mildest form of asthma (Step 1 and/or exercise-induced) would not require concurrent use based upon asthma guidelines. Patient must be instructed to seek medical attention in cases where acute symptoms are not relieved or a previous level of response is diminished. The need to increase frequency of use may indicate deterioration of asthma, and treatment must not be delayed.

Immediate hypersensitivity reactions (urticaria, angioedema, rash, bronchospasm) have been reported. Do not exceed recommended dose; serious adverse events including fatalities, have been associated with excessive use of inhaled sympathomimetics. Rarely, paradoxical bronchospasm may occur with use of inhaled bronchodilating agents; this should be distinguished from inadequate response.

Adverse Reactions

>10%:

Central nervous system: Nervousness, restlessness

Endocrine & metabolic: Serum glucose increased, serum potassium decreased

Neuromuscular & skeletal: Trembling

1% to 10%:

Cardiovascular: Tachycardia, hypertension, pounding heartbeat

Central nervous system: Dizziness, lightheadedness, drowsiness, headache, insomnia

Gastrointestinal: Dry mouth, nausea, vomiting, bad taste in mouth

Neuromuscular & skeletal: Muscle cramps, weakness

Miscellaneous: Diaphoresis

<1% (Limited to important or life-threatening): Arrhythmia, chest pain, hypokalemia, paradoxical bronchospasm

Overdosage/Toxicology

Symptoms of overdose include tachycardia, tremor, hypertension, angina, and seizures. Hypokalemia also may occur. Cardiac arrest and death may be associated with abuse of beta-agonist bronchodilators. Treatment includes immediate discontinuation and symptomatic and supportive therapies. Cautious use of beta-adrenergic blocking agents may be considered in severe cases.

Drug Interactions

Increased Effect/Toxicity: Increased toxicity with MAO inhibitors, tricyclic antidepressants.

Decreased Effect: Decreased effect with beta-blockers.

Ethanol/Nutrition/Herb Interactions Herb/Nutraceutical: Avoid ephedra, yohimbe (may cause CNS stimulation).

Stability Store injection at room temperature; do not freeze. Protect from heat and light. Use only clear solutions. Store powder for inhalation (Bricanyl® Turbuhaler [CAN]) at room temperature between 15°C and 30°C (58°F and 86°F).

Mechanism of Action Relaxes bronchial smooth muscle by action on beta$_2$-receptors with less effect on heart rate

Pharmacodynamics/Kinetics

Onset of action: Oral: 30-45 minutes; SubQ: 6-15 minutes

Protein binding: 25%

Metabolism: Hepatic to inactive sulfate conjugates

Bioavailability: SubQ doses are more bioavailable than oral

Half-life elimination: 11-16 hours

Excretion: Urine

Dosage

Children <12 years: Bronchoconstriction:

Oral: Initial: 0.05 mg/kg/dose 3 times/day, increased gradually as required; maximum: 0.15 mg/kg/dose 3-4 times/day or a total of 5 mg/24 hours

SubQ: 0.005-0.01 mg/kg/dose to a maximum of 0.3 mg/dose; may repeat in 15-20 minutes

Children ≥6 years and Adults: Bronchospasm (acute): Inhalation (Bricanyl® [CAN] MDI: 500 mcg/puff, *not labeled for use in the U.S.*): One puff as needed; may repeat with 1 inhalation (after 5 minutes); more than 6 inhalations should not be necessary in any 24 hour period. **Note:** If a previously effective dosage regimen fails to provide the usual relief, or the effects of a dose last for >3 hours, medical advice should be sought immediately; this is a sign of seriously worsening asthma that requires reassessment of therapy.

Children >12 years and Adults: Bronchoconstriction:

Oral:

12-15 years: 2.5 mg every 6 hours 3 times/day; not to exceed 7.5 mg in 24 hours

>15 years: 5 mg/dose every 6 hours 3 times/day; if side effects occur, reduce dose to 2.5 mg every 6 hours; not to exceed 15 mg in 24 hours

SubQ: 0.25 mg/dose; may repeat in 15-30 minutes (maximum: 0.5 mg/4-hour period)

Adults: Premature labor (tocolysis; unlabeled use):

Acute: I.V. 2.5-10 mcg/minute; increased gradually every 10-20 minutes; effective maximum dosages from 17.5-30 mcg/minute have been used with caution. Duration of infusion is at least 12 hours.

Maintenance: Oral: 2.5-10 mg every 4-6 hours for as long as necessary to prolong pregnancy depending on patient tolerance

Dosing adjustment/comments in renal impairment:

Cl_{cr} 10-50 mL/minute: Administer at 50% of normal dose

Cl_{cr} <10 mL/minute: Avoid use

Administration

I.V.: Use infusion pump.

Oral: Administer around-the-clock to promote less variation in peak and trough serum levels

Monitoring Parameters Serum potassium, glucose; heart rate, blood pressure, respiratory rate; monitor for signs and symptoms of pulmonary edema (when used as a tocolytic); monitor FEV_1, peak flow, and/or other pulmonary function tests (when used as bronchodilator)

Dosage Forms [CAN] = Canadian brand name

Injection, solution, as sulfate: 1 mg/mL (1 mL)

Powder for oral inhalation:

Bricanyl® Turbuhaler [CAN]: 500 mcg/actuation [50 or 200 metered actuations] [not available in U.S.]

Tablet, as sulfate: 2.5 mg, 5 mg

Extemporaneous Preparations A 1 mg/mL suspension made from terbutaline tablets in simple syrup NF is stable 30 days when refrigerated

Horner RK and Johnson CE, "Stability of An Extemporaneously Compounded Terbutaline Sulfate Oral Liquid," *Am J Hosp Pharm*, 1991, 48(2):293-5.

Terconazole (ter KONE a zole)

U.S. Brand Names Terazol® 3; Terazol® 7
Canadian Brand Names Terazol®
Index Terms Triaconazole
Pharmacologic Category Antifungal Agent, Vaginal
Additional Appendix Information
Treatment of Sexually Transmitted Infections *on page 2007*
Use Local treatment of vulvovaginal candidiasis
Pregnancy Risk Factor C
Lactation Excretion in breast milk unknown/not recommended
Medication Safety Issues
Sound-alike/look-alike issues:
Terconazole may be confused with tioconazole

International issues:
Terazol® may be confused with Theradol® which is a brand name for tramadol in the Netherlands
Contraindications Hypersensitivity to terconazole or any component of the formulation
Warnings/Precautions Should be discontinued if sensitization or irritation occurs. Microbiological studies (KOH smear and/or cultures) should be repeated in patients not responding to terconazole in order to confirm the diagnosis and rule out other pathogens.
Adverse Reactions
1% to 10%:
Central nervous system: Fever, chills
Gastrointestinal: Abdominal pain
Genitourinary: Vulvar/vaginal burning, dysmenorrhea
<1% (Limited to important or life-threatening): Burning or itching of penis of sexual partner, flu-like syndrome, polyuria; vulvar itching, soreness, edema, or discharge
Stability Store at room temperature of 13°C to 30°C (59°F to 86°F).
Mechanism of Action Triazole ketal antifungal agent; involves inhibition of fungal cytochrome P450. Specifically, terconazole inhibits cytochrome P450-dependent 14-alpha-demethylase which results in accumulation of membrane disturbing 14-alpha-demethylsterols and ergosterol depletion.
Pharmacodynamics/Kinetics Absorption: Extent of systemic absorption after vaginal administration may be dependent on presence of a uterus; 5% to 8% in women who had a hysterectomy versus 12% to 16% in nonhysterectomy women
Dosage Adults: Female:
Terazol® 3 vaginal cream: Insert 1 applicatorful intravaginally at bedtime for 3 consecutive days
Terazol® 7 vaginal cream: Insert 1 applicatorful intravaginally at bedtime for 7 consecutive days
Terazol® 3 vaginal suppository: Insert 1 suppository intravaginally at bedtime for 3 consecutive days
Additional Information Watch for local irritation; assist patient in administration, if necessary; assess patient's ability to self-administer, may be difficult in patients with arthritis or limited range of motion
Dosage Forms
Cream, vaginal:
Terazol® 7: 0.4% (45 g) [packaged with measured-dose applicator]
Terazol® 3: 0.8% (20 g) [packaged with measured-dose applicator]
Suppository, vaginal (Terazol® 3): 80 mg (3s) [may contain coconut and/or palm kernel oil]

♦ **Terfluzine (Can)** *see* Trifluoperazine *on page 1740*

Teriparatide (ter i PAR a tide)

U.S. Brand Names Forteo™
Canadian Brand Names Forteo™
Index Terms Parathyroid Hormone (1-34); Recombinant Human Parathyroid Hormone (1-34); rhPTH(1-34)
Pharmacologic Category Parathyroid Hormone Analog
Use Treatment of osteoporosis in postmenopausal women at high risk of fracture; treatment of primary or hypogonadal osteoporosis in men at high risk of fracture
Restrictions An FDA-approved medication guide must be distributed when dispensing an outpatient prescription (new or refill) where this medication is to be used without direct supervision of a healthcare provider. Medication guides are available at http://www.fda.gov/cder/Offices/ODS/medication_guides.htm.
Pregnancy Risk Factor C
Pregnancy Implications Effect on human fetal development has not been studied; not indicated for use in pregnant women
Lactation Excretion in breast milk unknown/not recommended
Contraindications Hypersensitivity to teriparatide or any component of the formulation
Warnings/Precautions [U.S. Boxed Warning]: **In animal studies, teriparatide has been associated with an increase in osteosarcoma;** risk was dependent on both dose and duration. Use of teriparatide for longer than 2 years is not recommended. Avoid use in patients with an increased risk of osteosarcoma (including Paget's disease, prior radiation, unexplained elevation of alkaline phosphatase, or in patients with open epiphyses). Do not use in patients with a history of skeletal metastases, hyperparathyroidism, or pre-existing hypercalcemia. Exclude metabolic bone disease other than osteoporosis prior to initiating therapy. Use caution in patients with active or recent urolithiasis. Use caution in patients at risk of orthostasis (including concurrent antihypertensive therapy), or in patients who may not tolerate transient hypotension (cardiovascular or cerebrovascular disease). Use caution in

patients with renal or hepatic impairment (limited data available concerning safety and efficacy). Not approved for use in pediatric patients.

Adverse Reactions 1% to 10%:
Cardiovascular: Chest pain (3%), syncope (3%)
Central nervous system: Dizziness (8%), depression (4%), vertigo (4%)
Dermatologic: Rash (5%)
Endocrine & metabolic: Hypercalcemia (transient increases noted 4-6 hours postdose in 11% of women and 6% of men)
Gastrointestinal: Nausea (9%), dyspepsia (5%), vomiting (3%), tooth disorder (2%)
Genitourinary: Hyperuricemia (3%)
Neuromuscular & skeletal: Arthralgia (10%), weakness (9%), leg cramps (3%)
Respiratory: Rhinitis (10%), pharyngitis (6%), dyspnea (4%), pneumonia (4%)
Miscellaneous: Antibodies to teriparatide (3% of women in long-term treatment; hypersensitivity reactions or decreased efficacy were not associated in preclinical trials)

Overdosage/Toxicology No specific experience in overdose. Symptoms may include hypercalcemia, hypotension, headache, nausea, vomiting, and hypotension. Treatment is supportive (monitor serum calcium and phosphorus).

Drug Interactions
Increased Effect/Toxicity: Digitalis serum concentrations are not affected, however, transient hypercalcemia may increase risk of digitalis toxicity (case reports).

Ethanol/Nutrition/Herb Interactions
Ethanol: Excessive intake may increase risk of osteoporosis.
Herb/Nutraceutical: Ensure adequate calcium and vitamin D intake.

Stability Store at 2°C to 8°C (36°F to 46°F); do not freeze. Protect from light. Discard pen 28 days after first injection.

Mechanism of Action Teriparatide is a recombinant formulation of endogenous parathyroid hormone (PTH), containing a 34-amino-acid sequence which is identical to the N-terminal portion of this hormone. The pharmacologic activity of teriparatide is similar to the physiologic activity of PTH, stimulating osteoblast function, increasing gastrointestinal calcium absorption, increasing renal tubular reabsorption of calcium. Treatment with teriparatide increases bone mineral density, bone mass, and strength. In postmenopausal women, it has been shown to decrease osteoporosis-related fractures.

Pharmacodynamics/Kinetics
Distribution: V_d: 0.12 L/kg
Metabolism: Hepatic (nonspecific proteolysis)
Bioavailability: 95%
Half-life elimination: Serum: I.V.: 5 minutes; SubQ: 1 hour
Excretion: Urine (as metabolites)

Dosage SubQ: Adults: 20 mcg once daily; **Note:** Initial administration should occur under circumstances in which the patient may sit or lie down, in the event of orthostasis.
Dosage adjustment in renal impairment: No dosage adjustment required. Bioavailability and half-life increase with Cl_{cr} <30 mL/minute.

Administration Administer by subcutaneous injection into the thigh or abdominal wall. Initial administration should occur under circumstances in which the patient may sit or lie down, in the event of orthostasis.

Monitoring Parameters Serum calcium, serum phosphorus, uric acid; blood pressure; bone mineral density

Additional Information Teriparatide was formerly marketed as a diagnostic agent (Perithar™); that agent was withdrawn from the market in 1997. Teriparatide (Forteo™) is manufactured from recombinant DNA technology using a strain of *E. coli*.

Dosage Forms Injection, solution: 250 mcg/mL (3 mL) [prefilled syringe, delivers teriparatide 20 mcg/dose]

- **Terramycin® (Can)** *see* Oxytetracycline *on page 1293*
- **Terramycin® I.M. [DSC]** *see* Oxytetracycline *on page 1293*
- **Teslac®** *see* Testolactone *on page 1653*
- **TESPA** *see* Thiotepa *on page 1674*
- **Tessalon®** *see* Benzonatate *on page 207*
- **Testim®** *see* Testosterone *on page 1653*

Testolactone (tes toe LAK tone)

U.S. Brand Names Teslac®
Canadian Brand Names Teslac®
Pharmacologic Category Androgen
Use Palliative treatment of advanced or disseminated breast carcinoma
Restrictions C-III
Pregnancy Risk Factor C
Medication Safety Issues
Sound-alike/look-alike issues:
Testolactone may be confused with testosterone
Dosage Adults: Female: Oral: 250 mg 4 times/day for at least 3 months; desired response may take as long as 3 months
Additional Information Complete prescribing information for this medication should be consulted for additional detail.
Dosage Forms Tablet: 50 mg

- **Testopel®** *see* Testosterone *on page 1653*

Testosterone (tes TOS ter one)

U.S. Brand Names Androderm®; AndroGel®; Delatestryl®; Depo®-Testosterone; First® Testosterone; First® Testosterone MC; Striant®; Testim®; Testopel®
(Continued)

Testosterone *(Continued)*

Canadian Brand Names Andriol®; Androderm®; AndroGel®; Andropository; Delatestryl®; Depotest® 100; Everone® 200; Virilon® IM

Index Terms Testosterone Cypionate; Testosterone Enanthate

Pharmacologic Category Androgen

Use

Injection: Androgen replacement therapy in the treatment of delayed male puberty; male hypogonadism (primary or hypogonadotropic); inoperable female breast cancer (enanthate only)

Pellet: Androgen replacement therapy in the treatment of delayed male puberty; male hypogonadism (primary or hypogonadotropic)

Buccal, topical: Male hypogonadism (primary or hypogonadotropic)

Capsule (not available in U.S.): Management of congenital or acquired primary hypogonadism and hypogonadotropic hypogonadism; development and maintenenance of secondary sexual characteristics in males with testosterone deficiency; stimulation of puberty in carefully selected males with clearly delayed puberty not secondary to a pathological disorder; replacement therapy in syndromes with symptoms of deficiency or absence of endogenous testosterone; replacement therapy in impotence or for male climacteric symptoms when the conditions are due to a measured or documented androgen deficiency

Restrictions C-III

Pregnancy Risk Factor X

Pregnancy Implications Testosterone may cause adverse effects, including masculinization of the female fetus, if used during pregnancy. Females who are or may become pregnant should also avoid skin-to-skin contact to areas where testosterone has been applied topically on another person.

Lactation Enters breast milk/contraindicated

Medication Safety Issues

Sound-alike/look-alike issues:

Testosterone may be confused with testolactone

Testoderm® may be confused with Estraderm®

Transdermal patch may contain conducting metal (eg, aluminum); remove patch prior to MRI.

Contraindications Hypersensitivity to testosterone, soy, or any component of the formulation; males with carcinoma of the breast or prostate; pregnancy or women who may become pregnant

Systemic use is contraindicated in hepatic, renal, or cardiac disease; benign prostatic hyperplasia with obstruction; undiagnosed genital bleeding; hypercalcemia

Warnings/Precautions When used to treat delayed male puberty, perform radiographic examination of the hand and wrist every 6 months to determine the rate of bone maturation. May cause hypercalcemia in patients with prolonged immobilization. May accelerate bone maturation without producing compensating gain in linear growth. Has both androgenic and anabolic activity, the anabolic action may enhance hypoglycemia. Use caution in elderly patients or patients with other demographic factors which may increase the risk of prostatic carcinoma; careful monitoring is required. May cause fluid retention; use caution in patients with cardiovascular disease or other edematous conditions. Prolonged use of orally-active androgens has been associated with serious hepatic effects (hepatitis, hepatic neoplasms, cholestatic hepatitis, jaundice). May potentiate sleep apnea in some male patients (obesity or chronic lung disease). Transdermal patch may contain conducting metal (eg, aluminum); remove patch prior to MRI. Gels and buccal system have not been evaluated in males <18 years of age; safety and efficacy of injection have not been established in males <12 years of age.

Adverse Reactions Frequency rarely defined.

Cardiovascular: Edema, flushing, hypertension, vasodilation

Central nervous system: Aggressive behavior, amnesia, anxiety, dizziness, emotional lability, excitation, headache, mental depression, nervousness, sleeplessness

Dermatologic: Acne, allergic contact dermatitis (transdermal 4%), alopecia, burn-like blisters (transdermal 12%), dry skin, erythema (transdermal 7%), hirsutism (increase in pubic hair growth), pruritus

Endocrine & metabolic: Breast soreness, gynecomastia, hypercalcemia, hypoglycemia, menstrual problems (amenorrhea), virilism

Gastrointestinal: GI irritation, nausea, vomiting

Following buccal administration: Bitter taste, gum edema, gum or mouth irritation, gum tenderness, taste perversion

Genitourinary: Bladder irritability, epididymitis, impotence, priapism, prostatic carcinoma, prostatic hyperplasia, PSA increased (up to 18%), testicular atrophy, urination impaired

Hepatic: Cholestatic hepatitis, hepatic dysfunction, hepatic necrosis

Hematologic: Leukopenia, polycythemia, suppression of clotting factors

Neuromuscular & skeletal: Paresthesia, weakness

Miscellaneous: Diaphoresis, hypersensitivity reactions

Drug Interactions

Cytochrome P450 Effect: Substrate (minor) of CYP2B6, 2C9, 2C19, 3A4; **Inhibits** CYP3A4 (weak)

Increased Effect/Toxicity: Testosterone may increase the effects warfarin.

Ethanol/Nutrition/Herb Interactions Herb/Nutraceutical: St John's wort may decrease testosterone levels.

Stability

Androderm®: Store at room temperature. Do not store outside of pouch. Excessive heat may cause system to burst.

AndroGel®, Delatestryl®, Striant®, Testim®: Store at room temperature.

Depo® Testosterone: Store at room temperature. Protect from light.

Testopel®: Store in a cool location.

Mechanism of Action Principal endogenous androgen responsible for promoting the growth and development of the male sex organs and maintaining secondary sex characteristics in androgen-deficient males

Pharmacodynamics/Kinetics

Duration (route and ester dependent): I.M.: Cypionate and enanthate esters have longest duration, ≤2-4 weeks

Absorption: Transdermal gel: ~10% of applied dose

Distribution: Crosses placenta; enters breast milk

Protein binding: 98%; bound to sex hormone-binding globulin (40%) and albumin

Metabolism: Hepatic; forms metabolites, including dihydrotestosterone (DHT) and estradiol (both active)

Half-life elimination: 10-100 minutes

Excretion: Urine (90%); feces (6%)

Dosage

Adolescents: I.M.:

Male hypogonadism:

Initiation of pubertal growth: 40-50 mg/m^2/dose (cypionate or enanthate ester) monthly until the growth rate falls to prepubertal levels

Terminal growth phase: 100 mg/m^2/dose (cypionate or enanthate ester) monthly until growth ceases

Maintenance virilizing dose: 100 mg/m^2/dose (cypionate or enanthate ester) twice monthly

Delayed male puberty: 40-50 mg/m^2/dose monthly (cypionate or enanthate ester) for 6 months

Adolescents and Adults:

Pellet (for subcutaneous implantation): Delayed male puberty, male hypogonadism: 150-450 mg every 3-6 months

Oral: Hypogonadism or hypogonadotropic hypogonadism:

Buccal: 30 mg twice daily (every 12 hours) applied to the gum region above the incisor tooth

Capsule (Andriol®; not available in U.S.): Initial: 120-160 mg/day in 2 divided doses for 2-3 weeks; adjust according to individual response; usual maintenance dose: 40-120 mg/day (in divided doses)

Adults:

I.M.:

Female: Inoperable breast cancer: Testosterone enanthate: 200-400 mg every 2-4 weeks

Male: Long-acting formulations: Testosterone enanthate (in oil)/testosterone cypionate (in oil):

Hypogonadism: 50-400 mg every 2-4 weeks

Delayed puberty: 50-200 mg every 2-4 weeks for a limited duration

Transdermal: Primary male hypogonadism **or** hypogonadotropic hypogonadism:

Androderm®: Initial: Apply 5 mg/day once nightly to clean, dry area on the back, abdomen, upper arms, or thighs (do **not** apply to scrotum); dosing range: 2.5-7.5 mg/day; in nonvirilized patients, dose may be initiated at 2.5 mg/day

AndroGel®, Testim®: 5 g (to deliver 50 mg of testosterone with 5 mg systemically absorbed) applied once daily (preferably in the morning) to clean, dry, intact skin of the shoulder and upper arms. AndroGel® may also be applied to the abdomen. Dosage may be increased to a maximum of 10 g (100 mg). **Do not apply testosterone gel to the genitals**.

Dosing adjustment/comments in hepatic disease: Reduce dose

Dietary Considerations Testosterone USP may be synthesized from soy. Food and beverages have not been found to interfere with buccal system; ensure system is in place following eating, drinking, or brushing teeth.

Administration

I.M.: Warm to room temperature; shaking vial will help redissolve crystals that have formed after storage. Administer by deep I.M. injection into the upper outer quadrant of the gluteus maximus.

Oral, buccal application (Striant®): One mucoadhesive for buccal application (buccal system) should be applied to a comfortable area above the incisor tooth. Apply flat side of system to gum. Rotate to alternate sides of mouth with each application. Hold buccal system firmly in place for 30 seconds to ensure adhesion. The buccal system should adhere to gum for 12 hours. If the buccal system falls out, replace with a new system. If the system falls out within 4 hours of next dose, the new buccal system should remain in place until the time of the following scheduled dose. System will soften and mold to shape of gum as it absorbs moisture from mouth. Do not chew or swallow the buccal system. The buccal system will not dissolve; gently remove by sliding downwards from gum; avoid scratching gum.

Oral, capsule (Andriol®; not available in the U.S.): Should be administered with meals. Should be swallowed whole; do not crush or chew.

Transdermal patch (Androderm®): Apply patch to clean, dry area of skin on the arm, back, or upper buttocks. Following patch removal, mild skin irritation may be treated with OTC hydrocortisone cream. A small amount of triamcinolone acetonide 0.1% cream may be applied under the system to decrease irritation; do not use ointment. Patch should be applied nightly. Rotate administration sites, allowing 7 days between applying to the same site.

Topical gel: AndroGel®, Testim®: Apply (preferably in the morning) to clean, dry, intact skin of the shoulder and upper arms (AndroGel® may also be applied to the abdomen). Upon opening the packet(s), the entire contents should be squeezed into the palm of the hand and immediately applied to the application site(s). Alternatively, a portion may be squeezed onto palm of hand and applied, repeating the process until entire packet has been applied. Application sites should be allowed to dry for a few minutes prior to dressing. Hands should be washed with soap and water after application. **Do not apply testosterone gel to the genitals**. For optimal absorption, after application wait at least 5-6 hours prior to showering or swimming; however waiting at least 1 hour should have minimal affect on absorption if done infrequently. Alcohol-based gels are flammable; avoid fire or smoking until gel has dried.

(Continued)

Testosterone *(Continued)*

Monitoring Parameters Periodic liver function tests, PSA, cholesterol, hemoglobin and hematocrit; radiologic examination of wrist and hand every 6 months (when using in prepubertal children)

Androderm®: Morning serum testosterone levels following application the previous evening

Gel: Morning serum testosterone levels 14 days after start of therapy

Reference Range Testosterone, urine: Male: 100-1500 ng/24 hours; Female: 100-500 ng/24 hours

Test Interactions May cause a decrease in creatinine and creatine excretion and an increase in the excretion of 17-ketosteroids, thyroid function tests

Dosage Forms [CAN] = Canadian brand name

Capsule, gelatin, as deconate (Andriol™ [CAN]): 40 mg (10s) [not available in U.S.]

Gel, topical:

AndroGel®:

1.25 g/actuation (75 g) [1% metered-dose pump; delivers 5 g/4 actuations; provides 60 1.25 g actuations; contains ethanol]

2.5 g (30s) [1% unit dose packets; contains ethanol]

5 g (30s) [1% unit dose packets; contains ethanol]

Testim®: 5 g (30s) [1% unit-dose tube; contains ethanol]

Injection, in oil, as cypionate: 200 mg/mL (10 mL)

Depo®-Testosterone: 100 mg/mL (10 mL); 200 mg/mL (1 mL, 10 mL) [contains benzyl alcohol, benzyl benzoate, and cottonseed oil]

Injection, in oil, as enanthate: 200 mg/mL (5 mL)

Delatestryl®: 200 mg/mL (1 mL) [prefilled syringe; contains sesame oil]; (5 mL) [multidose vial; contains sesame oil]

Kit [for prescription compounding testosterone 2%; kits also contain mixing jar and stirrer]:

First® Testosterone:

Injection, in oil: Testosterone propionate 100 mg/mL (12 mL) [contains sesame oil and benzyl alcohol]

Ointment: White petroleum (48 g)

First® Testosterone MC:

Injection, in oil: Testosterone propionate 100 mg/mL (12 mL) [contains sesame oil and benzyl alcohol]

Cream: Moisturizing cream (48 g)

Mucoadhesive, for buccal application [buccal system] (Striant®): 30 mg (10s)

Pellet, for subcutaneous implantation (Testopel®): 75 mg (1 pellet/vial)

Transdermal system (Androderm®): 2.5 mg/day (60s); 5 mg/day (30s) [contains ethanol]

- ◆ **Testosterone Cypionate** *see* Testosterone *on page 1653*
- ◆ **Testosterone Enanthate** *see* Testosterone *on page 1653*
- ◆ **Testred®** *see* MethylTESTOSTERone *on page 1125*
- ◆ **Tetanus and Diphtheria Toxoid** *see* Diphtheria and Tetanus Toxoid *on page 519*

Tetanus Immune Globulin (Human)
(TET a nus i MYUN GLOB yoo lin HYU man)

U.S. Brand Names BayTet™ [DSC]; HyperTET™ S/D

Canadian Brand Names BayTet™

Index Terms TIG

Pharmacologic Category Immune Globulin

Additional Appendix Information

Immunization Recommendations *on page 1929*

Use Passive immunization against tetanus; tetanus immune globulin is preferred over tetanus antitoxin for treatment of active tetanus; part of the management of an unclean, wound in a person whose history of previous receipt of tetanus toxoid is unknown or who has received less than three doses of tetanus toxoid; elderly may require TIG more often than younger patients with tetanus infection due to declining antibody titers with age

Pregnancy Risk Factor C

Contraindications Hypersensitivity to tetanus immune globulin, thimerosal, or any component of the formulation

Warnings/Precautions Have epinephrine 1:1000 available for anaphylactic reactions. Use caution in patients with isolated immunoglobulin A deficiency or a history of systemic hypersensitivity to human immunoglobulins. As a product of human plasma, this product may potentially transmit disease; screening of donors, as well as testing and/or inactivation of certain viruses reduces this risk. Use caution in patients with thrombocytopenia or coagulation disorders (I.M. injections may be contraindicated). Not for intravenous administration.

Adverse Reactions

>10%: Local: Pain, tenderness, erythema at injection site

1% to 10%:

Central nervous system: Fever (mild)

Dermatologic: Urticaria, angioedema

Neuromuscular & skeletal: Muscle stiffness

Miscellaneous: Anaphylaxis reaction

<1% (Limited to important or life-threatening): Sensitization to repeated injections

Stability Refrigerate

Mechanism of Action Passive immunity toward tetanus

Pharmacodynamics/Kinetics Absorption: Well absorbed

Dosage I.M.:

Prophylaxis of tetanus:

Children: 4 units/kg; some recommend administering 250 units to small children

Adults: 250 units

Treatment of tetanus:

Children: 500-3000 units; some should infiltrate locally around the wound

Adults: 3000-6000 units

Administration Do not administer I.V.; I.M. use only

Additional Information Tetanus immune globulin (TIG) must not contain <50 units/mL. Protein makes up 10% to 18% of TIG preparations. The great majority of this (≥90%) is IgG. TIG has almost no color or odor and it is a sterile, nonpyrogenic, concentrated preparation of immunoglobulins that has been derived from the plasma of adults hyperimmunized with tetanus toxoid. The pooled material from which the immunoglobulin is derived may be from fewer than 1000 donors. This plasma has been shown to be free of hepatitis B surface antigen.

Dosage Forms
Injection, solution [preservative free]:
  BayTet™[DSC], HyperTET™ S/D: 250 units/mL (1 mL) [prefilled syringe]

Tetanus Toxoid (Adsorbed) (TET a nus TOKS oyd, ad SORBED)

Pharmacologic Category Toxoid

Additional Appendix Information
Immunization Recommendations *on page 1929*

Use Active immunization against tetanus when combination antigen preparations are not indicated. **Note:** Tetanus and diphtheria toxoids for adult use (Td) is the preferred immunizing agent for most adults and for children after their seventh birthday. Young children should receive trivalent DTaP (diphtheria/tetanus/acellular pertussis), as part of their childhood immunization program, unless pertussis is contraindicated, then TD is warranted.

Pregnancy Risk Factor C

Pregnancy Implications Animal studies have not been conducted. The ACIP recommends vaccination in previously unvaccinated women or in women with an incomplete vaccination series, whose child may be born in unhygienic conditions. Vaccination using Td is preferred.

Medication Safety Issues
Sound-alike/look-alike issues:
  Tetanus toxoid products may be confused with influenza virus vaccine and tuberculin products. Medication errors have occurred when tetanus toxoid products have been inadvertently administered instead of tuberculin skin tests (PPD) and influenza virus vaccine. These products are refrigerated and often stored in close proximity to each other.

Contraindications Hypersensitivity to tetanus toxoid or any component of the formulation

Warnings/Precautions Not equivalent to tetanus toxoid fluid; the tetanus toxoid adsorbed is the preferred toxoid for immunization and Td, TD or DTaP are the preferred adsorbed forms; avoid injection into a blood vessel; allergic reactions may occur; epinephrine 1:1000 must be available; elderly may not mount adequate antibody titers following immunization. Patients who are immunocompromised may have reduced response; may be used in patients with HIV infection. May defer elective immunization during febrile illness or acute infection; defer elective immunization during outbreaks of poliomyelitis. In patients with a history of severe local reaction (Arthus-type) or temperature of >39.4°C (>103°F) following previous dose, do not give further routine or emergency doses of tetanus and diphtheria toxoids for 10 years. Use caution in patients on anticoagulants, with thrombocytopenia, or bleeding disorders (bleeding may occur following intramuscular injection). Contains thimerosal; vial stopper may contain natural latex rubber. This product is not indicated for use in children <7 years of age.

Adverse Reactions All serious adverse reactions must be reported to the U.S. Department of Health and Human Services (DHHS) Vaccine Adverse Event Reporting System (VAERS) 1-800-822-7967.
  Frequency not defined.
    Cardiovascular: Hypotension
    Central nervous system: Brachial neuritis, fever, malaise, pain
    Gastrointestinal: Nausea
    Local: Edema, induration (with or without tenderness), rash, redness, urticaria, warmth
    Neuromuscular: Arthralgia, Guillain-Barré syndrome
    Miscellaneous: Anaphylactic reaction, Arthus-type hypersensitivity reaction

Drug Interactions
  Decreased Effect: When used in greater than physiologic doses, corticosteroids lead to decreased effect of vaccine (consider deferring immunization for 1 month after steroid is discontinued). Consider deferring immunization for 1 month after immunosuppressive agent is discontinued (decreased response to vaccine).

Stability Refrigerate; do not freeze.

Mechanism of Action Tetanus toxoid preparations contain the toxin produced by virulent tetanus bacilli (detoxified growth products of *Clostridium tetani*). The toxin has been modified by treatment with formaldehyde so that it has lost toxicity but still retains ability to act as antigen and produce active immunity; the aluminum salt, a mineral adjuvant, delays the rate of absorption and prolongs and enhances its properties; duration ~10 years.

Pharmacodynamics/Kinetics Duration: Primary immunization: ~10 years

Dosage Children ≥7 years and Adults: I.M.:
  Primary immunization: 0.5 mL; repeat 0.5 mL at 4-8 weeks after first dose and at 6-12 months after second dose
  Routine booster dose: Recommended every 10 years
  Note: In most patients, Td is the recommended product for primary immunization, booster doses, and tetanus immunization in wound management (refer to Diphtheria and Tetanus Toxoid monograph)

Administration Inject intramuscularly in the area of the vastus lateralis (midthigh laterally) or deltoid. Do not inject into gluteal area. Shake well prior to withdrawing dose; do not use if product does not form a suspension.

For patients at risk of hemorrhage following intramuscular injection, the ACIP recommends "it should be administered intramuscularly if, in the opinion of the physician familiar with the patients bleeding risk, the vaccine can be administered with reasonable safety by this route. If the patient receives antihemophilia or other similar therapy, intramuscular vaccination can be (Continued)

Tetanus Toxoid (Adsorbed) *(Continued)*

scheduled shortly after such therapy is administered. A fine needle (23 gauge or smaller) can be used for the vaccination and firm pressure applied to the site (without rubbing) for at least 2 minutes. The patient should be instructed concerning the risk of hematoma from the injection."

Additional Information Federal law requires that the date of administration, the vaccine manufacturer, lot number of vaccine, and the administering person's name, title and address be entered into the patient's permanent medical record.

Dosage Forms Injection, suspension: Tetanus 5 Lf units per 0.5 mL (0.5 mL) [contains trace amounts of thimerosal]; (5 mL) [contains thimerosal; vial stopper contains latex]

Tetanus Toxoid (Fluid) (TET a nus TOKS oyd FLOO id)

Index Terms Tetanus Toxoid Plain

Pharmacologic Category Toxoid

Additional Appendix Information
Immunization Recommendations *on page 1929*

Use Indicated as booster dose in the active immunization against tetanus in the rare adult or child who is allergic to the aluminum adjuvant (a product containing adsorbed tetanus toxoid is preferred); not indicated for primary immunization

Unlabeled/Investigational Use Anergy testing (no longer recommended)

Pregnancy Risk Factor C

Pregnancy Implications Reproduction studies have not been conducted and effects to the fetus are not known. Deferring immunization until the 2nd trimester may be considered.

Medication Safety Issues
Sound-alike/look-alike issues:
Tetanus toxoid products may be confused with influenza virus vaccine and tuberculin products. Medication errors have occurred when tetanus toxoid products have been inadvertently administered instead of tuberculin skin tests (PPD) and influenza virus vaccine. These products are refrigerated and often stored in close proximity to each other.

Contraindications Hypersensitivity to tetanus toxoid or any component of the formulation

Warnings/Precautions Epinephrine 1:1000 should be readily available; skin test responsiveness may be delayed or reduced in elderly patients. Patients who are immunocompromised may have reduced response; may be used in patients with HIV infection. May defer elective immunization during febrile illness or acute infection; defer elective immunization during outbreaks of poliomyelitis. In patients with a history of severe local reaction (Arthus-type) following previous dose, do not give further routine or emergency doses of tetanus and diphtheria toxoids for 10 years. Use caution in patients on anticoagulants, with thrombocytopenia, or bleeding disorders (bleeding may occur following intramuscular injection). Contains thimerosal; vial stopper contains natural latex rubber. Safety and efficacy in children <6 weeks of age have not been established; this product is not indicated for use in children <7 years of age.

Adverse Reactions All serious adverse reactions must be reported to the U.S. Department of Health and Human Services (DHHS) Vaccine Adverse Event Reporting System (VAERS) 1-800-822-7967.

Frequency not defined.
Cardiovascular: Hypotension
Central nervous system: Brachial neuritis, fever, Guillain-Barré syndrome, malaise
Dermatologic: Rash, urticaria
Gastrointestinal: Nausea
Local: Edema, induration (with or without tenderness), redness, warmth
Neuromuscular & skeletal: Arthralgia
Miscellaneous: Anaphylaxis, Arthus-type hypersensitivity reactions (severe local reaction developing 2-8 hours following injection)

Drug Interactions
Increased Effect/Toxicity: Increased bleeding and bruising may occur from I.M. injection in patients on anticoagulants.
Decreased Effect: Decreased effect of vaccine may occur with corticosteroids (greater than physiologic doses) or immunosuppressive agents

Stability Refrigerate 2°C to 8°C (35°F to 46°F); do not freeze.

Mechanism of Action Tetanus toxoid preparations contain the toxin produced by virulent tetanus bacilli (detoxified growth products of *Clostridium tetani*). The toxin has been modified by treatment with formaldehyde so that is has lost toxicity but still retains ability to act as antigen and produce active immunity.

Dosage
Primary immunization: Not indicated for this use.
Booster doses: I.M., SubQ: 0.5 mL every 10 years
Anergy testing (unlabeled use; no longer recommended for this indication): Intradermal: 0.1 mL; doses that have been used range from 0.1 mL of a 1:10 dilution to 0.1 mL of the undiluted product

Administration
I.M. Shake well prior to use. Administer I.M. in lateral aspect of midthigh or deltoid muscle of upper arm
For patients at risk of hemorrhage following intramuscular injection, the ACIP recommends "it should be administered intramuscularly if, in the opinion of the physician familiar with the patients bleeding risk, the vaccine can be administered with reasonable safety by this route. If the patient receives antihemophilia or other similar therapy, intramuscular vaccination can be scheduled shortly after such therapy is administered. A fine needle (23 gauge or smaller) can be used for the vaccination and firm pressure applied to the site (without rubbing) for at least 2 minutes. The patient should be instructed concerning the risk of hematoma from the injection."

SubQ: Shake well prior to use. Administer in area of the lateral aspect of midthigh or deltoid.
SubQ route may be preferred in patients with thrombocytopenia or coagulation disorders.

Additional Information Federal law requires that the date of administration, the vaccine manufacturer, lot number of vaccine, and the administering person's name, title and address be entered into the patient's permanent medical record.

Dosage Forms Injection, solution: Tetanus 4 Lf units per 0.5 mL (7.5 mL) [contains thimerosal; vial stopper contains dry natural latex rubber]

♦ **Tetanus Toxoid Plain** see Tetanus Toxoid (Fluid) on page 1658

♦ **Tetanus Toxoid, Reduced Diphtheria Toxoid, and Acellular Pertussis, Adsorbed** see Diphtheria, Tetanus Toxoids, and Acellular Pertussis Vaccine on page 521

Tetracaine (TET ra kane)

U.S. Brand Names Pontocaine®; Pontocaine® Niphanoid®
Canadian Brand Names Ametop™; Pontocaine®
Index Terms Amethocaine Hydrochloride; Tetracaine Hydrochloride
Pharmacologic Category Local Anesthetic
Use Spinal anesthesia; local anesthesia in the eye for various diagnostic and examination purposes; topically applied to nose and throat for various diagnostic procedures
Pregnancy Risk Factor C
Dosage Adults:

Ophthalmic: Short-term anesthesia of the eye: 0.5% solution: Instill 1-2 drops; prolonged use (especially for at-home self-medication) is not recommended

Injection: Spinal anesthesia: **Note:** Dosage varies with the anesthetic procedure, the degree of anesthesia required, and the individual patient response; it is administered by subarachnoid injection for spinal anesthesia.

Perineal anesthesia: 5 mg

Perineal and lower extremities: 10 mg

Anesthesia extending up to costal margin: 15 mg; doses up to 20 mg may be given, but are reserved for exceptional cases

Low spinal anesthesia (saddle block): 2-5 mg

Topical mucous membranes (rhinolaryngology): Used as a 0.25% or 0.5% solution by direct application or nebulization; total dose should not exceed 20 mg

Additional Information Complete prescribing information for this medication should be consulted for additional detail.

Dosage Forms

Injection, solution, as hydrochloride [preservative free] (Pontocaine®): 1% [10 mg/mL] (2 mL) [contains sodium bisulfite]

Injection, powder for reconstitution, as hydrochloride [preservative free] (Pontocaine® Niphanoid®): 20 mg

Solution, ophthalmic, as hydrochloride: 0.5% [5 mg/mL] (15 mL)

Solution, topical, as hydrochloride (Pontocaine®): 2% [20 mg/mL] (30 mL, 118 mL) [for rhinolaryngology]

♦ **Tetracaine and Lidocaine** see Lidocaine and Tetracaine on page 1016

♦ **Tetracaine, Benzocaine, and Butamben** see Benzocaine, Butamben, and Tetracaine on page 207

♦ **Tetracaine Hydrochloride** see Tetracaine on page 1659

♦ **Tetracaine Hydrochloride, Benzocaine, Butyl Aminobenzoate, and Benzalkonium Chloride** see Benzocaine, Butyl Aminobenzoate, Tetracaine, and Benzalkonium Chloride on page 207

♦ **Tetracosactide** see Cosyntropin on page 422

Tetracycline (tet ra SYE kleen)

U.S. Brand Names Sumycin® [DSC]
Canadian Brand Names Apo-Tetra®; Nu-Tetra
Index Terms Achromycin; TCN; Tetracycline Hydrochloride
Pharmacologic Category Antibiotic, Tetracycline Derivative
Additional Appendix Information

Antimicrobial Drugs of Choice on page 1981

Helicobacter pylori Treatment on page 2056

Malaria Treatment on page 2003

Treatment of Sexually Transmitted Infections on page 2007

Use Treatment of susceptible bacterial infections of both gram-positive and gram-negative organisms; also infections due to *Mycoplasma*, *Chlamydia*, and *Rickettsia*; indicated for acne, exacerbations of chronic bronchitis, and treatment of gonorrhea and syphilis in patients that are allergic to penicillin; as part of a multidrug regimen for *H. pylori* eradication to reduce the risk of duodenal ulcer recurrence

Pregnancy Risk Factor D

Pregnancy Implications Tetracyclines cross the placenta and enter fetal circulation; may cause permanent discoloration of teeth if used during the last half of pregnancy.

Lactation Enters breast milk/not recommended (AAP rates "compatible")

Medication Safety Issues

Sound-alike/look-alike issues:

Tetracycline may be confused with tetradecyl sulfate

Achromycin may be confused with actinomycin, Adriamycin PFS®

Contraindications Hypersensitivity to tetracycline or any component of the formulation; do not administer to children ≤8 years of age; pregnancy

Warnings/Precautions Use of tetracyclines during tooth development may cause permanent discoloration of the teeth and enamel, hypoplasia and retardation of skeletal development and bone growth with risk being the greatest for children <4 years and those receiving high (Continued)

Tetracycline *(Continued)*

doses; use with caution in patients with renal or hepatic impairment (eg, elderly); dosage modification required in patients with renal impairment since it may increase BUN as an antianabolic agent; pseudotumor cerebri has been reported with tetracycline use (usually resolves with discontinuation); outdated drug can cause nephropathy; superinfection possible; use protective measure to avoid photosensitivity

Adverse Reactions Frequency not defined.

Cardiovascular: Pericarditis

Central nervous system: Intracranial pressure increased, bulging fontanels in infants, pseudotumor cerebri, paresthesia

Dermatologic: Photosensitivity, pruritus, pigmentation of nails, exfoliative dermatitis

Endocrine & metabolic: Diabetes insipidus syndrome

Gastrointestinal: Discoloration of teeth and enamel hypoplasia (young children), nausea, diarrhea, vomiting, esophagitis, anorexia, abdominal cramps, antibiotic-associated pseudomembranous colitis, staphylococcal enterocolitis, pancreatitis

Hematologic: Thrombophlebitis

Hepatic: Hepatotoxicity

Renal: Acute renal failure, azotemia, renal damage

Miscellaneous: Superinfection, anaphylaxis, hypersensitivity reactions, candidal superinfection

Overdosage/Toxicology Symptoms include nausea, anorexia, and diarrhea. Following GI decontamination, supportive care only.

Drug Interactions

Cytochrome P450 Effect: Substrate of CYP3A4 (major); **Inhibits** CYP3A4 (moderate)

Increased Effect/Toxicity: Methoxyflurane anesthesia when concurrent with tetracycline may cause fatal nephrotoxicity. Warfarin with tetracyclines may cause increased anticoagulation. Tetracycline may increase the levels/effects of selected benzodiazepines, calcium channel blockers, cisapride, cyclosporine, ergot alkaloids, selected HMG-CoA reductase inhibitors, mirtazapine, nateglinide, nefazodone, pimozide, quinidine, sildenafil (and other PDE-5 inhibitors), tacrolimus, venlafaxine, and other CYP3A4 substrates.

Decreased Effect: Calcium, magnesium- or aluminum-containing antacids, iron, zinc, sodium bicarbonate, sucralfate, didanosine, or quinapril may decrease tetracycline absorption. Therapeutic effect of penicillins may be reduced with coadministration of tetracycline. Although anecdotal reports suggest oral contraceptive efficacy could be reduced by tetracyclines, this has been refuted by more rigorous scientific and clinical data. The levels/effects of tetracycline may be decreased by aminoglutethimide, carbamazepine, nafcillin, nevirapine, phenobarbital, phenytoin, rifamycins, and other CYP3A4 inducers.

Ethanol/Nutrition/Herb Interactions

Food: Tetracycline serum concentrations may be decreased if taken with dairy products.

Herb/Nutraceutical: Avoid dong quai, St John's wort (may also cause photosensitization)

Stability Outdated tetracyclines have caused a Fanconi-like syndrome. Protect oral dosage forms from light.

Mechanism of Action Inhibits bacterial protein synthesis by binding with the 30S and possibly the 50S ribosomal subunit(s) of susceptible bacteria; may also cause alterations in the cytoplasmic membrane

Pharmacodynamics/Kinetics

Absorption: Oral: 75%

Distribution: Small amount appears in bile

Relative diffusion from blood into CSF: Good only with inflammation (exceeds usual MICs)

CSF:blood level ratio: Inflamed meninges: 25%

Protein binding: ~65%

Half-life elimination: Normal renal function: 8-11 hours; End-stage renal disease: 57-108 hours

Time to peak, serum: Oral: 2-4 hours

Excretion: Urine (60% as unchanged drug); feces (as active form)

Dosage

Usual dosage range:

Children >8 years: Oral: 25-50 mg/kg/day in divided doses every 6 hours

Adults: Oral: 250-500 mg/dose every 6 hours

Indication-specific dosing:

Adults: Oral:

Acne: 250-500 twice daily

Chronic bronchitis, acute exacerbation: 500 mg 4 times/day

Erlichiosis: 500 mg 4 times/day for 7-14 days

Peptic ulcer disease: Eradication of *Helicobacter pylori*: 500 mg 2-4 times/day depending on regimen; requires combination therapy with at least one other antibiotic and an acid-suppressing agent (proton pump inhibitor or H_2 blocker)

Periodontitis: 250 mg every 6 hours until improvement (usually 10 days)

Vibrio cholerae: 500 mg 4 times/day for 3 days

Dosing interval in renal impairment:

Cl_{cr} 50-80 mL/minute: Administer every 8-12 hours

Cl_{cr} 10-50 mL/minute: Administer every 12-24 hours

Cl_{cr} <10 mL/minute: Administer every 24 hours

Dialysis: Slightly dialyzable (5% to 20%) via hemo- and peritoneal dialysis or via continuous arteriovenous or venovenous hemofiltration; no supplemental dosage necessary

Dosing adjustment in hepatic impairment: Avoid use or maximum dose is 1 g/day

Administration Should be administered on an empty stomach (ie, 1 hour prior to, or 2 hours after meals) to increase total absorption. Administer at least 1-2 hours prior to, or 4 hours after antacid because aluminum and magnesium cations may chelate with tetracycline and reduce its total absorption.

Monitoring Parameters Renal, hepatic, and hematologic function test, temperature, WBC, cultures and sensitivity, appetite, mental status

Test Interactions False-negative urine glucose with Clinistix®

Dosage Forms

Capsule, as hydrochloride: 250 mg, 500 mg

Suspension, oral, as hydrochloride:

Sumycin®: 125 mg/5 mL (480 mL) [contains sodium benzoate and sodium metabisulfite; fruit flavor] [DSC]

Tablet, as hydrochloride:

Sumycin®: 250 mg, 500 mg [DSC]

♦ **Tetracycline Hydrochloride** see Tetracycline on page 1659

♦ **Tetracycline, Metronidazole, and Bismuth Subsalicylate** see Bismuth Subsalicylate, Metronidazole, and Tetracycline on page 225

♦ **Tetrahydroaminoacrine** see Tacrine on page 1625

♦ **Tetrahydrocannabinol** see Dronabinol on page 558

♦ **Tetra Tannate Pediatric** see Chlorpheniramine, Ephedrine, Phenylephrine, and Carbetapentane on page 351

♦ **Teveten®** see Eprosartan on page 600

♦ **Teveten® HCT** see Eprosartan and Hydrochlorothiazide on page 601

♦ **Teveten® Plus (Can)** see Eprosartan and Hydrochlorothiazide on page 601

♦ **Tev-Tropin®** see Somatropin on page 1586

♦ **Texacort®** see Hydrocortisone on page 852

♦ **TG** see Thioguanine on page 1669

♦ **6-TG (error-prone abbreviation)** see Thioguanine on page 1669

♦ **THA** see Tacrine on page 1625

Thalidomide (tha LI doe mide)

U.S. Brand Names Thalomid®

Canadian Brand Names Thalomid®

Index Terms NSC-66847

Pharmacologic Category Angiogenesis Inhibitor; Immunosuppressant Agent; Tumor Necrosis Factor (TNF) Blocking Agent

Use Treatment of multiple myeloma; treatment and maintenance of cutaneous manifestations of erythema nodosum leprosum (ENL)

Unlabeled/Investigational Use Treatment of Crohn's disease; graft-versus-host reactions after bone marrow transplantation; AIDS-related aphthous stomatitis; Behçet's syndrome; Waldenström's macroglobulinemia; Langerhans cell histiocytosis; may be effective in rheumatoid arthritis, discoid lupus erythematosus, and erythema multiforme

Restrictions Thalidomide is approved for marketing only under a special distribution program. This program, called the "System for Thalidomide Education and Prescribing Safety" (STEPS® 1-888-423-5436), has been approved by the FDA. Prescribers and pharmacists must be registered with the program. No more than a 4-week supply should be dispensed. Blister packs should be dispensed intact (do not repackage capsules). Prescriptions must be filled within 7 days. Subsequent prescriptions may be filled only if fewer than 7 days of therapy remain on the previous prescription. A new prescription is required for further dispensing (a telephone prescription may not be accepted.)

Pregnancy Risk Factor X

Pregnancy Implications Embryotoxic with limb defects noted from the 27th to 40th gestational day of exposure; all cases of phocomelia occur from the 27th to 42nd gestational day; fetal cardiac, gastrointestinal, bone, external ear, eye, and genitourinary tract abnormalities have also been described. Mortality at or shortly after birth has also been reported. Either abstinence or two forms of effective contraception must be used for at least 4 weeks before initiating therapy, during therapy, and for 4 weeks following discontinuation of thalidomide. A negative pregnancy test (sensitivity of at least 50 mIU/mL) within 24 hours prior to beginning therapy, weekly during the first 4 weeks, and every 4 weeks (every 2 weeks for women with irregular menstrual cycles) thereafter is required for women of childbearing potential. Males (even those vasectomized) must use a latex condom during any sexual contact with women of childbearing age. Risk to the fetus from semen of male patients is unknown. Thalidomide must be immediately discontinued and the patient referred to a reproductive toxicity specialist if pregnancy occurs during treatment. Any suspected fetal exposure to thalidomide must be reported to the FDA via the MedWatch program (1-800-FDA-1088) and to Celgene Corporation (1-888-423-5436).

Lactation Excretion in breast milk unknown/not recommended

Medication Safety Issues

Sound-alike/look-alike issues:

Thalidomide may be confused with flutamide

High alert medication: The Institute for Safe Medication Practices (ISMP) includes this medication among its list of drugs which have a heightened risk of causing significant patient harm when used in error.

International issues:

Thalomid® may be confused with Thilomide® which is a brand name for Iodoxamide in Greece and Turkey

Contraindications Hypersensitivity to thalidomide or any component of the formulation; neuropathy (peripheral); patient unable to comply with STEPS® program (including males); women of childbearing potential unless alternative therapies are inappropriate and adequate precautions are taken to avoid pregnancy; pregnancy

Warnings/Precautions Hazardous agent - use appropriate precautions for handling and disposal. **[U.S. Boxed Warning]: Thalidomide is a known teratogen; effective contraception must be used for at least 4 weeks before initiating therapy, during therapy, and for 4 weeks following discontinuation of thalidomide for women of childbearing potential.** Use caution with drugs which may decrease the efficacy of hormonal contraceptives. (Continued)

Thalidomide *(Continued)*

[U.S. Boxed Warning]: Thrombotic events have been reported, generally in patients with other risk factors for thrombosis (neoplastic disease, inflammatory disease, or concurrent therapy with combination chemotherapy. Use in combination with dexamethasone is associated with increased risk for deep vein thrombosis (DVT) and pulmonary embolism (PE), monitor for signs and symptoms of thromboembolism; patients at risk may benefit from prophylactic anticoagulation or aspirin.

May cause sedation; patients must be warned to use caution when performing tasks which require alertness. Use caution in patients with renal or hepatic impairment, neurological disorders, or constipation. Thalidomide has been associated with the development of peripheral neuropathy, which may be irreversible; use caution with other medications which may cause peripheral neuropathy. Consider immediate discontinuation (if clinically appropriate) in patients who develop neuropathy. May cause seizures; use caution in patients with a history of seizures, concurrent therapy with drugs which alter seizure threshold, or conditions which predispose to seizures. May cause neutropenia; discontinue therapy if absolute neutrophil count decreases to <750/mm³. Use caution in patients with HIV infection; has been associated with increased viral loads. May cause orthostasis and/or bradycardia; use with caution in patients with cardiovascular disease or in patients who would not tolerate transient hypotensive episodes. Hypersensitivity, Stevens-Johnson syndrome (SJS) and toxic epidermal necrolysis (TEN) have been reported; withhold therapy and evaluate with skin rashes; permanently discontinue if rash is exfoliative, purpuric, bullous or if SJS or TEN is suspected. Safety and efficacy have not been established in children <12 years of age.

Adverse Reactions

>10%:

Cardiovascular: Edema (57%), thrombosis/embolism (23%; grade 3: 13%, grade 4: 9%), hypotension (16%)

Central nervous system: Fatigue (79%; grade 3: 3%, grade 4: 1%), somnolence (36% to 38%), dizziness (4% to 20%), sensory neuropathy (54%), confusion (28%), anxiety/agitation (9% to 26%), fever (19% to 23%), motor neuropathy (22%), headache (13% to 19%)

Dermatologic: Rash (21% to 31%), rash/desquamation (30%; grade 3: 4%), dry skin (21%), maculopapular rash (4% to 19%), acne (3% to 11%)

Endocrine & metabolic: Hypocalcemia (72%)

Gastrointestinal: Constipation (3% to 55%), anorexia (3% to 28%), nausea (4% to 24%), weight loss (23%), weight gain (22%), diarrhea (4% to 19%), oral moniliasis (4% to 11%)

Hematologic: Leukopenia (17% to 35%), neutropenia (31%), anemia (6% to 13%), lymphadenopathy (6% to 13%)

Hepatic: AST/SGOT increased (3% to 25%), bilirubin increased (14%)

Neuromuscular & skeletal: Muscle weakness (40%), tremor (4% to 26%), weakness (6% to 22%), myalgia (17%), paresthesia (6% to 16%), arthralgia (13%)

Renal: Hematuria (11%)

Respiratory: Dyspnea (42%)

Miscellaneous: Diaphoresis (13%)

1% to 10%:

Cardiovascular: Facial edema (4%), peripheral edema (3% to 8%)

Central nervous system: Insomnia (9%), nervousness (3% to 9%), malaise (8%), vertigo (8%), pain (3% to 8%)

Dermatologic: Dermatitis (fungal 4% to 9%), pruritus (3% to 8%), nail disorder (3% to 4%)

Endocrine & metabolic: Hyperlipemia (6% to 9%)

Gastrointestinal: Xerostomia (8% to 9%), flatulence (8%), tooth pain (4%)

Genitourinary: Impotence (3% to 8%)

Hepatic: LFTs abnormal (9%)

Neuromuscular & skeletal: Neuropathy (8%), back pain (4% to 6%), neck pain (4%), neck rigidity (4%)

Renal: Albuminuria (3% to 8%)

Respiratory: Pharyngitis (4% to 8%), rhinitis (4%), sinusitis (4% to 8%)

Miscellaneous: Infection (6% to 8%)

Postmarketing and/or case reports (limited to important or life-threatening): Acute renal failure, alkaline phosphatase increased, amenorrhea, aphthous stomatitis, arrhythmia, atrial fibrillation, bile duct obstruction, bradycardia, BUN increased, carpal tunnel, CML, creatinine clearance decreased, creatinine increased, deafness, depression, diplopia, dysesthesia, ECG abnormalities, electrolyte imbalances, enuresis, eosinophilia, epistaxis, erythema multiforme, erythema nodosum, erythroleukemia, exfoliative dermatitis, febrile neutropenia, foot drop, galactorrhea, granulocytopenia, gynecomastia, hepatomegaly, Hodgkin's disease, hypercalcemia, hyper-/hypokalemia, hypersensitivity, hypertension, hyper-/hypothyroidism, hyperuricemia, hypomagnesemia, hyponatremia, hypoproteinemia, intestinal obstruction, intestinal perforation, interstitial pneumonitis, LDH increased, lethargy, leukocytosis, lymphedema, lymphopenia, mental status changes, metrorrhagia, migraine, myxedema, nystagmus, oliguria, orthostatic hypotension, pancytopenia, paresthesia, petechiae, peripheral neuritis, photosensitivity, pleural effusion, prothrombin time changes, psychosis, pulmonary embolus, pulmonary hypertension, purpura, Raynaud's syndrome, seizure, SGPT increased, status epilepticus, Stevens-Johnson syndrome, stomach ulcer, stupor, suicide attempt, syncope, tachycardia, thrombocytopenia, toxic epidermal necrolysis, tumor lysis syndrome

Overdosage/Toxicology Doses of up to 14.4 g have been reported (in suicide attempts) without fatalities. Treatment is symptom-directed and supportive.

Drug Interactions

Increased Effect/Toxicity: Thalidomide may enhance the sedative activity of other drugs such as ethanol, barbiturates, reserpine, and chlorpromazine. Thalidomide may be associated with increased risk of serious infection when used in combination with abatacept or anakinra. Thalidomide may increase the risk of vaccinal infection with vaccine (live attenuated).

Decreased Effect: Thalidomide may decrease the effect of vaccines (killed).

Ethanol/Nutrition/Herb Interactions

Ethanol: Avoid ethanol (may increase sedation).

Herb/Nutraceutical: Avoid cat's claw and echinacea (have immunostimulant properties; consider therapy modifications).

Stability Store at 15°C to 30°C (59°F to 86°F). Protect from light. Keep in original package.

Mechanism of Action Has immunomodulatory and antiangiogenic characteristics. Immunologic effects may vary based on conditions; may suppress excessive tumor necrosis factor-alpha production in patients with ENL, yet may increase plasma tumor necrosis factor-alpha levels in HIV-positive patients. In multiple myeloma, thalidomide is associated with an increase in natural killer cells and increased levels of interleukin-2 and interferon gamma. Other proposed mechanisms of action include suppression of angiogenesis, prevention of free-radical-mediated DNA damage, increased cell mediated cytotoxic effects, and altered expression of cellular.

Pharmacodynamics/Kinetics

Distribution: V_d: 120 L

Protein binding: 55% to 66%

Metabolism: Nonenzymatic hydrolysis in plasma; forms multiple metabolites

Half-life elimination: 5-7 hours

Time to peak, plasma: 3-6 hours

Excretion: Urine (<1% as unchanged drug)

Dosage Oral:

Multiple myeloma: 200 mg once daily (with dexamethasone 40 mg daily on days 1-4, 9-12, and 17-20 of a 28-day treatment cycle)

Cutaneous ENL:

Initial: 100-300 mg/day taken once daily at bedtime with water (at least 1 hour after evening meal)

Patients weighing <50 kg: Initiate at lower end of the dosing range

Severe cutaneous reaction or patients previously requiring high dose may be initiated at 400 mg/day; doses may be divided, but taken 1 hour after meals

Maintenance: Dosing should continue until active reaction subsides (usually at least 2 weeks), then tapered in 50 mg decrements every 2-4 weeks

Patients who flare during tapering or with a history or requiring prolonged maintenance should be maintained on the minimum dosage necessary to control the reaction. Efforts to taper should be repeated every 3-6 months, in increments of 50 mg every 2-4 weeks.

Behçet's syndrome (unlabeled use): 100-400 mg/day

Graft-vs-host reactions (unlabeled use): 100-1600 mg/day; usual initial dose: 200 mg 4 times/day for use up to 700 days

AIDS-related aphthous stomatitis (unlabeled use): 200 mg twice daily for 5 days, then 200 mg/day for up to 8 weeks

Discoid lupus erythematosus (unlabeled use): 100-400 mg/day; maintenance dose: 25-50 mg

Dietary Considerations Should be taken at least 1 hour after the evening meal.

Administration Oral: Administer with water, preferably at bedtime once daily on an empty stomach, at least 1 hour after the evening meal. Doses >400 mg/day may be given in 2-3 divided doses. Avoid extensive handling of capsules; capsules should remain in blister pack until ingestion. If exposed to the powder content from broken capsules or body fluids from patients receiving thalidomide, the exposed area should be washed with soap and water.

Monitoring Parameters CBC with differential, platelets; signs of neuropathy monthly for the first 3 months, then periodically during treatment; consider monitoring of sensory nerve application potential amplitudes (at baseline and every 6 months) to detect asymptomatic neuropathy. In HIV-seropositive patients: viral load after 1 and 3 months, then every 3 months. Pregnancy testing (sensitivity of at least 50 mIU/mL) is required within 24 hours prior to initiation of therapy, weekly during the first 4 weeks, then every 4 weeks in women with regular menstrual cycles or every 2 weeks in women with irregular menstrual cycles.

Reference Range Therapeutic plasma thalidomide levels in graft-vs-host reactions are 5-8 mcg/mL, although it has been suggested that lower plasma levels (0.5-1.5 mcg/mL) may be therapeutic; peak serum thalidomide level after a 200 mg dose: 1.2 mcg/mL

Dosage Forms

Capsule:

Thalomid®: 50 mg, 100 mg, 200 mg

- ◆ **Thalitone®** see Chlorthalidone on page 359
- ◆ **Thalomid®** see Thalidomide on page 1661
- ◆ **THAM®** see Tromethamine on page 1752
- ◆ **THC** see Dronabinol on page 558
- ◆ **Theo-24®** see Theophylline Salts on page 1664
- ◆ **Theochron®** see Theophylline Salts on page 1664
- ◆ **Theolair™** see Theophylline Salts on page 1664
- ◆ **Theolair-SR® [DSC]** see Theophylline Salts on page 1664

Theophylline and Guaifenesin (thee OFF i lin & gwye FEN e sin)

U.S. Brand Names Elixophyllin-GG®; Quibron® [DSC]

Index Terms Guaifenesin and Theophylline

Pharmacologic Category Theophylline Derivative

Use Symptomatic treatment of bronchospasm associated with bronchial asthma, chronic bronchitis, and pulmonary emphysema

Pregnancy Risk Factor C

Dosage Adults: Oral: 16 mg/kg/day or 400 mg theophylline/day, in divided doses, every 6-8 hours

Additional Information Complete prescribing information for this medication should be consulted for additional detail.

(Continued)

Theophylline and Guaifenesin (Continued)

Dosage Forms [DSC] = Discontinued product
Capsule:
Quibron®: Theophylline 150 mg and guaifenesin 90 mg [DSC]
Liquid:
Elixophyllin-GG®: Theophylline 100 mg and guaifenesin 100 mg per 15 mL (240 mL, 480 mL) [alcohol free, dye free, sugar free; cherry-berry flavor]

♦ **Theophylline Anhydrous** see Theophylline Salts on page 1664
♦ **Theophylline Ethylenediamine** see Theophylline Salts on page 1664

Theophylline Salts (thee OFF i lin salts)

U.S. Brand Names Elixophyllin®; Quibron®-T; Quibron®-T/SR; Theo-24®; Theochron®; Theolair™; Theolair-SR® [DSC]; T-Phyl®; Uniphyl®
Index Terms Aminophylline; Theophylline Anhydrous; Theophylline Ethylenediamine
Pharmacologic Category Bronchodilator; Theophylline Derivative
Additional Appendix Information
Asthma on page 2029
Toxicology Information on page 2081
Use Bronchodilator in reversible airway obstruction due to asthma, chronic bronchitis, and emphysema; for neonatal apnea/bradycardia
Pregnancy Risk Factor C
Pregnancy Implications Theophylline crosses the placenta; adverse effects may be seen in the newborn. Theophylline metabolism may change during pregnancy; monitor serum levels.
Lactation Enters breast milk/compatible (AAP rates "compatible")
Medication Safety Issues
Sound-alike/look-alike issues:
Aminophylline may be confused with amitriptyline, ampicillin
Theolair™ may be confused with Thiola™, Thyrolar®
Contraindications Hypersensitivity to theophylline, ethylenediamine, or any component of the formulation
Warnings/Precautions If a patient develops signs and symptoms of theophylline toxicity (eg, persistent, repetitive vomiting), a serum theophylline level should be measured and subsequent doses held. Due to potential saturation of theophylline clearance at serum levels in or (in some patients) less than the therapeutic range, dosage adjustment should be made in small increments (maximum: 25%). Due to wider interpatient variability, theophylline serum level measurements must be used to optimize therapy and prevent serious toxicity. Use with caution in patients with peptic ulcer, hyperthyroidism, seizure disorders, hypertension, and patients with cardiac arrhythmias (excluding bradyarrhythmias).
Adverse Reactions See table.

Theophylline Serum Levels (mcg/mL)*	Adverse Reactions
15-25	GI upset, diarrhea, N/V, abdominal pain, nervousness, headache, insomnia, agitation, dizziness, muscle cramp, tremor
25-35	Tachycardia, occasional PVC
>35	Ventricular tachycardia, frequent PVC, seizure

*Adverse effects do not necessarily occur according to serum levels. Arrhythmia and seizure can occur without seeing the other adverse effects.

Uncommon at serum theophylline concentrations ≤20 mcg/mL
1% to 10%:
Cardiovascular: Tachycardia
Central nervous system: Nervousness, restlessness
Gastrointestinal: Nausea, vomiting
<1%: Insomnia, irritability, rash, seizures, tremor, gastric irritation, allergic reactions
Drug Interactions
Cytochrome P450 Effect:
Theophylline: **Substrate** of CYP1A2 (major), 2C8/9 (minor), 2D6 (minor), 2E1 (major), 3A4 (major); **Inhibits** CYP1A2 (weak)
Increased Effect/Toxicity:
Theophylline: Changes in diet may affect the elimination of theophylline. The following may increase serum theophylline levels: propranolol, allopurinol (>600 mg/day), erythromycin, cimetidine, troleandomycin, ciprofloxacin (other quinolone antibiotics), oral contraceptives, beta-blockers, calcium channel blockers, corticosteroids, disulfiram, ephedrine, influenza virus vaccine, interferon, macrolides, mexiletine, thiabendazole, thyroid hormones, carbamazepine, isoniazid, and loop diuretics. Other inhibitors of cytochrome P450 1A2 (eg, amiodarone, fluvoxamine, ketoconazole, quinolone antibiotics) may increase theophylline levels.
Decreased Effect:
Theophylline: Changes in diet may affect the elimination of theophylline. Charcoal-broiled foods may increase elimination, reducing half-life by 50%. The following factors decrease theophylline serum levels: Smoking (cigarettes, marijuana), high protein/low carbohydrate diet, charcoal, phenytoin, CYP 1A2 inducers: (eg, aminoglutethimide, phenobarbital, carbamazepine, rifampin), ritonavir, I.V. isoproterenol, aminoglutethimide, barbiturates, hydantoins, ketoconazole, sulfinpyrazone, isoniazid, loop diuretics, and sympathomimetics.
Ethanol/Nutrition/Herb Interactions Food: Food does not appreciably affect the absorption of liquid, fast-release products, or most sustained release products; however, food may induce a sudden release (dose-dumping) of once-daily sustained release products resulting

in an increase in serum drug levels and potential toxicity. Avoid excessive amounts of caffeine. Avoid extremes of dietary protein and carbohydrate intake. Limit charcoal-broiled foods.

Stability Do not use solutions if discolored or if crystals are present.

Mechanism of Action Causes bronchodilatation, diuresis, CNS and cardiac stimulation, and gastric acid secretion by blocking phosphodiesterase which increases tissue concentrations of cyclic adenine monophosphate (cAMP) which in turn promotes catecholamine stimulation of lipolysis, glycogenolysis, and gluconeogenesis and induces release of epinephrine from adrenal medulla cells

Pharmacodynamics/Kinetics Theophylline:

Absorption: Oral: Dosage form dependent. Aminophylline is the ethylene diamine salt of theophylline and contains 80% theophylline.

Distribution: 0.45 L/kg based on ideal body weight

Protein binding: 40%, primarily to albumin

Metabolism: Children >1 year and Adults: Hepatic; involves CYP1A2, 2E1 and 3A4; forms active metabolites (caffeine and 3-methylxanthine)

Half-life elimination: Highly variable and dependent upon age, liver function, cardiac function, lung disease, and smoking history

Time to peak, serum:

Oral: Immediate release: 1-2 hours

I.V.: Within 30 minutes

Excretion: Urine

Neonates: 50% unchanged

Children >3 months and Adults: 10% unchanged

Dosage Use ideal body weight for obese patients

I.V.: Initial: Maintenance infusion rates:

Infants 6-52 weeks: 0.008 (age in weeks) + 0.21 mg/kg/hour **theophylline**

Children >1 year and Adults:

Treatment of acute bronchospasm: I.V.: Loading dose (in patients not currently receiving aminophylline or theophylline): 6 mg/kg (based on aminophylline) given I.V. over 20-30 minutes; administration rate should not exceed 25 mg/minute (aminophylline). See table.

Approximate I.V. Theophylline Dosage for Treatment of Acute Bronchospasm

Group	Dosage for Next 12 h[1]	Dosage After 12 h[1]
Infants 6 wk - 6 mo	0.5 mg/kg/h	
Children 6 mo - 1 y	0.6-0.7 mg/kg/h	
Children 1-9 y	0.95 mg/kg/h (1.2 mg/kg/h)	0.79 mg/kg/h (1 mg/kg/h)
Children 9-16 y and young adult smokers	0.79 mg/kg/h (1 mg/kg/h)	0.63 mg/kg/h (0.8 mg/kg/h)
Healthy, nonsmoking adults	0.55 mg/kg/h (0.7 mg/kg/h)	0.39 mg/kg/h (0.5 mg/kg/h)
Older patients and patients with cor pulmonale	0.47 mg/kg/h (0.6 mg/kg/h)	0.24 mg/kg/h (0.3 mg/kg/h)
Patients with congestive heart failure or liver failure	0.39 mg/kg/h (0.5 mg/kg/h)	0.08-0.16 mg/kg/h (0.1-0.2 mg/kg/h)

[1]Equivalent hydrous aminophylline dosage indicated in parentheses.

Approximate I.V. maintenance dosages are based upon continuous infusions; bolus dosing (often used in children <6 months of age) may be determined by multiplying the hourly infusion rate by 24 hours and dividing by the desired number of doses/day; see table.

Maintenance Dose for Acute Symptoms

Population Group	Oral Theophylline (mg/kg/day)	I.V. Aminophylline
Premature infant or newborn - 6 wk (for apnea/bradycardia)	4	5 mg/kg/day
6 wk - 6 mo	10	12 mg/kg/day or continuous I.V. infusion[1]
Infants 6 mo - 1 y	12-18	15 mg/kg/day or continuous I.V. infusion[1]
Children 1-9 y	20-24	1 mg/kg/h
Children 9-12 y, and adolescent daily smokers of cigarettes or marijuana, and otherwise healthy adult smokers <50 y	16	0.9 mg/kg/h
Adolescents 12-16 y (nonsmokers)	13	0.7 mg/kg/h
Otherwise healthy nonsmoking adults (including elderly patients)	10 (not to exceed 900 mg/day)	0.5 mg/kg/h
Cardiac decompensation, cor pulmonale, and/or liver dysfunction	5 (not to exceed 400 mg/day)	0.25 mg/kg/h

[1]For continuous I.V. infusion divide total daily dose by 24 = mg/kg/h.

Dosage should be adjusted according to serum level measurements during the first 12- to 24-hour period; see table on next page.

(Continued)

Theophylline Salts *(Continued)*

Dosage Adjustment After Serum Theophylline Measurement

Serum Theophylline		Guidelines
Within normal limits	10-20 mcg/mL	Maintain dosage if tolerated. Recheck serum theophylline concentration at 6- to 12-month intervals.[1]
Too high	20-25 mcg/mL	Decrease doses by about 10%. Recheck serum theophylline concentration after 3 days and then at 6- to 12-month intervals.[1]
	25-30 mcg/mL	Skip next dose and decrease subsequent doses by about 25%. Recheck serum theophylline.
	>30 mcg/mL	Skip next 2 doses and decrease subsequent doses by 50%. Recheck serum theophylline.
Too low	7.5-10 mcg/mL	Increase dose by about 25%.[2] Recheck serum theophylline concentration after 3 days and then at 6- to 12-month intervals.[1]
	5-7.5 mcg/mL	Increase dose by about 25% to the nearest dose increment[2] and recheck serum theophylline for guidance in further dosage adjustment (another increase will probably be needed, but this provides a safety check).

[1]Finer adjustments in dosage may be needed for some patients.
[2]Dividing the daily dose into 3 doses administered at 8-hour intervals may be indicated if symptoms occur repeatedly at the end of a dosing interval.
From Weinberger M and Hendeles L, "Practical Guide to Using Theophylline," *J Resp Dis*, 1981,2:12-27.

Oral theophylline: Initial dosage recommendation: Loading dose (to achieve a serum level of about 10 mcg/mL; loading doses should be given using a rapidly absorbed oral product **not** a sustained release product):
If no theophylline has been administered in the previous 24 hours: 4-6 mg/kg theophylline
If theophylline has been administered in the previous 24 hours: administer 1/2 loading dose or 2-3 mg/kg theophylline can be given in emergencies when serum levels are not available
On the average, for every 1 mg/kg theophylline given, blood levels will rise 2 mcg/mL
Ideally, defer the loading dose if a serum theophylline concentration can be obtained rapidly. However, if this is not possible, exercise clinical judgment. If the patient is not experiencing theophylline toxicity, this is unlikely to result in dangerous adverse effects. See table.

Oral Theophylline Dosage for Bronchial Asthma[1]

Age (y)	Initial 3 Days	Second 3 Days	Steady-State Maintenance
<1	0.2 x (age in weeks) + 5		0.3 x (age in weeks) + 8
1-9	16 up to a maximum of 400 mg/24 h	20	22
9-12	16 up to a maximum of 400 mg/24 h	16 up to a maximum of 600 mg/24 h	20 up to a maximum of 800 mg/24 h
12-16	16 up to a maximum of 400 mg/24 h	16 up to a maximum of 600 mg/24 h	18 up to a maximum of 900 mg/24 h
Adults	400 mg/24 h	600 mg/24 h	900 mg/24 h

[1]Dose in mg/kg/24 hours of theophylline.

Increasing dose: The dosage may be increased in approximately 25% increments at 2- to 3-day intervals so long as the drug is tolerated or until the maximum dose is reached
Maintenance dose: In newborns and infants, a fast-release oral product can be used. The total daily dose can be divided every 12 hours in newborns and every 6-8 hours in infants. In children and healthy adults, a slow-release product can be used. The total daily dose can be divided every 8-12 hours.

Administration
Aminophylline: Dilute with I.V. fluid to a concentration of 1 mg/mL and infuse over 20-30 minutes; maximum concentration: 25 mg/mL; maximum rate of infusion: 0.36 mg/kg/ minute, and no greater than 25 mg/minute. I.M. administration is not recommended. Oral and I.V. should be administered around-the-clock rather than 4 times/day, 3 times/day, etc (ie, 12-6-12-6, not 9-1-5-9) to promote less variation in peak and trough serum levels.
Theophylline: Oral: Long-acting preparations should be taken with a full glass of water, swallowed whole, or cut in half if scored. Do **not** crush. Extended release capsule forms may be opened and the contents sprinkled on soft foods; do **not** chew beads.

Monitoring Parameters
Aminophylline: Monitor vital signs, I & O, serum concentrations, and CNS effects (insomnia, irritability)
Theophylline: Monitor heart rate, CNS effects (insomnia, irritability); respiratory rate (COPD patients often have resting controlled respiratory rates in low 20s), serum theophylline level, arterial or capillary blood gases (if applicable)

Reference Range
Sample size: 0.5-1 mL serum (red top tube)
Saliva levels are approximately equal to 60% of plasma levels

Therapeutic levels: 10-20 µg/mL
  Neonatal apnea 6-13 µg/mL
  Pregnancy: 3-12 µg/mL
  Toxic concentration: >20 µg/mL

Timing of serum samples: If toxicity is suspected, draw a level any time during a continuous I.V. infusion, or 2 hours after an oral dose; if lack of therapeutic is effected, draw a trough immediately before the next oral dose.

Test Interactions May elevate uric acid levels
Additional Information See table for theophylline content.

Salt	% Theophylline Content
Theophylline anhydrous (eg, most oral solids)	100%
Theophylline monohydrate (eg, oral solutions)	91%
Aminophylline (theophylline) (eg, injection)	80% (79% to 86%)
Oxtriphylline (choline theophylline) (eg, Choledyl®)	64%

Dosage Forms
  Aminophylline:
    Injection, solution: 25 mg/mL (10 mL, 20 mL)
    Liquid, oral: 105 mg/5 mL (240 mL, 500 mL)
    Tablet: 100 mg, 200 mg
  Theophylline:
    Capsule, extended release (Theo-24®): 100 mg, 200 mg, 300 mg, 400 mg [24 hours]
    Elixir (Elixophyllin®): 80 mg/15 mL (480 mL) [contains alcohol 20%; fruit flavor]
    Infusion [premixed in D₅W]: 0.8 mg/mL (500 mL, 1000 mL); 1.6 mg/mL (250 mL, 500 mL); 2
      mg/mL (100 mL); 3.2 mg/mL (250 mL); 4 mg/mL (50 mL, 100 mL)
    Solution, oral: 80 mg/15 mL (15 mL, 18.75 mL, 500 mL) [dye free, sugar free; contains
      alcohol 0.4% and benzoic acid; orange flavor]
    Tablet, controlled release:
      T-Phyl®: 200 mg [12 hours; contains cetostearyl alcohol]
      Uniphyl®: 400 mg, 600 mg [24 hours; contains cetostearyl alcohol]
    Tablet, extended release: 100 mg, 200 mg, 300 mg, 450 mg
      Theochron®: 100 mg, 200 mg, 300 mg [12-24 hours]
    Tablet, immediate release:
      Quibron®-T: 300 mg
      Theolair™: 125 mg, 250 mg
    Tablet, sustained release (Quibron®-T/SR): 300 mg [8-12 hours]
    Tablet, timed release (Theolair™-SR [DSC]): 300 mg, 500 mg
♦ **TheraCys®** *see* BCG Vaccine *on page 197*
♦ **Thera-Flur-N®** *see* Fluoride *on page 722*
♦ **Theramycin Z®** *see* Erythromycin *on page 609*
♦ **Thermazene®** *see* Silver Sulfadiazine *on page 1567*

Thiabendazole (thye a BEN da zole)

U.S. Brand Names Mintezol®
Index Terms Tiabendazole
Pharmacologic Category Anthelmintic
Use Treatment of strongyloidiasis, cutaneous larva migrans, visceral larva migrans, dracunculiasis, trichinosis, and mixed helminthic infections
Unlabeled/Investigational Use Cutaneous larva migrans (topical application)
Pregnancy Risk Factor C
Pregnancy Implications Cleft palate and skeletal defects were observed in some animal studies. There are no adequate and well-controlled studies in pregnant women.
Lactation Excretion in breast milk unknown/not recommended
Contraindications Hypersensitivity to thiabendazole or any component of the formulation; not for use as prophylactic treatment of enterobiasis (pinworm) infestation
Warnings/Precautions Use with caution in patients with renal or hepatic impairment, malnutrition or anemia, or dehydration. Causes sedation; caution must be used in performing tasks which require alertness. Not suitable treatment for mixed infections with *Ascaris*. Ophthalmic changes may occur and persist >1 year. Safety and efficacy are limited in children <14 kg (30 lb).
Adverse Reactions Frequency not defined.
  Central nervous system: Chills, delirium, dizziness, drowsiness, hallucinations, headache, seizures
  Dermatologic: Angioedema, pruritus, rash, Stevens-Johnson syndrome
  Endocrine & metabolic: Hyperglycemia
  Gastrointestinal: Abdominal pain, anorexia, diarrhea, drying of mucous membranes, nausea, vomiting
  Genitourinary: Crystalluria, enuresis, hematuria, malodor of urine
  Hematologic: Leukopenia
  Hepatic: Cholestasis, hepatic failure, hepatotoxicity, jaundice
  Neuromuscular & skeletal: Incoordination, numbness
  Ocular: Abnormal sensation in eyes, blurred vision, dry eyes, Sicca syndrome, vision decreased, xanthopsia
  Otic: Tinnitus
  Renal: Nephrotoxicity
  Miscellaneous: Anaphylaxis, hypersensitivity reactions, lymphadenopathy
Overdosage/Toxicology Symptoms include altered mental status and visual problems. Supportive care only following GI decontamination.
Drug Interactions
  Cytochrome P450 Effect: Substrate of CYP1A2 (minor); **Inhibits** CYP1A2 (strong)
  Increased Effect/Toxicity: Thiabendazole may increase the levels/effects of aminophylline, fluvoxamine, mexiletine, mirtazapine, ropinirole, theophylline, trifluoperazine, and other CYP1A2 substrates.
Mechanism of Action Inhibits helminth-specific mitochondrial fumarate reductase
Pharmacodynamics/Kinetics
  Absorption: Rapid and well absorbed
  Metabolism: Rapidly hepatic; metabolized to 5-hydroxy form
  Half-life elimination: 1.2 hours
  Time to peak, plasma: Oral suspension: Within 1-2 hours
(Continued)

Thiabendazole *(Continued)*

Excretion: Urine (90%) and feces (5%) primarily as conjugated metabolites

Dosage Purgation is not required prior to use; drinking of fruit juice aids in expulsion of worms by removing the mucous to which the intestinal tapeworms attach themselves.

Children and Adults:

Oral: 50 mg/kg/day divided every 12 hours (if >68 kg: 1.5 g/dose); maximum dose: 3 g/day
Treatment duration:
Strongyloidiasis, ascariasis, uncinariasis: For 2 consecutive days
Cutaneous larva migrans: For 2 consecutive days; if active lesions are still present 2 days after completion, a second course of treatment is recommended.
Visceral larva migrans: For 7 consecutive days
Trichinosis: For 2-4 consecutive days; optimal dosage not established
Dracunculosis: 50-75 mg/kg/day divided every 12 hours for 3 days

Topical (unlabeled): Cutaneous larva migrans: Apply directly to larval tracks 2-3 times/day for up to 2 weeks; application frequencies may range from 2-6 times/day. **Note:** Not available as a topical formulation; oral suspension (10% to 15%) has been used topically, as well as a number of extemporaneous formulations.

Dosing comments in renal/hepatic impairment: Use with caution

Monitoring Parameters Periodic renal and hepatic function tests

Dosage Forms [DSC] = Discontinued product
Suspension, oral: 500 mg/5 mL (120 mL) [DSC]
Tablet, chewable: 500 mg [orange flavor]

Extemporaneous Preparations Topical application of thiabendazole has been recommended for the treatment of cutaneous larva migrans (*Redbook*, 2003; *Med Letter*, 2002). In some cases, the commercially-available 10% oral suspension has been used for topical application. Alternatively, a number of extemporaneous preparations have used crushed tablets to prepare distinct formulations. These include a 10% ointment (in white petrolatum), a 15% topical lotion (suspended with compound tragacanth powder 250 mg/40 mL), a 15% cream (in either hydrophilic or fat-based creams), and topical solutions (2% to 4% in DMSO). The stability of these formulations has not been established, and there are no comparative studies evaluating different formulations. All preparations have been applied between 2-6 times daily for up to 2 weeks.

♦ **Thiamazole** see Methimazole *on page 1108*
♦ **Thiamin** see Thiamine *on page 1668*

Thiamine (THYE a min)

Canadian Brand Names Betaxin®

Index Terms Aneurine Hydrochloride; Thiamin; Thiamine Hydrochloride; Thiaminium Chloride Hydrochloride; Vitamin B_1

Pharmacologic Category Vitamin, Water Soluble

Use Treatment of thiamine deficiency including beriberi, Wernicke's encephalopathy, Korsakoff's syndrome, neuritis associated with pregnancy, or in alcoholic patients; dietary supplement

Pregnancy Risk Factor A/C (dose exceeding RDA recommendation)

Pregnancy Implications
Thiamine requirements are increased during pregnancy. Severe nausea and vomiting (hyperemesis gravidarum) may lead to thiamine deficiency manifested as Wernicke's encephalopathy.

Lactation Enters breast milk/use caution (AAP rates "compatible")

Medication Safety Issues
Sound-alike/look-alike issues:
Thiamine may be confused with Tenormin®, Thorazine®

International issues:
Doxal® [Brazil] may be confused with Doxil® which is a brand name for doxorubicin in the U.S.
Doxal® [Brazil]: Brand name for doxycycline in Austria; brand name for pyridoxine in Brazil; brand name for doxepin in Finland

Contraindications Hypersensitivity to thiamine or any component of the formulation

Warnings/Precautions Use with caution with parenteral route (especially I.V.) of administration. Hypersensitivity reactions have been reported following repeated parenteral doses; consider skin test in individuals with history of allergic reactions. Single vitamin deficiency is rare; evaluate for other deficiencies. Dextrose administration may precipitate acute symptoms of thiamine deficiency; use caution when thiamine status is marginal or suspect.

Adverse Reactions Adverse reactions reported with injection. Frequency not defined.
Cardiovascular: Cyanosis
Central nervous system: Restlessness
Dermatologic: Angioneurotic edema, pruritus, urticaria
Gastrointestinal: Hemorrhage into GI tract, nausea, tightness of the throat
Local: Induration and/or tenderness at the injection site (following I.M. administration)
Neuromuscular & skeletal: Weakness
Respiratory: Pulmonary edema
Miscellaneous: Anaphylactic/hypersensitivity reactions (following I.V. administration), diaphoresis, warmth

Overdosage/Toxicology Anorexia, headache, insomnia, irritability, nausea, nervousness, palpitations, tremor, and vomiting have been rarely reported as an overdose response.

Ethanol/Nutrition/Herb Interactions
Ethanol: May decrease thiamine absorption.
Food: High carbohydrate diets may increase thiamine requirement.

Stability Injection: Store at 15°C to 30°C (59°F to 86°F). Protect from light

Mechanism of Action An essential coenzyme in carbohydrate metabolism by combining with adenosine triphosphate to form thiamine pyrophosphate

Pharmacodynamics/Kinetics

Absorption: Oral: Adequate; I.M.: Rapid and complete

Distribution: Highest concentrations found in brain, heart, kidney, liver; crosses the placenta, enters breast milk

Excretion: Urine (as unchanged drug and as pyrimidine after body storage sites become saturated)

Dosage

Adequate Intake:

0-6 months: 0.2 mg/day

7-12 months: 0.3 mg/day

Recommended daily intake:

1-3 years: 0.5 mg

4-8 years: 0.6 mg

9-13 years: 0.9 mg

14-18 years: Female: 1 mg; Male: 1.2 mg

≥19 years: Female: 1.1 mg; Male: 1.2 mg

Pregnancy, lactation: 1.4 mg

Parenteral nutrition supplementation:

Infants: 1.2 mg/day

Adults: 6 mg/day; may be increased to 25-50 mg/day with history of alcohol abuse

Thiamine deficiency (beriberi):

Children: 10-25 mg/dose I.M. or I.V. daily (if critically ill), or 10-50 mg/dose orally every day for 2 weeks, then 5-10 mg/dose orally daily for 1 month

Adults: 5-30 mg/dose I.M. or I.V. 3 times/day (if critically ill); then orally 5-30 mg/day in single or divided doses 3 times/day for 1 month

Alcohol withdrawal syndrome: Adults: 100 mg/day I.M. or I.V. for several days, followed by 50-100 mg/day orally

Wernicke's encephalopathy: Adults: Treatment: Initial: 100 mg I.V., then 50-100 mg/day I.M. or I.V. until consuming a regular, balanced diet. Larger doses may be needed in patients with alcohol abuse.

Dietary Considerations Dietary sources include legumes, pork, beef, whole grains, yeast, and fresh vegetables. A deficiency state can occur in as little as 3 weeks following total dietary absence.

Administration Parenteral form may be administered by I.M. or I.V. injection. Various rates of administration have been reported. Local injection reactions may be minimized by slow administration (~30 minutes) into larger, more proximal veins. Thiamine should be administered prior to parenteral glucose solutions to prevent the precipitation of heart failure.

Reference Range Normal, serum: 1.1-1.6 mg/dL

Test Interactions False-positive for uric acid using the phosphotungstate method and for urobilinogen using the Ehrlich's reagent; large doses may interfere with the spectrophotometric determination of serum theophylline concentration

Dosage Forms

Injection, solution, as hydrochloride: 100 mg/mL (2 mL)

Tablet, as hydrochloride: 50 mg, 100 mg, 250 mg, 500 mg

♦ **Thiamine Hydrochloride** *see* Thiamine *on page 1668*

♦ **Thiaminium Chloride Hydrochloride** *see* Thiamine *on page 1668*

Thioguanine (thye oh GWAH neen)

U.S. Brand Names Tabloid®

Canadian Brand Names Lanvis®

Index Terms 2-Amino-6-Mercaptopurine; NSC-752; TG; 6-TG (error-prone abbreviation); 6-Thioguanine (error-prone abbreviation); Tioguanine

Pharmacologic Category Antineoplastic Agent, Antimetabolite (Purine Antagonist)

Use Treatment of acute myelogenous (nonlymphocytic) leukemia; treatment of chronic myelogenous leukemia and granulocytic leukemia

Restrictions The I.V. formulation is not available in U.S.

Pregnancy Risk Factor D

Lactation Excretion in breast milk unknown

Medication Safety Issues

High alert medication: The Institute for Safe Medication Practices (ISMP) includes this medication among its list of drugs which have a heightened risk of causing significant patient harm when used in error.

6-thioguanine and 6-TG are error-prone abbreviations (associated with six-fold overdoses of thioguanine)

Contraindications Hypersensitivity to thioguanine or any component of the formulation; pregnancy

Warnings/Precautions Hazardous agent - use appropriate precautions for handling and disposal. Use with caution and reduce dose in patients with renal or hepatic impairment. Not recommended for long-term continuous therapy due to potential for hepatotoxicity (hepatic veno-occlusive disease). Discontinue in patients with evidence of hepatotoxicity. Thioguanine is potentially carcinogenic and teratogenic; myelosuppression may be delayed. Caution with history of previous therapy resistance with either thioguanine or mercaptopurine (there is usually complete cross resistance between these two). Patients with genetic deficiency of thiopurine methyltransferase (TPMT) or who are receiving drugs which inhibit this enzyme (mesalazine, olsalazine, sulfasalazine) may be highly sensitive to myelosuppressive effects.

Adverse Reactions

>10%: Hematologic: Myelosuppressive:

WBC: Moderate

Platelets: Moderate

(Continued)

Thioguanine *(Continued)*

Onset: 7-10 days
Nadir: 14 days
Recovery: 21 days
1% to 10%:
Dermatologic: Skin rash
Endocrine & metabolic: Hyperuricemia
Gastrointestinal: Mild nausea or vomiting, anorexia, stomatitis, diarrhea
Neuromuscular & skeletal: Unsteady gait
<1% (Limited to important or life-threatening): Ascites, esophageal varices, hepatic necrosis, hepatitis, jaundice, LFTs increased, neurotoxicity, photosensitivity, portal hypertension, splenomegaly, thrombocytopenia, veno-occlusive hepatic disease

Overdosage/Toxicology Symptoms include bone marrow suppression, nausea, vomiting, malaise, hypertension, and sweating. Treatment is supportive and dialysis is not useful.

Drug Interactions
Increased Effect/Toxicity: Allopurinol can be used in full doses with thioguanine unlike mercaptopurine. Use with busulfan may cause hepatotoxicity and esophageal varices. Aminosalicylates (olsalazine, mesalamine, sulfasalazine) may inhibit TPMT, increasing toxicity/myelosuppression of thioguanine.

Ethanol/Nutrition/Herb Interactions Food: Enhanced absorption if administered between meals.

Stability Store tablet at room temperature.

Mechanism of Action Purine analog that is incorporated into DNA and RNA resulting in the blockage of synthesis and metabolism of purine nucleotides

Pharmacodynamics/Kinetics
Absorption: 30% (highly variable)
Distribution: Crosses placenta
Metabolism: Hepatic; rapidly and extensively via TPMT to 2-amino-6-methylthioguanine (active) and inactive compounds
Half-life elimination: Terminal: 11 hours
Time to peak, serum: Within 8 hours
Excretion: Urine

Dosage Total daily dose can be given at one time.
Oral (refer to individual protocols):
Infants and Children <3 years: Combination drug therapy for acute nonlymphocytic leukemia: 3.3 mg/kg/day in divided doses twice daily for 4 days
Children and Adults: 2-3 mg/kg/day calculated to nearest 20 mg or 75-200 mg/m^2/day in 1-2 divided doses for 5-7 days or until remission is attained
Dosing comments in renal or hepatic impairment: Reduce dose

Monitoring Parameters CBC with differential and platelet count; liver function tests (weekly when beginning therapy then monthly, more frequently in patients with liver disease or concurrent hepatotoxic drugs); hemoglobin, hematocrit, serum uric acid; some laboratories offer testing for TPMT deficiency

Hepatotoxicity may present with signs of portal hypertension (splenomegaly, esophageal varices, thrombocytopenia) or veno-occlusive disease (fluid retention, ascites, hepatomegaly with tenderness, or hyperbilirubinemia)

Dosage Forms
Tablet [scored]:
Tabloid®: 40 mg

Extemporaneous Preparations A 20 mg/mL oral suspension can be prepared by crushing fifteen 40 mg tablets in a mortar, and then adding 10 mL of methylcellulose 1% (in small amounts). Transfer to a graduate, then add a sufficient quantity of syrup to make 30 mL of suspension. Label "shake well." Room temperature stability is 60 days.
Dressman JB and Poust RI, "Stability of Allopurinol and Five Antineoplastics in Suspension," *Am J Hosp Pharm*, 1983, 40:616-8.
Nahata MC, Morosco RS, and Hipple TF, 4th ed, *Pediatric Drug Formulations*, Cincinnati, OH: Harvey Whitney Books Co, 2000.

♦ 6-Thioguanine (error-prone abbreviation) *see* Thioguanine *on page 1669*

Thiopental *(thye oh PEN tal)*

U.S. Brand Names Pentothal®
Canadian Brand Names Pentothal®
Index Terms Thiopental Sodium
Pharmacologic Category Anticonvulsant, Barbiturate; Barbiturate; General Anesthetic
Use Induction of anesthesia; adjunct for intubation in head injury patients; control of convulsive states; treatment of elevated intracranial pressure
Restrictions C-III
Pregnancy Risk Factor C
Contraindications Hypersensitivity to thiopental, barbiturates, or any component of the formulation; status asthmaticus; severe cardiovascular disease; porphyria (variegate or acute intermittent); should not be administered by intra-arterial injection
Warnings/Precautions Laryngospasm or bronchospasms may occur; use with extreme caution in patients with reactive airway diseases (asthma or COPD). Use with caution when the hypnotic may be prolonged or potentiated (excessive premedication, Addison's disease, hepatic or renal dysfunction, myxedema, increased blood urea, severe anemia, or myasthenia gravis). Potential for drug dependency exists, abrupt cessation may precipitate withdrawal, including status epilepticus in epileptic patients. Use caution in patients with unstable aneurysms, cardiovascular disease, renal impairment, or hepatic disease. Use caution in elderly, debilitated, or pediatric patients. May cause paradoxical responses, including agitation and hyperactivity, particularly in acute pain and pediatric patients. Effects with other

sedative drugs or ethanol may be potentiated. May cause respiratory depression or hypotension; use with caution in hemodynamically unstable patients (hypotension or shock) or patients with respiratory disease. Repeated dosing or continuous infusions may cause cumulative effects. Extravasation or intra-arterial injection causes necrosis due to pH of 10.6, ensure patient has intravenous access.

Adverse Reactions Frequency not defined.

Cardiovascular: Bradycardia, hypotension, syncope

Central nervous system: Drowsiness, lethargy, CNS excitation or depression, impaired judgment, "hangover" effect, confusion, somnolence, agitation, hyperkinesia, ataxia, nervousness, headache, insomnia, nightmares, hallucinations, anxiety, dizziness, shivering

Dermatologic: Rash, exfoliative dermatitis, Stevens-Johnson syndrome

Gastrointestinal: Nausea, vomiting, constipation

Hematologic: Agranulocytosis, thrombocytopenia, megaloblastic anemia, immune hemolytic anemia (rare)

Local: Pain at injection site, thrombophlebitis with I.V. use

Renal: Oliguria

Respiratory: Laryngospasm, respiratory depression, apnea (especially with rapid I.V. use), hypoventilation, sneezing, cough, bronchospasm

Miscellaneous: Gangrene with inadvertent intra-arterial injection, anaphylaxis, anaphylactic reactions

Overdosage/Toxicology Symptoms include respiratory depression, hypotension, shock. Hypotension should respond to I.V. fluids and Trendelenburg positioning. If necessary, pressors such as norepinephrine may be used. Ventilatory support may be required.

Drug Interactions

Increased Effect/Toxicity: In chronic use, barbiturates are potent inducers of CYP isoenzymes resulting in multiple interactions with medication groups. When used for limited periods, thiopental is not likely to interact via this mechanism. Sedative effects and/or respiratory depression with barbiturates may be additive with other CNS depressants; includes ethanol, sedatives, antidepressants, opioid analgesics, and benzodiazepines. Felbamate may inhibit the metabolism of barbiturates and barbiturates may increase the metabolism of felbamate. Barbiturates may enhance the nephrotoxic effects of methoxyflurane

Stability Reconstituted solutions remain stable for 3 days at room temperature and 7 days when refrigerated.

Mechanism of Action Short-acting barbiturate with sedative, hypnotic, and anticonvulsant properties. Barbiturates depress the sensory cortex, decrease motor activity, alter cerebellar function, and produce drowsiness, sedation, and hypnosis. In high doses, barbiturates exhibit anticonvulsant activity; barbiturates produce dose-dependent respiratory depression.

Pharmacodynamics/Kinetics

Onset of action: Anesthetic: I.V.: 30-60 seconds

Duration: 5-30 minutes

Distribution: V_d: 1.4 L/kg

Protein binding: 72% to 86%

Metabolism: Hepatic, primarily to inactive metabolites but pentobarbital is also formed

Half-life elimination: 3-11.5 hours; decreased in children

Dosage I.V.:

Induction anesthesia:

Infants: 5-8 mg/kg

Children 1-12 years: 5-6 mg/kg

Adults: 3-5 mg/kg

Maintenance anesthesia:

Children: 1 mg/kg as needed

Adults: 25-100 mg as needed

Increased intracranial pressure: Children and Adults: 1.5-5 mg/kg/dose; repeat as needed to control intracranial pressure

Seizures:

Children: 2-3 mg/kg/dose; repeat as needed

Adults: 75-250 mg/dose; repeat as needed

Dosing adjustment in renal impairment: Cl_{cr} <10 mL/minute: Administer at 75% of normal dose

Note: Accumulation may occur with chronic dosing due to lipid solubility; prolonged recovery may result from redistribution of thiopental from fat stores

Dietary Considerations Sodium content of 1 g (injection): 86.8 mg (3.8 mEq)

Administration Administer slowly over 20-30 seconds. Rapid I.V. injection may cause hypotension or decreased cardiac output; avoid extravasation, necrosis may occur. Check I.V. catheter placement prior to administration.

Monitoring Parameters Respiratory rate, heart rate, blood pressure

Reference Range Therapeutic: Hypnotic: 1-5 mcg/mL (SI: 4.1-20.7 µmol/L); Coma: 30-100 mcg/mL (SI: 124-413 µmol/L); Anesthesia: 7-130 mcg/mL (SI: 29-536 µmol/L); Toxic: >10 mcg/mL (SI: >41 µmol/L)

Additional Information Thiopental switches from linear to nonlinear pharmacokinetics following prolonged continuous infusions.

Dosage Forms Injection, powder for reconstitution, as sodium: 250 mg, 400 mg, 500 mg, 1 g

♦ **Thiopental Sodium** see Thiopental on page 1670

♦ **Thiophosphoramide** see Thiotepa on page 1674

Thioridazine (thye oh RID a zeen)

Canadian Brand Names Mellaril®
Index Terms Thioridazine Hydrochloride
Pharmacologic Category Antipsychotic Agent, Typical, Phenothiazine
Additional Appendix Information
Antipsychotic Agents *on page 1872*
Use Management of schizophrenic patients who fail to respond adequately to treatment with other antipsychotic drugs, either because of insufficient effectiveness or the inability to achieve an effective dose due to intolerable adverse effects from those medications
Unlabeled/Investigational Use Psychosis
Pregnancy Risk Factor C
Lactation Excretion in breast milk unknown/not recommended
Medication Safety Issues
Sound-alike/look-alike issues:
Thioridazine may be confused with thiothixene, Thorazine®
Mellaril® may be confused with Elavil®, Mebaral®

Contraindications Hypersensitivity to thioridazine or any component of the formulation (cross-reactivity between phenothiazines may occur); severe CNS depression; circulatory collapse; severe hypotension; bone marrow suppression; blood dyscrasias; coma; in combination with other drugs that are known to prolong the QT_c interval; in patients with congenital long QT syndrome or a history of cardiac arrhythmias; concurrent use with medications that inhibit the metabolism of thioridazine (fluoxetine, paroxetine, fluvoxamine, propranolol, pindolol); patients known to have genetic defect leading to reduced levels of activity of CYP2D6

Warnings/Precautions Oral formulations may cause stomach upset; may cause thermoregulatory changes; use caution in patients with narrow-angle glaucoma; doses of 1 g/day frequently cause pigmentary retinopathy. **[U.S. Boxed Warning]: Thioridazine has dose-related effects on ventricular repolarization leading to QT_c prolongation, a potentially life-threatening effect.** As a result, it should be reserved for patients whose schizophrenia has failed to respond to adequate trials of other antipsychotic drugs. Use with caution in Parkinson's disease; hemodynamic instability; bone marrow suppression; predisposition to seizures; subcortical brain damage; severe cardiac, hepatic, renal, or respiratory disease. Esophageal dysmotility and aspiration have been associated with antipsychotic use - use with caution in patients at risk of pneumonia (ie, Alzheimer's disease). Caution in breast cancer or other prolactin-dependent tumors (may elevate prolactin levels). May alter temperature regulation or mask toxicity of other drugs due to antiemetic effects.

Phenothiazines may cause anticholinergic effects (confusion, agitation, constipation, xerostomia, blurred vision, urinary retention); therefore, they should be used with caution in patients with decreased gastrointestinal motility, urinary retention, BPH, xerostomia, or visual problems. Conditions which also may be exacerbated by cholinergic blockade include narrow-angle glaucoma (screening is recommended) and worsening of myasthenia gravis. Relative to other neuroleptics, thioridazine has a high potency of cholinergic blockade.

May cause extrapyramidal reactions, including pseudoparkinsonism, acute dystonic reactions, akathisia, and tardive dyskinesia (risk of these reactions is low relative to other neuroleptics). May be associated with neuroleptic malignant syndrome (NMS).

Adverse Reactions Frequency not defined.
Cardiovascular: Hypotension, orthostatic hypotension, peripheral edema, ECG changes
Central nervous system: EPS (pseudoparkinsonism, akathisia, dystonias, tardive dyskinesia), dizziness, drowsiness, neuroleptic malignant syndrome (NMS), impairment of temperature regulation, lowering of seizure threshold
Dermatologic: Increased sensitivity to sun, rash, discoloration of skin (blue-gray)
Endocrine & metabolic: Changes in menstrual cycle, libido (changes in), breast pain, galactorrhea, amenorrhea
Gastrointestinal: Constipation, weight gain, nausea, vomiting, stomach pain, xerostomia, diarrhea
Genitourinary: Difficulty in urination, ejaculatory disturbances, urinary retention, priapism
Hematologic: Agranulocytosis, leukopenia
Hepatic: Cholestatic jaundice, hepatotoxicity
Neuromuscular & skeletal: Tremor, seizure
Ocular: Pigmentary retinopathy, blurred vision, cornea and lens changes
Respiratory: Nasal congestion

Overdosage/Toxicology Symptoms include deep sleep, coma, extrapyramidal symptoms, abnormal involuntary muscle movements, hypotension, and arrhythmias. Immediate cardiovascular monitoring, including continuous ECG monitoring, to detect arrhythmias.

Following initiation of essential overdose management, toxic symptom treatment and supportive treatment should be initiated. **Avoid use of other medications that may also prolong the QT_c interval, such as disopyramide, procainamide and quinidine.** Hypotension usually responds to I.V. fluids or Trendelenburg positioning. If unresponsive to these measures, the use of a parenteral inotrope may be required (eg, norepinephrine 0.1-0.2 mcg/kg/minute titrated to response); do not use epinephrine. Seizures commonly respond to diazepam (I.V. 5-10 mg bolus in adults every 15 minutes if needed up to a total of 30 mg; I.V. 0.25-0.4 mg/kg/dose up to a total of 10 mg in children) or to phenytoin. Neuroleptics often cause extrapyramidal symptoms (eg, dystonic reactions) requiring management with diphenhydramine 1-2 mg/kg (adults) up to a maximum of 50 mg I.M. or slow I.V. push followed by a maintenance dose for 48-72 hours. When these reactions are unresponsive to diphenhydramine, anticholinergic agents such as benztropine mesylate I.V. 1-2 mg (adults) may be effective. These agents are generally effective within 2-5 minutes. Avoid barbiturates; may potentiate respiratory depression.

Drug Interactions
Cytochrome P450 Effect: **Substrate** of CYP2C19 (minor), 2D6 (major); **Inhibits** CYP1A2 (weak), 2C9 (weak), 2D6 (moderate), 2E1 (weak)

Increased Effect/Toxicity: Concurrent use fluvoxamine, propranolol, and pindolol. The levels/effects of thioridazine may be increased by chlorpromazine, delavirdine, fluoxetine, miconazole, paroxetine, pergolide, quinidine, quinine, ritonavir, ropinirole, and other CYP2D6 inhibitors. **Thioridazine is contraindicated with strong inhibitors of this enzyme.**

Drugs which alter the QT_c interval may be additive with thioridazine, increasing the risk of malignant arrhythmias; includes type Ia antiarrhythmics, TCAs, and some quinolone antibiotics (sparfloxacin, moxifloxacin and gatifloxacin). **These agents are contraindicated with thioridazine.** Potassium depleting agents may increase the risk of serious arrhythmias with thioridazine (includes many diuretics, aminoglycosides, and amphotericin).

Phenothiazines inhibit the ability of bromocriptine to lower serum prolactin concentrations. The sedative effects of CNS depressants or ethanol may be additive with phenothiazines. Phenothiazines and trazodone may produce additive hypotensive effects. Metoclopramide may increase risk of extrapyramidal symptoms (EPS). Acetylcholinesterase inhibitors (central) may increase the risk of antipsychotic-related EPS. Concurrent use of antihypertensives may result in additive hypotensive effects (particularly orthostasis).

Thioridazine may increase the levels/effects of amphetamines, beta-blockers, dextromethorphan, fluoxetine, lidocaine, mirtazapine, nefazodone, paroxetine, risperidone, ritonavir, tricyclic antidepressants, venlafaxine, and other CYP2D6 substrates. **Concurrent use with fluvoxamine is contraindicated.**

Phenothiazines may produce neurotoxicity with lithium; this is a rare event. Rare cases of respiratory paralysis have been reported with concurrent use of phenothiazines and polypeptide antibiotics. Naltrexone in combination with thioridazine has been reported to cause lethargy and somnolence. Phenylpropanolamine has been reported to result in cardiac arrhythmias when combined with thioridazine.

Decreased Effect: Aluminum salts may decrease the absorption of phenothiazines. The efficacy of amphetamines may be diminished by antipsychotics; in addition, amphetamines may increase psychotic symptoms; avoid concurrent use. Anticholinergics may inhibit the therapeutic response to phenothiazines and excess anticholinergic effects may occur (includes benztropine, trihexyphenidyl, biperiden, and drugs with significant anticholinergic activity). Chlorpromazine (and possibly other low potency antipsychotics) may diminish the pressor effects of epinephrine. The antihypertensive effects of guanethidine or guanadrel may be inhibited by phenothiazines. Phenothiazines may inhibit the antiparkinsonian effect of levodopa. Enzyme inducers may enhance the hepatic metabolism of phenothiazines; larger doses may be required; includes rifampin, rifabutin, barbiturates, phenytoin, and cigarette smoking. Thioridazine may decrease the levels/effects of CYP2D6 prodrug substrates (eg, codeine, hydrocodone, oxycodone, tramadol).

Ethanol/Nutrition/Herb Interactions

Ethanol: Avoid ethanol (may increase CNS depression).

Herb/Nutraceutical: Avoid kava kava, valerian, St John's wort, gotu kola (may increase CNS depression). Avoid dong quai, St John's wort (may also cause photosensitization).

Stability Protect from light.

Mechanism of Action Thioridazine is a piperidine phenothiazine which blocks postsynaptic mesolimbic dopaminergic receptors in the brain; exhibits a strong alpha-adrenergic blocking effect and depresses the release of hypothalamic and hypophyseal hormones

Pharmacodynamics/Kinetics

Duration: 4-5 days

Half-life elimination: 21-25 hours

Time to peak, serum: ~1 hour

Dosage Oral:

Children >2-12 years: Range: 0.5-3 mg/kg/day in 2-3 divided doses; usual: 1 mg/kg/day; maximum: 3 mg/kg/day

Behavior problems: Initial: 10 mg 2-3 times/day, increase gradually

Severe psychoses: Initial: 25 mg 2-3 times/day, increase gradually

Children >12 years and Adults:

Schizophrenia/psychoses: Initial: 50-100 mg 3 times/day with gradual increments as needed and tolerated; maximum: 800 mg/day in 2-4 divided doses

Depressive disorders/dementia: Initial: 25 mg 3 times/day; maintenance dose: 20-200 mg/day

Elderly: Behavioral symptoms associated with dementia: Oral: Initial: 10-25 mg 1-2 times/day; increase at 4- to 7-day intervals by 10-25 mg/day; increase dose intervals (once daily, twice daily, etc) as necessary to control response or side effects. Maximum daily dose: 400 mg; gradual increases (titration) may prevent some side effects or decrease their severity.

Hemodialysis: Not dialyzable (0% to 5%)

Administration Do not take antacid within 2 hours of taking drug.

Monitoring Parameters Baseline and periodic ECG; vital signs; serum potassium, lipid profile, fasting blood glucose and Hgb A_{1c}; BMI; mental status, abnormal involuntary movement scale (AIMS); periodic eye exam; do not initiate if QT_c >450 msec

Reference Range Toxic: >1 mg/mL; lethal: 2-8 mg/dL

Test Interactions False-positives for phenylketonuria, urinary amylase, uroporphyrins, urobilinogen

Dosage Forms Tablet, as hydrochloride: 10 mg, 15 mg, 25 mg, 50 mg, 100 mg, 150 mg, 200 mg

- **Thioridazine Hydrochloride** see Thioridazine on page 1672
- **Thiosulfuric Acid Disodium Salt** see Sodium Thiosulfate on page 1584

Thiotepa (thye oh TEP a)

Index Terms TESPA; Thiophosphoramide; Triethylenethiophosphoramide; TSPA

Pharmacologic Category Antineoplastic Agent, Alkylating Agent

Use Treatment of superficial tumors of the bladder; palliative treatment of adenocarcinoma of breast or ovary; lymphomas and sarcomas; controlling intracavitary effusions caused by metastatic tumors; I.T. use: CNS leukemia/lymphoma, CNS metastases

Pregnancy Risk Factor D

Pregnancy Implications Animal studies have demonstrated teratogenicity and fetal loss. There are no adequate and well-controlled studies in pregnant women. May cause harm if administered during pregnancy. Effective contraception is recommended for men and women of childbearing potential.

Lactation Enters breast milk/not recommended

Medication Safety Issues

High alert medication: The Institute for Safe Medication Practices (ISMP) includes this medication among its list of drugs which have a heightened risk of causing significant patient harm when used in error.

Contraindications Hypersensitivity to thiotepa or any component of the formulation; pregnancy

Warnings/Precautions Hazardous agent - use appropriate precautions for handling and disposal. Myelosuppression is common. Potentially mutagenic, carcinogenic, and teratogenic. Reduce dosage and use extreme caution in patients with hepatic, renal, or bone marrow damage. Use should be limited to cases where benefit outweighs risk.

Adverse Reactions

>10%:

Hematopoietic: Myelosuppression (dose related and cumulative): Anemia and pancytopenia may become fatal; careful hematologic monitoring is required; intravesical administration may cause bone marrow suppression as well.

Hematologic: Myelosuppression (WBC: moderate; platelets: severe; onset: 7-10 days, nadir: 14 days, recovery: 28 days)

Local: Injection site pain

1% to 10%:

Central nervous system: Dizziness, fatigue, fever, headache

Dermatologic: Alopecia, depigmentation (with topical treatment), hyperpigmentation (with high-dose therapy), pruritus, rash, urticaria

Endocrine & metabolic: Amenorrhea, hyperuricemia

Gastrointestinal: Anorexia, nausea and vomiting rarely occur

Emetic potential: Low (<10%)

Genitourinary: Dysuria, hemorrhagic cystitis (intravesicular administration: rare), urinary retention

Neuromuscular & skeletal: Weakness

Ocular: Conjunctivitis

Renal: Hematuria

Miscellaneous: Tightness of the throat, allergic reactions

<1% (Limited to important or life-threatening): Carcinogenesis: Like other alkylating agents, this drug is carcinogenic.

BMT:

Central nervous system: Confusion, inappropriate behavior, somnolence

Dermatologic: Hyperpigmentation

Gastrointestinal: Mucositis, mild nausea and vomiting

Hepatic: Serum transaminitis, hyperbilirubinemia

Overdosage/Toxicology Symptoms of overdose include nausea, vomiting, precipitation of uric acid in kidney tubules, bone marrow suppression, and bleeding. Treatment is symptom-directed and supportive. Thiotepa is dialyzable. Transfusions of whole blood or platelets have been proven beneficial.

Drug Interactions

Cytochrome P450 Effect: Inhibits CYP2B6 (strong)

Increased Effect/Toxicity: Phenytoin may increase the levels/effects of TEPA (active metabolite). Thiotepa may increase the levels/effects of CYP2B6 substrates; example substrates include bupropion, promethazine, propofol, selegiline, and sertraline.

Decreased Effect: Phenytoin may decrease the levels/effects of thiotepa.

Ethanol/Nutrition/Herb Interactions

Ethanol: Avoid ethanol (due to GI irritation).

Herb/Nutraceutical: Avoid black cohosh, dong quai in estrogen-dependent tumors.

Stability Store intact vials under refrigeration (2°C to 8°C). Protect from light. Reconstitute each vial to 10 mg/mL. Reconstituted solutions (10 mg/mL) are stable for up to 28 days under refrigeration (4°C to 8°C) or 7 days at room temperature (25°C). Filter through a 0.22 micron filter prior to administration.

Solutions for infusion should be diluted to a concentration ≥5 mg/mL in 5% dextrose or 1, 3, or 5 mg/mL in 0.9% sodium chloride injection:

Diluted in D_5W (≥5 mg/mL): Stable for 14 days under refrigeration (4°C) or 3 days at room temperature (23°C).

Diluted in NS:

1, 3, or 5 mg/mL concentration: Stable for 48 hours under refrigeration (4°C to 8°C) or 24 hours at room temperature (25°C).

≤0.5 mg/mL concentration: Stable for <1 hour.

Intrathecal: Dilute in 1-5 mL NS or Elliott's B solution.

Intravesicular: Dilute in 30-60 mL SWFI or NS.

Mechanism of Action Alkylating agent that reacts with DNA phosphate groups to produce cross-linking of DNA strands leading to inhibition of DNA, RNA, and protein synthesis; mechanism of action has not been explored as thoroughly as the other alkylating agents, it is presumed that the aziridine rings open and react as nitrogen mustard; reactivity is enhanced at a lower pH

Pharmacodynamics/Kinetics

Absorption: Intracavitary instillation: Unreliable (10% to 100%) through bladder mucosa; I.M.: variable

Metabolism: Extensively hepatic; major metabolite (active): TEPA

Half-life elimination: Terminal (dose-dependent clearance): 109 minutes

Excretion: Urine (as metabolites and unchanged drug)

Dosage Refer to individual protocols.

Children: Sarcomas: I.V.: 25-65 mg/m² as a single dose every 21 days

Adults:

I.M., I.V., SubQ: 30-60 mg/m² once weekly

I.V.: 0.3-0.4 mg/kg by rapid I.V. administration every 1-4 weeks, **or** 0.2 mg/kg or 6-8 mg/m²/day for 4-5 days every 2-4 weeks

High-dose therapy for bone marrow transplant: I.V.: 500 mg/m², up to 900 mg/m²

I.M.: 15-30 mg in various schedules have been given

Intracavitary: 0.6-0.8 mg/kg or 30-60 mg weekly

Intrapericardial: 15-30 mg

Intrathecal: 10-15 mg or 5-11.5 mg/m²

Dosing comments/adjustment in renal impairment: Use with extreme caution, reduced dose may be warranted.

Administration

I.V.: Administer either as a short (10-60 minute) infusion or 1-2 minute push; a 1 mg/mL solution is considered isotonic; not a vesicant

Intravesical lavage: Instill directly into the bladder and retain for at least 2 hours; patient should be repositioned every 15-30 minutes for maximal exposure

Monitoring Parameters CBC with differential and platelet count (monitor for at least 3 weeks after treatment); uric acid, urinalysis

Additional Information A 1 mg/mL solution is considered isotonic.

Dosage Forms Injection, powder for reconstitution: 15 mg, 30 mg

---

Thiothixene (thye oh THIKS een)

U.S. Brand Names Navane®

Canadian Brand Names Navane®

Index Terms Tiotixene

Pharmacologic Category Antipsychotic Agent, Typical

Additional Appendix Information

Antipsychotic Agents *on page 1872*

Use Management of schizophrenia

Unlabeled/Investigational Use Psychotic disorders

Pregnancy Risk Factor C

Lactation Excretion in breast milk unknown/not recommended

Medication Safety Issues

Sound-alike/look-alike issues:

Thiothixene may be confused with thioridazine

Navane® may be confused with Norvasc®, Nubain®

Contraindications Hypersensitivity to thiothixene or any component of the formulation; severe CNS depression; circulatory collapse; blood dyscrasias; coma

Warnings/Precautions Safety in children <12 years of age has not been established. May be sedating. Use with caution in Parkinson's disease; hemodynamic instability; predisposition to seizures; subcortical brain damage; bone marrow suppression; severe cardiac, hepatic, renal, or respiratory disease. Esophageal dysmotility and aspiration have been associated with antipsychotic use - use with caution in patients at risk of pneumonia (ie, Alzheimer's disease). Caution in breast cancer or other prolactin-dependent tumors (may elevate prolactin levels). May alter temperature regulation or mask toxicity of other drugs due to antiemetic effects. May alter cardiac conduction - life-threatening arrhythmias have occurred with therapeutic doses of neuroleptics. May cause orthostatic hypotension - use with caution in patients at risk of this effect or those who would tolerate transient hypotensive episodes (cerebrovascular disease, cardiovascular disease, or other medications which may predispose).

Phenothiazines may cause anticholinergic effects (confusion, agitation, constipation, xerostomia, blurred vision, urinary retention); therefore, they should be used with caution in patients with decreased gastrointestinal motility, urinary retention, BPH, xerostomia, or visual problems. Conditions which also may be exacerbated by cholinergic blockade include narrow-angle glaucoma (screening is recommended) and worsening of myasthenia gravis. Relative to other neuroleptics, thiothixene has a low potency of cholinergic blockade.

May cause extrapyramidal reactions, including pseudoparkinsonism, acute dystonic reactions, akathisia, and tardive dyskinesia (risk of these reactions is high relative to other neuroleptics). May be associated with neuroleptic malignant syndrome (NMS) or pigmentary retinopathy.

Adverse Reactions Frequency not defined.

Cardiovascular: Hypotension, nonspecific ECG changes, syncope, tachycardia

Central nervous system: Agitation, dizziness, drowsiness, extrapyramidal symptoms (akathisia, dystonias, lightheadedness, pseudoparkinsonism, tardive dyskinesia), insomnia restlessness

Dermatologic: Discoloration of skin (blue-gray), photosensitivity, pruritus, rash, urticaria

Endocrine & metabolic: Amenorrhea, breast pain, libido (changes in), changes in menstrual cycle, galactorrhea, gynecomastia, hyper-/hypoglycemia, lactation

Gastrointestinal: Constipation, nausea, salivation increased, stomach pain, vomiting, weight gain, xerostomia

Genitourinary: Difficulty in urination, ejaculatory disturbances, Impotence

Hematologic: Leukocytes, leukopenia

Neuromuscular & skeletal: Tremors

(Continued)

Thiothixene *(Continued)*

Ocular: Blurred vision, pigmentary retinopathy
Respiratory: Nasal congestion
Miscellaneous: Diaphoresis

Overdosage/Toxicology Symptoms include muscle twitching, drowsiness, dizziness, rigidity, tremor, hypotension, and cardiac arrhythmias. Following initiation of essential overdose management, toxic symptom treatment and supportive treatment should be initiated. Hypotension usually responds to I.V. fluids or Trendelenburg positioning. If unresponsive to these measures, the use of a parenteral inotrope may be required (eg, norepinephrine 0.1-0.2 mcg/kg/minute titrated to response). Seizures commonly respond to diazepam (I.V. 5-10 mg bolus in adults every 15 minutes if needed up to a total of 30 mg; I.V. 0.25-0.4 mg/kg/dose up to a total of 10 mg in children) or to phenytoin or phenobarbital. Neuroleptics often cause extrapyramidal symptoms (eg, dystonic reactions) requiring management with diphenhydramine 1-2 mg/kg (adults) up to a maximum of 50 mg I.M. or slow I.V. push, followed by a maintenance dose for 48-72 hours. When these reactions are unresponsive to diphenhydramine, anticholinergic agents such as benztropine mesylate I.V. 1-2 mg (adults) may be effective. These agents are generally effective within 2-5 minutes.

Drug Interactions

Cytochrome P450 Effect: Substrate of CYP1A2 (major); **Inhibits** CYP2D6 (weak)

Increased Effect/Toxicity: CYP1A2 inhibitors may increase the levels/effects of thiothixene; example inhibitors include ciprofloxacin, fluvoxamine, ketoconazole, norfloxacin, ofloxacin, and rofecoxib. Thiothixene and CNS depressants (ethanol, opioid analgesics) may produce additive CNS depressant effects. Thiothixene may increase the effect/toxicity of antihypertensives, benztropine (and other anticholinergic agents), lithium, trazodone, and TCAs. Thiothixene's concentrations may be increased by chloroquine, sulfadoxine-pyrimethamine, and propranolol. Metoclopramide may increase risk of extrapyramidal symptoms (EPS). Acetylcholinesterase inhibitors (central) may increase the risk of antipsychotic-related EPS.

Decreased Effect: CYP1A2 inducers may decrease the levels/effects of thiothixene; example inducers include aminoglutethimide, carbamazepine, phenobarbital, and rifampin. Thiothixene inhibits the activity of guanadrel, guanethidine, levodopa, and bromocriptine. Benztropine (and other anticholinergics) may inhibit the therapeutic response to thiothixene. Thiothixene and low potency antipsychotics may reverse the pressor effects of epinephrine.

Ethanol/Nutrition/Herb Interactions

Ethanol: Avoid ethanol (may increase CNS depression).
Herb/Nutraceutical: Avoid kava kava, valerian, St John's wort, gotu kola (may increase CNS depression).

Mechanism of Action Thiothixene is a thioxanthene antipsychotic which elicits antipsychotic activity by postsynaptic blockade of CNS dopamine receptors resulting in inhibition of dopamine-mediated effects; also has alpha-adrenergic blocking activity

Pharmacodynamics/Kinetics

Metabolism: Extensively hepatic
Half-life elimination: >24 hours with chronic use

Dosage Oral:

Children <12 years (unlabeled use): Schizophrenia/psychoses: 0.25 mg/kg/24 hours in divided doses (dose not well established; use not recommended)

Children >12 years and Adults:

Mild to moderate psychosis: 2 mg 3 times/day, up to 20-30 mg/day; more severe psychosis: Initial: 5 mg 2 times/day, may increase gradually, if necessary; maximum: 60 mg/day

Rapid tranquilization of the agitated patient (administered every 30-60 minutes): 5-10 mg; average total dose for tranquilization: 15-30 mg

Hemodialysis: Not dialyzable (0% to 5%)

Monitoring Parameters Vital signs; lipid profile, fasting blood glucose/Hgb A$_{1c}$; BMI; mental status, abnormal involuntary movement scale (AIMS), extrapyramidal symptoms (EPS)

Test Interactions May cause false-positive pregnancy test

Dosage Forms [DSC] = Discontinued product

Capsule: 1 mg, 2 mg, 5 mg, 10 mg
Navane®: 1 mg [DSC], 2 mg, 5 mg, 10 mg, 20 mg

♦ **Thonzonium, Neomycin, Colistin, and Hydrocortisone** *see* Neomycin, Colistin, Hydrocortisone, and Thonzonium *on page 1211*

♦ **Thorets [OTC]** *see* Benzocaine *on page 204*

♦ **Thrombate III®** *see* Antithrombin III *on page 137*

♦ **Thymocyte Stimulating Factor** *see* Aldesleukin *on page 59*

♦ **Thymoglobulin®** *see* Antithymocyte Globulin (Rabbit) *on page 140*

♦ **Thyrogen®** *see* Thyrotropin Alpha *on page 1677*

Thyroid *(THYE roid)*

U.S. Brand Names Armour® Thyroid; Nature-Throid® NT; Westhroid®

Index Terms Desiccated Thyroid; Thyroid Extract; Thyroid USP

Pharmacologic Category Thyroid Product

Use Replacement or supplemental therapy in hypothyroidism; pituitary TSH suppressants (thyroid nodules, thyroiditis, multinodular goiter, thyroid cancer), thyrotoxicosis, diagnostic suppression tests

Pregnancy Risk Factor A

Lactation Enters breast milk/compatible

Contraindications Hypersensitivity to beef or pork or any component of the formulation; recent myocardial infarction; thyrotoxicosis uncomplicated by hypothyroidism; uncorrected adrenal insufficiency

Warnings/Precautions [U.S. Boxed Warning]: Ineffective and potentially toxic for weight reduction. High doses may produce serious or even life-threatening toxic effects particularly when used with some anorectic drugs. Use with caution and reduce dosage in patients with angina pectoris or other cardiovascular disease and elderly since they may be more likely to have compromised cardiovascular function; chronic hypothyroidism predisposes patients to coronary artery disease. Use with caution in patients with adrenal insufficiency, diabetes mellitus or insipidus, and myxedema; symptoms may be exaggerated or aggravated. Desiccated thyroid contains variable amounts of T_3, T_4, and other triiodothyronine compounds which are more likely to cause cardiac signs or symptoms due to fluctuating levels. Should avoid use in the elderly for this reason. Many clinicians consider levothyroxine to be the drug of choice for thyroid replacement.

Adverse Reactions <1% (Limited to important or life-threatening): Alopecia, cardiac arrhythmia, chest pain, dyspnea, excessive bone loss with overtreatment (excess thyroid replacement), hand tremor, myalgia, palpitation, tachycardia, tremor

Drug Interactions

Increased Effect/Toxicity: Thyroid may potentiate the hypoprothrombinemic effect of oral anticoagulants. Tricyclic antidepressants (TAD) coadministered with thyroid hormone may increase potential for toxicity of both drugs.

Decreased Effect: Thyroid hormones increase the therapeutic need for oral hypoglycemics or insulin. Cholestyramine can bind thyroid and reduce its absorption. Phenytoin may decrease thyroxine serum levels. Thyroid hormone may decrease effect of oral sulfonylureas.

Mechanism of Action The primary active compound is T_3 (triiodothyronine), which may be converted from T_4 (thyroxine) and then circulates throughout the body to influence growth and maturation of various tissues; exact mechanism of action is unknown; however, it is believed the thyroid hormone exerts its many metabolic effects through control of DNA transcription and protein synthesis; involved in normal metabolism, growth, and development; promotes gluconeogenesis, increases utilization and mobilization of glycogen stores and stimulates protein synthesis, increases basal metabolic rate

Pharmacodynamics/Kinetics

Absorption: T_4: 48% to 79%; I_3: 95%; desiccated thyroid contains thyroxine, liothyronine, and iodine (primarily bound)

Metabolism: Thyroxine: Largely converted to liothyronine

Half-life elimination, serum: Liothyronine: 1-2 days; Thyroxine: 6-7 days

Dosage Oral:

Children: See table.

Recommended Pediatric Dosage for Congenital Hypothyroidism

Age	Daily Dose (mg)	Daily Dose/kg (mg)
0-6 mo	15-30	4.8-6
6-12 mo	30-45	3.6-4.8
1-5 y	45-60	3-3.6
6-12 y	60-90	2.4-3
>12 y	>90	1.2-1.8

Adults: Initial: 15-30 mg; increase with 15 mg increments every 2-4 weeks; use 15 mg in patients with cardiovascular disease or myxedema. Maintenance dose: Usually 60-120 mg/day; monitor TSH and clinical symptoms.

Thyroid cancer: Requires larger amounts than replacement therapy

Dietary Considerations Should be taken on an empty stomach.

Additional Information Equivalent doses: The following statement on relative potency of thyroid products is included in a joint statement by American Thyroid Association (ATA), American Association of Clinical Endocrinologists (AACE) and The Endocrine Society (TES): For purposes of conversion, levothyroxine sodium (T_4) 100 mcg is usually considered equivalent to desiccated thyroid 60 mg, thyroglobulin 60 mg, or liothyronine sodium (T_3) 25 mcg. However, these are rough guidelines only and do not obviate the careful re-evaluation of a patient when switching thyroid hormone preparations, including a change from one brand of levothyroxine to another. Joint position statement is available at http://www.thyroid.org/professionals/advocacy/04_12_08_thyroxine.html.

Dosage Forms

Tablet: 30 mg, 32.5 mg, 60 mg, 65 mg, 90 mg, 120 mg, 130 mg, 180 mg, 240 mg, 300 mg

Armour® Thyroid: 15 mg, 30 mg, 60 mg, 90 mg, 120 mg, 180 mg, 240 mg, 300 mg

Nature-Throid® NT, Westhroid®: 32.5 mg, 65 mg, 130 mg, 195 mg

♦ **Thyroid Extract** see Thyroid on page 1676
♦ **Thyroid USP** see Thyroid on page 1676
♦ **Thyrolar®** see Liotrix on page 1020
♦ **ThyroSafe™ [OTC]** see Potassium Iodide on page 1399
♦ **ThyroShield™ [OTC]** see Potassium Iodide on page 1399

Thyrotropin Alpha (thye roe TROH pin AL fa)

U.S. Brand Names Thyrogen®
Canadian Brand Names Thyrogen®
Index Terms Human Thyroid Stimulating Hormone; TSH
Pharmacologic Category Diagnostic Agent
Use As an adjunctive diagnostic tool for serum thyroglobulin (Tg) testing with or without radioiodine imaging in the follow-up of patients with well-differentiated thyroid cancer

(Continued)

Thyrotropin Alpha *(Continued)*

Potential clinical use:

1. Patients with an undetectable Tg on thyroid hormone suppressive therapy to exclude the diagnosis of residual or recurrent thyroid cancer
2. Patients requiring serum Tg testing and radioiodine imaging who are unwilling to undergo thyroid hormone withdrawal testing and whose treating physician believes that use of a less sensitive test is justified
3. Patients who are either unable to mount an adequate endogenous TSH response to thyroid hormone withdrawal or in whom withdrawal is medically contraindicated

Pregnancy Risk Factor C

Pregnancy Implications

No animal studies have been conducted. Effects on the fetus or pregnant woman are unknown.

Lactation

Excretion in breast milk unknown/use caution

Medication Safety Issues

Sound-alike/look-alike issues:

Thyrogen® may be confused with Thyrolar®

Contraindications Hypersensitivity to thyrotropin alpha or any component of the formulation

Warnings/Precautions For I.M. use only. Caution should be exercised when administered to patients who have been previously treated with bovine TSH and, in particular, to those patients who have experienced hypersensitivity reactions to bovine TSH. Thyrotropin will cause significant increases in thyroid hormone levels; use caution in patients with known history of heart disease and/or significant residual thyroid tissue. Safety and efficacy in children <16 years of age have not been established.

Considerations in the use of Thyrogen®:

1. There remains a meaningful risk of a diagnosis of thyroid cancer or of an underestimating the extent of disease when Thyrogen®-stimulated Tg testing is performed and in combination with radioiodine imaging
2. Thyrogen® Tg levels are generally lower than, and do not correlate with, Tg levels after thyroid hormone withdrawal
3. Newly detectable Tg level or a Tg level rising over time after Thyrogen® or a high index of suspicion of metastatic disease, even in the setting of a negative or low-stage Thyrogen® radioiodine scan, should prompt further evaluation such as thyroid hormone withdrawal to definitively establish the location and extent of thyroid cancer.
4. Decision to perform a Thyrogen® radioiodine scan in conjunction with a Thyrogen® serum Tg test and whether or when to withdraw a patient from thyroid hormones are complex. Pertinent factors in this decision include the sensitivity of the Tg assay used, the Thyrogen® Tg level obtained, and the index of suspicion of recurrent or persistent local or metastatic disease.
5. Thyrogen® is not recommended to stimulate radioiodine uptake for the purposes of ablative radiotherapy of thyroid cancer
6. The signs and symptoms of hypothyroidism which accompany thyroid hormone withdrawal are avoided with Thyrogen® use
7. May cause edema and/or hemorrhage at metastatic sites, leading to impingement of vital anatomic structures. Pretreatment with corticosteroids may be considered.

Adverse Reactions

>10 %: Gastrointestinal: Nausea (11%)

1% to 10%:

Central nervous system: Headache (7%), dizziness (2%), chills (1%), fever (1%)

Gastrointestinal: Vomiting (2%)

Neuromuscular & skeletal: Weakness (3%), paresthesia (2%)

Miscellaneous: Flu-like syndrome (1%)

Adverse reactions which may be related to local edema or hemorrhage at metastatic sites: Acute visual loss, enlargement of locally-recurring papillary carcinoma, laryngeal edema with respiratory distress, stridor

Postmarketing and/or case reports: Hypersensitivity reactions, hyperthyroidism, MI (case report; suspected hyperthyroidism)

Overdosage/Toxicology There has been no reported experience of overdose in humans. However, experience with higher than recommended doses and/or inadvertent I.V. administration suggest the following possible adverse reactions: Nausea, vomiting, diaphoresis, headache, hypotension, and tachycardia. Treatment is symptom-directed and supportive.

Stability Store intact vials at 2°C to 8°C (36°F to 46°F). Reconstitute each vial with 1.2 mL of sterile water for injection. Each vial should be reconstituted immediately prior to use with diluent provided. If necessary, the reconstituted solution can be stored for up to 24 hours at 2°C to 8°C. Protect from light.

Mechanism of Action A recombinant DNA source of human TSH that serves as an additional diagnostic tool in the follow-up of patients with a history of well-differentiated thyroid cancer. Binding of thyrotropin alpha to TSH receptors on normal thyroid epithelial cells or on well-differentiated thyroid cancer tissue stimulates iodine uptake and organification, and synthesis and secretion of thyroglobulin, triiodothyronine, and thyroxine. In thyroid cancer patients with near total thyroidectomy, thyrotropin is used to stimulate thyroglobulin from residual or remnant thyroid cancer tissue, which prevents the need for thyroid hormone therapy withdrawal.

Pharmacodynamics/Kinetics

Half-life elimination: 25 ± 10 hours

Time to peak: Median: 10 hours (range: 3-24 hours)

Dosage Children >16 years and Adults: I.M.: 0.9 mg every 24 hours for 2 doses or every 72 hours for 3 doses

For radioiodine imaging, radioiodine administration should be given 24 hours following the final Thyrogen® injection. Scanning should be performed 48 hours after radioiodine administration (72 hours after the final injection of Thyrogen®).

For serum testing, serum Tg should be obtained 72 hours after final injection of Thyrogen®.

Administration After reconstitution with 1.2 mL sterile water for injection, 1 mL of the resulting solution (0.9 mg/mL) should be administered into the buttock.

Dosage Forms Injection, powder for reconstitution: Four-vial kit: 1.1 mg [supplied as two vials of Thyrogen® and two 10 mL vials of SWFI]

♦ **L-Thyroxine Sodium** *see* Levothyroxine *on page 1007*
♦ **Tiabendazole** *see* Thiabendazole *on page 1667*

Tiagabine (tye AG a been)

U.S. Brand Names Gabitril®
Canadian Brand Names Gabitril®
Index Terms Tiagabine Hydrochloride
Pharmacologic Category Anticonvulsant, Miscellaneous
Additional Appendix Information
  Anticonvulsants by Seizure Type *on page 1865*
  Epilepsy *on page 2048*
Use Adjunctive therapy in adults and children ≥12 years of age in the treatment of partial seizures
Pregnancy Risk Factor C
Lactation Enters breast milk/not recommended
Medication Safety Issues
  Sound-alike/look-alike issues:
  Tiagabine may be confused with tizanidine
Contraindications Hypersensitivity to tiagabine or any component of the formulation
Warnings/Precautions New-onset seizures and status epilepticus have been associated with tiagabine use when taken for unlabeled indications. Often these seizures have occurred shortly after the initiation of treatment or shortly after a dosage increase. Seizures have also occurred with very low doses or after several months of therapy. In most cases, patients were using concomitant medications (eg, antidepressants, antipsychotics, stimulants, narcotics). In these instances, the discontinuation of tiagabine, followed by an evaluation for an underlying seizure disorder, is suggested. Use for unapproved indications, however, has not been proven to be safe or effective and is not recommended. When tiagabine is used as an adjunct in partial seizures (an FDA-approved indication), it should not be abruptly discontinued because of the possibility of increasing seizure frequency, unless safety concerns require a more rapid withdrawal. Rarely, nonconvulsive status epilepticus has been reported following abrupt discontinuation or dosage reduction.

Use with caution in patients with hepatic impairment. Experience in patients not receiving enzyme-inducing drugs has been limited; caution should be used in treating any patient who is not receiving one of these medications (decreased dose and slower titration may be required). Weakness, sedation, and confusion may occur with tiagabine use. Patients must be cautioned about performing tasks which require mental alertness (eg, operating machinery or driving). Effects with other sedative drugs or ethanol may be potentiated. Animal studies suggest that tiagabine may bind to retina and uvea; however, no treatment-related ophthalmoscopic changes were seen long-term; periodic monitoring may be considered. May cause serious rash, including Stevens-Johnson syndrome. Safety and efficacy have not been established in children <12 years of age.

Adverse Reactions
  >10%:
    Central nervous system: Concentration decreased, dizziness, nervousness, somnolence
    Gastrointestinal: Nausea
    Neuromuscular & skeletal: Weakness, tremor
  1% to 10%:
    Cardiovascular: Chest pain, edema, hypertension, palpitation, peripheral edema, syncope, tachycardia, vasodilation
    Central nervous system: Agitation, ataxia, chills, confusion, difficulty with memory, confusion, depersonalization, depression, euphoria, hallucination, hostility, insomnia, malaise, migraine, paranoid reaction, personality disorder, speech disorder
    Dermatologic: Alopecia, bruising, dry skin, pruritus, rash
    Gastrointestinal: Abdominal pain, diarrhea, gingivitis, increased appetite, mouth ulceration, stomatitis, vomiting, weight gain/loss
    Neuromuscular & skeletal: Abnormal gait, arthralgia, dysarthria, hyper-/hypokinesia, hyper-/hypotonia, myasthenia, myalgia, myoclonus, neck pain, paresthesia, reflexes decreased, stupor, twitching, vertigo
    Ocular: Abnormal vision, amblyopia, nystagmus
    Otic: Ear pain, hearing impairment, otitis media, tinnitus
    Respiratory: Bronchitis, cough, dyspnea, epistaxis, pneumonia
    Miscellaneous: Allergic reaction, cyst, diaphoresis, flu-like syndrome, lymphadenopathy
  <1% (Limited to important or life-threatening): Abortion, abscess, anemia, angina, apnea, asthma, blepharitis, blindness, cellulitis, cerebral ischemia, cholelithiasis, CNS neoplasm, coma, deafness, dehydration, dysphagia, dystonia, electrocardiogram abnormal, encephalopathy, hemorrhage, erythrocytes abnormal, leukopenia, fecal incontinence, herpes simplex/zoster, glossitis, goiter, hematuria, hemoptysis, hepatomegaly, hypercholesteremia, hyper-/hypoglycemia, hyperlipemia, hypokalemia, hyponatremia, hypotension, hypothyroidism, impotence, kidney failure, liver function tests abnormal, MI, neoplasm, peripheral vascular disorder, paralysis, photophobia, psychosis, petechia, photosensitivity, seizure (when used for unlabeled uses), sepsis, spasm, suicide attempt, thrombocytopenia, thrombophlebitis, urinary retention, urinary urgency, urticaria, visual field defect

Drug Interactions
  Cytochrome P450 Effect: Substrate of 3A4 (major)
  Increased Effect/Toxicity: Sedative effects may be additive with other CNS depressants. CYP3A4 inhibitors may increase the levels/effects of tiagabine; example inhibitors include azole antifungals, clarithromycin, diclofenac, doxycycline, erythromycin, imatinib, isoniazid,
  (Continued)

Tiagabine *(Continued)*

nefazodone, nicardipine, propofol, protease inhibitors, quinidine, telithromycin, and verap-amil. Valproate increased free tiagabine concentrations (*in vitro*) by 40%.

Decreased Effect: CYP3A4 inducers may decrease the levels/effects of tiagabine; example inducers include aminoglutethimide, carbamazepine, nafcillin, nevirapine, phenobarbital, phenytoin, and rifamycins.

Ethanol/Nutrition/Herb Interactions

Ethanol: Avoid ethanol (may increase CNS depression).

Food: Food reduces the rate but not the extent of absorption.

Herb/Nutraceutical: St John's wort may decrease tiagabine levels. Avoid valerian, St John's wort, kava kava, gotu kola (may increase CNS depression).

Mechanism of Action The exact mechanism by which tiagabine exerts antiseizure activity is not definitively known; however, *in vitro* experiments demonstrate that it enhances the activity of gamma aminobutyric acid (GABA), the major neuroinhibitory transmitter in the nervous system; it is thought that binding to the GABA uptake carrier inhibits the uptake of GABA into presynaptic neurons, allowing an increased amount of GABA to be available to postsynaptic neurons; based on *in vitro* studies, tiagabine does not inhibit the uptake of dopamine, norepinephrine, serotonin, glutamate, or choline

Pharmacodynamics/Kinetics

Absorption: Rapid (45 minutes); prolonged with food

Protein binding: 96%, primarily to albumin and α_1-acid glycoprotein

Metabolism: Hepatic via CYP (primarily 3A4)

Bioavailability: Oral: Absolute: 90%

Half-life elimination: 2-5 hours when administered with enzyme inducers; 7-9 hours when administered without enzyme inducers

Time to peak, plasma: 45 minutes

Excretion: Feces (63%); urine (25%); 2% as unchanged drug; primarily as metabolites

Dosage Oral (administer with food):

Patients receiving enzyme-inducing AED regimens:

Children 12-18 years: 4 mg once daily for 1 week; may increase to 8 mg daily in 2 divided doses for 1 week; then may increase by 4-8 mg weekly to response or up to 32 mg daily in 2-4 divided doses

Adults: 4 mg once daily for 1 week; may increase by 4-8 mg weekly to response or up to 56 mg daily in 2-4 divided doses; usual maintenance: 32-56 mg/day

Patients **not** receiving enzyme-inducing AED regimens: The estimated plasma concentra-tions of tiagabine in patients not taking enzyme-inducing medications is twice that of patients receiving enzyme-inducing AEDs. Lower doses are required; slower titration may be necessary.

Dietary Considerations Take with food.

Monitoring Parameters A reduction in seizure frequency is indicative of therapeutic response to tiagabine in patients with partial seizures; complete blood counts, renal function tests, liver function tests, and routine blood chemistry should be monitored periodically during therapy

Reference Range Maximal plasma level after a 24 mg/dose: 552 ng/mL

Dosage Forms

Tablet, as hydrochloride:

Gabitril®: 2 mg, 4 mg, 12 mg, 16 mg

- ♦ **Tiagabine Hydrochloride** *see* Tiagabine *on page 1679*
- ♦ **Tiamol® (Can)** *see* Fluocinonide *on page 721*
- ♦ **Tiazac®** *see* Diltiazem *on page 509*
- ♦ **Tiazac® XC (Can)** *see* Diltiazem *on page 509*
- ♦ **Ticar®** *see* Ticarcillin *on page 1680*

Ticarcillin *(tye kar SIL in)*

U.S. Brand Names Ticar®

Index Terms Ticarcillin Disodium

Pharmacologic Category Antibiotic, Penicillin

Additional Appendix Information

Antimicrobial Drugs of Choice *on page 1981*

Use Treatment of susceptible infections such as septicemia, acute and chronic respiratory tract infections, skin and soft tissue infections, and urinary tract infections due to susceptible strains of *Pseudomonas*, and other gram-negative bacteria

Pregnancy Risk Factor B

Lactation Enters breast milk/compatible

Medication Safety Issues

Sound-alike/look-alike issues:

Ticar® may be confused with Tigan®

Contraindications Hypersensitivity to ticarcillin, any component of the formulation, or penicil-lins

Warnings/Precautions Due to sodium load and adverse effects (anemia, neuropsychological changes), use with caution and modify dosage in patients with renal impairment; serious and occasionally severe or fatal hypersensitivity (anaphylactoid) reactions have been reported in patients on penicillin therapy (especially with a history of beta-lactam hypersensitivity and/or a history of sensitivity to multiple allergens); use with caution in patients with seizures

Adverse Reactions Frequency not defined.

Central nervous system: Confusion, convulsions, drowsiness, fever, Jarisch-Herxheimer reaction

Dermatologic: Rash

Endocrine & metabolic: Electrolyte imbalance

Gastrointestinal: *Clostridium difficile* colitis

Hematologic: Bleeding, eosinophilia, hemolytic anemia, leukopenia, neutropenia, positive Coombs' reaction, thrombocytopenia

Hepatic: Hepatotoxicity, jaundice

Local: Thrombophlebitis

Neuromuscular & skeletal: Myoclonus

Renal: Interstitial nephritis (acute)

Miscellaneous: Anaphylaxis, hypersensitivity reactions

Overdosage/Toxicology Symptoms of penicillin overdose include neuromuscular hypersensitivity (agitation, hallucinations, asterixis, encephalopathy, confusion, and seizures) and electrolyte imbalance (with potassium or sodium salts), especially in renal failure. Hemodialysis may be helpful to aid in the removal of the drug from the blood, otherwise most treatment is supportive or symptom-directed.

Drug Interactions

Increased Effect/Toxicity: Probenecid may increase penicillin levels. Neuromuscular blockers may have an increased duration of action (neuromuscular blockade). Penicillins may increase the exposure to methotrexate during concurrent therapy; monitor.

Decreased Effect: Tetracyclines may decrease penicillin effectiveness. Aminoglycosides may cause physical inactivation of aminoglycosides in the presence of high concentrations of ticarcillin and potential toxicity in patients with mild-moderate renal dysfunction. Although anecdotal reports suggest oral contraceptive efficacy could be reduced by penicillins, this has been refuted by more rigorous scientific and clinical data.

Stability Reconstituted solution is stable for 72 hours at room temperature and 14 days when refrigerated. For I.V. infusion in NS or D_5W, solution is stable for 72 hours at room temperature, 14 days when refrigerated, or 30 days when frozen. After freezing, thawed solution is stable for 72 hours at room temperature or 14 days when refrigerated.

Mechanism of Action Inhibits bacterial cell wall synthesis by binding to one or more of the penicillin binding proteins (PBPs); which in turn inhibits the final transpeptidation step of peptidoglycan synthesis in bacterial cell walls, thus inhibiting cell wall biosynthesis. Bacteria eventually lyse due to ongoing activity of cell wall autolytic enzymes (autolysins and murein hydrolases) while cell wall assembly is arrested.

Pharmacodynamics/Kinetics

Absorption: I.M.: 86%

Distribution: Blister fluid, lymph tissue, and gallbladder; low concentrations into CSF increasing with inflamed meninges, otherwise widely distributed; crosses placenta; enters breast milk (low concentrations)

Protein binding: 45% to 65%

Half-life elimination:

Neonates: <1 week old: 3.5-5.6 hours; 1-8 weeks old: 1.3-2.2 hours

Children 5-13 years: 0.9 hour

Adults: 66-72 minutes; prolonged with renal and/or hepatic impairment

Time to peak, serum: I.M.: 30-75 minutes

Excretion: Almost entirely urine (as unchanged drug and metabolites); feces (3.5%)

Dosage Note: Ticarcillin is generally given I.V., I.M. injection is only for the treatment of uncomplicated urinary tract infections and dose should not exceed 2 g/injection when administered I.M.

Usual dosage range:

Neonates: I.M., I.V.:

Postnatal age <7 days:

<2000 g: 75 mg/kg/dose every 12 hours

>2000 g: 75 mg/kg/dose every 8 hours

Postnatal age >7 days:

<1200 g: 75 mg/kg/dose every 12 hours

1200-2000 g: 75 mg/kg/dose every 8 hours

>2000 g: 75 mg/kg/dose every 6 hours

Infants and Children:

I.M.: 50-100 mg/kg/day in divided doses every 6-8 hours

I.V.: 50-300 mg/kg/day in divided doses every 4-8 hours (maximum dose: 24 g/day)

Adults: I.M., I.V.: 1-4 g every 4-6 hours

Indication-specific dosing:

Infants and Children:

Cystic fibrosis (acute pulmonary exacerbations): I.V.: 100 mg/kg every 6 hours

Systemic infection: I.V.: 200-300 mg/kg/day in divided doses every 4-6 hours

Urinary tract infections: I.M., I.V.: 50-100 mg/kg/day in divided doses every 6-8 hours

Adults:

Otitis externa (malignant): I.V.: 3 g every 4 hours with tobramycin

***Pseudomonas* infections:** I.V.: 3 g every 4 hours

Dosing adjustment in renal impairment: Adults:

Cl_{cr} 30-60 mL/minute: 2 g every 4 hours or 3 g every 8 hours

Cl_{cr} 10-30 mL/minute: 2 g every 8 hours or 3 g every 12 hours

Cl_{cr} <10 mL/minute: 2 g every 12 hours

Moderately dialyzable (20% to 50%)

Continuous arteriovenous or venovenous hemodiafiltration effects: Dose as for Cl_{cr} 10-50 mL/minute

Dietary Considerations Sodium content of 1 g: 119.6-149.5 mg (5.2-6.5 mEq)

Administration Intermittent infusion, over 30 minutes to 2 hours. Too rapid of infusion may cause seizures.

Some penicillins (eg, carbenicillin, ticarcillin and piperacillin) have been shown to inactivate aminoglycosides *in vitro*. This has been observed to a greater extent with tobramycin and gentamicin, while amikacin has shown greater stability against inactivation. Concurrent use of these agents may pose a risk of reduced antibacterial efficacy *in vivo*, particularly in the setting of profound renal impairment. However, definitive clinical evidence is lacking. If combination penicillin/aminoglycoside therapy is desired in a patient with renal dysfunction, separation of doses (if feasible), and routine monitoring of aminoglycoside levels, CBC, and clinical response should be considered.

(Continued)

Ticarcillin *(Continued)*

Monitoring Parameters Serum electrolytes, bleeding time, and periodic tests of renal, hepatic, and hematologic function; monitor for signs of anaphylaxis during first dose

Test Interactions May interfere with urinary glucose tests using cupric sulfate (Benedict's solution, Clinitest®); false-positive urinary or serum protein, positive Coombs' test

Some penicillin derivatives may accelerate the degradation of aminoglycosides *in vitro*, leading to a potential underestimation of aminoglycoside serum concentration.

Dosage Forms Injection, powder for reconstitution, as disodium: 3 g

---

Ticarcillin and Clavulanate Potassium
(tye kar SIL in & klav yoo LAN ate poe TASS ee um)

U.S. Brand Names Timentin®

Canadian Brand Names Timentin®

Index Terms Ticarcillin and Clavulanic Acid

Pharmacologic Category Antibiotic, Penicillin

Additional Appendix Information
Antimicrobial Drugs of Choice *on page 1981*

Use Treatment of infections of lower respiratory tract, urinary tract, skin and skin structures, bone and joint, and septicemia caused by susceptible organisms. Clavulanate expands activity of ticarcillin to include beta-lactamase producing strains of *S. aureus*, *H. influenzae*, *Bacteroides* species, and some other gram-negative bacilli

Pregnancy Risk Factor B

Lactation Enters breast milk (other penicillins are compatible with breast-feeding)

Contraindications Hypersensitivity to ticarcillin, clavulanate, any penicillin, or any component of the formulation

Warnings/Precautions Not approved for use in children <12 years of age; use with caution and modify dosage in patients with renal impairment; use with caution in patients with a history of allergy to cephalosporins and in patients with CHF due to high sodium load

Adverse Reactions Frequency not defined.

Central nervous system: Confusion, convulsions, drowsiness, fever, Jarisch-Herxheimer reaction

Dermatologic: Rash, erythema multiforme, toxic epidermal necrolysis, Stevens-Johnson syndrome

Endocrine & metabolic: Electrolyte imbalance

Gastrointestinal: *Clostridium difficile* colitis

Hematologic: Bleeding, hemolytic anemia, leukopenia, neutropenia, positive Coombs' reaction, thrombocytopenia

Hepatic: Hepatotoxicity, jaundice

Local: Thrombophlebitis

Neuromuscular & skeletal: Myoclonus

Renal: Interstitial nephritis (acute)

Miscellaneous: Anaphylaxis, hypersensitivity reactions

Overdosage/Toxicology Symptoms include neuromuscular hypersensitivity and seizures. Many beta-lactam containing antibiotics have the potential to cause neuromuscular hyperirritability or convulsive seizures. Hemodialysis may be helpful to aid in removal of the drug from the blood, otherwise most treatment is supportive or symptom-directed.

Drug Interactions

Increased Effect/Toxicity: Probenecid may increase penicillin levels. Neuromuscular blockers may have an increased duration of action (neuromuscular blockade). Penicillins may increase the exposure to methotrexate during concurrent therapy; monitor.

Decreased Effect: Tetracyclines may decrease penicillin effectiveness. Aminoglycosides may cause physical inactivation of aminoglycosides in the presence of high concentrations of ticarcillin and potential toxicity in patients with mild-moderate renal dysfunction. Although anecdotal reports suggest oral contraceptive efficacy could be reduced by penicillins, this has been refuted by more rigorous scientific and clinical data.

Stability Reconstituted solution is stable for 6 hours at room temperature and 72 hours when refrigerated. I.V. infusion in NS or LR is stable for 24 hours at room temperature, 7 days when refrigerated, or 30 days when frozen. I.V. infusion in D_5W solution is stable for 24 hours at room temperature, 3 days when refrigerated, or 7 days when frozen. After freezing, thawed solution is stable for 8 hours at room temperature. Darkening of drug indicates loss of potency of clavulanate potassium.

Mechanism of Action Inhibits bacterial cell wall synthesis by binding to one or more of the penicillin binding proteins (PBPs); which in turn inhibits the final transpeptidation step of peptidoglycan synthesis in bacterial cell walls, thus inhibiting cell wall biosynthesis. Bacteria eventually lyse due to ongoing activity of cell wall autolytic enzymes (autolysins and murein hydrolases) while cell wall assembly is arrested.

Pharmacodynamics/Kinetics

Ticarcillin: See Ticarcillin monograph.

Clavulanic acid:

Protein binding: 9% to 30%

Metabolism: Hepatic

Half-life elimination: 66-90 minutes

Excretion: Urine (45% as unchanged drug)

Clearance: Does not affect clearance of ticarcillin

Dosage

Usual dosage range:

Children and Adults <60 kg: I.V.: 75-300 mg of ticarcillin component/kg/day in divided doses every 4-6 hours

Children ≥60 kg and Adults: I.V.: 3.1 g (ticarcillin 3 g plus clavulanic acid 0.1 g) every 4-6 hours (maximum: 24 g/day)

Indication-specific dosing:

Children: I.V.:

Bite wounds (animal): 200 mg/kg/day in divided doses

Neutropenic fever: 75 mg/kg every 6 hours (maximum 3.1 g)

Pneumonia (nosocomial): 300 mg/kg/day in 4 divided doses (maximum: 18-24 g/day)

Children ≥60 kg and Adults: I.V.:

Amnionitis, cholangitis, diverticulitis, endometritis, epididymo-orchitis, mastoiditis, orbital cellulitis, peritonitis, pneumonia (aspiration): 3.1 g every 6 hours

Liver abscess, parafascial space infections, septic thrombophlebitis: 3.1 g every 4 hours

***Pseudomonas* infections:** 3.1 g every 4 hours

Urinary tract infections: 3.1 g every 6-8 hours

Dosing adjustment in renal impairment:

Cl_{cr} 30-60 mL/minute: Administer 2 g every 4 hours or 3.1 g every 8 hours

Cl_{cr} 10-30 mL/minute: Administer 2 g every 8 hours or 3.1 g every 12 hours

Cl_{cr} <10 mL/minute: Administer 2 g every 12 hours

Moderately dialyzable (20% to 50%)

Continuous arteriovenous or venovenous hemodiafiltration effects: Dose as for Cl_{cr} 10-50 mL/minute

Peritoneal dialysis: 3.1 g every 12 hours

Hemodialysis: 2 g every 12 hours; supplemented with 3.1 g after each dialysis

Dosing adjustment in hepatic dysfunction: Cl_{cr} <10 mL/minute: 2 g every 24 hours

Dietary Considerations Sodium content of 1 g: 4.51 mEq; potassium content of 1 g: 0.15 mEq

Administration Infuse over 30 minutes.

Some penicillins (eg, carbenicillin, ticarcillin and piperacillin) have been shown to inactivate aminoglycosides *in vitro*. This has been observed to a greater extent with tobramycin and gentamicin, while amikacin has shown greater stability against inactivation. Concurrent use of these agents may pose a risk of reduced antibacterial efficacy *in vivo*, particularly in the setting of profound renal impairment. However, definitive clinical evidence is lacking. If combination penicillin/aminoglycoside therapy is desired in a patient with renal dysfunction, separation of doses (if feasible), and routine monitoring of aminoglycoside levels, CBC, and clinical response should be considered.

Monitoring Parameters Observe for signs and symptoms of anaphylaxis during first dose.

Test Interactions Positive Coombs' test, false-positive urinary proteins

Some penicillin derivatives may accelerate the degradation of aminoglycosides *in vitro*, leading to a potential underestimation of aminoglycoside serum concentration.

Dosage Forms

Infusion [premixed, frozen]: Ticarcillin 3 g and clavulanic acid 0.1 g (100 mL) [contains sodium 4.51 mEq and potassium 0.15 mEq per g]

Injection, powder for reconstitution: Ticarcillin 3 g and clavulanic acid 0.1 g (3.1 g, 31 g) [contains sodium 4.51 mEq and potassium 0.15 mEq per g]

♦ **Ticarcillin and Clavulanic Acid** *see* Ticarcillin and Clavulanate Potassium *on page 1682*

♦ **Ticarcillin Disodium** *see* Ticarcillin *on page 1680*

♦ **TICE® BCG** *see* BCG Vaccine *on page 197*

♦ **Ticlid®** *see* Ticlopidine *on page 1683*

Ticlopidine (tye KLOE pi deen)

U.S. Brand Names Ticlid®

Canadian Brand Names Alti-Ticlopidine; Apo-Ticlopidine®; Gen-Ticlopidine; Novo-Ticlopidine; Nu-Ticlopidine; Rhoxal-ticlopidine; Sandoz-Ticlopidine; Ticlid®

Index Terms Ticlopidine Hydrochloride

Pharmacologic Category Antiplatelet Agent

Use Platelet aggregation inhibitor that reduces the risk of thrombotic stroke in patients who have had a stroke or stroke precursors. **Note:** Due to its association with life-threatening hematologic disorders, ticlopidine should be reserved for patients who are intolerant to aspirin, or who have failed aspirin therapy. Adjunctive therapy (with aspirin) following successful coronary stent implantation to reduce the incidence of subacute stent thrombosis.

Unlabeled/Investigational Use Protection of aortocoronary bypass grafts, diabetic microangiopathy, ischemic heart disease, prevention of postoperative DVT, reduction of graft loss following renal transplant

Pregnancy Risk Factor B

Lactation Excretion in breast milk unknown

Contraindications Hypersensitivity to ticlopidine or any component of the formulation; active pathological bleeding such as PUD or intracranial hemorrhage; severe liver dysfunction; hematopoietic disorders (neutropenia, thrombocytopenia, a past history of TTP)

Warnings/Precautions Use with caution in patients who may be at risk of increased bleeding. Consider discontinuing 10-14 days before elective surgery. Use caution in mixing with other antiplatelet drugs. Use with caution in patients with severe liver disease (experience is limited). **[U.S. Boxed Warning]: May cause life-threatening hematologic reactions, including neutropenia, agranulocytosis, thrombotic thrombocytopenia purpura (TTP), and aplastic anemia.** Routine monitoring is required (see Monitoring Parameters). Monitor for signs and symptoms of neutropenia including WBC count. Discontinue if the absolute neutrophil count falls to <1200/mm³ or if the platelet count falls to <80,000/mm³.

Adverse Reactions As with all drugs which may affect hemostasis, bleeding is associated with ticlopidine. Hemorrhage may occur at virtually any site. Risk is dependent on multiple variables, including the use of multiple agents which alter hemostasis and patient susceptibility.

(Continued)

Ticlopidine *(Continued)*

>10%:

Endocrine & metabolic: Increased total cholesterol (increases of ~8% to 10% within 1 month of therapy)

Gastrointestinal: Diarrhea (13%)

1% to 10%: Central nervous system: Dizziness (1%)

Dermatological: Rash (5%), purpura (2%), pruritus (1%)

Gastrointestinal: Nausea (7%), dyspepsia (7%), gastrointestinal pain (4%), vomiting (2%), flatulence (2%), anorexia (1%)

Hematologic: Neutropenia (2%)

Hepatic: Abnormal liver function test (1%)

<1% (Limited to important or life-threatening): Agranulocytosis, anaphylaxis, angioedema, aplastic anemia, arthropathy, bone marrow suppression, bronchiolitis obliterans-organized pneumonia, chronic diarrhea, conjunctival bleeding, eosinophilia, erythema multiforme, erythema nodosum, exfoliative dermatitis, gastrointestinal bleeding, hematuria, hemolytic anemia, hepatic necrosis, hepatitis, hyponatremia, intracranial bleeding (rare), jaundice, maculopapular rash, menorrhagia, myositis, nephrotic syndrome, pancytopenia, peptic ulcer, peripheral neuropathy, pneumonitis (allergic), positive ANA, renal failure, sepsis, serum creatinine increased, serum sickness, Stevens-Johnson syndrome, systemic lupus erythematosus, thrombocytopenia (immune), thrombocytosis, thrombotic thrombocytopenic purpura, urticaria, vasculitis

Overdosage/Toxicology Symptoms include ataxia, seizures, vomiting, abdominal pain, and hematologic abnormalities. Specific treatments are lacking; after decontamination. Treatment is symptomatic and supportive.

Drug Interactions

Cytochrome P450 Effect: Substrate of CYP3A4 (major); **Inhibits** CYP1A2 (weak), 2C9 (weak), 2C19 (strong), 2D6 (moderate), 2E1 (weak), 3A4 (weak)

Increased Effect/Toxicity: Ticlopidine may increase effect/toxicity of aspirin, anticoagulants, theophylline, and NSAIDs. Cimetidine may increase ticlopidine blood levels. Ticlopidine may increase the levels/effects of amphetamines, selected beta-blockers, citalopram, dextromethorphan, diazepam, fluoxetine, lidocaine, methsuximide, mirtazapine, nefazodone, paroxetine, phenytoin, sertraline, risperidone, ritonavir, thioridazine, tricyclic antidepressants, venlafaxine, and other CYP2C19 or 2D6 substrates.

Decreased Effect: Decreased effect of ticlopidine with antacids (decreased absorption). Ticlopidine may decrease the effect of digoxin or cyclosporine. The levels/effects of ticlopidine may be decreased by aminoglutethimide, carbamazepine, nafcillin, nevirapine, phenobarbital, phenytoin, rifamycins, and other CYP3A4 inducers. Ticlopidine may decrease the levels/effects of CYP2D6 prodrug substrates (eg, codeine, hydrocodone, oxycodone, tramadol).

Ethanol/Nutrition/Herb Interactions

Food: Ticlopidine bioavailability may be increased (20%) if taken with food. High-fat meals increase absorption, antacids decrease absorption.

Herb/Nutraceutical: Avoid cat's claw, dong quai, evening primrose, feverfew, garlic, ginkgo, ginger, red clover, horse chestnut, green tea, ginseng (all have additional antiplatelet activity).

Mechanism of Action Ticlopidine is an inhibitor of platelet function with a mechanism which is different from other antiplatelet drugs. The drug significantly increases bleeding time. This effect may not be solely related to ticlopidine's effect on platelets. The prolongation of the bleeding time caused by ticlopidine is further increased by the addition of aspirin in *ex vivo* experiments. Although many metabolites of ticlopidine have been found, none have been shown to account for *in vivo* activity.

Pharmacodynamics/Kinetics

Onset of action: ~6 hours

Peak effect: 3-5 days; serum levels do not correlate with clinical antiplatelet activity

Metabolism: Extensively hepatic; has at least one active metabolite

Half-life elimination: 24 hours

Dosage Oral: Adults:

Stroke prevention: 250 mg twice daily with food

Coronary artery stenting (initiate after successful implantation): 250 mg twice daily with food (in combination with antiplatelet doses of aspirin) for up to 30 days

Dietary Considerations Should be taken with food to reduce stomach upset.

Administration Oral: Administer with food.

Monitoring Parameters Signs of bleeding; CBC with differential every 2 weeks starting the second week through the third month of treatment; more frequent monitoring is recommended for patients whose absolute neutrophil counts have been consistently declining or are 30% less than baseline values. The peak incidence of TTP occurs between 3-4 weeks, the peak incidence of neutropenia occurs at approximately 4-6 weeks, and the incidence of aplastic anemia peaks after 4-8 weeks of therapy. Few cases have been reported after 3 months of treatment. Liver function tests (alkaline phosphatase and transaminases) should be performed in the first 4 months of therapy if liver dysfunction is suspected.

Test Interactions Increased cholesterol (S), increased alkaline phosphatase, increased transaminases (S)

Dosage Forms Tablet, as hydrochloride: 250 mg

♦ **Ticlopidine Hydrochloride** *see* Ticlopidine *on page 1683*

♦ **TIG** *see* Tetanus Immune Globulin (Human) *on page 1656*

♦ **Tigan**® *see* Trimethobenzamide *on page 1743*

Tigecycline (tye ge SYE kleen)

U.S. Brand Names Tygacil™
Index Terms GAR-936
Pharmacologic Category Antibiotic, Glycylcycline
Use Treatment of complicated skin and skin structure infections caused by susceptible organisms, including methicillin-resistant *Staphylococcus aureus* and vancomycin-sensitive *Enterococcus faecalis*; treatment of complicated intra-abdominal infections
Pregnancy Risk Factor D
Pregnancy Implications Tigecycline has been shown to cross the placenta in animal studies. Decreased fetal weight, minor skeletal abnormalities, and increased fetal loss were observed. There are no adequate and well-controlled studies in pregnant women. Due to structural similarity to tetracyclines, permanent discoloration of the teeth (brown-gray) may occur if used during tooth development (fetal stage through children up to 8 years of age). Should only be used in pregnancy if the potential benefit to the mother justifies risk to the fetus.
Lactation
Excretion in breast milk unknown/use caution
Contraindications Hypersensitivity to tigecycline or any component of the formulation
Warnings/Precautions Due to structural similarity with tetracyclines, use caution in patients with prior hypersensitivity and/or severe adverse reactions associated with tetracycline use. Due to structural similarities with tetracyclines, may be associated with photosensitivity, pseudotumor cerebri, pancreatitis, and antianabolic effects (including increased BUN, azotemia, acidosis, and hyperphosphatemia) observed with this class. May cause fetal harm if used during pregnancy; patients should be advised of potential risks associated with use. Permanent discoloration of the teeth may occur if used during tooth development (fetal stage through children up to 8 years of age). Use caution in hepatic impairment; dosage adjustment may be required with severe impairment.

Prolonged use may result in superinfection, including pseudomembranous colitis. Use with caution if using as monotherapy for patients with intestinal perforation (in the small sample of available cases, septic shock occurred more frequently than patients treated with imipenem/cilastatin comparator). Safety and efficacy in children <18 years of age have not been established.
Adverse Reactions Note: Frequencies relative to placebo are not available; some frequencies are lower than those experienced with comparator drugs.
>10%: Gastrointestinal: Nausea (25% to 30%; severe in 1%), vomiting (20%; severe in 1%), diarrhea (13%)
2% to 10%:
  Cardiovascular: Hypertension (5%), peripheral edema (3%), hypotension (2%), phlebitis (2%)
  Central nervous system: Fever (7%), headache (6%), dizziness (4%), pain (4%), insomnia (2%)
  Dermatologic: Pruritus (3%), rash (2%)
  Endocrine & metabolic: Hypoproteinemia (5%), hyperglycemia (2%), hypokalemia (2%)
  Gastrointestinal: Abdominal pain (7%), constipation (3%), dyspepsia (3%)
  Hematologic: Thrombocythemia (6%), anemia (4%), leukocytosis (4%)
  Hepatic: SGPT increased (6%), SGOT increased (4%), alkaline phosphatase increased (4%), amylase increased (3%), bilirubin increased (2%), LDH increased (4%)
  Local: Reaction to procedure (9%)
  Neuromuscular & skeletal: Weakness (3%)
  Renal: BUN increased (2%)
  Respiratory: Cough increased (4%), dyspnea (3%), pulmonary physical finding (2%)
  Miscellaneous: Abnormal healing (4%), infection (8%), abscess (3%), diaphoresis increased (2%)
<2% or postmarketing (Limited to important or life-threatening): Allergic reaction, bradycardia, creatinine increased, eosinophilia, injection site reaction, INR increased, jaundice, pancreatitis (acute), septic shock, taste perversion
Overdosage/Toxicology No specific experience in overdose. May experience increased nausea/vomiting. Not significantly removed by hemodialysis.
Drug Interactions
  Increased Effect/Toxicity: Retinoic acid derivatives may increase risk of pseudotumor cerebri (reported with tetracyclines). Hypoprothrombinemic response of warfarin may be increased with tigecycline; monitor INR closely during initiation or discontinuation.
  Decreased Effect: Anecdotal reports of oral contraceptives suggesting decreased contraceptive efficacy with tetracyclines have been refuted by more rigorous scientific and clinical data.
Stability Store at 20°C to 25°C prior to reconstitution; excursions permitted to 15°C to 30°C. Add 5.3 mL NS or D_5W to each 50 mg vial. Swirl gently to dissolve. Resulting solution is 10 mg/mL. Reconstituted solution must be immediately transferred (and further diluted) to allow I.V. administration. Transfer immediately to 100 mL I.V. bag for infusion (final concentration should not exceed 1 mg/mL). Following dilution, may be stored at room temperature for up to 6 hours, or up to 24 hours under refrigeration. Reconstituted solution is red-orange.
Mechanism of Action Binds to the 30S ribosomal subunit of susceptible bacteria, inhibiting protein synthesis.
Pharmacodynamics/Kinetics Note: Systemic clearance is reduced by 55% and half-life increased by 43% in moderate hepatic impairment.
Distribution: V_d: 7-9 L/kg; extensive tissue distribution
Protein binding: 71% to 89%
Metabolism: Hepatic, via glucuronidation, N-acetylation, and epimerization to several metabolites, each <10% of the dose
Half-life elimination: Single dose: 27 hours; following multiple doses: 42 hours
Excretion: Urine (33%; with 22% as unchanged drug); feces (59%; primarily as unchanged drug)
(Continued)

Tigecycline *(Continued)*

Dosage I.V.: Adults:

Initial: 100 mg as a single dose

Maintenance dose: 50 mg every 12 hours

Recommended duration of therapy: Intra-abdominal infections or complicated skin/skin structure infections: 5-14 days.

Dosage adjustment in renal impairment: No dosage adjustment required

Dosage adjustment in hepatic impairment:

Mild-to-moderate hepatic disease: No dosage adjustment required

Severe hepatic impairment (Child-Pugh class C): Initial dose of 100 mg should be followed
with 25 mg every 12 hours

Administration

Infuse over 30-60 minutes through dedicated line or via Y-site

Additional Information Generally considered bacteriostatic. Tigecycline is a derivative of
minocycline (9-t-butylglycylamido minocycline), but is not classified as a tetracycline. It has
demonstrated activity against a variety of Gram-positive and -negative bacterial pathogens.

Dosage Forms Injection, powder for reconstitution: 50 mg

♦ **Tikosyn®** *see* Dofetilide *on page 534*

♦ **Tilade®** *see* Nedocromil *on page 1205*

Tiludronate *(tye LOO droe nate)*

U.S. Brand Names Skelid®

Index Terms Tiludronate Disodium

Pharmacologic Category Bisphosphonate Derivative

Use Treatment of Paget's disease of the bone in patients who have a level of serum alkaline
phosphatase (SAP) at least twice the upper limit of normal, or who are symptomatic, or who
are at risk for future complications of their disease

Pregnancy Risk Factor C

Pregnancy Implications Teratogenic and nonteratogenic embryo/fetal effects have been
reported in animal studies. There are no adequate and well-controlled studies in pregnant
women. Bisphosphonates are incorporated into the bone matrix and gradually released over
time. Theoretically, there may be a risk of fetal harm when pregnancy follows the completion
of therapy. Based on limited case reports with pamidronate, serum calcium levels in the
newborn may be altered if administered during pregnancy.

Lactation Excretion in breast milk unknown/use caution

Medication Safety Issues

International issues:

Skelid® may be confused with Skaelud® which is a brand name for pyrithione zinc in
Denmark

Contraindications Hypersensitivity to bisphosphonates or any component of the formulation

Warnings/Precautions Not recommended in patients with severe renal impairment (Cl$_{cr}$ <30
mL/minute). Use with caution in patients with active upper GI problems (eg, dysphagia,
symptomatic esophageal diseases, gastritis, duodenitis, ulcers).

Bisphosphonate therapy has been associated with osteonecrosis, primarily of the jaw; this
has been observed mostly in cancer patients, but also in patients with postmenopausal
osteoporosis and other diagnoses. Dental exams and preventative dentistry should be
performed prior to placing patients with risk factors on chronic bisphosphonate therapy.
Invasive dental procedures should be avoided during treatment.

Infrequently, severe (and occasionally debilitating) bone, joint, and/or muscle pain have been
reported during bisphosphonate treatment. The onset of pain ranged from a single day to
several months. Symptoms usually resolve upon discontinuation. Some patients experienced
recurrence when rechallenged with same drug or another bisphosphonate; avoid use in
patients with a history of these symptoms in association with bisphosphonate therapy. Safety
and efficacy have not been established in children.

Adverse Reactions The following events occurred >2% and at a frequency > placebo:

1% to 10%:

Cardiovascular: Chest pain (3%), edema (3%)

Central nervous system: Dizziness (4%), paresthesia (4%)

Dermatologic: Rash (3%), skin disorder (3%)

Gastrointestinal: Nausea (9%), diarrhea (9%), heartburn (5%), vomiting (4%), flatulence
(3%)

Neuromuscular & skeletal: Arthrosis (3%)

Ocular: Cataract (3%), conjunctivitis (3%), glaucoma (3%)

Respiratory: Rhinitis (5%), sinusitis (5%), cough (3%), pharyngitis (3%)

<1% (Limited to important or life-threatening): Osteonecrosis, Stevens-Johnson syndrome

Overdosage/Toxicology Hypocalcemia is a potential consequence of tiludronate overdose.
No specific information on overdose treatment is available. Dialysis would not be beneficial.
Standard medical practices may be used to manage renal insufficiency or hypocalcemia, if
signs of these occur.

Drug Interactions

Increased Effect/Toxicity: Aminoglycosides may lower serum calcium levels with
prolonged administration; concomitant use may have an additive hypocalcemic effect.
NSAIDs may enhance the gastrointestinal adverse/toxic effects (increased incidence of GI
ulcers) of bisphosphonate derivatives. Bisphosphonate derivatives may enhance the hypocalcemic effect of phosphate supplements.

Decreased Effect: The following agents may decrease the absorption of oral
bisphosphonate derivatives: Antacids (aluminum, calcium, magnesium), oral calcium salts,
oral iron salts, and oral magnesium salts.

Ethanol/Nutrition/Herb Interactions Food: In single-dose studies, the bioavailability of
tiludronate was reduced by 90% when an oral dose was administered with, or 2 hours after, a

standard breakfast compared to the same dose administered after an overnight fast and 4 hours before a standard breakfast.

Stability Do not remove tablets from foil strips until they are to be used.

Mechanism of Action Inhibition of normal and abnormal bone resorption. Inhibits osteoclasts through at least two mechanisms: disruption of the cytoskeletal ring structure, possibly by inhibition of protein-tyrosine-phosphatase, thus leading to the detachment of osteoclasts from the bone surface area and the inhibition of the osteoclast proton pump.

Pharmacodynamics/Kinetics
Onset of action: Delayed, may require several weeks
Absorption: Rapid
Distribution: Widely to bone and soft tissue
Protein binding: 90%, primarily to albumin
Metabolism: Little, if any
Bioavailability: 6%; reduced by food
Half-life elimination: Healthy volunteers: 50 hours; Pagetic patients: 150 hours
Time to peak, plasma: ~2 hours
Excretion: Urine (60% as unchanged drug) within 13 days

Dosage Tiludronate should be taken with 6-8 oz of plain water and not taken within 2 hours of food
Adults: Oral: 400 mg (2 tablets of tiludronic acid) daily for a period of 3 months; allow an interval of 3 months to assess response
Dosing adjustment in renal impairment: Cl_{cr} <30 mL/minute: **Not recommended**
Dosing adjustment in hepatic impairment: Adjustment is not necessary

Dietary Considerations Do not take within 2 hours of food.

Administration Administer as a single oral dose, take with 6-8 oz of plain water. Beverages other than plain water (including mineral water), food, and some medications (see Drug Interactions) are likely to reduce the absorption of tiludronate. Do not take within 2 hours of food. Take calcium or mineral supplements at least 2 hours before or after tiludronate. Take aluminum- or magnesium-containing antacids at least 2 hours after taking tiludronate. Do not take tiludronate within 2 hours of indomethacin.

Test Interactions Bisphosphonates may interfere with diagnostic imaging agents such as technetium-99m-diphosphonate in bone scans.

Dosage Forms Tablet, tiludronic acid: 200 mg [equivalent to 240 mg tiludronate disodium]

♦ **Tiludronate Disodium** see Tiludronate on page 1686
♦ **Tim-AK (Can)** see Timolol on page 1687
♦ **Timentin®** see Ticarcillin and Clavulanate Potassium on page 1682

Timolol (TIM oh lol)

U.S. Brand Names Betimol®; Blocadren®; Istalol™; Timoptic®; Timoptic® in OcuDose®; Timoptic-XE®

Canadian Brand Names Alti-Timolol; Apo-Timol®; Apo-Timop®; Gen-Timolol; Nu-Timolol; Phoxal-timolol; PMS-Timolol; Sandoz-Timolol; Tim-AK; Timoptic®; Timoptic-XE®

Index Terms Timolol Hemihydrate; Timolol Maleate

Pharmacologic Category Beta-Adrenergic Blocker, Nonselective; Ophthalmic Agent, Antiglaucoma

Additional Appendix Information
Beta-Blockers on page 1875
Glaucoma Drug Therapy on page 2050

Use
Ophthalmic: Treatment of elevated intraocular pressure such as glaucoma or ocular hypertension
Oral: Treatment of hypertension and angina; to reduce mortality following myocardial infarction; prophylaxis of migraine

Pregnancy Risk Factor C (manufacturer); D (2nd and 3rd trimesters - expert analysis)

Pregnancy Implications Timolol was shown to cross the placenta in an in vitro perfusion study. Beta-blockers have been associated with bradycardia, hypotension, hypoglycemia, and intrauterine growth rate (IUGR); IUGR is probably related to maternal hypertension. Available evidence suggests beta-blockers are generally safe during pregnancy (JNC 7). Cases of neonatal hypoglycemia have been reported following maternal use of beta-blockers at parturition or during breast-feeding. Bradycardia and arrhythmia have been reported in an infant following ophthalmic administration of timolol during pregnancy.

Lactation Enters breast milk/use caution (AAP rates "compatible")

Medication Safety Issues
Sound-alike/look-alike issues:
Timolol may be confused with atenolol, Tylenol®
Timoptic® may be confused with Talacen®, Viroptic®

Bottle cap color change:
Timoptic®: Both the 0.25% and 0.5% strengths are now packaged in bottles with yellow caps; previously, the color of the cap on the product corresponded to different strengths.

International issues:
Betimol® may be confused with Betanol® which is a brand name for metipranolol in Monaco

Contraindications Hypersensitivity to timolol or any component of the formulation; sinus bradycardia; sinus node dysfunction; heart block greater than first degree (except in patients with a functioning artificial pacemaker); cardiogenic shock; uncompensated cardiac failure; bronchospastic disease; pregnancy (2nd and 3rd trimesters)

Warnings/Precautions Consider pre-existing conditions such as sick sinus syndrome before initiating. Administer cautiously in compensated heart failure and monitor for a worsening of the condition. **[U.S. Boxed Warning]: Beta-blocker therapy should not be withdrawn abruptly (particularly in patients with CAD), but gradually tapered to avoid acute tachycardia, hypertension, and/or ischemia.** Use caution with concurrent use of beta-blockers and either verapamil or diltiazem; bradycardia or heart block can occur. (Continued)

Timolol (Continued)

Beta-blockers can aggravate symptoms in patients with PVD. Patients with bronchospastic disease should generally not receive beta-blockers - monitor closely if used in patients with potential risk of bronchospasm. Use cautiously in diabetics because it can mask prominent hypoglycemic symptoms. Use cautiously in severe renal impairment: marked hypotension can occur in patients maintained on hemodialysis. Use care with anesthetic agents which decrease myocardial function. Can worsen myasthenia gravis. Use with caution in patients with a history of psychiatric illness; may cause or exacerbate CNS depression. Similar reactions found with systemic administration may occur with topical administration. Adequate alpha-blockade is required prior to use of any beta-blocker for patients with untreated pheochromocytoma. Safety and efficacy have not been established in children.

Ophthalmic: Systemic absorption and adverse effects may occur, including bradycardia and/or hypotension. Should not be used alone in angle-closure glaucoma (has no effect on pupillary constriction). Multidose vials have been associated with development of bacterial keratitis; avoid contamination. Some product do contain benzalkonium chloride which may be absorbed by soft contact lenses; do not administer while wearing soft contact lenses.

Adverse Reactions

Ophthalmic:
>10%: Ocular: Burning, stinging

1% to 10%:
Cardiovascular: Hypertension
Central nervous system: Headache
Ocular: Blurred vision, cataract, conjunctival injection, itching, visual acuity decreased
Miscellaneous: Infection

Systemic:
1% to 10%:
Cardiovascular: Bradycardia
Central nervous system: Fatigue, dizziness
Respiratory: Dyspnea

Frequency not defined (reported with any dosage form):
Cardiovascular: Angina pectoris, arrhythmia, bradycardia, cardiac failure, cardiac arrest, cerebral vascular accident, cerebral ischemia, edema, hypotension, heart block, palpitation, Raynaud's phenomenon
Central nervous system: Anxiety, confusion, depression, disorientation, dizziness, hallucinations, insomnia, memory loss, nervousness, nightmares, somnolence
Dermatologic: Alopecia, angioedema, pseudopemphigoid, psoriasiform rash, psoriasis exacerbation, rash, urticaria
Endocrine & metabolic: Hypoglycemia masked, libido decreased
Gastrointestinal: Anorexia, diarrhea, dyspepsia, nausea, xerostomia
Genitourinary: Impotence, retroperitoneal fibrosis
Hematologic: Claudication
Neuromuscular & skeletal: Myasthenia gravis exacerbation, paresthesia
Ocular: Blepharitis, conjunctivitis, corneal sensitivity decreased, cystoid macular edema, diplopia, dry eyes, foreign body sensation, keratitis, ocular discharge, ocular pain, ptosis, refractive changes, tearing, visual disturbances
Otic: Tinnitus
Respiratory: Bronchospasm, cough, dyspnea, nasal congestion, pulmonary edema, respiratory failure
Miscellaneous: Allergic reactions, cold hands/feet, Peyronie's disease, systemic lupus erythematosus

Overdosage/Toxicology
Symptoms of intoxication include cardiac disturbances, CNS toxicity, bronchospasm, hypoglycemia, and hyperkalemia. The most common cardiac symptoms include hypotension and bradycardia. Atrioventricular block, intraventricular conduction disturbances, cardiogenic shock, and asystole may occur with severe overdose, especially with membrane-depressant drugs (eg, propranolol). CNS effects include convulsions, coma, and respiratory arrest (commonly seen with propranolol and other membrane-depressant and lipid-soluble drugs). Treatment is symptomatic for seizures, hypotension, hyperkalemia, and hypoglycemia. Bradycardia and hypotension resistant to atropine, isoproterenol or pacing may respond to glucagon. Wide QRS defects caused by membrane-depressant poisoning may respond to hypertonic sodium bicarbonate. Repeat-dose charcoal, hemoperfusion, or hemodialysis may be helpful in removal of only those beta-blockers with a small V_d, long half-life, or low intrinsic clearance (acebutolol, atenolol, nadolol, sotalol). Timolol is not readily dialyzable.

Drug Interactions
Cytochrome P450 Effect: Substrate of CYP2D6 (major); **Inhibits** CYP2D6 (weak)

Increased Effect/Toxicity: CYP2D6 inhibitors may increase the levels/effects of timolol; example inhibitors include chlorpromazine, delavirdine, fluoxetine, miconazole, paroxetine, pergolide, quinidine, quinine, ritonavir, and ropinirole. The heart rate-lowering effects of timolol are additive with other drugs which slow AV conduction (digoxin, verapamil, diltiazem). Reserpine increases the effects of timolol. Concurrent use of timolol may increase the effects of alpha-blockers (prazosin, terazosin), alpha-adrenergic stimulants (epinephrine, phenylephrine), and the vasoconstrictive effects of ergot alkaloids. Timolol may mask the tachycardia from hypoglycemia caused by insulin and oral hypoglycemics. In patients receiving concurrent therapy, the risk of hypertensive crisis is increased when either clonidine or the beta-blocker is withdrawn. Beta-blockers may increase the action or levels of ethanol, disopyramide, nondepolarizing muscle relaxants, and theophylline although the effects are difficult to predict.

Decreased Effect: Decreased effect of timolol with aluminum salts, barbiturates, calcium salts, cholestyramine, colestipol, NSAIDs, penicillins (ampicillin), rifampin, salicylates, and sulfinpyrazone due to decreased bioavailability and plasma levels. Beta-blockers may decrease the effect of sulfonylureas. Beta-blockers may affect the action or levels of ethanol, disopyramide, nondepolarizing muscle relaxants, and theophylline, although the effects are difficult to predict.

Stability Ophthalmic drops: Store at room temperature; do not freeze. Protect from light.
Timoptic Occudose®: Store in the protective foil wrap and use within 1 month after opening foil package.

Mechanism of Action Blocks both beta$_1$- and beta$_2$-adrenergic receptors, reduces intraocular pressure by reducing aqueous humor production or possibly outflow; reduces blood pressure by blocking adrenergic receptors and decreasing sympathetic outflow; produces a negative chronotropic and inotropic activity through an unknown mechanism

Pharmacodynamics/Kinetics
Onset of action:
Hypotensive: Oral: 15-45 minutes
Peak effect: 0.5-2.5 hours
Intraocular pressure reduction: Ophthalmic: 30 minutes
Peak effect: 1-2 hours
Duration: ~4 hours; Ophthalmic: Intraocular: 24 hours
Protein binding: 60%
Metabolism: Extensively hepatic; extensive first-pass effect
Half-life elimination: 2-2.7 hours; prolonged with renal impairment
Excretion: Urine (15% to 20% as unchanged drug)

Dosage
Ophthalmic:
Children and Adults:
Solution: Initial: Instill 1 drop (0.25% solution) into affected eye(s) twice daily; increase to 0.5% solution if response not adequate; decrease to 1 drop/day if controlled; do not exceed 1 drop twice daily of 0.5% solution
Gel-forming solution (Timoptic-XE®): Instill 1 drop (either 0.25% or 0.5% solution) once daily
Adults: Solution (Istalol®): Instill 1 drop (0.5% solution) once daily in the morning
Oral: Adults:
Hypertension: Initial: 10 mg twice daily, increase gradually every 7 days, usual dosage: 20-40 mg/day in 2 divided doses; maximum: 60 mg/day
Prevention of myocardial infarction: 10 mg twice daily initiated within 1-4 weeks after infarction
Migraine headache: Initial: 10 mg twice daily, increase to maximum of 30 mg/day

Dietary Considerations Oral product should be administered with food at the same time each day.

Administration Ophthalmic: Administer other topically-applied ophthalmic medications at least 10 minutes before Timoptic-XE®; wash hands before use; invert closed bottle and shake once before use; remove cap carefully so that tip does not touch anything; hold bottle between thumb and index finger; use index finger of other hand to pull down the lower eyelid to form a pocket for the eye drop and tilt head back; place the dispenser tip close to the eye and gently squeeze the bottle to administer 1 drop; remove pressure after a single drop has been released; **do not allow the dispenser tip to touch the eye**; replace cap and store bottle in an upright position in a clean area; do **not** enlarge hole of dispenser; do **not** wash tip with water, soap, or any other cleaner. Some ophthalmic solutions contain benzalkonium chloride; wait at least 10 minutes after instilling solution before inserting soft contact lenses.

Monitoring Parameters Blood pressure, apical and radial pulses, fluid I & O, daily weight, respirations, mental status, and circulation in extremities before and during therapy; monitor for systemic effect of beta-blockade even when administering ophthalmic product

Dosage Forms Note: Unless otherwise specified, strength expressed as base.
Gel-forming solution, ophthalmic, as maleate: 0.25% (5 mL); 0.5% (2.5 mL, 5 mL)
Timoptic-XE®: 0.25% (5 mL); 0.5% (5 mL)
Solution, ophthalmic, as hemihydrate:
Betimol®: 0.25% (5 mL, 10 mL, 15 mL); 0.5% (5 mL, 10 mL, 15 mL) [contains benzalkonium chloride]
Solution, ophthalmic, as maleate: 0.25% (5 mL, 10 mL, 15 mL); 0.5% (5 mL, 10 mL, 15 mL) [contains benzalkonium chloride]
Istalol™: 0.5% (10 mL) [contains benzalkonium chloride and potassium sorbate]
Timoptic®: 0.25% (5 mL); 0.5% (5 mL, 10 mL) [contains benzalkonium chloride]
Solution, ophthalmic, as maleate [preservative free]:
Timoptic® in OcuDose®: 0.25% (0.2 mL); 0.5% (0.2 mL) [single use]
Tablet, as maleate: 5 mg, 10 mg, 20 mg [strength expressed as salt]
Blocadren®: 20 mg [strength expressed as salt]

♦ **Timolol and Dorzolamide** see Dorzolamide and Timolol on page 542
♦ **Timolol Hemihydrate** see Timolol on page 1687
♦ **Timolol Maleate** see Timolol on page 1687
♦ **Timoptic®** see Timolol on page 1687
♦ **Timoptic® in OcuDose®** see Timolol on page 1687
♦ **Timoptic-XE®** see Timolol on page 1687
♦ **Tinactin® Antifungal [OTC]** see Tolnaftate on page 1704
♦ **Tinactin® Antifungal Jock Itch [OTC]** see Tolnaftate on page 1704
♦ **Tinaderm [OTC]** see Tolnaftate on page 1704
♦ **Ting® Cream [OTC]** see Tolnaftate on page 1704
♦ **Ting® Spray Liquid [OTC]** see Tolnaftate on page 1704

Tinzaparin (tin ZA pa rin)

U.S. Brand Names Innohep®
Canadian Brand Names Innohep®
Index Terms Tinzaparin Sodium
Pharmacologic Category Low Molecular Weight Heparin
Additional Appendix Information
Anticoagulants, Injectable on page 1864
(Continued)

Tinzaparin *(Continued)*

Use Treatment of acute symptomatic deep vein thrombosis, with or without pulmonary embolism, in conjunction with warfarin sodium

Pregnancy Risk Factor B

Pregnancy Implications Teratogenic events were not observed in animal studies. Tinzaparin does not cross the human placenta. A pharmacokinetic study in pregnant women found no dose adjustment was needed during pregnancy. Pregnancy may increase the risk of thromboembolism; risk may be further increased with certain pre-existing conditions. As with all anticoagulants, bleeding is the major adverse effect of tinzaparin. Vaginal bleeding was reported in ~10% of pregnant patients during tinzaparin therapy.

Lactation Excretion in breast milk unknown/use caution

Contraindications Hypersensitivity to tinzaparin sodium, heparin, or any component of the formulation; active major bleeding; heparin-induced thrombocytopenia (current or history of)

Warnings/Precautions [U.S. Boxed Warning]: Patients with recent or anticipated neuraxial anesthesia (epidural or spinal anesthesia) are at risk of spinal or epidural hematoma and subsequent paralysis. Consider risk versus benefit prior to neuraxial anesthesia; risk is increased by concomitant agents that may alter hemostasis, as well as traumatic or repeated epidural or spinal puncture, and indwelling epidural catheters. Patient should be observed closely for signs and symptoms of neurological impairment. Not to be used interchangeably (unit for unit) with heparin or any other low molecular weight heparins.

Monitor patient closely for signs or symptoms of bleeding. Certain patients are at increased risk of bleeding. Risk factors include bacterial endocarditis; congenital or acquired bleeding disorders; active ulcerative or angiodysplastic GI diseases; severe uncontrolled hypertension; hemorrhagic stroke; use shortly after brain, spinal, or ophthalmologic surgery; patients treated concomitantly with platelet inhibitors; recent GI bleeding; thrombocytopenia or platelet defects; severe liver disease; hypertensive or diabetic retinopathy; or in patients undergoing invasive procedures. Monitor platelet count closely. Rare cases of thrombocytopenia have occurred. Manufacturer recommends discontinuation of therapy if platelets are <100,000/ mm^3. Rare cases of thrombocytopenia with thrombosis have occurred.

Safety and efficacy in pediatric patients have not been established. Use with caution in the elderly (delayed elimination may occur). Patients with severe renal impairment may show reduced elimination of tinzaparin

Heparin can cause hyperkalemia by affecting aldosterone; similar reactions could occur with LMWHs. Monitor for hyperkalemia. Do not administer intramuscularly or intravenously. Clinical experience is limited in patients with BMI >40 kg/m^2. Derived from porcine intestinal mucosa. Contains benzyl alcohol and sodium metabisulfite

Adverse Reactions As with all anticoagulants, bleeding is the major adverse effect of tinzaparin. Hemorrhage may occur at virtually any site. Risk is dependent on multiple variables.

>10%:
    Hepatic: Increased ALT (13%)
    Local: Injection site hematoma (16%)
1% to 10%:
    Cardiovascular: Angina pectoris, chest pain (2%), hyper-/hypotension, tachycardia
    Central nervous system: Confusion, dizziness, fever (2%), headache (2%), insomnia, pain (2%)
    Dermatologic: Bullous eruption, pruritus, rash (1%), skin disorder
    Gastrointestinal: Constipation (1%), dyspepsia, flatulence, nausea (2%), nonspecified gastrointestinal disorder, vomiting (1%)
    Genitourinary: Dysuria, urinary retention, urinary tract infection (4%)
    Hematologic: Anemia, hematoma, hemorrhage (2%), thrombocytopenia (1%)
    Hepatic: Increased AST (9%)
    Local: Thrombophlebitis (deep)
    Neuromuscular & skeletal: Back pain (2%)
    Renal: Hematuria (1%)
    Respiratory: Dyspnea (1%), epistaxis (2%), pneumonia, pulmonary embolism (2%), respiratory disorder
    Miscellaneous: Impaired healing, infection, unclassified reactions
<1% (Limited to important or life-threatening): Agranulocytosis, allergic purpura, allergic reaction, angioedema, arrhythmia, cholestatic hepatitis, epidermal necrolysis, gastrointestinal hemorrhage, granulocytopenia, hemarthrosis, hematoma, hemoptysis, intracranial hemorrhage, ischemic necrosis, major bleeding, MI, ocular hemorrhage, pancytopenia, priapism, purpura, rash, retroperitoneal/intra-abdominal bleeding, severe thrombocytopenia, skin necrosis, spinal epidural hematoma, Stevens-Johnson syndrome, urticaria, vaginal hemorrhage

Overdosage/Toxicology Overdose may lead to bleeding; bleeding may occur at any site. In case of overdose, discontinue medication, apply pressure to the bleeding site if possible, and replace volume and hemostatic blood elements as required. If these measures are ineffective, or if bleeding is severe, protamine sulfate may be administered by slow infusion at 1 mg per every 100 anti-Xa int. units of tinzaparin administered. However, protamine does not completely neutralize tinzaparin anti-Xa activity.

Drug Interactions
    Increased Effect/Toxicity: Drugs which affect platelet function (eg, aspirin, NSAIDs, dipyridamole, ticlopidine, clopidogrel, sulfinpyrazone, dextran) may potentiate the risk of hemorrhage. Thrombolytic agents increase the risk of hemorrhage.
        Warfarin: Risk of bleeding may be increased during concurrent therapy. Tinzaparin is commonly continued during the initiation of warfarin therapy to assure anticoagulation and to protect against possible transient hypercoagulability

Stability Store at 15°C to 30°C (59°F to 86°F).

Mechanism of Action Standard heparin consists of components with molecular weights ranging from 4000-30,000 daltons with a mean of 16,000 daltons. Heparin acts as an anticoagulant by enhancing the inhibition rate of clotting proteases by antithrombin III, impairing normal hemostasis and inhibition of factor Xa. Low molecular weight heparins have a small effect on the activated partial thromboplastin time and strongly inhibit factor Xa. The primary inhibitory activity of tinzaparin is through antithrombin. Tinzaparin is derived from porcine heparin that undergoes controlled enzymatic depolymerization. The average molecular weight of tinzaparin ranges between 5500 and 7500 daltons which is distributed as (<10%) 2000 daltons (60% to 72%) 2000-8000 daltons, and (22% to 36%) >8000 daltons. The antifactor Xa activity is approximately 100 int. units/mg.

Pharmacodynamics/Kinetics
Onset of action: 2-3 hours
Distribution: 3-5 L
Half-life elimination: 3-4 hours
Metabolism: Partially metabolized by desulphation and depolymerization
Bioavailability: 87%
Time to peak: 4-5 hours
Excretion: Urine

Dosage SubQ:
Adults: 175 anti-Xa int. units/kg of body weight once daily. Warfarin sodium should be started when appropriate. Administer tinzaparin for at least 6 days and until patient is adequately anticoagulated with warfarin.

Note: To calculate the volume of solution to administer per dose: Volume to be administered (mL) = patient weight (kg) x 0.00875 mL/kg (may be rounded off to the nearest 0.05 mL)

Elderly: No significant differences in safety or response were seen when used in patients ≥65 years of age. However, increased sensitivity to tinzaparin in elderly patients may be possible due to a decline in renal function.

Dosage adjustment in renal impairment: Patients with severe renal impairment (Cl_{cr} <30 mL/minute) had a 24% decrease in clearance, use with caution.

Dosage adjustment in hepatic impairment: No specific dosage adjustment has been recommended.

Administration Patient should be lying down or sitting. Administer by deep SubQ injection, alternating between the left and right anterolateral and left and right posterolateral abdominal wall. Vary site daily. The entire needle should be introduced into the skin fold formed by the thumb and forefinger. Hold the skin fold until injection is complete. To minimize bruising, do not rub the injection site.

Monitoring Parameters CBC including platelet count and hematocrit or hemoglobin, and stool for occult blood; the monitoring of PT and/or aPTT is not of clinical value. Patients receiving both warfarin and tinzaparin should have their INR drawn just prior to the next scheduled dose of tinzaparin.

Dosage Forms
Injection, solution, as solution:
Innohep®: 20,000 anti-Xa int. units/mL (2 mL) [contains benzyl alcohol and sodium metabisulfite]

♦ **Tinzaparin Sodium** see Tinzaparin on page 1689

Tioconazole (tye oh KONE a zole)

U.S. Brand Names 1-Day™ [OTC]; Vagistat®-1 [OTC]
Pharmacologic Category Antifungal Agent, Vaginal
Additional Appendix Information
Treatment of Sexually Transmitted Infections on page 2007
Use Local treatment of vulvovaginal candidiasis
Pregnancy Risk Factor C
Lactation Excretion in breast milk unknown/not recommended
Medication Safety Issues
Sound-alike/look-alike issues:
Tioconazole may be confused with terconazole
Contraindications Hypersensitivity to tioconazole or any component of the formulation
Warnings/Precautions For vaginal use only. Petrolatum-based vaginal products may damage rubber or latex condoms or diaphragms. Separate use by 3 days.
Drug Interactions
Cytochrome P450 Effect: Inhibits CYP1A2 (weak), 2A6 (weak), 2C9 (weak), 2C19 (weak), 2D6 (weak), 2E1 (weak)
Stability Store at room temperature.
Mechanism of Action A 1-substituted imidazole derivative with a broad antifungal spectrum against a wide variety of dermatophytes and yeasts, including *Trichophyton mentagrophytes, T. rubrum, T. erinacei, T. tonsurans, Microsporum canis, Microsporum gypseum,* and *Candida albicans.* Both agents appear to be similarly effective against *Epidermophyton floccosum.*
Pharmacodynamics/Kinetics
Onset of action: Some improvement: Within 24 hours; Complete relief: Within 7 days
Absorption: Intravaginal: Systemic (small amounts)
Distribution: Vaginal fluid: 24-72 hours
Excretion: Urine and feces
Dosage Adults: Vaginal: Insert 1 applicatorful in vagina, just prior to bedtime, as a single dose
Administration Insert high into vagina
Dosage Forms Ointment, vaginal: 6.5% (4.6 g) [with applicator]

♦ **Tioguanine** see Thioguanine on page 1669
♦ **Tiotixene** see Thiothixene on page 1675

Tipranavir (tip RA na veer)

U.S. Brand Names Aptivus®
Canadian Brand Names Aptivus®
Index Terms PNU-140690E; TPV
Pharmacologic Category Antiretroviral Agent, Protease Inhibitor
Additional Appendix Information
Antiretroviral Therapy for HIV Infection: Adults and Adolescents *on page 1988*
Management of Healthcare Worker Exposures to HBV, HCV, and HIV *on page 1941*
Use Treatment of HIV-1 infections in combination with ritonavir and other antiretroviral agents; limited to highly treatment-experienced or multiprotease inhibitor-resistant patients.
Pregnancy Risk Factor C
Pregnancy Implications It is not known if tipranavir crosses the human placenta. Pregnancy and protease inhibitors are both associated with an increased risk of hyperglycemia. Glucose levels should be closely monitored. Women receiving estrogen (as hormonal contraception or replacement therapy) have an increased incidence of rash. Alternative forms of contraception may be needed. Health professionals are encouraged to contact the antiretroviral pregnancy registry to monitor outcomes of pregnant women exposed to antiretroviral medications (1-800-258-4263 or www.APRegistry.com).
Lactation Excretion in breast milk unknown/contraindicated
Contraindications Hypersensitivity to tipranavir or any component of the formulation; concurrent therapy of tipranavir/ritonavir with amiodarone, cisapride, dihydroergotamine, ergonovine, ergotamine, flecainide, lovastatin, methylergonovine, midazolam, pimozide, propafenone, quinidine, simvastatin, and triazolam; patients with hepatic insufficiency (Child-Pugh Class B and C)
Warnings/Precautions Coadministration with ritonavir is required. **[U.S. Boxed Warning]: In combination with ritonavir, may cause hepatitis or exacerbate pre-existing hepatic dysfunction;** use with caution in patients with hepatitis B or C and in hepatic disease. May be associated with fat redistribution (buffalo hump, increased abdominal girth, breast engorgement, facial atrophy). Use caution in hemophilia. May increase cholesterol and/or triglycerides; hypertriglyceridemia may increase risk of pancreatitis. May cause hyperglycemia. Use with caution in patients with sulfonamide allergy. Tipranavir has been associated with dermatological adverse effects, including rash (sometimes accompanied by joint pain, throat tightness, or generalized pruritus) and photosensitivity. Immune reconstitution syndrome, including inflammatory responses to indolent infections, has been associated with antiretroviral therapy; additional evaluation and treatment may be required.

[U.S. Boxed Warning]: Tipranavir has been associated with rare reports of fatal and nonfatal intracranial hemorrhage; causal relationship not established. Events often occurred in patients with medical conditions or concurrent therapy which may have influenced these events. Tipranavir may inhibit platelet aggregation. Use with caution in patients who may be at risk for increased bleeding (trauma, surgery or other medical conditions) or in patients receiving concurrent medications which may increase the risk of bleeding, including antiplatelet agents and anticoagulants.

Use with caution in patients taking strong CYP3A4 inhibitors, moderate or strong CYP3A4 inducers and major CYP3A4 substrates (see drug interactions); consider alternative agents that avoid or lessen the potential for CYP-mediated interactions. Safety and efficacy have not been established in children.
Adverse Reactions Protease inhibitors cause dyslipidemia which includes elevated cholesterol and triglycerides and a redistribution of body fat centrally to cause increased abdominal girth, buffalo hump, facial atrophy, and breast enlargement. These agents also cause hyperglycemia.
>10%:
    Endocrine & metabolic: Hypercholesterolemia (>300 mg/dL: 11%), hypertriglyceridemia (>400 mg/dL: 26%)
    Gastrointestinal: Diarrhea (11%)
    Hepatic: Transaminase increased (ALT or AST: 24%)
2% to 10%:
    Central nervous system: Fever (5%), fatigue (4%), headache (3%), depression (2%)
    Dermatologic: Rash (2%)
    Endocrine & metabolic: Amylase increased (3%)
    Gastrointestinal: Nausea (7%), vomiting (3%), abdominal pain (3%), amylase increased (3%)
    Hematologic: WBC decreased (grade 3-4: 4%)
    Neuromuscular & skeletal: Weakness (2%)
    Respiratory: Bronchitis (3%)
<2% (Limited to important or life-threatening): Abdominal distension, anemia, anorexia, appetite decreased, cough, dehydration, diabetes mellitus, dizziness, dyspepsia, dyspnea, exanthem, facial wasting, flatulence, gastroesophageal reflux, hepatic failure, hepatitis, hyperglycemia, hypersensitivity, insomnia, intracranial hemorrhage, lipase increased, lipoatrophy, lipodystrophy (acquired), lipohypertrophy, muscle cramp, myalgia, neuropathy (peripheral), neutropenia, pancreatitis, pruritus, renal insufficiency, sleep disorder, somnolence, thrombocytopenia, viral infection (reactivation of herpes/varicella infection), weight loss
Drug Interactions
  Cytochrome P450 Effect: Substrate of CYP3A4 (major; minimal metabolism when coadministered with ritonavir)
  Increased Effect/Toxicity: Note: Listed interactions include interactions resulting from coadministration with ritonavir. Refer to Ritonavir monograph *on page 1520* for additional interaction concerns. The serum concentrations of tipranavir may be increased by ritonavir. This combination is recommended to enhance the effect ("boost") tipranavir.

  Tipranavir/ritonavir may increase the levels/effects of CYP3A4 substrates. Tipranavir/ritonavir may increase the toxicity of benzodiazepines; concurrent use of midazolam and triazolam is specifically contraindicated. Tipranavir may increase serum concentrations of cisapride, increasing the risk of malignant arrhythmias; use is contraindicated. Toxicity of pimozide is significantly increased by tipranavir/ritonavir; concurrent use is contraindicated. Tipranavir/ritonavir may increase serum concentrations/toxicity of several antiarrhythmic agents; contraindicated with amiodarone, flecainide, propafenone, and quinidine (use extreme caution with lidocaine). Tipranavir/ritonavir may also increase serum concentrations/effects of calcium channel blockers and immunosuppressants (cyclosporine, sirolimus, tacrolimus).

Serum concentrations of HMG-CoA reductase inhibitors (atorvastatin, cerivastatin, lovastatin, simvastatin) may be increased by tipranavir/ritonavir, increasing the risk of myopathy/rhabdomyolysis. Lovastatin and simvastatin are not recommended. Use lowest possible dose of atorvastatin. Fluvastatin and pravastatin may be safer alternatives. Serum concentrations of rifabutin may be increased by tipranavir/ritonavir; dosage adjustment of rifabutin is required.

The toxicity of ergot alkaloids (dihydroergotamine, ergotamine, ergonovine, methylergonovine) is increased by tipranavir; concurrent use is contraindicated. Effects of hypoglycemic agents may be altered by tipranavir/ritonavir. Concurrent therapy with tipranavir may increase serum concentrations of normeperidine, and decrease serum concentrations of meperidine. The serum concentrations of sildenafil, tadalafil, and vardenafil may be increased by tipranavir/ritonavir; dose adjustment and limitations related to ritonavir coadministration must be recognized.

Concurrent use of disulfiram with tipranavir oral solution is contraindicated due to risk of adverse reaction (due to alcohol content of formulation). Clarithromycin may increase serum concentrations of tipranavir. Tipranavir/ritonavir may increase serum concentrations of clarithromycin. Use with caution and adjust dose of clarithromycin during concurrent therapy in renally impaired patients.

Decreased Effect: CYP3A4 inducers may decrease the levels/effects of tipranavir. Example inducers include aminoglutethimide, carbamazepine, nafcillin, nevirapine, phenobarbital, phenytoin, and rifamycins. When coadministered with ritonavir, reduction of tipranavir serum concentrations is unlikely. Rifampin may decrease serum concentrations of tipranavir. Concurrent use of rifampin is not recommended. The effect of methadone may be reduced by tipranavir (dosage increase may be required).

Serum concentrations of protease inhibitors may be decreased by tipranavir. Concurrent therapy with amprenavir, lopinavir, or saquinavir is not recommended. Tipranavir/ritonavir may decrease serum concentrations of nucleoside reverse transcriptase inhibitors (NRTIs, including abacavir, didanosine, and zidovudine); administer tipranavir/ritonavir 2 hours before or after didanosine.

Ethanol/Nutrition/Herb Interactions
Ethanol: Capsules contain dehydrated alcohol 7% w/w (0.1g per capsule)
Food: Bioavailability is increased with a high-fat meal.

Stability Prior to opening bottle, store under refrigeration at 2°C to 8°C (36°F to 46°F). After bottle is opened, may be stored at 25°C (77°F); excursions permitted to 15°C to 30°C (59°F to 86°F) for up to 60 days.

Mechanism of Action Tipranavir is a nonpeptide inhibitor of HIV-1 protease. It binds to the protease activity site and inhibits the activity of the enzyme. HIV protease is required for the cleavage of viral polyprotein precursors into individual functional proteins found in infectious HIV. Inhibition prevents cleavage of these polyproteins, resulting in the formation of immature, noninfectious viral particles.

Pharmacodynamics/Kinetics
Absorption: Incomplete (percentage not established)
Protein binding: 99%
Metabolism: Hepatic, via CYP3A4 (minimal when coadministered with ritonavir)
Bioavailability: Not established
Half-life elimination: 6 hours
Excretion: Feces (82%); urine (4%); primarily as unchanged drug (when coadministered with ritonavir)

Dosage Oral: Adults: 500 mg twice daily with a high-fat meal. **Note:** Coadministration with ritonavir (200 mg twice daily) is required.
Dosage adjustment in renal impairment: No adjustment required
Dietary Considerations Contains dehydrated alcohol 7% w/w (0.1 g per capsule)
Administration Should be administered with food (bioavailability is increased); coadministration with ritonavir is standard
Monitoring Parameters Viral load, CD4, serum glucose, liver function tests, bilirubin
Dosage Forms Capsule, gelatin: 250 mg [contains dehydrated ethanol 7% per capsule]

Tirofiban (tye roe FYE ban)

U.S. Brand Names Aggrastat®
Canadian Brand Names Aggrastat®
Index Terms MK383; Tirofiban Hydrochloride
Pharmacologic Category Antiplatelet Agent, Glycoprotein IIb/IIIa Inhibitor
Additional Appendix Information
Glycoprotein Antagonists *on page 1884*
Use In combination with heparin, is indicated for the treatment of acute coronary syndrome, including patients who are to be managed medically and those undergoing PTCA or atherectomy. In this setting, it has been shown to decrease the rate of a combined endpoint of death, new myocardial infarction or refractory ischemia/repeat cardiac procedure.
Pregnancy Risk Factor B
Lactation Excretion in breast milk unknown/contraindicated
(Continued)

Tirofiban *(Continued)*

Medication Safety Issues

Sound-alike/look-alike issues:

Aggrastat® may be confused with Aggrenox®, argatroban

Contraindications Hypersensitivity to tirofiban or any component of the formulation; active internal bleeding or a history of bleeding diathesis within the previous 30 days; history of intracranial hemorrhage, intracranial neoplasm, arteriovenous malformation, or aneurysm; history of thrombocytopenia following prior exposure; history of CVA within 30 days or any history of hemorrhagic stroke; major surgical procedure or severe physical trauma within the previous month; history, symptoms, or findings suggestive of aortic dissection; severe hypertension (systolic BP >180 mm Hg and/or diastolic BP >110 mm Hg); concomitant use of another parenteral GP IIb/IIIa inhibitor; acute pericarditis

Warnings/Precautions Bleeding is the most common complication encountered during this therapy; most major bleeding occurs at the arterial access site for cardiac catheterization. Caution in patients with platelets <150,000/mm^3; patients with hemorrhagic retinopathy; chronic dialysis patients; when used in combination with other drugs impacting on coagulation. To minimize bleeding complications, care must be taken in sheath insertion/removal. Sheath hemostasis should be achieved at least 4 hours before hospital discharge. Other trauma and vascular punctures should be minimized. Avoid obtaining vascular access through a noncompressible site (eg, subclavian or jugular vein). Patients with severe renal insufficiency require dosage reduction. Safety and efficacy have not been established in children.

Adverse Reactions Bleeding is the major drug-related adverse effect. Patients received background treatment with aspirin and heparin. Major bleeding was reported in 1.4% to 2.2%; minor bleeding in 10.5% to 12%; transfusion was required in 4% to 4.3%.

>1% (nonbleeding adverse events):

Cardiovascular: Bradycardia (4%), coronary artery dissection (5%), edema (2%)

Central nervous system: Dizziness (3%), fever (>1%), headache (>1%), vasovagal reaction (2%)

Gastrointestinal: Nausea (>1%)

Genitourinary: Pelvic pain (6%)

Hematologic: Thrombocytopenia: <90,000/mm^3 (1.5%), <50,000/mm^3 (0.3%)

Neuromuscular & skeletal: Leg pain (3%)

Miscellaneous: Diaphoresis (2%)

<1% (Limited to important or life-threatening): Acutely decreased platelets in association with fever, anaphylaxis, GI bleeding (0.1% to 0.2%), GU bleeding (up to 0.1%), hemopericardium, intracranial bleeding (up to 0.1%), pulmonary alveolar hemorrhage, rash, retroperitoneal bleeding (up to 0.6%), severe (<10,000/mm^3) thrombocytopenia (rare), spinal-epidural hematoma

Overdosage/Toxicology The most frequent manifestation of overdose is bleeding. Treatment is cessation of therapy and assessment of transfusion. Tirofiban has a relatively short half-life and its platelet effects dissipate rather quickly. However, when immediate reversal is required, platelet transfusions can be useful. Tirofiban is dialyzable.

Drug Interactions

Increased Effect/Toxicity: Use of tirofiban with aspirin and heparin is associated with an increase in bleeding over aspirin and heparin alone; however, efficacy of tirofiban is improved. Risk of bleeding is increased when used with thrombolytics, oral anticoagulants, NSAIDs, dipyridamole, ticlopidine, and clopidogrel. Avoid concomitant use of other IIb/IIIa antagonists. Cephalosporins which contain the MTT side chain may theoretically increase the risk of hemorrhage.

Decreased Effect: Levothyroxine and omeprazole decrease tirofiban levels; however, the clinical significance of this interaction remains to be demonstrated.

Stability Store at 25°C (77°F); do not freeze. Protect from light during storage.

Tirofiban Dosing (Using 50 mcg/mL Concentration)

Patient Weight (kg)	Patients With Normal Renal Function		Patients With Renal Dysfunction	
	30-Min Loading Infusion Rate (mL/h)	Maintenance Infusion Rate (mL/h)	30-Min Loading Infusion Rate (mL/h)	Maintenance Infusion Rate (mL/h)
30-37	16	4	8	2
38-45	20	5	10	3
46-54	24	6	12	3
55-62	28	7	14	4
63-70	32	8	16	4
71-79	36	9	18	5
80-87	40	10	20	5
88-95	44	11	22	6
96-104	48	12	24	6
105-112	52	13	26	7
113-120	56	14	28	7
121-128	60	15	30	8
128-137	64	16	32	8
138-145	68	17	34	9
146-153	72	18	36	9

Mechanism of Action A reversible antagonist of fibrinogen binding to the GP IIb/IIIa receptor, the major platelet surface receptor involved in platelet aggregation. When administered intravenously, it inhibits *ex vivo* platelet aggregation in a dose- and concentration-dependent manner. When given according to the recommended regimen, >90% inhibition is attained by the end of the 30-minute infusion. Platelet aggregation inhibition is reversible following cessation of the infusion.

Pharmacodynamics/Kinetics

Distribution: 35% unbound

Metabolism: Minimally hepatic

Half-life elimination: 2 hours

Excretion: Urine (65%) and feces (25%) primarily as unchanged drug

Clearance: Elderly: Reduced by 19% to 26%

Dosage Adults: I.V.: Initial rate of 0.4 mcg/kg/minute for 30 minutes and then continued at 0.1 mcg/kg/minute; dosing should be continued through angiography and for 12-24 hours after angioplasty or atherectomy. See table on previous page.

Dosing adjustment in severe renal impairment: Cl_{cr} <30 mL/minute: Reduce dose to 50% of normal rate.

Administration Intended for intravenous delivery using sterile equipment and technique. Do not add other drugs or remove solution directly from the bag with a syringe. Do not use plastic containers in series connections; such use can result in air embolism by drawing air from the first container if it is empty of solution. Discard unused solution 24 hours following the start of infusion. May be administered through the same catheter as heparin. Tirofiban injection must be diluted to a concentration of 50 mcg/mL (premixed solution does not require dilution). Infuse over 30 minutes.

Monitoring Parameters Platelet count. Hemoglobin and hematocrit should be monitored prior to treatment, within 6 hours following loading infusion, and at least daily thereafter during therapy. Platelet count may need to be monitored earlier in patients who received prior glycoprotein IIb/IIa antagonists. Persistent reductions of platelet counts <90,000/mm^3 may require interruption or discontinuation of infusion. Because tirofiban requires concurrent heparin therapy, aPTT levels should also be followed. Monitor vital signs and laboratory results prior to, during, and after therapy. Assess infusion insertion site during and after therapy (every 15 minutes or as institutional policy). Observe and teach patient bleeding precautions (avoid invasive procedures and activities that could result in injury). Monitor closely for signs of unusual or excessive bleeding (eg, CNS changes, blood in urine, stool, or vomitus, unusual bruising or bleeding). Breast-feeding is contraindicated.

Dosage Forms

Infusion [premixed in sodium chloride]: 50 mcg/mL (100 mL, 250 mL)

Injection, solution: 250 mcg/mL (50 mL)

- ♦ **Tirofiban Hydrochloride** *see* Tirofiban *on page 1693*
- ♦ **Tisit® [OTC]** *see* Pyrethrins and Piperonyl Butoxide *on page 1461*
- ♦ **Tisit® Blue Gel [OTC]** *see* Pyrethrins and Piperonyl Butoxide *on page 1461*
- ♦ **Titralac™ [OTC]** *see* Calcium Carbonate *on page 269*
- ♦ **Ti-U-Lac® H (Can)** *see* Urea and Hydrocortisone *on page 1759*

Tizanidine (tye ZAN i deen)

U.S. Brand Names Zanaflex®

Canadian Brand Names Apo-Tizanidine®; Gen-Tizanidine; Zanaflex®

Index Terms Sirdalud®

Pharmacologic Category Alpha$_2$-Adrenergic Agonist

Use Skeletal muscle relaxant used for treatment of muscle spasticity

Unlabeled/Investigational Use Tension headaches, low back pain, and trigeminal neuralgia

Pregnancy Risk Factor C

Lactation Excretion in breast milk unknown/not recommended

Medication Safety Issues

Sound-alike/look-alike issues:

Tizanidine may be confused with tiagabine

Contraindications Hypersensitivity to tizanidine or any component of the formulation; concomitant therapy with ciprofloxacin or fluvoxamine or other potent inhibitors of CYP1A2

Warnings/Precautions

Reduce dose in patients with liver or renal disease. May cause significant orthostatic hypotension or bradycardia; use with caution in patients with hypotension or cardiac disease. Tizanidine clearance is reduced by more than 50% in elderly patients with renal insufficiency (Cl_{cr} <25 mL/minute) compared to healthy elderly subjects; this may lead to a longer duration of effects and, therefore, should be used with caution in renally impaired patients. Due to extensive hepatic metabolism, avoid use or use extreme caution in patents with hepatic impairment.

Adverse Reactions

>10%:

Cardiovascular: Hypotension (16% to 33%)

Central nervous system: Somnolence (48%), dizziness (16%)

Gastrointestinal: Xerostomia (49%)

Neuromuscular & skeletal: Weakness (41%)

1% to 10%:

Cardiovascular: Bradycardia (2% to 10%)

Central nervous system: Nervousness (3%), speech disorder (3%)

Gastrointestinal: Constipation (4%), vomiting (3%), pharyngitis (3%)

Genitourinary: UTI (10%), urinary frequency (3%)

Hepatic: Liver enzymes increased (3%)

Neuromuscular & skeletal: Dyskinesia (3%)

Ocular: Blurred vision (3%)

Respiratory: Rhinitis (3%)

Miscellaneous: Infection (6%), flu-like syndrome (3%)

<1%, frequency not defined, and postmarketing experience (limited to important or life-threatening): Adrenal insufficiency, allergic reaction, anemia, angina, arrhythmia,

(Continued)

Tizanidine *(Continued)*

asthma, carcinoma, cellulitis, cholelithiasis, coronary artery disorder, deafness, dementia, dyslipidemias, fecal impaction, fever, gastrointestinal, glaucoma, heart failure, hepatomegaly, hemiplegia, hepatic failure, hepatitis, hepatoma, hyperglycemia, hypokalemia, hyponatremia, hypoproteinemia, hypothyroidism, jaundice, leukopenia, leukocytosis, MI, optic neuritis, palpitation, personality disorder (various), pneumonia, postural hypotension, psychotic-like symptoms, pulmonary embolus, respiratory acidosis, retinal hemorrhage, sepsis, suicide attempt, syncope, thrombocythemia, thrombocytopenia, ventricular extrasystoles, ventricular tachycardia

Overdosage/Toxicology Symptoms include dry mouth, bradycardia, and hypotension. Lavage (within 2 hours of ingestion) with activated charcoal; benzodiazepines for seizure control. Atropine can be given for treatment of bradycardia. Flumazenil has been used to reverse coma successfully. Forced diuresis is not helpful. Multiple dosing of activated charcoal may be helpful. Following attempts to enhance drug elimination, hypotension should be treated with I.V. fluids and/or Trendelenburg positioning.

Drug Interactions

Cytochrome P450 Effect:

Substrate of CYP1A2 (major)

Increased Effect/Toxicity: Additive hypotensive effects may be seen with diuretics, other alpha adrenergic agonists, ciprofloxacin, or antihypertensives; CNS depression with baclofen or other CNS depressants. Potent CYP1A2 inhibitors may increase the levels/effects of tizanidine; example inhibitors include ciprofloxacin (contraindicated), fluvoxamine (contraindicated), ketoconazole, norfloxacin, ofloxacin, and rofecoxib. Oral contraceptives may decrease the clearance of tizanidine.

Ethanol/Nutrition/Herb Interactions

Ethanol: Avoid ethanol (may increase CNS depression).

Food: The tablet and capsule dosage forms are not bioequivalent when administered with food. Food increases both the time to peak concentration and the extent of absorption for both the tablet and capsule. However, maximal concentrations of tizanidine achieved when administered with food were increased by 30% for the tablet, but decreased by 20% for the capsule. Under fed conditions, the capsule is approximately 80% bioavailable relative to the tablet.

Herb/Nutraceutical: Avoid valerian, St John's wort, kava kava, gotu kola (may increase CNS depression). Avoid black cohosh, California poppy, coleus, golden seal, hawthorn, mistletoe, periwinkle, quinine, shepherd's purse (may increase hypotensive effects).

Mechanism of Action An alpha$_2$-adrenergic agonist agent which decreases excitatory input to alpha motor neurons; an imidazole derivative chemically-related to clonidine, which acts as a centrally acting muscle relaxant with alpha$_2$-adrenergic agonist properties; acts on the level of the spinal cord

Pharmacodynamics/Kinetics

Duration: 3-6 hours

Bioavailability: 40%

Metabolism: Extensively hepatic

Half-life elimination: 2 hours

Time to peak, serum:

Fasting state: Capsule, tablet: 1 hour

Fed state: Capsule: 3-4 hours, Tablet: 1.5 hours

Excretion: Urine (60%); feces (20%)

Dosage

Adults: 2-4 mg 3 times/day

Usual initial dose: 4 mg, may increase by 2-4 mg as needed for satisfactory reduction of muscle tone every 6-8 hours to a maximum of three doses in any 24 hour period

Maximum dose: 36 mg/day

Dosing adjustment in renal impairment: May require dose reductions or less frequent dosing

Dosing adjustment in hepatic impairment: Avoid use in hepatic impairment; if used, lowest possible dose should be used initially with close monitoring for adverse effects (eg, hypotension).

Administration Capsules may be opened and contents sprinkled on food; however, extent of absorption is increased up to 20% relative to administration of the capsule under fasted conditions.

Monitoring Parameters Monitor liver function (aminotransferases) at baseline, 1, 3, 6 months and then periodically thereafter; monitor ophthalmic function

Dosage Forms

Capsule:

Zanaflex®: 2 mg, 4 mg, 6 mg

Tablet: 2 mg, 4 mg

Zanaflex®: 2 mg [DSC], 4 mg

- **TMC-114** *see* Darunavir *on page 457*
- **TMP** *see* Trimethoprim *on page 1744*
- **TMP-SMZ** *see* Sulfamethoxazole and Trimethoprim *on page 1613*
- **TMZ** *see* Temozolomide *on page 1642*
- **TNKase™** *see* Tenecteplase *on page 1643*
- **TOBI®** *see* Tobramycin *on page 1696*
- **TobraDex®** *see* Tobramycin and Dexamethasone *on page 1700*
- **Tobradex® (Can)** *see* Tobramycin and Dexamethasone *on page 1700*

Tobramycin *(toe bra MYE sin)*

U.S. Brand Names AKTob®; TOBI®; Tobrex®

Canadian Brand Names PMS-Tobramycin; Sandoz-Tobramycin; TOBI®; Tobramycin Injection, USP; Tobrex®

Index Terms Tobramycin Sulfate

Pharmacologic Category Antibiotic, Aminoglycoside; Antibiotic, Ophthalmic

Additional Appendix Information
Aminoglycoside Dosing and Monitoring *on page 1858*
Antimicrobial Drugs of Choice *on page 1981*
Prevention of Wound Infection and Sepsis in Surgical Patients *on page 1964*

Use Treatment of documented or suspected infections caused by susceptible gram-negative bacilli including *Pseudomonas aeruginosa*; topically used to treat superficial ophthalmic infections caused by susceptible bacteria. Tobramycin solution for inhalation is indicated for the management of cystic fibrosis patients (>6 years of age) with *Pseudomonas aeruginosa*.

Pregnancy Risk Factor D (injection, inhalation); B (ophthalmic)

Pregnancy Implications Aminoglycosides, including tobramycin, cross the placenta. The manufacturers of Nebcin® and TOBI® have a labeled pregnancy category of D based on reports of bilateral congenital deafness in children whose mothers used streptomycin during pregnancy. The risk of teratogenic effects and deafness following *in utero* exposure to tobramycin is considered to be small and some resources consider the pregnancy risk factor to be C. The manufacturer of Tobrex® states that animal studies have not shown harm to the fetus; however, no adequate and well-controlled studies have been conducted in pregnant women.

Lactation Enters breast milk/not recommended

Medication Safety Issues
Sound-alike/look-alike issues:
Tobramycin may be confused with Trobicin®
AKTob® may be confused with AK-Trol®
Nebcin® may be confused with Inapsine®, Naprosyn®, Nubain®
Tobrex® may be confused with TobraDex®

Contraindications Hypersensitivity to tobramycin, other aminoglycosides, or any component of the formulation; pregnancy (injection/inhalation)

Warnings/Precautions [U.S. Boxed Warning]: Aminoglycosides may cause neurotoxicity and/or nephrotoxicity; usual risk factors include pre-existing renal impairment, concomitant neuro-/nephrotoxic medications, advanced age and dehydration. Ototoxicity may be directly proportional to the amount of drug given and the duration of treatment; tinnitus or vertigo are indications of vestibular injury and impending hearing loss; renal damage is usually reversible. May cause neuromuscular blockade and respiratory paralysis; especially when given soon after anesthesia or muscle relaxants.

Not intended for long-term therapy due to toxic hazards associated with extended administration; use caution in pre-existing renal insufficiency, vestibular or cochlear impairment, myasthenia gravis, hypocalcemia, conditions which depress neuromuscular transmission. Dosage modification required in patients with impaired renal function. Prolonged use may result in superinfection, including pseudomembranous colitis. Solution may contain sodium metabisulfate; use caution in patients with sulfite allergy.

Adverse Reactions
Injection: Frequency not defined:
Central nervous system: Confusion, disorientation, dizziness, fever, headache, lethargy, vertigo
Dermatologic: Exfoliative dermatitis, itching, rash, urticaria
Endocrine & metabolic: Serum calcium, magnesium, potassium, and/or sodium decreased
Gastrointestinal: Diarrhea, nausea, vomiting
Hematologic: Anemia, eosinophilia, granulocytopenia, leukocytosis, leukopenia, thrombocytopenia
Hepatic: ALT, AST, bilirubin, and/or LDH increased
Local: Pain at the injection site
Otic: Hearing loss, tinnitus, ototoxicity (auditory), ototoxicity (vestibular), roaring in the ears
Renal: BUN increased, cylindruria, serum creatinine increased, oliguria, proteinuria

Inhalation:
>10%:
Gastrointestinal: Sputum discoloration (21%)
Respiratory: Voice alteration (13%)
1% to 10%:
Central nervous system: Malaise (6%)
Otic: Tinnitus (3%)
Postmarketing and/or case reports: Hearing loss

Ophthalmic: <1% (Limited to important or life-threatening): Ocular: Conjunctival erythema, lid itching, lid swelling

Overdosage/Toxicology Symptoms include ototoxicity, nephrotoxicity, and neuromuscular toxicity. The treatment of choice following a single acute overdose appears to be the maintenance of urine output of at least 3 mL/kg/hour. Dialysis is of questionable value in the enhancement of aminoglycoside elimination. If required, hemodialysis is preferred over peritoneal dialysis in patients with normal renal function. Careful hydration may be all that is required to promote diuresis and therefore enhance elimination.

Drug Interactions
Increased Effect/Toxicity: Increased antimicrobial effect of tobramycin with extended spectrum penicillins (synergistic). Neuromuscular blockers may have an increased duration of action (neuromuscular blockade). Amphotericin B, cephalosporins, and loop diuretics may increase the risk of nephrotoxicity.

Stability
Injection: Stable at room temperature both as the clear, colorless solution and as the dry powder. Reconstituted solutions remain stable for 24 hours at room temperature and 96 hours when refrigerated. Dilute in 50-100 mL NS, D_5W for I.V. infusion.
Separate administration of extended-spectrum penicillins (eg, carbenicillin, ticarcillin, piperacillin) from tobramycin in patients with severe renal impairment; tobramycin's efficacy may be reduced if given concurrently.
Ophthalmic solution: Store at 8°C to 27°C (46°F to 80°F).
(Continued)

Tobramycin *(Continued)*

Solution, for inhalation (TOBI®): Store under refrigeration at 2°C to 8°C (36°F to 46°F). May be stored in foil pouch at room temperature of 25°C (77°F) for up to 28 days. Avoid intense light. Solution may darken over time; however, do not use if cloudy or contains particles.

Mechanism of Action Interferes with bacterial protein synthesis by binding to 30S and 50S ribosomal subunits resulting in a defective bacterial cell membrane

Pharmacodynamics/Kinetics

Absorption:

Oral: Poorly absorbed

I.M.: Rapid and complete

Inhalation: Peak serum concentrations are ~1 mcg/mL following a 300 mg dose

Distribution: V_d: 0.2-0.3 L/kg; Pediatrics: 0.2-0.7 L/kg; to extracellular fluid including serum, abscesses, ascitic, pericardial, pleural, synovial, lymphatic, and peritoneal fluids; crosses placenta; poor penetration into CSF, eye, bone, prostate

Inhalation: Tobramycin remains concentrated primarily in the airways

Protein binding: <30%

Half-life elimination:

Neonates: ≤1200 g: 11 hours; >1200 g: 2-9 hours

Adults: 2-3 hours; directly dependent upon glomerular filtration rate

Adults with impaired renal function: 5-70 hours

Time to peak, serum: I.M.: 30-60 minutes; I.V.: ~30 minutes

Excretion: Normal renal function: Urine (~90% to 95%) within 24 hours

Dosage Note: Dosage individualization is **critical** because of the low therapeutic index.

Use of ideal body weight (IBW) for determining the mg/kg/dose appears to be more accurate than dosing on the basis of total body weight (TBW). In morbid obesity, dosage requirement may best be estimated using a dosing weight of IBW + 0.4 (TBW - IBW).

Initial and periodic plasma drug levels (eg, peak and trough with conventional dosing) should be determined, particularly in critically-ill patients with serious infections or in disease states known to significantly alter aminoglycoside pharmacokinetics (eg, cystic fibrosis, burns, or major surgery).

Usual dosage range:

Infants and Children <5 years: I.M., I.V.: 2.5 mg/kg/dose every 8 hours

Children ≥5 years: I.M., I.V.: 2-2.5 mg/kg/dose every 8 hours

Note: Higher individual doses and/or more frequent intervals (eg, every 6 hours) may be required in selected clinical situations (cystic fibrosis) or serum levels document the need.

Children and Adults:

Inhalation:

Children: 40-80 mg 2-3 times/day

Adults: 60-80 mg 3 times/day

High-dose regimen: Children ≥6 years and Adults: 300 mg every 12 hours (do not administer doses <6 hours apart); administer in repeated cycles of 28 days on drug followed by 28 days off drug

Intrathecal: 4-8 mg/day

Ophthalmic: Children ≥2 months and Adults:

Ointment: Instill ½' (1.25 cm) 2-3 times/day every 3-4 hours

Solution: Instill 1-2 drops every 2-4 hours, up to 2 drops every hour for severe infections

Topical: Apply 3-4 times/day to affected area

Adults: I.M., I.V.:

Conventional: 1-2.5 mg/kg/dose every 8-12 hours; to ensure adequate peak concentrations early in therapy, higher initial dosage may be considered in selected patients when extracellular water is increased (edema, septic shock, postsurgical, and/or trauma)

Once-daily: 4-7 mg/kg/dose once daily; some clinicians recommend this approach for all patients with normal renal function; this dose is at least as efficacious with similar, if not less, toxicity than conventional dosing.

Indication-specific dosing:

Neonates: I.M., I.V.:

Meningitis:

0-7 days: <2000 g: 2.5 mg/kg every 18-24 hours; >2000 g: 2.5 mg/kg every 12 hours

8-28 days: <2000 g: 2.5 mg/kg every 8-12 hours; >2000 g: 2.5 mg/kg every 8 hours

Children:

Cystic fibrosis:

I.M., I.V.: 2.5-3.3 mg/kg every 6-8 hours; **Note:** Some patients may require larger or more frequent doses if serum levels document the need (eg, cystic fibrosis or febrile granulocytopenic patients).

Inhalation:

Standard aerosolized tobramycin: 40-80 mg 2-3 times/day

High-dose regimen (TOBI®): Children ≥6 years: See adult dosing.

Adults: I.M., I.V.:

Brucellosis: 240 mg (I.M.) daily or 5 mg/kg (I.V.) daily for 7 days; either regimen recommended in combination with doxycycline

Cholangitis: 4-6 mg/kg once daily with ampicillin

Diverticulitis, complicated: 1.5-2 mg/kg every 8 hours (with ampicillin and metronidazole)

Endocarditis prophylaxis (dental, oral, upper respiratory procedures, GI/GU procedures): 1.5 mg/kg with ampicillin (50 mg/kg) 30 minutes prior to procedure

Endocarditis or synergy (for gram-positive infections): 1 mg/kg every 8 hours (with ampicillin)

Meningitis *(Enterococcus or Pseudomonas aeruginosa)*: I.V.: Loading dose: 2 mg/kg, then 1.7 mg/kg/dose every 8 hours (administered with another bacteriocidal drug)

Pelvic inflammatory disease: Loading dose: 2 mg/kg, then 1.5 mg/kg every 8 hours **or** 4.5 mg/kg once daily

Plague *(Yersinia pestis):* Treatment: 5 mg/kg/day, followed by postexposure prophylaxis with doxycycline

Pneumonia, hospital- or ventilator-associated: 7 mg/kg/day (with antipseudomonal beta-lactam or carbapenem)

Tularemia: 5 mg/kg/day divided every 8 hours for 1-2 weeks

Urinary tract infection: 1.5 mg/kg/dose every 8 hours

Dosing interval in renal impairment: I.M., I.V.:

Conventional dosing:

Cl_{cr} ≥60 mL/minute: Administer every 8 hours

Cl_{cr} 40-60 mL/minute: Administer every 12 hours

Cl_{cr} 20-40 mL/minute: Administer every 24 hours

Cl_{cr} 10-20 mL/minute: Administer every 48 hours

Cl_{cr} <10 mL/minute: Administer every 72 hours

High-dose therapy: Interval may be extended (eg, every 48 hours) in patients with moderate renal impairment (Cl_{cr} 30-59 mL/minute) and/or adjusted based on serum level determinations.

Hemodialysis: Dialyzable; 30% removal of aminoglycosides occurs during 4 hours of HD - administer dose after dialysis and follow levels

Continuous arteriovenous or venovenous hemofiltration: Dose as for Cl_{cr} of 10-40 mL/minute and follow levels

Administration in CAPD fluid:

Gram-negative infection: 4-8 mg/L (4-8 mcg/mL) of CAPD fluid

Gram-positive infection (ie, synergy): 3-4 mg/L (3-4 mcg/mL) of CAPD fluid

Administration IVPB/I.M.: Dose as for Cl_{cr} <10 mL/minute and follow levels

Dosing adjustment/comments in hepatic disease: Monitor plasma concentrations

Dietary Considerations May require supplementation of calcium, magnesium, potassium.

Administration

I.V.: Infuse over 30-60 minutes. Flush with saline before and after administration.

Inhalation (TOBI®): To be inhaled over ~15 minutes using a handheld nebulizer.

Ophthalmic: Contact lenses should not be worn during treatment of ophthalmic infections.

Ointment: Do not touch tip of tube to eye. Instill ointment into pocket between eyeball and lower lid; patient should look downward before closing eye.

Solution: Allow 5 minutes between application of "multiple-drop" therapy.

Suspension: Shake well before using; Tilt head back, instill suspension in conjunctival sac and close eye(s). Do not touch dropper to eye. Apply light finger pressure on lacrimal sac for 1 minute following instillation.

Some penicillins (eg, carbenicillin, ticarcillin and piperacillin) have been shown to inactivate aminoglycosides *in vitro*. This has been observed to a greater extent with tobramycin and gentamicin, while amikacin has shown greater stability against inactivation. Concurrent use of these agents may pose a risk of reduced antibacterial efficacy *in vivo*, particularly in the setting of profound renal impairment. However, definitive clinical evidence is lacking. If combination penicillin/aminoglycoside therapy is desired in a patient with renal dysfunction, separation of doses (if feasible), and routine monitoring of aminoglycoside levels, CBC, and clinical response should be considered.

Monitoring Parameters Urinalysis, urine output, BUN, serum creatinine, peak and trough plasma tobramycin levels; be alert to ototoxicity; hearing should be tested before and during treatment

Some penicillin derivatives may accelerate the degradation of aminoglycosides *in vitro*. This may be clinically-significant for certain penicillin (ticarcillin, piperacillin, carbenicillin) and aminoglycoside (gentamicin, tobramycin) combination therapy in patients with significant renal impairment. Close monitoring of aminoglycoside levels is warranted.

Reference Range

Timing of serum samples: Draw peak 30 minutes after 30-minute infusion has been completed or 1 hour following I.M. injection or beginning of infusion; draw trough immediately before next dose

Therapeutic levels:

Peak:

Serious infections: 6-8 mcg/mL (SI: 12-17 µmol/L)

Life-threatening infections: 8-10 mcg/mL (SI: 17-21 µmol/L)

Urinary tract infections: 4-6 mcg/mL (SI: 7-12 µmol/L)

Synergy against gram-positive organisms: 3-5 mcg/mL

Trough:

Serious infections: 0.5-1 mcg/mL

Life-threatening infections: 1-2 mcg/mL

The American Thoracic Society (ATS) recommends trough levels of <1 mcg/mL for patients with hospital-acquired pneumonia.

Monitor serum creatinine and urine output; obtain drug levels after the third dose unless otherwise directed

Inhalation: Serum levels are ~1 mcg/mL one hour following a 300 mg dose in patients with normal renal function.

Test Interactions Some penicillin derivatives may accelerate the degradation of aminoglycosides *in vitro*, leading to a potential underestimation of aminoglycoside serum concentration.

Additional Information Once-daily dosing: Higher peak serum drug concentration to MIC ratios, demonstrated aminoglycoside postantibiotic effect, decreased renal cortex drug uptake, and improved cost-time efficiency are supportive reasons for the use of once daily dosing regimens for aminoglycosides. Current research indicates these regimens to be as effective for nonlife-threatening infections, with no higher incidence of nephrotoxicity, than those requiring multiple daily doses. Doses are determined by calculating the entire day's dose via usual multiple dose calculation techniques and administering this quantity as a single dose. Doses are then adjusted to maintain mean serum concentrations above the MIC(s) of the causative organism(s). (Example: 2.5-5 mg/kg as a single dose; expected Cp_{max}: 10-20 mcg/mL and Cp_{min}: <1 mcg/mL). Further research is needed for universal (Continued)

Tobramycin *(Continued)*

recommendation in all patient populations and gram-negative disease; exceptions may include those with known high clearance (eg, children, patients with cystic fibrosis, or burns who may require shorter dosage intervals) and patients with renal function impairment for whom longer than conventional dosage intervals are usually required.

Dosage Forms

Infusion [premixed in NS]: 60 mg (50 mL); 80 mg (100 mL)

Injection, powder for reconstitution: 1.2 g

Injection, solution: 10 mg/mL (2 mL, 8 mL); 40 mg/mL (2 mL, 30 mL, 50 mL) [may contain sodium metabisulfite]

Ointment, ophthalmic (Tobrex®): 0.3% (3.5 g)

Solution for nebulization [preservative free] (TOBI®): 60 mg/mL (5 mL)

Solution, ophthalmic (AKTob®, Tobrex®): 0.3% (5 mL) [contains benzalkonium chloride]

Tobramycin and Dexamethasone *(toe bra MYE sin & deks a METH a sone)*

U.S. Brand Names TobraDex®

Canadian Brand Names Tobradex®

Index Terms Dexamethasone and Tobramycin

Pharmacologic Category Antibiotic/Corticosteroid, Ophthalmic

Use Treatment of external ocular infection caused by susceptible gram-negative bacteria and steroid responsive inflammatory conditions of the palpebral and bulbar conjunctiva, lid, cornea, and anterior segment of the globe

Pregnancy Risk Factor C

Medication Safety Issues

Sound-alike/look-alike issues:

TobraDex® may be confused with Tobrex®

Dosage Children and Adults: Ophthalmic: Instill 1-2 drops of solution every 4 hours; apply ointment 2-3 times/day; for severe infections apply ointment every 3-4 hours, or solution 2 drops every 30-60 minutes initially, then reduce to less frequent intervals

Additional Information Complete prescribing information for this medication should be consulted for additional detail.

Dosage Forms

Ointment, ophthalmic: Tobramycin 0.3% and dexamethasone 0.1% (3.5 g)

Suspension, ophthalmic: Tobramycin 0.3% and dexamethasone 0.1% (2.5 mL, 5 mL, 10 mL) [contains benzalkonium chloride]

♦ **Tobramycin and Loteprednol Etabonate** *see* Loteprednol and Tobramycin *on page 1039*

♦ **Tobramycin Injection, USP (Can)** *see* Tobramycin *on page 1696*

♦ **Tobramycin Sulfate** *see* Tobramycin *on page 1696*

♦ **Tobrex®** *see* Tobramycin *on page 1696*

♦ **Today® Sponge [OTC]** *see* Nonoxynol 9 *on page 1239*

♦ **Tofranil®** *see* Imipramine *on page 888*

♦ **Tofranil-PM®** *see* Imipramine *on page 888*

TOLAZamide *(tole AZ a mide)*

U.S. Brand Names Tolinase® [DSC]

Canadian Brand Names Tolinase®

Pharmacologic Category Antidiabetic Agent, Sulfonylurea

Additional Appendix Information

Hyperglycemia- or Hypoglycemia-Causing Drugs *on page 2057*

Sulfonamide Derivatives *on page 1897*

Use Adjunct to diet for the management of mild to moderately severe, stable, type 2 diabetes mellitus (noninsulin dependent, NIDDM)

Pregnancy Risk Factor D

Medication Safety Issues

Sound-alike/look-alike issues:

TOLAZamide may be confused with tolazoline, TOLBUTamide

Tolinase® may be confused with Orinase®

Dosage Oral (doses >1000 mg/day normally do not improve diabetic control):

Adults:

Initial: 100-250 mg/day with breakfast or the first main meal of the day

Fasting blood sugar <200 mg/dL: 100 mg/day

Fasting blood sugar >200 mg/dL: 250 mg/day

Patient is malnourished, underweight, elderly, or not eating properly: 100 mg/day

Adjust dose in increments of 100-250 mg/day at weekly intervals to response. If >500 mg/day is required, give in divided doses twice daily; maximum daily dose: 1 g (doses >1 g/day are not likely to improve control)

Conversion from insulin to tolazamide

10 units day = 100 mg/day

20-40 units/day = 250 mg/day

>40 units/day = 250 mg/day and 50% of insulin dose

Doses >500 mg/day should be given in 2 divided doses

Dosing adjustment in renal impairment: Conservative initial and maintenance doses are recommended because tolazamide is metabolized to active metabolites, which are eliminated in the urine

Dosing comments in hepatic impairment: Conservative initial and maintenance doses and careful monitoring of blood glucose are recommended

Additional Information Complete prescribing information for this medication should be consulted for additional detail.

Dosage Forms [DSC] = Discontinued product
Tablet: 100 mg, 250 mg, 500 mg
   Tolinase® [DSC]: 100 mg, 250 mg

Tolazoline (tole AZ oh leen)

U.S. Brand Names Priscoline® [DSC]
Index Terms Benzazoline Hydrochloride; Tolazoline Hydrochloride
Pharmacologic Category Vasodilator
Use Treatment of persistent pulmonary vasoconstriction and hypertension of the newborn (persistent fetal circulation), peripheral vasospastic disorders
Pregnancy Risk Factor C
Medication Safety Issues
Sound-alike/look-alike issues:
   Tolazoline may be confused with TOLAZamide
   Priscoline® may be confused with Apresoline®
Dosage
Neonates: Initial: I.V.: 1-2 mg/kg over 10-15 minutes via scalp vein or upper extremity; maintenance: 1-2 mg/kg/hour; use lower maintenance doses in patients with decreased renal function. Also used in neonates for acute vasospasm "cath toes" at 0.25 mg/kg/hour (no load); maximum dose: 6-8 mg/kg/hour.
  Dosing interval in renal impairment in newborns: Urine output <0.9 mL/kg/hour: Decrease dose to 0.08 mg/kg/hour for every 1 mg/kg of loading dose
Adults: Peripheral vasospastic disorder: I.M., I.V., SubQ: 10-50 mg 4 times/day
Additional Information Complete prescribing information for this medication should be consulted for additional detail.
Dosage Forms [DSC] = Discontinued product
Injection, solution, as hydrochloride [DSC]: 25 mg/mL (4 mL)
♦ **Tolazoline Hydrochloride** *see* Tolazoline *on page 1701*

TOLBUTamide (tole BYOO ta mide)

Canadian Brand Names Apo-Tolbutamide®
Index Terms Tolbutamide Sodium
Pharmacologic Category Antidiabetic Agent, Sulfonylurea
Additional Appendix Information
Hyperglycemia- or Hypoglycemia-Causing Drugs *on page 2057*
Sulfonamide Derivatives *on page 1897*
Use Adjunct to diet for the management of mild to moderately severe, stable, type 2 diabetes mellitus (noninsulin dependent, NIDDM)
Pregnancy Risk Factor D
Medication Safety Issues
Sound-alike/look-alike issues:
   TOLBUTamide may be confused with terbutaline, TOLAZamide
   Orinase® may be confused with Orabase®, Ornex®, Tolinase®
Dosage Divided doses may improve gastrointestinal tolerance
Adults: Oral: Initial: 1-2 g/day as a single dose in the morning or in divided doses throughout the day. Total doses may be taken in the morning; however, divided doses may allow increased gastrointestinal tolerance. Maintenance dose: 0.25-3 g/day; however, a maintenance dose >2 g/day is seldom required.
Elderly: Oral: Initial: 250 mg 1-3 times/day; usual: 500-2000 mg; maximum: 3 g/day
  Dosing adjustment in renal impairment: Adjustment is not necessary
Hemodialysis: Not dialyzable (0% to 5%)
  Dosing adjustment in hepatic impairment: Reduction of dose may be necessary in patients with impaired liver function
Additional Information Complete prescribing information for this medication should be consulted for additional detail.
Dosage Forms Tablet: 500 mg
♦ **Tolbutamide Sodium** *see* TOLBUTamide *on page 1701*

Tolcapone (TOLE ka pone)

U.S. Brand Names Tasmar®
Pharmacologic Category Anti-Parkinson's Agent, COMT Inhibitor
Additional Appendix Information
Parkinson's Agents *on page 1895*
Use Adjunct to levodopa and carbidopa for the treatment of signs and symptoms of idiopathic Parkinson's disease
Restrictions A patient signed consent form acknowledging the risks of hepatic injury should be obtained by the treating physician.
Pregnancy Risk Factor C
Pregnancy Implications Tolcapone may be teratogenic based on animal studies. There are no adequate and well-controlled studies in pregnant women. Use only if benefit outweighs risk.
Lactation Excretion in breast milk unknown/contraindicated
Contraindications Hypersensitivity to tolcapone or any component of the formulation; history of liver disease or tolcapone-induced hepatocellular injury; nontraumatic rhabdomyolysis or hyperpyrexia and confusion
Warnings/Precautions [U.S. Boxed Warning]: Due to reports of fatal liver injury associated with use of this drug, the manufacturer is advising that tolcapone be reserved for patients who are experiencing inadequate symptom control or who are not appropriate
(Continued)

Tolcapone *(Continued)*

candidates for other available treatments. Patients must provide written consent acknowledging the risks of hepatic injury. Use with caution in patients with pre-existing dyskinesias, hepatic impairment, or severe renal impairment. Exacerbation of pre-existing dyskinesia and severe rhabdomyolysis has been reported. Has been associated with a syndrome resembling neuroleptic malignant syndrome (hyperpyrexia and confusion- some fatal) on abrupt withdrawal or dosage reduction. Patients receiving tolcapone are predisposed to orthostatic hypotension, diarrhea (usually within the first 6-12 weeks of therapy), transient hallucinations (most commonly within the first 2 weeks of therapy), and new onset or worsened dyskinesia.

Concomitant use of tolcapone and nonselective MAO inhibitors should be avoided. Selegiline is a selective MAO type B inhibitor (when given orally at ≤10 mg/day) and can be taken with tolcapone. Has also been associated with fibrotic complications, such as retroperitoneal fibrosis, pulmonary infiltrates or effusion and pleural thickening. Safety and efficacy in pediatric patients have not been established.

Adverse Reactions
>10%:
Cardiovascular: Orthostatic hypotension (17%)
Central nervous system: Sleep disorder (24% to 25%), excessive dreaming (16% to 21%), somnolence (14% to 18%), dizziness (6% to 13%), headache (10% to 11%), confusion (10% to 11%)
Gastrointestinal: Nausea (30% to 35%), anorexia (19% to 23%), diarrhea (16% to 18%)
Neuromuscular & skeletal: Dyskinesia (42% to 51%), dystonia (19% to 22%), muscle cramps (17% to 18%)
1% to 10%:
Cardiovascular: Syncope (4% to 5%), chest pain (1% to 3%), hypotension (2%), palpitation
Central nervous system: Hallucinations (8% to 10%), fatigue (3% to 7%), loss of balance (2% to 3%), agitation (1%), euphoria (1%), hyperactivity (1%), malaise (1%), panic reaction (1%), irritability (1%), mental deficiency (1%), fever (1%), depression, hypoesthesia, tremor, speech disorder, vertigo, emotional lability, hyperkinesia
Dermatologic: Alopecia (1%), bleeding (1%), tumor (1%), rash
Gastrointestinal: Vomiting (8% to 10%), constipation (6% to 8%), xerostomia (5% to 6%), abdominal pain (5% to 6%), dyspepsia (3% to 4%), flatulence (2% to 4%), tooth disorder
Genitourinary: UTI (5%), hematuria (4% to 5%), urine discoloration (2% to 3%), urination disorder (1% to 2%), uterine tumor (1%), incontinence, impotence
Hepatic: Transaminases increased (1% to 3%; 3 times ULN, usually with first 6 months of therapy)
Neuromuscular & skeletal: Paresthesia (1% to 3%), hyper-/hypokinesia (1% to 3%), arthritis (1% to 2%), neck pain (2%), stiffness (2%), myalgia, rhabdomyolysis
Ocular: Cataract (1%), eye inflammation (1%)
Otic: Tinnitus
Respiratory: Upper respiratory infection (5% to 7%), dyspnea (3%), sinus congestion (1% to 2%), bronchitis, pharyngitis
Miscellaneous: Diaphoresis (4% to 7%), influenza (3% to 4%), burning (1% to 2%), flank pain, injury, infection
<1% (Limited to important or life-threatening): Abnormal stools, abscess, allergic reaction, amnesia, anemia, antisocial reaction, apathy, apnea, arteriosclerosis, arthrosis, asthma, bladder calculus, breast neoplasm, carcinoma, cardiovascular disorder, cellulitis, cerebral ischemia, cerebrovascular accident, chills, cholecystitis, cholelithiasis, choreoathetosis, colitis, cough increased, death, dehydration, delirium, delusions, diabetes mellitus, diplopia, duodenal ulcer, dysphagia, dysuria, ear pain, eczema, edema, encephalopathy, epistaxis, erythema multiforme, esophagitis, extrapyramidal syndrome, eye hemorrhage, eye pain, facial edema, furunculosis, gastroenteritis, gastrointestinal carcinoma, gastrointestinal hemorrhage, glaucoma, hemiplegia, hernia, herpes simplex, herpes zoster, hiccup, hostility, hypercholesteremia, hyperventilation, hypoxia, infection (bacterial), infection (fungal), joint disorder, kidney calculus, lacrimation disorder, laryngitis, leukemia, libido changes, lung edema, manic reaction, meningitis, mouth ulceration, myoclonus, neoplasm, nervousness, neuralgia, neuropathy, nocturia, oliguria, otitis media, ovarian carcinoma, pain, paranoid reaction, parosmia, pericardial effusion, polyuria, prostatic carcinoma, prostatic disorder, pruritus, psychosis, rectal disorder, rhinitis, salivation increased, seborrhea, skin discoloration, skin disorder, stomach atony, surgical procedure, tenosynovitis, thinking abnormal, thirst, thrombocytopenia, thrombosis, tongue disorder, twitching, urinary retention, urinary tract disorder, urticaria, uterine atony, uterine disorder, uterine hemorrhage, vaginitis, viral infection

Overdosage/Toxicology No information is available regarding intentional overdose with tolcapone. The highest dose evaluated clinically was 800 mg 3 times/day, with side effects consisting primarily of nausea/vomiting, and dizziness. Treatment should be supportive and symptom-directed. Dialysis not likely to benefit.

Drug Interactions
Cytochrome P450 Effect: Inhibits CYP2C9 (weak)
Increased Effect/Toxicity: Tolcapone may decrease the metabolism and increase the side effects of COMT substrates (eg, apomorphine, bitolterol, dobutamine, dopamine, epinephrine, norepinephrine, isoproterenol, isoetharine, and methyldopa). Effects on mental status may be additive with other CNS depressants; includes barbiturates, benzodiazepines, TCAs, antipsychotics, ethanol, opioid analgesics, and other sedative-hypnotics. Concurrent use of nonselective MAO inhibitors with tolcapone may increase the risk of cardiovascular side effects; selective MAO inhibitors (eg, selegiline ≤10 mg/day) appear to pose limited risk.

Ethanol/Nutrition/Herb Interactions
Ethanol: Avoid ethanol (may increase CNS depression).
Food: Tolcapone, taken with food within 1 hour before or 2 hours after the dose, decreases bioavailability by 10% to 20%.
Avoid valerian, St John's wort, kava kava, gotu kola (may increase CNS depression).
Stability Store at 20°C to 25°C (68°F to 77°F).

Mechanism of Action Tolcapone is a selective and reversible inhibitor of cate-chol-o-methyltransferase (COMT). In the presence of a decarboxylase inhibitor (eg, carbidopa), COMT is the major degradation pathway for levodopa. Inhibition of COMT leads to more sustained plasma levels of levodopa and enhanced central dopaminergic activity.

Pharmacodynamics/Kinetics
Absorption: Rapid
Distribution: 9 L
Protein binding: >99.0%
Metabolism: Glucuronidation to inactive metabolite
Bioavailability: 65%
Half-life elimination: 2-3 hours
Time to peak: ~2 hours
Excretion: Urine (60% as metabolites); feces (40%)

Dosage Oral: Adults: Initial: 100 mg 3 times/day; may increase as tolerated to 200 mg 3 times/day; levodopa dose may need to be decreased upon initiation of tolcapone (average reduction in clinical trials was 30%)

Note: If clinical improvement is not observed after 3 weeks of therapy (regardless of dose), tolcapone treatment should be discontinued.

Dosage adjustment in renal impairment: No adjustment necessary for mild-moderate impairment. Use caution with severe impairment; no safety information available in patients with Cl_{cr}<25 mL/minute.

Dosage adjustment in hepatic impairment: Do not use.

Dietary Considerations May be taken without regard to food.

Administration May be administered with or without food. In clinical studies, the first dose of the day was administered with carbidopa/levodopa, and the subsequent doses were administered 6 hours and 12 hours later.

Monitoring Parameters Blood pressure, symptoms of Parkinson's disease, liver enzymes at baseline and then every 2-4 weeks for the first 6 months of therapy; thereafter, periodic monitoring should be conducted as deemed clinically relevant. If the dose is increased to 200 mg 3 times/day, reinitiate LFT monitoring every 2-4 weeks for 6 months, and then resume periodic monitoring. Discontinue therapy if the ALT or AST exceeds 2 times ULN or if the clinical signs and symptoms suggest the onset of liver failure.

Dosage Forms Tablet: 100 mg, 200 mg

- ◆ **Tolectin®** see Tolmetin on page 1703
- ◆ **Tolinase® [DSC]** see TOLAZamide on page 1700
- ◆ **Tolinase® (Can)** see TOLAZamide on page 1700

Tolmetin (TOLE met in)

U.S. Brand Names Tolectin®
Index Terms Tolmetin Sodium
Pharmacologic Category Nonsteroidal Anti-inflammatory Drug (NSAID), Oral
Additional Appendix Information
Nonsteroidal Anti-inflammatory Agents on page 1894
Use Treatment of rheumatoid arthritis and osteoarthritis, juvenile rheumatoid arthritis
Restrictions An FDA-approved medication guide must be distributed when dispensing an oral outpatient prescription (new or refill) where this medication is to be used without direct supervision of a healthcare provider. Medication guides are available at http://www.fda.gov/cder/Offices/ODS/medication_guides.htm.
Pregnancy Risk Factor C/D (3rd trimester)
Lactation Enters breast milk/not recommended (AAP rates "compatible")
Contraindications Hypersensitivity to tolmetin, aspirin, other NSAIDs, or any component of the formulation; perioperative pain in the setting of coronary artery bypass surgery (CABG); pregnancy (3rd trimester or near term)
Warnings/Precautions [U.S. Boxed Warning]: NSAIDs are associated with an increased risk of adverse cardiovascular events, including MI, stroke, and new onset or worsening of pre-existing hypertension. Risk may be increased with duration of use or pre-existing cardiovascular risk-factors or disease. Carefully evaluate individual cardiovascular risk profiles prior to prescribing. Use caution with fluid retention, CHF or hypertension. Concurrent administration of ibuprofen, and potentially other nonselective NSAIDs, may interfere with aspirin's cardioprotective effect.

Use of NSAIDs can compromise existing renal function. Renal toxicity can occur in patient with impaired renal function, dehydration, heart failure, liver dysfunction, those taking diuretics and ACEI and the elderly. Rehydrate patient before starting therapy. Monitor renal function closely. Use caution in patients with advanced renal disease.

[U.S. Boxed Warning]: NSAIDs may increase risk of gastrointestinal irritation, ulceration, bleeding, and perforation. These events may occur at any time during therapy and without warning. Use caution with a history of GI disease (bleeding or ulcers), concurrent therapy with aspirin, anticoagulants and/or corticosteroids, smoking, use of alcohol, the elderly or debilitated patients.

Use the lowest effective dose for the shortest duration of time, consistent with individual patient goals, to reduce risk of cardiovascular or GI adverse events. Alternate therapies should be considered for patients at high risk.

NSAIDs may cause serious skin adverse events including exfoliative dermatitis, Stevens-Johnson syndrome (SJS) and toxic epidermal necrolysis (TEN). Anaphylactoid reactions may occur, even without prior exposure; patients with "aspirin triad" (bronchial asthma, aspirin intolerance, rhinitis) may be at increased risk. Do not use in patients who experience bronchospasm, asthma, rhinitis, or urticaria with NSAID or aspirin therapy.

Use with caution in patients with decreased hepatic function. Closely monitor patients with any abnormal LFT. Severe hepatic reactions (eg, fulminant hepatitis, liver failure) have (Continued)

Tolmetin *(Continued)*

occurred with NSAID use, rarely; discontinue if signs or symptoms of liver disease develop, or if systemic manifestations occur.

The elderly are at increased risk for adverse effects (especially peptic ulceration, CNS effects, renal toxicity) from NSAIDs even at low doses.

Withhold for at least 4-6 half-lives prior to surgical or dental procedures. Safety and efficacy have not been established in children <2 years of age.

Adverse Reactions

1% to 10%:
Cardiovascular: Chest pain, hypertension, edema
Central nervous system: Headache, dizziness, drowsiness, depression
Dermatologic: Skin irritation
Endocrine & metabolic: Weight gain/loss
Gastrointestinal: Heartburn, abdominal pain, diarrhea, flatulence, vomiting, constipation, gastritis, peptic ulcer, nausea
Genitourinary: Urinary tract infection
Hematologic: Elevated BUN, transient decreases in hemoglobin/hematocrit
Ocular: Visual disturbances
Otic: Tinnitus
<1% (Limited to important or life-threatening): Abnormal LFTs, agranulocytosis, bronchospasm, CHF, dyspnea, erythema multiforme, GI bleeding, granulocytopenia, hematuria, hemolytic anemia, hepatitis, proteinuria, renal failure, thrombocytopenia, toxic epidermal necrolysis

Overdosage/Toxicology Symptoms include lethargy, mental confusion, dizziness, leukocytosis, and renal failure. Management of nonsteroidal anti-inflammatory drug (NSAID) intoxication is primarily supportive and symptomatic. Fluid therapy is commonly effective in managing hypotension that may occur following an acute NSAID overdose, except when due to acute blood loss. Seizures tend to be very short-lived and often do not require drug treatment; although, recurrent seizures should be treated with I.V. diazepam. Since many of the NSAIDs undergo enterohepatic cycling, multiple doses of charcoal may be needed to reduce the potential for delayed toxicities.

Drug Interactions

Increased Effect/Toxicity: Increased toxicity of digoxin, methotrexate, cyclosporine, lithium, insulin, sulfonylureas, potassium-sparing diuretics, and aspirin. Concomitant use with fluoroquinolones may rarely increase risk of seizure.

Decreased Effect: Decreased effect with aspirin. Salicylates' antiplatelet effect may be reduced. Decreased effect of thiazides and furosemide. NSAIDs may decrease the antihypertensive effect of ACE inhibitors, beta-blockers, hydralazine, and angiotensin antagonists. Cholestyramine (and other bile acid sequestrants) may decrease the absorption of NSAIDs; separate by at least 2 hours.

Ethanol/Nutrition/Herb Interactions

Ethanol: Avoid ethanol (may enhance gastric mucosal irritation).
Food: Tolmetin peak serum concentrations may be decreased if taken with food or milk.
Herb/Nutraceutical: Avoid alfalfa, anise, bilberry, bladderwrack, bromelain, cat's claw, celery, coleus, cordyceps, dong quai, evening primrose, feverfew, fenugreek, garlic, ginger, ginkgo biloboa, red clover, horse chestnut, grapeseed, green tea, ginseng, guggul, horse chestnut seed, horseradish, licorice, prickly ash, red clover, reishi, SAMe, sweet clover, turmeric, white willow (all have additional antiplatelet activity).

Mechanism of Action Inhibits prostaglandin synthesis by decreasing the activity of the enzyme, cyclooxygenase, which results in decreased formation of prostaglandin precursors

Pharmacodynamics/Kinetics

Onset of action: Analgesic: 1-2 hours; Anti-inflammatory: Days to weeks
Absorption: Well absorbed
Bioavailability: Reduced 16% with food or milk
Half-life elimination: Biphasic: Rapid: 1-2 hours; Slow: 5 hours
Time to peak, serum: 30-60 minutes
Excretion: Urine (as inactive metabolites or conjugates) within 24 hours

Dosage Oral:

Children ≥2 years:
Anti-inflammatory: Initial: 20 mg/kg/day in 3 divided doses, then 15-30 mg/kg/day in 3 divided doses
Analgesic: 5-7 mg/kg/dose every 6-8 hours
Adults: 400 mg 3 times/day; usual dose: 600 mg to 1.8 g/day; maximum: 2 g/day

Dietary Considerations Should be taken with food, milk, or antacids to decrease GI adverse effects. Sodium content of 200 mg: 0.8 mEq.

Monitoring Parameters Occult blood loss, CBC, liver enzymes, BUN, serum creatinine, periodic liver function test

Dosage Forms

Capsule: 400 mg
Tablet: 200 mg, 600 mg
Tolectin®: 600 mg [contains sodium 54 mg (2.35 mEq)]

♦ **Tolmetin Sodium** *see* Tolmetin *on page 1703*

Tolnaftate *(tole NAF tate)*

U.S. Brand Names Blis-To-Sol® [OTC]; Fungi-Guard [OTC]; Gold Bond® Antifungal [OTC] [DSC]; Mycocide® NS [OTC]; Podactin Powder [OTC]; Q-Naftate [OTC]; Tinactin® Antifungal [OTC]; Tinactin® Antifungal Jock Itch [OTC]; Tinaderm [OTC]; Ting® Cream [OTC]; Ting® Spray Liquid [OTC]

Canadian Brand Names Pitrex
Pharmacologic Category Antifungal Agent, Topical
Use Treatment of tinea pedis, tinea cruris, tinea corporis
Pregnancy Risk Factor C
Medication Safety Issues
  Sound-alike/look-alike issues:
    Tolnaftate may be confused with Tornalate®
    Tinactin® may be confused with Talacen®
Dosage Children ≥2 years and Adults: Topical: Wash and dry affected area; spray aerosol or apply 1-3 drops of solution or a small amount of cream, or powder and rub into the affected areas 2 times/day
  Note: May use for up to 4 weeks for tinea pedis or tinea corporis, and up to 2 weeks for tinea cruris
Additional Information Complete prescribing information for this medication should be consulted for additional detail.
Dosage Forms [DSC] = Discontinued product
  Aerosol, liquid, topical:
    Tinactin® Antifungal: 1% (60 mL, 150 mL) [contains alcohol]
    Ting®: 1% (90 mL)
  Aerosol, powder, topical:
    Tinactin® Antifungal: 1% (133 g) [contains alcohol]
    Tinactin® Antifungal Jock Itch: 1% (100 g, 133 g) [contains alcohol]
  Cream, topical: 1% (15 g, 30 g)
    Fungi-Guard, Tinactin® Antifungal Jock Itch, Ting®: 1% (15 g)
    Q-Naftate, Tinactin® Antifungal: 1% (15 g, 30 g)
  Liquid, topical:
    Blis-To-Sol®: 1% (30 mL, 55 mL)
    Fungi-Guard: 1% (30 mL) [contains vitamin E and aloe; brush applicator provided]
  Powder, topical: 1% (45 g)
    Podactin: 1% (45 g)
    Tinactin® Antifungal: 1% (108 g)
  Solution, topical: 1% (10 mL)
    Mycocide® NS: 1% (30 mL)
    Tinaderm: 1% (10 mL)
  Swab, topical [liquid filled swabstick]:
    Gold Bond® Antifungal: 1% (24s) [DSC]

Tolterodine (tole TER oh deen)

U.S. Brand Names Detrol®; Detrol® LA
Canadian Brand Names Detrol®; Detrol® LA; Unidet®
Index Terms Tolterodine Tartrate
Pharmacologic Category Anticholinergic Agent
Use Treatment of patients with an overactive bladder with symptoms of urinary frequency, urgency, or urge incontinence
Pregnancy Risk Factor C
Pregnancy Implications Teratogenic effects were observed in some animal studies. There are no adequate and well-controlled studies in pregnant women. Use during pregnancy only if the potential benefit to the mother outweighs the possible risk to the fetus.
Lactation Excretion in breast milk unknown/not recommended
Medication Safety Issues
  Sound-alike/look-alike issues:
    Detrol® may be confused with Ditropan®

  International issues:
    Detrol® may be confused with Desurol® which is a brand name for oxolinic acid in the Czech Republic
Contraindications Hypersensitivity to tolterodine or any component of the formulation; urinary retention; gastric retention; uncontrolled narrow-angle glaucoma; myasthenia gravis
Warnings/Precautions Use with caution in patients with bladder flow obstruction, may increase the risk of urinary retention. Use with caution in patients with gastrointestinal obstructive disorders (ie, pyloric stenosis), may increase the risk of gastric retention. Use with caution in patients with controlled (treated) narrow-angle glaucoma; metabolized in the liver and excreted in the urine and feces, dosage adjustment is required for patients with renal or hepatic impairment. Tolterodine has been associated with QT_c prolongation at high (supratherapeutic) doses. The manufacturer recommends caution in patients with congenital prolonged QT or in patients receiving concurrent therapy with QT_c-prolonging drugs (class Ia or III antiarrhythmics). However, the mean change in QT_c even at supratherapeutic dosages was less than 15 msec. Individuals who are poor metabolizers via CYP2D6 or in the presence of inhibitors of CYP2D6 and CYP3A4 may be more likely to exhibit prolongation. Dosage adjustment is recommended in patients receiving CYP3A4 inhibitors (a lower dose of tolterodine is recommended). Safety and efficacy in pediatric patients have not been established.
Adverse Reactions As reported with immediate release tablet, unless otherwise specified
  >10%: Gastrointestinal: Dry mouth (35%; extended release capsules 23%)
  1% to 10%:
    Cardiovascular: Chest pain (2%)
    Central nervous system: Headache (7%; extended release capsules 6%), somnolence (3%; extended release capsules 3%), fatigue (4%; extended release capsules 2%), dizziness (5%; extended release capsules 2%), anxiety (extended release capsules 1%)
    Dermatologic: Dry skin (1%)
  (Continued)

Tolterodine *(Continued)*

Gastrointestinal: Abdominal pain (5%; extended release capsules 4%), constipation (7%; extended release capsules 6%), dyspepsia (4%; extended release capsules 3%), diarrhea (4%), weight gain (1%)

Genitourinary: Dysuria (2%; extended release capsules 1%)

Neuromuscular & skeletal: Arthralgia (2%)

Ocular: Abnormal vision (2%; extended release capsules 1%), dry eyes (3%; extended release capsules 3%)

Respiratory: Bronchitis (2%), sinusitis (extended release capsules 2%)

Miscellaneous: Flu-like syndrome (3%), infection (1%)

<1% (Limited to important or life-threatening): Anaphylactoid reactions, angioedema, hallucinations, palpitation, peripheral edema, QT_c prolongation, tachycardia

Overdosage/Toxicology Overdosage can potentially result in severe central anticholinergic effects and should be treated accordingly. ECG monitoring is recommended in the event of overdosage. QT_c prolongation has been observed at supratherapeutic doses, particularly in CYP2D6 poor metabolizers.

Drug Interactions

Cytochrome P450 Effect: Substrate of CYP2C9 (minor), 2C19 (minor), 2D6 (major), 3A4 (major)

Increased Effect/Toxicity: CYP2D6 inhibitors may increase the levels/effects of tolterodine, which may include QT_c prolongation; example inhibitors include chlorpromazine, delavirdine, fluoxetine, miconazole, paroxetine, pergolide, quinidine, quinine, ritonavir, and ropinirole. No dosage adjustment was needed in patients coadministered tolterodine and fluoxetine. CYP3A4 inhibitors may increase the levels/effects of tolterodine, which may include QT_c prolongation; example inhibitors include azole antifungals, clarithromycin, diclofenac, doxycycline, erythromycin, imatinib, isoniazid, nefazodone, nicardipine, propofol, protease inhibitors, quinidine, telithromycin, and verapamil. Concomitant use with systemic anticholinergic agents may increase the risk of anticholinergic side effects. Use with pramlintide may result in increased slowing of gut motility. Additive effects on QT_c prolongation may occur with concurrent therapy with QT_c prolonging agents. Tolterodine may increase the effects of warfarin.

Decreased Effect: CYP3A4 inducers may decrease the levels/effects of tolterodine; example inducers include aminoglutethimide, carbamazepine, nafcillin, nevirapine, phenobarbital, phenytoin, and rifamycins. Use with acetylcholinesterase inhibitors may result in reduced therapeutic efficacy.

Ethanol/Nutrition/Herb Interactions

Food: Increases bioavailability (~53% increase) of tolterodine tablets, but does not affect the pharmacokinetics of tolterodine extended release capsules; adjustment of dose is not needed. As a CYP3A4 inhibitor, grapefruit juice may increase the serum level and/or toxicity of tolterodine, but unlikely secondary to high oral bioavailability.

Herb/Nutraceutical: St John's wort (*Hypericum*) appears to induce CYP3A enzymes.

Stability Store at 15°C to 30°C (59°F to 86°F). Protect from light.

Mechanism of Action Tolterodine is a competitive antagonist of muscarinic receptors. In animal models, tolterodine demonstrates selectivity for urinary bladder receptors over salivary receptors. Urinary bladder contraction is mediated by muscarinic receptors. Tolterodine increases residual urine volume and decreases detrusor muscle pressure.

Pharmacodynamics/Kinetics

Absorption: Immediate release tablet: Rapid; ≥77%

Distribution: I.V.: V_d: 113 ± 27 L

Protein binding: >96% (primarily to alpha$_1$-acid glycoprotein)

Metabolism: Extensively hepatic, primarily via CYP2D6 (some metabolites share activity) and 3A4 usually (minor pathway). In patients with a genetic deficiency of CYP2D6, metabolism via 3A4 predominates. Forms three active metabolites.

Bioavailability: Immediate release tablet: Increased 53% with food

Half-life elimination:

Immediate release tablet: Extensive metabolizers: ~2 hours; Poor metabolizers: ~10 hours

Extended release capsule: Extensive metabolizers: ~7 hours; Poor metabolizers: ~18 hours

Time to peak: Immediate release tablet: 1-2 hours; Extended release tablet: 2-6 hours

Excretion: Urine (77%); feces (17%); excreted primarily as metabolites (<1% unchanged drug) of which the active 5-hydroxymethyl metabolite accounts for 5% to 14% (<1% in poor metabolizers)

Dosage

Oral: Adults: Treatment of overactive bladder:

Immediate release tablet: 2 mg twice daily; the dose may be lowered to 1 mg twice daily based on individual response and tolerability

Dosing adjustment in patients concurrently taking CYP3A4 inhibitors: 1 mg twice daily

Extended release capsule: 4 mg once a day; dose may be lowered to 2 mg daily based on individual response and tolerability

Dosing adjustment in patients concurrently taking CYP3A4 inhibitors: 2 mg daily

Elderly: Safety and efficacy in patients >64 years was found to be similar to that in younger patients; no dosage adjustment is needed based on age

Dosing adjustment in renal impairment: Use with caution (studies conducted in patients with Cl_{cr} 10-30 mL/minute):

Immediate release tablet: 1 mg twice daily

Extended release capsule: 2 mg daily

Dosing adjustment in hepatic impairment:

Immediate release tablet: 1 mg twice daily

Extended release capsule: 2 mg daily

Administration Extended release capsule: Swallow whole; do not crush, chew, or open

Dosage Forms

Capsule, extended release, as tartrate (Detrol® LA): 2 mg, 4 mg

Tablet, as tartrate (Detrol®): 1 mg, 2 mg

TOPIRAMATE

♦ **Tolterodine Tartrate** *see* Tolterodine *on page 1705*

♦ **Tomoxetine** *see* Atomoxetine *on page 169*

♦ **Topamax®** *see* Topiramate *on page 1707*

♦ **Topicaine®** [OTC] *see* Lidocaine *on page 1010*

♦ **Topicort®** *see* Desoximetasone *on page 479*

♦ **Topicort®-LP** *see* Desoximetasone *on page 479*

♦ **Topilene® (Can)** *see* Betamethasone *on page 211*

Topiramate (toe PYRE a mate)

U.S. Brand Names Topamax®

Canadian Brand Names Dom-Topiramate; Gen-Topiramate; Novo-Topiramate; PHL-Topiramate; PMS-Topiramate; ratio-Topiramate; Rhoxal-topiramate; Sandoz-Topiramate; Topamax®

Pharmacologic Category Anticonvulsant, Miscellaneous

Additional Appendix Information

Anticonvulsants by Seizure Type *on page 1865*

Use Monotherapy or adjunctive therapy for partial onset seizures and primary generalized tonic-clonic seizures; adjunctive treatment of seizures associated with Lennox-Gastaut syndrome; prophylaxis of migraine headache

Unlabeled/Investigational Use Infantile spasms, neuropathic pain, cluster headache

Pregnancy Risk Factor C

Pregnancy Implications Topiramate was found to be teratogenic in animal studies; however, there is limited information in pregnant women; use only if benefit to the mother outweighs the risk to the fetus. Based on limited data, topiramate was found to cross the placenta. Postmarketing experience includes reports of hypospadias following *in vitro* exposure to topiramate.

Lactation Enters breast milk/not recommended

Medication Safety Issues

Sound-alike/look-alike issues:

Topamax® may be confused with Tegretol®, Tegretol®-XR, Toprol-XL®

Contraindications Hypersensitivity to topiramate or any component of the formulation

Warnings/Precautions Use with caution in patients with hepatic, respiratory, or renal impairment. Topiramate may decrease serum bicarbonate concentrations (up to 67% of patients); treatment-emergent metabolic acidosis is less common. Risk may be increased in patients with a predisposing condition (organ dysfunction, ketogenic diet, or concurrent treatment with other drugs which may cause acidosis). Metabolic acidosis may occur at dosages as low as 50 mg/day. Monitor serum bicarbonate as well as potential complications of chronic acidosis (nephrolithiasis, osteomalacia, and reduced growth rates in children). The risk of kidney stones is about 2-4 times that of the untreated population, the risk of this event may be reduced by increasing fluid intake.

Cognitive dysfunction, psychiatric disturbances (mood disorders), and sedation (somnolence or fatigue) may occur with topiramate use; incidence may be related to rapid titration and higher doses. Topiramate may also cause paresthesia and ataxia. Topiramate has been associated with secondary angle-closure glaucoma in adults and children, typically within 1 month of initiation; discontinue in patients with acute onset of decreased visual acuity or ocular pain. Hyperammonemia with or without encephalopathy may occur with concomitant valproate administration; use with caution in patients with inborn errors of metabolism or decreased hepatic mitochondrial activity. Topiramate may be associated (rarely) with severe oligohydrosis and hyperthermia, most frequently in children; use caution and monitor closely during strenuous exercise, during exposure to high environmental temperature, or in patients receiving drugs with anticholinergic activity.

Avoid abrupt withdrawal of topiramate therapy, it should be withdrawn/tapered slowly to minimize the potential of increased seizure frequency. Safety and efficacy have not been established in children <2 years of age for adjunctive treatment and <10 years of age for monotherapy. No adequate and well-controlled studies have been conducted in pregnant women; use only if benefit clearly outweighs risk.

Adverse Reactions Adverse events are reported for placebo-controlled trials of adjunctive therapy in adult and pediatric patients. Unless otherwise noted, the percentages refer to incidence in epilepsy trials. Note: A wide range of dosages were studied; incidence of adverse events was frequently lower in the pediatric population studied.

>10%:

Central nervous system: Dizziness (4% to 32%), ataxia (6% to 16%), somnolence (15% to 29%), psychomotor slowing (3% to 21%), nervousness (9% to 19%), memory difficulties (2% to 14%), speech problems (2% to 13%), fatigue (9% to 30%), difficulty concentrating (5% to 14%), depression (9% to 13%), confusion (4% to 14%)

Endocrine & metabolic: Serum bicarbonate decreased (dose-related: 7% to 67%; marked reductions [to <17 mEq/L] 1% to 11%)

Gastrointestinal: Nausea (6% to 12%; migraine trial: 14%), weight loss (8% to 13%), anorexia (4% to 24%)

Neuromuscular & skeletal: Paresthesia (1% to 19%; migraine trial: 35% to 51%)

Ocular: Nystagmus (10% to 11%), abnormal vision (<1% to 13%)

Respiratory: Upper respiratory infection (migraine trial: 12% to 13%)

Miscellaneous: Injury (6% to 14%)

1% to 10%:

Cardiovascular: Chest pain (2% to 4%), edema (1% to 2%), bradycardia (1%), pallor (up to 1%), hypertension (1% to 2%)

Central nervous system: Abnormal coordination (4%), hypoesthesia (1% to 2%; migraine trial: 8%), convulsions (1%), depersonalization (1% to 2%), apathy (1% to 3%), cognitive problems (3%), emotional lability (3%), agitation (3%), aggressive reactions (2% to 9%),

(Continued)

Topiramate *(Continued)*

tremor (3% to 9%), stupor (1% to 2%), mood problems (4% to 9%), anxiety (2% to 10%), insomnia (4% to 8%), neurosis (1%), vertigo (1% to 2%)

Dermatologic: Pruritus (migraine trial: 2% to 4%), skin disorder (1% to 3%), alopecia (2%), dermatitis (up to 2%), hypertrichosis (up to 2%), rash erythematous (up to 2%), eczema (up to 1%), seborrhea (up to 1%), skin discoloration (up to 1%)

Endocrine & metabolic: Hot flashes (1% to 2%); metabolic acidosis (hyperchloremia, nonanion gap), dehydration, breast pain (up to 4%), menstrual irregularities (1% to 2%), hypoglycemia (1%), libido decreased (<1% to 2%)

Gastrointestinal: Dyspepsia (2% to 7%), abdominal pain (5% to 7%), constipation (3% to 5%), xerostomia (2% to 4%), fecal incontinence (1%), gingivitis (1%), diarrhea (2%; migraine trial: 11%), vomiting (1% to 3%), gastroenteritis (1% to 3%), appetite increased (1%), GI disorder (1%), (2% to 4%; migraine trial: 12% to 15%), dysphagia (1%), flatulence (1%), GERD (1%), glossitis (1%), gum hyperplasia (1%), weight increase (1%)

Genitourinary: Impotence, dysuria/incontinence (<1% to 4%), prostatic disorder (2%), UTI (2% to 3%), premature ejaculation (migraine trial: 3%), cystitis (1%)

Hematologic: Leukopenia (1% to 2%), purpura (8%), hematoma (1%), prothrombin time increased (1%), thrombocytopenia (1%)

Neuromuscular & skeletal: Myalgia (2%), weakness (3% to 6%), back pain (1% to 5%), leg pain (2% to 4%), rigors (1%), hypertonia, arthralgia (1% to 7%), gait abnormal (2% to 8%), involuntary muscle contractions (2%; migraine trial: 4%), skeletal pain (1%), hyperkinesia (up to 5%), hyporeflexia (up to 2%)

Ocular: Conjunctivitis (1%), diplopia (2% to 10%), myopia (up to 1%)

Otic: Hearing decreased (1% to 2%), tinnitus (1% to 2%), otitis media (migraine trial: 1% to 2%)

Renal: Nephrolithiasis, renal calculus (migraine trial: 2%), hematuria (<1% to 4%)

Respiratory: Pharyngitis (3% to 6%), sinusitis (4% to 6%; migraine trial: 8% to 10%), epistaxis (1% to 4%), rhinitis (4% to 7%), dyspnea (1% to 2%), pneumonia (5%), coughing (migraine trial: 2% to 3%), bronchitis (migraine trial: 3%)

Miscellaneous: Flu-like syndrome (3% to 7%), allergy (2% to 3%), body odor (up to 1%), fever (migraine trial: 1% to 2%), viral infection (migraine trial: 3% to 4%), infection (<1% to 2%), diaphoresis (≤1%), thirst (2%)

<1% (Limited to important or life-threatening): Accommodation abnormality, allergic reactions, alopecia, anemia, angina, apraxia, AV block, bone marrow depression, deep vein thrombosis, dehydration, delirium, diabetes mellitus, dyskinesia, electrolyte imbalance, encephalopathy (with valproate therapy), eosinophilia, erythema multiforme, euphoria, eye pain, granulocytopenia, hepatic failure, hepatitis, hyperammonemia (with valproate therapy), hyperthermia (severe), hypotension, liver enzymes increased, lymphadenopathy, lymphopenia, manic reaction, migraine aggravated, neuropathy, oligohydrosis, pancreatitis, pancytopenia, paranoid reaction, pemphigus, photosensitivity, psychosis, pulmonary embolism, rash, renal tubular acidosis, Stevens-Johnson syndrome, suicidal behavior, syncope, syndrome of acute myopia/secondary angle-closure glaucoma, tongue edema, toxic epidermal necrolysis, tremor, vertigo

Overdosage/Toxicology Signs and symptoms of overdose include convulsions, drowsiness, speech disturbance, blurred vision, diplopia, impaired mentation, lethargy, and metabolic acidosis. Activated charcoal has not been shown to adsorb topiramate and is, therefore, not recommended; gastric contents should be emptied via lavage or emesis. Hemodialysis can remove approximately ~30% of the drug; however, most cases do not require removal and instead are best treated with supportive measures.

Drug Interactions

Cytochrome P450 Effect: Inhibits CYP2C19 (weak); **Induces** CYP3A4 (weak)

Increased Effect/Toxicity: Concomitant administration with other CNS depressants will increase its sedative effects. Coadministration with acetazolamide: may increase the chance of nephrolithiasis and/or hyperthermia. Topiramate may increase phenytoin concentration by 25%. Concurrent administration with anticholinergic drugs may increase the risk of oligohydrosis and/or hyperthermia (includes drugs with high anticholinergic activity such as antihistamines, cyclic antidepressants, and antipsychotics); use caution.

Decreased Effect: Phenytoin can decrease topiramate levels by as much as 48%, carbamazepine reduces it by 40%. Digoxin levels and ethinyl estradiol blood levels are decreased when coadministered with topiramate. Hyperammonemia (with or without encephalopathy) has been reported in patients who tolerated valproic acid or topiramate alone; these drugs may modestly decrease the serum concentrations of the other drug.

Ethanol/Nutrition/Herb Interactions

Ethanol: Avoid ethanol (may increase CNS depression).

Food: Ketogenic diet may increase the possibility of acidosis.

Herb/Nutraceutical: Avoid evening primrose (seizure threshold decreased).

Stability Store at room temperature of 15°C to 30°C (59°F to 86°F). Protect from moisture.

Mechanism of Action Anticonvulsant activity may be due to a combination of potential mechanisms: Blocks neuronal voltage-dependent sodium channels, enhances GABA(A) activity, antagonizes AMPA/kainate glutamate receptors, and weakly inhibits carbonic anhydrase.

Pharmacodynamics/Kinetics

Absorption: Good, rapid; unaffected by food

Protein binding: 15% to 41% (inversely related to plasma concentrations)

Metabolism: Hepatic via P450 enzymes

Bioavailability: 80%

Half-life elimination: Mean: Adults: Normal renal function: 21 hours; shorter in pediatric patients; clearance is 50% higher in pediatric patients

Time to peak, serum: ~2-4 hours

Excretion: Urine (~70% to 80% as unchanged drug)

Dialyzable: ~30%

Dosage Oral: **Note:** Do not abruptly discontinue therapy; taper dosage gradually to prevent rebound seizure.

Monotherapy: Children ≥10 years and Adults: Partial onset seizure and primary generalized tonic-clonic seizure: Initial: 25 mg twice daily; may increase weekly by 50 mg/day up to 100 mg twice daily (week 4 dose); thereafter, may further increase weekly by 100 mg/day up to the recommended maximum of 200 mg twice daily.

Adjunctive therapy:

Children 2-16 years:

Partial onset seizure or seizure associated with Lennox-Gastaut syndrome: Initial dose titration should begin at 25 mg (or less, based on a range of 1-3 mg/kg/day) nightly for the first week; dosage may be increased in increments of 1-3 mg/kg/day (administered in 2 divided doses) at 1- or 2-week intervals to a total daily dose of 5-9 mg/kg/day

Primary generalized tonic-clonic seizure: Use initial dose listed above, but use slower initial titration rate; titrate to recommended maintenance dose by the end of 8 weeks

Adolescents ≥17 years and Adults:

Partial onset seizures: Initial: 25-50 mg/day (given in 2 divided doses) for 1 week; increase at weekly intervals by 25-50 mg/day until response; usual maintenance dose: 100-200 mg twice daily. Doses >1600 mg/day have not been studied.

Primary generalized tonic-clonic seizures: Use initial dose as listed above for partial onset seizures, but use slower initial titration rate; titrate upwards to recommended dose by the end of 8 weeks; usual maintenance dose: 200 mg twice daily. Doses >1600 mg/day have not been studied.

Adults:

Migraine prophylaxis: Initial: 25 mg/day (in the evening), titrated at weekly intervals in 25 mg increments, up to the recommended total daily dose of 100 mg/day given in 2 divided doses

Cluster headache (unlabeled use): Initial: 25 mg/day, titrated at weekly intervals in 25 mg increments, up to 200 mg/day

Neuropathic pain (unlabeled use): Initial: 25 mg/day, titrated at weekly intervals in 25-50 mg increments to target dose of 400 mg daily in 2 divided doses. Reported dosage range studied: 25-800 mg/day

Dosing adjustment in renal impairment: Cl_{cr} <70 mL/minute: Administer 50% dose and titrate more slowly

Hemodialysis: Supplemental dose may be needed during hemodialysis

Dosing adjustment in hepatic impairment: Clearance may be reduced

Administration Oral: May be administered without regard to meals

Capsule sprinkles: May be swallowed whole or opened to sprinkle the contents on soft food (drug/food mixture should not be chewed).

Tablet: Because of bitter taste, tablets should not be broken.

Monitoring Parameters Seizure frequency, hydration status; electrolytes (recommended monitoring includes serum bicarbonate at baseline and periodically during treatment); monitor for symptoms of acute acidosis and complications of long-term acidosis (nephrolithiasis, osteomalacia, and reduced growth rates in children); ammonia level in patients with unexplained lethargy, vomiting, or mental status changes; symptoms of secondary angle closure glaucoma

Additional Information May be associated with weight loss in some patients

Dosage Forms

Capsule, sprinkle: 15 mg, 25 mg

Tablet: 25 mg, 50 mg, 100 mg, 200 mg

♦ **Topisone® (Can)** see Betamethasone on page 211

♦ **TOPO** see Topotecan on page 1709

♦ **Toposar®** see Etoposide on page 670

Topotecan (toe poe TEE kan)

U.S. Brand Names Hycamtin®

Canadian Brand Names Hycamtin®

Index Terms Hycamptamine; NSC-609699; SK and F 104864; SKF 104864; SKF 104864-A; TOPO; Topotecan Hydrochloride; TPT

Pharmacologic Category Antineoplastic Agent, Natural Source (Plant) Derivative

Use Treatment of ovarian cancer and small cell lung cancer; cervical cancer (in combination with cisplatin)

Unlabeled/Investigational Use Investigational: Treatment of nonsmall cell lung cancer, sarcoma (pediatrics)

Pregnancy Risk Factor D

Pregnancy Implications Animal studies found reduced fetal body weight, eye, brain, skull, and vertebrae malformations. May cause fetal harm in pregnant women. Use during pregnancy is contraindicated.

Lactation Excretion in breast milk unknown/contraindicated

Medication Safety Issues

Sound-alike/look-alike issues:

Hycamtin® may be confused with Hycomine®

High alert medication: The Institute for Safe Medication Practices (ISMP) includes this medication among its list of drugs which have a heightened risk of causing significant patient harm when used in error.

Contraindications Hypersensitivity to topotecan or any component of the formulation; severe bone marrow depression; pregnancy; breast-feeding

Warnings/Precautions Hazardous agent - use appropriate precautions for handling and disposal. The dose-limiting toxicity is bone marrow suppression (neutropenia, thrombocytopenia, anemia); monitor bone marrow function. **[U.S. Boxed Warning]: Should only administer to patients with adequate bone marrow reserves, baseline neutrophils at least 1500 cells/mm³ and platelet counts at least 100,000/mm³.** Use caution in renal impairment; may require dose adjustment. **[U.S. Boxed Warning]: Should be administered under the** (Continued)

Topotecan *(Continued)*

supervision of an experienced cancer chemotherapy physician. Safety and efficacy in children have not been established.

Adverse Reactions

>10%:

Central nervous system: Fatigue (29%), fever (28%), pain (23%), headache (18%)

Dermatologic: Alopecia (31% to 49%), rash (16%)

Gastrointestinal: Nausea (64%), vomiting (45%), diarrhea (32%), constipation (29%), abdominal pain (22%), anorexia (19%), stomatitis (18%)

Hematologic: Neutropenia (97%; grade 4: 70% to 80%; nadir 8-11 days; recovery <21 days), leukopenia (97%), anemia (89%), thrombocytopenia (69%; grade 4: 27% to 29%), neutropenic fever/sepsis (43%; grade 4: 23% to 28%)

Neuromuscular & skeletal: Weakness (25%)

Respiratory: Dyspnea (22%), cough (15%)

1% to 10%:

Hepatic: Transient increases in liver enzymes (8%)

Neuromuscular & skeletal: Paresthesia (7%)

Miscellaneous: Sepsis (grades 3/4: 5%)

<1% (Limited to important or life-threatening): Allergic reactions, anaphylactoid reactions, angioedema, bleeding (severe, associated with thrombocytopenia), dermatitis (severe), injection-site reactions (mild erythema, bruising), pruritus (severe)

Overdosage/Toxicology Anticipated effects of overdose include bone marrow suppression. Treatment is symptom-directed and supportive.

Drug Interactions

Increased Effect/Toxicity: Myelosuppression was more severe when given in combination with cisplatin. Filgrastim may cause prolonged and severe neutropenia and thrombocytopenia if administered concurrently with topotecan; initiate filgrastim at least 24 hours after topotecan.

Ethanol/Nutrition/Herb Interactions Ethanol: Avoid ethanol (due to GI irritation).

Stability Store intact vials of lyophilized powder for injection at room temperature of 20°C to 25°C (68°F to 77°F); protect from light. Reconstitute with 4 mL SWFI. This solution is stable for up to 28 days at room temperature of 20°C to 25°C (68°F to 77°F). Topotecan should be further diluted in 50-100 mL D_5W or NS. This solution is stable for 24 hours at room temperature or up to 7 days under refrigeration.

Mechanism of Action Binds to topoisomerase I and stabilizes the cleavable complex so that religation of the cleaved DNA strand cannot occur. This results in the accumulation of cleavable complexes and single-strand DNA breaks. Topotecan acts in S phase.

Pharmacodynamics/Kinetics

Absorption: Oral: ~30%

Distribution: V_{dss} of the lactone is high (mean: 87.3 L/mm²; range: 25.6-186 L/mm²), suggesting wide distribution and/or tissue sequestering

Protein binding: 35%

Metabolism: Undergoes a rapid, pH-dependent opening of the lactone ring to yield a relatively inactive hydroxy acid in plasma; metabolized in the liver to N-demethylated metabolite

Half-life elimination: 2-3 hours; renal impairment: 5 hours

Excretion: Urine (51%; 3% as desmethyl topotecan); feces (18%; 2% as desmethyl topotecan)

Dosage Adults (refer to individual protocols):

Metastatic ovarian cancer and small cell lung cancer:

IVPB: 1.5 mg/m²/day for 5 days; repeated every 21 days (baseline neutrophil count should be >1500/mm³ and platelet count should be >100,000/mm³)

I.V. continuous infusion (unlabeled dose) 0.2-0.7 mg/m²/day for 7-21 days

Cervical cancer: IVPB: 0.75 mg/m²/day for 3 days (followed by cisplatin 50 mg/m² on day 1 only, [with hydration]); repeated every 21 days (baseline neutrophil count should be >1500/mm³ and platelet count should be >100,000/mm³)

Dosage adjustment for toxicity:

Ovarian and small cell lung cancer: Dosage adjustment for hematological effects: Severe neutropenia or platelet count <25,000/mm³: Reduce dose to 1.25 mg/m²/day for subsequent cycles (may consider G-CSF support [beginning on day 6] prior to instituting dose reduction for neutropenia)

Cervical cancer: Severe febrile neutropenia (ANC <1000/mm³ with temperature of 38°C) or platelet count <10,000/mm³: Reduce topotecan to 0.6 mg/m²/day for subsequent cycles (may consider C-CSF support [beginning on day 4] prior to instituting dose reduction for neutropenic fever.

For neutropenic fever despite G-CSF use, reduce dose to 0.45 mg/m²/day for subsequent cycles). **Note:** Cisplatin may also require dose adjustment.

Dosing adjustment in renal impairment:

Cl_{cr} 20-39 mL/minute: Administer 0.75 mg/m²

Cl_{cr} <20 mL/minute: Insufficient data available for dosing recommendation.

Note: For topotecan in combination with cisplatin for cervical cancer, do not initiate treatment in patients with serum creatinine >1.5 mg/dL; consider discontinuing treatment in patients with serum creatinine >1.5 mg/dL in subsequent cycles.

Hemodialysis: Supplemental dose is not necessary

CAPD effects: Unknown

CAVH effects: Unknown

Dosing adjustment in hepatic impairment: Bilirubin 1.5-10 mg/dL: Adjustment is not necessary

Administration Administer IVPB over 30 minutes or by 24-hour continuous infusion. For combination chemotherapy with cisplatin, administer pretreatment hydration.

Monitoring Parameters CBC with differential and platelet count, renal function tests, bilirubin

Test Interactions None known

Dosage Forms
Injection, powder for reconstitution, as hydrochloride:
Hycamtin®: 4 mg [base]

♦ **Topotecan Hydrochloride** *see* Topotecan *on page 1709*
♦ **Toprol-XL®** *see* Metoprolol *on page 1129*
♦ **Topsyn® (Can)** *see* Fluocinonide *on page 721*
♦ **Toradol®** *see* Ketorolac *on page 963*
♦ **Toradol® IM (Can)** *see* Ketorolac *on page 963*

Toremifene (tore EM i feen)

U.S. Brand Names Fareston®
Canadian Brand Names Fareston®
Index Terms FC1157a; Toremifene Citrate
Pharmacologic Category Antineoplastic Agent, Estrogen Receptor Antagonist
Use Treatment of advanced breast cancer; management of desmoid tumors and endometrial carcinoma
Pregnancy Risk Factor D
Lactation Excretion in breast milk unknown/contraindicated
Contraindications Hypersensitivity to toremifene or any component of the formulation; pregnancy
Warnings/Precautions Hazardous agent - use appropriate precautions for handling and disposal. Hypercalcemia and tumor flare have been reported in some breast cancer patients with bone metastases during the first weeks of treatment. Tumor flare is a syndrome of diffuse musculoskeletal pain and erythema with increased size of tumor lesions that later regress. It is often accompanied by hypercalcemia. Tumor flare does not imply treatment failure or represent tumor progression. Institute appropriate measures if hypercalcemia occurs, and if severe, discontinue treatment. Drugs that decrease renal calcium excretion (eg, thiazide diuretics) may increase the risk of hypercalcemia in patients receiving toremifene. Use cautiously in patients with anemia, hepatic failure, or thromboembolic disease.
Adverse Reactions
>10%:
Endocrine & metabolic: Hot flashes, vaginal discharge
Gastrointestinal: Nausea, vomiting
Emetic potential: Moderate
Miscellaneous: Diaphoresis
1% to 10%:
Cardiovascular: Thromboembolism (venous thrombosis, pulmonary embolism, arterial thrombosis), cardiac failure, MI, angina, edema
Central nervous system: Dizziness
Endocrine & metabolic: Hypercalcemia (patients with bone metastases), galactorrhea, vitamin deficiency, menstrual irregularities
Gastrointestinal: Transaminases increased
Genitourinary: Vaginal bleeding or discharge, endometriosis, priapism, possible endometrial cancer
Ocular: Ophthalmologic effects (visual acuity changes, cataracts, or retinopathy), corneal opacities, dry eyes, blurred vision
Other events observed with unclear association with toremifene: Alopecia, anorexia, asthenia, dermatitis, dyspnea, jaundice, paresis, pruritus, rigors, skin discoloration, tremor
Overdosage/Toxicology Theoretically, overdose may be manifested as an increase of antiestrogenic effects such as hot flashes; estrogenic effects such as vaginal bleeding; or nervous system disorders such as vertigo, dizziness, ataxia and nausea. No specific antidote exists and treatment is symptomatic.
Drug Interactions
Cytochrome P450 Effect: Substrate of CYP1A2 (minor), 3A4 (major)
Increased Effect/Toxicity: Concurrent therapy with warfarin results in significant enhancement of anticoagulant effects; has been speculated that a decrease in antitumor effect of tamoxifen may also occur due to alterations in the percentage of active tamoxifen metabolites.
Decreased Effect: CYP3A4 inducers may decrease the levels/effects of toremifene; example inducers include aminoglutethimide, carbamazepine, nafcillin, nevirapine, phenobarbital, phenytoin, and rifamycins.
Stability Store at 25°C (77°F); excursions permitted to 15°C to 30°C (59°F to 86°F). Protect from heat and light.
Mechanism of Action Nonsteroidal, triphenylethylene derivative. Competitively binds to estrogen receptors on tumors and other tissue targets, producing a nuclear complex that decreases DNA synthesis and inhibits estrogen effects. Nonsteroidal agent with potent antiestrogenic properties which compete with estrogen for binding sites in breast and other tissues; cells accumulate in the G_0 and G_1 phases; therefore, toremifene is cytostatic rather than cytocidal.
Pharmacodynamics/Kinetics
Absorption: Well absorbed
Distribution: V_d: 580 L
Protein binding, plasma: >99.5%, primarily to albumin
Metabolism: Extensively hepatic, principally by CYP3A4 to N-demethyltoremifene, which is also antiestrogenic but with weak *in vivo* antitumor potency
Half-life elimination: ~5 days
Time to peak, serum: ~3 hours
Excretion: Primarily feces; urine (10%) during a 1-week period
Dosage Refer to individual protocols.
Adults: Oral: 60 mg once daily, generally continued until disease progression is observed
(Continued)

Toremifene *(Continued)*

Dosage adjustment in renal impairment: No dosage adjustment necessary

Dosage adjustment in hepatic impairment: Toremifene is extensively metabolized in the liver and dosage adjustments may be indicated in patients with liver disease; however, no specific guidelines have been developed

Administration Orally, usually as a single daily dose; occasionally in 2 or 3 divided doses

Monitoring Parameters Obtain periodic complete blood counts, calcium levels, and liver function tests. Closely monitor patients with bone metastases for hypercalcemia during the first few weeks of treatment. Leukopenia and thrombocytopenia have been reported rarely; monitor leukocyte and platelet counts during treatment.

Additional Information Increase of bone pain usually indicates a good therapeutic response

Dosage Forms Tablet: 60 mg

♦ **Toremifene Citrate** *see* Toremifene *on page 1711*

Torsemide *(TORE se mide)*

U.S. Brand Names Demadex®

Pharmacologic Category Diuretic, Loop

Additional Appendix Information

Heart Failure (Systolic) *on page 2051*

Sulfonamide Derivatives *on page 1897*

Use Management of edema associated with congestive heart failure and hepatic or renal disease; used alone or in combination with antihypertensives in treatment of hypertension; I.V. form is indicated when rapid onset is desired

Pregnancy Risk Factor B

Pregnancy Implications A decrease in fetal weight, an increase in fetal resorption, and delayed fetal ossification has occurred in animal studies.

Lactation Excretion in breast milk unknown/use caution

Medication Safety Issues

Sound-alike/look-alike issues:

Torsemide may be confused with furosemide

Demadex® may be confused with Denorex®

Contraindications Hypersensitivity to torsemide, any component of the formulation, or any sulfonylureas; anuria

Warnings/Precautions Loop diuretics are potent diuretics; excess amounts can lead to profound diuresis with fluid and electrolyte loss; close medical supervision and dose evaluation are required. Watch for and correct electrolyte disturbances; adjust dose to avoid dehydration. In cirrhosis, avoid electrolyte and acid/base imbalances that might lead to hepatic encephalopathy. Coadministration of antihypertensives may increase the risk of hypotension.

Monitor fluid status and renal function in an attempt to prevent oliguria, azotemia, and reversible increases in BUN and creatinine; close medical supervision of aggressive diuresis required. Rapid I.V. administration (associated with other loop diuretics), renal impairment, excessive doses, and concurrent use of other ototoxins is associated with ototoxicity; has been seen with oral torsemide.

Chemical similarities are present among sulfonamides, sulfonylureas, carbonic anhydrase inhibitors, thiazides, and loop diuretics (except ethacrynic acid). Use in patients with sulfonylurea allergy is specifically contraindicated in product labeling, however, a risk of cross-reaction exists in patients with allergy to any of these compounds; avoid use when previous reaction has been severe. Discontinue if signs of hypersensitivity are noted.

Adverse Reactions

1% to 10%:

Cardiovascular: Edema (1.1%), ECG abnormality (2%), chest pain (1.2%)

Central nervous system: Headache (7.3%), dizziness (3.2%), insomnia (1.2%), nervousness (1%)

Endocrine & metabolic: Hyperglycemia, hyperuricemia, hypokalemia

Gastrointestinal: Diarrhea (2%), constipation (1.8%), nausea (1.8%), dyspepsia (1.6%), sore throat (1.6%)

Genitourinary: Excessive urination (6.7%)

Neuromuscular & skeletal: Weakness (2%), arthralgia (1.8%), myalgia (1.6%)

Respiratory: Rhinitis (2.8%), cough increase (2%)

<1% (Limited to important or life-threatening): Angioedema, atrial fibrillation, GI hemorrhage, hypernatremia hypotension, hypovolemia, rash, rectal bleeding, shunt thrombosis, syncope, ventricular tachycardia

Overdosage/Toxicology Symptoms include electrolyte depletion, volume depletion, hypotension, dehydration, and circulatory collapse. Electrolyte depletion may be manifested by weakness, dizziness, mental confusion, anorexia, lethargy, vomiting, and cramps. Following GI decontamination, treatment is supportive. Hypotension responds to fluids and Trendelenburg positioning.

Drug Interactions

Cytochrome P450 Effect: Substrate of CYP2C8 (miinor), 2C9 (major); **Inhibits** CYP2C19 (weak)

Increased Effect/Toxicity: Torsemide-induced hypokalemia may predispose to digoxin toxicity and may increase the risk of arrhythmia with drugs which may prolong QT interval, including type Ia and type III antiarrhythmic agents, cisapride, and some quinolones (sparfloxacin, gatifloxacin, and moxifloxacin). The risk of toxicity from lithium and salicylates (high dose) may be increased by loop diuretics. Hypotensive effects and/or adverse renal effects of ACE inhibitors and NSAIDs are potentiated by bumetanide-induced hypovolemia. The effects of peripheral adrenergic-blocking drugs or ganglionic blockers may be increased by bumetanide.

Torsemide may increase the risk of ototoxicity with other ototoxic agents (aminoglycosides, cis-platinum), especially in patients with renal dysfunction. Synergistic diuretic effects occur with thiazide-type diuretics. Diuretics tend to be synergistic with other antihypertensive agents, and hypotension may occur.

Decreased Effect: Torsemide action may be reduced with probenecid. Diuretic action may be impaired in patients with cirrhosis and ascites if used with salicylates. Glucose tolerance may be decreased when used with sulfonylureas. CYP2C9 inducers may decrease the levels/effects of torsemide; example inducers include carbamazepine, phenobarbital, phenytoin, rifampin, rifapentine, and secobarbital. Torsemide efficacy may be decreased with NSAIDs.

Ethanol/Nutrition/Herb Interactions Herb/Nutraceutical: Avoid dong quai if using for hypertension (has estrogenic activity). Avoid ephedra, yohimbe, ginseng (may worsen hypertension). Avoid garlic (may have increased antihypertensive effect).

Stability If torsemide is to be administered via continuous infusion, stability has been demonstrated through 24 hours at room temperature in plastic containers for the following fluids and concentrations:

200 mg torsemide (10 mg/mL) added to 250 mL D_5W, 250 mL NS or 500 mL 0.45% sodium chloride.

50 mg torsemide (10 mg/mL) added to 500 mL D_5W, 250 mL NS or 500 mL 0.45% sodium chloride.

Mechanism of Action Inhibits reabsorption of sodium and chloride in the ascending loop of Henle and distal renal tubule, interfering with the chloride-binding cotransport system, thus causing increased excretion of water, sodium, chloride, magnesium, and calcium; does not alter GFR, renal plasma flow, or acid-base balance

Pharmacodynamics/Kinetics

Onset of action: Diuresis: 30-60 minutes
Peak effect: 1-4 hours
Duration: ~6 hours
Absorption: Oral: Rapid
Protein binding, plasma: ~97% to 99%
Metabolism: Hepatic (80%) via CYP
Bioavailability: 80% to 90%
Half-life elimination: 2-4; Cirrhosis: 7-8 hours
Excretion: Urine (20% as unchanged drug)

Dosage Adults: Oral, I.V.:

Congestive heart failure: 10-20 mg once daily; may increase gradually for chronic treatment by doubling dose until the diuretic response is apparent (for acute treatment, I.V. dose may be repeated every 2 hours with double the dose as needed). **Note:** ACC/AHA 2005 guidelines for chronic heart failure recommend a maximum daily oral dose of 200 mg; maximum single I.V. dose of 100-200 mg

Continuous I.V. infusion: 20 mg I.V. load then 5-20 mg/hour

Chronic renal failure: 20 mg once daily; increase as described above

Hepatic cirrhosis: 5-10 mg once daily with an aldosterone antagonist or a potassium-sparing diuretic; increase as described above

Hypertension: 2.5-5 mg once daily; increase to 10 mg after 4-6 weeks if an adequate hypotensive response is not apparent; if still not effective, an additional antihypertensive agent may be added

Administration I.V. injections should be administered over ≥2 minutes; the oral form may be administered regardless of meal times; patients may be switched from the I.V. form to the oral and vice-versa with no change in dose; no dosage adjustment is needed in the elderly or patients with hepatic impairment

To administer as a continuous infusion: 50 mg or 200 mg torsemide should be diluted in 250 mL or 500 mL of compatible solution in plastic containers

Monitoring Parameters Renal function, electrolytes, and fluid status (weight and I & O), blood pressure

Additional Information 10-20 mg torsemide is approximately equivalent to furosemide 40 mg or bumetanide 1 mg.

Dosage Forms

Injection, solution: 10 mg/mL (2 mL, 5 mL)
Tablet: 5 mg, 10 mg, 20 mg, 100 mg

- **Tositumomab I-131** *see* Tositumomab and Iodine I 131 Tositumomab *on page 1713*

Tositumomab and Iodine I 131 Tositumomab
(toe si TYOO mo mab & EYE oh dyne eye one THUR tee one toe si TYOO mo mab)

U.S. Brand Names Bexxar®

Index Terms Anti-CD20-Murine Monoclonal Antibody I-131; B1; B1 Antibody; 131 I Anti-B1 Antibody; 131 I-Anti-B1 Monoclonal Antibody; Iodine I 131 Tositumomab and Tositumomab; Tositumomab I-131

Pharmacologic Category Antineoplastic Agent, Monoclonal Antibody; Radiopharmaceutical

Use Treatment of relapsed or refractory CD20 positive, low-grade, follicular, or transformed non-Hodgkin's lymphoma

Pregnancy Risk Factor X

Pregnancy Implications Iodine-131 crosses the placenta and may cause severe and irreversible hypothyroidism in neonates. Pregnancy should be ruled out prior to therapy. Males and females should be instructed to use effective contraception for 12 months following treatment.

Lactation Enters breast milk/contraindicated

Medication Safety Issues

High alert medication: The Institute for Safe Medication Practices (ISMP) includes this medication among its list of drugs which have a heightened risk of causing significant patient harm when used in error.

Contraindications Hypersensitivity to murine proteins or any component of the formulation; pregnancy; breast-feeding
(Continued)

Tositumomab and Iodine I 131 Tositumomab *(Continued)*

Warnings/Precautions Hazardous agent - use appropriate precautions for handling and disposal. **[U.S. Boxed Warning]: Hypersensitivity reactions (including anaphylaxis) have been reported.** Patients should be screened for human antimouse antibodies (HAMA); may be at increased risk of allergic or serious hypersensitivity reactions. Hematologic toxicity was reported to be the most common adverse effect with 27% patients requiring supportive care. **[U.S. Boxed Warning]: Severe or life-threatening cytopenias (NCI CTC grade 3 or 4) have been reported in a large number of patients; may be prolonged and severe.** Secondary malignancies have been reported following use.

[U.S. Boxed Warning]: Treatment involves radioactive isotopes; appropriate precautions in handling and administration must be followed. Patients must be instructed in measures to minimize exposure of others. **[U.S. Boxed Warning]: Women of childbearing potential should be advised of potential fetal risk;** effective contraceptive measures should be used for 12 months following treatment (males and females). Treatment may lead to hypothyroidism; patients should receive thyroid-blocking medications prior to the start of therapy. Patients should be premedicated to prevent infusion related reactions. For a single course of therapy only; multiple courses or use in combination with other chemotherapy or irradiation have not been studied.

Safety has not been established in patients with >25% lymphoma marrow involvement, platelet count <100,000 cells/mm^3 or neutrophil count <1500 cells/mm^3. Use caution with cardiovascular disease, renal, or hepatic impairment. Safety and efficacy have not been established with impaired renal function or in pediatric patients.

Adverse Reactions
>10%:
Central nervous system: Fever (37%), pain (19%), chills (18%), headache (16%)
Dermatologic: Rash (17%)
Endocrine & metabolic: Hypothyroidism (7% to 19%)
Gastrointestinal: Nausea (36%), abdominal pain (15%), vomiting (15%), anorexia (14%), diarrhea (12%)
Hematologic:
Neutropenia (grade 3 or 4, 63%); thrombocytopenia (grade 3 or 4, 53%)
Time to nadir: 4-7 weeks
Duration: 30 days (>90 days in 5% to 7% of patients)
Neuromuscular & skeletal: Weakness (46%), myalgia (13%)
Respiratory: Cough (21%), pharyngitis (12%), dyspnea (11%)
Miscellaneous: Infusion-related reactions (26%, occurred within 14 days of infusion, included bronchospasm, chills, dyspnea, fever, hypotension, nausea, rigors, diaphoresis), infection (21%), HAMA-positive seroconversion (11%; up to 21% at 1 year)
1% to 10%:
Cardiovascular: Hypotension (7% to 10%), peripheral edema (9%), chest pain (7%), vasodilation (5%)
Central nervous system: Dizziness (5%), somnolence (5%)
Dermatologic: Pruritus (10%)
Gastrointestinal: Constipation (6%), dyspepsia (6%), weight loss (6%)
Local: Injection site hypersensitivity
Neuromuscular & skeletal: Arthralgia (10%), back pain (8%), neck pain (6%)
Respiratory: Rhinitis (10%), pneumonia (6%), laryngismus
Miscellaneous: Diaphoresis (8%), hypersensitivity reaction (6%), secondary leukemia/myelodysplastic syndrome (3%; up to 6% at 5 years), anaphylactoid reaction, secondary malignancies, serum sickness

Overdosage/Toxicology Grade 4 hematologic toxicity lasting 18 days was reported in one patient accidentally receiving a total body dose of 88 cGy. Monitor for cytopenias and radiation-related toxicity.

Drug Interactions
Increased Effect/Toxicity: No formal drug interaction studies have been conducted.
Decreased Effect: No formal drug interaction studies have been conducted. The ability of patients receiving tositumomab to generate humoral response (primary or anamnestic) to vaccination is unknown; safety of live vaccines has not been established.

Stability
Tositumomab: Store under refrigeration at 2°C to 8°C (36°F to 46°F); do not freeze. Protect from strong light. Withdraw and discard 32 mL of saline from a 50 mL bag of NS. Add contents of both 225 mg vials of tositumomab (total 32 mL) to remaining NS to make a final volume of 50 mL. Gently mix by inverting bag; do not shake. Following dilution, tositumomab is stable for 24 hour when refrigerated or 8 hours at room temperature.
Iodine I 131 tositumomab: Store frozen at less than or equal to -20°C in the original lead pots. Allow 60 minutes for thawing at ambient temperature. Calculate volume required for an iodine I 131 tositumomab activity of 5 mCi (specification sheet provided with product). If the amount of tositumomab contained in the iodine I 131 tositumomab solution contains <35 mg of tositumomab, use the 35 mg vial of tositumomab to prepare a final concentration of tositumomab 35 mg. Using NS, the final volume should equal 30 mL. Solutions for infusion are stable for up to 8 hours at 2°C to 8°C (36°F to 46°F) or room temperature.

Mechanism of Action Tositumomab is a murine IgG2a lambda monoclonal antibody which binds to the CD20 antigen, expressed on B-lymphocytes and on >90% of B-cell non-Hodgkin's lymphomas. Iodine I 131 tositumomab is a radio-iodinated derivative of tositumomab covalently linked to iodine 131. The possible actions of the regimen include apoptosis, complement-dependent cytotoxicity, antibody-dependent cellular cytotoxicity, and cell death. Administration results in depletion of CD20 positive cells.

Pharmacodynamics/Kinetics
Distribution: Tositumomab: V_d increased with high tumor burden, splenomegaly, or bone marrow involvement
Half-life elimination: Tositumomab:
Elimination: 36-48 hours

Terminal half-life decreased with high tumor burden, splenomegaly, or bone marrow involvement

Clearance: Blood: 68.2 mg/hour

Excretion: Iodine-131: Urine (98%) and decay

Dosage I.V.: Adults: Dosing consists of four components administered in 2 steps. Thyroid protective agents (SSKI, Lugol's solution or potassium iodide), acetaminophen and diphenhydramine should be given prior to or with treatment. Refer to Additional Information.

Step 1: Dosimetric step (Day 0):

Tositumomab 450 mg in NS 50 mL administered over 60 minutes

Iodine I 131 tositumomab (containing I-131 5.0 mCi and tositumomab 35mg) in NS 30 mL administered over 20 minutes

Note: Whole body dosimetry and biodistribution should be determined on Day 0; days 2, 3, or 4; and day 6 or 7 prior to administration of Step 2. If biodistribution is not acceptable, do not administer the therapeutic step. On day 6 or 7, calculate the patient specific activity of iodine I 131 tositumomab to deliver 75 cGy TBD or 65 cGy TBD (in mCi).

Step 2: Therapeutic step (Day 7):

Tositumomab 450 mg in NS 50 mL administered over 60 minutes

Iodine I 131 tositumomab:

Platelets ≥150,000/mm^3: Iodine I 131 calculated to deliver 75 cGy total body irradiation and tositumomab 35 mg over 20 minutes

Platelets ≥100,000/mm^3 and <150,000/mm^3: Iodine I 131 calculated to deliver 65 cGy total body irradiation and tositumomab 35 mg over 20 minutes

Administration I.V.:

Tositumomab: Infuse over 60 minutes

Iodine I 131 tositumomab: Infuse over 20 minutes

Reduce the rate of tositumomab or iodine 131 tositumomab infusion by 50% for mild-to-moderate infusion-related toxicities; interrupt for severe toxicity. Once severe toxicity has resolved, infusion may be restarted at half the previous rate. Prior to infusion, patients should be premedicated and a thyroid-protective agent should be started.

Monitoring Parameters CBC with differential (prior to therapy and at least weekly for a minimum of 10 weeks); TSH (prior to therapy and yearly); serum creatinine (immediately prior to administration)

Following infusion of the iodine I 131 tositumomab dosimetric dose, the total body gamma camera counts and whole body images should be taken within 1 hour of the infusion and prior to urination, and 2-4 days after the infusion and following urination, and 6-7 days after the infusion and following urination.

Test Interactions May interfere with tests using murine antibody technology.

Additional Information Thyroid protective agent: One of the following agents should be used starting at least 24 hours prior to the dosimetric dose and continued for 2 weeks after the therapeutic dose. Therapy should not begin without using one of the following agents:

SSKI: 4 drops 3 times/day

Lugol's solution: 20 drops 3 times/day

Potassium iodide: 130 mg once daily

Dosage Forms Note: Not all components are shipped from the same facility. When ordering, ensure that all will arrive on the same day.

Kit [dosimetric package]: Tositumomab 225 mg/16.1 mL [2 vials], tositumomab 35 mg/2.5 mL [1 vial], and iodine I 131 tositumomab 0.1 mg/mL and 0.61mCi/mL (20 mL) [1 vial]

Kit [therapeutic package]: Tositumomab 225 mg/16.1 mL [2 vials], tositumomab 35 mg/2.5 mL [1 vial], and iodine I 131 tositumomab 1.1 mg/mL and 5.6 mCi/mL (20 mL) [1 or 2 vials]

Total Parenteral Nutrition (TOE tal par EN ter al noo TRISH un)

Index Terms Hyperal; Hyperalimentation; Parenteral Nutrition; PN; TPN

Pharmacologic Category Caloric Agent; Intravenous Nutritional Therapy

Use Infusion of nutrient solutions into the bloodstream to support nutritional needs during a time when patient is unable to absorb nutrients via the gastrointestinal tract, cannot take adequate nutrition orally or enterally, or have had (or are expected to have) inadequate oral intake for 7-14 days

Contraindications Varies by composition:

Lipid-containing formulations are contraindicated in patients with hypersensitivity to fat emulsion or any component of the formulation; severe egg or legume (soybean) allergies; pathologic hyperlipidemia, lipoid nephrosis, pancreatitis with hyperlipemia

Dextrose is contraindicated in patients with hypersensitivity to corn or corn products; hypertonic solutions in patients with intracranial or intraspinal hemorrhage; glucose-galactose malabsorption syndrome

Amino acids are contraindicated in patients with hypersensitivity to one or more amino acids; severe liver disease or hepatic coma

Warnings/Precautions Monitor fluid and electrolyte status carefully. Use with caution in patients at risk for refeeding syndrome. Refeeding syndrome is a medical emergency; it can consist of electrolyte disturbances (eg, potassium, phosphorus), respiratory distress, and cardiac arrhythmias, resulting in cardiopulmonary arrest. It is usually seen in patients with long-standing or severe malnutrition; initiate cautiously; approach goals slowly. Do not overfeed patients; caloric replacement should match as closely as possible to intake. Use caution in patients with diabetes or insulin resistance. Use caution in patients who may be sensitive to volume overload (eg, CHF, renal failure, hepatic failure). Use caution and limit protein in patients with hepatic disease. If TPN is discontinued abruptly, infuse 10% dextrose at same rate and monitor blood glucose for hypoglycemia.

Adverse Reactions Frequency not defined (unless noted).

Endocrine & metabolic: Fluid overload, hypercapnia, hyperglycemia, hyper-/hypokalemia, hyper-/hypophosphatemia, metabolic bone disease, nonanion gap metabolic acidosis, refeeding syndrome

Hepatic: Cholestasis, cirrhosis (<1%), gallstones, liver function tests increased, pancreatitis, steatosis, triglycerides increased

Renal: Azotemia, BUN increased

(Continued)

Total Parenteral Nutrition *(Continued)*

Miscellaneous: Bacteremia, catheter-induced infection, exit-site infections

Stability USP Chapter 797 Guidelines consider TPN a medium-risk preparation and state that (in the absence of passing a sterility test) storage period should not exceed 30 hours at room temperature, 7 days at cold temperature, and 45 days in a solid frozen state at -20°C or colder. For patients on home TPN, multiple vitamins should be added prior to TPN administration, due to limited stability of multiple vitamins.

Dosage PN is a highly-individualized therapy. The following general guidelines may be used in the estimation of needs. Electrolytes, vitamins, and trace minerals should be added to TPN mixtures based on patients individualized needs.

Neonates: I.V.: **Note:** When indicated for premature neonates, start on day 1 of life if possible.
Total calories:
Term: 85-105 kcal/kg/day
Preterm (stable): 90-120 kcal/kg/day
Fluid:
<1.5 kg: 130-150 mL/kg/day
1.5-2 kg: 110-130 mL/kg/day
2-10 kg: 100 mL/kg/day
Carbohydrate (dextrose): 40% to 50 % of caloric intake; advance as tolerated
Term: Initial: 6-8 mg/kg/minute; goal: 10-14 mg/kg/minute
Premature: Initial: 6 mg/kg/minute; goal: 10-13 mg/kg/minute
Protein (amino acids):
Term: Initial: 2.5 g/kg/day; goal: 3 g/kg/day
Extremely (<1000 g) and very (<1500 g) low-birth-weight (stable): Initial: 1-1.5 g/kg/day; goal: 3.5-3.85 g/kg/day to promote utero growth rates.
Sepsis, hypoxia: Initial: 1 g/kg/day; goal: 3-3.85 g/kg/day
Fat:
Term: Initial: 0.5-1 g/kg/day (maximum: 3 g/kg/day); administer over 24 hours
Preterm: Initial: 0.25-0.5 g/kg/day (maximum: 3 g/kg/day or 1 g/kg/day if on phototherapy); administer over 24 hours
Note: Monitor triglycerides while receiving intralipids. If triglycerides >200 mg/dL, stop infusion and restart at 0.5-1g/kg/day
Heparin: 1 unit/mL of parenteral nutrition fluids should be added to enhance clearance of lipid emulsions

Children: I.V.: **Note:** Give within 5-7 days if unable to meet needs orally or with enteral nutrition:
Total calories:
<6 months: 85-105 kcal/kg/day
6-12 months: 80-100 kcal/kg/day
1-7 years: 75-90 kcal/kg/day
7-12 years: 50-75 kcal/kg/day
12-18 years: 30-50 kcal/kg/day
Fluid:
2-10 kg: 100 mL/kg
>10-20 kg: 1000 mL for 10 kg plus 50 mL/kg for each kg >10
>20 kg: 1500 mL for 10 kg plus 20 mL/kg for each kg >20
Carbohydrate (dextrose): 40% to 50% of caloric intake
<1 year: Initial: 6-8 mg/kg/minute; goal: 10-14 mg/kg/minute
1-10 years: Initial: 10% to 12.5%; daily increase: 5% increments (maximum: 15 mg/kg/minute)
>10 years: Initial: 10% to 15%; daily increase: 5% increments (maximum: 8.5 mg/kg/minute)
Protein (amino acids):
1-12 months: Initial: 2-3 g/kg/day; daily increase: 1 g/kg/day (maximum: 3 g/kg/day)
1-10 years: Initial: 1-2 g/kg/day; daily increase: 1 g/kg/day (maximum: 2-2.5 g/kg/day)
>10 years: Initial: 0.8-1.5 g/kg/day; daily increase: 1 g/kg/day (maximum: 1.5-2 g/kg/day)
Fat: Initial: 1 g/kg/day; daily increase: 1 g/kg/day (maximum: 3 g/kg/day); **Note:** Monitor triglycerides while receiving intralipids.

Adults: I.V.:
Total calories: Calculate using Harris-Benedict equation or based on stress level as indicated below:
Harris-Benedict Equation (BEE):
Females: $655.1 + [(9.56 \times W) + (1.85 \times H) - (4.68 \times A)]$
Males: $66.47 + [(13.75 \times W) + (5 \times H) - (6.76 \times A)]$
Then multiply BEE x (activity factor) x (stress factor)
W = weight in kg; H = height in cm; A = age in years
Activity factor = 1.2 sedentary, 1.3 normal activity, 1.4 active, 1.5 very active
Stress factor = 1.5 for trauma, stressed, or surgical patients and underweight (to promote weight gain); 2.0 for severe burn patients
Stress level:
Normal/mild stress level: 20-25 kcal/kg/day
Moderate stress level: 25-30 kcal/kg/day
Severe stress level: 30-40 kcal/kg/day
Pregnant women in second or third trimester: Add an additional 300 kcal/day
Fluid: mL/day = 30-40 mL/kg
Carbohydrate (dextrose):
5 g/kg/day or 3.5 mg/kg/minute (maximum rate: 4-7 mg/kg/minute)
Minimum recommended amount: 400 calories/day or 100 g/day
Protein (amino acids):
Maintenance: 0.8-1 g/kg/day
Normal/mild stress level: 1-1.2 g/kg/day
Moderate stress level: 1.2-1.5 g/kg/day

Severe stress level: 1.5-2 g/kg/day
Burn patients (severe): Increase protein until significant wound healing achieved
Solid organ transplant: Perioperative: 1.5-2 g/kg/day
Renal failure:
  Acute (severely malnourished or hypercatabolic): 1.5-1.8 g/kg/day
  Chronic, with dialysis: 1.2-1.3 g/kg/day
  Chronic, without dialysis: 0.6-0.8 g/kg/day
  Continuous hemofiltration: ≥1 g/kg/day
Hepatic failure:
  Acute management when other treatments have failed:
    With encephalopathy: 0.6-1 g/kg/day
    Without encephalopathy: 1-1.5 g/kg/day
  Chronic encephalopathy: Use branch chain amino acid enriched diets only if unresponsive to pharmacotherapy
Pregnant women in second or third trimester: Add an additional 10-14 g/day
Fat:
Initial: 20% to 40 % of total calories (maximum: 60% of total calories or 2.5 g/kg/day);
  Note: Monitor triglycerides while receiving intralipids.
Safe for use in pregnancy
I.V. lipids are safe in adults with pancreatitis if triglyceride levels <400 mg/dL

Administration For I.V. administration only, usually via a central venous catheter; can be administered by continuous infusion over 24 hours or cyclic infusion over 12-14 hours. Cyclic infusion is used with a tapering-up period at the beginning and a tapering-down period at the end to avoid hyper-/hypoglycemia. For infants <2 years, taper over 1-2 hours. Change tubing after each infusion. Hang fat emulsion higher than other fluids (has low specific gravity and could run up into other lines). Infuse via pump using either peripheral or central venous line. Do not use in-line filter.

Monitoring Parameters

Electrolytes: Sodium, potassium, chloride, and bicarbonate should be monitored frequently upon initiation and until stable; phosphate should be monitored closely in patients with pulmonary disease.
Efficacy: Nutrition and outcome parameters should be measured serially.
Glucose: In diabetics or patients with glucose intolerance risk factors, monitor closely. Monitor frequently upon initiation of therapy and with any changes in insulin dose or renal function.
Line site: Monitor for signs and symptoms of infection.
Liver function tests: Monitor periodically.
Triglycerides: Before initiation of lipid therapy and at least weekly during therapy.
Refeeding syndrome: Patients at risk should have phosphorus, magnesium, potassium, and glucose levels monitored closely at initiation.
Bone densitometry: Perform upon initiation of long-term therapy.
Vitamin A status: Should be carefully monitored in patients with chronic renal failure.
Neonates: Sodium, calcium and phosphate should be monitored closely. Frequent (some advise daily) platelet counts should be performed in neonatal patients receiving parenteral lipids.

Additional Information

Diabetes: Avoid excess calories.
Burns: Assess nutrition requirements with indirect calorimetry if possible.
Obesity: Assess nutrition requirements with indirect calorimetry if possible and give hypocaloric nutrition with supplemental protein.
Pulmonary disease: Use a fluid-restricted formula for ARDS. Energy (carbohydrate) intake should be kept at or below estimated needs in patients with pulmonary disease and hypercapnia.

1 g protein = 4 kcal
1 g dextrose = 3.4 kcal
1 g fat = 9 kcal
10% fat emulsion = 1.1 kcal
20% fat emulsion = 2 kcal
30% fat emulsion = 3 kcal

Adult standard daily electrolyte requirements:
  Acetate: As needed to maintain acid-base balance
  Calcium: 10-15 mEq
  Chloride: As needed to maintain acid-base balance
  Magnesium 8-20 mEq
  Phosphorus: 20-40 mmol
  Potassium: 1-2 mEq/kg
  Sodium: 1-2 mEq/kg

Adult daily requirements for parenteral vitamins:
  Ascorbic acid (C): 200 mg
  Biotin: 60 mcg
  Cyanocobalamin (B_{12}): 5 mcg
  Folic acid: 600 mcg
  Niacin (B_3): 40 mg
  Pantothenic acid: 15 mg
  Pyridoxine (B_6): 6 mg
  Riboflavin (B_2): 3.6 mg
  Thiamine (B_1): 6 mg
  Vitamin A: 3300 int. units
  Vitamin D: 200 int. units
  Vitamin E: 10 int. units
  Vitamin K: 150 mcg

Adult daily requirements for parenteral trace elements:
  Chromium: 10-15 mcg
(Continued)

Total Parenteral Nutrition (Continued)

          Copper: 0.3-0.5 mg
          Iron: Not routinely added
          Manganese: 60-100 mcg
          Selenium: 20-60 mcg
          Zinc: 2.5-5 mg

Dosage Forms TPN is usually compounded from optimal combinations of macronutrients (water, protein, dextrose, and lipids) and micronutrients (electrolytes, trace elements, and vitamins) to meet the specific nutritional requirements of a patient. Individual hospitals may have designated standard TPN formulas. There are a few commercially-available amino acids with electrolytes solutions; however, these products may not meet an individual's specific nutrition requirements.

♦ **Touro® CC** *see* Guaifenesin, Pseudoephedrine, and Dextromethorphan *on page 821*
♦ **Touro® CC-LD** *see* Guaifenesin, Pseudoephedrine, and Dextromethorphan *on page 821*
♦ **Touro™ Allergy** *see* Brompheniramine and Pseudoephedrine *on page 243*
♦ **Touro® DM** *see* Guaifenesin and Dextromethorphan *on page 816*
♦ **Touro® HC** *see* Hydrocodone and Guaifenesin *on page 849*
♦ **Touro LA®** *see* Guaifenesin and Pseudoephedrine *on page 819*
♦ **tPA** *see* Alteplase *on page 79*
♦ **T-Phyl®** *see* Theophylline Salts *on page 1664*
♦ **TPN** *see* Total Parenteral Nutrition *on page 1715*
♦ **TPT** *see* Topotecan *on page 1709*
♦ **TPV** *see* Tipranavir *on page 1692*
♦ **tRA** *see* Tretinoin (Oral) *on page 1730*
♦ **Tracleer®** *see* Bosentan *on page 232*
♦ **Tramacet (Can)** *see* Acetaminophen and Tramadol *on page 34*

Tramadol (TRA ma dole)

U.S. Brand Names Ultram®; Ultram® ER
Canadian Brand Names Ultram®
Index Terms Tramadol Hydrochloride
Pharmacologic Category Analgesic, Nonopioid
Use Relief of moderate to moderately-severe pain
Pregnancy Risk Factor C
Pregnancy Implications Tramadol has been shown to cross the placenta. Postmarketing reports following tramadol use during pregnancy include neonatal seizures, withdrawal syndrome, fetal death and stillbirth. Not recommended for use during labor and delivery.
Lactation Enters breast milk/contraindicated
Medication Safety Issues
    Sound-alike/look-alike issues:
        Tramadol may be confused with Toradol®, Trandate®, Voltaren®
        Ultram® may be confused with Ultane®, Voltaren®

    International issues:
        Theradol® [Netherlands] may be confused with Foradil® which is a brand name for formoterol in the U.S.
        Theradol® [Netherlands] may be confused with Terazol® which is a brand name for terconazole in the U.S.
        Theradol® [Netherlands] may be confused with Toradol® which is a brand name for keto-rolac in the U.S.
Contraindications Hypersensitivity to tramadol, opioids, or any component of the formulation; opioid-dependent patients; acute intoxication with alcohol, hypnotics, centrally-acting analgesics, opioids, or psychotropic drugs
    Ultram® ER (extended release formulation): Additional contraindications: Severe (Cl$_{cr}$ <30 mL/minute) renal dysfunction, severe (Child-Pugh Class C) hepatic dysfunction
Warnings/Precautions May cause CNS depression, which may impair physical or mental abilities; patients must be cautioned about performing tasks which require mental alertness (eg, operating machinery or driving). Should be used only with extreme caution in patients receiving MAO inhibitors. May cause CNS depression and/or respiratory depression, particularly when combined with other CNS depressants. Use with caution and reduce dosage when administered to patients receiving other CNS depressants. An increased risk of seizures may occur in patients receiving serotonin reuptake inhibitors (SSRIs or anorectics), tricyclic antidepressants, other cyclic compounds (including cyclobenzaprine, promethazine), neuroleptics, MAO inhibitors, or drugs which may lower seizure threshold. Patients with a history of seizures, or with a risk of seizures (head trauma, metabolic disorders, CNS infection, or malignancy, or during ethanol/drug withdrawal) are also at increased risk.

Elderly, debilitated patients and patients with chronic respiratory disorders may be at greater risk of adverse events. Use with caution in patients with increased intracranial pressure or head injury. Avoid use in patients who are suicidal or addiction prone. Use caution in heavy alcohol users. Use caution in treatment of acute abdominal conditions; may mask pain. Use tramadol with caution and reduce dosage in patients with liver disease or renal dysfunction. Tolerance or drug dependence may result from extended use (withdrawal symptoms have been reported); abrupt discontinuation should be avoided. Tapering of dose at the time of discontinuation limits the risk of withdrawal symptoms. Safety and efficacy in pediatric patients <18 years of age have not been established.
Adverse Reactions
    >10%:
        Cardiovascular: Flushing (8% to 16%)

Central nervous system: Dizziness (16% to 33%), headache (8% to 32%), insomnia (7% to 11%), somnolence (7% to 25%)

Dermatologic: Pruritus (6% to 12%)

Gastrointestinal: Constipation (12% to 46%), nausea (15% to 40%)

Neuromuscular & skeletal: Weakness (4% to 12%)

1% to 10%:

Cardiovascular: Chest pain (1% to <5%), postural hypotension (2% to 5%), vasodilation (1% to <5%)

Central nervous system: Agitation, anxiety (1% to <5%), confusion (1% to <5%), coordination impaired (1% to <5%), depression (1% to <5%), emotional lability, euphoria, hallucinations, hypoesthesia, lethargy, malaise, nervousness (1% to <5%), pain, pyrexia, restlessness

Dermatologic: Dermatitis, rash

Endocrine & metabolic: Hot flashes (2% to 9%), menopausal symptoms (1% to <5%)

Gastrointestinal: Abdominal pain, anorexia (<6%), diarrhea (5% to 10%), dry mouth (5% to 10%), dyspepsia, flatulence, vomiting (5% to 9%), weight loss

Genitourinary: Urinary frequency (1% to <5%), urinary retention (1% to <5%), urinary tract infection (1% to <5%)

Neuromuscular & skeletal: Arthralgia (1% to <5%), hypertonia (1% to <5%), rigors (<4%), paresthesia (1% to <5%), spasticity (1% to <5%), tremor (1% to <5%), creatinine phosphokinase increased

Ocular: Blurred vision (1% to <5%), miosis (1% to <5%)

Respiratory: Bronchitis (1% to <5%), cough (1% to <5%), dyspnea (1% to <5%), pharyngitis (1% to <5%), rhinorrhea (1% to <5%), sinusitis (1% to <5%)

Miscellaneous: Diaphoresis (2% to 6%), flu-like syndrome (<2%)

<1% (Limited to important or life-threatening): Allergic reaction, amnesia, anaphylactoid reactions, anaphylaxis, angioedema, bronchospasm, cataracts, cholecystitis, cholelithiasis, cognitive dysfunction, concentration difficulty, creatinine increased, deafness, gastrointestinal bleeding, hepatitis, hyper-/hypotension, liver failure, MI, migraine, myocardial ischemia, night sweats, pancreatitis, peripheral ischemia, pulmonary edema, pulmonary embolism, seizure, serotonin syndrome, Stevens-Johnson syndrome, suicidal tendency, syncope, toxic epidermal necrolysis, vertigo

A withdrawal syndrome may occur with abrupt discontinuation; includes anxiety, diarrhea, hallucinations (rare), nausea, pain, piloerection, rigors, sweating, and tremor. Uncommon discontinuation symptoms may include severe anxiety, panic attacks, or paresthesia.

Overdosage/Toxicology Symptoms of overdose include CNS and respiratory depression, lethargy, coma, miosis, seizure, cardiac arrest, and death. Treatment may be symptom-directed and supportive. Naloxone may reverse some overdose symptoms, but may increase the risk of seizures. Hemodialysis is not helpful in removal of tramadol.

Drug Interactions

Cytochrome P450 Effect: Substrate of CYP2D6 (major), 3A4 (minor)

Increased Effect/Toxicity: Tramadol may enhance the CNS depressant effect of ethanol and other CNS depressants. Cyclobenzaprine, MAO inhibitors, SSRIs, and tricyclic antidepressants may enhance the neuroexcitatory and/or seizure-potentiating effects of tramadol. Naloxone may increase the risk of seizures in tramadol overdose. Quinidine may increase tramadol serum concentrations. Naloxone may increase risk of seizures if administered in tramadol overdose. Serotonin modulators and sibutramine may enhance the serotonergic effects of tramadol.

Decreased Effect: Carbamazepine may decrease analgesic efficacy of tramadol (increased metabolism) and tramadol may increase the risk of in patients on carbamazepine. CYP2D6 inhibitors may decrease the effects of tramadol; examples include chlorpromazine, delavirdine, fluoxetine, miconazole, paroxetine, pergolide, quinidine, quinine, ritonavir, and ropinirole. Quinidine may decrease M1 (active metabolite) serum concentrations.

Ethanol/Nutrition/Herb Interactions

Ethanol: Avoid ethanol (may increase CNS depression).

Food:

Immediate release: Does not affect the rate or extent of absorption.

Extended release: Reduced C_{max} and AUC and T_{max} occurred 3 hours earlier when taken with a high-fat meal.

Herb/Nutraceutical: Avoid valerian, St John's wort, kava kava, gotu kola (may increase CNS depression).

Stability Store at 15°C to 30°C (59°F to 86°F).

Mechanism of Action Binds to μ-opiate receptors in the CNS causing inhibition of ascending pain pathways, altering the perception of and response to pain; also inhibits the reuptake of norepinephrine and serotonin, which also modifies the ascending pain pathway

Pharmacodynamics/Kinetics

Onset of action: ~1 hour

Duration of action: 9 hours

Absorption: Rapid and complete

Distribution: V_d: 2.5-3 L/kg

Protein binding, plasma: 20%

Metabolism: Extensively hepatic via demethylation, glucuronidation, and sulfation; has pharmacologically active metabolite formed by CYP2D6 (M1; O-desmethyl tramadol)

Bioavailability: Immediate release: 75%; Extended release: 85% to 90% as compared to immediate release.

Half-life elimination: Tramadol: ~6-8 hours; Active metabolite: 7-9 hours; prolonged in elderly, hepatic or renal impairment

Time to peak: Immediate release: 2 hours; Extended release: 12 hours

Excretion: Urine (30% as unchanged drug; 60% as metabolites)

Dosage Moderate-to-severe chronic pain: Oral:

Adults:

Immediate release formulation: 50-100 mg every 4-6 hours (not to exceed 400 mg/day)

(Continued)

Tramadol (Continued)

For patients not requiring rapid onset of effect, tolerability may be improved by starting dose at 25 mg/day and titrating dose by 25 mg every 3 days, until reaching 25 mg 4 times/day. Dose may then be increased by 50 mg every 3 days as tolerated, to reach dose of 50 mg 4 times/day.

Extended release formulation: 100 mg once daily; titrate every 5 days (maximum: 300 mg/day)

Elderly: >75 years:

Immediate release: 50 mg every 6 hours (not to exceed 300 mg/day); see dosing adjustments for renal and hepatic impairment.

Extended release formulation: Use with great caution. See adult dosing.

Dosing adjustment in renal impairment:

Immediate release: Cl_{cr} <30 mL/minute: Administer 50-100 mg dose every 12 hours (maximum: 200 mg/day)

Extended release: Should not be used in patients with Cl_{cr} < 30 mL/minute

Dosing adjustment in hepatic impairment:

Immediate release: Cirrhosis: Recommended dose: 50 mg every 12 hours

Extended release: Should not be used in patients with severe (Child-Pugh Class C) hepatic dysfunction

Dietary Considerations May be taken with or without food. Extended release formulation: Be consistent; always give with food or always give on an empty stomach.

Administration Do not crush or chew extended release tablet.

Monitoring Parameters Pain relief, respiratory rate, blood pressure, and pulse; signs of tolerance or abuse

Reference Range 100-300 ng/mL; however, serum level monitoring is not required

Dosage Forms

Tablet, as hydrochloride: 50 mg

Ultram®: 50 mg

Tablet, extended release, as hydrochloride:

Ultram® ER: 100 mg, 200 mg, 300 mg

- ◆ **Tramadol Hydrochloride** see Tramadol on page 1718
- ◆ **Tramadol Hydrochloride and Acetaminophen** see Acetaminophen and Tramadol on page 34
- ◆ **Trandate**® see Labetalol on page 967

Trandolapril (tran DOE la pril)

U.S. Brand Names Mavik®

Canadian Brand Names Mavik™

Pharmacologic Category Angiotensin-Converting Enzyme (ACE) Inhibitor

Additional Appendix Information

Angiotensin Agents on page 1860

Heart Failure (Systolic) on page 2051

Use Management of hypertension alone or in combination with other antihypertensive agents; treatment of left ventricular dysfunction after myocardial infarction

Unlabeled/Investigational Use As a class, ACE inhibitors are recommended in the treatment of systolic congestive heart failure

Pregnancy Risk Factor C (1st trimester)/D (2nd and 3rd trimesters)

Pregnancy Implications Decreased placental blood flow, low birth weight, fetal hypotension, preterm delivery, and fetal death have been noted with the use of some ACE inhibitors (ACEIs) in animal studies. Neonatal hypotension, skull hypoplasia, anuria, renal failure, oligohydramnios (associated with fetal limb contractures, craniofacial deformities, hypoplastic lung development), prematurity, intrauterine growth retardation, and patent ductus arteriosus have been reported with the use of ACEIs, primarily in the 2nd and 3rd trimesters. The risk of neonatal toxicity has been considered less when ACEIs have been used in the 1st trimester; however, major congenital malformations have been reported. The cardiovascular and/or central nervous systems are most commonly affected. Unless alternative agents are not appropriate, ACEIs should be discontinued as soon as possible once pregnancy is detected.

Lactation Excretion in breast milk unknown/not recommended

Contraindications Hypersensitivity to trandolapril or any component of the formulation; history of angioedema-related to previous treatment with an ACE inhibitor; bilateral renal artery stenosis; pregnancy (2nd and 3rd trimesters)

Warnings/Precautions Anaphylactic reactions can occur. Angioedema can occur at any time during treatment (especially following first dose). It may involve head and neck (potentially affecting the airway) or the intestine (presenting with abdominal pain). Prolonged monitoring may be required especially if tongue, glottis, or larynx are involved as they are associated with airway obstruction. Patients with a history of airway surgery in this situation have a higher risk. Careful blood pressure monitoring with first dose (hypotension can occur especially in volume-depleted patients). **[U.S. Boxed Warning]: Based on human data, ACEIs can cause injury and death to the developing fetus when used in the second and third trimesters. ACEIs should be discontinued as soon as possible once pregnancy is detected.** Dosage adjustment needed in severe renal dysfunction (Cl_{cr} <30 mL/minute) or in hepatic cirrhosis. Use with caution in hypovolemia; collagen vascular diseases; valvular stenosis (particularly aortic stenosis); hyperkalemia; or before, during, or immediately after anesthesia. Avoid rapid dosage escalation, which may lead to renal insufficiency. Hyperkalemia may rarely occur. Rare toxicities associated with ACE inhibitors include cholestatic jaundice (which may progress to hepatic necrosis) and neutropenia/agranulocytosis with myeloid hyperplasia. May be associated with deterioration of renal function and/or increases in serum creatinine, particularly in patients dependent on renin-angiotensin-aldosterone system. Use with caution in unilateral renal artery stenosis and pre-existing renal insufficiency; if patient has renal impairment then a baseline WBC with differential and serum creatinine should be evaluated and monitored closely during the first 3 months of therapy. Safety and efficacy have not been established in children.

Adverse Reactions Note: Frequency ranges include data from hypertension and heart failure trials. Higher rates of adverse reactions have generally been noted in patients with CHF. However, the frequency of adverse effects associated with placebo is also increased in this population.

>1%:
  Cardiovascular: Hypotension (<1% to 11%), bradycardia (<1% to 4.7%), intermittent claudication (3.8%), stroke (3.3%), syncope (5.9%)
  Central nervous system: Dizziness (1.3% to 23%), asthenia (3.3%)
  Endocrine & metabolic: Elevated uric acid (15%), hyperkalemia (5.3%), hypocalcemia (4.7%)
  Gastrointestinal: Dyspepsia (6.4%), gastritis (4.2%)
  Neuromuscular & skeletal: Myalgia (4.7%)
  Renal: Elevated BUN (9%), elevated serum creatinine (1.1% to 4.7%)
  Respiratory: Cough (1.9% to 35%)
<1% (Limited to important or life-threatening): Angina, angioedema, anxiety, AV block (first-degree), dyspnea, gout, impotence, increased ALT, increased serum creatinine, insomnia, laryngeal edema, muscle pain, neutropenia, pancreatitis, paresthesia, pruritus, rash, symptomatic hypotension, thrombocytopenia, vertigo. Worsening of renal function may occur in patients with bilateral renal artery stenosis or in hypovolemic patients. In addition, a syndrome which may include fever, myalgia, arthralgia, interstitial nephritis, vasculitis, rash, eosinophilia and positive ANA, and elevated ESR has been reported with ACE inhibitors.

Overdosage/Toxicology Symptoms may include hypotension, bradycardia, vertigo, and dizziness. Hyperkalemia occurs even with therapeutic doses, especially in patients with renal insufficiency and those taking NSAIDs. Following initiation of essential overdose management, toxic symptom treatment and supportive treatment should be initiated.

Hypotension usually responds to I.V. fluids or Trendelenburg positioning. If unresponsive to these measures, the use of a parenteral vasopressor may be required (eg, norepinephrine 0.1-0.2 mcg/kg/minute titrated to response). Seizures commonly respond to diazepam (I.V. 5-10 mg bolus in adults every 15 minutes, if needed, up to a total of 30 mg) or to phenytoin or phenobarbital.

Drug Interactions
  Increased Effect/Toxicity: Potassium supplements, co-trimoxazole (high dose), angiotensin II receptor antagonists (eg, candesartan, losartan, irbesartan), or potassium-sparing diuretics (amiloride, spironolactone, triamterene) may result in elevated serum potassium levels when combined with trandolapril. ACE inhibitor effects may be increased by phenothiazines or probenecid (increases levels of captopril). ACE inhibitors may increase serum concentrations/effects of lithium. ACE inhibitors may enhance the adverse/toxic effects (nitritoid reaction) of gold sodium thiomalate.

  Diuretics have additive hypotensive effects with ACE inhibitors, and hypovolemia increases the potential for adverse renal effects of ACE inhibitors. In patients with compromised renal function, coadministration with NSAIDs may result in further deterioration of renal function. Allopurinol and ACE inhibitors may cause a higher risk of hypersensitivity reaction when taken concurrently.

  Decreased Effect: Aspirin (high dose) may reduce the therapeutic effects of ACE inhibitors; at low dosages this does not appear to be significant. Rifampin may decrease the effect of ACE inhibitors. Antacids may decrease the bioavailability of ACE inhibitors (may be more likely to occur with captopril); separate administration times by 1-2 hours. NSAIDs, specifically indomethacin, may reduce the hypotensive effects of ACE inhibitors. More likely to occur in low renin or volume dependent hypertensive patients.

Ethanol/Nutrition/Herb Interactions Herb/Nutraceutical: Avoid dong quai if using for hypertension (has estrogenic activity). Avoid ephedra, yohimbe, ginseng (may worsen hypertension). Avoid garlic (may have increased antihypertensive effect).

Mechanism of Action Trandolapril is an ACE inhibitor which prevents the formation of angiotensin II from angiotensin I. Trandolapril must undergo enzymatic hydrolysis, mainly in liver, to its biologically active metabolite, trandolaprilat. A CNS mechanism may also be involved in the hypotensive effect as angiotensin II increases adrenergic outflow from the CNS. Vasoactive kallikrein's may be decreased in conversion to active hormones by ACE inhibitors, thus, reducing blood pressure.

Pharmacodynamics/Kinetics
  Onset of action: 1-2 hours
    Peak effect: Reduction in blood pressure: 6 hours
  Duration: Prolonged; 72 hours after single dose
  Absorption: Rapid
  Distribution: Trandolaprilat (active metabolite) is very lipophilic in comparison to other ACE inhibitors
  Protein binding: 80%
  Metabolism: Hepatically hydrolyzed to active metabolite, trandolaprilat
  Half-life elimination:
    Trandolapril: 6 hours; Trandolaprilat: Effective: 10 hours, Terminal: 24 hours
  Time to peak: Parent: 1 hour; Active metabolite trandolaprilat: 4-10 hours
  Excretion: Urine (as metabolites)
    Clearance: Reduce dose in renal failure; creatinine clearances ≤30 mL/minute result in accumulation of active metabolite

Dosage Adults: Oral:
  Hypertension: Initial dose in patients not receiving a diuretic: 1 mg/day (2 mg/day in black patients). Adjust dosage according to the blood pressure response. Make dosage adjustments at intervals of ≥1 week. Most patients have required dosages of 2-4 mg/day. There is a little experience with doses >8 mg/day. Patients inadequately treated with once daily dosing at 4 mg may be treated with twice daily dosing. If blood pressure is not adequately controlled with trandolapril monotherapy, a diuretic may be added.

(Continued)

Trandolapril *(Continued)*

Usual dose range (JNC 7): 1-4 mg once daily

Heart failure postmyocardial infarction or left ventricular dysfunction postmyocardial infarction: Initial: 1 mg/day; titrate patients (as tolerated) towards the target dose of 4 mg/day. If a 4 mg dose is not tolerated, patients can continue therapy with the greatest tolerated dose.

Dosing adjustment in renal impairment: Cl_{cr} ≤30 mL/minute: Recommended starting dose: 0.5 mg/day.

Dosing adjustment in hepatic impairment: Cirrhosis: Recommended starting dose: 0.5 mg/day.

Monitoring Parameters Serum potassium, renal function, serum creatinine, BUN, CBC; observe for hypotensive effects within 1-3 hours of first dose or new higher dose

Dosage Forms Tablet: 1 mg, 2 mg, 4 mg

Trandolapril and Verapamil *(tran DOE la pril & ver AP a mil)*

U.S. Brand Names Tarka®
Canadian Brand Names Tarka®
Index Terms Verapamil and Trandolapril
Pharmacologic Category Antihypertensive Agent, Combination
Use Combination drug for the treatment of hypertension, however, not indicated for initial treatment of hypertension; replacement therapy in patients receiving separate dosage forms (for patient convenience); when monotherapy with one component fails to achieve desired antihypertensive effect, or when dose-limiting adverse effects limit upward titration of monotherapy

Pregnancy Risk Factor C/D (2nd and 3rd trimesters)
Dosage Dose is individualized
Additional Information Complete prescribing information for this medication should be consulted for additional detail.
Dosage Forms Tablet, variable release:
1/240: Trandolapril 1 mg [immediate release] and verapamil hydrochloride 240 mg [sustained release]
2/180: Trandolapril 2 mg [immediate release] and verapamil hydrochloride 180 mg [sustained release]
2/240: Trandolapril 2 mg [immediate release] and verapamil hydrochloride 240 mg [sustained release]
4/240: Trandolapril 4 mg [immediate release] and verapamil hydrochloride 240 mg [sustained release]

Tranexamic Acid *(tran eks AM ik AS id)*

U.S. Brand Names Cyklokapron®
Canadian Brand Names Cyklokapron®; Tranexamic Acid Injection BP
Pharmacologic Category Antihemophilic Agent
Use Short-term use (2-8 days) in hemophilia patients during and following tooth extraction to reduce or prevent hemorrhage
Unlabeled/Investigational Use Has been used as an alternative to aminocaproic acid for subarachnoid hemorrhage
Pregnancy Risk Factor B
Medication Safety Issues
Sound-alike/look-alike issues:
Cyklokapron® may be confused with cycloSPORINE
Dosage Children and Adults: I.V.: 10 mg/kg immediately before surgery, then 25 mg/kg/dose orally 3-4 times/day for 2-8 days

Alternatively:
Oral: 25 mg/kg 3-4 times/day beginning 1 day prior to surgery
I.V.: 10 mg/kg 3-4 times/day in patients who are unable to take oral
Dosing adjustment/interval in renal impairment:
Cl_{cr} 50-80 mL/minute: Administer 50% of normal dose or 10 mg/kg twice daily I.V. or 15 mg/kg twice daily orally
Cl_{cr} 10-50 mL/minute: Administer 25% of normal dose or 10 mg/kg/day I.V. or 15 mg/kg/day orally
Cl_{cr} <10 mL/minute: Administer 10% of normal dose or 10 mg/kg/dose every 48 hours I.V. or 15 mg/kg/dose every 48 hours orally
Additional Information Complete prescribing information for this medication should be consulted for additional detail.
Dosage Forms
Injection, solution: 100 mg/mL (10 mL)
Tablet: 500 mg [Not marketed in U.S.; available from manufacturer for select cases]

♦ **Tranexamic Acid Injection BP (Can)** *see* Tranexamic Acid *on page 1722*
♦ **Transamine Sulphate** *see* Tranylcypromine *on page 1723*
♦ **Transderm-V® (Can)** *see* Scopolamine Derivatives *on page 1550*
♦ **Transderm-Nitro® (Can)** *see* Nitroglycerin *on page 1234*
♦ **Transderm Scōp®** *see* Scopolamine Derivatives *on page 1550*
♦ *trans*-**Retinoic Acid** *see* Tretinoin (Oral) *on page 1730*
♦ *trans*-**Retinoic Acid** *see* Tretinoin (Topical) *on page 1732*
♦ **Tranxene® SD™** *see* Clorazepate *on page 403*
♦ **Tranxene® SD™-Half Strength** *see* Clorazepate *on page 403*
♦ **Tranxene T-Tab®** *see* Clorazepate *on page 403*
♦ **Tranxene® T-Tab®** *see* Clorazepate *on page 403*

Tranylcypromine (tran il SIP roe meen)

U.S. Brand Names Parnate®
Canadian Brand Names Parnate®
Index Terms Transamine Sulphate; Tranylcypromine Sulfate
Pharmacologic Category Antidepressant, Monoamine Oxidase Inhibitor
Additional Appendix Information
Antidepressant Agents *on page 1866*
Tyramine Content of Foods *on page 2115*
Use Treatment of major depressive episode without melancholia
Unlabeled/Investigational Use Post-traumatic stress disorder
Restrictions An FDA-approved medication guide concerning the use of antidepressants in children and teenagers must be distributed when dispensing an outpatient prescription (new or refill) where this medication is to be used without direct supervision of a healthcare provider. Medication guides are available at http://www.fda.gov/cder/Offices/ODS/medication_guides.htm. Dispense to parents or guardians of children and teenagers receiving this medication.
Pregnancy Risk Factor C
Lactation Enters breast milk/not recommended
Contraindications Hypersensitivity to tranylcypromine, other MAO inhibitors, dibenzazepine derivatives, or any component of the formulation; cardiovascular disease; cerebrovascular defect; headache history; hepatic disease; hypertension; pheochromocytoma; renal disease; concurrent use of antihistamines, antiparkinson drugs, antihypertensives, bupropion, buspirone, CNS depressants, dexfenfluramine, dextromethorphan, diuretics, ethanol, meperidine, and SSRIs; general anesthesia (discontinue 10 days prior to elective surgery); local vasoconstrictors; spinal anesthesia (hypotension may be exaggerated); sympathomimetics (and related compounds); foods high in tyramine content; supplements containing tyrosine, phenylalanine, tryptophan, or caffeine
Warnings/Precautions Risk of suicide: [U.S. Boxed Warning]: Antidepressants increase the risk of suicidal thinking and behavior in children and adolescents with major depressive disorder (MDD) and other depressive disorders; consider risk prior to prescribing. Closely monitor for clinical worsening, suicidality, or unusual changes in behavior. The child's family or caregiver should be instructed to closely observe the patient and communicate condition with healthcare provider. Such observation would generally include at least weekly face-to-face contact with patients or their family members or caregivers during the first 4 weeks of treatment, then every other week visits for the next 4 weeks, then at 12 weeks, and as clinically indicated beyond 12 weeks. Additional contact by telephone may be appropriate between face-to-face visits. A medication guide should be dispensed with each prescription. **Tranylcypromine is not FDA approved for treatment of children and adolescents.**

Adults treated with antidepressants should be observed similarly for clinical worsening and suicidality, especially during the initial few months of a course of drug therapy, or at times of dose changes (increases or decreases). The possibility of a suicide attempt is inherent in major depression and may persist until remission occurs. Use caution in high-risk patients. Prescriptions should be written for the smallest quantity.

Disease state precautions: Use with caution in patients who are hyperactive, hyperexcitable, or who have glaucoma, hyperthyroidism, diabetes or hypotension. May cause orthostatic hypotension (especially at dosages >30 mg/day). Use with caution in patients at risk of seizures, or in patients receiving other drugs which may lower seizure threshold. Discontinue at least 48 hours prior to myelography. May increase the risks associated with electroconvulsive therapy. Consider discontinuing, if possible, prior to elective surgery. Use with caution in patients with renal impairment. May worsen psychosis in some patients or precipitate a shift to mania or hypomania in patients with bipolar disorder. **Tranylcypromine is not FDA approved for the treatment of bipolar depression.**

Elderly patients: Interactions with tyramine or tryptophan-containing foods and orthostasis have limited tranylcypromine's use.
Adverse Reactions Frequency not defined.
Cardiovascular: Edema, orthostatic hypotension, palpitations, tachycardia
Central nervous system: Agitation, akinesia, anxiety, ataxia, chills, confusion, disorientation, dizziness, drowsiness, fatigue, headache, hyper-reflexia, insomnia, mania, memory loss, restlessness, sleep disturbances, twitching
Dermatologic: Alopecia, cystic acne (flare), pruritus, rash, urticaria, scleroderma (localized)
Endocrine & metabolic: Hypernatremia, hypermetabolic syndrome; sexual dysfunction (anorgasmia, ejaculatory disturbances, impotence); SIADH
Gastrointestinal: Abdominal pain, anorexia, constipation, diarrhea, nausea, vomiting, weight gain, xerostomia
Genitourinary: Incontinence, urinary retention
Hematologic: Agranulocytosis, anemia, leukopenia, thrombocytopenia
Hepatic: Hepatitis
Neuromuscular & skeletal: Akinesis, muscle spasm, myoclonus, numbness, paresthesia, tremor, weakness
Ocular: Blurred vision, glaucoma
Otic: Tinnitus
Miscellaneous: Diaphoresis
Overdosage/Toxicology Symptoms of overdose include headache, tachycardia or bradycardia, neck stiffness, nausea, vomiting, chest pain, sweating, photophobia, palpitations, muscle twitching, seizures, insomnia, orthostatic hypotension, hypertension, hypertensive crisis, hyperpyrexia, and coma. Treatment is symptom-directed and supportive. The manufacturer suggests phentolamine (5 mg given slowly I.V.) for treatment of hypertensive crisis. Other useful agents may be labetalol or nitroprusside.
(Continued)

Tranylcypromine *(Continued)*

Drug Interactions

Cytochrome P450 Effect: Inhibits CYP1A2 (moderate), 2A6 (strong), 2C8 (weak), 2C9 (weak), 2C19 (moderate), 2D6 (moderate), 2E1 (weak), 3A4 (weak)

Increased Effect/Toxicity: Tranylcypromine may enhance the adverse effects of ethanol (CNS depression), amphetamines (hypertension), general anesthetics (hypotension), atomoxetine (CNS toxicity), buspirone (hypertension), CYP1A2 substrates, CYP2A6 substrates, CYP2C19 substrates, CYP2D6 substrates, dexmethylphenidate (hypertension), disulfiram (delirium), levodopa (hypertension), lithium (CNS toxicity), methylphenidate (hypertension), mirtazapine (CNS toxicity), rauwolfia alkaloids, and thioridazine. Tranylcypromine may enhance the vasopressor effects of alpha-/beta-agonists and enhance the hypertensive effects of alpha$_1$-agonists. Altretamine may enhance the orthostatic effects of tranylcypromine. Anticholinergics may enhance the side effects of tranylcypromine. Concurrent use of anorexiants, cyclobenzaprine, dextromethorphan, meperidine, SSRIs/SNRIs, serotonin 5-HT$_{1D}$ receptor agonist, sibutramine, and tricyclic antidepressants may result in a serotonin syndrome. Concurrent use of bupropion may lead to hypertensive crisis. COMT inhibitors may cause adverse/toxic effects. Pramlintide may increase anticholinergic effects of tranylcypromine. Serotonin modulators may enhance the adverse/toxic effects of tranylcypromine. Tramadol may increase the neuroexcitatory and seizure-potentiating effects of tranylcypromine.

Decreased Effect: Acetylcholinesterase inhibitors decrease tranylcypromine's anticholinergic side effects. Tranylcypromine may decrease the effects of CYP2D6 prodrug substrates, and false neurotransmitters (guanadrel, methyldopa).

Ethanol/Nutrition/Herb Interactions

Ethanol: Avoid ethanol (based on CNS depressant effects and potential tyramine content)

Food: Concurrent ingestion of foods rich in tyramine may cause sudden and severe high blood pressure (hypertensive crisis). Avoid tyramine-containing foods with MAOIs. Food's freshness is also an important concern; improperly stored or spoiled food can create an environment where tyramine concentrations may increase.

Herb/Nutraceuticals: Avoid valerian, St John's wort, SAMe. Avoid supplements containing caffeine, gingko, yohimbime, ephedra, tyrosine, tryptophan or phenylalanine. Ingestion of large quantities may increase the risk of severe side effects (eg, hypertensive reactions, serotonin syndrome).

Mechanism of Action Tranylcypromine is a nonhydrazine monoamine oxidase inhibitor. It increases endogenous concentrations of epinephrine, norepinephrine, dopamine, and serotonin through inhibition of the enzyme (monoamine oxidase) responsible for the breakdown of these neurotransmitters.

Pharmacodynamics/Kinetics

Onset of action: Therapeutic: 2 days to 3 weeks continued dosing

Half-life elimination: 90-190 minutes

Time to peak, serum: ~2 hours

Excretion: Urine

Dosage Adults: Oral: 10 mg twice daily, increase by 10 mg increments at 1- to 3-week intervals; maximum: 60 mg/day; usual effective dose: 30 mg/day

Dietary Considerations Avoid foods containing tryptophan and caffeine. Avoid tyramine-containing foods/beverages. Some examples include aged or matured cheese, air-dried or cured meats (including sausages and salamis), fava or broad bean pods, tap/draft beers, Marmite concentrate, sauerkraut, soy sauce and other soybean condiments.

Monitoring Parameters Blood pressure, mental status

Additional Information Tranylcypromine has a more rapid onset of therapeutic effect than other MAO inhibitors, but causes more severe hypertensive reactions.

Dosage Forms Tablet: 10 mg

♦ **Tranylcypromine Sulfate** *see* Tranylcypromine *on page 1723*

Trastuzumab *(tras TU zoo mab)*

U.S. Brand Names Herceptin®

Canadian Brand Names Herceptin®

Index Terms NSC-688097

Pharmacologic Category Antineoplastic Agent, Monoclonal Antibody; Monoclonal Antibody

Use Treatment of HER-2/*neu* overexpressing metastatic breast cancer; adjuvant treatment of HER-2/*neu* overexpressing node- positive breast cancer

Unlabeled/Investigational Use Treatment of ovarian, gastric, colorectal, endometrial, lung, bladder, prostate, and salivary gland tumors

Pregnancy Risk Factor B

Pregnancy Implications Reproductive studies in cynomolgus monkeys showed no evidence of impaired fertility or fetal harm. There are no adequate and well-controlled studies in pregnant women. Reversible anhydramnios and oligohydramnios have been reported with use during pregnancy.

Lactation Excretion in breast milk unknown/not recommended

Medication Safety Issues

High alert medication: The Institute for Safe Medication Practices (ISMP) includes this medication among its list of drugs which have a heightened risk of causing significant patient harm when used in error.

Contraindications Hypersensitivity to trastuzumab, Chinese hamster ovary cell proteins, or any component of the formulation

Warnings/Precautions Hazardous agent - use appropriate precautions for handling and disposal. **[U.S. Boxed Warning]: Congestive heart failure associated with trastuzumab may be severe and has been associated with disabling cardiac failure, death, mural thrombus, and stroke.** Left ventricular function should be evaluated in all patients prior to and during treatment with trastuzumab. Discontinuation should be strongly considered in patients who develop a clinically significant decrease in ejection fraction during therapy.

Combination therapy with anthracyclines increases the risk of cardiac dysfunction. Prior or concurrent use of antihypertensive medications may increase the risk of cardiac toxicity. Extreme caution should be used when treating patients with pre-existing cardiac disease or dysfunction, and in patients with previous exposure to anthracyclines or radiation therapy. Advanced age may also predispose to cardiac toxicity.

[U.S. Boxed Warning]: Serious adverse events, including hypersensitivity reaction (anaphylaxis), infusion reactions (including fatalities), and pulmonary events (including acute respiratory distress syndrome) have been associated with trastuzumab. Most of these events occur with the first infusion; pulmonary events may occur during or within 24 hours of administration; delayed reactions have occurred. Discontinuation of trastuzumab should be strongly considered in any patient who develops anaphylaxis, angioedema, or acute respiratory distress syndrome. Retreatment of patients who experienced severe hypersensitivity reactions has been attempted (with premedication). Some patients tolerated retreatment, while others experienced a second severe reaction. When used in combination with myelosuppressive chemotherapy, trastuzumab may increase the incidence of neutropenia (moderate-to-severe) and febrile neutropenia. May cause serious pulmonary toxicity (pneumonitis, pulmonary infiltrates, pleural effusion, noncardiogenic pulmonary edema, pulmonary insufficiency, acute respiratory distress syndrome, and/or pulmonary fibrosis); use caution in patients with pre-existing pulmonary disease or patients with extensive pulmonary tumor involvement. Safety and efficacy in children have not been established.

Adverse Reactions Note: Percentages reported with single-agent therapy.
>10%:
Central nervous system: Pain (47%), fever (36%), chills (32%), headache (26%), insomnia (14%), dizziness (13%)
Dermatologic: Rash (18%)
Gastrointestinal: Nausea (8% to 33%), diarrhea (25%), vomiting (8% to 23%), abdominal pain (22%), anorexia (14%)
Neuromuscular & skeletal: Weakness (42%), back pain (22%)
Respiratory: Cough (26%), dyspnea (22%), rhinitis (14%), pharyngitis (12%)
Miscellaneous: Infusion reaction (21% to 40%, chills and fever most common; severe: 1%), infection (20%)
1% to 10%:
Cardiovascular: Peripheral edema (10%), edema (8%), CHF (7%), tachycardia (5%)
Central nervous system: Depression (6%)
Dermatologic: Acne (2%)
Genitourinary: Urinary tract infection (5%)
Hematologic: Anemia (4%), leukopenia (3%)
Neuromuscular & skeletal: Paresthesia (9%), bone pain (7%), arthralgia (6%), peripheral neuritis (2%), neuropathy (1%)
Respiratory: Sinusitis (9%)
Miscellaneous: Flu syndrome (10%), accidental injury (6%), allergic reaction (3%), herpes simplex (2%)
<1% (Limited to important or life-threatening): Acute respiratory distress syndrome (ARDS), amblyopia, anaphylaxis, anaphylactoid reaction, angioedema, apnea, arrhythmia, ascites, asthma, ataxia, bone necrosis, bronchospasm, cardiac arrest, cardiomyopathy, cellulitis, coagulopathy, colitis, confusion, deafness, esophageal ulcer, gastroenteritis, glomerulonephritis (membranous and fibrillary), glomerulosclerosis, hematemesis, hemorrhage, hemorrhagic cystitis, hepatic failure, hepatitis, herpes zoster, hydrocephalus, hydronephrosis, hypercalcemia, hypotension, hypothyroidism, hypoxia, ileus, intestinal obstruction, laryngitis, leukemia (acute), lymphangitis, mania, mural thrombosis, myopathy, nephritic syndrome, neutropenia, pancreatitis, pancytopenia, paroxysmal nocturnal dyspnea, pathological fracture, pericardial effusion, pleural effusion, pneumonitis, pneumothorax, pulmonary edema (noncardiogenic), pulmonary fibrosis, pulmonary infiltrate, pyelonephritis, radiation injury, renal failure, respiratory distress, respiratory failure, seizure, sepsis, severe infusion reaction, shock, skin ulcers, stroke, syncope, stomatitis, vascular thrombosis, volume overload

Overdosage/Toxicology There is no experience with overdosage in human trials. Single doses >500 mg have not been tested. Treatment is symptom-directed and supportive.

Drug Interactions
Increased Effect/Toxicity: Paclitaxel may result in a decrease in clearance of trastuzumab, increasing serum concentrations. Combined use with anthracyclines may increase the incidence/severity of cardiac dysfunction. Monoclonal antibodies may increase the risk for allergic reactions to trastuzumab due to the presence of HACA antibodies. Trastuzumab may increase the incidence of neutropenia and/or febrile neutropenia when used in combination with myelosuppressive chemotherapy.

Stability Store intact vials under refrigeration at 2°C to 8°C (36°F to 46°F) prior to reconstitution. Reconstitute each vial with 20 mL of bacteriostatic sterile water for injection. Swirl gently; do not shake. Allow vial to rest for ~5 minutes. Avoid rapid expulsion from syringe. The concentration of this solution is 21 mg/mL and is stable for 28 days from the date of reconstitution under refrigeration. If sterile water for injection without preservative is used for reconstitution, it must be used immediately. Further dilute in 250 mL NS prior to administration. If the patient has a known hypersensitivity to benzyl alcohol, trastuzumab may be reconstituted with sterile water for injection which must be used immediately.

Determine the dose of trastuzumab and further dilute to an infusion bag containing 0.9% sodium chloride. This solution is stable for 24 hours at room temperature or refrigerated. However, since diluted trastuzumab contains no effective preservative, the reconstituted and diluted solution should be stored under refrigeration (2°C to 8°C).

Mechanism of Action Trastuzumab is a monoclonal antibody which binds to the extracellular domain of the human epidermal growth factor receptor 2 protein (HER-2); it mediates antibody-dependent cellular cytotoxicity against cells which overproduce HER-2

Pharmacodynamics/Kinetics
Distribution: V_d: 44 mL/kg
Half-life elimination: Mean: 5.8 days (range: 1-32 days)
(Continued)

Trastuzumab *(Continued)*

Dosage Refer to individual protocols. Adults: I.V. infusion:

Metastatic breast cancer:

Initial loading dose: 4 mg/kg infused over 90 minutes

Maintenance dose: 2 mg/kg infused over 90 minutes (can be administered over 30 minutes if prior infusions are well tolerated) weekly until disease progression

Node-positive breast cancer:

Initial loading dose: 4 mg/kg infused over 90 minutes

Maintenance dose: 2 mg/kg infused over 90 minutes (can be administered over 30 minutes if prior infusions are well tolerated) weekly for 51 weeks (total of 52 weeks)

Every 3-week schedule (unlabeled schedule):

Initial loading dose: 8 mg/kg infused over 90 minutes

Maintenance dose: 6 mg/kg infused over 90 minutes every 3 weeks

Dosage adjustment for toxicity:

Cardiotoxicity: LVEF ≥16% decrease from baseline within normal limits or LVEF below normal limits and ≥10% decrease from baseline: Withhold treatment for 4 weeks and repeat LVEF every 4 weeks. May resume trastuzumab treatment if LVEF returns to normal limits within 4-8 weeks and remains at ≤15% decrease from baseline value. Discontinue permanently for persistent LVEF decline or for >3 incidents of treatment interruptions for cardiomyopathy.

Infusion-related events:

Mild-moderate infusion reactions: Decrease infusion rate

Dyspnea, hypotension: Interrupt infusion

Severe reactions: Consider permanent discontinuation

Dosing adjustment in renal impairment: Data suggest that the disposition of trastuzumab is not altered based on age or serum creatinine (up to 2 mg/dL); however, no formal interaction studies have been performed

Dosing adjustment in hepatic impairment: No data is currently available

Administration Administered by I.V. infusion; loading doses are infused over 90 minutes; maintenance doses may be infused over 30 minutes if tolerated. Do not administer I.V. push or by rapid bolus. Treatment with acetaminophen, diphenhydramine, and/or meperidine is usually effective for managing infusion-related events.

Monitoring Parameters Signs and symptoms of cardiac dysfunction; monitor vital signs during infusion; LVEF (baseline & periodic)

Dosage Forms

Injection, powder for reconstitution:

Herceptin®: 440 mg [packaged with bacteriostatic water for injection; diluent contains benzyl alcohol]

♦ **Trasylol®** *see* Aprotinin *on page 146*

♦ **Travatan®** *see* Travoprost *on page 1726*

♦ **Travatan® Z** *see* Travoprost *on page 1726*

Travoprost *(TRA voe prost)*

U.S. Brand Names Travatan®; Travatan® Z

Canadian Brand Names Travatan®

Pharmacologic Category Ophthalmic Agent, Antiglaucoma; Prostaglandin, Ophthalmic

Additional Appendix Information

Glaucoma Drug Therapy *on page 2050*

Use Reduction of elevated intraocular pressure in patients with open-angle glaucoma or ocular hypertension who are intolerant of the other IOP-lowering medications or insufficiently responsive (failed to achieve target IOP determined after multiple measurements over time) to another IOP-lowering medication

Pregnancy Risk Factor C

Pregnancy Implications May interfere with the maintenance of pregnancy. Do not use during pregnancy or in women attempting to become pregnant. Teratogenic effects in humans are not known.

Lactation Excretion in breast milk unknown/use caution

Medication Safety Issues

Sound-alike/look-alike issues:

Travatan® may be confused with Xalatan®

Contraindications Hypersensitivity to travoprost or any component of the formulation; pregnancy

Warnings/Precautions May permanently change/increase brown pigmentation of the iris, the eyelid skin, and eyelashes. In addition, may increase the length and/or number of eyelashes (may vary between eyes); changes occur slowly and may not be noticeable for months or years. Bacterial keratitis, caused by inadvertent contamination of multiple-dose ophthalmic solutions, has been reported. Use caution in patients with intraocular inflammation, aphakic patients, pseudophakic patients with a torn posterior lens capsule, or patients with risk factors for macular edema. Contact with contents of vial should be avoided in women who are pregnant or attempting to become pregnant; in case of accidental exposure to the skin, wash the exposed area with soap and water immediately. Safety and efficacy have not been determined for use in patients with renal or hepatic impairment, angle-closure-, inflammatory-, or neovascular glaucoma. Safety and efficacy in pediatric patients have not been established.

Travatan®: Contains benzalkonium chloride which may be adsorbed by contact lenses; remove contacts prior to administration and wait 15 minutes before reinserting.

Adverse Reactions

>10%: Ocular: Hyperemia (35% to 50%)

5% to 10%: Ocular: Decreased visual acuity, eye discomfort, foreign body sensation, pain, pruritus

1% to 5%:
    Cardiovascular: Angina pectoris, bradycardia, hyper-/hypotension
    Central nervous system: Depression, pain, anxiety, headache
    Endocrine & metabolic: Hypercholesterolemia
    Gastrointestinal: Dyspepsia
    Genitourinary: Prostate disorder, urinary incontinence
    Neuromuscular & skeletal: Arthritis, back pain, chest pain
    Ocular (1% to 4%): Abnormal vision, blepharitis, blurred vision, conjunctivitis, dry eye, iris discoloration, keratitis, lid margin crusting, photophobia, subconjunctival hemorrhage, cataract, tearing, periorbital skin discoloration (darkening), eyelash darkening, eyelash growth increased
    Respiratory: Bronchitis, sinusitis
    Postmarketing and/or case reports: Bacterial keratitis (due to solution contamination)
Stability Store between 2°C to 25°C (36°F to 77°F).
Mechanism of Action A selective FP prostanoid receptor agonist which lowers intraocular pressure by increasing trabecular meshwork and outflow
Pharmacodynamics/Kinetics
Onset of action: ~2 hours
    Peak effect: 12 hours
Duration: Plasma levels decrease to <10 pg/mL within 1 hour
Absorption: Absorbed via cornea
Metabolism: Hydrolyzed by esterases in the cornea to active free acid; systemically; the free acid is metabolized to inactive metabolites
Dosage Ophthalmic: Adults: Glaucoma (open angle) or ocular hypertension: Instill 1 drop into affected eye(s) once daily in the evening; do not exceed once-daily dosing. (may decrease IOP-lowering effect). If used with other topical ophthalmic agents, separate administration by at least 5 minutes.
Administration May be used with other eye drops to lower intraocular pressure. If using more than one ophthalmic product, wait at least 5 minutes in between application of each medication. Travatan®: Remove contact lenses prior to administration and wait 15 minutes before reinserting.
Additional Information The IOP-lowering effect was shown to be 7-8 mm Hg in clinical studies. The mean IOP reduction in African-American patients was up to 1.8 mm Hg greater than in non-African-American patients. The reason for this effect is unknown.
Dosage Forms
Solution, ophthalmic:
    Travatan®: 0.004% (2.5 mL, 5 mL) [contains benzalkonium chloride]
    Travatan® Z: 0.004% (2.5 mL, 5 mL)

Trazodone (TRAZ oh done)

U.S. Brand Names Desyrel® [DSC]
Canadian Brand Names Alti-Trazodone; Apo-Trazodone®; Apo-Trazodone D®; Desyrel®; Gen-Trazodone; Novo-Trazodone; Nu-Trazodone; PMS-Trazodone; ratio-Trazodone; Trazorel®
Index Terms Trazodone Hydrochloride
Pharmacologic Category Antidepressant, Serotonin Reuptake Inhibitor/Antagonist
Additional Appendix Information
Antidepressant Agents *on page 1866*
Use Treatment of depression
Unlabeled/Investigational Use Potential augmenting agent for antidepressants, hypnotic
Restrictions An FDA-approved medication guide concerning the use of antidepressants in children and teenagers must be distributed when dispensing an outpatient prescription (new or refill) where this medication is to be used without direct supervision of a healthcare provider. Medication guides are available at http://www.fda.gov/cder/Offices/ODS/medication_guides.htm. Dispense to parents or guardians of children and teenagers receiving this medication.
Pregnancy Risk Factor C
Lactation Enters breast milk/use caution (AAP rates "of concern")
Medication Safety Issues
Sound-alike/look-alike issues:
    Desyrel® may be confused with Demerol®, Delsym®, Zestril®

International issues:
    Desyrel® may be confused with Deseril® which is a brand name for methysergide in multiple international markets
Contraindications Hypersensitivity to trazodone or any component of the formulation
Warnings/Precautions [U.S. Boxed Warning]: Antidepressants increase the risk of suicidal thinking and behavior in children and adolescents with major depressive disorder (MDD) and other depressive disorders; consider risk prior to prescribing. All patients must be closely monitored for clinical worsening, suicidality, or unusual changes in behavior, especially during the initiation of therapy or following an increase or decrease in dosage. When used in children, the child's family or caregiver must be instructed to closely observe the patient and communicate condition with healthcare provider. A medication guide should be dispensed with each prescription. **Trazodone is not FDA approved for use in children.**

The possibility of a suicide attempt is inherent in major depression and may persist until remission occurs. Use caution in high-risk patients. Worsening depression and severe abrupt suicidality that are not part of the presenting symptoms may require discontinuation or modification of drug therapy. The patient's family or caregiver should be alerted to monitor patients for the emergence of suicidality and associated behaviors (such as agitation, irritability, hostility, impulsivity, and hypomania) and call healthcare provider.
(Continued)

Trazodone *(Continued)*

May worsen psychosis in some patients or precipitate a shift to mania or hypomania in patients with bipolar disorder. Patients presenting with depressive symptoms should be screened for bipolar disorder. Monotherapy in patients with bipolar disorder should be avoided. **Trazodone is not FDA approved for the treatment of bipolar depression.**

Priapism, including cases resulting in permanent dysfunction, has occurred with the use of trazodone. Not recommended for use in a patient during the acute recovery phase of MI. Trazodone should be initiated with caution in patients who are receiving concurrent or recent therapy with a MAO inhibitor.

The risks of sedation and/or postural hypotension are high relative to other antidepressants. Trazodone frequently causes sedation, which may result in impaired performance of tasks requiring alertness (eg, operating machinery or driving). Sedative effects may be additive with other CNS depressants and ethanol. Use with caution in patients with a history of cardiovascular disease (including previous MI, stroke, tachycardia, or conduction abnormalities). The risk of conduction abnormalities with this agent is low relative to other antidepressants.

Consider discontinuing, when possible, prior to elective surgery. Therapy should not be abruptly discontinued in patients receiving high doses for prolonged periods. Use caution in patients with a previous seizure disorder or condition predisposing to seizures such as brain damage, alcoholism, or concurrent therapy with other drugs which lower the seizure threshold. Use with caution in patients with hepatic or renal dysfunction and in elderly patients.

Adverse Reactions

>10%:

Central nervous system: Dizziness, headache, sedation

Gastrointestinal: Nausea, xerostomia

Ocular: Blurred vision

1% to 10%:

Cardiovascular: Syncope, hyper-/hypotension, edema

Central nervous system: Confusion, decreased concentration, fatigue, incoordination

Gastrointestinal: Diarrhea, constipation, weight gain/loss

Neuromuscular & skeletal: Tremor, myalgia

Respiratory: Nasal congestion

<1% (Limited to important or life-threatening): Agitation, allergic reactions, alopecia, anxiety, bradycardia, extrapyramidal symptoms, hepatitis, priapism, rash, seizure, speech impairment, tachycardia, urinary retention

Overdosage/Toxicology Symptoms include drowsiness, vomiting, hypotension, tachycardia, incontinence, coma, and priapism. Following initiation of essential overdose management, toxic symptoms should be treated. Ventricular arrhythmias often respond to lidocaine 1.5 mg/kg bolus, followed by 2 mg/minute infusion with concurrent systemic alkalinization (sodium bicarbonate 0.5-2 mEq/kg I.V.). Seizures usually respond to diazepam I.V. boluses (5-10 mg for adults up to 30 mg or 0.25-0.4 mg/kg/dose for children up to 10 mg/dose). If seizures are unresponsive or recur, phenytoin or phenobarbital may be required. Hypotension is best treated by I.V. fluids and by Trendelenburg positioning.

Drug Interactions

Cytochrome P450 Effect: Substrate of CYP2D6 (minor), 3A4 (major); **Inhibits** CYP2D6 (moderate), 3A4 (weak)

Increased Effect/Toxicity: Sedative effects may be additive with other CNS depressants. Trazodone, in combination with other serotonergic agents (buspirone, MAO inhibitors), may produce additive serotonergic effects, including serotonin syndrome. Trazodone, in combination with other psychotropics (low potency antipsychotics), may result in additional hypotension. Fluoxetine may inhibit the metabolism of trazodone resulting in elevated plasma levels.

Trazodone may increase the levels/effects of amphetamines, beta-blockers, dextromethorphan, fluoxetine, lidocaine, mirtazapine, nefazodone, paroxetine, risperidone, ritonavir, thioridazine, tricyclic antidepressants, venlafaxine, and other CYP2D6 substrates. The levels/effects of trazodone may be increased by azole antifungals, clarithromycin, diclofenac, doxycycline, erythromycin, imatinib, isoniazid, nefazodone, nicardipine, propofol, protease inhibitors, quinidine, telithromycin, verapamil, and other CYP3A4 inhibitors.

Decreased Effect: Trazodone inhibits the hypotensive response to clonidine. The levels/effects of trazodone may be decreased by aminoglutethimide, carbamazepine, nafcillin, nevirapine, phenobarbital, phenytoin, rifamycins, and other CYP3A4 inducers. Trazodone may decrease the levels/effects of CYP2D6 prodrug substrates (eg, codeine, hydrocodone, oxycodone, tramadol).

Ethanol/Nutrition/Herb Interactions

Ethanol: Avoid ethanol (may increase CNS depression).

Food: Time to peak serum levels may be increased if trazodone is taken with food.

Herb/Nutraceutical: Avoid valerian, St John's wort, SAMe, kava kava (may increase risk of serotonin syndrome and/or excessive sedation).

Mechanism of Action Inhibits reuptake of serotonin, causes adrenoreceptor subsensitivity, and induces significant changes in 5-HT presynaptic receptor adrenoreceptors. Trazodone also significantly blocks histamine (H_1) and alpha$_1$-adrenergic receptors.

Pharmacodynamics/Kinetics

Onset of action: Therapeutic (antidepressant): 1-3 weeks; sleep aid: 1-3 hours

Protein binding: 85% to 95%

Metabolism: Hepatic via CYP3A4 to an active metabolite (mCPP)

Half-life elimination: 7-8 hours, two compartment kinetics

Time to peak, serum: 30-100 minutes; delayed with food (up to 2.5 hours)

Excretion: Primarily urine; secondarily feces

Dosage Oral: Therapeutic effects may take up to 6 weeks to occur; therapy is normally maintained for 6-12 months after optimum response is reached to prevent recurrence of depression

Children 6-12 years: Depression (unlabeled use): Initial: 1.5-2 mg/kg/day in divided doses; increase gradually every 3-4 days as needed; maximum: 6 mg/kg/day in 3 divided doses

Adolescents: Depression (unlabeled use): Initial: 25-50 mg/day; increase to 100-150 mg/day in divided doses

Adults:

Depression: Initial: 150 mg/day in 3 divided doses (may increase by 50 mg/day every 3-7 days); maximum: 600 mg/day

Sedation/hypnotic (unlabeled use): 25-50 mg at bedtime (often in combination with daytime SSRIs); may increase up to 200 mg at bedtime

Elderly: 25-50 mg at bedtime with 25-50 mg/day dose increase every 3 days for inpatients and weekly for outpatients, if tolerated; usual dose: 75-150 mg/day

Administration Dosing after meals may decrease lightheadedness and postural hypotension

Reference Range

Plasma levels do not always correlate with clinical effectiveness

Therapeutic: 0.5-2.5 mcg/mL

Potentially toxic: >2.5 mcg/mL

Toxic: >4 mcg/mL

Dosage Forms [DSC] = Discontinued product

Tablet: 50 mg, 100 mg, 150 mg, 300 mg

Desyrel®: 50 mg, 100 mg, 150 mg, 300 mg [DSC]

- ◆ **Trazodone Hydrochloride** see Trazodone on page 1727
- ◆ **Trazorel® (Can)** see Trazodone on page 1727
- ◆ **Trecator®** see Ethionamide on page 664
- ◆ **Trelstar™ (Can)** see Triptorelin on page 1750
- ◆ **Trelstar™ Depot** see Triptorelin on page 1750
- ◆ **Trelstar™ LA** see Triptorelin on page 1750
- ◆ **Trental®** see Pentoxifylline on page 1343

Treprostinil (tre PROST in il)

U.S. Brand Names Remodulin®

Canadian Brand Names Remodulin®

Index Terms Treprostinil Sodium

Pharmacologic Category Vasodilator

Additional Appendix Information

Heart Failure (Systolic) on page 2051

Use Treatment of pulmonary arterial hypertension (PAH) in patients with NYHA Class II-IV symptoms to decrease exercise-associated symptoms; to diminish clinical deterioration when transitioning from epoprostenol (I.V.)

Pregnancy Risk Factor B

Pregnancy Implications Some skeletal malformations and maternal toxicity noted in animal studies. There are no adequate and well-controlled studies in pregnant women. Use with caution and only if clearly needed.

Lactation Excretion in breast milk unknown/use caution

Contraindications Hypersensitivity to treprostinil or any component of formulation

Warnings/Precautions Use caution in hepatic insufficiency, dose modification may be warranted; use caution in renal impairment; abrupt withdrawal/large dosage reductions may worsen symptoms of PAH. Safety and efficacy have not been established in patients ≤16 years of age.

Adverse Reactions

>10%:

Cardiovascular: Vasodilation (11%)

Central nervous system: Headache (27%)

Dermatologic: Rash (14%)

Gastrointestinal: Diarrhea (25%), nausea (22%)

Local: Infusion site pain (SubQ 85%, may improve after several months of therapy); infusion site reaction (SubQ 83%)

Miscellaneous: Jaw pain (13%)

1% to 10%:

Cardiovascular: Edema (9%), hypotension (4%)

Central nervous system: Dizziness (9%)

Dermatologic: Pruritus (8%)

Postmarketing and/or case reports: Arm swelling, hematoma, I.V. line infections, pain, paresthesia, sepsis

Overdosage/Toxicology Symptoms of overdose may include flushing, headache, hypotension, nausea, vomiting, diarrhea and seizure-like activity. Dosage reduction will likely coincide with symptom resolution. Treatment is symptom-directed and supportive.

Drug Interactions

Increased Effect/Toxicity: Concomitant use of treprostinil with other agents that inhibit platelet aggregation (eg, NSAIDs, ASA, antiplatelet agents, salicylates) or promote anticoagulation (eg, warfarin) may increase the risk of bleeding.

Stability Store at 15°C to 30°C (59°F to 86°F). Product does not need dilution prior to SubQ use. For I.V. infusion, dilute in SWFI or NS to a final volume of either 50 mL or 100 mL (dependent on system reservoir and calculated dose). Stability for up to 48 hours has been shown for concentrations as low as 4000 ng/mL. Contents of a single-reservoir syringe of treprostinil can be administered up to 72 hours at 37°C. Diluted solutions can be used up to 48 hours at 37°C. Contents of a vial should not be used past 30 days after the initial needle access into the vial.

Mechanism of Action Treprostinil is a direct dilator of both pulmonary and systemic arterial vascular beds; also inhibits platelet aggregation.

Pharmacodynamics/Kinetics

Absorption: SubQ: Rapidly and completely

(Continued)

Treprostinil *(Continued)*

Distribution: 14 L/70 kg lean body weight
Protein binding: 91%
Metabolism: Hepatic (enzymes unknown); forms metabolites
Bioavailability: 100%
Half-life elimination: Terminal: 2-4 hours
Excretion: Urine (79% — 4% as unchanged drug, 64% as metabolites); feces (13%)

Dosage SubQ or I.V. infusion:

Adults: PAH:

Initial: New to prostacyclin therapy: 1.25 ng/kg/minute continuous; if dose cannot be tolerated, reduce to 0.625 ng/kg/minute. Increase at rate not >1.25 ng/kg/minute per week for first 4 weeks, and not >2.5 ng/kg/minute per week for remainder of therapy. Limited experience with doses >40 ng/kg/minute. **Note:** Dose must be carefully and individually titrated (symptom improvement with minimal adverse effects). Avoid abrupt withdrawal.

Transitioning from epoprostenol (see table): I.V. Infusion: **Note:** Transition should occur in a hospital setting to follow response (eg, walking distance, sign/symptoms of disease progression). May take 24-48 hours to transition. Transition is accomplished by initiating the infusion of treprostinil, and increasing it while simultaneously reducing the dose of intravenous epoprostenol.

Transitioning From Epoprostenol to Treprostinil

Step	Epoprostenol Dose	Treprostinil Dose
1	Maintain current dose	Initiate at 10% initial epoprostenol dose
2	Decrease to 80% initial dose	Increase to 30% initial epoprostenol dose
3	Decrease to 60% initial dose	Increase to 50% initial epoprostenol dose
4	Decrease to 40% initial dose	Increase to 70% initial epoprostenol dose
5	Decrease to 20% initial dose	Increase to 90% initial epoprostenol dose
6	Decrease to 5% initial dose	Increase to 110% initial epoprostenol dose
7	Discontinue epoprostenol	Maintain current dose plus additional 5% to 10% as needed

Elderly: Limited experience in patients >65 years; refer to adult dosing; use caution

Dosage adjustment in renal impairment: No specific dosage adjustment recommended; use with caution.

Dosage adjustment in hepatic impairment:

Mild to moderate: Initial: 0.625 ng/kg/minute; increase with caution.

Severe: No data available.

Dietary Considerations Sodium chloride content of solution for injection:

1 mg/mL, 2.5 mg/mL, and 5 mg/mL each contain sodium chloride 5.3 mg/mL

10 mg/mL contains sodium chloride 4 mg/mL

Administration

I.V. infusion: Solution must be diluted in SWFI or NS prior to use and administered by continuous infusion using a central indwelling catheter and infusion pump. A backup infusion pump and infusion set should be immediately available in order to avoid therapy interruption. I.V. use is recommended when SubQ infusion is not tolerated. Infusion site reactions may be helped by moving the infusion site every 3 days, local application of topical hot and cold packs, topical or oral analgesics. Injection site pain and erythema may improve after several months of therapy.

SubQ infusion: Administer via continuous SubQ infusion using an appropriately-designed infusion pump. Patients must be assessed regarding their ability to manage such a delivery system.

Monitoring Parameters Dyspnea, fatigue, activity tolerance, symptoms of excessive dose (eg, headache, nausea, vomiting)

Dosage Forms Injection, solution: 1 mg/mL (20 mL) [contains sodium chloride 5.3 mg/mL]; 2.5 mg/mL (20 mL) [contains sodium chloride 5.3 mg/mL]; 5 mg/mL (20 mL) [contains sodium chloride 5.3 mg/mL]; 10 mg/mL (20 mL) [contains sodium chloride 4 mg/mL]

♦ **Treprostinil Sodium** *see* Treprostinil *on page 1729*
♦ **Tretinoin and Clindamycin** *see* Clindamycin and Tretinoin *on page 391*
♦ **Tretinoin and Mequinol** *see* Mequinol and Tretinoin *on page 1085*
♦ **Tretinoin, Fluocinolone Acetonide, and Hydroquinone** *see* Fluocinolone, Hydroquinone, and Tretinoin *on page 721*

Tretinoin (Oral) *(TRET i noyn, oral)*

U.S. Brand Names Vesanoid®
Canadian Brand Names Vesanoid®
Index Terms All-*trans*-Retinoic Acid; ATRA; NSC-122758; Ro 5488; tRA; *trans*-Retinoic Acid
Pharmacologic Category Antineoplastic Agent, Miscellaneous
Use Induction of remission in patients with acute promyelocytic leukemia (APL), French American British (FAB) classification M3 (including the M3 variant)
Pregnancy Risk Factor D
Pregnancy Implications Oral tretinoin is teratogenic and fetotoxic in rats at doses 1000 and 500 times the topical human dose, respectively.

Lactation Enters breast milk/not recommended

Medication Safety Issues

Sound-alike/look-alike issues:

Tretinoin may be confused with trientine

High alert medication: The Institute for Safe Medication Practices (ISMP) includes this medication among its list of drugs which have a heightened risk of causing significant patient harm when used in error.

Contraindications Sensitivity to parabens, vitamin A, other retinoids, or any component of the formulation; pregnancy

Warnings/Precautions Hazardous agent - use appropriate precautions for handling and disposal. [U.S. Boxed Warning]: **Patients with acute promyelocytic leukemia (APL) are at high risk and can have severe adverse reactions to tretinoin.**

[U.S. Boxed Warning]: **About 25% of patients with APL and treated with tretinoin, have experienced retinoic acid-APL (RA-APL) syndrome, characterized by fever, dyspnea, acute respiratory distress, weight gain, radiographic pulmonary infiltrates and pleural or pericardial effusions, edema, and hepatic, renal, and/or multiorgan failure.** This syndrome has occasionally been accompanied by impaired myocardial contractility and episodic hypotension. It has been observed with or without concomitant leukocytosis. Endotracheal intubation and mechanical ventilation have been required in some cases due to progressive hypoxemia, and several patients have expired with multiorgan failure. The syndrome usually occurs during the first month of treatment, with some cases reported following the first dose.

Management of the syndrome has not been defined, but high-dose steroids given at the first suspicion of RA-APL syndrome appear to reduce morbidity and mortality. At the first signs suggestive of the syndrome, immediately initiate high-dose steroids (dexamethasone 10 mg I.V.) every 12 hours for 3 days or until resolution of symptoms, regardless of the leukocyte count. The majority of patients do not require termination of tretinoin therapy during treatment of the RA-APL syndrome.

[U.S. Boxed Warning]: **During treatment, ~40% of patients will develop rapidly evolving leukocytosis;** may be associated with a higher risk of life-threatening complications.

If signs and symptoms of the RA-APL syndrome are present together with leukocytosis, initiate treatment with high-dose steroids immediately. Consider adding full-dose chemotherapy (including an anthracycline, if not contraindicated) to the tretinoin therapy on day 1 or 2 for patients presenting with a WBC count of >5 x 10^9/L or immediately, for patients presenting with a WBC count of <5 x 10^9/L, if the WBC count reaches ≥6 x 10^9/L by day 5, or ≥10 x 10^9/L by day 10 or ≥15 x 10^9/L by day 28.

[U.S. Boxed Warning]: **High risk of teratogenicity; not to be used in women of child-bearing potential** unless the woman is capable of complying with effective contraceptive measures. Repeat pregnancy testing and contraception counseling monthly throughout the period of treatment.

Retinoids have been associated with pseudotumor cerebri (benign intracranial hypertension), especially in children. Concurrent use of other drugs associated with this effect (eg, tetracyclines) may increase risk. Early signs and symptoms include papilledema, headache, nausea, vomiting and visual disturbances.

Up to 60% of patients experienced hypercholesterolemia or hypertriglyceridemia, which were reversible upon completion of treatment. Elevated liver function test results occur in 50% to 60% of patients during treatment. Carefully monitor liver function test results during treatment and give consideration to a temporary withdrawal of tretinoin if test results reach >5 times the upper limit of normal. [U.S. Boxed Warning]: **Should be administered under the supervision of an experienced cancer chemotherapy physician.**

Adverse Reactions Virtually all patients experience some drug-related toxicity, especially headache, fever, weakness and fatigue. These adverse effects are seldom permanent or irreversible nor do they usually require therapy interruption.

>10%:

Cardiovascular: Peripheral edema (52%), chest discomfort (32%), edema (29%), arrhythmias (23%), flushing (23%), hypotension (14%), hypertension (11%)

Central nervous system: Headache (86%), fever (83%), malaise (66%), pain (37%), dizziness (20%), anxiety (17%), insomnia (14%), depression (14%), confusion (11%)

Dermatologic: Skin/mucous membrane dryness (77%), pruritus (20%), rash (54%), alopecia (14%)

Endocrine & metabolic: Hypercholesterolemia and/or hypertriglyceridemia (60%)

Gastrointestinal: Nausea/vomiting (57%), liver function tests increased (50% to 60%), GI hemorrhage (34%), abdominal pain (31%), mucositis (26%), diarrhea (23%), constipation (17%), dyspepsia (14%), abdominal distention (11%), weight gain (23%), weight loss (17%), xerostomia, anorexia (17%)

Hematologic: Hemorrhage (60%), leukocytosis (40%), disseminated intravascular coagulation (DIC) (26%)

Local: Phlebitis (11%), injection site reactions (17%)

Neuromuscular & skeletal: Bone pain (77%), myalgia (14%), paresthesia (17%)

Ocular: Visual disturbances (17%)

Otic: Earache/ear fullness (23%)

Renal: Renal insufficiency (11%)

Respiratory: Upper respiratory tract disorders (63%), dyspnea (60%), respiratory insufficiency (26%), pleural effusion (20%), pneumonia (14%), rales (14%), expiratory wheezing (14%), dry nose

Miscellaneous: Infection (58%), shivering (63%), retinoic acid-acute promyelocytic leukemia syndrome (25%), diaphoresis increased (20%)

1% to 10%:

Cardiovascular: Cerebral hemorrhage (9%), pallor (6%), cardiac failure (6%), cardiac arrest (3%), enlarged heart (3%), heart murmur (3%), ischemia, stroke (3%), MI (93%),

(Continued)

Tretinoin (Oral) *(Continued)*

myocarditis (3%), pericarditis (3%), pulmonary hypertension (3%), secondary cardiomyopathy (3%)

Central nervous system: Intracranial hypertension (9%), agitation (9%), hallucination (6%), agnosia (3%), aphasia (3%), cerebellar edema (3%), cerebral hemorrhage (9%), seizures (3%), coma (3%), CNS depression (3%), dysarthria (3%), encephalopathy (3%), hypotaxia (3%), light reflex absent (3%), spinal cord disorder (3%), unconsciousness (3%), dementia (3%), forgetfulness (3%), somnolence (3%), slow speech (3%), hypothermia (3%)

Dermatologic: Cellulitis (8%), photosensitivity

Endocrine & metabolic: Acidosis (3%)

Gastrointestinal: Hepatosplenomegaly (9%), hepatitis (3%), ulcer (3%)

Genitourinary: Dysuria (9%), acute renal failure (3%), micturition frequency (3%), renal tubular necrosis (3%), enlarged prostate (3%)

Hepatic: Ascites (3%), hepatitis

Neuromuscular & skeletal: Tremor (3%), leg weakness (3%), hyporeflexia, dysarthria, facial paralysis, hemiplegia, flank pain, asterixis, abnormal gait (3%), bone inflammation (3%)

Ocular: Dry eyes, visual acuity change (6%), visual field deficit (3%)

Otic: Hearing loss

Renal: Acute renal failure, renal tubular necrosis

Respiratory: Lower respiratory tract disorders (9%), pulmonary infiltration (6%), bronchial asthma (3%), pulmonary/larynx edema

Miscellaneous: Face edema

<1% (Limited to important or life-threatening): Arterial thrombosis, basophilia, cataracts, conjunctivitis, erythema nodosum, hypercalcemia, hyperuricemia, inflammatory bowel syndrome, irreversible hearing loss, pancreatitis, pseudomotor cerebri, renal infarct, Sweet's syndrome, vasculitis, venous thrombosis

Overdosage/Toxicology The maximum tolerated dose in adult patients with myelodysplastic syndrome in solid tumors was 195 mg/m²/day; the maximum tolerated dose in pediatric patients was lower at 60 mg/m²/day. Overdosage with other retinoids has been associated with transient headache, facial flushing, cheilosis, abdominal pain, dizziness, and ataxia. These symptoms resolved quickly without residual effects.

Drug Interactions

Cytochrome P450 Effect: Substrate (minor) of CYP2A6 (minor), 2B6 (minor), 2C8 (major), 2C9 (minor); **Inhibits** CYP2C9 (weak); **Induces** CYP2E1 (weak)

Increased Effect/Toxicity: Ketoconazole increases the mean plasma AUC of tretinoin. Concurrent use with antifibrinolytic agents (eg, aminocaproic acid, aprotinin, tranexamic acid) may increase risk of thrombosis. Concurrent use with tetracyclines may increase risk of pseudotumor cerebri. CYP2C8 Inhibitors may increase the levels/effects of tretinoin; example inhibitors include atazanavir, gemfibrozil, and ritonavir.

Ethanol/Nutrition/Herb Interactions

Ethanol: Avoid ethanol (may increase CNS depression).

Food: Absorption of retinoids has been shown to be enhanced when taken with food.

Herb/Nutraceutical: St John's wort may decrease tretinoin levels. Avoid dong quai, St John's wort (may also cause photosensitization). Avoid additional vitamin A supplementation. May lead to vitamin A toxicity.

Stability Store capsule at 15°C to 30°C (59°F to 86°F);. Protect from light.

Mechanism of Action Tretinoin appears to bind one or more nuclear receptors and inhibits clonal proliferation and/or granulocyte differentiation

Pharmacodynamics/Kinetics

Protein binding: >95%

Metabolism: Hepatic via CYP; primary metabolite: 4-oxo-all-*trans*-retinoic acid

Half-life elimination: Terminal: Parent drug: 0.5-2 hours

Time to peak, serum: 1-2 hours

Excretion: Urine (63%); feces (30%)

Dosage Oral: Children and Adults:

Remission induction: 45 mg/m²/day in 2-3 divided doses for up to 30 days after complete remission (maximum duration of treatment: 90 days)

Remission maintenance: 45-200 mg/m²/day in 2-3 divided doses for up to 12 months.

Dietary Considerations To enhance absorption, some clinicians recommend giving with a fatty meal. Capsule contains soybean oil.

Administration Administer with meals; do not crush capsules

Monitoring Parameters Monitor the patient's hematologic profile, coagulation profile, liver function test results and triglyceride and cholesterol levels frequently

Dosage Forms Capsule: 10 mg [contains soybean oil and parabens]

Tretinoin (Topical) (TRET i noyn, TOP i kal)

U.S. Brand Names Avita®; Renova®; Retin-A®; Retin-A® Micro

Canadian Brand Names Rejuva-A®; Retin-A®; Retin-A® Micro; Retinova®

Index Terms Retinoic Acid; *trans*-Retinoic Acid; Vitamin A Acid

Pharmacologic Category Acne Products; Retinoic Acid Derivative; Topical Skin Product, Acne

Use Treatment of acne vulgaris; photodamaged skin; palliation of fine wrinkles, mottled hyperpigmentation, and tactile roughness of facial skin as part of a comprehensive skin care and sun avoidance program

Unlabeled/Investigational Use Some skin cancers

Pregnancy Risk Factor C

Pregnancy Implications Oral tretinoin is teratogenic and fetotoxic in rats at doses 1000 and 500 times the topical human dose, respectively. Tretinoin does not appear to be teratogenic when used topically since it is rapidly metabolized by the skin; however, there are rare reports of fetal defects. Use for acne only if benefit to mother outweighs potential risk to fetus. During pregnancy, do not use for palliation of fine wrinkles, mottled hyperpigmentation, and tactile roughness of facial skin.

Lactation Enters breast milk/compatible

Medication Safety Issues
Sound-alike/look-alike issues:
Tretinoin may be confused with trientine

International issues:
Renova® may be confused with Remov® which is a brand name for nimesulide in Italy

Contraindications Hypersensitivity to tretinoin or any component of the formulation; sunburn

Warnings/Precautions Use with caution in patients with eczema; avoid excessive exposure to sunlight and sunlamps; avoid contact with abraded skin, mucous membranes, eyes, mouth, angles of the nose. Palliation of fine wrinkles, mottled hyperpigmentation, and tactile roughness of facial skin: Do not use the 0.05% cream for longer than 48 weeks or the 0.02% cream for longer than 52 weeks. Not for use on moderate- to heavily-pigmented skin. Gel is flammable; do not expose to high temperatures or flame.

Adverse Reactions
>10%: Dermatologic: Excessive dryness, erythema, scaling of the skin, pruritus
1% to 10%:
Dermatologic: Hyperpigmentation or hypopigmentation, photosensitivity, initial acne flare-up
Local: Edema, blistering, stinging

Overdosage/Toxicology Excessive application may lead to marked redness, peeling or discomfort. Oral ingestion of the topical product may lead to the same adverse reactions seen with excessive vitamin A intake (increased intracranial pressure, jaundice, ascites, cutaneous desquamation; symptoms of acute overdose [12,000 units/kg] include nausea, vomiting, and diarrhea). Toxic signs of an overdose commonly respond to drug discontinuation, and generally return to normal spontaneously within a few days to weeks. When confronted with signs of increased intracranial pressure, treatment with mannitol (0.25 g/kg I.V. up to 1 g/kg/dose repeated every 5 minutes as needed), dexamethasone (1.5 mg/kg I.V. load followed with 0.375 mg/kg every 6 hours for 5 days), and/or hyperventilation should be employed.

Drug Interactions
Cytochrome P450 Effect: Substrate of CYP2A6 (minor), 2B6 (minor), 2C8 (major), 2C9 (minor); **Inhibits** CYP2C9 (weak); **Induces** CYP2E1 (weak)

Increased Effect/Toxicity: Topical application of sulfur, benzoyl peroxide, salicylic acid, resorcinol, or any product with strong drying effects potentiates adverse reactions with tretinoin.

Photosensitizing medications (thiazides, tetracyclines, fluoroquinolones, phenothiazines, sulfonamides) augment phototoxicity and should not be used when treating palliation of fine wrinkles, mottled hyperpigmentation, and tactile roughness of facial skin.

Ethanol/Nutrition/Herb Interactions
Food: Avoid excessive intake of vitamin A (cod liver oil, halibut fish oil).
Herb/Nutraceutical: Avoid dong quai, St John's wort (may also cause photosensitization). Avoid excessive amounts of vitamin A supplements.

Stability Store at 25°C (77°F). Gel is flammable; keep away from heat and flame.

Mechanism of Action Keratinocytes in the sebaceous follicle become less adherent which allows for easy removal; inhibits microcomedone formation and eliminates lesions already present

Pharmacodynamics/Kinetics
Absorption: Minimal
Metabolism: Hepatic for the small amount absorbed
Excretion: Urine and feces

Dosage Topical:
Children >12 years and Adults: Acne vulgaris: Begin therapy with a weaker formulation of tretinoin (0.025% cream, 0.04% microsphere gel, or 0.01% gel) and increase the concentration as tolerated; apply once daily to acne lesions before retiring or on alternate days; if stinging or irritation develop, decrease frequency of application

Adults ≥18: Palliation of fine wrinkles, mottled hyperpigmentation, and tactile roughness of facial skin: Pea-sized amount of the 0.02% or 0.05% cream applied to entire face once daily in the evening

Elderly: Use of the 0.02% cream in patients 65-71 years of age showed similar improvement in fine wrinkles as seen in patients <65 years. Safety and efficacy of the 0.02% cream have not been established in patients >71 years of age. Safety and efficacy of the 0.05% cream have not been established in patients >50 years of age.

Administration Palliation of fine wrinkles, mottled hyperpigmentation, and tactile roughness of facial skin: Cream: Prior to application, gently wash face with a mild soap. Pat dry. Wait 20-30 minutes to apply cream. Avoid eyes, ears, nostrils, and mouth.

Dosage Forms [DSC] = Discontinued product
Cream, topical: 0.025% (20 g, 45 g); 0.05% (20 g, 45 g); 0.1% (20 g, 45 g)
Avita®: 0.025% (20 g, 45 g)
Renova®: 0.02% (40 g); 0.05% (40 g, 60 g) [DSC]
Retin-A®: 0.025% (20 g, 45 g); 0.05% (20 g, 45 g); 0.1% (20 g, 45 g)
Gel, topical: 0.025% (15 g, 45 g)
Avita®: 0.025% (20 g, 45 g) [contains ethanol 83%]
Retin-A®: 0.01% (15 g, 45 g); 0.025% (15 g, 45 g) [contains alcohol 90%]
Retin-A® Micro [microsphere gel]: 0.04% (20 g, 45 g); 0.1% (20 g, 45 g) [contains benzyl alcohol]
Liquid, topical (Retin-A®): 0.05% (28 mL) [contains alcohol 55%] [DSC]

♦ **Trexall**™ see Methotrexate on page 1111
♦ **Triacin-C**® **[DSC]** see Triprolidine, Pseudoephedrine, and Codeine on page 1750
♦ **Triaconazole** see Terconazole on page 1652
♦ **Triaderm (Can)** see Triamcinolone on page 1734

Triamcinolone (trye am SIN oh lone)

U.S. Brand Names Aristocort® [DSC]; Aristocort® A [DSC]; Aristospan®; Azmacort®; Kenalog®; Kenalog-10®; Kenalog-40®; Nasacort® AQ; Triderm®; Tri-Nasal®

Canadian Brand Names Aristospan®; Kenalog®; Kenalog® in Orabase; Nasacort® AQ; Oracort; Triaderm®; Trinasal®

Index Terms Triamcinolone Acetonide, Aerosol; Triamcinolone Acetonide, Parenteral; Triamcinolone Diacetate, Oral; Triamcinolone Diacetate, Parenteral; Triamcinolone Hexacetonide; Triamcinolone, Oral

Pharmacologic Category Corticosteroid, Adrenal; Corticosteroid, Inhalant (Oral); Corticosteroid, Nasal; Corticosteroid, Systemic; Corticosteroid, Topical

Additional Appendix Information
Asthma *on page 2029*
Corticosteroids *on page 1879*

Use
Nasal inhalation: Management of seasonal and perennial allergic rhinitis in patients ≥6 years of age

Oral inhalation: Control of bronchial asthma and related bronchospastic conditions

Oral topical: Adjunctive treatment and temporary relief of symptoms associated with oral inflammatory lesions and ulcerative lesions resulting from trauma

Systemic: Adrenocortical insufficiency, rheumatic disorders, allergic states, respiratory diseases, systemic lupus erythematosus (SLE), and other diseases requiring anti-inflammatory or immunosuppressive effects

Topical: Inflammatory dermatoses responsive to steroids

Pregnancy Risk Factor C

Pregnancy Implications There are no adequate and well-controlled studies in pregnant women, however, triamcinolone is teratogenic in animals; use during pregnancy with caution. Increased incidence of cleft palate, neonatal adrenal suppression, low birth weight, and cataracts in the infant has been reported following corticosteroid use during pregnancy. In general, the use of large amounts, or prolonged use, of topical corticosteroids during pregnancy should be avoided. In the mother, corticosteroids may increase calcium and potassium excretion, elevate blood pressure, and cause salt and water retention.

Lactation Excretion in breast milk unknown/use caution

Medication Safety Issues
Sound-alike/look-alike issues:
Kenalog® may be confused with Ketalar®
Nasacort® may be confused with NasalCrom®

TAC (occasional abbreviation for triamcinolone) is an error-prone abbreviation (mistaken as tetracaine-adrenaline-cocaine)

Contraindications Hypersensitivity to triamcinolone or any component of the formulation; systemic fungal infections; serious infections (except septic shock or tuberculous meningitis); primary treatment of status asthmaticus; fungal, viral, or bacterial infections of the mouth or throat (oral topical formulation)

Warnings/Precautions May cause hypercorticism or suppression of hypothalamic-pituitary-adrenal (HPA) axis, particularly in younger children or in patients receiving high doses for prolonged periods. HPA suppression may lead to adrenal crisis. Withdrawal and discontinuation of a corticosteroid should be done slowly and carefully. Particular care is required when patients are transferred from systemic corticosteroids to inhaled products due to possible adrenal insufficiency or withdrawal from steroids, including an increase in allergic symptoms. Patients receiving >20 mg per day of prednisone (or equivalent) may be most susceptible. Fatalities have occurred due to adrenal insufficiency in asthmatic patients during and after transfer from systemic corticosteroids to aerosol steroids; aerosol steroids do not provide the systemic steroid needed to treat patients having trauma, surgery, or infections.

Bronchospasm may occur with wheezing after inhalation; if this occurs stop steroid and treat with a fast-acting bronchodilator. Supplemental steroids (oral or parenteral) may be needed during stress or severe asthma attacks. Not to be used in status asthmaticus or for the relief of acute bronchospasm. Acute myopathy has been reported with high dose corticosteroids, usually in patients with neuromuscular transmission disorders; may involve ocular and/or respiratory muscles; monitor creatine kinase; recovery may be delayed. Corticosteroid use may cause psychiatric disturbances, including depression, euphoria, insomnia, mood swings, and personality changes. Pre-existing psychiatric conditions may be exacerbated by corticosteroid use. Prolonged use of corticosteroids may also increase the incidence of secondary infection, mask acute infection (including fungal infections), prolong or exacerbate viral infections, or limit response to vaccines. Exposure to chickenpox should be avoided; corticosteroids should not be used to treat ocular herpes simplex. Corticosteroids should not be used for cerebral malaria. Close observation is required in patients with latent tuberculosis and/or TB reactivity; restrict use in active TB (only in conjunction with antituberculosis treatment). Prolonged treatment with corticosteroids has been associated with the development of Kaposi's sarcoma (case reports); if noted, discontinuation of therapy should be considered.

Use with caution in patients with thyroid disease, hepatic impairment, renal impairment, cardiovascular disease, diabetes, glaucoma, cataracts, myasthenia gravis, patients at risk for osteoporosis, patients at risk for seizures, or GI diseases (diverticulitis, peptic ulcer, ulcerative colitis) due to perforation risk. Use caution following acute MI (corticosteroids have been associated with myocardial rupture). Because of the risk of adverse effects, systemic corticosteroids should be used cautiously in the elderly in the smallest possible effective dose for the shortest duration. Azmacort® (metered dose inhaler) comes with its own spacer device attached and may be easier to use in older patients. Avoid nasal corticosteroid use in patients with recent nasal septal ulcers, nasal surgery or nasal trauma until healing has occurred. Do not use occlusive dressings on weeping or exudative lesions and general caution with occlusive dressings should be observed; discontinue if skin irritation or contact dermatitis should occur; do not use in patients with decreased skin circulation; avoid the use of high potency steroids on the face.

Orally-inhaled and intranasal corticosteroids may cause a reduction in growth velocity in pediatric patients (~1 centimeter per year [range 0.3-1.8 cm per year] and related to dose and duration of exposure). To minimize the systemic effects of orally-inhaled and intranasal corticosteroids, each patient should be titrated to the lowest effective dose. Growth should be routinely monitored in pediatric patients. Withdraw systemic therapy with gradual tapering of dose. There have been reports of systemic corticosteroid withdrawal symptoms (eg, joint/muscle pain, lassitude, depression) when withdrawing oral inhalation therapy. Injection suspension contains benzyl alcohol; benzyl alcohol has been associated with the "gasping syndrome" in neonates and low-birth-weight infants.

Oral topical: Discontinue if local irritation or sensitization should develop. If significant regeneration or repair of oral tissues has not occurred in seven days, re-evaluation of the etiology of the oral lesion is advised.

Adverse Reactions

Systemic: Frequency not defined:

Cardiovascular: Angioedema, bradycardia, CHF, hypertension, myocardial rupture (following recent MI), thrombophlebitis, vasculitis

Central nervous system: Convulsions, depression, emotional instability, fever, headache, intracranial pressure increased, neuropathy, paresthesia, personality changes, vertigo

Dermatologic: Acne, allergic dermatitis, bruising, cutaneous atrophy, dry/scaly skin, ecchymoses, facial erythema, petechiae, photosensitivity, rash, striae, thin/fragile skin, wound healing impaired

Endocrine & metabolic: Adrenocortical/pituitary unresponsiveness (particularly during stress), carbohydrate tolerance decreased, cushingoid state, diabetes mellitus (manifestations of latent disease), fluid retention, growth suppression (children), hirsutism, hypokalemic alkalosis, menstrual irregularities, negative nitrogen balance, potassium loss, sodium retention

Gastrointestinal: Abdominal distention, bowel perforation, diarrhea, dyspepsia, nausea, oral *Monilia* (oral inhaler), pancreatitis, peptic ulcer, ulcerative esophagitis, weight gain

Hepatic: Hepatomegaly

Local: Skin atrophy (at the injection site)

Neuromuscular & skeletal: Calcinosis (following intra-articular or intralesional injection), Charcot-like arthropathy, femoral/humeral head aseptic necrosis, muscle mass decreased, muscle weakness, osteoporosis, pathologic fracture of long bones, steroid myopathy, tendon rupture, vertebral compression fractures

Ocular: Blindness (periocular injections), cataracts, intraocular pressure increased, exophthalmos, glaucoma, subcapsular cataract

Respiratory: Cough increased (nasal spray), epistaxis (nasal inhaler/spray), pharyngitis (nasal spray/oral inhaler), sinusitis (oral inhaler), voice alteration (oral inhaler)

Miscellaneous: Abnormal fat deposition (moon face), anaphylactoid reaction, anaphylaxis, diaphoresis increased, suppression to skin tests

Topical: Frequency not defined:

Dermatologic: Itching, allergic contact dermatitis, dryness, folliculitis, skin infection (secondary), itching, hypertrichosis, acneiform eruptions, hypopigmentation, skin maceration, skin atrophy, striae, miliaria, perioral dermatitis, atrophy of oral mucosa

Local: Burning, irritation

Overdosage/Toxicology When consumed in excessive quantities, systemic hypercorticism and adrenal suppression may occur; in those cases, discontinuation and withdrawal of the corticosteroid should be done judiciously.

Drug Interactions

Increased Effect/Toxicity: Salicylates or NSAIDs coadministered oral corticosteroids may increase risk of GI ulceration.

Decreased Effect: Decreased effect with barbiturates and phenytoin. Rifampin increased metabolism of triamcinolone. Vaccine and toxoid effects may be reduced.

Ethanol/Nutrition/Herb Interactions

Ethanol: Avoid ethanol (may enhance gastric mucosal irritation).

Food: Triamcinolone interferes with calcium absorption.

Herb/Nutraceutical: Avoid cat's claw, echinacea (have immunostimulant properties).

Stability Store at room temperature; do not freeze.

Injection, suspension: Shake well prior to use.

Hexacetonide suspension: Avoid diluents containing parabens or preservatives (may cause flocculation). Diluted suspension stable ~1 week. Suspension for intralesional use may be diluted with D_5NS, $D_{10}NS$ or SWFI to a 1:1, 1:2, or 1:4 concentration. Solutions for intra-articular use, may be diluted with lidocaine 1% or 2%.

Topical spray: Avoid excessive heat.

Mechanism of Action Decreases inflammation by suppression of migration of polymorphonuclear leukocytes and reversal of increased capillary permeability; suppresses the immune system by reducing activity and volume of the lymphatic system; suppresses adrenal function at high doses

Pharmacodynamics/Kinetics

Duration: Oral: 8-12 hours

Absorption: Topical: Systemic

Time to peak: I.M.: 8-10 hours

Half-life elimination: Biologic: 18-36 hours

Dosage The lowest possible dose should be used to control the condition; when dose reduction is possible, the dose should be reduced gradually. Parenteral dose is usually $1/3$ to $1/2$ the oral dose given every 12 hours. In life-threatening situations, parenteral doses larger than the oral dose may be needed.

(Continued)

Triamcinolone *(Continued)*

Injection:
Acetonide:
Intra-articular, intrabursal, tendon sheaths: Adults: Initial: Smaller joints: 2.5-5 mg, larger joints: 5-15 mg
Intradermal: Adults: Initial: 1 mg
I.M.: Range: 2.5-60 mg/day
Children 6-12 years: Initial: 40 mg
Children >12 years and Adults: Initial: 60 mg
Hexacetonide: Adults:
Intralesional, sublesional: Up to 0.5 mg/square inch of affected skin
Intra-articular: Range: 2-20 mg

Triamcinolone Dosing

	Acetonide	Hexacetonide
Intrasynovial	5-40 mg	
Intralesional	1-30 mg (usually 1 mg per injection site); 10 mg/mL suspension usually used	Up to 0.5 mg/sq inch affected area
Sublesional	1-30 mg	
Systemic I.M.	2.5-60 mg/dose (usual adult dose: 60 mg; may repeat with 20-100 mg dose when symptoms recur)	
Intra-articular	2.5-40 mg	2-20 mg average
large joints	5-15 mg	10-20 mg
small joints	2.5-5 mg	2-6 mg
Tendon sheaths	2.5-10 mg	
Intradermal	1 mg/site	

Intranasal: Perennial allergic rhinitis, seasonal allergic rhinitis:
Nasal spray:
Children 6-11 years: 110 mcg/day as 1 spray in each nostril once daily
Children ≥12 years and Adults: 220 mcg/day as 2 sprays in each nostril once daily
Nasal inhaler:
Children 6-11 years: Initial: 220 mcg/day as 2 sprays in each nostril once daily
Children ≥12 years and Adults: Initial: 220 mcg/day as 2 sprays in each nostril once daily; may increase dose to 440 mcg/day (given once daily or divided and given 2 or 4 times/day)

Oral: Adults:
Acute rheumatic carditis: Initial: 20-60 mg/day; reduce dose during maintenance therapy
Acute seasonal or perennial allergic rhinitis: 8-12 mg/day
Adrenocortical insufficiency: Range 4-12 mg/day
Bronchial asthma: 8-16 mg/day
Dermatological disorders, contact/atopic dermatitis: Initial: 8-16 mg/day
Ophthalmic disorders: 12-40 mg/day
Rheumatic disorders: Range: 8-16 mg/day
SLE: Initial: 20-32 mg/day, some patients may need initial doses ≥48 mg; reduce dose during maintenance therapy

Oral inhalation: Asthma:
Children 6-12 years: 100-200 mcg 3-4 times/day **or** 200-400 mcg twice daily; maximum dose: 1200 mcg/day
Children >12 years and Adults: 200 mcg 3-4 times/day **or** 400 mcg twice daily; maximum dose: 1600 mcg/day

Oral topical: Oral inflammatory lesions/ulcers: Press a small dab (about ¼ inch) to the lesion until a thin film develops. A larger quantity may be required for coverage of some lesions. For optimal results use only enough to coat the lesion with a thin film; do not rub in.

Topical:
Cream, Ointment: Apply thin film to affected areas 2-4 times/day
Spray: Apply to affected area 3-4 times/day

Dietary Considerations May be taken with food to decrease GI distress.

Administration
Injection: Avoid injecting into a previously infected joint; do not inject into unstable joints
I.M.: Inject deep in large muscle mass, avoid deltoid.
SubQ: Avoid subcutaneous administration.
Nasal spray, inhalation: Shake well prior to use. Gently blow nose to clear nostrils.
Oral inhalation: Shake well prior to use. Rinse mouth and throat after using inhaler to prevent candidiasis. Use spacer device provided with Azmacort®.
Oral topical: Apply small dab to lesion until a thin film develops; do not rub in. Apply at bedtime or after meals if applications are needed throughout the day.
Tablet: Once-daily doses should be given in the morning.
Topical: Apply a thin film sparingly and avoid topical application on the face. Do not use on open skin or wounds. Do not occlude area unless directed.

Additional Information 16 mg triamcinolone is equivalent to 100 mg cortisone (no mineralo-corticoid activity).

Effects of inhaled/intranasal steroids on growth have been observed in the absence of laboratory evidence of HPA axis suppression, suggesting that growth velocity is a more sensitive indicator of systemic corticosteroid exposure in pediatric patients than some commonly used tests of HPA axis function. The long-term effects of this reduction in growth velocity associated with orally-inhaled and intranasal corticosteroids, including the impact on final adult height, are unknown. The potential for "catch up" growth following discontinuation of treatment with inhaled corticosteroids has not been adequately studied.

Dosage Forms

[DSC] = Discontinued product

Aerosol for oral inhalation, as acetonide:
  Azmacort®: 100 mcg per actuation (20 g) [240 actuations]

Aerosol, topical, as acetonide:
  Kenalog®: 0.2 mg/2-second spray (63 g)

Cream, as acetonide: 0.025% (15 g, 80 g, 454 g); 0.1% (15 g, 80 g, 454 g, 2270 g); 0.5% (15 g)
  Aristocort® A: 0.025% (15 g, 60 g); 0.1% (15 g, 60 g); 0.5% (15 g) [DSC]
  Triderm®: 0.1% (30 g, 85 g)

Injection, suspension, as acetonide:
  Kenalog-10®: 10 mg/mL (5 mL) [contains benzyl alcohol; not for I.V. or I.M. use]
  Kenalog-40®: 40 mg/mL (1 mL, 5 mL, 10 mL) [contains benzyl alcohol; not for I.V. or intradermal use]

Injection, suspension, as hexacetonide:
  Aristospan®: 5 mg/mL (5 mL); 20 mg/mL (1 mL, 5 mL) [contains benzyl alcohol; not for I.V. use]

Lotion, as acetonide: 0.025% (60 mL); 0.1% (60 mL)

Ointment, topical, as acetonide: 0.025% (15 g, 80 g, 454 g); 0.1% (15 g, 80 g, 454 g); 0.5% (15 g)
  Aristocort® A: 0.1% (15 g, 60 g) [DSC]

Paste, oral, topical, as acetonide: 0.1% (5 g)

Solution, intranasal, as acetonide [spray]:
  Tri-Nasal®: 50 mcg/inhalation (15 mL) [120 actuations]

Suspension, intranasal, as acetonide [spray]:
  Nasacort® AQ: 55 mcg/inhalation (16.5 g) [120 actuations]

Tablet:
  Aristocort®: 4 mg [DSC]

♦ **Triamcinolone Acetonide, Aerosol** see Triamcinolone on page 1734
♦ **Triamcinolone Acetonide, Parenteral** see Triamcinolone on page 1734
♦ **Triamcinolone and Nystatin** see Nystatin and Triamcinolone on page 1251
♦ **Triamcinolone Diacetate, Oral** see Triamcinolone on page 1734
♦ **Triamcinolone Diacetate, Parenteral** see Triamcinolone on page 1734
♦ **Triamcinolone Hexacetonide** see Triamcinolone on page 1734
♦ **Triamcinolone, Oral** see Triamcinolone on page 1734
♦ **Triaminic® Allerchews™ [OTC]** see Loratadine on page 1033
♦ **Triaminic® Cold & Allergy (Can)** see Chlorpheniramine and Pseudoephedrine on page 350
♦ **Triaminic® Cold and Allergy [OTC] [DSC]** see Chlorpheniramine and Pseudoephedrine on page 350
♦ **Triaminic® Cold and Cough [OTC] [DSC]** see Chlorpheniramine, Pseudoephedrine, and Dextromethorphan on page 355
♦ **Triaminic® Cough [OTC] [DSC]** see Pseudoephedrine and Dextromethorphan on page 1455
♦ **Triaminic® Cough and Sore Throat Formula [OTC] [DSC]** see Acetaminophen, Dextromethorphan, and Pseudoephedrine on page 35
♦ **Triaminic® Cough & Nasal Congestion [OTC] [DSC]** see Pseudoephedrine and Dextromethorphan on page 1455
♦ **Triaminic® Night Time Cough and Cold [OTC] [DSC]** see Chlorpheniramine, Pseudoephedrine, and Dextromethorphan on page 355
♦ **Triaminic® Thin Strips™ Cough and Runny Nose [OTC]** see DiphenhydrAMINE on page 515

Triamterene (trye AM ter een)

U.S. Brand Names Dyrenium®

Pharmacologic Category Diuretic, Potassium-Sparing

Additional Appendix Information
  Heart Failure (Systolic) on page 2051

Use Alone or in combination with other diuretics in treatment of edema and hypertension; decreases potassium excretion caused by kaliuretic diuretics

Pregnancy Risk Factor B (manufacturer); D (expert analysis)

Medication Safety Issues
  Sound-alike/look-alike issues:
    Triamterene may be confused with trimipramine
    Dyrenium® may be confused with Pyridium®

Dosage Adults: Oral: 100-300 mg/day in 1-2 divided doses; maximum dose: 300 mg/day; usual dosage range (JNC 7): 50-100 mg/day
  Dosing comments in renal impairment: Cl$_{cr}$ <10 mL/minute: Avoid use.
  Dosing adjustment in hepatic impairment: Dose reduction is recommended in patients with cirrhosis.

Additional Information Complete prescribing information for this medication should be consulted for additional detail.

Dosage Forms Capsule: 50 mg, 100 mg [contains benzyl alcohol]

♦ **Triamterene and Hydrochlorothiazide** see Hydrochlorothiazide and Triamterene on page 847

♦ **Triatec-8 (Can)** *see* Acetaminophen and Codeine *on page 31*
♦ **Triatec-8 Strong (Can)** *see* Acetaminophen and Codeine *on page 31*
♦ **Triatec-30 (Can)** *see* Acetaminophen and Codeine *on page 31*

Triazolam (trye AY zoe lam)

U.S. Brand Names Halcion® [DSC]
Canadian Brand Names Apo-Triazo®; Gen-Triazolam; Halcion®
Pharmacologic Category Hypnotic, Benzodiazepine
Additional Appendix Information
Benzodiazepines *on page 1874*
Use Short-term treatment of insomnia
Restrictions C-IV
Pregnancy Risk Factor X
Pregnancy Implications Other benzodiazepines are known to cross the placenta and accumulate in the fetus. Teratogenic effects have been reported. Use of triazolam is contraindicated in pregnancy.
Lactation Excretion in breast milk unknown/not recommended
Medication Safety Issues
Sound-alike/look-alike issues:
Triazolam may be confused with alprazolam
Halcion® may be confused with halcinonide, Haldol®
Contraindications Hypersensitivity to triazolam or any component of the formulation (cross-sensitivity with other benzodiazepines may exist); concurrent therapy with atazanavir, ketoconazole, itraconazole, nefazodone, and ritonavir; pregnancy
Warnings/Precautions Should be used only after evaluation of potential causes of sleep disturbance. Failure of sleep disturbance to resolve after 7-10 days may indicate psychiatric or medical illness. A worsening of insomnia or the emergence of new abnormalities of thought or behavior may represent unrecognized psychiatric or medical illness and requires immediate and careful evaluation. Prescription should be written for a maximum of 7-10 days and should not be prescribed in quantities exceeding a 1-month supply. Abrupt discontinuation after sustained use (generally >10 days) may cause withdrawal symptoms.

An increase in daytime anxiety may occur after as few as 10 days of continuous use, which may be related to withdrawal reaction in some patients. Anterograde amnesia may occur at a higher rate with triazolam than with other benzodiazepines. Use with caution in elderly or debilitated patients, patients with hepatic disease (including alcoholics), or renal impairment. Use with caution in patients with respiratory disease or impaired gag reflex. Avoid use in patients with sleep apnea.

Causes CNS depression (dose-related) resulting in sedation, dizziness, confusion, or ataxia which may impair physical and mental capabilities. Patients must be cautioned about performing tasks which require mental alertness (eg, operating machinery or driving). Use with caution in patients receiving other CNS depressants or psychoactive agents. Effects with other sedative drugs or ethanol may be potentiated. Benzodiazepines have been associated with falls and traumatic injury and should be used with extreme caution in patients who are at risk of these events (especially the elderly).

Use caution with potent CYP3A4 inhibitors, as they may significantly decreased the clearance of triazolam. Use caution in patients with suicidal risk. Use with caution in patients with a history of drug dependence. Benzodiazepines have been associated with dependence and acute withdrawal symptoms on discontinuation or reduction in dose. Acute withdrawal, including seizures, may be precipitated after administration of flumazenil to patients receiving long-term benzodiazepine therapy.

Paradoxical reactions, including hyperactive or aggressive behavior have been reported with benzodiazepines, particularly in adolescent/pediatric or psychiatric patients. Does not have analgesic, antidepressant, or antipsychotic properties.

Adverse Reactions
>10%: Central nervous system: Drowsiness, anteriograde amnesia
1% to 10%:
Central nervous system: Headache, dizziness, nervousness, lightheadedness, ataxia
Gastrointestinal: Nausea, vomiting
<1% (Limited to important or life-threatening): Confusion, depression, euphoria, memory impairment

Overdosage/Toxicology Symptoms include somnolence, confusion, coma, diminished reflexes, dyspnea, and hypotension. Treatment for benzodiazepine overdose is supportive. Rarely is mechanical ventilation required. Flumazenil has been shown to selectively block the binding of benzodiazepines to CNS receptors, resulting in reversal of benzodiazepine-induced CNS depression, but not always respiratory depression.

Drug Interactions
Cytochrome P450 Effect: Substrate of CYP3A4 (major); **Inhibits** CYP2C8 (weak), 2C9 (weak)
Increased Effect/Toxicity: Sedative and/or respiratory depressive effects may be additive with other CNS depressants. CYP3A4 inhibitors may increase the levels/effects of triazolam; example inhibitors include azole antifungals, clarithromycin, diclofenac, doxycycline, erythromycin, imatinib, isoniazid, nefazodone, nicardipine, propofol, protease inhibitors, quinidine, telithromycin, and verapamil. Concurrent use of some strong CYP3A4 inhibitors (including azole antifungals, nefazodone, and protease inhibitors) has been contraindicated by the manufacturers. Oral contraceptives may decrease the clearance and increase the half-life of triazolam (monitor for increased triazolam effect). Disulfiram, isoniazid and proton pump inhibitors may increase the levels/effects of triazolam. Benzodiazepines may enhance the adverse/toxic effect of clozapine.

Decreased Effect: CYP3A4 inducers may decrease the levels/effects of triazolam; example inducers include aminoglutethimide, carbamazepine, nafcillin, nevirapine, phenobarbital, phenytoin, and rifamycins. Theophylline may decrease the levels/effects of triazolam.

Ethanol/Nutrition/Herb Interactions

Ethanol: Avoid ethanol (may increase CNS depression).

Food: Food may decrease the rate of absorption. Triazolam serum concentration may be increased by grapefruit juice; avoid concurrent use.

Herb/Nutraceutical: St John's wort may decrease levels. Avoid valerian, St John's wort, kava kava, gotu kola (may increase CNS depression).

Mechanism of Action Binds to stereospecific benzodiazepine receptors on the postsynaptic GABA neuron at several sites within the central nervous system, including the limbic system, reticular formation. Enhancement of the inhibitory effect of GABA on neuronal excitability results by increased neuronal membrane permeability to chloride ions. This shift in chloride ions results in hyperpolarization (a less excitable state) and stabilization.

Pharmacodynamics/Kinetics

Onset of action: Hypnotic: 15-30 minutes

Duration: 6-7 hours

Distribution: V_d: 0.8-1.8 L/kg

Protein binding: 89%

Metabolism: Extensively hepatic

Half-life elimination: 1.7-5 hours

Excretion: Urine as unchanged drug and metabolites

Dosage Oral (onset of action is rapid, patient should be in bed when taking medication):

Children <18 years: Dosage not established

Adults:

Hypnotic: 0.125-0.25 mg at bedtime (maximum dose: 0.5 mg/day)

Preprocedure sedation (dental): 0.25 mg taken the evening before oral surgery; or 0.25 mg 1 hour before procedure

Elderly: Insomnia (short-term use): 0.0625-0.125 mg at bedtime; maximum dose: 0.25 mg/day

Dosing adjustment/comments in hepatic impairment: Reduce dose or avoid use in cirrhosis

Administration May take with food. Tablet may be crushed or swallowed whole. Onset of action is rapid, patient should be in bed when taking medication.

Monitoring Parameters Respiratory and cardiovascular status

Dosage Forms

Tablet: 0.125 mg, 0.25 mg

Halcion®: 0.125 mg, 0.25 mg [DSC]

- **Tribavirin** see Ribavirin on page 1503
- **Tricardio B** see Folic Acid, Cyanocobalamin, and Pyridoxine on page 750
- **Trichloroacetaldehyde Monohydrate** see Chloral Hydrate on page 339
- **Trichloromonofluoromethane and Dichlorodifluoromethane** see Dichlorodifluoromethane and Trichloromonofluoromethane on page 492
- **TriCor®** see Fenofibrate on page 689
- **Tricosal** see Choline Magnesium Trisalicylate on page 361
- **Tri-Cyclen® (Can)** see Ethinyl Estradiol and Norgestimate on page 660
- **Tri-Cyclen® Lo (Can)** see Ethinyl Estradiol and Norgestimate on page 660
- **Triderm®** see Triamcinolone on page 1734

Trientine (TRYE en teen)

U.S. Brand Names Syprine®

Canadian Brand Names Syprine®

Index Terms Trientine Hydrochloride

Pharmacologic Category Chelating Agent

Use Treatment of Wilson's disease in patients intolerant to penicillamine

Pregnancy Risk Factor C

Medication Safety Issues

Sound-alike/look-alike issues:

Trientine may be confused with Trental®, tretinoin

Contraindications Hypersensitivity to trientine or any component of the formulation; rheumatoid arthritis, biliary cirrhosis, cystinuria

Warnings/Precautions May cause iron-deficiency anemia; monitor closely; use with caution in patients with reactive airway disease

Adverse Reactions Frequency not defined.

Central nervous system: Dystonia, malaise

Dermatologic: Thickening and fissuring of skin

Endocrine & metabolic: Iron deficiency

Gastrointestinal: Epigastric pain, heartburn

Hematologic: Anemia

Local: Tenderness

Neuromuscular & skeletal: Muscle cramps, muscular spasm, myasthenia gravis

Miscellaneous: Systemic lupus erythematosus

Overdosage/Toxicology Overdosage is unknown. A single 30 g ingestion resulted in no toxicity. Following GI decontamination, treatment is supportive.

Drug Interactions

Decreased Effect: Iron and possibly other mineral supplements may decrease effect.

Mechanism of Action Trientine hydrochloride is an oral chelating agent structurally dissimilar from penicillamine and other available chelating agents; an effective oral chelator of copper used to induce adequate cupriuresis

(Continued)

Trientine *(Continued)*

Dosage Oral (administer on an empty stomach):
Children <12 years: 500-750 mg/day in divided doses 2-4 times/day; maximum: 1.5 g/day
Adults: 750-1250 mg/day in divided doses 2-4 times/day; maximum dose: 2 g/day

Dietary Considerations Should be taken 1 hour before or 2 hours after meals and at least 1 hour apart from any drug, food, or milk.

Administration Do not chew capsule, swallow whole followed by a full glass of water; notify physician of any fever or skin changes; any skin exposed to the contents of a capsule should be promptly washed with water

Dosage Forms Capsule, as hydrochloride: 250 mg

♦ **Trientine Hydrochloride** *see* Trientine *on page 1739*

Triethanolamine Polypeptide Oleate-Condensate
(trye eth a NOLE a meen pol i PEP tide OH lee ate-KON den sate)

U.S. Brand Names Cerumenex® [DSC]
Canadian Brand Names Cerumenex®
Pharmacologic Category Otic Agent, Cerumenolytic
Use Removal of ear wax (cerumen)
Pregnancy Risk Factor C
Dosage Children and Adults: Otic: Fill ear canal, insert cotton plug; allow to remain 15-30 minutes; flush ear with lukewarm water as a single treatment; if a second application is needed for unusually hard impactions, repeat the procedure
Additional Information Complete prescribing information for this medication should be consulted for additional detail.
Dosage Forms [DSC] = Discontinued product
Solution, otic: 10% (6 mL, 12 mL) [DSC]

♦ **Triethylenethiophosphoramide** *see* Thiotepa *on page 1674*

Trifluoperazine (trye floo oh PER a zeen)

Canadian Brand Names Apo-Trifluoperazine®; Novo-Trifluzine; PMS-Trifluoperazine; Terfluzine
Index Terms Trifluoperazine Hydrochloride
Pharmacologic Category Antipsychotic Agent, Typical, Phenothiazine
Additional Appendix Information
Antipsychotic Agents *on page 1872*
Use Treatment of schizophrenia
Unlabeled/Investigational Use Management of psychotic disorders
Pregnancy Risk Factor C
Lactation Enters breast milk/not recommended (AAP rates "of concern")
Medication Safety Issues
Sound-alike/look-alike issues:
Trifluoperazine may be confused with triflupromazine, trihexyphenidyl
Stelazine® may be confused with selegiline
Contraindications Hypersensitivity to trifluoperazine or any component of the formulation (cross-reactivity between phenothiazines may occur); severe CNS depression; bone marrow suppression; blood dyscrasias; severe hepatic disease; coma
Warnings/Precautions Safety in children <6 months of age has not been established; use with caution in patients with cardiovascular disease, seizures, hepatic dysfunction, narrow-angle glaucoma, or bone marrow suppression; use with caution in patients with myasthenia gravis or Parkinson's disease
Adverse Reactions Frequency not defined.
Cardiovascular: Hypotension, orthostatic hypotension, cardiac arrest
Central nervous system: Extrapyramidal symptoms (pseudoparkinsonism, akathisia, dystonias, tardive dyskinesia), dizziness, headache, neuroleptic malignant syndrome (NMS), impairment of temperature regulation, lowering of seizure threshold
Dermatologic: Increased sensitivity to sun, rash, discoloration of skin (blue-gray), photosensitivity
Endocrine & metabolic: Changes in menstrual cycle, libido (changes in), breast pain, hyperglycemia, hypoglycemia, gynecomastia, lactation, galactorrhea
Gastrointestinal: Constipation, weight gain, nausea, vomiting, stomach pain, xerostomia
Genitourinary: Difficulty in urination, ejaculatory disturbances, urinary retention, priapism
Hematologic: Agranulocytosis, leukopenia, pancytopenia, thrombocytopenic purpura, eosinophilia, hemolytic anemia, aplastic anemia
Hepatic: Cholestatic jaundice, hepatotoxicity
Neuromuscular & skeletal: Tremor
Ocular: Pigmentary retinopathy, cornea and lens changes
Respiratory: Nasal congestion
Overdosage/Toxicology Symptoms include deep sleep, coma, extrapyramidal symptoms, abnormal involuntary muscle movements, hypo- or hypertension, and cardiac arrhythmias. Following initiation of essential overdose management, toxic symptom treatment and supportive treatment should be initiated. Hypotension usually responds to I.V. fluids or Trendelenburg positioning. If unresponsive to these measures, the use of a parenteral inotrope may be required (eg, norepinephrine 0.1-0.2 mcg/kg/minute titrated to response). Seizures commonly respond to diazepam (I.V. 5-10 mg bolus in adults every 15 minutes if needed up to a total of 30 mg; I.V. 0.25-0.4 mg/kg/dose up to a total of 10 mg in children) or to phenytoin or phenobarbital. Neuroleptics often cause extrapyramidal symptoms (eg, dystonic reactions) requiring management with diphenhydramine 1-2 mg/kg (adults) up to a maximum of 50 mg I.M. or slow I.V. push followed by a maintenance dose for 48-72 hours. When these reactions are unresponsive to diphenhydramine, anticholinergic agents such as benztropine

mesylate I.V. 1-2 mg (adults) may be effective. These agents are generally effective within 2-5 minutes. Cardiac arrhythmias are treated with lidocaine 1-2 mg/kg bolus followed by a maintenance infusion.

Drug Interactions

Cytochrome P450 Effect: Substrate of CYP1A2 (major)

Increased Effect/Toxicity: CYP1A2 inhibitors may increase the levels/effects of trifluoperazine; example inhibitors include ciprofloxacin, fluvoxamine, ketoconazole, norfloxacin, ofloxacin, and rofecoxib. Trifluoperazine's effects on CNS depression may be additive when trifluoperazine is combined with CNS depressants (opioid analgesics, ethanol, barbiturates, cyclic antidepressants, antihistamines, or sedative-hypnotics). Trifluoperazine may increase the effects/toxicity of anticholinergics, antihypertensives, lithium (rare neurotoxicity), trazodone, or valproic acid. Concurrent use with TCA may produce increased toxicity or altered therapeutic response. Chloroquine and propranolol may increase trifluoperazine concentrations. Hypotension may occur when trifluoperazine is combined with epinephrine. May increase the risk of arrhythmia when combined with antiarrhythmics, cisapride, pimozide, sparfloxacin, or other drugs which prolong QT interval. Metoclopramide may increase risk of extrapyramidal symptoms (EPS). Acetylcholinesterase inhibitors (central) may increase the risk of antipsychotic-related EPS.

Decreased Effect: CYP1A2 inducers may decrease the levels/effects of trifluoperazine; example inducers include aminoglutethimide, carbamazepine, phenobarbital, and rifampin. Phenothiazines inhibit the effects of levodopa, guanadrel, guanethidine, and bromocriptine. Benztropine (and other anticholinergics) may inhibit the therapeutic response to trifluoperazine and excess anticholinergic effects may occur. Cigarette smoking may enhance the hepatic metabolism of trifluoperazine. Trifluoperazine and possibly other low potency antipsychotics may reverse the pressor effects of epinephrine.

Ethanol/Nutrition/Herb Interactions

Ethanol: Avoid ethanol (may increase CNS depression).

Herb/Nutraceutical: Avoid kava kava, gotu kola, valerian, St John's wort (may increase CNS depression). Avoid dong quai, St John's wort (may also cause photosensitization).

Mechanism of Action Trifluoperazine is a piperazine phenothiazine antipsychotic which blocks postsynaptic mesolimbic dopaminergic receptors in the brain; exhibits alpha-adrenergic blocking effect and depresses the release of hypothalamic and hypophyseal hormones

Pharmacodynamics/Kinetics

Metabolism: Extensively hepatic

Half-life elimination: >24 hours with chronic use

Dosage Oral:

Children 6-12 years: Schizophrenia/psychoses: Hospitalized or well-supervised patients: Initial: 1 mg 1-2 times/day, gradually increase until symptoms are controlled or adverse effects become troublesome; maximum: 15 mg/day

Adults:

Schizophrenia/psychoses:

Outpatients: 1-2 mg twice daily

Hospitalized or well-supervised patients: Initial: 2-5 mg twice daily with optimum response in the 15-20 mg/day range; do not exceed 40 mg/day

Nonpsychotic anxiety: 1-2 mg twice daily; maximum: 6 mg/day; therapy for anxiety should not exceed 12 weeks; do not exceed 6 mg/day for longer than 12 weeks when treating anxiety; agitation, jitteriness, or insomnia may be confused with original neurotic or psychotic symptoms

Elderly:

Schizophrenia/psychoses:

Refer to adult dosing. Dose selection should start at the low end of the dosage range and titration must be gradual.

Behavioral symptoms associated with dementia behavior: Initial: 0.5-1 mg 1-2 times/day; increase dose at 4- to 7-day intervals by 0.5-1 mg/day; increase dosing intervals (bid, tid, etc) as necessary to control response or side effects. Maximum daily dose: 40 mg. Gradual increases (titration) may prevent some side effects or decrease their severity.

Hemodialysis: Not dialyzable (0% to 5%)

Dietary Considerations May be taken with food to decrease GI distress.

Monitoring Parameters Vital signs; lipid profile, fasting blood glucose/Hgb A$_{1c}$; BMI; mental status, abnormal involuntary movement scale (AIMS)

Reference Range Therapeutic response and blood levels have not been established

Test Interactions False-positive for phenylketonuria

Additional Information Do not exceed 6 mg/day for longer than 12 weeks when treating anxiety. Agitation, jitteriness, or insomnia may be confused with original neurotic or psychotic symptoms.

Dosage Forms Tablet: 1 mg, 2 mg, 5 mg, 10 mg

♦ **4'-Nitro-3'-Trifluoromethylisobutyrantide** see Flutamide on page 737

♦ **Trifluoperazine Hydrochloride** see Trifluoperazine on page 1740

♦ **Trifluorothymidine** see Trifluridine on page 1741

Trifluridine (trye FLURE i deen)

U.S. Brand Names Viroptic®

Canadian Brand Names SAB-Trifluridine; Sandoz-Trifluridine; Viroptic®

Index Terms F$_3$T; Trifluorothymidine

Pharmacologic Category Antiviral Agent, Ophthalmic

Use Treatment of primary keratoconjunctivitis and recurrent epithelial keratitis caused by herpes simplex virus types I and II

Pregnancy Risk Factor C

Lactation Excretion in breast milk unknown

(Continued)

Trifluridine *(Continued)*

Medication Safety Issues
Sound-alike/look-alike issues:
Viroptic® may be confused with Timoptic®

Contraindications Hypersensitivity to trifluridine or any component of the formulation

Warnings/Precautions Mild local irritation of conjunctival and cornea may occur when instilled but usually transient effects

Adverse Reactions
>10%: Local: Burning, stinging
<1% (Limited to important or life-threatening): Epithelial keratopathy, increased intraocular pressure, keratitis, palpebral edema, stromal edema

Stability Refrigerate at 2°C to 8°C (36°F to 46°F). Storage at room temperature may result in a solution altered pH which could result in ocular discomfort upon administration and/or decreased potency.

Mechanism of Action Interferes with viral replication by incorporating into viral DNA in place of thymidine, inhibiting thymidylate synthetase resulting in the formation of defective proteins

Pharmacodynamics/Kinetics Absorption: Ophthalmic: Systemic absorption negligible, corneal penetration adequate

Dosage Adults: Instill 1 drop into affected eye every 2 hours while awake, to a maximum of 9 drops/day, until re-epithelialization of corneal ulcer occurs; then use 1 drop every 4 hours for another 7 days; do **not** exceed 21 days of treatment; if improvement has not taken place in 7-14 days, consider another form of therapy

Monitoring Parameters Ophthalmologic exam (test for corneal staining with fluorescein or rose bengal)

Dosage Forms Solution, ophthalmic: 1% (7.5 mL)

♦ **Triglide™** *see* Fenofibrate *on page 689*

Trihexyphenidyl *(trye heks ee FEN i dil)*

Canadian Brand Names Apo-Trihex®

Index Terms Artane; Benzhexol Hydrochloride; Trihexyphenidyl Hydrochloride

Pharmacologic Category Anti-Parkinson's Agent, Anticholinergic; Anticholinergic Agent

Additional Appendix Information
Parkinson's Agents *on page 1895*

Use Adjunctive treatment of Parkinson's disease; treatment of drug-induced extrapyramidal symptoms

Pregnancy Risk Factor C

Lactation Excretion in breast milk unknown/use caution

Medication Safety Issues
Sound-alike/look-alike issues:
Trihexyphenidyl may be confused with trifluoperazine
Artane may be confused with Altace®, Anturane®, Aramine®

Contraindications Hypersensitivity to trihexyphenidyl or any component of the formulation; narrow-angle glaucoma; pyloric or duodenal obstruction; stenosing peptic ulcers; bladder neck obstructions; achalasia; myasthenia gravis

Warnings/Precautions Use with caution in hot weather or during exercise, especially when administered concomitantly with other atropine-like drugs to chronically-ill patients, alcoholics, patients with CNS disease, or persons during manual labor in a hot environment. Elderly patients require strict dosage regulation. Use with caution in patients with tachycardia, cardiac arrhythmias, hypertension, hypotension, prostatic hyperplasia or any tendency toward urinary retention, liver or kidney disorders, and obstructive disease of the GI or GU tract. May exacerbate mental symptoms when used to treat extrapyramidal symptoms. When given in large doses or to susceptible patients, may cause weakness.

Adverse Reactions Frequency not defined.
Cardiovascular: Tachycardia
Central nervous system: Confusion, agitation, euphoria, drowsiness, headache, dizziness, nervousness, delusions, hallucinations, paranoia
Dermatologic: Dry skin, increased sensitivity to light, rash
Gastrointestinal: Constipation, xerostomia, dry throat, ileus, nausea, vomiting, parotitis
Genitourinary: Urinary retention
Neuromuscular & skeletal: Weakness
Ocular: Blurred vision, mydriasis, increase in intraocular pressure, glaucoma, blindness (long-term use in narrow-angle glaucoma)
Respiratory: Dry nose
Miscellaneous: Diaphoresis (decreased)

Overdosage/Toxicology Symptoms include blurred vision, urinary retention, and tachycardia. Anticholinergic toxicity is caused by strong binding of the drug to cholinergic receptors. Anticholinesterase inhibitors reduce acetylcholinesterase. For anticholinergic overdose with severe life-threatening symptoms, physostigmine 1-2 mg (0.5 mg or 0.02 mg/kg for children) SubQ or slow I.V. may be given to reverse these effects.

Drug Interactions
Increased Effect/Toxicity: Central and/or peripheral anticholinergic syndrome can occur when administered with amantadine, rimantadine, opioid analgesics, phenothiazines and other antipsychotics (especially with high anticholinergic activity), tricyclic antidepressants, MAO inhibitors, quinidine and some other antiarrhythmics, and antihistamines. CNS depressants (cannabinoids, ethanol, barbiturates, and opioid analgesics) may have additive effects with trihexyphenidyl; an abuse potential exits.
Decreased Effect: May increase gastric degradation of levodopa and decrease the amount of levodopa absorbed by delaying gastric emptying; the opposite may be true for digoxin. Therapeutic effects of cholinergic agents (tacrine, donepezil, rivastigmine, galantamine) and neuroleptics may be antagonized.

Ethanol/Nutrition/Herb Interactions Ethanol: Avoid ethanol (may increase CNS depression).

Mechanism of Action Exerts a direct inhibitory effect on the parasympathetic nervous system. It also has a relaxing effect on smooth musculature; exerted both directly on the muscle itself and indirectly through parasympathetic nervous system (inhibitory effect)

Pharmacodynamics/Kinetics
Onset of action: Peak effect: ~1 hour
Half-life elimination: 3.3-4.1 hours
Time to peak, serum: 1-1.5 hours
Excretion: Primarily urine

Dosage Adults: Oral: Initial: 1-2 mg/day, increase by 2 mg increments at intervals of 3-5 days; usual dose: 5-15 mg/day in 3-4 divided doses

Administration Tolerated best if given in 3 daily doses and with food. High doses may be divided into 4 doses, at meal times and at bedtime. Patients may be switched to sustained-action capsules when stabilized on conventional dosage forms.

Monitoring Parameters IOP monitoring and gonioscopic evaluations should be performed periodically

Additional Information Incidence and severity of side effects are dose related. Patients may be switched to sustained-action capsules when stabilized on conventional dosage forms.

Dosage Forms
Elixir, as hydrochloride: 2 mg/5 mL (480 mL)
Tablet, as hydrochloride: 2 mg, 5 mg

- **Trihexyphenidyl Hydrochloride** *see* Trihexyphenidyl *on page 1742*
- **TriHIBit®** *see* Diphtheria, Tetanus Toxoids, and Acellular Pertussis Vaccine and *Haemophilus influenzae* b Conjugate Vaccine *on page 524*
- **Trikacide (Can)** *see* Metronidazole *on page 1132*
- **Trileptal®** *see* Oxcarbazepine *on page 1282*
- **Tri-Levlen®** *see* Ethinyl Estradiol and Levonorgestrel *on page 653*
- **Trilisate® [DSC]** *see* Choline Magnesium Trisalicylate *on page 361*
- **Tri-Luma™** *see* Fluocinolone, Hydroquinone, and Tretinoin *on page 721*
- **TriLyte™** *see* Polyethylene Glycol-Electrolyte Solution *on page 1387*
- **Trimazide [DSC]** *see* Trimethobenzamide *on page 1743*

Trimethobenzamide (trye meth oh BEN za mide)

U.S. Brand Names Tebamide™; Tigan®; Trimazide [DSC]
Canadian Brand Names Tigan®
Index Terms Trimethobenzamide Hydrochloride
Pharmacologic Category Anticholinergic Agent; Antiemetic
Use Treatment of nausea and vomiting
Pregnancy Risk Factor C
Pregnancy Implications Teratogenic effects were not observed in animal studies. Safety and efficacy have not been established in pregnant patients. Trimethobenzamide has been used to treat nausea and vomiting of pregnancy.
Lactation Excretion in breast milk unknown
Medication Safety Issues
Sound-alike/look-alike issues:
Tigan® may be confused with Tiazac®, Ticar®
Contraindications Hypersensitivity to trimethobenzamide, benzocaine (or similar local anesthetics), or any component of the formulation; injection contraindicated in children; suppositories contraindicated in premature infants or neonates
Warnings/Precautions May mask emesis due to Reye's syndrome or mimic CNS effects of Reye's syndrome in patients with emesis of other etiologies; use in patients with acute vomiting should be avoided. Risk of adverse effects (eg, EPS, seizure) may be increased in patients with acute febrile illness, dehydration, or electrolyte imbalance; use caution.
Adverse Reactions Frequency not defined.
Cardiovascular: Hypotension
Central nervous system: Coma, depression, disorientation, dizziness, drowsiness, EPS, headache, opisthotonos, Parkinson-like syndrome, seizure
Gastrointestinal: Diarrhea
Hematologic: Blood dyscrasias
Hepatic: Jaundice
Neuromuscular & skeletal: Muscle cramps
Ocular: Blurred vision
Miscellaneous: Hypersensitivity reactions
Overdosage/Toxicology Symptoms include hypotension, seizures, CNS depression, cardiac arrhythmias, disorientation, and confusion. Following initiation of essential overdose management, toxic symptom and supportive treatment should be initiated. Hypotension usually responds to I.V. fluids or Trendelenburg positioning. If unresponsive to these measures, the use of a parenteral inotrope may be required (eg, norepinephrine 0.1-0.2 mcg/kg/minute titrated to response). Seizures commonly respond to diazepam (I.V. 5-10 mg bolus in adults every 15 minutes, if needed, up to a total of 30 mg; I.V. 0.25-0.4 mg/kg/dose up to a total of 10 mg in children) or to phenytoin or phenobarbital. Critical cardiac arrhythmias often respond to lidocaine 1-2 mg/kg bolus followed by a maintenance infusion. Extrapyramidal symptoms (eg, dystonic reactions) may be managed with diphenhydramine 1-2 mg/kg (adults) up to a maximum of 50 mg I.M. or slow I.V. push followed by a maintenance dose for 48-72 hours. When these reactions are unresponsive to diphenhydramine, anticholinergic agents such as benztropine mesylate I.V. 1-2 mg (adults) may be effective. These agents are generally effective within 2-5 minutes.
Ethanol/Nutrition/Herb Interactions Ethanol: Concomitant use should be avoided (sedative effects may be additive).
(Continued)

Trimethobenzamide *(Continued)*

Stability Store capsules, injection solution, and suppositories at room temperature.

Mechanism of Action Acts centrally to inhibit the medullary chemoreceptor trigger zone

Pharmacodynamics/Kinetics

Onset of action: Antiemetic: Oral: 10-40 minutes; I.M.: 15-35 minutes

Duration: 3-4 hours

Absorption: Rectal: ~60%

Bioavailability: Oral: 60% to 100%

Half-life elimination: 7-9 hours

Time to peak: Oral: 45 minutes; I.M.: 30 minutes

Excretion: Urine (30% to 50%)

Dosage Rectal use is contraindicated in neonates and premature infants

Children:

<14 kg: Rectal: 100 mg 3-4 times/day

14-40 kg: Rectal: 100-200 mg 3-4 times/day

>40 kg:

Oral: 300 mg 3-4 times/day

Rectal: 200 mg 3-4 times/day

Adults:

Oral: 300 mg 3-4 times/day

I.M., rectal: 200 mg 3-4 times/day

Postoperative nausea and vomiting (PONV): I.M.: 200 mg, followed 1 hour later by a second 200 mg dose

Administration Administer I.M. only; not for I.V. administration. Inject deep into upper outer quadrant of gluteal muscle.

Dosage Forms

Capsule, as hydrochloride (Tigan®): 300 mg

Injection, solution, as hydrochloride: 100 mg/mL (2 mL)

Tigan®: 100 mg/mL (2 mL [preservative free], 20 mL)

Suppository, rectal, as hydrochloride: 100 mg, 200 mg

Tebamide™: 100 mg, 200 mg [contains benzocaine]

Tigan®, Trimazide [DSC]: 200 mg [contains benzocaine]

♦ **Trimethobenzamide Hydrochloride** see Trimethobenzamide *on page 1743*

Trimethoprim *(trye METH oh prim)*

U.S. Brand Names Primsol®; Proloprim®

Canadian Brand Names Apo-Trimethoprim®

Index Terms TMP

Pharmacologic Category Antibiotic, Miscellaneous

Use Treatment of urinary tract infections due to susceptible strains of *E. coli, P. mirabilis, K. pneumoniae, Enterobacter* sp and coagulase-negative *Staphylococcus* including *S. saprophyticus*; acute otitis media in children; acute exacerbations of chronic bronchitis in adults; in combination with other agents for treatment of toxoplasmosis, *Pneumocystis carinii*; treatment of superficial ocular infections involving the conjunctiva and cornea

Pregnancy Risk Factor C

Pregnancy Implications There are no well-controlled studies on the use of trimethoprim during pregnancy. Because trimethoprim may interfere with folic acid metabolism, consider using only if the potential benefit to the mother outweighs the possible risk to the fetus.

Lactation Enters breast milk/use caution (AAP rates "compatible")

Medication Safety Issues

Sound-alike/look-alike issues:

Trimethoprim may be confused with trimethaphan

Proloprim® may be confused with Prolixin®, Protropin®

Contraindications Hypersensitivity to trimethoprim or any component of the formulation; megaloblastic anemia due to folate deficiency

Warnings/Precautions Use with caution in patients with impaired renal or hepatic function or with possible folate deficiency

Adverse Reactions Frequency not defined.

Central nervous system: Aseptic meningitis (rare), fever

Dermatologic: Maculopapular rash (3% to 7% at 200 mg/day; incidence higher with larger daily doses), erythema multiforme (rare), exfoliative dermatitis (rare), pruritus (common), phototoxic skin eruptions, Stevens-Johnson syndrome (rare), toxic epidermal necrolysis (rare)

Endocrine & metabolic: Hyperkalemia, hyponatremia

Gastrointestinal: Epigastric distress, glossitis, nausea, vomiting

Hematologic: Leukopenia, megaloblastic anemia, methemoglobinemia, neutropenia, thrombocytopenia

Hepatic: Liver enzyme elevation, cholestatic jaundice (rare)

Renal: BUN and creatinine increased

Miscellaneous: Anaphylaxis, hypersensitivity reactions

Overdosage/Toxicology Symptom of acute toxicity includes nausea, vomiting, confusion, and dizziness. Chronic overdose results in bone marrow suppression. Treatment of acute overdose is supportive following GI decontamination. Treatment of chronic overdose includes the use of oral leucovorin 5-15 mg/day. Hemodialysis is only moderately effective in eliminating drug.

Drug Interactions

Cytochrome P450 Effect: Substrate (major) of CYP2C9, 3A4; **Inhibits** CYP2C8 (moderate), 2C9 (moderate)

Increased Effect/Toxicity: Increased effect/toxicity/levels of phenytoin. Concurrent use with ACE inhibitors increases risk of hyperkalemia. Increased myelosuppression with methotrexate. May increase levels of digoxin. Concurrent use with dapsone may increase levels of dapsone and trimethoprim. Concurrent use with procainamide may increase levels of procainamide and trimethoprim. Trimethoprim may increase the levels/effects of amiodarone, fluoxetine, glimepiride, glipizide, nateglinide, phenytoin, pioglitazone, rosiglitazone, sertraline, warfarin, and other CYP2C8 and 2C9 substrates.

Decreased Effect: The levels/effects of trimethoprim may be decreased by aminoglutethimide, carbamazepine, nafcillin, nevirapine, phenobarbital, phenytoin, rifampin, rifapentine, secobarbital, and other CYP2C9 or 3A4 inducers.

Stability Protect the 200 mg tablet from light.

Mechanism of Action Inhibits folic acid reduction to tetrahydrofolate, and thereby inhibits microbial growth

Pharmacodynamics/Kinetics

Absorption: Readily and extensive

Distribution: Widely into body tissues and fluids (middle ear, prostate, bile, aqueous humor, CSF); crosses placenta; enters breast milk

Protein binding: 42% to 46%

Metabolism: Partially hepatic

Half-life elimination: 8-14 hours; prolonged with renal impairment

Time to peak, serum: 1-4 hours

Excretion: Urine (60% to 80%) as unchanged drug

Dosage Oral:

Children: 4 mg/kg/day in divided doses every 12 hours

Adults: 100 mg every 12 hours or 200 mg every 24 hours for 10 days; longer treatment periods may be necessary for prostatitis (ie, 4-16 weeks); in the treatment of *Pneumocystis carinii* pneumonia; dose may be as high as 15-20 mg/kg/day in 3-4 divided doses

Dosing interval in renal impairment:

Cl_{cr} 15-30 mL/minute: Administer 100 mg every 18 hours or 50 mg every 12 hours

Cl_{cr} <15 mL/minute: Administer 100 mg every 24 hours or avoid use

Hemodialysis: Moderately dialyzable (20% to 50%)

Dietary Considerations May cause folic acid deficiency, supplements may be needed. Should be taken with milk or food.

Administration Administer with milk or food.

Reference Range Therapeutic: Peak: 5-15 mg/L; Trough: 2-8 mg/L

Dosage Forms [DSC] = Discontinued product

Solution, oral (Primsol®): 50 mg (base)/5 mL (480 mL) [contains sodium benzoate; bubble gum flavor]

Tablet: 100 mg

Proloprim®: 100 mg, 200 mg [DSC]

Trimethoprim and Polymyxin B (trye METH oh prim & pol i MIKS in bee)

U.S. Brand Names Polytrim®

Canadian Brand Names PMS-Polytrimethoprim; Polytrim™

Index Terms Polymyxin B and Trimethoprim

Pharmacologic Category Antibiotic, Ophthalmic

Use Treatment of surface ocular bacterial conjunctivitis and blepharoconjunctivitis

Pregnancy Risk Factor C

Dosage Instill 1-2 drops in eye(s) every 4-6 hours

Elderly: No overall differences observed between elderly and other adults

Additional Information Complete prescribing information for this medication should be consulted for additional detail.

Dosage Forms Solution, ophthalmic: Trimethoprim 1 mg and polymyxin B sulfate 10,000 units per mL (10 mL) [contains benzalkonium chloride]

♦ **Trimethoprim and Sulfamethoxazole** see Sulfamethoxazole and Trimethoprim on page 1613

Trimetrexate (tri me TREKS ate)

U.S. Brand Names NeuTrexin®

Index Terms NSC-352122; Trimetrexate Glucuronate

Pharmacologic Category Antineoplastic Agent, Miscellaneous

Use Alternative therapy for the treatment of moderate-to-severe *Pneumocystis jiroveci* pneumonia (PCP) in immunocompromised patients, including patients with acquired immunodeficiency syndrome (AIDS), who are intolerant of, or are refractory to, sulfamethoxazole/trimethoprim therapy or for whom sulfamethoxazole/trimethoprim and pentamidine are contraindicated

Unlabeled/Investigational Use Treatment of nonsmall cell lung cancer, metastatic colorectal cancer, metastatic head and neck cancer, pancreatic adenocarcinoma, cutaneous T-cell lymphoma

Pregnancy Risk Factor D

Pregnancy Implications Teratogenic effects and fetal loss were observed in animal studies. May cause fetal harm when administered to pregnant women. Women of childbearing potential should avoid becoming pregnant while receiving treatment. If used in pregnancy, or if patient becomes pregnant during treatment, the patient should be apprised of potential hazard to the fetus.

Lactation Excretion in breast milk unknown/not recommended

Medication Safety Issues

High alert medication: The Institute for Safe Medication Practices (ISMP) includes this medication among its list of drugs which have a heightened risk of causing significant patient harm when used in error.

Contraindications Hypersensitivity to trimetrexate, methotrexate, leucovorin, or any component of the formulation; severe existing myelosuppression; pregnancy

(Continued)

Trimetrexate *(Continued)*

Warnings/Precautions Hazardous agent - use appropriate precautions for handling and disposal. **[U.S. Boxed Warning]: Must be administered with concurrent leucovorin to avoid potentially serious or life-threatening toxicities.** Leucovorin therapy must extend for 72 hours past the last dose of trimetrexate. Hypersensitivity/allergic-type reactions have been reported, primarily when given as a bolus infusion, at higher than recommended doses for PCP, or in combination with fluorouracil or leucovorin. May cause anaphylactoid reactions (rarely) including acute hypotension and loss of consciousness. Epinephrine should be available for treatment of acute allergic symptoms. Use with caution in patients with mild myelo-suppression, severe hepatic or renal dysfunction, hypoproteinemia, hypoalbuminemia, or previous extensive myelosuppressive therapies. Withhold zidovudine during trimetrexate treatment.

Adverse Reactions

>10%:

Hematologic: Neutropenia (30%)

Hepatic: AST increased (14%), ALT increased (11%)

1% to 10%:

Central nervous system: Fever (8%), confusion (3%), fatigue (2%)

Dermatologic: Rash/pruritus (6%)

Endocrine & metabolic: Hyponatremia (5%), hypocalcemia (2%)

Gastrointestinal: Nausea/vomiting (5%), stomatitis

Hematologic: Thrombocytopenia (10%), anemia (7%)

Hepatic: Alkaline phosphatase increased (5%), bilirubin increased (2%)

Neuromuscular & skeletal: Peripheral neuropathy

Miscellaneous: Flu-like illness; hypersensitivity/allergic reactions (chills, rigors); anaphylactoid reactions (acute hypotension, loss of consciousness)

<1% (Limited to important or life-threatening): Seizure, serum creatinine increased

Overdosage/Toxicology Administration of trimetrexate without leucovorin may cause lethal complications. Toxicities observed at I.V. doses of 90 mg/m²/day with concurrent leucovorin were primarily hematologic. In the event of an overdose, trimetrexate should be discontinued and leucovorin should be administered at a dose of 40 mg/m² I.V. every 6 hours for 3 days.

Drug Interactions

Increased Effect/Toxicity: Zidovudine may increase the myelotoxicity of trimetrexate; discontinue zidovudine during trimetrexate treatment. Trimetrexate may increase toxicity (infections) of live virus vaccines.

Stability Prior to reconstitution, vials should be stored at controlled room temperature of 20°C to 25°C (68°F to 77°F). Protect from light. Reconstitute with D₅W or SWFI to a concentration of 12.5 mg/mL. Do not use if cloudy or if precipitate forms. Reconstituted solution is stable for 6 hours at room temperature and 24 hours under refrigeration. Prior to administration, solution should be further diluted with D₅W to a concentration of 0.25 mg/mL to 2 mg/mL. Diluted solutions for infusion are stable under refrigeration or at room temperature for 24 hours. Do not freeze. Precipitate occurs with leucovorin or any solution containing chloride ion.

Mechanism of Action Trimetrexate is a folate antimetabolite that inhibits DNA synthesis by inhibition of dihydrofolate reductase (DHFR); DHFR inhibition reduces the formation of reduced folates and thymidylate synthetase, resulting in inhibition of purine and thymidylic acid synthesis.

Pharmacodynamics/Kinetics

Distribution: V_d: 0.62 L/kg

Protein binding: 80% to 90% (concentration dependent)

Metabolism: Extensively hepatic: O-demethylation followed by conjugation to glucuronide or sulfate (major); N-demethylation and oxidation (minor)

Half-life elimination: 9-18 hours (11 hours with leucovorin)

Excretion: Urine (10% to 40% as unchanged drug); feces (<1% to 8%)

Dosage Note: Concurrent leucovorin 20 mg/m² every 6 hours must be administered daily (oral or I.V.) during treatment and for 72 hours past the last dose of trimetrexate.

Dosage Adjustment in Hematologic Toxicity

Toxicity Grade	Neutrophils (Polys/Bands)	Platelets	Dosage Recommendations	
			Trimetrexate	Leucovorin
1	>1000/mm³	>75,000/mm³	45 mg/m² once daily	20 mg/m² every 6 h
2	750-1000/mm³	50,000-75,000/mm³	45 mg/m² once daily	40 mg/m² every 6 h
3	500-749/mm³	25,000-49,999/mm³	22 mg/m² once daily	40 mg/m² every 6 h
4	<500/mm³	<25,000/mm³	Day 1-9: Discontinue Day 10-21: Interrupt up to 96 hours (see **Note**)	40 mg/m² every 6 h

Note:

If Grade 4 hematologic toxicity occurs prior to day 10: Trimetrexate should be discontinued and leucovorin administered for an additional 72 hours.

If Grade 4 hematologic toxicity occurs at day 10 or later: Trimetrexate may be held up to 96 hours to allow counts to recover.

If counts recover to Grade 3 within 96 hours, trimetrexate should be administered at a dose of 22 mg/m² and leucovorin 40 mg/m² every 6 hours.

When counts recover to Grade 2 toxicity, trimetrexate may be increased to 45 mg/m². Continue leucovorin at 40 mg/m² for duration of treatment.

Discontinue trimetrexate if counts do not improve to less than or equal to Grade 3 toxicity within 96 hours. Continue leucovorin at 40 mg/m² every 6 hours for 72 hours following last dose.

Adults: I.V.:
Pneumocystis jiroveci pneumonia (PCP): 45 mg/m² once daily for 21 days; **alternative dosing based on weight:**
  <50 kg:Trimetrexate 1.5 mg/kg/day; leucovorin 0.6 mg/kg 4 times/day
  50-80 kg:Trimetrexate 1.2 mg/kg/day; leucovorin 0.5 mg/kg/4 times/day
  >80 kg: Trimetrexate 1 mg/kg/day; leucovorin 0.5 mg/kg/4 times/day
  Note: Oral doses of leucovorin should be rounded up to the next higher 25 mg increment.

Antineoplastic (unlabeled use): 6-16 mg/m² once daily for 5 days every 21-28 days **or** 150-200 mg/m² every 2 weeks

Dosage adjustment in hepatic impairment: Although it may be necessary to reduce the dose in patients with liver dysfunction, no specific dosage recommendations exist for treatment initiation with hepatic impairment.

Hepatic toxicity (during treatment): Hold drug therapy if transaminase levels or alkaline phosphatase levels increase to >5 times the upper limit of normal.

Renal toxicity (during treatment): Hold drug therapy if serum creatinine levels increase to >2.5 mg/dL and elevation is considered secondary to trimetrexate.

Other toxicities: Hold drug therapy in patients experiencing severe mucosal toxicity that interferes with oral intake. Treatment should be discontinued for fever that cannot be controlled with antipyretics (oral temperature ≥40.5°C/105°F).

In addition: If trimetrexate treatment is interrupted for toxicity, leucovorin therapy must continue for 72 hours past the last administered dose of trimetrexate.

Administration I.V. infusion: Over 60-90 minutes; must be used with concurrent leucovorin; trimetrexate and leucovorin solutions **must** be administered separately; intravenous lines should be flushed with at least 10 mL of D_5W before and after trimetrexate and between trimetrexate and leucovorin

Monitoring Parameters Check and record patient's temperature daily; absolute neutrophil counts (ANC), platelet count, renal function tests (serum creatinine, BUN), and hepatic function tests (ALT, AST, alkaline phosphatase) twice weekly

Additional Information Not a vesicant; methotrexate derivative

Dosage Forms Injection, powder for reconstitution [preservative free]: 25 mg, 200 mg

♦ **Trimetrexate Glucuronate** *see* Trimetrexate *on page 1745*

Trimipramine (trye MI pra meen)

U.S. Brand Names Surmontil®
Canadian Brand Names Apo-Trimip®; Nu-Trimipramine; Rhotrimine®; Surmontil®
Index Terms Trimipramine Maleate
Pharmacologic Category Antidepressant, Tricyclic (Tertiary Amine)
Additional Appendix Information
Antidepressant Agents *on page 1866*
Use Treatment of depression
Restrictions An FDA-approved medication guide concerning the use of antidepressants in children and teenagers must be distributed when dispensing an outpatient prescription (new or refill) where this medication is to be used without direct supervision of a healthcare provider. Medication guides are available at http://www.fda.gov/cder/Offices/ODS/medication_guides.htm. Dispense to parents or guardians of children and teenagers receiving this medication.
Pregnancy Risk Factor C
Lactation Enters breast milk/contraindicated
Medication Safety Issues
Sound-alike/look-alike issues:
Trimipramine may be confused with triamterene, trimeprazine
Contraindications Hypersensitivity to trimipramine, any component of the formulation, or other dibenzodiazepines; use of MAO inhibitors within 14 days; use in a patient during the acute recovery phase of MI
Warnings/Precautions [U.S. Boxed Warning]: Antidepressants increase the risk of suicidal thinking and behavior in children and adolescents with major depressive disorder (MDD) and other depressive disorders; consider risk prior to prescribing. All patients must be closely monitored for clinical worsening, suicidality, or unusual changes in behavior, especially during the initiation of therapy or following an increase or decrease in dosage. When used in children, the child's family or caregiver should be instructed to closely observe the patient and communicate condition with healthcare provider. A medication guide should be dispensed with each prescription. **Trimipramine is not FDA approved for use in children.**

The possibility of a suicide attempt is inherent in major depression and may persist until remission occurs. Use caution in high-risk patients. Worsening depression and severe abrupt suicidality that are not part of the presenting symptoms may require discontinuation or modification of drug therapy. The patient's family or caregiver should be alerted to monitor patients for the emergence of suicidality and associated behaviors (such as agitation, irritability, hostility, impulsivity, and hypomania) and call healthcare provider.

May worsen psychosis in some patients or precipitate a shift to mania or hypomania in patients with bipolar disorder. Patients presenting with depressive symptoms should be screened for bipolar disorder. Monotherapy in patients with bipolar disorder should be avoided. **Trimipramine is not FDA approved for the treatment of bipolar depression.**

The degree of sedation, anticholinergic effects, orthostasis, and conduction abnormalities are high relative to other antidepressants. Trimipramine often causes drowsiness/sedation, resulting in impaired performance of tasks requiring alertness (eg, operating machinery or driving). Sedative effects may be additive with other CNS depressants and/or ethanol. Use with caution in patients with a history of cardiovascular disease (including previous MI, stroke, tachycardia, or conduction abnormalities). Use with caution in patients with urinary retention,
(Continued)

Trimipramine (Continued)

benign prostatic hyperplasia, narrow-angle glaucoma, xerostomia, visual problems, constipation, or a history of bowel obstruction.

May alter glucose control - use with caution in patients with diabetes. Consider discontinuing, when possible, prior to elective surgery. Therapy should not be abruptly discontinued in patients receiving high doses for prolonged periods. May lower seizure threshold - use caution in patients with a previous seizure disorder or condition predisposing to seizures such as brain damage, alcoholism, or concurrent therapy with other drugs which lower the seizure threshold. May increase the risks associated with electroconvulsive therapy. Use with caution in hyperthyroid patients or those receiving thyroid supplementation. Use with caution in patients with hepatic or renal dysfunction and in elderly patients.

Adverse Reactions Frequency not defined.

Cardiovascular: Arrhythmias, hyper-/hypotension, tachycardia, palpitation, heart block, stroke, MI

Central nervous system: Headache, exacerbation of psychosis, confusion, delirium, hallucinations, nervousness, restlessness, delusions, agitation, insomnia, nightmares, anxiety, seizure, drowsiness

Dermatologic: Photosensitivity, rash, petechiae, itching

Endocrine & metabolic: Sexual dysfunction, breast enlargement, galactorrhea, SIADH

Gastrointestinal: Xerostomia, constipation, increased appetite, nausea, unpleasant taste, weight gain, diarrhea, heartburn, vomiting, anorexia, trouble with gums, decreased lower esophageal sphincter tone may cause GE reflux

Genitourinary: Difficult urination, urinary retention, testicular edema

Hematologic: Agranulocytosis, eosinophilia, purpura, thrombocytopenia

Hepatic: Cholestatic jaundice, increased liver enzymes

Neuromuscular & skeletal: Tremors, numbness, tingling, paresthesia, incoordination, ataxia, peripheral neuropathy, extrapyramidal symptoms

Ocular: Blurred vision, eye pain, disturbances in accommodation, mydriasis, increased intraocular pressure

Otic: Tinnitus

Miscellaneous: Allergic reactions

Overdosage/Toxicology Symptoms include agitation, confusion, hallucinations, urinary retention, hypothermia, hypotension, tachycardia, and cardiac arrhythmias. Following initiation of essential overdose management, toxic symptoms should be treated. Sodium bicarbonate is indicated when the QRS interval is >0.10 seconds or the QT_c >0.42 seconds. Ventricular arrhythmias and ECG changes (QRS widening) often respond to systemic alkalinization (sodium bicarbonate 0.5-2 mEq/kg I.V.). Arrhythmias unresponsive to this therapy may respond to lidocaine 1 mg/kg I.V. followed by a titrated infusion. Physostigmine (1-2 mg slow I.V. for adults or 0.5 mg slow I.V. for children) may be indicated in reversing life-threatening cardiac arrhythmias. Seizures usually respond to diazepam I.V. boluses (5-10 mg for adults up to 30 mg or 0.25-0.4 mg/kg/dose for children up to 10 mg/dose). If seizures are unresponsive or recur, phenytoin or phenobarbital may be required.

Drug Interactions

Cytochrome P450 Effect: Substrate (major) of CYP2C19, 2D6, 3A4

Increased Effect/Toxicity: Pressor response to I.V. epinephrine, norepinephrine, and phenylephrine may be enhanced in patients receiving TCAs (**Note:** Effect is unlikely with epinephrine or levonordefrin dosages typically administered as infiltration in combination with local anesthetics). Trimipramine increases the effects of amphetamines, anticholinergics, other CNS depressants (sedatives, hypnotics, or ethanol), chlorpropamide, tolazamide, and warfarin. When used with MAO inhibitors, hyperpyrexia, hypertension, tachycardia, confusion, seizures, and **deaths have been reported** (serotonin syndrome). Serotonin syndrome has also been reported with ritonavir (rare).

CYP2C19 inhibitors may increase the levels/effects of trimipramine; example inhibitors include delavirdine, fluconazole, fluvoxamine, gemfibrozil, isoniazid, omeprazole, and ticlopidine. CYP2D6 inhibitors may increase the levels/effects of trimipramine; example inhibitors include chlorpromazine, delavirdine, fluoxetine, miconazole, paroxetine, pergolide, quinidine, quinine, ritonavir, and ropinirole. CYP3A4 inhibitors may increase the levels/effects of trimipramine; example inhibitors include azole antifungals, clarithromycin, diclofenac, doxycycline, erythromycin, imatinib, isoniazid, nefazodone, nicardipine, propofol, protease inhibitors, quinidine, telithromycin, and verapamil. Use of lithium with a TCA may increase the risk for neurotoxicity. Phenothiazines may increase concentration of some TCAs and TCAs may increase concentration of phenothiazines. Combined use of beta-agonists or drugs which prolong QT_c (including quinidine, procainamide, disopyramide, cisapride, sparfloxacin, gatifloxacin, moxifloxacin) with TCAs may predispose patients to cardiac arrhythmias.

Decreased Effect: CYP2C19 inducers may decrease the levels/effects of trimipramine; example inducers include aminoglutethimide, carbamazepine, phenytoin, and rifampin. Trimipramine inhibits the antihypertensive response to bethanidine, clonidine, debrisoquin, guanadrel, guanethidine, guanabenz, and guanfacine. Cholestyramine and colestipol may bind TCAs and reduce their absorption; monitor for altered response. CYP3A4 inducers may decrease the levels/effects of trimipramine; example inducers include aminoglutethimide, carbamazepine, nafcillin, nevirapine, phenobarbital, phenytoin, and rifamycins.

Ethanol/Nutrition/Herb Interactions

Ethanol: Avoid ethanol (may increase CNS depression).

Food: Grapefruit juice may inhibit the metabolism of some TCAs and clinical toxicity may result.

Herb/Nutraceutical: Avoid valerian, St John's wort, SAMe, kava kava (may increase risk of serotonin syndrome and/or excessive sedation).

Stability Solutions stable at a pH of 4-5. Turns yellowish or reddish on exposure to light. Slight discoloration does not affect potency; marked discoloration is associated with loss of potency. Capsules stable for 3 years following date of manufacture.

Mechanism of Action Increases the synaptic concentration of serotonin and/or norepinephrine in the central nervous system by inhibition of their reuptake by the presynaptic neuronal membrane

Pharmacodynamics/Kinetics
Distribution: V_d: 17-48 L/kg
Protein binding: 95%; free drug: 3% to 7%
Metabolism: Hepatic; significant first-pass effect
Bioavailability: 18% to 63%
Half-life elimination: 16-40 hours
Excretion: Urine

Dosage Oral:
Adults: 50-150 mg/day as a single bedtime dose up to a maximum of 200 mg/day outpatient and 300 mg/day inpatient
Elderly: Adequate studies have not been done in the elderly. In general, dosing should be cautious, starting at the lower end of dosing range.

Monitoring Parameters Blood pressure and pulse rate prior to and during initial therapy; evaluate mental status; monitor weight; ECG in older adults

Additional Information May cause alterations in bleeding time.

Dosage Forms Capsule: 25 mg, 50 mg, 100 mg

♦ **Trimipramine Maleate** *see Trimipramine on page 1747*
♦ **Tri-Nasal®** *see Triamcinolone on page 1734*
♦ **Trinasal®** (Can) *see Triamcinolone on page 1734*
♦ **TriNessa™** *see Ethinyl Estradiol and Norgestimate on page 660*
♦ **Trinipatch® 0.2** (Can) *see Nitroglycerin on page 1234*
♦ **Trinipatch® 0.4** (Can) *see Nitroglycerin on page 1234*
♦ **Trinipatch® 0.6** (Can) *see Nitroglycerin on page 1234*
♦ **Tri-Norinyl®** *see Ethinyl Estradiol and Norethindrone on page 655*
♦ **Triostat®** *see Liothyronine on page 1020*
♦ **Tripedia®** *see Diphtheria, Tetanus Toxoids, and Acellular Pertussis Vaccine on page 521*
♦ **Triphasil®** *see Ethinyl Estradiol and Levonorgestrel on page 653*
♦ **Triple Antibiotic** *see Bacitracin, Neomycin, and Polymyxin B on page 192*
♦ **Tri-Previfem™** *see Ethinyl Estradiol and Norgestimate on page 660*

Triprolidine and Pseudoephedrine (trye PROE li deen & soo doe e FED rin)

U.S. Brand Names Actifed® Cold and Allergy [OTC] [DSC]; Allerfrim® [OTC]; Aprodine® [OTC]; Genac® [OTC]; Silafed® [OTC]; Sudafed® Maximum Strength Sinus Nighttime [OTC] [DSC]; Tri-Sudo® [OTC] [DSC]; Zymine®-D

Canadian Brand Names Actifed®

Index Terms Pseudoephedrine and Triprolidine

Pharmacologic Category Alpha/Beta Agonist; Antihistamine

Use Temporary relief of nasal congestion, decongest sinus openings, running nose, sneezing, itching of nose or throat and itchy, watery eyes due to common cold, hay fever, or other upper respiratory allergies

Pregnancy Risk Factor C

Medication Safety Issues
Sound-alike/look-alike issues:
Aprodine® may be confused with Aphrodyne®

Dosage Oral:
Liquid (Zymine®-D):
Children:
2-4 years: 1.25 mL every 4-6 hours (maximum pseudoephedrine: 60 mg/24 hours)
4-6 years: 2.5 mL every 4-6 hours (maximum pseudoephedrine: 60 mg/24 hours)
6-12 years: 2.5-5 mL every 4-6 hours (maximum pseudoephedrine: 120 mg/24 hours)
Children ≥12 years and Adults: 5-10 mL every 4-6 hours (maximum pseudoephedrine: 240 mg/24 hours)
Syrup (Allerfrim, Aprodine):
Children 6-12 years: 5 mL every 4-6 hours; do not exceed 4 doses in 24 hours
Children >12 years and Adults: 10 mL every 4-6 hours; do not exceed 4 doses in 24 hours
Tablet (Aprodine):
Children 6-12 years: ½ tablet every 4-6 hours; do not exceed 4 doses in 24 hours
Children >12 years and Adults: One tablet every 4-6 hours; do not exceed 4 doses in 24 hours

Additional Information Complete prescribing information for this medication should be consulted for additional detail.

Dosage Forms [DSC] = Discontinued product
Liquid:
Zymine®-D: Triprolidine hydrochloride 1.25 mg and pseudoephedrine hydrochloride 45 mg per 5 mL (480 mL)
Syrup: Triprolidine hydrochloride 1.25 mg and pseudoephedrine hydrochloride 30 mg per 5 mL (120 mL)
Allerfrim®: Triprolidine hydrochloride 1.25 mg and pseudoephedrine hydrochloride 30 mg per 5 mL (120 mL, 480 mL) [contains sodium benzoate]
Aprodine®: Triprolidine hydrochloride 1.25 mg and pseudoephedrine hydrochloride 30 mg per 5 mL (120 mL)
Silafed®: Triprolidine hydrochloride 1.25 mg and pseudoephedrine hydrochloride 30 mg per 5 mL (120 mL, 240 mL)
Tablet:
Actifed® Cold and Allergy [DSC], Allerfrim® [DSC], Aprodine®, Genac®, Sudafed® Maximum Strength Sinus Nighttime, Tri-Sudo® [DSC]: Triprolidine hydrochloride 2.5 mg and pseudoephedrine hydrochloride 60 mg

♦ **Triprolidine, Codeine, and Pseudoephedrine** *see* Triprolidine, Pseudoephedrine, and Codeine *on page 1750*

Triprolidine, Pseudoephedrine, and Codeine
(trye PROE li deen, soo doe e FED rin, & KOE deen)

U.S. Brand Names Triacin-C® [DSC]

Canadian Brand Names CoActifed®; Covan®; ratio-Cotridin

Index Terms Codeine, Pseudoephedrine, and Triprolidine; Codeine, Triprolidine, and Pseudoephedrine; Pseudoephedrine, Codeine, and Triprolidine; Pseudoephedrine, Triprolidine, and Codeine; Triprolidine, Codeine, and Pseudoephedrine

Pharmacologic Category Antihistamine/Decongestant/Antitussive

Use Symptomatic relief of upper respiratory symptoms and cough

Restrictions C-V (CDSA-I)

Pregnancy Risk Factor C

Medication Safety Issues
Sound-alike/look-alike issues:
Triacin-C® may be confused with triacetin

Dosage Oral:
Children:
2-6 years: 2.5 mL 4 times/day
7-12 years: 5 mL 4 times/day **or** ½ tablet 4 times/day
Children >12 years and Adults: 10 mL 4 times/day **or** 1 tablet 4 times/day

Additional Information Complete prescribing information for this medication should be consulted for additional detail.

Dosage Forms
Syrup:
Triprolidine hydrochloride 1.25 mg, pseudoephedrine hydrochloride 30 mg, and codeine phosphate 10 mg per 5 mL [contains alcohol 4.3%]
CoActifed®, CoVan®, ratio-Cotridin: Triprolidine hydrochloride 2 mg, pseudoephedrine hydrochloride 30 mg, and codeine phosphate 10 mg per 5 mL [available in Canada; not available in U.S.]
Tablet (CoActifed®): Triprolidine hydrochloride 4 mg, pseudoephedrine hydrochloride 60 mg, and codeine phosphate 20 mg (50s) [available in Canada; not available in U.S.]

♦ **TripTone® [OTC] [DSC]** *see* DimenhyDRINATE *on page 511*
♦ **Triptoraline** *see* Triptorelin *on page 1750*

Triptorelin (trip toe REL in)

U.S. Brand Names Trelstar™ Depot; Trelstar™ LA

Canadian Brand Names Trelstar™; Trelstar™ Depot; Trelstar™ LA

Index Terms AY-25650; CL-118,532; D-Trp(6)-LHRH; Triptoraline; Triptorelin Pamoate; Tryptoreline

Pharmacologic Category Gonadotropin Releasing Hormone Agonist

Use Palliative treatment of advanced prostate cancer as an alternative to orchiectomy or estrogen administration

Unlabeled/Investigational Use Treatment of endometriosis, growth hormone deficiency, hyperandrogenism, *in vitro* fertilization, ovarian carcinoma, pancreatic carcinoma, precocious puberty, uterine leiomyomata

Pregnancy Risk Factor X

Pregnancy Implications Contraindicated in women who are or may become pregnant.

Lactation Excretion in breast milk unknown/contraindicated

Contraindications Hypersensitivity to triptorelin or any component of the formulation, other LHRH agonists or LHRH; pregnancy

Warnings/Precautions Hazardous agent - use appropriate precautions for handling and disposal. Transient increases in testosterone can lead to worsening symptoms (bone pain, hematuria, bladder outlet obstruction) of prostate cancer during the first few weeks of therapy. Cases of spinal cord compression have been reported with LHRH agonists. Hypersensitivity reactions including angioedema and anaphylaxis have rarely occurred. Rare cases of pituitary apoplexy (frequently secondary to pituitary adenoma) have been observed with leuprolide administration (onset from 1 hour to usually <2 weeks); may present as sudden headache, vomiting, visual or mental status changes, and infrequently cardiovascular collapse; immediate medical attention required. Safety and efficacy not established in pediatric population.

Adverse Reactions As reported with Trelstar™ Depot and Trelstar™ LA; frequency of effect may vary by product:

>10%:
Central nervous system: Headache (30% to 50%)
Endocrine & metabolic: Hot flashes (95% to 100%), glucose increased
Hematologic: Hemoglobin decreased, RBC count decreased
Hepatic: Alkaline phosphatase increased, ALT increased, AST increased
Neuromuscular & skeletal: Skeletal pain (12% to 13%)
Renal: BUN increased

1% to 10%:
Cardiovascular: Leg edema (6%), hypertension (4%), chest pain (2%), peripheral edema (1%)
Central nervous system: Dizziness (1% to 3%), pain (2% to 3%), emotional lability (1%), fatigue (2%), insomnia (2%)
Dermatologic: Rash (2%), pruritus (1%)
Endocrine & metabolic: Alkaline phosphatase increased (2%), breast pain (2%), gynecomastia (2%), libido decreased (2%), tumor flare (8%)
Gastrointestinal: Nausea (3%), anorexia (2%), constipation (2%), dyspepsia (2%), vomiting (2%), abdominal pain (1%), diarrhea (1%)
Genitourinary: Dysuria (5%), impotence (2% to 7%), urinary retention (1%), urinary tract infection (1%)
Hematologic: Anemia (1%)
Local: Injection site pain (4%)
Neuromuscular & skeletal: Leg pain (2% to 5%), back pain (3%), arthralgia (2%), leg cramps (2%), myalgia (1%), weakness (1%)
Ocular: Conjunctivitis (1%), eye pain (1%)
Respiratory: Cough (2%), dyspnea (1%), pharyngitis (1%)
Postmarketing and/or case reports (limited to important or life-threatening): Anaphylaxis, angioedema, hypersensitivity reactions, pituitary apoplexy, renal dysfunction, spinal cord compression

Overdosage/Toxicology Accidental or intentional overdose unlikely. If it were to occur, supportive and symptomatic treatment would be indicated.

Drug Interactions
Increased Effect/Toxicity: Not studied. Hyperprolactinemic drugs (dopamine antagonists such as antipsychotics, and metoclopramide) are contraindicated.
Decreased Effect: Not studied. Hyperprolactinemic drugs (dopamine antagonists such as antipsychotics, and metoclopramide) are contraindicated.

Stability
Trelstar™ Depot: Store at 15°C to 30°C (59°F to 86°F).
Trelstar™ LA: Store at 20°C to 25°C (68°F to 77°F).

Reconstitution: Reconstitute with 2 mL sterile water for injection. Shake well to obtain a uniform suspension.
Debioclip™: Follow manufacturer's instructions for mixing prior to use.

Mechanism of Action Causes suppression of ovarian and testicular steroidogenesis due to decreased levels of LH and FSH with subsequent decrease in testosterone (male) and estrogen (female) levels. After chronic and continuous administration, usually 2-4 weeks after initiation, a sustained decrease in LH and FSH secretion occurs.

Pharmacodynamics/Kinetics
Absorption: Oral: Not active
Distribution: V_d: 30-33 L
Protein binding: None
Metabolism: Unknown; unlikely to involve CYP; no known metabolites
Half-life elimination: 2.8 ± 1.2 hours
Moderate to severe renal impairment: 6.5-7.7 hours
Hepatic impairment: 7.6 hours
Time to peak: 1-3 hours
Excretion: Urine (42% as intact peptide); hepatic

Dosage I.M.: Adults: Prostate cancer:
Trelstar™ Depot: 3.75 mg once every 28 days
Trelstar™ LA: 11.25 mg once every 84 days
Dosage adjustment in renal/hepatic impairment: Although this drug is excreted renally, no guidelines for adjustments are available.

Administration Administer by I.M. injection into the buttock; alternate injection sites.

Monitoring Parameters Serum testosterone levels, prostate-specific antigen

Test Interactions Pituitary-gonadal function may be suppressed with chronic administration and for up to 8 weeks after triptorelin therapy has been discontinued.

Dosage Forms Injection, powder for reconstitution, as pamoate [also available packaged with Debioclip™ (prefilled syringe containing sterile water)]:
Trelstar™ Depot: 3.75 mg
Trelstar™ LA: 11.25 mg

♦ **Triptorelin Pamoate** *see* Triptorelin *on page 1750*
♦ **Triquilar® (Can)** *see* Ethinyl Estradiol and Levonorgestrel *on page 653*
♦ **Tris Buffer** *see* Tromethamine *on page 1752*
♦ **Trisenox®** *see* Arsenic Trioxide *on page 154*
♦ **Tris(hydroxymethyl)aminomethane** *see* Tromethamine *on page 1752*
♦ **Tri-Sprintec™** *see* Ethinyl Estradiol and Norgestimate *on page 660*
♦ **Tri-Sudo® [OTC] [DSC]** *see* Triprolidine and Pseudoephedrine *on page 1749*
♦ **Trivagizole-3® (Can)** *see* Clotrimazole *on page 404*
♦ **Trivalent Inactivated Influenza Vaccine (TIV)** *see* Influenza Virus Vaccine *on page 906*
♦ **Tri-Vent™ DM** *see* Guaifenesin, Pseudoephedrine, and Dextromethorphan *on page 821*
♦ **Tri-Vent™ DPC** *see* Chlorpheniramine, Phenylephrine, and Dextromethorphan *on page 352*
♦ **Tri-Vent™ HC** *see* Hydrocodone, Carbinoxamine, and Pseudoephedrine *on page 851*
♦ **Trivora®** *see* Ethinyl Estradiol and Levonorgestrel *on page 653*
♦ **Trizivir®** *see* Abacavir, Lamivudine, and Zidovudine *on page 19*
♦ **Trobicin® [DSC]** *see* Spectinomycin *on page 1595*
♦ **Trocaine® [OTC]** *see* Benzocaine *on page 204*
♦ **Trombovar® (Can)** *see* Sodium Tetradecyl *on page 1583*

Tromethamine (troe METH a meen)

U.S. Brand Names THAM®
Index Terms Tris Buffer; Tris(hydroxymethyl)aminomethane
Pharmacologic Category Alkalinizing Agent, Parenteral
Use Correction of metabolic acidosis associated with cardiac bypass surgery or cardiac arrest; to correct excess acidity of stored blood that is preserved with acid citrate dextrose (ACD); indicated in infants needing alkalinization after receiving maximum sodium bicarbonate (8-10 mEq/kg/24 hours)
Pregnancy Risk Factor C
Pregnancy Implications Animal studies have not been conducted. There are no adequate and well-controlled studies in pregnant women. Use only if potential benefit outweighs possible risk to the fetus.
Lactation Excretion in breast milk unknown/use caution
Medication Safety Issues
Sound-alike/look-alike issues:
Tromethamine may be confused with TrophAmine®
Contraindications Hypersensitivity to tromethamine or any component of the formulation; uremia or anuria; chronic respiratory acidosis (neonates); salicylate intoxication (neonates)
Warnings/Precautions Reduce dose and monitor pH carefully in renal impairment; drug should not be given for a period of longer than 24 hours unless for a life-threatening situation. May cause respiratory depression. May cause hypoglycemia. Avoid extravasation.
Adverse Reactions Frequency not defined.
Cardiovascular: Hypervolemia, venospasm
Endocrine and Metabolic: Hyperkalemia, hypoglycemia (usually doses >500 mg/kg administered over <1 hour)
Hepatic: Hepatic necrosis (resulted during delivery via umbilical venous catheter)
Local: Necrosis with extravasation, phlebitis, tissue irritation
Respiratory: Apnea, pulmonary edema, respiratory depression
Overdosage/Toxicology Symptoms of overdose include metabolic alkalosis, hyper-/hypokalemia, respiratory depression, hypoglycemia; supportive therapy is required to correct electrolyte, osmolality, and abnormalities
Stability Store at 20°C to 25°C (68°F to 77°F); protect from freezing
Mechanism of Action Acts as a proton acceptor, which combines with hydrogen ions, liberating bicarbonate buffer, to correct acidosis. It buffers both metabolic and respiratory acids, limiting carbon dioxide generation. Also an osmotic diuretic.
Pharmacodynamics/Kinetics
Distribution: Distributes quickly into extracellular space; at steady state distributes into a volume slightly greater than total body water; penetrates slowly intracellularly
Half-life elimination: 5.6 hours
Excretion: Urine (>75%) within 8 hours
Dosage
Neonates and Infants: Metabolic acidosis associated with RDS: Initial: Approximately 1 mL/kg for each pH unit below 7.4; additional doses determined by changes in PaO_2, pH, and pCO_2; **Note:** Although THAM® solution does not raise pCO_2 when treating metabolic acidosis with concurrent respiratory acidosis, bicarbonate may be preferred because the osmotic effects of THAM® are greater.

Adults: Dose depends on buffer base deficit; when deficit is known: tromethamine (mL of 0.3 M solution) = body weight (kg) x base deficit (mEq/L) x 1.1
Metabolic acidosis with cardiac arrest:
I.V.: 3.6-10.8 g (111-333 mL); additional amounts may be required to control acidosis after arrest reversed
Open chest: Intraventricular: 2-6 g (62-185 mL). **Note:** Do not inject into cardiac muscle
Acidosis associated with cardiac bypass surgery: Average dose: 9 mL/kg (2.7 mEq/kg); 500 mL is adequate for most adults; maximum dose: 500 mg/kg in ≤1 hour
Excess acidity of acid citrate dextrose (ACD) blood in coronary artery surgery: 15-77 mL of 0.3 molar solution added to each 500 mL of blood

Dosing comments in renal impairment: Use with caution; monitor for toxicity
Administration Maximum concentration: 0.3 molar; infuse slowly over at least 1 hour; to avoid glucose or potassium changes, should not exceed 16.5 mL/kg in 1 hour
Monitoring Parameters Serum electrolytes (especially potassium, blood glucose); renal function, arterial blood gases, ECG monitoring, fluid status, ventilation rate
Check infusion site frequently during administration.
Reference Range Blood pH (physiologic): 7.38-7.42
Additional Information 1 mM = 120 mg = 3.3 mL = 1 mEq of THAM®
Dosage Forms
Injection, solution:
THAM®: 18 g [0.3 molar] (500 mL)

♦ Tronolane® **Suppository [OTC]** see Phenylephrine on page 1358
♦ Tropicacyl® see Tropicamide on page 1752

Tropicamide (troe PIK a mide)

U.S. Brand Names Mydral™; Mydriacyl®; Tropicacyl®
Canadian Brand Names Diotrope®; Mydriacyl®
Index Terms Bistropamide
Pharmacologic Category Ophthalmic Agent, Mydriatic
Additional Appendix Information
Cycloplegic Mydriatics on page 1882

Use Short-acting mydriatic used in diagnostic procedures; as well as preoperatively and post-operatively; treatment of some cases of acute iritis, iridocyclitis, and keratitis

Pregnancy Risk Factor C

Dosage Ophthalmic: Children and Adults (individuals with heavily pigmented eyes may require larger doses):

Cycloplegia: Instill 1-2 drops (1%); may repeat in 5 minutes
Exam must be performed within 30 minutes after the repeat dose; if the patient is not examined within 20-30 minutes, instill an additional drop

Mydriasis: Instill 1-2 drops (0.5%) 15-20 minutes before exam; may repeat every 30 minutes as needed

Additional Information Complete prescribing information for this medication should be consulted for additional detail.

Dosage Forms

Solution, ophthalmic: 0.5% (15 mL); 1% (2 mL, 15 mL) [contains benzalkonium chloride]
Mydriacyl®: 1% (3 mL, 15 mL) [contains benzalkonium chloride]
Mydral™, Tropicacyl®: 0.5% (15 mL); 1% (15 mL) [contains benzalkonium chloride]

♦ **Trosec (Can)** *see* Trospium *on page 1753*

Trospium (TROSE pee urn)

U.S. Brand Names Sanctura®

Canadian Brand Names Trosec

Index Terms Trospium Chloride

Pharmacologic Category Anticholinergic Agent

Use Treatment of overactive bladder with symptoms of urgency, incontinence, and urinary frequency

Pregnancy Risk Factor C

Pregnancy Implications Maternal toxicity and decreased fetal survival was seen in animal studies when given 10 times the expected clinical exposure. There are no adequate or well-controlled studies in pregnant women; use only if clearly needed.

Lactation Excretion in breast milk unknown/use caution

Contraindications Hypersensitivity to trospium or any component of the formulation; urinary retention; gastric retention; uncontrolled narrow-angle glaucoma

Warnings/Precautions Use with caution in patients with bladder flow obstruction, may increase the risk of urinary retention. Use with caution in patients with gastrointestinal obstructive disorders (eg, pyloric stenosis); may increase the risk of gastric retention. Use caution in patients with decreased GI motility (eg, myasthenia gravis, ulcerative colitis). Use with caution in renal dysfunction; dosage adjustment is required. Active tubular secretion (ATS) is a route of elimination; use caution with other medications that are eliminated by ATS (eg, procainamide, pancuronium, vancomycin, morphine). Use with extreme caution in patients with controlled (treated) narrow-angle glaucoma. Use caution in patients with moderate-to-severe hepatic dysfunction. Use caution in Alzheimer's patients. Use caution in the elderly (≥75 years); increased anticholinergic side effects are seen. Safety and efficacy in pediatric patients have not been established.

Adverse Reactions

>10%: Gastrointestinal: Xerostomia (20%)

1% to 10%:
Cardiovascular: Tachycardia, heart rate increase
Central nervous system: Headache (4%), fatigue (2%)
Dermatologic: Dry skin
Gastrointestinal: Constipation (10%), abdominal pain (2%), dyspepsia (1%), flatulence (1%), abdominal distention, vomiting, dysgeusia
Genitourinary: Urinary retention (1%)
Ocular: Dry eyes (1%), blurred vision

<1% (Limited to important or life-threatening): Anaphylaxis, angioneurotic edema, chest pain, delirium, gastritis, hallucinations, hypertensive crisis, palpitation, rhabdomyolysis, Stevens-Johnson syndrome, supraventricular tachycardia, syncope, T-wave inversion

Overdosage/Toxicology ECG monitoring is recommended. Treatment is symptom-directed and supportive.

Drug Interactions

Increased Effect/Toxicity: Trospium anticholinergic effects may be increased when administered with other anticholinergics and pramlintide.

Decreased Effect: Trospium anticholinergic effect may be decreased when administered with acetylcholinesterase inhibitors (central).

Ethanol/Nutrition/Herb Interactions

Ethanol: Avoid use.
Food: Administration with a fatty meal reduced absorption 70% to 80%.

Stability Store at 20°C to 25°C (68°F to 77°F).

Mechanism of Action Trospium antagonizes the effects of acetylcholine on muscarinic receptors in cholinergically innervated organs. It reduces the smooth muscle tone of the bladder.

Pharmacodynamics/Kinetics

Absorption: <10%; decreased with food
Distribution: V_d: 395 L, primarily in plasma
Protein binding: 50% to 85% *in vitro*
Metabolism: Hypothesized to be via esterase hydrolysis and conjugation; forms metabolites
Bioavailability: ~10%
Half-life elimination: 20 hours; severe renal insufficiency (Cl_{cr} <30 mL/minute): ~33 hours
Time to peak, plasma: 5-6 hours
Excretion: Feces (85%); urine (~6%; mostly as unchanged drug) primarily via active tubular secretion

(Continued)

Trospium *(Continued)*

Dosage Oral:

Adults: 20 mg twice daily

Elderly ≥75 years: Consider initial dose of 20 mg once daily (based on tolerability) at bedtime

Dosage adjustment in renal impairment: Cl$_{cr}$ ≤30 mL/minute: 20 mg once daily at bedtime

Dietary Considerations Give 1 hour prior to meals or on an empty stomach. Avoid alcohol.

Administration Administer 1 hour before meals or on an empty stomach.

Dosage Forms

Tablet, as chloride:

Sanctura™: 20 mg

♦ **Trospium Chloride** *see Trospium on page 1753*

♦ **Trusopt®** *see Dorzolamide on page 542*

♦ **Truvada®** *see Emtricitabine and Tenofovir on page 578*

Trypsin, Balsam Peru, and Castor Oil

(TRIP sin, BAL sam pe RUE, & KAS tor oyl)

U.S. Brand Names Granulex®; Optase™; Xenaderm™

Index Terms Balsam Peru, Trypsin, and Castor Oil; Castor Oil, Trypsin, and Balsam Peru

Pharmacologic Category Protectant, Topical

Use Treatment of decubitus ulcers, varicose ulcers, debridement of eschar, dehiscent wounds and sunburn; promote wound healing; reduce odor from necrotic wounds

Medication Safety Issues

Sound-alike/look-alike issues:

Granulex® may be confused with Regranex®

Dosage Topical: Apply a minimum of twice daily or as often as necessary

Additional Information Complete prescribing information for this medication should be consulted for additional detail.

Dosage Forms

Aerosol, topical: Trypsin 0.12 mg, balsam Peru 87 mg, and castor oil 788 mg per gram (120 g)

Granulex®: Trypsin 0.12 mg, balsam Peru 87 mg, and castor oil 788 mg per gram (60 g, 120 g)

Gel, topical:

Optase™: Trypsin 0.12 mg, balsam Peru 87 mg, and castor oil 788 mg per gram (95 g)

Ointment, topical:

Xenaderm™: Trypsin 90 USP units, balsam Peru 87 mg, and castor oil 788 mg per gram (30 g, 60 g)

♦ **Tryptoreline** *see Triptorelin on page 1750*

♦ **TSH** *see Thyrotropin Alpha on page 1677*

♦ **TSPA** *see Thiotepa on page 1674*

♦ **TST** *see Tuberculin Tests on page 1754*

♦ **T-Stat® [DSC]** *see Erythromycin on page 609*

♦ **Tuberculin Purified Protein Derivative** *see Tuberculin Tests on page 1754*

♦ **Tuberculin Skin Test** *see Tuberculin Tests on page 1754*

Tuberculin Tests (too BER kyoo lin tests)

U.S. Brand Names Aplisol®; Tubersol®

Index Terms Mantoux; PPD; TB Skin Test; TST; Tuberculin Purified Protein Derivative; Tuberculin Skin Test

Pharmacologic Category Diagnostic Agent

Use Skin test in diagnosis of tuberculosis

Pregnancy Risk Factor C

Pregnancy Implications Reproduction studies have not been conducted. Pregnancy is not a contraindication to testing.

Medication Safety Issues

Sound-alike/look-alike issues:

Aplisol® may be confused with Anusol®, A.P.L.®, Aplitest®, Atropisol®

Tuberculin products may be confused with tetanus toxoid products and influenza virus vaccine. Medication errors have occurred when tuberculin skin tests (PPD) have been inadvertently administered instead of tetanus toxoid products and influenza virus vaccine. These products are refrigerated and often stored in close proximity to each other.

Administration issues:

Tuberculin products may be confused with tetanus toxoid products and influenza virus vaccine. Medication errors have occurred when tuberculin skin tests (PPD) have been inadvertently administered instead of tetanus toxoid products and influenza virus vaccine. These products are refrigerated and often stored in close proximity to each other.

Contraindications Hypersensitivity to tuberculin purified protein derivative (PPD) or any component of the formulation; previous severe reaction to tuberculin PPD skin test (TST)

Warnings/Precautions Patients with a previous severe reaction to TST (vesiculation, ulceration, necrosis) at the injection site should not receive tuberculin PPD again. Tuberculous or viral infection, live virus vaccination, bacterial infections, malignancy, immunosuppressive agents, and conditions which impair immune response may cause a decreased response to test. Very young children may also have an absent or delayed response. For intradermal administration only; do not administer I.V. or SubQ. Epinephrine (1:1000) should be available to treat possible allergic reactions.

Adverse Reactions Frequency not defined.

Dermatologic: Rash

Local: Injection site reactions: Erythematous reaction, necrosis, scarring, ulceration, vesiculation

Miscellaneous: Anaphylaxis

Drug Interactions

Decreased Effect: Reaction may be depressed or suppressed in patients receiving systemic corticosteroids, immunosuppressants, live viral vaccines.

Stability Aplisol®, Tubersol®: Store under refrigeration at 2°C to 8°C (36°F to 46°F); do not freeze. Protect from light. Opened vials should be discarded after 30 days.

Mechanism of Action Tuberculosis results in individuals becoming sensitized to certain antigenic components of the *M. tuberculosis* organism. Culture extracts called tuberculins are contained in tuberculin skin test preparations. Upon intracutaneous injection of these culture extracts, a classic delayed (cellular) hypersensitivity reaction occurs. This reaction is characteristic of a delayed course (peak occurs >24 hours after injection, induration of the skin secondary to cell infiltration, and occasional vesiculation and necrosis). Delayed hypersensitivity reactions to tuberculin may indicate infection with a variety of nontuberculosis mycobacteria, or vaccination with the live attenuated mycobacterial strain of *M. bovis* vaccine, BCG, in addition to previous natural infection with *M. tuberculosis*.

Pharmacodynamics/Kinetics

Onset of action: Delayed hypersensitivity reactions: 5-6 hours

Peak effect: 48-72 hours

Duration: Reactions subside over a few days

Dosage Children and Adults: Intradermal: 0.1 mL

Note: A two-step testing is recommended for healthcare workers when the TST is used as the baseline test. If the first test is negative, a second TST should be administered 1-3 weeks after the first test was read.

TST interpretation (CDC guidelines):

Baseline test: ≥10 mm is positive (either first or second step)

Serial testing without known exposure: Increase of ≥10 mm is positive

Known exposure:

≥5 mm is positive in patients with baseline of 0 mm

≥10 mm is positive in patients with negative baseline or previous screening result of ≥0mm

Read test at 48-72 hours following placement. Test results with 0 mm induration or measured induration less than the defined cutoff point are considered to signify absence of infection with *M. tuberculosis*. Test results should be documented in millimeters even if classified as negative.

Administration For intradermal administration only. Administer to upper third of forearm (palm up) ≥2 inches from elbow, wrist, or other injection site. If neither arm can be used, may administer to back of shoulder. Administer using inch ¼ to½ inch 27-gauge needle or finer tuberculin syringe. Should form wheal (6-10 mm in diameter) as liquid is injected which will remain ~10 minutes. Avoid pressure or bandage at injection site. Document date and time of injection, person placing TST, location of injection site and lot number of solution.

Monitoring Parameters Monitor for immediate hypersensitivity reactions for ~15 minutes following injection.

Dosage Forms

Injection, solution:

Aplisol®, Tubersol®: 5 TU/0.1 mL (1 mL, 5 mL) [contains polysorbate 80]

♦ **Tubersol®** *see* Tuberculin Tests *on page 1754*

♦ **Tucks® Anti-Itch [OTC]** *see* Hydrocortisone *on page 852*

♦ **Tuinal® [DSC]** *see* Amobarbital and Secobarbital *on page 108*

♦ **Tums® [OTC]** *see* Calcium Carbonate *on page 269*

♦ **Tums® E-X [OTC]** *see* Calcium Carbonate *on page 269*

♦ **Tums® Extra Strength Sugar Free [OTC]** *see* Calcium Carbonate *on page 269*

♦ **Tums® Smoothies™ [OTC]** *see* Calcium Carbonate *on page 269*

♦ **Tums® Ultra [OTC]** *see* Calcium Carbonate *on page 269*

♦ **Tusnel Pediatric®** *see* Guaifenesin, Pseudoephedrine, and Dextromethorphan *on page 821*

♦ **Tussafed® [DSC]** *see* Carbinoxamine, Pseudoephedrine, and Dextromethorphan *on page 291*

♦ **Tussend® Expectorant [DSC]** *see* Hydrocodone, Pseudoephedrine, and Guaifenesin *on page 852*

♦ **Tussigon®** *see* Hydrocodone and Homatropine *on page 850*

♦ **Tussin [OTC]** *see* Guaifenesin *on page 814*

♦ **Tussionex®** *see* Hydrocodone and Chlorpheniramine *on page 849*

♦ **Tussi-Organidin® NR** *see* Guaifenesin and Codeine *on page 815*

♦ **Tussi-Organidin® S-NR** *see* Guaifenesin and Codeine *on page 815*

♦ **Tusso-DF®** *see* Hydrocodone and Guaifenesin *on page 849*

♦ **TVP-1012** *see* Rasagiline *on page 1488*

♦ **Twelve Resin-K** *see* Cyanocobalamin *on page 425*

♦ **Twilite® [OTC]** *see* DiphenhydrAMINE *on page 515*

♦ **Twinject™** *see* Epinephrine *on page 589*

♦ **Twinrix®** *see* Hepatitis A Inactivated and Hepatitis B (Recombinant) Vaccine *on page 832*

♦ **Ty21a Vaccine** *see* Typhoid Vaccine *on page 1756*

♦ **Tycolene [OTC]** *see* Acetaminophen *on page 28*

♦ **Tycolene Maximum Strength [OTC]** *see* Acetaminophen *on page 28*

♦ **Tygacil™** *see* Tigecycline *on page 1685*

♦ **Tylenol® [OTC]** *see* Acetaminophen *on page 28*

♦ **Tylenol® (Can)** *see* Acetaminophen *on page 28*

♦ **Tylenol® 8 Hour [OTC]** *see* Acetaminophen *on page 28*

♦ **Tylenol® Allergy Complete [OTC] [DSC]** *see* Acetaminophen, Chlorpheniramine, and Pseudoephedrine *on page 35*

♦ **Tylenol® Allergy Sinus (Can)** *see* Acetaminophen, Chlorpheniramine, and Pseudoephedrine *on page 35*

♦ **Tylenol® Arthritis Pain [OTC]** *see* Acetaminophen *on page 28*

♦ **Tylenol® Children's [OTC]** *see* Acetaminophen *on page 28*

♦ **Tylenol® Children's with Flavor Creator [OTC]** *see* Acetaminophen *on page 28*

♦ **Tylenol® Children's Plus Cold Nighttime [OTC]** *see* Acetaminophen, Chlorpheniramine, and Pseudoephedrine *on page 35*

♦ **Tylenol® Cold Day Non-Drowsy [OTC]** *see* Acetaminophen, Dextromethorphan, and Pseudoephedrine *on page 35*

♦ **Tylenol® Cold Daytime (Can)** *see* Acetaminophen, Dextromethorphan, and Pseudoephedrine *on page 35*

♦ **Tylenol® Cold Daytime, Children's [OTC]** *see* Acetaminophen and Pseudoephedrine *on page 33*

♦ **Tylenol® Cold, Infants [OTC]** *see* Acetaminophen and Pseudoephedrine *on page 33*

♦ **Tylenol® Decongestant (Can)** *see* Acetaminophen and Pseudoephedrine *on page 33*

♦ **Tylenol Elixir with Codeine (Can)** *see* Acetaminophen and Codeine *on page 31*

♦ **Tylenol® Extra Strength [OTC]** *see* Acetaminophen *on page 28*

♦ **Tylenol® Flu Non-Drowsy Maximum Strength [OTC]** *see* Acetaminophen, Dextromethorphan, and Pseudoephedrine *on page 35*

♦ **Tylenol® Infants [OTC]** *see* Acetaminophen *on page 28*

♦ **Tylenol® Junior [OTC]** *see* Acetaminophen *on page 28*

♦ **Tylenol No. 1 (Can)** *see* Acetaminophen and Codeine *on page 31*

♦ **Tylenol No. 1 Forte (Can)** *see* Acetaminophen and Codeine *on page 31*

♦ **Tylenol No. 2 with Codeine (Can)** *see* Acetaminophen and Codeine *on page 31*

♦ **Tylenol No. 3 with Codeine (Can)** *see* Acetaminophen and Codeine *on page 31*

♦ **Tylenol No. 4 with Codeine (Can)** *see* Acetaminophen and Codeine *on page 31*

♦ **Tylenol® PM [OTC]** *see* Acetaminophen and Diphenhydramine *on page 31*

♦ **Tylenol® Severe Allergy [OTC]** *see* Acetaminophen and Diphenhydramine *on page 31*

♦ **Tylenol® Sinus (Can)** *see* Acetaminophen and Pseudoephedrine *on page 33*

♦ **Tylenol® Sinus Daytime [OTC]** *see* Acetaminophen and Pseudoephedrine *on page 33*

♦ **Tylenol® With Codeine** *see* Acetaminophen and Codeine *on page 31*

♦ **Tylox®** *see* Oxycodone and Acetaminophen *on page 1289*

♦ **Typhim Vi®** *see* Typhoid Vaccine *on page 1756*

Typhoid Vaccine (TYE foid vak SEEN)

U.S. Brand Names Typhim Vi®; Vivotif®

Index Terms Ty21a Vaccine; Typhoid Vaccine Live Oral Ty21a; Vi Vaccine

Pharmacologic Category Vaccine

Additional Appendix Information

Immunization Recommendations *on page 1929*

Use Active immunization against typhoid fever caused by *Salmonella typhi*

Not for routine vaccination. In the United States, use should be limited to:
— Travelers to areas with risk of exposure to *S. typhi*
— Persons with intimate exposure to a *S. typhi* carrier
— Laboratory technicians with exposure to *S. typhi*

Pregnancy Risk Factor C

Pregnancy Implications Reproduction studies have not been conducted. The manufacturer of the injection suggests delaying vaccination until the 2nd or 3rd trimester if possible. Untreated typhoid fever may lead to miscarriage or vertical intrauterine transmission causing neonatal typhoid (rare).

Lactation Excretion in breast milk unknown/use caution

Contraindications Hypersensitivity to any component of the vaccine. In addition, the oral vaccine is contraindicated with congenital or acquired immunodeficient state, acute febrile illness, acute GI illness

Warnings/Precautions Not all recipients of typhoid vaccine will be fully protected against typhoid fever. Travelers should take all necessary precautions to avoid contact or ingestion of potentially contaminated food or water sources. Should not be used to treat typhoid fever.

Injection: Administer at least 2 weeks prior to expected exposure. Vaccination may be deferred during acute infection or febrile illness. Immune response may be decreased in those receiving immunosuppressive therapy or are otherwise immunocompromised. Use caution with coagulation disorders (including thrombocytopenia) where intramuscular injections should not be used. Epinephrine 1:1000 should be readily available. Safety and efficacy have not been established in children <2 years of age.

Oral: Full immunization schedule should be completed at least 1 week prior to expected exposure. The complete immunization schedule must be followed to achieve optimum immune response. Vaccination may be deferred with persistent diarrhea or vomiting. Safety and efficacy have not been established in children <6 years of age.

Adverse Reactions All serious adverse reactions must be reported to the U.S. Department of Health and Human Services (DHHS) Vaccine Adverse Event Reporting System (VAERS) 1-800-822-7967.

Oral:
1% to 10%:
Central nervous system: Headache (5%), fever (3%)
Dermatologic: Rash (1%)
Gastrointestinal: Abdominal pain (6%), diarrhea (3%), nausea (6%), vomiting (2%)

Postmarketing and/or case reports: Anaphylactic reaction, demyelinating disease, myalgia, pain, RA, urticaria, sepsis, weakness

Injection:

>10%:

Central nervous system: Headache (16% to 20%), fever <100°F (3% to 11%), malaise (4% to 24%)

Local: Tenderness (97% to 98%), induration (5% to 15%), pain at injection site (27% to 41%)

1% to 10%:

Central nervous system: Fever ≥100°F (2%)

Gastrointestinal: Nausea (2% to 8%), vomiting (2%)

Local: Erythema at injection site (4% to 5%)

Neuromuscular & skeletal: Myalgia (3% to 7%)

Postmarketing and/or case reports: Abdominal pain, allergic reactions, arthralgia, cervical pain, diarrhea, dizziness, flu-like syndrome, Guillain-Barré syndrome, hypotension, injection site inflammation (including angioedema and urticaria), loss of consciousness, lymphadenopathy, malaise, perforated jejunum, rash, serum sickness, tremor, vasodilation, weakness

Drug Interactions

Increased Effect/Toxicity: Immunosuppressants may enhance the adverse/toxic effect of live vaccines; vaccinial infections may develop.

Decreased Effect: Antibiotics (systemic) may decrease the effect of oral live attenuated Ty21a vaccine (Vivotif®); delay vaccine administration for at least 24 hours after administration of these drugs. Mefloquine may decrease the effect of oral live attenuated Ty21a vaccine (Vivotif®); the CDC recommends delaying vaccine administration for at least 24 hours after administration of mefloquine (the manufacturer notes that no delay is needed). Proguanil may decrease the effect of oral live attenuated Ty21a vaccine (Vivotif®); separate dosing by at least 10 days. Immune globulins may diminish the therapeutic effect of live vaccines.

Ethanol/Nutrition/Herb Interactions Ethanol: Avoid alcohol within 2 hours of taking the capsule; may disrupt the enteric coating

Stability

Typhim Vi®: Store between 2°C to 8°C (35°F to 46°F); do not freeze.

Vivotif®: Store between 2°C to 8°C (35°F to 46°F).

Mechanism of Action Virulent strains of *Salmonella typhi* cause disease by penetrating the intestinal mucosa and entering the systemic circulation via the lymphatic vasculature. One possible mechanism of conferring immunity may be the provocation of a local immune response in the intestinal tract induced by oral ingesting of a live strain with subsequent aborted infection. The ability of *Salmonella typhi* to produce clinical disease (and to elicit an immune response) is dependent on the bacteria having a complete lipopolysaccharide. The live attenuate Ty21a strain lacks the enzyme UDP-4-galactose epimerase so that lipopolysaccharide is only synthesized under conditions that induce bacterial autolysis. Thus, the strain remains avirulent despite the production of sufficient lipopolysaccharide to evoke a protective immune response. Despite low levels of lipopolysaccharide synthesis, cells lyse before gaining a virulent phenotype due to the intracellular accumulation of metabolic intermediates.

Pharmacodynamics/Kinetics

Onset of action: Immunity to *Salmonella typhi*: Oral: ~1 week

Duration: Immunity: Oral: ~4-7 years; Parenteral: >17-21 months

Dosage Immunization:

Oral: Children ≥6 years and Adults:

Primary immunization: One capsule on alternate days (day 1, 3, 5, and 7) for a total of 4 doses; all doses should be complete at least 1 week prior to potential exposure

Booster immunization: Repeat full course of primary immunization every 5 years

I.M.: Children ≥2 years and Adults: 0.5 mL given at least 2 weeks prior to expected exposure

Reimmunization: 0.5 mL; optimal schedule has not been established; a single dose every 2 years is currently recommended for repeated or continued exposure

Administration Injection: Typhim Vi® may be given I.M. and is indicated for children ≥2 years of age; administer as a single 0.5 mL (25 mcg) injection in deltoid muscle. **Note:** For patients at risk of hemorrhage following intramuscular injection, the ACIP recommends "it should be administered intramuscularly if, in the opinion of the physician familiar with the patients bleeding risk, the vaccine can be administered with reasonable safety by this route. If the patient receives antihemophilia or other similar therapy, intramuscular vaccination can be scheduled shortly after such therapy is administered. A fine needle (23 gauge or smaller) can be used for the vaccination and firm pressure applied to the site (without rubbing) for at least 2 minutes. The patient should be instructed concerning the risk of hematoma from the injection."

Oral: Swallow capsule whole soon after placing into mouth; do not chew or open capsule. Capsule should be taken with a cold or lukewarm beverage (≤37°C/98.6°F). Take one hour prior to a meal. Avoid alcohol within 2 hours of administration.

Additional Information Federal law requires that the date of administration, the vaccine manufacturer, lot number of vaccine, and the administering person's name, title, and address be entered into the patient's permanent medical record.

Dosage Forms

Capsule, enteric coated:

Vivotif®: Viable *S. typhi* Ty21a 2-6 x 10^9 colony-forming units and nonviable *S. typhi* Ty21a 5-50 x 10^9 bacterial cells [contains lactose and sucrose]

Injection, solution:

Typhim Vi®: Purified Vi capsular polysaccharide 25 mcg/0.5 mL (0.5 mL, 10 mL) [derived from *S. typhi* Ty2 strain]

◆ **Typhoid Vaccine Live Oral Ty21a** see Typhoid Vaccine on page 1756

◆ **Tysabri®** see Natalizumab on page 1203

◆ **506U78** see Nelarabine on page 1207

- **U-90152S** *see* Delavirdine *on page 468*
- **UCB-P071** *see* Cetirizine *on page 334*
- **UK** *see* Urokinase *on page 1761*
- **UK-88,525** *see* Darifenacin *on page 455*
- **UK92480** *see* Sildenafil *on page 1564*
- **UK109496** *see* Voriconazole *on page 1797*
- **Ulcidine (Can)** *see* Famotidine *on page 683*
- **Ultane®** *see* Sevoflurane *on page 1561*
- **Ultiva®** *see* Remifentanil *on page 1493*
- **Ultracaps MT** *see* Pancrelipase *on page 1302*
- **Ultracet™** *see* Acetaminophen and Tramadol *on page 34*
- **Ultram®** *see* Tramadol *on page 1718*
- **Ultram® ER** *see* Tramadol *on page 1718*
- **Ultra Mide® [OTC]** *see* Urea *on page 1758*
- **UltraMide 25™ (Can)** *see* Urea *on page 1758*
- **Ultramop™ (Can)** *see* Methoxsalen *on page 1115*
- **Ultraprin [OTC]** *see* Ibuprofen *on page 873*
- **Ultraquin™ (Can)** *see* Hydroquinone *on page 859*
- **Ultrase®** *see* Pancrelipase *on page 1302*
- **Ultrase® MT** *see* Pancrelipase *on page 1302*
- **Ultravate®** *see* Halobetasol *on page 826*
- **Umecta®** *see* Urea *on page 1758*
- **Unasyn®** *see* Ampicillin and Sulbactam *on page 124*
- **Unidet® (Can)** *see* Tolterodine *on page 1705*
- **Unipen® (Can)** *see* Nafcillin *on page 1190*
- **Uniphyl®** *see* Theophylline Salts *on page 1664*
- **Uniretic®** *see* Moexipril and Hydrochlorothiazide *on page 1164*
- **Unisom® Maximum Strength SleepGels® [OTC]** *see* DiphenhydrAMINE *on page 515*
- **Unithroid®** *see* Levothyroxine *on page 1007*
- **Univasc®** *see* Moexipril *on page 1162*
- **Unna's Boot** *see* Zinc Gelatin *on page 1817*
- **Unna's Paste** *see* Zinc Gelatin *on page 1817*
- **Urasal® (Can)** *see* Methenamine *on page 1106*

Urea (yoor EE a)

U.S. Brand Names Amino-Cerv™; Aquacare® [OTC]; Aquaphilic With Carbamide [OTC]; Carmol® 10 [OTC]; Carmol® 20 [OTC]; Carmol® 40; Carmol® Deep Cleaning; Cerovel™; DPM™ [OTC]; Gormel® [OTC]; Keralac™; Keralac™ Nailstik; Lanaphilic® [OTC]; Nutraplus® [OTC]; Rea-Lo®; Ultra Mide® [OTC]; Umecta®; Ureacin® [OTC]; Vanamide™
Canadian Brand Names UltraMide 25™; Uremol®; Urisec®
Index Terms Carbamide
Pharmacologic Category Diuretic, Osmotic; Keratolytic Agent; Topical Skin Product
Use
Topical: Keratolytic agent to soften nails or skin; OTC: Moisturizer for dry, rough skin
Vaginal: Treatment of cervicitis
Pregnancy Risk Factor C
Dosage Adults:
Hyperkeratotic conditions, dry skin: Topical: Apply 1-3 times/day
Cervicitis: Vaginal: Insert 1 applicatorful in vagina at bedtime for 2-4 weeks
Additional Information Complete prescribing information for this medication should be consulted for additional detail.
Dosage Forms
Cream: 40% (30 g, 85 g, 199 g)
Aquacare®: 10% (75 g)
Carmol® 20: 20% (90 g)
Carmol® 40: 40% (30 g, 90 g, 210 g)
Cerovel™: 40% (133 g)
DPM™: 20% (118 g) [contains menthol and peppermint oil]
Gormel®: 20% (75 g, 120 g, 454 g, 2270 g)
Keralac™: 50% (142 g, 255 g) [contains lactic acid, vitamin E, and zinc]
Nutraplus®: 10% (90 g, 454 g)
Rea-Lo®: 30% (60 g, 240 g)
Ureacin®-20: 20% (120 g)
Vanamide™: 40% (85 g, 199 g)
Cream, vaginal (Amino-Cerv™): 8.34% (83.4 mg/g) (82.5 g)
Emulsion, topical (Umecta®): 40% (120 mL, 480 mL)
Gel: 40% (15 mL)
Carmol® 40: 40% (15 mL)
Cerovel™: 40% (25 mL)
Keralac™: 50% (18 mL) [contains lactic acid and zinc]
Lotion: 40% (240 mL)
Aquacare®: 10% (240 mL)
Carmol® 10: 10% (180 mL)
Carmol® 40: 40% (240 mL)
Cerovel™: 40% (325 mL)
Keralac™: 35% (207 mL, 325 mL) [contains lactic acid, vitamin E, and zinc]
Nutraplus®: 10% (240 mL, 480 mL)
Ultra Mide®: 25% (120 mL, 240 mL)

Ureacin®-10: 10% (240 mL)
Ointment:
Aquaphilic® with Carbamide: 10% (180 g, 480 g); 20% (480 g)
Keralac™: 50% (90 g)
Lanaphilic®: 10% (454 g); 20% (454 g)
Shampoo (Carmol® Deep Cleaning): 10% (240 mL)
Solution, topical (Keralac™ Nailstick): 50% (2.4 mL)
Suspension, topical (Umecta®): 40% (18 mL) [nail film with applicator], (300 mL)

Urea and Hydrocortisone (yoor EE a & hye droe KOR ti sone)

U.S. Brand Names Carmol-HC®
Canadian Brand Names Ti-U-Lac® H; Uremol® HC
Index Terms Hydrocortisone and Urea
Pharmacologic Category Corticosteroid, Topical
Use Inflammation of corticosteroid-responsive dermatoses
Pregnancy Risk Factor C
Dosage Apply thin film and rub in well 1-4 times/day. Therapy should be discontinued when control is achieved; if no improvement is seen, reassessment of diagnosis may be necessary.
Additional Information Complete prescribing information for this medication should be consulted for additional detail.
Dosage Forms Cream: Urea 10% and hydrocortisone acetate 1% (30 g) [in water soluble vanishing cream base]

♦ **Urea, Chlorophyllin, and Papain** see Chlorophyllin, Papain, and Urea on page 345
♦ **Ureacin® [OTC]** see Urea on page 1758
♦ **Urea Peroxide** see Carbamide Peroxide on page 287
♦ **Urecholine®** see Bethanechol on page 216
♦ **Urelle®** see Methenamine, Sodium Biphosphate, Phenyl Salicylate, Methylene Blue, and Hyoscyamine on page 1107
♦ **Uremol® (Can)** see Urea on page 1758
♦ **Uremol® HC (Can)** see Urea and Hydrocortisone on page 1759
♦ **Urex®** see Methenamine on page 1106
♦ **Urimar-T** see Methenamine, Sodium Biphosphate, Phenyl Salicylate, Methylene Blue, and Hyoscyamine on page 1107
♦ **Urisec® (Can)** see Urea on page 1758
♦ **Urispas®** see Flavoxate on page 710
♦ **Uristat® [OTC]** see Phenazopyridine on page 1351

Urofollitropin (yoor oh fol li TROE pin)

U.S. Brand Names Bravelle®
Canadian Brand Names Bravelle®; Fertinorm® H.P.
Index Terms Follicle-Stimulating Hormone, Human; FSH; hFSH
Pharmacologic Category Gonadotropin; Ovulation Stimulator
Use Ovulation induction in patients who previously received pituitary suppression; development of multiple follicles with Assisted Reproductive Technologies (ART)
Pregnancy Risk Factor X
Pregnancy Implications Ectopic pregnancy, congenital abnormalities, spontaneous abortion and multiple births have been reported. The incidence of congenital abnormality may be slightly higher after ART than with spontaneous conception; higher incidence may be related to parenteral characteristics (maternal age, sperm characteristics).
Lactation Excretion in breast milk unknown/not recommended
Contraindications Hypersensitivity to follitropins or any component of the formulation; high levels of FSH indicating primary ovarian failure; uncontrolled thyroid or adrenal dysfunction; the presence of any cause of infertility other than anovulation; presence of an organic intracranial lesion (eg, pituitary tumor); abnormal vaginal bleeding of undetermined origin; ovarian cysts or enlargement not due to polycystic ovary syndrome; pregnancy
Warnings/Precautions These medications should only be used by physicians who are thoroughly familiar with infertility problems and their management. To minimize risks, use only at the lowest effective dose. Monitor ovarian response with serum estradiol and vaginal ultrasound on a regular basis.

Ovarian enlargement which may be accompanied by abdominal distention or abdominal pain, occurs in ~20% of those treated with urofollitropin and hCG, and generally regresses without treatment within 2-3 weeks. If ovaries are abnormally enlarged on the last day of treatment, withhold hCG to reduce the risk of ovarian hyperstimulation syndrome (OHSS). OHSS is reported in about 6% of patients; it is characterized by severe ovarian enlargement, abdominal pain/distention, nausea, vomiting, diarrhea, dyspnea, and oliguria, and may be accompanied by ascites, pleural effusion, hypovolemia, electrolyte imbalance, hemoperitoneum, and thromboembolic events. If hyperstimulation occurs, stop treatment and hospitalize patient. This syndrome develops rapidly within 24 hours to several days and generally occurs during the 7-10 days immediately following treatment. Hemoconcentration associated with fluid loss into the abdominal cavity has occurred and should be assessed by fluid intake & output, weight, hematocrit, serum & urinary electrolytes, urine specific gravity, BUN and creatinine, and abdominal girth. Determinations should be performed daily or more often if the need arises. Treatment is primarily symptomatic and consists of bed rest, fluid and electrolyte replacement and analgesics. The ascitic, pleural and pericardial fluids should not be removed unless needed to relieve symptoms of cardiopulmonary distress.

Serious pulmonary conditions (atelectasis, acute respiratory distress syndrome and exacerbation of asthma) have been reported. Thromboembolic events, both in association with and separate from ovarian hyperstimulation syndrome, have been reported.
(Continued)

Urofollitropin *(Continued)*

Multiple births may result from the use of these medications, including triplet and quintuplet gestations. Advise patient of the potential risk of multiple births before starting the treatment.

Adverse Reactions Percentage may vary by indication, route of administration.

>10%:

Central nervous system: Headache

Endocrine & metabolic: Ovarian enlargement, ovarian hyperstimulation syndrome

Gastrointestinal: Abdominal cramps

1% to 10%:

Cardiovascular: Hypertension

Central nervous system: Depression, emotional lability, fever, pain

Dermatologic: Acne, exfoliative dermatitis, rash

Endocrine & metabolic: Breast tenderness, hot flashes, ovarian disorder (pain, cyst)

Gastrointestinal: Abdomen enlarged, abdominal pain, constipation, diarrhea, dehydration, nausea, vomiting, weight gain

Genitourinary: Cervical disorder, urinary tract infection, pelvic pain/cramps, uterine spasms, vaginal discharge, vaginal hemorrhage, vaginal spotting

Local: Injection site reaction

Neuromuscular & skeletal: Neck pain

Respiratory: Respiratory disorder, sinusitis

Miscellaneous: Infection, post retrieval pain

Postmarketing, case reports, or events reported with gonadotropins: Acute respiratory distress syndrome, adnexal torsion, anaphylactic reactions, arterial occlusion, atelectasis, cerebral vascular occlusion, deep vein thrombosis, hemoperitoneum, hypersensitivity reactions, ovarian neoplasms, pulmonary embolism

Overdosage/Toxicology Aside from possible ovarian hyperstimulation and multiple gestations, little is known concerning the consequences of an acute overdose. Treatment is symptomatic.

Stability Lyophilized powder may be stored in the refrigerator or at room temperature of 3°C to 25°C (37°F to 77°F). Protect from light. Dissolve contents of vial in sterile saline 1 mL; gently swirl (do not shake); do not use if solution is not clear or contains particles. If more than 1 vial is required for a single dose, up to 6 vials can be reconstituted with 1 mL sterile saline and administered as a single injection. This is done by first reconstituting 1 vial with sterile saline as previously described, withdrawing the entire contents of the reconstituted vial and (using this as the diluent for the second vial) injecting into the second vial, etc. Use immediately after reconstitution.

Mechanism of Action Urofollitropin is a preparation of highly purified follicle-stimulating hormone (FSH) extracted from the urine of postmenopausal women. Follitropins stimulate ovarian follicular growth in women who do not have primary ovarian failure. FSH is required for normal follicular growth, maturation, gonadal steroid production, and spermatogenesis.

Pharmacodynamics/Kinetics

Half-life elimination

I.M.: 37 hours, 15 hours following multiple doses

SubQ: 32 hours, 21 hours following multiple doses

Time to peak, plasma:

I.M.: 17 hours, 11 hours following multiple doses

SubQ: 21 hours, 10 hours following multiple doses

Dosage Note: Dose should be individualized. Use the lowest dose consistent with the expectation of good results. Over the course of treatment, doses may vary depending on individual patient response.

Adults: Female:

Ovulation induction: I.M., SubQ: Initial: 150 int. units daily for the first 5 days of treatment. Dose adjustments of ≤75-150 int. units can be made every ≥2 days; maximum daily dose: 450 int. units; treatment >12 days is not recommended. If response to follitropin is appropriate, hCG is given 1 day following the last dose. Withhold hCG if serum estradiol is >2000 pg/mL, if the ovaries are abnormally enlarged, or if abdominal pain occurs.

ART: SubQ: 225 int. units daily for the first 5 days; dose may be adjusted based on patient response, but adjustments should not be made more frequently than once every 2 days; maximum adjustment: 75-150 int. units; maximum daily dose: 450 int. units; maximum duration of treatment: 12 days. When a sufficient number of follicles of adequate size are present, the final maturation of the follicles is induced by administering hCG. Withhold hCG in cases where the ovaries are abnormally enlarged on the last day of therapy.

Administration Administer I.M. or SubQ; gently massage site after administration.

I.M.: Administer in upper quadrant of buttock near hip

SubQ: Administer on lower abdomen; thigh is not recommended unless abdomen cannot be used

Monitoring Parameters Monitor sufficient follicular maturation. This may be directly estimated by sonographic visualization of the ovaries and endometrial lining or measuring serum estradiol levels. The combination of both ultrasonography and measurement of estradiol levels is useful for monitoring for the growth and development of follicles and timing hCG administration.

The clinical evaluation of estrogenic activity (changes in vaginal cytology and changes in appearance and volume of cervical mucus) provides an indirect estimate of the estrogenic effect upon the target organs and, therefore, it should only be used adjunctively with more direct estimates of follicular development (ultrasonography and serum estradiol determinations).

The clinical confirmation of ovulation is obtained by direct and indirect indices of progesterone production. The indices most generally used are: rise in basal body temperature, increase in serum progesterone, and menstruation following the shift in basal body temperature.

Monitor for signs and symptoms of OHSS for at least 2 weeks following hCG administration.

Dosage Forms

Injection, powder for reconstitution [human origin]:

Bravelle® : 75 int. units [contains lactose; packaged with diluent]

Urokinase (ur oh KYE nase)

U.S. Brand Names Abbokinase® [DSC]

Index Terms UK

Pharmacologic Category Thrombolytic Agent

Use Thrombolytic agent for the lysis of acute massive pulmonary emboli or pulmonary emboli with unstable hemodynamics

Unlabeled/Investigational Use Thrombolytic agent used in treatment of recent severe or massive deep vein thrombosis, myocardial infarction, and occluded I.V. or dialysis cannulas

Pregnancy Risk Factor B

Pregnancy Implications Urokinase was not found to be teratogenic in animal studies; it is not known if it crosses the human placenta. Placental separation and hemorrhage have been reported in one patient treated at 3 months gestation. Use during pregnancy only if clearly needed.

Lactation Excretion in breast milk unknown/use caution

Contraindications Hypersensitivity to urokinase or any component of the formulation; active internal bleeding; history of CVA; recent (within 2 months) intracranial or intraspinal surgery or trauma; intracranial neoplasm, arteriovenous malformation, or aneurysm; known bleeding diathesis; severe uncontrolled hypertension

Warnings/Precautions Concurrent heparin anticoagulation can contribute to bleeding; careful attention to all potential bleeding sites. I.M. injections and nonessential handling of the patient should be avoided. Venipunctures should be performed carefully and only when necessary. If arterial puncture is necessary, use an upper extremity vessel that can be manually compressed. If serious bleeding occurs, then the infusion of urokinase and heparin should be stopped.

For the following conditions the risk of bleeding is higher with use of anistreplase and should be weighed against the benefits of therapy: recent (within 10 days) major surgery (eg, CABG, obstetrical delivery, organ biopsy, previous puncture of noncompressible vessels), cerebrovascular disease, recent (within 10 days) gastrointestinal or genitourinary bleeding, recent trauma (within 10 days) including CPR, hypertension (systolic BP >180 mm Hg and/or diastolic BP >110 mm Hg), high likelihood of left heart thrombus (eg, mitral stenosis with atrial fibrillation), acute pericarditis, subacute bacterial endocarditis, hemostatic defects including ones caused by severe renal or hepatic dysfunction, significant hepatic dysfunction, pregnancy, diabetic hemorrhagic retinopathy or other hemorrhagic ophthalmic conditions, septic thrombophlebitis or occluded AV cannula at seriously infected site, advanced age (eg, >75 years), patients receiving oral anticoagulants, any other condition in which bleeding constitutes a significant hazard or would be particularly difficult to manage because of location.

Coronary thrombolysis may result in reperfusion arrhythmias. Follow standard MI management. Rare anaphylactoid reactions can occur. Safety and efficacy in pediatric patients have not been established.

Adverse Reactions As with all drugs which may affect hemostasis, bleeding is the major adverse effect associated with urokinase. Hemorrhage may occur at virtually any site. Risk is dependent on multiple variables, including the dosage administered, concurrent use of multiple agents which alter hemostasis, and patient predisposition.

>10%: Local: Injection site: Bleeding (5% decrease in hematocrit reported in 37% patients; most bleeding occurring at external incisions or injection sites, but also reported in other areas)

<1% (Limited to important or life-threatening): Allergic reaction (includes bronchospasm, orolingual edema, urticaria, skin rash, pruritus); cardiac arrest, cerebral vascular accident, chest pain, cholesterol embolism, diaphoresis, hemiplegia, intracranial hemorrhage, retroperitoneal hemorrhage, MI, pulmonary edema, recurrent pulmonary embolism, reperfusion ventricular arrhythmia, stroke, substernal pain, thrombocytopenia, vascular embolization (cerebral and distal); infusion reactions (most occurring within 1 hour) including acidosis, back pain, chills, cyanosis, dyspnea, fever, hyper-/hypotension, hypoxia, nausea, rigors, tachycardia, vomiting

Overdosage/Toxicology Symptoms include epistaxis, bleeding gums, hematoma, spontaneous ecchymoses, and oozing at the catheter site. In case of overdose, stop the infusion reverse bleeding with blood products that contain clotting factors.

Drug Interactions

Increased Effect/Toxicity: Oral anticoagulants (warfarin), heparin, low molecular weight heparins, and drugs which affect platelet function (eg, NSAIDs, dipyridamole, ticlopidine, clopidogrel, IIb/IIIa antagonists) may potentiate the risk of hemorrhage.

Decreased Effect: Aminocaproic acid (an antifibrinolytic agent) may decrease the effectiveness of thrombolytic therapy.

Stability Prior to reconstitution, store in refrigerator at 2°C to 8°C (36°F to 46°F). Reconstitute vial with 5 mL sterile water for injection (preservative free) by gently rolling and tilting; do not shake. Contains no preservatives. Should not be reconstituted until immediately before using. Discard unused portion. Solution will look pale and straw colored. May filter through ≤0.45 micron filter. Prior to infusion, solution should be further diluted in D₅W or NS.

Mechanism of Action Promotes thrombolysis by directly activating plasminogen to plasmin, which degrades fibrin, fibrinogen, and other procoagulant plasma proteins

Pharmacodynamics/Kinetics

Onset of action: I.V.: Fibrinolysis occurs rapidly

Duration: 24 hours

Distribution: 11.5 L

Half-life elimination: 6.4-18.8 minutes

Excretion: Urine and feces (small amounts)

(Continued)

Urokinase *(Continued)*

Dosage

Children and Adults: Deep vein thrombosis (unlabeled use): I.V.: Loading: 4400 units/kg over 10 minutes, then 4400 units/kg/hour for 12 hours

Adults:

Acute pulmonary embolism: I.V.: Loading: 4400 int. units/kg over 10 minutes; maintenance: 4400 int. units/kg/hour for 12 hours. Following infusion, anticoagulation treatment is recommended to prevent recurrent thrombosis. Do not start anticoagulation until aPTT has decreased to less than twice the normal control value. If heparin is used, do not administer loading dose. Treatment should be followed with oral anticoagulants.

Myocardial infarction (unlabeled use): Intracoronary: 750,000 units over 2 hours (6000 units/minute over up to 2 hours)

Occluded I.V. catheters (unlabeled use):

5000 units in each lumen over 1-2 minutes, leave in lumen for 1-4 hours, then aspirate; may repeat with 10,000 units in each lumen if 5000 units fails to clear the catheter; **do not infuse into the patient**; volume to instill into catheter is equal to the volume of the catheter

I.V. infusion: 200 units/kg/hour in each lumen for 12-48 hours at a rate of at least 20 mL/hour

Dialysis patients: 5000 units is administered in each lumen over 1-2 minutes; leave urokinase in lumen for 1-2 days, then aspirate

Administration Solution may be filtered using a 0.22 or 0.45 micron filter during I.V. therapy. Administer using a pump which can deliver a total volume of 195 mL. The loading dose should be administered at 90 mL/hour over 10 minutes. The maintenance dose should be administered at 15 mL/hour over 12 hours. I.V. tubing should be flushed with NS or D_5W to ensure total dose is administered.

Monitoring Parameters Blood pressure, pulse; CBC, platelet count, aPTT, urinalysis

Dosage Forms [DSC] = Discontinued product

Injection, powder for reconstitution: 250,000 int. units [contains human albumin 250 mg and mannitol 25 mg] [DSC]

♦ **Uro-KP-Neutral®** *see* Potassium Phosphate and Sodium Phosphate *on page 1403*
♦ **Urolene Blue®** *see* Methylene Blue *on page 1118*
♦ **Uro-Mag® [OTC]** *see* Magnesium Oxide *on page 1050*
♦ **Uromax® (Can)** *see* Oxybutynin *on page 1285*
♦ **Uromitexan (Can)** *see* Mesna *on page 1091*
♦ **Uroqid-Acid® No. 2** *see* Methenamine and Sodium Acid Phosphate *on page 1107*
♦ **Uroxatral®** *see* Alfuzosin *on page 68*
♦ **Urso® (Can)** *see* Ursodiol *on page 1762*
♦ **Urso 250™** *see* Ursodiol *on page 1762*
♦ **Ursodeoxycholic Acid** *see* Ursodiol *on page 1762*

Ursodiol *(ur soe DYE ol)*

U.S. Brand Names Actigall®; Urso 250™; Urso Forte™
Canadian Brand Names Urso®; Urso® DS
Index Terms Ursodeoxycholic Acid
Pharmacologic Category Gallstone Dissolution Agent
Use Actigall®: Gallbladder stone dissolution; prevention of gallstones in obese patients experiencing rapid weight loss; Urso®: Primary biliary cirrhosis
Unlabeled/Investigational Use Liver transplantation
Pregnancy Risk Factor B
Dosage Adults: Oral:

Gallstone dissolution: 8-10 mg/kg/day in 2-3 divided doses; use beyond 24 months is not established; obtain ultrasound images at 6-month intervals for the first year of therapy; 30% of patients have stone recurrence after dissolution

Gallstone prevention: 300 mg twice daily

Primary biliary cirrhosis: 13-15 mg/kg/day in 2-4 divided doses (with food)

Additional Information Complete prescribing information for this medication should be consulted for additional detail.

Dosage Forms

Capsule (Actigall®): 300 mg

Tablet:

Urso 250™: 250 mg

Urso Forte™: 500 mg

♦ **Urso® DS (Can)** *see* Ursodiol *on page 1762*
♦ **Urso Forte™** *see* Ursodiol *on page 1762*
♦ **UTI Relief® [OTC]** *see* Phenazopyridine *on page 1351*
♦ **Utradol™ (Can)** *see* Etodolac *on page 666*
♦ **Uvadex®** *see* Methoxsalen *on page 1115*

Vaccinia Immune Globulin (Intravenous)
(vax IN ee a i MYUN GLOB yoo lin IN tra VEE nus)

U.S. Brand Names CNJ-016™
Index Terms VIGIV
Pharmacologic Category Immune Globulin
Use Treatment of infectious complications of smallpox (vaccinia virus) vaccination, such as eczema vaccinatum, progressive vaccinia, and severe generalized vaccinia; vaccinia infections in individuals with concurrent skin conditions or accidental virus exposure to eyes

(except vaccinia keratitis), mouth, or other areas where viral infection would pose significant risk

Pregnancy Risk Factor C

Pregnancy Implications Immune globulins cross the placenta in increased amounts after 30 weeks gestation. There are no adequate and well-controlled studies in pregnant women; use only if benefits outweigh the risks.

Lactation Excretion in breast milk unknown/use caution

Contraindications Hypersensitivity to immune globulin or any component of the formulation; isolated vaccinia keratitis; selective IgA deficiency

Warnings/Precautions Anaphylactic hypersensitivity reactions can occur; epinephrine 1:1000 should be readily available; aseptic meningitis may occur with high doses (≥2 g/kg). Use with caution in the elderly, patients with renal disease, diabetes mellitus, volume depletion, sepsis, paraproteinemia, and nephrotoxic medications due to risk of renal dysfunction. Patients should be adequately hydrated prior to therapy. Contains trace amounts of IgA. Use caution in patients with a history of thrombotic events or cardiovascular disease; monitor for signs of hemolytic anemia or transfusion-related, noncardiogenic pulmonary edema. For intravenous administration only.

Adverse Reactions Note: Actual frequency varies by dose, rate of infusion and specific product used

Cardiovascular: Flushing

Central nervous system: Cold or hot feeling, dizziness, fatigue, headache, pain, pallor, pyrexia

Dermatologic: Erythema, urticaria

Gastrointestinal: Abdominal pain, appetite decreased, nausea, vomiting

Local: Injection site reaction

Neuromuscular & skeletal: Arthralgia, back pain, paraesthesia, muscle cramp, rigors, tremor, weakness

Miscellaneous: Diaphoresis

Postmarketing and/or case reports (as reported with other IVIG products): Apnea, acute respiratory distress syndrome, bronchospasm, bullous dermatitis, cardiac arrest, coma, Coombs' test positive, cyanosis, dyspnea, epidermolysis, erythema multiforme, hemolysis, hepatic dysfunction, hypoxemia, hypotension, leukopenia, loss of consciousness, lung injury (transfusion-associated), pancytopenia, pulmonary edema, seizure, Stevens-Johnson syndrome, syncope, thromboembolism, vascular collapse

Overdosage/Toxicology Symptoms primarily related to volume overload; treatment should be supportive

Drug Interactions

Decreased Effect: Vaccina immune globulin may interfere with immune response to live virus vaccines (eg, polio, measles, mumps, and rubella); live virus vaccinations should be deferred until 6 months after administration of VIGIV; if given shortly before receiving VIGIV, revaccination with the live virus may be necessary (consult individual products for guidance)

Stability Store between 2°C and 8°C (35.6°F to 46.4°F).

CNJ-016™ (Cangene product): If frozen, use within 60 days of thawing at 2°C and 8°C. Infusion should begin within 4 hours after entering vial.

DynPort product: Use within 6 hours of piercing vial stopper; complete infusion within 12 hours of spiking vial.

Mechanism of Action Antibodies obtained from pooled human plasma of individuals immunized with the smallpox vaccine provide passive immunity

Pharmacodynamics/Kinetics

Distribution: V_d: CNJ-016™ (Cangene product): 6630 L

Half-life elimination:

CNJ-016™ (Cangene product): 30 days (range 13-67 days)

DynPort product: 22 days

Dosage I.V.:

Adults:

CNJ-016™ (Cangene product): 6000 units/kg; 9000 units/kg may be considered if patient does not respond to initial dose.

DynPort product: Total dose: 2 mL/kg (100 mg/kg); higher doses (200-500 mg/kg) may be considered if patient does not respond to initial recommended dose (sucrose-related renal impairment is worsened at doses ≥400 mg/kg)

Elderly: Safety and efficacy have not been established

Dosage adjustment in renal impairment: Use caution. Dose ≥400 mg/kg of the DynPort product are not recommended.

Dietary Considerations DynPort solution for injection contains sodium 0.02-0.03 mEq/mL.

Administration Do not shake; avoid foaming. For intravenous use only. Predilution not recommended; if dedicated line not available, flush with NS prior to administration of VIGIV. Do not exceed recommended rates of infusion.

CNJ-016™ (Cangene product): Patients ≥50 kg: Infuse at ≤2 mL/minute; Patients < 50 kg: Infuse at 0.04 mL/kg/minute. Maximum assessed rate of infusion: 4 mL/minute. Decrease rate of infusion if minor adverse reactions develop, in patients with risk factors for thrombosis/thromboembolism, and/or renal insufficiency.

DynPort product: Infuse at 1 mL/kg/hour for 30 minutes, then 2 mL/kg/hour for 30 minutes, then 3 mL/kg/hour until complete. Administer through 0.22 micron filtered set; use of infusion pump recommended.

Monitoring Parameters During infusion, monitor patient for signs of infusion-related reactions, including (but not limited to) flushing, fever, chills, respiratory distress, blood pressure or heart rate changes

Test Interactions CNJ-016™ contains maltose. Falsely-elevated blood glucose levels may occur when glucose monitoring devices and test strips utilizing the glucose dehydrogenase pyrroloquinolinequinone (GDH-PQQ) based methods are used. Glucose monitoring devices and test strips which utilize the glucose-specific method are recommended.

(Continued)

Vaccinia Immune Globulin (Intravenous) *(Continued)*

Dosage Forms Injection, solution [preservative free; solvent-detergent treated]:
CNJ-016™ (Cangene product): ≥50,000 units/15 mL (15 mL) [contains maltose 10% and polysorbate 80 0.03%]
DynPort product: 50 mg/mL (50 mL) [contains sucrose 50 mg/mL, human albumin 10 mg/mL, sodium 0.02-0.03 mEq/mL]

♦ **Vaccinia Vaccine** *see Smallpox Vaccine on page 1573*
♦ **Vagifem®** *see Estradiol on page 620*
♦ **Vagi-Gard® [OTC]** *see Povidone-Iodine on page 1404*
♦ **Vagistat®-1 [OTC]** *see Tioconazole on page 1691*

Valacyclovir *(val ay SYE kloe veer)*

U.S. Brand Names Valtrex®
Canadian Brand Names Valtrex®
Index Terms Valacyclovir Hydrochloride
Pharmacologic Category Antiviral Agent, Oral
Additional Appendix Information
Treatment of Sexually Transmitted Infections *on page 2007*
Use Treatment of herpes zoster (shingles) in immunocompetent patients; treatment of first-episode genital herpes; episodic treatment of recurrent genital herpes; suppression of recurrent genital herpes and reduction of heterosexual transmission of genital herpes in immunocompetent patients; suppression of genital herpes in HIV-infected individuals; treatment of herpes labialis (cold sores)
Pregnancy Risk Factor B
Pregnancy Implications Teratogenicity registry has shown no increased rate of birth defects than that of the general population; however, the registry is small and use during pregnancy is only warranted if the potential benefit to the mother justifies the risk of the fetus.
Lactation Enters breast milk/use caution
Medication Safety Issues
Sound-alike/look-alike issues:
Valtrex® may be confused with Valcyte™
Valacyclovir may be confused with valganciclovir
Contraindications Hypersensitivity to valacyclovir, acyclovir, or any component of the formulation
Warnings/Precautions Hazardous agent - use appropriate precautions for handling and disposal. Thrombotic thrombocytopenic purpura/hemolytic uremic syndrome has occurred in immunocompromised patients; use caution and adjust the dose in elderly patients or those with renal insufficiency; safety and efficacy in prepubertal patients have not been established
Adverse Reactions
>10%: Central nervous system: Headache (14% to 35%)
1% to 10%:
Central nervous system: Dizziness (2% to 4%), depression (0% to 7%)
Endocrine: Dysmenorrhea (≤1% to 8%)
Gastrointestinal: Abdominal pain (2% to 11%), vomiting (<1% to 6%), nausea (6% to 15%)
Hematologic: Leukopenia (≤1%), thrombocytopenia (≤1%)
Hepatic: AST increased (1% to 4%)
Neuromuscular & skeletal: Arthralgia (≤1 to 6%)
<1% (Limited to important or life-threatening): Acute hypersensitivity reactions (angioedema, anaphylaxis, dyspnea, pruritus, rash, urticaria); aggression, agitation, alopecia, aplastic anemia, ataxia, coma, confusion, dysarthria, encephalopathy, erythema multiforme, hallucinations (auditory and visual), hemolytic uremic syndrome (HUS), hepatitis, leukocytoclastic vasculitis, mania, photosensitivity reaction, psychosis, rash, renal failure, seizure, thrombotic thrombocytopenic purpura/hemolytic uremic syndrome, tremor
Overdosage/Toxicology Symptoms include elevated serum creatinine, renal failure, encephalitis, and precipitation in renal tubules. Hemodialysis has resulted in up to 60% reduction in serum acyclovir levels after administration of acyclovir.
Drug Interactions
Increased Effect/Toxicity: Valacyclovir and acyclovir have increased CNS side effects with zidovudine and probenecid.
Decreased Effect: Cimetidine and/or probenecid has decreased the rate but not the extent of valacyclovir conversion to acyclovir leading to decreased effectiveness of valacyclovir.
Stability Store at 15°C to 25°C (59°F to 77°F).
Mechanism of Action Valacyclovir is rapidly and nearly completely converted to acyclovir by intestinal and hepatic metabolism. Acyclovir is converted to acyclovir monophosphate by virus-specific thymidine kinase then further converted to acyclovir triphosphate by other cellular enzymes. Acyclovir triphosphate inhibits DNA synthesis and viral replication by competing with deoxyguanosine triphosphate for viral DNA polymerase and being incorporated into viral DNA.
Pharmacodynamics/Kinetics
Absorption: Rapid
Distribution: Acyclovir is widely distributed throughout the body including brain, kidney, lungs, liver, spleen, muscle, uterus, vagina, and CSF
Protein binding: 13.5% to 17.9%
Metabolism: Hepatic; valacyclovir is rapidly and nearly completely converted to acyclovir and L-valine by first-pass effect; acyclovir is hepatically metabolized to a very small extent by aldehyde oxidase and by alcohol and aldehyde dehydrogenase (inactive metabolites)
Bioavailability: ~55% once converted to acyclovir
Half-life elimination: Normal renal function: Adults: Acyclovir: 2.5-3.3 hours, Valacyclovir: ~30 minutes; End-stage renal disease: Acyclovir: 14-20 hours

Excretion: Urine, primarily as acyclovir (88%); **Note:** Following oral administration of radiolabeled valacyclovir, 46% of the label is eliminated in the feces (corresponding to nonabsorbed drug), while 47% of the radiolabel is eliminated in the urine.

Dosage Oral:

Adolescents and Adults: Herpes labialis (cold sores): 2 g twice daily for 1 day (separate doses by ~12 hours)

Adults:

Herpes zoster (shingles): 1 g 3 times/day for 7 days

Genital herpes:

Initial episode: 1 g twice daily for 10 days

Recurrent episode: 500 mg twice daily for 3 days

Reduction of transmission: 500 mg once daily (source partner)

Suppressive therapy:

Immunocompetent patients: 1000 mg once daily (500 mg once daily in patients with <9 recurrences per year)

HIV-infected patients (CD4 ≥100 cells/mm^3): 500 mg twice daily

Dosing interval in renal impairment:

Herpes zoster: Adults:

Cl$_{cr}$ 30-49 mL/minute: 1 g every 12 hours

Cl$_{cr}$ 10-29 mL/minute: 1 g every 24 hours

Cl$_{cr}$ <10 mL/minute: 500 mg every 24 hours

Genital herpes: Adults:

Initial episode:

Cl$_{cr}$ 10-29 mL/minute: 1 g every 24 hours

Cl$_{cr}$ <10 mL/minute: 500 mg every 24 hours

Recurrent episode: Cl$_{cr}$ <10-29 mL/minute: 500 mg every 24 hours

Suppressive therapy: Cl$_{cr}$ <10-29 mL/minute:

For usual dose of 1 g every 24 hours, decrease dose to 500 mg every 24 hours

For usual dose of 500 mg every 24 hours, decrease dose to 500 mg every 48 hours

HIV-infected patients: 500 mg every 24 hours

Herpes labialis: Adolescents and Adults:

Cl$_{cr}$ 30-49 mL/minute: 1 g every 12 hours for 2 doses

Cl$_{cr}$ 10-29 mL/minute: 500 mg every 12 hours for 2 doses

Cl$_{cr}$ <10 mL/minute: 500 mg as a single dose

Hemodialysis: Dialyzable (~33% removed during 4-hour session); administer dose postdialysis

Chronic ambulatory peritoneal dialysis/continuous arteriovenous hemofiltration dialysis: Pharmacokinetic parameters are similar to those in patients with ESRD; supplemental dose not needed following dialysis

Dietary Considerations May be taken with or without food.

Administration If GI upset occurs, administer with meals.

Monitoring Parameters Urinalysis, BUN, serum creatinine, liver enzymes, and CBC

Dosage Forms Caplet: 500 mg, 1000 mg

♦ **Valacyclovir Hydrochloride** *see* Valacyclovir *on page 1764*

♦ **Valcyte™** *see* Valganciclovir *on page 1765*

♦ **23-Valent Pneumococcal Polysaccharide Vaccine** *see* Pneumococcal Polysaccharide Vaccine (Polyvalent) *on page 1384*

Valganciclovir *(val gan SYE kloh veer)*

U.S. Brand Names Valcyte™

Canadian Brand Names Valcyte™

Index Terms Valganciclovir Hydrochloride

Pharmacologic Category Antiviral Agent

Use Treatment of cytomegalovirus (CMV) retinitis in patients with acquired immunodeficiency syndrome (AIDS); prevention of CMV disease in high-risk patients (donor CMV positive/recipient CMV negative) undergoing kidney, heart, or kidney/pancreas transplantation

Pregnancy Risk Factor C

Pregnancy Implications Valganciclovir is converted to ganciclovir and shares its reproductive toxicity. Ganciclovir may adversely affect spermatogenesis and fertility; due to its mutagenic potential, contraceptive precautions for female and male patients need to be followed during and for at least 90 days after therapy with this drug.

Lactation Excretion in breast milk unknown/contraindicated

Medication Safety Issues

Sound-alike/look-alike issues:

Valcyte™ may be confused with Valium®, Valtrex®

Valganciclovir may be confused with valacyclovir

Contraindications Hypersensitivity to valganciclovir, ganciclovir, acyclovir, or any component of the formulation; absolute neutrophil count <500/mm^3; platelet count <25,000/mm^3; hemoglobin <8 g/dL

Warnings/Precautions [U.S. Boxed Warning]: May cause dose or therapy limiting granulocytopenia, anemia, and/or thrombocytopenia; use caution in patients with impaired renal function (dose adjustment required). **[U.S. Boxed Warning]: Ganciclovir may adversely affect spermatogenesis and fertility;** due to its mutagenic potential, contraceptive precautions for female and male patients need to be followed during and for at least 90 days after therapy with the drug. Due to differences in bioavailability, valganciclovir tablets (Continued)

Valganciclovir *(Continued)*

cannot be substituted for ganciclovir capsules on a one-to-one basis. Not indicated for use in liver transplant patients (higher incidence of tissue-invasive CMV relative to oral ganciclovir was observed in trials). Safety and efficacy not established in pediatric patients.

Adverse Reactions
>10%:
Central nervous system: Fever (31%), headache (9% to 22%), insomnia (16%)
Gastrointestinal: Diarrhea (16% to 41%), nausea (8% to 30%), vomiting (21%), abdominal pain (15%)
Hematologic: Granulocytopenia (11% to 27%), anemia (8% to 26%)
Ocular: Retinal detachment (15%)
1% to 10%:
Central nervous system: Peripheral neuropathy (9%), paresthesia (8%), seizure (<5%), psychosis, hallucinations (<5%), confusion (<5%), agitation (<5%)
Hematologic: Thrombocytopenia (8%), pancytopenia (<5%), bone marrow depression (<5%), aplastic anemia (<5%), bleeding (potentially life-threatening due to thrombocytopenia <5%)
Renal: Decreased renal function (<5%)
Miscellaneous: Local and systemic infection, including sepsis (<5%); allergic reaction (<5%)
<1% (Limited to important or life-threatening): Valganciclovir is expected to share the toxicities which may occur at a low incidence or due to idiosyncratic reactions which have been associated with ganciclovir

Overdosage/Toxicology Symptoms of overdose with ganciclovir include neutropenia, vomiting, hypersalivation, bloody diarrhea, cytopenia, and testicular atrophy. Treatment is supportive. Hemodialysis removes 50% of the drug. Hydration may be of some benefit.

Drug Interactions
Increased Effect/Toxicity: Reported for ganciclovir: Immunosuppressive agents may increase hematologic toxicity of ganciclovir. Imipenem/cilastatin may increase seizure potential. Oral ganciclovir increases blood levels of zidovudine, although zidovudine decreases steady-state levels of ganciclovir. Since both drugs have the potential to cause neutropenia and anemia, some patients may not tolerate concomitant therapy with these drugs at full dosage. Didanosine levels are increased with concurrent ganciclovir. Other nephrotoxic drugs (eg, amphotericin and cyclosporine) may have additive nephrotoxicity with ganciclovir.
Decreased Effect: Reported for ganciclovir: A decrease in blood levels of ganciclovir AUC may occur when used with didanosine.

Ethanol/Nutrition/Herb Interactions Food: Coadministration with a high-fat meal increased AUC by 30%.

Stability Store at 25°C (77°F); excursions permitted to 15°C to 30°C (59°F to 86°F).

Mechanism of Action Valganciclovir is rapidly converted to ganciclovir in the body. The bioavailability of ganciclovir from valganciclovir is increased 10-fold compared to the oral ganciclovir. A dose of 900 mg achieved systemic exposure of ganciclovir comparable to that achieved with the recommended doses of intravenous ganciclovir of 5 mg/kg. Ganciclovir is phosphorylated to a substrate which competitively inhibits the binding of deoxyguanosine triphosphate to DNA polymerase resulting in inhibition of viral DNA synthesis.

Pharmacodynamics/Kinetics
Absorption: Well absorbed; high-fat meal increases AUC by 30%
Distribution: Ganciclovir: V_d: 15.26 L/1.73 m^2; widely to all tissues including CSF and ocular tissue
Protein binding: 1% to 2%
Metabolism: Converted to ganciclovir by intestinal mucosal cells and hepatocytes
Bioavailability: With food: 60%
Half-life elimination: Ganciclovir: 4.08 hours; prolonged with renal impairment; Severe renal impairment: Up to 68 hours
Excretion: Urine (primarily as ganciclovir)

Dosage
Oral: Adults:
CMV retinitis:
Induction: 900 mg twice daily for 21 days (with food)
Maintenance: Following induction treatment, or for patients with inactive CMV retinitis who require maintenance therapy: Recommended dose: 900 mg once daily (with food)
Prevention of CMV disease following transplantation: 900 mg once daily (with food) beginning within 10 days of transplantation; continue therapy until 100 days post-transplantation
Dosage adjustment in renal impairment:
Induction dose:
Cl_{cr} 40-59 mL/minute: 450 mg twice daily
Cl_{cr} 25-39 mL/minute: 450 mg once daily
Cl_{cr} 10-24 mL/minute: 450 mg every 2 days
Maintenance dose:
Cl_{cr} 40-59 mL/minute: 450 mg once daily
Cl_{cr} 25-39 mL/minute: 450 mg every 2 days
Cl_{cr} 10-24 mL/minute: 450 mg twice weekly
Note: Valganciclovir is not recommended in patients receiving hemodialysis. For patients on hemodialysis (Cl_{cr} <10 mL/minute), it is recommended that ganciclovir be used (dose adjusted as specified for ganciclovir).

Dietary Considerations Should be taken with meals.

Administration Avoid direct contact with broken or crushed tablets. Consideration should be given to handling and disposal according to guidelines issued for antineoplastic drugs. However, there is no consensus on the need for these precautions.

Monitoring Parameters Retinal exam (at least every 4-6 weeks), CBC, platelet counts, serum creatinine

Dosage Forms Tablet, as hydrochloride: 450 mg [valganciclovir hydrochloride 496.3 mg equivalent to valganciclovir 450 mg]

- ◆ **Valganciclovir Hydrochloride** *see* Valganciclovir *on page 1765*
- ◆ **Valisone® Scalp Lotion (Can)** *see* Betamethasone *on page 211*
- ◆ **Valium®** *see* Diazepam *on page 488*
- ◆ **Valorin [OTC]** *see* Acetaminophen *on page 28*
- ◆ **Valorin Extra [OTC]** *see* Acetaminophen *on page 28*
- ◆ **Valproate Semisodium** *see* Valproic Acid and Derivatives *on page 1767*
- ◆ **Valproate Sodium** *see* Valproic Acid and Derivatives *on page 1767*
- ◆ **Valproic Acid** *see* Valproic Acid and Derivatives *on page 1767*

Valproic Acid and Derivatives (val PROE ik AS id & dah RIV ah tives)

U.S. Brand Names Depacon®; Depakene®; Depakote®; Depakote® ER; Depakote® Sprinkle

Canadian Brand Names Alti-Divalproex; Apo-Divalproex®; Apo-Valproic®; Depakene®; Epival® I.V.; Gen-Divalproex; Novo-Divalproex; Nu-Divalproex; PMS-Valproic Acid; PMS-Valproic Acid E.C.; Rhoxal-valproic; Sandoz-Valproic

Index Terms Dipropylacetic Acid; Divalproex Sodium; DPA; 2-Propylpentanoic Acid; 2-Propylvaleric Acid; Valproate Semisodium; Valproate Sodium; Valproic Acid

Pharmacologic Category Anticonvulsant, Miscellaneous

Additional Appendix Information
Anticonvulsants by Seizure Type *on page 1865*
Epilepsy *on page 2048*

Use
Depacon®, Depakene®, Depakote®, Depakote® ER, Depakote® Sprinkle: Monotherapy and adjunctive therapy in the treatment of patients with complex partial seizures; monotherapy and adjunctive therapy of simple and complex absence seizures; adjunctive therapy in patients with multiple seizure types that include absence seizures

Depakote®, Depakote® ER: Mania associated with bipolar disorder; migraine prophylaxis

Unlabeled/Investigational Use Status epilepticus

Pregnancy Risk Factor D

Pregnancy Implications Teratogenic effects have been reported in animals and humans. Valproic acid crosses the placenta. Neural tube, cardiac, facial (characteristic pattern of dysmorphic facial features), skeletal, multiple other defects reported. Epilepsy itself, number of medications, genetic factors, or a combination of these probably influence the teratogenicity of anticonvulsant therapy. Information from the North American Antiepileptic Drug Pregnancy Registry notes a fourfold increase in congenital malformations with exposure to valproic acid monotherapy during the 1st trimester of pregnancy when compared to monotherapy with other antiepileptic drugs (AED). The risk of neural tube defects is ~1% to 2% (general population risk estimated to be 0.14% to 0.2%). The effect of folic acid supplementation to decrease this risk is unknown, however, folic acid supplementation is recommended for all women contemplating pregnancy.

Nonteratogenic effects have also been reported. Afibrinogenemia leading to fatal hemorrhage and hepatotoxicity have been noted in case reports of infants following in utero exposure to valproic acid. Use in women of childbearing potential requires that benefits of use in mother be weighed against the potential risk to fetus, especially when used for conditions not associated with permanent injury or risk of death (eg, migraine). Health professionals and patients are encouraged to contact the North American Antiepileptic Drug Pregnancy registry to monitor outcomes of pregnant women exposed to valproic acid and other AEDs (1-888-233-2334).

Lactation Enters breast milk/not recommended (AAP considers "compatible")

Medication Safety Issues
Sound-alike/look-alike issues:
Depakene® may be confused with Depakote®
Depakote® may be confused with Depakene®, Depakote® ER, Senokot®

Contraindications Hypersensitivity to valproic acid, derivatives, or any component of the formulation; hepatic dysfunction; urea cycle disorders

Warnings/Precautions
[U.S. Boxed Warning]: Hepatic failure resulting in fatalities has occurred in patients; children <2 years of age are at considerable risk. Other risk factors include organic brain disease, mental retardation with severe seizure disorders, congenital metabolic disorders, and patients on multiple anticonvulsants. Hepatotoxicity has been reported within 6 months of therapy. Monitor patients closely for appearance of malaise, weakness, facial edema, anorexia, jaundice, and vomiting.

[U.S. Boxed Warning]: Cases of life-threatening pancreatitis, occurring at the start of therapy or following years of use, have been reported in adults and children. Some cases have been hemorrhagic with rapid progression of initial symptoms to death. Evaluate symptoms of abdominal pain, nausea, vomiting and/or anorexia.

[U.S. Boxed Warning]: May cause teratogenic effects such as neural tube defects (eg, spina bifida). Use in women of childbearing potential requires that benefits of use in mother be weighed against the potential risk to fetus, especially when used for conditions not associated with permanent injury or risk of death (eg, migraine).

May cause severe thrombocytopenia, inhibition of platelet aggregation and bleeding. Tremors may indicate overdosage; use with caution in patients receiving other anticonvulsants. Hypersensitivity reactions affecting multiple organs have been reported in association with valproic acid use; may include dermatologic and/or hematologic changes (eosinophilia, neutropenia, thrombocytopenia) or symptoms of organ dysfunction.

Hyperammonemia and/or encephalopathy, sometimes fatal, have been reported following the initiation of valproic acid therapy and may be present with normal transaminase levels. Ammonia levels should be measured in patients who develop unexplained lethargy and vomiting, or changes in mental status. Discontinue therapy if ammonia levels are increased and evaluate for possible urea cycle disorder (UCD). Although rare genetic disorders, UCD (Continued)

Valproic Acid and Derivatives *(Continued)*

evaluation should be considered for the following patients, prior to the start of therapy: History of unexplained encephalopathy or coma; encephalopathy associated with protein load; pregnancy or postpartum encephalopathy; unexplained mental retardation; history of elevated plasma ammonia or glutamine; history of cyclical vomiting and lethargy; episodic extreme irritability, ataxia; low BUN or protein avoidance; family history of UCD or unexplained infant deaths (particularly male); signs or symptoms of UCD (hyperammonemia, encephalopathy, respiratory alkalosis).

In vitro studies have suggested valproic acid stimulates the replication of HIV and CMV viruses under experimental conditions. The clinical consequence of this is unknown, but should be considered when monitoring affected patients.

Use of Depacon® injection is not recommended for post-traumatic seizure prophylaxis following acute head trauma. Anticonvulsants should not be discontinued abruptly because of the possibility of increasing seizure frequency; valproic acid should be withdrawn gradually to minimize the potential of increased seizure frequency, unless safety concerns require a more rapid withdrawal. Concomitant use with clonazepam may induce absence status. Patients treated for bipolar disorder should be monitored closely for clinical worsening or suicidality; prescriptions should be written for the smallest quantity consistent with good patient care.

CNS depression may occur with valproic acid use. Patients must be cautioned about performing tasks which require mental alertness (operating machinery or driving). Effects with other sedative drugs or ethanol may be potentiated.

Adverse Reactions

Adverse reactions reported when used as monotherapy for complex partial seizure:

>10%:

Central nervous system: Somnolence (18% to 30%), dizziness (13% to 18%), insomnia (9% to 15%), nervousness (7% to 11%)

Dermatologic: Alopecia (13% to 24%)

Gastrointestinal: Nausea (26% to 34%), vomiting (15% to 23%), diarrhea (19% to 23%), abdominal pain (9% to 12%), dyspepsia (10% to 11%), anorexia (4% to 11%)

Hematologic: Thrombocytopenia (1% to 24%)

Neuromuscular & skeletal: Tremor (19% to 57%), weakness (10% to 21%)

Miscellaneous: Infection (13% to 20%)

1% to 10%:

Cardiovascular: Chest pain, hypertension, palpitation, peripheral edema, tachycardia

Central nervous system: Abnormal dreams, amnesia, anxiety, confusion, coordination abnormal, depression, headache, malaise, personality disorder

Dermatologic: Bruising, dry skin, petechia, pruritus, rash

Endocrine & metabolic: Amenorrhea, dysmenorrhea

Gastrointestinal: Appetite increased, eructation, flatulence, hematemesis, pancreatitis, periodontal abscess, taste perversion, weight gain

Genitourinary: Urinary frequency, urinary incontinence, vaginitis

Hepatic: AST/ALT increased

Neuromuscular & skeletal: Abnormal gait, arthralgia, back pain, hypertonia, leg cramps, myalgia, myasthenia, paresthesia, twitching

Ocular: Abnormal vision, amblyopia/blurred vision, nystagmus

Otic: Deafness, otitis media, tinnitus

Respiratory: Dyspnea, epistaxis, increased cough, pharyngitis, pneumonia, sinusitis

Additional adverse effects: Frequency not defined:

Cardiovascular: Bradycardia, edema

Central nervous system: Aggression, ataxia, behavioral deterioration, cerebral atrophy (reversible), coma (rare), dementia, encephalopathy (rare), fever, hallucinations, hostility, hyperactivity, hypoesthesia, hypothermia, parkinsonism, psychosis, sedation, vertigo

Dermatologic: Cutaneous vasculitis, erythema multiforme, photosensitivity, Stevens-Johnson syndrome, toxic epidermal necrolysis (rare)

Endocrine & metabolic: Breast enlargement, galactorrhea, hyperammonemia, hyponatremia, inappropriate ADH secretion, parotid gland swelling, polycystic ovary disease (rare), abnormal thyroid function tests

Gastrointestinal: Abdominal cramps, constipation, indigestion, weight loss

Genitourinary: Enuresis, urinary tract infection

Hematologic: Agranulocytosis, anemia, aplastic anemia, bone marrow suppression, eosinophilia, hematoma formation, hemorrhage, hypofibrinogenemia, intermittent porphyria, leukopenia, lymphocytosis, macrocytosis, pancytopenia

Hepatic: Bilirubin increased, hyperammonemic encephalopathy (in patients with UCD)

Neuromuscular & skeletal: Asterixis, bone pain, dysarthria

Ocular: Diplopia, seeing "spots before the eyes"

Otic: Ear pain

Renal: Fanconi-like syndrome (rare, in children)

Miscellaneous: Allergic reaction, anaphylaxis, carnitine decreased, hyperglycinemia, lupus

Postmarketing and/or case reports: Pancreatitis (life-threatening), severe hypersensitivity reactions with organ dysfunction

Overdosage/Toxicology Symptoms include coma, deep sleep, motor restlessness, heart block, and visual hallucinations. Supportive treatment is necessary. Naloxone has been used to reverse CNS depressant effects, but may block the action of other anticonvulsants. In overdose, the fraction of unbound valproic acid is high. Hemodialysis or tandem hemodialysis plus hemoperfusion may lead to significant removal of the drug.

Drug Interactions

Cytochrome P450 Effect: For valproic acid: **Substrate** (minor) of CYP2A6, 2B6, 2C9, 2C19, 2E1; **Inhibits** CYP2C9 (weak), 2C19 (weak), 2D6 (weak), 3A4 (weak); **Induces** CYP2A6 (weak)

Increased Effect/Toxicity: Absence seizures have been reported in patients receiving VPA and clonazepam. Valproic acid may increase, decrease, or have no effect on carbamazepine and phenytoin levels. Valproic acid may increase serum concentrations of carbamazepine - epoxide (active metabolite). Valproic acid may increase serum concentrations of lamotrigine, phenobarbital, and zidovudine. Macrolide antibiotics (clarithromycin, erythromycin, troleandomycin), felbamate, and isoniazid may inhibit the metabolism of valproic acid. Aspirin or other salicylates may displace valproic acid from protein-binding sites, leading to acute toxicity. When combined with topiramate, hyperammonemia with or without encephalopathy has been reported in patients who tolerated either drug alone. Valproic acid may enhance the adverse/toxic effect of risperidone; monitor for the development of peripheral edema.

Decreased Effect: Carbapenem antibiotics (ertapenem, imipenem, meropenem) may decrease valproic acid concentrations to subtherapeutic levels; monitor. Valproic acid may decrease the serum concentration of oxcarbazepine.

Ethanol/Nutrition/Herb Interactions

Ethanol: Avoid ethanol (may increase CNS depression).

Food: Food may delay but does not affect the extent of absorption. Valproic acid serum concentrations may be decreased if taken with food. Milk has no effect on absorption.

Herb/Nutraceutical: Avoid evening primrose (seizure threshold decreased)

Stability

Depakote® tablet, Depakene® solution: Store below 30°C (86°F)

Depakote® Sprinkles: Store below 25°C (77°F)

Depakote® ER: Store at 15°C to 30°C (59°F to 86°F)

Depakene® capsule: Store at 15°C to 25°C (59°F to 77°F)

Depacon®: Store vial at room temperature of 15°C to 30°C (59°F to 86°F). Injection should be diluted in 50 mL of a compatible diluent. Stable in D_5W, NS, and LR for at least 24 hours when stored in glass or PVC.

Mechanism of Action Causes increased availability of gamma-aminobutyric acid (GABA), an inhibitory neurotransmitter, to brain neurons or may enhance the action of GABA or mimic its action at postsynaptic receptor sites

Pharmacodynamics/Kinetics

Distribution: Total valproate: 11 L/1.73 m²; free valproate 92 L/1.73 m²

Protein binding (dose dependent): 80% to 90%; decreased in the elderly and with hepatic or renal dysfunction

Metabolism: Extensively hepatic via glucuronide conjugation and mitochondrial beta-oxidation. The relationship between dose and total valproate concentration is nonlinear; concentration does not increase proportionally with the dose, but increases to a lesser extent due to saturable plasma protein binding. The kinetics of unbound drug are linear.

Bioavailability: Depakote® ER: 90% of I.V. dose and ~89% of delayed release formulation

Half-life elimination: (increased in neonates and with liver disease): Children >2 months: 7-13 hours; Adults: 9-16 hours

Time to peak, serum: Depakote® tablet: ~4 hours; Depakote® ER: 4-17 hours

Excretion: Urine (30% to 50% as glucuronide conjugate, 3% as unchanged drug)

Dosage

Seizure disorders: **Note:** Administer doses >250 mg/day in divided doses.

Oral:

Simple and complex absence seizures: Children and Adults: Initial: 15 mg/kg/day; increase by 5-10 mg/kg/day at weekly intervals until therapeutic levels are achieved; maximum: 60 mg/kg/day. Larger maintenance doses may be required in younger children.

Complex partial seizures: Children ≥10 years and Adults: Initial: 10-15 mg/kg/day; increase by 5-10 mg/kg/day at weekly intervals until therapeutic levels are achieved; maximum: 60 mg/kg/day. Larger maintenance doses may be required in younger children.

Note: Regular release and delayed release formulations are usually given in 2-4 divided doses/day; extended release formulation (Depakote® ER) is usually given once daily. Conversion to Depakote® ER from a stable dose of Depakote® may require an increase in the total daily dose between 8% and 20% to maintain similar serum concentrations.

I.V.: Administer as a 60-minute infusion (≤20 mg/minute) with the same frequency as oral products; switch patient to oral products as soon as possible. Rapid infusions of ≤15 mg/kg over 5-10 minutes (1.5-3 mg/kg/minute) were generally well tolerated in a clinical trial.

Rectal (unlabeled): Dilute syrup 1:1 with water for use as a retention enema; loading dose: 17-20 mg/kg one time; maintenance: 10-15 mg/kg/dose every 8 hours

Status epilepticus (unlabeled use): Adults:

Loading dose: I.V.: 15-25 mg/kg administered at 3 mg/kg/minute.

Maintenance dose: I.V. infusion: 1-4 mg/kg/hour; titrate dose as needed based upon patient response and evaluation of drug-drug interactions

Mania: Adults: Oral: Initial: 750 mg/day in divided doses; dose should be adjusted as rapidly as possible to desired clinical effect; maximum recommended dosage: 60 mg/kg/day

Depakote® ER: Initial: 25 mg/kg/day given once daily; dose should be adjusted as rapidly as possible to desired clinical effect; maximum recommended dose: 60 mg/kg/day.

Migraine prophylaxis: Children ≥16 years and Adults: Oral:

Depakote® ER: 500 mg once daily for 7 days, then increase to 1000 mg once daily; adjust dose based on patient response; usual dosage range 500-1000 mg/day

Depakote® tablet: 250 mg twice daily; adjust dose based on patient response, up to 1000 mg/day

Elderly: Elimination is decreased in the elderly. Studies of elderly patients with dementia show a high incidence of somnolence. In some patients, this was associated with weight loss. Starting doses should be lower and increases should be slow, with careful monitoring of nutritional intake and dehydration. Safety and efficacy for use in patients >65 years have not been studied for migraine prophylaxis.

Dosing adjustment in renal impairment: A 27% reduction in clearance of unbound valproate is seen in patients with Cl_{cr} <10 mL/minute. Hemodialysis reduces valproate (Continued)

Valproic Acid and Derivatives *(Continued)*

concentrations by 20%, therefore no dose adjustment is needed in patients with renal failure. Protein binding is reduced, monitoring only total valproate concentrations may be misleading.

Dosing adjustment/comments in hepatic impairment: Reduce dose. Clearance is decreased with liver impairment. Hepatic disease is also associated with decreased albumin concentrations and 2- to 2.6-fold increase in the unbound fraction. Free concentrations of valproate may be elevated while total concentrations appear normal.

Dietary Considerations Valproic acid may cause GI upset; take with large amount of water or food to decrease GI upset. May need to split doses to avoid GI upset.

Depakote® Sprinkle capsule contents may be mixed with semisolid food (eg, applesauce or pudding) in patients having difficulty swallowing; particles should be swallowed and not chewed

Valproate sodium oral solution will generate valproic acid in carbonated beverages and may cause mouth and throat irritation; do not mix valproate sodium oral solution with carbonated beverages

Administration

Depakote® ER: Swallow whole, do not crush or chew. Patients who need dose adjustments smaller than 500 mg/day for migraine prophylaxis should be changed to Depakote® delayed release tablets.

Depakote® Sprinkle capsules may be swallowed whole or open capsule and sprinkle on small amount (1 teaspoonful) of soft food and use immediately (do not store or chew).

Depacon®: Following dilution to final concentration, administer over 60 minutes at a rate of ≤20 mg/minute. Alternatively, single doses up to 15 mg/kg have been administered as a rapid infusion over 5-10 minutes (1.5-3 mg/kg/minute).

Depakene® capsule: Swallow whole; do not chew

Monitoring Parameters Liver enzymes (at baseline and during therapy), CBC with platelets, PT/PTT (especially prior to surgery), serum ammonia (with symptoms of lethargy, mental status change), serum valproate levels

Reference Range

Therapeutic:

Epilepsy: 50-100 mcg/mL (SI: 350-690 µmol/L)

Mania: 50-125 mcg/mL (SI: 350-860 µmol/L)

Toxic: Some laboratories may report >200 mcg/mL (SI: >1390 µmol/L) as a toxic threshold, although clinical toxicity can occur at lower concentrations. Probability of thrombocytopenia increases with total valproate levels of ≥110 mcg/mL in females or ≥135 mcg/mL in males.

Seizure control: May improve at levels >100 mcg/mL (SI: 690 µmol/L), but toxicity may occur at levels of 100-150 mcg/mL (SI: 690-1040 µmol/L)

Mania: Clinical response seen with trough levels between 50-125 mcg/mL; risk of toxicity increases at levels >125 mcg/mL

Test Interactions False-positive result for urine ketones; accuracy of thyroid function tests

Additional Information Extended release tablets have 10% to 20% less fluctuation in serum concentration than delayed release tablets. Extended release tablets are not bioequivalent to delayed release tablets.

Dosage Forms Note: Strength expressed as valproic acid

Capsule, as valproic acid: 250 mg

Depakene®: 250 mg

Capsule, sprinkles, as divalproex sodium:

Depakote® Sprinkle: 125 mg

Injection, solution, as valproate sodium: 100 mg/mL (5 mL)

Depacon®: 100 mg/mL (5 mL) [contains edetate disodium]

Syrup, as valproic acid: 250 mg/5 mL (5 mL, 480 mL)

Depakene®: 250 mg/5 mL (480 mL)

Tablet, delayed release, as divalproex sodium:

Depakote®: 125 mg, 250 mg, 500 mg

Tablet, extended release, as divalproex sodium:

Depakote® ER: 250 mg, 500 mg

Valrubicin *(val ROO bi sin)*

U.S. Brand Names Valstar® [DSC]

Canadian Brand Names Valstar®; Valtaxin®

Index Terms AD3L; *N*-trifluoroacetyladriamycin-14-valerate

Pharmacologic Category Antineoplastic Agent, Anthracycline

Use Intravesical therapy of BCG-refractory carcinoma *in situ* of the urinary bladder

Pregnancy Risk Factor C

Pregnancy Implications There are no adequate and well-controlled studies in pregnant women. All patients of reproductive age should use an effective method of contraception during the treatment period.

Lactation Excretion in breast milk unknown/not recommended

Medication Safety Issues

Sound-alike/look-alike issues:

Valstar® may be confused with valsartan

High alert medication: The Institute for Safe Medication Practices (ISMP) includes this medication among its list of drugs which have a heightened risk of causing significant patient harm when used in error.

Contraindications Hypersensitivity to anthracyclines, Cremophor® EL, or any component of the formulation; concurrent urinary tract infection or small bladder capacity (unable to tolerate a 75 mL instillation)

Warnings/Precautions

Hazardous agent - use appropriate precautions for handling and disposal. Do not administer if mucosal integrity of bladder has been compromised or bladder perforation is present. Irritable bladder symptoms may occur during instillation and retention. Use caution in patients with severe irritable bladder symptoms. Do not clamp urinary catheter. Red-tinged urine is typical for the first 24 hours after instillation. Prolonged symptoms or discoloration should prompt contact with the physician.

Adverse Reactions

>10%: Genitourinary: Frequency (61%), dysuria (56%), urgency (57%), bladder spasm (31%), hematuria (29%), bladder pain (28%), urinary incontinence (22%), cystitis (15%), urinary tract infection (15%)

1% to 10%:

Cardiovascular: Chest pain (2%), vasodilation (2%), peripheral edema (1%)

Central nervous system: Headache (4%), malaise (4%), dizziness (3%), fever (2%)

Dermatologic: Rash (3%)

Endocrine & metabolic: Hyperglycemia (1%)

Gastrointestinal: Abdominal pain (5%), nausea (5%), diarrhea (3%), vomiting (2%), flatulence (1%)

Genitourinary: Nocturia (7%), burning symptoms (5%), urinary retention (4%), urethral pain (3%), pelvic pain (1%), hematuria (microscopic) (3%)

Hematologic: Anemia (2%)

Neuromuscular & skeletal: Weakness (4%), back pain (3%), myalgia (1%)

Respiratory: Pneumonia (1%)

<1% (Limited to important or life-threatening): Decreased urine flow, pruritus, skin irritation, taste disturbance, tenesmus, urethritis

Overdosage/Toxicology Inadvertent paravenous extravasation has not been associated with skin ulceration or necrosis. Myelosuppression is possible following inadvertent systemic administration or following significant systemic absorption from intravesical instillation.

Drug Interactions

Increased Effect/Toxicity: No specific drug interactions studies have been performed. Systemic exposure to valrubicin is negligible, and interactions are unlikely.

Decreased Effect: No specific drug interactions studies have been performed. Systemic exposure to valrubicin is negligible, and interactions are unlikely.

Stability Store unopened vials under refrigeration at 2°C to 8°C (36°F to 48°F). Stable for 12 hours when diluted in 0.9% sodium chloride. Allow vial to warm to room temperature without heating. Dilute 800 mg (20 mL) with 55 mL NS.

Mechanism of Action Blocks function of DNA topoisomerase II; inhibits DNA synthesis, causes extensive chromosomal damage, and arrests cell development; unlike other anthracyclines, does not appear to intercalate DNA

Pharmacodynamics/Kinetics

Absorption: Well absorbed into bladder tissue, negligible systemic absorption. Trauma to mucosa may increase absorption, and perforation greatly increases absorption with significant systemic myelotoxicity.

Metabolism: Negligible after intravesical instillation and 2 hour retention

Excretion: Urine when expelled from urinary bladder (98.6% as intact drug; 0.4% as N-trifluoroacetyladriamycin)

Dosage Adults: Intravesical: 800 mg once weekly for 6 weeks

Dosing adjustment in renal impairment: No specific adjustment recommended

Dosing adjustment in hepatic impairment: No specific adjustment recommended

Administration Intravesicular bladder lavage, usually in 75 mL of 0.9% sodium chloride injection. Retain in the bladder for 2 hours, then void. Due to the Cremophor® EL diluent, valrubicin should be administered through non-PVC tubing.

Monitoring Parameters Cystoscopy, biopsy, and urine cytology every 3 months for recurrence or progression

Dosage Forms [DSC] = Discontinued product

Injection, solution [DSC]: 40 mg/mL (5 mL) [contains Cremophor® EL 50% (polyoxyethyleneglycol triricinoleate) and dehydrated alcohol 50%]

Valsartan (val SAR tan)

U.S. Brand Names Diovan®

Canadian Brand Names Diovan®

Pharmacologic Category Angiotensin II Receptor Blocker

Additional Appendix Information

Angiotensin Agents on page 1860

Use Alone or in combination with other antihypertensive agents in the treatment of essential hypertension; treatment of heart failure (NYHA Class II-IV); reduction of cardiovascular mortality in patients with left ventricular dysfunction postmyocardial infarction

Pregnancy Risk Factor C/D (2nd and 3rd trimesters)

Pregnancy Implications Medications which act on the renin-angiotensin system are reported to have the following fetal/neonatal effects: Hypotension, neonatal skull hypoplasia, anuria, renal failure, and death; oligohydramnios is also reported. These effects are reported to occur with exposure during the 2nd and 3rd trimesters. Valsartan should be discontinued as soon as possible after pregnancy is detected.

Lactation Excretion in breast milk unknown/contraindicated

Medication Safety Issues

Sound-alike/look-alike issues:

Valsartan may be confused with losartan, Valstar™

Diovan® may be confused with Darvon®, Dioval®, Zyban®

Contraindications Hypersensitivity to valsartan or any component of the formulation; hypersensitivity to other A-II receptor antagonists; bilateral renal artery stenosis; pregnancy

Warnings/Precautions [U.S. Boxed Warning]: Based on human data, drugs that act on the angiotensin system can cause injury and death to the developing fetus when used

(Continued)

Valsartan *(Continued)*

in the second and third trimesters. **Angiotensin receptor blockers should be discontinued as soon as possible once pregnancy is detected.** May cause hyperkalemia; avoid potassium supplementation unless specifically required by healthcare provider. During the initiation of therapy, hypotension may occur, particularly in patients with heart failure or post-MI patients. Use extreme caution with concurrent administration of potassium-sparing diuretics or potassium supplements, in patients with mild to moderate hepatic dysfunction (adjust dose), in those who may be sodium/water depleted (eg, on high-dose diuretics), and in the elderly; avoid use in patients with CHF, unilateral renal artery stenosis, aortic/mitral valve stenosis, coronary artery disease, or hypertrophic cardiomyopathy, if possible. May be associated with deterioration of renal function and/or increases in serum creatinine, particularly in patients dependent on renin-angiotensin-aldosterone system. Safety and efficacy have not been established in children.

Adverse Reactions

>10%:

Central nervous system: Dizziness (heart failure 17%)

Renal: Bun increased >50% (heart failure 17%)

1% to 10%:

Cardiovascular: Hypotension (1% to 7%), postural hypotension (2%), syncope (up to >1%)

Central nervous system: Fatigue (2% to 3%), headache (heart failure >1%)

Endocrine & metabolic: Serum potassium increased by >20% (4% to 10%), hyperkalemia (heart failure 2%)

Gastrointestinal: Diarrhea (heart failure 5%), abdominal pain (2%), nausea (>1%)

Hematologic: Neutropenia (2%)

Neuromuscular & skeletal: Arthralgia (3%), back pain (up to 3%)

Ocular: Blurred vision (heart failure >1%)

Otic: Vertigo (up to >1%)

Renal: Creatinine doubled (MI 4%), creatinine increased >50% (heart failure 4%), renal dysfunction (up to >1%)

Respiratory: Cough (1% to 3%)

Miscellaneous: Viral infection (3%)

All indications: <1% (Limited to important or life-threatening): Allergic reactions, alopecia, anemia, angioedema, anorexia, anxiety, chest pain, constipation, dyspepsia, dyspnea, flatulence, hematocrit/hemoglobin decreased, hepatitis, impotence, insomnia, liver function tests increased, microcytic anemia, muscle cramps, myalgia, palpitation, paresthesia, pruritus, rhabdomyolysis, rash, somnolence, thrombocytopenia, vomiting, weakness, xerostomia

Overdosage/Toxicology Symptoms of toxicity may include: Hypotension, bradycardia, hyperkalemia, tachycardia, decreased mental status, circulatory collapse and shock. Treatment is symptom-directed and supportive. Not removed by hemodialysis.

Drug Interactions

Cytochrome P450 Effect: Inhibits CYP2C9 (weak)

Increased Effect/Toxicity: Lithium toxicity may be increased by valsartan. Concurrent use of eplerenone, potassium salts/supplements, and potassium-sparing diuretics (amiloride, spironolactone, triamterene) may increase the risk of hyperkalemia.

Decreased Effect: NSAIDs may decrease the efficacy of valsartan

Ethanol/Nutrition/Herb Interactions

Food: Decreases rate and extent of absorption by 50% and 40%, respectively.

Herb/Nutraceutical: Avoid dong quai if using for hypertension (has estrogenic activity). Avoid ephedra, yohimbe, ginseng (may worsen hypertension). Avoid garlic (may have increased antihypertensive effect).

Stability Store at controlled room temperature of 15°C to 30°C (59°F to 86°F). Protect from moisture.

Mechanism of Action Valsartan produces direct antagonism of the angiotensin II (AT2) receptors, unlike the ACE inhibitors. It displaces angiotensin II from the AT1 receptor and produces its blood pressure lowering effects by antagonizing AT1-induced vasoconstriction, aldosterone release, catecholamine release, arginine vasopressin release, water intake, and hypertrophic responses. This action results in more efficient blockade of the cardiovascular effects of angiotensin II and fewer side effects than the ACE inhibitors.

Pharmacodynamics/Kinetics

Onset of antihypertensive effect: 2 weeks (maximal: 4 weeks)

Distribution: V_d: 17 L (adults)

Protein binding: 95%, primarily albumin

Metabolism: To inactive metabolite

Bioavailability: 25% (range 10% to 35%)

Half-life elimination: 6 hours

Time to peak, serum: 2-4 hours

Excretion: Feces (83%) and urine (13%) as unchanged drug

Dosage Adults: Oral:

Hypertension: Initial: 80 mg or 160 mg once daily (in patients who are not volume depleted); dose may be increased to achieve desired effect; maximum recommended dose: 320 mg/day

Heart failure: Initial: 40 mg twice daily; titrate dose to 80-160 mg twice daily, as tolerated; maximum daily dose: 320 mg

Left ventricular dysfunction after MI: Initial: 20 mg twice daily; titrate dose to target of 160 mg twice daily as tolerated; may initiate ≥12 hours following MI

Dosing adjustment in renal impairment: No dosage adjustment necessary if Cl_{cr} >10 mL/minute.

Dialysis: Not significantly removed

Dosing adjustment in hepatic impairment In mild-to-moderate liver disease no adjustment is needed. Use caution in patients with liver disease. Patients with mild to moderate chronic disease have twice the exposure as healthy volunteers.

Dietary Considerations Avoid salt substitutes which contain potassium. May be taken with or without food.

Administration Administer with or without food.

Monitoring Parameters Baseline and periodic electrolyte panels, renal function, BP; in CHF, serum potassium during dose escalation and periodically thereafter

Additional Information Valsartan may have an advantage over losartan due to minimal metabolism requirements and consequent use in mild to moderate hepatic impairment.

Dosage Forms
Tablet:
Diovan®: 40 mg, 80 mg, 160 mg, 320 mg

Valsartan and Hydrochlorothiazide
(val SAR tan & hye droe klor oh THYE a zide)

U.S. Brand Names Diovan HCT®

Canadian Brand Names Diovan HCT®

Index Terms Hydrochlorothiazide and Valsartan

Pharmacologic Category Angiotensin II Receptor Blocker Combination; Antihypertensive Agent, Combination; Diuretic, Thiazide

Use Treatment of hypertension (not indicated for initial therapy)

Pregnancy Risk Factor C/D (2nd and 3rd trimester)

Medication Safety Issues
Sound-alike/look-alike issues:
Diovan® may be confused with Darvon®, Dioval®, Zyban®

Dosage Oral: Adults: Dose is individualized (combination substituted for individual components); dose may be titrated after 3-4 weeks of therapy.
Usual recommended starting dose of valsartan: 80 mg or 160 mg once daily (maximum: 320 mg/day) when used as monotherapy in patients who are not volume depleted
Usual recommended starting dose of hydrochlorothiazide: 12.5-25 mg once daily (maximum: 25 mg/day)

Dosage adjustment in renal impairment: Cl_{cr} ≤30 mL/minute: Use of combination not recommended. Contraindicated in patients with anuria.

Dosage adjustment in hepatic impairment: Use with caution

Additional Information Complete prescribing information for this medication should be consulted for additional detail.

Dosage Forms Tablet:
Diovan HCT® 80 mg/12.5 mg: Valsartan 80 mg and hydrochlorothiazide 12.5 mg
Diovan HCT® 160 mg/12.5 mg: Valsartan 160 mg and hydrochlorothiazide 12.5 mg
Diovan HCT® 160 mg/25 mg: Valsartan 160 mg and hydrochlorothiazide 25 mg
Diovan HCT® 320 mg/12.5 mg: Valsartan 320 mg and hydrochlorothiazide 12.5 mg
Diovan HCT® 320 mg/25 mg: Valsartan 320 mg and hydrochlorothiazide 25 mg

♦ **Valstar® [DSC]** see Valrubicin on page 1770
♦ **Valstar® (Can)** see Valrubicin on page 1770
♦ **Valtaxin® (Can)** see Valrubicin on page 1770
♦ **Valtrex®** see Valacyclovir on page 1764
♦ **Vanamide™** see Urea on page 1758
♦ **Vanceril® AEM (Can)** see Beclomethasone on page 198
♦ **Vancocin®** see Vancomycin on page 1773

Vancomycin (van koe MYE sin)

U.S. Brand Names Vancocin®

Canadian Brand Names Vancocin®

Index Terms Vancomycin Hydrochloride

Pharmacologic Category Antibiotic, Miscellaneous

Additional Appendix Information
Antibiotic Treatment of Adults With Infective Endocarditis on page 1977
Antimicrobial Drugs of Choice on page 1981
Community-Acquired Pneumonia in Adults on page 1999
Desensitization Protocols on page 1913
Prevention of Bacterial Endocarditis on page 1960
Prevention of Wound Infection and Sepsis in Surgical Patients on page 1964

Use Treatment of patients with infections caused by staphylococcal species and streptococcal species; used orally for staphylococcal enterocolitis or for antibiotic-associated pseudomembranous colitis produced by *C. difficile*

Pregnancy Risk Factor C

Lactation Enters breast milk/use caution

Medication Safety Issues
Sound-alike/look-alike issues:
I.V. vancomycin may be confused with Invanz®
Vancomycin may be confused with vecuronium

Contraindications Hypersensitivity to vancomycin or any component of the formulation; avoid in patients with previous severe hearing loss

Warnings/Precautions May cause nephrotoxicity; usual risk factors include pre-existing renal impairment, concomitant nephrotoxic medications, advanced age and dehydration. Discontinue treatment if signs of nephrotoxicity occur; renal damage is usually reversible. May cause neurotoxicity; usual risk factors include pre-existing renal impairment, concomitant neuro-/nephrotoxic medications, advanced age and dehydration. Ototoxicity is proportional to the amount of drug given and the duration of treatment. Tinnitus or vertigo may be indications of vestibular injury and impending bilateral irreversible damage. Discontinue treatment if signs of ototoxicity occur. Prolonged therapy (>1 week) or total doses exceeding 25 g
(Continued)

Vancomycin *(Continued)*

may increase the risk of neutropenia; prompt reversal of neutropenia is expected after discontinuation of therapy. Prolonged use may result in superinfection, including pseudomembranous colitis. Use with caution in patients with renal impairment or those receiving other nephrotoxic or ototoxic drugs; dosage modification required in patients with impaired renal function (especially elderly). Rapid I.V. administration may result in hypotension, flushing, erythema, urticaria, and/or pruritus; rate of infusion should be ≥60 minutes.

Adverse Reactions

Oral:

>10%: Gastrointestinal: Bitter taste, nausea, vomiting, stomatitis

1% to 10%:

Central nervous system: Chills, drug fever

Hematologic: Eosinophilia

<1% (Limited to important or life-threatening): Interstitial nephritis, ototoxicity, renal failure, skin rash, thrombocytopenia, vasculitis

Parenteral:

>10%:

Cardiovascular: Hypotension accompanied by flushing

Dermatologic: Erythematous rash on face and upper body (red neck or red man syndrome)

1% to 10%:

Central nervous system: Chills, drug fever

Hematologic: Eosinophilia

<1% (Limited to important or life-threatening): Ototoxicity, renal failure, thrombocytopenia, vasculitis

Overdosage/Toxicology Symptoms include ototoxicity and nephrotoxicity. There is no specific therapy for vancomycin overdose. Care is symptomatic and supportive. Peritoneal filtration and hemofiltration (not dialysis) have been shown to reduce the serum concentration of vancomycin. High flux dialysis may remove up to 25%.

Drug Interactions

Increased Effect/Toxicity: Increased toxicity with other ototoxic or nephrotoxic drugs. Increased neuromuscular blockade with most neuromuscular blocking agents.

Stability Reconstituted 500 mg and 1 g vials are stable for at either room temperature or under refrigeration for 14 days. **Note:** Vials contain no bacteriostatic agent. Solutions diluted for administration in either D₅W or NS are stable under refrigeration for 14 days or at room temperature for 7 days. Reconstitute vials with 20 mL of SWFI for each 1 g of vancomycin (10 mL/500 mg vial; 20 mL/1 g vial; 100 mL/5 g vial; 200 mL/10 g vial). The reconstituted solution must be further diluted with at least 100 mL of a compatible diluent per 500 mg of vancomycin prior to parenteral administration.

Intrathecal: Vancomycin is available as a powder for injection and may be diluted to 1-5 mg/mL concentration in preservative free 0.9% sodium chloride for administration into the CSF.

Mechanism of Action Inhibits bacterial cell wall synthesis by blocking glycopeptide polymerization through binding tightly to D-alanyl-D-alanine portion of cell wall precursor

Pharmacodynamics/Kinetics

Absorption: Oral: Poor; I.M.: Erratic; Intraperitoneal: ~38%

Distribution: Widely in body tissues and fluids, except for CSF

Relative diffusion from blood into CSF: Good only with inflammation (exceeds usual MICs)

CSF:blood level ratio: Normal meninges: Nil; Inflamed meninges: 20% to 30%

Protein binding: 10% to 50%

Half-life elimination: Biphasic: Terminal:

Newborns: 6-10 hours

Infants and Children 3 months to 4 years: 4 hours

Children >3 years: 2.2-3 hours

Adults: 5-11 hours; significantly prolonged with renal impairment

End-stage renal disease: 200-250 hours

Time to peak, serum: I.V.: 45-65 minutes

Excretion: I.V.: Urine (80% to 90% as unchanged drug); Oral: Primarily feces

Dosage Initial dosage recommendation:

Neonates: I.V.:

Postnatal age ≤7 days:

<1200 g: 15 mg/kg/dose every 24 hours

1200-2000 g: 10 mg/kg/dose every 12 hours

>2000 g: 15 mg/kg/dose every 12 hours

Postnatal age >7 days:

<1200 g: 15 mg/kg/dose every 24 hours

≥1200 g: 10 mg/kg/dose every 8 hours

Infants >1 month and Children: I.V.:

40 mg/kg/day in divided doses every 6 hours

Prophylaxis for bacterial endocarditis:

Dental, oral, or upper respiratory tract surgery: 20 mg/kg 1 hour prior to the procedure

GI/GU procedure: 20 mg/kg plus gentamicin 2 mg/kg 1 hour prior to surgery

Infants >1 month and Children with staphylococcal central nervous system infection: I.V.: 60 mg/kg/day in divided doses every 6 hours

Adults: I.V.:

With normal renal function: 1 g **or** 10-15 mg/kg/dose every 12 hours

Hospital-acquired pneumonia (HAP): 15 mg/kg/dose every 12 hours (American Thoracic Society/ATS guidelines)

Meningitis *(Pneumococcus* or *Staphylococcus)*: 30-45 mg/kg/day in divided doses every 8-12 hours **or** 500-750 mg every 6 hours (with third-generation cephalosporin for PCN-resistant *Streptococcus pneumoniae)*; maximum dose: 2-3 g/day

Prophylaxis for bacterial endocarditis:

Dental, oral, or upper respiratory tract surgery: 1 g 1 hour before surgery

GI/GU procedure: 1 g plus 1.5 mg/kg gentamicin 1 hour prior to surgery

Antibiotic lock technique (for catheter infections): 2 mg/mL in SWI/NS or D$_5$W; instill 3-5 mL into catheter port as a flush solution instead of heparin lock (**Note:** Do not mix with any other solutions)

Intrathecal: Vancomycin is available as a powder for injection and may be diluted to 1-5 mg/mL concentration in preservative-free 0.9% sodium chloride for administration into the CSF

Neonates: 5-10 mg/day

Children: 5-20 mg/day

Adults: Up to 20 mg/day

Oral: Pseudomembranous colitis produced by *C. difficile*:

Neonates: 10 mg/kg/day in divided doses

Children: 40 mg/kg/day in divided doses, added to fluids

Adults: 125 mg 4 times/day for 10 days

Dosing interval in renal impairment (vancomycin levels should be monitored in patients with any renal impairment):

Cl$_{cr}$ >60 mL/minute: Start with 1 g or 10-15 mg/kg/dose every 12 hours

Cl$_{cr}$ 40-60 mL/minute: Start with 1 g or 10-15 mg/kg/dose every 24 hours

Cl$_{cr}$ <40 mL/minute: Will need longer intervals; determine by serum concentration monitoring

Hemodialysis: Not dialyzable (0% to 5%); generally not removed; exception minimal-moderate removal by some of the newer high-flux filters; dose may need to be administered more frequently; monitor serum concentrations

Continuous ambulatory peritoneal dialysis (CAPD): Not significantly removed; administration via CAPD fluid: 15-30 mg/L (15-30 mcg/mL) of CAPD fluid

Continuous arteriovenous hemofiltration: Dose as for Cl$_{cr}$ 10-40 mL/minute

Dietary Considerations May be taken with food.

Administration Administer vancomycin by I.V. intermittent infusion over at least 60 minutes at a final concentration not to exceed 5 mg/mL. If a maculopapular rash appears on the face, neck, trunk, and/or upper extremities (Red man syndrome), slow the infusion rate to over 1½ to 2 hours and increase the dilution volume. Hypotension, shock, and cardiac arrest (rare) have also been reported with too rapid of infusion. Reactions are often treated with antihistamines and steroids.

Extravasation treatment: Monitor I.V. site closely; extravasation will cause serious injury with possible necrosis and tissue sloughing. Rotate infusion site frequently.

Monitoring Parameters Periodic renal function tests, urinalysis, serum vancomycin concentrations, WBC, audiogram

Reference Range

Timing of serum samples: Draw peak 1 hour after 1-hour infusion has completed; draw trough just before next dose

Therapeutic levels: Peak: 25-40 mcg/mL; Trough: 5-12 mcg/mL

Toxic: >80 mcg/mL (SI: >54 µmol/L)

The ATS guidelines recommend trough levels of 15-20 mcg/mL for hospital-acquired pneumonia. The Infectious Disease Society of America (ISDA) meningitis guidelines recommend trough levels of 15-20 mcg/mL.

Additional Information Because of its long half-life, vancomycin should be dosed on an every 12 hour basis; monitoring of peak and trough serum levels is advisable. The "red man syndrome" characterized by skin rash and hypotension is not an allergic reaction but rather is associated with too rapid infusion of the drug. To alleviate or prevent the reaction, infuse vancomycin at a rate of ≥30 minutes for each 500 mg of drug being administered (eg, 1 g over ≥60 minutes); 1.5 g over ≥90 minutes.

Dosage Forms

Capsule (Vancocin®): 125 mg, 250 mg

Infusion [premixed in iso-osmotic dextrose] (Vancocin®): 500 mg (100 mL); 1 g (200 mL)

Injection, powder for reconstitution: 500 mg, 1 g, 5 g, 10 g

♦ **Vancomycin Hydrochloride** *see Vancomycin on page 1773*

♦ **Vandazole™** *see Metronidazole on page 1132*

♦ **Vaniqa™** *see Eflornithine on page 573*

♦ **Vanos™** *see Fluocinonide on page 721*

♦ **Vanoxide-HC®** *see Benzoyl Peroxide and Hydrocortisone on page 208*

♦ **Vanquish® Extra Strength Pain Reliever [OTC]** *see Acetaminophen, Aspirin, and Caffeine on page 34*

♦ **Vantas™** *see Histrelin on page 839*

♦ **Vantin®** *see Cefpodoxime on page 317*

♦ **Vaprisol®** *see Conivaptan on page 417*

♦ **VAQTA®** *see Hepatitis A Vaccine on page 833*

Vardenafil (var DEN a fil)

U.S. Brand Names Levitra®

Canadian Brand Names Levitra®

Index Terms Vardenafil Hydrochloride

Pharmacologic Category Phosphodiesterase-5 Enzyme Inhibitor

Use Treatment of erectile dysfunction

Pregnancy Risk Factor B

Pregnancy Implications Teratogenic effects were not observed in animal studies; however, vardenafil is not indicated for use in women. No effects on sperm motility or morphology were observed in healthy males.

Lactation Excretion in breast milk unknown/not indicated for use in women.

Medication Safety Issues

Sound-alike/look-alike issues:

Levitra® may be confused with Lexiva®

(Continued)

Vardenafil (Continued)

Contraindications Hypersensitivity to vardenafil or any component of the formulation; concurrent use of organic nitrates (nitroglycerin; scheduled dosing or as needed)

Warnings/Precautions There is a degree of cardiac risk associated with sexual activity; therefore, physicians may wish to consider the patient's cardiovascular status prior to initiating any treatment for erectile dysfunction. Use caution in patients with anatomical deformation of the penis (angulation, cavernosal fibrosis, or Peyronie's disease) and in patients who have conditions which may predispose them to priapism (sickle cell anemia, multiple myeloma, leukemia). Patients should be instructed to seek medical attention if erection persists >4 hours.

Not recommended for use in patients with congenital QT prolongation or those taking Class Ia or III antiarrhythmics. Concomitant use with alpha blockers may cause hypotension; safety of this combination may be affected by other antihypertensives and intravascular volume depletion. Patients should be hemodynamically stable prior to initiating therapy. Use caution with alpha blockers, effective CYP3A4 inhibitors, the elderly, or those with hepatic impairment (Child-Pugh class B); dosage adjustment is needed.

Rare cases of nonarteritic ischemic optic neuropathy (NAION) have been reported; risk may be increased with history of vision loss. Other risk factors for NAION include heart disease, diabetes, hypertension, smoking, age >50 years, or history of certain eye problems.

Safety and efficacy have not been studied in patients with the following conditions, therefore, use in these patients is not recommended at this time: Hypotension, uncontrolled hypertension, unstable angina, severe cardiac failure; a life-threatening arrhythmia, myocardial infarction, or stroke within the last 6 months; severe hepatic impairment (Child-Pugh class C); end-stage renal disease requiring dialysis; retinitis pigmentosa or other degenerative retinal disorders. The safety and efficacy of vardenafil with other treatments for erectile dysfunction have not been studied and are not recommended as combination therapy.

Adverse Reactions
>10%:
- Cardiovascular: Flushing (11%)
- Central nervous system: Headache (15%)

2% to 10%:
- Central nervous system: Dizziness (2%)
- Gastrointestinal: Dyspepsia (4%), nausea (2%)
- Neuromuscular & skeletal: CPK increased (2%)
- Respiratory: Rhinitis (9%), sinusitis (3%)
- Miscellaneous: Flu-like syndrome (3%)

<2% (Limited to important or life-threatening): Abnormal ejaculation, anaphylactic reaction, angina, arthralgia, dyspnea, hyper-/hypotension, insomnia, liver function tests abnormal, MI, myalgia, nonarteritic ischemic optic neuropathy (NAION), pain, photophobia, photosensitivity, postural hypotension, priapism, pruritus, rash, somnolence, syncope, tachycardia, tinnitus, vertigo, vision changes (including blurred vision, color changes, dimming)

Overdosage/Toxicology Doses of up to 120 mg caused back pain, myalgia, and/or abnormal vision in healthy volunteers. Treatment should be symptomatic and supportive.

Drug Interactions
Cytochrome P450 Effect: Substrate of CYP2C (minor), 3A5 (minor), 3A4 (major)

Increased Effect/Toxicity: CYP3A4 inhibitors may increase the levels/effects of vardenafil; example inhibitors include azole antifungals, clarithromycin, diclofenac, doxycycline, erythromycin, imatinib, isoniazid, nefazodone, nicardipine, propofol, protease inhibitors, quinidine, telithromycin, and verapamil. Nitroglycerin may lead to excessive hypotension; concomitant use is contraindicated. Alpha-blockers may also lead to excessive hypotension; initiate vardenafil at lowest possible dose if patient is stabilized on alpha blocker; initiate alpha-blocker at lowest possible dose and titrate cautiously in patients on a stable dose of vardenafil.

Ethanol/Nutrition/Herb Interactions
Food: High-fat meals decrease maximum serum concentration 18% to 50%. Serum concentrations/toxicity may be increased with grapefruit juice; avoid concurrent use.

Stability Store at controlled room temperature of 15°C to 30°C (59°F to 86°F).

Mechanism of Action Does not directly cause penile erections, but affects the response to sexual stimulation. The physiologic mechanism of erection of the penis involves release of nitric oxide (NO) in the corpus cavernosum during sexual stimulation. NO then activates the enzyme guanylate cyclase, which results in increased levels of cyclic guanosine monophosphate (cGMP), producing smooth muscle relaxation and inflow of blood to the corpus cavernosum. Vardenafil enhances the effect of NO by inhibiting phosphodiesterase type 5 (PDE-5), which is responsible for degradation of cGMP in the corpus cavernosum; when sexual stimulation causes local release of NO, inhibition of PDE-5 by vardenafil causes increased levels of cGMP in the corpus cavernosum, resulting in smooth muscle relaxation and inflow of blood to the corpus cavernosum; at recommended doses, it has no effect in the absence of sexual stimulation.

Pharmacodynamics/Kinetics
Absorption: Rapid

Distribution: V_d: 208 L; <0.01% found in semen 1.5 hours after dose

Metabolism: Hepatic via CYP3A4 (major), CYP2C and 3A5 (minor); forms metabolite (active)

Bioavailability: 15%; Elderly (≥65 years): 52%; Hepatic impairment (Child-Pugh class B): 160%

Half-life elimination: Terminal: Vardenafil and metabolite: 4-5 hours

Time to peak, plasma: 0.5-2 hours

Excretion: Feces (91% to 95% as metabolites); urine (2% to 6%)

Clearance: 56 L/hour

Dosage Oral: Adults: Erectile dysfunction: 10 mg 60 minutes prior to sexual activity; dosing range: 5-20 mg; to be given as one single dose and not given more than once daily

Dosing adjustment with concomitant medications:

Alpha blocker (dose should be stable at time of vardenafil initiation): Initial vardenafil dose: 5 mg/24 hours; if an alpha blocker is added to vardenafil therapy, it should be initiated at the smallest possible dose, and titrated carefully.

Erythromycin: Maximum vardenafil dose: 5 mg/24 hours

Indinavir: Maximum vardenafil dose: 2.5 mg/24 hours

Itraconazole:

200 mg/day: Maximum vardenafil dose: 5 mg/24 hours

400 mg/day: Maximum vardenafil dose: 2.5 mg/24 hours

Ketoconazole:

200 mg/day: Maximum vardenafil dose: 5 mg/24 hours

400 mg/day: Maximum vardenafil dose: 2.5 mg/24 hours

Ritonavir: Maximum vardenafil dose: 2.5 mg/72 hours

Elderly ≥65 years: Initial: 5 mg 60 minutes prior to sexual activity; to be given as one single dose and not given more than once daily

Dosage adjustment in renal impairment: Dose adjustment not needed for mild, moderate, or severe impairment; use has not been studied in patients on renal dialysis

Dosage adjustment in hepatic impairment: Child-Pugh class B: Initial: 5 mg 60 minutes prior to sexual activity (maximum dose: 10 mg); to be given as one single dose and not given more than once daily

Dietary Considerations May take with or without food

Administration May be administered with or without food, 60 minutes prior to sexual activity.

Monitoring Parameters Monitor for response and adverse reactions.

Dosage Forms Tablet: 2.5 mg, 5 mg, 10 mg, 20 mg

♦ **Vardenafil Hydrochloride** see Vardenafil on page 1775

Varenicline (var e NI kleen)

U.S. Brand Names Chantix™

Index Terms Varenicline Tartrate

Pharmacologic Category Partial Nicotine Agonist; Smoking Cessation Aid

Use Treatment to aid in smoking cessation

Pregnancy Implications Teratogenic effects were not observed in animal studies, but decreased fertility, decreased fetal weight, and increased auditory startle response were observed in the offspring. There are no adequate or well-controlled studies in pregnant women. Use only if benefit outweighs the potential risk to fetus.

Lactation Excretion in breast milk unknown/not recommended

Contraindications Hypersensitivity to varenicline tartrate or any component of the formulation

Warnings/Precautions Use caution in renal dysfunction; dosage adjustment required. Safety and efficacy of varenicline with other smoking cessation therapies have not been established; increased adverse events when used concurrently with nicotine replacement therapy. Safety and efficacy have not been established in children.

Adverse Reactions

>10%:

Central nervous system: Insomnia (18% to 19%), headache (15% to 19%), abnormal dreams (9% to 13%)

Gastrointestinal: Nausea (16% to 40%; dose related)

1% to 10%:

Central nervous system: Somnolence (3%), nightmares (1% to 2%), lethargy (1% to 2%), malaise (≤7%)

Dermatologic: Rash (≤3%)

Gastrointestinal: Flatulence (6% to 9%), abdominal pain (6% to 7%), constipation (5% to 8%), dysgeusia (5% to 8%), xerostomia (5% to 6%), dyspepsia (5%), vomiting (1% to 5%), appetite increased (3% to 4%), anorexia (≤2%), gastroesophageal reflux (1%)

Respiratory: Dyspnea (≤2%), rhinorrhea (≤1%)

<1% (Limited to important or life-threatening): Acne, acute coronary syndrome, acute renal failure, aggression, agitation, amnesia, anemia, angina pectoris, anxiety, arrhythmia, arthralgia, arthritis, asthma, atrial fibrillation, back pain, blindness (transient), blurred vision, bradycardia, cataract, cerebrovascular accident, chest pain, chills, conjunctivitis, coronary artery disease, cor pulmonale, deafness, depression, dermatitis, diabetes mellitus, diarrhea, disorientation, dizziness, dry eye, dry skin, dysarthria, dysphagia, eczema, edema, enterocolitis, epistaxis, erectile dysfunction, eructation, erythema, esophagitis, euphoria, eye irritation, eye pain, facial palsy, flu-like syndrome, flushing, gastritis, gastric ulcer, gastrointestinal hemorrhage, gingivitis, hallucinations, hyperhidrosis, hyper-/hypokalemia, hyperlipidemia, hypersensitivity, hyper-/hypotension, hypoglycemia, intestinal obstruction, irritability, leukocytosis, libido decreased, lymphadenopathy, Ménière's disease, mental impairment, MI, migraine, mood swings, mouth ulceration, muscle cramps, muscle enzyme increased, musculoskeletal pain, multiple sclerosis, myalgia, myositis, nephrolithiasis, night blindness, nocturia, nystagmus, palpitations, pancreatitis, parosmia, peripheral ischemia, photophobia, photosensitivity, pleurisy, polyuria, psoriasis, psychomotor hyperactivity, pulmonary embolism, pyrexia, osteoporosis, restless leg syndrome, restlessness, seizure, sexual dysfunction, splenomegaly, suicidal ideation, syncope, tachycardia, thrombocytopenia, thrombosis, tinnitus, transient ischemic attack, tremor, urinary retention, urticaria, ventricular extrasystoles, vertigo, vitreous floaters, weight gain

Overdosage/Toxicology There is no experience with overdose. Treatment is symptom-directed and supportive. Varenicline is effectively removed by hemodialysis.

Drug Interactions

Increased Effect/Toxicity: Successful cessation of smoking may alter pharmacokinetic properties of other medications (eg, theophylline, warfarin, insulin).

Stability Store at controlled room temperature of 15°C to 30°C (59°F to 86°F).

Mechanism of Action Partial neuronal alpha$_4$ β_2 nicotinic receptor agonist; prevents nicotine stimulation of mesolimbic dopamine system associated with nicotine addiction. Also binds to 5 HT$_3$ receptor (significance not determined) with moderate affinity. Varenicline stimulates (Continued)

Varenicline *(Continued)*

dopamine activity but to a much smaller degree than nicotine does, resulting in decreased craving and withdrawal symptoms.

Pharmacodynamics/Kinetics
Absorption: Well absorbed; unaffected by food
Protein binding: ≤20%
Half-life elimination: 24 hours
Time to peak, plasma: 3-4 hours
Excretion: Primarily urine (92% as unchanged drug)

Dosage Oral: Adults:
Initial:
Days 1-3: 0.5 mg once daily
Days 4-7: 0.5 mg twice daily
Maintenance (week 2-12): 1 mg twice daily
Note: Start 1 week before target quit date. Patients who cannot tolerate adverse events may require temporary reduction in dose. If patient successfully quits smoking during the 12 weeks, may continue for another 12 weeks to help maintain success. If not successful in first 12 weeks, then stop medication and reassess factors contributing to failure.
Dosage adjustment for toxicity: Lower dose for a period of time, then increase again
Dosage adjustment in renal impairment:
Cl_{cr} ≥30 mL/minute: No adjustment required
Cl_{cr} <30 mL/minute: Initial: 0.5 mg once daily; maximum dose: 0.5 mg twice daily
Hemodialysis: Maximum dose: 0.5 mg once daily
Dosage adjustment in hepatic impairment: No adjustment required

Dietary Considerations Should be given with food and a full glass of water to decrease gastric upset.

Administration Administer with food and glass of water.

Additional Information In all studies, patients received an educational booklet on smoking cessation and received up to 10 minutes of counseling at each weekly visit. Dosing started 1 week before target quit date. Successful cessation of smoking may alter pharmacokinetic properties of other medications (eg, theophylline, warfarin, insulin).

Dosage Forms
Tablet, as tartrate:
Chantix™: 0.5 mg, 1 mg

♦ **Varenicline Tartrate** *see* Varenicline *on page 1777*

♦ **Varicella, Measles, Mumps, and Rubella Vaccine** *see* Measles, Mumps, Rubella, and Varicella Virus Vaccine *on page 1057*

Varicella Virus Vaccine *(var i SEL a VYE rus vak SEEN)*

U.S. Brand Names Varivax®
Canadian Brand Names Varilrix®; Varivax® III
Index Terms Chicken Pox Vaccine; Varicella-Zoster Virus (VZV) Vaccine (Varicella); VZV Vaccine (Varicella)
Pharmacologic Category Vaccine
Additional Appendix Information
Immunization Recommendations *on page 1929*
Use Immunization against varicella in children ≥12 months of age and adults
Pregnancy Risk Factor C
Pregnancy Implications Animal reproduction studies have not been conducted. Varivax® should not be administered to pregnant females and pregnancy should be avoided for 3 months following vaccination. A pregnancy registry has been established for pregnant women exposed to varicella virus vaccine (800-986-8999).
Lactation Excretion in breast milk unknown/use caution
Medication Safety Issues
Sound-alike/look-alike issues:
Varicella virus vaccine has been given in error (instead of the indicated varicella immune globulin) to pregnant women exposed to varicella.

Both varicella vaccine and zoster vaccine are live, attenuated strains of varicella-zoster virus. Their indications, dosing, and composition are distinct. Varicella is indicated in children to prevent chickenpox, while zoster vaccine is indicated in older individuals to prevent reactivation of the virus which causes shingles. Zoster vaccine is **not** a substitute for varicella vaccine and should not be used in children.

Contraindications Hypersensitivity to any component of the vaccine; individuals with blood dyscrasias, leukemia, lymphomas, or other malignant neoplasms affecting the bone marrow or lymphatic systems; those receiving immunosuppressive therapy; primary and acquired immunodeficiency states; family history of congenital or hereditary immunodeficiency; active, untreated tuberculosis; current febrile illness; pregnancy

Warnings/Precautions Immediate treatment for anaphylactoid reaction should be available during vaccine use. Defer vaccination for at least 5 months following blood or plasma transfusions, immune globulin (IgG), or VZIG (avoid IgG or IVIG use for 2 months following vaccination); salicylates should be avoided for 6 weeks after vaccination. Vaccinated individuals should not have close association with susceptible high risk individuals (newborns, pregnant women, immunocompromised persons) following vaccination. Products may contain gelatin, neomycin, or albumin.

Adverse Reactions All serious adverse reactions must be reported to the U.S. Department of Health and Human Services (DHHS) Vaccine Adverse Event Reporting System (VAERS) 1-800-822-7967.
>10%:
Central nervous system: Fever (10% to 15%)
Local: Injection site reaction (19% to 33%)

1% to 10%:

Central nervous system: Chills, fatigue, headache, irritability, malaise, nervousness, sleep disturbance

Dermatologic: Generalized varicella-like rash (1% to 6%), contact rash, dermatitis, diaper rash, dry skin, eczema, heat rash, itching

Gastrointestinal: Abdominal pain, appetite decreased, cold/canker sore, constipation, diarrhea, nausea, vomiting

Hematologic: Lymphadenopathy

Local: Varicella-like rash at the injection site (1% to 3%)

Neuromuscular & skeletal: Arthralgia, myalgia, stiff neck

Otic: Otitis

Respiratory: Cough, lower/upper respiratory illness

Miscellaneous: Allergic reactions, teething

<1%: Febrile seizure, pneumonitis

<1% (Limited to important or life-threatening) Anaphylaxis, Bell's palsy, cellulitis, cerebrovascular accident, dizziness, encephalitis, erythema multiforme, febrile seizure, Guillain-Barré syndrome, Henoch-Schönlein purpura, nonfebrile seizure, pneumonia, Stevens-Johnson syndrome, thrombocytopenia, transverse myelitis

Drug Interactions

Increased Effect/Toxicity: Salicylates may increase the risk of Reye's following varicella vaccination (avoid salicylate use for 6 weeks following vaccination).

Decreased Effect: The effect of the vaccine may be decreased and the risk of varicella disease in individuals who are receiving immunosuppressant drugs (including high dose systemic corticosteroids) may be increased. Effect of vaccine may be decreased if given within 5 months of immune globulins. Effectiveness of varicella vaccine may be decreased if given within 30 days of MMR vaccine (effectiveness not decreased when administered simultaneously).

Stability Store powder in freezer at -15°C (5°F) or colder; protect from light. Store diluent separately at room temperature or in refrigerator. Powder may be stored under refrigeration for up to 72 continuous hours prior to reconstitution; if not used within 72 hours, vaccine should be discarded. Use 0.7 mL of the provided diluent to reconstitute vaccine. Gently agitate to mix thoroughly. (Total volume of reconstituted vaccine will be ~0.5 mL.) Following reconstitution, discard reconstituted vaccine if not used within 30 minutes.

Canadian formulations: **Note:** Varicella vaccine has been reformulated to produce a refrigerator-stable preparation. Previously, the product required storage in a freezer prior to reconstitution. The new Canadian formulation may be stored in a freezer, but if transferred to a refrigerator, may not be refrozen. Individual product labeling should be consulted to confirm proper conditions.

Mechanism of Action As a live, attenuated vaccine, varicella virus vaccine offers active immunity to disease caused by the varicella-zoster virus

Pharmacodynamics/Kinetics

Onset of action: Seroconversion: ~4-6 weeks

Duration: Antibody titers detectable at 10 years postvaccination

Dosage SubQ:

Children 12 months to 12 years: 0.5 mL; a second dose may be administered ≥3 months later

Children ≥13 years to Adults: 2 doses of 0.5 mL separated by 4-8 weeks

Administration Do not administer I.V.; inject immediately after reconstitution; inject SubQ into the outer aspect of the upper arm, if possible. Federal law requires that the date of administration, the vaccine manufacturer, lot number of vaccine, and the administering person's name, title and address be entered into the patient's permanent medical record.

Monitoring Parameters Rash, fever

Additional Information Federal law requires that the date of administration, the vaccine manufacturer, lot number of vaccine, and the administering person's name, title and address be entered into the patient's permanent medical record.

Dosage Forms [CAN] = Canadian brand name

Injection, powder for reconstitution [preservative free]:

Varivax®: 1350 plaque-forming units (PFU) [contains gelatin and trace amounts of neomycin; packaged with diluent]

Varivax® III [CAN]: 1350 plaque-forming units (PFU) [contains gelatin and trace amounts of neomycin; packaged with diluent; not available in U.S.]

Injection, powder for reconstitution (Valrilix® [CAN]): $10^{3.3}$ plaque-forming units (PFU) [contains albumin and gelatin; packaged with diluent; not available in U.S.]

♦ **Varicella-Zoster Virus (VZV) Vaccine (Varicella)** see Varicella Virus Vaccine on page 1778

♦ **Varicella-Zoster (VZV) Vaccine (Zoster)** see Zoster Vaccine on page 1827

♦ **Varilrix® (Can)** see Varicella Virus Vaccine on page 1778

♦ **Varivax®** see Varicella Virus Vaccine on page 1778

♦ **Varivax® III (Can)** see Varicella Virus Vaccine on page 1778

♦ **Vaseretic®** see Enalapril and Hydrochlorothiazide on page 581

♦ **Vasocon® (Can)** see Naphazoline on page 1198

♦ **Vasodilan® [DSC]** see Isoxsuprine on page 950

Vasopressin (vay soe PRES in)

U.S. Brand Names Pitressin®

Canadian Brand Names Pressyn®; Pressyn® AR

Index Terms ADH; Antidiuretic Hormone; 8-Arginine Vasopressin

Pharmacologic Category Antidiuretic Hormone Analog; Hormone, Posterior Pituitary

Use Treatment of diabetes insipidus; prevention and treatment of postoperative abdominal distention; differential diagnosis of diabetes insipidus

(Continued)

Vasopressin *(Continued)*

Unlabeled/Investigational Use Adjunct in the treatment of GI hemorrhage and esophageal varices; pulseless arrest (ventricular tachycardia [VT]/ventricular fibrillation [VF], asystole/pulseless electrical activity [PEA]); vasodilatory shock (septic shock)

Pregnancy Risk Factor C

Medication Safety Issues
Sound-alike/look-alike issues:
Pitressin® may be confused with Pitocin®

Dosage
Diabetes insipidus (highly variable dosage; titrated based on serum and urine sodium and osmolality in addition to fluid balance and urine output):
I.M., SubQ:
Children: 2.5-10 units 2-4 times/day as needed
Adults: 5-10 units 2-4 times/day as needed (dosage range 5-60 units/day)
Continuous I.V. infusion: Children and Adults: 0.5 milliunit/kg/hour (0.0005 unit/kg/hour); double dosage as needed every 30 minutes to a maximum of 0.01 unit/kg/hour
Intranasal: Administer on cotton pledget, as nasal spray, or by dropper
Abdominal distention: Adults: I.M.: 5 units stat, 10 units every 3-4 hours
GI hemorrhage (unlabeled use): I.V. infusion: Dilute in NS or D_5W to 0.1-1 unit/mL
Children: Initial: 0.002-0.005 units/kg/minute; titrate dose as needed; maximum: 0.01 unit/kg/minute; continue at same dosage (if bleeding stops) for 12 hours, then taper off over 24-48 hours
Adults: Initial: 0.2-0.4 unit/minute, then titrate dose as needed, if bleeding stops; continue at same dose for 12 hours, taper off over 24-48 hours
Pulseless arrest (unlabeled use) [ACLS protocol]: Adults: I.V; I.O.: 40 units; may give one dose to replace first or second dose of epinephrine. I.V./I.O. drug administration is preferred, but if no access, may give endotracheally at 2 to 2 ½ times the I.V. dose. Mix with 5-10 mL of water or normal saline, and administer down the endotracheal tube.
Vasodilatory shock/septic shock (unlabeled use): Adults: I.V.: 0.01-0.04 units/minute for the treatment of septic shock. Doses >0.04 units/minute may have more cardiovascular side effects. Most case reports have used 0.04 units/minute continuous infusion as a fixed dose.
Dosing adjustment in hepatic impairment: Some patients respond to much lower doses with cirrhosis

Additional Information Complete prescribing information for this medication should be consulted for additional detail.

Dosage Forms
Injection, solution: 20 units/mL (0.5 mL, 1 mL, 10 mL)
Pitressin®: 20 units/mL (1 mL)

♦ **Vasotec®** *see* Enalapril *on page 578*

♦ **Vaxigrip® (Can)** *see* Influenza Virus Vaccine *on page 906*

♦ **VCF™ [OTC]** *see* Nonoxynol 9 *on page 1239*

♦ **VCR** *see* VinCRIStine *on page 1789*

♦ **Vectibix™** *see* Panitumumab *on page 1305*

Vecuronium *(vek ue ROE nee um)*

U.S. Brand Names Norcuron® [DSC]
Canadian Brand Names Norcuron®
Index Terms ORG NC 45
Pharmacologic Category Neuromuscular Blocker Agent, Nondepolarizing
Additional Appendix Information
Neuromuscular Blocking Agents *on page 1890*
Use Adjunct to general anesthesia to facilitate endotracheal intubation and to relax skeletal muscles during surgery; to facilitate mechanical ventilation in ICU patients; does not relieve pain or produce sedation
Pregnancy Risk Factor C
Pregnancy Implications Use in cesarean section has been reported. Umbilical venous concentrations were 11% of maternal.
Lactation Excretion in breast milk unknown/use caution
Medication Safety Issues
Sound-alike/look-alike issues:
Vecuronium may be confused with vancomycin
Norcuron® may be confused with Narcan®

High alert medication: The Institute for Safe Medication Practices (ISMP) includes this medication among its list of drugs which have a heightened risk of causing significant patient harm when used in error.
Contraindications Hypersensitivity to vecuronium or any component of the formulation
Warnings/Precautions Ventilation must be supported during neuromuscular blockade; certain clinical conditions may result in potentiation or antagonism of neuromuscular blockade:
Potentiation: Electrolyte abnormalities, severe hyponatremia, severe hypocalcemia, severe hypokalemia, hypermagnesemia, neuromuscular diseases, acidosis, acute intermittent porphyria, renal failure, hepatic failure
Antagonism: Alkalosis, hypercalcemia, demyelinating lesions, peripheral neuropathies, diabetes mellitus

Increased sensitivity in patients with myasthenia gravis, Eaton-Lambert syndrome; resistance in burn patients (>30% of body) for period of 5-70 days postinjury; resistance in patients with muscle trauma, denervation, immobilization, infection; use with caution in patients with hepatic or renal impairment; does not counteract bradycardia produced by anesthetics/vagal stimulation. Cross-sensitivity with other neuromuscular-blocking agents may occur; use extreme caution in patients with previous anaphylactic reactions. **[U.S. Boxed Warning]: Should be administered by adequately trained individuals familiar with its use.**

Adverse Reactions <1% (Limited to important or life-threatening): Bradycardia, circulatory collapse, edema, flushing, hypersensitivity reaction, hypotension, itching, rash, tachycardia, acute quadriplegic myopathy syndrome (prolonged use), myositis ossificans (prolonged use)

Overdosage/Toxicology Symptoms include prolonged skeletal muscle weakness, apnea, and cardiovascular collapse. Use neostigmine, edrophonium, or pyridostigmine with atropine to antagonize skeletal muscle relaxation. Mechanical cardiovascular and respiratory support, fluids, and pressors may be necessary.

Drug Interactions

Increased Effect/Toxicity: Increased effects are possible with aminoglycosides, beta-blockers, clindamycin, calcium channel blockers, halogenated anesthetics, imipenem, ketamine, lidocaine, loop diuretics (furosemide), macrolides (case reports), magnesium sulfate, procainamide, quinidine, quinolones, tetracyclines, and vancomycin. May increase risk of myopathy when used with high- dose corticosteroids for extended periods.

Stability Store intact vials of powder for injection at room temperature 15°C to 30°C (59°F to 86°F). Vials reconstituted with bacteriostatic water for injection (BWFI) may be stored for 5 days under refrigeration or at room temperature. Vials reconstituted with other compatible diluents (nonbacteriostatic) should be stored under refrigeration and used within 24 hours. Reconstitute with compatible solution for injection to final concentration of 1 mg/mL.

Mechanism of Action Blocks acetylcholine from binding to receptors on motor endplate inhibiting depolarization

Pharmacodynamics/Kinetics
Onset of action:
Good intubation conditions: Within 2.5-3 minutes
Maximum neuromuscular blockade: Within 3-5 minutes
Duration: 20-40 minutes
Metabolism: Active metabolite: 3-desacetyl vecuronium ($1/2$ the activity of parent drug)
Half-life elimination: 51-80 minutes
Excretion: Primarily feces (40% to 75%); urine (30% as unchanged drug and metabolites)

Dosage Administer I.V.; dose to effect; doses will vary due to interpatient variability; use ideal body weight for obese patients
Surgery:
Neonates: 0.1 mg/kg/dose; maintenance: 0.03-0.15 mg/kg every 1-2 hours as needed
Infants >7 weeks to 1 year: Initial: 0.08-0.1 mg/kg/dose; maintenance: 0.05-0.1 mg/kg every 60 minutes as needed
Children >1 year and Adults: Initial: 0.08-0.1 mg/kg or 0.04-0.06 mg/kg after initial dose of succinylcholine for intubation; maintenance: 0.01-0.015 mg/kg 25-40 minutes after initial dose, then 0.01-0.015 mg/kg every 12-15 minutes (higher doses will allow less frequent maintenance doses); may be administered as a continuous infusion at 0.8-2 mcg/kg/minute
Pretreatment/priming: Adults: 10% of intubating dose given 3-5 minutes before initial dose
ICU: Adults: 0.05-0.1 mg/kg bolus followed by 0.8-1.7 mcg/kg/minute once initial recovery from bolus observed or 0.1-0.2 mg/kg/dose every 1 hour

Note: Children (1-10 years) may require slightly higher initial doses and slightly more frequent supplementation; infants >7 weeks to 1 year may be more sensitive to vecuronium and have a longer recovery time

Dosing adjustment in renal impairment: Prolongation of blockade

Dosing adjustment in hepatic impairment: Dose reductions are necessary in patients with cirrhosis or cholestasis

Administration Concentration of 1 mg/mL may be administered by rapid I.V. injection. May further dilute reconstituted vial to 0.1-0.2 mg/mL in a compatible solution for I.V. infusion. Concentration of 1 mg/mL may be used for I.V. infusion in fluid-restricted patients.

Monitoring Parameters Blood pressure, heart rate

Additional Information Vecuronium is classified as an intermediate-duration neuromuscular-blocking agent. It produces minimal, if any, histamine release; does not relieve pain or produce sedation. It may produce cumulative effect on duration of blockade.

Dosage Forms Injection, powder for reconstitution, as bromide: 10 mg, 20 mg [may be supplied with diluent containing benzyl alcohol]

♦ **Velcade**® *see* Bortezomib *on page 230*
♦ **Velivet**™ *see* Ethinyl Estradiol and Desogestrel *on page 645*
♦ **Velosef**® *see* Cephradine *on page 332*

Venlafaxine (ven la FAX een)

U.S. Brand Names Effexor®; Effexor® XR
Canadian Brand Names Effexor® XR
Pharmacologic Category Antidepressant, Serotonin/Norepinephrine Reuptake Inhibitor
Additional Appendix Information
Antidepressant Agents *on page 1866*
Use Treatment of major depressive disorder; generalized anxiety disorder (GAD), social anxiety disorder (social phobia); panic disorder
Unlabeled/Investigational Use Obsessive-compulsive disorder (OCD); hot flashes; neuropathic pain; attention-deficit/hyperactivity disorder (ADHD)
Restrictions An FDA-approved medication guide concerning the use of antidepressants in children and teenagers must be distributed when dispensing an outpatient prescription (new or refill) where this medication is to be used without direct supervision of a healthcare provider. Medication guides are available at http://www.fda.gov/cder/Offices/ODS/medication_guides.htm. Dispense to parents or guardians of children and teenagers receiving this medication.
Pregnancy Risk Factor C
(Continued)

Venlafaxine *(Continued)*

Pregnancy Implications Teratogenic effects were not observed in animal studies. Nonteratogenic effects including respiratory distress, cyanosis, apnea, seizures, temperature instability, feeding difficulty, vomiting, hypoglycemia, hypo- or hypertonia, hyper-reflexia, jitteriness, irritability, constant crying, and tremor have been reported in the neonate immediately following delivery after exposure late in the third trimester. Exposure to SSRIs late in pregnancy has also been associated with persistent pulmonary hypertension of the newborn (PPHN). Adverse effects may be due to toxic effects of SNRI or drug discontinuation. In some cases, effects may present clinically as serotonin syndrome. There are no adequate and well-controlled studies in pregnant women. Use during pregnancy only if the potential benefit to the mother outweighs the possible risk to the fetus. If treatment during pregnancy is required, consider tapering therapy during the third trimester.

Lactation Enters breast milk/not recommended

Contraindications Hypersensitivity to venlafaxine or any component of the formulation; use of MAO inhibitors within 14 days; should not initiate MAO inhibitor within 7 days of discontinuing venlafaxine

Warnings/Precautions **[U.S. Boxed Warning]: Antidepressants increase the risk of suicidal thinking and behavior in children and adolescents with major depressive disorder (MDD) and other depressive disorders;** consider risk prior to prescribing. All patients must be closely monitored for clinical worsening, suicidality, or unusual changes in behavior, especially during the initiation of therapy or following an increase or decrease in dosage. When used in children, the child's family or caregiver should be instructed to closely observe the patient and communicate condition with healthcare provider. Reduced growth rate has been observed with venlafaxine therapy in children. A medication guide should be dispensed with each prescription. **Venlafaxine is not FDA approved for use in children.**

The possibility of a suicide attempt is inherent in major depression and may persist until remission occurs. Use caution in high-risk patients. Worsening depression and severe abrupt suicidality that are not part of the presenting symptoms may require discontinuation or modification of drug therapy. The patient's family or caregiver should be alerted to monitor patients for the emergence of suicidality and associated behaviors (such as agitation, irritability, hostility, impulsivity, and hypomania) and call healthcare provider.

May worsen psychosis in some patients or precipitate a shift to mania or hypomania in patients with bipolar disorder. Patients presenting with depressive symptoms should be screened for bipolar disorder. Monotherapy in patients with bipolar disorder should be avoided. **Venlafaxine is not FDA approved for the treatment of bipolar depression.**

The potential for severe reactions exists when used with MAO inhibitors, SSRIs/SNRIs or triptans (myoclonus, diaphoresis, hyperthermia, NMS features, seizures, and death). May cause sustained increase in blood pressure or tachycardia; dose related and increases are generally modest (12-15 mm Hg diastolic). Control pre-existing hypertension prior to initiation of venlafaxine. Use caution in patients with recent history of MI, unstable heart disease, or hyperthyroidism; may cause increase in anxiety, nervousness, insomnia; may cause weight loss (use with caution in patients where weight loss is undesirable); may cause increases in serum cholesterol. Use caution with hepatic or renal impairment. Venlafaxine has been associated with the development of SIADH and hyponatremia.

May increase the risks associated with electroconvulsive therapy. Use cautiously in patients with a history of seizures. The risks of cognitive or motor impairment, as well as the potential for anticholinergic effects are very low. May cause or exacerbate sexual dysfunction. May impair platelet aggregation, resulting in bleeding.

Abrupt discontinuation or dosage reduction after extended (≥6 weeks) therapy may lead to agitation, dysphoria, nervousness, anxiety, and other symptoms. When discontinuing therapy, dosage should be tapered gradually over at least a 2-week period. If intolerable symptoms occur following a decrease in dosage or upon discontinuation of therapy, then resuming the previous dose with a more gradual taper should be considered. Use caution in patients with increased intraocular pressure or at risk of acute narrow-angle glaucoma.

Adverse Reactions

>10%:
- Central nervous system: Headache (25% to 34%), insomnia (15% to 23%), somnolence (12% to 23%), dizziness (11% to 20%), nervousness (6% to 13%)
- Gastrointestinal: Nausea (21% to 37%), xerostomia (12% to 22%), anorexia (8% to 20%), constipation (8% to 15%)
- Genitourinary: Abnormal ejaculation/orgasm (2% to 16%)
- Neuromuscular & skeletal: Weakness (8% to 17%)
- Miscellaneous: Diaphoresis (10% to 14%)

1% to 10%:
- Cardiovascular: Hypertension (dose related; 3% in patients receiving <100 mg/day, up to 13% in patients receiving >300 mg/day); vasodilation (3% to 4%); palpitation (3%), tachycardia (2%), chest pain (2%), postural hypotension (1%), edema
- Central nervous system: Abnormal dreams (3% to 7%), anxiety (5% to 6%), yawning (3% to 5%), agitation (2% to 4%), chills (3%), confusion (2%), abnormal thinking (2%), depersonalization (1%), depression (1% to 3%), fever, migraine, amnesia, hypoesthesia, trismus, vertigo
- Dermatologic: Rash (3%), pruritus (1%), bruising
- Endocrine & metabolic: Libido decreased (3% to 9%)
- Gastrointestinal: Diarrhea (6% to 8%), vomiting (3% to 6%), dyspepsia (5%), abdominal pain (4%), flatulence (3% to 4%), taste perversion (2%), weight loss (1% to 4%), appetite increased, weight gain
- Genitourinary: Impotence (4% to 10%), urinary frequency (3%), impaired urination (2%), urinary retention (1%), prostatic disorder
- Neuromuscular & skeletal: Tremor (4% to 5%), hypertonia (3%), paresthesia (2% to 3%), twitching (1% to 2%), neck pain, arthralgia
- Ocular: Abnormal or blurred vision (4% to 6%), mydriasis (2%)
- Otic: Tinnitus (2%)

Respiratory: Pharyngitis (7%), sinusitis (2%), cough increased, dyspnea

Miscellaneous: Infection (6%), flu-like syndrome (6%), trauma (2%)

<1% (Limited to important or life-threatening): Agranulocytosis, anaphylaxis, aplastic anemia, aneurysm, angina pectoris, anuria; arrhythmia (including atrial and ventricular tachycardia, fibrillation and torsade de pointes); arteritis, asthma, ataxia, atelectasis, atrioventricular block, bacteremia, basophilia, bigeminy, biliary pain, bilirubinemia, bleeding time increased, bradycardia, bradykinesia, BUN increased, bundle branch block, carcinoma, cardiovascular disorder (mitral valve and circulatory disturbance), cataract, catatonia, cellulitis, cerebral ischemia, cholelithiasis, congestive heart failure, coronary artery disease, creatinine increased, crystalluria, cyanosis, deafness, DVT, dehydration, delusions, dementia, diabetes mellitus, dystonia, EKG abnormalities (including QT prolongation), electrolyte abnormalities, embolus, eosinophilia, exfoliative dermatitis, erythema multiforme, extrapyramidal symptoms, extrasystoles, facial paralysis, fasciitis, gastrointestinal ulcer, glaucoma, Guillain-Barré syndrome, heart arrest, hematemesis, hematoma; hemorrhage (eye, GI, mucocutaneous, rectal); hepatitis, homicidal ideation, hostility, hyperacusis, hypercalcinuria, hyperchlorhydria, hyper-/hypocholesteremia, hyper-/hypoglycemia, hyperlipemia, hyper-/hypothyroidism, hyperuricemia, hypokalemia, hyponatremia, hypophosphatemia, hypoproteinemia, hypotension, intestinal obstruction, jaundice, kidney function abnormal, larynx edema, leukocytosis, leukoderma, leukopenia, liver enzymes increased, loss of consciousness, lymphadenopathy, lymphocytosis, maculopapular rash, menstrual abnormalities, miliaria, moniliasis, multiple myeloma, myasthenia, myocardial infarct, myoclonus, myopathy, neck rigidity, neuroleptic malignant-like syndrome, neuropathy, neutropenia, osteoporosis, pancytopenia, pleurisy, pneumonia, pyelonephritis, pyuria, rhabdomyolysis, rheumatoid arthritis, seizure, serotonin syndrome, SIADH, skin atrophy, Stevens-Johnson syndrome, suicidal ideation (reported at a frequency up to 2% in children/adolescents with major depressive disorder), suicide attempt, syncope, tendon rupture, thrombocythemia, thrombocytopenia, thrombophlebitis, toxic epidermal necrolysis, withdrawal syndrome

Overdosage/Toxicology Symptoms of overdose include altered consciousness (somnolence to coma), tachycardia, mydriasis, seizures, and vomiting. Predominantly occurs in combination with ethanol and/or other drug use. Most overdoses resolve with only supportive treatment, though ECG monitoring would be prudent considering the risk of arrhythmia. Postmarketing experience suggests that the risk of fatal outcome associated with overdose may be higher than that observed with SSRI-associated overdoses. Use of activated charcoal, inductions of emesis, or gastric lavage should be considered for acute ingestion. Forced diuresis, dialysis, and hemoperfusion not effective due to large volume of distribution.

Drug Interactions

Cytochrome P450 Effect: Substrate of CYP2C9 (minor), 2C19 (minor), 2D6 (major), 3A4 (major); **Inhibits** CYP2B6 (weak), 2D6 (weak), 3A4 (weak)

Increased Effect/Toxicity: Concurrent use of MAO inhibitors (phenelzine, isocarboxazid), or drugs with MAO inhibitor activity (linezolid) may result in serotonin syndrome; should not be used within 2 weeks of each other. Selegiline may have a lower risk of this effect, particularly at low dosages, due to selectivity for MAO type B. In addition, concurrent use of buspirone, lithium, meperidine, nefazodone, selegiline, serotonin agonists (sumatriptan, naratriptan), sibutramine, SSRIs/SNRIs, trazodone, or tricyclic antidepressants may increase the risk of serotonin syndrome. Serum levels of haloperidol may be increased by venlafaxine. CYP2D6 inhibitors may increase the levels/effects of venlafaxine; example inhibitors include chlorpromazine, delavirdine, fluoxetine, miconazole, paroxetine, pergolide, quinidine, quinine, ritonavir, and ropinirole. CYP3A4 inhibitors may increase the levels/effects of venlafaxine; example inhibitors include azole antifungals, clarithromycin, diclofenac, doxycycline, erythromycin, imatinib, isoniazid, nefazodone, nicardipine, propofol, protease inhibitors, quinidine, telithromycin, and verapamil.

Decreased Effect: Serum levels of indinavir may be reduced be venlafaxine (AUC reduced by 28%); clinical significance not determined. CYP3A4 inducers may decrease the levels/effects of venlafaxine; example inducers include aminoglutethimide, carbamazepine, nafcillin, nevirapine, phenobarbital, phenytoin, and rifamycins.

Ethanol/Nutrition/Herb Interactions

Ethanol: Avoid ethanol (may increase CNS effects).

Herb/Nutraceutical: Avoid valerian, St John's wort, SAMe, kava kava, tryptophan (may increase risk of serotonin syndrome and/or excessive sedation).

Mechanism of Action Venlafaxine and its active metabolite o-desmethylvenlafaxine (ODV) are potent inhibitors of neuronal serotonin and norepinephrine reuptake and weak inhibitors of dopamine reuptake. Venlafaxine and ODV have no significant activity for muscarinic cholinergic, H_1-histaminergic, or alpha$_2$-adrenergic receptors. Venlafaxine and ODV do not possess MAO-inhibitory activity.

Pharmacodynamics/Kinetics

Absorption: Oral: 92% to 100%; food has no significant effect on the absorption of venlafaxine or formation of the active metabolite O-desmethylvenlafaxine (ODV)

Distribution: At steady state: Venlafaxine 7.5 ± 3.7 L/kg, ODV 5.7 ± 1.8 L/Kg

Protein binding: Bound to human plasma protein: Venlafaxine 27%, ODV 30%

Metabolism: Hepatic via CYP2D6 to active metabolite, O-desmethylvenlafaxine (ODV); other metabolites include N-desmethylvenlafaxine and N,O-didesmethylvenlafaxine

Bioavailability: Absolute: ~45%

Half-life elimination: Venlafaxine: 3-7 hours; ODV: 9-13 hours; Steady-state, plasma: Venlafaxine/ODV: Within 3 days of multiple-dose therapy; prolonged with cirrhosis (Adults: Venlafaxine: ~30%, ODV: ~60%) and with dialysis (Adults: Venlafaxine: ~180%, ODV: ~142%)

Time to peak:

Immediate release: Venlafaxine: 2 hours, ODV: 3 hours

Extended release: Venlafaxine: 5.5 hours, ODV: 9 hours

Excretion: Urine (~87%, 5% as unchanged drug, 29% as unconjugated ODV, 26% as conjugated ODV, 27% as minor inactive metabolites) within 48 hours

Clearance at steady state: Venlafaxine: 1.3 ± 0.6 L/hour/kg, ODV: 0.4 ± 0.2 L/hour/kg

(Continued)

Venlafaxine *(Continued)*

Clearance decreased with:
  Cirrhosis: Adults: Venlafaxine: ~50%, ODV: ~30%
  Severe cirrhosis: Adults: Venlafaxine: ~90%
  Renal impairment (Cl$_{cr}$ 10-70 mL/minute): Adults: Venlafaxine: ~24%
  Dialysis: Adults: Venlafaxine: ~57%, ODV: ~56%; due to large volume of distribution, a
    significant amount of drug is not likely to be removed.

Dosage Oral:
Children and Adolescents:
  ADHD (unlabeled use): Initial: 12.5 mg/day
    Children <40 kg: Increase by 12.5 mg/week to maximum of 50 mg/day in 2 divided doses
    Children ≥40 kg: Increase by 25 mg/week to maximum of 75 mg/day in 3 divided doses.
    Mean dose: 60 mg or 1.4 mg/kg administered in 2-3 divided doses
Adults:
  Depression:
    Immediate-release tablets: 75 mg/day, administered in 2 or 3 divided doses, taken with
      food; dose may be increased in 75 mg/day increments at intervals of at least 4 days,
      up to 225-375 mg/day
    Extended-release capsules: 75 mg once daily taken with food; for some new patients, it
      may be desirable to start at 37.5 mg/day for 4-7 days before increasing to 75 mg once
      daily; dose may be increased by up to 75 mg/day increments every 4 days as toler-
      ated, up to a recommended maximum of 225 mg/day
  GAD, social anxiety disorder: Extended-release capsules: 75 mg once daily taken with
    food; for some new patients, it may be desirable to start at 37.5 mg/day for 4-7 days
    before increasing to 75 mg once daily; dose may be increased by up to 75 mg/day
    increments every 4 days as tolerated, up to a maximum of 225 mg/day
  Panic disorder: Extended-release capsules: 37.5 mg once daily for 1 week; may increase
    to 75 mg daily, with subsequent weekly increases of 75 mg/day up to a maximum of 225
    mg/day.
  Obsessive-compulsive disorder (unlabeled use): Titrate to usual dosage range of 150-300
    mg/day; however, doses up to 375 mg daily have been used; response may be seen in 4
    weeks
  Neuropathic pain (unlabeled use): Dosages evaluated varied considerably based on
    etiology of chronic pain, but efficacy has been shown for many conditions in the range of
    75-225 mg/day; onset of relief may occur in 1-2 weeks, or take up to 6 weeks for full
    benefit.
  Hot flashes (unlabeled use): Doses of 37.5-75 mg/day have demonstrated significant
    improvement of vasomotor symptoms after 4-8 weeks of treatment; in one study, doses
    >75 mg/day offered no additional benefit; however, higher doses (225 mg/day) may be
    beneficial in patients with perimenopausal depression.
  Attention-deficit disorder (unlabeled use): Initial: Doses vary between 18.75 to 75 mg/day;
    may increase after 4 weeks to 150 mg/day; if tolerated, doses up to 225 mg/day have
    been used
  Note: When discontinuing this medication after more than 1 week of treatment, it is
    generally recommended that the dose be tapered. If venlafaxine is used for 6 weeks or
    longer, the dose should be tapered over 2 weeks when discontinuing its use.
  Dosing adjustment in renal impairment: Cl$_{cr}$ 10-70 mL/minute: Decrease dose by 25%;
    decrease total daily dose by 50% if dialysis patients; dialysis patients should receive dosing
    after completion of dialysis
  Dosing adjustment in moderate hepatic impairment: Reduce total daily dosage by 50%

Dietary Considerations Should be taken with food.

Administration Administer with food.
  Extended release capsule: Swallow capsule whole; do not crush or chew. Alternatively,
    contents may be sprinkled on a spoonful of applesauce and swallowed immediately without
    chewing; followed with a glass of water to ensure complete swallowing of the pellets.

Monitoring Parameters Blood pressure should be regularly monitored, especially in patients
  with a high baseline blood pressure; may cause mean increase in heart rate of 4-9 beats/
  minute; cholesterol; mental status for depression, suicidal ideation (especially at the beginning of therapy or when doses are increased or decreased), anxiety, social functioning,
  mania, panic attacks; height and weight should be monitored in children

Reference Range Peak serum level of 163 ng/mL (325 ng/mL of ODV metabolite) obtained
  after a 150 mg oral dose

Dosage Forms
  Capsule, extended release:
    Effexor® XR: 37.5 mg, 75 mg, 150 mg
  Tablet: 25 mg, 37.5 mg, 50 mg, 75 mg, 100 mg
    Effexor®: 25 mg, 37.5 mg, 50 mg, 75 mg, 100 mg

- ♦ **Venofer®** *see* Iron Sucrose *on page 941*
- ♦ **Ventavis™** *see* Iloprost *on page 881*
- ♦ **Ventolin® (Can)** *see* Albuterol *on page 57*
- ♦ **Ventolin® Diskus (Can)** *see* Albuterol *on page 57*
- ♦ **Ventolin® HFA** *see* Albuterol *on page 57*
- ♦ **Ventrodisk (Can)** *see* Albuterol *on page 57*
- ♦ **VePesid®** *see* Etoposide *on page 670*
- ♦ **Veracolate [OTC]** *see* Bisacodyl *on page 223*

Verapamil *(ver AP a mil)*

U.S. Brand Names Calan®; Calan® SR; Covera-HS®; Isoptin® SR; Verelan®; Verelan® PM
Canadian Brand Names Alti-Verapamil; Apo-Verap®; Apo-Verap® SR; Calan®; Chronovera®;
  Covera®; Covera-HS®; Gen-Verapamil; Gen-Verapamil SR; Isoptin® SR; Novo-Veramil SR;
  Nu-Verap; Riva-Verapamil SR; Verapamil Hydrochloride Injection, USP

Index Terms Iproveratril Hydrochloride; Verapamil Hydrochloride

Pharmacologic Category Antiarrhythmic Agent, Class IV, Calcium Channel Blocker

Additional Appendix Information
Calcium Channel Blockers *on page 1878*
Hypertension *on page 2063*

Use Orally for treatment of angina pectoris (vasospastic, chronic stable, unstable) and hypertension; I.V. for supraventricular tachyarrhythmias (PSVT, atrial fibrillation, atrial flutter)

Unlabeled/Investigational Use Migraine; hypertrophic cardiomyopathy; bipolar disorder (manic manifestations)

Pregnancy Risk Factor C

Pregnancy Implications Use in pregnancy only when clearly needed and when the benefits outweigh the potential risk to the fetus. Crosses the placenta. One report of suspected heart block when used to control fetal supraventricular tachycardia. May exhibit tocolytic effects.

Lactation Enters breast milk (small amounts)/not recommended

Medication Safety Issues
Sound-alike/look-alike issues:
Verapamil may be confused with Verelan®
Calan® may be confused with Colace®
Covera-HS® may be confused with Provera®
Isoptin® may be confused with Isopto® Tears
Verelan® may be confused with verapamil, Virilon®, Voltaren®

Significant differences exist between oral and I.V. dosing. Use caution when converting from one route of administration to another.

International issues:
Calan®: Brand name for vinpocetine in Japan

Contraindications Hypersensitivity to verapamil or any component of the formulation; severe left ventricular dysfunction; hypotension (systolic pressure <90 mm Hg) or cardiogenic shock; sick sinus syndrome (except in patients with a functioning artificial pacemaker); second- or third-degree AV block (except in patients with a functioning artificial pacemaker); atrial flutter or fibrillation and an accessory bypass tract (WPW, Lown-Ganong-Levine syndrome)

Warnings/Precautions Use with caution in sick-sinus syndrome, severe left ventricular dysfunction, hepatic or renal impairment, hypertrophic cardiomyopathy (especially obstructive), abrupt withdrawal may cause increased duration and frequency of chest pain; avoid I.V. use in neonates and young infants due to severe apnea, bradycardia, or hypotensive reactions; elderly may experience more constipation and hypotension. Monitor ECG and blood pressure closely in patients receiving I.V. therapy particularly in patients with supraventricular tachycardia. May prolong recovery from nondepolarizing neuromuscular-blocking agents.

Adverse Reactions
>10%: Gastrointestinal: Gingival hyperplasia (up to 19%), constipation (12% up to 42% in clinical trials)

1% to 10%:
Cardiovascular: Bradycardia (1.2 to 1.4%), first-, second-, or third-degree AV block (1.2%), CHF (1.8%), hypotension (2.5% to 3%), peripheral edema (1.9%), symptomatic hypotension (1.5% I.V.), severe tachycardia (1%)
Central nervous system: Dizziness (1.2% to 3.3%), fatigue (1.7%), headache (1.2% to 2.2%)
Dermatologic: Rash (1.2%)
Gastrointestinal: Nausea (0.9% to 2.7%)
Respiratory: Dyspnea (1.4%)

<1% (Limited to important or life-threatening): Alopecia, angina, arthralgia, asystole, atrioventricular dissociation, bronchial/laryngeal spasm, cerebrovascular accident, chest pain, claudication, confusion, diarrhea, dry mouth, ecchymosis, electrical mechanical dissociation (EMD), emotional depression, eosinophilia, equilibrium disorders, erythema multiforme, exanthema, exfoliative dermatitis, galactorrhea/hyperprolactinemia, GI obstruction, gingival hyperplasia, gynecomastia, hair color change, impotence, muscle cramps, MI, myoclonus, paresthesia, Parkinsonian syndrome, psychotic symptoms, purpura (vasculitis), rash, respiratory failure, rotary nystagmus, shakiness, shock, somnolence, Stevens-Johnson syndrome, syncope, urticaria, ventricular fibrillation, vertigo

Overdosage/Toxicology Primary cardiac symptoms of calcium blocker overdose include hypotension and bradycardia. Hypotension is caused by peripheral vasodilation, myocardial depression, and bradycardia. Bradycardia results from sinus bradycardia, second- or third-degree atrioventricular block, or sinus arrest with junctional rhythm. Intraventricular conduction is usually not affected, so QRS duration is normal (verapamil prolongs the PR interval and bepridil prolongs the QT interval and may cause ventricular arrhythmias, including torsade de pointes).

The noncardiac symptoms include confusion, stupor, nausea, vomiting, metabolic acidosis and hyperglycemia.

Following initial gastric decontamination, if possible, repeated calcium administration may promptly reverse depressed cardiac contractility (but not sinus node depression or peripheral vasodilation). Glucagon, epinephrine, and inamrinone (amrinone) may treat refractory hypotension. Glucagon and epinephrine also increase the heart rate (outside the U.S., 4-aminopyridine may be available as an antidote). Dialysis and hemoperfusion are not effective in enhancing elimination, although repeat-dose activated charcoal may serve as an adjunct with sustained-release preparations.

In a few reported cases, overdose with calcium channel blockers has been associated with hypotension and bradycardia, initially refractory to atropine, but becoming more responsive to this agent when larger doses (approaching 1 g/hour for more than 24 hours) of calcium chloride were administered.

Drug Interactions
Cytochrome P450 Effect: Substrate of CYP1A2 (minor), 2B6 (minor), 2C9 (minor), 2C18 (minor), 2E1 (minor), 3A4 (major); **Inhibits** CYP1A2 (weak), 2C9 (weak), 2D6 (weak), 3A4 (moderate)

(Continued)

Verapamil *(Continued)*

Increased Effect/Toxicity: Use of verapamil with amiodarone, beta-blockers, or flecainide may lead to bradycardia and decreased cardiac output. Aspirin and concurrent verapamil use may increase bleeding times. Lithium neurotoxicity may result when verapamil is added. Effect of nondepolarizing neuromuscular blocker is prolonged by verapamil. Grapefruit juice may increase verapamil serum concentrations. Blood pressure-lowering effects may be additive with sildenafil, tadalafil, and vardenafil (use caution).

Cisapride levels may be increased by verapamil, potentially resulting in life-threatening arrhythmias; avoid concurrent use. Verapamil may increase the levels/effects of selected benzodiazepines, other calcium channel blockers, cyclosporine, ergot alkaloids, selected HMG-CoA reductase inhibitors, mirtazapine, nateglinide, nefazodone, pimozide, quinidine, risperidone, sildenafil (and other PDE-5 inhibitors), tacrolimus, telithromycin, venlafaxine, and other CYP3A4 substrates. In addition, serum concentrations of the following drugs may be increased by verapamil: Alfentanil, digoxin, doxorubicin, ethanol, prazosin, and theophylline. Verapamil may increase colchicine toxicity (especially nephrotoxicity).

The levels/effects of verapamil may be increased by azole antifungals, clarithromycin, diclofenac, doxycycline, erythromycin, imatinib, isoniazid, nefazodone, nicardipine, propofol, protease inhibitors, quinidine, telithromycin, and other CYP3A4 inhibitors.

Decreased Effect: The levels/effects of verapamil may be decreased by aminoglutethimide, carbamazepine, nafcillin, nevirapine, phenobarbital, phenytoin, rifamycins, and other CYP3A4 inducers. Lithium levels may be decreased by verapamil. Nafcillin decreases plasma concentration of verapamil.

Ethanol/Nutrition/Herb Interactions

Ethanol: Avoid or limit ethanol (may increase ethanol levels).

Food: Grapefruit juice may increase the serum concentration of verapamil; avoid concurrent use.

Herb/Nutraceutical: St John's wort may decrease levels. Avoid dong quai if using for hypertension (has estrogenic activity). Avoid ephedra, yohimbe, ginseng (may worsen arrhythmia or hypertension). Avoid garlic (may have increased antihypertensive effect).

Stability Store injection at room temperature; do not freeze. Protect from heat. Use only clear solutions. Physically compatible in solutions of pH of 3-6, but may precipitate in solutions having a pH ≥6. Protect I.V. solution from light.

Mechanism of Action Inhibits calcium ion from entering the "slow channels" or select voltage-sensitive areas of vascular smooth muscle and myocardium during depolarization; produces a relaxation of coronary vascular smooth muscle and coronary vasodilation; increases myocardial oxygen delivery in patients with vasospastic angina; slows automaticity and conduction of AV node.

Pharmacodynamics/Kinetics

Onset of action: Peak effect: Oral: Immediate release: 1-2 hours; I.V.: 1-5 minutes

Duration: Oral: Immediate release tablets: 6-8 hours; I.V.: 10-20 minutes

Protein binding: 90%

Metabolism: Hepatic via multiple CYP isoenzymes; extensive first-pass effect

Bioavailability: Oral: 20% to 35%

Half-life elimination: Infants: 4.4-6.9 hours; Adults: Single dose: 2-8 hours, Multiple doses: 4.5-12 hours; prolonged with hepatic cirrhosis

Excretion: Urine (70%, 3% to 4% as unchanged drug); feces (16%)

Dosage

Children: SVT:

I.V.:

<1 year: 0.1-0.2 mg/kg over 2 minutes; repeat every 30 minutes as needed

1-15 years: 0.1-0.3 mg/kg over 2 minutes; maximum: 5 mg/dose, may repeat dose in 15 minutes if adequate response not achieved; maximum for second dose: 10 mg/dose

Oral (dose not well established):

1-5 years: 4-8 mg/kg/day in 3 divided doses **or** 40-80 mg every 8 hours

>5 years: 80 mg every 6-8 hours

Adults:

SVT: I.V.: 2.5-5 mg (over 2 minutes); second dose of 5-10 mg (~0.15 mg/kg) may be given 15-30 minutes after the initial dose if patient tolerates, but does not respond to initial dose; maximum total dose: 20 mg

Angina: Oral: Initial dose: 80-120 mg 3 times/day (elderly or small stature: 40 mg 3 times/day); range: 240-480 mg/day in 3-4 divided doses

Hypertension: Oral:

Immediate release: 80 mg 3 times/day; usual dose range (JNC 7): 80-320 mg/day in 2 divided doses

Sustained release: 240 mg/day; usual dose range (JNC 7): 120-360 mg/day in 1-2 divided doses; 120 mg/day in the elderly or small patients (no evidence of additional benefit in doses >360 mg/day).

Extended release:

Covera-HS®: Usual dose range (JNC 7): 120-360 mg once daily (once-daily dosing is recommended at bedtime)

Verelan® PM: Usual dose range: 200-400 mg once daily at bedtime

Dosing adjustment in renal impairment: Cl_{cr} <10 mL/minute: Administer at 50% to 75% of normal dose.

Dialysis: Not dialyzable (0% to 5%) via hemo- or peritoneal dialysis; supplemental dose is not necessary.

Dosing adjustment/comments in hepatic disease: Reduce dose in cirrhosis, reduce dose to 20% to 50% of normal and monitor ECG.

Dietary Considerations Calan® SR and Isoptin® SR products may be taken with food or milk, other formulations may be administered without regard to meals; sprinkling contents of Verelan® or Verelan® PM capsule onto applesauce does not affect oral absorption.

Administration

Oral: Do not crush or chew sustained or extended release products.

Calan® SR, Isoptin® SR: Administer with food.

Verelan®, Verelan® PM: Capsules may be opened and the contents sprinkled on 1 table-spoonful of applesauce, then swallowed without chewing.

I.V.: Rate of infusion: Over 2 minutes.

Monitoring Parameters Monitor blood pressure closely

Reference Range Therapeutic: 50-200 ng/mL (SI: 100-410 nmol/L) for parent; under normal conditions norverapamil concentration is the same as parent drug. Toxic: >90 mcg/mL

Dosage Forms

Caplet, sustained release: 120 mg, 180 mg, 240 mg
  Calan® SR: 120 mg, 180 mg, 240 mg
Capsule, extended release, controlled onset, as hydrochloride:
  Verelan® PM: 100 mg, 200 mg, 300 mg
Capsule, sustained release, as hydrochloride: 120 mg, 180 mg, 240 mg, 360 mg
  Verelan®: 120 mg, 180 mg, 240 mg, 360 mg
Injection, solution, as hydrochloride: 2.5 mg/mL (2 mL, 4 mL)
Tablet, as hydrochloride: 80 mg, 120 mg
  Calan®: 40 mg, 80 mg, 120 mg
Tablet, extended release: 120 mg, 180 mg, 240 mg
Tablet, extended release, controlled onset, as hydrochloride:
  Covera-HS®: 180 mg, 240 mg
Tablet, sustained release, as hydrochloride: 120 mg, 180 mg, 240 mg
  Isoptin® SR: 120 mg, 180 mg, 240 mg

Extemporaneous Preparations A 50 mg/mL oral suspension may be made using twenty 80 mg verapamil tablets, 3 mL of purified water USP, 8 mL of methylcellulose 1% and simple syrup qs ad to 32 mL; the expected stability is 30 days under refrigeration; shake well before use. A mixture of verapamil 50 mg/mL plus hydrochlorothiazide 5 mg/mL was stable 60 days in refrigerator in a 1:1 preparation of Ora-Sweet® and Ora-Plus®, of Ora-Sweet® SF and Ora-Plus®, and of cherry syrup.

Allen LV and Erickson III MA, "Stability of Labetalol Hydrochloride, Metoprolol Tartrate, Verapamil Hydrochloride, and Spironolactone With Hydrochlorothiazide in Extempora-neously Compounded Oral Liquids," *Am J Health Syst Pharm*, 1996, 53:304-9.

Nahata MC and Hipple TF, *Pediatric Drug Formulations*, 2nd ed, Cincinnati, OH: Harvey Whitney Books Co, 1992.

- **Verapamil and Trandolapril** see Trandolapril and Verapamil *on page 1722*
- **Verapamil Hydrochloride** see Verapamil *on page 1784*
- **Verapamil Hydrochloride Injection, USP (Can)** see Verapamil *on page 1784*
- **Verdeso™** see Desonide *on page 478*
- **Verelan®** see Verapamil *on page 1784*
- **Verelan® PM** see Verapamil *on page 1784*
- **Vermox® [DSC]** see Mebendazole *on page 1059*
- **Vermox® (Can)** see Mebendazole *on page 1059*
- **Versed** see Midazolam *on page 1139*
- **Versel® (Can)** see Selenium Sulfide *on page 1555*
- **Versiclear™** see Sodium Thiosulfate *on page 1584*
- **Vesanoid®** see Tretinoin (Oral) *on page 1730*
- **VESIcare®** see Solifenacin *on page 1585*
- **Vexol®** see Rimexolone *on page 1514*
- **VFEND®** see Voriconazole *on page 1797*
- **Viadur®** see Leuprolide *on page 991*
- **Viagra®** see Sildenafil *on page 1564*
- **Vibramycin®** see Doxycycline *on page 555*
- **Vibra-Tabs®** see Doxycycline *on page 555*
- **Vicks® 44D Cough & Head Congestion [OTC] [DSC]** see Pseudoephedrine and Dextromethorphan *on page 1455*
- **Vicks® 44E [OTC]** see Guaifenesin and Dextromethorphan *on page 816*
- **Vicks® Casero™ [OTC]** see Guaifenesin *on page 814*
- **Vicks® Children's NyQuil® [OTC] [DSC]** see Chlorpheniramine, Pseudoephedrine, and Dextromethorphan *on page 355*
- **Vicks® DayQuil® Multi-Symptom Cold and Flu [OTC] [DSC]** see Acetaminophen, Dextromethorphan, and Pseudoephedrine *on page 35*
- **Vicks® Pediatric 44®m [OTC] [DSC]** see Chlorpheniramine, Pseudoephedrine, and Dextromethorphan *on page 355*
- **Vicks® Pediatric Formula 44E [OTC]** see Guaifenesin and Dextromethorphan *on page 816*
- **Vicks® Sinex® Nasal Spray [OTC]** see Phenylephrine *on page 1358*
- **Vicks® Sinex® UltraFine Mist [OTC]** see Phenylephrine *on page 1358*
- **Vicodin®** see Hydrocodone and Acetaminophen *on page 848*
- **Vicodin® ES** see Hydrocodone and Acetaminophen *on page 848*
- **Vicodin® HP** see Hydrocodone and Acetaminophen *on page 848*
- **Vicoprofen®** see Hydrocodone and Ibuprofen *on page 851*
- **Vidaza™** see Azacitidine *on page 181*
- **Videx®** see Didanosine *on page 496*
- **Videx® EC** see Didanosine *on page 496*
- **Vigamox™** see Moxifloxacin *on page 1175*
- **VIGIV** see Vaccinia Immune Globulin (Intravenous) *on page 1762*

VinBLAStine (vin BLAS teen)

Index Terms NSC-49842; Vinblastine Sulfate; VLB

Pharmacologic Category Antineoplastic Agent, Natural Source (Plant) Derivative; Antineoplastic Agent, Vinca Alkaloid

Use Treatment of Hodgkin's and non-Hodgkin's lymphoma, testicular, lung, head and neck, breast, and renal carcinomas, Mycosis fungoides, Kaposi's sarcoma, histiocytosis, choriocarcinoma, and idiopathic thrombocytopenic purpura

Pregnancy Risk Factor D

Lactation Enters breast milk/not recommended

Medication Safety Issues
Sound-alike/look-alike issues:
VinBLAStine may be confused with vinCRIStine, vinorelbine

High alert medication: The Institute for Safe Medication Practices (ISMP) includes this medication among its list of drugs which have a heightened risk of causing significant patient harm when used in error.

Note: Must be dispensed in overwrap which bears the statement **"Do not remove covering until the moment of injection. Fatal if given intrathecally. For I.V. use only."** Syringes should be labeled: **"Fatal if given intrathecally. For I.V. use only."**

Contraindications For I.V. use only; **I.T. use may result in death**; hypersensitivity to vinblastine or any component of the formulation; pregnancy

Warnings/Precautions Hazardous agent - use appropriate precautions for handling and disposal. **[U.S. Boxed Warning]: Vinblastine is a moderate vesicant; avoid extravasation.** Dosage modification required in patients with impaired liver function and neurotoxicity. **[U.S. Boxed Warning]: For I.V. use only. Intrathecal administration may result in death.** Monitor closely for shortness of breath or bronchospasm in patients receiving in combination with mitomycin C. **[U.S. Boxed Warning]: Should be administered under the supervision of an experienced cancer chemotherapy physician.**

Adverse Reactions
>10%:
Dermatologic: Alopecia
Endocrine & metabolic: SIADH
Gastrointestinal: Diarrhea (less common), stomatitis, anorexia, metallic taste
Hematologic: May cause severe bone marrow suppression and is the dose-limiting toxicity of vinblastine (unlike vincristine); severe granulocytopenia and thrombocytopenia may occur following the administration of vinblastine and nadir 5-10 days after treatment
Myelosuppression (primarily leukopenia, may be dose limiting)
Onset: 4-7 days
Nadir: 5-10 days
Recovery: 4-21 days
1% to 10%:
Cardiovascular: Hypertension, Raynaud's phenomenon
Central nervous system: Depression, malaise, headache, seizure
Dermatologic: Rash, photosensitivity, dermatitis
Endocrine & metabolic: Hyperuricemia
Gastrointestinal: Constipation, abdominal pain, nausea (mild), vomiting (mild), paralytic ileus, stomatitis
Genitourinary: Urinary retention
Neuromuscular & skeletal: Jaw pain, myalgia, paresthesia
Respiratory: Bronchospasm
<1% (Limited to important or life-threatening): Hemorrhagic colitis, neurotoxicity (rare; symptoms may include peripheral neuropathy, loss of deep tendon reflexes, headache, weakness, urinary retention, GI symptoms, tachycardia, orthostatic hypotension, convulsions), rectal bleeding

Overdosage/Toxicology Symptoms include bone marrow suppression, mental depression, paresthesias, loss of deep reflexes, and neurotoxicity. There is no information regarding the effectiveness of dialysis. There are no antidotes for vinblastine. Treatment is supportive and symptomatic, including fluid restriction or administration of hypertonic saline (3% sodium chloride) for drug-induced secretion of inappropriate antidiuretic hormone (SIADH), diazepam or phenytoin for seizures, laxatives for constipation, and antiemetics for toxic emesis. Inadvertent intrathecal administration requires emergent neurosurgical intervention.

Drug Interactions
Cytochrome P450 Effect: Substrate of CYP2D6 (minor), 3A4 (major); **Inhibits** CYP2D6 (weak), 3A4 (weak)
Increased Effect/Toxicity: CYP3A4 inhibitors may increase the levels/effects of vinblastine; example inhibitors include azole antifungals, clarithromycin, diclofenac, doxycycline, erythromycin, imatinib, isoniazid, nefazodone, nicardipine, propofol, protease inhibitors, quinidine, telithromycin, and verapamil.

Previous or simultaneous use with mitomycin-C has resulted in acute shortness of breath and severe bronchospasm within minutes or several hours after vinca alkaloid injection and may occur up to 2 weeks after the dose of mitomycin. Mitomycin-C in combination with administration of vinblastine may cause acute shortness of breath and severe bronchospasm, onset may be within minutes or several hours after vinblastine injection.

Decreased Effect: CYP3A4 inducers may decrease the levels/effects of vinblastine; example inducers include aminoglutethimide, carbamazepine, nafcillin, nevirapine, phenobarbital, phenytoin (may reduce vinblastine serum concentrations), and rifamycins.

Ethanol/Nutrition/Herb Interactions Herb/Nutraceutical: St John's wort may decrease vinblastine levels. Avoid black cohosh, dong quai in estrogen-dependent tumors.

Stability Store intact vials under refrigeration (2°C to 8°C). Protect from light. Reconstitute to a concentration of 1 mg/mL with bacteriostatic water, bacteriostatic NS, SWFI, NS, or D_5W. For infusion, may be diluted with 50-1000 mL Ns or D_5W. Solutions reconstituted in bacteriostatic water or bacteriostatic NS are stable for 21 days at room temperature or under refrigeration.

Note: **Must be dispensed in overwrap which bears the statement "Do not remove covering until the moment of injection. Fatal if given intrathecally. For I.V. use only." Syringes should be labeled: "Fatal if given intrathecally. For I.V. use only."**

Mechanism of Action Vinblastine binds to tubulin and inhibits microtubule formation, therefore, arresting the cell at metaphase by disrupting the formation of the mitotic spindle; it is specific for the M and S phases. Vinblastine may also interfere with nucleic acid and protein synthesis by blocking glutamic acid utilization.

Pharmacodynamics/Kinetics

Distribution: V_d: 27.3 L/kg; binds extensively to tissues; does not penetrate CNS or other fatty tissues; distributes to liver

Protein binding: 99%

Metabolism: Hepatic to active metabolite

Half-life elimination: Biphasic: Initial: 0.164 hours; Terminal: 25 hours

Excretion: Feces (95%); urine (<1% as unchanged drug)

Dosage Refer to individual protocols.

Children and Adults: I.V.: 4-20 mg/m² (0.1-0.5 mg/kg) every 7-10 days **or** 5-day continuous infusion of 1.5-2 mg/m²/day **or** 0.1-0.5 mg/kg/week

Dosing adjustment in hepatic impairment:

Serum bilirubin 1.5-3.0 mg/dL or AST 60-180 units: Administer 50% of normal dose

Serum bilirubin 3.0-5.0 mg/dL: Administer 25% of dose

Serum bilirubin >5.0 mg/dL or AST >180 units: Omit dose

Administration FATAL IF GIVEN INTRATHECALLY. For I.V. administration only, usually as a slow (2-3 minutes) push, or a bolus (5- to 15-minute) infusion. It is occasionally given as a 24-hour continuous infusion.

Monitoring Parameters CBC with differential and platelet count, serum uric acid, hepatic function tests

Dosage Forms

Injection, powder for reconstitution, as sulfate: 10 mg

Injection, solution, as sulfate: 1 mg/mL (10 mL) [contains benzyl alcohol]

♦ **Vinblastine Sulfate** see VinBLAStine on page 1788
♦ **Vincasar PFS®** see VinCRIStine on page 1789
♦ **Vincasar® PFS® (Can)** see VinCRIStine on page 1789

VinCRIStine (vin KRIS teen)

U.S. Brand Names Vincasar PFS®

Canadian Brand Names Vincasar® PFS®

Index Terms LCR; Leurocristine Sulfate; NSC-67574; VCR; Vincristine Sulfate

Pharmacologic Category Antineoplastic Agent, Natural Source (Plant) Derivative; Antineoplastic Agent, Vinca Alkaloid

Use Treatment of leukemias, Hodgkin's disease, non-Hodgkin's lymphomas, Wilms' tumor, neuroblastoma, rhabdomyosarcoma

Pregnancy Risk Factor D

Lactation Enters breast milk/not recommended

Medication Safety Issues

Sound-alike/look-alike issues:

VinCRIStine may be confused with vinBLAStine

Oncovin® may be confused with Ancobon®

High alert medication: The Institute for Safe Medication Practices (ISMP) includes this medication among its list of drugs which have a heightened risk of causing significant patient harm when used in error.

To prevent fatal inadvertent intrathecal injection, it is recommended that all doses be dispensed in a small minibag. When dispensing vincristine in a syringe, vincristine must be packaged in the manufacturer-provided overwrap which bears the statement **"Do not remove covering until the moment of injection. For intravenous use only. Fatal if given intrathecally."**

Contraindications Hypersensitivity to vincristine or any component of the formulation; **for I.V. use only, fatal if given intrathecally;** patients with demyelinating form of Charcot-Marie-Tooth syndrome; pregnancy

Warnings/Precautions Hazardous agent - use appropriate precautions for handling and disposal. **[U.S. Boxed Warning]: Vincristine is a vesicant; avoid extravasation. (Individuals administering should be experienced in vincristine administration.)**

Dosage modification required in patients with impaired hepatic function or who have pre-existing neuromuscular disease. Use with caution in the elderly; avoid eye contamination; observe closely for shortness of breath, bronchospasm, especially in patients treated with mitomycin C. Alterations in mental status such as depression, confusion, or insomnia; constipation, paralytic ileus, and urinary tract disturbances may occur. All patients should be on a prophylactic bowel management regimen.

[U.S. Boxed Warning]: Intrathecal administration of vincristine has uniformly caused severe neurologic damage and/or death; vincristine should never be administered by this route. For I.V. use only. Neurologic effects of vincristine may be additive with those of other neurotoxic agents and spinal cord irradiation.

Adverse Reactions

>10%: Dermatologic: Alopecia (20% to 70%)

1% to 10%:

Cardiovascular: Orthostatic hypotension or hypertension, hyper-/hypotension

Central nervous system: CNS depression, confusion, cranial nerve paralysis, fever, headache, insomnia, motor difficulties, seizure

Intrathecal administration of vincristine has uniformly caused death; vincristine should never be administered by this route. Neurologic effects of vincristine may be additive with those of other neurotoxic agents and spinal cord irradiation.

Dermatologic: Rash

(Continued)

VinCRIStine (Continued)

Endocrine & metabolic: Hyperuricemia

Gastrointestinal: Abdominal cramps, anorexia, bloating, constipation (and possible para-lytic ileus secondary to neurologic toxicity), diarrhea, metallic taste, nausea (mild), oral ulceration, vomiting, weight loss

Genitourinary: Bladder atony (related to neurotoxicity), dysuria, polyuria, urinary retention

Hematologic: Leukopenia (mild), thrombocytopenia, myelosuppression (onset: 7 days; nadir: 10 days; recovery: 21 days)

Local: Phlebitis, tissue irritation and necrosis if infiltrated

Neuromuscular & skeletal: Cramping, jaw pain, leg pain, myalgia, numbness, weakness

Peripheral neuropathy: Frequently the dose-limiting toxicity of vincristine. Most frequent in patients >40 years of age; occurs usually after an average of 3 weekly doses, but may occur after just one dose. Manifested as loss of the deep tendon reflexes in the lower extremities, numbness, tingling, pain, paresthesia of the fingers and toes (stocking glove sensation), and "foot drop" or "wrist drop."

Ocular: Optic atrophy, photophobia

<1% (Limited to important or life-threatening): SIADH (rare), stomatitis

Overdosage/Toxicology Symptoms include bone marrow suppression, mental depression, paresthesias, loss of deep reflexes, alopecia, and nausea. Severe symptoms may occur with 3-4 mg/m^2. There are no antidotes for vincristine. Treatment is supportive and symptomatic, including fluid restriction or administration of hypertonic saline (3% sodium chloride) for drug-induced secretion of inappropriate antidiuretic hormone (SIADH), diazepam or phenytoin for seizures, laxatives for constipation, and antiemetics for toxic emesis. Case reports suggest that folinic acid may be helpful in treating vincristine overdose. It is suggested that 100 mg folinic acid be given I.V. every 3 hours for 24 hours, then every 6 hours for 48 hours; this is in addition to supportive care. The use of pyridoxine, leucovorin factor, cyanocobalamin, or thiamine have been used with little success for drug-induced peripheral neuropathy.

Drug Interactions

Cytochrome P450 Effect: Substrate of CYP3A4 (major); **Inhibits** CYP3A4 (weak)

Increased Effect/Toxicity: Vincristine should be given 12-24 hours before asparaginase to minimize toxicity (may decrease the hepatic clearance of vincristine). Acute pulmonary reactions may occur with mitomycin-C. Previous or simultaneous use with mitomycin-C has resulted in acute shortness of breath and severe bronchospasm within minutes or several hours after vinca alkaloid injection and may occur up to 2 weeks after the dose of mitomycin. Intraconazole may enhance the neurotoxicity of vincristine.

CYP3A4 inhibitors may increase the levels/effects of vincristine. Example inhibitors include azole antifungals, clarithromycin, diclofenac, doxycycline, erythromycin, imatinib, isoniazid, nefazodone, nicardipine, propofol, protease inhibitors, quinidine, telithromycin, and verapamil. Digoxin plasma levels and renal excretion may decrease with combination chemotherapy including vincristine. Nifedipine may increase the levels/effects of vincristine.

Decreased Effect: Digoxin levels may decrease with combination chemotherapy. CYP3A4 inducers may decrease the levels/effects of vincristine; example inducers include aminoglutethimide, carbamazepine, nafcillin, nevirapine, phenobarbital, phenytoin, and rifamycins.

Ethanol/Nutrition/Herb Interactions Herb/Nutraceutical: St John's wort may decrease vincristine levels.

Stability

Undiluted vials: Store under refrigeration. May be stable for up to 30 days at room temperature.

I.V. solution: Diluted in 20-50 mL NS or D$_5$W, stable for 7 days under refrigeration, or 2 days at room temperature. In ambulatory pumps, solution is stable for 7-10 days at room temperature.

Mechanism of Action Binds to tubulin and inhibits microtubule formation; therefore arresting the cell at metaphase by disrupting the formation of the mitotic spindle; it is specific for the M and S phases. Vincristine may also interfere with nucleic acid and protein synthesis by blocking glutamic acid utilization.

Pharmacodynamics/Kinetics

Absorption: Oral: Poor

Distribution: V$_d$: 163-165 L/m^2; Poor penetration into CSF; rapidly removed from bloodstream and tightly bound to tissues; penetrates blood-brain barrier poorly

Protein binding: 75%

Metabolism: Extensively hepatic

Half-life elimination: Terminal: 24 hours

Excretion: Feces (~80%); urine (<1% as unchanged drug)

Dosage Note: Doses are often capped at 2 mg; however, this may reduce the efficacy of the therapy and may not be advisable. Refer to individual protocols; orders for single doses >2.5 mg or >5 mg/treatment cycle should be verified with the specific treatment regimen and/or an experienced oncologist prior to dispensing. I.V.:

Children ≤10 kg or BSA <1 m^2: Initial therapy: 0.05 mg/kg once weekly then titrate dose

Children >10 kg or BSA ≥1 m^2: 1-2 mg/m^2, may repeat once weekly for 3-6 weeks; maximum single dose: 2 mg

Neuroblastoma: I.V. continuous infusion with doxorubicin: 1 mg/m^2/day for 72 hours

Adults: 0.4-1.4 mg/m^2, may repeat every week **or**

0.4-0.5 mg/day continuous infusion for 4 days every 4 weeks **or**

0.25-0.5 mg/m^2/day for 5 days every 4 weeks

Dosing adjustment in hepatic impairment:

Serum bilirubin 1.5-3.0 mg/dL or AST 60-180 units: Administer 50% of normal dose

Serum bilirubin 3.0-5.0 mg/dL: Administer 25% of dose

Serum bilirubin >5.0 mg/dL or AST >180 units: Omit dose

Administration FATAL IF GIVEN INTRATHECALLY.

I.V.: Usually administered as slow (1-2 minutes) push or as short (10-15 minutes) infusion; 24-hour continuous infusions are occasionally used

Intralesional injection has been reported for Kaposi's sarcoma.

Monitoring Parameters Serum electrolytes (sodium), hepatic function tests, neurologic examination, CBC, serum uric acid

Dosage Forms Injection, solution, as sulfate: 1 mg/mL (1 mL, 2 mL)

♦ **Vincristine Sulfate** *see* VinCRIStine *on page 1789*

Vinorelbine (vi NOR el been)

U.S. Brand Names Navelbine®

Canadian Brand Names Navelbine®; Vinorelbine Injection, USP; Vinorelbine Tartrate for Injection

Index Terms Dihydroxydeoxynorvinkaleukoblastine; NVB; Vinorelbine Tartrate

Pharmacologic Category Antineoplastic Agent, Natural Source (Plant) Derivative; Antineoplastic Agent, Vinca Alkaloid

Use Treatment of nonsmall cell lung cancer

Unlabeled/Investigational Use Treatment of breast cancer, ovarian carcinoma, Hodgkin's disease, non-Hodgkin's lymphoma

Pregnancy Risk Factor D

Lactation Excretion in breast milk unknown/contraindicated

Medication Safety Issues
Sound-alike/look-alike issues:
Vinorelbine may be confused with vinBLAStine

High alert medication: The Institute for Safe Medication Practices (ISMP) includes this medication among its list of drugs which have a heightened risk of causing significant patient harm when used in error.

Contraindications For I.V. use only; **I.T. use may result in death**; hypersensitivity to vinorelbine or any component of the formulation; pregnancy

Warnings/Precautions Hazardous agent - use appropriate precautions for handling and disposal. **[U.S. Boxed Warning]: Avoid extravasation**; dosage modification required in patients with impaired liver function and neurotoxicity. Frequently monitor patients for myelosuppression both during and after therapy. **[U.S. Boxed Warnings]: Granulocytopenia is dose-limiting. Intrathecal administration may result in death.** Use with caution in patients with cachexia or ulcerated skin.

Acute shortness of breath and severe bronchospasm have been reported, most commonly when administered with mitomycin. Fatal cases of interstitial pulmonary changes and ARDS have also been reported. May cause severe constipation (grade 3-4), paralytic ileus, intestinal obstruction, necrosis, and/or perforation. **[U.S. Boxed Warning]: Should be administered under the supervision of an experienced cancer chemotherapy physician.**

Adverse Reactions
>10%:
    Central nervous system: Fatigue (27%)
    Dermatologic: Alopecia (12%)
    Gastrointestinal: Nausea (44%, severe <2%), constipation (35%), vomiting (20%), diarrhea (17%)
        Emetic potential: Moderate (30% to 60%)
    Hematologic: May cause severe bone marrow suppression and is the dose-limiting toxicity of vinorelbine; severe granulocytopenia (90%) may occur following the administration of vinorelbine; leukopenia (92%), anemia (83%)
    Myelosuppressive:
        WBC: Moderate - severe
        Onset: 4-7 days
        Nadir: 7-10 days
        Recovery: 14-21 days
    Hepatic: SGOT (67%) increased, total bilirubin increased (13%)
    Local: Injection site reaction (28%), injection site pain (16%)
    Neuromuscular & skeletal: Weakness (36%), peripheral neuropathy (20% to 25%)
1% to 10%:
    Cardiovascular: Chest pain (5%)
    Gastrointestinal: Paralytic ileus (1%)
    Hematologic: Thrombocytopenia (5%)
    Local: Phlebitis (7%)
    Neuromuscular & skeletal: Mild to moderate peripheral neuropathy manifested by paresthesia and hyperesthesia, loss of deep tendon reflexes (<5%); myalgia (<5%), arthralgia (<5%), jaw pain (<5%)
    Respiratory: Dyspnea (3% to 7%)
<1% (Limited to important or life-threatening): Anaphylaxis, angioedema, deep vein thrombosis, dysphagia, esophagitis, gait instability, hemorrhagic cystitis, pancreatitis, pulmonary edema, pulmonary embolus, radiation recall (dermatitis, esophagitis), severe peripheral neuropathy (generally reversible), SIADH

Overdosage/Toxicology Symptoms include bone marrow suppression, mental depression, paresthesias, loss of deep reflexes, and neurotoxicity. Overdoses involving quantities of up to 10 times the recommended dose (30 mg/m^2) have been reported. The toxicities described were consistent with those listed in the Adverse Reactions section including paralytic ileus, stomatitis, and esophagitis. Bone marrow aplasia, sepsis, and paresis have also been reported. Fatalities have occurred following overdose of vinorelbine. There are no antidotes for vinorelbine. Treatment is supportive and symptomatic, including fluid restriction or administration of hypertonic saline (3% sodium chloride) for drug-induced secretion of inappropriate antidiuretic hormone (SIADH), diazepam or phenytoin for seizures, laxatives for constipation, blood transfusions, growth factors, antibiotics, and antiemetics for toxic emesis.

Drug Interactions
Cytochrome P450 Effect: Substrate of CYP2D6 (minor), 3A4 (major); **Inhibits** CYP2D6 (weak), 3A4 (weak)
(Continued)

Vinorelbine *(Continued)*

Increased Effect/Toxicity: Previous or simultaneous use with mitomycin-C has resulted in acute shortness of breath and severe bronchospasm within minutes or several hours after vinca alkaloid injection and may occur up to 2 weeks after the dose of mitomycin. CYP3A4 inhibitors may increase the levels/effects of vinorelbine; example inhibitors include azole antifungals, clarithromycin, diclofenac, doxycycline, erythromycin, imatinib, isoniazid, nefazodone, nicardipine, propofol, protease inhibitors, quinidine, telithromycin, and verapamil. Incidence of granulocytopenia is significantly higher in cisplatin/vinorelbine combination therapy than with single-agent vinorelbine.

Decreased Effect: CYP3A4 inducers may decrease the levels/effects of vinorelbine; example inducers include aminoglutethimide, carbamazepine, nafcillin, nevirapine, phenobarbital, phenytoin, and rifamycins.

Ethanol/Nutrition/Herb Interactions Herb/Nutraceutical: St John's wort may decrease vinorelbine levels.

Stability Store intact vials under refrigeration (2°C to 8°C). Protect from ligh. Vals are stable at room temperature for up to 72 hours. Dilute in 10-50 mL D$_5$W or NS. Dilutions in D$_5$W or NS are stable for 24 hours at room temperature.

Mechanism of Action Semisynthetic vinca alkaloid which binds to tubulin and inhibits microtubule formation, therefore, arresting the cell at metaphase by disrupting the formation of the mitotic spindle; it is specific for the M and S phases. Vinorelbine may also interfere with nucleic acid and protein synthesis by blocking glutamic acid utilization.

Pharmacodynamics/Kinetics

Absorption: Unreliable; must be given I.V.

Distribution: V$_d$: 25.4-40.1 L/kg; binds extensively to human platelets and lymphocytes (79.6% to 91.2%)

Protein binding: 80% to 90%

Metabolism: Extensively hepatic to two metabolites, deacetylvinorelbine (active) and vinorelbine N-oxide

Bioavailability: Oral: 26% to 45%

Half-life elimination: Triphasic: Terminal: 27.7-43.6 hours

Excretion: Feces (46%); urine (18%, 10% to 12% as unchanged drug)

Clearance: Plasma: Mean: 0.97-1.26 L/hour/kg

Dosage Refer to individual protocols.

Adults: I.V.:

Single-agent therapy: 30 mg/m^2 every 7 days

Combination therapy with cisplatin: 25 mg/m^2 every 7 days (with cisplatin 100 mg/m^2 every 4 weeks); **Alternatively:** 30 mg/m^2 in combination with cisplatin 120 mg/m^2 on days 1 and 29, then every 6 weeks

Dosage adjustment in hematological toxicity: Granulocyte counts should be ≥1000 cells/mm^3 prior to the administration of vinorelbine. Adjustments in the dosage of vinorelbine should be based on granulocyte counts obtained on the day of treatment as follows:

Granulocytes ≥1500 cells/mm^3 on day of treatment: Administer 100% of starting dose

Granulocytes 1000-1499 cells/mm^3 on day of treatment: Administer 50% of starting dose

Granulocytes <1000 cells/mm^3 on day of treatment: Do not administer. Repeat granulocyte count in one week; if 3 consecutive doses are held because granulocyte count is <1000 cells/mm^3, discontinue vinorelbine

For patients who, during treatment, have experienced fever and/or sepsis while granulocytopenic or had 2 consecutive weekly doses held due to granulocytopenia, subsequent doses of vinorelbine should be:

75% of starting dose for granulocytes ≥1500 cells/mm^3

37.5% of starting dose for granulocytes 1000-1499 cells/mm^3

Dosage adjustment in renal impairment: No dose adjustments are required for renal insufficiency.

Dosing adjustment in hepatic impairment: Vinorelbine should be administered with caution in patients with hepatic insufficiency. In patients who develop hyperbilirubinemia during treatment with vinorelbine, the dose should be adjusted for total bilirubin as follows:

Serum bilirubin ≤2 mg/dL: Administer 100% of starting dose

Serum bilirubin 2.1-3 mg/dL: Administer 50% of starting dose

Serum bilirubin >3 mg/dL: Administer 25% of starting dose

Dosing adjustment in patients with concurrent hematologic toxicity and hepatic impairment: Administer the lower doses determined from the above recommendations

Administration FATAL IF GIVEN INTRATHECALLY. Administer as a direct intravenous push or rapid bolus, over 6-10 minutes (up to 30 minutes). Longer infusions may increase the risk of pain and phlebitis. Intravenous doses should be followed by 150-250 mL of saline or dextrose to reduce the incidence of phlebitis and inflammation.

Monitoring Parameters CBC with differential and platelet count, hepatic function tests

Dosage Forms Injection, solution [preservative free]: 10 mg/mL (1 mL, 5 mL)

♦ **Vinorelbine Injection, USP (Can)** *see* Vinorelbine *on page 1791*
♦ **Vinorelbine Tartrate** *see* Vinorelbine *on page 1791*
♦ **Vinorelbine Tartrate for Injection (Can)** *see* Vinorelbine *on page 1791*
♦ **Viokase®** *see* Pancrelipase *on page 1302*
♦ **Viosterol** *see* Ergocalciferol *on page 603*
♦ **Viracept®** *see* Nelfinavir *on page 1208*
♦ **Viramune®** *see* Nevirapine *on page 1217*
♦ **Virazole®** *see* Ribavirin *on page 1503*
♦ **Viread®** *see* Tenofovir *on page 1645*
♦ **Virilon®** *see* MethylTESTOSTERone *on page 1125*
♦ **Virilon® IM (Can)** *see* Testosterone *on page 1653*
♦ **Viroptic®** *see* Trifluridine *on page 1741*
♦ **Viscoat®** *see* Chondroitin Sulfate and Sodium Hyaluronate *on page 362*
♦ **Visine-A® [OTC]** *see* Naphazoline and Pheniramine *on page 1199*

- ♦ **Visine® Advanced Allergy (Can)** *see* Naphazoline and Pheniramine *on page 1199*
- ♦ **Visken® (Can)** *see* Pindolol *on page 1371*
- ♦ **Vistaril®** *see* HydrOXYzine *on page 865*
- ♦ **Vistide®** *see* Cidofovir *on page 367*
- ♦ **Vita-C® [OTC]** *see* Ascorbic Acid *on page 156*
- ♦ **Vitamin C** *see* Ascorbic Acid *on page 156*
- ♦ **Vitamin D₂** *see* Ergocalciferol *on page 603*
- ♦ **Vitamin D₃** *see* Alendronate and Cholecalciferol *on page 67*
- ♦ **Vitamin D and Calcium Carbonate** *see* Calcium and Vitamin D *on page 268*

Vitamin A (VYE ta min aye)

U.S. Brand Names Aquasol A®; Palmitate-A® [OTC]
Index Terms Oleovitamin A
Pharmacologic Category Vitamin, Fat Soluble
Use Treatment and prevention of vitamin A deficiency; parenteral (I.M.) route is indicated when oral administration is not feasible or when absorption is insufficient (malabsorption syndrome)
Pregnancy Risk Factor A/X (dose exceeding RDA recommendation)
Pregnancy Implications Excessive use of vitamin A shortly before and during pregnancy could be harmful to babies.
Lactation Enters breast milk/compatible at normal daily doses
Medication Safety Issues
Sound-alike/look-alike issues:
Aquasol® may be confused with Anusol®
Contraindications Hypersensitivity to vitamin A or any component of the formulation; hypervitaminosis A; pregnancy (dose exceeding RDA)
Warnings/Precautions Evaluate other sources of vitamin A while receiving this product; patients receiving >25,000 units/day should be closely monitored for toxicity. Parenteral vitamin A: In low birth weight infants, polysorbates have been associated with thrombocytopenia, renal dysfunction, hepatomegaly, cholestasis, ascites, hypotension, and metabolic acidosis (E-Ferol syndrome).
Adverse Reactions Systemic: 1% to 10%:
Central nervous system: Fever, headache, irritability, lethargy, malaise, vertigo
Dermatologic: Drying or cracking of skin
Endocrine & metabolic: Hypercalcemia
Gastrointestinal: Weight loss
Ocular: Visual changes
Miscellaneous: Hypervitaminosis A
Overdosage/Toxicology
Toxic manifestations are dependent on age, dose, and duration of administration. General manifestations of hypervitaminosis A syndrome include fatigue, malaise, lethargy, abdominal discomfort, anorexia, and vomiting. Systemic manifestations occurring with plasma levels >1200 units/mL include hepatotoxicity, hypomenorrhea, hepatosplenomegaly, jaundice, and leukopenia. Skeletal, CNS, and dermatologic effects also occur.
Acute toxicity: Single dose of 25,000 units/kg
Chronic toxicity: 4000 units/kg for 6-15 months
Treat intracranial hypertension from chronic exposure, if needed. For acute exposure, use gut decontamination, otherwise treatment is symptomatic and supportive.
Drug Interactions
Increased Effect/Toxicity: Retinoids may have additive adverse effects.
Decreased Effect: Cholestyramine resin decreases absorption of vitamin A. Neomycin and mineral oil may also interfere with vitamin A absorption.
Stability Protect from light.
Mechanism of Action Needed for bone development, growth, visual adaptation to darkness, testicular and ovarian function, and as a cofactor in many biochemical processes
Pharmacodynamics/Kinetics
Absorption: Vitamin A in dosages **not** exceeding physiologic replacement is well absorbed after oral administration; water miscible preparations are absorbed more rapidly than oil preparations; large oral doses, conditions of fat malabsorption, low protein intake, or hepatic or pancreatic disease reduces oral absorption
Distribution: Large amounts concentrate for storage in the liver; enters breast milk
Metabolism: Conjugated with glucuronide; undergoes enterohepatic recirculation
Excretion: Feces
Dosage
RDA:
<1 year: 375 mcg
1-3 years: 400 mcg
4-6 years: 500 mcg*
7-10 years: 700 mcg*
>10 years: 800-1000 mcg*
Male: 1000 mcg
Female: 800 mcg
* mcg retinol equivalent (0.3 mcg retinol = 1 unit vitamin A)
Vitamin A supplementation in measles (recommendation of the World Health Organization): Children: Oral: Administer as a single dose; repeat the next day and at 4 weeks for children with ophthalmologic evidence of vitamin A deficiency:
6 months to 1 year: 100,000 units
>1 year: 200,000 units
Note: Use of vitamin A in measles is recommended only for patients 6 months to 2 years of age hospitalized with measles and its complications **or** patients >6 months of age who have any of the following risk factors and who are not already receiving vitamin A: immunodeficiency, ophthalmologic evidence of vitamin A deficiency including night blindness, *(Continued)*

Vitamin A *(Continued)*

Bitot's spots or evidence of xerophthalmia, impaired intestinal absorption, moderate to severe malnutrition including that associated with eating disorders, or recent immigration from areas where high mortality rates from measles have been observed

Note: Monitor patients closely; dosages >25,000 units/kg have been associated with toxicity

Severe deficiency with xerophthalmia: Oral:

Children 1-8 years: 5000-10,000 units/kg/day for 5 days or until recovery occurs

Children >8 years and Adults: 500,000 units/day for 3 days, then 50,000 units/day for 14 days, then 10,000-20,000 units/day for 2 months

Deficiency (without corneal changes): Oral:

Infants <1 year: 100,000 units every 4-6 months

Children 1-8 years: 200,000 units every 4-6 months

Children >8 years and Adults: 100,000 units/day for 3 days then 50,000 units/day for 14 days

Deficiency: I.M.: **Note:** I.M. route is indicated when oral administration is not feasible or when absorption is insufficient (malabsorption syndrome):

Infants: 7500-15,000 units/day for 10 days

Children 1-8 years: 17,500-35,000 units/day for 10 days

Children >8 years and Adults: 100,000 units/day for 3 days, followed by 50,000 units/day for 2 weeks

Note: Follow-up therapy with an oral therapeutic multivitamin (containing additional vitamin A) is recommended:

Low Birth Weight Infants: Additional vitamin A is recommended, however, no dosage amount has been established

Children ≤8 years: 5000-10,000 units/day

Children >8 years and Adults: 10,000-20,000 units/day

Malabsorption syndrome (prophylaxis): Children >8 years and Adults: Oral: 10,000-50,000 units/day of water miscible product

Dietary supplement: Oral:

Infants up to 6 months: 1500 units/day

Children:

6 months to 3 years: 1500-2000 units/day

4-6 years: 2500 units/day

7-10 years: 3300-3500 units/day

Children >10 years and Adults: 4000-5000 units/day

Administration Do not give by I.V. push.

Reference Range 1 RE = 1 retinol equivalent; 1 RE = 1 mcg retinol or 6 mcg beta-carotene; Normal levels of Vitamin A in serum = 80-300 units/mL

Additional Information 1 mg = 3333 units

Dosage Forms

Capsule [softgel]: 10,000 units; 25,000 units

Injection, solution (Aquasol A®): 50,000 units/mL (2 mL) [contains polysorbate 80]

Tablet (Palmitate-A®): 5000 units, 15,000 units

♦ **Vitamin A Acid** *see* Tretinoin (Topical) *on page 1732*

Vitamin A and Vitamin D (VYE ta min aye & VYE ta min dee)

U.S. Brand Names A and D® Original [OTC]; Baza® Clear [OTC]; Sween Cream® [OTC]

Index Terms Cod Liver Oil

Pharmacologic Category Topical Skin Product

Use Temporary relief of discomfort due to chapped skin, diaper rash, minor burns, abrasions, as well as irritations associated with ostomy skin care

Pregnancy Risk Factor B

Dosage Topical: Apply locally with gentle massage as needed

Additional Information Complete prescribing information for this medication should be consulted for additional detail.

Dosage Forms

Capsule, softgel: Vitamin A 1250 int. units and vitamin D 135 int. units; vitamin A 1250 int. units and vitamin D 130 int. units; vitamin A 5,000 int. units and vitamin D 400 int. units; vitamin A 10,000 int. units and vitamin D 400 int. units; vitamin A 10,000 int. units and vitamin D 5000 int. units; vitamin A 25,000 int. units and vitamin D 1000 int. units

Cream:

Sween Cream®: 2 g, 85 g, 184 g, 339 g [original]

Sween Cream®: 57 g, 142 g [fresh scent]

Sween Cream®: 57 g [fragrance free]

Ointment: 0.9 g, 5 g, 60 g, 120 g, 454 g [in lanolin-petrolatum base]

A and D® Original: 45 g, 120 g, 454 g

Baza® Clear: 50 g, 150 g, 240 g

Tablet: Vitamin A 10,000 int. units and vitamin D 400 int. units

♦ **Vitamin B₁** *see* Thiamine *on page 1668*

♦ **Vitamin B₂** *see* Riboflavin *on page 1506*

♦ **Vitamin B₃** *see* Niacin *on page 1219*

♦ **Vitamin B₃** *see* Niacinamide *on page 1220*

♦ **Vitamin B₆** *see* Pyridoxine *on page 1463*

♦ **Vitamin B₁₂** *see* Cyanocobalamin *on page 425*

♦ **Vitamin B₁₂ₐ** *see* Hydroxocobalamin *on page 860*

Vitamin E (VYE ta min ee)

U.S. Brand Names Alph-E [OTC]; Alph-E-Mixed [OTC]; Aquasol E® [OTC]; Aquavit-E [OTC]; d-Alpha-Gems™ [OTC]; E-Gems® [OTC]; E-Gems Elite® [OTC]; E-Gems Plus® [OTC];

Ester-E™ [OTC]; Gamma E-Gems® [OTC]; Gamma-E Plus [OTC]; High Gamma Vitamin E Complete™ [OTC]; Key-E® [OTC]; Key-E® Kaps [OTC]

Index Terms d-Alpha Tocopherol; dl-Alpha Tocopherol

Pharmacologic Category Vitamin, Fat Soluble

Use Dietary supplement

Unlabeled/Investigational Use To reduce the risk of bronchopulmonary dysplasia or retrolental fibroplasia in infants exposed to high concentrations of oxygen; prevention and treatment of tardive dyskinesia and Alzheimer's disease; prevention and treatment of hemolytic anemia secondary to vitamin E deficiency

Pregnancy Risk Factor A/C (dose exceeding RDA recommendation)

Lactation Enters breast milk/compatible

Medication Safety Issues
Sound-alike/look-alike issues:
Aquasol E® may be confused with Anusol®

Contraindications Hypersensitivity to vitamin E or any component of the formulation

Warnings/Precautions May induce vitamin K deficiency; necrotizing enterocolitis has been associated with oral administration of large dosages (eg, >200 units/day) of a hyperosmolar vitamin E preparation in low birth weight infants

Adverse Reactions Frequency not defined.
Central nervous system: Fatigue, headache, weakness
Dermatologic: Contact dermatitis with topical preparation
Endocrine & metabolic: Gonadal dysfunction
Gastrointestinal: Diarrhea, intestinal cramps, nausea
Neuromuscular & skeletal: Weakness
Ocular: Blurred vision

Drug Interactions
Increased Effect/Toxicity: Vitamin E may alter the effect of vitamin K actions on clotting factors resulting in an increase hypoprothrombinemic response to warfarin; monitor.
Decreased Effect: Vitamin E may impair the hematologic response to iron in children with iron-deficiency anemia; monitor.

Stability Protect from light.

Mechanism of Action Prevents oxidation of vitamin A and C; protects polyunsaturated fatty acids in membranes from attack by free radicals and protects red blood cells against hemolysis

Pharmacodynamics/Kinetics
Absorption: Oral: Depends on presence of bile; reduced in conditions of malabsorption, in low birth weight premature infants, and as dosage increases; water miscible preparations are better absorbed than oil preparations
Distribution: To all body tissues, especially adipose tissue, where it is stored
Metabolism: Hepatic to glucuronides
Excretion: Feces

Dosage Vitamin E may be expressed as alpha-tocopherol equivalents (ATE), which refer to the biologically active (R) stereoisomer content. Oral:
Recommended daily allowance (RDA):
Infants (adequate intake; RDA not establshed):
≤6 months: 4 mg
7-12 months: 6 mg
Children:
1-3 years: 6 mg; upper limit of intake should not exceed 200 mg/day
4-8 years: 7 mg; upper limit of intake should not exceed 300 mg/day
9-13 years: 11 mg; upper limit of intake should not exceed 600 mg/day
14-18 years: 15 mg; upper limit of intake should not exceed 800 mg/day
Adults: 15 mg; upper limit of intake should not exceed 1000 mg/day
Pregnant female:
≤18 years: 15 mg; upper level of intake should not exceed 800 mg/day
19-50 years: 15 mg; upper level of intake should not exceed 1000 mg/day
Lactating female:
≤18 years: 19 mg; upper level of intake should not exceed 800 mg/day
19-50 years: 19 mg; upper level of intake should not exceed 1000 mg/day

Vitamin E deficiency:
Children (with malabsorption syndrome): 1 unit/kg/day of water miscible vitamin E (to raise plasma tocopherol concentrations to the normal range within 2 months and to maintain normal plasma concentrations)
Adults: 60-75 units/day
Prevention of vitamin E deficiency: Adults: 30 units/day
Cystic fibrosis, beta-thalassemia, sickle cell anemia may require higher daily maintenance doses:
Children:
Cystic fibrosis: 100-400 units/day
Beta-thalassemia: 750 units/day
Adults:
Sickle cell: 450 units/day
Alzheimer's disease (unlabeled use): 1000 units twice daily
Tardive dyskinesia (unlabeled use): 1600 units/day

Administration Swallow capsules whole, do not crush or chew.

Monitoring Parameters Monitor plasma tocopherol concentrations (normal range: 6-14 mcg/mL)

Reference Range Therapeutic: 0.8-1.5 mg/dL (SI: 19-35 µmol/L), some method variation

Additional Information The 2R-stereoisomeric forms of α-tocopherol are used to define vitamine E intake and RDA. While international units are no longer recognized, many fortified foods and supplements continue to use this term although USP units are now used by the pharmaceutical industry when labeling vitamin E supplements. Both IUs and USP units are based on the same equivalency. The following can be used to convert international units (IU)
(Continued)

Vitamin E *(Continued)*

of vitamin E (and esters) to milligrams α-tocopherol in order to meet recommended daily intake:

Synthetic (eg, all-racemic α-tocopherol):
dl-α-tocopherol:
  USP: 1.10 IU / mg; 0.91 mg / IU
  Molar: 2.12 µmol / IU
  α-tocopherol: 0.45 mg / IU
dl-α-tocopherol acetate:
  USP: 1 IU / mg; 1 mg / IU
  Molar: 2.12 µmol / IU
  α-tocopherol: 0.45 mg / IU
dl-α-tocopherol succinate:
  USP: 0.89 IU / mg; 1.12 mg / IU
  Molar: 2.12 µmol / IU
  α-tocopherol: 0.45 mg / IU

Natural (eg, RRR-α-tocopherol):
d-α-tocopherol:
  USP: 1.49 IU / mg; 0.67 mg / IU
  Molar: 1.56 µmol / IU
  α-tocopherol: 0.67 mg / IU
d-α-tocopherol acetate:
  USP: 1.36 IU / mg; 0.74mg / IU
  Molar: 1.56 µmol / IU
  α-tocopherol: 0.67 mg / IU
d-α-tocopherol succinate:
  USP: 1.21 IU / mg; 0.83 mg / IU
  Molar: 1.56 µmol / IU
  α-tocopherol: 0.67 mg / IU

Historically, vitamin E supplements have been labeled (incorrectly) as *d*- or *dl*-α-tocopherol. Synthetic vitamin E compounds are racemic mixtures, and may be designated as all-racemic (all rac-α-tocopherol). The natural form contains the only RRR-α-tocopherol. All of these compounds may be present in fortified foods and multivitamins. Not all stereoisomers are capable of performing physiological functions in humans; therefore, cannot be considered to meet vitamin E requirements.

Dosage Forms
Capsule: 400 int. units, 1000 int. units
  Key-E® Kaps: 200 int. units, 400 int. units
Capsule, softgel: 200 int. units, 400 int. units, 600 int. units, 1000 int. units
  Alph-E: 200 int. units, 400 int. units
  Alph-E-Mixed: 200 int. units [contains mixed tocopherols]; 400 int. units [contains mixed tocopherols], 1000 int. units [sugar free; contains mixed tocopherols]
  Aqua Gem E®: 200 int. units, 400 int. units
  d-Alpha-Gems™: 400 int. units [derived from soybean oil]
  E-Gems®: 30 int. units, 100 int. units, 200 int. units, 400 int. units, 600 int. units, 800 int. units, 1000 int. units, 1200 int. units [derived from soybean oil]
  E-Gems Plus®: 200 int. units, 400 int. units, 800 int. units [contains mixed tocopherols]
  E-Gems Elite®: 400 int. units [contains mixed tocopherols]
  Ester-E™: 400 int. units
  Gamma E-Gems®: 90 int. units [also contains mixed tocopherols]
  Gamma-E Plus: 200 int. units [contains soybean oil]
  High Gamma Vitamin E Complete™: 200 int. units [contains soybean oil, mixed tocopherols]
Cream: 50 int. units/g (60 g), 100 int. units/g (60 g), 1000 int. units/120 g (120 g), 30,000 int. units/57 g (57 g)
  Key-E®: 30 int. units/g (60 g, 120 g, 600 g)
Lip balm (E-Gem® Lip Care): 1000 int. units/tube [contains vitamin A and aloe]
Oil, oral/topical: 100 int. units/0.25 mL (60 mL, 75 mL); 1150 units/0.25 mL (30 mL, 60 mL, 120 mL); 28,000 int. units/30 mL (30 mL)
  Alph-E: 28,000 int. units/30 mL (30 mL) [topical]
  E-Gems®: 100 units/10 drops (15 mL, 60 mL)
Ointment, topical (Key-E®): 30 units/g (60 g, 120 g, 480 g)
Powder (Key-E®): 700 int. units per 1/4 teaspoon (15 g, 75 g, 1000 g) [derived from soybean oil]
Solution, oral drops: 15 int. units/0.3 mL (30 mL)
  Aquasol E®: 15 int. units/0.3 mL (12 mL, 30 mL) [latex free]
  Aquavit-E: 15 int. units/0.3 mL (30 mL) [butterscotch flavor]
Suppository, rectal/vaginal (Key-E®): 30 int. units (12s, 24s) [contains coconut oil]
Tablet: 100 int. units, 200 int. units, 400 int. units, 500 int. units
  Key-E®: 200 int. units, 400 int. units

♦ **Vitamin G** *see* Riboflavin *on page 1506*
♦ **Vitamin K₁** *see* Phytonadione *on page 1366*
♦ **Vitelle™ Irospan® [OTC] [DSC]** *see* Ferrous Sulfate and Ascorbic Acid *on page 705*
♦ **Vitrasert®** *see* Ganciclovir *on page 779*
♦ **Vitravene™ [DSC]** *see* Fomivirsen *on page 756*
♦ **Vitravene™ (Can)** *see* Fomivirsen *on page 756*
♦ **Vitrax®** *see* Hyaluronate and Derivatives *on page 841*
♦ **Vitussin** *see* Hydrocodone and Guaifenesin *on page 849*
♦ **Vi Vaccine** *see* Typhoid Vaccine *on page 1756*
♦ **Vivactil®** *see* Protriptyline *on page 1452*
♦ **Vivaglobin®** *see* Immune Globulin (Subcutaneous) *on page 896*

♦ **Vivelle®** *see* Estradiol *on page 620*
♦ **Vivelle-Dot®** *see* Estradiol *on page 620*
♦ **Vivitrol™** *see* Naltrexone *on page 1195*
♦ **Vivotif®** *see* Typhoid Vaccine *on page 1756*
♦ **VLB** *see* VinBLAStine *on page 1788*
♦ **VM-26** *see* Teniposide *on page 1645*
♦ **Voltaren®** *see* Diclofenac *on page 492*
♦ **Voltaren Ophtha® (Can)** *see* Diclofenac *on page 492*
♦ **Voltaren Ophthalmic®** *see* Diclofenac *on page 492*
♦ **Voltaren Rapide® (Can)** *see* Diclofenac *on page 492*
♦ **Voltaren®-XR** *see* Diclofenac *on page 492*
♦ **Voluven® (Can)** *see* Hetastarch *on page 838*

Voriconazole (vor i KOE na zole)

U.S. Brand Names VFEND®
Canadian Brand Names VFEND®
Index Terms UK109496
Pharmacologic Category Antifungal Agent, Oral; Antifungal Agent, Parenteral
Additional Appendix Information
Antifungal Agents *on page 1869*
Use Treatment of invasive aspergillosis; treatment of esophageal candidiasis; treatment of candidemia (in non-neutropenic patients); treatment of *Candida* deep tissue infections; treatment of serious fungal infections caused by *Scedosporium apiospermum* and *Fusarium* spp (including *Fusarium solani*) in patients intolerant of, or refractory to, other therapy
Pregnancy Risk Factor D
Pregnancy Implications Voriconazole can cause fetal harm when administered to a pregnant woman. Voriconazole was teratogenic in animal studies, and lowered plasma estradiol in animal models. Should be used in pregnant woman only if benefit to mother justifies potential risk to the fetus.
Lactation Excretion in breast milk unknown/not recommended
Contraindications Hypersensitivity to voriconazole or any component of the formulation (cross-reaction with other azole antifungal agents may occur but has not been established, use caution); coadministration of CYP3A4 substrates which may lead to QT$_c$ prolongation (cisapride, pimozide, or quinidine); coadministration with barbiturates (long acting), carbamazepine, efavirenz, ergot alkaloids, rifampin, rifabutin, ritonavir (≥800 mg/day), and sirolimus; pregnancy (unless risk:benefit justifies use)
Warnings/Precautions Visual changes are commonly associated with treatment. Patients should be warned to avoid tasks which depend on vision, including operating machinery or driving. Changes are reversible on discontinuation following brief exposure/treatment regimens (≤28 days).

Serious hepatic reactions (including hepatitis, cholestasis, and fulminant hepatic failure) have occurred during treatment, primarily in patients with serious concomitant medical conditions. However, hepatotoxicity has occurred in patients with no identifiable risk factors. Use caution in patients with pre-existing hepatic impairment (dose adjustment required).

Voriconazole tablets contain lactose; avoid administration in hereditary galactose intolerance, Lapp lactase deficiency, or glucose-galactose malabsorption. Suspension contains sucrose; use caution with fructose intolerance, sucrose-isomaltase deficiency, or glucose-galactose malabsorption. Avoid/limit use of intravenous formulation in patients with renal impairment; intravenous formulation contains excipient sulfobutyl ether beta-cyclodextrin (SBECD), which may accumulate in renal insufficiency. Infusion-related reactions may occur with intravenous dosing. Consider discontinuation of infusion if reaction is severe.

Use caution in patients with an increased risk of arrhythmia (concurrent QT$_c$-prolonging drugs, hypokalemia, cardiomyopathy, or prior cardiotoxic therapy). Correct electrolyte abnormalities before initiating therapy. Use caution in patients receiving concurrent non-nucleoside reverse transcriptase inhibitors (efavirenz is contraindicated).

Avoid use in pregnancy, unless an evaluation of the potential benefit justifies possible risk to the fetus. Safety and efficacy have not been established in children <12 years of age.
Adverse Reactions
>10%: Ocular: Visual changes (photophobia, color changes, increased or decreased visual acuity, or blurred vision occur in ~21%)
1% to 10%:
  Cardiovascular: Tachycardia (2% to 3%), hyper-/hypotension (2%), vasodilation (2%), peripheral edema (1%)
  Central nervous system: Fever (6%), chills (4%), headache (3%), hallucinations (3%), dizziness (1%)
  Dermatologic: Rash (6%), pruritus (1%)
  Endocrine & metabolic: Hypokalemia (2%), hypomagnesemia (1%)
  Gastrointestinal: Nausea (5% to 6%), vomiting (4% to 5%), abdominal pain (2%), diarrhea (1%), xerostomia (1%)
  Hematologic: Thrombocytopenia (1%)
  Hepatic: Alkaline phosphatase increased (4%), transaminases increased (2% to 3%), AST increased (2%), ALT increased (2%), cholestatic jaundice (1%)
  Ocular: Chromatopsia (1%), photophobia (2% to 3%)
<1% (Limited to important or life-threatening): Acute tubular necrosis, adrenal cortical insufficiency, agranulocytosis, allergic reaction, anaphylactoid reaction; anemia (aplastic, macrocytic, megaloblastic, or microcytic); angioedema, ataxia, atrial arrhythmia, atrial fibrillation, AV block, bone marrow depression, bone necrosis, bradycardia, brain edema, bundle branch block, cardiac arrest, cerebral hemorrhage, cholecystitis, cholelithiasis, coma, CHF, convulsion, delirium, dementia, depression, DIC, discoid lupus erythematosus, duodenal
(Continued)

Voriconazole *(Continued)*

ulcer perforation, encephalopathy, erythema multiforme, exfoliative dermatitis, extrapyramidal symptoms, fixed drug eruption, gastrointestinal hemorrhage, grand mal seizure, Guillain-Barré syndrome, hematemesis, hemolytic anemia, hepatic coma, hepatic failure, hepatitis, intestinal perforation, intracranial hypertension, kidney dysfunction, lung edema, myasthenia, MI, neuropathy, night blindness, optic atrophy, optic neuritis, pancreatitis, pancytopenia, papilledema, paresthesia, photosensitivity, psychosis, pulmonary embolus, QT-interval prolongation, renal failure (acute), respiratory distress syndrome, sepsis, Stevens-Johnson syndrome, suicidal ideation, supraventricular tachycardia, syncope, thrombotic thrombocytopenic purpura, toxic epidermal necrolysis, ventricular arrhythmia, ventricular fibrillation, ventricular tachycardia, torsade de pointes, vertigo

Overdosage/Toxicology Visual changes may occur; one patient had photophobia for 10 minutes. Treatment is symptom-directed and supportive. Following intravenous overdose, toxicity from the vehicle, SBECD, may also occur. Both voriconazole and the intravenous vehicle may be eliminated via hemodialysis.

Drug Interactions

Cytochrome P450 Effect: Substrate of CYP2C9 (major), 2C19 (major), 3A4 (minor); **Inhibits** CYP2C9 (weak), 2C19 (weak), 3A4 (moderate)

Increased Effect/Toxicity: Voriconazole increases serum levels/effects of efavirenz, ergot alkaloids, pimozide, quinidine, rifabutin, and sirolimus; concurrent use contraindicated. Voriconazole increases serum levels/effects of benzodiazepines (metabolized by oxidation; eg, alprazolam, diazepam, triazolam, midazolam), buspirone, busulfan, calcium channel blockers (eg, felodipine, nifedipine, verapamil), cisapride, CYP2C9 substrates, CYP3A4 substrates, cyclosporine, HMG-CoA reductase inhibitors (except pravastatin and fluvastatin), methadone, omeprazole, phenytoin, sulfonylureas, tacrolimus, trimetrexate, warfarin, and vinca alkaloids. Voriconazole may increase the levels of ethinyl estradiol and/or norethindrone; conversely, hormonal contraceptive agents may increase the levels/effects of voriconazole. Use with QT_c-prolonging agents may increase risk of malignant arrhythmia.

Decreased Effect: Barbiturates (phenobarbital, secobarbital), carbamazepine, efavirenz, rifampin, and ritonavir (≥800 mg/day) decrease serum levels/effects of voriconazole; concurrent use is contraindicated. Use caution with smaller doses (<800 mg/day) of ritonavir. CYP2C9 inducers, CYP2C19 inducers, and phenytoin decrease serum levels/effects of voriconazole.

Ethanol/Nutrition/Herb Interactions

Food: May decrease voriconazole absorption. Voriconazole should be taken 1 hour before or 1 hour after a meal.

Herb/Nutraceutical: St John's wort may decrease voriconazole levels.

Stability

Powder for injection: Store at 15°C to 30°C (59°F to 86°F). Reconstitute 200 mg vial with 19 mL of sterile water for injection (use of automated syringe is not recommended). Resultant solution (20 mL) has a concentration of 10 mg/mL. Prior to infusion, must dilute to 0.5-5 mg/mL with NS, LR, D_5WLR, $D_5\frac{1}{2}NS$, D_5W, D_5W with KCl 20 mEq, $\frac{1}{2}NS$, or D_5WNS. Do not dilute with 4.2% sodium bicarbonate infusion. Reconstituted solutions are stable for up to 24 hours under refrigeration at 2°C to 8°C (36°F to 46°F).

Powder for oral suspension: Store at 2°C to 8°C (36°F to 46°F). Add 46 mL of water to the bottle to make 40 mg/mL suspension. Reconstituted oral suspension may be stored at 15°C to 30°C (59°F to 86°F). Discard after 14 days.

Tablets: Store at 15°C to 30°C (59°F to 86°F).

Mechanism of Action Interferes with fungal cytochrome P450 activity, decreasing ergosterol synthesis (principal sterol in fungal cell membrane) and inhibiting fungal cell membrane formation.

Pharmacodynamics/Kinetics

Absorption: Well absorbed after oral administration

Distribution: V_d: 4.6 L/kg

Protein binding: 58%

Metabolism: Hepatic, via CYP2C19 (major pathway) and CYP2C9 and CYP3A4 (less significant); saturable (may demonstrate nonlinearity)

Bioavailability: 96%

Half-life elimination: Variable, dose-dependent

Time to peak: 1-2 hours

Excretion: Urine (as inactive metabolites)

Dosage

Usual dosage ranges:

Children <12 years: Dosage not established

Children ≥12 years and Adults:

Oral: 100-300 mg every 12 hours

I.V.: 6 mg/kg every 12 hours for 2 doses; followed by maintenance dose of 4 mg/kg every 12 hours

Indication-specific dosing: Children ≥12 years and Adults:

Aspergillosis (invasive) and other serious fungal infections: I.V.: Initial: Loading dose: 6 mg/kg every 12 hours for 2 doses; followed by maintenance dose of 4 mg/kg every 12 hours

Candidemia and other deep tissue *Candida* infections: I.V.: Initial: Loading dose 6 mg/kg every 12 hours for 2 doses; followed by maintenance dose of 3-4 mg/kg every 12 hours

Note: Conversion to oral dosing:

Patients <40 kg: 100 mg every 12 hours; increase to 150 mg every 12 hours in patients who fail to respond adequately

Patients ≥40 kg: 200 mg every 12 hours; increase to 300 mg every 12 hours in patients who fail to respond adequately

Endophthalmitis, fungal: I.V.: 6 mg/kg every 12 hours for 2 doses, then 200 mg orally twice daily

Esophageal candidiasis: Oral:
Patients <40 kg: 100 mg every 12 hours
Patients ≥40 kg: 200 mg every 12 hours
Note: Treatment should continue for a minimum of 14 days, and for at least 7 days following resolution of symptoms.

Dosage adjustment in patients unable to tolerate treatment:
I.V.: Dose may be reduced to 3 mg/kg every 12 hours
Oral: Dose may be reduced in 50 mg increments to a minimum dosage of 200 mg every 12 hours in patients weighing ≥40 kg (100 mg every 12 hours in patients <40 kg)

Dosage adjustment in patients receiving concomitant phenytoin:
I.V.: Increase maintenance dosage to 5 mg/kg every 12 hours
Oral: Increase dose from 200 mg to 400 mg every 12 hours in patients ≥40 kg (100 mg to 200 mg every 12 hours in patients <40 kg)

Dosage adjustment in patients receiving concomitant cyclosporine: Reduce cyclosporine dose by $1/2$ and monitor closely.

Dosage adjustment in renal impairment: In patients with Cl_{cr} <50 mL/minute, accumulation of the intravenous vehicle (SBECD) occurs. After initial loading dose, oral voriconazole should be administered to these patients, unless an assessment of the benefit:risk to the patient justifies the use of I.V. voriconazole. Monitor serum creatinine and change to oral voriconazole therapy when possible.
Hemodialysis: Oral dosage adjustment not required; for I.V. dosing, see dosage adjustment in renal impairment

Dosage adjustment in hepatic impairment:
Mild-to-moderate hepatic dysfunction (Child-Pugh Class A and B): Following standard loading dose, reduce maintenance dosage by 50%
Severe hepatic impairment: Should only be used if benefit outweighs risk; monitor closely for toxicity

Dietary Considerations Oral: Should be taken 1 hour before or 1 hour after a meal. Voriconazole tablets contain lactose; avoid administration in hereditary galactose intolerance, Lapp lactase deficiency, or glucose-galactose malabsorption. Suspension contains sucrose; use caution with fructose intolerance, sucrose-isomaltase deficiency, or glucose-galactose malabsorption.

Administration
Oral: Administer 1 hour before or 1 hour after a meal.
I.V.: Infuse over 1-2 hours (rate not to exceed 3 mg/kg/hour). Do not infuse concomitantly into same line or cannula with other drug infusions, including TPN.

Monitoring Parameters Hepatic function at initiation and during course of treatment; visual function if treatment course continues >28 days; renal function

Dosage Forms
Injection, powder for reconstitution: 200 mg [contains SBECD 3200 mg]
Powder for oral suspension: 200 mg/5 mL (70 mL) [contains sodium benzoate and sucrose; orange flavor]
Tablet: 50 mg, 200 mg [contains lactose]

Vorinostat (vor IN oh stat)

U.S. Brand Names Zolinza™
Index Terms NSC-701852; SAHA; Suberoylanilide Hydroxamic Acid
Pharmacologic Category Antineoplastic Agent, Histone Deacetylase Inhibitor
Use Treatment of relapsed or refractory cutaneous T-cell lymphoma (CTCL)
Pregnancy Risk Factor D
Pregnancy Implications Animal studies have demonstrated adverse fetal effects, including fetal loss, decreased fetal weight, and skeletal malformation. There are no adequate and well-controlled studies in pregnant women. Inform patient of potential hazard if used during pregnancy or if pregnancy occurs during treatment.
Lactation Excretion in breast milk unknown/not recommended
Medication Safety Issues
High alert medication: The Institute for Safe Medication Practices (ISMP) includes this medication among its list of drugs which have a heightened risk of causing significant patient harm when used in error.
Contraindications Hypersensitivity to vorinostat or any component of the formulation
Warnings/Precautions Hazardous agent - use appropriate precautions for handling and disposal. Pulmonary embolism and deep vein thrombosis (DVT) have been reported; monitor; use caution in patients with a history of thrombotic events. Dose related thrombocytopenia and/or anemia may occur. QT_c prolongation has been observed; a baseline and periodic 12-lead ECG should be obtained; correct electrolyte abnormalities prior to treatment and monitor and correct potassium, calcium and magnesium levels during therapy; use caution in patients with a history of QT_c prolongation or with medications known to prolong the QT interval. May cause hyperglycemia; monitor and use with caution in diabetics; may require diet and/or therapy modifications. Safety and efficacy in children have not been established.

Adverse Reactions
>10%:
Cardiovascular: Peripheral edema (13%)
Central nervous system: Fatigue (52% to 73%), chills (16%), dizziness (15%), headache (12%), fever (11%)
Dermatologic: Alopecia (19%), pruritus (12%)
Endocrine & metabolic: Hyperglycemia (8% to 69%; grade 3: 5%), dehydration (16%)
Gastrointestinal: Diarrhea (49% to 52%), nausea (41% to 49%), taste perversion (28% to 46%), xerostomia (16% to 35%), weight loss (21% to 27%), anorexia (22% to 24%), vomiting (15% to 24%), appetite decreased (14% to 22%), constipation (15%)
Hematologic: Thrombocytopenia (26% to 54%; grades 3/4: 6% to 19%), anemia (2% to 14%; grades 3/4: 2% to 3%)
(Continued)

Vorinostat *(Continued)*

Neuromuscular & skeletal: Muscle spasm (20%)
Renal: Proteinuria (51%), creatinine increased (16% to 47%)
Respiratory: Dyspnea (34%), cough (11%), upper respiratory infection (11%)
1% to 10%:
Cardiovascular: QT$_c$ prolongation (3% to 6%)
Dermatologic: Squamous cell carcinoma (4%)
Respiratory: Pulmonary embolism (5%)
<1% (Limited to important or life-threatening): Angioneurotic edema, blurred vision, chest pain, cholecystitis, creatine phosphokinase (CPK) increased, DVT, enterococcal infection, exfoliative dermatitis, gastrointestinal hemorrhage, hemoptysis, hypertension, hypocalcemia, hypokalemia, hyponatremia, hypophosphatemia, infection, lethargy, leukopenia, MI, neutropenia, pneumonia, renal failure, sepsis, spinal cord injury, streptococcal bacteremia, stroke (ischemic), syncope, T-cell lymphoma, transaminases increased, tumor hemorrhage, ureteric obstruction, ureteropelvic junction obstruction, urinary retention, vasculitis, weakness

Overdosage/Toxicology Treatment is symptom-directed and supportive. The benefit of dialysis is unknown.

Drug Interactions
Increased Effect/Toxicity:
Concomitant QT$_c$ prolonging agents may increase the risk of arrhythmia. Valproic acid may enhance thrombocytopenia or gastrointestinal bleeding. Vorinostat may enhance the anticoagulant effect of warfarin.

Stability Store at 15°C to 30°C (59°F to 86°F).

Mechanism of Action Inhibition of histone deacetylase enzymes HDAC1, HDAC2, HDAC3, and HDAC6, which catalyze acetyl group removal from protein lysine residues (including histones and transcription factors). Inhibition of histone deacetylase results in accumulation of acetyl groups, leading to alterations in chromatin structure and transcription factor activation causing termination of cell growth leading to cell death.

Pharmacodynamics/Kinetics
Protein binding: ~71%
Metabolism: Glucuronidated and hydrolyzed (followed by beta-oxidation) to inactive metabolites
Bioavailability: Fasting: ~43%
Half-life elimination: ~2 hours
Time to peak, plasma: With high-fat meal: ~4 hours
Excretion: Urine: 52% (<1% as unchanged drug, ~52% as inactive metabolites)

Dosage Oral: Adults: Cutaneous T-cell lymphoma: 400 mg once daily
Dosage adjustment for intolerance: Reduce dose to 300 mg once daily; may further reduce to 300 mg daily for 5 consecutive days per week
In clinical trials, **dose reductions** were instituted for the following adverse events: Increased serum creatinine, decreased appetite, hypokalemia, leukopenia, nausea, neutropenia, thrombocytopenia and vomiting. Vorinostat was **discontinued** for the following adverse events: Anemia, angioneurotic edema, weakness, chest pain, exfoliative dermatitis, DVT, ischemic stroke, lethargy, pulmonary embolism and spinal cord injury.

Dosage adjustment in renal impairment: Not studied, however, based on the minimal renal elimination, adjustment may not be required.

Dosage adjustment in hepatic impairment: Not studied minimal.

Dietary Considerations Take with food.

Administration Administer with food. Do not open, crush, or chew capsules.

Monitoring Parameters Baseline, then periodic 12-lead ECG; baseline, then every other week serum electrolytes (including calcium, magnesium and potassium), CBC with differential, serum creatinine and blood glucose for 2 months, then monthly

Dosage Forms
Capsule:
Zolinza™: 100 mg

♦ **VoSol® [DSC]** *see* Acetic Acid *on page 38*
♦ **VoSol® HC** *see* Acetic Acid, Propylene Glycol Diacetate, and Hydrocortisone *on page 38*
♦ **VoSpire ER®** *see* Albuterol *on page 57*
♦ **VP-16** *see* Etoposide *on page 670*
♦ **VP-16-213** *see* Etoposide *on page 670*
♦ **Vumon®** *see* Teniposide *on page 1645*
♦ **Vusion™** *see* Miconazole and Zinc Oxide *on page 1139*
♦ **Vytone®** *see* Iodoquinol and Hydrocortisone *on page 931*
♦ **Vytorin®** *see* Ezetimibe and Simvastatin *on page 678*
♦ **VZV Vaccine (Varicella)** *see* Varicella Virus Vaccine *on page 1778*
♦ **VZV Vaccine (Zoster)** *see* Zoster Vaccine *on page 1827*

Warfarin *(WAR far in)*

U.S. Brand Names Coumadin®; Jantoven™
Canadian Brand Names Apo-Warfarin®; Coumadin®; Gen-Warfarin; Novo-Warfarin; Taro-Warfarin
Index Terms Warfarin Sodium
Pharmacologic Category Anticoagulant, Coumarin Derivative
Additional Appendix Information
Anticoagulants, Injectable *on page 1864*

Use Prophylaxis and treatment of venous thrombosis, pulmonary embolism and thromboembolic disorders; atrial fibrillation with risk of embolism and as an adjunct in the prophylaxis of systemic embolism after myocardial infarction

Unlabeled/Investigational Use Prevention of recurrent transient ischemic attacks and to reduce risk of recurrent myocardial infarction

Restrictions

An FDA-approved medication guide must be distributed when dispensing an outpatient prescription (new or refill) where this medication is to be used without direct supervision of a healthcare provider. Medication guides are available at http://www.fda.gov/cder/Offices/ODS/medication_guides.htm.

Pregnancy Risk Factor X

Pregnancy Implications Oral anticoagulants cross the placenta and produce fetal abnormalities. May also cause fatal fetal hemorrhage. Warfarin should not be used during pregnancy because of significant risks. Adjusted-dose heparin can be given safely throughout pregnancy in patients with venous thromboembolism.

Lactation Does not enter breast milk, only metabolites are excreted (AAP rates "compatible")

Medication Safety Issues

Sound-alike/look-alike issues:

Coumadin® may be confused with Avandia®, Cardura®, Compazine®, Kemadrin®

High alert medication: The Institute for Safe Medication Practices (ISMP) includes this medication among its list of drugs which have a heightened risk of causing significant patient harm when used in error.

Contraindications Hypersensitivity to warfarin or any component of the formulation; hemorrhagic tendencies; hemophilia; thrombocytopenia purpura; leukemia; recent or potential surgery of the eye or CNS; major regional lumbar block anesthesia or surgery resulting in large, open surfaces; patients bleeding from the GI, respiratory, or GU tract; threatened abortion; aneurysm; ascorbic acid deficiency; history of bleeding diathesis; prostatectomy; continuous tube drainage of the small intestine; polyarthritis; diverticulitis; emaciation; malnutrition; cerebrovascular hemorrhage; eclampsia/pre-eclampsia; blood dyscrasias; severe uncontrolled or malignant hypertension; severe hepatic disease; pericarditis or pericardial effusion; subacute bacterial endocarditis; visceral carcinoma; following spinal puncture and other diagnostic or therapeutic procedures with potential for significant bleeding; history of warfarin-induced necrosis; an unreliable, noncompliant patient; alcoholism; patient who has a history of falls or is a significant fall risk; unsupervised senile or psychotic patient; pregnancy

Warnings/Precautions Use care in the selection of patients appropriate for this treatment. Ensure patient cooperation especially from the alcoholic, illicit drug user, demented, or psychotic patient. Use with caution in trauma, acute infection, moderate-severe renal insufficiency, prolonged dietary insufficiencies, moderate-severe hypertension, polycythemia vera, vasculitis, open wound, active TB, history of PUD, anaphylactic disorders, indwelling catheters, severe diabetes, thyroid disease, and menstruating and postpartum women. Use with caution in protein C deficiency. Use with caution in patients with heparin-induced thrombocytopenia and DVT. Warfarin monotherapy is contraindicated in the initial treatment of active HIT.

[U.S. Boxed Warning]: May cause major or fatal bleeding. Risk factors for bleeding include high intensity anticoagulation, age, variable INRs, history of GI bleeding, hypertension, cerebrovascular disease, serious heart disease, anemia, malignancy, trauma, renal insufficiency, drug-drug interactions and long duration of therapy. Patient must be instructed to report bleeding, accidents, or falls. Patient must also report any new or discontinued medications, herbal or alternative products used, significant changes in smoking or dietary habits. Necrosis or gangrene of the skin and other tissues can occur. "Purple toes syndrome" may rarely occur. Women may be at risk of developing ovarian hemorrhage at the time of ovulation. The elderly may be more sensitive to anticoagulant therapy. Safety and efficacy have not been established in children.

Adverse Reactions Bleeding is the major adverse effect of warfarin. Hemorrhage may occur at virtually any site. Risk is dependent on multiple variables, including the intensity of anticoagulation and patient susceptibility.

Cardiovascular: Angina, edema, hemorrhagic shock, hypotension, pallor, syncope, vasculitis
Central nervous system: Asthenia, dizziness, fever, headache, lethargy, malaise, pain, stroke
Dermatologic: Alopecia, bullous eruptions, dermatitis, rash, pruritus, urticaria
Gastrointestinal: Abdominal cramps, abdominal pain, anorexia, diarrhea, flatulence, gastrointestinal bleeding, mouth ulcers, nausea, taste disturbance, vomiting
Genitourinary: Hematuria, priapism
Hematologic: Agranulocytosis, anemia, hemorrhage, leukopenia, retroperitoneal hematoma, unrecognized bleeding sites (eg, colon cancer) may be uncovered by anticoagulation
Hepatic: Hepatic injury, hepatitis, jaundice, transaminases increased
Neuromuscular & skeletal: Osteoporosis, paresthesia, weakness
Respiratory: Epistaxis, hemoptysis, pulmonary hemorrhage, tracheobronchial calcification
Miscellaneous: Hypersensitivity/allergic reactions

Skin necrosis/gangrene (<0.1%), due to paradoxical local thrombosis, is a known but rare risk of warfarin therapy. Its onset is usually within the first few days of therapy and is frequently localized to the limbs, breast or penis. The risk of this effect is increased in patients with protein C or S deficiency.

"Purple toes syndrome," caused by cholesterol microembolization, also occurs rarely. Typically, this occurs after several weeks of therapy, and may present as a dark, purplish, mottled discoloration of the plantar and lateral surfaces. Other manifestations of cholesterol microembolization may include rash; livedo reticularis; gangrene; abrupt and intense pain in lower extremities; abdominal, flank, or back pain; hematuria, renal insufficiency; hypertension; cerebral ischemia; spinal cord infarction; or other symptom of vascular compromise.

Overdosage/Toxicology Symptoms include internal or external hemorrhage and hematuria. Avoid emesis and lavage to avoid possible trauma and incidental bleeding. When an overdose occurs, the drug should be immediately discontinued and vitamin K_1 (phytonadione) may be administered. When hemorrhage occurs, fresh frozen plasma transfusions (Continued)

Warfarin *(Continued)*

have been used to help control bleeding by replacing clotting factors. In urgent bleeding, prothrombin complex concentrates may be needed. **Management of elevated INR:** See table.

Management of Elevated INR

INR	Symptom	Action
Above therapeutic range to <5	No significant bleeding	Lower or hold the next dose and monitor frequently; when INR approaches desired range, may resume dosing with a lower dose if INR was significantly above therapeutic range.
≥5 and <9	No significant bleeding	Omit the next 1or 2 doses; monitor INR and resume with a lower dose when the INR approaches the desired range. Alternatively, if there are other risk factors for bleeding, omit the next dose and give vitamin K_1 orally ≤5 mg; resume with a lower dose when the INR approaches the desired range. If rapid reversal is required for surgery, then given vitamin K_1 orally 2-4 mg and hold warfarin. Expect a response within 24 hours; another 1-2 mg may be given orally if needed.
≥9	No significant bleeding	Hold warfarin, give vitamin K_1 orally 5-10 mg, expect the INR to be reduced within 24-48 hours; monitor INR and administer additional vitamin K if necessary. Resume warfarin at lower doses when INR is in the desired range.
Any INR elevation	Serious bleeding	Hold warfarin, give vitamin K_1 (10 mg by slow I.V. infusion), and supplement with fresh plasma transfusion or prothrombin complex concentrate (Factor X complex); recombinant factor VIIa is an alternative to prothrombin complex concentrate. Vitamin K_1 injection can be repeated every 12 hours.
Any INR elevation	Life-threatening bleeding	Hold warfarin, give prothrombin complex concentrate, supplemented with vitamin K_1 (10 mg by slow I.V. infusion); repeat if necessary. Recombinant factor VIIa is an alternative to prothrombin complex concentrate.

Note: Use of high doses of vitamin K_1 (10.0-15.0) may cause resistance to warfarin for up to a week. Heparin or low molecular weight heparin can be given until the patient becomes responsive to warfarin.

Reference: Ansell J, Hirsh J, Poller L et al. "The Pharmacology and Management of the Vitamin K Antagonists," *Chest,* 2004, 126 (3 Suppl):204-33.

Drug Interactions

Cytochrome P450 Effect: Substrate of CYP1A2 (minor), 2C9 (major), 2C19 (minor), 3A4 (minor); **Inhibits** CYP2C9 (moderate), 2C19 (weak)

Increased Effect/Toxicity: Serum levels/effects of warfarin may be increased by acetaminophen (>1.3 g for >1 week), allopurinol, amiodarone, androgens, other anticoagulants, antifungal agents (imidazole), antiplatelet agents, capecitabine, cephalosporins, cimetidine, CYP2C9 inhibitors, disulfiram, drotrecogin alfa, etoposide, fibric acid derivatives, fluconazole, fluorouracil, gefitinib, glucagon, HMG-CoA reductase inhibitors, ifosfamide, leflunomide, macrolide antibiotics, mefloquine, metronidazole, NSAIDs (COX-2 inhibitors and nonselective), omega-3-acids, orlistat, phenytoin, propafenone, propoxyphene, proton pump inhibitors (omeprazole), quinidine, quinolone antibiotics, ropinirole, salicylates, SSRIs, sulfinpyrazone, sulfonamide derivatives, tetracycline derivatives, thyroid products, tigecycline, tolterodine, treprostinil, tricyclic antidepressants, vitamin A, vitamin E, voriconazole, zafirlukast, and zileuton.

Decreased Effect: Serum levels/effects of warfarin may be decreased by aminoglutethimide, antithyroid agents, aprepitant, azathioprine, barbiturates, bile acid sequestrants, bosentan, carbamazepine, CYP2C9 inducers, dicloxacillin, griseofulvin, hormonal contraceptives (estrogens and progestins), mercaptopurine, mitotane, nafcillin, phytonadione, rifamycin derivatives, and sulfasalazine.

Ethanol/Nutrition/Herb Interactions

Ethanol: Avoid ethanol. Acute ethanol ingestion (binge drinking) decreases the metabolism of warfarin and increases PT/INR. Chronic daily ethanol use increases the metabolism of warfarin and decreases PT/INR.

Food: The anticoagulant effects of warfarin may be decreased if taken with foods rich in vitamin K. Vitamin E may increase warfarin effect. Cranberry juice may increase warfarin effect.

Herb/Nutraceutical: Cranberry, fenugreek, ginkgo biloba, glucosamine, may enhance bleeding or increase warfarin's effect. Ginseng (American), coenzyme Q_{10}, and St John's wort may decrease warfarin levels and effects. Avoid alfalfa, anise, bilberry, bladderwrack, bromelain, cat's claw, celery, coleus, cordyceps, dong quai, evening primrose oil, fenugreek, feverfew, garlic, ginger, ginkgo biloba, ginseng (American), ginseng (Panax), ginseng (Siberian), grape seed, green tea, guggul, horse chestnut seed, horseradish, licorice, omega-3-acids, prickly ash, red clover, reishi, same (s-adenosylmethionine), sweet clover, turmeric,and white willow (all have additional antiplatelet activity).

Stability

Injection: Prior to reconstitution, store at 15°C to 30°C (59°F to 86°F). Following reconstitution with 2.7 mL of sterile water (yields 2 mg/mL solution), stable for 4 hours at 15°C to 30°C (59°F to 86°F). Protect from light.

Tablet: Store at 15°C to 30°C (59°F to 86°F). Protect from light.

Mechanism of Action Interferes with hepatic synthesis of vitamin K-dependent coagulation factors (II, VII, IX, X).

Pharmacodynamics/Kinetics

Onset of action: Anticoagulation: Oral: 36-72 hours

Peak effect: Full therapeutic effect: 5-7 days; INR may increase in 36-72 hours

Duration: 2-5 days

Absorption: Oral: Rapid, complete

Distribution: 0.14 L/kg

Protein binding: 99%

Metabolism: Hepatic, primarily via CYP2C9; minor pathways include CYP2C19, 1A2, and 3A4

Half-life elimination: 20-60 hours; Mean: 40 hours; highly variable among individuals

Dosage

Oral:

Infants and Children: 0.05-0.34 mg/kg/day; infants <12 months of age may require doses at or near the high end of this range; consistent anticoagulation may be difficult to maintain in children <5 years of age

Adults: Initial dosing must be individualized. Consider the patient (hepatic function, cardiac function, age, nutritional status, concurrent therapy, risk of bleeding) in addition to prior dose response (if available) and the clinical situation. Start 5-10 mg daily for 2 days. Adjust dose according to INR results; usual maintenance dose ranges from 2-10 mg daily (individual patients may require loading and maintenance doses outside these general guidelines).

Note: Lower starting doses may be required for patients with hepatic impairment, poor nutrition, CHF, elderly, high risk of bleeding, or patients that are debilitated. Higher initial doses may be reasonable in selected patients (ie, receiving enzyme-inducing agents and with low risk of bleeding).

I.V. (administer as a slow bolus injection): 2-5 mg/day

Dosing adjustment in renal disease: No adjustment required, however, patients with renal failure have an increased risk of bleeding complications. Monitor closely.

Dosing adjustment in hepatic disease: Monitor effect at usual doses; the response to oral anticoagulants may be markedly enhanced in obstructive jaundice (due to reduced vitamin K absorption) and also in hepatitis and cirrhosis (due to decreased production of vitamin K-dependent clotting factors); INR should be closely monitored

Dietary Considerations Foods high in vitamin K (eg, beef liver, pork liver, green tea and leafy green vegetables) inhibit anticoagulant effect. Do not change dietary habits once stabilized on warfarin therapy; a balanced diet with a consistent intake of vitamin K is essential; avoid large amounts of alfalfa, asparagus, broccoli, Brussels sprouts, cabbage, cauliflower, green teas, kale, lettuce, spinach, turnip greens, watercress decrease efficacy of warfarin. It is recommended that the diet contain a CONSISTENT vitamin K content of 70-140 mcg/day. Check with healthcare provider before changing diet.

Administration

Oral: Do not take with food. Take at the same time each day.

I.V.: Administer as a slow bolus injection over 1-2 minutes; avoid all I.M. injections

Monitoring Parameters Prothrombin time, hematocrit, INR

Reference Range

INR = patient prothrombin time/mean normal prothrombin time

ISI = international sensitivity index

INR should be increased by 2-3.5 times depending upon indication. An INR >4 does not generally add additional therapeutic benefit and is associated with increased risk of bleeding.

INR ranges based upon indication: See table.

INR Ranges Based Upon Indication

Indication	Targeted INR	Targeted INR Range
Acute myocardial infarction (high-risk)	2.5	2.0-3.0 [1,2,3]
Atrial fibrillation	2.5	2.0-3.0
St Jude Medical bileaflet mechanical aortic valve	2.5	2.0-3.0
Bileaflet or tilting disk mechanical aortic valve	3	2.5-3.5
Caged ball or caged disk mechanical valve	3	2.5-3.5 [1]
Mechanical prosthetic valve with systemic embolism despite adequate anticoagulation	3	2.5-3.5 [1]
Carbomedics bileaflet/Medtronic Hall tilting disk mechanical aortic valve (NSR, NI LA size)	2.5	2.0-3.0
Mechanical valve and risk factors (atrial fibrillation, MI, left atrial enlargement, low EF, endocardial damage)	3	2.5-3.5 [1]
Bioprosthetic mitral valve	2.5	2.0-3.0 [2]
Bioprosthetic aortic valve	2.5	2.0-3.0 [2] (or aspirin 81 mg/day)
Bioprosthetic mitral or aortic valve with atrial fibrillation	2.5	2.0-3.0
Rheumatic mitral valve disease and NSR (left atrial diameter >5.5 cm)	2.5	2.0-3.0
Venous thromboembolism	2.5	2.0-3.0
Lupus inhibitor (no other risk factors)	2.5	2.0-3.0
Lupus inhibitor and recurrent thromboembolism	3	2.5-3.5

[1]Combine with aspirin 81 mg/day

[2]Maintain anticoagulation for 3 months

[3]High-risk includes a large anterior MI, significant heart failure, intracardiac thrombus, thromboembolism

Warfarin levels are not used for monitoring degree of anticoagulation. They may be useful if a patient with unexplained coagulopathy is using the drug surreptitiously or if it is unclear whether clinical resistance is due to true drug resistance or lack of drug intake.

(Continued)

Warfarin *(Continued)*

Normal prothrombin time (PT): 10.9-12.9 seconds. Healthy premature newborns have prolonged coagulation test screening results (eg, PT, aPTT, TT) which return to normal adult values at approximately 6 months of age. Healthy prematures, however, do not develop spontaneous hemorrhage or thrombotic complications because of a balance between procoagulants and inhibitors

Dosage Forms

Injection, powder for reconstitution, as sodium:
  Coumadin®: 5 mg
Tablet, as sodium: 1 mg, 2 mg, 2.5 mg, 3 mg, 4 mg, 5 mg, 6 mg, 7.5 mg, 10 mg
  Coumadin®, Jantoven™: 1 mg, 2 mg, 2.5 mg, 3 mg, 4 mg, 5 mg, 6 mg, 7.5 mg, 10 mg

- ◆ **Warfarin Sodium** *see* Warfarin *on page 1800*
- ◆ **4-Way® Saline Moisturizing Mist [OTC]** *see* Sodium Chloride *on page 1576*
- ◆ **WelChol®** *see* Colesevelam *on page 414*
- ◆ **Wellbutrin®** *see* BuPROPion *on page 252*
- ◆ **Wellbutrin XL™** *see* BuPROPion *on page 252*
- ◆ **Wellbutrin SR®** *see* BuPROPion *on page 252*
- ◆ **Westcort®** *see* Hydrocortisone *on page 852*
- ◆ **Westhroid®** *see* Thyroid *on page 1676*
- ◆ **Winpred™ (Can)** *see* PredniSONE *on page 1416*
- ◆ **WinRho® SDF** *see* Rh₀(D) Immune Globulin *on page 1499*
- ◆ **Winstrol®** *see* Stanozolol *on page 1598*
- ◆ **Wound Wash Saline™ [OTC]** *see* Sodium Chloride *on page 1576*
- ◆ **WR-2721** *see* Amifostine *on page 89*
- ◆ **WR-139007** *see* Dacarbazine *on page 442*
- ◆ **WR-139013** *see* Chlorambucil *on page 340*
- ◆ **WR-139021** *see* Carmustine *on page 296*
- ◆ **Wycillin [DSC]** *see* Penicillin G Procaine *on page 1335*
- ◆ **Wycillin® (Can)** *see* Penicillin G Procaine *on page 1335*
- ◆ **Wytensin® (Can)** *see* Guanabenz *on page 823*
- ◆ **Xalatan®** *see* Latanoprost *on page 981*
- ◆ **Xanax®** *see* Alprazolam *on page 75*
- ◆ **Xanax TS™ (Can)** *see* Alprazolam *on page 75*
- ◆ **Xanax XR®** *see* Alprazolam *on page 75*
- ◆ **Xatral (Can)** *see* Alfuzosin *on page 68*
- ◆ **Xeloda®** *see* Capecitabine *on page 278*
- ◆ **Xenaderm™** *see* Trypsin, Balsam Peru, and Castor Oil *on page 1754*
- ◆ **Xenical®** *see* Orlistat *on page 1272*
- ◆ **Xibrom™** *see* Bromfenac *on page 240*
- ◆ **Xifaxan™** *see* Rifaximin *on page 1511*
- ◆ **Xigris®** *see* Drotrecogin Alfa *on page 561*
- ◆ **Xodol®** *see* Hydrocodone and Acetaminophen *on page 848*
- ◆ **Xodol® 5/300** *see* Hydrocodone and Acetaminophen *on page 848*
- ◆ **Xolair®** *see* Omalizumab *on page 1262*
- ◆ **Xolegel™** *see* Ketoconazole *on page 959*
- ◆ **Xopenex®** *see* Levalbuterol *on page 993*
- ◆ **Xopenex HFA™** *see* Levalbuterol *on page 993*
- ◆ **XPECT™ [OTC]** *see* Guaifenesin *on page 814*
- ◆ **Xpect-HC™** *see* Hydrocodone and Guaifenesin *on page 849*
- ◆ **XPECT-PE™** *see* Guaifenesin and Phenylephrine *on page 818*
- ◆ **Xylocaine®** *see* Lidocaine *on page 1010*
- ◆ **Xylocaine® MPF** *see* Lidocaine *on page 1010*
- ◆ **Xylocaine® MPF With Epinephrine** *see* Lidocaine and Epinephrine *on page 1014*
- ◆ **Xylocaine® Viscous** *see* Lidocaine *on page 1010*
- ◆ **Xylocaine® With Epinephrine** *see* Lidocaine and Epinephrine *on page 1014*
- ◆ **Xylocard® (Can)** *see* Lidocaine *on page 1010*
- ◆ **Xyrem®** *see* Sodium Oxybate *on page 1580*
- ◆ **Y-90 Zevalin** *see* Ibritumomab *on page 871*
- ◆ **Yasmin®** *see* Ethinyl Estradiol and Drospirenone *on page 646*
- ◆ **Yaz** *see* Ethinyl Estradiol and Drospirenone *on page 646*

Yellow Fever Vaccine *(YEL oh FEE ver vak SEEN)*

U.S. Brand Names YF-VAX®
Canadian Brand Names YF-VAX®
Pharmacologic Category Vaccine
Additional Appendix Information
  Immunization Recommendations *on page 1929*
Use Induction of active immunity against yellow fever virus, primarily among persons traveling or living in areas where yellow fever infection exists
Pregnancy Risk Factor C
Pregnancy Implications Animal reproduction studies have not been conducted. Adverse effects to the mother or fetus have not been noted in case reports, however, safety and efficacy for use during pregnancy have not been established. Vaccine should be administered if travel to an endemic area is unavoidable and the infant should be monitored after birth. Seroconversion after vaccination is reduced during pregnancy. Tests to verify immune

response should be considered. If a pregnant woman is to be vaccinated only to satisfy an international requirement (as opposed to decreasing risk of infection), efforts should be made to obtain a waiver letter.

Lactation Excretion in breast milk unknown/use caution

Contraindications Hypersensitivity to egg or chick embryo protein, or any component of the formulation; children <9 months of age unless in high risk area; children <6 months of age; immunosuppressed patients

Warnings/Precautions Do not use in immunodeficient persons (including patients <24 months after hematopoietic stem cell transplant) or patients receiving immunosuppressants (eg, steroids, radiation). Patients who are immunosuppressed have a theoretical risk of encephalitis with yellow fever vaccine administration; consider delaying travel or obtaining a waiver letter. Patients on low-dose or short-term corticosteroids, or with asymptomatic HIV infection are not considered immunosuppressed and may receive the vaccine. Chicken embryos are used in the manufacture of this vaccine; have epinephrine available in persons with previous history of egg allergy if the vaccine must be used. The vial stopper contains latex. Avoid use in infants <9 months and pregnant women unless travel to high-risk areas are unavoidable; use in infants <6 months of age is contraindicated due to risk of encephalitis.

Adverse Reactions All serious adverse reactions must be reported to the U.S. Department of Health and Human Services (DHHS) Vaccine Adverse Event Reporting System (VAERS) 1-800-822-7967.

Frequency not defined (adverse reactions may be increased in patients <9 months or ≥65 years of age)

Central nervous system: Headache, myalgia, fever (incidence of these reactions have been reported to be as low as <5% and as high as 10% to 30% depending on the study)

Local: Injection site reactions (edema, hypersensitivity, mass, pain)

Neuromuscular & skeletal: Weakness

Miscellaneous: Hypersensitivity (immediate), vaccine-associated neurotropic disease (rare), viscerotropic disease (rare)

Drug Interactions

Decreased Effect: Decreased effect of live vaccines may occur; use of yellow fever vaccine in immunosuppressed patients is contraindicated due to possible risk of encephalitis or other serious adverse reactions.

Stability Yellow fever vaccine is shipped with dry ice. Do not use vaccine unless shipping case contains some dry ice on arrival. Maintain vaccine continuously at a temperature between 0°C to 5°C (32°F to 41°F); do not freeze. Reconstitute only with diluent provided. Inject diluent slowly into vial and allow to stand for 1-2 minutes. Gently swirl until a uniform suspension forms; swirl well before withdrawing dose. Avoid vigorous shaking to prevent foaming of suspension. Vaccine must be used within 60 minutes of reconstitution. Keep suspension refrigerated until used.

Pharmacodynamics/Kinetics

Onset: Seroconversion: 10-14 days

Duration: ≥30 years

Dosage Children ≥9 months and Adults: SubQ: One dose (0.5 mL) ≥10 days before travel; Booster: Every 10 years

Administration For SubQ injection only. Do not administer I.M. or I.V.

Monitoring Parameters Monitor for adverse effects up to 10 days after vaccination.

Additional Information Federal law requires that the date of administration, the vaccine manufacturer, lot number of vaccine, and the administering person's name, title, and address be entered into the patient's permanent medical record. A desensitization procedure is available for persons with severe egg sensitivity. Consult manufacturer's labeling for details. Some countries require a valid international Certification of Vaccination showing receipt of vaccine. The WHO requires revaccination every 10 years to maintain traveler's vaccination certificate.

The following CDC agencies may be contacted if serologic testing is needed or for advice when administering yellow fever vaccine to pregnant women, children < 9 months or patients with altered immune status:

Division of Vector-Borne Infectious Diseases: 970-221-6400

Division of Global Migration and Quarantine: 404-498-1600

Dosage Forms Injection, powder for reconstitution [17D-204 strain]: ≥4.74 Log$_{10}$ plaque-forming units (PFU) per 0.5 mL dose [single-dose or 5-dose vial; produced in chicken embryos; packaged with diluent; vial stopper contains latex]

♦ **YF-VAX**® *see* Yellow Fever Vaccine *on page 1804*

♦ **YM087** *see* Conivaptan *on page 417*

♦ **YM-08310** *see* Amifostine *on page 89*

♦ **Yodoxin**® *see* Iodoquinol *on page 930*

♦ **Z4942** *see* Ifosfamide *on page 880*

♦ **Zaditen**® **(Can)** *see* Ketotifen *on page 965*

♦ **Zaditor**® **[OTC]** *see* Ketotifen *on page 965*

♦ **Zaditor**® **(Can)** *see* Ketotifen *on page 965*

Zafirlukast (za FIR loo kast)

U.S. Brand Names Accolate®

Canadian Brand Names Accolate®

Index Terms ICI-204,219

Pharmacologic Category Leukotriene-Receptor Antagonist

Additional Appendix Information

Asthma *on page 2029*

Use Prophylaxis and chronic treatment of asthma in adults and children ≥5 years of age

Pregnancy Risk Factor B

(Continued)

Zafirlukast *(Continued)*

Pregnancy Implications There are no adequate and well-controlled trials in pregnant women. Teratogenic effects not observed in animal studies; fetal defects were observed when administered in maternally toxic doses.

Lactation Enters breast milk/contraindicated

Medication Safety Issues
Sound-alike/look-alike issues:
Accolate® may be confused with Accupril®, Accutane®, Aclovate®

Contraindications Hypersensitivity to zafirlukast or any component of the formulation

Warnings/Precautions Zafirlukast is not FDA approved for use in the reversal of broncho-spasm in acute asthma attacks, including status asthmaticus. Therapy with zafirlukast can be continued during acute exacerbations of asthma.

Hepatic adverse events (including hepatitis, hyperbilirubinemia, and hepatic failure) have been reported; female patients may be at greater risk. Discontinue immediately if liver dysfunction is suspected. Periodic testing of liver function may be considered. If hepatic dysfunction is suspected, liver function tests should be measured immediately. Do not resume or restart if hepatic function studies are consistent with dysfunction. Use caution in patients with alcoholic cirrhosis; clearance is reduced.

Rare cases of eosinophilic vasculitis (Churg-Strauss) have been reported in patients receiving zafirlukast. No causal relationship established. Monitor for eosinophilic vasculitis, rash, pulmonary symptoms, cardiac symptoms, or neuropathy. Safety and efficacy have not been established in patients <5 years of age.

Adverse Reactions
>10%: Central nervous system: Headache (13%)
1% to 10%:
Central nervous system: Dizziness (2%), pain (2%), fever (2%)
Gastrointestinal: Nausea (3%), diarrhea (3%), abdominal pain (2%), vomiting (2%), dyspepsia (1%)
Hepatic: SGPT increased (2%)
Neuromuscular & skeletal: Back pain (2%), myalgia (2%), weakness (2%)
Miscellaneous: Infection (4%)
<1% (Limited to important or life-threatening): Agranulocytosis, angioedema, arthralgia, bleeding, bruising, edema, eosinophilia (systemic), eosinophilic pneumonia, hepatic failure, hepatitis, hyperbilirubinemia, hypersensitivity reactions, insomnia, malaise, pruritus, rash, urticaria, vasculitis with clinical features of Churg-Strauss syndrome (rare)

Overdosage/Toxicology Ingestions of up to 200 mg have been reported. Rash and upset stomach were the predominant symptoms. Treatment should be symptomatic and supportive.

Drug Interactions
Cytochrome P450 Effect: Substrate of CYP2C9 (major); **Inhibits** CYP1A2 (weak), 2C8 (weak), 2C9 (moderate), 2C19 (weak), 2D6 (weak), 3A4 (weak)
Increased Effect/Toxicity: Zafirlukast concentrations are increased by aspirin. Zafirlukast may increase theophylline levels. Zafirlukast may increase the levels/effects of bosentan, dapsone, fluoxetine, glimepiride, glipizide, losartan, montelukast, nateglinide, paclitaxel, phenytoin, warfarin, zafirlukast, and other CYP2C9 substrates.
Decreased Effect: The levels/effects of zafirlukast may be decreased by carbamazepine, phenobarbital, phenytoin, rifampin, rifapentine, secobarbital, and other CYP2C9 inducers. Zafirlukast concentrations may be reduced by erythromycin.

Ethanol/Nutrition/Herb Interactions Food: Decreases bioavailability of zafirlukast by 40%.

Stability Store tablets at controlled room temperature (20°C to 25°C; 68°F to 77°F). Protect from light and moisture; dispense in original airtight container.

Mechanism of Action Zafirlukast is a selectively and competitive leukotriene-receptor antagonist (LTRA) of leukotriene D4 and E4 (LTD4 and LTE4), components of slow-reacting substance of anaphylaxis (SRSA). Cysteinyl leukotriene production and receptor occupation have been correlated with the pathophysiology of asthma, including airway edema, smooth muscle constriction and altered cellular activity associated with the inflammatory process, which contribute to the signs and symptoms of asthma.

Pharmacodynamics/Kinetics
Protein binding: >99%, primarily to albumin
Metabolism: Extensively hepatic via CYP2C9
Bioavailability: Reduced 40% with food
Half-life elimination: 10 hours
Time to peak, serum: 3 hours
Excretion: Urine (10%); feces

Dosage Oral:
Children <5 years: Safety and effectiveness have not been established
Children 5-11 years: 10 mg twice daily
Children ≥12 years and Adults: 20 mg twice daily
Elderly: The mean dose (mg/kg) normalized AUC and C_{max} increase and plasma clearance decreases with increasing age. In patients >65 years of age, there is a two- to threefold greater C_{max} and AUC compared to younger adults.
Dosing adjustment in renal impairment: Dosage adjustment not required.
Dosing adjustment in hepatic impairment: In patients with hepatic impairment (ie, biopsy-proven cirrhosis), there is a 50% to 60% greater C_{max} and AUC compared to normal subjects.

Dietary Considerations Should be taken on an empty stomach (1 hour before or 2 hours after meals).

Administration Administer at least 1 hour before or 2 hours after a meal

Monitoring Parameters Monitor for improvements in air flow; monitor closely for sign/symptoms of hepatic injury; periodic monitoring of LFTs may be considered (not proved to prevent serious injury, but early detection may enhance recovery)

Dosage Forms Tablet: 10 mg, 20 mg

Zalcitabine (zal SITE a been)

U.S. Brand Names Hivid® [DSC]
Canadian Brand Names Hivid®
Index Terms ddC; Dideoxycytidine
Pharmacologic Category Antiretroviral Agent, Reverse Transcriptase Inhibitor (Nucleoside)
Additional Appendix Information
Antiretroviral Therapy for HIV Infection: Adults and Adolescents *on page 1988*
Management of Healthcare Worker Exposures to HBV, HCV, and HIV *on page 1941*
Use In combination with at least two other antiretrovirals in the treatment of patients with HIV infection; it is not recommended that zalcitabine be given in combination with didanosine, stavudine, or lamivudine due to overlapping toxicities, virologic interactions, or lack of clinical data
Pregnancy Risk Factor C
Pregnancy Implications It is not known if zalcitabine crosses the human placenta. Animal studies have shown zalcitabine to be teratogenic, developmental toxicities were also observed. Cases of lactic acidosis/hepatic steatosis syndrome have been reported in pregnant women receiving nucleoside analogue drugs. It is not known if pregnancy itself potentiates this known side effect; however, pregnant women may be at increased risk of lactic acidosis and liver damage. Hepatic enzymes and electrolytes should be monitored frequently during the 3rd trimester of pregnancy in women receiving nucleoside analogues. Health professionals are encouraged to contact the antiretroviral pregnancy registry to monitor outcomes of pregnant women exposed to antiretroviral medications (1-800-258-4263 or www.APRegistry.com).
Lactation Excretion in breast milk unknown/contraindicated
Contraindications Hypersensitivity to zalcitabine or any component of the formulation
Warnings/Precautions Careful monitoring of pancreatic enzymes and liver function tests in patients with a history of pancreatitis, increased amylase, those on parenteral nutrition or with a history of ethanol abuse. **[U.S. Boxed Warning]: Discontinue use immediately if pancreatitis is suspected. [U.S. Boxed Warning]: Lactic acidosis and severe hepatomegaly and failure have rarely occurred with zalcitabine resulting in fatality (stop treatment if lactic acidosis or hepatotoxicity occurs); some cases may possibly be related to underlying hepatitis B;** use with caution in patients on digitalis, CHF, renal failure, hyperphosphatemia. **[U.S. Boxed Warning]: Zalcitabine can cause severe peripheral neuropathy;** avoid use, if possible, in patients with pre-existing neuropathy

Adverse Reactions
>10%:
Central nervous system: Fever (5% to 17%), malaise (2% to 13%)
Neuromuscular & skeletal: Peripheral neuropathy (28%)
1% to 10%:
Central nervous system: Headache (2%), dizziness (1%), fatigue (4%), seizure (1.3%)
Dermatologic: Rash (2% to 11%), pruritus (3% to 5%)
Endocrine & metabolic: Hypoglycemia (2% to 6%), hyponatremia (4%), hyperglycemia (1% to 6%)
Gastrointestinal: Nausea (3%), dysphagia (1% to 4%), anorexia (4%), abdominal pain (3% to 8%), vomiting (1% to 3%), diarrhea (<1% to 10%), weight loss, oral ulcers (3% to 7%), increased amylase (3% to 8%)
Hematologic: Anemia (occurs as early as 2-4 weeks), granulocytopenia (usually after 6-8 weeks)
Hepatic: Abnormal hepatic function (9%), hyperbilirubinemia (2% to 5%)
Neuromuscular & skeletal: Myalgia (1% to 6%), foot pain
Respiratory: Pharyngitis (2%), cough (6%), nasal discharge (4%)
<1% (Limited to important or life-threatening): Anaphylaxis, atrial fibrillation, constipation, hepatic failure, hepatitis, hypocalcemia, jaundice, lactic acidosis, night sweats, pancreatitis, redistribution/accumulation of body fat, syncope
Overdosage/Toxicology Symptoms include delayed peripheral neurotoxicity. Following oral decontamination, treatment is supportive.

Drug Interactions
Increased Effect/Toxicity: Amphotericin, foscarnet, and aminoglycosides may potentiate the risk of developing peripheral neuropathy or other toxicities associated with zalcitabine by interfering with the renal elimination of zalcitabine. Other drugs associated with peripheral neuropathy include chloramphenicol, cisplatin, dapsone, disulfiram, ethionamide, gold, hydralazine, iodoquinol, isoniazid, metronidazole, nitrofurantoin, phenytoin, ribavirin, and vincristine. Concomitant use with zalcitabine may increase risk of peripheral neuropathy. Concomitant use of zalcitabine with didanosine is not recommended. Concomitant use of ribavirin with or without interferon alfa and nucleoside analogues may increase the risk of developing hepatic decompensation or other signs of mitochondrial toxicity, including pancreatitis or lactic acidosis.
Decreased Effect: It is not recommended that zalcitabine be given in combination with didanosine, stavudine, or lamivudine due to overlapping toxicities, virologic interactions, or lack of clinical data. Doxorubicin and lamivudine have been shown *in vitro* to decrease zalcitabine phosphorylation. Magnesium/aluminum-containing antacids and metoclopramide may decrease the absorption of zalcitabine.
Ethanol/Nutrition/Herb Interactions Food: Food decreases peak plasma concentrations by 39%. Extent and rate of absorption may be decreased with food.
Stability Tablets should be stored in tightly closed bottles at 59°F to 86°F.
Mechanism of Action Purine nucleoside (cytosine) analog, zalcitabine or 2',3'-dideoxycytidine (ddC) is converted to active metabolite ddCTP; lack the presence of the 3'-hydroxyl group necessary for phosphodiester linkages during DNA replication. As a result viral replication is prematurely terminated. ddCTP acts as a competitor for binding sites on the HIV-RNA dependent DNA polymerase (reverse transcriptase) to further contribute to inhibition of viral replication.
(Continued)

Zalcitabine *(Continued)*

Pharmacodynamics/Kinetics

Absorption: Well, but variable; decreased 39% with food

Distribution: Minimal data available; variable CSF penetration

Protein binding: <4%

Metabolism: Intracellularly to active triphosphorylated agent

Bioavailability: >80%

Half-life elimination: 2.9 hours; Renal impairment: ≤8.5 hours

Excretion: Urine (>70% as unchanged drug)

Dosage Oral:

Neonates: Dose unknown

Infants and Children <13 years: Safety and efficacy have not been established; investigational dose: 0.01 mg/kg every 8 hours

Adolescents and Adults: 0.75 mg 3 times/day

Dosing adjustment in renal impairment: Adults:

Cl_{cr} 10-40 mL/minute: 0.75 mg every 12 hours

Cl_{cr} <10 mL/minute: 0.75 mg every 24 hours

Moderately dialyzable (20% to 50%)

Administration Food decreases absorption; take on an empty stomach. Administer around-the-clock. Do not take at the same time with dapsone.

Monitoring Parameters Renal function, viral load, liver function tests, CD4 counts, CBC, serum amylase, triglycerides, calcium

Additional Information Potential compliance problems, frequency of administration and adverse effects should be discussed with patients before initiating therapy to help prevent the emergence of resistance.

Dosage Forms [DSC] = Discontinued product

Tablet:

Hivid®: 0.375 mg, 0.75 mg [DSC]

Zaleplon (ZAL e plon)

U.S. Brand Names Sonata®

Canadian Brand Names Sonata®; Starnoc®

Pharmacologic Category Hypnotic, Nonbenzodiazepine

Use Short-term (7-10 days) treatment of insomnia (has been demonstrated to be effective for up to 5 weeks in controlled trial)

Restrictions C-IV

Pregnancy Risk Factor C

Pregnancy Implications Not recommended for use during pregnancy

Lactation Enters breast milk/not recommended

Contraindications Hypersensitivity to zaleplon or any component of the formulation

Warnings/Precautions Symptomatic treatment of insomnia should be initiated only after careful evaluation of potential causes of sleep disturbance. Failure of sleep disturbance to resolve after 7-10 days may indicate psychiatric and/or medical illness.

Use with caution in patients with depression, particularly if suicidal risk may be present. Use with caution in patients with a history of drug dependence. Abrupt discontinuance may lead to withdrawal symptoms. Hypnotics/sedatives have been associated with abnormal thinking and behavior changes including decreased inhibition, aggression, bizarre behavior, agitation, hallucinations, and depersonalization. These changes may occur unpredictably and may indicate previously unrecognized psychiatric disorders; evaluate appropriately. May impair physical and mental capabilities. Patients must be cautioned about performing tasks which require mental alertness (operating machinery or driving). Amnesia can occur. Use with caution in patients receiving other CNS depressants or psychoactive medications. Effects with other sedative drugs or ethanol may be potentiated.

Use with caution in the elderly, those with compromised respiratory function, or renal and hepatic impairment. Because of the rapid onset of action, zaleplon should be administered immediately prior to bedtime or after the patient has gone to bed and is having difficulty falling asleep. Capsules contain tartrazine (FDC yellow #5); avoid in patients with sensitivity (caution in patients with asthma). Safety and efficacy have not been established in children.

Adverse Reactions

1% to 10%:

Cardiovascular: Chest pain, peripheral edema

Central nervous system: Amnesia, anxiety, depersonalization, depression, dizziness, fever, hallucination, hypoesthesia, impaired coordination, lightheadedness, malaise, migraine, somnolence, vertigo

Dermatologic: Photosensitivity reaction, pruritus, rash

Gastrointestinal: Abdominal pain, anorexia, colitis, constipation, dyspepsia, nausea, xerostomia

Genitourinary: Dysmenorrhea

Neuromuscular & skeletal: Arthralgia, back pain, myalgia, paresthesia, tremor, weakness

Ocular: Abnormal vision, eye pain

Otic: Hyperacusis

Miscellaneous: Parosmia

<1% (Limited to important or life-threatening): Alopecia, angina, ataxia, bundle branch block, circumoral paresthesia, dysarthria, dystonia, eosinophilia, facial paralysis, glaucoma, intestinal obstruction, pericardial effusion, ptosis, pulmonary embolus, syncope, urinary retention, ventricular tachycardia

Overdosage/Toxicology Symptoms include CNS depression, ranging from drowsiness to coma. Mild overdose is associated with drowsiness, confusion, and lethargy. Serious cases may result in ataxia, respiratory depression, hypotension, hypotonia, coma, and rarely death. Treatment is supportive.

Drug Interactions

Cytochrome P450 Effect: Substrate of CYP3A4 (minor)

Increased Effect/Toxicity: Zaleplon potentiates the CNS effects of CNS depressants, including anticonvulsants, antipsychotics, barbiturates, benzodiazepines, opioid agonists, and other sedative agents. Cimetidine increases concentrations of zaleplon; Use or use 5 mg zaleplon as starting dose in patient receiving cimetidine.

Decreased Effect:

Flumazenil and rifamycin derivatives may decrease the effect of zaleplon.

Ethanol/Nutrition/Herb Interactions

Ethanol: Avoid ethanol (may increase CNS depression).

Food: High fat meal prolonged absorption; delayed t_{max} by 2 hours, and reduced C_{max} by 35%.

Herb/Nutraceutical: St John's wort may decrease zaleplon levels. Avoid valerian, St John's wort, kava kava, gotu kola (may increase CNS depression).

Stability Store at controlled room temperature of 20°C to 25°C (68°F to 77°F). Protect from light.

Mechanism of Action Zaleplon is unrelated to benzodiazepines, barbiturates, or other hypnotics. However, it interacts with the benzodiazepine GABA receptor complex. Nonclinical studies have shown that it binds selectively to the brain omega-1 receptor situated on the alpha subunit of the GABA-A receptor complex.

Pharmacodynamics/Kinetics

Onset of action: Rapid

Peak effect: ~1 hour

Duration: 6-8 hours

Absorption: Rapid and almost complete

Distribution: V_d: 1.4 L/kg

Protein binding: 60% ± 15%

Metabolism: Extensive, primarily via aldehyde oxidase to form 5-oxo-zaleplon and to a lesser extent by CYP3A4 to desethylzaleplon; all metabolites are pharmacologically inactive

Bioavailability: 30%

Half-life elimination: 1 hour

Time to peak, serum: 1 hour

Excretion: Urine (primarily metabolites, <1% as unchanged drug)

Clearance: Plasma: Oral: 3 L/hour/kg

Dosage Oral:

Adults: 10 mg at bedtime (range: 5-20 mg); has been used for up to 5 weeks of treatment in controlled trial setting

Elderly: 5 mg at bedtime

Dosage adjustment in renal impairment: No adjustment for mild to moderate renal impairment; use in severe renal impairment has not been adequately studied

Dosage adjustment in hepatic impairment: Mild to moderate impairment: 5 mg; not recommended for use in patients with severe hepatic impairment

Administration Immediately before bedtime or when the patient is in bed and cannot fall asleep

Additional Information Prescription quantities should not exceed a 1-month supply.

Dosage Forms Capsule: 5 mg, 10 mg [contains tartrazine]

♦ **Zanaflex®** see Tizanidine on page 1695

Zanamivir (za NA mi veer)

U.S. Brand Names Relenza®

Canadian Brand Names Relenza®

Pharmacologic Category Antiviral Agent; Neuraminidase Inhibitor

Additional Appendix Information

Community-Acquired Pneumonia in Adults on page 1999

Use Treatment of uncomplicated acute illness due to influenza virus A and B; treatment should only be initiated in patients who have been symptomatic for no more than 2 days. Prophylaxis against influenza virus A and B

Pregnancy Risk Factor C

Pregnancy Implications Zanamivir has been shown to cross the placenta in animal models, however, no evidence of fetal malformations has been demonstrated. There are no adequate and well-controlled studies in pregnant women.

Lactation Excretion in breast milk unknown/use caution

Contraindications Hypersensitivity to zanamivir or any component of the formulation

Warnings/Precautions Patients must be instructed in the use of the delivery system. No data are available to support the use of this drug in patients who begin use for treatment after 48 hours of symptoms. Effectiveness has not been established in patients with significant underlying medical conditions or for prophylaxis of influenza in nursing home patients. Not recommended for use in patients with underlying respiratory disease, such as asthma or COPD, due to lack of efficacy and risk of serious adverse effects. Bronchospasm, decreased lung function, and other serious adverse reactions, including those with fatal outcomes, have been reported in patients with and without airway disease; discontinue with bronchospasm or signs of decreased lung function. For a patient with an underlying airway disease where a medical decision has been made to use zanamivir, a fast-acting bronchodilator should be made available, and used prior to each dose. Not a substitute for the flu vaccine. Consider primary or concomitant bacterial infections. Powder for oral inhalation contains lactose. Safety and efficacy of repeated courses or use with severe renal impairment have not been established; efficacy in children <5 years of age have not been established.

Adverse Reactions Most adverse reactions occurred at a frequency which was less than or equal to the control (lactose vehicle).

>10%:

Central nervous system: Headache (prophylaxis 13% to 24%; treatment 2%)

Gastrointestinal: Throat/tonsil discomfort/pain (prophylaxis 8% to 19%)

(Continued)

Zanamivir *(Continued)*

Respiratory: Cough (prophylaxis 7% to 17%; treatment ≤2%), nasal signs and symptoms (prophylaxis 12%; treatment 2%)

Miscellaneous: Viral infection (prophylaxis 3% to 13%)

1% to 10%:

Central nervous system: Fever/chills (prophylaxis 5% to 9%; treatment <1.5%), fatigue (prophylaxis 5% to 8%; treatment <1.5%), malaise (prophylaxis 5% to 8%; treatment <1.5%), dizziness (treatment 1% to 2%)

Dermatologic: Urticaria (treatment <1.5%)

Gastrointestinal: Anorexia/appetite decreased (prophylaxis 2% to 4%), nausea (prophylaxis 1% to 2%; treatment ≤3%), diarrhea (prophylaxis 2%; treatment 2% to 3%), vomiting (prophylaxis 1% to 2%; treatment 1% to 2%) abdominal pain (treatment <1.5%)

Neuromuscular & skeletal: Muscle pain (prophylaxis 3% to 8%), musculoskeletal pain (prophylaxis 6%), arthralgia/articular rheumatism (prophylaxis 2%), arthralgia (treatment <1.5%), myalgia (treatment <1.5%)

Respiratory: Infection (ear/nose/throat; prophylaxis 2%; treatment 2% to 5%), sinusitis (treatment 3%), bronchitis (treatment 2%), nasal inflammation (prophylaxis 1%)

<1% (Limited to important or life-threatening): Allergic or allergic-like reaction (including oropharyngeal edema), arrhythmia, asthma, bronchospasm, dyspnea, facial edema, hemorrhage (ear/nose/throat), rash (including serious cutaneous reactions), seizure, syncope

Overdosage/Toxicology Information is limited, and symptoms appear similar to reported adverse events from clinical studies. Treatment should be symptom-directed and supportive

Drug Interactions

Decreased Effect: Zanamivir may diminish the therapeutic effect of live, attentuated influenza virus vaccine (FluMist™). The manufacturer of FluMist™ recommends that the administration of anti-influenza virus medications be avoided during the period beginning 48 hours prior to vaccine administration and ending 2 weeks after vaccine.

Stability Store at room temperature (25°C) 77°F. Do not puncture blister until taking a dose using the Diskhaler®.

Mechanism of Action Zanamivir inhibits influenza virus neuraminidase enzymes, potentially altering virus particle aggregation and release.

Pharmacodynamics/Kinetics

Absorption: Inhalation: 4% to 17%

Protein binding, plasma: <10%

Metabolism: None

Half-life elimination, serum: 2.5-5.1 hours

Excretion: Urine (as unchanged drug); feces (unabsorbed drug)

Dosage Oral inhalation:

Children ≥5 years and Adults: Prophylaxis (household setting): Two inhalations (10 mg) once daily for 10 days. Begin within 1 ½ days following onset of signs or symptoms of index case.

Children ≥7 years and Adults: Treatment: Two inhalations (10 mg total) twice daily for 5 days. Doses on first day should be separated by at least 2 hours; on subsequent days, doses should be spaced by ~12 hours. Begin within 2 days of signs or symptoms.

Adolescents and Adults: Prophylaxis (community outbreak): Two inhalations (10 mg) once daily for 28 days. Begin within 5 days of outbreak.

Administration Inhalation: Must be used with Diskhaler® delivery device. Patients who are scheduled to use an inhaled bronchodilator should use their bronchodilator prior to zanamivir. With the exception of the initial dose when used for treatment, administer at the same time each day.

Additional Information Majority of patients included in clinical trials were infected with influenza A, however, a number of patients with influenza B infections were also enrolled. Patients with lower temperature or less severe symptoms appeared to derive less benefit from therapy. No consistent treatment benefit was demonstrated in patients with chronic underlying medical conditions.

Dosage Forms Powder for oral inhalation: 5 mg/blister (20s) [4 blisters per Rotadisk® foil pack, 5 Rotadisk® per package; packaged with Diskhaler® inhalation device; contains lactose]

- **Zantac®** *see* Ranitidine *on page 1485*
- **Zantac 75®** **[OTC]** *see* Ranitidine *on page 1485*
- **Zantac 75®** **(Can)** *see* Ranitidine *on page 1485*
- **Zantac 150™** **[OTC]** *see* Ranitidine *on page 1485*
- **Zantac® EFFERdose®** *see* Ranitidine *on page 1485*
- **Zarontin®** *see* Ethosuximide *on page 665*
- **Zaroxolyn®** *see* Metolazone *on page 1128*
- **Zavesca®** *see* Miglustat *on page 1147*
- **Z-Cof™ DM** *see* Guaifenesin, Pseudoephedrine, and Dextromethorphan *on page 821*
- **Z-Cof LA™** *see* Guaifenesin and Dextromethorphan *on page 816*
- **ZD1033** *see* Anastrozole *on page 129*
- **ZD1839** *see* Gefitinib *on page 784*
- **ZDV** *see* Zidovudine *on page 1812*
- **ZDV, Abacavir, and Lamivudine** *see* Abacavir, Lamivudine, and Zidovudine *on page 19*
- **Zeasorb®-AF [OTC]** *see* Miconazole *on page 1137*
- **Zebeta®** *see* Bisoprolol *on page 226*
- **Zebutal™** *see* Butalbital, Acetaminophen, and Caffeine *on page 259*
- **Zegerid®** *see* Omeprazole and Sodium Bicarbonate *on page 1266*
- **Zelapar™** *see* Selegiline *on page 1552*
- **Zeldox** *see* Ziprasidone *on page 1818*
- **Zelnorm®** *see* Tegaserod *on page 1636*

♦ **Zemplar®** *see* Paricalcitol *on page 1312*
♦ **Zemuron®** *see* Rocuronium *on page 1529*
♦ **Zenapax®** *see* Daclizumab *on page 443*
♦ **Zeneca 182,780** *see* Fulvestrant *on page 772*
♦ **Zephrex LA® [DSC]** *see* Guaifenesin and Pseudoephedrine *on page 819*
♦ **Zerit®** *see* Stavudine *on page 1599*
♦ **Zestoretic®** *see* Lisinopril and Hydrochlorothiazide *on page 1023*
♦ **Zestril®** *see* Lisinopril *on page 1021*
♦ **Zetacet®** *see* Sulfur and Sulfacetamide *on page 1618*
♦ **Zetia™** *see* Ezetimibe *on page 677*
♦ **Zevalin®** *see* Ibritumomab *on page 871*
♦ **Ziac®** *see* Bisoprolol and Hydrochlorothiazide *on page 227*
♦ **Ziagen®** *see* Abacavir *on page 18*
♦ **Ziana™** *see* Clindamycin and Tretinoin *on page 391*

Ziconotide (zi KOE no tide)

U.S. Brand Names Prialt®
Pharmacologic Category Analgesic, Nonopioid; Calcium Channel Blocker, N-Type
Use Management of severe chronic pain in patients requiring intrathecal (I.T.) therapy and are intolerant or refractory to other therapies
Pregnancy Risk Factor C
Pregnancy Implications Teratogenic effects were not observed in animal studies, but increased postimplantation pup loss was reported. Maternal toxicity was also noted. There are no adequate and well-controlled studies in pregnant women.
Lactation Excretion in breast milk unknown/not recommended
Contraindications Hypersensitivity to ziconotide or any component of the formulation; history of psychosis; I.V. administration
I.T. administration is contraindicated in patients with infection at the injection site, uncontrolled bleeding, or spinal canal obstruction that impairs CSF circulation
Warnings/Precautions [U.S Boxed Warning]: Severe psychiatric symptoms and neurological impairment have been reported; interrupt or discontinue therapy if cognitive impairment, hallucinations, mood changes, or changes in consciousness occur. Cognitive impairment may appear gradually during treatment and is generally reversible after discontinuation. Use caution in the elderly; may experience confusion. Patients should be instructed to use caution in performing tasks which require alertness (eg, operating machinery or driving). May have additive effects with opiates or other CNS-depressant medications. Does not potentiate opiate-induced respiratory depression. Will not prevent or relieve symptoms associated with opiate withdrawal and opiates should not be abruptly discontinued. Unlike opioids, ziconotide therapy can be interrupted abruptly or discontinued without evidence of withdrawal. Meningitis may occur with use of I.T. pumps and treatment may require removal of system and discontinuation of therapy. Elevated serum creatine kinase can occur. Safety and efficacy have not been established with renal or hepatic dysfunction, or in pediatric patients.
Adverse Reactions Percentages reported when using the slow (21-day) titration schedule; frequencies may be higher with faster titration.
>10%:
Central nervous system: Dizziness (47%), somnolence (22%), confusion (18%), ataxia (16%), headache (15%), memory impairment (12%), pain (11%)
Gastrointestinal: Nausea (41%), diarrhea (19%), vomiting (15%)
Neuromuscular & skeletal: Weakness (22%), gait disturbances (15%), hypertonia (11%)
2% to 10%:
Cardiovascular: Chest pain, edema, hyper-/hypotension, postural hypotension, tachycardia, vasodilation
Central nervous system: Anxiety (9%), speech disorder (9%), aphasia (8%), dysesthesia (7%), fever (7%), hallucinations (7%), nervousness (7%), vertigo (7%), agitation, chills, depression, dreams abnormal, emotional lability, hostility, hyperesthesia, insomnia, malaise, meningitis, paranoid reaction, stupor
Dermatologic: Bruising, cellulitis, dry skin, pruritus, rash
Endocrine & metabolic: Hypokalemia
Gastrointestinal: Anorexia (10%), abdominal pain, constipation, dehydration, dyspepsia, taste perversion, weight loss, xerostomia
Genitourinary: Urinary retention (9%), dysuria, urinary incontinence, urinary tract infection, urination impaired
Hematologic: Anemia
Local: Catheter complication, catheter site pain, pump site complication, pump site mass, pump site pain
Neuromuscular & skeletal: Paresthesia (7%), arthralgia, arthritis, back pain, incoordination, leg cramps, myalgia, myasthenia, neck pain, neck rigidity, neuralgia, reflexes decreased, tremor
Ocular: Vision abnormal (10%), nystagmus (8%), diplopia, photophobia,
Otic: Tinnitus
Respiratory: Bronchitis, cough, dyspnea, pharyngitis, pneumonia, rhinitis, sinusitis
Miscellaneous: CSF abnormalities, diaphoresis, flu-like syndrome, infection
<2% (Limited to important or life-threatening): Aspiration pneumonia (<1%), atrial fibrillation, cerebral vascular accident, convulsions, CPK increased (<2%), ECG abnormalities, kidney failure (acute), myoclonus, psychosis, respiratory distress, rhabdomyolysis, sepsis, suicidal ideation, suicide (<1%)
Overdosage/Toxicology Exaggerated pharmacological effects, including ataxia, confusion, dizziness, garbled speech, hypotension, nausea, nystagmus, sedation, spinal myoclonus, stupor, unresponsiveness, vomiting and word-finding difficulty, are reported at doses >19.2 mcg/day. Respiratory depression was not observed. In case of overdose, ziconotide can be discontinued temporarily or withdrawn; additional treatment should be symptom directed and (Continued)

Ziconotide *(Continued)*

supportive. Opioid antagonists are not effective. Most patients recover within 24 hours of discontinuing ziconotide therapy.

Drug Interactions

Increased Effect/Toxicity: May enhance the adverse/toxic effects of other CNS depressants

Stability Prior to use, store vials at 2°C to 8°C (36°F to 46°F). Once diluted, may be stored at 2°C to 8°C (36°F to 46°F) for 24 hours. Do not freeze. Protect from light.

Preservative free NS should be used when dilution is needed.

CADD-Micro® ambulatory infusion pump: Initial fill: Dilute to final concentration of 5 mcg/mL.

When using the Medtronic SynchroMed® EL or SynchroMed® II Infusion System, solutions expire as follows:

25 mcg/mL: Undiluted:
Initial fill: Use within 14 days.
Refill: Use within 60 days.

100 mcg/mL
Undiluted: Refill: Use within 60 days.
Diluted: Refill: Use within 40 days.

Mechanism of Action Ziconotide selectively binds to N-type voltage sensitive calcium channels located on the afferent nerves of the dorsal horn in the spinal cord. This binding is thought to block N-type calcium channels, leading to a blockade of excitatory neurotransmitter release and reducing sensitivity to painful stimuli.

Pharmacodynamics/Kinetics

Distribution: I.T.: V_d: ~140 mL

Protein binding: 50%

Metabolism: Metabolized via endopeptidases and exopeptidases present on multiple organs including kidney, liver, lung; degraded to peptide fragments and free amino acids

Half-life elimination: I.V.: 1-1.6 hours (plasma); I.T.: 2.9-6.5 hours (CSF)

Excretion: I.V.: Urine (<1%)

Dosage I.T.:

Adults: Chronic pain: Initial dose: 2.4 mcg/day (0.1 mcg/hour)

Dose may be titrated by ≤2.4 mcg/day (0.1 mcg/hour) at intervals ≥2-3 times/week to a maximum dose of 19.2 mcg/day (0.8 mcg/hour) by day 21; average dose at day 21: 6.9 mcg/day (0.29 mcg/hour). A faster titration should be used only if the urgent need for analgesia outweighs the possible risk to patient safety.

Dosage adjustment for toxicity: Cognitive impairment: Reduce dose or discontinue. Effects are generally reversible within 2 weeks of discontinuation.

Elderly: Refer to Adults dosing; use with caution

Administration Not for I.V. administration. For I.T. administration only using Medtronic SynchroMed® EL, SynchroMed® II Infusion System, or CADD-Micro® ambulatory infusion pump.

Medtronic SynchroMed® EL or SynchroMed® II Infusion Systems:

Naive pump priming (first time use with ziconotide): Use 2 mL of undiluted ziconotide 25 mcg/mL solution to rinse the internal surfaces of the pump; repeat twice for a total of 3 rinses

Initial pump fill: Use only undiluted 25 mcg/mL solution and fill pump after priming. Following the initial fill only, adsorption on internal device surfaces will occur, requiring the use of the undiluted solution and refill within 14 days.

Pump refills: Contents should be emptied prior to refill. Subsequent pump refills should occur at least every 40 days if using diluted solution or every 60 days if using undiluted solution

CADD-Micro® ambulatory infusion pump: Refer to manufacturers' manual for initial fill and refill instructions

Monitoring Parameters Monitor for psychiatric or neurological impairment; signs and symptoms of meningitis or other infection; serum CPK (every other week for first month then monthly); pain relief

Dosage Forms Injection, solution, as acetate [preservative free]: 25 mcg/mL (20 mL); 100 mcg/mL (1 mL, 2 mL, 5 mL)

Zidovudine *(zye DOE vyoo deen)*

U.S. Brand Names Retrovir®

Canadian Brand Names Apo-Zidovudine®; AZT™; Retrovir®

Index Terms Azidothymidine; AZT (error-prone abbreviation); Compound S; ZDV

Pharmacologic Category Antiretroviral Agent, Reverse Transcriptase Inhibitor (Nucleoside)

Additional Appendix Information

Antiretroviral Therapy for HIV Infection: Adults and Adolescents *on page 1988*

Management of Healthcare Worker Exposures to HBV, HCV, and HIV *on page 1941*

Prevention of Perinatal HIV-1 Transmission *on page 1953*

Use Treatment of HIV infection in combination with at least two other antiretroviral agents; prevention of maternal/fetal HIV transmission as monotherapy

Unlabeled/Investigational Use Postexposure prophylaxis for HIV exposure as part of a multidrug regimen

Pregnancy Risk Factor C

Pregnancy Implications Zidovudine crosses the placenta. No increased risk of overall birth defects has been observed following 1st trimester exposure according to data collected by the antiretroviral pregnancy registry. The use of zidovudine reduces the maternal-fetal transmission of HIV by ~70% and should be considered for antenatal and intrapartum therapy whenever possible. The Perinatal HIV Guidelines Working Group considers zidovudine the preferred NRTI for use in combination regimens during pregnancy. In HIV infected mothers not previously on antiretroviral therapy, treatment may be delayed until after 10-12 weeks gestation. Cases of lactic acidosis/hepatic steatosis syndrome have been reported in pregnant women receiving nucleoside analogues. It is not known if pregnancy itself potentiates this known side effect; however, pregnant women may be at increased risk of lactic acidosis and liver damage. Hepatic enzymes and electrolytes should be monitored frequently during the 3rd trimester of pregnancy in women receiving nucleoside analogues. Health professionals are encouraged to contact the antiretroviral pregnancy registry to monitor outcomes of pregnant women exposed to antiretroviral medications (1-800-258-4263 or www.APRegistry.com).

Lactation Enters breast milk/contraindicated

Medication Safety Issues
Sound-alike/look-alike issues:
Azidothymidine may be confused with azathioprine, aztreonam
Retrovir® may be confused with ritonavir

AZT is an error-prone abbreviation (mistaken as azathioprine, aztreonam)

Contraindications Life-threatening hypersensitivity to zidovudine or any component of the formulation

Warnings/Precautions [U.S. Boxed Warning]: Often associated with hematologic toxicity including granulocytopenia, severe anemia requiring transfusions, or (rarely) pancytopenia. Use with caution in patients with bone marrow compromise (granulocytes <1000 cells/mm³ or hemoglobin <9.5 mg/dL); dosage adjustment may be required in patients who develop anemia or neutropenia. **[U.S. Boxed Warning]: Lactic acidosis and severe hepatomegaly with steatosis have been reported, including fatal cases;** use with caution in patients with risk factors for liver disease (risk may be increased in obese patients or prolonged exposure) and suspend treatment with zidovudine in any patient who develops clinical or laboratory findings suggestive of lactic acidosis (transaminase elevation may/may not accompany hepatomegaly and steatosis). Use caution in combination with interferon alfa with or without ribavirin in HIV/HBV coinfected patients; monitor closely for hepatic decompensation, anemia, or neutropenia; dose reduction or discontinuation of interferon and/or ribavirin may be required if toxicity evident. **[U.S. Boxed Warning]: Prolonged use has been associated with symptomatic myopathy and myositis.** Immune reconstitution syndrome may develop resulting in the occurrence of an inflammatory response to an indolent or residual opportunistic infection; further evaluation and treatment may be required. Reduce dose in patients with severe renal impairment.

Adverse Reactions As reported in adult patients with asymptomatic HIV infection. Frequency and severity may increase with advanced disease.
>10%:
Central nervous system: Headache (63%), malaise (53%)
Gastrointestinal: Nausea (51%), anorexia (20%), vomiting (17%)
1% to 10%:
Gastrointestinal: Constipation (6%)
Hematologic: Granulocytopenia (2%; onset 6-8 weeks), anemia (1%; onset 2-4 weeks)
Hepatic: Transaminases increased (1% to 3%)
Neuromuscular & skeletal: Weakness (9%)

Frequency not defined:
Cardiovascular: Cardiomyopathy, chest pain, syncope, vasculitis
Central nervous system: Anxiety, chills, confusion, depression, dizziness, fatigue, insomnia, loss of mental acuity, mania, seizures, somnolence, vertigo
Dermatologic: Pruritus, rash, skin/nail pigmentation changes, Stevens-Johnson syndrome, toxic epidermal necrolysis, urticaria
Endocrine & metabolic: Body fat redistribution, gynecomastia
Gastrointestinal: Abdominal cramps, abdominal pain, dyspepsia, dysphagia, flatulence, mouth ulcer, oral mucosa pigmentation, pancreatitis, taste perversion
Genitourinary: Urinary frequency, urinary hesitancy
Hematologic: Aplastic anemia, hemolytic anemia, leukopenia, lymphadenopathy, pancytopenia with marrow hypoplasia, pure red cell aplasia
Hepatic: Hepatitis, hepatomegaly with steatosis, hyperbilirubinemia, jaundice, lactic acidosis
Neuromuscular & skeletal: Arthralgia, back pain, CPK increased, LDH increased, musculoskeletal pain, myalgia, neuropathy, muscle spasm, myopathy, myositis, paresthesia, rhabdomyolysis, tremor
Ocular: Amblyopia, macular edema, photophobia
Otic: Hearing loss
Respiratory: Cough, dyspnea, rhinitis, sinusitis
Miscellaneous: Allergic reactions, anaphylaxis, angioedema, diaphoresis, flu-like syndrome, immune reconstitution syndrome

Overdosage/Toxicology Acute overdoses up to 50 g have been reported. Symptoms of overdose include nausea, vomiting, ataxia, and granulocytopenia. Treatment is symptom-directed and supportive. Dialysis does not appear to significantly remove zidovudine, but does improve clearance of the primary metabolite.

Drug Interactions
Cytochrome P450 Effect: Substrate (minor) of CYP2A6, 2C9, 2C19, 3A4
Increased Effect/Toxicity: Coadministration of zidovudine with drugs that are nephrotoxic (amphotericin B), cytotoxic (flucytosine, vincristine, vinblastine, doxorubicin, interferon), inhibit glucuronidation or excretion (acetaminophen, cimetidine, indomethacin, lorazepam, probenecid, aspirin), or interfere with RBC/WBC number or function (acyclovir, ganciclovir, pentamidine, dapsone). Clarithromycin may increase blood levels of zidovudine (although total body exposure was unaffected, peak plasma concentrations were increased). Methadone may increase the levels/effects of zidovudine. Valproic acid significantly increases zidovudine's blood levels (believed due to inhibition first pass metabolism). Concomitant use of acyclovir/valacyclovir may increase the CNS depressant effects of zidovudine. Concomitant use of ribavirin with or without interferon alfa and nucleoside analogues may increase the risk of developing hepatic decompensation or other signs of mitochondrial

(Continued)

Zidovudine *(Continued)*

toxicity, including pancreatitis or lactic acidosis. Zidovudine may increase the myelosuppressive effects of trimetrexate; avoid concomitant use.

Decreased Effect: Zidovudine may decrease the antiviral activity of stavudine (based on *in vitro* data); avoid concurrent use. Rifampin may decrease the levels of zidovudine.

Stability Store undiluted vials at 15°C to 25°C (59°F to 77°F). Protect from light. Solution for injection should be diluted with D_5W to a concentration ≤4 mg/mL. The solution is physically and chemically stable for 24 hours at room temperature and 48 hours if refrigerated. Attempt to administer diluted solution within 8 hours if stored at room temperature or 24 hours if refrigerated to minimize potential for microbially-contaminated solutions.

Mechanism of Action Zidovudine is a thymidine analog which interferes with the HIV viral RNA dependent DNA polymerase resulting in inhibition of viral replication; nucleoside reverse transcriptase inhibitor

Pharmacodynamics/Kinetics

Distribution: Significant penetration into the CSF; crosses placenta

V_d: 1-2.2 L/kg

Relative diffusion from blood into CSF: Adequate with or without inflammation (exceeds usual MICs)

CSF:blood level ratio: Normal meninges: ~60%

Protein binding: 25% to 38%

Metabolism: Hepatic via glucuronidation to inactive metabolites; extensive first-pass effect

Bioavailability: 54% to 74%

Half-life elimination: Terminal: 0.5-3 hours

Time to peak, serum: 30-90 minutes

Excretion:

Oral: Urine (72% to 74% as metabolites, 14% to 18% as unchanged drug)

I.V.: Urine (45% to 60% as metabolites, 18% to 29% as unchanged drug)

Dosage

Prevention of maternal-fetal HIV transmission:

Neonatal: **Note:** Dosing should begin 8-12 hours after birth and continue for the first 6 weeks of life.

Oral:

Full-term infants: 2 mg/kg/dose every 6 hours

Infants ≥30 weeks and <35 weeks gestation at birth: 2 mg/kg/dose every 12 hours; at 2 weeks of age, advance to 2 mg/kg/dose every 8 hours

Infants <30 weeks gestation at birth: 2 mg/kg/dose every 12 hours; at 4 weeks of age, advance to 2 mg/kg/dose every 8 hours

I.V.: Infants unable to receive oral dosing:

Full term: 1.5 mg/kg/dose every 6 hours

Infants ≥30 weeks and <35 weeks gestation at birth: 1.5 mg/kg/dose every 12 hours; at 2 weeks of age, advance to 1.5 mg/kg/dose every 8 hours

Infants <30 weeks gestation at birth: 1.5 mg/kg/dose every 12 hours; at 4 weeks of age, advance to 1.5 mg/kg/dose every 8 hours

Maternal: Oral (per AIDSinfo guidelines): 100 mg 5 times/day **or** 200 mg 3 times/day or 300 mg twice daily. Begin at 14-34 weeks gestation and continue until start of labor. During labor and delivery, administer zidovudine I.V. at 2 mg/kg as loading dose followed by a continuous I.V. infusion of 1 mg/kg/hour until the umbilical cord is clamped

Treatment of HIV infection:

Children 6 weeks to 12 years:

Oral: 160 mg/m² 3 times/day every 8 hours (maximum: 200 mg every 8 hours); some Working Group members use a dose of 180 mg/m² to 240 mg/m² every 12 hours when using in drug combinations with other antiretroviral compounds, but data on this dosing in children is limited

I.V. continuous infusion: 20 mg/m²/hour

I.V. intermittent infusion: 120 mg/m²/dose every 6 hours

Adults:

Oral: 300 mg twice daily or 200 mg 3 times/day

I.V.: 1 mg/kg/dose administered every 4 hours around-the-clock (5-6 doses/day)

Prevention of HIV following needlesticks (unlabeled use): Oral: Adults: 200 mg 3 times/day plus lamivudine 150 mg twice daily; a protease inhibitor (eg, indinavir) may be added for high risk exposures; begin therapy within 2 hours of exposure if possible

Patients should receive I.V. therapy only until oral therapy can be administered

Dosing adjustment for hematologic toxicity: Consider dose interruption for significant anemia (hemoglobin <7.5 g/dL or >25% reduction from baseline) and/or neutropenia (granulocyte count <750 cells/mm³ or >50% reduction from baseline) until evidence of recovery. Anemia associated with chronic zidovudine may warrant dose reduction.

Dosing adjustment in renal impairment: Cl_{cr} <15 mL/minute including hemo-/peritoneal dialysis: 100 mg (oral) or 1 mg/kg (I.V.) every 6-8 hours

Continuous arteriovenous or venovenous hemodiafiltration effects: Administer 100 mg every 8 hours

Dosing adjustment in hepatic impairment: Reduce dose by 50% or double dosing interval in patients with cirrhosis

Dietary Considerations May be taken without regard to food.

Administration

Oral: Administer around-the-clock to promote less variation in peak and trough serum levels; may be administered without regard to food

I.M.: Do not administer I.M.

I.V.: Avoid rapid infusion or bolus injection

Neonates: Infuse over 30 minutes

Adults: Infuse loading dose over 1 hour, followed by continuous infusion

Monitoring Parameters Monitor CBC and platelet count at least every 2 weeks, liver function tests, MCV, serum creatinine kinase, viral load, and CD4 count; observe for appearance of opportunistic infections

Additional Information Potential compliance problems, frequency of administration and adverse effects should be discussed with patients before initiating therapy to help prevent the emergence of resistance.

Dosage Forms
Capsule:
Retrovir®: 100 mg
Injection, solution [preservative free]:
Retrovir®: 10 mg/mL (20 mL)
Syrup:
Retrovir®: 50 mg/5 mL (240 mL) [contains sodium benzoate; strawberry flavor]
Tablet: 300 mg
Retrovir®: 300 mg

♦ **Zidovudine, Abacavir, and Lamivudine** see Abacavir, Lamivudine, and Zidovudine on page 19

Zidovudine and Lamivudine (zye DOE vyoo deen & la MI vyoo deen)

U.S. Brand Names Combivir®
Canadian Brand Names Combivir®
Index Terms AZT + 3TC (error-prone abbreviation); Lamivudine and Zidovudine
Pharmacologic Category Antiretroviral Agent, Reverse Transcriptase Inhibitor (Nucleoside)
Additional Appendix Information
Antiretroviral Therapy for HIV Infection: Adults and Adolescents on page 1988
Management of Healthcare Worker Exposures to HBV, HCV, and HIV on page 1941
Use Treatment of HIV infection when therapy is warranted based on clinical and/or immunological evidence of disease progression
Pregnancy Risk Factor C
Medication Safety Issues
Sound-alike/look-alike issues:
Combivir® may be confused with Combivent®, Epivir®

AZT is an error-prone abbreviation (mistaken as azathioprine, aztreonam)
Dosage Children ≥12 years and Adults: Oral: One tablet twice daily
Note: Because this is a fixed-dose combination product, avoid use in patients requiring dosage reduction including children <12 years of age, renally-impaired patients with a creatinine clearance ≤50 mL/minute, hepatic impairment, or those patients experiencing dose-limiting adverse effects.
Additional Information Complete prescribing information for this medication should be consulted for additional detail.
Dosage Forms
Tablet:
Combivir®: Zidovudine 300 mg and lamivudine 150 mg

♦ **Zilactin® (Can)** see Lidocaine on page 1010
♦ **Zilactin-L® [OTC]** see Lidocaine on page 1010
♦ **Zilactin®-B [OTC]** see Benzocaine on page 204
♦ **Zilactin-B® (Can)** see Benzocaine on page 204
♦ **Zilactin Baby® (Can)** see Benzocaine on page 204
♦ **Zilactin Toothache and Gum Pain® [OTC]** see Benzocaine on page 204

Zileuton (zye LOO ton)

U.S. Brand Names Zyflo®
Pharmacologic Category 5-Lipoxygenase Inhibitor
Additional Appendix Information
Asthma on page 2029
Use Prophylaxis and chronic treatment of asthma in children ≥12 years of age and adults
Pregnancy Risk Factor C
Pregnancy Implications Clinical effects on the fetus: Developmental studies indicated adverse effects (reduced body weight and increased skeletal variations) in rats at an oral dose of 300 mg/kg/day. There are no adequate and well-controlled studies in pregnant women.
Lactation Excretion in breast milk unknown/not recommended
Contraindications Hypersensitivity to zileuton or any component of the formulation; active liver disease or transaminase elevations greater than or equal to three times the upper limit of normal (≥3 times ULN)
Warnings/Precautions Not FDA approved for the reversal of bronchospasm in acute asthma attacks, including status asthmaticus; therapy may be continued during acute asthma exacerbations. Hepatic adverse effects have been reported; females >65 years and patients with pre-existing elevated transaminases may be at greater risk. Use caution with history of liver disease or alcoholic cirrhosis. Safety and efficacy have not been established in children <12 years of age.
Adverse Reactions
>10%: Central nervous system: Headache (25%)
1% to 10%:
Central nervous system: Pain (8%)
Gastrointestinal: Dyspepsia (8%), nausea (6%), abdominal pain (5%)
Hematologic: Leukopenia (1%)
Hepatic: ALT increased (2%)
Neuromuscular & skeletal: Asthenia (4%), myalgia (3%)
Frequency not defined:
Cardiovascular: Chest pain
Central nervous system: Dizziness, fever, insomnia, malaise, nervousness, somnolence
(Continued)

Zileuton *(Continued)*

Dermatologic: Pruritus
Gastrointestinal: Constipation, flatulence, vomiting
Genitourinary: Urinary tract infection, vaginitis
Neuromuscular & skeletal: Arthralgia, hypertonia, neck pain/rigidity
Ocular: Conjunctivitis
Miscellaneous: Lymphadenopathy
Postmarketing and/or case reports: Rash, urticaria

Overdosage/Toxicology Symptoms of overdose in humans are limited. Oral minimum lethal doses in mice and rats were 500-1000 and 300-1000 mg/kg, respectively (providing >3 and 9 times the systemic exposure achieved at the maximum recommended human daily oral dose, respectively). No deaths occurred, but nephritis was reported in dogs at an oral dose of 1000 mg/kg. Treat symptomatically. Institute supportive measures as required. If indicated, achieve elimination of unabsorbed drug by emesis or gastric lavage. Observe usual precautions to maintain the airway. Zileuton is NOT removed by dialysis.

Drug Interactions
Cytochrome P450 Effect: Substrate (minor) of CYP1A2, 2C9, 3A4; **Inhibits** CYP1A2 (moderate)

Increased Effect/Toxicity: Zileuton may increase the serum concentration/effects of theophylline, propranolol, and warfarin; monitor and reduce doses accordingly. Zileuton may increase the levels/effects of CYP1A2 substrates; example substrates include aminopylline, fluvoxamine, mexiletine, mirtazapine, ropinirole, and trifluoperazine.

Ethanol/Nutrition/Herb Interactions
Ethanol: Avoid ethanol (may increase CNS depression; may increase risk of hepatic toxicity).
Herb/Nutraceutical: St John's wort may decrease zileuton levels.

Stability Store tablets at controlled room temperature of 20°C to 25°C (68°F to 77°F). Protect from light.

Mechanism of Action Specific 5-Lipoxygenase inhibitor which inhibits leukotriene formation. Leukotrienes augment neutrophil and eosinophil migration, neutrophil and monocyte aggregation, leukocyte adhesion, increased capillary permeability and smooth muscle contraction (which contribute to inflammation, edema, mucous secretion, and bronchoconstriction in the airway of the asthmatic.)

Pharmacodynamics/Kinetics
Absorption: Rapid
Distribution: 1.2 L/kg
Protein binding: 93%
Metabolism: Several metabolites in plasma and urine; metabolized by CYP1A2, 2C9, and 3A4
Bioavailability: Unknown
Half-life elimination: 2.5 hours
Time to peak, serum: 1.7 hours
Excretion: Urine (~95% primarily as metabolites); feces (~2%)

Dosage Oral:
Children <12 years: Safety and effectiveness have not been established
Children ≥12 years and Adults: 600 mg 4 times/day
Dosing adjustment in renal impairment: Adjustment not required.
Dosing adjustment in hepatic impairment: Contraindicated with hepatic dysfunction

Dietary Considerations May be taken with or without food.

Administration May be administered without regard to meals (eg, with or without food)

Monitoring Parameters Evaluate hepatic transaminases at initiation of and during therapy with zileuton. Monitor serum ALT before treatment begins, once-a-month for the first 3 months, every 2-3 months for the remainder of the first year, and periodically thereafter for patients receiving long-term zileuton therapy. If symptoms of liver dysfunction (right upper quadrant pain, nausea, fatigue, lethargy, pruritus, jaundice or "flu-like" symptoms) develop or transaminase elevations >5 times ULN occur, discontinue therapy and follow transaminase levels until normal.

Dosage Forms Tablet: 600 mg

♦ **Zinacef**® see Cefuroxime *on page 326*
♦ **Zincate**® see Zinc Sulfate *on page 1817*

Zinc Chloride *(zink KLOR ide)*

Pharmacologic Category Trace Element

Use Cofactor for replacement therapy to different enzymes helps maintain normal growth rates, normal skin hydration and senses of taste and smell

Pregnancy Risk Factor C

Dosage Clinical response may not occur for up to 6-8 weeks
Supplemental to I.V. solutions:
Premature Infants <1500 g, up to 3 kg: 300 mcg/kg/day
Full-term Infants and Children ≤5 years: 100 mcg/kg/day
Adults:
Stable with fluid loss from small bowel: 12.2 mg zinc/liter TPN or 17.1 mg zinc/kg (added to 1000 mL I.V. fluids) of stool or ileostomy output
Metabolically stable: 2.5-4 mg/day, add 2 mg/day for acute catabolic states

Additional Information Complete prescribing information for this medication should be consulted for additional detail.

Dosage Forms Injection, solution: 1 mg/mL (10 mL, 50 mL)

Zinc Gelatin (zink JEL ah tin)

U.S. Brand Names Gelucast®
Index Terms Dome Paste Bandage; Unna's Boot; Unna's Paste; Zinc Gelatin Boot
Pharmacologic Category Topical Skin Product
Use As a protectant and to support varicosities and similar lesions of the lower limbs
Dosage Apply externally as an occlusive boot
Additional Information Complete prescribing information for this medication should be consulted for additional detail.
Dosage Forms Bandage: 3" x 10 yards; 4" x 10 yards

♦ **Zinc Gelatin Boot** see Zinc Gelatin on page 1817
♦ **Zincofax® (Can)** see Zinc Oxide on page 1817

Zinc Oxide (zink OKS ide)

U.S. Brand Names Ammens® Medicated Deodorant [OTC]; Balmex® [OTC]; Boudreaux's® Butt Paste [OTC]; Critic-Aid Skin Care® [OTC]; Desitin® [OTC]; Desitin® Creamy [OTC]
Canadian Brand Names Zincofax®
Index Terms Base Ointment; Lassar's Zinc Paste
Pharmacologic Category Topical Skin Product
Use Protective coating for mild skin irritations and abrasions, soothing and protective ointment to promote healing of chapped skin, diaper rash
Dosage Infants, Children, and Adults: Topical: Apply as required for affected areas several times daily
Additional Information Complete prescribing information for this medication should be consulted for additional detail.
Dosage Forms
Cream:
Balmex®: 11.3% (60 g, 120 g, 480 g) [contains aloe and vitamin E]
Ointment, topical: 20% (30 g, 60 g, 454 g); 40% (120 g)
Desitin®: 40% (30 g, 60 g, 90 g, 120 g, 270 g, 480 g) [contains cod liver oil and lanolin]
Desitin® Creamy: 10% (60 g, 120 g)
Paste, topical:
Boudreaux's® Butt Paste: 16% (30 g, 60 g, 120 g, 480 g) [contains castor oil, boric acid, mineral oil, and Peruvian balsam]
Critic-Aid Skin Care®: 20% (71 g, 170 g)
Powder, topical (Ammens® Medicated Deodorant): 9.1% (187.5 g, 330 g) [original and shower fresh scent]

♦ **Zinc Oxide and Miconazole Nitrate** see Miconazole and Zinc Oxide on page 1139

Zinc Sulfate (zink SUL fate)

U.S. Brand Names Orazinc® [OTC]; Zincate®
Canadian Brand Names Anuzinc; Rivasol
Index Terms ZnSO₄ (error-prone abbreviation)
Pharmacologic Category Trace Element
Use Zinc supplement (oral and parenteral); may improve wound healing in those who are deficient
Pregnancy Risk Factor C
Medication Safety Issues
Sound-alike/look-alike issues:
$ZnSO_4$ is an error-prone abbreviation (mistaken as morphine sulfate)
Dosage
RDA: Oral:
Birth to 6 months: 3 mg elemental zinc/day
6-12 months: 5 mg elemental zinc/day
1-10 years: 10 mg elemental zinc/day
≥11 years: 15 mg elemental zinc/day

Zinc deficiency: Oral:
Infants and Children: 0.5-1 mg elemental zinc/kg/day divided 1-3 times/day; somewhat larger quantities may be needed if there is impaired intestinal absorption or an excessive loss of zinc
Adults: 110-220 mg zinc sulfate (25-50 mg elemental zinc)/dose 3 times/day
Parenteral TPN: I.V.:
Infants (premature, birth weight <1500 g up to 3 kg): 300 mcg/kg/day
Infants (full-term) and Children ≤5 years: 100 mcg/kg/day
Adults:
Acute metabolic states: 4.5-6 mg/day
Metabolically stable: 2.5-4 mg/day
Stable with fluid loss from the small bowel: 12.2 mg zinc/L of TPN solution, or an additional 17.1 mg zinc (added to 1000 mL I.V. fluids) per kg of stool or ileostomy output
Additional Information Complete prescribing information for this medication should be consulted for additional detail.
Dosage Forms
Capsule (Orazinc®, Zincate®): 220 mg [elemental zinc 50 mg]
Injection, solution [preservative free]: 1 mg elemental zinc/mL (10 mL), 5 mg elemental zinc/mL (5 mL)
Tablet (Orazinc®): 110 mg [elemental zinc 25 mg]

♦ **Zinecard®** see Dexrazoxane on page 485

ZIPRASIDONE

* Ziox™ [DSC] *see* Chlorophyllin, Papain, and Urea *on page 345*
* Ziox 405™ *see* Chlorophyllin, Papain, and Urea *on page 345*

Ziprasidone (zi PRAS i done)

U.S. Brand Names Geodon®
Index Terms Zeldox; Ziprasidone Hydrochloride; Ziprasidone Mesylate
Pharmacologic Category Antipsychotic Agent, Atypical
Additional Appendix Information
Antipsychotic Agents *on page 1872*
Use Treatment of schizophrenia; treatment of acute manic or mixed episodes associated with bipolar disorder with or without psychosis; acute agitation in patients with schizophrenia
Unlabeled/Investigational Use Tourette's syndrome
Pregnancy Risk Factor C
Pregnancy Implications Developmental toxicity demonstrated in animals. There are no adequate and well-controlled studies in pregnant women. Use only if potential benefit justifies risk to the fetus.
Lactation Excretion in breast milk unknown/not recommended
Contraindications Hypersensitivity to ziprasidone or any component of the formulation; history (or current) prolonged QT; congenital long QT syndrome; recent myocardial infarction; history of arrhythmias; uncompensated heart failure; concurrent use of other QT$_c$-prolonging agents including amiodarone, arsenic trioxide, bretylium, chlorpromazine, cisapride, class Ia antiarrhythmics (quinidine, procainamide), dofetilide, dolasetron, droperidol, ibutilide, levomethadyl, mefloquine, mesoridazine, pentamidine, pimozide, probucol, some quinolone antibiotics (moxifloxacin, sparfloxacin, gatifloxacin), sotalol, tacrolimus, and thioridazine
Warnings/Precautions [U.S. Boxed Warning]: Patients with dementia-related behavioral disorders treated with atypical antipsychotics are at an increased risk of death compared to placebo. An increased incidence of cerebrovascular adverse events (including fatalities) has been reported in elderly patients with dementia-related psychosis. Risk may be increased by dehydration; use caution with concurrent diuretics. Ziprasidone is not approved for this indication.
May result in QT$_c$ prolongation (dose-related), which has been associated with the development of malignant ventricular arrhythmias (torsade de pointes). Avoid hypokalemia, hypomagnesemia. Use caution in patients with bradycardia. Discontinue in patients found to have persistent QT$_c$ intervals >500 msec. Patients with symptoms of dizziness, palpitations, or syncope should receive further cardiac evaluation. May cause orthostatic hypotension.

May cause extrapyramidal symptoms. Impaired core body temperature regulation may occur; caution with strenuous exercise, heat exposure, dehydration, and concomitant medication possessing anticholinergic effects; not reported in premarketing trials of ziprasidone. Antipsychotic use may also be associated with neuroleptic malignant syndrome (NMS). Use with caution in patients at risk of seizures.

Atypical antipsychotics have been associated with development of hyperglycemia. There is limited documentation with ziprasidone and specific risk associated with this agent is not known. Use caution in patients with diabetes or other disorders of glucose regulation; monitor for worsening of glucose control.

Cognitive and/or motor impairment (sedation) is common with ziprasidone. Use with caution in disorders where CNS depression is a feature. Use with caution in Parkinson's disease. Antipsychotic use has been associated with esophageal dysmotility and aspiration; use with caution in patients at risk of pneumonia (ie, Alzheimer's disease). Caution in breast cancer or other prolactin-dependent tumors, Use caution in renal or hepatic impairment. Ziprasidone has been associated with a fairly high incidence of rash (5%). Significant weight gain has been observed with antipsychotic therapy; incidence varies with product. Safety and efficacy have not been established in pediatric patients.

The possibility of a suicide attempt is inherent in psychotic illness or bipolar disorder; use caution in high-risk patients during initiation of therapy. Prescriptions should be written for the smallest quantity consistent with good patient care.
Adverse Reactions Note: Although minor QT$_c$ prolongation (mean 10 msec at 160 mg/day) may occur more frequently (incidence not specified), clinically-relevant prolongation (>500 msec) was rare (0.06%) and less than placebo (0.23%).

>10%:
Central nervous system: Extrapyramidal symptoms (2% to 31%), somnolence (8% to 31%), headache (3% to 18%), dizziness (3% to 16%)
Gastrointestinal: Nausea (4% to 12%)
1% to 10%:
Cardiovascular: Chest pain (5%), postural hypotension (5%), hypertension (2% to 3%), bradycardia (2%), tachycardia (2%), vasodilation (1%), facial edema, orthostatic hypotension
Central nervous system: Akathisia (2% to 10%), anxiety (2% to 5%) insomnia (3%), agitation (2%), speech disorder (2%), personality disorder (2%), psychosis (1%), akinesia, amnesia, ataxia, chills, confusion, coordination abnormal, delirium, dystonia, fever, hostility, hypothermia, oculogyric crisis, vertigo
Dermatologic: Rash (4%), fungal dermatitis (2%)
Endocrine & metabolic: Dysmenorrhea (2%)
Gastrointestinal: Weight gain (10%), constipation (2% to 9%), dyspepsia (1% to 8%), diarrhea (3% to 5%), vomiting (3% to 5%), salivation increased (4%), xerostomia (1% to 5%), tongue edema (3%), abdominal pain (2%), anorexia (2%), dysphagia (2%), rectal hemorrhage (2%), tooth disorder (1%), buccoglossal syndrome
Genitourinary: Priapism (1%)
Local: Injection site pain (7% to 9%)
Neuromuscular & skeletal: Weakness (2% to 6%), hypoesthesia (2%), myalgia (2%), paresthesia (2%), back pain (1%), cogwheel rigidity (1%), hypertonia (1%), abnormal

gait, choreoathetosis, dysarthria, dyskinesia, hyper-/hypokinesia, hypotonia, neuropathy, tremor, twitching

Ocular: Vision abnormal (3% to 6%), diplopia

Respiratory: Infection (8%), rhinitis (1% to 4%), cough (3%), pharyngitis (3%), dyspnea (2%)

Miscellaneous: Diaphoresis (2%), furunculosis (2%), flu-like syndrome (1%), photosensitivity reaction, withdrawal syndrome

<1% (Limited to important or life-threatening): Akinesia, allergic reaction, angina, atrial fibrillation, ataxia, AV block (first degree), bundle branch block, cerebral infarction, cholestatic jaundice, choreoathetosis, delirium, dysarthria, dysphagia, eosinophilia, exfoliative dermatitis, galactorrhea, gout, gynecomastia, hemorrhage, hepatitis, jaundice, myocarditis, neuroleptic malignant syndrome, neuropathy, opisthotonos, photophobia, pneumonia, pulmonary embolism, QT_c prolongation >500 msec (0.06%), seizure (0.4%), sexual dysfunction (male and female), stroke, syncope (0.6%), tenosynovitis, thrombocytopenia, thyroiditis, torsade de pointes, torticollis, urinary retention

Overdosage/Toxicology Reported symptoms include somnolence, slurring of speech, tremor, and anxiety. Acute extrapyramidal symptoms may also occur. Cardiac monitoring should be initiated immediately. Treatment is symptom-directed and supportive. Not removed by dialysis.

Drug Interactions

Cytochrome P450 Effect: Substrate (minor) of CYP1A2, 3A4; **Inhibits** CYP2D6 (weak), 3A4 (weak)

Increased Effect/Toxicity:

Ketoconazole may increase serum concentrations of ziprasidone. Other CYP3A4 inhibitors may share this potential.

Concurrent use with QT_c-prolonging agents may result in additive effects on cardiac conduction, potentially resulting in malignant or lethal arrhythmias. Concurrent use is contraindicated; includes amiodarone, arsenic trioxide, bretylium, chlorpromazine, cisapride; class Ia antiarrhythmics (quinidine, procainamide); dofetilide, dolasetron, droperidol, ibutilide, levomethadyl, mefloquine, mesoridazine, pentamidine, pimozide, probucol; some quinolone antibiotics (moxifloxacin, sparfloxacin, gatifloxacin); sotalol, tacrolimus, and thioridazine. Potassium- or magnesium-depleting agents (diuretics, aminoglycosides, cyclosporine, and amphotericin B) may increase the risk of QT_c prolongation. Antihypertensive agents may increase the risk of orthostatic hypotension. CNS depressants may increase the degree of sedation caused by ziprasidone. Metoclopramide may increase risk of extrapyramidal symptoms (EPS). Acetylcholinesterase inhibitors (central) may increase the risk of antipsychotic-related EPS.

Decreased Effect: Carbamazepine may decrease serum concentrations of ziprasidone. Other enzyme-inducing agents may share this potential. Amphetamines may decrease the efficacy of ziprasidone. Ziprasidone may inhibit the efficacy of levodopa.

Ethanol/Nutrition/Herb Interactions

Ethanol: Avoid ethanol (may increase CNS depression).

Food: Administration with food increases serum levels twofold. Grapefruit juice may increase serum concentration of ziprasidone.

Herb/Nutraceutical: St John's wort may decrease serum levels of ziprasidone, due to a potential effect on CYP3A4. This has not been specifically studied. Avoid kava kava, chamomile (may increase CNS depression).

Stability

Capsule: Store at controlled room temperature of 15°C to 30°C (59°F to 86°F).

Vials for injection: Store at controlled room temperature of 15°C to 30°C (59°F to 86°F). Protect from light. Each vial should be reconstituted with 1.2 mL SWI. Shake vigorously. Will form a pale, pink solution containing 20 mg/mL ziprasidone. Following reconstitution, injection may be stored at room temperature up to 24 hours or up to 7 days if refrigerated. Protect from light.

Mechanism of Action Ziprasidone is a benzylisothiazolylpiperazine antipsychotic. The exact mechanism of action is unknown. However, in vitro radioligand studies show that ziprasidone has high affinity for D_2, D_3, $5-HT_{2A}$, $5-HT_{1A}$, $5-HT_{2C}$, $5-HT_{1D}$, and alpha$_1$ adrenergic; moderate affinity for histamine H_1 receptors; and no appreciable affinity for alpha$_2$ adrenergic receptors, beta adrenergic, $5-HT_3$, $5-HT_4$, cholinergic, mu, sigma, or benzodiazepine receptors. Ziprasidone functions as an antagonist at the D_2, $5-HT_{2A}$, and $5-HT_{1D}$ receptors and as an agonist at the $5-HT_{1A}$ receptor. Ziprasidone moderately inhibits the reuptake of serotonin and norepinephrine.

Pharmacodynamics/Kinetics

Absorption: Well absorbed

Distribution: V_d: 1.5 L/kg

Protein binding: 99%, primarily to albumin and alpha$_1$-acid glycoprotein

Metabolism: Extensively hepatic, primarily via aldehyde oxidase; less than 1/3 of total metabolism via CYP3A4 and CYP1A2 (minor)

Bioavailability: Oral (with food): 60% (up to twofold increase with food); I.M.: 100%

Half-life elimination: Oral: 7 hours; I.M.: 2-5 hours

Time to peak: Oral: 6-8 hours; I.M.: ≤60 minutes

Excretion: Feces (66%) and urine (20%) as metabolites; little as unchanged drug (1% urine, 4% feces)

Clearance: 7.5 mL/minute/kg

Dosage

Children and Adolescents: Tourette's syndrome (unlabeled use): Oral: 5-40 mg/day

Adults:

Bipolar mania: Oral: Initial: 40 mg twice daily (with food)

Adjustment: May increase to 60 or 80 mg twice daily on second day of treatment; average dose 40-80 mg twice daily

Schizophrenia: Oral: Initial: 20 mg twice daily (with food)

Adjustment: Increases (if indicated) should be made no more frequently than every 2 days; ordinarily patients should be observed for improvement over several weeks before adjusting the dose

(Continued)

Ziprasidone *(Continued)*

Maintenance: Range 20-100 mg twice daily; however, dosages >80 mg twice daily are generally not recommended

Acute agitation (schizophrenia): I.M.: 10 mg every 2 hours **or** 20 mg every 4 hours; maximum: 40 mg/day; oral therapy should replace I.M. administration as soon as possible

Elderly: No dosage adjustment is recommended; consider initiating at a low end of the dosage range, with slower titration

Dosage adjustment in renal impairment:

Oral: No dosage adjustment is recommended

I.M.: Cyclodextrin, an excipient in the I.M. formulation, is cleared by renal filtration; use with caution.

Ziprasidone is not removed by hemodialysis.

Dosage adjustment in hepatic impairment: No dosage adjustment is recommended

Administration

Oral: Administer with food.

Injection: For I.M. administration only.

Monitoring Parameters Vital signs; serum potassium and magnesium; fasting lipid profile and fasting blood glucose/Hgb A_{1c} (prior to treatment, at 3 months, then annually); BMI, personal/family history of obesity, waist circumference; blood pressure; mental status, abnormal involuntary movement scale (AIMS), extrapyramidal symptoms. Weight should be assessed prior to treatment, at 4 weeks, 8 weeks, 12 weeks, and then at quarterly intervals. Consider titrating to a different antipsychotic agent for a weight gain ≥5% of the initial weight. The value of routine ECG screening or monitoring has not been established.

Additional Information The increased potential to prolong QT_c, as compared to other available antipsychotic agents, should be considered in the evaluation of available alternatives.

Dosage Forms

Capsule, as hydrochloride: 20 mg, 40 mg, 60 mg, 80 mg

Injection, powder for reconstitution, as mesylate: 20 mg

♦ **Ziprasidone Hydrochloride** *see* Ziprasidone *on page 1818*
♦ **Ziprasidone Mesylate** *see* Ziprasidone *on page 1818*
♦ **Zithromax®** *see* Azithromycin *on page 186*
♦ **Zithromax® TRI-PAK™** *see* Azithromycin *on page 186*
♦ **Zithromax® Z-PAK®** *see* Azithromycin *on page 186*
♦ **ZM-182,780** *see* Fulvestrant *on page 772*
♦ **Zmax™** *see* Azithromycin *on page 186*
♦ **ZnSO₄ (error-prone abbreviation)** *see* Zinc Sulfate *on page 1817*
♦ **Zocor®** *see* Simvastatin *on page 1567*
♦ **Zofran®** *see* Ondansetron *on page 1267*
♦ **Zofran® ODT** *see* Ondansetron *on page 1267*
♦ **Zoladex®** *see* Goserelin *on page 810*
♦ **Zoladex® LA (Can)** *see* Goserelin *on page 810*
♦ **Zoledronate** *see* Zoledronic Acid *on page 1820*

Zoledronic Acid *(zoe le DRON ik AS id)*

U.S. Brand Names Zometa®

Canadian Brand Names Aclasta®; Zometa®

Index Terms CGP-42446; NSC-721517; Zoledronate

Pharmacologic Category Antidote; Bisphosphonate Derivative

Use Treatment of hypercalcemia of malignancy, multiple myeloma, bone metastases of solid tumors

Unlabeled/Investigational Use Treatment of metabolic bone diseases

Pregnancy Risk Factor D

Pregnancy Implications Animal studies resulted in embryotoxicity and losses. May cause fetal harm when administered to a pregnant woman. Bisphosphonates are incorporated into the bone matrix and gradually released over time. Theoretically, there may be a risk of fetal harm when pregnancy follows the completion of therapy. Based on limited case reports with pamidronate, serum calcium levels in the newborn may be altered if administered during pregnancy.

Lactation Excretion in breast milk unknown/not recommended

Contraindications Hypersensitivity to zoledronic acid, other bisphosphonates, or any component of the formulation; pregnancy

Warnings/Precautions Bisphosphonate therapy has been associated with osteonecrosis, primarily of the jaw; this has been observed mostly in cancer patients, but also in patients with postmenopausal osteoporosis and other diagnoses. Dental exams and preventative dentistry should be performed prior to placing patients with risk factors on chronic bisphosphonate therapy. Invasive dental procedures should be avoided during treatment.

Infrequently, severe (and occasionally debilitating) bone, joint, and/or muscle pain have been reported during bisphosphonate treatment. The onset of pain ranged from a single day to several months. Symptoms usually resolve upon discontinuation. Some patients experienced recurrence when rechallenged with same drug or another bisphosphonate; avoid use in patients with a history of these symptoms in association with bisphosphonate therapy.

Use caution in renal dysfunction; dosage adjustment required. In cancer patients, renal toxicity has been reported with doses >4 mg or infusions administered over 15 minutes. Risk factors for renal deterioration include pre-existing renal insufficiency and repeated doses of zoledronic acid and other bisphosphonates. Dehydration and the use of other nephrotoxic drugs which may contribute to renal deterioration should be identified and managed. Use is not recommended in patients with severe renal impairment (serum creatinine >3 mg/dL) and bone metastases (limited data); use in patients with hypercalcemia of malignancy and severe renal impairment should only be done if the benefits outweigh the risks. Renal function should be assessed prior to treatment; if decreased after treatment, additional treatments should be withheld until renal function returns to within 10% of baseline. Adequate hydration is required during treatment (urine output ~2 L/day); avoid overhydration, especially in patients with heart failure; diuretics should not be used before correcting hypovolemia. Renal deterioration, resulting in renal failure and dialysis has occurred in patients treated with zoledronic acid after single and multiple infusions at recommended doses of 4 mg over 15 minutes. **Note:** When used in the treatment of Paget's disease (Aclasta® - not available in the U.S.), significant renal deterioration has not been observed with the usual 5 mg unit-dose.

Use caution in patients with aspirin-sensitive asthma (may cause bronchoconstriction), hepatic dysfunction, and the elderly. Women of childbearing age should be advised against becoming pregnant. Safety and efficacy in pediatric patients have not been established.

Adverse Reactions
>10%:
  Cardiovascular: Leg edema (5% to 21%), hypotension (11%)
  Central nervous system: Fatigue (39%), fever (32% to 44%), headache (5% to 19%), dizziness (18%), insomnia (15% to 16%), anxiety (11% to 14%), depression (14%), agitation (13%), confusion (7% to 13%), hypoesthesia (12%)
  Dermatologic: Alopecia (12%), dermatitis (11%)
  Endocrine & metabolic: Dehydration (5% to 14%), hypophosphatemia (12% to 13%), hypokalemia (12%), hypomagnesemia (11%)
  Gastrointestinal: Nausea (29% to 46%), constipation (27% to 31%), vomiting (14% to 32%), diarrhea (17% to 24%), anorexia (9% to 22%), abdominal pain (14% to 16%), weight loss (16%), appetite decreased (13%)
  Genitourinary: Urinary tract infection (12% to 14%)
  Hematologic: Anemia (22% to 33%), neutropenia (12%)
  Neuromuscular & skeletal: Bone pain (55%), weakness (5% to 24%), myalgia (23%), arthralgia (5% to 21%), back pain (15%), paresthesia (15%), limb pain (14%), skeletal pain (12%), rigors (11%)
  Renal: Renal deterioration (8% to 17%; up to 40% in patients with abnormal baseline creatinine)
  Respiratory: Dyspnea (22% to 27%), cough (12% to 22%)
  Miscellaneous: Cancer progression (16%), moniliasis (12%)
1% to 10%:
  Cardiovascular: Chest pain (5% to 10%)
  Central nervous system: Somnolence (5% to 10%)
  Endocrine & metabolic: Hypocalcemia (1% to 10%), hypermagnesemia (2%)
  Gastrointestinal: Dysphagia (5% to 10%), dyspepsia (10%), mucositis (5% to 10%), stomatitis (8%), sore throat (8%)
  Hematologic: Thrombocytopenia (5% to 10%), pancytopenia (5% to 10%), granulocytopenia (5% to 10%)
  Renal: Serum creatinine increased (grades 3/4: 2%)
  Respiratory: Pleural effusion, upper respiratory tract infection (10%)
  Miscellaneous: Metastases (5% to 10%), nonspecifc infection (5% to 10%)
<1% (Limited to important or life-threatening): Angioneurotic edema, blurred vision, bradycardia, conjunctivitis, diaphoresis, episcleritis; flu-like syndrome (fever, chills, flushing, bone pain, arthralgia, myalgia); hematuria, hyperesthesia, hyperkalemia, hypernatremia, hypersensitivity, hypertension, injection site reaction, joint and/or muscle pain, muscle cramps, osteonecrosis (primarily of the jaws), proteinuria, pruritus, rash, renal failure, renal impairment, taste perversion, tremor, uveitis, weight gain, xerostomia

Overdosage/Toxicology Clinically-significant hypocalcemia, hypophosphatemia, and hypomagnesemia may occur. Doses >4 mg and infusion times <15 minutes are associated with a risk of renal toxicity. Treatment is symptom-directed and supportive.

Drug Interactions
  Increased Effect/Toxicity: Aminoglycosides may lower serum calcium levels with prolonged administration; concomitant use may have an additive hypocalcemic effect. NSAIDs may enhance the gastrointestinal adverse/toxic effects (increased incidence of GI ulcers) of bisphosphonate derivatives. Bisphosphonate derivatives may enhance the hypocalcemic effect of phosphate supplements.
  Decreased Effect: The following agents may decrease the absorption of oral bisphosphonate derivatives: Antacids (aluminum, calcium, magnesium), oral calcium salts, oral iron salts, and oral magnesium salts.

Stability Store vials at 15°C to 30°C (59°F to 86°F). Dilute solution for injection in 100 mL NS or D_5W prior to administration. Solutions for infusion may be stored for 24 hours at 15°C to 30°C (59°F to 86°F). Infusion of solution must be completed within 24 hours.

Mechanism of Action A bisphosphonate which inhibits bone resorption via actions on osteoclasts or on osteoclast precursors; inhibits osteoclastic activity and skeletal calcium release induced by tumors. Decreases serum calcium and phosphorus, and increases their elimination.

Pharmacodynamics/Kinetics
  Onset of action: Maximum effect may not been seen for 7 days
  Distribution: Binds to bone
  Protein binding: ~22%
  Half-life elimination: Triphasic; Terminal: 146 hours
  Excretion: Urine (39% ± 16% as unchanged drug) within 24 hours; feces (<3%)

Dosage I.V.: Adults:
  Hypercalcemia of malignancy (albumin-corrected serum calcium ≥12 mg/dL): 4 mg (maximum) given as a single dose. Wait at least 7 days before considering retreatment. Dosage adjustment may be needed in patients with decreased renal function following treatment.
  Multiple myeloma or metastatic bone lesions from solid tumors: 4 mg every 3-4 weeks
    Note: Patients should receive a daily calcium supplement and multivitamin containing vitamin D
(Continued)

Zoledronic Acid *(Continued)*

Paget's disease (Aclasta®, not available in U.S.): 5 mg infused over at least 15 minutes.
Note: Data concerning retreatment is not available.

Dosage adjustment in renal impairment (at treatment initiation):
Zometa®: Multiple myeloma and bone metastases:
Cl$_{cr}$ >60 mL/minute: 4 mg
Cl$_{cr}$ 50-60 mL/minute: 3.5 mg
Cl$_{cr}$ 40-49 mL/minute: 3.3 mg
Cl$_{cr}$ 30-39 mL/minute: 3 mg
Cl$_{cr}$ <30 mL/minute: Not recommended
Zometa®: Hypercalcemia of malignancy:
Mild-to-moderate impairment: No adjustment necessary
Severe impairment (serum creatinine >4.5 mg/dL): Evaluate risk versus benefit
Aclasta® [not available in U.S.]: Cl$_{cr}$ >30 mL/minute: No adjustment recommended

Dosage adjustment for renal toxicity (during treatment):
Hypercalcemia of malignancy: Evidence of renal deterioration: Evaluate risk versus benefit.
Multiple myeloma and bone metastases: Evidence of renal deterioration: Withhold dose
until renal function returns to within 10% of baseline: renal deterioration defined as
follows:
Normal baseline creatinine: Increase of 0.5 mg/dL
Abnormal baseline creatinine: Increase of 1 mg/dL
Reinitiate dose at the same dose administered prior to treatment interruption.

Dosage adjustment in hepatic impairment: Specific guidelines are not available.

Dietary Considerations Multiple myeloma or metastatic bone lesions from solid tumors:
Take daily calcium supplement (500 mg) and daily multivitamin (with 400 int. units vitamin D).

Administration Infuse over 15-30 minutes; do not infuse over <15 minutes. Infuse in a line
separate from other medications. Patients should be appropriately hydrated prior to treatment.

Monitoring Parameters Prior to initiation of therapy, dental exam and preventative dentistry
for patients at risk for osteonecrosis; serum creatinine prior to each dose; serum electrolytes,
phosphate, magnesium, and hemoglobin/hematocrit should be evaluated regularly. Monitor
serum calcium to assess response and avoid overtreatment.

Test Interactions Bisphosphonates may interfere with diagnostic imaging agents such as
technetium-99m-diphosphonate in bone scans.

Dosage Forms [CAN] = Canadian brand name
Infusion, solution [premixed]:
Aclasta® [CAN]: 5 mg (100 mL) [not available in U.S.]
Injection, solution:
Zometa®: 4 mg/5 mL (5 mL) [as monohydrate 4.264 mg]

♦ **Zolinza**™ *see* Vorinostat *on page 1799*

Zolmitriptan *(zohl mi TRIP tan)*

U.S. Brand Names Zomig®; Zomig-ZMT™
Canadian Brand Names Zomig®; Zomig® Nasal Spray; Zomig® Rapimelt
Index Terms 311C90
Pharmacologic Category Antimigraine Agent; Serotonin 5-HT$_{1B, 1D}$ Receptor Agonist
Additional Appendix Information
Antimigraine Drugs: 5-HT$_1$ Receptor Agonists *on page 1871*
Use Acute treatment of migraine with or without aura
Pregnancy Risk Factor C
Pregnancy Implications There are no adequate and well-controlled studies using suma-
triptan in pregnant women. Use only if potential benefit to the mother outweighs the potential
risk to the fetus. In animal studies, administration was associated with embryolethality, fetal
abnormalities, and pup mortality.
Lactation Excretion in breast milk unknown/use caution
Medication Safety Issues
Sound-alike/look-alike issues:
Zolmitriptan may be confused with sumatriptan
Contraindications Hypersensitivity to zolmitriptan or any component of the formulation;
ischemic heart disease or Prinzmetal's angina; signs or symptoms of ischemic heart disease;
uncontrolled hypertension; symptomatic Wolff-Parkinson-White syndrome or arrhythmias
associated with other cardiac accessory conduction pathway disorders; use with ergotamine
derivatives (within 24 hours of); use within 24 hours of another 5-HT$_1$ agonist; concurrent
administration or within 2 weeks of discontinuing an MAO inhibitor; management of hemiplegic or basilar migraine
Warnings/Precautions Zolmitriptan is indicated only in patient populations with a clear diagnosis of migraine. Not for prophylactic treatment of migraine headaches. Cardiac events
(coronary artery vasospasm, transient ischemia, myocardial infarction, ventricular tachy-
cardia/fibrillation, cardiac arrest, and death) have been reported with 5-HT$_1$ agonist administration. Should not be given to patients who have risk factors for CAD (eg, hypertension,
hypercholesterolemia, smoker, obesity, diabetes, strong family history of CAD, menopause,
male >40 years of age) without adequate cardiac evaluation. Patients with suspected CAD
should have cardiovascular evaluation to rule out CAD before considering zolmitriptan's use;
if cardiovascular evaluation negative, first dose would be safest if given in the healthcare
provider's office. Periodic evaluation of those without cardiovascular disease, but with
continued risk factors should be done. Significant elevation in blood pressure, including
hypertensive crisis, has also been reported on rare occasions in patients with and without a
history of hypertension. Vasospasm-related reactions have been reported other than coronary artery vasospasm. Peripheral vascular ischemia and colonic ischemia with abdominal
pain and bloody diarrhea have occurred. Cerebral/subarachnoid hemorrhage and stroke
have been reported with 5-HT$_1$ agonist administration. Use with caution in patients with

hepatic impairment. Zomig-ZMT™ tablets contain phenylalanine. Symptoms of agitation, confusion, hallucinations, hyperreflexia, myoclonus, shivering, and tachycardia (serotonin syndrome) may occur with concomitant proserotonergic drugs (ie, SSRIs/SNRIs or triptans) or agents which reduce zolmitriptan's metabolism. Concurrent use of serotonin precursors (eg, tryptophan) is not recommended. Safety and efficacy not established in patients <18 years of age.

Adverse Reactions Percentages noted from oral preparations.

1% to 10%:

Cardiovascular: Chest pain (2% to 4%), palpitation (up to 2%)

Central nervous system: Dizziness (6% to 10%), somnolence (5% to 8%), pain (2% to 3%), vertigo (≤2%)

Gastrointestinal: Nausea (4% to 9%), xerostomia (3% to 5%), dyspepsia (1% to 3%), dysphagia (≤2%)

Neuromuscular & skeletal: Paresthesia (5% to 9%), weakness (3% to 9%), warm/cold sensation (5% to 7%), hypoesthesia (1% to 2%), myalgia (1% to 2%), myasthenia (up to 2%)

Miscellaneous: Neck/throat/jaw pain (4% to 10%), diaphoresis (up to 3%), allergic reaction (up to 1%)

<1% (Limited to important or life-threatening): Anaphylactoid reaction, anaphylaxis, angina, apnea, arrhythmia, ataxia, bronchospasm, cerebral ischemia, coronary artery vasospasm, cyanosis, eosinophilia, esophagitis, gastrointestinal infarction/necrosis, hallucinations, headache, hematemesis, hypertension, hypertensive crisis, ischemic colitis, melena, miscarriage, MI, myocardial ischemia, pancreatitis, photosensitivity, QT prolongation, rash, splenic infarction, syncope, tetany, thrombocytopenia, tinnitus, ulcer, urticaria

Events related to other serotonin 5-HT$_{1D}$ receptor agonists: Cardiac arrest, cerebral hemorrhage, peripheral vascular ischemia, stroke, subarachnoid hemorrhage, ventricular fibrillation

Overdosage/Toxicology Treatment is symptom-directed and supportive. It is not known if hemodialysis or peritoneal dialysis is effective.

Drug Interactions

Cytochrome P450 Effect: Substrate of CYP1A2 (minor)

Increased Effect/Toxicity: Ergot-containing drugs may lead to vasospasm; cimetidine, MAO inhibitors, oral contraceptives, propranolol increase levels of zolmitriptan; concurrent use with sibutramaine, SSRIs/SNRIs or other serotonin agonists may lead to serotonin syndrome.

Ethanol/Nutrition/Herb Interactions Ethanol: Limit use (may have additive CNS toxicity).

Stability Store at 20°C to 25°C (68°F to 77°F). Protect from light and moisture.

Mechanism of Action Selective agonist for serotonin (5-HT$_{1B}$ and 5-HT$_{1D}$ receptors) in cranial arteries to cause vasoconstriction and reduce sterile inflammation associated with antidromic neuronal transmission correlating with relief of migraine

Pharmacodynamics/Kinetics

Onset of action: 0.5-1 hour

Absorption: Well absorbed

Distribution: V$_d$: 7 L/kg

Protein binding: 25%

Metabolism: Converted to an active N-desmethyl metabolite (2-6 times more potent than zolmitriptan)

Half-life elimination: 2.8-3.7 hours

Bioavailability: 40%

Time to peak, serum: Tablet: 1.5 hours; Orally-disintegrating tablet and nasal spray: 3 hours

Excretion: Urine (~60% to 65% total dose); feces (30% to 40%)

Dosage Oral:

Children: Safety and efficacy have not been established

Adults: Migraine:

Tablet: Initial: ≤2.5 mg at the onset of migraine headache; may break 2.5 mg tablet in half

Orally-disintegrating tablet: Initial: 2.5 mg at the onset of migraine headache

Nasal spray: Initial: 1 spray (5 mg) at the onset of migraine headache

Note: Use the lowest possible dose to minimize adverse events. If the headache returns, the dose may be repeated after 2 hours; do not exceed 10 mg within a 24-hour period. Controlled trials have not established the effectiveness of a second dose if the initial one was ineffective

Elderly: No dosage adjustment needed but elderly patients are more likely to have underlying cardiovascular disease and should have careful evaluation of cardiovascular system before prescribing.

Dosage adjustment in renal impairment: No dosage adjustment recommended. There is a 25% reduction in zolmitriptan's clearance in patients with severe renal impairment (Cl$_{cr}$ 5-25 mL/minute)

Dosage adjustment in hepatic impairment: Administer with caution in patients with liver disease, generally using doses <2.5 mg. Patients with moderate-to-severe hepatic impairment may have decreased clearance of zolmitriptan, and significant elevation in blood pressure was observed in some patients.

Administration Administer as soon as migraine headache starts.

Tablet: May be broken

Orally-disintegrating tablet: Must be taken whole; do not break, crush or chew; place on tongue and allow to dissolve; administration with liquid is not required

Nasal spray: Blow nose gently prior to use. After removing protective cap, instill device into nostril. Block opposite nostril; breathe in gently through nose while pressing plunger of spray device. One dose (5 mg) is equal to 1 spray in 1 nostril.

Additional Information Not recommended if the patient has risk factors for heart disease (high blood pressure, high cholesterol, obesity, diabetes, smoking, strong family history of heart disease, postmenopausal woman, or a male >40 years of age).

This agent is intended to relieve migraine, but not to prevent or reduce the number of attacks. Use only to treat an actual migraine attack.

(Continued)

Zolmitriptan *(Continued)*

Dosage Forms

Solution, nasal spray [single dose] (Zomig®): 5 mg/0.1 mL (0.1 mL)

Tablet (Zomig®): 2.5 mg, 5 mg

Tablet, orally disintegrating (Zomig-ZMT™): 2.5 mg [contains phenylalanine 2.81 mg/tablet; orange flavor]; 5 mg [contains phenylalanine 5.62 mg/tablet; orange flavor]

♦ **Zoloft®** *see* Sertraline *on page 1557*

Zolpidem *(zole Pl dem)*

U.S. Brand Names Ambien®; Ambien CR™

Index Terms Zolpidem Tartrate

Pharmacologic Category Hypnotic, Nonbenzodiazepine

Use Short-term treatment of insomnia (sleep onset and/or sleep maintenance)

Restrictions C-IV; not available in Canada

Pregnancy Risk Factor C

Pregnancy Implications Teratogenic effects were not observed in animal studies. Children born of mothers taking sedative/hypnotics may be at risk for withdrawal; neonatal flaccidity has been reported in infants following maternal use of sedative/hypnotics during pregnancy.

Lactation Enters breast milk/not recommended (AAP rates "compatible")

Medication Safety Issues

Sound-alike/look-alike issues:

Ambien® may be confused with Ambi 10®

Contraindications Hypersensitivity to zolpidem or any component of the formulation

Warnings/Precautions Should be used only after evaluation of potential causes of sleep disturbance. Failure of sleep disturbance to resolve after 7-10 days may indicate psychiatric or medical illness. Use with caution in patients with depression. Hypnotics/sedatives have been associated with abnormal thinking and behavior changes including decreased inhibition, aggression, bizarre behavior, agitation, hallucinations, and depersonalization. These changes may occur unpredictably and may indicate previously unrecognized psychiatric disorders; evaluate appropriately. Sedative/hypnotics may produce withdrawal symptoms following abrupt discontinuation. Causes CNS depression, which may impair physical and mental capabilities. Effects with other sedative drugs or ethanol may be potentiated. Use caution in the elderly; dose adjustment recommended. Closely monitor elderly or debilitated patients for impaired cognitive or motor performance. Avoid use in patients with sleep apnea or a history of sedative-hypnotic abuse. Use caution with respiratory disease. Use caution with hepatic impairment; dose adjustment required. Prescriptions should be written for the smallest effective dose (especially in the elderly) and for the smallest quantity consistent with good patient care (especially with depression). Because of the rapid onset of action, administer immediately prior to bedtime or after the patient has gone to bed and is having difficulty falling asleep. Safety and efficacy have not been established in pediatric patients.

Adverse Reactions Actual frequency may be dosage form, dose and/or age dependent

>10%: Central nervous system: Dizziness, headache, somnolence

1% to 10%:

Cardiovascular: Blood pressure increased, chest discomfort, palpitation

Central nervous system: Anxiety, apathy, amnesia, ataxia, attention disturbance, body temperature increased, confusion, depersonalization, depression, disinhibition, disorientation, drowsiness, drugged feeling, euphoria, fatigue, fever, hallucinations, hypoesthesia, insomnia, memory disorder, lethargy, lightheadedness, mood swings, stress

Dermatologic: Rash, urticaria, wrinkling

Endocrine & metabolic: Menorrhagia

Gastrointestinal: Abdominal discomfort, abdominal pain, abdominal tenderness, appetite disorder, constipation, diarrhea, dyspepsia, flatulence, gastroenteritis, gastroesophageal reflux, hiccup, nausea, vomiting, xerostomia

Genitourinary: Urinary tract infection

Neuromuscular & skeletal: Arthralgia, back pain, balance disorder, myalgia, neck pain, paresthesia, psychomotor retardation, tremor, weakness

Ocular: Asthenopia, blurred vision, depth perception altered, diplopia, red eye, visual disturbance

Otic: Labyrinthitis, tinnitus, vertigo

Renal: Dysuria

Respiratory: Pharyngitis, sinusitis, throat irritation, upper respiratory tract infection

Miscellaneous: Allergy, binge eating, flu-like syndrome

<1% (Limited to important or life-threatening): Abnormal dreams, agitation, anorexia, arthritis, bronchitis, chest pain, cognition decreased, concentrating difficulty, constipation, cough, cystitis, diaphoresis increased, dysarthria, dysphagia, edema, emotional lability, eye irritation, falling, hepatic function abnormalities, hyperglycemia, hypoesthesia, illusion, leg cramps, menstrual disorder, nervousness, pallor, postural hypotension, pruritus, scleritis, somnambulism (sleepwalking), speech disorder, stupor, syncope, tachycardia, taste perversion, thirst, urinary incontinence, vaginitis

Overdosage/Toxicology Symptoms include coma and hypotension. Treatment for overdose is supportive. Rarely is mechanical ventilation required. Flumazenil has been shown to selectively block binding to CNS receptors, resulting in reversal of CNS depression but not always respiratory depression. Hemodialysis is not likely to be of benefit.

Drug Interactions

Cytochrome P450 Effect: Substrate of CYP1A2 (minor), 2C9 (minor), 2C19 (minor), 2D6 (minor), 3A4 (major)

Increased Effect/Toxicity: Use of zolpidem in combination with other centrally-acting drugs may produce additive CNS depression. CYP3A4 inhibitors may increase the levels/effects of zolpidem; example inhibitors include azole antifungals, clarithromycin, diclofenac, doxycycline, erythromycin, imatinib, isoniazid, nefazodone, nicardipine, propofol, protease inhibitors, quinidine, telithromycin, troleandomycin, and verapamil.

Decreased Effect: CYP3A4 inducers may decrease the levels/effects of zolpidem; example inducers include aminoglutethimide, carbamazepine, nafcillin, nevirapine, phenobarbital, phenytoin, and rifamycins.

Ethanol/Nutrition/Herb Interactions

Ethanol: Avoid ethanol (may increase CNS depression).

Food: Maximum plasma concentration and bioavailability are decreased with food; time to peak plasma concentration is increased; half-life remains unchanged.

Herb/Nutraceutical: St John's wort may decrease zolpidem levels. Avoid valerian, St John's wort, kava kava, gotu kola (may increase CNS depression).

Mechanism of Action Structurally dissimilar to benzodiazepines. Selective hypnotic effects (with minor anxiolytic, myorelaxant and anticonvulsant properties) mediated through selective affinity for the alpha-1 subunit of the omega-1 (benzodiazepine) receptor located on the $GABA_A$ receptor complex. Agonism at this site enhances GABA-ergic chloride conductance hyperpolarizing neuronal membranes thereby reducing the responsiveness to excitatory signals.

Pharmacodynamics/Kinetics

Onset of action: 30 minutes

Duration: 6-8 hours

Absorption: Rapid

Distribution: Very low amounts enter breast milk

Protein binding: 92%

Metabolism: Hepatic, primarily via CYP3A4 (~60%), to inactive metabolites

Half-life elimination: 2.5-2.8 hours (range 1.4-4.5 hours); Cirrhosis: Up to 9.9 hours

Time to peak, plasma: 2 hours; 4 hours with food

Excretion: As metabolites in urine, bile, feces

Dosage Oral:

Adults:

Ambien®: 10 mg immediately before bedtime; maximum dose: 10 mg

Ambien CR™: 12.5 mg immediately before bedtime

Elderly:

Ambien®: 5 mg immediately before bedtime

Ambien CR™: 6.25 mg immediately before bedtime

Dosing adjustment in renal impairment: Dose adjustment not required; monitor closely

Hemodialysis: Not dialyzable

Dosing adjustment in hepatic impairment:

Ambien®: 5 mg

Ambien CR™: 6.25 mg

Dietary Considerations For faster sleep onset, do not administer with (or immediately after) a meal.

Administration Ingest immediately before bedtime due to rapid onset of action. Ambien CR™ tablets should not be divided, crushed, or chewed.

Monitoring Parameters Daytime alertness; respiratory and cardiac status; behavior profile

Reference Range 80-150 ng/mL

Additional Information Causes less disturbances in sleep stages as compared to benzodiazepines. Time spent in sleep stages 3 and 4 are maintained; decreases sleep latency. Should not be prescribed in quantities exceeding a 1-month supply.

Dosage Forms [DSC] = Discontinued product

Tablet, as tartrate:

Ambien®: 5 mg, 10 mg

Ambien® PAK™ [dose pack]: 5 mg (30s); 10 mg (30s) [DSC]

Tablet, extended release, as tartrate (Ambien CR™): 6.25 mg, 12.5 mg

♦ **Zolpidem Tartrate** see Zolpidem on page 1824

♦ **Zometa®** see Zoledronic Acid on page 1820

♦ **Zomig®** see Zolmitriptan on page 1822

♦ **Zomig® Nasal Spray (Can)** see Zolmitriptan on page 1822

♦ **Zomig® Rapimelt (Can)** see Zolmitriptan on page 1822

♦ **Zomig-ZMT™** see Zolmitriptan on page 1822

♦ **Zomorph® (Can)** see Morphine Sulfate on page 1171

♦ **Zonalon®** see Doxepin on page 545

♦ **Zone-A®** see Pramoxine and Hydrocortisone on page 1409

♦ **Zone-A Forte®** see Pramoxine and Hydrocortisone on page 1409

♦ **Zonegran®** see Zonisamide on page 1825

Zonisamide (zoe NIS a mide)

U.S. Brand Names Zonegran®

Canadian Brand Names Zonegran®

Pharmacologic Category Anticonvulsant, Miscellaneous

Additional Appendix Information

Anticonvulsants by Seizure Type on page 1865

Epilepsy on page 2048

Sulfonamide Derivatives on page 1897

Use Adjunct treatment of partial seizures in children >16 years of age and adults with epilepsy

Unlabeled/Investigational Use Bipolar disorder

Pregnancy Risk Factor C

Pregnancy Implications Fetal abnormalities and death have been reported in animals, however, there are no studies in pregnant women. Based on limited case reports, it appears zonisamide crosses the placenta. Use during pregnancy only if the potential benefits outweigh the potential risks.

Lactation Excretion in breast milk unknown/contraindicated

(Continued)

Zonisamide *(Continued)*

Contraindications Hypersensitivity to zonisamide, sulfonamides, or any component of the formulation

Warnings/Precautions Rare, but potentially fatal sulfonamide reactions have occurred following the use of zonisamide. These reactions include Stevens-Johnson syndrome and toxic epidermal necrolysis, usually appearing within 2-16 weeks of drug initiation. Discontinue zonisamide if rash develops. Chemical similarities are present among sulfonamides, sulfonylureas, carbonic anhydrase inhibitors, thiazides, and loop diuretics (except ethacrynic acid). Use in patients with sulfonamide allergy is specifically contraindicated in product labeling, however, a risk of cross-reaction exists in patients with allergy to any of these compounds; avoid use when previous reaction has been severe.

Decreased sweating (oligohydrosis) and hyperthermia requiring hospitalization have been reported in children. Discontinue zonisamide in patients who develop acute renal failure or a significant sustained increase in creatinine/BUN concentration. Kidney stones have been reported. Use cautiously in patients with renal or hepatic dysfunction. Significant CNS effects include psychiatric symptoms, psychomotor slowing, and fatigue or somnolence. Fatigue and somnolence occur within the first month of treatment, most commonly at doses of 300-500 mg/day. Abrupt withdrawal may precipitate seizures; discontinue or reduce doses gradually. Safety and efficacy in children <16 years of age has not been established.

Adverse Reactions Adjunctive Therapy: Frequencies noted in patients receiving other anticonvulsants:

>10%:
  Central nervous system: Somnolence (17%), dizziness (13%)
  Gastrointestinal: Anorexia (13%)
1% to 10%:
  Central nervous system: Headache (10%), agitation/irritability (9%), fatigue (8%), tiredness (7%), ataxia (6%), confusion (6%), decreased concentration (6%), memory impairment (6%), depression (6%), insomnia (6%), speech disorders (5%), mental slowing (4%), anxiety (3%), nervousness (2%), schizophrenic/schizophreniform behavior (2%), difficulty in verbal expression (2%), status epilepticus (1%), tremor (1%), convulsion (1%), hyperesthesia (1%), incoordination (1%)
  Dermatologic: Rash (3%), bruising (2%), pruritus (1%)
  Gastrointestinal: Nausea (9%), abdominal pain (6%), diarrhea (5%), dyspepsia (3%), weight loss (3%), constipation (2%), dry mouth (2%), taste perversion (2%), vomiting (1%)
  Neuromuscular & skeletal: Paresthesia (4%), weakness (1%), abnormal gait (1%)
  Ocular: Diplopia (6%), nystagmus (4%), amblyopia (1%)
  Otic: Tinnitus (1%)
  Respiratory: Rhinitis (2%), pharyngitis (1%), increased cough (1%)
  Miscellaneous: Flu-like syndrome (4%) accidental injury (1%)
<1% (Limited to important or life threatening symptoms): Agranulocytosis, allergic reaction, alopecia, aplastic anemia, apnea, atrial fibrillation, bladder calculus, cholangitis, cholecystitis, cholestatic jaundice, colitis, deafness, duodenitis, dysarthria, dyskinesia, dyspnea, dystonia, encephalopathy, esophagitis, facial paralysis, gingival hyperplasia, glaucoma, gum hemorrhage, gynecomastia, heart failure, hematemesis, hemoptysis, hirsutism, hyperthermia, impotence, leukopenia, lupus erythematosus, menorrhagia, movement disorder, myoclonus, nephrolithiasis, neuropathy, oculogyric crisis, oligohydrosis, peripheral neuritis, pulmonary embolus, rash, rectal hemorrhage, Stevens-Johnson syndrome, stroke, syncope, thrombocytopenia, toxic epidermal necrolysis, urinary retention, urticaria

Overdosage/Toxicology No specific antidotes are available, experience with doses >800 mg/day are limited. Emesis or gastric lavage, with airway protection, should be done following a recent overdose. General supportive care and close observation are indicated. Renal dialysis may not be effective due to low protein binding (40%).

Drug Interactions
  Cytochrome P450 Effect: Substrate of CYP2C19 (minor), 3A4 (major)
  Increased Effect/Toxicity: Sedative effects may be additive with other CNS depressants; monitor for increased effect (includes barbiturates, benzodiazepines, opioid analgesics, ethanol, and other sedative agents). CYP3A4 inhibitors may increase the levels/effects of zonisamide; example inhibitors include azole antifungals, clarithromycin, diclofenac, doxycycline, erythromycin, imatinib, isoniazid, nefazodone, nicardipine, propofol, protease inhibitors, quinidine, telithromycin, and verapamil.
  Decreased Effect: CYP3A4 inducers may decrease the levels/effects of zonisamide; example inducers include aminoglutethimide, carbamazepine, nafcillin, nevirapine, phenobarbital, phenytoin, and rifamycins.

Ethanol/Nutrition/Herb Interactions
  Ethanol: Avoid ethanol (may increase CNS depression).
  Food: Food delays time to maximum concentration, but does not affect bioavailability.

Stability Store at controlled room temperature 25°C (77°F). Protect from moisture and light.

Mechanism of Action The exact mechanism of action is not known. May stabilize neuronal membranes and suppress neuronal hypersynchronization through action at sodium and calcium channels. Does not affect GABA activity.

Pharmacodynamics/Kinetics
  Distribution: V_d: 1.45 L/kg
  Protein binding: 40%
  Metabolism: Hepatic via CYP3A4; forms N-acetyl zonisamide and 2-sulfamoylacetyl phenol (SMAP)
  Half-life elimination: 63 hours
  Time to peak: 2-6 hours
  Excretion: Urine (62%, 35% as unchanged drug, 65% as metabolites); feces (3%)

Dosage Oral:
  Children >16 years and Adults:
    Adjunctive treatment of partial seizures: Initial: 100 mg/day; dose may be increased to 200 mg/day after 2 weeks. Further dosage increases to 300 mg/day and 400 mg/day can

then be made with a minimum of 2 weeks between adjustments, in order to reach steady state at each dosage level. Doses of up to 600 mg/day have been studied, however, there is no evidence of increased response with doses above 400 mg/day.

Mania (unlabeled use): Initial: 100-200 mg/day; maximum: 600 mg/day (Kanba, 1994)

Elderly: Data from clinical trials is insufficient for patients >65 years; begin dosing at the low end of the dosing range.

Dosage adjustment in renal/hepatic impairment: Slower titration and frequent monitoring are indicated in patients with renal or hepatic disease. There is insufficient experience regarding dosing/toxicity in patients with estimated GFR <50 mL/minute. Marked renal impairment (Cl_{cr} <20 mL/minute) was associated with a 35% increase in AUC.

Dietary Considerations May be taken with or without food.

Administration Capsules should be swallowed whole. Dose may be administered once or twice daily. Doses of 300 mg/day and higher are associated with increased side effects. Steady-state levels are reached in 14 days.

Monitoring Parameters Monitor BUN and serum creatinine

Dosage Forms
Capsule: 25 mg, 50 mg, 100 mg
Zonegran®: 25 mg, 100 mg

♦ **Zorbtive®** see Somatropin on page 1586
♦ **ZORprin®** see Aspirin on page 160
♦ **Zostavax®** see Zoster Vaccine on page 1827

Zoster Vaccine (ZOS ter vak SEEN)

U.S. Brand Names Zostavax®

Index Terms Shingles Vaccine; Varicella-Zoster (VZV) Vaccine (Zoster); VZV Vaccine (Zoster)

Pharmacologic Category Vaccine

Use Prevention of herpes zoster (shingles) in patients ≥60 years of age

Pregnancy Risk Factor C

Pregnancy Implications Animal reproduction studies have not been conducted. Should not be administered to pregnant females and pregnancy should be avoided for 3 months following vaccination. Exposure to the vaccine during pregnancy should be reported to 800-986-8999.

Lactation Excretion in breast milk unknown/use caution

Medication Safety Issues
Both varicella vaccine and zoster vaccine are live, attenuated strains of varicella-zoster virus. Their indications, dosing, and composition are distinct. Varicella is indicated in children to prevent chickenpox, while zoster vaccine is indicated in older individuals to prevent reactivation of the virus which causes shingles. Zoster vaccine is **not** a substitute for varicella vaccine and should not be used in children.

Contraindications Hypersensitivity to any component of the vaccine, including a history of anaphylactic/anaphylactoid reaction to gelatin or neomycin; individuals with blood dyscrasias, leukemia, lymphomas, or other malignant neoplasms affecting the bone marrow or lymphatic systems; primary and acquired immunodeficiency states; those receiving immunosuppressive therapy (including high-dose corticosteroids); active untreated tuberculosis; pregnancy; I.V. injection.

Warnings/Precautions Zoster vaccine is not a substitute for varicella vaccine and should not be used in children. Not for use in the treatment of active zoster outbreak or in the treatment of postherpetic neuropathy (PHN). Contact dermatitis to neomycin is not a contraindication to the vaccine. Avoid administration in patients with acute febrile illness; consider deferral of vaccination.

Immediate treatment for anaphylactoid reaction should be available during vaccine use; defer vaccination for at least 5 months following blood or plasma transfusions, immune globulin (IgG), or VZIG (avoid IgG or IVIG use for 2 months following vaccination); vaccinated individuals should not have close association with susceptible high-risk individuals (newborns, pregnant women, immunocompromised persons) for 6 weeks following vaccination.

Safety and efficacy in immunosuppressed patients or in patients receiving corticosteroid therapy (including inhaled steroids) have not been evaluated. Vaccination of immunosuppressed individuals may result in more severe manifestations of the attenuated virus (extensive rash or disseminated disease). Concurrent administration with antiviral medications with activity against VZV has not been evaluated. Use in patients with previous history of zoster has not been evaluated. Not for use in patients <60 years of age.

Adverse Reactions All serious adverse reactions must be reported to the U.S. Department of Health and Human Services (DHHS) Vaccine Adverse Event Reporting System (VAERS) 1-800-822-7967.
>10%: Local: Injection site reaction (48%; includes erythema, tenderness, swelling, hematoma, pruritus, and/or warmth)
1% to 10%:
Central nervous system: Fever (2%), headache (1%)
Dermatologic: Skin disorder (1%)
Gastrointestinal: Diarrhea (2%)
Neuromuscular & skeletal: Weakness (1%)
Respiratory: Respiratory tract infection (2%), rhinitis (1%)
Miscellaneous: Flu-like syndrome (2%)
<1%, postmarketing, and/or case reports following varicella vaccine have included (not reported specifically following zoster vaccine): Anaphylaxis, ataxia, Bell's palsy, cellulitis, cerebrovascular accident, dizziness, encephalitis, erythema multiforme, Guillain-Barré syndrome, Henoch-Schönlein purpura, herpes zoster, impetigo, nonfebrile seizure, paresthesia, pharyngitis, secondary skin infection, Stevens-Johnson syndrome, thrombocytopenia, transverse myelitis

(Continued)

Zoster Vaccine *(Continued)*

Drug Interactions

Decreased Effect: The effect of the vaccine may be decreased and the risk of varicella disease in individuals who are receiving immunosuppressant drugs (including high-dose systemic corticosteroids) may be increased. Effect of vaccine may be decreased in given within 5 months of immune globulins.

Stability During shipment, should be maintained at -20°C (-4°F) or colder. Store powder in freezer at -15°C (5°F). Protect from light. Store diluent separately at room temperature or in refrigerator. Withdraw entire contents of the vial containing the provided diluent to reconstitute vaccine. Gently agitate to mix thoroughly. Withdraw entire contents of reconstituted vaccine vial for administration. Discard if reconstituted vaccine is not used within 30 minutes. Do not freeze reconstituted vaccine.

Mechanism of Action As a live, attenuated vaccine (Oka/Merck strain of varicella-zoster virus), zoster virus vaccine stimulates active immunity to disease caused by the varicella-zoster virus. Administration has been demonstrated to protect against the development of herpes zoster, with the highest efficacy in patients 60-69 years of age. It may also reduce the severity of complications, including postherpetic neuralgia, in patients who develop zoster following vaccination.

Pharmacodynamics/Kinetics

Onset of action: Seroconversion: ~6 weeks

Duration: Not established; protection has been demonstrated for at least 4 years

Dosage SubQ: Adults ≥65 years: 0.65 mL administered as a single dose; there is no data to support readministration of the vaccine

Dosage adjustment in renal impairment: No adjustment required

Administration Do not administer I.V.; inject immediately after reconstitution. Inject SubQ into the outer aspect of the upper arm, if possible. Federal law requires that the date of administration, the vaccine manufacturer, lot number of vaccine, and the administering person's name, title and address be entered into the patient's permanent medical record.

Monitoring Parameters Fever, rash

Additional Information Federal law requires that the date of administration, the vaccine manufacturer, lot number of vaccine, and the administering person's name, title and address be entered into the patient's permanent medical record.

The varicella-zoster virus (VZV) is capable of causing two distinct manifestations of infection. Primary infection results in chickenpox (varicella). These infections tend to occur in young children or younger adults. Reactivation of latent infection (painful vesicular cutaneous eruption usually in a dermatomal pattern) occurs in older patients or in immunosuppressed populations. This is commonly referred to as shingles (herpes zoster). Although the vaccines are directed against the same causative organism, healthcare workers should be aware of differences in indications, dosing, populations, and composition of the vaccine. Neither vaccine is intended for administration during active outbreaks.

Dosage Forms

Injection, powder for reconstitution [preservative free]

Zostavax®: 19,400 plaque-forming units (PFU) [contains gelatin, sucrose, and trace amounts of neomycin]

♦ **Zosyn®** *see* Piperacillin and Tazobactam Sodium *on page 1375*

♦ **Zovia™** *see* Ethinyl Estradiol and Ethynodiol Diacetate *on page 648*

♦ **Zovirax®** *see* Acyclovir *on page 44*

♦ **Ztuss™ Tablet** *see* Hydrocodone, Pseudoephedrine, and Guaifenesin *on page 852*

♦ **Ztuss™ ZT** *see* Hydrocodone and Guaifenesin *on page 849*

♦ **Zyban®** *see* BuPROPion *on page 252*

♦ **Zydone®** *see* Hydrocodone and Acetaminophen *on page 848*

♦ **Zyflo®** *see* Zileuton *on page 1815*

♦ **Zylet™** *see* Loteprednol and Tobramycin *on page 1039*

♦ **Zyloprim®** *see* Allopurinol *on page 71*

♦ **Zymar™** *see* Gatifloxacin *on page 781*

♦ **Zymine®-D** *see* Triprolidine and Pseudoephedrine *on page 1749*

♦ **Zyprexa®** *see* Olanzapine *on page 1257*

♦ **Zyprexa Zydis** *see* Olanzapine *on page 1257*

♦ **Zyprexa® Zydis®** *see* Olanzapine *on page 1257*

♦ **Zyrtec®** *see* Cetirizine *on page 334*

♦ **Zyvox™** *see* Linezolid *on page 1018*

♦ **Zyvoxam® (Can)** *see* Linezolid *on page 1018*

APPENDIX TABLE OF CONTENTS

ABBREVIATIONS AND MEASUREMENTS
Abbreviations, Acronyms, and Symbols 1832
APACHE II Scoring System 1836
Apothecary / Metric Equivalents 1838
Average Weights and Surface Areas 1839
Body Mass Index (BMI) 1839
Body Surface Area of Adults and Children 1840
Ideal Body Weight Calculation 1840
Milliequivalent and Millimole Calculations and Conversions 1841
Pediatric Dosage Estimations 1845
Pounds / Kilograms Conversion 1846
Temperature Conversion 1846
Reference Values for Children 1847
Reference Values for Adults 1849

ASSESSMENT OF LIVER FUNCTION
Liver Disease 1853

ASSESSMENT OF RENAL FUNCTION
Creatinine Clearance Estimating Methods in Patients With Stable
    Renal Function 1854
Renal Function Tests 1856

COMPARATIVE DRUG CHARTS
Aminoglycoside Dosing and Monitoring 1858
Angiotensin Agents 1860
Anticoagulants, Injectable 1864
Anticonvulsants by Seizure Type 1865
Antidepressant Agents 1866
Antifungal Agents 1869
Antimigraine Drugs: 5-HT$_1$ Receptor Agonists 1871
Antipsychotic Agents 1872
Benzodiazepines 1874
Beta-Blockers 1875
Bronchodilators 1877
Calcium Channel Blockers 1878
Corticosteroids 1879
Cycloplegic Mydriatics 1882
Fosphenytoin and Phenytoin 1883
Glycoprotein Antagonists 1884
Hemodynamic Support, Intravenous 1885
Laxatives, Classification and Properties 1886
Lipid-Lowering Agents 1887
Narcotic Agonists 1888
Neuromuscular-Blocking Agents 1890
Nicotine Products 1892
Nitrates 1893
Nonsteroidal Anti-inflammatory Agents 1894
Parkinson's Agents 1895
Selective Serotonin Reuptake Inhibitors (SSRIs)
    Pharmacokinetics 1896
Sulfonamide Derivatives 1897
Thiazolidinediones 1898

CYTOCHROME P450 AND DRUG INTERACTIONS
Cytochrome P450 Enzymes: Substrates, Inhibitors, and Inducers 1899

DESENSITIZATION AND SKIN TESTING GUIDELINES
Desensitization Protocols 1913
    Ampicillin 1913
    Penicillin G 1914
    Penicillin 1914
    Allopurinol 1914
    Amphotericin B 1915
    Bactrim™ 1915
    Vancomycin 1917
    Ceftriaxone 1921
    Ciprofloxacin 1922
    Imipenem 1922
    Insulin 1923
    Nelfinavir 1923
    Rifampin and Ethambutol 1923

Skin Tests 1924
    Penicillin Allergy 1924
    Penicillin Skin Testing Protocol 1925
    Scratch / Skin Testing Protocol 1925
    Delayed Hypersensitivity (Anergy) 1926

IMMUNIZATIONS AND VACCINATIONS
Immunization Recommendations
    Recommended Immunization Schedule for Ages 0-6 years –
        United States, 2007 1929
    Recommended Immunization Schedule for Ages 7-8 years –
        United States, 2007 1930
    Recommended Immunization Schedule for Children and
        Adolescents Who Start Late or Who Are >1 Month
        Behind – United States, 2007 1931
    Recommended Adult Immunization Schedule, by Vaccine
        and Age Group – United States, 2006-2007 1934
    Recommended Adult Immunization Schedule, by Vaccine
        and Medical and Other Indications – United States,
        2006-2007 1934
Prevention of Hepatitis A Through Active or Passive
    Immunization: Recommendations of the Advisory Committee
    on Immunization Practices (ACIP) 1939
Adverse Events and Vaccination 1940

INFECTIOUS DISEASE – PROPHYLAXIS
Management of Healthcare Worker Exposures to HBV, HCV, and
    HIV 1941
Perinatal HIV 1953
Prevention of Bacterial Endocarditis 1960
Prevention of Wound Infection and Sepsis in Surgical Patients 1964
USPHS / IDSA Guidelines for the Prevention of Opportunistic Infections
    in Persons Infected With HIV
    Drug Regimens for Adults and Adolescents 1966
    Drug Regimens for Infants and Children 1972

INFECTIOUS DISEASE – TREATMENT
Animal and Human Bites 1976
Antibiotic Treatment of Adults With Infective Endocarditis 1977
Antimicrobial Drugs of Choice 1981
Antiretroviral Therapy for HIV Infection: Adults and Adolescents 1988
Community-Acquired Pneumonia in Adults 1999
Malaria Treatment 2003
Treatment of Sexually Transmitted Infections 2007
Tuberculosis 2010

PARENTERAL NUTRITION
Calculations for Total Parenteral Nutrition Therapy –
    Adult Patients 2021
Median Heights and Weights and Recommended Energy Intake 2022

THERAPY RECOMMENDATIONS
Pediatric ALS Algorithms 2023
Adult ACLS Algorithms 2026
Asthma 2029
Contrast Media Reactions, Premedication for Prophylaxis 2036
Depression 2038
Diabetes Mellitus Management, Adults 2040
Epilepsy 2048
    Convulsive Status Epilepticus 2048
Glaucoma Drug Therapy 2050
Heart Failure (Systolic) 2051
Helicobacter pylori Treatment 2056
Hyperglycemia- or Hypoglycemia-Causing Drugs 2057
Hyperlipidemia Management 2058
Hypertension 2063
Obesity Treatment Guidelines for Adults 2073

TOXICOLOGY
Management of Overdosages 2075
Salicylates 2080
Toxicology Information 2081
Toxidromes 2090

MISCELLANEOUS

Breast-Feeding and Drugs 2095
Discoloration of Feces Due to Drugs 2098
Discoloration of Urine Due to Drugs 2099
Drugs in Pregnancy..2101
Fever Due to Drugs..2104
Herb-Drug Interactions / Cautions..............................2105
Laboratory Detection of Drugs 2108
Low Potassium Diet 2109
Oral Dosages That Should Not Be Crushed 2110
Top 200 Prescribed Drugs 2111
Tyramine Content of Foods 2115
Vitamin K Content in Selected Foods........................2116

ABBREVIATIONS, ACRONYMS, AND SYMBOLS

Abbreviation	Meaning
<	less than
>	greater than
≤	less than or equal to
≥	greater than or equal to
$\overline{aa}$, aa	of each
AA	Alcoholics Anonymous
ABG	arterial blood gases
ac	before meals or food
ACA	Adult Children of Alcoholics
ACLS	advanced cardiac life support
ad	to, up to
a.d.	right ear
ADHD	attention-deficit/hyperactivity disorder
ADLs	activities of daily living
ad lib	at pleasure
AIDS	acquired immune deficiency syndrome
AIMS	Abnormal Involuntary Movement Scale
a.l.	left ear
ALS	amyotrophic lateral sclerosis
AM	morning
AMA	against medical advice
amp	ampul
amt	amount
aq	water
aq. dest.	distilled water
ARC	AIDS-related complex
ARDS	adult respiratory distress syndrome
ARF	acute renal failure
a.s.	left ear
ASAP	as soon as possible
a.u.	each ear
AUC	area under the curve
BDI	Beck Depression Inventory
bid	twice daily
BLS	basic life support
bm	bowel movement
BMI	body mass index
bp	blood pressure
BPH	benign prostatic hyperplasia
BPRS	Brief Psychiatric Rating Scale
BSA	body surface area
c	a gallon
$\overline{c}$	with
CA	cancer
CABG	coronary artery bypass graft
CAD	coronary artery disease
cal	calorie
cap	capsule
CBT	cognitive behavioral therapy
cc	cubic centimeter
CCL	creatinine clearance
CF	cystic fibrosis
CGI	Clinical Global Impression
CIE	chemotherapy-induced emesis
cm	centimeter
CIV	continuous I.V. infusion
CNS	central nervous system
comp	compound
cont	continue
COPD	chronic obstructive pulmonary disease
CRF	chronic renal failure
CT	computed tomography

Abbreviation	Meaning
d	day
DBP	diastolic blood pressure
d/c	discontinue
dil	dilute
disp	dispense
div	divide
DOE	dyspnea on exertion
DSC	discontinued
DSM-IV	Diagnostic and Statistical Manual
DTs	delirium tremens
dtd	give of such a dose
DVT	deep vein thrombosis
Dx	diagnosis
ECG	electrocardiogram
ECT	electroconvulsive therapy
EEG	electroencephalogram
elix, el	elixir
emp	as directed
EPS	extrapyramidal side effects
ESRD	end stage renal disease
et	and
EtOH	alcohol
ex aq	in water
f, ft	make, let be made
FDA	Food and Drug Administration
FMS	fibromyalgia syndrome
g	gram
GA	Gamblers Anonymous
GAD	generalized anxiety disorder
GAF	Global Assessment of Functioning Scale
GABA	gamma-aminobutyric acid
GERD	gastroesophageal reflux disease
GFR	glomerular filtration rate
GITS	gastrointestinal therapeutic system
gr	grain
gtt	a drop
GVHD	graft versus host disease
h	hour
HAM-A	Hamilton Anxiety Scale
HAM-D	Hamilton Depression Scale
hs	at bedtime
HSV	herpes simplex virus
HTN	hypertension
IBD	inflammatory bowel disease
IBS	irritable bowel syndrome
ICH	intracranial hemorrhage
IHSS	idiopathic hypertrophic subaortic stenosis
I.M.	intramuscular
IOP	intraocular pressure
IU	international unit
I.V.	intravenous
kcal	kilocalorie
kg	kilogram
KIU	kallikrein inhibitor unit
L	liter
LAMM	L-α-acetyl methadol
liq	a liquor, solution
LVH	left ventricular hypertrophy
M	mix; Molar
MADRS	Montgomery Asbery Depression Rating Scale
MAOIs	monamine oxidase inhibitors
mcg	microgram
MDEA	3,4-methylene-dioxy amphetamine
m. dict	as directed
MDMA	3,4-methylene-dioxy methamphetamine

ABBREVIATIONS, ACRONYMS, AND SYMBOLS *(Continued)*

Abbreviation	Meaning
mEq	milliequivalent
mg	milligram
mixt	a mixture
mL	milliliter
mm	millimeter
mM	millimolar
MMSE	mini mental status examination
MPPP	l-methyl-4-proprionoxy-4-phenyl pyridine
MR	mental retardation
MRI	magnetic resonance imaging
MS	multiple sclerosis
NF	National Formulary
NKA	no known allergies
NMS	neuroleptic malignant syndrome
no.	number
noc	in the night
non rep	do not repeat, no refills
NPO	nothing by mouth
NSAID	nonsteroidal anti-inflammatory drug
NV	nausea and vomiting
O, Oct	a pint
OA	osteoarthritis
OCD	obsessive-compulsive disorder
o.d.	right eye
o.l.	left eye
o.s.	left eye
o.u.	each eye
PANSS	Positive and Negative Symptom Scale
PAT	paroxysmal artrial tachycardia
pc, post cib	after meals
PCP	phencyclidine
PD	Parkinson's disease
PE	pulmonary embolus
per	through or by
PID	pelvic inflammatory disease
PM	afternoon or evening
P.O.	by mouth
PONV	postoperative nausea and vomiting
P.R.	rectally
prn	as needed
PSVT	paroxysmal superventricular tachycardia
PTA	prior to admission
PTSD	post-traumatic stress disorder
PUD	peptic ulcer disease
pulv	a powder
PVD	peripheral vascular disease
q	every
qad	every other day
qd	every day, daily
qh	every hour
qid	four times a day
qod	every other day
qs	a sufficient quantity
qs ad	a sufficient quantity to make
qty	quantity
qv	as much as you wish
RA	rheumatoid arthritis
REM	rapid eye movement
Rx	take, a recipe
rep	let it be repeated
$\bar{s}$	without
sa	according to art
SAH	subarachnoid hemorrhage

Abbreviation	Meaning
sat	saturated
SBE	subacute bacterial endocarditis
SBP	systolic blood pressure
SIADH	syndrome of inappropriate antidiuretic hormone secretion
sig	label, or let it be printed
SL	sublingual
SLE	systemic lupus erythematosus
SOB	shortness of breath
sol	solution
solv	dissolve
$\overline{ss}$	one-half
sos	if there is need
SSKI	saturated solution of potassium iodide
SSRIs	selective serotonin reuptake inhibitors
stat	at once, immediately
STD	sexually transmitted disease
SubQ	subcutaneous
supp	suppository
SVT	supraventricular tachycardia
Sx	symptom
syr	syrup
tab	tablet
tal	such
TCA	tricyclic antidepressant
TD	tardive dyskinesia
tid	three times a day
TKO	to keep open
TPN	total parenteral nutrition
tr, tinct	tincture
trit	triturate
tsp	teaspoonful
Tx	treatment
ULN	upper limits of normal
ung	ointment
URI	upper respiratory infection
USAN	United States Adopted Names
USP	United States Pharmacopeia
UTI	urinary tract infection
u.d., ut dict	as directed
v.o.	verbal order
VTE	venous thromboembolism
VZV	varicella zoster virus
w.a.	while awake
x3	3 times
x4	4 times
YBOC	Yale Brown Obsessive-Compulsive Scale
YMRS	Young Mania Rating Scale

APACHE II SCORING SYSTEM

The APACHE II score is the sum of the total acute physiology score (APS), age points, and chronic health points. Determination of these scores/points are outlined in the following tables. For an online scoring calculator, see http://www.sfar.org/scores2/scores2.html.

APACHE II Score	Points
APS points	
+ Age points	
+ Chronic health points	
Total APACHE II Score	

Glasgow Coma Scale
(circle appropriate response)

Eyes open
4 - Spontaneously
3 - To verbal
2 - To painful stimuli
1 - No response

Verbal - nonintubated
5 - Oriented and controversed
4 - Disoriented and talks
3 - Inappropriate words
2 - Incomprehensible sounds
1 - No response

Motor response
6 - To verbal command
5 - Localizes to pain
4 - Withdraws to pain
3 - Decorticate
2 - Decerebrate
1 - No response

Verbal - intubated
5 - Seems able to talk
3 - Questionable ability to talk
1 - Generally unresponsive

Age Points

Assign points to age as follows:	Points
≤44	0
45-54	2
55-64	3
65-74	5
≥75	6

Chronic Health Points

| Liver
Cardiovascular
Pulmonary
Kidney
Immune | If the patient has a history of severe organ system insufficiency or is immunocompromised assign points as follows:
a. for nonoperative or emergency postoperative patients - 5 points
or
b. for elective postoperative patients - 2 points
DEFINITIONS
Organ insufficiency or immunocompromised state must have been evident prior to this hospital admission and conform to the following criteria:
Liver: Biopsy proven cirrhosis and documented portal hypertension; episodes of past upper GI bleeding attributed to portal hypertension; or prior episodes of hepatic failure/encephalopathy/coma
Cardiovascular: New York Heart Association Class IV
Respiratory: Chronic restrictive, obstructive, or vascular disease resulting in severe exercise restriction, ie, unable to climb stairs or perform household duties; or documented chronic hypoxia, hypercapnia, secondary polycythemia, severe pulmonary hypertension (>40 mm Hg), or respirator dependency
Renal: Receiving chronic dialysis
Immunocompromised: The patient has received therapy that suppresses resistance to infection, eg, immunosuppression, chemotherapy, radiation, long term or recent high dose steroids, or has a disease that is sufficiently advanced to suppress resistance to infection, eg, leukemia, lymphoma, AIDS
Chronic Health Points = |

Reference: Knaus WA, Draper EA, Wagner DP, et al, "APACHE II: A Severity of Disease Classification System," *Crit Care Med*, 1985, 13(10):818-29.

Total Acute Physiology Score (APS)
(Choose the worst value in the past 24 hours)

	Physiologic Variable	High Abnormal Range				0	Low Abnormal Range			
		+4	+3	+2	+1	0	+1	+2	+3	+4
1	Temperature rectal (°C)[1]	≥41	39-40.9		38.5-38.9	36-38.4	34-35.9	32-33.9	30-31.9	≤29.9
2	Mean arterial pressure (mm Hg)	≥160	130-159	110-129		70-109		50-69		≤49
3	Heart rate (ventricular response)	≥180	140-179	110-139		70-109		55-69	40-54	≤39
4	Respiratory rate (nonventilated or ventilated)	≥50	35-49		25-34	12-24	10-11	6-9		≤5
5	Oxygenation: A-aDO2 or PaO2 (mm Hg) a) FiO2 ≥0.5: record A-aDO2 b) FiO2 <0.5: record only PaO2	≥500	350-499	200-349		<200 / PO2 >70	PO2 61-70		PO2 55-60	PO2 <55
6*	Arterial pH	≥7.7	7.6-7.69		7.5-7.59	7.33-7.49		7.25-7.32	7.15-7.24	<7.15
7	Serum sodium (mmol/L)	≥180	160-179	155-159	150-154	130-149		120-129	111-119	≤110
8	Serum potassium (mmol/L)	≥7	6-6.9		5.5-5.9	3.5-5.4	3-3.4	2.5-2.9		<2.5
9	Serum creatinine (mg/100 mL) double point score for acute renal failure	≥3.5	2-3.4	1.5-1.9		0.6-1.4		<0.6		
10	Hematocrit (%)	≥60		50-59.9	46-49.9	30-45.9		20-29.9		<20
11	White blood count (total/mm³) (in 1000s)	≥40		20-39.9	15-19.9	3-14.9		1-2.9		<1
12	Glasgow coma score (GCS): Score = 15 minus actual GCS [see Glasgow Coma Scale table]									
A	Total acute physiology score (APS): Sum of the 12 individual variable points									
*	Serum HCO3 (venous-mmol/L) Not preferred, use if no ABGs	≥52	41-51.9	32-40.9		22-31.9	18-21.9		15-17.9	<15

[1]Temperature may also be obtained by the following methods: Swan-Ganz core, bladder, tympanic membrane.

APOTHECARY / METRIC EQUIVALENTS

Approximate Liquid Measures

Basic equivalent: 1 fluid ounce = 30 mL

Examples:

1 gallon	3800 mL	1 gallon	128 fluid ounces
1 quart	960 mL	1 quart	32 fluid ounces
1 pint	480 mL	1 pint	16 fluid ounces
8 fluid oz	240 mL	15 minims	1 mL
4 fluid oz	120 mL	10 minims	0.6 mL

Approximate Household Equivalents

1 teaspoonful	5 mL	1 tablespoonful	15 mL

Weights

Basic equivalents:

1 oz	30 g	15 gr	1 g

Examples:

4 oz	120 g	1 gr	60 mg
2 oz	60 g	1/100 gr	600 mcg
10 gr	600 mg	1/150 gr	400 mcg
7½ gr	500 mg	1/200 gr	300 mcg
16 oz	1 lb		

Metric Conversions

Basic equivalents:

1 g	1000 mg	1 mg	1000 mcg

Examples:

5 g	5000 mg	5 mg	5000 mcg
0.5 g	500 mg	0.5 mg	500 mcg
0.05 g	50 mg	0.05 mg	50 mcg

Exact Equivalents

1 g	=	15.43 gr	0.1 mg	=	1/600 gr
1 mL	=	16.23 minims	0.12 mg	=	1/500 gr
1 minim	=	0.06 mL	0.15 mg	=	1/400 gr
1 gr	=	64.8 mg	0.2 mg	=	1/300 gr
1 pint (pt)	=	473.2 mL	0.3 mg	=	1/200 gr
1 oz	=	28.35 g	0.4 mg	=	1/150 gr
1 lb	=	453.6 g	0.5 mg	=	1/120 gr
1 kg	=	2.2 lb	0.6 mg	=	1/100 gr
1 qt	=	946.4 mL	0.8 mg	=	1/80 gr
			1 mg	=	1/65 gr

Solids[1]

¼ grain	=	15 mg
½ grain	=	30 mg
1 grain	=	60 mg
1½ grains	=	90 mg
5 grains	=	300 mg
10 grains	=	600 mg

[1]Use exact equivalents for compounding and calculations requiring a high degree of accuracy.

AVERAGE WEIGHTS AND SURFACE AREAS

Average Weight and Surface Area of Preterm Infants, Term Infants, and Children

Age	Average Weight (kg)[1]	Approximate Surface Area (m^2)
Weeks Gestation		
26	0.9-1	0.1
30	1.3-1.5	0.12
32	1.6-2	0.15
38	2.9-3	0.2
40 (term infant at birth)	3.1-4	0.25
Months		
3	5	0.29
6	7	0.38
9	8	0.42
Year		
1	10	0.49
2	12	0.55
3	15	0.64
4	17	0.74
5	18	0.76
6	20	0.82
7	23	0.90
8	25	0.95
9	28	1.06
10	33	1.18
11	35	1.23
12	40	1.34
Adults	70	1.73

[1]Weights from age 3 months and older are rounded off to the nearest kilogram.

BODY MASS INDEX (BMI)

$$BMI = \frac{weight \ (kg)}{[height \ (m)]^2}$$

See "Obesity Treatment Guidelines for Adults" in Therapy Recommendations section.

BODY SURFACE AREA OF ADULTS AND CHILDREN

Calculating Body Surface Area in Children

In a child of average size, find weight and corresponding surface area on the boxed scale to the left; or, use the nomogram to the right. Lay a straightedge on the correct height and weight points for the child, then read the intersecting point on the surface area scale.

FOR CHILDREN OF NORMAL HEIGHT AND WEIGHT

NOMOGRAM

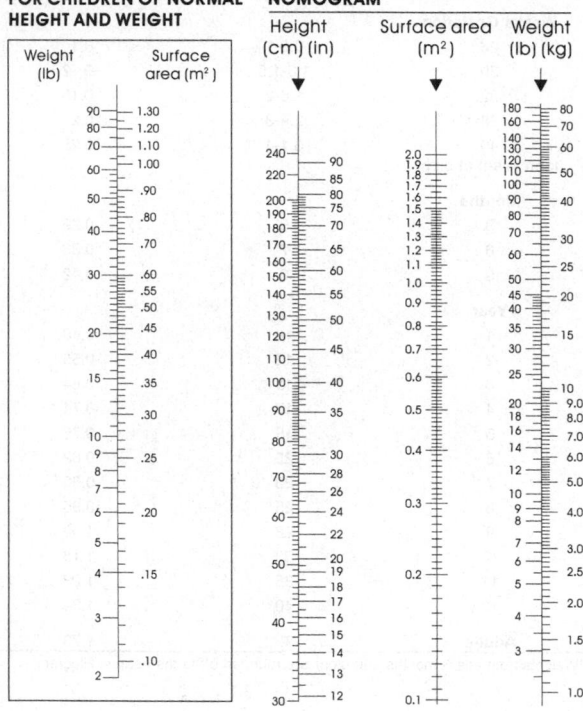

BODY SURFACE AREA FORMULA
(Adult and Pediatric)

$$BSA\ (m^2) = \sqrt{\frac{ht\ (in)\ x\ wt\ (lb)}{3131}}\quad \text{or, in metric: } BSA\ (m^2) = \sqrt{\frac{ht\ (cm)\ x\ wt\ (kg)}{3600}}$$

References

Lam TK and Leung DT, "More on Simplified Calculation of Body Surface Area," *N Engl J Med*, 1988, 318(17):1130 (letter).

Mosteller RD, "Simplified Calculation of Body Surface Area," *N Engl J Med*, 1987, 317(17):1098 (letter).

IDEAL BODY WEIGHT CALCULATION

Adults (18 years and older) (IBW is in kg)

IBW (male) = 50 + (2.3 x height in inches over 5 feet)

IBW (female) = 45.5 + (2.3 x height in inches over 5 feet)

Children (IBW is in kg; height is in cm)

a. 1-18 years

$$IBW = \frac{(height^2\ x\ 1.65)}{1000}$$

b. 5 feet and taller

IBW (male) = 39 + (2.27 x height in inches over 5 feet)

IBW (female) = 42.2 + (2.27 x height in inches over 5 feet)

MILLIEQUIVALENT AND MILLIMOLE CALCULATIONS AND CONVERSIONS

DEFINITIONS AND CALCULATIONS

Definitions

mole	=	gram molecular weight of a substance (aka molar weight)
millimole (mM)	=	milligram molecular weight of a substance (a millimole is 1/1000 of a mole)
equivalent weight	=	gram weight of a substance which will combine with or replace 1 gram (1 mole) of hydrogen; an equivalent weight can be determined by dividing the molar weight of a substance by its ionic valence
milliequivalent (mEq)	=	milligram weight of a substance which will combine with or replace 1 milligram (1 millimole) of hydrogen (a milliequivalent is 1/1000 of an equivalent)

Calculations

moles	=	$\dfrac{\text{weight of a substance (grams)}}{\text{molecular weight of that substance (grams)}}$
millimoles	=	$\dfrac{\text{weight of a substance (milligrams)}}{\text{molecular weight of that substance (milligrams)}}$
equivalents	=	moles x valence of ion
milliequivalents	=	millimoles x valence of ion
moles	=	$\dfrac{\text{equivalents}}{\text{valence of ion}}$
millimoles	=	$\dfrac{\text{milliequivalents}}{\text{valence of ion}}$
millimoles	=	moles x 1000
milliequivalents	=	equivalents x 1000

Note: Use of equivalents and milliequivalents is valid only for those substances which have fixed ionic valences (eg, sodium, potassium, calcium, chlorine, magnesium bromine, etc). For substances with variable ionic valences (eg, phosphorous), a reliable equivalent value cannot be determined. In these instances, one should calculate millimoles (which are fixed and reliable) rather than milliequivalents.

MILLIEQUIVALENT CONVERSIONS

To convert mg/100 mL to mEq/L the following formula may be used:

$$\frac{\text{(mg/100 mL) x 10 x valence}}{\text{atomic weight}} = \text{mEq/L}$$

To convert mEq/L to mg/100 mL the following formula may be used:

$$\frac{\text{(mEq/L) x atomic weight}}{\text{10 x valence}} = \text{mg/100 mL}$$

To convert mEq/L to volume of percent of a gas the following formula may be used:

$$\frac{\text{(mEq/L) x 22.4}}{10} = \text{volume percent}$$

MILLIEQUIVALENT AND MILLIMOLE CALCULATIONS AND CONVERSIONS *(Continued)*

Valences and Atomic Weights of Selected Ions

Substance	Electrolyte	Valence	Molecular Wt
Calcium	Ca^{++}	2	40
Chloride	Cl^-	1	35.5
Magnesium	Mg^{++}	2	24
Phosphate	HPO_4^{--} (80%)	1.8	96[1]
pH = 7.4	$H_2PO_4^-$ (20%)	1.8	96[1]
Potassium	K^+	1	39
Sodium	Na^+	1	23
Sulfate	SO_4^{--}	2	96[1]

[1]The molecular weight of phosphorus only is 31, and sulfur only is 32.

Approximate Milliequivalents — Weights of Selected Ions

Salt	mEq/g Salt	mg Salt/mEq
Calcium carbonate [$CaCO_3$]	20	50
Calcium chloride [$CaCl_2 \cdot 2H_2O$]	14	74
Calcium gluceptate [$Ca(C_7H_{13}O_8)_2$]	4	245
Calcium gluconate [$Ca(C_6H_{11}O_7)_2 \cdot H_2O$]	5	224
Calcium lactate [$Ca(C_3H_5O_3)_2 \cdot 5H_2O$]	7	154
Magnesium gluconate [$Mg(C_6H_{11}O_7)_2 \cdot H_2O$]	5	216
Magnesium oxide [MgO]	50	20
Magnesium sulfate [$MgSO_4$]	17	60
Magnesium sulfate [$MgSO_4 \cdot 7H_2O$]	8	123
Potassium acetate [$K(C_2H_3O_2)$]	10	98
Potassium chloride [KCl]	13	75
Potassium citrate [$K_3(C_6H_5O_7) \cdot H_2O$]	9	108
Potassium iodide [KI]	6	166
Sodium acetate [$Na(C_2H_3O_2)$]	12	82
Sodium acetate [$Na(C_2H_3O_2) \cdot 3H_2O$]	7	136
Sodium bicarbonate [$NaHCO_3$]	12	84
Sodium chloride [$NaCl$]	17	58
Sodium citrate [$Na_3(C_6H_5O_7) \cdot 2H_2O$]	10	98
Sodium iodine [NaI]	7	150
Sodium lactate [$Na(C_3H_5O_3)$]	9	112
Zinc sulfate [$ZnSO_4 \cdot 7H_2O$]	7	144

CORRECTED SODIUM

Corrected Na^+ = measured Na^+ + [1.5 x (glucose – 150 divided by 100)]

Note: Do not correct for glucose <150.

WATER DEFICIT

Water deficit = 0.6 x body weight [1 – (140 divided by Na^+)]

Note: Body weight is estimated weight in kg when fully hydrated; Na^+ is serum or plasma sodium. Use corrected Na^+ if necessary. Consult medical references for recommendations for replacement of deficit.

TOTAL SERUM CALCIUM CORRECTED FOR ALBUMIN LEVEL

[(Normal albumin – patient's albumin) x 0.8] + patient's measured total calcium

ACID-BASE ASSESSMENT

Henderson-Hasselbalch Equation

$$pH = 6.1 + \log (HCO_3^- / (0.03) (pCO_2))$$

Alveolar Gas Equation

PIO_2 = FiO_2 x (total atmospheric pressure − vapor pressure of H_2O at 37°C)

= FiO_2 x (760 mm Hg − 47 mm Hg)

PAO_2 = $PIO_2 - PACO_2 / R$

Alveolar/arterial oxygen gradient = $PAO_2 - PaO_2$

Normal ranges:

Children	15-20 mm Hg
Adults	20-25 mm Hg

where:

PIO_2 = Oxygen partial pressure of inspired gas (mm Hg) (150 mm Hg in room air at sea level)

FiO_2 = Fractional pressure of oxygen in inspired gas (0.21 in room air)

PAO_2 = Alveolar oxygen partial pressure

$PACO_2$ = Alveolar carbon dioxide partial pressure

PaO_2 = Arterial oxygen partial pressure

R = Respiratory exchange quotient (typically 0.8, increases with high carbohydrate diet, decreases with high fat diet)

Acid-Base Disorders

Acute metabolic acidosis:
$PaCO_2$ expected = 1.5 (HCO_3^-) + 8 ± 2 **or**
Expected decrease in $PaCO_2$ = 1.3 (1-1.5) x decrease in HCO_3^-

Acute metabolic alkalosis:
Expected increase in $PaCO_2$ = 0.6 (0.5-1) x increase in HCO_3^-

Acute respiratory acidosis (<6 h duration):
For every $PaCO_2$ increase of 10 mm Hg, HCO_3 increases by 1 mEq/L

Chronic respiratory acidosis (>6 h duration):
For every $PaCO_2$ increase of 10 mm Hg, HCO_3 increases by 4 mEq/L

Acute respiratory alkalosis (<6 h duration):
For every $PaCO_2$ decrease of 10 mm Hg, HCO_3 decreases by 2 mEq/L

Chronic respiratory alkalosis (>6 h duration):
For every $PaCO_2$ decrease of 10 mm Hg, HCO_3 increases by 5 mEq/L

ACID-BASE EQUATION

H^+ (in mEq/L) = (24 x $PaCO_2$) divided by HCO_3^-

Aa GRADIENT

Aa gradient [(713)(FiO_2 − ($PaCO_2$ divided by 0.8))] − PaO_2

Aa gradient = alveolar-arterial oxygen gradient

FiO_2 = inspired oxygen (expressed as a fraction)

$PaCO_2$ = arterial partial pressure carbon dioxide (mm Hg)

PaO_2 = arterial partial pressure oxygen (mm Hg)

OSMOLALITY

Definition: The summed concentrations of all osmotically active solute particles.

Predicted serum osmolality =
2 Na^+ + glucose (mg/dL) / 18 + BUN (mg/dL) / 2.8

The normal range of serum osmolality is 285-295 mOsm/L.

Differential diagnosis of increased serum osmolal gap (>10 mOsm/L)

Medications and toxins
Alcohols (ethanol, methanol, isopropanol, glycerol, ethylene glycol)
Mannitol

MILLIEQUIVALENT AND MILLIMOLE CALCULATIONS AND CONVERSIONS *(Continued)*

Calculated Osm

Osmolal gap = measured Osm − calculated Osm

> 0 to +10: Normal
> >10: Abnormal
> <0: Probable lab or calculation error

For drugs causing increased osmolar gap, see "Toxicology Information" section in this Appendix.

BICARBONATE DEFICIT

HCO_3^- deficit = (0.4 x wt in kg) x (HCO_3^- desired − HCO_3^- measured)

Note: In clinical practice, the calculated quantity may differ markedly from the actual amount of bicarbonate needed or that which may be safely administered.

ANION GAP

Definition: The difference in concentration between unmeasured cation and anion equivalents in serum.

Anion gap = Na^+ − (Cl^- + HCO_3^-)
        (The normal anion gap is 10-14 mEq/L)

Differential Diagnosis of Increased Anion Gap Acidosis

Organic anions

> Lactate (sepsis, hypovolemia, seizures, large tumor burden)
> Pyruvate
> Uremia
> Ketoacidosis (β-hydroxybutyrate and acetoacetate)
> Amino acids and their metabolites
> Other organic acids

Inorganic anions

> Hyperphosphatemia
> Sulfates
> Nitrates

Differential Diagnosis of Decreased Anion Gap

Organic cations

> Hypergammaglobulinemia

Inorganic cations

> Hyperkalemia
> Hypercalcemia
> Hypermagnesemia

Medications and toxins

> Lithium

Hypoalbuminemia

RETICULOCYTE INDEX

(% retic divided by 2) x (patient's Hct divided by normal Hct) **or**
(% retic divided by 2) x (patient's Hgb divided by normal Hgb)

Normal index: 1.0
Good marrow response: 2.0-6.0

PEDIATRIC DOSAGE ESTIMATIONS

Dosage Estimations Based on Weight:

Augsberger's rule:

$$(1.5 \times \text{weight in kg} + 10) \% \text{ of adult dose} = \text{child's approximate dose}$$

Clark's rule:

$$\frac{\text{weight (in pounds)}}{150} \times \text{adult dose} = \text{child's approximate dose}$$

Dosage Estimations Based on Age:

Augsberger's rule:

$$(4 \times \text{age in years} + 20) \% \text{ of adult dose} = \text{child's approximate dose}$$

Bastedo's rule:

$$\frac{\text{age in years} + 3}{30} \times \text{adult dose} = \text{child's approximate dose}$$

Cowling's rule:

$$\frac{\text{age at next birthday (in years)}}{24} \times \text{adult dose} = \text{child's approximate dose}$$

Dilling's rule:

$$\frac{\text{age (in years)}}{20} \times \text{adult dose} = \text{child's approximate dose}$$

Fried's rule for infants (younger than 1 year):

$$\frac{\text{age (in months)}}{150} \times \text{adult dose} = \text{infant's approximate dose}$$

Young's rule:

$$\frac{\text{age (in years)}}{\text{age} + 12} \times \text{adult dose} = \text{child's approximate dose}$$

POUNDS / KILOGRAMS CONVERSION

1 pound = 0.45359 kilograms
1 kilogram = 2.2 pounds

lb =	kg	lb =	kg	lb =	kg
1	0.45	70	31.75	140	63.50
5	2.27	75	34.02	145	65.77
10	4.54	80	36.29	150	68.04
15	6.80	85	38.56	155	70.31
20	9.07	90	40.82	160	72.58
25	11.34	95	43.09	165	74.84
30	13.61	100	45.36	170	77.11
35	15.88	105	47.63	175	79.38
40	18.14	110	49.90	180	81.65
45	20.41	115	52.16	185	83.92
50	22.68	120	54.43	190	86.18
55	24.95	125	56.70	195	88.45
60	27.22	130	58.91	200	90.72
65	29.48	135	61.24		

TEMPERATURE CONVERSION

Celsius to Fahrenheit = (°C x 9/5) + 32 = °F
Fahrenheit to Celsius = (°F – 32) x 5/9 = °C

°C =	°F	°C =	°F	°C =	°F
100.0	212.0	39.0	102.2	36.8	98.2
50.0	122.0	38.8	101.8	36.6	97.9
41.0	105.8	38.6	101.5	36.4	97.5
40.8	105.4	38.4	101.1	36.2	97.2
40.6	105.1	38.2	100.8	36.0	96.8
40.4	104.7	38.0	100.4	35.8	96.4
40.2	104.4	37.8	100.1	35.6	96.1
40.0	104.0	37.6	99.7	35.4	95.7
39.8	103.6	37.4	99.3	35.2	95.4
39.6	103.3	37.2	99.0	35.0	95.0
39.4	102.9	37.0	98.6	0	32.0
39.2	102.6				

REFERENCE VALUES FOR CHILDREN

Chemistry

Albumin	0-1 y	2-4 g/dL
	1 y to adult	3.5-5.5 g/dL
Ammonia	Newborns	90-150 µg/dL
	Children	40-120 µg/dL
	Adults	18-54 µg/dL
Amylase	Newborns	0-60 units/L
	Adults	30-110 units/L
Bilirubin, conjugated, direct	Newborns	<1.5 mg/dL
	1 mo to adult	0-0.5 mg/dL
Bilirubin, total	0-3 d	2-10 mg/dL
	1 mo to adult	0-1.5 mg/dL
Bilirubin, unconjugated, indirect		0.6-10.5 mg/dL
Calcium	Newborns	7-12 mg/dL
	0-2 y	8.8-11.2 mg/dL
	2 y to adult	9-11 mg/dL
Calcium, ionized, whole blood		4.4-5.4 mg/dL
Carbon dioxide, total		23-33 mEq/L
Chloride		95-105 mEq/L
Cholesterol	Newborns	45-170 mg/dL
	0-1 y	65-175 mg/dL
	1-20 y	120-230 mg/dL
Creatinine	0-1 y	≤0.6 mg/dL
	1 y to adult	0.5-1.5 mg/dL
Glucose	Newborns	30-90 mg/dL
	0-2 y	60-105 mg/dL
	Children to adults	70-110 mg/dL
Iron	Newborns	110-270 µg/dL
	Infants	30-70 µg/dL
	Children	55-120 µg/dL
	Adults	70-180 µg/dL
Iron binding	Newborns	59-175 µg/dL
	Infants	100-400 µg/dL
	Adults	250-400 µg/dL
Lactic acid, lactate		2-20 mg/dL
Lead, whole blood		<10 µg/dL
Lipase	Children	20-140 units/L
	Adults	0-190 units/L
Magnesium		1.5-2.5 mEq/L
Osmolality, serum		275-296 mOsm/kg
Osmolality, urine		50-1400 mOsm/kg
Phosphorus	Newborns	4.2-9.0 mg/dL
	6 wk to ≤18 mo	3.8-6.7 mg/dL
	18 mo to 3 y	2.9-5.9 mg/dL
	3-15 y	3.6-5.6 mg/dL
	>15 y	2.5-5.0 mg/dL
Potassium, plasma	Newborns	4.5-7.2 mEq/L
	2 d to 3 mo	4.0-6.2 mEq/L
	3 mo to 1 y	3.7-5.6 mEq/L
	1-16 y	3.5-5.0 mEq/L
Protein, total	0-2 y	4.2-7.4 g/dL
	>2 y	6-8 g/dL
Sodium		136-145 mEq/L
Triglycerides	Infants	0-171 mg/dL
	Children	20-130 mg/dL
	Adults	30-200 mg/dL
Urea nitrogen, blood	0-2 y	4-15 mg/dL
	2 y to adult	5-20 mg/dL

REFERENCE VALUES FOR CHILDREN (Continued)

Chemistry (continued)

Uric acid	Male	3-7 mg/dL
	Female	2-6 mg/dL

ENZYMES

Alanine aminotransferase (ALT)	0-2 mo	8-78 units/L
(SGPT)	>2 mo	8-36 units/L
Alkaline phosphatase (ALKP)	Newborns	60-130 units/L
	0-16 y	85-400 units/L
	>16 y	30-115 units/L
Aspartate aminotransferase (AST)	Infants	18-74 units/L
(SGOT)	Children	15-46 units/L
	Adults	5-35 units/L
Creatine kinase (CK)	Infants	20-200 units/L
	Children	10-90 units/L
	Adult male	0-206 units/L
	Adult female	0-175 units/L
Lactate dehydrogenase (LDH)	Newborns	290-501 units/L
	1 mo to 2 y	110-144 units/L
	>16 y	60-170 units/L

BLOOD GASES

	Arterial	Capillary	Venous
pH	7.35-7.45	7.35-7.45	7.32-7.42
pCO_2 (mm Hg)	35-45	35-45	38-52
pO_2 (mm Hg)	70-100	60-80	24-48
HCO_3 (mEq/L)	19-25	19-25	19-25
TCO_2 (mEq/L)	19-29	19-29	23-33
O_2 saturation (%)	90-95	90-95	40-70
Base excess (mEq/L)	-5 to +5	-5 to +5	-5 to +5

THYROID FUNCTION TESTS

T_4 (thyroxine)	1-7 d	10.1-20.9 µg/dL
	8-14 d	9.8-16.6 µg/dL
	1 mo to 1 y	5.5-16.0 µg/dL
	>1 y	4-12 µg/dL
FTI	1-3 d	9.3-26.6
	1-4 wks	7.6-20.8
	1-4 mo	7.4-17.9
	4-12 mo	5.1-14.5
	1-6 y	5.7-13.3
	>6 y	4.8-14.0
T_3 by RIA	Newborns	100-470 ng/dL
	1-5 y	100-260 ng/dL
	5-10 y	90-240 ng/dL
	10 y to adult	70-210 ng/dL
T_3 uptake		35%-45%
TSH	Cord	3-22 µU/mL
	1-3 d	<40 µU/mL
	3-7 d	<25 µU/mL
	>7 d	0-10 µU/mL

REFERENCE VALUES FOR ADULTS

CHEMISTRY

Test	Values	Remarks
Serum / Plasma		
Acetone	Negative	
Albumin	3.2-5 g/dL	
Alcohol, ethyl	Negative	
Aldolase	1.2-7.6 IU/L	
Ammonia	20-70 mcg/dL	Specimen to be placed on ice as soon as collected.
Amylase	30-110 units/L	
Bilirubin, direct	0-0.3 mg/dL	
Bilirubin, total	0.1-1.2 mg/dL	
Calcium	8.6-10.3 mg/dL	
Calcium, ionized	2.24-2.46 mEq/L	
Chloride	95-108 mEq/L	
Cholesterol, total	≤200 mg/dL	Fasted blood required – normal value affected by dietary habits. This reference range is for a general adult population.
HDL cholesterol	40-60 mg/dL	Fasted blood required – normal value affected by dietary habits.
LDL cholesterol	<160 mg/dL	If triglyceride is >400 mg/dL, LDL cannot be calculated accurately (Friedewald equation). Target LDL-C depends on patient's risk factors.
CO_2	23-30 mEq/L	
Creatine kinase (CK) isoenzymes		
CK-BB	0%	
CK-MB (cardiac)	0%-3.9%	
CK-MM (muscle)	96%-100%	
CK-MB levels must be both ≥4% and 10 IU/L to meet diagnostic criteria for CK-MB positive result consistent with myocardial injury.		
Creatine phosphokinase (CPK)	8-150 IU/L	
Creatinine	0.5-1.4 mg/dL	
Ferritin	13-300 ng/mL	
Folate	3.6-20 ng/dL	
GGT (gamma-glutamyltranspeptidase)		
male	11-63 IU/L	
female	8-35 IU/L	
GLDH	To be determined	
Glucose (preprandial)	<115 mg/dL	Goals different for diabetics.
Glucose, fasting	60-110 mg/dL	Goals different for diabetics.
Glucose, nonfasting (2-h postprandial)	<120 mg/dL	Goals different for diabetics.
Hemoglobin A_{1c}	<8	
Hemoglobin, plasma free	<2.5 mg/100 mL	
Hemoglobin, total glycosolated (Hb A_1)	4%-8%	
Iron	65-150 mcg/dL	
Iron binding capacity, total (TIBC)	250-420 mcg/dL	
Lactic acid	0.7-2.1 mEq/L	Specimen to be kept on ice and sent to lab as soon as possible.
Lactate dehydrogenase (LDH)	56-194 IU/L	
Lactate dehydrogenase (LDH) isoenzymes		
LD_1	20%-34%	
LD_2	29%-41%	
LD_3	15%-25%	
LD_4	1%-12%	
LD_5	1%-15%	
Flipped LD_1/LD_2 ratios (>1 may be consistent with myocardial injury) particularly when considered in combination with a recent CK-MB positive result.		
Lipase	23-208 units/L	
Magnesium	1.6-2.5 mg/dL	Increased by slight hemolysis.
Osmolality	289-308 mOsm/kg	
Phosphatase, alkaline		
adults 25-60 y	33-131 IU/L	
adults ≥61 y	51-153 IU/L	

REFERENCE VALUES FOR ADULTS *(Continued)*

CHEMISTRY *(continued)*

Test	Values	Remarks
infancy-adolescence	Values range up to 3-5 times higher than adults	
Phosphate, inorganic	2.8-4.2 mg/dL	
Potassium	3.5-5.2 mEq/L	Increased by slight hemolysis.
Prealbumin	>15 mg/dL	
Protein, total	6.5-7.9 g/dL	
SGOT (AST)	<35 IU/L (20-48)	
SGPT (ALT) (10-35)	<35 IU/L	
Sodium	134-149 mEq/L	
Thyroid stimulating hormone (TSH)		
adult ≤20 y	0.7-6.4 mIU/L	
21-54 y	0.4-4.2 mIU/L	
55-87 y	0.5-8.9 mIU/L	
Transferrin	>200 mg/dL	
Triglycerides	45-155 mg/dL	Fasted blood required.
Troponin I	<1.5 ng/mL	
Urea nitrogen (BUN)	7-20 mg/dL	
Uric acid		
male	2-8 mg/dL	
female	2-7.5 mg/dL	

Cerebrospinal Fluid

Glucose	50-70 mg/dL	
Protein	15-45 mg/dL	CSF obtained by lumbar puncture.

Note: Bloody specimen gives erroneously high value due to contamination with blood proteins

Urine
(24-hour specimen is required for all these tests unless specified)

Amylase	32-641 units/L	The value is in units/L and **not** calculated for total volume.
Amylase, fluid (random samples)		Interpretation of value left for physician, depends on the nature of fluid.
Calcium	Depends upon dietary intake	
Creatine		
male	150 mg/24 h	Higher value on children and during pregnancy.
female	250 mg/24 h	
Creatinine	1000-2000 mg/24 h	
Creatinine clearance (endogenous)		
male	85-125 mL/min	A blood sample must accompany urine specimen.
female	75-115 mL/min	
Glucose	1 g/24 h	
5-hydroxyindoleacetic acid	2-8 mg/24 h	
Iron	0.15 mg/24 h	Acid washed container required.
Magnesium	146-209 mg/24 h	
Osmolality	500-800 mOsm/kg	With normal fluid intake.
Oxalate	10-40 mg/24 h	
Phosphate	400-1300 mg/24 h	
Potassium	25-120 mEq/24 h	Varies with diet; the interpretation of urine electrolytes and osmolality should be left for the physician.
Sodium	40-220 mEq/24 h	
Porphobilinogen, qualitative	Negative	
Porphyrins, qualitative	Negative	
Proteins	0.05-0.1 g/24 h	
Salicylate	Negative	
Urea clearance	60-95 mL/min	A blood sample must accompany specimen.
Urea N	10-40 g/24 h	Dependent on protein intake.
Uric acid	250-750 mg/24 h	Dependent on diet and therapy.
Urobilinogen	0.5-3.5 mg/24 h	For qualitative determination on random urine, send sample to urinalysis section in Hematology Lab.

CHEMISTRY *(continued)*

Test	Values	Remarks
Xylose absorption test children	16%-33% of ingested xylose	
Feces		
Fat, 3-day collection	<5 g/d	Value depends on fat intake of 100 g/d for 3 days preceding and during collection.
Gastric Acidity		
Acidity, total, 12 h	10-60 mEq/L	Titrated at pH 7.

Blood Gases

	Arterial	Capillary	Venous
pH	7.35-7.45	7.35-7.45	7.32-7.42
pCO_2 (mm Hg)	35-45	35-45	38-52
pO_2 (mm Hg)	70-100	60-80	24-48
HCO_3 (mEq/L)	19-25	19-25	19-25
TCO_2 (mEq/L)	19-29	19-29	23-33
O_2 saturation (%)	90-95	90-95	40-70
Base excess (mEq/L)	-5 to +5	-5 to 15	-5 to +5

HEMATOLOGY

Complete Blood Count

Age	Hgb (g/dL)	Hct (%)	RBC (mill/mm^3)	RDW
0-3 d	15.0-20.0	45-61	4.0-5.9	<18
1-2 wk	12.5-18.5	39-57	3.6-5.5	<17
1-6 mo	10.0-13.0	29-42	3.1-4.3	<16.5
7 mo to 2 y	10.5-13.0	33-38	3.7-4.9	<16
2-5 y	11.5-13.0	34-39	3.9-5.0	<15
5-8 y	11.5-14.5	35-42	4.0-4.9	<15
13-18 y	12.0-15.2	36-47	4.5-5.1	<14.5
Adult male	13.5-16.5	41-50	4.5-5.5	<14.5
Adult female	12.0-15.0	36-44	4.0-4.9	<14.5

Age	MCV (fL)	MCH (pg)	MCHC (%)	Plts (x 10^3/mm^3)
0-3 d	95-115	31-37	29-37	250-450
1-2 wk	86-110	28-36	28-38	250-450
1-6 mo	74-96	25-35	30-36	300-700
7 mo to 2 y	70-84	23-30	31-37	250-600
2-5 y	75-87	24-30	31-37	250-550
5-8 y	77-95	25-33	31-37	250-550
13-18 y	78-96	25-35	31-37	150-450
Adult male	80-100	26-34	31-37	150-450
Adult female	80-100	26-34	31-37	150-450

REFERENCE VALUES FOR ADULTS *(Continued)*

WBC and Differential

Age	WBC (x 10^3/mm^3)	Segs	Bands	Lymphs	Monos
0-3 d	9.0-35.0	32-62	10-18	19-29	5-7
1-2 wk	5.0-20.0	14-34	6-14	36-45	6-10
1-6 mo	6.0-17.5	13-33	4-12	41-71	4-7
7 mo to 2 y	6.0-17.0	15-35	5-11	45-76	3-6
2-5 y	5.5-15.5	23-45	5-11	35-65	3-6
5-8 y	5.0-14.5	32-54	5-11	28-48	3-6
13-18 y	4.5-13.0	34-64	5-11	25-45	3-6
Adults	4.5-11.0	35-66	5-11	24-44	3-6

Age	Eosinophils	Basophils	Atypical Lymphs	No. of NRBCs
0-3 d	0-2	0-1	0-8	0-2
1-2 wk	0-2	0-1	0-8	0
1-6 mo	0-3	0-1	0-8	0
7 mo to 2 y	0-3	0-1	0-8	0
2-5 y	0-3	0-1	0-8	0
5-8 y	0-3	0-1	0-8	0
13-18 y	0-3	0-1	0-8	0
Adults	0-3	0-1	0-8	0

Segs = segmented neutrophils.
Bands = band neutrophils.
Lymphs = lymphocytes.
Monos = monocytes.

Erythrocyte Sedimentation Rates and Reticulocyte Counts

Sedimentation rate, Westergren	Children	0-20 mm/h
	Adult male	0-15 mm/h
	Adult female	0-20 mm/h
Sedimentation rate, Wintrobe	Children	0-13 mm/h
	Adult male	0-10 mm/h
	Adult female	0-15 mm/h
Reticulocyte count	Newborns	2%-6%
	1-6 mo	0%-2.8%
	Adults	0.5%-1.5%

LIVER DISEASE

Pugh's Modification of Child's Classification for Severity

Parameter	Points for Increasing Abnormality		
	1	2	3
Encephalopathy	None	1 or 2	3 or 4
Ascites	Absent	Slight	Moderate
Bilirubin (mg/dL)	<2.9	2.9-5.8	>5.8
Albumin (g/dL)	>3.5	2.8-3.5	<2.8
Prothrombin time (seconds over control)	1-4	4-6	>6

Scores:
  Mild hepatic impairment = <6 points.
  Moderate hepatic impairment = 6-10 points.
  Severe hepatic impairment = >10 points.

Considerations for Drug Dose Adjustment

Extent of Change in Drug Dose	Conditions or Requirements to Be Satisfied
None or minor change	Mild liver disease
	Extensive elimination of drug by kidneys and no renal dysfunction
	Elimination by pathways of metabolism spared by liver disease
	Drug is enzyme-limited and given acutely
	Drug is flow/enzyme-sensitive and only given acutely by I.V. route
	No alteration in drug sensitivity
Decrease in dose up to 25%	Elimination by the liver does not exceed 40% of the dose; no renal dysfunction
	Drug is flow-limited and given by I.V. route, with no large change in protein binding
	Drug is flow/enzyme-limited and given acutely by oral route
	Drug has a large therapeutic ratio
>25% decrease in dose	Drug metabolism is affected by liver disease; drug administered chronically
	Drug has a narrow therapeutic range; protein binding altered significantly
	Drug is flow-limited and given orally
	Drug is eliminated by kidneys and renal function severely affected
	Altered sensitivity to drug due to liver disease

Reference

Arns PA, Wedlund PJ, and Branch RA, "Adjustment of Medications in Liver Failure," *The Pharmacologic Approach to the Critically Ill Patient*, 2nd ed, Chernow B, ed, Baltimore, MD: Williams & Wilkins, 1988, 85-111.

CREATININE CLEARANCE ESTIMATING METHODS IN PATIENTS WITH STABLE RENAL FUNCTION

These formulas provide an acceptable estimate of the patient's creatinine clearance **except** in the following instances.

- Patient's serum creatinine is changing rapidly (either increasing or decreasing).
- Patient is markedly emaciated.

In above situations, certain assumptions have to be made.

- In a patient with rapidly rising serum creatinine (ie, >0.5-0.7 mg/dL/day), it is best to assume that the patient's creatinine clearance is probably <10 mL/minute.
- In an emaciated patient, although their actual creatinine clearance is less than their calculated creatinine clearance (because of decreased creatinine production), it is not possible to easily predict how much less.

Infants

Estimation of creatinine clearance using serum creatinine and body length (to be used when an adequate timed specimen cannot be obtained). **Note:** This formula may not provide an accurate estimation of creatinine clearance for infants younger than 6 months of age and for patients with severe starvation or muscle wasting.

$$Cl_{cr} = K \times L/S_{cr}$$

where:

Cl_{cr} = creatinine clearance in mL/minute/1.73 m²
K = constant of proportionality that is age specific

Age	K
Low birth weight ≤1 y	0.33
Full-term ≤1 y	0.45
2-12 y	0.55
13-21 y female	0.55
13-21 y male	0.70

L = length in cm
S_{cr} = serum creatinine concentration in mg/dL

Reference

Schwartz GJ, Brion LP, and Spitzer A, "The Use of Plasma Creatinine Concentration for Estimating Glomerular Filtration Rate in Infants, Children and Adolescents," *Pediatr Clin North Am*, 1987, 34(3):571-90.

Children (1-18 years)

Method 1: (Traub SL and Johnson CE, *Am J Hosp Pharm*, 1980, 37(2):195-201)

$$Cl_{cr} = \frac{0.48 \times (height)}{S_{cr}}$$

where:

Cl_{cr} = creatinine clearance in mL/min/1.73 m²
S_{cr} = serum creatinine in mg/dL
Height = height in cm

<u>Method 2</u>: Nomogram (Traub SL and Johnson CE, *Am J Hosp Pharm*, 1980, 37(2):195-201)

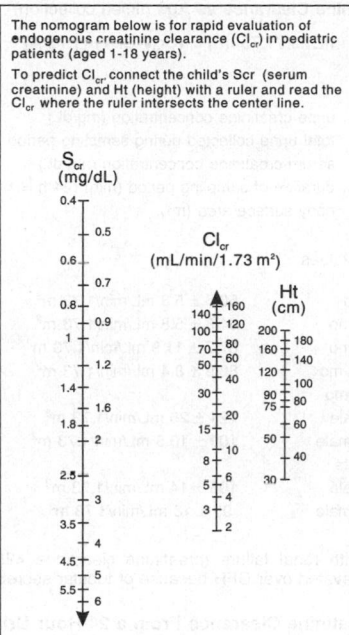

The nomogram below is for rapid evaluation of endogenous creatinine clearance (Cl_{cr}) in pediatric patients (aged 1-18 years).

To predict Cl_{cr}, connect the child's Scr (serum creatinine) and Ht (height) with a ruler and read the Cl_{cr} where the ruler intersects the center line.

Adults (18 years and older)

<u>Method 1</u>: (Cockroft DW and Gault MH, *Nephron*, 1976, 16:31-41)

Estimated creatinine clearance (Cl_{cr}) (mL/min):

$$\text{Male} = \frac{(140 - \text{age}) \times \text{BW (kg)}}{72 \times S_{cr}}$$

$$\text{Female} = \text{male} \times 0.85$$

Note: Use of actual body weight (BW) in obese patients (and possibly patients with ascites) may significantly overestimate creatinine clearance. Some clinicians prefer to use an adjusted ideal body weight (IBW) in such cases [eg, IBW + 0.4(ABW-IBW)], especially when calculating dosages for aminoglycoside antibiotics.

<u>Method 2</u>: (Jelliffe RW, *Ann Intern Med*, 1973, 79:604)

Estimated creatinine clearance (Cl_{cr}) (mL/min/1.73 m²):

$$\text{Male} = \frac{98 - 0.8 (\text{age} - 20)}{S_{cr}}$$

$$\text{Female} = \text{male} \times 0.90$$

RENAL FUNCTION TESTS

Endogenous Creatinine Clearance vs Age (timed collection)

Creatinine clearance (mL/min/1.73 m²) = (Cr_uV/Cr_sT) (1.73/A)

where:

Cr_u	=	urine creatinine concentration (mg/dL)
V	=	total urine collected during sampling period (mL)
Cr_s	=	serum creatinine concentration (mg/dL)
T	=	duration of sampling period (min) (24 h = 1440 min)
A	=	body surface area (m²)

Age-specific normal values

5-7 d	50.6 ± 5.8 mL/min/1.73 m²
1-2 mo	64.6 ± 5.8 mL/min/1.73 m²
5-8 mo	87.7 ± 11.9 mL/min/1.73 m²
9-12 mo	86.9 ± 8.4 mL/min/1.73 m²
≥18 mo	
male	124 ± 26 mL/min/1.73 m²
female	109 ± 13.5 mL/min/1.73 m²
Adults	
male	105 ± 14 mL/min/1.73 m²
female	95 ± 18 mL/min/1.73 m²

Note: In patients with renal failure (creatinine clearance <25 mL/min), creatinine clearance may be elevated over GFR because of tubular secretion of creatinine.

Calculation of Creatinine Clearance From a 24-Hour Urine Collection

Equation 1:

$$Cl_{cr} = \frac{U \times V}{P}$$

where:

Cl_{cr}	=	creatinine clearance
U	=	urine concentration of creatinine
V	=	total urine volume in the collection
P	=	plasma creatinine concentration

Equation 2:

$$Cl_{cr} = \frac{(\text{total urine volume [mL]}) \times (\text{urine Cr concentration [mg/dL]})}{(\text{serum creatinine [mg/dL]}) \times (\text{time of urine collection [minutes]})}$$

Occasionally, a patient will have a 12- or 24-hour urine collection done for direct calculation of creatinine clearance. Although a urine collection for 24 hours is best, it is difficult to do since many urine collections occur for a much shorter period. A 24-hour urine collection is the desired duration of urine collection because the urine excretion of creatinine is diurnal and thus the measured creatinine clearance will vary throughout the day as the creatinine in the urine varies. When the urine collection is less than 24 hours, the total excreted creatinine will be affected by the time of the day during which the collection is performed. A 24-hour urine collection is sufficient to be able to accurately average the diurnal creatinine excretion variations. If a patient has 24 hours of urine collected for creatinine clearance, equation 1 can be used for calculating the creatinine clearance. To use equation 1 to calculate the creatinine clearance, it will be necessary to know the duration of urine collection, the urine collection volume, the urine creatinine concentration, and the serum creatinine value that reflects the urine collection period. In most cases, a serum creatinine concentration is drawn anytime during the day, but it is best to have the value drawn halfway through the collection period.

Amylase:Creatinine Clearance Ratio

$$\frac{\text{Amylase}_u \times \text{creatinine}_p}{\text{Amylase}_p \times \text{creatinine}_u} \times 100$$

u = urine; p = plasma

Serum BUN:Serum Creatinine Ratio

Serum BUN (mg/dL:serum creatinine (mg/dL))

Normal BUN:creatinine ratio is 10-15

BUN:creatinine ratio >20 suggests prerenal azotemia (also seen with high urea-generation states such as GI bleeding)

BUN:creatinine ratio <5 may be seen with disorders affecting urea biosynthesis such as urea cycle enzyme deficiencies and with hepatitis.

Fractional Sodium Excretion

Fractional sodium secretion (FENa) = Na_uCr_s/Na_sCr_u x 100%

where:

Na_u = urine sodium (mEq/L)
Na_s = serum sodium (mEq/L)
Cr_u = urine creatinine (mg/dL)
Cr_s = serum creatinine (mg/dL)

FENa <1% suggests prerenal failure

FENa >2% suggest intrinsic renal failure
(for newborns, normal FENa is approximately 2.5%)

Note: Disease states associated with a falsely elevated FENa include severe volume depletion (>10%), early acute tubular necrosis, and volume depletion in chronic renal disease. Disorders associated with a lowered FENa include acute glomerulonephritis, hemoglobinuric or myoglobinuric renal failure, nonoliguric acute tubular necrosis, and acute urinary tract obstruction. In addition, FENa may be <1% in patients with acute renal failure **and** a second condition predisposing to sodium retention (eg, burns, congestive heart failure, nephrotic syndrome).

Urine Calcium:Urine Creatinine Ratio (spot sample)

Urine calcium (mg/dL): urine creatinine (mg/dL)

Normal values <0.21 (mean values 0.08 males, 0.06 females)

Premature infants show wide variability of calcium:creatinine ratio, and tend to have lower thresholds for calcium loss than older children. Prematures without nephrolithiasis had mean Ca:Cr ratio of 0.75 ± 0.76. Infants with nephrolithiasis had mean Ca:Cr ratio of 1.32 ± 1.03 (Jacinto JS, Modanlou HD, Crade M, et al, "Renal Calcification Incidence in Very Low Birth Weight Infants," *Pediatrics*, 1988, 81:31.)

Urine Protein:Urine Creatinine Ratio (spot sample)

P_u/Cr_u	Total Protein Excretion (mg/m²/d)
0.1	80
1	800
10	8000

where:

P_u = urine protein concentration (mg/dL)
Cr_u = urine creatinine concentration (mg/dL)

AMINOGLYCOSIDE DOSING AND MONITORING

All aminoglycoside therapy should be individualized for specific patients in specific clinical situation. The following are guidelines for initiating therapy.

1. Loading dose based on estimated ideal body weight (IBW). **All patients require a loading dose independent of renal function.**

Agent	Dose
Gentamicin	2 mg/kg
Tobramycin	2 mg/kg
Amikacin	7.5 mg/kg

Significantly higher loading doses may be required in severely ill intensive care unit patients.

2. Initial maintenance doses as a percent of loading dose according to desired dosing interval and creatinine clearance (Cl_{cr}):

$$\text{Male } Cl_{cr} \text{ (mL/min)} = \frac{(140 - \text{age}) \times \text{IBW}}{72 \times \text{serum creatinine}}$$

$$\text{Female} = 0.85 \times Cl_{cr} \text{ males}$$

Cl_{cr} (mL/min)	Dosing Interval (h)		
	8	12	24
90	84%	—	—
80	80%	—	—
70	76%	88%	—
60	—	84%	—
50	—	79%	—
40	—	72%	92%
30	—	—	86%
25	—	—	81%
20	—	—	75%

Patients >65 years of age should not receive initial aminoglycoside maintenance dosing more often than every 12 hours.

3. Serum concentration monitoring

- Serum concentration monitoring is necessary for **safe** and **effective** therapy, particularly in patients with serious infections and those with risk factors for toxicity.

- Peak serum concentrations should be drawn 30 minutes after the completion of a 30-minute infusion. Trough serum concentrations should be drawn within 30 minutes prior to the administered dose.

- Serum concentrations should be drawn after 5 half-lives, usually around the third dose or thereafter.

4. Desired measured serum concentrations

	Peak (mcg/mL)	Trough (mcg/mL)
Gentamicin	6-10	0.5-2.0
Tobramycin	6-10	0.5-2.0
Amikacin	20-30	<5

5. For patients receiving hemodialysis:

- administer the **same** loading dose
- administer $2/3$ of the loading dose after each dialysis
- **serum concentrations must be monitored**
- watch for ototoxicity from accumulation of drug

6. For individual clinical situations the prescribing physician should feel free to consult Infectious Disease, the Pharmacology Service, or the Pharmacy.

"Once Daily" Aminoglycosides

High dose, "once daily" aminoglycoside therapy for treatment of gram-negative bacterial infections has been studied and remains controversial. The pharmacodynamics of aminoglycosides reveal dose-dependent killing which suggests an efficacy advantage of "high" peak serum concentrations. It is also suggested that allowing troughs to fall to unmeasurable levels decreases the risk of nephrotoxicity without detriment to efficacy. Because of a theoretical saturation of tubular cell uptake of aminoglycosides, decreasing the number of times the drug is administered in a particular time period may play a role in minimizing the risk of nephrotoxicity. Ototoxicity has not been sufficiently formally evaluated through audiometry or vestibular testing comparing "once daily" to standard therapy. Over 100 letters, commentaries, studies and reviews have been published on the topic of "once daily" aminoglycosides with varying dosing regimens, monitoring parameters, inclusion and exclusion criteria, and results (most of which have been favorable for the "once daily" regimens). The caveats of this simplified method of dosing are several, including assurance that creatinine clearances be calculated, that all patients are not candidates and should not be considered for this regimen, and that "once daily" is a semantic misnomer.

Because of the controversial nature of this method, it is beyond the scope of this book to present significant detail and dosing regimen recommendations. Considerable experience with two methods warrants mention. The Hartford Hospital has experience with over 2000 patients utilizing a 7 mg/kg dose, a dosing scheme for various creatinine clearance estimates, and a serum concentration monitoring nomogram.[1] Providence Medical Center utilizes a 5 mg/kg dosing regimen but only in patients with excellent renal function; serum concentrations are monitored 4-6 hours prior to the dose administered.[2] Two excellent reviews discuss the majority of studies and controversies regarding these dosing techniques.[3,4] An editorial accompanies one of the reviews and is worth examination.[5]

"Once daily" dosing may be a safe and effective method of providing aminoglycoside therapy to a large number of patients who require these efficacious yet toxic agents. As with any method of aminoglycoside administration, dosing must be individualized and the caveats of the method considered.

Footnotes

1. Nicolau DP, Freeman CD, Belliveau PP, et al, "Experience With a Once-Daily Aminoglycoside Program Administered to 2,184 Patients," *Antimicrob Agents Chemother*, 1995, 39:650-5.
2. Gilbert DN, "Once-Daily Aminoglycoside Therapy," *Antimicrob Agents Chemother*, 1991, 35:399-405.
3. Preston SL and Briceland LL, "Single Daily Dosing of Aminoglycosides," *Pharmacotherapy*, 1995, 15:297-316.
4. Bates RD and Nahata MC, "Once-Daily Administration of Aminoglycosides," *Ann Pharmacother*, 1994, 28:757-66.
5. Rotschafer JC and Rybak MJ, "Single Daily Dosing of Aminoglycosides: A Commentary," *Ann Pharmacother*, 1994, 28:797-801.

Aminoglycoside Penetration Into Various Tissues

Site	Extent of Distribution
Eye	Poor
CNS	Poor (<25%)
Pleural	Excellent
Bronchial secretions	Poor
Sputum	Fair (10%-50%)
Pulmonary tissue	Excellent
Ascitic fluid	Variable (43%-132%)
Peritoneal fluid	Poor
Bile	Variable (25%-90%)
Bile with obstruction	Poor
Synovial fluid	Excellent
Bone	Poor
Prostate	Poor
Urine	Excellent
Renal tissue	Excellent

From Neu HC, "Pharmacology of Aminoglycosides," *The Aminoglycosides*, Whelton E and Neu HC, eds, New York, NY: Marcel Dekker, Inc, 1981.

ANGIOTENSIN AGENTS

ACE Inhibitors: Comparison of Indications and Adult Dosages

Drug	Hypertension	CHF	Renal Dysfunction	Dialyzable	Strengths (mg)
Benazepril (Lotensin®)	10-40 mg/day	Not FDA approved	Cl_{cr} <30 mL/min: 5 mg/day initially Maximum: 40 mg/day	Yes	Tablets 5, 10, 20, 40
Captopril (Capoten®)	25-100 mg/day bid-tid	6.25-100 mg tid Maximum: 450 mg/day	Cl_{cr} 10-50 mL/min: 75% of usual dose Cl_{cr} <10 mL/min: 50% of usual dose	Yes	Tablets 12.5, 25, 50, 100
Enalapril (Vasotec®)	2.5-40 mg/day qd-bid	2.5-20 mg bid Maximum: 20 mg bid	Cl_{cr} 30-80 mL/min: 5 mg/day initially Cl_{cr} <30 mL/min: 2.5 mg/day initially	Yes	Tablets 2.5, 5, 10, 20
Enalaprilat[1]	0.625 mg, 1.25 mg, 2.5 mg q6h Maximum: 5 mg q6h	Not FDA approved	Cl_{cr} <30 mL/min: 0.625 mg q6h	Yes	1.25 mg/mL (1 mL, 2 mL vials)
Fosinopril (Monopril®)	10-40 mg/day	10-40 mg/day	No dosage reduction necessary	Not well dialyzed	Tablets 10, 20, 40
Lisinopril (Prinivil®, Zestril®)	10-40 mg/day Maximum: 40 mg/day	5-40 mg/day	Cl_{cr} 10-30 mL/min: 5 mg/day initially Cl_{cr} <10 mL/min: 2.5 mg/day initially	Yes	Tablets 2.5, 5, 10, 20, 30, 40
Moexipril (Univasc®)	7.5-30 mg/day qd-bid Maximum: 30 mg/day	LV dysfunction (post-MI): 7.5-30 mg/day	Cl_{cr} <40 mL/min: 3.75 mg/day initially Maximum: 15 mg/day	Unknown	Tablets 7.5, 15
Perindopril (Aceon®)	4-8 mg/day	4-8 mg/day Maximum: 16 mg/day	Cl_{cr} 30-60 mL/min: 2 mg/day Cl_{cr} 15-29 mL/min: 2 mg qod Cl_{cr} <15 mL/min: 2 mg on dialysis days	Yes	Tablets 2, 4, 8
Quinapril (Accupril®)	10-40 mg/day qd-bid	5-20 mg bid	Cl_{cr} 30-60 mL/min: 5 mg/day initially Cl_{cr} <10-30 mL/min: 2.5 mg/day initially	Not well dialyzed	Tablets 5, 10, 20, 40
Ramipril (Altace®)	2.5-20 mg/day qd-bid	2.5-10 mg/day	Cl_{cr} <40 mL/min: 25% of normal dose	Unknown	Capsules 1.25, 2.5, 5, 10
Trandolapril (Mavik®)	1-4 mg/day Maximum: 8 mg/day qd-bid	LV dysfunction (post-MI): 1-4 mg/day	Cl_{cr} <30 mL/min: 0.5 mg/day initially	No	Tablets 1, 2, 4

Dosage is based on 70 kg adult with normal hepatic and renal function.

[1] Enalaprilat is the only available ACE inhibitor in a parenteral formulation.

Angiotensin II Receptor Blockers: Comparison of Indications and Adult Dosages

Drug	Hypertension	CHF	Renal Dysfunction	Dialyzable	Strengths (mg)
Candesartan (Atacand®)	8-32 mg/day	Target: 32 mg once daily	No dosage adjustment necessary	No	Tablets 4, 8, 16, 32
Eprosartan (Teveten®)	400-800 mg/day qd-bid	Not FDA approved	No dosage adjustment necessary	Unknown	Tablets 400, 600
Irbesartan (Avapro®)	150-300 mg/day	Not FDA approved	No dosage reduction necessary	No	Tablets 75, 150, 300
Losartan (Cozaar®)	25-100 mg qd or bid	Not FDA approved	No dosage adjustment necessary	No	Tablets 25, 50, 100
Olmesartan (Benicar®)	20-40 mg/day	Not FDA approved	No dosage adjustment necessary	Unknown	Tablets 5, 20, 40
Telmisartan (Micardis®)	20-80 mg/day	Not FDA approved	No dosage reduction necessary	No	Tablets 20, 40, 80
Valsartan (Diovan®)	80-320 mg/day	Target: 160 mg bid	Decrease dose only if Cl_{cr} <10 mL/minute	No	Tablets 40, 80, 160, 320

Dosage is based on 70 kg adult with normal hepatic and renal function.

ANGIOTENSIN AGENTS *(Continued)*

ACE Inhibitors: Comparative Pharmacokinetics

Drug	Prodrug	Absorption (%)	Serum $t_{1/2}$ (h) Normal Renal Function	Serum Protein Binding (%)	Elimination	Onset of BP Lowering Action (h)	Peak BP Lowering Effects (h)	Duration of BP Lowering Effects (h)
Benazepril	Yes	37	10-11 (effective)	~97	Renal (32%), biliary (~12%)	1	2-4	24
Benazeprilat				~95%				
Captopril	No	60-75 (fasting)	1.9 (elimination)	25-30	Renal	0.25-0.5	1-1.5	~6
Enalapril	Yes	55-75	2	50-60	Renal (60%-80%), fecal	1	4-6	12-24
Enalaprilat			11 (effective)					
Fosinopril		36	12 (effective)	>99	Renal (~50%), biliary (~50%)	1		24
Fosinoprilat								
Moexipril	Yes		1	90	Fecal (53%), renal (8%)		1-2	>24
Moexiprilat			2-10	50				
Perindopril	Yes		1.5-3	60	Renal		3-7	
Perindoprilat			3-10 (effective)	10-20				
Quinapril	Yes	>60	0.8	97	Renal (~60%) as metabolite, fecal	1	2-4	24
Quinaprilat			2					
Ramipril	Yes	50-60	1-2	73	Renal (60%), fecal (40%)	1-2	3-6	24
Ramiprilat			13-17 (effective)	56				
Trandolapril	Yes		6	80	Renal (33%), fecal (66%)	1-2	6	≥24
Trandolaprilat			10	65-94				

Angiotensin II Receptor Blockers: Comparative Pharmacokinetics

	Candesartan (Atacand®)	Eprosartan (Teveten®)	Irbesartan (Avapro®)	Losartan (Cozaar®)	Olmesartan (Benicar®)	Telmisartan (Micardis®)	Valsartan (Diovan®)
Prodrug	Yes[1]	No	No	Yes[2]	Yes	No	No
Time to peak	3-4 h	1-2 h	1.5-2	1 h / 3-4 h[2]	1-2 h	0.5-1 h	2-4 h
Bioavailability	15%	13%	60%-80%	33%	26%	42%-58%	25%
Food – area-under-the-curve	No effect	No effect	No effect	9%-10%	No effect	9.6%-20%	9%-40%
Elimination half-life	9 h	5-9 h	11-15 h	1.5-2 h / 6-9 h[2]	13 h	24 h	6 h
Elimination altered in renal dysfunction	Yes[3]	No	No	No	Yes	No	No
Precautions in severe renal dysfunction	Yes	Yes	Yes	Yes	Yes	Yes	Yes
Elimination altered in hepatic dysfunction	No	No	No	No	Yes	Yes	Yes
Precautions in hepatic dysfunction	No	Yes	No	No	No	Yes	No
Protein binding	>99%	98%	90%	~99%	99%	>99.5%	95%

[1]Candesartan cilexetil: Active metabolite candesartan.
[2]Losartan: Active metabolite E-3174.
[3]Dosage adjustments are not necessary.

ANTICOAGULANTS, INJECTABLE

Name	Use	Limitation	Dose (SubQ unless otherwise noted)	Average MW (in daltons)
Low Molecular Weight Heparins				
Dalteparin (Fragmin®)	Prophylaxis	Abdominal surgery[1] Abdominal surgery[2]	2500 units/d 5000 units/d	4000-6000
		Hip surgery[1]	5000 units/d postoperatively	
	Treatment	DVT[3]	100 units/kg bid 200 units/kg qd	4000-6000
		Unstable[4] angina Non-Q-wave MI	120 units/kg (max: 10,000 units) q12h for 5-8 d	
Enoxaparin (Lovenox®)	Prophylaxis	Hip or knee replacement	30 mg twice daily[5]	3500-5500
		High-risk hip replacement or abdominal surgery	40 mg once daily	
	Treatment	DVT or PE	1 mg/kg q12h	
		Acute coronary	1 mg/kg q12h	
Tinzaparin (Innohep®)	Treatment	DVT or PE	175 anti-Xa int. units/ kg/day	5500-7500
Heparin				
Heparin (Hep-Lock®)	Prophylaxis	Risk of thromboembolic disease	5000 units q8-12h	3000-30,000
	Treatment	Thrombosis or embolization	80 units/kg IVP then 20,000-40,000 units daily as continuous I.V. infusion	
	Treatment[3]	Unstable angina[3]	80 units/kg IVP then 20,000-40,000 units daily as continuous I.V. infusion	
Heparinoid				
Danaparoid	Prophylaxis	Hip replacement	750 units bid	6500
	Treatment[3]		2000 units q12h	
Selective Anti-Xa Inhibitor				
Fondaparinux[6] (Arixtra®)	Prophylaxis	Hip fracture Hip or knee replacement	2.5 mg once daily	1728
Coumarin Derivatives				
Warfarin (Coumadin®)	Prophylaxis	NS	Variable	NS
	Treatment		2-5 mg/d	

NS = not stated.

[1]Patients with low risk of DVT.
[2]Patients with high risk of DVT.
[3]Not FDA approved.
[4]Patients >60 years of age may require a lower dose of heparin.
[5]Patients weighing <100 lb or ≥65 years of age may receive 0.5 mg/kg/dose every 12 hours.
[6]Synthetic pentasaccharide.

ANTICONVULSANTS, BY SEIZURE TYPE

Antiepileptic Drugs for Children and Adolescents by Seizure Type and Epilepsy Syndrome

Seizure Type or Epilepsy Syndrome	First Line Therapy	Alternatives
Partial seizures (with or without secondary generalization)	Carbamazepine, oxcarbazepine, or phenytoin	**Second choice:** Gabapentin, lamotrigine, topiramate, or valproate **Third choice:** Tiagabine, zonisamide, phenobarbital, or primidone **Consider:** Benzodiazepine, acetazolamide, vigabatrin, or felbamate
Generalized tonic-clonic seizures	Valproate, carbamazepine, or phenytoin	**Second choice:** Topiramate or lamotrigine **Third choice:** Phenobarbital or primidone **Consider:** Zonisamide
Childhood absence epilepsy Before 10 years of age	Ethosuximide (only if no convulsive seizures) or valproate	**Second choice:** Lamotrigine **Third choice:** Methsuximide, acetazolamide, benzodiazepine, topiramate, or zonisamide
After 10 years of age	Valproate	**Second choice:** Lamotrigine **Third choice:** Ethosuximide, methsuximide, acetazolamide, benzodiazepine, topiramate or zonisamide
Juvenile myoclonic epilepsy	Valproate	**Second choice:** Lamotrigine, topiramate, or clonazepam **Third choice:** Phenobarbital, primidone, carbamazepine, or phenytoin **Consider:** Felbamate
Progressive myoclonic epilepsy	Valproate	**Second choice:** Valproate plus clonazepam, or phenobarbital
Lennox-Gastaut and related syndromes	Valproate	**Second choice:** Topiramate, lamotrigine **Third choice:** Ketogenic diet, vagal nerve stimulation, felbamate, benzodiazepine, or phenobarbital **Consider:** Ethosuximide, methsuximide, ACTH or steroids, pyridoxine or vigabatrin
Infantile spasms	ACTH (or steroids), vigabatrin, or valproate	**Second choice:** Topiramate **Third choice:** Lamotrigine, tiagabine, or benzodiazepine **Consider:** Pyridoxine, felbamate, or zonisamide
Benign epilepsy of childhood with centrotemporal spikes	Gabapentin or valproate	**Second choice:** Carbamazepine or phenytoin **Third choice:** Phenobarbital, primidone, or benzodiazepine **Consider:** Lamotrigine or topiramate
Neonatal seizures	Phenobarbital	**Second choice:** Phenytoin **Consider:** Clonazepam, primidone, valproate, or pyridoxine

Adapted from Bourgeois BF, "Antiepileptic Drugs in Pediatric Practice," *Epilepsia*, 1995, 36(Suppl 2):S34-S45 and Bourgeois BF, "New Antiepileptic Drugs in Children: Which Ones for Which Seizures?" *Clin Neuropharmacol*, 2000, 23(3):119-32.

ANTIDEPRESSANT AGENTS

Comparison of Usual Dosage, Mechanism of Action, and Adverse Effects

Drug	Initial Dose	Usual Dosage (mg/d)	Dosage Forms	ACH	Drowsiness	Orthostatic Hypotension	Conduction Abnormalities[1]	GI Distress	Weight Gain	Comments
						Adverse Effects				
				Tricyclic Antidepressants and Related Compounds[1]						
Amitriptyline	25-75 mg qhs	100-300	T, I	4+	4+	3+	3+	1	4+	Also used in chronic pain, migraine, and as a hypnotic; contraindicated with cisapride
Amoxapine	50 mg bid	100-400	T	2+	2+	2+	2+	0	2+	May cause extrapyramidal symptom (EPS)
Clomipramine (Anafranil[®])	25-75 mg qhs	100-250	C	4+	4+	2+	3+	1+	4+	Approved for OCD
Desipramine[2] (Norpramin[®])	25-75 mg qhs	100-300	T	1+	2+	2+	2+	0	1+	Blood levels useful for therapeutic monitoring
Doxepin (Sinequan[®], Zonalon[®])	25-75 mg qhs	100-300	C, L	3+	4+	2+	2+	0	4+	
Imipramine (Tofranil[®], Tofranil-PM[®])	25-75 mg qhs	100-300	T, C	3+	3+	4+	3+	1+	4+	Blood levels useful for therapeutic monitoring
Maprotiline	25-75 mg qhs	100-225	T	2+	3+	2+	2+	0	2+	
Nortriptyline (Pamelor[®])	25-50 mg qhs	50-150	C, L	2+	2+	1+	2+	0	1+	Blood levels useful for therapeutic monitoring
Protriptyline (Vivactil[®])	15 mg qAM	15-60	T	2+	1+	2+	3+	1+	1+	Blood levels useful for therapeutic
Trimipramine (Surmontil[®])	25-75 mg qhs	100-300	C	4+	4+	3+	3+	0	4+	

Comparison of Usual Dosage, Mechanism of Action, and Adverse Effects *(continued)*

Drug	Initial Dose	Usual Dosage (mg/d)	Dosage Forms	ACH	Drowsiness	Orthostatic Hypotension	Conduction Abnormalities	GI Distress	Weight Gain	Comments
						Adverse Effects				
					Selective Serotonin Reuptake Inhibitors[3]					
Citalopram (Celexa™)	20 mg qAM	20–50	T	0	0	0	0	3+⁴	1+	
Escitalopram (Lexapro™)	10 mg qAM	10–20	T	0	0	0	0	3+	1+	S-enantiomer of citalopram
Fluoxetine (Prozac®, Prozac® Weekly™, Sarafem™)	10–20 mg qAM	20–80	C, L, T	0	0	0	0	3+⁴	1+	CYP2B6 and 2D6 inhibitor
Fluvoxamine[2]	50 mg qhs	100–300	T	0	0	0	0	3+⁴	1+	Contraindicated with pimozide, thioridazine, mesoridazine, CYP1A2, 2B6, 2C19, and 3A4 inhibitors
Paroxetine (Paxil®, Paxil® CR™)	10–20 mg qAM	20–50	T, L	1+	1+	0	0	3+⁴	2+	CYP2B6 and 2D6 inhibitor
Sertraline (Zoloft®)	25–50 mg qAM	50–200	T	0	0	0	0	3+⁴	1+	CYP2B6 and 2C19 inhibitor
					Dopamine-Reuptake Blocking Compounds					
Bupropion (Wellbutrin®, Wellbutrin SR®, Wellbutrin XL™, Zyban®)	100 mg bid-tid IR[5] 150 mg bid SR[6] qAM-bid	300–450[7]	T	0	0	0	1+/0	1+	0	Contraindicated with seizures, bulimia, and anorexia; low incidence of sexual dysfunction IR: A 6-h interval between doses preferred SR: An 8-h interval between doses preferred
					Serotonin / Norepinephrine Reuptake Inhibitors[8]					
Duloxetine (Cymbalta®)	40–60 mg qd	40–60	C	1+	1+	0	1+	3+⁴	0	
Venlafaxine (Effexor®, Effexor® XR)	25 mg bid-tid IR 37.5 mg qd XR	75–375	T	1+	1+	0	1+	3+⁴	0	High-dose is useful to treat refractory depression; frequency of hypertension increases with dosage >225 mg/d

ANTIDEPRESSANT AGENTS *(Continued)*

Comparison of Usual Dosage, Mechanism of Action, and Adverse Effects *(continued)*

Drug	Initial Dose	Usual Dosage (mg/d)	Dosage Forms	ACH	Drowsiness	Orthostatic Hypotension	Conduction Abnormalities	GI Distress	Weight Gain	Comments
5-HT$_2$ Receptor Antagonist Properties										
Nefazodone	100 mg bid	300–600	T	1+	1+	2+	1+	1+	0	Contraindicated with carbamazepine, pimozide, astemizole, cisapride, and terfenadine; caution with triazolam and alprazolam; low incidence of sexual dysfunction
Trazodone (Desyrel®)	50 mg tid	150–600	T	0	4+	3+	1+	1+	2+	
Noradrenergic Antagonist										
Mirtazapine (Remeron®, Remeron® SolTab®)	15 mg qhs	15–45	T	1+	3+	1+	1+	0	3+	Dose >15 mg/d less sedating, low incidence of sexual dysfunction
Monoamine Oxidase Inhibitors										
Isocarboxazid (Marplan®)	10 mg tid	10–30	T	2+	2+	2+	1+	1+	2+	Diet must be low in tyramine; contraindicated with sympathomimetics and other antidepressants
Phenelzine (Nardil®)	15 mg tid	15–90	T	2+	2+	2+	0	1+	3+	
Tranylcypromine (Parnate®)	10 mg bid	10–60	T	2+	1+	2+	1+	1+	2+	

ACH = anticholinergic effects (dry mouth, blurred vision, urinary retention, constipation); 0 - 4+ = absent or rare - relatively common. T = tablet, L = liquid, I = injectable, C = capsule; IR = immediate release, SR = sustained release.

[1]**Important note:** A 1-week supply taken all at once in a patient receiving the maximum dose can be fatal.

[2]Not approved by FDA for depression. Approved for OCD.

[3]Flat dose response curve. Approved for OCD.

[4]Nausea is usually mild and transient.

[5]IR: 100 mg bid, may be increased to 100 mg tid no sooner than 3 days after beginning therapy.

[6]SR: 150 mg qAM, may be increased to 150 mg bid as early as day 4 of dosing.

[7]To minimize seizure risk, do not exceed IR 150 mg/dose or SR 200 mg/dose.

[8]Do not use with sibutramine; relatively safe in overdose.

ANTIFUNGAL AGENTS

Activities of Various Agents Against Specific Fungi

Organisms	Amphotericin B[1]	Caspofungin	Fluconazole	Flucytosine
Aspergillus spp	FA	FA	N	?
Blastomyces dermatitidis	FA	?	A	N
Candida albicans	FA	FA	FA	FA
Candida glabrata	A	A	?	A
Candida krusei	FA	A	?	A
Candida tropicalis	FA	A	?	A
Coccidioides immitis	FA	?	A	N
Cryptococcus spp	FA	N	FA	FA
Dermatophytes	A	?	A	?
Fusarium spp	A	N	N	N
Histoplasma capsulatum	FA	A?	A	N
Penicillium spp	A	?	?	A
Pseudoallescheria boydii	?	A	N	N
Sporothrix schenckii	A	?	?	?
Zygomycetes (Mucor, Rhizopus)	A	N	N	N

Organisms	Griseofulvin	Itraconazole	Ketoconazole	Micafungin
Aspergillus spp	N	FA	N	A
Blastomyces dermatitidis	N	FA	FA	?
Candida albicans	N	FA	FA	FA
Candida glabrata	N	?	?	FA
Candida krusei	N	A	?	A
Candida tropicalis	N	?	?	A
Coccidioides immitis	N	A	FA	?
Cryptococcus spp	N	A	A	N
Dermatophytes	FA	A	A	?
Fusarium spp	N	N	N	?
Histoplasma capsulatum	N	FA	FA	?
Penicillium spp	N	?	N	?
Pseudoallescheria boydii	N	N	N	?
Sporothrix schenckii	N	?	N	?
Zygomycetes (Mucor, Rhizopus)	N	N	N	N

Organisms	Miconazole	Nystatin	Terbinafine	Voriconazole
Aspergillus spp	N	A	N	FA
Blastomyces dermatitidis	N	A	N	A
Candida albicans	FA	FA	A	A
Candida glabrata	?	A	?	A
Candida krusei	?	A	?	A
Candida tropicalis	?	A	?	A
Coccidioides immitis	A	N	N	A
Cryptococcus spp	A	N	N	A
Dermatophytes	N	N	FA	?
Fusarium spp	N	N	N	FA
Histoplasma capsulatum	N	N	N	A
Penicillium spp	N	N	N	?
Pseudoallescheria boydii	N	N	N	FA
Sporothrix schenckii	?	N	N	?
Zygomycetes (Mucor, Rhizopus)	N	N	N	N?

Organisms	Anidulafungin	Posaconazole
Aspergillus spp	A	FA
Blastomyces dermatitidis	N	A
Candida albicans	FA	FA
Candida glabrata	FA	A
Candida krusei	A	A
Candida tropicalis	FA	A
Coccidioides immitis	?	A
Cryptococcus spp	N	A
Dermatophytes	N?	A
Fusarium spp	N	A
Histoplasma capsulatum	?	A
Penicillium spp	A	A
Pseudoallescheria boydii	?	A
Sporothrix schenckii	?	A
Zygomycetes (Mucor, Rhizopus)	N?	A

FA = FDA approved indication. A = active. ? = unknown or questionable. N = not active.
[1] Various lipid products have differing indications, but all have activity against the same organisms.

ANTIFUNGAL AGENTS *(Continued)*

References

Espinel-Ingroff A, "Comparison of *In Vitro* Activities of the New Triazole SCH56592 and the Echinocandins MK-0991 (L-743,872) and LY303366 Against Opportunistic Filamentous and Dimorphic Fungi and Yeasts," *J Clin Microbiol*, 1998, 36(10):2950-6.

Sabatelli F, Patel R, Mann PA, et al, "*In Vitro* Activities of Posaconazole, Fluconazole, Itraconazole, Voriconazole, and Amphotericin B Against a Large Collection of Clinically Important Molds and Yeasts," *Antimicrob Agents Chemother*, 2006, 50(6):2009-15.

Torres HA, Hachem RY, Chemaly RF, et al, "Posaconazole: A Broad-Spectrum Triazole Antifungal," *Lancet Infect Dis*, 2005, 5(12):775-85.

Vazquez JA, "Anidulafungin: A New Echinocandin With a Novel Profile," *Clin Ther*, 2005, 27(6):657-73.

Zhanel GG, Karlowsky JA, Harding GA, et al, "*In Vitro* Activity of a New Semisynthetic Echinocandin, LY-303366, Against Systemic Isolates of *Candida* Species, *Cryptococcus neoformans*, *Blastomyces dermatitidis*, and *Aspergillus* Species," *Antimicrob Agents Chemother*, 1997, 41(4):863-5.

ANTIMIGRAINE DRUGS: 5-HT$_1$ RECEPTOR AGONISTS

Pharmacokinetic Differences

Pharmacokinetic Parameter	Almotriptan (Axert™) Oral (6.25 mg)	Eletriptan (Relpax®) Tablets	Frovatriptan (Frova®) Oral	Naratriptan (Amerge®) Oral	Rizatriptan (Maxalt®, Maxalt-MLT®) Tablets	Rizatriptan Disintegrating Tablets	Sumatriptan (Imitrex®) SubQ (6 mg)	Sumatriptan Oral (100 mg)	Sumatriptan Nasal (20 mg)	Zolmitriptan (Zomig®, Zomig-ZMT™) Oral (5 mg)	Zolmitriptan Oral (10 mg)
Onset	<60 min	<2 h	<2 h	30 min	~30 min	~30 min	10 min	30-60 min	<60 min	0.5-1 h	
Duration	Short	Short	Long	Long	Short	Short	Short	Short	Short	Short	
Time to peak serum concentration (h)	1-3	1.5-2	2-4	2-4	1-1.5	1.6-2.5	5-20	1.5-2.5	1	1.5	2-3.5
Average bioavailability (%)	70	50	20-30	70	45	—	97	15	17	40-46	46-49
Volume of distribution (L)	180-200	138	210-280	170	110-140	110-140	170	170	NA	—	402
Half-life (h)	3-4	4	26	6	2-3	2-3	2	2-2.5[1]	2	2.8-3.4	2.5-3.7
Fraction excreted unchanged in urine (%)	40	—	32	50	14	14	22	3	3	8	8

[1]With extended dosing, the half-life extends to 7 hours.

ANTIPSYCHOTIC AGENTS

Antipsychotic Agent	Dosage Forms	I.M./P.O. Potency	Equiv. Dosages (approx) (mg)	Usual Adult Daily Maint. Dose (mg)	Sedation (Incidence)	Extrapyramidal Side Effects	Anticholinergic Side Effects	Orthostatic Hypotension	Comments
Aripiprazole (Abilify™)	Soln, tab		4	10-30	Low	Very low	Very low	Very low	Low weight gain; activating
Chlorpromazine (Thorazine® [DSC])	Conc, inj, supp, syr, tab	4:1	100	200-1000	High	Moderate	Moderate	Moderate / high	
Clozapine (Clozaril®)	Tab		100	75-900	High	Very low	High	High	~1% incidence of agranulocytosis; weekly-biweekly CBC required; potential for weight gain, lipid abnormalities, and diabetes
Fluphenazine (Permitil®, Prolixin®, Prolixin Decanoate®, Prolixin Enanthate®)	Conc, elix, inj, tab	2:1	2	0.5-20	Low	High	Low	Low	
Haloperidol (Haldol®, Haldol® Decanoate)	Conc, inj, tab	2:1	2	0.5-20	Low	High	Low	Low	
Loxapine (Loxitane®, Loxitane® C, Loxitane® I.M.)	Cap, conc, inj		10	25-250	Moderate	Moderate	Low	Low	
Mesoridazine (Serentil®)	Inj, liq, tab	3:1	50	30-400	High	Low	High	Moderate	Prolongs QTc; use only in treatment of refractory illness
Molindone (Moban®)	Conc, tab		15	15-225	Low	Moderate	Low	Low	May cause less weight gain
Olanzapine (Zyprexa®, Zyprexa® Zydis®)	Inj, tab, tab (oral-disintegrating)		4	5-20	Moderate / high	Low	Moderate	Moderate	Potential for weight gain, lipid abnormalities, diabetes
Perphenazine (Trilafon®)	Conc, inj, tab		10	16-64	Low	Moderate	Low	Low	
Pimozide (Orap™)	Tab		2	1-20	Moderate	High	Moderate	Low	Contraindicated with CYP3A inhibitors
Quetiapine (Seroquel®)	Tab		125	50-800	Moderate / high	Very low	Moderate	Moderate	Moderate weight gain; potential for lipid abnormalities; diabetes
Risperidone (Risperdal®)	Inj, soln, tab, tab (oral-disintegrating)		1	0.5-6	Low / moderate	Low	Very low	Moderate	Low to moderate weight gain; potential for diabetes

Antipsychotic Agent	Dosage Forms	I.M./P.O. Potency	Equiv. Dosages (approx) (mg)	Usual Adult Daily Maint. Dose (mg)	Sedation (Incidence)	Extrapyramidal Side Effects	Anticholinergic Side Effects	Orthostatic Hypotension	Comments
Thioridazine (Mellaril®)	Conc, tab		100	200-800	High	Low	High	Moderate / high	May cause irreversible retinitis pigmentosa at doses >800 mg/d; prolongs QTc; use only in treatment of refractory illness
Thiothixene (Navane®)	Cap, conc, powder for inj	4:1	4	5-40	Low	High	Low	Low / moderate	
Trifluoperazine (Stelazine® [DSC])	Conc, inj, tab		5	2-40	Low	High	Low	Low	
Ziprasidone (Geodon®)	Cap, powder for inj	2:1	40	40-160	Low / moderate	Low	Very low	Low / moderate	Low weight gain; contraindicated with QTc-prolonging agents

BENZODIAZEPINES

Agent	Dosage Forms	Approximate Equivalent Dose (mg)	Peak Blood Levels (oral) (h)	Protein Binding (%)	Volume of Distribution (L/kg)	Major Active Metabolite	Half-Life (parent) (h)	Half-Life[1] (metabolite) (h)	Usual Initial Dose	Adult Oral Dosage Range
Anxiolytic										
Alprazolam (Alprazolam Intensol®, Xanax®)	Sol, tab	0.5	1-2	80	0.9-1.2	No	12-15	—	0.25-0.5 mg tid	0.75-4 mg/d
Chlordiazepoxide (Librium®)	Cap, powder for inj	10	2-4	90-98	0.3	Yes	5-30	24-96	5-25 mg tid-qid	15-100 mg/d
Diazepam (Diastat® Rectal Delivery System, Diazepam Intensol®, Valium®)	Gel, inj, sol, tab	5	0.5-2	98	1.1	Yes	20-80	50-100	2-10 mg bid-qid	4-40 mg/d
Lorazepam (Ativan®)[2]	Inj, sol, tab	1	1-6	88-92	1.3	No	10-20	—	0.5-2 mg tid-qid	2-4 mg/d
Oxazepam (Serax®)	Cap, tab	15-30	2-4	86-99	0.6-2	No	5-20	—	10-30 mg tid-qid	30-120 mg/d
Sedative / Hypnotic										
Estazolam (ProSom®)	Tab	0.3	2	93	—	No	10-24	—	1 mg qhs	1-2 mg
Flurazepam (Dalmane®)	Cap	5	0.5-2	97	—	Yes	Not significant	40-114	15 mg qhs	15-60 mg
Quazepam (Doral®)	Tab	5	2	95	5	Yes	25-41	28-114	15 mg qhs	7.5-15 mg
Temazepam (Restoril®)	Cap	5	2-3	96	1.4	No	10-40	—	15-30 mg qhs	15-30 mg
Triazolam (Halcion®)	Tab	0.1	1	89-94	0.8-1.3	No	2.3	—	0.125-0.25 mg qhs	0.125-0.25 mg
Miscellaneous										
Clonazepam (Klonopin®)	Tab	0.25-0.5	1-2	86	1.8-4	No	18-50 h	—	0.5 mg tid	1.5-20 mg/d
Clorazepate (Tranxene®)	Cap, tab	7.5	1-2	80-95	—	Yes	Not significant	50-100 h	7.5-15 mg bid-qid	15-60 mg
Midazolam	Inj	NA	0.4-0.7[3]	95	0.8-6.6	No	2-5 h	—	NA	NA

[1]Significant metabolite.

[2]Reliable bioavailability when given I.M.

[3]I.V. only.

NA = not available.

BETA-BLOCKERS

Agent	Adrenergic Receptor Blocking Activity	Lipid Solubility	Protein Bound (%)	Half-Life (h)	Bioavailability (%)	Primary (Secondary) Route of Elimination	Indications	Usual Dosage
Acebutolol (Sectral®)	beta₁	Low	15-25	3-4	40 7-fold[1]	Hepatic (renal)	Hypertension, arrhythmias	P.O.: 400-1200 mg/d
Atenolol (Tenormin®)	beta₁	Low	<5-10	6-9[2]	50-60 4-fold[1]	Renal (hepatic)	Hypertension, angina pectoris, acute MI	P.O.: 50-200 mg/d I.V.: 5 mg x 2 doses
Betaxolol (Kerlone®)	beta₁	Low	50-55	14-22	84-94	Hepatic (renal)	Hypertension	P.O.: 10-20 mg/d
Bisoprolol (Zebeta®)	beta₁	Low	26-33	9-12	80	Renal (hepatic)	Hypertension, heart failure	P.O.: 2.5-5 mg
Carteolol (Cartrol®)	beta₁, beta₂	Low	20-30	6	80-85	Renal	Hypertension	P.O.: 2.5-10 mg/d
Carvedilol (Coreg®)	beta₁, beta₂, alpha₁	ND	98	7-10	25-35	Bile into feces	Hypertension, heart failure (mild to severe)	P.O.: 6.25 mg twice daily
Esmolol (Brevibloc®)	beta₁	Low	55	0.15	NA 5-fold[1]	Red blood cell	Supraventricular tachycardia, sinus tachycardia	I.V. infusion: 25-300 mcg/kg/min
Labetalol (Trancate®)	alpha₁, beta₁, beta₂	Moderate	50	5.5-8	18-30 10-fold[1]	Renal (hepatic)	Hypertension	P.O.: 200-2400 mg/d I.V.: 20-80 mg at 10-min intervals up to a maximum of 300 mg or continuous infusion of 2 mg/min
Metoprolol (Lopressor®, Toprol-XL®)	beta₁	Moderate	10-12	3-7	50 10-fold[1] (Toprol XL®: 77)	Hepatic/renal	Hypertension, angina pectoris, acute MI, heart failure (mild to moderate; XL formulation only)	P.O.: 100-450 mg/d I.V.: Post-MI 15 mg Angina: 15 mg then 2-5 mg/hour Arrhythmias: 0.2 mg/kg
Nadolol (Corgard®)	beta₁, beta₂	Low	25-30	20-24	30 5- to 8-fold[1]	Renal	Hypertension, angina pectoris	P.O.: 40-320 mg/d
Penbutolol (Levatol®)	beta₁, beta₂	High	80-98	5	≅100	Hepatic (renal)	Hypertension	P.O.: 20-80 mg/d
Pindolol	beta₁, beta₂	Moderate	57	3-4[2]	90 4-fold[1]	Hepatic (renal)	Hypertension	P.O.: 20-60 mg/d
Propranolol (Inderal®, various)	beta₁, beta₂	High	90	3-5[2]	30 20-fold[1]	Hepatic	Hypertension, angina pectoris, arrhythmias	P.O.: 40-480 mg/d I.V.: Reflex tachycardia 1-10 mg
Propranolol long-acting (Inderal-LA®)	beta₁, beta₂	High	90	9-18	20- to 30-fold[1]	Hepatic	Hypertrophic subaoric stenosis, prophylax's (post-MI)	P.O.: 180-240 mg/d

BETA-BLOCKERS *(Continued)*

Agent	Adrenergic Receptor Blocking Activity	Lipid Solubility	Protein Bound (%)	Half-Life (h)	Bioavailability (%)	Primary (Secondary) Route of Elimination	Indications	Usual Dosage
Sotalol (Betapace®, Betapace AF®, Sorine®)	beta₁ beta₂	Low	0	12	90-100	Renal	Ventricular arrhythmias/ tachyarrhythmias	P.O. 160-320 mg/d
Timolol (Blocadren®)	beta₁ beta₂	Low to moderate	<10	4	75 7-fold¹	Hepatic (renal)	Hypertension, prophylaxis (post-MI)	P.O.: 20-60 mg/d P.O.: 20 mg/d

Dosage is based on 70 kg adult with normal hepatic and renal function.

Note: All beta₁-selective agents will inhibit beta₂ receptors at higher doses.

¹Interpatient variations in plasma levels.

²Half-life increased to 16-27 hours in creatinine clearance of 15-35 mL/minute and >27 hours in creatinine clearance <15 mL/minute.

BRONCHODILATORS

Comparison of Inhaled Sympathomimetic Bronchodilators

Drug	Adrenergic Receptor	Onset (min)	Duration Activity (h)
Albuterol (Proventil®)	Beta$_1$ < Beta$_2$	<5	3-8
Arformoterol (Brovana™)	Beta$_1$ < Beta$_2$	7-20	
Epinephrine (various)	Alpha and Beta$_1$ and Beta$_2$	1-5	1-3
Formoterol (Foradil®)	Beta$_1$ < Beta$_2$	3-5	12
Isoproterenol (Isuprel®)	Beta$_1$ and Beta$_2$	2-5	0.5-2
Levalbuterol (Xopenex®)	Beta$_1$ < Beta$_2$	10-17	5-6
Metaproterenol (Alupent®)	Beta$_1$ < Beta$_2$	5-30	2-6
Pirbuterol (Maxair™)	Beta$_1$ < Beta$_2$	<5	5
Salmeterol (Serevent®)	Beta$_1$ < Beta$_2$	5-14	12
Terbutaline	Beta$_1$ < Beta$_2$	5-30	3-6

CALCIUM CHANNEL BLOCKERS

Comparative Pharmacokinetics

Agent	Bioavailability (%)	Protein Binding (%)	Onset of BP Effect (min)	Duration of BP Effect (h)	Half-Life (h)	Volume of Distribution	Route of Metabolism	Route of Excretion
Dihydropyridines								
Amlodipine (Norvasc®)	64-90	93-98	30-50	24	30-50	21 L/kg	Hepatic; inactive metabolites	Urine; 10% as parent
Felodipine (Plendil®)	20	>99	2-5 h	24	11-16	10 L/kg	Hepatic; CYP3A4 substrate (major); inactive metabolites; extensive first pass	Urine (70%; as metabolites); feces 10%
Isradipine (DynaCirc® [DSC]) (immediate release)	15-24	95	20	>12	8	3 L/kg	Hepatic; CYP3A4 substrate (major); inactive metabolites; extensive first pass	Urine as metabolites
Nicardipine (Cardene®) (immediate release)	35	>95	30	≤8	2-4		Hepatic; CYP3A4 substrate (major); saturable first pass	Urine (60%; as metabolites); feces 35%
Nifedipine (Procardia®) (immediate release)	40-77	92-98	Within 20		2-5		Hepatic; CYP3A4 substrate (major); inactive metabolites	Urine as metabolites
Nimodipine (Nimotop®)	13	>95	ND	4-6	1-2		Hepatic; CYP3A4 substrate (major); metabolites inactive or less active than parent; extensive first pass	Urine (50%; as metabolites); feces 32%
Nisoldipine (Sular®)	5	>99	ND	6-12	7-12		Hepatic; CYP3A4 substrate (major); 1 active metabolite (10% of parent); extensive first pass	Urine as metabolites
Phenylalkylamines								
Verapamil (Calan®) (immediate release)	20-35	90	30	6-8	4.5-12		Hepatic; CYP3A4 substrate (major); 1 active metabolite (20% of parent); extensive first pass	Urine (70%; 3%-4% as unchanged drug); feces 16%
Benzothiazepines								
Diltiazem (Cardizem®) (immediate release)	~40	70-80	30-60	6-8	3-4.5	3-13 L/kg	Hepatic; CYP3A4 substrate (major); 1 major metabolite (20%-50% of parent); extensive first pass	Urine as metabolites

CORTICOSTEROIDS

Corticosteroids, Systemic Equivalencies

Glucocorticoid	Pregnancy Category	Approximate Equivalent Dose (mg)	Routes of Administration	Relative Anti-inflammatory Potency	Relative Mineralocorticoid Potency	Protein Binding (%)	Half-life Plasma (min)	Half-life Biologic (h)
Short-Acting								
Cortisone	D	25	P.O., I.M.	0.8	2	90	30	8-12
Hydrocortisone	C	20	I.M., I.V.	1	2	90	80-118	8-12
Intermediate-Acting								
Methylprednisolone[1]	—	4	P.O., I.M., I.V.	5	0	—	78-188	18-36
Prednisolone	B	5	P.O., I.M., I.V., intra-articular, intradermal, soft tissue injection	4	1	90-95	115-212	18-36
Prednisone	B	5	P.O.	4	1	70	60	18-36
Triamcinolone[1]	C	4	P.O., I.M., intra-articular, intradermal, intrasynovial, soft tissue injection	5	0	—	200+	18-36
Long-Acting								
Betamethasone	C	0.6-0.75	P.O., I.M., intra-articular, intradermal, intrasynovial, soft tissue injection	25	0	64	300+	36-54
Dexamethasone	C	0.75	P.O., I.M., I.V., intra-articular, intradermal, soft tissue injection	25-30	0	—	110-210	36-54
Mineralocorticoids								
Fludrocortisone	C	—	P.O.	10	125	42	210+	18-36

[1]May contain propylene glycol as an excipient in injectable forms.

CORTICOSTEROIDS *(Continued)*

GUIDELINES FOR SELECTION AND USE OF TOPICAL CORTICOSTEROIDS

The quantity prescribed and the frequency of refills should be monitored to reduce the risk of adrenal suppression. In general, short courses of high-potency agents are preferable to prolonged use of low potency. After control is achieved, control should be maintained with a low potency preparation.

1. Low-to-medium potency agents are usually effective for treating thin, acute, inflammatory skin lesions; whereas, high or super-potent agents are often required for treating chronic, hyperkeratotic, or lichenified lesions.
2. Since the stratum corneum is thin on the face and intertriginous areas, low-potency agents are preferred but a higher potency agent may be used for 2 weeks.
3. Because the palms and soles shave a thick stratum corneum, high or super-potent agents are frequently required.
4. Low potency agents are preferred for infants and the elderly. Infants have a high body surface area to weight ratio; elderly patients have thin, fragile skin.
5. The vehicle in which the topical corticosteroid is formulated influences the absorption and potency of the drug. Ointment bases are preferred for thick, lichenified lesions; they enhance penetration of the drug. Creams are preferred for acute and subacute dermatoses; they may be used on moist skin areas or intertriginous areas. Solutions, gels, and sprays are preferred for the scalp or for areas where a nonoil-based vehicle is needed.
6. In general, super-potent agents should not be used for longer than 2-3 weeks unless the lesion is limited to a small body area. Medium-to-high potency agents usually cause only rare adverse effects when treatment is limited to 3 months or less, and use on the face and intertriginous areas are avoided. If long-term treatment is needed, intermittent vs continued treatment is recommended.
7. Most preparations are applied once or twice daily. More frequent application may be necessary for the palms or soles because the preparation is easily removed by normal activity and penetration is poor due to a thick stratum corneum. Every-other-day or weekend-only application may be effective for treating some chronic conditions.

Corticosteroids, Topical

	Steroid	Vehicle
Very High Potency		
0.05%	Betamethasone dipropionate, augmented	Ointment, lotion
0.05%	Clobetasol propionate	Cream, foam, gel, lotion, ointment, shampoo, spray
0.05%	Diflorasone diacetate	Ointment
0.05%	Halobetasol propionate	Cream, ointment
High Potency		
0.1%	Amcinonide	Cream, ointment, lotion
0.05%	Betamethasone dipropionate, augmented	Cream
0.05%	Betamethasone dipropionate	Cream, ointment
0.1%	Betamethasone valerate	Ointment
0.05%	Desoximetasone	Gel
0.25%	Desoximetasone	Cream, ointment
0.05%	Diflorasone diacetate	Cream, ointment
0.05%	Fluocinonide	Cream, ointment, gel
0.1%	Halcinonide	Cream, ointment
0.5%	Triamcinolone acetonide	Cream
Intermediate Potency		
0.05%	Betamethasone dipropionate	Lotion
0.1%	Betamethasone valerate	Cream
0.1%	Clocortolone pivalate	Cream
0.05%	Desoximetasone	Cream
0.025%	Fluocinolone acetonide	Cream, ointment
0.05%	Flurandrenolide	Cream, ointment, lotion, tape
0.005%	Fluticasone propionate	Ointment
0.05%	Fluticasone propionate	Cream
0.1%	Hydrocortisone butyrate[1]	Ointment, solution
0.2%	Hydrocortisone valerate[1]	Cream, ointment
0.1%	Mometasone furoate[1]	Cream, ointment, lotion

Corticosteroids, Topical *(continued)*

	Steroid	Vehicle
0.1%	Prednicarbate	Cream, ointment
0.025%	Triamcinolone acetonide	Cream, ointment, lotion
0.1%	Triamcinolone acetonide	Cream, ointment, lotion
Low Potency		
0.05%	Alclometasone dipropionate[1]	Cream, ointment
0.05%	Desonide	Cream
0.01%	Fluocinolone acetonide	Cream, solution
0.5%	Hydrocortisone[1]	Cream, ointment, lotion
0.5%	Hydrocortisone acetate[1]	Cream, ointment
1%	Hydrocortisone acetate[1]	Cream, ointment
1%	Hydrocortisone	Cream, ointment, lotion, solution
2.5%	Hydrocortisone	Cream, ointment, lotion

[1] Not fluorinated.

CYCLOPLEGIC MYDRIATICS

Agent	Peak Mydriasis	Peak Cycloplegia	Time to Recovery
Atropine	30-40 min	1-3 h	>14 d
Cyclopentolate	25-75 min	25-75 min	24 h
Homatropine	30-90 min	30-90 min	6 h - 4 d
Scopolamine	20-30 min	30 min - 1 h	5-7 d
Tropicamide	20-40 min	20-35 min	1-6 h

FOSPHENYTOIN AND PHENYTOIN

Comparison of Parenteral Fosphenytoin and Phenytoin

	Fosphenytoin (Cerebyx®)	Phenytoin (Dilantin®)
Parenteral dosage forms available	50 mg PE/mL in 2 mL and 10 mL vials	50 mg phenytoin sodium/mL in 2 mL and 5 mL vials
Intravenous Administration	Recommended	Recommended
Loading dose	10-20 mg PE[1]/kg	10-15 mg/kg
Maintenance dose	4-7 mg/kg/day	100 mg I.V. q6-8h (oral form available)
Maximum infusion rate	Up to 150 mg PE/min	Up to 50 mg/min
Minimum infusion time for 1000 mg	6.7 min	20 min
Compatible with saline	Yes	Yes
Compatible with D$_5$W	Yes	No
Saline flush recommended after infusion	No	Yes
Intramuscular Administration	Recommended	Not recommended
Loading dose	10-20 mg PE/kg	10-15 mg/kg
Maintenance dose	4-7 mg/kg	Not recommended

[1]PE = phenytoin equivalents.

GLYCOPROTEIN ANTAGONISTS

Comparison of Glycoprotein IIb / IIIa Receptor Antagonists

	Abciximab (ReoPro®)	Tirofiban (Aggrastat®)	Eptifibatide (Integrilin®)
Type	Monoclonal antibody	Nonpeptide	Peptide
Mechanism of action	Steric hindrance and conformational changes	Mimics native protein sequence in receptor	Mimics native protein sequence in receptor
Biologic half-life	12-24 h	4-8 h	4-8 h
Reversible with platelet infusions	Yes	No (effect dissipates within 4-8 h)	No (effect dissipates within 4-8 h)
Speed of reversibility (return of platelet function)	Slow (>48 h)	Fast (2 h)	Fast (2 h)
Vitronectin activity	Yes	No	No
FDA-approved labeling			
Percutaneous coronary intervention (PCI)	Yes	No	Yes
Coronary stents	Yes	No	No
Unstable angina pre-PCI	When PCI planned	When PCI planned	When PCI planned
Unstable angina, medical stabilization	No	Yes	Yes
FDA-approved dosing for percutaneous coronary intervention	0.25 mg/kg bolus followed by 0.125 mcg/kg/min infusion (max: 10 mcg/min) x 12 h	Not approved for use in planned PCI	180 mcg/kg bolus immediately before the initiation of PCI, followed by 2 mcg/kg/min infusion until discharge or 18-24 hours. Repeat bolus 10 minutes after initial bolus.
FDA-approved dosing for unstable angina stabilization	0.25 mg/kg bolus followed by 10 mcg/min infusion x 18-24 h, concluding 1 h post-PCI	0.4 mcg/kg/min x 30 min followed by 0.1 mcg/kg/min infusion through angiography or 12-24 h after subsequent PCI	180 mcg/kg/bolus followed by 2 mcg/kg/min infusion until discharge, CABG procedure or up to 72 h
How supplied – volume of injectable (total drug contents/vial)	5 mL vial (10 mg)	50 mL vial (12.5 mg) 100 mL premixed solution (5 mg) 250 mL premixed solution (12.5 mg)	10 mL vial (20 mg) 100 mL vial (75 mg) 100 mL vial (200 mg)
Storage requirements	Refrigerate, do not freeze and do not shake	Can store at room temperature, do not freeze, protect from light during storage	Refrigerate and protect from light until administered

HEMODYNAMIC SUPPORT, INTRAVENOUS

Drug	Dose	Hemodynamic Effects				
		HR	MAP	PAOP	CI	SVR
Dopamine	1-3 mcg/kg/min	↑	0	↓	0/↑	0/↓
	3-10 mcg/kg/min	↑	↑	0	↑	0
	>10-20 mcg/kg/min	↑↑	↑↑	0	↑	↑
Epinephrine	0.01-0.05 mcg/kg/min	↑	↑	0/↓	↑↑	0/↓
	>0.05 mcg/kg/min	↑↑	↑↑	↑	↑↑	↑↑
Norepinephrine	0.02-3 mcg/kg/min	0/↑	↑↑↑	↑↑	0/↓/↑	↑↑↑
Phenylephrine	0.5-9 mcg/kg/min	0/↓	↑	↑	0/↓/↑	↑↑↑
Vasopressin	0.04 units/min	0/↓	↑↑	↑	0/↓	↑↑
Dobutamine	2-10 mcg/kg/min	0/↑	↑	↓	↑	0/↓
	>10-20 mcg/kg/min	↑↑	↓/↑	↓	↑	↓
Milrinone	0.375-0.75 mcg/kg/min	↑↑	0/↓/↑	↓	↑	↓↓
Nesiritide	2 mcg/kg bolus; 0.01-0.03 mcg/kg/min	0	↓	↓	0/↑	↓
Nitroglycerin	0.1-2 mcg/kg/min	0/↑	0/↓	↓	0/↑	↓
Nitroprusside	0.25-3 mcg/kg/min	0/↑	0/↓	↓	↑	↓

HR = heart rate; MAP = mean arterial pressure; PAOP = pulmonary artery occlusion pressure; CI = cardiac index; SVR = systemic vascular resistance

↑ = increase; ↓ = decrease; 0 = no change.

Drug	Dose	Receptor Activity				
		α_1	α_2	β_1	β_2	DA_1
Dobutamine	2-10 mcg/kg/min	+	0	+++	++	0
	>10-20 mcg/kg/min	++	0	++++	+++	0
Dopamine	1-3 mcg/kg/min	0	0	+	0	++++
	3-10 mcg/kg/min	0/+	0	++++	++	++++
	>10-20 mcg/kg/min	+++	0	++++	+	0
Epinephrine	0.01-0.05 mcg/kg/min	++	++	++++	+++	0
	>0.05 mcg/kg/min	++++	++++	+++	+	0
Norepinephrine	0.02-3 mcg/kg/min	++++	++	++	0	0
Phenylephrine	0.5-9 mcg/kg/min	++++	+	0	0	0
Vasopressin	0.04 units/min	0	0	0	0	0

Activity ranges from no activity (0) to maximal activity (++++).

DA = dopaminergic.

Reference
Sypniewski ES, "Hypovolemic and Cardigenic Shock," *Pharmacotherapy: A Pathophysiologic Approach*, 3rd ed, Dipiro JT, Talbert RL, Hayes PE, et al, eds, Stamford, CT: McGraw-Hill, 1997, 522-3.

LAXATIVES, CLASSIFICATION AND PROPERTIES

Laxative	Onset of Action	Site of Action	Mechanism of Action
Saline			
Magnesium citrate Magnesium hydroxide (Phillips'® Milk of Magnesia)	30 min to 3 h	Small and large intestine	Attract/retain water in intestinal lumen increasing intraluminal pressure; cholecystokinin release
Sodium phosphates (Fleet® Enema)	2-15 min	Colon	
Irritant / Stimulant			
Senna (Senokot®)	6-10 h	Colon	Direct action on intestinal mucosa; stimulate myenteric plexus; alter water and electrolyte secretion
Bisacodyl (Dulcolax®) tablets, suppositories	15 min to 1 h	Colon	
Castor oil	2-6 h	Small intestine	
Bulk-Producing			
Methylcellulose (Citrucel®) Psyllium (Metamucil®)	12-24 h (up to 72 h)	Small and large intestine	Holds water in stool; mechanical distention; malt soup extract reduces fecal pH
Lubricant			
Mineral oil	6-8 h	Colon	Lubricates intestine; retards colonic absorption of fecal water; softens stool
Surfactants / Stool Softener			
Docusate sodium (Colace®) Docusate calcium (Surfak®)	24-72 h	Small and large intestine	Detergent activity; facilitates admixture of fat and water to soften stool
Miscellaneous and Combination Laxatives			
Glycerin suppository	15-30 min	Colon	Local irritation; hyperosmotic action
Lactulose	24-48 h	Colon	Delivers osmotically active molecules to colon
Docusate/senna (Peri-Colace®)	8-12 h	Small and large intestine	Senna – mild irritant; docusate – stool softener
Polyethylene glycol 3350 (GlycoLax™, MiraLax™)	48 h	Small and large intestine	Nonabsorbable solution which acts as an osmotic agent
Sorbitol 70%	24-48 h	Colon	Delivers osmotically active molecules to colon

LIPID-LOWERING AGENTS

Effects on Lipoproteins

Drug	Total Cholesterol (%)	LDLC (%)	HDLC (%)	TG (%)
Bile-acid resins	↓20-25	↓20-35	→	↑5-20
Fibric acid derivatives	↓10	↓10 (↑)	↑10-20	↓40-55
HMG-CoA RI (statins)	↓15-60	↓20-40	↑2-15	↓7-25
Nicotinic acid	↓25	↓20	↑20	↓40
Probucol	↓10-15	↓<10	↓30	→
Ezetimibe	↓12-13	↓16-18	↑1-4	↓5-6

Lipid-Lowering Agents

Drug	Dose / Day	Effect on LDL (%)	Effect on HDL (%)	Effect on TG (%)
HMG-CoA Reductase Inhibitors				
Atorvastatin	10 mg	-39	+6	-19
	20 mg	-43	+9	-26
	40 mg	-50	+6	-29
	80 mg	-60	+5	-37
Fluvastatin	20 mg	-22	+3	-12
	40 mg	-25	+4	-14
	80 mg	-36	+6	-18
Lovastatin	10 mg	-21	+5	-10
	20 mg	-27	+6	-8
	40 mg	-31	+5	-8
	80 mg	-40	+9.5	-19
Pravastatin	10 mg	-22	+7	-15
	20 mg	-32	+2	-11
	40 mg	-34	+12	-24
	80 mg	-37	+3	-19
Rosuvastatin	5 mg	-45	+13	-35
	10 mg	-52	+14	-10
	20 mg	-55	+8	-23
	40 mg	-63	+10	-28
Simvastatin	5 mg	-26	+10	-12
	10 mg	-30	+12	-15
	20 mg	-38	+8	-19
	40 mg	-41	+13	-28
	80 mg	-47	+16	-33
Bile Acid Sequestrants				
Cholestyramine	4-24 g	-15 to -30	+3 to +5	+0 to +20
Colestipol	7-30 g	-15 to -30	+3 to +5	+0 to +20
Colesevelam	6 tablets	-15	+3	+10
	7 tablets	-18	+3	+9
Fibric Acid Derivatives				
Fenofibrate	67-200 mg	-20 to -25	+1 to +20	-30 to -50
Gemfibrozil	600 mg twice daily	-5 to -10[1]	+10 to +20	-40 to -60
Niacin	1.5-6 g	-21 to -27	+10 to +35	-10 to -50
2-Azetidinone				
Ezetimibe	10 mg	-18	+1	-8
Omega-3-Acid Ethyl Esters	4 g	+44.5	+9.1	-44.9
Combination Products				
Ezetimibe and fenofibrate	10/160 mg	-20	+19	-44
Ezetimibe and simvastatin	10/10 mg	-45	+8	-23
	10/20 mg	-52	+10	-24
	10/40 mg	-55	+6	-23
	10/80 mg	-60	+6	-31
Niacin and lovastatin	1000/20 mg	-30	+20	-32
	1000/40 mg	-36	+20	-39
	1500/40 mg	-37	+27	-44
	2000/40 mg	-42	+30	-44

[1]May increase LDL in some patients.

Recommended Liver Function Monitoring for HMG-CoA Reductase Inhibitors

Agent	Initial and After Elevation in Dose	6 Weeks[1]	12 Weeks[1]	Periodically
Atorvastatin (Lipitor®)	x		x	x
Fluvastatin (Lescol®)	x		x	x
Lovastatin (Mevacor®)	x	x	x	x
Pravastatin (Pravachol®)	x			x
Simvastatin (Zocor®)	x			x

[1]After initiation of therapy or any elevation in dose.

NARCOTIC AGONISTS

Comparative Pharmacokinetics

Drug	Onset (min)	Peak (h)	Duration (h)	Half-Life (h)	Average Dosing Interval (h)	Equianalgesic Doses[1] (mg) I.M.	Equianalgesic Doses[1] (mg) Oral
Alfentanil	Immediate	ND	ND	1-2	—	ND	NA
Buprenorphine	15	1	4-8	2-3	—	0.4	—
Butorphanol	I.M.: 30-60; I.V.: 4-5	0.5-1	3-5	2.5-3.5	3 (3-6)	2	—
Codeine	P.O.: 30-60; I.M.: 10-30	0.5-1	4-6	3-4	3 (3-6)	120	200
Fentanyl	I.M.: 7-15 I.V.: Immediate	ND	1-2	1.5-6	1 (0.5-2)	0.1	NA
Hydrocodone	ND	ND	4-8	3.3-4.4	6 (4-8)	ND	ND
Hydromorphone	P.O.: 15-30	0.5-1	4-6	2-4	4 (3-6)	1.5	7.5
Levorphanol	P.O.: 10-60	0.5-1	4-8	12-16	6 (6-24)	2 (A) 1 (C)	4 (A) 1 (C)
Meperidine	P.O./I.M./SubQ: 10-15 I.V.: ≤5	0.5-1	2-4	3-4	3 (2-4)	75	300
Methadone	P.O.: 30-60; I.V.: 10-20	0.5-1	4-6 (A) >8 (C)	15-30	8 (6-12)	10 (A) 2-4 (C)	20 (A) 2-4 (C)
Morphine	P.O.: 15-60 I.V.: ≤5	P.O./I.M./SubQ: 0.5-1; I.V.: 0.3	3-6	2-4	4 (3-6)	10	60[2] (A) 30 (C)
Nalbuphine	I.M.: 30; I.V.: 1-3	1	3-6	5	—	10	—
Oxycodone	P.O.: 10-15	0.5-1	4-6	3-4	4 (3-6)	NA	20
Oxymorphone	5-15	0.5-1	3-6	—	—	1	10
Pentazocine	15-20	0.25-1	3-4	2-3	3 (3-6)		
Propoxyphene	P.O.: 30-60	2-2.5	4-6	3.5-15	6 (4-8)	ND	130[3]-200[4]
Remifentanil	1-3	<0.3	0.1-0.2	0.15-0.3	—	ND	ND
Sufentanil	1.3-3	ND	ND	2.5-3	—	0.02	NA

ND = no data available. NA = not applicable. (A) = acute, (C) = chronic.

[1] Based on acute, short-term use. Chronic administration may alter pharmacokinetics and decrease the oral parenteral dose ratio. The morphine oral-parenteral ratio decreases to ~1.5-2.5:1 upon chronic dosing.

[2] Extensive survey data suggest that the relative potency of I.M.:P.O. morphine of 1:6 changes to 1:2-3 with chronic dosing.

[3] HCl salt.

[4] Napsylate salt.

Adapted from *Principles of Analgesic Use in the Treatment of Acute Pain and Cancer Pain*, 4th ed, Skokie, IL: The American Pain Society, 1999.

Comparative Pharmacology

Drug	Analgesic	Antitussive	Constipation	Respiratory Depression	Sedation	Emesis
Phenanthrenes						
Codeine	+	+++	+	+	+	+
Hydrocodone	+	+++		+		
Hydromorphone	++	+++	+	++	+	+
Levorphanol	++	++	++	++	++	+
Morphine	++	+++	++	++	++	++
Oxycodone	++	+++	++	++	++	++
Oxymorphone	++	+	++	+++		+++
Phenylpiperidines						
Alfentanil	++					
Fentanyl	++			+		+
Meperidine	++	+	+	++	+	
Remifentanil	++			++	++	++
Sufentanil	+++					
Diphenylheptanes						
Methadone	++	++	++	++	+	+
Propoxyphene	+			+	+	+
Agonist / Antagonist						
Buprenorphine	++	N/A	++	++	++	++
Butorphanol	++	N/A	++	+++	++	+
Nalbuphine	++	N/A	+++	+++	++	++
Pentazocine	++	N/A	+	++	++ or stimulation	++

NEUROMUSCULAR-BLOCKING AGENTS

Suggested Dosing Guidelines for the Use of Neuromuscular-Blocking Agents in the Intensive Care Unit

Agent	Intermittent Injection	Continuous Infusion
Short Duration		
Mivacurium	0.15-0.25 mg/kg followed by 0.1 mg/kg every 15 minutes	1-15 mcg/kg/min
Intermediate Duration		
Atracurium	0.4-0.5 mg/kg every 25-35 minutes	0.4-1 mg/kg/h
Cisatracurium (Nimbex®)	0.15-0.2 mg/kg every 40-60 minutes	0.03-0.6 mg/kg/h
Rocuronium (Zemuron®)	0.6 mg/kg every 30 minutes	0.6 mg/kg/h
Vecuronium	0.1 mg/kg every 35-45 minutes	0.05-0.1 mg/kg/h
Long Duration		
Doxacurium (Nuromax®)	0.025 mg/kg every 2-3 hours	0.015-0.045 mg/kg/h
Pancuronium	0.1 mg/kg every 90-100 minutes	0.05-0.1 mg/kg/h

Pharmacokinetic and Pharmacodynamic Properties of Neuromuscular Blocking Agents

Agent	Clearance (mL/kg/min)	V_{dss} (L/kg)	Half-life (min)	ED95[1] (mg/kg)	Initial Adult Dose[2,3] (mg/kg)	Onset (min)	Clinical Duration of Action of Initial Dose (min)	Administration as an Intraoperative Infusion (mcg/kg/min)
Ultra-Short Duration								
Succinylcholine	Unknown	Unknown	Unknown	0.2	1-1.5	0.5-1	4-8	10-100
Short Duration								
Mivacurium	50-100[2]	0.2	2[4]	0.07	0.15-0.25	1.5-3	12-20	1-15
Intermediate Duration								
Atracurium	5-7	0.2	20	0.2	0.4-0.5	2-3	20-45	4-12
Cisatracurium	4.6	0.15	22-29	0.05	0.15-0.2	2-3	40-60	1-3
Rocuronium	4	0.17-0.29	60-70	0.3	0.6-1.2	1-1.5	31-67	4-16
Vecuronium	4.5	0.16-0.27	51-80	0.05	0.08-0.1	2-3	20-40	0.8-2
Long Duration								
Doxacurium	1-2.5	0.2	100-200	0.025	0.05-0.08	4-6	100-160	n/a
Pancuronium	1-2	0.18-0.26	107-169	0.07	0.08-0.1	3-5	60-100	n/a

[1]ED95: Effective dose causing 95% blockade.

[2]Initial dose (intubation dose) is usually 2 x ED95 with the exception of cisatracurium where the recommended initial dose is 3-4 x ED95.

[3]Prior administration of succinylcholine generally enhances the magnitude and duration of nondepolarizing NMB agents; initial doses should be lower.

[4]Values reflect contribution of cis-trans and trans-trans isomers only.

NICOTINE PRODUCTS

Dosage Form	Brand Name	Dosing	Recommended Treatment Duration	Strengths Available
Lozenge	Commit™ (OTC)	Patients who smoke their first cigarette within 30 minutes of waking should use the 4 mg strength; otherwise the 2 mg strength is recommended. 1-6 wk: One lozenge q1-2h 7-9 wk: One lozenge q2-4h 10-12 wk: One lozenge q4-8h	~12 wk	2 mg, 4 mg
Chewing gum	Nicorette® (OTC)	Chew 1 piece q1-2h for 6 wk, then decrease to 1 piece q2-4h for 3 wk, then 1 piece q4-8h for 3 wk, then discontinue.	~12 wk	2 mg, 4 mg
Transdermal	Nicoderm CQ® (OTC)	One 21 mg/d patch qd for 6 wk, then one 14 mg/d patch qd for 2 wk, then one 7 mg/d patch qd for 2 wk, then discontinue. Low-dose regimen[1]: One 14 mg/d patch qd for 6 wk, then one 7 mg/d patch qd for 2 wk, then discontinue.	~10 wk	Patch: 21 mg/d 14 mg/d 7 mg/d
	Nicotrol®	One 15 mg patch qd, worn for 16 h/d and removed for 8 h/d for a total of 6 wk, then discontinue.	~6 wk	Patch: 15 mg/16 h 10 mg/16 h 5 mg/16 h
Nasal spray	Nicotrol® NS	One dose is 2 sprays (1 spray in each nostril). Initial dose: 1-2 sprays q1h, should not exceed 10 sprays (5 doses)/h or 80 sprays (40 doses)/d.	~12 wk	10 mL spray 0.5/mg spray (200 actuations)
Inhaler	Nicotrol®	Inhaler releases 4 mg nicotine (the equivalent of 2 cigarettes smoked) for 20 min of active inhaler puffing. Usual dose: 6-16 cartridges/d for up to 12 wk, then reduce dose gradually over ensuing 12 wk, then discontinue.	~18-24 wk	10 mg/ cartridge: releases 4 mg/ cartridge

[1]Transdermal low-dose regimens are intended for patients <100 lb, smoke <10 cigarettes/day, and/or have a history of cardiovascular disease.

NITRATES

Nitrates[1]	Dosage Form	Onset (min)	Duration
Nitroglycerin	I.V.	1-2	3-5 min
	Sublingual	1-3	30-60 min
	Translingual spray	2	30-60 min
	Oral, sustained release	40	4-8 h
	Topical ointment	20-60	2-12 h
	Transdermal	40-60	18-24 h
Isosorbide dinitrate	Sublingual and chewable	2-5	1-2 h
	Oral	20-40	4-6 h
	Oral, sustained release	Slow	8-12 h
Isosorbide mononitrate	Oral	60-120	5-12 h

[1]Hemodynamic and antianginal tolerance often develops within 24-48 hours of continuous nitrate administration.

Adapted from Corwin S and Reiffel JA, "Nitrate Therapy for Angina Pectoris," *Arch Intern Med*, 1985, 145:538-43 and Franciosa JA, "Nitroglycerin and Nitrates in Congestive Heart Failure," *Heart and Lung*, 1980, 9(5):873-82.

NONSTEROIDAL ANTI-INFLAMMATORY AGENTS

Comparative Dosages and Pharmacokinetics

Drug	Maximum Recommended Daily Dose (mg)	Time to Peak Levels (h)[1]	Half-life (h)
Acetic Acids			
Diclofenac potassium immediate release (Cataflam®)	200	1	1-2
Diclofenac sodium delayed release (Voltaren®)	225	2-3	1-2
Etodolac	1200	1-2	7.3
Indomethacin (Indocin®)	200	1-2	4.5
Indomethacin sustained release (Indocin® SR)	150	2-4	4.5-6
Ketorolac (Toradol®)	I.M.: 120[2] P.O.: 40	0.5-1	3.8-8.6
Sulindac (Clinoril®)	400	2-4	7.8 (16.4)[3]
Tolmetin (Tolectin®)	2000	0.5-1	1-1.5
Fenamates (Anthranilic Acids)			
Meclofenamate	400	0.5-1	2 (3.3)[4]
Mefenamic acid (Ponstel®)	1000	2-4	2-4
Propionic Acids			
Fenoprofen (Nalfon®)	3200	1-2	2-3
Flurbiprofen	300	1.5	5.7
Ibuprofen (various)	3200	1-2	1.8-2.5
Ketoprofen	300	0.5-2	2-4
Naproxen (Naprosyn®)	1500	2-4	12-15
Naproxen sodium (Anaprox®, others)	1375	1-2	12-13
Oxaprozin (Daypro®)	1800	3-5	42-50
Nonacidic Agent			
Nabumetone	2000	3-6	24
Salicylic Acid Derivative			
Diflunisal	1500	2-3	8-12
Salsalate	3000	2-3	7-8
COX-2 Inhibitor			
Celecoxib (Celebrex®)	400	3	11
Oxicam			
Meloxicam (Mobic®)	15	4-5	15-20
Piroxicam (Feldene®)	20	3-5	30-86

Dosage is based on 70 kg adult with normal hepatic and renal function.

[1]Food decreases the rate of absorption and may delay the time to peak levels.

[2]150 mg on the first day.

[3]Half-life of active sulfide metabolite.

[4]Half-life with multiple doses.

PARKINSON'S AGENTS

Drugs Used for the Treatment of Parkinson's Disease

Drug	Receptor Affinity	Initial Dose	Titration Schedule	Usual Daily Dosage	Recommended Dosing Schedule
Amantadine (Symmetrel®)	NMDA receptor antagonist and inhibits neuronal reuptake of dopamine	100 mg every other day	100 mg/dose every week, up to 300 mg 3 times/d	100–200 mg	Twice daily
Apomorphine (Apokyn™)	D_2 receptors (caudate-putamen)	1–2 mg	Complex; based or tolerance and response to test dose(s)	Variable; <20 mg	Individualized; 3–5 times/d prn
Benztropine (Cogentin®)	Cholinergic receptors, also has antihistamine effects	0.5–2 mg/d in 1–4 divided doses	0.5 mg/dose every 5–6 d	2–6 mg	1–2 times/d
Bromocriptine (Parlodel®)	Moderate affinity for D_2 and D_3 dopamine receptors	1.25 mg twice daily	2.5 mg/d every 2–4 wk	2.5–100 mg	3 times/d
Cabergoline (Dostinex®)[1]	Selective to D_2 dopamine receptors	0.5 mg once daily	0.25–0.5 mg/d every 4 wk	0.5–5 mg	Once daily
Entacapone (Comtan®)	COMT enzyme inhibitor	200 mg 3 times/d	Titrate down the doses of levodopa/carbidopa as required	600–1600 mg	3 times/d; up to 8 times/d
Levodopa/carbidopa (Sinemet® CR)	Converts to dopamine; binds to all CNS dopamine receptors	10–25/100 mg 2–4 times/d	0.5–1 tablet (10 or 25/100 mg) every 1–2 d	50/200 to 200/2000 mg (3–8 tablets)	3 times/d or twice daily (for controlled release)
Pergolide (Permax®)	Low affinity for D_1 and maximal affinity for D_2 and D_3 dopamine receptors	0.05 mg/night	0.1–0.15 mg/d every 3 d for 12 d, then 0.25 mg/d every 3 d	0.05–5 mg	3 times/d
Pramipexole (Mirapex®)	High affinity for D_2 and D_3 dopamine receptors	0.125 mg 3 times/d	0.125 mg/dose every 5–7 d	1.5–4.5 mg	3 times/d
Ropinirole (Requip®)	High affinity for D_2 and D_3 dopamine receptors	0.25 mg 3 times/d	0.25 mg/dose weekly for 4 wk, then 1.5 mg/d every week up to 9 mg/d; 3 mg/d up to a max of 24 mg/d	0.75–24 mg	3 times/d
Selegiline (Eldepryl®)	No receptor effects, inhibits monoamine oxidase	5–10 mg twice daily	Titrate down the doses of levodopa/carbidopa as required	5–10 mg	Twice daily
Tolcapone (Tasmar®)	COMT enzyme inhibitor	100 mg 3 times/d	Titrate down the doses of levodopa/carbidopa as required	300–600 mg	3 times/d
Trihexyphenidyl	Cholinergic receptors; also some direct effect	1–2 mg/d	2 mg/d at intervals of 3–5 d	5–15 mg	3–4 times/d

[1]Cabergoline is not FDA approved for the treatment of Parkinson's disease.

SELECTIVE SEROTONIN REUPTAKE INHIBITORS (SSRIs) PHARMACOKINETICS

SSRI	Half-life (h)	Metabolite Half-life	Peak Plasma Level (h)	% Protein Bound	Bioavailability (%)	Initial Dose
Citalopram (Celexa™)	35	S-desmethyl-citalopram 59 hours	4	80	80	20 mg qAM
Escitalopram (Lexapro™)	27-32	S-desmethyl-citalopram 59 hours	5	56	80	10 mg qAM
Fluoxetine (Prozac®, Prozac® Weekly™, Sarafem™)	Initial: 24-72 Chronic: 96-144	Norfluoxetine: 4-16 days	6-8	95	72	10-20 mg qAM
Fluvoxamine	16	N/A	3	80	53	50 mg qhs
Paroxetine (Paxil®, Paxil® CR™)	21	N/A	5	95	>90	10-20 mg qAM
Sertraline (Zoloft®)	26	N-desmethyl-sertraline: 62-104 hours	5-8	98	88	25-50 mg qAM

SULFONAMIDE DERIVATIVES

The following table lists commonly prescribed drugs which are either sulfonamide derivatives or are structurally similar to sulfonamides. Please note that the list may not be all inclusive. **Note:** The degree of cross-reaction between antibiotic sulfonamides (arylamine sulfonamides) and nonantibiotic sulfonamides is controversial.

Commonly Prescribed Drugs

Classification	Specific Drugs
Antimicrobial Agents	Mafenide acetate (Sulfamylon®) Silver sulfadiazine (Silvadene®) Sodium sulfacetamide Sulfadiazine Sulfamethoxazole (ie, Bactrim™ and co-trimoxazole) Sulfisoxazole (Gantrisin®)
Diuretics, Carbonic Anhydrase Inhibitors	Acetazolamide (Diamox®) Dichlorphenamide (Daranide®) Methazolamide
Diuretics, Loop	Bumetanide (Bumex®) Furosemide (Lasix®) Torsemide (Demadex®)
Diuretics, Thiazide	Chlorothiazide (Diuril®) Chlorthalidone (Thalitone®) Hydrochlorothiazide (various and combinations, eg, Dyazide®, Maxzide®) Indapamide Methyclothiazide Metolazone (Zaroxolyn®) Polythiazide (Renese®)
Hypoglycemic Agents, Oral	Chlorpropamide (Diabinese®) Glimepiride (Amaryl®) Glipizide (Glucotrol®) Glyburide (DiaBeta®, Glynase®, Micronase®) Tolazamide Tolbutamide
Other Agents	Celecoxib (Celebrex®) Dapsone Sulfasalazine (Azulfidine®) Sumatriptan (Imitrex®) Zonisamide (Zonegran®)

THIAZOLIDINEDIONES

Lipid Effects

Parameter	Pioglitazone (Actos®)	Rosiglitazone (Avandia®)
LDL	No significant change	↑ up to 12.1%
HDL	↑ up to 13%	↑ up to 18.5%
Total cholesterol	No significant change	↑
Total cholesterol/HDL ratio	–	–
LDL/HDL ratio	–	No change
Triglycerides	↓ up to 28%	Variable effects

Thiazolidinedione Pharmacokinetics

Parameter	Pioglitazone (Actos®)	Rosiglitazone (Avandia®)
Absorption	Food slightly delays but does not alter the extent of absorption	Absolute bioavailability is 99% Food ↓ C_{max} and delays T_{max}, but not change in AUC
C_{max}	156-342 ng/mL	–
T_{max}	2 hours	1 hour
Distribution	0.63 ± 0.41 L/kg	17.6 L
Plasma protein binding	>99% to serum albumin	99.8% to serum albumin
Metabolism	Extensive liver metabolism by hydroxylation and oxidation. Some metabolites are pharmacologically active. CYP2C8 and CYP3A4 metabolism	Extensive metabolism via N-demethylation and hydroxylation with no unchanged drug excreted in the urine CYP2C8 and some CYP2C9 metabolism
Excretion	Urine (15% to 30%) and bile	Urine (64%) and feces (23%)
Half-life	3-6 hours (pioglitazone) 16-24 hours (pioglitazone and metabolites)	3.15-3.59 hours
Effect of hemodialysis	Not removed	Not removed

Thiazolidinedione Derivatives Approved Indications

Indication	Pioglitazone (Actos®)	Rosiglitazone (Avandia®)
Monotherapy	x	x
Combination Therapy – Dual Therapy		
Combination with sulfonylureas	x	x
Combination therapy with metformin (Glucophage®)	x	x
Combination therapy with insulin	x	x
Combination Therapy – Triple Therapy		
Combination therapy with sulfonylureas and metformin (Glucophage®)	–	x

CYTOCHROME P450 ENZYMES: SUBSTRATES, INHIBITORS, AND INDUCERS

INTRODUCTION

Most drugs are eliminated from the body, at least in part, by being chemically altered to less lipid-soluble products (ie, metabolized), and thus are more likely to be excreted via the kidneys or the bile. Phase I metabolism includes drug hydrolysis, oxidation, and reduction, and results in drugs that are more polar in their chemical structure, while Phase II metabolism involves the attachment of an additional molecule onto the drug (or partially metabolized drug) in order to create an inactive and/or more water soluble compound. Phase II processes include (primarily) glucuronidation, sulfation, glutathione conjugation, acetylation, and methylation.

Virtually any of the Phase I and II enzymes can be inhibited by some xenobiotic or drug. Some of the Phase I and II enzymes can be induced. Inhibition of the activity of metabolic enzymes will result in increased concentrations of the substrate (drug), whereas induction of the activity of metabolic enzymes will result in decreased concentrations of the substrate. For example, the well-documented enzyme-inducing effects of phenobarbital may include a combination of Phase I and II enzymes. Phase II glucuronidation may be increased via induced UDP-glucuronosyltransferase (UGT) activity, whereas Phase I oxidation may be increased via induced cytochrome P450 (CYP) activity. However, for most drugs, the primary route of metabolism (and the primary focus of drug-drug interaction) is Phase I oxidation, and specifically, metabolism.

CYP enzymes may be responsible for the metabolism (at least partial metabolism) of approximately 75% of all drugs, with the CYP3A subfamily responsible for nearly half of this activity. Found throughout plant, animal, and bacterial species, CYP enzymes represent a superfamily of xenobiotic metabolizing proteins. There have been several hundred CYP enzymes identified in nature, each of which has been assigned to a family (1, 2, 3, etc), subfamily (A, B, C, etc), and given a specific enzyme number (1, 2, 3, etc) according to the similarity in amino acid sequence that it shares with other enzymes. Of these many enzymes, only a few are found in humans, and even fewer appear to be involved in the metabolism of xenobiotics (eg, drugs). The key human enzyme subfamilies include CYP1A, CYP2A, CYP2B, CYP2C, CYP2D, CYP2E, and CYP3A.

CYP enzymes are found in the endoplasmic reticulum of cells in a variety of human tissues (eg, skin, kidneys, brain, lungs), but their predominant sites of concentration and activity are the liver and intestine. Though the abundance of CYP enzymes throughout the body is relatively equally distributed among the various subfamilies, the relative contribution to drug metabolism is (in decreasing order of magnitude) CYP3A4 (nearly 50%), CYP2D6 (nearly 25%), CYP2C8/9 (nearly 15%), then CYP1A2, CYP2C19, CYP2A6, and CYP2E1. Owing to their potential for numerous drug-drug interactions, those drugs that are identified in preclinical studies as substrates of CYP3A enzymes are often given a lower priority for continued research and development in favor of drugs that appear to be less affected by (or less likely to affect) this enzyme subfamily.

Each enzyme subfamily possesses unique selectivity toward potential substrates. For example, CYP1A2 preferentially binds medium-sized, planar, lipophilic molecules, while CYP2D6 preferentially binds molecules that possess a basic nitrogen atom. Some CYP subfamilies exhibit polymorphism (ie, multiple allelic variants that manifest differing catalytic properties). The best described polymorphisms involve CYP2C9, CYP2C19, and CYP2D6. Individuals possessing "wild type" gene alleles exhibit normal functioning CYP capacity. Others, however, possess allelic variants that leave the person with a subnormal level of catalytic potential (so called "poor metabolizers"). Poor metabolizers would be more likely to experience toxicity from drugs metabolized by the affected enzymes (or less effects if the enzyme is responsible for converting a prodrug to it's active form as in the case of codeine). The percentage of people classified as poor metabolizers varies by enzyme and population group. As an example, approximately 7% of Caucasians and only about 1% of Orientals appear to be CYP2D6 poor metabolizers.

CYP enzymes can be both inhibited and induced by other drugs, leading to increased or decreased serum concentrations (along with the associated effects), respectively. Induction occurs when a drug causes an increase in the amount of smooth endoplasmic reticulum, secondary to increasing the amount of the affected CYP enzymes in the tissues. This "revving up" of the CYP enzyme system may take several days to reach peak activity, and likewise, may take several days, even months, to return to normal following discontinuation of the inducing agent.

CYP inhibition occurs via several potential mechanisms. Most commonly, a CYP inhibitor competitively (and reversibly) binds to the active site on the enzyme, thus preventing the substrate from binding to the same site, and preventing the substrate from being metabolized. The affinity of an inhibitor for an enzyme may be expressed by an inhibition constant (Ki) or IC50 (defined as the concentration of the inhibitor required to cause 50% inhibition under a given set of conditions). In addition to reversible

CYTOCHROME P450 ENZYMES: SUBSTRATES, INHIBITORS, AND INDUCERS *(Continued)*

competition for an enzyme site, drugs may inhibit enzyme activity by binding to sites on the enzyme other than that to which the substrate would bind, and thereby cause a change in the functionality or physical structure of the enzyme. A drug may also bind to the enzyme in an irreversible (ie, "suicide") fashion. In such a case, it is not the concentration of drug at the enzyme site that is important (constantly binding and releasing), but the number of molecules available for binding (once bound, always bound).

Although an inhibitor or inducer may be known to affect a variety of CYP subfamilies, it may only inhibit one or two in a clinically important fashion. Likewise, although a substrate is known to be at least partially metabolized by a variety of CYP enzymes, only one or two enzymes may contribute significantly enough to its overall metabolism to warrant concern when used with potential inducers or inhibitors. Therefore, when attempting to predict the level of risk of using two drugs that may affect each other via altered CYP function, it is important to identify the relative effectiveness of the inhibiting/inducing drug on the CYP subfamilies that significantly contribute to the metabolism of the substrate. The contribution of a specific CYP pathway to substrate metabolism should be considered not only in light of other known CYP pathways, but also other nonoxidative pathways for substrate metabolism (eg, glucuronidation) and transporter proteins (eg, P-glycoprotein) that may affect the presentation of a substrate to a metabolic pathway.

HOW TO USE THE TABLES

The following CYP SUBSTRATES, INHIBITORS, and INDUCERS tables provide a clinically relevant perspective on drugs that are affected by, or affect, cytochrome P450 (CYP) enzymes. Not all human, drug-metabolizing CYP enzymes are specifically (or separately) included in the tables. Some enzymes have been excluded because they do not appear to significantly contribute to the metabolism of marketed drugs (eg, CYP2C18). In the case of CYP3A4, the industry routinely uses this single enzyme designation to represent all enzymes in the CYP3A subfamily. CYP3A7 is present in fetal livers. It is effectively absent from adult livers. CYP3A4 (adult) and CYP3A7 (fetal) appear to share similar properties in their respective hosts. The impact of CYP3A7 in fetal and neonatal drug interactions has not been investigated.

The **CYP Substrates table** contains a list of drugs reported to be metabolized, at least in part, by one or more CYP enzymes. An enzyme that appears to play a clinically significant (major) role in a drug's metabolism is indicated by "●", and an enzyme whose role appears to be clinically insignificant (minor) is indicated by "○". A clinically significant designation is the result of a two-phase review. The first phase considered the contribution of each CYP enzyme to the overall metabolism of the drug. The enzyme pathway was considered potentially clinically relevant if it was responsible for at least 30% of the metabolism of the drug. If so, the drug was subjected to a second phase. The second phase considered the clinical relevance of a substrate's concentration being increased twofold, or decreased by one-half (such as might be observed if combined with an effective CYP inhibitor or inducer, respectively). If either of these changes was considered to present a clinically significant concern, the CYP pathway for the drug was designated "major." If neither change would appear to present a clinically significant concern, or if the CYP enzyme was responsible for a smaller portion of the overall metabolism (ie, <30%), the pathway was designated "minor."

The **CYP Inhibitors table** contains a list of drugs that are reported to inhibit one or more CYP enzymes. Enzymes that are strongly inhibited by a drug are indicated by "●". Enzymes that are moderately inhibited are indicated by "◑". Enzymes that are weakly inhibited are indicated by "○". The designations are the result of a review of published clinical reports, available Ki data, and assessments published by other experts in the field. As it pertains to Ki values set in a ratio with achievable serum drug concentrations ([I]) under normal dosing conditions, the following parameters were employed: $[I]/K_i \geq 1$ = strong; $[I]/K_i$ 0.1-1 = moderate; $[I]/K_i$ <0.1 = weak.

The **CYP Inducers table** contains a list of drugs that are reported to induce one or more CYP enzymes. Enzymes that appear to be effectively induced by a drug are indicated by "●", and enzymes that do not appear to be effectively induced are indicated by "○". The designations are the result of a review of published clinical reports and assessments published by experts in the field.

In general, clinically significant interactions are more likely to occur between substrates and either inhibitors or inducers of the same enzyme(s), all of which have been indicated by "●". However, these assessments possess a degree of subjectivity, at times based on limited indications regarding the significance of CYP effects of particular agents. An attempt has been made to balance a conservative, clinically-sensitive presentation of the data with a desire to avoid the numbing effect of a "beware of everything" approach. Even so, other potential interactions (ie, those involving enzymes indicated by "○") may warrant consideration in some cases. It is important to note that information related to CYP metabolism of drugs is expanding at a rapid pace, and thus, the contents of this table should only be considered to represent a "snapshot" of the information available at the time of publication.

Selected Readings

Bjornsson TD, Callaghan JT, Einolf HJ, et al, "The Conduct of *in vitro* and *in vivo* Drug-Drug Interaction Studies: A PhRMA Perspective," *J Clin Pharmacol*, 2003, 43(5):443-69.

Drug-Drug Interactions, Rodrigues AD, ed, New York, NY: Marcel Dekker, Inc, 2002.

Levy RH, Thummel KE, Trager WF, et al, eds, *Metabolic Drug Interactions*, Philadelphia, PA: Lippincott Williams & Wilkins, 2000.

Michalets EL, "Update: Clinically Significant Cytochrome P-450 Drug Interactions," *Pharmacotherapy*, 1998, 18(1):84-112.

Thummel KE and Wilkinson GR, "*In vitro* and *in vivo* Drug Interactions Involving Human CYP3A," *Annu Rev Pharmacol Toxicol*, 1998, 38:389-430.

Zhang Y and Benet LZ, "The Gut as a Barrier to Drug Absorption: Combined Role of Cytochrome P450 3A and P-Glycoprotein," *Clin Pharmacokinet*, 2001, 40(3):159-68.

Selected Websites

http://www.gentest.com
http://www.imm.ki.se/CYPalleles
http://medicine.iupui.edu/flockhart
http://www.mhc.com/Cytochromes

CYP Substrates

● = major substrate
○ = minor substrate

Drug	1A2	2A6	2B6	2C8	2C9	2C19	2D6	2E1	3A4
Acenocoumarol	●				●	○			
Acetaminophen	○	○			○		○	○	○
Albendazole	○								○
Albuterol									●
Alfentanil									●
Almotriptan							○		○
Alosetron	○				●				○
Alprazolam									●
Aminophylline	●						○		○
Amiodarone	○			●		○	○		
Amitriptyline	○		○		○	○	●		○
Amlodipine									●
Amoxapine							●		
Amphetamine							○		
Amprenavir					○				●
Aprepitant	○					○			●
Argatroban									○
Aripiprazole							●		●
Aspirin					○				
Atazanavir									●
Atomoxetine							○	●	
Atorvastatin									●
Azelastine	○						○	○	○
Azithromycin									○
Benzphetamine			○						●
Benztropine							○		
Betaxolol	●						●		
Bexarotene									○
Bezafibrate									○
Bisoprolol							○		●
Bortezomib	○				○	○	○		●
Bosentan					●				●
Brinzolamide									○
Bromazepam									●
Bromocriptine									●
Budesonide									●
Bupivacaine	○						○	○	○
Buprenorphine									●
BuPROPion	○	○	●		○		○	○	○
BusPIRone							○		●
Busulfan									●
Caffeine	●				○		○	○	○
Candesartan					○				
Capsaicin								○	
Captopril							●		
Carbamazepine			○						●
Carisoprodol						●			
Carteolol							○		
Carvedilol	○				●		●	○	○
Celecoxib					●				○
Cerivastatin									●
Cetirizine									○
Cevimeline							○		●
Chlordiazepoxide									●

CYTOCHROME P450 ENZYMES: SUBSTRATES, INHIBITORS, AND INDUCERS (Continued)

CYP Substrates (continued)

Drug	1A2	2A6	2B6	2C8	2C9	2C19	2D6	2E1	3A4
Chloroquine							●		●
Chlorpheniramine							○		●
ChlorproMAZINE	○						●		○
ChlorproPAMIDE					○				
Chlorzoxazone	○	○					○	●	○
Cilostazol	○					●	○		●
Cinacalcet	○						○		○
Cisapride	○	○	○		○	○			●
Citalopram						●	○		●
Clarithromycin									●
Clobazam						●			●
Clofibrate									○
ClomiPRAMINE	●					●	●		○
Clonazepam									●
Clopidogrel	○								○
Clorazepate									●
Clozapine	●	○			○	○	○		○
Cocaine									●
Codeine[1]							●		○
Colchicine									●
Conivaptan									●
Cyclobenzaprine	●						○		○
Cyclophosphamide[2]		○	●		○	○			●
CycloSPORINE									●
Dacarbazine	●							●	
Dantrolene									●
Dapsone				○	●	○		○	●
Delavirdine							○		●
Desipramine	○						●		
Desogestrel						●			
Dexamethasone									○
Dexmedetomidine		●							
Dextroamphetamine							●		
Dextromethorphan		○			○	○	●		○
Diazepam	○		○		○	●			●
Diclofenac	○		○	○	○	○	○		○
Digoxin									○
Dihydrocodeine[1]							●		
Dihydroergotamine									●
Diltiazem					○		○		●
Dirithromycin									○
Disopyramide									●
Disulfiram	○	○	○				○	○	○
Docetaxel									●
Dofetilide									○
Dolasetron						○			○
Domperidone									○
Donepezil							○		○
Dorzolamide					○				○
Doxepin	●						●		●
DOXOrubicin							●		●
Doxycycline									●
Drospirenone									○
Duloxetine	●						●		
Dutasteride									○
Efavirenz			●						●
Eletriptan									●
Enalapril									●
Enflurane								●	
Eplerenone									●
Ergoloid mesylates									●
Ergonovine									●
Ergotamine									●
Erythromycin			○						●
Escitalopram						●			●
Esomeprazole						●			○
Estazolam									○
Estradiol	●	○	○		○	○	○	○	●
Estrogens, conjugated A/synthetic	●	○	○		○	○	○	○	●

1902

CYP Substrates (continued)

Drug	1A2	2A6	2B6	2C8	2C9	2C19	2D6	2E1	3A4
Estrogens, conjugated equine	●	○	○		○	○	○	○	●
Estrogens, conjugated esterified	●		○		○			○	●
Estrone	●		○		○			○	●
Estropipate	●		○		○			○	●
Ethinyl estradiol					○				●
Ethosuximide									●
Etonogestrel									○
Etoposide	○						○		●
Exemestane									●
Felbamate							○		●
Felodipine									●
Fenofibrate									○
Fentanyl									●
Fexofenadine									○
Finasteride									○
Flecainide	○						●		
Fluoxetine	○		○		●	○	●	○	○
Fluphenazine							●		
Flurazepam									●
Flurbiprofen					○				
Flutamide	●								●
Fluticasone									●
Fluvastatin					○		○		○
Fluvoxamine	●						●		
Formoterol		○			○	○	○		
Fosamprenavir (as amprenavir)					○				●
Fosphenytoin (as phenytoin)					●	●			○
Frovatriptan	○								
Fulvestrant									○
Galantamine							○		○
Gefitinib									●
Gemfibrozil									○
Glimepiride					●				
GlipiZIDE					●				
Granisetron									○
Guanabenz	●								
Halazepam									○
Haloperidol	○						●		●
Halothane		○	○		○		○	●	○
Hydrocodone[1]							●		
Hydrocortisone									○
Ibuprofen					○	○			
Ifosfamide[3]		○	○	○	○	○			●
Imatinib	○				○	○	○		●
Imipramine	○		○			●	●		○
Imiquimod	○								○
Indinavir							○		●
Indomethacin					○	○			
Irbesartan					○				
Irinotecan			●						●
Isoflurane								●	
Isoniazid								●	
Isosorbide									●
Isosorbide dinitrate									●
Isosorbide mononitrate									●
Isradipine									●
Itraconazole									●
Ivermectin									○
Ketamine			●		●				●
Ketoconazole									●
Labetalol							●		
Lansoprazole					○	●			●
Letrozole		○							●
Levobupivacaine	○								○
Levonorgestrel									●
Lidocaine	○	○	○		○		●		●
Lomustine							●		
Lopinavir									○
Loratadine							○		○
Losartan					●				●
Lovastatin									●

CYTOCHROME P450 ENZYMES: SUBSTRATES, INHIBITORS, AND INDUCERS (Continued)

CYP Substrates (continued)

Drug	1A2	2A6	2B6	2C8	2C9	2C19	2D6	2E1	3A4
Maprotiline							●		
MedroxyPROGESTERone									●
Mefenamic acid					○				
Mefloquine									●
Meloxicam					○				○
Mephobarbital			○		○	●			
Mestranol[4]					●				●
Methadone					○	○	○		●
Methamphetamine							●		
Methoxsalen		○							
Methsuximide						●			
Methylergonovine									●
Methylphenidate							●		
MethylPREDNISolone									○
Metoclopramide	○						○		
Metoprolol						○	●		
Mexiletine	●						●		
Miconazole									●
Midazolam			○						●
Mifepristone									○
Miglustat									●
Mirtazapine	●				○		●		●
Moclobemide						●	●		
Modafinil									●
Mometasone furoate									○
Montelukast					●				●
Moricizine									●
Morphine sulfate							○		
Naproxen	○				○				
Nateglinide					●				●
Nefazodone							●		●
Nelfinavir					○	●	○		●
Nevirapine			○				○		●
NiCARdipine	○				○		○	○	●
Nicotine	○	○	○		○	○	○	○	○
NIFEdipine							○		●
Nilutamide							●		
Nimodipine									●
Nisoldipine									●
Norelgestromin									○
Norethindrone									●
Norgestrel									●
Nortriptyline	○					○	●		○
Olanzapine	○						○		
Omeprazole		○			○	●	○		○
Ondansetron	○				○		○	○	●
Orphenadrine	○		○				○		○
Oxybutynin									○
Oxycodone[1]							●		
Paclitaxel				●	●				●
Palonosetron	○						○		○
Pantoprazole						●			○
Paroxetine							●		
Pentamidine							●		
Pergolide									●
Perphenazine	○				○	○	●		○
Phencyclidine									●
Phenobarbital					○	●		○	
Phenytoin					●	●			○
Pimecrolimus									○
Pimozide	●								●
Pindolol							●		
Pioglitazone				●					○
Pipotiazine							●		●
Piroxicam					○				
Pravastatin									○
PrednisoLONE									○
PredniSONE									○
Primaquine									●
Procainamide							●		

CYP Substrates *(continued)*

Drug	1A2	2A6	2B6	2C8	2C9	2C19	2D6	2E1	3A4
Progesterone	○	○			○	●	○		●
Proguanil	○					○			○
Promethazine			●				●		
Propafenone	○						●		○
Propofol	○	○	●		●	○	○	○	○
Propranolol	●					○	●		○
Protriptyline							●		
Quazepam									○
Quetiapine							○		●
Quinidine					○			○	●
Quinine	○					○			○
Rabeprazole						●			●
Ranitidine	○					○	○		
Ranolazine							○		●
Repaglinide				●					●
Rifabutin									●
Riluzole	●								
Risperidone							●		○
Ritonavir	○		○				○		●
Rofecoxib					○				
Ropinirole	●								○
Ropivacaine	○		○				○		○
Rosiglitazone				●	○				
Rosuvastatin					○				○
Salmeterol									●
Saquinavir							○		●
Selegiline	○	○	●	○		○	○		○
Sertraline			○		○	●	○		○
Sevoflurane		○	○					●	○
Sibutramine									●
Sildenafil					○				●
Simvastatin									●
Sirolimus									●
Sorafenib									○
Spiramycin									●
Sufentanil									●
SulfaDIAZINE					●			○	○
Sulfamethoxazole					●				○
Sulfinpyrazone					●				○
SulfiSOXAZOLE					●				
Sunitinib									●
Tacrine	●								
Tacrolimus									●
Tamoxifen		○	○		●		●	○	●
Tamsulosin							●		●
Telithromycin	○								●
Temazepam			○		○	○			○
Teniposide									●
Terbinafine	○				○	○			○
Testosterone			○		○	○			○
Tetracycline									●
Theophylline	●				○		○	●	●
Thiabendazole	○								
Thioridazine						○	●		
Thiothixene	●								
Tiagabine									●
Ticlopidine									●
Timolol							●		
Tinidazole									○
Tiotropium							○		○
Tipranavir									●
TOLBUTamide					●	○			
Tolcapone		○							○
Tolterodine						○	●		●
Toremifene	○								●
Torsemide				○	●				
Tramadol[1]			○				●		○
Trazodone							○		●
Tretinoin		○	○	●	○				
Triazolam									●
Trifluoperazine	●								
Trimethadione					○	○		●	○
Trimethoprim					●				●

CYTOCHROME P450 ENZYMES: SUBSTRATES, INHIBITORS, AND INDUCERS (Continued)

CYP Substrates (continued)

Drug	1A2	2A6	2B6	2C8	2C9	2C19	2D6	2E1	3A4
Trimipramine						●	●		●
Troleandomycin									●
Valdecoxib					○				○
Valproic acid		○	○		○	○		○	
Vardenafil									●
Venlafaxine					○	○	●		●
Verapamil	○		○				○		●
VinBLAStine							○		●
VinCRIStine									●
Vinorelbine							○		●
Voriconazole					●	●			○
Warfarin	○				●	○			○
Yohimbine							○		
Zafirlukast					●				
Zaleplon									○
Zidovudine		○			○	○			○
Zileuton	○				○				○
Ziprasidone	○								○
Zolmitriptan	○								
Zolpidem	○				○	○	○		●
Zonisamide						○			●
Zopiclone					●				●
Zuclopenthixol							●		

[1]This opioid analgesic is bioactivated in vivo via CYP2D6. Inhibiting this enzyme would decrease the effects of the analgesic. The active metabolite might also affect, or be affected by, CYP enzymes.
[2]Cyclophosphamide is bioactivated in vivo to acrolein via CYP2B6 and 3A4. Inhibiting these enzymes would decrease the effects of cyclophosphamide.
[3]Ifosfamide is bioactivated in vivo to acrolein via CYP3A4. Inhibiting this enzyme would decrease the effects of ifosfamide.
[4]Mestranol is bioactivated in vivo to ethinyl estradiol via CYP2C8/9. See Ethinyl Estradiol for additional CYP information.

CYP Inhibitors

● = strong inhibitor
◐ = moderate inhibitor
○ = weak inhibitor

Drug	1A2	2A6	2B6	2C8	2C9	2C19	2D6	2E1	3A4
Acebutolol							○		
Acetaminophen									○
AcetaZOLAMIDE									○
Albendazole	○								
Alosetron	○							○	
Amiodarone	○	◐	○		◐	○	◐		◐
Amitriptyline	○				○	○	○	○	
Amlodipine	◐	○		○	○		○		○
Amphetamine							○		
Amprenavir						○			●
Anastrozole	○			○	○				○
Aprepitant					○	○			◐
Atazanavir	○			●	○				●
Atorvastatin									○
Azelastine			○		○	○	○		○
Azithromycin									○
Bepridil							○		
Betamethasone									○
Betaxolol							○		
Biperiden							○		
Bortezomib	○				○	◐	○		○
Bromazepam								○	
Bromocriptine	○								○
Buprenorphine	○	○					○		○
BuPROPion							○		
Caffeine	●								◐
Candesartan				○	○				
Celecoxib				◐			○		
Cerivastatin									○
Chloramphenicol					○				○
Chloroquine							◐		
Chlorpheniramine							○		
ChlorproMAZINE							●	○	
Chlorzoxazone							○	○	○
Cholecalciferol					○	○	○		
Cimetidine	◐				○	◐	◐	○	◐
Cinacalcet							○		
Ciprofloxacin	●								○
Cisapride							○		○
Citalopram	○		○			○	○		
Clarithromycin	○								●
Clemastine							○		○
Clofazimine									○
Clofibrate		○							
ClomiPRAMINE							◐		
Clopidogrel					○				
Clotrimazole	○	○	○	○	○	○	○	○	◐
Clozapine	○				○	○	◐	○	○
Cocaine							●		○
Codeine							○		
Conivaptan									●
Cyclophosphamide									○
CycloSPORINE					○				◐
Danazol									○
Delavirdine	○				●	●	●		◐
Desipramine		◐	◐				◐		◐
Dexmedetomidine	○				○		●		○
Dextromethorphan							○		
Diazepam						○			○
Diclofenac	◐				○			○	○
Dihydroergotamine									○
Diltiazem					○		○		◐
Dimethyl sulfoxide					○	○			
DiphenhydrAMINE							◐		
Disulfiram	○	○	○		○		○	●	○

CYTOCHROME P450 ENZYMES: SUBSTRATES, INHIBITORS, AND INDUCERS (Continued)

CYP Inhibitors (continued)

Drug	1A2	2A6	2B6	2C8	2C9	2C19	2D6	2E1	3A4
Docetaxel									○
Dolasetron							○		
DOXOrubicin			◐				○		○
Doxycycline									◐
Drospirenone	○				○	○			○
Duloxetine							◐		
Econazole								○	
Efavirenz					○	○			○
Enoxacin	●								●
Entacapone	○	○			○	○	○	○	○
Eprosartan					○				
Ergotamine									○
Erythromycin	○								◐
Escitalopram							○		
Estradiol	○			○					
Estrogens, conjugated A/synthetic	○								
Estrogens, conjugated equine	○								
Ethinyl estradiol	○		○	○		○			○
Ethotoin						○			
Etoposide					○				○
Felbamate						○			
Felodipine				◐	○		○		○
Fenofibrate		○		◐	◐	○			
Fentanyl									○
Fexofenadine							○		
Flecainide							○		
Fluconazole	○				●	●			◐
Fluoxetine	◐		○		○	◐	●		○
Fluphenazine	○				○		○	○	
Flurazepam								○	
Flurbiprofen					●				
Flutamide	○								
Fluvastatin	○			○	◐		○		○
Fluvoxamine	●		○		○	●	○		○
Fosamprenavir (as amprenavir)						○			●
Gefitinib						○	○		
Gemfibrozil	◐			●	●	◐			
Glyburide				○					○
Grapefruit juice									◐
Haloperidol							◐		◐
HydrALAZINE									○
HydrOXYzine							○		
Ibuprofen					●				
Ifosfamide									○
Imatinib					○		○		●
Imipramine	○					○	◐	○	
Indinavir					○	○	○		●
Indomethacin					●	○			
Interferon alfa-2a	○								
Interferon alfa-2b	○								
Interferon gamma-1b	○							○	
Irbesartan				◐	◐		○		○
Isoflurane			○						
Isoniazid	○	◐			○		●	◐	●
Isradipine									○
Itraconazole									●
Ketoconazole	●	◐	○	○	●	○	◐		●
Ketoprofen					○				
Labetalol							○		
Lansoprazole					○	◐	○		○
Leflunomide					○				
Letrozole		●				○			
Lidocaine	●						◐		◐
Lomefloxacin	○								

CYP Inhibitors *(continued)*

Drug	1A2	2A6	2B6	2C8	2C9	2C19	2D6	2E1	3A4
Lomustine							○		○
Loratadine				○		◐	○		
Losartan	○			◐	◐	○			○
Lovastatin					○		○		○
Mefenamic acid					●				
Mefloquine							○		○
Meloxicam					○				
Mephobarbital						○			
Mestranol	○		○			○			○
Methadone							◐		○
Methimazole	○	○	○		○	○	◐	○	
Methotrimeprazine							○		
Methoxsalen	●	●			○	○	○	○	○
Methsuximide						○			
Methylphenidate							○		
MethylPREDNISolone				○					○
Metoclopramide							○		
Metoprolol							○		
Metronidazole					○				◐
Metyrapone		○							
Mexiletine	●								
Miconazole	◐	●	○		●	●	●	◐	●
Midazolam				○	○				○
Mifepristone							○		○
Mirtazapine	○								○
Mitoxantrone									○
Moclobemide	○					○	○		
Modafinil	○	○			○	●		○	○
Montelukast				○	○				
Nalidixic acid	○								
Nateglinide					○				
Nefazodone	○		○	○			○		●
Nelfinavir	○		○		○	○	○		●
Nevirapine	○						○		○
NiCARdipine					●	◐	◐		●
Nicotine		○						○	
NIFEdipine	◐				○		○		○
Nilutamide						○			
Nisoldipine	○								○
Nizatidine									○
Norfloxacin	●								◐
Nortriptyline							○	○	
Ofloxacin	●								
Olanzapine	○				○	○	○		○
Omeprazole	○				◐	●	○		○
Ondansetron	○				○		○		
Orphenadrine	○	○	○		○		○	○	○
Oxcarbazepine						○			
Oxprenolol							○		
Oxybutynin				○			○		○
Pantoprazole						◐			
Paroxetine	○		◐		○	○	●		○
Peginterferon alfa-2a	○								
Peginterferon alfa-2b	○								
Pentamidine					○	○			○
Pentoxifylline	○								
Pergolide							●		○
Perphenazine	○						○		
Phencyclidine									○
Pilocarpine		○						○	○
Pimozide						○	○	○	○
Pindolol							○		
Pioglitazone				◐	○	○	◐		
Piroxicam					●				
Pravastatin					○		○		○
Praziquantel							○		
PrednisoLONE									○
Primaquine	●						○		○
Probenecid						○			

CYTOCHROME P450 ENZYMES: SUBSTRATES, INHIBITORS, AND INDUCERS *(Continued)*

CYP Inhibitors *(continued)*

Drug	1A2	2A6	2B6	2C8	2C9	2C19	2D6	2E1	3A4
Progesterone					O	O			O
Promethazine							O		
Propafenone	O						O		
Propofol	◐				O	◐	O	O	●
Propoxyphene					O		O		O
Propranolol	O						O		
Pyrimethamine					◐		◐		
Quinidine					O		●		●
Quinine				◐	◐		●		O
Quinupristin									O
Rabeprazole				◐		◐	O		O
Ranitidine	O						O		
Ranolazine							O		O
Risperidone							O		O
Ritonavir			●	O	O	O	●	O	●
Rofecoxib	O								
Ropinirole	O						●		
Rosiglitazone				◐	O	O	O		
Saquinavir					O	O	O		◐
Selegiline	O	O			O	O	O	O	O
Sertraline	O		◐	O	O	◐	◐		◐
Sildenafil	O				O	O	O	O	O
Simvastatin				O	O		O		
Sirolimus									O
Sorafenib			O	O					
Sulconazole	O	O			O	O	O	O	
SulfaDIAZINE					●				
Sulfamethoxazole					◐				
Sulfinpyrazone					◐				
SulfiSOXAZOLE					●				
Tacrine	O								
Tacrolimus									O
Tamoxifen				O	◐	O			O
Telithromycin							O		●
Telmisartan						O			
Teniposide					O				O
Tenofovir	O								
Terbinafine							●		
Testosterone									O
Tetracycline									◐
Theophylline	O								
Thiabendazole	●								
Thioridazine	O				O		◐	O	
Thiotepa			O						
Thiothixene							O		
Ticlopidine	O				O	●	◐	O	O
Timolol							O		
Tioconazole	O	O			O	O	O	O	
Tocainide	O								
TOLBUTamide				O	●				
Tolcapone					O				
Topiramate						O			
Torsemide						O			
Tranylcypromine	◐	●		O	O	◐	◐	O	O
Trazodone							◐		O
Tretinoin					O				
Triazolam				O	O				
Trimethoprim				◐	◐				
Tripelennamine							◐		
Triprolidine							O		
Troleandomycin									◐
Valdecoxib				O	O	O			
Valproic acid					O	O	O		O
Valsartan					O				
Venlafaxine			O				O		O
Verapamil	O				O		O		◐

CYP Inhibitors *(continued)*

Drug	1A2	2A6	2B6	2C8	2C9	2C19	2D6	2E1	3A4
VinBLAStine							○		○
VinCRIStine									○
Vinorelbine							○		○
Voriconazole					○	○			◑
Warfarin					◑	○			
Yohimbine							○		
Zafirlukast	○			○	◑	○	○		○
Zileuton	◑								
Ziprasidone							○		○

CYTOCHROME P450 ENZYMES: SUBSTRATES, INHIBITORS, AND INDUCERS *(Continued)*

CYP Inducers

● = effectively induced
○ = not effectively induced

Drug	1A2	2A6	2B6	2C8	2C9	2C19	2D6	2E1	3A4
Aminoglutethimide	●					●			●
Amobarbital		●							
Aprepitant					○				○
Bexarotene									○
Bosentan					○				○
Calcitriol									○
Carbamazepine	●		●	●	●	●			●
Clofibrate			○					○	○
Colchicine				○	○			○	○
Cyclophosphamide			○	○	○				
Dexamethasone		○	○	○	○				○
Dicloxacillin									○
Efavirenz (in liver only)			○						○
Estradiol									○
Estrogens, conjugated A/synthetic									○
Estrogens, conjugated equine									○
Exemestane									○
Felbamate									○
Fosphenytoin (as phenytoin)			●	●	●	●			●
Griseofulvin	○			○	○				○
Hydrocortisone									○
Ifosfamide				○	○				
Insulin preparations	○								
Isoniazid (after D/C)								○	
Lansoprazole	○								
MedroxyPROGESTERone									○
Mephobarbital		○							
Metyrapone									○
Modafinil	○		○						○
Moricizine	○								○
Nafcillin									●
Nevirapine			●						●
Norethindrone						○			
Omeprazole	○								
Oxcarbazepine									●
Paclitaxel									○
Pantoprazole	○								○
Pentobarbital			●						●
Phenobarbital	●	●	●	●	●				●
Phenytoin			●	●	●	●			●
Pioglitazone									○
PredniSONE						○			○
Primaquine	○								
Primidone[1]	●		●	●	●				●
Rifabutin									●
Rifampin	●	●	●	●	●	●			●
Rifapentine				●	●				●
Ritonavir (long-term)	○			○	○				○
Rofecoxib									○
Secobarbital			●		●	●			
Sulfinpyrazone									○
Terbinafine									○
Topiramate									○
Tretinoin								○	
Troglitazone									○
Valproic acid		○							

[1]Primidone is partially metabolized to phenobarbital. See Phenobarbital for additional CYP information.

DESENSITIZATION PROTOCOLS

PENICILLIN DESENSITIZATION PROTOCOL: MUST BE DONE BY PHYSICIAN!

Acute penicillin desensitization should only be performed in an intensive care setting. Any remedial risk factor should be corrected. All β-adrenergic antagonists such as propranolol or even timolol ophthalmic drops should be discontinued. Asthmatic patients should be under optimal control. An intravenous line should be established, baseline electrocardiogram (ECG) and spirometry should be performed, and continuous ECG monitoring should be instituted. Premedication with antihistamines or steroids is not recommended, as these drugs have not proven effective in suppressing severe reactions but may mask early signs of reactivity that would otherwise result in a modification of the protocol.

Protocols have been developed for penicillin desensitization using both the oral and parenteral route. As of 1987 there were 93 reported cases of oral desensitization, 74 of which were done by Sullivan and his collaborators. Of these 74 patients, 32% experienced a transient allergic reaction either during desensitization (one-third) or during penicillin treatment after desensitization (two-thirds). These reactions were usually mild and self-limited in nature. Only one IgE-mediated reaction (wheezing and bronchospasm) required discontinuation of the procedure before desensitization could be completed. It has been argued that oral desensitization may be safer than parenteral desensitization, but most patients can also be safely desensitized by parenteral route.

During desensitization any dose that causes mild systemic reactions such as pruritus, fleeting urticaria, rhinitis, or mild wheezing should be repeated until the patient tolerates the dose without systemic symptoms or signs. More serious reactions such as hypotension, laryngeal edema, or asthma require appropriate treatment, and if desensitization is continued, the dose should be decreased by at least 10-fold and withheld until the patient is stable.

Once desensitized, the patient's treatment with penicillin must not lapse or the risk of an allergic reaction increases. If the patient requires a β-lactam antibiotic in the future and still remains skin test-positive to penicillin reagents, desensitization would be required again.

Several patients have been maintained on long-term, low-dose penicillin therapy (usually bid-tid) to sustain a chronic state of desensitization. Such individuals usually require chronic desensitization because of continuous occupationally related exposure to β-lactam drugs.

Order for placement/availability at the bedside in the event of a hypersensitivity reaction during scratch/skin testing and desensitization:

Hydrocortisone: 100 mg IVP
Diphenhydramine: 50 mg IVP
Epinephrine: 1:1000 SubQ

Several investigators have demonstrated that penicillin can be administered to history positive, skin test positive patients if initially small but gradually increasing doses are given. However, patients with a history of exfoliative dermatitis secondary to penicillin should not be re-exposed to the drug, even by desensitization.

Desensitization is a potentially dangerous procedure and should be only performed in an area where immediate access to emergency drugs and equipment can be assured.

Begin between 8-10 AM in the morning.

Follow desensitization as indicated for penicillin G or ampicillin.

AMPICILLIN
Oral Desensitization Protocol

1. Begin 0.03 mg of ampicillin
2. Double the dose administered every 30 minutes until complete
3. Example of oral dosing regimen:

Dose #	Ampicillin (mg)
1	0.03
2	0.06
3	0.12
4	0.23
5	0.47
6	0.94
7	1.87
8	3.75
9	7.5
10	15
11	30
12	60
13	125
14	250
15	500

DESENSITIZATION PROTOCOLS *(Continued)*

PENICILLIN G
Parenteral Desensitization Protocol: Typical Schedule

Injection No.	Benzylpenicillin Concentration (units/mL)	Volume and Route (mL)[1]
1[2]	100	0.1 I.D.
2	↓	0.2 SubQ
3		0.4 SubQ
4		0.8 SubQ
5[2]	1,000	0.1 I.D.
6	↓	0.3 SubQ
7		0.6 SubQ
8[2]	10,000	0.1 I.D.
9	↓	0.2 SubQ
10		0.4 SubQ
11		0.8 SubQ
12[2]	100,000	0.1 I.D.
13	↓	0.3 SubQ
14		0.6 SubQ
15[2]	1,000,000	0.1 I.D.
16	↓	0.2 SubQ
17		0.2 I.M.
18		0.4 I.M.
19	Continuous I.V. infusion (1,000,000 units/h)	

[1]Administer progressive doses at intervals of not less than 20 minutes.
[2]Observe and record skin wheal and flare response to intradermal dose.

Abbreviations: I.D. = intradermal, SubQ = subcutaneous, I.M. = intramuscular, I.V. = intravenous.

PENICILLIN
Oral Desensitization Protocol

Step[1]	Phenoxymethyl Penicillin (units/mL)	Amount (mL)	Dose (units)	Cumulative Dosage (units)
1	1000	0.1	100	100
2	1000	0.2	200	300
3	1000	0.4	400	700
4	1000	0.8	800	1500
5	1000	1.6	1600	3100
6	1000	3.2	3200	6300
7	1000	6.4	6400	12,700
8	10,000	1.2	12,000	24,700
9	10,000	2.4	24,000	48,700
10	10,000	4.8	48,000	96,700
11	80,000	1	80,000	176,700
12	80,000	2	160,000	336,700
13	80,000	4	320,000	656,700
14	80,000	8	640,000	1,296,700
	Observe patient for 30 minutes			
Change to benzylpenicillin G I.V.				
15	500,000	0.25	125,000	
16	500,000	0.50	250,000	
17	500,000	1	500,000	
18	500,000	2.25	1,125,000	

[1]Interval between steps, 15 min

ALLOPURINOL
Successful Desensitization for Treatment of a Fixed Drug Eruption

	Oral Dose of Allopurinol
Days 1-3	50 mcg/day
Days 4-6	100 mcg/day
Days 7-9	200 mcg/day
Days 10-12	500 mcg/day
Days 13-15	1 mg/day
Days 16-18	5 mg/day
Days 19-21	10 mg/day
Days 22-24	25 mg/day
Days 25-27	50 mg/day
Day 28	100 mg/day

Prednisone 10 mg/day through desensitization and 1 month after reaching dose of 100 mg allopurinol

Modified from *J Allergy Clin Immunol*, 1996, 97:1171-2.

AMPHOTERICIN B
Challenge and Desensitization Protocol

1. Procedure supervised by physician
2. Epinephrine, 1:1000 wt/vol, multidose vial at bedside
3. Premixed albuterol solution at bedside for nebulization
4. Endotracheal intubation supplies at bedside with anesthesiologist on standby
5. Continuous cardiac telemetry with electronic monitoring of blood pressure
6. Continuous pulse oximetry
7. Premedication with methylprednisolone, 60 mg, I.V. and diphenhydramine, 25 mg I.V.
8. Amphotericin B (Fungizone®)[1] administration schedule

   a. 10^{-6} dilution, infused over 10 minutes

   b. 10^{-5} dilution, infused over 10 minutes

   c. 10^{-4} dilution, infused over 10 minutes

   d. 10^{-3} dilution, infused over 10 minutes

   e. 10^{-2} dilution, infused over 10 minutes

   f. 10^{-1} dilution (1 mg), infused over 30 minutes

   g. 30 mg in 250 mL 5% dextrose, infused over 4 hours

[1]Mixtures were prepared in 10 mL 5% dextrose by hospital intensive care unit pharmacy, unless otherwise noted.

From Kemp SF and Lockey RF, "Amphotericin B: Emergency Challenge in a Neutropenic, Asthmatic Patient With Fungal Sepsis," *J Allergy Clin Immunol*, 1995, 96(3):425-7.

BACTRIM™
Oral Desensitization Protocol

(Adapted from Gluckstein D and Ruskin J, "Rapid Oral Desensitization to Trimethoprim-Sulfamethoxazole (TMP-SMZ): Use in Prophylaxis for *Pneumocystis carinii* Pneumonia in Patients With AIDS Who Were Previously Intolerant to TMP-SMZ," *Clin Infect Dis*, 1995, 20:849-53.)

Please read the directions carefully before starting the protocol!

1. There must be a clear cut need for a sulfa drug or a sulfa drug combination product such as Bactrim™. The decision to use sulfa must be made prior to skin testing.
2. Informed consent from the patient or an appropriate relative must have been obtained.
3. A trained individual, physician, nurse, or aide, **must be with the patient** at all times.
4. A physician **must** be on the floor at all times.
5. Injectable epinephrine 0.3 mL 1:1000, diphenhydramine (Benadryl®) 50 mg, corticosteroids and oral ibuprofen 400 mg solution should be drawn up and available at the bedside.
6. Appropriate resuscitative equipment must be available.
7. All dilution of oral Bactrim™ should be made up prior to beginning procedure.
8. Patient should drink 180 mL of water after each Bactrim™ dose.

Dilution for Bactrim™ Desensitization

Final Concentration	Bottle #	Procedure
Oral Bactrim™ 40/200 mg/5 mL	A	Conventional oral Bactrim™ suspension 5 mL = 40/200 mg
Oral Bactrim™ 0.4/2 mg/mL	B	1. Add 5 mL conventional oral Bactrim™ suspension or A (concentration = 40/200 mg/5 mL) to 95 mL of sterile water 2. Shake well. This will give 100 mL of 40/200 mg Bactrim™; each mL = 0.4/2 mg Bactrim™. 3. Dispense 20 mL for use
Oral Bactrim™ 0.004/0.02 mg/mL	C	1. Add 1 mL of the 0.4/2 mg/mL Bactrim™ or B to 99 mL of sterile water 2. Shake well. This will give 100 mL of 0.4/2 mg Bactrim™; each mL = 0.004/0.02 mg Bactrim™. 3. Dispense 20 mL for use

Adverse Reactions and Response During the Protocol

Types of Reactions	Alteration of Protocol
Mild reactions (rash, fever, nausea)	I.V. diphenhydramine (Benadryl®) 50 mg and oral ibuprofen suspension 400 mg
Urticaria, dyspnea, severe vomiting, or hypotension	**STOP** the protocol IMMEDIATELY

- If patient tolerates up to Bactrim™ DS, he/she is desensitized.
- Assuming that there were no complications, the procedure will take up to 6 hours.

DESENSITIZATION PROTOCOLS *(Continued)*

Sample Bactrim™ Desensitization Flow Sheet

Patient Name _____   Age _____ Gender _____ Hospital # _____

Diagnosis _____   Physician _____   Pager _____ History of sulfa reaction _____

# Hour	Actual Time	Suggested Dose	Form	Suggested Volume	Actual Dose	Form	Actual Volume	Reaction/ Notes	Initial
0		Bactrim™ 0.004/0.02 mg (use **0.004/0.02 mg/mL** bottle or bottle C)	Susp (C)	1 mL					
1		Bactrim™ 0.04/0.2 mg (use 0.004/0.02 mg/mL bottle or bottle C)	Susp (C)	10 mL					
2		Bactrim™ 0.4/2 mg (use **0.4/2 mg/mL bottle** or bottle B)	Susp (B)	1 mL					
3		Bactrim™ 4/20 mg (use 0.4/2 mg/mL bottle or bottle B)	Susp (B)	10 mL					
4		Bactrim™ 40/200 mg (use **40/200 mg/5 mL unit dose** Bactrim™ or A)	Susp (A)	5 mL					
5		Bactrim™ 80/400 mg (use 40/200 mg/5 mL unit dose Bactrim™ or A)	Susp (A)	10 mL					
6		Bactrim™ DS tablet	Tablet	1 DS pill					

Note: Drink 180 mL of water after each Bactrim™ dose.

ALTERNATIVE BACTRIM™ PROTOCOL

Adapted from Leung GS, Stanford JF, Giordano MF, et al, "Trimethoprim-Sulfamethoxazole (TMP-SMZ) Dose Escalation Versus Direct Rechallenge for *Pneumocystis carinii* Pneumonia, Prophylaxis in Human Immunodeficiency Virus-Infected Patients With Previous Adverse Reaction to TMP-SMZ," *J Infect Dis*, 2001, 184(8):992-7.

Trimethoprim-Sulfamethoxazole (TMP-SMZ) Dose-Escalation Regimen in Human Immunodeficiency Virus-Infected Patients With Previous Mild-to-Moderate Treatment-Limiting Rash and/or Fever

Dosing Level	Portion of Single-Strength TMP-SMZ (%)	Amount (Frequency) of Pediatric Suspension (mL)	Total TMP Dose (mg)	Total SMZ Dose (mg)
1	12.5	1.25 qd	10	50
2	25	1.25 bid	20	100
3	37.5	1.25 tid	30	150
4	50	2.5 bid	40	200
5	75	2.5 tid	60	300
6	100	1 single-strength tablet	80	400

Note: Each dosing level is a daily dose. For successful completion of the reintroduction phase, patients must have taken each dose level at least once. Patients were permitted to repeat dose levels once; dose levels were completed in increasing increments, and the level 6 dose was taken no later than day 13 of the reintroduction phase. Patients were permitted to withhold study drug for 2 days during the reintroduction phase (withholding study drug for >2 days during reintroduction resulted in permanent discontinuation). Patients were required to take an antihistamine during dose escalation.

VANCOMYCIN DESENSITIZATION PROTOCOL

(Adapted from Wong JT, Ripple RE, MacLean JA, et al, "Vancomycin Hypersensitivity: Synergism with Narcotics and Desensitization by a Rapid Continuous Intravenous Protocol," *J Allergy Clin Immunol*, 1994, 94(2 Pt 1):189-94.)

Please read the directions carefully before starting the protocol!

1. Vancomycin desensitization is indicated only for cases with a definitive need for vancomycin and persistent allergic reaction despite slowing of infusion rate and the addition of Benadryl® or cases with reported vancomycin anaphylactic reactions.
2. Informed consent from the patient or an appropriate relative must have been obtained.
3. A trained individual, physician, nurse, or aide, **must be with the patient** at all times.
4. A physician **must** be on the floor at all times.
5. Injectable epinephrine 0.3 mL 1:1000, diphenhydramine (Benadryl®) 50 mg, corticosteroids and oral ibuprofen 400 mg solution should be drawn up and available at the bedside.
6. Appropriate resuscitative equipment must be available.
7. All dilution of I.V. vancomycin should be made up prior to beginning procedure.
8. All patients are pretreated with 25-50 mg Benadryl®.
9. Infusion rates are to be tightly regulated with **syringe pump**.

Dilution for Vancomycin Desensitization

Final Concentration	Bottle #	Procedure
10 mg/mL	A	1. Dilute 1 g of vancomycin in 10 mL of sterile water 2. Shake well until the drug is completely dissolved 3. Add 2 mL of solution to 18 mL of 0.9% normal saline 4. Mix well 5. This will give 20 mL of 10 mg/mL concentration of vancomycin or (Bottle A) 6. Dispense 10-15 mL in a syringe for syringe pump. Label the syringe as "SYR A: conc = 10 mg/mL" with patient's name, ID, room number, date, and dispensor's initial/pharmacist's initial.
1 mg/mL	B	1. Add 2 mL of bottle A vancomycin (10 mg/mL) to 18 mL of 0.9% normal saline 2. Mix well 3. This will give 20 mL of 1 mg/mL concentration vancomycin or (Bottle B) 4. Dispense 10-15 mL in a syringe for syringe pump. Label the syringe as "SYR B: conc = 1 mg/mL" with patient's name, ID, room number, date, and dispensor's initial/pharmacist's initial.
0.1 mg/mL	C	1. Add 2 mL of Bottle B vancomycin (1 mg/mL) to 18 mL of 0.9% normal saline 2. Mix well 3. This will give 20 mL of 0.1 mg/mL concentration vancomycin or (Bottle C) 4. Dispense 10-15 mL in a syringe for syringe pump. Label the syringe as "SYR C: conc = 0.1 mg/mL" with patient's name, ID, room number, date, and dispensor's initial/pharmacist's initial.

DESENSITIZATION PROTOCOLS (Continued)

Dilution for Vancomycin Desensitization (continued)

Final Concentration	Bottle #	Procedure
0.01 mg/mL	D	1. Add 2 mL of Bottle C vancomycin (0.1 mg/mL) to 18 mL of 0.9% normal saline 2. Mix well 3. This will give 20 mL of 0.01 mg/mL concentration vancomycin or (Bottle D) 4. Dispense 10-15 mL in a syringe for syringe pump. Label the syringe as "SYR D: conc = 0.01 mg/mL" with patient's name, ID, room number, date, and dispensor's initial/pharmacist's initial.
0.001 mg/mL	E	1. Add 2 mL of Bottle D vancomycin (0.01 mg/mL) to 18 mL of 0.9% normal saline 2. Mix well 3. This will give 20 mL of 0.001 mg/mL concentration vancomycin or (Bottle E) 4. Dispense 10-15 mL in a syringe for syringe pump. Label the syringe as "SYR E: conc = 0.001 mg/mL" with patient's name, ID, room number, date, and dispensor's initial/pharmacist's initial.
0.0001 mg/mL	F	1. Add 2 mL of Bottle E vancomycin (0.001 mg/mL) to 18 mL of 0.9% normal saline 2. Mix well 3. This will give 20 mL of 0.0001 mg/mL concentration vancomycin or (Bottle F) 4. Dispense 10-15 mL in a syringe for syringe pump. Label the syringe as "SYR F: conc = 0.0001 mg/mL" with patient's name, ID, room number, date, and dispensor's initial/pharmacist's initial.

Sample Vancomycin Desensitization Flow Sheet

Patient Name _____ Physician _____ Age _____ Gender _____ Pager _____ Hospital # _____

Diagnosis _____ History of vancomycin reaction _____

Time (h/min)	Actual Time	Vancomycin concentration (mg/mL)	Syr #	Fluid infusion rate (mL/min)	VIR (mg/min)	Actual concentration (mg/mL)	Syr #	Infusion rate (mL/min)	Reaction/Notes	Initial
0:00		0.0001	F	1	0.0001					
0:10		0.001	E	0.33	0.00033					
0:20		0.001	E	1.0	0.001					
0:30		0.01	D	0.33	0.0033					
0:40		0.01	D	1.0	0.010					
0:50		0.1	C	0.33	0.033					
1:00		0.1	C	0.33	0.033					
1:10		1.0	B	0.33	0.33					
1:20		1.0	B	1	1					
1:30		10.0	A	0.22	2.2[1]					
1:30		10.0	A	0.44	4.4[1]					

[1] After a VIR of 2.2-4.4 mg/min is achieved, full dose of vancomycin can be administered at the VIR for the first day. The rate can be gradually advanced over the next few days as tolerated.

Patients in whom a VIF of 2.2-4.4 mg/min cannot be achieved, continue to receive vancomycin at the highest tolerated infusion rate for the first day. The rate is to be gradually advanced over the next few days as tolerated.

DESENSITIZATION PROTOCOLS *(Continued)*

ALTERNATIVE VANCOMYCIN PROTOCOL

Adapted from Wazny LD and Daghigh B, "Desensitization Protocols for Vancomycin Hypersensitivity," *Ann Pharmacother*, 2001, 35(11):1458-64.

Rapid Vancomycin Desensitization Protocol
(Lerner and Dwyer)

Premedication

Diphenhydramine 50 mg I.V. and hydrocortisone 100 mg I.V. 15 minutes prior to initiation of protocol, then q6h throughout protocol.

Infusion No.	Dilution	Vancomycin Dose (mg)	Concentration (mg/mL)
1	1:10,000	0.02	0.0002
2	1:1000	0.20	0.002
3	1:100	2	0.02
4	1:10	20	0.2
5	Standard	500	2

Preparation

1. Prepare a standard bag of 500 mg vancomycin in 250 mL NS or D_5W; label as infusion no. 5, vancomycin 2 mg/mL.

2. Draw up 10 mL of the standard vancomycin 2 mg/mL preparation and place in 100 mL bag of NS or D_5W; label as infusion no. 4, vancomycin 0.2 mg/mL.

3. Draw up 10 mL of the 0.2 mg/mL solution and place in a 100 mL bag of NS or D_5W; label as infusion no. 3, vancomycin 0.02 mg/mL.

4. Draw up 10 mL of the 0.02 mg/mL solution and place in a 100 mL bag of NS or D_5W; label as infusion no. 2, vancomycin 0.002 mg/mL.

5. Draw up 10 mL of the 0.002 mg/mL solution and place in a 100 mL bag of NS or D_5W; label as infusion no. 1, vancomycin 0.0002 mg/mL.

Infusion Rate Directions

Initiate infusion rate at 0.5 mL/min (30 mL/h) and increase by 0.5 mL/min (30 mL/h) as tolerated every 5 minutes to a maximum rate of 5 mL/min (300 mL/h). If pruritus, hypotension, rash, or difficulty breathing occurs, stop infusion and reinfuse the previously tolerated infusion at the highest tolerated rate. This step may be repeated up to three times for any given concentration.

Upon completion of infusion no. 5, immediately administer the required dose of vancomycin in the usual dilution of NS or D_5W over 2 hours. Decrease rate if patient becomes symptomatic or, alternatively, increase rate if patient tolerates dose. Administer diphenhydramine 50 mg P.O. 60 minutes prior to each dose.

CEFTRIAXONE DESENSITIZATION PROTOCOL

Dose	Concentration (mg/mL)	Volume (mL)	Dose (mg)
Subcutaneous Route: 15-minute intervals between all doses			
1	0.2	0.5	0.1
2	0.2	1	0.2
3	2	0.25	0.5
4	2	0.5	1
5	2	1	2
6	16	0.25	4
7	16	0.5	8
8	16	1	16
Intravenous Route: Infuse over 20-30 minutes; 15 minutes between doses			
9	20	1.5 mL qs to 50 mL	30 mg/50 mL
10	20	3 mL qs to 50 mL	60 mg/50 mL
11	20	6 mL qs to 50 mL	120 mg/50 mL
12	20	12.5 mL qs to 50 mL	250 mg/50 mL
13	–	–	1 g/50 mL

Pharmacy Admixture Instructions

1. Mix ceftriaxone 1 g/50 mL NS (concentration 20 mg/mL); label **Bag A**.

2. Remove 1 mL from Bag A and add 99 mL NS (concentration 0.2 mg/mL); label **Bag B**.

3. Use **Bag B** to make doses 1 and 2.

4. Remove 1 mL from Bag A and add 9 mL NS (concentration 2 mg/mL); label **Bag C**.

5. Use Bag C to make doses 3, 4, and 5.

6. Remove 1 mL from Bag A and add 0.25 mL NS (concentration 16 mg/mL); label **Bag D**.

7. Use Bag D to make doses 6 and 7.

8. Repeat step 6 to make dose 8 (step 6 only makes 1.25 mL; therefore need to repeat to make dose 8).

9. Take a 50 mL bag of NS and remove overfill plus 1.5 mL; add 1.5 mL from Bag A to NS bag (30 mg/50 mL); this is dose 9.

10. Take a 50 mL bag of NS and remove overfill plus 3 mL; add 3 mL from Bag A to NS bag (60 mg/50 mL); this is dose 10.

11. Take a 50 mL bag of NS and remove overfill plus 6 mL; add 6 mL from Bag A to NS bag (120 mg/50 mL); this is dose 11.

12. Take a 50 mL bag of NS and remove overfill plus 12.5 mL; add 12.5 mL from Bag A to NS bag (250 mg/50 mL); this is dose 12.

13. Dispense 1 g/50 mL for dose 13.

DESENSITIZATION PROTOCOLS (Continued)

CIPROFLOXACIN

Modified from *J Allergy Clin Immunol*, 1996, 97:1426-7.

Premedicated with diphenhydramine hydrochloride, ranitidine, and prednisone 1 hour before the desensitization.

The individual doses were administered at 15-minute intervals. Because the patient was intubated in the intensive care unit, vital signs were continually monitored. The patient's skin was inspected for development of urticaria, and his chest was auscultated for wheezing every 10 minutes. No rash, hypotension, or wheezing developed during desensitization. The procedure took 4 hours, and once finished, the patient had received an equivalent to his first scheduled dose (400 mg twice daily). The second dose was given 4 hours later, followed by routine administration of 400 mg every 12 hours, with a small dose (25 mg intravenously) between therapeutic doses to maintain a drug level in the blood. The patient subsequently received 4 weeks of ciprofloxacin treatment without difficulty.

Desensitization Regimen for Ciprofloxacin

Ciprofloxacin Concentration (mg/mL)	Volume Given (mL)	Absolute Amount (mg)	Cumulative Total Dose (mg)
0.1	0.1	0.01	0.01
0.1	0.2	0.02	0.03
0.1	0.4	0.04	0.07
0.1	0.8	0.08	0.15
1	0.16	0.16	0.31
1	0.32	0.32	0.63
1	0.64	0.64	1.27
2	0.6	1.2	2.47
2	1.2	2.4	4.87
2	2.4	4.8	9.67
2	5	10	19.67
2	10	20	39.67
2	20	40	79.67
2	40	80	159.67
2	120	240	399.67

Drug volumes <1 mL were mixed with normal saline solution to a final volume of 3 mL and then slowly infused; the other doses were administered over 10 minutes, except the last dose (240 mg in 120 mL), which was given with an infusion pump over 20 minutes.

IMIPENEM DESENSITIZATION PROTOCOL

Adapted from Saxon A, Adelman DC, Patel A, et al, "Imipenem Cross-Reactivity With Penicillin in Humans," *J Allergy Clin Immunol*, 1988, 82(2):213-7.

Indication: Need for imipenem in the setting of anaphylactic potential to penicillin. Cross-reactivity between imipenem and penicillin is high.

Subcutaneous Route: 15-minute intervals between all doses

Dose	Solution No.	Concentration (mg/mL)	SubQ Injections q15min	
			Volume (mL)	Dosage (mg)
1	3	0.05	0.5	0.025
2		0.05	1	0.05
3	2	0.5	0.2	0.1
4		0.5	0.4	0.2
5		0.5	0.8	0.4
6	1	5	0.12	0.6
7		5	0.25	1.25
8		5	0.5	2.5
9		5	1	5

-------------------- Wait 30 minutes --------------------

Intravenous Route: Infuse over 20-30 minutes; 15 minutes between doses

Dose	Solution No.	I.V. Imipenem Dose (using 50 mL NSS)	Concentration (mg/mL)	Total Dosage (mg)
10	1	2 mL in 50 mL NSS	10 mg/50 mL	10
11		4 mL in 50 mL NSS	20 mg/50 mL	20
12		8 mL in 50 mL NSS	40 mg/50 mL	40
13		12 mL in 50 mL NSS	60 mg/50 mL	60
	Add 10 mL NSS to 500 mg vial Primaxin®			
14		2.5 mL in 50 mL NSS	125 mg/50 mL	125
15		5 mL in 50 mL NSS	250 mg/50 mL	250

INSULIN

Lilly's appropriate diluting fluid, sterile saline, or distilled water, to which 1 mL of the patient's blood or the addition of 1 mL of 1% serum albumin (making a 0.1% solution) for each 10 mL of stock diluent, is a satisfactory diluent. The albumin in the blood or serum albumin solution is necessary to retain the integrity of the higher dilutions by preventing adsorption to glass or plastic. Dilution is stable 30 days under refrigeration or room temperature, but should be used within 24 hours due to a lack of preservative.

1. Make a 1:1 dilution of single species (beef, pork, or human) insulin (50 units/mL).
2. Add 0.5 mL of the above dilution to 4.5 mL of diluent (5 units/mL).
3. Add 0.5 mL of the 5 units/mL dilution to 4.5 mL of diluent (0.5 unit/mL).
4. Add 0.5 mL of the 0.5 unit/mL dilution to 4.5 mL of diluent (0.05 unit/mL).
5. Add 0.5 mL of the 0.05 unit/mL dilution to 4.5 mL of diluent (0.005 unit/mL).

The 5 vials containing 50, 5, 0.5, 0.05, and 0.005 unit/mL are ready for skin testing or desensitization procedures.

One may start desensitization by giving 0.02 mL of 0.05 unit/mL concentration (1/1000 unit) intradermally. If no reaction occurs, administer 0.04 and 0.08 mL of the same concentration at 30-minute intervals.

The procedure continues proceeding to the next greater concentration (0.5 unit/mL) and giving 0.02, 0.04, and 0.08 mL at 30-minute intervals.

In the same manner proceed through the 5 units/mL and 50 units/mL concentrations with the exception that these injections should be given subcutaneously.

Note: If a reaction is noted, back up 2 steps and try to proceed forward again.

If the patient reacts to the initial injection, it will be necessary to utilize the lower concentration (0.005 unit/mL) to initiate the procedure.

It is essential that manifestations of allergic reactions not be obscured. Therefore, antihistamines or steroids should not be used during desensitization except to treat severe allergic reactions. The use of these agents may obscure mild to moderate reactions to the lower doses and result in more severe reactions as doses increase, leading to failure of the desensitization program.

NELFINAVIR DESENSITIZATION PROTOCOL

Adapted from Abraham PE, Sorensen SJ, Baker WH, et al, "Nelfinavir Desensitization," *Ann Pharmacother*, 2001, 35(5):553-6.

Step	Time (min)	Nelfinavir Dose (mg)	
		q30min	Total
1	0	0.5	0.5
2	30	1	1.5
3	60	2	3.5
4	90	5	8.5
5	120	10	18.5
6	150	20	38.5
7	180	40	78.5
8	210	80	158.5
9	240	160	318.5
10	270	250	568.5
11	300	500	1068.5
12	330	750	1818.5
Observe patient in ICU for 2 hours before discharge			

RIFAMPIN and ETHAMBUTOL
Oral Desensitization in Mycobacterial Disease

Time from Start (h:min)	Rifampin (mg)	Ethambutol (mg)
0	0.1	0.1
00:45	0.5	0.5
01:30	1	1
02:15	2	2
03:00	4	4
03:45	8	8
04:30	16	16
05:15	32	32
06:00	50	50
06:45	100	100
07:30	150	200
11:00	300	400
Next day		
6:30 AM	300 mg twice daily	400 mg 3 times/day

From *Am J Respir Crit Care Med*, 1994, 149:815-7.

SKIN TESTS

Penicillin Allergy

The recommended battery of major and minor determinants used in penicillin skin testing will disclose those individuals with circulating IgE antibodies. This procedure is therefore useful to identify patients at risk for immediate or accelerated reactions. Skin tests are of no value in predicting the occurrence of non-IgE-mediated hypersensitivity reactions to penicillin such as delayed exanthem, drug fever, hemolytic anemia, interstitial nephritis, or exfoliative dermatitis. Based on large scale trials, skin testing solutions have been standardized.

Antihistamines, tricyclic antidepressants, and adrenergic drugs, all of which may inhibit skin test results, should be discontinued at least 24 hours prior to skin testing. Antihistamines with long half-lives (hydroxyzine, terfenadine, astemizole, etc) may attenuate skin test results up to a week, or longer after discontinuation.

When properly performed with due consideration for preliminary scratch tests and appropriate dilutions, skin testing with penicillin reagents can almost always be safely accomplished. Systemic reactions accompany about 1% of positive skin tests; these are usually mild but can be serious. **Therefore skin tests should be done in the presence of a physician and with immediate access to medications and equipment needed to treat anaphylaxis.**

History of Penicillin Allergy

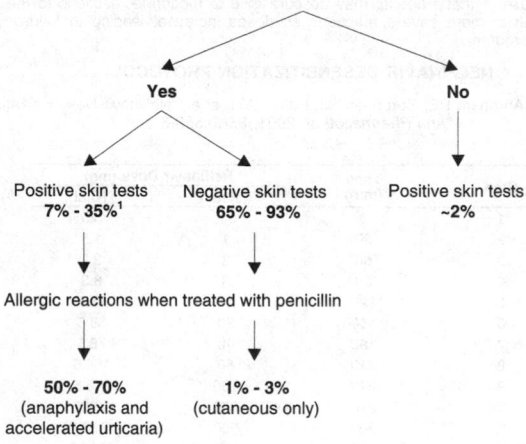

[1]One study found 65% positive.
Prevalence of positive and negative skin tests and subsequent allergic reactions in patients treated with penicilin (based on studies using both penicilloyl-polylysine and minor determinant mixture as skin test reagents).

Penicillin Skin Testing Protocol

Skin tests evaluate the patient for the presence of penicillin IgE — sensitive mast cells which are responsible for anaphylaxis and other immediate hypersensitivity reactions. Local or systemic allergic reactions rarely occur due to skin testing, therefore, a tourniquet, I.V., and epinephrine should be at the bedside. The breakdown products of penicillin provide the antigen which is responsible for the allergy. Testing is performed with benzylpenicilloyl-polylysine (Pre-Pen®), the major determinant, penicillin G which provides the minor determinants, and the actual penicillin which will be administered.

Controls are important if the patient is extremely ill or is taking antihistamines, codeine, or morphine. Normal saline is the negative control. Morphine sulfate, a mast cell degranulator, can be used as a positive control, if the patient is not on morphine or codeine. Histamine is the preferred positive control, however, is not manufactured in a pharmaceutical formulation anymore. A false-positive or false-negative will make further skin testing invalid.

Control Solutions

Normal saline = negative control
Morphine sulfate (10 mg/100 mL 0.9% NaCl, 0.1 mg/mL) = positive control

Test Solutions

Order the necessary solutions as 0.5 mL in a tuberculin syringe. **Note:** May need to order 2 syringes of each — one for scratch testing and one for intradermal skin testing.

I. **Pre-Pen®: Benzylpenicilloyl-polylysine (0.25 mL ampul) = MAJOR DETERMINANT**
    A. Undiluted Pre-Pen®
    B. 1:100 concentration
        To make: Dilute 0.1 mL of Pre-Pen® in 10 mL of 0.9% NaCl
    C. 1:10,000 concentration
        (Only necessary in patients with a history of anaphylaxis)
        To make: Dilute 1 mL of the 1:100 solution in 100 mL of 0.9% NaCl

II. **Penicillin G sodium/potassium = MINOR DETERMINANT**
    A. 5000 units/mL concentration
    B. 5 units/mL concentration
        (Only necessary in patients with a history of anaphylaxis)
        To make: Dilute 0.1 mL of a 5000 units/mL solution in 100 mL of 0.9% NaCl

III. **Penicillin product to be administered — if not penicillin G**
    A. **Ampicillin** 2.5 mg/mL concentration
        To make: Dilute 250 mg in 100 mL of 0.9% NaCl
    B. **Nafcillin** 2.5 mg/mL concentration
        To make: Dilute 250 mg in 100 mL of 0.9% NaCl

Order for placement/availability at the bedside in the event of a hypersensitivity reaction during scratch/skin testing and desensitization:

Hydrocortisone: 100 mg IVP
Diphenhydramine: 50 mg IVP
Epinephrine: 1:1000 SubQ

Scratch / Skin Testing Protocol: Must Be Done by Physician!

1. Begin with the control solutions (ie, normal saline and morphine).

2. Administer **scratch tests** in the following order (beginning with the most dilute solution):

Pre-Pen®	Syringes: C,B,A
Penicillin G	Syringes: E,D
Ampicillin/Nafcillin	Syringe: F

The inner volar surface of the forearm is usually used.

A nonbleeding scratch of 3-5 mm in length is made in the epidermis with a 20-gauge needle.

If bleeding occurs, another site should be selected and another scratch made using less pressure.

A small drop of the test solution is then applied and rubbed gently into the scratch using an applicator, toothpick, or the side of the needle.

The scratch test site should be observed for the appearance of a wheal, erythema, and pruritus.

A positive reaction is signified by the appearance within 15 minutes of a pale wheal (usually with pseudopods) ranging from 5-15 mm or more in diameter.

As soon as a positive response is elicited, or 15 minutes has elapsed, the solution should be wiped off the scratch.

If the scratch test is negative or equivocal (ie, a wheal of <5 mm in diameter with little or no erythema or itching appears), an intradermal test may be performed.

If significant reaction, treat and proceed to desensitization.

SKIN TESTS *(Continued)*

3. Administer **intradermal tests** in the following order (beginning with the most dilute solution):

Pre-Pen®	Syringes: C,B,A
Penicillin G	Syringes: E,D
Ampicillin/Nafcillin	Syringe: F

Intradermal tests are usually performed on a sterilized area of the upper outer arm at a sufficient distance below the deltoid muscle to permit proximal application of a tourniquet if a severe reaction occurs.

Using a tuberculin syringe with a $^3/_8$-$^5/_8$ inch 26- to 30-gauge needle, an amount of each test solution sufficient to raise the smallest perceptible bleb (usually 0.01-0.02 mL) is injected immediately under the surface of the skin.

A separate needle and syringe must be used for each solution.

Each test and control site should be at least 15 cm apart.

Positive reactions are manifested as a wheal at the test site with a diameter at least 5 mm larger than the saline control, often accompanied by itching and a marked increase in the size of the bleb.

Skin responses to penicillin testing will develop within 15 minutes.

If no significant reaction, may challenge patient with reduced dosage of the penicillin to be administered.

Physician should be at the bedside during this challenge dose!

If significant reaction, treat and begin desensitization.

Delayed Hypersensitivity (Anergy)

Delayed cutaneous hypersensitivity (DCH) is a cell-mediated immunological response which has been used diagnostically to assess previous infection (eg, purified protein derivative (PPD) and coccidioidin) or as an indicator of the status of the immune system by using mumps, *Candida*, tetanus toxoid, or trichophyton to test for anergy. Anergy is a defect in cell-mediated immunity that is characterized by an impaired response, or lack of a response to DCH testing with injected antigens. Anergy has been associated with several disease states, malnutrition, and immunosuppressive therapy, and has been correlated with increased risk of infection, morbidity, and mortality.

Many of the skin test antigens have not been approved by the FDA as tests for anergy, and so the directions for use and interpretation of reactions to these products may differ from that of the product labeling. There is also disagreement in the published literature as to the selection and interpretation of these tests for anergy assessment, leading to different recommendations for use of these products.

General Guidelines

Read these guidelines before using any skin test.

Administration

1. Use a separate sterile TB syringe for each antigen. Immediately after the antigen is drawn up, make the injection intradermally in the flexor surface of the forearm.
2. A small bleb 6-10 mm in diameter will form if the injection is made at the correct depth. If a bleb does not form or if the antigen solution leaks from the site, the injection must be repeated.
3. When applying more than one skin test, make the injections at least 5 cm apart.
4. Do any serologic blood tests before testing or wait 48-96 hours.

Reading

1. Read all tests at 24, 48, and 72 hours. Reactions occurring before 24 hours are indicative of an immediate rather than a delayed hypersensitivity.
2. Measure the diameter of the induration in two directions (at right angles) with a ruler and record each diameter in millimeters. Ballpoint pen method of measurement is the most accurate.
3. Test results should be recorded by the nurse in the Physician's Progress Notes section of the chart, and should include the millimeters of induration present, and a picture of the arm showing the location of the test(s).

Factors Causing False-Negative Reactions

1. Improper administration, interpretation, or use of outdated antigen
2. Test is applied too soon after exposure to the antigen (DCH takes 2-20 weeks to develop)
3. Concurrent viral illnesses (eg, rubeola, influenza, mumps, and probably others) or recent administration of live attenuated virus vaccines (eg, measles)
4. Anergy may be associated with:
    a. Immune suppressing chronic illnesses such as diabetes, uremia, sarcoidosis, metastatic carcinomas, Hodgkin's, acute lymphocytic leukemia, hypothyroidism, chronic hepatitis, and cirrhosis.

b. Some antineoplastic agents, radiation therapy, and corticosteroids. If possible, discontinue steroids at least 48 hours prior to DCH skin testing.

c. Congenital immune deficiencies.

d. Malnutrition, shock, severe burns, and trauma.

e. Severe disseminated infections (miliary or cavitary TB, cocci granuloma, and other disseminated mycotic infections, gram-negative bacillary septicemia).

f. Leukocytosis (>15,000 cells/mm^3).

Factors Causing False-Positive Reactions

1. Improper interpretation

2. Patient sensitivity to minor ingredients in the antigen solutions such as the phenol or thimerosal preservatives

3. Cross-reactions between similar antigens

***Candida* 1:1000**

Dose = 0.1 mL intradermally (30% of children <18 months of age and 50% >18 months of age respond)

Can be used as a control antigen

Coccidioidin 1:1000

Dose = 0.1 mL intradermally (apply with PPD **and** a control antigen)

Mercury derivative used as a preservative for Spherulin®.

Multitest CMI (*Candida*, diphtheria toxoid, tetanus toxoid, *Streptococcus*, old tuberculin, *Trichophyton, Proteus* antigen, and negative control)

Press loaded unit into the skin with sufficient pressure to puncture the skin and allow adequate penetration of all points.

Mumps 40 cfu/mL

Dose = 0.1 mL intradermally (contraindicated in patients allergic to eggs, egg products, or thimerosal)

Dosage as Part of Disease Diagnosis

Tuberculin Testing

Purified Protein Derivative (PPD)

Preparation	Dilution	Units/0.1 mL
First strength	1:10,000	1
Intermediate strength	1:2000	5
Second strength	1:100	250

The usual initial dose is 0.1 mL of the intermediate strength. The first strength should be used in the individuals suspected of being highly sensitive. The second strength is used only for individuals who fail to respond to a previous injection of the first or intermediate strengths.

A positive reaction is ≥10 mm induration except in HIV-infected individuals where a positive reaction is ≥5 mm of induration.

Adverse Reactions

In patients who are highly sensitive, or when higher than recommended doses are used, exaggerated local reactions may occur, including erythema, pain, blisters, necrosis, and scarring. Although systemic reactions are rare, a few cases of lymph node enlargement, fever, malaise, and fatigue have been reported.

To prevent severe local reactions, never use second test strengths as the initial agent. Use diluted first strengths in patients with known or suspected hypersensitivity to the antigen.

Have epinephrine and antihistamines on hand to treat severe allergic reactions that may occur.

Treatment of Adverse Reactions

Severe reactions to intradermal skin tests are rare and treatment consists of symptomatic care.

Skin Testing

All skin tests are given intradermally into the flexor surface of one arm.

Purified protein derivative (PPD) is used most often in the diagnosis of tuberculosis. *Candida, Trichophyton*, and mumps skin tests are used most often as controls for anergy.

SKIN TESTS *(Continued)*

Dose: The usual skin test dose is as follows:

Antigen		Standard Dose	Concentration
PPD	1 TU	0.1 mL	1 TU — highly sensitive patients
	5 TU	0.1 mL	5 TU — standard dose
	250 TU	0.1 mL	250 TU — anergic patients in whom TB is suspected
Candida		0.02 mL	
Mumps		0.1 mL	
Trichophyton		0.02 mL	

Interpretation:

Skin Test	Reading Time	Positive Reaction
PPD	48-72 h	**≥5 mm considered positive for:** • close contacts to an infectious case • persons with abnormal chest x-ray indicating old healed TB • persons with known or suspected HIV infection **≥10 mm considered positive for:** • other medical risk factors • foreign born from high prevalence areas • medically underserved, low income populations • alcoholics and intravenous drug users • residents of long-term care facilities (including correctional facilities and nursing homes) • staff in settings where disease would pose a hazard to large number of susceptible persons **≥15 mm considered positive for:** • persons without risk factors for TB
Candida	24-72 h	≥5 mm induration
Mumps	24-36 h	≥5 mm
Trichophyton	24-72 h	≥5 mm induration

Recommended Interpretation of Skin Test Reactions

Reaction	Local Reaction	
	After Intradermal Injections of Antigens	**After Dinitrochlorobenzene**
1+	Erythema >10 mm and/or induration >1-5 mm	Erythema and/or induration covering <¹/₂ area of dose site
2+	Induration 6-10 mm	Induration covering >¹/₂ area of dose site
3+	Induration 11-20 mm	Vesiculation and induration at dose site or spontaneous flare at days 7-14 at the site
4+	Induration >20 mm	Bulla or ulceration at dose site or spontaneous flare at days 7-14 at the site

IMMUNIZATION RECOMMENDATIONS

Recommended Immunization Schedule for Ages 0-6 Years
United States, 2007

Age ► Vaccine ▼	Birth	1 mo	2 mo	4 mo	6 mo	12 mo	15 mo	18 mo	19-23 mo	2-3 y	4-6 y
Hepatitis B[1]	HepB	HepB	See footnote		HepB					HepB series	
Rotavirus[2]			Rota	Rota	Rota						
Diphtheria, tetanus, pertussis[3]			DTaP	DTaP	DTaP		DTaP				DTaP
Haemophilus influenzae type b[4]			Hib	Hib	Hib[4]	Hib			Hib		
Pneumococcal[5]			PCV	PCV	PCV	PCV				PCV PPV	
Inactivated poliovirus			IPV	IPV		IPV					IPV
Influenza[6]						Influenza (yearly)					
Measles, mumps, rubella[7]						MMR					MMR
Varicella[8]						Varicella					Varicella
Hepatitis A[9]						HepA (2 doses)				HepA series	
Meningococcal[10]										MPSV4	

☐ Range of recommended ages	☐ Catch-up immunization	☐ Certain high-risk groups

This schedule indicates the recommended ages for routine administration of currently licensed childhood vaccines, as of December 1, 2006, for children through age 6 years. For additional information see **www.cdc.gov/nip/recs/child-schedule.htm**. Any dose not administered at the recommended age should be administered at any subsequent visit when indicated and feasible. Additional vaccines may be licensed and recommended during the year. Licensed combination vaccines may be used whenever any components of the combination are indicated and other components of the vaccine are not contraindicated and if approved by the Food and Drug Administration for that dose of the series. Providers should consult the respective Advisory Committee on Immunization Practices (ACIP) statement for detailed recommendations. Clinically significant adverse events that follow immunization should be reported to the Vaccine Adverse Event Reporting System (VAERS). Guidance about how to obtain and complete a VAERS form is available at **http://www.vaers.hhs.gov** or by telephone, **800-822-7967**.

[1] **Hepatitis B vaccine (HepB).** *(Minimum age: birth)*
At birth:
- Administer monovalent HepB to all newborns prior to hospital discharge.
- If mother is HBsAg-positive, administer HepB and 0.5 mL of hepatitis B immune globulin (HBIG) within 12 hours of birth.
- If mother's HBsAg status is unknown, administer HepB within 12 hours of birth. Determine the HBsAg status as soon as possible and if HBsAg-positive, administer HBIG (no later than age 1 week).
- If mother is HBsAg-negative, the birth dose can only be delayed with physician's order and mothers' negative HBsAg laboratory report documented in the infant's medical record.
Following the birth dose:
- The HepB series should be completed with either monovalent HepB or a combination vaccine containing HepB. The second dose should be administered at age 1–2 months. The final dose should be administered at age ≥24 weeks. Infants born to HBsAg-positive mothers should be tested for HBsAg and antibody to HBsAg after completion of 3 or more doses in a licensed HepB series, at age 9–18 months (generally at the next well-child visit).
4-month dose of HepB:
- It is permissible to administer 4 doses of HepB when combination vaccines are given after the birth dose. If monovalent HepB is used for doses after the birth dose, a dose at age 4 months is not needed.

[2] **Rotavirus vaccine (Rota).** *(Minimum age: 6 weeks)*
- Administer the first dose between 6 and 12 weeks of age. Do not start the series later than age 12 weeks.
- Administer the final dose in the series by 32 weeks of age. Do not administer a dose later than age 32 weeks.
- There are insufficient data on safety and efficacy outside of these age ranges.

[3] **Diphtheria, tetanus toxoids, and acellular pertussis vaccine (DTaP).** *(Minimum age: 6 weeks)*
- The fourth dose of DTaP may be administered as early as age 12 months, provided 6 months have elapsed since the third dose.
- Administer the final dose in the series at age 4-6 years.

[4] **Haemophilus influenzae type b conjugate vaccine (Hib).** *(Minimum age: 6 weeks)*
- If PRP-OMP (PedvaxHIB® or ComVax® [Merck]) is administered at ages 2 and 4 months, a dose at age 6 months is not required.
- TriHiBit® DTaP/Hib combination products should not be used for primary immunization but can be used as boosters following any Hib vaccine in ≥12 months olds.

[5] **Pneumococcal vaccine.** *(Minimum age: 6 weeks for Pneumococcal Conjugate Vaccine (PCV); 2 years for Pneumococcal Polysaccharide Vaccine (PPV))*
- Administer PCV at ages 24-59 months in certain high-risk groups. Administer PPV to certain high-risk groups aged ≥2 years. See *MMWR*, 2000, 49(RR-9):1-35.

[6] **Influenza vaccine.** *(Minimum age: 6 months for trivalent inactivated influenza vaccine (TIV); 5 years for live, attenuated influenza vaccine (LAIV))*
- All children aged 6–59 months and close contacts of all children aged 0–59 months are recommended to receive influenza vaccine.
- Influenza vaccine is recommended annually for children aged ≥59 months with certain risk factors, healthcare workers, and other persons (including household members) in close contact with persons in groups at high risk. See *MMWR*, 2006, 55(RR-10):1-41.
- For healthy persons aged 5–49 years, LAIV may be used as an alternative to TIV.
- Children receiving TIV should receive 0.25 mL if aged 6–35 months or 0.5 mL if aged ≥3 years.
- Children aged <9 years who are receiving influenza vaccine for the first time should receive 2 doses (separated by ≥4 weeks for TIV and ≥6 weeks for LAIV).

[7] **Measles, mumps, and rubella vaccine (MMR).** *(Minimum age: 12 months)*
- Administer the second dose of MMR at age 4-6 years. MMR may be administered prior to age 4-6 years, provided ≥4 weeks have elapsed since the first dose and both doses are administered ≥12 months.

[8] **Varicella vaccine.** *(Minimum age: 12 months)*
- Administer the second dose of varicella vaccine at age 4-6 years. Varicella vaccine may be administered prior to age 4-6 years, provided that ≥3 months have elapsed since the first dose and both doses are administered at age ≥12 months. If second dose was administered ≥28 days following the first dose, the second dose does not need to be repeated.

[9] **Hepatitis A vaccine (HepA).** *(Minimum age: 12 months)*
- HepA is recommended for all children at 1 year of age (ie, 12-23 months). The 2 doses in the series should be administered at least 6 months apart.
- Children not fully vaccinated by age 2 years can be vaccinated at subsequent visits.
- HepA is recommended for certain other groups of children including in areas where vaccination programs target older children. See *MMWR*, 2006, 55(RR-7):1-23.

[10] **Meningococcal polysaccharide vaccine (MPSV4).** *(Minimum age: 2 years)*
- Administer MPSV4 to children age 2-10 years with terminal complement deficiencies or anatomic or functional asplenia and certain other high risk groups. See *MMWR*, 2005, 54(RR-7):1:21.

Approved by the Advisory Committee on Immunization Practices (**www.cdc.gov/nip/acip**), the American Academy of Pediatrics (**www.aap.org**), and the American Academy of Family Physicians (**www.aafp.org**).

Reference:
"Recommended Immunization Schedules for Persons Aged 0-18 Years — United States, 2007," *MMWR*, 2007, 55(51):Q1-4.

IMMUNIZATION RECOMMENDATIONS *(Continued)*

Recommended Immunization Schedule for Ages 7-18 Years
United States, 2007

Age ▶ Vaccine ▼	7-10 y	11-12 y	13-14 y	15 y	16-18 y
Tetanus, diphtheria, pertussis[1]	See footnote 1	Tdap	Tdap		
Human papillomavirus[2]	See footnote 2	HPV (3 doses)	HPV series		
Meningococcal[3]	MPSV4	MCV4	MCV4[3] MCV4		
Pneumococcal[4]	PPV				
Influenza[5]	Influenza (yearly)				
Hepatitis A[6]	HepA series				
Hepatitis B[7]	HepB series				
Inactivated poliovirus[8]	IPV series				
Measles, mumps, rubella[9]	MMR series				
Varicella[10]	Varicella series				

☐ Range of recommended ages   ▨ Catch-up immunization   ▪ Certain high-risk groups

This schedule indicates the recommended ages for routine administration of currently licensed childhood vaccines, as of December 1, 2006, for children aged 7-18 years. For additional information see www.cdc.gov/nip/recs/child-schedule.htm. Any dose not administered at the recommended earlier age should be administered at any subsequent visit when indicated and feasible. Additional vaccines may be licensed and recommended during the year. Licensed combination vaccines may be used whenever any components of the combination are indicated and other components of the vaccine are not contraindicated and if approved by the Food and Drug Administration for that dose of the series. Providers should consult the respective Advisory Committee on Immunization Practices (ACIP) statement for detailed recommendations. Clinically significant adverse events that follow immunization should be reported to the Vaccine Adverse Event Reporting System (VAERS). Guidance about how to obtain and complete a VAERS form is available at **www.vaers.hhs.org** or by telephone, **800-822-7967**.

[1]**Tetanus and diphtheria toxoids and acellular pertussis vaccine (Tdap).** *(Minimum age: 10 years for BOOSTRIX® and 11 years for ADACEL™)*
- Administer at age 11-12 years for those who have completed the recommended childhood DTP/DTaP vaccination series and have not received a Td booster dose.
- Adolescents 13-18 years who missed the 11-12 year Td/Tdap booster dose should also receive a single dose of Tdap if they have completed the recommended childhood DTP/DTaP vaccination series.

[2]**Human papillomavirus vaccine (HPV).** *(Minimum age: 9 years)*
- Administer the first dose of the HPV vaccine series to females at age 11-12 years.
- Administer the second dose 2 months after the first dose and the third dose 6 months after the first dose.
- Administer the HPV vaccine series to females at age 13-18 years if not previously vaccinated.

[3]**Meningococcal vaccine.** *(Minimum age: 11 years for meningococcal conjugate vaccine (MCV4); 2 years for meningococcal polysaccharide vaccine (MPSV4))*
- Administer MCV4 at age 11-12 years and to previously unvaccinated adolescents at high school entry (~15 years of age).
- Administer MCV4 to previously unvaccinated college freshmen living in dormitories; MPSV4 is an acceptable alternative.
- Vaccination against invasive meningococcal disease is recommended for children and adolescents aged ≥2 years with terminal complement deficiencies or anatomic or functional asplenia and certain other high-risk groups. See MMWR, 2005, 54(RR-7):1-21. Use MPSV4 for children aged 2-10 years and MCV4 or MPSV4 for older children.

[4]**Pneumococcal polysaccharide vaccine (PPV).** *(Minimum age: 2 years)*
- Administer for certain high-risk groups. See MMWR, 1997, 46(RR-08), 1-24 and MMWR, 2000, 49(RR-9):1-35.

[5]**Influenza vaccine.** *(Minimum age: 6 months for trivalent inactivated influenza vaccine (TIV); 5 years for live, attenuated influenza vaccine (LAIV))*
- Influenza vaccine is recommended annually for persons with certain risk factors, healthcare workers, and other persons (including household members) in close contact with persons in groups at high risk. See MMWR, 2006, 55(RR-10);1-41.
- For healthy persons aged 5-49 years, LAIV may be used as an alternative to TIV.
- Children aged <9 years who are receiving influenza vaccine for the first time should receive 2 doses (separated by ≥4 weeks for TIV and ≥6 weeks for LAIV).

[6]**Hepatitis A vaccine (HepA).** *(Minimum age: 12 months)*
- The 2 doses in the series should be administered at least 6 months apart.
- HepA is recommended for certain other groups of children including in areas where vaccination programs target older children. See MMWR, 2006, 55(RR-7):1:23.

[7]**Hepatitis B vaccine (HepB).** *(Minimum age: birth)*
- Administer the 3-dose series to those who were not previously vaccinated.
- A 2-dose series of Recombivax HB® is licensed for 11-15 year olds.

[8]**Inactivated poliovirus vaccine (IPV).** *(Minimum age: 6 weeks)*
- For children who received an all-IPV or all-oral poliovirus (OPV) series, a fourth dose is not necessary if third dose was administered at age ≥4 years.
- If both OPV and IPV were administered as part of a series, a total of 4 doses should be given, regardless of the child's current age.

[9]**Measles, mumps, and rubella vaccine (MMR).** *(Minimum age: 12 months)*
- If not previously vaccinated, administer 2 doses of MMR during any visit with ≥4 weeks between the doses.

[10]**Varicella vaccine.** *(Minimum age: 12 months)*
- Administer 2 doses of varicella vaccine to persons without evidence of immunity.
- Administer 2 doses of varicella vaccine to persons aged ≤13 years at least 3 month apart. Do not repeat the second dose, if administered ≥28 days following the first dose.
- Administer 2 doses of varicella vaccine to persons aged ≥13 years at least 4 weeks apart.

Approved by the Advisory Committee on Immunization Practices (**www.cdc.gov/nip/acip**), the American Academy of Pediatrics (**www.aap.org**), and the American Academy of Family Physicians (**www.aafp.org**).

Reference:
"Recommended Immunization Schedules for Persons Aged 0-18 Years — United States, 2007," MMWR , 2007, 55(51):Q1-4.

Recommended Immunization Schedule for Children and Adolescents Who Start Late or Who Are >1 Month Behind – United States, 2007

Tables 1 and 2 give catch-up schedules and minimum intervals between doses for children who have delayed immunizations. There is no need to restart a vaccine series regardless of the time that has elapsed between doses. Use the table appropriate for the childs age.

Table 1. Catch-up Schedule for Ages 4 Months - 6 Years

Vaccine (Minimum Age for Dose 1)	Minimum Interval Between Doses			
	Dose 1 to Dose 2	Dose 2 to Dose 3	Dose 3 to Dose 4	Dose 4 to Dose 5
HepB[1] (birth)	4 weeks	8 weeks (and 16 weeks after 1st dose)		
Rotavirus[2] (6 wk)	4 weeks	4 weeks		
DTaP[3] (6 wk)	4 weeks	4 weeks	6 months	6 months[3]
Hib[4] (6 wk)	**4 weeks** if 1st dose given at age <12 months **8 weeks (as final dose)** if 1st dose given at age 12-14 months **No further doses needed** if 1st dose given at age ≥15 months	**4 weeks[4]** if current age <12 months **8 weeks (as final dose)[4]** if current age ≥12 months and 2nd dose given at age <15 months **No further doses needed** if previous dose given at age ≥15 months	**8 weeks (as final dose)** This dose only necessary for children age 12 months - 5 years who received 3 doses before age 12 months	
PCV[5] (6 wk)	**4 weeks** if 1st dose given at age <12 months and current age <24 months **8 weeks (as final dose)** if 1st dose given at age ≥12 months or current age 24-59 months **No further doses needed** for healthy children if 1st dose given at age ≥24 months	**4 weeks** if current age <12 months **8 weeks (as final dose)** if current age ≥12 months **No further doses needed** for healthy children if previous dose given at age ≥24 months	**8 weeks (as final dose)** This dose only necessary for children age 12 months - 5 years who received 3 doses before age 12 months	
IPV[6] (6 wk)	4 weeks	4 weeks	4 weeks[6]	
MMR[7] (12 mo)	4 weeks			
Varicella[8] (12 mo)	3 months			
HepA[9] (12 mo)	6 months			

IMMUNIZATION RECOMMENDATIONS *(Continued)*

Table 2. Catch-up Schedule for Ages 7-18 Years

Vaccine (Minimum Age for Dose 1)	Minimum Interval Between Doses			
	Dose 1 to Dose 2	Dose 2 to Dose 3	Dose 3 to Dose 4	Dose 4 to Dose 5
Td/TdaP[10] (7 y[10])	4 weeks	**8 months** if first dose given at age <12 months **6 months** if first dose given at age ≥12 months	**6 months** if first dose given at age <12 months	
HPV[11] (9 y)	4 weeks	12 weeks		
HepA[9] (12 mo)	6 months			
HepB[1] (birth)	4 weeks	8 weeks (and 16 weeks after first dose)		
IPV[6] (6 wk)	4 weeks	4 weeks	4 weeks[6]	
MMR[7] (12 mo)	4 weeks			
Varicella[8] (12 mo)	**4 weeks** if first dose given at age ≥13 years **3 months** if first dose given at age <13 years			

Footnotes to Table 1 and Table 2

[1]**HepB (hepatitis B).** *(Minimum age: birth)*

- Administer the 3-dose series to those who were not previously vaccinated.
- A 2-dose series of Recombivax HB® is licensed for 11-15 year olds.

[2]**Rotavirus (Rota).** *(Minimum age: 6 weeks)*

- Do not start the series later than age 12 weeks.
- Administer the final dose in the series by 32 weeks of age. Do not administer a dose later than age 32 weeks.
- There are insufficient data on safety and efficacy outside of these age ranges.

[3]**DTaP (diphtheria and tetanus toxoids and acellular pertussis).** *(Minimum age: 6 weeks)*

- The fifth dose is not necessary if the fourth dose was administered at age ≥4 years.
- DTaP is not indicated for persons age ≥7 years.

[4]**Hib** *(Haemophilus influenzae type b conjugate).* *(Minimum age: 6 weeks)*

- Vaccine is not generally recommended for children age ≥5 years.
- If current age <12 months and the first 2 doses were PRP-OMP (PedvaxHIB® or ComVax® [Merck]), the third (and final) dose should be administered at age 12-15 months and at least 8 weeks after the second dose.
- If first dose given at age 7-11 months, give 2 doses separated by 4 weeks plus a booster at age 12-15 months.

[5]**PCV (pneumococcal conjugate vaccine).** *(Minimum age: 6 weeks)*

- Vaccine is not generally recommended for children age ≥5 years.

[6]**IPV (inactivated poliovirus).** *(Minimum age: 6 weeks)*

- For children who received an all-IPV or all-oral poliovirus (OPV) series, a fourth dose is not necessary if third dose was administered at age ≥4 years.
- If both OPV and IPV were administered as part of a series, a total of 4 doses should be given, regardless of the child's current age.

[7]**MMR (measles, mumps, and rubella).** *(Minimum age: 12 months)*

- The second dose of MMR is recommended routinely at age 4-6 years, but may be administered earlier if desired.
- If not previously vaccinated, administer 2 doses of MMR during any visit with ≥4 weeks between the doses.

[8]**Varicella.** *(Minimum age: 12 months)*

- The second dose of varicella vaccine is recommended routinely at age 4-6 years but may be administered earlier if desired.
- Do not repeat the second dose in persons age <13 years, if administered ≥28 days following the first dose.

[9]**HepA (hepatitis A).** *(Minimum age: 12 months)*

- HepA is recommended for certain groups of children including in areas where vaccination programs target older children. See *MMWR*, 2006, SS(RR-7):1-23.

[10]**Td (tetanus and diphtheria toxoids) and Tdap (tetanus and diphtheria toxoids and acellular pertussis).** *(Minimum ages: 7 years for Td, 10 years for BOOSTRIX®, and 11 years for ADACEL™)*

- Tdap should be substituted for a single dose of Td in the primary catch-up series or as a booster if age-appropriate; use Td for other doses.
- A 5-year interval from the last Td dose is encouraged when Tdap is used as a booster dose. A booster (fourth) dose is needed if any of the previous doses were administered at age <12 months. Refer to ACIP recommendations for further information. See *MMWR*, 2006, SS(RR-3):L34.

[11] **HPV (human papillomavirus).** *(Minimum age: 9 years)*

- Administer the HPV vaccine series to females at age 13-18 years if not previously vaccinated.

Reporting Adverse Reactions

For information on reporting reactions following immunization, visit **www.vaers.hhs.gov** or call the 24-hour national toll-free information line **800-822-7967**. Report suspected cases of vaccine-preventable diseases to your state or local health department. For additional information including precautions and contraindications for immunization, visit the National Center for Immunization and Respiratory Diseases at **www.cdc.gov/ncird** or contact **800-CDC-INFO (800-232-4636)**.

IMMUNIZATION RECOMMENDATIONS *(Continued)*

Recommended Adult Immunization Schedule, by Vaccine and Age Group
United States, October 2006 - September 2007

Vaccine	Age Group (years)		
	19-49	50-64	≥65
Tetanus, diphtheria, pertussis (Td/Tdap)[1]*	1-dose Td booster every 10 years		
	Substitute 1 dose of Tdap for Td		
Human papilloma-virus (HPV)[2]*	3 doses (females)		
Measles, mumps, rubella (MMR)[3]*	1 or 2 doses	1 dose	
Varicella[4]*	2 doses (0, 4-8 weeks)	2 doses (0, 4-8 weeks)	
Influenza[5]*	1 dose annually	1 dose annually	
Pneumococcal (polysaccharide)[6,7]	1-2 doses		1 dose
Hepatitis A[8]*	2 doses (0, 6-12 months, or 0, 6-18 months)		
Hepatitis B[9]*	3 doses (0, 1-2, 4-6 months)		
Meningococcal[10]	1 or more doses		

For all persons in this category who meet the age requirements and who lack evidence of immunity (eg, lack documentation of vaccination or have no evidence of prior infection)

Recommended if some other risk factor is present (eg, on the basis of medical, occupational, lifestyle, or other indications)

*Covered by the Vaccine Injury Compensation Program.
Note: These recommendations must be read along with the footnotes, which can be found following this schedule.

Recommended Adult Immunization Schedule, by Vaccine and Medical and Other Indications — United States, October 2006 - September 2007

Vaccine	Indication							
	Pregnancy	Congenital immunodeficiency, leukemia,[11] lymphoma, generalized malignancy, cerebrospinal fluid leaks, therapy with alkylating agents, antimetabolites, radiation, or high-dose, long-term corticosteroids	Diabetes, heart disease, chronic pulmonary disease, chronic alcoholism	Asplenia[11] (including elective splenectomy and terminal complement component deficiencies)	Chronic liver disease, recipients of clotting factor concentrates	Kidney failure, end-stage renal disease, recipients of hemodialysis	Human immuno-deficiency virus (HIV) infection[3,11]	Healthcare workers
Tetanus, diphtheria, pertussis (Td/Tdap)[1]*	1-dose Td booster every 10 years							
	Substitute 1 dose of Tdap for Td							
Human papilloma-virus (HPV)[2]*	3 doses for women ≤26 years of age (0, 2, 6 months)							
Measles, mumps, rubella (MMR)[3]*			1 or 2 doses					
Varicella[4]*			2 doses (0, 4-8 weeks)					2 doses
Influenza[5]*	1 dose annually		1 dose annually	1 dose annually				
Pneumococcal (polysaccharide)[6,7]	1-2 doses	1-2 doses						1-2 doses
Hepatitis A[8]*	2 doses (0, 6-12 months, or 0, 6-18 months)				2 doses (0, 6-12 months, or 0, 6-18 months)			
Hepatitis B[9]*	3 doses (0, 1-2, 4-6 months)				3 doses (0, 1-2, 4-6 months)			
Meningococcal[10]	1 dose		1 dose		1 dose			

For all persons in this category who meet the age requirements and who lack evidence of immunity (eg, lack documentation of vaccination or have no evidence of prior infection)

Recommended if some other risk factor is present (eg, on the basis of medical, occupational, lifestyle, or other indications)

Contraindicated

*Covered by the Vaccine Injury Compensation Program.
Note: These recommendations must be read along with the footnotes, which can be found following this schedule.

Footnotes to Recommended Adult Immunization Schedule

[1]**Tetanus, diphtheria, and acellular pertussis (Td/Tdap) vaccination.** Adults with uncertain histories of a complete primary vaccination series with diphtheria and tetanus toxoid-containing vaccines should begin or complete a primary vaccination series. A primary series for adults is 3 doses; administer the first 2 doses at least 4 weeks apart and the third dose 6-12 months after the second. Administer a booster dose to adults who have completed a primary series and if the last vaccination was received ≥10 years previously. Tdap or tetanus and diphtheria (Td) vaccine may be used; Tdap should replace a single dose of Td for adults aged <65 years who have not previously received a dose of Tdap (either in the primary series, as a booster or for wound management). Only one of two Tdap products (Adacel™ [sanofi pasteur, Swiftwater, Pennsylvania]) is licensed for use in adults. If the person is pregnant and received the last Td vaccination ≥10 years previously, administer Td during the second or third trimester; if the person received the last Td vaccination in <10 years, administer Tdap during the immediate postpartum period. A one-time administration of 1-dose of Tdap with an interval as short as 2 years from a previous Td vaccination is recommended for postpartum women, close contacts of infants aged <12 months, and all healthcare workers with direct patient contact. In certain situations, Td can be deferred during pregnancy and Tdap substituted in the immediate postpartum period, or Tdap can be given instead of Td to a pregnant woman after an informed discussion with the woman (see http://www.cdc.gov/nip/publications/acip-list.htm). Consult the ACIP statement for recommendations for administering Td as prophylaxis in wound management (http://www.cdc.gov/mmwr/preview/mmwrhtml/00001645.htm).

[2]**Human papillomavirus (HPV) vaccination.** HPV vaccination is recommended for all women aged ≤26 years who have not completed the vaccine series. Ideally, vaccine should be administered before potential exposure to HPV through sexual activity; however, women who are sexually active should still be vaccinated. Sexually active women who have not been infected with any of the HPV vaccine types receive the full benefit of the vaccination. Vaccination is less beneficial for women who have already been infected with one or more of the four HPV vaccine types. A complete series consists of 3 doses. The second dose should be administered 2 months after the first dose; the third dose should be administered 6 months after the first dose. Vaccination is not recommended during pregnancy. If a woman is found to be pregnant after initiating the vaccination series, the remainder of the 3-dose regimen should be delayed until after completion of the pregnancy.

[3]**Measles, mumps, rubella (MMR) vaccination.** *Measles component:* Adults born before 1957 can be considered immune to measles. Adults born during or after 1957 should receive ≥1 dose of MMR unless they have a medical contraindication, documentation of ≥1 dose, history of measles based on healthcare provider diagnosis, or laboratory evidence of immunity. A second dose of MMR is recommended for adults who 1) have been recently exposed to measles or in an outbreak setting; 2) have been previously vaccinated with killed measles vaccine; 3) have been vaccinated with an unknown type of measles vaccine during 1963-1967; 4) are students in postsecondary educational institutions; 5) work in a healthcare facility; or 6) plan to travel internationally. Withhold MMR or other measles-containing vaccines from HIV-infected persons with severe immunosuppression. *Mumps component:* Adults born before 1957 can generally be considered immune to mumps. Adults born during or after 1957 should receive 1 dose of MMR unless they have a medical contraindication, history of mumps based on healthcare provider diagnosis, or laboratory evidence of immunity. A second dose of MMR is recommended for adults who 1) are in an age group that is affected during a mumps outbreak; 2) are students in postsecondary educational institutions; 3) work in a healthcare facility; or 4) plan to travel internationally. For unvaccinated healthcare workers born before 1957 who do not have other evidence of mumps immunity, consider giving 1 dose on a routine basis and strongly consider giving a second dose during an outbreak. *Rubella component:* Administer 1 dose of MMR vaccine to women whose rubella vaccination history is unreliable or who lack laboratory evidence of immunity. For women of childbearing age, regardless of birth year, routinely determine rubella immunity and counsel women regarding congenital rubella syndrome. Do not vaccinate women who are pregnant or who might become pregnant within 4 weeks of receiving vaccine. Women who do not have evidence of immunity should receive MMR vaccine upon completion or termination of pregnancy and before discharge from the healthcare facility.

[4]**Varicella vaccination.** All adults without evidence of immunity to varicella should receive 2 doses of varicella vaccine. Special consideration should be given to those who 1) have close contact with persons at high risk for severe disease (eg, healthcare workers and family contacts of immunocompromised persons) or 2) are at high risk for exposure or transmission (eg, teachers of young children; child care employees; residents and staff members of institutional settings, including correctional institutions; college students; military personnel; adolescents and adults living in households with children; nonpregnant women of childbearing age; and international travelers). Evidence of immunity to varicella in adults includes any of the following: 1) documentation of 2 doses of varicella vaccine at least 4 weeks apart; 2) U.S.-born before 1980 (although for healthcare workers and pregnant women, birth before 1980 should not be considered evidence of immunity); 3) history of varicella based on diagnosis or verification of varicella by a healthcare provider (for a patient reporting a history of or presenting with an atypical case, a mild case, or both, healthcare providers should seek either an epidemiologic link with a typical varicella case or evidence of laboratory confirmation, if it was performed at the time of acute disease); 4) history of herpes zoster based on healthcare provider diagnosis; or 5) laboratory evidence of immunity or laboratory confirmation of disease. Do not vaccinate women who are pregnant or might become pregnant within 4 weeks of receiving the vaccine. Assess pregnant women for evidence of varicella immunity. Women who do not have evidence of immunity should receive dose 1 of varicella vaccine upon completion or termination of pregnancy and before discharge from the healthcare facility. Dose 2 should be administered 4-8 weeks after dose 1.

[5]**Influenza vaccination.** *Medical indications:* Chronic disorders of the cardiovascular or pulmonary systems, including asthma; chronic metabolic diseases, including diabetes mellitus, renal dysfunction, hemoglobinopathies, or immunosuppression (including immunosuppression caused by medications or HIV); any condition that compromises respiratory function or the handling of respiratory secretions or that can increase the risk of aspiration (eg, cognitive dysfunction, spinal cord injury, or seizure disorder or other neuromuscular disorder); and pregnancy during the influenza season. No data exist on the risk for severe or complicated influenza disease among persons with asplenia; however, influenza is a risk factor for secondary bacterial infections that can cause severe disease among persons with asplenia. *Occupational indications:* Healthcare workers and employees of long-term care and assisted living facilities. *Other indications:* Residents of nursing homes and other long-term care and assisted living facilities; persons likely to transmit influenza to persons at high risk (ie, in-home household contacts and caregivers of children aged 0-59 months, or persons of all ages with high-risk conditions); and anyone who would like to be vaccinated. Healthy, nonpregnant persons aged 5-49 years without high-risk medical conditions who are not contacts of severely immunocompromised persons in special care units can receive either intranasally administered influenza vaccine (fluMist®) or inactivated vaccine. Other persons should receive the inactivated vaccine.

[6]**Pneumococcal polysaccharide vaccination.** *Medical indications:* Chronic disorders of the pulmonary system (excluding asthma); cardiovascular diseases; diabetes mellitus; chronic liver diseases, including liver disease as a result of alcohol abuse (eg, cirrhosis); chronic renal failure or nephrotic syndrome;

IMMUNIZATION RECOMMENDATIONS *(Continued)*

functional or anatomic asplenia (eg, sickle cell disease or splenectomy [if elective splenectomy is planned, vaccinate at least 2 weeks before surgery]); immunosuppressive conditions (eg, congenital immunodeficiency, HIV infection [vaccinate as close to diagnosis as possible when CD4 cell counts are highest], leukemia, lymphoma, multiple myeloma, Hodgkin disease, generalized malignancy, or organ or bone marrow transplantation); chemotherapy with alkylating agents, antimetabolites, or high-dose, long-term corticosteroids; and cochlear implants. *Other indications:* Alaska Natives and certain American Indian populations and residents of nursing homes or other long-term care facilities.

[7]**Revaccination with pneumococcal polysaccharide vaccine.** One-time revaccination after 5 years for persons with chronic renal failure or nephrotic syndrome; functional or anatomic asplenia (eg, sickle cell disease or splenectomy); immunosuppressive conditions (eg, congenital immunodeficiency, HIV infection, leukemia, lymphoma, multiple myeloma, Hodgkin disease, generalized malignancy, or organ or bone marrow transplantation); or chemotherapy with alkylating agents, antimetabolites, or high-dose, long-term corticosteroids. For persons aged ≥65 years, one-time revaccination if they were vaccinated ≥5 years previously and were aged <65 years at the time of primary vaccination.

[8]**Hepatitis A vaccination.** *Medical indications:* Persons with chronic liver disease and persons who receive clotting factor concentrates. *Behavioral indications:* Men who have sex with men and persons who use illegal drugs. *Occupational indications:* Persons working with hepatitis A virus (HAV)-infected primates or with HAV in a research laboratory setting. *Other indications:* Persons traveling to or working in countries that have high or intermediate endemicity of hepatitis A (a list of countries is available at http://www.cdc.gov/travel/diseases.htm) and any person who would like to obtain immunity. Current vaccines should be administered in a 2-dose schedule at either 0 and 6-12 months, or 0 and 6-18 months. If the combined hepatitis A and hepatitis B vaccine is used, administer 3 doses at 0, 1, and 6 months.

[9]**Hepatitis B vaccination.** *Medical indications:* Persons with end-stage renal disease, including patients receiving hemodialysis; persons seeking evaluation or treatment for a sexually transmitted disease (STD); persons with HIV infection; persons with chronic liver disease; and persons who receive clotting factor concentrates. *Occupational indications:* Healthcare workers and public-safety workers who are exposed to blood or other potentially infectious body fluids. *Behavioral indications:* Sexually active persons who are not in a long-term, mutually monogamous relationship (ie, persons with >1 sex partner during the previous 6 months); current or recent injection-drug users; and men who have sex with men. *Other indications:* Household contacts and sex partners of persons with chronic hepatitis B virus (HBV) infection; clients and staff members of institutions for persons with developmental disabilities; all clients of STD clinics; international travelers to countries with high or intermediate prevalence of chronic HBV infection (a list of countries is available at http://www.cdc.gov/travel/diseases.htm); and any adult seeking protection from HBV infection. Settings where hepatitis B vaccination is recommended for all adults: STD treatment facilities; HIV testing and treatment facilities; facilities providing drug-abuse treatment and prevention services; healthcare settings providing services for injection-drug users or men who have sex with men; correctional facilities; end-stage renal disease programs and facilities for chronic hemodialysis patients; and institutions and nonresidential daycare facilities for persons with developmental disabilities. *Special formulation indications:* For adult patients receiving hemodialysis and other immunocompromised adults, 1 dose of 40 mcg/mL (Recombivax HB®) or 2 doses of 20 mcg/mL (Engerix-B®).

[10]**Meningococcal vaccination.** *Medical indications:* Adults with anatomic or functional asplenia, or terminal complement component deficiencies. *Other indications:* First-year college students living in dormitories; microbiologists who are routinely exposed to isolates of *Neisseria meningitidis*; military recruits; and persons who travel to or live in countries in which meningococcal disease is hyperendemic or epidemic (eg, the "meningitis belt" of sub-Saharan Africa during the dry season [December-June]), particularly if their contact with local populations will be prolonged. Vaccination is required by the government of Saudi Arabia for all travelers to Mecca during the annual Hajj. Meningococcal conjugate vaccine is preferred for adults with any of the preceding indications who are aged ≤55 years, although meningococcal polysaccharide vaccine (MPSV4) is an acceptable alternative. Revaccination after 5 years might be indicated for adults previously vaccinated with MPSV4 who remain at high risk for infection (eg, persons residing in areas in which disease is epidemic).

[11]**Selected conditions for which *Haemophilus influenzae* type b (Hib) vaccine may be used.** Hib conjugate vaccines are licensed for children aged 6 weeks to 71 months. No efficacy data are available on which to base a recommendation concerning use of Hib vaccine for older children and adults with the chronic conditions associated with an increased risk for Hib disease. However, studies suggest good immunogenicity in patients who have sickle cell disease, leukemia, or HIV infection or who have had splenectomies; administering vaccine to these patients is not contraindicated.

Adapted from "Centers for Disease Control and Prevention. Recommended Adult Immunization Schedule – United States, October 2006 - September 2007," *MMWR*, 2006, 55(40):Q1-4.

The Recommended Adult Immunization Schedule has been approved by the Advisory Committee on Immunization Practices (ACIP), the American College of Obstetricians and Gynecologists (ACOG), and the American Academy of Family Physicians (AAFP).

This schedule indicates the recommended age groups and medical indications for routine administration of currently licensed vaccines for persons ≥19 years of age, as of October 1, 2006. Licensed combination vaccines may be used whenever any components of the combination are indicated and when the vaccine's other components are not contraindicated. For detailed recommendations on **all** vaccines, including those used primarily for travelers or that are issued during the year, consult the manufacturers' package inserts and the complete statements from the Advisory Committee on Immunization Practices (http://www.cdc.gov/nip/publications/acip-list.htm).

Additional information about the vaccines in this schedule and contraindications for vaccination is also available at http://www.cdc.gov/nip or from the CDC-INFO Contact Center at 800-CDC-INFO (800-232-4636) in English and Spanish, 24 hours a day, 7 days a week.

Immunization in HIV-Infected Persons

Vaccination of immunocompromised patients depends on the characteristics of the vaccine and the patient. Vaccines are typically divided into two broad categories: those which contain live virus/bacteria or those which are derived from a component of the organism (or an inactivated organism). Live virus or live bacterial vaccines have been associated with severe complications in immunocompromised patients, and should generally be avoided [(except in selected circumstances (noted below)]. Inactivated, recombinant, subunit, polysaccharide, and conjugate vaccines and toxoids can be administered to all immunocompromised patients. However, it should be recognized that the response to these vaccines may be suboptimal. If indicated, all inactivated vaccines are recommended in usual doses and according to prescribed schedules. Pneumococcal, meningococcal, and Hib vaccines are recommended only for specific subpopulations, including functional or anatomic asplenia.

Special consideration must be given to immunization with measles and/or varicella vaccines. Persons with HIV are at a higher risk for severe complications from measles infection. In patients without severe immunocompromise, measles vaccination in HIV-infected persons has not been reported to cause severe and/or unusual adverse events. MMR vaccination is recommended for all HIV-infected persons who do not have evidence of severe immunocompromise (defined as a low age-specific total CD4+ T-lymphocyte count or a low CD4+ T-lymphocyte count as a percentage of total lymphocytes).

Varicella and/or herpes zoster infections are also associated with an increased risk of severe complications in children with HIV infection. Asymptomatic or mildly symptomatic HIV-infected children receiving varicella vaccination have demonstrated adequate response to the vaccine without evidence of severe and/or unusual events. However, experience has been limited. Varicella vaccine should be considered for children who are classified as CDC class N1, N2, A1, A2, B1, or B2 with age-specific CD4+ T-lymphocyte percentages >15%.

HIV-infected persons who are receiving IVIG may not respond to MMR or varicella vaccines (or an individual component) due to the presence of a passively acquired antibody. Measles vaccine should be considered approximately 2 weeks before the next scheduled dose of IVIG (unless otherwise contraindicated). Unless serologic testing confirms the production of specific antibodies, the vaccination should be repeated at the recommended interval. In patients receiving maintenance IVIG therapy, an additional dose of IVIG should be considered if the exposure to measles occurs ≥3 weeks following a standard dose. Persons with cellular immunodeficiency should not receive varicella vaccine; however, persons with humoral immunodeficiency should be vaccinated (including persons with dysgammaglobulinemia or hypogammaglobulinemia).

Summarized/adapted from Centers for Disease Control and Prevention, "General Recommendations on Immunization. Recommendations of the Advisory Committee on Immunization Practices (ACIP), *MMWR Recomm Rep*, 2006, 55(RR-15):1-56.

IMMUNIZATION RECOMMENDATIONS *(Continued)*

Recommendations for Pneumococcal Conjugate Vaccine Use Among Healthy Children During Moderate and Severe Shortages

Age at First Vaccination (mo)	No Shortage[1]	Moderate Shortage	Severe Shortage
<6	2, 4, 6, and 12-15 months	2, 4, and 6 months (defer fourth dose)	2 doses at 2-month interval in first 6 months of life (defer third and fourth doses)
7-11	2 doses at 2-month interval; 12-15 month dose	2 doses at 2-month interval; 12-15-month dose	2 doses at 2-month interval (defer third dose)
12-23	2 doses at 2-month interval	2 doses at 2-month interval	1 dose (defer second dose)
>24	1 dose should be considered	No vaccination	No vaccination
Reduction in vaccine doses used[2]		21%	46%

[1]The vaccine schedule for no shortage is included as a reference. Providers should not use the no shortage schedule regardless of their vaccine supply until the national shortage is resolved.

[2]Assumes that approximately 85% of vaccine is administered to healthy infants beginning at age <7 months; approximately 5% is administered to high-risk infants beginning at age <7 months; and approximately 10% is administered to healthy children beginning at age 7-24 months. Actual vaccine savings will depend on a provider's vaccine use.

Adapted from the Advisory Committee on Immunization Practices, "Updated Recommendations on Use of Pneumococcal Conjugate Vaccine in a Setting of Vaccine Shortage," *MMWR Morb Mortal Wkly Rep*, 2001, 50(50):1140-2.

Recommended Regimens for Pneumococcal Conjugate Vaccine Among Children With a Late Start or Lapse in Vaccine Administration

Age at Examination (mo)	Previous Pneumococcal Conjugate Vaccination History	Recommended Regimen[1]
2-6	0 doses	3 doses 2 months apart, 4th dose at 12-15 months
	1 dose	2 doses 2 months apart, 4th dose at 12-15 months
	2 doses	1 dose, 4th dose at 12-15 months
7-11	0 doses	2 doses 2 months apart, 3rd dose at 12-15 months
	1 or 2 doses before age 7 months	1 dose at 7-11 months, with another dose at 12-15 months (≥2 months later)
12-23	0 doses	2 doses ≥2 months apart
	1 dose before age 12 months	2 doses ≥2 months apart
	1 dose at ≥12 months	1 dose ≥2 months after the most recent dose
	2 or 3 doses before age 12 months	1 dose ≥2 months after the most recent dose
24-59		
Healthy children[2]	Any incomplete schedule	Consider 1 dose ≥2 months after the most recent dose
High risk[3]	<3 doses	1 dose ≥2 months after the most recent dose and another dose ≥2 months later
	3 doses	1 dose ≥2 months after the most recent dose

[1]For children vaccinated at age <1 year, the minimum interval between doses is 4 weeks. Doses administered at ≥12 months should be at least 8 weeks apart.

[2]Providers should consider 1 dose for healthy children 24-59 months, with priority to children 24-35 months, American Indian/Alaska native and black children, and those who attend group child care centers.

[3]Children with sickle cell disease, asplenia, human immunodeficiency virus infection, chronic illness, cochlear implant, or immunocompromising condition.

Adapted from "CDC. Notice to Readers: Pneumococcal Conjugate Vaccine Shortage Resolved," *MMWR Morb Mortal Wkly Rep*, 2003, 52(19):446-7.

PREVENTION OF HEPATITIS A THROUGH ACTIVE OR PASSIVE IMMUNIZATION: RECOMMENDATIONS OF THE ADVISORY COMMITTEE ON IMMUNIZATION PRACTICES (ACIP)

PROPHYLAXIS AGAINST HEPATITIS A VIRUS INFECTION

Recommended Doses of Immune Globulin (IG) for Hepatitis A Pre-exposure and Postexposure Prophylaxis[1]

Setting	Duration of Coverage	IG Dose[2]
Pre-exposure	Short-term (1-2 months)	0.02 mL/kg
	Long-term (3-5 months)	0.06 mL/kg[3]
Postexposure	—	0.02 mL/kg

[1]Infants and pregnant women should receive a preparation that does not include thimerosal.

[2]IG should be administered by intramuscular injection into either the deltoid or gluteal muscle. For children <24 months of age, IG can be administered in the anterolateral thigh muscle.

[3]Repeat every 5 months if continued exposure to HAV occurs.

Recommended Dosages of Havrix®[1]

Vaccinee's Age (y)	Dose (EL.U.)[2]	Volume (mL)	No. Doses	Schedule (mo)[3]
2-18	720	0.5	2	0, 6-12
≥19	1440	1.0	2	0, 6-12

[1]Hepatitis A vaccine, inactivated, SmithKline Beecham Biologicals.

[2]Enzyme-linked immunosorbent assay (ELISA) units.

[3]0 months represents timing of the initial dose; subsequent numbers represent months after the initial dose.

Recommended Dosages of VAQTA®[1]

Vaccinee's Age (y)	Dose (units)	Volume (mL)	No. Doses	Schedule (mo)[2]
2-18	25	0.5	2	0, 6-18
≥19	50	1.0	2	0, 6

[1]Hepatitis A vaccine, inactivated, Merck & Company, Inc.

[2]0 months represents timing of the initial dose; subsequent numbers represent months after the initial dose.

Adapted from "Prevention of Hepatitis A Through Active or Passive Immunization: Recommendations of the Advisory Committee on Immunization Practices (ACIP)," *MMWR Recomm Rep*, 2006, 55(RR-07):1-23.

Recommended Dosages of Twinrix®[1]

Vaccinee's Age (y)	Dose (HepA / HepB)	Volume (mL)	No. Doses	Schedule (mo)[2]
≥18	720 EL.U./20 mcg	1	3	0, 1, 6

[1]Combined hepatitis A and hepatitis B vaccine manufactured by GlaxoSmithKline (Rixensart, Belgium).

[2]0 months represents timing of the initial dose; subsequent numbers represent months after the initial dose.

IMMUNIZATION RECOMMENDATIONS (Continued)

ADVERSE EVENTS AND VACCINATION

Reportable Events Following Vaccination[1]

Vaccine / Toxoid		Event	Onset Interval
Tetanus in any combination; DTaP, DTP, DTP-Hib, DT, Td, TT	A.	Anaphylaxis or anaphylactic shock	7 days
	B.	Brachial neuritis	28 days
	C.	Any sequela (including death) of above events	Not applicable
	D.	Events described in manufacturer's package insert as contraindications to additional doses of vaccine	See package insert
Pertussis in any combination; DTaP, DTP, DTP-Hib, P	A.	Anaphylaxis or anaphylactic shock	7 days
	B.	Encephalopathy (or encephalitis)	7 days
	C.	Any sequela (including death) of above events	Not applicable
	D.	Events described in manufacturer's package insert as contraindications to additional doses of vaccine	See package insert
Measles, mumps, and rubella in any combination; MMR, MR, M, R	A.	Anaphylaxis or anaphylactic shock	7 days
	B.	Encephalopathy (or encephalitis)	15 days
	C.	Any sequela (including death) of above events	Not applicable
	D.	Events described in manufacturer's package insert as contraindications to additional doses of vaccine	See package insert
Rubella in any combination; MMR, MR, R	A.	Chronic arthritis	42 days
	B.	Any sequela (including death) of above events	Not applicable
	C.	Events described in manufacturer's package insert as contraindications to additional doses of vaccine	See package insert
Measles in any combination; MMR, MR, M	A.	Thrombocytopenic purpura	7-30 days
	B.	Vaccine-strain measles viral infection in an immunodeficient recipient	6 months
	C.	Any sequela (including death) of above events	Not applicable
	D.	Events described in manufacturer's package insert as contraindications to additional doses of vaccine	See package insert
Inactivated polio (IPV)	A.	Anaphylaxis or anaphylactic shock	7 days
	B.	Any sequela (including death) of above events	Not applicable
	C.	Events described in manufacturer's package insert as contraindications to additional doses of vaccine	See package insert
Hepatitis B	A.	Anaphylaxis or anaphylactic shock	7 days
	B.	Any sequela (including death) of above events	Not applicable
	C.	Events described in manufacturer's package insert as contraindications to additional doses of vaccine	See package insert
Haemophilus influenzae type b (conjugate)	A.	Events described in manufacturer's package insert as contraindications to additional doses of vaccine	See package insert
Varicella	A.	Events described in manufacturer's package insert as contraindications to additional doses of vaccine	See package insert
Rotavirus	A.	Intussusception	30 days
	B.	Any sequela (including death) of above events	Not applicable
	C.	Events described in manufacturer's package insert as contraindications to additional doses of vaccine	See package insert
Pneumococcal conjugate	A.	Events described in manufacturer's package insert as contraindications to additional doses of vaccine	See package insert

[1]Effective date: July 1, 2005.

The Reportable Events Table (RET) reflects what is reportable by law (42 USC 300aa-25) to the Vaccine Adverse Event Reporting System (VAERS), including conditions found in the manufacturer's package insert. In addition, individuals are encouraged to report **any** clinically significant or unexpected events (even if you are not certain the vaccine caused the event) for **any** vaccine, whether or not it is listed on the RET. Manufacturers are also required by regulation (21CFR 600.80) to report to the VAERS program all adverse events made known to them for any vaccine.

Adapted from the website **http://www.vaers.org/reportable.htm**. For further information, contact VAERS at 1-800-822-7967.

MANAGEMENT OF HEALTHCARE WORKER EXPOSURES TO HBV, HCV, AND HIV

Adapted from Updated U.S. Public Health Service Guidelines for the Management of Occupational Exposures to HIV and Recommendations for Postexposure Prophylaxis, "Recommended HIV Postexposure Prophylaxis (PEP) for Percutaneous Injuries," *MMWR Recomm Rep*, 2005, 54(RR-9):3-17.

Factors to Consider in Assessing the Need for Follow-up of Occupational Exposures

- **Type of exposure**
  - Percutaneous injury
  - Mucous membrane exposure
  - Nonintact skin exposure
  - Bites resulting in blood exposure to either person involved
- **Type and amount of fluid/tissue**
  - Blood
  - Fluids containing blood
  - Potentially infectious fluid or tissue (semen; vaginal secretions; and cerebrospinal, synovial, pleural, peritoneal, pericardial, and amniotic fluids)
  - Direct contact with concentrated virus
- **Infectious status of source**
  - Presence of HB_sAg
  - Presence of HCV antibody
  - Presence of HIV antibody
- **Susceptibility of exposed person**
  - Hepatitis B vaccine and vaccine response status
  - HBV, HCV, HIV immune status

Evaluation of Occupational Exposure Sources

Known sources

- Test known sources for HB_sAg, anti-HCV, and HIV antibody
  - Direct virus assays for routine screening of source patients are **not** recommended
  - Consider using a rapid HIV-antibody test
  - If the source person is **not** infected with a blood-borne pathogen, baseline testing or further follow-up of the exposed person is **not** necessary
- For sources whose infection status remains unknown (eg, the source person refuses testing), consider medical diagnoses, clinical symptoms, and history of risk behaviors
- Do not test discarded needles for blood-borne pathogens

Unknown sources

- For unknown sources, evaluate the likelihood of exposure to a source at high risk for infection
  - Consider the likelihood of blood-borne pathogen infection among patients in the exposure setting

MANAGEMENT OF HEALTHCARE WORKER EXPOSURES TO HBV, HCV, AND HIV *(Continued)*

Recommended Postexposure Prophylaxis for Exposure to Hepatitis B Virus

Vaccination and Antibody Response Status of Exposed Workers[1]	Treatment		
	Source HB$_s$Ag[2]-Positive	Source HB$_s$Ag[2]-Negative	Source Unknown or Not Available for Testing
Unvaccinated	HBIG[3] x 1 and initiate HB vaccine series[4]	Initiate HB vaccine series	Initiate HB vaccine series
Previously vaccinated			
Known responder[5]	No treatment	No treatment	No treatment
Known nonresponder[6]	HBIG[3] x 1 and initiate revaccination or HBIG x 2[7]	No treatment	If known high risk source, treat as if source was HB$_s$Ag-positive
Antibody response unknown	Test exposed person for anti-HB$_s$[8] 1. If adequate,[5] no treatment is necessary 2. If inadequate,[6] administer HBIG[3] x 1 and vaccine booster	No treatment	Test exposed person for anti-HB$_s$ 1. If adequate,[4] no treatment is necessary 2. If inadequate,[4] administer vaccine booster and recheck titer in 1-2 months

[1]Persons who have previously been infected with HBV are immune to reinfection and do not require postexposure prophylaxis.

[2]Hepatitis B surface antigen.

[3]Hepatitis B immune globulin; dose is 0.06 mL/kg intramuscularly.

[4]Hepatitis B vaccine.

[5]A responder is a person with adequate levels of serum antibody to HB$_s$Ag (ie, anti-HB$_s$ ≥10 mIU/mL).

[6]A nonresponder is a person with inadequate response to vaccination (ie, serum anti-HB$_s$ <10 mIU/mL).

[7]The option of giving one dose of HBIG and reinitiating the vaccine series is preferred for nonresponders who have not completed a second 3-dose vaccine series. For persons who previously completed a second vaccine series but failed to respond, two doses of HBIG are preferred.

[8]Antibody to HB$_s$Ag.

Recommended HIV Postexposure Prophylaxis (PEP) for Percutaneous Injuries

Exposure Type	HIV-Positive, Class 1[1]	HIV-Positive, Class 2[1]	Source of Unknown HIV Status[2]	Unknown Source[3]	HIV-Negative
			Infection Status of Source		
Less severe[4]	Recommend basic 2-drug PEP	Recommend expanded ≥3-drug PEP	Generally, no PEP warranted; however, consider basic 2-drug PEP[5] for source with HIV risk factors[6]	Generally, no PEP warranted; however, consider basic 2-drug PEP[5] in settings in which exposure to HIV-infected persons is likely	No PEP warranted
More severe[7]	Recommend expanded 3-drug PEP	Recommend expanded ≥3-drug PEP	Generally, no PEP warranted; however consider basic 2-drug PEP[5] for source with HIV risk factors[6]	Generally, no PEP warranted; however, consider basic 2-drug PEP[5] in settings in which exposure to HIV-infected persons is likely	No PEP warranted

[1]HIV-positive, class 1 – asymptomatic HIV infection or known low viral load (eg, <1500 ribonucleic acid copies/mL). HIV-positive, class 2 – symptomatic HIV infection, AIDS, acute seroconversion, or known high viral load. If drug resistance is a concern, obtain expert consultation. Initiation of PEP should not be delayed pending expert consultation, and, because expert consultation alone cannot substitute for face-to-face counseling, resources should be available to provide immediate evaluation and follow-up care for all exposures.

[2]For example, deceased source person with no samples available for HIV testing.

[3]For example, a needle from a sharps disposal container.

[4]For example, solid needle or superficial injury.

[5]The recommendation "consider PEP" indicates that PEP is optional; a decision to initiate PEP should be based on a discussion between the exposed person and the treating clinician regarding the risks versus benefits of PEP.

[6]If PEP is offered and administered and the source is later determined to be HIV-negative, PEP should be discontinued.

[7]For example, large-bore hollow needle, deep puncture, visible blood on device, or needle used in patient's artery or vein.

MANAGEMENT OF HEALTHCARE WORKER EXPOSURES TO HBV, HCV, AND HIV (Continued)

Recommended HIV Postexposure Prophylaxis (PEP) for Mucous Membrane Exposures and Nonintact Skin[1] Exposures

Exposure Type	HIV-Positive, Class 1[2]	HIV-Positive, Class 2[2]	Source of Unknown HIV Status[3]	Unknown Source[4]	HIV-Negative
			Infection Status of Source		
Small volume[5]	Consider basic 2-drug PEP[6]	Recommend basic 2-drug PEP	Generally, no PEP warranted[7]	Generally, no PEP warranted	No PEP warranted
Large volume[8]	Recommend basic 2-drug PEP	Recommend expanded ≥3-drug PEP	Generally, no PEP warranted; however consider basic 2-drug PEP[6] for source with HIV risk factors[7]	Generally, no PEP warranted; however, consider basic 2-drug PEP[6] in settings in which exposure to HIV-infected persons is likely	No PEP warranted

[1]For skin exposures, follow-up is indicated only if evidence exists of compromised skin integrity (eg, dermatitis, abrasion, or open wound).

[2]HIV-positive, class 1 – asymptomatic HIV infection or known low viral load (eg, <1500 ribonucleic acid copies/mL). HIV-positive, class 2 – symptomatic HIV infection, AIDS, acute seroconversion, or known high viral load. If drug resistance is a concern, obtain expert consultation. Initiation of PEP should not be delayed pending expert consultation, and, because expert consultation alone cannot substitute for face-to-face counseling, resources should be available to provide immediate evaluation and follow-up care for all exposures.

[3]For example, deceased source person with no samples available for HIV testing.

[4]For example, splash from inappropriately disposed blood.

[5]For example, a few drops.

[6]The recommendation "consider PEP" indicates that PEP is optional; a decision to initiate PEP should be based on a discussion between the exposed person and the treating clinician regarding the risks versus benefits of PEP.

[7]If PEP is offered and administered and the source is later determined to be HIV-negative, PEP should be discontinued.

[8]For example, a major blood splash.

Situations for Which Expert[1] Consultation for HIV Postexposure Prophylaxis Is Advised

- **Delayed (ie, later than 24-36 hours) exposure report**
    - The interval after which there is no benefit from postexposure prophylaxis (PEP) is undefined

- **Unknown source (eg, needle in sharps disposal container or laundry)**
    - Decide use of PEP on a case-by-case basis
    - Consider the severity of the exposure and the epidemiologic likelihood of HIV exposure
    - Do not test needles or sharp instruments for HIV

- **Known or suspected pregnancy in the exposed person**
    - Does not preclude the use of optimal PEP regimens
    - Do not deny PEP solely on the basis of pregnancy

- **Breast-feeding in the exposed person**
    - Use of optimal PEP regimen not precluded
    - PEP should not be denied solely on the basis of breast-feeding

- **Resistance of the source virus to antiretroviral agents**
    - Influence of drug resistance on transmission risk is unknown
    - Selection of drugs to which the source person's virus is unlikely to be resistant is recommended, if the source person's virus is unknown or suspected to be resistant to ≥1 of the drugs considered for the PEP regimen
    - Resistance testing of the source person's virus at the time of the exposure is not recommended
    - Initiation of PEP not to be delayed while awaiting results of resistance testing

- **Toxicity of the initial PEP regimen**
    - Adverse symptoms, such as nausea and diarrhea, are common with PEP
    - Symptoms can often be managed without changing the PEP regimen by prescribing antimotility and/or antiemetic agents
    - Modification of dose intervals (ie, administering a lower dose of drug more frequently throughout the day, as recommended by the manufacturer), in other situations, might help alleviate symptoms

[1]Local experts and/or the National Clinicians' Postexposure Prophylaxis Hotline (PEPline 1-888-448-4911).

MANAGEMENT OF HEALTHCARE WORKER EXPOSURES TO HBV, HCV, AND HIV *(Continued)*

Occupational Exposure Management Resources

National Clinicians' Postexposure Prophylaxis Hotline (PEPline)
Run by University of California-San Francisco/San Francisco General Hospital staff; supported by the Health Resources and Services Administration Ryan White CARE Act, HIV/AIDS Bureau, AIDS Education and Training Centers, and CDC

Phone: (888) 448-4911
Internet: http://www.ucsf.edu/hivcntr

Needlestick!
A website to help clinicians manage and document occupational blood and body fluid exposures. Developed and maintained by the University of California, Los Angeles (UCLA), Emergency Medicine Center, UCLA School of Medicine, and funded in part by CDC and the Agency for Healthcare Research and Quality.

Internet: http://www.needlestick.mednet.ucla.edu

Hepatitis Hotline

Phone: (888) 443-7232
Internet: http://www.cdc.gov/hepatitis

Reporting to CDC:
Occupationally acquired HIV infections and failures of PEP

Phone: (800) 893-0485

HIV Antiretroviral Pregnancy Registry

Phone: (800) 258-4263
Fax: (800) 800-1052
Address: 1410 Commonwealth Drive, Suite 215
Wilmington, NC 28405
Internet: http://www.glaxowellcome.com/preg_reg/antiretroviral

Food and Drug Administration
Report unusual or severe toxicity to antiretroviral agents

Phone: (800) 332-1088
Address: MedWatch
HF-2, FDA
5600 Fishers Lane
Rockville, MD 20857
Internet: http://www.fda.gov/medwatch

HIV / AIDS Treatment Information Service

Internet: http://www.aidsinfo.nih.gov

Management of Occupational Blood Exposures

Provide immediate care to the exposure site

- Wash wounds and skin with soap and water
- Flush mucous membranes with water

Determine risk associated with exposure by:

- Type of fluid (eg, blood, visibly bloody fluid, other potentially infectious fluid or tissue, and concentrated virus)
- Type of exposure (ie, percutaneous injury, mucous membrane or nonintact skin exposure, and bites resulting in blood exposure)

Evaluate exposure source

- Assess the risk of infection using available information
- Test known sources for HB$_s$Ag, anti-HCV, and HIV antibody (consider using rapid testing)
- For unknown sources, assess risk of exposure to HBV, HCV, or HIV infection
- Do not test discarded needle or syringes for virus contamination

Evaluate the exposed person

- Assess immune status for HBV infection (ie, by history of hepatitis B vaccination and vaccine response)

Give PEP for exposures posing risk of infection transmission

- HBV: See Recommended Postexposure Prophylaxis for Exposure to Hepatitis B Virus Table
- HCV: PEP not recommended
- HIV: See Recommended HIV Postexposure Prophylaxis for Percutaneous Injuries Table and Recommended HIV Postexposure Prophylaxis for Mucous Membrane Exposures and Nonintact Skin Exposures Table

  - Initiate PEP as soon as possible, preferably within hours of exposure
  - Offer pregnancy testing to all women of childbearing age not known to be pregnant
  - Seek expert consultation if viral resistance is suspected
  - Administer PEP for 4 weeks if tolerated

Perform follow-up testing and provide counseling

- Advise exposed persons to seek medical evaluation for any acute illness occurring during follow-up

HBV exposures

  - Perform follow-up anti-HB$_s$ testing in persons who receive hepatitis B vaccine

    - Test for anti-HB$_s$ 1-2 months after last dose of vaccine
    - Anti-HB$_s$ response to vaccine cannot be ascertained if HBIG was received in the previous 3-4 months

HCV exposures

  - Perform baseline and follow-up testing for anti-HCV and alanine amino-transferase (ALT) 4-6 months after exposures
  - Perform HCV RNA at 4-6 months if earlier diagnosis of HCV infection is desired
  - Confirm repeatedly reactive anti-HCV enzyme immunoassays (EIAs) with supplemental tests

HIV exposures

  - Perform HIV antibody testing for at least 6 months postexposure (eg, at baseline, 6 weeks, 3 months, and 6 months)
  - Perform HIV antibody testing if illness compatible with an acute retroviral syndrome occurs
  - Advise exposed persons to use precautions to prevent secondary transmission during the follow-up period
  - Evaluate exposed persons taking PEP within 72 hours after exposure and monitor for drug toxicity for at least 2 weeks

MANAGEMENT OF HEALTHCARE WORKER EXPOSURES TO HBV, HCV, AND HIV *(Continued)*

Basic and Expanded HIV Postexposure Prophylaxis Regimens

BASIC REGIMENS

Zidovudine (Retrovir®; ZDV; AZT) + lamivudine (Epivir®; 3TC); available as Combivir®
Preferred dosing
- ZDV: 300 mg twice daily or 200 mg three times daily, with food; total: 600 mg daily
- 3TC: 300 mg once daily or 150 mg twice daily
- Combivir®: One tablet twice daily

Advantages
- ZDV associated with decreased risk for HIV transmission
- ZDV used more often than other drugs for PEP for healthcare personnel (HCP)
- Serious toxicity rare when used for PEP
- Side effects predictable and manageable with antimotility and antiemetic agents
- Can be used by pregnant HCP
- Can be given as a single tablet (Combivir®) twice daily

Disadvantages
- Side effects (especially nausea and fatigue) common and might result in low adherence
- Source-patient virus resistance to this regimen possible
- Potential for delayed toxicity (oncogenic/teratogenic) unknown

Zidovudine (Retrovir®; ZDV; AZT) + emtricitabine (Emtriva®; FTC)
Preferred dosing
- ZDV: 300 mg twice daily or 200 mg three times daily, with food; total: 600 mg/day, in 2-3 divided doses
- FTC: 200 mg (one capsule) once daily

Advantages
- ZDV: See above
- FTC
  - Convenient (once daily)
  - Well tolerated
  - Long intracellular half-life (~40 hours)

Disadvantages
- ZDV: See above
- FTC
  - Rash perhaps more frequent than with 3TC
  - No long-term experience with this drug
  - Cross resistance to 3TC
  - Hyperpigmentation among non-Caucasians with long-term use: 3%

Tenofovir DF (Viread®; TDF) + lamivudine (Epivir®; 3TC)
Preferred dosing
- TDF: 300 mg once daily
- 3TC: 300 mg once daily or 150 mg twice daily

Advantages
- 3TC: See above
- TDF
  - Convenient dosing (single pill once daily)
  - Resistance profile activity against certain thymidine analogue mutations
  - Well tolerated

Disadvantages
- TDF
  - Same class warnings as nucleoside reverse transcriptase inhibitors (NRTIs)
  - Drug interactions
  - Increased TDF concentrations among persons taking atazanavir and lopinavir/ritonavir; need to monitor patients for TDF-associated toxicities
- Preferred dosage of atazanavir if used with TDF: 300 mg + ritonavir 100 mg once daily + TDF 300 mg once daily

Tenofovir DF (Viread®; TDF) + emtricitabine (Emtriva®; FTC); available as Truvada®
Preferred dosing
- TDF: 300 mg once daily
- FTC: 200 mg once daily
- As Truvada®: One tablet daily

Advantages
- FTC: See above
- TDF
  - Convenient dosing (single pill once daily)
  - Resistance profile activity against certain thymidine analogue mutations
  - Well tolerated

Disadvantages
- TDF
  - Same class warnings as NRTIs
  - Drug interactions
  - Increased TDF concentrations among persons taking atazanavir and lopinavir/ritonavir; need to monitor patients for TDF-associated toxicities
  - Preferred dosing of atazanavir if used with TDF: 300 mg + ritonavir 100 mg once daily + TDF 300 mg once daily

ALTERNATE BASIC REGIMENS

Lamivudine (Epivir®; 3TC) + stavudine (Zerit®; d4T)
Preferred dosing
- 3TC: 300 mg once daily or 150 mg twice daily
- d4T: 40 mg twice daily (can use lower doses of 20-30 mg twice daily if toxicity occurs; equally effective but less toxic among HIV-infected patients with peripheral neuropathy); 30 mg twice daily if body weight is <60 kg

Advantages
- 3TC: See above
- d4T: Gastrointestinal (GI) side effects rare

Disadvantages
- Possibility that source-patient virus is resistant to this regimen
- Potential for delayed toxicity (oncogenic/teratogenic) unknown

Emtricitabine (Emtriva®; FTC) + stavudine (Zerit®; d4T)
Preferred dosing
- FTC: 200 mg daily
- d4T: 40 mg twice daily (can use lower doses of 20-30 mg twice daily if toxicity occurs; equally effective but less toxic among HIV-infected patients who developed peripheral neuropathy); if body weight is <60 kg, 30 mg twice daily

Advantages
- 3TC and FTC: See above; d4T's GI side effects rare

Disadvantages
- Potential that source-patient virus is resistant to this regimen
- Unknown potential for delayed toxicity (oncogenic/teratogenic) unknown

Lamivudine (Epivir®; 3TC) + didanosine (Videx®; ddI)
Preferred dosing
- 3TC: 300 mg once daily or 150 mg twice daily
- ddI: Videx® chewable/dispersible buffered tablets can be administered on an empty stomach as either 200 mg twice daily or 400 mg once daily. Patients must take at least two of the appropriate strength tablets at each dose to provide adequate buffering and prevent gastric acid degradation of ddI. Because of the need for adequate buffering, the 200 mg strength tablet should be used only as a component of a once-daily regimen. The dose is either 200 mg twice daily or 400 mg once daily for patients weighing >60 kg and 125 mg twice daily or 250 mg once daily for patients weighing >60 kg.

Advantages
- ddI: Once-daily dosing option
- 3TC: See above

Disadvantages
- Tolerability: Diarrhea more common with buffered preparation than with enteric-coated preparation
- Associated with toxicity: Peripheral neuropathy, pancreatitis, and lactic acidosis
- Must be taken on empty stomach except with TDF
- Drug interactions
- 3TC: See above

Emtricitabine (Emtriva®; FTC) + didanosine (Videx®; ddI)
Preferred dosing
- FTC: 200 mg once daily
- ddI: See above

MANAGEMENT OF HEALTHCARE WORKER EXPOSURES TO HBV, HCV, AND HIV *(Continued)*

Advantages
- ddI: See above
- FTC: See above

Disadvantages
- Tolerability: Diarrhea more common with buffered than with enteric-coated preparation
- Associated with toxicity: Peripheral neuropathy, pancreatitis, and lactic acidosis
- Must be taken on empty stomach except with TDF
- Drug interactions
- FTC: See above

PREFERRED EXPANDED REGIMEN

Basic regimen plus:

Lopinavir / Ritonavir (Kaletra®; LPV/RTV)
Preferred dosing
- LPV/RTV: 400 mg/100 mg = twice daily with food

Advantages
- Potent HIV protease inhibitor
- Generally well-tolerated

Disadvantages
- Potential for serious or life-threatening drug interactions
- Might accelerate clearance of certain drugs, including oral contraceptives (requiring alternative or additional contraceptive measures for women taking these drugs)
- Can cause severe hyperlipidemia, especially hypertriglyceridemia
- GI (eg, diarrhea) events common

ALTERNATE EXPANDED REGIMEN

Basic regimen plus one of the following:

Atazanavir (Reyataz®; ATV) ± ritonavir (Norvir®; RTV)
Preferred dosing
- ATV: 400 mg once daily, unless used in combination with TDF, in which case ATV should be boosted with RTV, preferred dosing of ATV 300 mg + RTV: 100 mg once daily

Advantages
- Potent HIV protease inhibitor
- Convenient dosing – once daily
- Generally well tolerated

Disadvantages
- Hyperbilirubinemia and jaundice common
- Potential for serious or life-threatening drug interactions
- Avoid coadministration with proton pump inhibitors
- Separate antacids and buffered medications by 2 hours and H_2-receptor antagonists by 12 hours to avoid decreasing ATV levels
- Caution should be used with ATV and products known to induce PR prolongation (eg, diltiazem)

Fosamprenavir (Lexiva™; FOSAPV) ± ritonavir (Norvir®; RTV)
Preferred dosing
- FOSAPV: 1400 mg twice daily (without RTV)
- FOSAPV: 1400 mg once daily + RTV 200 mg once daily
- FOSAPV: 700 mg twice daily + RTV 100 mg twice daily

Advantages
- Once daily dosing when given with ritonavir

Disadvantages
- Tolerability: GI side effects common
- Multiple drug interactions. Oral contraceptives decrease fosamprenavir concentrations.
- Incidence of rash in healthy volunteers, especially when used with low doses of ritonavir. Differentiating between early drug-associated rash and acute seroconversion can be difficult and cause extraordinary concern for the exposed person.

Indinavir (Crixivan®; IDV) ± ritonavir (Norvir®; RTV)
Preferred dosing
- IDV 800 mg + RTV 100 mg twice daily without regard to food

Alternative dosing
- IDV: 800 mg every 8 hours, on an empty stomach

Advantages
- Potent HIV inhibitor

Disadvantages
- Potential for serious or life-threatening drug interactions
- Serious toxicity (eg, nephrolithiasis) possible; consumption of 8 glasses of fluid/day required
- Hyperbilirubinemia common; must avoid this drug during late pregnancy
- Requires acid for absorption and cannot be taken simultaneously with ddI, chewable/dispersible buffered tablet formulation (doses must be separated by ≥1 hour)

Saquinavir (Invirase®; SQV) + ritonavir (Norvir®; RTV)
Preferred dosing
- SQV: 1000 mg (given as Invirase®) + RTV 100 mg, twice daily
- SQV: Five capsules twice daily + RTV: One capsule twice daily

Advantages
- Generally well-tolerated, although GI events common

Disadvantages
- Potential for serious or life-threatening drug interactions
- Substantial pill burden

Nelfinavir (Viracept®; NFV)
Preferred dosing
- NFV: 1250 mg (2 x 625 mg or 5 x 250 mg tablets), twice daily with a meal

Advantages
- Generally well-tolerated

Disadvantages
- Diarrhea or other GI events common
- Potential for serious and/or life-threatening drug interactions

Efavirenz (Sustiva®; EFV)
Preferred dosing
- EFV: 600 mg daily, at bedtime

Advantages
- Does not require phosphorylation before activation and might be active earlier than other antiretroviral agents (a theoretic advantage of no demonstrated clinical benefit)
- Once daily dosing

Disadvantages
- Drug associated with rash (early onset) that can be severe and might rarely progress to Stevens-Johnson syndrome
- Differentiating between early drug-associated rash and acute seroconversion can be difficult and cause extraordinary concern for the exposed person
- Central nervous system side effects (eg, dizziness, somnolence, insomnia, or abnormal dreaming) common; severe psychiatric symptoms possible (dosing before bedtime might minimize these side effects)
- Teratogen; should not be used during pregnancy
- Potential for serious or life-threatening drug interactions

ANTIRETROVIRAL AGENTS GENERALLY NOT RECOMMENDED FOR USE AS PEP

Nevirapine (Viramune®; NVP)

Disadvantages
- Associated with severe hepatotoxicity (including at least one case of liver failure requiring liver transplantation in an exposed person taking PEP)
- Associated with rash (early onset) that can be severe and progress to Stevens-Johnson syndrome
- Differentiating between early drug-associated rash and acute seroconversion can be difficult and cause extraordinary concern for the exposed person
- Drug interactions: Can lower effectiveness of certain antiretroviral agents and other commonly used medicines

Delavirdine (Rescriptor®; DLV)

Disadvantages
- Drug associated with rash (early onset) that can be severe and progress to Stevens-Johnson syndrome
- Multiple drug interactions

MANAGEMENT OF HEALTHCARE WORKER EXPOSURES TO HBV, HCV, AND HIV *(Continued)*

Abacavir (Ziagen®; ABC)

Disadvantages

- Severe hypersensitivity reactions can occur, usually within the first 6 weeks
- Differentiating between early drug-associated rash/hypersensitivity and acute seroconversion can be difficult

Zalcitabine (Hivid®; ddC)

Disadvantages

- Three times a day dosing
- Tolerability
- Weakest antiretroviral agent

ANTIRETROVIRAL AGENT FOR USE AS PEP ONLY WITH EXPERT CONSULTATION

Enfuvirtide (Fuzeon™; T20)

Preferred dosing

- T20: 90 mg (1 mL) twice daily by subcutaneous injection

Advantages

- New class
- Unique viral target; to block cell entry
- Prevalence of resistance low

Disadvantages

- Twice-daily injection
- Safety profile: Local injection site reactions
- Never studied among antiretroviral-naive or HIV-negative patients
- False-positive EIA HIV antibody tests might result from formation of anti-T20 antibodies that cross-react with anti-gp41 antibodies

PERINATAL HIV

Selected tables from the Perinatal HIV Guidelines Working Group, Public Health Service Task Force, "Recommendations for Use of Antiretroviral Drugs in Pregnant HIV-1-Infected Women for Maternal Health and Interventions to Reduce Perinatal HIV-1 Transmission in the United States," November 17, 2005, located at (URL) http://www.aidsinfo.nih.gov.

Pediatric AIDS Clinical Trials Group (PACTG) 076 Zidovudine (ZDV) Regimen

ZDV Perinatal Transmission Prophylaxis Regimen

Time of ZDV Administration	Regimen
Antepartum	Oral administration (to the pregnant woman) of 100 mg ZDV 5 times daily,[1] initiated at 14-34 weeks gestation and continued throughout the pregnancy.
Intrapartum	During labor, intravenous administration (to the pregnant women) of ZDV in a 1-hour initial dose of 2 mg/kg body weight, followed by a continuous infusion of 1 mg/kg body weight/hour until delivery.
Postpartum	Oral administration of ZDV to the newborn infant (ZDV syrup at 2 mg/kg body weight/dose every 6 hours) for the first 6 weeks of life, beginning at 8-12 hours after birth.[2]

[1]Oral ZDV administered as 200 mg 3 times daily or 300 mg twice daily is currently used in general clinical practice and is an acceptable alternative regimen to 100 mg orally 5 times daily.

[2]Intravenous dosage for full-term infants who cannot tolerate oral intake is 1.5 mg/kg body weight intravenously every 6 hours. ZDV dosing for infants <35 weeks gestation at birth is 1.5 mg/kg/dose intravenously, or 2 mg/kg/dose orally, every 12 hours, advancing to every 8 hours at 2 weeks of age if >30 weeks gestation at birth or at 4 weeks of age if <30 weeks gestation at birth.

Clinical Scenarios and Recommendations for the Use of Antiretroviral Drugs to Reduce Perinatal Human Immunodeficiency Virus Type (HIV-1) Transmission

SCENARIO #1
HIV-1-infected pregnant women who have not received prior antiretroviral therapy

- Pregnant women with HIV-1 infection must receive standard clinical, immunologic, and virologic evaluation. Recommendations for initiation and choice of antiretroviral therapy should be based on the same parameters used for persons who are not pregnant, although the known and unknown risks and benefits of such therapy during pregnancy must be considered and discussed.

- The three-part ZDV chemoprophylaxis regimen, initiated after the first trimester, is recommended for all pregnant women with HIV-1 regardless of antenatal HIV RNA copy number to reduce the risk for perinatal transmission.

- The combination of ZDV chemoprophylaxis with additional antiretroviral drugs for treatment of HIV-1 infection is recommended for infected women whose clinical, immunologic, or virologic status requires treatment or who have HIV-1 RNA over 1000 copies/mL regardless of clinical or immunologic status, and can be considered for women with HIV-1 RNA <1000 copies/mL.

- Women who are in the first trimester of pregnancy may consider delaying initiation of therapy until after 10-12 weeks' gestation.

PERINATAL HIV *(Continued)*

SCENARIO #2
HIV-1-infected women receiving antiretroviral therapy during the current pregnancy

- HIV-1-infected women receiving antiretroviral therapy in whom pregnancy is identified after the first trimester should continue therapy. ZDV should be a component of the antenatal antiretroviral treatment regimen after the first trimester whenever possible, although this may not always be feasible.

- For women receiving antiretroviral therapy in whom pregnancy is recognized during the first trimester, the woman should be counseled regarding the benefits and potential risks of antiretroviral administration during this period, and continuation of therapy should be considered. If therapy is discontinued during the first trimester, all drugs should be stopped and reintroduced simultaneously to avoid the development of drug resistance.

- Regardless of the antepartum antiretroviral regimen, ZDV administration is recommended during the intrapartum period and for the newborn.

SCENARIO #3
HIV-1-infected women in labor who have had no prior therapy

Several effective regimens are available (see Comparison of Intrapartum / Postpartum Regimens). These include:

- intrapartum intravenous ZDV followed by 6 weeks of ZDV for the newborn

- oral ZDV and 3TC during labor, followed by 1 week of oral ZDV-3TC for the newborn

- a single-dose nevirapine at the onset of labor followed by a single dose of nevirapine for the newborn at age 48 hours, and

- the single-dose maternal/infant nevirapine regimen combined with intrapartum intravenous ZDV and 6-week ZDV for the newborn

If single-dose nevirapine is given to the mother, alone or in combination with ZDV, consideration should be given to adding maternal ZDV/3TC starting as soon as possible (intrapartum or immediately postpartum) and continuing for 3-7 days, which may reduce development of nevirapine resistance.

In the immediate postpartum period, the woman should have appropriate assessments (eg, CD4+ count and HIV-1 RNA copy number) to determine whether antiretroviral therapy is recommended for her own health.

SCENARIO #4
Infants born to mothers who have received no antiretroviral therapy during pregnancy or intrapartum

- The 6-week neonatal ZDV component of the ZDV chemoprophylactic regimen should be discussed with the mother and offered for the newborn.

- ZDV should be initiated as soon as possible after delivery – preferably within 6-12 hours of birth.

- Some clinicians may choose to use ZDV in combination with other antiretroviral drugs, particularly if the mother is known or suspected to have ZDV-resistant virus. However, the efficacy of this approach for prevention of transmission has not been proven in clinical trials, and appropriate dosing regimens for neonates are incompletely defined for many drugs.

- In the immediate postpartum period, the woman should undergo appropriate assessments (eg, CD4+ count and HIV-1 RNA copy number) to determine whether antiretroviral therapy is required for her own health. The infant should undergo early diagnostic testing so that if HIV-1-infected, treatment can be initiated as soon as possible.

Note: Discussion of treatment options and recommendations should be noncoercive, and the final decision regarding the use of antiretroviral drugs is the responsibility of the woman. A decision to not accept treatment with ZDV or other drugs should not result in punitive action or denial of care. Use of ZDV should not be denied to a woman who wishes to minimize exposure of the fetus to other antiretroviral drugs and who, therefore, chooses to receive only ZDV during pregnancy to reduce the risk for perinatal transmission.

Comparison of Intrapartum / Postpartum Regimens for HIV-1-Infected Women in Labor Who Have Had No Prior Antiretroviral Therapy (Scenario #3)

ZDV

Source of Evidence: Epidemiologic data, U.S.; compared to no ZDV treatment

Maternal Intrapartum: 2 mg/kg intravenous bolus, followed by continuous infusion of 1 mg/kg/h until delivery

Infant Postpartum: 2 mg/kg orally every 6 hours for 6 weeks[1]

Data on Transmission: Transmission 10% with ZDV compared to 27% with no ZDV treatment, a 62% reduction (95% CI, 19% to 82%)

Advantages: Has been standard recommendation

Disadvantages:

- Requires intravenous administration and availability of ZDV intravenous formulation
- Adherence to 6-week infant regimen
- Reversible, mild anemia with 6-week infant ZDV regimen

ZDV / 3TC

Source of Evidence: Clinical trial, Africa; compared to placebo

Maternal Intrapartum: ZDV 600 mg orally at onset of labor, followed by 300 mg orally every 3 hours until delivery **and** 3TC 150 mg orally at onset of labor, followed by 150 mg orally every 12 hours until delivery

Infant Postpartum: ZDV 4 mg/kg orally every 12 hours **and** 3TC 2 mg/kg orally every 12 hours for 7 days

Data on Transmission: Transmission at 6 weeks 9% with ZDV-3TC vs 15% with placebo, a 42% reduction

Advantages: Oral regimen; adherence easier than 6 weeks of ZDV

Disadvantages: Requires administration of two drugs

Nevirapine

Source of Evidence: Clinical trial, Africa; compared to oral ZDV given intrapartum and for 1 week to the infant

Maternal Intrapartum: Single 200 mg oral dose at onset of labor; consider adding intrapartum ZDV/3TC and 3-7 days of ZDV/3TC postpartum to reduce nevirapine resistance

Infant Postpartum: Single 2 mg/kg oral dose at age 48-72 hours[2]

Data on Transmission: Transmission at 6 weeks 12% with nevirapine compared to 21% with ZDV, a 47% reduction (95% CI,[1] 20% to 64%)

Advantages: Inexpensive; oral regimen; simple, easy to administer; can give directly observed treatment

Disadvantages:

- Unknown efficacy if mother has nevirapine-resistant virus
- Nevirapine resistance mutations have been detected postpartum in some women and in infants who became infected despite prophylaxis

ZDV-Nevirapine

Source of Evidence: Theoretical

Maternal Intrapartum: ZDV 2 mg/kg intravenous bolus, followed by continuous infusion of 1 mg/kg/h until delivery **and** nevirapine single 200 mg oral dose at onset of labor; consider adding intrapartum ZDV/3TC and 3-7 days of ZDV/3TC postpartum to reduce nevirapine resistance

Infant Postpartum: ZDV 2 mg/kg orally every 6 hours for 6 weeks **and** nevirapine single 2 mg/kg oral dose at age 48-72 hours[2]

Data on Transmission: No data

Advantages: Potential benefit if maternal virus is resistant to either nevirapine or ZDV; synergistic inhibition of HIV replication with combination *in vitro*

Disadvantages:

- Requires intravenous administration and availability of ZDV intravenous formulation
- Adherence to 6-week infant ZDV regimen
- Unknown if additive efficacy with combination
- Nevirapine resistance mutations have been detected postpartum in some women and in infants who became infected despite prophylaxis

ZDV = zidovudine, CI = confidence interval, 3TC = lamivudine.

Footnotes

[1]ZDV dosing for infants <35 weeks gestation at birth is 1.5 mg/kg/dose intravenously, or 2 mg/kg orally, every 12 hours, advancing to every 8 hours at 2 weeks of age if ≥30 weeks gestation at birth or at 4 weeks of age if <30 weeks gestation at birth.

[2]If the mother received nevirapine <1 hour prior to delivery, the infant should be given 2 mg/kg oral nevirapine as soon as possible after birth and again at 48-72 hours.

PERINATAL HIV *(Continued)*

Recommendations Related to Antiretroviral Drug Resistance and Drug Resistance Testing for Pregnant Women With HIV-1 Infection

- All pregnant HIV-1-infected women should be offered highly active antiretroviral therapy to maximally suppress viral replication, reduce the risk of perinatal transmission, and minimize the risk of development of resistant virus.

- For women for whom combination antiretroviral therapy would be considered optional (HIV-1 RNA <1000 copies/mL) and who wish to restrict their exposure to antiretroviral drugs during pregnancy, monotherapy with the three-part zidovudine (ZDV) prophylaxis regimen (or in selected circumstances, dual nucleosides) should be offered. In these circumstances, the development of resistance should be minimized by limited viral replication (assuming HIV-1 RNA levels remain low) and the time-limited exposure to ZDV. Monotherapy with ZDV does not suppress HIV-1 replication to undetectable levels in most cases, theoretically, such therapy might select for ZDV-resistant viral variants, potentially limiting future treatment options. These considerations should be discussed with the pregnant woman.

- Recommendations for resistance testing for HIV-1-infected pregnant women are the same as for nonpregnant patients: Acute HIV-1 infection, virologic failure, suboptimal viral suppression after initiation of antiretroviral therapy, or high likelihood of exposure to resistant virus based on community prevalence or source characteristics.

- Women who have a history of presumed or documented ZDV resistance and are on antiretroviral regimens that do not include ZDV for their own health should still receive intravenous ZDV intrapartum and oral ZDV for their infants according to the PACTG 076 protocol whenever possible. A key mechanism by which ZDV reduce perinatal transmission is likely through pre- and postexposure prophylaxis of the infant, which may be less dependent on drug sensitivity than is reduction of viral replication. However, these women are not good candidates for ZDV alone.

- Optimal antiretroviral prophylaxis of the infant born to a woman with HIV-1 known to be resistant to ZDV or other agents should be determined in consultation with pediatric infectious disease specialists, taking into account resistance patterns, available drug formulations, and infant pharmacokinetic data, when available.

- If women receiving combination therapy require temporary discontinuation for any reason during pregnancy, all drugs should be stopped and reintroduced simultaneously to reduce the potential for emergence of resistance.

- Optimal adherence to antiretroviral medications is a key part of the strategy to reduce the development of resistance.

- Because the prevalence of drug-resistant virus is an evolving phenomenon, surveillance is needed to monitor the prevalence of drug-resistant virus in pregnant women over time and the risk of transmission of resistant viral strains.

Clinical Scenarios and Recommendations Regarding Mode of Delivery to Reduce Perinatal Human Immunodeficiency Virus Type (HIV-1) Transmission

SCENARIO A

HIV-1-infected women presenting in late pregnancy (after about 36 weeks of gestation), known to be HIV-1-infected but not receiving antiretroviral therapy, and who have HIV-1 RNA level and lymphocyte subsets pending but unlikely to be available before delivery.

Recommendations

Therapy options should be discussed in detail. The woman should be started on antiretroviral therapy including at least the PACTG 076 ZDV regimen. The woman should be counseled that scheduled cesarean section is likely to reduce the risk of transmission to her infant. She should also be informed of the increased risks to her of cesarean section, including increased rates of postoperative infection, anesthesia risks, and other surgical risks.

If cesarean section is chosen, the procedure should be scheduled at 38 weeks of gestation based on the best available clinical information. When scheduled cesarean section is performed, the woman should receive continuous intravenous ZDV infusion beginning 3 hours before surgery and her infant should receive 6 weeks of ZDV therapy after birth. Options for continuing or initiating combination antiretroviral therapy after delivery should be discussed with the woman as soon as her viral load and lymphocyte subset results are available.

SCENARIO B

HIV-1-infected women who initiated prenatal care early in the third trimester, are receiving highly active combination antiretroviral therapy, and have an initial virologic response, but have HIV-1 RNA levels that remain substantially over 1000 copies/mL at 36 weeks of gestation.

Recommendations

The current combination antiretroviral regimen should be continued as the HIV-1 RNA level is dropping appropriately. The woman should be counseled that although she is responding to the antiretroviral therapy, it is unlikely that her HIV-1 RNA level will fall below 1000 copies/mL before delivery. Therefore, scheduled cesarean section may provide additional benefit in preventing intrapartum transmission of HIV-1. She should also be informed of the increased risks to her of cesarean section, including increased rates of postoperative infection, anesthesia risks, and surgical risks.

If she chooses scheduled cesarean section, it should be performed at 38 weeks' gestation according to the best available dating parameters, and intravenous ZDV should be begun at least 3 hours before surgery. Other antiretroviral medications should be continued on schedule as much as possible before and after surgery. The infant should receive oral ZDV for 6 weeks after birth. The importance of adhering to therapy after delivery for her own health should be emphasized.

SCENARIO C

HIV-1-infected women on highly active combination antiretroviral therapy with an undetectable HIV-1 RNA level at 36 weeks of gestation.

Recommendations

The woman should be counseled that her risk of perinatal transmission of HIV-1 with a persistently undetectable HIV-1 RNA level is low, probably 2% or less, even with vaginal delivery. There is currently no information to evaluate whether performing a scheduled cesarean section will lower her risk further.

Cesarean section has an increased risk of complications for the woman compared to vaginal delivery, and these risks must be balanced against the uncertain benefit of cesarean section in this case.

SCENARIO D

HIV-1-infected women who have elected scheduled cesarean section but present in early labor or shortly after rupture of membranes.

Recommendations

Intravenous ZDV should be started immediately since the woman is in labor or has ruptured membranes.

If labor is progressing rapidly, the woman should be allowed to deliver vaginally. If cervical dilatation is minimal and a long period of labor is anticipated, some clinicians may choose to administer the loading dose of intravenous ZDV and proceed with cesarean section to minimize the duration of membrane rupture and avoid vaginal delivery. Others might begin Pitocin® augmentation to enhance contractions and potentially expedite delivery.

If the woman is allowed to labor, scalp electrodes and other invasive monitoring and operative delivery should be avoided if possible. The infant should be treated with 6 weeks of ZDV therapy after birth.

PERINATAL HIV *(Continued)*

Recommended Antiretroviral Therapy in Pregnant HIV-Infected Women

Drug	Recommended	Alternative	Not Recommended	Insufficient Data	Rationale / Concerns
Nucleoside Reverse Transcriptase Inhibitors (NRTIs)					
Zidovudine	X				Based on efficacy studies and experience showing well-tolerated and safe (short-term)
Lamivudine	X				Based on extensive experience showing well-tolerated and safe (short-term)
Didanosine		X			Cases of lactic acidosis; do not use with stavudine if possible
Emtricitabine		X			No studies in pregnant women
Stavudine		X			Lactic acidosis noted in pregnant women in combination with didanosine; avoid use with didanosine; do not use with zidovudine due to antagonism
Abacavir		X			Hypersensitivity reactions in 5% to 8% nonpregnant individuals
Tenofovir				X	No studies in pregnant women; fetal effects in animal studies; demineralization noted in children
Zalcitabine			X		No studies in pregnant women; teratogenicity noted in animal studies
Non-nucleoside Reverse Transcriptase Inhibitors (NNRTIs)					
Nevirapine	X				Possible increased risk of liver toxicity; use if benefit outweighs risk and only when CD4 counts >250
Efavirenz			X		No studies in pregnant women; teratogenic effects noted in animal studies and human clinical experience
Delavirdine			X		No studies in pregnant women; carcinogenic and teratogenic in animal studies

Recommended Antiretroviral Therapy in Pregnant HIV-Infected Women *(continued)*

Drug	Recommended	Alternative	Not Recommended	Insufficient Data	Rationale / Concerns
Protease Inhibitors (PIs)					
Nelfinavir	X				No evidence of teratogenicity; well-tolerated and short-term safety demonstrated in mother and infant
Saquinavir	X				No evidence of teratogenicity; well-tolerated and short-term safety demonstrated in mother and infant; use with ritonavir boosting
Indinavir		X			Possible increased bilirubin levels; use with ritonavir boosting
Lopinavir/ritonavir		X			Limited experience in human pregnancy; monitor response closely
Ritonavir		X			Minimal experience in human pregnancy; recommended as part of boosted regimen
Amprenavir				X	Oral solution contraindicated; insufficient safety/kinetic data available
Fosamprenavir				X	No experience in human pregnancy; insufficient safety/kinetic data available
Atazanavir				X	Possible increased bilirubin levels; insufficient safety/kinetic data available
Tipranavir				X	No experience in human pregnancy; insufficient safety/kinetic data available
Fusion Inhibitor					
Enfuvirtide				X	No studies in pregnant women

PREVENTION OF BACTERIAL ENDOCARDITIS

Recommendations by the American Heart Association
(*JAMA*, 1997, 277:1794-801)

Consensus Process – The recommendations were formulated by the writing group after specific therapeutic regimens were discussed. The consensus statement was subsequently reviewed by outside experts not affiliated with the writing group and by the Science Advisory and Coordinating Committee of the American Heart Association. These guidelines are meant to aid practitioners but are not intended as the standard of care or as a substitute for clinical judgment.

Table 1. Cardiac Conditions[1]

Endocarditis Prophylaxis Recommended

High-Risk Category

    Prosthetic cardiac valves, including bioprosthetic and homograft valves

    Previous bacterial endocarditis

    Complex cyanotic congenital heart disease (eg, single ventricle states, transposition of the great arteries, tetralogy of Fallot)

    Surgically constructed systemic pulmonary shunts or conduits

Moderate-Risk Category

    Most other congenital cardiac malformations (other than above and below)

    Acquired valvar dysfunction (eg, rheumatic heart disease)

    Hypertrophic cardiomyopathy

    Mitral valve prolapse with valvar regurgitation and/or thickened leaflets

Endocarditis Prophylaxis Not Recommended

Negligible-Risk Category (no greater risk than the general population)

    Isolated secundum atrial septal defect

    Surgical repair of atrial septal defect, ventricular septal defect, or patent ductus arteriosus (without residua beyond 6 months)

    Previous coronary artery bypass graft surgery

    Mitral valve prolapse without valvar regurgitation

    Physiologic, functional, or innocent heart murmurs

    Previous Kawasaki disease without valvar dysfunction

    Previous rheumatic fever without valvar dysfunction

    Cardiac pacemakers (intravascular and epicardial) and implanted defibrillators

[1]This table lists selected conditions but is not meant to be all-inclusive.

Patient With Suspected Mitral Valve Prolapse

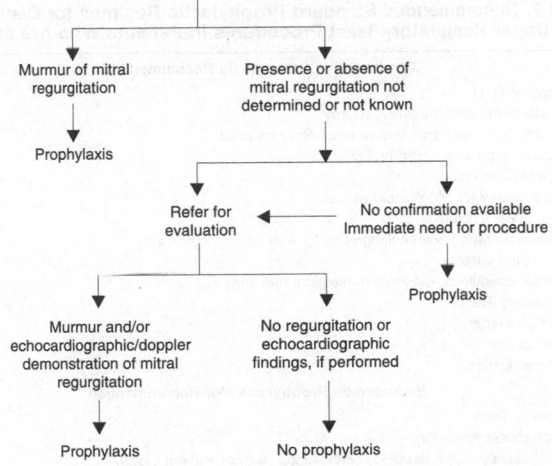

Table 2. Dental Procedures and Endocarditis Prophylaxis

Endocarditis Prophylaxis Recommended[1]

Dental extractions

Periodontal procedures including surgery, scaling and root planing, probing, and recall maintenance

Dental implant placement and reimplantation of avulsed teeth

Endodontic (root canal) instrumentation or surgery only beyond the apex

Subgingival placement of antibiotic fibers or strips

Initial placement of orthodontic bands but not brackets

Intraligamentary local anesthetic injections

Prophylactic cleaning of teeth or implants where bleeding is anticipated

Endocarditis Prophylaxis Not Recommended

Restorative dentistry[2] (operative and prosthodontic) with or without retraction cord[3]

Local anesthetic injections (nonintraligamentary)

Intracanal endodontic treatment; post placement and buildup[3]

Placement of rubber dams[3]

Postoperative suture removal

Placement of removable prosthodontic or orthodontic appliances

Taking of oral impressions[3]

Fluoride treatments

Taking of oral radiographs

Orthodontic appliance adjustment

Shedding of primary teeth

[1]Prophylaxis is recommended for patients with high- and moderate-risk cardiac conditions.

[2]This includes restoration of decayed teeth (filling cavities) and replacement of missing teeth.

[3]Clinical judgment may indicate antibiotic use in selected circumstances that may create significant bleeding.

PREVENTION OF BACTERIAL ENDOCARDITIS *(Continued)*

Table 3. Recommended Standard Prophylactic Regimen for Dental, Oral, or Upper Respiratory Tract Procedures in Patients Who Are at Risk

Endocarditis Prophylaxis Recommended

Respiratory Tract
  Tonsillectomy and/or adenoidectomy
  Surgical operations that involve respiratory mucosa
  Bronchoscopy with a rigid bronchoscope
Gastrointestinal Tract[1]
  Sclerotherapy for esophageal varices
  Esophageal stricture dilation
  Endoscopic retrograde cholangiography with biliary obstruction
  Biliary tract surgery
  Surgical operations that involve intestinal mucosa
Genitourinary Tract
  Prostatic surgery
  Cystoscopy
  Urethral dilation

Endocarditis Prophylaxis Not Recommended

Respiratory Tract
  Endotracheal intubation
  Bronchoscopy with a flexible bronchoscope, with or without biopsy[2]
  Tympanostomy tube insertion
Gastrointestinal Tract
  Transesophageal echocardiography[2]
  Endoscopy with or without gastrointestinal biopsy[2]
Genitourinary Tract
  Vaginal hysterectomy[2]
  Vaginal delivery[2]
  Cesarean section
  In uninfected tissues:
    Urethral catheterization
    Uterine dilatation and curettage
    Therapeutic abortion
    Sterilization procedures
    Insertion or removal of intrauterine devices
Other
  Cardiac catheterization, including balloon angioplasty
  Implanted cardiac pacemakers, implanted defibrillators, and coronary stents
  Incision or biopsy or surgically scrubbed skin
  Circumcision

[1]Prophylaxis is recommended for high-risk patients, optional for medium-risk patients.
[2]Prophylaxis is optional for high-risk patients.

Table 4. Prophylactic Regimens for Dental, Oral, Respiratory Tract, or Esophageal Procedures

Situation	Agent	Regimen[1]	
		Adults	Children
Standard general prophylaxis	Amoxicillin	2 g P.O. 1 h before procedure	50 mg/kg P.O. 1 h before procedure
Unable to take oral medications	Ampicillin	2 g I.M./I.V. within 30 min before procedure	50 mg/kg I.M./I.V. within 30 min before procedure
Allergic to penicillin	Clindamycin or	600 mg P.O. 1 h before procedure	20 mg/kg P.O. 1 h before procedure
	Cephalexin[2] or cefadroxil[2] or	2 g P.O 1 h before procedure	50 mg/kg P.O. 1 h before procedure
	Azithromycin or clarithromycin	500 mg P.O. 1 h before procedure	15 mg/kg P.O. 1 h before procedure
Allergic to penicillin and unable to take oral medications	Clindamycin or	600 mg I.V. within 30 min before procedure	20 mg/kg I.V. within 30 min before procedure
	Cefazolin[2]	1 g I.M./I.V. within 30 min before procedure	25 mg/kg I.M./I.V. within 30 min before procedure

[1]Total children's dose should not exceed adult dose.

[2]Cephalosporins should not be used in individuals with immediate-type hypersensitivity reaction (urticaria, angioedema, or anaphylaxis) to penicillins.

Table 5. Prophylactic Regimens for Genitourinary / Gastrointestinal (Excluding Esophageal) Procedures

Situation	Agents	Regimen[1,2]	
		Adults	Children
High-risk[3] patients	Ampicillin plus gentamicin	Ampicillin 2 g I.M. or I.V. plus gentamicin 1.5 mg/kg (not to exceed 120 mg) within 30 min of starting the procedure; 6 h later, ampicillin 1 g I.M./I.V. or amoxicillin 1 g orally	Ampicillin 50 mg/kg I.M./I.V. (not to exceed 2 g) plus gentamicin 1.5 mg/kg within 30 min of starting the procedure; 6 h later, ampicillin 25 mg/kg I.M./I.V. or amoxicillin 25 mg/kg orally
High-risk[3] patients allergic to ampicillin/ amoxicillin	Vancomycin plus gentamicin	Vancomycin 1 g I.V. over 1-2 h plus gentamicin 1.5 mg/kg I.M./I.V. (not to exceed 120 mg); complete injection/infusion within 30 min of starting the procedure	Vancomycin 20 mg/kg I.V. over 1-2 h plus gentamicin 1.5 mg/kg I.M./I.V.; complete injection/infusion within 30 min of starting the procedure
Moderate-risk[4] patients	Amoxicillin or ampicillin	Amoxicillin 2 g orally 1 h before procedure, or ampicillin 2 g I.M./I.V within 30 min of starting the procedure	Amoxicillin 50 mg/kg orally 1 h before procedure, or ampicillin 50 mg/kg I.M./I.V. within 30 min of starting the procedure
Moderate-risk[4] patients allergic to ampicillin/amoxicillin	Vancomycin	Vancomycin 1 g I.V. over 1-2 h; complete infusion within 30 min of starting the procedure	Vancomycin 20 mg/kg I.V. over 1-2 h; complete infusion within 30 min of starting the procedure

[1]Total children's dose should not exceed adult dose.

[2]No second dose of vancomycin or gentamicin is recommended.

[3]High-risk: Patients are those who have prosthetic valves, a previous history of endocarditis (even in the absence of other heart disease, complex cyanotic congenital heart disease, or surgically constructed systemic pulmonary shunts or conduits).

[4]Moderate-risk: Individuals with certain other underlying cardiac defects. Congenital cardiac conditions include the following uncorrected conditions: Patent ductus arteriosus, ventricular septal defect, ostium primum atrial septal defect, coarctation of the aorta, and bicuspid aortic valve. Acquired valvar dysfunction and hypertrophic cardiomyopathy are also moderate risk conditions.

PREVENTION OF WOUND INFECTION AND SEPSIS IN SURGICAL PATIENTS

Nature of Operation	Likely Pathogens	Recommended Drugs	Adult Dosage Before Surgery[1]
Cardiac	S. aureus, S. epidermidis	Cefazolin or cefuroxime or vancomycin[3]	1-2 g I.V.[2] 1.5 g I.V.[2] 1 g I.V.
Gastrointestinal			
Esophageal, gastroduodenal	Enteric gram-negative bacilli, gram-positive cocci	*High risk[4] only:* Cefazolin[5]	1-2 g I.V.
Biliary tract	Enteric gram-negative bacilli, enterococci, clostridia	*High risk[6] only:* Cefazolin[5]	1-2 g I.V.
Colorectal	Enteric gram-negative bacilli, anaerobes, enterococci	*Oral:* Neomycin + erythromycin base[7] or neomycin + metronidazole[7]	1 g of each x 3 doses 2 g of each x 2 doses
		Parenteral: Cefoxitin[5] or cefazolin[5] + metronidazole[5]	1-2 g I.V. 1-2 g I.V. 0.5-1 g I.V.
Appendectomy, nonperforated	Enteric gram-negative bacilli, anaerobes, enterococci	Cefoxitin[5] or cefazolin[5] + metronidazole or ampicillin/sulbactam	1-2 g I.V. 1-2 g I.V. 0.5 g I.V. 3 g I.V.
Ruptured viscus	Enteric gram-negative bacilli, anaerobes, enterococci	Cefoxitin ± gentamicin[5,8]	1-2 g I.V. q6h 1.5 mg/kg I.V. q8h
Genitourinary	Enteric gram-negative bacilli, enterococci	*High risk[9] only:* Ciprofloxacin	500 mg P.O. or 400 mg I.V.
Gynecologic and Obstetric			
Vaginal, abdominal, or laparoscopic hysterectomy	Enteric gram-negative bacilli, anaerobes, group B streptococci, enterococci	Cefoxitin[5] or cefazolin[5] or ampicillin/sulbactam[5]	1-2 g I.V 1-2 g I.V. 3 g I.V.
Cesarean section	Same as for hysterectomy	Cefazolin[5]	1-2 g I.V. after cord clamping
Abortion	Same as for hysterectomy	*First trimester, high-risk[10]:* Aqueous penicillin G or doxycycline	2 mill units I.V. or 300 mg P.O.[11]
		Second trimester: Cefazolin[5]	1-2 g I.V.
Head and Neck			
Incisions through oral or pharyngeal mucosa	Anaerobes, enteric gram-negative bacilli, S. aureus	Clindamycin + gentamicin OR cefazolin	600-900 mg I.V. 1.5 mg/kg I.V. 1-2 g I.V.
Neurosurgery	S. aureus, S. epidermidis	Cefazolin OR vancomycin[3]	1-2 g I.V. 1 g I.V.
Ophthalmic	S. epidermidis, S. aureus, streptococci, enteric gram-negative bacilli, Pseudomonas	Gentamicin, tobramycin, ciprofloxacin, levofloxacin, moxifloxacin, ofloxacin, or neomycin-gramicidin-polymyxin B	Multiple drops topically over 2-24 hours
		Cefazolin	100 mg subconjunctivally
Orthopedic	S. aureus, S. epidermidis	Cefazolin[12] or cefuroxime[12] or vancomycin[3,12]	1-2 g I.V. 1.5 g I.V. 1 g I.V.
Thoracic (Noncardiac)	S. aureus, S. epidermidis, streptococci, enteric gram-negative bacilli	Cefazolin or cefuroxime or vancomycin[3]	1-2 g I.V. 1.5 g I.V. 1 g I.V.
Vascular			
Arterial surgery involving a prosthesis, the abdominal aorta, or a groin incision	S. aureus, S. epidermidis, enteric gram-negative bacilli	Cefazolin or vancomycin[3]	1-2 g I.V. 1 g I.V.
Lower extremity amputation for ischemia	S. aureus, S. epidermidis, enteric gram-negative bacilli, clostridia	Cefazolin or vancomycin[3]	1-2 g I.V. 1 g I.V.

[1]Parenteral prophylactic antimicrobials can be given as a single I.V. dose begun 60 minutes or less before the operation. For prolonged operations, additional intraoperative doses should be given at intervals 1-2 times the half-life of the drug for the duration of the procedure. If vancomycin or a fluoroquinolone is used, the infusion should be started 60-120 minutes before incision in order to minimize the possibility of an infusion reaction close to the time of induction of anesthesia and to have adequate tissue levels at the time of incision.

[2]Some consultants recommend an additional dose when patients are removed from bypass during open-heart surgery.

[3]For hospitals in which methicillin-resistant *S. aureus* and *S. epidermidis* are a frequent cause of postoperative wound infection, for patients previously colonized with MRSA, or for patients allergic to penicillins or cephalosporin. Rapid I.V. administration may cause hypotension, which could be especially dangerous during induction of anesthesia. Even if the drug is given over 60 minutes, hypotension may occur; treatment with diphenhydramine (Benadryl® and others) and further slowing of the infusion rate may be helpful. For procedures in which enteric gram-negative bacilli are likely pathogens, such as vascular surgery involving a groin incision, cefazolin or cefuroxime should be included in the prophylaxis regimen for patients not allergic to cephalosporins; ciprofloxacin, levofloxacin (750 mg), gentamicin, or aztreonam, each one in combination with vancomycin, can be used in patients who cannot tolerate a cephalosporin.

[4]Morbid obesity, esophageal obstruction, decreased gastric acidity, or gastrointestinal motility.

[5]For patients allergic to cephalosporins, clindamycin with either gentamicin, ciprofloxacin, levofloxacin (750 mg), or aztreonam is a reasonable alternative.

[6]Age >70 years, acute cholecystitis, nonfunctioning gallbladder, obstructive jaundice, or common duct stones.

[7]After appropriate diet and catharsis, 1 g of neomycin plus 1 g of erythromycin at 1 PM, 2 PM, and 11 PM or 2 g of neomycin plus 2 g of metronidazole at 7 PM and 11 PM the day before an 8 AM operation.

[8]Therapy is often continued for about 5 days. Ruptured viscus in postoperative setting (dehiscence) requires antibacterials to include coverage of nosocomial pathogens.

[9]Urine culture positive or unavailable, preoperative catheter, transrectal prostatic biopsy, placement of prosthetic material.

[10]Patients with previous pelvic inflammatory disease, previous gonorrhea, or multiple sex partners.

[11]Divided into 100 mg 1 hour before the abortion and 200 mg 30 minutes after.

[12]If a tourniquet is to be used in the procedure, the entire dose of antibiotic must be infused prior to its inflation.

References

Adapted with permission from "Antimicrobial Prophylaxis for Surgery," *Treatment Guidelines From The Medical Letter®*, 2006, 4(52):83-8.

Bratzler DW, Houck PM, Surgical Infection Prevention Guideline Writers Workgroup, et al, "Antimicrobial Prophylaxis for Surgery: An Advisory Statement From the National Surgical Infection Prevention Project," *Clin Infect Dis*, 2004, 38(12):1706-15.

USPHS / IDSA GUIDELINES FOR THE PREVENTION OF OPPORTUNISTIC INFECTIONS IN PERSONS INFECTED WITH HIV

Adapted from "2002 USPHS/IDSA Guidelines for the Prevention of Opportunistic Infections in Persons Infected With Human Immunodeficiency Virus. USPHS/IDSA Prevention of Opportunistic Infections Working Group" (www.aidsinfo.nih.gov)

DRUG REGIMENS FOR ADULTS AND ADOLESCENTS

Prophylaxis to Prevent First Episode of Opportunistic Disease in HIV-Infected Adults and Adolescents

Pathogen	Indication	Preventive Regimens	
		First Choice	Alternatives
I. Strongly Recommended as Standard of Care			
Pneumocystis jiroveci[1]	CD4+ count <200/µL or oropharyngeal candidiasis	TMP-SMZ, 1 DS P.O. every day; TMP-SMZ, 1 SS P.O. every day	Dapsone, 50 mg P.O. twice daily *or* 100 mg P.O. every day; dapsone, 50 mg P.O. every day *plus* pyrimethamine, 50 mg P.O. weekly *plus* leucovorin, 25 mg P.O. weekly; dapsone, 200 mg P.O. *plus* pyrimethamine, 75 mg P.O. *plus* leucovorin, 25 mg P.O. weekly; aerosolized pentamidine, 300 mg monthly via Respirgard II™ nebulizer; atovaquone, 1500 mg P.O. every day; TMP-SMZ, 1 DS P.O. 3 times/week
Mycobacterium tuberculosis			
Isoniazid-sensitive[2]	TST reaction ≥5 mm *or* prior positive TST result without treatment or contact with case of active tuberculosis **regardless of TST result**	Isoniazid, 300 mg P.O. *plus* pyridoxine, 50 mg P.O. every day x 9 months or isoniazid, 900 mg P.O. *plus* pyridoxine, 100 mg P.O. twice a week x 9 months	Rifampin, 600 mg P.O. every day x 4 months or rifampin, 300 mg P.O. every day x 4 months Pyrazinamide, 15-20 mg/kg P.O. every day x 2 months *plus* either rifampin, 600 mg P.O. every day x 2 months or rifabutin, 300 mg P.O. every day x 2 months
Isoniazid-resistant	Same as above; high probability of exposure to isoniazid-resistant tuberculosis	Rifampin, 600 mg P.O. or rifabutin, 300 mg P.O. every day x 4 months	Pyrazinamide, 15-20 mg/kg P.O. every day *plus* either rifampin, 600 mg P.O. or rifabutin, 300 mg P.O. every day x 2 months
Multidrug (isoniazid and rifampin)-resistant	Same as above; high probability of exposure to multidrug-resistant tuberculosis	Choice of drugs requires consultation with public health authorities. **Depends on susceptibility of isolate from source patient.**	None
Toxoplasma gondii[3]	IgG antibody to *Toxoplasma* and CD4+ count <100/µL	TMP-SMZ, 1 DS P.O. every day	TMP-SMZ, 1 SS P.O. every day; dapsone, 50 mg P.O. every day *plus* pyrimethamine, 50 mg P.O. once weekly *plus* leucovorin, 25 mg P.O. weekly; dapsone, 200 mg P.O. *plus* pyrimethamine, 75 mg P.O. *plus* leucovorin, 25 mg P.O. weekly; atovaquone, 1500 mg P.O. every day with or without pyrimethamine, 25 mg P.O. every day *plus* leucovorin, 10 mg P.O. every day
Mycobacterium avium complex	CD4+ count <50/µL	Azithromycin, 1200 mg P.O. weekly or clarithromycin,[4] 500 mg P.O. twice daily	Rifabutin, 300 mg P.O. every day; azithromycin, 1200 mg P.O. weekly *plus* rifabutin, 300 mg P.O. every day

Prophylaxis to Prevent First Episode of Opportunistic Disease in HIV-Infected Adults and Adolescents *(continued)*

Pathogen	Indication	Preventive Regimens	
		First Choice	Alternatives
Varicella zoster virus (VZV) **Note:** VZIG has been discontinued; an investigational product VariZIG™ is available under an IND. IRB approval required for access to product.	Significant exposure to chickenpox or shingles for patients who have no history of either condition or, if available, negative antibody to VZV	Varicella zoster immune globulin (VZIG), 5 vials (1.25 mL each) I.M., administered ≤96 hours after exposure, ideally within 48 hours	

II. Generally Recommended

Pathogen	Indication	First Choice	Alternatives
Streptococcus pneumoniae[5]	CD4+ count ≥200/μL	23 valent polysaccharide vaccine, 0.5 mL I.M.	None
Hepatitis B virus[6,7]	All susceptible (anti-HB$_c$-negative) patients	Hepatitis B vaccine: 3 doses	None
Influenza virus[6,8]	All patients (annually, before influenza season)	Inactivated trivalent influenza virus vaccine: One annual dose (0.5 mL) I.M.	Oseltamivir, 75 mg P.O. every day (influenza A or B); while not formally endorsed in the guideline document, zanamivir 10 mg (2 inhalations) once daily for 10 days is indicated for treatment/prevention of influenza A and B
Hepatitis A virus[6,7]	All susceptible (anti-HAV-negative) patients at increased risk for HAV infection (eg, illicit drug users, men who have sex with men, hemophiliacs) or with chronic liver disease, including chronic hepatitis B or hepatitis C	Hepatitis A vaccine: 2 doses	None

III. Evidence for Efficacy but Not Routinely Indicated

Pathogen	Indication	First Choice	Alternatives
Bacteria	Neutropenia	Granulocyte-colony-stimulating factor (G-CSF), 5-10 mcg/kg SubQ every day x 2-4 weeks or granulocyte-macrophage colony-stimulating factor (GM-CSF), 250 mcg/m² SubQ, I.V. x 2-4 weeks	None
Cryptococcus neoformans	CD4+ count <50/μL	Fluconazole, 100-200 mg P.O. every day	Itraconazole capsule, 200 mg P.O. every day
Histoplasma capsulatum[9]	CD4+ count <100/μL, endemic geographic area	Itraconazole capsule, 200 mg P.O. every day	None
Cytomegalovirus (CMV)[10]	CD4+ count <50/μL and CMV antibody positivity	Oral ganciclovir, 1 g P.O. 3 times/day	None

Note: Information included in these guidelines may not represent Food and Drug Administration (FDA) approval or approved labeling for the particular products or indications in question. Specifically, the terms "safe" and "effective" may not be synonymous with the FDA-defined legal standards for product approval.

Abbreviations: Anti-HB$_c$ = antibody to hepatitis B core antigen; CMV = cytomegalovirus; DS = double-strength tablet; HAART = highly active antiretroviral therapy; HAV = hepatitis A virus; SS = single-strength tablet; TMP-SMZ = trimethoprim-sulfamethoxazole; and TST = tuberculin skin test. The Respirgard II™ nebulizer is manufactured by Marquest, Englewood, CO.

[1]Prophylaxis should also be considered for persons with a CD4+ percentage <14%, for persons with a history of an AIDS-defining illness, and possibly for those with CD4+ count >200 but <250 cells/μL. TMP-SMZ also reduces the frequency of toxoplasmosis and some bacterial infections. Patients receiving dapsone should be tested for glucose-6-phosphate dehydrogenase deficiency. A dosage of 50 mg every day is probably less effective than 100 mg every day. The efficacy of parenteral pentamidine (eg, 4 mg/kg/month) is uncertain. Fansidar® (sulfadoxine-pyrimethamine) is rarely used because of severe hypersensitivity reactions. Patients who are being administered therapy for toxoplasmosis with sulfadiazine-pyrimethamine are protected against *Pneumocystis jiroveci* pneumonia and do not need additional prophylaxis against PCP.

[2]Directly observed therapy is recommended for isoniazid (eg, 900 mg twice weekly); INH regimens should include pyridoxine to prevent peripheral neuropathy. If rifampin or rifabutin are administered concurrently with protease inhibitors or non-nucleoside reverse transcriptase inhibitors, careful consideration should be given to potential pharmacokinetic interactions. There have been reports of fatal and severe liver injury associated with the treatment of latent TB infection in HIV-uninfected persons treated with the 2 month regimen of daily rifampin and pyrazinamide; therefore it may be prudent to use regimens that do not contain pyrazinamide in HIV-infected persons whose completion of treatment can

USPHS / IDSA GUIDELINES FOR THE PREVENTION OF OPPORTUNISTIC INFECTIONS IN PERSONS INFECTED WITH HIV *(Continued)*

be assured (CDC. "Update: Fatal and Severe Liver Injuries Associated with Rifampin and Pyrazinamide for Latent Tuberculosis Infection and Revisions in American Thoracic Society/CDC Recommendations, United States 2001," *MMWR*, 2001, 50(34). Exposure to multidrug-resistant tuberculosis might require prophylaxis with two drugs; consult public health authorities. Possible regimens include pyrazinamide plus either ethambutol or a fluoroquinolone.

[3]Protection against toxoplasmosis is provided by TMP-SMZ, dapsone plus pyrimethamine, and possibly by atovaquone. Atovaquone may be used with or without pyrimethamine. Pyrimethamine alone probably provides little, if any, protection.

[4]**During pregnancy, azithromycin is preferred over clarithromycin because of the teratogenicity in animals of clarithromycin.**

[5]Vaccination **may** be offered to persons who have a CD4[+] T-lymphocyte count <200 cells/µL, although the efficacy **is likely to** be diminished. Revaccination 5 years after the first dose or sooner if the initial immunization was given when the CD4[+] count was <200 cells/µL and if the CD4[+] count has increased to >200 cells/µL on HAART is considered optional. Some authorities are concerned that immunizations may stimulate the replication of HIV.

[6]Although data demonstrating clinical benefit of these vaccines in HIV-infected persons are not available, it is logical to assume that those patients who develop antibody responses will derive some protection. Some authorities are concerned that immunizations may stimulate HIV replication, although for influenza vaccination, a large observational study of HIV-infected persons in clinical care showed no adverse effect of this vaccine, including multiple doses, on patient survival (J. Ward, CDC, personal communication). Also, this concern may be less relevant in the setting of HAART. However, because of the theoretical concern that increases in HIV plasma RNA following vaccination during pregnancy might increase the risk of perinatal transmission of HIV, providers may wish to defer vaccination for such patients until after HAART is initiated.

[7]Hepatitis B vaccine has been recommended for all children and adolescents and for all adults with risk factors for hepatitis B virus (HBV). For persons requiring vaccination against both hepatitis A and hepatitis B, a combination vaccine is now available. For additional information regarding vaccination against hepatitis A and B, see CDC, "Hepatitis B Virus: A Comprehensive Strategy for Eliminating Transmission in the United States Through Universal Childhood Vaccination. Recommendations of the Advisory Committee on Immunization Practices (ACIP)," *MMWR Morb Mortal Wkly Rep*, 1991, 40(RR13).

[8]Oseltamivir or zanamivir are appropriate during outbreaks of either influenza A or influenza B. The CDC announced in January, 2006, that rimantadine and amantadine are no longer recommended due to increased rates of resistance. Dosage reduction for antiviral chemoprophylaxis against influenza might be indicated for decreased renal or hepatic function, and for persons with seizure disorders. Physicians should consult the drug package inserts and the annual CDC influenza guidelines for more specific information about adverse effects and dosage adjustments. For additional information about vaccinations, antiviral chemoprophylaxis, and therapy against influenza, see CDC, "Prevention and Control of Influenza: Recommendations of the Advisory Committee on Immunization Practices (ACIP)," *MMWR Morb Mortal Wkly Rep*, 2001, 50(RR-4).

[9]In a few unusual occupational or other circumstances, prophylaxis should be considered; consult a specialist.

[10]Acyclovir is not protective against CMV. Valacyclovir is not recommended because of an unexplained trend toward increased mortality observed in persons with AIDS who were being administered this drug for prevention of CMV disease.

Prophylaxis to Prevent Recurrence of Opportunistic Disease (After Chemotherapy for Acute Disease) in HIV-Infected Adults and Adolescents

Pathogen	Indication	Preventive Regimens	
		First Choice	Alternatives
I. Recommended as Standard of Care			
Pneumocystis jiroveci	Prior *P. jiroveci* pneumonia	TMP-SMZ, 1 DS P.O. every day; TMP-SMZ, 1 SS P.O. every day	Dapsone, 50 mg P.O. twice daily or 100 mg P.O. every day; dapsone, 50 mg P.O. every day *plus* pyrimethamine, 50 mg P.O. weekly *plus* leucovorin, 25 mg P.O. weekly; dapsone, 200 mg P.O. *plus* pyrimethamine, 75 mg P.O. *plus* leucovorin, 25 mg P.O. weekly; aerosolized pentamidine. 300 mg monthly via Respirgard II™ nebulizer; atovaquone, 1500 mg P.O. every day; TMP-SMZ, 1 DS P.O. 3 times/week
Toxoplasma gondii[1]	Prior toxoplasmic encephalitis	Sulfadiazine, 500-1000 mg P.O. 4 times/day *plus* pyrimethamine 25-50 mg P.O. every day *plus* leucovorin, 10-25 mg P.O. every day	Clindamycin, 300-450 mg P.O. every 6-8 hours *plus* pyrimethamine, 25-50 mg P.O. every day *plus* leucovorin, 10-25 mg P.O. every day; atovaquone, 750 mg P.O. every 6-12 hours with or without pyrimethamine, 25 mg P.O. every day *plus* leucovorin 10 mg P.O. every day
Mycobacterium avium complex[2]	Documented disseminated disease	Clarithromycin,[2] 500 mg P.O. twice daily *plus* ethambutol, 15 mg/kg P.O. every day; with or without rifabutin, 300 mg P.O. every day	Azithromycin, 500 mg P.O. every day *plus* ethambutol, 15 mg/kg P.O. every day; with or without rifabutin, 300 mg P.O. every day
Cytomegalovirus	Prior end-organ disease	Ganciclovir, 5-6 mg/kg I.V. 5-7 days/week or 1000 mg P.O. 3 times/day; or foscarnet, 90-120 mg/kg I.V. every day; or (for retinitis) ganciclovir sustained-release implant, every 6-9 months *plus* ganciclovir, 1-1.5 g P.O. 3 times/day	Cidofovir, 5 mg/kg I.V. every other week with probenecid 2 g P.O. 3 hours before the dose followed by 1 g P.O. given 2 hours after the dose, and 1 g P.O. 8 hours after the dose (total of 4 g); fomivirsen [DSC], 1 vial (330 mcg) injected into the vitreous, then repeated every 2-4 weeks; valganciclovir 900 mg P.O. every day
Cryptococcus neoformans	Documented disease	Fluconazole, 200 mg P.O. every day	Amphotericin B, 0.6-1 mg/kg I.V. weekly to 3 times/week; itraconazole capsule, 200 mg P.O. every day
Histoplasma capsulatum	Documented disease	Itraconazole capsule, 200 mg P.O. twice daily	Amphotericin B, 1 mg/kg I.V. weekly
Coccidioides immitis	Documented disease	Fluconazole, 400 mg P.O. every day	Amphotericin B, 1 mg/kg I.V. weekly; itraconazole capsule, 200 mg P.O. twice daily
Salmonella species (non-*typhi*)[3]	Bacteremia	Ciprofloxacin, 500 mg P.O. twice daily for several months	Antibiotic chemoprophylaxis with another active agent
II. Recommended Only if Subsequent Episodes Are Frequent or Severe			
Herpes simplex virus	Frequent/ severe recurrences	Acyclovir, 200 mg P.O. 3 times/ day or 400 mg P.O. twice daily; famciclovir, 250 mg P.O. twice daily	Valacyclovir, 500 mg P.O. twice daily
Candida (oropharyngeal or vaginal)	Frequent/ severe recurrences	Fluconazole, 100-200 mg P.O. every day	Itraconazole solution, 200 mg P.O. every day

USPHS / IDSA GUIDELINES FOR THE PREVENTION OF OPPORTUNISTIC INFECTIONS IN PERSONS INFECTED WITH HIV *(Continued)*

Prophylaxis to Prevent Recurrence of Opportunistic Disease (After Chemotherapy for Acute Disease) in HIV-Infected Adults and Adolescents *(continued)*

Pathogen	Indication	Preventive Regimens	
		First Choice	**Alternatives**
Candida (esophageal)	Frequent/ severe recurrences	Fluconazole, 100-200 mg P.O. every day	Itraconazole solution, 200 mg P.O. every day

Note: Information included in these guidelines may not represent Food and Drug Administration (FDA) approval or approved labeling for the particular products or indications in question. Specifically, the terms "safe" and "effective" may not be synonymous with the FDA-defined legal standards for product approval.

DS = double-strength tablet; SS = single-strength tablet; and TMP-SMZ = trimethoprim-sulfamethoxazole. The Respirgard II™ nebulizer is manufactured by Marquest, Englewood, CO.

[1]Pyrimethamine/sulfadiazine confers protection against PCP as well as toxoplasmosis; clindamycin-pyrimethamine does **not offer protection against PCP.**

[2]Many multiple-drug regimens are poorly tolerated. Drug interactions (eg, those seen with clarithromycin/rifabutin) can be problematic; rifabutin has been associated with uveitis, especially when administered at daily doses of >300 mg or concurrently with fluconazole or clarithromycin. **During pregnancy, azithromycin is recommended instead of clarithromycin because clarithromycin is teratogenic in animals.**

[3]Efficacy of eradication of *Salmonella* has been demonstrated only for ciprofloxacin.

Criteria for Starting, Discontinuing, and Restarting Opportunistic Infection Prophylaxis for Adult Patients With HIV Infection[1]

Opportunistic Illness	Criteria for Initiating Primary Prophylaxis	Criteria for Discontinuing Primary Prophylaxis	Criteria for Restarting Primary Prophylaxis	Criteria for Initiating Secondary Prophylaxis	Criteria for Discontinuing Secondary Prophylaxis	Criteria for Restarting Secondary Prophylaxis
Pneumocystis jiroveci pneumonia	CD4$^+$ <200 cells/μL or oropharyngeal candidiasis	CD4$^+$ >200 cells/μL for ≥3 months	CD4$^+$ <200 cells/μL	Prior *Pneumocystis jiroveci* pneumonia	CD4$^+$ >200 cells/μL for ≥3 months	CD4$^+$ <200 cells/μL
Toxoplasmosis	IgG antibody to *Toxoplasma* and CD4$^+$ <100 cells/μL	CD4$^+$ >200 cells/μL for ≥3 months	CD4$^+$ <100-200 cells/μL	Prior toxoplasmic encephalitis	CD4$^+$ >200 cells/μL sustained (eg, ≥6 months) and completed initial therapy, and asymptomatic for toxoplasmosis	CD4$^+$ <200 cells/μL
Disseminated *Mycobacterium avium* complex	CD4$^+$ <50 cells/μL	CD4$^+$ >100 cells/μL for ≥3 months	CD4$^+$ <50-100 cells/μL	Documented disseminated disease	CD4$^+$ >100 cells/μL sustained (eg, ≥6 months) and completed 12 months of MAC therapy, and asymptomatic for MAC	CD4$^+$ <100 cells/μL
Cryptococcosis	None	Not applicable	Not applicable	Documented disease	CD4$^+$ >100-200 cells/μL sustained (eg, ≥6 months) and completed initial therapy, and asymptomatic for cryptococcosis	CD4$^+$ <100-200 cells/μL
Histoplasmosis	None	Not applicable	Not applicable	Documented disease	No criteria recommended for stopping	Not applicable
Coccidioidomycosis	None	Not applicable	Not applicable	Documented disease	No criteria recommended for stopping	Not applicable
Cytomegalovirus retinitis	None	Not applicable	Not applicable	Documented end-organ disease	CD4$^+$ >100-150 cells/μL sustained (eg, ≥6 months) and no evidence of active disease, and regular ophthalmic examination	CD4$^+$ <100-150 cells/μL

[1]The safety of discontinuing prophylaxis in children whose CD4$^+$ counts have increased in response to HAART has not been studied.

USPHS / IDSA GUIDELINES FOR THE PREVENTION OF OPPORTUNISTIC INFECTIONS IN PERSONS INFECTED WITH HIV *(Continued)*

DRUG REGIMENS FOR INFANTS AND CHILDREN

Prophylaxis to Prevent First Episode of Opportunistic Disease in HIV-Infected Infants and Children

Pathogen	Indication	Preventive Regimens	
		First Choice	Alternatives
I. Strongly Recommended as Standard of Care			
Pneumocystis jiroveci[1]	HIV-infected or HIV-indeterminate infants 1-12 mo of age HIV-infected children 1-5 y of age with CD4+ count <500/μL or CD4+ percentage <15% HIV-infected children 6-12 y of age with CD4+ count <200/μL or CD4+ percentage <15%	TMP-SMZ, 150/750 mg/m²/day in 2 divided doses P.O. 3 times/week on consecutive days Acceptable alternative dosage schedules: • Single dose P.O. 3 times/week on consecutive days • 2 divided doses P.O. every day; 2 divided doses P.O. 3 times/week on alternate days	Dapsone (children ≥1 mo), 2 mg/kg (max: 100 mg) P.O. every day or 4 mg/kg (max: 200 mg) P.O. once weekly) Aerosolized pentamidine (children ≥5 y), 300 mg/mo via Respigard II™ nebulizer Atovaquone (1-3 mo and >24 mo, 30 mg/kg P.O. every day; 4-24 mo, 45 mg/kg P.O. every day)
Mycobacterium tuberculosis[2]			
Isoniazid-sensitive	TST reaction, ≥5 mm *or* prior positive TST result without treatment **or** **contact** with any case of active tuberculosis **regardless of TST result**	Isoniazid, 10-15 mg/kg (max: 300 mg) P.O. every day x 9 mo or 20-30 mg/kg (max: 900 mg) P.O. twice weekly x 9 mo	Rifampin, 10-20 mg/kg (max: 600 mg) P.O. every day x 4-6 mo
Isoniazid-resistant	Same as above; high probability of exposure to isoniazid-resistant tuberculosis	Rifampin, 10-20 mg/kg (max: 600 mg) P.O. every day x 4-6 mo	Uncertain
Multidrug (isoniazid and rifampin)-resistant	Same as above; high probability of exposure to multidrug-resistant tuberculosis	Choice of drug requires consultation with public health authorities and depends on susceptibility of isolate from source patient	
Mycobacterium avium complex[2]	For children ≥6 y, CD4+ count <50/μL; 2-6 y, CD4+ count <75/μL; 1-2 y, CD4+ count <500/μL; <1 y, CD4+ count <750/μL	Clarithromycin, 7.5 mg/kg (max: 500 mg) P.O. twice daily, or azithromycin, 20 mg/kg (max: 1200 mg) P.O. weekly	Azithromycin, 5 mg/kg (max: 250 mg) P.O. every day; children ≥6 y, rifabutin, 300 mg P.O. every day
Varicella zoster virus[3] **Note:** VZIG has been discontinued; an investigational product VariZIG™ is available under an IND. IRB approval required for access to product.	Significant exposure to varicella or shingles with no history of chickenpox or shingles	Varicella zoster immune globulin (VZIG), 1 vial (1.25 mL)/10 kg (max: 5 vials) I.M., administered ≤96 hours after exposure, ideally within 48 hours	None
Vaccine-preventable pathogens[4]	HIV exposure/infection	Routine immunizations	None
II. Generally Recommended			
Influenza virus	All patients (annually, before influenza season)	Inactivated split trivalent influenza vaccine	Oseltamivir (during outbreaks of influenza A or B) for children ≥13 y, 75 mg P.O. every day; while not formally endorsed in the guideline document, zanamivir 10 mg (2 inhalations) once daily for 10 days is indicated for treatment/prevention of influenza A and B in children ≥5 years
Varicella zoster virus	HIV-infected children who are asymptomatic and not immunosuppressed	Varicella zoster vaccine	None

Prophylaxis to Prevent First Episode of Opportunistic Disease in HIV-Infected Infants and Children (continued)

Pathogen	Indication	Preventive Regimens	
		First Choice	Alternatives
Toxoplasma gondii[5]	IgG antibody to Toxoplasma and severe immunosuppression	TMP-SMZ, 150/750 mg/m²/d in 2 divided doses P.O. every day	Dapsone (≥1 mo of age), 2 mg/kg or 15 mg/m² (max: 25 mg) P.O. every day plus pyrimethamine, 1 mg/kg P.O. every day plus leucovorin, 5 mg P.O. every 3 days
			Atovaquone (aged 1-3 mo and >24 mo, 30 mg/kg P.O. every day; aged 14-24 mo, 45 mg/kg P.O. every day)

III. Not Recommended for Most Children; Indicated for Use Only in Unusual Circumstances

Pathogen	Indication	First Choice	Alternatives
Invasive bacterial infections[6]	Hypogamma-globulinemia (ie, IgG <400 mg/dL)	IVIG (400 mg/kg every 2-4 weeks)	None
Cryptococcus neoformans	Severe immunosuppression	Fluconazole, 3-6 mg/kg P.O. every day	Itraconazole, 2-5 mg/kg P.O. every 12-24 hours
Histoplasma capsulatum	Severe immunosuppression, endemic geographic area	Itraconazole, 2-5 mg/kg P.O. every 12-24 hours	None
Cytomegalovirus (CMV)[7]	CMV antibody positivity and severe immunosuppression	Oral ganciclovir 30 mg/kg P.O. 3 times/day	None

Note: Information included in these guidelines may not represent FDA approval or approved labeling for the particular products or indications in question. Specifically, the terms "safe" and "effective" may not be synonymous with the FDA-defined legal standards for product approval. CMV = cytomegalovirus; IVIG = intravenous immune globulin; TMP-SMZ = trimethoprim-sulfamethoxazole; and VZIG = varicella zoster immune globulin. The Respirgard II™ nebulizer is manufactured by Marquest, Englewood, CO.

[1]Daily TMP-SMZ reduces frequency of some bacterial infections. TMP-SMZ, dapsone-pyrimethamine, and possibly atovaquone (with or without pyrimethamine) appear to protect against toxoplasmosis, although data have not been prospectively collected. When compared with weekly dapsone, daily dapsone is associated with lower incidence of Pneumocystis jiroveci pneumonia (PCP) but higher hematologic toxicity and mortality (McIntosh K, Cooper E, Xu J, et al, "Toxicity and Efficacy of Daily vs Weekly Dapsone for Prevention of Pneumocystis carinii Pneumonia in Children Infected With HIV," Ped Infect Dis J 1999, 18:432-9.). Efficacy of parenteral pentamidine (eg, 4 mg/kg/every 2-4 weeks) is controversial. Patients receiving therapy for toxoplasmosis with sulfadiazine-pyrimethamine are protected against PCP and do not need TMP-SMZ.

[2]Significant drug interactions may occur between rifamycins (rifampin and rifabutin) and protease inhibitors, and non-nucleoside reverse transcriptase inhibitors. Consult a specialist.

[3]Children routinely being administered intravenous immune globulin (IVIG) should receive VZIG if the last dose of IVIG was administered >21 days before exposure.

[4]HIV-infected and HIV-exposed children should be immunized according to the childhood immunization schedule, which has been adapted from the January-December 2001 schedule recommended for immunocompetent children by the Advisory Committee on Immunization Practices, the American Academy of Pediatrics, and the American Academy of Family Physicians. This schedule differs from that for immunocompetent children in that both the conjugate pneumococcal vaccine (PCV-7) and the pneumococcal polysaccharide vaccine (PPV-23) are recommended and vaccination against influenza should be offered. MMR should not be administered to severely immunocompromised children. Vaccination against varicella is indicated only for asymptomatic nonimmunosuppressed children. Once an HIV-exposed child is determined not to be HIV infected, the schedule for immunocompetent children applies.

[5]Protection against toxoplasmosis is provided by the preferred antipneumocystis regimens and possibly by atovaquone. Atovaquone may be used with or without pyrimethamine. Pyrimethamine alone probably provides little, if any, protection.

[6]If available, respiratory syncytial virus (RSV) IVIG (750 mg/kg), not monoclonal RSV antibody, may be substituted for IVIG during RSV season to provide broad anti-infective protection.

[7]Oral ganciclovir and perhaps valganciclovir results in reduced CMV shedding in CMV-infected children. Acyclovir is not protective against CMV.

USPHS / IDSA GUIDELINES FOR THE PREVENTION OF OPPORTUNISTIC INFECTIONS IN PERSONS INFECTED WITH HIV *(Continued)*

Prophylaxis to Prevent Recurrence of Opportunistic Disease (After Chemotherapy for Acute Disease) in HIV-Infected Infants and Children

Pathogen	Indication	Preventive Regimens	
		First Choice	**Alternatives**
I. Recommended for Life as Standard of Care			
Pneumocystis jiroveci	Prior *P. jiroveci* pneumonia	TMP-SMZ, 150/750 mg/m^2/d in 2 divided doses P.O. 3 times/week on consecutive days Acceptable alternative schedules for same dosage Single dose P.O. 3 times/week on consecutive days; 2 divided doses P.O. daily; 2 divided doses P.O. 3 times/week on alternate days	Dapsone (children ≥1 mo of age), 2 mg/kg (max: 100 mg) P.O. once daily *or* 4 mg/kg (max: 200 mg) P.O. weekly; aerosolized pentamidine (children ≥5 y of age), 300 mg monthly via Respirgard II™ nebulizer; atovaquone (children 1-3 mo and >24 mo of age, 30 mg/kg P.O. every day; children 4-24 mo, 45 mg/kg P.O. every day)
Toxoplasma gondii[1]	Prior toxoplasmic encephalitis	Sulfadiazine, 85-120 mg/kg/d in 2-4 divided doses P.O. daily *plus* pyrimethamine, 1 mg/kg *or* 15 mg/m^2 (max: 25 mg) P.O. every day *plus* leucovorin, 5 mg P.O. every 3 days	Clindamycin, 20-30 mg/kg/d in 4 divided doses P.O. every day *plus* pyrimethamine, 1 mg/kg P.O. every day *plus* leucovorin, 5 mg P.O. every 3 days
Mycobacterium avium complex[2]	Prior disease	Clarithromycin, 7.5 mg/kg (max: 500 mg) P.O. twice daily *plus* ethambutol, 15 mg/kg (max: 900 mg) P.O. every day; with or without rifabutin, 5 mg/kg (max: 300 mg) P.O. once daily	Azithromycin, 5 mg/kg (max: 250 mg) P.O. every day *plus* ethambutol, 15 mg/kg (max: 900 mg) P.O. every day; with or without rifabutin, 5 mg/kg (max: 300 mg) P.O. once daily
Cryptococcus neoformans	Documented disease	Fluconazole, 3-6 mg/kg P.O. every day	Amphotericin B, 0.5-1 mg/kg I.V. 1-3 times/ week; itraconazole, 2-5 mg/kg P.O. every 12-24 hours
Histoplasma capsulatum	Documented disease	Itraconazole, 2-5 mg/kg P.O. every 12-48 hours	Amphotericin B, 1 mg/kg I.V. weekly
Coccidioides immitis	Documented disease	Fluconazole, 6 mg/kg P.O. every day	Amphotericin B, 1 mg/kg I.V. weekly; itraconazole, 2-5 mg/kg P.O. every 12-48 hours
Cytomegalovirus	Prior end-organ disease	Ganciclovir, 5 mg/kg I.V. every day, *or* foscarnet, 90-120 mg/kg I.V. every day	(For retinitis) — ganciclovir sustained-release implant, every 6-9 mo *plus* ganciclovir, 30 mg/kg P.O. every 3 times/d
Salmonella species (non-*typhi*)[3]	Bacteremia	TMP-SMZ, 150/750 mg/m^2 in 2 divided doses P.O. every day for several months	Antibiotic chemoprophylaxis with another active agent
II. Recommended Only if Subsequent Episodes Are Frequent or Severe			
Invasive bacterial infections[4]	>2 infections in 1-year period	TMP-SMZ, 150/750 mg/m^2 in 2 divided doses P.O. every day; *or* IVIG, 400 mg/kg every 2-4 weeks	Antibiotic chemoprophylaxis with another active agent
Herpes simplex virus	Frequent/ severe recurrences	Acyclovir, 80 mg/kg/d in 3-4 divided doses P.O. daily	
Candida (oropharyngeal)	Frequent/ severe recurrences	Fluconazole, 3-6 mg/kg P.O. every day	

Prophylaxis to Prevent Recurrence of Opportunistic Disease (After Chemotherapy for Acute Disease) in HIV-Infected Infants and Children (continued)

Pathogen	Indication	Preventive Regimens	
		First Choice	Alternatives
Candida (esophageal)	Frequent/ severe recurrences	Fluconazole, 3-6 mg/kg P.O. every day	Itraconazole solution, 5 mg/kg P.O. every day; ketoconazole, 5-10 mg/kg P.O. every 12-24 hours

Note: Information included in these guidelines may not represent Food and Drug Administration (FDA) approval or approved labeling for the particular products or indications in question. Specifically, the terms "safe" and "effective" may not be synonymous with the FDA-defined legal standards for product approval. IVIG = intravenous immune globulin and TMP-SMZ = trimethoprim-sulfamethoxazole. The Respirgard II™ nebulizer is manufactured by Marquest, Englewood, CO.

[1]Only pyrimethamine plus sulfadiazine confers protection against PCP as well as toxoplasmosis. Although the clindamycin plus pyrimethamine regimen is the preferred alternative in adults, it has not been tested in children. However, these drugs are safe and are used for other infections.

[2]Significant drug interactions may occur between rifabutin and protease inhibitors and non-nucleoside reverse transcriptase inhibitors. Consult an expert.

[3]Drug should be determined by susceptibilities of the organism isolated. Alternatives to TMP-SMZ include ampicillin, chloramphenicol, or ciprofloxacin. However, ciprofloxacin is not approved for use in persons aged <18 years; therefore, it should be used in children with caution and only if no alternatives exist.

[4]Antimicrobial prophylaxis should be chosen based on the microorganism and antibiotic sensitivities. TMP-SMZ, if used, should be administered daily. Providers should be cautious about using antibiotics solely for this purpose because of the potential for development of drug-resistant microorganisms. IVIG may not provide additional benefit to children receiving daily TMP-SMZ, but may be considered for children who have recurrent bacterial infections despite TMP-SMZ prophylaxis. Choice of antibiotic prophylaxis vs IVIG should also involve consideration of adherence, ease of intravenous access, and cost. If IVIG is used, RSV-IVIG (750 mg/kg), not monoclonal RSV antibody, may be substituted for IVIG during the RSV season to provide broad anti-infective protection, if this product is available.

ANIMAL AND HUMAN BITES

Bite Wound Antibiotic Regimens

	Dog Bite	Cat Bite	Human Bite
Prophylactic Antibiotics			
Prophylaxis	No routine prophylaxis, consider if involves face or hand, or immunosuppressed or asplenic patients	Routine prophylaxis	Routine prophylaxis
Prophylactic antibiotic	Amoxicillin	Amoxicillin	Amoxicillin
Penicillin allergy	Doxycycline if >10 y or co-trimoxazole	Doxycycline if >10 y or co-trimoxazole	Doxycycline if >10 y or erythromycin and cephalexin[1]
Outpatient Oral Antibiotic Treatment (mild to moderate infection)			
Established infection	Amoxicillin and clavulanic acid	Amoxicillin and clavulanic acid	Amoxicillin and clavulanic acid
Penicillin allergy (mild infection only)	Doxycycline if >10 y	Doxycycline if >10 y	Cephalexin[1] or clindamycin
Outpatient Parenteral Antibiotic Treatment (moderate infections – single drug regimens)			
	Ceftriaxone	Ceftriaxone	Cefotetan
Inpatient Parenteral Antibiotic Treatment			
Established infection	Ampicillin + cefazolin	Ampicillin + cefazolin	Ampicillin + clindamycin
Penicillin allergy	Cefazolin[1]	Ceftriaxone[1]	Cefotetan[1] or imipenem
Duration of Prophylactic and Treatment Regimens			
Prophylaxis: 5 days			
Treatment: 10-14 days			

[1]Contraindicated if history of immediate hypersensitivity reaction (anaphylaxis) to penicillin.

ANTIBIOTIC TREATMENT OF ADULTS WITH INFECTIVE ENDOCARDITIS

Table 1. Suggested Regimens for Therapy of Native Valve Endocarditis Due to Penicillin-Susceptible Viridans Streptococci and *Streptococcus bovis* (Minimum Inhibitory Concentration ≤0.12 mcg/mL)[1]

Antibiotic	Dosage and Route	Duration (wk)	Comments
Aqueous crystalline penicillin G sodium or	12-18 million units/24 h I.V. either continuously or in 4-6 equally divided doses	4	Preferred in most patients older than 65 y and in those with impairment of the 8th cranial nerve or renal function
Ceftriaxone sodium	2 g once daily I.V. or I.M.[2]	4	
Either penicillin or ceftriaxone regimen above with gentamicin sulfate[3]	3 mg/kg/24 h I.M./I.V. as single daily dose	2	When using combination therapy, both β-lactam and aminoglycoside regimen duration is 2 weeks; 2-week regimen not intended if known cardiac or extracardiac abscess, Cl$_{cr}$ <20 mL/min, 8th cranial nerve impairment or *Abiotrophia, Granulicatella,* or *Gemella* spp
Vancomycin hydrochloride[4]	30 mg/kg/24 h I.V. in 2 equally divided doses, not to exceed 2 g/24 h unless serum levels are monitored	4	Vancomycin therapy is recommended for patients allergic to β-lactams; peak serum concentrations of vancomycin should be obtained 1 h after completion of the infusion and should be in the range of 30-45 mcg/mL and trough of 10-15 mcg/mL for twice-daily dosing

[1]Dosages recommended are for patients with normal renal function. For nutritionally variant streptococci, see Table 3. I.V. indicates intravenous; I.M., intramuscular.

[2]Patients should be informed that I.M. injection of ceftriaxone is painful.

[3]Dosing of gentamicin on a mg/kg basis will produce higher serum concentrations in obese patients that in lean patients. Therefore, in obese patients, dosing should be based on ideal body weight. (Ideal body weight for men is 50 kg + 2.3 kg per inch over 5 feet, and ideal body weight for women is 45.5 kg + 2.3 kg per inch over 5 feet.) Relative contraindications to the use of gentamicin are age >65 years, renal impairment, or impairment of the eighth nerve. Other potentially nephrotoxic agents (eg, nonsteroidal anti-inflammatory drugs) should be used cautiously in patients receiving gentamicin.

[4]Vancomycin dosage should be reduced in patients with impaired renal function. Vancomycin given on a mg/kg basis will produce higher serum concentrations in obese patients than in lean patients. Therefore, in obese patients, dosing should be based on ideal body weight. Each dose of vancomycin should be infused over at least 1 hour to reduce the risk of the histamine-release "red man" syndrome.

Table 2. Therapy for Native Valve Endocarditis Due to Strains of Viridans Streptococci and *Streptococcus bovis* Relatively Resistant to Penicillin G (Minimum Inhibitory Concentration >0.12 mcg/mL and ≤0.5 mcg/mL)[1]

Antibiotic	Dosage and Route	Duration (wk)	Comments
Aqueous crystalline penicillin G sodium	24 million units/24 h I.V. either continuously or in 4-6 equally divided doses	4	Cefazolin or other first-generation cephalosporins may be substituted for penicillin in patients whose penicillin hypersensitivity is not of the immediate type.
With gentamicin sulfate[2]	3 mg/kg/24 h I.M./I.V. as single daily dose	2	
Ceftriaxone sodium	2 g once daily I.V. or I.M.[2]	4	
With gentamicin sulfate[2]	3 mg/kg/24 h I.M./I.V. as single daily dose	2	
Vancomycin hydrochloride[3]	30 mg/kg/24 h I.V. in 2 equally divided doses, not to exceed 2 g/24 h unless serum levels are monitored	4	Vancomycin therapy is recommended for patients allergic to β-lactams.

[1]Dosages recommended are for patients with normal renal function. I.V. indicates intravenous; I.M., intramuscular.

[2]For specific dosing adjustment and issues concerning gentamicin (obese patients, relative contraindications), see Table 1 footnotes.

[3]For specific dosing adjustment and issues concerning vancomycin (obese patients, length of infusion), see Table 1 footnotes.

ANTIBIOTIC TREATMENT OF ADULTS WITH INFECTIVE ENDOCARDITIS *(Continued)*

Table 3. Standard Therapy for Endocarditis Due to Enterococci[1]

Antibiotic	Dosage and Route	Duration (wk)	Comments
Aqueous crystalline penicillin G sodium	18-30 million units/24 h I.V. either continuously or in 6 equally divided doses	4-6	Native valve: 4-week therapy recommended for patients with symptoms ≤3 months in duration; 6-week therapy recommended for patients with symptoms >3 months in duration.
With gentamicin sulfate[2]	1 mg/kg I.M. or I.V. every 8 h	4-6	
Ampicillin sodium	12 g/24 h I.V. in 6 equally divided doses	4-6	Prosthetic valve or other prosthetic material: 6-week minimum therapy recommended
With gentamicin sulfate[2]	1 mg/kg I.M. or I.V. every 8 hours	4-6	Target gentamicin peak concentration of 3-4 mcg/mL and trough of <1 mcg/mL
Vancomycin hydrochloride[2,3]	30 mg/kg/24 h I.V. in 2 equally divided doses, not to exceed 2 g/24 h unless serum levels are monitored	6	Vancomycin therapy is recommended for patients allergic to β-lactams; cephalosporins are not acceptable alternatives for patients allergic to penicillin.
With gentamicin sulfate[2]	1 mg/kg I.M. or I.V. every 8 h	6	

[1]All enterococci causing endocarditis must be tested for antimicrobial susceptibility in order to select optimal therapy. This table is for endocarditis due to penicillin-, gentamicin-, and vancomycin-susceptible enterococci, viridans streptococci with a minimum inhibitory concentration of >0.5 mcg/mL, nutritionally variant viridans streptococci, or prosthetic valve endocarditis caused by viridans streptococci or *Streptococcus bovis*. If penicillin-resistant organisms, use vancomycin/gentamicin regimen above, or may use ampicillin/sulbactam (12 g/24 h in 4 divided doses) with gentamicin for 6 weeks. Antibiotic dosages are for patients with normal renal function. I.V. indicates intravenous; I.M., intramuscular.

[2]For specific dosing adjustment and issues concerning gentamicin (obese patients, relative contraindications), see Table 1 footnotes.

[3]For specific dosing adjustment and issues concerning vancomycin (obese patients, length of infusion), see Table 1 footnotes.

Table 4. Therapy for Native or Prosthetic Valve Endocarditis Due to Enterococci[1] Resistant to Vancomycin, Aminoglycosides, and Penicillin[2]

Antibiotic	Dosage and Route	Duration (wk)	Comments
E. faecium			
Linezolid	1200 mg/24 h P.O./I.V. in 2 divided doses	≥8	May cause severe, but reversible thrombocytopenia, particularly with extended therapy >2 weeks.
Quinupristin-dalfopristin	22.5 mg/kg/24 h I.V. in 3 divided doses	≥8	May cause severe myalgia; not effective against *E. faecalis*.
E. faecalis			
Imipenem/cilastatin	2 g/24 h I.V. in 4 divided doses	≥8	Limited patient experience with these regimens.
With ampicillin sodium	12 g/24 h in 6 divided doses	≥8	
or			
Ceftriaxone sodium	2 g/24 h I.V./I.M.[3] once daily	≥8	Limited patient experience with these regimens.
With ampicillin sodium	12 g/24 h in 6 divided doses	≥8	

[1]Endocarditis caused by the organisms should be treated in consultation with an infectious disease specialist; bacteriologic cure with antimicrobial therapy alone may be <50% and valve replacement may be required.

[2]Dosages recommended are for patients with normal renal function. I.V. = intravenous; I.M. = intramuscular.

[3]Patients should be informed that I.M. injection of ceftriaxone is painful.

Table 5. Therapy for Endocarditis Due to *Staphylococcus* in the Absence of Prosthetic Material[1]

Antibiotic	Dosage and Route	Duration	Comments
Methicillin-Susceptible Staphylococci			
Regimens for non-β-lactam-allergic patients			
Nafcillin sodium or oxacillin sodium	12 g/24 h I.V. in 4-6 divided doses	6 wk	Uncomplicated right side endocarditis may be treated for 2 weeks.
With optional addition of gentamicin sulfate[2]	3 mg/kg/24 h I.M./I.V. in 2-3 divided doses	3-5 d	Benefit of additional aminoglycosides has not been established.
Regimens for β-lactam-allergic patients (nonanaphylactic)			
Cefazolin (or other first-generation cephalosporins in equivalent dosages)	2 g I.V. every 8 h	6 wk	Cephalosporins should be avoided in patients with immediate-type hypersensitivity to penicillin; if penicillin-sensitive, vancomycin should be used.
With optional addition of gentamicin[2]	3 mg/kg/24 h I.M./I.V. in 2-3 divided doses	3-5 d	Benefit of additional aminoglycosides has not been established.
Methicillin-Resistant Staphylococci			
Vancomycin hydrochloride[3]	30 mg/kg/24 h I.V. in 2 equally divided doses; not to exceed 2 g/24 h unless serum levels are monitored	4-6 wk	Vancomycin therapy is recommended for patients allergic to β-lactams; peak serum concentrations of vancomycin should be obtained 1 h after completion of the infusion and should be in the range of 30-45 mcg/mL and trough of 10-15 mcg/mL for twice-daily dosing.

[1]For treatment of endocarditis due to penicillin-susceptible staphylococci (minimum inhibitory concentration ≤0.1 mcg/mL and non-beta-lactamase producing), aqueous crystalline penicillin G sodium 24 million units/24 h can be used instead of nafcillin or oxacillin. Shorter antibiotic courses have been effective in some drug addicts with right-sided endocarditis due to *Staphylococcus aureus*. I.V. indicates intravenous; I.M., intramuscular.

[2]For specific dosing adjustment and issues concerning gentamicin (obese patients, relative contraindications), see Table 1 footnotes.

[3]For specific dosing adjustment and issues concerning vancomycin (obese patients, length of infusion), see Table 1 footnotes.

Table 6. Treatment of Staphylococcal Endocarditis in the Presence of a Prosthetic Valve or Other Prosthetic Material[1]

Antibiotic	Dosage and Route	Duration (wk)	Comments
Methicillin-Susceptible Staphylococci			
Nafcillin sodium or oxacillin sodium[2]	12 g/24 h I.V. in 6 divided doses	≥6	First-generation cephalosporins or vancomycin should be used in patients allergic to β-lactam. Cephalosporins should be avoided in patients with immediate-type hypersensitivity to penicillin or with methicillin-resistant staphylococci.
With rifampin[3]	300 mg P.O./I.V. every 8 h	≥6	–
And with gentamicin sulfate[4,5]	3 mg/kg I.M./I.V. in 2-3 divided doses	2	Aminoglycoside should be administered in close proximity to vancomycin, nafcillin, or oxacillin.
Methicillin-Resistant Staphylococci			
Vancomycin hydrochloride[6]	30 mg/kg/24 h I.V. in 2 equally divided doses, not to exceed 2 g/24 h unless serum levels are monitored	≥6	–
With rifampin[3]	300 mg P.O./I.V. every 8 h	≥6	Rifampin increases the amount of warfarin sodium required for antithrombotic therapy.
And with gentamicin sulfate[4,5]	3 mg/kg I.M./I.V. in 2-3 divided doses	2	Aminoglycoside should be administered in close proximity to vancomycin, nafcillin, or oxacillin.

[1]Dosages recommended are for patients with normal renal function. I.V. indicates intravenous; I.M., intramuscular.

[2]May use aqueous penicillin G 24 million units/24 h in 4-6 divided doses if strain is penicillin susceptible (MIC ≤0.1 mcg/mL and non-beta-lactamase producing).

[3]Rifampin plays a unique role in the eradication of staphylococcal infection involving prosthetic material; combination therapy is essential to prevent emergence of rifampin resistance.

[4]For a specific dosing adjustment and issues concerning gentamicin (obese patients, relative contraindications), see Table 1 footnotes.

[5]Use during initial 2 weeks.

[6]For specific dosing adjustment and issues concerning vancomycin (obese patients, relative contraindications), see Table 1 footnotes.

ANTIBIOTIC TREATMENT OF ADULTS WITH INFECTIVE ENDOCARDITIS (Continued)

Table 7. Therapy for Native or Prosthetic Valve Endocarditis Due to HACEK Microorganisms (Haemophilus parainfluenzae, Haemophilus aphrophilus, Actinobacillus actinomycetemcomitans, Cardiobacterium hominus, Eikenella corrodens, and Kingella kingae)[1]

Antibiotic	Dosage and Route	Duration (wk)	Comments
Ceftriaxone sodium[2]	2 g once daily I.V. or I.M.[2]	4	Cefotaxime sodium or other third- or fourth-generation cephalosporins may be substituted.
Ampicillin/ sulbactam	12 g/24 h I.V. in 6 equally divided doses	4	
Ciprofloxacin	1000 mg/24 h orally or 800 mg/ 24 h I.V. in 2 divided doses	4	Use of fluoroquinolone recommended only if patient intolerant to ampicillin or cephalosporins; may substitute fluoroquinolone with equivalent coverage (eg, levofloxacin, moxifloxacin); if prosthetic material involved, treatment duration should be 6 weeks.

[1]Antibiotic dosages are for patients with normal renal function. I.V. indicates intravenous; I.M. intramuscular.

[2]Patients should be informed that I.M. injection of ceftriaxone is painful.

[3]Ampicillin should not be used if laboratory tests show β-lactamase production.

Reference

Baddour LM, Wilson WR, Bayer AS, et al, "Infective Endocarditis. Diagnosis, Antimicrobial Therapy, and Management of Complications. A Statement for Healthcare Professionals from the Committee on Rheumatic Fever, Endocarditis, and Kawasaki Disease, Council on Cardiovascular Disease in the Young, and the Councils on Clinical Cardiology, Stroke, and Cardiovascular Surgery and Anesthesia, American Heart Association," Circulation, 2005, 111(23):e394-434.

ANTIMICROBIAL DRUGS OF CHOICE

Empirical treatment of some common infecting organisms is listed below. These recommendations are based on results of susceptibility studies, clinical trials, and the opinions of *Medical Letter* consultants. The site and severity of the infection, pharmacokinetic characteristics of antibiotics, local resistance patterns, potential drug interactions, and specific patient factors should be taken into account in choosing an appropriate regimen.

Infecting Organism	Drug of First Choice	Alternative Drugs
GRAM-POSITIVE COCCI		
Enterococcus[1]		
endocarditis or other severe infection	Penicillin G or ampicillin + gentamicin or streptomycin[2]	Vancomycin + gentamicin or streptomycin[2]; linezolid; daptomycin[3]; quinupristin/dalfopristin[4]
uncomplicated urinary tract infection	Ampicillin or amoxicillin	Nitrofurantoin; a fluoroquinolone[5]; fosfomycin
Staphylococcus aureus or *epidermidis*		
methicillin-susceptible	A penicillinase-resistant penicillin[6]	A cephalosporin[7,8]; vancomycin; imipenem or meropenem; clindamycin; linezolid; daptomycin[3]; a fluoroquinolone[5]
methicillin-resistant[9]	Vancomycin ± gentamicin ± rifampin	Linezolid; daptomycin[3]; a fluoroquinolone[5]; quinupristin/dalfopristin; a tetracycline[10]; trimethoprim-sulfamethoxazole
Streptococcus pyogenes (group A[11]) and groups C and G	Penicillin G or V[12]	Clindamycin; erythromycin; a cephalosporin[7,8]; vancomycin; clarithromycin[13]; azithromycin[13]; linezolid; daptomycin[3]
Streptococcus, group B	Penicillin G or ampicillin	A cephalosporin[7,8]; vancomycin; daptomycin[3]; erythromycin
Streptococcus, viridans group[1]	Penicillin G ± gentamicin	A cephalosporin[7,8]; vancomycin
Streptococcus bovis	Penicillin G	A cephalosporin[7,8]; vancomycin
Streptococcus, anaerobic or *Peptostreptococcus*	Penicillin G	Clindamycin; a cephalosporin[7,8]; vancomycin
Streptococcus pneumoniae[14] (pneumococcus)		
penicillin-susceptible (MIC <0.1 mcg/mL)	Penicillin G or V[12]; amoxicillin	A cephalosporin[7,8]; erythromycin; azithromycin; clarithromycin[13]; levofloxacin, gatifloxacin or moxifloxacin[16]; meropenem; imipenem or ertapenem; trimethoprim-sulfamethoxazole; clindamycin; a tetracycline[10]; vancomycin
penicillin-intermediate resistance (MIC 0.1-≤2 mcg/mL)	Penicillin G I.V. (12 million units/day for adults); ceftriaxone or cefotaxime	Levofloxacin, gatifloxacin or moxifloxacin[16]; vancomycin; clindamycin
penicillin-high level resistance (MIC >2 mcg/mL)	**Meningitis:** Vancomycin ± rifampin + ceftriaxone or cefotaxime	
	Other Infections: Vancomycin + ceftriaxone or cefotaxime; levofloxacin, gatifloxacin, or moxifloxacin[16]	Linezolid; quinupristin/dalfopristin
GRAM-NEGATIVE COCCI		
Moraxella (Branhamella) catarrhalis	Cefuroxime[7]; a fluoroquinolone[5]	Trimethoprim-sulfamethoxazole; amoxicillin/clavulanate; erythromycin; clarithromycin[13]; azithromycin; a tetracycline[10]; cefotaxime[7]; ceftizoxime[7]; ceftriaxone[7]; cefpodoxime[7]
Neisseria gonorrhoeae (gonococcus)[17]	Ceftriaxone[7]; ciprofloxacin, gatifloxacin, or ofloxacin[15,16]	Cefotaxime[7]; penicillin G

ANTIMICROBIAL DRUGS OF CHOICE *(Continued)*

Infecting Organism	Drug of First Choice	Alternative Drugs
Neisseria meningitidis[18] (meningococcus)	Penicillin G	Cefotaxime[7]; ceftizoxime[7]; ceftriaxone[7]; chloramphenicol[19]; a sulfonamide[20]; a fluoroquinolone[5]
GRAM-POSITIVE BACILLI		
*Bacillus anthracis[21] (anthrax)	Ciprofloxacin[16]; a tetracycline[10]	Penicillin G, amoxicillin; erythromycin; imipenem; clindamycin; levofloxacin[16]
Bacillus cereus, subtilis	Vancomycin	Imipenem or meropenem; clindamycin
Clostridium perfringens[22]	Penicillin G; clindamycin	Metronidazole; imipenem, meropenem, or ertapenem; chloramphenicol[19]
Clostridium tetani[23]	Metronidazole	Penicillin G; a tetracycline[10]
Clostridium difficile[24]	Metronidazole (oral)	Vancomycin (oral)
Corynebacterium diphtheriae[25]	Erythromycin	Penicillin G
Corynebacterium, JK group	Vancomycin	Penicillin G + gentamicin; erythromycin
*Erysipelothrix rhusiopathiae	Penicillin G	Erythromycin, a cephalosporin[7,8]; a fluoroquinolone[5]
Listeria monocytogenes	Ampicillin ± gentamicin	Trimethoprim-sulfamethoxazole
ENTERIC GRAM-NEGATIVE BACILLI		
*Campylobacter fetus	A third-generation cephalosporin[8]; gentamicin	Ampicillin; imipenem or meropenem
*Campylobacter jejuni	Erythromycin or azithromycin	A fluoroquinolone[5]; a tetracycline[10]; gentamicin
*Citrobacter freundii	Imipenem or meropenem[26]	A fluoroquinolone[5];ertapenem; amikacin; a tetracycline[10]; trimethoprim-sulfamethoxazole; cefotaxime[7,26]; ceftizoxime[7,26]; ceftriaxone[7,26]; cefepime[7,26] or ceftazidime[7,26]
*Enterobacter	Imipenem or meropenem[26]; cefepime[7,26]	Gentamicin, tobramycin or amikacin; trimethoprim-sulfamethoxazole; ciprofloxacin[16]; ticarcillin/clavulanate[27] or piperacillin/sulbactam[27]; aztreonam[26]; cefotaxime, ceftizoxime, ceftriaxone, or ceftazidime[7,26]
*Escherichia coli[28]	Cefotaxime, ceftriaxone, cefepime, or ceftazidime[7,26]	Ampicillin ± gentamicin, tobramycin or amikacin; gentamicin, tobramycin, or amikacin; amoxicillin/clavulanate[26]; ticarcillin/clavulanate[27]; piperacillin/tazobactam[27]; ampicillin/sulbactam[26]; trimethoprim-sulfamethoxazole; imipenem, meropenem, or ertapenem[26]; aztreonam[26]; a fluoroquinolone[5]; another cephalosporin[7,8]
*Klebsiella pneumoniae[28]	Cefotaxime, ceftriaxone, cefepime, or ceftazidime[7,26]	Imipenem, meropenem, or ertapenem[26]; gentamicin, tobramycin or amikacin; amoxicillin/clavulanate[26]; ticarcillin/clavulanate[27]; piperacillin/tazobactam[27]; ampicillin/sulbactam[26]; trimethoprim-sulfamethoxazole; aztreonam[26]; a fluoroquinolone[5]; another cephalosporin[7,8]
*Proteus mirabilis[28]	Ampicillin[29]	A cephalosporin[7,8,26]; ticarcillin/clavulanate or piperacillin/tazobactam[27]; gentamicin, tobramycin, or amikacin; trimethoprim-sulfamethoxazole; imipenem, meropenem, or ertapenem[26]; aztreonam[26]; a fluoroquinolone[5]; chloramphenicol[19]

Infecting Organism	Drug of First Choice	Alternative Drugs
*Proteus, indole-positive (including Providencia rettgeri, Morganella morganii, and Proteus vulgaris)	Cefotaxime, ceftriaxone, cefepime, or ceftazidime[7,26]	Imipenem, meropenem, or ertapenem[28]; gentamicin, tobramycin, or amikacin; amoxicillin/ clavulanate[26]; ticarcillin/ clavulanate[27]; piperacillin/ tazobactam[27]; ampicillin/ sulbactam[26]; aztreonam[26]; trimethoprim-sulfamethoxazole; a fluoroquinolone[5]
*Providencia stuartii	Cefotaxime, ceftriaxone, cefepime, or ceftazidime[7,26]	Imipenem, meropenem, or ertapenem[26]; ticarcillin/clavulanate[27]; piperacillin/tazobactam[27]; gentamicin, tobramycin, or amikacin; aztreonam[26]; trimethoprim-sulfamethoxazole; a fluoroquinolone[5]
*Salmonella typhi (typhoid fever)[30]	A fluoroquinolone[5] or ceftriaxone[7]	Chloramphenicol[19]; trimethoprim-sulfamethoxazole; ampicillin; amoxicillin; azithromycin[31]
*Other Salmonella[32]	Cefotaxime[7] or ceftriaxone[7] or a fluoroquinolone[5]	Ampicillin or amoxicillin; trimethoprim-sulfamethoxazole; chloramphenicol[19]
*Serratia	Imipenem or meropenem[26]	Gentamicin or amikacin; cefotaxime, ceftizoxime, ceftriaxone, cefepime, or ceftazidime[7,26]; aztreonam[26]; trimethoprim-sulfamethoxazole; a fluoroquinolone[5]
*Shigella	A fluoroquinolone[5]	Azithromycin; trimethoprim-sulfamethoxazole; ampicillin; ceftriaxone[7]
*Yersinia enterocolitica	Trimethoprim-sulfamethoxazole	A fluoroquinolone[5]; gentamicin, tobramycin, or amikacin; cefotaxime[7]

OTHER GRAM-NEGATIVE BACILLI

Infecting Organism	Drug of First Choice	Alternative Drugs
*Acinetobacter	Imipenem or meropenem[26]	An aminoglycoside; ciprofloxacin[16]; trimethoprim-sulfamethoxazole; ticarcillin/clavulanate,[27] or piperacillin/tazobactam[27]; ceftazidime[26]; minocycline[10]; doxycycline[10]; sulbactam[33]; polymyxin
*Aeromonas	Trimethoprim-sulfamethoxazole	Gentamicin or tobramycin; imipenem; a fluoroquinolone[5]
*Bacteroides	Metronidazole	Clindamycin; imipenem, meropenem or ertapenem; amoxicillin/ clavulanate; ticarcillin/clavulanate; piperacillin/tazobactam or ampicillin/ sulbactam; cefoxitin[7]; chloramphenicol[19]
Bartonella henselae or quintana (bacillary angiomatosis, trench fever)	Erythromycin	Azithromycin; doxycycline[10]
Bartonella henselae[34] (cat scratch bacillus)	Azithromycin	Erythromycin; ciprofloxacin[16]; trimethoprim-sulfamethoxazole; gentamicin; rifampin
Bordetella pertussis (whooping cough)	Erythromycin; clarithromycin[13]	Azithromycin; trimethoprim-sulfamethoxazole
*Brucella	A tetracycline[10] + rifampin	A tetracycline[10] + streptomycin or gentamicin; chloramphenicol[19] ± streptomycin; trimethoprim-sulfamethoxazole ± gentamicin; ciprofloxacin[16] + rifampin
*Burkholderia cepacia	Trimethoprim-sulfamethoxazole	Ceftazidime[7]; chloramphenicol[19]; imipenem
Burkholderia (Pseudomonas) mallei (glanders)	Streptomycin + a tetracycline[10]	Streptomycin + chloramphenicol[19]; imipenem
*Burkholderia (Pseudomonas) pseudomallei (melioidosis)	Imipenem; ceftazidime[7]	Meropenem; chloramphenicol[19] + doxycycline[10] + trimethoprim-sulfamethoxazole; amoxicillin/clavulanate
Calymmatobacterium granulomatis (granuloma inguinale)	Trimethoprim-sulfamethoxazole	Doxycycline[10] or ciprofloxacin[16] ± gentamicin
Capnocytophaga canimorsus[35]	Penicillin G	Cefotaxime, ceftizoxime, or ceftriaxone[7]; imipenem or meropenem; vancomycin; a fluoroquinolone[5]; clindamycin

ANTIMICROBIAL DRUGS OF CHOICE (Continued)

Infecting Organism	Drug of First Choice	Alternative Drugs
Eikenella corrodens	Ampicillin	Erythromycin; azithromycin; clarithromycin[13]; a tetracycline[10]; amoxicillin/clavulanate; ampicillin/sulbactam; ceftriaxone[7]
Francisella tularensis (tularemia)	Gentamicin or streptomycin either + a tetracycline[10]	Chloramphenicol[19]; ciprofloxacin[16]
Fusobacterium	Penicillin G; metronidazole	Clindamycin; cefoxitin[7]; chloramphenicol[19]
Gardnerella vaginalis (bacterial vaginosis)	Oral metronidazole[37]	Topical clindamycin or metronidazole; oral clindamycin
Haemophilus ducreyi (chancroid)	Azithromycin or ceftriaxone	Ciprofloxacin[16] or erythromycin
Haemophilus influenzae		
meningitis, epiglottitis, arthritis, and other serious infections	Cefotaxime or ceftriaxone[7]	Cefuroxime[7] (not for meningitis); chloramphenicol[19]; meropenem
upper respiratory infections and bronchitis	Trimethoprim-sulfamethoxazole	Cefuroxime[7]; amoxicillin/clavulanate; cefuroxime axetil[7]; cefpodoxime[7]; cefaclor[7]; cefotaxime[7]; ceftizoxime[7]; ceftriaxone[7]; cefixime[7]; a tetracycline[10]; clarithromycin[13]; azithromycin; a fluoroquinolone[5]; ampicillin or amoxicillin
Helicobacter pylori[38]	Proton pump inhibitor[39] + clarithromycin[13] + either amoxicillin or metronidazole	Bismuth subsalicylate + metronidazole + tetracycline HCl[10] + either a proton pump inhibitor[39] or H₂-blocker[39]
Legionella species	Azithromycin or a fluoroquinolone[5] ± rifampin	Doxycycline[10] ± rifampin; trimethoprim-sulfamethoxazole; erythromycin
Leptotrichia buccalis	Penicillin G	A tetracycline[10]; clindamycin; erythromycin
Pasteurella multocida	Penicillin G	A tetracycline[10]; a second- or third-generation cephalosporin[7,8]; amoxicillin/clavulanate; ampicillin/sulbactam
Pseudomonas aeruginosa		
urinary tract infection	Ciprofloxacin[16]	Levofloxacin[16]; ticarcillin/clavulanate or piperacillin/tazobactam; ceftazidime[7]; cefepime[7]; imipenem or meropenem; aztreonam; tobramycin; gentamicin or amikacin
other infections	Piperacillin/tazobactam or ticarcillin/clavulanate **each** + tobramycin, gentamicin, or amikacin[40]	Ceftazidime,[7] ciprofloxacin[16]; imipenem or meropenem, aztreonam, cefepime[7] **each** + tobramycin, gentamicin, or amikacin
Spirillum minus (rat bite fever)	Penicillin G	A tetracycline[10]; streptomycin
Stenotrophomonas maltophilia	Trimethoprim-sulfamethoxazole	Minocycline[10]; a fluoroquinolone[5]
Streptobacillus moniliformis (rat bite fever, Haverhill fever)	Penicillin G	A tetracycline[10]; streptomycin
Vibrio cholerae (cholera)[41]	A tetracycline[10]	A fluoroquinolone[5]; trimethoprim-sulfamethoxazole
Vibrio vulnificus	A tetracycline[10]	Cefotaxime[7]; ciprofloxacin[13]
Yersinia pestis (plague)	Streptomycin ± a tetracycline[10]	Chloramphenicol[19]; gentamicin; trimethoprim-sulfamethoxazole; ciprofloxacin[13]
ACID-FAST BACILLI		
Mycobacterium tuberculosis	Isoniazid + rifampin + pyrazinamide ± ethambutol or streptomycin[19]	A fluoroquinolone[5]; cycloserine[19]; capreomycin[19] or kanamycin[19] or amikacin[19]; ethionamide[19]; para-aminosalicylic acid[19]
Mycobacterium kansasii	Isoniazid + rifampin ± ethambutol or streptomycin[19]	Clarithromycin[13] or azithromycin; ethionamide[19]; cycloserine[19]

Infecting Organism	Drug of First Choice	Alternative Drugs
Mycobacterium avium complex		
treatment	Clarithromycin[13] or azithromycin + ethambutol ± rifabutin	Ciprofloxacin[16]; amikacin[19]
prophylaxis	Clarithromycin[13] or azithromycin ± rifabutin	
Mycobacterium fortuitum/ chelonae complex	Amikacin + clarithromycin[13]	Cefoxitin[7]; rifampin; a sulfonamide; doxycycline[10]; ethambutol; linezolid
Mycobacterium marinum (balnei)[42]	Minocycline[10]	Trimethoprim-sulfamethoxazole; rifampin; clarithromycin[13]; doxycycline[10]
Mycobacterium leprae (leprosy)	Dapsone + rifampin ± clofazimine	Minocycline[10]; ofloxacin[16]; clarithromycin[13]
ACTINOMYCETES		
Actinomyces israelii (actinomycosis)	Penicillin G	A tetracycline[10]; erythromycin; clindamycin
Nocardia	Trimethoprim-sulfamethoxazole	Sulfisoxazole; amikacin[19]; a tetracycline[10]; ceftriaxone; imipenem or meropenem; cycloserine[19]; linezolid
Rhodococcus equi	Vancomycin ± a fluoroquinolone,[5] rifampin, imipenem, or meropenem; amikacin	Erythromycin
Tropheryma whippelii (Whipple's disease)	Trimethoprim-sulfamethoxazole	Penicillin G; a tetracycline[10]; ceftriaxone
CHLAMYDIAE		
Chlamydia trachomatis		
trachoma	Azithromycin	A tetracycline[10] (topical plus oral); a sulfonamide (topical plus oral)
inclusion conjunctivitis	Erythromycin (oral or I.V.)	A sulfonamide
pneumonia	Erythromycin	A sulfonamide
urethritis, cervicitis	Azithromycin or doxycycline[10]	Erythromycin; ofloxacin[16]; amoxicillin
lymphogranuloma venereum	A tetracycline[10]	Erythromycin
Chlamydophilia (formerly Chlamydia) pneumoniae (TWAR strain)	Erythromycin; a tetracycline[10]; clarithromycin[13] or azithromycin	A fluoroquinolone[5]
Chlamydophilia (formerly Chlamydia) psittaci (psittacosis, ornithosis)	A tetracycline[10]	Chloramphenicol[19]
EHRLICHIA		
Anaplasma phagocytophilum (formerly Ehrlichia phagocytophila)	Doxycycline[10]	Rifampin
Ehrlichia chaffeensis	Doxycycline[10]	Chloramphenicol[19]
Ehrlichia ewingii	Doxycycline[10]	
MYCOPLASMA		
Mycoplasma pneumoniae	Erythromycin; a tetracycline[10]; clarithromycin[13] or azithromycin	A fluoroquinolone[5]
Ureaplasma urealyticum	Azithromycin	Erythromycin; a tetracycline[10]; clarithromycin[13]; ofloxacin[16]
RICKETTSIOSES		
Coxiella burnetii (Q fever)	Doxycycline[10]	Chloramphenicol[19]; a fluoroquinolone[5]
Orientia tsutsugamushi (scrub typhus)	Doxycycline[10]	Chloramphenicol[19]; a fluoroquinolone[5]
Rickettsia prowazekii (epidemic typhus – louse-borne)	Doxycycline[10]	Chloramphenicol[19]; a fluoroquinolone[5]
Rickettsia rickettsii Rocky Mountain spotted fever)	Doxycycline[10]	Chloramphenicol[19]; a fluoroquinolone[5]
Rickettsia typhi (endemic typhus – murine)	Doxycycline[10]	Chloramphenicol[19]; a fluoroquinolone[5]

ANTIMICROBIAL DRUGS OF CHOICE *(Continued)*

Infecting Organism	Drug of First Choice	Alternative Drugs
SPIROCHETES		
Borrelia burgdorferi (Lyme disease)[43]	Doxycycline[10]; amoxicillin; cefuroxime axetil[7]	Ceftriaxone[7]; cefotaxime[7]; penicillin G; azithromycin; clarithromycin[13]
Borrelia recurrentis (relapsing fever)	A tetracycline[10]	Penicillin G; erythromycin
Leptospira	Penicillin G	A tetracycline[10]; ceftriaxone[7,44]
Treponema pallidum (syphilis)	Penicillin G[12]	A tetracycline[10]; ceftriaxone[7]
Treponema pertenue (yaws)	Penicillin G	A tetracycline[10]

*Resistance may be a problem; susceptibility tests should be used to guide therapy.

[1]Disk sensitivity testing may not provide adequate information; beta-lactamase assays, "E" tests, and dilution tests for susceptibility should be used in serious infections.

[2]Aminoglycoside resistance is increasingly common among enterococci; treatment options include ampicillin 2 g I.V. every 4 hours, continuous infusion of ampicillin, a combination of ampicillin plus a fluoroquinolone, or a combination of ampicillin, imipenem, and vancomycin.

[3]Daptomycin should not be used to treat pneumonia.

[4]Quinupristin/dalfopristin is not active against *Enterococcus faecalis*.

[5]Among the fluoroquinolones, levofloxacin, gatifloxacin, and moxifloxacin have excellent *in vitro* activity against *S. pneumoniae*, including penicillin- and cephalosporin-resistant strains. Levofloxacin, gatifloxacin, and moxifloxacin also have good activity against many strains of *S. aureus*, but resistance has become frequent among methicillin-resistant strains. Ciprofloxacin has the greatest activity against *Pseudomonas aeruginosa*. For urinary tract infections, norfloxacin, lomefloxacin, or enoxacin can be used. For tuberculosis, levofloxacin, ofloxacin, ciprofloxacin, gatifloxacin, or moxifloxacin could be used. Ciprofloxacin, ofloxacin, levofloxacin, moxifloxacin, and gatifloxacin are available for intravenous use. None of these agents are recommended for pregnant women. Ciprofloxacin has FDA approval for use in children.

[6]For oral use against staphylococci, cloxacillin or dicloxacillin is preferred; for severe infections, a parenteral formulation of nafcillin or oxacillin should be used. Ampicillin, amoxicillin, carbenicillin, ticarcillin, and piperacillin are not effective against penicillinase-producing staphylococci. The combinations of clavulanate with amoxicillin or ticarcillin, sulbactam with ampicillin, and tazobactam with piperacillin may be active against these organisms.

[7]Cephalosporins have been used as alternatives to penicillins in patients allergic to penicillins, but such patients may also have allergic reactions to cephalosporins.

[8]For parenteral treatment of staphylococcal or nonenterococcal streptococcal infections, a first-generation cephalosporin such as cefazolin can be used. For oral therapy, cephalexin or cephradine can be used. The second-generation cephalosporins cefamandole, cefprozil, cefuroxime, cefotetan, cefoxitin, and loracarbef are more active than the first-generation drugs against gram-negative bacteria. Cefuroxime is active against ampicillin-resistant strains of *H. influenzae*. Cefoxitin and cefotetan are the most active of the cephalosporins against *B. fragilis*, but cefotetan has been associated with prothrombin deficiency. The third-generation cephalosporins cefotaxime, cefoperazone, ceftizoxime, ceftriaxone, and ceftazidime, and the fourth-generation cefepime have greater activity than the second-generation drugs against enteric gram-negative bacilli. Ceftazidime has poor activity against many gram-positive cocci and anaerobes, and ceftizoxime has poor activity against penicillin-resistant *S. pneumoniae*. Cefepime has *in vitro* activity against gram-positive cocci similar to cefotaxime and ceftriaxone and somewhat greater activity against enteric gram-negative bacilli. The activity of cefepime against *Pseudomonas aeruginosa* is similar to that of ceftazidime. Cefixime, cefpodoxime, cefdinir, ceftibuten, and cefditoren are oral cephalosporins with more activity than second-generation cephalosporins against facultative gram-negative bacilli; they have no useful activity against anaerobes or *P. aeruginosa*, and cefixime and ceftibuten have no useful activity against staphylococci. With the exception of cefoperazone (which, like cefamandole, can cause bleeding), ceftazidime and cefepime, the activity of all currently available cephalosporins against *P. aeruginosa* is poor or inconsistent.

[9]Many strains of coagulase-positive and coagulase-negative staphylococci are resistant to penicillinase-resistant penicillins; these strains are also resistant to cephalosporins, imipenem, and meropenem, and are often resistant to fluoroquinolones, trimethoprim-sulfamethoxazole, and clindamycin. Community-acquired MRSA often is susceptible to clindamycin and trimethoprim-sulfamethoxazole.

[10]Tetracyclines are generally not recommended for pregnant women or children younger than 8 years of age.

[11]For serious soft-tissue infection due to group A streptococci, clindamycin may be more effective than penicillin. Group A streptococci may, however, be resistant to clindamycin; therefore, some *Medical Letter* consultants suggest using both clindamycin and penicillin, with or without I.V. immune globulin, to treat serious soft-tissue infections. Surgical debridement is usually needed for necrotizing soft tissue infections due to group A streptococcus. Group A streptococci may also be resistant to erythromycin, azithromycin, and clarithromycin.

[12]Penicillin V (or amoxicillin) is preferred for oral treatment of infections caused by nonpenicillinase-producing streptococci. For initial therapy of severe infections, penicillin G, administered parenterally, is first choice. For somewhat longer action in less severe infections due to group A streptococci, pneumococci or *Treponema pallidum*, procaine penicillin G, an intramuscular formulation, can be given once or twice daily, but is seldom used now. Benzathine penicillin G, a slowly absorbed preparation, is usually given in a single monthly injection for prophylaxis of rheumatic fever, once for treatment of group A streptococcal pharyngitis and once or more for treatment of syphilis.

[13]Not recommended for use in pregnancy.

[14]Some strains of *S. pneumoniae* are resistant to erythromycin, clindamycin, trimethoprim-sulfamethoxazole, clarithromycin, azithromycin, and chloramphenicol, and resistance to the newer fluoroquinolones is rare but increasing (Davidson R, Cavalcanti R, Brunton JL, et al, "Resistance to Levofloxacin and Failure of Treatment of Pneumococcal Pneumonia," *N Engl J Med*, 2002, 346(10):747-50). Nearly all strains tested so far are susceptible to linezolid and quinupristin/dalfopristin *in vitro*.

[15]Fluoroquinolone-resistant strains of gonococcus are increasingly common (*MMWR, Morb Mortal Wkly Rep*, 2002, 51:1041; Fenton KA, Ison C, Johnson AP, et al, "Ciprofloxacin Resistance in *Neisseria gonorrhoeae* in England and Wales in 2002," *Lancet*, 2003, 361(9372):1867-9.

[16]Usually not recommended for use in children or pregnant women.

[17]Patients with gonorrhea should be treated presumptively for coinfection with *C. trachomatis* with azithromycin or doxycycline.

[18]Rare strains of *N. meningitidis* are resistant or relatively resistant to penicillin. A fluoroquinolone or rifampin is recommended for prophylaxis after close contact with infected patients.

[19]Because of the possibility of serious adverse effects, this drug should be used only for severe infections when less hazardous drugs are ineffective.

[20]Sulfonamide-resistant strains are frequent in the U.S.A; sulfonamides should be used only when susceptibility is established by susceptibility tests.

[21]For postexposure prophylaxis, ciprofloxacin for 4 weeks if given with vaccination, and 60 days if not given with vaccination, might prevent disease; if the strain is susceptible, doxycycline is an alternative (Bartlett JG, Inglesby TV Jr, and Borio L, "Management of Anthrax," *Clin Infect Dis*, 2002, 35(7):851-8; *Medical Letter*, 2001, 43:87.

[22]Debridement is primary. Large doses of penicillin G are required. Hyperbaric oxygen therapy may be a useful adjunct to surgical debridement in management of the spreading, necrotizing type of infection.

[23]For prophylaxis, a tetanus toxoid booster and, for some patients, tetanus immune globulin (human) are required.

[24]In order to decrease the emergence of vancomycin-resistant enterococci in hospitals and to reduce costs, most clinicians now recommend use of metronidazole first in treatment of patients with *C. difficile* colitis, with oral vancomycin used only for seriously ill patients or those who do not respond to metronidazole.

[25]Antitoxin is primary; antimicrobials are used only to halt further toxin production and to prevent the carrier state.

[26]In severely ill patients, most *Medical Letter* consultants would add gentamicin, tobramycin, or amikacin.

[27]In severely ill patients, most *Medical Letter* consultants would add gentamicin, tobramycin, or amikacin (but see footnote 40).

[28]For an acute, uncomplicated urinary tract infection, before the infecting organism is known, the drug of first choice is trimethoprim-sulfamethoxazole.

[29]Large doses (6 g or more daily) are usually necessary for systemic infections. In severely ill patients, some *Medical Letter* consultants would add gentamicin, tobramycin, or amikacin.

[30]A fluoroquinolone or amoxicillin is the drug of choice for *S. typhi* carriers (Parry CM, Hien TT, Dougan G, "Typhoid Fever," *N Engl J Med*, 2002, 347(22):1770-82).

[31]Frenck RW Jr, Nakhla I, Sultan Y, et al, "Azithromycin Versus Ceftriaxone for the Treatment of Uncomplicated Typhoid Fever in Children," *Clin Infect Dis*, 2000, 31(5):1134-8.

[32]Most cases of *Salmonella* gastroenteritis subside spontaneously without antimicrobial therapy. Immunosuppressed patients, young children, and the elderly may benefit the most from antibacterials.

[33]Sulbactam may be useful to treat multidrug resistant *Acinetobacter*. It is only available in combination with ampicillin as Unasyn®. *Medical Letter* consultants recommend 3 g I.V. every 4 hours (Urban C, Segal-Maurer S, and Rahal JJ, "Considerations in Control and Treatment of Nosocomial Infections Due to Multidrug-Resistant *Acinetobacter baumannii*," *Clin Infect Dis*, 2003, 36(10):1268-74; Levin AS, Levy CE, Manrique AE, et al, "Severe Nosocomial Infections With Imipenem-Resistant *Acinetobacter baumannii* Treated With Ampicillin/Sulbactam," *Int J Antimicrob Agents*, 2003, 21(1):58-62.

[34]Role of antibiotics is not clear (Conrad DA, "Treatment of Cat-Scratch Disease," *Curr Opin Pediatr*, 2001, 13(1):56-9).

[35]Pers C, Gahrn-Hansen B, Frederiksen W, et al, "*Capnocytophaga canimorsus* Septicemia in Denmark, 1982-1995: Review of 39 Cases," *Clin Infect Dis*, 1996, 23(1):71-5.

[36]For postexposure prophylaxis, doxycycline, or ciprofloxacin begun during the incubation period and continued for 14 days might prevent disease (*Medical Letter*, 2001, 43:87).

[37]Metronidazole is effective for bacterial vaginosis even though it is not usually active *in vitro* against *Gardnerella*.

[38]Eradication of *H. pylori* with various antibacterial combinations, given concurrently with a proton pump inhibitor or H2-blockerr, has led to rapid healing of active peptic ulcers and low recurrence rates (Mégraud F and Marshall BJ, "How to Treat *Helicobacter pylori*: First-line, Second-line, and Future Therapies," *Gastroenterol Clin North Am*, 2000, 29(4):759-73; *Treatment Guidelines*, 2004, 2:9.).

[39]Proton pump inhibitors available in the U.S.A. are omeprazole (Prilosec®, and others) lansoprazole (Prevacid®), pantoprazole (Protonix®), esomeprazole (Nexium®), and rabeprazole (Aciphex®). Available H2-blockers include cimetidine (Tagamet®, and others), famotidine (Pepcid®, and others), nizatidine (Axid®, and others), and ranitidine (Zantac®, and others).

[40]Neither gentamicin, tobramycin, netilmicin, or amikacin should be mixed in the same bottle with carbenicillin, ticarcillin, mezlocillin, or piperacillin for intravenous administration. When used in high doses or in patients with renal impairment, these penicillins may inactivate the aminoglycosides.

[41]Antibiotic therapy is an adjunct to and not a substitute for prompt fluid and electrolyte replacement.

[42]Most infections are self-limited without drug treatment.

[43]For treatment of erythema migrans, uncomplicated facial nerve palsy, mild cardiac disease, and arthritis, oral therapy is satisfactory; for other neurologic or more serious cardiac disease, parenteral therapy with ceftriaxone, cefotaxime, or penicillin G is recommended. For recurrent arthritis after an oral regimen, another course of oral therapy or a parenteral drug may be given (Wormser GP, Nadelman RB, Dattwyler RJ, et al, "Practice Guidelines for the Treatment of Lyme Disease. The Infectious Diseases Society of America," *Clin Infect Dis*, 2000, 31(Suppl 1):1-14).

[44]Vinetz JM, "A Mountain Out of a Molehill: Do We Treat Acute Leptospirosis, and if so, With What?" *Clin Infect Dis*, 2003, 36(12):1514-5; Panaphot T et al, *Clin Infect Dis*, 2003, 36:1507.

Adapted with permission from "Choice of Antibacterial Drugs," *Treatment Guidelines*, 2004, 2(19):18-23.

ANTIRETROVIRAL THERAPY FOR HIV INFECTION: ADULTS AND ADOLESCENTS

Adapted from the "Guidelines for the Use of Antiretroviral Agents in HIV-1-Infected Adults and Adolescents," developed by the Panel on Clinical Practices for Treatment of HIV Infection, Department of Health and Human Services, updated October 10, 2006; available at www.aidsinfo.nih.gov.

GOALS OF THERAPY

Goals of Therapy

- Maximal and durable suppression of viral load
- Restoration and/or preservation of immunologic function
- Improvement of quality of life
- Reduction of HIV-related morbidity and mortality

Tools to Achieve Goals of Therapy

- Maximize adherence to the antiretroviral regimen
- Rational selection and sequencing of drugs
- Preservation of future treatment options
- Use of pretreatment testing and therapeutic drug monitoring in selected clinical settings

WHEN TO TREAT

Indications for Viral Load Assessment

Indications for Plasma HIV RNA Testing[1]

Clinical Indication	Information	Use
Syndrome consistent with acute HIV infection	Establishes diagnosis when HIV antibody test is negative or indeterminate	Diagnosis[2]
Initial evaluation of newly diagnosed HIV infection	Baseline viral load "set point"	Decision to start or defer therapy (in conjunction with CD4+ T-cell counts)
Every 3-4 months in patients not on therapy	Changes in viral load	Decision to start therapy (in conjunction with CD4+ T-cell counts)
2-8 weeks after initiation or change in antiretroviral therapy	Initial assessment of drug efficacy	Decision to continue or change therapy
3-4 months after start of therapy	Virologic effect of therapy	Decision to continue or change therapy
Every 3-4 months in patients on therapy	Durability of antiretroviral effect	Decision to continue or change therapy
Clinical event or significant decline in CD4+ T cells	Association with changing or stable viral load	Decision to continue, initiate, or change therapy

[1]Acute illness (eg, bacterial pneumonia, tuberculosis, HSV, PCP) and immunizations can cause increases in plasma HIV RNA for 2-4 weeks; viral load testing should not be performed during this time. Plasma HIV RNA results should usually be verified with a repeat determination before starting or making changes in therapy.

[2]Diagnosis of HIV infection determined by HIV RNA testing should be confirmed by standard methods (eg, Western blot serology) performed 2-4 months after the initial indeterminate or negative test.

Criteria for Initiating Treatment

The optimal time to initiate therapy in asymptomatic individuals with >200 CD4+ T cells is not known. This table provides general guidance rather than absolute recommendations for an individual patient. Recent literature suggests that a CD4+ cell count may be a more important prognostic indicator than viral load and that a significantly increased risk of progression occurs when viral load exceeds 100,000 copies/mL. All decisions to initiate therapy should be based on prognosis as determined by the CD4+ T-cell count and viral load, the potential benefits and risks of therapy, and the willingness of the patient to accept therapy.

Indications for the Initiation of Antiretroviral Therapy in the Chronically HIV-1 Infected Patient

Clinical Category	CD4+ T-Cell Count	Plasma HIV RNA	Recommendation
AIDS-defining illness or severe symptoms[1]	Any value	Any value	Treat
Asymptomatic[2]	CD4+ T cells <200/mm³	Any value	Treat
Asymptomatic	CD4+ T cells >200/mm³ but ≤350/mm³	Any value	Treatment should be offered following full discussion of pros and cons with each patient
Asymptomatic	CD4+ T cells >350/mm³	≥100,000 copies/mL	Most clinicians recommend deferring therapy, but some clinicians will treat
Asymptomatic	CD4+ T cells >350/mm³	<100,000 copies/mL	Defer therapy

[1]AIDS-defining illness per Centers for Disease Control, 1993. Severe symptoms include unexplained fever or diarrhea >2-4 weeks, oral candidiasis, or >10% unexplained weight loss.

[2]Clinical benefit has been demonstrated in controlled trials only for patients with CD4+ T cells <200/mm³; however, the majority of clinicians would offer therapy at a CD4+ T-cell threshold <350/mm³. A collaborative analysis of data from 13 cohort studies from Europe and North America found that lower CD4+ count, higher HIV viral load, injection drug use, and age >50 were all predictors of progression to AIDS or death in antiretroviral-naive patients beginning combination antiretroviral therapy. These data indicate that the prognosis is better for patients who initiate therapy at >200 cells/mm³, but risk after initiation of therapy does not vary considerably at >200 cells/mm³.

Early vs Delayed Treatment

Benefits and Risks of Delayed Initiation of Therapy in the Asymptomatic HIV-Infected Patient[1]

Benefits	Risks
• Avoid treatment-related negative quality of life effects (ie, inconvenience) • Avoid drug-related adverse events • Delay development of drug resistance • Preserve maximum number of available and future drug options • More time for patient to understand treatment demands	• Possibly irreversible immune system depletion • Possibly greater difficulty in suppressing viral replication • Possibly increased risk of HIV transmission[2] • Control of viral replication more difficult to achieve and maintain

[1]See table, "Indications for the Initiation of Antiretroviral Therapy in the Chronically HIV-1 Infected Patient," for consensus recommendations regarding when to initiate therapy.

[2]Antiretroviral therapy cannot substitute for primary HIV prevention measures (eg, use of condoms and safer sex practices).

ANTIRETROVIRAL THERAPY FOR HIV INFECTION: ADULTS AND ADOLESCENTS *(Continued)*

TREATMENT OPTIONS

Recommended Antiretroviral Agents for Initial Treatment of Established HIV Infection

The following tables provide a guide to treatment regimens for patients who have no previous experience with HIV therapy. Regimens should be individualized based on the advantages and disadvantages of each combination such as pill burden, dosing frequency, toxicities, drug-drug interactions, patient variables (such as pregnancy), comorbid conditions, and level of plasma HIV-RNA. Regimens are designated as "preferred" for use in treatment-naive patients when clinical trial data suggest optimal efficacy and durability with acceptable tolerability and ease of use. Alternative regimens are those in which clinical trial data show efficacy, but may be disadvantageous compared to the preferred regimens in terms of antiviral activity, demonstrated durable effect, tolerability, or ease of use. Based on individual patient characteristics, a regimen listed as an alternative may actually be the preferred regimen for a selected patient. Of note, the designation of preferred or alternative regimens may change as new safety and efficacy data emerge, which, in the opinion of the Panel, warrants reassignment of regimens in these categories. Revisions will be updated on an ongoing basis. Clinicians initiating antiretroviral regimens in pregnant women or pediatric patients should refer to the specific guidelines found at http://www.aidsinfo.nih.gov/guidelines. Additional guidelines are available for postexposure prophylaxis (occupational and nonoccupational) as well as management of opportunistic infections.

NNRTI-Based Regimens

Preferred Regimens	Efavirenz + (lamivudine or emtricitabine) + (zidovudine or tenofovir) – except in 1st trimester pregnancy or women with high pregnancy potential[1]
Alternative Regimens	Efavirenz + (lamivudine or emtricitabine) + (abacavir or didanosine) – except in 1st trimester pregnancy or women with high pregnancy potential[1]
	Nevirapine[2] + (lamivudine or emtricitabine) + (zidovudine or didanosine or abacavir or tenofovir). **Note:** Nevirapine should only be used if CD4$^+$ T-cell counts are ≤250 cells/mm^3 in women or ≤400 cells/mm^3 in men.

[1]Women with high pregnancy potential implies women who want to conceive or those who are not using effective contraception.

[2]High incidence (11%) of hepatotoxicity and skin reactions; close clinical monitoring advised, especially during first 18 months of therapy. Do not use if CD4$^+$ T-cell counts are >250 cells/mm^3 in women or >400 cells/mm^3 in men.

PI-Based Regimens

Preferred Regimens	Lopinavir / ritonavir (twice-daily regimen) + (lamivudine or emtricitabine) + (zidovudine or tenofovir)
	Fosamprenavir and ritonavir[1] (twice-daily regimen) + (lamivudine or emtricitabine) + (zidovudine or tenofovir)
	Atazanavir and ritonavir[1] + (lamivudine or emtricitabine) + (zidovudine or tenofovir)
Alternative Regimens	Fosamprenavir and ritonavir[1] (once-daily regimen) + (lamivudine or emtricitabine) + (zidovudine or abacavir or tenofovir or didanosine)
	Fosamprenavir + (lamivudine or emtricitabine) + (zidovudine or abacavir or tenofovir or didanosine)
	Atazanavir + (lamivudine or emtricitabine) + (zidovudine or abacavir or didanosine) or (tenofovir + ritonavir 100 mg/day)
	Lopinavir / ritonavir (once-daily regimen) + (emtricitabine or lamivudine) + (abacavir or tenofovir or didanosine or zidovudine)
	Lopinavir / ritonavir (twice-daily regimen) + (emtricitabine or lamivudine) + (abacavir or didanosine)
	Fosamprenavir and ritonavir[1] (twice-daily regimen) + (lamivudine or emtricitabine) + (abacavir or didanosine)
	Atazanavir and ritonavir[1] + (lamivudine or emtricitabine) + (abacavir or didanosine)
Additional Regimens Considered Acceptable but Inferior to Alternatives	Nelfinavir + (lamivudine or emtricitabine) + (zidovudine or abacavir or tenofovir or didanosine)
	Saquinavir and ritonavir[1] + (lamivudine or emtricitabine) + (zidovudine or abacavir or tenofovir or didanosine)
	Any PI with stavudine + lamivudine as 2NRTI component

[1]Low-dose ritonavir (100-400 mg/day).

Triple NRTI Regimen

Only as alternative to NNRTI- or PI-based regimen – should not be used first-line	Abacavir + lamivudine + zidovudine

ANTIRETROVIRAL THERAPY FOR HIV INFECTION: ADULTS AND ADOLESCENTS *(Continued)*

TREATMENT LIMITATIONS

Antiretroviral Drugs Not Recommended as Initial Therapy

Drugs	Reasons for Not Recommending as Initial Therapy
Darunavir (ritonavir-boosted)	• Lack of data in treatment-naive patients
Delavirdine	• Inferior virologic efficacy • Inconvenient dosing (3 times/day)
Didanosine + tenofovir	• High rate of early virological failure in combination with efavirenz or nevirapine • Rapid selection of resistant mutations • Potential for immunologic nonresponse
Enfuvirtide	• No clinical trial experience in treatment-naive patients • Requires twice-daily subcutaneous injections
Indinavir (ritonavir-boosted)	• High incidence of nephrolithiasis
Indinavir (unboosted)	• Inconvenient dosing (3 times/day with meal restrictions)
Ritonavir as sole PI	• High pill burden • Gastrointestinal intolerance
Saquinavir (unboosted)	• High pill burden • Inferior virologic efficacy
Tipranavir (ritonavir-boosted)	• Lack of data in treatment-naive patients
Zalcitabine + zidovudine	• Inferior virologic efficacy • Higher rate of adverse effects than other two-NRTI alternatives

Antiretroviral Regimens or Components That Should Not Be Offered at Any Time

	Rationale	Exception
Antiretroviral Regimens Not Recommended		
Monotherapy with NRTI or NNRTI	• Rapid development of resistance • Inferior antiretroviral activity when compared to combination with three or more antiretrovirals	Pregnant women with HIV-RNA <1000 copies/mL using zidovudine monotherapy for prevention of perinatal HIV transmission[1] and not for HIV treatment for the mother
Two-NRTI drug combinations	• Rapid development of resistance • Inferior antiretroviral activity when compared to combination with three or more antiretrovirals	For patients currently on this treatment, it is reasonable to continue if virologic goals are achieved
Triple-NRTI combinations	High rate of early virologic nonresponse seen when this triple-NRTI combination was used as initial regimen in treatment-naive patients	May consider (abacavir or possibly tenofovir) + zidovudine + lamivudine
Antiretroviral Components Not Recommended as Part of Antiretroviral Regimen		
Amprenavir oral solution in: • pregnant women • children <4 y • patients with renal or hepatic failure • patients treated with metronidazole or disulfiram	Oral liquid contains large amount of the excipient propylene glycol, which may be toxic in the patients at risk	No exception
Amprenavir + fosamprenavir	Fosamprenavir is a prodrug for amprenavir, so no additional benefit	No exception
Amprenavir oral solution + ritonavir oral solution	Propylene glycol in amprenavir may compete metabolically with ethanol (vehicle in ritonavir) leading to accumulation of either vehicle	No exception
Atazanavir + indinavir	Potential additive hyperbilirubinemia	No exception
Didanosine + stavudine	• High incidence of toxicities – peripheral neuropathy, pancreatitis, and hyperlactatemia • Reports of serious, even fatal cases of lactic acidosis with hepatic steatosis with or without pancreatitis in pregnant women	When no other antiretroviral options are available and potential benefits outweigh the risks[1]
Didanosine + zalcitabine	Additive peripheral neuropathy	No exception
Efavirenz in 1st trimester pregnancy or in women with significant high pregnancy potential[2]	Teratogenic in nonhuman primates	When no other antiretroviral options are available and potential benefits outweigh the risks[1]
Emtricitabine + lamivudine	• Similar resistance profile • No potential benefit	No exception
Lamivudine + zalcitabine	*In vitro* antagonism demonstrated	No exception
Nevirapine initiation with CD4+ T-cell count >250 cells/mm³ in women or >400 cells/mm³ in men	Higher incidence of symptomatic (including serious or fatal) hepatic events	Only if benefit clearly outweighs risk
Saquinavir hard gel capsule (Invirase®) as **single** protease inhibitor	• Poor oral bioavailability (4%) • Inferior antiretroviral activity when compared to other protease inhibitors	No exception

ANTIRETROVIRAL THERAPY FOR HIV INFECTION: ADULTS AND ADOLESCENTS *(Continued)*

Antiretroviral Regimens or Components That Should Not Be Offered at Any Time *(continued)*

	Rationale	Exception
Stavudine + zalcitabine	Additive peripheral neuropathy	No exception
Stavudine + zidovudine	Antagonistic	No exception

[1] When constructing an antiretroviral regimen for an HIV-infected pregnant woman, please consult "Public Health Service Task Force Recommendations for the Use of Antiretroviral Drugs in Pregnant HIV-1-Infected Women for Maternal Health and Interventions to Reduce Perinatal HIV-1 Transmission in the United States" in http://www.aidsinfo.nih.gov/guidelines.

[2] Women with high pregnancy potential implies women who want to conceive or those who are not using effective contraception.

SPECIAL CONSIDERATIONS

Resistance Testing

Viral drug resistance is generally determined by one of two methods: genotypic assays or phenotypic assays. Genotypic assays involve sequencing techniques to identify the presence of specific drug-resistant genes. While these assays produce relatively rapid results (1-2 weeks) they require knowledge of specific drug-resistance mutations for appropriate interpretation. Alternatively, phenotypic assays measure the ability of the patient's virus (as monitored by recombination with a reporter gene) to replicate in the presence of antiretroviral drugs. These assays can be more time-consuming and costly, and also suffer from the drawback that resistance level breakpoints are unknown.

Despite these methodological limitations, resistance testing can assist in designing an appropriate therapeutic regimen, by identifying, and thus avoiding less effective antiretroviral drugs in the setting of virologic failure. In addition, prior knowledge of specific drug-resistant viral phenotypes can guide selection of initial therapy which offers a greater likelihood of success.

The following table identifies the appropriate settings for the use of resistance testing.

Clinical Setting[1]	Drug-Resistance Assay Recommendation	Rationale
Virologic failure during combination antiretroviral therapy	Recommended	Determine the role of resistance in drug failure and maximize selection of active drugs.
Suboptimal suppression of viral load after antiretroviral therapy initiation	Recommended	Determine the role of resistance and maximize selection of active drugs.
Acute HIV infection, if initiating therapy[2]	Recommended	Determine if drug-resistant virus was transmitted to assist in designing initial regimen.
Acute HIV infection, if treatment deferred	Should be considered	
Chronic HIV infection before initiation of therapy[2]	Recommended	Baseline resistance may be present in up to 16% of patients, leading to suboptimal virologic response.
Chronic HIV infection during early course of therapy	Should be considered	Greater likelihood that transmitted resistance-associated mutations will be detected earlier
After discontinuation of drugs	Not usually recommended	Assays may not detect minor drug-resistant species which may occur in the absence of selective drug pressure.
Plasma viral load <1000 HIV RNA copies/mL	Not usually recommended	Assays may not reliably detect low numbers of viral RNA.

[1] Genotypic resistance testing should be conducted in all pregnant women prior to initiation of therapy, or in women entering pregnancy with detectable HIV RNA levels, despite antiretroviral therapy.

[2] Genotypic assays are recommended due to more rapid turnaround time.

Summary of Guidelines for Changing an Antiretroviral Regimen for Suspected Treatment Regimen Failure

Patient Assessment

- Review antiretroviral treatment history.
- Assess for evidence of clinical progression (eg, physical exam, laboratory and/or radiologic tests).
- Assess adherence, tolerability, and pharmacokinetic issues.
- Distinguish between limited, intermediate, and extensive prior therapy and drug resistance.
- Perform resistance testing while patient is taking therapy (or within 4 weeks after regimen discontinuation).
- Identify active drugs and drug classes to use in designing new regimen.

Patient Management: Specific Clinical Scenarios

- **Limited or intermediate prior treatment with low (but not suppressed) HIV RNA level (eg, up to 5000 copies/mL):** The goal of treatment is to resuppress HIV RNA to below level of assay detection. Consider intensifying with one drug (eg, tenofovir) or pharmacokinetic enhancement (use of ritonavir boosting of a protease inhibitor), perform resistance testing if possible, or most aggressively, change two or more drugs in the regimen. If continuing the same treatment regimen, HIV RNA levels should be followed closely because ongoing viral replication will lead to accumulation of additional resistance mutations.

- **Limited or intermediate prior treatment with resistance to one drug:** Consider changing the one drug, pharmacokinetic enhancement (few data available), or, most aggressively, change two or more drugs in the regimen.

- **Limited or intermediate prior treatment resistance to more than one drug:** The goal of treatment is to suppress viremia to prevent further selection of resistance mutations. Consider optimizing the regimen by changing classes (eg, PI-based to NNRTI-based and vice versa) and/or adding new active drugs. (See table Treatment Options Following Virologic Failure on Initial Recommended Therapy Regimens.)

- **Prior treatment with no resistance identified:** Consider the timing of the drug resistance test (eg, was the patient off antiretroviral medications?) and/or nonadherence. Consider resuming the same regimen or starting a new regimen and then repeating genotypic testing early (eg, 2-4 weeks) to determine if a resistant virus becomes evident.

- **Extensive prior treatment and drug resistance:** In patients with active antiretroviral agents available (eg, an active ritonavir-boosted PI with enfuvirtide), the goal of therapy is suppression of viremia. In patients without active antiretroviral agent available and with ongoing viremia, the goal of therapy is preservation of immune response and delay of clinical progression. It is reasonable to continue the same antiretroviral regimen if there are few or no treatment options. In general, avoid adding a single active drug because of the risk for the rapid development of resistance to that drug. In advanced HIV disease with a high likelihood of clinical progression (eg, CD4+ cell count <100 cells/mm^3), adding a single drug may reduce the risk of immediate clinical progression. In this complicated scenario, expert advise should be sought.

ANTIRETROVIRAL THERAPY FOR HIV INFECTION: ADULTS AND ADOLESCENTS *(Continued)*

- **Immunologic failure (or blunted CD4 response) with virologic suppression:** Immunologic failure (or blunted CD4+ cell response) may not warrant a change in therapy in the setting of suppressed viremia. Assess for other causes of immunosuppression (eg, HIV-2, HTLV-1, drug toxicity). The combination of didanosine and tenofovir has been associated with CD4+ cell declines or blunted CD4+ cell responses. In the setting of immunologic failure (or blunted CD4+ response), it would be reasonable to change one of these drugs. Intensifying with additional antiretroviral drugs or the use of immune-based therapies (eg, interleukin-2) to improve immunologic responses remain unproven strategies and generally should not be offered.

Treatment Options Following Virologic Failure on Initial Recommended Therapy Regimens

Antiretroviral therapy regimens should be selected on the basis of treatment history and drug-resistance testing to optimize antiretroviral potency in the second regimen. This is particularly important in selecting NRTIS for an NNRTI-based regimen where drug resistance may occur rapidly to the NNRTI if the NRTIs are not sufficiently potent.

First Virologic Failure

Regimen Class	Initial Regimen	Recommended Change[1]
NNRTI	2 NRTIs + NNRTI	• 2 NRTIs (based on resistance testing) + PI (with or without low-dose ritonavir)
PI	2 NRTIs + PI (with or without low-dose ritonavir)	• 2 NRTIs (based on resistance testing) + NNRTI • 2 NRTIs (based on resistance testing) + alternative PI (with low-dose ritonavir; based on resistance testing) • NRTI(s) (based on resistance testing) + NNRTI + alternative PI (with low-dose ritonavir; based on resistance testing)
Triple-NRTI	3 nucleosides	• 2 NRTIs (based on resistance testing) + NNRTI or PI (with or without low-dose ritonavir) • NNRTI + PI (with or without low-dose ritonavir) • NRTI(s) (based on resistance testing) + NNRTI + PI (with or without low-dose ritonavir)
Three-class[2]	NRTI + NNRTI + PI	• >1 NRTIs (based on resistance testing) + a newer PI (with low-dose ritonavir; based on resistance testing) ± enfuvirtide

[1]Antiretroviral therapy regimens should be selected on the basis of treatment history and drug-resistance testing to optimize antiretroviral potency in the second regimen. This is particularly important in selecting NRTIs for an NNRTI-based regimen where drug resistance may occur rapidly to the NNRTI if the NRTIs are not sufficiently potent. **Note:** NNRTIs generally should not be used following the development of NNRTI-resistance because of the risk for selection of additional NNRTI-associated mutations.

[2]Insufficient evidence to recommend the use of this combination approach.

Discontinuation or Interruption of Therapy

Short-term Interruption

- Planned or unplanned interruption of therapy may occur due to a number of situations including, but not limited to, adverse drug reactions, intercurrent illness, and surgical procedures. Generally, short-term therapy interruptions (as with elective surgery) can be managed by simultaneously stopping all drug therapy, as long as all components of the regimen exhibit similar half-lives. Accordingly, all drugs would be resumed simultaneously when clinically appropriate.

- However, in the event that the medication regimen includes drugs exhibiting different biological half-lives, there is a risk of inducing functional monotherapy when discontinuing all of the medications at once. There is no clear guidance on how best to address this situation. One option may involve discontinuing the drug with the longest half-life first (typically an NRTI such as nevirapine or efavirenz), while continuing the other components of therapy, ideally for the duration of detectable plasma levels of the first drug. Given the polymorphic nature of drug metabolism, this "endpoint" is difficult to ascertain. Thus, some experts recommend substituting the NNRTI with a PI, and continuing with the other components of the regimen for approximately 4 weeks.

- In the event of a severe or life-threatening toxicity, all components of the drug regimen should be discontinued, regardless of half-life.

Long-term Discontinuation

- A number of strategies have been considered as a basis for treatment inter-ruption. These include preservation of virologic response in patients with few treatment options, patients who have achieved virologic suppression, or who have maintained a CD4 count above recommended treatment initiation threshold levels. Additionally, planned discontinuation has been proposed as a method for reducing the overall costs, inconvenience, and/or toxicities of therapy. However, data are conflicting with respect to optimal discontinuation/ reinitiation parameters and current clinical trials data have generally shown worsened outcomes in those who have experienced a planned interruption compared to patients on continuous therapy. Therefore, planned long-term treatment interruptions are **not** recommended under any circumstance outside of a controlled, clinical trial setting. Nevertheless, if discontinuation is going to be implemented, both the patient and physician must be aware of the potential complications or consequences of this action, including, but not limited to viral rebound, disease progression, and opportunistic infection.

Recommendations for Treatment of Hepatitis B (HBV) or Hepatitis C (HCV) Coinfection

HBV

- All patients should be advised to avoid alcohol and receive hepatitis A vaccine (if not previously immunized).

- Use more than one antiretroviral agent with activity against hepatitis B virus. Recommended first-line therapy should consist of tenofovir + lamivudine or tenofovir + emtricitabine as the NRTI backbone. Lamivudine, emtricitabine, or tenofovir should **not** be the sole agent with anti-IBV activity in an antiretroviral regimen due to the risk for resistance.

- Discontinuation of antiviral agents with activity against HBV has been associ-ated with hepatocellular damage due to flare of HBV infection.

- HBV coinfection increases the risk of medication-related transaminase eleva-tions. Generally, it is recommended to withhold the causative agent when ALT is ≥5-10 times ULN, but one should recognize that transaminase eleva-tions may signify HB_eAg seroconversion.

HCV

- All patients should be advised to avoid alcohol and receive hepatitis A and B vaccines (if not previously immunized).

- Initiate treatment according to standard guidelines, preferentially in patients with a higher CD4 count (>200 cells/mm^3); in those with lower CD4 counts, HCV treatment may be deferred in favor of antiretroviral therapy.

- Monitor closely for drug interactions.

- Growth factors may be necessary to manage HCV treatment-related anemia or neutropenia.

ANTIRETROVIRAL THERAPY FOR HIV INFECTION: ADULTS AND ADOLESCENTS *(Continued)*

Therapeutic Drug Monitoring

As with other notable drug classes (eg, antibiotics, anticonvulsants), the goal of therapeutic drug monitoring (TDM) is to maximize therapeutic efficacy and minimize drug-related toxicities. The utility of TDM in the setting of antiretroviral drug therapy is supported by data showing considerable interpatient variability with respect to drug concentrations among patients taking similar doses, as well as data demonstrating concentration/effect and concentration/toxicity correlations. The optimal plasma concentrations of many antiretroviral drugs have yet to be determined (eg, NRTIs). Those drugs for which target trough levels are defined are shown below.

Suggested Minimum Target Trough Concentrations for Persons With Wild-Type HIV-1

Drug	Concentration (ng/mL)
Amprenavir	400
or	
Fosamprenavir	(concentration assayed as amprenavir)
Atazanavir	150
Indinavir	100
Lopinavir / ritonavir (Kaletra®)	1000
Nelfinavir[1]	800
Ritonavir[2]	2100
Saquinavir	100-250
Efavirenz	1000
Nevirapine	3400

[1]Measurable active M8 metabolite.

[2]Ritonavir given as a single PI.

COMMUNITY-ACQUIRED PNEUMONIA IN ADULTS

The initial site of treatment should be based on a 3-step process:

1. assessment of pre-existing conditions that compromise safety of home care
2. calculation of the pneumonia PORT (Pneumonia Outcome Research Team) Severity Index with recommendation for home care for risk classes I, II, and III, and
3. clinical judgment

Algorithm

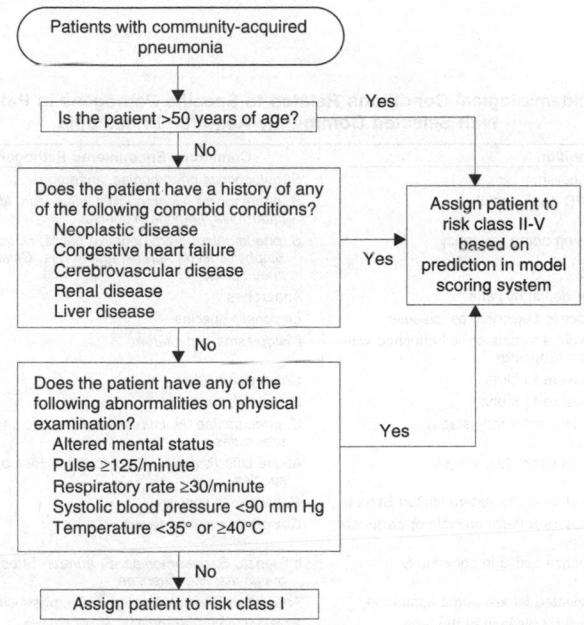

Stratification of Risk Score

Risk	Risk Class	Based on
	I	Algorithm
Low	II	≤70 total points
	III	71-90 total points
Moderate	IV	91-130 total points
High	V	>130 total points

COMMUNITY-ACQUIRED PNEUMONIA IN ADULTS *(Continued)*

Risk-Class Mortality Rates for Patients With Pneumonia

Risk Class	No. of Points	Validation Cohort		Recommended Site of Care
		No. of Patients	Mortality (%)	
I	No predictors	3034	0.1	Outpatient
II	≤70	5778	0.6	Outpatient
III	71-90	6790	2.8	Outpatient or brief inpatient
IV	91-130	13,104	8.2	Inpatient
V	>130	9333	29.2	Inpatient

Epidemiological Conditions Related to Specific Pathogens in Patients With Selected Community-Acquired Pneumonia

Condition	Commonly Encountered Pathogens
Alcoholism	*Streptococcus pneumoniae*, anaerobes
COPD and/or smoker	*S. pneumoniae, Haemophilus influenzae, Moraxella catarrhalis, Legionella* species
Nursing home residency	*S. pneumoniae*, gram-negative bacilli, *H. influenzae, Staphylococcus aureus*, anaerobes, *Chlamydia pneumoniae*
Poor dental hygiene	Anaerobes
Epidemic Legionnaires' disease	*Legionella* species
Exposure to bats or soil enriched with bird droppings	*Histoplasma capsulatum*
Exposure to birds	*Chlamydia psittaci*
Exposure to rabbits	*Francisella tularensis*
HIV infection (early stage)	*S. pneumoniae, H. influenzae, Mycobacterium tuberculosis*
HIV infection (late stage)	Above plus *P. carinii, Cryptococcus, Histoplasma* species
Travel to southwestern United States	*Coccidioides* species
Exposure to farm animals or parturient cats	*Coxiella burnetii* (Q fever)
Influenza active in community	Influenza, *S. pneumoniae, S. aureus, Streptococcus pyogenes, H. influenzae*
Suspected large-volume aspiration	Anaerobes (chemical pneumonitis, obstruction)
Structural disease of the lung (bronchiectasis, cystic fibrosis, etc)	*Pseudomonas aeruginosa, Burkholderia (Pseudomonas) cepacia, S. aureus*
Injection drug use	*S. aureus*, anaerobes, *M. tuberculosis, S. pneumoniae*
Airway obstruction	Anaerobes, *S. pneumoniae, H. influenzae, S. aureus*

COPD = chronic obstructive pulmonary disease.

Scoring System: Assignment to Risk Classes II-V

Patient Characteristic	Points Assigned[1]
Demographic factors	
Age	
Male	No. of years
Female	No. of years -10
Nursing home resident	+10
Comorbid illnesses	
Neoplastic disease[2]	+30
Liver disease[3]	+20
Congestive heart failure[4]	+10
Cerebrovascular disease[5]	+10
Renal disease[6]	+10
Physical examination findings	
Altered mental status[7]	+20
Respiratory rate >30 breaths/minute	+20
Systolic blood pressure <90 mm Hg	+20
Temperature <35°C or >40°C	+15
Pulse >125 beats/minute	+10
Laboratory or radiographic findings	
Arterial pH <7.35	+30
BUN >30 mg/dL	+20
Sodium <130 mEq/L	+20
Glucose >250 mg/dL	+10
Hematocrit <30%	+10
pO$_2$ <60 mm Hg[8]	+10
Pleural effusion	+10

[1]A total point score for a given patient is obtained by adding the patient's age in years (age -10, for females) and the points for each applicable patient characteristic.

[2]Any cancer, except basal or squamous cell cancer of the skin, that was active at the time of presentation or diagnosed within 1 year of presentation.

[3]A clinical or histologic diagnosis of cirrhosis or other form of chronic liver disease such as chronic active hepatitis.

[4]Systolic or diastolic ventricular dysfunction documented by history and physical examination, as well as chest radiography, echocardiography, Muga scanning, or left ventriculography.

[5]A clinical diagnosis of stroke, transient ischemic attack, or stroke documented by MRI or computed axial tomography.

[6]A history of chronic renal disease or abnormal blood urea nitrogen (BUN) and creatinine values documented in the medical record.

[7]Disorientation (to person, place, or time; not known to be chronic), stupor, or coma.

[8]In the Pneumonia Patient Outcome Research Team cohort study, an oxygen saturation value <90% on pulse oximetry or intubation before admission was also considered abnormal.

COMMUNITY-ACQUIRED PNEUMONIA IN ADULTS *(Continued)*

Initial Empiric Therapy for Suspected Bacterial Community-Acquired Pneumonia (CAP) in Immunocompetent Adults

Patient Variable	Preferred Treatment Options
Outpatient	
Previously healthy	
No recent antibiotic therapy	A macrolide[1] or doxycycline
Recent antibiotic therapy[2]	A respiratory fluoroquinolone[3] alone, an advanced macrolide[4] plus high-dose amoxicillin,[5] or an advanced macrolide plus high-dose amoxicillin-clavulanate[6]
Comorbidities (COPD, diabetes, renal or congestive heart failure, or malignancy)	
No recent antibiotic therapy	An advanced macrolide[4] or a respiratory fluoroquinolone
Recent antibiotic therapy	A respiratory fluoroquinolone[3] alone or an advanced macrolide plus a β-lactam[7]
Suspected aspiration with infection	Amoxicillin-clavulanate or clindamycin
Influenza with bacterial superinfection	A β-lactam[7] or a respiratory fluoroquinolone
Inpatient	
Medical ward	
No recent antibiotic therapy	A respiratory fluoroquinolone alone or an advanced macrolide plus a β-lactam[8]
Recent antibiotic therapy	An advanced macrolide plus a β-lactam or a respiratory fluoroquinolone alone (regimen selected will depend on nature of recent antibiotic therapy)
ICU	
Pseudomonas infection is not an issue	A β-lactam[8] plus either an advanced macrolide or a respiratory fluoroquinolone
Pseudomonas infection is not an issue but patient has a β-lactam allergy	A respiratory fluoroquinolone, with or without clindamycin
Pseudomonas infection is an issue[9]	Either (1) an antipseudomonal agent[10] plus ciprofloxacin, or (2) an antipseudomonal agent plus an aminoglycoside[11] plus a respiratory fluoroquinolone or a macrolide
Pseudomonas infection is an issue but the patient has a β-lactam allergy	Either (1) aztreonam plus levofloxacin,[12] or (2) aztreonam plus moxifloxacin or gatifloxacin, with or without an aminoglycoside
Nursing home	
Receiving treatment in nursing home	A respiratory fluoroquinolone alone or amoxicillin-clavulanate plus an advanced macrolide
Hospitalized	Same as for medical ward and ICU

COPD = chronic obstructive pulmonary disease; ICU = intensive care unit.

[1]Erythromycin, azithromycin, or clarithromycin.

[2]That is, the patient was given a course of antibiotic(s) for treatment of any infection within the past 3 months, excluding the current episode of infection. Such treatment is a risk factor for drug-resistant *Streptococcus pneumoniae* and possibly for infection with gram-negative bacilli. Depending on the class of antibiotics recently given, one or other of the suggested options may be selected. Recent use of a fluoroquinolone should dictate selection of a nonfluoroquinolone regimen, and vice versa.

[3]Moxifloxacin, gatifloxacin, levofloxacin, or gemifloxacin (oral gemifloxacin only, which was approved by the U.S. Food and Drug Administration on April 4, 2003 and which is the only fluoroquinolone approved for multidrug-resistant *S. pneumoniae*; not yet marketed).

[4]Azithromycin or clarithromycin.

[5]Dosage, 1 g P.O. 3 times/day.

[6]Dosage, 2 g P.O. twice daily.

[7]High-dose amoxicillin, high-dose amoxicillin-clavulanate, cefpodoxime, cefprozil, or cefuroxime.

[8]Cefotaxime, ceftriaxone, ampicillin-sulbactam, or ertapenem; ertapenem was recently approved for such use (in once-daily parenteral treatment), but there is little experience thus far.

[9]The antipseudomonal agents chosen reflect this concern. Risk factors for *Pseudomonas* infection include severe structural lung disease (eg, bronchiectasis), and recent antibiotic therapy or stay in hospital (especially in the ICU). For patients with CAP in the ICU, coverage for *S. pneumoniae* and *Legionella* species must always be assured. Piperacillin-tazobactam, imipenem, meropenem, and cefepime are excellent β-lactams and are adequate for most *S. pneumoniae* and *Haemophilus influenzae* infections. They may be preferred when there is concern for relatively unusual CAP pathogens, such as *Pseudomonas aeruginosa*, *Klebsiella* species, and other gram-negative bacteria.

[10]Piperacillin, piperacillin-tazobactam, imipenem, meropenem, or cefepime.

[11]Data suggest that elderly patients receiving aminoglycosides have worse outcomes.

[12]Dosage for hospitalized patients, 750 mg daily.

References

Bartlett JG, Breiman RF, Mandell LA, et al, "Community-Acquired Pneumonia in Adults: Guidelines for Management. The Infectious Diseases Society of America," *Clin Infect Dis*, 1998, 26(4):811-38.

Mandell LA, Bartlett JG, Dowell SF, et al, "Update of Practice Guidelines for the Management of Community-Acquired Pneumonia in Immunocompetent Adults," *Clin Infect Dis*, 2003, 37(11):1405-33.

MALARIA TREATMENT

Recommended Drug	Adult Dose[1,7]	Pediatric Dose[1,7]†	Region Infection Acquired
	Uncomplicated Malaria / *P. falciparum* or Species Not Identified†		
Chloroquine phosphate (Aralen™ and generics)	600 mg base (= 1000 mg salt) P.O. immediately, followed by 300 mg base (= 500 mg salt) P.O. at 6, 24, and 48 hours Total dose: 1500 mg base (= 2500 mg salt)	10 mg base/kg P.O. immediately, followed by 5 mg base/kg P.O. at 6, 24, and 48 hours Total dose: 25 mg base/kg	**Chloroquine-sensitive** (Central America west of Panama Canal; Haiti; the Dominican Republic; and most of the Middle East)
A. Quinine sulfate[2] plus one of the following: Doxycycline,[3] tetracycline,[3] or clindamycin	**Quinine sulfate[2]:** 542 mg base (= 650 mg salt) P.O. tid x 3-7 days **Doxycycline:** 100 mg P.O. bid x 7 days **Tetracycline:** 250 mg P.O. qid x 7 days **Clindamycin:** 20 mg base/kg/day P.O. divided tid x 7 days	**Quinine sulfate[2]:** 8.3 mg base/kg (= 10 mg salt/kg) P.O. tid x 3-7 days **Doxycycline:** 2.2 mg/kg P.O. bid x 7 days **Tetracycline:** 25 mg/kg/day P.O. divided qid x 7 days **Clindamycin:** 20 mg base/kg/day P.O. divided tid x 7 days	**Chloroquine-resistant or unknown resistance[1]** (All malarious regions except those specified as chloroquine-sensitive listed in the box above. Middle Eastern countries with chloroquine-resistant *P. falciparum* include Iran, Oman, Saudi Arabia, and Yemen. Of note, infections acquired in the Newly Independent States of the former Soviet Union and Korea to date have been uniformly caused by *P. vivax* and should therefore be treated as chloroquine-sensitive infections.)
B. Atovaquone-proguanil (Malarone™)[4]	**Adult tab = 250 mg atovaquone/100 mg proguanil** 4 adult tabs P.O. qd x 3 days	**Adult tab = 250 mg atovaquone/100 mg proguanil** **Peds tab = 62.5 mg atovaquone/25 mg proguanil** 5-8 kg: 2 peds tabs P.O. qd x 3 d 9-10 kg: 3 peds tabs P.O. qd x 3 d 11-20 kg: 1 adult tab P.O. qd x 3 d 21-30 kg: 2 adult tabs P.O. qd x 3 d 31-40 kg: 3 adult tabs P.O. qd x 3 d >40 kg: 4 adult tabs P.O. qd x 3 d	
C. Mefloquine (Lariam™ and generics)[5]	684 mg base (= 750 mg salt) P.O. as initial dose, followed by 456 mg base (= 500 mg salt) P.O. given 6-12 hours after initial dose Total dose = 1250 mg salt	13.7 mg base/kg (= 15 mg salt/kg) P.O. as initial dose, followed by 9.1 mg base/kg (= 10 mg salt/kg) P.O. given 6-12 hours after initial dose Total dose = 25 mg salt/kg	
	Uncomplicated Malaria / *P. malariae*		
Chloroquine phosphate	Treatment as above	Treatment as above	All regions
	Uncomplicated Malaria / *P. vivax* or *P. ovale*		
Chloroquine phosphate plus primaquine phosphate[6]	**Chloroquine phosphate:** Treatment as above **Primaquine phosphate:** 30 mg base P.O. qd x 14 days	**Chloroquine phosphate:** Treatment as above **Primaquine phosphate:** 0.6 mg base/kg P.O. qd x 14 days	**All regions[7]** **Note:** For suspected chloroquine-resistant *P. vivax*, see row below

MALARIA TREATMENT *(Continued)*

Recommended Drug	Adult Dose[1,7]	Pediatric Dose[1,7]	Region Infection Acquired
Uncomplicated Malaria / *P. vivax*			
A. Quinine sulfate[2] plus either doxycycline[3] or tetracycline[3] plus primaquine phosphate[6]	**Quinine sulfate:** Treatment as above **Doxycycline or tetracycline:** Treatment as above **Primaquine phosphate:** Treatment as above	**Quinine sulfate:** Treatment as above **Doxycycline or tetracycline:** Treatment as above **Primaquine phosphate:** Treatment as above	**Chloroquine-resistant[7]** (Papua New Guinea and Indonesia)
B. Mefloquine plus primaquine phosphate[6]	**Mefloquine:** Treatment as above **Primaquine phosphate:** Treatment as above	**Mefloquine:** Treatment as above **Primaquine phosphate:** Treatment as above	
Uncomplicated Malaria: Alternatives for Pregnant Women[8,9,10,11]			
Chloroquine phosphate	**Chloroquine phosphate:** Treatment as above	Not applicable	**Chloroquine-sensitive[11]** (See uncomplicated malaria sections above for chloroquine-sensitive *Plasmodium* species by region)
Quinine sulfate[2] plus clindamycin	**Quinine sulfate:** Treatment as above **Clindamycin:** Treatment as above	Not applicable	**Chloroquine-resistant** ***P. falciparum*[8,9,10]** (See uncomplicated malaria sections above for regions with known chloroquine resistant *P. falciparum*)
Quinine sulfate	**Quinine sulfate:** 650 mg salt P.O. tid x 7 days	Not applicable	**Chloroquine-resistant** ***P. vivax*[8,9,10,11]** (See uncomplicated malaria sections above for regions with chloroquine-resistant *P. vivax*)

Recommended Drug	Adult Dose[1,7]	Pediatric Dose[1,7]	Region Infection Acquired
	Severe Malaria[12,13,14,15]		
Quinidine gluconate[13] plus one of the following: Doxycycline,[3] tetracycline,[3] or clindamycin	**Quinidine gluconate:** 6.25 mg base/kg (= 10 mg salt/kg) loading dose I.V. over 1-2 hours, then 0.0125 mg base/kg/min (= 0.02 mg salt/kg/min) continuous infusion for at least 24 hours. An alternative regimen is 15 mg base/kg (= 24 mg salt/kg) loading dose I.V. infused over 4 hours, followed by 7.5 mg base/kg (= 12 mg salt/kg) infused over 4 hours every 8 hours, starting 8 hours after the loading dose (see package insert). Once parasite density <1% and patient can take oral medication, complete treatment with oral quinine, dose as above. Quinidine/quinine course = 7 days in Southeast Asia; = 3 days in Africa or South America. **Doxycycline:** Treatment as above. If patient not able to take oral medication, give 100 mg I.V. every 12 hours and then switch to oral doxycycline (as above) as soon as patient can take oral medication. For I.V. use, avoid rapid administration. Treatment course = 7 days. **Tetracycline:** Treatment as above **Clindamycin:** Treatment as above. If patient not able to take oral medication, give 10 mg base/kg loading dose I.V. followed by 5 mg base/ kg I.V. every 8 hours. Switch to oral clindamycin (oral dose as above) as soon as patient can take oral medication. For I.V. use, avoid rapid administration. Treatment course = 7 days.	**Quinidine gluconate:** Same mg/kg dosing and recommendations as for adults. **Doxycycline:** Treatment as above. If patient not able to take oral medication, may give I.V.. For children <45 kg, give 2.2 mg/kg I.V. every 12 hours and then switch to oral doxycycline (dose as above) as soon as patient can take oral medication. For children >45 kg, use same dosing as for adults. For I.V. use, avoid rapid administration. Treatment course = 7 days. **Tetracycline:** Treatment as above **Clindamycin:** Treatment as above. If patient not able to take oral medication, give 10 mg base/kg loading dose I.V. followed by 5 mg base/kg I.V. every 8 hours. Switch to oral clindamycin (oral dose as above) as soon as patient can take oral medication. For I.V. use, avoid rapid administration. Treatment course = 7 days.	All regions

*Pediatric dose should NEVER exceed adult dose

†If "species not identified" is subsequently diagnosed as *P. vivax* or *P. ovale*, see *P. vivax* and *P. ovale* (below) regarding treatment with primaquine.

[1] **Note:** There are three options (A, B, or C) available for treatment of uncomplicated malaria caused by chloroquine-resistant *P. falciparum*. Options A and B are equally recommended. Because of a higher rate of severe neuropsychiatric reactions seen at treatment doses, we do not recommend option C (mefloquine) unless options A and B cannot be used. For option A, because there is more data on the efficacy of quinine in combination with doxycycline or tetracycline, these treatment combinations are generally preferred to quinine in combination with clindamycin.

[2] For infections acquired in Southeast Asia, quinine treatment should continue for 7 days. For infections acquired in Africa and South America, quinine treatment should continue for 3 days.

[3] Doxycycline and tetracycline are not indicated for use in children less than 8 years old. For children less than 8 years old with chloroquine-resistant *P. falciparum*, quinine (given alone for 7 days or given in combination with clindamycin) and atovaquone-proguanil are recommended treatment options; mefloquine can be considered if no other options are available. For children less than 8 years old with chloroquine-resistant *P. vivax*, quinine (given alone for 7 days) or mefloquine are recommended treatment options. If none of these treatment options are available or are not being tolerated and if the treatment benefits outweigh the risks, doxycycline or tetracycline may be given to children less than 8 years old.

[4] Give atovaquone-proguanil with food. If patient vomits within 30 minutes of taking a dose, then they should repeat the dose.

[5]Treatment with mefloquine is not recommended in persons who have acquired infections from the Southeast Asian region of Burma, Thailand, and Cambodia due to resistant strains.

[6]Primaquine is used to eradicate any hypnozoite forms that may remain dormant in the liver, and thus prevent relapses, in P. vivax and P. ovale infections. Because primaquine can cause hemolytic anemia in persons with G6PD deficiency, patients must be screened for G6PD deficiency prior to starting treatment with primaquine. For persons with borderline G6PD deficiency or as an alternate to the above regimen, primaquine may be given 45 mg orally one time per week for 8 weeks; consultation with an expert in infectious disease and/or tropical medicine is advised if this alternative regimen is considered in G6PD-deficient persons. Primaquine must not be used during pregnancy.

Note: There are two options (A or B) available for treatment of uncomplicated malaria caused by chloroquine-resistant P. vivax. High treatment failure rates due to chloroquine-resistant P. vivax have been well documented in Papua New Guinea and Indonesia. Rare case reports of chloroquine-resistant P. vivax have also been documented in Burma (Myanmar), India, and Central and South America. Persons acquiring P. vivax infections outside of Papua New Guinea or Indonesia should be started on chloroquine. If the patient does not respond, the treatment should be changed to a chloroquine-resistant P. vivax regimen and CDC should be notified (Malaria Hotline number listed above). For treatment of chloroquine-resistant P. vivax infections, options A and B are equally recommended.

[8]For pregnant women diagnosed with uncomplicated malaria caused by chloroquine-resistant P. falciparum or chloroquine-resistant P. vivax infection, treatment with doxycycline or tetracycline is generally not indicated. However, doxycycline or tetracycline may be used in combination with quinine (as recommended for nonpregnant adults) if other treatment options are not available or are not being tolerated, and the benefit is judged to outweigh the risks.

[9]Because there are no adequate, well-controlled studies of atovaquone and/or proguanil hydrochloride in pregnant women, atovaquone-proguanil is generally not recommended for use in pregnant women. For pregnant women diagnosed with uncomplicated malaria caused by chloroquine-resistant P. falciparum infection, atovaquone-proguanil may be used if other treatment options are not available or are not being tolerated, and if the potential benefit is judged to outweigh the potential risks. There are no data on the efficacy of atovaquone-proguanil in the treatment of chloroquine-resistant P. vivax infections.

[10]Because of a possible association with mefloquine treatment during pregnancy and an increase in stillbirths, mefloquine is generally not recommended for treatment in pregnant women. However, mefloquine may be used if it is the only treatment option available and if the potential benefit is judged to outweigh the potential risks.

[11]For P. vivax and P. ovale infections, primaquine phosphate for radical treatment of hypnozoites should not be given during pregnancy. Pregnant patients with P. vivax and P. ovale infections should be maintained on chloroquine prophylaxis for the duration of their pregnancy. The chemoprophylactic dose of chloroquine phosphate is 300 mg base (= 500 mg salt) orally once per week. After delivery, pregnant patients who do not have G6PD deficiency should be treated with primaquine.

[12]Persons with a positive blood smear OR history of recent possible exposure and no other recognized pathology who have one or more of the following clinical criteria (impaired consciousness/coma, severe normocytic anemia, renal failure, pulmonary edema, acute respiratory distress syndrome, circulatory shock, disseminated intravascular coagulation, spontaneous bleeding, acidosis, hemoglobinuria, jaundice, repeated generalized convulsions, and/or parasitemia of >5%) are considered to have manifestations of more severe disease. Severe malaria is practically always due to P. falciparum.

[13]Patients diagnosed with severe malaria should be treated aggressively with parenteral antimalarial therapy. Treatment with I.V. quinidine should be initiated as soon as possible after the diagnosis has been made. Patients with severe malaria should be given an intravenous loading dose of quinidine unless they have received more than 40 mg/kg of quinine in the preceding 48 hours or if they have received mefloquine within the preceding 12 hours. Consultation with a cardiologist and a physician with experience treating malaria is advised when treating malaria patients with quinidine. During administration of quinidine, blood pressure monitoring (for hypotension) and cardiac monitoring (for widening of the QRS complex and/or lengthening of the QTc interval) should be monitored continuously and blood glucose (for hypoglycemia) should be monitored periodically. Cardiac complications, if severe, may warrant temporary discontinuation of the drug or slowing of the intravenous infusion.

[14]Consider exchange transfusion if the parasite density (i.e. parasitemia) is >10% OR if the patient has altered mental status, nonvolume overload pulmonary edema, or renal complications. The parasite density can be estimated by examining a monolayer of red blood cells (RBCs) on the thin smear under oil immersion magnification. The slide should be examined where the RBCs are more or less touching (approximately 400 RBCs per field). The parasite density can then be estimated from the percentage of infected RBCs and should be monitored every 12 hours. Exchange transfusion should be continued until the parasite density is <1% (usually requires 8-10 units). I.V. quinidine administration should not be delayed for an exchange transfusion and can be given concurrently throughout the exchange transfusion.

[15]Pregnant women diagnosed with severe malaria should be treated aggressively with parenteral antimalarial therapy.

TREATMENT OF SEXUALLY TRANSMITTED INFECTIONS

Type or Stage	Drugs of Choice / Dosage	Alternatives
CHLAMYDIAL INFECTION AND RELATED CLINICAL SYNDROMES[1]		
Urethritis, cervicitis, conjunctivitis, or proctitis (except lymphogranuloma venereum)		
	Azithromycin 1 g oral once **or** Doxycycline[2,3] 100 mg oral bid x 7 d	Ofloxacin[3] 300 mg oral bid x 7 d **or** Levofloxacin[3] 500 mg oral once/d x 7 d **or** Erythromycin[4] 500 mg oral qid x 7 d
Infection in pregnancy		
	Azithromycin 1 g oral once **or** Amoxicillin 500 mg oral tid x 7 d	Erythromycin[4] 500 mg oral qid x 7 d
Neonatal ophthalmia or pneumonia		
	Azithromycin 20 mg/kg once daily x 3 d	Erythromycin 12.5 mg/kg oral qid x 14 d[5]
Lymphogranuloma venereum		
	Doxycycline[2,3] 100 mg oral bid x 21 d	Erythromycin[4] 500 mg oral qid x 21 d
EPIDIDYMITIS		
	Ofloxacin 300 mg bid x 10 d **or** Levofloxacin 500 mg oral once daily x 10 d	Ceftriaxone 250 mg I.M. once **followed by** doxycycline[2] 100 mg oral bid x 10 d
GONORRHEA[6]		
Disseminated gonococcal infection		
	Ceftriaxone 1 g I.M. or I.V. q24h	Cefotaxime 1 g I.V. q8h **or** Ceftizoxime 1 g I.V. q8h **or** **For persons allergic to β-lactam drugs:** Ciprofloxacin 400 mg I.V. q12h **or** Levofloxacin 250 mg I.V. once daily **or** Ofloxacin 400 mg I.V. q12h **or** Spectinomycin 2 g I.M. q12h
		All regimens should be continued for 24-48 hours after improvement begins, at which time therapy may be switched to one of the following regimens to complete a full week of antimicrobial therapy:
		Cefixime 400 mg oral bid **or** Ciprofloxacin 500 mg oral bid **or** Levofloxacin 500 mg oral once daily **or** Ofloxacin 400 mg oral bid
Gonococcal meningitis and endocarditis		
	Ceftriaxone 1-2 g I.V. q12h	
Urethral, cervical, rectal, or pharyngeal		
	Cefixime 400 mg oral once **or** Ceftriaxone 125 mg I.M. once	Cefpodoxime 400 mg oral once **or** Ciprofloxacin[3,7] 500 mg oral once **or** Ofloxacin[3,7] 400 mg oral once **or** Levofloxacin[3,7] 250 mg oral once **or** Spectinomycin 2 g I.M. once[8]
PELVIC INFLAMMATORY DISEASE		
– parenteral	Cefotetan 2 g I.V. q12h **or** cefoxitin 2 g I.V. q6h **plus** doxycycline[3] 100 mg oral or I.V. q12h, until improved **followed by** doxycycline[3] 100 mg oral bid to complete 14 d[10] **or** Clindamycin 900 mg I.V. q8h **plus** gentamicin 2 mg/kg I.V. once, then 1.5 mg/kg I.V. q8h,[11] until improved **followed by** doxycycline[3] 100 mg oral bid to complete 14 d[10]	Ofloxacin[3] 400 mg I.V. q12h **or** levofloxacin[3] 500 mg I.V. once daily **plus** metronidazole 500 mg I.V. q8h[9] **or** Ampicillin/sulbactam 3 g I.V. q6h **plus** doxycycline[3] 100 mg oral or I.V. q12h **All continued until improved, then followed by** doxycycline[3] 100 mg oral bid to complete 14 d[10]

TREATMENT OF SEXUALLY TRANSMITTED INFECTIONS
(Continued)

Type or Stage	Drugs of Choice / Dosage	Alternatives
– oral	Ofloxacin[3] 400 mg bid x 14 d **or** Levofloxacin[3] 500 mg once daily x 14 d ± metronidazole[9] 500 mg bid x 14 d **or** Ceftriaxone 250 mg I.M. once **followed by** doxycycline[3,12] 100 mg bid x 14 d	Cefoxitin 2 g once **plus** probenecid 1 g oral once **followed by** doxycycline[3,12] 100 mg bid x 14 d

TRICHOMONIASIS

	Metronidazole 2 g oral once **or** Tinidazole 2 g oral once	Metronidazole 375 or 500 mg oral bid x 7 d

BACTERIAL VAGINOSIS

	Metronidazole 500 mg oral bid x 7 d **or** Metronidazole gel 0.75%[14] 5 g intravaginally once or twice daily x 5 d **or** Clindamycin 2% cream[14] 5 g intravaginally qhs x 3-7 d	Metronidazole 2 g oral once[13] or Flagyl ER® 750 mg once daily x 7 d **or** Clindamycin 300 mg oral bid x 7 d **or** Clindamycin ovules[14] 100 mg intravaginally once daily x 3 d

VULVOVAGINAL CANDIDIASIS

	Intravaginal butoconazole, clotrimazole, miconazole, terconazole, or tioconazole[15] **or** Fluconazole 150 mg oral once	Nystatin 100,000 unit vaginal tablet once daily x 14 d

SYPHILIS

Early (primary, secondary, or latent <1 y)

	Penicillin G benzathine 2.4 million units I.M. once[16]	Doxycycline[3] 100 mg oral bid x 14 d

Late (>1 year's duration, cardiovascular, gumma, late-latent)

	Penicillin G benzathine 2.4 million units I.M. weekly x 3 wk	Doxycycline[3] 100 mg oral bid x 4 wk

Neurosyphilis[17]

	Penicillin G 3-4 million units I.V. q4h or 24 million units continuous I.V. infusion x 10-14 d	Penicillin G procaine 2.4 million units I.M. daily **plus** probenecid 500 mg qid oral, both x 10-14 d **or** Ceftriaxone 2 g I.V. once daily x 10-14 d

Congenital

	Penicillin G 50,000 units/kg I.V. q8-12h for 10-14 d **or** Penicillin G procaine 50,000 units/kg I.M. daily for 10-14 d	

CHANCROID[18]

	Azithromycin 1 g oral once **or** Ceftriaxone 250 mg I.M. once	Ciprofloxacin[3] 500 mg oral bid x 3 d **or** Erythromycin[4] 500 mg oral qid x 7 d

GENITAL WARTS[19]

	Trichloroacetic or bichloroacetic acid, or podophyllin[3] or liquid nitrogen 1-2 times/wk until resolved **or** Imiquimod 5% 3 times/wk x 16 wk **or** Podofilox 0.5% bid x 3 d, 4 days rest, then repeated up to 4 times	Surgical removal **or** Laser surgery **or** Intralesional interferon

GENITAL HERPES

First episode

	Acyclovir 400 mg oral tid x 7-10 d **or** Famciclovir 250 mg oral tid x 7-10 d **or** Valacyclovir 1 g oral bid x 7-10 d	Acyclovir 200 mg oral 5 times/d x 7-10 d

Severe (hospitalized patients)

	Acyclovir 5-10 mg/kg I.V. q8h x 5-7 d	

Suppression of recurrences[20]

	Acyclovir 400 mg oral bid **or** Famciclovir 250 mg oral bid **or** Valacyclovir 500 mg - 1 g once daily[21]	Acyclovir 200 mg oral, 2-5 times/d

Episodic treatment of recurrences[22]

	Acyclovir 800 mg oral tid x 2 d or 400 mg oral tid x 3-5 d[23] **or** Famciclovir 125 mg oral bid x 3-5 d[23] **or** Valacyclovir 500 mg oral bid x 3 d	

Type or Stage	Drugs of Choice / Dosage	Alternatives
GRANULOMA INGUINALE		
	TMP-SMZ 1 double-strength tablet oral bid for a minimum of 3 wk **or** Doxycycline 100 oral bid for a minimum of 3 wk	Ciprofloxacin 750 mg oral bid for a minimum of 3 wk **or** Erythromycin base 500 mg oral qid for a minimum of 3 wk **or** Azithromycin 1 g oral once per week for a minimum of 3 weeks

[1] Related clinical syndromes include nonchlamydial nongonococcal urethritis and cervicitis.

[2] Or oral tetracycline 500 mg qid.

[3] Not recommended in pregnancy.

[4] Erythromycin ethylsuccinate 800 mg may be substituted for erythromycin base 500 mg; erythromycin estolate is contraindicated in pregnancy.

[5] Pyloric stenosis has been associated with use of erythromycin in newborns.

[6] All patients should also receive a course of treatment effective for *Chlamydia*.

[7] Fluoroquinolones should not be used to treat gonorrhea acquired in Asia, Hawaii, Israel, or other areas where fluoroquinolone-resistant strains of *N. gonorrhoeae* are common.

[8] Recommended only for use during pregnancy in patients allergic to β-lactams. Not effective for pharyngeal infection.

[9] Some clinicians believe the addition of metronidazole is not required.

[10] Or clindamycin 450 mg oral qid to complete 14 days.

[11] A single daily dose of 3 mg/kg is likely to be effective, but has not been studied in pelvic inflammatory disease.

[12] Some experts would add metronidazole 500 mg bid.

[13] Higher relapse rate with single dose, but useful for patients who may not comply with multiple-dose therapy.

[14] In pregnancy, topical preparations have not been effective in preventing premature delivery; oral metronidazole has been effective in some studies.

[15] For preparations and dosage of topical products, see *Med Lett Drugs Ther*, 1994, 36:81; single-dose therapy is not recommended.

[16] Some experts recommend a repeat dose after 7 days, especially in patients with HIV infection or pregnant women.

[17] Patients allergic to penicillin should be desensitized and treated with penicillin.

[18] All regimens, especially single-dose ceftriaxone, are less effective in HIV-infected patients.

[19] Recommendations for external genital warts. Liquid nitrogen can also be used for vaginal, urethral, and oral warts. Podofilox or imiquimod can be used for urethral meatus warts. Trichloroacetic or bichloroacetic acid can be used for anal warts.

[20] Some Medical Letter consultants discontinue preventive treatment for 1-2 months once a year to reassess the frequency of recurrence.

[21] Use 500 mg once daily in patients with <10 recurrences per year and 500 mg bid or 1 g daily in patients with <10 recurrences per year.

[22] Antiviral therapy is variably effective for episodic treatment of recurrences; only effective if started early.

[23] No published data are available to support 3 days' use.

Adapted from "Sexually Transmitted Diseases Treatment Guidelines 2002," *MMWR Morb Mortal Wkly Rep*, 2002, 51(RR-6).

Adapted from "Drugs for Sexually Transmitted Infections," *Treatment Guidelines From The Medical Letter®*, 2004, 2(26):70-2.

TUBERCULOSIS

Tuberculin Skin Test Recommendations[1]

Children for whom immediate skin testing is indicated:

- Contacts of persons with confirmed or suspected infectious tuberculosis (contact investigation); this includes children identified as contacts of family members or associates in jail or prison in the last 5 years

- Children with radiographic or clinical findings suggesting tuberculosis

- Children immigrating from endemic countries (eg, Asia, Middle East, Africa, Latin America)

- Children with travel histories to endemic countries and/or significant contact with indigenous persons from such countries

Children who should be tested annually for tuberculosis[2]:

- Children infected with HIV or living in household with HIV-infected persons

- Incarcerated adolescents

Children who should be tested every 2-3 years[2]:

- Children exposed to the following individuals: HIV-infected, homeless, residents of nursing homes, institutionalized adolescents or adults, users of illicit drugs, incarcerated adolescents or adults, and migrant farm workers. Foster children with exposure to adults in the preceding high-risk groups are included.

Children who should be considered for tuberculin skin testing at ages 4-6 and 11-16 years:

- Children whose parents immigrated (with unknown tuberculin skin test status) from regions of the world with high prevalence of tuberculosis; continued potential exposure by travel to the endemic areas and/or household contact with persons from the endemic areas (with unknown tuberculin skin test status) should be an indication for repeat tuberculin skin testing

- Children without specific risk factors who reside in high-prevalence areas; in general, a high-risk neighborhood or community does not mean an entire city is at high risk; rates in any area of the city may vary by neighborhood, or even from block to block; physicians should be aware of these patterns in determining the likelihood of exposure; public health officials or local tuberculosis experts should help clinicians identify areas that have appreciable tuberculosis rates

Children at increased risk of progression of infection to disease: Those with other medical risk factors, including diabetes mellitus, chronic renal failure, malnutrition, and congenital or acquired immunodeficiencies deserve special consideration. Without recent exposure, these persons are not at increased risk of acquiring tuberculosis infection. Underlying immune deficiencies associated with these conditions theoretically would enhance the possibility for progression to severe disease. Initial histories of potential exposure to tuberculosis should be included on all of these patients. If these histories or local epidemiologic factors suggest a possibility of exposure, immediate and periodic tuberculin skin testing should be considered. An initial Mantoux tuberculin skin test should be performed before initiation of immunosuppressive therapy in any child with an underlying condition that necessitates immunosuppressive therapy.

---

[1]BCG immunization is not a contraindication to tuberculin skin testing.

[2]Initial tuberculin skin testing is at the time of diagnosis or circumstance, beginning as early as at age 3 months.

Adapted from "Report of the Committee on Infectious Diseases," *2003 Red Book*®, 26th ed, 646.

Table 1. Tuberculosis Prophylaxis
Infection Without Disease (Positive Tuberculin Test)[1]

Specific Circumstances/ Organism	Comments	Regimen
Regardless of age (see INH Preventive Therapy)	Rx indicated	INH (5 mg/kg/d, maximum: 300 mg/d for adults, 10 mg/kg/d not to exceed 300 mg/d for children). Results with 6 months of treatment are nearly as effective as 12 months (65% vs 75% reduction in disease). *Am Thoracic Society* (6 months), *Am Acad Pediatrics*, 1991 (9 months). If CXR is abnormal, treat for 12 months. In HIV-positive patient, treatment for a minimum of 12 months, some suggest longer. Monitor transaminases monthly (*MMWR Morb Mortal Wkly Rep* 1989, 38:247).
Age <35 y	Rx indicated	Reanalysis of earlier studies favors INH prophylaxis for 6 months (if INH-related hepatitis case fatality rate is <1% and TB case fatality is ≥6.7%, which appears to be the case, monitor transaminases monthly (*Arch Int Med*, 1990, 150:2517).
INH-resistant organisms likely	Rx indicated	Data on efficacy of alternative regimens is currently lacking. Regimens include ETB + RIF daily for 6 months. PZA + RIF daily for 2 months, then INH + RIF daily until sensitivities from index case (if available) known, then if INH-CR, discontinue INH and continue RIF for 9 months, otherwise INH + RIF for 9 months (this latter is *Am Acad Pediatrics*, 1991 recommendation).
INH + RIF resistant organisms likely	Rx indicated	Efficacy of alternative regimens is unknown; PZA (25-30 mg/kg P.O.) + ETB (15-25 mg/kg P.O.) (at 25 mg/kg ETB, monitoring for retrobulbar neuritis required), for 6 months unless HIV-positive, then 12 months; PZA + ciprofloxacin (750 mg P.O. bid) or ofloxacin (400 mg P.O. bid) x 6-12 months (*MMWR Morb Mortal Wkly Rep*, 1992, 41(RR11):68).

INH = isoniazid; RIF = rifampin; KM = kanamycin; ETB = ethambutol
SM = streptomycin; CXR = chest x-ray; Rx = treatment
See also guidelines for interpreting PPD in "Skin Testing for Delayed Hypersensitivity."
[1]Tuberculin test (TBnT). The standard is the Mantoux test, 5 TU PPD in 0.1 mL diluent stabilized with Tween 80. Read at 48-72 hours measuring maximum diameter of induration. A reaction ≥5 mm is defined as positive in the following: positive HIV or risk factors, recent close case contacts, CXR consistent with healed TBc. ≥10 mm is positive in foreign-born in countries of high prevalence, injection drug users, low income populations, nursing home residents, patients with medical conditions which increase risk (see above, preventive treatment). ≥15 mm is positive in all others (*Am Rev Resp Dis*, 1990, 142:725). Two-stage TBnT: Use in individuals to be tested regularly (ie, healthcare workers). TBn reactivity may decrease over time but be boosted by skin testing. If unrecognized, individual may be incorrectly diagnosed as recent converter. If first TBnT is reactive but <10 mm, repeat 5 TU in 1 week, if then ≥10 mm = positive, not recent conversion (*Am Rev Resp Dis*, 1979, 119:587).

TUBERCULOSIS *(Continued)*

Changes From Prior Recommendations on Tuberculin Testing and Treatment of Latent Tuberculosis Infection (LTBI)

Tuberculin Testing

- Emphasis on targeted tuberculin testing among persons at high risk for recent LTBI or with clinical conditions that increase the risk for tuberculosis (TB), regardless of age; testing is discouraged among persons at lower risk

- For patients with organ transplants and other immunosuppressed patients (eg, persons receiving the equivalent of ≥15 mg/day prednisone for 1 month or more), 5 mm of induration rather than 10 mm of induration rather than 10 mm of induration as a cut-off level for tuberculin positivity

- A tuberculin skin test conversion is defined as in increase of ≥10 mm of induration within a 2-year period, regardless of age

Treatment of Latent Tuberculosis Infection

- For human immunodeficiency virus (HIV)-negative persons, isoniazid given for 9 months is preferred over 6-month regimens

- For HIV-positive persons and those with fibrotic lesions on chest x-ray consistent with previous TB, isoniazid should be given for 9 months instead of 12 months

- For HIV-negative and HIV-positive persons, rifampin and pyrazinamide should be given for 2 months

- For HIV-negative and HIV-positive persons, rifampin should be given for 4 months

Clinical and Laboratory Monitoring

- Routine baseline and follow-up laboratory monitoring can be eliminated in most persons with LTBI, except for those with HIV infection, pregnant women (or those in the immediate postpartum period), and persons with chronic liver disease or those who use alcohol regularly

- Emphasis on clinical monitoring for signs and symptoms of possible adverse effects, with prompt evaluation and changes in treatment, as indicated

Adapted from *MMWR*, 2000, 49(RR-6).

Table 2. Recommended Treatment Regimens for Drug-Susceptible Tuberculosis in Infants, Children, and Adolescents

Infection or Disease Category	Regimen	Remarks
Latent tuberculosis infection (positive tuberculin skin test, no disease):		
• Isoniazid-susceptible	9 months of isoniazid once a day	If daily therapy is not possible, directly observed therapy twice a week may be used for 9 months.
• Isoniazid-resistant	6 months of rifampin once a day	
• Isoniazid-rifampin-resistant[1]	Consult a tuberculosis specialist	
Pulmonary and extrapulmonary (except meningitis)	2 months of isoniazid, rifampin, and pyrazinamide daily, followed by 4 months of isoniazid and rifampin[2]	If possible drug resistance is a concern, another drug (ethambutol or aminoglycoside) is added to the initial 3-drug therapy until drug susceptibilities are determined. Directly observed therapy is highly desirable.
		If hilar adenopathy only, a 6-month course of isoniazid and rifampin is sufficient.
		Drugs can be given 2 or 3 times/week under directly observed therapy in the initial phase if nonadherence is likely.
Meningitis	2 months of isoniazid, rifampin, pyrazinamide, and aminoglycoside or ethionamide, once a day, followed by 7-10 months of isoniazid and rifampin once a day or twice a week (9-12 months total)	A fourth drug, usually an aminoglycoside, is given with initial therapy until drug susceptibility is known.
		For patients who may have acquired tuberculosis in geographic areas where resistance to streptomycin is common, capreomycin, kanamycin, or amikacin may be used instead of streptomycin.

[1]Duration of therapy is longer for human immunodeficiency virus (HIV)-infected people, and additional drugs may be indicated.

[2]Medications should be administered daily for the first 2 weeks to 2 months of treatment and then can be administered 2-3 times/week by directly observed therapy.

Adapted from "Report of the Committee on Infectious Diseases," *2003 Red Book*®, 26th ed, 649.

TUBERCULOSIS *(Continued)*

Table 3. Recommended Drug Regimens for Treatment of Latent Tuberculosis Infection in Children

Drug	Interval and Duration	Comments
Isoniazid	Daily for 9 mo Twice weekly for 9 mo	This includes treatment for any child <5 years old who is exposed to household members or other close contacts who are potentially infectious even if skin test is negative
Rifampin	Daily for 4-9 mo	No controlled trials; only to be used in INH intolerant or resistant
Rifampin-pyrazinamide	Daily for 3 mo	No controlled trials; only to be used in INH intolerant or resistant

Modified from *MMWR*, 2000, 14(RR-6).

Table 4. Recommended Drug Regimens for Treatment of Latent Tuberculosis Infection in Adults

Drug	Interval and Duration	Comments	Rating[1] (Evidence)[2]	
			HIV⁻	HIV⁺
Isoniazid	Daily for 9 months[3,4]	In HIV-infected patients, isoniazid may be administered concurrently with nucleoside reverse transcriptase inhibitors (NRTIs), protease inhibitors, or non-nucleoside reverse transcriptase inhibitors (NNRTIs)	A (II)	A (II)
	Twice weekly for 9 months[3,4]	Directly observed therapy (DOT) must be used with twice-weekly dosing	B (II)	B (II)
Isoniazid	Daily for 6 months[4]	Not indicated for HIV-infected persons, those with fibrotic lesions on chest radiographs, or children	B (I)	C (I)
	Twice weekly for 6 months[4]	DOT must be used with twice-weekly dosing	B (II)	C (I)
Rifampin	Daily for 4 months	For persons who cannot tolerate pyrazinamide	B (II)	B (III)
		For persons who are contacts of patients with isoniazid-resistant, rifampin-susceptible TB who cannot tolerate pyrazinamide		
Rifampin plus pyrazinamide	Daily for 2 months	May also be offered to persons who are contacts of pyrazinamide patients with isoniazid-resistant, rifampin-susceptible TB	B (II)	A (I)
		In HIV-infected patients, protease inhibitors or NNRTIs should generally not be administered concurrently with rifampin. Rifabutin can be used as an alternative for patients treated with indinavir, nelfinavir, amprenavir, ritonavir, or efavirenz, and possibly with nevirapine or soft-gel saquinavir[5]		
	Twice weekly for 2-3 months	DOT must be used with twice-weekly dosing	C (II)	C (I)

[1]Strength of recommendation: A = preferred; B = acceptable alternative; C = offer when A and B cannot be given.

[2]Quality of evidence: I = randomized clinical trial data; II = data from clinical trials that are not randomized or were conducted in other populations; III = expert opinion.

[3]Recommended regimen for children <18 years of age.

[4]Recommended regimens for pregnant women. Some experts would use rifampin and pyrazinamide for 2 months as an alternative regimen in HIV-infected pregnant women, although pyrazinamide should be avoided during the first trimester.

[5]Rifabutin should not be used with hard-gel saquinavir or delavirdine. When used with other protease inhibitors or NNRTIs, dose adjustment of rifabutin may be required.

Adapted from *MMWR Recomm Rep*, 2000, 49(RR6).

Table 5. TB Drugs in Special Situations

Drug	Pregnancy[1]	CNS TB Disease	Renal Insufficiency
Isoniazid	Safe	Good penetration	Normal clearance
Rifampin	Safe	Fair penetration Penetrates inflamed meninges (10% to 20%)	Normal clearance
Pyrazinamide	Avoid	Good penetration	Clearance reduced Decrease dose or prolong interval
Ethambutol	Safe	Penetrates inflamed meninges only (4% to 64%)	Clearance reduced Decrease dose or prolong interval
Streptomycin	Avoid	Penetrates inflamed meninges only	Clearance reduced Decrease dose or prolong interval
Capreomycin	Avoid	Penetrates inflamed meninges only	Clearance reduced Decrease dose or prolong interval
Kanamycin	Avoid	Penetrates inflamed meninges only	Clearance reduced Decrease dose or prolong interval
Ethionamide	Do not use	Good penetration	Normal clearance
Para-amino-salicylic acid	Safe	Penetrates inflamed meninges only (10% to 50%)	Incomplete data on clearance
Cycloserine	Avoid	Good penetration	Clearance reduced Decrease dose or prolong interval
Ciprofloxacin	Do not use	Fair penetration (5% to 10%) Penetrates inflamed meninges (50% to 90%)	Clearance reduced Decrease dose or prolong interval
Ofloxacin	Do not use	Fair penetration (5% to 10%) Penetrates inflamed meninges (50% to 90%)	Clearance reduced Decrease dose or prolong interval
Amikacin	Avoid	Penetrates inflamed meninges only	Clearance reduced Decrease dose or prolong interval
Clofazimine	Avoid	Penetration unknown	Clearance probably normal

[1]Safe = the drug has not been demonstrated to have teratogenic effects.

Avoid = data on the drug's safety are limited, or the drug is associated with mild malformations (as in the aminoglycosides).

Do not use = studies show an association between the drug and premature labor, congenital malformations, or teratogenicity.

TUBERCULOSIS *(Continued)*

Table 6. Recommendations for Coadministering Different Antiretroviral Drugs With the Antimycobacterial Drugs Rifabutin and Rifampin

Antiretroviral	Use in Combination with Rifabutin	Use in Combination with Rifampin	Comments
Saquinavir[1] Hard-gel capsules (HGC)	Possibly[2], if antiretroviral regimen also includes ritonavir	Possibly, if antiretroviral regimen also includes ritonavir	Coadministration of saquinavir SGC with usual-dose rifabutin (300 mg/day or 2-3 times/week) is a possibility. However, the pharmacokinetic data and clinical experience for this combination are limited.
Soft-gel capsules (SGC)	Probably[3]	Possibly, if antiretroviral regimen also includes ritonavir	The combination of saquinavir SGC or saquinavir HGC and ritonavir, coadministered with 1) usual-dose rifampin (600 mg/day or 2-3 times/week), or 2) reduced-dose rifabutin (150 mg 2-3 times/week) is a possibility. However, the pharmacokinetic data and clinical experience for these combinations are limited. Coadministration of saquinavir or saquinavir SGC with rifampin is not recommended because rifampin markedly decreases concentrations of saquinavir.
Ritonavir	Probably	Probably	If the combination of ritonavir and rifabutin is used, then a substantially reduced-dose rifabutin regimen (150 mg 2-3 times/week) is recommended. Coadministration of ritonavir with usual-dose rifampin (600 mg/day or 2-3 times/week) is a possibility, though pharmacokinetic data and clinical experience are limited.
Indinavir	Yes	No	There is limited, but favorable, clinical experience with coadministration of indinavir[4] with a reduced daily dose of rifabutin (150 mg) or with the usual dose of rifabutin (300 mg 2-3 times/week). Coadministration of indinavir with rifampin is not recommended because rifampin markedly decreases concentrations of indinavir.
Nelfinavir	Yes	No	There is limited, but favorable, clinical experience with coadministration of nelfinavir[5] with a reduced daily dose of rifabutin (150 mg) or with the usual dose of rifabutin (300 mg 2-3 times/week). Coadministration of nelfinavir with rifampin is not recommended because rifampin markedly decreases concentrations of nelfinavir.
Amprenavir	Yes	No	Coadministration of amprenavir with a reduced daily dose of rifabutin (150 mg) or with the usual dose of rifabutin (300 mg 2-3 times/week) is a possibility, but there is no published clinical experience. Coadministration of amprenavir with rifampin is not recommended because rifampin markedly decreases concentrations of amprenavir.
Nevirapine	Yes	Possibly	Coadministration of nevirapine with usual-dose rifabutin (300 mg/day or 2-3 times/week) is a possibility based on pharmacokinetic study data. However, there is no published clinical experience for this combination. Data are insufficient to assess whether dose adjustments are necessary when rifampin is coadministered with nevirapine. Therefore, rifampin and nevirapine should be used only in combination if clearly indicated and with careful monitoring.

Table 6. Recommendations for Coadministering Different Antiretroviral Drugs With the Antimycobacterial Drugs Rifabutin and Rifampin (continued)

Antiretroviral	Use in Combination with Rifabutin	Use in Combination with Rifampin	Comments
Delavirdine	No	No	Contraindicated because of the marked decrease in concentrations of delavirdine when administered with either rifabutin or rifampin.
Efavirenz	Probably	Probably	Coadministration of efavirenz with increased-dose rifabutin (450 mg/day or 600 mg/day, or 600 mg 2-3 times/week) is a possibility, though there is no published clinical experience. Coadministration of efavirenz[6] with usual-dose rifampin (600 mg/day or 2-3 times/week) is a possibility, though there is no published clinical experience.

[1]Usual recommended doses are 400 mg twice daily for each of these protease inhibitors and 400 mg of ritonavir.

[2]Despite limited data and clinical experience, the use of this combination is potentially successful.

[3]Based on available data and clinical experience, the successful use of this combination is likely.

[4] Usual recommended dose is 800 mg every 8 hours; some experts recommend increasing the indinavir dose to 1000 mg every 8 hours if indinavir is used in combination with rifabutin.

[5]Usual recommended dose is 750 mg 3 times/day or 1250 mg twice daily; some experts recommend increasing the nelfinavir dose to 1000 mg if the 3-times/day dosing is used and nelfinavir is used in combination with rifabutin.

[6]Usual recommended dose is 600 mg/day; some experts recommend increasing the efavirenz dose to 800 mg/day if efavirenz is used in combination with rifampin.

Updated March 2000 from www.aidsinfo.nih.gov -"Updated Guidelines for the Use of Rifabutin or Rifampin for the Treatment and Prevention of Tuberculosis Among HIV-Infected Patients Taking Protease Inhibitors or Non-nucleoside Reverse Transcriptase Inhibitors," *MMWR,* March 10, 2000, 49(09):185-9.

Table 7. Criteria for Tuberculin Positivity, by Risk Group

Reaction ≥5 mm of Induration	Reaction ≥10 mm of Induration	Reaction ≥15 mm of Induration
HIV-positive persons	Recent immigrants (ie, within the last 5 years) from high prevalence countries	Persons with no risk factors for TB
Recent contacts of tuberculosis (TB) case patients	Injection drug users	
Fibrotic changes on chest radiograph consistent with prior TB	Residents and employees[1] of the following high risk congregate settings: prisons and jails, nursing homes and other long-term facilities for the elderly, hospitals and other healthcare facilities, residential facilities for patients with AIDS, and homeless shelters	
Patients with organ transplant and other immunosuppressed patients (receiving the equivalent of ≥15 mg/day of prednisone for 1 month)[2]	Mycobacteriology laboratory personnel	
	Persons with the following clinical conditions that place them at high risk: silicosis, diabetes mellitus, chronic renal failure, some hematologic disorders (eg, leukemias and lymphomas), other specific malignancies (eg, carcinoma of the head and neck and lung), weight loss of ≥10% of ideal body weight, gastrectomy, and jejunoileal bypass	
	Children <4 years of age or infants, children, and adolescents exposed to adults at high-risk	

[1]For persons who are otherwise at low risk and are tested at the start of employment, a reaction of ≥15 mm induration is considered positive.

[2]Risk of TB in patients treated with corticosteroids increases with higher dose and longer duration.

Modified from *MMWR Morb Mortal Wkly Rep,* 2000, 49(RR-6).

TUBERCULOSIS (Continued)

Table 8. Recommendations, Rankings, and Performance Indicators for Treatment of Patients With Tuberculosis (TB)

Recommendation	Ranking[1] (Evidence)[2]	Performance Indicator
Obtain bacteriologic confirmation and susceptibility testing for patients with TB or suspected of having TB	A (II)	90% of adults with or suspected of having TB have 3 cultures for mycobacteria obtained before initiation of antituberculosis therapy (50% of children 0-12 y)
Place persons with suspected or confirmed smear-positive pulmonary or laryngeal TB in respiratory isolation until noninfectious	A (II)	90% of persons with sputum smear-positive TB remain in respiratory isolation until smear converts to negative
Begin treatment of patients with confirmed or suspected TB disease with one of the following drug combinations, depending on local resistance patterns: INH + RIF + PZA **or** INH + RIF + PZA + EMB **or** INH + RIF + PZA + SM	A (III)	90% of all patients with TB are started on INH + RIF + PZA + SM in geographic areas where >4% of TB isolates are resistant to INH
Report each case of TB promptly to the local public health department	A (III)	100% of persons with active TB are reported to the local public health department within 1 week of diagnosis
Perform HIV testing for all patients with TB	A (III)	80% of all patients with TB have HIV status determined within 2 months of a diagnosis of TB
Treat patients with TB caused by a susceptible organism for 6 months, using an ATS/CDC-approved regimen	A (I)	90% of all patients with TB complete 6 months of therapy within 12 months of beginning treatment
Re-evaluate patients with TB who are smear positive at 3 months for possible nonadherence or infection with drug-resistant bacilli	A (III)	90% of all patients with TB who are smear positive at 3 months have sputum culture/susceptibility testing performed within 1 month of the 3-month visit
Add ≥2 new antituberculosis agents when TB treatment failure is suspected	A (II)	100% of patients with TB with suspected treatment failure are prescribed ≥2 new antituberculosis agents
Perform tuberculin skin testing on all patients with a history of ≥1 of the following: HIV infection, I.V. drug use, homelessness, incarceration, or contact with a person with pulmonary TB	A (II)	80% of persons in the indicated population groups receive tuberculin skin test and return for reading
Administer treatment for latent TB infection to all persons with latent TB infection, unless it can be documented that they received such treatment previously	A (I)	75% of patients with positive tuberculin skin tests who are candidates for treatment for latent TB infection complete a course of therapy within 12 months of initiation

Note: ATS/CDC = American Thoracic Society and Centers for Disease Control and Prevention; EMB = ethambutol; INH = isoniazid; PZA = pyrazinamide; RIF = rifampin; SM = streptomycin.

[1]Strength of recommendation: A = preferred; B = acceptable alternative; C = offer when A and B cannot be given.

[2]Quality of evidence: I = randomized clinical trial data; II = data from clinical trials that are not randomized or were conducted in other populations; III = expert opinion.

Adapted from the Infectious Diseases Society of America, *Clinical Infectious Diseases*, 2000, 31:633-9.

Table 9. Drug Regimens for Culture-Positive Pulmonary Tuberculosis Caused by Drug-Susceptible Organisms

Initial Phase			Continuation Phase			Range of Total Doses (minimal duration)	Rating[1] (Evidence)[2]	
Regimen	Drugs	Interval and Doses[3] (minimal duration)	Regimen	Drugs	Interval and Doses[3,4] (minimal duration)		HIV-	HIV+
1	INH RIF PZA EMB	Seven days per week for 56 doses (8 wk) or 5 d/wk for 40 doses (8 wk)[5]	1a	INH/RIF	Seven days per week for 126 doses (18 wk) or 5 d/wk for 90 doses (18 wk)[5]	182-130 (26 wk)	A (I)	A (II)
			1b	INH/RIF	Twice weekly for 36 doses (18 wk)	92-76 (26 wk)	A (I)	A (II)[6]
			1c[7]	INH/RPT	Once weekly for 18 doses (18 wk)	74-58 (25 wk)	B (I)	E (I)
2	INH RIF PZA EMB	Seven days per week for 14 doses (2 wk), then twice weekly for 12 doses (6 wk) or 5 d/wk for 10 doses (2 wk)[5], then twice weekly for 12 doses (6 wk)	2a	INH/RIF	Twice weekly for 36 doses (18 wk)	62-58 (25 wk)	A (II)	B (II)[6]
			2b[7]	INH/RPT	Once weekly for 18 doses (18 wk)	44-40 (25 wk)	B (I)	E (I)
3	INH RIF PZA EMB	Three times weekly for 24 doses (8 wk)	3a	INH/RIF	Three times weekly for 54 doses (18 wk)	78 (26 wk)	B (I)	B (II)
4	INH RIF EMB	Seven days per week for 56 doses (8 wk) or 5 d/wk for 40 doses (8 wk)[5]	4a	INH/RIF	Seven days per week for 217 doses (31 wk) or 5 d/wk for 155 doses (31 wk)[5]	273-195 (39 wk)	C (I)	C (II)
			4b	INH/RIF	Twice weekly for 62 doses (31 wk)	118-102 (39 wk)	C (I)	C (II)

Definition of abbreviations: EMB = ethambutol; INH = isoniazid; PZA = pyrazinamide; RIF = rifampin; RPT = rifapentine.

[1]Definitions of evidence ratings: A = preferred; B = acceptable alternative; C = offer when A and B cannot be given; E = should never be given.

[2]Definitions of evidence ratings: I = randomized clinical trial; II = data from clinical trials that were not randomized or were conducted in other populations; III = expert opinion.

[3]When directly observed therapy (DOT) is used, drugs may be given 5 days/week and the necessary number of doses adjusted accordingly. Although there are no studies that compare five with seven daily doses, extensive experience indicates this would be an effective practice.

[4]Patients with cavitation on initial chest radiograph and positive cultures at completion of 2 months of therapy should receive a 7-month (31-week; either 217 doses daily) or 62 doses [twice weekly]) continuation phase.

[5]Five-day/week administration is always given by DOT. Rating for 5 day/week regimens is AIII.

[6]Not recommended for HIV-infected patients with CD4+ cell counts <100 cells/μL.

[7]Options 1c and 2b should be used only in HIV-negative patients who have negative sputum smears at the time of completion of 2 months of therapy and who do not have cavitation on initial chest radiograph. For patients started on this regimen and found to have a positive culture from the 2-month specimen, treatment should be extended an extra 3 months.

Adapted from *MMWR*, 2003, 52(RR11).

TUBERCULOSIS (Continued)

Table 10. Suggested Pyrazinamide Doses, Using Whole Tablets, for Adults Weighing 40-90 kg

	Weight (kg)[1]		
	40-55	56-75	76-90
Daily, mg (mg/kg)	1000 (18.2-25)	1500 (20-26.8)	2000[2] (22.2-26.3)
Thrice weekly, mg (mg/kg)	1500 (27.3-37.5)	2500 (33.3-44.6)	3000[2] (33.3-39.5)
Twice weekly, mg (mg/kg)	2000 (36.4-50)	3000 (40-53.6)	4000[2] (44.4-52.6)

[1]Based on estimated lean body weight

[2]Maximum dose regardless of weight.

Table 11. Suggested Ethambutol Doses, Using Whole Tablets, for Adults Weighing 40-90 kg

	Weight (kg)[1]		
	40-55	56-75	76-90
Daily, mg (mg/kg)	800 (14.5-20)	1200 (16-21.4)	1600[2] (17.8-21.1)
Thrice weekly, mg (mg/kg)	1200 (21.8-30)	2000 (26.7-35.7)	2400[2] (26.7-31.6)
Twice weekly, mg (mg/kg)	2000 (36.4-50)	2800 (37.3-50)	4000[2] (44.4-52.6)

[1]Based on estimated lean body weight

[2]Maximum dose regardless of weight.

CALCULATIONS FOR TOTAL PARENTERAL NUTRITION THERAPY – ADULT PATIENTS

Condition	Calorie Requirement (kcal/kg/d)	Protein Requirement (g/kg/d)
Resting state (adult medical patient)	20-30	0.8-1
Uncomplicated postop patients	25-35	1-1.3
Depleted patients	30-40	1.3-1.7
Hypermetabolic patients (trauma, sepsis, burns)	35-45	1.5-2

1 g protein yields 4 kcal/g
1 g fat yields 9 kcal/g
1 g dextrose yields 3.4 kcal/g
1 g nitrogen = 6.25 g protein

Electrolytes Required/Day

	mEq/d
Sodium	60-120
Potassium	60-120
Chloride	100-150
Magnesium	10-24
Calcium	10-20
Phosphate	20-50 mmol/d
Sulfate	10-24
Acetate	60-150
Bicarbonate	Should not be added

Estimated Energy Requirements

Basal Energy Expenditure (BEE)	
Harris Benedict equation	
males	$BEE_{mal} = 66.67 + (13.75 \times kg) + (5 \times cm) - (6.76 \times y)$
females	$BEE_{fem} = 665.1 + (9.56 \times kg) + (1.85 \times cm) - (4.68 \times y)$
Total daily energy expenditure (TDE)	TDE = BEE x activity factor x injury factor
Activity factor	Confined to bed = 1.2
	Out of bed = 1.3
Injury factor	Surgery:
	Minor operations = 1-1.1
	Major operations = 1.1-1.2
	Infection:
	Mild = 1-1.2
	Moderate = 1.2-1.4
	Severe = 1.4-1.6
	Skeletal trauma = 1.2-1.35
	Head injury (treated with corticosteroids) = 1.6
	Blunt trauma = 1.15-1.35
	Burns
	≤20% body surface area (BSA) = 2
	20%-30% BSA = 2-2.2
	>30% BSA = 2.2

Estimated Fluid Requirements

30-35 mL/kg/d
or
mL/d = 1500 mL for first 20 kg of body weight + 20 mL/kg for body weight >20 kg

MEDIAN HEIGHTS AND WEIGHTS AND RECOMMENDED ENERGY INTAKE[1]

Age (y) or Condition	Weight (kg)	Weight (lb)	Height (cm)	Height (in)	REE[2] (kcal/d)	Average Energy Allowance (kcal)[3] Multiples of REE	Average Energy Allowance (kcal)[3] /kg	Average Energy Allowance (kcal)[3] /d[4]
Infants								
0-0.5	6	13	60	24	320		108	650
0.5-1	9	20	71	28	500		98	850
Children								
1-3	13	29	90	35	740		102	1300
4-6	20	44	112	44	950		90	1800
7-10	28	62	132	52	1130		70	2000
Male								
11-14	45	99	157	62	1440	1.70	55	2500
15-18	66	145	176	69	1760	1.67	45	3000
19-24	72	160	177	70	1780	1.67	40	2900
25-50	79	174	176	70	1800	1.60	37	2900
51+	77	170	173	68	1530	1.50	30	2300
Female								
11-14	46	101	157	62	1310	1.67	47	2200
15-18	55	120	163	64	1370	1.60	40	2200
19-24	58	128	164	65	1350	1.60	38	2200
25-50	63	138	163	64	1380	1.55	36	2200
51+	65	143	160	63	1280	1.50	30	1900
Pregnant								+0
1st trimester								+300
2nd trimester								+300
3rd trimester								+300
Lactating								
1st 6 months								+500
2nd 6 months								+500

[1]From *Recommended Dietary Allowances*, 10th ed, Washington, DC: National Academy Press, 1989.
[2]Calculation based on FAO equations, then rounded.
[3]In the range of light to moderate activity, the coefficient of variation is ±20%.
[4]Figure is rounded.

PEDIATRIC ALS ALGORITHMS

PALS Bradycardia Algorithm

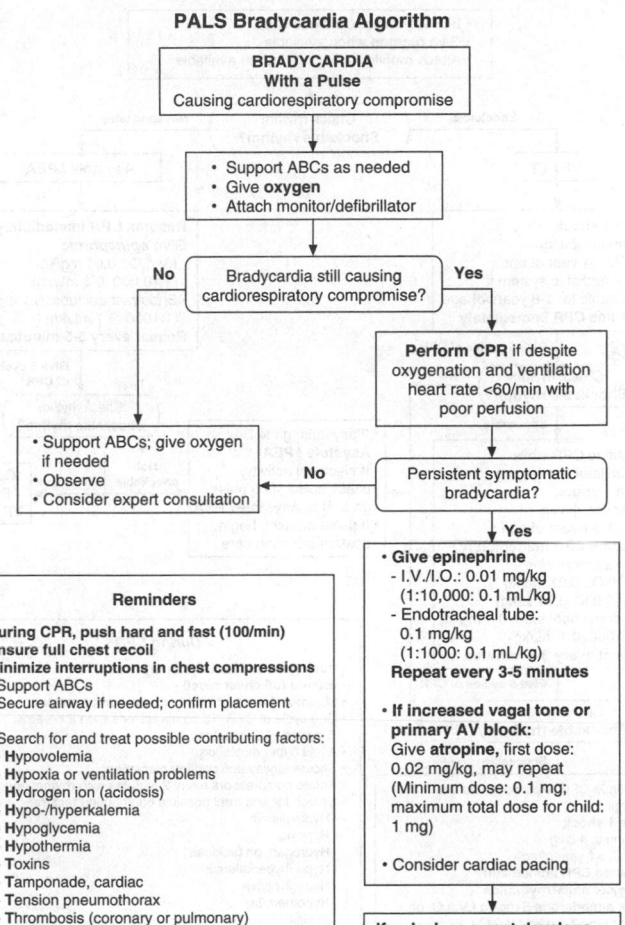

BRADYCARDIA
With a Pulse
Causing cardiorespiratory compromise

- Support ABCs as needed
- Give **oxygen**
- Attach monitor/defibrillator

No ← Bradycardia still causing cardiorespiratory compromise? → **Yes**

Perform CPR if despite oxygenation and ventilation heart rate <60/min with poor perfusion

- Support ABCs; give oxygen if needed
- Observe
- Consider expert consultation

No ← Persistent symptomatic bradycardia?

↓ **Yes**

- **Give epinephrine**
  - I.V./I.O.: 0.01 mg/kg (1:10,000: 0.1 mL/kg)
  - Endotracheal tube: 0.1 mg/kg (1:1000: 0.1 mL/kg)
  Repeat every 3-5 minutes

- **If increased vagal tone or primary AV block:**
  Give **atropine,** first dose: 0.02 mg/kg, may repeat (Minimum dose: 0.1 mg; maximum total dose for child: 1 mg)

- Consider cardiac pacing

If pulseless arrest develops, go to Pulseless Arrest Algorithm

Reminders

During CPR, push hard and fast (100/min)
Ensure full chest recoil
Minimize interruptions in chest compressions
- Support ABCs
- Secure airway if needed; confirm placement

- Search for and treat possible contributing factors:
  - Hypovolemia
  - Hypoxia or ventilation problems
  - Hydrogen ion (acidosis)
  - Hypo-/hyperkalemia
  - Hypoglycemia
  - Hypothermia
  - Toxins
  - Tamponade, cardiac
  - Tension pneumothorax
  - Thrombosis (coronary or pulmonary)
  - Trauma (hypovolemia, increased ICP)

PEDIATRIC ALS ALGORITHMS *(Continued)*

PALS Pulseless Arrest Algorithm

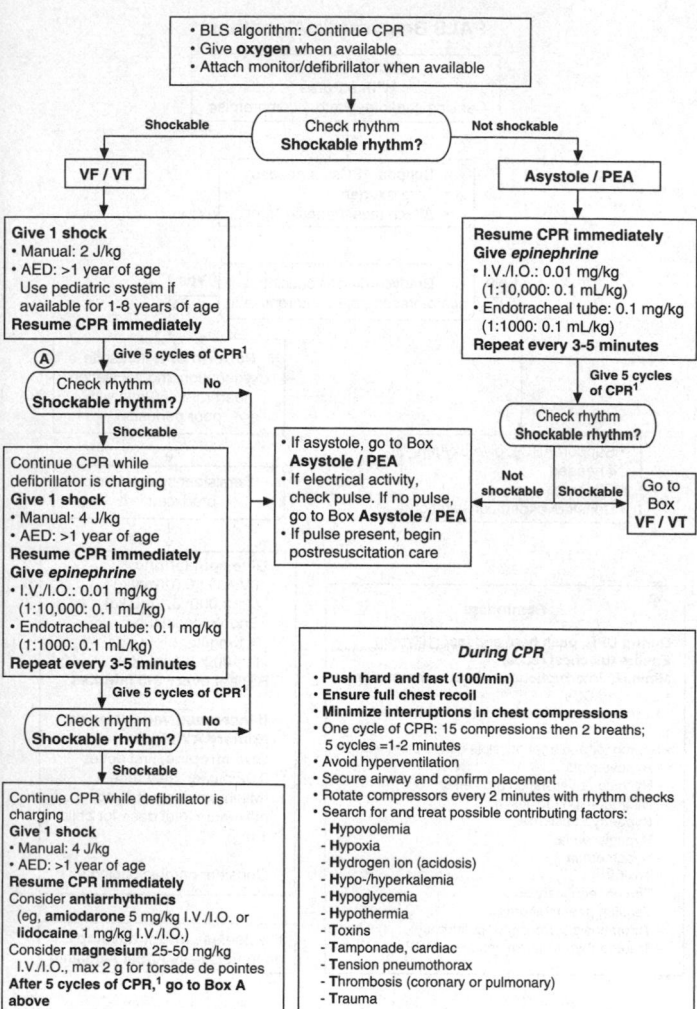

VF = ventricular fibrillation; VT = ventricular tachycardia; PEA = pulseless electrical activity; AED = automated external defibrillator.

[1]After an advanced airway is placed, rescuers no longer deliver "cycles" of CPR. Give continuous chest compressions without pauses for breaths. Give 8-10 breaths/min. Check rhythm every 2 minutes.

PALS Tachycardia Algorithm
With Pulses and Poor Perfusion

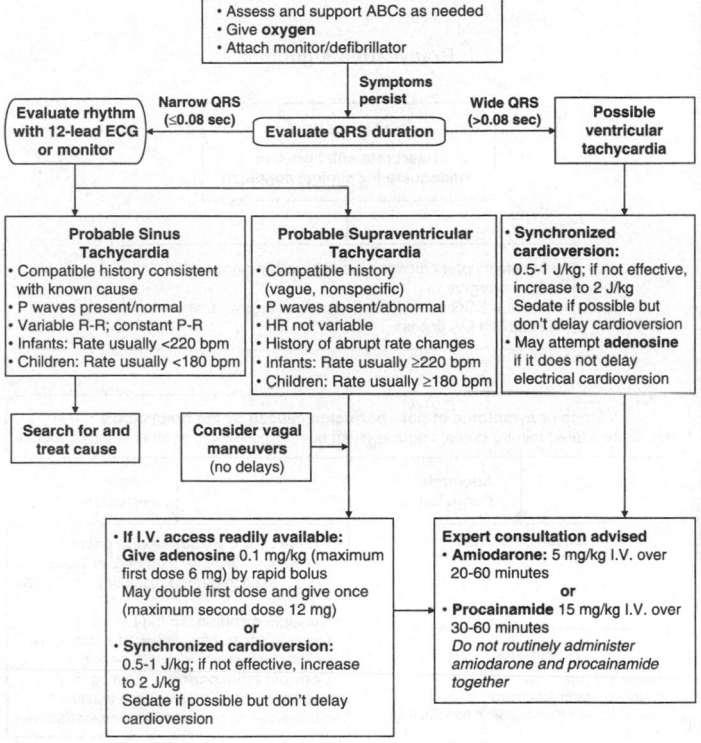

During Evaluation	Treat possible contributing factors:	
• Secure, verify airway and vascular access when possible • Consider expert consultation • Prepare for cardioversion	• Hypovolemia • Hypoxia • Hydrogen ion (acidosis) • Hypo-/hyperkalemia • Hypoglycemia • Hypothermia	• Toxins • Tamponade, cardiac • Tension pneumothorax • Thrombosis (coronary or pulmonary) • Trauma (hypovolemia)

ADULT ACLS ALGORITHMS

Bradycardia Algorithm

BRADYCARDIA
Heart rate <60 bpm and
inadequate for clinical condition

- Maintain patent **airway**; assist **breathing** as needed
- Give **oxygen**
- Monitor ECG (identify rhythm), blood pressure, oximetry
- Establish I.V. access

Signs or symptoms of poor perfusion caused by the bradycardia?
(eg, acute altered mental status, ongoing chest pain, hypotension, or other signs of shock)

Adequate Perfusion

Observe / Monitor

Poor Perfusion

- **Prepare for transcutaneous pacing;**
  use without delay for high-degree block
  (type II second-degree block or third-degree
  AV block)
- Consider **atropine** 0.5 mg I.V. while
  awaiting pacer. May repeat to a total dose
  of 3 mg. If ineffective, begin pacing.
- Consider **epinephrine** (2-10 mcg/min) or
  dopamine (2-10 mcg/kg/min) infusion
  while awaiting pacer or if pacing ineffective

- Prepare for **transvenous pacing**
- Treat contributing causes
- Consider expert consultation

Reminders

- If pulseless arrest develops, *see*
  Pulseless Arrest Algorithm
- Search for and treat possible contributing
  factors:
  - Hypovolemia
  - Hypoxia
  - Hydrogen ion (acidosis)
  - Hypo-/hyperkalemia
  - Hypoglycemia
  - Hypothermia
  - Toxins
  - Tamponade, cardiac
  - Tension pneumothorax
  - Thrombosis (coronary or pulmonary)
  - Trauma (hypovolemia, increased ICP)

ACLS Pulseless Arrest Algorithm

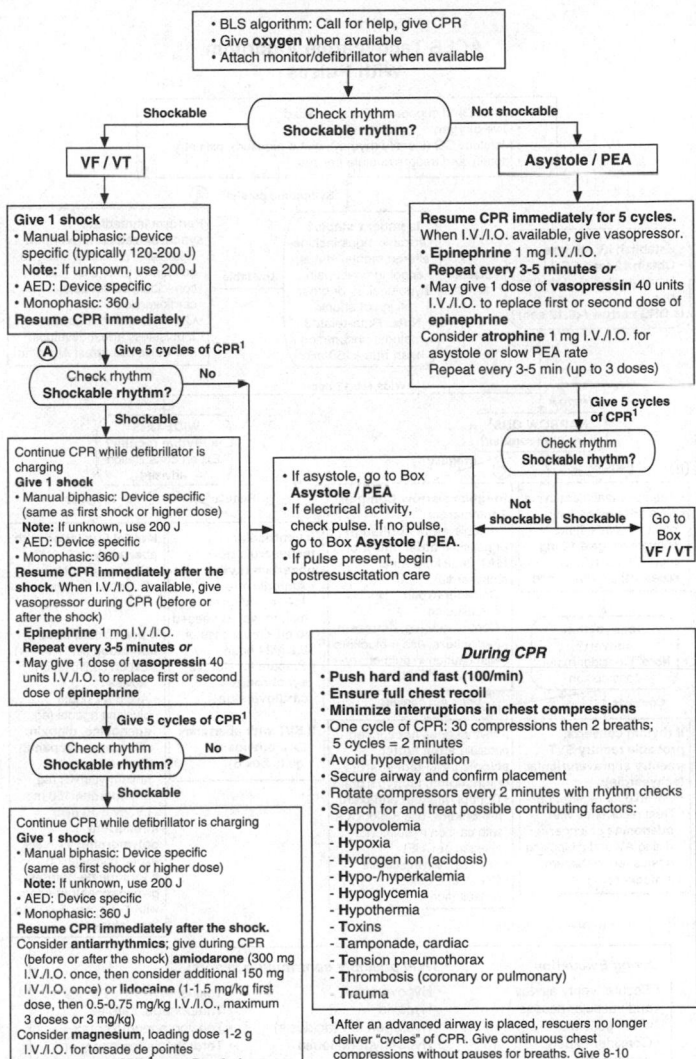

VF = ventricular fibrillation; VT = ventricular tachycardia; PEA = pulseless electrical activity; AED = automated external defibrillator.

ACLS Tachycardia Algorithm
With Pulses

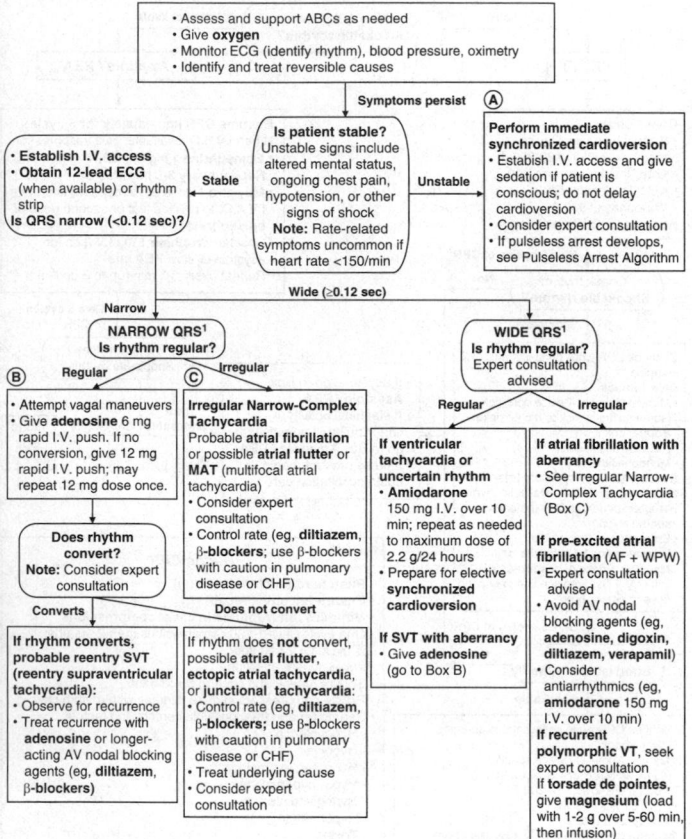

- Assess and support ABCs as needed
- Give **oxygen**
- Monitor ECG (identify rhythm), blood pressure, oximetry
- Identify and treat reversible causes

Symptoms persist Ⓐ

Is patient stable?
Unstable signs include altered mental status, ongoing chest pain, hypotension, or other signs of shock
Note: Rate-related symptoms uncommon if heart rate <150/min

Stable →

- **Establish I.V. access**
- **Obtain 12-lead ECG** (when available) or rhythm strip
Is QRS narrow (<0.12 sec)?

← Unstable

Perform immediate synchronized cardioversion
- Establish I.V. access and give sedation if patient is conscious; do not delay cardioversion
- Consider expert consultation
- If pulseless arrest develops, see Pulseless Arrest Algorithm

Narrow

Wide (≥0.12 sec)

NARROW QRS[1]
Is rhythm regular? Ⓑ

Regular

Ⓑ
- Attempt vagal maneuvers
- Give **adenosine** 6 mg rapid I.V. push. If no conversion, give 12 mg rapid I.V. push; may repeat 12 mg dose once.

Does rhythm convert?
Note: Consider expert consultation

Converts

If rhythm converts, probable reentry SVT (reentry supraventricular tachycardia):
- Observe for recurrence
- Treat recurrence with **adenosine** or longer-acting AV nodal blocking agents (eg, **diltiazem**, β-**blockers**)

Irregular Ⓒ

Ⓒ
Irregular Narrow-Complex Tachycardia
Probable **atrial fibrillation** or possible **atrial flutter** or **MAT** (multifocal atrial tachycardia)
- Consider expert consultation
- Control rate (eg, **diltiazem**, β-**blockers**; use β-blockers with caution in pulmonary disease or CHF)

Does not convert

If rhythm does **not** convert, possible **atrial flutter**, **ectopic atrial tachycardia**, or **junctional tachycardia**:
- Control rate (eg, **diltiazem**, β-**blockers**; use β-blockers with caution in pulmonary disease or CHF)
- Treat underlying cause
- Consider expert consultation

WIDE QRS[1]
Is rhythm regular?
Expert consultation advised

Regular

If ventricular tachycardia or uncertain rhythm
- **Amiodarone** 150 mg I.V. over 10 min; repeat as needed to maximum dose of 2.2 g/24 hours
- Prepare for elective **synchronized cardioversion**

If SVT with aberrancy
- Give **adenosine** (go to Box B)

Irregular

If atrial fibrillation with aberrancy
- See Irregular Narrow-Complex Tachycardia (Box C)

If pre-excited atrial fibrillation (AF + WPW)
- Expert consultation advised
- Avoid AV nodal blocking agents (eg, **adenosine**, **digoxin**, **diltiazem**, **verapamil**)
- Consider antiarrhythmics (eg, **amiodarone** 150 mg I.V. over 10 min)

If recurrent polymorphic VT, seek expert consultation
If torsade de pointes, give **magnesium** (load with 1-2 g over 5-60 min, then infusion)

During Evaluation	*Treat possible contributing factors:*	
- Secure, verify airway and vascular access when possible - Consider expert consultation - Prepare for cardioversion	- Hypovolemia - Hypoxia - Hydrogen ion (acidosis) - Hypo-/hyperkalemia - Hypoglycemia - Hypothermia	- Toxins - Tamponade, cardiac - Tension pneumothorax - Thrombosis (coronary or pulmonary) - Trauma (hypovolemia)

SVT = supraventricular tachycardia; VT = ventricular tachycardia.

[1]If patient becomes unstable, go to Box A.

ASTHMA

MANAGEMENT OF ASTHMA IN ADULTS AND CHILDREN >5 YEARS OF AGE

Goals of Asthma Treatment

- Minimal or no chronic symptoms day or night
- Minimal or no exacerbations
- No limitations on activities; no school/work missed
- Minimal use of inhaled short-acting beta$_2$-agonist (<1 time/day, <1 canister/month)
- Minimal or no adverse effects from medications
- Children >5 years of age and adults only: PEF >80% of personal best

All Patients

- Short-acting bronchodilator: **Inhaled beta$_2$-agonists** as needed for symptoms.
- Intensity of treatment will depend on severity of exacerbation; see "Management of Asthma Exacerbations".
- Use of short-acting inhaled beta$_2$-agonists on a daily basis, or increasing use, indicates the need to initiate or titrate long-term control therapy.

Education

- Teach self-management.
- Teach about controlling environmental factors (avoidance of allergens or other factors that contribute to asthma severity).
- Review administration technique and compliance with patient.
- May use a written action plan to help educate.

Stepwise Approach for Managing Asthma in Adults and Children >5 Years of Age: Treatment[1]

Symptoms[2]	Lung Function[3]	Long-Term Control (Daily Medications)
STEP 4: Severe Persistent		
Day: Continual Night: Frequent	PEF/FEV$_1$ ≤60% PEF variability >30%	• **Preferred treatment:** – **High dose inhaled corticosteroid AND** – **Long-acting inhaled beta$_2$-agonist** AND, if needed – Long-term oral corticosteroids (2 mg/kg/day, generally do not exceed 60 mg/day). (Make repeated attempts to reduce systemic corticosteroids and maintain control with high-dose inhaled corticosteroids.)
STEP 3: Moderate Persistent		
Day: Every day Night: >1 night/week	PEF/FEV$_1$ >60% - <80% PEF variability >30%	• **Preferred treatment:** – **Low-medium dose inhaled corticosteroid AND** – **Long-acting inhaled beta$_2$-agonist** • Alternatives: – Increase inhaled corticosteroids within medium-dose range OR – Low-medium dose inhaled corticosteroids and either leukotriene receptor antagonist or theophylline
		If needed (especially with recurring severe exacerbations): • **Preferred treatment:** – Increase inhaled corticosteroids within medium-dose range, and add long-acting inhaled beta$_2$-agonist • Alternatives: – Increase inhaled corticosteroids in medium-dose range, and add either leukotriene receptor antagonist or theophylline

ASTHMA *(Continued)*

Stepwise Approach for Managing Asthma in Adults and Children >5 Years of Age: Treatment[1]

Symptoms[2]	Lung Function[3]	Long-Term Control (Daily Medications)
STEP 2: Mild Persistent		
Day: >2 days/week but <1 time/day Night: >2 nights/month	PEF/FEV$_1$ ≥80% PEF variability 20%-30%	• **Preferred treatment:** – Low-dose inhaled corticosteroid • Alternatives: Cromolyn, leukotriene receptor antagonist, nedocromil, or sustained release theophylline (serum concentration 5-15 mcg/mL)
STEP 1: Mild Intermittent		
Day: ≤2 days/week Night: ≤2 nights/month	PEF/FEV$_1$ ≥80% PEF variability <20%	No daily medication needed. A course of systemic corticosteroids is recommended for severe exacerbations.

[1]Classify severity. The presence of one of the features of severity is sufficient to place a patient in that category. An individual should be assigned to the most severe grade in which any feature occurs. The characteristics noted are general and may overlap because asthma is highly variable. Furthermore, an individual's classification may change over time.

[2]Patients at any level of severity can have mild, moderate, or severe exacerbations. Some patients with intermittent asthma experience severe and life-threatening exacerbations separated by long periods of normal lung function and no symptoms.

[3]PEF is % of personal best and FEV$_1$ is % predicted.

↓ Step down
Review treatment every 1-6 months; a gradual stepwise reduction in treatment may be possible.

↑Step up
If control is not maintained, consider step up. First, review patient medication technique, adherence, and environmental control.

Notes:

- **The stepwise approach presents general guidelines to assist clinical decision making; it is not intended to be a specific prescription. Asthma is highly variable; clinicians should tailor specific medication plans to the needs and circumstances of individual patients.**

- Gain control as quickly as possible; then decrease treatment to the least medication necessary to maintain control.

- A rescue course of systemic corticosteroids may be needed at any time and at any step.

- Some patients with intermittent asthma experience severe and life-threatening exacerbations separated by long periods of normal lung function and no symptoms. This may be especially common with exacerbations provoked by respiratory infections. A short course of systemic corticosteroids is recommended.

- At each step, patients should control their environment to avoid or control factors that make their asthma worse.

- Antibiotics are not recommended for treatment of acute asthma exacerbations except where there is evidence or suspicion of bacterial infection.

- Consultation with an asthma specialist is recommended for moderate or severe persistent asthma.

- Peak flow monitoring for patients with moderate-severe asthma should be considered.

MANAGEMENT OF ASTHMA IN INFANTS AND YOUNG CHILDREN

All Patients

- Bronchodilator as needed for symptoms ≤2 times/week. Intensity of treatment will depend upon severity of exacerbation (see "Management of Asthma Exacerbations"). Either:

    – Preferred treatment: Inhaled short-acting beta$_2$-agonist by nebulizer or face mask and spacer/holding chamber

    or

    – Alternative treatment: Oral beta$_2$-agonist

- With viral respiratory infection:

    – Bronchodilator q4-6h up to 24 hours (longer with physician consult) but, in general, repeat no more than once every 6 weeks.

    – Consider systemic corticosteroid if current exacerbation is severe or patient has history of severe exacerbations.

- Use of short-acting inhaled beta$_2$-agonist on a daily basis, or increasing use, indicates the need to initiate or titrate long-term control therapy.

Education

- Teach self-management or caregiver management.
- Teach about controlling environmental factors.
- Review administration technique and compliance with patient.
- May use a written action plan to help educate.

Stepwise Approach for Managing Infants and Young Children (≤5 Years of Age) With Acute or Chronic Asthma[1]

Symptoms[2]	Long-Term Control (Daily Medications)
STEP 4: Severe Persistent	
Day: Continual Night: Frequent	• **Preferred treatment:** – **High dose inhaled corticosteroid** **AND** – **Long-acting inhaled beta$_2$-agonist** AND, if needed – Long-term oral corticosteroids (2 mg/kg/day, generally do not exceed 60 mg/day). (Make repeated attempts to reduce systemic corticosteroids and maintain control with high-dose inhaled corticosteroids.)
STEP 3: Moderate Persistent	
Day: Every day Night: >1 night/week	• **Preferred treatment:** – **Low-dose inhaled corticosteroid** **AND** **Long-acting inhaled beta$_2$-agonist** **OR** **Medium-dose inhaled corticosteroid** • Alternatives: – Low-dose inhaled corticosteroid and either leukotriene receptor antagonist or theophylline
	If needed (especially with recurring severe exacerbations): • **Preferred treatment:** – **Medium-dose inhaled corticosteroid and long-acting inhaled beta$_2$-agonist** • Alternatives: – Medium-dose inhaled corticosteroid and either leukotriene receptor antagonist or theophylline
STEP 2: Mild Persistent	
Day: >2 days/week but <1 time/day Night: >2 nights/month	• **Preferred treatment:** – **Low-dose inhaled corticosteroid (with nebulizer or MDI with holding chamber with or without face mask or DPI)** • Alternatives: Cromolyn (nebulizer is preferred or MDI with holding chamber) **OR** Leukotriene receptor antagonist
STEP 1: Mild Intermittent	
Day: ≤2 days/week Night: ≤2 nights/month	No daily medication needed

[1]Classify severity. The presence of one of the features of severity is sufficient to place a patient in that category. An individual should be assigned to the most severe grade in which any feature occurs. The characteristics noted in this figure are general and may overlap because asthma is highly variable. Furthermore, an individual's classification may change over time.

[2]Patients at any level of severity can have mild, moderate, or severe exacerbations. Some patients with intermittent asthma experience severe and life-threatening exacerbations separated by long periods of normal lung function and no symptoms.

↓ **Step Down**
Review treatment every 1-6 month; a gradual stepwise reduction in treatment may be possible.

↑ **Step Up**
If control is not achieved, consider step up. But first: review patient medication technique, adherence, and environmental control (avoidance of allergens or other precipitant factors)

ASTHMA *(Continued)*

Notes:

- **The stepwise approach presents guidelines to assist clinical decision making. Asthma is highly variable; clinicians should tailor specific medication plans to the needs and circumstances of individual patients.**
- Gain control as quickly as possible; then decrease treatment to the least medication necessary to maintain control.
- A rescue course of systemic corticosteroid may be needed at any time and step.
- In general, use of a short-acting beta$_2$-agonist on a daily basis indicates the need for additional long-term control therapy.
- There are very few studies on asthma therapy for infants.
- Studies comparing medications in children <5 years of age are not available.
- Consultation with an asthma specialist is recommended for moderate or severe persistent asthma. Consider consultation for patient with mild persistent asthma.
- Initiation of long-term control therapy should be considered in infants and young children who have had >3 episodes of wheezing in the past year that lasted >1 day and affected sleep and who have risk factors for asthma.
- Inhaled corticosteroids improve health outcomes for children with mild-moderate persistent asthma. Monitor growth of children taking corticosteroids by any route. If growth appears slowed, weigh the benefits against the risks.
- Antibiotics are not recommended for treatment of acute asthma exacerbations except where there is evidence or suspicion of bacterial infection.

Management of Asthma Exacerbations: Home Treatment[1]

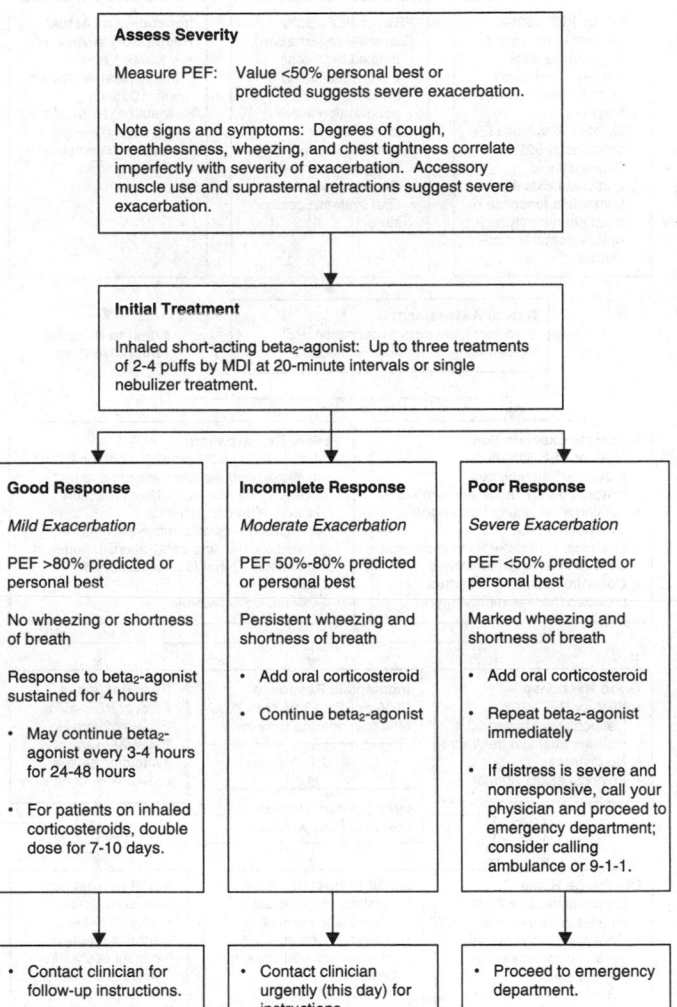

Assess Severity

Measure PEF: Value <50% personal best or predicted suggests severe exacerbation.

Note signs and symptoms: Degrees of cough, breathlessness, wheezing, and chest tightness correlate imperfectly with severity of exacerbation. Accessory muscle use and suprasternal retractions suggest severe exacerbation.

Initial Treatment

Inhaled short-acting beta$_2$-agonist: Up to three treatments of 2-4 puffs by MDI at 20-minute intervals or single nebulizer treatment.

Good Response	**Incomplete Response**	**Poor Response**
Mild Exacerbation	*Moderate Exacerbation*	*Severe Exacerbation*
PEF >80% predicted or personal best	PEF 50%-80% predicted or personal best	PEF <50% predicted or personal best
No wheezing or shortness of breath	Persistent wheezing and shortness of breath	Marked wheezing and shortness of breath
Response to beta$_2$-agonist sustained for 4 hours	• Add oral corticosteroid	• Add oral corticosteroid
• May continue beta$_2$-agonist every 3-4 hours for 24-48 hours	• Continue beta$_2$-agonist	• Repeat beta$_2$-agonist immediately
• For patients on inhaled corticosteroids, double dose for 7-10 days.		• If distress is severe and nonresponsive, call your physician and proceed to emergency department; consider calling ambulance or 9-1-1.
• Contact clinician for follow-up instructions.	• Contact clinician urgently (this day) for instructions.	• Proceed to emergency department.

[1]Patients at high risk of asthma-related death should receive immediate clinical attention after initial treatment. Additional therapy may be required.

ASTHMA *(Continued)*

Management of Asthma Exacerbations: Emergency Department and Hospital-Based Care

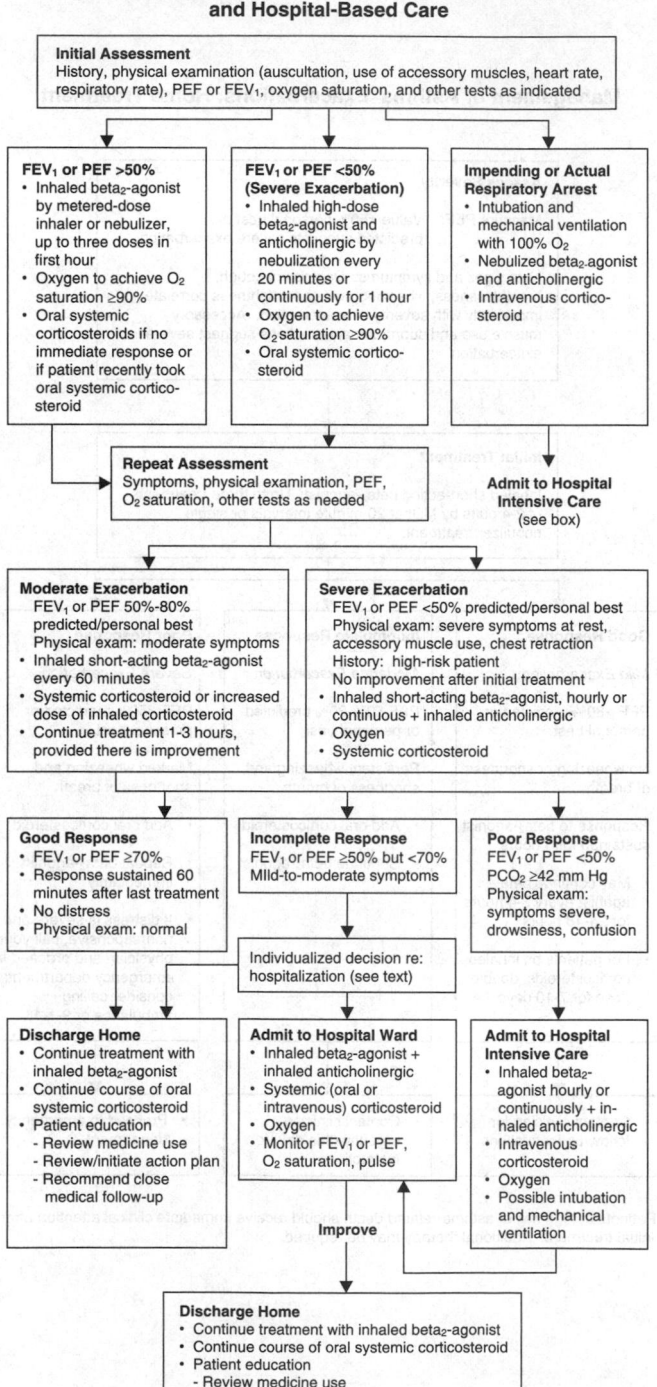

Initial Assessment
History, physical examination (auscultation, use of accessory muscles, heart rate, respiratory rate), PEF or FEV_1, oxygen saturation, and other tests as indicated

FEV_1 or PEF >50%
- Inhaled beta$_2$-agonist by metered-dose inhaler or nebulizer, up to three doses in first hour
- Oxygen to achieve O_2 saturation ≥90%
- Oral systemic corticosteroids if no immediate response or if patient recently took oral systemic corticosteroid

FEV_1 or PEF <50% (Severe Exacerbation)
- Inhaled high-dose beta$_2$-agonist and anticholinergic by nebulization every 20 minutes or continuously for 1 hour
- Oxygen to achieve O_2 saturation ≥90%
- Oral systemic corticosteroid

Impending or Actual Respiratory Arrest
- Intubation and mechanical ventilation with 100% O_2
- Nebulized beta$_2$-agonist and anticholinergic
- Intravenous corticosteroid

Repeat Assessment
Symptoms, physical examination, PEF, O_2 saturation, other tests as needed

Admit to Hospital Intensive Care (see box)

Moderate Exacerbation
FEV_1 or PEF 50%-80% predicted/personal best
Physical exam: moderate symptoms
- Inhaled short-acting beta$_2$-agonist every 60 minutes
- Systemic corticosteroid or increased dose of inhaled corticosteroid
- Continue treatment 1-3 hours, provided there is improvement

Severe Exacerbation
FEV_1 or PEF <50% predicted/personal best
Physical exam: severe symptoms at rest, accessory muscle use, chest retraction
History: high-risk patient
No improvement after initial treatment
- Inhaled short-acting beta$_2$-agonist, hourly or continuous + inhaled anticholinergic
- Oxygen
- Systemic corticosteroid

Good Response
- FEV_1 or PEF ≥70%
- Response sustained 60 minutes after last treatment
- No distress
- Physical exam: normal

Incomplete Response
FEV_1 or PEF ≥50% but <70%
Mild-to-moderate symptoms

Poor Response
FEV_1 or PEF <50%
PCO_2 ≥42 mm Hg
Physical exam: symptoms severe, drowsiness, confusion

Individualized decision re: hospitalization (see text)

Discharge Home
- Continue treatment with inhaled beta$_2$-agonist
- Continue course of oral systemic corticosteroid
- Patient education
  - Review medicine use
  - Review/initiate action plan
  - Recommend close medical follow-up

Admit to Hospital Ward
- Inhaled beta$_2$-agonist + inhaled anticholinergic
- Systemic (oral or intravenous) corticosteroid
- Oxygen
- Monitor FEV_1 or PEF, O_2 saturation, pulse

Admit to Hospital Intensive Care
- Inhaled beta$_2$-agonist hourly or continuously + inhaled anticholinergic
- Intravenous corticosteroid
- Oxygen
- Possible intubation and mechanical ventilation

Improve

Discharge Home
- Continue treatment with inhaled beta$_2$-agonist
- Continue course of oral systemic corticosteroid
- Patient education
  - Review medicine use
  - Review/initiate action plan
  - Recommend close medical follow-up

ESTIMATED COMPARATIVE DAILY DOSAGES FOR INHALED CORTICOSTEROIDS

Adults

Drug	Low Dose	Medium Dose	High Dose
Beclomethasone dipropionate	168-504 mcg	504-840 mcg	>840 mcg
42 mcg/puff	4-12 puffs	12-20 puffs	>20 puffs
84 mcg/puff	2-6 puffs	6-10 puffs	>10 puffs
Beclomethasone dipropionate HFA	80-240 mcg	240-480 mcg	>480 mcg
40 mcg/puff	2-6 puffs	6-12 puffs	>12 puffs
80 mcg/puff	1-3 puffs	3-6 puffs	>6 puffs
Budesonide Turbuhaler®	200-600 mcg	600-1200 mcg	>1200 mcg
200 mcg/inhalation	1-3 inhalations	3-6 inhalations	>6 inhalations
Flunisolide	500-1000 mcg	1000-2000 mcg	>2000 mcg
250 mcg/puff	2-4 puffs	4-8 puffs	>8 puffs
Fluticasone MDI	88-264 mcg	264-660 mcg	>660 mcg
44, 110, 220 mcg/ puff			
Fluticasone DPI	100-300 mcg	300-600 mcg	>600 mcg
50, 100, 250 mcg/ dose			
Triamcinolone acetonide	400-1000 mcg	1000-2000 mcg	>2000 mcg
100 mcg/puff	4-10 puffs	10-20 puffs	>20 puffs

Children

Drug	Low Dose	Medium Dose	High Dose
Beclomethasone dipropionate	84-336 mcg	336-672 mcg	>672 mcg
42 mcg/puff	2-8 puffs	8-16 puffs	>16 puffs
84 mcg/puff	1-4 puffs	4-8 puffs	>8 puffs
Beclomethasone dipropionate HFA	80-160 mcg	160-320 mcg	>320 mcg
40 mcg/puff	2-4 puffs	4-8 puffs	>8 puffs
80 mcg/puff	1-2 puffs	2-4 puffs	>4 puffs
Budesonide Turbuhaler®	200-400 mcg	400-800 mcg	>800 mcg
200 mcg/inhalation	1-2 inhalations	2-4 inhalations	>4 inhalations
Budesonide inhalation suspension for nebulization	0.5 mg	1 mg	2 mg
Flunisolide	500-750 mcg	1000-1250 mcg	>1250 mcg
250 mcg/puff	2-3 puffs	4-5 puffs	>5 puffs
Fluticasone MDI	88-176 mcg	176-440 mcg	>440 mcg
44, 110, 220 mcg/ puff			
Fluticasone DPI	100-200 mcg	200-400 mcg	>400 mcg
50, 100, 250 mcg/ dose			
Triamcinolone acetonide	400-800 mcg	800-1200 mcg	>1200 mcg
100 mcg/puff	4-8 puffs	8-12 puffs	>12 puffs

Reference

National Asthma Education and Prevention Program (NAEPP), Clinical Practice Guidelines, Expert Panel Report 2, "Guidelines for the Diagnosis and Management of Asthma," NIH Publication No. 97-4051, July 1997.

National Asthma Education and Prevention Program (NAEPP) Expert Panel Report, "Guidelines for the Diagnosis and Management of Asthma – Update on Selected Topics 2002," NIH Publication No. 02-5075 (www.nhlbi.nih.gov/guidelines/asthma/index.html).

CONTRAST MEDIA REACTIONS, PREMEDICATION FOR PROPHYLAXIS

American College of Radiology Guidelines for Use of Nonionic Contrast Media

It is estimated that approximately 5% to 10% of patients will experience adverse reactions to administration of contrast dye (less for nonionic contrast). In approximately 1000-2000 administrations, a life-threatening reaction will occur.

A variety of premedication regimens have been proposed, both for pretreatment of "at risk" patients who require contrast media and before the routine administration of the intravenous high osmolar contrast media. Such regimens have been shown in clinical trials to decrease the frequency of all forms of contrast medium reactions. Pretreatment with a 2-dose regimen of methylprednisolone 32 mg, 12 and 2 hours prior to intravenous administration of HOCM (ionic), has been shown to decrease mild, moderate, and severe reactions in patients at increased risk and perhaps in patients without risk factors. Logistical and feasibility problems may preclude adequate premedication with this or any regimen for all patients. It is unclear at this time that steroid pretreatment prior to administration of ionic contrast media reduces the incidence of reactions to the same extent or less than that achieved with the use of nonionic contrast media alone. Information about the efficacy of nonionic contrast media combined with a premedication strategy, including steroids, is preliminary or not yet currently available. For high-risk patients (ie, previous contrast reactors), the combination of a pretreatment regimen with nonionic contrast media has empirical merit and may warrant consideration. Oral administration of steroids appears preferable to intravascular routes, and the drug may be prednisone or methylprednisolone. Supplemental administration of H_1 and H_2 antihistamine therapies, orally or intravenously, may reduce the frequency of urticaria, angioedema, and respiratory symptoms. Additionally, ephedrine administration has been suggested to decrease the frequency of contrast reactions, but caution is advised in patients with cardiac disease, hypertension, or hyperthyroidism. No premedication strategy should be a substitute for the ABC approach to preadministration preparedness listed above. Contrast reactions do occur despite any and all premedication prophylaxis. The incidence can be decreased, however, in some categories of "at risk" patients receiving high osmolar contrast media plus a medication regimen. For patients with previous contrast medium reactions, there is a slight chance that recurrence may be more severe or the same as the prior reaction, however, it is more likely that there will be no recurrence.

General Premedication Regimen

Methylprednisolone	32 mg orally 12 and 2 hours prior to procedure
Diphenhydramine	50 mg orally 1 hour prior to the procedure

Alternative Premedication Regimen

Prednisone	50 mg orally 13, 7, and 1 hour before the procedure
Diphenhydramine	50 mg orally 1 hour before the procedure
Ephedrine	25 mg orally 1 hour before the procedure (except when contraindicated)

Unlabeled Use (Nephroprotective)

N-acetylcysteine, P.O.	600 mg orally twice daily on the day before and the day of the scan in addition to hydration with 0.45% saline intravenously

Indications for Nonionic Contrast

- Previous reaction to contrast – premedicate[1]
- Known allergy to iodine or shellfish
- Asthma, especially if on medication
- Myocardial instability or CHF
- Risk for aspiration or severe nausea and vomiting
- Difficulty communicating or inability to give history
- Patients taking beta-blockers
- Small children at risk for electrolyte imbalance or extravasation
- Renal failure with diabetes, sickle cell disease, or myeloma
- At physician or patient request

[1]Life-threatening reactions (throat swelling, laryngeal edema, etc), consider omitting the intravenous contrast.

DEPRESSION

Criteria for Major Depressive Episode

A. Five (or more) of the following symptoms have been present during the same 2-week period and represent a change from previous functioning; at least one of the symptoms is either (1) depressed mood or (2) loss of interest or pleasure.

   1. Depressed mood most of the day, nearly every day

   2. Marked diminished interest or pleasure in all, or almost all, activities

   3. Significant weight loss (not dieting) or weight gain, or decrease or increase in appetite nearly every day

   4. Insomnia or hypersomnia nearly every day

   5. Psychomotor agitation or retardation nearly every day

   6. Fatigue or loss of energy nearly every day

   7. Feelings of worthlessness or excessive or inappropriate guilt (may be delusional) nearly every day

   8. Diminished ability to think or concentrate, or indecisiveness

   9. Recurrent thoughts of death, recurrent suicidal ideation without a specific plan, or a suicide attempt or a specific suicide plan

B. The symptoms cause clinically significant distress or impairment in social, occupational or other important areas of functioning.

C. The symptoms are not due to the direct physiologic effects of a substance or a general medical condition (eg, hypothyroidism).

Medications That May Precipitate Depression

Anticancer agents	Vinblastine, vincristine, interferon, procarbazine, asparaginase, tamoxifen, cyproterone
Anti-inflammatory & analgesic agents	Indomethacin, pentazocine, phenacetin, phenylbutazone
Antimicrobial agents	Cycloserine, ethambutol, sulfonamides, select gram-negative antibiotics
Cardiovascular/ antihypertensive agents	Clonidine, digitalis, diuretics, guanethidine, hydralazine, indapamide, methyldopa, prazosin, procainamide, propranolol, reserpine
CNS agents	Alcohol, amantadine, amphetamine & derivatives, barbiturates, benzodiazepines, chloral hydrate, carbamazepine, cocaine, haloperidol, L-dopa, phenothiazines, succinimide derivatives
Hormonal agents	ACTH, corticosteroids, estrogen, melatonin, oral contraceptives, progesterone
Miscellaneous	Cimetidine, disulfiram, organic pesticides, physostigmine

Medical Disorders & Psychiatric Disorders Associated With Depression

Endocrine diseases	Acromegaly, Addison's disease, Cushing's disease, diabetes mellitus, hyperparathyroidism, hypoparathyroidism, hyperthyroidism, hypothyroidism, insulinoma, pheochromocytoma, pituitary dysfunction
Deficiency states	Pernicious anemia, severe anemia, Wernicke's encephalopathy
Infections	Encephalitis, fungal infections, meningitis, neurosyphilis, influenza, mononucleosis, tuberculosis, AIDS
Collagen disorders	Rheumatoid arthritis
Systemic lupus erythematosus	
Metabolic disorders	Electrolyte imbalance, hypokalemia, hyponatremia, hepatic encephalopathy, Pick's disease, uremia, Wilson's disease
Cardiovascular disease	Cerebral arteriosclerosis, chronic bronchitis, congestive heart failure, emphysema, myocardial infarction, paroxysmal dysrhythmia, pneumonia
Neurologic disorders	Alzheimer's disease, amyotrophic lateral sclerosis, brain tumors, chronic pain syndrome, Creutzfeldt-Jakob disease, Huntington's disease, multiple sclerosis, myasthenia gravis, Parkinson's disease, poststroke, trauma (postconcussion)
Malignant disease	Breast, gastrointestinal, lung, pancreas, prostate
Psychiatric disorders	Alcoholism, anxiety disorders, eating disorders, schizophrenia

Somatic Treatments of Depression in the Patient With Medical Illness

Condition	First Choice	Second-Line Options	Alternatives
Thyroid Hypothyroid	Thyroid (T)	T_4 or T_3 + antidepressant (SSRIs , TCAs, new generation agents)	ECT, other antidepressants psychostimulants
Hyperthyroid	Antidepressant and antihyperthyroid medications	Select a different group of antidepressants	
Diabetes mellitus	SSRIs, other new generation antidepressants	TCAs (second amine or low-dose tertiary amino) MAOIs	ECT, buspirone, psychostimulants, thyroid supplements, mood stabilizers
Cardiovascular disorders	SSRIs, bupropion	ECT, psychostimulants B-blockers, buspirone	ECT, TCAs, MAOIs, mood stabilizers
Renal disease	Fluoxetine, sertraline	TCAs, other new generation antidepressants, psychostimulants	ECT, anticonvulsants, lithium (if dialysis or CLOSELY monitored)
Hepatic disease (reduced dose ALL)	Sertraline	Other new generation antidepressants, TCAs-secondary amines	TCAs-tertiary amines
HIV	Bupropion, SSRIs, psychostimulants	TCAs	ECT
Transplant	**Closely monitor.** See cardiovascular, renal, liver, pulmonary, new antidepressant agents, TCAs-secondary amines		
Neurologic	Newer generation antidepressants, TCAs-secondary amines	Selegiline, anticonvulsants	Bromocriptine
Malignancy	Newer generation antidepressants, TCAs-secondary amines psychostimulants	TCAs-tertiary amines of pain MAOIs	ECT
Respiratory	Activating antidepressants, buspirone		More sedating antidepressants, ECT
Gastrointestinal	TCAs-secondary amines, new generation antidepressants	TCAs-tertiary amines	ECT

DIABETES MELLITUS MANAGEMENT, ADULTS

OVERVIEW

Diabetes represents a significant health care problem in the United States and worldwide. Of the nearly 16 million Americans with diabetes, the majority (90% to 95%) have type 2 diabetes. Of this number, roughly one-third are undiagnosed. The incidence of type 2 diabetes is increasing around the world. There is strong evidence to support an interaction between a genetic predisposition and behavioral or environmental factors, such as obesity and physical inactivity, in the development of this disease. In individuals at high risk of developing type 2 diabetes, it has been shown that the development of diabetes may be prevented or delayed by changes in lifestyle or pharmacologic intervention.

Within the United States, type 1 diabetes is estimated to affect 5% to 10% of those with diabetes and therefore represents the minority of individuals with diabetes. In addition to type 1 and type 2 diabetes, approximately 4% of pregnancies are complicated by the development of gestational diabetes. Gestational diabetes mellitus is defined as the first onset or recognition of glucose intolerance during pregnancy. Women who have had gestational diabetes are at an increased risk for later development of type 2 diabetes. In addition to the causes noted above, diabetes may result from genetic syndromes, surgery (pancreatectomy), chemicals and/or drugs, recurrent pancreatitis, malnutrition, and viral infections.

COMPLICATIONS OF DIABETES

Complications due to diabetes comprise the seventh leading cause of death in the United States. The greatest number of these deaths are related to cardiovascular complications (myocardial infarction, CHF, and stroke), which have been estimated to result in more than 77,000 deaths annually.

In addition to cardiovascular effects, diabetes is the leading cause of new blindness in people 20-74 years of age, and diabetic nephropathy is the most common cause of end-stage renal disease. Mild to severe forms of diabetic neuropathy are common. Neuropathy and circulatory insufficiency combine to make diabetes the most frequent cause of nontraumatic lower-limb amputations. The rate of impotence in diabetic males over 50 years of age has been estimated to be as high as 50% to 60%. Control of hyperglycemia may significantly decrease the rate at which diabetic complications develop, and provides compelling justification for early diagnosis and management of this disorder.

DIAGNOSIS

Diabetes

Diagnosis of diabetes is made by any of the three criteria described below. In the absence of unequivocal hyperglycemia with acute metabolic decompensation, these criteria should be confirmed by repeat testing on a different day. The third method, (OGTT), is not recommended for routine clinical use. The use of Hb A_{1c} for diagnosis is not recommended. Screening should be considered in patients ≥45 years of age, especially those with a BMI ≥25 kg/m². Consider screening in patients <45 years of age if they are overweight or have other risk factors. Testing should be repeated every 3 years.

1. Symptoms of diabetes (polydipsia, polyuria, unexplained weight loss) plus casual plasma glucose concentration ≥200 mg/dL (11.1 mmol/L)
   Note: Casual plasma glucose is defined as any time of day without regard to time of last meal.

OR

2. Fasting plasma glucose (no caloric intake for at least 8 hours) ≥126 mg/dL (7 mmol/L)

OR

3. A 2-hour plasma glucose ≥200 mg/dL (11.1 mmol/L) during an oral glucose tolerance test (OGTT)

Prediabetes

Patients with impaired fasting glucose (IFG) or impaired glucose tolerance (IGT) are considered to be in an intermediate group whose glucose levels do not meet the criteria for diabetes, yet are higher than normal. Patients with IFG or IGT are considered to be at high risk for developing diabetes and are referred to as having "prediabetes."

Prediabetes Categories using Fasting Plasma Glucose (FPG) or the Oral Glucose Tolerance Test (OGTT)

	FPG	OGTT[1]
Normal	<100 mg/dL (5.6 mmol/L)	<140 mg/dL (<7.8 mmol/L)
Impaired	100-125 mg/dL (5.6-6.9 mmol/L) [IFG]	≥140 mg/dL (≥7.8 mmol/L) and <200 mg/dL (<11.1 mmol/L) [IGT]
Provisional diagnosis of diabetes		≥200 mg/dL (≥11.1 mmol/L); diagnosis must then be confirmed

[1]Value corresponds to a 2-hour postload glucose.

Gestational Diabetes Mellitus (GDM)

Assessment of risk should be undertaken at the first prenatal visit. Women with GDM should be screened for diabetes at 6-12 weeks postpartum.

Low risk: Women who fulfill **all** of the following criteria are considered at lower risk for the development of GDM and do not require routine screening.

- <25 years of age
- normal body weight
- no family history of diabetes (ie, first-degree relatives)
- no history of abnormal glucose metabolism
- no history of poor obstetric outcome
- not a member of an ethnic/racial group with a high prevalence of diabetes (Hispanic, Native American, Asian, African, Pacific Islander)

Average risk: Testing at 24-28 weeks gestation is recommended.

High risk: The following are characteristics considered to be high risk for GDM. Perform the initial screening (OGTT) as soon as feasible; repeat at 24-28 weeks gestation.

- marked obesity
- personal history of GDM
- glycosuria
- strong family history

DIABETES MELLITUS MANAGEMENT, ADULTS *(Continued)*

GOALS

The goals of diabetes treatment include normalization of hyperglycemia, avoidance of hypoglycemia, and slowing the development of diabetic complications. The following is a summary of recommendations for adults with diabetes.

2006 ADA Summary of Recommendations for Adults With Diabetes

Glycemic control	
Hb A_{1c}	<7%[1]
Preprandial capillary plasma glucose	90-130 mg/dL
Peak postprandial capillary plasma glucose[2]	<180 mg/dL
Blood pressure	<130/80 mm Hg
Lipids[3]	
LDL	<100 mg/dL
Triglycerides	<150 mg/dL
HDL[4]	>40 mg/dL

Key concepts in setting glycemic goals:

- Hb A_{1c} is the primary target for glycemic control.

- Goals should be individualized.

- Certain populations (children, pregnant women, and elderly) require special considerations.

- Less intensive glycemic goals may be indicated in patients with severe or frequent hypoglycemia.

- More stringent glycemic goals (ie, a normal Hb A_{1c}, <6%) may further reduce complications at the cost of increased risk of hypoglycemia (particularly in those with type 1 diabetes).

- Postprandial glucose may be targeted if Hb A_{1c} goals are not met despite reaching preprandial glucose goals.

[1]Referenced to a nondiabetic range of 4% to 6% using a DCCT-based assay. **Note:** The Hb A_{1c} goal for patients in general is <7%; the goal for the individual patient is an Hb A_{1c} as close to normal without significant hypoglycemia (<6%)

[2]Postprandial glucose measurements should be made 1-2 hours after the beginning of the meal, generally peak levels in patients with diabetes.

[3]Current NCEP/ATP III guidelines suggest that in patients with triglycerides ≥200 mg/dL, the "non-HDL cholesterol" (total cholesterol minus HDL) be used. The goal is ≤130 mg/dL.

[4]For women, it has been suggested that the HDL goal be increased by 10 mg/dL.

MANAGEMENT

Current American Diabetes Association (ADA) recommendations emphasize a multidisciplinary approach to the management of diabetes, with an emphasis on the participation of the patient and/or caregivers in the monitoring and management of the disease. Consultation with a diabetes educator and dietitian may help to prepare the patient to manage his/her disease and adjust to the necessary changes in diet and lifestyle. Patients must be educated about disease monitoring procedures, including blood glucose self-monitoring equipment and tests. Patients should be encouraged to wear or carry appropriate identification to inform health care providers of the disease in the event of an emergency. Issues related to possible complications (eg, foot care, eye care) should be addressed. It is extremely important to educate patients concerning the recognition and management of hypoglycemic symptoms. Weight management, which may include diet and exercise, should be considered in overweight and obese patients. Weight loss not only improves glycemic control, but decreases cardiovascular risk and can prevent development of type 2 diabetes. The management of diabetes is constantly adapting to new information, techniques, and technologies. For the most current information on diabetes diagnosis and management, visit the ADA website at http://diabetes.org.

Additional Management Issues

Recommendations by the ADA include glycemic control as well as the following:

1. Use an ACEI or ARB in diabetics with hypertension and micro- or macroalbuminuria to slow the progression of nephropathy, unless contraindicated.
2. Consider statin use in all diabetics, irrespective of lipoprotein levels.
3. Immunize against pneumococcal disease and influenza.
4. Daily ASA use 75-162 mg daily in all diabetics ≥21 years of age, unless contraindicated.
5. Patients should be advised not to smoke.

DRUG TREATMENT

Insulin

Insulin therapy is required in type 1 diabetes, and may be necessary in some individuals with type 2 diabetes. The general objective of insulin replacement therapy is to approximate the physiologic pattern of insulin secretion. This requires a basal level of insulin throughout the day, supplemented by additional insulin at mealtimes.

Multiple daily doses guided by blood glucose monitoring are the standard of diabetes care. Combinations of insulin are commonly used. The number and size of daily doses, time of administration, and diet and exercise require continuous medical supervision. In addition, specific formulations may require distinct administration procedures/timing (refer to individual monographs).

There is solid scientific documentation of the benefit of tight glucose control, either by insulin pump or multiple daily injections (4-6 times daily). However, the benefits must be balanced against the risk of hypoglycemia, the patient's ability to adhere to the regimen, and other issues regarding the complexity of management. Diabetic education and nutritional counseling are essential to maximize the effectiveness of therapy. In addition to the educational issues outlined above, patients should be instructed in administration techniques, timing of administration, and sick-day management.

The initial dose of insulin in type 1 diabetes is typically 0.2-0.6 units/kg/day in divided doses. Conservative initial doses of 0.2-0.4 units/kg/day are often recommended to avoid the potential for hypoglycemia. Generally, one-half to three-fourths of the daily insulin dose is given as an intermediate or long-acting form of insulin (in 1-2 daily injections). The remaining portion of the 24-hour insulin requirement is divided and administered as a rapid-acting or short-acting form of insulin. These may be given with meals (before or at the time of meals depending on the form of insulin) or at the same time as injections of intermediate forms (some premixed combinations are intended for this purpose).

Since combinations of agents are frequently used, dosage adjustment must address the individual component of the insulin regimen which most directly influences the blood glucose value in question, based on the known onset and duration of the insulin component (see table). The frequency of doses and monitoring must also be individualized in consideration of the patient's ability to manage therapy.

Types of Insulin	Onset (h)	Peak (h)	Duration (h)
Rapid-Acting			
Insulin lispro (Humalog®)	0.2-0.5	0.5-1.5	3-4
Insulin aspart (NovoLog®)	0.2-0.5	1-3	3-5
Insulin glulisine (Apidra™)	0.2-0.5	0.5-1.5	3-4
Short-Acting			
Insulin, regular (Humulin® R, Novolin® R)	0.5-1	2-4	6-8
Intermediate-Acting			
Insulin NPH (isophane suspension) (Humulin® N, Novolin® N)	1-2	6-12	18-24
Insulin zinc suspension (Lente®)	1-2.5	8-12	18-24
Intermediate- to Long-Acting			
Insulin detemir (Levemir®)	3-4	6-8	6-23
Long-Acting			
Insulin glargine (Lantus®)	3-4	*	24
Combinations			
Insulin aspart protamine suspension and insulin aspart (NovoLog® Mix 70/30)	0.2-0.5	1-4	18-24
Insulin lispro protamine and insulin lispro (Humalog® Mix 75/25™)	0.2-0.5	2-12	18-24
Insulin NPH suspension and insulin regular solution (Novolin® 70/30)	0.5	2-12	18-24

*Insulin glargine has no pronounced peak.

DIABETES MELLITUS MANAGEMENT, ADULTS *(Continued)*

Maintenance Dosing

Typical maintenance insulin doses are between 0.5 and 1.2 units/kg/day in divided doses. Adolescents may require ≤1.5 units/kg/day during growth spurts. Nonobese patients typically require 0.4-0.6 units/kg/day while obese patients may require 0.8-1.2 units/kg/day. In renally impaired patients, insulin requirements are reduced due to changes in insulin clearance or metabolism. Renally impaired patients may require <0.2 units/kg/day.

As stated above, the general objective of insulin replacement therapy is to approximate the physiologic pattern of insulin secretion. This requires a basal level of insulin throughout the day, supplemented by additional insulin at mealtimes. Combination regimens which exploit differences in the onset and duration of different insulin products are commonly used to approximate physiologic secretion. Frequently, split mixed or basal bolus regimens are used to approximate physiologic secretion.

Split-mixed regimens: In split-mixed regimens, an intermediate-acting insulin (such as NPH insulin) is administered once or twice daily and supplemented by short-acting (regular) or rapid-acting (lispro, aspart, or glulisine) insulin. Blood glucose measurements are completed several times daily. Dosages are adjusted emphasizing the individual component of the regimen which most directly influences the blood sugar in question (either the intermediate-acting component or the shorter-acting component). Fixed-ratio formulations (eg, 70/30 mix) may be used as twice daily injections in this scenario; however, the ability to titrate the dosage of an individual component is limited. An example of a "split-mixed" regimen is 21 units of NPH plus 9 units of regular in the morning and an evening meal dose consisting of 14 units of NPH plus 6 units of regular insulin.

Basal-bolus regimens: Basal-bolus regimens are designed to more closely mimic physiologic secretion. These employ a long-acting insulin (eg, glargine) to simulate basal insulin secretion. The basal component is frequently administered at bedtime or in the early morning. This is supplemented by multiple daily injections of very rapid-acting products (lispro or aspart) immediately prior to a meal, which provides insulin at the time when nutrients are absorbed. An example of basal-bolus regimen would be 30 units of glargine at bedtime and 12 units of lispro insulin prior to each meal.

Adjustment of Insulin Dose

Dosage must be titrated to achieve glucose control and avoid hypoglycemia. In general, dosage is adjusted to maintain premeal and bedtime glucose of 80-140 mg/dL (children <5 years: 100-200 mg/dL). Since combinations of agents are frequently used, dosage adjustment must address the individual component of the insulin regimen which most directly influences the blood glucose value in question, based on the known onset and duration of the insulin component. Individual insulin products have specific dosage recommendations.

Estimation of the effect per unit: A "Rule of 1500" has been frequently used as a means to estimate the change in blood sugar relative to each unit of insulin administered. In fact, the recommended values used in these calculations may vary from 1500-2200 (a value of at least 1800 is recommended for lispro). The higher values lead to more conservative estimates of the effect per unit of insulin, and therefore lead to more cautious adjustments. The effect per unit of insulin is approximated by dividing the selected numerical value (eg, 1500-2200) by the number of units/day received by the patient. This may be used as a crude approximation of the patient's insulin sensitivity as adjustments to individual components of the regimen are made. Each additional unit of insulin added to the corresponding insulin dose may be expected to lower the blood glucose by this amount.

To illustrate, in the "basal-bolus" regimen which includes 30 units of glargine at bedtime and 12 units of lispro insulin prior to each meal, the rule of 1800 would indicate an expected change of 27 mg/dL per unit of insulin (the total daily insulin dose is 66 units; using the formula: 1800/66 = 27). A patient may be instructed to add additional insulin if the preprandial glucose is >125 mg/dL. For a prelunch glucose of 195 mg/dL (70 mg/dL higher than goal), this would mean the patient would administer the scheduled 12 units of lispro along with an additional "correctional" 3 units (70 divided by the value of 27 derived from the formula) for a total of 15 units prior to the meal. If correctional doses are required on a consistent basis, an adjustment of the patient's diet and/or scheduled insulin dose may be necessary.

Insulin Therapy in Type 2 Diabetes Mellitus

Insulin may be used in type 2 diabetes as a means to augment response to oral hypoglycemic agents or it may be used as monotherapy in some patients. As augmentation, it may be administered when residual beta-cell function is present, as a supplemental agent when oral hypoglycemics have not achieved goal glucose control. Twice daily NPH, or an evening dose of NPH, lente, or glargine insulin may be added to oral therapy with metformin or a sulfonylurea. Augmentation to control postprandial glucose may be accomplished with regular, glulisine, aspart, or lispro insulin. Dosage must be carefully adjusted.

When used as monotherapy, the requirements for insulin are highly variable. An empirically defined scheme for dosage estimation based on fasting plasma glucose and degree of obesity has been published with recommended doses ranging from 6-77 units/day (Holman, 1995). In the setting of glucose toxicity (loss of beta-cell sensitivity to glucose concentrations), insulin therapy may be used for short-term management to restore sensitivity of beta-cells; in these cases, the dose may need to be rapidly reduced/withdrawn when sensitivity is re-established.

Oral Agents

A large number of drugs for oral administration have become available for diabetic management. Oral hypoglycemic agents include sulfonylureas, meglitinides, alpha-glucosidase inhibitors, biguanides, and thiazolidinediones (TZDs). The drug classes vary in terms of their magnitude of effect on glycemic control, mechanism of action, and adverse effect profiles. In many cases, the adverse effect profile may influence the selection of a particular drug. The risk of hypoglycemia is higher for drugs which prompt insulin secretion (particularly sulfonylureas or insulin secretagogues). Drug selection is based on patient-specific factors and anticipated tolerance of adverse effects.

At least two drugs have been withdrawn from the U.S. market due to toxicities. Phenformin was removed many years ago after a number of cases of fatal lactic acidosis were reported. Metformin (a drug similar to phenformin) carries some risk of this reaction, but it is lower than the risk associated with phenformin. Troglitazone, a prototype thiazolidinedione, was associated with hepatic failure and several deaths, and it was withdrawn shortly after introduction. Currently, marketed drugs from this class appear to have a lower risk of these reactions.

Combination therapy may be necessary to achieve glycemic goals. The risk of additive or additional adverse effects must be balanced with the desire to achieve goals of glycemic control as well as normalization of other metabolic parameters. In particular, weight gain and lipid disturbances may complicate drug treatment.

DIABETES MELLITUS MANAGEMENT, ADULTS *(Continued)*

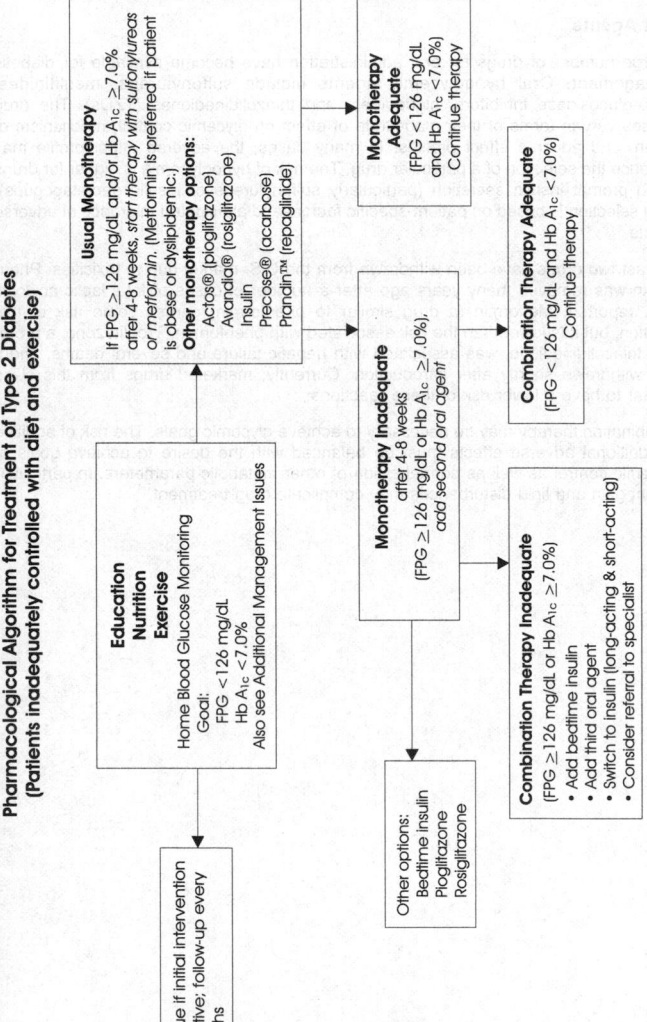

Pharmacological Algorithm for Treatment of Type 2 Diabetes
(Patients inadequately controlled with diet and exercise)

Modified from DeFronzo RA, "Pharmacological Treatment for Type 2 Diabetes Mellitus," *Ann Intern Med*, 2000, 133(1):73-4.

Oral Antidiabetic Agents for Type 2 Diabetes

Generic Name (Brand Name)	Effect on Hb A_{1c} as Monotherapy	Key Adverse Effects
Alpha-Glucosidase Inhibitors		
Acarbose (Precose®)	-0.44 to -1.0	GI distress, bloating, flatulence
Miglitol (Glyset®)	-0.26 to -0.81	
Biguanide		
Metformin (Fortamet™; Glucophage® XR; Glucophage®; Riomet™)	-0.4 to -1.4	GI distress, lactic acidosis (rare)
Meglitinide Derivatives		
Nateglinide (Starlix®)	-0.3 to -0.5	Hypoglycemia
Repaglinide (Prandin®)	-0.6	
Sulfonylurea, 1st Generation		
Acetohexamide	-0.8 to -2.0	Dizziness, headache, GI distress, SIADH
Chlorpropramide (Diabinese®)		
Tolazamide		
Tolbutamide		
Sulfonylurea, 2nd Generation		
Glimepiride (Amaryl®)	-0.8 to -2.0	Dizziness, headache, GI distress, SIADH
Glipizide® (Glucotrol® XL, Glucotrol®)		
Glyburide (Diaβeta®, Glynase® PresTab®, Micronase®)		
Thiazolidinediones		
Pioglitazone (Actos®)	0.0 to -1.9	Hepatic dysfunction, hepatic failure, weight gain, edema, CHF, lipid changes
Rosiglitazone (Avandia®)	0.0 to -0.7	

Injectable Agents (Noninsulin)

In addition to insulin and oral agents, two injectable products are available for the management of diabetes. Exanatide (Byetta™) is FDA approved for the treatment of type 2 diabetes in patients previously treated with a sulfonylurea, metformin, or a combination of these agents but still do not have adequate glycemic control. Exanatide increases insulin secretion, increases B-cell growth/replication, slows gastric emptying, and may decrease food intake.

Pramlintide (Symlin®) is FDA approved for the treatment of type 1 and type 2 diabetes. In type 1 diabetes, it is approved for use in patients who have failed to achieve glucose control despite optimal insulin therapy. When used for type 2 diabetes, pramlintide is approved for use in patients who have failed to achieve desired glucose control despite optimal insulin therapy, with or without concurrent sulfonylurea and/or metformin. Pramlintide is a synthetic analog of human amylin cosecreted with insulin by pancreatic beta cells. It reduces postprandial glucose increases by prolonging gastric emptying time, reducing postprandial glucagon secretion, and reducing caloric intake through centrally-mediated appetite suppression. It should be noted that the concentration of this product is in mcg/mL; patients and healthcare providers should exercise caution when administering this product to avoid inadvertent calculation of the dose based on "units," which could result in a sixfold overdose.

References

American Diabetes Association, "Clinical Practice Recommendations 2006," *Diabetes Care*, 2006, 29(Suppl 1):S3-42.

Colhoun HM, Betteridge DJ, Durrington PN, et al, "Primary Prevention of Cardiovascular Disease With Atorvastatin in Type 2 Diabetes in the Collaborative Atorvastatin Diabetes Study (CARDS): Multicentre Randomised Placebo-Controlled Trial," *Lancet*, 2004, 364(9435):685-96.

Dailey G, "New Strategies for Basal Insulin Treatment in Type 2 Diabetes Mellitus," *Clin Ther*, 2004, 26(6):889-901.

DeFronzo RA, "Pharmacologic Therapy for Type 2 Diabetes Mellitus," *Ann Intern Med*, 2000; 133(1):73-4

Heart Protection Study Collaborative Group, "MRC/BHF Heart Protection Study of Cholesterol Lowering With Simvastatin in 20,536 High-Risk Individuals: A Randomised Placebo-Controlled Trial," *Lancet*, 2002, 360(9326):7-22.

Holman RR and Turner RC, "Insulin Therapy in Type II Diabetes," *Diabetes Res Clin Pract*, 1995, (28 Suppl):S179-84.

Joint Commission on Accreditation of Healthcare Organizations, "2005 National Patient Safety Goals," available at http://www.jcaho.org/accredited+organizations/patient+safety/05_npsg_guidelines.

Kitabchi AE, Umpierrez GE, Murphy MB, et al, "Hyperglycemic Crises in Diabetes," *Diabetes Care*, 2004, 27(Suppl 1):S94-102.

Oiknine R, Bernbaum M, and Mooradian AD, "A Critical Appraisal of the Role of Insulin Analogues in the Management of Diabetes Mellitus," *Drugs*, 2005, 65(3):325-40.

Silverstein J, Klingensmith G, Copeland K, et al, "Care of Children and Adolescents With Type 1 Diabetes: A Statement of the American Diabetes Association," *Diabetes Care*, 2005, 28(1):186-212.

The Diabetes Control and Complications Trial Research Group, "The Effect of Intensive Treatment of Diabetes on the Development and Progression of Long-Term Complications in Insulin-dependent Diabetes Mellitus," *N Engl J Med*, 1993, 329(14):977-86.

The Expert Committee on the Diagnosis and Classification of Diabetes Mellitus, "Report of the Expert Committee on the Diagnosis and Classification of Diabetes Mellitus," *Diabetes Care*, 2002, 25 (Suppl 1).

Tuomilehto J, Lindstrom J, Eriksson JG, et al, "Prevention of Type 2 Diabetes Mellitus by Changes in Lifestyle Among Subjects With Impaired Glucose Tolerance," *N Engl J Med*, 2001, 344(18):1343-50.

UK Prospective Diabetes Study Group, " Intensive Blood Glucose Control With Sulphonylureas or Insulin Compared With Conventional Treatment and Risk of Complications in Patients With Type 2 Diabetes (UKPDS 33)," *Lancet*, 1998, 352(9131):837-53.

EPILEPSY

CONVULSIVE STATUS EPILEPTICUS

Recommendations of the Epilepsy Foundation of America's Working Group on Status Epilepticus
(*JAMA*, 1993, 270:854-9)

Convulsive status epilepticus is an emergency that is associated with high morbidity and mortality. The outcome largely depends on etiology, but prompt and appropriate pharmacological therapy can reduce morbidity and mortality. Etiology varies in children and adults and reflects the distribution of disease in these age groups. Antiepileptic drug administration should be initiated whenever a seizure has lasted 10 minutes. Immediate concerns include supporting respiration, maintaining blood pressure, gaining intravenous access, and identifying and treating the underlying cause. Initial therapeutic and diagnostic measures are conducted simultaneously. The goal of therapy is rapid termination of clinical and electrical seizure activity; the longer a seizure continues, the greater the likelihood of an adverse outcome. Several drug protocols now in use will terminate status epilepticus. Common to all patients is the need for a clear plan, prompt administration of appropriate drugs in adequate doses, and attention to the possibility of apnea, hypoventilation, or other metabolic abnormalities.

Figure 1. Algorithm for the Initial Management of Status Epilepticus

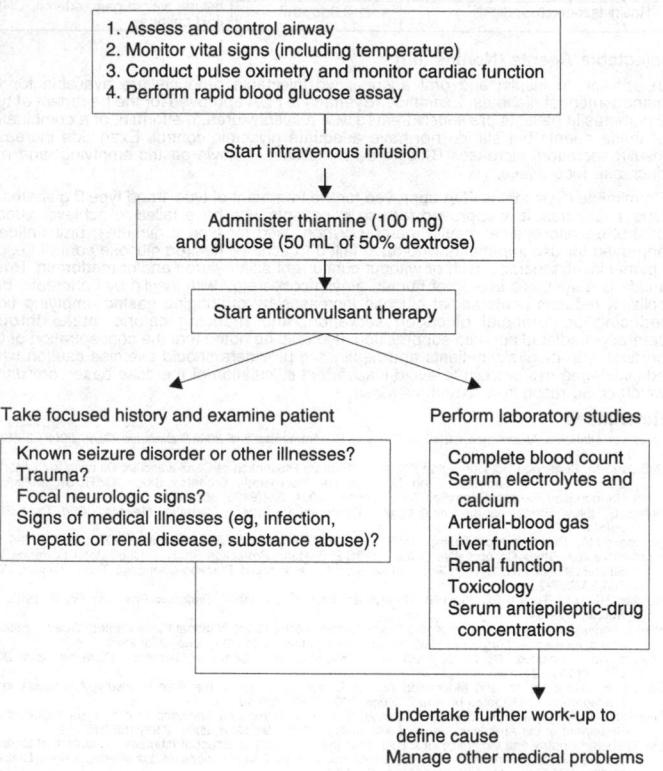

1. Assess and control airway
2. Monitor vital signs (including temperature)
3. Conduct pulse oximetry and monitor cardiac function
4. Perform rapid blood glucose assay

Start intravenous infusion

Administer thiamine (100 mg)
and glucose (50 mL of 50% dextrose)

Start anticonvulsant therapy

Take focused history and examine patient

Known seizure disorder or other illnesses?
Trauma?
Focal neurologic signs?
Signs of medical illnesses (eg, infection, hepatic or renal disease, substance abuse)?

Perform laboratory studies

Complete blood count
Serum electrolytes and calcium
Arterial-blood gas
Liver function
Renal function
Toxicology
Serum antiepileptic-drug concentrations

Undertake further work-up to define cause
Manage other medical problems

Adapted from Lowenstein A, "Current Concepts: Status Epilepticus," *N Engl J Med*, 1998, 338:970-6 with permission.

Figure 2. Antiepileptic Drug Therapy for Status Epilepticus

I.V. denotes intravenous and PE denotes phenytoin equivalents. The horizontal bars indicate the approximate duration of drug infusions.

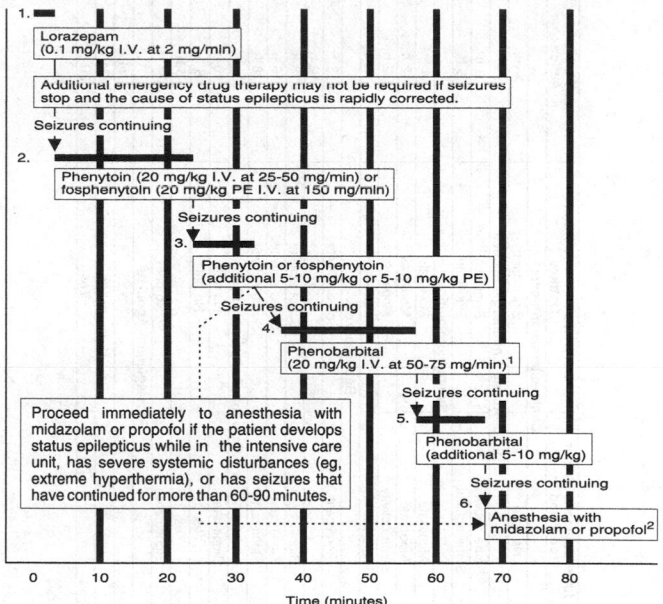

[1]Or pentobarbital (10-20 mg/kg over 1-2 hours).
[2]Or valproate sodium (15-25 mg/kg administered at 3 mg/kg/minute).

Adapted from Lowenstein A, "Current Concepts: Status Epilepticus," *N Engl J Med*, 1998, 338:970-6 with permission.

GLAUCOMA DRUG THERAPY

Ophthalmic Agent (Brand)	Reduces Aqueous Humor Production	Increases Aqueous Humor Outflow[1]	Average Duration of Action	Strengths Available
Cholinesterase Inhibitor[1]				
Echothiophate (Phospholine Iodide®)	No data	Significant	2 wk	0.125%
Direct-Acting Cholinergic Miotics				
Carbachol	Some activity	Significant	8 h	0.75% to 3%
Pilocarpine (various)	Some activity	Significant	5 h	0.5%, 1%, 2%, 3%, 4%
Sympathomimetics				
Apraclonidine (Iopidine®)	Moderate	Moderate	4 h	0.5%, 1%
Brimonidine (Alphagan®, Alphagan® P)	Moderate	Moderate	12 h	0.1%, 0.15%
Dipivefrin (Propine®)	Some activity	Moderate	12 h	0.1%
Epinephrine	Some activity	Moderate	18 h	0.25% to 2%
Beta-Blockers				
Betaxolol (Betoptic® S)	Significant	Some activity	12 h	0.5%
Carteolol	Yes	No	12 h	1%
Levobunolol (Betagan®)	Significant	Some activity	18 h	0.5%
Metipranolol (OptiPranolol®)	Significant	Some activity	18 h	0.3%
Timolol (Betimol®, Timoptic®)	Significant	Some activity	18 h	0.25%, 0.5%
Carbonic Anhydrase Inhibitors				
Acetazolamide (Diamox®)	Significant	No data	10 h	125 mg, 250 mg tab; 500 mg cap
Brinzolamide (Azopt®)	Yes	No data	8 h	1%
Dorzolamide (Trusopt®)	Yes	No	8 h	2%
Methazolamide	Significant	No data	14 h	25 mg, 50 mg
Prostaglandin Agonists				
Bimatoprost (Lumigan®)		Yes	≥24 h	0.03%
Latanoprost (Xalatan®)		Yes	≥24 h	0.005%
Travoprost (Travatan®)		Yes	20 h	0.004%

[1] All miotic drugs significantly affect accommodation.

HEART FAILURE (SYSTOLIC)

INTRODUCTORY COMMENTS

This chapter summarizes the pharmacotherapy of patients with systolic heart failure with respect to treating mild-moderate exacerbations and chronic therapy. A more detailed discussion is available at: www.acc.org/clinical/guidelines/failure;index.pdf.

It should be recognized that the most common cause for exacerbations of patents' heart failure is poor adherence to therapy (medications and diet restriction). Healthcare providers need to educate patients about the importance of adherence to medical regimens.

For many years, therapy of heart failure focused on correcting the hemodynamic imbalances that occurred in heart failure. It is now recognized that heart failure triggers the release of several neurohormones that, in the short-run, help the patient; but, in the long-run, are detrimental. Newer pharmacotherapeutic approaches address counteracting the actions of these harmful neurohormones as well as address hemodynamic issues.

Diuretics

Although data have yet to demonstrate that diuretics reduce the mortality associated with heart failure, they relieve symptoms seen in heart failure. Diuretics should only be used in patients experiencing congestion with their heart failure. Although not usually the case, some patients do have heart failure without any congestion. In such rare instances, diuretic therapy is not indicated since they further stimulate the deleterious neurohormonal responses seen.

Although some heart failure patients with congestion can be controlled with thiazide diuretics, most will require the more potent loop diuretics, either because a strong diuretic effect is needed or the renal function of the patients is compromised (thus limiting the effectiveness of the thiazide diuretic). When patients with heart failure are discovered to have mild-moderate worsening congestion, they often can be controlled by adjusting their oral loop diuretic dose or, if applicable, initiating a loop diuretic regimen. If a more aggressive diuresis is indicated, especially if the patient is suffering from pulmonary congestion, intravenous loop diuretics would be indicated. When loop diuretics are given intravenously, before any diuretic effect occurs, they benefit the patient by dilating veins and reducing preload, thus relieving pulmonary congestion. Intravenous loop diuresis may also be considered in a patient where concerns exist about the ability of the patient to absorb the orally administered medication.

If already on an oral loop diuretic, the dosage should be increased (generally, 1.5-2 times their current regimen) in an effort for the patient to lose about 1-1.5 liters of fluid per day (about equivalent to 1-1.5 kg of weight per day). If the patient had yet to be started on a diuretic or was previously receiving a thiazide diuretic, initiating furosemide at 20-40 mg once or twice daily is a reasonable consideration. If the initial increase (or initiation) in dosage fails to induce a diuretic response, the dosage may be increased. If the initial increase (or initiation) does induce a diuretic response but the patient fails to lose weight or is not losing more fluids than taking in, the frequency of giving the loop diuretic can be increased. When an effective regimen is achieved, this regimen should be continued until the patient achieves a goal "dry" weight. Once this weight is attained, a decision needs to be made on how to continue the patient on diuretic therapy. If the patient had not been on a diuretic at home, continuation of the loop diuretic at a reduced dose is a worthy consideration. If the exacerbation was related to noncompliance with the diuretic or diet, the previous home dose might be continued with education on compliance. If the exacerbation was caused by an inadequate pharmacotherapeutic regimen (such as vasodilator was not being use), the previous home dose might be continued in conjunction with a more complete pharmacotherapeutic regimen. If the patient was compliant and on an acceptable pharmacotherapeutic regimen, the patient's original diuretic dose would be increased to some dosage greater than their home regimen, yet generally less than what was just used to achieve their dry weight.

The use of loop diuretics can lead to hypokalemia and/or hypomagnesemia. Electrolyte disturbances can predispose a patient to serious cardiac arrhythmias particularly if the patient is concurrently receiving digoxin. Fluid depletion, hypotension, and azotemia can also result from excessive use of diuretics. In contrast to thiazide diuretics, a loop diuretic can also lower serum calcium concentrations. For some patients, despite higher doses of loop diuretic treatment, an adequate diuretic response cannot be attained. Diuretic resistance can usually be overcome by intravenous administration (including continuous infusion), the use of 2 diuretics together (eg, furosemide and metolazone), or the use of a diuretic with a positive inotropic agent. When such combinations are used, serum electrolytes need to be monitored even more closely.

When loop diuretics are used in patients with renal dysfunction, to achieve the desired diuretic response, dosages typically will need to be greater than what is used in patients with normal renal function.

HEART FAILURE (SYSTOLIC) *(Continued)*

Due to its long existence and inexpensive price, furosemide tends to be the loop diuretic most commonly used. Bumetanide is now available as a generic and its use has been increasing consequently. The oral bioavailability of bumetanide and torsemide are nearly 100%; whereas, furosemide's oral bioavailability averages about 50%. A useful rule of thumb for conversion of intravenous loop diuretics is 40 mg of furosemide is equal to 1 mg bumetanide is equal to 15 mg torsemide. A few patients have allergies to diuretics because many contain a sulfur element. The only loop diuretic that lacks a sulfur element is ethacrynic acid.

Vasodilators

Vasodilator therapy, specifically the combination of hydralazine and isosorbide dinitrate, was the first pharmacotherapeutic treatment demonstrated to enhance survival of heart failure patients. The use of hydralazine 75 mg (which reduces afterload) and isosorbide dinitrate 40 mg four times a day (which reduces preload) demonstrated enhanced survival compared to placebo and prazosin. Unfortunately, many patients were unable to tolerate this regimen (primarily due to headaches and gastrointestinal disturbances) and the magnitude of benefit in survival dissipated with time.

Later, a series of investigations demonstrated that enalapril (which reduces both after-load and preload) enhances the survival of heart failure patients. Dosages used in these trials averaged about 10 mg twice daily. Since these trials, other ACE inhibitors were proven to benefit heart failure patients.

ACE Inhibitors

This led to the question, which is superior, ACE inhibitor or the combination of hydralazine and isosorbide dinitrate? In a comparative trial, using doses described above, enalapril was superior to the combination of hydralazine and isosorbide dinitrate, making an ACE inhibitor the vasodilator of choice in heart failure patients. An ACE inhibitor can alleviate symptoms, improve clinical status, and enhance a patient's quality of life. In addition an ACE inhibitor can reduce the risk of death and the combined risk of death or hospitalization.

Adverse effects associated with ACE inhibitors include hyperkalemia, rash, dysgeusia, dry cough, and (rarely) angioedema. Patients sometime develop renal dysfunction with the initiation of ACE inhibitors. This is not due to direct nephrotoxicity of the kidney but related to the ACE inhibitor dilating the efferent renal artery of the kidney, thus shunting blood away from being filtered in the glomerulus. The risk for renal dysfunction is increased when the ACE inhibitor is introduced to a patient who is hypovolemic, is being aggressively diuresed, is on an NSAID, or has bilateral renal artery stenosis (unilateral if only one kidney is present). Avoid NSAIDs in heart failure patients. ACE inhibitors should be avoided in patients with known renal artery stenosis. Monitor renal function and serum potassium within 1 to 2 weeks of initiation of therapy and routinely thereafter especially in patients with pre-existing hypotension, hyponatremia, diabetes, azotemia, or in those taking potassium supplements. Some patients will have an exaggerated hypotensive response following the initial doses (especially the first dose) of an ACE inhibitor.

A major limitation to using ACE inhibitors treatment in heart failure can be the dry cough that some patients develop. Lowering the ACE inhibitor dose sometimes can control it, but this may limit the effectiveness of the ACE inhibitor treatment. The development of angiotensin receptor blockers (ARBs) has helped address this issue. ARBs were demonstrated to enhance survival of heart failure patients. Although they are not the vasodilator of first choice in heart failure, they are a reasonable alternative in patients who cannot tolerate an ACE inhibitor due to the cough or some other adverse effect (with the exception of hyperkalemia and renal dysfunction; ARBs can induce as well). ARBs do not cause an accumulation of kinins as ACE inhibitors do.

Can ARBs can be used in patients who suffer angioedema with ACE inhibitors. Reports are available in the literature describing patients who experienced angioedema with both ACE inhibitors and ARBs. These cases do not indicate how safe an ARB is in a patient who has experienced ACE inhibitor-induced angioedema. The CHARM-Alternative trial confirmed that only one of 39 patients (~2.6%) who experienced angioedema with an ACE inhibitors also experienced it with an ARB.

Concurrent Use of an ACE Inhibitor and an ARB

In Val-HeFT, valsartan added to conventional treatment (included ACE inhibitor treatment) did not impact survival but did reduce morbidity. Of note, a subgroup analysis of this trial suggested the combination of valsartan and an ACE inhibitor may be detrimental to patients also receiving a beta-blocker. In CHARM-Added, candesartan added to ACE inhibitor therapy was of benefit to heart failure patients (modest reduction in hospitalization; increased risk of hyperkalemia and renal dysfunction), even for those receiving a beta-blocker. As a result, the recently released ACC/AHA Practice Guidelines do not speak against using the combination of ACE inhibitors and ARBs. However, few patients in these trials were receiving an aldosterone blocker (such as spironolactone), which is now known to be of benefit to heart failure patients. Since there is enhanced risk for hyperkalemia and outcome data are currently unknown, the ACC/AHA

Practice Guidelines for heart failure do not advocate the combined use of ACE inhibitors, ARBs, and an aldosterone inhibitor.

In summary, vasodilator therapy should initially consist of an ACE inhibitor. If such therapy cannot be tolerated due to renal failure or hyperkalemia, the combination of hydralazine and isosorbide dinitrate may be considered as ARBs can also cause renal failure and hyperkalemia. If the ACE inhibitor cannot be tolerated due to adverse effects such as dry cough, an ARB may be considered. If an ACE inhibitor and beta blocker have been maximized yet heart failure symptoms persist, consider adding hydralazine and isosorbide dinitrate. This approach, in fact, has been demonstrated to enhance the survival of African-American patients with heart failure. Another approach may be to add an ARB to the ACE inhibitor; but caution should occur, due to the risk of hyperkalemia.

Beta-Blockers

Despite being negative inotropes, beta-blockers have been demonstrated to enhance the survival of systolic heart failure patients. Their benefit is attributed to their ability to protect the myocardium from the "bombardment" of catecholamines present in heart failure that can lead to ventricular remodeling. Bisoprolol, metoprolol succinate (extended release), and carvedilol have been demonstrated in trials to improve survival. At present, superiority of one agent over another has not been definitively demonstrated. For patients to be able to tolerate this therapy, beta-blocker treatment needs to be initiated at low doses and titrated slowly (generally, the dose is double every two weeks). Following the initiation of treatment and the increase in dosage, patients may feel that their disease is worsening but this should dissipate after a few days. If this ill feeling continues beyond a few days, consideration should be given to regimen adjustments. If the patient is congested, increase the diuretic dosage. If the patient's discomfort is related to hypotension, staggering the beta-blocker dose with the vasodilator dose and/or lowering the vasodilator dosage may be helpful. If these approaches are ineffective or cannot explain the patient's ill feeling, consideration should be given to lowering the beta-blocker dosage and attempt a titration later on. Sometimes, a patient may not be able to tolerate "goal" doses of both beta-blockers and concurrent vasodilator treatment due to hypotension. It is the consensus opinion that a reduced dose of each agent is better than a goal dose of just one agent. Beta-blockers are not necessarily contraindicated but need to be used cautiously in patients with bronchospastic disease, peripheral artery disease, or diabetes mellitus.

Aldosterone Blockers

Of the pharmacotherapeutic treatments of heart failure demonstrated to benefit patients, the use of aldosterone blockers is the newest. It has been demonstrated, especially in the more severe forms of heart failure, that spironolactone, at an average dose of 25 mg daily, enhances the survival of heart failure patients. In patients who suffer hyperkalemia at this relatively low dosage, lowering the dose to 25 mg every other day may be attempted. In patients who are still symptomatic with their heart failure and have maximized the other proven treatments of heart failure and whose potassium concentrations can tolerate it, the spironolactone dose may be increased to 50 mg daily.

Obviously, hyperkalemia is a concern with this treatment, especially since patients generally will also be on an ACE inhibitor or ARB. It has been demonstrated that the number of emergency visits related to hyperkalemia in heart failure has increased with the introduction of aldosterone blocking therapy in treating heart failure. About 10% of patients will experience endocrinological effects with spironolactone. In men, breast tenderness and gynecomastic can occur. In women, menstrual irregularities may occur. In such instances, the use of eplerenone may be considered. Eplerenone is less apt to induce endocrinological effects but it is more expensive. A typical dose is 25-50 mg daily. Eplerenone has been demonstrated to enhance survival of post-MI patients with reduced ejection fractions. Spironolactone has not been studied in this patient group.

These medications should not be started in patients with renal insufficiency. These medications should be avoided if the serum creatinine exceeds 2.5 mg/dL in men (2 mg/dL in women) or if baseline potassium $\geq$5 mEq/L.

Digoxin

The value of digoxin in heart failure has crossed the spectrum. In the late 1980s further investigation with digoxin suggested that indeed it may have a role in heart failure treatment, but the methods of these trials were not ideal (digoxin was taken away from stabilized patients to see if the condition of patients worsened – it did). Finally, digoxin was studied in a prospective manner where patients were on known optimal heart failure treatment at the time and randomized to placebo or digoxin. The digoxin dosage used resulted in digoxin steady-state concentrations of 1 mcg/L. This trial revealed that digoxin did not impact survival but reduced the number of patient hospitalizations, suggesting digoxin has a morbidity benefit. Many are of the opinion that digoxin's benefit is unrelated to its positive inotropic activity but related to inhibiting neurohormal activity. Healthcare providers may consider adding digoxin in patients with persistent heart failure symptoms as a fourth line agent.

HEART FAILURE (SYSTOLIC) *(Continued)*

Digoxin is primarily renally eliminated; therefore, renal function of patients should be closely monitored and the dose adjusted. Digoxin does become difficult to use in patients whose renal function is unstable. In the DIG trial, effective digoxin steady-state concentrations were around 0.7-1 mcg/L. Levels much beyond 1 mcg/L were associated with worsened outcomes, especially in women. Since digoxin's benefit is long-term, a loading dose is not necessary. When checking a digoxin serum concentration, the sample should not be obtained until 12 hours after a dose, especially if it was oral, since digoxin has a relatively long distribution phase. It should also be assured that the patient is at steady-state (recall that the half-life of digoxin in a patient with normal renal function is 36 hours and that patients with heart failure generally have worsened renal function).

Hypokalemia, hypomagnesia, and hypercalcemia can precipitate digoxin toxicity in the presence of a therapeutic digoxin concentration. This toxicity can be alleviated by correcting the electrolyte abnormality. In acute digoxin overdoses, hyperkalemia can occur since digoxin inhibits the sodium-potassium ATPase pump. For this reason, one should not assume potassium is given to just **any** patient with digoxin toxicity. Digoxin toxicity can present as bradyarrhythmias, heart blocks, ventricular tachyarrhythmias, and atrial tachyarrhythmias (PAT with block is pathognomic). Other toxic manifestations include visual disturbances (including greenish-yellowish vision and halos around lights), gastrointestinal disturbances, anorexia, and altered mental status. Many medications elevate digoxin concentrations and a patient's regimen should be assessed for potential interactions.

Other Heart Failure Therapeutic Considerations

- If a calcium channel blocker is desired, amlodipine and felodipine are preferred choices.

- To treat arrhythmias, amiodarone and dofetilide are best documented to lack much proarrhythmic propensity in heart failure patients.

- In heart failure patients with diabetes mellitus, metformin should not be used and "glitazones" should not be used in severe heart failure (NYHA III and IV) and used cautiously, if at all, in mild-moderate heart failure.

- The use of cilostazol, because it has type III phosphodiesterase-inhibiting properties, is contraindicated in heart failure. This is because the chronic use of oral milrinone and inamrinone, also type III phosphodiesterase inhibitors, resulted in enhanced mortality in heart failure patients (and therefore, these two agents were never FDA-approved for oral use).

- NSAID use should be avoided or used minimally as these agents antagonize the effects of diuretics and ACE inhibitors.

- Retrospective data suggests that daily aspirin may also negate the effects of ACE inhibitors but this has yet to be definitively proven in prospective trials. Using the lowest possible aspirin dose with the highest possible ACE inhibitor dose has been suggested as a way to best circumvent this issue.

- Routine intermittent infusions of positive inotropes are not recommended. Can be used as palliation in end-stage disease.

Dosing of ACE Inhibitors in Heart Failure[1]

ACEI	Initial Dose	Maximum Dose
Captopril	6.25 mg tid	50 mg tid
Enalapril	2.5 mg bid	10-20 mg bid
Fosinopril	5-10 mg daily	40 mg daily
Lisinopril	2.5-5 mg daily	20-40 mg daily
Perindopril	2 mg daily	8-16 mg daily
Quinapril	5 mg bid	20 mg bid
Ramipril	1.25-2.5 mg daily	10 mg daily
Trandolapril	1 mg daily	4 mg daily

[1]From ACC/AHA Guidelines.

Dosing of ARBs in Heart Failure[1]

ARB	Initial Dose	Maximum Dose
Candesartan	4-8 mg daily	32 mg daily
Losartan	25-50 mg daily	50-100 mg daily
Valsartan	20-40 mg bid	160 mg bid

[1]From ACC/AHA Guidelines.

Initial and Target Doses for Beta-Blocker Therapy in Heart Failure[1]

Beta-Blocker	Starting Dose	Target Dose	Comment
Bisoprolol	1.25 mg daily	10 mg daily	β_1-Selective blocker Inconvenient dosage forms for initial dose titration
Carvedilol	3.125 mg bid	25 mg bid (≤85 kg) 50 mg bid >85 kg)	β-Nonselective blocker α-Blocking properties
Metoprolol succinate, extended release	12.5-25 mg daily	200 mg daily	β_1-Selective blocker

[1]From ACC/AHA Guidelines.

References

Brater DC, "Diuretic Therapy," N Engl J Med, 1998, 339(6):387-95.

Granger CB, McMurray JJ, Yusuf S, et al, "Effects of Candesartan in Patients With Chronic Heart Failure and Reduced Left-Ventricular Systolic Function Intolerant to Angiotensin-Converting-Enzyme Inhibitors: The CHARM-Alternative Trial," Lancet, 2003, 362(9386):772-6.

Hunt SA, Abraham WT, Chin MH, et al, "ACC/AHA 2005 Guideline Update for the Diagnosis and Management of Chronic Heart Failure in the Adult. A Report of the American College of Cardiology/American Heart Association Task Force on Practice Guidelines (Writing Committee to Update the 2001 Guidelines for the Evaluation and Management of Heart Failure), J Am Coll Cardiol, 2005, 46(6):1116-43. Available online at www.acc.org.

McMurray JJ, Ostergren J, Swedberg K, et al, "Effects of Candesartan in Patients With Chronic Heart Failure and Reduced Left-Ventricular Systolic Function Taking Angiotensin-Converting-Enzyme Inhibitors: The CHARM-Added Trial," Lancet, 2003, 362(9386):767-71.

Taylor AL, Ziesche S, Yancy C, et al, "Combination of Isosorbide Dinitrate and Hydralazine in Blacks With Heart Failure," N Engl J Med, 2004, 351(20):2049-57.

HELICOBACTER PYLORI TREATMENT

Multiple Drug Regimens for the Treatment of *H. pylori* Infection

Drug	Dosages	Duration of Therapy
H₂-receptor antagonist[1] *plus*	Any one given at appropriate dose	4 weeks
Bismuth subsalicylate *plus*	525 mg 4 times/day	2 weeks
Metronidazole *plus*	250 mg 4 times/day	2 weeks
Tetracycline	500 mg 4 times/day	2 weeks
Proton pump inhibitor[1] *plus*	Esomeprazole 40 mg once daily	10 days
Clarithromycin *plus*	500 mg twice daily	10 days
Amoxicillin	1000 mg twice daily	10 days
Proton pump inhibitor[1] *plus*	Lansoprazole 30 mg twice daily or Omeprazole 20 mg twice daily	10-14 days
Clarithromycin *plus*	500 mg twice daily	10-14 days
Amoxicillin	1000 mg twice daily	10-14 days
Proton pump inhibitor[1] *plus*	Rabeprazole 20 mg twice daily	7 days
Clarithromycin *plus*	500 mg twice daily	7 days
Amoxicillin	1000 mg twice daily	7 days
Proton pump inhibitor *plus*	Lansoprazole 30 mg twice daily or Omeprazole 20 mg twice daily	2 weeks
Clarithromycin *plus*	500 mg twice daily	2 weeks
Metronidazole	500 mg twice daily	2 weeks
Proton pump inhibitor *plus*	Lansoprazole 30 mg once daily or Omeprazole 20 mg once daily	2 weeks
Bismuth *plus*	525 mg 4 times/day	2 weeks
Metronidazole *plus*	500 mg 3 times/day	2 weeks
Tetracycline	500 mg 4 times/day	2 weeks

[1]FDA-approved regimen.

Modified from Howden CS and Hunt RH, "Guidelines for the Management of *Helicobacter pylori* Infection," *AJG*, 1998, 93:2336.

HYPERGLYCEMIA- OR HYPOGLYCEMIA-CAUSING DRUGS

Hyperglycemia	Hypoglycemia	Hyperglycemia or Hypoglycemia
Caffeine	Anabolic steroids	Beta-blockers (also may mask symptoms of hypoglycemia)
Calcitonin	ACE inhibitors	Alcohol
Corticosteroids	Chloramphenicol	Lithium
Diltiazem	Clofibrate	Phenothiazines
Estrogens	Disopyramide	Rifampin
Isoniazid	MAO inhibitors	Octreotide
Morphine	Miconazole (oral form)	Fluoxetine
Nifedipine	Probenecid	
Nicotine	Pyridoxine	
Nicotinic acid	Salicylates	
Oral contraceptives	Sulfonamides	
Phenytoin	Tetracycline	
Sympathomimetic amines	Verapamil	
Theophylline	Warfarin	
Thiazide diuretics		
Thyroid products		

Adapted from American Association of Diabetes Educators, *A Core Curriculum for Diabetes Education*, 3rd ed, Vol 10, Chicago, IL, 1998, 338-41.

HYPERLIPIDEMIA MANAGEMENT

MORTALITY

There is a strong link between serum cholesterol and cardiovascular mortality. This association becomes stronger in patients with established coronary artery disease. Lipid-lowering trials show that reductions in LDL cholesterol are followed by reductions in mortality. In general, each 1% fall in LDL cholesterol confers a 2% reduction in cardiovascular events. The aim of therapy for hyperlipidemia is to decrease cardiovascular morbidity and mortality by lowering cholesterol to a target level using safe and cost-effective treatment modalities. The target LDL cholesterol is determined by the number of patient risk factors (see the following Risk Factors and Goal LDL Cholesterol tables). The goal is achieved through diet, lifestyle modification, and drug therapy. The basis for these recommendations is provided by longitudinal interventional studies, demonstrating that lipid-lowering in patients with prior cardiovascular events (secondary prevention) and in patients with hyperlipidemia but no prior cardiac event (primary prevention) lowers the occurrence of future cardiovascular events, including stroke.

Major Risk Factors That Modify LDL Goals

Positive risk factors	Male ≥45 years
	Female ≥55 years
	Family history of premature coronary heart disease, defined as CHD in male first-degree relative <55 years; CHD in female first-degree relative <65 years
	Cigarette smoking
	Hypertension (blood pressure ≥140/90 mm Hg) or taking antihypertensive medication
	Low HDL (<40 mg/dL [1.03 mmol/L])
Negative risk factors	High HDL (≥60 mg/dL [1.6 mmol/L])[1]

[1]If HDL is ≥60 mg/dL, may subtract one positive risk factor.

Adult Treatment Panel (ATP) III LDL-C Goals and Cutpoints for Therapeutic Lifestyle Changes (TLC) and Drug Therapy in Different Risk Categories

Risk Category	LDL-C Goal	Initiate TLC	Consider Drug Therapy[1]
High risk: CHD[2] or CHD risk equivalents[3] (10-year risk >20%)	<100 mg/dL (optional goal: <70 mg/dL)[4]	≥100 mg/dL[5]	≥100 mg/dL[6] (<100 mg/dL: Consider drug options)[1]
Moderately high risk: 2+ risk factors[7] (10-year risk 10% to 20%)[8]	<130 mg/dL[9]	≥130 mg/dL[5]	≥130 mg/dL (100-120 mg/dL: Consider drug options)[10]
Moderate risk: 2+ risk factors[7] (10-year risk <10%)[8]	<130 mg/dL	≥130 mg/dL	≥160 mg/dL
Lower risk: 0-1 risk factor[11]	<160 mg/dL	≥160 mg/dL	≥190 mg/dL (160-189 mg/dL: LDL-lowering drug optional)

[1]When LDL-lowering drug therapy is employed, it is advised that intensity of therapy be sufficient to achieve at least a 30% to 40% reduction in LDL-C levels.

[2]CHD includes history of myocardial infarction, unstable angina, stable angina, coronary artery procedures (angioplasty or bypass surgery), or evidence of clinically significant myocardial ischemia.

[3]CHD risk equivalents include clinical manifestations of noncoronary forms of atherosclerotic disease (peripheral arterial disease, abdominal aortic aneurysm, and carotid artery disease [transient ischemic attacks or stroke of carotid origin or >50% obstruction of a carotid artery]), diabetes, and 2+ risk factors with 10-year risk for hard CHD >20%.

[4]Very high risk favors the optional LDL-C goal of <70 mg/dL, and in patients with high triglycerides, non-HDL-C <100 mg/dL.

[5]Any person at high risk or moderately high risk who has lifestyle-related risk factors (eg, obesity, physical inactivity, elevated triglyceride, low HDL-C, or metabolic syndrome) is a candidate for therapeutic lifestyle changes to modify these risk factors regardless of LDL-C level.

[6]If baseline LDL-C is <100 mg/dL, institution of an LDL-lowering drug is a therapeutic option on the basis of available clinical trial results. If a high-risk person has high triglycerides or low HDL-C, combining a fibrate or nicotinic acid with an LDL-lowering drug can be considered.

[7]Risk factors include cigarette smoking, hypertension (BP ≥140/90 mm Hg or on antihypertensive medication), low HDL cholesterol (<40 mg/dL), family history of premature CHD (CHD in male first-degree relative <55 years of age; CHD in female first-degree relative <65 years of age), and age (men ≥45 years; women ≥55 years).

[8]Electronic 10-year risk calculators are available at www.nhlbi.nih.gov/guidelines/cholesterol.

[9]Optional LDL-C goal <100 mg/dL.

[10]For moderately high-risk persons, when LDL-C level is 100-129 mg/dL, at baseline or on lifestyle therapy, initiation of an LDL-lowering drug to achieve an LDL-C level <100 mg/dL is a therapeutic option on the basis of available clinical trial results.

[11]Almost all people with zero or 1 risk factor have a 10-year risk <10%, and 10-year risk assessment in people with zero or 1 risk factor thus not necessary.

Any person with elevated LDL cholesterol or other form of hyperlipidemia should undergo evaluation to rule out secondary dyslipidemia. Causes of secondary dyslipidemia include diabetes, hypothyroidism, obstructive liver disease, chronic renal failure, and drugs that increase LDL and decrease HDL (progestins, anabolic steroids, corticosteroids).

Elevated Serum Triglyceride Levels

Elevated serum triglyceride levels may be an independent risk factor for coronary heart disease. Factors that contribute to hypertriglyceridemia include obesity, inactivity, cigarette smoking, excess alcohol intake, high carbohydrate diets (>60% of energy intake), type 2 diabetes, chronic renal failure, nephrotic syndrome, certain medications (corticosteroids, estrogens, retinoids, higher doses of beta-blockers), and genetic disorders. Non-HDL cholesterol (total cholesterol minus HDL cholesterol) is a secondary focus for clinicians treating patients with high serum triglyceride levels (≥200 mg/dL). The goal for non-HDL cholesterol in patients with high serum triglyceride levels can be set 30 mg/dL higher than usual LDL cholesterol goals. Patients with serum triglyceride levels <200 mg/dL should aim for the target LDL cholesterol goal.

ATP classification of serum triglyceride levels:

- Normal triglycerides: <150 mg/dL
- Borderline-high: 150-199 mg/dL
- High: 200-499 mg/dL
- Very high: ≥500 mg/dL

NONDRUG THERAPY

Dietary therapy and lifestyle modifications should be individualized for each patient. A total lifestyle change is recommended for all patients. Dietary and lifestyle modifications should be tried for 3 months, if deemed appropriate. Nondrug and drug therapy should be initiated simultaneously in patients with highly elevated cholesterol (see LDL Cholesterol Goals and Cutpoints for Therapeutic Lifestyle Changes and Drug Therapy in Different Risk Categories table). Increasing physical activity and smoking cessation will aid in the treatment of hyperlipidemia and improve cardiovascular health.

Note: Refer to the National Cholesterol Education Program reference for details concerning the calculation of 10-year risk of CHD using Framingham risk scoring. Risk assessment tool is available on-line at http://hin.nhlbi.nih.gov/atpiii/calculator.asp?usertype=prof, last accessed March 14, 2002.

Total Lifestyle Change (TLC) Diet

	Recommended Intake
Total fat	25%-35% of total calories
Saturated fat[1]	<7% of total calories
Polyunsaturated fat	≤10% of total calories
Monounsaturated fat	≤20% of total calories
Carbohydrates[2]	50%-60% of total calories
Fiber	20-30 g/day
Protein	~15% of total calories
Cholesterol	<200 mg/day
Total calories[3]	Balance energy intake and expenditure to maintain desirable body weight/prevent weight gain

[1]*Trans* fatty acids (partially hydrogenated oils) intake should be kept low. These are found in potato chips, other snack foods, margarines and shortenings, and fast-foods.

[2]Complex carbohydrates including grains (especially whole grains, fruits, and vegetables).

[3]Daily energy expenditure should include at least moderate physical activity.

DRUG THERAPY

Drug therapy should be selected based on the patient's lipid profile, concomitant disease states, and the cost of therapy. The following table lists specific advantages and disadvantages for various classes of lipid-lowering medications. The expected reduction in lipids with therapy is listed in the Lipid-Lowering Agents table. Refer to individual drug monographs for detailed information.

Advantages and Disadvantages of Specific Lipid-Lowering Therapies

	Advantages	Disadvantages
Bile acid sequestrants	Good choice for ↑ LDL, especially when combined with a statin (↓ LDL ≤50%); low potential for systemic side effects; good choice for younger patients	May increase triglycerides; higher incidence of adverse effects; moderately expensive; drug interactions; inconvenient dosing

HYPERLIPIDEMIA MANAGEMENT *(Continued)*

	Advantages	Disadvantages
Niacin	Good choice for almost any lipid abnormality; inexpensive; greatest increase in HDL	High incidence of adverse effects; may adversely affect NIDDM and gout; sustained release niacin may decrease the incidence of flushing and circumvent the need for multiple daily dosing; sustained release niacin may not increase HDL cholesterol or decrease triglycerides as well as immediate release niacin
HMG-CoA reductase inhibitors	Produces greatest ↓ in LDL; generally well-tolerated; convenient once-daily dosing; proven decrease in mortality	Expensive
Gemfibrozil	Good choice in patients with ↑ triglycerides where niacin is contraindicated or not well-tolerated; gemfibrozil is well tolerated	Variable effects on LDL
Ezetimibe	Additional cholesterol-lowering effects when combined with HMG-CoA reductase inhibitors	Effects similar to bile acid sequestrants

Lipid-Lowering Agents

Drug	Dose / Day	Effect on LDL (%)	Effect on HDL (%)	Effect on TG (%)
HMG-CoA Reductase Inhibitors				
Atorvastatin	10 mg	-39	+6	-19
	20 mg	-43	+9	-26
	40 mg	-50	+6	-29
	80 mg	-60	+5	-37
Fluvastatin	20 mg	-22	+3	-12
	40 mg	-25	+4	-14
	80 mg	-36	+6	-18
Lovastatin	10 mg	-21	+5	-10
	20 mg	-27	+6	-8
	40 mg	-31	+5	-8
	80 mg	-40	+9.5	-19
Pravastatin	10 mg	-22	+7	-15
	20 mg	-32	+2	-11
	40 mg	-34	+12	-24
	80 mg	-37	+3	-19
Rosuvastatin	5 mg	-45	+13	-35
	10 mg	-52	+14	-10
	20 mg	-55	+8	-23
	40 mg	-63	+10	-28
Simvastatin	5 mg	-26	+10	-12
	10 mg	-30	+12	-15
	20 mg	-38	+8	-19
	40 mg	-41	+13	-28
	80 mg	-47	+16	-33
Bile Acid Sequestrants				
Cholestyramine	4-24 g	-15 to -30	+3 to +5	+0 to +20
Colestipol	7-30 g	-15 to -30	+3 to +5	+0 to +20
Colesevelam	6 tablets	-15	+3	+10
	7 tablets	-18	+3	+9
Fibric Acid Derivatives				
Fenofibrate	67-200 mg	-20 to -25	+1 to +20	-30 to -50
Gemfibrozil	600 mg twice daily	-5 to -10[1]	+10 to +20	-40 to -60
Niacin	1.5-6 g	-21 to -27	+10 to +35	-10 to -50
2-Azetidinone				
Ezetimibe	10 mg	-18	+1	-8
Omega-3-Acid Ethyl Esters	4 g	+44.5	+9.1	-44.9
Combination Products				
Ezetimibe and simvastatin	10/10 mg	-45	+8	-23
	10/20 mg	-52	+10	-24
	10/40 mg	-55	+6	-23
	10/80 mg	-60	+6	-31
Niacin and lovastatin	1000/20 mg	-30	+20	-32
	1000/40 mg	-36	+20	-39
	1500/40 mg	-37	+27	-44
	2000/40 mg	-42	+30	-44

[1]May increase LDL in some patients.

Recommended Liver Function Monitoring for HMG-CoA Reductase Inhibitors

Agent	Initial and After Elevation in Dose	6 Weeks[1]	12 Weeks[1]	Periodically
Atorvastatin (Lipitor®)	x		x	x
Fluvastatin (Lescol®)	x		x	x
Lovastatin (Mevacor®)	x	x	x	x
Pravastatin (Pravachol®)	x			x
Simvastatin (Zocor®)	x			x

[1]After initiation of therapy or any elevation in dose.

DRUG SELECTION

Lipid Profile	Monotherapy	Combination Therapies
Increased LDL with normal HDL and triglycerides (TG)	Resin Niacin[1] Statin	Resin plus niacin[1] or statin Statin plus niacin[1,2]
Increased LDL and increased TG (200-499 mg/dL)[2]	Intensify LDL-lowering therapy	Statin plus niacin[1,3] Statin plus fibrate[3]
Increased LDL and increased TG (≥500 mg/dL)[2]	Consider combination therapy (niacin,[1] fibrates, statin)	
Increased TG	Niacin[1] Fibrates	Niacin[1] plus fibrates
Increased LDL and low HDL	Niacin[1] Statin	Statin plus niacin[1,2]

[1]Avoid in diabetics.

[2]Emphasize weight reduction and increased physical activity.

[3]Risk of myopathy with combination.

Resins = bile acid sequestrants; statins = HMG-CoA reductase inhibitors; fibrates = fibric acid derivatives (eg, gemfibrozil, fenofibrate).

COMBINATION DRUG THERAPY

If after at least 6 weeks of therapy at the maximum recommended or tolerated dose, the patient's LDL cholesterol is not at target, consider optimizing nondrug measures, prescribing a higher dose of current lipid-lowering drug, or adding another lipid-lowering medication to the current therapy. Successful drug combinations include statin and niacin, statin and bile acid sequestrant, or niacin and bile acid sequestrant. At maximum recommended doses, LDL cholesterol may be decreased by 50% to 60% with combination therapy. This is the same reduction achieved by atorvastatin 40 mg twice daily. If a bile acid sequestrant is used with other lipid-lowering agents, space doses 1 hour before or 4 hours after the bile acid sequestrant administration. Statins combined with either fenofibrate, clofibrate, gemfibrozil, or niacin increase the risk of rhabdomyolysis. In this situation, patient education (muscle pain/weakness) and careful follow-up are warranted.

Progression of Drug Therapy in Primary Prevention

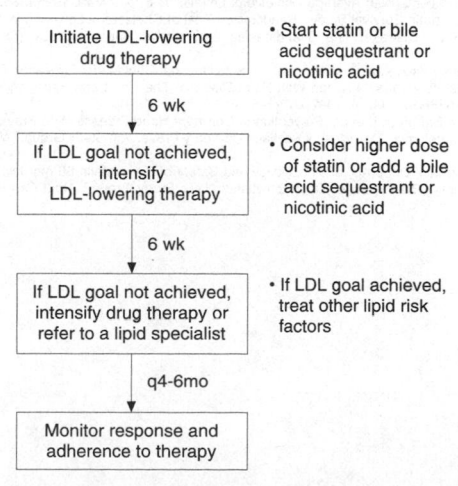

Initiate LDL-lowering drug therapy	• Start statin or bile acid sequestrant or nicotinic acid
↓ 6 wk	
If LDL goal not achieved, intensify LDL-lowering therapy	• Consider higher dose of statin or add a bile acid sequestrant or nicotinic acid
↓ 6 wk	
If LDL goal not achieved, intensify drug therapy or refer to a lipid specialist	• If LDL goal achieved, treat other lipid risk factors
↓ q4-6mo	
Monitor response and adherence to therapy	

HYPERLIPIDEMIA MANAGEMENT *(Continued)*

References

Guidelines

Gavin JR, Alberti KGMM, Davidson MB, et al, for the Members of the Expert Committee on the Diagnosis and Classification of Diabetes Mellitus, "American Diabetes Association: Clinical Practice Recommendations," *Diabetes Care*, 1999, 22(Suppl 1):S1-S114.

National Cholesterol Education Program, "Third Report of the Expert Panel on Detection, Evaluation, and Treatment of High Blood Cholesterol in Adults (Adult Treatment Panel III)," *JAMA*, 2001, 285:2486-97.

Grundy SM, Cleeman JI, Merz CN, et al, "Implications of Recent Clinical Trials for the National Cholesterol Education Program Adult Treatment Panel III Guidelines," *JACC*, 2004, 44(3):729.

Mosca L, Appel LJ, Benjamin EJ, et al, "Evidence-Based Guidelines for Cardiovascular Disease Prevention in Women," *J Am Coll Cardiol*, 2004, 43(5):900-21.

Others

Berthold HK, Sudhop T, and von Bergmann K, "Effect of a Garlic Oil Preparation on Serum Lipoproteins and Cholesterol Metabolism: A Randomized Controlled Trial," *JAMA*, 1998, 279:1900-2.

Bertolini S, Bon GB, Campbell LM, et al, "Efficacy and Safety of Atorvastatin Compared to Pravastatin in Patients With Hypercholesterolemia," *Atherosclerosis*, 1997, 130:191-7.

Blankenhorn DH, Nessim SA, Johnson RL, et al, "Beneficial Effects of Combined Colestipol-Niacin Therapy on Coronary Atherosclerosis and Venous Bypass Grafts," *JAMA*, 1987, 257:3233-40.

Brown G, Albers JJ, Fisher LD, et al, "Regression of Coronary Artery Disease as a Result of Intensive Lipid-Lowering Therapy in Men With High Levels of Apolipoprotein B," *N Engl J Med*, 1990, 323:1289-98.

Capuzzi DM, Guyton JR, Morgan JM, et al, "Efficacy and Safety of an Extended-Release Niacin (Niaspan®): A Long-Term Study," *Am J Cardiol*, 1998, 82:74U-81U.

Coronary Drug Project Research Program, "Clofibrate and Niacin in Coronary Heart Disease," *JAMA*, 1975, 231:360-81.

Dart A, Jerums G, Nicholson G, et al, "A Multicenter, Double-Blind, One-Year Study Comparing Safety and Efficacy of Atorvastatin Versus Simvastatin in Patients With Hypercholesterolemia," *Am J Cardiol*, 1997, 80:39-44.

Davidson MH, Dillon MA, Gordon B, et al, "Colesevelam Hydrochloride (Cholestagel): A New Potent Bile Acid Sequestrant Associated With a Low Incidence of Gastrointestinal Side Effects," *Arch Intern Med*, 1999, 159(16):1893-900.

Davidson M, McKenney J, Stein E, et al, "Comparison of One-Year Efficacy and Safety of Atorvastatin Versus Lovastatin in Primary Hypercholesterolemia," *Am J Cardiol*, 1997, 79:1475-81.

Frick MH, Heinonen OP, Huttunen JK, et al, "Helsinki Heart Study: Primary-Prevention Trial With Gemfibrozil in Middle-Aged Men With Dyslipidemia," *N Engl J Med*, 1987, 317:1237-45.

Garber AM, Browner WS, and Hulley SB, "Clinical Guideline, Part 2: Cholesterol Screening in Asymptomatic Adults, Revisited," *Ann Intern Med*, 1995, 124:518-31.

Johannesson M, Jonsson B, Kjekshus J, et al, "Cost-Effectiveness of Simvastatin Treatment to Lower Cholesterol Levels in Patients With Coronary Heart Disease. Scandinavian Simvastatin Survival Study Group," *N Engl N Med*, 1997, 336:332-6.

Jones P, Kafonek S, Laurora I, et al, "Comparative Dose Efficacy Study of Atorvastatin Versus Simvastatin, Pravastatin, Lovastatin, and Fluvastatin in Patients With Hypercholesterolemia," *Am J Cardiol*, 1998, 81:582-7.

Kasiske BL, Ma JZ, Kalil RS, et al, "Effects of Antihypertensive Therapy on Serum Lipids," *Ann Intern Med*, 1995, 133-41.

Lipid Research Clinics Program, "The Lipid Research Clinics Coronary Primary Prevention Trial Results: I. Reduction in Incidence of Coronary Heart Disease," *JAMA*, 1984, 251:351-64.

Mauro VF and Tuckerman CE, "Ezetimibe for Management of Hypercholesterolemia," *Ann Pharmacother*, 2003, 37(6):839-48.

Multiple Risk Factor Intervention Trial Research Group, "Multiple Risk Factor Intervention Trial: Risk Factor Changes and Mortality Results," *JAMA*, 1982, 248:1465-77.

Pitt B, Waters D, Brown WV, et al, "Aggressive Lipid-Lowering Therapy Compared With Angioplasty in Stable Coronary Artery Disease. Atorvastatin Versus Revascularization Treatment Investigators," *N Engl J Med*, 1999, 341(2):70-6.

Ross SD, Allen IE, Connelly JE, et al, "Clinical Outcomes in Statin Treatment Trials: A Meta-Analysis," *Arch Intern Med*, 1999, 159:1793-802.

Sacks FM, Pfeffer MA, Moye LA, et al, "The Effect of Pravastatin on Coronary Events After Myocardial Infarction in Patients With Average Cholesterol Levels," *N Engl J Med*, 1996, 335:1001-9.

Scandinavian Simvastatin Survival Study, "Randomized Trial of Cholesterol Lowering in 4444 Patients With Coronary Heart Disease: The Scandinavian Simvastatin Survival Study (4S)," *Lancet*, 1994, 344:1383-9.

Schrott HG, Bittner V, Vittinghoff E, et al, "Adherence to National Cholesterol Education Program Treatment Goals in Postmenopausal Women With Heart Disease. The Heart and Estrogen/Progestin Replacement Study (HERS)," *JAMA*, 1997, 277:1281-6.

Shepherd J, Cobbe SM, Ford I, et al, "Prevention of Coronary Heart Disease With Pravastatin in Men With Hypercholesterolemia, The West of Scotland Coronary Prevention Study Group," *N Engl J Med*, 1995, 333:1301-7.

Stein EA, Davidson MH, Dobs AS, et al, "Efficacy and Safety of Simvastatin 80 mg/day in Hypercholesterolemic Patients. The Expanded Dose Simvastatin U.S. Study Group," *Am J Cardiol*, 1998, 82:311-6.

HYPERTENSION

The optimal blood pressure for adults is <120/80 mm Hg. Consistent systolic pressure ≥140 mm Hg or a diastolic pressure ≥90 mm Hg, in the absence of a secondary cause, defines hypertension. Hypertension affects approximately 25% (50 million people) in the United States. Of those patients on antihypertensive medication, only one in three have their blood pressure controlled (<140/90 mm Hg).

Controlling systolic hypertension has been much more difficult than controlling diastolic hypertension. Educating patients in lifestyle management, cardiovascular risk reduction, and drug therapy aids in improving the morbidity and mortality of patients with hypertension.

The Seventh Report of the Joint National Committee (JNC VII) is an excellent reference and guide for the treatment of hypertension (Chobanian AV, Bakris GL, Black HR, et al, "The Seventh Report of the Joint National Committee on Prevention, Detection, Evaluation, and Treatment of High Blood Pressure: The JNC 7 Report," *JAMA*, 2003, 289(19):2560-71). For adults, hypertension is classified in stages (see following table).

Adult Classification of Blood Pressure

Category	Systolic (mm Hg)		Diastolic (mm Hg)
Normal	<120	and	<80
Prehypertension	120-139	or	80-89
Hypertension			
Stage 1	140-159	or	90-99
Stage 2	≥160	or	≥100

Adapted from Chobanian AV, Bakris GL, Black HR, et al, "The Seventh Report of the Joint National Committee on Prevention, Detection, Evaluation, and Treatment of High Blood Pressure: The JNC 7 Report," *JAMA*, 2003, 289(19):2560-71.

Normal Blood Pressure in Children

Age (y)	Girls' SBP / DBP (mm Hg)		Boys' SBP / DBP (mm Hg)	
	50th Percentile for Height	75th Percentile for Height	50th Percentile for Height	75th Percentile for Height
1	104/58	105/59	102/57	104/58
6	111/73	112/73	114/74	115/75
12	123/80	124/81	123/81	125/82
17	129/84	130/85	136/87	138/88

SBP = systolic blood pressure.

DBP = diastolic blood pressure.

Adapted from the report by the NHBPEP Working Group on Hypertension Control in Children and Adolescents, *Pediatrics*, 1996, 98(4 Pt 1):649-58.

PATIENT ASSESSMENT

- **Cardiovascular Risk Factors:** Hypertension, cigarette smoking, obesity (BMI ≥30), inactive lifestyle, dyslipidemia, diabetes mellitus, microalbuminuria or estimated GFR <60 mL/minute, age (>55 years for men, >65 years for women), family history of premature cardiovascular disease (men <55 years or women >65 years).

  Components of metabolic syndrome include hypertension, obesity, dyslipidemia, diabetes mellitus.

- Identify causes of high BP.

- Assess target-organ damage and CVD.

Target-Organ Disease

Organ System	Manifestation
Cardiac	Clinical, ECG, or radiologic evidence of coronary artery disease; prior MI, angina, post-CABG; left ventricular hypertrophy (LVH); left ventricular dysfunction or cardiac failure, prior coronary revascularization
Cerebrovascular	Transient ischemic attack or stroke
Peripheral vascular	Absence of pulses in extremities (except dorsalis pedis), claudication, aneurysm, peripheral arterial disease
Renal	Serum creatinine ≥130 µmol/L (1.5 mg/dL); proteinuria (≥1+); microalbuminuria, chronic kidney disease

HYPERTENSION *(Continued)*

Target-Organ Disease *(continued)*

Organ System	Manifestation
Eye	Hemorrhages or exudates, with or without papilledema; retinopathy

Adapted from Chobanian AV, Bakris GL, Black HR, et al, "The Seventh Report of the Joint National Committee on Prevention, Detection, Evaluation, and Treatment of High Blood Pressure: The JNC 7 Report," *JAMA*, 2003, 289(19):2560-71.

BLOOD PRESSURE MEASUREMENT

At an office visit, patients should be seated quietly for ≥5 minutes in a chair with feet on the floor and arm supported at heart level. At least two measurements should be made. Patients should be given their results and their goal BP.

Ambulatory BP monitoring is useful in evaluating "white coat hypertension" (no end-organ damage), drug resistance, hypotensive symptoms, episodic hypertension, and autonomic dysfunction. Ambulatory BP monitoring correlates better with end-organ damage than office measurements.

Having patients monitor their own BP helps to improve compliance and provides information on response to therapeutic interventions.

Based on these initial assessments, treatment strategies for patients with hypertension are stratified based on their blood pressure and comorbidities (compelling indications).

Management of Blood Pressure

BP Classification	Management: Based upon highest BP category		
	Lifestyle Modification	Initial Therapy Without Compelling Indication	Initial Therapy With Compelling Indication[1]
Normal	Encourage	None	None
Prehypertensive	Yes	None	Treat patients with chronic kidney disease or diabetes to BP goal of <130/80 mm Hg
Hypertension Stage 1	Yes	Thiazide-type diuretic for most; consider ACEI, ARB, β-blocker, CCB, or combination	Drugs for the compelling indications; other antihypertensives as needed
Hypertension Stage 2	Yes	Two drug combos (typically a thiazide-type diuretic and ACEI or ARB or β-blocker or CCB). Use combo cautiously in patients at risk for orthostasis.	Drugs for the compelling indications; other antihypertensives as needed

[1]Compelling Indication: Conditions for which specific classes of antihypertensive drugs have proven beneficial.

Adapted from Chobanian AV, Bakris GL, Black HR, et al, "The Seventh Report of the Joint National Committee on Prevention, Detection, Evaluation, and Treatment of High Blood Pressure: The JNC 7 Report," *JAMA*, 2003, 289(19):2560-71.

ACHIEVING BLOOD PRESSURE CONTROL

Treatment of hypertension should be individualized. Lower blood pressure (goal <130/80 mm Hg) should be achieved in patients with diabetes or chronic renal disease. The following Hypertension Treatment Algorithm may be used to select specific antihypertensives based on compelling indications.

Special consideration for starting combination therapy should be made in each patient.

Starting drug therapy at a low dose and titrating upward if blood pressure is not controlled is recommended.

Most patients with hypertension will require two or more drugs to achieve their BP goals.

Adding a second drug from a different class will help when a single drug at reasonable doses has failed to achieve the goal.

If the untreated BP is >20/10 mm Hg away from the goal, consider initiating therapy with two drugs. Use caution in those at risk for orthostasis (eg, diabetics, geriatrics, and those with autonomic dysfunction).

Low-dose aspirin therapy should be considered when BP is controlled; use in uncontrolled hypertension can increase the risk of hemorrhagic stroke.

Lifestyle modification and risk reduction should always be reviewed and reinforced.

MONITORING THERAPY

Generally, monthly follow-up is recommended until BP control is reached.

More frequent monitoring is required for those patients with Stage 2 hypertension or those with complications.

Serum potassium and serum creatinine should be monitored at least twice yearly.

When BP is at goal and stable, follow-up can be maintained every 3-6 months. Treat other cardiovascular risk factors if present.

HYPERTENSION *(Continued)*

Hypertension Treatment Algorithm

Begin or continue lifestyle modifications

↓

Not at goal blood pressure (<140/90 mm Hg or <130/80 mm Hg for patients with diabetes or chronic renal disease)

↓

Initial Drug Choice

Hypertension

Stage I
Thiazide-type diuretic for most.
Consider ACEI, ARB, β-blocker,
CCB, or combo.

Stage 2
Two-drug combo for most
(typically thiazide-type diuretic +
ACEI or ARB or β-blocker or CCB)

Compelling Indications
Chronic kidney disease
- ACEI
- ARB
Diabetes mellitus
- ACEI
- ARB
- β-blocker
- CCB
- Diuretic
Heart failure
- ACEI
- Aldosterone blocker
- ARB
- β-blocker
- Diuretic
High coronary risk
- ACEI
- β-blocker
- CCB
- Diuretic
Myocardial infarction
- ACEI
- Aldosterone blocker
- β-blocker
Recurrent stroke prevention
- ACEI
- Diuretic

↓

Not at goal blood pressure

↓ ↓

Optimize dosages or add additional
drugs until goal BP achieved.

Consider consultation with
hypertension specialist.

Additional Considerations for Specific Therapies

Indication	Drug Therapy
Atrial tachyarrhythmias	β-blocker, CCB (non-DHP)
Chronic kidney disease	
Cl_{cr} <60 mL/min or albuminuria	ACEI or ARB
Cl_{cr} <30 mL/min	Increase loop diuretic
Diabetes	Thiazide diuretic, β-blocker, ACEI, ARB, CCB
Nephropathy	ACEI, ARB
Essential tremor	β-blocker (noncardioselective)
Heart failure	
Ventricular dysfunction (asymptomatic)	ACEI, β-blocker
Ventricular dysfunction (symptomatic)	ACEI, β-blocker, ARB, aldosterone blocker, loop diuretic
Hypertensive women who are pregnant	Methyldopa, β-blocker, vasodilator
Ischemic heart disease	
Angina	β-blocker, CCB (long-acting)
Acute coronary syndromes	β-blocker, ACEI
Migraine	β-blocker (noncardioselective), CCB (long-acting, non-DHP)
Osteoporosis	Thiazide diuretic
Perioperative hypertension	β-blocker
Prostatism (BPH)	Alpha-adrenergic blocking agent
Raynaud syndrome	CCB
Thyrotoxicosis	β-blocker

Note: ACEI = angiotensin-converting enzyme inhibitor; ARB = angiotensin receptor blocker; CCB = calcium channel blocker; DHP = dihydropyridine.

May Have Unfavorable Effects on Comorbid Conditions

Condition	Drug Therapy to Avoid
Angioedema	ACEI
Bronchospastic disease	β-blocker
Gout	Thiazide diuretic
Heart block (second or third degree)	β-blocker, CCB (non-DHP)
Hyponatremia	Thiazide diuretic
Potassium >5 mEq/L before treatment	Potassium-sparing diuretic, aldosterone antagonist
Pregnancy or those likely to become pregnant	ACEI, ARB

Note: ACEI = angiotensin-converting enzyme inhibitor; ARB = angiotensin receptor blocker; CCB = calcium channel blocker; DHP = dihydropyridine.

HYPERTENSION *(Continued)*

HYPERTENSIVE EMERGENCIES AND URGENCIES

General Treatment Principles in the Treatment of Hypertensive Emergencies

Principle	Considerations
Admit the patient to the hospital, preferably in the ICU. Monitor vital signs appropriately.	Establish I.V. access and place patient on a cardiac monitor. Place a femoral intra-arterial line and pulmonary arterial catheter, if indicated, to assess cardiopulmonary function and intravascular volume status.
Perform rapid but thorough history and physical examination.	Determine cause of, or precipitating factors to, hypertensive crisis if possible (remember to obtain a medication history including Rx, OTC, and illicit drugs). Obtain details regarding any prior history of hypertension (severity, duration, treatment), as well as other coexisting illnesses. Assess the extent of hypertensive end organ damage. Determine if a hypertensive urgency or emergency exists.
Determine goal blood pressure based on premorbid level, duration, severity and rapidity of increase of blood pressure, concomitant medical conditions, race, and age.	Acute decreases in blood pressure to normal or subnormal levels during the initial treatment period may reduce perfusion to the brain, heart, and kidneys, and must be avoided except in specific instances (ie, dissecting aortic aneurysm). Gradually establish a normal (or reasonable) blood pressure over the next 1-2 weeks.
Select an appropriate antihypertensive regimen depending on the individual patient and clinical setting.	Initiate a controlled decrease in blood pressure. Avoid concomitant administration of multiple agents that may cause precipitous falls in blood pressure. Select the agent with the best hemodynamic profile based on the primary treatment goal. Avoid diuretics and sodium restriction during the initial treatment period unless there is a clear clinical indication (ie, CHF, pulmonary edema). Avoid sedating antihypertensives in patients with hypertensive encephalopathy, CVA, or other CNS disorders in whom mental status must be monitored. Use caution with direct vasodilating agents that induce reflex tachycardia or increase cardiac output in patients with coronary heart disease, history of angina or myocardial infarction, or dissecting aortic aneurysm. Preferably choose an agent that does not adversely affect glomerular filtration rate or renal blood flow and also agents that have favorable effects on cerebral blood flow and its autoregulation, especially for patients with hypertensive encephalopathy or CVAs. Select the most efficacious agent with the fewest adverse effects based on the underlying cause of the hypertensive crisis and other individual patient factors.
Initiate a chronic antihypertensive regimen after the patient's blood pressure is stabilized	Begin oral antihypertensive therapy once goal blood pressure is achieved before gradually tapering parenteral medications. Select the best oral regimen based on cost, ease of administration, adverse effect profile, and concomitant medical conditions.

Oral Agents Used in the Treatment of Hypertensive Urgencies

Drug	Dose	Onset	Cautions
Captopril[1]	P.O.: 25 mg, repeat as required	15-30 min	Hypotension, renal failure in bilateral renal artery stenosis
Clonidine	P.O.: 0.1-0.2 mg, repeated every hour as needed to a total dose of 0.6 mg	30-60 min	Hypotension, drowsiness, dry mouth
Labetalol	P.O.: 200-400 mg, repeat every 2-3 h	30 min to 2 h	Bronchoconstriction, heart block, orthostatic hypotension

[1]There is no clearly defined clinical advantage in the use of sublingual over oral routes of administration with these agents.

Recommendations for the Use of Intravenous Antihypertensive Drugs in Selected Hypertensive Emergencies

Condition	Agent(s) of Choice	Agent(s) to Avoid or Use With Caution	General Treatment Principles
Hypertensive encephalopathy	Nitroprusside, labetalol, diazoxide	Methyldopa, reserpine	Avoid drugs with CNS-sedating effects.
Acute intracranial or subarachnoid hemorrhage	Nicardipine,[1] nitroprusside	β-blocker	Careful titration with a short-acting agent.
Cerebral infarction	Nicardipine,[1] nitroprusside, labetalol	β-blocker, minoxidil, diazoxide	Careful titration with a short-acting agent. Avoid agents that may decrease cerebral blood flow.
Head trauma	Esmolol, labetalol	Methyldopa, reserpine, nitroprusside, nitroglycerin, hydralazine	Avoid drugs with CNS-sedating effects, or those that may increase intracranial pressure.
Acute myocardial infarction, myocardial ischemia	Nitroglycerin, nicardipine[1] (calcium channel blocker), labetalol	Hydralazine, diazoxide, minoxidil	Avoid drugs which cause reflex tachycardia and increased myocardial oxygen consumption.
Acute pulmonary edema	Nitroprusside, nitroglycerin, loop diuretics	β-blocker (labetalol), minoxidil, methyldopa	Avoid drugs which may cause sodium and water retention and edema exacerbation.
Renal dysfunction	Hydralazine, calcium channel blocker	Nitroprusside, ACE inhibitors, β-blocker (labetalol)	Avoid drugs with increased toxicity in renal failure and those that may cause decreased renal blood flow.
Eclampsia	Hydralazine, labetalol, nitroprusside[2]	Diuretics, diazoxide (diazoxide may cause cessation of labor)	Avoid drugs that may cause adverse fetal effects, compromise placental circulation, or decrease cardiac output.
Pheochromocytoma	Phentolamine, nitroprusside, β-blocker (eg, esmolol) only after alpha blockade (phentolamine)	β-blocker in the absence of alpha blockade, methyldopa, minoxidil	Use drugs of proven efficacy and specificity. Unopposed beta blockade may exacerbate hypertension.
Dissecting aortic aneurysm	Nitroprusside and beta blockade	Hydralazine, diazoxide, minoxidil	Avoid drugs which may increase cardiac output.
Postoperative hypertension	Nitroprusside, nicardipine,[1] labetalol		Avoid drugs which may exacerbate postoperative ileus.

[1]The use of nicardipine in these situations is by the recommendation of the author based on a review of the literature.

[2]Reserve nitroprusside for eclamptic patients with life-threatening hypertension unresponsive to other agents due to the potential risk to the fetus (cyanide and thiocyanate metabolites may cross the placenta).

HYPERTENSION (Continued)

Selected Intravenous Agents for Hypertensive Emergencies

Drug	Dose[1]	Onset of Action	Duration of Action	Adverse Effects[2]	Special Indications
Vasodilators					
Sodium nitroprusside	0.25-10 mcg/kg/min as I.V. infusion[3] (max: 10 min only)	Immediate	1-2 min	Nausea, vomiting, muscle twitching, sweating, thiocyanate and cyanide intoxication	Most hypertensive emergencies; caution with high intracranial pressure or azotemia
Nicardipine hydrochloride	5-15 mg/h I.V.	5-10 min	1-4 h	Tachycardia, headache, flushing, local phlebitis	Most hypertensive emergencies except acute heart failure; caution with coronary ischemia
Fenoldopam mesylate	0.1-0.3 mcg/kg/min as I.V. infusion	<5 min	30 min	Tachycardia, headache, nausea, flushing	Most hypertensive emergencies; caution with glaucoma
Nitroglycerin	5-100 mcg/min as I.V. infusion[3]	2-5 min	3-5 min	Headache, vomiting, methemoglobinemia, tolerance with prolonged use	Coronary ischemia
Enalaprilat	1.25-5 mg every 6 hours I.V.	15-30 min	6 h	Precipitous fall in pressure in high-renin states; response variable	Acute left ventricular failure; avoid in acute myocardial infarction
Hydralazine hydrochloride	10-20 mg I.V. 10-50 mg I.M.	10-20 min 20-30 min	3-8 h	Tachycardia, flushing, headache, vomiting, aggravation of angina	Eclampsia
Diazoxide	50-100 mg I.V. bolus repeated, or 15-30 mg/min infusion	2-4 min	6-12 h	Nausea, flushing, tachycardia, chest pain	Now obsolete; when no intensive monitoring available
Adrenergic Inhibitors					
Labetalol hydrochloride	20-80 mg I.V. bolus every 10 min; 0.5-2 mg/min as I.V. infusion	5-10 min	3-6 h	Vomiting, scalp tingling, burning in throat, dizziness, nausea, heart block, orthostatic hypotension	Most hypertensive emergencies except acute heart failure
Esmolol hydrochloride	250-500 mcg/kg/min for 1 min, then 50-100 mcg/kg/min for 4 min; may repeat	1-2 min	10-20 min	Hypotension, nausea	Aortic dissection, perioperative
Phentolamine	5-15 mg I.V.	1-2 min	3-10 min	Tachycardia, flushing, headache	Catecholamine excess

[1]These doses may vary from those in the *Physicians' Desk Reference* (51st edition).
[2]Hypotension may occur with all agents.
[3]Require special delivery system.

References

Guidelines

1999 World Health Organization-International Society of Hypertension Guidelines for the Management of Hypertension. Guidelines Subcommittee, *J Hypertens*, 1999, 17:151-83.

Chobanian AV, Bakris GL, Black HR, et al, "The Seventh Report of the Joint National Committee on Prevention, Detection, Evaluation, and Treatment of High Blood Pressure: The JNC 7 Report," *JAMA*, 2003, 289(19):2560-71.

National High Blood Pressure Education Program Working Group on Hypertension Control in Children and Adolescents. Update on the 1987 Task Force Report on High Blood Pressure in Children and Adolescents: A Working Group Report From the National High Blood Pressure Education Program, *Pediatrics*, 1996, 98(4 Pt 1):649-58.

National High Blood Pressure Education Program Working Group. 1995 Update of the Working Group Reports on Chronic Renal Failure and Renovascular Hypertension, *Arch Intern Med*, 1996, 156:1938-47.

"The Sixth Report of the National Committee on Detection, Evaluation, and Treatment of High Blood Pressure (JNC-VI)," *Arch Intern Med*, 1997, 157:2413-46.

Others

Appel LJ, Moore TJ, Obarzanek E, et al, "A Clinical Trial of the Effect of Dietary Patterns on Blood Pressure. The DASH Collaborative Research Group," *N Engl J Med*, 1997, 336:1117-24.

Epstein M and Bakris G, "Newer Approaches to Antihypertensive Therapy: Use of Fixed-Dose Combination Therapy," *Arch Intern Med*, 1996, 156:1969-78.

Estacio RO and Schrier RW, "Antihypertensive Therapy in Type II Diabetes: Implications of the Appropriate Blood Pressure Control in Diabetes (ABCD) Trial," *Am J Cardiol*, 1998, 82:9R-14R.

Flack JM, Neaton J, Grimm RJ, et al, "Blood Pressure and Mortality Among Men With Prior Myocardial Infarction. The Multiple Risk Factor Intervention Trial Research Group," *Circulation*, 1995, 92:2437-45.

Frishman WH, Bryzinski BS, Coulson LR, et al, "A Multifactorial Trial Design to Assess Combination Therapy in Hypertension: Treatment With Bisoprolol and Hydrochlorothiazide," *Arch Intern Med*, 1994, 154:1461-8.

Furberg CD, Psaty BM, and Meyer JV, "Nifedipine: Dose-Related Increase in Mortality in Patients With Coronary Heart Disease," *Circulation*, 1995, 92:1326-31.

Glynn RJ, Brock DB, Harris T, et al, "Use of Antihypertensive Drugs and Trends in Blood Pressure in the Elderly," *Arch Intern Med*, 1995, 155:1855-60.

Gradman AH, Cutler NR, Davis PJ, et al, "Combined Enalapril and Felodipine Extended Release (ER) for Systemic Hypertension. The Enalapril-Felodipine ER Factorial Study Group," *Am J Cardiol*, 1997, 79:431-5.

Grim RH Jr, Flack JM, Grandits GA, et al, "Long-Term Effects on Plasma Lipids of Diet and Drugs to Treat Hypertension. The Treatment of Mild Hypertension Study (TOMHS) Research Group," *JAMA*, 1996, 275:1549-56.

Grim RH Jr, Grandits GA, Cutler JA, et al, "Relationships of Quality-of-Life Measures to Long-Term Lifestyle and Drug Treatment in the Treatment of Mild Hypertension Study. The TOMHS Research Group," *Arch Intern Med*, 1997, 157:638-48.

Grossman E, Messerli FH, Grodzicki T, et al, "Should a Moratorium Be Placed on Sublingual Nifedipine Capsules Given for Hypertensive Emergencies and Pseudoemergencies?" *JAMA*, 1996, 276:1328-31.

Hansson L, Zanchetti A, Carruthers SG, et al, "Effects of Intensive Blood Pressure Lowering and Low-Dose Aspirin in Patients With Hypertension: Principal Results of the Hypertension Optimal Treatment (HOT) Randomized Trial. HOT Study Group," *Lancet*, 1998, 351:1755-62.

Kaplan NM and Gifford RW Jr, "Choice of Initial Therapy for Hypertension," *JAMA*, 1996, 275:1577-80.

Kasiske BL, Ma JZ, Kalil RSN, et al, "Effects of Antihypertensive Therapy in Serum Lipids," *Ann Intern Med*, 1995, 122:133-41.

Kostis JB, Davis BR, Cutler J, et al, "Prevention of Heart Failure by Antihypertensive Drug Treatment in Older Persons With Isolated Systolic Hypertension. SHEP Cooperative Research Group," *JAMA*, 1997, 278:212-6.

Lazarus JM, Bourgoignie JJ, Buckalew VM, et al, "Achievement and Safety of a Low Blood Pressure Goal in Chronic Renal Disease: The Modification of Diet in Renal Disease Study Group," *Hypertension*, 1997, 29:641-50.

Lindheimer MD, "Hypertension in Pregnancy," *Hypertension*, 1993, 22:127-37.

Materson BJ, Reda DJ, Cushman WC, et al, "Single-Drug Therapy for Hypertension in Men: A Comparison of Six Antihypertensive Agents With Placebo. The Department of Veterans Affairs Cooperative Study Group on Antihypertensive Agents," *N Engl J Med*, 1993, 328:914-21.

Miller NH, Hill M, Kottke T, et al, "The Multi-Level Compliance Challenge: Recommendations for a Call to Action; A Statement for Healthcare Professionals," *Circulation*, 1997, 95:1085-90.

Neaton JD and Wentworth D, "Serum Cholesterol, Blood Pressure, Cigarette Smoking, and Death From Coronary Heart Disease: Overall Findings and Differences by Age for 316,099 White Men. The Multiple Risk Factor Intervention Trial Research Group," *Arch Intern Med*, 1992, 152:56-64.

Neaton JD, Grim RH, Prineas RJ, et al, "Treatment of Mild Hypertension Study (TOHMS). Final Results," *JAMA*, 1993, 270:721-31.

Oparil S, Levine JH, Zuschke CA, et al, "Effects of Candesartan Cilexetil in Patients With Severe Systemic Hypertension," *Am J Cardiol*, 1999, 84:289-93.

Perloff D, Grim C, Flack J, et al, "Human Blood Pressure Determination by Sphygmomanometry," *Circulation*, 1993, 88:2460-7.

Perry HM Jr, Bingham S, Horney A, et al, "Antihypertensive Efficacy of Treatment Regimens Used in Veterans Administration Hypertension Clinics. Department of Veterans Affairs Cooperative Study Group on Antihypertensive Agents," *Hypertension*, 1998, 31:771-9.

Preston RA, Materson BJ, Reda DJ, et al, "Age-Race Subgroup Compared With Renin Profile as Predictors of Blood Pressure Response to Antihypertensive Therapy," *JAMA*, 1998, 280:1168-72.

HYPERTENSION *(Continued)*

Psaty BM, Smith NL, Siscovick DS, et al, "Health Outcomes Associated With Antihypertensive Therapies Used as First-Line Agents. A Systemic Review and Meta-analysis," *JAMA*, 1997, 277:739-45.

Radevski IV, Valtchanova SP, Candy GP, et al, "Comparison of Acebutolol With and Without Hydrochlorothiazide Versus Carvedilol With and Without Hydrochlorothiazide in Black Patients With Mild to Moderate Systemic Hypertension," *Am J Cardiol*, 1999, 84(1):70-5.

Setaro JF and Black HR, "Refractory Hypertension," *N Engl J Med*, 1992, 327:543-7.

SHEP Cooperative Research Group, "Prevention of Stroke by Antihypertensive Drug Treatment in Older Persons With Isolated Systolic Hypertension: Final Results of the Systolic Hypertension in the Elderly Program (SHEP)," *JAMA*, 1991, 265:3255-64.

Sibai BM, "Treatment of Hypertension in Pregnant Women," *N Engl J Med*, 1996, 335:257-65.

Sowers JR, "Comorbidity of Hypertension and Diabetes: The Fosinopril Versus Amlodipine Cardiovascular Events Trial," *Am J Cardiol*, 1998, 82:15R-19R.

Sternberg H, Rosenthal T, Shamiss A, et al, "Altered Circadian Rhythm of Blood Pressure in Shift Workers," *J Hum Hypertens*, 1995, 9:349-53.

"The Hypertension Prevention Trial: Three-Year Effects of Dietary Changes on Blood Pressure. Hypertension Prevention Trial Research Group," *Arch Intern Med*, 1990, 150:153-62.

Trials of Hypertension Prevention Collaborative Research Group, "Effects of Weight Loss and Sodium Reduction Intervention on Blood Pressure and Hypertension Incidence in Overweight People With High-Normal Blood Pressure: The Trials of Hypertension Prevention, Phase II," *Arch Intern Med*, 1997, 157:657-67.

Tuomilehto J, Rastenyte D, Birkenhager WH, et al, "Effects of Calcium Channel Blockade in Older Patients With Diabetes and Systolic Hypertension," *N Engl J Med*, 1999, 340:677-84.

Veelken R and Schmieder RE, "Overview of Alpha-1 Adrenoceptor Antagonism and Recent Advances in Hypertensive Therapy," *Am J Hypertens*, 1996, 9:139S-49S.

White WB, Black HR, Weber MA, et al, "Comparison of Effects of Controlled Onset Extended Release Verapamil at Bedtime and Nifedipine Gastrointestinal Therapeutic System on Arising on Early Morning Blood Pressure, Heart Rate, and the Heart Rate-Blood Pressure Product," *Am J Cardiol*, 1998, 81:424-31.

OBESITY TREATMENT GUIDELINES FOR ADULTS

SUMMARY OF CLINICAL PRACTICE GUIDELINES

Note: Weight loss treatment for children and adolescents is not covered by these guidelines.

ASSESSMENT

Assessment of weight involves evaluating body mass index, waist circumference, and the patient's risk factors.

- A. Body Mass Index (BMI)
  1. BMI should be calculated for all adults (see table). Those with normal BMI should be reassessed in 2 years. A very muscular person may have a high BMI without the additional health risks. A BMI calculator is available through LEXI-Calc.
  2. Normal body weight is defined as a BMI of 18.5-24.9 kg/m². Overweight is defined as a BMI of 25-29.9 kg/m².
  3. Obesity is defined as a BMI of ≥30 kg/m². There are 3 classes of obesity: Class I (BMI 30-34.9), Class II (BMI 35-39.9), Class III (BMI ≥40).

- B. Abdominal Fat
  1. Excess abdominal fat, not proportional to total body fat, is an independent predictor for risk and morbidity.
  2. Waist circumference for men >40 inches or women >35 inches is an increased risk for those with a BMI of 25-34.9.

- C. Risk Factors
  1. Coronary heart disease, hypertension, stroke, or other atherosclerotic diseases, type 2 diabetes, gallbladder disease, osteoarthritis, sleep apnea, and other respiratory problems are associated with a very high risk of developing disease complications and higher mortality in an obese individual.
  2. Obesity is also associated with complications of pregnancy, menstrual irregularities, stress incontinence, and psychological disorders (eg, depression).
  3. **Cardiovascular Risk Factors:** Hypertension, cigarette smoking, obesity (BMI ≥30), inactive lifestyle, dyslipidemia, diabetes mellitus, microalbuminuria or estimated GFR <60 mL/minute, age (>55 years for men, >65 years for women), family history of premature cardiovascular disease (men <55 years or women >65 years).

     Weight loss is recommended for those who are obese and for those who are classified as overweight or have a high waist circumference and increased disease risks.

Body Mass Index (BMI), kg/m²
Height (feet, inches)

Weight (lb)	5'0"	5'3"	5'6"	5'9"	6'0"	6'3"
140	27	25	23	21	19	18
150	29	27	24	22	20	19
160	31	28	26	24	22	20
170	33	30	28	25	23	21
180	35	32	29	27	25	23
190	37	34	31	28	26	24
200	39	36	32	30	27	25
210	41	37	34	31	29	26
220	43	39	36	33	30	28
230	45	41	37	34	31	29
240	47	43	39	36	33	30
250	49	44	40	37	34	31

Note: For BMI calculations see "Body Mass Index" in Abbreviations and Measurements section.

OBESITY TREATMENT GUIDELINES FOR ADULTS *(Continued)*

TREATMENT

Patients who are overweight or obese, but are not candidates for weight loss (eg, those with serious psychiatric illness) or do not wish to lose weight loss, should be counseled to avoid further weight gain. Women who are overweight or obese at the onset of pregnancy are advised to gain less total weight during pregnancy.

A. Goals of Treatment

   1. Prevent further weight gain.

   2. Reduce body weight. The initial goal is to reduce body weight by 10% from baseline over the suggested time period of 6 months.

   3. Maintain a lower body weight, long term.

B. Nonpharmacologic treatment should include:

   1. An individually-planned diet which includes a decrease in fat as well as total calories.

   2. An increase in physical activity. Physical activity should be gradually increased to a goal of 30 minutes per day of moderate-intensity activity.

   3. Behavior therapy, which should include tools to help overcome individual barriers to weight loss.

C. Drug Therapy

   In select patients with BMI ≥30, or BMI ≥27 with other risk factors (eg, hypertension, diabetes, dyslipidemia), who did not lose weight or maintain weight loss, drug therapy can be started along with dietary therapy and physical activity.

D. Surgery

   Patients with severe clinical obesity, BMI ≥40 or BMI ≥35 with coexisting conditions, can be considered for weight loss surgery when other methods have failed. Lifelong surveillance after surgery is necessary.

Medications Approved for Long-Term Use in the Treatment of Obesity

Generic (Trade) Name	Therapeutic Category / Mechanism of Action	Usual Adult Dosage
Orlistat (Xenical®)	Lipase inhibitor; a reversible inhibitor of gastric and pancreatic lipases thus inhibiting absorption of dietary fats by 30% (at doses of 120 mg 3 times/day)	120 mg 3 times/day with each main meal containing fat (during or up to 1 hour after the meal); omit dose if meal is occasionally missed or contains no fat.
Sibutramine (Meridia®)	Anorexiant; blocks the neuronal uptake of norepinephrine and, to a lesser extent, serotonin and dopamine	Initial: 10 mg once daily; after 4 weeks may titrate up to 15 mg once daily as needed and tolerated

References:

McTigue KM, Harris R, Hemphill B, et al, "Screening and Interventions for Obesity in Adults: Summary of the Evidence for the U.S. Preventive Services Task Force," *Ann Intern Med*, 2003, 139(11):933-49.

National Heart, Lung, and Blood Institute Obesity Education Initiative, "Clinical Guidelines on the Identification, Evaluation, and Treatment of Overweight and Obesity in Adults. The Evidence Report," NIH Publication No. 98-4083, Bethesda, MD: U.S. Department of Health and Human Services, Public Health Service, National Institutes of Health, National Heart, Lung, and Blood Institute, 1998.

Snow V, Barry P, Fitterman N, et al, "Pharmacologic and Surgical Management of Obesity in Primary Care: A Clinical Practice Guideline From the American College of Physicians," *Ann Intern Med*, 2005, 142(7):525-31.

MANAGEMENT OF OVERDOSAGES

Antidote	Poison / Drug	Indications	Dosage	Comments
Acetylcysteine (Mucomyst®)	Acetaminophen	Unknown quantity ingested and <24 hours have elapsed since the time of ingestion or unable to obtain serum acetaminophen levels within 12 hours of ingestion. >7.5 g acetaminophen acutely ingested. Serum acetaminophen level >140 mcg/mL at 4 hours postingestion. Ingested dose >140 mg/kg.	Dilute to 5% solutions with carbonated beverage, fruit juice, or water and administer orally. **Loading:** 140 mg/kg for 1 dose **Maintenance:** 70 mg/kg for 17 doses, starting 4 hours after the loading dose and given every 4 hours	SGOT, SGPT, bilirubin, prothrombin time, creatinine, BUN, blood sugar, and electrolytes should be obtained daily if a toxic serum acetaminophen level has been determined. **Note:** Activated charcoal has been shown to absorb acetylcysteine *in vitro* and may do so in patients. Serum acetaminophen levels may not peak until 4 hours postingestion, and therefore, serum levels should not be drawn earlier.
Amyl nitrate, sodium nitrate, sodium thiosulfate (cyanide antidote package)	Cyanide	Begin treatment at the first sign of toxicity if exposure is known or strongly expected.	Break ampul of amyl nitrate and allow patient to inhale for 15 seconds, then take away for 15 seconds. Use a fresh ampul every 3 minutes. Continue until injection of sodium nitrate (3% solution) 300 mg (0.15-0.33 mL/kg over 5 minutes in pediatric patients) can be injected at 2.5-5 mL/min. Then immediately inject 12.5 g 25% sodium thiosulfate, slow I.V. (1.65 mL/kg in children).	If symptoms return, treatment may be repeated at half the normal dosages. For pediatric dosing see package insert. Do **not** use methylene blue to reduce elevated methemoglobin levels. Oxygen therapy may be useful when combined with sodium thiosulfate therapy.
Antivenin (*Crotalidae*) polyvalent (equine origin)	Pit viper bites (rattlesnakes, cotton-mouths, copperheads)	Mild, moderate, or severe symptoms and history of envenomation by a pit viper **Mild:** Local swelling (progressive), pain, no systemic systems **Moderate:** Ecchymosis and swelling beyond the bite site, some systemic symptoms and/or lab changes **Severe:** Profound edema involving entire extremity, cyanosis, serious systemic involvement, significant lab changes	**Mild:** 3-5 vials of antivenin in 250-500 mL NS **Moderate:** 6-10 vials of antivenin in 500 mL NS **Severe:** Minimum of 10 vials in 500-1000 mL NS Administer over 4-6 hours. Additional antivenin should be given on the basis of clinical response and continuing assessment of severity of the poisoning.	Draw blood for type and crossmatch, hematocrit, BUN, electrolytes, CBC, platelets, coagulation profile. Do **not** administer heparin for possible allergic reaction. A tetanus shot should also be given.

MANAGEMENT OF OVERDOSAGES *(Continued)*

Antidote	Poison / Drug	Indications	Dosage	Comments
Atropine	Organophosphate and carbamate insecticides, mushrooms containing muscarine (inocybe or clitocybe)	Myoclonic seizures, severe hallucinations, weakness, arrhythmias, excessive salivation, involuntary urination, and defecation	**Children:** I.V.: 0.05 mg/kg **Adults:** I.V.: 1-2 mg Repeat dosage every 10 minutes until patient is atropinized (normal pulse, dilated pupils, absence of rales, dry mouth)	Caution should be used in patients with narrow-angle glaucoma, cardiovascular disease, or pregnancy. Plasma and/or erythrocyte cholinesterase levels will be depressed from normal. Atropine should only be used when indicated; otherwise, use may result in anticholinergic poisoning. For organophosphate poisoning, large doses of atropine may be required.
Calcium EDTA (calcium disodium versenate)	Lead	Symptomatic patients or asymptomatic children with blood levels >50 mcg/dL	50-75 mg/kg/day deep I.M. or slow I.V. infusion in 3-6 divided doses for up to 5 days	If urine flow is not established, hemodialysis must accompany calcium EDTA dosing. In most cases, the I.M. route is preferred.
Calcium gluconate	Hydrofluoric acid (HF), magnesium	Calcium gluconate gel 2.5% for dermal exposures of HF <20% concentration. Sub-Q injections of calcium gluconate for dermal exposures of HF in >20% concentration or failure to respond to calcium gluconate gel.	Massage 2.5% gel into exposed area for 15 minutes. Infiltrate each square centimeter of exposed area with 0.5 mL of 10% calcium gluconate Sub-Q using a 30-gauge needle. 1 mL/kg I.V. of a 10% solution for magnesium toxicity (intra-arterial injection).	Injections of calcium gluconate should not be used in digital area. With exposures to dilute concentrations of HF, symptoms may take several hours to develop. Calcium gluconate gel is not currently available. Contact your regional poison control center for compounding instructions.
Deferoxamine (Desferal®)	Iron	Serum iron >350 mcg/dL. Inability to obtain serum iron in a reasonable time and patient is symptomatic.	**Mild symptoms:** I.M.: 10 mg/kg up to 1 g every 8 hours **Severe symptoms:** I.V.: 10-15 mg/kg/hour not to exceed 6 g in 24 hours; rates up to 35 mg/kg have been given.	Passing of vin rose-colored urine indicates free iron was present. Therapy should be discontinued when urine returns to normal color. Monitor for hypotension, especially when giving deferoxamine I.V.
Digoxin immune fab (ovine), (Digibind®)	Digoxin, digitoxin, oleander, foxglove, lily-of-the-valley (?), red squill (?)	Life-threatening cardiac arrhythmias, progressive bradyarrhythmias, second or third degree heart block unresponsive to atropine, serum digoxin level >5 ng/mL, potassium levels >5 mEq/L, or ingestion >10 mg in adults (or 4 mg in children).	Multiply serum digoxin concentration at steady-state level by 5.6 and multiply the result by the patient's weight in kilograms, divide this by 1000 and divide the result by 0.6. This gives the dose in number of vials to use. For other dosing methods, see package insert.	Monitor potassium levels, continuous ECG. **Note:** Digibind® interferes with serum digoxin/digitoxin levels.

Antidote	Poison / Drug	Indications	Dosage	Comments
Dimercaprol (BAL in oil®)	Arsenic, lead, mercury, gold, trivalent antimony, methyl bromide, methyl iodide	Any symptoms due to arsenic exposure. All patients with symptoms or asymptomatic children with blood levels >70 mcg/dL Any symptoms due to mercury and patient unable to take D-penicillamine.	3-5 mg/kg/dose deep I.M. every 4 hours until GI symptoms subside and patient switched to D-penicillamine. 3-5 mg/kg/dose deep I.M. every 4 hours for 2 days then every 4-12 hours for up to 7 additional days. 3-5 mg/kg/dose deep I.M. every 4 hours for 48 hours, then 3 mg/kg/dose every 6 hours, then 3 mg/kg/dose every 12 hours for 7 more days.	Patients receiving dimercaprol should be monitored for hypertension, tachycardia, hyperpyrexia, and urticaria. Used in conjunction with calcium EDTA in lead poisoning.
Ethanol	Ethylene glycol or methanol	Ethylene glycol or methanol blood levels >20 mg/dL. Blood levels not readily available and suspected ingestion of toxic amounts. Any asymptomatic patient with a history of ethylene glycol or methanol ingestion.	**Loading dose:** I.V.: 7.5-10 mL/kg 10% ethanol in D_5W over 1 hour **Maintenance dose:** I.V.: 1.4 mL/kg/hour of 10% ethanol in D_5W. Maintain blood ethanol level of 100-200 mg/dL.	Monitor blood glucose, especially in children, as ethanol may cause hypoglycemia. Do not use 5% ethanol in D_5W as excessive amounts of fluid would be required to maintain adequate ethanol blood levels. If dialysis is performed, adjustment of ethanol dosing is required.
Flumazenil (Romazicon®)	Benzodiazepine	As adjunct to conventional management/ diagnosis of benzodiazepine overdose.	I.V.: 0.2 mg over 30 seconds; wait another 30 seconds, and then give an additional 0.3 mg over 30 seconds. Additional doses of 0.5 mg over 30 seconds at 1-minute intervals up to a cumulative dose of 3 mg.	Onset of reversal usually within 1-2 minutes. Contraindicated in patients with epilepsy, increased intracranial pressure, or coingestion of seizuregenic agents (ie, cyclic antidepressant).
Glucagon	Propranolol: Hypoglycemic agents	Propranolol-induced cardiac dysfunction. Treatment of hypoglycemia.	Sub-Q, I.M., or I.V.: 0.5-1 mg May repeat after 15 minutes	Requires liver glycogen stores for hyperglycemic response. Intravenous glucose must also be given in treatment of hypoglycemia.
Hydroxocobalamin	Cyanide	Treatment if exposure is known or highly suspected.	I.V.: 5 g over 15 minutes; may repeat 5 g dose over 15 minutes to 2 hours, if clinically needed.	Monitor blood pressure during infusion; elevations usually noted at beginning of infusion, peak toward the end of infusion and return to baseline within 4 hours of infusion; chromaturia and erythema common and can persist for weeks after administration.
Leucovorin (citrovorum factor, folinic acid)	Methotrexate, trimethoprim, pyrimethamine, methanol, trimetrexate	Methotrexate-induced bone marrow depression (methotrexate serum level >1 x 10^{-5} mmol/L); may also be useful in pyrimethamine-trimethoprim bone marrow depression	Dose should be equal to or greater than the dose of methotrexate ingested. Usually 10-100 mg/m² is given I.V. or orally every 6 hours for 72 hours.	Most effective if given within 1 hour after exposure. May not be effective to prevent liver toxicity. Monitor methotrexate levels. May enhance the toxicity of fluorouracil.

MANAGEMENT OF OVERDOSAGES *(Continued)*

Antidote	Poison / Drug	Indications	Dosage	Comments
Methylene blue	Methemoglobin inducers (ie, nitrites, phenazopyridine)	Cyanosis Methemoglobin level >30% in an asymptomatic patient	I.V.: 1-2 mg/kg (0.1-0.2 mL/kg) per dose over 2-3 minutes. May repeat doses as needed clinically. Injection can be given as 1% solution or diluted in normal saline.	Treatment can result in falsely elevated methemoglobin levels when measured by a co-oximeter. Large doses (>15 mg/kg) may cause hemolysis.
Naloxone (Narcan®)	Opiates (eg, heroin, morphine, codeine)	Coma or respiratory depression from unknown cause or from opiate overdose	Give 0.4-2.0 mg I.V. bolus. Doses may be repeated if there is no response, up to 10 mg.	For prolonged intoxication, a continuous infusion may be used.
D-penicillamine (Cuprimine®)	Arsenic, lead, mercury	Following BAL therapy in symptomatic acutely poisoned patients Asymptomatic patients with excess lead burden Patient symptomatic from mercury exposure or excessive levels	100 mg/kg/day up to 2 g in 4 divided doses for 5 days 1-2 g/day in 4 divided doses for 5 days **Children:** 100 mg/kg/day up to 1 g/day in 4 divided doses. Given for 3-10 days. **Adults:** P.O.: 250 mg 4 times/day	Possible contraindication for patients with penicillin allergy. Monitor heavy metal levels daily in severely poisoned patients. Monitor CBC and renal function in patients receiving chronic D-penicillamine therapy. Dosages given are for short-term acute therapy only.
Physostigmine salicylate	Atropine and anticholinergic agents, cyclic antidepressants, intrathecal baclofen	Myoclonic seizures, severe arrhythmias Refractory seizures or arrhythmias unresponsive to conventional therapies	**Children:** Slow I.V. push: 0.5 mg. Repeat as required for life-threatening symptoms **Adults:** Slow I.V. push: 0.5-2 mg Same as above	Dramatic reversal of anticholinergic symptoms after I.V. use. Should not be used just to keep patient awake. **Contraindications:** Asthma, gangrene; physostigmine use in cyclic antidepressant-induced cardiac toxicity it controversial. **Extreme caution** is advised — should be considered only in the presence of life-threatening anticholinergic symptoms.
Pralidoxime (2-PAM, Protopam®)	Organophosphate, insecticides, tacrine	An adjunct to atropine therapy for treatment of profound muscle weakness, respiratory depression, muscle twitching	**Children:** 25-50 mg/kg in 250 mL saline over 30 minutes **Adults:** I.V.: 2 g at 0.5 g/minute or infused in 250 mL NS over 30 minutes	Most effective when used in initial 24-36 hours after the exposure. Dosage may be repeated in 1 hour followed by every 8 hours if indicated.
Phytonadione (vitamin K₁)	Coumarin derivatives, indandione derivatives	Large acute ingestion of warfarin rodenticides; chronic exposure or greater than normal prothrombin time	**Children:** I.M.: 1-5 mg. With severe toxicity, vitamin K₁ may be given I.V. **Adults:** I.M.: 10 mg	Vitamin K therapy is relatively contraindicated for patients with prosthetic heart valves unless toxicity is life-threatening.
Protamine sulfate	Heparin	Severe hemorrhage	Maximum rate of 5 mg/minute up to a total dose of 200 mg in 2 hours. 1 mg of protamine neutralizes 90 units of beef lung heparin or 115 units of pork intestinal heparin.	Monitor partial thromboplastin time or activated coagulation time. Effect may be immediate and can last for 2 hours. Monitor for hypotension.

Antidote	Poison / Drug	Indications	Dosage	Comments
Pyridoxine (vitamin B_6)	Isoniazid monomethyl-hydrazine-containing mushrooms (Gyromitra); acrylamide, hydrazine	Unknown overdose or ingested isoniazid (INH) amount >80 mg/kg	I.V. pyridoxine in the amount of INH ingested or 5 g if amount is unknown given over 30-60 minutes.	Cumulative dose of pyridoxine is arbitrarily limited to 40 g in adults and 20 g in children.
Succimer (Chemet®)	Lead, arsenic, mercury	Asymptomatic children with venous blood lead 45-69 mcg/dL. Not FDA approved for adult lead exposure or other metals.	P.O.: 10 mg/kg or 350 mg/m² every 8 hours for 5 days. Reduce to 10 mg/kg or 350 mg/m² every 12 hours for an additional 2 weeks.	Monitor liver function; emits "rotten egg" sulfur odor.

Adapted from Rush Poison Control Center, Rush-Presbyterian-St Luke's Medical Center, Chicago, IL 60612.

SALICYLATES

Toxic Symptoms	Treatment
Overdose	Induce emesis with ipecac, and/or lavage with saline, followed with activated charcoal
Dehydration	I.V. fluids with KCl (no D_5W only)
Metabolic acidosis (must be treated)	Sodium bicarbonate
Hyperthermia	Cooling blankets or sponge baths
Coagulopathy/hemorrhage	Vitamin K I.V.
Hypoglycemia (with coma, seizures, or change in mental status)	Dextrose 25 g I.V.
Seizures	Diazepam 5-10 mg I.V.

TOXICOLOGY INFORMATION

Initial Stabilization of the Patients

The recommended treatment plan for the poisoned patient is not unlike general treatment plans taught in advanced cardiac life support (ACLS) or advanced trauma life support (ATLS) courses. In this manner, the initial approach to the poisoned patient should be essentially similar in every case, irrespective of the toxin ingested, just as the initial approach to the trauma patient is the same irrespective of the mechanism of injury. This approach, which can be termed as routine poison management, essentially includes the following aspects.

- Stabilization: ABCs (airway, breathing, circulation; administration of glucose, thiamine, oxygen, and naloxone
- History, physical examination leading toward the identification of class of toxin (toxidrome recognition)
- Prevention of absorption (decontamination)
- Specific antidote, if available
- Removal of absorbed toxin (enhancing excretion)
- Support and monitoring for adverse effects

Drug	Effect	Comment
25-50 g **dextrose** ($D_{50}W$) intravenously to reverse the effects of drug-induced hypoglycemia (adult) 1 mL/kg $D_{50}W$ diluted 1:1 (child)	This can be especially effective in patients with limited glycogen stores (ie, neonates and patients with cirrhosis)	Extravasation into the extremity of this hyperosmolar solution can cause Volkmann's contractures
50-100 mg intravenous **thiamine**	Prevent Wernicke's encephalopathy	A water-soluble vitamin with low toxicity; rare anaphylactoid reactions have been reported
Initial dosage of **naloxone** should be 2 mg in adult patients preferably by the intravenous route, although intramuscular, subcutaneous, intralingual, and endotracheal routes may also be utilized. Pediatric dose is 0.1 mg/kg from birth until 5 years of age	Specific opioid antagonist without any agent properties	It should be noted that some semisynthetic opiates (such as meperidine or propoxyphene) may require higher initial doses for reversal, so that a total dose of 6-10 mg is not unusual for the adults. If the patient responds to a bolus dose and then relapses to a lethargic or comatose state, a naloxone drip can be considered. This can be accomplished by administering two-thirds of the bolus dose that revives the patient per hour or injecting 4 mg naloxone in 1 L crystalloid solution and administering at a rate of 100 mL/hour 0.4 mg/hour)
Oxygen, utilized in 100% concentration	Useful for carbon monoxide, hydrogen, sulfide, and asphyxiants	While oxygen is antidotal for carbon monoxide intoxication, the only relative toxic contraindication is in paraquat intoxication (in that it can promote pulmonary fibrosis)
Flumazenil	Benzodiazepine antagonist	Not routinely recommended due to increased risk of seizures

Laboratory Evaluation of Overdose

Unknown ingestion: Electrolytes, anion gap, serum osmolality, arterial blood gases, serum drug concentration

Known ingestion: Labs tailored to agent

TOXICOLOGY INFORMATION *(Continued)*

Toxins Affecting the Anion Gap

Drugs Causing Increased Anion Gap (>12 mEq/L)

Nonacidotic

Carbenicillin   Sodium salts

Metabolic Acidosis

Acetaminophen (ingestion >75-100 g)	Isoniazid
Acetazolamide	Ketamine
Amiloride	Ketoprofen
Ascorbic acid	Metaldehyde
Benzalkonium chloride	Metformin
Benzyl alcohol	Methanol
Beta-adrenergic drugs	Methenamine mandelate
Bialaphos	Monochloracetic acid
2-Butanone	Nalidixic acid
Carbon monoxide	Naproxen
Centrimonium bromide	Niacin
Chloramphenicol	Papaverine
Colchicine	Pennyroyal oil
Cyanide	Pentachlorophenol
Dapsone	Phenelzine
Dimethyl sulfate	Phenformin (off the market)
Dinitrophenol	Phenol
Endosulfan	Phenylbutazone
Epinephrine (I.V. overdose)	Phosphoric acid
Ethanol	Potassium chloroplatinite
Ethylene dibromide	Propylene glycol
Ethylene glycol	Salicylates
Fenoprofen	Sorbitol (I.V.)
Fluoroacetate	Strychnine
Formaldehyde	Surfactant herbicide
Fructose (I.V.)	Tetracycline (outdated)
Glycol ethers	Theophylline
Hydrogen sulfide	Tienilic acid
Ibuprofen (ingestion >300 mg/kg)	Toluene
Inorganic acid	Tranylcypromine
Iodine	Vacor
Iron	Verapamil

Drugs Causing Decreased Anion Gap (<6 mEq/L)

Acidosis

Ammonium chloride	Lithium
Bromide	Polymyxin B
Iodide	Tromethamine

Drugs Causing Increased Osmolar Gap

(by freezing-point depression, gap is >10 mOsm)

Ethanol[1]

Ethylene glycol[1]

Glycerol

Hypermagnesemia (>9.5 mEq/L)

Isopropanol[1] (acetone)

Iodine (questionable)

Mannitol

Methanol[1]

Propylene glycol

Severe alcoholic ketoacidosis or lactic acidosis

Sorbitol[1]

[1]Toxins increasing both anion and osmolar gap.

Toxins Associated With Oxygen Saturation Gap

(>5% difference between measured and calculated value)

Carbon monoxide

Cyanide (questionable)

Hydrogen sulfide (possible)

Methemoglobin

Acetaminophen Toxicity

The Toxicology Laboratory is also very useful for determining levels of toxin in body fluids. Often these drug levels will guide therapy. For example, use of the Rumack-Matthew nomogram for acute acetaminophen poisoning can direct N-acetylcysteine therapy if the serum acetaminophen level falls above the treatment line.

Acetaminophen Toxicity Nomogram

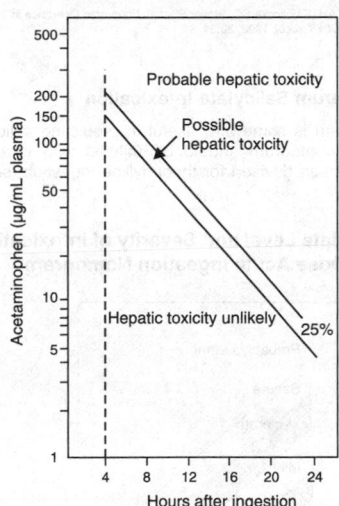

The Rumack-Matthew nomogram, relating expected severity of liver toxicity to serum acetaminophen concentrations.

From Smilkstein MJ, Bronstein AC, Linden C, et al, "Acetaminophen Overdose: A 48-Hour Intravenous N-Acetylcysteine Treatment Protocol," *Ann Emerg Med*, 1991, 20(10):1058, with permission.

TOXICOLOGY INFORMATION *(Continued)*

Ibuprofen Toxicity Nomogram

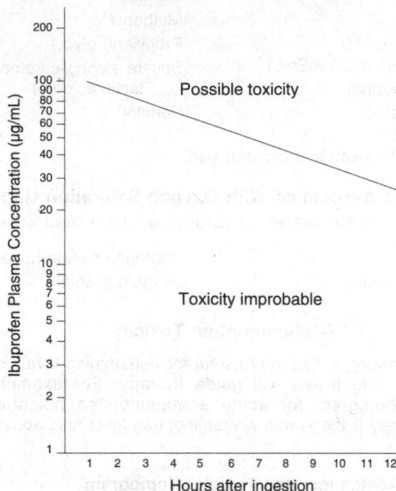

Adapted from Hall AH, Smolinske SC, Stover B, et al, "Ibuprofen Overdose in Adults," *J Toxicol Clin Toxicol*, 1992, 30:34.

Serum Salicylate Intoxication

Similarly, the Done nomogram is somewhat useful in predicting salicylate toxicity in pediatric patients. Neither nomogram should be utilized with chronic ingestions. Recently, a nomogram has been devised for theophylline ingestion; see the following nomogram.

Serum Salicylate Level and Severity of Intoxication
Single Dose Acute Ingestion Nomogram

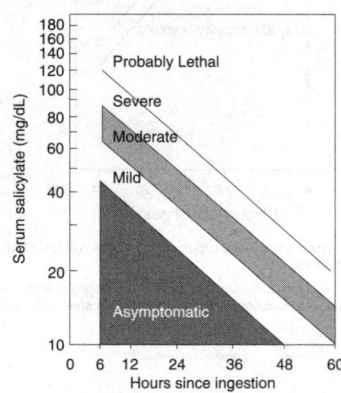

Done nomogram for salicylate poisoning. Note that this nomogram is not accurate for chronic ingestions nor for acute ingestions with enteric coated tabs. Clinical laboratory signs and symptoms are best indicators for assessments. (From Done AK, "Salicylate Intoxication: Significance of Measurements of Salicylate in Blood in Cases of Acute Ingestions," *Pediatrics*, 1960, 26:800; copyright American Academy of Pediatrics, 1960.)

Serum Theophylline Overdose
Nonsmokers

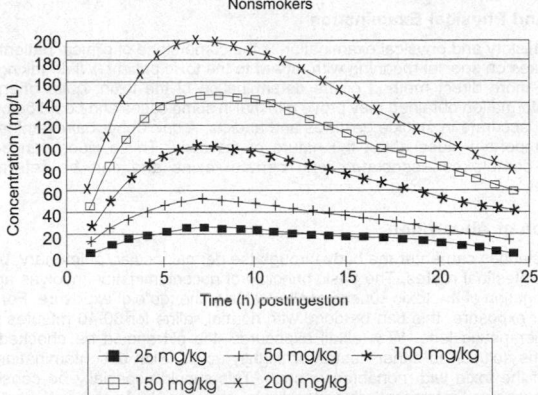

Serum Theophylline Overdose
Smokers and Children

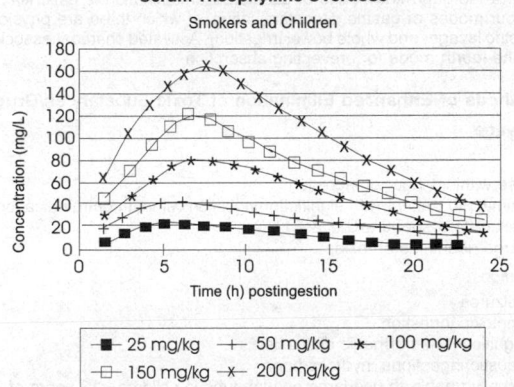

Nomogram for overdose of sustained-release theophylline in 1) nonsmoking adults, and 2) smokers and children. (Courtesy of Frank Paloucek, PharmD, College of Pharmacy, University of Illinois, Chicago.)

TOXICOLOGY INFORMATION *(Continued)*

History and Physical Examination

While the history and physical examination is the cornerstone of clinical patient management, it takes on special meaning with regard to the toxic patient. While taking a history may be a more direct method of the determination of the toxin, quite often is is not reliable. Information obtained may prove minimal in some cases and could be considered partial or inaccurate in suicide gestures and addicts. A quick physical examination often leads to important clues about the nature of the toxin. These clues can be specific symptom complexes associated with certain toxins and can be referred to as "toxidromes".

Prevention of Absorption

Toxic substances can enter the body through the dermal, ocular, pulmonary, parenteral, and gastrointestinal routes. The basic principle of decontamination involves appropriate copious irrigation of the toxic substances relatable to the route of exposure. For example, with ocular exposure, this can be done with normal saline for 30-40 minutes through a Morgan therapeutic lens. With alkali exposures, the pH should be checked until the runoff of the solution is either neutral or slightly acidic. Skin decontamination involves removal of the toxin with nonabrasive soap. This should especially be considered for organophosphates, methylene chloride, dioxin, radiation, hydrocarbons, and herbicide exposure. Separate drainage areas should be obtained for the contaminated runoff.

Since >80% of incidents of accidental poisoning in children occur through the gastrointestinal tract, a thorough knowledge of gastric decontamination is essential. There are essentially four modes of gastric decontamination, of which three are physical removal (emesis, gastric lavage, and whole bowel irrigation). Activated charcoal associated with a cathartic is the fourth mode for preventing absorption.

Methods of Enhanced Elimination of Toxic Substances/Drugs

Gastric Lavage

Indications

- Use within 1 hour of ingestion
- Comatose patient with significant ingestion without contraindications
- Failure to respond to ipecac
- Large quantities of toxins

Contraindications

- Seizures
- Nontoxic ingestion
- Significant hemorrhagic diathesis
- Caustic ingestions, hydrocarbons
- Usually unable to use large enough tube in children <12 years of age

Note: Lavage is not routinely recommended except for recent and very large ingestions of noncontraindicated toxins since it is believed to actually push a significant portion of drug into the intestine and may delay administration of activated charcoal.

Enhancement of Elimination

Only recently has this aspect of poison management received more than cursory attention in practice and in the literature. The standard practice for enhancement of elimination consisted primarily of forced diuresis in order to excrete the toxin. However, the past 10 years experience has produced a radical change in the approach to this and therefore, a more focused methodology to eliminating absorbed toxins. Essentially, there are three methods by which absorbed toxins may be eliminated: recurrent adsorption with multiple dosings of activated charcoal, use of forced diuresis in combination with possible alkalinization of the urine, and use of dialysis or charcoal hemoperfusion.

Activated Charcoal Indications

Indications

- Single dose for agents known to be bound

- Multiple dose for drugs with favorable characteristics: Small volume of distribution (<1 L/kg), low plasma protein binding, biliary or gastric secretion, active metabolites that recirculate, drugs that exhibit a large free fraction (eg, dapsone, carbamazepine, digitalis, methotrexate, phenobarbital, salicylates, theophylline, tricyclic antidepressants), unchanged, lipophilic, long half-life

Recently, multiple dosing of activated charcoal ("pulse dosing") has been advocated as a method for removal of absorbed drug. This procedure has been demonstrated to be efficacious in drugs that re-enter the gastrointestinal tract through enterohepatic circulation (ie, carbamazepine) and with drugs that diffuse from the systemic circulation into the gastrointestinal tract due to formation of a concentration gradient ("the infinite sink" hypothesis).

Toxins Eliminated by Multiple Dosing of Activated Charcoal (MDAC)

Acetaminophen
Amitriptyline
Amoxapine
Baclofen (?)
Benzodiazepines (?)
Bupropion (?)
Carbamazepine[1]
Chlordecone
Cyclosporine
Diazepam
Digoxin
Disopyramide
Maprotiline
Meprobamate

Methotrexate
Methyprylon
Nadolol
Nortriptyline
Phencyclidine
Phenobarbital[1]
Phenylbutazone
Phenytoin (?)
Piroxicam
Propoxyphene
Propranolol
Salicylates (?)[1]
Theophylline[1]
Valproic acid[1]

[1]Only agents routinely recommended for removal with MDAC.

Contraindications

- Absence of hypoactive bowel sounds
- Caustic ingestions
- Drugs without effect: Acids, alkalis, alcohols, cyanide, iron, heavy metals, lithium, insecticides

Dose

Children and Adults: 50-100 g initially or 1 g/kg weight; repeat doses of 25 g or 0.5 g/kg every 2-4 hours

Most effective at 1-hour postingestion but can remove at >1-hour postingestion

Doses subsequent to first may be admixed with water rather than a cathartic such as sorbitol to avoid diarrhea and consequent electrolyte disturbances.

Whole Bowel Irrigation – propylene glycol based solutions

Initial dose of charcoal is necessary prior to use. Avoid pretreatment with ipecac.

Indications

- Iron, lead, lithium
- Agents not bound by charcoal
- Modified or sustained release dosage forms
- Body packers

Contraindications

- Bowel perforation
- Obstruction
- Ileus
- Gastrointestinal bleed

Dose

Maximum: 5-10 L
Toddlers/preschool: 250-500 mL/hour or 35 mL/kg
Adults: 1-2 L/hour
Terminate when rectal effluent = infusate = clear

Urinary Ion Trapping – to alkalinize the urine

Indications

- Salicylates
- Phenobarbital

Toxins Eliminated by Forced Saline Diuretics	Toxins Eliminated by Alkaline Diuresis
Bromidex	2,4-D chlorphenoxyacetic acid
Chromium	Fluoride
Cimetidine (?)	Isoniazid (?)
Cis-platinum	Mephobarbital
Cyclophosphamide	Methotrexate
Hydrazine	Phenobarbital
Iodide	Primidone
Iodine	Quinolones antibiotic
Isoniazid (?)	Salicylates
Lithium	Uranium
Methyl iodide	
Potassium chloroplatinite	
Thallium	

TOXICOLOGY INFORMATION *(Continued)*

Dose

Sodium bicarbonate 1-2 mEq/kg every 3-4 hours or 100 mEq NaHCO$_3$ in 1 L D$_5$¼NS at 200 mL/hour (desired urine pH: 7.6-7.8)

A urine flow of 3-5 mL/kg/hour should be achieved with a combination of isotonic fluids or diuretics. Although several drugs can exhibit enhanced elimination through an acidic urine (quinine, amphetamines, PCP, nicotine, bismuth, ephedrine, flecainide), the practice of acidifying the urine should be discouraged in that it can produce metabolic acidosis and promote renal failure in the presence of rhabdomyolysis. **Note:** Use caution in alkalinizing urine of children to avoid fluid overdose.

Hemodialysis

Indications

Drugs with favorable characteristics

- Low molecular weight (<500 daltons)
- Ionically charged
- H$_2$O soluble
- Low plasma protein binding (<70%-80%)
- Small volume of distribution (<1 L/kg)
- Low tissue binding
- Methanol, ethylene glycol

Drugs and Toxins Removed by Hemodialysis

Acetaminophen	Iodides
Acyclovir	Isoniazid
Amanita phalloides (?)	Isopropanol
Amantadine (?)	Ketoprofen
Ammonium chloride	Lithium
Amphetamine	Magnesium
Anilines	Meprobamate
Atenolol	Metal-chelate compounds
Bromides	Metformin (?)
Bromisoval	Methanol
Calcium	Methaqualone
Captopril (?)	Methotrexate
Carbromal	Methyldopa
Carisoprodol	Methylprylone
Chloral hydrate	Monochloroacetic acid
Chlorpropamide	Nadolol
Chromium	Oxalic acid
Cimetidine (?)	Phenelzine (?)
Cyclophosphamide	Phenobarbital
Dapsone	Phosphoric acid
Disopyramide	Potassium
Enalapril (?)	Procainamide
Ethanol	Quinidine
Ethylene glycol	Ranitidine (?)
Famotidine (?)	Rifabutin
Fluoride	Salicylates
Folic acid	Sotalol
Formaldehyde	Strychnine
Foscarnet sodium	Thallium
Gabapentin	Theophylline
Glycol ethers	Thiocyanates
Hydrazine (?)	Tranylcypromine sulfate (?)
Hydrochlorothiazide	Verapamil (?)

Hemoperfusion

Indications

Drugs with favorable characteristics:

- Affinity for activated charcoal
- Tissue binding
- High rate of equilibration from peripheral tissues to blood

Examples: Barbiturates, carbamazepine, ethchlorvynol, methotrexate, phenytoin, theophylline

Drugs and Toxins Removed by Hemoperfusion (Charcoal)

Aconitine	Meprobamate
Amanita phalloides (?)	Methaqualone
Atenolol (?)	Methotrexate
Bromisoval	Methsuximide
Bromoethylbutyramide	Methyprylon (?)
Caffeine	Metoprolol (?)
Carbamazepine	Nadolol (?)
Carbon tetrachloride (?)	Oxalic acid (?)
Carbromal	Paraquat
Chloral hydrate (trichloroethanol)	Phenelzine (?)
Chloramphenicol	Phenobarbital
Chlorpropamide	Phenytoin
Colchicine (?)	Podophyllin (?)
Creosote (?)	Procainamide (?)
Dapsone	Quinidine (?)
Diltiazem (?)	Rifabutin (?)
Disopyramide	Sotalol (?)
Ethchlorvynol	Thallium
Ethylene oxide	Theophylline
Lindane	Verapamil (?)

Exchange transfusion is another mode of extracorporeal removal of toxins that can be utilized in neonatal infant drug toxicity. It may be especially useful for barbiturate, iron, caffeine, sodium nitrite, or theophylline overdose.

TOXIDROMES

Overdose Signs and Symptoms

Toxin	Vital Signs	Mental Status	Symptoms	Physical Exam	Laboratories
Acetaminophen	Normal	Normal	Anorexia, nausea, vomiting	RUQ tenderness, jaundice	Elevated LFTs
Cocaine	Hypertension, tachycardia, hyperthermia	Anxiety, agitation, delirium	Hallucinations	Mydriasis, tremor, diaphoresis, seizures, perforated nasal septum	ECG abnormalities, increased CPK
Cyclic antidepressants	Tachycardia, hypotension, hyperthermia	Decreased, including coma	Confusion, dizziness	Mydriasis, dry mucous membranes, distended bladder, decreased bowel sounds, flushed, seizures	Long QRS complex, cardiac dysrhythmias
Iron	Early: Normal Late: Hypotension, tachycardia	Normal; lethargic if hypotensive	Nausea, vomiting, diarrhea, abdominal pain, hematemesis	Abdominal tenderness	Heme + stool and vomit, metabolic acidosis, ECG and x-ray findings, elevated serum iron (early); child: hyperglycemia, leukocytosis
Opioids	Hypotension, bradycardia, hypoventilation, hypothermia	Decreased, including coma	Intoxication	Miosis, absent bowel sounds	Abnormal ABGs
Salicylates	Hyperventilation, hyperthermia	Agitation; lethargy; including coma	Tinnitus, nausea, vomiting, confusion	Diaphoresis, tender abdomen	Anion gap metabolic acidosis, respiratory alkalosis, abnormal LFTs, and coagulation studies
Theophylline	Tachycardia, hypotension, hyperventilation, hyperthermia	Agitation, lethargy, including coma	Nausea, vomiting, diaphoresis, tremor, confusion	Seizures, arrhythmias	Hypokalemia, hyperglycemia, metabolic acidosis, abnormal ECG

Examples of Toxidromes

Toxidromes	Pattern	Example of Drugs	Treatment Approach
Anticholinergic	Fever, ileus, flushing, tachycardia, urinary retention, inability to sweat, visual blurring, and mydriasis. Central manifestations include myoclonus, choreoathetosis, toxic psychosis with lilliputian hallucinations, seizures, and coma.	Antihistamines Baclofen Benztropine Jimson weed Methylpyroline Phenothiazines Propantheline Tricyclic antidepressants	Physostigmine for life-threatening symptoms only; may predispose to arrhythmias[1]
Cholinergic	Characterized by salivation, lacrimation, urination, defecation, gastrointestinal cramps, and emesis ("sludge"). Bradycardia and bronchoconstriction may also be seen.	Carbamate Organophosphates Pilocarpine	• Atropine[1] • Pralidoxime for organophosphate insecticides[1]
Extrapyramidal	Choreoathetosis, hyperreflexia, trismus, opisthotonos, rigidity, and tremor	Haloperidol Phenothiazines	• Diphenhydramine • Benztropine
Hallucinogenic	Perceptual distortions, synthesis, depersonalization, and derealization	Amphetamines Cannabinoids Cocaine Indole alkaloids Phencyclidine	Benzodiazepine
Narcotic	Altered mental status, unresponsiveness, shallow respirations, slow respiratory rate or periodic breathing, miosis, bradycardia, hypothermia	Opiates Dextromethorphan Pentazocine Propoxyphene	Naloxone[1]

TOXIDROMES *(Continued)*

Examples of Toxidromes *(continued)*

Toxidromes	Pattern	Example of Drugs	Treatment Approach
Sedative/Hypnotic	Manifested by sedation with progressive deterioration of central nervous system function. Coma, stupor, confusion, apnea, delirium, or hallucinations may accompany this pattern.	Anticonvulsants Antipsychotics Barbiturates Benzodiazepines Ethanol Ethchlorvynol Fentanyl Glutethimide Meprobamate Methadone Methocarbamol Opiates Quinazolines Propoxyphene Tricyclic antidepressants	• Naloxone[1] • Flumazenil; usually not recommended due to increased risk of seizures[1] • Urinary alkalinization (barbiturates)
Seizuregenic	May mimic stimulant pattern with hyperthermia, hyperreflexia, and tremors being prominent signs	Anticholinergics Camphor Chlorinated hydrocarbons Cocaine Isoniazid Lidocaine Lindane Nicotine Phencyclidine Strychnine Xanthines	• Antiseizure medications • Pyridoxine for isoniazid[1] • Extracorporeal removal of drug (ie, lindane, camphor, xanthines) • Physostigmine for anticholinergic agents[1]

Examples of Toxidromes *(continued)*

Toxidromes	Pattern	Example of Drugs	Treatment Approach
Serotonin	Confusion, myoclonus, hyperreflexia, diaphoresis, tremor, facial flushing, diarrhea, fever, trismus	Clomipramine Fluoxetine Isoniazid L-tryptophan Paroxetine Phenelzine Sertraline Tranylcypromine Drug combinations include: • MAO inhibitors with L-tryptophan • Fluoxetine or meperidine • Fluoxetine with carbamazepine or sertraline • Clomipramine and meclobemide • Trazodol and buspirone • Paroxetine and dextromethorphan	Withdrawal of drug/benzodiazepine
Solvent	Lethargy, confusion, dizziness, headache, restlessness, incoordination, derealization, depersonalization	Acetone Chlorinated hydrocarbons Hydrocarbons Naphthalene Trichloroethane Toluene	Avoid catecholamines
Stimulant	Restlessness, excessive speech and motor activity, tachycardia, tremor, and insomnia — may progress to seizure. Other effects noted include euphoria, mydriasis, anorexia, and paranoia.	Amphetamines Caffeine (xanthines) Cocaine Ephedrine/pseudoephedrine Methylphenidate Nicotine Phencyclidine	Benzodiazepines

TOXIDROMES (Continued)

Examples of Toxidromes (continued)

Toxidromes	Pattern	Example of Drugs	Treatment Approach
Uncoupling of oxidative phosphylation	Hyperthermia, tachypnea, diaphoresis, metabolic acidosis (usually)	Aluminum phosphide Aspirin/salicylates 2,4-Dichlorophenol Di-n-Butyl phthalate Dinitrophenols Dinitro-o-cresols Hexachlorobutadiene Phosphorus Pentachlorophenol Tin (?) Zinc phosphide	Sodium bicarbonate to treat metabolic acidosis; patient cooling techniques; avoidance of atropine or salicylate agents; hemodialysis may be required for acidosis treatment

¹See the Poison Control Center Antidote Chart.

From Nice A, Leikin JB, Maturen A, et al, "Toxidrome Recognition to Improve Efficiency of Emergency Urine Drug Screens," *Ann Emerg Med*, 1988, 17:676-80.

BREAST-FEEDING AND DRUGS

Prior to recommending or prescribing medications to a lactating woman, the following should be considered:

- Is drug therapy necessary?
- Can drug exposure to the infant be minimized? (Using a different route of administration, timing of the dose in relation to breast-feeding, length of therapy, using breast milk stored prior to treatment, etc)
- The infants age and health status (their own ability to metabolize the medication)
- The pharmacokinetics of the drug
- Will the drug interact with a medication the infant is prescribed?
- If medications must be used, pick the safest drug possible.
- In situations where the only drug available may have adverse effects in the nursing infant, consider measuring the infants blood levels.

The tables presented below have been adapted from the American Academy of Pediatrics Committee on Drugs report "Transfer of Drugs and Other Chemicals Into Human Milk," September 2001. It should not be inferred that if a medication is not in the tables it is considered safe for administration to a lactating woman; only that published reports concerning their use were not available at the time the report was published.

Table 1. Cytotoxic Drugs

Cyclophosphamide	Doxorubicin
Cyclosporine	Methotrexate

These are medications thought to interfere with cellular metabolism in the nursing infant. Immune suppression may be possible; effects on growth or carcinogenesis are not known. In addition, doxorubicin is concentrated in human milk; methotrexate is associated with neutropenia in the nursing infant.

Table 2. Drugs of Abuse

Amphetamine	Marijuana
Cocaine	Phencyclidine
Heroin	

Drugs of abuse are not only dangerous to the nursing infant, but also to the mother. Women should be encouraged to avoid their use completely. Effects to the infant reported with amphetamine use in the mother include irritability and poor sleeping; it is also a substance that is concentrated in human milk. Cocaine may cause irritability, vomiting, diarrhea, tremors, or seizures in the infant. Heroin may also cause tremors as well as restlessness, vomiting, and poor feeding.

Nicotine, which was previously on this list, is associated with decreased milk production, decreased weight gain in the infant, and possible increased respiratory illness in the infant. Although there are still questions outstanding regarding smoking and breast-feeding, women should be counseled on the possible effects to their infants and offered aid to smoking cessation if appropriate.

BREAST-FEEDING AND DRUGS *(Continued)*

Table 3. Radioactive Compounds That Require Temporary Cessation of Breast-Feeding

Drug	Recommended Time for Cessation of Breast-Feeding
Copper 64 (^{64}Cu)	Radioactivity in milk present at 50 h
Gallium 67 (^{67}Ga)	Radioactivity in milk present for 2 wk
Indium 111 (^{111}In)	Very small amount present at 20 h
Iodine 123 (^{123}I)	Radioactivity in milk present up to 36 h
Iodine 125 (^{125}I)	Radioactivity in milk present for 12 d
Iodine 131 (^{131}I)	Radioactivity in milk present 2-14 d, depending on study
Iodine^{131}	If used for thyroid cancer, high radioactivity may prolong exposure to infant
Radioactive sodium	Radioactivity in milk present 96 h
Technetium-99m (^{99m}Tc), ^{99m}Tc macroaggregates, ^{99m}Tc O4	Radioactivity in milk present 15 h to 3 d

Consider pumping and storing milk prior to study for use during the radioactive period. Pumping should continue after the study to maintain milk production; however, this milk should be discarded until radioactivity is gone. Notify nuclear medicine physician prior to study that the mother is breast-feeding; a short-acting radionuclide may be appropriate. Contact Radiology Department after testing is complete to screen milk samples before resuming feeding.

Table 4a. Psychotropic Drugs Whose Effect on Nursing Infants Is Unknown But May Be of Concern

Antianxiety	Antidepressant	Antipsychotic
Alprazolam	Amitriptyline	Chlorpromazine
Diazepam	Amoxapine	Clozapine[1]
Lorazepam	Bupropion	Haloperidol
Midazolam	Clomipramine	Mesoridazine
Perphenazine	Desipramine	Trifluoperazine
Quazepam	Doxepin	
Temazepam	Fluoxetine	
	Fluvoxamine	
	Imipramine	
	Nortriptyline	
	Paroxetine	
	Sertraline[1]	
	Trazodone	

[1]Drug is concentrated in human milk.

Psychotropic medications usually appear in the breast milk in low concentrations. Although adverse effects in the infant may be limited to a few case reports, the long half-life of these medications and their metabolites should be considered. In addition, measurable amounts may be found in the infants plasma and also brain tissue. Long-term effects are not known. Colic, irritability, feeding and sleep disorders, and slow weight gain are effects reported with fluoxetine. Chlorpromazine may cause galactorrhea in the mother, while drowsiness and lethargy have been reported in the nursing infant. A decline in developmental scores has been reported with chlorpromazine and haloperidol.

Table 4b. Additional Drugs Whose Effect on Nursing Infants Is Unknown But May Be of Concern

Drug	Reported Effect in Nursing Infant
Amiodarone	Hypothyroidism
Chloramphenicol	Idiosyncratic bone marrow suppression
Clofazimine	Increase in skin pigmentation; high transfer of mothers dose to infant is possible
Lamotrigine	Therapeutic serum concentrations in infant
Metoclopramide[1]	
Metronidazole	
Tinidazole	

[1]Drug is concentrated in human milk.

No adverse effects to the infant have been reported for metoclopramide; however, it should be recognized that it is a dopaminergic agent. Metronidazole and tinidazole are *in vitro* mutagenic agents. In cases where single dose therapy is appropriate for the mother, breast-feeding may be discontinued for 12-24 hours to allow excretion of the medication.

Table 5. Drugs That Have Been Associated With Significant Effects on Some Nursing Infants and Should Be Given to Nursing Mothers With Caution[1]

Drug	Reported Effect
Acebutolol	Hypotension, bradycardia, tachypnea
5-Aminosalicylic acid	Diarrhea (one case)
Atenolol	Cyanosis, bradycardia
Bromocriptine	Suppresses lactation; may be hazardous to the mother
Aspirin (salicylates)	Metabolic acidosis (one case)
Clemastine	Drowsiness, irritability, refusal to feed, high-pitched cry, neck stiffness (one case)
Ergotamine	Vomiting, diarrhea, convulsions (doses used in migraine medications
Lithium	One-third to one-half therapeutic blood concentration in infants
Phenindone	Anticoagulant: increased prothrombin and partial thromboplastin time in one infant; not used in the United States
Phenobarbital	Sedation; infantile spasms after weaning from milk-containing phenobarbital, methemoglobinemia (one case)
Primidone	Sedation, feeding problems
Sulfasalazine (salicylazosulfapyridine)	Bloody diarrhea (one case)

[1]Blood concentration in the infant may be of clinical importance; measure when possible.

References

American Academy of Pediatrics Committee on Drugs, "Transfer of Drugs and Other Chemicals Into Human Milk," *Pediatrics*, 2001, 108(3): 776-89.

2000 Red Book: Report of the Committee on Infectious Diseases, 25th ed, Elk Grove Village, IL: American Academy of Pediatrics, 2000, 98-104.

DISCOLORATION OF FECES
DUE TO DRUGS

Black

Acetazolamide
Alcohols
Alkalies
Aluminum hydroxide
Aminophylline
Aminosalicylic acid
Amphetamine
Amphotericin
Antacids
Anticoagulants
Aspirin
Betamethasone
Bismuth
Charcoal
Chloramphenicol
Chlorpropamide
Clindamycin
Corticosteroids
Cortisone
Cyclophosphamide
Cytarabine
Digitalis
Ethacrynic acid
Ferrous salts
Floxuridine
Fluorides
Fluorouracil
Halothane
Heparin
Hydralazine
Hydrocortisone
Ibuprofen
Indomethacin
Iodine drugs
Iron salts
Levarterenol
Levodopa
Manganese
Melphalan
Methylprednisolone
Methotrexate

Methylene blue
Oxyphenbutazone
Phenacetin
Phenolphthalein
Phenylbutazone
Phenylephrine
Phosphorous
Potassium salts
Prednisolone
Procarbazine
Pyrvinium
Reserpine
Salicylates
Sulfonamides
Tetracycline
Theophylline
Thiotepa
Triamcinolone
Warfarin

Blue

Chloramphenicol
Methylene blue

Dark Brown

Dexamethasone

Gray

Colchicine

Green

Indomethacin
Iron
Medroxyprogesterone

Greenish Gray

Oral antibiotics
Oxyphenbutazone
Phenylbutazone

Light Brown

Anticoagulants

Orange-Red

Phenazopyridine
Rifampin

Pink

Anticoagulants
Aspirin
Heparin
Oxyphenbutazone
Phenylbutazone
Salicylates

Red

Anticoagulants
Aspirin
Heparin
Oxyphenbutazone
Phenolphthalein
Phenylbutazone
Pyrvinium
Salicylates
Tetracycline syrup

Red-Brown

Oxyphenbutazone
Phenylbutazone
Rifampin

Tarry

Ergot preparations
Ibuprofen
Salicylates
Warfarin

White/Speckling

Aluminum hydroxide
Antibiotics (oral)
Indocyanine green

Yellow

Senna

Yellow-Green

Senna

Adapted from Drugdex® — Drug Consults, Micromedex, Vol 62, Denver, CO: Rocky Mountain Drug Consultation Center, 1998.

DISCOLORATION OF URINE
DUE TO DRUGS

Black
Cascara
Cotrimoxazole
Ferrous salts
Iron dextran
Levodopa
Methocarbamol
Methyldopa
Naphthalene
Pamaquine
Phenacetin
Phenols
Quinine
Sulfonamides

Blue
Anthraquinone
DeWitt's pills
Indigo blue
Indigo carmine
Methocarbamol
Methylene blue
Mitoxantrone
Nitrofurans
Resorcinol
Triamterene

Blue-Green
Amitriptyline
Anthraquinone
DeWitt's pills
Doan's® pills
Indigo blue
Indigo carmine
Magnesium salicylate
Methylene blue
Resorcinol

Brown
Anthraquinone dyes
Cascara
Chloroquine
Hydroquinone
Levodopa
Methocarbamol
Methyldopa
Metronidazole
Nitrofurans
Nitrofurantoin
Pamaquine
Phenacetin
Phenols
Primaquine
Quinine
Rifabutin
Rifampin
Senna
Sodium diatrizoate
Sulfonamides

Brown-Black
Isosorbide mono- or dini-
  trate
Methyldopa
Metronidazole
Nitrates
Nitrofurans
Phenacetin
Povidone iodine
Quinine
Senna

Dark
p-Aminosalicylic acid
Cascara
Levodopa
Metronidazole
Nitrites
Phenacetin
Phenol
Primaquine
Quinine
Resorcinol
Riboflavin
Senna

Green
Amitriptyline
Anthraquinone
DeWitt's pills
Indigo blue
Indigo carmine
Indomethacin
Methocarbamol
Methylene blue
Nitrofurans
Phenols
Propofol
Resorcinol
Suprofen

Green-Yellow
DeWitt's pills
Methylene blue

Milky
Phosphates

Orange
Chlorzoxazone
Dihydroergotamine mesy-
  late
Heparin sodium
Phenazopyridine
Phenindione
Rifabutin
Rifampin
Sulfasalazine
Warfarin

Orange-Red-Brown
Chlorzoxazone
Doxidan
Phenazopyridine
Rifampin
Warfarin

Orange-Yellow
Fluorescein sodium
Rifampin
Sulfasalazine

Pink
Aminopyrine
Anthraquinone dyes
Aspirin
Cascara
Danthron
Deferoxamine
Methyldopa
Phenazopyridone
Phenolphthalein
Phenothiazines
Phenytoin
Salicylates
Senna

Purple
Phenolphthalein

Red
Anthraquinone
Cascara
Chlorpromazine
Daunorubicin
Deferoxamine
Dihydroergotamine mesy-
  late
Dimethyl sulfoxide
DMSO
Doxorubicin
Heparin
Ibuprofen
Methyldopa
Oxyphenbutazone
Phenacetin
Phenazopyridine
Phenolphthalein
Phenothiazines
Phensuximide
Phenylbutazone
Phenytoin
Rifampin
Senna

Red-Brown
Cascara
Deferoxamine
Methyldopa
Oxyphenbutazone
Pamaquine
Phenacetin
Phenazopyridine
Phenolphthalein
Phenothiazines
Phenylbutazone
Phenytoin
Quinine
Senna

Red-Purple
Chlorzoxazone
Ibuprofen
Phenacetin
Senna

Rust
Cascara
Chloroquine
Metronidazole
Nitrofurantoin
Pamaquine
Phenacetin
Quinacrine
Riboflavin
Senna
Sulfonamides

Yellow
Nitrofurantoin
Phenacetin
Quinacrine
Riboflavin
Sulfasalazine

DISCOLORATION OF URINE DUE TO DRUGS *(Continued)*

Yellow-Brown
Aminosalicylate acid
Bismuth
Cascara
Chloroquine
DeWitt's pills
Methylene blue
Metronidazole
Nitrofurantoin
Pamaquine
Primaquine
Quinacrine
Senna
Sulfonamides

Yellow-Pink
Cascara
Senna

Adapted from Drugdex® — Drug Consults, Micromedex, Vol 62, Denver, CO: Rocky Mountain Drug Consultation Center, 1998.

DRUGS IN PREGNANCY

Medications Known to Be Teratogens

Alcohol
Androgens
Anticonvulsants
Antineoplastics
Cocaine
Diethylstilbestrol
Etretinate
Iodides (including radioactive iodine)

Isotretinoin
Lithium
Live vaccines
Methimazole
Penicillamine
Tetracyclines
Warfarin

Medications Suspected to Be Teratogens

ACE inhibitors
Benzodiazepines
Estrogens

Oral hypoglycemic drugs
Progestogens
Quinolones

Medications With No Known Teratogenic Effects[1]

Acetaminophen
Cephalosporins
Corticosteroids
Docusate sodium
Erythromycin
Multiple vitamins

Narcotic analgesics
Penicillins
Phenothiazines
Thyroid hormones
Tricyclic antidepressants

[1]No drug is absolutely without risk during pregnancy. These drugs appear to have a minimal risk when used judiciously in usual doses under the supervision of a medical professional.

Medications With Nonteratogenic Adverse Effects in Pregnancy

Antithyroid drugs
Aminoglycosides
Aspirin
Barbiturates (chronic use)
Benzodiazepines
Beta-blockers
Caffeine
Chloramphenicol
Cocaine

Diuretics
Isoniazid
Narcotic analgesics (chronic use)
Nicotine
Nonsteroidal anti-inflammatory agents
Oral hypoglycemic agents
Propylthiouracil
Sulfonamides

Adapted from DiPiro JT, Talbert RL, Hayes PE, et al, "Therapeutic Considerations During Pregnancy and Lactation," *Pharmacotherapy: A Pathophysiologic Approach*, 4th ed, Stamford, CT: Appleton & Lange, 1999.

DRUGS IN PREGNANCY *(Continued)*

MATERNAL / FETAL MEDICATIONS

Adapted from Briggs GG, "Medication Use During the Perinatal Period,"
J Am Pharm Assoc, 1998, 38:717-27.

Antibiotics in Pregnancy

Antibiotic	Comments
Antibiotics to Be Avoided	
Aminoglycosides (prolonged use)	Eighth cranial nerve damage (hearing loss, vestibulotoxicity)
Erythromycin estolate	Hepatotoxic in mother
Fluoroquinolones	Potentially mutagenic, cartilage damage, arthropathy, and teratogenicity
Ribavirin	Possibly fetotoxic
Tetracyclines	Staining of deciduous teeth (4th month through term)
Antibiotics Which Are Generally Regarded as Safe	
Aminoglycosides (limited use)	
Cephalosporins	
Clindamycin	
Erythromycin	
Penicillins	

Treatment and Prevention of Infection

Prophylaxis	
Preterm premature rupture of membranes	Ampicillin, amoxicillin, cefazolin, amoxicillin/clavulanate, ampicillin/sulbactam, erythromycin
Prevention of bacterial endocarditis	Ampicillin 2 g and gentamicin 1.5 mg/kg (max 120 mg) within 30 minutes of delivery, followed by 1 g ampicillin (I.V.) or amoxicillin (oral) 6 hours later
Cesarean section	Cefazolin (I.V. or uterine irrigation) or clindamycin/gentamicin
Treatment	
Bacterial vaginosis	Clindamycin (oral or gel) in first trimester (gel has been associated with higher rate of preterm deliveries) Metronidazole (oral) for 7 days or gel for 5 days (after first trimester)
Chorioamnionitis	Ampicillin plus gentamicin (clindamycin, erythromycin, or vancomycin if PCN allergic)
Genital herpes	First episode: Oral acyclovir Near term treatment may reduce Cesarian sections I.V. therapy for disseminated infection
Group B streptococci	Penicillin G 5 million units once, then 2.5 million units q4h Ampicillin 2 g once, then 1 g q4h Clindamycin or erythromycin if PCN allergic
HIV*	*Note: Always consult HIV guidelines (www.hivatis.org) Zidovudine (limits maternal-fetal transmission) Oral dosing during pregnancy/I.V. prior to delivery Other antiretroviral agents – effects unknown Lamivudine during labor used in combination with zidovudine in women who have not received prior antiretroviral therapy
Postpartum endometritis	Ampicillin (vancomycin if PCN allergic) plus clindamycin (or metronidazole) plus gentamicin until afebrile
Pyelonephritis	Ampicillin-gentamicin Cefazolin Co-trimoxazole
Urinary tract infection	Amoxicillin/ampicillin (resistance has increased) Co-trimoxazole Nitrofurantoin Cephalexin
Vaginal candidiasis	Buconizole for 7 days Clotrimazole for 7 days Miconazole for 7 days Terconazole for 7 days

Preterm Labor: Tocolytic Agents

Drug Class	Route	Fetal / Neonatal Toxicities	Maternal Toxicities
Beta-adrenergic agonists			
Ritodrine, terbutaline	Oral, I.V., Sub-Q	Fetal tachycardia, intraventricular septal hypertrophy, neonatal hyperinsulinemia/hypoglycemia	Pulmonary, edema, myocardial infarction, hypokalemia, hypotension, hyperglycemia, tachycardia
Magnesium	I.V.	Neurologic depression in newborn (loss of reflexes, hypotonia, respiratory depression); fetal hypocalcemia and hypercalcuria; abnormal fetal bone mineralization and enamel hypoplasia	Hypotension, respiratory depression, ileus/constipation, hypocalcemia, pulmonary edema, hypotension, headache/dizziness
NSAIDs			
Indomethacin	Oral, P.R.	Ductus arteriosis: premature closure, tricuspid regurgitation, primary pulmonary hypertension of the newborn, PDA; intraventricular hemorrhage, necrotizing enterocolitis, renal failure	GI bleeding, oligohydramnios, pulmonary edema, acute renal failure
Calcium channel blockers			
Nifedipine	Oral	Hypoxia secondary to maternal hypotension	Hypotension, flushing, tachycardia, headache
Nitrates			
Nitroglycerin	I.V./S.L.	Hypoxia secondary to maternal hypotension	Hypotension, headache, dizziness

Pregnancy-Induced Hypertension[1]

Drug Class	Maternal / Fetal Effects
Antihypertensives Contraindicated in PIH	
Diuretics	Reduction of maternal plasma volume exacerbates disease; use in chronic hypertension acceptable (if no superimposed pregnancy-induced hypertension)
ACE inhibitors	Teratogenic in second and third trimester; fetal/newborn anuria and hypotension, fetal oligohydramnios; neonatal death (congenital abnormalities of skull and renal failure)
Hypertension Treatment[2]	
Central-acting	
Methyldopa	Relatively safe in second/third trimester
Beta-blockers	
Acebutolol, atenolol, metoprolol, pindolol, propranolol	Increased risk of IUGR
Alpha-/beta-blockers	
Labetolol	See beta-blockers
Vasodilators	
Hydralazine	
Nitrates	
Nitroglycerin	Relatively safe in second/third trimester
Calcium channel blockers	
Nifedipine	

[1]Includes management of pre-eclampsia/eclampsia and HELLP syndrome.
Note: Prevention may include low-dose aspirin (81 mg/day) or calcium supplementation (2 g/day).
[2]All agents must be carefully titrated to avoid fetal hypoxia.

FEVER DUE TO DRUGS

Most Common

Atropine

Amphotericin B

Asparaginase

Barbiturates

Bleomycin

Cephalosporins

Interferon

Methyldopa

Penicillins

Phenytoin

Procainamide

Quinidine

Salicylates (high doses)

Streptomycin

Sulfonamides

Less Common

Allopurinol

Antihistamines

Azathioprine

Carbamazepine

Cimetidine

Cisplatin

Colistimethate

Diazoxide

Folic acid

Hydralazine

Hydroxyurea

Imipenem

Iodides

Isoniazid

Mercaptopurine

Metoclopramide

Nifedipine

NSAIDs

Nitrofurantoin

Pentazocine

Procarbazine

Propylthiouracil

Rifampin

Streptokinase

Triamterene

Vancomycin

References

Cunha BA, "Antibiotic Side Effects," *Med Clin North Am*, 2001, 85(1):149-85.

Mackowiak PA and LeMaistre CF, "Drug Fever: A Critical Appraisal of Conventional Concepts. An Analysis of 51 Episodes in Two Dallas Hospitals and 97 Episodes Reported in the English Literature," *Ann Intern Med*, 1987, 106(5):728-33.

Tabor PA, "Drug-Induced Fever," Table 2, "Drugs Implicated in Causing a Fever," *Drug Intell Clin Pharm*, 1986, 20(6):416.

HERB–DRUG INTERACTIONS / CAUTIONS

Herb	Drug Interaction / Caution
Acidophilus / bifidobacterium	Antibiotics (oral)
Activated charcoal	Vitamins or oral medications may be adsorbed
Alfalfa	Do not use with lupus due to amino acid L-canavanine; causes pancytopenia at high doses; warfarin (alfalfa contains a large amount of vitamin K)
Aloe vera	Caution in pregnancy, may cause uterine contractions; digoxin, diuretics (hypokalemia)
Ashwagandha	May cause sedation and other CNS effects
Asparagus root	Causes diuresis
Barberry	Normal metabolism of vitamin B may be altered with high doses
Birch	If taking a diuretic, drink plenty of fluids
Black cohosh	Estrogen-like component; pregnant and nursing women should probably avoid this herb; also women with estrogen-dependent cancer and women who are taking birth control pills or estrogen supplements after menopause; caution also in people taking sedatives or blood pressure medications
Black haw	Do not give to children <6 years of age (salicin content) with flu or chickenpox due to potential Reye's syndrome; do not take if allergic to aspirin
Black pepper (*Piper nigrum*)	Antiasthmatic drugs (decreases metabolism)
Black tea	May inhibit body's utilization of thiamine
Blessed thistle	Do not use with gastritis, ulcers, or hyperacidity since herb stimulates gastric juices
Blood root	Large doses can cause nausea, vomiting, CNS sedation, low BP, shock, coma, and death
Broom (*Cytisus scoparius*)	MAO inhibitors lead to sudden blood pressure changes
Bugleweed (*Lycopus virginicus*)	May interfere with nuclear imaging studies of the thyroid gland (thyroid uptake scan)
Cat's claw (*Uncaria tomentosa*)	Avoid in organ transplant patients or patients on ulcer medications, antiplatelet drugs, NSAIDs, anticoagulants, immunosuppressive therapy, intravenous immunoglobulin therapy
Chaste tree berry (*Vitex agnus-castus*)	Interferes with actions of oral contraceptives, HRT, and other endocrine therapies; may interfere with metabolism of dopamine-receptor antagonists
Chicory (*Cichorium intybus*)	Avoid with gallstones due to bile-stimulating properties
Chlorella (*Chlorella vulgaris*)	Contains significant amounts of vitamin K
Chromium picolinate	Picolinic acid causes notable changes in brain chemicals (serotonin, dopamine, norepinephrine); do not use if patient has behavioral disorders or diabetes
Cinnabar root (*Salviae miltiorrhizae*)	Warfarin (increases INR)
Deadly nightshade (*Atropa belladonna*)	Contains atropine
Dong quai	Warfarin (increases INR), estrogens, oral contraceptives, photosensitizing drugs, histamine replacement therapy, anticoagulants, antiplatelet drugs, antihypertensives
Echinacea	Caution with other immunosuppressive therapies; stimulates TNF and interferons
Evening primrose oil	May lower seizure threshold; do not combine with anticonvulsants or phenothiazines
Fennel	Do not use in women who have had breast cancer or who have been told not to take birth control pills
Fenugreek	Practice moderation in patients on diabetes drugs, MAO inhibitors, cardiovascular agents, hormonal medicines, or warfarin due to the many components of fenugreek
Feverfew	Antiplatelets, anticoagulants, NSAIDs

HERB–DRUG INTERACTIONS / CAUTIONS (Continued)

Herb	Drug Interaction / Caution
Forskolin, coleonol	This herb lowers blood pressure (vasodilator) and is a bronchodilator and increases the contractility of the heart, inhibits platelet aggregation, and increases gastric acid secretion
Foxglove	Digitalis-containing herb
Garlic	Blood sugar-lowering medications, warfarin, and aspirin at medicinal doses of garlic
Ginger	May inhibit platelet aggregation by inhibiting thromboxane synthetase at large doses; *in vitro* and animal studies indicate that ginger may interfere with diabetics; has anticoagulant effect, so avoid in medicinal amounts in patients on warfarin or heart medicines
Ginkgo biloba	Warfarin (ginkgo decreases blood clotting rate); NSAIDs, MAO inhibitors
Ginseng	Blood sugar-lowering medications (additive effects) and other stimulants
Ginseng (American, Korean)	Furosemide (decreases efficacy)
Ginseng (Siberian)	Digoxin (increases digoxin level)
Glucomannan	Diabetics (herb delays absorption of glucose from intestines, decreasing mean fasting sugar levels)
Goldenrod	Diuretics (additive properties)
Gymnema	Blood sugar-lowering medications (additive effects)
Hawthorn	Digoxin or other heart medications (herb dilates coronary vessels and other blood vessels, also inotropic)
Hibiscus	Chloroquine (reduced effectiveness of chloroquine)
Hops	Those with estrogen-dependent breast cancer should not take hops (contains estrogen-like chemicals); patients with depression (accentuate symptoms); alcohol or sedative (additive effects)
Horehound	May cause arrhythmias at high doses
Horseradish	In medicinal amounts with thyroid medications
Kava	CNS depressants (additive effects, eg, alcohol, barbiturates, etc); benzodiazepines
Kelp	Thyroid medications (additive effects or opposite effects by negative feedback); kelp contains a high amount of sodium
Labrador tea	Plant has narcotic properties, possible additive effects with other CNS depressants
Lemon balm	Do not use with Graves disease since it inhibits certain thyroid hormones
Licorice	Acts as a corticosteroid at high doses (about 1.5 lbs candy in 9 days) which can lead to hypertension, edema, hypernatremia, and hypokalemia (pseudoaldosteronism); do not use in persons with hypertension, glaucoma, diabetes, kidney or liver disease, or those on hormonal therapy; may interact with digitalis (due to hypokalemia)
Lobelia	Contains lobeline which has nicotinic activity; may mask withdrawal symptoms from nicotine; it can act as a polarizing neuromuscular blocker
Lovage	Is a diuretic
Ma huang	MAO inhibitors, digoxin, beta-blockers, methyldopa, caffeine, theophylline, decongestants (increases toxicity)
Marshmallow	May delay absorption of other drugs taken at the same time; may interfere with treatments of lowering blood sugar
Meadowsweet	Contains salicylates
Melatonin	Acts as contraceptive at high doses; antidepressants (decreases efficacy)
Mistletoe	May interfere with medications for blood pressure, depression, and heart disease
L-phenylalanine	MAO inhibitors

Herb	Drug Interaction / Caution
Pleurisy root	Digoxin (plant contains cardiac glycosides); also contains estrogen-like compounds; may alter amine concentrations in the brain and interact with antidepressants
Prickly ash (Northern)	Contains coumarin-like compounds
Prickly ash (Southern)	Contains neuromuscular blockers
Psyllium	Digoxin (decreases absorption)
Quassia	High doses may complicate heart or blood-thinning treatments (quassia may be inotropic)
Red clover	May have estrogen-like actions; avoid when taking birth control pills, HRT, people with heart disease or at risk for blood clots, patients who suffer from estrogen-dependent cancer; do not take with warfarin
Red pepper	May increase liver metabolism of other medications and may interfere with high blood pressure medications or MAO inhibitors
Rhubarb, Chinese	Do not use with digoxin (enhanced effects)
St John's wort	Indinavir, cyclosporine, SSRIs or any antidepressants, tetracycline (increases sun sensitivity); digoxin (decreases digoxin concentration); may also interact with diltiazem, nicardipine, verapamil, etoposide, paclitaxel, vinblastine, vincristine, glucocorticoids, cyclosporine, dextromethorphan, ephedrine, lithium, meperidine, pseudoephedrine, selegiline, yohimbine, ACE inhibitors (serotonin syndrome, hypertension, possible exacerbation of allergic reaction)
Saw palmetto	Acts an antiandrogen; do not take with prostate medicines or HRT
Squill	Digoxin or persons with potassium deficiency; also not with quinidine, calcium, laxatives, saluretics, prednisone (long-term)
Tonka bean	Contains coumarin, interacts with warfarin
Vervain	Avoid large amounts of herb with blood pressure medications or HRT
Wild Oregon grape	High doses may alter metabolism of vitamin B
Wild yam	May interfere with hormone precursors
Wintergreen	Warfarin, increased bleeding
Sweet woodruff	Contains coumarin
Yarrow	Interferes with anticoagulants and blood pressure medications
Yohimbe	Do not consume tyramine-rich foods; do not take with nasal decongestants, PPA-containing diet aids, antidepressants, or mood-altering drugs

LABORATORY DETECTION OF DRUGS

Agent	Time Detectable in Urine[1]
Amobarbital	2-4 d
Amphetamine	2-4 d[2]
Butalbital	2-4 d
Cannabinoids	
Occasional use	2-7 d
Regular use	30 d
Cocaine (benzoylecgonine)	12-96 h
Codeine	2-4 d
Chlordiazepoxide	30 d
Diazepam	30 d
Dilaudid®	2-4 d
Ethanol	12-24 h
Heroin (6-monoacetyl morphine)	12 h
Hydromorphone	2-4 d
Librium®	30 d
Marijuana	
Occasional use	1-5 d
Regular use	30 d[2]
Methamphetamine	2-7 d
Methaqualone	2-4 d
Morphine	2-4 d
Pentobarbital	2-4 d
Phencyclidine (PCP)	
Occasional use	2-7 d[2]
Regular use	30 d[2]
Phenobarbital	30 d[2]
Quaalude®	2-4 d
Secobarbital	2-4 d
Valium®	30 d

[1]The periods of detection for the various abused drugs listed above should be taken as estimates since the actual figures will vary due to metabolism, user, laboratory, and excretion.

[2]Urine pH dependent.

Modified from Chang JY, "Drug Testing and Interpretation of Results," *Pharmchem Newsletter*, 1989, 17:1.

LOW POTASSIUM DIET

Potassium is a mineral found in most all foods except sugar and lard. It plays a role in maintaining normal muscle activity and helps to keep body fluids in balance. Too much potassium in the blood can lead to changes in heartbeat and can lead to muscle weakness. The kidneys normally help to keep blood potassium controlled, but in kidney disease or when certain drugs are taken, dietary potassium must be limited to maintain a normal level of potassium in the blood.

The following guideline includes 2-3 g of potassium per day.

1. **Milk Group:** Limit to one cup serving of milk or milk product (yogurt, cottage cheese, ice cream, pudding).

2. **Fruit Group:** Limit to two servings daily from the low potassium choices. Watch serving sizes. Avoid the high potassium choices.

> **Low Potassium**
> Apple, 1 small
> Apple juice, applesauce 1/2 cup
> Apricot, 1 medium or 1/2 cup canned in syrup
> Blueberries, 1/2 cup
> Cherries, canned in syrup 1/3 cup
> Cranberries, cranberry juice 1/2 cup
> Fruit cocktail, canned in syrup 1/2 cup
> Grapes, 10 fresh
> Lemon, lime 1 fresh
> Mandarin orange, canned in syrup 1/2 cup
> Nectar: apricot, pear, peach 1/2 cup
> Peach, 1 small or 1/2 cup canned with syrup
> Pear, 1 small or 1/2 cup canned with syrup
> Pineapple, 1/2 cup raw or canned with syrup
> Plums, 1 small or 1/2 cup canned with syrup
> Tangerine, 1 small
> Watermelon, 1/2 cup
> **High Potassium**
> Avocado
> Banana
> Cantaloupe
> Cherries, fresh
> Dried fruits
> Grapefruit, fresh and juice
> Honeydew melon
> Kiwi
> Mango
> Nectarine
> Orange, fresh and juice
> Papaya
> Prunes, prune juice
> Raisins

3. Avoid use of the following salt substitutes due to their high potassium contents: Adolph's, Lawry's Season Salt Substitute, No Salt, Morton Season Salt Free, Nu Salt, Papa Dash, and Morton Lite Salt.

ORAL DOSAGES THAT SHOULD NOT BE CRUSHED

There are a variety of reasons for crushing tablets or capsule contents prior to administering to the patient. Patients may have nasogastric tubes which do not permit the administration of tablets or capsules; an oral solution for a particular medication may not be available from the manufacturer or readily prepared by pharmacy; patients may have difficulty swallowing capsules or tablets; or mixing of powdered medication with food or drink may make the drug more palatable.

Generally, medications which should not be crushed fall into one of the following categories:

- **Extended-Release Products.** The formulation of some tablets is specialized as to allow the medication within it to be slowly released into the body. This is sometimes accomplished by centering the drug within the core of the tablet, with a subsequent shedding of multiple layers around the core. Wax melts in the GI tract. Slow-K® is an example of this. Capsules may contain beads which have multiple layers which are slowly dissolved with time.

- **Medications Which Are Irritating to the Stomach.** Tablets which are irritating to the stomach may be enteric coated which delays release of the drug until the time when it reaches the small intestine. Enteric-coated aspirin is an example of this.

- **Foul Tasting Medication.** Some drugs are quite unpleasant in their taste and the manufacturer, to increase their palatability will coat the tablet in a sugar coating. By crushing the tablet, this sugar coating is lost and the patient tastes the unpleasant tasting medication.

- **Sublingual Medication.** Medication intended for use under the tongue should not be crushed. While it appears to be obvious, it is not always easy to determine if a medication is to be used sublingually. Sublingual medications should indicate on the package that they are intended for sublingual use.

- **Effervescent Tablets.** These are tablets which, when dropped into a liquid, quickly dissolve to yield a solution. Many effervescent tablets, when crushed, lose their ability to quickly dissolve.

Recommendations

1. It is not advisable to crush certain medications.

2. Consult individual monographs prior to crushing capsule or tablet.

3. If crushing a tablet or capsule is contraindicated, consult with your pharmacist to determine whether an oral solution exists or can be compounded.

4. Refer to individual drug monograph for crushing information.

Summary of Drug Formulations That Preclude Crushing

Type	Reason(s) for the Formulation
Enteric-coated	Designed to pass through the stomach intact with drug released in the intestines to: • prevent destruction of drug by stomach acids • prevent stomach irritation • delay onset of action
Extended release	Designed to release drug over an extended period of time. Such products include: • multiple layered tablets releasing drug as each layer is dissolved • mixed release pellets that dissolve at different time intervals • special matrixes that are themselves inert but slowly release drug from the matrix
Sublingual buccal	Designed to dissolve quickly in oral fluids for rapid absorption by the abundant blood supply of the mouth
Miscellaneous	Drugs that: • produce oral mucosa irritation • are extremely bitter • contain dyes or inherently could stain teeth and mucosal tissue

TOP 200 PRESCRIBED DRUGS

Brand Name (if appropriate)	Generic Name	Rank
Accupril®	quinapril	118
—	acetaminophen and codeine	43
Aciphex®	rabeprazole	110
Actonel®	risedronate	81
Actos®	pioglitazone	79
—	acyclovir	158
Adderall XR™	dextroamphetamine and amphetamine	89
Advair™ Diskus®	fluticasone and salmeterol	34
—	albuterol (aerosol)	10
—	albuterol (nebulization solution)	108
Allegra®	fexofenadine	56
Allegra-D® 12 Hour	fexofenadine and pseudoephedrine	132
—	allopurinol	76
—	alprazolam	8
Altace®	ramipril	65
Amaryl®	glimepiride	127
Ambien®	zolpidem	19
—	amitriptyline	50
—	amoxicillin	3
—	amoxicillin and clavulanate potassium	33
Aricept®	donepezil	161
—	atenolol	6
—	atenolol chlorthalidone	199
Avalide®	irbesartan and hydrochlorothiazide	176
Avandia®	rosiglitazone	71
Avapro®	irbesartan	126
Aviane™	ethinyl estradiol and levonorgestrel	186
—	azithromycin	164
—	benazepril	124
Benicar®	olmesartan	146
Benicar HTC®	olmesartan and hydrochlorothiazide	171
—	benzonatate	180
—	betamethasone and clotrimazole	174
—	bisoprolol and hydrochlorothiazide	148
—	buspirone SR	179
—	buspirone	166
—	butalbital, acetaminophen, and caffeine	162
—	carisoprodol	74
Cartia® XT	diltiazem	183
Celebrex®	celecoxib	67
—	cephalexin	18
Cialis®	tadalafil	175
—	ciprofloxacin	53
—	citalopram	83
Clarinex®	desloratadine	149
—	clindamycin	119
—	clonazepam	39
—	clonidine	77
Combivent®	ipratropium and albuterol	123
Concerta™	methylphenidate	96
Coreg®	carvedilol	95

TOP 200 PRESCRIBED DRUGS *(Continued)*

Brand Name (if appropriate)	Generic Name	Rank
Coumadin®	warfarin	134
Cozaar®	losartan	93
Crestor®	rosuvastatin	102
Cymbalta®	duloxetine	143
—	cyclobenzaprine	49
Depakote®	valproic acid and derivatives	165
Detrol® LA	tolterodine	139
—	dextroamphetamine and amphetamine	188
—	diazepam	60
—	diclofenac	136
Digitek®	digoxin	111
—	digoxin	190
—	diltiazem CD	138
Diovan®	valsartan	58
Diovan HCT®	valsartan and hydrochlorothiazide	73
—	doxazosin	133
—	doxycycline	69
Effexor® XR	venlafaxine	36
—	enalapril	59
Endocet®	oxycodone and acetaminophen	197
—	estradiol	129
—	etodolac	198
Evista®	raloxifene	137
—	famotidine	189
—	fexofenadine	177
Flomax®	tamsulosin	101
Flonase®	fluticasone	47
—	fluconazole	62
—	fluoxetine	29
—	folic acid	91
Fosamax®	alendronate	35
—	furosemide	7
—	gabapentin	45
—	gemfibrozil	125
—	glipizide	135
—	glipizide ER	103
—	glyburide	87
—	glyburide and metformin	141
GlycoLax™	polethylene glycol 3350	157
Humalog®	insulin preparations	184
—	hydrochlorothiazide	5
—	hydrochlorothiazide and triamterene	23
—	hydrocodone and acetaminophen	1
—	hydroxyzine	130
Hyzaar®	losartan and hydrochlorothiazide	116
—	ibuprofen	17
Imitrex®	sumatriptan	152
—	isosorbide mononitrate	85
Klor-Con®	potassium chloride	64
Lamictal®	lamotrigine	155
Lanoxin®	digoxin	187
Lantus®	insulin glargine	98
Levaquin®	levofloxacin	51
Levothroid®	levothyroxine	191
—	levothyroxine	12
Levoxyl®	levothyroxine	57

Brand Name (if appropriate)	Generic Name	Rank
Lexapro®	escitalopram	16
Lipitor®	atorvastatin	2
—	lisinopril	4
—	lisinopril and hydrochlorothiazide	63
—	lorazepam	30
Lotrel®	amlodipine and benazepril	54
—	lovastatin	72
—	meclizine	140
—	metformin	14
—	metformin ER	115
—	methylprednisolone	78
—	methotrexate	168
—	metoclopramide	131
—	metoprolol	28
—	metronidazole	120
—	minocycline	151
—	mirtazapine	147
Mobic®	meloxicam	100
—	nabumetone	153
—	naproxen	61
Nasacort® AQ	triamcinolone	160
Nasonex®	mometasone	90
Nexium™	esomeprazole	22
Niaspan®	niacin	163
—	nifedipine ER	192
—	nitrofurantoin	144
Nitroquick®	nitroglycerin	195
—	nortriptyline	193
Norvasc®	amlodipine	11
—	omeprazole	106
Omnicef®	cefdinir	107
Ortho Evra®	ethinyl estradiol and norelgestromin	82
Ortho Tri-Cyclen®	ethinyl estradiol and norgestimate	178
Ortho Tri-Cyclen® Lo	ethinyl estradiol and norgestimate	104
—	oxycodone	150
—	oxycodone and acetaminophen	32
Oxycontin®	oxycodone	169
Patanol®	olopatadine	181
—	paroxetine	38
Paxil® CR	paroxetine	185
—	penicillin V potassium	86
—	phentermine	200
—	phenytoin	196
Plavix®	clopidogrel	31
—	potassium chloride	42
Pravachol®	pravastatin	80
—	prednisone	21
Premarin®	estrogens (conjugated)	46
Prevacid®	lansoprazole	27
—	promethazine	99
—	promethazine and codeine	145
—	propoxyphene and acetaminophen	24
—	propranolol	159
Protonix®	pantoprazole	41
—	quinine	182
—	ranitidine	55
Rhinocort® Aqua™	budesonide	170
Risperdal®	risperidone	109

TOP 200 PRESCRIBED DRUGS *(Continued)*

Brand Name (if appropriate)	Generic Name	Rank
Seroquel®	quetiapine	92
Singulair®	montelukast	26
Skelaxin®	metaxalone	173
—	spironolactone	112
—	sulfamethoxazole and trimethoprim	44
Strattera®	atomoxetine	142
Synthroid®	levothyroxine	13
—	temazepam	105
—	terazosin	172
Topamax®	topiramate	122
Toprol-XL®	metoprolol	9
—	tramadol	52
—	trazodone	48
—	triamcinolone acetonide	121
TriCor®	fenofibrate	94
TriNessa™	ethinyl estradiol and norgestimate	128
Tri-Sprintec®	ethinyl estradiol and norgestimate	167
Tussionex®	hydrocodone and chlorpheniramine	194
Valtrex®	valacyclovir	113
—	verapamil	84
Viagra®	sildenafil	68
Vytorin™	ezetimibe and simvastatin	97
—	warfarin	37
Wellbutrin XL™	bupropion	66
Xalatan®	latanoprost	114
Yasmin® 28	ethinyl estradiol and drospirenone	75
Zetia™	ezetimibe	70
Zithromax® Z-Pak®	azithromycin	20
Zithromax® Tablets	azithromycin	117
Zithromax® Suspension	azithromycin	88
Zocor®	simvastatin	25
Zoloft®	sertraline	15
Zyprexa®	olanzapine	154
Zyrtec® Tablets	cetirizine	40
Zyrtec® Syrup	cetirizine	156

NDC Health, "The Top 200 Prescriptions for 2005 by Number of US Prescriptions Dispensed," Available at: http://www.rxlist.com//top200.htm

TYRAMINE CONTENT OF FOODS

Food[1]	Allowed	Minimize Intake	Not Allowed
Beverages	Decaffeinated beverages (eg, coffee, tea, soda); milk, soy milk, chocolate beverage	Caffeine-containing drinks, clear spirits, wine, bottled/canned beers	**Tap** beer
Breads/cereals	All except those containing cheese	None	Cheese bread and crackers
Dairy products	Cottage cheese, farmers or pot cheese, cream cheese, ricotta cheese, all milk, eggs, ice cream, pudding, yogurt, sour cream, processed cheese, mozzarella	None	All other cheeses (**aged** cheese, American, Camembert, cheddar, Gouda, gruyere, parmesan, provolone, romano, Roquefort, stilton)
Meat, fish, and poultry	All fresh packaged or pressed (eg, hotdogs, bologna), or frozen	Pepperoni	**Aged** chicken and beef liver, dried and pickled fish, shrimp paste, summer or dry sausage, dried meats (eg, salami, cacciatore), meat extracts, liverwurst
Starches — potatoes/rice	All	None	Soybean (including paste), tofu
Vegetables	All fresh, frozen, canned, or dried vegetable juices except those not allowed	Chili peppers, Chinese pea pods	Sauerkraut, broad or fava bean pods (not beans)
Fruit	Fresh, frozen, or canned fruits and fruit juices	Avocado, figs	Banana peel, avocado (over-ripened)
Soups	All soups not listed to limit or avoid	None	Soups which contain **aged** cheese, **tap** beer, any made with flavor cubes or meat extract, miso soup, broad or fava bean pods (not beans)
Fats	All except fermented	None	None
Sweets	Sugar, hard candy, honey, molasses, syrups, chocolate candy	None	None
Desserts	Cakes, cookies, gelatin, pastries, sherbets, sorbets, chocolate desserts	None	None
Miscellaneous	Salt, nuts, spices, herbs, flavorings, Worcestershire sauce, Bewer's or Baker's yeast, monosodium glutamate, vitamins with Brewer's yeast	Peanuts	Soy sauce, all aged and fermented products, marmite and other concentrated yeast extracts

[1] Freshness is of primary importance. Food that is spoiled or imporperly stored should be avoided.

References

Shulman KI and Walker SE, "A Reevaluation of Dietary Restrictions for Irreversible Monoamine Oxidase Inhibitors," *Psychiatr Ann*, 2001, 31(6):378-84.

Shulman KI and Walker SE, "Refining the MAOI Diet: Tyramine Content of Pizza and Soy Products," *J Clin Psychiatry*, 1999, 60(3):191-3.

Walker SE, Shulman KI, Tailor SAN, et al, "Tyramine Content of Previously Restricted Foods in Monoamine Oxidase Inhibitor Diets," *J Clin Psychopharmacol*, 1996, 16(5):383-8.

VITAMIN K CONTENT IN SELECTED FOODS

The following lists describe the relative amounts of vitamin K in selected foods. The abbreviations for vitamin K is "H" for high amounts, "M" for medium amounts, and "L" for low amounts.

Foods[1]	Portion Size[2]	Vitamin K Content
Coffee brewed	10 cups	L
Cola, regular and diet	3½ fl oz	L
Fruit juices, assorted types	3½ fl oz	L
Milk	3½ fl oz	L
Tea, black, brewed	3½ fl oz	L
Bread, assorted types	4 slices	L
Cereal, assorted types	3½ oz	L
Flour, assorted types	1 cup	L
Oatmeal, instant, dry	1 cup	L
Rice, white	½ cup	L
Spaghetti, dry	3½ oz	L
Butter	6 Tbsp	L
Cheddar cheese	3½ oz	L
Eggs	2 large	L
Margarine	7 Tbsp	M
Mayonnaise	7 Tbsp	H
Oils		
Canola, salad, soybean	7 Tbsp	H
Olive	7 Tbsp	M
Corn, peanut, safflower, sesame, sunflower	7 Tbsp	L
Sour cream	8 Tbsp	L
Yogurt	3½ oz	L
Apple	1 medium	L
Banana	1 medium	L
Blueberries	⅔ cup	L
Cantaloupe pieces	⅔ cup	L
Grapes	1 cup	L
Grapefruit	½ medium	L
Lemon	2 medium	L
Orange	1 medium	L
Peach	1 medium	L
Abalone	3½ oz	L
Beef, ground	3½ oz	L
Chicken	3½ oz	L
Mackerel	3½ oz	L
Meatloaf	3½ oz	L
Pork, meat	3½ oz	L
Tuna	3½ oz	L
Turkey, meat	3½ oz	L
Asparagus, raw	7 spears	M
Avocado, peeled	1 small	M
Beans, pod, raw	1 cup	M
Broccoli, raw and cooked	½ cup	H
Brussel sprout, sprout and top leaf	5 sprouts	H
Cabbage, raw	1½ cups shredded	H
Cabbage, red, raw	1½ cups shredded	M
Carrot	⅔ cup	L
Cauliflower	1 cup	L
Celery	2½ stalks	L
Coleslaw	¾ cup	M
Collard greens	½ cup chopped	H
Cucumber peel, raw	1 cup	H
Cucumber, peel removed	1 cup	L
Eggplant	1¼ cups pieces	L
Endive, raw	2 cups chopped	H
Green scallion, raw	⅔ cup chopped	H
Kale, raw leaf	¾ cup	H
Lettuce, raw, heading, bib, red leaf	1¾ cups shredded	H
Mushroom	1½ cups	L
Mustard greens, raw	1½ cups	H

Foods[1]	Portion Size[2]	Vitamin K Content
Onion, white	⅔ cup chopped	L
Parsley, raw and cooked	1½ cups chopped	H
Peas, green, cooked	⅔ cup	M
Pepper, green, raw	1 cup chopped	L
Potato	1 medium	L
Pumpkin	½ cup	L
Spinach, raw leaf	1½ cups	H
Tomato	1 medium	L
Turnip greens, raw	1½ cups chopped	H
Watercress, raw	3 cups chopped	H
Honey	5 Tbsp	L
Jell-O® Gelatin	⅓ cup	L
Peanut butter	6 Tbsp	L
Pickle, dill	1 medium	M
Sauerkraut	1 cup	M
Soybean, dry	½ cup	M

[1]This list is a partial listing of foods. For more complete information, refer to references 1-2.

[2]Portions in chart are calculated from estimated portions provided in reference 4.

References

Booth SL, Sadowski JA, Weihrauch JL, et al, "Vitamin K₁ (Phylloquinone) Content of Foods a Provisional Table," *J Food Comp Anal*, 1993, 6:109-20.

Ferland G, MacDonald DL, and Sadowski JA, "Development of a Diet Low in Vitamin K₁ (Phylloquinone)," *J Am Diet Assoc*, 1992, 92, 593-7.

Hogan RP, "Hemorrhagic Diathesis Caused by Drinking an Herbal Tea," *JAMA*, 1983, 249:2679-80.

Pennington JA, *Bowes and Church's Food Values of Portions Commonly Used*, 15th ed, JP Lippincott Co, 1985.

PHARMACOLOGIC CATEGORY INDEX

Abortifacient
Carboprost Tromethamine 293
Dinoprostone 513
Mifepristone 1143

Acetylcholinesterase Inhibitor
Echothiophate Iodide 566
Neostigmine 1213
Physostigmine 1365
Pyridostigmine 1462

Acetylcholinesterase Inhibitor (Central)
Donepezil 538
Galantamine 777
Rivastigmine 1526
Tacrine 1625

Acne Products
Adapalene 49
Benzoyl Peroxide and Hydrocortisone 208
Clindamycin and Tretinoin 391
Erythromycin 609
Erythromycin and Benzoyl Peroxide 613
Isotretinoin 948
Sulfacetamide 1609
Sulfur and Sulfacetamide 1618
Tazarotene 1635
Tretinoin (Topical) 1732

Activated Prothrombin Complex Concentrate (aPCC)
Anti-inhibitor Coagulant Complex 137

Adhesiolytic
Icodextrin 877

Adjuvant, Chemoprotective Agent (Cytoprotective)
Amifostine 89

Adrenergic Agonist Agent
Carbinoxamine and Pseudoephedrine 290
DOBUTamine 529
DOPamine 539

Aldehyde Dehydrogenase Inhibitor
Disulfiram 528

Alkalinizing Agent
Sodium Bicarbonate 1575

Alkalinizing Agent, Oral
Citric Acid, Sodium Citrate, and Potassium Citrate 383
Potassium Citrate and Citric Acid 1398
Sodium Citrate and Citric Acid 1579

Alkalinizing Agent, Parenteral
Tromethamine 1752

Alpha$_1$ Agonist
Midodrine 1142
Naphazoline 1198

Alpha$_1$ Blocker
Alfuzosin 68
Doxazosin 544
Phenoxybenzamine 1355
Phentolamine 1357
Prazosin 1411
Tamsulosin 1633
Terazosin 1647

Alpha$_1$ Blocker, Ophthalmic
Dapiprazole 450

Alpha$_2$-Adrenergic Agonist
Clonidine 399
Dexmedetomidine 483
Guanabenz 823
Guanfacine 823
Tizanidine 1695

Alpha$_2$ Agonist, Ophthalmic
Apraclonidine 144
Brimonidine 239

Alpha-Adrenergic Inhibitor
Methyldopa 1117

Alpha/Beta Agonist
Acetaminophen and Pseudoephedrine 33
Chlorpheniramine and Pseudoephedrine 350
Dexchlorpheniramine and Pseudoephedrine 483
Dipivefrin 524
Ephedrine 587
Epinephrine 589
Guaifenesin and Pseudoephedrine 819
Norepinephrine 1240
Phenylephrine 1358
Pseudoephedrine 1454
Triprolidine and Pseudoephedrine 1749

5 Alpha-Reductase Inhibitor
Dutasteride 565
Finasteride 708

Amebicide
Diloxanide Furoate 508
Iodoquinol 930
Metronidazole 1132
Paromomycin 1314

Amino Acid
Glutamine 803

Aminoquinoline (Antimalarial)
Chloroquine 347
Hydroxychloroquine 862
Primaquine 1421

5-Aminosalicylic Acid Derivative
Balsalazide 194
Mesalamine 1089
Olsalazine 1262
Sulfasalazine 1615

Ammonium Detoxicant
Lactulose 971
Neomycin 1210

Amylinomimetic
Pramlintide 1407

Anabolic Steroid
Oxymetholone 1290
Stanozolol 1598

Analgesic Combination (Opioid)
Belladonna and Opium 200
Hydrocodone and Acetaminophen 848
Hydrocodone and Aspirin 849
Meperidine and Promethazine 1083
Propoxyphene and Acetaminophen 1445
Propoxyphene, Aspirin, and Caffeine 1446

Analgesic, Miscellaneous
Acetaminophen 28
Acetaminophen and Diphenhydramine 31
Acetaminophen and Phenyltoloxamine 32
Acetaminophen and Pseudoephedrine 33
Acetaminophen and Tramadol 34
Acetaminophen, Aspirin, and Caffeine 34
Acetaminophen, Chlorpheniramine, and Pseudoephedrine 35
Acetaminophen, Isometheptene, and Dichloralphenazone 36
Butalbital and Acetaminophen 259
Pregabalin 1418

Analgesic, Nonopioid
Acetaminophen and Tramadol 34
Tramadol 1718
Ziconotide 1811

Analgesic, Opioid
Acetaminophen and Codeine 31
Alfentanil 67
Buprenorphine 250
Buprenorphine and Naloxone 252
Butorphanol 261
Codeine 410
Dihydrocodeine, Aspirin, and Caffeine 506
Fentanyl 693
Hydrocodone and Ibuprofen 851
Hydromorphone 856
Levorphanol 1006
Meperidine 1081
Methadone 1100
Morphine Sulfate 1171
Nalbuphine 1191
Opium Tincture 1269
Oxycodone 1286
Oxycodone and Acetaminophen 1289
Oxycodone and Aspirin 1289
Oxycodone and Ibuprofen 1290
Oxymorphone 1290
Paregoric 1311
Pentazocine 1339
Propoxyphene 1444
Remifentanil 1493
Sufentanil 1608

Analgesic, Topical
Dichlorodifluoromethane and Trichloromonofluoromethane 492
Lidocaine 1010
Lidocaine and Tetracaine 1016

Analgesic, Urinary
Pentosan Polysulfate Sodium 1342
Phenazopyridine 1351

Androgen
Danazol 447
(Continued)

Androgen *(Continued)*
Fluoxymesterone 730
MethylTESTOSTERone 1125
Nandrolone 1197
Oxandrolone 1278
Testolactone 1653
Testosterone 1653

Anesthetic/Corticosteroid
Pramoxine and Hydrocortisone 1409

Angiogenesis Inhibitor
Lenalidomide 984
Thalidomide 1661

Angiotensin II Receptor Blocker
Candesartan 276
Eprosartan 600
Irbesartan 934
Losartan 1037
Olmesartan 1260
Telmisartan 1639
Valsartan 1771

Angiotensin II Receptor Blocker Combination
Candesartan and Hydrochlorothiazide 278
Eprosartan and Hydrochlorothiazide 601
Irbesartan and Hydrochlorothiazide 935
Losartan and Hydrochlorothiazide 1039
Olmesartan and Hydrochlorothiazide 1261
Telmisartan and Hydrochlorothiazide 1640
Valsartan and Hydrochlorothiazide 1773

Angiotensin-Converting Enzyme (ACE) Inhibitor
Benazepril 202
Captopril 281
Enalapril 578
Fosinopril 766
Lisinopril 1021
Moexipril 1162
Perindopril Erbumine 1346
Quinapril 1469
Quinapril and Hydrochlorothiazide 1471
Ramipril 1482
Trandolapril 1720

Anorexiant
Diethylpropion 499
Phentermine 1356
Sibutramine 1562

Antacid
Aluminum Hydroxide 83
Aluminum Hydroxide and Magnesium Carbonate 84
Aluminum Hydroxide and Magnesium Hydroxide 85
Aluminum Hydroxide and Magnesium Trisilicate 85
Aluminum Hydroxide, Magnesium Hydroxide, and Simethicone 85
Calcium Carbonate 269
Calcium Carbonate and Magnesium Hydroxide 271
Famotidine, Calcium Carbonate, and Magnesium Hydroxide 685
Magaldrate and Simethicone 1045
Magnesium Hydroxide 1047
Sodium Bicarbonate 1575

Anthelmintic
Albendazole 54
Ivermectin 955
Mebendazole 1059
Praziquantel 1411
Pyrantel Pamoate 1459
Thiabendazole 1667

Antiandrogen
Nilutamide 1228

Antianxiety Agent, Miscellaneous
Aspirin and Meprobamate 164
BusPIRone 256
Meprobamate 1085

Antiarrhythmic Agent, Class I
Moricizine 1169

Antiarrhythmic Agent, Class Ia
Disopyramide 526
Procainamide 1424
Quinidine 1471

Antiarrhythmic Agent, Class Ib
Lidocaine 1010
Mexiletine 1135
Phenytoin 1361

Antiarrhythmic Agent, Class Ic
Flecainide 710
Propafenone 1439

Antiarrhythmic Agent, Class II
Acebutolol 27

Esmolol 616
Propranolol 1446
Sotalol 1592

Antiarrhythmic Agent, Class III
Amiodarone 97
Dofetilide 534
Ibutilide 876
Sotalol 1592

Antiarrhythmic Agent, Class IV
Adenosine 50
Digoxin 501
Verapamil 1784

Antibiotic, Aminoglycoside
Amikacin 90
Gentamicin 793
Kanamycin 957
Neomycin 1210
Streptomycin 1602
Tobramycin 1696

Antibiotic, Carbacephem
Loracarbef 1032

Antibiotic, Carbapenem
Ertapenem 607
Imipenem and Cilastatin 885
Meropenem 1087

Antibiotic, Cephalosporin
Cefditoren 309

Antibiotic, Cephalosporin (First Generation)
Cefadroxil 305
Cefazolin 306
Cephalexin 331
Cephradine 332

Antibiotic, Cephalosporin (Second Generation)
Cefaclor 303
Cefotetan 315
Cefoxitin 316
Cefprozil 319
Cefuroxime 326

Antibiotic, Cephalosporin (Third Generation)
Cefdinir 307
Cefixime 312
Cefotaxime 313
Cefpodoxime 317
Ceftazidime 320
Ceftibuten 322
Ceftizoxime 323
Ceftriaxone 324

Antibiotic, Cephalosporin (Fourth Generation)
Cefepime 310

Antibiotic/Corticosteroid, Ophthalmic
Loteprednol and Tobramycin 1039
Neomycin, Polymyxin B, and Dexamethasone 1211
Neomycin, Polymyxin B, and Hydrocortisone 1212
Neomycin, Polymyxin B, and Prednisolone 1212
Prednisolone and Gentamicin 1416
Sulfacetamide and Prednisolone 1610
Sulfacetamide Sodium and Fluorometholone 1610
Tobramycin and Dexamethasone 1700

Antibiotic/Corticosteroid, Otic
Ciprofloxacin and Dexamethasone 376
Ciprofloxacin and Hydrocortisone 377
Neomycin, Colistin, Hydrocortisone, and Thonzonium 1211
Neomycin, Polymyxin B, and Hydrocortisone 1212

Antibiotic, Cyclic Lipopeptide
Daptomycin 452

Antibiotic, Glycylcycline
Tigecycline 1685

Antibiotic, Irrigation
Polymyxin B 1389

Antibiotic, Ketolide
Telithromycin 1637

Antibiotic, Lincosamide
Clindamycin 389

Antibiotic, Macrolide
Azithromycin 186
Clarithromycin 385
Dirithromycin 526
Erythromycin 609
Erythromycin and Sulfisoxazole 613

Antibiotic, Macrolide Combination
Erythromycin and Sulfisoxazole 613
Lansoprazole, Amoxicillin, and Clarithromycin 979

Antibiotic, Miscellaneous
Aztreonam 189
Bacitracin 191
Capreomycin 280
Chloramphenicol 341
Colistimethate 415
CycloSERINE 430
Dapsone 450
Fosfomycin 765
Methenamine 1106
Methenamine and Sodium Acid Phosphate 1107
Methenamine, Sodium Biphosphate, Phenyl Salicylate, Methylene Blue, and
    Hyoscyamine 1107
Metronidazole 1132
Nitrofurantoin 1233
Pentamidine 1338
Polymyxin B 1389
Rifabutin 1507
Rifampin 1508
Rifaximin 1511
Spectinomycin 1595
Sulfamethoxazole and Trimethoprim 1613
Trimethoprim 1744
Vancomycin 1773

Antibiotic, Ophthalmic
Bacitracin 191
Bacitracin and Polymyxin B 192
Bacitracin, Neomycin, and Polymyxin B 192
Bacitracin, Neomycin, Polymyxin B, and Hydrocortisone 192
Ciprofloxacin 372
Erythromycin 609
Gatifloxacin 781
Gentamicin 793
Moxifloxacin 1175
Neomycin, Polymyxin B, and Gramicidin 1212
Sulfacetamide 1609
Tobramycin 1696
Trimethoprim and Polymyxin B 1745

Antibiotic, Oral Rinse
Chlorhexidine Gluconate 344

Antibiotic, Otic
Bacitracin, Neomycin, Polymyxin B, and Hydrocortisone 192

Antibiotic, Oxazolidinone
Linezolid 1018

Antibiotic, Penicillin
Amoxicillin 110
Amoxicillin and Clavulanate Potassium 112
Ampicillin 122
Ampicillin and Sulbactam 124
Carbenicillin 288
Dicloxacillin 495
Lansoprazole, Amoxicillin, and Clarithromycin 979
Nafcillin 1190
Oxacillin 1276
Penicillin V Potassium 1336
Penicillin G Benzathine 1332
Penicillin G Benzathine and Penicillin G Procaine 1333
Penicillin G (Parenteral/Aqueous) 1333
Penicillin G Procaine 1335
Piperacillin 1375
Piperacillin and Tazobactam Sodium 1375
Ticarcillin 1680
Ticarcillin and Clavulanate Potassium 1682

Antibiotic, Quinolone
Ciprofloxacin 372
Gatifloxacin 781
Gemifloxacin 788
Levofloxacin 1001
Moxifloxacin 1175
Norfloxacin 1241
Ofloxacin 1254

Antibiotic, Streptogramin
Quinupristin and Dalfopristin 1476

Antibiotic, Sulfonamide Derivative
Erythromycin and Sulfisoxazole 613
Sulfacetamide 1609
SulfaDIAZINE 1610
Sulfamethoxazole and Trimethoprim 1613
SulfiSOXAZOLE 1617
Sulfur and Sulfacetamide 1618

Antibiotic, Tetracycline Derivative
Bismuth Subsalicylate, Metronidazole, and Tetracycline 225
Demeclocycline 469
Doxycycline 555
Minocycline 1149
Oxytetracycline 1293
Tetracycline 1659

Antibiotic, Topical

Bacitracin 191
Bacitracin and Polymyxin B 192
Bacitracin, Neomycin, and Polymyxin B 192
Bacitracin, Neomycin, Polymyxin B, and Hydrocortisone 192
Chlorhexidine Gluconate 344
Erythromycin 609
Gentamicin 793
Gentian Violet 796
Hexachlorophene 838
Mafenide 1045
Metronidazole 1132
Mupirocin 1179
Neomycin 1210
Neomycin and Polymyxin B 1211
Silver Nitrate 1566
Silver Sulfadiazine 1567

Anticholinergic/Adrenergic Agonist

Phenylephrine and Scopolamine 1360

Anticholinergic Agent

Atropine 176
Benztropine 208
Chlordiazepoxide and Methscopolamine 344
Darifenacin 455
Dicyclomine 496
Edrophonium and Atropine 570
Glycopyrrolate 807
Hyoscyamine 866
Hyoscyamine, Atropine, Scopolamine, and Phenobarbital . . . 868
Ipratropium 932
Procyclidine 1432
Propantheline 1440
Scopolamine Derivatives 1550
Solifenacin 1585
Tolterodine 1705
Trihexyphenidyl 1742
Trimethobenzamide 1743
Trospium 1753

Anticholinergic Agent, Ophthalmic

Atropine 176
Cyclopentolate 428
Homatropine 840

Anticoagulant

Antithrombin III 137
Heparin 829

Anticoagulant, Coumarin Derivative

Warfarin 1800

Anticoagulant, Thrombin Inhibitor

Argatroban 149
Bivalirudin 227
Lepirudin 986

Anticonvulsant, Barbiturate

Pentobarbital 1340
Phenobarbital 1353
Thiopental 1670

Anticonvulsant, Hydantoin

Fosphenytoin 768
Phenytoin 1361

Anticonvulsant, Miscellaneous

AcetaZOLAMIDE 37
Carbamazepine 284
Felbamate 687
Gabapentin 775
Lamotrigine 974
Levetiracetam 995
Magnesium Sulfate 1052
Oxcarbazepine 1282
Pregabalin 1418
Primidone 1422
Tiagabine 1679
Topiramate 1707
Valproic Acid and Derivatives 1767
Zonisamide 1825

Anticonvulsant, Succinimide

Ethosuximide 665
Methsuximide 1116

Anticystine Agent

Cysteamine 437

Antidepressant, Alpha-2 Antagonist

Mirtazapine 1152

Antidepressant, Dopamine-Reuptake Inhibitor

BuPROPion 252

Antidepressant, Monoamine Oxidase Inhibitor

Phenelzine 1351
Selegiline 1552
(Continued)

Antidepressant, Monoamine Oxidase Inhibitor *(Continued)*
Tranylcypromine 1723

Antidepressant, Selective Serotonin Reuptake Inhibitor
Citalopram 381
Escitalopram 613
Fluoxetine 727
Fluvoxamine 747
Olanzapine and Fluoxetine 1259
Paroxetine 1314
Sertraline 1557

Antidepressant, Serotonin/Norepinephrine Reuptake Inhibitor
Duloxetine 562
Venlafaxine 1781

Antidepressant, Serotonin Reuptake Inhibitor/Antagonist
Nefazodone 1206
Trazodone 1727

Antidepressant, Tetracyclic
Maprotiline 1056

Antidepressant, Tricyclic (Secondary Amine)
Amoxapine 108
Desipramine 473
Nortriptyline 1243
Protriptyline 1452

Antidepressant, Tricyclic (Tertiary Amine)
Amitriptyline 101
Amitriptyline and Chlordiazepoxide 103
Amitriptyline and Perphenazine 103
ClomiPRAMINE 395
Doxepin 545
Imipramine 888
Trimipramine 1747

Antidiabetic Agent
Pramlintide 1407

Antidiabetic Agent, Alpha-Glucosidase Inhibitor
Acarbose 25
Miglitol 1146

Antidiabetic Agent, Biguanide
Glipizide and Metformin 801
Glyburide and Metformin 805
Metformin 1098
Pioglitazone and Metformin 1374
Rosiglitazone and Metformin 1537

Antidiabetic Agent, Dipeptidyl Peptidase IV (DPP-IV) Inhibitor
Sitagliptin 1572

Antidiabetic Agent, Incretin Mimetic
Exenatide 676

Antidiabetic Agent, Insulin
Insulin Aspart 909
Insulin Aspart Protamine and Insulin Aspart 910
Insulin Detemir 910
Insulin Glargine 911
Insulin Glulisine 911
Insulin Inhalation 911
Insulin Lispro 913
Insulin Lispro Protamine and Insulin Lispro 913
Insulin NPH 913
Insulin NPH and Insulin Regular 914
Insulin Regular 914

Antidiabetic Agent, Meglitinide Derivative
Nateglinide 1204
Repaglinide 1494

Antidiabetic Agent, Sulfonylurea
ChlorproPAMIDE 358
Glimepiride 797
GlipiZIDE 799
Glipizide and Metformin 801
GlyBURIDE 803
Glyburide and Metformin 805
Pioglitazone and Glimepiride 1374
Rosiglitazone and Glimepiride 1536
TOLAZamide 1700
TOLBUTamide 1701

Antidiabetic Agent, Thiazolidinedione
Pioglitazone 1372
Pioglitazone and Glimepiride 1374
Pioglitazone and Metformin 1374
Rosiglitazone 1535
Rosiglitazone and Glimepiride 1536
Rosiglitazone and Metformin 1537

Antidiarrheal
Bismuth 224
Bismuth Subsalicylate, Metronidazole, and Tetracycline 225
Difenoxin and Atropine 499

Diphenoxylate and Atropine 518
Loperamide 1027
Loperamide and Simethicone 1029
Octreotide 1252
Opium Tincture 1269
Psyllium 1458

Antidiuretic Hormone Analog
Vasopressin 1779

Antidote
Acetylcysteine 39
Aluminum Hydroxide 83
Amifostine 89
Amyl Nitrite 127
Atropine 176
Calcitonin 264
Calcium Acetate 267
Calcium Carbonate 269
Charcoal 338
Deferasirox 465
Deferoxamine 466
Digoxin Immune Fab 504
Dimercaprol 512
Edrophonium 569
Edrophonium and Atropine 570
Epinephrine 589
Ferric Hexacyanoferrate 701
Flumazenil 718
Fomepizole 755
Glucagon 802
Hydroxocobalamin 860
Insulin Regular 914
Ipecac Syrup 932
Leucovorin 990
Mesna 1091
Methylene Blue 1118
Nalmefene 1193
Naloxone 1194
Naltrexone 1195
Pamidronate 1300
Pralidoxime 1405
Protamine Sulfate 1451
Sodium Phenylacetate and Sodium Benzoate 1582
Sodium Polystyrene Sulfonate 1582
Sodium Thiosulfate 1584
Succimer 1604
Zoledronic Acid 1820

Antiemetic
Aprepitant 144
Dexamethasone 479
Dolasetron 536
Dronabinol 558
Droperidol 559
Granisetron 811
HydrOXYzine 865
Meclizine 1063
Metoclopramide 1126
Ondansetron 1267
Palonosetron 1299
Prochlorperazine 1429
Promethazine 1435
Trimethobenzamide 1743

Antiflatulent
Aluminum Hydroxide, Magnesium Hydroxide, and Simethicone 85
Loperamide and Simethicone 1029
Magaldrate and Simethicone 1045

Antifungal Agent, Ophthalmic
Natamycin 1203

Antifungal Agent, Oral
Fluconazole 712
Flucytosine 714
Griseofulvin 813
Itraconazole 952
Ketoconazole 959
Posaconazole 1393
Terbinafine 1648
Voriconazole 1797

Antifungal Agent, Oral Nonabsorbed
Clotrimazole 404
Nystatin 1250

Antifungal Agent, Parenteral
Amphotericin B Cholesteryl Sulfate Complex 115
Amphotericin B (Conventional) 116
Amphotericin B (Lipid Complex) 118
Amphotericin B (Liposomal) 119
Anidulafungin 131
Caspofungin 302
Fluconazole 712
Micafungin 1136
(Continued)

Antifungal Agent, Parenteral *(Continued)*
Voriconazole 1797

Antifungal Agent, Topical
Betamethasone and Clotrimazole 214
Butenafine 260
Ciclopirox 366
Clotrimazole 404
Econazole 566
Gentian Violet 796
Iodoquinol and Hydrocortisone 931
Ketoconazole 959
Miconazole 1137
Miconazole and Zinc Oxide 1139
Naftifine 1191
Nystatin 1250
Nystatin and Triamcinolone 1251
Oxiconazole 1284
Sertaconazole 1557
Sulconazole 1609
Terbinafine 1648
Tolnaftate 1704

Antifungal Agent, Vaginal
Butoconazole 260
Clotrimazole 404
Miconazole 1137
Nystatin 1250
Terconazole 1652
Tioconazole 1691

Antigout Agent
Colchicine and Probenecid 414

Antihemophilic Agent
Antihemophilic Factor (Human) 133
Antihemophilic Factor (Recombinant) 135
Antihemophilic Factor/von Willebrand Factor Complex (Human) 136
Anti-inhibitor Coagulant Complex 137
Desmopressin 476
Factor IX 679
Factor IX Complex (Human) 681
Factor VIIa (Recombinant) 678
Tranexamic Acid 1722

Antihistamine
Acetaminophen, Chlorpheniramine, and Pseudoephedrine 35
Acetaminophen, Dextromethorphan, and Pseudoephedrine 35
Acrivastine and Pseudoephedrine 43
Azelastine 185
Brompheniramine 242
Carbinoxamine 289
Cetirizine 334
Chlorpheniramine and Pseudoephedrine 350
Clemastine 387
Cyproheptadine 436
Dexchlorpheniramine 483
Dexchlorpheniramine and Pseudoephedrine 483
Dihydrocodeine, Chlorpheniramine, and Phenylephrine 506
DimenhyDRINATE 511
DiphenhydrAMINE 515
HydrOXYzine 865
Meclizine 1063
Olopatadine 1261
Promethazine 1435
Triprolidine and Pseudoephedrine 1749

Antihistamine/Analgesic
Chlorpheniramine and Acetaminophen 349

Antihistamine/Antitussive
Hydrocodone and Chlorpheniramine 849
Promethazine and Codeine 1437
Promethazine and Dextromethorphan 1437

Antihistamine/Decongestant/Anticholinergic
Chlorpheniramine, Phenylephrine, and Methscopolamine 353

Antihistamine/Decongestant/Antitussive
Carbinoxamine, Pseudoephedrine, and Dextromethorphan 291
Chlorpheniramine, Ephedrine, Phenylephrine, and Carbetapentane 351
Chlorpheniramine, Phenylephrine, and Dextromethorphan 352
Chlorpheniramine, Pseudoephedrine, and Codeine 355
Chlorpheniramine, Pseudoephedrine, and Dextromethorphan 355
Dihydrocodeine, Chlorpheniramine, and Phenylephrine 506
Hydrocodone, Carbinoxamine, and Pseudoephedrine 851
Promethazine, Phenylephrine, and Codeine 1438
Triprolidine, Pseudoephedrine, and Codeine 1750

Antihistamine/Decongestant/Antitussive/Expectorant
Chlorpheniramine, Phenylephrine, Codeine, and Potassium Iodide 354

Antihistamine/Decongestant Combination
Brompheniramine and Pseudoephedrine 243
Chlorpheniramine and Phenylephrine 349
Chlorpheniramine, Phenylephrine, and Phenyltoloxamine 354
Dexbrompheniramine and Pseudoephedrine 482

Diphenhydramine and Pseudoephedrine 517
Fexofenadine and Pseudoephedrine 706
Loratadine and Pseudoephedrine 1034
Promethazine and Phenylephrine 1438

Antihistamine/Decongestant Combination, Nonsedating
Desloratadine and Pseudoephedrine 476

Antihistamine, H₁ Blocker
Carbinoxamine and Pseudoephedrine 290

Antihistamine, H₁ Blocker, Ophthalmic
Epinastine 589
Ketotifen 965
Levocabastine 997

Antihistamine, Nonsedating
Desloratadine 475
Fexofenadine 705
Loratadine 1033

Antihypertensive
Diazoxide 491
Quinapril and Hydrochlorothiazide 1471

Antihypertensive Agent, Combination
Amlodipine and Benazepril 106
Atenolol and Chlorthalidone 169
Benazepril and Hydrochlorothiazide 203
Bisoprolol and Hydrochlorothiazide 227
Candesartan and Hydrochlorothiazide 278
Captopril and Hydrochlorothiazide 284
Clonidine and Chlorthalidone 401
Enalapril and Felodipine 581
Enalapril and Hydrochlorothiazide 581
Eprosartan and Hydrochlorothiazide 601
Hydralazine and Hydrochlorothiazide 845
Hydrochlorothiazide and Spironolactone 847
Hydrochlorothiazide and Triamterene 847
Irbesartan and Hydrochlorothiazide 935
Lisinopril and Hydrochlorothiazide 1023
Losartan and Hydrochlorothiazide 1039
Methyldopa and Hydrochlorothiazide 1117
Moexipril and Hydrochlorothiazide 1164
Olmesartan and Hydrochlorothiazide 1261
Prazosin and Polythiazide 1413
Propranolol and Hydrochlorothiazide 1449
Telmisartan and Hydrochlorothiazide 1640
Trandolapril and Verapamil 1722
Valsartan and Hydrochlorothiazide 1773

Antihypoglycemic Agent
Diazoxide 491

Anti-inflammatory Agent
Balsalazide 194
Colchicine and Probenecid 414
Dexamethasone 479

Anti-inflammatory Agent, Ophthalmic
Dexamethasone 479

Anti-inflammatory, Locally Applied
Amlexanox 103
Carbamide Peroxide 287

Antilipemic Agent, 2-Azetidinone
Ezetimibe 677
Ezetimibe and Simvastatin 678

Antilipemic Agent, Bile Acid Sequestrant
Cholestyramine Resin 360
Colesevelam 414
Colestipol 415

Antilipemic Agent, Fibric Acid
Fenofibrate 689
Gemfibrozil 787

Antilipemic Agent, HMG-CoA Reductase Inhibitor
Amlodipine and Atorvastatin 105
Aspirin and Pravastatin 164
Atorvastatin 171
Ezetimibe and Simvastatin 678
Fluvastatin 745
Lovastatin 1040
Niacin and Lovastatin 1221
Pravastatin 1409
Rosuvastatin 1537
Simvastatin 1567

Antilipemic Agent, Miscellaneous
Niacin 1219
Niacin and Lovastatin 1221
Omega-3-Acid Ethyl Esters 1264

Antimalarial Agent
Atovaquone and Proguanil 173
Mefloquine 1069
Pyrimethamine 1464
(Continued)

Antimalarial Agent *(Continued)*
Quinine 1474
Sulfadoxine and Pyrimethamine 1611

Antimigraine Agent
Almotriptan 73
Dihydroergotamine 507
Eletriptan 575
Ergotamine 605
Frovatriptan 771
Naratriptan 1202
Rizatriptan 1528
Sumatriptan 1620
Zolmitriptan 1822

Antineoplastic Agent
Bortezomib 230
Carmustine 296
Lenalidomide 984

Antineoplastic Agent, Alkylating Agent
Busulfan 257
Carboplatin 291
Chlorambucil 340
Cisplatin 379
Cyclophosphamide 428
Estramustine 626
Ifosfamide 880
Lomustine 1026
Melphalan 1074
Oxaliplatin 1277
Procarbazine 1428
Temozolomide 1642
Thiotepa 1674

Antineoplastic Agent, Alkylating Agent (Nitrogen Mustard)
Ifosfamide 880
Mechlorethamine 1061

Antineoplastic Agent, Alkylating Agent (Nitrosourea)
Carmustine 296

Antineoplastic Agent, Alkylating Agent (Triazene)
Dacarbazine 442

Antineoplastic Agent, Anthracenedione
Mitoxantrone 1157

Antineoplastic Agent, Anthracycline
DAUNOrubicin Citrate (Liposomal) 460
DAUNOrubicin Hydrochloride 462
DOXOrubicin 549
DOXOrubicin (Liposomal) 552
Epirubicin 592
Idarubicin 878
Valrubicin 1770

Antineoplastic Agent, Antiandrogen
Bicalutamide 221
Flutamide 737
Nilutamide 1228

Antineoplastic Agent, Antibiotic
Bleomycin 229
Dactinomycin 444
Idarubicin 878
Mitomycin 1155
Pentostatin 1342

Antineoplastic Agent, Antimetabolite
Capecitabine 278
Cladribine 383
Cytarabine 437
Cytarabine (Liposomal) 439
Hydroxyurea 863
Mercaptopurine 1086
Nelarabine 1207
Pemetrexed 1328

Antineoplastic Agent, Antimetabolite (Antifolate)
Methotrexate 1111
Pemetrexed 1328

Antineoplastic Agent, Antimetabolite (Purine Antagonist)
Cladribine 383
Clofarabine 393
Cytarabine 437
Fludarabine 716
Pentostatin 1342
Thioguanine 1669

Antineoplastic Agent, Antimetabolite (Pyrimidine)
Azacitidine 181
Decitabine 463

Antineoplastic Agent, Antimetabolite (Pyrimidine Antagonist)
Capecitabine 278
Fluorouracil 725
Gemcitabine 785

Antineoplastic Agent, Antimicrotubular
Paclitaxel 1295
Paclitaxel (Protein Bound) 1297

Antineoplastic Agent, Aromatase Inactivator
Exemestane 674

Antineoplastic Agent, Aromatase Inhibitor
Aminoglutethimide 95
Anastrozole 129
Letrozole 988

Antineoplastic Agent, DNA Adduct-Forming Agent
Carmustine 296

Antineoplastic Agent, DNA Binding Agent
Carmustine 296

Antineoplastic Agent, Estrogen Receptor Antagonist
Fulvestrant 772
Tamoxifen 1631
Toremifene 1711

Antineoplastic Agent, Histone Deacetylase Inhibitor
Vorinostat 1799

Antineoplastic Agent, Hormone
Estramustine 626
Megestrol 1071

Antineoplastic Agent, Hormone Antagonist
Mifepristone 1143

Antineoplastic Agent, Hormone (Estrogen/Nitrogen Mustard)
Estramustine 626

Antineoplastic Agent, Miscellaneous
Alitretinoin 70
Altretamine 82
Arsenic Trioxide 154
Asparaginase 157
Bexarotene 219
Denileukin Diftitox 471
Mitotane 1156
Pegaspargase 1320
Porfimer 1391
Teniposide 1645
Tretinoin (Oral) 1730
Trimetrexate 1745

Antineoplastic Agent, Monoclonal Antibody
Alemtuzumab 63
Bevacizumab 217
Cetuximab 336
Gemtuzumab Ozogamicin 790
Ibritumomab 871
Panitumumab 1305
Rituximab 1523
Tositumomab and Iodine I 131 Tositumomab 1713
Trastuzumab 1724

Antineoplastic Agent, Natural Source (Plant) Derivative
Docetaxel 530
Irinotecan 935
Paclitaxel 1295
Paclitaxel (Protein Bound) 1297
Topotecan 1709
VinBLAStine 1788
VinCRIStine 1789
Vinorelbine 1791

Antineoplastic Agent, Podophyllotoxin Derivative
Etoposide 670
Etoposide Phosphate 673

Antineoplastic Agent, Tyrosine Kinase Inhibitor
Dasatinib 458
Erlotinib 606
Gefitinib 784
Imatinib 881
Sorafenib 1590
Sunitinib 1622

Antineoplastic Agent, Vinca Alkaloid
VinBLAStine 1788
VinCRIStine 1789
Vinorelbine 1791

Antiparasitic Agent, Topical
Lindane 1016
Malathion 1053
Permethrin 1348
Pyrethrins and Piperonyl Butoxide 1461

Anti-Parkinson's Agent, Anticholinergic
Benztropine 208
Orphenadrine 1273
Procyclidine 1432
Trihexyphenidyl 1742

Anti-Parkinson's Agent, COMT Inhibitor
Entacapone 585
Levodopa, Carbidopa, and Entacapone 1001
Tolcapone 1701

Anti-Parkinson's Agent, Dopamine Agonist
Amantadine 86
Bromocriptine 240
Carbidopa 289
Levodopa and Carbidopa 999
Levodopa, Carbidopa, and Entacapone 1001
Pergolide 1345
Pramipexole 1406
Ropinirole 1531

Anti-Parkinson's Agent, MAO Type B Inhibitor
Rasagiline 1488
Selegiline 1552

Antiplatelet Agent
Aspirin and Dipyridamole 163
Cilostazol 368
Clopidogrel 401
Dipyridamole 525
Ticlopidine 1683

Antiplatelet Agent, Glycoprotein IIb/IIIa Inhibitor
Abciximab 22
Eptifibatide 601
Tirofiban 1693

Antiprogestin
Mifepristone 1143

Antiprotozoal
Atovaquone 173
Eflornithine 573
Nitazoxanide 1232

Antiprotozoal, Nitroimidazole
Metronidazole 1132

Antipsoriatic Agent
Anthralin 132

Antipsychotic Agent, Atypical
Aripiprazole 151
Clozapine 406
Olanzapine 1257
Olanzapine and Fluoxetine 1259
Quetiapine 1467
Risperidone 1517
Ziprasidone 1818

Antipsychotic Agent, Typical
Droperidol 559
Haloperidol 826
Loxapine 1042
Molindone 1164
Pimozide 1370
Thiothixene 1675

Antipsychotic Agent, Typical, Phenothiazine
Amitriptyline and Perphenazine 103
ChlorproMAZINE 356
Fluphenazine 731
Mesoridazine 1091
Perphenazine 1349
Prochlorperazine 1429
Thioridazine 1672
Trifluoperazine 1740

Antiretroviral Agent, Fusion Protein Inhibitor
Enfuvirtide 581

Antiretroviral Agent, Protease Inhibitor
Amprenavir 125
Atazanavir 165
Darunavir 457
Fosamprenavir 761
Indinavir 899
Lopinavir and Ritonavir 1029
Nelfinavir 1208
Ritonavir 1520
Saquinavir 1546
Tipranavir 1692

Antiretroviral Agent, Reverse Transcriptase Inhibitor (Non-nucleoside)
Delavirdine 468
Efavirenz 571
Efavirenz, Emtricitabine, and Tenofovir 573
Nevirapine 1217

Antiretroviral Agent, Reverse Transcriptase Inhibitor (Nucleoside)
Abacavir 18
Abacavir and Lamivudine 19
Abacavir, Lamivudine, and Zidovudine 19
Adefovir 49
Didanosine 496

Efavirenz, Emtricitabine, and Tenofovir 573
Emtricitabine 576
Emtricitabine and Tenofovir 578
Entecavir 586
Lamivudine 971
Stavudine 1599
Zalcitabine 1807
Zidovudine 1812
Zidovudine and Lamivudine 1815

Antiretroviral Agent, Reverse Transcriptase Inhibitor (Nucleotide)
Efavirenz, Emtricitabine, and Tenofovir 573
Emtricitabine and Tenofovir 578
Tenofovir 1645

Antirheumatic, Disease Modifying
Abatacept 21
Adalimumab 47
Anakinra 128
Etanercept 641
Infliximab 904
Leflunomide 982
Methotrexate 1111

Antirheumatic Miscellaneous
Hyaluronate and Derivatives 841

Antiseborrheic Agent, Topical
Sulfur and Sulfacetamide 1618

Antiseptic, Ophthalmic
Povidone-Iodine 1404

Antiseptic, Topical
Povidone-Iodine 1404

Antiseptic, Vaginal
Povidone-Iodine 1404

Antispasmodic Agent, Gastrointestinal
Atropine 176
Clidinium and Chlordiazepoxide 388
Hyoscyamine, Atropine, Scopolamine, and Phenobarbital 868

Antispasmodic Agent, Urinary
Belladonna and Opium 200
Flavoxate 710
Oxybutynin 1285

Antithyroid Agent
Methimazole 1108
Potassium Iodide 1399
Potassium Iodide and Iodine 1401
Propylthiouracil 1449

Antitubercular Agent
Capreomycin 280
CycloSERINE 430
Ethambutol 643
Ethionamide 664
Isoniazid 942
Pyrazinamide 1460
Rifabutin 1507
Rifampin 1508
Rifapentine 1510
Streptomycin 1602

Antitussive
Acetaminophen, Dextromethorphan, and Pseudoephedrine 35
Benzonatate 207
Carbetapentane and Phenylephrine 289
Codeine 410
Dihydrocodeine, Chlorpheniramine, and Phenylephrine 506
Guaifenesin and Codeine 815
Guaifenesin and Dextromethorphan 816
Hydrocodone and Homatropine 850

Antitussive/Decongestant
Carbetapentane and Phenylephrine 289
Carbetapentane and Pseudoephedrine 289
Hydrocodone and Pseudoephedrine 851
Hydrocodone, Chlorpheniramine, Phenylephrine, Acetaminophen, and Caffeine 852
Pseudoephedrine and Dextromethorphan 1455

Antitussive/Decongestant/Expectorant
Dihydrocodeine, Pseudoephedrine, and Guaifenesin 506
Guaifenesin, Pseudoephedrine, and Codeine 820
Guaifenesin, Pseudoephedrine, and Dextromethorphan 821
Hydrocodone, Pseudoephedrine, and Guaifenesin 852

Antitussive/Expectorant
Hydrocodone and Guaifenesin 849

Antiviral Agent
Acyclovir 44
Cidofovir 367
Famciclovir 682
Foscarnet 762
Ganciclovir 779
Interferon Alfa-2b and Ribavirin 923
(Continued)

Antiviral Agent *(Continued)*
Oseltamivir 1274
Penciclovir 1329
Ribavirin 1503
Valganciclovir 1765
Zanamivir 1809

Antiviral Agent, Adamantane
Amantadine 86
Rimantadine 1513

Antiviral Agent, Ophthalmic
Fomivirsen 756
Trifluridine 1741

Antiviral Agent, Oral
Valacyclovir 1764

Antiviral Agent, Topical
Docosanol 533

Appetite Stimulant
Dronabinol 558
Megestrol 1071

Barbiturate
Amobarbital 107
Amobarbital and Secobarbital 108
Butabarbital 259
Butalbital, Acetaminophen, and Caffeine 259
Butalbital and Acetaminophen 259
Butalbital, Aspirin, and Caffeine 260
Mephobarbital 1083
Methohexital 1110
Pentobarbital 1340
Phenobarbital 1353
Primidone 1422
Secobarbital 1552
Thiopental 1670

Benzodiazepine
Alprazolam 75
Amitriptyline and Chlordiazepoxide 103
Chlordiazepoxide 342
Chlordiazepoxide and Methscopolamine 344
Clidinium and Chlordiazepoxide 388
Clonazepam 397
Clorazepate 403
Diazepam 488
Estazolam 619
Lorazepam 1035
Midazolam 1139
Oxazepam 1281
Quazepam 1466

Beta$_1$- & Beta$_2$-Adrenergic Agonist Agent
Isoproterenol 944

Beta$_2$-Adrenergic Agonist
Albuterol 57
Arformoterol 148
Budesonide and Formoterol 247
Fluticasone and Salmeterol 742
Formoterol 759
Levalbuterol 993
Metaproterenol 1096
Pirbuterol 1378
Salmeterol 1543
Terbutaline 1650

Beta-Adrenergic Blocker, Nonselective
Dorzolamide and Timolol 542
Levobunolol 996
Metipranolol 1126
Nadolol 1187
Propranolol 1446
Sotalol 1592
Timolol 1687

Beta Blocker, Beta$_1$ Selective
Atenolol 167
Betaxolol 214
Bisoprolol 226
Esmolol 616
Metoprolol 1129
Metoprolol and Hydrochlorothiazide 1132

Beta Blocker With Alpha-Blocking Activity
Carvedilol 299
Labetalol 967

Beta Blocker With Intrinsic Sympathomimetic Activity
Acebutolol 27
Carteolol 298
Pindolol 1371

Biological, Miscellaneous
Glatiramer Acetate 796

Biological Response Modulator
Aldesleukin 59
BCG Vaccine 197
Oprelvekin 1270

Bisphosphonate Derivative
Alendronate 65
Alendronate and Cholecalciferol 67
Etidronate Disodium 665
Ibandronate 869
Pamidronate 1300
Risedronate 1515
Risedronate and Calcium 1517
Tiludronate 1686
Zoledronic Acid 1820

Blood Product Derivative
Albumin 55
Antihemophilic Factor (Human) 133
Antihemophilic Factor/von Willebrand Factor Complex (Human) 136
Anti-inhibitor Coagulant Complex 137
Antithrombin III 137
Aprotinin 146
Factor IX 679
Factor IX Complex (Human) 681
Factor VIIa (Recombinant) 678

Blood Viscosity Reducer Agent
Pentoxifylline 1343

Bronchodilator
Ipratropium and Albuterol 934
Theophylline Salts 1664

Calcimimetic
Cinacalcet 371

Calcium Channel Blocker
Amlodipine 104
Amlodipine and Atorvastatin 105
Diltiazem 509
Felodipine 687
Isradipine 950
NiCARdipine 1222
NIFEdipine 1226
Nimodipine 1229
Nisoldipine 1231
Verapamil 1784

Calcium Channel Blocker, N-Type
Ziconotide 1811

Calcium Salt
Calcium Acetate 267
Calcium and Vitamin D 268
Calcium Carbonate 269
Calcium Chloride 271
Calcium Citrate 272
Calcium Glubionate 273
Calcium Gluconate 273
Risedronate and Calcium 1517

Caloric Agent
Fat Emulsion 686
Total Parenteral Nutrition 1715

Carbonic Anhydrase Inhibitor
AcetaZOLAMIDE 37
Brinzolamide 240
Dorzolamide 542
Dorzolamide and Timolol 542
Methazolamide 1105

Cardiac Glycoside
Digoxin 501

Cardioprotectant
Dexrazoxane 485

Cardiovascular Agent, Miscellaneous
Ranolazine 1487

Cauterizing Agent, Topical
Silver Nitrate 1566

Central Monoamine-Depleting Agent
Reserpine 1496

Central Nervous System Depressant
Sodium Oxybate 1580

Central Nervous System Stimulant
Dexmethylphenidate 484
Methylphenidate 1119

Chelating Agent
Deferasirox 465
Edetate Calcium Disodium 566
Edetate Disodium 568
Penicillamine 1330
Trientine 1739

Cholinergic Agonist
Acetylcholine 38
Bethanechol 216
Carbachol 284
Cevimeline 338
Edrophonium 569
Edrophonium and Atropine 570
Pilocarpine 1368

Colchicine
Colchicine 412

Colony Stimulating Factor
Darbepoetin Alfa 453
Epoetin Alfa 595
Filgrastim 707
Pegfilgrastim 1321
Sargramostim 1548

Contraceptive
Ethinyl Estradiol and Desogestrel 645
Ethinyl Estradiol and Drospirenone 646
Ethinyl Estradiol and Ethynodiol Diacetate 648
Ethinyl Estradiol and Etonogestrel 650
Ethinyl Estradiol and Levonorgestrel 653
Ethinyl Estradiol and Norelgestromin 655
Ethinyl Estradiol and Norethindrone 655
Ethinyl Estradiol and Norgestimate 660
Ethinyl Estradiol and Norgestrel 663
Levonorgestrel 1004
MedroxyPROGESTERone 1065
Mestranol and Norethindrone 1093
Nonoxynol 9 1239

Corticosteroid, Adrenal
Triamcinolone 1734

Corticosteroid, Inhalant (Oral)
Beclomethasone 198
Budesonide 244
Budesonide and Formoterol 247
Flunisolide 720
Fluticasone 738
Fluticasone and Salmeterol 742
Mometasone Furoate 1165
Triamcinolone 1734

Corticosteroid, Nasal
Beclomethasone 198
Budesonide 244
Ciclesonide 365
Flunisolide 720
Fluticasone 738
Mometasone Furoate 1165
Triamcinolone 1734

Corticosteroid, Ophthalmic
Bacitracin, Neomycin, Polymyxin B, and Hydrocortisone 192
Dexamethasone 479
Fluocinolone 721
Fluorometholone 724
Loteprednol 1039
Medrysone 1067
PrednisoLONE 1413
Rimexolone 1514

Corticosteroid, Otic
Bacitracin, Neomycin, Polymyxin B, and Hydrocortisone 192
Dexamethasone 479

Corticosteroid, Rectal
Hydrocortisone 852

Corticosteroid, Systemic
Betamethasone 211
Budesonide 244
Cortisone 420
Dexamethasone 479
Fludrocortisone 717
Hydrocortisone 852
MethylPREDNISolone 1122
PrednisoLONE 1413
PredniSONE 1416
Triamcinolone 1734

Corticosteroid, Topical
Alclometasone 59
Amcinonide 88
Bacitracin, Neomycin, Polymyxin B, and Hydrocortisone 192
Betamethasone 211
Betamethasone and Clotrimazole 214
Calcipotriene and Betamethasone 264
Clobetasol 391
Clocortolone 392
Desonide 478
Desoximetasone 479
Diflorasone 499

Fluocinolone 721
Fluocinolone, Hydroquinone, and Tretinoin 721
Fluocinonide 721
Flurandrenolide 733
Fluticasone 738
Halcinonide 825
Halobetasol 826
Hydrocortisone 852
Iodoquinol and Hydrocortisone 931
Mometasone Furoate 1165
Nystatin and Triamcinolone 1251
Prednicarbate 1413
Triamcinolone 1734
Urea and Hydrocortisone 1759

Corticosteroid, Topical (Medium Potency)

Fluticasone 738

Cosmetic Agent, Implant

Poly-L-Lactic Acid 1388

Cough Preparation

Guaifenesin and Codeine 815
Guaifenesin and Dextromethorphan 816

Decongestant

Carbinoxamine and Pseudoephedrine 290
Dihydrocodeine, Chlorpheniramine, and Phenylephrine 506
Guaifenesin and Phenylephrine 818

Decongestant/Analgesic

Naproxen and Pseudoephedrine 1201
Pseudoephedrine and Ibuprofen 1456

Decongestant/Anticholingeric Combination

Pseudoephedrine and Methscopolamine 1457

Depigmenting Agent

Fluocinolone, Hydroquinone, and Tretinoin 721
Hydroquinone 859

Diagnostic Agent

Adenosine 50
Arginine 151
Benzylpenicilloyl-polylysine 209
Cosyntropin 422
Edrophonium 569
Fluorescein Sodium 722
Glucagon 802
Gonadorelin 809
Methacholine 1100
Perflutren Protein Type A 1345
Proparacaine and Fluorescein 1441
Sermorelin Acetate 1556
Thyrotropin Alpha 1677
Tuberculin Tests 1754

Diagnostic Agent, ACTH-Dependent Hypercortisolism

Corticorelin 419

Dietary Supplement

Lactobacillus 969
Levocarnitine 997

Disinfectant, Antibacterial (Topical)

Sodium Hypochlorite Solution 1579

Diuretic, Carbonic Anhydrase Inhibitor

AcetaZOLAMIDE 37
Methazolamide 1105

Diuretic, Combination

Amiloride and Hydrochlorothiazide 93

Diuretic, Loop

Bumetanide 247
Ethacrynic Acid 642
Furosemide 773
Torsemide 1712

Diuretic, Osmotic

Mannitol 1055
Urea 1758

Diuretic, Potassium-Sparing

Amiloride 92
Eplerenone 594
Hydrochlorothiazide and Triamterene 847
Spironolactone 1596
Triamterene 1737

Diuretic, Thiazide

Candesartan and Hydrochlorothiazide 278
Chlorothiazide 349
Chlorthalidone 359
Eprosartan and Hydrochlorothiazide 601
Hydrochlorothiazide 845
Hydrochlorothiazide and Triamterene 847
Irbesartan and Hydrochlorothiazide 935
Losartan and Hydrochlorothiazide 1039
(Continued)

Diuretic, Thiazide *(Continued)*
Methyclothiazide 1116
Metoprolol and Hydrochlorothiazide 1132
Olmesartan and Hydrochlorothiazide 1261
Polythiazide 1391
Quinapril and Hydrochlorothiazide 1471
Telmisartan and Hydrochlorothiazide 1640
Valsartan and Hydrochlorothiazide 1773

Diuretic, Thiazide-Related
Indapamide 898
Metolazone 1128

Dopamine Agonist
Fenoldopam 691

Echinocandin
Anidulafungin 131
Caspofungin 302
Micafungin 1136

Electrolyte Supplement
Magnesium L-lactate 1050

Electrolyte Supplement, Oral
Calcium and Vitamin D 268
Calcium Carbonate 269
Calcium Gluconate 273
Magnesium L-aspartate Hydrochloride 1049
Magnesium Chloride 1046
Magnesium Gluconate 1047
Magnesium Oxide 1050
Potassium Bicarbonate and Potassium Chloride 1396
Potassium Bicarbonate and Potassium Citrate 1396
Potassium Chloride 1396
Potassium Gluconate 1399
Potassium Phosphate 1402
Potassium Phosphate and Sodium Phosphate 1403
Sodium Bicarbonate 1575

Electrolyte Supplement, Parenteral
Ammonium Chloride 106
Calcium Chloride 271
Calcium Gluconate 273
Magnesium Chloride 1046
Magnesium Sulfate 1052
Potassium Acetate 1394
Potassium Chloride 1396
Potassium Phosphate 1402
Sodium Acetate 1575
Sodium Bicarbonate 1575
Sodium Chloride 1576

Endothelin Antagonist
Bosentan 232

Enzyme
Agalsidase Beta 53
Alglucerase 69
Alglucosidase Alfa 70
Alpha-Galactosidase 74
Dornase Alfa 541
Idursulfase 879
Imiglucerase 885
Laronidase 980
Pancrelipase 1302
Pegademase Bovine 1319
Rasburicase 1490

Enzyme, Gastrointestinal
Sacrosidase 1542

Enzyme Inhibitor
Aminoglutethimide 95
Miglustat 1147

Enzyme, Topical Debridement
Chlorophyllin, Papain, and Urea 345
Collagenase 416
Papain and Urea 1309

Enzyme, Urate-Oxidase (Recombinant)
Rasburicase 1490

Epidermal Growth Factor Receptor (EGFR) Inhibitor
Cetuximab 336
Erlotinib 606
Panitumumab 1305

Ergot Derivative
Belladonna, Phenobarbital, and Ergotamine 201
Bromocriptine 240
Cabergoline 263
Dihydroergotamine 507
Ergoloid Mesylates 604
Ergonovine 604
Ergotamine 605
Methylergonovine 1118

Pergolide 1345

Estrogen and Progestin Combination
Estradiol and Levonorgestrel 624
Estradiol and Norethindrone 624
Estrogens (Conjugated/Equine) and Medroxyprogesterone 634
Estrogens (Esterified) and Methyltestosterone 637
Ethinyl Estradiol and Desogestrel 645
Ethinyl Estradiol and Drospirenone 646
Ethinyl Estradiol and Ethynodiol Diacetate 648
Ethinyl Estradiol and Etonogestrel 650
Ethinyl Estradiol and Levonorgestrel 653
Ethinyl Estradiol and Norelgestromin 655
Ethinyl Estradiol and Norethindrone 655
Ethinyl Estradiol and Norgestimate 660
Ethinyl Estradiol and Norgestrel 663
Mestranol and Norethindrone 1093

Estrogen Derivative
Estradiol 620
Estrogens (Conjugated A/Synthetic) 627
Estrogens (Conjugated B/Synthetic) 629
Estrogens (Conjugated/Equine) 631
Estrogens (Esterified) 635
Estropipate 637

Expectorant
Guaifenesin 814
Guaifenesin and Codeine 815
Guaifenesin and Dextromethorphan 816
Guaifenesin and Phenylephrine 818
Guaifenesin and Pseudoephedrine 819
Potassium Iodide 1399

Factor Xa Inhibitor
Fondaparinux 757

GABA Agonist/Glutamate Antagonist
Acamprosate 24

Gallstone Dissolution Agent
Ursodiol 1762

Ganglionic Blocking Agent
Mecamylamine 1059

Gastrointestinal Agent, Miscellaneous
Infliximab 904
Lansoprazole, Amoxicillin, and Clarithromycin 979
Lubiprostone 1044
Sucralfate 1606

Gastrointestinal Agent, Prokinetic
Cisapride 377
Metoclopramide 1126

Gastrointestinal Agent, Stimulant
Dexpanthenol 485

General Anesthetic
Etomidate 668
Fentanyl 693
Ketamine 958
Propofol 1441
Sufentanil 1608
Thiopental 1670

General Anesthetic, Inhalation
Sevoflurane 1561

Genitourinary Irrigant
Mannitol 1055
Neomycin and Polymyxin B 1211
Sodium Chloride 1576
Sorbitol 1592

Glutamate Inhibitor
Riluzole 1512

Gold Compound
Auranofin 179
Gold Sodium Thiomalate 808

Gonadotropin
Chorionic Gonadotropin (Human) 363
Chorionic Gonadotropin (Recombinant) 364
Follitropin Alfa 751
Follitropin Beta 753
Gonadorelin 809
Lutropin Alfa 1044
Menotropins 1079
Urofollitropin 1759

Gonadotropin Releasing Hormone Agonist
Goserelin 810
Histrelin 839
Leuprolide 991
Nafarelin 1188
Triptorelin 1750

Gonadotropin Releasing Hormone Antagonist
Abarelix 20
Cetrorelix 335
Ganirelix 780

Growth Factor
Darbepoetin Alfa 453

Growth Factor, Platelet-Derived
Becaplermin 198

Growth Hormone
Mecasermin 1060
Sermorelin Acetate 1556
Somatropin 1586

Growth Hormone Receptor Antagonist
Pegvisomant 1327

Hemostatic Agent
Aminocaproic Acid 93
Aprotinin 146
Collagen Hemostat 416
Desmopressin 476

Histamine H₂ Antagonist
Cimetidine 369
Famotidine 683
Famotidine, Calcium Carbonate, and Magnesium Hydroxide 685
Nizatidine 1238
Ranitidine 1485

Homocystinuria, Treatment Agent
Betaine Anhydrous 211

Hormone
Calcitonin 264

Hormone Antagonist, Anti-Adrenal
Aminoglutethimide 95

Hormone, Posterior Pituitary
Vasopressin 1779

Human Growth Factor
Oprelvekin 1270

4-Hydroxyphenylpyruvate Dioxygenase Inhibitor
Nitisinone 1233

Hypnotic, Benzodiazepine
Flurazepam 733
Temazepam 1640
Triazolam 1738

Hypnotic, Nonbenzodiazepine
Chloral Hydrate 339
Eszopiclone 639
Ramelteon 1481
Zaleplon 1808
Zolpidem 1824

Hypoglycemic Agent, Oral
Pioglitazone and Glimepiride 1374

Imidazoline Derivative
Naphazoline 1198

Immune Globulin
Antithymocyte Globulin (Rabbit) 140
Botulism Immune Globulin (Intravenous-Human) 238
Cytomegalovirus Immune Globulin (Intravenous-Human) 441
Hepatitis B Immune Globulin 834
Immune Globulin (Intramuscular) 891
Immune Globulin (Intravenous) 892
Immune Globulin (Subcutaneous) 896
Rabies Immune Globulin (Human) 1478
Respiratory Syncytial Virus Immune Globulin (Intravenous) 1497
Rh₀(D) Immune Globulin 1499
Tetanus Immune Globulin (Human) 1656
Vaccinia Immune Globulin (Intravenous) 1762

Immunosuppressant Agent
Antithymocyte Globulin (Equine) 138
Azathioprine 183
CycloSPORINE 431
Daclizumab 443
Efalizumab 570
Lenalidomide 984
Mercaptopurine 1086
Muromonab-CD3 1179
Mycophenolate 1181
Pimecrolimus 1369
Sirolimus 1569
Tacrolimus 1626
Thalidomide 1661

Interferon
Interferon Alfa-2a 918
Interferon Alfa-2b 920
Interferon Alfa-2b and Ribavirin 923

Interferon Alfacon-1 924
Interferon Alfa-n3 926
Interferon Beta-1a 926
Interferon Beta-1b 928
Interferon Gamma-1b 929
Peginterferon Alfa-2a 1322
Peginterferon Alfa-2b 1325

Interleukin-1 Receptor Antagonist
Anakinra 128

Intravenous Nutritional Therapy
Total Parenteral Nutrition 1715

Iodinated Contrast Media
Ioxilan 931

Iron Salt
Ferric Gluconate 699
Ferrous Fumarate 702
Ferrous Gluconate 703
Ferrous Sulfate 704
Ferrous Sulfate and Ascorbic Acid 705
Iron Dextran Complex 939
Iron Sucrose 941
Polysaccharide-Iron Complex 1390

Irrigant
Sodium Chloride 1576

Keratinocyte Growth Factor
Palifermin 1298

Keratolytic Agent
Anthralin 132
Podophyllum Resin 1385
Tazarotene 1635
Urea 1758

Laxative
Magnesium Hydroxide and Mineral Oil 1048

Laxative, Bulk-Producing
Psyllium 1458

Laxative, Osmotic
Lactulose 971
Polyethylene Glycol 3350 1387
Polyethylene Glycol-Electrolyte Solution 1387
Sorbitol 1592

Laxative, Saline
Magnesium Citrate 1046
Magnesium Sulfate 1052

Laxative, Stimulant
Bisacodyl 223
Docusate and Senna 534

Leukotriene-Receptor Antagonist
Montelukast 1168
Zafirlukast 1805

Lipase Inhibitor
Orlistat 1272

5-Lipoxygenase Inhibitor
Zileuton 1815

Lithium
Lithium 1023

Local Anesthetic
Benzocaine 204
Benzocaine, Butamben, and Tetracaine 207
Benzocaine, Butyl Aminobenzoate, Tetracaine, and Benzalkonium Chloride 207
Bupivacaine 249
Chloroprocaine 346
Cocaine 409
Levobupivacaine 997
Lidocaine 1010
Lidocaine and Bupivacaine 1014
Lidocaine and Epinephrine 1014
Lidocaine and Prilocaine 1015
Lidocaine and Tetracaine 1016
Mepivacaine 1084
Procaine 1427
Proparacaine and Fluorescein 1441
Ropivacaine 1533
Tetracaine 1659

Local Anesthetic, Ophthalmic
Proparacaine 1440

Local Anesthetic, Oral
Dyclonine 565

Low Molecular Weight Heparin
Dalteparin 446
Enoxaparin 583
Tinzaparin 1689

Lubricant, Ocular
Sodium Chloride 1576

Lung Surfactant
Beractant 210
Calfactant 275

Magnesium Salt
Magnesium L-aspartate Hydrochloride 1049
Magnesium L-lactate 1050
Magnesium Chloride 1046
Magnesium Citrate 1046
Magnesium Gluconate 1047
Magnesium Hydroxide 1047
Magnesium Oxide 1050
Magnesium Sulfate 1052

Mast Cell Stabilizer
Cromolyn 423
Lodoxamide 1026
Nedocromil 1205
Pemirolast 1329

Monoclonal Antibody
Adalimumab 47
Alefacept 62
Basiliximab 195
Efalizumab 570
Infliximab 904
Palivizumab 1299
Ranibizumab 1484
Rituximab 1523
Trastuzumab 1724

Monoclonal Antibody, Anti-Asthmatic
Omalizumab 1262

Monoclonal Antibody, Selective Adhesion-Molecule Inhibitor
Natalizumab 1203

Mucolytic Agent
Acetylcysteine 39

Natriuretic Peptide, B-Type, Human
Nesiritide 1215

Neuraminidase Inhibitor
Oseltamivir 1274
Zanamivir 1809

Neuromuscular Blocker Agent, Depolarizing
Succinylcholine 1605

Neuromuscular Blocker Agent, Nondepolarizing
Atracurium 175
Cisatracurium 377
Doxacurium 542
Mivacurium 1159
Pancuronium 1304
Rocuronium 1529
Vecuronium 1780

Neuromuscular Blocker Agent, Toxin
Botulinum Toxin Type A 235
Botulinum Toxin Type B 237

N-Methyl-D-Aspartate Receptor Antagonist
Memantine 1076

Nonsteroidal Anti-inflammatory Drug (NSAID)
Diclofenac 492

Nonsteroidal Anti-inflammatory Drug (NSAID), COX-2 Selective
Celecoxib 329

Nonsteroidal Anti-inflammatory Drug (NSAID), Ophthalmic
Bromfenac 240
Diclofenac 492
Flurbiprofen 735
Ketorolac 963
Nepafenac 1214

Nonsteroidal Anti-inflammatory Drug (NSAID), Oral
Diclofenac 492
Diclofenac and Misoprostol 494
Diflunisal 500
Etodolac 666
Fenoprofen 692
Flurbiprofen 735
Hydrocodone and Ibuprofen 851
Ibuprofen 873
Indomethacin 901
Ketoprofen 961
Ketorolac 963
Lansoprazole and Naproxen 980
Meclofenamate 1063
Mefenamic Acid 1068
Meloxicam 1072
Nabumetone 1185
Naproxen 1199

Oxaprozin 1279
Oxycodone and Ibuprofen 1290
Piroxicam 1378
Sulindac 1618
Tolmetin 1703

Nonsteroidal Anti-inflammatory Drug (NSAID), Parenteral
Ibuprofen 873
Indomethacin 901
Ketorolac 963

Nonsteroidal Aromatase Inhibitor
Aminoglutethimide 95

Norepinephrine Reuptake Inhibitor, Selective
Atomoxetine 169

Nutritional Supplement
Fluoride 722

Ophthalmic Agent
Pegaptanib 1319
Ranibizumab 1484

Ophthalmic Agent, Antiglaucoma
AcetaZOLAMIDE 37
Bimatoprost 222
Brimonidine 239
Brinzolamide 240
Carbachol 284
Carteolol 298
Cyclopentolate and Phenylephrine 428
Dipivefrin 524
Dorzolamide 542
Dorzolamide and Timolol 542
Echothiophate Iodide 566
Latanoprost 981
Levobunolol 996
Methazolamide 1105
Metipranolol 1126
Phenylephrine 1358
Pilocarpine 1368
Timolol 1687
Travoprost 1726

Ophthalmic Agent, Miotic
Acetylcholine 38
Carbachol 284
Echothiophate Iodide 566
Pilocarpine 1368

Ophthalmic Agent, Miscellaneous
Olopatadine 1261
Pemirolast 1329

Ophthalmic Agent, Mydriatic
Atropine 176
Homatropine 840
Phenylephrine 1358
Tropicamide 1752

Ophthalmic Agent, Toxin
Botulinum Toxin Type A 235

Ophthalmic Agent, Vasoconstrictor
Dipivefrin 524
Naphazoline 1198
Naphazoline and Pheniramine 1199

Ophthalmic Agent, Viscoelastic
Chondroitin Sulfate and Sodium Hyaluronate 362
Hyaluronate and Derivatives 841

Otic Agent, Analgesic
Antipyrine and Benzocaine 137

Otic Agent, Anti-infective
Acetic Acid 38
Acetic Acid, Propylene Glycol Diacetate, and Hydrocortisone 38

Otic Agent, Cerumenolytic
Antipyrine and Benzocaine 137
Carbamide Peroxide 287
Triethanolamine Polypeptide Oleate-Condensate 1740

Ovulation Stimulator
Chorionic Gonadotropin (Human) 363
Chorionic Gonadotropin (Recombinant) 364
ClomiPHENE 394
Follitropin Alfa 751
Follitropin Beta 753
Lutropin Alfa 1044
Menotropins 1079
Urofollitropin 1759

Oxytocic Agent
Oxytocin 1293

Parathyroid Hormone Analog
Teriparatide 1652

Partial Nicotine Agonist
Varenicline 1777

Pediculocide
Lindane 1016
Malathion 1053
Pyrethrins and Piperonyl Butoxide 1461

Peritoneal Dialysate, Osmotic
Icodextrin 877

Phenothiazine Derivative
Promethazine 1435

Phosphate Binder
Calcium Acetate 267
Sevelamer 1560

Phosphodiesterase-5 Enzyme Inhibitor
Sildenafil 1564
Tadalafil 1629
Vardenafil 1775

Phosphodiesterase Enzyme Inhibitor
Cilostazol 368
Inamrinone 897
Milrinone 1148

Phospholipase A$_2$ Inhibitor
Anagrelide 128

Photosensitizing Agent, Topical
Aminolevulinic Acid 95

Plasma Volume Expander
Dextran 485
Dextran 1 486

Plasma Volume Expander, Colloid
Albumin 55
Hetastarch 838

Probiotic
Lactobacillus 969

Progestin
Levonorgestrel 1004
MedroxyPROGESTERone 1065
Megestrol 1071
Progesterone 1433

Prostaglandin
Alprostadil 77
Carboprost Tromethamine 293
Diclofenac and Misoprostol 494
Dinoprostone 513
Epoprostenol 598
Iloprost 881
Misoprostol 1154

Prostaglandin, Ophthalmic
Bimatoprost 222
Latanoprost 981
Travoprost 1726

Proteasome Inhibitor
Bortezomib 230

Protectant, Topical
Aluminum Hydroxide 83
Trypsin, Balsam Peru, and Castor Oil 1754

Protein C (Activated)
Drotrecogin Alfa 561

Proton Pump Inhibitor
Esomeprazole 618
Lansoprazole 977
Lansoprazole and Naproxen 980
Omeprazole 1264
Omeprazole and Sodium Bicarbonate 1266
Pantoprazole 1307
Rabeprazole 1477

Psoralen
Methoxsalen 1115

Radiological/Contrast Media, Nonionic
Ioxilan 931

Radiopharmaceutical
Ibritumomab 871
Strontium-89 1604
Tositumomab and Iodine I 131 Tositumomab 1713

Rauwolfia Alkaloid
Reserpine 1496

Recombinant Human Erythropoietin
Darbepoetin Alfa 453

Respiratory Stimulant
Doxapram 543

Retinoic Acid Derivative
Clindamycin and Tretinoin 391
Fluocinolone, Hydroquinone, and Tretinoin 721
Isotretinoin 948
Mequinol and Tretinoin 1085
Tretinoin (Topical) 1732

Retinoid-Like Compound
Acitretin 41

Salicylate
Aminosalicylic Acid 96
Aspirin 160
Aspirin and Pravastatin 164
Choline Magnesium Trisalicylate 361
Magnesium Salicylate 1051
Salsalate 1544

Scabicidal Agent
Crotamiton 424
Lindane 1016
Malathion 1053
Permethrin 1348

Sclerosing Agent
Ethanolamine Oleate 644
Morrhuate Sodium 1175
Sodium Tetradecyl 1583

Sedative
Dexmedetomidine 483
Promethazine 1435

Selective 5-HT$_3$ Receptor Antagonist
Dolasetron 536
Granisetron 811
Ondansetron 1267
Palonosetron 1299

Selective Aldosterone Blocker
Eplerenone 594
Spironolactone 1596

Selective Estrogen Receptor Modulator (SERM)
Raloxifene 1480

Serotonin 5-HT$_{1B, 1D}$ Receptor Agonist
Almotriptan 73
Eletriptan 575
Frovatriptan 771
Naratriptan 1202
Rizatriptan 1528
Sumatriptan 1620
Zolmitriptan 1822

Serotonin 5-HT$_4$ Receptor Agonist
Tegaserod 1636

Shampoo, Pediculocide
Pyrethrins and Piperonyl Butoxide 1461

Skeletal Muscle Relaxant
Baclofen 193
Carisoprodol 294
Carisoprodol and Aspirin 295
Carisoprodol, Aspirin, and Codeine 295
Chlorzoxazone 359
Cyclobenzaprine 427
Dantrolene 449
Metaxalone 1097
Methocarbamol 1109
Orphenadrine 1273
Orphenadrine, Aspirin, and Caffeine 1273

Skin and Mucous Membrane Agent
Imiquimod 890

Skin and Mucous Membrane Agent, Miscellaneous
Hyaluronate and Derivatives 841

Smoking Cessation Aid
BuPROPion 252
Nicotine 1223
Varenicline 1777

Sodium Salt
Sodium Chloride 1576

Somatostatin Analog
Octreotide 1252

Spermicide
Nonoxynol 9 1239

Stimulant
Dextroamphetamine 486
Dextroamphetamine and Amphetamine 487
Doxapram 543
Methamphetamine 1104
Modafinil 1161

Stool Softener
Docusate 533
Docusate and Senna 534

Substance P/Neurokinin 1 Receptor Antagonist
Aprepitant 144

Substituted Benzimidazole
Esomeprazole 618
Lansoprazole 977
Omeprazole 1264
Omeprazole and Sodium Bicarbonate 1266
Pantoprazole 1307
Rabeprazole 1477

Sympathomimetic
Carbetapentane and Phenylephrine 289

Theophylline Derivative
Theophylline and Guaifenesin 1663
Theophylline Salts 1664

Thrombolytic Agent
Alteplase 79
Reteplase 1498
Streptokinase 1600
Tenecteplase 1643
Urokinase 1761

Thyroid Product
Levothyroxine 1007
Liothyronine 1020
Liotrix 1020
Thyroid 1676

Topical Skin Product
Acetic Acid 38
Aluminum Sulfate and Calcium Acetate 86
Aminolevulinic Acid 95
Becaplermin 198
Bentoquatam 204
Benzoyl Peroxide and Hydrocortisone 208
Calcipotriene 264
Clindamycin and Tretinoin 391
Dexpanthenol 485
Doxepin 545
Eflornithine 573
Erythromycin 609
Gelatin, Pectin, and Methylcellulose 785
Imiquimod 890
Minoxidil 1151
Neomycin, Polymyxin B, and Hydrocortisone 1212
Pimecrolimus 1369
Povidone-Iodine 1404
Selenium Sulfide 1555
Tacrolimus 1626
Urea 1758
Vitamin A and Vitamin D 1794
Zinc Gelatin 1817
Zinc Oxide 1817

Topical Skin Product, Acne
Adapalene 49
Azelaic Acid 184
Benzoyl Peroxide and Hydrocortisone 208
Clindamycin 389
Clindamycin and Tretinoin 391
Dapsone 450
Erythromycin 609
Erythromycin and Benzoyl Peroxide 613
Sulfacetamide 1609
Sulfur and Sulfacetamide 1618
Tazarotene 1635
Tretinoin (Topical) 1732

Topical Skin Product, Antibacterial
Silver Nitrate 1566

Toxoid
Botulinum Pentavalent (ABCDE) Toxoid 234
Diphtheria and Tetanus Toxoid 519
Diphtheria, Tetanus Toxoids, and Acellular Pertussis Vaccine 521
Diphtheria, Tetanus Toxoids, and Acellular Pertussis Vaccine and *Haemophilus
    influenzae* b Conjugate Vaccine 524
Tetanus Toxoid (Adsorbed) 1657
Tetanus Toxoid (Fluid) 1658

Trace Element
Zinc Chloride 1816
Zinc Sulfate 1817

Trace Element, Parenteral
Manganese 1054
Selenium 1555

Tumor Necrosis Factor (TNF) Blocking Agent
Adalimumab 47
Etanercept 641

Infliximab 904
Lenalidomide 984
Thalidomide 1661

Tyrosine Hydroxylase Inhibitor
Metyrosine 1134

Urea Cycle Disorder (UCD) Treatment Agent
Sodium Phenylacetate and Sodium Benzoate 1582
Sodium Phenylbutyrate 1582

Uricosuric Agent
Colchicine and Probenecid 414
Probenecid 1423

Urinary Acidifying Agent
Potassium Acid Phosphate 1395

Urinary Tract Product
Cysteamine 437

Vaccine
Anthrax Vaccine Adsorbed 132
BCG Vaccine 197
Diphtheria, Tetanus Toxoids, Acellular Pertussis, Hepatitis B (Recombinant), and
   Poliovirus (Inactivated) Vaccine 521
Haemophilus b Conjugate and Hepatitis B Vaccine 823
Haemophilus b Conjugate Vaccine 824
Hepatitis A Inactivated and Hepatitis B (Recombinant) Vaccine 832
Hepatitis A Vaccine 833
Hepatitis B Vaccine 835
Influenza Virus Vaccine 906
Japanese Encephalitis Virus Vaccine (Inactivated) 956
Meningococcal Polysaccharide (Groups A / C / Y and W-135) Diphtheria Toxoid
   Conjugate Vaccine 1077
Meningococcal Polysaccharide Vaccine (Groups A / C / Y and W-135) 1078
Mumps Virus Vaccine (Live/Attenuated) 1178
Papillomavirus (Types 6, 11, 16, 18) Recombinant Vaccine 1310
Pneumococcal Conjugate Vaccine (7-Valent) 1382
Pneumococcal Polysaccharide Vaccine (Polyvalent) 1384
Poliovirus Vaccine (Inactivated) 1385
Rabies Virus Vaccine 1479
Rotavirus Vaccine 1539
Rubella Virus Vaccine (Live) 1540
Smallpox Vaccine 1573
Typhoid Vaccine 1756
Varicella Virus Vaccine 1778
Yellow Fever Vaccine 1804
Zoster Vaccine 1827

Vaccine, Inactivated Bacteria
Diphtheria, Tetanus Toxoids, and Acellular Pertussis Vaccine and *Haemophilus*
   influenzae b Conjugate Vaccine 524

Vaccine, Live Virus
Measles, Mumps, and Rubella Vaccines (Combined) 1057
Measles, Mumps, Rubella, and Varicella Virus Vaccine 1057
Measles Virus Vaccine (Live) 1058

Vascular Endothelial Growth Factor (VEGF) Inhibitor
Bevacizumab 217
Pegaptanib 1319
Ranibizumab 1484
Sorafenib 1590
Sunitinib 1622

Vasodilator
Amyl Nitrite 127
Dipyridamole 525
HydrALAZINE 843
Isosorbide Dinitrate 945
Isosorbide Dinitrate and Hydralazine 947
Isosorbide Mononitrate 947
Isoxsuprine 950
Minoxidil 1151
Nesiritide 1215
Nitroglycerin 1234
Nitroprusside 1237
Papaverine 1309
Tolazoline 1701
Treprostinil 1729

Vasopressin Analog, Synthetic
Desmopressin 476

Vasopressin Antagonist
Conivaptan 417

Vitamin
Ferrous Sulfate and Ascorbic Acid 705
Folic Acid, Cyanocobalamin, and Pyridoxine 750

Vitamin D Analog
Alendronate and Cholecalciferol 67
Calcipotriene 264
Calcipotriene and Betamethasone 264
Calcitriol 266
Dihydrotachysterol 508
Doxercalciferol 548
(Continued)

Vitamin D Analog *(Continued)*
Ergocalciferol 603
Paricalcitol 1312

Vitamin A Derivative
Mequinol and Tretinoin 1085

Vitamin, Fat Soluble
Beta-Carotene 211
Calcium and Vitamin D 268
Phytonadione 1366
Vitamin A 1793
Vitamin E 1794

Vitamin, Topical
Mequinol and Tretinoin 1085

Vitamin, Water Soluble
Ascorbic Acid 156
Cyanocobalamin 425
Folic Acid 749
Hydroxocobalamin 860
Leucovorin 990
Niacin 1219
Niacinamide 1220
Pyridoxine 1463
Riboflavin 1506
Thiamine 1668

Xanthine Oxidase Inhibitor
Allopurinol 71

NOTES

NOTES

Other Products Offered by Lexi-Comp®

Anesthesiology & Critical Care Drug Handbook

Designed for anesthesiologists, critical care practitioners, and all healthcare professionals involved in the care of surgical or ICU patients.

Includes: Comprehensive drug information to ensure the appropriate clinical management of patients; Intensivist and Anesthesiologist perspective; Over 2000 medications most commonly used in the preoperative and critical care setting; and Special Topics/Issues section with frequently encountered patient conditions

Clinician's Guide to Diagnosis

A reference with a practical approach to commonly-encountered symptoms, designed to follow the logical thought process of a seasoned clinician.

Includes: Evidence-based, easy-to-find answers to the questions that commonly arise in the symptom evaluation process; Over 35 algorithms that provide parallel references to the information in each chapter

Clinician's Guide to Internal Medicine

Quick access to essential information covering diagnosis, treatment, and management of commonly-encountered patient conditions in Internal Medicine.

Includes: Practical approaches ideal for point-of-care use; Algorithms to establish a diagnosis and select the appropriate therapy; and Tables to summarize diagnostic and therapeutic strategies

Clinician's Guide to Laboratory Medicine

A resource providing a logical step-by-step process from an abnormal lab test to diagnosis. This two-book set provides you with a full size guide and a portable pocket version for convenient referencing.

Includes: 137 chapters; 700 charts, tables, and algorithms; and sections such as neurology, infectious diseases, and obstetrics/gynecology

Other Products Offered by Lexi-Comp®

Drug Information Handbook with International Brand Names

Drug Information Handbook with International Brand Names includes the same content of our Drug Information Handbook, plus International drug monographs for use worldwide! Published in cooperation with APhA, this easy-to-use drug reference is compiled especially for the pharmacist, physician, or other healthcare professional seeking quick access to comprehensive drug information.

Drug Information Handbook for Advanced Practice Nursing

Designed to assist the Advanced Practice Nurse with prescribing, monitoring, and educating patients.

Includes: Over 4800 generic and brand names, cross-referenced by page number; Drug names and important Nursing fields highlighted in RED; Labeled and investigational indications; Adult, Geriatric, and Pediatric dosing; and Up to 58 fields including critical information on Patient Education and Physical Assessment

Drug Information Handbook for Nursing

Designed for registered professional nurses and upper-division nursing students requiring dosing, administration, monitoring, and patient education information.

Includes: Over 4800 generic and brand drug names cross-referenced by page number; Drug names and Nursing fields in RED; Fields of information include: Nursing Actions: Physical Assessment, and Patient Education; and Administration: I.V. Detail, Storage, Reconstitution, and Compatibility; and Labeled and investigational indications

Drug Information Handbook for Oncology

Designed for oncology professionals requiring information on combination chemotherapy regimens and dosing protocols.

Includes: Monographs containing warnings, adverse reaction profiles, drug interactions, dosing for specific indications, vesicant, emetic potential, combination regimens, and more; Where applicable, a special Combination Chemotherapy field that will link you to specific oncology monographs; Special Topics such as Cancer Treatment Related Complications, Bone Marrow Transplantation, and Drug Development

To order call Customer Service at 1-866-397-3433 or go to www.lexi.com.
Outside of the U.S. call: 330-650-6506 or www.lexi.com

Other Products Offered by Lexi-Comp®

Drug Information Handbook for Perioperative Nursing

Designed especially for perioperative nurses, Registered Nurses practicing in operative and interventional procedure settings, and upper-division nursing students seeking a distinctive reference for dosing, administration, monitoring, and patient education criteria for perioperative patient care environments

Includes: Up to 40 fields per monograph including Medication Safety data; Adult, Pediatric, and Geriatric Dosing guidelines; and information on each phase of the perioperative encounter and how it is addressed, with emphasis on special situations central to perioperative patient care

Drug Information Handbook for Psychiatry

Designed for any healthcare professional requiring quick access to comprehensive drug information as it relates to mental health issues.

Includes: Detailed drug monographs for psychotropic, nonpsychotropic, and herbal medications; Special fields such as Mental Health Comment (useful clinical pearls), Medication Safety Issues, Effects on Mental Status, and Effects on Psychiatric Treatment

Geriatric Dosage Handbook

Designed for any healthcare professional managing geriatric patients.

Includes: Complete adult and geriatric dosing; Special geriatric considerations; Up to 36 key fields of information in each monograph including Medication Safety Issues; and Extensive information on drug interactions as well as dosing for patients with renal/hepatic impairment.

Infectious Diseases Handbook

Comprehensive and easy-to-use reference for the diagnosis and treatment of infectious diseases, providing detailed information on diagnostic tests and antimicrobial agents used in treatment.

Includes: 244 Disease Syndromed Organism Monographs including West Nile and Ebola viruses; 248 diagnostic tests/procedures; 329 antimicrobial agents; and over 160 pages of Appendices

Other Products Offered by Lexi-Comp®

Laboratory Test Handbook

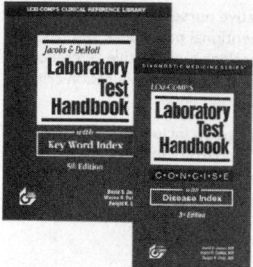

An invaluable source of information for anyone interested in diagnostic laboratory testing.

Includes: 960 tests; Up to 25 fields per test; Extensive cross-referencing; Over 12,000 references; and Key Word Index: test result, disease, organ system and syndrome

Clinicians, nurse practitioners, residents, nurses, and students will appreciate the Concise version of the *Laboratory Test Handbook* for its convenience as a quick reference. This abridged version includes 876 tests.

Pediatric Dosage Handbook

This book is designed for any healthcare professional requiring quick access to comprehensive pediatric drug information. Each monograph contains multiple field of content, including usual dosage by age group, indication and route of administration. Drug interactions, adverse reactions, extemporaneous preparations, pharmacodynamics/pharmacokinetics data, and medication safety issue are covered.

Pediatric Dosage Handbook with International Brand Names also available.

Pharmacogenomics Handbook

Ideal for any healthcare professional or student wishing to gain insight into the emerging field of pharmacogenomics.

Includes: Information concerning key genetic variations that may influence drug disposition and/or sensitivity; brief introductions to fundamental concepts in genetics and genomics. A foundation for all clinicians who will be called on to integrate rapidly-expanding genomic knowledge into the management of drug therapy,

Pharmacology Companion Guides

Our Pharmacology Companion Guide series supplies the best of Lexi-Comp's comparative charts, therapy guidelines, and supplemental data. Ideal for healthcare providers who require a quick reference resource for the key appendix information found in the *Drug Information Handbook* and *Pediatric Dosage Handbook*. An excellent companion to our PDA software.